MACMILLAN
CONTEMPORARY
DICTIONARY

MACMILLAN
CONTEMPORARY
DICTIONARY

William D. Halsey, Editorial Director

Previously published in hardcover as the Macmillan Dictionary.

MACMILLAN PUBLISHING CO., INC.
New York

COLLIER MACMILLAN PUBLISHERS
London

Macmillan Publishing Co., Inc.
866 Third Avenue, New York, N.Y. 10022
Collier Macmillan Canada, Ltd.

Library of Congress Catalog Card Number: 79-89820

ISBN 0-02-080780-5

First Macmillan Paperback Edition 1979

Printed in the United States of America

Introduction

The *Macmillan Contemporary Dictionary* is the best paperback dictionary available today. Based on the *Macmillan Dictionary*, compiled by the Macmillan Educational Corporation, it is an all-purpose dictionary made especially clear and complete for everyone. Its more than 90,000 main items (called entries) include more than 100,000 different definitions. Unlike most other paperback dictionaries, the *Macmillan Contemporary Dictionary* offers numerous illustrative sentences. There are also more than 2,000 synonym studies and over 19,000 etymologies (word origins). These features, along with 1,900 illustrations covering its 1,100 pages, put this dictionary in a league with the larger, more expensive hardcover lexicons—and make the *Macmillan Contemporary Dictionary* an excellent addition to a home, a school, or an office collection of handy, economical reference books.

The entries in the dictionary reflect current American usage. The first definition given under each entry is usually the most common one—reflecting the way the word is most frequently used. The sentences and phrases illustrating the definitions are written in the language of today, except when these examples include quotations from famous writers of the past—a special feature of this dictionary.

Language is always changing. Perhaps today more words and phrases are being added to American English than ever before. We have given special attention, therefore, both to words that have come into our language in recent years and to the new meanings that old words have acquired with the changes in society. Our language is rich in new idioms and scientific names and terms; we have included important new words or meanings to make this dictionary up-to-date and useful to the modern reader.

The synonym studies, which follow many of the main entries, will be particularly useful in helping you make selections among words that have essentially the same meaning. The usage notes in many entries, indicated by a ▲, also help you pick the right word or phrase for use in a particular situation. Scientific names of plants and animals are given as part of their definitions. The many detailed illustrations that make the *Macmillan Contemporary Dictionary* attractive as well as informative also frequently convey important definitions more clearly than do lengthy written explanations.

Sample Page

See
Section

Main Entry — ① *

jab (jab) **jabbed, jab·bing.** *v.t., v.i.* **1.** to poke or thrust sharply, as with something pointed; stab. **2.** to punch or strike with short, quick blows. —*n.* sharp, quick thrust or blow. [Form of archaic *job* to strike; possibly imitative.]

Syllable Division — ②

jab·ber (jab′ər) *v.i., v.t.* to talk rapidly, unintelligibly, or nonsensically; chatter. —*n.* rapid, unintelligible, or nonsensical talk; gibberish. [Imitative.] —**jab′ber·er,** *n.*

Pronunciation — ③

ja·bot (zha bō′, ja-) *n.* ruffle or similar ornamentation of lace or other material, usually worn down the front of a dress or shirt. [French *jabot* originally, crop of a bird; of uncertain origin.]

Definition — ④

jack·al (jak′əl, -ôl) *n.* **1.** any of various foxlike mammals, genus *Thos,* of Africa, Asia, and southeastern Europe, having a pointed face, bushy tail, and usually gray, buff, or reddish-black fur. Jackals often feed on the remains of another animal's prey. Length: 32–38 inches including the tail. **2.** one who does menial or dishonest work for another. [Turkish *chakāl* the animal, from Persian *shaghāl*.]

jack·daw (jak′dô′) *n.* glossy black crow, *Corvus monedula,* of Europe, Asia, and northern Africa, having a gray band around the throat and a gray underside. Length: 13 inches. Also, **daw.**

Variants — ⑤

jack-in-the-box (jak′in thə boks′) *also,* **jack′-in-a-box′.** *n.* toy consisting of a box containing a grotesque figure, often that of a clown, that springs up when the lid of the box is opened.

Part of Speech — ⑥

jack·pot (jak′pot′) *n.* **1.** top prize or cumulative stakes in any of various games and contests: *a quiz show that offers a $100,000 jackpot. Nick played the slot machine until he won the jackpot.* **2.** **to hit the jackpot. a.** to win a jackpot. **b.** to have great success or unexpected good fortune.

Idiom — ⑧

Subentry — ⑦

jack·straw (jak′strô′) *n.* **1.** **jackstraws.** game in which a number of objects, usually thin sticks or light strips of wood or other material, are thrown into a pile and must be picked up one at a time without disturbing the rest of the pile. ▲ construed as singular. **2.** one of the sticks or other objects used in this game.

Usage Note — ⑮

Usage Labels — ⑩

jail·er (jā′lər) *also,* **jail·or;** *British,* **gaol·er.** *n.* keeper of a jail.

ja·lop·y (jə lop′ē) *pl.,* **-lop·ies.** *n.* *Informal.* old or broken-down automobile. [Of uncertain origin.]

Scientific Name — ⑪

Japanese beetle, small destructive beetle, *Popillia japonica,* introduced into the United States from Japan, that has red wings and a greenish oval body, and feeds on various plants.

Homographs with Superscript Numbers

jar¹ (jär) *n.* **1.** wide-mouthed, usually cylindrical container or vessel that is usually made of glass or earthenware. **2.** amount contained in a jar; contents of a jar: *The boy ate a whole jar of jam.* [French *jarre* large earthen vessel, from Arabic *jarrah*.]

jar² (jär) **jarred, jar·ring.** *v.t.* **1.** to cause to shake or vibrate; cause to move suddenly by impact or shock: *The explosion jarred the building.* **2.** to have a harsh, disturbing, or unpleasant effect on: *The sudden clatter jarred her nerves.* —*v.i.* **1.** to shake, vibrate, or move suddenly from impact or shock. **2.** to have an irritating or upsetting effect: *His snide laugh jars on my nerves.* **3.** to clash; conflict: *This verse . . . jars with the words which precede and follow* (Arnold, 1873). **4.** to make a harsh or discordant sound. —*n.* **1.** shake or sudden movement; shock; jolt. **2.** sudden disturbing effect on the mind or senses.

Illustrative Sentence — ⑫

Quotation — ⑬

at; āpe; cär; end; mē; it; īce; hot; ōld; fôrk; wood; fōol; oil; out; up; ūse;

See
Section

3. harsh or discordant sound or combination of sounds. [Probably imitative.] —**jar'ring·ly,** *adv.*

⑰ * ——— Run-on Entry

jeu d'es·prit (zhœ′ des prē′) *pl.,* **jeux d'es·prit.** *French.* witty remark or piece of writing; witticism.

⑩ ——— Language Label

jigsaw puzzle, puzzle consisting of a set of irregularly shaped cardboard or wood pieces that can be fitted together to form a picture.

① ——— Compound Entry

Jo·cas·ta (jō kas′tə) *n.* *Greek Mythology.* queen of Thebes who unknowingly married her own son, Oedipus. When she later discovered his identity, she committed suicide.

⑩ ——— Subject Label

Jo·han·nes·burg (jō han′is burg′, yō hä′nis-) *n.* largest city and commercial and industrial center of the Republic of South Africa, in the northeastern part of the country. Pop. (1967 est.), 1,294,800.

① ——— Geographical Entry

Jones, John Paul (jōnz) 1747–92, Scottish-born U.S. naval hero in the American Revolution; born John Paul.

① ——— Biographical Entry

jour·ney (jur′nē) *pl.,* **-neys.** *n.* **1.** trip, esp. one over a considerable distance or taking considerable time: *a journey across the United States.* **2.** distance traveled, or that can be traveled, in a specified time: *a four days' journey from here.* —*v.i.* **-neyed, -ney·ing.** to make a trip; travel. —*v.t.* to travel over or through. [Old French *journee* day, a day's travel, a day's work, going back to Latin *diurnus* daily, from *diēs* day.] —**jour'ney·er,** *n.*

④ ——— Inflected Forms
④

Syn. *n.* **1. Journey, voyage, trip, tour** denote travel from one place to another. **Journey** implies that the travel is for a somewhat lengthy period, often over land: *The New Yorkers' journey to California was uneventful.* **Voyage** also implies length of time but is used esp. in reference to travel by ship: *Columbus made four voyages to the new world.* **Trip** indicates a relatively short period of travel, esp. for a specified purpose: *The salesman makes two trips to Seattle every week.* **Tour** suggests a circular trip with a planned itinerary, as for sightseeing: *The travel agent suggested a ninety-day tour of Europe.*

⑱ ——— Synonym Study

jo·vi·al (jō′vē əl) *adj.* characterized by hearty, good-natured humor and conviviality; merry; jolly. [Late Latin *Joviālis* relating to Jove or Jupiter, from Latin *Jov-.* See JOVE. From the belief that people born under the sign of the planet Jupiter were happy and jolly.] —**jo'vi·al·ly,** *adv.* —**jo'vi·al·ness,** *n.*

⑯ ——— Etymology

jr., junior.

① ——— Abbreviation

Judeo- *also,* **Judaeo-.** *combining form* Jewish: *Judeo-Christian.* [Latin *Jūdaeus* Jewish, Jew. See JEW.]

① ——— Combining Form

Ju·go·sla·vi·a (ū′gō slä′vē ə) *n.* *Yugoslavia.* —**Ju'go·sla'vi·an,** *adj., n.*

⑭ ——— Cross Reference

June (joon) *n.* sixth month of the year, containing thirty days. [Latin *Jūnius,* from *Jūnō,* the queen of the gods in Roman mythology.]

June·ber·ry (joon′ber′ē) *pl.,* **-ries.** *n.* the shadbush or its fruit.

June bug 1. any of several stout, brown beetles, family Scarabaeidae, that emerge as adults in late spring or early summer and are destructive to shrubs and trees. Their larvae feed on the roots of many crops. Also, **June beetle. 2.** figeater.

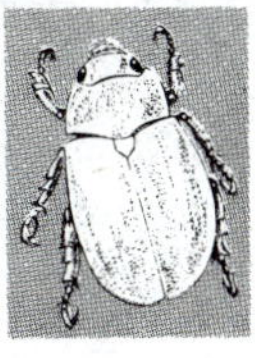

June bug

⑲ ——— Illustration

Jung, Carl Gus·tav (yoong; goos′täf) 1875–1961, Swiss psychiatrist.

③ ——— Pronunciation Key

Guide to the Dictionary

The *Macmillan Contemporary Dictionary* contains many different kinds of information to help you in your reading, writing, and speaking. In order to gain the greatest possible benefit from this book, you need to know just what information it contains, how this information is arranged, and how it can be put to use. The following sections present a step-by-step description of the various features of the book, following the order in which you will find these items when you look up a word. The *Macmillan Contemporary Dictionary* can be a highly valuable language tool.

How to Look Up a Word

Main Entry   Homographs
Alphabetical Order   Secondary Entries
Guide Words

The Entry

Kinds of Main Entries   Scientific Names
Dividing a Word into Syllables   Illustrative Sentences
Pronunciation   and Phrases
Inflected Forms   Quotations
Variants   Cross-references
Parts of Speech   Usage Notes
Subentries   The Etymology
Idioms   Run-on Entries
Definitions   Synonym Study
Labels   Illustrations

How to Look Up a Word

The Main Entry The words defined in this dictionary are called main entries. These *main entries* are printed in **boldface type** and appear at the left-hand margin of each column, followed by a body of information.

Alphabetical Order Main entries are arranged alphabetically. The *Macmillan Contemporary Dictionary*'s entries are all contained in a single list, so that you may locate the word you want as easily as possible. There are no separate sections for special kinds of words, such as names of persons and places. Entries are listed alphabetically letter by letter, whether they consist of a single word or of two or more different words.

ice floe	**pollster**
ice hockey	**poll tax**
icehouse	**pollutant**

A small number of entries do not follow this letter-by-letter pattern. Entries for famous people are placed alphabetically according to the person's last name; the first name is not considered in alphabetizing.

mendacity
Mendel, Gregor
mendelevium

Names of places are alphabetized by their specific proper name only, rather than by *Lake, Mount, Cape,* or any other such word that describes what they are. Thus you would find **Lake Superior** under the letter *s*, not the letter *l*.

horn	**rush hour**
Horn, Cape	**Rushmore, Mount**
hornbeam	**rusk**

Guide Words The two words that appear in large boldface type at the top of each outside column are called *guide words*. They indicate the alphabetical range of the words to be found on that particular page. They are placed on the outside of the page, so that you can see them easily as you leaf through the book. The first guide word shows the first main entry word that appears on the page, and the second guide word shows the last main entry on the page. For example, the word **forceps** can be found on the page whose guide words are **forced/ foremast.**

Homographs Sometimes you may find that the main entry you are looking up is not really the word you want, even though it looks exactly like your word. That's because many words in English are *homographs*—they are spelled the same way as other words. A homograph

Secondary Entries is a word that has the same spelling as another word or words, but a different meaning and origin, such as **bass** meaning "a kind of fish" and **bass** meaning "male singing voice." In this dictionary, words that are homographs are entered separately, and they are identified by a small numeral after the main entry.

> **kind**[1] . . . **1.** gentle, considerate, and friendly in nature or behavior . . .
> **kind**[2] . . . **1.** class, sort, or grouping; variety; type . . .

Even if the word or phrase you are looking for does not appear as a main entry, it's still very likely that it is explained in the dictionary. Many words are included as *secondary entries*. Secondary entries are printed in **secondary boldface** type within the body of material following a main entry. They appear with the main entry to which they are most closely related. A detailed description of each of the different kinds of secondary entries is included in the section entitled **The Entry.**

The Entry

All the information in the *Macmillan Contemporary Dictionary* is contained in, or relates to, various entries in the book. Now that you have learned how to locate the entry you want, this section will tell you exactly what you will find when you arrive at that entry.

Kinds of Main Entries Most of the main entries in this dictionary are single words, such as **water, energy, boutique, cassette, scofflaw,** and **nectarine.** But there are certain kinds of main entries that do not fall into this single-word group.

A. Compound Entries

A *compound entry* is a main entry that is made up of a combination of two or more words, rather than a single word. Each of the individual words in such a combination may have its own entry in the dictionary, but often the combination must also be included as a separate main entry. A compound entry is necessary whenever the meanings of the individual words in a phrase do not clearly explain the meaning of the phrase. For example, looking up the meanings of the words **blind** and **date** would not enable you to fully understand the informal expression "blind date," so there is a separate entry for **blind date.** The phrase **long house** has its own entry because it is the name of a certain type of American Indian dwelling, rather than a general term meaning "any house that is long." If a phrase can be clearly understood from the meanings of its individual words, as is the case with such combinations as *hand lotion, motor oil, baseball glove,* or *solar telescope,* it does not have its own separate entry. Even though such phrases occur quite frequently in the language, you can understand them by looking up the individual words and combining their meanings.

B. Prefixes, Suffixes, and Combining Forms

Prefixes, suffixes, and combining forms are not actually words, but they appear in the dictionary because they are very important in the formation of words. All of these forms are groups of letters. *Prefixes* appear at the beginning of a word, *suffixes* appear at the end, and *combining forms* may appear in either place. The word **postwar** is composed of the prefix **post-** plus the word **war.** The words **creation, creative,** and **creator** are formed by adding various suffixes to the word **create.** In this dictionary combining forms that

appear at the beginning of a word and prefixes are identified by a hyphen following the entry form.

dia- *prefix* **1.** through; between; across . . .
centi- *combining form* **1.** hundred . . . .

Combining forms that appear at the end of a word and suffixes are identified by a hyphen preceding the entry form.

-ative *suffix* . . . **1.** tending to . . .
-cide[1] *combining form* killing of . . .

Many of the new words formed in English are created by adding a prefix, suffix, or combining form to a word that already exists in the language. There is no limit to the number of possible new words that can be made in this way. So you may occasionally encounter certain formations of this type that do not appear in your dictionary. By using the information in the *Macmillan Contemporary Dictionary*, however, you can understand the meaning of words even when they are not actually defined in the book. Suppose you encountered the unfamiliar word **thermomotor** in your reading. **Thermomotor** does not appear in this dictionary, since it is a very rare term. But there is an entry for the combining form **thermo-**, which means "heat." If you take this information and combine it with your knowledge of the word **motor**, it is not hard to gain an understanding of **thermomotor**. The word means "an engine driven by heat."

C. Abbreviations

This dictionary includes the abbreviations that occur frequently in writing. In general, only one form of a particular abbreviation is entered here, the form that is most commonly used. Abbreviations vary so widely in form that it would not be possible to record all the different ways a particular abbreviation may be written. The abbreviation given here for "direct current" is **DC**, but the forms **D.C., d.c., dc, d-c,** or **d.-c.** might also occur.

D. Geographical Entries

The names of countries, states, major cities, lakes, mountains, and the like are entered in the main entry list. Important statistics, such as the area and population figures, are listed under all geographical entries.

O·kla·ho·ma . . . state in the south-central United States. Capital, Oklahoma City. Area, 69,919 sq. mi. Pop. (1970), 2,559,253. Abbreviation, **Okla.**

E. Biographical Entries

The names of important persons are entered in the main entry list alphabetically according to the last name. Such biographical entries include the years of a person's birth and death, his or her nationality, and a phrase describing the person's occupation or main area of contribution.

Dick·in·son, Emily . . . 1830–86, U.S. poet.

Dividing A Word Into Syllables

Entry words are divided into syllables by centered black dots.

fer·men·ta·tion
re·pu·di·ate

These dots show where the word should be divided in writing or printing if it occurs at the end of a line and part of the word must be carried over to the next line. If you were using the word **fermentation** and had to write part of it on the next line, it could be broken after **fer-, fermen-,** or **fermenta-,** depending on how much space you had available at the

end of the first line. Not all main entry words are divided into syllables. The individual words of a compound entry are not broken into syllables if they have their own separate main entries. Thus the entry **second lieutenant** is not divided, since the entry **sec·ond** and the entry **lieu·ten·ant** show the proper division for these words. Words that are pronounced as one syllable, such as **length** or **schnapps,** should not be divided in writing. This dictionary shows all the syllables of a word, but sometimes in writing it is not proper to break a word at a syllable division. When a syllable of one letter begins or ends a word, it should not be separated from the rest of the word. Words such as **bus·y, e·lect,** and **a·wake** should not be divided in writing.

③

Pronunciation The pronunciation of a word is printed in roman type (the same kind of type this sentence is written in). It is enclosed in parentheses and follows immediately after the boldface spelling of the entry to which it applies.

> **jeep** (jēp) . . .

Pronunciations are shown by a respelling of the entry word according to a special system of letter symbols. These symbols represent the sounds of American English. The system which the symbols follow is presented in a pronunciation key on page G26, along with common words that show how each symbol is sounded. A shorter version of this pronunciation key is printed at the bottom of each page of the dictionary itself. The syllables of the pronunciation are divided by a space. Some syllables of a word are spoken with more *stress,* or force, than others. A syllable that is stressed is followed by an accent mark. Primary, or strong, stress indicates a syllable spoken with a great degree of force, and is represented by a heavy mark (′). Secondary, or weak, stress indicates a syllable spoken with a lesser degree of force and is represented by a lighter mark (′). Syllables that are spoken without any stress at all have no accent mark.

> **cen·ten·ni·al** (sen ten′ ē əl) . . .
> **klep·to·ma·ni·a** (klep′tə mā′nē ə) . . .

The syllables of the pronunciation are not always the same as the syllables of the main entry word. The pronunciation syllables are divided according to the way the word is spoken, in order to make it easy for you to sound out the pronunciation given.

> **Dar·win·ism** (där′wi niz′əm) . . .
> **prac·ti·cal·ly** (prak′tik lē) . . .

You can see that **Darwinism** has three syllables in its written form, but four in its spoken form. **Practically** is just the opposite—it has four in its written form, and three in its spoken form. Just remember that the syllable division of the boldface main entry word applies only to the way the word is written. The syllables of the pronunciation apply to the way the word is spoken. Therefore, the two sets of syllables won't always agree.

You will often find that an entry has more than one pronunciation. The alternate pronunciations are set off from the first pronunciation by a comma.

> **a·dult** (ə dult′, ad′ult) . . .

Each pronunciation is given in complete form once, but often alternate pronunciations do not appear in full. When a part of an alternate pronunciation does not change from the first pronunciation, it may be omitted and replaced by a hyphen.

> **ma·chet·e** (mə shet′e, -chet′ē) . . .
> **shib·bo·leth** (shib′ əlith, -leth′) . . .

The hyphen indicates that you should apply the missing part of the first pronunciation in sounding the second pronunciation. In the case of **machete,** for example, the second pronunciation would be (mə chet′ē). Sometimes a pronunciation is preceded by an itali-

xii

cized label. This label usually means that this pronunciation is not used for all the definitions of the word. It may apply to only one part of speech, or to only one definition, as indicated by the label.

ap·prox·i·mate (*adj.,* ə prok′sə mit; *v.,* ə prok′sə māt′) . . .
suite (swēt; *def.* 2 *also* so͞ot) . . .

Any pronunciation that does not have a label of any kind applies to all the definitions of the word. Each one-word main entry is given a pronunciation, no matter how simple the word may be.

big (big) . . .
hut (hut) . . .

However, some main entries that consist of more than one word are not followed by a pronunciation.

theater of the absurd, . . .

This means that the individual words of the compound entry are pronounced at their own separate entries. The dictionary has entries for the words **theater, of, the,** and **absurd.** The pronunciations given at those entries tell you how to pronounce the compound **theater of the absurd.** On the other hand, a word in a compound entry is given a pronunciation if it does not have a pronunciation anywhere else in the book.

Do·ber·man pin·scher (dō′bər mən pin′shər) . . .

Sometimes a word in a compound entry has the same pronunciation as a one-word entry, except for the addition of *-s, -ed, -ing,* or another such ending. In such cases no pronunciation is given for that word in the compound.

sol·dier (sōl′jər) . . .
Soldier's Medal, U.S. military decoration . . .

A word in a compound entry is pronounced whenever there is some doubt as to its pronunciation, even if it does have its own main entry.

lead¹ (lēd)
lead² (led)

lead line (led)

Because our language is spoken in different ways in different parts of the United States, many words have more than one acceptable pronunciation. These alternate pronunciations may reflect either a certain way of speaking used in one part of the country, or a pronunciation used by some speakers in all parts of the country. The first pronunciation shown for a word is often the most common, but frequently the other pronunciations are used just as often. You should not consider the first pronunciation given to be more correct than the others. All the pronunciations in the *Macmillan Contemporary Dictionary* are an accepted part of American English as it is actually spoken today.

4

Inflected Forms An important characteristic of the English language is that it frequently shows a change in the meaning of a word by *inflection*—a changing of the form of the word. These changed forms—called *inflected forms*—give such information as the tense of the word (*do, doing, done, did*), its number (*man, men; is, are*), or its degree (*good, better, best*). Inflected forms

are printed in secondary boldface type and are placed after the pronunciation. Syllable division is shown.

dub¹ (dub) **dubbed, dub·bing.**

If part of the syllable division of an inflected form is not shown, this means that the division of that part is the same as in the main entry. For example, in the main entry **grad·u·ate**. . . **-at·ed, -at·ing**. . ., the past participle would be divided **grad·u·at·ed.** Pronunciation is not shown unless the pronunciation of the inflected form is not clear from that of the main entry. Also, any inflected form that also appears as a separate main entry is given a pronunciation only at its own entry.

break (brāk) **broke** or . . .
broke (brōke) *v.* past tense of **break.** . . .

When inflected forms belong to a part of speech other than the one that is defined first, they follow immediately after the appropriate part-of-speech label, rather than being placed at the beginning of the entry.

drug (drug) *n.* **1.** any chemical agent that affects living cells . . . —*v.t.,* **drugged, drug·ging.** . . .

For *verbs* the inflected forms usually shown are the *past tense,* (The bird *flew* away), the *past participle* (The geese have *flown* south), and the *present participle* (The plane is *flying* too low). They are listed in that order.

grow (grō) **grew, grown, grow·ing.**

Often the past tense and the past participle have the same form (We *lost* the game; She has *lost* her summer tan). In such cases, only one form is given for both, followed by the present participle.

teach (tēch) **taught, teach·ing.**

Most English verbs form their past tense and past participle by adding the letters **-ed,** and their present participle by adding the letters **-ing.** Inflected forms that follow this regular pattern are not listed here, since they present no special problem in spelling or pronunciation.

jump (jump) *v.i.* **1.** . . .

All forms that are irregular in any way are shown, even if the irregularity is only the dropping of a single letter.

cen·sure (sen′shər) **-sured, -sur·ing.**

For *nouns* the inflected form shown is the *plural.* Most nouns in English form their plural by adding the letter **-s** (book, book*s;* wire, wire*s*), or the letters **-es** when the singular ends in *-s, -sh, -ch, -x,* or *-z* (moss, moss*es;* box, box*es;* porch, porch*es*). Inflected forms that follow this regular *-s* or *-es* pattern are not listed in the dictionary. The plural form of a noun is shown whenever it departs from this regular pattern in any way.

half (haf) *pl.,* **halves.**
a·lum·na (əlum′nə) *pl.,* **-nae** . . .

The plurals are also shown for words whose singular form ends in *-o*, since some such nouns form their plural by adding *-es*, and others by adding only *-s*.

> **po·ta·to** (pə tā′tō) *pl.*, **-toes.**
> **jun·to** (jun′tō) *pl.*, **-toes.**

Plurals are also shown when the singular form of the entry might create confusion about the formation of the plural.

> **mon·goose** (mong′gōōs′) *pl.*, **-goos·es.**
> **adjutant general,** *pl.*, **adjutants general.**

The plural is shown for **mongoose** because it might otherwise be assumed to be "mongeese," and for **adjutant general** because it might be assumed to be "adjutant generals."

For *adjectives* and *adverbs* the inflected forms shown are the *comparative* and *superlative* degrees. In English the regular pattern for forming the comparative and superlative is to add **-er** and **-est** to the basic word (high*er*, high*est;* warm*er,* warm*est*). Inflected forms that follow this regular pattern are not shown. Inflected forms are given wherever there is any departure from the regular *-er, -est* pattern.

> **hot** (hot) **hot·ter, hot·test.**
> **good** (good) **bet·ter, best.**

The comparative and superlative degrees of an adjective may also be indicated by the use of *more* and *most* (*happier* or *more happy; happiest* or *most happy*). You may use either style, depending on which one sounds more natural. There are many words, particularly longer ones, for which the *-er, -est* pattern is awkward (*more courageous* is more suitable than *courageouser*). Regular inflected forms are given if a word has both regular and irregular forms.

> **ban·dit** (ban′dit) *pl.*, **ban·dits** or **ban·dit·ti.** . . .

If an irregular form is so different in spelling from its main entry that it would not appear within a short distance of it in alphabetical order, it is given its own main entry at the appropriate alphabetical place.

> **drank** (drangk) past tense of **drink.**

⑤

Variants Many words in our language have more than one acceptable spelling, such as *judgment, judgement* or *theater, theatre.* In such a case, the spelling that occurs more frequently or is generally preferred is given as the main entry. The acceptable variant or variants appear after the pronunciation and inflected forms. A variant spelling is preceded by *"also"* and is printed in secondary boldface type. The syllable division of a variant is shown, but a variant spelling is not given a separate pronunciation if its pronunciation is the same as that of the main entry.

> **czar** (zär) *also,* **tsar, tzar.**
> **gas·o·line** (gas′ə lēn) *also,* **gas·o·lene.**

If the variant is not pronounced in exactly the same way as the main entry, it does have its own pronunciation.

> **an·i·line** (an′əl in, -īn) *also,* **an·i·lin** (an′əl in).

The variant spellings given in this dictionary are all part of standard English language. The fact that one spelling of a word is given as a main entry, while another spelling appears as a variant, does not mean that you would be entirely wrong if you used the variant.

It simply means that the first spelling is generally preferred by most users of the American language. Sometimes two or more different forms have the same meaning, such as *cougar, puma, mountain lion,* and *catamount.* The form that occurs most frequently is given as the main entry. The other forms, which are called *variant terms,* appear at the end of the entry. A variant term is preceded by "Also" and is printed in secondary boldface type. Variant terms are not given a pronunciation, since they are pronounced at their own main entry.

    scatter rug, small rug used to cover part of a floor. Also, **throw rug.**

If a variant spelling or variant term does not fall close to the defined entry in alphabetical order, it has its own separate entry referring you to the main entry.

    es·thet·ic (əs thet′ik) *adj.* aesthetic.
    cot·ton·mouth (kot′ən mouth′) *n.* water moccasin.

⑥

Parts of Speech This dictionary uses the traditional parts of speech in classifying words. The names of parts of speech are indicated by the following abbreviations:

n.	noun	*adj.*	adjective
pron.	pronoun	*adv.*	adverb
v.	verb	*prep.*	preposition
v.t.	transitive verb	*conj.*	conjunction
v.i.	intransitive verb	*interj.*	interjection

All the definitions of a word that have the same part of speech are grouped together. The part-of-speech label precedes the first definition in the group. There is only one main entry for each word, no matter how many parts of speech it may have. Each additional part of speech is introduced by the appropriate label, preceded by a dash.

    safe (sāf) **saf·er, saf·est.** *adj.* **1.** free from harm or danger . . . —*n.* **1.** strong container of metal or other material . . .

In general, the different parts of speech of a particular word are arranged according to how frequently they occur in the language. For a particular word, the part of speech which occurs most commonly is defined first, the one which occurs second most frequently is defined second, and so on.

    flat[1] (flat) **flat·ter, flat·test.** *adj.* **1.** extending horizontally with little or no slope or inclination . . . —*n.* **1.** flat part or surface . . . —*adv.* **1.** in a flat manner; flatly. —*v.t.,* **flat·ted, flat·ting. 1.** to make flat . . . —*v.i.* to become flat.

This dictionary does not give a part-of-speech label to an entry that consists of more than one word.

    end zone, area at either end . . .

You should not assume that the parts of speech assigned to a word in the dictionary cover all the possible uses of the word. A word may function as a certain part of speech in a particular sentence, without really belonging to that part of speech. For example, a word entered here as a noun may also be used to modify other nouns, and thus function as an adjective, as in "an *asphalt* driveway," "*kitchen* furniture," or "a *progress* report." The most common example of a grammatical form not defined in this book is the use of verbs as adjectives or nouns. Verbs are often used in the present and past participles as adjectives (*recurring* pains, a *rejected* suitor), and in the present participle as nouns (*Gambling* is legal in Nevada). Such forms are not entered separately, unless their meaning is not fully explained by the definitions given for the verb from which they are derived.

⑦

Subentries A *subentry* is a word, or sometimes a phrase, that is very closely related to a main word, but is slightly different in form. A subentry appears under the main entry to which it is related and is printed in secondary boldface type. A subentry may be the plural of a singular entry, or the capitalized form of an entry that begins with a small letter.

> **clas·sic** . . . *n*. . . . **2. the classics.** literature of ancient Greece and Rome.
> **cyn·ic** . . . *n*. . . . **2. Cynic.** member of a group of Greek philosophers . . .

Another basic type of subentry is a word or phrase that is so closely related to an important main entry that it is clearer and more meaningful to define it there than to give it its own main entry.

> **e·clipse** . . . *n*. **1.** apparent partial or total darkening of one celestial body by its passage through the shadow of another. In a **solar eclipse** the moon passes between the sun and the earth . . . In a **lunar eclipse** the earth moves between the sun and the moon . . .

⑧

Idioms An *idiom* is a group of words whose meaning cannot be understood from the meanings of its individual words. For example, the idiom **to hit the sack** means "to go to bed," a meaning that cannot be understood from the separate words of the phrase. Idioms are entered in secondary boldface type under the main entry of their key word. Thus **to hit the sack** would appear under **sack** with the noun definitions. If an entry has five or more idioms for one part of speech, they are entered in an indented column under that part of speech. If there are fewer than five idioms, they appear as numbered definitions within the body of the entry. Some idioms have more than one form in which they are used. Rather than each variant being repeated in full, the variant words are put in parentheses in secondary boldface type. This indicates that the variant words may each be substituted in the idiom. For example, under **set** the idiom "**to set on** (or **upon**). to attack or urge to attack." appears. The words in the parentheses show that this idiom may appear as **to set on** or **to set upon** without any change in meaning.

⑨

Definitions The definitions of an entry are grouped according to part of speech. They are numbered consecutively in secondary boldface type.

> **mid·dle** (mid′əl) *adj*. **1.** equally distant from the sides, extremities, or exterior points: *The middle office is his. We sat in the middle row.* **2.** being or occurring halfway between two things . . .

Related senses of one basic meaning are grouped together under one number and lettered in secondary boldface type.

> **al·bum** . . . *n*. . . . **2.a.** booklike holder with envelopes for phonograph records. **b.** long-playing phonograph record, or set of records sold as a unit. . . .

In some definitions the abbreviation "esp.", meaning "especially," is used to indicate a sense that is not different enough to be a separate definition.

> **ap·pel·lant** . . . *n*. one who appeals, esp. to a higher court. . . .

In general, the individual definitions are arranged according to the frequency with which they occur in the language. The meaning that is used most commonly is placed first. The other definitions follow according to their relative frequency. This is done so that you

can locate the meaning that you are looking for as quickly and as easily as possible.

ba·by (bā′bē) *pl.,* **-bies.** *n.* **1.** newborn or very young child. **2.** youngest member of a family or group. **3.** one who behaves like a child; childish or immature person. **4.** newborn or very young animal. **5.** *Slang.* object of special attention or pride . . .

Within a particular definition, there may appear one or more statements or synonymous words separated by semicolons which serve to point out different ways of describing the same basic meaning. In the example below, "to irritate greatly," "provoke to anger," and "infuriate" are all different ways of explaining the word **exasperate.**

ex·as·per·ate . . . *v.t.* to irritate greatly; provoke to anger; infuriate . . .

⑩

Labels

Labels such as *Informal, British,* and *Chemistry* provide additional information about a word, form, or definition. The labels used in this dictionary fall into two basic categories: *subject labels* and *usage labels.*

A. Subject Labels

Subject labels indicate the field of knowledge. They are especially helpful when the wording of a definition does not clearly show that it applies to a particular field.

green . . . **4.** *Golf.* area around a cup, having very thick, closely cut grass.

When a word has a large number of definitions, the presence of a subject label makes it much easier to locate a specialized definition.

run . . . *v.i.* **1.** . . . **32.** *Law.* to have legal validity or force . . .

B. Usage Labels

Many words and meanings in English are not used throughout the entire range of the language. Some are not common in all parts of the English-speaking world; others rarely appear in modern speech and writing; still others are not suitable to be used in certain kinds of speech and writing. This dictionary employs usage labels to indicate that a particular word or definition is restricted to a certain area or level of language. If a word or meaning does not have a usage label, you may consider it appropriate to be used in any kind of speech or writing.   **Informal:** The style of language that a person uses varies according to the situation. You would not use the same language in writing an essay that you use in talking on the telephone to a friend. The label *Informal* indicates that a word or meaning is not suitable to be used in a formal context, such as a legal contract, a technical article, or a scientific lecture. An *Informal* label does not mean that a word or definition is incorrect. But just as certain clothing is considered to be more appropriate for a picnic or a trip to the beach than for a wedding ceremony, certain words are more suited to informal contexts than to formal ones. Any word or meaning labeled *Informal* in this book may be used freely in ordinary conversation, and in writing that is intended to have the same feeling as actual speech. But you should remember that the use of an informal word can affect the tone of formal writing or speech.   **Slang:** The label *Slang* is applied to words or meanings that are extremely informal. Slang is composed mostly of new words or of unusual uses of existing words, and it is usually used to produce a certain effect, such as humor or exaggeration. New slang terms are constantly being added to the language, and many existing slang terms pass out of use after having enjoyed only a brief period of popularity.   **British:** The label *British* indicates that a word, meaning, spelling, or the like is common in Great Britain but is not generally used by American speakers and writers. This does not mean that something labeled *British* in this book will never be found in American usage. Today the two cultures influence one another to such an extent that an absolute distinction between British and American English is not really possible.

Archaic: The label *Archaic* indicates that a word or meaning was once frequently used but is no longer common in our language. You wouldn't want to use such a word in your own speech or writing unless you were trying to achieve an old-fashioned effect. But archaic terms are included in the dictionary because you will encounter them in the works of great writers of the past, such as Shakespeare and Milton. In this dictionary a word or phrase occasionally has a foreign language label, such as *Latin, French,* or *Spanish.* This indicates that the entry, although actually part of a foreign language, is used enough in English contexts to justify its being included in an English-language dictionary.

⑪
Scientific Names

The *Macmillan Dictionary* tries to give you the most complete descriptions possible of plants and animals. As part of this effort, the scientific name of a plant or animal is given in the definition.

> **cou·gar** (kōō′gər) *n.* tawny or grayish-brown wild cat, *Felis concolor,* of North, Central, and South America, having a small, round head, long limbs, and a slender, muscular body. Length: 6–8 feet including tail. . . .

If the entry refers to a grouping that is more general than a species, the designation of the grouping (such as genus, family, or order) is indicated.

> **cock·roach** (kok′rōch′) *n.* any of a group of brown or black insects, family Blattidae. . . .

When the genus name of a particular species has been mentioned previously in the definition, the full name is not repeated. The genus is abbreviated after the first letter, followed by the full species name.

> **gar·de·nia** (gär dēn′yə, -dē nē ə) *n.* **1.** fragrant yellow or white flower of any of a group of evergreen shrubs and small trees, genus *Gardenia,* as the **cape jasmine,** *G. jasminoides* . . .

Scientific names are especially helpful in identifying an organism when there is disagreement about its common name. The animal defined here under *cougar,* for example, is also known as the "puma," "mountain lion," or "catamount," as well as by various other names. But it is known by only one scientific name, *Felis concolor.*

⑫
Illustrative Sentences and Phrases

Following many of the definitions in this dictionary, there are sentences and phrases printed in *italic type.* These sentences and phrases show the meaning of the word in context, and they serve several purposes. For example, they may be employed to clarify a meaning by showing it in its most familiar use.

> **old** . . . **10.** experienced, skilled, or practiced: *He is an old hand at making speeches.*

They may also distinguish between two slightly different senses of the same meaning.

> **bar·ren** . . . **1.a.** having little or no vegetation; producing poor crops: *barren soil, the barren Siberian wastes.*

Or they may indicate the way a meaning is used. The illustrative phrases under definition **3** of **barren** show that this meaning is used in a figurative sense.

> **bar·ren** . . . **3.** not leading to any gain; fruitless; unprofitable: *barren endeavors, barren prospects.*

⑬
Quotations

This book includes quotations from literature to illustrate definitions. The quotation is accompanied by the author's last name and the date of publication of the work from which the quotation is taken. These quotations provide you with an understanding of how the English language has been used by distinguished writers throughout history.

teach . . . —*v.i.* to act or be employed as a teacher; give instruction: *Gladly would he learn, and gladly teach* (Chaucer, c.1387).

noon . . . **2.** highest point: *in the bright wisdom of youth's breathless noon* (Shelley, 1817).

void . . . *n.* **1.** an empty space; vacuum: *No nightmare of hostile objects could be as terrible as this void* (Auden, 1944).

Quotations from William Shakespeare are followed by the name of the play rather than the year of publication.

round . . . —*v.t.* . . . **3.** to make complete; finish or perfect . . . *We are such stuff as dreams are made on, and our little life is rounded with a sleep* (Shakespeare, *The Tempest*).

When the Bible is the source of a quotation, the King James version is used, and the book, chapter, and verse are cited.

seek . . . —*v.i.* to search; make inquiry: *Seek and ye shall find* (Matthew 7:7).

⑭

Cross References Often, information about an entry is provided under another main entry. In such cases it is necessary to have a *cross reference*—an instruction directing you to refer to another part of the dictionary. When an entry is a variant of another main entry, the definition of the variant form consists simply of a reference to the preferred form.

giant panda, panda *(def. 1).*

When a word is defined under another entry but is not actually a variant of that entry, the cross reference is introduced by "see," and the defined entry is printed in boldface.

St. Pe·ters·burg . . . **1.** see **Leningrad.** . . .

⑮

Usage Notes Usage notes provide information about the way a particular word or expression is used in current English. The usage notes in this dictionary do not make subjective judgments as to how language should be used, based on the personal feelings of the editors. These notes describe how our language actually is used by educated speakers and writers. The editors hope that this information will guide you in your own use of the language. Usage notes are introduced by a dark triangle (▲) and are printed in roman type, the same kind of type used for definitions. The usage note follows immediately after the definition to which it applies. When a usage note applies to all the definitions of a part of speech, it is placed after the last definition.

none . . . *pron.* **1.** . . . **2.** . . . **3.** . . . ▲ Because *none* originally meant "no one," it has traditionally been construed as singular: *None of his friends has ever been to Paris.* However, since the word is usually used with a plural noun, in current usage it is more often considered to be plural: *None of the passengers were aware of the danger.* —*adv.* . . .

A usage note that applies to the entire word is placed at the end of the text for the main entry. Usage notes are often used when there may be some doubt as to whether a noun form takes a plural or singular verb.

a·cous·tics . . . *n., pl.* **1.** properties, as of a room, theater, or auditorium, that determine how well sound is carried and heard in it. **2.** science that deals with the production, transmission, effects, and reception of sound. ▲ construed as plural in def. 1, singular in def. 2.

⑯

The Etymology An etymology in this dictionary traces the history of a word from its Modern English form back to its original form and includes the changes in spelling and meaning that have taken place in the word over the years. The etymologies are placed between square brackets and follow the definitions. A feature of this book is the presentation of the etymologies without the customary abbreviations and symbols that so often make word histories difficult to read. The words that an English word comes from are called its *sources,* or *ancestors.* These foreign words are printed in italic type. The names of the languages for these word ancestors and the explanatory material are printed in roman type. The *glosses* (explanations of a foreign word's meaning) are also in roman type.

con·sid·er . . . [Old French *considerer* to observe closely, from Latin *cōnsiderāre* originally, to observe the stars, from *con-* with + *sīdus* star; from the ancient astrological practice of consulting the stars when trying to make a decision.]

If the first ancestor word of an entry has basically the same meanings as the entry, no gloss is given. Glosses are furnished only if the meanings differ significantly. When a foreign word in an etymology has the same meaning as the word that precedes it, the gloss is not repeated.

hol·ster . . . [Dutch *holster.*]
vi·a·ble . . . [French *viable* capable of living, from *vie* life, from Latin *vīta.*]

Since there is no gloss after Dutch *holster* in the first of the above examples, you can assume that it has basically the same meaning as the English word **holster** that is derived from it. In the same way, the absence of a gloss after the Latin word *vita* indicates that it has the same meaning as the French word *vie.* The name of a language is shown only before its first appearance in an etymology. It is not repeated for stages of development within the same language.

jo·cose . . . [Latin *jocōsus,* from *jocus* jest, game.]

A plus sign (+) is used to connect the parts of a word that is formed from two or more words or word elements.

bi·ol·o·gy . . . [BIO- + -LOGY.]

When a word has an interesting history, full information is provided about its origin in the form of an anecdote. Very often the current meaning of a word is made clearer by an etymology.

boy·cott (boi′kot) *v.t.* **1.** to combine in refusing to patronize, associate with, participate in, or have any dealings with: *to boycott a store* . . . [From Captain Charles *Boycott,* 1832–97, agent for an absentee Irish landlord, who was ostracized and harassed by Irish farmers for his harsh actions against them.]

red tape, attention to or following of official rules, forms, and procedures, esp. as involving inaction and delay. [From the practice that began in the seventeenth century in England of using *red tape* to tie official documents.]

An etymology is not given for every entry. When the elements of a derived word, compound, or phrase are easy to recognize, it is not necessary to provide an etymology, for you can look up the separate elements where they are entered. For example, since there is an etymology for **extreme,** there is no need for one under **extremely, extremism,** or **extremist.** You can find sufficient information in the word histories provided for the elements of these words—**extreme, -ly¹, -ism,** and **-ist.** Also, the source of compound entries like **coffeepot** and **greenhouse** and of phrases like **box seat** is obvious. Again, etymologies can be found where the separate elements are entered.

⑰
Run-on Entries

Many words in English are formed by the addition of a suffix to an existing word, called a *root word.* The adverb **cheerfully** and the noun **cheerfulness** are formed by adding suffixes to the adjective **cheerful.** A word formed in this way is called a *derived word.* It usually has the same essential meaning as its root word, but a different grammatical form. The noun **deliciousness** is formed from the adjective **delicious** and the suffix **-ness,** which means "quality, state, or condition of being delicious." When the meaning of a derived word is equal to the meaning of the root word plus that of the attached suffix, it is not necessary to have a separate main entry for the derived word. The derived word can be understood without a definition, since the root word and the suffix are both fully defined. Such derived words appear in this dictionary as *run-on entries*—they are "run on" at the end of the text dealing with the root word. Run-on entries are set in secondary boldface type and are introduced by a dash. Run-ons are divided into syllables, and stress is shown by accent marks. The part of speech of a run-on is indicated following the form.

> **keen¹** (kēn) *adj.* **1.** having a fine cutting edge or point . . . [Old English *cēne* wise, brave.] —**keen′ly,** *adv.* —**keen′ness,** *n.*

A run-on is not given a pronunciation unless its pronunciation cannot be understood from that of the main entry.

> **cen·tric** (sen′trik) *adj.* . . . —**cen·tric·i·ty** (sen tris′ə te), *n.*

A derived word is not run on unless all its meanings can be understood from the definitions given for the root word. The word **catcher** is a main entry because, although its basic meaning can be understood from **catch** plus **-er** ("one who catches"), it has a specialized sense (the player in baseball) that is not fully covered by **catch.**

⑱
The Synonym Study

Because the English language draws its words from many different sources, it has an unusually large number of synonyms. Although several words may mean almost the same thing, usually each one has particular characteristics that make it more suitable for a certain situation than its synonyms. The purpose of a synonym study is to show subtle distinctions among words that are very close in meaning, so that a careful writer or speaker may choose the word that is most appropriate in a particular statement. The synonym study appears as a separate paragraph beneath the rest of the main entry. It is introduced by the boldface abbreviation **Syn.** and a notation indicating which definition of the main entry is being discussed.

> **cor·rect** . . . **Syn.** *adj.* **1.** Correct, precise, accurate, exact . . .

In general, the synonym study appears under the most common or most comprehensive word in the group of synonyms being discussed. The other words in the synonym study have a cross-reference to the study at the end of their own main entry.

> **o·rig·i·nal** . . . —**Syn.** *adj.* **1.** see **new.**

The synonym study usually begins with a general statement expressing the essential meaning that the words listed have in common, followed by a discussion of the special, finer distinctions suggested by each word.

> **dan·ger** . . . **Syn. 1. Danger, hazard, peril, risk** mean a threat of damage or harm. **Danger,** the general term, gives no indication of how immediate the threat is or whether it is inevitable: *There is danger in climbing a high mountain.* **Hazard** suggests chance and implies a greater or lesser probability of harm in the very nature of a situation: *He became accustomed to the hazards of driving in heavy traffic.* **Peril** suggests a high probability of harm and implies an impending threat: *The present generation lives in greater peril of nuclear war.* **Risk** suggests both the probability of harm and a voluntary acceptance of the chances: *There is a risk involved in stock market speculation.*

⑲

Illustrations Illustrations serve to provide a fuller understanding of a word than is possible through the use of definitions alone. Often a fact, idea, or principle that would require a long and complicated verbal explanation can be expressed much more clearly by an illustration. The illustrations in this dictionary are extremely detailed, and the great majority of them are enhanced by the use of color. This color makes the illustrations—and the entire page—lively and appealing to the eye. It also serves a practical purpose, in that it often depicts or points out the key feature of an illustration. The following example will show you how greatly your knowledge of a word can be increased by an illustration.

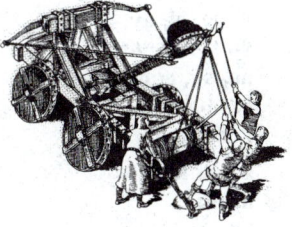

> **cat·a·pult** (kat′ ə pult′, -poolt′) *n.* **1.** war machine, similar to a ballista, used to shoot or hurl projectiles. **2.** track-mounted device used to launch an airplane from the deck of a ship. **3.** *British.* slingshot. —*v.t.* to hurl or shoot (something) from or as from a catapult. —*v.i.* to leap or be ejected. [Late Latin *catapulta* this war machine, from Greek *katapaltēs*.]

Catapult

The Abbreviations Used In This Dictionary The *Macmillan Contemporary Dictionary* has made a special effort to limit the number of abbreviations used. To make this book clear to you, all words have been spelled out in full except when demands of space make this impossible. No abbreviations at all are used in etymologies. The abbreviations that are used in definitions are explained below.

A.D.	Anno Domini (after Christ)	pl.	plural
adj.	adjective	pop.	population
adv.	adverb	prep.	preposition
approx.	approximately	pron.	pronoun
B.C.	before Christ	sing.	singular
c.	circa (about; approximately)	sq. mi.	square miles
conj.	conjunction	St.	Saint
def.	definition	syn.	synonym
esp.	especially	U.S.	United States
est.	estimated	v.	verb
interj.	interjection	v.i.	intransitive verb
n.	noun	v.t.	transitive verb

Table of English Spellings

This table shows the more common spellings for the different sounds in English. It is meant to be used as a guide to help find words you know how to pronounce but don't know how to spell.

SOUND	SPELLING	EXAMPLE
a	a, ai, au	hand, plaid, aunt
ā	a, ai, au, ay, ea, eh, ei, eigh, ey	rate, rain, gauge, pay, steak, eh, veil, eight, obey
ä	a, ah, e, ea, ua	art, hah, sergeant, heart, guard
b	b, bb	bit, rabbit
ch	c, ch, t, tch, te, ti	cello, chin, nature, batch, righteous, mention
d	d, dd, ed	dive, ladder, failed
e	a, ae, ai, ay, e, ea, ei, eo, ie, u, ue	many, aesthetic, said, says, met, weather, heifer, jeopardy, friend, bury, guess
ē	ae, ay, e, ea, ee, ei, eo, ey, i, ie, oe, y	Caesar, quay, he, beach, bee, deceive, people, key, machine, field, amoeba, city
f	f, ff, gh, ph	fine, off, laugh, physical
g	g, gg, gh, gue	go, stagger, ghost, catalogue
h	h, wh	he, whom
hw	wh	wheel
i	a, e, ee, ei, i, ia, ie, o, u, ui, y	damage, pretty, been, counterfeit, bit, carriage, sieve, women, busy, build, myth
ī	ai, aye, ei, eigh, ey, eye, i, ie, igh, uy, y, ye	aisle, aye, stein, height, geyser, eye, rice, tie, high, buy, try, dye
j	d, dg, dge, di, g, gg, j	graduate, ledger, judge, soldier, magic, exaggerate, jump
k	c, cc, ch, ck, cq, cque, cu, k, q, qu, que	cat, account, chord, tack, acquaint, sacque, biscuit, key, Iraq, liquor, bisque
l	l, ll	line, hall
m	m, mb, mm, mn	mine, climb, hammer, hymn
n	n, gn, kn, nn, pn	nice, gnome, knee, funny, pneumonia
ng	n, ng, ngue	link, sing, tongue

SOUND	SPELLING	EXAMPLE
o	a, o	watch, lock
ō	au, eau, eo, ew, o, oa, oe, oh, oo, ou, ow, owe	mauve, beau, yeoman, sew, so, boat, foe, oh, brooch, soul, know, owe
ô	a, au, augh, aw, eo, o, oa, ough, ow	fall, author, caught, jaw, George, order, broad, bought, toward
oi	aw, oi, oy, uoy	lawyer, foil, toy, buoy
oo	o, oo, ou, u	wolf, look, should, full
ōo	eu, ew, ieu, o, oe, oo, ou, u, ue, ug, ui	maneuver, jewel, lieu, prove, canoe, tool, soup, luminous, true, impugn, fruit
ou	ou, ough, ow	out, bough, now
p	p, pp	pill, happy
r	r, rh, rr, wr	ray, rhyme, parrot, wrong
s	c, ps, s, sc, sch, ss	city, psychology, song, scene, schism, mess
sh	ce, ch, ci, s, sch, sci sh, si, ss, ssi, ti	ocean, machine, special, sugar, schist, conscience, shin, expansion, tissue, mission, nation
t	t, tt, ed, th, pt	ten, bitter, topped, thyme, ptomaine
th	th	thin
t̲h	th, the	them, bathe
u	o, oe, oo, ou, u	come, does, flood, touch, sun
ur	ear, er, err, eur, ir, or, our, ur, yr, yrrh	earth, fern, err, amateur, thirst, worst, courage, turn, myrtle, myrrh
ū	eau, eu, ew, ieu, iew, ou, u, ue, ueu, yu	beautiful, feud, new, adieu, view, you, use, cue, queu, yule
v	f, ph, v, vv	of, Stephen, vine, flivver
w	o, ou, u, w	choir, ouija, queen, we
y	i, j, y	onion, hallelujah, yes
z	s, ss, x, z, zz	has, scissors, xylophone, zoo, fuzz
zh	ge, s, si, z, zi	garage, treasure, division, azure, brazier
ə	a, ai, e, i, o, ou, u	ago, bargain, taken, pencil, lemon, furious, circus

Pronunciation Key

a	a as in **at, bad**
ā	a as in **ape**, ai as in **pain**, ay as in **day**
ä	a as in **father, car**
e	e as in **end, pet**
ē	e as in **me**, ee as in **feet**, ea as in **meat**, ie as in **piece**, y as in **finally**
i	i as in **it, pig**
ī	i as in **ice, fine**, ie as in **lie**, y as in **my**
o	o as in **odd, hot**
ō	o as in **old**, oa as in **oat**, ow as in **low**, oe as in **toe**
ô	o as in **coffee, fork**, au as in **author**, aw as in **law**, a as in **all**
oo	oo as in **wood**, u as in **put**
ōo	oo as in **fool**, ue as in **true**
oi	oi as in **oil**, oy as in **boy**
ou	ou as in **out**, ow as in **cow**
u	u as in **up, mud**, o as in **oven, love**
ū	u as in **use**, ue as in **cue**, ew as in **few**, eu as in **feud**
ur	ur as in **turn**, er as in **term**, ir as in **bird**, or as in **word**
ə	a as in **ago**, e as in **taken**, i as in **pencil**, o as in **lemon**, u as in **helpful**
b	b as in **bat, above, job**
ch	ch as in **chin, such**, tch as in **hatch**
d	d as in **dear, soda, bad**
f	f as in **five, defend, leaf**, ff as in **off**
g	g as in **game, ago, fog**
h	h as in **hit, ahead**
j	j as in **joke, enjoy**, g as in **gem**, dge as in **edge**
k	k as in **kit, baking, seek**, ck as in **tack**, c as in **cat**
l	l as in **lid, sailor, feel**, ll as in **ball, allow**
m	m as in **man, family, dream**
n	n as in **not, final, on**
ng	ng as in **singer, long**, n as in **sink**
p	p as in **pail, repair, soap**
r	r as in **ride, parent, four**
s	s as in **sat, aside, cats**, c as in **cent**, ss as in **pass**
sh	sh as in **shoe, wishing, fish**
t	t as in **tag, pretend, hat**
th	th as in **thin, ether, both**
th	th as in **this, mother, smooth**
v	v as in **very, favor, salve**
w	w as in **wet, reward**
y	y as in **yes**
z	z as in **zoo, gazing**, zz as in **jazz**, s as in **rose, dogs**
zh	s as in **treasure**, z as in **seizure**, ge as in **garage**
N	on as in French **bon**; indicates that the vowel preceding N is nasalized
KH	ch as in **loch**, German **ach** or **ich**
oe	eu as in French **feu**, ö as in German **schön**; similar to oo in **wood**

a, A (ā) *pl.* **a's, A's.** *n.* **1.** first letter of the English alphabet. **2.** shape of this letter or something having such a shape. **3.** first item in a series or group. **4.** *Music.* **a.** sixth note or tone of the diatonic scale of C major. See **do²** for illustration. **b.** scale or key that has this note or tone as its tonic. **5. from a to z.** from beginning to end.

a¹ (ə; stressed ā) *indefinite article* **1.** any: *A child could understand this problem.* **2.** one: *He won a hundred dollars.* **3.** one single: *There was not a person in sight.* [Short for Old English *an* one, an.]

a² (ə; stressed ā) *prep.* to, in, or for each; per: *three times a year, two dollars a pound.* [Short for Old English *an, on* on, to.]

A 1. angstrom. **2.** argon. **3.** answer. **4.** artillery.

a-¹ *prefix* in; on; to; at: *atop, apart, aboard, afoot.* [From Old English preposition *an, on* on, to.]

a-², form of **ab-¹** before *m, p, v,* as in *avert.*

a-³, form of **ad-** before *sc, sp, st,* as in *ascend, aspect, aspire.*

a-⁴, form of **an-¹** before consonants except *h,* as in *asexual, amorphous.*

a. 1. about. **2.** acre; acres. **3.** adjective. **4.** *Baseball.* assist; assists.

A-1 *also* **A-one, A number 1.** *adj. Informal.* first-rate; first-class; excellent: *He's in A-1 shape.* [From the rating *A-1* used in an annual registry of ships published by Lloyd's, the London insurers, to indicate that a ship is in first-class condition as to seaworthiness.]

AA 1. Alcoholics Anonymous. **2.** antiaircraft.

AAA 1. Agricultural Adjustment Administration. **2.** American Automobile Association.

AAAS, American Association for the Advancement of Science.

Aa·chen (ä′kən, ä′KHən) *n.* city in West Germany, west of the Rhine, once the capital of Charlemagne's empire. Pop. (1968 est.), 176,204. Also, **Aix-la-Chapelle.**

Aardvark

aard·vark (ärd′värk′) *n.* burrow-dwelling mammal, *Orycteropus afer,* of southern and east-central Africa, that has a long, sticky tongue and powerful claws and feeds on ants and termites. It constitutes the only genus of the order Tubulidentata. Average length: 6 feet including the tail. [Afrikaans *aardvark,* from Dutch *aarde* earth + *vark* pig.]

aard·wolf (ärd′woolf′) *n.* carnivorous mammal, *Proteles cristatus,* of southern and east-central Africa, related to the hyena. It feeds mainly on carrion but also on termites. Average length: 2½ feet including the tail. [Afrikaans *aardwolf,* from Dutch *aarde* earth + *wolf* wolf.]

Aar·hus (ôr′hōōs′) *n.* port city in Denmark, on the eastern coast of Jutland. Pop. (1966), 115,804.

Aar·on (ar′ən) *n.* in the Old Testament, elder brother of Moses and the first high priest of the Hebrews.

ab-¹ *prefix* from; departing from; away from: *abnormal, abduct, abjure.* [Latin *ab* from, away.]

ab-², form of **ad-** before *b,* as in *abbreviate.*

a.b., able-bodied seaman.

Ab, alabamine.

A.B., Bachelor of Arts. Also, **B.A.**

ab·a·ca (ab′ə kä′) *n.* **1.** treelike tropical plant, *Musa textilis,* of the banana family, from whose leaves Manila hemp is made. **2.** Manila hemp. [Spanish *abacá,* from Tagalog *abaka* this plant.]

a·back (ə bak′) *adv.* **1. taken aback.** suddenly surprised or startled. **2.** *Archaic.* backward; at the back. [Old English *on bæc.*]

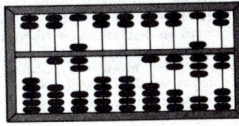

Abacus

ab·a·cus (ab′ə kəs, ə bak′əs) *pl.,* **ab·a·cus·es** or **ab·a·ci** (ab′ə sī′). *n.* **1.** counting device consisting of a frame with balls or beads that slide back and forth in grooves or on wires. **2.** flat slab forming the top of the capital of a column. [Latin *abacus* counting board, slab, through Greek *abax,* from Hebrew *ābāq* dust. The Greco-Roman abacus was a board covered with dust or sand, on which figures could be drawn and then erased.]

A·ba·dan (ä′bä dän′) *n.* city in southwestern Iran. Pop. (1966), 272,962.

a·baft (ə baft′) *prep.* in the stern or rear of; behind. *—adv.* at or toward the stern. [A-¹ + Middle English *baft* behind, from Old English *beæftan.*]

a·ba·lo·ne (ab′ə lō′nē) *n.* any of a group of edible marine mollusks, genus *Haliotis,* in which the ear-shaped shell is lined with mother-of-pearl and perforated along part of the outer rim. The **red abalone,** *H. rufescens,* of Californian and Mexican Pacific waters, is the largest species and is valued for its meat. [Spanish *abulón;* of uncertain origin.]

Abalone

a·ban·don (ə ban′dən) *v.t.* **1.** to desert or forsake completely: *to abandon a child, to abandon ship.* **2.** to give up (something) completely: *He abandoned all hope.* **3.** to yield or surrender (with *to*): *The king abandoned the city to the conquering army.* **4.** to yield (oneself) without restraint, as to an emotion or influence: *to abandon oneself to grief.* *—n.* complete surrender to one's impulses; freedom from constraint: *The child cried with abandon.* [Old French *abandoner* to give up, from (*mettre*) *a bandon* (to put) in the power of (someone else), from *bandon* power; of Germanic origin.] **—a·ban′don·er, a·ban′don·ment,** *n.* **—Syn.** *v.t.* **1.** see **desert².**

a·ban·doned (ə ban′dənd) *adj.* **1.** deserted; forsaken. **2.** given up to immorality: *a cruel, wicked, and abandoned woman.*

a·base (ə bās′) *v.,* **a·based, a·bas·ing.** *v.t.* **1.** to lower in rank, condition, or esteem; humiliate; humble: *The proud man refused to abase himself.* [Old French *abaisser* to lower, going back to Latin *ad* to + Late Latin *bassus* low.] **—a·base′ment,** *n.*

a·bash (ə bash′) *v.t.* to make self-conscious or ashamed; disconcert. [Anglo-Norman *abaiss-,* form of Old French *esbaiss-* to astound, going back to Latin *ex* utterly + Late Latin *badāre* to gape (possibly imitative).] **—a·bash′ment,** *n.*

a·bate (ə bāt′) *v.,* **a·bat·ed, a·bat·ing.** *v.i.* to become less in force, intensity, or amount; subside: *The hurricane winds have abated.* *—v.t.* **1.** to lessen or reduce in force, intensity, or amount: *to abate a pain. Nothing could abate his rage.* **2.** *Law.* to put a stop to; nullify. [Old French *abat(t)re* to beat down, going back to Latin *ad* to + *battuere* to strike, beat.] **—a·bat′a·ble,** *adj.* **—a·bat′er,** *n.* **—Syn.** *v.i.* see **decrease.**

a·bate·ment (ə bāt′mənt) *n.* **1.** action or process of lessening or subsiding. **2.** *Law.* putting a stop to; annulment. **3.** amount by which something is abated; reduction.

ab·at·toir (ab′ə twär′) *n.* slaughterhouse. [French *abattoir,* from Old French *abat(t)re.* See ABATE.]

ab·ba·cy (ab′ə sē) *pl.,* **-cies.** *n.* office, term of office, or jurisdiction of an abbot. [Late Latin *abbātia,* from *abbās.* See ABBOT.]

Ab·bas (ä′bäs, ə bäs′) *n.* A.D. 566–652, uncle of Muhammad.

Ab·bas·side (ab′ə sīd′, ə bas′īd) *also,* **Ab·bas·sid** (ab′ə sid, ə bas′id). *n.* any of the caliphs of the dynasty that claimed descent from Abbas and who ruled the Muslim empire from A.D. 750 to 1258.

ab·bé (ăb′ā, ă bā′) *n. French.* **1.** member of the clergy, esp. a priest. ▲ used as a title of respect. **2.** abbot.

ab·bess (ăb′ĭs) *n.* female superior of a convent. [Old French *ab-(b)esse,* from Late Latin *abbātissa,* feminine of *abbās.* See ABBOT.]

ab·bey (ăb′ē) *pl.,* **-beys.** *n.* **1.a.** monastery under the rule of an abbot. **b.** convent under the rule of an abbess. **2.** church of an abbey. **3.** church or other building, as the residence of an abbot or abbess, that was originally part of an abbey. [Old French *abbaie* monastery, from Late Latin *abbātia,* abbacy, from *abbās.* See ABBOT.]

ab·bot (ăb′ət) *n.* male superior of a monastery. [Old English *abbad,* from Late Latin *abbās,* through Greek, from Aramaic *abbā* father.]

abbr., abbrev., abbreviation; abbreviated. Also, **abbrev.**

ab·bre·vi·ate (ə brē′vē āt′) **-at·ed, -at·ing.** *v.t.* **1.** to shorten (a word or phrase) so that one or more characters stand for the whole, as *Feb.* for *February, no.* for *number,* and *m.p.h.* for *miles per hour.* **2.** to reduce in length, size, or duration; shorten. [Latin *abbreviātus,* past participle of *abbreviāre* to shorten. Doublet of ABRIDGE.] —**ab·bre′vi·a′tor,** *n.*

ab·bre·vi·a·tion (ə brē′vē ā′shən) *n.* **1.** one or more letters representing the whole of a word or phrase. **2.** act of abbreviating; being abbreviated.

ABC (ā′bē′sē′) *also,* **ABC's.** *n.* **1.** the alphabet. **2.** the basic principles (of a subject); rudiments.

Ab·di·as (ăb dī′əs) *n.* in the Douay Bible, Obadiah.

ab·di·cate (ăb′də kāt′) **-cat·ed, -cat·ing.** *v.t.* to renounce or relinquish formally (power, rights, or responsibility). —*v.i.* to renounce or relinquish power or a position of power, as a throne; step down formally: *In 1936, King Edward VIII abdicated.* [Latin *abdicātus,* past participle of *abdicāre* to renounce.] —**ab′di·ca′tion, ab′di·ca′tor,** *n.*

ab·do·men (ăb′də mən, ăb dō′-) *n.* **1.** largest of the body cavities of a mammal, situated between the diaphragm and the pelvis, containing many vital organs such as the stomach, the intestines, the kidneys, and the liver; belly. **2.** corresponding body region or cavity in vertebrates lower than mammals. **3.** hindmost section of the body of an insect, spider, or crustacean, situated behind the thorax or cephalothorax. [Latin *abdōmen* belly.]

ab·dom·i·nal (ăb dom′ən əl) *adj.* of, in, on, or relating to the abdomen. —**ab·dom′i·nal·ly,** *adv.*

ab·duct (ăb dukt′) *v.t.* **1.** to carry off (someone) unlawfully by force or fraud; kidnap. **2.** to move (a digit or a limb) away from the body or body part to which the digit or limb is attached. [Latin *abductus,* past participle of *abdūcere* to lead away.] —**ab·duc′tion,** *n.* —**Syn. 1.** see kidnap.

ab·duc·tor (ăb duk′tər) *n.* **1.** one who abducts; kidnaper. **2.** muscle that abducts.

a·beam (ə bēm′) *adv.* **1.** alongside a ship, esp. directly opposite the middle of a ship's side. **2.** at right angles to a ship's keel.

a·bed (ə bĕd′) *adv.* in bed.

A·bel (ā′bəl) *n.* in the Old Testament, second son of Adam and Eve, killed by his older brother Cain.

Ab·é·lard, Peter (ăb′ə lärd′) 1079–1142, French philosopher, theologian, and teacher.

Ab·er·deen (ăb′ər dēn′) *n.* city on the east coast of central Scotland. Pop. (1968), 183,875.

ab·er·rant (ə bĕr′ənt, ăb′ər-) *adj.* **1.** deviating from that which is usual, normal, or correct. **2.** deviating from an ordinary or normal type; atypical: *an aberrant rock formation.* [Latin *aberrāns,* present participle of *aberrāre* to stray from.]

ab·er·ra·tion (ăb′ə rā′shən) *n.* **1.** deviation from the usual, normal, or correct course or mode of action. **2.** deviation from a normal or ordinary type; abnormal structure or development. **3.** slight mental disorder or lapse. **4.** failure of a lens or mirror to focus the light rays from a single point on an object at a corresponding single point on its image, causing the formation of a blurred or otherwise imperfect image. **5.** *Astronomy.* apparent displacement of a heavenly body caused by the joint effect of the earth's motion and the noninstantaneous transmission of light. [Latin *aberrātiō* a wandering.]

a·bet (ə bĕt′) *v.t.* **a·bet·ted, a·bet·ting.** to encourage or assist, esp. in wrongdoing. [Old French *abeter* to exite, arouse, from *a* to (from Latin *ad* to) + *beter* to bait (a bear), from Old Norse *beita* to cause to bite.] —**a·bet′ment, a·bet′tor;** *also,* **a·bet′ter,** *n.*

a·bey·ance (ə bā′əns) *n.* **1.** temporary inactivity or suspension: *Hold the matter in abeyance until later.* **2.** *Law.* state of being undetermined or unsettled, as of an estate without a legal heir. [Old French *abeance* suspension; literally, gaping at, from *abaer* to gape, going back to Latin *ad* to + Late Latin *badāre* to gape (possibly imitative).]

ab·hor (ăb hôr′) *v.t.* **-horred, -hor·ring.** to regard with repugnance, disgust, or hatred; loathe: *The pacifist abhorred all violence.* [Latin *abhorrēre* to shrink back, from *ab* from, away + *horrēre* to have one's hair stand on end, bristle.] —**ab·hor′rer,** *n.* —**Syn.** see hate.

ab·hor·rence (ăb hôr′əns, -hŏr′-) *n.* **1.** feeling of disgust, repugnance, or loathing. **2.** something repugnant or loathsome.

ab·hor·rent (ăb hôr′ənt, -hŏr′-) *adj.* **1.** causing disgust, repugnance, or loathing; detestable: *abhorrent criminal acts.* **2.** in opposition; contrary (with *to*): *a suggestion abhorrent to their principles.* **3.** feeling abhorrence (with *of*): *abhorrent of violence.* —**ab·hor′rent·ly,** *adv.*

a·bide (ə bīd′) **a·bode** or **a·bid·ed, a·bid·ing.** *v.i.* **1.** to continue to reside; dwell. **2.** to continue to exist; endure: *What was, and is, and will abide* (Wordsworth, 1819). **3.** to continue to stay; remain: *Abide with me from morn till eve* (Keble, 1827). **4. to abide by. a.** to comply with: *You must abide by the rules.* **b.** to live up to; carry out; fulfill: *John failed to abide by his promise.* —*v.t.* **1.** to put up with; bear patiently; tolerate: *The critic could not abide a bad performance.* ▲ used with the negative. **2.** *Archaic.* to await; wait for: *I will abide the coming of my lord* (Tennyson, 1859). [Old English *abīdan* to remain on.] —**a·bid′er,** *n.*

a·bid·ing (ə bī′ding) *adj.* continuing; enduring; permanent.

Ab·i·djan (ăb′i jän′) *n.* port city and capital of the Ivory Coast, in the southeastern part of the country. Pop., metropolitan area (1965), 282,000.

Ab·i·lene (ăb′ə lēn′) *n.* city in west-central Texas. Pop. (1970), 89,653.

a·bil·i·ty (ə bĭl′ə tē) *pl.,* **-ties.** *n.* **1.** power or capacity (to do or act): *the ability to walk, the ability to learn.* **2.** competence; skill: *He displayed great ability as a carpenter.* **3.** natural gift or endowment; talent: *His abilities were evident in the high quality of his musical compositions.* [Old French *ablete, (h)abilite* aptitude, from Latin *habilitās.*]

Syn. 3. Ability, talent, skill, aptitude refer to personal competence for doing something well. **Ability** indicates a proved and demonstrated power, innate or acquired, to do something well: *Dick shows a lot of ability in his work on automobile engines.* **Talent** indicates an innate power in a special area, as in one of the arts: *The award was usually given in recognition of talent.* **Skill** suggests proficiency and competence as a result of practice: *It is in writing sonnets that he best displays his poetic skill.* **Aptitude** implies both skill and inclination toward doing something: *Barbara has a definite aptitude for the life sciences.*

-ability *suffix* (used to form nouns) capability or likelihood of being or causing: *movability.*

ab in·i·ti·o (ăb′ i nish′ē ō′) *Latin.* from the beginning.

ab·ject (ăb′jekt, ăb jekt′) *adj.* **1.** utterly miserable; hopeless; humiliating; disheartening: *abject slavery.* **2.** low in character; servile; groveling: *an abject liar.* [Latin *abjectus,* past participle of *abicere* to throw away.] —**ab·jec′tion,** *n.* —**ab′ject·ly,** *adv.*

ab·jure (ăb joor′) **-jured, -jur·ing.** *v.t.* **1.** to renounce or give up on oath: *The traitor abjured all allegiance to the king.* **2.** to recant or retract (a belief or opinion); repudiate. [Latin *abjūrāre* to deny on oath.] —**ab′ju·ra′tion, ab·jur′er,** *n.*

abl., ablative.

ab·la·tive (ăb′lə tiv) *n.* **1.** grammatical case in Latin and certain other Indo-European languages that indicates movement, direction, source, cause, and the like. **2.** word or construction in this case. —*adj.* of, relating to, or designating this case. [Latin *ablātīvus* this case, from *ablātus* taken away; with reference to its frequent use to express something taken away.]

a·blaze (ə blāz′) *adv.* on fire. —*adj.* **1.** in flames. **2.** brilliantly lit; gleaming: *a Christmas tree ablaze with colored lights.* **3.** in a state of excitement, anger, or desire: *He was ablaze with jealousy.*

a·ble (ā′bəl) **a·bler, a·blest.** *adj.* **1.** having sufficient power, skill, or qualifications: *able to read and write.* **2.** having or showing unusual competence or intelligence; talented; skillful: *an able politician, an able performance.* [Old French *able,* from Latin *habilis* easy to handle, apt, skillful.] —**a′bly,** *adv.*

Syn. 1. Able, capable, competent refer to personal faculties or powers. **Able** indicates a power to accomplish something, without reference to efficiency: *He is able to run several miles.* **Capable** suggests some potential force, either demonstrated already or merely latent: *He is capable of running the mile in less than four minutes.* **Competent** points to some efficiency already made manifest: *She is a competent dressmaker.*

-able *suffix* **1.** (used to form adjectives from verbs) **a.** able to or capable of being: *eatable, tolerable.* **b.** worthy of being: *laudable, commendable, believable.* **c.** likely to: *perishable.* **2.** (used to form adjectives from nouns) **a.** worthy of or able to cause: *objectionable, comfortable.* **b.** tending toward: *peaceable.* [French *-able,* from Latin *-ābilis.*]

a·ble-bod·ied (ā′bəl bŏd′ēd) *adj.* having a strong, healthy body; capable of doing physical work.

able-bodied seaman, experienced and skilled sailor.

a·bloom (ə bloom′) *adj.* in bloom; flowering.

ab·lu·tion (ə bloo′shən) *n.* **1.** *also,* **ablutions.** a washing or cleansing, esp. of one's body: *one's morning ablutions.* **2.a.** ceremonial washing as part of a religious rite or observance. **b.** liquid used for this. [Latin *ablūtiō* a washing off.]

ab·ne·gate (ăb′nə gāt′) **-gat·ed, -gat·ing.** *v.t.* to deny (something) to oneself; renounce. [Latin *abnegātus,* past participle of *abnegāre* to refuse, deny.] —**ab′ne·ga′tion, ab′ne·ga′tor,** *n.*

ăt; āpe; cär; end; mē; ĭt; īce; hot; ōld; fôrk; wood; fōōl; oil; out; up; ūse; turn; sing; thin; this; zh in treasure; ə in ago, taken, pencil, lemon, circus.

ab·nor·mal (ab nôr′məl) *adj.* deviating markedly from the normal, usual, or average; not conforming to a type or standard; irregular: *abnormal structure of a plant, an abnormal situation.* [Latin *abnōrmis* irregular, from *ab* away + *nōrma* carpenter's square, rule.] —**ab·nor′mal·ly**, *adv.*

ab·nor·mal·i·ty (ab′nôr mal′ə tē) *pl.*, **-ties.** *n.* **1.** state or quality of being abnormal. **2.** that which is abnormal.

a·board (ə bôrd′) *adv.* **1.** in, on, or into a ship, train, bus, or airplane. **2.** *Nautical.* alongside (of a ship or shore). **3. all aboard.** get in, get on. ▲ call used to warn passengers that a bus or train is about to depart. —*prep.* in, on, or into (a ship, train, or other vehicle).

a·bode (ə bōd′) *n.* place where one lives; dwelling; home. [Middle English *abad* remaining, stay, from *abiden* to abide.]

a·bol·ish (ə bol′ish) *v.t.* to put an end to; do away with completely: *to abolish poverty.* [French *aboliss-*, a stem of *abolir*, from Latin *abolēre* to destroy.] —**a·bol′ish·a·ble**, *adj.* —**a·bol′ish·er, a·bol′ish·ment**, *n.*
Syn. Abolish, annihilate, exterminate refer to making an end of something. **Abolish** applies more to human usages, as laws, traditions, customs, and ideas, than to physical things: *Slavery was abolished in the British Empire in 1807.* **Annihilate** indicates the complete destruction of the object of the verb; it means to wipe out beyond hope of being revived: *One cannot really conceive of the human race being annihilated.* **Exterminate** also indicates complete destruction, but is usually used of things considered to be bad: *They succeeded in their effort to exterminate the termites.*

ab·o·li·tion (ab′ə lish′ən) *n.* **1.** act or process of abolishing; being abolished. **2.** the abolishing of Negro slavery in the United States. [Latin *abolitiō* an annulling.]

ab·o·li·tion·ism (ab′ə lish′-ə niz′əm) *n.* principles or measures of those who advocated the abolition of Negro slavery in the United States. —**ab′o·li′tion·ist**, *n.*

ab·o·ma·sum (ab′ə mā′səm) *pl.*, **-sa.** *n.* the fourth and true digestive stomach of a cud-chewing animal, as a cow or camel. [Modern Latin *abomasum*, from Latin *ab* away from + *omasum* bullock's tripe.] —**ab′o·ma′sal**, *adj.*

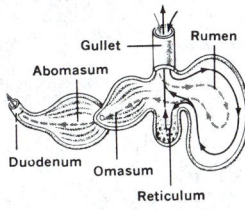

Abomasum of a cow

A-bomb (ā′bom′) *n.* atomic bomb. —*v.t.* to attack with an atomic bomb.

a·bom·i·na·ble (ə bom′ə nəbəl) *adj.* **1.** disgusting; loathsome; detestable: *abominable crimes.* **2.** very unpleasant, disagreeable, or distasteful: *abominable manners.* [French *abominable*, from Latin *abōminā*bilis abhorrent, from Latin *abōmināri* to abhor. See ABOMINATE.] —**a·bom′i·na·bly**, *adv.*

abominable snowman, legendary creature of the Himalayas, variously believed to resemble a bear, ape, or primitive man. Also, **yet′i.**

a·bom·i·nate (ə bom′ə nāt′) -nat·ed, -nat·ing. *v.t.* **1.** to feel disgust, loathing, or hatred for; abhor; detest. **2.** to dislike strongly. [Latin *abōminātus*, past participle of *abōmināri* literally, to turn away from a bad omen.] —**a·bom′i·na′tor**, *n.*

a·bom·i·na·tion (ə bom′ə nā′shən) *n.* **1.** that which is disgusting or loathsome; detestable action or practice: *Cruelty to animals is an abomination to her.* **2.** intense disgust, hatred, or loathing.

ab·o·rig·i·nal (ab′ə rij′ən əl) *adj.* **1.** existing in a place from the earliest known time; native; indigenous: *aboriginal people.* **2.** of, relating to, or characteristic of aborigines; primitive: *The boomerang was an aboriginal weapon.* —*n.* an aboriginal person, plant, or animal.

ab·o·rig·i·ne (ab′ə rij′ə nē) *n.* **1.** one of the original or earliest known inhabitants of a country. **2.** any one of the original flora and fauna of a region. [Latin *aborigines* original inhabitants of a country, from *ab origine* from the beginning.]

a·bort (ə bôrt′) *v.i.* **1.** to give birth before the fetus is able to live; miscarry. **2.** to terminate something, as a mission or project, before completion: *The pilots were given orders to abort.* —*v.t.* **1.** to cause an abortion of. **2.** to terminate before completion: *The space shot was aborted because of bad weather.* [Latin *abortus*, past participle of *aborīrī* to miscarry, disappear.]

a·bor·tion (ə bôr′shən) *n.* **1.** artificially induced termination of a pregnancy before a fetus is viable. **2.** spontaneous expulsion of a nonviable fetus in the early phases of pregnancy, before the fetus has become well formed, roughly before the fourth month. **3.** product of a prematurely terminated pregnancy. **4.** something that fails to succeed: *His first novel was an abortion.*

a·bor·tion·ist (ə bôr′shə nist) *n.* person who performs an abortion or abortions, esp. one who does so illegally.

a·bor·tive (ə bôr′tiv) *adj.* **1.** failing to succeed; fruitless: *Until 1953*

all attempts to climb Mount Everest were abortive. **2.** *Medicine.* **a.** causing an abortion: *abortive drugs.* **b.** checking the progress of a disease. —**a·bor′tive·ly**, *adv.* —**a·bor′tive·ness**, *n.*

A·bou·kir (ä′boo kēr′) Abukir.

a·bound (ə bound′) *v.i.* **1.** to exist in great quantity or large numbers; be plentiful: *Buffalo used to abound on the Western plains.* **2. to abound in.** to be rich in: *Some languages abound in idioms.* **3. to abound with.** to be filled with; teem with: *The jungle abounds with wild game.* [Old French *abonder*, from Latin *abundāre* to overflow, going back to Latin *ab* from + *unda* wave.]

a·bout (ə bout′) *prep.* **1.** in regard to; of; concerning: *We know about the plan.* **2.** attached to as an attribute; connected with: *He has a certain way about him.* **3.** somewhat near; in the vicinity of: *Autograph-seekers stood about the stage door.* **4.** on every side of; around: *A moat runs about the castle.* **5.** on or near (one's person); on hand; with: *He kept his wits about him.* **6.** on the point of; ready (with the infinitive): *about to jump from the window.* **7.** around or over the parts of; here and there in or on: *Wind scattered the leaves about the yard.* **8.** concerned or occupied with: *to go about one's business.* —*adv.* **1.** approximately; nearly: *about a thousand people in the crowd.* **2.** all but; almost: *We are about ready to go.* **3.** in several directions; all around: *to look about.* **4.** here and there; to and fro: *to wander about.* **5.** in or to the opposite direction or reversed position: *Hearing her name, she turned about.* **6.** in rotation or succession. —*adj.* on the move; astir: *He was up and about in two days.* [Old English *onbūtan, ābūtan* on the outside of, around.]

a·bout-face (ə bout′fās′) *n.* **1.** action of turning around and facing the opposite direction. **2.** command to perform this action. **3.** sudden reversal, as of attitude or opinion. —*v.i.*, **-faced, -fac·ing.** to execute an about-face.

a·bove (ə buv′) *adv.* **1.** in, at, or to a higher place; overhead: *Stars glittered above.* **2.** in heaven: *He prayed to the Lord above.* **3.** in an earlier part of a book or other piece of writing: *See the examples given above.* ▲ hyphenated in combinations as in *above-mentioned* and *above-cited.* **4.** in a higher rank or position: *Take your complaint to the powers above.* —*prep.* **1.** on top of; over: *Clouds hung above the water.* **2.** higher than; rising beyond: *a voice heard above the roar, a building towering above the city.* **3.** superior to the influence of; not liable to stoop to: *He was above such pettiness.* **4.** superior to in rank, position, degree, or quality: *to stand above the crowd.* **5.** in preference to: *I chose this above the others.* **6.** more than; in excess of: *Anything above fifty dollars will be too expensive.* **7.** farther north than. —*adj.* placed, written, or mentioned earlier: *the above explanation.* —*n.* **the above.** that which is placed, written, or mentioned earlier: *The above will be used to illustrate the theory.* [Old English *ābūfan* over, higher up, earlier.]

a·bove·board (ə buv′bôrd′) *adv., adj.* without deception, dishonesty, or concealment: *The controversy was resolved fairly because everyone acted aboveboard. All his dealings were open and aboveboard.* [ABOVE + BOARD; from playing cards with the hands above the table to prevent cheating by changing cards under the table.]

ab o·vo (ab ō′vō) *Latin.* from the beginning; literally, from the egg.

abp., archbishop.

ab·ra·ca·dab·ra (ab′rə kə dab′rə) *n.* **1.** secret word once supposed to have magic power when written in a triangular arrangement or used in incantations. **2.** any magical spell or incantation. **3.** gibberish; jargon. [Late Latin *abracadabra* a magic word, transliteration of Greek *abrasadabra* a magic word.]

a·brade (ə brād′) **a·brad·ed, a·brad·ing.** *v.t.* to wear away by friction; rub or scrape off. [Latin *abrādere*, from *ab* away + *rādere* to scrape off.]

A·bra·ham (ā′brə ham′, -həm) *n.* patriarch and ancestor of the Hebrew people.

a·bra·sion (ə brā′zhən) *n.* **1.** wearing or rubbing off or away by friction. **2.** abraded area or spot: *painful skin abrasions caused by a fall.* [Medieval Latin *abrasio* a scraping off, going back to Latin *abrādere* to scrape off.]

a·bra·sive (ə brā′siv, -ziv) *n.* any of a group of natural or synthetic substances used for cleaning, grinding, or polishing. Corundum, emery, and sand are abrasives. —*adj.* **1.** causing or capable of causing abrasion. **2.** causing irritation or annoyance; provoking: *abrasive humor.*

a·breast (ə brest′) *adv., adj.* **1.** side by side and facing or moving in the same direction; parallel: *They walked two abreast.* **2. abreast of (or with).** **a.** advancing equally with; up with: *The reporter must keep abreast of new developments.* **b.** parallel to or alongside of: *The ship was abreast of the shore.*

a·bridge (ə brij′) **a·bridged, a·bridg·ing.** *v.t.* **1.** to shorten (as a written work) by leaving out less important parts; condense. **2.** to lessen or curtail: *The Magna Carta abridged the king's powers.* **3.** *Archaic.* to deprive (with *of*). [Old French *abregier* to shorten, from Latin *abbreviāre.* Doublet of ABBREVIATE.] —**a·bridg′a·ble;** also, **a·bridge′a·ble**, *adj.*

at; āpe; cär; end; mē; it; īce; hot; ōld; fôrk; wood; fōōl; oil; out; up; ūse; turn; sing; thin; this; zh in treasure; ə in ago, taken, pencil, lemon, circus.

3

a·bridg·ment (ə brij′mənt) *also*, **a·bridge·ment**. *n.* **1.** act of abridging; being abridged. **2.** shortened version of a work; condensation: *He read an abridgment of the long novel.*

a·broad (ə brôd′) *adv.* **1.** out of one's country; in or into foreign lands: *to travel abroad.* **2.** in circulation; current; prevalent: *Rumors of victory were abroad.* **3.** out of one's house or abode; out of doors: *that domestic sort which never stirs abroad at all* (Sheridan, 1777). **4.** over a large area; far and wide.

ab·ro·gate (ab′rə gāt′) -gat·ed, -gat·ing. *v.t.* to abolish or repeal by authority; annul: *to abrogate a law.* [Latin *abrogātus*, past participle of *abrogāre* to repeal.] —**ab′ro·ga′tion, ab′ro·ga′tor,** *n.*

a·brupt (ə brupt′) *adj.* **1.** sudden; unexpected; hasty: *an abrupt change of heart, an abrupt departure.* **2.** curt or unceremonious; brusque: *an abrupt manner.* **3.** steep; precipitous: *an abrupt descent.* **4.** lacking continuity or smooth transitions; disconnected: *an abrupt literary style.* [Latin *abruptus*, past participle of *abrumpere* to break off.] —**a·brupt′ly,** *adv.* —**a·brupt′ness,** *n.*

Syn. 2. Abrupt, brusque, curt mean short and without embellishment in speech or conduct. **Abrupt** suggests directness with no time or effort wasted: *His abrupt replies indicated that an explanation of his actions would have to be forced from him.* **Brusque** suggests lack of social polish: *His reply was so brusque as to cause her to turn away.* **Curt** suggests discourtesy in its abruptness: *His curt note of acknowledgment was all the reply I ever got.*

abs-, form of **ab-**¹ before *c* and *t*, as in *abscond, abstract.*

Ab·sa·lom (ab′sə ləm) *n.* in the Old Testament, favorite son of David who was killed after waging a war of rebellion against his father.

ab·scess (ab′ses) *n.* localized collection of pus resulting from infection in the tissues of some part of the body. [Latin *abscessus* literally, a going away.] —**ab′scessed,** *adj.*

ab·scis·sa (ab sis′ə) *pl.*, **-scis·sas** or **-scis·sae** (-sis′ē). *n.* **1.** on a line graph, the distance of a point from the vertical axis measured parallel to the horizontal axis, used to define the point in the system of Cartesian coordinates. Distinguished from **ordinate.** **2.** line, number, or algebraic expression representing this distance. [Latin *(linea) abscissa* (line) cut off, from *abscindere* to cut off.]

ab·scond (ab skond′) *v.i.* to flee secretly and conceal oneself, esp. to avoid the law: *The treasurer absconded with the club's funds.* [Latin *abscondere* to hide, put away.] —**ab·scond′er,** *n.*

ab·sence (ab′səns) *n.* **1.** being away or not present. **2.** period of being away: *an absence of a year.* **3.** being without; lack: *Black is the absence of color.*

absence of mind, absent-mindedness.

ab·sent (*adj.*, ab′sənt; *v.*, ab sent′) *adj.* **1.** not in a certain place at a given time; not present; away: *She was absent because of illness.* **2.** nonexistent; lacking. **3.** inattentive; preoccupied: *an absent expression on her face.* —*v.t.* to take or keep (oneself) away: *He absented himself from the conference.* [French *absent* away, from Latin *absēns* being away, present participle of *abesse* to be away.]

ab·sen·tee (ab′sən tē′) *n.* one who is absent. —*adj.* designating an absentee; by an absentee: *absentee ownership.*

absentee ballot, ballot that enables a voter who cannot be present at the polls to vote by mail.

ab·sen·tee·ism (ab′sən tē′iz′əm) *n.* habitual or repeated absence, as from work or school.

absentee landlord, one who owns land or buildings in a place or country in which he does not reside.

ab·sent·ly (ab′sənt lē) *adv.* absent-mindedly; inattentively.

ab·sent-mind·ed (ab′sənt mīn′did) *adj.* **1.** unaware of one's immediate surroundings or actions; lost in thought; preoccupied. **2.** chronically forgetful. —**ab′sent-mind′ed·ly,** *adv.* —**ab′sent-mind′ed·ness,** *n.*

ab·sinthe (ab′sinth) *also*, **ab·sinth.** *n.* bitter, green liqueur with a licorice taste, flavored with wormwood and anise. Excessive drinking of absinthe may damage nerve centers, causing delirium and insanity. [French *absinthe*, through Latin, from Greek *apsinthion* wormwood.]

ab·so·lute (ab′sə lōōt′) *adj.* **1.** complete; utter: *absolute purity.* **2.** free from all restrictions or qualifications; unconditional: *absolute power.* **3.** certain; infallible; positive: *absolute proof.* **4.** having power that is not limited by constitutional or other restraints; despotic; arbitrary: *absolute monarchy, absolute ruler.* **5.** without reference to anything else; not relative or comparative: *the absolute merits of the case.* **6.** self-existent or self-evident; ultimate: *an absolute principle.* **7.** *Grammar.* **a.** not connected to the rest of the sentence by the usual relations of syntax. In the sentence *It being Sunday, we slept late,* the phrase *It being Sunday* is an absolute construction. **b.** (of a verb that is usually

transitive) having an object implied but not expressed. In the sentence *The violinist played well,* the word *played* is an absolute verb. **c.** (of an adjective or pronoun) standing alone with the noun understood but not stated. In the phrase *his selection and mine,* the word *mine* is an absolute pronoun. **8.a.** of or relating to absolute temperature. **b.** relating to or derived from the fundamental notions or units of time, space, and mass: *absolute units of velocity.* —*n.* **1. the Absolute.** the ultimate reality thought of as a single, all-inclusive system of being. **2.** something that exists independently of all relations and conditions; that which has reality or validity in and of itself. [Latin *absolūtus,* past participle of *absolvere* to loosen, free.] —**ab′so·lute′ness,** *n.*

absolute alcohol, ethyl alcohol that is at least ninety-nine percent pure.

ab·so·lute·ly (ab′sə lōōt′lē, ab′sə lōōt′-) *adv.* **1.** to the fullest extent or highest degree; completely: *absolutely beautiful.* **2.** positively; definitely: *Are you absolutely sure?*

absolute pitch 1. pitch of a tone as determined by its rate of vibration. **2.** ability to identify the pitch of any tone heard, or to sing a given tone without reference to any previously sounded pitch.

absolute temperature, temperature measured from absolute zero.

absolute value, positive value of a real number. The absolute value of negative 3, written |−3|, is 3.

absolute zero, theoretical temperature at which substances would have no molecular motion and no heat. Absolute zero is zero on the Kelvin temperature scale and is equal to −273.15 degrees centigrade or −459.67 degrees Fahrenheit.

ab·so·lu·tion (ab′sə lōō′shən) *n.* **1.a.** formal remission of sins and accompanying penalties, esp. as pronounced by a priest in the sacrament of penance. **b.** formula declaring this remission. **2.** release or freedom from obligation, guilt, or penalty.

ab·so·lut·ism (ab′sə lōō tiz′əm) *n.* system or principles of government in which the power of the ruler is unlimited; despotism. —**ab′so·lut′ist,** *n., adj.* —**ab′so·lu·tis′tic,** *adj.*

ab·solve (ab zolv′, -solv′) -solved, -solv·ing. *v.t.* **1.** to free from guilt or blame: *His confession had the effect of absolving all the other suspects.* **2.** to set (someone) free, as from an obligation, duty, or responsibility. **3.** to give absolution to: *The priest absolved the penitent.* [Latin *absolvere* to loosen, free. Doublet of ASSOIL.]

Syn. 1. Absolve, exonerate, acquit refer to a freeing from blame. **Absolve** suggests the lifting of a charge or of the burden of guilt: *If he reports the accident, he is absolved of more serious charges, though he may still be accused of negligence.* **Exonerate** implies the removal of a charge or burden so as to eliminate it completely: *He was exonerated when the real thief confessed.* **Acquit** indicates that some specific charge has failed because of lack of proof: *After a short trial, he was acquitted by the jury.*

ab·sorb (ab sôrb′, -zôrb′) *v.t.* **1.** to soak up (liquid): *A sponge absorbs water.* **2.** to engage completely: *The book absorbed his attention.* **3.** to take in and incorporate: *The Roman Empire absorbed many territories.* **4.** to take up and retain (energy) without reflection or echo: *Acoustic tile absorbs sound.* **5.** to take up (a substance) by chemical or molecular action: *Water absorbs oxygen.* [Latin *absorbēre* to suck up, swallow up.] —**ab·sorb′a·bil′i·ty, ab·sorb′er,** *n.* —**ab·sorb′a·ble,** *adj.*

Syn. 1. Absorb, assimilate mean to take in something. **Absorb** refers to the process of taking in and retaining something thoroughly and quickly: *A blotter absorbs ink.* **Assimilate** refers to a slower process of converting what is absorbed into an essential part of the substance or system: *Vitamin pills are easily assimilated by the body.*

ab·sorbed (ab sôrbd′, -zôrbd′) *adj.* entirely engrossed; preoccupied; rapt: *an absorbed look.*

ab·sorb·ent (ab sôr′bənt, -zôr′-) *adj.* absorbing or capable of absorbing: *absorbent cotton.* —*n.* material that absorbs: *Blotting paper is an absorbent.* —**ab·sor′ben·cy,** *n.*

ab·sorb·ing (ab sôr′bing, -zôr′-) *adj.* very interesting; engrossing: *an absorbing play.* —**ab·sorb′ing·ly,** *adv.* —**Syn. see interesting.**

ab·sorp·tion (ab sôrp′shən, -zôrp′-) *n.* **1.** act or process of absorbing; being absorbed. **2.** entire engrossment or engagement: *absorption in his work.* **3.** process by which a substance, as a gas or liquid, is taken up and made a part of another substance by chemical or molecular action. In absorption the substance taken up is distributed throughout the material or substance that receives it. See **adsorption** for illustration. **4.** process by which energy is received by a substance without reflection or echo: *the absorption of light rays.* **5.** process by which digested proteins and carbohydrates are taken into the blood capillaries and digested fats are taken into the lymphatics. [Latin *absorptiō* a swallowing.] —**ab·sorp′tive,** *adj.*

ab·stain (ab stān′) *v.i.* **1.** to hold oneself back; refrain voluntarily (with *from*): *A teetotaler abstains from drink.* **2.** to refrain voluntarily from voting: *In the UN voting, three neutral countries abstained.* [Middle French *abstenir* to refrain from, from Latin *abstinēre* to withhold, from *abs* from + *tenēre* to hold.] —**ab·stain′er,** *n.*

at; āpe; cär; end; mē; it; īce; hot; ōld; fôrk; wood; fōōl; oil; out; up; ūse; turn; sing; thin; this; zh in treasure; ə in ago, taken, pencil, lemon, circus.

ab·ste·mi·ous (ab stē′mē əs) *adj.* moderate or sparing, esp. in the use of food and drink. [Latin *abstēmius,* from *abs* away from + *tēmētum* intoxicating drink.] **—ab·ste′mi·ous·ly,** *adv.* **—ab·ste′mi·ous·ness,** *n.*

ab·sten·tion (ab sten′shən) *n.* act or practice of abstaining. [Late Latin *abstentiō* holding back.] **—ab·sten′tious,** *adj.*

ab·sti·nence (ab′stə nəns) *n.* **1.** act or practice of abstaining from the indulgence of appetites or pleasures. **2.** abstention for religious reasons from certain kinds of food or drink, esp. in observance of specified holy days. **3.** practice of abstaining from alcoholic beverages. **4.** self-denial; forbearance. [Latin *abstinentia* self-restraint.] **—ab′sti·nent,** *adj.*

ab·stract (*adj.* ab′strakt, ab strakt′; *v., defs. 1, 3, 4, 5* ab strakt′, *def. 2* ab′strakt; *n.,* ab′strakt) *adj.* **1.** considered apart from matter, material objects, or particular examples; not concrete: *the abstract concepts of geometry.* **2.** expressing a quality or attribute without relation to a particular object or example. *Goodness* and *purity* are abstract nouns. **3.** theoretical or ideal, as distinguished from real or practical: *He was motivated by an abstract sense of duty.* **4.** difficult to understand; abstruse. **5.** of, relating to, or characteristic of a style in the arts that does not imitate reality directly, but uses lines, geometric forms, and colors to express emotion or an aesthetic idea. *—v.t.* **1.** to isolate (a quality or attribute) from particular objects or instances; derive as a general idea from a specific instance or group of instances: *to abstract the common qualities of mankind from a group of individuals, to abstract the notion of time.* **2.** to make an abstract of; summarize: *The author abstracted his book.* **3.** to take away secretly or dishonestly; purloin. **4.** to withdraw or divert the attention of. **5.** to remove; take away: *to abstract water from a solution. —n.* **1.** summary; epitome. **2.** that which concentrates in itself the essential qualities of something more extensive or more general; essence: *An individual is an abstract of humanity.* **3.** that which is abstracted; abstract idea or term. **4. in the abstract.** without reference to the concrete; theoretically rather than practically: *The wealthy know poverty only in the abstract.* [Latin *abstractus,* past participle of *abstrahere* to draw away, from *abs* away from + *trahere* to draw.] **—ab·stract′ly,** *adv.* **—ab·stract′ness,** *n.*

Syn. *n.* **1. Abstract, abridgment, epitome, summary** denote condensation of a larger work. **Abstract** denotes a condensed statement of the substantial features of a text: *The journal contained abstracts of articles on medicine.* **Abridgment** suggests a reduction in compass by omitting the less important parts without change in the style or manner of the original: *The concise dictionary is an abridgment of the desk dictionary.* **Epitome** suggests a miniature version that distills the essence of a large work: *The Nicene Creed is an epitome of the Gospels.* **Summary** is an organized but skeletal presentation or recapitulation of the outlines of a text, often as a preliminary aid to a more detailed study: *Every chapter was preceded by a summary of its contents.*

ab·stract·ed (ab strak′tid) *adj.* lost in thought; preoccupied. **—ab·stract′ed·ly,** *adv.* **—ab·stract′ed·ness,** *n.*

abstract expressionism, nonrepresentational style of painting, first developed in the United States around 1945, characterized esp. by the spontaneous and impulsive application of paint and the free use of accidental effects.

ab·strac·tion (ab strak′shən) *n.* **1.** process of isolating an attribute or quality from particular objects or instances; formation of a general concept from specific instances. **2.** concept thus formed; abstract idea: *The idea of redness is an abstraction.* **3.** state of being lost in thought; preoccupation. **4.** work of art that is partly or totally abstract. **5.** act of withdrawing or removing; separation: *The abstraction of heat from a surface will make that surface cold.*

ab·struse (ab strōōs′) *adj.* hard to understand; recondite. [Latin *abstrūsus,* past participle of *abstrūdere* to thrust away, conceal.] **—ab·struse′ly,** *adv.* **—ab·struse′ness,** *n.*

ab·surd (ab surd′, -zurd′) *adj.* contrary to reason, common sense, or truth; irrational; ridiculous. [Latin *absurdus* out of tune, senseless.] **—ab·surd′ly,** *adv.* **—ab·surd′ness,** *n.*

ab·surd·i·ty (ab sur′də tē, -zur′-) *pl.,* **-ties.** *n.* **1.** state or quality of being absurd. **2.** something absurd: *the absurdity of our situation.* **2.** something absurd: *the absurdities he uttered at dinner.*

A·bu·kir (ä′bōō kēr′) also, **A·bou·kir.** *n.* bay in northern Egypt where the British, under Admiral Nelson, defeated the French in 1798.

a·bun·dance (ə bun′dəns) *n.* **1.** plentiful or overflowing supply; number or amount that is more than enough: *abundance of food.* **2.** wealth; affluence. **3.** overflowing fullness: *abundance of heart.* [Old French *abundance* plenty, from Latin *abundantia,* from *abundāns* overflowing, going back to *ab* from + *unda* wave.]

a·bun·dant (ə bun′dənt) *adj.* **1.** more than sufficient; plentiful: *an abundant supply.* **2. abundant in,** possessing in great quantity: *abundant in goodness and truth* (Exodus 24:6). **—a·bun′dant·ly,** *adv.*

Syn. **1. Abundant, plentiful, ample, copious** signify a quantity more than sufficient. **Abundant** implies a very large amount and often approaches the idea of overflow and profusion: *The rivers and forests of the New World were abundant with fish and game.* **Plentiful** suggests

a more than adequate quantity: *They stacked up a plentiful supply of firewood.* **Ample** indicates fullness and generosity in terms of some requirement: *The amount of the check is ample payment for the work they did.* **Copious** connotes a supply approaching the point of overabundance: *The diary provided copious information about life at the court.*

a·buse (*v.,* ə būz′; *n.,* ə būs′) **a·bused, a·bus·ing.** *v.t.* **1.** to use improperly or wrongly; misuse: *to abuse rights or privileges.* **2.** to hurt by treating wrongly; mistreat; injure: *a camp where the prisoners were abused.* **3.** to attack with coarse or insulting language; revile. *—n.* **1.** wrong or improper use; misuse: *abuse of power.* **2.** ill-treatment; injury: *Our car has taken much abuse.* **3.** corrupt practice or custom: *the abuses of tyranny.* **4.** insulting, rude, or maligning language. [Old French *abuser* to misuse, from Latin *abūsus,* past participle of *abūtī* to use up, misuse.] **—a·bus′er,** *n.*

a·bu·sive (ə bū′siv, -ziv) *adj.* **1.** characterized by, containing, or using verbal abuse: *an abusive slander, an abusive article.* **2.** wrongly or improperly used; corrupt: *an abusive exercise of power.* **3.** involving ill-treatment; injurious: *Abusive handling can ruin the camera.* **—a·bu′sive·ly,** *adv.* **—a·bu′sive·ness,** *n.*

a·but (ə but′) **a·but·ted, a·but·ting.** *v.i.* to touch at one end or side; adjoin; border (with *on, upon,* to or *against*): *Our land abuts on the forest. The two buildings abut.* [Old French *abouter* to border on, from *a* to (from Latin *ad* to) + *bouter* to thrust (of Germanic origin).]

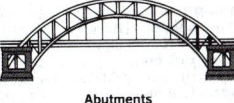
Abutments

a·but·ment (ə but′mənt) *n.* **1.** supporting part designed to withstand thrust or lateral pressure, as one of the end supports of an arch or bridge or the part of a bridge pier against which the water flows. **2.** that which abuts on something else. **3.** point or place where abutting parts meet; junction. **4.** act of abutting.

a·bysm (ə biz′əm) *n.* *Archaic.* abyss. [Old French *abisme,* going back to Latin *abyssus.* See ABYSS.]

a·bys·mal (ə biz′məl) *adj.* **1.** extremely deep; immeasurable; fathomless: *abysmal sorrow.* **2.** wretched; miserable; dreary: *living under abysmal conditions. We had an abysmal time.* **—a·bys′mal·ly,** *adv.*

a·byss (ə bis′) *n.* **1.** immeasurably deep or bottomless chasm. **2.** anything unfathomable or immeasurable: *the abyss of time.* [Latin *abyssus* bottomless pit, from Greek *abyssos* bottomless.]

Ab·ys·sin·i·a (ab′ə sin′ē ə) *n.* Ethiopia. **—Ab′ys·sin′i·an,** *adj., n.*

ac-, form of **ad-** before *c* and *q,* as in *accent, acquire.*

-ac *suffix* **1.** affected by or having: *hypochondriac.* **2.** of, relating to, or characteristic of: *cardiac, elegiac.*

Ac, actinium.

AC, alternating current.

a·ca·cia (ə kā′shə) *n.* **1.** any of a group of trees or shrubs, genus *Acacia,* of the mimosa family, found in warm regions throughout the world, many of which bear delicate, fernlike leaves and clusters of white, yellow, or orange flowers. Some species yield useful products, such as gum arabic or tannic acid. **2.** any of several other trees, esp. certain locusts. **3.** gum arabic. [Latin *acācia* acacia tree, from Greek *akakiā* thorny Egyptian acacia, from *akis* thorn.]

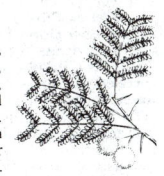
Acacia leaves and flowers

ac·a·deme (ak′ə dēm′) *n.* **1.** academic world; scholarly life. **2. Academe.** Plato's Academy. **3. Archaic.** school.

ac·a·dem·ic (ak′ə dem′ik) *adj.* **1.** of or relating to an academy or institution of higher education or to advanced study in general; scholarly: *academic pursuits, academic robes.* **2.** giving or relating to liberal or general education, esp. to that which prepares the student for college. Distinguished from **commercial, technical,** or **vocational. 3.** without practical application; theoretical; speculative. *What came before time?* is an academic question. **4.** conforming to set rules and traditions; conventional: *an academic style of painting.* Also, **ac′a·dem′i·cal. —ac′a·dem′i·cal·ly,** *adv.*

ac·a·dem·i·cals (ak′ə dem′i kəlz) *n.,pl.* academic robes; cap and gown.

academic freedom, freedom of persons at educational institutions to study, teach, and discuss any subject without fear of interference or dismissal.

a·cad·e·mi·cian (ə kad′ə mish′ən, ak′ə də-) *n.* **1.** member of an academy for advancing literature, science, or the arts. **2.** one who rigidly adheres to the formalized rules or traditions of a school of thought.

a·cad·e·my (ə kad′ə mē) *pl.,* **-mies.** *n.* **1.** private secondary school. **2.** school for instruction in a particular subject: *a military academy, an academy of music.* **3.** institution of higher learning. **4.** society or institution for the cultivation and advancement of literature, science, or the arts. **5. the Academy. a.** place for sports and leisure activities near ancient Athens, at which Plato established his school. **b.** this school

itself. **c.** Plato and his followers. **d.** the philosophy taught at this school. [French *académie*, going back to Greek *akadēmeia* Plato's Academy, from *Akadēmos* Greek mythological hero, whose shrine became the site of the Academy.]

A·ca·di·a (ə kā′dē ə) *n.* former French colony in eastern Canada, consisting of the present Maritime Provinces. —**A·ca′di·an,** *adj., n.*

a·can·thus (ə kan′thəs) *pl.* **-thus·es** or **-thi** (-thī). *n.* **1.** any of a group of thistlelike plants, genus *Acanthus,* native to the Mediterranean region, Africa, and Asia, bearing large spiny or sharply notched leaves and clusters of pink, red, white, or purple flowers. **2.** conventionalized, ornamental representation of the acanthus leaf, used on the capitals of Corinthian columns. The Greeks patterned their decoration after the spiny leaves of the *A. spinosus;* the Romans copied the fuller leaves of the *A. mollis.* [Latin *acanthus* acanthus plant, from Greek *akanthos,* from *akantha* thorn.]

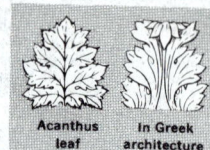

Acanthus leaf / In Greek architecture

Acanthus

a cap·pel·la (ä′ kə pel′ə) (of vocal music) without instrumental accompaniment. [Italian *a cappella* (music) in the chapel style, from Latin *ad* to + Late Latin *cappella* cloak. See CHAPEL.]

A·ca·pul·co (ä′kə pool′kō, ä′kä pool′kō) *n.* resort city on the southwestern coast of Mexico. Pop. (1960), 49,149.

acc. 1. accusative. **2.** account.

Ac·cad (ak′ad, ä′käd) Akkad.

ac·cede (ak sēd′) **-ced·ed, -ced·ing.** *v.i.* **1.** to give one's agreement or adherence; assent; yield (with *to*): *to accede to demand, to accede to a treaty.* **2.** to gain and take control or possession of (an office, dignity, or position): *Queen Elizabeth II acceded to the throne in 1952.* [Latin *accēdere* to go to, approach.] —**Syn. 1.** see **consent.**

accel., accelerando.

ac·ce·le·ran·do (ak se′lə rän′dō) *adv., adj. Music.* gradually increasing in speed. [Italian *accelerando,* going back to Latin *accelerāre* to hasten.]

ac·cel·er·ate (ak sel′ə rāt′) **-at·ed, -at·ing.** *v.t.* **1.** to increase the speed of; cause to move or advance faster: *to accelerate the heartbeat, to accelerate a bright student.* **2.** to cause to happen sooner; hasten: *The bad weather accelerated our departure.* **3.** *Physics.* to change the speed or direction of (a moving body); cause to undergo acceleration. —*v.i.* to go faster; increase in speed: *The car accelerated as it went down the hill.* [Latin *accelerātus,* past participle of *accelerāre* to hasten.] —**ac·cel′er·a′tive,** *adj.* —**Syn. 2.** see **quicken.**

ac·cel·er·a·tion (ak sel′ə rā′shən) *n.* **1.** act or process of accelerating; being accelerated. **2.** *Physics.* **a.** change in the speed or direction of movement. **Positive acceleration** causes an increase in speed; **negative acceleration** causes a decrease. **b.** rate of such change per unit of time.

ac·cel·er·a·tor (ak sel′ə rā′tər) *n.* **1.** device for increasing the speed of a machine, esp. the foot throttle of an automobile. **2.** *Physics.* any of various devices that accelerate subatomic particles to high speeds and high energies, as a cyclotron or synchrotron. **3.** anything that causes an increase in speed.

ac·cent (*n.,* ak′sent; *v.,* ak′sent, ak sent′) *n.* **1.** stress given to a particular syllable or word in speech. In the sentence *I heard you,* the accent could be on the *I,* the *heard,* or the *you.* The meaning of the sentence would vary according to the position of the accent. **2.** mark (as ′ or ′) used to indicate a stressed syllable. **3.** any one of various marks used in certain languages to indicate variant pronunciations or meanings. In French, the accents are acute (′), grave (`), and circumflex (^). **4.** characteristic mode of pronunciation peculiar to a particular region or group within a single language or to an individual speaking a language not his own: *British accent, Southern accent, to speak English with a German accent.* **5.** stress or importance; emphasis (with *on*): *a biology course with an accent on laboratory work.* **6.** stress on certain words or syllables marking the rhythm of verse, usually occurring at fixed intervals; ictus. In the line *While joy gave clouds the light of stars,* the words *joy, clouds, light,* and *stars* have the accent. **7.** *Music.* **a.** stress given to certain notes or chords. **b.** mark used to indicate this. **8. accents.** *Archaic.* speech; language. **9.** small ornamental detail or part: *a green room with accents of blue.* —*v.t.* **1.** to pronounce (a syllable, word, or words) with particular stress. **2.** to emphasize; accentuate. **3.** to mark with a written or printed accent. [Latin *accentus* accentuation of a word, tone, from *ac-,* for *ad* to + *cantus* song; literally, a song added to (speech).] —**Syn. v.t. 4.** see **inflection. 5.** see **emphasis.**

ac·cen·tu·al (ak sen′chŏō əl) *adj.* of, relating to, or formed by accent. —**ac·cen′tu·al·ly,** *adv.*

ac·cen·tu·ate (ak sen′chŏō āt′) **-at·ed, -at·ing.** *v.t.* **1.** to heighten the effect of; emphasize; stress: *The boy's height accentuated his thinness.* **2.** to mark or pronounce with an accent. —**ac·cen′tu·a′tion,** *n.*

ac·cept (ak sept′) *v.t.* **1.** to agree to take (something offered); receive willingly: *to accept a present.* **2.** to receive with favor or approval: *The girls quickly accepted their new roommate.* **3.** to agree or assent to: *to accept the referee's decision.* **4.** to respond affirmatively to: *to accept an invitation.* **5.** to submit to; accommodate oneself to: *to accept a situation.* **6.** to receive as true, satisfactory, or sufficient; believe in: *to accept the evidence.* **7.** to undertake formally; take on the responsibility of: *to accept the office.* **8.** to acknowledge by signature and undertake to pay (a bill or draft). —*v.i.* to take something offered; respond affirmatively. [Latin *acceptāre* to receive.] —**ac·cept′er,** *n.* —**Syn. v.t. 1.** see **receive.**

ac·cept·a·ble (ak sep′tə bəl) *adj.* worthy of being accepted; pleasing or satisfactory: *His work is acceptable.* —**ac·cept′a·bil′i·ty,** *n.* —**ac·cept′a·bly,** *adv.*

ac·cept·ance (ak sep′təns) *n.* **1.** act of accepting; being accepted or acceptable. **2.** favorable reception; approval. **3.** belief in; assent. **4.a.** written agreement to pay a draft or bill according to contracted terms. **b.** accepted draft or bill of exchange.

ac·cep·ta·tion (ak′sep tā′shən) *n.* **1.** generally accepted meaning (of a word, expression, or statement). **2.** *Archaic.* favorable reception.

ac·cep·tor (ak sep′tər) *n.* one who accepts a draft or bill of exchange.

ac·cess (ak′ses) *n.* **1.** right or permission to approach, enter, or use; admittance: *We had access to his private files.* **2.** way of approaching; means of approach: *The only access to the farm was a dirt road.* **3.** condition of being approachable: *Access to their house in the hills was difficult during the winter.* **4.** sudden outburst or onset. [Latin *accessus* approach.]

ac·ces·si·ble (ak ses′ə bəl) *adj.* **1.** capable of being approached or entered; easy to reach: *The new airport will be accessible from all directions.* **2.** obtainable; attainable: *Such information is not readily accessible.* **3.** accessible **to.** open to the influence of: *accessible to bribery.* —**ac·ces′si·bil′i·ty,** *n.* —**ac·ces′si·bly,** *adv.*

ac·ces·sion (ak sesh′ən) *n.* **1.** act of coming to and taking control or possession of (an office, dignity, or position): *his accession to the throne.* **2.** increase by something added; addition: *The library collection was enlarged by the accession of fifty volumes.* **3.** thing added: *The new books were a valuable accession.* **4.** assent; agreement: *accession to a proposal.* [Latin *accessiō* a going to, addition.]

ac·ces·so·ry (ak ses′ər ē) *pl.* **-ries.** *also,* **ac·ces·sa·ry,** *n.* **1.** something subordinate that aids or adds to a general effect or effectiveness; additional device or object: *new car accessories.* **2.** *Law.* **a.** one who, without being present at the commission of a felony, assists or instigates the offense. Also, **accessory before the fact. b.** one who knowingly conceals a felon from the law. Also, **accessory after the fact.** —*adj.* **1.** contributing subordinately; additional; supplemental. **2.** *Law.* giving help as an accessory.

ac·ci·dence (ak′sə dəns) *n.* part of grammar that deals with the inflection of words.

ac·ci·dent (ak′sə dənt) *n.* **1.** something that happens unexpectedly or without apparent cause or reason: *The discovery was a happy accident.* **2.** unfortunate event that is unexpected or caused unintentionally, usually involving harm or injury; mishap: *traffic accident.* **3.** chance; fortune: *I was there by accident.* **4.** nonessential quality or characteristic: *accident of birth.* **5.** *Geology.* irregularity of surface. [Latin *accident-,* stem of *accidēns* chance, happening.]

ac·ci·den·tal (ak′sə dent′əl) *adj.* **1.** happening by chance; unexpected; unintentional. **2.** nonessential; subsidiary; incidental. **3.** *Music.* of or indicating an accidental. —*n.* **1.** nonessential or incidental feature or quality. **2.** *Music.* **a.** sign, as a flat, sharp, or natural, appearing outside the key signature, altering the pitch of the note or notes it precedes. **b.** note so altered.

ac·ci·den·tal·ly (ak′sə dent′lē) *adv.* by chance.

ac·claim (ə klām′) *v.t.* **1.** to greet or salute, with loud or enthusiastic approval; hail; applaud: *Parisians acclaimed Lindbergh when he landed.* **2.** to announce or declare with strong approval: *The judges acclaimed her the winner.* —*n.* emphatic or enthusiastic praise or welcome: *The book was greeted with critical acclaim.* [Latin *acclāmāre* to shout applause.]

ac·cla·ma·tion (ak′lə mā′shən) *n.* **1.** enthusiastic demonstration of approval. **2.** oral vote of approval, esp. an enthusiastic or unanimous one: *The motion was passed by acclamation.* —**Syn. 1.** see **praise.**

ac·cli·mate (ə klī′mit, ak′lə māt′) **-mat·ed, -mat·ing.** *v.t., v.i.* to adjust or adapt to a new climate, environment, or situation. [French *acclimater* to adapt to a climate, going back to Latin *ad* to + *clima.* See CLIMATE.] —**ac·cli·ma·tion** (ak′lə mā′shən), *n.*

ac·cli·ma·tize (ə klī′mə tīz′) **-tized, -tiz·ing.** *v.t., v.i.* to acclimate. —**ac·cli′ma·ti·za′tion,** *n.*

ac·cliv·i·ty (ə kliv′ə tē) *pl.* **-ties.** *n.* upward or ascending slope. [Latin *acclīvitās* steepness.]

ac·co·lade (ak′ə lād′, -läd′) *n.* **1.** praise; award; honor. **2.** ceremony used in conferring knighthood, formerly an embrace or kiss and now a light tap on the shoulder with the flat side of a sword. [French

at; āpe; cär; end; mē; it; īce; hot; ōld; fôrk; wood; fōōl; oil; out; up; ūse; turn; sing; thin; this; zh in treasure; ə in ago, taken, pencil, lemon, circus.

accolade accolade of knighthood, from Italian *accolata* embrace about the neck, going back to Latin *ad* to, at + *collum* neck.]

ac·com·mo·date (ə kom′ə dāt′) -dat·ed, -dat·ing. *v.t.* **1.** to have or make room or facilities for: *The car can accommodate five passengers.* **2.** to furnish or supply with lodgings or with room and board. **3.** to do a favor or service for; oblige; help: *When we asked for help, the policeman accommodated us.* **4.** to supply or provide (with *with*). **5.** to make suitable; adapt (with *to*): *Accommodate yourself to the new situation.* **6.** to bring into agreement; reconcile: *to accommodate differences of opinion.* —*v.i.* to adjust or come into adjustment: *The lens of the eye accommodates to distance.* [Latin *accommodātus,* past participle of *accommodāre* to adapt.] —**Syn.** *v.t.* **1.** see contain. **5.** see adapt.

ac·com·mo·dat·ing (ə kom′ə dā′ting) *adj.* readily obliging; compliant; helpful. —**ac·com′mo·dat′ing·ly,** *adv.*

ac·com·mo·da·tion (ə kom′ə dā′shən) *n.* **1.** act or process of accommodating; being accommodated. **2.** *also,* **accommodations.** facilities for passage or lodging, often with food: *tourist accommodations on a boat, motel accommodations.* **3.** aid, comfort, or convenience: *Buses are for the accommodation of travelers.* **4.** willingness to help; obligingness; complaisance. **5.** loan. **6.** *Physiology.* automatic adjustment of the lens of the eye for focusing at different distances.

ac·com·pa·ni·ment (ə kum′pə ni mənt) *n.* **1.** something that accompanies; complement; concomitant. **2.** *Music.* subordinate part or parts, instrumental or vocal, providing a background or complement for a principal part.

ac·com·pa·nist (ə kum′pə nist) *n.* one who plays or sings a musical accompaniment.

ac·com·pa·ny (ə kum′pə nē) -nied, -ny·ing. *v.t.* **1.** to go along or in company with; attend as a companion or escort: *I'll accompany you to the theater.* **2.** to exist or occur in association or combination; be an adjunct to: *the slides which accompanied the lecture.* **3.** to cause (something) to be supplemented or associated (with *with*): *He accompanied his speech with gestures.* **4.** to play or sing a musical accompaniment for or to. —*v.i.* to perform a musical accompaniment. [Old French *accompaigner* to associate with, from *a* to + *compaing, compaignon.* See COMPANION.] —**ac·com′pa·ni·er,** *n.*

Syn. *v.t.* **1. Accompany, attend, escort** refer to association of one person or thing with another. **Accompany** suggests close association of people, companionship, and equality: *She often accompanied her husband to the ball game.* **Attend** suggests that the person or thing attending another is subordinate: *The nobles attended the king on his journey through the realm.* **Escort** suggests protection, sometimes implying armed force and always implying diligent care: *Destroyers escorted the convoy through the straits. Cynthia's brother escorted her to many social events.*

ac·com·plice (ə kom′plis) *n.* one who participates in a crime; associate in wrongdoing. [Earlier *a complice* a confederate, through French *complice,* from Latin *complex* literally, woven together.] —**Syn.** see **confederate.**

ac·com·plish (ə kom′plish) *v.t.* to succeed in completing or carrying out; perform: *to accomplish a task.* [Old French *acompliss-* a stem of *acomplir* to complete, going back to Latin *ad* to, at + *complēre* to fulfill, complete.] —**ac·com′plish·er,** *n.*

Syn. Accomplish, achieve, effect include the idea of carrying an undertaking through to the end. **Accomplish** stresses the result rather than the process: *What did he accomplish by bringing a lawyer into the argument?* **Achieve** implies obstacles overcome in reaching the result: *He was achieving, amongst a very wretched population, a world of active good* (Charlotte Brontë, 1853). **Effect** emphasizes the result of applying energy or force to reach the required end: *Only total national effort can effect a victory.*

ac·com·plished (ə kom′plisht) *adj.* **1.** successfully completed; done; effected. **2.** skilled; proficient; expert: *an accomplished performer.* **3.** skilled or trained in social arts and graces; polished: *An accomplished person moves gracefully without thinking of it* (Cowper, 1786).

ac·com·plish·ment (ə kom′plish mənt) *n.* **1.** act of accomplishing; being accomplished; completion. **2.** something done successfully; achievement. **3.** skill, art, or facility, esp. one that is acquired.

ac·cord (ə kôrd′) *n.* **1.** state of agreement; conformity: *The decision was in accord with popular sentiment.* **2.** an agreement between parties, esp. one between nations. **3.** correspondence or harmony, as of color, pitch, or tone. **4.** of (or **on**) **one's own accord.** by one's own choice or will; voluntarily. **5. with one accord.** with complete agreement; with unanimity. —*v.t.* **1.** to grant, give, or concede: *He was accorded the praise due him.* **2.** *Archaic.* to bring into agreement or harmony; reconcile. —*v.i.* to be consistent or in harmony; agree (with *with*): *Her actions accorded with their wishes.* [Old French *acorder* to agree, going back to Latin *ad* to, at + *cor* heart.]

ac·cord·ance (ə kôrd′əns) *n.* **1.** state of agreement; conformity: *Act in accordance with our wishes.* **2.** act of according, granting, or giving.

ac·cord·ant (ə kôrd′ənt) *adj.* in harmony; agreeing; corresponding (with *with*): *accordant with our principles.* —**ac·cord′ant·ly,** *adv.*

ac·cord·ing (ə kôr′ding) *adj.* in harmony; agreeing. —*adv.* **1.** accordingly. **2. according to. a.** in agreement or conformity with: *Everything went according to plan.* **b.** in proportion to; in relation to: *each according to his ability.* **c.** on the authority of; as stated by: *according to the teacher.*

ac·cord·ing·ly (ə kôr′ding lē) *adv.* **1.** in accordance; correspondingly; conformably. **2.** consequently; therefore.

ac·cor·di·on (ə kôr′dē ən) *n.* portable musical wind instrument with keys, metallic reeds, and a bellows, which produces tones when the player compresses or expands the bellows, forcing air through the reeds. —*adj.* resembling the folds of the bellows of an accordion: *accordion pleats.* [German *Akkordion,* from Italian *accordare* to tune (an instrument), going back to Latin *ad* to, at + *chorda.* See CHORD².]

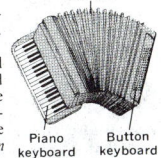

Bellows

Piano keyboard   Button keyboard

Accordion

ac·cost (ə kôst′) *v.t.* to approach and speak to; address. [French *accoster,* from Italian *accostare* to approach, going back to Latin *ad* to, at + *costa* side, rib.]

ac·couche·ment (ə koosh′mənt, -mänt′, *French* ä koosh mäN′) *n.* confinement for childbirth; childbirth. [French *accouchement,* from *accoucher* to give birth to; literally, to be brought to bed, going back to Latin *ad* to + *collocāre* to lay together.]

ac·count (ə kount′) *n.* **1.** oral or written statement; report; description: *a detailed account of the invasion.* **2.** statement of reasons, causes, or grounds; explanation: *Give an account of your behavior.* **3.a.** record or statement of business or financial transactions. **b.** any record or enumeration. **4.** business relation requiring the keeping of financial records: *bank account.* **5.** worth; importance: *a man of no account.*

on account. **a.** as part of a final payment. **b.** on credit.
on account of. **a.** because of. **b.** for the sake of; in consideration of.
on no account. under no circumstances; never.
on (someone's) account. for (someone's) sake or benefit.
to call (someone) to account. a. to demand an explanation of. **b.** to reprimand; rebuke.
to give (a good or poor) account of oneself. to behave or perform (well or poorly).
to take account of or **take into account. a.** to take into consideration; allow for. **b.** to take note of.
to turn to account. to make advantageous, useful, or profitable.

—*v.i.* **1.** to provide a reckoning; be responsible (with *for*): *Account for the money spent on office supplies.* **2.** to give a satisfactory reason or cause; explain (with *for*): *How do you account for your lateness?* **3.** to cause the death, capture, or destruction of (with *for*). —*v.t.* to consider to be; deem; value. [Old French *aconter, acompter* to count up, reckon, from *a* to (from Latin *ad* to) + *conter, compter.* See COUNT¹.]

Syn. *n.* **1. Account, story¹, version, report** refer to a description of events. **Account** is used of a circumstantial statement, usually of personal experience: *His brief account of the voyage has become a classic.* **Story** implies nothing more than a statement of alleged facts, but often is used when a distortion of the truth is hinted at: *Few people really believed Colter's story of what he had seen up the Yellowstone.* **Version** suggests two or more statements covering the same events, but it carries no implication of truth or untruth: *The jury apparently believed his version of the origin of the quarrel.* **Report** indicates a statement of facts, either personally experienced or compiled by research, often submitted to a superior or to a group: *The report on public acceptance of the new design was discouraging.*

ac·count·a·ble (ə koun′tə bəl) *adj.* **1.** liable to be called to account; responsible: *He must be held accountable for his actions.* **2.** capable of being explained. —**ac·count′a·bil′i·ty, ac·count′a·ble·ness,** *n.* —**ac·count′a·bly,** *adv.*

ac·count·an·cy (ə koun′tən sē) *n.* work or profession of an accountant.

ac·count·ant (ə koun′tənt) *n.* one who has charge of or verifies business records and accounts; one trained in accounting.

ac·count·ing (ə koun′ting) *n.* **1.** principles, procedures, or profession concerned with the systematic recording, analyzing, and verifying of business and financial transactions. **2.** formal report or statement of transactions by one responsible for property, money, or the execution of some task.

ac·cou·ter (ə kōō′tər) *also,* **ac·cou·tre.** *v.t.* to attire, equip, or outfit, esp. for military service. [Middle French *accoutrer,* from *a* to + *cousture* sewing, going back to Latin *cōnsuere* to sew together.]

ac·cou·ter·ments (ə kōō′tər mənts) *also,* **ac·cou·tre·ments.** *n.,pl.* personal equipment or accessories, esp. the equipment of a soldier other than arms and clothing; trappings.

Ac·cra (ak′rə, ə krä′) *also,* **Ak·kra.** *n.* capital and largest city of Ghana, on the southern coast of the country. Pop. (1966), 615,800.

ac·cred·it (ə kred′it) *v.t.* **1.** to regard (someone) as having; give credit for (with *with*): *They accredit the mayor with having made great improvements.* **2.** to ascribe or attribute (with *to*). **3.** to certify as meeting certain official standards or requirements: *to accredit a college.* **4.** to send or provide with authorization or credentials: *to accredit a diplomat.* **5.** to accept as true; believe: *We accredited her account of the accident.* **6.** to provide authority for. [French *accréditer*, from *à* to + *crédit*. See CREDIT.] —**ac·cred′i·ta′tion**, *n.*

ac·cre·tion (ə krē′shən) *n.* **1.** increase in size by natural growth or external addition. **2.** product of such a process. **3.** something that is added; external addition. **4.** growing together of separate parts. [Latin *accrētiō* increase, increment.]

ac·cru·al (ə krōō′əl) *n.* **1.** act or process of accruing. **2.** something accruing or accrued; amount accrued.

ac·crue (ə krōō′) -**crued**, -**cru·ing.** *v.i.* **1.** to come as a result of natural growth or addition (with *to*): *benefits that accrue to a community from new construction.* **2.** to grow in amount; accumulate: *Interest accrues from the day of deposit.* —*v.t.* to accumulate (something): *The account accrues interest at the rate of five percent a year.* [Middle French *accrue* increase, from Old French *accreistre* to increase, from Latin *accrēscere* to grow.] —**ac·crue′ment**, *n.*

acct. **1.** account. **2.** accountant.

ac·cul·tur·a·tion (ə kul′chə rā′shən) *n.* process or result of adopting traits or patterns of another culture.

ac·cu·mu·late (ə kū′myə lāt′) -**lat·ed**, -**lat·ing.** *v.t.* to gather or pile up (something); collect; amass: *to accumulate a large collection of books.* —*v.i.* to grow in size, quantity, or number; increase gradually: *A pile of work accumulated on his desk.* [Latin *accumulātus*, past participle of *accumulāre* to pile up.]

Syn. *v.t.* **Accumulate, amass** both mean to gather together some amount. **Accumulate** suggests addition, by small amounts over a period of time to a growing pile, not always large: *Judicious investment permitted him to accumulate a considerable fortune during his lifetime. Dust and cobwebs accumulating in the corners gave the place a dingy look.* **Amass** suggests the gathering of a considerable mass, as of wealth, treasure, or facts, with the stress on the large amount rather than on the process of gathering: *The store of knowledge he has amassed about the Elizabethan era is remarkable.*

ac·cu·mu·la·tion (ə kū′myə lā′shən) *n.* **1.** action or process of accumulating; being accumulated: *Little things grow by continual accumulation* (Johnson, 1750). **2.** that which is accumulated or has accumulated; mass; collection: *accumulations of snow.* —**ac·cu′mu·la′tive,** *adj.*

ac·cu·mu·la·tor (ə kū′myə lā′tər) *n.* **1.** person or thing that accumulates. **2.** *British.* storage battery.

ac·cu·ra·cy (ak′yər ə sē) *n.* condition or quality of being accurate; correctness; exactness; precision.

ac·cu·rate (ak′yər it) *adj.* **1.** making few or no errors; careful; exact: *an accurate typist.* **2.** conforming exactly to a truth, standard, or model; without error; correct: *an accurate report.* [Latin *accūrātus*, past participle of *accūrāre* to do with care, take care of.] —**ac′cu·rate·ly,** *adv.* —**ac′cu·rate·ness,** *n.* —**Syn. 1.** see correct.

ac·curs·ed (ə kur′sid, ə kurst′) *also,* **ac·curst** (ə kurst′). *adj.* **1.** under a curse; ill-fated; doomed. **2.** worthy of curses; damnable; hateful.

accus., accusative.

ac·cu·sa·tion (ak′yə zā′shən) *n.* **1.** charge of wrongdoing. **2.** crime, offense, or error charged. **3.** act of accusing; being accused.

ac·cu·sa·tive (ə kū′zə tiv) *n.* **1.** grammatical case in Latin, Greek, and other Indo-European languages that indicates the direct object of a verb or the object of certain prepositions. It corresponds to the objective case in English. **2.** word or construction in this case. —*adj.* of, relating to, or designating this case.

ac·cu·sa·to·ry (ə kū′zə tôr′ē) *adj.* containing an accusation; accusing: *an accusatory tone of voice.*

ac·cuse (ə kūz′) -**cused**, -**cus·ing.** *v.t.* **1.** to bring charges against (with *of*): *The police accused him of larceny.* **2.** to find at fault or in error; blame. [Old French *acuser*, from Latin *accūsāre* to call to account.] —**ac·cus′er,** *n.* —**ac·cus′ing·ly,** *adv.*

Syn. **1.** **Accuse, denounce, charge, blame** apply to stating that someone is at fault. **Accuse** points the finger directly at someone: *I accuse them of extreme negligence.* **Denounce** suggests an open and public condemnation: *They were denounced in the press and over the air.* **Charge** imputes a definite and formal statement of a specific infraction: *The article charged that he had accepted several bribes.* **Blame** implies not only wrongdoing but often suggests an underlying rather than an immediate cause: *It is the owners and not the dogs themselves who must be blamed for the damage.*

ac·cused (ə kyūzd′) *adj.* subjected to an accusation. —*n.* **the accused.** person or persons charged with an offense, esp. the defendant or defendants in a criminal case.

ac·cus·tom (ə kus′təm) *v.t.* to familiarize by use, custom, or habit; habituate (with *to*): *to accustom oneself to new surroundings.* [Old French *acostumer*, from *a* to (from Latin *ad* to) + *costume* custom, going back to Latin *cōnsuētūdō* custom.]

Syn. **Accustom, habituate, familiarize** indicate a becoming used to new or changed circumstances. **Accustom** simply implies repeated exposure: *He became accustomed to the noise of the hammers.* **Habituate** suggests a certain deadening as a result of frequent repetition of an experience: *Mark had become habituated to the rude treatment and hardly noticed it any more.* **Familiarize** indicates a deliberate effort to learn (or to teach), by repeated exposure, something hitherto unknown: *He took long walks to familiarize himself with the new neighborhood.*

ac·cus·tomed (ə kus′təmd) *adj.* **1.** usual; customary; habitual: *in their accustomed manner.* **2.** accustomed to. in the habit of; used to: *accustomed to rising with the dawn.*

ace (ās) *n.* **1.a.** playing card having a single symbol of the suit it represents. **b.** face of a die having one spot. **2.** one who excels at something; expert: *tennis ace.* **3.** fighter pilot who has shot down five or more enemy planes. **4.a.** in tennis and similar games, a served ball which the opponent fails to return. **b.** a hole in one in golf. **5. ace in the hole.** *Slang.* hidden advantage. **6. within an ace of.** at the very point of; close to: *I came within an ace of making my fortune* (Irving, 1824). —*v.t.* **aced, ac·ing.** **1.** to make (a golf hole) in one stroke. **2.** to score a point on an unreturned serve, as in tennis. **3. to ace out.** *Slang.* to beat or surpass (someone): *to ace out an opponent.* —*adj.* of the highest quality; expert: *an ace performance.* [Old French *as* face of a die having one spot, from Latin *ās* unit, coin.]

a·cer·bi·ty (ə sur′bə tē) *pl.*, -**ties.** *n.* **1.** harshness, bitterness, or severity of temper or manner. **2.** sourness, bitterness, or acidity of taste. [French *acerbité*, from Latin *acerbitās.*] —**a·cerb′,** *adj.*

ac·e·tab·u·lum (as′ə tab′yə ləm) *pl.*, -**la** (-lə). *n.* cup-shaped socket in the hipbone into which the head of the thighbone fits. [Latin *acetābulum* cup for vinegar, from *acētum* vinegar.]

ac·et·al·de·hyde (as′ə tal′də hīd′) *n.* colorless flammable liquid with a pungent, fruity odor, widely used in the making of organic compounds and as an organic solvent. Formula: CH_3CHO

ac·et·an·i·lide (as′ə tan′l id′, -id) *also,* **ac·et·an·i·lid** (as′ə tan′l id). *n.* white crystalline compound, used as a drug to relieve pain and reduce fever. Formula: $CH_3CONHC_6H_5$

ac·e·tate (as′ə tāt′) *n.* **1.** salt or ester of acetic acid. **2.** cellulose acetate or any of its products, esp. a cellulose acetate fabric, fiber, or yarn.

a·ce·tic (ə sē′tik, ə set′ik) *adj.* of, relating to, like, or producing vinegar or acetic acid. [Latin *acētum* vinegar + -ic.]

acetic acid, colorless liquid acid having a pungent odor and sour taste. It is the acid in vinegar and is used widely in the production of textile fibers, plastics, and drugs. Formula: CH_3COOH

ac·e·tone (as′ə tōn′) *n.* colorless, volatile, flammable liquid with a minty odor, used widely as a solvent for fats, cellulose compounds, and other organic substances. Formula: CH_3COCH_3

a·ce·tyl (ə sēt′əl, as′ət əl) *n.* univalent radical of acetic acid. Formula: CH_3CO

a·cet·y·lene (ə set′əl ēn′, -in) *n.* colorless, highly flammable gas of the alkyne series, used in the synthesis of many organic compounds and, in combination with oxygen, in the cutting and welding of metals. Formula: C_2H_2

a·ce·tyl·sal·i·cyl·ic acid (ə set′əl sal′ə sil′ik) aspirin.

A·chae·a (ə kē′ə) *also,* **A·cha·ia** (ə kā′ə, ə kī′ə). *n.* region of ancient Greece in the northern Peloponnesus.

A·chae·an (ə kē′ən) *also,* **A·cha·ian** (ə kā′ən, ə kī′ən). *adj.* of or relating to Achaea, its people, or their culture. —*n.* member of one of the four major Greek tribes of antiquity. The Achaeans settled in the Peloponnesus, establishing the Mycenaean civilization, and later fled to Asia Minor during the Dorian invasion.

A·cha·tes (ə kā′tēz) *n.* **1.** *Roman Legend.* the faithful companion and friend of Aeneas. **2.** any loyal friend.

ache (āk) **ached, ach·ing.** *v.i.* **1.** to have or be in pain, esp. dull or continuous pain. **2.** *Informal.* to long for; yearn (with *for* or the infinitive): *The homesick children ached to go home.* —*n.* continuous, usually dull pain. [Old English *acan* to ache.] —**ach′ing·ly,** *adv.* —**Syn.** *n.* see pain.

a·chene (ā kēn′) *also* **a·kene.** *n.* small, dry, one-seeded fruit, as of a dandelion or sunflower, whose thin outer covering does not burst open at maturity. [Modern Latin *achaenium*, from A-⁴ + Greek *chainein* to gape.] —**a·che′ni·al,** *adj.*

A·cher·nar (ā′kər när′) *n.* star in the constellation Eridanus and one of the brightest in the sky.

Ach·er·on (ak′ə ron′) *n.* *Greek and Roman Mythology.* **1.** one of the rivers of the lower world. **2.** the lower world; Hades; hell.

a·chieve (ə chēv′) **a·chieved, a·chiev·ing.** *v.t.* **1.** to carry out successfully; accomplish. **2.** to succeed in gaining; attain: *to achieve the rank of major.* —*v.i.* to be successful in something; bring about an intended

at; āpe; cär; end; mē; it; īce; hot; ōld; fôrk; wood; fōōl; oil; out; up; ūse; turn; sing; thin; this; zh in treasure; ə in ago, taken, pencil, lemon, circus.

result: *He achieved because he was a hard worker.* [Old French *achever* to bring to an end, accomplish, from a phrase *a chief* to a head, to an end, from Latin phrase *ad caput* to a head.] —**a·chiev′a·ble,** *adj.* —**a·chiev′er,** *n.* —**Syn.** *v.t.* **1.** see **accomplish.**

a·chieve·ment (ə chēv′mənt) *n.* **1.** something achieved, esp. by great exertion or skill; feat; accomplishment. **2.** act of achieving.

achievement test, test for measuring how much a person has learned in a particular subject.

A·chil·les (ə kil′ēz) *n.* the most valiant Greek warrior in the Trojan War. Achilles was killed by Paris, who wounded him in his only vulnerable spot, his heel.

Achilles′ heel, vulnerable spot; weak point.

Achilles′ tendon, tendon which joins the muscles of the calf to the bone of the heel.

ach·ro·mat·ic (ak′rə mat′ik) *adj.* **1.** refracting white light without separating it into the colors of the spectrum. **2.** without hue. [Greek *achrōmatos* colorless.] —**ach′ro·mat′i·cal·ly,** *adv.* —**a·chro·ma·tism** (ə krō′mə tiz′əm), *n.*

ac·id (as′id) *n.* **1.** *Chemistry* **a.** compound containing hydrogen and having a sour taste in water solution. Acids react with bases to form salts. **b.** compound that gives up protons to a base. **c.** compound capable of accepting an unshared pair of electrons from a base. **2.** any sour substance. —*adj.* **1.** of, relating to, yielding, or like an acid. **2.** sharp and biting to the taste; sour. **3.** sharp, as in tone or manner; ill-tempered; biting: *acid remarks.* [Latin *acidus* sour.] —**ac′id·ly,** *adv.* —**ac′id·ness,** *n.*

a·cid·ic (ə sid′ik) *adj.* **1.** acid-forming. **2.** (of rock) containing a large percentage of silica.

a·cid·i·fy (ə sid′ə fī′) **-fied, -fy·ing.** *v.t., v.i.* **1.** to make or become acid or sour. **2.** to change into an acid. —**a·cid′i·fi′a·ble,** *adj.* —**a·cid′i·fi·ca′tion, a·cid′i·fi′er,** *n.*

a·cid·i·ty (ə sid′ə tē) *pl.* **-ties.** *n.* **1.** quality or state of being acid; sourness; tartness. **2.** degree of being acid. **3.** hyperacidity.

ac·i·do·sis (as′ə dō′sis) *n.* abnormal condition of the body resulting from increased acidity or reduced alkalinity in the blood and tissues. [ACID + -OSIS.]

acid test, something that tests the real or essential quality, character, or worth of a person or thing.

a·cid·u·late (ə sij′ə lāt′) **-lat·ed, -lat·ing.** *v.t.* to make somewhat acid or sour. —**a·cid′u·la′tion,** *n.*

a·cid·u·lous (ə sij′ə ləs) *adj.* slightly acid or sour. Also, **a·cid′u·lent.**

ack-ack (ak′ak′) *n. Informal.* antiaircraft fire; antiaircraft gun. [British signalman's code for *AA,* abbreviation of *antiaircraft.*]

ac·knowl·edge (ak nol′ij) **-edged, -edg·ing.** *v.t.* **1.** to admit the truth or fact of; confess: *He acknowledged his error.* **2.** to recognize the authority, validity, or claims of: *The government acknowledged his right to petition.* **3.** to express appreciation or gratitude for: *to acknowledge a favor.* **4.** to make known the receipt or arrival of: *She acknowledged the letter.* **5.** to express recognition of; take notice of: *The host acknowledged our greeting.* **6.** *Law.* to recognize as valid or true; certify legally: *to acknowledge a deed.* [Probably blend of obsolete *aknow* to recognize (from Old English *oncnāwan*) and obsolete *knowledge* to confess, admit (going back to Old English *cnāwan* to know).] —**ac·knowl′edge·a·ble,** *adj.* —**Syn.** *v.t.* **1.** see **admit.**

ac·knowl·edged (ak nol′ijd) *adj.* generally accepted; recognized: *the acknowledged leader in the field.* —**ac·knowl′edged·ly,** *adv.*

ac·knowl·edg·ment (ak nol′ij mənt) *also,* **ac·knowl·edge·ment.** **1.** act of admitting or confessing; avowal: *acknowledgment of his misdeeds.* **2.** recognition, as of authority, validity, or claims: *acknowledgment of his right to rule.* **3.** thing given or done in recognition of the arrival or receipt of (something): *Their letter was an acknowledgment of the shipment.* **4.** expression of gratitude, recognition, or appreciation. **5.** *Law.* sworn declaration of the truth or validity of an action or fact; certificate of such a declaration.

a·clin·ic line (ā klin′ik) magnetic equator.

ac·me (ak′mē) *n.* highest point; zenith. [Greek *akmē* point, highest point.]

ac·ne (ak′nē) *n.* skin disorder characterized by pimples or other blemishes on the face, back, or chest resulting from clogged and inflamed pores of the sebaceous glands. [Modern Latin *acne,* mistaken reading of Greek *akmē* point, pimple.]

ac·o·lyte (ak′ə līt′) *n.* **1.** one who assists a minister or priest at certain religious services; altar boy. **2.** attendant; assistant. [Medieval Latin *acolitus, acolythus* follower, attendant, from Greek *akolouthos* follower.]

A·con·ca·gua (ak′ən kog′wə; *Spanish* ä′kông kä′gwä) *n.* mountain in western Argentina, in the Andes, highest in the Western Hemisphere.

ac·o·nite (ak′ə nīt′) *n.* **1.** any of a group of poisonous plants, genus *Aconitum,* of the Northern Hemisphere, bearing blue, white, purple, or yellow hood-shaped flowers. Also, **wolfs′bane′, monks′hood′.** **2.** drug obtained from any of several species of these plants, esp. from *A. napel-*

lus, used as a cardiac and respiratory depressant and as an analgesic. [French *aconit* the plant, through Latin, from Greek *akoniton.*]

a·corn (ā′kôrn, ā′kərn) *n.* nut of the oak, the base of which is surrounded by a woody cup. [Old English *æcern* fruit of the field, from *æcer* field.]

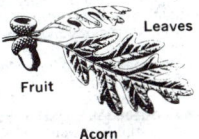
Leaves
Fruit
Acorn

a·cous·tic (ə kōōs′tik) *adj.* **1.** relating to the sense or organs of hearing, to sound, or to the science of sound. **2.** serving to absorb and deaden sound: *acoustic tile.* Also, **a·cous′ti·cal.** [Greek *akoustikos* relating to hearing, from *akouein* to hear.] —**a·cous′ti·cal·ly,** *adv.*

a·cous·tics (ə kōōs′tiks) *n.,pl.* **1.** properties, as of a room, theater, or auditorium, that determine how well sound is carried and heard in it. **2.** science that deals with the production, transmission, effects, and reception of sound. ▲ construed as plural in def. 1, singular in def. 2.

ac·quaint (ə kwānt′) *v.t.* **1.** to make (someone) familiar or conversant (with *with*): *Misery acquaints a man with strange bedfellows* (Shakespeare, *The Tempest*). *Acquaint yourself with the new procedures.* **2.** to make known to; inform (with *with*): *Shall we acquaint him with our decision before going on?* [Old French *acointer,* from Late Latin *adcognitāre* to make known, going back to Latin *ad* to + *cognitus,* past participle of *cognōscere* to know.]

ac·quaint·ance (ə kwānt′əns) *n.* **1.** person whom one knows, but who is not a close friend. **2.** state of being acquainted: *a brief acquaintance one summer. Ours was only a nodding acquaintance.* **3.** knowledge of something, esp. as a result of much experience or contact; familiarity (with *with*): *Long and careful study gave him a thorough acquaintance with Shakespeare's works.* —**ac·quaint′ance·ship′,** *n.*

ac·quaint·ed (ə kwān′tid) *adj.* **1.** knowing someone, or each other, but not intimately: *Are you two acquainted?* **2. to get** (or **become**) **acquainted,** to come to know (someone or each other): *Let's get acquainted.* **3.** familiar or conversant: *I'm acquainted with the new rules.*

ac·qui·esce (ak′wē es′) **-esced, -esc·ing.** *v.i.* to consent or agree tacitly; comply passively (with *in* or *to*): *They acquiesced to our proposal.* [Latin *acquiēscere* to rest, repose in, assent.] —**Syn.** see **consent.**

ac·qui·es·cence (ak′wē es′əns) *n.* act of acquiescing; tacit agreement; silent submission.

ac·qui·es·cent (ak′wē es′ənt) *adj.* disposed to acquiesce or yield; submissive; acquiescing. —**ac′qui·es′cent·ly,** *adv.*

ac·quire (ə kwīr′) **-quired, -quir·ing.** *v.t.* **1.** to come into possession of: *The idler acquires weight by lying still* (Johnson, 1758). **2.** to gain or obtain as one's own; to acquire wealth and property. [Latin *acquīrere* to obtain, get in addition.] —**ac·quir′a·bil′i·ty,** *n.* —**ac·quir′a·ble,** *adj.* —**Syn.** see **gain.**

ac·quire·ment (ə kwīr′mənt) *n.* **1.** act of acquiring. **2.** that which is acquired; attainment: *a girl with many social acquirements.*

ac·qui·si·tion (ak′wə zish′ən) *n.* **1.** act of acquiring: *the acquisition of new colonies for the empire.* **2.** that which is received or acquired: *The museum displayed its recent acquisitions.* [Latin *acquīsītiō.*]

ac·quis·i·tive (ə kwiz′ə tiv) *adj.* eager or tending to acquire, esp. to acquire and own; grasping: *a greedy and acquisitive person.* —**ac·quis′i·tive·ly,** *adv.* —**ac·quis′i·tive·ness,** *n.*

ac·quit (ə kwit′) **-quit·ted, -quit·ting.** *v.t.* **1.** to free or clear from an accusation or charge of crime; declare not guilty; exonerate: *The jury acquitted him after a short trial.* **2.** to relieve or release, as from a duty or obligation: *to acquit him of responsibility.* **3.** to conduct (oneself); behave: *The team acquitted itself well in its first game.* [Old French *aquiter* to set free, save, going back to Latin *ad* to + *quiētāre* to quiet.] —**ac·quit′ter,** *n.* —**Syn.** see **absolve.**

ac·quit·tal (ə kwit′əl) *n.* **1.** a setting free from a criminal charge by a verdict or other legal process. **2.** act of acquitting; being acquitted.

ac·quit·tance (ə kwit′əns) *n.* **1.** discharge from or settlement of a debt or obligation. **2.** written statement confirming this settlement or discharge; receipt in full.

a·cre (ā′kər) *n.* **1.** a measure of land equal to 43,560 square feet or 160 square rods. See **weights and measures** for table. **2. acres. a.** lands; estate. **b.** *Informal.* large quantity or amount. [Old English *æcer* originally, field; later, a measure of land.]

A·cre (ä′kər, ā′kər) *n.* port town in northwestern Israel, important during the Crusades. Pop. (1962 est.), 28,100.

a·cre·age (ā′kər ij) *n.* area of land measured in acres; acres collectively: *How much acreage do you own?*

ac·rid (ak′rid) *adj.* **1.** burning, biting, or irritating to the taste or smell; bitterly pungent: *acrid smell of smoke.* **2.** biting or cutting in manner, temper, or tone. [Alteration of Latin *ācer* sharp; possibly influenced by ACID.] —**a·crid′i·ty** (ə krid′ə tē), **ac′rid·ness,** *n.* —**ac′rid·ly,** *adv.*

ac·ri·mo·ni·ous (ak′rə mō′nē əs) *adj.* caustic, bitter, or sarcastic in disposition, manner, or tone. —**ac′ri·mo′ni·ous·ly,** *adv.* —**ac′ri·mo′ni·ous·ness,** *n.*

at; āpe; cär; end; mē; it; īce; hot; ōld; fôrk; wood; fōōl; oil; out; up; ūse; turn; sing; thin; this; zh in treasure; ə in ago, taken, pencil, lemon, circus.

9

ac·ri·mo·ny (ak′rə mō′nē) *pl.*, **-nies.** *n.* sharpness or bitterness in disposition, manner, or tone. [Latin *ācrimōnia.*]

ac·ro·bat (ak′rə bat′) *n.* one skilled in performing feats of agility requiring great muscular coordination and control, as a trapeze artist, tightrope walker, or tumbler. [French *acrobate,* from Greek *akrobatēs,* from *akrobatos* walking on tiptoe.] —**ac′ro·bat′ic,** *adj.* —**ac′ro·bat′·i·cal·ly,** *adv.*

ac·ro·bat·ics (ak′rə bat′iks) *n.pl.* **1.** feats or skills of an acrobat. **2.** any display of great skill or agility: *The pianist performed musical acrobatics.*

ac·ro·gen (ak′rə jən) *n.* plant having a perennial stem that grows only at the tip. Ferns and mosses are acrogens. [Greek *akros* topmost + -GEN.] —**ac·ro·gen·ic** (ak′rə jen′ik), **a·crog·e·nous** (ə kroj′ə nəs), *adj.*

ac·ro·me·gal·ic (ak′rō mə gal′ik) *adj.* relating to or afflicted with acromegaly. —*n.* person afflicted with acromegaly.

ac·ro·meg·a·ly (ak′rə meg′ə lē) *n.* disease characterized by the permanent enlargement of the bones and soft parts of the head, hands, and feet, caused by overactivity of the pituitary gland. [French *acromégalie,* from Greek *akros* at the end + *megas* big.]

ac·ro·nym (ak′rə nim′) *n.* word formed by combining the first letters or syllables of other words. *Radar* is an acronym for *radio detecting and ranging.* [Greek *akros* at the end + *onyma* (dialectal form) name, word.]

A·crop·o·lis (ə krop′ə lis) *n.* **1.** the ancient citadel on the highest hill of Athens, Greece, famous for its temples and monuments. **2.** **acropolis.** the citadel in any ancient Greek city, usually built on the highest part. [Greek *akropolis,* from *akros* topmost + *polis* city.]

a·cross (ə krôs′) *adv.* **1.** from one side to the other: *We came across in a boat.* **2.** on or to the other side: *We'll soon be across.* **3.** crossed; crosswise: *He stood with arms across.* —*prep.* **1.** from one side to the other; over: *He drove across the bridge.* **2.** on the other side of; beyond: *He lives across the street.* **3.** in a direction so as to cross; at right angles with: *The cat walked across our path.*

a·cros·tic (ə krôs′tik) *n.* poem or other arrangement of words in which the first, last, or certain other letters in each line, taken in order, form a word, phrase, or sequence of the alphabet. [French *acrostiche,* from Greek *akrostichis,* from *akros* at the end + *stichos* line of verse.]

> **F**ew plants grow when it is cold,
> **L**ocked up in the ground's stronghold.
> **O**ver them the snowflakes fall,
> **W**inter white till April's call.
> **E**arth wakes up, it's almost May,
> **R**ain brings blossoms every day.
>
> **Acrostic**

a·cryl·ic fiber (ə kril′ik) any of a group of synthetic textile fibers, made from acrylic resins. They resemble wool but when woven make a lighter-weight, wrinkle-resistant fabric that wears well and is used for such items as sweaters, blankets, and carpets.

acrylic resin, any one of a group of synthetic, thermoplastic, polymeric compounds used esp. in paints and textiles.

act (akt) *n.* **1.** something done; deed: *act of a madman.* **2.** process of doing something: *The smugglers were caught in the act.* **3.** formal decision or law, as of a legislative body or sovereign: *act of Congress.* **4.** one of the main divisions of a dramatic or theatrical work. **5.** short theatrical performance, usually one of several on a program: *The magician's act follows the acrobats.* **6.** display of feigned or insincere behavior: *Her crying was just an act.* —*v.t.* **1.** to behave in a manner befitting: *Act your age.* **2.** to play the part of; perform on the stage: *He acts Romeo with great passion.* **3.** to feign or simulate the character of: *He acts the lover.* —*v.i.* **1.** to do or perform something: *We must act quickly.* **2.** to conduct oneself; behave: *He acted like a gentleman.* **3.** to perform on the stage; be an actor: *How long have you been acting?* **4.** to produce an effect (often with *on*): *Wait until the drug acts.* **5.** to assume the appearance of; pretend to be: *She acted calm, although she was very worried.* **6.a.** to have a certain effect: *The chemical acted as a catalyst.* **b.** to perform certain duties or functions: *Jones acted as president.* **7.** to serve as an agent; substitute: *Please act for me during my absence.* **8. to act on** (or **upon**). **a.** to behave in accordance with; follow: *Act on his orders.* **b.** to have an effect upon; influence: *This acid acts on metal.* **9. to act up.** *Informal.* **a.** to behave mischievously or playfully: *The children were acting up again.* **b.** to cause trouble: *His stomach acted up after dinner.* [Partly from Latin *āctus* a doing, partly from Latin *āctum* a thing done; both forms are noun uses of the past participle of *agere* to do.]

Syn. *n.* **1. Act, action, deed** refer to something done. An **act** is an isolated occurrence, complete in itself and with limited purpose behind it: *His act of kindness was held up as an example to follow.* An **action** is usually thought of as something taking time or as a sequence of related acts, each contributing to the whole: *The action of the legislature in levying a new tax was widely resented.* A **deed** is also isolated and limited, but it is noteworthy on a broader basis than an act and likely

to be widely recognized: *whose bloody deeds shall make all Europe quake* (Shakespeare, *Henry VI,* part 2). Idiomatically, *deed* is most often contrasted with word, and *act* (or *action*) with thought.

Ac·te·on (ak tē′ən) *also,* **Ac·tae·on.** *n. Greek Legend.* the hunter who accidentally saw Artemis bathing and was changed by her into a stag, then torn to pieces by his own dogs.

ACTH, hormone that is produced by the pituitary gland and stimulates the cortex of the human adrenal gland to secrete its hormones. It can be extracted from the pituitary gland of hogs and other animals for use in the treatment of certain diseases, as arthritis, rheumatic fever, and asthma. [*A(dreno)-c(ortico)-t(rophic) h(ormone)*.]

act·ing (ak′ting) *adj.* **1.** performing the duties or functions of another: *the acting mayor.* **2.** of, relating to, or suitable for theatrical performance: *an acting company, an acting script.* —*n.* **1.** art or occupation of an actor; act of performing on the stage or before cameras. **2.** feigned or simulated behavior.

ac·tin·ic (ak tin′ik) *adj.* of, relating to, or having actinism. [Greek *aktin-,* stem of *aktīs* ray + -IC.]

ac·tin·ism (ak′tə niz′əm) *n.* property of ultraviolet rays, X rays, and other forms of radiant energy that produces chemical changes.

ac·tin·i·um (ak tin′ē əm) *n.* rare, radioactive metallic element found in pitchblende and other uranium ores. Symbol: **Ac** See **element** for table.

ac·ti·no·zo·an (ak′tə nō zō′ən) *n.* anthozoan. [Modern Latin *actinozoan,* from Greek *aktis* ray + *zōia* animals.]

ac·tion (ak′shən) *n.* **1.** process of acting or doing; operation: *the action of throwing a ball.* **2.** exertion of energy; activity: *man of action.* **3.** thing done; act; deed: *Actions speak louder than words.* **4. actions.** habitual behavior; conduct: *He couldn't explain his actions.* **5.** effect; influence: *the action of water on rock.* **6.** manner of moving or operating: *a washing machine with gentle action.* **7.** mechanism by which something operates: *the action of a rifle.* **8.** battle; combat. **9.** events or progress of events in a story or play; plot. **10.** suit in a court of law. **11. in action.** in a state of activity; at work; in operation. **12. to see action.** to engage in military combat. **13. to take action. a.** to become active; start to act: *He took action immediately.* **b.** to institute a lawsuit. [French *action* process of doing, motion, battle, lawsuit, from Latin *āctiō* a doing.] —**ac′tion·less,** *adj.* —**Syn.** **3.** see **act.**

ac·tion·a·ble (ak′shə nə bəl) *adj.* giving grounds for a lawsuit.

Ac·ti·um (ak′tē əm, -shē əm) *n.* promontory in the northwestern part of ancient Greece where Octavian's forces under Agrippa defeated Antony and Cleopatra in 31 B.C.

ac·ti·vate (ak′tə vāt′) **-vat·ed, -vat·ing.** *v.t.* **1.** to make active; cause to work or operate. **2.** *Physics.* to make radioactive. **3.** *Chemistry.* to accelerate a reaction in; make more reactive. **4.** *Military.* **a.** to create (a unit or installation) officially so that it can be organized to function in its assigned capacity. **b.** to mobilize (an inactive unit or installation). —**ac′ti·va′tion,** *n.*

ac·ti·va·tor (ak′tə vā′tər) *n.* **1.** one who or that which activates. **2.** *Chemistry.* catalyst.

ac·tive (ak′tiv) *adj.* **1.** constantly engaged in action or movement; busy: *an active child.* **2.** moving or working quickly; lively; vigorous: *active trading on the stock market, an active mind.* **3.** requiring action or exertion; producing real effects: *active participation.* **4.** acting or capable of acting; working; functioning: *an active volcano.* **5.** causing action, motion, or change. **6.a.** relating to or designating the voice of a verb whose subject is represented as performing the action expressed by the verb. In the sentence *The boy called his sister,* the verb *called* is in the active voice. Distinguished from **passive. b.** designating verbs expressing action rather than state or being. *Throw, run,* and *jump* are active verbs. —*n.* the active voice. [Latin *āctīvus* practical, denoting the active voice.] —**ac·tive·ly,** *adv.* —**ac′tive·ness,** *n.*

active duty, full-time military service.

ac·tiv·ist (ak′tə vist) *n.* one who believes in and uses vigorous and direct action, as for political ends. —**ac′tiv·ism,** *n.* —**ac′ti·vis′tic,** *adj.*

ac·tiv·i·ty (ak tiv′ə tē) *pl.,* **-ties.** *n.* **1.** quality or state of being active; movement; action: *the activity of the mind.* **2.** brisk or vigorous action; energy; liveliness: *There was little activity in the quiet town.* **3.** specific action or sphere of action: *extracurricular activities.*

act of God, natural occurrence, as lightning or an earthquake, beyond the control of man; event that could not have been reasonably foreseen or prevented.

ac·tor (ak′tər) *n.* **1.** one who plays a role or performs, as in a play or motion picture. **2.** one who acts; doer.

ac·tress (ak′tris) *n.* female actor.

Acts (akts) *n.* book of the New Testament, attributed to Saint Luke. Also, **Acts of the Apostles.**

ac·tu·al (ak′chōō əl) *adj.* in existence; existing; real: *The actual result differed from our predictions.* [Old French *actuel* active, from Late Latin *āctuālis,* from Latin *āctus* a doing.] —**ac′tu·al·ness,** *n.* —**Syn.** see **real¹.**

at; āpe; cär; end; mē; it; īce; hot; ōld; fôrk; wood; fōōl; oil; out; up; ūse; turn; sing; thin; **th**is; zh in treasure; ə in ago, taken, pencil, lemon, circus.

ac·tu·al·i·ty (ak′chŏŏ al′ə tē) *pl.*, **-ties.** *n.* **1.** state or quality of being actual; reality. **2.** actual condition or circumstance; fact.

ac·tu·al·ize (ak′chŏŏ ə līz′) **-ized, -iz·ing.** *v.t.* to make actual; realize in action or fact. —**ac′tu·al·i·za′tion,** *n.*

ac·tu·al·ly (ak′chŏŏ ə lē) *adv.* in reality or fact; really: *He actually told the truth.*

ac·tu·ar·i·al (ak′chŏŏ ār′ē əl) *adj.* **1.** of actuaries or their work. **2.** determined by actuaries: *actuarial tables.*

ac·tu·ar·y (ak′chŏŏ er′ē) *pl.*, **-ar·ies.** *n.* one skilled in the mathematics and statistics of insurance. An actuary computes insurance risks and determines premiums, rates, and dividends. [Latin *āctuārius* keeper of accounts, from *āctus* a doing.]

ac·tu·ate (ak′chŏŏ āt′) **-at·ed, -at·ing.** *v.t.* **1.** to put into action or motion: *A spring actuates the trap.* **2.** to incite or influence to act; motivate: *He was actuated by desire for fame.* [Medieval Latin *actuatus,* past participle of *actuare* to perform, put in action, from Latin *āctus* doing.] —**ac′tu·a′tion, ac′tu·a′tor,** *n.*

a·cu·i·ty (ə kū′ə tē) *n.* sharpness; acuteness: *acuity of vision.* [French *acuité,* going back to Latin *acūtus* sharp. See ACUTE.]

a·cu·men (ə kū′mən) *n.* keenness of insight or judgment; mental sharpness: *the entrepreneur's great business acumen.* [Latin *acūmen* sharpness.]

a·cu·mi·nate (ə kū′mə nit) *adj.* tapering to a point; pointed. [Latin *acūmināatus,* past participle of *acūmināre* to make pointed.]

a·cute (ə kūt′) *adj.* **1.** having or exhibiting keenness of discernment or insight; penetrating: *an acute author, an acute mind.* **2.** sensitive to impressions or stimuli: *acute hearing.* **3.** acting keenly; intense; poignant: *acute jealousy, acute pain.* **4.** (of a disease) having a rapid onset and short duration: *acute pleurisy.* Distinguished from **chronic.** **5.** of utmost importance; severe; crucial: *an acute need.* **6.** ending in a sharp point; pointed. **7.** high in pitch; shrill: *Dogs can hear acute sounds that men cannot hear.* **8.** marked or pronounced with an acute accent ′. **9.** (of an angle) less than ninety degrees. [Latin *acūtus,* past participle of *acuere* to sharpen.] —**a·cute′ly,** *adv.* —**a·cute′ness,** *n.*

acute accent, mark (′) indicating the stress, quality, length, or pitch of a vowel, as in French *lycée,* or a difference in meaning, as in Spanish *quién.*

ad¹ (ad) *n.* advertisement.

ad² (ad) *n.* advantage in tennis.

ad- *prefix* used to express direction or motion toward or nearness to: *adverb.* [Latin *ad* to, at.]

A.D., anno Domini.

ad·age (ad′ij) *n.* familiar saying expressing popular wisdom; proverb. [French *adage,* from Latin *adagium.*] —**Syn.** see **proverb.**

a·da·gio (ə dä′jō, -zhē ō′) *adv. Music.* slowly; leisurely and gracefully. —*adj. Music.* slow. —*n. pl.,* **-gi·os. 1.** musical composition, movement, or part in adagio tempo. **2.** ballet dance in slow tempo. [Italian *ad agio* at ease, *agio* going back to Latin *adjacēns* nearby place (suggesting ease of access).]

Ad·am (ad′əm) *n.* in the Old Testament, the first man who, with his wife Eve, began the human race.

ad·a·mant (ad′ə mənt, -mant′) *adj.* totally unyielding: *The judge was adamant in his refusal to change his decision.* —*n.* legendary substance so hard that it could not be cut or broken. [Old French *adamant* diamond, hardest metal, going back to Greek *adamās,* from *a-* not + *damân* to tame.] —**ad′a·mant·ly,** *adv.*

ad·a·man·tine (ad′ə man′tin, -tēn, -tīn) *adj.* **1.** made of or like adamant in quality: *the adamantine chain of the logic* (Coleridge, 1817). **2.** *Mineralogy.* like a diamond in hardness or luster.

Ad·ams (ad′əmz) **1.** John. 1735-1826, second president of the United States, from 1797 to 1801. **2.** John Quin·cy. (kwin′sē). 1767-1848, his son; sixth president of the United States, from 1825 to 1829.

Adam's apple, projection in the throat just below the chin, formed by the largest cartilage of the larynx. [From the belief that a piece of the apple of the tree of knowledge stuck in Adam's throat.]

a·dapt (ə dapt′) *v.i., v.t.* **1.** to change (oneself) to meet particular circumstances. **2.** to alter or change to meet new requirements. [French *adapter* to adjust, fit, from Latin *adaptāre.*]

Syn. 2. Adapt, adjust, accommodate indicate a fitting together of things or persons. **Adapt** suggests relative ease in obtaining a fit: *The mechanic adapted American-made parts for the foreign car.* **Adjust** implies bringing into close or exact correspondence without major changes and, often, through the use of skill: *The tall man adjusted the microphone to his height.* **Accommodate** may be preferred when there is a marked variance between the objects brought into agreement and implies a special adaptation or compromise: *The office was redesigned to accommodate the bank and the restaurant.*

a·dapt·a·ble (ə dap′tə bəl) *adj.* **1.** capable of being adapted. **2.** capable of adapting. —**a·dapt′a·bil′i·ty, a·dapt′a·ble·ness,** *n.*

ad·ap·ta·tion (ad′əp tā′shən) *n.* **1.** act or process of adapting; being adapted. **2.** thing produced by adapting: *an adaptation of an old folk tale.* **3.** genetic modification of a species as a result of which it is better suited to survive in its environment.

a·dapt·er (ə dap′tər) *n.* **1.** one who adapts. **2.a.** device for modifying an apparatus for a new use. **b.** device for connecting unmatched parts of an apparatus.

a·dapt·ive (ə dap′tiv) *adj.* **1.** characterized by adaptation: *adaptive behavior.* **2.** tending to adapt: *adaptive power of the mind.*

add (ad) *v.t.* **1.a.** to put (something) with (another or others of the same kind): *to add a record to a collection.* **b.** to join (something to another or others); attach: *to add a porch to a house.* **2.** to combine (mathematical quantities) into a single sum (often with *up*). **3.** to say or write further. —*v.i.* **1.** to perform the arithmetical operation of addition: *He learned to add before he learned to multiply.* **2.** to make or serve as an addition; augment (with *to*): *The balloons added to the festive atmosphere.* **3. to add up. a.** to equal an established or desired total: *These figures don't add up.* **b.** to be meaningful or consistent: *The facts don't add up in this case.* **4. to add up to.** to amount to or mean: *Their actions added up to a deliberate flouting of the rules.* [Latin *addere* to add, from *ad-* to, at + *dare* to give. See DATE¹. The sense "to say or write further" is a development of the sense "to join, augment."] —**add′a·ble;** *also,* **add′i·ble,** *adj.*

ad·dax (ad′aks) *n.* antelope, *Addax nasomaculatus,* of the desert regions of Arabia, Syria, and North Africa. [Latin *addax;* of African origin (according to the Roman author Pliny).]

added line, ledger line.

ad·dend (ad′end, ə dend′) *n.* number or algebraic expression to be added to another.

Addax

ad·den·dum (ə den′dəm) *pl.,* **-da** (-də). *n.* **1.** something added; addition. **2.** appendix to a written work. [Latin *addendum* something to be added, from *addere* to add.]

ad·der (ad′ər) *n.* **1.** poisonous snake, *Vipera berus,* of northern Europe and Asia, brown with black markings. Length: 2 feet. **2.** North American hognose snake. **3.** any of various snakes of Africa, esp. the puff adder. [Middle English *naddre* viper, from Old English *nǣdre.* The initial *n* was lost by being joined to the preceding indefinite article: *a naddre* became *an adder.*]

ad·der's-tongue (ad′ərz tung′) *n.* **1.** fern, *Ophioglossum vulgatum,* whose spike resembles a snake's tongue. **2.** dogtooth violet.

ad·dict (*n.,* ad′ikt; *v.,* ə dikt′) *n.* **1.** one who is compulsively dependent on something, as drugs. **2.** devotee: *a TV addict.* —*v.t.* to cause (someone) to become compulsively dependent or devoted (with *to*). [Latin *addictus,* past participle of *addicere* to assign to, sentence; *addictus* implies "assigned to, as by a court of law," and thus, "bound to."]

ad·dic·tion (ə dik′shən) *n.* condition of being addicted; compulsive dependence.

Ad·dis Ab·a·ba (ad′is ab′ə bə) capital and largest city of Ethiopia, in the central part of the country. Pop. (1964), 644,120.

Ad·di·son, Joseph (ad′ə sən) 1672-1719, English essayist.

ad·di·tion (ə dish′ən) *n.* **1.** act or process of adding or joining. **2.** process of combining numbers into one sum. The symbol for the process is +. **3.** something added: *A new wing is an addition to a building.* **4. in addition.** besides; moreover. **5. in addition to.** as well as. [Latin *additiō* an adding.]

ad·di·tion·al (ə dish′ən əl) *adj.* added; further. —**ad·di′tion·al·ly,** *adv.* —**Syn.** see **extra.**

ad·di·tive (ad′ə tiv) *n.* substance used in relatively small quantities to improve or alter another substance or thing: *a fuel additive, a food additive.* —*adj.* involving or characterized by addition: *an additive compound.*

ad·dle (ad′əl) **-dled, -dling.** *v.t., v.i.* **1.** to make or become confused. **2.** (of an egg) to make or become rotten. —*adj.* muddled; confused. ▲ used only in combination, as in *addle-brained.* [The Greek noun *ourion ōion* wind egg (used for an egg that did not hatch) passed into Latin as *ōvum urīnum* wind egg, mistakenly thought to mean *ōvum urīnae* egg of urine, rotten egg, and was in turn translated into Middle English as *adel* egg (later *addle* egg), from Old English *adela* urine.]

ad·dress (*n.,* ə dres′, ad′res; *v.,* ə dres′) *n.* **1.** a formal speech: *a commencement address.* **2.** location of a building or place at which a person or organization can be reached: *a street address, a mailing address.* **3.** inscription on a letter, package, or other item to be delivered indicating its destination. **4.** personal manner in conversation; deportment: *the poise and elegance of an experienced actress.* **5.** adroitness: *to accomplish a job with address.* **6. addresses.** acts of courteous attention: *to pay one's addresses to a lady.* **7.** the place in a computer where a particular piece of information may be found. —*v.t.* **1.** to speak formally to: *to address a convention.* **2.** to direct (writing or speech) toward (with *to*): *He addressed his remarks to the jury.* **3.** to direct (oneself) in speech or writing (with *to*): *He addressed himself to the crowd.*

at; āpe; cär; end; mē; it; īce; hot; ōld; fôrk; wood; fŏŏl; oil; out; up; ūse; turn; sing; thin; this; zh in treasure; ə in ago, taken, pencil, lemon, circus.

11

4. to write the destination on (something to be delivered). **5.** to use proper forms in speaking or writing to: *How should one address a senator?* **6.** to apply (oneself); direct one's energies or attention. **7. to address the ball.** to assume a preparatory position in order to hit the ball in golf. [Old French *adresser, adrecier* to straighten, direct, convey, going back to Latin *ad* to, at + *dīrēctus* straight, direct.]

ad·dress·ee (ad′res ē′, ə dres′ē′) *n.* one to whom anything is addressed.

Ad·dres·so·graph (ə dres′ə graf′) *n. Trademark.* machine that prints addresses on mail by means of stencils.

ad·duce (ə dōōs′, ə dūs′) **-duced, -duc·ing.** *v.t.* to present as proof, reason, or example in argument. [Latin *addūcere* to lead to.]

ad·duct (ə dukt′) *v.t.* to move (a limb) toward the median axis of the body or (a finger or toe) toward the axis of the hand or foot. [Latin *adductus,* past participle of *addūcere* to lead to.]

ad·duc·tion (ə duk′shən) *n.* **1.** act of adducing; presenting as evidence. **2.** act of adducting; being adducted.

ad·duc·tor (ə duk′tər) *n.* muscle that adducts.

Ad·e·laide (ad′əl ād′) *n.* city in southern Australia. Pop. (1968), 747,700.

A·den (äd′ən, ād′ən) *n.* **1.** region and port on the southeastern coast of Southern Yemen, formerly a British dependency. Area, 80 sq. mi. Pop. (1966 est.), 250,000. **2. Gulf of.** western inlet of the Arabian Sea, between southern Arabia and eastern Africa.

ad·e·nine (ad′ən ēn′, -in) *n.* purine base that is an essential constituent of DNA and RNA. Formula: $C_5H_5N_5$

ad·e·noid (ad′ən oid′) *adj.* **1.** relating to lymphoid tissue. **2.** relating to or resembling a gland; glandular. —*n. usually,* **adenoids.** overgrowth of glandular tissue in the upper part of the throat, behind the nose, esp. noticeable in children. See **nose** for illustration. [Greek *adenoeidēs* glandular, from *adēn* gland.]

ad·e·noi·dal (ad′ən oid′əl) *adj.* **1.** adenoid. **2.** of inflamed adenoids or the speech and breathing attendant on them.

a·dept (*adj.* ə dept′; *n.* ad′ept) *adj.* highly skilled; proficient: *adept in his work.* —*n.* one who is proficient; an expert: *an adept in music.* [Medieval Latin *adeptus* a title given to alchemists who supposedly had achieved the transmutation of lesser metals into gold, from Latin *adeptus,* past participle of *adipiscī* to attain.] —**a·dept′ly,** *adv.* —**a·dept′ness,** *n.* —**Syn.** *adj.* see **expert.**

ad·e·qua·cy (ad′ə kwə sē) *n.* quality or state of being adequate.

ad·e·quate (ad′ə kwət) *adj.* **1.** sufficient; suitable. **2.** just passable; mediocre. [Latin *adaequātus,* past participle of *adaequāre* to make equal.] —**ad′e·quate·ly,** *adv.* —**ad′e·quate·ness,** *n.* —**Syn. 1.** see **enough.**

Ad·ha·ra (ad här′ə) *n.* star in the constellation Canis Major and one of the brightest in the sky.

ad·here (ad hēr′) **-hered, -her·ing.** *v.i.* **1.** to stick or hold fast: *This glue adheres under the worst conditions.* **2.** to keep by; observe closely (with *to*): *They adhered to the contract.* **3.** to attach oneself; support firmly (with *to*): *to adhere to a doctrine.* [Latin *adhaerēre* to stick to.]

ad·her·ence (ad hēr′əns) *n.* **1.** firm attachment; faithful support: *adherence to a cause.* **2.** close observance: *adherence to tradition.*

ad·her·ent (ad hēr′ənt) *n.* firm supporter; advocate: *an adherent of free trade.* —*adj.* **1.** sticking or able to stick. **2.** connected: *parties adherent to the agreement.*

ad·he·sion (ad hē′zhən) *n.* **1.** act or state of sticking or holding fast. **2.** faithful attachment; adherence. **3.** abnormal growing together of separate organs or their parts, as after an operation. **4.** fibrous tissue by which such parts are abnormally connected. **5.** attraction, and the result of the attraction, between dissimilar particles in contact which causes them to cling to each other. [Latin *adhaesiō* a sticking to.]

ad·he·sive (ad hē′siv, -ziv) *adj.* **1.** tending to stick or hold fast; clinging: *Wet snow has adhesive properties.* **2.** having a sticky surface that will hold fast to something; gummed: *adhesive labels.* —*n.* **1.** an adhesive substance: *Glue is an adhesive.* **2.** adhesive tape. —**ad·he′sive·ly,** *adv.* —**ad·he′sive·ness,** *n.*

adhesive tape, tape coated on one side with a sticky substance.

ad hoc (ad hok′) for a specific and limited purpose: *an ad hoc committee.* [Latin *ad hoc* literally, to this.]

ad hom·i·nem (ad hom′ə nem′) (of an argument) attacking the person who holds opposing views, rather than dealing with those views on their own merit. [Latin *ad hominem* literally, to the man.]

a·dieu (ə dōō′, ə dū′) *pl.* **a·dieus** or **a·dieux** (ə dōōz′, ə dūz′). *interj., n.* good-by; farewell. [Old French *adieu,* standing for *à Dieu* (I commend you) to God, going back to Latin *ad Deum* to God.]

ad in·fi·ni·tum (ad′ in′fə nī′təm) without limit; endlessly. [Latin *ad infinītum* literally, to the infinite.]

ad in·ter·im (ad in′tər im) *Latin.* in the meantime.

a·di·os (ä′dē ōs′, ad′ē-) *interj., n.* good-by; farewell. [Spanish *adiós,* standing for *a Dios* (I commend you) to God, going back to Latin *ad Deum* to God.]

ad·i·pose (ad′ə pōs′) *adj.* relating to animal fat; fatty. [Modern Latin *adiposus,* from Latin *adeps* fat.]

adipose tissue, loose connective tissue, found throughout an animal's body, in which fat cells are deposited.

ad·i·pos·i·ty (ad′ə pos′ə tē) *n.* **1.** fatness; obesity. **2.** tendency to become corpulent or obese.

Ad·i·ron·dacks (ad′ə ron′daks) *n.,pl.* mountain range in northeastern New York. Also, **Adirondack Mountains.**

ad·it (ad′it) *n.* **1.** entrance. **2.** nearly horizontal tunnel leading from the surface into a mine. [Latin *aditus* approach.]

adj. 1. adjective. **2.** adjourned. **3.** adjustment. **4.** adjunct.

ad·ja·cen·cy (ə jā′sən sē) *n.* **1.** nearness; proximity: *the adjacency of the land to water.* **2.** something that lies near.

ad·ja·cent (ə jā′sənt) *adj.* lying next to or near; neighboring: *The fire spread to the adjacent farmland.* [Latin *adjacēns,* present participle of *adjacēre* to lie near.] —**ad·ja′cent·ly,** *adv.*

Syn. Adjacent, contiguous, adjoining describe close physical proximity. **Adjacent** is used of things near each other that may or may not be touching: *The auditorium is adjacent to the dining rooms.* **Contiguous** indicates more or less extensive contact between two bodies: *France and Spain are contiguous where the Pyrenees form a natural border.* **Adjoining** usually implies direct contact, though it may also suggest that the things are separated slightly: *From the terrace, an adjoining lawn slopes gently toward the bay.*

adjacent angles, two angles having the same vertex and a common side.

ad·jec·ti·val (aj′ik tī′vəl) *adj.* **1.** of, belonging to, or resembling an adjective: *adjectival form.* **2.** functioning as an adjective: *adjectival phrase.*

ad·jec·ti·val·ly (aj′ik tī′və lē) *adv.* as an adjective: *a noun used adjectivally.*

Adjacent angles *XWY* and *YWZ* are adjacent angles

ad·jec·tive (aj′ik tiv) *n.* word belonging to that part of speech in many languages which modifies a noun or pronoun. An adjective may describe the word it modifies (*red* car, *sad* boy) or in some way limit the word (*that* pen, *his* bat, *many* books, *three* dogs). —*adj.* **1.** having the quality of or functioning as an adjective. **2.** dependent; secondary. [Late Latin *adjectīvum (verbum)* added (word), going back to Latin *adjectus,* past participle of *adicere* to cast beside, place beside.]

ad·join (ə join′) *v.t.* **1.** to be next to; touch on; be contiguous to: *The garage adjoins the house.* **2.** *Archaic.* to attach or append. —*v.i.* to be close together or touching: *Their farms adjoin.* [Old French *ajoindre* to join, from Latin *adjungere* to join to.]

ad·join·ing (ə joi′ning) *adj.* located next to; adjacent. —**Syn.** adjacent.

ad·journ (ə jurn′) *v.t.* **1.** to postpone; defer: *The case was adjourned until next week.* **2.** to suspend the work or proceedings (of a group or formal body). —*v.i.* **1.** to suspend work or proceedings: *The Senate adjourned for the summer.* **2.** to leave in order to go (to another place): *Let's adjourn to the sitting room.* [Old French *ajorner* to postpone (to an appointed day), going back to Latin *ad* to + Late Latin *diurnum* day, from Latin *diurnus* daily.]

ad·journ·ment (ə jurn′mənt) *n.* **1.** act of adjourning: *The chairman called for a vote on adjournment.* **2.a.** state of being adjourned: *The adjournment of the case lasted for two weeks.* **b.** interval during which a group or formal body is adjourned: *a month's adjournment.*

ad·judge (ə juj′) **-judged, -judg·ing.** *v.t.* **1.** to decide or settle judicially; adjudicate. **2.** to pronounce or decree judicially. **3.** to condemn or sentence (with *to*): *adjudged to life in prison.* **4.** to award or grant judicially: *The money was adjudged to the defendant.* **5.** to deem; consider. [Old French *ajuger* to bring to trial, sentence, decide, from Latin *adjūdicāre* to award, assign. Doublet of ADJUDICATE.]

ad·ju·di·cate (ə jōō′də kāt′) **-cat·ed, -cat·ing.** *v.t.* to consider and decide judicially: *to adjudicate a case in civil court.* —*v.i.* to sit in judgment; pronounce judgment: *to adjudicate in a dispute.* [Latin *adjūdicātus,* past participle of *adjūdicāre* to award, assign. Doublet of ADJUDGE.]

ad·ju·di·ca·tion (ə jōō′də kā′shən) *n.* **1.** act or process of adjudicating. **2.** decision or decree of a judge or court.

ad·junct (aj′ungkt) *n.* **1.** auxiliary or secondary thing. **2.** person acting as a subordinate or assistant to someone else. **3.** dependent word or phrase added to another word or phrase as a modifier. [Latin *adjūnctus,* past participle of *adjungere* to join to.]

ad·ju·ra·tion (aj′ə rā′shən) *n.* **1.** solemn charge or order. **2.** earnest request or appeal.

ad·jure (ə joor′) **-jured, -jur·ing.** *v.t.* **1.** to order or charge solemnly, esp. on oath or threat of penalty: *to adjure a witness to testify truthfully.* **2.** to urge seriously; request earnestly: *His friend adjured him to be careful.* [Latin *adjūrāre* to swear to.]

ad·just (ə just′) *v.t.* **1.** to arrange or alter to fit or accommodate: *He*

at; āpe; cär; end; mē; it; īce; hot; ōld; fôrk; wood; fŏŏl; oil; out; up; ūse; turn; sing; thin; this; zh in treasure; ə in ago, taken, pencil, lemon, circus.

adjusted his position for a clearer view. **2.** to arrange properly or regulate for proper functioning: *to adjust your tie, to adjust the brakes.* **3.a.** to arrange satisfactory terms of agreement or settlement: *to adjust a claim.* **b.** to correct; rectify: *to adjust an account.* —*v.i.* to adapt oneself; become accustomed: *to adjust to a new climate.* [Obsolete French *adjuster* to settle, adapt, going back to Latin *ad* to + *juxtā* near, close.] —**ad·just'a·ble,** *adj.* —**Syn.** *v.t.* **1.** see **adapt.**

ad·just·er (ə jus'tər) *also,* **ad·jus·tor.** *n.* **1.** thing or part used to make an adjustment, as a mechanical device. **2.** one who rectifies or settles: *a claims adjuster.*

ad·just·ment (ə just'mənt) *n.* **1.** process of adjusting; an adapting: *a slow adjustment to a new situation.* **2.** state of being adjusted for proper functioning: *a perfect adjustment of an instrument.* **3.** method or device by which something is adjusted or regulated: *the adjustments on a microscope.* **4.a.** process of determining the amount to be paid in settling a claim. **b.** the amount paid. **5.** rectification; modification: *to make adjustments for new statistical data.*

ad·ju·tant (aj'ə tənt) *n.* **1.** military staff officer who acts as administrative assistant to a commanding officer. **2.** an aide; assistant. [Latin *adjūtāns,* present participle of *adjūtāre* to assist.] —**ad'ju·tan·cy,** *n.*

adjutant bird, marabou. Also, **adjutant stork.** [Because of the bird's erect and seemingly military bearing.]

adjutant general *pl.* **adjutants general.** **1.** chief officer of the administrative branch of the U.S. Army. **2.** adjutant of any U.S. Army unit having a general staff.

ad·ju·vant (aj'ə vənt) *n.* one who or that which helps or assists, esp. a substance added to a drug to facilitate its action. —*adj. Archaic.* helping; auxiliary. [Latin *adjuvāns,* present participle of *adjuvāre* to help, assist.]

Ad·ler, Alfred (ad'lər) 1870–1937, Austrian psychiatrist.

ad-lib (ad'lib') **ad-libbed, ad-lib-bing.** *v.t., v.i.* **1.** (of an actor, entertainer, or the like) to say or do something not in the script. **2.** to engage in any performance not previously planned; improvise. —*n.* something improvised, esp. repartee on the stage. —*adj.* improvised. [From AD LIBITUM.]

ad lib, in an improvised way; by improvising.

ad lib., ad libitum.

ad lib·i·tum (ad lib'ə təm) *Music.* as one wishes. ▲ used to indicate that the performer may vary, expand, or omit a passage at his own discretion. [Modern Latin *ad libitum* at (one's) pleasure; *libitum* from neuter past participle of Latin *libet* it pleases.]

adm., administrator; administrative.

Adm. **1.** Admiral. **2.** Admiralty.

Ad·me·tus (ad mē'təs) *n.* *Greek Legend.* king of Thessaly and husband of Alcestis.

ad·min·is·ter (ad min'is tər) *v.t.* **1.** to control the operation of; manage; direct. **2.** to apply; use: *to administer medicine.* **3.** to dispense; provide; supply: *The Red Cross administers aid in disaster areas.* **4.** to give or offer formally, as an oath. **5.** *Law.* to manage or settle (an estate). —*v.i.* **1.** to be of beneficial service; contribute (with *to*): *to administer to the well-being of the community.* **2.** to act as administrator or executor. [Old French *aministrer* to take care of, manage, from Latin *administrāre* to manage.] —**Syn.** *v.t.* **1.** see **manage.**

ad·min·is·trate (ad min'is trāt') **-trat·ed, -trat·ing.** *v.t., v.i.* to administer.

ad·min·is·tra·tion (ad min'is trā'shən) *n.* **1.** act or method of managing or directing. **2.** group of persons empowered to manage and direct; officials: *school administration.* **3.** operation and execution of governmental affairs. **4.a.** executive branch of a government, esp. one in power for a certain period. **b.** *also,* **Administration.** the president of the United States and his cabinet. **5.** period during which a chief executive holds office. **6.** act of administering something to others, as an oath, medicine, or justice.

ad·min·is·tra·tive (ad min'is trā'tiv) *adj.* pertaining to administration or management. —**ad·min'is·tra'tive·ly,** *adv.*

ad·min·is·tra·tor (ad min'is trā'tər) *n.* **1.** one who administers. **2.** one appointed by a law court to manage or settle the estate of a deceased person. Distinguished from **executor.**

ad·min·is·tra·trix (ad min'is trā'triks) *pl.* **-tra·tri·ces** (-trā'trə-sēz', -trə trī'sēz), **-trixes.** *n.* woman administrator.

ad·mi·ra·ble (ad'mər ə bəl) *adj.* **1.** deserving admiration. **2.** excellent. [French *admirable,* from Latin *admirābilis.*] —**ad'mi·ra·ble·ness,** *n.* —**ad'mi·ra·bly,** *adv.*

ad·mi·ral (ad'mər əl) *n.* **1.** commander in chief of a fleet. **2.** *U.S. Navy.* **a.** officer of the second highest rank. **b.** fleet admiral, vice admiral, or rear admiral. **3.** either of two species of brightly colored butterflies: the **red admiral,** *Vanessa atalanta,* or the **white admiral,** *Limenitis arthemis.* [Middle French *amiral* high-ranking naval officer, going back to Arabic *amīr-al-* commander of the sea (as in *amīr-al-bahr* commander of the sea.)]

ad·mi·ral·ty (ad'mər əl tē) *pl.* **-ties.** *n.* **1.a.** branch of law that deals with maritime affairs. **b.** court that administers it. **2.** *also,* **Admiralty.** British government department or officials appointed for the administration of naval affairs.

ad·mi·ra·tion (ad'mə rā'shən) *n.* **1.** feeling of high regard or esteem: *She earned the admiration of all who knew her.* **2.** act of viewing something with appreciation and delight: *admiration of a beautiful painting.* **3.** object of appreciation or respect. **4.** *Archaic.* wonder. [Latin *admirātiō* an admiring.]

ad·mire (ad mīr') **-mired, -mir·ing.** *v.t.* **1.** to feel high regard or esteem for. **2.** to regard with delight and pleasurable appreciation. **3.** *Archaic.* to marvel at. —*v.i. Informal.* to be pleased: *I'd admire to walk with you.* [Latin *admīrārī* to marvel at.]

ad·mir·er (ad mīr'ər) *n.* **1.** one who admires. **2.** man who is in love with, or courts, a woman.

ad·mis·si·bil·i·ty (ad mis'ə bil'ə tē) *n.* quality or state of being admissible.

ad·mis·si·ble (ad mis'ə bəl) *adj.* **1.** that can be allowed or properly considered; an admissible argument. **2.** qualifying for admission (to something). —**ad·mis'si·ble·ness,** *n.* —**ad·mis'si·bly,** *adv.*

ad·mis·sion (ad mish'ən) *n.* **1.a.** act of granting or being granted entrance or formal acceptance: *the admission of students to college.* **b.** permission to function, as in some professional capacity: *admission to medical practice.* **2.** privilege of entrance or use: *to have admission to a club.* **3.** fee required for entrance: *The admission is two dollars.* **4.** acknowledgment; confession. **5.** an allowing or granting as valid or relevant: *the admission of an argument in debate.* [Latin *admissiō* a letting in.]

Syn. **2. Admission, admittance** refer to right of entry. **Admission** is the more general term, referring to figurative as well as physical entry; it further implies privileges and duties entailed in such entry: *Admission to the fellowship followed long investigation by committees as well as an initiation ceremony.* **Admittance** refers only to physical entry into places: *Only by showing his ticket could he gain admittance.*

ad·mit (ad mit') **-mit·ted, -mit·ting.** *v.t.* **1.a.** to grant entrance to; let in: *The ushers admitted only one person at a time. John was admitted to the inner circle.* **b.** to allow to function, as in some professional capacity: *to admit an attorney to practice before the Supreme Court.* **2.** to acknowledge; confess; grant: *to admit one's guilt. I'll admit you're right.* **3.** to recognize as valid or relevant: *to admit evidence in a trial.* **4.** to be the means of entrance for: *This pass will admit you to the show.* **5.** to have the room to hold; accommodate. —*v.i.* **1.** to allow the possibility (with *of*): *His outrageous behavior admits of no apology.* **2.** to open access to; open on (with *to*): *The hatchway admits to the engine room.* [Latin *admittere* to let in.]

Syn. *v.t.* **2. Admit, acknowledge, confess** indicate disclosure. **Admit** suggests an impelling force, generally an outside force, causing the disclosure of fact: *Under interrogation he admitted his presence at the scene.* **Acknowledge** stresses disclosure of what one knows but has previously concealed: *He acknowledged that they had been married for more than a year.* **Confess** indicates disclosure of something one knows to be wrong, esp. something discreditable to oneself: *He confessed that he was the one who had broken the flowerpot.*

ad·mit·tance (ad mit'əns) *n.* **1.** permission to enter; privilege of entrance. **2.** act of admitting; being admitted. —**Syn.** **1.** see **admission.**

ad·mit·ted·ly (ad mit'id lē) *adv.* **1.** by common acknowledgment. **2.** by confession.

ad·mix (ad miks') *v.t., v.i.* to mix into something else; blend.

ad·mix·ture (ad miks'chər) *n.* **1.** something added in mixing; an additive, alloy, or adulterant. **2.** act of mixing. **3.** mixture. [Latin *admixtus,* past participle of *admiscēre* to mix with.]

ad·mon·ish (ad mon'ish) *v.t.* **1.** to caution, as against specific action; warn: *He was admonished not to cut class again.* **2.** to reprimand, usually mildly. **3.** to advise strongly: *They were admonished to repent.* [Old French *amonester* to warn, going back to Latin *admonēre* to remind, warn.] —**ad·mon'ish·er,** *n.* —**ad·mon'ish·ment,** *n.*

ad·mo·ni·tion (ad'mə nish'ən) *n.* **1.** warning. **2.** advice or counsel. **3.** reprimand. [Latin *admonitiō* a calling to mind.]

ad·mon·i·to·ry (ad mon'ə-tôr'ē) *adj.* cautioning; warning: *an admonitory tone of voice.* —**ad·mon'i·to'ri·ly,** *adv.*

ad nau·se·am (ad nô'zē əm) to a disgusting extent. [Latin *ad nauseam* to the point of nausea.]

a·do (ə dōō') *n.* **1.** fuss; bustle; difficulty: *much ado about nothing.* [Middle English *at do* to do.]

Adobe house

a·do·be (ə dō'bē) *n.* **1.** sun-dried brick, used as a building material. **2.** clay or soil from which these

bricks are made. —*adj.* constructed of adobe: *adobe hacienda.* [Spanish *adobe* sun-dried brick, through Arabic *attōb* the brick, from Coptic *tōb* brick.]

ad·o·les·cence (ad'əl es'əns) *n.* **1.** period or process of growing from puberty to adulthood. **2.** state or condition of being adolescent.

ad·o·les·cent (ad'əl es'ənt) *n.* person between puberty and adulthood. —*adj.* **1.** growing from puberty to adulthood. **2.** characteristic of or having to do with adolescence or an adolescent; youthful; immature: *adolescent behavior.* [Latin *adolēscēns,* present participle of *adolēscere* to grow up.]

A·don·is (ə don'is, ə dō'nis) *n.* **1.** *Greek Mythology.* a handsome youth who was loved by Aphrodite and Persephone. **2.** any handsome young man. [Latin *Adōnis,* through Greek, from Phoenician *adōn* lord, a title given to some of the Phoenicians' gods.]

a·dopt (ə dopt') *v.t.* **1.** to accept and take as one's own; embrace. **2.** to accept by formal vote: *The board adopted the proposal after much debate.* **3.** to take into one's family (a child of other parents), esp. by a formal legal act. **4.** to select, esp. a textbook, for required use in a U.S. school system. [Latin *adoptāre* to choose for oneself.]

Syn. **1.** Adopt, assume are used of taking some thing as one's own. **Adopt** implies no pretense but rather a taking that is completely in character: *The fraternity adopted the uniform of German university students.* **Assume** often suggests dissembling and acting as if one were someone else: *He assumed the role of the protective father.*

a·dop·tion (ə dop'shən) *n.* **1.** act of adopting; being adopted. **2.** legal act of assuming parenthood of a child who is not one's own.

a·dop·tive (ə dop'tiv) *adj.* **1.** tending to adopt. **2.** related by adoption. **3.** associated with adoption. —**a·dop'tive·ly,** *adv.*

a·dor·a·ble (ə dôr'ə bəl) *adj.* **1.** worthy of adoration. **2.** charming: *an adorable child.* —**a·dor'a·bly,** *adv.*

ad·o·ra·tion (ad'ə rā'shən) *n.* **1.** act of honoring or worshiping as divine: *the adoration of the Magi.* **2.** reverent love and devotion.

a·dore (ə dôr') **a·dored, a·dor·ing.** *v.t.* **1.** to have love and admiration for; idolize: *Her students adored her.* **2.** to honor as divine; worship. **3.** *Informal.* to have a great liking for: *I adore your hat.* [Latin *adōrāre* to address, worship, going back to *ad* to + *ōs* (stem *ōr-*) mouth (in the sense of using the mouth, or kissing, in religious observance).] —**a·dor'er,** *n.* —**a·dor'ing·ly,** *adv.*

a·dorn (ə dôrn') *v.t.* **1.** to add or lend beauty, honor, or distinction to; enhance: *Her face has adorned many magazine covers.* **2.** to make beautiful or decorate: *to adorn the room with flowers.* [Old French *adorner* to provide, decorate, from Latin *adōrnāre.*] —**a·dorn'er,** *n.* —**Syn.** **2.** see decorate.

a·dorn·ment (ə dôrn'mənt) *n.* **1.** that which adorns; ornament: *adornments for her hair.* **2.** act of adorning; being adorned.

a·down (ə doun') *adv., prep. Archaic.* down.

ad·re·nal (ə drēn'əl) *adj.* **1.** near or on the kidneys. **2.** relating to or from the adrenal glands. —*n.* an adrenal gland. [Latin *ad* at + Late Latin *rēnālis* of the kidneys, from Latin *rēnēs* kidneys.]

adrenal gland, one of a pair of small ductless glands above the kidneys, that secrete several hormones. Also, **suprarenal gland.**

ad·ren·a·lin (ə dren'əl in) *also,* **ad·ren·a·line.** *n.* **1.** hormone secreted by the medulla of the adrenal glands that affects the body as a stimulant. **2.** drug used as a stimulant, esp. for the heart. Trademark: Adrenalin. Also, **ep'in·eph'rine.**

A·dri·at·ic (ā'drē at'ik) *n.* sea between Italy and Yugoslavia, an arm of the Mediterranean.

a·drift (ə drift') *adv., adj.* **1.** (of a ship or other floating object) without mooring; moving with the current. **2.** without direction or aim.

a·droit (ə droit') *adj.* smoothly skillful; deft: *adroit in the use of tools.* [French *adroit,* from *à droit* rightly, properly, going back to Latin *ad* to + *dīrēctus* straight, right.] —**a·droit'ness,** *n.* —**Syn.** see clever, dexterous.

ad·sorb (ad sôrb', -zôrb') *v.t.* to retain (a gas, liquid, or dissolved substance) on the surface as opposed to absorbing it. [Latin *ad* to + *sorbēre* to suck.]

ad·sor·bate (ad sôr'bāt, -bit, -zôr'-) *n.* solid, liquid, or gas which is adsorbed.

ad·sor·bent (ad sôr'bənt, -zôr'-) *adj.* able to adsorb. —*n.* liquid or solid that adsorbs.

ad·sorp·tion (ad sôrp'shən, -zôrp'-) *n.* process of adsorbing; state of being adsorbed.

ad·sorp·tive (ad sôrp'tiv, -zôrp'-) *adj.* **1.** connected with adsorption. **2.** able to adsorb. —*n.* substance that adsorbs.

ad·u·late (aj'ə lāt') **-lat·ed, -lat·ing.** *v.t.* to praise or admire lavishly. [Latin *adūlātus,* past participle of *adūlārī* to flatter.] —**ad'u·la'tor,** *n.*

Charcoal particle

Sponge

Adsorption of gas molecules

Absorption of water

Adsorption

ad·u·la·tion (aj'ə lā'shən) *n.* lavish praise or flattery.

ad·u·la·to·ry (aj'ə lə tôr'ē) *adj.* lavishly praising or flattering.

a·dult (ə dult', ad'ult) *adj.* **1.** having attained maturity; fully grown. **2.** of, characteristic of, or for adults. —*n.* **1.** grown man or woman; mature person. **2.** plant or animal that has reached full growth. **3.** one who is legally of age. Opposed to **minor.** [Latin *adultus* grown up, past participle of *adolescere* to grow up.] —**a·dult'hood',** *n.*

a·dul·ter·ant (ə dul'tər ənt) *n.* substance or element that adulterates.

a·dul·ter·ate (ə dul'tə rāt') **-at·ed, -at·ing.** *v.t.* to lessen the quality of (something) by including in it inferior or inappropriate substances, esp. to debase commercial goods in this way. [Latin *adulterātus,* past participle of *adulterāre* to corrupt; literally, to change to something other (for the worse), going back to Latin *ad* to + *alter* other.]

a·dul·ter·a·tion (ə dul'tə rā'shən) *n.* **1.** act or process of adulterating. **2.** adulterated substance or product.

a·dul·ter·er (ə dul'tər ər) *n.* one who commits adultery, esp. a man.

a·dul·ter·ess (ə dul'tər is, -tris) *n.* woman who commits adultery.

a·dul·ter·ous (ə dul'tər əs) *adj.* **1.** inclined to or guilty of adultery. **2.** characterized by or concerning adultery. —**a·dul'ter·ous·ly,** *adv.*

a·dul·ter·y (ə dul'tər ē) *pl.,* **-ter·ies.** *n.* voluntary sexual intercourse of a married person with anyone except his or her spouse. [Modification of Old French *avouterie,* influenced by Latin *adulterium.*]

ad·um·brate (ad'əm brāt', ə dum'-) **-brat·ed, -brat·ing.** *v.t.* **1.** to suggest faintly or sketchily. **2.** to foreshadow. **3.** to overshadow. [Latin *adumbrātus,* past participle of *adumbrāre* to overshadow, cast a shadow over.] —**ad'um·bra'tion,** *n.*

adv. **1.** adverb. **2.** adverbial. **3.** advertisement.

ad val. ad valorem.

ad va·lo·rem (ad və lôr'əm) (of merchandise) in proportion to the value: *an ad valorem tax.* [Latin phrase *ad valorem* (according to value.)]

ad·vance (əd vans') **-vanced, -vanc·ing.** *v.t.* **1.** to move (something) forward: *to advance the hands on a clock.* **2.** to help the progress of; further: *His work advanced the science of microbiology.* **3.** to offer; propose: *to advance a theory.* **4.** to raise to a higher or more favorable position or rank: *to advance an actor to stardom.* **5.** to increase (the rate or price). **6.a.** to make earlier, as a time, date, or event: *to advance the wedding from June 30 to June 12.* **b.** to hasten. **7.** to pay on credit or in expectation of being repaid. **8.** to lend (on credit or security): *Advance him five dollars.* —*v.i.* **1.** to move forward; proceed: *He advanced through the crowd.* **2.** to progress; improve; grow. **3.** to move up (in position, rank, or esteem): *to advance in the community.* **4.** to increase in price, rate, or value: *Railroad stocks advanced two points.* **5.** (of color) to appear to move toward the viewer: *Red advances while black recedes.* —*n.* **1.** movement forward in space. **2.a.** progress; growth. **b.** improvement. **3.** an increase in price or value. **4. advances.** attempts to establish friendship, accord, or understanding; personal overtures. **5.** payment or provision given before due or without immediate return of goods, services, or other repayment. **6. in advance. a.** ahead of time: *Pay in advance.* **b.** in front: *a boy far in advance of his friends.* —*adj.* **1.** ahead of time; early: *advance sale.* **2.** situated in front; preceding: *an advance scout.* [Old French *avancier* to set out before (someone), going back to Latin *abante* away before.]

Syn. *v.i.* **1.** Advance, proceed, progress indicate forward motion. **Advance** indicates motion toward a definite goal, or motion for a definite time, or over a definite space: *The hands of the clock seemed not to advance.* **Proceed** implies a steady motion ahead, despite pauses or obstacles: *Plans for the meeting of the heads of state proceeded throughout the tense period of border conflicts.* **Progress** indicates forward motion in a regular, methodical way, as if following some law of nature: *At every visit to the site, they could see that the building was progressing.*

ad·vanced (ad vanst') *adj.* **1.a.** ahead of others; modern; progressive: *the most advanced social concepts.* **b.** past the elementary; not primary: *advanced algebra.* **2.** near the end in development or time: *at an advanced age.* **3.** situated in front; moved forward: *an advanced pawn.*

advanced standing, credit given to a student by a college for work done in another school.

advance guard, body of troops going before the main force.

ad·vance·ment (ad vans'mənt) *n.* **1.** progression; furtherance. **2.** promotion to a higher rank or position: *a job with opportunities for advancement.* **3.** movement forward in space. —**Syn.** see promotion.

ad·van·tage (ad van'tij) *n.* **1.** useful or beneficial circumstance, factor, or event; asset: *Nearby shopping is an advantage of living in the city.* **2.** benefit; gain: *More practice will be to your advantage.* **3.** better position; superiority (often with *of* or *over*): *The invaders had an overwhelming advantage over the natives.* **4.** *Tennis.* first point after deuce. **5. to advantage.** favorably; effectively: *to display a painting to advantage.* **6. to take advantage of. a.** to use profitably. **b.** to exploit unfairly. —*v.t.* **-taged, -tag·ing.** *Archaic.* to be of aid to; benefit. [Old French

at; āpe; cär; end; mē; it; īce; hot; ōld; fôrk; wood; fool; oil; out; up; ūse; turn; sing; thin; this; zh in treasure; ə in ago, taken, pencil, lemon, circus.

avantage advance, head start, going back to Latin *abante* away before.]

Syn. *n.* **2. Advantage, benefit, profit** have similar meanings when some kind of increase to the good is indicated. **Advantage** implies a change that puts someone in a better position relative to others: *Voice training will be to your advantage if you plan to go into the theater.* **Benefit** refers broadly to any improvement in the welfare of a person or group: *The benefits of town planning became clear to all.* **Profit** stresses the value or usefulness, often material, of the change for the better: *The voter may study the booklet on election procedures with profit.*

ad·van·ta·geous (ad van tā′jəs) *adj.* affording advantage; favorable; beneficial. —**ad′van·ta′geous·ly,** *adv.* —**ad′van·ta′geous·ness,** *n.*

ad·vent (ad′vent) *n.* **1.** arrival: *the advent of old age.* **2. Advent. a.** the birth of Christ. **b.** period of devotion just before Christmas, which includes four Sundays. **c.** Second Coming. [Latin *adventus* arrival.]

Ad·vent·ist (ad′ven tist) *n.* member of a Christian denomination believing that the Second Coming of Christ will soon occur. —**Ad′vent·ism,** *n.*

ad·ven·ti·tious (ad′ven tish′əs) *adj.* **1.** not essential or intrinsic. **2.** (of part of a plant or animal) appearing out of the usual or normal place, as buds growing from roots of a plant. [Latin *adventīcius* coming from abroad, foreign.] —**ad′ven·ti′tious·ly,** *adv.* —**ad′ven·ti′tious·ness,** *n.*

ad·ven·tive (ad ven′tiv) *adj.* (of plants or animals) in a new environment; not native or not yet naturalized; exotic.

Advent Sunday, first Sunday in Advent.

ad·ven·ture (ad ven′chər) *n.* **1.** difficult and perilous undertaking; speculative venture: *I would hesitate to get involved in this adventure.* **2.** thrilling or unusual experience: *A day in the city was always an adventure for her.* —*v.i.,* **-tured, -tur·ing. 1.** to venture. **2.** to seek hazardous or thrilling experiences. —*v.t.* to venture. [Old French *aventure* chance, mischance, from Latin *(rēs) adventūra* (thing) about to happen, feminine future participle of *advenīre* to happen.]

ad·ven·tur·er (ad ven′chər ər) *n.* **1.** one who engages in or seeks adventures. **2.** soldier of fortune. **3.** one who uses questionable or deceitful means to advance oneself.

ad·ven·ture·some (ad ven′chər səm) *adj.* adventurous.

ad·ven·tur·ess (ad ven′chər is) *n.* **1.** woman who schemes or uses her charms to obtain wealth or social position. **2.** female adventurer (defs. 1, 3).

ad·ven·tur·ous (ad ven′chər əs) *adj.* **1.** eager for adventure; willing to encounter danger: *an adventurous knight.* **2.** full of danger; hazardous. —**ad·ven′tur·ous·ly,** *adv.* —**ad·ven′tur·ous·ness,** *n.*

ad·verb (ad′vurb′) *n.* word belonging to that part of speech in many languages which modifies a verb, adjective, or another adverb, indicating such ideas as time, place, degree, or manner. [Latin *adverbium.*]

ad·ver·bi·al (ad vur′bē əl) *adj.* **1.** of or belonging to an adverb: *an adverbial suffix.* **2.** functioning as an adverb: *an adverbial clause.* —**ad·ver′bi·al·ly,** *adv.*

ad·ver·sar·y (ad′vər ser′ē) *pl.,* **-sar·ies.** *n.* person or group that is hostile or competing; opponent; enemy. [Old French *adversarie,* from Latin *adversārius.*] —**Syn.** see **opponent.**

ad·ver·sa·tive (ad vur′sə tiv) *adj.* (of words or propositions) expressing opposition or antithesis. *But* is an adversative conjunction. —*n.* adversative word or proposition. —**ad·ver′sa·tive·ly,** *adv.*

ad·verse (ad vurs′, ad′vurs) *adj.* **1.** unfavorable; difficult: *adverse circumstances.* **2.** antagonistic; hostile: *an adverse attitude.* **3.** acting so as to hinder; opposite: *adverse winds.* [Old French *advers* opposite, hostile, from Latin *adversus* opposite, hostile, past participle of *advertere* to turn to.] —**ad·verse′ly,** *adv.*

Syn. 1. Adverse, averse, antagonistic imply being against something or someone. **Adverse** suggests opposition and hostility, esp. in action: *The settlers had an adverse reaction to the idea of granting water rights to those outside the valley.* **Averse** suggests reluctance and disinclination, esp. in terms of action: *He was averse to bringing in a left-handed pinch hitter against Smith.* **Antagonistic** suggests openly hostile action or complete estrangement: *His deep hurt left him antagonistic to the very idea of a truce.*

ad·ver·si·ty (ad vur′sə tē) *pl.,* **-ties.** *n.* condition or instance of misfortune, hardship, or suffering.

ad·vert (ad vurt′) *v.i.* to refer. [Middle French *advertir* to call attention to, going back to Latin *advertere* to turn to.]

ad·ver·tise (ad′vər tīz′) **-tised, -tis·ing.** *v.t.* to make known publicly, as through a communication medium, esp. to publicize (a product or service) in a way that makes it seem attractive and promotes its sale or use. —*v.i.* **1.** to inquire or seek by public notice (with *for*): *to advertise for a car.* **2.** to issue or pay for advertisements: *a company that advertises nationally.* [Middle French *advertir* to turn to, call attention to, going back to Latin *advertere* to turn to.] —**ad′ver·tis′er,** *n.*

ad·ver·tise·ment (ad′vər tīz′mənt, ə vur′tiz mənt, -tis-) *n.* public announcement, usually printed or broadcast, esp. one promoting a product or service.

ad·ver·tis·ing (ad′vər tī′zing) *n.* **1.** business of preparing and placing advertisements, esp. in print, on television, or on the radio. **2.** advertisements collectively: *to buy advertising.* —**Syn. 1.** see **publicity.**

ad·vice (əd vīs′) *n.* **1.** opinion offered as guidance; counsel: *I was acting on my lawyer's advice.* **2.** *also,* **advices.** information; notification. [Old French *avis* opinion, earlier *a vis* according to one's view, from Latin *ad* according to + *vīsus* something seen.]

Syn. 1. Advice, counsel indicate the expression of views for the guidance of someone else. **Advice** is the more general term, indicating that the one giving the advice has experience or knowledge which the recipient of the advice should weigh carefully: *We took his advice on which route to follow when we drove west.* **Counsel** indicates wisdom, balance, and depth of knowledge on the part of the one giving counsel, and suggests that the occasion is a more serious one than would simply require advice: *The president listened carefully to the counsel of his cabinet.*

ad·vis·a·bil·i·ty (əd vī′zə bil′ə tē) *n.* quality of being advisable; propriety; suitability.

ad·vis·a·ble (əd vī′zə bəl) *adj.* that can be recommended; wise; fitting. —**ad·vis′a·bly,** *adv.*

ad·vise (əd vīz′) **-vised, -vis·ing.** *v.t.* **1.** to give advice to; counsel. **2.** to suggest as a sound or expedient course; recommend. **3.** to notify; inform. —*v.i.* **1.** to give advice: *I'll do as you advise.* **2.** to confer; discuss (with *with*). [Old French *aviser, adviser* to be of the opinion, give an opinion, from Old French *avis* opinion. See ADVICE.] —**Syn.** *v.i.* **2.** see **consult.**

ad·vised (əd vīzd′) *adj.* thought out; considered. ▲ chiefly used in combination, as in *ill-advised, well-advised.*

ad·vis·ed·ly (əd vī′zid lē) *adv.* by design; deliberately.

ad·vise·ment (əd vīz′mənt) *n.* serious consideration or consultation: *to take the matter under advisement.*

ad·vis·er (əd vī′zər) *also,* **ad·vi·sor.** *n.* one who advises, esp. one appointed to advise: *a faculty adviser.*

ad·vis·o·ry (əd vī′zər ē) *adj.* **1.** empowered to advise: *an advisory board.* **2.** giving advice: *an advisory report.* —**ad·vi′so·ri·ly,** *adv.*

ad·vo·ca·cy (ad′və kə sē) *n.* act of advocating; support.

ad·vo·cate (*v.,* ad′və kāt′; *n.,* ad′və kit, -kāt′) **-cat·ed, -cat·ing.** *v.t.* to plead in favor of; urge; support: *The council advocated a change of policy.* —*n.* **1.** one who publicly supports or urges; proponent: *an advocate of free trade.* **2.** one who pleads the cause of another: *The advocates of the younger candidate failed to convince many voters.* **3.** lawyer practicing before certain courts, esp. Scottish or English. [Latin *advocātus* witness, attorney; noun use of past participle of *advocāre* to summon, call to (the bar).]

advt., advertisement.

adz (adz) *also,* **adze.** *n.* tool for dressing timber, having a blade set at right angles to the handle and curving inward. [Old English *adesa* ax, hatchet.]

AEC, Atomic Energy Commission.

ae·dile (ē′dīl) *also,* **e·dile.** *n.* magistrate in ancient Rome in charge of municipal functions and public works, such as buildings, games, streets, and markets. [Latin *aedīlis,* from *aedēs* building.]

Ae·ge·an (i jē′ən) *n.* sea between Greece and Turkey, an arm of the Mediterranean. Also, **Aegean Sea.**

ae·gis (ē′jis) *also,* **e·gis.** *n.* **1.** protection; guard. **2.** sponsorship; guidance. [Latin *aegis* shield of Jupiter, from Greek *aigis* shield of Zeus, goatskin, possibly from Greek *aix* goat, since shields in earlier times were often covered with goatskin.]

Ae·gis·thus (i jis′thəs) *n. Greek Legend.* nephew of Atreus and lover of Clytemnestra. Aegisthus and Clytemnestra murdered Agamemnon and were killed by Orestes.

Ae·ne·as (i nē′əs) *n. Classical Legend.* Trojan warrior who was the hero of Virgil's *Aeneid* and whose descendants are said to have founded Rome.

Ae·ne·id (i nē′id) *n.* Latin epic poem by Virgil, describing the adventures of Aeneas.

Ae·o·li·an¹ (ē ō′lē ən) *adj.* **1.** of or relating to Aeolus. **2.** *aeolian. also,* **eolian.** of or produced by wind. [Going back to Greek *Aiolos* god of the winds.]

Ae·o·li·an² (ē ō′lē ən) *also,* **E·o·li·an.** *adj.* relating to a principal branch of the ancient Greek peoples. —*n.* member of one of the four major Greek tribes of antiquity. The Aeolians settled in Thessaly, Boetia, Lesbos, and along the northwestern coast of Asia Minor. [From Greek *Aiolis* an ancient region of Asia Minor.]

aeolian harp, instrument over whose opening are stretched strings or wires that produce musical sounds when a current of air passes over them.

Ae·ol·ic (ē ol′ik) *also,* **E·ol·ic.** *adj.* Aeolian².

Ae·o·lus (ē′ə ləs) *n.* **1.** *Classical Mythology.* god of the winds. **2.** *Greek Legend.* king of Thessaly and ancestor of the Aeolians.

---

ae·on (ē′ən, ē′on) eon.

aer·ate (âr′āt, ā′ə rāt′) -at·ed, -at·ing. v.t. **1.** to mix with air: to aerate drinking water. **2.** to expose to air: It is possible to aerate soil by plowing. **3.** to charge or fill (a liquid) with gas: Soda water is aerated with carbon dioxide. **4.** to expose to the chemical action of oxygen; oxygenate: The blood is aerated in respiration. [AER(O)- + -ATE¹.] —**aer·a′tion**, **aer′a·tor**, n.

aer·i·al (adj. âr′ē·əl, ā ēr′ē əl; n., âr′ē əl) adj. **1.** of or in the air: aerial ascent. **2.** like air; thin; ethereal: aerial being. **3.** imaginary; fanciful; unsubstantial: aerial dreams. **4.** high in the air; lofty: aerial spires. **5.** occurring in the air: aerial acrobatics. **6.** of, for, or from aircraft: aerial photography. **7.** growing in the air rather than in soil or water: aerial roots of some trees. —n. antenna (def. 2). [Latin āerius relating to air, from Greek āerios + -AL¹.] —**aer′i·al·ly**, adv.

aer·i·a·list (âr′ē ə list, ā ēr′ē-) n. one who performs in the air, as on a trapeze or high wire.

ae·rie (âr′ē, ēr′ē) also, **ae·ry, ey·rie, ey·ry**. n. **1.** nest built high on a cliff or mountainside by an eagle, hawk, or other bird of prey. **2.** brood of a bird of prey. **3.** dwelling or stronghold standing on a height. [Medieval Latin aerea nest of a bird, through Old French aire, from Latin ārea open space.]

aero- combining form **1.** of the air; air: aerospace. **2.** of gas or gases: aeromechanics. **3.** of aircraft or flying: aeronautics. [Greek āēr air.]

aer·o·bat·ics (âr′ə bat′iks) n.pl. **1.** performance of feats or stunts with an aircraft in flight. ▲ construed as singular. **2.** the feats or stunts performed.

aer·obe (âr′ōb) n. microorganism that requires free oxygen for life. Opposed to **anaerabe.**

aer·o·bic (ā rō′bik) adj. **1.** requiring or living in the presence of free oxygen: aerobic bacteria. **2.** having to do with or produced by microorganisms requiring oxygen. [AERO- + BI(O)- + -IC.]

aer·o·drome (âr′ə drōm′) n. British. airdrome.

aer·o·dy·nam·ics (âr′ō dī nam′iks) n.pl. branch of physics that deals with the laws of motion of gases, esp. the atmosphere, and with the forces exerted by such gases on bodies moving in them. ▲ construed as singular.

aer·o·me·chan·ics (âr′ō mi kan′iks) n.pl. science of air and other gases in motion (aerodynamics) and in equilibrium (aerostatics). ▲ construed as singular.

aer·o·naut (âr′ə nôt′) n. pilot of a lighter-than-air craft. [French aéronaute, from Greek āēr air + nautēs sailor.]

aer·o·nau·tic (âr′ə nô′tik) adj. of aeronautics or aeronauts. Also, **aer′o·nau′ti·cal.** —**aer′o·nau′ti·cal·ly**, adv.

aer·o·nau·tics (âr′ə nô′tiks) n.pl. **1.** science or art of flight. **2.** branch of engineering concerned with creating and flying aircraft. ▲ construed as singular in both definitions.

aer·o·pause (âr′ō pôz′) n. region where outer space is considered to begin and where the atmosphere will not support aircraft.

aer·o·plane (âr′ə plān′) n. British. airplane.

aer·o·sol (âr′ə sôl′) n. colloidal suspension of a solid or liquid in a gas.

aerosol bomb, container fitted with a spray and filled with an aerosol under pressure. Aerosol bombs are used for spreading insecticide, paint, and other materials.

aer·o·space (âr′ō spās′) n. the earth's atmosphere and outer space, considered as the region in which aircraft or spacecraft are operated. —adj. having to do with aerospace and all aspects of human activity in or for this region, as science, engineering, medicine, or industry.

aer·o·stat (âr′ō stat′) n. any lighter-than-air craft, as a dirigible. [French aérostat, from Greek āēr air + statos standing.]

aer·o·stat·ics (âr′ō stat′iks) n.pl. branch of physics that deals with the equilibrium of air and other gases and of solid objects immersed in them. ▲ construed as singular.

ae·ry (âr′ē) adj. pl., -ries. n. aerie.

Aes·chi·nes (es′kə nēz′) n. 389–314 B.C., orator of ancient Athens, rival of Demosthenes.

Aes·chy·lus (es′kə ləs) n. 525–456 B.C., Greek tragic dramatist.

Aes·cu·la·pi·us (es′kyə lā′pē əs) n. Roman god of medicine and healing. His Greek counterpart is Asclepius.

Ae·sop (ē′səp, ē′sop) n. c.620–c.560 B.C., Greek writer of fables.

aes·thete (es′thēt) also, **es·thete.** n. **1.** one particularly sensitive to and appreciative of beauty. **2.** one who affects a sensitivity to art and beauty. [Greek aisthētēs one who perceives.]

aes·thet·ic (es thet′ik) also, **es·thet·ic.** adj. **1.** of or relating to the

---

principles of art or the sense of the beautiful: aesthetic values. **2.** highly sensitive to or preoccupied with art and beauty.

aes·thet·i·cal·ly (es thet′ik lē) also, **es·thet·i·cal·ly.** adv. **1.** according to aesthetic standards: a pursuit aesthetically rather than financially satisfying. **2.** in an aesthetic manner: a room decorated aesthetically.

aes·thet·i·cism (es thet′ə siz′əm) also, **es·thet·i·cism.** n. **1.** belief in the supreme importance of aesthetic values. **2.** strong appreciation of and devotion to beauty and art.

aes·thet·ics (es thet′iks) also, **es·thet·ics.** n.,pl **1.a.** branch of philosophy that studies beauty in art and nature to formulate principles and criteria for its evaluation. **b.** theory or principles thus deduced. **2.** theory and description of emotional and intellectual responses to beauty, esp. as studied by psychology. ▲ construed as singular. [German Ästhetik, going back to Greek aisthētikos pertaining to aisthēta things perceived by the senses.]

aes·ti·val (es′tə vəl, es tī′-) estival.

aes·ti·vate (es′tə vāt′) estivate.

aet., at the age of. Also, **aetat.** [Abbreviation of Latin aetātis, genitive of aetās age.]

ae·ther (ē′thər) ether (defs. 2, 3).

ae·ther·i·al (i thēr′ē əl) etherial.

ae·ti·ol·o·gy (ē′tē ol′ə jē) etiology.

Aet·na, Mount (et′nə) see Etna, Mount.

af-, form of **ad-** before f, as in affront.

AF, audio frequency.

a·far (ə fär′) adv. from, at, or to a distance; far away.

a·feard (ə fērd′) also, **a·feared.** adj. Archaic. afraid.

af·fa·ble (af′ə bəl) adj. easy to approach and speak to; pleasant; friendly. [French affable gracious, kindly, from Latin affābilis easily spoken to, from affārī to speak to.] —**af′fa·bil′i·ty**, n.

af·fair (ə fâr′) n. **1.** matter or business done or to be done: Making a reservation can be a trying affair. **2.** affairs. totality of practical matters with which a person or group is involved: The affairs of the church left the minister no time for scholarly pursuits. **3.** private or personal concern: That's none of your affair. **4.** thing: Her first soufflé was a sad affair. **5.** amorous relationship, esp. a temporary one. **6.** public controversy or scandal. **7.** social gathering or party. [Old French afaire matter, concern, thing, from à faire to do, to be done, from Latin ad to + facere to do.]

af·fect¹ (v., ə fekt′; n., af′ekt, ə fekt′) v.t. **1.** to act upon; produce an effect in. **2.** to influence the emotions of; move. —n. the subjective emotional content of an idea. [Latin affectus, past participle of afficere to act upon.]

af·fect² (ə fekt′) v.t. **1.** to put on a pretense of; feign: to affect boldness although really assumed. **2.** to put on; assume: to affect a haughty manner. **3.** to be partial to: She affects old clothes. [Latin affectāre to aim at, pretend to have.]

af·fec·ta·tion (af′ek tā′shən) n. **1.** artificiality of manner or conduct, usually to impress others: Her Southern accent is an affectation. **2.** studied show or pretense: an affectation of innocence. —**Syn.** **1.** see pose¹.

af·fect·ed¹ (ə fek′tid) adj. **1.** acted upon; materially affected. **2.** influenced emotionally; moved. **3.** impaired; afflicted: an affected limb, affected by a disease. [From AFFECT¹.]

af·fect·ed² (ə fek′tid) adj. **1.** assumed for show; artificial: affected behavior. **2.** assuming or displaying artificality in manner or conduct: an affected dandy. **3.** inclined; disposed: well affected toward the proposals. [From AFFECT².] —**af·fect′ed·ly**, adv. —**af·fect′ed·ness**, n.

af·fect·ing (ə fek′ting) adj. emotionally moving; stirring.

af·fec·tion (ə fek′shən) n. **1.** tender feeling or fondness; warm attachment. **2.** Psychology. the element of emotion or feeling in experience. **3.** disease or diseased condition. [Latin affectiō feeling.]

af·fec·tion·ate (ə fek′shə nit) adj. full of, expressing, or displaying affection; loving; tender. —**af·fec′tion·ate·ly**, adv.

af·fec·tive (ə fek′tiv) adj. **1.** having to do with or acting upon the feelings; emotional. **2.** Psychology. having to do with or caused by the emotions rather than by thought.

af·fer·ent (af′ər ənt) adj. leading or conducting to a central organ or point: afferent nerve fibers. Opposed to **efferent.** [Latin afferēns, present participle of afferre to bring to.]

af·fi·ance (ə fī′əns) -anced, -anc·ing. v.t. to pledge (someone) to be married; betroth. —n. Archaic. pledge of faith; betrothal. [Old French afiancer to promise, through Medieval latin affidāre to pledge one's faith, going back to Latin ad to + fidēs faith.]

af·fi·da·vit (af′ə dā′vit) n. written declaration sworn to or affirmed, usually before a judge or other recognized authority. [Medieval Latin affidavit he has made an oath (used as the first word in certain legal documents), from affidāre. See AFFIANCE.]

af·fil·i·ate (v., ə fil′ē āt′; n., ə fil′ē it, -āt′) -at·ed, -at·ing. v.t. **1.** to join in close association; unite: The merger affiliates two major manufacturers. **2.** to associate (oneself) as a member or supporter (with

Cap

Valve

Spring

Gas

Solution

Container

Aerosol bomb

at; āpe; cär; end; mē; it; īce; hot; ōld; fôrk; wood; fōōl; oil; out; up; ūse; turn; sing; thin; this; zh in treasure; ə in ago, taken, pencil, lemon, circus.

with). **3.a.** *Law.* to determine the paternity of. **b.** to trace the origins and connections of. —*v.i.* to join or associate oneself. —*n.* **1.** subsidiary or branch organization or firm. **2.** one who is affiliated; associate. [Medieval Latin *affiliatus,* past participle of *affiliare* to adopt, from Latin *ad* to + *filius* son.]

af·fil·i·a·tion (ə fil′ē ā′shən) *n.* act or condition of being affiliated; alliance; connection.

af·fin·i·ty (ə fin′ə tē) *pl.,* **-ties.** *n.* **1.** natural attraction or liking. **2.** close relation or similarity. **3.** relationship by marriage rather than by birth. Distinguished from **consanguinity. 4.** resemblance in the structure or physiology of organisms indicating common origin. **5.** *Chemistry.* property or force of attraction by which the atoms of certain elements unite with those of certain others to form compounds. [Old French *afinite* proximity, relationship, from Latin *affīnitās* relationship.]

af·firm (ə furm′) *v.t., v.i.* **1.** to state positively; declare firmly. **2.** to confirm; ratify; uphold. [Old French *afermer,* from Latin *affirmāre.*]

af·fir·ma·tion (af′ər mā′shən) *n.* **1.** act of stating positively or confirming. **2.** that which is asserted. **3.** confirmation; ratification. **4.** *Law.* solemn declaration in place of an oath made by one who conscientiously objects to taking oaths.

af·firm·a·tive (ə fur′mə tiv) *adj.* **1.** asserting that something is true or valid; assenting: *an affirmative reply.* **2.** positive: *affirmative outlook.* —*n.* **1.** word or expression of assent or agreement. **2.** the side that argues in favor of the proposition in a debate. —**af·firm′a·tive·ly,** *adv.*

af·fix (*v.,* ə fiks′; *n.,* af′iks) *v.t.* **1.** to attach or fasten: *to affix stamps to an envelope.* **2.** to add; append: *He affixed his name to the document.* —*n.* **1.** linguistic form or element attached to a word, root, or stem so as to modify the meaning. Affixes may be prefixes or suffixes. **2.** that which is added or attached. [Medieval Latin *affixare* to fasten onto, going back to Latin *affixus.*]

af·fla·tus (ə flā′təs) *n.* inspirational impulse, as of a poet or a prophet. ▲ rare except in the phrase *divine afflatus.* [Latin *afflātus* a breathing upon, inspiration.]

af·flict (ə flikt′) *v.t.* to cause great suffering and pain to; distress severely. [Latin *afflīctāre* to injure, torment.]

af·flic·tion (ə flik′shən) *n.* **1.** state of being afflicted; misery; suffering: *Comfort them in their affliction.* **2.** any cause of pain or suffering; misfortune. —**Syn.** *see* **distress.**

af·flic·tive (ə flik′tiv) *adj.* causing or characterized by pain or distress. —**af·flic′tive·ly,** *adv.*

af·flu·ence (af′lōō əns) *n.* **1.** abundant material wealth. **2.** any abundant supply; profusion. **3.** a flowing toward. [French *affluence* flowing, abundance, from Latin *affluentia,* going back to *affluere* to flow toward, abound in.]

af·flu·ent (af′lōō ənt) *adj.* **1.** materially wealthy; prosperous: *the affluent society.* **2.** abundant; copious; profuse: *an affluent imagination.* —*n.* tributary stream. [Latin *affluēns,* present participle of *affluere* to flow toward, abound in.]

af·flux (af′luks) *n.* a flow or flowing to. [Medieval Latin *affluxus* a flowing toward, from Latin *affluxus,* past participle of *affluere* to flow toward.]

af·ford (ə fôrd′) *v.t.* **1.** to be able to bear the expense of; have the money for. **2.** to be able to spare or give: *I can't afford the time.* **3.** to be able to bear the consequences of: *He can afford to try new methods.* **4.** to yield; provide. [Old English *geforthian* to further, accomplish.]

af·for·est (ə fôr′ist, ə for′-) *v.t.* to convert unwooded land into forest. —**af·for′es·ta′tion,** *n.*

af·fran·chise (ə fran′chīz) **-chised, -chis·ing.** *v.t. Archaic.* to set free; liberate.

af·fray (ə frā′) *n.* noisy brawl or quarrel; public disturbance. [Anglo-Norman *affrai* uproar, tumult, from *afrayer* to frighten, going back to Latin *ex* out of + an unrecorded Germanic word meaning "peace."]

af·fri·cate (af′rə kit) *n.* speech sound composed of a stop followed by a fricative. The affricates in English are *ch* as in *chew* and *j* as in *jaw.* [Latin *affricātus,* past participle of *affricāre* to rub against.]

af·fright (ə frīt′) *Archaic. v.t.* to frighten. —*n.* sudden fear; terror. [Old English *āfyrht,* past participle of *āfyrhtan* to terrify.]

af·front (ə frunt′) *n.* insulting act or remark, esp. one that is open and deliberate. —*v.t.* **1.** to insult openly; offend. **2.** to face defiantly; confront. [Old French *afronter* to strike in the face, insult, going back to Latin *ad frontem* to the face.] —**Syn.** *n. see* **insult.** *v.t. see* **offend.**

Af·ghan (af′gan, -gən) *adj.* of Afghanistan or its people, language, or culture. —*n.* **1.a.** a citizen of Afghanistan. **b.** member of the close descendant of the people of Afghanistan. **2.** Pashto. **3.** long-headed dog of a breed originally from Afghanistan, having a coat of long, silky hair, usually tan, large, drooping ears, and a long tail. Height: 27 inches at

the shoulder. **4. afghan.** knitted or crocheted wool blanket or shawl, made in colored squares, stripes, or other, usually geometric, patterns.

Af·ghan·i·stan (af gan′ə stan′) *n.* landlocked country in south-central Asia. Capital, Kabul. Area, 250,000 sq. mi. Pop. (1969 est.), 16,516,000.

a·fi·ci·o·na·do (ə fish′ē ə nä′dō, ə fē′sē-) *pl.,* **-dos.** *n.* devotee or fan, esp. of bullfighting. [Spanish *aficionado,* from *aficionar* to inspire affection, going back to Latin *affectiō* feeling.]

a·field (ə fēld′) *adv.* **1.** off the beaten path; astray. **2.** away from home; abroad. **3.** on, in, or to the field.

a·fire (ə fīr′) *adv., adj.* on fire.

AFL, American Federation of Labor. Also, **AF of L.**

Afghan

a·flame (ə flām′) *adv., adj.* flaming.

AFL-CIO, the American Federation of Labor and the Congress of Industrial Organizations.

a·float (ə flōt′) *adv., adj.* **1.** floating on or as if in water. **2.** out of difficulty, esp. insolvency. **3.** at sea; on board ship. **4.** in circulation: *There are strange rumors afloat.* **5.** covered by water; flooded. **6.** adrift; unsettled.

a·flut·ter (ə flut′ər) *adv., adj.* **1.** fluttering. **2.** nervously confused or agitated.

a·fo·cal (ā fō′kəl) *adj. Physics.* having infinitely distant focal points or none at all.

a·foot (ə foot′) *adv., adj.* **1.** on foot: *We proceeded afoot.* **2.** in progress or motion; stirring: *There's an evil plot afoot.*

a·fore (ə fôr′) *adv., prep., conj. Archaic.* before. [Old English *onforan* in front, in advance.]

a·fore·men·tioned (ə fôr′men′shənd) *adj.* mentioned before.

a·fore·said (ə fôr′sed′) *adj.* said or mentioned before.

a·fore·thought (ə fôr′thôt′) *adj.* planned beforehand; premeditated. ▲ rare except in the phrase *malice aforethought.*

a for·ti·o·ri (ā fôr′shē ôr′ī) for a still stronger reason. [Latin *ā fortiōrī* from the stronger (argument).]

a·foul (ə foul′) *adv., adj.* **1.** in collision or entanglement. **2. to run (or fall) afoul of.** to become entangled with; get into trouble with.

Afr., Africa; African.

a·fraid (ə frād′) *adj.* **1.** feeling fear or apprehension; frightened. **2.** averse; wary: *afraid of physical exercise, afraid to inconvenience anyone.* **3.** *Informal.* regretful; sorry. ▲ often used to moderate a statement that might otherwise sound harsh: *I'm afraid you'll have to give up your seat.* [Middle English *affraied,* past participle of *affraien* to frighten, from Anglo-Norman *afrayer.* See AFFRAY.]

Syn. 1. Afraid, frightened indicate a mental state in which there is urgent recognition of danger. **Afraid** implies constricted action or thought because of fear: *I heard thy voice in the garden, and I was afraid . . . and I hid myself* (Genesis 3:10). **Frightened** also implies a physical reaction to fear and usually suggests that the fear is of short duration: *The frightened horse shied and then bolted.*

a·fresh (ə fresh′) *adv.* anew; again.

Af·ri·ca (af′ri kə) *n.* continent south of Europe, between the Atlantic and Indian oceans. Area, 11,677,000 sq. mi. Pop. (1966 est.), 318,- 000,000. [Latin *Africa,* going back to *Afer* inhabitant of North Africa.]

Af·ri·can (af′ri kən) *adj.* **1.** of, from, or characteristic of Africa or its people. **2.** relating to the black race of Africa; Negro. —*n.* **1.** native or inhabitant of Africa. **2.** member of the black African race; Negro.

Af·ri·kaans (af′ri käns′) *n.* one of the two official languages of South Africa, a dialect of Dutch from that of seventeenth-century Dutch settlers. [Afrikaans *afrikaans* African, going back to Latin *Africānus.*]

Af·ri·ka·ner (af′ri kä′nər) *n.* descendant of Dutch settlers in South Africa.

Afro- *combining form* African and: *Afro-Asian.*

Af·ro-A·mer·i·can (af′rō ə mer′i kən) *adj.* of or relating to American Negroes. —*n.* American Negro.

Af·ro-A·sian (af′rō ā′zhən, -shən) *adj.* of or made up of Africans and Asians or the countries of Africa and Asia: *Afro-Asian bloc.*

aft (aft) *adv.* at, near, or toward the stern of a ship or the tail of an aircraft. [Old English *æftan* behind.]

af·ter (af′tər) *prep.* **1.** in or at the rear of; behind: *The boy trailed after his father.* **2.** in quest of; with desire for: *to seek after success.* **3.** subsequent to or following; later than: *after dark.* **4.** as a consequence of: *After that remark, you'll have to apologize.* **5.** in spite of; regardless of: *After all we've said, he still won't change his mind.* **6.** in repeated succession to: *time after time.* **7.** concerning: *He inquired after your health.* **8.** in imitation of; in the style of: *a building designed after the Parthenon.* **9.** in honor of; with a name like; for: *Name him*

after your uncle. **10.** in agreement with the nature of: *a man after my own heart.* **11.** below in rank, order, or importance: *After the prima donna come a number of lesser singers.* **12.** (of time) past: *half after one.* —*adv.* **1.** in the rear; behind: *Jill came tumbling after.* **2.** later; subsequently: *two days after.* —*conj.* subsequent to the time that: *It happened after you left.* —*adj.* **1.** later; subsequent: *in after years.* **2.** toward the stern; farther aft. **3.** rear; hindmost. [Old English *æfter* behind in place or time.] —**Syn.** *prep.* **1.** see **behind.**

af·ter·birth (af'tǝr burth') *n.* the placenta and other matter expelled from the uterus after childbirth.

af·ter·burn·er (af'tǝr bur'nǝr) *n.* device that injects fuel into the hot exhaust of a jet engine, thereby creating additional thrust.

af·ter·deck (af'tǝr dek') *n.* deck at a ship's stern.

af·ter·ef·fect (af'tǝr i fekt') *n.* secondary effect, occurring after the primary one: *the aftereffects of a drug.*

af·ter·glow (af'tǝr glō') *n.* **1.** glow remaining after a source of brightness has gone, as in the western sky after sunset. **2.** good feeling lingering after a pleasant experience: *The afterglow she felt from winning the award lasted for a week.*

af·ter·im·age (af'tǝr im'ij) *n.* persistence or recurrence of a retinal image or other sensation after withdrawal of, or end of exposure to, an external stimulus.

af·ter·math (af'tǝr math') *n.* **1.** resulting situation; consequence or consequences: *the aftermath of a hurricane.* **2. in the aftermath of.** in the wake of; after. **3.** second mowing of grass for hay from the same land in the same season.

af·ter·most (af'tǝr mōst') *adj.* **1.** nearest the stern of a ship; farthest aft. **2.** rearmost; last.

af·ter·noon (af'tǝr nōōn') *n.* part of the day from noon until evening. —*adj.* in, for, or characteristic of the afternoon.

af·ter·taste (af'tǝr tāst') *n.* **1.** taste that remains after what caused it is gone; taste occurring after the initial one. **2.** sensation left after an experience, esp. an unpleasant one.

af·ter·thought (af'tǝr thôt') *n.* **1.** later or second thought or statement. **2.** thought that comes too late. **3.** something not thought of originally that is added to a planned or completed whole.

af·ter·ward (af'tǝr wǝrd) *also,* **af·ter·wards.** *adv.* at a later time; subsequently.

ag-, form of **ad-** before *g,* as in *aggravate.*

Ag, silver. [Abbreviation of Latin *argentum* silver.]

a·gain (ǝ gen') *adv.* **1.** once more; another time: *Say it again.* **2.** on the other hand: *We might go, and again we might not.* **3.** moreover; besides; furthermore. **4.** back into a former position or state: *Here we go again.* **5.** again and again. many times. **6. as much again.** quantity equal to the original. **7. now and again.** occasionally; sometimes. [Old English *ongegn* against, back.]

a·gainst (ǝ genst') *prep.* **1.** in opposition to: *They were against the reform.* **2.** (of motion or direction) **a.** meeting head on; toward: *against the current.* **b.** toward, so as to strike: *He drove his fist against the wall.* **3.** on a background of: *bright figures against a pale background.* **4.** in contact with: *The man leaned against the tree.* **5.** in preparation for; as a provision for: *to save against an emergency.* **6.** as a defense or protection from: *Shade trees are used against the heat.* **7.** expressing hostility toward: *Everyone is against him.* **8.** in competition with: *a race against time.* **9.** in balance or account for: *an advance against next week's salary.* [Going back to Old English *ongegn* opposite, back.]

Ag·a·mem·non (ag'ǝ mem'non) *n. Greek Legend.* king of Mycenae who led the Greeks in the Trojan War. He was later murdered by his wife, Clytemnestra.

a·gape (ǝ gāp', ǝ gap') *adv., adj.* **1.** with the mouth wide open esp. expressing wonder or disbelief. **2.** wide open.

a·gar (ä'gär, ag'ǝr) *n.* culture medium containing agar-agar.

a·gar·a·gar (ä'gär ä'gär, ag'ǝr ag'ǝr) *n.* gelatinous product obtained from certain seaweeds, used esp. for growing bacteria cultures. [Malay *agar-agar* a seaweed.]

ag·a·ric (ag'ǝ rik, ǝ gar'ik) *n.* any fungus of the family Agaricaceae, including the common edible mushroom and the shelflike fungus that grows on trees. [Latin *agaricum* a tree fungus, from Greek *agarikon,* possibly from *Agaria,* a settlement in Sarmatia (now part of Poland and Russia), where it abounded.]

ag·ate (ag'it) *n.* **1.** semiprecious variety of quartz (chalcedony) typically with varicolored layers or bands. **2.** playing marble made of or resembling agate. **3.** small size of printing type (5½ point). [Middle French *agate* this stone, from Latin *achātēs,* from Greek *achátēs;* supposedly because it was found near the Sicilian river *Achates.*]

Polished agate (def. 1)

agate line, standard measure for newspaper advertising space, one column wide and ¹⁄₁₄ inch deep (approximately the depth of agate type).

ag·ate·ware (ag'it wâr') *n.* **1.** steel or iron ware for kitchen use,

enameled to resemble agate. **2.** pottery mottled and veined to resemble agate.

a·ga·ve (ǝ gä'vē) *n.* any of a group of desert plants, genus *Agave,* of the amaryllis family, typically found in warm, dry regions of the Western Hemisphere. The most familiar is the century plant. [Modern Latin *agave,* from Greek *agauē,* feminine of *agauos* noble; possibly called this because of its impressive height.]

age (āj) *n.* **1.** length of existence since coming into being. **2.** average duration of existence; whole life span. **3.** period or stage of life. **4.** particular period of life which, naturally or conventionally, qualifies or disqualifies: *under the age for a driver's license. Act your age.* **5.** latter part of life; old age: *weary with age.* **6.a.** particular period of history or of mankind's development: *atomic age.* **b.** people who live at a particular period. **7.** period or epoch in the earth's history: *the age of mammals.* **8.** *also,* **ages.** *Informal.* a very long time. **9. of age.** at an age when certain rights or responsibilities become applicable. —*v.i.* **aged, ag·ing** or **age·ing. 1.** to make old. **2.** to bring to a state for use; ripen: *He aged the wood for several months.* —*v.i.* to grow old or mature. [Old French *age, aäge* life-time, majority, going back to Latin *aetas* time period, time of life.] —**Syn.** *n.* **6.a.** see **era.**

-age *suffix* (used to form nouns) **1.** collection of: *luggage.* **2.** that which relates to the act of: *tutelage.* **3.** condition of: *wreckage.* **4.** home or place of: *orphanage.* **5.** fee for or cost of: *wharfage.* **6.** amount of: *yardage*¹. [Old French *-age,* from Late Latin *-āticum* related to.]

a·ged (*adj., defs. 1, 3* ā'jid, *defs. 2, 4* ājd; *n.,* ā'jid) *adj.* **1.** grown old; old. **2.** of the age of: *a boy aged three.* **3.** characteristic of old age: *an aged walk.* **4.** having a desired quality as the result of aging: *aged cheese.* —*n.* **the aged.** old people: *medical care for the aged.* —**a'ged·ness,** *n.* **Syn.** *adj.* **1. Aged, old, elderly** indicate a late stage in life. **Aged** suggests extreme old age with signs of physical and, sometimes, mental decline: *She helped take care of her aged grandfather.* **Old** implies merely that maturity is past; it has no connotation of physical or mental deterioration: *The old man had a full head of white hair.* **Elderly** indicates an age well past maturity: *He was an elderly man, but still vigorous enough to take long daily hikes.*

age·less (āj'lis) *adj.* **1.** not growing old or showing signs of old age. **2.** never-ending; eternal.

age·long (āj'lông') *adj.* lasting a very long time.

a·gen·cy (ā'jǝn sē) *pl.,* **-cies.** *n.* **1.** means, action, or power by or through which a thing is effected. **2.** company or business empowered to act for others. **3.** location in which the business of an agency or agent takes place. —**Syn. 1.** see **mean**³.

a·gen·da (ǝ jen'dǝ) *n.* list of things to be done: *The reading of the minutes was the first item on the agenda.* ▲ Although by derivation *agenda* is the plural of *agendum,* the word *agenda* is now generally treated as singular: *My agenda for today starts with cleaning out the cellar.* The regular English plural *agendas* is therefore permissible: *the agendas of the last four meetings.* [Latin *agenda* things to be done, from *agere* to do.] —**Syn.** see **program.**

a·gent (ā'jǝnt) *n.* **1.** person vested with authority to represent or act for another. **2.** one who or that which acts or has the power to act: *a free agent.* **3.** that which produces or is used to produce an effect: *a cleansing agent.* **4.** means; instrument. **5.** *Informal.* salesman. [Latin *agēns,* present participle of *agere* to do.]

Syn. 1. Agent, representative, delegate, deputy apply to someone acting for another. **Agent** is the general word: *Public officers are the servants and agents of the people* (Cleveland, 1882). **Representative** is one who takes the place of someone or of a group, supposedly embodying their characteristics in himself: *He is the representative of a whole school of poets.* **Delegate** is one empowered to act for another: *Each of the state societies sent one voting delegate to the national convention.* **Deputy** is one acting with all the authority of his principal: *As the company grew, he was forced to appoint deputies for many of the jobs he would have preferred doing himself.*

a·gent pro·vo·ca·teur (ā'jǝnt prǝ vok'ǝ toor'; *French* ä zhän prō vō kä toer') *pl.,* **a·gents pro·vo·ca·teurs** (ā'jǝnts prǝ vok'ǝ toor'; *French* ä zhän prō vō kä toer'). *French.* someone secretly placed in an opponent organization or group to provoke illegal or reprehensible acts for which that group can then be prosecuted or blamed.

ag·er·a·tum (aj'ǝ rā'tǝm, ǝ jer'ǝ-) *n.* **1.** ornamental plant, genus *Ageratum,* of the composite family, having clustered flower heads of blue, white, or pink. **2.** any of several similar plants of the genus *Eupatorium.* [Modern Latin *Ageratum,* through Latin *agēraton* a plant that withers slowly, from Greek *agēraton* literally, (something) ageless.]

ag·glom·er·ate (*v.,* ǝ glom'ǝ rāt'; *n., adj.,* ǝ glom'ǝr it, -ǝ rāt') **-at·ed, -at·ing.** *v.i., v.t.* to gather in a mass or cluster. —*n.* **1.** things gathered together in a mass or cluster. **2.** rock formed of a mass of angular volcanic fragments in ash. —*adj.* gathered together in a mass or cluster: *an agglomerate whole.* —**an agglomerate whole.** of agglomerate to heap up, from *ag-,* for *ad-,* to, at + *glomerāre* to gather into a ball, from *glomus* ball.]

ag·glom·er·a·tion (ə glom'ə rā'shən) *n.* **1.** act of agglomerating; being agglomerated. **2.** collection of things gathered indiscriminately.

ag·glu·ti·nant (ə gloō'tin ənt) *n.* substance causing agglutination —*adj.* tending to cause agglutination.

ag·glu·ti·nate (*v.,* ə gloōt'ən āt'; *adj.,* ə gloōt'ən it, -āt') **-nat·ed, -nat·ing.** *v.i., v.t.* **1.** to stick together; unite with or as with glue: *to agglutinate sand and pebbles into one mass.* **2.** to form (words) by agglutination. **3.** to clump together, as bacteria or blood cells. —*adj.* joined by or as by glue. [Latin *agglūtinātus,* past participle of *agglūtināre* to glue to, going back to *ad* to + *glūten* glue.]

ag·glu·ti·na·tion (ə gloōt'ən ā'shən) *n.* **1.** process of sticking together; state of being stuck together. **2.** process by which words or word elements are combined to form new words in which the constituent parts remain apparent without loss of meaning. **3.** clumping together of bacteria or blood cells in the body due to the presence of an antibody. **4.** collection of parts stuck together.

ag·glu·ti·na·tive (ə gloōt'ən ā'tiv) *adj.* **1.** tending to agglutinate. **2.** forming words by agglutination.

ag·glu·tin·in (ə gloōt'ən in) *n.* substance, as an antibody, which causes agglutination.

ag·glu·tin·o·gen (ag'loō tin'ə jən) *n.* antigen which, when present in the body, causes the formation of agglutinin.

ag·gran·dize (ə gran'dīz, ag'rən dīz') **-dized, -diz·ing.** *v.t.* **1.** to increase or make greater: *the king's efforts to aggrandize his empire.* **2.** to increase in scope or intensity. **3.** to cause to appear greater: *to aggrandize a mediocre subject.* [French *agrandir* to enlarge, increase, going back to Latin *ag-,* for *ad-* to + *grandīre* to increase, grow.] —**ag·gran'dize·ment, ag·gran'diz·er,** *n.*

ag·gra·vate (ag'rə vāt') **-vat·ed, -vat·ing.** *v.t.* **1.** to make worse or more severe. **2.** *Informal.* to annoy; irritate. [Latin *aggravātus,* past participle of *aggravāre* to make heavier. Doublet of AGGRIEVE.] —**ag'gra·vat'ing·ly,** *adv.* —**ag'gra·va'tor,** *n.*

ag·gra·va·tion (ag'rə vā'shən) *n.* **1.** an extending or deepening of severity; a worsening. **2.** that which causes a worsening. **3.** *Informal.* annoyance; irritation.

ag·gre·gate (*v.,* ag'rə gāt'; *n., adj.,* ag'rə git, -gāt') **-gat·ed, -gat·ing.** *v.t.* **1.** to collect or gather (something) into a mass or group. **2.** to amount to; total: *Admission charges aggregated $250.* —*v.i.* to come together; collect. —*n.* **1.** whole composed of distinguishable parts. **2.** sum total. **3. in the aggregate.** taken together; as a whole. —*adj.* composed of parts gathered together. [Latin *aggregātus,* past participle of *aggregāre* to add to a flock, going back to Latin *ad-* to + *grex* flock.] —**ag'gre·gate·ly,** *adv.* —**ag'gre·gate·ness,** *n.*

ag·gre·ga·tion (ag'rə gā'shən) *n.* collection of distinguishable things into or as into a single mass or whole.

ag·gres·sion (ə gresh'ən) *n.* **1.** offensive or unprovoked assault or attack. **2.** habitual practice of making assaults or attacks. [Latin *aggressiō* a going toward, attack.]

ag·gres·sive (ə gres'iv) *adj.* **1.** of or characterized by aggression. **2.** forceful; bold: *an aggressive salesman, an aggressive public campaign.* —**ag·gres'sive·ly,** *adv.* —**ag·gres'sive·ness,** *n.*

ag·gres·sor (ə gres'ər) *n.* one who engages in aggression.

ag·grieve (ə grēv') **-grieved, -griev·ing.** *v.t.* **1.** to cause grief or trouble to; distress. **2.** *Law.* to cause to suffer loss or injury. [Old French *agrever* to make heavier, render more severe, going back to Latin *aggravāre* to make heavier. Doublet of AGGRAVATE.]

a·ghast (ə gast') *adj.* stricken with fear, horror, or amazement. [Middle English *agast,* past participle of *agasten* to terrify, from Old English *ā-* (for emphasis) + *gæstan* to terrify.]

ag·ile (aj'əl) *adj.* able to move or think quickly and easily; nimble. [French *agile,* from Latin *agilis.*] —**ag'ile·ly,** *adv.* —**ag'ile·ness,** *n.*

a·gil·i·ty (ə jil'ə tē) *n.* quickness and ease in motion or thought; nimbleness.

Ag·in·court (aj'in kôrt') *n.* village in northern France, site of an English victory over the French in 1415.

ag·i·tate (aj'ə tāt') **-tat·ed, -tat·ing.** *v.t.* **1.** to move or shake roughly or irregularly; stir up: *The wind agitated the trees.* **2.** to move to and fro with a regular motion: *The washing machine agitates the clothes.* **3.** to perturb; disturb; excite: *The unruliness of the members agitated the chairman.* —*v.i.* to arouse or maintain public interest, as in an effort to bring about change: *to agitate for higher wages.* [Latin *agitātus,* past participle of *agitāre* to move to and fro, drive.] —**ag'i·tat'ed·ly,** *adv.* —**Syn.** *v.t.* **3.** see **disturb.**

ag·i·ta·tion (aj'ə tā'shən) *n.* **1.** act of agitating; being agitated. **2.** state of being emotionally upset or shaken. **3.** action or argument to arouse or maintain public interest in some matter.

ag·i·ta·tor (aj'ə tā'tər) *n.* **1.** one who agitates for change, esp. political or social change. **2.** device for shaking or stirring.

A·gla·ia (ə glā'ə) *n.* Greek Mythology. one of the three Graces.

a·gleam (ə glēm') *adv., adj.* gleaming.

a·gley (ə glē', ə glī') *adv. Scottish.* out of line; awry.

a·glit·ter (ə glit'ər) *adv., adj.* glittering.

a·glow (ə glō') *adv., adj.* glowing.

ag·nos·tic (ag nos'tik) *n.* one who holds that nothing can be known about the existence of God or of any but material things. ▲ **Agnostic** is sometimes mistaken as a synonym for **atheist.** The difference is that while the **atheist** openly denies the existence of God, the **agnostic** merely denies that it is possible to know one way or the other. —*adj.* characteristic of agnostics or their beliefs. [Coined in 1869 by the English biologist Thomas Huxley, from Greek *agnōstos* unknown, unknowing; modified by GNOSTIC.] —**ag·nos'ti·cism,** *n.*

Ag·nus De·i (ag'nəs dē'ī, ä'nyoos dā'ē) **1.** prayer in the Mass starting with the words "Agnus Dei" or "O Lamb of God." **2.** music for this prayer. **3.** image of a lamb, esp. one with a halo and the banner of the Cross, emblematic of Christ. [Latin *Agnus Deī* Lamb of God.]

a·go (ə gō') *adj.* before now; past. ▲ always placed after the noun: *three days ago.* —*adv.* in the past. ▲ used only in *long ago.* [Middle English *ago,* past participle of *agon* to go away, from Old English *āgān.*]

a·gog (ə gog') *adj., adv.* in a state of excitement or eager expectation. [French phrase *en gogues* lively, in a merry mood; of uncertain origin.]

ag·o·nize (ag'ə nīz') **-nized, -niz·ing.** *v.i.* **1.** to feel great pain or anguish; suffer greatly. **2.** to strive painfully; struggle. —*v.t.* to cause to suffer great pain or agony; torture. [French *agoniser* to be in agony, be dying, through Late Latin *agonizāre* to strive, contend, suffer, from Greek *agōnizesthai* to contend for a prize, struggle.] —**ag'o·niz'ing·ly,** *adv.*

ag·o·ny (ag'ə nē) *pl.,* **-nies.** *n.* **1.** great pain, suffering, or anguish of mind or body. **2.** the often unconscious movements of the body, resembling a struggle, that sometimes precede death. **3.** any intense emotion: *an agony of indecision.* [Late Latin *agōnia* anguish, from Greek *agōniā* anguish, struggle, contest.]

ag·o·ra (ag'ər ə) *pl.,* **ag·o·rae** (ag'ər ē). *n.* market place of an ancient Greek city, usually the center of civic and commercial life. [Greek *agorā* assembly, market place.]

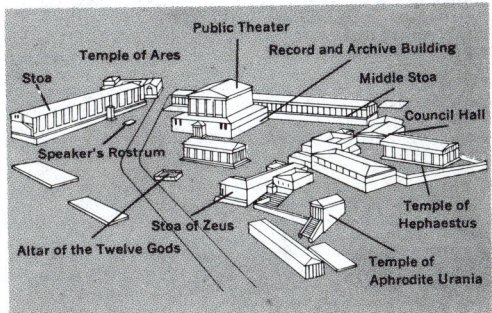

The Agora of Athens

(labels: Public Theater; Temple of Ares; Record and Archive Building; Stoa; Middle Stoa; Council Hall; Speaker's Rostrum; Temple of Hephaestus; Stoa of Zeus; Altar of the Twelve Gods; Temple of Aphrodite Urania)

a·gou·ti (ə goō'tē) *pl.,* **-tis** or **-ties.** *n.* West Indian and South American rodent, genus *Dasyprocta,* related to the guinea pig. [French *agouti* or Spanish *aguti,* from Tupi-Guarani *aguti.*]

A·gra (ä'grə) *n.* city in north-central India, site of the Taj Mahal. Pop. (1969), 610,328.

a·grar·i·an (ə grâr'ē ən) *adj.* **1.** concerning land, its cultivation, or its ownership. **2.** concerning the furthering of the interests of farmers. **3.** one who favors agrarianism. [Latin *agrārius* relating to land, from *ager* land, field.]

a·grar·i·an·ism (ə grâr'ē ə niz'əm) *n.* **1.** doctrine advocating the equal distribution of land. **2.** political activity aimed at securing equal distribution of land.

Agouti

a·gree (ə grē') **a·greed, a·gree·ing.** *v.i.* **1.** to have the same opinion; concur. **2.** to be in harmony; coincide. **3.** to consent (with *to*): *We can agree to that proposal.* **4.** to reach an understanding; come to terms, esp. in ending a dispute: *The negotiators finally agreed on every point.* **5.** *Grammar.* to have an inflected form that corresponds in case, number, gender, or person (with another word or phrase in a sentence): *In English, a verb must agree with its subject.* **6. to agree with.** to produce no ill effect on; suit: *Long plane trips do not agree with me.* —*v.t.* to acknowledge; accept; grant (with a noun clause as object): *I agree that*

at; āpe; cär; end; mē; it; īce; hot; ōld; fôrk; wood; fōōl; oil; out; up; ūse; turn; sing; thin; this; zh in treasure; ə in ago, taken, pencil, lemon, circus.

19

the terms are most generous. [Old French *agreer* to please, from phrase *a gre* to (one's) pleasure, going back to Latin *ad* to + *grātus* pleasing.] **Syn.** *v. i.* **2. Agree, coincide, correspond** indicate a being in or reaching harmony on some matter. **Agree** suggests a matching of position on all basic points with no serious divergences anywhere: *The candidates agreed on what the country's foreign policy should be.* **Coincide** indicates a matching at all points: *The ambassador's desire to influence policy coincided with his rare ability to make his influence felt.* **Correspond** indicates a general matching of positions but recognizes that differences remain: *The House of Commons corresponds to our House of Representatives.*

a·gree·a·ble (ə grē'ə bəl) *adj.* **1.** to one's liking; pleasant. **2.** willing to consent. **3.** suitable (with *to*). —**a·gree'a·bil'i·ty, a·gree'a·ble·ness,** *n.* —**a·gree'a·bly,** *adv.*

a·greed (ə grēd') *adj.* settled by common consent: *to stick to the agreed route.*

a·gree·ment (ə grē'mənt) *n.* **1.** understanding reached by two or more parties, as a treaty or contract. **2.** harmony; accord. **3.** the agreeing of words in a phrase or sentence.

agric., agriculture.

ag·ri·cul·tur·al (ag'rə kul'chər əl) *adj.* relating to farms or farming; of agriculture. —**ag'ri·cul'tur·al·ly,** *adv.*

ag·ri·cul·ture (ag'rə kul'chər) *n.* **1.** business or practice of raising crops and livestock; farming. **2.** science of farming, esp. with regard to improving the amount or quality of yield. [Latin *agricultūra,* from *agrī cultūra* cultivation of the land.]

ag·ri·cul·tur·ist (ag'rə kul'chər ist) *n.* **1.** farmer. **2.** expert in the science of agriculture. Also, **ag'ri·cul'tur·al·ist.**

ag·ri·mo·ny (ag'rə mō'nē) *pl.,* **-nies.** *n.* any of a group of plants, genus *Agrimonia,* of the rose family, bearing aromatic, bitter leaves, yellow flowers, and burrs. [Latin *agrimōnia,* a false reading of Latin *argemōnia* a plant, from Greek *argemōne* poppy, possibly from Hebrew *argāmān* purple.]

A·grip·pa, Mar·cus Vip·sa·ni·us (ə grip'ə; mär'kəs vip sā'nē əs) 63–12 B.C., Roman general and statesman.

ag·ro·nom·ic (ag'rə nom'ik) *adj.* concerning agronomy.

a·gron·o·mist (ə gron'ə mist) *n.* student of or expert in agronomy.

a·gron·o·my (ə gron'ə mē) *n.* branch of agriculture concerned with all aspects of field-crop production, including the cultivation of farm land and conservation and improvement of soil. [Greek *agros* field + *-nomiā* management.]

a·ground (ə ground') *adv., adj.* with the bottom stuck, as in shallow water: *He ran the boat aground on the sand bar.*

agt., agent.

a·gue (ā'gū) *n.* **1.** chills and fever, esp. the chilly stage of a recurrent fever. **2.** malarial fever marked by regularly recurring cold, hot, and sweating stages. **3.** any fit of shivering; chill. [Old French *ague* sharp fever, from Latin *acūta (febris)* sharp or severe (fever).]

A·gui·nal·do, E·mi·lio (ä'gē näl'dō; ä mēl'yō) c.1870–1964, Filipino revolutionary leader.

a·gu·ish (ā'gū ish) *adj.* **1.** having the qualities of ague. **2.** tending to cause ague. **3.** subject to ague.

ah (ä) *interj.* used to show any of various feelings from pain or sorrow (*Ah, how pitiful!*) to joy or admiration (*Ah, how beautiful!*).

a·ha (ä hä') *interj.* used variously, but esp. to indicate discovery.

A·hab (ā'hab) *n.* in the Old Testament, king of Israel in the ninth century B.C. who was influenced by his wife, Jezebel, to become a worshiper of idols.

a·head (ə hed') *adv.* **1.** in front: *The American runner was now ahead.* **2.** onward: *They went ahead with their plans.* **3. ahead of.** in advance: *ahead of his time.* **4. to be ahead.** *Informal.* to have gained a profit or advantage. **5. to get ahead.** *Informal.* to advance one's position in the social or business world. **6. to get ahead of.** to surpass; overtake.

a·hem (ə hem') *interj.* used esp. to attract attention or give warning, as by clearing the throat.

Ah·med·a·bad (ä'məd ä bäd') *also,* **Ah·mad·a·bad.** *n.* city in west-central India. Pop. (1969), 1,507,921.

a·hoy (ə hoi') *interj.* used to greet or catch the attention, esp. of persons on another ship.

Ah·ri·man (är'i mən) *n.* in Zoroastrian religion, the spirit of evil opposing Ahura Mazda.

A·hu·ra Maz·da (ä'hoor ə maz'də) in Zoroastrian religion, the spirit of goodness, light, and truth, in ceaseless conflict with Ahriman. Also, **Or'mazd.**

aid (ād) *v. t., v. i.* to help; assist. —*n.* **1.** help; assistance. **2.** one who or that which helps; assistant; helper. [Old French *aider* to help, assist, going back to Latin *adjutāre.*] —**Syn.** *v. t.* see **help.**

aide (ād) *n.* **1.** aide-de-camp. **2.** assistant.

aide-de-camp (ād'də kamp') *pl.,* **aides-de-camp.** *n.* officer who serves as an assistant to a superior officer. [French *aide-de-camp* literally, camp assistant.]

ai·grette (ā'gret, ā gret') *also,* **ai·gret.** *n.* **1.** ornamental plume or tuft of feathers worn on the head. **2.** plume or feathers of the egret. **3.** ornamental jewelry imitating such feathers. **4.** egret. [French *aigrette* egret, plume, from Provençal *aigreta* from *aigron* heron; of Germanic origin.]

ail (āl) *v. t.* to cause illness, trouble, or discomfort to: *What ails you?* —*v. i.* to be ill or indisposed, esp. chronically. [Old English *eglan* to trouble, pain.]

ai·lan·thus (ā lan'thəs) *pl.,* **-es.** *n.* any tree of the genus *Ailanthus,* bearing pinnate leaves and clusters of small, greenish flowers, valued esp. as a shade tree. The best-known species is *A. altissima,* tree of heaven. [Modern Latin *ailanthus,* from native term of the Moluccas *ai lanto* tree of heaven; spelling influenced by Greek *anthos* flower.]

Ailanthus

ai·le·ron (ā'lə ron') *n.* movable section in the trailing edge of an airplane wing used to control movement of the airplane about its nose-to-tail axis, as in banking or rolling. See **airplane** for illustration. [French *aileron* bird's wing, diminutive of *aile* wing, from Latin *āla.*]

ail·ment (āl'mənt) *n.* illness or affliction, esp. a mild one.

aim (ām) *v. t.* to point, as a weapon, or direct, as a remark or blow, for the purpose of hitting a target. —*v. i.* **1.** to try: *We aim to please.* **2.** *Informal.* to intend: *We aim to be visiting you soon.* —*n.* **1.** act of pointing or directing something at a target. **2.** direction in which something is aimed. **3.** thing or person aimed at; target. **4.** purpose; intention; object. [Old French *(a)esmer* to estimate, intend, going back to Latin *ad* to + *aestimāre* to value.] —**Syn.** *n.* **4.** see **purpose.**

aim·less (ām'lis) *adj.* without purpose or direction. —**aim'less·ly,** *adv.* —**aim'less·ness,** *n.*

ain't (ānt) is (am, are) not; has (have) not. ▲ This form is now frowned on in any use except where the aim is deliberately to show departure from standard speech as for humor or characterization: *We ain't got a barrel of money.*

Ai·nu (ī'nōō) *pl.,* **-nus** or **-nu.** *n.* **1.** member of a primitive, aboriginal race of northern Japan, having light skin and hairy bodies. **2.** language of the Ainus, apparently unrelated to any other known language.

air (âr) *n.* **1.** mixture of gases that surrounds and envelops the earth, forming its atmosphere. **2.** space surrounding and above the earth's surface. **3.** moving current of air; light wind. **4.** public exposure; circulation: *He gave air to his grievances.* **5.** impression, mood, or feeling as imparted by exterior appearance or surroundings. **6.** (of a person) demeanor; appearance; attitude: *There was a furtive air about the little man.* **7.** *usually,* **airs.** pretentious or affected manner: *Don't put on airs.* **8.** medium through which radio waves are transmitted. **9.a.** melody; tune. **b.** main part of a harmonized musical composition. **in the air. a.** in circulation. **b.** undecided (usually preceded by *up*). **off the air.** not broadcasting or being broadcast. **on the air.** broadcasting or being broadcast. **to clear the air.** to remove disagreements or tension. **to take the air. a.** to go outside. **b.** to begin to broadcast. **to vanish (or disappear) into thin air.** to vanish quickly. **to walk on air.** to be very happy. —*v. t.* **1.** to freshen, ventilate, or dry by exposing to air. **2.** to expose to public notice; publicize. [Old French *air* atmospheric air, through Latin *āēr,* from Greek *āēr* atmospheric air, mist.] —**Syn.** *n.* **7.** see **air.**

air bag, safety device in an automobile, consisting of a plastic bag that inflates in front of passengers upon the impact of collision to protect them from injury.

air base, place from which military airplanes operate.

air bladder, sac filled with air, esp. as found in most fish. It aids in maintaining equilibrium in the water. Also, **swim bladder, swimming bladder.**

air·borne (âr'bôrn') *adj.* **1.** carried by the air: *airborne pollen.* **2.** transported by airplanes or gliders: *airborne artillery.* **3.** off the ground; in flight: *By midnight we were airborne.*

air brake 1. mechanical braking system in which compressed air drives a piston or pistons. **2.** flaps on airplane wings used to reduce speed in the air.

air brush, atomizer operated by compressed air used to spray paint or other liquids on a surface.

air chamber, compartment or part filled with air, esp. one used to equalize the flow of a liquid in a hydraulic device.

air coach, coach (def. 3).

air cock, valve used to control air flow.

air-con·di·tion (âr'kən dish'ən) *v. t.* to provide apparatus for air conditioning. —**air'-con·di'tioned,** *adj.*

air conditioner, machine used for air conditioning.
air conditioning, system or process for controlling the temperature, humidity, purity, and circulation of the air in some enclosed area, such as a building, room, or vehicle.
air-cool (âr′kōōl′) v.t. **1.** to reduce heat in a mechanical device, as an automobile engine, by air circulation. **2.** to blow air into (a room) and cool by causing the air to circulate.
air corridor, route followed by an aircraft in flight, esp. one established by international agreement.
air-craft (âr′kraft′) pl., **-craft.** n. **1.** machine for flight in air designed to be supported by buoyancy (lighter-than-air craft) or by aerodynamic action (heavier-than-air craft). **2.** such vehicles collectively.
aircraft carrier, warship with a large open top deck, used as a floating air base.
air cushion vehicle, hovercraft.
air-drome (âr′drōm′) n. airport.

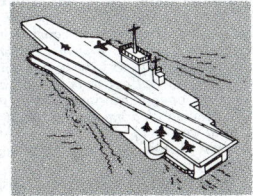

Aircraft carrier

air-drop (âr′drop′) -dropped, -drop·ping. v.t. to drop (food, supplies, or personnel) by parachute from airborne aircraft. —n. act of airdropping.
Aire-dale (âr′dāl′) n. largest breed of terrier, having a wiry tan coat with dark markings on the back and shoulders. [From the valley or DALE of the Aire River in Yorkshire, England.]
air-field (âr′fēld′) n. **1.** landing field of an airport. **2.** airport, esp. a small one.
air-foil (âr′foil′) n. **1.** any part, such as a wing, aileron, or rudder, designed to help lift or control an aircraft by controlling the flow of air over or around its surface. **2.** any body or surface which serves to control the direction of the flow of air.

Airedale

air force 1. the air branch of a country's armed forces. **2. Air Force.** the air force of the United States. Its responsibilities include land-based guided missile systems. Before June 26, 1947, it was part of the Army.
air gun 1. rifle or pistol using compressed air as propellant. **2.** hand tool operating by the force of compressed air.
air hammer, automatic hammer driven by compressed air.
air hole 1. hole through which air is permitted to pass in or out. **2.** natural opening in the ice on a river, pond, or the like. **3.** air pocket. **4.** imperfection formed by gas in a clay or metal casting.
air-i-ly (âr′ə lē) adv. in an airy manner; lightly; gaily.
air-i-ness (âr′ē nis) n. quality or state of being airy.
air-ing (âr′ing) n. **1.** exposure to air for the purpose of drying or freshening. **2.** exposure to public knowledge or discussion. **3.** walk or ride in the open air.
air lane, route used by aircraft, esp. a route used regularly because of steady winds.
air-less (âr′lis) adj. **1.** without air, esp. fresh air; stuffy. **2.** without any wind; still.
air-lift (âr′lift′) n. emergency system of transporting people, supplies, or animals by aircraft when land approaches are closed. —v.t. to transport by airlift.
air-line (âr′līn′) n. **1.** system and equipment for transporting people and goods by air. **2.** business organization owning and managing such a system. **3.** shortest route between two places.
air-lin-er (âr′lī′nər) n. large passenger plane.
air lock 1. airtight chamber, in which air pressure can be varied, affording passage between two places having differing air pressures. **2.** hindrance to the flow of a liquid in a system caused by the pressure of an air bubble.
air-mail (âr′māl′) v.t. to send by air mail. —adj. of or relating to air mail.
air mail 1. mail carried by airplane between cities. **2.** system of transporting mail by airplane.
air-man (âr′mən) pl., -men. n. **1.** pilot of an aircraft; aviator. **2.** enlisted man in the U.S. Air Force.
air mass, widespread body of air that is approximately uniform in its horizontal extent, particularly with reference to its temperature and moisture distribution.
air mattress, inflatable mattress made of rubber, plastic, or other airtight material.

air mile, unit of distance in air navigation equal to 6,076.1155 feet.
air-mind-ed (âr′mīn′did) adj. **1.** interested in things connected with airplanes, air travel, aviation, or the like. **2.** disposed to travel by air. —air′-mind′ed·ness, n.
air-plane (âr′plān′) n. aircraft that is heavier-than-air and has fixed wings, supported in flight by the action of air against its wings and driven by an engine or engines.
air plant, epiphyte.
air pocket, downward current of air causing an airplane to drop suddenly.
air police, members of the Air Force assigned to police duties.
air-port (âr′pôrt′) n. area equipped with facilities necessary for the landing, take-off, maintenance, and storage of aircraft and for the loading and discharge of passengers and cargo.

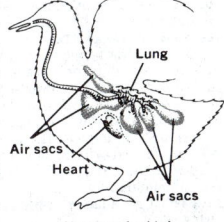

Airplane

air pressure 1. atmospheric pressure. **2.** force of compressed air.
air pump, machine for drawing in, exhausting, or compressing air in a container, or for forcing it through pipes or other apparatus.
air raid, attack by aircraft, esp. one involving the dropping of bombs on populated or industrial areas by organized groups of airplanes.
air-raid shelter, place intended to provide cover during an air raid.
air rifle, rifle powered by compressed air, esp. one that shoots BB's.
air sac, one of a number of membranous sacs of air in the body of a bird which are connected with the lungs.
air service, air traffic regularly available for commercial use.
air shaft, passage, usually vertical, to permit fresh air to reach into a mine, building, or the like.
air-ship (âr′ship′) n. any lighter-than-air craft, commonly made buoyant by such gases as helium or hydrogen, that is motor driven and can be steered, such as a blimp or dirigible.
air-sick (âr′sik′) adj. nauseated as a result of the motion of an aircraft. —air′sick′ness, n.
air-space (âr′spās′) n. space above a country, or some part of it, esp. such space considered as subject to certain laws of that country.
air speed, speed of an aircraft relative to the air through which it is moving. Distinguished from **ground speed.**
air-strip (âr′strip′) n. paved or cleared area from which planes land and take off.
air-tight (âr′tīt′) adj. **1.** so tight as to prevent air or gas from entering or escaping. **2.** free of weak points that could easily be criticized or refuted.
air-to-air (âr′tōō âr′, -tə-) adj. launched from an airborne carrier at an airborne target: air-to-air missiles.
air valve, valve designed to control the flow of air, as in a pipe.
air-waves (âr′wāvz′) n.,pl. radio or television broadcasting: the highest-paid performer of the airwaves.
air-way (âr′wā′) n. **1.** air route along which beacons and other aids to aircraft navigation are maintained. **2.** passage used for ventilation, as in a mine.
air-wor-thy (âr′wur′thē) adj. (of an aircraft) in good or safe condition for flying. —air′wor′thi·ness, n.
air-y (âr′ē) air-i·er, air-i·est. adj. **1.** immaterial; unsubstantial: an airy phantom. **2.** light as air in appearance and movement; thin; delicate. **3.** vivacious; buoyant: Her charmingly airy manner lifted their spirits. **4.** open to the flow of air; breezy: an airy apartment. **5.** high in the air; lofty. **6.** taking place in the air.
aisle (īl) n. **1.** passage between sections of seats in a place of assembly. **2.** any similar passageway: department store aisle, an aisle through the forest. **3.** wing or side division of a church alongside the nave, choir, or transept, set off by pillars or arches. See basilica for illustration. **4. on the aisle.** (seat or seats) closest to an aisle: He bought two on the aisle for himself and his date. **5. to roll in the aisles.** to laugh uproariously and uncontrollably. **6. to walk down the aisle.** to get married. [Old French ele wing, from Latin āla wing; later influenced by French aile wing, wing of a building.] —Syn. **1.** see passage.

Aix-en-Pro·vence (āks′än prō väNs′) *n.* resort in southeastern France, northeast of Marseilles. Pop. (1968), 89,566. Also, **Aix.**

Aix-la-Cha·pelle (āks′lä shä pel′) *n.* Aachen.

A·jac·cio (ä yät′chō) *n.* city on the west coast of Corsica, noted as the birthplace of Napoleon Bonaparte. Pop. (1962), 41,006.

a·jar¹ (ə jär′) *adj., adv.* partly open: *The door was left ajar.* [Middle English *on char* on the turn, from Old English *on cerre* on the turn.]

a·jar² (ə jär′) *adv., adj.* shaken up; unsettled: *My nerves are all ajar.* [AT + JAR².]

A·jax (ā′jaks) *n.* **1.** *Greek Legend.* son of Telamon, second only to Achilles in bravery in the Trojan War. Also, **Ajax the Greater. 2.** warrior in the Trojan War, one of the swiftest of the Greeks. Also, **Ajax the Lesser.**

a·kene (ā kēn′) achene.

a·kim·bo (ə kim′bō) *adj., adv.* (of arms) with the hands on the hips and elbows out. [Middle English *in kenebowe* in a sharp curve; of uncertain origin.]

a·kin (ə kin′) *adj.* **1.a.** related by blood: *Your aunt and my mother are akin.* **b.** of the same class or family: *The dog is akin to the wolf.* **2.** similar in character or properties: *Love and friendship are akin.* [Contraction of KIN.]

Ak·kad (ak′ad) *also,* **Ac·cad.** *n.* **1.** ancient region in the northern part of Mesopotamia. **2.** ancient city in central Mesopotamia, on the Euphrates River.

Ak·ka·di·an (ə kā′dē ən, ə kä′-) *also,* **Ac·ca·di·an.** *n.* **1.** member of an ancient Semitic people who inhabited the region of Akkad. The Akkadians conquered the Sumerians of Mesopotamia and established one of the first empires of history. **2.** extinct Semitic language of these people from which the Babylonian and Assyrian languages were derived. —*adj.* of or relating to the Akkadians, their empire, language, or culture.

Ak·kra (ak′rə) Accra.

Ak·ron (ak′rən) *n.* city in northeastern Ohio. Pop. (1970), 275,425.

al-, form of *ad-* before *l,* as in *allegation, alliteration.*

-al¹ *suffix* **1.** (used to form adjectives from nouns) of, relating to, or characterized by: *medicinal, historical.* **2.** (used to form nouns from adjectives) that which is characterized by (what is indicated by the stem): *animal, annual.* [Latin *-ālis* relating to.]

-al² *suffix* used to form nouns from verbs: act, process, or result: *recital, denial, arrival.* [Latin *-ālia,* neuter plural of *-ālis* relating to.]

Al, aluminum.

a·la (ā′lə) *pl.,* **a·lae.** *n.* wing or winglike part or structure. [Latin *āla* wing.]

a la (ä′ lə, ä′ lä) *also,* **à la.** in the manner of: *He writes a la Dickens.* [Shortened from À LA MODE.]

Ala., Alabama.

ALA, American Library Association.

Al·a·bam·a (al′ə bam′ə) *n.* state in the southeastern United States, at the southern end of the Appalachian Mountains and on the Gulf of Mexico. Capital, Montgomery. Area, 51,609 sq. mi. Pop. (1970), 3,444,165. Abbreviation, **Ala.** [Choctaw *alba amo* thicket clearers.] —**Al′a·bam′an,** **Al′a·bam′i·an,** *adj., n.*

al·a·bam·ine (al′ə bam′ēn, -in) *n.* astatine.

al·a·bas·ter (al′ə bas′tər) *n.* **1.** smooth, whitish stone used esp. in sculpture, a fine-grained, translucent variety of gypsum. **2.** calcite of a semitranslucent, hard variety, often having bandlike markings. —*adj.* resembling alabaster; smooth, translucent, and pale: *her alabaster arms.* [Old French *alabastre* these minerals, going back to Greek *alabastron,* possibly from *Alabastron* an ancient Egyptian town having alabaster quarries.]

a la carte (ä′lə kärt′) *also,* **à la carte.** with a separate price for each item on the menu. [French *à la carte* literally, according to the menu.]

a·lack (ə lak′) *interj. Archaic.* exclamation expressing regret, dismay, or disappointment. Also, **a·lack·a·day** (ə lak′ə dā′).

a·lac·ri·ty (ə lak′rə tē) *n.* **1.** eager willingness: *He accepted the position with alacrity.* **2.** swiftness; celerity: *to pursue with alacrity.* [Latin *alacritās* liveliness.]

a·lae (ā′lē) plural of ala.

a la king (ä′ lə king′) *also,* **à la king.** cooked in cream sauce with mushrooms and pimentos or green peppers. [A LA + KING.]

al·a·me·da (al′ə mē′də, -mä′-) *n.* shaded public walk lined with poplar or other trees.

Al·a·me·da (al′ə mē′də, -mä′-) *n.* city in western California, a residential suburb of Oakland. Pop. (1970), 70,968.

a·la·mo (al′ə mō′, ä′lə mō′) *pl.,* **-mos.** *n.* poplar tree, esp. a cottonwood. [Spanish *álamo* poplar; of uncertain origin.]

Al·a·mo (al′ə mō′) *n.* fortified mission in San Antonio, Texas, besieged and taken by Mexican troops in 1836.

a la mode (ä′ lə mōd′) *also,* **à la mode. 1.** *Cooking.* **a.** served with ice cream: *pie a la mode.* **b.** braised with vegetables and served with

a rich brown sauce: *beef a la mode.* **2.** in style; fashionable. [French *à la mode* in the manner or fashion of.]

Å·land Islands (ō′länd) group of Finnish islands in the Baltic Sea. Land area, 572 sq. mi. Pop. (1968), 21,600.

a·lar (ā′lər) *adj.* **1.** of or relating to an ala or wing. **2.** having alae or wings. **3.** winglike or wing-shaped. [Latin *alāris* relating to a wing, from *āla* wing.]

Al·a·ric (al′ər ik) *n.* c.370–410, king of the Visigoths and first Germanic leader to capture Rome.

a·larm (ə lärm′) *n.* **1.** fear and excitement, esp. over sudden danger: *The clap of thunder filled him with alarm.* **2.** warning of danger: *Give the alarm.* **3.** device or signal that warns, rouses, or calls to action: *burglar alarm.* **4.** *Archaic.* alarum. **5. false alarm.** something that deceptively appears to be genuine, impending, or accurate: *The forecast for rain turned out to be a false alarm.* —*v.t.* to cause to feel fear, anxiety, or apprehension. [Old French *alarme* warning of danger, from Old Italian *all'arme* to arms, going back to Latin *ad* to + *ille* that + *arma* weapons.]

alarm clock, clock that has an alarm that can be set to go off at any given time.

a·larm·ing (ə lär′ming) *adj.* causing fear and excitement; disturbing. —**a·larm′ing·ly,** *adv.*

a·larm·ist (ə lär′mist) *n.* one inclined to alarm others or become alarmed needlessly or on slight grounds. —**a·larm′ism,** *n.*

a·lar·um (ə lar′əm, ə lär′-) *n. Archaic.* call to action or to arms.

a·la·ry (ā′lər ē, al′ər ē) *adj.* **1.** of or relating to wings. **2.** wing-shaped. [Latin *ālārius* relating to wings, from *āla* wing.]

a·las (ə las′) *interj.* exclamation expressing disappointment, sorrow, or regret. [Old French *a las* ah wretched, ah weary, from *a* ah (imitative) + *las* weary (from Latin *lassus*).]

Alas., Alaska.

A·las·ka (ə las′kə) *n.* largest state of the United States, on the extreme northwestern peninsula of North America. Capital, Juneau. Area, 586,-400 sq. mi. Pop. (1970), 302,173. Abbreviation, **Alas.** [Eskimo *Alakshak* mainland.] —**A·las′kan,** *adj. n.*

Alaska Highway, road running from eastern British Columbia, in Canada, to Fairbanks, Alaska. Also, **Alcan Highway.**

Alaskan malamute, wolflike dog of a breed native to northwestern Alaska, having a thick, coarse coat and large, bushy tail, used to pull sleds. Height: 25 inches at the shoulder.

Alaskan malamute

a·late (ā′lāt) *adj.* having wings or wing-like parts. [Latin *ālātus,* from *āla* wing.]

alb (alb) *n.* floor-length white linen robe with narrow sleeves, worn girded at the waist by Roman Catholic and some Anglican priests at the celebration of the Mass and other ceremonies. [Old English *albe,* from Late Latin *alba (vestis)* white (garment), from Latin *alba,* feminine of *albus* white.]

al·ba·core (al′bə kôr′) *pl.,* **-cores** or **-core.** *n.* important food and game fish, *Thunnus alalunga,* of the tuna family, found mostly in temperate seas and distinguished from other tunas by its long pectoral fin. Weight: under 40 pounds. [Portuguese *albacora,* from Arabic *al* the + *bukr* young camel.]

Al·ba Lon·ga (al′bə lông′gə) ancient city in Latium, southeast of Rome, and legendary birthplace of Romulus and Remus.

Al·ba·ni·a (al bā′nē ə, -bän′yə) *n.* small country in southeastern Europe, on the Balkan Peninsula. Capital, Tirana. Area, 11,100 sq. mi. Pop. (1969 est.), 2,075,000.

Al·ba·ni·an (al bā′nē ən, -bän′yən) *adj.* of or relating to Albania, its people, their language or culture. —*n.* **1.** member or close descendant of the people of Albania. **2.** the language of these people, a branch of the Indo-European language family.

Al·ba·ny (ôl′bə nē) *n.* **1.** capital of New York, in the eastern part of the state. Pop. (1970), 114,-873. **2.** city in southwestern Georgia. Pop. (1970), 72,623.

al·ba·tross (al′bə trôs′, -tros′) *n.* any of various web-footed sea birds, family Diomedeidae, found chiefly in the southern oceans, having a long hooked beak and capable of prolonged flight. One species, the **wandering albatross,** has a wing span of up to eleven feet, the largest of any living bird. Length: 28–53 inches. Also, **goo′ney.** [Modification (influenced by Latin *albus* white) of earlier *aicatras* pelican, from Portuguese *alcatraz* pelican, originally bucket (with reference to its pouch for carrying water), from Arabic *al* the + *qādūs* pitcher, from Greek *kados* jar; of Semitic origin.]

Albatross

at; āpe; cär; end; mē; it; īce; hot; ōld; fôrk; wood; fōol; oil; out; up; ūse; turn; sing; thin; this; zh in treasure; ə in ago, taken, pencil, lemon, circus.

al·be·it (ôl bē′it) *conj.* although; notwithstanding; even though. [Short for *although it be that.*]

Al·ber·ich (al′bər ik) *n. Germanic Legend.* the king of the dwarfs and chief of the Nibelungs.

Al·bert (al′bərt) **1. Prince.** 1819–61, consort of Queen Victoria of Great Britain. **2. Lake.** lake in east-central Africa, on the border between Uganda and the Democratic Republic of the Congo.

Al·ber·ta (al bur′tə) *n.* province of Canada, in the western part of the country. Area, 255,285 sq. mi. Pop. (1969 est.) 1,561,000.

Al·ber·tus Mag·nus, Saint (al bur′təs mag′nəs) c.1193–1280, German monk and medieval philosopher who instructed St. Thomas Aquinas.

Al·bi·gen·ses (al′bi jen′sēz) *n.,pl.* members of a religious sect existing in southern France from the eleventh to the thirteenth centuries, suppressed for heresy. —**Al′bi·gen′si·an,** *adj., n.*

al·bi·nism (al′bə niz′əm) *n.* condition of an albino; state of being an albino.

al·bi·no (al bī′nō) *pl.,* **-nos.** *n.* **1.** person with a congenital deficiency in pigmentation characterized by pale, milky skin, very light hair, and pink eyes. **2.** any plant or animal with deficient coloration. [Spanish *albino,* from *albo* snow white, from Latin *albus* white.]

Al·bi·on (al′bē ən) *n.* England. ▲ used primarily in literature.

al·bite (al′bīt) *n.* white, translucent sodium aluminum silicate, a variety of feldspar, used esp. as a glaze in ceramics. Moonstone, an opalescent variety, is used as a gemstone. Formula: NaAlSi₃O₈.

al·bum (al′bəm) *n.* **1.** book with blank pages or transparent envelopes in which to keep collected items: *stamp album, autograph album, photograph album.* **2.a.** booklike holder with envelopes for phonograph records. **b.** long-playing phonograph record, or set of records sold as a unit. [Latin *album* blank tablet on which notices were recorded.]

al·bu·men (al bū′mən) *n.* **1.** white of an egg. **2.** albumin. **3.** endosperm. [Latin *albūmen* white of an egg.]

al·bu·min (al bū′min) *n.* any of a group of water-soluble proteins found in many plant and animal tissues and fluids. Albumin occurs in its purest natural form in the white of an egg. [French *albumine,* from Latin *albūmen* white of an egg.]

al·bu·mi·nous (al bū′mə nəs) *adj.* of, like, or containing albumin.

Al·bu·quer·que (al′bə kur′kē) *n.* largest city of New Mexico, in the north-central part of the state. Pop. (1970), 243,751.

al·bur·num (al bur′nəm) *n.* sapwood.

al·caide (al kād′) *also,* **al·cayde.** *n.* **1.** governor of a Spanish, Portuguese, or Moorish fortress. **2.** jailer or warden of a Spanish prison. [Spanish *alcaide* governor of a castle, from Arabic *al-qā′īd* the leader.]

al·cal·de (al käl′dē) *n.* mayor of a Spanish or Spanish-American town who has judicial as well as administrative powers and functions. [Spanish *alcalde,* from Arabic *al-qāḍī* the judge.]

Al·can Highway (al′kan′) Alaska Highway.

Al·ca·traz (al′kə traz′) *n.* island in San Francisco Bay, site of a former U.S. penitentiary of the same name.

al·ca·zar (al kaz′ər, al′kə zär′) *n.* **1.** castle or fortress of the Moors in Spain. **2. the Alcazar.** palace of the Moorish kings in Seville, Spain, later occupied by the Spanish royal family. [Spanish *alcázar,* from Arabic *al* the + *qaçr* castle, from Latin *castrum* fortified place.]

Al·ces·tis (al ses′tis) *n. Greek Legend.* Thessalian queen who sacrificed her life to save that of her husband, King Admetus. She was later rescued from Hades by Hercules.

al·che·mist (al′kə mist) *n.* one who studies or practices alchemy. —**al′che·mis′tic;** *also,* **al·che·mis′ti·cal,** *adj.*

al·che·my (al′kə mē) *n.* **1.** chemistry of the Middle Ages, concerned primarily with attempts to transmute base metals into gold and the search for an elixir of life. **2.** any seemingly magical power or process of transforming one thing into another. [Old French *alchemie, alquemie,* going back to Arabic *al* the + *kīmīā,* presumably from Late Greek *chēmīā* transmutation of metals, chemistry; of uncertain origin.] —**al·chem·ic** (al kem′ik); *also,* **al·chem′i·cal·ly,** *adv.*

Al·ci·bi·a·des (al′sə bī′ə dēz′) *n.* c.450–404 B.C., Athenian politician and general.

Al·ci·des (al sī′dēz) *n.* Hercules.

Alc·me·ne (alk mē′nē) *n. Greek Legend.* the mother of Hercules by Zeus.

al·co·hol (al′kə hôl′) *n.* **1.** odorless, flammable, volatile liquid that is produced synthetically or by the fermentation of grain, fruit, or other starch or sugary substances; grain alcohol; ethyl alcohol. It is the intoxicating agent in liquor and is used widely in the manufacture of drugs and other chemicals. Formula: C₂H₅OH Also, **eth·a·nol.** **2.** any beverage containing this liquid. **3.** *Chemistry.* any of the group of colorless, flammable, organic compounds to which ethyl alcohol belongs, distinguished by the presence of one or more hydroxyl groups. The simplest alcohol is methyl alcohol or wood alcohol, CH₃OH. [Modern Latin *alcohol* distilled liquid, from Medieval Latin *alcohol* powder for decorating the eyelids, from Arabic *al-koh'l* the powdered antimony used to stain the eyelids.]

al·co·hol·ic (al′kə hô′lik, -hol′ik) *adj.* **1.** of alcohol. **2.** containing or using alcohol: *alcoholic mixture.* **3.** caused by alcohol: *wandering in an alcoholic haze.* **4.** suffering from alcholism. —*n.* one who suffers from alcoholism or is addicted to excessive use of alcoholic beverages.

al·co·hol·ism (al′kə hô liz′əm) *n.* **1.** chronic disease characterized by an uncontrollable urge to drink alcoholic beverages. **2.** diseased condition of the body caused by the excessive or prolonged use of alcoholic beverages.

Al·co·ran (al′kō rän′, -ran′) *n.* the Koran.

Al·cott, Louisa May (ôl′kət, -kot) 1832–88, U.S. author.

al·cove (al′kōv′) *n.* **1.** small room or recess opening off a larger room. **2.** any recessed space or secluded bower: *an alcove in the garden.* [French *alcove* recess, from Spanish *alcoba,* from Arabic *al* the + *qobbah* vaulted area.]

Ald., Alderman. Also, **Aldm.**

Al·deb·a·ran (al deb′ər ən) *n.* giant red star, one of the brightest in the sky, and the brightest in the constellation Taurus.

al·de·hyde (al′də hīd′) *n.* **1.** any of a group of organic compounds which yield acids when oxidized and alcohols when reduced. General formula: R-CHO **2.** acetaldehyde. [Short for Modern Latin *al(cohol) de·hyd(rogenatum)* alcohol deprived of its hydrogen.]

Al·den, John (ôl′dən) c.1599–1687, Puritan settler in Plymouth Colony.

al·der (ôl′dər) *n.* any of a group of trees or shrubs, genus *Alnus,* found in cool, moist regions of the Northern Hemisphere, most of which have scaly bark, saw-toothed oval leaves, and bear both male and female catkins. [Old English *alr, alor.*]

Alder

al·der·man (ôl′dər mən) *pl.,* **-men.** *n.* **1.** in the United States, a member of a municipal governing body, often representing a certain ward or district. **2.** in England and Ireland, one of the members of a municipal or borough council. **3.** in Anglo-Saxon England, chief magistrate of a county or group of counties. [Old English *ealdorman* high-ranking nobleman, official, member of a council, from *ealdor* head of a family, elder, chief + MAN.] —**al·der·man·ic** (ôl′dər man′ik), *adj.*

Al·der·ney (ôl′dər nē) *n.* British island in the English Channel. Area, 3 sq. mi. Pop. (1961), 1449.

ale (āl) *n.* fermented beverage made from hops and malt, similar to beer, but heavier and more bitter. [Old English *alu.*]

a·lee (ə lē′) *adv., adj.* on or toward the lee side of a ship; leeward. [A¹ + LEE.]

ale·house (āl′hous′) *n.* **1.** tavern where ale is served. **2.** any tavern.

a·lem·bic (ə lem′bik) *n.* **1.** gourd-shaped glass or metal container with a beaked top, formerly used in distilling. **2.** anything that purifies, refines, or transforms. [French *alambic* still², going back to Arabic *al* the + *anbīq* still², from Greek *ambix* cup.]

A·lep·po (ə lep′ō) *n.* city in northwestern Syria. Pop. (1968), 566,-770.

a·lert (ə lurt′) *adj.* **1.** watchful; vigilant: *an alert sentinel.* **2.** quick to act or learn; lively; active: *an alert mind.* **3.** aware of; conscious of: *He was alert to all the possibilities.* —*n.* **1.** warning of possible danger: *an air alert.* **2.** length of time an alert lasts: *They were quiet during the alert.* **3.** signal to be ready: *The captain gave the alert an hour before sailing.* **4. on alert,** on notice to be ready. **5. on the alert,** on the lookout; vigilant: *He was on the alert for any sign of danger.* —*v.t.* **1.** to notify to be ready; warn: *to alert the town before the hurricane.* **2.** to make aware of; inform: *He alerted his friends to the fact that the fishing boats had come in.* [French *alerte* to arms, from Italian *all'erta* on the watch, on the watchtower, going back to Latin *ad* to + *erta,* past participle of *ērigere* to erect.] —**a·lert′ly,** *adv.* —**a·lert′ness,** *n.*

A·leu·tian Islands (ə lōō′shən) chain of U.S. islands in the North Pacific extending southwest from Alaska. Land area, 6391 sq. mi. Pop. (1960 est.), 6,000. Also, **A·leu′tians.**

ale·wife¹ (āl′wīf′) *pl.,* **-wives.** *n.* small bony fish, *Alosa pseudoharengus,* of the herring family, abundant along the Atlantic coast of the United States. It swims upstream in large numbers to spawn and has survived in landlocked waters, esp. the Great Lakes. Length: 6–15 inches. [Of uncertain origin.]

ale·wife² (āl′wīf′) *pl.,* **-wives.** *n.* woman who runs an alehouse.

Al·ex·an·der I (al′ig zan′dər) 1777–1825, czar of Russia from 1801 to 1825.

Alexander II, 1818–88, czar of Russia from 1855 to 1881.

at; āpe; cär; end; mē; it; īce; hot; ōld; fôrk; wood; fōōl; oil; out; up; ūse; turn; sing; thin; this; zh in treasure; ə in ago, taken, pencil, lemon, circus.

23

Alexander III, 1845–94, czar of Russia from 1881 to 1894.

Alexander VI, 1431–1503, pope from 1492 to 1503.

Alexander the Great, 356–323 B.C., king of Macedonia from 336 to 323 B.C., general of Greece, and conqueror of Persia.

Al·ex·an·dri·a (al'ig zan'drē ə) n. **1.** port city in the U.A.R., in ancient times, the capital of Egypt, on the Mediterranean in the northeastern part of the country. It was founded by Alexander the Great in 332 B.C. Pop. (1967 est.), 1,801,056. **2.** city in central Louisiana. Pop. (1970), 41,557. **3.** city in northern Virginia, a residential suburb of Washington, D.C. Pop. (1970), 110,938.

Al·ex·an·dri·an (al'ig zan'drē ən) adj. **1.** of Alexandria, Egypt. **2.** of or relating to the Alexandrian school or its influence. **3.** of Alexander the Great or his reign. **4.** Alexandrine.

Alexandrian school, school of literature, science, and philosophy that flourished in Alexandria, Egypt, during the first few centuries A.D.

Al·ex·an·drine (al'ig zan'drin, -drēn) n. line of poetry having six iambic feet. —adj. designating or composed of an Alexandrine or Alexandrines. [French alexandrin, referring to its use in Old French poems about Alexander the Great.]

al·ex·i·a (ə lek'sē ə) n. form of aphasia marked by the inability to recognize or understand written or printed words. [Modern Latin alexia, from Greek a- without + lexis speech (confused with Latin legere to read).]

al·fal·fa (al fal'fə) n. any of a group of bushy, cloverlike plants, genus Medicago, several varieties of which are widely cultivated as forage and fodder crops. [Spanish alfalfa, from Arabic al-façaçah the best kind of fodder.]

al fi·ne (äl fē'nā) Italian. to the end.

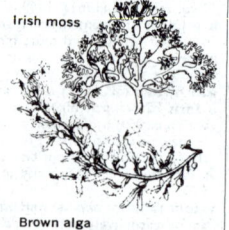

Flower

Leaflet

Root

Alfalfa

Al·fred the Great (al'frid) 849–889, king of the West Saxons from 871 to 899 and the most famous figure in early English history.

al·fres·co (al fres'kō) also, **al fres·co.** adv., adj. in the open air; outdoors. [Italian.]

alg., algebra.

al·gae (al'jē) sing., **al·ga** (al'gə) n.,pl. large group of rootless, non-flowering plants, including scums formed in ponds and most seaweeds, classified in the lowest seven divisions of the plant kingdom. Although algae range from microscopic, one-celled organisms, such as diatoms, to giant marine seaweeds and kelps, the best-known kinds have chlorophyll and are found in water. [Latin algae, plural of alga seaweed.] —**al·gal** (al'gəl), adj.

Irish moss

al·ge·bra (al'jə brə) n. branch of mathematics in which the relationships and properties of numbers are expressed and analyzed in terms of letters, numerals, and abstract symbols. [Italian algebra, from Arabic aljebr the reduction, repair of broken parts, bone setting.]

Brown alga

Algae

al·ge·bra·ic (al'jə brā'ik) adj. of, used in, or involving algebra: an algebraic equation. Also, **al'ge·bra'i·cal.** —**al'ge·bra'i·cal·ly,** adv.

al·ge·bra·ist (al'jə brā'ist) n. one who is skilled in algebra.

Al·ge·ri·a (al jēr'ē ə) n. country in northern Africa, on the Mediterranean, formerly a French possession. Capital, Algiers. Area, 919,515 sq. mi. Pop. (1970), 11,821,679. —**Al·ge'ri·an,** adj., n.

Al·giers (al jērz') n. **1.** capital and port city of Algeria, on the Mediterranean, in the northern part of the country. Pop. (1966 est.), 1,-100,000. **2.** Algeria.

Al·gol (al'gol, -gōl) n. multiple star system in the constellation Perseus, including an eclipsing double star. [Arabic al-ghūl literally, the demon, the ghoul; because its periodic variation in brightness may have suggested the existence of an evil force.]

ALGOL (al'gol) computer coding system used for scientific purposes.

Al·gon·qui·an (al gong'kē ən, -kwē ən) pl., **-qui·ans** or **-qui·an.** n. **1.** one of the most widespread of North American Indian language families, including Cree, Delaware, Shawnee, Ojibwa, Blackfoot, and Cheyenne. **2.** member of any Algonquian-speaking tribe. —adj. of or relating to this linguistic family.

Al·gon·quin (al gong'kin, -kwin) pl., **-quins** or **-quin.** n. **1.** member of a group of Algonquian-speaking Indian tribes formerly living along the Ottawa River and in the region of the St. Lawrence River. **2.** Algonquian language spoken by these tribes. **3.** any Algonquian-speaking Indian. [Possibly from Micmac algoomeaking at the place to spear fish.]

Al·ham·bra (al ham'brə) n. **1.** palace in Granada, Spain, built by Moorish princes in the thirteenth century, an outstanding example of Moorish architecture. **2.** city in southern California, a residential suburb of Los Angeles. Pop. (1970), 62,125.

A·li (ä'lē) n. c.600–661, caliph of Islam, from 656 to 661.

a·li·as (ā'lē əs) pl., **-as·es.** n. assumed name; other name: William H. Bonney's alias was Billy the Kid. —adv. also known as; under the assumed name of: Brown alias Bell. [Latin aliās otherwise, from alius another.] —**Syn.** n. see **pseudonym.**

al·i·bi (al'ə bī') pl., **-bis.** n. **1.** claim or proof of having been elsewhere at the time an act or offense was committed. **2.** any excuse. —v.i., **-bied, -bi·ing.** to offer an excuse (with for): His brother alibied for him. [Latin alibī elsewhere.]

Al·i·can·te (al'ə kan'tē, Spanish ä'lē kän'tä) n. port city in southeastern Spain, on the Mediterranean. Pop. (1968), 135,566.

al·ien (āl'yən, ā'lē ən) n. **1.** foreign-born person who is not a naturalized citizen of the country in which he lives. **2.** foreigner; stranger. —adj. **1.** of or belonging to another country or people; foreign. **2.** strange; unfamiliar: alien patterns of behavior. **3.** alien to. incompatible or inconsistent with; foreign to: actions alien to our democratic tradition. [Latin aliēnus strange, stranger.]

al·ien·a·ble (āl'yə nə bəl, ā'lē ə-) adj. capable of being transferred to another.

al·ien·ate (āl'yə nāt', ā'lē ə-) **-at·ed, -at·ing.** v.t. **1.** to cause (someone) to feel unfriendly, indifferent, or hostile: His conduct alienated the whole family. **2.** to cause to be removed or withdrawn: youth alienated from society. **3.** to transfer or convey to another owner: to alienate property.

al·ien·a·tion (āl'yə nā'shən, ā'lē ə-) n. **1.** act of alienating; being alienated. **2.** Psychiatry. loss or derangement of mental faculties.

al·ien·ist (āl'yə nist, ā'lē ə-) n. psychiatrist, esp. one who specializes in giving legal testimony. [French aliéniste, going back to Latin aliēnāre to estrange, make insane.]

al·i·form (al'ə fôrm', ā'lə-) adj. wing-shaped.

a·light[1] (ə līt') **a·light·ed** or **a·lit, a·light·ing.** v.i. **1.** to step down from; get off: The passengers alighted from the plane. **2.** to land on: The bee alighted on the flower. **3.** to alight on (or upon). Archaic. to happen upon by chance; discover. [Old English ālīhtan to remove weight from, descend.]

a·light[2] (ə līt') adv., adj. aglow; brightly illuminated: a church alight with candles. [Past participle of obsolete alight to light up, from Old English ālīhtan.]

a·lign (ə līn') also, **a·line.** v.t. **1.** to bring into line: He aligned the putter with the ball. **2.** to ally (oneself) with others for a common cause: Republicans aligned themselves with the Southern Democrats. **3.** to adjust (the wheels of a vehicle) to their proper position. **4.** to adjust (parts of an electric circuit or a mechanical device) so that they function properly. —v.i. **1.** to fall into line. **2.** to join in common cause. [French aligner to line up, from à to (from Latin ad-) + ligne line (from Latin līnea).]

a·lign·ment (ə līn'mənt) also, **a·line·ment.** n. **1.** act of aligning; state of being aligned. **2.** line or lines formed by aligning.

a·like (ə līk') adv. in the same manner; equally; similarly: They all talk alike. —adj. like one another; having resemblance; similar: He thinks all dogs are alike. [Old English onlīc.]

al·i·ment (al'ə mənt) n. that which nourishes; food. [Latin alimentum.]

al·i·men·ta·ry (al'ə men'tər ē, -trē) adj. **1.** of or relating to food and nutrition. **2.** nourishing.

alimentary canal, continuous tube extending from mouth to anus through which food passes as it is digested, absorbed, and eliminated as waste matter.

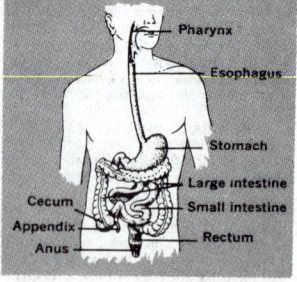

Pharynx
Esophagus
Stomach
Large intestine
Cecum
Small intestine
Appendix
Rectum
Anus

Alimentary canal

al·i·men·ta·tion (al'ə men tā'shən) n. **1.** act or process of nourishing; state of being nourished. **2.** that which nourishes; nourishment.

al·i·mo·ny (al'ə mō'nē) n. court-ordered allotment of part of a hus-

at; āpe; cär; end; mē; it; īce; hot; ōld; fôrk; wood; fōol; oil; out; up; ūse; turn; sing; thin; this; zh in treasure; ə in ago, taken, pencil, lemon, circus.

band's estate or income to be paid for his wife's support after they are divorced or while they are separated or awaiting settlement of their case. [Latin *alimōnia* nourishment, support.]

a·line (ə līn′) a-lined, a-lin·ing. *v.t., v.i.* to align.

a·line·ment (ə līn′mənt) alignment.

al·i·phat·ic (al′ə fat′ik) *adj.* (of a hydrocarbon) consisting of a straight or branched chain, rather than a ring, of carbon atoms, to which hydrogen atoms are attached. Aliphatic hydrocarbons occur in three principal homologous series: alkanes, alkenes, and alkynes.

al·i·quant (al′ə kwənt) *adj.* contained in, but not dividing evenly into another number. The number three is an aliquant part of seven. Distinguished from **aliquot**. [Latin *aliquantum* in some degree.]

al·i·quot (al′ə kwət) *adj.* contained in and dividing evenly into another number. The number two is an aliquot part of four. Distinguished from **aliquant**. [French *aliquote* proportionate, from Latin *aliquot* several.]

a·lit (ə lit′) a past tense and past participle of **alight**[1].

a·live (ə līv′) *adj.* 1. having life; animate. 2. in force or operation; active: *to keep old memories alive.* 3. full of life; animated; lively: *alive with excitement.* 4. of all living: *the proudest girl alive.* 5. **alive to.** alert to; aware of; sensitive to: *He was alive to the changes going on around him.* 6. **alive with.** filled or swarming with: *The station was alive with rushing commuters.* 7. **look alive.** be alert; move quickly. [Old English *on līfe* having life.] **—a·live′ness,** *n.*

a·liz·a·rin (ə liz′ər in) *n.* orange-red or red compound prepared from aniline, used in making dyes. It was formerly obtained from madder. Formula: C₁₄H₈O₄ [French *alizarine*, from *alizari* madder, going back to Arabic *al-ʿaçarah* the extract.]

al·ka·li (al′kə lī′) *pl.,* -lis or -lies. *n.* 1. any of a group of strong, water-soluble bases or their salts. Most alkalis are compounds of the alkali metals. 2. any water-soluble mineral salt or mixture of such salts. Alkalis are found in soils, esp. desert soils. [French *alcali,* going back to Arabic *al-qalīy* the ashes of the saltwort (an early source of alkali).]

alkali metal, any of the soft, metallic elements lithium, sodium, potassium, rubidium, cesium, and francium.

al·ka·line (al′kə līn′, -lin) *adj.* of or like an alkali; having the properties of an alkali. **—al·ka·lin·i·ty** (al′kə lin′ə tē), *n.*

alkaline earth, an oxide of any of the alkaline-earth metals.

alkaline-earth metal, any of the metallic elements beryllium, magnesium, calcium, strontium, barium, and radium.

al·ka·lize (al′kə līz′) -lized, -liz·ing. *v.t., v.i.* to make or become alkaline.

al·ka·loid (al′kə loid′) *n.* any of a group of organic alkaline substances, including atropine, morphine, caffeine, and quinine, obtained chiefly from higher plants and widely used in medicine.

al·kane (al′kān) *n.* member of one of the three principal series of aliphatic hydrocarbons. General formula: CₙH₂ₙ ₊ ₂ Also, **par′af·fin.**

al·kene (al′kēn) *n.* member of one of the three principal series of aliphatic hydrocarbons. Ethylene is an alkene. General formula: CₙH₂ₙ Also, **o′le·fin.**

Al·ko·ran (al′kô rän′, -ran′) *n.* the Koran.

al·kyl group (al′kəl) any univalent group or radical formed when one of the hydrocarbons of the alkane series loses a hydrogen atom. CH₃ is an alkyl group. [ALK(ALI) + Greek *hylē* matter.]

al·kyne (al′kīn) *n.* member of one of the three principal series of aliphatic hydrocarbons. General formula: CₙH₂ₙ ₋ ₂

all (ôl) *adj.* 1. whole of: *all Asia.* 2. entire number of: *all nations.* 3. greatest possible: *with all due speed.* 4. any; whatever: *beyond all hope.* 5. nothing but; only: *This is all fantasy.* 6. every: *all sorts of people.* ▲ used chiefly in the phrases *all sorts of, all kinds of, all manner of.* **—n.** 1. everything one has: *to give one's all.* 2. everything: *All is lost.*
above all. before everything else; most of all.
after all. all things considered; despite everything.
all in all. everything considered; on the whole.
all out. *Informal.* with the greatest effort possible: *We went all out to help him.*
at all. a. in any degree: *no luck at all.* **b.** in any way: *He can't sing at all.* **c.** under any circumstances: *He refuses to drive at all.*
for all (that). a. in spite of; notwithstanding. **b.** as far as: *For all we know, he's lying.*
in all. everyone or everything included; altogether: *In all, about fifty attended.*
—pron. 1. whole quantity, amount, or number: *All of the cake is gone.* 2. each: *All answered yes.* **—adv.** 1. wholly; completely; entirely: *all agog.* 2. each; apiece: *a score of seven all.* 3. **all but.** almost; nearly. 4. **all in.** *Informal.* exhausted; weary. 5. **all of.** no less than; no more than: *He's all of six years old.* 6. **all over. a.** finished; ended. **b.** many places; everywhere. **c.** *Informal.* in every way; typically: *That's Henry all over.* [Old English *all, eall.*]

al·la bre·ve (ä′lä brā′vä) *Music.* tempo in duple time in which the

rhythmic beat is on the half note, rather than the quarter note, causing the notes to be played twice as quickly. Symbol: ₵ . [Italian *alla breve* literally, according to the breve.]

Al·lah (al′ə, ä′lə) *n.* the one God of Islam. [Arabic *allāh*.]

Al·la·ha·bad (al′ə hə bad′, ä′lə hä bäd′) *n.* city in north-central India, on the Ganges. Pop. (1968), 521,568.

all-A·mer·i·can (ôl′ə mer′i kən) *adj.* 1. representative or typical of the United States. 2. selected as the best or composed of the best players in any type in the United States. **—n.** all-American player or athlete.

al·lar·gan·do (äl′lär gän′dō) *adj., adv. Music.* gradually slower and more dignified, with the same or greater volume. [Italian *allargando* literally, making slow.]

all-a·round (ôl′ə round′) *adj.* good at many things; good for many purposes; versatile: *an all-around athlete, an all-around education.* Also, **all′-round′.**

al·lay (ə lā′) -layed, -lay·ing. *v.t.* 1. to put at rest; quiet; calm: *to allay a child's fears.* 2. to make less severe; relieve: *The ice pack allayed the pain in his ankle.* [Old English *ālecgan* to suppress.]

all clear, signal indicating that an air raid is over.

al·le·ga·tion (al′ə gā′shən) *n.* 1. assertion without proof. 2. assertion to be proven in a court of law. [French *allégation* assertion, from Latin *allēgātiō* alleging.]

al·lege (ə lej′) -leged, -leg·ing. *v.t.* 1. to assert or declare without proof: *He alleged his innocence before the court.* 2. to give as an excuse or defense. [Anglo-Norman *alegier*, equivalent to Old French *esligier* to clear at law, going back to Latin *ex* out of + *lītigāre* to sue; influenced by Middle French *alleguer* to urge, from Latin *allēgāre* to bring forward.] **—al·lege′a·ble,** *adj.* **—al·leg′er,** *n.*

al·leged (ə lejd′) *adj.* presumed; supposed: *The alleged murderer was proved innocent.* **—al·leg·ed·ly** (ə lej′id lē), *adv.*

Al·le·ghe·ny (al′ə gā′nē) *n.* river in western Pennsylvania and southwestern New York joining the Monongahela at Pittsburgh to form the Ohio River.

Allegheny Mountains, mountain range extending from north-central Pennsylvania through western Maryland, eastern West Virginia, and western Virginia. It is part of the Appalachian mountain system. Also, **Al′le·ghe′nies.**

al·le·giance (ə lē′jəns) *n.* 1. obligation of loyalty to a government, country, or sovereign. 2. loyalty or devotion to a person, cause, or thing. 3. *Archaic.* obligation of a vassal to his feudal lord. [A⁻³ + Old French *ligeance* homage, from *lige.* See LIEGE.] **—Syn.** 1. see **loyalty.**

al·le·gor·i·cal (al′ə gôr′i kəl, -gor′-) *adj.* of, relating to, or containing allegory; figurative. Also, **al′le·gor′ic. —al′le·gor′i·cal·ly,** *adv.*

al·le·go·rize (al′ə gə rīz′) -rized, -riz·ing. *v.t.* to make allegorical; treat as an allegory. **—v.i.** to use or make allegorical.

al·le·go·ry (al′ə gôr′ē) *pl.,* -ries. *n.* 1. literary device of presenting abstract ideas or moral principles in the form of symbolic characters, events, or objects; extended metaphor. 2. narrative form in which allegory is used extensively. [Latin *allēgoria,* from Greek *allēgoriā.*]

al·le·gret·to (al′ə gret′ō) *Music. adj., adv.* faster than andante but slower than allegro; rather lively. **—n. pl.,** -tos. piece, movement, or passage in such tempo. [Italian *allegretto,* diminutive of *allegro* fast. See ALLEGRO.]

al·le·gro (ə lā′grō, ə leg′rō) *Music. adj., adv.* faster than allegretto but slower than presto; lively; fast. **—n. pl.,** -gros. piece, movement, or passage in such tempo. [Italian *allegro* fast, from Latin *alacer* lively.]

al·le·lu·ia (al′ə lōō′ yə) hallelujah.

al·le·mande (al′ə mand′) *n.* 1. any of various German processional dances of the seventeenth and eighteenth centuries. 2. music for any of these dances. 3. piece of music resembling this in rhythm, formerly used as the movement preceding the prelude in a suite. [French *allemande* feminine of *allemand* German, from Latin *Alemannī* ancient German tribe; of Germanic origin.]

Al·len, E·than (al′ən; ē′thən) 1738–89, leader of American irregulars in Vermont during the Revolutionary War.

Allen Park (al′ən) city in southeastern Michigan, a residential suburb of Detroit. Pop. (1970), 40,747.

Al·len·town (al′ən toun′) *n.* city in southeastern Pennsylvania. Pop. (1970), 109,527.

al·ler·gen (al′ər jən) *n.* substance that induces allergy.

al·ler·gen·ic (al′ər jen′ik) *adj.* inducing allergy.

al·ler·gic (ə lûr′jik) *adj.* 1. of or produced by allergy: *an allergic reaction.* 2. having an allergy. 3. *Informal.* having a strong distaste or aversion (with *to*): *allergic to homework.*

al·ler·gy (al′ər jē) *pl.,* -gies. *n.* 1. hypersensitivity of the body tissues to a specific substance, such as pollen, dust, or certain fruits, resulting in various reactions affecting the skin, respiratory system, and the nose, including hives, rashes, sneezing, and asthma. Such substances cause no reaction in those who have no such hypersensitivity. 2. *Informal.* strong distaste or aversion. [Modern Latin *allergia,* from Greek *allos* other + *ergon* work.]

al·le·vi·ate (ə lē′vē āt′) -at·ed, -at·ing. v.t. to make easier to bear; relieve; lessen: to alleviate pain. [Latin alleviātus, past participle of alleviāre to lighten.] —al·le′vi·a′tion, n.

al·le·vi·a·tive (ə lē′vē ā′tiv) adj. capable of alleviating.

al·ley¹ (al′ē) pl., -leys. n. 1. narrow street or passageway between buildings, esp. one giving access to rear entrances or garages. 2. bowling alley. 3. path or walk, as in a garden or park, bordered by trees or shrubbery. 4. Slang. up one's alley. to one's liking; suited to one's talents. [Old French alee passage, walk, from aler to go, going back to Latin ambulāre to walk.]

al·ley² (al′ē) pl., -leys. n. large playing marble, esp. a white one. [Short for ALABASTER.]

alley cat, stray, mongrel cat.

al·ley·way (al′ē wā′) n. narrow or short passageway between buildings.

All Fools' Day, April Fools' Day.

all hail Archaic. greeting or welcome.

All·hal·lows (ôl hal′ōz) n. All Saints' Day.

al·li·ance (ə lī′əns) n. 1. union of nations joined in common cause. 2. any union, association, or close connection: an alliance between government and industry. 3. something that allies or connects, as a treaty between nations or a marriage that joins families. 4. state of being allied. 5. close relationship; affinity: the alliance between math and physics. [Old French aliance connection, from alier to bind to, going back to Latin alligāre.]

Syn. 2. Alliance, league¹, coalition, association mean a union of persons or parties for a common purpose. **Alliance** refers to such a group having an identity of interests and organized to pool their resources for furthering common objectives: An alliance of minorities was formed to fight for their civil rights. **League** refers to a union of persons for the achievement of more limited and more clearly defined goals: War veterans in this state have organized themselves into a league. **Coalition** refers to a temporary alliance of otherwise rival or opposing interests, as in a time of emergency: Democrats and liberals formed a coalition to defeat the bill. **Association** refers to a voluntary organization of people sharing common professional or social interests: The local automobile association helps motorists.

al·lied (ə līd′, al′īd) adj. 1. united by treaty, alliance, or common purpose: allied railroad unions, allied nations. 2. related or similar: Painting and sculpture are allied arts. 3. Allied. of or relating to the Allies of World Wars I or II: Allied Expeditionary Force.

Al·lies (al′īz, ə līz′) n.,pl. 1. nations allied against Germany and the other Central Powers in World War I, esp. the nations of the Triple Entente (Great Britain, Russia, and France). 2. nations allied against the Axis Powers in World War II, esp. the United States, Great Britain, and the Soviet Union.

al·li·ga·tor (al′ə gā′tər) n. 1. reptile of the crocodile family, Alligator mississipiensis, native to the southern United States, and distinguished from the crocodile, esp. by its broader snout. Another species of alligator, A. sinensis, found near Shanghai, China, is almost extinct. Length: 9 feet. Weight: 250 pounds. 2. leather made from the alligator's skin. 3. caiman. [Spanish el lagerto the lizard, going back to Latin lacertus lizard.]

Alligator

Crocodile

alligator pear, avocado.

all-im·por·tant (ôl′im pôr′tənt) adj. very important; essential; indispensable.

all-in·clu·sive (ôl′in klōō′siv) adj. including or covering everything; comprehensive.

al·lit·er·ate (ə lit′ə rāt′) -at·ed, -at·ing. v.i. 1. to display alliteration. 2. to use alliteration. —v.t. to cause to have alliteration. [AL- + Latin littera letter + -ATE¹.]

al·lit·er·a·tion (ə lit′ə rā′shən) n. repetition of the same initial letter, sound, or group of sounds in a series of words, for example: The furrow followed free (Coleridge, 1798).

al·lit·er·a·tive (ə lit′ə rā′tiv) adj. of or characterized by alliteration. —al·lit′er·a′tive·ly, adv. —al·lit′er·a′tive·ness, n.

al·lo·cate (al′ə kāt′) -cat·ed, -cat·ing. v.t. to set aside, as for a specific purpose; designate: to allocate funds for housing. [Medieval Latin allocatus, past participle of allocare to allot, from Latin ad to + locāre to place.]

al·lo·ca·tion (al′ə kā′shən) n. 1. that which is allocated. 2. act of allocating; being allocated.

al·lo·morph (al′ə môrf′) n. any of the variant forms of a particular

morpheme. The s in cats and the es in glasses are two allomorphs of the English morpheme indicating a plural. —al′lo·mor′phic, adj.

al·lo·path (al′ə path′) n. one who practices or advocates allopathy. Also, **al·lop·a·thist** (ə lop′ə thist).

al·lop·a·thy (ə lop′ə thē) n. method of treating a disease by using remedies to produce effects differing from or incompatible with those of the disease being treated. Opposed to **homeopathy.** [German Allopathie, from Greek allos other + -patheia, pathos suffering.] —al·lo·path·ic (al′ə path′ik), adj. —al′lo·path′i·cal·ly, adv.

al·lo·phone (al′ə fōn′) n. any of the variant forms of a particular phoneme. Two allophones of d are the d sound in down and the d sound in ladder. [Greek allos other + PHONE².]

al·lot (ə lot′) -lot·ted, -lot·ting. v.t. 1. to distribute or parcel out; apportion: to allot shares of stock. 2. to set aside; appropriate: to allot funds for a new library. [Old French aloter, from à to + loter to divide by lot (of Germanic origin).] —Syn. 1. see assign.

al·lot·ment (ə lot′mənt) n. 1. act of allotting. 2. that which is allotted; share; portion.

al·lo·trop·ic (al′ə trop′ik) adj. of, relating to, or exhibiting allotropy. Also, **al′lo·trop′i·cal.** —al′lo·trop′i·cal·ly, adv.

al·lot·ro·py (ə lo′trə pē) n. existence of a chemical element in two or more forms that have different molecular or crystalline structures. Also, **al·lot′ro·pism.** [Greek allotropia variation.]

all-out (ôl′out′) adj. maximum; complete; total: all-out war.

all-o·ver (ôl′ō′vər) adj. covering the whole extent or surface: an all-over pattern.

al·low (ə lou′) v.t. 1. to grant permission to; permit: His father allows him to drive the car. 2. to let have; give: She is allowed five dollars a week for lunch money. 3. to permit through oversight or neglect: to allow the prisoner to escape. 4. to take into account; count on: to allow one week extra for third class mail. 5. to accept as true or valid; acknowledge; concede: The tax agent allowed the deduction. 6. Informal. to think; assert: I allow she'll be late again. 7. to allow for. to make provision or concession for: to allow for errors. 8. to allow of. to permit; admit: The problem allows of only one solution. [Old French alouer to grant, from Medieval Latin allocare to allot, going back to Latin ad-to + locāre to place; associated with Old French alouer to approve, from Latin adlaudāre to praise.] —Syn. 1. see let¹.

al·low·a·ble (ə lou′ə bəl) adj. that can be allowed; legitimate; permissible. —al·low′a·ble·ness, n. —al·low′a·bly, adv.

al·low·ance (ə lou′əns) n. 1. quantity granted or set apart, esp. a sum of money given regularly: an officer's clothing allowance, a child's weekly allowance. 2. compensation made for contingencies or modifying circumstances: depreciation allowance. 3. deduction or discount given in return for something: trade-in allowance on a used car. 4. acceptance; admission: allowance of a claim. 5. Archaic. tolerance; sanction. 6. to make allowance (or allowances) for. to take into consideration; allow for; excuse: They made allowance for his youth and inexperience.

al·loy (n., al′oi, ə loi′; v., ə loi′) n. 1. metallic substance formed by adding to a pure metallic element, called the base, some proportion of another metal or metals or, sometimes, nonmetallic elements. Alloys tend to increase the malleability, hardness, or heat resistance of the base metal. 2. less valuable metal mixed with a finer one. 3. something that debases or reduces quality; adulterant. —v.t. 1. to mix (metals) so as to form an alloy. 2. to reduce the purity of (a metal) by mixture with a less valuable metal. 3. to debase or modify by mixture with something inferior; adulterate. [Old French alei combination, from aleier to combine, from Latin alligāre to join together.]

all-pur·pose (ôl′pur′pəs) adj. useful for many things: all-purpose detergent.

all right 1. satisfactory: His work's all right. It's all right with me. 2. safe; uninjured; well: Are you all right? 3. yes; agreed: All right, I'll do it. 4. satisfactorily: He's doing all right. 5. without fail; certainly: I'll be there, all right.

all-right (ôl′rīt′) adj. Slang. good; dependable; admirable: an all-right guy.

all-round (ôl′round′) all-around.

All Saints' Day, church festival celebrated in honor of all the saints. November 1. Also **All′hal′lows.**

All Souls' Day, in the Roman Catholic Church, a day of services and prayer for the souls in purgatory. November 2.

all·spice (ôl′spīs′) n. 1. aromatic spice made from dried and ground berries of the evergreen pimento tree, Pimenta officinalis, of the myrtle family, native to the West Indies. 2. the berry itself. [ALL + SPICE; because it was thought to have the flavors of cloves, cinnamon, and nutmeg.]

all-star (ôl′stär′) adj. comprised of exceptional or star players or performers.

al·lude (ə lōōd′) -lud·ed, -lud·ing. v.i. to refer to indirectly; mention

casually and in passing (with *to*): *He alluded to her absence without actually mentioning her name.* [Latin *allūdere* to touch on.]

al·lure (ə loŏr′) *-lured, -lur·ing. v.t., v.i.* to fascinate or attract with something desirable; entice. —*n.* power to allure or attract; fascination. [Old French *alurer, aleurrer* to attract, from *à* to + *lure* bait (of Germanic origin).] —**al·lur′er,** *n.*

al·lure·ment (ə loŏr′mənt) *n.* **1.** something that allures; enticement. **2.** attractiveness; fascination; charm. **3.** act or process of alluring.

al·lur·ing (ə loŏr′ing) *adj.* tempting; enticing; attractive: *an alluring prospect.*

al·lu·sion (ə loō′zhən) *n.* indirect or casual reference; incidental mention: *allusions to his misbehavior.* [Latin *allūsiō* a touching on.]

al·lu·sive (ə loō′siv) *adj.* containing, using, or characterized by allusions; referring indirectly.

al·lu·vi·al (ə loō′vē əl) *adj.* of, relating to, or composed of alluvium: *alluvial deposit.* —*n.* alluvial soil.

al·lu·vi·um (ə loō′vē əm) *pl.* **-vi·ums** or **-vi·a** (-vē ə). *n.* accumulation, as of mud or sand, carried and deposited by flowing water. [Latin *alluvium,* neuter of *alluvius* alluvial.]

al·ly (*v.* ə lī′; *n.,* al′ī, ə lī′) **-lied, -ly·ing.** *v.t.* **1.** to unite or associate (oneself) for a common purpose (with *to* or *with*): *England allied itself with the United States during World War II.* **2.** to connect by some similarity or common feature; relate: *Men are allied to apes.* —*v.i.* to become allied; unite. —*n. pl.* **-lies. 1.** person, nation, or group united or leagued with another for a common purpose. **2.** supporter; partisan. **3.** something akin to another in structure or descent. [Old French *alier* to bind to, from Latin *alligāre* to join together.]

Al·ma-A·ta (al′mä ä′tä) *n.* city in Soviet Central Asia, capital of Kazakhstan. Pop. (1970), 730,000.

al·ma ma·ter (äl′mə mä′tər, mā′tər, al′mə) *also,* **Al·ma Ma·ter. 1.** institution of learning that one has attended. **2.** its anthem. [Latin *alma māter* bountiful mother.]

al·ma·nac (ôl′mə nak′) *n.* **1.** reference book of statistical and general information compiled annually. **2.** book arranged by days, weeks, and months, containing astronomical and meteorological data, and tables of other useful information. [Medieval Latin *almanach* diary, account; of uncertain origin.]

al·might·y (ôl mī′tē) *adj.* **1.** all-powerful; omnipotent. **2.** *Informal.* great; inordinate. —*n.* **the Almighty.** God. —**al·might′i·ly,** *adv.* —**al·might′i·ness,** *n.*

al·mond (ä′mənd, am′ənd) *n.* **1.** edible, nutlike kernel of the fruit of a tree, *Prunus amygdalus,* of the rose family, the sweet variety of which is widely used in desserts, candy, and cooking. **2.** tree that bears this fruit, found in the Mediterranean region and cultivated in California and other areas for the seeds and as an ornamental. [Old French *almande,* from Medieval Latin *amandula,* modification of Latin *amygdala,* from Greek *amygdalē.*]

Almonds

al·mond-eyed (ä′mənd īd′, am′ənd-) *adj.* having oval-shaped eyes with tapering ends.

al·mon·er (al′mə nər, ä′mən-) *n.* one who distributes alms as an official duty, as for a church or royal court. [Old French *almosnier,* from *almosne* alms, going back to Latin *eleēmosyna* alms. See ALMS.]

al·mon·ry (al′mən rē, ä′mən-) *pl.,* **-ries.** *n.* **1.** place where alms are distributed. **2.** residence of an almoner.

al·most (ôl′mōst, ôl mōst′) *adv.* very nearly; all but. [Old English *ealmǣst.*]

Syn. Almost, nearly, practically indicate close approximation. **Almost** implies effort just short of success: *He had almost completed the painting.* **Nearly** suggests not quite as close an approach: *He was nearly there when the car ran into the ditch.* **Practically** suggests lacking by very little in being exactly or totally: *The bottle is practically empty. It snowed practically all day.*

alms (ämz) *n.,pl.* money or gifts for the poor; charity. ▲ construed as singular or plural. [Old English *ælmysse,* going back to Latin *eleēmosyna,* from Greek *eleēmosynē* pity.]

alms·giv·ing (ämz′giv′ing) *n.* giving of alms. —**alms′giv′er,** *n.*

alms·house (ämz′hous′) *n.* publicly supported home for the poor; poorhouse.

al·oe (al′ō) *pl.* **-oes.** *n.* **1.** any of a group of cactuslike plants, genus *Aloe,* of the lily family, found chiefly in tropical and southern Africa, most of which have thick, fleshy leaves edged with spines and red or yellow tube-shaped flowers that grow at the top of tall, leafless stalks.

Aloe

2. aloes. bitter drug made from the juice of the leaves of certain aloe plants. ▲ construed as singular. **3.** the century plant of North America. [Latin *aloē* the cactuslike plant, from Greek *aloē.*]

a·loft (ə lôft′) *adv.* **1.** in or to a place far above the ground; high up. **2.** in, at, or into the rigging of a ship; far above the deck. [Old Norse *ā lopt* in the air.]

a·lo·ha (ə lō′ə, ä lō′hä) *n., interj.* **1.** greetings; hello. **2.** good-by; farewell. [Hawaiian *aloha* literally, love.]

a·lone (ə lōn′) *adj., adv.* **1.** without other persons; unaccompanied; solitary: *The widow lived alone. She was alone in the world.* **2.** excluding all other persons or things; only; solely: *Man cannot live by bread alone. He alone can do it.* **3. let alone.** not to mention: *She didn't even have a fur collar, let alone a fur coat.* **4. to leave** (or **let**) **alone. a.** to allow (someone) to be by himself. **b.** to refrain from bothering or interfering with. **5. to leave** (or **let**) **well enough alone.** to be content with things the way they are. **6. to stand alone.** to be unique or without equal: *He stands alone as a conductor of modern symphonic music.* [Middle English *al one,* from *al* all + *one* one; wholly one. See ALL, ONE.]

Syn. adj. 1. Alone, lone, solitary mean separated from others. **Alone** implies a lack of companions, with the suggestion of cheerlessness: *He alone remained.* **Lone** implies that nothing else of a similar kind is near: *The lone cypress stands on the bleak headland.* **Solitary** implies physical or emotional distance, often deliberately maintained, from others of one's kind: *While a student, he led a solitary life.*

a·long (ə lông′) *prep.* **1.** through or by the whole length of; from one end to the other of; following the line of: *Walk along the road.* —*adv.* **1.** progressively onward; forward: *We walked along swiftly. They worked along diligently.* **2.** near or on one's person; with someone: *She brought her umbrella along. You can come along.* **3.** advanced in its course: *The party was well along when he arrived.* **4. all along.** from the start; throughout; continuously: *He knew about the plan all along.* **5. along about** (or **toward**). (of time) somewhere near or approaching: *along about midnight.* **6. along with.** in company or association with; together with: *Let her go along with you to the market.* **7. to get along. a.** to manage to make do. **b.** to be compatible; agree: *The children got along together.* **c.** to go away; move on. **d.** to advance; progress: *The man was getting along in years.* [Old English *andlang* from end to end, following the line of.]

a·long·shore (ə lông′shôr′) *adv.* near, beside, or parallel to the shore.

a·long·side (ə lông′sīd′) *adv.* **1.** at, close to, or by the side: *They brought the rescue boat alongside.* **2. alongside of.** side by side with; next to: *The soldiers stood at attention alongside of each other. The boat docked alongside of the wharf.* —*prep.* by or at the side of; beside: *The car was parked alongside the curb.*

a·loof (ə loōf′) *adv.* at a distance; without involvement; apart: *She stood aloof from the crowd. One boy stood aloof from all the others.* —*adj.* reserved and disinterested; removed: *The queen had an aloof manner toward her subjects.* [A⁻¹ + *loof,* form of LUFF, probably from Dutch *te loef* to windward.] —**a·loof′ly,** *adv.* —**a·loof′ness,** *n.*

a·loud (ə loud′) *adv.* **1.** in a voice that can be heard; audibly. **2.** loudly.

alp (alp) *n.* high mountain or mountain peak. [Latin *Alpēs* the Alps. See ALPINE.]

al·pac·a (al pak′ə) *n.* **1.** cud-chewing mammal, *Lama pacos,* of the camel family, closely related to and resembling the llama and guanaco, raised in the Andes for its fine, silky wool. Height: about 3 feet at the shoulder. **2.** its wool. **3.** silky lightweight fabric woven from or containing this wool, used esp. for coats and suits. [Spanish *alpaca;* of Quechuan origin.]

Alpaca (def. 1)

al·pen·horn (al′pən hôrn′) *n.* long, slightly curved, wooden horn, used by herdsmen in the Alps often ranging from seven to fifteen feet in length. [German *Alpenhorn,* going back to Latin *Alpēs* the Alps + German *Horn* horn.]

al·pen·stock (al′pən stok′) *n.* strong iron-pointed staff used in mountain climbing. [German *Alpenstock,* going back to Latin *Alpēs* the Alps + German *Stock* staff.]

al·pha (al′fə) *n.* **1.** first letter of the Greek alphabet (Α, α), corresponding to the English letter *A, a.* **2.** first in a group or series, esp. in scientific classification; beginning.

alpha and omega, the beginning and the end; the first and the last.

al·pha·bet (al′fə bet′, -bət) *n.* **1.** series of letters or characters used to write a language, esp. as arranged in a customary order. **2.** any

system of characters or symbols representing sounds or words. **3.** basic principles; rudiments. [Latin *alphabētum* the letters of a language, from Greek *alphabētos,* from *alpha* A + *bēta* B, the first two letters of the Greek alphabet.]

al·pha·bet·i·cal (al′fə bet′i kəl) *adj.* **1.** in the order of the letters of the alphabet. **2.** of, relating to, or using an alphabet. Also, **al′pha·bet′ic.** —**al′pha·bet′i·cal·ly,** *adv.*

al·pha·bet·ize (al′fə bə tīz′) **-ized, -iz·ing,** *v.t.* **1.** to arrange in alphabetical order. **2.** to express by or furnish with an alphabet. —**al·pha·bet·i·za·tion** (al′fə bet′ə zā′shən), **al′pha·bet·i′zer,** *n.*

Al·pha Cen·tau·ri (al′fə sen tôr′ē) giant star, one of the brightest in the sky, and the brightest in the constellation Centaurus. Although it appears as a single star to the naked eye, it actually consists of the three stars **Proxima Centauri,** the closest star to our solar system, **Alpha Centauri A,** and **Alpha Centauri B.**

alpha particle, positively charged particle, equivalent to the nucleus of the helium atom, consisting of two protons and two neutrons. Alpha particles are emitted from certain radioactive substances.

alpha ray, stream of alpha particles.

Al·phe·us (al fē′əs) *n.* Greek river god who pursued the nymph Arethusa and changed into an underground river to be near her after she was turned into a spring by Artemis.

al·pine (al′pīn) *adj.* **1.** of or like high mountains; very high. **2.** Alpine, of, relating to, or characteristic of the Alps. **3.** growing on or situated in high mountains: *alpine flowers.*

Alps (alps) *n.,pl.* mountain system in south-central Europe, extending in an arc from the Mediterranean coast near the French-Italian border to the Balkan Peninsula.

al·read·y (ôl red′ē) *adv.* **1.** before or by this or that time; previously: *It's already been done.* **2.** so soon: *Are you finished already?* [Middle English *al redy.* See ALL, READY.]

al·right (ôl rīt′) *Informal.* all right.

Al·sace (al säs′, al′sas) *n.* historic region and former province in eastern France, bordering West Germany and Switzerland.

Al·sace-Lor·raine (al′sás lô rän′, al′sas-) *n.* historic region in eastern France, on the German and Swiss borders, the subject of dispute between France and Germany during the nineteenth and twentieth centuries.

Al·sa·tian (al sā′shən) *adj.* of or relating to Alsace or its people. —*n.* **1.** member or recent descendant of the people of Alsace. **2.** German shepherd dog.

al·so (ôl′sō) *adv.* in addition; as well; too. [Old English *eealswā* wholly so.]

al·so-ran (ôl′sō ran′) *n. Informal.* **1.** horse that fails to finish in first, second, or third place in a race. **2.** any unsuccessful competitor.

alt. 1. alternate; alternating. **2.** altitude.

Al·ta·de·na (al′tə dē′nə) *n.* city in southwestern California. Pop. (1970), 42,380.

Al·tai Mountains (al tī′, äl-, al′tī, äl′-) mountain system in central Asia, in the southern Soviet Union, northwestern China, and the northwestern part of the Mongolian People's Republic.

Al·tair (al′tãr) *n.* one of the brightest stars in the sky and the brightest in the constellation Aquila.

Al·ta·mi·ra (al′tə mēr′ə) *n.* cave near the northern coast of Spain, containing outstanding examples of paleolithic cave art.

al·tar (ôl′tər) *n.* **1.** consecrated, usually raised structure where sacrifices and other sacred rites are performed. **2.** in Christian churches, the table where Communion services are held. **3. to lead to the altar,** to marry. [Old English *altar,* going back to Latin *altāria* burnt offerings; altar; possibly from *altus* high.]

altar boy, boy or man who aids the priest during religious services, as during Mass.

al·tar·piece (ôl′tər pēs′) *n.* decorative hanging or panel attached to an altar, ornamenting the space behind and above it.

al·ter (ôl′tər) *v.t.* **1.** to make different in some degree; modify: *to alter a suit.* **2.** to castrate or spay (an animal). —*v.i.* to become different; change: *His attitude has altered in the past year.* [Middle French *altérer* to change, from Medieval Latin *alterare,* from Latin *alter* other.] —**al′ter·a·ble,** *adj.* —**al′ter·a·bly,** *adv.* —**Syn.** *v.t.* **1.** see **change.**

al·ter·a·tion (ôl′tə rā′shən) *n.* **1.** change; modification: *There's been an alteration in our plans.* **2.** act or process of altering; being altered.

al·ter·a·tive (ôl′tə rā′tiv) *adj.* **1.** causing or capable of causing change. **2.** *Archaic.* gradually restoring the body to a normal state of health. —*n. Archaic.* medicine that modifies the nutritional processes of the body and gradually restores health.

al·ter·cate (ôl′tər kāt′, al′-) **-cat·ed, -cat·ing,** *v.i.* to argue noisily; wrangle. [Latin *altercātus,* past participle of *altercārī.*]

al·ter·ca·tion (ôl′tər kā′shən, al′-) *n.* noisy or heated dispute. [Old French *altercation,* going back to Latin *altercārī* to dispute with another.]

al·ter e·go (ôl′tər ē′gō, eg′ō, al′tər) **1.** person who is an extension

of oneself; another self. **2.** constant companion; intimate friend. [Latin *alter ego* literally, another I.]

al·ter·nate (*v.,* ôl′tər nāt′, al′-; *adj., n.,* ôl′tər nit, al′-) **-nat·ed, -nat·ing** *v.i.* **1.** to succeed each other by turns; happen or appear in turn: *Day alternates with night. They alternated at waxing the floor.* **2.** to pass back and forth from one condition, action, or place to another: *He alternates between hope and despair.* **3.** *Electricity.* to reverse direction regularly. —*v.t.* **1.** to do or perform by turns: *He alternated singing and dancing.* **2.** to cause to follow one another by turns; interchange successively: *He alternated the blue lines with the red.* —*adj.* **1.** occurring or following by turns: *alternate layers of rock and sand.* **2.** every other: *to sit in alternate rows.* **3.** substitute; alternative: *alternate delegates, alternate routes.* **4.** (of leaves) arranged singly at different heights on either side of a stem. Distinguished from **opposite.** —*n.* one who takes the place of another; substitute. [Latin *alternātus,* past participle of *alternāre* to do a thing by turns.] —**al′ter·nate·ly,** *adv.*

alternate angles, two nonadjacent angles formed on opposite sides of a line that crosses two other lines.

alternating current, electric current in which the flow of electrons reverses direction in regular cycles. Distinguished from **direct current.**

al·ter·na·tion (ôl′tər nā′shən, al′-) *n.* act of alternating; being alternated.

alternation of generations, life cycle of any organism that reproduces first sexually and then asexually.

al·ter·na·tive (ôl tur′nə tiv, al-) *adj.* providing or expressing a choice: *an alternative solution.* —*n.* **1.** choice between two or more things. **2.** one of the things that may be chosen: *The alternative to death was dishonor.* **3.** other or remaining choice: *no alternative but to sue.* ▲ Tradionally the adjective **alternative** referred to one of only two possibilities and **alternate** was reserved for cases where there were more than two. **Alternative** now commonly refers to a remaining possibility after others have been eliminated and **alternate** refers simply to any of several. —**al·ter′na·tive·ly,** *adv.* —**Syn.** *n.* **1.** see **choice.**

al·ter·na·tor (ôl′tər nā′tər, al′-) *n.* generator for producing alternating electric current.

al·the·a (al thē′ə) *also,* **al·thae·a.** *n.* **1.** rose of Sharon. **2.** any plant of the genus *Althea,* including the marsh mallow and the hollyhock. [Latin *althaea* marsh mallow, from Greek *althaiā.*]

alt·horn (alt′hôrn′) *n.* alto member of the saxhorn class, often used in bands in place of the French horn. Also, **alto horn.**

al·though (ôl thō′) *also,* **al·tho.** *conj.* in spite of the fact that; even though; though. [Middle English *although.*]

al·tim·e·ter (al tim′ə tər, al′tə mē′tər) *n.* instrument for measuring altitude above sea level or ground, esp. an aneroid barometer calibrated for that purpose, used in aircraft. [Latin *altus* high + -METER.]

al·ti·tude (al′tə tōōd′, -tūd′) *n.* **1.** elevation above any given point, esp. above the earth's surface or sea level; height: *He kept the plane at an altitude of 8000 feet.* **2. altitudes.** great heights; elevated regions: *mountain altitudes.* **3.** perpendicular distance or line segment from the base of a geometrical figure to its highest point. **4.** *Astronomy.* (of a celestial body) angle of elevation, or number of degrees, above the horizon. [Latin *altitūdō* height.] —**al′ti·tu′di·nal,** *adj.* —**Syn.** **1.** see **height.**

al·to (al′tō) *pl.* **-tos.** *n.* **1.** lowest female voice; contralto. **2.** highest male voice; countertenor. **3.** singer who has an alto voice. **4.** instrument having the second highest range in a family of musical instruments, as the viola or althorn. **5.** musical part for an alto voice or instrument. —*adj.* **1.** able to sing alto: *an alto voice.* **2.** for the alto: *an alto score.* **3.** having the second highest range in a family of instruments: *an alto saxophone.* [Italian *alto* high, from Latin *altus* high.]

al·to·geth·er (ôl′tə geth′ər) *adv.* **1.** entirely; wholly; completely: *He missed the bull's eye altogether.* **2.** with everything included; in all: *There were twelve of us altogether.* **3.** on the whole; everything considered: *Altogether, it was a good paper.* —*n.* **in the altogether.** *Informal.* nude. [Middle English *al* ALL + *togedere* TOGETHER.]

alto horn, althorn.

Al·ton (ôl′tən) *n.* city in southwestern Illinois. Pop. (1970), 39,700.

Al·too·na (al tōō′nə) *n.* city in southwestern Pennsylvania. Pop. (1970), 62,900.

al·to-re·lie·vo (al′tō ri lē′vō) *pl.,* **-vos.** *n.* high relief. [Italian *alto-rilievo,* going back to Latin *altus* high + *relevāre* to raise.]

al·tru·ism (al′trōō iz′əm) *n.* unselfish concern for or devotion to the welfare of others. [French *altruisme,* term created by Auguste Comte from Latin *alter* other; influenced by French *autrui* another.]

al·tru·ist (al′trōō ist) *n.* one who professes or exhibits altruism. —**al′tru·is′tic,** *adj.* —**al′tru·is′ti·cal·ly,** *adv.*

al·um (al′əm) *n.* **1.** any of a group of hydrated double salts with the general formula M M (SO$_4$)$_2$·12H$_2$O, where M represents a univalent positive ion and M represents a trivalent positive ion. **2.** hydrated double salt of potassium and aluminum, used esp. as a medical astringent and in dyeing and water purification. Formula:

KAl(SO₄)₂·12H₂O Also, **potash alum.** [Old French *alum,* from Latin *alūmen.*]

a·lu·mi·na (ə loo′mə nə) *n.* oxide of aluminum, occurring in pure form as the mineral corundum and also widely found in clays and bauxite. Formula: Al₂O₃ [Modern Latin *alumina,* from Latin *alūmen* alum.]

a·lu·mi·nous (ə loo′mə nəs) *adj.* of or containing alum or aluminum.

a·lu·mi·num (ə loo′mə nəm) *n.* light, soft, silvery-white metallic element obtained from bauxite. Symbol: **Al** See **element** for table. Also, British, **al·u·min·i·um** (al′yə min′ē əm).

a·lum·na (ə lum′nə) *pl.,* **-nae** (-nē). *n.* female graduate or former student of an educational institution. [Latin *alumna,* feminine of *alumnus* foster child, pupil.]

a·lum·nus (ə lum′nəs) *pl.,* **-ni** (-nī). *n.* male graduate or former student of an educational institution. [Latin *alumnus* foster child, pupil.]

al·ve·o·lar (al vē′ə lər) *adj.* **1.** of or relating to that part of the mouth that contains the sockets of the teeth. **2.** *Phonetics.* formed by placing the tip of the tongue on the ridge just behind the teeth. In English, *s, z, t, d, n,* and *l* are alveolar sounds. —*n.* an alveolar sound.

al·ve·o·lus (al vē′ə ləs) *pl.,* **-li** (-lī′). *n. Anatomy.* **1.** small cavity or pit. **2.** socket in the jawbone in which a tooth is inserted. **3.** one of the small air sacs of the lungs. [Latin *alveolus,* diminutive of *alveus* cavity.]

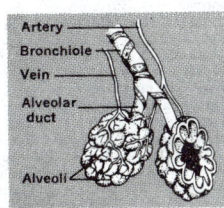

Artery
Bronchiole
Vein
Alveolar duct
Alveoli

Alveolus (def. 3)

al·way (ôl′wā) *adv. Archaic.* always.

al·ways (ôl′wāz, -wēz) *adv.* **1.** at all times; on every occasion; invariably: *Paul always comes late.* **2.** all the time; continuously: *It's always raining there.* **3.** throughout all time; forever: *I'll remember you always.* **4.** *Informal.* in any case; as a last resort: *If there are no seats left, we can always stand.* [Originally ALL + WAY.]

a·lys·sum (ə lis′əm) *n.* **1.** any of a group of low, branching plants, genus *Alyssum,* of the mustard family, found chiefly in the Mediterranean region, bearing clusters of small white or yellow flowers. **2.** sweet alyssum. [Modern Latin *alyssum,* from Latin *alysson* plant used to cure rabies, from Greek *alysson,* possibly neuter of *alyssos* curing madness.]

am (am, əm) first person singular, present indicative, of **be.** [Old English *eom.*]

Am, americium.

Am., America; American.

AM **1.** method of radio broadcasting by which a signal is transmitted over radio carrier waves by altering the amplitude of the waves. **2.** broadcasting system using this method. **3.** of, relating to, or using an AM broadcasting system: *an AM radio, an AM station.* Distinguished from **FM.** [Abbreviation of *amplitude modulation.*]

A.M. **1.** before noon; time from midnight to noon. [Latin ANTE MERIDIEM.] **2.** Master of Arts; M.A.

AMA, American Medical Association.

a·mah (ä′mə, am′ə) *n.* in the Orient, a female servant or nurse, esp. a wet nurse. [Portuguese *ama,* from Medieval Latin *amma.*]

a·main (ə mān′) *adv. Archaic.* **1.** with full force. **2.** at full speed. **3.** hastily. [A-¹ + MAIN force.]

a·mal·gam (ə mal′gəm) *n.* **1.** alloy of mercury with another metal or metals. Silver amalgam is used for filling teeth. **2** any mixture or combination. [French *amalgame* alloy of mercury, probably going back to Latin *malagma* emollient, from Greek *malagma.*]

a·mal·ga·mate (ə mal′gə māt′) **-mat·ed, -mat·ing.** *v.t.* **1.** to unite so as to form a combination; merge: *to amalgamate several school districts into one.* **2.** to combine (a metal or metals) with mercury. —*v.i.* **1.** to unite together; combine; merge: *The two unions amalgamated.* **2.** to unite with another metal.

a·mal·gam·a·tion (ə mal′gə mā′shən) *n.* **1.** act of amalgamating; being amalgamated. **2.** result of amalgamating; union; blend. **3.** merger of two or more business firms.

a·man·u·en·sis (ə man′ū en′sis) *pl.,* **-ses** (-sēz). *n.* one employed to take dictation or copy manuscript; secretary. [Latin *āmanuēnsis* secretary, from *ā manū* short for *servus ā manū* servant for writing + *-ēnsis* belonging to.]

am·a·ranth (am′ə ranth′) *n.* **1.** imaginary flower that never fades or wilts. **2.** any of a group of weeds and garden plants, genus *Amaranthus,* several species of which are cultivated for their colorful leaves or showy blossoms. [Alteration (influenced in spelling by Greek *anthos* flower) of Latin *amarantus* never-fading flower, from Greek *amarantos* never-fading flower (noun), unfading, everlasting (adjective).]

am·a·ran·thine (am′ə ran′thin, -thīn) *adj.* **1.** of or resembling amaranth. **2.** never-fading; everlasting.

Am·a·ril·lo (am′ə ril′ō) *n.* city in northwestern Texas. Pop. (1970), 127,010.

am·a·ryl·lis (am ə ril′is) *n.* **1.** any of a group of plants, genus *Amaryllis,* found chiefly in tropical America, bearing large, bright-colored, lilylike flowers. **2.** any of various related plants, esp. of the genus *Bransvigia,* as *B. rosea,* the belladonna lily, native to South Africa. [Modern Latin *amaryllis,* from Latin *Amaryllis* country girl in the poems of Virgil and Ovid, from Greek *Amaryllis* country girl in the poems of Theocritus.]

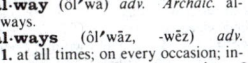

Amaryllis

a·mass (ə mas′) *v.t.* to collect (a great quantity); accumulate: *to amass great wealth.* [Old French *amasser* to gather, heap, going back to Latin *ad* to + *massa* mass (from Greek *maza* lump).] —**a·mass′er, a·mass′ment,** *n.* —Syn. see **accumulate.**

am·a·teur (am′ə char, -tər, -tyər) *n.* **1.** one who does something as a pastime rather than as a vocation or profession. **2.** one who does something with less than professional skill. **3.** athlete who has never competed for money or earned money through athletic skill. —*adj.* **1.** done by or relating to an amateur or amateurs: *amateur sports.* **2.** composed of amateurs; nonprofessional: *an amateur cast, amateur actor.* **3.** characteristic of amateurs; amateurish. [French *amateur* lover of something, dilettante, from Latin *amātor* lover.]

am·a·teur·ish (am′ə choor′ish, -toor′-, -tyoor′-) *adj.* performed like an amateur; inexpert. —**am′a·teur′ish·ly,** *adv.* —**am′a·teur′ish·ness,** *n.*

am·a·teur·ism (am′ə chə riz′əm, am′ə tə-, -tyə-) *n.* amateurish method or character.

A·ma·ti (ä mä′tē) **1.** Ni·co·lò (nē′kō lō′). 1596–1684, Italian violin maker. **2.** violin made by him or a member of his family.

am·a·to·ry (am′ə tôr′ē) *adj.* of, relating to, or expressing love: *amatory notes.* [Latin *amātōrius* loving, from *amātor* lover.]

a·maze (ə māz′) **a·mazed, a·maz·ing.** *v.t.* to overwhelm with sudden wonder or surprise; astound. —*n. Archaic.* amazement; wonder. [Old English *āmasian* to bewilder.] —**a·maz′ed·ly** (ə mā′zid lē), *adv.*

a·maze·ment (ə māz′mənt) *n.* overwhelming wonder or surprise; astonishment.

a·maz·ing (ə mā′zing) *adj.* causing amazement; wonderful; astonishing. —**a·maz′ing·ly,** *adv.*

Am·a·zon (am′ə zon′, -zən) *n.* **1.** longest river in South America and, by volume, the largest in the world, flowing from the Andes, across Brazil, into the Atlantic. **2.** *Greek Legend.* one of a race of female warriors said to have lived in Scythia, near the Black Sea. **3.** *also,* **amazon.** any woman of notable size or strength or who possesses some other supposedly masculine characteristic. [Latin *Amāzon* woman warrior, from Greek *Amazōn;* river so called because of South American Indian women warriors who fought in a battle near it in 1541.]

Am·a·zo·ni·an (am′ə zō′nē ən) *adj.* **1.** of or relating to the Amazon River or the region it drains. **2.** *also,* **amazonian.** of, like, or characteristic of an Amazon.

Amb., Ambassador.

am·bas·sa·dor (am bas′ə dər) *n.* **1.** diplomat of the highest rank. An **ambassador extraordinary and plenipotentiary** is accredited to a foreign country or government and is the ranking diplomat residing in that country. Other ambassadors can be given special, often temporary, assignments, as to the United Nations or other international bodies. **2.** any authorized representative or messenger. [Old French *ambassadeur,* from Old Italian *ambasciatore,* going back to Medieval Latin *ambactia* mission, embassy, from Latin *ambactus* vassal, servant sent on a mission; of Celtic origin.] —**am·bas·sa·do·ri·al** (am bas′ə dôr′ē əl), *adj.* —**am·bas′sa·dor·ship′,** *n.*

am·bas·sa·dor-at-large (am bas′ə dər ət lärj′) *pl.,* **ambassadors-at-large.** *n.* ambassador assigned to no particular country or specific task.

am·bas·sa·dress (am bas′ə dris) *n.* **1.** female ambassador. **2.** wife of an ambassador.

am·ber (am′bər) *n.* **1.** hard, translucent fossil resin from pine trees, yellow to brown in color, used esp. for carvings, jewelry, and electrical insulation. **2.** the color of amber; yellowish-orange or yellowish-brown. —*adj.* made of or having this color. [Old French *ambre* this resin, ambergris, from Arabic *'anbar.*]

am·ber·gris (am′bər grēs′, -gris) *n.* grayish, waxy substance formed in the intestines of sperm whales, usually found floating on tropical seas or washed ashore, used in making perfume. [French *ambre gris* literally, gray amber, from *ambre* (see AMBER) + *gris* gray (of Germanic origin). The Arabic word *'anbar* originally meant only ambergris but was extended to cover amber, apparently because the fossil resin too was often found washed up on seashores. In French the whale product

came to be called gray amber to distinguish it from the yellow-brown resinous substance of the same name.]

am·bi- *combining form* around; both: *ambiguous.* [Latin *ambi-* about, around, both.]

am·bi·dex·ter·i·ty (am′bi deks ter′ə tē) *n.* quality or state of being ambidextrous.

am·bi·dex·trous (am′bi deks′trəs) *adj.* **1.** able to use both hands with equal ease. **2.** very skillful or versatile; adroit. **3.** *Archaic.* deceitful. [Medieval Latin *ambidexter,* from Latin *ambi-* both + *dexter* right hand.] —**am′bi·dex′trous·ly,** *adv.* —**am′bi·dex′trous·ness,** *n.*

am·bi·ence (am′bē əns) *also,* **am·bi·ance.** *n.* pervading atmosphere; surroundings; milieu. [French *ambiance,* going back to Latin *ambīre* to go around.]

am·bi·ent (am′bē ənt) *adj.* completely surrounding; encompassing. [Latin *ambiēns,* present participle of *ambīre* to go around.]

am·bi·gu·i·ty (am′bə gū′ə tē) *pl.,* **-ties.** *n.* **1.** something that is open to more than one interpretation; unclear, uncertain, or equivocal instance or feature: *the ambiguities in his book.* **2.** doubtfulness or uncertainty of purpose or meaning; vagueness: *Bob's ambiguity about his future plans worried his wife.*

am·big·u·ous (am big′ū əs) *adj.* **1.** open to more than one interpretation; having a double meaning; equivocal: *an ambiguous statement.* **2.** unclear; uncertain; vague: *an ambiguous attitude.* [Latin *ambiguus* uncertain, from *ambigere* to wander about, waver.] —**am·big′u·ous·ly,** *adv.* —**am·big′u·ous·ness,** *n.*

am·bi·tion (am bish′ən) *n.* **1.** strong desire or drive to succeed or to achieve something. **2.** object of such desire: *His ambition was to break the track record.* [Latin *ambitiō* going around (to solicit votes).]

Syn. 1. Ambition, aspiration mean effort toward improvement of one's position. **Ambition** suggests desire to get ahead, to become famous or rich, to achieve power, sometimes with the implication of offensive aggression, but often with completely neutral moral connotation: *He has more ambition than any other boy we have ever hired.* **Aspiration** implies a reaching beyond what is usual; it has almost no derogatory connotation, but sometimes suggests criticism of what might be considered overreaching: *Her aspirations as a writer received a blow when the manuscript was rejected.*

am·bi·tious (am bish′əs) *adj.* **1.** full of, guided by, or showing ambition: *an ambitious politician, an ambitious effort.* **2.** strongly desirous; eager for (with *of* or the infinitive): *ambitious of power. He is ambitious to win first prize.* **3.** requiring great ability or effort; arduous; demanding: *an ambitious program.* **4.** overly aspiring; presumptuous. —**am·bi′tious·ly,** *adv.* —**am·bi′tious·ness,** *n.*

am·biv·a·lence (am biv′ə ləns) *n.* simultaneous existence of conflicting feelings or attitudes about an object, person, or idea. [AMBI- + VALENCE.] —**am·biv′a·lent** *adj.* —**am·biv′a·lent·ly,** *adv.*

am·ble (am′bəl) **-bled, -bling.** *v.i.* to walk at a relaxed, leisurely pace. —*n.* **1.** slow, leisurely pace in walking: *moving at an amble.* **2.** leisurely stroll or walk: *We decided to take an amble down the boardwalk.* [Old French *ambler* to amble, from Latin *ambulāre* to walk.] —**am′·bler,** *n.*

am·bro·sia (am brō′zhə) *n.* **1.** *Classical Mythology.* the food of the gods, capable of imparting immortality. **2.** something particularly delicious or delightful to taste or smell. [Latin *ambrosia* food of the gods, from Greek *ambrosiā,* from *ambrotos* immortal.]

am·bro·sial (am brō′zhəl) *adj.* **1.** of or like ambrosia; delicious; fragrant. **2.** belonging to or worthy of the gods; divine.

am·bu·lance (am′byə ləns) *n.* specially equipped vehicle for carrying persons who are sick or wounded. [French *ambulance,* for earlier *(hôpital) ambulant* literally, walking or moving (hospital), going back to Latin *ambulāre* to walk.]

am·bu·lant (am′byə lənt) *adj.* moving about; walking.

am·bu·late (am′byə lāt) **-lat·ed, -lat·ing.** *v.i.* to move about; walk. [Latin *ambulātus,* past participle of *ambulāre.*] —**am′bu·la′tion,** *n.*

am·bu·la·to·ry (am′byə lə tôr′ē) *adj.* **1.** able to walk: *ambulatory patient.* **2.** of or fitted for walking: *ambulatory exercise.* **3.** moving from place to place; not stationary. **4.** *Law.* not fixed; alterable: *an ambulatory will.* —*n. pl.,* **-ries.** sheltered place for walking in a building, as the cloisters of a monastery.

am·bus·cade (am′bəs kād′) *n.* ambush. —*v.t.,* **-cad·ed, -cad·ing.** to ambush. [French *embuscade* an ambush, from Italian *imboscata,* going back to Latin *in* in + Late Latin *boscus* wood (possibly of Germanic origin).] —**am′bus·cad′er,** *n.*

am·bush (am′boosh) *n.* **1.** surprise attack from a concealed position. **2.** concealed position for surprise attack. **3.** state of lying in wait. —*v.t.* to make a surprise attack on from a concealed position. [Old French *embuscher* to place in ambush, going back to Latin *in* in + Late Latin *boscus* wood (possibly of Germanic origin).] —**am′bush·er,** *n.*

a·me·ba (ə mē′bə) *pl.,* **-bas** or **-bae** (-bē) *also,* **a·moe·ba.** *n.* any of a group of protozoans of the class Sarcodina that move and feed by sending out temporary projections, or pseudopods. Amebas reproduce by binary fission and may be found in fresh or salt water, moist soils, or as parasites on animals. [Greek *amoibē* change; because it is continually changing shape.]

a·me·bic (ə mē′bik) *also,* **a·moe·bic.** *adj.* **1.** of, like, or relating to an ameba. **2.** caused by an ameba or amebas.

a·me·boid (ə mē′boid) *also,* **a·moe·boid.** *adj.* resembling an ameba, esp. in its flowing movement or change of shape.

Ameba

a·meer (ə mēr′) *amir.*

a·me·lio·rate (ə mēl′yə rāt′) **-rat·ed, -rat·ing.** *v.t.* to make better; improve. —*v.i.* to grow or become better. [Middle French *améliorer* to make better, going back to Latin *ad* to + Late Latin *meliōrāre.* See MELIORATE.] —**a·mel·io·ra·ble** (ə mēl′yər ə bəl), **a·mel′io·ra′tive,** *adj.* —**a·mel′io·rant, a·mel′io·ra′tor,** *n.*

a·me·lio·ra·tion (ə mēl′yə rā′shən) *n.* act of ameliorating; being ameliorated; improvement.

a·men (ā′men′, ä′men′) *interj.* may it be so; so be it. ▲ used to express assent or approval, esp. after a prayer. —*adv.* verily; truly. —*n.* **1.** uttering of this word. **2.** any expression of assent or approval. [Latin *āmēn* so be it, verily, from Greek *āmēn,* from Hebrew *āmēn.*]

A·men (ä′mən) *also,* **A·mon, Am·mon.** *n.* local god of ancient Egypt, represented as having a ram's head, later identified with the sun god Ra as the supreme deity and called **Amen-Ra.**

a·me·na·ble (ə mē′nə bəl, ə men′ə-) *adj.* **1.** open and willing; capable of being persuaded. **2.** *Archaic.* liable to be called to account; answerable. [Old French *amener* to lead to, going back to Latin *ad* to + Late Latin *mināre* to drive out, from Latin *minārī* to threaten.] —**a·me′na·bil′i·ty, a·me′na·ble·ness,** *n.* —**a·me′na·bly,** *adv.*

a·mend (ə mend′) *v.t.* **1.** to modify; revise. **2.** to alter formally by modification, addition, or deletion: *to amend the Constitution.* **3.** *Archaic.* to change for the better; improve; correct: *Amend your ways.* [Old French *amender* to make better, from Latin *ēmendāre* to correct, from *ex* out of + *menda* fault.] —**a·mend′a·ble,** *adj.* —**a·mend′er,** *n.*

a·mend·a·to·ry (ə men′də tôr′ē) *adj.* tending or serving to amend.

a·mend·ment (ə mend′mənt) *n.* **1.** act of amending; being amended. **2.** result of amending or being amended; change. **3.a.** formal change or revision, as by parliamentary or constitutional procedure: *He proposed an amendment to that statute.* **b.** text of such a change.

a·mends (ə mendz′) *n.,pl.* **1. to make amends.** to compensate (for loss, injury, or insult); recompense. **2.** *Archaic.* payment or satisfaction; compensation. ▲ construed as singular or plural.

a·men·i·ty (ə men′ə tē, ə mē′nə-) *pl.,* **-ties.** *n.* **1. amenities. a.** polite acts, esp. certain standard or accepted ones; civilities. **b.** agreeable features or circumstances: *all the amenities of home life.* **2.** pleasantness of climate or situation. [Latin *amoenitās* pleasantness.]

am·ent (am′ənt, ā′mənt) *n.* catkin. [Latin *amentum* thong.]

Amer., America; American.

a·merce (ə murs′) **a·merced, a·merc·ing.** *v.t.* **1.** to punish with an arbitrary fine. **2.** *Archaic.* to punish. [Anglo-Norman *amercier* to fine, from phrase *estre amercié* to be fined, from phrase *à merci* at the mercy of, going back to Latin *ad* to + *mercēs* cost.] —**a·merce′a·ble,** *adj.* —**a·merce′ment, a·merc′er,** *n.*

A·mer·i·ca (ə mer′i kə) *n.* **1.** United States. **2.** North and South America; the Western Hemisphere. **3.** North America or South America. **4.** *Also,* **the Americas.** North, Central, and South America considered as a whole. [From the Italian explorer *Amerigo* (in Latin, *Americus*) Vespucci, mistakenly believed to have discovered the Western Hemisphere.]

A·mer·i·can (ə mer′i kən) *adj.* **1.** of, relating to, or characteristic of the United States or its people: *the American flag, American ingenuity.* **2.** of, relating to, or characteristic of the Americas or their people. —*n.* **1.** citizen of the United States. **2.** member or close descendant of one of the peoples of the Americas. **3.** American English.

A·mer·i·ca·na (ə mer′i kan′ə, -kä′nə, -kā′nə) *n.,pl.* **1.** materials, as books, papers, and relics, of or relating to America, its history, and its culture. **2.** collection of such materials.

American Beauty, variety of red rose.

American cheese, any of several mild, white or yellow cheddar or processed cheeses, popular in the United States.

American eagle, North American bald eagle, shown on the coat of arms of the United States.

American English, the English language as spoken and written in the United States.

at; āpe; cär; end; mē; it; īce; hot; ōld; fôrk; wood; fōōl; oil; out; up; ūse; turn; sing; thin; this; zh in treasure; ə in ago, taken, pencil, lemon, circus.

American Federation of Labor, federation of trade unions founded in 1886. In 1955 it merged with the Congress of Industrial Organizations to form the AFL–CIO.

American Indian, Indian *(def. 1).*

A·mer·i·can·ism (ə mer′i kə niz′əm) *n.* **1.** word, phrase, or usage originating in the United States or peculiar to American English. *Cow-catcher* is an Americanism. **2.** custom, trait, or belief characteristic of and peculiar to the United States and its people. **3.** devotion to or support of the United States and its institutions.

A·mer·i·can·ize (ə mer′i kə nīz′) **-ized, -iz·ing.** *v.t.* to cause to conform to or acquire American traits or beliefs. —*v.i.* to conform to or acquire American characteristics. —**A·mer′i·can·i·za′tion,** *n.*

American larch, tamarack.

American Legion, organization of veterans of the U.S. armed forces of World Wars I and II, the Korean War, and the war in Vietnam, founded in 1919.

American plan, in hotels, system of charging at a fixed rate that includes both room and meals. Distinguished from **European plan.**

American Revolution, war fought from 1775 to 1783 between England and her American colonies, in which the colonies gained their independence. Also, **Revolutionary War.**

American Samoa, island group in Samoa, administered by the United States. Land area, 76 sq. mi. Pop. (1968 est.) 33,000.

am·er·i·ci·um (am′ə rish′ē əm) *n.* man-made radioactive metallic element of a silvery-white color, resulting from the bombardment of uranium and plutonium by high-energy helium ions. Symbol: **Am** See **element** for table. [Modern Latin *americium,* from AMERICA.]

Am·er·ind (am′ə rind) *n.* American Indian or Eskimo. Also, **Am′-er·in′di·an.** [AMER(ICAN) + IND(IAN).]

Ames (āmz) *n.* city in central Iowa. Pop. (1970), 39,505.

am·e·thyst (am′ə thist) *n.* **1.** purple or violet quartz, used as a gem. **2.** violet-colored corundum, used as a gem. **3.** purple; violet. [Latin *amethystus* this gem or stone, from Greek *amethystos* literally, not drunken; because this stone was believed to remedy drunkenness.] —**am·e·thys·tine** (am′ə this′tin), *adj.*

a·mi·a·ble (ā′mē ə bəl) *adj.* **1.** (of persons) having a pleasing and kindly disposition; good-natured; friendly: *The amiable gentleman smiled when he was hit with a snowball.* **2.** agreeable; pleasant: *amiable surroundings.* [Old French *amiable,* from Late Latin *amīcābilis,* from Latin *amīcus* friend. Doublet of AMICABLE.] —**a′mi·a·bil′i·ty,** *n.* —**a′mi·a·bly,** *adv.*

am·i·ca·ble (am′ə kə bəl) *adj.* characterized by friendliness and good will; peaceable: *an amicable settlement of a dispute.* [Late Latin *amīc-ābilis* from Latin *amīcus* friend. Doublet of AMIABLE.] —**am′i·ca·bil′i·ty,** *n.* —**am′i·ca·bly,** *adv.*

am·ice (am′is) *n.* vestment worn under the alb by a priest at Mass, made of an oblong piece of white linen that falls around the neck and shoulders. [Old French *amis,* going back to Latin *amictus* cloak.]

a·mi·cus cu·ri·ae (ə mē′kəs kyoor·ē ī′) one who advises or offers arguments to the court regarding a suit to which he is not a party. An individual, group, or institution can act as an amicus curiae. [Modern Latin *amicus curiae* friend of the court.]

a·mid (ə mid′) *prep.* in the middle or midst of; surrounded by; among. [Old English *on middan* in the middle.]

a·mid·ships (ə mid′ships′) *adv.* in or toward the middle of a ship, either halfway between the bow and stern or between the sides.

a·midst (ə midst′) *prep.* amid.

Am·i·ens (am′ē ənz; *French* ä myaṅ′) *n.* city in north-central France. Pop. (1968), 117,888.

a·mi·go (ə mē′gō) *pl.* **-gos.** *n.* friend. [Spanish *amigo,* from Latin *amīcus.*]

a·mine (ə mēn′, am′in) *n.* any of a class of organic compounds containing nitrogen, formed from ammonia by replacing hydrogen atoms with organic radicals.

a·mi·no acid (ə mē′nō, am′ə nō′) any of a group of organic acids found in plant and animal cells, essential for protein synthesis.

a·mir (ə mēr′) *also,* **a·meer.** *n.* a commander, native ruler, or prince in a Muslim country. [Arabic *amīr* commander.]

Am·ish (ä′mish, am′ish) *n.,pl.* Protestant denomination, closely related to the Mennonites, founded in Switzerland in the seventeenth century. The Amish, most of whom live in the United States, follow simple customs and refuse to take oaths or perform military service. —*adj.* of, belonging to, or relating to this sect. [From Jacob *Am(mann),* founder of the sect.]

a·miss (ə mis′) *adj.* **1.** faulty; wrong; improper. ▲ used only predicatively: *What is amiss?* **2. to take (something) amiss. a.** to take offense at; resent. **b.** to understand wrongly; interpret mistakenly. —*adv.* out of proper course or order; improperly; wrongly. [A-⁴ + MISS¹ failure.]

a·mi·to·sis (ā′mī tō′sis, am′ə-) *n.* direct cell division by simple division of the nucleus without the formation of chromosomes. [A-⁴ + MITOSIS.]

am·i·ty (am′ə tē) *pl.* **-ties.** *n.* peaceful, friendly relations; friendship; *amity between nations.* [Middle French *amitié,* going back to Latin *amīcus* friend.]

Am·man (ä män′, a man′) *n.* ancient city in northwestern Jordan, now the capital of the country. Pop. (1968 est.), 342,000.

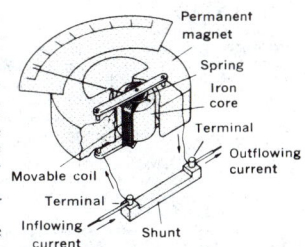

Ammeter

am·me·ter (am′mē′tər, am′ē′tər) *n.* instrument used for measuring the strength of an electric current in amperes. [AM(PERE) + -METER.]

am·mo (am′ō) *n.* Informal. ammunition.

Am·mon (am′ən) *n.* the god Amen.

am·mo·ni·a (ə mōn′yə, ə mō′nē ə) *n.* **1.** colorless, gaseous compound of nitrogen and hydrogen having a highly pungent odor. Ammonia is used esp. in fertilizers and in the production of other chemicals. Formula: NH_3. **2.** water solution of ammonia, used as a cleaning agent. Also *(def. 2),* **ammonia water.** [From SAL AMMONIAC, from which ammonia was first isolated as a gas, in 1774, by heating it when mixed with lime.]

am·mo·ni·ac (ə mō′nē ak′) *n.* pungent gum resin used in medicine and in plasters and cements. Also, **gum ammoniac.** [Latin *ammoniacum* (gum) of Amen; probably by parallel with *sal ammoniacus* literally, salt of Amen, because the gum had the same strong-smelling, medicinally useful properties as the salt. See SAL AMMONIAC.]

am·mo·nite (am′ə nīt′) *n.* coiled, chambered fossil shell of an extinct mollusk, found esp. in the Mesozoic age. [Modern Latin *Ammonites,* from Medieval Latin *cornu Ammonis* horn of Amen; because of its resemblance to the horns of this ram-headed Egyptian god.]

am·mo·ni·um (ə mō′nē əm) *n.* univalent radical consisting of nitrogen and hydrogen atoms which acts as an alkali metal in chemical reactions. Formula: NH_4.

ammonium chloride, colorless or white crystalline compound, a salt of ammonia, used esp. in medicine, dry cells, and dyes. Formula: NH_4CL Also, **sal ammoniac.**

ammonium hydroxide, compound formed when ammonia gas dissolves in water. It exists only in solution. Formula: NH_4OH

ammonium nitrate, colorless, crystalline compound used esp. in fertilizers, explosives, and propellants. Formula: NH_4NO_3

am·mu·ni·tion (am′yə nish′ən) *n.* **1.** bullets, shells, and other projectiles with their fuses, charges, and propellants for use in firearms and artillery. **2.** any type of explosive weapon, as a bomb. **3.** resources for any type of attack or defense: *The scandal provided new ammunition for the senator's foes.* [Middle French *amunition* provisions for an army, modification of *munition,* from Latin *mūnītiō* defense.]

am·ne·sia (am nē′zhə) *n.* partial or total loss of memory, esp. as caused by brain injury, mental illness, disease, or shock. [Modern Latin *amnesia,* from Greek *amnēsia* forgetfulness.]

am·nes·ty (am′nis tē) *pl.* **-ties.** *n.* general pardon, esp. as given by a government to prisoners, outlaws, or rebels. —*v.t.,* **-tied, -ty·ing.** to grant amnesty to; pardon. [Latin *amnēstia* forgetfulness, from Greek *amnēstia* forgetfulness; supposedly with reference to a Greek general's offering to forget the wrongs done by his enemies.]

am·ni·o·cen·te·sis (am′nē ō sen te′səs) *n.* the insertion of a hollow needle into the uterus of a pregnant woman to obtain a sample of the fetal cells contained in the amnion, used to determine sex or detect possible genetic diseases.

am·ni·on (am′nē ən) *pl.,* **-ni·ons** or **-ni·a** (-nē ə). *n.* membrane forming the fluid-filled sac surrounding the embryo in reptiles, birds, and mammals. [Greek *amnion* caul, diminutive of *amnos* lamb.]

a·moe·ba (ə mē′bə) ameba.

a·moe·bic (ə mē′bik) amebic.

a·moe·boid (ə mē′boid) ameboid.

a·mok (ə muk′, ə mok′) amuck.

A·mon (ä′mən) Amen.

a·mong (ə mung′) *prep.* **1.** in the midst of **2.** in association with; in the company of: *He lived among the poor.* **3.** in the number or class of: *the best among the new playwrights.* **4.** by, with, or through many or all of: *popular among college students.* **5.** in shares to; for each of: *He divided the prize among the winners.* **6.** by the concerted or joint action of: *Among us, we can raise the money.* **7.** mutually; between: *They quarreled among themselves.* ▲ In careful usage **among** is distinguished from **between.** **Between** is most precisely limited to two persons or things: *There was a yard between the house and the barn.* **Between** may also be used of the relation of someone or

something to a number of other persons or things each considered individually: *The profits were shared between the four partners.* **Among,** however, is preferred when three or more persons or things are considered collectively and is never used of two: *He is happy when he is among friends.* [Old English *on gemang* in a crowd.]

a·mongst (ə mungst′) *prep.* also, **among.**

a·mor·al (ā môr′əl, ā mor′-, ă mor′-) *adj.* 1. not subject to moral considerations; neither moral nor immoral. 2. not having or concerned with moral standards. [A-¹ + MORAL.] —**a·mor·al·i·ty** (ā′mə ral′ə tē, ă′mə-), *n.* —**a·mor′al·ly,** *adv.* —**Syn.** 1. see **immoral.**

am·o·rous (am′ər əs) *adj.* 1. inclined to love or to fall in love: *an amorous nature.* 2. produced by or exhibiting love: *an amorous glance.* 3. of or relating to love. 4. *Archaic.* enamored or fond (with *of*): *Thy roses amorous of the moon* (Keats, 1821). [Old French *amorous* in love, from Late Latin *amōrōsus* full of love, from Latin *amor* love.] —**am′o·rous·ly,** *adv.* —**am′o·rous·ness,** *n.*

a·mor pa·tri·ae (ā′môr pā′trē ē′, ä′môr pä′trē ĭ′) *Latin.* love of one's country; patriotism.

a·mor·phous (ə môr′fəs) *adj.* 1. without definite form or shape; shapeless. 2. of no particular kind or character; unorganized. 3. *Chemistry.* without crystalline form. [Greek *amorphos* shapeless.] —**a·mor′phous·ly,** *adv.* —**a·mor′phous·ness,** *n.*

am·or·ti·za·tion (am′ər ti zā′shən, ə môr′-) *n.* 1. act of amortizing; being amortized. 2. money used for this purpose.

am·or·tize (am′ər tīz′, ə môr′tīz) **-tized, -tiz·ing.** *v.t.* to extinguish (a debt) gradually by periodic payments, usually in equal installments at equal intervals of time. [Old French *amortiss-,* stem of *amortir* to bring to death, going back to Latin *ad* to + *mors* death.] —**am′or·tize′ment,** *n.*

A·mos (ā′məs) *n.* 1. Hebrew prophet and social reformer of the eighth century B.C. 2. book of the Old Testament containing his prophecies.

a·mount (ə mount′) *n.* 1.a. numerical quantity; sum: *Please pay the full amount.* b. any quantity: *the amount of work we turned out.* 2. *Archaic.* full effect, significance, or extent. —*v.i.* 1. to equal in number or quantity; add up (with *to*): *The bill amounts to ten dollars.* 2. to be equivalent in value, significance, or effect (with *to*): *That remark amounts to a threat.* 3. (of a person) to develop into; become (with *to*): *He'll never amount to anything.* [Old French *amonter* to amount to, from *â mont* toward a mountain, going back to Latin *ad* to + *mōns* mountain.] —**Syn.** 1. 1.a. see **quantity.**

a·mour (ə moor′) *n.* love affair, esp. one of an illicit or secret nature. [Old French *amour* love.]

a·mour-pro·pre (ə moor′prō′prə) *French.* self-love; self-esteem.

A·moy (ä moi′) *n.* 1. city on an island in a harbor on the southeast coast of China opposite Taiwan. Pop. (1953), 224,300. 2. the island itself.

amp. 1. ampere; amperes. 2. amperage.

am·per·age (am′pər ij, am pēr′-) *n.* strength of an electric current measured in amperes.

am·pere (am′pēr) *n.* standard unit of strength of an electric current, equal to the amount of current produced by one volt acting through a resistance of one ohm. [From the French physicist André Marie Ampère, 1775–1836.]

am·pere-hour (am′pēr our′) *n.* quantity of electricity produced in one hour by a current of one ampere, equal to 3600 coulombs.

am·per·sand (am′pər sand′) *n.* the character (&) representing the word "and." [Modification of the phrase *and per se and* and by itself means *and* (used in hornbooks).]

am·phet·a·mine (am fet′ə mēn′, -min) *n.* colorless liquid compound, used as a drug to relieve nasal congestion and as a stimulant to the central nervous system. Formula: C₉H₁₃N [Short for *a(lpha)-m(ethyl)-ph(enyl)-et(hyl)-amine*.]

amphi- *combining form* 1. around: *amphitheater.* 2. on two or all sides; at both ends: *amphistylar.* 3. of two kinds: *amphibian.* [Greek *amphi* on both sides, around.]

am·phib·i·an (am fib′ē ən) *n.* 1. any animal of the class Amphibia, of cold-blooded vertebrates, including frogs, toads, and salamanders, usually living in or near water and typically having moist, scaleless skin. Generally, their eggs are laid in water or moist places and hatch into legless, gilled larvae which develop into adults with lungs and two pairs of limbs. 2. anything that lives both on land and in water. 3. aircraft designed to take off from and land on either land or water; seaplane. 4. tank or other vehicle that can travel on both land and water. —*adj.* 1. of, relating to, or characteristic of the class Amphibia. 2. amphibious. [Modern Latin *Amphibia,* plural of *amphibium* amphibious creature, from Greek *amphibios* living a double life, from *amphi* both + *bios* life.]

am·phib·i·ous (am fib′ē əs) *adj.* 1. capable of living on land or in water. 2. adapted or suitable for use on land or water: *an amphibious plane.* 3. carried out by the action of both land and naval forces: *an*

amphibious attack. [Greek *amphibios,* from *amphi* both + *bios* life.] —**am·phib′i·ous·ly,** *adv.* —**am·phib′i·ous·ness,** *n.*

am·phi·sty·lar (am′fə stī′lər) *adj.* having columns on both ends or on both sides. [AMPHI- + Greek *stylos* pillar.]

am·phi·the·a·ter (am′fə thē′ə tər) *n.* 1. elliptical or circular structure with rising tiers of seats around a central open space. 2. something resembling an amphitheater in shape, as a lecture hall having tiers of seats arranged around a central area or a level area of ground surrounded by rising slopes. [Latin *amphitheātrum,* from Greek *amphitheātron.*]

Amphitheater

Am·phi·tri·te (am′fə trī′tē) *n. Greek Mythology.* one of the Nereids, goddess of the sea and wife of Poseidon.

am·pho·ra (am′fər ə) *pl.,* **-pho·rae** (-fər ē) or **-pho·ras.** *n.* two-handled jar or vase with a narrow neck, broad body, and tapering base, used by the ancient Greeks and Romans. [Latin *amphora,* from Greek *amphoreus,* short for *amphiphoreus,* from *am-phi-* on both sides + *phoreus* bearer.]

am·ple (am′pəl) **-pler, -plest.** *adj.* 1. of great size, extent, or capacity; roomy: *The car has an ample trunk.* 2. more than enough; abundant: *ample time in which to finish the job.* 3. sufficient; enough; adequate: *an income ample for his needs.* [French *ample* full, wide, from Latin *am-plus* large.] —**am′ple·ness,** *n.* —**am′ply,** *adv.* —**Syn.** 2. see **abundant.**

am·pli·fi·ca·tion (am′plə fi kā′shən) *n.* 1. act of amplifying; being amplified; expansion. 2. that which is used to amplify; additional matter: *The footnotes were an amplification of the treatise.* 3. something so expanded. 4. increase in the strength of an electronic signal. —**am·plif·i·ca·to·ry** (am plif′ə kə tôr′ē), *adj.*

am·pli·fi·er (am′plə fī′ər) *n.* 1. any of various devices for increasing the strength of an electronic signal by the use of power from a source other than the signal. 2. component of a sound-reproduction system that contains such a device. 3. one who or that which amplifies.

Amphora

am·pli·fy (am′plə fī′) **-fied, -fy·ing.** *v.t.* 1. to add to or expand, as speech or thought; enlarge on: *He amplified his statement with various illustrations.* 2. to increase the strength of (an electronic signal). 3. to increase in scope, significance, or power; extend. —*v.i.* to make additions to speech or writing; expatiate: *He amplified for the sake of clarity.* [French *amplifier* to enlarge, develop, from Latin *amplificāre* to enlarge.]

am·pli·tude (am′plə tōōd′, -tūd′) *n.* 1. greatness of size; largeness; breadth. 2. abundance; fullness. 3. distance that a vibrating body moves from the mean position. 4. highest value reached by an electromagnetic or other kind of current during a complete cycle, as measured from the average value. [Latin *amplitūdō* breadth.]

amplitude modulation, see **AM.**

am·pu·tate (am′pyə tāt′) **-tat·ed, -tat·ing.** *v.t., v.i.* to cut off, esp. to remove (an extremity) surgically: *Because of the seriousness of the infection, the doctor was forced to amputate his patient's leg below the knee.* [Latin *amputātus,* past participle of *amputāre* to cut around, prune.] —**am′pu·ta′tion, am′pu·ta′tor,** *n.*

am·pu·tee (am′pyoo tē′) *n.* one who has had a limb amputated.

Am·rit·sar (əm rit′sər) *n.* city in northwestern India. Pop. (1969), 424,961.

Am·ster·dam (am′stər dam′) *n.* capital and largest city of the Netherlands, in the west-central part of the country. Pop. (1968), 852,479.

amt., amount.

a·muck (ə muk′) *also,* **a·mok.** *adv.* 1. to go awry or amiss: *My plans have gone amuck.* 2. to run amuck. to lose control of oneself and rush about wildly, esp. with intent to attack or kill. [Malay *amok* frenzied to the point of killing.]

A·mu Dar·ya (ä mōō′ där′yə) river in central Asia, principally in the Soviet Union, flowing into the Aral Sea. In ancient times it was known as the Oxus.

am·u·let (am′yə lit) *n.* object worn or placed in a house to bring good fortune or to protect against disease, bad luck, or evil; charm. [Latin *amulētum.*] —**Syn.** see **charm.**

A·mund·sen, Ro·ald (ä′mən sən; rō′äl) 1872–1928, Norwegian explorer who discovered the South Pole in 1911.

A·mur (ä moor′) *n.* river in northeastern Asia, forming part of the boundary between the Soviet Union and China.

a·muse (ə mūz′) **a·mused, a·mus·ing.** *v.t.* **1.** to please the sense of humor of: *His jokes amused all of us.* **2.** to keep pleasantly occupied or interested; entertain; divert: *He amused himself by reading.* [Old French *amuser,* from *à* to (from Latin *ad* to) + *muser* to ponder. See MUSE.] —**a·mus′er,** *n.*

a·mused (ə mūzd′) *adj.* **1.** feeling mirth or enjoyment: *an amused spectator.* **2.** expressing enjoyment or mirth: *an amused smile.* —**a·mus·ed·ly** (ə mū′zid lē), *adv.*

a·muse·ment (ə mūz′mənt) *n.* **1.** state of being amused; enjoyment. **2.** something that amuses or entertains; diversion.

Syn. **2.** **Amusement, entertainment, diversion, pastime, recreation** indicate pleasant undertakings and their effects. **Amusement** implies conscious attention to something pleasant: *The theater was one of the principal amusements of the Elizabethans.* **Entertainment** suggests a passive occupation, in which others do the performing: *The circus clowns provided entertainment for the patients at the hospital.* **Diversion** implies turning the attention away from worries or everyday cares: *He wanted some better diversion than watching cars race by.* **Pastime** suggests some occupation that uses up leisure hours: *Fishing and similar pastimes did not interest him.* **Recreation** indicates a pursuit that invigorates by virtue of being a change of occupation: *His recreation was to grow beans and tomatoes in the back yard.*

amusement park, commercially operated area with various games, rides, and entertainment devices, such as a Ferris wheel, merry-go-round, and shooting gallery.

a·mus·ing (ə mū′zing) *adj.* **1.** causing laughter or mirth. **2.** entertaining; diverting. —**a·mus′ing·ly,** *adv.* —**Syn.** **2.** see **funny.**

am·yl (am′əl) *n.* univalent alcohol radical derived from pentane. Formula: C_5H_{11} [Latin *amylum* starch (from Greek *amylon* starch) + Greek *hȳlē* substance.]

am·yl·ase (am′ə lās′) *n.* enzyme that converts starch to sugar, used esp. in laundry products.

am·y·lop·sin (am′ə lop′sin) *n.* enzyme in the pancreatic juice that breaks down starch molecules into sugar molecules. [AMYL + (TRY)PSIN.]

an¹ (an; *unstressed* ən) indefinite article form of *a* before words with an initial vowel sound: *an artichoke, an hour.* [Old English *ān.*]

an² (an; *unstressed* ən) *conj.* *Archaic.* if. [Form of AND.]

an-¹, prefix not; without: *anemia, anarchy, anhydrous.* [Greek *a-, an-*.]

an-², form of **ad-** before *n,* as in *annul.*

-an *suffix* **1.** used to form adjectives and nouns indicating relationships, membership, or characteristics: *Mexican, Elizabethan, republican.* **2.** used to form adjectives and nouns indicating belief, adherence, or a following: *Lutheran, Mohammadan.* **3.** used to form nouns indicating skill or specialization: *mathematician, magician.* [Latin *-ānus* of, belonging to.]

ana- *prefix* **1.** up; upward: *anadromous.* **2.** back; backward; against: *anachronism.* **3.** again; anew: *Anabaptist.* **4.** throughout; thoroughly: *analysis.* [Greek *ana* on, up, again.]

An·a·bap·tist (an′ə bap′tist) *n.* any of a group of radically fundamentalist Protestants in Switzerland, Germany, and Holland in the sixteenth century who rejected infant baptism, advocated communal property and separation of church and state, and were persecuted by Catholics and other Protestants alike. [Modern Latin *anabaptista* literally, one who baptizes again, going back to Greek *ana* again + *baptistēs* one that dips or baptizes.]

a·nab·o·lism (ə nab′ə liz′əm) *n.* a phase of metabolism in which food molecules and energy are utilized in the chemical processes of building protoplasm. Opposed to **catabolism.** [ANA- + (META)BOLISM.] —**an·a·bol·ic** (an′ə bol′ik), *adj.*

a·nach·ro·nism (ə nak′rə niz′əm) *n.* **1.** something out of its proper time. **2.** placement of something in a time to which it does not belong; chronological error. [Greek *anachronismos,* from *ana* back + *chronos* time.]

a·nach·ro·nis·tic (ə nak′rə nis′tik) *adj.* containing or involving an anachronism. Also, **a·nach′ro·nis′ti·cal.** —**a·nach′ro·nis′ti·cal·ly,** *adv.*

a·nach·ro·nous (ə nak′rə nəs) *adj.* anachronistic. —**a·nach′ro·nous·ly,** *adv.*

an·a·co·lu·thon (an′ə kə lōō′thon) *pl.,*-**tha** (-thə) or -**thons.** *n.* interruption in a sentence followed by a change from one grammatical construction to another. The sentence *I wanted to go—never mind, there's no use in saying it* contains an anacoluthon. [Greek *anakolouthon* inconsistency, from *anakolouthos* inconsistent.]

an·a·con·da (an′ə kon′də) *n.* **1.** constrictor snake, genus *Eunectes,* native to tropical South America, feeding mostly on fish, water birds, and small mammals. The **giant anaconda,** *E. murinus,* probably the

largest snake in the world, may grow to a length of more than thirty feet. **2.** any large constrictor, such as the python or boa. [Possibly Singhalese *henakandayā* large snake of Ceylon; literally, lightning stem.]

A·nac·re·on (ə nak′rē ən) *n.* c.572– c.488 B.C., Greek lyric poet.

a·nad·ro·mous (ə nad′rə məs) *adj.* (of fish) swimming upstream from the sea to spawn. Opposed to **catadromous.** [Greek *anadromos* running upward, from *ana* up + *dromos* a running.]

a·nae·mi·a (ə nē′mē ə) anemia.

a·nae·mic (ə nē′mik) anemic.

an·aer·obe (an ār′ōb, an′ə rōb′) *n.* microorganism that can live in an environment lacking free oxygen. Distinguished from **aerobe.** [AN¹ + Greek *āēr* air + *bios* life.]

Anaconda

an·aer·o·bic (an′ā rō′bik, an′ə-) *adj.* **1.** able to live or grow where free oxygen is lacking. **2.** of or caused by anaerobes.

an·aes·the·sia (an′is thē′zhə) anesthesia.

an·aes·the·si·ol·o·gist (an′is thē′zē ol′ə jist) anesthesiologist.

an·aes·the·si·ol·o·gy (an′is thē′zē ol′ə jē) anesthesiology.

an·aes·thet·ic (an′is thet′ik) anesthetic. —**an′aes·thet′i·cal·ly,** *adv.*

an·aes·the·tist (ə nes′thə tist) anesthetist.

an·aes·the·tize (ə nes′thə tīz′) anesthetize. —**a·naes′the·ti·za′tion,** *n.*

an·a·gram (an′ə gram′) *n.* **1.** word or phrase created by transposing the letters of another word or phrase. The word *veil* is an anagram of the word *evil.* **2.** **anagrams.** game in which the players form words by rearranging given letters or by arranging letters taken in turn from a pile of cards or tiles. [French *anagramme,* going back to Greek *ana-* backwards + *gramma* letter.]

An·a·heim (an′ə hīm′) *n.* city in southwestern California. Pop. (1970), 166,701.

a·nal (ān′əl) *adj.* of, relating to, or near the anus.

an·al·ge·si·a (an′əl jē′zē ə, -sē ə) *n.* insensibility to pain without the loss of consciousness. [Modern Latin *analgesia,* from Greek *analgēsia,* from *an-¹* without + *algēsiā* sense of pain.]

an·al·ge·sic (an′əl jē′zik, -sik) *adj.* relating to or causing analgesia. —*n.* remedy used to relieve or remove pain. Aspirin is one of the most common analgesics.

analog computer *also,* **analogue computer.** computer that directly represents quantities by physical entities of analogous value. A slide rule is a simple analog computer, with scales that represent numerical quantities. An electronic analog computer utilizes such things as voltage, current, or electric impulses to represent the given quantities. Distinguished from **digital computer.**

an·a·log·i·cal (an′ə loj′i kəl) *adj.* related to, using, or based on analogy: *analogical reasoning.* —**an′a·log′i·cal·ly,** *adv.*

a·nal·o·gous (ə nal′ə gəs) *adj.* **1.** alike or similar in certain respects; comparable. **2.** *Biology.* having the same function, but differing in structure and origin. The gills of a fish and the lungs of a mammal are analogous. Distinguished from **homologous** in def. 2. —**a·nal′o·gous·ly,** *adv.* —**a·nal′o·gous·ness,** *n.*

an·a·logue (an′ə ôg′, -og′) *also,* **an·a·log.** *n.* **1.** something analogous to something else. **2.** *Biology.* organ, part, or system that is analogous to one in another organism. **3.** word in one language corresponding to one in another.

a·nal·o·gy (ə nal′ə jē) *pl.* -**gies.** *n.* **1.** resemblance in certain aspects between things otherwise unlike; partial similarity: *the analogy between the heart and a pump.* **2.** any similarity or correspondence: *There's no analogy between his position and yours.* **3.** *Biology.* similarity in function of parts dissimilar in structure and origin. **4.** *Logic.* form of reasoning in which similarities are inferred from others that are already known and observed. [Latin *analogia* resemblance, from Greek *analogiā* resemblance, proportion.]

a·nal·y·sis (ə nal′ə sis) *pl.* -**ses** (-sēz′). *n.* **1.** method of determining the nature and essential features of something by separating it into its parts; critical examination. **2.** statement of the results of such an examination. **3.** separation of a whole into its constituent parts or elements. Opposed to **synthesis.** **4.** psychoanalysis. **5.** *Chemistry.* **a.** intentional separation or decomposition of a substance into its constituent compounds or elements. **Quantitative analysis** determines the amount of the ingredients; **qualitative analysis** determines their nature. **b.** determination of the nature or amount of one or more constituents of a substance, whether obtained in separate form or not. [Modern Latin *analysis,* from Greek *analysis* releasing, solution.]

an·a·lyst (an′əl ist) *n.* **1.** one who analyzes or is skilled in analysis. **2.** psychoanalyst.

an·a·lyt·i·cal (an′əl it′i kəl) *adj.* of, relating to, or using analysis. Also, **an′a·lyt′ic.** —**an′a·lyt′i·cal·ly,** *adv.*

analytic geometry, branch of mathematics in which geometric figures are described and analyzed in algebraic terms and plotted in space by means of coordinates.

an·a·lyt·ics (an′əl it′iks) *n.,pl.* branch of logic concerned with analysis. ▲ construed as singular.

an·a·lyze (an′əl īz′) **-lyzed, -lyz·ing.** *v.t.* **1.** to separate into constituent parts, esp. so as to determine the nature or essential features of the whole: *to analyze a sentence grammatically.* **2.** to examine critically or in detail: *to analyze one's reasons for refusing.* **3.** to psychoanalyze. **4.** to subject to chemical or mathematical analysis. —**an′a·lyz′a·ble,** *adj.* —**an′a·lyz′er,** *n.*

An·a·ni·as (an′ə nī′əs) *n.* **1.** in the New Testament, man who was struck dead after lying to Peter. **2.** any liar.

an·a·pest (an′ə pest′) *n.* **1.** metrical foot in verse consisting of two unaccented or short syllables followed by an accented or long syllable. The line *And the sheen′ / of their spears′ / was like stars′ / on the sea′ /* (Byron, 1815) contains four anapests. **2.** line of verse made up of such feet. [Latin *anapaestus* anapest *(def. 1),* from Greek *anapaistos (pous)* reversed (metrical foot); because it is the opposite of a dactyl.] —**an′a·pes′tic,** *adj.*

an·a·pho·ra (ə naf′ər ə) *n.* repetition of a word or phrase at the beginning of two or more successive clauses, verses, or sentences. [Latin *anaphora,* from Greek *anaphorā* repetition.]

an·a·phy·lax·is (an′ə fə lak′sis) *n.* hypersensitivity to a foreign protein or other substance following a first injection of it into the blood. [Modern Latin *anaphylaxis,* from ANA- + Greek *phylaxis* guarding.] —**an′a·phy·lac′tic,** *adj.*

an·arch (an′ärk′) *n. Archaic.* anarchist.

an·ar·chic (an är′kik) *adj.* **1.** of, like, or involving anarchy. **2.** advocating anarchy. **3.** causing or provoking anarchy. Also **an·ar′chi·cal.** —**an·ar′chi·cal·ly,** *adv.*

an·ar·chism (an′ər kiz′əm) *n.* **1.** political theory that all forms of government and governmental restraint are morally wrong and must be abolished if absolute individual and social liberty is to be achieved. **2.** advocacy of this theory or practices characteristic of its advocates.

an·ar·chist (an′ər kist) *n.* **1.** one who promotes, believes in, or advocates anarchy or anarchism, esp. by the violent overthrow of the established political and social order. **2.** one who promotes disorder or incites revolt against any kind of established rule and order. —**an′ar·chis′tic,** *adj.*

an·ar·chy (an′ər kē) *n.* **1.** absence of government and law. **2.** lawless confusion and political disorder due to the absence of governmental authority. **3.** general disorder and confusion; chaos. [French *anarchie,* from Greek *anarchiā* lack of a ruler, lawlessness.]

a·nas·tro·phe (ə nas′trə fē) *n.* inversion of the usual order of words or parts of a sentence, for example: *echoed the hills.* [Greek *anastrophē* inversion.]

a·nath·e·ma (ə nath′ə mə) *pl.,* **-mas.** *n.* **1.** in the Roman Catholic and Orthodox churches, the formal denunciation of a person or the condemnation of a practice or doctrine. **2.** any strong denunciation or imprecation; curse. **3.** person or thing that is accursed or denounced. **4.** person or thing that is detested or abhorred. [Latin *anathema* accursed person, curse, from Greek *anathema* thing devoted (to evil).]

a·nath·e·ma·tize (ə nath′ə mə tīz′) **-tized, -tiz·ing.** *v.t.* to pronounce an anathema against; denounce; curse.

An·a·to·li·a (an′ə tō′lē ə) *n.* Asia Minor. —**An′a·to′li·an,** *adj., n.*

an·a·tom·i·cal (an′ə tom′i kəl) *adj.* of or relating to anatomy or its study. Also, **an′a·tom′ic.** —**an′a·tom′i·cal·ly,** *adv.*

a·nat·o·mist (ə nat′ə mist) *n.* one skilled in anatomy or dissection.

a·nat·o·mize (ə nat′ə mīz′) **-mized, -miz·ing.** *v.t.* **1.** to dissect (an animal or plant) in order to study or display the structure and relationships of its parts. **2.** to analyze closely. —**a·nat′o·mi·za′tion,** *n.*

a·nat·o·my (ə nat′ə mē) *pl.,* **-mies.** *n.* **1.** science of the physical structure of organisms and the interrelationships of their parts. **2.** physical structure of an organism or any of its parts. **3.** structure: *anatomy of a problem.* **4.** detailed examination; analysis: *anatomy of a crime.* **5.** anatomical model or cast. **6.** *Informal.* human body. [French *anatomie* science of the physical structure of organisms, dissection, from Late Latin *anatomia* dissection, from Greek *anatomē* cutting up.]

An·ax·ag·o·ras (an′ak sag′ər əs) *n.* c.500–428 B.C., Greek philosopher.

anc., ancient.

-ance *suffix* **1.** (used to form nouns directly from verbs): **a.** process or action of: *continuance, utterance.* **b.** state, quality, or condition of: *resemblance, complaisance.* **c.** result of an action: *contrivance.* **d.** agent of: *conveyance.* **2.** (used to form nouns from adjectives ending in *-ant*): **a.** state, quality, or condition: *ignorance, brilliance, vigilance.* **b.** that which is in or exhibits such a state, quality, or condition. [Latin *-antia, -entia,* often through French *-ance.*]

an·ces·tor (an′ses′tər) *n.* **1.** one from whom a person is descended;

forefather. ▲ usually used to designate one more remote than a grandparent. **2.** something that precedes or influences the development of (something else); forerunner; prototype: *the ancestor of the modern automobile.* **3.** organism from which higher or later organisms have evolved. [Old French *ancestre* forefather, from Latin *antecessor* one who goes before, predecessor.]

an·ces·tral (an ses′trəl) *adj.* of, relating to, or inherited from ancestors: *an ancestral estate.* —**an·ces′tral·ly,** *adv.*

an·ces·tress (an′ses′tris) *n.* female from whom a person is descended.

an·ces·try (an′ses′trē) *pl.,* **-tries.** *n.* **1.** family lineage or descent. **2.** ancestors collectively. **3.** honorable or aristocratic descent: *He was possessed of wealth and ancestry.*

An·chi·ses (an kī′sēz) *n.* *Roman Legend.* a prince of Troy and the father of Aeneas.

an·chor (ang′kər) *n.* **1.** device for preventing a boat or other floating structure from drifting on water. An anchor usually grips the bottom under water and is attached to the boat by a chain or cable. **2.** any device that holds something in place. **3.** source or means of support, stability, or security: *Hope was his anchor.* **4. at anchor.** held fast by the anchor. **5. to drop** (or **cast**) **anchor.** to lower the anchor overboard. **6. to ride at anchor.** to be held fast by the anchor. **7. to weigh anchor.** to take up the anchor. —*v.t.* **1.** to hold (a floating structure) in place by an anchor. **2.** to fasten in place; secure firmly: *Anchor the shelf to the wall.* **3.** to position or fix (oneself) firmly: *He anchored himself near the door.* —*v.i.* to lower the anchor overboard and remain held fast: *We anchored in the bay.* [Old English *ancor* mooring device, from Latin *anc(h)ora,* from Greek *ankūra.*]

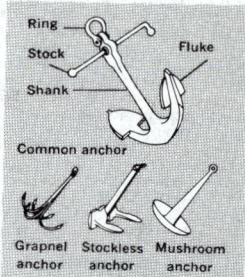

Ring
Fluke
Stock
Shank
Common anchor
Grapnel anchor
Stockless anchor
Mushroom anchor

an·chor·age (ang′kər ij) *n.* **1.** place for anchoring. **2.** fee charged for anchoring. **3.** act of anchoring; being anchored. **4.** something that fastens or holds securely: *The ropes were used as anchorage.*

An·chor·age (ang′kər ij) *n.* port city in southern Alaska, the largest city in the state and the chief center of transportation. Pop. (1970), 48,029.

an·cho·rite (ang′kə rīt′) *also,* **an·cho·ret** (ang′kər it, -kə ret′). *n.* one who lives in seclusion, esp. for religious reasons; hermit. [Medieval Latin *anachorita,* through Late Latin, from Greek *anachōrētēs* literally, one who has withdrawn.] —**an′cho·ress,** *n.*

anchor man, key man or main support of a team or group, as the last runner in a relay race or the principal announcer on a newscast.

an·cho·vy (an′chō vē, an chō′-) *pl.,* **-vies.** *n.* any of various saltwater and freshwater fish, family Engraulidae, closely related to the herring. The European anchovy, *Engraulis encrasicholus,* is caught commercially, esp. in the Mediterranean area, and canned as fillets or processed into a paste. Length: 3–4 inches. [Spanish *anchova,* possibly from Basque *anchu,* anchovy, dried fish, from *antzua* dry.]

an·cienne no·blesse (äN syaN nō bles′) *French.* the old nobility, esp. that of France before the revolution of 1789.

an·cien ré·gime (äN syaN rā zhēm′) *French.* the old political and social system, esp. that of France before the revolution of 1789.

an·cient¹ (ān′shənt, -chənt) *adj.* **1.** of or relating to times long past, esp. before the fall of the Western Roman Empire in A.D. 476: *the ancient philosophers.* **2.** of great age; very old: *an ancient tradition.* —*n.* **1.** aged or venerable person. **2. the ancients** (or **Ancients**). **a.** civilized peoples of antiquity, esp. the Greeks and Romans: *a custom common among the ancients.* **b.** authors of ancient Greece and Rome: *Cicero, Livy, and the other ancients.* [Old French *ancien* old, going back to Latin *ante* before.] —**an′cient·ly,** *adv.* —**an′cient·ness,** *n.*

an·cient² (ān′shənt, -chənt) *n. Archaic.* **1.** flag or banner; ensign. **2.** bearer of a flag or banner; standard-bearer. [Modification of ENSIGN.]

ancient history 1. history from the beginning of recorded events to the fall of the Western Roman Empire in A.D. 476. **2.** *Informal.* recent information or event that is no longer pertinent or interesting.

an·cil·lar·y (an′sə ler′ē) *adj.* supplementary or subsidiary; auxiliary. [Latin *ancillāris* relating to a maidservant, from *ancilla* maidservant.]

an·con (ang′kon) *pl.,* **an·co·nes** (ang-kō′nēz). *n.* **1.** upper end of the

Ancons

at; āpe; cär; end; mē; it; īce; hot; ōld; fôrk; wood; fōol; oil; out; up; ūse; turn; sing; thin; this; zh in treasure; ə in ago, taken, pencil, lemon, circus.

ulna; elbow. **2.** projection used to support a cornice or other structure; console. [Latin *ancōn* projecting stone support, from Greek *ankōn* bend, elbow.] **—an·co·nal** (ang kōn′əl), **an·co′ne·al,** *adj.*

-ancy, form of **-ance,** as in *vacancy.*

and (and; *unstressed* ənd, ən) *conj.* **1.** as well as; also; moreover: *paper, pen, and ink, big and strong.* **2.** added to; plus: *four and twenty blackbirds. Two and two make four.* **3.** as a result or consequence; then: *Give him an inch and he'll take a mile.* **4.** *Informal.* to: *Come and see us sometime.* **5.** *Archaic.* if: *and it please you.* [Old English *and* also, plus.]

and., andante.

An·da·lu·sia (an′də lōō′zhə, -shē ə) *n.* historic region of southern Spain, now divided into eight provinces. **—An′da·lu′sian,** *adj., n.*

An·da·man and Nic·o·bar Islands (an′də mən; nik′ə bär′) two island groups belonging to India, located in the eastern part of the Bay of Bengal. Land area, 3215 sq. mi. Pop. (1961), 63,548.

an·dan·te (än dän′tā, an dan′tē) *Music. adv., adj.* slower than moderato but faster than adagio; moderately slow. *—n.* composition, movement, or part in such a tempo. [Italian *andante* slow; literally, going; possibly going back to Latin *ambulāre* to walk.]

an·dan·ti·no (än′dän tē′nō, an′dan-) *Music. adv., adj.* slightly faster than andante. *—n. pl., -nos.* composition, movement, or part in such a tempo. [Italian *andantino,* diminutive of *andante* slow. See ANDANTE.]

An·de·an (an dē′ən, an′dē-) *adj.* of, relating to, or characteristic of the Andes.

An·der·sen, Hans Christian (an′dər sən; hanz) 1805–75, Danish author known esp. for his fairy tales.

An·der·son (an′dər sən) **1. Maxwell.** 1888–1959, U.S. playwright. **2. Sherwood.** 1876–1941, U.S. novelist and short-story writer. **3.** city in central Indiana. Pop. (1970), 70,787.

An·der·son·ville (an′dər sən vil′) *n.* village in west-central Georgia, site of a Confederate prison during the Civil War.

An·des (an′dēz) *n.pl.* longest mountain system in the world, extending along the west coast of South America.

and·i·ron (and′ī′ərn) *n.* either of two metal supports for holding wood in a fireplace. Also, **fire′dog′.** [Old French *andier,* influenced by *iron;* of uncertain origin.]

and/or, both or either. ▲ used to indicate that either *and* or *or* may connect two words, phrases, or clauses depending on what is meant: *insurance that covers fire and/or theft.*

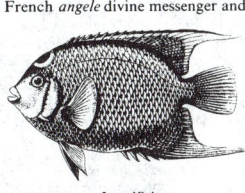

Andirons

An·dor·ra (an dôr′ə, -dor′ə) *n.* **1.** small country in southwestern Europe, between France and Spain. Area, 175 sq. mi. Pop. (1969 est.), 19,000. **2.** its capital. Pop. (approx.), 1000.

An·dre·a del Sar·to (än drā′ə del sär′tō) 1486–1531, Italian Renaissance painter; born Andrea Vanucci.

An·drew (an′drōō) *n.* in the New Testament, one of the twelve Apostles of Jesus, and brother of Peter.

An·dro·cles (an′drə klēz′) *also,* **An·dro·clus** (an′drə kləs). *n. Roman Legend.* a slave spared in the arena by a lion because he had once removed a thorn from its paw.

an·dro·gen (an′drə jən) *n.* any of various hormones that control and stimulate the development of masculine characteristics. **—an·dro·gen·ic** (an′drə jen′ik), *adj.*

an·drog·y·nous (an drog′ə nəs) *adj.* **1.** uniting the characteristics of both sexes; hermaphroditic. **2.** (of a flower cluster) having both male and female flowers. [Latin *androgynus* hermaphrodite, from Greek *androgynos,* from *andr-,* stem of *anēr* man + *gynē* woman.] **—androg′y·ny,** *n.*

an·droid (an′droid) *n. Science Fiction.* nonhuman being that is human in form or appearance.

An·drom·a·che (an drom′ə kē) *n. Greek Legend.* wife of Hector and mother of Astyanax. She was captured by the Greeks after the fall of Troy.

An·drom·e·da (an drom′ə də) *n.* **1.** *Greek Mythology.* Ethiopian princess whom Perseus rescued from a sea monster and then took as his wife. **2.** constellation in the northern sky, conventionally depicted as a woman with outstretched arms.

-ane *suffix* designating a hydrocarbon compound of the alkane, or paraffin, series: *methane.* [Form of -ENE, -INE, or -ONE.]

an·ec·do·tal (an′ik dōt′əl) *adj.* relating to, consisting of, or resembling anecdotes. **—an′ec·do′tal·ly,** *adv.*

an·ec·dote (an′ik dōt′) *n.* short account of some incident or event, esp. one intended to amuse or illustrate: *He repeated several anecdotes about his first years as a congressman.* [French *anecdote,* from Greek *anekdota* things unpublished (suggesting a private story or gossip).]

an·ec·dot·ist (an′ik dō′tist) *n.* one who tells or is given to telling anecdotes.

a·ne·mi·a (ə nē′mē ə) *also,* **a·nae·mi·a.** *n.* deficiency in the amount of hemoglobin or the number of red corpuscles in the blood, characterized by pallor, weakness, and fatigue. [Modern Latin *anaemia,* from Greek *anaimiā* lack of blood.]

a·ne·mic (ə nē′mik) *also,* **a·nae·mic.** *adj.* **1.** of, having, or characteristic of anemia. **2.** lacking vitality or spirit; bloodless.

an·e·mom·e·ter (an′ə mom′ə tər) *n.* instrument for measuring the velocity of the wind. [Greek *anemos* wind + -METER.] **—an·e·mo·met·ric** (an′ə mō met′rik); *also,* **an′e·mo·met′ri·cal,** *adj.*

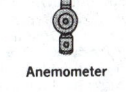

Anemometer

a·nem·o·ne (ə nem′ə nē) *n.* **1.** any plant of the genus *Anemone,* usually having slender stems, lobed or notched leaves, and small flowers. Also, **wind′flow′er. 2.** sea anemone. [Latin *anemōnē* windflower, from Greek *anemōnē.*]

a·nent (ə nent′) *prep. Archaic.* in regard to; concerning. [Old English *on efen* near.]

an·er·oid (an′ə roid′) *adj.* not using or containing liquid. **—***n.* aneroid barometer. [French *anéroïde,* from Greek *a-* without + *nēros* wet + -OID.]

aneroid barometer, barometer in which a flexible metal box containing a partial vacuum contracts and expands in response to changes in air pressure. When the box expands, it pushes a spring attached to a pointer, which registers the change.

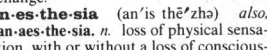
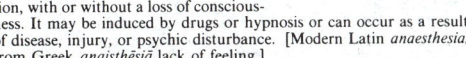

Cross section Front view

Aneroid barometer

an·es·the·sia (an′is thē′zhə) *also,* **an·aes·the·sia.** *n.* loss of physical sensation, with or without a loss of consciousness. It may be induced by drugs or hypnosis or can occur as a result of disease, injury, or psychic disturbance. [Modern Latin *anaesthesia,* from Greek *anaisthēsiā* lack of feeling.]

an·es·the·si·ol·o·gist (an′is thē′zē ol′ə jist) *also,* **an·aes·the·si·ol·o·gist.** *n.* physician specializing in anesthesiology.

an·es·the·si·ol·o·gy (an′is thē′zē ol′ə jē) *also,* **an·aes·the·si·ol·o·gy.** *n.* branch of medicine that deals with anesthesia and the administration of anesthetics.

an·es·thet·ic (an′is thet′ik) *also,* **an·aes·thet·ic.** *n.* substance that produces anesthesia. *—adj.* **1.** producing anesthesia. **2.** of, relating to, or characteristic of anesthesia. **—an′es·thet′i·cal·ly,** *adv.*

a·nes·the·tist (ə nes′thə tist) *also,* **a·naes·the·tist.** *n.* one who is trained and licensed to administer anesthetics, esp. a registered nurse.

a·nes·the·tize (ə nes′thə tīz′) **-tized, -tiz·ing.** *also,* **a·naes·the·tize.** *v.t.* to produce anesthesia in; make insensible, esp. to pain. **—a·nes′the·ti·za′tion,** *n.*

an·eu·rysm (an′yə riz′əm) *also,* **an·eu·rism.** *n.* sac formed by the dilation of the wall of an artery weakened by disease, injury, or infection. [Greek *aneurysma* dilation.] **—an′eu·rys′mal;** *also,* **an′eu·ris′mal,** *adj.*

a·new (ə nōō′, ə nū′) *adv.* in a new or different way; over again: *to begin life anew.* [Old English *of-niowe* over again.]

an·gel (ān′jəl) *n.* **1.** one of the group of immortal, spiritual beings who serve as the attendants and messengers of God. Traditionally, angels are ranked in nine orders: seraphim, cherubim, thrones, dominions or dominations, virtues, powers, principalities, archangels, and angels. **2.** attendant or guardian spirit: *Her good angel watched over her.* **3.** one of the fallen immortal spiritual beings; Satan or one of his attendants. **4.** conventional representation of one of these beings, usually a human form with wings and a halo. **5.** person regarded as resembling an angel in goodness, beauty, or kindliness. **6.** *Informal.* one who provides funds for a theatrical production; financial backer. **7.** English gold coin minted between 1465 and 1634, having on its face the Archangel Michael defeating Satan. [Old French *angele* divine messenger and spirit (replacing Old English *engel*), from Latin *angelus* messenger, divine messenger, from Greek *angelos.*]

an·gel·fish (ān′jəl fish′) *pl.,* **-fish** or **-fish·es.** *n.* **1.** any of various saltwater and freshwater fish which have filamentous extensions on their fins and often have striking markings or coloration. Two freshwater angelfish, *Pterophyllum scalare* and *P. eimekei,*

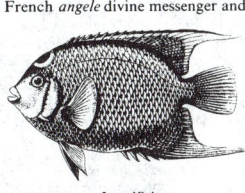

Angelfish

having flattened silver bodies, vertical black bands, and fan-shaped rear fins, are popular aquarium fish. **2.** any of several sharks, genus *Squatina*, found in warm and temperate shore waters and having large, winglike pectoral fins and a flat body.

an·gel·ic (an jel′ik) *adj.* **1.** like or characteristic of an angel; beautiful; pure; saintly: *an angelic temperament.* **2.** of or relating to the angels. Also, **an·gel′i·cal.** —**an·gel′i·cal·ly,** *adv.*

an·gel·i·ca (an jel′i kə) *n.* **1.** any of a large group of plants, genus *Angelica,* of the parsley family, native to the Northern Hemisphere, esp. *A. archangelica,* some parts of which are used in medicine and in cooking. **2.** candied angelica. young stems and leafstalks of *A. archangelica,* cooked in sugar syrup and used as a confection, esp. to decorate cakes and cookies. [Medieval Latin (*herba*) *angelica* angelic (herb); because of its medicinal uses.]

An·ge·li·co, Fra (an jel′i kō′; frä) 1387–1455, Italian painter of religious subjects and Dominican monk; born Guido di Pietro.

An·ge·lus (an′jə ləs) *also,* **an·ge·lus.** *n.* **1.** in the Roman Catholic Church, prayer said in commemoration of the Annunciation. **2.** bell rung at morning, noon, and night to announce the time for saying this prayer. Also, **Angelus bell.** [Latin *angelus* angel; the first word of the prayer.]

an·ger (ang′gər) *n.* feeling of great displeasure, annoyance, or irritation, often accompanied by antagonism; ire. —*v.t.* to make angry. —*v.i.* to become angry. [Old Norse *angr* grief.]

Syn. *n.* **Anger, indignation, wrath, ire** indicate great displeasure. **Anger,** the least specific of these words, simply refers to the presence of the emotion with no indication of its depth or manifestation: *He managed to control his anger.* **Indignation** carries the implication of moral displeasure, as over something considered improper or blameworthy: *The demonstration expressed the widespread public indignation against the judges' decision.* **Wrath** implies the desire to impose punishment on its object: *Only by fleeing the country could they escape the king's wrath.* **Ire,** a rarer and more rhetorical word, is sometimes used humorously to suggest great annoyance: *The constant noise aroused the sleeping man's ire.*

An·ge·vin (an′jə vin) *also,* **An·ge·vine** (an′jə vin, -vīn′) *adj.* **1.** of or from Anjou. **2.** of or relating to the Plantagenet line of English kings or the period of their rule. —*n.* **1.** member of the people of Anjou. **2.** member of the Plantagenet royal house.

an·gi·na (an jī′nə, an′jə nə) *n.* **1.** angina pectoris. **2.** any disease characterized by attacks of spasmodic suffocation, esp. with an inflammation of the throat or chest. [Latin *angina* quinsy; literally, choking.]

angina pec·to·ris (pek′tər is) condition marked by paroxysms of constricting chest pains caused by a temporary inadequacy of blood flow to the heart muscle. [Modern Latin *angina pectoris* angina of the chest.]

an·gi·o·sperm (an′jē ə-spurm′) *n.* flowering plant.

an·gle[1] (ang′gəl) *n.* **1.a.** figure formed by two lines diverging from a common point or by two planes diverging from a common straight line. **b.** space between these lines or planes. **c.** amount of divergence between these lines or planes, measured in degrees: *The tree stood at a 90° angle to the ground.* **2.** pointed projection or sharp corner: *The sculpture consisted of contrasting angles and curves.* **3.** point of view; aspect: *Look at the problem from this angle.* **4.** *Slang.* motive or interest; way of operating or profiting: *What's your angle in all this?* —*v.t.* **-gled, -gling. 1.** to cause to move or turn at an angle: *to angle a billiard ball.* **2.** to present from a particular or prejudiced point of view; slant. —*v.i.* to move or bend at an angle: *The road angles up the hill.* [Latin *angulus* corner.]

an·gle[2] (ang′gəl) **-gled, -gling.** *v.i.* **1.** to fish with a hook and line. **2. to angle for.** to use artful or wily means to obtain (something): *He angled for the girl's affection.* [Old English *angel* fishhook.]

angle iron, piece of metal in the form of an angle, esp. a right angle, used to join or strengthen structural pieces.

angle of incidence, angle that a ray, as of light, striking a surface forms with a line perpendicular to that surface at the point of striking.

angle of reflection, angle that a ray, as of light, reflected from a surface forms with a line perpendicular to that surface at the point of reflection.

Obtuse angle (150°)

Acute angles

Right angle 90° 60° 30°

Types of angles

Angle of incidence | **Angle of reflection**

Incident ray | **Reflected ray**

Angle of incidence

an·gler (ang′glər) *n.* **1.** one who fishes with a hook and line. **2.** one who schemes to gain an objective. **3.** anglerfish.

an·gler·fish (ang′glər fish′) *n.* any of various saltwater fish, family Lophiidae, having a large head, wide mouth, and a rod extending from the head with which it lures its prey. Length: to 4 feet.

An·gles (ang′gəlz) *n.,pl.* Germanic tribe that settled in Britain in the fifth and sixth centuries.

an·gle·worm (ang′gəl wurm′) *n.* earthworm.

An·gli·a (ang′glē ə) *n.* England. [Latin.]

An·gli·an (ang′glē ən) *adj.* of or relating to the Angles or to their language or culture. —*n.* **1.** one of the Angles. **2.** Old English as spoken by the Angles.

An·gli·can (ang′gli kən) *adj.* of or relating to the Church of England or a church affiliated with it. —*n.* member of the Church of England or a church affiliated with it.

An·gli·can·ism (ang′gli kə niz′əm) *n.* body of doctrines and practices of the Church of England.

An·gli·cism (ang′glə siz′əm) *n.* **1.** word, phrase, or usage peculiar to British English. **2.** quality characteristic of the English; state of being English.

an·gli·cize (ang′glə sīz′) **-cized, -ciz·ing.** *also,* **An·gli·cize.** *v.t.* **1.** to adopt (a foreign word or phrase) into English, sometimes with a slight change in pronunciation, form, or meaning. *Chauffeur* is a French word that has been anglicized. **2.** to cause to adapt to or acquire English traits, institutions, or beliefs. —*v.i.* to conform to or acquire English characteristics or institutions. —**an′gli·ci·za′tion;** *also,* **An′gli·ci·za′tion,** *n.*

an·gling (ang′gling) *n.* act or art of fishing with a hook and line.

Anglo- *combining form* **1.** English: *Anglo-Norman, Anglophobia.* **2.** English and: *Anglo-American relations.* [From Latin *Anglī* the Angles.]

An·glo-A·mer·i·can (ang′glō ə mer′i kən) *adj.* **1.** English and American: *Anglo-American trade.* **2.** of or relating to Anglo-Americans. —*n.* American citizen or inhabitant of English birth or descent.

An·glo-E·gyp·tian Sudan (ang′glō i jip′shən) former territory in northern Africa under joint British and Egyptian control, now the independent country of Sudan.

An·glo-French (ang′glō french′) *adj.* English and French. —*n.* Anglo-Norman.

An·glo·ma·ni·a (ang′glə mā′nē ə) *n.* excessive admiration for or imitation of English institutions, manners, or customs. —**An′glo·ma′ni·ac,** *n.*

An·glo-Nor·man (ang′glō nôr′mən) *n.* **1.** one of the Normans who settled in England after the Norman Conquest in 1066. **2.** dialect of Old French brought into England by the Norman conquerers and spoken by the upper classes in England from the Norman Conquest through the fourteenth century. —*adj.* of or relating to the Anglo-Normans or their language.

An·glo·phile (ang′glə fīl′) *n.* one who is extremely fond of England, its people, traditions, manners, or customs.

An·glo·pho·bi·a (ang′glə fō′bē ə) *n.* intense hatred or fear of England or of what is English. —**An′glo·phobe′,** *n.* —**An′glo·pho′bic,** *adj.*

An·glo-Saxon (ang′glō sak′sən) *n.* **1.** member or descendant of one of the Germanic tribes that invaded England in the fifth and sixth centuries. **2.** any Englishman of the period from the fifth century to the Norman Conquest in 1066. **3.** person of English nationality or descent. **4.** Old English. **5.** direct, plain English. —*adj.* **1.** of or relating to the Anglo-Saxons or their culture. **2.** of or relating to Anglo-Saxon.

An·go·la (ang gō′lə) *n.* country on the west coast of southern Africa, formerly Portuguese West Africa. Area, 481,350 sq. mi. Pop. (1975 est.), 6,400,000.

An·go·ra (ang gôr′ə) *n.* **1.** Ankara. **2.a.** Angora cat. **b.** Angora goat. **c.** Angora rabbit. **3.** *also,* **angora. a.** mohair. **b.** yarn or knitted fabric made from the hair of the Angora rabbit.

Angora cat 1. any domestic cat with long, silky hair. The Angora cat, in this sense, is not a distinct breed. **2.** cat of a former breed, originally from Turkey, having a long body, nose, and ears, a ruff around the neck, and a bushy tail.

Angora goat, goat of a breed that originated in Asia Minor, raised for its long, silky hair, which is called mohair.

Angora rabbit, domestic rabbit bred for its long, silky hair.

Angora goat

an·gos·tu·ra (ang′gəs toor′ə, -tyoor′ə) *n.* aromatic, bitter bark of certain South American trees, used esp. for making a kind of bitters. [From *Angostura* (now Ciudad Bolivar), town in Venezuela.]

at; āpe; cär; end; mē; it; īce; hot; ōld; fôrk; wood; fo͞ol; oil; out; up; ūse; turn; sing; thin; this; zh in treasure; ə in ago, taken, pencil, lemon, circus.

an·gry (ang′grē) -gri·er, -gri·est. *adj.* **1.** feeling or showing anger; irate: *angry with his boss, angry about the situation.* **2.** resulting from or exhibiting anger: *an angry look.* **3.** threatening and raging, as if in anger: *an angry sea.* **4.** painfully inflamed: *an angry rash.* [From AN-GER.] —**an′gri·ly,** *adv.* —**an′gri·ness,** *n.*

ang·strom (ang′strəm) *also,* **Ang·strom.** *n.* unit of measurement equal to one hundred-millionth of a centimeter, used to express the wavelength of light or other radiations. Also, **angstrom unit.** [From the Swedish physicist Anders J. *Ångström,* 1814–74.]

an·guish (ang′gwish) *n.* extreme mental or physical suffering; agony: *the anguish of unrequited love.* [Old French *anguisse,* from Latin *angustia* narrowness.]

an·guished (ang′gwisht) *adj.* **1.** having or affected by anguish: *an anguished conscience.* **2.** resulting from or exhibiting anguish: *an anguished moan.*

an·gu·lar (ang′gyə lər) *adj.* **1.** having or forming an angle or angles; sharp-cornered: *an angular drawing, an angular piece of rock.* **2.** measured by an angle: *angular distance.* **3.** having prominent bones; gaunt. **4.** (of movement) not smooth or flowing; stiff; jerky. [Latin *angulāris* having corners or angles, from *angulus* corner, angle.] —**an′gu·lar·ly,** *adv.*

an·gu·lar·i·ty (ang′gyə lar′ə tē) *pl.,* **-ties.** *n.* **1.** quality or state of being angular. **2.** angularities. angular parts or forms.

An·gus (ang′gəs) *n.* Celtic god of love.

an·hy·dride (an hī′drīd, -drid) *n.* **1.** oxide that forms an acid or base when it is added to water. A nonmetal oxide that so reacts is called an **acid anhydride,** and a metal oxide is called a **basic anhydride.** **2.** any compound from which water has been removed.

an·hy·drous (an hī′drəs) *adj.* (of a chemical compound) having no water, esp. water of crystallization. Opposed to **hydrous.** [Greek *anydros* waterless, from *an-* without + *hydōr* water.]

an·il (an′əl) *n.* **1.** West Indian indigo plant, *Indigofera anil.* **2.** indigo. [French *anil,* through Spanish, Arabic, and Persian, from Sanskrit *nīlī* indigo plant, from *nēla* dark blue.]

an·ile (an′īl, ā′nīl) *adj.* like a doddering old woman; foolish; feeble-minded. [Latin *anīlis,* from *anus* old woman.] —**a·nil′i·ty,** *n.*

an·i·line (an′əl in, -īn′) *also,* **an·i·lin** (an′əl in) *n.* toxic, oily liquid derived chiefly from nitrobenzene and used in making rubber, dyes, and drugs. Formula: $C_6H_5NH_2$ —*adj.* made of, derived from, or relating to aniline. [German *Anilin,* from *Anil* indigo. See ANIL.]

aniline dye **1.** any of a number of dyes made from aniline. **2.** any synthetic dye.

an·i·ma (an′ə mə) *n.* vital principle; life; soul. [Latin *anima* life, breath.]

an·i·mad·ver·sion (an′ə mad′vur′zhən, -shən) *n.* **1.** unfavorable remark; adverse criticism. **2.** dislike or antipathy; aversion: *He became a vegetarian because of his animadversion toward meat.* [Latin *animadversiō* observation, censure.]

an·i·mad·vert (an′ə mad′vurt′) *v.i.* to comment unfavorably or critically (with *on* or *upon*). [Latin *animadvertere* to observe, censure.]

an·i·mal (an′ə məl) *n.* **1.** any living organism distinguished from plants by its ability to move about in its environment or move some parts of its body, its inability to produce its own food by photosynthesis, and the presence of sense organs. **2.** any of these except man; beast. **3.** mammal. **4.** bestial or brutish human being. —*adj.* **1.** of, relating to, or derived from animals: *animal fats, animal instincts.* **2.** relating to the physical or sensual rather than the spiritual or intellectual nature of man: *animal appetites.* [Latin *animal* living creature, from *anima* breath, life.]

Syn. **2. Animal, beast, brute** denote a creature considered lower in the scale of living beings than man, all three words sometimes being used to contrast some quality in man with something lacking (or present) in the lower order. **Animal** is the broadest of these words: *The animals of the forest are shy.* **Beast** is usually simply a four-legged animal: *I went to the animal fair; the birds and the beasts were there.* **Brute** stresses the lack in an animal of those faculties, such as intellect and speech, setting man apart: *Head down, the brute awaited the death stroke.*

an·i·mal·cule (an′ə mal′kūl′) *n.* minute or microscopic animal. [Modern Latin *animalculum,* diminutive of Latin *animal* living creature.]

animal husbandry, branch of agriculture dealing with the breeding, raising, and care of livestock.

an·i·mal·ism (an′ə mə liz′əm) *n.* **1.** qualities regarded as typical of animals, esp. vigorous health and uninhibited vitality. **2.** preoccupation with physical appetites; sensuality. **3.** doctrine that man is a mere animal, having no soul or spiritual qualities. —**an′i·mal·ist,** *n.* —**an′i·mal·is′tic,** *adj.*

an·i·mal·i·ty (an′ə mal′ə tē) *n.* animal nature of man, as distinguished from his moral and spiritual nature.

animal spirits, exuberant liveliness and vigor; vivacity.

an·i·mate (*v.,* an′ə māt′; *adj.,* an′ə mit) -mat·ed, -mat·ing. *v.t.* **1.** to impart liveliness, vividness, or interest to; enliven: *Delight animated her face.* **2.** to move to action; inspire; incite: *actions animated by patriotism.* **3.** to give life to; make alive: *The soul animates the body.* —*adj.* having life; alive: *animate beings and inanimate objects.* [Latin *animātus,* past participle of *animāre* to give life to.]

an·i·mat·ed (an′ə mā′tid) *adj.* **1.** full of life, activity, or spirit; lively; vivacious: *an animated debate. The animated speaker easily held the attention of her audience.* **2.** made to appear alive: *animated puppets.* —**an′i·mat′ed·ly,** *adv.*

animated cartoon, motion picture consisting of a series of drawings, each of which shows a successive stage of movement. When the drawings are photographed and projected in rapid succession, an illusion of movement is created.

an·i·ma·tion (an′ə mā′shən) *n.* **1.** liveliness; spirit; vivacity: *a story told with great animation.* **2.** act of animating; being animated. **3.** process and technique of preparing animated cartoons.

a·ni·ma·to (ä′nə mä′tō, an′ə-) *Music. adj.* lively; animated. —*adv.* in a spirited, lively manner. [Italian *animato* enlivened, brisk, going back to Latin *animāre* to quicken.]

an·i·ma·tor (an′ə mā′tər) *n.* artist who prepares the drawings for animated cartoons.

an·i·mism (an′ə miz′əm) *n.* **1.** belief that inanimate objects and natural phenomena possess living souls. **2.** belief in the existence of the soul as independent of matter. [Latin *anima* life, breath + -ISM.] —**an′i·mist,** *n.* —**an′i·mis′tic,** *adj.*

an·i·mos·i·ty (an′ə mos′ə tē) *pl.,* **-ties.** *n.* open or vehement hostility or hatred; enmity. [Late Latin *animōsitās* vehemence, going back to Latin *animus* spirit.] —**Syn.** see **hostility.**

an·i·mus (an′ə məs) *n.* **1.** animating spirit or purpose; intention. **2.** feeling of hostility; enmity; animosity. [Latin *animus* spirit.]

an·i·on (an′ī′ən) *n.* negatively charged ion of an electrolyte, attracted to the anode in electrolysis. Opposed to **cation.** [Greek *anion* (thing) going up, neuter present participle of *anienai* to go up.] —**an·i·on·ic** (an′ī on′ik), *adj.*

an·ise (an′is) *n.* **1.** aromatic herb, *Pimpinella anisum,* of the parsley family, widely cultivated in the Mediterranean region, India, and South America. **2.** aniseed. [Old French *anis,* from Latin *anisum* anise plant, from Greek *anison* anise plant.]

an·i·seed (an′i sēd′, an′is sēd′) *n.* seed of anise, having a spicy, licoricelike taste, used as a flavoring in cookies, pastries, and other food. Aniseed oil is used in some medicines and perfumes and as a flavor in some candies and liqueurs.

An·jou (an′jōō; *French* äⁿ zhōō′) *n.* region and former province in western France, in the Loire valley.

An·ka·ra (ang′kər ə) *n.* capital of Turkey, in the west-central part of the country. Pop. (1965), 905,660. Also, **An·go′ra.**

ankh (angk) *n.* simple cross with a loop at the top, an ancient Egyptian symbol of life.

an·kle (ang′kəl) *n.* **1.** joint that connects the foot and the leg. **2.** part of the leg at and just above this joint. [Of Scandinavian origin.]

an·kle·bone (ang′kəl bōn′) *n.* bone of the ankle. Also, **ta′lus.**

an·klet (ang′klit) *n.* **1.** short sock reaching just above the ankle. **2.** ornamental band or chain worn around the ankle. **3.** *Archaic.* fetter or shackle for the ankle.

an·ky·lo·sis (ang′ki lō′sis) *n.* **1.** fusion or consolidation of bones or the different parts of a bone. **2.** stiffness or immovability of a joint caused by abnormal adhesion of the joint bones. [Modern Latin *ankylosis,* from Greek *ankylōsis* stiffening of the joints, from *ankyloein* to bend, stiffen.] —**an·ky·lot·ic** (ang′ki lot′ik), *adj.*

an·na (an′ə) *n.* former coin of India equal to one-sixteenth of a rupee. [Hindustani *ānā.*]

an·nal·ist (an′əl ist) *n.* one who writes annals; chronicler.

an·nals (an′əlz) *n.,pl.* **1.** written account of events in chronological order recorded year by year. **2.** historical records; chronicles. **3.** periodical publication of an organization or learned society containing accounts of its activities and articles pertinent to its interests. [Latin *annālēs (librī)* yearly (books), chronicles, from *annus* year.]

An·nam (ə nam′) *n.* former protectorate in French Indochina, now Vietnam. —**An·nam·ese** (an′ə mēz′, -mēs′), *adj., n.*

An·nap·o·lis (ə nap′ə lis) *n.* **1.** capital and port city of Maryland, in the central part of the state. Pop. (1970), 29,592. **2.** officially, United States Naval Academy, an accredited four-year institution at Annapolis, Maryland, providing college-level instruction and officer training for careers in the U.S. Navy.

An·na·pur·na (an′ə poor′nə, -pur′-) *n.* mountain of the Himalayas, in west-central Nepal.

Ann Ar·bor (an′ är′bər) city in southeastern Michigan. Pop. (1970), 99,797.

Anne (an) *n.* 1665–1714, queen of Great Britain, from 1702 to 1714.

an·neal (ə nēl′) *v.t.* **1.** to heat and then slowly cool (metal or glass)

to reduce brittleness and increase toughness. **2.** to toughen or temper: *to strengthen and anneal the mind.* [Old English *onǣlan* to burn.]

an·ne·lid (an′əl id) *n.* any of various segmented worms of the phylum Annelida, including earthworms, marine worms, and leeches. [French *annélide*, going back to Old French *annel* ring, going back to Latin *ānulus* ring.]

an·nex (*v.*, ə neks′; *n.*, an′eks) *v.t.* **1.** to add or attach as an additional or subordinate part: *to annex a province to a kingdom.* **2.** to attach as an attribute, condition, or consequence: *the privileges annexed to nobility.* —*n.* **1.** building used as an addition to another; supplementary wing of a building: *annex of a hospital.* **2.** addition to a document; addendum. [French *annexer* to join, from Latin *annexus*, past participle of *annectere* to bind to.]

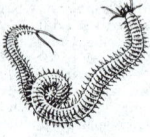

Annelid

an·nex·a·tion (an′ek sā′shən) *n.* **1.** act of annexing; being annexed. **2.** something annexed.

an·ni·hi·late (ə nī′ə lāt′) -**lat·ed**, -**lat·ing**. *v.t.* **1.** to reduce to nothing; destroy totally; obliterate: *The bombers annihilated the city.* **2.** to defeat completely; rout: *Their players annihilated our team.* [Latin *annihilātus*, past participle of *annihilāre* to bring to nothing.] —**an·ni·hi·la·tion**, **an·ni′hi·la·tor**, *n.* —**an·ni′hi·la′tive**, *adj.* —**Syn. 1.** see **abolish.**

An·nis·ton (an′is tən) *n.* city in northeastern Alabama. Pop. (1970), 31,533.

an·ni·ver·sa·ry (an′ə vur′sər ē) *pl.,* -**ries.** *n.* **1.** yearly recurring date of some past event: *the anniversary of the founding of the republic.* **2.** celebration of this date. —*adj.* of or relating to an anniversary: *an anniversary gift.* [Latin *anniversārius* returning every year, from *annus* year + *versus*, past participle of *vertere* to turn.]

an·no Dom·i·ni (an′ō dom′i nī′) in the (given) year since the birth of Christ. Abbreviation, **A.D.** [Medieval Latin *anno Domini* in the year of the Lord.]

an·no·tate (an′ə tāt′, an′ō-) -**tat·ed**, -**tat·ing.** *v.t.* to provide with or make critical or explanatory notes. [Latin *annotātus*, past participle of *annotāre* to note down.] —**an′no·ta′tor,** *n.*

an·no·ta·tion (an′ə tā′shən, an′ō-) *n.* **1.** critical or explanatory note or comment. **2.** act of annotating; being annotated.

an·nounce (ə nouns′) -**nounced,** -**nounc·ing.** *v.t.* **1.** to make known publicly or officially; proclaim: *His appointment was announced at the press conference.* **2.** to make known the approach, arrival, or presence of: *The butler announced every guest.* **3.** to make manifest; indicate: *Gathering clouds announced the oncoming storm.* —*v.i.* to serve as a radio or television announcer. [Old French *anoncer* to proclaim, from Latin *annūntiāre.* Doublet of **ANNUNCIATE.**] —**Syn.** *v.t.* **1.** see **declare.**

an·nounce·ment (ə nouns′mənt) *n.* **1.** act of announcing; being announced. **2.** that which is announced: *Your announcement was well received.* **3.** printed declaration: *engraved engagement announcements.*

an·nounc·er (ə noun′sər) *n.* **1.** person on radio or television who introduces programs and people, identifies the station, or presents advertisements, bulletins, or news items. **2.** one who announces anything.

an·noy (ə noi′) *v.t.* to be troublesome or irritating to; vex; bother: *His thoughtlessness annoyed her.* [Old French *anoier,* from *anoi* vexation, from Latin phrase *in odiō* in hatred.] —**an·noy′er,** *n.*

an·noy·ance (ə noi′əns) *n.* **1.** person or thing that annoys; nuisance. **2.** state or feeling of being annoyed; vexation. **3.** act of annoying.

an·noy·ing (ə noi′ing) *adj.* irritating; vexing. —**an·noy′ing·ly,** *adv.*

an·nu·al (an′ū əl) *adj.* **1.** relating to or measured by the year: *annual growth, annual income.* **2.** occurring or returning once a year: *annual stockholders' meeting, annual sale.* **3.** performed during a year: *the earth's annual course around the sun.* **4.** (of a plant) completing its entire life cycle within a single growing season. —*n.* **1.** publication issued once a year. **2.** an annual plant that sprouts, flowers, produces seed, and dies within one growing season. [Old French *annuel,* from Late Latin *annuālis,* from Latin *annus* year.] —**an′nu·al·ly,** *adv.*

annual ring, any of the rings of wood visible in the cross section of a stem, or trunk, of a tree or shrub. Each ring represents a year's growth.

an·nu·i·tant (ə nōō′ət ənt, ə nū′-) *n.* one who receives, or is entitled to receive, an annuity.

an·nu·i·ty (ə nōō′ə tē, ə nū′-) *pl.,* -**ties.** *n.* **1.** specified amount paid yearly or at other fixed intervals. **2.** right to receive or obligation to pay such an amount. **3.** investment, usually made with an insurance company, whereby a guaranteed annual return is paid during the investor's lifetime or for a contracted number of years. [French *annuité* annual payment, from Medieval Latin *annuitas,* from Latin *annuus* yearly.]

an·nul (ə nul′) -**nulled,** -**nul·ling.** *v.t.* to make void or of no effect; declare invalid: *to annul a law, to annul a marriage.* [Old French *anuller* to regard as nothing, from Late Latin *annūllāre* to make into nothing, going back to Latin *ad* to + *nūllus* none.]

an·nu·lar (an′yə lər) *adj.* relating to, consisting of, or shaped like a ring or rings. [Latin *an(n)ulāris* relating to a ring, from *an(n)ulus* ring.]

annular eclipse, solar eclipse in which a portion of the sun is visible as a ring surrounding the dark body of the moon.

an·nu·let (an′yə lit) *n.* **1.** little ring. **2.** narrow, ringlike molding encircling a column.

an·nul·ment (ə nul′mənt) *n.* act of annulling; being annulled; invalidation: *the annulment of a marriage.*

an·nu·lus (an′yə ləs) *pl.,* -**li** (-lī′) or -**lus·es.** *n.* ring or ringlike part, space, or marking. [Latin *an(n)ulus* ring.]

an·num (an′əm) *n. Latin.* year.

an·nun·ci·ate (ə nun′sē āt′) -**at·ed,** -**at·ing.** *v.t. Archaic.* to announce. [Latin *annuntiatus,* past participle of *annuntiare* to proclaim. Doublet of ANNOUNCE.]

an·nun·ci·a·tion (ə nun′sē ā′shən) *n.* **1. the Annunciation.** announcement brought by the angel Gabriel to the Virgin Mary that she was to give birth to Christ. **2. Annunciation.** church festival commemorating this announcement. March 25. Also, **Lady Day. 3.** *Archaic.* announcement.

an·nun·ci·a·tor (ə nun′sē ā′tər) *n.* **1.** device used to register signals and indicate their source. **2.** *Archaic.* announcer.

an·ode (an′ōd) *n.* **1.** electrode through which electrons leave an electrical device or medium. When electricity is used to produce a chemical reaction, the positive electrode is the anode; when a chemical reaction is used to produce electricity, the negative electrode is the anode. **2.** in electrolysis, electrode that has a comparative lack of electrons and is positively charged. Negatively charged ions are oxidized at the anode. **3.** in an electron tube, electrode or plate that attracts electrons. Opposed to **cathode** in all definitions. [Greek *anodos* way up.]

an·o·dyne (an′ə dīn′) *n.* **1.** medicine that relieves pain; analgesic. **2.** anything that soothes or calms: *Time is often an anodyne for sorrow.* [Latin *anōdynos* (drug) relieving pain, from Greek *anōdynos* painless.]

a·noint (ə noint′) *v.t.* **1.** to cover or smear with oil or any oily substance; apply ointment to. **2.** to put oil on as an act of consecration. [Old French *enoint,* past participle of *enoindre,* from Latin *inunguere* to cover with oil.] —**a·noint′er, a·noint′ment,** *n.*

anointing of the sick, sacrament of the Roman Catholic Church given by a priest to a person presumed to be dying, intended to absolve the person of his sins. Also, **extreme unction.**

a·nom·a·lous (ə nom′ə ləs) *adj.* deviating from the usual or normal; irregular; abnormal. [Late Latin *anōmalus,* from Greek *anōmalos* uneven, irregular.] —**a·nom′a·lous·ly,** *adv.* —**a·nom′a·lous·ness,** *n.*

a·nom·a·ly (ə nom′ə lē) *pl.,* -**lies.** *n.* **1.** something anomalous: *A capital without a country is an anomaly* (Disraeli, 1870). **2.** deviation from the usual or normal; irregularity; abnormality.

a·non (ə non′) *adv. Archaic.* **1.** in a little while; soon. **2.** at another time; again. **3. ever and anon.** again and again; now and then. [Old English *on ān* into one, *on āne* in one.]

anon., anonymous.

a·non·y·mous (ə non′ə məs) *adj.* **1.** of unknown or unavowed authorship or origin: *an anonymous book, an anonymous phone call.* **2.** with no name known or acknowledged: *an anonymous author.* **3.** lacking individuality, personality, or distinction: *a sea of anonymous faces.* [Greek *anōnymos* nameless.] —**an·o·nym·i·ty** (an′ə nim′ə tē), *n.* —**a·non′y·mous·ly,** *adv.*

a·noph·e·les (ə nof′ə lēz′) *pl.,* -**les.** *n.* mosquito, genus *Anopheles,* the female of which can transmit malaria by its bite. [Modern Latin *Anopheles,* from Greek *anōphelēs* hurtful.]

an·oth·er (ə nuth′ər) *adj.* **1.** one more; an additional: *Here's another example.* **2.** different: *Try another place.* **3.** similar or the same in character or achievements: *He thinks he's another Caesar.* —*pron.* **1.** one more; an additional one. **2.** a similar or identical one: *He's a scoundrel, and you're another.* [Middle English *an other,* from AN¹, OTHER.]

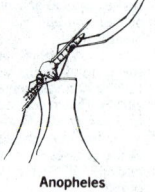

Anopheles

an·ox·i·a (an ok′sē ə, ə nok′-) *n.* condition in which the body cells fail either to receive or to use a sufficient amount of oxygen.

An·schluss (än′shloos) *n.* political and economic union of two countries, esp. that of Germany and Austria in 1938. [German *Anschluss* union.]

An·selm, Saint (an′selm) 1033–1109, Italian-born theologian and archbishop of Canterbury.

an·ser·ine (an′sə rīn′, -sər in) *adj.* of, resembling, or related to a goose or geese. [Latin *ānserīnus,* from *ānser* goose.]

an·swer (an′sər) *n.* **1.** something spoken or written as a reply: *Ask a silly question and you get a silly answer. The editorial was in answer to the reader's angry letter.* **2.** something done in reply or return: *Further bombing was the enemy's answer to our peace offerings.* **3.a.** solution

to a mathematical problem: *To find the answer, multiply by two.* **b.** any solution or explanation: *seeking the answer to the puzzle of history.* **4.** *Law.* statement of a defendant in response to the charges made by a plaintiff. —*v.t.* **1.** to speak or write in reply to: *She answered my letter. Can you answer the question?* **2.** to act in response to: *She ran to answer the phone.* **3.** to be suitable or sufficient for; serve: *This money should answer your needs.* **4.** to conform or correspond to: *He answers the description.* —*v.i.* **1.** to speak or write in reply: *Answer in a loud and clear voice.* **2.** to act in response; respond: *He answered with a wink. The dog answered to his master's nudge.* **3.** to be responsible or accountable (with *for*). **4.** to correspond or conform (with *to*): *You answer to his description.* **5.** to make amends; atone (with *for*): *He has answered for his crimes.* **6.** to be sufficient or satisfactory; serve. **7. to answer back.** *Informal.* to reply impertinently or rudely; talk back. [Old English *andswaru* sworn statement in reply (to an accusation), from *and*- in reply + *swerian* to swear.]

Syn. *n.* **1. Answer, reply, response** refer to something said or written in reaction to something asked or requested. **Answer** is the most general term and indicates a reaction directly corresponding to what induced it: *Would you repeat your answer, please.* **Reply** has a tone of formality and deliberation: *We have not received a reply to our inquiry.* **Response** suggests a predictable or expected answer and stresses the manner of answering rather than what is said: *"Sorry, can't help you" was Henry's response to the panhandler.*

an·swer·a·ble (an′sər ə bəl) *adj.* **1.** accountable; responsible. **2.** capable of being answered.

ant (ant) *n.* any of numerous social insects of the family Formicidae, found in all temperate and tropical regions. They live in colonies which may contain as few as several dozen or as many as 1.5 million individuals. [Old English *ǣmet(t)e.*]

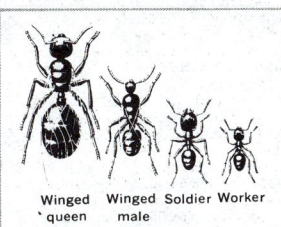

Winged Winged Soldier Worker
queen male

Types of ants

ant-, form of **anti-** before vowels and *h*, as in *ant- acid.*

-ant *suffix* **1.** (used to form adjectives) doing or being (what is indicated by the stem): *defiant, radiant.* **2.** (used to form nouns) person or thing that does (what is indicated by the stem): *servant, lubricant.* [French *-ant,* from Latin *-āns* (stem *-ant-*), present participial ending used as a suffix.]

ant., antonym.

ant·ac·id (ant′as′id) *n.* chemical substance that neutralizes acids, esp. a remedy for stomach acidity. —*adj.* neutralizing acids; counteracting acidity.

An·tae·us (an tē′əs) *n. Greek Mythology.* giant who was invincible as long as he was touching the earth. He was finally killed by Hercules who crushed him while holding him in the air.

an·tag·o·nism (an tag′ə niz′əm) *n.* active opposition, antipathy, or enmity; hostility: *class antagonisms that ended in civil war. Mark felt great antagonism toward his rival.* —**Syn.** see **hostility.**

an·tag·o·nist (an tag′ə nist) *n.* **1.** one who opposes, fights, or competes with another; adversary. **2.** muscle that acts in opposition to another. —**Syn. 1.** see **opponent.**

an·tag·o·nis·tic (an tag′ə nis′tik) *adj.* acting or being in opposition; contending; hostile. —**an·tag′o·nis′ti·cal·ly,** *adv.*

an·tag·o·nize (an tag′ə nīz′) -**nized, -niz·ing.** *v.t.* to provoke dislike or hostility; make unfriendly: *His bad manners soon antagonized everyone present.* [Greek *antagōnizesthai* to struggle against.] —**an·tag′o·niz′er,** *n.*

An·ta·kya (än′tä kyä′) *n.* city in the southernmost part of central Turkey, on the site of ancient Antioch. Pop. (1965), 57,600.

ant·arc·tic (ant ärk′tik, -är′tik) *adj.* of or relating to the South Pole or to the south polar regions. —*n.* **the Antarctic.** Antarctica. [Latin *antarcticus* southern, from Greek *antarktikos* opposite to the north. See ANTI-, ARCTIC.]

Ant·arc·ti·ca (ant ärk′ti kə, -är′ti-) *n.* ice-covered region surrounding the South Pole and lying mainly within the Antarctic Circle. Area, (approx.) 5,500,000 sq. mi. Also, **the Antarctic, Antarctic Continent.**

Antarctic Circle *also,* **antarctic circle.** imaginary line around the earth at 66°33′ south latitude, or about 1600 miles from the South Pole.

Antarctic Ocean, body of water surrounding Antarctica, consisting of the southernmost parts of the Atlantic, Pacific, and Indian oceans.

An·tar·es (an tār′ēz) *n.* giant red star, one of the brightest and largest in the sky, and the brightest in the constellation Scorpio.

ant bear, gray anteater, *Myrmecophaga tridactyla,* of tropical Central and South America. It is the largest of the anteaters. Length: to 8 feet, including the tail.

an·te (an′tē) *n.* **1.** *Poker.* stake that each player must put up before receiving a hand or drawing new cards. **2.** *Slang.* any amount required as a share. —*v.t., v.i.,* **-ted** or **-teed, te·ing. 1.** *Poker.* to put up (one's ante). **2.** *Slang.* to pay one's share (often with *up*). [Latin *ante* before.]

Ant bear

ante- *prefix* **1.** previous in time; prior to: *antebellum, antenatal.* **2.** before in position; in front of: *antepenult, antechamber.* [Latin *ante* before.]

ant·eat·er (ant′ē′tər) *n.* **1.** any of various toothless mammals, family Myrmecophagidae, of tropical Central and South America, that feed on ants and termites. They have long narrow heads, long, sticky tongues, and powerful front claws. **2.** any of various other animals that feed on ants, as the aardvark, pangolin, and echidna.

an·te·bel·lum (an′tē bel′əm) *adj.* before the war, esp. before the Civil War: *the antebellum South.* [Latin *ante bellum* before the war.]

an·te·ced·ence (an′tə sēd′əns) *n.* **1.** act of going before or state of being before; precedence. **2.** apparent retrograde motion of a planet.

an·te·ced·ent (an′tə sēd′ənt) *n.* **1.** thing, event, or circumstance that goes before: *the antecedents of the war.* **2.** substantive to which a pronoun refers. In the sentence *He found a dime, but lost it later,* the noun *dime* is the antecedent of the pronoun *it.* **3. antecedents.** previous events or influences in a person's life; ancestry. **4.** first term of a mathematical ratio; first or third term of a mathematical proportion. —*adj.* going or being before; preceding; prior: *the conditions antecedent to the Industrial Revolution.* [Latin *antecēdēns,* present participle of *antecēdere* to go before.] —**an′te·ced′ent·ly,** *adv.* —**Syn.** *n.* **1.** see **cause.**

an·te·cham·ber (an′tē chām′bər) *n.* anteroom.

an·te·date (an′ti dāt′) -**dat·ed, -dat·ing.** *v.t.* **1.** to be or occur earlier than; precede in time. **2.** to give (something) a date earlier than the correct one: *to antedate a check.*

an·te·di·lu·vi·an (an′tē di loo′vē ən) *adj.* **1.** of or relating to the period before the Flood. **2.** very old or old-fashioned. —*n.* **1.** one who lived before the Flood. **2.** very old or old-fashioned person. [ANTE- + Latin *dīluvium* flood.]

an·te·lope (ant′əl ōp′) *pl.,* **-lope** or **-lopes.** *n.* **1.** any of various cud-chewing mammals, family Bovidae, closely related to goats, having unbranched horns and cloven hoofs. Antelopes are native to Africa and southern Asia. Height: 10 inches to 6 feet at the shoulder. **2.** pronghorn. [Old French *antelop* savage mythical beast with sawlike horns; of uncertain origin.]

Antelope

an·te me·rid·i·em (an′tē mə rid′ē əm) between midnight and noon. Abbreviation, A.M. [Latin *ante* before + *merīdiēs* noon.]

an·te·na·tal (an′tē nāt′əl) *adj.* prenatal.

an·ten·na (an ten′ə) *pl.,* **-ten·nas** (def. 1) or **-ten·nae** (-ten′ē) (def. 2). *n.* **1.** metal structure, wire, or set of wires used to receive or transmit electromagnetic waves, as in television or radio; aerial. **2.** one of two or four jointed sense organs, or feelers, on the heads of centipedes, millipedes, insects, crustaceans, and some other arthropods. [Medieval Latin *antenna* horn (of an insect), from Latin *antenna* yard for a sail.]

an·te·pe·nult (an′tē pē′nult, -pə nult′) *n.* syllable preceding the last but one in a word. In *port·fo·li·o,* the syllable *fo* is the antepenult.

an·te·pe·nul·ti·mate (an′tē pi nul′tə mit) *adj.* second from the last. —*n.* antepenult.

an·te·ri·or (an tēr′ē ər) *adj.* **1.** at or toward the front or head; fore: *the anterior lobe of the brain.* Opposed to **posterior. 2.** preceding in time; prior; earlier. [Latin *anterior* former, comparative of *ante* before.]

an·te·room (an′tē rōōm′, -room′) *n.* room serving as a waiting room or entranceway to a larger or main room.

an·them (an′thəm) *n.* **1.** song of gladness, praise, devotion, or patriotism: *heavenly anthems, the national anthem.* **2.** piece of sacred choral music with words usually taken from a Biblical passage. [Old English *antefn* antiphon, from Late Latin *antiphōna,* going back to Greek *antiphōnos* responsive. Doublet of ANTIPHON.]

an·ther (an′thər) *n.* in a flower, the pollen-bearing part of the stamen. See **flower** for illustration. [Modern Latin *anthēra,* from Latin *anthēra* medicine composed of flowers, going back to Greek *anthēros* flowery.]

an·ther·id·i·um (an′thə rid′ē əm) *pl.,* **-i·a** (-ē ə). *n.* male sex organ

of nonflowering plants, such as mosses and ferns. [Modern Latin *antheridium*, diminutive of *anthera*. See ANTHER.]

ant hill, mound of dirt or other material heaped up by ants around the entrance to their underground nest.

an·thol·o·gist (an thol′ə jist) *n.* compiler of an anthology.

an·thol·o·gize (an thol′ə jīz′) -gized, -giz·ing. *v.i.* to compile an anthology. —*v.t.* to put in an anthology.

an·thol·o·gy (an thol′ə jē) *pl.,* -gies. *n.* 1. collection of varied written works or passages within a single book or set: *an anthology of French poetry, a folksong anthology.* 2. similar collection of recorded materials: *an anthology of baroque concertos.* [Greek *anthologia* a gathering of flowers, from *anthos* flower + *legein* to gather, speak.]

An·tho·ny, Susan B. (an′thə nē) 1820–1906, U.S. reformer and leader of the women's suffrage movement.

An·tho·ny of Egypt, Saint (an′thə nē, an′tə-) c.251–c.356, founder of Christian monasticism.

An·tho·ny of Padua, Saint (an′thə nē, an′tə-) 1195–1231, Franciscan preacher and teacher of theology.

an·tho·zo·an (an′thə zō′ən) *n.* any polyp of the class Anthozoa, including sea anemones and corals. They have both bilateral and radial symmetry and have no free-swimming jellyfish stage. [Greek *anthos* flower + *zōia* animals.]

an·thra·cene (an′thrə sēn′) *n.* crystalline hydrocarbon obtained from coal tar. Formula: $C_{14}H_{10}$ [Greek *anthrax* coal + -ENE.]

an·thra·cite (an′thrə sīt′) *n.* lustrous black coal with a high carbon content that burns with a low smokeless flame. Also, **hard coal.** [Greek *anthrakītis* a type of coal, from *anthrax* coal.]

an·thrax (an′thraks) *n.* infectious disease of animals, esp. hoofed animals, that may be transmitted to man. It is caused by a spore-forming bacterium, *Bacillus anthracis,* which produces inflamed pustules in man and blood poisoning in animals. [Late Latin *anthrax* carbuncle, from Greek *anthrax* coal, carbuncle.]

anthropo- *combining form* man; human being: *anthropomorphic, anthropoid.* [Greek *anthrōpos* man.]

an·thro·poid (an′thrə poid′) *adj.* 1. (of certain apes) resembling man; manlike. 2. resembling an ape. —*n.* ape (*def.*1). [Greek *anthrōpoeidēs* of human form, from *anthrōpos* man.]

an·thro·pol·o·gy (an′thrə pol′ə jē) *n.* science of the physical, cultural, and social development of man, his evolution, behavior, and geographic distribution from prehistoric times to the present. [ANTHROPO- + -LOGY.] —**an·thro·po·log·i·cal** (an′thrə pə loj′i kəl); *also,* **an′thro·po·log′ic,** *adj.* —**an′thro·po·log′i·cal·ly,** *adv.* —**an′·thro·pol′o·gist,** *n.*

an·thro·pom·e·try (an′thrə pom′ə trē) *n.* science of the measurement of the dimensions and proportions of the human body, esp. as a basis for comparing races or individuals. —**an·thro·po·met·ric** (an′thrə pə met′rik); *also,* **an′thro·po·met′ri·cal,** *adj.*

an·thro·po·mor·phic (an′thrə pə môr′fik) *adj.* of or characterized by anthropomorphism: *The Greeks worshiped anthropomorphic gods.* [Greek *anthrōpomorphos* of human form + -IC.]

an·thro·po·mor·phism (an′thrə pə môr′fiz′əm) *n.* attributing of human form or characteristics to gods, animals, or inanimate objects.

an·thro·po·mor·phous (an′thrə pə môr′fəs) *adj.* having or resembling human form.

an·ti (an′tī, an′tē) *pl.,* -tis. *n. Informal.* person opposed to something, as a policy, action, or political party. [From ANTI-.]

anti- *prefix* 1. opposed to; against: *antitrust, anti-Semitism.* 2. expressing the opposite or reverse of: *anticlimactic.* 3. operating against; counteracting: *antifreeze, antiaircraft.* 4. rival; false: *antipope, antichrist.* 5. *Medicine.* preventing, curing, or neutralizing: *antipyretic, antitoxin.* [Greek *anti* opposite, against.]

an·ti·air·craft (an′tē ār′kraft′ an′tī-) *adj.* for use against aircraft in flight: *antiaircraft guns.*

an·ti·bi·ot·ic (an′tē bī ot′ik, -bē-, an′tī-) *n.* any of a group of substances, as penicillin or streptomycin, produced by molds, bacteria, and other microorganisms and used in medicine to kill or slow the growth of disease-causing bacteria, viruses, or fungi. —*adj.* of or relating to antibiotics.

an·ti·bod·y (an′ti bod′ē, an′tē-) *pl.,* -bod·ies. *n.* any of various proteins in the blood serum produced by the body as a normal function, or induced by exposure to an antigen, that neutralize, destroy, or otherwise counteract specific disease-producing antigens.

an·tic (an′tik) *n.* 1. silly or comical act or action; caper; prank: *antics of a clown, antics of a puppy.* 2. *Archaic.* clown; buffoon. —*adj.* grotesque; bizarre; ludicrous: *To put an antic disposition on* (Shakespeare, *Hamlet*.) [Italian *antica* old, grotesque, from Latin *antīquus* old. Doublet of ANTIQUE.] —**Syn.** *n.* 1. see **prank**[1].

an·ti·christ (an′ti krīst′) *n.* 1. *also,* **An·ti·christ.** one who denies or opposes Christ or Christianity. 2. **Antichrist.** the antagonist of Christ, expected to fill the world with wickedness until he is vanquished by Christ on Judgment Day. 3. one who falsely claims to be Christ.

an·tic·i·pate (an tis′ə pāt′) -pat·ed, pat·ing. *v.t.* 1. to look forward to; expect: *I do not anticipate any trouble. I anticipate his arrival at four o'clock.* 2. to foresee and deal with in advance: *We anticipate your every desire. He anticipated my questions.* 3. to act so as to prevent or counter; forestall: *to anticipate the enemy's tactics.* 4. to take into consideration or deal with in advance: *Your question anticipates the material to be covered later.* 5. to be before (another) in doing something; precede: *The Vikings are reputed to have anticipated Columbus in the discovery of America.* 6. to use or expend (funds) in advance of actual possession. [Latin *anticipātus,* past participle of *anticipāre* to take before.] —**an·tic′i·pa′tor,** *n.* —**Syn.** 1. see **expect**.

an·tic·i·pa·tion (an tis′ə pā′shən) *n.* 1. act of anticipating; being anticipated. 2. feeling of excited expectation: *They awaited his arrival with eager anticipation.*

an·tic·i·pa·tive (an tis′ə pā′tiv) *adj.* characterized by, resulting from, or exhibiting anticipation.

an·tic·i·pa·to·ry (an tis′ə pə tôr′ē) *adj.* anticipative: *anticipatory dread.* —**an·tic′i·pa·to′ri·ly,** *adv.*

an·ti·cler·i·cal (an′tē kler′i kəl, an′tī-) *adj.* opposed to the influence and activities of the church or clergy. —**an′ti·cler′i·cal·ism, an′ti·cler′i·cal·ist,** *n.*

an·ti·cli·mac·tic (an′ti klī mak′tic) *adj.* of, having, or like an anticlimax. —**an′ti·cli·mac′ti·cal·ly,** *adv.*

an·ti·cli·max (an′ti klī′maks) *n.* 1. unexpected, often ludicrous change from the important or dignified to the trivial or absurd in speech and writing, for example: *My car was stolen, my house burned down, and I forgot to tie my shoes.* 2. anything that is much less important or interesting than what has preceded it; letdown after a high point: *The film's last scene was an anticlimax.*

an·ti·cli·nal (an′ti klīn′əl) *adj.* 1. inclining in opposite directions. 2. of, relating to, or forming an anticline.

an·ti·cline (an′ti klīn′) *n.* archlike fold of stratified rock having the layers sloping downward from the crest in opposite directions. Opposed to **syncline.** [ANTI- + Greek *klīnein* to lean; influenced in form by INCLINE.]

an·ti·cy·clone (an′ti sī′klōn) *n.* atmospheric condition consisting of a mass of air currents rotating about a center of high barometric pressure; high pressure area. —**an·ti·cy·clon·ic** (an′tē sī klon′ik), *adj.*

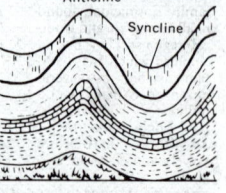
Anticline
Cross section of stratified rock

an·ti·do·tal (an′ti dōt′əl) *adj.* of, like, or acting as an antidote.

an·ti·dote (an′ti dōt′) *n.* 1. medicine or other remedy to counteract the effects of a poison. 2. any counteracting remedy: *Work is an antidote to boredom.* [Latin *antidotum,* from Greek *antidoton* literally, (thing) given against.]

An·tie·tam (an tē′təm) *n.* creek in northwestern Maryland, site of one of the bloodiest battles of the Civil War, in 1862.

An·ti·fed·er·al·ist (an′tē fed′ər ə list, an′tī-) *n.* member of the political party that opposed the adoption and ratification of the U.S. Constitution and later opposed the creation of a strong central government. —**An′ti·fed′er·al,** *adj.* —**An′ti·fed′er·al·ism,** *n.*

an·ti·freeze (an′ti frēz′, an′tē-) *n.* substance added to a liquid to prevent it from freezing at given temperatures by lowering its freezing point.

an·ti·gen (an′tə jən) *n.* substance usually harmful to the body, such as a toxin or bacterium, that stimulates the body to produce antibodies. [ANTI- + -GEN.] —**an·ti·gen·ic** (an′ti jen′ik), *adj.*

An·tig·o·ne (an tig′ə nē) *n. Greek Legend.* the daughter of Oedipus who was condemned to death for giving her brother a proper burial against the command of her uncle Creon.

An·ti·gua (an tē′gə, -gwə) *n.* one of the Leeward Islands, in the West Indies. Capital, St. John's. Area, 108 sq. mi. Pop. (est. 1967) 62,000.

an·ti·his·ta·mine (an′ti his′tə mēn, -min) *n.* any of several drugs that neutralize the effect of histamine in the body and are used chiefly in the treatment of allergic reactions and colds.

an·ti·knock (an′tē nok′, an′tī-) *n.* chemical substance added to gasoline to reduce knocking in the engine.

An·til·les (an til′ēz) *n.,pl.* islands of the West Indies excluding the Bahamas, divided into the Greater Antilles and the Lesser Antilles.

an·ti·log·a·rithm (an′ti lô′gə rith′əm, -log′ə-) *n.* number corresponding to a given logarithm.

an·ti·ma·cas·sar (an′ti mə kas′ər) *n.* small ornamental covering put over the back of a chair, originally to prevent soiling. [ANTI- + earlier *macassar* nineteenth-century hair oil from *Macassar,* a district of Celebes.]

at; āpe; cär; end; mē; it; īce; hot; ōld; fôrk; wood; fōōl; oil; out; up; ūse; turn; sing; thin; this; zh in treasure; ə in ago, taken, pencil, lemon, circus.

an·ti·mat·ter (an′tē mat′ər, an′tī-) *n.* *Physics.* theoretical form of matter consisting of antiparticles.

an·ti·mis·sile (an′tē mis′əl, an′tī-) *adj.* designed or used for defense against ballistic and guided missiles.

an·ti·mo·ny (an′ti mō′nē) *n.* crystalline metallic element with a silver or bluish-white luster, used chiefly as an alloying element to increase the hardness and brittleness of other metals. Also, **stib′i·um.** Symbol: Sb See **element** for table. [Medieval Latin *antimonium;* of uncertain origin.]

an·ti·neu·tri·no (an′tē nōō trē′nō, -nū-, an′tī-) *pl.* **-nos.** *n.* antiparticle of the neutrino.

an·ti·neu·tron (an′tē nōō′tron, -nū′-, an′tī-) *n.* antiparticle of the neutron.

an·ti·node (an′ti nōd′) *n.* *Physics.* any point of a wave where the amplitude is at maximum.

An·ti·och (an′tē ok′) *n.* capital of ancient Syria. It is the site of present-day Antakya, Turkey.

an·ti·par·ti·cle (an′tē pär′ti kəl, an′tī-) *n.* any of a group of subatomic particles, each of which corresponds to another subatomic particle in mass and magnitude of spin but is its opposite in direction of spin and, in the case of charged particles, in electric charge. When a particle and its antiparticle collide, they annihilate each other and energy appears in their place. See **subatomic particle** for table.

an·ti·pas·to (an′ti päs′tō, än′tē-) *pl.* **-tos** or **-ti** (-tē). *n.* Italian dish served as an appetizer or first course consisting of small portions of various foods. [Italian *antipasto,* going back to Latin *ante* before + *pastus* food.]

an·ti·pa·thet·ic (an′ti pə thet′ik, an tip′ə-) *adj.* having an aversion; opposed in nature or disposition: *a strange group composed of people antipathetic to each other.* Also, **an′ti·pa·thet′i·cal.** —**an′ti·pa·thet′·i·cal·ly,** *adv.*

an·tip·a·thy (an tip′ə thē) *pl.* **-thies.** *n.* feeling of strong dislike; distaste; aversion. [Latin *antipathīa,* from Greek *antipatheia* literally, a feeling against.]

an·ti·phon (an′tə fon′) *n.* **1.** verse of a psalm, hymn, or prayer sung or chanted in alternation, or in response to one another. **2.** any composition consisting of passages for responsive singing or chanting. [Late Latin *antiphōna* sacred song sung responsively, going back to Greek *antiphōnos* responsive. Doublet of ANTHEM.]

an·tiph·o·nal (an tif′ə nəl) *adj.* **1.** book of antiphons. Also, **an·tiph·o·nar·y** (an tif′ə ner′ē). —*adj.* of or like an antiphon or antiphony; responsive. —**an·tiph′o·nal·ly,** *adv.*

an·tiph·o·ny (an tif′ə nē) *pl.* **-nies.** *n.* **1.** singing or playing of music by alternate groups of performers. **2.** music so performed; antiphon.

an·tip·o·dal (an tip′əd əl) *adj.* **1.** of or relating to antipodes; situated on opposite sides of the earth. **2.** diametrically opposed or opposite: *antipodal points of view.*

an·ti·pode (an′tə pōd′) *n.* exact or direct opposite. [From ANTIPODES.]

an·tip·o·des (an tip′ə dēz) *n.,pl.* **1.** two places on the earth's surface diametrically opposite one another. **2.** two opposite or contrary things: *Love and hate are antipodes.* [Latin *antipodēs* geographic antipodes, from Greek *antipodes* people having their feet down.] —**an·tip′o·de′an,** *adj.*

an·ti·pope (an′ti pōp′) *n.* one elected as or claiming to be pope in opposition to a pope canonically chosen.

an·ti·pro·ton (an′tē prō′ton, an′tī-) *n.* antiparticle of the proton.

an·ti·py·ret·ic (an′tē pī ret′ik, an′tī-) *adj.* reducing or preventing fever. —*n.* drug or other agent for reducing or preventing fever.

an·ti·quar·i·an (an′tə kwâr′ē ən) *adj.* of or relating to antiquities. —*n.* antiquary.

an·ti·quar·y (an′tə kwer′ē) *pl.* **-quar·ies.** *n.* one who collects, studies, or deals in antiquities. [Latin *antīquārius,* from *antīquus* old.]

an·ti·quate (an′tə kwāt′) -quat·ed, -quat·ing. *v.t.* to cause to become old-fashioned; make obsolete. [Latin *antīquātus,* past participle of *antīquāre* to make old.]

an·ti·quat·ed (an′tə kwā′tid) *adj.* old-fashioned; out-of-date; obsolete: *antiquated ideas, an antiquated style of dress.*

an·tique (an tēk′) *adj.* **1.** of, belonging to, or in the style of a former period: *antique furniture, an antique watch.* **2.** of, belonging to, or in the style of classical antiquity; of ancient Greece or Rome. **3.** *Archaic.* old-fashioned; antiquated: *an antique custom.* —*n.* **1.** object of an earlier period that is valued for its age, scarcity, craftsmanship, or historical significance. ▲ In common usage, an antique is an object made in an earlier time. Strictly, an antique is an article at least a hundred years old or, in the United States, made before 1830. **2.** *Informal.* any object of great age; relic: *His jalopy is an antique.* **3.** **the antique.** style of ancient Greco-Roman art. **4.** *Printing.* style of type in which all lines are of equal thickness. —*v.t.,* **an·tiqued,** **an·ti·quing.** to make (something) appear old: *to antique a chair.* [Latin *antīquus* old. Doublet of ANTIC.] —**an·tique′ly,** *adv.* —**an·tique′ness,** *n.*

an·tiq·ui·ty (an tik′wə tē) *pl.,* **-ties.** *n.* **1.** early ages of history, esp. the period preceding the Middle Ages; ancient times: *Archaeologists study ruins surviving from antiquity to learn about ancient civilizations.* **2.** people and cultures of ancient times collectively: *the heritage left to us by antiquity.* **3.** quality of being ancient; great age: *a ring valued for its antiquity.* **4.** **antiquities.** objects belonging to or remaining from ancient times; ancient relics.

an·ti·ra·chit·ic (an′tē rə kit′ik, an′tī-) *adj.* relieving or curing rickets. —*n.* remedy for rickets.

an·ti·scor·bu·tic (an′tē skôr bū′tik, an′tī-) *adj.* relieving or curing scurvy. —*n.* remedy for scurvy.

an·ti·Sem·i·tism (an′tē sem′ə tiz′əm, an′tī-) *n.* prejudice or discrimination against, or persecution of, Jews. —**an·ti·Sem·ite** (an′tē sem′īt, an′tī-), *n.* —**an·ti·Se·mit·ic** (an′tē sə mit′ik, an′tī-), *adj.* —**an′ti·Se·mit′i·cal·ly,** *adv.*

an·ti·sep·sis (an′ti sep′sis) *n.* antiseptic condition or methods.

an·ti·sep·tic (an′ti sep′tik) *adj.* **1.** preventing infection, putrefaction, or decay; inhibiting the growth of microorganisms: *antiseptic solutions and other germicides.* **2.** like or caused by an antiseptic: *an antiseptic odor.* **3.** free from harmful bacteria or other microorganisms; sterile: *an antiseptic wound.* **4.** lacking warmth or interest; coldly impersonal: *an antiseptic smile.* —*n.* substance that inhibits the growth of harmful bacteria and other microorganisms, esp. in or on living tissue. [ANTI- + SEPTIC.] —**an′ti·sep′ti·cal·ly,** *adv.*

an·ti·so·cial (an′tē sō′shəl, an′tī-) *adj.* **1.** averse to companionship or to the society of others; unsociable. **2.** opposed to the general good or basic principles of society: *crimes and other antisocial acts.*

an·ti·spas·mod·ic (an′tē spaz mod′ik, an′tī-) *adj.* checking or relieving spasms. —*n.* drug or other agent that checks or relieves spasms.

an·tis·tro·phe (an tis′trə fē) *n.* **1.** part of an ancient Greek choral ode sung by a play's chorus in answer to the preceding strophe. **2.** stanza in a Pindaric ode which follows a strophe. It usually has the same metrical form as the strophe. [Latin *antistrophē,* from Greek *antistrophē* literally, a turning about.]

an·ti·tank (an′tē tangk′, an′tī-) *adj.* designed for or used against tanks or other armored vehicles.

an·tith·e·sis (an tith′ə sis) *pl.,* **-ses** (-sēz′). *n.* **1.** exact opposite: *Hope is the antithesis of despair.* **2.** opposition; contrast: *the antithesis of bravery and cowardice.* **3.** *Rhetoric.* **a.** opposition or contrast of ideas, esp. by means of parallel arrangements of words, clauses, or sentences, for example: *Ask not what your country can do for you—ask what you can do for your country* (John F. Kennedy, 1961). **b.** second part of such an expression. [Greek *antithesis* opposition; literally, a setting against.]

an·ti·thet·i·cal (an′ti thet′i kəl) *adj.* **1.** directly opposed; strongly contrasted: *This action is antithetical to my nature.* **2.** of, characterized by, or containing antithesis: *an antithetical construction.* Also, **an′ti·thet′ic.** —**an′ti·thet′i·cal·ly,** *adv.*

an·ti·tox·ic (an′ti tok′sik, an′tē-) *adj.* **1.** counteracting the effects of toxins. **2.** of, relating to, or serving as an antitoxin.

an·ti·tox·in (an′ti tok′sin, an′tē-) *n.* **1.** antibody formed in the body that provides protection against a specific poison released by invading bacteria. **2.** serum containing such an antibody, obtained from the blood of horses or other animals which have been injected with a toxin.

an·ti·trades (an′ti trādz′) *n.,pl.* winds that blow above, and in a direction opposite to, the trade winds.

an·ti·trust (an′tē trust′, an′tī-) *adj.* relating to the regulation of or opposition to monopolies, trusts, or other business combinations or practices that cause unlawful restraint of trade: *antitrust laws.*

ant·ler (ant′lər) *n.* **1.** one of the branched horns of various members of the deer family. Antlers are shed each year and replaced by new ones. **2.** any of the branches of such a horn. [Old French *antoillier,* going back to Latin *ante* before + *oculus* eye.] —**ant′lered,** *adj.*

ant lion, any of a group of insects, family Myrmeleontidae, whose larva, commonly called a *doodlebug,* feeds on ants and other wingless insects, esp. by digging a pit into which the prey falls.

An·to·ni·nus Pi·us (an′tə nī′nəs pī′əs) A.D. 86–161, Roman emperor from 138 to 161.

An·to·ny, Mark (an′tə nē) c.83–30 B.C., Roman general and political leader, friend of Caesar and lover of Cleopatra.

an·to·nym (an′tə nim′) *n.* word having a meaning opposite of another word. *Young* is an antonym of *old.* Opposed to **synonym.** [Greek *antōnymía* interchange of names.]

Ant·werp (ant′wurp) *n.* port city in northern Belgium, the largest city in the country. Pop. (1967), 289,000.

A·nu·bis (ə nōō′bis, ə nū′-) *n.* *Egyptian Mythology.* the son of Osiris and a god of the underworld, represented as a man with the head of a jackal. His Greek counterpart is Hermes.

A number 1, A-1.

a·nus (ā′nəs) *pl.,* **a·nus·es.** *n.* opening at the lower end of the alimentary canal, through which solid waste products are eliminated from the body. [Latin *ānus.*]

---

at; āpe; cär; end; mē; it; īce; hot; ōld; fôrk; wood; fōōl; oil; out; up; ūse; turn; sing; thin; this; zh in treasure; ə in ago, taken, pencil, lemon, circus.

an·vil (an′vəl) *n.* **1.** iron or steel block on which heat-softened metals are hammered into desired shapes. **2.** one of the three small bones of the middle ear, lying between the hammer and the stirrup and shaped like an anvil; incus. See **ear** for illustration. [Old English *anfilte* block for shaping metals.]

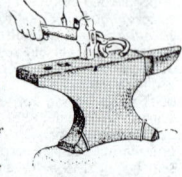

Anvil *(def. 1)*

anx·i·e·ty (ang zī′ə tē) *pl.* **-ties.** *n.* **1.** feeling of fearful uneasiness or apprehension, as over some impending or anticipated event; worry: *Your anxiety about your health is unfounded.* **2.** something that causes this feeling: *Lack of money is one of his chief anxieties.* **3.** strained or solicitous desire; eagerness: *Her anxiety to succeed hindered her performance.* **4.** *Psychiatry.* tense emotional state characterized by generalized or exaggerated apprehension and usually rooted in unconscious causes.
Syn. 1. Anxiety, worry, apprehension indicate a state of troubled concern. **Anxiety** implies nervous activity resulting from such concern: *The mother's anxiety increased as the hours passed.* **Worry** suggests fear that something has gone or will go wrong: *His worry about his ability is not warranted.* **Apprehension** suggests a continuing state of fear about what will happen: *It was still with considerable apprehension that he boarded airplanes.*

anx·ious (angk′shəs, ang′-) *adj.* **1.** having anxiety or anxieties; uneasy; apprehensive: *I'm anxious about our safety on the trip.* **2.** exhibiting, causing, or resulting from anxiety: *an anxious matter, anxious inquiries about her health.* **3.** eagerly or earnestly desiring: *anxious to please.* [Latin *anxius* distressed.] —**anx′ious·ly,** *adv.* —**anx′ious·ness,** *n.* —**Syn. 3.** see **eager.**

an·y (en′ē) *adj.* **1.** one, no matter which; some, whatever quality or kind: *Any information will help. Take any seat.* **2.** some, in whatever quantity or number: *Have you any apples?* **3.** every: *Any child can do it.* **4.** at all: *Has a coward any courage? I haven't any change.* —*pron.* any one or ones; any quantity or number: *We haven't any left. He scored better than any of the others.* —*adv.* to any extent or degree: *Stop before you go any farther.* [Old English *ænig* no matter which, at all.]

an·y·bod·y (en′ē bod′ē, -bud′ə) *pl.* **-bod·ies.** *pron.* any person whatever; anyone: *Has anybody seen him?* —*n.* person of importance: *Everybody who is anybody was there.*

an·y·how (en′ē hou′) *adv.* **1.** in any case; at any rate: *Anyhow, that is beside the point.* **2.** *Archaic.* in any way whatever.

an·y·one (en′ē wun′, -wən) *pron.* any person whatever; anybody.

an·y·place (en′ē plās′) *adv. Informal.* anywhere.

an·y·thing (en′ē thing′) *pron.* **1.** any thing whatever: *I'll do anything you say.* **2. anything but.** by no means; not at all: *He's anything but polite.* —*n.* thing of any sort. —*adv.* to any extent; at all. ▲ now used only in the expression *anything like,* as in: *Is this glove anything like the one you lost?*

an·y·way (en′ē wā′) *adv.* **1.** in any case; at any rate; nevertheless: *Anyway, I am glad it happened.* **2.** in any manner or way: *anyway you look at it.* ▲ now usually written as two separate words, as in *I'll accept it any way it's done.*

an·y·where (en′ē hwâr′, -wâr′) *adv.* **1.** in, at, or to any place: *Just put it down anywhere.* **2.** *Informal.* to any extent; at all: *Did you come anywhere near the right answer?* **3. to get** (or **go**) **anywhere.** to achieve success: *You'll never get anywhere with that attitude.*

an·y·wise (en′ē wīz′) *adv.* in any way; to any degree; at all.

A-OK (ā′ō kā′) *adj., adv., interj. also,* **A-o·kay.** *Informal.* excellent; perfect. [Attributed to Alan B. Shepard, Jr., first American astronaut in space.]

A-one (ā′wun′) A-1.

a·o·rist (ā′ər ist) *n.* tense of Greek verbs expressing action, usually past, without reference to its duration or completion. [Greek *aoristos* indefinite.]

a·or·ta (ā ôr′tə) *pl.* **-tas** or **-tae** (-tē). *n.* main artery or trunk of the arterial system that carries the blood from the left ventricle of the heart to all parts of the body except the lungs. See **heart** for illustration. [Modern Latin *aorta,* from Greek *aortē.*] —**a·or′tic, a·or′tic,** *adj.*

Aoudad

aou·dad (ou′dad) *n.* wild sheep, *Ammotragus lervia,* of northern Africa, which has a tawny coat, fringes of long hair on its neck, forelegs, and chest, and long, curving horns. Height: 40 inches at the shoulder. Also, **Barbary sheep.** [French *aoudad,* from Berber *audad.*]

ap-¹, form of **ad-** before *p,* as in *approbation.*

ap-², form of **apo-** before vowels and *h,* as in *aphorism.*

AP, Associated Press, U.S.-based cooperative agency that gathers and distributes news stories and pictures throughout the world.

a·pace (ə pās′) *adv. Archaic.* swiftly; quickly; rapidly: *Great weeds do grow apace* (Shakespeare, *Richard III*). [Old French *à pas* at a (fast) pace, going back to Latin *ad* to, at + *passus* step, pace.]

a·pache (ə päsh′, ə pash′) *n.* ruffian, gangster, or thug of Paris. [French *apache,* from *Apache* (in the sense of a fierce, ruthless fighter).]

A·pach·e (ə pach′ē) *pl.* **A·pach·es** or **A·pach·e,** *n.* **1.** member of a group of Indian tribes of Athapascan linguistic stock, inhabiting the southwestern United States. **2.** any of the Athapascan languages spoken by these people. [Spanish *apache* Apache Indian, from Zuñi *ápachu* enemy.]

ap·a·nage (ap′ə nij) appanage.

a·part (ə pärt′) *adv.* **1.** away from one another; separated in space or time: *Their houses are two miles apart. They left three hours apart.* **2.** into two or more parts; in or to pieces: *He tore the book apart.* **3.** at a distance; aside: *He sat apart from the others.* **4.** as a separate consideration; independently: *Viewed apart, the matter becomes clearer.* **5. apart from.** other than; besides. **6. to take apart. a.** to separate into component parts; disassemble: *He took the engine apart.* **b.** to criticize or upbraid severely: *He really took her apart for that mistake.* **7. to tell apart.** to distinguish between: *He couldn't tell the triplets apart.* —*adj.* having separate or unique features or characteristics; distinct: *a breed apart.* [French *à part* aside, singly, from *à* to (from Latin *ad* to) + *part* part, from Latin *pars* part.] —**a·part′ness,** *n.*

a·part·heid (ə pär′tīd, ə pärt′hāt′) *n.* official policy of racial segregation, as practiced in South Africa. [Afrikaans *apartheid* separateness, from *apart* separate, from French *à part* aside. See APART.]

a·part·ment (ə pärt′mənt) *n.* housing unit consisting of a room or set of rooms, usually in a building that contains other such units. [French *appartement,* from Italian *appartamento* separation, apartment, going back to Latin *ad* to + *pars* part.]

apartment house, building divided into a number of apartments.

ap·a·thet·ic (ap′ə thet′ik) *adj.* having or showing little interest, concern, or desire to act; indifferent: *apathetic voters who fail to go to the polls.* Also, **ap′a·thet′i·cal.** —**ap′a·thet′i·cal·ly,** *adv.*

ap·a·thy (ap′ə thē) *n.* lack of interest, concern, or desire to act; indifference. [French *apathie* lack of feeling, from Latin *apathīa,* from Greek *apatheia.*]

ape (āp) *n.* **1.** any of the several large, tail-less monkeys, family Pongidae, that are structurally similar to man and capable of standing or walking nearly erect, including the chimpanzee, gibbon, gorilla, and orang-utan. **2.** any monkey. **3.** one who imitates; mimic. —*v.t.,* **aped, ap·ing.** to imitate; mimic. [Old English *apa* ape, monkey.] —**ape′-like′,** *adj.* —**ap′er,** *n.* —**Syn.** *v.t.* see **imitate.**

Ap·en·nines (ap′ə nīnz′) *n.,pl.* mountain system in southern Europe, on the Italian peninsula.

a·pe·ri·ent (ə pēr′ē ənt) *adj., n.* laxative. [Latin *aperiēns,* present participle of *aperīre* to open.]

a·pe·ri·tif (ə per′ə tēf′, ä per′-) *n.* alcoholic drink taken before a meal as an appetizer. [French *apéritif* appetizer, going back to Latin *aperīre* to open.]

ap·er·ture (ap′ər chər) *n.* **1.** hole, gap, or other opening. **2.** *Optics.* **a.** opening in a lens through which light passes into a camera or other optical instrument. **b.** size of this opening. [Latin *apertūra* opening. Doublet of OVERTURE.]

a·pet·al·ous (ā pet′əl əs) *adj.* having no petals.

a·pex (ā′peks) *pl.* **a·pex·es** or **ap·i·ces.** *n.* **1.** uppermost point; tip; vertex: *the apex of a triangle.* **2.** highest or culminating point; climax: *the apex of his career.* [Latin *apex* point, summit.]

a·pha·sia (ə fā′zhə) *n.* total or partial loss of the ability to use or understand spoken or written language. It is a symptom of brain disease or injury. [Modern Latin *aphasia,* from Greek *aphasiā* speechlessness.] —**a·pha·sic** (ə fā′zik), *n., adj.*

a·phe·li·on (ə fē′lē ən) *pl.* **-li·ons** or **-li·a** (-lē ə). *n.* point in the orbit of a planet or other heavenly body farthest away from the sun. Opposed to **perihelion.** [Modification of Modern Latin *aphelium,* from Greek *apo* off, from + *hēlios* sun.] —**a·phe′li·an,** *adj.*

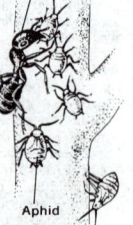

Ant

Aphid

a·phid (ā′fid, af′id) *n.* any of a group of small insects, family Aphididae, that live by sucking juices from plants. They are often nurtured by ants, which obtain a honeylike substance from aphids. [Modern Latin *aphis;* of uncertain origin.]

a·phis (ā′fis, af′is) *pl.* **aph·i·des** (af′ə dēz′) *n.* aphid.

aph·o·rism (af′ə riz′əm) *n.* short, pithy statement expressing a general truth or doctrine, for example: *A little learning is a dangerous thing*

(Pope, 1711). [Late Latin *aphorismus*, from Greek *aphorismos* definition, short sentence.] —**Syn.** see **proverb.**

aph·o·rist (af′ər ist) *n.* one who writes or uses aphorisms.

aph·o·ris·tic (af′ə ris′tik) *adj.* of, like, or containing aphorisms. —**aph′o·ris′ti·cal·ly,** *adv.*

aph·ro·dis·i·ac (af′rə diz′ē ak′) *n.* drug or other agent that stimulates or increases sexual desire and potency. —*adj.* stimulating or increasing sexual desire and potency.

Aph·ro·di·te (af′rə dī′tē) *n.* Greek goddess of love and beauty. Her Roman counterpart is Venus. [Greek *Aphrodite*, said to mean "foamborn."]

A·pi·a (ä pē′ə, ä′pē ä′) *n.* capital and port city of Western Samoa. Pop. (1967 est.), 26,000.

a·pi·a·rist (ā′pē ər ist) *n.* beekeeper.

a·pi·ar·y (ā′pē er′ē) *pl.,* **-ar·ies.** *n.* place where bees are kept; collection of beehives. [Latin *apiarium*, from *apis* bee.]

ap·i·cal (ap′i kəl, ā′pi-) *adj.* of, at, or forming the apex.

ap·i·ces (ap′ə sēz′, ā′pə-) plural of **apex.**

a·pi·cul·ture (ā′pə kul′chər) *n.* beekeeping. [Latin *apis* bee + CULTURE.] —**a′pi·cul′tur·al,** *adj.* —**a′pi·cul′tur·ist,** *n.*

a·piece (ə pēs′) *adv.* for or to each one; each: *They weigh fifty pounds apiece. Give them a napkin apiece.*

A·pis (ā′pis) *n. Egyptian Mythology.* sacred bull worshiped by the ancient Egyptians as representing the soul of their god Osiris.

ap·ish (ā′pish) *adj.* **1.** having the appearance, qualities, or mannerisms of an ape. **2.** stupidly or foolishly imitative. —**ap′ish·ly,** *adv.* —**ap′ish·ness,** *n.*

a·plomb (ə plom′, ə plum′) *n.* complete self-possession or assurance; poise. [French *aplomb* literally, perpendicularity, from *à plomb* according to the plummet, from *à* to + *plomb* lead. See PLUMB.]

apo- *prefix* off; from; away from: *apogee.* [Greek *apo* off, from.]

APO, Army Post Office.

a·poc·a·lypse (ə pok′ə lips′) *n.* **1.** stunning prophecy or disclosure; remarkable revelation. **2. the Apocalypse.** last book of the New Testament, attributed to Saint John. Also, **Rev′e·la′tion. 3.** cataclysmic end of the world; doomsday. [Latin *apocalypsis* revelation, from Greek *apokalypsis* uncovering, revelation.]

a·poc·a·lyp·tic (ə pok′ə lip′tik) *adj.* **1.** of, like, or containing an apocalyptic: *an apocalyptic vision.* **2.** of or relating to the Apocalypse. Also, **a·poc′a·lyp′ti·cal.** —**a·poc′a·lyp′ti·cal·ly,** *adv.*

a·poc·o·pe (ə pok′ə pē) *n.* cutting off or elision of the final sound, syllable, or letter of a word, as in *th′* for *the.* [Late Latin *apocope,* from Greek *apokope* cutting off.]

A·poc·ry·pha (ə pok′rə fə) *n.,pl.* **1.** fourteen books included in the Septuagint and Vulgate as an appendix to the Old Testament, but rejected as uncanonical by Protestants and Jews. **2.** collection of early Christian writings of uncertain origin, rejected as additions to the New Testament. **3. apocrypha.** writings or statements of doubtful authorship or authenticity. [Late Latin *apocrypha* not canonical, not authentic, neuter plural of *apocryphus* hidden, from Greek *apokryphos* hidden.]

a·poc·ry·phal (ə pok′rə fəl) *adj.* **1.** of doubtful authenticity; false; spurious. **2.** having no ecclesiastical authority; not canonical. **3. Apocryphal.** of or relating to the Apocrypha.

ap·o·gee (ap′ə jē) *n.* **1.** point in the orbit of the moon or other earth satellite which is farthest from the earth. Opposed to **perigee. 2.** highest or culminating point; climax. [French *apogée,* from Greek *apogaion,* neuter of *apogaios* far from earth.] —**ap′o·ge′al, ap′o·ge′an,** *adj.*

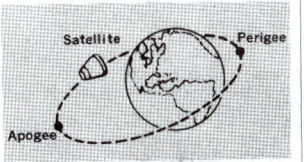

Apogee

A·pol·lo (ə pol′ō) *pl.* **-los.** *n.* **1.** *Classical Mythology.* god of manly beauty, poetry, music, prophecy, and healing. He was also considered god of the sun and, as such, was god of light and truth. **2.** *also,* **apollo.** any handsome or beautiful young man.

Ap·ol·lo·ni·an (ap′ə lō′nē ən) *adj.* **1.** of, like, or relating to Apollo. **2. apollonian.** rational, ordered, or disciplined in character or form.

A·pol·lyon (ə pol′yən) *n.* the angel of the bottomless pit; devil.

a·pol·o·get·ic (ə pol′ə jet′ik) *adj.* **1.** making an apology or excuse; expressing regret. **2.** of, relating to, or containing a defense. Also, **a·pol′o·get′i·cal.** —*n.* defense of a belief, cause, or the like. —**a·pol′o·get′i·cal·ly,** *adv.*

a·pol·o·get·ics (ə pol′ə jet′iks) *n.,pl.* branch of theology that deals with the grounds and defense of Christianity. ▲ construed as singular.

ap·o·lo·gi·a (ap′ə lō′jē ə) *n.* formal defense or justification.

a·pol·o·gist (ə pol′ə jist) *n.* one who argues in defense of a person or idea; champion.

a·pol·o·gize (ə pol′ə jīz′) **-gized, -giz·ing.** *v.i.* **1.** to acknowledge and express regret for a fault, error, or offense. **2.** to make a formal defense or justification. —**a·pol′o·giz′er,** *n.*

ap·o·logue (ap′ə lôg′, -log′) *n.* allegorical narrative or tale with a moral; fable. [French *apologue,* from Latin *apologus,* from Greek *apologos.*]

a·pol·o·gy (ə pol′ə jē) *pl.* **-gies.** *n.* **1.** expression of regret for a fault, error, or offense. **2.** formal defense or justification. **3.** poor substitute; makeshift: *The raft was a sad apology for a boat.* [Late Latin *apologia* defense, from Greek *apologia* speech in defense.]

ap·o·phthegm (ap′ə them′) *n.* apothegm.

ap·o·plec·tic (ap′ə plek′tik) *adj.* **1.** of, relating to, or causing apoplexy: *an apoplectic stroke.* **2.** suffering from or liable to have apoplexy: *an apoplectic patient. He was apoplectic with rage.* —*n.* person suffering from or liable to have apoplexy. Also, **ap′o·plec′ti·cal.** —**ap′o·plec′ti·cal·ly,** *adv.*

ap·o·plex·y (ap′ə plek′sē) *n.* sudden weakness or paralysis, with or without loss of consciousness, caused by rupture or blockage of blood vessels in the brain; stroke. [Old French *apoplexie,* from Late Latin *apoplexia,* from Greek *apoplexia.*]

a·pos·ta·sy (ə pos′tə sē) *pl.* **-sies.** *n.* desertion or renunciation of one's religion, cause, political party, or principles. [Late Latin *apostasia* desertion of one's religion, from Late Greek *apostasia* literally, standing away from.]

a·pos·tate (ə pos′tāt, -tit) *n.* one who commits apostasy. —*adj.* guilty of apostasy.

a·pos·ta·tize (ə pos′tə tīz′) **-tized, -tiz·ing.** *v.i.* to commit apostasy; become an apostate.

a pos·te·ri·o·ri (ā′ pos tēr′ē ôr′ī) **1.** proceeding from the particular to the general or from effect to cause; inductive: *a posteriori reasoning.* **2.** based on or derived from actual experience; empirical: *a posteriori knowledge.* Opposed to **a priori** in both definitions. [Latin *a posteriori* from what comes after.]

a·pos·tle (ə pos′əl) *n.* **1. Apostle.** early disciple of Christ, esp. one of the twelve originally chosen by Christ to preach His gospel. **2.** any early Christian leader or missionary. **3.** first or foremost Christian missionary to a country or other region. **4.** leader or early advocate of a movement or cause. **5.** one of the twelve members of the administrative council of the Mormon Church. [Old English *apostol* messenger of Christ, through Latin, from Greek *apostolos* messenger; literally, one sent forth.]

Apostles' Creed, formal statement of Christian faith that affirms the apostolic teachings. It begins with the statement *I believe in God the Father Almighty.*

ap·os·tol·ic (ap′əs tol′ik) *adj.* **1.** of or relating to the Apostles, their times, doctrines, or teachings. **2.** of or relating to an apostle. **3.** *also,* **Apostolic.** of the pope; papal. Also, **ap′os·tol′i·cal.**

Apostolic See, see of the pope, considered to have been founded at Rome by Saint Peter.

apostolic succession, belief that the spiritual authority of the clergy, esp. the bishops, has been handed down in direct and unbroken succession from Christ's Apostles.

a·pos·tro·phe¹ (ə pos′trə fē) *n.* punctuation mark (′) used to indicate the omission of one or more letters in a word, as in *you're* for *you are,* or *e'er* for *ever;* to indicate the possessive case of nouns or indefinite pronouns, as in *Paul's desk, anyone's concern, the boys' club;* and to indicate the plural of letters and figures, as in *the three R's, five 6's.* [Latin *apostrophus* mark of omission, from Greek *apostrophos* mark of omission.]

a·pos·tro·phe² (ə pos′trə fē) *n.* figure of speech in which an object, abstract quality, or person, often absent or imaginary, is directly addressed as if present. [Latin *apostrophe,* from Greek *apostrophe* turning away.]

a·pos·tro·phize (ə pos′trə fīz′) **-phized, -phiz·ing.** *v.t., v.i.* to speak or write an apostrophe (to).

apothecaries' measure, system of liquid measure used in pharmacy.

apothecaries' weight, system of weights used in pharmacy.

a·poth·e·car·y (ə poth′ə ker′ē) *pl.* **-car·ies.** *n.* one who prepares and sells drugs and medicines; druggist; pharmacist. [Late Latin *apothecarius* storekeeper, from Latin *apotheca* storehouse, from Greek *apotheke.*]

ap·o·thegm (ap′ə them′) *also,* **ap·o·phthegm.** *n.* terse, instructive, practical saying; maxim. [Greek *apophthegma.*]

a·poth·e·o·sis (ə poth′ē ō′sis, ap′ə thē′ə-) *pl.* **-ses** (-sēz) *n.* **1.** exaltation of a human being to the rank of a god; deification. **2.** glorified ideal; perfect example: *the very apotheosis of womanhood.* **3.** glorification of a person, principle, or thing. [Latin *apotheosis* deification, from Greek *apotheosis.*]

a·poth·e·o·size (ə poth′ē ə sīz′, ap′ə thē′ə-) **-sized, -siz·ing.** *v.t.* **1.** to deify. **2.** to glorify; exalt.

app. 1. apparent; apparently. 2. appendix. 3. appointed.

Ap·pa·la·chi·an Mountains (ap′ə lā′chē ən, -chən, -lach′ē ən, -lach′ən) principal mountain system in eastern North America, extending from southeastern Canada to north-central Alabama. Also, **Ap′pa·la′chi·ans.** [Possibly from Choctaw *A′palachi* people on the other side.]

ap·pall (ə pôl′) **-palled, -pall·ing.** *also,* **ap·pal.** *v.t.* to fill with horror or dismay; terrify; shock: *We were appalled by the news of the war.* [Old French *apallir* to make pale, from *a* to (from Latin *ad* to) + *pale* pale (from Latin *pallidus* pale).]

ap·pall·ing (ə pô′ling) *adj.* causing horror or dismay; shocking; dreadful. —**ap·pall′ing·ly,** *adv.*

ap·pa·nage (ap′ə nij) *also,* **a·pa·nage.** *n.* 1. land, money, or other provisions for the support of members of royal or noble families. 2. natural accompaniment or endowment; attribute. [French *apanage,* from *apaner* to nourish, give bread to, going back to Latin *ad* to + *pānis* bread.]

ap·pa·ra·tus (ap′ə rat′əs, -rā′təs) *pl.,* **-us** or **-us·es.** *n.* 1. device or appliance for a particular purpose: *an underwater breathing apparatus.* 2. organized set of instruments, materials, or equipment designed for a particular use: *Set up the surgical apparatus at once.* 3. method or means by which an organized activity is carried out; system: *the apparatus of government.* 4. *Physiology.* group of organs operating together to perform a particular function: *digestive apparatus.* [Latin *apparātus* preparation.]

ap·par·el (ə par′əl) *n.* clothing or garments; attire. —*v.t.,* **-eled, -el·ing;** *also, British,* **-elled, -el·ling.** to clothe; dress. [Old French *apareiller* to clothe, from *a* to + *pareiller* to put like with like, going back to Latin *ad* to + *pār* equal.]

ap·par·ent (ə par′ənt) *adj.* 1. easily seen or understood; plainly visible; evident: *It was apparent that he was lying.* 2. appearing or seeming real or true, although not necessarily so: *an apparent contradiction.* [Old French *aparant,* present participle of *aparoir* to appear, from Latin *appārēre* to appear.]

ap·par·ent·ly (ə par′ənt lē) *adv.* 1. clearly; plainly; obviously. 2. to all appearances; seemingly.

ap·pa·ri·tion (ap′ə rish′ən) *n.* 1. ghost; specter; phantom. 2. something strange, startling, or unexpected which comes suddenly into view. [Late Latin *appārītiō* appearance, from Latin *appārēre* to appear.] —**Syn.** 1. see **ghost.**

ap·peal (ə pēl′) *n.* 1. earnest request or entreaty; call for aid or sympathy: *an appeal for mercy, a nationwide television appeal.* 2. power or ability to attract, charm, or interest: *an actor with great audience appeal.* 3. resort to some authority for proof, aid, or corroboration. 4. *Law.* **a.** action of bringing a case before a higher court for review or retrial. **b.** request for this. —*v.i.* 1. to make an earnest request; entreat. 2. to arouse a favorable response; be attractive or interesting: *This menu doesn't appeal to me.* 3. to turn to a higher authority for a decision or settlement. 4. *Law.* to bring a case, or request that a case be brought, before a higher court for review or retrial. —*v.t. Law.* to institute proceedings for the appeal of (a case). [Old French *apeler* to call, from Latin *appellāre* to accost, call upon.]
Syn. *v.i.* 1. **Appeal, plead, sue** indicate earnest application to someone for help. **Appeal** asks that a request be examined and acted upon: *He appealed to the voters for their support.* **Plead** has a formal implication, as in court proceedings, or suggests desperation: *He pleaded for time to look into the facts of the case.* **Sue,** usually restricted to legal meanings, stresses that a higher power is being approached: *Columbus sued for the favor of an audience with the queen.*

ap·peal·ing (ə pē′ling) *adj.* 1. producing a pleasing response; charming. 2. earnestly imploring; entreating. —**ap·peal′ing·ly,** *adv.*

ap·pear (ə pēr′) *v.i.* 1. to come into view; be visible or perceivable: *He appeared in the doorway. The theme appears throughout his work.* 2. to give the impression of being; seem: *He appeared learned but was not.* 3. to be or become clear or obvious to the mind: *It does not appear that you are right.* 4. to come or be placed before the public: *The book appeared in June. He has often appeared on the stage.* 5. to come formally before an authoritative body: *He appeared as a witness in the committee hearings.* [Old French *aparoir* to show oneself, from Latin *appārēre* to come into sight.] —**Syn.** 2. see **seem.**

ap·pear·ance (ə pēr′əns) *n.* 1. act of appearing or coming into view: *the appearance of the sun above the horizon.* 2. external look or aspect: *the shabby appearance of his clothes. She has the appearance of a model.* 3. outward show as opposed to actual state; semblance: *In spite of his troubles, he gave the appearance of being happy.* 4. a coming before the public or an authoritative body. 5. **appearances.** circumstances or outward indications. 6. *Law.* a coming into court as a party or attorney in a suit. 7. something seen or perceived; phenomenon: *strange appearances in the evening sky.* 8. **to keep up appearances.** to maintain the outward signs of what is normal, conventional, or proper. 9. **to put in an appearance.** to appear briefly; attend for a short time.

Syn. 2. **Appearance, aspect** refer to the outward features, often as opposed to the essential nature, of someone or something. **Appearance** refers to what is visible to the observer: *In drawing, represent the appearances of things, never what you know the things to be* (Ruskin, 1872). **Aspect** refers to the way someone or something presents itself under specific conditions or at certain times: *The battle soon gave the field a different aspect from the quiet summer scene of an hour before.*

ap·pease (ə pēz′) **-peased, -peas·ing.** *v.t.* 1. to placate by yielding to demands or making concessions: *Churchill refused to appease Hitler.* 2. to bring to a state of peace or quiet; calm: *to appease the anger of the gods.* 3. to cause to subside; satisfy: *to appease one's hunger.* [Old French *apaisier* to pacify, from *a* to (from Latin *ad* to) + *pais* peace (from Latin *pāx* peace).] —**ap·peas′er,** *n.* —**ap·peas′ing·ly,** *adv.*
Syn. 2. **Appease, pacify, soothe** mean to make someone or something calm or quiet. **Appease** implies that someone has made a demand that has to be met before quiet can be restored; it is also applied to appetites or desires: *To appease his parents, he agreed to go to school part time. Only by making full restitution could he appease his conscience.* **Pacify** implies an open fight, quarrel, rebellion, or other manifestation of acute unrest that has to be quelled even if the underlying reason for the outbreak is not changed: *The arrival of the police soon pacified the milling students.* **Soothe** implies returning something or someone in an excited or uneasy state to normal equilibrium or calm: *She soothed the infant by singing a lullaby.*

ap·pease·ment (ə pēz′mənt) *n.* 1. act of appeasing; being appeased; pacification; satisfaction. 2. policy of making territorial or other concessions to a hostile or aggressive power in order to maintain peace.

ap·pel·lant (ə pel′ənt) *n.* one who appeals, esp. to a higher court. —*adj.* of or relating to judicial appeals; appellate.

ap·pel·late (ə pel′it) *adj.* 1. relating to legal appeals. 2. having the power to hear and rule on legal appeals: *an appellate court.* [Latin *appellātus,* past participle of *appellāre* to call upon.]

ap·pel·la·tion (ap′ə lā′shən) *n.* 1. name; title; designation. 2. act of naming.

ap·pel·la·tive (ə pel′ə tiv) *n.* 1. descriptive name, as *Lion-Hearted* in *Richard the Lion-Hearted.* 2. common noun. —*adj.* 1. of or designating a common noun. 2. of or relating to the giving of names.

ap·pend (ə pend′) *v.t.* to add as a supplement or accessory; attach: *to append explanatory notes to a text.* [Latin *appendere* to hang on.]

ap·pend·age (ə pen′dij) *n.* 1. that which is appended; addition. 2. subordinate part of a plant or animal attached to and extending from a larger part or the main body.

ap·pend·ant (ə pen′dənt) *adj.* added; attached. —*n.* something added or attached.

ap·pen·dec·to·my (ap′ən dek′tə mē) *pl.,* **-mies.** *n.* surgical removal of the appendix, esp. because of appendicitis. [APPENDIX + Greek *ek* out of + *tomē* cutting.]

ap·pen·di·ci·tis (ə pen′də sī′tis) *n.* inflammation of the appendix, esp. when accompanied by swelling of the appendix, severe abdominal pain, and the danger of a ruptured appendix, which can bring on peritonitis. [APPENDIX + -ITIS.]

ap·pen·dix (ə pen′diks) *pl.,* **-dix·es** or **-di·ces** (-də sēz′). *n.* **1.a.** thin saclike structure attached to the beginning of the large intestine. In man, it is two to three inches in length, is in the lower right abdomen, and has no apparent function. Also, **vermiform appendix. b.** any of various outgrowths or projections of bodily organs. 2. section of additional material supplementing a book or other piece of writing. [Latin *appendix* appendage.]

ap·per·ceive (ap′ər sēv′) **-ceived, ceiv·ing.** *v.t.* to comprehend (new ideas or ideas) in relation to past knowledge or experience.

ap·per·cep·tion (ap′ər sep′shən) *n.* 1. interpretation and assimilation of new ideas and experiences in relation to previously assimilated ones. 2. full and conscious perception. [French *aperception* clear perception, from Modern Latin *apperceptio.* See AP-¹, PERCEPTION.] —*ap′per·cep′tive,* *adj.*

ap·per·tain (ap′ər tān′) *v.i.* to belong as part, function, or attribute; pertain; relate (with *to*). [Old French *apartenir,* going back to Late Latin *appertinēre* for *ad-* to + *pertinēre* to belong, concern.]

ap·pe·tite (ap′ə tīt′) *n.* 1. desire for food. 2. natural or strong desire; craving. [Old French *apetit* desire, from Latin *appetītus* desire for, literally, assault upon, going back to *ad* to + *petere* to seek.]

ap·pe·tiz·er (ap′ə tī′zər) *n.* 1. food or drink served as a first course or before a meal, usually to stimulate the appetite. 2. anything that arouses interest in or desire for what is to follow.

ap·pe·tiz·ing (ap′ə tī′zing) *adj.* appealing to the appetite; savory: *an appetizing dinner.* —**ap′pe·tiz′ing·ly,** *adv.*

Ap·pi·an Way (ap′ē ən) ancient Roman road, begun in 312 B.C., that extended more than 350 miles, from Rome to Brundisium. Part of it exists today. [From the Roman censor *Appius* Claudius Caecus, who ordered its construction.]

at; āpe; cär; end; mē; it; īce; hot; ōld; fôrk; wood; fŏŏl; oil; out; up; ūse; turn; sing; thin; this; zh in treasure; ə in ago, taken, pencil, lemon, circus.

ap·plaud (ə plôd') *v.t.* **1.** to express approval or enjoyment of (something) by clapping the hands: *The audience applauded his performance.* **2.** to approve; commend; praise: *His efforts were applauded by all.* —*v.i.* to express approval or enjoyment by clapping the hands: *They kept applauding long after the curtain came down.* [Latin *applaudere* to clap the hands.]

ap·plause (ə plôz') *n.* **1.** approval or enjoyment expressed by clapping the hands: *Loud applause greeted his appearance.* **2.** any expression of approval or appreciation; praise: *His first novel was worthy of applause.* [Latin *applausus*, past participle of *applaudere.* See APPLAUD.]

ap·ple (ap'əl) *n.* **1.** roundish fruit with usually red, yellow, or green skin and a firm, edible outer part surrounding a core with small seeds. It is the most widely cultivated fruit. **2.a.** any of thousands of varieties of cultivated trees bearing this fruit, growing in temperate regions. Most varieties derive from two species, *Malus pumila* and *M. baccata.* **b.** any tree of the genus *Malus,* of the rose family. **3.** any of certain other plants, fruits, or fruitlike growths, as the custard apple or oak gall. **4. apple of (one's) eye.** person or thing that is most precious or dear (to one). [Old English *æppel* fruit of the apple tree.]

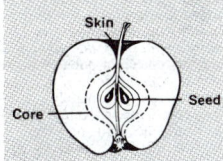

Cross section of an apple

apple butter, thick, brown, spiced applesauce used as a spread for bread.

apple cart 1. pushcart for peddling apples. **2. to upset the (or one's) apple cart.** to spoil plans or disrupt the established situation.

ap·ple·jack (ap'əl jak') *n.* brandy distilled from hard cider. Also, **apple brandy.** [APPLE + JACK.]

apple of discord 1. *Greek Legend.* a golden apple inscribed "For the fairest," thrown among the gods by Eris. It was claimed by Aphrodite, Athena, and Hera, but Paris, who acted as judge, awarded it to Aphrodite, because she promised him Helen. **2.** any cause of envy or dispute.

ap·ple-pie order (ap'əl pī') *Informal.* condition of perfect neatness; perfect order.

apple polisher *Slang.* one who flatters or seeks favor with servility; bootlicker.

ap·ple·sauce (ap'əl sôs') *n.* **1.** apples sweetened and stewed to a pulp. **2.** *Slang.* nonsense; bunk.

Ap·ple·ton (ap'əl tən) *n.* city in eastern Wisconsin. Pop. (1970), 57,143.

ap·pli·ance (ə plī'əns) *n.* **1.** device or piece of equipment for a particular use, esp. one for household use. **2.** *Archaic.* act of applying; being applied; application.

ap·pli·ca·ble (ap'li kə bəl, ə plik'ə-) *adj.* capable of being applied; relevant; suitable: *Your argument is not applicable in this case.* —**ap′pli·ca·bil′i·ty,** *n.* —**ap′pli·ca·bly,** *adv.*

ap·pli·cant (ap'li kənt) *n.* person who asks or applies (for something); candidate: *an applicant for a job.* —**Syn.** see **candidate.**

ap·pli·ca·tion (ap'lə kā'shən) *n.* **1.** a putting to use: *the application of science to industry.* **2.** a putting on: *the application of ointment to a burn.* **3.** something put on or applied: *This application will soothe the sore area.* **4.** capacity of being usable or suitable; relevance: *The testimony has no application to the case.* **5.** request made personally or in writing: *His application was denied.* **6.** written form used in making such a request: *Fill out this application.* **7.** close or diligent attention: *application to one's studies.* [Latin *applicātiō* a joining to.]

ap·plied (ə plīd') *adj.* used to work out actual problems; put to practical use: *applied science, applied mathematics.* Distinguished from **abstract, theoretical,** or **pure.**

ap·pli·qué (ap'lə kā') *n.* design or decoration made separately and then sewed or otherwise fastened to the background. —*adj.* decorated in this way. —*v.t.,* **-quéd, -qué·ing.** to decorate with or apply as appliqué. [French *appliqué,* past participle of *appliquer* to fasten to, from Latin *applicāre* to join to.]

ap·ply (ə plī') *v.t.* **-plied, -ply·ing.** *v.t.* **1.** to put into use or practice; employ: *Learn how to apply your knowledge. He applied pressure on the other committee members to make them vote against the proposal.* **2.** to bring into contact (with something); put on or to: *to apply a bandage, to apply paint.* **3.** to use (a word or statement) to refer to a particular person or thing: *That term is rarely applied to animals.* **4.** to devote (oneself) diligently; use (one's resources) fully: *He applied himself to his work.* —*v.i.* **1.** to make a request; ask (with *for*): *to apply for a loan.* **2.** to have relevance or reference; be suitable; fit: *That principle doesn't apply here.* [Old French *aplier* to bring to, present, from Latin *applicāre* to join to, turn toward.]

ap·pog·gia·tu·ra (ə poj'ə toor'ə, -tyoor'ə) *n.* musical note that precedes and ornaments an essential note of a melody. The **long appoggiatura** takes away a portion of the time value of the note it precedes, while the **short appoggiatura** does not. [Italian *appoggiatura* literally, support, from *appoggiare* to lean on, from Latin *ap-,* for *ad-* to + *podium* elevated place. See PODIUM.]

ap·point (ə point') *v.t.* **1.** to name or select for an office or position: *He was just appointed chairman.* **2.** to arrange or determine by agreement or authority; fix: *The judge appointed the trial date. They appointed a meeting place.* **3.** to furnish; equip. **4.** now commonly used chiefly in combination in the past participle: *a well-appointed ship, beautifully appointed lodgings.* **4.** *Archaic.* to ordain by decree; prescribe; command: *laws appointed by God.* [Old French *apointer* to fix, arrange, from *à point* to a point, going back to Latin *ad* to + *pūnctum* point.]

ap·point·ee (ə poin'tē', ap'oin tē') *n.* person named to an office or position: *a political appointee.*

ap·poin·tive (ə poin'tiv) *adj.* of or filled by appointment rather than election: *an appointive office.*

ap·point·ment (ə point'mənt) *n.* **1.** a naming or selecting for an office or position: *The vacancy was filled by appointment.* **2.** office or position so filled: *a high appointment in government.* **3.** arrangement to meet someone or to be somewhere; engagement: *I have an appointment at six o'clock.* **4. appointments.** furnishings; equipment.
Syn. 3. Appointment, engagement, rendezvous, date[1] refer to an understanding to meet with another or others, esp. at a given place and time. **Appointment** implies careful scheduling of time, as by a physician or business executive: *His appointment was for 3:15 the following afternoon.* **Engagement** suggests an obligation to attend the meeting arranged: *He has so many engagements this week that he must decline any new requests.* **Rendezvous** emphasizes the place rather than the time and often implies secrecy: *Our rendezvous will be at the fountain tomorrow night.* **Date** is quite informal and suggests entertainment rather than business or some other necessity: *We made a date to go bowling after work.*

Ap·po·mat·tox (ap'ə mat'əks) *n.* town in central Virginia where the Confederate command formally surrendered to the Union forces on April 9, 1865, ending the Civil War.

ap·por·tion (ə pôr'shən) *v.t.* to divide and distribute proportionally or according to a rule or plan; allot. [Middle French *apportionner,* from *a* to (from Latin *ad* to) + *portionner* to share (going back to Latin *portiō* a share).] —**Syn.** see **assign.**

ap·por·tion·ment (ə pôr'shən mənt) *n.* **1.** act of apportioning; being apportioned. **2.** assignment, based upon proportionate share of population, of the number of representatives that a state may have in the U.S. House of Representatives or that any other political division may have in its legislative body.

ap·pose (ə pōz') *v.t.* **-posed, -pos·ing.** *v.t.* **1.** to arrange side by side; juxtapose. **2.** *Archaic.* to put or apply (one thing) to another. [Middle French *ap(p)oser* to set beside, modification (influenced by French *poser* to place, put) of Latin *appōnere* to place, to apply.]

ap·po·site (ap'ə zit, ə poz'it) *adj.* well-suited or adapted; appropriate; pertinent. [Latin *appositus,* past participle of *appōnere* to place to, apply.] —**ap′po·site·ly,** *adv.* —**ap′po·site·ness,** *n.*

ap·po·si·tion (ap'ə zish'ən) *n.* **1.** *Grammar.* **a.** placing of a noun or a noun phrase near another noun or noun phrase so that the second explains or supplements and has the same grammatical construction as the first. **b.** syntactical relationship between such words. In the sentence *Susy, her sister, bought the dog,* the word *Susy* and the phrase *her sister* are in apposition. **2.** act of apposing; being apposed; juxtaposition. —**ap′po·si′tion·al,** *adj.* —**ap′po·si′tion·al·ly,** *adv.*

ap·pos·i·tive (ə poz'ə tiv) *n.* word, phrase, or clause in apposition. —*adj.* of, relating to, or placed in apposition. —**ap·pos′i·tive·ly,** *adv.*

ap·prais·al (ə prā'zəl) *n.* **1.** act of appraising; being appraised. **2.** price or value assigned; valuation; estimate: *What's your appraisal of his theory?* Also, **ap·praise′ment.**

ap·praise (ə prāz') *v.t.* **-praised, -prais·ing.** *v.t.* **1.** to estimate the monetary value of; fix a price for: *to appraise land for taxation, to appraise a diamond.* **2.** to evaluate the quality or significance of; judge: *to appraise a man's character, to appraise a situation.* [Modification of APPRIZE, influenced by PRAISE.] —**ap·prais′er,** *n.* —**ap·prais′ing·ly,** *adv.*

ap·pre·cia·ble (ə prē'shə bəl) *adj.* enough to be perceived or noticed; perceptible: *an appreciable increase in income.* —**ap·pre′cia·bly,** *adv.*

ap·pre·ci·ate (ə prē'shē āt') *v.t.* **-at·ed, -at·ing.** *v.t.* **1.** to recognize the worth or value of; value or regard highly: *His work was not appreciated by his own generation.* **2.** to be grateful for: *I appreciate your kindness.* **3.** to be keenly sensitive or sensible of: *He's incapable of appreciating the subtleties of your argument.* **4.** to perceive the full nature or effect of; be fully conscious of: *I appreciate all the dangers involved.* **5.** to raise in value: *This stock has appreciated twenty percent.* —*v.i.* to rise in value. [Latin *appretiātus,* past participle of *appretiāre* to value at a price, appraise.]

ap·pre·ci·a·tion (ə prē'shē ā'shən) *n.* **1.** act of recognizing the

worth or quality of: *an appreciation of the finer things in life.* **2.** sensitive or discriminating understanding: *a keen appreciation of classical literature.* **3.** gratitude: *I can't express my deep appreciation.* **4.** increase in value. Opposed to **depreciation.**

ap·pre·cia·tive (ə prē′shə tiv, -shē ā′tiv) *adj.* feeling or showing appreciation: *an appreciative audience.* —**ap·pre′cia·tive·ly,** *adv.* —**ap·pre′cia·tive·ness,** *n.* —**Syn.** see **grateful.**

ap·pre·hend (ap′ri hend′) *v.t.* **1.a.** to seize (someone) on legal or other authority; capture; detain: *The police apprehended the burglar. The king sent troops to apprehend his rival.* **b.** to catch and stop; intercept: *The messenger apprehended them as they were leaving the city.* **2.** to grasp mentally; be aware of: *a truth that we but dimly apprehend.* **3.** *Archaic.* to anticipate with fear; dread: *I sometimes apprehend that our institutions may perish* (Hawthorne, 1868). [Latin *apprehendere* to seize, grasp mentally.] —**Syn.** **2.** see **comprehend.**

ap·pre·hen·sion (ap′ri hen′shən) *n.* **1.** fear of what may happen; anxiety; foreboding: *a feeling of apprehension, apprehensions of disaster.* **2.** seizure on legal or other authority; capture. **3.** act of grasping mentally. [Late Latin *apprehēnsiō* seizing upon, understanding, from Latin *apprehendere.* See APPREHEND.] —**Syn.** **1.** see **anxiety.**

ap·pre·hen·sive (ap′ri hen′siv) *adj.* fearful about what may happen; uneasy. —**ap′pre·hen′sive·ly,** *adv.* —**ap′pre·hen′sive·ness,** *n.*

ap·pren·tice (ə pren′tis) *n.* **1.a.** one who was bound by contract to serve a medieval guild or master for a specified time, in return for maintenance and instruction in a craft or trade. **b.** beginner in a trade or art. An apprentice is usually so classified for a specified period of time, during which he works with skilled workers for reduced pay. **2.** one lacking skill or experience; novice. —*v.t.,* **-ticed, -tic·ing.** to take on or place as an apprentice. [Old French *aprentis* one who learns a trade, from *aprendre* to learn, from Latin *apprehendere* to seize, grasp mentally.]

ap·pren·tice·ship (ə pren′tis ship′) *n.* **1.** condition or state of being an apprentice. **2.** time period during which one works as an apprentice.

ap·prise (ə prīz′) **-prised, -pris·ing.** *also, British,* **ap·prize.** *v.t.* to inform; notify. [French *appris,* past participle of *apprendre* to inform, teach, learn, from Latin *apprehendere* to grasp mentally.]

ap·prize (ə prīz′) **-prized, -priz·ing.** *also, British,* **ap·prise.** *v.t.* to appraise. [Old French *apris(i)er,* going back to Latin *ad* to + *pretium* value, price.]

ap·proach (ə prōch′) *v.i.* to come near in space or time: *The horses approached swiftly. The hour of attack is approaching.* —*v.t.* **1.** to come near to (a time, place, quality, or condition): *to approach manhood, to approach perfection.* **2.** to make overtures to: *Why not approach him on the subject?* **3.** to deal with; try to understand: *We should approach the problem from this angle.* —*n.* **1.** a coming near or drawing near in space, time, quality, or condition. **2.** method used for dealing with: *a new approach to Shakespeare.* **3.** access: *The approach to the house was blocked.* **4.** advance or overture (to a person). **5.** stroke in golf intended to place the ball on the putting green. [Old French *aprochier* to come near to, going back to Latin *ad* to + *propius* nearer.] —**Syn.** *v.t.* **1.** **Approach, near, approximate** indicate convergence. **Approach** suggests closeness almost to the point of contact, physically or conceptually: *His theory approaches a thorough explanation of the data.* **Near** is used of a coming close in space or time: *As they neared the shore, the boats began to pitch in the surf.* **Approximate** implies coming close to something, as to a standard: *The appearance of this man-made diamond approximates that of a natural one.*

ap·proach·a·ble (ə prō′chə bəl) *adj.* **1.** possible to approach; accessible: *The town was approachable from only one direction.* **2.** friendly; affable. —**ap·proach′a·bil′i·ty,** *n.*

ap·pro·ba·tion (ap′rə bā′shən) *n.* **1.a.** praise; commendation. **b.** approval. **2.** *Archaic.* sanction. [Latin *approbātiō* an approving.]

ap·pro·pri·a·ble (ə prō′prē ə bəl) *adj.* capable of being appropriated.

ap·pro·pri·ate (*adj.,* ə prō′prē it; *v.,* ə prō′prē āt′) *adj.* particularly well-suited; fitting: *an appropriate remark, a dress appropriate for the occasion.* —*v.t.,* **-at·ed, -at·ing.** **1.** to set apart or assign for a particular use: *Congress appropriated funds for education.* **2.** to take for oneself, esp. without permission. [Late Latin *appropriātus,* past participle of *appropriāre* to make one's own, from Latin *ad* to + *proprius* one's own.] —**ap·pro′pri·ate·ly,** *adv.* —**ap·pro′pri·ate·ness,** *n.* —**Syn.** *adj.* see **fit[1], proper.**

ap·pro·pri·a·tion (ə prō′prē ā′shən) *n.* **1.** something appropriated, esp. a sum of money: *A government appropriation results from an act of the legislature.* **2.** act of appropriating; being appropriated.

ap·prov·al (ə prōō′vəl) *n.* **1.** favorable opinion; acceptance: *While the young people danced, their elders looked on with approval.* **2.** official consent; sanction: *We can't print your article without the editor's approval.* **3.** on approval. subject to a customer's trial or examination before final sale.

ap·prove (ə prōōv′) **-proved, -prov·ing.** *v.t.* **1.** to consider (something)

satisfactory or acceptable; be favorable toward: *I can't approve such methods.* **2.** to confirm officially; sanction: *Congress approved the budget.* —*v.i.* **to approve of.** to have a favorable opinion of: *My parents don't approve of him.* [Old French *aprover* from Latin *approbāre.*] —**ap·prov′ing·ly,** *adv.* —**ap·prov′er,** *n.*

Syn. *v.t.* **1.** **Approve, endorse, sanction** mean to be in favor of and to state that opinion. **Approve** goes no further than that; it expresses a formal definitive statement in favor of something: *The committee was asked to approve the secretary's action.* **Endorse** adds the suggestion of backing up the favorable opinion: *The policy was publicly endorsed by every member of the cabinet.* **Sanction** expresses, in addition, some weighty official or public action or authority: *Such conduct is not sanctioned in many parts of our country.*

approx., approximately.

ap·prox·i·mate (*adj.,* ə prok′sə mit; *v.,* ə prok′sə māt′) *adj.* **1.** nearly accurate or exact: *approximate length.* **2.** near to; close together. **3.** very similar. —*v.t.* **-mat·ed, -mat·ing.** **1.** to come close to (something) in quality, quantity, or degree: *Wind-tunnel conditions approximate those of actual flight.* **2.** to estimate: *Approximate the time it will take you to finish.* **3.** to bring (something) near (with *to*). —*v.i.* to come close in quality, quantity, degree, or condition (with *to*). [Latin *approximātus,* past participle of *approximāre* to come near to.] —**ap·prox′i·mate·ly,** *adv.* —**Syn.** *v.t.* **1.** see **approach.**

ap·prox·i·ma·tion (ə prok′sə mā′shən) *n.* **1.** act or process of approximating; something approximate. **2.** value that is not exact, but is accurate enough for a specified purpose: *The figure 3.14 is an approximation of the value of pi.*

ap·pur·te·nance (ə purt′ən əns) *n.* **1.** something added and subordinate; accessory. **2.** subordinate right, privilege, or improvement attached to a property. [Anglo-Norman *apurtenance* accessory, from Old French *apartenir* to belong to, going back to Latin *ad* to + *pertinēre* to belong.]

ap·pur·te·nant (ə purt′ən ənt) *adj.* appertaining or belonging, as a legal right. —*n.* appurtenance.

Apr., April.

a·pri·cot (ā′prə kot′, ap′rə-) *n.* **1.** orange-colored fruit of a tree, *Prunus armeniaca,* resembling a small peach but with a distinct aromatic flavor. **2.** the tree itself, native to eastern Asia and cultivated in mild climates. **3.** pale orange-yellow color. [French *abricot* this fruit, from Portuguese *albricoque,* from Arabic *al-birqūq* the apricot, through Late Greek, from Latin *(prūnum) praecoquum* early-ripe (plum), neuter variant of *praecox* early ripe; because it ripened before certain other fruits.]

Apricot leaves and fruit

A·pril (ā′prəl) *n.* fourth month of the year, containing thirty days. [Latin *Aprīlis,* possibly from Greek *Aphrō,* short for *Aphroditē* Greek goddess of love, this month of spring being associated with love.]

April Fool, person at whose expense a trick or joke is played on April Fool's Day.

April Fools' Day, the first day of April, traditional day for playing tricks and practical jokes. Also, **All Fool's Day.**

a pri·o·ri (ā′ prī ôr′ī) **1.** proceeding from the general to the particular, or from cause to effect; deductive. **2.** innate in the mind, rather than resulting from experience. Opposed to **a posteriori** in defs. 1, 2. **3.** previous to investigation or analysis: *an a priori judgment.* [Latin phrase *ā priori* from (something) before.]

a·pron (ā′prən) *n.* **1.** garment made in various ways and worn over the front of the body, for protection of one's clothes or person or as decoration: *chef's apron, leather apron.* **2.** any of various things resembling an apron in use, position, or shape, as a protective metal plate covering machine parts or the hard-surface area in front of a hangar. **3.** the part of a stage in front of the curtain. **4. tied to (someone's) apron strings.** dependent on or dominated, as by a mother or wife. [Earlier *napron,* from Old French *naperon* napkin, diminutive of *nape* tablecloth, from Latin *mappa* cloth. The phrase *a napron* came to be divided incorrectly as *an apron.* For a similar development, see ADDER.]

ap·ro·pos (ap′rə pō′) *adj.* pertinent; fitting: *an apropos remark.* —*adv.* **1.** to the purpose; pertinently. **2. apropos of.** with regard to; in relation to: *apropos of that matter.* ▲ **Apropos** sometimes appears in this meaning as a preposition, not followed by **of.** [French phrase *à propos* to the purpose, going back to Latin *ad* to + *prōpositum* plan, purpose.]

apse (aps) *n.* **1.** semicircular recess with vaulted ceiling in a building, esp. a church. **2.** similarly shaped end of a church or other building. **3.** altar end of a church, beyond the nave and transept, not necessarily semicircular in shape. **4.** apsis. [Latin *apsis* arch, vault. See APSIS.]

ap·sis (ap′sis) *pl.* **ap·si·des** (ap′sə dēz′) *n.* **1.** either of two points in an astronomical orbit. At the **lower apsis** the orbiting body is nearest to the center of attraction; at the **higher apsis** it is farthest away.

at; āpe; cär; end; mē; it; īce; hot; ōld; fôrk; wood; fŏŏl; oil; out; up; ūse; turn; sing; thin; this; zh in treasure; ə in ago, taken, pencil, lemon, circus.

2. line of apsides. line joining these two points. [Latin *apsis* arch, vault, from Greek *(h)apsis*.]

apt (apt) *adj.* **1.** predisposed; inclined: *He was apt to behave impulsively.* **2.** likely: *The store is apt to be closed.* **3.** appropriate; to the point: *an apt quotation.* **4.** quick to learn; gifted: *an apt student.* [Latin *aptus* fitted, suited.] —**apt'ly,** *adv.* —**apt'ness,** *n.*

apt. *pl.,* **apts.** apartment.

ap·ter·ous (ap'tər əs) *adj.* **1.** (of an insect) lacking wings. **2.** having no membranous extensions: *an apterous seed.* [Greek *apteros* wingless, from a- A-¹ + *pteron* wing.]

ap·ter·yx (ap'tər iks) *n.* kiwi. [Greek *a-* without + *pteryx* wing.]

ap·ti·tude (ap'tə tōōd', -tūd') *n.* **1.** natural ability or capacity; talent: *an aptitude for languages.* **2.** *Archaic.* suitability. [French *aptitude,* from Late Latin *aptitūdō* fitness, from Latin *aptus* fit, suited. Doublet of ATTITUDE.] —**Syn.** see **ability.**

aptitude test, test given to determine a person's capacity for learning or doing any of a number of specified types of work.

Ap·u·le·ius, Lucius (ap'yə lē'əs) Roman writer and philosopher of the second century A.D.

A·qa·ba, Gulf of (ä'kä bä') gulf at the northeastern end of the Red Sea, between the Sinai Peninsula and Saudi Arabia.

aq·ua for·tis (ak'wə fôr'tis, äk'-wə) nitric acid. [Latin *aqua* water + *fortis* strong.]

aq·ua·lung (ak'wə lung', äk'-) *n.* scuba having a valve that supplies air on demand. Trademark: Aqua-Lung.

Aqualung

aq·ua·ma·rine (ak'wə mə rēn', äk'-) *n.* **1.** transparent beryl of a pale blue or bluish-green variety, used as a gem. **2.** bluish-green color. [Latin *aqua marīna* sea water.]

aq·ua·naut (ak'wə nôt', äk'-) *n.* one who is trained to live in an underwater chamber and to conduct oceanographic research and experiments. [Latin *aqua* water + Greek *nautēs* sailor.]

aq·ua·plane (ak'wə plān', äk'-) *n.* board on which one who is standing can ride across the surface of the water while being towed by a motorboat. —*v.i.* **-planed, -plan·ing.** to ride an aquaplane. —**aq'ua·plan'er,** *n.*

aq·ua re·gi·a (ak'wə rē'jē ə, äk'wə) mixture of one part nitric acid and three parts hydrochloric acid, which can dissolve gold and platinum, although neither acid by itself can do so. [Latin *aqua regia* literally, royal water, because it dissolves "royal" metals.]

a·quar·i·um (ə kwâr'ē əm) *pl.* **-i·ums** or **-i·a** (-ē ə) *n.* **1.** tank, bowl, or similar container, partly of glass or other transparent material, in which aquatic animals and plants can be kept alive and easily observed. **2.** establishment where collections of living aquatic animals and plants are exhibited or studied. [Latin *aquārium* (thing) having to do with water, from *aqua* water.]

A·quar·i·us (ə kwâr'ē əs) *n.* **1.** constellation near the celestial equator, conventionally depicted as a man pouring water out of a vase. **2.** eleventh sign of the zodiac. See **zodiac** for illustration. [Latin *aquārius* water bearer.]

a·quat·ic (ə kwat'ik, ə kwot'-) *adj.* **1.** (of a plant or animal) growing or living in or near water. **2.** performed in or on water: *aquatic sports.* —*n.* **aquatics.** performances on or in water; water sports. [Latin *aquāticus* having to do with water, from *aqua* water.] —**a·quat'i·cally,** *adv.*

aq·ua·tint (ak'wə tint', äk'-) *n.* **1.** process in which spaces are etched on copperplate with acid so as to produce a print resembling an ink or wash drawing. **2.** print or plate made in this way. —*v.t.* to etch by this process. [French *aquatinte* kind of print, from Italian *acqua tinta,* from Latin *aqua* water + *tincta,* feminine past participle of *tingo* to dye.]

aq·ua vi·tae (ak'wə vī'tē, äk'wə) **1.** alcohol. **2.** strong liquor, as brandy or whiskey. [Medieval Latin *aqua vitae* water of life; possibly so called because strong liquor was used medicinally.]

aq·ue·duct (ak'wə dukt') *n.* **1.** conduit for carrying water, esp. over long distances.

2. structure supporting such a conduit. **3.** canal or passage for conducting fluids in the body. [Latin *aquae ductus* conveyance of water.]

a·que·ous (ã'kwē əs, ak'wē-) *adj.* **1.** diluted with or containing water: *an aqueous solution.* **2.** of, like, or having to do with water; watery. **3.** (of rock) sedimentary. [Medieval Latin *aqueus* relating to water, from Latin *aqua* water.]

Aqueduct

---

aqueous humor, in the eye, the clear watery fluid filling the space between the cornea and the lens.

Aq·ui·la (ak'wə lə) *n.* constellation in the northern sky containing the bright star Altair, conventionally depicted as a flying eagle, sometimes carrying a boy in its talons. [Latin *aquila* eagle.]

aq·ui·line (ak'wə līn', -lin) *adj.* **1.** (of the nose) curved, sharply defined, and prominent, like an eagle's beak. **2.** of or like an eagle. [Latin *aquilīnus* relating to the eagle, from *aquila* eagle.]

A·qui·nas, Saint Thomas (ə kwī'nəs) c.1225–74, Italian philosopher and theologian of the Roman Catholic Church.

Aq·ui·taine (ak'wə tān') *n.* historic region in southwestern France.

a·quiv·er (ə kwiv'ər) *adj.* trembling: *all aquiver with excitement.*

Ar, argon.

ar-, form of ad- before *r,* as in *array.*

-ar¹ *suffix* (used to form adjectives) of, like, or having the nature of (the stem): *lunar, angular, similar.* [Latin *-āris* belonging to, having the form of.]

-ar² *suffix* (used to form nouns) person or thing connected with (the stem): *vicar, scholar, pillar, collar.* [Latin *-ārius* relating to, or *-āris* belonging to.]

-ar³, form of *-er¹* or *-or,* as in *liar, beggar.*

Ar·ab (ar'əb) *n.* **1.a.** member or close descendant of any of the Arabic-speaking peoples inhabiting southwestern Asia and North Africa. **b.** before the Islamic expansion, a tribal people inhabiting Arabia and the Syrian desert. **2.** Bedouin. **3.** Arabian horse. —*adj.* of or characteristic of the Arabs. [Latin *Arabs* Arabian, from Greek *Araps,* from Arabic *'arab* Arabia.]

ar·a·besque (ar'ə besk') *n.* **1.** design consisting of elaborately intertwined patterns of scrollwork, flowers, leaves, or other figures. **2.** position in ballet in which the dancer stands with one leg lifted in full extension backward and, usually, with one arm extended forward and the other back. **3.** short musical piece in rondo form. —*adj.* **1.** relating to or done in the style of arabesque. **2.** resembling arabesque; full of ornamentation; fanciful. [French *arabesque,* from Italian *arabesco* in the Arabian manner, going back to Latin *Arabs.* See ARAB.]

Arabesque (def. 1)

A·ra·bi·a (ə rā'bē ə) *n.* peninsula constituting the southwestern extremity of Asia. Area, approx. 1,000,000 sq. mi.

A·ra·bi·an (ə rā'bē ən) *adj.* **1.** of or relating to Arabia or its people. **2.** relating to a breed of horses originally native to Arabia, noted for their speed, grace, and intelligence. —*n.* **1.** member or close descendant of the people of Arabia. **2.** Arab.

Arabian Desert, desert in eastern Egypt between the Nile River valley and the Red Sea. Area, 86,000 sq. mi.

Arabian Nights, collection of tales from Arabia, Persia, and India, dating from the tenth century.

Arabian Sea, northwestern part of the Indian Ocean, between Arabia and India.

Ar·a·bic (ar'ə bik) *adj.* of, relating to, or characteristic of the Arabs, their language, or their culture. —*n.* the Semitic language predominant in most of the Middle East and North Africa, originally spoken by the Arab tribesmen of the Arabian peninsula but extended to its present extent by the Islamic conquests.

Arabic numerals, the symbols 1, 2, 3, 4, 5, 6, 7, 8, 9, and 0.

ar·a·ble (ar'ə bəl) *adj.* (of land) fit for plowing or cultivation. [Latin *arābilis,* from *arāre* to plow.]

Arab League, organization of independent Arab states, formed in 1945 to promote Arab cultural, political, and economic unity. Founding members were the United Arab Republic (then Egypt), Iraq, Lebanon, Saudi Arabia, Syria, Jordan, and Yemen; they were joined later by Algeria, Kuwait, Tunisia, Morocco, Libya, and the Sudan.

A·ra·by (ar'ə bē) *n. Archaic.* Arabia.

A·rach·ne (ə rak'nē) *n. Greek Legend.* Lydian maiden changed into a spider by Athena for daring to challenge the goddess to a weaving contest. [Greek *arachnē* spider.]

a·rach·nid (ə rak'nid) *n.* any of a large group of air-breathing arthropods, class Arachnida, characteristically having four pairs of legs, no wings or antennas, and a body divided into two parts, an abdomen and a cephalothorax. Spiders, mites, scorpions, and ticks are arachnids. [Modern Latin *Arachnida,* from Greek *arachnē* spider + *-idēs* son of, descendant of.] —**a·rach'ni·dan,** *adj., n.*

a·rach·noid (ə rak'noid) *adj.* **1.** of or resembling the arachnids. **2.** designating the membrane covering the brain and the spinal cord that lies between the dura mater and the pia mater. **3.** (of a plant) covered with or consisting of long, slender hairs or fibers. —*n.* **1.** arachnoid membrane. **2.** an arachnid. [Greek *arachnoeidēs* like a spider's web, from *arachnē* spider.]

Ar·a·gon (ar′ə gon′) *n.* historic region and former kingdom in northeastern Spain.

Ar·al Sea (ar′əl) inland lake in the southwestern Soviet Union. Also, **Lake Aral.**

Ar·a·ma·ic (ar′ə mā′ik) *n.* ancient Semitic language, or group of dialects, widely used in the ancient Middle East, c.600 B.C.–A.D. 800, as a language of trade and government. It was spoken by many Palestinian Jews and was the language of Jesus.

Ar·a·rat (ar′ə rat′) *n.* mountain in eastern Turkey, traditionally identified as the landing place of Noah's Ark. Also, **Mount Ararat.**

Ar·au·ca·ni·an (ar′ô kā′nē ən) *n.* **1.** member of a group of related South American Indian tribes, living predominantly in central and southern Chile. **2.** any of the several closely related languages which are spoken by these people and constitute a separate language family. —*adj.* of or relating to the Araucanians, their culture, or their language. [Spanish *araucano* relating to the Araucanians, from *Arauco*, province in Chile, from Araucanian *rau* clay + *co* water.]

ar·ba·lest (är′bə ləst) *also,* **ar·ba·list.** *n.* crossbow of late medieval Europe, having a bow so strong that a special mechanism was needed to bend it. [Old French *arbaleste* crossbow, from Late Latin *arcubalista* ballista with a bow, from Latin *arcus* bow + *ballista*. See BALLISTA.]

ar·bi·ter (är′bə tər) *n.* **1.** person whose decision or opinion is authoritative or final: *an arbiter of taste.* **2.** arbitrator. [Latin *arbiter* judge; literally, one who goes to see (in order to judge), from *ad* to + *bītere* to go.] —**ar′bi·tress,** *n.* —*Syn.* **1.** see **judge.**

ar·bi·tra·ble (är′bə trə bəl) *adj.* capable of being arbitrated; suitable for arbitration.

ar·bi·tral (är′bə trəl) *adj.* of or relating to an arbiter or arbitration.

ar·bit·ra·ment (är bit′rə mənt) *n.* **1.** arbitration. **2.** decision or award made by an arbitrator. **3.** *Archaic.* power of absolute and final decision.

ar·bi·trar·y (är′bə trer′ē) *adj.* **1.** not determined by reason or principle; decided at random or by individual will or whim: *an arbitrary interpretation.* **2.** uncontrolled by law; despotic: *harsh and arbitrary government.* **3.** subject to a judge's decision; not fixed by law. [Latin *arbitrārius* relating to arbitration, uncertain, from *arbiter* judge (reflecting the uncertainty of judges' decisions).] —**ar′bi·trar′i·ly,** *adv.* —**ar′bi·trar′i·ness,** *n.*

ar·bi·trate (är′bə trāt′) -**trat·ed, -trat·ing.** *v.t., v.i.* **1.** to act or decide as arbitrator: *to arbitrate between contending parties. Who is arbitrating this dispute?* **2.** to settle by or submit to arbitration: *Both sides agreed to arbitrate. Neither party would arbitrate the dispute.* [Latin *arbitrātus,* past participle of *arbitrārī* to give judgment.] —**ar′bi·tra′tive,** *adj.*

ar·bi·tra·tion (är′bə trā′shən) *n.* hearing and settlement of a dispute by an arbitrator or arbitrators.

ar·bi·tra·tor (är′bə trā′tər) *n.* person empowered by parties in a dispute to settle or decide their differences. —*Syn.* see **judge.**

ar·bor¹ (är′bər) *also, British,* **ar·bour.** *n.* area covered over and partly enclosed on the sides by trees, shrubs, or a vine-covered trellis, esp. in a garden. [Anglo-Norman *erber* place where grass or herbs are grown, going back to Latin *herba* grass, herb.]

ar·bor² (är′bər) *n.* main shaft or beam of a machine; axle; spindle. [French *arbre* tree, pole, from Latin *arbor* tree, pole.]

Arbor Day, day set aside for tree planting, observed esp. by schools, civic groups, and conservationists in most states of the United States and in several other countries.

ar·bo·re·al (är bôr′ē əl) *adj.* **1.** of or relating to trees; treelike. **2.** inhabiting trees or adapted for living in trees. Squirrels and monkeys are arboreal animals. —**ar·bo′re·al·ly,** *adv.*

ar·bo·res·cent (är′bə res′ənt) *adj.* treelike in structure, appearance, or growth; branching. —**ar′bo·res′cence,** *n.* —**ar′bo·res′cent·ly,** *adv.*

ar·bo·re·tum (är′bə rē′təm) *pl.,* -**tums** or -**ta** (-tə). *n.* botanical garden devoted primarily to trees and shrubs. [Latin *arborētum* place grown with trees.]

ar·bor·vi·tae (är′bər vī′tē) *n.* any of various evergreen shrubs or trees, genus *Thuja,* of the pine family, characterized by scalelike aromatic leaves. Many varieties are used as ornamental trees, as hedges, or as windbreaks. [From Latin *arbor* tree + *vītae* of life.]

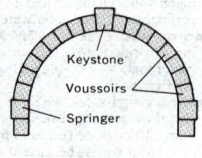

Arborvitae leaves

ar·bour, *arbor¹.*

ar·bu·tus (är bū′təs) *pl.,* -**tus·es.** *n.* **1.** trailing evergreen plant, *Epigaea repens,* found in North America, that bears fragrant pink or white flowers in early spring. Also, **may′flow′er, trailing arbutus. 2.** any of various evergreen shrubs or trees, genus *Arbutus,* of the heath family, bearing clusters of white or pink flowers and scarlet berries. [Latin *arbūtus* strawberry tree.]

arc (ärk) *n.* **1.** continuous curved line between any two points on a circle; any line curving in this way. **2.** intensely hot and bright electric current flowing in a curved path between two electrodes separated by a small space, used in arc lamps. **3.** part of the circular course that the sun or other heavenly body seems to follow as the earth rotates. —*v.i.* **arced** or **arcked, arc·ing** or **arck·ing. 1.** to form an electric arc. **2.** to move in a curved line. [Latin *arcus* bow, arch.]

Arc, Jeanne d' (därk; zhän) Joan of Arc.

ar·cade (är kād′) *n.* **1.** passageway covered by an arched roof. **2.** any covered passageway, street, or area opening onto a street, esp. one with shops along its sides. **3.** row of arches with their supporting columns and piers. An arcade may be ornamental, as a **blind arcade,** or it may function as an architectural support. —*v.t.* **-cad·ed, -cad·ing.** to provide with or form into an arcade. [French *arcade* arch, from Italian *arcata* arch, span, going back to Latin *arcus* bow, vault.]

Arcade

Ar·ca·di·a (är kā′dē ə) *n.* **1.** region of ancient Greece, in the central Peloponnesus, traditionally noted for the idyllic existence of its inhabitants. **2.** *also,* **arcadia.** any rural region of ideal calm, pleasantness, and simplicity.

Ar·ca·di·an (är kā′dē ən) *adj.* **1.** of Arcadia. **2.** *also,* **arcadian.** rustically simple, pleasant, and calm; pastoral. —*n.* **1.** native or inhabitant of Arcadia. **2.** *also,* **arcadian.** person who favors a simple and pleasant rural way of life.

Ar·ca·dy (är′kə dē) *n.* Arcadia.

ar·cane (är kān′) *adj.* secret; mysterious; obscure. [Latin *arcānus* hidden, secret.]

ar·ca·num (är kā′nəm) *pl.,* -**na** (-nə) or -**nums.** *n.* **1.** a secret or mystery: *the arcana of political intrigue.* **2.** secret remedy; elixir. [Latin *arcānum* a secret.]

Arc de Tri·omphe (ärk də trē ônf′) monumental arch in Paris built by Napoleon Bonaparte to commemorate the victories of his troops. Also, **Arch of Triumph.**

arch¹ (ärch) *n.* **1.** structural member, esp. a curved one, that rests on its two extremities and spans a space. It is usually constructed to support the weight of material above it, but may be merely ornamental. The traditional masonry arch consists of wedge-shaped blocks fitted together in a semicircle or similar shape. **2.** monument consisting of an arch or arches: *There is a giant steel arch in St. Louis, Missouri.* **3.a.** curved line or shape: *the arch of an eyebrow.* **b.** thing like an arch in shape or function. **4.** the raised, curved part of the foot between the ball and the heel; the curved bony structure of this part: *Good shoes give support to the arches.* **5.** archway. —*v.t.* **1.** to form (something) into an arch; curve: *The cat arched its back.* **2.** to cover or span with or as with an arch: *the rude bridge that arched the flood* (Emerson, 1837). —*v.i.* to have the form of an arch: *The sky arched overhead.* [Old French *arche* vault, chest, from Latin *arca* chest, confused with Latin *arcus* bow, vault.]

Keystone
Voussoirs
Springer

Masonry

Triangular   Segmental

Arches

arch² (ärch) *adj.* **1.** cunning; sly; mischievous. **2.** chief; pre-eminent; leading: *the arch criminal.* [From ARCH-.] —**arch′ly,** *adv.* —**arch′ness,** *n.*

arch- *prefix* **1.** chief; principal: *archbishop, archangel, archenemy.* **2.** original; primitive: *archenteron.* [Greek *arch(i)-,* from *archos* chief, *archē* beginning, often through Latin *arch(i)-.*]

arch. **1.** archaic; archaism. **2.** archery. **3.** architecture; architect; architectural. **4.** archipelago.

Arch. Archbishop.

Ar·chae·an (är kē′ən) Archean.

archaeo- *combining form* ancient; primitive: *archaeology, archaeopteryx.* [Greek *archaios* ancient.]

ar·chae·o·log·i·cal (är′kē ə loj′i kəl) *also,* **ar·che·o·log·i·cal.** *adj.* of or relating to archaeology.

ar·chae·ol·o·gist (är′kē ol′ə jist) *also,* **ar·che·ol·o·gist.** *n.* specialist in archaeology.

ar·chae·ol·o·gy (är′kē ol′ə jē) *also,* **ar·che·ol·o·gy.** *n.* scientific study of the human past through excavation of former dwelling sites or other places of activity and examination of the physical remains thus

discovered, such as tools, artifacts, or architecture. [Greek *archaiologiā* study of antiquity.]

ar·chae·op·ter·yx (är'kē op'tər iks) *n.* extinct primitive bird, genus *Archaeopteryx,* that had many reptilian characteristics along with wings and feathers. Found in European fossils from the Jurassic period, it is the earliest known bird. [Modern Latin *archaeopteryx,* from ARCHAEO- + Greek *pteryx* wing, bird.]

Ar·chae·o·zo·ic (är'kē ə zō'ik) *n.* Archean.

ar·cha·ic (är kā'ik) *adj.* **1.** no longer in common use in speech or writing. *Thou* and *thy* are archaic forms of *you* and *yours.* **2.** having the flavor of an earlier time; antiquated. [Greek *archaïkos* old-fashioned.] **—ar·cha'i·cal·ly,** *adv.*

ar·cha·ism (är'kē iz'əm, -kā-) *n.* **1.** something archaic, esp. an archaic word or phrase. **2.** use of something archaic, esp. in language or art; archaic style. **—ar'cha·ist,** *n.* **—ar'cha·is'tic,** *adj.*

arch·an·gel (ärk'ān'jəl) *n.* **1.** angel of the highest rank; chief angel. **2.** member of the eighth, or next-to-lowest, order of angels in Roman Catholic theology. [Late Latin *archangelus* chief angel, from Greek *archangelos.*]

Arch·an·gel (ärk'ān'jəl) *n.* port city in the northwestern Soviet Union. Pop. (1970), 343,000. Also, **Ar·khan'gelsk.**

arch·bish·op (ärch'bish'əp) *n.* bishop of the highest rank. An archbishop can be the chief bishop of an archdiocese or one holding an equivalent honorary rank. [Old English *ærcebiscop,* from Latin *archiepiscopus,* from Greek *archiepiskopos* literally, chief overseer.]

arch·bish·op·ric (ärch'bish'əp rik) *n.* **1.** archdiocese. **2.** office, rank, or jurisdiction of an archbishop.

arch·dea·con (ärch'dē'kən) *n.* clergyman in the Anglican or Episcopal Church who serves as chief administrative officer in a diocese. [Old English *archidiacon,* from Late Latin *archidiaconus* archdeacon, from Greek *archidiakonos.* See ARCH-, DEACON.]

arch·dea·con·ate (ärch'dē'kə nit) *n.* archdeaconry (*def. 1*).

arch·dea·con·ry (ärch'dē'kən rē) *pl.,* **-ries.** *n.* **1.** office, rank, or jurisdiction of an archdeacon. **2.** archdeacon's residence.

arch·di·o·cese (ärch'dī'ə sēz', -sis) *n.* church district consisting of several dioceses. An archdiocese is governed by an archbishop. **—arch·di·oc·e·san** (ärch'dī os'ə sən), *adj.*

arch·du·cal (ärch'dōō'kəl, -dū'-) *adj.* of or relating to an archduke or an archduchy.

arch·duch·ess (ärch'duch'is) *n.* **1.** wife or widow of an archduke. **2.** princess of the former royal family of Austria.

arch·duch·y (ärch'duch'ē) *pl.,* **-duch·ies.** *n.* territory ruled by an archduke or archduchess.

arch·duke (ärch'dōōk', -dūk') *n.* **1.** duke of superior authority or power. **2.** prince of the former royal house of Austria. [Old French *archiduc,* going back to Latin *archi-* chief + *dux* leader.]

Ar·che·an (är kē'ən) *also,* **Ar·chae·an.** *n.* earliest eon of geologic time, during which the earth was formed and life began. See **geology** for chart. **—adj.** of, relating to, or characteristic of the Archean eon. [Greek *archaios* ancient + -AN.]

arched (ärcht) *adj.* **1.** having the form of an arch. **2.** covered with or having an arch or arches.

ar·che·go·ni·um (är'kə gō'nē əm) *pl.,* **-ni·a** (-nē ə). *n.* female reproductive organ, as in ferns or mosses. [Modern Latin *archegonium,* diminutive of Greek *archegonos* original, primal, from *arche* beginning + *gonos* race.]

arch·en·e·my (ärch'en'ə mē) *pl.,* **-mies.** *n.* chief enemy.

ar·chen·ter·on (är ken'tə ron') *n.* digestive cavity of an animal embryo, formed during the gastrula stage. [Modern Latin *archenteron,* from ARCH- + Greek *enteron* intestine.]

archeo-, form of **archaeo-,** as in *archeology.*

ar·che·o·log·i·cal (är'kē ə loj'i kəl) *adj.* archaeological. **—ar'che·o·log'i·cal·ly,** *adv.*

ar·che·ol·o·gist (är'kē ol'ə jist) *n.* archaeologist.

ar·che·ol·o·gy (är'kē ol'ə jē) *n.* archaeology.

Ar·che·o·zo·ic (är'kē ə zō'ik) *also,* **Ar·chae·o·zo·ic.** *n.* Archean. [*Archeo-,* form of ARCHAEO- + Greek *zoē* life.]

arch·er (är'chər) *n.* one who shoots with a bow and arrow. [Anglo-Norman *archer,* from Late Latin *arcārius,* from Latin *arcus* bow.]

arch·er·fish (är'chər fish') *pl.,* **-fish** or **-fish·es.** *n.* any of a group of fish, family Toxotidae, esp. *Toxotes jaculatrix,* found in the waters of southeastern Asia, which shoot down their insect prey with a stream of water ejected from the mouth.

arch·er·y (är'chər ē) *n.* **1.** practice, skill, or sport of shooting with bow and arrow. **2.** body or company of archers.

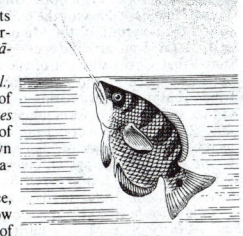

Archerfish

ar·che·typ·al (är'kə tī'pəl) *adj.* of, constituting, or having the nature of an archetype. Also, **ar·che·typ·i·cal** (är'kə tip'i kəl).

ar·che·type (är'kə tīp') *n.* **1.** original or ideal model or pattern from which all things of the same type are derived or copied. **2.** in the psychology of Carl Jung, unconscious way of thinking inherited from primitive ancestors. [Latin *archetypum* original pattern, from Greek *archetypon.*]

arch·fiend (ärch'fēnd') *n.* **1.** chief fiend. **2. the archfiend.** Satan.

archi-, form of **arch-,** as in *archiepiscopal.*

ar·chi·di·ac·o·nal (är'ki dī ak'ən əl) *adj.* of or relating to an archdeacon or his office. [Late Latin *archidiāconus* archdeacon, from Late Greek *archidiakonos.* See ARCH-, DEACON.]

ar·chi·e·pis·co·pal (är'kē i pis'kə pəl) *adj.* of or relating to an archbishop or his office. [Late Latin *archiepiscopus* archbishop, from Late Greek *archiepiskopos.* See ARCH-, BISHOP.]

Ar·chi·me·de·an screw (är'kə mē'dē ən, -mə dē'ən) ancient device for raising water, consisting of a spiral tube around or within an inclined cylinder. Also, **Archimedes' screw.**

Ar·chi·me·des (är'kə mē'dēz) *n.* c.287–212 B.C., Greek mathematician, physicist, and inventor.

ar·chi·pel·a·go (är'kə pel'ə gō') *pl.,* **-gos** or **-goes.** *n.* **1.** large group of islands. **2.** large body of water with many islands. [Italian *arcipelago,* going back to Greek *archi-* chief + *pelagos* sea; referring to the Aegean Sea with its many islands.]

ar·chi·tect (är'kə tekt') *n.* **1.** one whose profession is to design, draw plans for, and supervise the construction of buildings or other structures. **2.** creator, maker, or designer of anything: *the architects of their own happiness* (Milton, 1649). [French *architecte,* from Latin *architectus,* from Greek *architektōn* chief builder.]

ar·chi·tec·ton·ic (är'kə tek ton'ik) *adj.* **1.** of or relating to architecture. **2.** of or relating to construction or design of any kind. **3.** having the organized design or structural qualities of architecture: *an architectonic poem.* **4.** of or relating to the systematic classification of knowledge.

ar·chi·tec·ton·ics (är'kə tek ton'iks) *n.,pl.* **1.** structural design or system of structure, as of a work of art. **2.** science of systematic classification of knowledge. ▲ both definitions construed as singular.

ar·chi·tec·tur·al (är'kə tek'chər əl) *adj.* of, relating to, or characteristic of architecture: *an architectural effect.* **—ar'chi·tec'tur·al·ly,** *adv.*

ar·chi·tec·ture (är'kə tek'chər) *n.* **1.** science, art, or profession of planning, designing, and constructing buildings or other structures. Architecture includes plan, design, construction, and decoration of the structure and the surrounding space. **2.** style or method of building: *Byzantine architecture.* **3.** architectural work or works: *We saw some impressive architecture on the trip.* **4.** construction or design of anything: *the architecture of a novel.*

ar·chi·trave (är'kə trāv') *n.* **1.** lowest part of an entablature, resting directly on the capital of a column. See **entablature** for illustration. **2.** ornamental molding around a door or window. [French *architrave,* from Italian *architrave,* from *archi-* chief + *trave* beam, from Latin *trabs* beam.]

ar·chives (är'kīvz) *n.,pl.* **1.** place where public records or historical documents are kept. ▲ construed as singular. **2.** public records, papers, or documents so kept. [French *archives,* from Late Latin *archivum,* from Greek *archeion* public building.] **—ar·chi'val,** *adj.*

arch·ly (ärch'lē) *adv.* in an arch manner.

arch·ness (ärch'nis) *n.* quality of being arch.

Arch of Triumph, Arc de Triomphe.

ar·chon (är'kon) *n.* **1.** one of the nine chief magistrates in ancient Athens. **2.** *Archaic.* ruler. [Greek *archōn* ruler.]

arch·way (ärch'wā') *n.* **1.** entrance or passage under an arch. **2.** arch over a passage.

-archy *combining form* rule; government: *monarchy.* [Greek *-archiā* rule, from *archos* ruler, often through Latin *-archia.*]

arc lamp, lamp in which high intensity light is produced by an electric arc between carbon rods. Also, **arc light.**

arc·tic (ärk'tik, är'tik) *adj.* **1.** of, relating to, characteristic of, or near the North Pole, or the north polar regions. **2.** extremely cold; frigid. **—n. 1. the Arctic.** ice-covered region surrounding the North Pole. **2. arctics.** warm, waterproof overshoes. [Latin *arcticus* northern, from Greek *arktikos,* from *arktos* bear, with reference to the northern constellation of the Great Bear.]

Arctic Circle *also,* **arctic circle.** imaginary line around the earth at 66°33' north latitude, or about 1600 miles from the North Pole.

Arctic Ocean, ocean north of the Arctic Circle and surrounding the North Pole. Also, **Arctic Sea.**

Arc·tu·rus (ärk toor'əs, -tyoor'-) *n.* giant orange star, one of the brightest in the sky and brightest in the constellation Boötes.

-ard *suffix* (used to form nouns) one who does (something) to excess: *drunkard, coward.* ▲ used as an intensifier.

---

at; āpe; cär; end; mē; it; īce; hot; ōld; fôrk; wood; fōōl; oil; out; up; ūse; turn; sing; thin; this; zh in treasure; ə in ago, taken, pencil, lemon, circus.

ar·den·cy (ärd′ən sē) *n.* *Archaic.* ardor.

Ar·dennes (är den′) *n.* wooded region in southeastern Belgium, Luxembourg, and northern France, site of the Battle of the Bulge.

ar·dent (ärd′ənt) *adj.* characterized by intensity of feeling; passionate; enthusiastic: *an ardent supporter of the king.* [Old French *ardant* burning, from Latin *ārdēns,* present participle of *ārdēre* to burn.] —**ar′·dent·ly,** *adv.* —**Syn.** see **impassioned.**

ardent spirits *Archaic.* strong, distilled alcoholic liquors.

ar·dor (är′dər) *also, British,* **ar·dour.** *n.* intensity of emotion; fervor; enthusiasm; passion: *the ardor of a lover, revolutionary ardor.* [Old French *ardour,* from Latin *ardor* heat.] —**Syn.** see **passion.**

ar·du·ous (är′jōo əs) *adj.* requiring great exertion or endurance; difficult; strenuous: *an arduous effort, an arduous task.* [Latin *arduus* steep, difficult.] —**ar′du·ous·ly,** *adv.* —**ar′du·ous·ness,** *n.* —**Syn.** see **hard.**

are[1] (är; *unstressed* ər) present indicative plural and second person singular of **be.** [Old English (Northumbrian dialect) *aron* are.]

are[2] (âr, är) *n.* in the metric system, a unit of surface measure equal to 100 square meters, or 119.6 square yards. [French *are,* from Latin *ārea* open space.]

ar·e·a (âr′ē ə) *n.* **1.** amount of surface within given limits, esp. as measured in square units: *the area of a triangle.* **2.** particular surface, space, or tract; region: *a picnic area.* **3.** division or segment of activity, thought, or interest; field: *His education was weak in the area of math.* **4.** that which is included within limits; extent: *He covered a vast area in his talk.* **5.** *British.* areaway (*def. 1*). [Latin *ārea* open space.]

area code, combination of three numbers which represents any of the various geographic areas into which the United States and Canada are divided for purposes of telephone communication. This combination is dialed before the local number in calling from one area to another.

ar·e·a·way (âr′ē ə wā′) *n.* **1.** sunken space or passage in front of the windows or entrance of a cellar or basement. **2.** passageway, as between buildings.

a·re·na (ə rē′nə) *n.* **1.** central part of a Roman amphitheater, used for gladiatorial contests or other performances. **2.** any similar place used for public meetings or entertainment: *a boxing arena, a circus arena.* **3.** scene or sphere of conflict or activity: *the arena of politics.* [Latin *arēna* sand. Sand was used to cover the ground of Roman amphitheaters to absorb the blood shed in gladiatorial contests.]

ar·e·na·ceous (ar′ə nā′shəs) *adj.* **1.** like sand; sandy. **2.** living in or growing best in sand or sandy places. [Latin *arēnāceus* sandy, from *arēna* sand.]

arena theater, theater-in-the-round.

aren't (ärnt, är′ənt) **1.** are not. **2.** am not. ▲ used in the interrogative: *Aren't I allowed to come along?*

a·re·o·la (ə rē′ə lə) *pl.,* **-lae** (-lē) or **-las.** *n.* *Biology.* **1.** small space, as between the veins of a leaf or insect's wing. **2.** ring of color, as around a vesicle or a nipple. [Latin *āreola* small open place, diminutive of *ārea* open place.]

Ar·e·op·a·gus (ar′ē op′ə gəs) *n.* **1.** hill west of the Acropolis in Athens. **2.** court of ancient Athens, which met there. [Latin *Areopagus* this hill, from Greek *Areiopagos* literally, hill of Ares.]

A·re·qui·pa (ä′rə kē′pə, ä′rā–) *n.* city in southern Peru. Pop. (1969) 187,400.

A·res (âr′ēz) *n.* Greek god of war. His Roman counterpart is Mars.

Ar·e·thu·sa (ar′ə thōō′zə) *n.* *Greek Mythology.* a nymph who was transformed into a spring by Artemis to save her from her pursuer, the river god Alpheus.

ar·ga·li (är′gə lē) *pl.,* **-lis** or **-li.** *n.* wild sheep, *Ovis ammon,* of Central Asia, noted for its long, thick, curved horns. It is the largest of all sheep. Height: 4 feet at the shoulder. [Of Mongol origin.]

ar·gent (är′jənt) *Archaic. n.* silver. —*adj.* made of silver; silvery-white. Also, **ar′gen·tine′.** [French *argent* this metal, from Latin *argentum.*]

Ar·gen·ti·na (är′jən tē′nə; *Spanish* är′hen tē′nä) *n.* country in southern South America. Capital, Buenos Aires. Area, 1,072,072 sq. mi. Pop. (1969 est.), 23,983,000.

Ar·gen·tine (är′jən tīn′, -tēn′) *adj.* of or relating to Argentina, its people, or its culture. —*n.* **1.** member or close descendant of the people of Argentina. **2. the Argentine.** Argentina. Also (*n., adj., def. 1*), **Ar·gen·tin·e·an** (är′jən tin′ē ən).

ar·gil (är′jil) *n.* clay, esp. potter's clay. [French *argile,* through Latin, from Greek *argillos,* from *argēs* shining.]

Ar·give (är′jīv, -gīv) *adj.* **1.** of or relating to Argos or Argolis. **2.** Greek. —*n.* **1.** member or close descendant of the people of Argos or Argolis. **2.** any Greek.

Ar·go (är′gō) *n.* *Greek Legend.* the ship in which Jason and the Argonauts sailed in quest of the Golden Fleece.

Ar·go·lis (är′gə lis) *n.* district in the southeastern part of ancient Greece.

ar·gon (är′gon) *n.* colorless, inert gaseous element that forms approximately one percent of the earth's atmosphere. It is esp. noted for its use in electric light bulbs. Symbol: Ar See **element** for table. [Greek *argon,* neuter of *argos* idle.]

Ar·go·naut (är′gə nôt′) *n.* **1.** *Greek Legend.* one who sailed with Jason in search of the Golden Fleece. **2.** one who went to California in 1848–49 to search for gold. **3.** argonaut, paper nautilus. [Latin *Argonauta* Argonaut (of Greek legend), from Greek *Argonautēs,* from *Argō* ARGO + *nautēs* sailor.] —**Ar′go·nau′tic,** *adj.*

Ar·gonne (är′gon) *n.* forest in northeastern France, site of several battles of World War I and World War II.

Ar·gos (är′gos, -gəs) *n.* ancient Greek city in the eastern Peloponnesus.

ar·go·sy (är′gə sē) *pl.,* **-sies.** *n.* **1.** large merchant ship. **2.** fleet of such ships. [Modification of Italian *ragusea* ship of Ragusa, former name of the seaport Dubrovnik, Yugoslavia.]

ar·got (är′gō, -gət) *n.* specialized vocabulary or idiom used by a particular group or class, as the secret language of thieves. [French; of uncertain origin.]

ar·gue (är′gū) **-gued, -gu·ing.** *v.i.* **1.** to contend in argument; dispute: *to argue about politics.* **2.** to give reasons (for or against something): *He argued against the motion.* —*v.t.* **1.** to give reasons for or against; debate: *Let's not argue the matter.* **2.** to persuade (someone) by giving reasons (with *into* or *out of*): *Argue him out of selling his car.* **3.** to maintain; contend: *to argue that someone is wrong.* **4.** to give evidence of; indicate; prove: *Her accent argues that she was born abroad.* [Middle French *arguer* to reason, from Latin *argūtāre* to prattle, from *arguere* to prove, make clear.] —**ar′gu·a·ble,** *adj.* —**ar′gu·er,** *n.* —**Syn.** *v.t.* **1.** see **discuss.**

ar·gu·ment (är′gyə mənt) *n.* **1.a.** discussion of a disputed topic; debate: *for the sake of argument.* **b.** disagreement; quarrel: *They were friends before the argument.* **2.** reason or reasons given (to support or oppose something): *What are the arguments for accepting the proposal?* **3.** process or line of reasoning: *I couldn't follow his argument.* **4.** *Archaic.* summary of the chief points of a literary work.

Syn. **1.a. Argument, controversy, dispute** indicate a disagreement about which there is discussion. **Argument** suggests that each of the parties is trying to win his opponent over by an appeal to reason: *The long argument was resolved in the scientist's favor when the expedition returned with new evidence.* **Controversy** suggests a widespread disagreement on principle, as between groups or parties, in which the discussion is formal and often in the third person, as in correspondence in learned journals: *The controversy about the Darwinian theory is far from dead.* **Dispute** suggests a heated disagreement in which the appeal is to feeling rather than reason and in which the opposing argument is contradicted or challenged rather than refuted: *The boundary dispute was often close to breaking out into open conflict.*

ar·gu·men·ta·tion (är′gyə men tā′shən) *n.* **1.** process of forming and presenting reasons and of developing conclusions from them. **2.** argument; debate.

ar·gu·men·ta·tive (är′gyə men′tə tiv) *adj.* **1.** inclined to argue; quarrelsome. **2.** containing argument; controversial. —**ar′gu·men′·ta·tive·ly,** *adv.*

Ar·gus (är′gəs) *n.* **1.** *Greek Mythology.* giant with a hundred eyes that were put in the peacock's tail after he was killed by Hermes. **2.** any extremely observant or watchful person.

Ar·gus-eyed (är′gəs īd′) *adj.* extremely observant; vigilant.

ar·gyle (är′gīl) *also,* **ar·gyle.** *n.* **1.** diamond-shaped pattern of contrasting colors, used esp. in knitting. **2.** argyles. pair of socks having this pattern. —*adj.* having this pattern. [From *Argyll,* a branch of the Campbell clan of Scotland, whose tartan inspired the design.]

ar·gy·rol (är′jə rôl′) *n.* compound of silver and a protein, used as an antiseptic in treating inflammation of mucous membranes. Trademark: Argyrol. [Greek *argyros* silver.]

a·ri·a (är′ē ə, âr′ē ə) *n.* elaborate musical composition for solo voice with instrumental accompaniment. [Italian *aria* air (in all senses), from Latin *āēr* air, from Greek *āēr* air.]

Ar·i·ad·ne (ar′ē ad′nē) *n.* *Greek Legend.* the daughter of King Minos, who gave Theseus the ball of thread by which he found his way out of the labyrinth of the Minotaur.

Ar·i·an (âr′ē ən, ar′-) *adj.* of or relating to the doctrine of Arius that stated that Christ was not of the same substance as God the Father, but was created by and subordinate to Him. —*n.* believer in this doctrine. [Latin *Ariānus* relating to Arius.] —**Ar′i·an·ism,** *n.*

-arian *suffix* (used to form nouns): **1.** one who believes in: *humanitarian.* **2.** one whose work deals with: *grammarian.* **3.** one who is a member of: *Unitarian.* **4.** one who is an advocate of: *disciplinarian.* **5.** one who is of the age of: *octogenarian.* [-ARY[1] + -ON.]

ar·id (ar′id) *adj.* **1.** dry; parched or without rain. **2.** uninteresting; lifeless. [Latin *āridus* dry.] —**a·rid·i·ty** (ə rid′ə tē), **ar′id·ness,** *n.* —**ar′id·ly,** *adv.* —**Syn.** **1.** see **dry.**

Ar·i·el (âr′ē əl) *n.* **1.** airy spirit who used magic to help Prospero in Shakespeare's *The Tempest.* **2.** the inner satellite of Uranus. [Through

at; āpe; cär; end; mē; it; īce; hot; ōld; fôrk; wood; fōōl; oil; out; up; ūse; turn; sing; thin; this; zh in treasure; ə in ago, taken, pencil, lemon, circus.

Latin and Greek, going back to Hebrew *'ari̇'ēl* lion of God (a name of Jerusalem in the Old Testament); also influenced by English *airy*.]

Ar·ies (âr′ēz, âr′ē ēz) *n.* **1.** constellation in the northern sky, conventionally depicted as a ram. **2.** first sign of the zodiac. See **zodiac** for illustration. [Latin *ariēs* ram.]

a·right (ə rīt′) *adv.* *Archaic.* correctly; rightly.

ar·il (ar′il) *n.* outer, sometimes pulpy, covering or appendage of certain seeds. [Modern Latin *arillus*, from Medieval Latin *arillus* raisin; of uncertain origin.]

A·ri·os·to, Lu·do·vi·co (är′ē os′tō, -ôs′-; lⁿōⁿdō′ vē′kō) 1474–1533, Italian poet.

a·rise (ə rīz′) *a·rose, a·ris·en, a·ris·ing.* *v.i.* **1.** to come into being; appear; originate: *Questions arise as we read. We dealt with each problem as it arose.* **2.** to result or proceed (with *from*): *New problems arose from the war.* **3.** to get up; stand up: *The audience arose and remained standing.* **4.** to ascend. [Old English *ārīsan*.]

Ar·is·ti·des (ar′is tī′dēz) *n.* c.520–c.468 B.C., Athenian general and statesman. Also, **Aristides the Just.**

ar·is·toc·ra·cy (ar′is tok′rə sē) *pl.,* **-cies.** *n.* **1.** privileged upper class; hereditary nobility. **2.** government by an upper class minority or the nobility. **3.** state having this form of government. **4.** any outstanding or superior group: *the aristocracy of culture.* [French *aristocratie* rule of the nobly born, from Greek *aristokratiā* rule of the best.]

a·ris·to·crat (ə ris′tə krat′, ar′is tə-) *n.* **1.** member of an aristocracy; nobleman. **2.** one who has the tastes, manners, and attitudes associated with the aristocracy.

a·ris·to·crat·ic (ə ris′tə krat′ik, ar′is tə-) *adj.* **1.** characteristic of or befitting an aristocracy: *aristocratic bearing.* **2.** of or belonging to the aristocracy. **3.** of, relating to, or supporting government by aristocracy. —**a·ris′to·crat′i·cal·ly,** *adv.*

Ar·is·toph·a·nes (ar′is tof′ə nēz′) *n.* c.448–385 B.C., Greek comic dramatist.

Ar·is·to·te·li·an (ar′is tə tē′lē ən, -tēl′yən, ə ris′tə-) *adj.* of, relating to, or characteristic of Aristotle or his philosophy. —*n.* **1.** follower of Aristotle or his philosophy. **2.** one whose thinking or method tends to be deductive or empirical rather than intuitive or idealistic. —**Ar′is·to·te′li·an·ism,** *n.*

Aristotelian logic 1. deductive logic of Aristotle, characterized by the syllogism. **2.** formal symbolic logic developed from that of Aristotle, dealing with the relations between the form, rather than the content, of the propositions.

Ar·is·tot·le (ar′is tot′əl) *n.* 384–322 B.C., Greek philosopher.

arith., arithmetic; arithmetical.

a·rith·me·tic (*n.,* ə rith′mə tik′; *adj.,* ar′ith met′ik) *n.* science and technique of computing with positive, real numbers. Arithmetic deals with the four basic operations of addition, subtraction, multiplication, and division. —*adj.* *also,* **ar′ith·met′i·cal.** of, relating to, or according to the rules of arithmetic. [French *arithmétique,* from Latin *arithmētica* science of numbers, from Greek *arithmētikē,* from *arithmos* number.] —**ar′ith·met′i·cal·ly,** *adv.*

a·rith·me·ti·cian (ə rith′mə tish′ən) *n.* one skilled in arithmetic.

arithmetic mean, average.

arithmetic progression, series in which the difference between any two terms is a constant quantity. 1, 3, 5, 7, and 3, 1, −1, −3 are arithmetic progressions. Distinguished from **geometric progression.** Also, **arithmetic series.**

A·ri·us (ə rī′əs, âr′ē əs) *n.* A.D. c.250–336, Christian priest of Alexandria.

Ariz., Arizona.

Ar·i·zo·na (ar′ə zō′nə) *n.* state in the southwestern United States, bordering on Mexico. Capital, Phoenix. Area, 113,909 sq. mi. Pop. (1970), 1,772,482. Abbreviation, **Ariz.**

ark (ärk) *n.* **1.** Noah's Ark. **2.** any large, flat-bottomed, clumsy boat, esp. one formerly used for transport on American rivers. **3.** Ark of the Covenant. [Old English *arc,* from Latin *arca* chest, box.]

Ark., Arkansas.

Ar·kan·sas (är′kən sô′; *def. 2 also* är kan′zəs) *n.* **1.** state in the south-central United States. Capital, Little Rock. Area, 53,104 sq. mi. Pop. (1970), 1,923,295. Abbreviation, **Ark. 2.** major river flowing from west-central Colorado into the Mississippi.

Ar·khan·gelsk (är KHän′gelsk) *n.* Archangel.

Ark of the Covenant 1. sacred chest that held the two stone tablets containing the Ten Commandments. **2.** repository in a synagogue for the scrolls of the Torah and other sacred books.

Ark·wright, Sir Richard (ärk′rīt′) 1732–92, English inventor and industrialist.

Ar·ling·ton (är′ling tən) *n.* **1.** one of the largest national cemeteries in the United States, in northeastern Virginia. **2.** county in northern Virginia, a residential suburb of Washington, D.C. Pop. (1970), 174,-284. **3.** city in northeastern Texas. Pop. (1970), 90,643.

arm¹ (ärm) *n.* **1.** upper limb of the human body, esp. the part between the shoulder and wrist. **2.** forelimb of any vertebrate animal. **3.** something used to support or cover the human arm: *the arm of a chair, the arm of a coat.* **4.** anything branching out from a larger body: *an arm of the sea, the arm of a phonograph.* **5.** division of an organization: *an arm of government.* **6. arm in arm.** with arms interlinked. **7. long arm of the law.** reach or authority of the law. **8. to keep at arm's length.** to keep at a distance; prevent friendship or familiarity. **9. with open arms.** with an eager welcome; cordially. [Old English *earm* upper limb of the human body.]

arm² (ärm) *n.* **1.** weapon, esp. a firearm. **2.** combat branch of the armed forces. —*v.t.* **1.** to provide with or as with weapons or tools: *Arm the populace.* **2.** to provide with something that protects or strengthens; fortify: *The porcupine is armed with quills.* **3.** to furnish with whatever is necessary to meet the occasion; prepare: *Arm them with a good education.* **4.** to activate or supply (as a bomb or grenade) with a fuse or detonator so that it will explode at the desired time. —*v.i.* to prepare for war or hostility, esp. by equipping oneself with weapons. [Old French *armer* to furnish with weapons, from Latin *armāre,* from *arma* weapons.]

ar·ma·da (är mä′də, -mā′-) *n.* **1.** fleet of warships. **2. the Armada.** Spanish Armada. [Spanish *armada* fleet, from *armar* to arm, from Latin *armāre* to furnish with weapons.]

ar·ma·dil·lo (är′mə dil′ō) *pl.,* **-los.** *n.* any of several insect-eating, burrowing mammals, order Edentata, ranging from South America to the southern United States, having an armorlike shell of bony plates, a long snout, strong, sharp claws, and a long tail. Length: 5 inches–5 feet. [Spanish *armadillo* literally, little armed creature, from *armado,* past participle of *armar* to arm, from Latin *armāre* to furnish with arms.]

Armadillo

Ar·ma·ged·don (är′mə ged′ən) *n.* **1.** site of the world's great and final battle between the forces of good and evil, as prophesied in the Bible. **2.** any great and decisive battle. [Going back to Hebrew *Har Megiddō* literally, mountain of Megiddo; a district in ancient Israel where a number of important battles were fought in Biblical times.]

ar·ma·ment (är′mə mənt) *n.* **1.** armaments. military forces, equipment, and supplies, esp. considered as the entire military strength of a nation. **2.** *also,* **armaments.** weapons with which a military unit, ship, or plane is equipped. **3.** process of arming: *The country's armament took two months.*

ar·ma·ture (är′mə chər) *n.* **1.** rotating member of an electric motor or dynamo, consisting of a laminated iron core with wire coiled around it. See **dynamo** for illustration. **2.** piece of soft iron placed across the poles of a magnet to preserve magnetic power. **3.** vibrating iron part of an electric buzzer or relay. **4.** part or organ of an animal or plant serving for offense or defense, esp. a protective covering. **5.** framework used as a support around which clay or some other substance is modeled in sculpture. **6.** *Archaic.* military equipment, esp. defensive armor. [Latin *armātūra* armor. Doublet of ARMOR.]

arm·chair (ärm′châr′) *n.* chair with pieces at each side to support one's arms or elbows. —*adj.* dealing with problems indirectly or without actual experience: *armchair general.*

armed (ärmd) *adj.* **1.** having, bearing, or supported by arms or weapons: *armed neutrality, armed garrison.* **2.** having whatever is necessary to meet the occasion: *armed with statistics.* **3.** having an arm or arms. ▲ usually used in combination, as *one-armed, long-armed.*

armed forces, all of the military forces of a nation taken as a whole. In the United States it includes the Army, Navy, Marines, Air Force, and Coast Guard.

Ar·me·ni·a (ar mē′nē ə, -mēn′yə) *n.* **1.** republic in the southwestern Soviet Union, bordering on Turkey and Iran. Official name: **Armenian Soviet Socialist Republic.** Capital, Yerevan. Area, 11,500 sq. mi. Pop. (1969), 2,363,000. **2.** ancient country in northeastern Asia Minor, now a region consisting of Soviet Armenia and parts of eastern Turkey and northwestern Iran.

Ar·me·ni·an (ar mē′nē ən, -mēn′yən) *adj.* of Armenia, its people, language, or culture. —*n.* **1.** member or close descendant of the people of Armenia. **2.** the Indo-European language of the Armenians.

arm·ful (ärm′fool′) *pl.,* **-fuls.** *n.* **1.** as much as one or both arms can hold. **2.** that which one holds in one or both arms.

arm·hole (ärm′hōl′) *n.* opening in a garment for the arm.

Ar·min·i·an (är min′ē ən) *adj.* of or relating to Jacobus Arminius or his doctrines, esp. those which opposed the Calvinist doctrine of predestination. —*n.* believer in the doctrines of Arminius. —**Ar·min′i·an·ism,** *n.*

Ar·min·i·us, Ja·co·bus (är min′ē əs; jə kō′bəs) 1560–1609, Dutch Protestant theologian.

ar·mi·stice (är′mi stis) *n.* temporary suspension of fighting by mutual agreement; truce. [French *armistice,* going back to Latin *arma* weapons + *sistere* to stop.]

Armistice Day, see Veteran's Day.

arm·let (ärm′lit) *n.* **1.** ornamental band worn around the upper arm. **2.** small arm, as of the sea.

ar·moire (ärm wär′) *n.* large, movable cabinet or wardrobe with full-length doors.

ar·mor (är′mər) *also, British,* **ar·mour.** *n.* **1.** defensive covering for the body. **2.** protective metal covering as used on tanks, automobiles, or warships. **3.** armored military vehicles. **4.** any protective covering. —*v.t., v.i.* to cover or furnish with armor. [Old French *armeüre* defensive covering for the body, from Latin *armātūra,* from *armāre* to furnish with weapons. Doublet of AR·MATURE.]

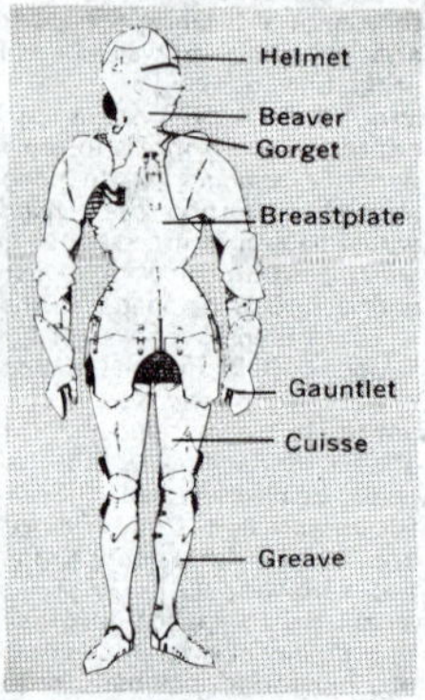

ar·mor-bear·er (är′mər bâr′ər) *n.* one who carries a warrior's armor or weapons.

ar·mored (är′mərd) *also, British,* **ar·moured.** *adj.* **1.** protected by armor. **2.** equipped with armored vehicles.

armored car 1. vehicle covered with armor plate, used to transport money or other valuable cargo. **2.** military vehicle sheathed in armor plate and usually equipped with a machine gun, used esp. for reconnaissance.

ar·mor·er (är′mər ər) *also, British,* **ar·mour·er.** *n.* **1.** *Military.* enlisted man in charge of small arms. **2.** one who made or repaired armor.

ar·mo·ri·al (är môr′ē əl) *adj.* relating to heraldry or coats of arms.

armor plate, specially hardened steel used for protective covering, as on a tank or automobile. —**ar′mor-plat′ed,** *adj.*

ar·mor·y (är′mər ē) *pl.,* **-mor·ies.** *n.* **1.** building that is the headquarters and training center of a National Guard or other military reserve unit. **2.** place where arms are kept; arsenal. **3.** place where arms are manufactured.

ar·mour (är′mər) *British.* armor.

arm·pit (ärm′pit′) *n.* hollow under the arm at the shoulder.

arm·rest (ärm′rest′) *n.* support for the arm, as on a chair.

arms (ärmz) *n.,pl.* **1.** weapons, esp. as considered collectively. **2.** coat of arms. **3. to arms.** to make ready to fight. **4. to bear arms. a.** to possess or carry weapons. **b.** to serve in the armed forces. **5. under arms.** furnished with weapons; ready for war: *The total of men under arms has reached a post-war high.* **6. up in arms.** aroused to fight; indignant: *Congress was up in arms about federal spending.* [Old French *armes* weapons, from Latin *arma.*]

Arm·strong, Neil (ärm′strông) 1930—, U.S. astronaut, the first man to set foot on the moon.

ar·my (är′mē) *pl.,* **-mies.** *n.* **1.** large, organized body of soldiers armed and trained for combat on land. **2.** *also,* **Army.** branch of the military forces of a nation trained primarily for land operations. In some countries it includes the air forces. **3.** large body of persons organized for a common cause: *an army of suffragettes.* **4.** any large group; multitude: *army of strap hangers.* [Old French *armee* armed forces, from *armer* to arm, from Latin *armāre* to furnish with arms.]

army ant, any of a group of nomadic social ants, subfamily Dorylinae, found in Africa and tropical America, which kills its prey by stinging. Hunting and migrating in huge swarms, it consumes all vegetation and nearly all the small animals in its path. Also, **driver ant.**

army of occupation, army stationed in a defeated country to keep order and enforce surrender terms.

army worm, voracious larva of a brown moth, *Cirphis unipuncta,* that travels in vast numbers, destroying grass, grain, and other crops.

ar·ni·ca (är′ni kə) *n.* **1.** any of a group of plants, genus *Arnica,* of the composite family, bearing clusters of yellow flower heads. **2.** tincture prepared from the dried flowers and roots of a species of this plant, *A. montana.* [Modern Latin *Arnica;* of unknown origin.]

Ar·no (är′nō) *n.* river in north-central Italy, flowing through Florence to the Mediterranean.

Ar·nold (är′nəld) **1. Benedict.** 1741–1801, U.S. Revolutionary general who turned traitor. **2. Matthew.** 1822–88, English poet and essayist.

a·ro·ma (ə rō′mə) *n.* **1.** distinctive odor, esp. an agreeable one; fragrance. **2.** distinctive or subtle quality; flavor. [Late Latin *arōma* spice, fragrance, from Greek *arōma.*] —**Syn. 1.** see smell.

ar·o·mat·ic (ar′ə mat′ik) *adj.* **1.** having an aroma; fragrant: *aromatic leaves of the clove tree.* **2.** of or relating to a group of organic

hydrocarbon compounds, including benzene and its derivatives, which contain at least one unsaturated benzene ring and generally have a pleasant odor. —*n.* aromatic plant, chemical, or other substance. —**ar′o·mat′i·cal·ly,** *adv.*

a·rose (ə rōz′) past tense of **arise.**

a·round (ə round′) *prep.* **1.** so as to encircle: *in orbit around the earth.* **2.** along the circumference or outer edge of: *Walk around the block.* **3.** so as to surround or envelop: *Her arms were around the children.* **4.** on all sides of: *Around us lay the ruins of a city.* **5.** here and there in or through: *Wander around the town.* **6.** somewhere in or near: *Stay around the theater.* **7.** somewhat near as in time or amount; about: *around six o'clock.* **8.** on another side of: *around the bend.* —*adv.* **1.** in a circle or circular course. **2.** in circumference: *The tree measures four feet around.* **3.** on all sides; in various directions: *with people all around.* **4.** here and there; about: *We spread the word around. Drive around until we get back.* **5.** *Informal.* somewhere near: *Stand around awhile.* **6.** to a (particular) place: *Come around again tomorrow.* **7.** in or to the opposite direction: *He spun around quickly.* **8.** to have been around. *Informal.* to be experienced or sophisticated. ▲ see **round** for usage note.

a·rouse (ə rouz′) **a·roused, a·rous·ing.** *v.t.* **1.** to stir up; excite: *a speech that aroused the crowd, to arouse curiosity.* **2.** to awaken (someone): *His friend aroused him from sleep.* —*v.i.* to wake up. [A-¹ + ROUSE.]

ar·peg·gi·o (är pej′ē ō′,-pej′ō) *pl.,* **-gi·os.** *n.* **1.** playing of the notes of a chord in succession instead of simultaneously. **2.** chord played in this way. [Italian *arpeggio,* from *arpeggiare* to play on the harp, from *arpa* harp; of Germanic origin; so called because of the resemblance to harp playing.]

ar·que·bus (är′kwə bəs) harquebus.

ar·raign (ə rān′) *v.t.* to formally state the charge against (someone) before a judge, and record an answer to the charge. [Anglo-Norman *arainer,* going back to Latin *ad* to + *ratiō* reason, account.]

ar·raign·ment (ə rān′mənt) *n.* act of arraigning or being arraigned.

ar·range (ə rānj′) **-ranged, -rang·ing.** *v.t.* **1.** to put in proper, convenient, or pleasing order: *to arrange the cards in alphabetical order, to arrange the furniture in a room.* **2.** to help to bring about; prepare for; plan: *to arrange a settlement. Who arranged their meeting?* **3.** to settle; determine: *to arrange the terms of payment.* **4.** to adapt or change (a musical composition) while preserving its essential nature, esp. by scoring it for instruments or voices for which it was not originally written. —*v.i.* **1.** to make plans or preparations: *I'll arrange for us to go.* **2.** to come to an agreement: *I'll arrange with him about the tickets.* [Old French *arengier* to put into a rank, from *à* to (from Latin *ad* to) + *rengier* to put in order, from *renc* line, row; of Germanic origin.] —**ar·rang′er,** *n.*

ar·range·ment (ə rānj′mənt) *n.* **1.** putting in order; being put in order: *The arrangement of the books took two hours.* **2.** result of arranging or ordering: *a flower arrangement.* **3.** style or manner in which something is ordered: *arrangement of electrons in an atom.* **4.** *also,* **arrangements.** plan; preparation: *arrangements for a dance.* **5.** settlement; adjustment: *an arrangement that pleased us all.* **6.a.** adaptation or changing of a musical composition, esp. by scoring it for instruments or voices for which it was not originally written. **b.** work so adapted.

ar·rant (ar′ənt) *adj.* unmitigated; downright; notorious: *an arrant fool.* [Form of ERRANT.]

ar·ras (ar′əs) *n.* **1.** type of tapestry. **2.** tapestry screen or wall hanging. [From *Arras,* a city in northern France, where the tapestry was produced.]

ar·ray (ə rā′) *n.* **1.** orderly grouping or arrangement, as of troops for battle. **2.** large, imposing collection; display: *an array of jewels.* **3.** persons or things on display or in order. **4.** attire; finery: *in rich array.* —*v.t.* **1.** to place in order; marshal: *The forces were arrayed against us.* **2.** to dress up; deck; adorn. [Anglo-Norman *arayer* to prepare, arrange, from *a-* to (from Latin *ad* to) + an unrecorded Germanic word.]

ar·rear·age (ə rēr′ij) *n.* **1.** state of being in arrears. **2.** amount in arrears; debt.

ar·rears (ə rērz′) *n.,pl.* **1.** debt that is due but unpaid. **2. in arrears.** behind in payments, duties, or obligations. [Old French *arere* backward, from Latin *ad* toward + *retrō* backward.]

ar·rest (ə rest′) *v.t.* **1.** to seize or take into custody by legal authority. **2.** to stop; check: *to arrest the progress of a disease.* **3.** to catch and hold; engage: *to arrest the attention.* —*n.* **1.** seizure by legal authority; taking into custody. **2.** check; stoppage. **3. under arrest.** held by legal authority. **4.** device for stopping or checking motion. [Old French *arester* to stay, from Latin *ad* + *restāre* to stop.] —**ar·rest′er, ar·res′tor,** *n.*

ar·rest·ing (ə res′ting) *adj.* demanding the attention; striking.

ar·ris (ar′is) *pl.,* **-ris** or **-ris·es.** *n.* sharp ridge or edge formed by the meeting of two surfaces at an angle, as between two flutings on the shaft of a Doric column. [Old French *areste* fishbone, from Latin *arista* ear of corn, fishbone.]

[Illustration labels:]
Helmet
Beaver
Gorget
Breastplate
Gauntlet
Cuisse
Greave

Armor

at; āpe; cär; end; mē; it; īce; hot; ōld; fôrk; wood; fōōl; oil; out; up; ūse; turn; sing; thin; this; zh in treasure; ə in ago, taken, pencil, lemon, circus.

ar·riv·al (ə rī′vəl) *n.* **1.** act of arriving: *arrival of a plane, arrival at a decision.* **2.** one who or that which arrives or has arrived.

ar·rive (ə rīv′) **-rived, -riv·ing.** *v.i.* **1.** to reach a destination; appear at a place. **2. to arrive at. a.** to come to or reach by traveling: *to arrive at home.* **b.** to come to or reach by any process or effort: *to arrive at a conclusion.* **3.** (of time) to come: *The moment of truth has arrived.* **4.** to attain success or fame: *to arrive as a poet.* [Old French *ariver* to come to land, going back to Latin *ad* to + *rīpa* shore.]

ar·ri·ve·der·ci (ä′rē ve der′chē, ə rē′və-) *interj.* until we meet again; good-by for now. [Italian *arrivederci,* going back to Latin *ad* to + *revidēre* to see again.]

ar·ro·gance (ar′ə gəns) *n.* display of feelings of superiority; overbearing pride; haughtiness.

ar·ro·gant (ar′ə gənt) *adj.* full of or proceeding from unwarranted pride; conceited and haughty: *an arrogant person, arrogant claims.* [Latin *arrogāns* insolent, present participle of *arrogāre* to claim for oneself.] **—ar′ro·gant·ly,** *adv.* **—Syn.** see **proud.**

ar·ro·gate (ar′ə gāt′) **-gat·ed, -gat·ing.** *v.t.* **1.** to claim or seize presumptuously or without right: *to arrogate judicial powers to oneself.* **2.** to ascribe (to another) without good reason. [Latin *arrogātus,* past participle of *arrogāre* to claim for good oneself.]

ar·ro·ga·tion (ar′ə gā′shən) *n.* **1.** act of arrogating. **2.** that which is arrogated; assumption.

ar·ron·disse·ment (ə ron′dis mənt; *French* a rôn dēs mäN′) *pl.* **-ments** (-mənts; *French* -mäN′). *n.* **1.** largest administrative division of a department in France. **2.** administrative district of a city, as in Paris. [French *arrondissement* literally, a rounding, going back to Latin *ad* to + *rotundus* round.]

ar·row (ar′ō) *n.* **1.** slender shaft, usually pointed at one end and feathered at the other, made to be shot from a bow. **2.** symbol in the shape of an arrow used to indicate direction or position, as in road signs. **3.** anything resembling an arrow, in form or function. [Old English *arwe* this shaft.]

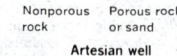

ONE WAY

Arrows

ar·row·head (ar′ō hed′) *n.* **1.** pointed tip of an arrow. **2.** any of a group of aquatic plants, genus *Sagittaria,* found in temperate and tropical regions, bearing arrow-shaped leaves and whorls of white flowers on a separate stem.

ar·row·root (ar′ō rōōt′, -root′) *n.* **1.** nutritious starch made from the roots of a tropical American plant, *Maranta arundinacea,* used as a thickening agent in cooking. **2.** the plant itself, widely cultivated in the West Indies and other tropical regions, bearing long, pointed leaves, and small, white flowers. [South American Indians used the *root* of this plant to absorb poison from *arrow* wounds.]

ar·row·wood (ar′ō wood′) *n.* any of several North American trees or shrubs, genus *Viburnum,* having slender, straight shoots which were used by Indians for making shafts, esp. *V. dentatum,* a tree often cultivated as an ornamental, bearing clusters of tiny, white flowers.

ar·roy·o (ə roi′ō) *pl.* **-roy·os.** *n.* **1.** bed of a stream; gully. **2.** small river or stream. [Spanish *arroyo* stream, gutter; of uncertain origin.]

ar·se·nal (är′sən əl) *n.* **1.** place for storing or manufacturing arms and munitions. **2.** collection or accumulation of firearms or other weapons. **3.** storehouse: *Our country is . . . the arsenal of democracy* (Franklin Roosevelt, 1941). [Italian *arsenale,* going back to Arabic *dâr aç çinâ 'ah* house of manufacture.]

ar·se·nate (är′sə nāt′, -nit) *n.* salt or ester of an arsenic acid.

ar·se·nic (*n.,* är′sə nik, ärs′nik; *adj.,* är sen′ik) *n.* **1.** white, tasteless, highly poisonous compound, used esp. in rat, insect, and weed poisons. Formula: As_2O_3 or As_4O_6 Also, **white arsenic. 2.** metallic element, usually in the form of silver-gray or blackish crystals, used esp. in alloys and poisonous compounds. Symbol: **As** See **element** for table. *—adj.* relating to or containing arsenic, esp. with a valence of five. [Latin *arsenicum* this element, from Greek *arsenikon* yellow arsenic, modification (influenced by Greek *arrhenikos* male, due to belief that some metals were either male or female) of Arabic *az-zernīk* the yellow arsenic, from Persian *zarnī(k)* yellow arsenic, from *zar* gold.]

arsenic acid, colorless, water-soluble, crystalline compound, used to derive arsenates. Formula: H_3AsO_4

ar·sen·i·cal (är sen′i kəl) *adj.* relating to or containing arsenic. *—n.* any preparation, as an insecticide or medicine, containing arsenic.

ar·se·nous (är′sə nəs) *adj.* relating to or containing arsenic, esp. with a valence of three. Also, **ar·se·ni·ous** (är sē′nē əs).

ar·son (är′sən) *n.* crime of setting fire intentionally to another's building or property, or to one's own, when insured, with intent to defraud the insurers. [Old French *arson,* going back to Latin *arsus,* past participle of *ardēre* to burn.] **—ar′son·ist,** *n.*

ars po·e·ti·ca (ärz′ pō et′i kə) art of poetry. [Latin *ars poētica.*]

art¹ (ärt) *n.* **1.** the application or exhibition of skill, aesthetic principles, and creative imagination in the production of the beautiful or the meaningful: *Art for art's sake.* **2.** form of activity characterized by such application or exhibition. Dance, music, literature, drama, painting, sculpture, and architecture are all forms of art. **3.** works produced by creative activity, esp. in the fine arts: *modern art.* **4.** special skill; knack: *the art of saying things well.* **5.a.** system of rules guiding any form of endeavor: *the art of self-defense.* **b.** skilled craft, occupation, or pursuit: *the navigator's art.* **6. the arts. a.** the several forms of creative activity considered together. **b.** the liberal arts. **7.** branch of learning or study. **8.** human skill or endeavor, opposed to nature. **9.** studied behavior; artifice: *More matter with less art* (Shakespeare, *Hamlet*). [Old French *art* skill, from Latin *ars* (stem *art-*).]

art² (ärt) *Archaic.* second person singular, present indicative of **be.** ▲ used with *thou.* [Old English *eart* (thou) art.]

-art, form of **-ard,** as in *braggart.*

art. **1.** article. **2.** artificial. **3.** artillery. **4.** artist.

ar·te·fact (är′tə fakt′) artifact.

Ar·te·mis (är′tə mis) *n.* Greek virgin goddess of the hunt and of the moon and twin sister of Apollo. Her Roman counterpart is Diana.

ar·te·ri·al (är tēr′ē əl) *adj.* **1.** of, relating to, or resembling an artery or arteries. **2.** of, relating to, or designating the blood, esp. in the arteries, which has become bright red as a result of oxygenation in the lungs or gills. **3.** having a main channel and many branches: *an arterial drainage system.* **—ar·te′ri·al·ly,** *adv.*

ar·te·ri·o·scle·ro·sis (är tēr′ē ō skli rō′sis) *n.* chronic disorder, esp. of old age, in which the walls of the arteries thicken and harden, and thereby hamper the flow of blood. [Modern Latin *arteriosclerosis,* from Greek *artēriā* artery + *sklerōsis* hardening.] **—ar·te·ri·o·scle·rot·ic** (är tēr′ē ō skli rot′ik), *adj.*

ar·ter·y (är′tər ē) *pl.* **-ter·ies.** *n.* **1.** one of the muscular elastic tubes that carry blood away from the heart to all parts of the body. **2.** main channel of communication or transportation: *Traffic is slow on all major arteries.* [Latin *artēria* this blood vessel, from Greek *artēriā.*]

ar·te·sian well (är tē′zhən) well from which water rises as a result of underground water pressure. [French *ar′tésien* of Artois, northern French province, where wells of this kind were first constructed.]

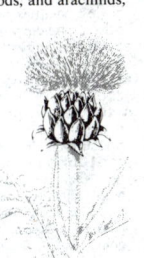

Rainfall · Topsoil · Artesian well · Nonporous rock · Porous rock or sand

Artesian well

art·ful (ärt′fəl) *adj.* **1.** crafty; cunning; deceitful: *an artful ruse.* **2.** skillful; ingenious; clever: *an artful invention.* **3.** done with or showing art or skill: *an artful performance.* **—art′ful·ly,** *adv.* **—art′ful·ness,** *n.*

ar·thrit·ic (är thrit′ik) *adj.* of, relating to, or affected with arthritis. *—n.* one who has arthritis.

ar·thri·tis (är thrī′tis) *n.* inflammation of a joint or joints. [Latin *arthrītis* gout, from Greek *arthrītis,* from *arthron* joint.]

ar·thro·pod (är′thrə pod′) *n.* any of a group of invertebrates, phylum Arthropoda, including crustaceans, insects, myriapods, and arachnids, characterized by jointed legs and segmented bodies. [Greek *arthron* joint + *pous* (stem *pod-*) foot.]

Ar·thur (är′thər) *n.* **1.** sixth-century British king about whom many legends were written. He was the hero and leader of the knights of the Round Table. **2. Chester A.** 1830–86, twenty-first president of the United States, from 1881 to 1885.

Ar·thu·ri·an (är thoor′ē ən) *adj.* of or relating to King Arthur or the legends connected with him and his knights.

ar·ti·choke (är′tə chōk′) *n.* **1.** yellowish-green flower head of a plant, *Cynara scolymus,* of the composite family, cooked and eaten as a vegetable. **2.** the hardy, thistlelike plant itself, widely cultivated in Mediterranean countries, Belgium, and the United States. **3.** Jerusalem artichoke. [Dialectal Italian *articiocco,* from Italian *carciofo,* through Spanish, from Arabic *al-kharshōf* the artichoke.]

Artichoke

ar·ti·cle (är′ti kəl) *n.* **1.** prose composition, forming an independent part of a larger publication, as of a periodical or encyclopedia: *The professor wrote an article on space for the magazine.* **2.a.** individual item (of a group or class): *an article of clothing.* **b.** particular thing or object; item: *Several articles were stolen from the house.* **3.** separate clause, provision, or division of a formal document, as in a treaty, constitution, or contract. **4.** one of the words *a, an,* or *the* or their equivalents in

other languages, used as modifiers for nouns. *A* and *an* are **indefinite articles** and *the* is the **definite article.** —*v.t.,* **-cled, -cling.** to bind by articles of an agreement: *to article an apprentice.* [Old French *article* clause, joint, from Latin *articulus* division, little joint, diminutive of *artus* joint.] —**Syn.** *n.* 1. see **essay.**

Articles for the Government of the Navy, code of regulations governing the U.S. Navy and Marines, superseded in 1951 by the Uniform Code of Military Justice.

Articles of Confederation, first constitution of the United States, adopted by the thirteen original colonies in 1781, superseded by the present Constitution in 1788.

Articles of War, code of regulations governing the U.S. Army and Air Force, superseded in 1951 by the Uniform Code of Military Justice.

ar·tic·u·lar (är tik′yə lər) *adj.* of or affecting a joint or the joints. [Latin *articulāris,* from *articulus* little joint. See ARTICLE.]

ar·tic·u·late (*adj.* är tik′yə lit; *v.,* är tik′yə lāt′) *adj.* **1.a.** spoken in distinct syllables and words. **b.** able to speak. **2.** able to express oneself well or effectively: *an articulate spokesman.* **3.** expressed or presented clearly and coherently: *an articulate discussion.* **4.** *Anatomy.* jointed or segmented. —*v.t.,* **-lat·ed, -lat·ing. 1.** to pronounce distinctly; enunciate. **2.** to put into words; express effectively: *to articulate a sentiment.* **3.** to unite by means of a joint; connect. **4.** to make distinct; define clearly. —*v.i.* **1.** to pronounce distinct syllables and words; enunciate. **2.** to form a joint or connection: *The bones did not articulate well.* [Latin *articulātus,* past participle of *articulāre* to pronounce distinctly, divide into joints.] —**ar·tic′u·late·ly,** *adv.* —**ar·tic′u·late·ness,** *n.*

ar·tic·u·la·tion (är tik′yə lā′shən) *n.* **1.** manner or process of articulating sounds; enunciation. **2.** an articulated sound, esp. a consonant. **3.** act or manner of jointing or connecting; being connected: *the articulation of the bones.* **4.** *Anatomy.* joint, as the movable segments of an arthropod. **5.** *Botany.* joint between two parts that separate naturally or easily, as at the base of a leafstalk. —**ar·tic′u·la′tive,** **ar·tic·u·la·to·ry** (är tik′yə lə tôr′ē), *adj.* —**Syn.** 1. see **pronunciation.**

ar·tic·u·la·tor (är tik′yə lā′tər) *n.* organ of speech, as the tongue, lips, or hard palate.

ar·ti·fact (är′tə fakt′) *also,* **ar·te·fact.** *n.* anything made or altered by man, esp. an object used in the daily life of an ancient civilization. [Latin *ars* skill + *factus,* past participle of *facere* to make.]

ar·ti·fice (är′tə fis) *n.* **1.** clever or ingenious device; contrivance. **2.** trickery; cunning; deception. [French *artifice* skill, cunning, from Latin *artificium* cunning, handicraft.]

ar·tif·i·cer (är tif′ə sər) *n.* **1.** one skilled in a craft or trade; craftsman. **2.** one who creates or devises; inventor.

ar·ti·fi·cial (är′tə fish′əl) *adj.* **1.** not natural; man-made: *artificial light.* **2.** made in imitation of something natural or real; simulated: *artificial flowers.* **3.** assumed; feigned: *artificial politeness.* **4.** (of a person) not natural; affected. **5.** not based on reality; forced; contrived: *an artificial distinction.* [Latin *artificiālis* relating to art, from *artificium* handicraft, cunning.] —**ar′ti·fi′cial·ly,** *adv.* —**ar′ti·fi′cial·ness,** *n.*

Syn. 1. Artificial, synthetic indicate human manufacture rather than natural origin. **Artificial** is used of things fashioned by man's art and skill, often in imitation of or as a likeness to things occurring naturally: *There was a bowl of artificial fruit on the table.* **Synthetic** is used of things made in scientific laboratories from natural substances and often having qualities not occurring in their natural counterparts, if those exist: *Synthetic fabrics like nylon have revolutionized the textile industry.*

artificial insemination, injection of semen into the female reproductive organs by artificial means, to induce pregnancy.

ar·ti·fi·ci·al·i·ty (är′tə fish′ē al′ə tē) *pl.,* **-ties.** *n.* **1.** artificial quality. **2.** that which is artificial.

artificial respiration, the forcing of air into and out of the lungs to restore or maintain proper breathing, as by applying rhythmical pressure on the back.

ar·til·ler·y (är til′ər ē) *n.* **1.** firearms, as cannon, howitzers, and mortars, that fire projectiles and are mounted on stationary or movable emplacements. Distinguished from **small arms. 2.** branch of military force utilizing these weapons. **3.** *Informal.* firearms of any sort. [Old French *artillerie* war equipment, from *artiller* to fortify, possibly going back to Latin *ars* skill.]

ar·til·ler·y·man (är til′ər ē mən) *pl.,* **-men.** *n.* soldier in the artillery; gunner. Also, **ar·til·ler·ist** (är til′ər ist).

ar·ti·san (är′tə zən) *n.* one skilled in a particular craft; craftsman. [French *artisan,* from Italian *artigiano,* going back to Latin *artītus* cunning, skilled in arts, from *ars* art.]

art·ist (är′tist) *n.* **1.** one who is skilled in or whose profession is one of the fine arts, esp. a painter or sculptor. **2.** skilled public performer. **3.** one who exhibits artistry and skill in his work: *a make-up artist.* [French *artiste,* from Italian *artista,* from Latin *ars* art, skill.]

ar·tiste (är tēst′) *n.* **1.** artist *(def. 2).* **2.** one who does anything with skill. ▲ used ironically. [French *artiste.* See ARTIST.]

ar·tis·tic (är tis′tik) *adj.* **1.** relating to or characteristic of art or

artists. **2.** skillfully and tastefully done; aesthetically pleasing: *an artistic arrangement.* —**ar·tis′ti·cal·ly,** *adv.*

art·ist·ry (är′tis trē) *pl.,* **-ries.** *n.* artistic quality, methods, or workmanship.

art·less (ärt′lis) *adj.* **1.** without guile or deceit; naive. **2.** not artificial; simple; natural: *artless grace.* **3.** lacking skill or knowledge; ignorant. —**art′less·ly,** *adv.* —**art′less·ness,** *n.*

Art Nou·veau (är′ nōō vō′, ärt′) *also,* **art nou·veau.** style of art which originated in the 1890s, characterized by elaborately curving patterns based on natural forms.

art·y (är′tē) **art·i·er, art·i·est.** *adj. Informal.* pretentiously pursuing or interested in the arts. —**art′i·ness,** *n.*

ar·um (âr′əm) *n.* **1.** any of a group of small, Eurasian plants, genus *Arum,* bearing a cluster of tiny flowers on a spike surrounded by a showy spathe. **2.** any of various related plants, as the calla lily. —*adj.* designating a family, Araceae, of chiefly tropical plants, with flowers typically crowded on a spike surrounded by a showy leaf, including the calla lily and the jack-in-the-pulpit. [Latin *arum,* from Greek *aron.*]

-ary¹ *suffix* **1.** (used to form nouns) **a.** place dealing with: *library, granary.* **b.** person doing or connected with: *functionary, antiquary.* **c.** thing or group of things relating to: *dictionary, formulary.* **2.** (used to form adjectives) being or characterized by: *secondary, honorary.* [Latin *-ārius, -āria, -ārium* relating to.]

-ary² *suffix* (used to form adjectives) like; relating to; connected with: *military, exemplary.* [See -AR¹.]

Ar·y·an (âr′ē ən, är′yən, ar′-) *n.* **1.** member or descendant of a group of prehistoric nomadic people who spoke an Indo-European language. **2.** formerly, an alternative term for the Indo-European family of languages. **3.** In Nazi terminology, a non-Jewish Caucasian of Nordic racial stock. —*adj.* **1.** of or relating to the Aryans or their culture. **2.** in Nazi terminology, of or relating to non-Jewish Caucasians of Nordic racial stock. [Sanskrit *ārya* noble.]

as¹ (az; *unstressed* əz) *adv.* **1.** to the same amount or degree; equally: *quick as a flash.* **2.** for example; for instance: *several colors, as red and blue.* —*conj.* **1.** to the same degree or extent that: *She was proud as proud can be.* **2.** in the same way or manner that: *Speak as I speak.* **3.** at the same time; while: *It occurred to me as I was waiting.* **4.** because; since: *As you are not ready yet, we will wait.* **5.** that the result is; with the intent (with *so* and an infinitive): *He told the story so as to please everyone. Be so good as to come.* **6.** though: *Late as it was, we left for the play.* —*prep.* in the manner, function, or role of: *I speak as a friend.* —*pron.* **1.** fact that; which: *It is true, as you can plainly see.* **2.** who; that; which (after *same* and *such*): *such a night as I had.*

as for (or to). with respect to; concerning.

as if (or **though**). as it would be if.

as is. in the present condition; just as it is.

as it were. as if it were so; so to speak.

as yet. up to this time; so far.

[Old English *ealswā* just so, just as.]

as² (as) *pl.,* **ass·es** (as′iz) *n.* **1.** copper or copper alloy coin of ancient Rome, originally weighing about twelve ounces. **2.** unit of weight in ancient Rome, equal to twelve ounces. [Latin *ās.*]

as-, form of **ad-** before *s,* as in *assume.*

As, arsenic.

as·a·fet·i·da (as′ə fet′ə də) *also,* **as·a·foet·i·da, as·sa·fet·i·da, as·sa·foet·i·da.** *n.* brown gum resin that smells like garlic, obtained from the roots of various central Asian plants, genus *Ferula,* of the parsley family, formerly used medicinally. [Medieval Latin *asafetida,* going back to Persian *azā* a gum resin + Latin *foetidus* ill-smelling.]

as·bes·tos (as bes′təs, az-) *also,* **as·bes·tus.** *n.* any of several varieties of a fibrous mineral whose fibers may be woven or pressed into material that is valued because it is incombustible and chemically resistant and does not conduct electricity. [Latin *asbestus* this mineral, from Greek *asbestos* unquenchable, from *a-* not + *sbennynai* to quench. The Greek word was mistakenly applied by Pliny to the incombustible fiber of a lamp wick used to keep an "unquenchable" eternal light burning in a temple of Athena. The Greeks had a different word for the incombustible fiber—*amiantos;* they used the term *asbestos* to refer to another mineral, probably unslaked lime, which was "unquenchable" in the way it steamed when cold water was thrown on it.]

As·bur·y Park (az′ber′ē, -bər ē) resort on the coast of east-central New Jersey. Pop., (1970), 16,533.

as·cend (ə send′) *v.i.* **1.** to move upward physically; rise: *The elevator ascended slowly.* **2.** to move upward from a lower degree or level, as in the musical scale. **3.** to go up; move upward along; climb: *to ascend a mountain.* [Latin *ascendere* to climb up to.] —**Syn.** *v.t.* see **climb.**

as·cen·dance (ə sen′dəns) *also,* **as·cen·dence.** *n.* ascendancy.

as·cen·dan·cy (ə sen′dən sē) *also,* **as·cen·den·cy.** *n.* quality or state of being in the ascendant; domination.

at; āpe; cär; end; mē; it; īce; hot; ōld; fôrk; wood; fōōl; oil; out; up; ūse; turn; sing; thin; this; zh in treasure; ə in ago, taken, pencil, lemon, circus.

as·cen·dant (ə sen′dənt) *also,* **as·cen·dent.** *adj.* **1.** ascending; rising. **2.** superior; preeminent; dominant: *an ascendant position in public life.* —*n.* **1.** position of dominant power; controlling influence: *to gain the ascendant.* **2.** *Astrology.* any sign of the zodiac or other influence that is rising above the eastern horizon, as at the time of one's birth. **3. in the ascendant.** in or approaching a dominant, influential, or superior position.

as·cen·sion (ə sen′shən) *n.* **1.** act or process of ascending. **2. Ascension. a.** passing of Christ from earth to heaven after His resurrection. **b.** Ascension Day. [Latin *ascēnsiō* ascending.]

As·cen·sion (ə sen′shən) *n.* British island in the south Atlantic, west of Africa. Area, 34 sq. mi. Pop. (1963), 478.

Ascension Day, day on which Christ passed from earth to heaven, now commemorated annually on the fortieth day after Easter. Also, **Ascension Thursday.**

as·cent (ə sent′) *n.* **1.** movement upward in space; rise: *the ascent of the balloon.* **2.** rise in status; advancement: *his recent ascent to high office.* **3.** act of climbing or going up: *Snow made ascent of the mountain impossible.* **4.** place or way that one ascends; upward slope: *a steep ascent.* [From ASCEND, formed to parallel DESCENT.]

as·cer·tain (as′ər tān′) *v.t.* to find out with certainty; determine. [Old French *acertener* to certify, from *à* to + *certain* sure, from Latin *certus* determined, sure.] —**as′cer·tain′a·ble,** *adj.* —**as′cer·tain′a·bly,** *adv.* —**as′cer·tain′ment,** *n.*

as·cet·ic (ə set′ik) *n.* **1.** one who, for religious reasons, practices rigorous self-discipline by leading a life of meditation and self-denial. **2.** one who leads an austerely abstinent and self-disciplined life. —*adj.* **1.** relating to or characteristic of ascetics or asceticism. **2.** severely abstinent; austere. Also, **as·cet′i·cal.** [Greek *askētikos* laborious, ascetic, from *askētēs* hermit, exerciser, from *askein* to exercise.] —**as·cet′i·cal·ly,** *adv.*

as·cet·i·cism (ə set′ə siz′əm) *n.* **1.** way of life of an ascetic; extreme self-denial. **2.** doctrine that one can attain conformity with the will of God through rigorous self-discipline, self-denial, and meditation.

as·cid·i·an (ə sid′ē ən) *n.* any of various saltwater animals, class Ascidiacea, having a leathery, saclike outer covering as the sea squirts. Ascidians attach themselves to the surfaces of rocks and ship bottoms.

as·cid·i·um (ə sid′ē um) *pl.,* **as·cid·i·a** (ə sid′ē ə) *n.* baglike or flask-shaped part of a plant, as the leaf of the pitcher plant. See *pitcher plant* for illustration. [Modern Latin *ascidium,* from Greek *askidion,* diminutive of *askos* leather bag.]

As·cle·pi·us (as klē′pē əs) *n.* Greek god of medicine and healing, son of Apollo. The Roman counterpart is Aesculapius.

as·co·my·cete (as′kə mī sēt′) *n.* any of a large group of fungi, class Ascomycetes, including yeasts, molds, and mildews, characterized by sexual spores formed in saclike cells. [Greek *askos* bag + *mykēs* fungus.] —**as′co·my·ce′tous,** *adj.*

a·scor·bic acid (ə skôr′bik) crystalline, water-soluble vitamin compound that aids in the formation of connective tissues, increases resistance to infection, and prevents scurvy. It is found in citrus fruits and made synthetically. Formula: $C_6H_8O_6$. Also, **vitamin C.** [A- + SCORB(UT)IC.]

as·cot (as′kət, -kot) *n.* scarf worn tied around the neck with one end placed over the other. [From *Ascot,* a racetrack in England, where this neckwear was fashionable.]

Ascot

as·cribe (əs krīb′)-**cribed, -crib·ing.** *v.t.* **1.** to attribute (something), as to a cause or source: *They ascribed the forest fire to carelessness.* **2.** to regard or allege (a quality or attribute) as belonging to: *to ascribe selfishness to others.* [Latin *ascrībere* to add to a writing, attribute to.] —**as·crib′a·ble,** *adj.* —Syn. 1. See ATTRIBUTE.

as·crip·tion (əs krip′shən) *n.* **1.** act of ascribing. **2.** expression that ascribes. [Latin *ascriptiō* an addition in writing, from *ascrībere.* See ASCRIBE.]

-ase *suffix* (used to form nouns) designating an enzyme: *amylase.* [From (DIAST)ASE, the first enzyme isolated.]

a·sep·sis (ā sep′sis, ə sep′-) *n.* **1.** state or condition of being aseptic. **2.** use of sterilized medical instruments or materials in preventing infection or inhibiting microorganisms that cause decay or disease.

a·sep·tic (ā sep′tik, ə sep′-) *adj.* free from or inhibiting decay or disease-causing microorganisms. [A-⁴ + SEPTIC.] —**a·sep′ti·cal·ly,** *adv.*

a·sex·u·al (ā sek′shōō əl) *adj. Biology.* **1.** without sex or distinct sexual organs. **2.** not involving the union of male and female germ cells. The simple cell division of amebas is a form of asexual reproduction. —**a·sex′u·al·ly,** *adv.*

As·gard (as′gärd, az′-) *also,* **As·garth** (äs′gärth), **As·gar·dhr** (äs′gär′thər). *n. Norse Mythology.* the home of the gods, and of heroes slain in battle.

ash¹ (ash) *n.* **1.** gray-white powdery residue left after a substance has burned completely. **2.** fine particles of lava, as erupted by a volcano. [Old English *asce* the powdery residue.]

ash² (ash) *n.* **1.** any of a group of valuable hardwood trees, genus *Fraxinus,* of the olive family, found chiefly in temperate regions of the Northern Hemisphere, usually bearing pinnate leaves and winged seeds. **2.** wood of any of these trees. —*adj.* relating to or made of the wood of an ash. [Old English *æsc* ash tree.]

a·shamed (ə shāmd′) *adj.* **1.** feeling shame, as through the recognition that one's actions or thoughts are foolish or improper: *John was ashamed that he had wept over such a foolish thing.* **2.** unwilling or deterred through fear of shame: *I am ashamed to say you told me so.* [Old English *āscamod,* past participle of *āscamian* to feel shame, to make ashamed.] —**a·sham·ed·ly** (ə shā′mid lē), *adv.*

A·shan·ti (ə shan′tē) *n.* **1.** historic region in central Ghana, once an independent kingdom and later a British possession. **2.** member of the people of this region. **3.** language of this people.

ash can 1. can or similar receptacle for ashes or trash. **2.** *Slang.* depth bomb.

ash·en (ash′ən) *adj.* **1.** ash-colored; pale. **2.** *Archaic.* of or resembling ashes. [ASH¹ + -EN².]

ash·es (ash′iz) *n.,pl.* **1.a.** gray-white powdery residue left after something has been burned. **b.** such residue together with partially burned remnants, as in a fireplace. **2.** bodily remains after cremation or decomposition. **3.** remains of something that has been destroyed; ruins.

Ashe·ville (ash′vil′) *n.* city in western North Carolina. Pop. (1970), 57,681.

Ash·ke·naz·i (ash′kə näz′ē) *pl.,* **-naz·im** (-naz′im). *n.* member or close descendant of the group of Jews who settled in northern or central Europe. Distinguished from **Sephardi.** [Hebrew *Ashkenazzīm,* plural of *Ashkenaz,* a Biblical name applied in the Middle Ages as a term for Germany.] —**Ash′ke·naz′ic,** *adj.*

Ash·kha·bad (äsh′kä bäd′) *n.* city in the southern part of the west-central Soviet Union, capital of the Turkmen Republic. Pop. (1970), 253,000.

ash·lar (ash′lər) *also,* **ash·ler.** *n.* **1.** square, hewn stone used in building. **2.** thin slab of stone used for facing a wall. **3.** masonry wall made of ashlars. [Old French *aiseler* crossbeam, going back to Latin *axilla,* diminutive of *axis* board.]

a·shore (ə shôr′) *adv., adj.* **1.** on or to the shore. **2.** on land.

Ash·to·reth (ash′tə reth′) *n.* Astarte.

ash tray, receptacle for smokers' tobacco ashes.

A·shur (ä′shoor) Assur.

Ash Wednesday, the first day of Lent, observed on the seventh Wednesday before Easter. [From the custom of placing ashes on the forehead as a symbol of penitence on this day.]

ash·y (ash′ē) **ash·i·er, ash·i·est.** *adj.* **1.** of, resembling, or covered with ashes. **2.** *Archaic.* ash-colored; pale.

A·sia (ā′zhə, ā′shə) *n.* largest continent, bounded on the west by the Ural Mountains, the Caucasus, the Black, Mediterranean, and Red seas, on the south by the Indian Ocean, and on the east by the Pacific. Area, (approx.) 17,124,000 sq. mi. Pop. (1967), 1,961,329,000.

Asia Minor, peninsula in western Asia, bounded by the Black and Mediterranean seas. It comprises Asiatic Turkey. Area, 287,000 sq. mi. Also, **An′a·to′li·a.**

A·sian (ā′zhən, ā′shən) *adj.* of, relating to, or characteristic of Asia or its people. —*n.* member or close descendant of any of the peoples historically inhabiting Asia.

Asian flu, influenza caused by a mutant strain of virus first recognized in Asia in 1957.

A·si·at·ic (ā′zhē at′ik, ā′shē-) *n., adj.* Asian. ▲ **Asiatic** is now generally considered offensive; **Asian** is preferred.

Asiatic cholera, cholera.

a·side (ə sīd′) *adv.* **1.** on or to one side; out of the way; away: *Step aside, please.* **2.** out of or apart from consideration or use: *my personal feelings aside.* **3.** in reserve; in keeping: *Hold that aside for me.* **4. aside from. a.** apart from; independent of. **b.** except for. —*n.* **1.** remark not intended to be heard by all those who are present, esp. an actor's remark intended for the audience but not the other characters. **2.** departure from a main theme; digression.

as·i·nine (as′ə nīn′) *adj.* stupid; silly. [Latin *asinīnus* of an ass, from *asinus* ass.] —**as′i·nine′ly,** *adv.*

as·i·nin·i·ty (as′ə nin′ə tē) *pl.,* **-ties.** *n.* **1.** quality of being asinine; silliness. **2.** something that is asinine, as a remark.

ask (ask) *v.t.* **1.** to put a question to; inquire of: *Ask the way.* **2.** to put a question to; inquire of: *Ask me if you're not sure.* **3.** to call for the answer to: *to ask a question.* **4.** to make a request of: *to ask him for directions. I'll ask her to advise us.* **b.** to make a request for: *to ask a favor.* **5.** to invite: *to ask him to dinner.* **6.** to set (as a price); demand: *to ask a high price for an old car.* **7.** to demand; require: *He asks too much from his workers.* **8.** *Archaic.* to publish (banns).

—*v.i.* **1.** to make inquiries (with *for*, *after*, or *about*). **2.** to make a request (with *for*): *to ask for bread.* **3. to ask for.** *Informal.* to invite or provoke (punishment or retaliation). [Old English *āscian* to question.]
Syn. *v.t.* **1. Ask, question, query** mean to attempt to get information. **Ask,** the general term, simply indicates seeking a direct answer: *If you have any doubts, ask me now.* **Question** implies a systematic interrogation aimed at getting certain information: *The police questioned him about his movements.* **Query,** a rarer and more formal word, means to seek an authoritative and substantive answer resolving a doubtful point: *The author queried the editor on some style rules.*

a·skance (ə skans′) *also,* **a·skant** (ə skant′). *adv.* **1.** with a side glance; sideways. **2. to look askance at.** to view with suspicion, distrust, or disapproval. [Of uncertain origin.]

a·skew (ə skū′) *adv., adj.* to one side; out of the proper position; awry [A-¹ + SKEW.]

a·slant (ə slant′) *adv.* in a slanting direction; on a slant. —*adj.* slanting. —*prep.* slantingly across or over.

a·sleep (ə slēp′) *adj.* **1.** in a state of sleep; sleeping. **2.** dormant; inactive; sluggish. **3.** (of an arm, leg, or other body part) numb. **4.** dead. —*adv.* into a sleeping condition: *to fall asleep.*

As·ma·ra (äs mär′ə) *n.* city in northern Ethiopia. Pop. (1968), 190,-500.

asp¹ (asp) *n.* **1.** a cobra native to Egypt, *Naja haje,* worshiped by the ancient Egyptians and said to have been used by Cleopatra to kill herself. **2.** any of several venomous snakes, esp. a viper of central Europe and the Mediterranean. [Latin *aspis,* from Greek *aspis.*]

asp² (asp) *n.* *Archaic.* aspen. [Old English *æspe* aspen tree.]

as·par·a·gus (əs par′ə gəs) *n.* **1.** young, green or white spears of the plant *Asparagus officinalis,* of the lily family, cooked and eaten as a vegetable. **2.** the plant itself, found in Eurasia, but raised in most parts of the world. The spears grow from horizontal, underground stems, called rhizomes, and bear scalelike leaves at the tip. [Latin *asparagus,* from Greek *asparagos.*]

Asparagus spears

As·pa·sia (as pā′zhə, -shə) *n.* c.470–c.410 B.C., Greek woman of outstanding intellect, the consort of Pericles.

ASPCA, American Society for the Prevention of Cruelty to Animals.

as·pect (as′pekt) *n.* **1.a.** any of the ways in which something appears or presents itself to the mind; facet: *a problem in all its aspects.* **b.** way in which to regard (a subject); viewpoint: *looked at from this aspect.* **2.** appearance presented to the eye; look: *the striking aspect of the mountains.* **3.** way in which one appears; countenance; mien: *the fierce aspect of the criminal.* **4.** side or surface facing a given direction: *dorsal aspect.* **5.** relative positions of the planets, thought to have favorable or unfavorable influence on human affairs. **6.** direction in which something faces; exposure. [Latin *aspectus* look, sight.] —**Syn.** 2. see **appearance.**

as·pen (as′pən) *n.* any of several poplar trees found in the Northern Hemisphere, bearing small, rounded, papery leaves. [ASP² + -EN²; originally an adjective, then a noun.]

As·pen (as′pən) *n.* ski resort in west-central Colorado. Pop. (1970), 2,404.

Aspen leaves

as·per·i·ty (as per′ə tē, əs-) *n.,* **-ties.** *n.* **1.** harshness of manner or temper; bitterness; severity. **2.** hardship; difficulty. **3.** roughness, as of surface; unevenness. [Latin *asperitās.*]

as·perse (əs purs′) **-persed, -pers·ing.** *v.t.* **1.** to spread false or damaging accusations against; slander. **2.** to sprinkle or scatter (holy water) over. [Latin *aspersus,* past participle of *aspergere* to sprinkle, bespatter.] —**as·pers′er,** *n.* —**as·per′sive,** *adj.*

as·per·sion (əs pur′zhən, -shən) *n.* **1.** damaging or false statement; slander: *to cast aspersions on his good name.* **2.** act of slandering; defaming. **3.** sprinkling with water in a religious service.

as·phalt (as′fôlt, -falt) *n.* **1.** brown or black bituminous substance, occurring in nature and also obtained as a by-product of petroleum refining. **2.** mixture of this with gravel, sand, or both of these, used esp. for paving. Also, **as·phal·tum** (as fal′təm). —*v.t.* to pave or cover with asphalt. [Late Latin *asphaltus* this bituminous substance, from Greek *asphaltos;* possibly of Semitic origin.]

as·pho·del (as′fə del′) *n.* any of several plants of the lily family, bearing showy, trumpet-shaped, white or yellow flowers on a spike. [Latin *asphodelus,* from Greek *asphodelos.*]

as·phyx·i·a (as fik′sē ə) *n.* unconsciousness resulting from a lack of

oxygen and an increase of carbon dioxide in the blood and body tissues. [Modern Latin *asphyxia,* from Greek *asphyxiā* stopping of the pulse, from *a-* not, without + *sphyxis* pulse.]

as·phyx·i·ate (as fik′sē āt′) **-at·ed, at·ing.** *v.t.* **1.** to cause asphyxia in; suffocate. —*v.i.* to undergo asphyxia. —**as·phyx′i·a′tion, as·phyx′-i·a′tor,** *n.*

as·pic (as′pik) *n.* **1.** jellied dish made from meat, poultry, fish, or vegetable juices chilled until firm. **2.** the jelly itself. [French *aspic* asp, through Latin, from Greek *aspis* asp; possibly from the French proverb *froid comme un aspic* cold as an asp.]

as·pi·dis·tra (as′pə dis′trə) *n.* any of several plants, genus *Aspidistra,* of the lily family, bearing large, glossy, evergreen leaves, esp. *A. elatior,* widely cultivated as a house plant. [Modern Latin *Aspidistra,* from Greek *aspis* shield; because of its shield-shaped leaves.]

as·pi·rant (as′pər ənt, əs pī′rənt) *n.* one who aspires or seeks advancement or honors. —*adj.* aspiring. —**Syn.** see **candidate.**

as·pi·rate (*v.,* as′pə rāt′; *adj., n.,* as′pər it) **-rat·ed, -rat·ing.** *v.t.* **1.** to precede the pronunciation of (a word of syllable) with a puff of breath or with an *h* sound. In the pronunciation of the word *when,* when the *wh* is aspirated, the word is pronounced *hwen.* **2.** to follow (the pronunciation of a consonant) with a puff of breath. The letters *p, t,* and *k* are aspirated when followed by a vowel, as in *palm, ton,* and *kid.* **3.** to remove (fluids or gases) from a body cavity with an aspirator. —*n.* **1.** sound of the letter *h.* **2.** consonant whose pronunciation is followed by a puff of breath. —*adj.* pronounced with an aspirate or followed by a puff of breath. Also, **as′pi·rat·ed.** [Latin *aspīrātus,* past participle of *aspīrāre* to breathe upon.]

as·pi·ra·tion (as′pə rā′shən) *n.* **1.a.** strong desire for attainment, as of something good or lofty; high ambition. **b.** object of this desire or ambition. **2.** act of breathing; a breath. **3.a.** articulation of an aspirate. **b.** an aspirate. **3.** removal of fluids or gases from a body cavity with an aspirator. —**Syn.** 1.a. see **ambition.**

as·pi·ra·tor (as′pə rā′tər) *n.* **1.** any apparatus or device employing suction. **2.** instrument for the removal of fluids and gases from a body cavity by the use of suction.

as·pire (əs pīr′) **-pired, -pir·ing.** *v.i.* **1.** to seek ambitiously to attain something; be earnestly desirous; aim: *to aspire after glory, to aspire to the presidency, to aspire to be made leader.* **2.** *Archaic.* to rise up; ascend. [Latin *aspīrāre* to breathe upon, desire to obtain.] —**as·pir′er,** *n.*

as·pi·rin (as′pər in) *n.* **1.** white, crystalline derivative of salicylic acid, used in tablet form for the relief of pain and fever. Formula: C₉H₈O₄. Also, **acetylsalicylic acid.** **2.** tablet of aspirin. [A(CETYL) + *spir(aeic acid)* (former name of SALICYLIC ACID) + -IN¹.]

As·quith, Herbert Henry (as′kwith) 1852–1928, prime minister of Great Britain, from 1908 to 1916.

ass (as) *n.* **1.** long-eared mammal, *Equus asinus,* of the horse family, native to Asia and Africa, esp. the domesticated ass, *Equus asinus osinus,* used as a beast of burden; donkey. **2.** any of several similar mammals of Asia and the Middle East. **3.** stupid person; fool. [Old English *assa* donkey, from Old Irish *assan,* from Latin *asinus;* probably of Semitic origin.]

as·sa·fet·i·da (as′ə fet′ə də) *also,* **as·sa·foet·i·da.** asafetida.

as·sa·gai (as′ə gī′) *pl.,* **-gais.** *also,* **as·se·gai.** *n.* slender spear of hard wood, used by some tribes of southern Africa. [Portuguese *azagaia* javelin, from Arabic *az-zaghāyah,* from *al* the + Berber *zaghāyah* javelin.]

as·sail (ə sāl′) *v.t.* **1.** to attack with physical violence. **2.** to attack vigorously with arguments or abuse. [Old French *assaillir,* going back to Latin *ad* to, at + *salīre* to leap.] —**as·sail′a·ble,** *adj.* —**as·sail′er, as·sail′ment,** *n.* —**Syn.** 1. see **attack.**

as·sail·ant (ə sā′lənt) *n.* one who assails: *The police rescued the man from his assailant.*

as·sas·sin (ə sas′in) *n.* murderer, esp. of a public figure. [French *assassin,* from Arabic *hashshāshīn* eaters of hashish; originally a Muslim society, members of which, under the influence of hashish, killed Christian crusaders.]

as·sas·si·nate (ə sas′ə nāt′) **-nat·ed, -nat·ing.** *v.t.* **1.** to murder, esp. a public figure; kill treacherously. **2.** to destroy or damage maliciously: *to assassinate a man's character.* —**as·sas′si·na′tion, as·sas′si·na′-tor,** *n.* —**Syn.** 1. see **kill.**

as·sault (ə sôlt′) *n.* **1.** violent or vigorous attack: *an assault on an old man in broad daylight, an assault on democratic institutions.* **2.** *Law.* unlawful attempt or threat to do physical violence to another without the actual accomplishment of the intended attack. Distinguished from **battery. 3.** *Military.* last stage of an attack; closing with the enemy in hand-to-hand fighting. **4.** rape. —*v.t., v.i.* to make an assault (on); attack. [Old French *asaut* an attack, going back to Latin *ad* to, at + *saltus* leap.] —**Syn.** *v.t.* see **attack.**

assault and battery *Law.* assault followed by the actual infliction of physical violence upon the one assaulted.

as·say (*v.,* ə sā′; *n.,* ə sā′, as′ā) *v.t.* **1.** to test (as an ore, mineral, or

at; āpe; cär; end; mē; it; īce; hot; ōld; fôrk; wood; fōol; oil; out; up; ūse; turn; sing; thin; this; zh in treasure; ə in ago, taken, pencil, lemon, circus.

alloy) by chemical means to determine the amount of a particular metal present in it. **2.** to put to trial; test; evaluate. —*v.i.* to prove that a substance, as an ore or mineral, contains a certain amount of a particular metal: *The ore sample assayed low in uranium.* —*n.* **1.** chemical analysis, as of an ore, mineral, or alloy, to determine the amount of a particular metal contained in it. **2.** the substance analyzed. **3.** report or results of an assaying. **4.** examination; test. [Old French *asaier,* form of *essaier* to try, test, from *essai* a test, from Latin *exagium* a weighing.] —**as·say′er,** *n.*

as·sem·blage (ə sem′blij) *n.* **1.** group of persons or things brought together; collection. **2.** putting or fitting together, as of parts of something to be constructed. **3.** act of assembling; being assembled.

as·sem·ble (ə sem′bəl) **-bled, -bling.** *v.t.* **1.** to gather or bring (a group) together; collect. **2.** to put or fit together, as the parts of something to be constructed. —*v.i.* to meet or come together; convene. [Old French *assembler* to gather, going back to Latin *ad* to + *simul* together.] —**as·sem′bler,** *n.* —**Syn.** *v.t.* **1.** see **gather.**

as·sem·bly (ə sem′blē) *n.* **1.** group of people gathered together for a common purpose. **2.** Assembly, in all states of the United States, except Nebraska, the lower house of the legislature. **3.** act or process of fitting together (parts) to make a whole: *the assembly of the airplane parts.* **4.** act of assembling; state of being assembled. **5.** signal for troops to fall in. —**Syn. 1.** see **meeting.**

assembly.line, arrangement of tools, machines, and workers, past which an unfinished product is moved, each worker or machine performing a specialized operation on it until it is put together completely.

as·sem·bly·man (ə sem′blē mən) *pl.,* **-men.** *n.* member of a legislative assembly, esp. of a lower house of a state or provincial legislature.

as·sent (ə sent′) *v.i.* to express agreement; concur (with *to*): *I assent to your proposals.* —*n.* **1.** agreement; concurrence. **2.** acquiescence; consent. [Old French *assentir* to assent, from Latin *assentīre.*] —**Syn.** *v.i.* see **consent.**

as·sert (ə surt′) *v.t.* **1.** to state positively; affirm: *to assert that something is true.* **2.** to put forward or maintain insistently; put into effect: *Assert your rights.* **3. to assert oneself.** **a.** to thrust oneself forward aggressively. **b.** to come into effect; exercise an influence: *The . . . firmness of his nature began to assert itself* (George Eliot, 1860). [Latin *assertus,* past participle of *asserere* claim, affirm.] —**as·sert′er,** *n.*

as·ser·tion (ə sur′shən) *n.* **1.** positive statement; declaration: *His assertion was proved false.* **2.** act of putting forward or maintaining.

as·ser·tive (ə sur′tiv) *adj.* characterized by self-assertion; positive; aggressive: *an assertive person, an assertive tone of voice.* —**as·ser′tive·ly,** *adv.* —**as·ser′tive·ness,** *n.*

as·sess (ə ses′) *v.t.* **1.** to set the official value of (property) for taxation. **2.** to determine the amount of (a tax, fine, or damages). **3.** to tax or charge (a person or property): *Assess each member fifty dollars for the building fund.* **4.** to evaluate: *Assess carefully your chances of winning.* [Old French *assesser* to determine, tax, from Late Latin *assessāre* to fix a tax, from Latin *assessus,* past participle of *assidēre* to sit beside, assist a judge.] —**as·sess′a·ble,** *adj.*

as·sess·ment (ə ses′mənt) *n.* **1.** act of assessing. **2.** amount or value assessed. **3.** estimation; evaluation: *What is your assessment of the situation?*

as·ses·sor (ə ses′ər) *n.* person who assesses property for taxation.

as·set (as′et) *n.* **1.** something valuable or useful; advantage: *Knowing a trade is a great asset.* **2.** anything owned having a money value. **3. assets. a.** property and resources of a business or person as listed on a balance sheet. Opposed to **liabilities. b.** property or effects applicable for payment of the owner's debts. [Anglo-Norman *assets,* earlier *asetz,* equivalent to Old French *asez* enough, going back to Latin *ad* toward + *satis* enough (in the sense of "enough for payment of debts").]

as·sev·er·ate (ə sev′ə rāt′) **-at·ed, -at·ing.** *v.t.* to declare solemnly or positively; affirm. [Latin *asseverātus,* past participle of *asseverāre* to affirm strongly.]

as·sev·er·a·tion (ə sev′ə rā′shən) *n.* **1.** act of asseverating. **2.** emphatic or solemn assertion.

as·si·du·i·ty (as′ə doo͞o′ə tē, -dū′-) *pl.,* **-ties.** *n.* perseverance; diligence.

as·sid·u·ous (ə sij′oo͞o əs) *adj.* characterized by persistence and diligence: *an assiduous student.* [Latin *assiduus* sitting by, busy, constant.] —**as·sid′u·ous·ly,** *adv.* —**as·sid′u·ous·ness,** *n.*

as·sign (ə sīn′) *v.t.* **1.** to give out; distribute; allot: *Work will be assigned daily.* **2.** to select for a duty or office; appoint: *A new principal was assigned to the school.* **3.** to fix definitely; designate. **4.** to ascribe, as to a period of time; attribute, as a reason. **5.** to transfer (a right, property, or interest). —*n. also,* **assigns,** assignee. [Old French *assigner,* from Latin *assignāre.*] —**as·sign′a·ble,** *adj.* —**as·sign′er,** *n.*

Syn. *v.t.* **1. Assign, allot, apportion** indicate that something is given as a share. **Assign** suggests that a plan with authority behind it is the basis of distribution, which may or may not be equal: *The recruits, as they*

answered the roll call, were assigned beds in order. **Allot** suggests distribution by chance, again with no equal division implied: *The colonists were allotted their acreage some time before the landing was made.* **Apportion** suggests an equitable distribution according to some principle: *Representatives are apportioned among the states according to the size of their populations.*

as·sig·nat (as′ig nat′) *n.* paper money issued by the French Revolutionary government from 1789 to 1796, based on the security of confiscated lands. [French *assignat,* from Latin *assignātus,* past participle of *assignāre* to allot.]

as·sig·na·tion (as′ig nā′shən) *n.* **1.** arrangement of a time and place for a meeting, esp. a secret or illicit one between lovers; tryst. **2.** an assigning.

as·sign·ee (ə sī′nē′, as′ə nē′) *n.* person to whom a right, property, or interest is legally transferred.

as·sign·ment (ə sīn′mənt) *n.* **1.** that which is assigned; task; job: *a difficult assignment.* **2.** act of assigning; being assigned: *His assignment to the new post was still not official.* **3.a.** transfer of a right, property, or interest. **b.** document by which the transfer is made.

as·sign·or (ə sī′nor, as′ə nôr′) *n.* one who legally assigns a right, property, or interest.

as·sim·i·la·ble (ə sim′ə lə bəl) *adj.* capable of being assimilated. —**as·sim′i·la·bil′i·ty,** *n.*

as·sim·i·late (ə sim′ə lāt′) **-lat·ed, -lat·ing.** *v.t.* **1.** to take in and incorporate as one's own: *He assimilated every fact in the textbook.* **2.** to absorb and convert into living tissue: *Food is assimilated in the small intestine.* **3.** to absorb a minority or immigrant group into a prevailing culture: *Scandinavians are easily assimilated in the United States.* **4.** to alter phonetically by assimilation. —*v.i.* **1.** to be absorbed by or incorporated into a system or culture. **2.** *Archaic.* to become similar; come to resemble. [Latin *assimilātus,* past participle of *assimilāre* to make like.] —**as·sim′i·la′tor,** *n.* —**Syn.** *v.t.* **2.** see **absorb.**

as·sim·i·la·tion (ə sim′ə lā′shən) *n.* **1.** act of assimilating; being assimilated. **2.** process whereby a minority or immigrant group is absorbed into an existing culture through contact. **3.** absorption and transformation of digested food into living tissue. **4.** process in which a sound becomes similar to or the same as an adjacent sound. *Grandma* pronounced *gramma* is an example of assimilation.

as·sim·i·la·tive (ə sim′ə lā′tiv) *adj.* capable of or causing assimilation.

As·si·si (ə sē′zē) *n.* historic town and religious center in central Italy, noted as the birthplace of Saint Francis. Pop. (1961), 5,100.

as·sist (ə sist′) *v.t.* **1.** to give help or aid to. **2.** to be associated with as an assistant: *The intern assisted the surgeon.* —*v.i.* **1.** to help; aid; support: **2.** to be present; participate: *to assist at a banquet, to assist at an operation.* —*n.* **1.** *Baseball.* **a.** play that aids a teammate in making an out. **b.** credit given for such a play. **2.** *Ice Hockey.* **a.** action of passing the puck to the teammate who makes the goal. **b.** credit given for such a play. [French *assister* to help, from Latin *assistere* to stand by, aid.] —**Syn.** *v.t.* **1.** see **help.**

as·sis·tance (ə sis′təns) *n.* act of assisting; aid or support given.

as·sist·ant (ə sis′tənt) *n.* subordinate; helper. —*adj.* assisting; present in an assistant capacity only.

assistant professor, teacher in a college or university who ranks above an instructor and below an associate professor.

as·size (ə sīz′) *n.* **1.** *Archaic.* session of a law court or legislative assembly. **2. assizes. a.** court sessions held periodically in the counties of England to try criminal and civil cases by jury. **b.** time or place of such sessions. [Old French *as (s)ise* sitting, from *asseoir* to sit at, from Latin *assidēre* to sit beside, assist a judge.]

assn., association.

assoc. 1. associate. **2.** association.

as·so·ci·ate (*v.,* ə sō′shē āt′, -sē-; *n., adj.,* ə sō′shē it, -āt′, -sē-) **-at·ed, -at·ing.** *v.t.* **1.** to connect in one's mind: *We often associate darkness with danger.* **2.** to join or connect (oneself) as a companion, partner, or friend; *He associated himself with the law firm.* **3.** to join together; combine; connect: *the misery that is always associated with poverty.* —*v.i.* **1.** to keep certain company, as a friend, companion, or partner: *He associates only with highbrows.* **2.** to form a union or combination; unite: *Hydrogen associates freely with oxygen.* —*n.* **1.** one who is frequently in the company of another; companion; friend. **2.** one who is connected with another or others in some enterprise or action; partner; colleague: *business associates.* **3.** member of a society, institution, or organization having partial rights or privileges. **4.** anything usually accompanying or connected with another. **5.** one who has received an associate's degree. —*adj.* **1.** having secondary membership, status, or privileges: *associate judge, associate partner.* **2.** connected; concomitant. [Latin *associātus,* past participle of *associāre* to join, from *ad* to + *socius* companion.]

Syn. *n.* **2. Associate, colleague, companion, comrade** are used of fellow workers. **Associate** is an equal in a common endeavor: *He chose his*

associates for their skills, his assistants for their accuracy. **Colleague** is one sharing similar interests: *His colleagues in the profession held a testimonial dinner for him.* **Companion** usually is in a close relationship, going along toward a common goal: *Ralph and his companions would explore the woods on the estate for days on end.* **Comrade** is one to whom there are close personal ties in addition to shared experiences or efforts: *He and his three comrades served together in the war.*

Associated Press, AP.

associate professor, teacher in a college or university who ranks above an assistant professor and below a professor.

as·so·ci·a·tion (ə sō′sē ā′shən, -shē-) *n.* **1.** organized group of people with common interests or purposes; society: *The association voted to revoke his membership.* **2.** state of being associated; relationship; connection. **3.** act of associating; being associated. **4.a.** connection of or between thoughts, images, or sensations, such that one brings the other to mind: *the association between "red" and "blood".* **b.** one of the thoughts or sensations so connected. —**as·so′ci·a′tion·al,** *adj.* —**Syn. 1.** see **alliance.**

association football, soccer.

as·so·ci·a·tive (ə sō′shē ā′tiv, -sē-, -shə tiv) *adj.* relating to, characterized by, or resulting from association, esp. of thoughts or sensations: *associative images.*

as·soil (ə soil′) *v.t. Archaic.* **1.** to absolve. **2.** to atone for. [Old French *a(s)soil,* present indicative of *a(s)soldre* to absolve, from Latin *absolvere* to free. Doublet of ABSOLVE.]

as·so·nance (as′ə nəns) *n.* poetic device in which the stressed vowel sounds are alike but the consonant sounds different. In the line *And grassy barrows of the happier dead,* the *a*'s in *grassy, barrows,* and *happier* are examples of assonance. [French *assonance,* from Latin *assonāre* to respond to.]

as·sort (ə sôrt′) *v.t.* to put into categories; classify: *Assort these cards into three piles.* —*v.i.* **1.** to fall into a category; be matched. **2.** to consort; associate (with *with*). [Old French *assorter* to match, going back to Latin *ad* to + Latin *sors* lot, share.] —**as·sort′er,** *n.*

as·sort·ed (ə sôr′tid) *adj.* **1.** of various kinds: *a pound of assorted cookies.* **2.** sorted according to kind; classified. **3.** matched; suited. —**Syn. 3.** see **miscellaneous.**

as·sort·ment (ə sôrt′mənt) *n.* **1.** varied or diversified collection. **2.** act of assorting; being assorted.

asst., assistant.

as·suage (ə swāj′) **-suaged, -suag·ing.** *v.t.* **1.** to lessen in intensity; mitigate: *to assuage pain.* **2.** to calm; mollify; pacify: *one difficult to assuage when angry.* **3.** to satisfy; appease: *to assuage the appetite.* [Old French *assouagier* to soften, appease, going back to Latin *ad* to + *suāvis* sweet.] —**as·suage′ment,** *n.*

as·sume (ə sōom′) **-sumed, -sum·ing.** *v.t.* **1.** to take for granted; suppose as a fact. **2.** to take upon oneself; undertake: *assume a post, assume responsibility.* **3.** to take on; adopt: *assume great proportions, assume an air of authority.* **4.** to seize; arrogate; usurp: *He assumed dictatorial powers.* **5.** to put on the guise of; pretend: *Assume a virtue if you have it not* (Shakespeare, *Hamlet*). **6.** *Archaic.* to take or receive into association or partnership. [Latin *assūmere* to take to oneself, adopt.] —**Syn. 3.** see **adopt.**

as·sumed (ə sōomd′) *adj.* **1.** pretended; fictitious: *an assumed name.* **2.** taken for granted. **3.** usurped: *assumed powers.*

as·sum·ing (ə sōo′ming) *adj.* presumptuous; arrogant.

as·sump·tion (ə sump′shən) *n.* **1.** act of assuming; being assumed. **2.** something taken for granted; supposition: *His assumption proved to be wrong.* **3.** *Archaic.* presumption; effrontery; arrogance. **4.** the **Assumption. a.** the taking up into heaven of the body and soul of the Virgin Mary after her death. **b.** church festival celebrated in honor of this event. August 15. [Latin *assūmptiō* a taking.]

As·sur (as′ər) *n.* early capital of Assyria, in what is now north-central Iraq. Also, **A′shur.**

as·sur·ance (ə shoor′əns) *n.* **1.** act of assuring; being assured. **2.** positive declaration intended to give confidence; guarantee: *We felt easy only after his repeated assurances.* **3.** freedom from doubt; certainty: *He had assurance of her loyalty.* **4.** confidence; aplomb. **5.** *Archaic.* impudence; effrontery. **6.** *British.* insurance. —**Syn. 4.** see **confidence.**

as·sure (ə shoor′) **-sured, -sur·ing.** *v.t.* **1.** to declare positively; tell with certainty: *I assure you that they will come.* **2.** to make certain the occurrence or accomplishment of something); guarantee: *Their agreement assured passage of the bill.* **3.** to make (someone) certain; convince: *He assured us of their honesty.* **4.** to give confidence to; reassure: *to assure a frightened child.* **5.** to make secure; ensure: *He assured his position in the firm.* **6.** to insure. [Old French *asseürer* to make sure, going back to Latin *ad* to + *sēcūrus* sure.] —**as·sur′er,** *n.*

as·sured (ə shoord′) *adj.* **1.** made certain; undoubted; guaranteed: *an assured victory.* **2.** self-possessed; confident: *He spoke in his usual assured tones.* **3.** insured. —*n.* **1.** one who is the beneficiary of an insur-

ance policy. **2.** one whose life or property is insured. —**as·sur·ed·ly** (ə shoor′id lē, ə shoord′-), *adv.* —**as·sur′ed·ness,** *n.*

As·syr·i·a (ə sir′ē ə) *n.* ancient empire in southwestern Asia, at its height extending into Egypt.

As·syr·i·an (ə sir′ē ən) *adj.* of or relating to Assyria, its people, culture, or language. —*n.* **1.** member of the people of Assyria. **2.** Semitic language of the Assyrians.

As·tar·te (as tär′tē) *n.* Syrian and Phoenician goddess of fertility and love, identified with the Babylonian and Assyrian Ishtar and later with the Greek Aphrodite.

as·ta·tine (as′tə tēn′) *n.* radioactive chemical element of the halogen family that is usually produced by bombarding bismuth with alpha particles but traces of which occur in nature as radioactive decay products. It was formerly called **alabamine.** Symbol: **At** See element for table. [Greek *astatos* unstable + -INF².]

as·ter (as′tər) *n.* **1.** daisylike flower head of any of a large group of plants of the genus *Aster,* consisting of many ray flowers around a yellow or orange disk of tubular flowers. **2.** plant bearing such flower heads, usually in clusters, found in most temperate regions of the world. **3.** any other plant of the genus *Aster,* of the composite family, such as the daisy. **4.** China aster. [Latin *astēr* from Greek *astēr;* because the shape of the flower head suggests a star.]

Asters

as·ter·isk (as′tə risk′) *n.* star-shaped mark (*) used in printing or writing to indicate a reference, footnote or omission. —*v.t.* to mark with an asterisk; star. [Latin *asteriscus* a typographical mark, from Greek *asteriskos* literally, little star.]

as·ter·ism (as′tə riz′əm) *n.* group of stars; constellation.

a·stern (ə sturn′) *adv., adj.* **1.** at or toward the rear of a ship. **2.** behind a ship. **3.** backward.

as·ter·oid (as′tə roid′) *n.* **1.** any of thousands of minor planets that revolve around the sun, chiefly between the orbits of Mars and Jupiter. Also, **plan′et·oid′. 2.** starfish. [Greek *asteroeidēs* starlike, from *astēr* star.]

asth·ma (az′mə) *n.* chronic or recurrent allergic disease characterized by attacks of difficult breathing, wheezing, and coughing, accompanied by a feeling of suffocation. [Greek *asthma* panting.]

asth·mat·ic (az mat′ik) *adj.* of, relating to, or having asthma. —*n.* one who has asthma.

a·stig·mat·ic (as′tig mat′ik) *adj.* **1.** of, relating to, or having astigmatism. **2.** correcting astigmatism.

a·stig·ma·tism (ə stig′mə tiz′əm) *n.* **1.** defect of the cornea or lens of an eye causing blurred vision because the light rays from a single point do not converge at one point on the retina. **2.** similar defect in any type of lens. [A- + Greek *stigma* mark + -ISM.]

a·stir (ə stur′) *adv., adj.* **1.** in motion; stirring; active. **2.** out of bed.

as·ton·ish (əs ton′ish) *v.t.* to surprise greatly; amaze. [Modification of Middle English *astonen* to stun, from Old French *estoner,* going back to Latin *ex* out + *tonāre* to thunder.]

as·ton·ish·ing (əs ton′i shing) *adj.* causing astonishment; amazing. —**as·ton′ish·ing·ly,** *adv.*

as·ton·ish·ment (əs ton′ish mənt) *n.* **1.** surprise; amazement. **2.** cause of amazement or surprise.

As·tor, John Jacob (as′tər) 1763-1848, U.S. financier and fur trader.

as·tound (əs tound′) *v.t.* to overwhelm with sudden surprise or amazement; stun. [Possibly from Middle English *astoned,* past participle of *astonen* to stun. See ASTONISH.] —**as·tound′ing·ly,** *adv.*

a·strad·dle (ə strad′əl) *adv., adj.* astride.

as·trag·al (as′trə gəl) *n.* **1.** small, convex molding shaped like a string of beads, used in classical architecture around the top of columns. **2.** any small, plain, convex molding. [Latin *astragalus* molding on a column, from Greek *astragalos* molding on a column, anklebone.] —**as·trag′a·lar** (əs trag′ə lər), *adj.*

as·trag·a·lus (əs trag′ə ləs) *pl.,* **-li** (lī′). *n.* talus. [Probably Modern Latin *astragalus,* from Greek *astragalos* anklebone, molding on a column.]

as·tra·khan (as′trə kən, -kan′) *also,* **as·tra·chan.** *n.* **1.** fur of young lambs, originally from the region of Astrakhan, a grade of karakul. **2.** woolen cloth woven to resemble this.

As·tra·khan (as′trə kən, -kan′) *n.* port city on the lower Volga River, in the southwestern Soviet Union. Pop. (1970), 411,000.

as·tral (as′trəl) *adj.* **1.** of, relating to, resembling, or from the stars; starry. **2.** *Biology.* of or relating to an aster; star-shaped. [Late Latin *astrālis* relating to the stars, from Latin *astrum* star, from Greek *astron.*]

at; āpe; cär; end; mē; it; īce; hot; ōld; fôrk; wood; fōōl; oil; out; up; ūse; turn; sing; thin; this; zh in treasure; ə in ago, taken, pencil, lemon, circus.

astral lamp, oil lamp designed to cast no downward shadow.

a·stray (ə strā′) *adj., adv.* **1.** off the right path; wandering. **2.** into error or evil.

a·stride (ə strīd′) *adj., adv.* **1.** with one leg on each side. **2.** with legs far apart. —*prep.* with one leg on each side of.

as·trin·gent (əs trin′jənt) *n.* substance that contracts the tissues of the body. Astringents can stop or decrease the flow of blood or other body secretions. —*adj.* **1.** tending to contract the tissues of the body: *an astringent lotion.* **2.** stern; severe; austere. [Latin *astringēns,* present participle of *astringere* to bind together.] —**as·trin′gen·cy,** *n.* —**as·trin′gent·ly,** *adv.*

as·tro·gate (as′trə gāt′) -gat·ed, -gat·ing. *v.t., v.i.* to navigate in space.

as·tro·labe (as′trə lāb′) *n.* instrument formerly used for measuring the altitudes of the heavenly bodies, superseded by the sextant. [Old French *astrelabe,* from Medieval Latin *astrolabium,* from Greek *astrolabos.*]

as·trol·o·gy (əs trol′ə jē) *n.* study and interpretation of the influence that the heavenly bodies supposedly exert on events and the lives of men. [Old French *astrologie,* from Latin *astrologia* astronomy, from Greek *astrologiā.*] —**as·trol′o·ger,** *n.* —**as·tro·log·i·cal** (as′trə loj′-i kəl), *adj.* —**as′tro·log′i·cal·ly,** *adv.*

astron., astronomer; astronomical; astronomy.

as·tro·naut (as′trə nôt′) *n.* one who flies in or navigates a spacecraft. [Greek *astron* star + *nautēs* sailor.]

as·tro·naut·ics (as′trə nô′tiks) *n.* science or art dealing with the design, construction, and operation of spacecraft. ▲ construed as singular. —**as′tro·naut′ic, as′tro·naut′i·cal,** *adj.*

as·tron·o·mer (əs tron′ə mər) *n.* expert in astronomy.

as·tro·nom·i·cal (as′trə nom′i kəl) *adj.* **1.** of or relating to astronomy. **2.** immensely or unbelievably large. *a budget of astronomical proportions.* Also, **as′tro·nom′ic.** —**as′tro·nom′i·cal·ly,** *adv.*

astronomical unit, unit of length used to measure distances in astronomy, equal to the average distance between the center of the earth and the center of the sun or about 93 million miles.

astronomical year, solar year.

as·tron·o·my (əs tron′ə mē) *n.* science that deals with the planets, stars, and other heavenly bodies, including the study of their physical characteristics, relative positions, and motions. [Old French *astrono-mie,* from Latin *astronomia,* from Greek *astronomiā.*]

as·tro·phys·ics (as′trō fiz′iks) *n.* branch of astronomy dealing with the physical and chemical nature of heavenly bodies, esp. through the analysis of their light and other forms of energy they emit. ▲ construed as singular. [Greek *astron* star + PHYSICS.] —**as′tro·phys′i·cal,** *adj.* —**as′tro·phys′i·cist,** *n.*

As·tu·ri·as (əs toor′ē əs) *n.* region and former kingdom in northwestern Spain. Area, 4207 sq. mi. Pop. (1960), 989,344.

as·tute (əs tōōt′, -tūt′) *adj.* keenly discerning; shrewd; sagacious: *an astute businessman, an astute observation.* [Latin *astūtus.*] —**as·tute′ly,** *adv.* —**as·tute′ness,** *n.*

As·ty·a·nax (əs tī′ə naks′) *n. Greek Legend.* the young son of Hector and Andromache, hurled from the walls of Troy by the victorious Greeks, so that he would not grow up and avenge the Trojan defeat.

A·sun·ción (ä sōōn syōn′) *n.* capital, inland port, and largest city of Paraguay, in the southwestern part of the country. Pop. (1962), 305,200.

a·sun·der (ə sun′dər) *adv.* **1.** in pieces; separate parts: *torn asunder.* **2.** apart in position or direction: *The leaves were scattered asunder.* [Old English *on sundran* apart.]

As·wan High Dam (as′wän) giant dam in southeastern Egypt, on the Nile.

a·sy·lum (ə sī′ləm) *n.* **1.** institution providing shelter and care, as for the mentally ill or orphaned. **2.a.** shelter or protection afforded as a refuge: *The fugitive sought asylum.* **b.** shelter or protection from punishment or extradition granted by a foreign country to fugitives or political refugees. Also, **political asylum. 3.** inviolable place of refuge, as a church; sanctuary. **4.** any place of refuge; retreat; haven. [Latin *asylum* sanctuary, from Greek *asylon,* from *a-* not, without + *sylē* right of seizure.]

a·sym·met·ri·cal (ā′si met′ri kəl, as′i-) *adj.* not symmetrical. Also, **a′sym·met′ric.** —**a′sym·met′-ri·cal·ly,** *adv.*

a·sym·me·try (ā sim′ə trē) *n.* lack of symmetry. [Greek *asymmetriā* lack of proportion.]

as·ymp·tote (as′im tōt′) *n.* straight line continually approached by a given curve but never met by it within a finite distance. [Greek *asymptōtos* not falling together.]

Symmetrical

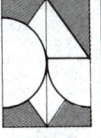

Asymmetrical

at (at; *unstressed* ət) *prep.* **1.** in; on; by; near: *at the top, at the door.* **2.** to or toward: *Look at the scenery.* **3.** in a place, state, or condition of: *at peace, at home.* **4.** on, near, or during the age or time of: *at noon. He died at seventy.* **5.** occupied with; engaged in: *at play, at dinner.* **6.** because of; resulting from: *She cringed at the sight of blood.* **7.** in the rate, degree, order, or position of: *at first, at ten miles per hour.* **8.** in the amount of; for: *The dress was sold at half price.* **9.** in the method or manner: *at ease, at random.* **10.** according to: *at one's beck and call. Proceed at your own risk.* **11.** present during the occurrence of; attending: *at the opera, at the birth.* **12.** from: *Get the book at the library. He warmed his hands at the fire.* **13.** through; by way of: *He entered at the back door.* [Old English *æt* in, near.]

at-, form of **ad-** before *t,* as in *attract.*

At, astatine.

at. **1.** atmosphere. **2.** atomic.

At·a·lan·ta (at′ə lan′tə) *n. Greek Legend.* maiden famed as a runner and as a huntress. After agreeing to wed any suitor who could beat her in a footrace, Atalanta was defeated by Hippomenes.

at·a·man (at′ə mən) *n.* pl. **-mans.** *n.* hetman.

at·a·vism (at′ə viz′əm) *n.* **1.** reversion to an earlier or primitive type of behavior. **2.** reappearance, usually after many generations, of a physical trait possessed by an ancestor. Also, **re·ver′sion.** [French *atavisme,* from Latin *atavus* remote ancestor.] —**at′a·vist,** *n.* —**at·a·vis′tic,** *adj.* —**at′a·vis′ti·cal·ly,** *adv.*

a·tax·i·a (ə tak′sē ə) *n.* **1.** impairment of coordination of the voluntary muscles, resulting from disorders affecting the cerebellum or the spinal cord. **2.** locomotor ataxia. [Modern Latin *ataxia,* from Greek *ataxiā* disorder.] —**a·tax′ic,** *adj., n.*

ate[1] (āt) past tense of eat.

a·te[2] (ā′tē) *n.* **1.** in ancient Greek thought, moral blindness, recklessness, or mental confusion which leads men to ruin. **2. Ate.** Greek goddess personifying and instigating such impulses. [Greek *atē.*]

-ate[1] *suffix* **1.** (used to form adjectives from nouns) of, relating to, or having: *vertebrate, collegiate.* **2.** (used to form verbs from certain stems) **a.** to become: *antiquate.* **b.** to cause to become: *consecrate, aggravate.* **c.** to produce: *substantiate.* **d.** to combine, impregnate, or treat with: *sulphurate.* **3.** used to form adjectives from certain verbs whose past participle ends in -ed: *situate, accumulate.* [Latin *-ātus, -āta, -ātum.*]

-ate[2] *suffix* used to form the names of salts made from an acid ending in *-ic: nitrate, acetate.* [Special use of -ATE[1].]

-ate[3] *suffix* (used to form nouns) **1.** denoting function, office, rule, or agent: *episcopate, magistrate.* **2.** denoting the object or result of an action: *delegate, mandate.* [Latin *-ātus.*]

at·el·ier (at′əl yā′) *n.* workshop or studio, esp. of an artist. [French *atelier,* from Old French carpenter's shop, pile of wood, from *astele* piece of wood, going back to Latin *astula,* diminutive of *assis* plank.]

a tem·po (ä tem′pō) *Music.* resuming the original rate of speed. [Italian *a tempo* in time, going back to Latin *ad* to + *tempus* time.]

Ath·a·na·sius, Saint (ath′ə nā′shəs) A.D. c.296–373, bishop of Alexandria and a leading figure of the early Christian church.

Ath·a·pas·can (ath′ə pas′kən) *n.* **1.** North American Indian language family, including languages of Alaska and northwestern Canada, the Pacific coast, and the southwestern United States. The Apaches and the Navahos are Athapascan-speaking tribes. **2.** member of a tribe speaking an Athapascan language. —*adj.* of or relating to this linguistic stock.

a·the·ism (ā′thē iz′əm) *n.* belief that there is no God. [French *athéisme,* from Greek *atheos* without God, denying the gods.]

a·the·ist (ā′thē ist) *n.* one who disbelieves in or denies the existence of God or gods.

a·the·is·tic (ā′thē is′tik) *adj.* of, relating to, or characteristic of atheism or atheists. Also, **a′the·is′ti·cal.** —**a′the·is′ti·cal·ly,** *adv.*

Ath·el·stan (ath′əl stan′) *n.* A.D. c.895–940, king of the English, from 925 to 940.

A·the·na (ə thē′nə) *also,* **A·the·ne** (ə thē′nē). *n.* Greek goddess of wisdom and the arts and crafts, the daughter of Zeus. Her Roman counterpart is Minerva. Also, **Pallas Athena.**

ath·e·nae·um (ath′ə nē′əm) *also,* **ath·e·ne·um.** *n.* **1. Athenaeum. a.** temple dedicated to Athena, esp. the one in ancient Athens where poets and scholars met to discuss their works. **b.** school founded in ancient Rome by Hadrian for the study of poetry, law, rhetoric, grammar, and philosophy. **2.** scientific or literary club. **3.** reading room; library. [Latin *Athēnaeum* temple of Athena, from Greek *Athēnaion,* from *Athēnē* Athena.]

A·the·ni·an (ə thē′nē ən) *adj.* of or relating to Athens, esp. ancient Athens, its people, art, or culture. —*n.* native, citizen, or inhabitant of Athens, esp. ancient Athens.

Ath·ens (ath′ənz) *n.* **1.** capital of Greece, in the eastern part of the country. It was once the most important and powerful of the ancient

---

ăt; āpe; cär; end; mē; ĭt; īce; hŏt; ōld; fôrk; wood; fōōl; oil; out; up; ūse; turn; sing; thin; this; zh in treasure; ə ago, taken, pencil, lemon, circus.

Greek city-states and for centuries the leading cultural center of the Mediterranean area. Pop. (1961), 627,564. **2.** any city considered a leading cultural center: *the Athens of the far West.* **3.** city in northeastern Georgia. Pop. (1970), 44,342.

a·thirst (ə thurst′) *adj.* **1.** having a strong desire; eager; longing. **2.** *Archaic.* thirsty.

ath·lete (ath′lēt) *n.* **1.** one trained for sports, games, or other competitive activities requiring physical strength, skill, agility, and stamina. **2.** one having an aptitude for such activities. [Latin *athlēta,* from Greek *athlētēs* contestant in sports, going back to *athlos* contest and *athlon* prize.]

athlete's foot, contagious fungus infection commonly occurring in the feet, particularly between the toes; ringworm of the foot.

ath·let·ic (ath let′ik) *adj.* **1.** of, relating to, characteristic of, or suited to an athlete or athletics. **2.** physically active and strong; vigorous. —**ath·let′i·cal·ly,** *adv.*

ath·let·ics (ath let′iks) *n.* **1.** athletic games, sports, or activities. **2.** practice or principles of athletic activities or training. ▲ usually construed as singular in def. 2, as plural in def. 1.

at-home (ət hōm′) *n.* informal reception given at one's home, usually in the afternoon.

Ath·os, Mount (ath′ōs, ā′thos) mountain on a peninsula of northeastern Greece, noted for the monasteries located there.

a·thwart (ə thwôrt′) *adv.* from side to side; crosswise. —*prep.* **1.** from side to side of; across. **2.** in opposition to; against. **3.** *Nautical.* across the line or course of: *The boat was athwart our bow.* [A-¹ + THWART (adverb).]

a·tilt (ə tilt′) *adj., adv.* **1.** tilted. **2.** in the manner of one tilting with a lance.

-ation *suffix* (used to form nouns) **1.** action or process of: *compilation.* **2.** condition or state of being: *isolation.* **3.** result of: *commendation.* [Latin *-ātiō,* genitive *-ātiōnis.*]

-ative *suffix* (used to form adjectives) **1.** tending to: *demonstrative.* **2.** of or relating to: *authoritative.* [Latin *-ātīvus.*]

At·lan·ta (at lan′tə) *n.* capital and largest city of Georgia, in the northwest-central part of the state. Pop. (1970), 496,973.

At·lan·te·an (at′lan tē′ən) *adj.* **1.** of, relating to, or like Atlas; strong. **2.** of or relating to Atlantis.

At·lan·tic (at lan′tik) *n.* ocean separating Europe and Africa from North America and South America. Also, **Atlantic Ocean.** —*adj.* **1.** of, relating to, or designating the Atlantic. **2.** on, along, or near the coast of the Atlantic.

Atlantic Charter, statement of postwar peace aims, issued on August 14, 1941, after a meeting at sea between President Roosevelt and Prime Minister Churchill.

Atlantic City, seashore resort city on the eastern coast of southern New Jersey. Pop. (1970), 47,859.

Atlantic Provinces, Canadian provinces of New Brunswick, Nova Scotia, Prince Edward Island, and Newfoundland and Labrador, in the eastern part of the nation, on the Atlantic.

At·lan·tis (at lan′tis) *n.* legendary island or continent in the Atlantic which had an advanced civilization but which sank into the sea because of the wickedness of its people. [Latin *Atlantis,* from Greek *Atlantis.*]

at·las (at′ləs) *n.* **1.** bound collection of maps. **2.** any similar collection containing illustrations, tables, or explanatory material relating to a particular subject. **3.** **Atlas.** *Greek Mythology.* a Titan condemned by Zeus to bear the weight of the heavens on his shoulders forever. [Greek *Atlās* the Titan. Pictures of Atlas supporting the heavens were used by sixteenth-century geographers to illustrate collections of maps.]

Atlas Mountains, mountain system along the northwestern coast of Africa, extending through most of Morocco and parts of Algeria and Tunisia.

at·man (ät′mən) *also,* **At·man.** *n. Hinduism.* eternal portion of Brahman that exists in every living thing. At death, the atman transmigrates to another body where it is reincarnated as a new life. [Sanskrit *ātman* breath, soul.]

at·mos·phere (at′məs fēr′) *n.* **1.** mass of gases that surrounds the earth or any other heavenly body. The earth's atmosphere is composed of air. **2.** air in a particular place: *suffocating atmosphere of the room.* **3.** pervading or surrounding environment or influence: *an atmosphere of hostility.* **4.** feeling, mood, or impression conveyed by surroundings or a work of art: *the cheerful atmosphere of a sunlit room, a restaurant with atmosphere.* **5.** unit of pressure equal to atmospheric pressure at sea level, or 14.69 pounds per square inch. [Modern Latin *atmosphaera,* from Greek *atmos* vapor + *sphaira* sphere.]

at·mos·pher·ic (at′məs fēr′ik) *adj.* **1.** of, in, relating to, or consisting of the atmosphere. **2.** caused or influenced by the atmosphere. Also, **at′mos·pher′i·cal.** —**at′mos·pher′i·cal·ly,** *adv.*

atmospheric pressure, pressure exerted by the weight of the earth's atmosphere. At sea level it is equal to 14.69 pounds per square inch.

at·mos·pher·ics (at′məs fer′iks) *n.* **1.** electrical disturbances in the atmosphere. **2.** radio interference caused by such disturbances; static. Also, **sfer′ics.** ▲ construed as singular in both definitions.

at. no., atomic number.

at·oll (at′ôl, a′tôl′, ā′tôl) *n.* circular or nearly circular coral reef or string of reefs rising above and surrounding a lagoon. [Malayalam *atolu* the Maldive Islands (which are typical atolls); literally, reef.]

at·om (at′əm) *n.* **1.** smallest particle of a chemical element that has the chemical properties of that element and is composed of a positively charged central nucleus around which negatively charged electrons travel in circular or elliptical paths. **2.** any extremely small particle; iota. [Latin *atomus* smallest particle, from Greek *atomos* indivisible; from the earlier belief that atoms could not be split.]

atom bomb, atomic bomb.

a·tom·ic (ə tom′ik) *adj.* **1.** of, relating to, or consisting of an atom or atoms. **2.** powered by atomic energy. **3.** extremely minute; microscopic. —**a·tom′i·cal·ly,** *adv.*

atomic bomb, nuclear bomb whose great destructive power is derived from the sudden release of energy by nuclear fission, as when atoms of heavy elements, such as uranium or plutonium, are split into atoms of lighter elements. Also, **A-bomb.**

atomic clock, electric clock regulated by the rapid and extremely regular movements within atoms or molecules. Atomic clocks are the most accurate timekeeping devices yet developed.

atomic energy, nuclear energy.

atomic number, number of positive charges in the nucleus of an atom of an element. The atomic number determines the place of an element in the periodic table.

atomic pile, nuclear reactor.

atomic reactor, nuclear reactor.

atomic theory, general theory that all matter is composed of atoms.

atomic weight, average weight of an atom of a chemical element, measured in terms of units equal to one-twelfth the mass of an atom of carbon-12.

at·om·ize (at′ə mīz′) **-ized, -iz·ing.** *v.t.* **1.** to reduce to atoms. **2.** to reduce (a liquid) to a fine spray. —**at′om·i·za′tion,** *n.*

at·om·iz·er (at′ə mī′zər) *n.* device for reducing a liquid to a fine spray.

atom smasher, accelerator *(def. 2).*

at·o·my (at′ə mē) *pl.* **-mies.** *n. Archaic.* **1.** minute particle; atom. **2.** tiny being; pygmy. [Latin *atomī.* plural of *atomus.* See ATOM.]

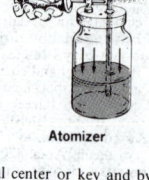
Atomizer

a·ton·al (ā tōn′əl) *adj.* **1.** without tonality. **2.** *Music.* characterized by the absence of tonal center or key and by the giving of equal emphasis to all twelve tones of the chromatic scale. —**a·to·nal·i·ty** (ā′tō nal′ə tē), *n.* —**a·ton′al·ly,** *adv.*

a·tone (ə tōn′) **a·toned, a·ton·ing.** *v.i.* to make amends or reparation (with *for*): *He atoned for his crime.* [Back formation from ATONEMENT.]

a·tone·ment (ə tōn′mənt) *n.* **1.** reparation for a wrong or injury; expiation; amends. **2. the Atonement.** reconciliation of God with man through the life, sufferings, and esp. the death of Christ. [From *at one* in sense of "at one with God" + -MENT.]

a·top (ə top′) *prep.* on the top of. —*adv. Archaic.* on or at the top.

at·ra·bil·ious (at′rə bil′yəs) *adj.* **1.** melancholy or gloomy; depressed. **2.** bad-tempered; choleric; acrimonious. [Latin *ātra bilis* black bile, melancholy, translation of Greek *melancholiā.* See MELANCHOLY.]

A·tre·us (ā′trē əs, ā′troos) *n. Greek Legend.* a king of Mycenae and the father of Agamemnon and Menelaus. Atreus brought a curse upon his house when he killed his brother's children and served them to him at a banquet.

a·tri·um (ā′trē əm) *pl.* **a·tri·a** (ā′trē ə) *or* **a·tri·ums.** *n.* **1.** principal room or entrance hall of an ancient Roman house, having an opening in the center of the roof, directly over a pool or fountain. **2.** colonnaded courtyard in front of the entrance of early Christian churches. **3.** auricle *(def. 1).* [Latin *ātrium* principal room in a Roman house.]

a·tro·cious (ə trō′shəs) *adj.* **1.** outrageous; heinous; despicable: *an atrocious crime.* **2.** *Informal.* very bad; distasteful; offensive: *an atrocious speech.* —**a·tro′cious·ly,** *adv.* —**a·tro′cious·ness,** *n.*

a·troc·i·ty (ə tros′ə tē) *pl.* **-ties.** *n.* **1.** state or quality of being atrocious: *the atrocity of his crime.* **2.** any outrageously cruel act: *The enslavement of human beings is an atrocity.* **3.** *Informal.* that which is distasteful or offensive: *The book is an atrocity.* [Latin *atrōcitās* cruelty.]

at·ro·phy (at′rə fē) *n.* **1.** wasting away of the body or its tissues or organs. **2.** withering away; decay; degeneration: *the atrophy of a nation.* —*v.i.* **-phied, -phy·ing.** to waste or wither away. —*v.t.* to cause to waste or wither away. [Late Latin *atrophia* lack of food, from Greek *atrophiā.*] —**a·troph·ic** (ə trof′ik), *adj.*

at·ro·pine (at′rə pēn′, -pin) *n.* poisonous, white crystalline alkaloid made synthetically or obtained from belladonna and similar plants and used in medicine to relieve spasms and to dilate the pupil of the eye. Formula: $C_{17}H_{23}NO_3$ [Modern Latin *atropa belladonna,* from Greek *Atropos.* See ATROPOS.]

At·ro·pos (at′rə pos′) *n.* Greek Mythology. one of the three Fates. She cuts the thread of life which is spun and measured by the other two. [Greek *Atropos* literally, inflexible.]

at·tach (ə tach′) *v.t.* **1.** to tack on or fasten; connect; affix. **2.** to join or connect as an associate or part of: *He was attached to the committee.* **3.** to bind by personal ties, as of affection. **4.** to attribute; ascribe: *They attached significance to his speech.* **5.** to appoint or assign in an official capacity: *He was attached to the American Embassy.* **6.** to add (with to): *He attached his name to the contract.* **7.** to take (a person or property) by legal authority: *His creditors attached his salary.* **8.** to place units or personnel under the command of a military organization on a temporary basis. —*v.i.* to belong; adhere. [Old French *attachier* to fasten, from *a* to (from Latin *ad* to) + Low German *takk* pointed thing (in the sense of "to nail to"). Doublet of ATTACK.] —**at·tach′a·ble,** *adj.*

at·ta·ché (at′ə shā′, a tash′ā) *n.* one who is attached to the staff of a diplomatic mission to act in a specialized capacity: *commercial attaché.* [French *attaché,* from past participle of *attacher* to attach. See ATTACH.]

attaché case, slim briefcase.

at·tach·ment (ə tach′mənt) *n.* **1.** act of attaching; being attached. **2.** binding affection; devotion. **3.** that which is attached: *vacuum cleaner attachments.* **4.** that which attaches; fastening; connection. **5.a.** act of taking a person or property by legal authority, esp. the taking of property as security for debts. **b.** writ or other process authorizing this.

at·tack (ə tak′) *v.t.* **1.** to set upon with force or arms; assault. **2.** to write or speak against vehemently; censure. **3.** to start to work on vigorously; undertake energetically: *He attacked the problem realistically.* **4.** to begin to act on or to affect destructively: *Locusts attacked the crops.* —*v.i.* to make an attack; begin combat: *The barbarians attacked at daybreak.* —*n.* **1.** act of attacking. **2.** sudden onset, fit, or occurrence of a disease: *an attack of asthma.* [French *attaquer* to attack, from Italian *attaccare (battaglia)* to join (battle), from Latin *ad* to + Low German *takk* pointed thing. (in the sense of "to fix a nail to"). Doublet of ATTACH.] —**at·tack′er,** *n.*

Syn. *v.t.* **1.** Attack, assault, assail mean to use violence against someone or something. Attack indicates a sudden, forceful onset, often without warning: *They attacked the entrenched enemy as soon as reinforcements arrived.* Assault stresses direct contact and the use of raw force: *The mob broke into shops and assaulted passers-by in its fury.* Assail suggests repeated blows rather than overwhelming force: *The defenders on the parapet were assailed by a constant rain of arrows.*

at·tain (ə tān′) *v.t.* **1.** to achieve or gain (something) through continued effort; accomplish. **2.** to arrive at; reach. —*v.i.* **to attain to.** to succeed in reaching or achieving: *He attained to great power.* [Old French *ataindre* to reach, convict, going back to Latin *attingere* to touch upon, reach.]

at·tain·a·ble (ə tān′nə bəl) *adj.* capable of being attained. —**at·tain′a·bil′i·ty, at·tain′a·ble·ness,** *n.*

at·tain·der (ə tān′dər) *n.* loss of civil rights which occurs when a person convicted of a felony or treason is sentenced to death. [Old French *ataindre,* noun use of infinitive *ataindre* to attain, convict. See ATTAIN.]

at·tain·ment (ə tān′mənt) *n.* **1.** act of attaining. **2.** something attained; accomplishment.

at·taint (ə tānt′) *v.t.* **1.** to condemn to attainder. **2.** *Archaic.* to disgrace; dishonor. —*n.* *Archaic.* stain upon honor or purity; disgrace. [Old French *ataint,* past participle of *ataindre* to attain, convict; sense in English influenced by confusion with *taint.* See ATTAIN.]

at·tar (at′ər) *n.* fragrant essential oil obtained from the petals of flowers, esp. roses, used in the making of perfume. [Persian *'atar,* Arabic *'itr* perfume.]

at·tempt (ə tempt′) *v.t.* **1.** to make an effort to do or accomplish (something); try. **2.** putting forth of effort to do or accomplish something; endeavor; effort. **2.** an assault or attack, esp. upon a person's life. [Old French *atempter* to try, from Latin *attemptāre.*] —**Syn.** *v.t.* **1.** see **try.**

at·tend (ə tend′) *v.t.* **1.** to be present at: *to attend church.* **2.** to take care of; minister to: *The doctor attended the patient.* **3.** to wait upon or accompany: *Two maids attend the queen.* **4.** to accompany as a circumstance or consequence: *Fever attends many diseases.* **5.** to listen to; pay heed to: *Attend my words.* —*v.i.* **1.** to be present: *She does not attend often.* **2.** **to attend to. a.** to devote one's energy to; apply oneself to: *Attend to your duties.* **b.** to take care of: *The nurse attended to her patients.* **c.** to give careful thought and consideration to; pay attention to: *Attend to the speech.* [Old French *atendre* to wait, from Latin *attendere* to give heed to.] —**Syn.** *v.t.* **3.** see **accompany.**

at·ten·dance (ə ten′dəns) *n.* **1.** act of attending; state of being present. **2.a.** persons or number of persons present. **b.** record of this. **3.** number of times attending: *He has perfect attendance.*

at·ten·dant (ə ten′dənt) *n.* **1.** one who waits upon or accompanies another: *the queen's attendants.* **2.** one who is present. **3.** accompanying circumstance; consequence. —*adj.* **1.** following as a consequence: *attendant circumstances.* **2.** being present; in attendance: *attendant crowds.* **3.** waiting upon another; accompanying. —**at·tend′ant·ly,** *adv.*

at·ten·tion (ə ten′shən) *n.* **1.** active focusing of the mind; giving heed: *The speaker had our undivided attention.* **2.** power or faculty of mental concentration: *His attention was distracted.* **3.** thoughtful consideration; observant care: *This matter will receive our immediate attention.* **4.** a good mother gives equal attention to each of her children. **4.a.** courtesy; civility: *attention to a stranger.* **b.** **attentions.** acts of courtesy, thoughtfulness, or devotion, esp. those of a suitor. **5.a.** regulation military stance, characterized by stiff, erect posture, esp. with arms at the sides and eyes front: *The soldiers snapped to attention.* **b.** any similar posture: *The children stood at attention as the flag was raised.* —*interj.* command to assume this posture. [Latin *attentiō* attentiveness, application.]

at·ten·tive (ə ten′tiv) *adj.* **1.** paying attention; observant; heedful. **2.** courteous; considerate; thoughtful: *an attentive host.* —**at·ten′tive·ly,** *adv.* —**at·ten′tive·ness,** *n.*

at·ten·u·ate (ə ten′ū āt′) *-at·ed, -at·ing. v.t.* **1.** to make thin or slender. **2.** to lessen or reduce, as in size, severity, or force. **3.** to reduce in density or consistency; dilute. —*v.i.* to become thin, slender, or less. —*adj.* **1.** slender; thin; lessened. **2.** *Botany.* tapering gradually to a slender point. [Latin *attenuātus,* past participle of *attenuāre* to make thin.]

at·ten·u·a·tion (ə ten′ū ā′shən) *n.* act of attenuating; being attenuated.

at·test (ə test′) *v.t.* **1.** to affirm to be correct, true, or genuine, esp. by oath or signature: *The witness attested the truth of the evidence.* **2.** to be proof or evidence of; manifest: *His good deeds attest his virtue.* **3.** to put on oath. —*v.i.* to bear witness; certify (with *to*). [Latin *attestārī* to bear witness to.] —**Syn.** *v.t.* **1.** see **certify.**

at·tes·ta·tion (at′əs tā′shən) *n.* **1.** act of attesting. **2.** testimony; evidence; proof.

at·tic (at′ik) *n.* space or story directly below the sloping roof of a building. [French *attique* referring to the space or story beneath the roof, which was usually decorated in a simple, elegant style, like the architecture of ancient Athens, from Latin *Atticus* pertaining to Attica or Athens. See ATTIC.]

At·tic (at′ik) *adj.* **1.** of or relating to Attica. **2.** of or relating to Athens, its people, or culture; Athenian. **3.** *also,* **attic.** characterized by simplicity, elegance, and refinement. —*n.* Ionic dialect of ancient Greek spoken predominantly in Attica. It was the major literary dialect of ancient Greece. [Latin *Atticus* pertaining to Attica or Athens, from Greek *Attikos.*]

At·ti·ca (at′i kə) *n.* historic region and province in east-central Greece, on the Aegean. Athens is its principal city and capital.

At·ti·la (at′əl ə, ə til′ə) *n.* A.D. c.406–453, king of the Huns from c.433 to 453.

at·tire (ə tīr′) *-tired, -tir·ing. v.t.* to clothe; dress; array. —*n.* **1.** clothes; apparel; dress. **2.** *attires. Heraldry.* horns of a stag. [Old French *atir(i)er* to arrange, dress, from phrase *a tire* in order; *a* to, from Latin *ad* to + *tire* order; possibly of Germanic origin.]

at·ti·tude (at′ə tōōd′, -tūd′) *n.* **1.** manner of thinking, acting, or feeling: *a hostile attitude.* **2.** position of the body implying or indicating an action or mental state. **3.** position of an aircraft in relation to some frame of reference, as the earth. [Italian *attitudine* disposition, posture, from Late Latin *aptitūdō* fitness, from Latin *aptus* fitted. Doublet of APTITUDE.]

Att·lee, Clem·ent Richard (at′lē; clem′ənt) 1883–1967, English statesman and Labour Party leader, prime minister from 1945 to 1951.

at·tor·ney (ə tur′nē) *pl.,* **-neys.** *n.* **1.** lawyer. **2.** person authorized by another to act in his place. [Old French *atorné* literally, one appointed, from *atorner* to appoint, turn to, going back to Latin *ad* to + *tornāre* to turn. See TURN.] —**Syn.** **1.** see **lawyer.**

attorney at law *pl.,* **attorneys at law.** lawyer.

attorney general *pl.,* **attorneys general** or **attorney generals.** chief law officer of a national or state government. He advises the chief executive and appears on behalf of the government in court.

at·tract (ə trakt′) *v.t.* **1.** to be appealing to; draw the attention or interest of; fascinate: *This scenery attracts many tourists.* **2.** to draw to oneself or itself by physical force. —*v.i.* to exert attraction; be attractive. [Latin *attractus,* past participle of *attrahere* to draw to.] —**at·tract′er, at·trac′tor,** *n.*

at·trac·tion (ə trak′shən) *n.* **1.** appealing quality or feature; allurement; charm. **2.** act or power of attracting: *the attraction of a magnet.* **3.** thing that attracts: *The juggler was the main attraction.* **4.** *Physics.*

---

at; āpe; cär; end; mē; it; īce; hot; ōld; fôrk; wood; fōōl; oil; out; up; ūse; turn; sing; thin; this; zh in treasure; ə in ago, taken, pencil, lemon, circus.

a. the force exerted by bodies on one another, tending to draw them together. **b.** the effect of this force; the tendency of bodies to draw together.

at·trac·tive (ə trak′tiv) *adj.* **1.** having an appealing quality or feature; alluring; pleasing. **2.** having the power or property of attracting. —**at·trac′tive·ly,** *adv.* —**at·trac′tive·ness,** *n.*

attrib. **1.** attribute. **2.** attributive.

at·trib·ute (*v.*, ə trib′ūt; *n.*, at′rə būt′) **-ut·ed, -ut·ing.** *v.t.* to designate or consider (something) as belonging to, caused by, or resulting from; assign. —*n.* **1.** quality or characteristic considered as belonging to a person or thing. **2.** object considered as a characteristic or symbol: *The moon was the attribute of Diana.* [Latin *attribūtus,* past participle of *attribuere* to assign.] —**at·trib′ut·a·ble,** *adj.*
Syn. *v.t.* **Attribute, ascribe, impute** indicate that someone or something is believed to be the cause of something. **Attribute** implies that the result is appropriate or natural to its originator: *Archaeologists attribute the ruins to a flourishing prehistoric kingdom.* **Ascribe** implies that something tentative remains in the reasoning, that the link with the cause is circumstantial: *Medical researchers ascribe much of the rise in the incidence of lung cancer to the widespread use of cigarettes.* **Impute** implies that what is ascribed in some way brands the cause in a negative way: *The motives they impute to Richard III appear to be political fictions of the Tudor court.* —*n.* **1. see quality.**

at·tri·bu·tion (at′rə bū′shən) *n.* **1.** act of attributing. **2.** quality or thing attributed; attribute.

at·trib·u·tive (ə trib′yə tiv) *adj.* **1.** of, relating to, or like an attribute. **2.** relating to an adjective, or a noun used as an adjective, preceding and modifying a noun. In the phrase *school bus,* the noun *school* is an attributive word. —*n.* attributive word. —**at·trib′u·tive·ly,** *adv.*

at·tri·tion (ə trish′ən) *n.* **1.** wearing away by friction; abrasion. **2.** gradual wearing down or weakening, as by continued abuse or attack: *a war of attrition.* [Latin *attrītiō* friction.] —**at·tri′tion·al,** *adj.*

At·tu Island (at′tōō) westernmost part of the United States, forming part of Alaska. It is one of the Aleutian Islands.

at·tune (ə tōōn′, ə tūn′) **-tuned, -tun·ing.** *v.t.* to bring into harmony or accord. —**at·tune′ment,** *n.*

atty., attorney.

at. wt., atomic weight.

a·typ·i·cal (ā tip′i kəl) *adj.* not conforming to a standard or type; not typical. —**a·typ′i·cal·ly,** *adv.*

Au, gold. [Abbreviation of Latin *aurum.*]

au·burn (ô′bərn) *n.* reddish brown color. —*adj.* of the color auburn. [Old French *auborne* light-colored, from Late Latin *alburnus* whitish, from *albus* white (somehow became confused with *brown*).]

Au·burn (ô′bərn) *n.* city in west-central New York. Pop. (1970), 34,599.

Auck·land (ôk′lənd) *n.* port city in northern New Zealand. Pop. (1969), 152,200.

auc·tion (ôk′shən) *n.* **1.** public sale at which articles or property are sold to the highest bidder. **2.** bidding in certain card games, as bridge. **3.** auction bridge. —*v.t.* to sell by or at auction. [Latin *auctiō* such a public sale, increase, from *augēre* to increase; because it is a sale in which buyers keep increasing their offers.]

auction bridge, type of bridge differing from contract bridge only in the number of points given, as for tricks or honors, and requiring only thirty points for game.

auc·tion·eer (ôk′shə nēr′) *n.* one who conducts sales by auction.

au·da·cious (ô dā′shəs) *adj.* **1.** bold; daring; intrepid. **2.** unrestrained, as by decorum or morality; insolent. —**au·da′cious·ly,** *adv.* —**au·da′cious·ness,** *n.*

au·dac·i·ty (ô das′ə tē) *n.* **1.** boldness; daring. **2.** shameless boldness; impudence. [Latin *audāx* bold + -ITY.]

au·di·ble (ô′də bəl) *adj.* capable of being heard; loud enough to be heard. [Late Latin *audibilis,* from Latin *audīre* to hear.] —**au′di·bil′i·ty,** *n.* —**au′di·bly,** *adv.*

au·di·ence (ô′dē əns) *n.* **1.** assembled group of listeners or spectators. **2.** those reached, as by a broadcast or publication. **3.** formal meeting, hearing, or interview with a person of rank or position: *an audience with the pope.* **4.** opportunity to be heard; hearing. **5.** act of hearing. [Old French *audience* hearing, from Latin *audientia.*]

au·di·o (ô′dē ō′) *adj.* **1.** of or relating to sound or audio frequencies. **2.** of or relating to the reproduction of sound or audio frequencies, esp. in high-fidelity reproduction. **3.** of, relating to, or used in the transmission or reception of sound or audio frequencies. —*n.* the audio part of television. Distinguished from *video.* [From AUDIO-.]

audio- *combining form* relating to hearing: *audiovisual.* [From Latin *audīre* to hear.]

audio frequency, any frequency at which a sound wave is normally audible, from about 15 to 20,000 cycles per second.

au·di·om·e·ter (ô′dē om′ə tər) *n.* machine which produces controlled sounds, used for measuring a person's hearing. [AUDIO- +

-METER.] —**au·di·o·met·ric** (ô′dē ō met′rik), *adj.* —**au′di·om′e·try,** *n.*

au·di·o·vis·u·al (ô′dē ō vizh′ōō əl) *adj.* **1.** of or relating to hearing and sight. **2.** of, relating to, or using educational materials other than books for teaching, as films, recordings, television, and photographs.

au·dit (ô′dit) *v.t.* **1.** to examine and verify (financial accounts and records) officially. **2.** to attend (a college course) as a listener without obligation to do required work or intention of receiving formal credit for attendance. —*v.i.* **1.** to examine and verify financial accounts and records officially. **2.** to attend a college course as an auditor. —*n.* **1.** official investigation and verification of financial accounts and records. **2.** final statement, prepared by an auditor, of the financial accounts and records that have been examined and verified. [Latin *audītus* a hearing. In earlier times, audits were made by hearing an oral presentation of accounts rather than by examining written statements.]

au·di·tion (ô dish′ən) *n.* **1.** test performance of the abilities of a singer, musician, actor, or other performer. **2.** act or sense of hearing. —*v.t.* to give an audition to (a performer): *We auditioned three actors for the part.* —*v.i.* to perform in an audition. [Latin *audītiō* hearing.]

au·di·tor (ô′də tər) *n.* **1.** one authorized to audit financial records and accounts. **2.** hearer; listener. **3.** one who audits a college course.

au·di·to·ri·um (ô′də tôr′ē əm) *pl.,* **-to·ri·ums** or **-to·ri·a** (-tôr′ē ə). *n.* **1.** large room, as in a church or school, in which an audience may assemble, usually with a stage or platform at one end. **2.** building used for public gatherings. [Latin *audītōrium* place where something is heard, going back to *audīre* to hear.]

au·di·to·ry (ô′də tôr′ē) *adj.* of or relating to the sense or organs of hearing.

Au·du·bon, John James (ô′də bon′) 1785–1851, American ornithologist and artist.

auf Wie·der·seh·en (ouf vē′dər zā′ən) *German.* until we meet again; good-by for now.

Aug., August.

Au·ge·an stables (ô jē′ən) *Greek Legend.* the stables of King Augeas which sheltered 3000 oxen and had not been cleaned for thirty years. Hercules cleaned them by changing the course of two rivers so that they flowed through the stables.

Au·ge·as (ô′jē əs, ô jē′as) *n.* king whose stables Hercules cleaned.

au·ger (ô′gər) *n.* **1.** tool for boring holes in wood. **2.** drill for boring holes in the earth. [Earlier *nauger,* from Old English *nafugār* auger, tool used to bore the nave of a wheel; *a nauger* being incorrectly written later as *an auger.* For a similar development, see ADDER.]

Augers

aught[1] (ôt) *also,* **ought.** *n. Archaic.* **1.** all: *for aught I care.* **2.** anything; any part. —*adv.* in any way; at all. [Old English *āwiht* anything; literally, ever a thing, from *ā* ever + *wiht* thing.]

aught[2] (ôt) *also,* **ought.** *n.* **1.** zero; cipher. **2.** *Archaic.* nothing; naught. [Earlier *naught,* from Old English *nāwiht* nothing; from *nā* no + *wiht* thing; *a naught* being incorrectly written later as *an aught.* For a similar development, see ADDER.]

aug·ment (ôg ment′) *v.t.* to make greater, as in size or amount; increase; enlarge: *John augmented his regular salary by working overtime.* —*v.i.* to become greater; increase; grow. [Latin *augmentāre* to increase.] —**aug·ment′a·ble,** *adj.* —**Syn.** *v.t.* **increase.**

aug·men·ta·tion (ôg′men tā′shən) *n.* **1.** act of augmenting; being augmented. **2.** that by which something is augmented; addition. —**aug·men·ta·tive** (ôg men′tə tiv), *adj.*

au grat·in (ō grat′ən, ō grät′ən) covered with bread crumbs or grated cheese and baked or grilled until brown. [French *au gratin.*]

Augs·burg (ôgz′bərg) *n.* city in southern West Germany. Pop. (1968), 210,610.

au·gur (ô′gər) *n.* **1.** any of a group of priests of ancient Rome who made predictions based on the interpretations of various omens. **2.** any soothsayer; diviner; fortuneteller. —*v.t.* **1.** to predict from signs or omens; prophesy. **2.** to be a sign or omen of; give promise of. —*v.i.* **1.** to predict from signs or omens. **2.** to augur ill; to be a bad sign or omen. **3. to augur well** to be a good sign or omen. [Latin *augur* soothsayer.]

au·gu·ry (ô′gyər ē) *pl.,* **-ries.** *n.* **1.** art or practice of prophesying by means of omens or signs; divination. **2.** prediction; sign; omen. **3.** rite or ceremony carried out by an augur.

au·gust (ô gust′) *adj.* **1.** inspiring awe, reverence, or admiration; magnificent; majestic; imposing: *the august beauty of the Sistine Chapel.* **2.** venerable; dignified; eminent: *an august assembly.* [Latin *augustus* venerable.] —**au·gust′ly,** *adv.* —**au·gust′ness,** *n.*

Au·gust (ô′gəst) *n.* eighth month of the year, containing thirty-one days. [Old English *August,* from Latin *Augustus* title of the first Roman

at; āpe; cär; end; mē; it; īce; hot; ōld; fôrk; wood; fōōl; oil; out; up; ūse; turn; sing; thin; this; zh in treasure; ə in ago, taken, pencil, lemon, circus.

emperor, from *augustus* venerable. The Emperor Augustus gave his name to the month of *Sextīlis* in the Roman calendar.]

Au·gus·ta (ô gus′tə) *n.* **1.** capital of Maine, in the southern part of the state. Pop. (1970), 21,945. **2.** city in northeastern Georgia. ·Pop. (1970), 59,864.

Au·gus·tan (ô gus′tən) *adj.* **1.** of, relating to, or characteristic of the Roman emperor Augustus, his times, or his reign. **2.** of, relating to, or characteristic of the late seventeenth to the middle eighteenth centuries in England, esp. the reign of Queen Anne. —*n.* writer during an Augustan age.

Augustan age 1. period of Latin literature during the reign of Augustus in which such writers as Horace, Virgil, and Ovid flourished. **2.** any similar period of literary productivity and excellence, esp. in England from the seventeenth to the middle eighteenth centuries.

Au·gus·tine (ô′gəs tēn′, ô gus′tin) **1.** Saint. A.D. 354–430, bishop of Hippo and most important of the Latin Church fathers. **2. of Canterbury, Saint.** died A.D. 604, first archbishop of Canterbury.

Au·gus·tin·i·an (ô′gəs tin′ē ən) *adj.* of or relating to Saint Augustine, his religious doctrines, or the religious orders following his rule. —*n.* **1.** adherent of the doctrines of Saint Augustine. **2.** member of any of several religious orders that follow the rule of Saint Augustine.

Au·gus·tus (ô gus′təs) *n.* 63 B.C.–A.D. 14, first emperor of Rome, from 27 B.C. to A.D. 14; full name Gaius Julius Caesar Octavianus. Also, **Oc·ta′vi·an.**

au jus (ō′ zhōōs′, ō jōōs′) (of meat) served with the gravy that forms naturally from the juices of the meat while it is cooking. [French.]

auk (ôk) *n.* any of several web-footed diving birds, family Alcidae, found chiefly in coastal waters of the Northern Hemisphere, resembling the penguin, and having a heavy body, short tail, and short wings. Length: up to 18 inches. [Old Norse *ālka.*]

Auk

au lait (ō lā′) *adj. French.* with milk.

auld lang syne (ôld′ lang zīn′, sīn′) days of long ago, esp. the happy times. [Scottish *auld lang syne* literally, old long ago.]

au na·tu·rel (ō nä tōō rel′) **1.** cooked plainly or served without garnish. **2.** in the natural state; nude. [French *au naturel* cooked plain, naturally.]

aunt (ant, änt) *n.* **1.** sister of one's father or mother. **2.** wife of one's uncle. [Old French *ante, aunte,* from Latin *amita* father's sister.]

au·ra (ôr′ə) *pl.,* **au·ras** or **au·rae** (ôr′ē). *n.* **1.** distinctive character or atmosphere arising from and surrounding a person or thing: *an aura of peace in the cathedral. An aura of incense filled the room.* [Latin *aura* breath, breeze, from Greek *aurā.*]

au·ral (ôr′əl) *adj.* of or relating to the ear or the sense of hearing. [Latin *auris* ear + -AL′.]

au·re·ate (ôr′ē it, -āt′) *adj.* **1.** golden; gilded. **2.** *Archaic.* brilliant or splendid, esp. in literary or rhetorical style. [Late Latin *aureātus* decorated with gold, from Latin *aurum* gold.]

Au·re·li·us (ô rē′lē əs, ô rēl′yəs) See **Marcus Aurelius.**

au·re·ole (ôr′ē ōl′) *also,* **au·re·o·la** (ô rē′ō lə) *n.* **1.** in art, radiance emanating from and encircling the entire body of a sacred figure; halo. **2.** luminous region surrounding the sun or moon, as seen in fog. [Latin *aureola (corōna)* golden (crown), feminine of *aureolus* golden, from *aurum* gold.]

Au·re·o·my·cin (ôr′ē ō mī′sin) *n. Trademark.* chlortetracycline, an antibiotic drug used against certain infections caused by bacteria and viruses. [Latin *aureus* golden + Greek *mykēs* fungus; name suggested by its color.]

au re·voir (ō rə vwär′) *French.* until we meet again.

au·ric (ôr′ik) *adj.* of, containing, or derived from gold. [Latin *aurum* gold.]

au·ri·cle (ôr′i kəl) *n.* **1.** upper cavity on either side of the heart, serving as a reservoir of blood flowing into the heart and as a transmitter of blood to the ventricles. Also, **a′tri·um.** See **heart** for diagram. **2.** external ear; pinna. **3.** ear-shaped part. [Latin *auricula* the external ear, diminutive of *auris* ear.]

au·ric·u·lar (ô rik′yə lər) *adj.* **1.** of or relating to the ear or the sense of hearing. **2.** spoken into or perceived by the ear. **3.** shaped like an ear. **4.** of or relating to an auricle of the heart. —**au·ric′u·lar·ly,** *adv.*

au·rif·er·ous (ô rif′ər əs) *adj.* containing or yielding gold. [Latin *aurifer,* from *aurum* gold + *ferre* to bear.]

Au·ri·ga (ô rī′gə) *n.* constellation near the northern celestial pole containing the bright star Capella, conventionally depicted as a charioteer kneeling in his chariot. [Latin *aurīga* charioteer.]

au·rist (ôr′ist) *n.* doctor who specializes in treating diseases of the ear. [Latin *auris* ear + -IST.]

au·rochs (ôr′oks) *pl.,* **-rochs.** *n.* **1.** extinct wild ox, *Bos primigenius,* that once inhabited Europe and North Africa. The aurochs is probably

the direct ancestor of modern domesticated cattle. Also, **u′rus.** **2.** European bison, *Bison bonasus,* which resembles the American buffalo. [Obsolete German *Aurochs.*]

Au·ro·ra (ə rôr′ə) *n.* **1.** Roman goddess of the dawn. Her Greek counterpart is Eos. **2.** city in northeastern Illinois. Pop. (1970), 74,182. **3.** city in north-central Colorado, a residential suburb of Denver. Pop. (1970), 74,974. **4.** **aurora. a.** luminous display appearing in the night sky in various forms, as in bands, streamers, or arches. **b.** dawn. [Latin *aurora* dawn, Roman goddess of the dawn.]

Aurochs

au·ro·ra aus·tra·lis (ə rôr′ə ôs trā′lis) aurora seen in the Southern Hemisphere. Also, **southern lights.** [Modern Latin *aurora australis* literally, southern aurora, from Latin *aurōra* dawn + *austrālis* southern, from *Auster* south wind.]

au·ro·ra bo·re·al·is (ə rôr′ə bôr′ē al′is) aurora seen in the Northern Hemisphere. Also, **northern lights.** [Modern Latin *aurora borealis* literally, northern aurora, from Latin *aurōra* dawn + *boreālis* northern, from *Boreās* north wind.]

au·ro·ral (ə rôr′əl) *adj.* **1.** relating to or resembling the dawn; dawning; roseate. **2.** relating to or resembling an aurora.

Ausch·witz (oush′vits) *n.* Nazi concentration camp built in 1940 near Krakow, Poland, where over 4 million prisoners, mostly Jews, were killed.

aus·cul·tate (ôs′kəl tāt′) *-tat·ed, -tat·ing. v.t., v.i.* to examine by auscultation. [Latin *auscultātus,* past participle of *auscultāre* to listen.]

aus·cul·ta·tion (ôs′kəl tā′shən) *n.* **1.** listening, as with a stethoscope, to sounds arising from various organs, esp. the heart and lungs, to help determine their condition. **2.** *Archaic.* act of listening. [Latin *auscultātiō* a listening.]

aus·pice (ôs′pis) *pl.,* **-pic·es** (-pə siz, -sēz′) *n.* **1.** omen or sign. **2.** divination or prophecy, esp. one made on the basis of the flight of birds. **3.** *also,* **auspices.** circumstance or condition, esp. one that indicates success. **4. under the auspices of.** under the patronage or guidance of: *a tour conducted under the auspices of the school board.* [Latin *auspicium* divination by observing the actions of birds, from *avis* bird + *specere* to look.]

aus·pi·cious (ô spish′əs) *adj.* **1.** promising; propitious; favorable. **2.** fortunate; prosperous. —**aus·pi′cious·ly,** *adv.* —**aus·pi′cious·ness,** *n.* —Syn. **1.** see **favorable.**

Aus·ten, Jane (ôs′tən) 1775–1817, English novelist.

aus·tere (ôs tēr′) *adj.* **1.** severe or stern, as in manner or appearance: *an austere master.* **2.** grave; serious; sober: *austere occasion.* **3.** morally strict; ascetic. **4.** severely simple; unadorned: *an austere room.* **5.** *Archaic.* sour to the taste. [Latin *austērus* harsh, from Greek *austēros;* originally, making the tongue dry.] —**aus·tere′ly,** *adv.* —**aus·tere′·ness,** *n.* —Syn. **1.** see **severe.**

aus·ter·i·ty (ôs ter′ə tē) *pl.,* **-ties.** *n.* **1.** quality or condition of being austere. **2.** *also,* **austerities.** severe or ascetic practices.

Aus·ter·litz (ôs′tər lits′) *n.* town in Czechoslovakia, site of Napoleon Bonaparte's victory over the Austrian and Russian armies in 1805.

Aus·tin (ôs′tin) *n.* capital of Texas, in the south-central part of the state. Pop. (1970), 251,808.

aus·tral (ôs′trəl) *adj.* southern. [Latin *austrālis,* from *Auster* south wind.]

Aus·tral·a·sia (ôs′trə lā′zhə, -shə) *n.* extensive area in the southwestern Pacific including Australia, Tasmania, New Zealand, New Guinea, New Britain, and certain lesser islands in the immediate vicinity. —**Aus′tral·a′sian,** *adj., n.*

Aus·tra·lia (ôs trāl′yə) *n.* **1.** continent southeast of Asia, between the Indian and Pacific oceans. It is the smallest of the continents. Area, 2,941,526 sq. mi. Pop. (1969 est.), 11,907,800. **2.** country comprising this continent and Tasmania. Capital, Canberra. Area, 2,967,909 sq. mi. Pop. (1969 est.), 12,296,300.

Aus·tra·lian (ôs trāl′yən) *adj.* of or relating to Australia, its people, its language, or its culture. —*n.* **1.** native or close descendant of the people inhabiting Australia. **2.** Australian aborigine. **3.** any of the languages of the aborigines of Australia.

Australian ballot, ballot containing the names of all candidates and any proposals to be voted on. It is marked in secrecy by the voter.

Aus·tri·a (ôs′trē ə) *n.* small, landlocked country in central Europe, mainly in the Alps. Prior to World War I, it was the center of the Austro-Hungarian empire. Capital, Vienna. Area, 32,374 sq. mi. Pop. (1969 est.), 7,371,000. —**Aus′tri·an,** *adj., n.*

Aus·tro-Hun·ga·ry (ôs′trō hung′gə rē) *also,* **Aus·tri·a-Hun·ga·ry.** *n.* former dual monarchy in central Europe, comprising what are now Austria, Hungary, Czechoslovakia, and parts of Poland, Romania,

---

at; āpe; cär; end; mē; it; īce; hot; ōld; fôrk; wood; fōōl; out; up; ūse; turn; sing; thin; this; zh in treasure; ə in ago, taken, pencil, lemon, circus.

Italy, and Yugoslavia. It collapsed at the end of World War I. —**Aus′tro-Hun·ga′ri·an,** *adj., n.*

aut-, form of **auto-** before vowels and *h,* as in *autarky.*

au·tar·chy (ô′tär kē) *pl.* **-chies.** *n.* absolute rule by one person, or a country so ruled; despotism; autocracy. [Greek *autarchiā,* going back to *autos* self + *archein* to rule.]

au·tar·ky (ô′tär kē) *pl.* **-kies.** *n.* **1.** national economic self-sufficiency. **2.** policy by which a nation produces all of its own needs, independent of imports. [Greek *autarkeia* self-sufficiency, going back to *autos* self + *arkein* to suffice.] —**au·tar′kic,** *adj.*

au·then·tic (ô then′tik) *adj.* **1.** deserving of acceptance or belief; reliable; trustworthy: *The eyewitness gave an authentic account of the accident.* **2.** being what it purports to be; genuine; real: *an authentic document.* [Old French *autentique,* from Late Latin *authenticus,* from Greek *authentiokos.*] —**au·then′ti·cal·ly,** *adv.* —**Syn. 2.** see **genuine.**

au·then·ti·cate (ô then′tə kāt′) **-cat·ed, -cat·ing.** *v.t.* **1.** to establish as authentic. **2.** to establish as legally valid, as claims or authorship. —**au·then′ti·ca′tion,** *n.* —**Syn. 1.** see **confirm.**

au·then·tic·i·ty (ô′then tis′ə tē) *n.* state or quality of being authentic.

au·thor (ô′thər) *n.* **1.** original writer of a book or other literary work. **2.** author's writings: *Do you read many French authors?* **3.** one who originates or begins (something); creator: *He was the author of the plot.* —*v.t.* to be the author of. [Old French *autor* writer, creator, from Latin *auctor* creator.] —**au′thor·ess,** *n.*

au·thor·i·tar·i·an (ə thôr′ə tār′ē ən, ə thor′-) *adj.* advocating total submission to authority, as opposed to individual freedom. —*n.* one who advocates complete submission to authority. —**au·thor′i·tar′i·an·ism,** *n.*

au·thor·i·ta·tive (ə thôr′ə tā′tiv, ə thor′-) *adj.* **1.** worthy of acceptance or belief; reliable: *The report of the incident came from authoritative sources.* **2.** proceeding from or having acknowledged authority: *authoritative statement.* **3.** exercising authority; commanding; dictatorial: *authoritative parents.* —**au·thor′i·ta′tive·ly,** *adv.* —**au·thor′i·ta′tive·ness,** *n.*

au·thor·i·ty (ə thôr′ə tē, ə thor′-) *pl.* **-ties.** *n.* **1.** power or right to act, command, enforce obedience, or make decisions: *The dictator had ultimate authority.* **2.** *also,* **authorities.** person or group of persons possessing and exercising such a right or a power: *We will report this incident to the military authorities.* **3.** power or right delegated to another; authorization: *He has our authority to publish the book.* **4.** acknowledged influence upon the actions of others: *the authority of age.* **5.** acknowledged or authoritative source of information or advice. **6.** an expert on a particular subject: *an authority on geology.* [Old French *autorite* power, from Latin *auctōritās.*]

Syn. 1. Authority, control, influence suggest power over others. **Authority** is used of sanctioned power, either legal or traditional: *By the authority invested in me, I pronounce you man and wife.* **Control** implies a position from which power over someone or something may be exercised: *A good driver maintains control of his automobile at all times.* **Influence** suggests power vested in a person, growing from his personal qualities or position: *His influence was always used toward some socially desirable end.*

au·thor·i·za·tion (ô′thər i zā′shən) *n.* **1.** act of authorizing. **2.** legal right or power.

au·thor·ize (ô′thə rīz′) **-ized, -iz·ing.** *v.t.* **1.** to give authority to; empower. **2.** to approve officially; sanction: *The mayor authorized the appointment of a new police chief.* **3.** to establish by authority; justify.

au·thor·ized (ô′thə rīzd′) *adj.* having authority; acknowledged as authoritative: *an authorized agent.*

Authorized Version, King James Version of the Bible, published in England in 1611.

au·thor·ship (ô′thər ship′) *n.* **1.** profession of a writer of books or other literary works. **2.** origin or source, esp. of a literary work: *a book of unknown authorship.*

au·tism (ô′tiz′əm) *n.* emotional disorder characterized by a profound withdrawal from contact with people, repetitive behavior, and fear of change in the environment. [Modern Latin *autismus,* from Greek *autos* self + -ISM.] —**au·tis′tic,** *adj.*

au·to (ô′tō) *pl.* **au·tos.** *n.* automobile.

auto- *combining form* by the or one's self; self-: *autocracy, automaton.* [Greek *autos* self.]

Au·to·bahn (ô′tə bän′) *pl.* **-bahns** or **-bah·nen** (-bä′nən). *n.* in Germany, superhighway with a central dividing strip. [German *Autobahn* literally, automobile road.]

au·to·bi·og·ra·phy (ô′tə bī og′rə fē, -bē-) *pl.* **-phies.** *n.* story of one's life written by oneself. [AUTO- + BIOGRAPHY.] —**au′to·bi·og′ra·pher,** *n.* —**au′to·bi·o·graph′ic** (-ə graf′ic, -bē′-); *also,* **au′to·bi·o·graph′i·cal,** *adj.* —**au′to·bi·o·graph′i·cal·ly,** *adv.*

au·toch·thon (ô tok′thən) *pl.* **-thons** or **-tho·nes** (-thə nēz′). *n.*

1. autochthons. original inhabitants of a place; aborigines. **2.** indigenous plant or animal. [Greek *autochthōn* sprung from the land itself, native, from *autos* self + *chthōn* earth.]

au·toch·tho·nous (ô tok′thə nəs) *adj.* native to a place; indigenous.

au·to·clave (ô′tə klāv′) *n.* apparatus used for sterilizing by steam under pressure. —*v.t.* **-claved, -clav·ing.** to sterilize in an autoclave. [French *autoclave* sterilizer; literally, self-locking, from Greek *autos* self + Latin *clāvis* key.]

au·toc·ra·cy (ô tok′rə sē) *pl.* **-cies.** *n.* **1.** form of government in which one person holds absolute power; the government or power of an autocrat. **2.** country ruled by an autocrat. **3.** unlimited authority or influence of one person over others.

au·to·crat (ô′tə krat′) *n.* **1.** ruler who has absolute power. **2.** one who is invested with or assumes unlimited authority or influence. [French *autocrate,* from Greek *autokratēs* ruling by oneself, absolute, from *autos* self + *kratos* power.]

au·to·crat·ic (ô′tə krat′ik) *adj.* relating to or of the nature of an autocrat or autocracy; holding independent and unlimited powers. —**au′to·crat′i·cal·ly,** *adv.*

au·to·da·fé (ô′tō də fā′) *pl.* **au·tos-da-fé** *n.* **1.** ceremony accompanying the passing of the final sentence imposed upon heretics by the Spanish Inquisition. **2.** execution of such a sentence, esp. burning at the stake. [Portuguese *auto-da-fé* act of the faith; *auto,* from Latin *āctus* act; *fé,* from Latin *fidēs* faith.]

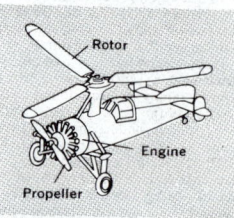

au·to·gi·ro (ô′tə jī′rō) *pl.* **-ros.** *also,* **au·to·gy·ro.** *n.* airplane which is lifted and supported in air by a large aerodynamically-driven rotor and is moved forward by an engine-driven propeller. It differs from a helicopter which has an engine-driven rotor and no propeller. Trademark: Autogiro. [Spanish *autogiro* helicopter, from Greek *autos* self + *gyros* circle.]

Autogiro

au·to·graph (ô′tə graf′) *n.* **1.** one's distinctive signature. **2.** something in one's own handwriting; original manuscript. —*v.t.* **1.** to write one's signature in or on. **2.** to write in one's own handwriting. [French *autographe* one's own signature or manuscript, from Latin *autographus* written with one's own hand, from Greek *autographos,* from *autos* self + *graphein* to write.] —**au′to·graph′ic,** *adj.* **au′to·graph′i·cal,** *adj.*

au·to·in·tox·i·ca·tion (ô′tō in tok′sə kā′shən) *n.* poisoning by toxic substances formed within the body.

au·to·mat (ô′tə mat′) *n.* cafeteria in which food is obtained from small compartments whose doors open when the proper coins are deposited in the slots. [Shortened form of AUTOMATIC.]

au·to·mate (ô′tə māt′) **-mat·ed, -mat·ing.** *v.t.* to convert to or operate by automation.

au·to·mat·ic (ô′tə mat′ik) *adj.* **1.** moving or acting from forces within itself; self-regulating; mechanical: *an automatic washing machine.* **2.** done without deliberate or conscious effort; reflex: *Her reaction was automatic.* **3.** (of firearms) using either the recoil or the gas from a fired cartridge to eject the empty cartridge, reload, and fire continuously until the trigger is released. —*n.* automatic weapon. [Greek *automatos* self-acting + -IC.] —**au′to·mat′i·cal·ly,** *adv.*

Syn. 2. Automatic, involuntary, spontaneous indicate reaction uncontrolled by the conscious mind. **Automatic** suggests a mechanism doing the same thing again and again and implies that the same cause will always evoke the same reaction: *As she thought of home, her replies to the officer's questions became automatic.* **Involuntary** means done without volition or will taking part: *Dirk emitted an involuntary gasp at the sight.* **Spontaneous** implies a natural reaction, unplanned and uninfluenced by thought: *A storm of spontaneous applause burst from the audience.*

au·to·ma·tion (ô′tə mā′shən) *n.* development and use of mechanical equipment in combination with automatic control systems. It involves the replacement of machines controlled by human operators with machines that are self-regulating or operated by other machines. [Greek *automatos* self-acting + -ION.]

au·tom·a·tism (ô tom′ə tiz′əm) *n.* state or quality of being automatic or like an automaton; automatic or involuntary action.

au·tom·a·ton (ô tom′ə ton′, -tən) *pl.* **-tons** or **-ta** (-tə). *n.* **1.** device that appears to function by itself through the use of concealed motive power. Also, **ro′bot. 2.** one whose behavior is purely mechanical. [Greek *automaton,* neuter of *automatos* self-acting.]

au·to·mo·bile (ô′tə mə bēl′, ô′tə mə bēl′, ô′tə mō′bēl) *n.* passenger vehicle, propelled by an engine, and usually having four wheels; car.

—*adj.* automotive. —*v.i.* **-biled, -bil·ing.** to ride in or drive an automobile. [French *automobile,* from Greek *autos* self + Latin *mōbilis* movable.] —**au′to·mo·bil′ist,** *n.*

au·to·mo·tive (ô′tə mō′tiv) *adj.* **1.** of, relating to, or for an automobile or automobiles. **2.** self-propelled; self-moving.

au·to·nom·ic (ô′tə nom′ik) *adj.* **1.** of or relating to the autonomic nervous system. **2.** autonomous (*def. 1*). **3.** *Botany.* produced by internal causes: *autonomic movement.* —**au′to·nom′i·cal·ly,** *adv.*

autonomic nervous system, that part of the nervous system of vertebrates consisting of the sympathetic and parasympathetic nervous systems. It controls and regulates the involuntary functions of the body, such as the activities of involuntary muscles that control the heart, lungs, or intestines.

au·ton·o·mous (ô ton′ə məs) *adj.* **1.** self-governing; independent. **2.** *Botany.* autonomic. —**au·ton′o·mous·ly,** *adv.*

au·ton·o·my (ô ton′ə mē) *pl.,* **-mies.** *n.* **1.** quality or condition of being autonomous; self-governing. **2.** power or right of self-government. **3.** self-governing state or community. [Greek *autonomiā* independence.]

au·top·sy (ô′top′sē, ô′təp-) *pl.,* **-sies.** *n.* dissection and examination of a dead body in order to discover the cause of death or the nature and extent of the cause; post-mortem. [Modern Latin *autopsia,* from Greek *autopsiā* seeing with one's own eyes.]

au·tumn (ô′təm) *n.* **1.** season of the year coming between summer and winter; fall. In the Northern Hemisphere it extends from the autumnal equinox, about September 23, to the winter solstice, about December 22. **2.** time of maturity, mellowing, and beginning decline. —*adj.* of, like, characteristic of, or occurring in autumn: *autumn haze.* [Old French *autompne* this season, from Latin *autumnus,* possibly of Etruscan origin.]

au·tum·nal (ô tum′nəl) *adj.* **1.** of, relating to, or characteristic of autumn. **2.** maturing or gathered in autumn: *autumnal fruits.* **3.** past maturity or the middle stage of one's life. —**au·tum′nal·ly,** *adv.*

autumnal equinox, see **equinox.**

aux·il·ia·ry (ôg zil′yər ē, -zil′ər ē) *adj.* **1.** giving aid or support; helping. **2.** additional; reserve; supplementary. **3.** subsidiary; secondary. —*n. pl.,* **-ries.** **1.** one who or that which aids or supports; helper. **2.** supplementary or subsidiary group or organization: *ladies' auxiliary.* **3.** auxiliary verb. **4. auxiliaries.** foreign or allied troops in the service of a nation at war. [Latin *auxiliārius* aiding, from *auxilium* aid.]

auxiliary verb, verb used in addition to the main verb to express the tense, mood, or voice. In the sentence *They will go,* the word *will* is an auxiliary verb.

av. **1.** avenue. **2.** average. **3.** avoirdupois.

A.V., Authorized Version.

a·vail (ə vāl′) *v.t.* **1.** to be of advantage or worth to; assist: *My presence will not avail you now.* **2. to avail oneself of.** to take advantage of; make use of: *He availed himself of the opportunity.* —*v.i.* to be of use or value; help: *In this matter, force will not avail.* —*n.* use; help; advantage: *Your effort would be of no avail.* [A-² + obsolete *vail* to prevail, from Old French *valoir* to be of value, from Latin *valēre* to be strong.]

a·vail·a·bil·i·ty (ə vā′lə bil′ə tē) *pl.,* **-ties.** *n.* **1.** state or quality of being available. **2.** that which is available.

a·vail·a·ble (ə vā′lə bəl) *adj.* **1.** that can be had; obtainable; accessible: *The dress is available in all sizes.* **2.** that can be used; at one's disposal: *The telephone is now available.* —**a·vail′a·bly,** *adv.*

av·a·lanche (av′ə lanch′) *n.* **1.** swift, sudden fall of a mass of snow, ice, earth, or rocks down a mountain slope. **2.** anything like an avalanche, as in size or suddenness. —*v.t.,* **-lanched, -lanch·ing.** to fall in or like an avalanche. —*v.t.* to overwhelm with an abundance of (something). [French *avalanche* snowslide, partly from dialectal French *lavanche* (of uncertain origin); partly from French *avaler* to descend, from Old French *a val* to the valley, from Latin phrase *ad vallem* to the valley.]

Av·a·lon (av′ə lon′) *n.* the island to which King Arthur was carried after being mortally wounded in battle.

a·vant-garde (ə vänt′gärd′, ə vant′-) *n.* group of people who are considered in the forefront in accepting or experimenting with new, daring, or extreme styles or ideas, esp. in the arts. —*adj.* new, daring, or extreme in styles or ideas: *an avant-garde movie.* [French *avant-garde* literally, advance guard.]

av·a·rice (av′ər is) *n.* inordinate desire for wealth or possessions; greed; cupidity. [Old French *avarice,* from Latin *avāritia.*]

av·a·ri·cious (av′ə rish′əs) *adj.* greedy for wealth or possessions; covetous; grasping. —**av′a·ri′cious·ly,** *adv.* —**av′a·ri′cious·ness,** *n.* —**Syn.** see **greedy.**

a·vast (ə vast′) *interj. Nautical.* stop; stay; cease. [Dutch *houd vast* hold fast.]

av·a·tar (av′ə tär′) *n.* **1.** the incarnation of a god in Hinduism: *Krishna is an avatar of Vishnu.* **2.** any incarnation or embodiment. [Sanskrit *avatāra* descent.]

a·vaunt (ə vônt′, ə vänt′) *interj. Archaic.* go away; begone. [Anglo-Norman *avaunt* before, from Latin *abante* from in front of.]

a·ve (ä′vā) *interj.* hail or farewell. —*n.* Ave Maria. [Latin *avē* hail, farewell, possibly from Punic *hwy* live.]

ave., avenue.

A·ve Ma·ri·a (ä′vā mə rē′ə) also, **A·ve Mar·y.** *n.* **1.** Roman Catholic prayer to the Virgin Mary, based on the Biblical salutations of Gabriel and Saint Elizabeth. Also, **Hail Mary. 2.** a salutation to the Virgin Mary. **3.** any of several musical compositions based on this prayer. [Medieval Latin *Ave Maria* hail Mary.]

a·venge (ə venj′) **a·venged, a·veng·ing.** *v.t.* to get revenge for or on behalf of: *He swore to avenge his father.* [Old French *avengier,* from *a* to (from Latin *ad* to) + *vengier* to take vengeance, from Latin *vindicāre* to punish.] —**a·veng′er,** *n.* —**Syn.** see **revenge.**

a·ven·tu·rine (ə ven′chər in) *n.* semiprecious stone that is a sparkling red, iridescent variety of feldspar, composed of sodium aluminum silicate. Also, **aventurin.**

av·e·nue (av′ə nū′ -nōō′) *n.* **1.** street or thoroughfare, esp. a wide one. **2.** means of access or attainment: *an avenue to success.* **3.** road or walk, often lined with trees. [French *avenue* approach, avenue, noun use of feminine past participle of *avenir* to come to, from Latin *advenīre* to come to.]

a·ver (ə vur′) **a·verred, a·ver·ring.** *v.t.* **1.** to declare positively; affirm; assert. **2.** *Law.* to assert or declare formally in a plea. [French *avérer,* going back to Latin *ad* to + *vērus* true.]

av·er·age (av′rij, -ər ij) *n.* **1.** single number which describes or typifies a set of numbers, found by dividing the sum of two or more quantities by the number of quantities; arithmetic mean: *The average of 2, 4, 6, and 8 is 5.* **2.** typical, ordinary, or usual quantity, rate, kind, or quality; anything approaching the norm: *This year's rainfall came close to the average.* —*adj.* **1.** arrived at by calculating the arithmetic mean; resembling or constituting an average: *average yield, average speed.* **2.** usual; typical; ordinary: *average height, an average American.* —*v.t.,* **-aged, -ag·ing. 1.** to find the arithmetic mean of: *He averaged their bridge scores for the week.* **2.** to do, take, yield, have, or amount to on the average: *His salary averages 200 dollars a week.* **3.** to apportion equally: *The boys averaged their meager profits.* —*v.i.* to be or amount to an average. [French *avarie* damage to ship or cargo, from Italian *avaria* damage at sea, from Arabic *'awārīya* damaged goods, from *'awār* damage; possibly because insurance on such damage was calculated and paid on the basis of an average.]

Syn. *adj.* **2. Average, mean, middling, medium** indicate an intermediate position. **Average** suggests lack of abnormality and approximation to everything held in common by members of a group: *She reacts just like the average housewife.* **Mean** implies a position at or very near to the middle of the group when its traits are measured against some scale of criteria: *Los Angeles' mean annual rainfall is considerably less than New York's.* **Middling** suggests a position, not at either end of the scale, but somewhere vaguely between: *He was a middling actor and played many supporting roles, without ever achieving fame.* **Medium** also suggests a position between the extremes, but implies some means of measuring so that the position can be marked on a scale: *She was of medium height.* —*n.* **2.** see **norm.**

a·ver·ment (ə vur′mənt) *n.* **1.** act of averring. **2.** that which is averred; assertion.

A·ver·nus (ə vur′nəs) *n.* **1.** *Roman Mythology.* the lower world; hell. **2. Lake.** small lake in the crater of an extinct volcano in southwestern Italy, near Naples. It was regarded by the ancients as the entrance to the lower world. [Latin *(lacus) Avernus* (Lake) Avernus, from Greek *aornos* without birds; it was believed that the fumes from this lake killed birds that came near it.]

a·verse (ə vurs′) *adj.* **1.** opposed; disinclined; reluctant; unwilling (with *to*): *averse to doing homework.* **2.** turned away from the axis or stem. Opposed to **adverse.** [Latin *āversus,* past participle of *āvertere* to turn away.] —**a·verse′ly,** *adv.* —**a·verse′ness,** *n.*

a·ver·sion (ə vur′zhən, -shən) *n.* **1.** deep-rooted opposition or dislike; antipathy: *an aversion to insects.* **2.** cause of dislike or opposition. —**Syn.** see **dislike.**

a·vert (ə vurt′) *v.t.* **1.** to turn away or aside: *to avert one's attention.* **2.** to ward off; prevent; avoid: *to avert disaster.* [Latin *āvertere* to turn away.] —**a·vert′i·ble;** also, **a·vert′a·ble,** *adj.*

A·ves·ta (ə ves′tə) *n.* sacred scriptures of Zoroastrianism.

a·vi·ar·y (ā′vē er′ē) *pl.,* **-ar·ies.** *n.* large cage, building, or enclosure in which birds are kept. [Latin *aviārium* place for birds, from *avis* bird.]

a·vi·a·tion (ā′vē ā′shən, av′ē-) *n.* **1.** science or art of flight in heavier-than-air aircraft. **2.** production and design of heavier-than-air aircraft. [French *aviation,* from Latin *avis* bird.]

a·vi·a·tor (ā′vē ā′tər, av′ē-) *n.* one who flies an airplane or other heavier-than-air aircraft.

a·vi·a·trix (ā′vē ā′triks, av′ē-) *pl.,* **-a·tri·ces** (-ā′trə sēz′, -ə trī′sēz). *n.* woman aviator. Also, **a′vi·a′tress.**

av·id (av′id) *adj.* ardent; eager; enthusiastic: *an avid scholar.* [Latin *avidus* greedy.] —**av′id·ly,** *adv.* —**av′id·ness,** *n.*

a·vid·i·ty (ə vid′ə tē) *n.* intense desire; extreme greed; eagerness.

A·vi·gnon (ä vē nyŌN′) *n.* historic city in southeastern France. It was the papal seat from 1309 to 1377. Pop. (1968), 86,096.

av·o·ca·do (av′ə kä′dō, ä′və-) *pl.* **-dos.** *n.* **1.** pulpy fruit of a tree, *Persea americana,* of the laurel family, having a buttery texture and a nutty flavor, eaten raw in salads, desserts, and other dishes. Also, **alligator pear. 2.** evergreen tree bearing this fruit, having dark green, oval-shaped leaves and clusters of small greenish flowers, widely cultivated in California and Florida. [Spanish *aguacate,* from Nahuatl *ahuacatl* testicle.]

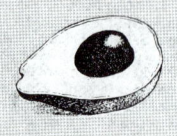

Halved avocado

av·o·ca·tion (av′ə kā′shən) *n.* **1.** interest or pastime that one has in addition to his regular occupation; hobby: *Our doctor's avocation is sculpturing.* **2.** one's usual occupation; vocation. ▲ rarely used in the second definition because of confusion with **vocation.** [Latin *āvocātiō* diverting of attention.] —**av′o·ca′tion·al,** *adj.*

av·o·cet (av′ə set′) *n.* any of several long-legged wading birds, genus *Recurvirostra,* having webbed feet and a long, slender, up-curving beak. Length: 15–18 inches from bill to tail. [French *avocette,* from Italian *avosetta* storklike bird; of uncertain origin.]

Avocet

A·vo·ga·dro's law (ä′və gä′drōz) law stating that equal volumes of gases at the same temperature and pressure contain the same number of molecules, regardless of the gases involved. [From Count Amadeo *Avogadro,* 1776–1856, Italian physicist who formulated it.]

a·void (ə void′) *v.t.* **1.** to keep away or refrain from; shun; evade: *He was inclined to avoid work.* **2.** *Law.* to make void, useless, or of no effect; annul. [Anglo-Norman *avoider,* from Old French *esvuidier* to empty, from *es-* out (from Latin *ex*) + *vuide* empty; of uncertain origin; possibly influenced in meaning by French *éviter* to avoid.] —**a·void′a·ble,** *adj.* —**a·void′a·bly,** *adv.*

Syn. 1. Avoid, evade, shun mean to actively stay away from someone or something. **Avoid** implies caution and deliberation in not encountering something undesirable or dangerous: *They managed to avoid meeting the Penningtons by staying at a different hotel.* **Evade** suggests clever ruses in staying clear of what is undesirable: *He evaded his pursuers by changing trains several times in the next half hour.* **Shun** has the connotation of dislike: *James shunned the company of others.*

a·void·ance (ə void′əns) *n.* **1.** act of avoiding. **2.** *Law.* a making void; annulment.

av·oir·du·pois (av′ər də poiz′) *n.* **1.** avoirdupois weight. **2.** *Informal.* heaviness or weight, esp. of a person. [Anglo-Norman *aveir de peis* goods of weight; *aveir* goods, noun use of *aveir* to have, from Latin *habēre;* *de* of, from Latin *dē; peis* weight, from Latin *pēnsum.*]

avoirdupois weight, in Great Britain, the United States, and Canada, a system of weights used for all goods except drugs or precious metals.

A·von (ā′ən, av′ən) *n.* river in central England. It flows past Stratford, the birthplace of Shakespeare.

a·vouch (ə vouch′) *v.t.* **1.** to declare positively; assert; affirm. **2.** to vouch for; guarantee. **3.** to acknowledge; admit; confess. [Old French *avochier* to call upon, from Latin *advocāre* to call to, summon. Doublet of AVOW.] —**a·vouch′ment,** *n.*

a·vow (ə vou′) *v.t.* **1.** to declare frankly or openly; admit; acknowledge. [Old French *avouer,* from Latin *advocāre.* See AVOUCH.]

a·vow·al (ə vou′əl) *n.* frank or open declaration, admission, or acknowledgment: *an avowal of his sentiments.*

a·vowed (ə voud′) *adj.* openly declared or acknowledged; *avowed enemies.* —**a·vow·ed·ly** (ə vou′id lē, ə voud′lē), *adv.*

a·vun·cu·lar (ə vung′kyə lər) *adj.* of, relating to, like, or belonging to an uncle. [Latin *avunculus* mother's brother + -AR¹.]

a·wait (ə wāt′) *v.t.* to wait for; anticipate: *She had long awaited this day.* **2.** to be ready or in store for: *Many surprises await him.* [Anglo-Norman *awaitier* to watch for, from *a-* to (from Latin *ad* to) + *waitier* to watch (of Germanic origin).] —**Syn. 1.** see **expect.**

a·wake (ə wāk′) **a·woke** or **a·waked, a·wak·ing.** *v.t.* **1.** to rouse from sleep; wake. **2.** to make active; stir up or excite: *to awake new interest.* —*v.i.* **1.** to cease to sleep. **2.** to become active or aroused. —*adj.* **1.** not asleep. **2.** alert; aware. [Blend of Old English *āwacian* and *onwæcnan* to waken.]

a·wak·en (ə wā′kən) *v.t., v.i.* to awake.

a·wak·en·ing (ə wā′kə ning) *n.* **1.** act of waking. **2.** awareness; realization. —*adj.* arousing; stirring: *an awakening sense of obligation.*

a·ward (ə wôrd′) *v.t.* **1.** to give as merited or due: *to award a good conduct medal.* **2.** to grant or bestow by judicial determination; adjudge: *The jury awarded damages to the plaintiff.* —*n.* **1.** that which is awarded, as a medal. **2.** decision or finding, as of a judge or arbitrator. [Anglo-Norman *awarder,* form of Old French *eswarder* to observe, decide, from *es*-out (from Latin *ex* out) + *warder* to observe (of Germanic origin).] —**Syn.** *n.* **1.** see **prize¹.**

a·ware (ə wâr′) *adj.* being conscious; in possession of information; cognizant; informed (often with *of*): *He was aware of our plans.* [Old English *gewær.*] —**a·ware′ness,** *n.*

Syn. Aware, conscious, cognizant mean recognizing the existence of something. **Aware** stresses knowing through the senses or, sometimes, by receiving information from someone else: *A soft patter made Don Carlos aware that the rain had come.* **Conscious** suggests a knowledge of something's existence, strongly or dimly, either through the senses or purely emotionally: *He slowly became conscious of a familiar face in the crowd at the foot of the scaffold.* **Cognizant** indicates definite information, usually received directly through the senses: *He was cognizant of his friends' return but did not care to speak with them.*

a·wash (ə wôsh′, -wosh′) *adv., adj.* **1.** covered with water: *The decks were awash.* **2.** level with or just above the surface of the water so that the water washes over it. **3.** tossed or washed about by waves; floating.

a·way (ə wā′) *adv.* **1.** from this or that place; off: *to sail away.* **2.** at a distance; far: *They stood several paces away from us.* **3.** in another place; absent: *He was away from his desk.* **4.** in another direction; aside: *Look away.* **5.** from or out of one's possession, attention, or use: *Throw away the old coat.* **6.** at or to an end; out of existence: *to wither away.* **7.** without interruption; continuously: *She pounded away at her typewriter.* **8.** without hesitation or delay; directly: *Fire away!* **9. away back.** *Informal.* far back in time; long ago: *away back before the war.* **10. away with.** take (someone or something) away: *Away with this man!* **11. away with you.** go away. **12. to do away with. a.** to put an end or stop to; get rid of: *He did away with the rules.* **b.** to eliminate by killing: *The king did away with his enemies.* —*adj.* **1.** distant; far. **2.** absent; gone. [Old English *onweg* literally, on the way.]

awe (ô) *n.* overwhelming wonderment combined with fear or reverence: *We stood in awe of the king.* —*v.t.,* **awed, aw·ing.** to inspire or fill with awe: *We were awed by the fury of the storm.* [Old Norse *agi* terror.]

a·wea·ry (ə wēr′ē) *adj.* weary; tired.

a·weigh (ə wā′) *adj.* *Nautical.* (of an anchor) raised clear of the bottom.

awe·some (ô′səm) *adj.* **1.** inspiring awe: *an awesome creature.* **2.** expressive of awe: *an awesome glance.* —**awe′some·ness,** *n.*

awe·struck (ô′struk′) *adj.* filled with awe. Also, **awe′-strick′en.**

aw·ful (ô′fəl) *adj.* **1.** terrible; frightening; appalling: *an awful disaster.* **2.** *Informal.* excessively bad, distasteful, or ugly: *awful handwriting.* **3.** worthy of or commanding respect and reverence: *his awful holiness.* **4.** inspiring awe. —*adv.* *Informal.* extremely; terribly: *He was awful glad.* [AWE + -FUL.] —**aw′ful·ness,** *n.*

aw·ful·ly (ô′fə lē, ô′flē) *adv.* **1.** dreadfully; terribly. **2.** *Informal.* very; extremely: *She was awfully depressed.*

a·while (ə wīl′, ə hwīl′) *adv.* for a short time; for a little.

awk·ward (ôk′wərd) *adj.* **1.** lacking ease or grace in bearing; ungainly: *an awkward child.* **2.** lacking dexterity or skill: *The dancer gave an awkward performance.* **3.** difficult or embarrassing: *an awkward situation.* **4.** ill-adapted for use or handling; unwieldy: *an awkward method.* **5.** hard to manage; difficult: *an awkward turn.* [Obsolete *awk* perverse, clumsy (from Old Norse *ǫfugr* turned the wrong way) + WARD.] —**awk′ward·ly,** *adv.* —**awk′ward·ness,** *n.*

Syn. 1. Awkward, clumsy, ungainly mean lacking grace or skill. **Awkward** indicates simply that grace, ease, or proficiency are absent: *He was quite awkward before large audiences, but very effective at small gatherings.* **Clumsy** implies stiffness, heaviness, and disinclination as the source of the lack of grace: *His clumsy attempts at humor failed to get a conversation started.* **Ungainly** stresses the lack of physical adroitness and suggests limbs and joints out of control: *The ungainly young man stumbled up to the door and rang.*

awl (ôl) *n.* pointed tool used for making small holes or for working designs into the surface of leather or wood. [Old English *æl.*]

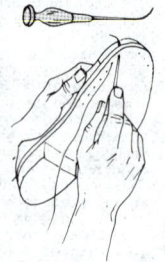

Awl

awn (ôn) *n.* bristlelike part that constitutes the beard in some grasses, as on a spike of barley or wheat. [Old Norse *ǫgn* chaff.]

at; āpe; cär; end; mē; it; īce; hot; ōld; fôrk; wood; fōōl; oil; out; up; ūse; turn; sing; thin; this; zh in treasure; ə in ago, taken, pencil, lemon, circus.

aw·ning (ô′ning) *n.* rooflike cover of canvas or other material, as over or before a door or window, used as a shelter from the sun or rain. [Of unknown origin.]

a·woke (ə wōk′) past tense and past participle of **awake.**

A·wol (ā′wôl′) *also,* **a·wol, AWOL, a.w.o.l.** *adv., adj. Military.* absent from one's post without official leave without intent to desert. —*n.* one who is absent without official leave. [*A(bsent) w(ith)o(ut) l(eave).*]

a·wry (ə rī′) *adv., adj.* **1.** twisted or turned to one side; askew. **2.** out of the right course; wrong; amiss. [A-¹ + WRY.]

ax (aks) *pl.,* **ax·es.** *also,* **axe.** *n.* **1.** tool with a bladed metal head on a handle, used esp. for felling trees and chopping wood. **2. to have an ax to grind.** *Informal.* **a.** to have a special purpose or end to attain. **b.** to have a grievance. **3. to get the ax.** *Informal.* to be dismissed from one's job. —*v.t.* to chop or cut with, or as with, an ax. [Old English *æx* this tool.]

ax·es¹ (ak′sēz) plural of **axis.**

ax·es² (ak′siz) plural of **ax.**

ax·i·al (ak′sē əl) *adj.* **1.** of, relating to, or forming an axis. **2.** situated on, around, or along an axis.

ax·il (ak′sil) *n.* upper angle formed where a leafstalk or stem joins the stem on which it is borne. [Latin *axilla* armpit.]

ax·il·la (ak sil′ə) *pl.,* **ax·il·lae** (ak sil′ē). *n.* **1.** armpit. **2.** axil. [Latin *axilla* armpit.]

ax·il·lar·y (ak′sə ler′ē) *adj.* **1.** of, relating to, or near the armpit. **2.** of, relating to, situated in, or growing from an axil.

ax·i·om (ak′sē əm) *n.* **1.** statement or principle accepted as true without proof; self-evident or universally accepted truth. **2.** established principle, rule, or law. [Latin *axiōma* principle, from Greek *axiōma.*]

ax·i·o·mat·ic (ak′sē ə mat′ik) *adj.* **1.** of, relating to, or like an axiom; self-evident. **2.** full of axioms or maxims; aphoristic. —**ax′i·o·mat′i·cal·ly,** *adv.*

ax·is (ak′sis) *pl.,* **ax·es** (ak′sēz) *n.* **1.** real or imaginary straight line passing through an object or body, as the earth, and around which it rotates or seems to rotate. **2.** straight, central line around which the parts of a plane or solid figure are symmetrically arranged. The axis of a cylinder is the line segment joining the center of the two bases. **3.** number line. **4.** *Anatomy.* **a.** any central line of a bodily structure, esp. the spinal column. **b.** the second cervical vertebra that acts as a pivot on which the head turns. **5.** main stem of a plant. **6.** central line around which parts of any system are regularly arranged. **7.** political and military alliance between two or more nations. **8. the Axis.** World War II coalition between Hitler and Mussolini that ultimately included Japan and several smaller countries. Also, **Axis Powers.** [Latin *axis* axis (of the earth), axle.]

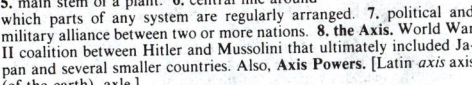

North Pole / South Pole / **Earth's axis**

ax·le (ak′səl) *n.* shaft or bar on which or with which a pair of wheels or one wheel turns. [Old Norse *öxull.*]

ax·le·tree (ak′səl trē′) *n.* fixed axle, usually wooden, connecting a pair of wheels, as on a cart or wagon. Each end of the axletree has a spindle or bearings on which the wheel turns.

ax·man (aks′mən) *pl.,* **-men.** *also,* **axe·man.** *n.* one who wields an ax.

Ax·min·ster (aks′min′stər) *n.* carpet of a type in which the tufts are individually inserted in order to achieve an almost unlimited variety of colors and intricate designs. [From *Axminster,* England, where originally made.]

ax·o·lotl (ak′sə lot′əl) *n.* larva of any of several salamanders, genus *Ambystoma,* of Mexico and the western United States. It breeds in the larval stage and usually does not metamorphose into the adult form. Length: 6–10 inches. [Nahuatl *axolotl* literally, water spirit.]

ax·on (ak′son) *also,* **ax·one** (ak′sōn). *n.* nerve fiber extending from a neuron and conducts impulses away from the body of the cell. [Modern Latin *axon,* from Greek *axōn* axis, axle.]

ay (ā) *also,* **aye.** *adv.* always; ever. [Old Norse *ei, ey* ever.]

a·yah (ä′yə) *n.* native nursemaid or maid in India. [Hindi *āyā,* from Portuguese *aia* nurse, governess, from Latin *avia* grandmother.]

aye (ī) *also,* **ay.** *n.* affirmative vote or voter. —*adv.* yes; yea. [Of uncertain origin.]

aye-aye (ī′ī′) *n.* squirrel-like lemur of Madagascar, *Daubentonia madagascariensis,* having brown fur, a long, bushy tail, rodentlike teeth, and sharp claws. It is about the size of a house cat. [French *aye-aye,* from Malagasy *aiay;* probably imitative of its cry.]

Aye-aye

Ayr·shire (âr′shēr, -shər) *n.* one of a Scottish breed of hardy, long-horned dairy cattle that may be white, red, or brown, or any combination of these colors. [From the county of *Ayr,* Scotland, where originally bred.]

a·za·lea (ə zāl′yə) *n.* any of a group of shrubs, genus *Rhododendron,* found in cool and temperate regions of the Northern Hemisphere, bearing clusters of funnel-shaped flowers. ▲ Azalea is no longer used as a name for a separate genus, but has remained a common term for certain plants that are technically rhododendrons. [Modern Latin *azalea,* from Greek *azalea,* feminine of *azaleos* dry; possibly because it thrives in dry soil.]

A·zer·bai·jan (ä′zər bī jän′, az′ər bī jan′) *also,* **A·zer·bai·dzhan.** *n.* **1.** republic of the Soviet Union, south of the Caucasus, on the west coast of the Caspian Sea, and bordering Iran. Official name: **Azerbaijan Soviet Socialist Republic.** Area, 33,446 sq. mi. Pop. (1969), 5,042,000. **2.** part of Iran bordering this republic.

az·i·muth (az′ə məth) *n.* **1.** measurement of angular distance of bearing. In astronomy it is used to plot the position of a celestial body; in navigation, to plot the position of an aircraft or ship. **2.** *Military.* angular distance that a weapon must be moved to the left or right in order to give it greater accuracy. [French *azimut* angular distance or bearing, going back to Arabic *as,* for *al* the + *samt* way, direction.]

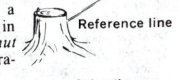

Object / Angle of azimuth / Reference line / **Azimuth**

A·zores (ə zōrz′, ā′zōrz) *n.,pl.* island group in the North Atlantic, west of and belonging to Portugal. Land area, 894 sq. mi. Pop. (1968 est.), 603,000.

A·zov, Sea of (ä zôf′) northern arm of the Black Sea, in the southwestern Soviet Union.

Az·tec (az′tek) *n.* **1.** member of a large group of Indian tribes having a well-developed civilization and controlling an empire in central Mexico at the time of the Spanish conquest in 1519. **2.** Nahuatl. —*adj.* of or relating to the Aztecs, their language, culture, or civilization. —**Az′tec·an,** *adj.*

az·ure (azh′ər, ā′zhər) *n.* **1.** clear sky-blue color. **2.** *Archaic.* unclouded sky. [Old French *azur* blue, from Arabic *lāzward* lapis lazuli, blue, from Persian *lāzhward.*]

az·u·rite (azh′ə rit) *n.* azure-blue basic carbonate of copper, often used to make jewelry or decorative objects. Formula: $2CuCO_3 \cdot Cu(OH)_2$

at; āpe; cär; end; mē; it; īce; hot; ōld; fôrk; wood; fōōl; oil; out; up; ūse; turn; sing; thin; this; zh in treasure; ə in ago, taken, pencil, lemon, circus.

b, B (bē) *pl.* **b's, B's.** *n.* **1.** second letter of the English alphabet. **2.** second item in a series or group. **3.** *Music.* **a.** seventh note or tone of the diatonic scale of C major. See **do²** for illustration. **b.** scale or key that has this note or tone as its tonic.

B, boron.

b. **1.** born. **2.** book. **3.** base. **4.** bass.

B. **1.** British. **2.** Bible. **3.** Bay.

Ba, barium.

B.A., Bachelor of Arts. Also, **A.B.**

baa (bä) **baaed, baa·ing.** *v.i.* to bleat, as a sheep. —*n.* cry of a sheep; bleat. [Imitative.]

Ba·al (bā′əl, bäl) *pl.,* **Ba·al·im** (bā′ə lim). *n.* **1.** chief god of the ancient Semites, esp. the Canaanites and Phoenicians. He served primarily as the god of fertility and was worshiped under various local names. **2.** false god; idol. [Hebrew *ba'al* lord.]

Baal·bek (bäl′bek, bäl′-) *n.* town in northeastern Lebanon, site of several ancient temples.

Bab·bitt (bab′it) *n.* conventionalized American businessman who conforms to provincial, middle-class ideas of respectability and success. [From George F. *Babbitt,* title character of Sinclair Lewis' satirical novel *Babbitt,* 1922.] —**Bab′bitt·ry,** *n.*

Babbitt metal, any of various alloys having a lead or tin base and smaller amounts of antimony or copper, used to reduce friction, as in bearings. Also, **bab′bitt.** [From the American inventor Isaac *Babbitt,* 1799–1862.]

bab·ble (bab′əl) **-bled, -bling.** *v.i.* **1.** to make indistinct or meaningless sounds; prattle: *The baby gurgled and babbled.* **2.** to talk foolishly or excessively; chatter. **3.** to make a continuous, murmuring sound: *The brook babbled.* —*v.t.* **1.** to utter incoherently or with meaningless repetition: *He kept babbling his name until the drug wore off.* **2.** to utter foolishly; jabber: *She babbled all kinds of gossip and other nonsense.* —*n.* **1.** confused or continuous murmur: *a babble of voices.* **2.** incoherent, unintelligible speech. [Imitative.] —**bab′bler,** *n.*

babe (bāb) *n.* **1.** baby or young child. **2.** naive, inexperienced, or helpless person. [Of uncertain origin.]

Ba·bel (bā′bəl, bab′əl) *n.* **1.** in the Old Testament, Babylon. **2. Tower of Babel.** tower begun in Babel by the descendants of Noah in order to reach heaven. God punished its builders and prevented the completion of the tower by changing their language into many different ones. **3.** *also,* **babel.** confused mixture of many voices or languages; tumult. [Hebrew *Bābel* Babylon; possibly for Assyrian *bābilu* gate of God.]

ba·bies'-breath (bā′bēz breth′) baby's breath.

bab·i·ru·sa (bab′ə rōō′sə, bä′bə-) *also,* **bab·i·rous·sa, bab·i·rus·sa.** *n.* wild hog, *Babirussa babirussa,* of the East Indies and southeast Asia. The male of the species has two pairs of upward-curving tusks. [Malay *bābīrūsa* hog like a deer, from *bābī* hog + *rūsa* deer.]

Ba·bism (bä′biz′əm) *n.* pantheistic religious movement founded in 1844 in Persia. Babism stresses abstinence from alcoholic liquors and forbids polygamy and slavery.

ba·boo (bä′bōō) *pl.,* **-boos.** *also,* **ba·bu.** *n.* **1.** Hindu gentleman. ▲ used as a Hindu form of address equivalent to *sir* or *Mr.* **2.** in India, a native clerk who can write English. [Hindi *bābū.*]

ba·boon (ba bōōn′) *n.* any of several African monkeys, family Cercopithecidae, that have long doglike muzzles, cheek pouches for storing food, front and back legs of almost equal length, and usually

Baboon

a short tail. [Old French *babouin* simpleton, ape, possibly from *baboue* grimace; of imitative origin.]

ba·bush·ka (bə boosh′kə) *n.* kerchief, often made or folded in a triangular shape, worn over the head and tied under the chin. [Russian *babushka* grandmother, diminutive of *baba* old woman.]

ba·by (bā′bē) *pl.,* **-bies.** *n.* **1.** newborn or very young child. **2.** youngest member of a family or group. **3.** one who behaves like a child; childish or immature person. **4.** newborn or very young animal. **5.** *Slang.* object of special affection or pride; beloved. —*adj.* **1.** for a baby: *a baby blanket.* **2.** of or like a baby; childish: *a baby face.* **3.** young. **4.** small for its kind; comparatively little. —*v.t.,* **-bied, -by·ing.** to treat as a baby; pamper; coddle. [Diminutive of BABE.] —**ba′by·hood′,** *n.*

baby carriage, small, four-wheeled carriage for a baby, usually with a folding top.

ba·by·ish (bā′bē ish) *adj.* like a baby; childish; infantile. —**ba′by·ish·ly,** *adv.* —**ba′by·ish·ness,** *n.*

Bab·y·lon (bab′ə lən, -lon′) *n.* **1.** ancient city of Mesopotamia on the Euphrates River, capital of Babylonia and later of the Chaldean empire. Babylon was noted for its wealth, magnificence, and wickedness. **2.** city or place of great wealth, luxury, or vice.

Bab·y·lo·ni·a (bab′ə lō′nē ə) *n.* ancient empire in lower Mesopotamia that flourished from about 1900 B.C. until 538 B.C., when it was conquered by the Persians.

Bab·y·lo·ni·an (bab′ə lō′nē ən) *adj.* of, like, or relating to Babylon or Babylonia. —*n.* **1.** member of the people of Babylonia. **2.** Semitic language of the Babylonians.

ba·by's breath (bā′bēz breth′) *also,* **ba·bies′-breath.** *n.* garden plant, *Gypsophila paniculata,* native to Europe and northern Asia, bearing thick clusters of tiny white or pink flowers.

ba·by·sit (bā′bē sit′) **-sat, -sit·ting.** *v.i.* to take care of young children during the temporary absence of their parents.

bac·ca·lau·re·ate (bak′ə lôr′ē it) *n.* **1.** bachelor's degree given by a college or university. **2.** sermon or address delivered to a graduating class at commencement. Also *(def. 2),* **baccalaureate sermon.** [Medieval Latin *baccalaureatus* rank of holder of a bachelor's degree, from *baccalaureus,* advanced student, possibly modification (influenced by Latin *bacca laureus* berry of the laurel) of *baccalarius* young man, farmer, going back to Late Latin *bacca* cow, from Latin *vacca* cow.]

bac·ca·rat (bä′kə rä′, bak′ə rä′) *also,* **bac·ca·ra.** *n.* card game in which one player acts as banker and two or more players bet against him. [French *baccara;* of uncertain origin.]

Bac·chae (bak′ē) *n.,pl.* **1.** female attendants or worshipers of Bacchus, esp. those taking part in the Bacchanalia. **2.** priestesses of Bacchus.

bac·cha·nal (bä′kə näl′, bak′ə nal′) *adj.* **1.** of or relating to Bacchus or his worship. **2.** indulging in or characterized by drunken revelry; carousing. —*n.* **1.** follower of Bacchus. **2.** drunken reveler; carouser. **3.** drunken revelry or carousal; orgy. **4. Bacchanals.** the Bacchanalia. [Latin *bacchānālis* of Bacchus, from *Bacchus.* See BACCHUS.]

Bac·cha·na·li·a (bak′ə nā′lē ə, -nāl′yə) *n.,pl.* **1.** ancient Roman festival in honor of Bacchus. **2. bacchanalia.** drunken revelry or carousal; orgy. —**bac′cha·na′li·an,** *adj., n.*

bac·chant (bak′ənt) *pl.,* **bac·chants** or **bac·chan·tes** (bə kan′tēz). *n.* **1.** priest or male worshiper of Bacchus. **2.** drunken reveler; carouser. [Latin *bacchāns,* present participle of *bacchārī* to celebrate the festival of Bacchus, from Greek *bacchān.*]

bac·chan·te (bə kan′tē, bə kant′, bak′ənt) *n.* priestess or female worshiper of Bacchus; maenad. [French *bacchante,* from Latin *bacchāns.* See BACCHANT.]

Bac·chic (bak′ik) *adj.* **1.** of or relating to Bacchus or his worship. **2.** *also,* **bacchic.** drunken; riotous; orgiastic.

Bac·chus (bak′əs) *n.* Roman god of wine. His Greek counterpart is Dionysus. [Latin *Bacchus,* from Greek *Bacchos.*]

at; āpe; cär; end; mē; it; īce; hot; ōld; fôrk; wood; fōōl; oil; out; up; ūse; turn; sing; thin; this; zh in treasure; ə in ago, taken, pencil, lemon, circus.

Bach (bäкн) **1. Jo·hann Se·bas·tian** (yō′hän sə bas′chən). 1685–1750, German composer and organist. **2. Carl Phillip Emanuel.** 1714–89, his second son; German composer. **3. Johann Christian.** 1735–82, youngest son of Johann Sebastian; German composer.

bach·e·lor (bach′ə lər, bach′lər) n. **1.** unmarried man. **2.** one who has received a bachelor's degree. **3.** young knight serving under another's banner. Also (def. 3), **bach′e·lor-at-arms′.** [Old French bacheler young man, squire, from Medieval Latin baccalarius. See BAC-CALAUREATE.] —**bach′e·lor·hood′,** n.

Bachelor of Arts, bachelor's degree granted by a college or university to a person who has completed an undergraduate course of study in the liberal arts or social sciences.

Bachelor of Science, bachelor's degree granted by a college or university to a person who has completed a course of study in science or mathematics.

bach·e·lor's-but·ton (bach′ə lərz but′ən, bach′lərz-) n. **1.** hardy field plant, Centaurea cyanus, of the aster family, bearing many slender branching stems and showy flower heads that are used as boutonnieres. **2.** any of several plants with button-shaped flowers or flower.heads.

bachelor's degree, undergraduate degree that represents completion of a four-year college program or its equivalent. The most commonly awarded forms of this degree are Bachelor of Arts and Bachelor of Science. Also, **bac′ca·lau′re·ate.**

bac·il·lar·y (bas′ə ler′ē, bə sil′ər ē) adj. **1.** (of bacteria) rod-shaped. **2.** relating to, caused by, or characterized by bacilli. **3.** consisting of or containing small rods. Also, **ba·cil·lar** (bə sil′ər, bas′ə lər).

ba·cil·lus (bə sil′əs) pl., **-cil·li** (-sil′ī). n. **1.** any rod-shaped or cylindrical bacterium, esp. one of the spore-forming family bacillaceae. **2.** any bacterium, esp. a pathogenic variety. [Late Latin bacillus small rod, diminutive of Latin baculus rod.]

back¹ (bak) n. **1.** rear part of the human body, esp. from the neck to the end of the spine. **2.** part of the body of animals corresponding to the human back. **3.** backbone: Be careful, or you'll injure your back. **4.** part opposite to or farthest from the front; rear or posterior part: the back of a room, the back of the head. **5.** farther or other side; the reverse: Hang them up on the back of the door. Sign the check on the back. **6.** part opposite to or behind the part that is normally used: the back of the hand, the back of a spoon. **7.** part of an object that protects or supports the human back: the back of a chair, the back of a bench. **8.** Sports. **a.** a player whose regular position is behind that of players making initial contact with the opposing team. **b.** position occupied by such a player. **9. behind one's back.** without one's knowledge or consent; in secret. **10. to be (flat) on one's back.** to be sick or helpless. **11. to get (or put) one's back up.** Informal. to become or make angry or annoyed. **12. to turn one's back on.** to ignore, neglect, or abandon. **13. with one's back to the wall.** in a difficult or desperate situation; cornered. —v.t. **1.** to approve, aid, or strengthen; support (often with up): to back a candidate. He backed up his argument with facts. **2.** to cause to move backward; reverse the action of (often with up): The driver backed up the truck. **3.** to furnish with a back or backing; strengthen at the back: to back a book with cardboard. **4.** to bet in favor of: to back a horse in a race. **5.** to lie at the back of; form a background for: a beach backed by cliffs. **6. to back up.** to bring (movement) to a halt; obstruct: The accident backed up traffic. The heavy rainfall backed up the sewers. **7. to back water.** to withdraw from a position or claim; retreat. —v.i. **1.** to move backward (often with up): He backed up to get a better view. **2. to back and fill.** to trim the sails of a boat so that it moves along with the current in midstream. **3. to back down.** Informal. to abandon a position, opinion, or claim; retreat. **4. to back off.** Informal. to withdraw or retreat. **5. to back out (of).** Informal. to withdraw from or abandon an engagement, undertaking, or commitment. —adj. **1.** at or in the rear: a back door, the back stairs. **2.** belonging to the past; not current: back files, a back copy of a book. **3.** outlying; remote: back roads, back settlements. **4.** in arrears; overdue: back pay, back taxes. **5.** in a backward direction; reversed: a back thrust, a back stroke. **6.** Phonetics. pronounced with the back part of the tongue arched toward the palate: a back vowel. [Old English bæc human and animal back.]

back² (bak) adv. **1.** at, to, or toward the rear; backward: to step back, to shrink back. **2.** in, to, or toward a previous place or position: Put them back on the shelf. I'm going back home. **3.** in, to, or toward a previous condition or state: My cold's come back. **4.** in or into the past: to look back on one's childhood. It happened back in 1950. **5.** in reply or return: to answer back, to pay back a loan. Don't hit him back. **6. back and forth.** first in one direction and then in the other; to and fro. **7. back of.** Informal. behind. **8. to go back on.** Informal. to refuse to fulfill a promise or commitment. [Short for ABACK.]

back·ache (bak′āk′) n. ache or pain in one's back.

back·band (bak′band′) n. band of a harness extending over the back of a horse's neck, used to hold up the shafts of a vehicle.

back·bite (bak′bīt′) **-bit, -bit·ten** or **-bit·ing.** v.t., v.i. to speak mali-

ciously about (an absent person or persons); slander. —**back′bit′er,** n.

back·board (bak′bôrd′) n. **1.** board forming or supporting the back of something. **2.** rectangular board in basketball to which the basket is attached.

back·bone (bak′bōn′) n. **1.** spinal or vertebral column; the spine. See spine for illustration. **2.** something resembling a backbone in shape, position, or function; axis, foundation, or mainstay: The courts are the backbone of our judicial system. **3.** strength of character; resoluteness.

back·break·ing (bak′brā′king) adj. physically exhausting.

back·door (bak′dôr′) adj. concealed; underhanded; clandestine.

back·drop (bak′drop′) n. **1.** curtain hung at the back of a stage, often painted to represent a scene. **2.** background of an event; setting.

back·er (bak′ər) n. one who supports a person or undertaking with money or influence; patron.

back·field (bak′fēld′) n. **1.** the four players in football whose regular positions are behind the linemen; the quarterback, two halfbacks, and fullback. **2.** position behind the linemen.

back·fire (bak′fīr′) n. **1.** explosion in the cylinder of an internal combustion engine resulting from a premature ignition of the fuel. **2.** fire built to check an advancing forest or prairie fire by burning off an area in its path. —v.i. **-fired, -fir·ing. 1.** to undergo a backfire: The truck backfired. **2.** to bring results opposite to those planned; boomerang: His scheme backfired. **3.** to build or use a backfire.

back·for·ma·tion (bak′fôr mā′shən) n. **1.** derivation of a new word from an existing word assumed to be its derivative, as sculpt from sculptor. **2.** word so derived.

back·gam·mon (bak′gam′ən, bak′gam′-) n. game for two played on a special board with dice and fifteen pieces for each player, the throw of the dice determining where the counters move. [BACK² + gammon, earlier form of GAME¹; because sometimes the pieces must go back to start again.]

back·ground (bak′ground′) n. **1.** part of a picture or scene perceived as furthest from the spectator's eye. Opposed to **foreground. 2.** surroundings or surface behind something seen or represented. **3.** information or past circumstances that help to explain some later event or situation: the background of the Civil War. **4.** conditions or environment in which an occurrence is perceived; setting: He assumed power against a background of civil anarchy. **5.** one's origin, experience, and education considered as a whole: He hasn't the right kind of background for the job. **6. in** (or **into) the background.** out of sight or notice; inconspicuous: He kept his shady dealings in the background.

background music, music or sound effects used as accompaniment to dialogue or action in a play, movie, or broadcast.

back·hand (bak′hand′) n. **1.** in sports, stroke made with the arm drawn across the body, the palm of the hand facing the body, and the back of the hand turned outward. Distinguished from **forehand. 2.** handwriting which slants toward the left. —adj. backhanded. —adv. with a backhand stroke.

back·hand·ed (bak′han′did) adj. **1.** performed or made with the back of the hand, or with the back of the hand turned forward: a backhanded blow, a backhanded stroke. **2.** slanting to the left: backhanded handwriting. **3.** insincere; equivocal: a backhanded compliment. —**back′hand′ed·ly,** adv. —**back′hand′ed·ness,** n.

back·ing (bak′ing) n. **1.** approval or assistance; support: financial backing. **2.** supporters or backers collectively. **3.** something used to support, form, or strengthen a back.

back·lash (bak′lash′) n. **1.** opposing action or trend in reaction to some force or event; sharp recoil: a reactionary backlash against liberal reforms. **2.** jarring recoil of loose or worn parts in a machine.

back·log (bak′lôg′, -log′) n. **1.** reserve supply: a backlog of business experience. **2.** accumulation of unfinished work: a backlog of orders that must be filled. **3.** large log placed at the back of a fireplace to sustain the fire and concentrate the heat.

back number 1. out-of-date issue of a magazine or newspaper. **2.** Informal. old-fashioned person or thing.

back·pack (bak′pak′) n. pack for camping supplies supported by a metal frame and carried on the back. —v.i. to go on a hike or a camping trip using a backpack. —**back′pack′er,** n.

back·rest (bak′rest′) n. support for or at the back.

back seat 1. seat to the rear. **2.** Informal. secondary or inferior position.

back-seat driver Informal. one who offers unwanted advice, esp. a passenger in a car who tells the driver how to drive the car.

back·side (bak′sīd′) n. rump; buttocks.

back·slide (bak′slīd′) **-slid, -slid** or **-slid·den, -slid·ing.** v.i. to return to former or undesirable ways; relapse. —**back′slid′er,** n.

back·spin (bak′spin′) n. backward rotation of a round object that is moving forward: backspin of a basketball, backspin of a wheel.

back·stage (bak′stāj′) n. area of a theater behind the curtain line, esp. that part behind the stage. —adj. **1.** related to, located, or occurring backstage: A backstage accident delayed the play. **2.** behind the

scenes; private; secret: *backstage negotiations for the merger.* —*adv.* in, to, or toward the backstage.

back·stay (bak′stā′) *n.* **1.** stay which extends aft from an upper masthead to the side or stern of a boat. **2.** *Mechanics.* piece or device used to strengthen or support something.

back·stitch (bak′stich′) *n.* stitching or stitch made by doubling the thread back each time on the preceding stitch. —*v.t., v.i.* to sew with backstitches.

back·stop (bak′stop′) *n.* **1.** fence, screen, or wall used in sports to stop the ball from going too far beyond the normal playing area. **2.** player who stops the ball, esp. the catcher in baseball.

back·stroke (bak′strōk′) *n.* stroke in swimming made by lying on the back and moving the arms alternately up and back into the water, accompanied by a flutter kick.

back talk *Informal.* insolent or argumentative retort; answering back.

back·track (bak′trak′) *v.i.* **1.** to return by the same route or path; retrace one's course: *to backtrack through the woods. Backtrack over your ideas and explain your conclusion.* **2.** to withdraw from an undertaking; reverse a position or stand: *The witness backtracked on his testimony.*

back·ward (bak′wərd) *adv.* also, **back·wards. 1.** toward the back; to the rear: *He threw his arms backward.* **2.** with the back foremost: *to walk backward.* **3.** opposite to the usual or right way; in reverse: *to count backward.* **4.** toward or into the past: *to look backward over the past centuries.* **5.** toward a worse or less advanced state. —*adj.* **1.** directed or turned toward the back or rear: *a backward glance, backward movement.* **2.** behind in growth or development; slow; retarded: *a backward learner, backward nations.* **3.** done with the back foremost: *a backward dive.* **4.** directed to or toward a previous point or position: *a backward journey.* **5.** done in a reverse or incorrect way: *backward rotation.* [Middle English *bakward* towards the back, from *bak* BACK + -WARD.] —**back′ward·ly,** *adv.* —**back′ward·ness,** *n.*

back·wash (bak′wŏsh′, -wosh′) *n.* **1.** water moved backward by the propelling force of a moving object. **2.** backward current of air from an airplane propeller. **3.** result of an event or condition; aftermath.

back·wa·ter (bak′wô′tər, -wot′ər) *n.* **1.** water turned or held back by an obstruction, tide, or opposing current: *the backwater created by the dam.* **2.** place or condition regarded as sluggish, stagnant, or backward. —*adj.* sluggish; stagnant; backward.

back·woods (bak′woodz′) *n.,pl.* **1.** wild, heavily wooded, or thinly settled areas that are remote from centers of population. **2.** area regarded as crude, provincial, or culturally backward. —*adj.* **1.** of, in, or relating to the backwoods: *a backwoods settlement.* **2.** crude; provincial; backward: *a backwoods approach.*

back·woods·man (bak′woodz′mən) *pl.* **-men.** *n.* one who lives in or comes from the backwoods.

back·yard (bak′yärd′) *n.* area behind a house, esp. one put to some domestic use. —*adj.* of or in a backyard: *a backyard fence.*

ba·con (bā′kən) *n.* **1.** salted and smoked meat from the back and sides of a hog. **2. to bring home the bacon.** *Informal.* **a.** to earn a living. **b.** to succeed. [Old French *bacon;* of Germanic origin.]

Ba·con (bā′kən) **1. Francis.** 1561–1626, English essayist, statesman, and philosopher. **2. Roger.** c.1214–94, English philosopher and scientist.

bac·te·ri·a (bak tēr′ē ə) *sing.,* **-ri·um,** *n.,pl.* of numerous one-celled microorganisms, class Schizomycetes, that exhibit both plant and animal characteristics. They may be beneficial, harmless, or pathogenic and are classified according to shape as bacilli, cocci, or spirilla. [Modern Latin *bacteria,* plural of *bacterium,* from Greek *baktērion,* diminutive of *baktron* stick.]

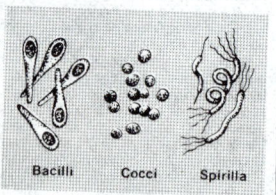

Bacilli   Cocci   Spirilla

Bacteria

bac·te·ri·al (bak tēr′ē əl) *adj.* relating to or produced by bacteria: *a bacterial infection, bacterial activity.*

bac·te·ri·cide (bak tēr′ə sīd′) *n.* agent that destroys bacteria. [BACTERI(A) + -CIDE².] —**bac·te′ri·ci′dal,** *adj.*

bac·te·ri·ol·o·gist (bak tēr′ē ol′ə jist) *n.* one who studies or specializes in bacteriology.

bac·te·ri·ol·o·gy (bak tēr′ē ol′ə jē) *n.* branch of microbiology concerned with the characteristics and activities of bacteria. —**bac·te·ri·o·log·i·cal** (bak tēr′ē ə loj′i kəl), *adj.*

bac·te·ri·o·phage (bak tēr′ē ə fāj′) *n.* any of a group of microscopic agents, possibly viruses, that destroy bacteria. [BACTERI(A) + -PHAGE.]

bac·te·ri·um (bak tēr′ē əm) singular of **bacteria.**

Bac·tri·an camel (bak′trē ən) two-humped camel, *Camelus bactrianus,* of central Asia. See **camel** for illustration.

bad¹ (bad) **worse, worst.** *adj.* **1.** having little quality or worth; below standard; poor: *bad health.* **2.** evil; wicked; immoral: *bad conduct, a bad influence.* **3.** severe: *a bad fall, a bad cold.* **4.** incorrect; faulty; erroneous: *bad aim, bad grammar.* **5.** unpleasant; disagreeable; offensive: *bad manners, a bad odor.* **6.** having a harmful effect; damaging; injurious: *bad for your health, bad for your reputation.* **7.** not valid or sound: *bad advice, bad judgment.* **8.** not sufficient or satisfactory for use; inadequate: *bad lighting.* **9.** distressing; unfavorable; unfortunate: *bad news.* **10.** lacking skill or proficiency; untalented: *a bad actor.* **11.** not functioning properly; defective: *bad wiring, a bad connection.* **12.** regretful; distressed: *He felt bad about causing such trouble.* **13.** in poor health; sick: *I've felt bad all week.* **14.** rotten; decayed; spoiled: *a bad apple.* **15. not (so or half) bad.** *Informal.* fairly good; not unsatisfactory; acceptable. **16. too bad.** disappointing; unfortunate. —*n.* **1.** that which is bad: *from bad to worse. Take the bad with the good.* **2. the bad.** those who are bad: *The good die early, and the bad die late* (Defoe, c.1715). **3. to be in bad.** *Informal.* to be in trouble or disfavor. **4. to go bad.** *Informal.* to become spoiled, rotten, or corrupt. —*adv. Informal.* badly. [Possibly from Old English *gebǣded* oppressed; hence, wretched, worthless.] —**bad′ness,** *n.*

Syn. *adj.* **2. Bad, evil, wicked** mean immoral or wrong. **Bad** has the widest application and suggests something reprehensible without reference to degree: *That dishonest grocer has earned a bad reputation.* **Evil** has a sinister connotation and suggests depravity and corruption: *Faust sold his soul to the evil Mephistopheles.* **Wicked** has stronger moral association and suggests sinfulness and moral transgression: *In the Bible, Ahab was a wicked king who was hated by his people.*

bad² (bad) *Archaic.* past tense of **bid.**

bad blood, mutual or long-standing animosity; enmity.

bade (bad, bād) past tense of **bid.**

Ba·den-Pow·ell, First Baron (bād′ən pō′əl) 1857–1941, English general who founded the Boy Scout movement; born Robert Stephenson Smyth Baden-Powell.

badge (baj) *n.* **1.** distinctive emblem or device worn to indicate rank, membership, or achievement: *a sheriff's badge, a merit badge.* **2.** symbol or sign; token: *He wore his scar as a badge of courage.* [Anglo-Norman *bage* the emblem; of uncertain origin.]

badg·er (baj′ər) *n.* **1.** any of a group of burrowing mammals of the weasel family, having a wide, flat body, short legs, long claws, and a short, thick tail. **2.** fur of a badger, often used in making brushes. —*v.t.* to annoy or harass persistently; torment; pester: *to badger a witness.* [Possibly from BADGE, with reference to the white mark on its head.] —**Syn.** *v.t.* see **bait.**

Badger

bad·i·nage (bad′ən äzh′, bad′ən ij) *n.* good-natured teasing or raillery; banter. [French *badinage,* from *badiner* to joke, from *badin* roguish, silly, going back to Late Latin *badāre* to gape. See BAY².]

Bad·lands (bad′landz′) *n.,pl.* **1.** barren, heavily eroded region in southwestern South Dakota. **2.** also, **badlands.** any barren region characterized by numerous ridges, mesas, and peaks cut by erosion.

bad·ly (bad′lē) *adv.* **1.** in a bad manner: *He acted his role badly.* **2.** *Informal.* very much; greatly: *He needs new shoes badly.*

bad·min·ton (bad′min′tən) *n.* game similar to tennis, in which a shuttlecock is volleyed instead of a ball. [From *Badminton,* estate of the English Duke of Beaufort, where the game was introduced.]

bad-tem·pered (bad′tem′pərd) *adj.* having a cross or quarrelsome disposition; irritable.

Bae·de·ker, Karl (bā′də kər) 1801–59, German publisher of travelers' guidebooks.

Baf·fin, William (baf′in) c.1584–1622, explorer of arctic North America.

Baffin Bay, inlet of the Atlantic west of Greenland and east of Baffin Island.

Baffin Island, large Canadian island west of Greenland, at the mouth of Hudson Bay. Area, approx. 200,000 sq. mi.

baf·fle (baf′əl) **-fled, -fling.** *v.t.* to bewilder or puzzle greatly; perplex; thwart: *a case that baffled the police. Algebra problems baffle me.* —*n.* rigid structure, as a wall or screen, for controlling or deflecting the flow of fluids or sound waves. [Possibly from French *beffler* to deceive, or Middle French *baffouer* to deceive; both probably of Germanic origin.] —**baf′fle·ment,** *n.* **baf′fler,** *n.*

bag (bag) *n.* **1.** receptacle made of paper, cloth, leather, or other flexible material: *a shopping bag, a mail bag.* **2.** something resembling a bag in shape: *bags under the eyes. Your trousers have bags at the knees.* **3.** woman's purse; handbag. **4.** suitcase or satchel; valise: *Pack your*

at; āpe; cär; end; mē; it; īce; hot; ōld; fôrk; wood; foŏl; oil; out; up; ūse; turn; sing; thin; **this**; zh in treasure; ə in ago, taken, pencil, lemon, circus.

bags. **5.** amount contained in a bag. **6.** sac or pouchlike part in various animals, as the udder of a cow. **7.** quantity of game killed or captured in hunting. **8.** *Baseball.* a base. **9.** *Slang.* slovenly, unattractive woman. **10. bag and baggage.** *Informal.* **a.** with all one's possessions. **b.** entirely; completely. **11. in the bag.** *Informal.* assured; certain: *His promotion was in the bag.* **12. to be left holding the bag.** *Informal.* to be left to take full blame or responsibility. —*v.t.,* **bagged, bag·ging. 1.** to kill or capture (game) in hunting: *He bagged three birds.* **2.** *Informal.* to seize or capture; trap: *The policeman bagged the thief.* **3.** to put into a bag. **4** *Slang.* to make off with; steal: *The robbers bagged a million dollars in furs.* —*v.i.* **1.** to hang loosely; sag: *His jacket bagged at the elbow.* **2.** to swell; bulge. [Old Norse *baggi* pack, bundle.]

ba·gasse (bə gas′) *n.* crushed sugarcane or sugar beet from which the juice has been extracted, used as a fuel and in the manufacture of paper. [French *bagasse,* from Spanish *bagazo,* from *baga* husk, pod, from Latin *bāca* berry.]

bag·a·telle (bag′ə tel′) *n.* **1.** something of little value or importance; trifle. **2.** game similar to billiards. [French *bagatelle* trifle, from Italian *bagatella,* diminutive of *bagata* small property; possibly of Germanic origin.]

ba·gel (bā′gəl) *n.* doughnut-shaped roll made of yeast dough, cooked in simmering water and then baked. [Yiddish *beygel,* going back to Middle High German *beuc* ring.]

bag·gage (bag′ij) *n.* **1.** luggage and other belongings that a traveler takes with him. **2.** portable equipment and supplies of an army. [Old French *bagage* collection of bundles, from *bague* bundle, possibly from Old Norse *baggi* bundle.]

bag·ging (bag′ing) *n.* coarse cloth used for making bags; sacking.

bag·gy (bag′ē) -**gi·er,** -**gi·est.** *adj.* hanging loosely; bulging. —**bag′·gi·ly,** *adv.* —**bag′gi·ness,** *n.*

Bagh·dad (bag′dad) *also,* **Bag·dad.** *n.* capital of Iraq, in the east-central part of the country, on the Tigris River. Pop. (1965), 1,745,328.

bagn·io (ban′yō, bän′-) *pl.,* -**ios.** *n.* house of prostitution; brothel. [Italian *bagno* bath, from Latin *balneum,* from Greek *balaneion.*]

bag·pipe (bag′pīp′) *also,* **bag·pipes.** *n.* shrill-toned, musical wind instrument, commonly identified with Scotland, consisting of a leather windbag, a chanter or melody pipe, and three drone pipes. —**bag′pip′er,** *n.*

bah (bä) *interj.* exclamation of contempt or disbelief.

Ba·ha·i (bə hä′ē, bə hī′) *pl.,* **Ba·ha·is.** *n.* follower of Bahaism.

Ba·ha·ism (bə hä′iz′əm, -hī′-) *n.* religious system developed from Babism that teaches that all religions are one. The faith rejects ritual and monasticism, and it has no official clergy.

Bagpipe

Ba·ha·mas (bə hä′məz, hä′-) island country in the West Indies, located off the southeastern coast of Florida. Land area, 4404 sq. mi. Pop. (1975 est.), 203,815. Also, **Bahama Islands.** —**Ba·ham·i·an** (bə hä′mē ən, -hä′-), *adj., n.*

Bah·rain (bä rān′) *also,* **Bah·rein.** *n.* island country in the Persian Gulf west of Qatar. Land Area, 240 sq. mi. Pop. (1975 est.), 300,000.

Bai·kal, Lake (bī käl′) lake in south-central Soviet Asia. It is the deepest freshwater lake in the world and the largest in Eurasia.

bail[1] (bāl) *n.* **1.** security given to the court to obtain the temporary release of a prisoner and guaranteeing his appearance at a designated time. **2.** temporary release granted on this security. **3.** person or persons giving the security. **4. to go** (or **stand**) **bail.** to furnish bail. —*v.t.* to obtain the temporary release of (a person under arrest) by providing bail (often with *out*). [Old French *bail* custody, from *baillier* to have in charge, from Latin *bājulāre* to carry.]

bail[2] (bāl) *n.* **1.** arched handle of a kettle, pail, or similar container. **2.** hooplike piece of sturdy material used for support, as that used for the top of a covered wagon. [Probably of Scandinavian origin.]

bail[3] (bāl) *v.t.* **1.** to remove (water) from a boat with a pail or similar container: *to bail water.* **2.** to clear of water with a pail or similar container (often with *out*): *to bail a boat out.* **3. to bail out.** *Informal.* to assist (a person or thing) in a financial crisis or other emergency: *The government hopes to bail out the railroad with a subsidy.* —*v.i.* **1.** to bail water: *We bailed desperately for an hour.* **2. to bail out.** to parachute from an aircraft. [French *baille* bucket, possibly from Late Latin *bacula,* diminutive of *baca* trough.]

bail[4] (bāl) *n.* in cricket, either of two pieces of wood that form the top of a wicket. [Old French *bail* crossbeam; of uncertain origin.]

bail·a·ble (bā′lə bəl) *adj.* **1.** capable of being bailed. **2.** admitting of bail: *a bailable offense.*

bail·ee (bā′lē′) *n.* one who receives goods for bailment.

bail·er (bā′lər) *n.* something used as a container to scoop water out of a boat.

bail·ie (bā′lē) *n.* in Scotland, a municipal officer or magistrate, corresponding to an alderman in England. [Old French *bailli,* form of *baillif* magistrate. See BAILIFF.]

bail·iff (bā′lif) *n.* **1.** court officer who guards the prisoners and the jurors in a courtroom. **2.** assistant to a sheriff, who serves processes, writs, and warrants of arrest. **3.** one who oversees an estate for the owner; steward. **4.** in certain English towns, a local administrative official or chief magistrate. [Old French *baillif* magistrate, from *baillir* to govern, from *bail* manager, from Latin *bājulus* porter.]

bail·i·wick (bā′lə wik′) *n.* **1.** office, jurisdiction, or district of a bailiff. **2.** field in which a person has special or superior competence, interest, or authority. [BAILIE + obsolete English *wick* town, going back to Latin *vīcus* village.]

bail·ment (bāl′mənt) *n.* delivery of goods to another for a specified purpose and limited time. The deposit of goods for storage in a warehouse is a bailment.

bail·out (bāl′out′) *n.* act of parachuting from an aircraft, esp. in an emergency.

bails·man (bālz′mən) *pl.,* -**men.** *n.* one who gives bail or serves as security for another.

bairn (bârn) *n.* *Scottish.* son or daughter; child. [Old English *bearn.*]

bait (bāt) *n.* **1.** food or any other lure used to attract fish or other animals so that they may be caught. **2.** anything that tempts or attracts; enticement. —*v.t.* **1.** to put food or any other lure on or in: *to bait a hook, to bait a trap.* **2.** to persecute or goad, esp. with insulting or exasperating remarks; torment; harass. **3.** to entice; lure. **4.** to set dogs upon (an animal) for sport: *to bait a bear.* [Partly from Old Norse *beit* pasture and *beita* food; partly from Old Norse *beita* to cause to bite.] —**bait′er,** *n.*

Syn. *v.t.* **2. Bait, badger, heckle, ride** all mean to harass or pester. **Bait** means to persecute or hound maliciously: *The guard was fired for baiting the prisoners.* **Badger** means to pester or exasperate so persistently as to bring to a state of frantic confusion: *The lawyer badgered the witness until he broke down.* **Heckle** means to annoy, vex, or disconcert a speaker by persistent questioning, gibes, and taunts: *A hostile audience heckled the candidate at the meeting.* **Ride** means to goad in a carping way by harsh criticism: *The coach rides the rookies mercilessly.* See also **pester.**

baize (bāz) *n.* woolen fabric with a long nap, chiefly used for such items as curtains and table covers. [French *baies,* feminine plural of *bai* the color bay; possibly because the fabric was originally of this color. See BAY[1].]

Ba·ja California (bä′hə) Lower California.

bake (bāk) **baked, bak·ing.** *v.t.* **1.** to cook (food) by dry indirect heat, esp. in an oven. **2.** to dry or harden by heating: *to bake bricks. The sun baked the sidewalk.* —*v.i.* **1.** to prepare food by baking: *She baked well.* **2.** to become dried or hardened by heat: *The cake baked too long.* [Old English *bacan* to cook by dry heat.]

Ba·ke·lite (bā′kə līt′, bāk′līt′) *n. Trademark.* any of a group of very hard, heat-resistant plastics made from formaldehyde and phenol and used esp. as a protective coating for appliances and floors and in a wide variety of commercial products. [From Leo H. *Baekeland,* 1863–1944, U.S. chemist who invented it.]

bak·er (bā′kər) *n.* one who makes and sells bread and other baked goods.

baker's dozen, thirteen. [From a former custom among bakers of giving an excess (thirteen for a dozen) as a safeguard against the penalties for short weights.]

Bak·ers·field (bā′kərs fēld′) *n.* city in southern California. Pop. (1970), 69,515.

bak·er·y (bā′kər ē) *pl.,* -**er·ies.** *n.* place where bread and other baked goods are made or sold.

bak·ing (bā′king) *n.* **1.** act of one who or that which bakes. **2.** amount or batch baked at one time.

baking powder, powder used as a leavening agent in baking, composed of sodium bicarbonate, an acid-producing chemical, and a starch or flour. When moistened, the mixture releases carbon dioxide, which causes the dough or batter to rise.

baking soda, sodium bicarbonate.

Ba·ku (bä kōō′) *n.* port city in the southwestern Soviet Union, on the west coast of the Caspian Sea, capital of Azerbaijan. Pop. (1970), 847,-000.

Ba·ku·nin, Mi·kha·il (bä kōō′nin; mi кнä ēl′) 1814–76, Russian anarchist and revolutionary.

bal., balance.

Ba·laam (bā′ləm) *n.* in the Old Testament, a prophet who was ordered to curse the Israelites. He blessed them instead after God caused his donkey to reproach him, and after an angel appeared, warning him to speak only as God commanded.

---

at; āpe; cär; end; mē; it; īce; hot; ōld; fôrk; wood; fōōl; oil; out; up; ūse; turn; sing; thin; this; zh in treasure; ə in ago, taken, pencil, lemon, circus.

bal·a·lai·ka (bal′ə lī′kə) *n.* Russian stringed musical instrument resembling a guitar and having a triangular body, three strings, and a fretted neck. [Russian *balalaika*.]

bal·ance (bal′əns) *n.* **1.** equality between opposing or contrasting forces or elements; equilibrium: *the balance between good and evil in his nature.* **2.** physical stability: *to lose one's balance and fall.* **3.** mental or emotional stability: *a man possessed of judgment, sanity, and balance.* **4.** something that counterbalances or offsets (something else); counterpoise: *Comic highlights were introduced in the play as a balance to its tragic ending.* **5.** aesthetically pleasing integration of elements or component parts; proportion; harmony: *a nice balance between light and shade in the painting.* **6.** *Bookkeeping.* **a.** equality between the debit and credit sides of an account. **b.** difference between these sides: *He had a debit balance of $10 after the purchase.*

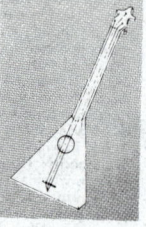

Balalaika

c. amount in excess on either side of an account. **7.** any of several instruments for determining the weight of an object, esp. by balancing it against known weights or forces, consisting in its simplest form of a horizontal bar having a pan suspended from each end, that pivots on a central point as weights are placed in the pans. **8.** balance wheel. **9.** *Informal.* that which is left over; remainder: *He completed the balance of the work later.* **10. to hang in the balance,** to be uncertain or undetermined: *The fate of the defendant hung in the balance.* **11. to strike a balance,** to find or assume an intermediate position; compromise. —*v.t.* **-anced, anc·ing. 1.** to bring into or keep in equilibrium; poise: *The seal balanced the ball on its nose.* **2.** to estimate the relative value, weight, or importance of;

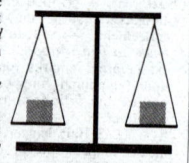

Balance

compare: *He balanced the pros and cons of the situation.* **3.** to counteract the effect of; compensate for; offset: *The good grade balances the poor one.* **4.** to place or keep in proportion; equalize: *to balance equations.* **5.** to be equal or in proportion to: *The white balances the black in the painting.* **6.** to weigh in a balance. **7.** *Bookkeeping.* **a.** to compute the difference between the credit and debit sides of an account. **b.** to equalize these sides. **c.** to settle (an account) by paying the amount due. —*v.i.* **1.** to be in or come into equilibrium: *He balanced on the tightrope.* **2.** to be equal: *Income and expenditures exactly balance.* **3.** (of an account) to have the debit and credit sides equal to each other: *My checking account doesn't balance.* [Old French *balance* weighing instrument, going back to Late Latin *bilanx* having two scales, from Latin *bi-* two + *lanx* scale.]

Syn. n. 9. Balance, remainder, rest², residue, surplus all denote what is left over. **Balance** is used in the simple sense of what remains after the removal of a part: *With the balance of the army, the general tried to hold off the enemy.* **Remainder** is a more formal word having the same meaning: *The remainder of the meal was put in the refrigerator.* **Rest** is used to suggest a part still considered in relation to a given whole: *John returned home while the rest of the party stayed in the camp.* **Residue** is what is left after some process is completed: *The burning chemical left a sticky residue.* **Surplus** suggests quantity or amount over and above what is needed: *The farmer kept some corn for his needs and sold the surplus.*

balance of payments, statement of all economic transactions between one country and all other countries in any given period. It is based on the movement of capital, including goods, services, and gold. Also, **international balance of payments.**

balance of power 1. an equilibrium of power among nations or groups of nations. It is maintained to prevent domination by any one nation or group of nations. **2.** ability to influence or change this equilibrium: *Germany held the balance of power in Europe.*

balance of trade, difference in value between the exports and imports of a nation.

balance sheet 1. itemized statement that shows the financial condition of a business at a given time by providing a summary of its assets, liabilities, and net worth. **2.** any overall summary or evaluation.

balance wheel, wheel that regulates the mechanism and rate of motion of a time-keeping instrument.

bal·a·ta (bal′ə tə) *n.* **1.** rubberlike gum obtained from the latex of a tropical American evergreen tree, *Mimusops balata,* used for machinery belting, golf ball covers, and other products. **2.** the tree itself. [Spanish *balata;* of Carib origin.]

bal·bo·a (bal bō′ə) *n.* silver coin of Panama.

Bal·bo·a (bal bō′ə), **Vas·co de** (bal bō′ə; väs′kō dā) c.1475–1517, Spanish conquistador who discovered the Pacific.

bal·brig·gan (bal brig′ən) *n.* knitted cotton cloth, chiefly used for hosiery or underwear. [From *Balbriggan,* Irish port where it was first made.]

bal·co·ny (bal′kə nē) *pl.* **-nies.** *n.* **1.** platform projecting from the wall of a building and enclosed by a parapet or railing of some kind. **2.** projecting gallery in a theater, auditorium, or other place of assembly. [Italian *balcone;* probably of Germanic origin.]

bald (bôld) *adj.* **1.** having little or no hair on the head. **2.** without usual or natural covering: *a bald mountain.* **3.** undisguised; unadorned; bare: *a bald lie, a bald statement of the facts.* **4.** (of animals) having white on the face or head. —*v.i.* to lose one's hair; become bald. ▲ The verb appears most commonly in the present participial form: *He is balding rapidly.* [Middle English *balled,* possibly from obsolete *ball* white spot.] —**bald′ness,** *n.*

Balcony

bald eagle, large eagle of North America, *Haliaeetus leucocephalus,* which, in the adult stage, is brown with a white head, neck, and tail; American eagle. Average wingspan: 6 feet.

Bal·der (bôl′dər) *also,* **Bal·dr, Bal·dur.** *n.* Scandinavian god of light, happiness, and peace; son of Odin and Frigg. His death was caused by the treachery of Loki.

bal·der·dash (bôl′dər dash′) *n., interj.* nonsense.

bald·pate (bôld′pāt′) *n.* **1.** one who has a bald head. **2.** migratory widgeon, *Mareca americana,* of Canada and the northern United States, which flies as far south as Central America in the winter.

bal·dric (bôl′drik) *n.* belt, often richly ornamented, worn over one shoulder and across the chest to support a sword or bugle. [Partly from Old French *baudre* belt; partly from Middle High German *balderich* girdle; possibly going back to Latin *balteus* belt.]

Bald·win (bôld′win) *n.* red winter apple.

bale¹ (bāl) *n.* large bundle of bulky merchandise compressed, corded, or otherwise prepared for transportation or storage: *a bale of hay.* —*v.t.* **baled, bal·ing.** to make into a bale or bales. [Old French *bale* round bundle; of Germanic origin.] —**bal′er,** *n.*

bale² (bāl) *n. Archaic.* **1.** that which causes ruin or sorrow; evil. **2.** sorrow; misery. [Old English *bealo* woe, evil.]

Bal·e·ar·ic Islands (bal′ē ar′ik) Spanish island group in the western Mediterranean. Land area, 1936 sq. mi. Pop. (1960), 443,327.

ba·leen (bə lēn′) *n.* whalebone. [Old French *baleine,* from Latin *balaena* whale, from Greek *phallaina.*]

bale·ful (bāl′fəl) *adj.* **1.** harmful or evil; malignant; sinister. **2.** *Archaic.* sorrowful; miserable; wretched. —**bale′ful·ly,** *adv.* —**bale′ful·ness,** *n.*

Ba·li (bä′lē) *n.* island in Indonesia, east of Java. Area, 2905 sq. mi. Pop. (1961 est.), 1,775,000.

Ba·li·nese (bä′lə nēz′, -nēs′) *pl.* **-nese.** *n.* **1.** member or close descendant of the people of Bali. **2.** language spoken by these people. —*adj.* of or relating to Bali, its people, or their language.

balk (bôk) *also,* **baulk.** *v.i.* **1.** to stop short and refuse to proceed or act (often with *at*): *I balked at the thought of it. My horse balked at the high jump.* **2.** to make a balk in baseball. —*v.t.* to hinder or check; thwart. —*n.* **1.** ridge between furrows; strip of unplowed land. **2.** large beam or timber; tie beam. **3.** failure of a baseball pitcher to complete his pitching motion when one or more runners are on base. [Old English *balca* ridge, beam, from old Norse *balkr* partition.] —**balk′er,** *n.*

Bal·kan (bôl′kən) *adj.* **1.** of or relating to the Balkan Peninsula. **2.** of or relating to the Balkan States or their people. **3.** of or relating to the Balkan Mountains. —*n.* **the Balkans.** Balkan States.

Balkan Mountains, mountain range on the Balkan Peninsula extending across the north-central part of Bulgaria.

Balkan Peninsula, peninsula in southern Europe, bordered by the Black and Aegean seas on the east and the Adriatic Sea on the west.

Balkan States, countries on the Balkan Peninsula: Yugoslavia, Romania, Bulgaria, Albania, and Greece.

bal·kan·ize (bôl′kə nīz′) **-ized, -iz·ing.** *also,* **Bal·kan·ize.** *v.t., v.i.* to break up into small, hostile political units or states. —**bal′kan·i·za′tion;** *also,* **Bal′kan·i·za′tion,** *n.*

balk·y (bô′kē) **balk·i·er, balk·i·est.** *also,* **baulk·y.** *adj.* given to balking: *a balky horse.*

ball¹ (bôl) *n.* **1.** any round or spherical body; globe: *a ball of yarn, the blazing ball of the sun.* **2.** round or spherical object used in playing various sports and games. **3.** ball put into motion or play in a specified manner: *a high ball, a curve ball.* **4.** game played with such a ball, esp. baseball. **5.** rounded protuberant part of something: *the ball of the foot.* **6.** *Baseball.* pitch which fails to pass over the home plate in the area

at; āpe; cär; end; mē; it; īce; hot; ōld; fôrk; wood; fōōl; oil; out; up; ūse; turn; sing; thin; this; zh in treasure; ə in ago, taken, pencil, lemon, circus.

between the batter's knees and shoulders and which is not struck at by him. **7.** *Military.* spherical or cylindrical projectile that is larger than shot. **8. to be** (or **to have something**) **on the ball.** *Slang.* to be alert, efficient, or capable. **9. to play ball.** *Informal.* **a.** to begin or resume a ball game or other activity. **b.** to work together; cooperate. —*v.t., v.i.* **1.** to form, wind, or gather into a ball or balls: *to ball cotton. The sweater has balled.* **2. to ball up.** *Slang.* to make or become hopelessly confused; muddle. [Old Norse *böllr* globe.]

Syn. *n.* **1. Ball, globe, sphere** all denote a round body. **Ball** is the most common word to describe a round object: *He wound the twine into a ball.* **Globe** and **sphere** are more dignified words to describe anything which is more or less round: *The pendant was a gold globe encrusted with jewels. Atlas is represented as carrying a sphere on his shoulders.*

ball² (bôl) *n.* **1.** large, formal dance. **2. to have a ball.** *Slang.* to have a thoroughly enjoyable time. [Old French *bal,* from *baler* to dance, from Late Latin *ballāre,* from Greek *ballizein.*]

bal·lad (bal′əd) *n.* **1.** sentimental or romantic song of two or more verses, each sung to the same melody. **2.** narrative poem or song written in simple verse and short stanzas that deals with a dramatic or exciting episode. Ballads of popular origin were usually altered as they were passed along orally through generations. [Old French *balade* dancing song, from Provençal *balada,* from *balar* to dance, going back to Late Latin *ballāre.* See BALL².]

bal·lade (bə läd′) *n.* **1.** verse form having three stanzas of eight or ten lines each, with an envoy of four or five lines, and the same rhyme scheme repeated throughout. The last lines of the three stanzas and of the envoy are the same. **2.** short, musical composition in the romantic mood of a ballad, for piano and orchestra. [French *ballade.* See BALLAD.]

ball-and-sock·et joint (bôl ən-sok′it) joint formed by a ball or knob in a socket, permitting limited rotary movement in every direction.

bal·last (bal′əst) *n.* **1.** weighty material placed in a floating or airborne vessel to maintain stability or control altitude. **2.** something lending stability or weight. **3.** gravel or crushed rock used as a bed for the ties of a railroad. —*v.t.* **1.** to fill or furnish with ballast: *to ballast a ship, to ballast a railroad bed.* **2.** to steady with ballast; stabilize. [Of Scandinavian origin.]

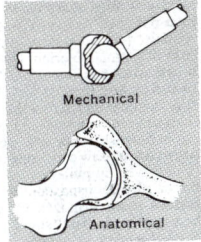

Mechanical

Anatomical

Ball-and-socket joints

ball bearing 1. bearing consisting of a number of metal balls on which the moving parts of a machine turn. **2.** any of these metal balls.

bal·le·ri·na (bal′ə rē′nə) *pl.,* **-nas.** *n.* female ballet dancer. [Italian *ballerina,* from *ballare* to dance, from Late Latin *ballāre,* from Greek *ballizein.*]

bal·let (ba lā′, bal′ā) *n.* **1.** style of dancing which combines conventionalized steps and positions in continuous, flowing movement. **2.** theatrical presentation in which a story or mood is conveyed by such dancing. **3.** company of dancers who perform in a ballet. [French *ballet* literally, little dance, from Italian *balletto,* diminutive of *ballo* dancing, from *ballare* to dance, from Late Latin *ballāre.* See BALL².]

bal·lis·ta (bə lis′tə) *pl.,* **-tae** (-tē). *n.* weapon used in ancient and medieval times to hurl stones, javelins, and other projectiles. [Latin *ballista,* going back to Greek *ballein* to throw.]

bal·lis·tic (bə lis′tik) *adj.* of, relating to, or used in ballistics.

ballistic missile, self-propelled missile that is controlled during the upward portion of its trajectory, but is a free-falling object in its descent.

bal·lis·tics (bə lis′tiks) *n.* study of the motion and impact of projectiles and the conditions that affect their motion. **Interior ballistics** studies a projectile's movement within the barrel of a weapon. **Exterior ballistics** studies the flight of a projectile after it has left the barrel and is used to calculate the path of rockets and ballistic missiles. —**bal·lis·ti·cian** (bal′is tish′ən), *n.*

bal·lo·net (bal′ə net′) *n.* flexible air-filled or gas-filled compartment inside a balloon or airship for maintaining and controlling buoyancy and shape. [French *ballonnet* small balloon, diminutive of *ballon.* See BALLOON.]

bal·loon (bə lōōn′) *n.* **1.** inflatable, often brightly colored, rubber bag, used as a toy or decoration. **2.** nonporous bag made of tough, light material, filled with a gas lighter than air, and designed to rise and float in the atmosphere. A car is often attached to its bottom for carrying scientific instruments or passengers. **3.** outline enclosing words represented as spoken by a character, as in a cartoon or comic strip. —*v.i.* **1.** to ascend or travel in a balloon. **2.** to swell out or expand like a balloon. —*v.t.* to inflate or distend (something). —*adj.* swelled or puffed out like a balloon. [Partly from French *ballon* child's air balloon,

aerostat, from *balle* ball; partly from Italian *ballone* large ball, from *balla* ball; of Germanic origin.] —**bal·loon′ist,** *n.*

balloon tire, pneumatic tire, containing air under low pressure.

balloon vine, climbing plant, *Cardiospermum halicacabum,* native to tropical regions and growing wild in the United States, having deeply-toothed leaflets and bearing small white flowers.

bal·lot (bal′ət) *n.* **1.** written or printed form used to cast a vote. **2.** total number of votes cast in an election: *The ballot was recorded.* **3.** system of voting by ballots or voting machines. —*v.i.* **-lot·ed, -lot·ing.** to cast a ballot or ballots; vote. [Italian *ballotta* little ball used in voting, diminutive of *balla* ball; of Germanic origin; from the ancient Greek method of voting by using small white and black balls to indicate approval and disapproval respectively.]

ballot box, box into which ballots are put.

ball·play·er (bôl′plā′ər) *n.* person who plays any of various ball games, esp. baseball.

ball-point pen (bôl′point′) pen whose point is a small metal ball that rolls the ink from a cartridge onto the writing surface.

ball·room (bôl′rōōm′, -rōm′) *n.* large room for dances or other social gatherings.

bal·ly·hoo (bal′ē hōō′) *pl.,* **-hoos.** *Informal. n.* **1.** exaggerated or sensational advertising or publicity. **2.** noisy uproar; clamor. —*v.t., v.i.* **-hooed, -hoo·ing.** to advertise or promote with ballyhoo. [Said to be named after *Ballyhooly,* an Irish village famous for its noisy quarrels.]

balm (bäm) *n.* **1.** fragrant gum resin obtained from certain trees or shrubs and used as salve; balsam. **2.** any fragrant ointment or oil: *to anoint with balm.* **3.** anything that heals or soothes: *Sleep was a balm to his troubled mind.* **4.** *Archaic.* sweet or pleasing fragrance. **5.** any of various aromatic plants of the mint family, esp. *Melissa officinalis,* a hardy herb, the leaves of which have a lemon flavor and are used for seasoning, esp. in liquors. [Old French *basme* balsam, from Latin *balsamum,* from Greek *balsamon;* probably of Semitic origin. Doublet of BALSAM.]

balm of Gilead 1. fragrant gum from a tree, formerly used as a soothing and healing ointment. **2.** small evergreen tree, *Commiphora opobalsamum,* of Asia and Africa, from which this gum was obtained. **3.** balsam fir (*def. 1*).

Bal·mung (bäl′mŏong) *n.* in the *Nibelungenlied,* Siegfried's sword.

balm·y¹ (bä′mē) **balm·i·er, balm·i·est.** *adj.* **1.** mild; soothing: *balmy spring weather.* **2.** *Archaic.* fragrant. [BALM + -Y¹.] —**balm′i·ly,** *adv.* —**balm′i·ness,** *n.*

balm·y² (bä′mē) **balm·i·er, balm·i·est.** *adj.* British. Slang. crazy; foolish. [Variant of BARMY.]

bal·sa (bôl′sə, bäl′-) *n.* **1.** strong, lightweight wood used esp. for making models and some water-sports equipment. **2.** any of a group of tropical American trees, genus *Ochroma,* from which this wood comes. [Spanish *balsa* raft; of Iberian origin.]

bal·sam (bôl′səm) *n.* **1.** any of a group of aromatic oily or gummy oleoresins used in cough drops, candies, and medicine. **2.** tree yielding such a substance, as the balsam fir. **3.** bushy plant, *Impatiens balsamina,* widely cultivated in tropical and subtropical gardens for its showy blossoms. Its mature pods burst open at a slight touch, scattering the seeds for several feet. Also, **garden balsam. 4.** *Archaic.* something that heals or soothes. [Latin *balsamum* resin, resin-yielding tree. See BALM.]

balsam fir 1. evergreen tree, *Abies balsamea,* of the pine family, found in North America, having resinous blisters on its bark from which a kind of balsam is made. Also, **balm of Gilead. 2.** wood of this tree, used esp. to make boxes, crates, and paper pulp.

Bal·tic (bôl′tik) *adj.* of or relating to the Baltic Sea or the Baltic States. —*n.* branch of the Indo-European language family, including Lithuanian and Lettish.

Baltic Sea, inland sea in northern Europe, bordered by Germany and Poland on the south, Denmark and Sweden on the west, and Finland and the Soviet Union on the east.

Baltic States, Estonia, Latvia, and Lithuania.

Bal·ti·more (bôl′tə môr′) *n.* **1.** largest city in Maryland, on the Chesapeake Bay. Pop. (1970), 905,759. **2. Lord.** see Calvert, Sir George.

Baltimore oriole, North American songbird, *Icterus galbula,* closely related to the meadowlark and blackbird. The male of the species has brilliant markings of orange and black. [From the family coat of arms of Lord *Baltimore,* which is orange and black.]

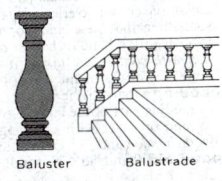

Baluster   Balustrade

bal·us·ter (bal′əs tər) *n.* upright support for the railing of a staircase, parapet, or similar structure. [French *balustre,* from Italian *balaustro*

at; āpe; cär; end; mē; it; īce; hot; ōld; fôrk; wood; fōōl; oil; out; up; ūse; turn; sing; thin; this; zh in treasure; ə in ago, taken, pencil, lemon, circus.

73

baluster, small pillar, going back to Latin *balaustium* pomegranate flower, from Greek *balaustion;* from its resemblance to the flower's shape.]

bal·us·trade (bal′əs trād′) *n.* row of balusters and the handrail they support. [French *balustrade,* from Italian *balaustrata,* from *balaustro* small pillar. See BALUSTER.]

Bal·zac, Honoré de (bal′zak, bôl′-, bal zak′; on′ə rā′ də) 1799–1850, French novelist.

Ba·ma·ko (bä′mä kō′) *n.* capital of Mali, in the southwestern part of the country. Pop. (1968 est.), 182,000.

bam·bi·no (bam bē′nō, bäm-) *pl.,* **-ni** (-nē). *n.* **1.** baby or child. **2.** figure of the baby Jesus. [Italian *bambino* baby, diminutive of *bambo* silly.]

bam·boo (bam bōō′) *pl.,* **-boos.** *n.* **1.a.** hollow, jointed woody stem or piece of a stem of any of a large group of plants, genus *Bambusa* and related genera, of the grass family. **b.** such stems collectively, esp. those used for furniture, shades, utensil handles, and similar items. **2.** the tall, fast-growing plant itself, having slender branches and sword-shaped leaves. Some may reach a height of 120 feet. [Probably from Malay *bambū* this plant.]

Bamboo trees

bam·boo·zle (bam bōō′zəl) **-zled, -zling.** *v.t. Informal.* to deceive or cheat by trickery; hoodwink: *He bamboozled us into buying the worthless car.* [Of uncertain origin.]

ban (ban) **banned, ban·ning.** *v.t.* **1.** to forbid or prohibit. **2.** to pronounce an ecclesiastical ban upon; condemn; curse. —*n.* **1.** formal or authoritative prohibition: *nuclear test ban.* **2.** denunciation or prohibition by public opinion. **3.** official denunciation by the church; excommunication. **4.** *Archaic.* sentence of outlawry or banishment. [Partly from Old English *bannan* to summon; partly from Old French *ban* edict, prohibition; of Germanic origin.]

ba·nal (bān′əl, bə nal′, -näl′) *adj.* commonplace or trite; hackneyed. [Old French *banal* relating to compulsory service to a feudal lord; hence, for everybody, commonplace, from *ban* edict (of a feudal lord); of Germanic origin.] —**ba′nal·ly,** *adv.*

ba·nal·i·ty (bə nal′ə tē) *pl.,* **-ties.** *n.* **1.** commonplace or trite remark or idea: *His conversation is full of clichés and other banalities.* **2.** triteness; triviality: *The banality of his ideas bored me.*

ba·nan·a (bə nan′ə) *n.* **1.** pulpy, crescent-shaped edible fruit of any of a group of large plants, genus *Musa,* found in nearly all tropical regions of the world. The most popular species in the United States is the yellow *M. paradisiaca,* variety *sapientum.* **2.** treelike plant bearing this fruit, having a high, thick stalk and large, deep-green, palmlike leaves. [Spanish *banana* this fruit; of West African origin.]

Ba·na·ras (bə när′əs) Benares.

Banana plant

band¹ (band) *n.* **1.** group of persons or animals; troop: *a band of gypsies, a band of sheep.* **2.** group of musicians organized to play together: *a marching band, a dance band.* —*v.t., v.i.* to unite in a group: *The cattle banded together for protection from the wind. The troops banded together for the attack.* [French *bande* troop; of Germanic origin.] —**Syn.** *n.* **1.** see **company.**

band² (band) *n.* **1.** flat strip of material used for binding, trimming, or some other purpose: *She wore a red band in her hair.* **2.** strip of contrasting color or material; stripe; bar: *The dog had bands of brown and gray in its coat.* **3.** range of wavelengths or frequencies between two specified limits. **4. bands.** pair of strips hanging from the front of the collar on certain clerical, legal, or academic garments. **5.** *Archaic.* something that ties, binds, or restrains. —*v.t.* to mark, decorate, or furnish with a band or bands: *to band the leg of a bird. He banded the box with cord before taking it to the post office..* [Old French *bande* bond, tie; of Germanic origin.]

band·age (ban′dij) *n.* strip of cloth or other material used in covering or binding part of the body, esp. an injured part. —*v.t., v.i.,* **-aged, -ag·ing.** to bind or cover with a bandage. [French *bandage* strip of material, from *bande* band²; of Germanic origin.]

band-aid (band′ād′) *n.* small, adhesive, gauze bandage. Trademark: Band-Aid.

ban·dan·na (ban dan′ə) *also,* **ban·dan·a,** *n.* large handkerchief, often brightly colored or patterned. [Hindi *bāndhnū* method of dyeing cloth in which certain parts of the cloth do not receive the dye.]

band·box (band′boks′) *n.* box of cardboard or other light material, used for holding hats and other articles of attire.

ban·deau (ban dō′, ban′dō) *pl.,* **-deaux** (-dōz′, -dōz). *n.* narrow band, esp. one worn about the hair; headband. [French *bandeau* headband, diminutive of *bande* band²; of Germanic origin.]

ban·de·ril·la (ban′də rē′ə, -rēl′yə) *n.* decorated sticks with metal points customarily thrust into the hump behind the bull's head at the beginning of a bullfight. [Spanish *banderilla,* diminutive of *bandera* banner, going back to Late Latin *bandum.* See BANNER.]

ban·de·ril·le·ro (ban′dər ē är′ō, -ēl yār′ō) *n.* bullfighter who thrusts banderillas into the bull's hump. [Spanish *banderillero,* from *banderilla.* See BANDERILLA.]

ban·de·role (ban′də rōl′) *also,* **ban·de·rol,** *n.* small flag or streamer; pennant. [French *banderole,* from Italian *banderuola,* diminutive of *bandiera* flag, banner, going back to Late Latin *bandum;* of Germanic origin.]

ban·di·coot (ban′də kōōt′) *n.* **1.** large rat, *Mus* or *Nesokia bandicota,* of India and Ceylon, which may grow to over a foot in length and often destroys gardens and rice fields. **2.** any of various marsupial mammals, family Peramelidae, native to Australia and neighboring islands, which resemble rats. They have large hind feet and slender forefeet with long, sharp claws. [Telugu *pandikokku* pig-rat.]

Bandicoot

ban·dit (ban′dit) *pl.,* **ban·dits** *or* **ban·dit·ti** (ban dit′ē). *n.* robber or outlaw. [Italian *bandito,* noun use of past participle of *bandire* to banish; of Germanic origin.] —**ban′dit·ry,** *n.*

band·mas·ter (band′mas′tər) *n.* conductor of a musical band.

ban·do·leer (ban′də lēr′) *also,* **ban·do·lier,** *n.* broad belt worn over the shoulder and across the chest, with loops or small pockets used for carrying ammunition and other small articles. [French *bandoulière,* from Spanish *bandolera,* from *banda* band; of Germanic origin.]

band saw, saw consisting of an endless serrated steel belt running over and driven by pulleys.

band shell, bandstand with shell-like, concave back.

bands·man (bandz′mən) *pl.,* **-men.** *n.* member of a musical band.

band·stand (band′stand′) *n.* platform for musical concerts, often roofed when outdoors.

Ban·dung (bän′dōōng) *n.* city in Indonesia, in western Java. Pop. (1961), 972,566.

band·wag·on (band′wag′ən) *n.* **1.** decorated wagon that carries a musical band in a parade or similar procession. **2.** enthusiasm and support for a person or cause: *The candidate's bandwagon started rolling early in the campaign.* **3. on** (or **aboard**) **the bandwagon.** *Informal.* on the successful or popular side: *to climb on the bandwagon.*

ban·dy (ban′dē) **-died, -dy·ing.** *v.t.* **1.** to give and take; exchange: *to bandy blows; to bandy words.* **2.** to discuss freely or carelessly; circulate: *to bandy a rumor.* **3.** to throw or knock back and forth: *to bandy a ball over a net.* —*adj.* (of legs) bent or curved outward; bowed. [Middle French *bander* to toss back and forth, bend; of uncertain origin.]

ban·dy-leg·ged (ban′dē leg′id, -legd′) *adj.* bowlegged.

bane (bān) *n.* **1.** cause of death, ruin, or injury. **2.** ruin; woe. [Old English *bana* murderer.]

bane·ber·ry (bān′ber′ē) *pl.,* **-ries.** *n.* **1.** any of a group of hardy woodland plants, genus *Actaea,* bearing showy clusters of small white flowers and white or red berries. **2.** one of these berries.

bane·ful (bān′fəl) *adj.* deadly or destructive; pernicious.

bang¹ (bang) *n.* **1.** loud, sudden, or explosive noise: *The door shut with a bang.* **2.** heavy, noisy blow; thump; whack: *I fell and gave my head a good bang on the floor.* **3.** *Informal.* sudden burst of energy or activity: *The racers started off with a bang.* **4.** *Slang.* thrill; kick: *He gets a bang out of skiing.* —*v.t.* **1.** to strike violently or noisily: *He banged his elbow on the chair.* **2.** to produce a loud noise by slamming (something): *He banged the window shut.* —*v.i.* **1.** to make a loud, sudden, or explosive noise. **2.** to strike noisily or violently. —*adv. Informal.* suddenly and loudly; abruptly. [Of Scandinavian origin.]

bang² (bang) *v.t.* to cut short and straight across. —*n. also,* **bangs.** hair worn over or across the forehead. [Of uncertain origin.]

Ban·ga·lore (bang′gə lôr′) *n.* city in southern India. Pop. (1969 est.), 1,027,327.

Bang·kok (bang′kok) *n.* capital, largest city, and chief port of Thailand, in the south-central part of the country. Pop. (1963 est.), 1,608,300.

Ban·gla·desh (bang′glə desh′, bäng′-) *also,* **Ban·gla Desh.** *n.* country located north of the Bay of Bengal and east of India, formerly the province of East Pakistan. Capital, Dacca. Area, 54,501 sq. mi. Pop. (1975 est.), 73,700,000.

ban·gle (bang′gəl) *n.* ornamental circular band worn around the wrist, arm, or ankle. [Hindi *bangri* bracelet.]

Ban·gor (bang′gôr, -gər) *n.* city in south-central Maine. Pop. (1970), 33,168.

Ban·gui (bäng′gē) *n.* capital of the Central African Republic, in the southwestern part of the country. Pop. (1966 est.), 150,000.

bang-up (bang′up′) *adj. Slang.* first-rate; excellent.

ban·ian (ban′yən) *n.* **1.** banyan. **2.** Hindu trader or merchant of a caste that eats no meat. [Portuguese *banian* trader, from Gujarati *vāniyo* member of the merchant caste, from Sanskrit *vānija* merchant.]

ban·ish (ban′ish) *v.t.* **1.** to force to leave a country by authoritative decree. **2.** to send or drive away; dismiss; expel: *Her reassuring words helped to banish my fears.* [Old French *baniss-,* a stem of *banir* to expel; of Germanic origin.] —**ban′ish·ment,** *n.*

Syn. 1. Banish, exile, deport, all mean to expel a person from a country or region. **Banish** means to force a person to leave a country for reasons of state: *The dictator banished his opponents from the country.* **Exile** means to banish someone from his native land either permanently or for a specified time: *The Russian government exiled political prisoners to Siberia in the nineteenth century.* **Deport** means to send an alien out of a country which he has illegally entered or where his presence is undesirable: *The government deported the foreigner who entered the country without a visa.*

ban·is·ter (ban′is tər) *also,* **ban·nis·ter.** *n.* handrail and its upright supports along the edge of a staircase, parapet, or other elevated structure. [Modification of BALUSTER.]

Ban·jer·ma·sin (bän′jər mä′sin) *n.* port city in Indonesia, on the southern coast of Borneo. Pop. (1961), 214,096.

ban·jo (ban′jō) *pl.* **-jos** or **-joes.** *n.* stringed musical instrument, usually having five strings, with a long fretted neck and a round, tambourinelike body. [Modification of earlier *bandore* a stringed instrument, from Spanish *bandurria,* through Late Latin, from Greek *pandoura* an ancient stringed instrument.] —**ban′jo·ist,** *n.*

Banjo

bank¹ (bangk) *n.* **1.** long pile or heap; mound: *cloud bank, bank of leaves.* **2.** rising ground bordering a body of water or any cut or hollow: *river bank, road bank.* **3.** slope. **4.** elevation in the sea floor or bed of a river; shoal: *banks of Dunkirk.* **5.** controlled lateral tilt made by an airplane in a turn. —*v.t.* **1.** to border with or along a bank; raise a bank around; embank: *They banked the river with sand during flood time.* **2.** to form into a bank; pile (often with *up*): *They banked up the cut logs.* **3.** to cover (a fire) with ashes, earth, or fuel so that it will burn slowly. **4.** to give a slope to: *The engineers banked the highway.* **5.** to tilt (an airplane) laterally when making a turn. —*v.i.* **1.** to lie or form in banks: *Snow banked all along the road.* **2.** to tilt an airplane laterally when turning: *The pilot banked too sharply.* [Of Scandinavian origin.]

bank² (bangk) *n.* **1.** institution that safeguards, lends, exchanges, and issues money and conducts a variety of other financial transactions. **2.** money held by the dealer or banker in some gambling games from which he pays the winners. **3.** any reserve supply. **4.** place that stores such a supply. —*v.t.* to deposit in a bank: *I banked $20 this week.* —*v.i.* **1.** to do business with (a bank): *We bank downtown.* **2.** to keep the bank in a game: *You deal, he'll bank.* **3. to bank on** (or **upon**). *Informal.* to depend on; be sure about: *You can bank on his going.* [Italian *banca* bench (of a banker or moneychanger); of Germanic origin.]

bank³ (bangk) *n.* **1.** group of objects arranged in a line or in tiers: *a bank of spotlights.* **2.** *Nautical.* **a.** bench for rowers in a galley. **b.** row or tier of oars. **3.** row of keys on an organ. —*v.t.* to arrange in a bank. [Old French *banc* bench, from Late Latin *bancus;* of Germanic origin.]

bank account, money deposited in a bank to the credit of, and subject to withdrawal by, the depositor.

bank·book (bangk′book′) *n.* book held by a depositor in which the transactions relating to his bank account are recorded. Also, **pass′book′.**

bank·er (bang′kər) *n.* **1.** officer or executive of a bank; banking company. **2.** keeper of the bank, esp. in a gambling game.

bank·ing (bang′king) *n.* business carried on by a bank; business of operating a bank.

bank note, promissory note issued by a bank, payable to bearer on demand and serving as currency.

bank·rupt (bangk′rupt′, -rəpt) *n.* **1.** debtor who is legally declared insolvent and whose property is distributed among or administered for the benefit of his creditors under bankruptcy laws. **2.** one who is without resources or unable to pay his debts. **3.** one who lacks a particular quality or thing: *an intellectual bankrupt.* —*adj.* **1.** subject to, or under, legal process because of insolvency; insolvent. **2.** lacking (in); destitute (of): *bankrupt of ethics, bankrupt in good manners.* —*v.t.* to

make bankrupt. [Italian *bancarotta* bankruptcy; literally, broken bench (from medieval custom of breaking the bench of an insolvent money-changer), from *banca* bench (of Germanic origin) + *rotta* feminine past participle of *rompere* to break, from Latin *rumpere* to break.]

bank·rupt·cy (bangk′rupt′sē, -rəp sē) *pl.,* **-cies.** *n.* **1.** state of being bankrupt; financial ruin. **2.** total ruin or failure.

ban·ner (ban′ər) *n.* **1.** piece of cloth bearing some emblem or motto: *Marchers in the parade carried colorful banners.* **2.** flag: *star-spangled banner.* **3.** something regarded or displayed as a symbol. **4.** headline extending across a newspaper page. Also (*def. 4*), **banner headline.** —*adj.* leading or outstanding; foremost: *a banner year.* [Old French *baniere* standard, flag, going back to Late Latin *bandum;* of Germanic origin.]

ban·ner·et (ban′ə ret′) *also,* **ban·ner·ette.** *n.* small banner.

ban·nis·ter (ban′is tər) banister.

ban·nock (ban′ək) *n. Scottish.* round, flattened cake made of oatmeal or flour. [Old English *bannuc* a cake, from Gaelic *bonnach,* possibly going back to Latin *pānicium* something baked.]

Ban·nock·burn (ban′ək burn′) *n.* village in central Scotland near which Scottish troops, under Robert the Bruce, defeated the English on June 24, 1314, thereby ending English control of Scotland until modern times.

banns (banz) *also,* **bans.** *n.,pl.* public announcement in church of an intended marriage. [Plural of *bann,* a form of BAN.]

ban·quet (bang′kwit) *n.* **1.** feast. **2.** formal or ceremonial dinner, often followed by speeches. —*v.t.,* **-quet·ed, -quet·ing.** to entertain at a banquet. —*v.i.* to eat sumptuously; feast. [French *banquet* feast, from Italian *banchetto* literally, little bench (as at a feast table), diminutive of *banco* bench; of Germanic origin.] —**Syn.** *n.* 2, see **feast.**

ban·quette (bang ket′) *n.* **1.** upholstered bench, as along a wall in a restaurant. **2.** platform along the inside of a parapet or trench for soldiers to stand on when firing. [French *banquette* bench, platform, from Provençal *banqueta,* diminutive of *banc* bench; of Germanic origin.]

ban·shee (ban′shē) *also,* **ban·shie.** *n.* female spirit in Celtic folklore whose wails mean that there will soon be a death in the family. [Irish *bean sidhe* woman of the fairies.]

ban·tam (ban′təm) *n.* **1.** *also,* **Ban·tam.** any of various miniature domestic fowl. **2.** small person who is cocky or quarrelsome. —*adj.* diminutive; small. [From *Bantam,* city of Java, from which the fowl was supposedly imported.]

ban·tam·weight (ban′təm wāt′) *n.* athlete competing in the next to lowest weight class in boxing or wrestling or the lowest weight class in weight lifting.

ban·ter (ban′tər) *n.* good-natured, witty jesting; raillery; repartee. —*v.i.* to exchange good-natured repartee. [Of uncertain origin.] —**ban′ter·ing·ly,** *adv.*

Ban·tu (ban′tōō) *pl.,* **-tu** or **-tus.** *n.* **1.** member of any of numerous Negroid tribes in central and southern Africa. **2.** family of languages spoken by these tribes and allied with the Sudanese-Guinean family. It includes Swahili and Zulu. —*adj.* of or relating to the Bantu or their languages.

ban·yan (ban′yən) *also,* **ban·ian.** *n.* any of several large trees, genus *Ficus,* of Asia, whose branches send down aerial roots that enter the ground and develop into new trunks. One tree will often cover a large expanse of ground. [Originally applied to a tree of this family, under which Hindu merchants (sometimes known as *banians*) had erected a temple. See BANIAN.]

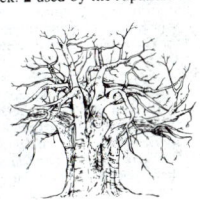

Banyan

ban·zai (bän′zī′) *interj.* **1.** forward; attack. ▲ used by the Japanese as a battle cry. **2.** used as a cheer to wish the emperor long life. [Japanese *banzai* literally, (may you live) ten thousand years.]

ba·o·bab (bā′ō bab′, bä′-) *n.* broad-trunked tree, *Adansonia digitata,* found mostly in tropical Africa, having thick spreading branches and large white flowers that develop into an edible gourdlike fruit. The fibers of its bark are used for making rope, cloth, and paper. [Of central-African origin.]

Baobab

Bapt., Baptist. Also, **Bap.**

bap·tism (bap′tiz′əm) *n.* **1.** act of baptizing, esp. the ceremonial initiation into the Christian church

through a ritualized use of water. **2.** any experience that purifies or initiates. —**bap·tis′mal,** *adj.*

baptism of fire 1. first time that a soldier is engaged in actual combat or under enemy fire. **2.** any severe ordeal that tests one's endurance for the first time.

Bap·tist (bap′tist) *n.* **1.** member of a Protestant denomination holding that baptism should be given by immersion and only to consenting believers. **2. the Baptist.** John the Baptist. —*adj.* of or relating to the Baptists, their doctrines, or their practices.

bap·tis·tery (bap′tis trē) *pl.*, **-ter·ies.** *n.* **1.** part of a church, or a separate building, in which baptism is performed. **2.** tank for baptism by immersion.

bap·tis·try (bap′tis trē) *pl.*, **-tries.** baptistery.

bap·tize (bap tīz′, bap′tīz) **-tized, -tiz·ing.** *v.t.* **1.** to ceremonially initiate into the Christian church by immersing in water or pouring or sprinkling water upon. **2.** to purify or initiate. **3.** to give a name to; christen. —*v.i.* to administer baptism. [Old French *baptiser,* from Late Latin *baptizāre,* from Greek *baptizein,* from *baptein* to dip.] —**bap·tiz′er,** *n.*

bar (bär) *n.* **1.** piece of metal, wood, or other sturdy material, longer than it is wide or thick, used as a barrier, fastening, lever, or support: *bars across a window, a ballet bar, bars on a bicycle.* **2.** oblong piece of solid material: *a bar of soap, a bar of gold.* **3.** amount of material contained in such a piece: *This statue contains seven bars of copper.* **4.** anything that obstructs or hinders; obstacle; barrier: *Poverty was a bar to their advancement.* **5.** stripe or band: *The painting consisted of bars of red and gold.* **6.** counter where food or drinks, esp. alcoholic drinks, are served. **7.** establishment containing such a counter: *a bar and grill.* **8.** legal profession: *He was a member of the bar.* **9.** lawyers collectively. **10.** law court; tribunal. **11.** any tribunal or place of judgment: *before the bar of divine justice.* **12.** bank of alluvium forming an obstruction to navigation or to the flow of water. **13.** *Music.* **a.** vertical line placed on a staff to mark the division between two measures. **b.** unit of music contained between two such lines; measure. **c.** two parallel vertical lines marking the end of a section or composition. Also, **double bar.** **14.** horizontal stripe covering one fifth or less of a heraldic shield or device. —*v.t.,* **barred, bar·ring. 1.** to fasten with or as with a bar: *Bar the windows.* **2.** to block or hinder; obstruct: *Armed guards barred the way.* **3.** to prevent or prohibit: *Smoking was barred.* **4.** to keep out; exclude: *He was barred from membership in the club.* **5.** to mark or provide with bars. —*prep.* except; excluding: *bar none.* [Old French *barre* rod, from Late Latin *barra;* of uncertain origin.]

bar. 1. barometer; barometric. **2.** barrel.

Ba·rab·bas (bə rab′əs) *n.* in the New Testament, the prisoner released instead of Jesus at the demand of the crowd, when Pilate asked which of the two should be spared from crucifixion.

barb (bärb) *n.* **1.** point or hook extending backward from the tip: *the barb of a fishhook.* **2.** any sharp pointed projection: *My sleeve ripped on the barbs of the wire.* **3.** pointedness; sharpness; sting: *the barb of his wit.* **4.** one of the hairlike projections growing from the shaft of a bird's feather. See **feather** for illustration. **5.** thin, beardlike growth near the mouth of certain animals. —*v.t.* to furnish with a barb or barbs: *to barb an arrow.* [French *barbe* beard, from Latin *barba.*]

Bar·ba·dos (bär bā′dōz, -dōs) *n.* island nation in the Lesser Antilles, easternmost island of the West Indies. Capital, Bridgetown. Area, 166 sq. mi. Pop. (1969 est.), 254,000.

bar·bar·i·an (bär bâr′ē ən) *n.* **1.** one who belongs to a primitive people, group, or tribe; uncivilized person. **2.** crude, coarse, or brutal person; brute. **3.** one who lacks understanding or appreciation of literary or artistic culture; unrefined or insensitive person; philistine. **4.** in ancient or medieval times, a foreigner, esp. one not Greek, Roman, or Christian, and therefore considered to be uncivilized. —*adj.* **1.** characteristic of or resembling a barbarian; uncivilized; savage. **2.** of or relating to a people or culture differing from one's own; in a way regarded as inferior; foreign; alien.

Syn. *adj.* **1. Barbarian, barbaric, barbarous, savage** all mean uncivilized or semicivilized. **Barbarian** means primitive and wild without further connotation: *The Goths and Huns were nomadic and barbarian peoples.* **Barbaric** suggests coarseness of spirit and lack of taste and refinement characteristic of barbarians: *The witch doctor was dressed in a barbaric costume.* **Barbarous** suggests cruelty and ferocity unworthy of advanced cultures: *Head-hunting is a barbarous custom.* **Savage** suggests the unrestrained violence and brutality of people untamed by or beyond the pale of civilization: *War brings out the savage instincts in man.*

bar·bar·ic (bär bar′ik) *adj.* **1.** relating to or characteristic of barbarians; uncivilized; savage; brutal: *barbaric tribes, barbaric rites.* **2.** crude or unrestrained in style or manner; having a primitive or unsophisticated quality: *the barbaric splendor of the decorations.* [Latin *barbaricus* foreign, uncivilized, from Greek *barbarikos,* from *barbaros* foreign. To the ancient Greeks foreign languages sounded as if they were made up of nonsense syllables, like "bar-bar." Hence, one who spoke a foreign language was called *barbaros.*] —**Syn. 2.** see **barbarian.**

bar·ba·rism (bär′bə riz′əm) *n.* **1.** uncivilized or primitive condition. **2.** act, custom, or trait characteristic of such a condition. **3.** use of words or forms not approved or current in the usage of a language. **4.** such a word or form.

bar·bar·i·ty (bär bar′ə tē) *pl.*, **-ties.** *n.* **1.** savage or merciless cruelty. **2.** act of savage or merciless cruelty.

bar·ba·rize (bär′bə rīz′) **-rized, -riz·ing.** *v.t., v.i.* to make or become barbarous.

Bar·ba·ros·sa (bär′bə ros′ə) *n.* Frederick Barbarossa.

bar·ba·rous (bär′bər əs) *adj.* **1.** uncivilized; primitive. **2.** brutally harsh or cruel. **3.** lacking refinement; crude. **4.** (of language) abounding in barbarisms. [Latin *barbarus* foreign, uncivilized, from Greek *barbaros.* See BARBARIC.] —**bar′ba·rous·ly,** *adv.* —**bar′ba·rous·ness,** *n.* —**Syn. 1.** see **barbarian.**

Bar·ba·ry (bär′bər ē) *n.* region in North Africa, comprising Libya, Tunisia, Algeria, and Morocco.

Barbary ape, tail-less monkey, *Macaca sylvana,* of northern Africa and Gibraltar. Average length: 2½ feet.

Barbary Coast, Mediterranean coast of the Barbary States.

Barbary sheep, aoudad.

Barbary States, Morocco, Algeria, Tunisia, and the region of Tripoli when under Turkish control, notorious for piracy from the sixteenth to the early nineteenth century.

bar·be·cue (bär′bə kū′) *n.* **1.** gathering, usually outdoors, at which meat and other foods are roasted over an open fire. **2.** spit, grill, or pit used for roasting food before or over an open fire. **3.** whole animal carcass or other food roasted over an open fire, esp. with a highly seasoned sauce. —*v.t.,* **-cued, -cu·ing.** to cook (meat) over an open fire or by direct heat, esp. with a highly seasoned sauce. [Spanish *barbacoa* frame for roasting an animal, from native West Indian word.]

barbed (bärbd) *adj.* **1.** having a barb or barbs. **2.** biting; cutting; stinging: *a barbed remark.*

barbed wire, wire or set of twisted wires to which barbs are attached at short intervals.

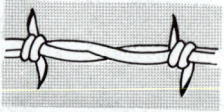

Barbed wire

bar·bel (bär′bəl) *n.* **1.** one of the threadlike feelers hanging from the mouths of certain fish. **2.** any of various freshwater fish, genus *Barbus,* of the carp family, having such feelers, esp. *B. barbus,* a European game fish which may grow to three feet in length. [Old French *barbel* barbel fish, from Late Latin *barbellus,* diminutive of *barbus,* from Latin *barba* beard.]

bar·bell (bär′bel′) *n.* bar with one or more weights at both ends, used for exercise and in weight lifting.

bar·ber (bär′bər) *n.* one whose business or trade is cutting or dressing hair, shaving or trimming beards, and providing related services. —*v.t.* to trim or dress the hair or beard of. [Anglo-Norman *barber* a barber, from Old French *barbe* beard, from Latin *barba.*]

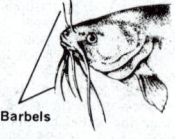

Barbels

bar·ber·ry (bär′ber′ē) *pl.*, **-ries.** *n.* **1.** any of a group of spiny shrubs, genus *Berberis,* having small, fragrant yellow flowers and inedible red or purple berries. **2.** the berry itself. [Old French *berberis* the barberry shrub, from Arabic *barbārīs.*]

bar·bette (bär bet′) *n.* platform in a fort which allowed guns to shoot over a parapet. [French *barbette,* diminutive of *barbe* beard, from Latin *barba.*]

bar·bi·can (bär′bi kən) *n.* defensive tower or other fortification at a bridge or gate leading into a castle or city. [Old French *barbacane* battlement; of uncertain origin.]

bar·bi·tal (bär′bə tôl′) *n.* white, crystalline barbiturate. Formula: $C_8H_{12}O_3N_2$.

bar·bi·tu·rate (bär bich′ər it, -rāt′) *n.* any of a group of barbituric acid derivatives, used as sedatives and hypnotics. They are often habit-forming.

bar·bi·tu·ric acid (bär′bə toor′ik, -tyoor′-) crystalline acid used chiefly as the basis of barbiturates. Formula: $C_4H_4O_3N_2$.

Bar·bi·zon (bär′bə zon′) *n.* village near Paris where a school of French painting originated in the nineteenth century.

at; āpe; cär; end; mē; it; īce; hot; ōld; fôrk; wood; fōōl; out; up; ūse; turn; sing; thin; this; zh in treasure; ə in ago, taken, pencil, lemon, circus.

Bar·ca (bär′ka) *n.* powerful family of ancient Carthage to which Hamilcar, Hannibal, and Hasdrubal belonged.

bar·ca·role (bär′ka rōl′) *also,* **bar·ca·rolle.** *n.* **1.** song sung by Venetian gondoliers. **2.** musical composition similar in style and rhythm to this song. [French *barcarolle* boatman's song, from Italian (Venetian dialect) *barcarola,* feminine of *barcarolo* gondolier, from Italian *barca* boat. See BARK¹.]

Bar·ce·lo·na (bär′sə lō′nə) *n.* port city in northeastern Spain. Pop. (1968 est.), 1,794,381.

bard (bärd) *n.* **1.** ancient Celtic poet and musician who composed and sang verses, esp. of heroes and heroic achievements. **2.** poet. [Of Celtic origin.] —**bard′ic,** *adj.*

Bard of Avon. William Shakespeare [From his birthplace, Stratford-on-Avon.]

bare¹ (bār) **bar·er, bar·est.** *adj.* **1.** without covering or clothing; naked: *bare arms. In winter the trees are bare.* **2.** exposed to view; unconcealed: *His motives were laid bare at the trial.* **3.** lacking or without furnishings; empty: *bare walls, a bare room.* **4.** unadorned or undisguised; plain: *bare facts.* **5.** just sufficient; mere: *bare necessities of life, the bare minimum.* —*v.t.,* **bared, bar·ing.** to make or lay bare; uncover; expose: *The poet bared his thoughts to the world. The dog bared its fangs.* [Old English *bær* without covering.] —**bare′ness,** *n.*

Syn. *adj.* **1. Bare, naked, nude** mean without clothing or covering. **Bare** suggests lack of surface or exterior covering: *He walked on the beach with bare feet.* **Naked** also means absence of covering but emphasizes physical covering and strongly conveys the sense of a natural state of being: *The boy swam naked in the river.* **Nude** is so close to **naked** in meaning as to be almost interchangeable but is usually used to describe an undraped figure in art: *He is a painter of nude figures.* **3.** see **empty.**

bare² (bār) *Archaic.* past tense of **bear¹.**

bare·back (bār′bak′) *adj.* on the unsaddled back of a horse or other animal: *a bareback rider.* —*adv.* without a saddle: *to ride bareback.*

bare·faced (bār′fāst′) *adj.* **1.** shameless or impudent; brazen: *barefaced disrespect.* **2.** unconcealed; open: *barefaced tyranny.* **3.** with the face uncovered. —**bare·fac·ed·ly** (bār′fā′sid lē, -fāst′lē), *adj.* —**bare′fac′ed·ness,** *n.*

bare·foot (bār′foot′) *adj., adv.* with the feet bare. Also, **bare′foot′ed.**

bare·hand·ed (bār′han′did) *adj., adv.* **1.** with hands uncovered: *They boxed barehanded.* **2.** without tools or other means.

bare·head·ed (bār′hed′id) *adj., adv.* with the head uncovered.

Ba·reil·ly (bə rā′lē) *n.* city in north-central India. Pop. (1969 est.), 325,560.

bare·leg·ged (bār′leg′id, -legd′) *adj., adv.* with the legs bare.

bare·ly (bār′lē) *adv.* hardly; scarcely: *barely enough food to go around.*

Bar·ents Sea (bar′ənts, bär′-) part of the Arctic Ocean north of Norway and the Soviet Union.

bar·gain (bär′gin) *n.* **1.** something bought or offered at a low price. **2.** agreement on the terms of a business transaction or other arrangement: *He didn't fulfill his part of the bargain.* **3.** terms of such an agreement, esp. as affecting one of the parties: *He drove a hard bargain. She made a bad bargain.* **4. into the bargain.** in addition to what was agreed upon; besides. **5. to strike a bargain.** to come to terms; reach an agreement. —*v.i.* **1.** to negotiate the terms of an agreement; haggle, esp. over a purchase price. **2. to bargain for** (or **on**). to count on; expect: *more than I bargained for. We didn't bargain on his arrival.* [Old French *bargaignier* to haggle; probably of Germanic origin.]

barge (bärj) *n.* **1.** flat-bottomed boat for transporting freight on inland waterways; lighter. **2.** large boat, often highly ornamented, used for recreation, pageants, or formal ceremonies. **3.** large launch used by the commanding officer of a flagship. —*v.i.,* **barged, barg·ing.** **1.** to move clumsily and abruptly: *He barged out of the room.* **2.** *Informal.* to enter or intrude rudely or heedlessly: *to barge into a meeting.* **3. to barge into.** *Informal.* to encounter or collide with: *I barged into him on the street.* —*v.t.* to transport by barge. [Old French *barge* flat boat, through Medieval Latin, from Greek *báris* Egyptian boat.]

barge·man (bärj′mən) *pl.,* **-men.** *n.* one who operates or works aboard a barge.

bar·ite (bār′īt, bar′-) *n.* mineral composed mainly of barium sulfate that is the main source of barium. Formula: BaSO₄. [Greek *barytes* weight, from *barys* heavy.]

bar·i·tone (bar′ə tōn′) *also, British,* **bar·y·tone.** *n.* **1.** male voice lower than tenor and higher than bass. **2.** singer who has a baritone voice. **3.** any of several brass or wind instruments with a similar range. **4.** musical part for a baritone. —*adj.* **1.** able to sing baritone: *baritone voice.* **2.** for the baritone: *baritone score.* [Italian *baritono* this male voice, from Greek *barytonos* deep-toned.]

bar·i·um (bar′ē əm, bar′-) *n.* soft, silver-white metallic element extracted from barite, used esp. in alloys, paints, rat poisons, and signal flares. Symbol: **Ba** See **element** for table. [Modern Latin *barium,* from Greek *barys* heavy; so called because it was found in BARITE.]

bark¹ (bärk) *n.* **1.** outer covering of the branches, stems, trunks, and roots of trees and other woody plants. **2.** such a covering as used for some specific purpose, as tanning, dyeing, or medication. —*v.t.* **1.** to rub the skin off of; scrape: *to bark one's shins.* **2.** to strip the bark off, esp. to girdle. **3.** to treat or tan with an infusion of bark. [Of Scandinavian origin.]

bark² (bärk) *n.* **1.** sharp, abrupt cry made by a dog. **2.** similar cry or sound: *the bark of a seal, the bark of a gun.* —*v.i.* **1.** to utter or give forth a bark. **2.** to speak loudly and sharply; snap: *He barked at us when we slammed the door.* **3.** *Informal.* to advertise by lively, persistent talking or shouting. **4. to bark up the wrong tree.** *Informal.* to mistake one's object or the means of attaining it. —*v.t.* to utter or advertise in a sharp, loud tone: *He barked orders at his staff. The street vendor barked his wares.* [Old English *beorcan* to utter a bark.]

Syn. *v.i.* **1. Bark, bay³, howl, yelp** all mean to make the sound of a dog. **Bark** means to make the harsh, abrupt, and explosive sound made by dogs: *Many dogs bark at strangers.* **Bay** means to utter the deep and prolonged cry of dogs in pursuit: *The dogs began to bay as they scented the quarry.* **Howl** means to utter the long, plaintive sound of dogs suggesting hunger or distress: *The wounded dog howled pathetically.* **Yelp** means to utter the short, high-pitched sound made by dogs in fear or pain: *The puppies yelped when the wolf came near them.*

bark³ (bärk) *also,* **barque.** *n.* **1.** ship with three or more masts, all square-rigged except for the aftermost one, which is fore-and-aft-rigged. **2.** *Archaic.* sailing vessel, esp. a small one. [Middle French *barque* small ship, from Italian *barca* boat, from Late Latin *barca* small ship.]

Bark³ (def. 1)

bar·keep·er (bär′kē′pər) *n.* one who owns, manages, or tends a bar where alcoholic liquors are served. Also, **bar′keep.′**

bar·ken·tine (bär′kən tēn′) *also,* **bar·quen·tine.** *n.* ship with three or more masts, the foremast square-rigged and the other masts fore-and-aft-rigged. [BARK³ + ending *-entine,* suggested by BRIGANTINE.]

bark·er¹ (bär′kər) *n.* **1.** one who or that which makes a barking sound. **2.** one who stands outside a show and attracts customers by lively, persistent talking: *a barker at a carnival.* [BARK² + -ER¹.]

bark·er² (bär′kər) *n.* one who or that which strips the bark off trees. [BARK¹ + -ER¹.]

bar·ley (bär′lē) *n.* **1.** grain of a hollow-stemmed plant, *Hordeum vulgare,* of the grass family. It is used mainly as animal feed, but is often made into malt and used for flavoring cereals and beverages. **2.** the plant itself, bearing short spear-shaped leaves and spikes with tightly packed rows of grain. [Old English *bærlic.*]

bar·ley·corn (bär′lē kôrn′) *n.* grain of barley.

barm (bärm) *n.* foamy yeast that forms on top of fermenting malt liquors. [Old English *beorma.*]

bar·maid (bär′mād′) *n.* woman who serves customers in a bar.

bar·man (bär′mən) *pl.,* **-men.** *n.* bartender.

Bar·me·ci·dal (bär′mə sīd′əl) *adj.* pretended or illusory; unreal. Also, **Bar′me·cide′.**

Barmecide feast, illusory or false show of hospitality or abundance. [From *Barmecide,* a Persian prince in *The Arabian Nights,* who served a beggar empty dishes, pretending they were an elaborate feast.]

bar mitz·vah (bär mits′və) **1.** ceremony signifying a Jewish boy's assumption of religious responsibilities upon his reaching the age of thirteen. **2.** boy for whom this ceremony is held. [Hebrew *bar mitzvāh* literally, son of the commandment.]

barm·y (bär′mē) **barm·i·er, barm·i·est.** *adj.* containing or resembling barm; frothy. [BARM + -Y¹.]

barn (bärn) *n.* **1.** building for storing farm produce and equipment and for sheltering cows, horses, and other livestock. **2.** *Informal.* large house or building, esp. one that is poorly built. [Old English *bern* literally, barley place, from *bere* barley + *ærn* place.]

Bar·na·bas (bär′nə bəs) *n.* in the New Testament, a companion of Saint Paul and one of the first Christian missionaries.

bar·na·cle (bär′nə kəl) *n.* any of various small marine crustaceans, order Cirripedia, that attach themselves to underwater objects and secrete a hard, cup-shaped shell. The **rock barnacle,** *Balanus balanoides,* is

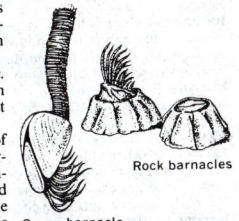

Rock barnacles

Goose barnacle

found on such objects as wharves or ship bottoms; the **goose barnacle,** *Lepas fasciularis,* on floating objects such as seaweed, attached by a long, fleshy stalk. [Possibly of Celtic origin.] —**bar'na·cled,** *adj.*

barn dance 1. social gathering, esp. one held in a barn, with square dances or other folk dances, and hoe-down music. **2.** folk dance resembling a slow polka.

barn·storm (bärn'stôrm') *v.i.* **1.** to tour rural or outlying areas, making brief stops, esp. to give campaign speeches or lectures or to present plays: *The presidential candidate barnstormed through five states.* **2.** to tour such areas as a stunt flyer or pilot. [When theatrical companies made tours in nineteenth-century America, they would *storm* through country districts, often performing their plays in *barns.*] —**barn'storm'er,** *n.*

barn swallow, fork-tailed swallow, *Hirundo rustica,* of North America and Eurasia, that usually builds a mud nest in chimneys or on the rafters inside barns.

Bar·num, P(hineas) T(aylor) (bär'nəm) 1810–91, U.S. showman.

barn·yard (bärn'yärd') *n.* yard surrounding or adjoining a barn.

Ba·ro·da (bə rō'də) *n.* city in western India. Pop. (1969 est.), 400,725.

bar·o·gram (bar'ə gram') *n.* record traced by a barograph.

bar·o·graph (bar'ə graf') *n.* aneroid barometer that automatically records its readings. [Greek *baros* weight + -GRAPH.]

ba·rom·e·ter (bə rom'ə tər) *n.* **1.** instrument for measuring atmospheric pressure, used in weather forecasting and to determine height above sea level. **2.** anything that indicates changes: *The stock market is a barometer of business activity.* [Greek *baros* weight + -METER.]

bar·o·met·ric (bar'ə met'rik) *adj.* of or indicated by a barometer: *barometric pressure.* Also, **bar'o·met'ri·cal.** —**bar'o·met'ri·cal·ly,** *adv.*

bar·on (bar'ən) *n.* **1.** feudal lord who held lands as a vassal of a king or other higher-ranking lord. **2.** British nobleman of the lowest rank. **3.** nobleman of certain European countries or of Japan having a similar rank. **4.** one who wields great power or dominates, esp. in business or industry: *an oil baron, a cattle baron.* [Old French *baron* man, warrior, from Medieval Latin *baro;* of uncertain origin.]

bar·on·age (bar'ə nij) *n.* **1.** the entire body of barons collectively. **2.** the rank, title, or territory of a baron.

bar·on·ess (bar'ə nis) *n.* **1.** wife or widow of a baron. **2.** noblewoman having baronial rank in her own right, as by inheritance.

bar·on·et (bar'ə nit, -net') *n.* member of the lowest hereditary order of honor in Great Britain. Although a baronet is not a nobleman, he is addressed as *Sir,* and may write *Bart.* after his name; for example: *Sir Thomas Beecham, Bart.*

bar·on·et·age (bar'ə nit ij, -net'-) *n.* **1.** the entire body of baronets collectively. **2.** the rank or title of a baronet.

bar·on·et·cy (bar'ə nit sē, -net'-) *pl.,* **-cies.** *n.* **1.** the rank or title of a baronet. **2.** document conferring such rank or title.

ba·ro·ni·al (bə rō'nē əl) *adj.* **1.** of or relating to a baron, barony, or the order of barons. **2.** befitting a baron; stately; magnificent: *a baronial mansion.*

bar·o·ny (bar'ə nē) *pl.,* **-nies.** *n.* **1.** the territory of a baron. **2.** the rank or title of a baron.

ba·roque (bə rōk') *adj.* **1.** of, characteristic of, or like a style of art and architecture, prevalent esp. in Europe from about 1550 to the end of the eighteenth century, that is distinguished by elaborate ornamentation and the use of curved rather than straight lines. **2.** of, characteristic of, or like a style of music prevalent in Europe from about 1600 to 1750 that is distinguished by elaborate ornamentation, strong rhythm, polyphony, and a figured bass. **3.** exaggeratedly showy or ornate. **4.** (of pearls) irregular in shape. —*n.* baroque style or period. [French *baroque* this style, from Italian *barocco,* probably from Federigo Barocci, 1528–1612, Italian painter who first painted in this style.]

ba·rouche (bə rōōsh') *n.* large four-wheeled carriage with two double seats facing each other and covered by a folding top, with a box seat in front for the driver. [German *barutsche,* from Italian *baroccio, biroccio* two-wheeled cart, going back to Latin *birotus* two-wheeled.]

barque (bärk) *bark*[1].

bar·quen·tine (bär'kən tēn') barkentine.

bar·rack (bar'ək) *n.* barracks.

bar·racks (bar'əks) *n.* **1.** building or set of buildings for housing soldiers or other military personnel, esp. at a permanent base. **2.** any plain, usually temporary housing for many people in close quarters: *refugee barracks, workmen's barracks.* ▲ construed as singular or plural. [French *baraque* hut, from Spanish *barraca;* of uncertain origin.]

bar·ra·cu·da (bar'ə kōō'də) *pl.,* **-das** or **-da.** *n.* any of a group of

long-bodied, predatory fish, genus *Sphyraena,* found in warm seas throughout the world and often caught for food. The possibly **great barracuda** of the southern United States and West Indies, with its large mouth, strong teeth, and aggressive nature, is known to attack swimmers. [Spanish *barracuda;* of uncertain origin.]

Barracuda

bar·rage[1] (bə räzh') *n.* **1.** heavy concentration of exploding shells, as from a number of cannon or mortars. **2.** any heavy concentration or massive outpouring: *a barrage of protest.* —*v.t.* **-raged, -rag·ing.** to subject to a barrage: *He was barraged with requests for autographs.* [From French *tir de barrage* curtain fire, from *barrage* barrier. See BARRAGE[2].]

bar·rage[2] (bär'ij) *n.* man-made bar in or across a watercourse; dam. [French *barrage* barrier, dam, from *barrer* to bar, from Old French *barre.* See BAR.]

Bar·ran·quil·la (bär'räng kē'yä) *n.* chief seaport of Colombia, in the northern part of the country. Pop. (1969 est.), 816,706.

bar·ra·try (bar'ə trē) *n.* **1.** fraud or negligence by captain or crew against the interest of the owner or insurer of a ship or its cargo, esp. destruction of the ship or cargo in order to collect insurance. **2.** the offense of repeatedly inciting quarrels or lawsuits. **3.** the offense of selling or buying positions of honor or profit, esp. in the church. [Old French *baraterie* deception, from *barater* to cheat. See BARTER.]

barred (bärd) *adj.* **1.** having bars: *a barred cell.* **2.** having stripes: *barred feathers.*

bar·rel (bar'əl) *n.* **1.a.** cylindrical wooden container having bulging sides and round, flat ends. It is made of staves bound by hoops. **b.** any of various other cylindrical containers: *an oil barrel, a trash barrel.* **2.** the capacity of a barrel, esp. a standard capacity used as a measure of weight or quantity, varying by country or commodity. See **weights and measures** for table. **3.** tube of a gun. **4.** any of various cylindrical parts or casings, esp. of mechanical devices: *a fountain-pen barrel, the barrel of a winch.* **5.** the hard, hollow part at the base of a feather. **6.** *Informal.* large quantity: *a barrel of laughs, a barrel of fun, a barrel of money.* **7. over a barrel.** in an awkward position; in a dilemma or quandary. —*v.t.* **-reled, -rel·ing;** *also, British.* **-relled, -rel·ling.** to put or pack in barrels. —*v.i.* *Informal.* to travel rapidly; move rapidly: *The train was barreling along.* [Old French *baril* cask, possibly from *barre* bar; in the sense that a barrel is constructed with "bars" of wood. See BAR.]

bar·rel·head (bar'əl hed') *n.* **1.** either round, flat end of a barrel. **2. on the barrelhead.** paying immediately and in full; without credit.

barrel organ, hand organ.

bar·ren (bar'ən) *adj.* **1.a.** having little or no vegetation; producing poor crops: *barren soil, the barren Siberian wastes.* **b.** desolate; bare; empty; dreary. **2.** incapable of reproduction; sterile: *a barren woman, a barren fruit tree.* **3.** not leading to any gain; fruitless; unprofitable: *barren endeavors, barren prospects.* **4. barren of.** devoid of; lacking in: *barren of interest, barren of any charm.* —*n., pl.* **barrens.** area of barren land. [Anglo-Norman *barai(g)ne* sterile; of uncertain origin.] —**bar'ren·ness,** *n.*

Syn. *adj.* **2. Barren, sterile** mean infertile or unfruitful. **Barren** denotes inability to produce fruit or offspring and is usually applied to the female of the species: *The barren woman adopted two children.* **Sterile** denotes lack of creative vigor because of some defect in the reproductive functions: *The worker bees are sterile.*

bar·rette (bə ret', bä-) *n.* clasp or clip, often in the shape of a bar, for holding the hair in place. [French *barrette,* diminutive of *barre.* See BAR.]

bar·ri·cade (bar'ə kād') *n.* **1.** hastily built rampart of make-shift materials, as in revolutionary street fighting: *to man the barricades.* **2.a.** temporary or hastily erected barrier of any kind: *a barricade of trucks across a highway, police barricades.* **b.** any barrier. —*v.t.* **-cad·ed, -cad·ing. 1.** to block; obstruct: *The way was barricaded with trees.* **2.** to shut in; close off; reinforce: *Barricade the doors with furniture. The rebels barricaded themselves in the center of the city.* [French *barricade* barrier, obstacle, from *barrique* barrel, from Spanish *barrica,* from *barril* cask, probably from *barra* bar; from the early use of *barrels* filled with earth and stones as makeshift ramparts in revolutionary street fighting in Paris. See BARREL.]

bar·ri·ca·do (bar'ə kā'dō) *pl.,* **-does.** *n. Archaic.* barricade.

Bar·rie, Sir James M. (bar'ē) 1860–1937, Scottish playwright and novelist.

bar·ri·er (bar'ē ər) *n.* **1.a.** something that blocks the way: *a defensive barrier, a mountain barrier.* **b.** something that restricts or hinders: *a barrier to industrial growth, a trade barrier.* **2.** something that divides or holds apart: *a highway barrier between opposing streams of traffic,*

at; āpe; cär; end; mē; it; īce; hot; ōld; fôrk; wood; fōōl; oil; out; up; ūse; turn; sing; thin; this; zh in treasure; ə in ago, taken, pencil, lemon, circus.

a barrier of mistrust between nations, language barrier. [Anglo-Norman *barrere* obstacle, from *barre.* See BAR.]

bar·ri·er reef 1. offshore coral reef roughly parallel to the shoreline, usually acting as a breakwater that leaves the landward channel, or lagoon, relatively still. It is the high outer edge of a coral shelf which, in turn, extends underwater from the shore. 2. any similar offshore reef, as of rock, usually acting as a breakwater.

bar·ring (bär'ing) *prep.* 1. excluding the possibility of: *Barring disaster, the ship will be docking here next week.* 2. with the exception of: *No one, barring the parties to the agreement, is to know of these plans.*

bar·ris·ter (bar'is tər) *n.* British lawyer who argues cases in court. Distinguished from solicitor. [BAR (the legal profession) + -STER.]

bar·room (bär'rōōm', -room') *n.* room or establishment having a bar where alcoholic drinks are sold.

bar·row¹ (bar'ō) *n.* 1. wheelbarrow. 2. handbarrow. [Old English *bearwe.*]

bar·row² (bar'ō) *n.* mound of earth or stones marking a prehistoric grave, esp. one in Britain. [Old English *beorg* hill, mound.]

Bar·row, Point (bar'ō) small Alaskan peninsula, northernmost point of the United States.

bar sinister, heraldic device erroneously supposed to indicate illegitimacy.

Bart., Baronet.

bar·tend·er (bär'ten'dər) *n.* one who makes and serves alcoholic drinks at a bar.

bar·ter (bär'tər) *v.t.* 1. to trade (goods for goods) without using money. 2. **to barter away.** to trade in return for something of less value. *– –v.i.* to engage in bartering goods. *—n.* 1. act or practice of bartering. 2. thing bartered. [Old French *barater* to exchange, cheat, from *barat* an exchange, cheating; possibly of Celtic origin.]

Bar·thol·di, Fre·de·ric Au·guste (bär thol'dē; frā'də rĕk'ō goost') 1834–1904, French sculptor.

Bar·thol·o·mew, Saint (bär thol'ə mū') one of the twelve Apostles.

bar·ti·zan (bär'ti zan, bär'ti zan') *n.* overhanging turret on a wall or tower. [Scottish *bartisane* parapet, going back to Old French *bretesque;* of uncertain origin.]

Bart·lett pear (bärt'lit) pear of a variety that is usually large, yellow, and juicy. [From Enoch *Bartlett,* 1779–1806, merchant who popularized it in the United States.]

Bar·tók, Be·la (bär'tok; bā'lə) 1881–1945, Hungarian composer and pianist.

Bar·ton, Clara (bärt'ən) 1821–1912, U.S. humanitarian and founder of the American Red Cross.

Bar·uch (bâr'ək) *n.* 1. book of the Old Testament Apocrypha. 2. this book's reputed author, who was the secretary and disciple of the Old Testament prophet Jeremiah.

bar·y·on (bar'ē on') *n.* any subatomic particle whose weight is equal to or greater than that of a proton. See **subatomic particle** for table. [Greek *barys* heavy.]

bar·y·tone (bar'ə tōn') baritone.

ba·sal (bā'səl, -zəl) *adj.* of or at the base; forming part or all of the base; fundamental. ▲ Basal is used most often in a scientific context or to give that effect; **basic** appears in both general and scientific contexts.

basal metabolism, amount of energy utilized by any organism when it is completely at rest. Basal metabolism is measured by the rate of oxygen consumption and heat output.

ba·salt (ba sôlt', bā'sôlt) *n.* dark, usually fine-grained volcanic rock, often found in striking columnar formations. [Latin *basaltēs* a variant of marble, form of *basanītēs (lapis)* touchstone, going back to Greek *basanos* touchstone.]

ba·sal·tic (bə sôl'tik) *adj.* of or like basalt.

bas·cule bridge (bas'kūl) drawbridge hinged at the bank so that it may be raised to allow ships to pass under it. [French *bascule* seesaw, from *battre* to beat (from Latin *battuere*) + *cul* backside (from Latin *cūlus*); influenced by French *bas* low.]

Bascule bridge

base¹ (bās) *n.* 1.a. part on which a thing rests or stands; underlying part that gives support: *a new base for a statue, a broad political base, a country's industrial base.* b. lowest part; bottom: *the base of a tree, the base of a mountain.* 2. main element or ingredient: *paint having an oil base.* 3. *Archaic.* fundamental principle; basis. 4.a. military area and facilities, esp. for particular purposes or activities; installation: *a training base, a supply base, a missile base.* b. any center of operations; headquarters. 5. *Chemistry.* a. compound that reacts with an acid to form a salt. b. compound capable of receiving protons from an acid.

c. compound able to give up an unshared pair of electrons to an acid. 6. *Mathematics.* fixed number from which all numbers in a numerical or logarithmic system are derived. Simple arithmetic is usually done in the decimal system, whose base is 10. Computers use the binary system, whose base is 2. 7.a. station, goal, or safety area in certain games. b. any of the four corners of the baseball diamond. 8. lower part of a column, building, or wall as a distinct architectural feature. 9. part of an organ in a plant or animal that is closest to the point of attachment to a larger or more central part: *the base of the thumb, the base of the skull.* 10. the line or plane in a geometrical figure on which it is thought to rest. 11. the form of a word to which affixes are added. *—v.t.* **based, bas·ing.** 1. to place on a basis or foundation: *Alice always bases her opinions on the facts.* 2. to derive from; model after: *to base a movie on a best seller.* 3. to locate; station: *to base troops in Europe.* [Latin *basis* foundation, pedestal, from Greek *basis* step, pedestal.]

Syn. *n.* 1. **Base, basis, foundation** denote the part which supports something. **Base** describes the bottom part which supports what is above it: *The lamp had a metal base.* **Basis** conveys the same idea of underlying support but is seldom applied to physical things: *The rumor had no basis.* **Foundation** refers to a solid groundwork on which something of greater magnitude is built and emphasizes permanence: *Mastery of the phonetic alphabet is a good foundation for learning to read.*

base² (bās) **bas·er, bas·est.** *adj.* 1. morally low; dishonorable; repugnant: *base motives.* 2. of low status; menial; degrading: *base servitude.* 3. (of coin) containing base metal; debased. 4. *Archaic.* Bastard. [Old French *bas* low, from Late Latin *bassus* low, short.] —**base'ly,** *adv.* —**base'ness,** *n.*

base·ball (bās'bôl') *n.* 1.a. game played with ball and bat between two teams, officially of nine players each, on a field having four bases that form a diamond. A player of the team at bat must hit the ball and reach at least first base without being put out. To score, he must then reach home base by way of second and third bases before he or his team are put out. b. any game played on a similar field with similar rules. 2. ball used in any of these games.

base·board (bās'bôrd') *n.* strip of board, molding, or the like at the bottom of a wall for covering the line where the wall meets the floor.

base·born (bās'bôrn') *adj.* 1. of humble birth. 2. born out of wedlock; illegitimate.

base·burn·er (bās'bur'nər) *n.* stove or furnace fed automatically from above as the fuel below is consumed.

base hit, the hitting of a pitched baseball by a batter in a way that enables him to get on base without benefit of an opponent's error and without anyone on his own team being forced out.

Ba·sel (bä'zəl) *also,* **Basle.** *n.* city in northwestern Switzerland, on the Rhine, Pop. (1969 est.), 213,200.

base·less (bās'lis) *adj.* having no basis in fact: *a baseless claim to fame.* —**Syn.** see **unfounded.**

base line 1. line serving as or representing a base. 2. *Baseball.* area within which a base runner must stay while running from one base to another. 3. line marking either end of a tennis or basketball court.

base·man (bās'mən) *pl.* **-men.** *n.* baseball player stationed near first, second, or third base. ▲ Now used only in the specific terms *first baseman, second baseman,* and *third baseman.*

base·ment (bās'mənt) *n.* 1. floor of a building below the ground floor. 2. lowest or fundamental portion of a structure, which serves as its support.

base metal, metal, such as iron or lead, that is not a precious metal.

ba·sen·ji (bə sen'jē) *n.* short-haired hound of a breed that originated in central Africa, usually having a reddish-brown or black coat with white markings. Does not bark but makes a chortling whine. Height: 17 inches at the shoulder. [Of Bantu origin.]

Basenji

base on balls, *Baseball.* walk.

base runner, member of the team at bat, who is on base or attempting to reach a base.

bas·es¹ (bā'siz) plural of **base**¹.

bas·es² (bā'sēz) plural of **basis.**

bash (bash) *v.t. Informal.* to strike with a smashing blow (often with *in*). *—n.* 1. *Informal.* such a blow. 2. *Slang.* exciting, lively party. 3. *British.* an attempt; try: *Have a bash at it.* [Possibly blend of BANG¹ and SMASH.]

ba·shaw (bə shô') *n.* 1. pasha. 2. important or pretentious person. [Form of PASHA.]

bash·ful (bash'fəl) *adj.* easily embarrassed; extremely modest; shy. [Short for ABASH + -FUL.] —**bash'ful·ly,** *adv.* —**bash'ful·ness,** *n.* —**Syn.** see **shy**¹.

ba·sic (bā'sik) *adj.* 1. of, at, or constituting the base; fundamental. 2. *Chemistry.* a. of or containing a base. b. alkaline. *—n. usually,* **basics.** that which is basic —**ba'si·cal·ly,** *adv.*

bas·il (baz′əl, bā′zəl) *n.* **1.** any of several aromatic plants, genus *Ocimum,* of the mint family, esp. the common cooking herb **sweet basil,** *O. basilicum,* whose dried leaves are used for seasoning food. **2.** the dried leaves themselves. [Old French *basile* the plant, from Late Latin *basilicum,* from Greek *basilikon (phyton)* literally, royal (plant); possibly because the plant was an ingredient in a medicine used by royalty.]

bas·i·lar (bas′ə lər) *adj.* of or at the base, esp. of the skull.

ba·sil·i·ca (bə sil′i kə) *n* **1.** in ancient Rome, a rectangular building composed of a broad central aisle ending in a semicircular area and separated from two or more side aisles by rows of columns. Basilicas were used chiefly for the transaction of business and the adjudication of legal matters. **2.** early Christian church built on the model of the Roman structure. [Latin *basilica* the building, from Greek *basilikē (oikia)* royal (house), palace.]

bas·i·lisk (bas′ə lisk′, baz′-) *n.* **1.** mythical monster that was supposedly hatched by a serpent from a rooster's egg and whose breath or gaze was deadly. Also, **cock′a·trice. 2.** any of a group of lizards of tropical America related to the iguanas and characterized by an inflatable sac upon the head and an erectile crest along the back and tail. [Latin *basiliscus* the mythical monster, from Greek *basiliskos* literally, little king (supposedly because it had a spot on its head resembling a crown).]

Bas·il the Great, Saint (baz′əl, bas′-) A.D. c.330–c.379, theologian and monastic leader of the Eastern Church, archbishop of Caesarea after 370.

ba·sin (bā′sin) *n.* **1.a.** a container that is usually round with a wide, flat bottom and sloping sides; shallow bowl, esp. for holding liquids. **b.** bathroom sink. **2.** contents or capacity of a basin. **3.** the entire region drained by a river and its tributaries. **4.** depression in the earth usually holding water, like a pond, but sometimes dry. [Old French *bacin* bowl, going back to Late Latin *bacca* water container; possibly of Celtic origin.]

bas·i·net (bas′ə net′) *n.* iron skullcap worn under the helmet in feudal Europe. It was gradually developed into a large headpiece with a movable facepiece or visor. [Old French *bacinet,* diminutive of *bacin* bowl. See BASIN.]

ba·sis (bā′sis) *pl.* **ba·ses.** *n.* **1.a.** fundamental supporting element; foundation; substance: *the basis of an argument.* **b.** underlying or guiding principle; premise. **2.** *Archaic.* base. [Latin *basis* foundation, pedestal, from Greek *basis* step, pedestal.] —**Syn. 1.a.** see **base**[1].

bask (bask) *v.i.* **1.** to lie and enjoy a warm glow: *to bask in the sun.* **2.** to take pleasure in favorable treatment or circumstances: *He basked in the glow of her smile.* [Of Scandinavian origin.]

bas·ket (bas′kit) *n.* **1.a.** container woven out of thin wooden strips, rods, or other flexible material: *a willow basket, a rope basket.* **b.** container made of thin wooden slats in which fruit, vegetables, or certain other foodstuffs are packed and shipped: *a bushel basket of peaches, a pint basket of strawberries.* **2.** something resembling a basket in shape or function: *the basket in a percolator, a wire bicycle basket.* **3.** amount contained in a basket. **4.a.** *Basketball.* the metal hoop and circular net through which the ball is thrown in order to score. **b.** any passing of the ball through the hoop. **c.** score, esp. the two-point score made when the ball is in open play. [Of uncertain origin.]

bas·ket·ball (bas′kit bôl′) *n.* **1.** game played with a large, air-filled ball on a hard-surface court between two teams, officially of five players each (for men) and six each (for women). To score, a player on one team must toss the ball through a raised basket at the opponent's end of the court. **2.** the ball used in this game.

basket case 1. person whose four limbs have all been amputated. **2.** *Informal.* completely incapable person.

bas·ket·ry (bas′ki trē) *n.* **1.** art or trade of weaving baskets. **2.** wickerwork.

basket weave, loose weave in cloth made by interlacing two or more threads at the same time. It resembles the weave in a basket.

bas·ket·work (bas′kit wurk′) *n.* wickerwork.

Basle (bäl) *n.* Basel.

Basque (bask) *n.* **1.** member of a people of uncertain origin living in the Pyrenees in southwestern France and in northern Spain. **2.** language of the Basque people, apparently having no relation to any other known language. **3.** **basque.** woman's close-fitting bodice that extends over the hips to form a short overskirt.

Bas·ra (bus′rə, bäs′-) *also,* **Bus·ra,** (-rə) *n.* port city in southeastern Iraq. Pop. (1965), 313,327.

bas-re·lief (bä′ri lēf′, bas′-) *n.* carving or sculpture on a flat surface, as a wall, in which the figures stand out only slightly from the background. Also, **low relief.** [French *bas-relief,* from Italian *basso rilievo,* going back to Late Latin *bassus* low + Latin *relevāre* to raise up.]

bass[1] (bās) *pl.* **bass·es.** *n.* **1.a.** lowest part in harmonic music. **b.** lower half of the audio frequency range. Opposed to **treble. 2.** lowest male singing voice. **3.** singer having such a voice. **4.** bass viol. —*adj.* **1.** able to sing or play bass: *a bass voice.* **2.** for the bass: *bass score.* **3.** having the lowest range in a class of instruments: *bass trombone.* **4.** deep or low in sound: *the bass rumble of thunder.* [Form of BASE[2]; influenced in spelling by Italian *basso* low.]

bass[2] (bas) *pl.* **bass·es** *or* **bass.** *n.* any of various edible fresh or saltwater fish, esp. of the families Serranidae and Centrarchidae. Some marine species, as the sea bass, are caught commercially for food; certain freshwater bass, as the **large-mouthed bass** and the **striped bass,** are highly favored game fish. [Modification of dialectal English *barse* perch, from Old English *bærs.*]

bass[3] (bas) *n.* **1.** basswood or linden. **2.** bast. [Modification of BAST.]

bass clef (bās) clef placed on the fourth line of the staff, indicating that that line corresponds to the note F below middle C. Also, **F clef.** See clef for illustration.

bass drum (bās) drum of the largest type. It gives off a deep, booming sound and is usually held so that both sides can be beaten.

bass horn (bās) tuba.

bas·si·net (bas′ə net′) *n.* **1.** basketlike cradle, often on legs and hooded at one end, used esp. for newborn babies. **2.** perambulator resembling this. [French *bassinet* small basin, diminutive of *bassin* basin, from Old French *bacin.* See BASIN.]

bas·so (bas′ō, bä′sō) *pl.* **bas·sos.** *n.* bass singer, voice, or part. [Italian *basso* low, from Late Latin *bassus.*]

bas·soon (bə soon′) *n.* wind instrument with a low range, the bass of the woodwind family, having a wooden tube so long that it doubles back on itself. It is played from the side through a curved metal mouthpiece containing the reed. [French *basson,* from Italian *bassone,* from *basso* low, from Late Latin *bassus.*]

bass vi·ol (bās′ vī′əl) the largest stringed instrument. It is shaped like a violin and gives a deep, thrumming sound when played by hand, as in jazz and popular music. When played with a bow, as in classical music, it sounds like a very deep cello. Also, **double bass, con′tra-bass′, string bass, bass fiddle, bass.**

bass·wood (bas′wood′) *n.* **1.** any of the several species of linden, genus *Tilia,* that grow in North America, esp. *T. americana.* Also, **lime, white′wood′. 2.** wood of such a tree, widely used in cabinetmaking and millwork. [BASS[3] + WOOD.]

bast (bast) *n.* **1.** strong, flexible fibers obtained from the inner bark of several trees and from the stems or leaves of certain plants, used esp. in making cloth, rope, and heavy paper. **2.** phloem. [Old English *bæst* inner bark.]

bas·tard (bas′tərd) *n.* **1.** illegitimate child. **2.** something irregular, inferior, or counterfeit. —*adj.* **1.** illegitimate in birth. **2.** not genuine or standard; counterfeit; inferior: *bastard hopes. He speaks a bastard French.* **3.** abnormal or irregular in shape, size, or proportion. [Old French *bastard* illegitimate child, equivalent to Old French *fils de bast* child of a packsaddle (implying out of the marriage bed), from *bast* packsaddle, from Late Latin *bastum;* of uncertain origin.] —**bas′tard·y,** *n.*

bas·tard·ize (bas′tər dīz′) **-ized, -iz·ing.** *v.t.* **1.** to lower or corrupt in condition or worth; debase. **2.** to declare (someone) to be of illegitimate birth. —*v.i.* to become debased. —**bas′tard·i·za′tion,** *n.*

baste[1] (bāst) **bast·ed, bast·ing.** *v.t.* to apply melted butter, gravy, or other liquid to (food) while cooking: *She used a large spoon to baste the turkey.* [Of uncertain origin.]

baste[2] (bāst) **bast·ed, bast·ing.** *v.t.* to sew with temporary stitches: *to baste a hem.* [Old French *bastir;* of Germanic origin.]

baste[3] (bāst) **bast·ed, bast·ing.** *v.t. Informal.* **1.** to beat soundly; thrash. **2.** to scold or abuse vigorously; berate. [Old Norse *beysta* to beat.]

Bas·tille (bas tēl′) *n.* **1.** fortress in Paris used as a prison before the French Revolution. Its destruction by the people on July 14, 1789, was one of the opening acts of the revolution. **2. bastille.** *also,* **bas·tile.** *Archaic.* prison. [Old French *bastille* fortress, from *bastir* to build; of Germanic origin.]

bas·ti·na·do (bas′tə nā′dō) *pl.* **-does.** *n.* **1.** blow or beating with a

Basilica

Basilisk

at; āpe; cär; end; mē; it; īce; hot; ōld; fôrk; wood; fŏŏl; oil; out; up; ūse; turn; sing; thin; this; zh in treasure; ə in ago, taken, pencil, lemon, circus.

stick, esp. on the soles of the feet. 2. stick; cudgel. —v.t., -doed, -do-
ing. to beat with a stick, esp. on the soles of the feet. [Spanish *bastonada*
blow with a cudgel, from *baston* cudgel, from Late Latin *bastum* stick.
See BATON.]

bas·tion (bas'chən, -tē ən) n. 1. part of
a rampart or fortification projecting
from the main body and forming an irregular pentagon. 2. any fortified or
firmly established place or position;
stronghold: *a bastion of academic freedom.* [French *bastion*, from *bastille.* See
BASTILLE.] —**bas'tioned,** adj.

Bastions

Ba·su·to·land (bə sōō'tō land') n.
see Lesotho.

bat¹ (bat) n. 1. wooden stick or club,
esp. one used for hitting the ball in baseball and other games. 2. act
of batting. 3. right or turn to bat. 4. *Informal.* blow. 5. *Slang.* spree;
binge. 6. **at bat.** in the act or position of batting. 7. **to go to bat for.**
Informal. to intercede for; defend. —v.i., **bat·ted, bat·ting.** 1. to use
a bat in baseball and other games. 2. to take a turn at bat: *He bats next.*
—v.t. 1. to hit with or as with a bat. 2. to have a batting average of
(a certain figure): *to bat .319 for
the season.* [Old English *batt*
cudgel, club.]

bat² (bat) n. 1. any of numerous
mouselike mammals, with winglike membranes supported by
elongated forelimbs, order Chiroptera. They are the only flying
mammals. Many bats, though
they can see, guide themselves by

Bat²

a kind of natural radar by which
the echo of their ultrasonic cries indicates the size and position of an
object. Wingspan: 2 inches to 5 feet. 2. **blind as a bat.** having very poor
vision; nearly or totally blind. 3. **to have bats in one's (or the) belfry.**
Slang. to be crazy. [Of Scandinavian origin.]

bat³ (bat) **bat·ted, bat·ting.** v.t. 1. to flutter; wink: *to bat
one's eyelashes.* 2. **to not bat an eye (or eyelash).** to fail to show any
emotion or surprise. [Old French *batre* to beat, from Latin *battuere.*]

bat., abbreviation.

Ba·taan (bə tän', -tan') n. peninsula in the Philippines, west of Manila, where U.S. troops surrendered to the Japanese in 1942.

Ba·ta·vi·a (bə tā'vē ə) n. see Djakarta.

batch (bach) n. 1. number of persons or things taken together; group:
a batch of newspapers, a batch of recruits. 2. quantity produced or done
at one time: *He just finished grading a batch of papers.* 3. quantity of
material prepared or required for one operation: *a batch of dough, a
batch of cement.* 4. amount baked at one time. [Middle English *bacche*
a baking, going back to Old English *bacan* to bake.]

bate (bāt) **bat·ed, bat·ing.** v.t.,v.i. 1. *Archaic.* to diminish or lessen;
abate. 2. **with bated breath.** with breath checked or held because of
anticipation, fear, or excitement: *I waited for his arrival with bated
breath.* [Short for ABATE.]

ba·teau (ba tō') n. any of various lightweight,
flat-bottomed boats used chiefly in the United States and Canada, esp.
one having flaring sides and a pointed bow and stern. [French *bateau*
boat, going back to Old English *bāt.*]

bath (bath, bäth) pl., **baths** (ba*th*z, bä*th*z). n. 1. the washing or immersing of something, esp. the body, in water or other liquid: *Give the dog
a bath.* 2. water or other liquid used for bathing: *His bath was too hot.*
3. container for such liquid: *Clean out the bath when you're done.*
4. room equipped for bathing; bathroom: *a room and bath.* 5. set of
rooms or building for bathing: *the public baths of the ancient Romans.*
6. also, **baths.** resort where bathing is part of a medical treatment; spa.
7. solution or other preparation in which something is immersed for
chemical treatment: *an electrolytic bath.* [Old English *bæth* washing of
the body, liquid for bathing.]

Bath (bath, bäth) n. historic city in southwestern England, once famous as a health resort. Pop. (1963 est.), 82,600.

bathe (bā*th*) **bathed, bath·ing.** v.i. 1. to take a bath. 2. to go into a
body of water, as the ocean, to swim for pleasure or cool oneself; go
swimming. 3. to become covered or enveloped as if with liquid.
—v.t. 1. to immerse in liquid to clean; give a bath to: *to bathe a baby.*
2. to wash or moisten with water or other liquid to cleanse or heal: *to
bathe the eyes, to bathe a wound.* 3. to make wet; moisten. 4. to cover
or envelop as if with liquid: *He pulled a switch and the stage was bathed
in light.* [Old English *bathian* to wash.] —**bath'er,** n.

ba·thet·ic (bə thet'ik) adj. characterized by bathos.

bath·house (bath'hous', bäth'-) n. 1. building equipped for bathing.
2. building having dressing rooms for swimmers.

bathing suit, a garment worn while swimming; swimsuit.

ba·thos (bā'thos) n. 1. sudden and ludicrous descent from the elevated
to the commonplace in speech or writing; anticlimax, for example: *The
senator pledged to oppose war, fight poverty, protect individual freedom,
and name a new state flower.* 2. triteness or dullness. 3. insincere or
excessive pathos; sentimentality. [Greek *bathos* depth.]

bath·robe (bath'rōb', bäth'-) n. loose, coatlike garment worn before
and after bathing or for lounging.

bath·room (bath'rōōm', -room', bäth'-) n. room usually equipped
with a toilet, sink, and a bathtub or shower.

bath salts, crystals or flakes of a salt used in bath water to perfume
and soften the skin.

Bath-she·ba (bath shē'bə, bath'shə-) n. in the Old Testament, the
wife of King David and mother of King Solomon. David married her
after he had sent her husband Uriah to death in battle.

bath·tub (bath'tub', bäth'-) n. tub in which to bathe, esp. one permanently fixed in a bathroom.

Bath·urst (bath'ərst) n. capital of Gambia, in the western part of the
country. Pop. (1967 est.), 31,800.

bath·y·scaph (bath'i skaf') also, **bath·y·scaphe** (bath'i skāf',
-skaf') n. craft for deep-sea exploration, consisting of a thick-walled
steel sphere suspended beneath a large hull. The crew and scientific
instruments are carried in the sphere and the hull is filled with gasoline,
which makes it buoyant. A bathyscaph has electric motors that enable
it to move horizontally. [Greek *bathys* deep + *skaphē* light boat.]

bath·y·sphere (bath'i sfēr') n. hollow, watertight steel globe having
heavy quartz observation windows and made to withstand great pressure, used for undersea exploration. A bathysphere is suspended by
cable from a surface vessel and cannot move independently. [Greek
bathys deep + *sphaira* ball, globe.]

ba·tik (bə tēk', bat'ik) n. 1. method of hand printing colored designs
on cloth by putting a wax coating on those parts which are not to be
dyed. 2. cloth decorated by this method. [Javanese *'mbatik* wax painting.]

ba·tiste (bə tēst') n. any of several fine, soft, sheer fabrics of plain
weave, made of cotton or other fibers. [French *batiste;* probably from
Baptiste of Cambrai, France, a thirteenth-century
weaver who is believed to have invented the fabric.]

ba·ton (bə ton', ba-) n. 1. wand with which a
conductor directs a musical performance. 2. rod
with a knob at one or both ends, as used by a drum
major. 3. short staff or truncheon used as a symbol
of office, command, or authority: *a field marshal's
baton.* 4. band on an escutcheon that is considered
a mark of illegitimacy in English heraldry. Also
(def. 4), **baton sinister.** [French *bâton* stick, from
Old French *baston,* from Late Latin *bastum;* of uncertain origin.]

Baton
(def. 4)

Bat·on Rouge (bat'ən rōōzh') capital of
Louisiana, in the south-central part of the state. Pop. (1970), 165,963.

ba·tra·chi·an (bə trā'kē ən) n. frog or toad. —adj. of or relating to
amphibians, esp. frogs and toads. [Greek *bátrachos* frog + -IAN.]

bats·man (bats'mən) pl., **-men.** n. batter, esp. in cricket.

bat·tal·ion (bə tal'yən) n. 1. military unit composed of two or more
companies or comparable units and a headquarters company and forming part of a brigade or regiment. 2. large group or force; host: *battalions of protesters, battalions of ants.* [French *battaillon,* from Italian
battaglione unit of an army, from *battaglia* battle, going back to Late
Latin *battuālia.* See BATTLE.]

bat·ten¹ (bat'ən) *Archaic.* v.i. to grow fat by or as by feeding; thrive.
—v.t. to make fat. [Old Norse *batna* to get better.]

bat·ten² (bat'ən) n. 1. piece of sawed timber used esp. for flooring.
2. light strip of wood used in construction, as to cover or reinforce
a joint between boards. 3. *Nautical.* long, narrow strip of wood or metal
used for various purposes, as to secure a tarpaulin over a hatch.
—v.t. 1. to fasten, furnish, or strengthen with battens. 2. **to batten down
the hatches. a.** *Nautical.* to fasten one or more tarpaulins over a ship's
hatches, esp. in preparation for bad weather. **b.** to prepare for any
difficult or trying situation. [Form of BATON.]

bat·ter¹ (bat'ər) v.t. 1. to strike with heavy, repeated blows.
2. to subject to rough, bruising usage; shatter; damage: *The winds
battered the trees.* —v.i. to deal heavy, repeated blows; pound; hammer:
He battered away at the door. [From BAT¹ + -ER¹.]

bat·ter² (bat'ər) n. mixture of flour, liquid, and other ingredients
beaten together, prepared for use in cooking and thin enough to be
poured or stirred. [Probably from BATTER¹.]

bat·ter³ (bat'ər) n. player who is batting or whose turn it is to bat
in baseball, softball, or cricket. [BAT¹ + -ER¹.]

battering ram, ancient military machine, esp. a long, massive beam,
used for battering down walls or gates.

bat·ter·y (bat'ər ē) pl., **-ter·ies.** n. 1. *Electricity.* cell or group of cells
producing and storing direct current by means of a chemical reaction.

2. group of things that are similar or related to one another and are assembled or used as a unit: *a battery of lights, to run through a battery of tests.* **3.** *Military.* **a.** two or more guns or other weapons operating as a unit. **b.** these guns or other weapons together with the men and equipment for them. **c.** the men operating these weapons. **4.** *Law.* unlawful beating, touching, or physical constraint of another person. Distinguished from *assault.* **5.** *Baseball.* pitcher and the catcher who is receiving his pitched balls. **6.** *Archaic.* platform or fortification on which artillery is mounted. [French *batterie* beating, from *battre* to beat, from Latin *battuere*.]

bat·ting (bat′ing) *n.* **1.** act or manner of using a bat, esp. in a game of ball. **2.** cotton or wool fibers that have been pressed into sheets or layers, used esp. in bandaging wounds or as padding for upholstery or quilts.

batting average, mathematical average indicating the hitting ability of a baseball player, obtained by dividing the number of base hits by the number of official times at bat and carrying the result to three decimal places.

bat·tle (bat′əl) *n.* **1.** fight between opposing armed forces, on land, at sea, or in the air: *The battle raged almost three days.* **2.** any fight or contest; conflict; struggle: *a battle against the elements, a battle for the custody of a child.* —*v.i.* **-tled, -tling. 1.** to engage in fighting: *The armies battled on the beach.* **2.** to struggle; contend: *to battle against temptation.* —*v.t.* to fight or struggle against: *The ship battled the waves.* [Old French *bataille* a fight, going back to Late Latin *battuālia* fighting exercises, from Latin *battuere* to beat.] —**bat′tler,** *n.*

bat·tle-ax (bat′əl aks′) *also,* **bat·tle-axe.** *n.* **1.** wide-bladed ax, formerly used as a weapon in war. Also, **broadax.** *n.* **2.** *Slang.* quarrelsome, domineering woman.

battle cruiser, cruiser (def. 1).

battle cry 1. shout or cry of troops in battle; war cry. **2.** motto or slogan used in any contest or conflict: *"Down with poverty" was their battle cry.*

bat·tle·dore (bat′əl dôr′) *n.* *Archaic.* small racket used to hit a shuttlecock. [Middle English *batyldore,* from Provençal *batedor* implement for beating laundry, from *batre* to beat, from Latin *battuere;* influenced by BATTLE.]

battle fatigue, type of hysteria or psychoneurosis arising during combat and often marked by depression, loss of self-control, and great anxiety. Also, **combat fatigue.**

bat·tle·field (bat′əl fēld′) *n.* scene of a battle: *The wounded lay everywhere upon the battlefield. His mind was a battlefield of conflicting thoughts.* Also, **bat′tle·ground′.**

bat·tle·ment (bat′əl mənt) *n.* parapet having a series of indentations along its upper edge, used originally for defense and later for ornamentation. —**bat·tle·ment·ed** (bat′əl men′tid), *adj.* [Old French *batailler* to fortify with battlements, from *bataille.* See BATTLE.]

battle royal 1. severe fight or struggle: *The police and the pickets had quite a battle royal.* **2.** vehement, heated argument: *The discussion soon became a battle royal.*

bat·tle-scarred (bat′əl skärd′) *adj.* **1.** scarred from wounds received in or as in battle: *a battle-scarred veteran.* **2.** showing the effects of many trying experiences or much hard usage: *a battle-scarred marriage, a battle-scarred desk.*

bat·tle·ship (bat′əl ship′) *n.* any of a class of heavily armored warships having the most powerful guns afloat.

battle wagon *Slang.* battleship.

bat·tue (ba tōō′, -tū′) *n.* **1.** act of beating the bushes and making loud noises to drive game out toward hunters. **2.** hunt in which this is done. **3.** wholesale slaughter, esp. of defenseless crowds. [French *battue* beating, from *battre* to beat, going back to Latin *battuere.*]

bat·ty (bat′ē) *-ti·er, -ti·est.* *adj.* *Slang.* crazy. [From *to have bats in one's belfry.* See BAT².]

Ba·tu·mi (bä tōō′mē) *n.* port city in the southwestern Soviet Union, in Georgia, on the Black Sea. Pop. (1970), 101,000. Also, **Ba·tum′.**

bau·ble (bô′bəl) *n.* **1.** showy, worthless trinket; trifle: *cheap bracelets and other baubles.* **2.** *Archaic.* jester's staff. [Old French *ba(u)bel* toy; of uncertain origin.]

Bau·cis (bô′sis) *n.* *Classical Mythology.* aged Phrygian woman who, along with her husband Philemon, was rewarded for showing hospitality to the disguised gods Zeus and Hermes.

Bau·de·laire, Charles (bōd′əl âr′) 1821–67, French poet and critic.

baulk (bôk) *balk.*

baux·ite (bôk′sīt, bō′zīt) *n.* claylike substance composed of several hydrous aluminum oxides. It is the chief ore of aluminum. [French *bauxite;* from Les *Baux,* a town in southeastern France where it was first found.]

Ba·var·i·a (bə vâr′ē ə) *n.* largest state of West Germany, in the southeastern part of the country. Area, 27,239 sq. mi. Pop. (1968 est.), 10,405,600. —**Ba·var′i·an,** *adj., n.*

baw·bee (bô bē′, bô′bē) *n.* *Scottish.* halfpenny.

bawd (bôd) *n.* **1.** prostitute. **2.** *Archaic.* one who runs a brothel. [Possibly from Old French *baud* bold; of Germanic origin.]

bawd·ry (bôd′rē) *n.* *Archaic.* obscenity or lewdness, esp. in language.

bawd·y (bô′dē) **bawd·i·er, bawd·i·est.** *adj.* indecent or lewd; obscene. —**bawd′i·ly,** *adv.* —**bawd′i·ness,** *n.*

bawd·y·house (bô′dē hous′) *n.* brothel.

bawl (bôl) *v.i.* **1.** to weep or sob loudly; wail: *The child bawled when his mother left him.* **2.** to shout or yell; bellow: *He bawled at them for coming in late.* —*v.t.* **1.** to call out or proclaim noisily; shout: *He bawled his orders at them.* **2. to bawl out.** *Informal.* to scold or reprimand severely. —*n.* loud shout or outcry: *He let out a bawl of rage.* [Possibly of Scandinavian origin.]

bay¹ (bā) *n.* arm of a sea or lake extending into the land; broad inlet. [Old French *baie,* from Spanish *bahia;* possibly of Iberian origin.]

bay² (bā) *n.* **1.** *Architecture.* **a.** space or section of a wall or building that separates the whole into corresponding parts, as that between two columns. **b.** internal recessed space forming an outward projection in a wall and containing a window or set of windows. **2.** compartment or area in a ship or aircraft that is used for a particular purpose. **3.** compartment in a barn for storing hay or grain. [Old French *baee* opening, from *baer* to stand open, from Late Latin *badāre* to gape; of uncertain origin.]

bay³ (bā) *n.* **1.** deep, prolonged barking of a dog or other canine animal: *the bay of the hounds.* **2.** position of or as of a cornered animal who is forced to turn and confront its pursuers: *The boar stood at bay. The police brought the convict to bay.* **3.** state of being held off by or as by one's quarry: *The bronco kept the cowboys at bay.* —*v.i.* to bark with a deep, prolonged howl: *a wolf baying at the moon.* —*v.t.* to utter or express by or as by such barking: *The dogs bayed their anger.* [Old French *(a)bai* barking, from *(a)baiier* to bark; possibly imitative.] —Syn. *v.i.* see bark².

bay⁴ (bā) *n.* **1.** small, ornamental tree, *Laurus nobilis,* of the laurel family, widely cultivated in Europe and the Americas, having stiff lance-shaped leaves, purple berries, and yellowish flowers. Also, **laur′el, sweet bay. 2.** any of various shrubs or trees resembling the laurel. [Old French *baie* berry, from Latin *bāca.*]

bay⁵ (bā) *n.* **1.** reddish-brown color. **2.** horse or other animal of this color. —*adj.* (of horses and other animals) reddish-brown. [Old French *bai* bay-colored, from Latin *badius.*]

bay·ber·ry (bā′ber′ē) *pl.,* **-ries.** *n.* **1.** North American shrub, *Myrica pensylvanica,* having fragrant oblong leaves and pale-blue, wax-coated berries. **2.** the small, round berry itself, used for making scented soaps and fragrant candles. **3.** tropical American tree, *Pimenta racemosa,* of the myrtle family, having large leathery leaves that yield an oil used in making bay rum.

Bay City, port city in eastern Michigan. Pop. (1960), 53,604.

Ba·yeux Tapestry (bä yōō′, bī′-) medieval embroidery believed to date from the eleventh century that depicts events leading to and including the Norman Conquest of England. [From *Bayeux,* the French town in which it is kept.]

bay leaf, dried, spicy leaf of the laurel tree, used as a seasoning in cooking.

bay·o·net (bā′ə nit, -net′) *n.* large knife or dagger that can be attached to the muzzle of a rifle and used for stabbing or slashing in hand-to-hand fighting. —*v.t.* **-net·ed, -net·ing.** to stab or slash with or as with a bayonet. [French *baïonnette* a knife, from *Bayonne,* a French city where bayonets were first made.]

Ba·yonne (bā ōn′) *n.* city in northeastern New Jersey. Pop. (1970), 72,743.

bay·ou (bī′ōō, bī′ō) *pl.,* **-ous.** *n.* marshy, sluggish, sometimes stagnant inlet, branch, or overflowing of a river or gulf, esp. in the southern United States. [French *bayou,* from Choctaw *bayuk* stream.]

Bay·reuth (bī roit′) *n.* city in east-central West Germany, famous for its annual Wagnerian music festival. Pop. (1963 est.), 61,600.

bay rum, fragrant liquid used in cosmetics and medicines, originally distilled from the leaves of the bayberry tree, but now prepared from a mixture of essential oils, alcohol, and water.

Bay State, Massachusetts.

Bay² (def. 1a)

Embrasure   **Merlons**

Battlement

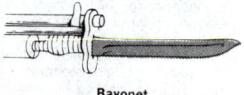

Bayonet

at; āpe; cär; end; mē; it; īce; hot; ōld; fôrk; wood; fōōl; oil; out; up; ūse; turn; sing; thin; **this;** zh in treasure; ə in ago, taken, pencil, lemon, circus.

bay window 1. window or set of windows projecting outward from the wall of a building and forming a recess within. 2. *Slang.* large protruding belly, esp. of a man; paunch.

ba·zaar (bə zär′) *also,* **ba·zar.** *n.* 1. sale of miscellaneous articles for some special purpose: *a charity bazaar.* 2. place for the sale of a variety of goods. 3. in Middle and Far Eastern countries, marketplace or street lined with shops or stalls. [Persian *bāzār* market.]

ba·zoo·ka (bə zoō′kə) *n.* portable tube-shaped weapon used for firing armor-piercing rockets, esp. against tanks. [From its resemblance to the *bazooka,* a long, slender musical instrument invented and named by the American comedian Bob Burns, 1890–1956, probably from (slang) bazoo mouth; of uncertain origin.]

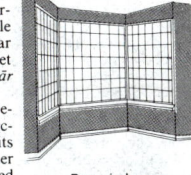

Bay window

BB *pl.,* **BB's.** *n.* small shot, 0.18 inches in diameter, used esp. in a type of air rifle.

BBC, British Broadcasting Corporation.

BB gun, air rifle that uses BB's.

bbl. *pl.,* **bbls.** barrel.

B.C. 1. before Christ. 2. British Columbia.

bd. 1. board. 2. bond. 3. bound.

bd. ft., board foot; board feet.

bdl., bundle.

be (bē) been, be·ing. Present indicative: *sing.,* first person, am; second, are or *(archaic)* art; third, is; *pl.,* are. Past indicative: *sing.,* first person, was; second, were or *(archaic)* wast or *art;* third, was; *pl.,* were. Present subjunctive: be. Past subjunctive: were. *v.i.* **1.a.** to live or exist: *There once was a princess. There is much evidence against you.* **b.** to take place; happen; occur: *The wedding was last month. It had to be.* **c.** to occupy a place, situation, or position: *Your coat is on the chair. He is in debt.* **d.** to remain or continue as before: *Let me be.* **e.** *Archaic.* to belong or attend; befall: *Peace be with you.* **2.a.** used to link the subject with its predicate adjective or nominative to describe, identify, or amplify the subject: *John is tall. Let x be 10. She was president last year.* **b.** used to form or introduce interrogative or imperative sentences: *Is that true? Be still!* **c.** used to form participial and infinitive phrases: *the sorrow of being lonely. He is to blame.* **3.a.** used with the present participle of another verb to express continuous or progressive action: *He is talking. They are building a dam.* **b.** used with the past participle of a transitive verb to form the passive voice: *It is being washed. The book was found by the teacher.* **c.** used with the infinitive or participle of another verb to express future time, duty, possibility, or purpose: *They were to appear before him. She is visiting them tomorrow.* **d.** used with the past participles of intransitive verbs to form the perfect tense: *I am done. They were gone.* [Old English *bēon.*]

Be, beryllium.

be- *prefix* 1. throughout; all around; all over: *besiege, besprinkle.* 2. about: *bemoan.* 3. make; cause to be: *betroth, bedazzle.* 4. furnish with: *bejewel, bespeckled.* [Old English *be-* about, unstressed form of *bi* by.]

beach (bēch) *n.* gently sloping shore of an ocean or other body of water, esp. that part covered by sand or pebbles. —*v.t., v.i.* to run or haul (a boat) up onto a beach. [Of uncertain origin.]

Syn. *n.* Beach, coast, shore[1] denote land along a large body of water. **Beach** denotes a level stretch of sandy land along the sea: *Children build sand castles on the beach.* **Coast** denotes the broad expanse of land along the sea regarded as a border: *The hurricane struck the coast of Florida.* **Shore** denotes land abutting on a sea, lake, or river: *Palm trees dotted the shore of the lake.*

beach·comb·er (bēch′kō′mər) *n.* 1. vagrant or loafer who lives on the seashore. 2. long wave that rolls in from the ocean and onto the beach.

beach·head (bēch′hed′) *n.* 1. area on an enemy shore first seized and held to secure further operations. 2. initial advance position or foothold; breakthrough: *The new vaccine established a beachhead in the fight against malaria.*

bea·con (bē′kən) *n.* 1. guiding or warning signal, esp. a light or fire. 2. lighthouse, buoy, or other object placed so as to guide or warn mariners. 3. radio beacon. 4. something that warns, signals, or guides. —*v.t.* 1. to furnish or mark with beacons. 2. to guide or warn by or as by beacons. —*v.i.* to serve or shine as a beacon. [Old English *bēacen* sign, signal.]

Bea·cons·field, Earl of (bē′kənz fēld′, bek′ənz-) see **Disraeli, Benjamin.**

bead (bēd) *n.* 1. small, pierced ball or piece of wood, glass, or other material, used for decoration or other purposes: *the beads of an abacus.*

Bazooka

She sewed white beads on her sweater. 2. **beads.** **a.** necklace of beads. **b.** rosary. 3. any small, roundish body: *Beads of sweat formed on his brow.* 4. small, metal knob used as the front sight of a gun. 5. *Architecture.* small, convex molding, often cut in the form of a string of beads. 6. **to draw a bead on.** to take careful aim at. 7. **to tell (count or say) one's beads.** to say prayers, esp. with a rosary. —*v.t.* to furnish or decorate with beads or beading: *The dressmaker beaded the dress.* —*v.i.* to collect in beads or drops: *Water beaded on the side of the glass.* [Old English *(ge)bed* prayer; later applied to rosary beads used in prayer and then to small balls or jewels strung together as ornaments.]

bead·ing (bē′ding) *n.* 1. decorative work made of or with beads. 2. material consisting of or decorated with beads. 3. lace or embroidery having open work through which ribbon may be run. 4. *Architecture.* narrow, convex molding.

bea·dle (bēd′l) *n.* 1. in the Church of England, a lay officer having such duties as ushering and keeping order during services. 2. minor official in a synagogue. [Middle English *bedel* herald, from Old French *bedel;* of Germanic origin.]

bead·work (bēd′wurk′) *n.* 1. decorative work made of or with beads. 2. *Architecture.* beads collectively.

bead·y (bē′dē) **bead·i·er, bead·i·est.** *adj.* 1. (of eyes) small, round, and glittering. 2. covered with or full of beads.

bea·gle (bē′gəl) *n.* smooth-coated hound having short legs, drooping ears, and usually white, tan, and black markings. Height: 9–15 inches at the shoulder. [Possibly from Old French *bee-gueule* noisy person; literally, open throat, going back to Late Latin *badāre* to gape + Latin *gula* throat; said to refer to the loud bark of this breed.]

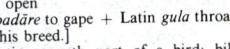

Beagle

beak (bēk) *n.* 1. horny, projecting mouth part of a bird; bill. 2. similar rigid, projecting part in other animals, as the horny jaws of turtles and certain cephalopods. 3. something resembling a bird's beak, as the spout of a pitcher or the pointed end of an anvil. 4. pointed projection at the prow of an ancient warship, used to ram or pierce enemy ships. 5. *Slang.* person's nose, esp. if large or prominent. [Old French *bec* bird's bill, from Latin *beccus;* of Celtic origin.] —**beaked,** *adj.* —**Syn.** 1. see **bill**[2].

beak·er (bē′kər) *n.* 1. cylindrical vessel of glass or other material, often having a lip for pouring, used esp. in laboratories. 2. large drinking cup or goblet with a wide mouth. 3. contents of a beaker. [Old Norse *bikarr* cup, from Late Latin *bīcārium* goblet, possibly from Greek *bīkos* jar.]

Beaks

beam (bēm) *n.* 1. large, heavy piece of wood, steel, or other material, used in construction: *At least ten beams were needed for the barn's frame.* 2. ray or shaft, as of light: *an x-ray beam. The sun's beams warmed us.* 3. *Nautical.* **a.** one of the heavy pieces of timber stretching across a ship to support the decks and stay the sides. **b.** greatest width of a ship. **c.** side of a ship, or the direction at right angles to the keel. 4. continuous radio signal transmitted in one direction to guide pilots. 5. suggestion or hint; gleam: *a beam of hope.* 6. transverse bar of a balance, from which the scales are suspended. 7. horizontal part of a plow from which the handles and share are attached and by which it is pulled. 8. *Slang.* hips or buttocks: *She is broad in the beam.* 9. **off the beam.** **a.** not following the course indicated by a radio beam. **b.** *Informal.* wrong; incorrect. 10. **on the beam.** **a.** following the course indicated by a radio beam. **b.** at right angles with a ship's keel. **c.** *Informal.* just right; correct. —*v.t.* 1. to emit in or as in beams or rays: *She beamed affection.* 2. to direct or transmit a broadcast or radio signal. 3. to guide (an airplane) by radio beams: *They beamed her down safely.* —*v.i.* 1. to shine brightly; radiate: *The sun beamed down. Her face beamed with smiles.* 2. to smile radiantly or joyfully: *The actress beamed with happiness as she accepted the award.* [Old English *bēam* tree, ray.]

Beaker

Syn. *n.* 2. Beam, ray[1] denote a shaft of light. **Beam** describes a long and wide column of light: *The beams of the searchlights scanned the sky.* **Ray** suggests a narrow beam of light which emanates from a radiant center or source: *When he opened the curtains the sun's rays streamed into the room.*

beam-ends (bēm′endz′) *n.* 1. ends of a ship's beams. 2. **on her**

at; āpe; cär; end; mē; it; īce; hot; ōld; fôrk; wood; fōōl; oil; out; up; ūse; turn; sing; thin; this; zh in treasure; ə in ago, taken, pencil, lemon, circus.

83

beam-ends. (of a ship) tipped so far over that the beams are almost vertical; almost capsizing.

beam·ing (bē'ming) *adj.* bright; shining; radiant: *a beaming smile, a beaming face.* —**beam'ing·ly,** *adv.*

bean (bēn) *n.* **1.** seed of any of various plants of the pea family, some varieties of which are edible, esp. genera *Phaseolus* or *Vicia.* **2.** elongated pod containing several such seeds. The pods of some varieties are cooked and eaten as a vegetable with the seed still inside. **3.** plant that produces these pods. **4.** beanlike seed of various other unrelated plants, as the coffee bean and the cacao bean. **5.** *Slang.* head. **6. to spill the beans.** *Informal.* to reveal a secret, esp. unintentionally. —*v.t. Slang.* to hit on the head, esp. with a pitched baseball. [Old English *bēan* common leguminous plant or its seed.]

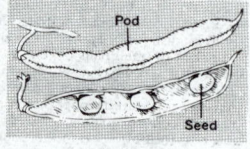

Bean (string bean)

bean·bag (bēn'bag') *n.* small cloth bag filled with beans and used in certain games.

bean·ball (bēn'bôl') *n.* baseball deliberately pitched at or near the batter's head.

bean·ie (bē'nē) *n.* small, brimless cap.

bean·pole (bēn'pōl') *n.* **1.** tall pole for a growing bean plant to climb on. **2.** *Slang.* tall, thin person.

bean·stalk (bēn'stôk') *n.* main stem of a bean plant.

bear¹ (bâr) *v.* bore or (*archaic*) bare, borne or born, bear·ing. *v.t.* **1.** to hold up; support: *Beams bear the weight of the roof.* **2.** to possess as a feature, characteristic, or attribute: *He bears the title of baron. The letter bears his signature.* **3.** to carry; transport: *to bear gifts.* **4.** to suffer or endure; undergo; abide: *He bore the brunt of the punishment. I can't bear his rudeness.* **5.** to bring forth or give birth to; produce: *to bear fruit, to bear young.* **6.** to hold in the mind; entertain: *to bear malice.* **7.** to accept or acknowledge; assume: *to bear the blame, to bear the expense.* **8.** to conduct or guide; escort: *They bore him to his quarters.* **9.** to communicate or spread; convey: *to bear tidings.* **10.** to move or push by pressing against; thrust: *The crowd bore him along.* **11.** to be fit for or worthy of; demand; require: *His behavior bears investigating. His behavior bears watching.* **12.** to give; render: *to bear testimony.* **13.** to carry or conduct (oneself): *She bears herself nobly.* **14.** to be able to withstand; allow: *This evidence won't bear scrutiny.* **15.** to have or stand in (a relationship): *Demand bears a relation to supply.* **16.** *Archaic.* to exercise; wield: *to bear sway.* —*v.i.* **1.** to lean or press; weigh: *Burdens bear heavily upon him.* **2.** to lie or move in a particular direction: *to bear east. Bear left at the intersection.* **3.** to bring forth young or fruit.

to bear down. a. to press or weigh down: *The heavy bundle bore him down.* **b.** to make a strong effort; exert oneself: *He bore down as he approached the finish line.*

to bear down on (or **upon**). **a.** to make a great effort towards; strive harder at: *He bore down on the task at hand.* **b.** to exert pressure on; press hard: *He bore down on the pencil and broke the point.* **c.** to approach rapidly: *The police bore down on the getaway car.*

to bear on (or **upon**). to affect or relate to; be relevant to: *This evidence bears on the testimony. This discovery will bear on later developments.*

to bear out. to confirm or support; corroborate: *The facts bear out my story.*

to bear up. to support a weight or strain; endure: *to bear up under hardship. The fabric bore up well during testing.*

to bear with. to be patient or tolerant toward: *Bear with my faults.*

to bring to bear. to apply or exert; employ: *to bring experience to bear, to bring pressure to bear.* [Old English *beran* to carry, support.]

Syn. *v.t.* **3.** see **carry. 4.** see **stand, endure** mean to sustain something painful or difficult. **Bear** emphasizes the strength or capacity to sustain something difficult rather than the way in which it is sustained: *The cavalry bore the brunt of the fighting.* **Stand** is so close to **bear** as to be interchangeable and means to put up with hardships and impositions without flinching: *John can stand both extreme heat and cold.* **Endure** means to withstand prolonged pain, distress, and affliction without giving in and suggests physical and mental stamina: *He endured the miseries of prison life for ten years.*

bear² (bâr) *n.* **1.** any of various thickset mammals, family Ursidae, of North and South America, Asia, Europe, and the Arctic, having coarse, thick fur, powerful legs and claws, and a short, stumpy tail. Bears, the largest carnivores, range in size from 3 to 11 feet long. **2.** any of various animals thought to resemble the bear, as the ant bear and the koala bear. **3.** gruff, surly, or clumsy person. **4.** speculator, esp. one in the stock market, who attempts to bring down prices or who anticipates a decline in prices and sells in order that he may buy back at a lower rate. Opposed to **bull.** [Old English *bera*, mammal of the family *Ursidae*.]

bear·a·ble (bâr'ə bəl) *adj.* capable of being borne or endured; tolerable. —**bear'a·bly,** *adv.*

bear-bait·ing (bâr'bā'ting) *n.* former sport of setting dogs on a chained bear.

bear·ber·ry (bâr'ber'ē) *pl.,* **-ries.** *n.* **1.** hardy, trailing evergreen shrub, *Arctostaphlos uva-ursi,* of the heath family, found on sandy or rocky soils in northern regions, having branched stems and clusters of small white flowers, and bearing red inedible fruit. **2.** related shrub, *Arctous alpina,* found in Arctic regions and mountains of the Northern Hemisphere, having edible black berries.

beard (bêrd) *n.* **1.** growth of hair on the cheeks, chin, and throat, esp. of a man. **2.** growth or appendage resembling a beard, as the hair on the chin of a goat or the bristles near the beak of certain birds. **3.** tuft or covering of awns or other hairlike growths, as on the head of a stalk of wheat. —*v.t.* **1.** to furnish with a beard. **2.** to confront or defy (an opponent or difficulty) resolutely. [Old English *beard* hair on the face.]

Beards·ley, Au·brey Vincent (bêrdz'lē; ô'brē) 1872–98, English illustrator.

bear·er (bâr'ər) *n.* **1.** one who or that which carries, supports, or brings: *flag bearer, bearer of good news.* **2.** one who holds or presents a check or other order for payment of money. **3.** pallbearer. **4.** tree or plant that yields fruit or flowers.

bear·ing (bâr'ing) *n.* **1.** manner of carrying or conducting oneself; carriage; behavior: *a regal bearing. He had a polite bearing toward women.* **2.** relevance or relation; connection: *Your complaints have no bearing on the matter.* **3.** bearings. awareness or comprehension of one's environment, situation, or relative position. **4.** direction or position in relation to another point or to the points of a compass. **5.** *Machinery.* part of a machine which holds or supports moving parts and reduces friction and wear. **6.** act or capacity of enduring; endurance: *His insolence is beyond bearing.* **7.** act, capacity, or period of producing or bringing forth: *a tree past bearing.* **8.** any single device in a coat of arms.

Syn. **1. Bearing, carriage, posture** denote the characteristic way a person manages or holds himself. **Bearing** is the most general of these words and suggests the manner of a person's deportment and gestures which reflect his personality: *The queen has a regal bearing.* **Carriage** refers to the way one holds one's body while walking: *The beauty contestant had a stately carriage.* **Posture** refers to the habitual or assumed attitude of the body while sitting or standing: *Many people who do desk work have poor posture.*

bear·ish (bâr'ish) *adj.* **1.** rough or cross; gruff. **2.** marked by, tending toward, or expecting a decline in the price of stocks. —**bear'ish·ly,** *adv.* —**bear'ish·ness,** *n.*

bear·skin (bâr'skin') *n.* **1.** skin of a bear. **2.** tall, black fur cap, as that worn by Buckingham Palace guards.

beast (bēst) *n.* **1.** any animal other than man, esp. a four-footed mammal: *the beasts of the forest.* **2.** coarse, brutal, or contemptible person. [Old French *beste* animal, going back to Latin *bēstia.*] —**Syn.** **1.** see **animal.**

beast·ly (bēst'lē) **-li·er, -li·est.** *adj.* **1.** brutal or coarse; bestial. **2.** *Informal.* disagreeable; nasty. —*adv. British. Informal.* very. —**beast'li·ness,** *n.*

beast of burden, animal used for carrying or pulling loads.

beat (bēt) **beat, beat·en** or **beat, beat·ing.** *v.t.* **1.** to deal repeated blows to; thrash: *He beat his brother for lying.* **2.** to strike or hit repeatedly; pound: *to beat a drum. He beat the door down.* **3.** to dash against: *The waves beat the shore.* **4.** to drive or force by or as by blows: *They beat back the invaders. He beat his way through the crowd.* **5.** to defeat: *I beat him at checkers.* **6.** to flap repeatedly or vigorously: *The bird beat its wings against the cage.* **7.** to form, shape, or flatten by hammering: *to beat a horseshoe into shape, to beat swords into plowshares.* **8.** to stir vigorously: *Beat the yolks and whites separately.* **9.** to sound or signal, as on a drum: *to beat a tattoo, to beat a steady rhythm.* **10.** to mark or measure with or as with a baton: *The metronome beat a waltz tempo.* **11.** to hunt through in order to flush or locate quarry; scour: *to beat the bushes for game. The men beat the countryside for the fugitive.* **12.** to surpass or be superior to; outdo: *This book beats all others in length. Riding beats walking.* **13.** to make (a path) by frequent treading or passage. **14.** to offset, avoid, or circumvent the effects of: *to beat the heat by going swimming. He beat the rap.* **15.** *Informal.* to bewilder or perplex; baffle: *It beats me.* **16.** to beat a retreat. to withdraw swiftly; retreat. **17. to beat around** (or **about**) **the bush.** to approach a matter in a roundabout way; avoid coming to the point. **18. to beat down.** *Informal.* to cause (a seller) to lower his price. **19. to beat it.** *Slang.* to leave hastily. **20. to beat up.** *Informal.* to give a beating to; thrash. —*v.i.* **1.** to strike repeatedly: *He beat at the door. The rain beat against the windows.* **2.** to throb; pulsate: *The heart beats rhythmically.* **3.** to smite as if with blows: *The sun beat into my face.* **4.** to sound upon being struck: *The drums beat in time to the march.* **5.** to strike a drum. **6.** to permit beating: *The batter doesn't beat smoothly.* **7.** *Nautical.* to

at; āpe; cär; end; mē; it; īce; hot; ōld; fôrk; wood; fōōl; oil; out; up; ūse; turn; sing; thin; this; zh in treasure; ə in ago, taken, pencil, lemon, circus.

move against the wind by tacking. —*n.* **1.** stroke or blow. **2.** rhythmic sequence of sounds or movements; pulsation: *the beat of the to:n-toms, the beat of the heart.* **3.** assigned or regular course; habitual round: *a policeman's beat, a reporter's beat.* **4.** *Music.* accent or unit of time. **5.** pattern of recurrence of stressed syllables in a line or stanza of poetry; rhythm. **6. beats.** *Physics.* regularly recurring pulsation heard when sound waves of slightly different frequencies combine. **7.** *Journalism. Slang.* reporting of news ahead of one's competitors; scoop. —*adj. Informal.* **1.** worn out; weary; exhausted. **2.** of, like, or relating to beatniks or to the beat generation. [Old English *bēatan* to strike repeatedly.]
Syn. *v.t.* **2. Beat, pound²** mean to strike or hit repeatedly. **Beat** means to deal repeated blows: *The woman beat the rug to clean it.* **Pound** means to deal heavy blows repeatedly or rhythmically: *The judge pounded the desk with a gavel.*

beat·en (bēt'ən) *v.* a past participle of **beat.** —*adj.* **1.** formed or shaped by blows; hammered: *beaten gold.* **2.** worn by use; commonly used: *a beaten path.* **3.** thwarted or vanquished; defeated: *a beaten man.* **4.** mixed or whipped by vigorous stirring: *Add a beaten egg.*
beat·er (bē'tər) *n.* **1.** implement or device for beating: *a rug beater.* **2.** one who flushes game during a hunt. **3.** one who beats.
beat generation, group of people belonging to the generation that reached adulthood after the Korean War, who expressed disillusionment with middle-class values. They were characterized by their unconventional dress and their interest in the arts, esp. jazz and poetry. [Supposedly coined by Jack Kerouac, 1922–70, U.S. novelist. See BEAT, GENERATION.]
be·a·tif·ic (bē'ə tif'ik) *adj.* imparting or expressing bliss or blessedness; blissful: *a beatific smile.* —**be'a·tif'i·cal·ly,** *adv.*
be·at·i·fi·ca·tion (bē at'ə fi kā'shən) *n.* **1.** act of beatifying; being beatified. **2.** in the Roman Catholic Church, act whereby the pope declares a deceased person to be one of the blessed in heaven and entitled to public reverence within a certain locality or group. It is one of the steps toward canonization.
be·at·i·fy (bē at'ə fī') -**fied,** -**fy·ing.** *v.t.* **1.** to make supremely happy. **2.** in the Roman Catholic Church, to declare the beatification of. [Late Latin *beātificāre* to make happy, from Latin *beātus* happy + *facere* to make.]
beat·ing (bē'ting) *n.* **1.** act of one who or that which beats. **2.** series of forceful blows; thrashing: *He got a beating from that bully.* **3.** throbbing; pulsation: *the beating of the heart.* **4.** severe loss or defeat: *He took a beating on the stock market. They gave our team quite a beating.* **5.** rough treatment; punishment: *The car took a beating on those unpaved roads.*
be·at·i·tude (bē at'ə tōōd', -tūd') *n.* **1.** supreme happiness or blessedness; bliss. **2. the Beatitudes.** in the New Testament, the pronouncements made by Jesus in the Sermon on the Mount blessing those who possess particular virtues. Each begins with "Blessed are." [Latin *beātitūdō* happiness.]
beat·nik (bēt'nik) *n.* member of the beat generation. [BEAT + -NIK.]
Be·a·trice (bē'ə tris) *n.* idealized and symbolic figure in Dante's *Divine Comedy* who was developed from the woman he loved.
beau (bō) *pl.,* **beaux** (bōz) or **beaus.** *n.* **1.** sweetheart or lover of a girl or woman; boyfriend. **2.** dandy. [French *beau* fine, handsome, from Latin *bellus.*]
Beau Brum·mell (bō' brum'əl) fop; dandy. [From George Bryan (Beau) Brummell, 1778–1840, English leader of society and men's fashion.]
Beau·fort scale (bō'fərt) internationally used scale of wind velocities, ranging from 0 for speeds of less than one mile per hour (calm) to 17 for speeds above 75 miles per hour (hurricane). [From Sir Francis Beaufort, 1774–1857, British admiral who originated it.]
Beaufort Sea, arm of the Arctic, bordering northern Alaska and northwestern Canada.
beau geste (bō zhest') *pl.,* **beaux gestes** (bō zhest'). **1.** gracious or noble gesture. **2.** such an act or gesture made only for selfish reasons or for effect. [French *beau geste* handsome gesture, from Latin *bellus* handsome + *gestus* gesture.]
Beau·har·nais, Josephine de (bō'är nā') see **Josephine.**
beau ideal *pl.,* **beaux ideals** or **beaus ideal.** type of excellence or beauty; perfect type or model. [French *beau idéal,* from Latin *bellus* handsome + Late Latin *ideālis.* See IDEAL.]
Beau·mar·chais, Pierre Au·gus·tin Ca·ron de (bō märshā'; pyer ō goos taN' kä rôN') 1732–99, French dramatist.
beau monde (bō' mônd') the fashionable world; society. [French *beau monde,* from Latin *bellus* handsome + *mundus* world.]
Beau·mont (bō'mənt) *n.* **1.** port city in southeastern Texas. Pop. (1965 est.), 126,000. **2. Francis.** 1584–1616, English dramatist.
Beau·re·gard, Pierre G. T. (bō'rə gärd'; pē är') 1818–93, Confederate general.
beau·te·ous (bū'tē əs) *adj.* beautiful. —**beau'te·ous·ly,** *adv.*

beau·ti·cian (bū tish'ən) *n.* hairdresser or cosmetologist.
beau·ti·ful (bū'tə fəl) *adj.* possessing qualities that delight the mind or senses; full of beauty. —**beau'ti·ful·ly,** *adv.* —**beau'ti·ful·ness,** *n.*
Syn. Beautiful, lovely, pretty, handsome mean pleasing or delightful to the senses or mind. **Beautiful** has the widest range of application and refers to that which most closely approaches an ideal standard of visual or aesthetic perfection: *Beethoven's fifth symphony is a beautiful piece of music.* **Lovely** refers especially to something having rich physical charms and implies that the delight inspired is emotional rather than intellectual: *His home overlooks one of the most lovely beaches on the entire coast.* **Pretty** stresses grace, delicacy, petiteness, and charm, and often implies a superficial appeal that falls short of perfection: *That's a very pretty scarf you're wearing.* **Handsome** suggests excellence of form and qualities of dignity, stateliness, or impressiveness: *Next to the table stood a handsome mahogany cabinet.*
beau·ti·fy (bū'tə fī') -**fied,** -**fy·ing.** *v.t.* to make beautiful or add beauty to. —**beau'ti·fi·ca'tion, beau'ti·fi'er,** *n.* —**Syn.** see decorate.
beau·ty (bū'tē) *pl.,* -**ties.** *n.* **1.** quality or combination of qualities that delights the senses or mind: *the beauty of a face, the beauty and harmony of brotherhood.* **2.** one who or that which is beautiful: *Your daughter is quite a beauty. That yacht is a beauty.* **3.** outstanding or particularly pleasing feature or part: *The beauty of the story was its subtle humor.* [Old French *beaute, balte* comeliness, going back to Latin *bellus* handsome.]
beauty mark, mole or other small mark on the skin.
beauty parlor, establishment for the hairdressing, manicuring, or other beauty treatment of women. Also, **beauty salon, beauty shop.**
beauty spot, beauty mark, esp. a patch put on the face to set off its whiteness.
beaux (bōz) alternative plural of **beau.**
beaux-arts (bō zär') *n. French.* fine arts.

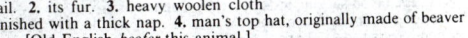

bea·ver¹ (bē'vər) *n.* **1.** aquatic rodent, genus *Castor,* having a stocky body, soft grayish fur, and a broad, flat tail. It builds its lodge in or on the banks of shallow streams and constructs a dam of branches, stones, and mud to protect it. There are two species, the American beaver, *C. canadensis,* and the Eurasian beaver, *C. fiber.* Length: 3–4 feet including tail. **2.** its fur. **3.** heavy woolen cloth finished with a thick nap. **4.** man's top hat, originally made of beaver fur. [Old English *beofor* this animal.]

Beaver

bea·ver² (bē'vər) *n.* movable part of a helmet that protected the mouth and chin. [Old French *baviere* beaver of a helmet, bib, from *bave* saliva (imitative); because it was thought to resemble a child's bib.]
bea·ver·board (bē'vər bôrd') *n.* thin, stiff material made of compressed wood fibers, used for partitions, ceilings, and temporary structures. Trademark: Beaverboard.
be·bop (bē'bop') *n.* style of jazz developed in the 1940s, characterized by complex harmony, extreme variation in rhythmic pattern, and very rapid tempos. [Imitative of a staccato two-beat phrase typical of this music.]
be·calm (bi käm') *v.t.* **1.** to keep motionless by lack of wind: *The fleet was becalmed in the Caribbean.* **2.** *Archaic.* to make calm or still; quiet.
be·came (bi kām') past tense of **become.**
be·cause (bi kôz', -kuz') *conj.* for the fact that; since: *He was cold because he forgot his sweater.* —*adv.* **because of.** by reason of; on account of: *I went swimming because of the heat.* [Middle English *bi cause* literally, by cause. See BY, CAUSE.]
be·chance (bi chans') -**chanced,** -**chanc·ing.** *v.t., v.i.* to befall.
Bech·u·a·na·land (bech'ōō ä'nə land') *n.* see **Botswana.**
beck (bek) *n.* **1.** *Archaic.* nod or other gesture given as a summons or command. **2. at one's beck and call.** subject to one's slightest wish; ready to do one's bidding. —*v.t., v.i. Archaic.* to beckon. [Short for BECKON.]
Beck·et, Saint Thomas à (bek'it) c.1118–70, archbishop of Canterbury.
Beck·ett, Samuel (bek'it) 1906–, Irish playwright, novelist, and poet.
beck·on (bek'ən) *v.t., v.i.* **1.** to signal, summon, or direct by a sign or gesture: *She beckoned me aside. He beckoned with his hand.* **2.** to be inviting or enticing (to); attract: *The smell of bread beckoned the hungry boy. The sea beckons.* [Old English *bīecnan, bēcnan* to indicate, signify.]
be·cloud (bi kloud') *v.t.* to obscure with or as with clouds: *to becloud an issue.*
be·come (bi kum') **be·came, be·come, be·com·ing.** *v.i.* **1.** to come to be; grow to be: *The tired child became cranky. The tadpole becomes a*

at; āpe; cär; end; mē; it; īce; hot; ōld; fôrk; wood; fōōl; oil; out; up; ūse; turn; s·ng; thin; this; zh in treasure; ə in ago, taken, pencil, lemon, circus.

85

frog. **2. to become of.** to be the condition or fate of; happen to: *Whatever became of him? What has become of my umbrella?* —*v.t.* **1.** to look well on; suit: *A blue shirt becomes your brother.* **2.** to be appropriate for; befit: *Impertinence does not become you.* [Old English *becuman* to happen.]

be·com·ing (bi kum′ing) *adj.* **1.** flattering: *a becoming hat.* **2.** suitable; appropriate: *conduct not becoming to an officer.* —**be·com′ing·ly,** *adv.*

Becque·rel rays (bek′rel) any of the electromagnetic rays given off by radioactive substances. ▲ This term was replaced by various other terms as the different types of rays were distinguished and identified. [From the French physicist Antoine H. *Becquerel.* 1852–1908, who discovered them.]

bed (bed) *n.* **1.** piece of furniture upon which to sleep or rest, often consisting of a mattress, bedstead, and spring. **2.** any place or thing used for sleeping or resting: *The hayloft was his bed.* **3.** something resembling a bed in shape or function: *a bed of leaves.* **4.** sleeping accommodation for the night; lodging. **5.** piece of ground used for planting: *beds of roses and tulips.* **6.** ground at the bottom of a body of water: *the bed of a stream.* **7.** part or surface serving as a foundation or support: *a railroad bed. They built the road on a bed of gravel.* **8.** layer; stratum: *They drilled through beds of sand and clay.* **9. bed and board (of someone).** support and security offered by marriage (to someone): *She left her husband's bed and board.* **10. to get up on the wrong side of the bed.** to be irritable or cross. **11. to make one's bed and lie in it.** to create a situation and suffer its consequences. **12. to put to bed.** *Slang.* to complete work on an edition (of a newspaper or other publication). **13. to take to one's bed.** to go to bed because of illness. —*v.t.,* **bed·ded, bed·ding. 1.** to provide with a place to sleep: *The host bedded his guests. The farmer bedded his mules.* **2.** to put or take to bed: *The mother was busy getting her sleepy daughter bedded.* **3.** to set or plant in the ground: *She bedded her rose bushes.* **4.** to fix or set firmly; embed: *They bedded the cobblestones in mortar.* **5.** to lay flat or arrange in layers: *to bed oysters.* —*v.i.* **1.** to go to bed. **2.** to form a layer; stratify. **3. to bed down. a.** to provide with a place to sleep: *to bed down cattle.* **b.** to go to bed; sleep: *We bedded down after the hike.* [Old English *bed* couch to sleep on, ground for planting.]

be·daub (bi dôb′) *v.t.* to smear with something dirty.

be·daz·zle (bi daz′əl) **-zled, -zling.** *v.t.* **1.** to impress or charm forcefully; overwhelm: *He was bedazzled by her smile.* **2.** to blind, as by excessive light.

bed·bug (bed′bug′) *n.* any of a widespread group of wingless, blood-sucking insects, family Cimicidae, esp. *Cimex lectularius,* a common parasite of man which often infests beds and upholstery.

bed·cham·ber (bed′chām′bər) *n.* bedroom.

bed·clothes (bed′klōz′, -klō̄z′) *n.,pl.* coverings, as sheets and blankets, used on a bed.

bed·ding (bed′ing) *n.* **1.** bedclothes: *I changed the bedding and sent some to the laundry.* **2.** materials for a bed: *He used straw for the oxen's bedding.* **3.** bottom layer; foundation: *First, lay down a bedding of concrete.* **4.** *Geology.* stratification.

Bede, Saint (bēd) c.673–c.735, English historian and scholastic theologian. Also, **the Venerable Bede.**

be·deck (bi dek′) *v.t.* to adorn.

be·dev·il (bi dev′əl) **-iled, -il·ing;** *also, British,* **-illed, il·ling.** *v.t.* **1.** to worry or harass; plague; torment. **2.** *Archaic.* to bewitch. —**be·dev′il·ment,** *n.*

be·dew (bi dōō′, -dyōō′) *v.t. Archaic.* to moisten with or as with dew.

bed·fast (bed′fast′) *adj. Archaic.* bedridden.

bed·fel·low (bed′fel′ō) *n.* **1.** one who shares a bed with another. **2.** companion or ally; associate: *Politics makes strange bedfellows.*

Bed·ford cord (bed′fərd) heavy durable cloth having lengthwise ribs, used in coats, uniforms, and riding habits.

be·dight (bi dīt′) **-dight, -dight** or **-dight·ed, -dight·ing.** *v.t. Archaic.* to dress or adorn; array. [BE- + DIGHT.]

be·dim (bi dim′) **-dimmed, -dim·ming.** *v.t.* to make dim; obscure.

Bed·i·vere (bed′ə vēr′) *n.* in Arthurian legend, loyal knight who brought the dying King Arthur to the barge which then bore him to Avalon.

be·di·zen (bi dī′zən, -diz′ən) *v.t. Archaic.* to dress or adorn gaudily. [BE- + DIZEN.]

bed jacket, short, loose robe for the upper part of the body, usually worn over a nightgown.

bed·lam (bed′ləm) *n.* **1.** scene or situation marked by wild uproar and confusion: *It was bedlam at the department store during the sale.* **2. Bedlam.** Hospital of St. Mary of Bethlehem in London, used since 1547 as an insane asylum. **3.** *Archaic.* insane asylum; madhouse. [Modification of *Bethlehem* in Hospital of St. Mary of Bethlehem.]

bed·lam·ite (bed′lə mīt′) *n. Archaic.* madman; lunatic.

bed linen, bedclothes, esp. sheets and pillowcases.

Bed·ou·in (bed′ōō in, bed′win) *n.* **1.** member of a large group of nomadic Arab tribes who inhabit the desert regions of North Africa and the Middle East. **2.** wanderer; nomad. —*adj.* of, relating to, or like the Bedouins. [French *bédouin,* from Arabic *badāwīn* literally, desert dwellers.]

bed·pan (bed′pan′) *n.* pan used as a toilet by one who is confined to bed.

bed·post (bed′pōst′) *n.* one of the vertical supports at the corners of certain beds.

be·drag·gle (bi drag′əl) **-gled, -gling.** *v.t.* to make wet, soiled, or disheveled, as with rain or dirt.

bed·rid·den (bed′rid′ən) *adj.* confined to bed: *Pneumonia kept him bedridden for weeks.* Also, **bed′rid′.** [Old English *bedrida* paralyzed person, from *bed* bed + *rida* rider.]

bed·rock (bed′rok′) *n.* **1.** solid rock underlying the looser materials of the earth's surface. **2.** foundation; basis. **3.** lowest point or level; bottom.

bed·room (bed′rōōm′, -room′) *n.* room for sleeping.

bed·side (bed′sīd′) *n.* side of a bed, esp. of a sick person: *He hurried to his friend's bedside.*

bedside manner, attitude or manner that a doctor assumes toward his patients.

bed·sore (bed′sôr′) *n.* ulceration caused by prolonged pressure against a bed, occurring among persons bedridden for long periods.

bed·spread (bed′spred′) *n.* covering placed on a bed for protective or decorative purposes.

bed·stead (bed′sted′) *n.* framework which supports the springs and mattress of a bed.

bed·straw (bed′strô′) *n.* any of a group of plants, genus *Galium,* having a square, slender stem, whorled leaves, and clusters of tiny yellow or white flowers. It was formerly used as a mattress stuffing.

bed·time (bed′tīm′) *n.* time for going to bed.

bee (bē) *n.* **1.a.** any of a great variety of relatively thick-bodied, hairy, winged insects, superfamily Apoidea, that feed on nectar and pollen and are related to wasps and ants. The best-known bees, the honeybees and bumblebees, of the family Apidae, live in colonies and may sting, but most kinds of bees are not social and many bees, esp. in the tropics, are stingless. **b.** the common honeybee, *Apis mellifera,* that lives in colonies, or hives, of many thousands and is widely domesticated for the honey and beeswax produced. **2.** gathering or meeting combining work, pleasure, and often, competition: *a spelling bee, a quilting bee.* **3. to have a bee in one's bonnet.** to be excessively concerned about or preoccupied with some notion. [Old English *bēo* the insect.]

bee balm, North American plant, *Monarda didyma,* of the mint family, that grows in moist soils and bears aromatic leaves and showy flower heads that are usually bright red in color.

bee·bread (bē′bred′) *n.* mixture of pollen and honey or nectar, made by bees to feed their young.

beech (bēch) *n.* **1.** any of a group of ornamental trees, genus *Fagus,* found in cooler regions of the Northern Hemisphere, having light-gray bark and bearing small, edible nuts. **2.** the close-grained wood of this tree. —*adj.* designating a family, Fagaceae, of trees and shrubs chiefly of the temperate regions of the Northern Hemisphere, including important timber and ornamental trees, as the beech, oak, and chestnut. —**beech′en,** *adj.* [Old English *bēce* beech tree.]

Bee·cher, Henry Ward (bē′chər) 1813–87, U.S. clergyman, lecturer, and author.

beech·nut (bēch′nut′) *n.* small, edible, triangular nut of the beech tree, used to make cooking oil and flavorings.

bee eater, any of various insect-eating birds, family Meropidae, of the warmer regions of Europe, Africa, Asia, and Australia, having a slim body and slender, curved bill. Length: 6–14 inches.

Bee eater

beef (bēf) *pl.,* (*def. 2*) **beeves** (bēvz) *or* **beefs;** (*def. 3*) **beefs.** *n.* **1.** meat of a mature steer, cow, or bull. **2.** fully-grown steer, cow, or bull that is raised for meat. **3.** *Slang.* complaint. **4.** *Slang.* flesh; muscle; brawn. —*v.i.* **1.** *Slang.* to complain. **2. to beef up.** *Informal.* to add force or vigor to; strengthen. [Old French *boef, buef* ox or its meat, from Latin *bōs* ox.]

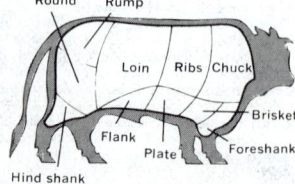

Cuts of beef

at; āpe; cär; end; mē; it; īce; hot; ōld; fôrk; wood; fōōl; oil; out; up; ūse; turn; sing; thin; this; zh in treasure; ə in ago, taken, pencil, lemon, circus.

beef cattle, cattle raised for meat.

beef·eat·er (bēf′ē′tər) *n.* yeoman of the English royal guard or a warder of the Tower of London.

beef·steak (bēf′stāk′) *n.* slice of beef suitable for broiling or frying.

beef tea, broth made from beef extract or by boiling lean beef in water.

beef·y (bē′fē) beef·i·er, beef·i·est. *adj.* fleshy; brawny. —**beef′i·ness,** *n.*

bee·hive (bē′hīv′) *n.* **1.** hive for a colony of bees, either man-made or natural. See **hive** for illustration. **2.** busy, crowded place: *The office was a beehive of activity.*

bee·keep·er (bē′kē′pər) *n.* one who raises bees.

bee·keep·ing (bē′kē′ping) *n.* the raising of bees for honey or wax.

bee·line (bē′līn′) *n.* **1.** the direct course a honeybee follows to its hive after collecting nectar or pollen. **2.** any direct line or course. **3. to make a beeline for** (or **to**). to go directly to.

Be·el·ze·bub (bē el′zə bub′) *n.* **1.** the Devil; Satan. **2.** fallen angel ranking second to Satan in Milton's *Paradise Lost.* [Latin *Beelzebūb,* transliteration of Hebrew *ba'al-z'būb* Philistine god of pestilence and flies mentioned in the Old Testament; literally, lord of flies; also, transliteration of Greek *Beelzeboub* Satan in the New Testament.]

been (bin) past participle of **be.**

beer (bēr) *n.* alcoholic beverage made from malt and hops. [Old English *bēor,* going back to Church Latin *biber* beverage.]

beer and skittles, carefree pleasure or enjoyment.

Beer·she·ba (bēr shē′bə, bēr′shə-) *n.* town in central Israel. It was the southernmost city of ancient Palestine. Pop. (1969 est.), 72,000.

beest·ings (bēs′tingz) *also,* **biest·ings.** *n.,pl.* colostrum, esp. of a cow. [Old English *bȳsting,* from *bēost.*]

bees·wax (bēz′waks′) *n.* yellow wax secreted by honeybees to make their honeycombs, used commercially in candles, cosmetics, floor wax, and other products.

bees·wing (bēz′wing′) *n.* **1.** fine film that often forms on certain old wines, as port. **2.** wine that has such a film.

beet (bēt) *n.* **1.** fleshy root of any of a group of leafy plants, genus *Beta,* esp. the common red beet, a variety of *B. vulgaris,* cooked and eaten as a vegetable. **2.** the plant itself, having leaves that may be eaten either cooked or raw. **3.** sugar beet. [Old English *bēte,* from Latin *bēta.*]

Bee·tho·ven, Lud·wig van (bā′tō′vən; *loud* wig) 1770–1827, German composer.

bee·tle[1] (bēt′əl) *n.* **1.** any insect of the order Coleoptera, having biting mouth parts and hard, sheathlike front wings that, when folded back, cover the membranous hind wings. The order is the largest in the insect class, containing some 300,000 species, and includes the boll weevil and Japanese beetle. **2.** any insect resembling a beetle. [Old English *bitela* literally, biting insect, from *bītan* to bite.]

bee·tle[2] (bēt′əl) *n.* **1.** heavy hammering implement, usually with a wooden head, used for driving wedges, pounding paving stones, and for other similar purposes. **2.** wooden mallet for household purposes, as mashing. —*v.t.,* **-tled, -tling.** to pound with a beetle. [Old English *bīetel* hammer, from *bēatan* to beat.]

bee·tle[3] (bēt′əl) **-tled, -tling.** *v.i.* to project or jut out; overhang: *The crags beetled over the shore.* —*adj.* (of eyebrows) protruding; prominent. [From BEETLE-BROWED.] —**bee′tling,** *adj.*

bee·tle-browed (bēt′əl broud′) *adj.* **1.** having protruding eyebrows. **2.** scowling; frowning. [Middle English *bitel-browed,* from *bitel* projecting (of uncertain origin) + BROW + -ED[2].]

beet sugar, sugar obtained from the sugar beet.

beeves (bēvz) *n.* a plural of **beef.**

be·fall (bi fôl′) **-fell, -fall·en, -fall·ing.** *v.t.* to happen to: *the awful misfortune that befell him.* —*v.i.* to come to pass; happen. [Old English *befeallan* to fall.]

be·fit (bi fit′) **-fit·ted, -fit·ting.** *v.t.* to be suitable or appropriate for: *The brigadier general expects to be treated with the dignity that befits his rank.*

be·fit·ting (bi fit′ing) *adj.* suitable; appropriate; proper. —**be·fit′ting·ly,** *adv.*

be·fog (bi fôg′, -fog′) **-fogged, -fog·ging.** *v.t.* to envelop in or as if in a fog; obscure; confuse: *Mist befogged the skyline.*

be·fool (bi fōōl′) *v.t.* to fool; delude; dupe.

be·fore (bi fôr′) *prep.* **1.** in front of; in advance of; ahead of: *The prisoner marched before the guard.* **2.** previous to; earlier than: *He awoke before dawn.* **3.** in preference to; rather than: *death before dishonor. I would die before leaving you.* **4.** in the presence, notice, or sight of: *to appear before an audience. He stood before the jury.* **5.** in precedence of in development, importance, or rank: *Put his welfare before all else.* **6.** under the consideration or cognizance of; occupying: *the problem before us.* **7.** in store for; awaiting: *His best years were still before him.* —*adv.* **1.** in front; in advance; ahead: *Several soldiers went before to scout.* **2.** in time preceding; previously: *He has more money*

than he had before. **3.** earlier; sooner: *They had married three years before.* —*conj.* **1.** previous to the time when: *He spoke to me before he left.* **2.** rather than; sooner than: *I would starve before I tell.* [Old English *beforan* ahead (of), in the presence of.]

be·fore·hand (bi fôr′hand′) *adv., adj.* ahead of time; in advance: *She prepared the dessert beforehand.*

be·foul (bi foul′) *v.t.* to make dirty or foul; soil.

be·friend (bi frend′) *v.t.* to act as a friend to; assist: *to befriend a stranger.*

be·fud·dle (bi fud′əl) **-dled, -dling.** *v.t.* to confuse or bewilder utterly: *The liquor he drank befuddled his senses.*

beg (beg) **begged, beg·ging.** *v.t.* **1.** to ask for as charity: *to beg alms.* **2.** to ask for or of earnestly; entreat: *to beg a favor. I beg your pardon.* **3. to beg the question. a.** to evade or sidestep the issue. **b.** to assume the truth of the very matter in dispute. —*v.i.* **1.** to ask alms or charity; be a beggar. **2.** to ask humbly or earnestly: *He begged for mercy.* **3. to beg off.** to be excused or released (from): *He promised to go, but then begged off.* **4. to go begging.** to go unwanted, unclaimed, or unused: *four scholarships that went begging.* [Possibly from Anglo-Norman *begger* to ask for alms, from Old French *begard.* See BEGGAR.]

Syn. *v.t.* **2.** Beg, beseech, entreat, implore mean to appeal or plead earnestly and humbly. **Beg** means to request or ask a favor of someone earnestly and with a measure of self-abasement: *The child begged her mother for some candy.* **Beseech** adds to beg a sense of urgency and anxiety about the outcome: *We beseech thee, O Lord, to hear our prayer.* **Entreat** means to ask in an ingratiating and persuasive way so as to overcome resistance: *He entreated the girl to marry him.* **Implore** means to make an urgent and anguished plea: *The prisoner implored the judge to grant him pardon.*

be·gan (bi gan′) past tense of **begin.**

be·get (bi get′) **be·got** or *(archaic)* **be·gat** (bi gat′), **be·got·ten** or **be·got** (bi got′), **be·get·ting.** *v.t.* **1.** to be the father of; sire: *Abraham begat Isaac.* **2.** to give rise to; produce: *Jealousy begets hatred.* [Old English *begitan* to get.] —**be·get′ter,** *n.*

beg·gar (beg′ər) *n.* **1.** one who asks for alms, esp. one who does so for a living. **2.** very poor person; pauper. **3.** fellow; rascal. —*v.t.* **1.** to reduce to poverty; impoverish. **2.** to exhaust the resources of; surpass: *His wealth beggars comparison.* [Possibly from Old French *begard* one who begs, member of a western European order of friars said to be named after Lambert le Bègue, a medieval priest. Since many of these friars frequently begged alms, *begard* became associated primarily with begging.]

beg·gar·ly (beg′ər lē) *adj.* poor; inadequate; mean. —**beg′gar·li·ness,** *n.*

beg·gar's-lice (beg′ərz līs′) *also,* **beg·gar·lice.** *n.* beggar's-ticks.

beg·gar's-ticks (beg′ər tiks′) *also,* **beg·gar·ticks.** *n.* **1.** any of a group of plants, genus *Desmodium,* bearing barbed pods that stick to clothing and to animal fur. **2.** the dry, bristly pods themselves. ▲ construed as singular or plural in def. 1, as plural in def. 2.

beg·gar·y (beg′ər ē) *n.* **1.** extreme poverty. **2.** beggars collectively.

be·gin (bi gin′) **be·gan, be·gun, be·gin·ning.** *v.i.* **1.** to set about (doing or being something); take the first step; start: *Where should I begin?* **2.** to come into existence; arise: *The epidemic began last month.* **3.** to do or be in the slightest degree: *His highway begins at the border.* **3.** to do or be in the slightest degree: *His second book doesn't begin to compare with his first.* —*v.t.* **1.** to do the first act or part of; start to do: *They began their homework.* **2.** to bring into existence; create; originate: *He began the reform movement after the war.* [Old English *beginnan* to start.]

Syn. *v.t.* **1.** Begin, commence, start mean to enter on a particular course of action. **Begin** means to take the first step toward a given end: *Paul began to read the letter aloud.* **Commence** is identical in meaning but is preferred in formal language: *The court commenced its work with a prayer.* **Start** means to set out from a definite point and implies that there was or will be a stop: *The ship started on its voyage.*

be·gin·ner (bi gin′ər) *n.* one who is just beginning to do or learn something; novice: *He drives better than most beginners.* **2.** one who begins or originates anything; founder.

be·gin·ning (bi gin′ing) *n.* **1.** first part: *The beginning of the trip was dull.* **2.** point at which something begins: *They signaled the beginning of the race.* **3.** act of starting: *A ceremony was held to commemorate the beginning of the library's construction.* **4.** first cause; source; origin: *The beginning of the dispute is unknown.* **5.** *also,* **beginnings.** initial or rudimentary stage: *the beginnings of medical science.*

be·gird (bi gûrd′) **-girt** (-gûrt′) or **-gird·ed, -gird·ing.** *v.t.* to gird; encircle; surround.

be·gone (bi gôn′, -gon′) *v.i. Archaic.* to go away; depart. ▲ appears most frequently in the imperative.

be·gon·ia (bi gōn′yə, -gō′nē ə) *n.* **1.** large showy flower of certain plants, genus *Begonia,* now widely cultivated in temperate zones. The flowers may be white, yellow, red, purple, or pink. **2.** plant bearing this flower. **3.** any other flowering or nonflowering plant of the genus *Be-*

gonia. [Modern Latin *begonia,* from Michel *Bégon,* 1638–1710, a French botanist.]

be·got (bi got') past tense and past participle of **beget.**

be·got·ten (bi got'ən) a past participle of **beget.**

be·grime (bi grīm') -grimed, -grim·ing. *v.t.* to make grimy; soil.

be·grudge (bi gruj') -grudged, -grudg·ing. *v.t.* **1.** to envy (someone) the possession or pleasure of: *Don't begrudge him his good fortune.* **2.** to give or allow reluctantly: *He begrudged the beggar a few pennies.* —**be·grudg'ing·ly,** *adv.*

be·guile (bi gīl') -guiled, -guil·ing. *v.t.* **1.** to influence by guile; mislead; deceive. **2.** to amuse or delight; charm. **3.** to pass (time) pleasantly. —**be·guile'ment, be·guil'er,** *n.*

be·guine (bə gēn') *n.* **1.** social dance similar to the rumba. **2.** music for this dance.

be·gum (bē'gəm) *n.* Muslim woman of high rank. [Urdu *begam* lady; of Turkic origin.]

be·gun (bi gun') past participle of **begin.**

be·half (bi haf') *n.* **1. in** (or **on**) **behalf of. a.** in the interest of; for the benefit of: *A carnival was planned in behalf of the church.* **b.** in the name of; as a representative of: *The minister accepted the contribution on behalf of his congregation.* **2. in** (or **on**) **one's behalf.** in the interest of or aid of (someone); for one's benefit: *He intervened in my behalf.* [From Middle English phrase *on behalve* on the side of, from blend of Old English *on healfe* on the side of and *be healfe* by the side of.]

be·have (bi hāv') -haved, -hav·ing. *v.i.* **1.** to act in a particular way: *He behaved admirably under stress.* **2.** to conduct oneself properly: *Did he behave while I was out?* **3.** to perform, function, or react in a particular way: *This substance behaves like mercury.* —*v.t.* to conduct (oneself), esp. in a proper manner: *Sit up and behave yourself.*

be·hav·ior (bi hāv'yər) *also, British,* **be·hav·iour.** *n.* **1.** manner of behaving or acting; conduct; deportment: *His behavior was disgraceful.* **2.** manner in which something acts under given circumstances: *the behavior of coal under pressure.* **3.** *Psychology.* actions or responses of an organism.
Syn. 1. Behavior, conduct denote the manner in which one acts or manages oneself. **Behavior** denotes the social acts of men and animals which express their personality or breeding: *The man apologized for his rude behavior.* **Conduct** denotes behavior as influenced by discipline or in accordance with one's duties and obligations: *The officer was commended for his good conduct.*

be·hav·ior·ism (bi hāv'yə riz'əm) *n.* system of psychology emphasizing openly observable behavior, rather than mental activity, as a valid source of scientific data. —**be·hav'ior·ist,** *n., adj.* —**be·hav'ior·is'tic,** *adj.*

be·head (bi hed') *v.t.* to cut off the head of; decapitate.

be·held (bi held') past tense and past participle of **behold.**

be·he·moth (bi hē'məth, bē'ə mŏth') *n.* **1.** in the Bible, an enormous animal, assumed to be the hippopotamus. **2.** any creature or thing of monstrous size or power. [Hebrew *b'hēmôth,* plural of *b'hēmāh* beast, possibly from Egyptian *p-ehe-mau,* hippopotamus.]

be·hest (bi hest') *n.* authoritative or insistent request; command; bidding. [Old English *behǣs* vow, promise.]

be·hind (bi hīnd') *prep.* **1.** at or toward the back of; in the rear of: *I sat behind a very tall man. Look behind you.* **2.** at or on the farther side of; beyond: *The path runs behind these hedges.* **3.** not on or up to: *Production was running behind schedule.* **4.** later than; after: *Our truck came ten minutes behind the first one.* **5.** less advanced than; inferior to: *a nation far behind its neighbors in technology.* **6.** hidden by: *Fear lay behind her show of bravery.* **7.** causing or contributing to: *What were the reasons behind his resignation?* **8.** in support of; supporting; backing: *The senators are fully behind his welfare policy.* **9.** remaining after: *Leave your cares behind you.* —*adv.* **1.** in a place or condition departed from: *He left a great legacy behind. She wished to remain behind.* **2.** at or toward the rear; in the rear: *They grabbed him from behind. Unable to keep up, he dropped behind.* **3.** not on time; slow: *They are behind in their work.* **4.** in or into arrears; overdue: *He fell behind in his payments.* —*n. Informal.* buttocks. [Old English *behindan* in the rear (of).]
Syn. prep. 1. Behind, after mean following upon in space or in time. **Behind** denotes a position to the rear or back of something and when applied to movement suggests backwardness: *They live in a pretty cottage behind an orchard.* **After** implies behind in place or in time and is usually used with verbs implying motion, order, and sequence: *The actors entered the stage, one after another.*

be·hind·hand (bi hīnd'hand') *adv., adj.* behind schedule; late.

be·hold (bi hōld') **be·held, be·hold·ing.** *v.t.* **1.** to look at; gaze upon; see. —*interj.* look; see. [Old English *behealdan* to hold, see.] —**be·hold'er,** *n.*

be·hold·en (bi hōl'dən) *adj.* obligated; indebted.

be·hoof (bi hōōf') *n. Archaic.* advantage; benefit. [Old English *behôf.*]

be·hoove (bi hōōv') -hooved, -hoov·ing. *v.t.* to be necessary, fitting,

or advantageous for: *It behooves a gentleman to stand when a lady enters. It behooves you to be on good terms with him.* [Old English *behôfian* to need.]

beige (bāzh) *n.* pale-brown or grayish-tan color. [French *beige;* of uncertain origin.]

be·ing (bē'ing) *n.* **1.** existence; life: *to come into being.* **2.** creature: *a human being, a celestial being.* **3.** essential nature; essence: *His essay examined the very being of literature.* **4.** *Philosophy.* that which exists or is logically conceivable. **5.** one's whole being. all of one's capacities: *He responded with his whole being.*

Bei·rut (bā rōōt') *n.* capital, largest city, and chief port of Lebanon, in the west-central part of the country, on the Mediterranean. Pop. (1964 est.), 700,000. Also, **Bey·routh'.**

be·jew·el (bi jōō'əl) -eled, -el·ing; *also, British,* -elled, -el·ling. *v.t.* to adorn with or as with jewels.

bel (bel) *n. Physics.* unit expressing the ratio of the values of two amounts of power, used to measure sound intensity. One bel equals ten decibels. [From Alexander Graham Bell.]

Bel (bāl, bel) *n.* Assyrian and Babylonian god of the earth and of nature. [Akkadian *Belu* literally, master, lord.]

be·la·bor (bi lā'bər) *also, British,* **be·la·bour.** *v.t.* **1.** to beat soundly; thrash. **2.** to assail verbally: *She constantly belabored and nagged her husband.* **3.** to deal with (something) for an excessive amount of time: *He belabored the point long after the audience had lost interest.*

be·lat·ed (bi lā'tid) *adj.* delayed; late: *his belated arrival, a belated birthday present.* —**be·lat'ed·ly,** *adv.* —**be·lat'ed·ness,** *n.*

be·lay (bi lā') **be·layed, be·lay·ing.** *v.t., v.i. Nautical.* **1.** to secure (a rope) by winding around a belaying pin, cleat, or similar object. **2.** *Informal.* to stop; hold. ▲ used chiefly in the imperative: *Belay there!* [Dutch *beleggen* to wind around.]

belaying pin *Nautical.* removable pin around which running rigging is made fast.

belch (belch) *v.i.* **1.** to expel gas noisily from the stomach through the mouth. **2.** to issue forth; gush: *Flames belched from the windows of the burning house.* **3.** to expel its contents violently: *The geyser rumbled and belched.* —*v.t.* to eject or emit violently or spasmodically: *The chimney belched smoke and sparks.* —*n.* act of belching. [Old English *bealcan* to eructate, give vent to.]

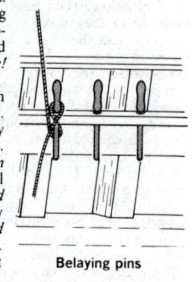
Belaying pins

bel·dam (bel'dəm) *also,* **bel·dame** (bel'dəm, -dām'). *n.* old woman, esp. one who is ugly; hag. [Middle English *beldam,* from *bel-* grand (going back to Latin *bellus* handsome) + *dam* mother, lady (going back to Latin *domina* lady).]

be·lea·guer (bi lē'gər) *v.t.* **1.** to surround or shut in with troops; besiege: *to beleaguer a castle.* **2.** to surround or harass; beset: *He was beleaguered with annoyances.* [Dutch *belegeren* to besiege with troops; literally, to camp beside, from *be-* by + *leger* camp.]

Be·lém (bə lem') *n.* port city in northeastern Brazil. Pop. (1968 est.), 563,996.

Bel·fast (bel'fast) *n.* capital, largest city, and chief port of Northern Ireland, on the eastern coast of the country. Pop. (1968 est.), 390,700.

bel·fry (bel'frē) *pl.,* -fries. *n.* **1.** bell tower, esp. one attached to a church or other structure. **2.** that part of a steeple or tower in which a bell or bells are hung. [Middle English *berfrey* siege tower (influenced by *bell*), from Old French *berfrei,* from Middle High German *bercfrit* protecting tower. A *berfrey,* originally a movable tower used in attacks, was later used as a watch tower and had an alarm *bell.*]

Belg., Belgian; Belgium.

Bel·gian (bel'jən) *adj.* of or relating to Belgium, its people, or their culture. —*n.* member or close descendant of the people of Belgium.

Belfry

Belgian Congo, former Belgian colony in central Africa, now the Democratic Republic of the Congo, officially named **Zaire.** It was originally known as the Congo Free State.

Belgian hare, reddish-brown domestic rabbit, raised in Europe for meat.

Bel·gium (bel'jəm) *n.* country in northwestern Europe, on the North Sea. Capital, Brussels. Area, 11,779 sq. mi. Pop. (1969 est.), 9,660,000.

Bel·grade (bel'grād, bel grād') *n.* capital, largest city, and major port of Yugoslavia, in the eastern part of the country. Pop. (1966), 697,000.

Be·li·al (bē′lē əl, bēl′yəl) *n.* **1.** in the New Testament, a figure thought of as representing evil; the Devil. **2.** one of the fallen angels in Milton's *Paradise Lost.* [Hebrew *b'liya'al* Satan, literally, worthlessness.]

be·lie (bi lī′) **-lied, -ly·ing.** *v. t.* **1.** to misrepresent; disguise: *His face belies his thoughts.* **2.** to show to be false; contradict: *His trembling hands belied his profession of innocence.* **3.** to fail to come up to; disappoint: *to belie expectations.* [Old English *belēogan* to deceive by lies.]

be·lief (bi lēf′) *n.* **1.** acceptance of the truth or reality of: *a belief in life on other planets.* **2.** that which is believed; opinion; conviction: *We must uphold our democratic beliefs.* **3.** confidence, esp. in another person; faith; trust: *I have great belief in his ability to succeed.* [Middle English *bileafe* faith, opinion, from Old English *gelēafa* faith (with substitution of BE- for *ge-*).]

Syn. 1. **Belief, faith** denote acceptance of the truth or validity of something. **Belief,** the more general term, denotes acceptance with or without proof or reasoning: *Nothing can shake my belief in his honesty.* **Faith** suggests blind and unquestioning belief for which there is no rational proof or material evidence: *The old woman has a deep faith in miracles.* **2.** see **opinion.**

be·lieve (bi lēv′) **-lieved, -liev·ing.** *v. t.* **1.** to accept as true or real: *I believe your story.* **2.** to credit (somebody) with truthfulness: *I don't believe you.* **3.** to be of the opinion; think; suppose: *I believe she went out shopping.* **4.** to make believe, to imagine; pretend. —*v. i.* **1.** to have religious faith. **2. to believe in. a.** to be convinced of the truth, existence, or worth of (something): *to believe in ghosts, to believe in freedom of speech.* **b.** to have confidence or faith in: *We believe in our government. I believe in him.* [Old English *belīefan.*] —**be·liev′a·ble,** *adj.* —**be·liev′er,** *n.*

be·like (bi līk′) *adv. Archaic.* perhaps; probably.

be·lit·tle (bi lit′əl) **-tled, -tling.** *v. t.* to cause to seem small or less important; disparage: *He belittled his opponent's arguments.* —**be·lit′tler,** *n.* —**Syn.** see **disparage.**

Be·lize (bē lēz′) *n.* **1.** country on the northeastern coast of Central America, on the Caribbean, formerly British Honduras. Capital, Belize. Area, 8,867 sq. mi. Pop. (1974 est.), 130,000. **2.** its capital, on the eastern coast. Pop. (1970), 39,332.

bell¹ (bel) *n.* **1.** hollow, metallic instrument, usually cup-shaped, that rings when struck by a clapper, hammer, or similar object. **2.** sound produced by a bell. **3.** something resembling a bell in shape or function, as the flared lower end of a musical instrument or a doorbell. **4.** *Nautical.* **a.** stroke of a bell sounded aboard ship to mark intervals during the watches, which begin at 4:00, 8:00, and 12:00. One bell signals the end of the first half hour of a watch, and an additional bell is struck for each succeeding half hour, so that eight bells signal the end of a four-hour watch. **b.** half-hour interval thus indicated. **5. to ring** (or **strike**) **a bell,** to evoke a response of recognition; remind one of something: *The name rings a bell.* —*v. t.* **1.** to put a bell on. **2.** to cause to swell out like a bell. **3. to bell the cat,** to perform a daring or dangerous feat. [Old English *belle* hollow metallic instrument that rings when struck.]

bell² (bel) *v. i.* to bellow or cry, as a stag or hound. —*n.* bellow; cry. [Old English *bellan* to make a loud noise.]

Bell, Alexander Gra·ham (bel; grā′əm) 1847–1922, American inventor of the telephone, born in Scotland.

bel·la·don·na (bel′ə don′ə) *n.* **1.** plant, genus *Atropa,* of the nightshade family, native to the Mediterranean areas of Europe and Asia, having bell-shaped purplish or reddish flowers and poisonous black berries. Also, **deadly nightshade. 2.** drug derived from this plant, chiefly used to dilate the pupil of the eye, to stimulate the heart, and to relieve spasms. [Italian *bella donna* literally, beautiful lady (with reference to a beauty preparation obtained from its berries and leaves), going back to Latin *bellus* handsome + *domina* lady.]

belladonna lily, ornamental plant, *Brunsvigia rosea,* of the amaryllis family, widely cultivated throughout the world, having long strap-shaped leaves and bearing large fragrant red, white, or purple flowers.

bell-bot·tom (bel′bot′əm) *also,* **bell-bot·tomed.** *adj.* (of trousers) gradually flaring from below the knee to the bottom of each leg.

bell-bot·toms (bel′bot′əmz) *n.* bell-bottom trousers.

bell·boy (bel′boi′) *n.* man or boy employed, as in a hotel or club, to carry luggage, attend to guests, and run errands.

bell buoy, buoy with a bell mounted on it that is rung by the motion of the sea or by electric batteries.

bell captain, employee, as in a hotel, who supervises the bellboys.

belle (bel) *n.* **1.** beautiful woman or girl: *a Southern belle.* **2.** most beautiful, popular, or admired woman or girl (in a certain place or situation). [French *belle,* feminine of *beau* handsome. See BEAU.]

Bel·leau Wood (bel′ō) forest northeast of Paris, site of a World War I battle in June, 1918. It is a memorial to the United States marines who died there.

Bel·ler·o·phon (bə ler′ə fon′) *n. Greek Legend.* Corinthian hero who killed the monstrous Chimera.

belles-let·tres (bel′let′rə) *n., pl.* literature, including fiction, drama, poetry, and criticism, having artistic rather than didactic value or appeal. [French *belles-lettres* (plural). See BELLE, LETTER.]

bell·flow·er (bel′flou′ər) *n.* **1.** bell-shaped flower of any of a large group of plants, genus *Campanula,* found throughout the Northern Hemisphere and ranging in color from lavender to blue. **2.** plant bearing this flower, having narrow, scalloped or toothed leaves.

bell·hop (bel′hop′) *n.* bellboy.

bel·li·cose (bel′ə kōs′) *adj.* exhibiting a tendency or eagerness to fight; warlike: *a bellicose people, a bellicose disposition.* [Latin *bellicōsus.*] —**bel·li·cos·i·ty** (bel′ə kos′ə tē), *n.*

bel·lig·er·ence (bə lij′ər əns) *n.* **1.** state or quality of being belligerent: *His belligerence is provoking.* **2.** fighting; warfare.

bel·lig·er·en·cy (bə lij′ər ən sē) *n.* **1.** status of a belligerent country; state of being at war. **2.** belligerence.

bel·lig·er·ent (bə lij′ər ənt) *adj.* **1.** eager or willing to fight; hostile: *a belligerent attitude. He's a belligerent young man.* **2.** engaged in warfare; at war: *belligerent countries.* —*n.* country or person engaged in warfare or fighting. [Latin *belligerāns,* present participle of *belligerāre* to wage war.] —**bel·lig′er·ent·ly,** *adv.*

Bel·li·ni (be lē′nē) **1.** Ja·co·po (yä′kō pō). c.1400–c.1470, Venetian painter. **2.** Gio·van·ni (jō vän′nē). c.1430–1516, son of Jacopo; Venetian painter. **3.** Gen·ti·le (jen tē′lā). c.1429–1507, son of Jacopo; Venetian painter. **4.** Vin·cen·zo (vēn chen′zō). 1801–35, composer of operas.

bell jar, bell-shaped glass vessel used to cover objects, to contain gases, or to create a vacuum. Also, **bell glass.**

bell·man (bel′mən) *pl.,* **-men.** *n. Archaic.* town crier.

bel·low (bel′ō) *v. i.* **1.** to emit a loud, hollow sound: *wild beasts bellowing and roaring.* **2.** to cry out in a loud, deep voice; roar: *The injured man bellowed with pain.* —*v. t.* to utter (words or sounds) loudly and deeply. —*n.* **1.** loud, hollow sound: *the bellow of an angry man, the bellow of a bull, the bellow of a foghorn.* **2.** loud, deep outcry. [Old English *bylgean* to roar like a bull, or Old English *bellan* to make a loud noise.]

Bell jar

bel·lows (bel′ōz, -əs) *n.* **1.** device for producing an air current, as for making a fire burn faster or for sounding a musical instrument, consisting of an expansible air chamber into which air is drawn and from which it is expelled under pressure. **2.** anything that resembles a bellows, as the collapsible connection between the lens and body of a folding camera. ▲ construed as singular or plural in both definitions. [Old English *belga,* plural of *bel(i)g* bag.]

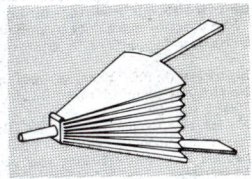

Bellows

bell pepper, sweet pepper.

bell·weth·er (bel′weth′ər) *n.* **1.** male sheep that leads the flock, usually having a bell around its neck. **2.** someone or something that leads or signifies a trend: *That city is a bellwether in state elections.*

bel·ly (bel′ē) *pl.,* **-lies.** *n.* **1.** abdomen (*def.* 1). **2.** underside of the body of an animal. **3.** stomach, esp. in its capacity or appetite for food. **4.** internal cavity; interior: *the belly of a ship.* **5.** curved or bulging surface or part: *the belly of a laboratory flask.* **6.** front or under surface of anything: *The plane landed on its belly.* Distinguished from **back.** **7.** fleshy part of a muscle. —*v. t., v. i.,* **-lied, -ly·ing.** to swell or billow out; bulge. [Old English *belig* bag.]

bel·ly·ache (bel′ē āk′) *n.* pain in the abdomen, esp. the stomach. —*v. i.* **-ached, -ach·ing.** *Slang.* to complain peevishly; whine.

bel·ly·band (bel′ē band′) *n.* strap running under an animal's belly forming part of a harness. See **harness** for illustration.

bel·ly·but·ton (bel′ē but′ən) *n. Informal.* navel.

belly flop, dive in which the front of the diver's body lands forcefully, in a horizontal position. —*v. i.,* **flopped, flop·ping.** to make a belly flop.

bel·ly·ful (bel′ē fool′) *n.* **1.** enough to fill the stomach or satiate the appetite. **2.** *Informal.* enough or more than enough: *We've had a bellyful of her antics.*

belly laugh 1. hearty laugh. **2.** cause of such a laugh.

Be·lo Ho·ri·zon·te (bel′ō hôr′ə zon′tē) city in southeastern Brazil. Pop. (1968 est.), 1,167,026.

be·long (bi lông′) *v. i.* **1.** to have a proper place; be suitable or right: *The lamp belongs on that table. You don't belong in the beginner's class.* **2. to belong to. a.** to be the property of: *This book belongs to me.* **b.** to be an adjunct, attribute, or part of; be connected with. **c.** to be

at; āpe; cär; end; mē; it; īce; hot; ōld; fôrk; wood; fōōl; oil; out; up; ūse; turn; sing; thin; this; zh in treasure; ə in ago, taken, pencil, lemon, circus.

89

a member of: *He belongs to a club.* [Middle English *belongen,* from BE- + *longen* to concern, pertain, going back to Old English *langian* to desire.]

be·long·ings (bi lông'ingz) *n.,pl.* personal property; possessions.

be·lov·ed (bi luv'id, -luvd') *adj.* much loved. —*n.* one who is dearly loved.

be·low (bi lō') *adv.* **1.** in or to a lower place: *in the valley below.* **2.** on or to a lower floor or deck: *We stowed the gear below.* **3.** in a lower rank. **4.** in a later part of a book or other piece of writing: *A detailed description is given below.* **5.** on earth. **6.** in or to hell. —*prep.* **1.** in a lower place or position than: *below the neck.* **2.** lower in rank, degree, or amount than; less than: *five dollars below cost.* **3.** unworthy of; beneath: *It is below her to speak to the peasants.* [*Be,* form of BY + LOW[1].]

Bel·sen (bel'zən) *n.* Nazi concentration camp of World War II, in north-central Germany, near Hanover.

Bel·shaz·zar (bel shaz'ər) *n.* in the Old Testament, the son of Nebuchadnezzar and last Chaldean king of Babylon, whose doom was prophesied by the writing on the wall.

belt (belt) *n.* **1.** strip or band of leather or other pliant material worn around the body as a support for clothing or tools, as an ornament or identification, or for safety. **2.** any strip or band that encircles something: *radiation belt.* **3.** region or zone characterized by or noted for something distinctive: *a wheat belt.* **4.** *Mechanics.* **a.** unbroken flexible band passing around two or more wheels or pulleys, used to transmit power or motion. **b.** conveyor belt. **5.** *Informal.* strong or powerful blow. **6. below the belt. a.** in boxing, below the waist. **b.** unfair; unfairly. **7. to tighten one's belt.** to live in a more thrifty way; reduce expenses. **8. under (one's) belt. a.** in the stomach. **b.** assimilated, as of past experience. —*v.t.* **1.** to encircle or fasten with a belt. **2.** to beat or strike with a belt or strap. **3.** *Informal.* to strike forcefully. **4.** *Informal.* to sing in a loud, forceful style: *She belted out a lively blues song.* [Old English *belt* girdle, going back to Latin *balteus;* probably of Etruscan origin.]

belt·ing (bel'ting) *n.* **1.** material used for belts. **2.** belts. **3.** *Informal.* beating; thrashing.

be·lu·ga (bə lōō'gə) *n.* **1.** freshwater sturgeon, *Huso huso,* of the Black Sea, Caspian Sea, and Volga River, whose eggs are processed to be eaten as caviar. **2.** white whale, *Delphinapterus leucas,* of the shallow coastal waters of Arctic seas. Length: 18 feet. [Russian *byeluga* sturgeon, and Russian *byelukha* white whale; both from *byelyi* white.]

be·mire (bi mīr') *-mired, -mir·ing.* *v.t.* **1.** to sink in mud or mire. **2.** to cover or make dirty with mud.

be·moan (bi mōn') *v.t.* to grieve over; bewail; lament: *to bemoan one's fate.*

be·muse (bi mūz') *-mused, -mus·ing.* *v.t.* to confuse; stupefy.

be·mused (bi mūzd') *adj.* lost in thought; preoccupied. **2.** confused; stupefied.

Be·na·res (bə när'is, -ēz) *also,* **Ba·na·ras.** *n.* Hindu holy city in northeastern India. Official name: **Varanasi.** Pop. (1969 est.), 619,822.

bench (bench) *n.* **1.** long seat, with or without a back. **2.** sturdy worktable: *a cobbler's bench.* **3.a.** seat for judges in a law court. **b.** office or position of a judge: *He was appointed to the bench.* **c.** judge or judges who sit in a law court. **4.** strip of elevated, relatively level land on a slope or along a coast. **5.** platform used for exhibiting animals, esp. dogs, at a show. **6. on the bench. a.** serving as judge in a law court. **b.** *Sports.* (of a player) not participating in the game. —*v.t.* **1.** to keep (a player) from participating in a game or games: *He was benched for the rest of the season.* **2.** to exhibit on or as on a bench: *to bench a dog.* **3.** to seat (someone) on a bench. [Old English *benc* long seat.]

bench·er (ben'chər) *n.* *British.* one who sits on an official bench, as a judge or a member of Parliament.

bench mark, identifying mark made on a fixed object of known elevation, used in surveying as a starting point or reference.

bench warrant, warrant issued by a judge or a court of law for the apprehension or arrest of a person.

bend[1] (bend) *bent, bend·ing.* *v.t.* **1.** to change the shape of, esp. by making curved or crooked. **2.** to cause to yield; make submissive: *She could bend him to her will.* **3.** to direct or apply (one's mind or energies to or toward): *He bent all his energies toward building his business.* **4.** to direct or turn from a straight line; deflect. **5.** *Nautical.* to tie; secure: *to bend a sail to the mast.* —*v.i.* **1.** to become curved or crooked: *The branch bent under the weight of its fruit.* **2.** to assume a stooping posture; bow: *He bent over to tie his shoe.* **3.** to turn in a particular direction: *The river bends westward.* **4.** to yield in submission or deference; yield. **5. to bend over backward** (or **backwards**). to make a determined effort; do one's best. —*n.* **1.** thing or part of a thing that is curved or bent; crook: *a bend in the river.* **2.** act of bending; being bent. **3.** *Nautical.* **a.** any of several knots used to join two ropes or to fasten a rope to something else. **b.** bends. wales. **4. the bends.**

painful condition caused by nitrogen gas bubbles in the body, resulting from a rapid decrease in external pressure on the body. Also, **caisson disease.** [Old English *bendan* to stretch a bow, bind.]

Syn. *v.t.* **1.** Bend, bow[1], crook, twist mean to cause something to deviate from a straight line. Bend usually implies a smooth curve, but may involve sharp angles: *You can bend that pipe without breaking it, but the metal strip will snap if you try to bend it.* Bow implies a curve like that of an archer's bow: *The weight of the books bowed the shelf.* Crook suggests a somewhat circular curve, like that of a shepherd's staff: *He crooked a finger at the waiter.* Twist suggests a distorted, unnatural turning: *He twisted his ankle coming down the stairs, causing a bad sprain.*

bend[2] (bend) *n.* diagonal band on a heraldic shield. [Partly from Old English *bend* band, bond; partly from Old French *bende* bond, heraldic band (of Germanic origin).]

bend·er (ben'dər) *n.* **1.** one who or that which bends. **2.** *Slang.* drinking spree.

be·neath (bi nēth') *prep.* **1.** lower than; below: *as we stood beneath the stars.* **2.** directly under; underneath: *firm earth beneath my feet.* **3.** not fitting the dignity of; unworthy of: *Lying is beneath him.* **4.** under the influence or pressure of: *to sink beneath the weight of oppression.* —*adv.* below; underneath. [Old English *beneothan* below.]

ben·e·di·ci·te (ben'ə dis'ə tē) *interj.* **1.** invocation of a blessing, esp. one said before a meal. **2. Benedicite.** canticle that begins *Benedicite omnia opera Domini* in Latin and *O all ye works of the Lord, bless ye the Lord* in English. —*interj.* bless you. [Latin *benedicite,* plural imperative of *benedicere* to bless, praise.]

ben·e·dict (ben'ə dikt') *n.* newly married man, esp. one who had seemed to be a confirmed bachelor. [From *Benedick,* a character in Shakespeare's *Much Ado About Nothing,* a bachelor who eventually marries.]

Ben·e·dict XIV (ben'ə dikt') 1675–1758, pope from 1740 to 1758.

Benedict XV, 1854–1922, pope from 1914 to 1922.

Ben·e·dic·tine (*n. def. 1,* ben'ə dik'tin, -tēn; *n. def. 2, adj.,* ben'ə dik'tēn) *n.* **1.** monk or nun following the rules of the order founded by Saint Benedict in the sixth century. **2.** herb-flavored liqueur. —*adj.* of or relating to Saint Benedict or his religious order. [French *bénédictin* monk of the order of Saint Benedict, from Late Latin *Benedictus* (Saint) Benedict.]

Benedictine rule, set of rules stressing useful employment and frugality that governs life in Benedictine monasteries.

ben·e·dic·tion (ben'ə dik'shən) *n.* **1.** invocation of a divine blessing upon a person or persons, esp. at the close of a church service. **2.** blessing so invoked. **3.** result of a blessing; blessedness. [Latin *benedictio* praising, blessing. Doublet of BENISON.]

Benedict of Nur·sia, Saint (nûr'shə) c.480–c.550, Italian founder of the Benedictine order.

Ben·e·dic·tus (ben'ə dik'təs) *n.* **1.** canticle of praise beginning *Benedictus qui venit in nomine Domini* in Latin and *Blessed is He that cometh in the name of the Lord* in English. **2.** canticle of thanksgiving beginning *Benedictus Dominus Deus Israel* in Latin and *Blessed be the Lord God of Israel* in English. **3.** musical setting of either of these canticles. [Latin *benedictus* blessed, past participle of *benedicere* to bless.]

ben·e·fac·tion (ben'ə fak'shən) *n.* **1.** act of conferring a benefit; kind or generous act. **2.** benefit conferred; charitable gift, esp. of money.

ben·e·fac·tor (ben'ə fak'tər) *n.* one who gives help or financial aid; patron. [Latin *benefactor,* going back to *bene* well + *facere* to do.] —**ben'e·fac'tress,** *n.*

ben·e·fice (ben'ə fis) *n.* endowed church office, esp. that of a rector or vicar. [Old French *benefice,* from Latin *beneficium* kindness.]

be·nef·i·cence (bə nef'ə səns) *n.* **1.** active kindness or generosity; doing good. **2.** charitable gift or act. [Latin *beneficentia* kindness.] —**Syn. 1.** see benevolence.

be·nef·i·cent (bə nef'ə sənt) *adj.* **1.** doing or effecting good; being charitable. **2.** resulting in good: *a beneficent gift.*

ben·e·fi·cial (ben'ə fish'əl) *adj.* having a good effect; advantageous; helpful: *Some insects are harmful, others are beneficial.* —**ben'e·fi'cial·ly,** *adv.*

ben·e·fi·ci·ar·y (ben'ə fish'ē er'ē, -fish'ər ē) *pl.,* **-ar·ies.** *n.* **1.** one who receives anything as a benefit: *He was the beneficiary of a generous scholarship.* **2.** person named to receive the money or proceeds from a will, trust, or insurance policy.

ben·e·fit (ben'ə fit) *n.* **1.** something that helps or betters a person or thing; advantage. **2.a.** money or other services given by an insurance company, government agency, or other institution, as to the sick, disabled, or aged: *Social Security benefits.* **b.** fringe benefit. **3.** social or theatrical event held to raise money for some charity or cause. **4.** *Archaic.* act of kindness; good deed. —*v.t.* to be useful, profitable, or helpful to: *Rain will benefit the crops.* —*v.i.* to gain or profit; receive help: *We can all benefit from his knowledge.* [Anglo-Norman *benfet* good deed, from Latin *benefactum* benefit.] —**Syn. 1.** see advantage.

at; āpe; cär; end; mē; it; īce; hot; ōld; fôrk; wood; fōōl; oil; out; up; ūse; turn; sing; thin; this; zh in treasure; ə in ago, taken, pencil, lemon, circus.

benefit of clergy **1.** former privilege allowing a member of the clergy accused of serious crimes to be tried in ecclesiastic rather than secular courts. **2.** services administered or sanction given by a church.

Ben·e·lux (ben′ə luks′) *n.* the economic union of Belgium, the Netherlands, and Luxembourg.

Be·nét, Stephen Vincent (bə nā′) 1898–1943, U.S. poet, novelist, and short-story writer.

be·nev·o·lence (bə nev′ə ləns) *n.* **1.** disposition to do good; kindliness; generosity. **2.** forced loan or contribution formerly levied by some English kings on their subjects. **3.** *Archaic.* act of kindness. [Old French *benevolence* good will, from Latin *benevolentia* kindness.]
Syn. 1. Benevolence, beneficence, kindness refer to sympathy and feeling for others. **Benevolence** implies a deep-rooted character trait that causes one to care about others: *His benevolence caused him to work for many charities.* **Beneficence**, on the other hand, is the actual performing of good: *His beneficence helped the families left homeless by the flood.* **Kindness** combines both warm feelings and doing good: *Kindness does not consist in gifts, but in gentleness and generosity of spirit* (Smiles, 1871).

be·nev·o·lent (bə nev′ə lənt) *adj.* doing or desiring to do good; kindly: *a benevolent despot, his benevolent acts.* **—be·nev′o·lent·ly,** *adv.*

Ben·gal (ben gôl′, beng-) **1.** former province and historic region of northeastern British India, divided between India and Pakistan in 1947. **2. Bay of.** northeastern part of the Indian Ocean, between Burma and the peninsula of India.

Ben·ga·lese (ben gə lēz′, -lēs′ beng-′) *adj.* of or relating to Bengal or its people. **—n.** *pl.,* **-lese.** native or inhabitant of Bengal.

Ben·ga·li (ben gô′lē, beng-) *adj.* of or relating to Bengal, its people, or their language. **—n. 1.** Bengalese. **2.** modern Indic language of the Indo-European family spoken predominantly in Bengal.

ben·ga·line (beng′gə lēn′) *n.* durable corded fabric of silk or rayon with wool or cotton in it. [French *bengaline,* from *Bengal,* source of a fabric it resembles.]

Ben·gha·zi (ben gä′zē) *also,* **Ben·ga·si.** *n.* one of the two capitals of Libya, a port city in the northeastern part of the country. Pop. (1964), 137,295.

be·night·ed (bi nī′tid) *adj.* **1.** morally or intellectually unaware; unenlightened; ignorant. **2.** *Archaic.* overtaken by night. [Past participle of obsolete *benight* to be overtaken by night, from BE- + NIGHT.]

be·nign (bi nīn′) *adj.* **1.** of a kindly or gentle disposition: *a benign old man.* **2.** caused by or exhibiting gentleness or kindness: *a benign smile.* **3.** favorable; beneficial: *a benign climate.* **4.** *Medicine.* not malignant: *a benign tumor.* [Old French *benigne* kind, from Latin *benīgnus* kind; literally, well-born.] **—be·nign′ly,** *adv.*

be·nig·nan·cy (bi nig′nən sē) *n.* quality or condition of being benignant.

be·nig·nant (bi nig′nənt) *adj.* **1.** kindly or gracious, esp. toward inferiors: *a benignant sovereign.* **2.** favorable; beneficial: *The sun sheds its benignant rays.* **—be·nig′nant·ly,** *adv.*

be·nig·ni·ty (bi nig′nə tē) *pl.,* **-ties. 1.** kindliness; benignancy. **2.** kind or gracious act.

Ben·in (ben in′) *n.* country in western Africa, formerly called Dahomey. Capital, Porto-Novo. Area, 44,713 sq. mi. Pop. (1975 est.), 3,100,000.

ben·i·son (ben′ə zən, -sən) *n.* blessing; benediction. [Old French *beneison,* from Latin *benedictiō.* Doublet of BENEDICTION.]

Ben·ja·min (ben′jə min) *n.* **1.** in the Old Testament, the youngest son of Jacob. **2.** tribe of Israel descended from him.

Ben·nett, Arnold (ben′ət) 1867–1931, English novelist and playwright.

bent¹ (bent) *v.* past tense and past participle of **bend.** **—adj. 1.** not straight; curved. **2. bent on.** with the fixed purpose of; determined to: *bent on avenging his father's death.* **—n.** inclination or ability; leaning: *a bent for dancing. He has a natural bent for fixing things.*

bent² (bent) *n.* **1.** any of various grasses that make up the genus *Agrostis,* found esp. in the north temperate zone. Certain varieties are cultivated as lawn and pasture grasses. Also, **bent grass. 2.** *Archaic.* heath. [Old English *beonet-* (found only in compounds) stiff grass.]

Ben·tham, Jeremy (ben′thəm, -təm) 1748–1832, English philosopher, lawyer, and reformer.

be·numb (bi num′) *v.t.* **1.** to make numb; deprive of sensation. **2.** to render inactive; stupefy. [Old English *benumen,* past participle of *beniman* to deprive.]

ben·ze·drine (ben′zə drēn′) *n.* sulfate of amphetamine, a drug used as a stimulant, esp. for staying awake. Trademark: Benzedrine. Formula: $(C_9H_{13}N)_2 \cdot H_2SO_4$

ben·zene (ben′zēn, ben zēn′) *n.* colorless liquid hydrocarbon which is toxic, volatile, and flammable. It is obtained from coal tar and the refining of petroleum and is used as a solvent for waxes and oils and in the manufacture of other chemicals and synthetic materials. Formula: C_6H_6 [BENZ(OIC ACID) + -ENE.]

benzene ring **1.** molecular structure that exists in benzene and other aromatic compounds. In benzene it consists of six carbon atoms linked in a six-sided ring, with a hydrogen atom attached to each carbon atom. Different atoms or groups replace the hydrogen atoms to form different aromatic compounds. **2.** representation of such a structure.

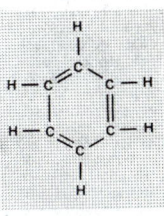
Benzene ring

ben·zine (ben′zēn, ben zēn′) *n.* colorless, volatile, flammable mixture of hydrocarbons obtained in petroleum distillation, used as a solvent and as a motor fuel; ligroin. [BENZ(OIC ACID) + -INE².]

ben·zo·ate (ben′zō āt′) *n.* salt or ester of benzoic acid.

ben·zo·ic acid (ben zō′ik) colorless or white crystalline organic acid occurring in certain plants and produced commercially, used esp. in flavoring tobacco, fixing dyes, and in certain antiseptics and pharmaceuticals. Formula: C_6H_5COOH [BENZO(IN)¹ + -IC + ACID.]

ben·zo·in¹ (ben′zō in, -zoin) *n.* **1.** fragrant resin obtained from the tree *Styrax benzoin* of southeast Asia, used esp. in medicine and perfume. **2.** spicebush. [French *benjoin* the resin, through Spanish and Italian, from Arabic *lubān jāwī* frankincense of Java.]

ben·zo·in² (ben′zō in, -zoin) *n.* white or yellowish crystalline compound with an odor like camphor, used esp. as an antiseptic and food flavoring. [BENZO(IC ACID) + -IN¹.]

ben·zol (ben′zôl) *n.* **1.** benzene. **2.** crude form of benzene consisting of about 70 percent benzene and 20 to 30 percent other hydrocarbons.

Be·o·wulf (bā′ə woolf′) *n.* **1.** Old English epic in alliterative verse, composed by an unknown poet, probably early in the eighth century. **2.** hero of this epic.

be·queath (bi kwēth′, -kwēth′) *v.t.* **1.** to give or leave (property) by will. **2.** to hand down; transmit: *to bequeath a heritage of freedom to future generations.* [Old English *becwethan* to leave by will.]

be·queath·al (bi kwē′thəl, -thal) *n.* act of bequeathing.

be·quest (bi kwest′) *n.* **1.** that which is bequeathed; legacy: *The will contained a bequest for each of his relatives.* **2.** act of bequeathing. [Middle English *biqueste,* going back to Old English *bī* by + *-cwiss* saying.]

be·rate (bi rāt′) **-rat·ed, -rat·ing.** *v.t.* to scold; upbraid. **—Syn.** see **scold.**

Ber·ber (bûr′bər) *n.* **1.** member of a non-Arab people living in North Africa, esp. in Morocco, Algeria, and Ifni. **2.** Hamitic language spoken by the Berbers. **—adj.** of or relating to the Berbers, their culture, or their language. [Arabic *Barbar* one of the people of Barbary, possibly from Greek *barbaros* foreign, uncivilized. See BARBARIC.]

ber·ceuse (ber scez′) *French.* lullaby.

be·reave (bi rēv′) **be·reaved** or **be·reft** (bi reft′), **be·reav·ing.** *v.t.* **1.** to deprive, rob, or strip, as of hope or a loved one. **2.** to make desolate or forlorn, as by death or loss. ▲ **Bereaved** is used most often when dealing with the death of a loved one; **bereft** is used in other contexts. [Old English *berēafian* to rob.]

be·reave·ment (bi rēv′mənt) *n.* condition of being bereaved or left desolate, esp. by the death of a loved one.

be·ret (bə rā′, ber′ā) *n.* soft, round cap, usually without a brim. [French *béret,* from Provençal *berret,* from Late Latin *birrus* hooded cloak; possibly of Celtic origin.]

Beret

berg (burg) *n.* iceberg.

ber·ga·mot (bûr′gə mot′) *n.* **1.** round yellow fruit of a tree, *Citrus bergamia,* related to the lemon and orange, widely cultivated in Italy and southern Europe for the oil extracted from its thin peel. **2.** the honey-colored oil so extracted, used in making perfume. **3.** the small, spiny evergreen tree that bears this fruit. **4.** any of various aromatic plants of the mint family, native to northern temperate areas, esp. the genera *Monarda* and *Mentha.* [French *bergamote* this fruit, through Italian, from Turkish *beg-armūdī* prince's pear.]

Ber·gen (bur′gən) *n.* port city in southwestern Norway. Pop. (1968 est.), 116,609.

Berg·son, Hen·ri (burg′sən, berg′-; äN rē′) 1859–1941, French philosopher.

be·rib·boned (bi rib′ənd) *adj.* covered or decorated with ribbons.

ber·i·ber·i (ber′ē ber′ē) *n.* disease affecting the nervous system, muscles, and heart, caused by a deficiency of vitamin B_1, or thiamine. It occurs mainly in Asia and is treated by administering vitamin B_1 or by improving the diet. [Singhalese *beriberi,* repetition of *beri* weakness.]

Ber·ing Sea (bēr′ing, ber′-) northernmost arm of the Pacific, between Siberia and Alaska.

at; āpe; cär; end; mē; it; īce; hot; ōld; fôrk; wood; fōōl; oil; out; up; ūse; turn; sing; thin; this; zh in treasure; ə in ago, taken, pencil, lemon, circus.

91

Bering Strait, strait connecting the Bering Sea with the Arctic Ocean.

Berke·ley (burk′lē) n. city in western California, on the eastern shore of San Francisco Bay. Pop. (1970), 116,716.

ber·ke·li·um (bər kē′lē əm) n. man-made radioactive element produced by bombarding americium with alpha particles. Symbol: **Bk** See **element** for table. [From *Berkeley*, California, site of the University of California where it was first isolated.]

ber·lin (bər lin′, bur′lin) n. **1.** closed four-wheeled, two-seated carriage with a suspended body, a rear platform for footmen, and a raised front seat for the driver. **2.** soft woolen yarn. Also (def. 2), **berlin**

Berlin

wool. [From *Berlin*, Germany, where this type of coach flourished in the seventeenth century.]

Ber·lin (bər lin′) n. former capital of Germany, now in East Germany and divided into West Berlin and East Berlin.

Ber·li·oz, Louis Hector (bâr′lē ōz′) 1803–69, French composer.

Ber·mu·da (bər mū′də) n. British island group in the North Atlantic, about 600 miles east of North Carolina. Land area, 21 sq. mi. Pop. (1969 est.), 52,000. Also, **Ber·mu′das.** [From the Spanish sea captain Juan de *Bermúdez*, who discovered these islands in the early sixteenth century.]

Bermuda onion, large flattened onion with a mild, slightly sweet taste, cultivated in Bermuda, Texas, and California. They may be red, yellow, or white.

Bermuda shorts, shorts reaching almost to the knees. Also, **Bermu′das.** [From *Bermuda*, where American tourists in the 1920s had local tailors adapt for civilian wear the regulation army shorts of British soldiers stationed there.]

Bern (burn) also, **Berne.** n. capital of Switzerland, in the west-central part of the country. Pop. (1969 est.), 166,800.

Ber·nard (bur′nərd, bər närd′) **1. of Men·thon, Saint.** (mäN tōN′) c.996–c.1081, founder of the alpine hospices of St. Bernard. **2. of Clair·vaux, Saint.** (klâr vō′) 1090–1153, monk and theologian.

Ber·nese Alps (bur′nēz, -nēs) mountain range in southwestern and south-central Switzerland.

Bern·hardt, Sar·ah (burn′härt′) 1844–1923, French actress.

Ber·noul·li's principle (bər nŏŏ′lēz′) principle stating that the pressure exerted by a moving fluid decreases as the fluid moves faster. [From Daniel *Bernoulli*, eighteenth-century Swiss physicist.]

ber·ry (ber′ē) pl., **-ries.** n. **1.** any of several small, pulpy fruits with numerous seeds, such as huckleberries and strawberries. **2.** *Botany.* any fleshy, indehiscent fruit that develops from a single pistil and contains one or more seeds, such as tomatoes, grapes, and cranberries. **3.** dry seed or kernel of various plants, as the bean of the coffee plant. —v.i., **-ried, -ry·ing.** **1.** to look for or gather berries. **2.** to bear berries. [From English *beri(g)e* small pulpy fruit with seeds, grape.]

ber·serk (bər surk′, -zurk′) adj., adv. in or into a crazed, violent rage; frenzied; mad. [See BERSERKER.]

ber·serk·er (bər sur′kər, -zur′-) n. ancient Norse warrior of a type known for frenzied fury in battle and reputed to be invulnerable. [Old Norse *berserkr* literally, bear shirt; referring to the bearskins often worn by Norse warriors.]

berth (burth) n. **1.** built-in bed or bunk, esp. on a ship or train. **2.** *Nautical.* **a.** place for a ship to moor; a slip at a dock. **b.** enough space to maneuver a ship safely. **3.** position; job. **4. to give a wide berth to.** to steer clear of; avoid. —v.t. **1.** to bring a (ship) into a berth. **2.** to provide with a berth. —v.i. **1.** to come into or occupy a berth. [Possibly from BEAR¹.]

Upper berth

Lower berth

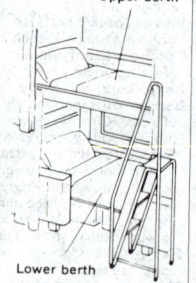

ber·tha (bur′thə) n. wide collar, worn by women, which covers the shoulders. [French *berthe*, from *Berthe*, mother of Charlemagne, known for her modesty.]

Ber·til·lon system (burt′əl on′) system of identifying persons, esp. criminals, by the recording of body measurements and other distinguishing physical characteristics. It was later replaced by fingerprinting. [From the French police official Alphonse *Bertillon*, 1853–1914, who introduced it.]

Ber·wyn (bur′win) n. city in northeastern Illinois, principally a residential suburb of Chicago. Pop. (1970), 52,502.

ber·yl (ber′əl) n. hard, opaque or transparent mineral occurring in various colors, but usually bluish or light yellow. Beryl is a silicate of beryllium and aluminum and the principal ore of beryllium. Emeralds and aquamarines are varieties of beryl. [Latin *bēryllus*, from Greek *bēryllos*, going back to a Dravidian word.]

be·ryl·li·um (bə ril′ē əm) n. strong, light, silvery-white metallic element, used chiefly in alloys and as a reflecting and moderating material in atomic piles. Symbol: **Be** See **element** for table. [Modern Latin *beryllium*; because it was first obtained from beryl.]

be·seech (bi sēch′) **-sought, -seeched, -seech·ing.** v.t. **1.** to beg; entreat; implore: *I beseech you, help us before it's too late.* **2.** to ask for earnestly; plead for: *I beseech your mercy.* **3.** to cover or stud: *a gown beset with jewels.* [Old English *besettan* to set near, surround.] —**be·seech′ing·ly,** adv. —Syn. **1.** see **beg.**

be·seem (bi sēm′) v.t. *Archaic.* to be appropriate for or to; suit: *Your behavior does not beseem a person of your rank.*

be·set (bi set′) **-set, -set·ting.** v.t. **1.** to attack from all sides; harass: *troops beset by enemy fire, beset with difficulties.* **2.** to hem in; surround: *a camp beset by enemy troops.* **3.** to cover or stud: *a gown beset with jewels.* [Old English *besettan* to set near, surround.]

be·set·ting (bi set′ing) adj. constantly attacking or harassing.

be·shrew (bi shrōō′) v.t. *Archaic.* to wish evil upon; curse. [BE- + SHREW.]

be·side (bi sīd′) prep. **1.** at or by the side of; near: *Sit beside me.* **2.** in comparison with: *His work seems poor beside yours.* **3.** in addition to; other than: *There will be six, beside me, for dinner.* **4.** apart from; not connected with: *beside the point.* **5. beside oneself.** extremely agitated or excited; beyond self-control. —adv. *Archaic.* besides. [Old English *be sīdan* by the side.]

be·sides (bi sīdz′) adv. **1.** moreover; furthermore: *I don't want to go; besides, it's too late.* **2.** in addition; also: *I brought two others besides.* **3.** otherwise; else: *Whatever you do besides, keep my advice in mind.* —prep. also, **beside.** in addition to; other than: *Besides you, no one is qualified.*

be·siege (bi sēj′) **-sieged, -sieg·ing.** v.t. **1.** to surround with armed forces in order to capture; lay siege to: *Indians besieged the isolated fort.* **2.** to crowd around; hem in: *Autograph seekers besieged the singer.* **3.** to overwhelm or harass: *The community besieged the newspaper with letters about its recent editorial.* —**be·sieg′er,** n.

be·smear (bi smēr′) v.t. to smear over; soil.

be·smirch (bi smurch′) v.t. to make dirty; soil.

be·som (bē′zəm) n. broom, esp. one made of bound twigs. [Old English *besma.*]

be·sot (bi sot′) **-sot·ted, -sot·ting.** v.t. **1.** to make into a sot; stupefy with drink. **2.** to make foolish, esp. by infatuation.

be·sought (bi sôt′) past tense and past participle of **beseech.**

be·spake (bi spāk′) *Archaic.* past tense of **bespeak.**

be·span·gle (bi spang′gəl) **-gled, -gling.** v.t. to adorn or cover with or as with spangles.

be·spat·ter (bi spat′ər) v.t. **1.** to spatter with or as with mud; soil; sully. **2.** to slander.

be·speak (bi spēk′) **-spoke** or (archaic) **-spake, -spo·ken** or **-spoke, -speak·ing.** v.t. **1.** to give evidence of; indicate: *His way of life bespeaks great wealth.* **2.** to be an omen of; foreshadow: *events that bespeak coming danger.* **3.** *Archaic.* to engage or arrange for in advance; order; reserve. **4.** *Archaic.* to speak to. [Old English *besprecan* to speak to, complain.]

be·spec·ta·cled (bi spek′tə kəld) adj. wearing eyeglasses.

be·spoke (bi spōk′) v. a past tense and past participle of **bespeak.** —adj. *British.* made to order; custom-made: *the bespoke overcoat.*

be·spread (bi spred′) **-spread, -spread·ing.** v.t. to spread over or cover thickly: *Daffodils bespread the field below.*

be·sprent (bi sprent′) adj. *Archaic.* besprinkled. [Middle English *bespreynt*, going back to Old English *besprengan* to besprinkle.]

be·sprin·kle (bi spring′kəl) **-kled, -kling.** v.t. to sprinkle over; scatter over: *grass besprinkled with dew.*

Bes·sa·ra·bi·a (bes′ə rä′bē ə) n. historic region of eastern Europe, now in the southwestern part of the Soviet Union, on the Black Sea.

Bes·se·mer, Sir Henry (bes′ə mər) 1813–98, English inventor and industrialist.

Bessemer converter, pear-shaped steel vessel with air inlets at the bottom, used in the Bessemer process.

Bessemer process, method of making steel in which a blast of air blown through molten iron oxidizes and removes the carbon and impurities in the iron. [From Sir Henry *Bessemer.*]

best (best) superlative of **good.** adj. **1.** of the highest quality or excellence; superior to all others: *the best speaker in the class.* **2.** most advantageous, desirable, or appropriate: *the best approach to the problem.* **3.** largest; most: *It took the best part of a day to get there.*

at; āpe; cär; end; mē; it; īce; hot; ōld; fôrk; wood; fōōl; oil; out; up; ūse; turn; sing; thin; this; zh in treasure; ə in ago, taken, pencil, lemon, circus.

—*adv.*, superlative of **well¹. 1.** in the most excellent way; most successfully or advantageously: *I work best when by myself.* **2.** in or to the highest degree; to the fullest extent; most fully: *according to those best qualified.* **3. had best.** would be wise to; ought to; should: *You had best get home before midnight.* —*n.* **1.** that which is of the highest quality or excellence: *My uncle can afford the best.* **2.** people of the highest repute or capability: *That poet is one of the best in his field.* **3. all for the best.** more favorable than could have been expected. **4. at best. a.** under the most favorable or advantageous circumstances. **b.** at most. **5. one's best. a.** one's greatest effort; utmost: *The young boy did his best to overcome his handicap.* **b.** one's highest point; one's greatest degree of excellence: *The singer was at her best during the performance.* **c.** finest clothes: *We wore our Sunday best to the party.* **6. to get (or have) the best of.** to defeat or outwit. **7. to make the best of.** to adapt oneself to or use as well as possible. —*v.t.* to outdo; defeat; surpass. [Old English *betst* of highest excellence, in the most excellent way.]
be·stead (bi sted´) **-stead·ed, -stead·ed** or **-stead, -stead·ing.** *Archaic. v.t.* to help; serve; avail. —*adj.* placed; situated. [BE- + STEAD.]
bes·tial (bes´chəl, bēs´-) *adj.* **1.** having the qualities of a beast; savage; brutish; inhuman. **2.** of or relating to beasts. [Latin *bēstiālis* like a beast, from *bēstia* beast.] —**bes´tial·ly,** *adv.*
bes·ti·al·i·ty (bes´chē al´ə tē, bēs´-) *pl.*, **-ties.** *n.* **1.** bestial quality, character, or nature. **2.** bestial act or behavior.
bes·ti·ar·y (bes´chē er´ē, bēs´-) *n.* collection of allegorical fables and stories about animals, particularly popular during the Middle Ages. [Medieval Latin *bestiarium,* going back to Latin *bēstia* beast.]
be·stir (bi stur´) **-stirred, -stir·ring.** *v.t.* to stir up; rouse to action or activity.
best man, chief attendant of the bridegroom at a wedding.
be·stow (bi stō´) *v.t.* **1.** to present as a gift; give; confer: *to bestow honors on a hero.* **2.** *Archaic.* to apply or devote. **3.** *Archaic.* to provide for safekeeping. **4.** *Archaic.* to provide quarters for. [BE- + STOW.] —**be·stow´al,** *n.* —**Syn. 1.** see donate.
be·strew (bi strōō´) **-strewed, -strewed** or **-strewn, -strew·ing.** *v.t.* **1.** to scatter or strew over: *The onlookers bestrewed the motorcade with confetti.* **2.** to scatter around. **3.** to lie scattered over or about: *Fallen leaves bestrewed the ground.* [Old English *bestrēowian* to cover.]
be·stride (bi strīd´) **-strode** (-strōd´), **-strid** (-strid´), **-strid·den** (-strid´ən) or **-strid, -strid·ing.** *v.t.* **1.** to mount, sit on, or stand over (something) with one leg on each side; straddle. **2.** *Archaic.* to stride over or across. [Old English *bestrīdan* to sit astride.]
best seller, book or other article that sells or has sold in very large quantities.
bet (bet) *n.* **1.** pledge that one will pay money or some other specified thing if the outcome of an event is other than one predicts or if a statement one makes is proved untrue. **2.** that which is pledged or wagered. **3.** that on which a wager is or can be made: *That horse is a good bet.* —*v.t.* **1.** to pledge or risk (money or some other specified thing) in a bet. **2.** to assert in or as in a bet: *I bet he won't be surprised.* **3.** to make a bet with: *I'll bet you he won't come.* —*v.i.* **1.** to make a bet: *Yesterday we bet on a horse that lost.* **2. you bet.** *Slang.* of course; certainly. [Probably short for ABET.]
be·ta (bā´tə, bē´-) *n.* **1.** second letter of the Greek alphabet (B, β). **2.** second in a group or series, esp. in scientific classification.
be·take (bi tāk´) **-took, -tak·en, -tak·ing.** *v.t.* to cause to go: *The boy betook himself to the store.* **2.** *Archaic.* to apply (oneself).
beta particle, electron ejected from a radioactive atomic nucleus.
beta ray, stream of beta particles.
be·ta·tron (bā´tə tron´, bē´-) *n.* device in which electrons are accelerated to high speeds by a varying magnetic field. [BETA (RAYS) + (ELEC)TRON.]
be·tel (bēt´əl) *n.* climbing plant, *Piper betle,* of the pepper family, native to Eastern tropic regions. Its dark-green heart-shaped leaves are chewed with betel nuts. [Portuguese *betel,* from Malayalam *vettila.*]
Be·tel·geuse (bēt´əl jōōz´, bet´əl jœz´) *n.* giant red star that varies in size and brightness in a regular cycle and is the brightest star in the constellation Orion. [French *Bételgeuse,* apparently from Arabic *bīt al-jauzā'* shoulder of the giant (Orion), with reference to its position in the constellation Orion.]
betel nut, red or orange seed of the betel palm, having a mottled brown, fibrous husk. Betel nuts are wrapped in leaves from the betel plant and chewed for their mild narcotic effect.
betel palm, tall Asian tree, *Areca catechu,* of the palm family, native to India and Malaya and widely cultivated for its nuts.
bête noire (bāt´ nwär´) thing or person that is particularly dreaded or disliked; bugbear. [French *bête noire* literally, black beast, going back to Latin *bēstia* beast + *niger* black.]
Beth·a·ny (beth´ə nē) *n.* ancient Palestinian community just east of Jerusalem.
beth·el (beth´əl) *n.* **1.** hallowed place. **2.** place of worship for seamen. [Hebrew *bēth Ēl* house of God.]

Beth·el (beth´əl) *n.* ancient town in Palestine, near Jerusalem, referred to in the Bible.
Be·thes·da (bə thez´də) *n.* unincorporated community in south-central Maryland, principally a residential suburb of Washington, D.C. Pop. (1970), 71, 621.
be·think (bi thingk´) **-thought, -think·ing.** *v.t. Archaic.* **1.** to consider; reflect. **2.** remind (oneself): *He bethought himself of younger days.* [Old English *bithencan* to consider.]
Beth·le·hem (beth´lə hem´, -lē əm) *n.* **1.** Palestinian town near Jerusalem, in what is now western Jordan. It was the birthplace of Jesus Christ. Pop. (1961), 21,700. **2.** city in eastern Pennsylvania. Pop. (1970), 72,686.
be·thought (bi thôt´) past tense and past participle of **bethink.**
be·tide (bi tīd´) **-tid·ed, -tid·ing.** *v.t., v.i.* to happen (to); befall. [BE- + TIDE.]
be·times (bi tīmz´) *adv.* **1.** in good time; early: *The boy arose betimes to finish his chores.* **2.** in a short time; soon; quickly. [Earlier *betime,* from *be* BY + TIME.]
be·to·ken (bi tō´kən) *v.t.* **1.** to be a sign of; foreshadow: *Cloudy skies betoken rain.* **2.** to give evidence of; show; indicate.
be·tray (bi trā´) *v.t.* **1.** to aid the enemy of; be a traitor to: *to betray one's country.* **2.** to be unfaithful or false to; fail to live up to: *to betray one's ideals.* **3.** to disclose (something secret): *to betray confidential plans.* **4.** to reveal unintentionally or unknowingly: *The child's eyes betrayed his fear.* **5.** to show; point to; indicate: *Footprints betrayed the presence of an intruder.* **6.** to deceive; mislead; seduce. [BE- + Middle English *traien* to be a traitor, from Old French *traïr* to hand over, from Latin *trādere.*] —**be·tray´al, be·tray´er,** *n.*
be·troth (bi trōth´, -trôth´) *v.t.* to promise to give in marriage. [Middle English *betreuthien,* from BE- + *treuthe* troth, from Old English *trēowth.*]
be·troth·al (bi trō´thəl, -trô´thəl) *n.* act of betrothing; being betrothed; engagement.
be·trothed (bi trōthd´, -trôtht´) *n.* one who is engaged to be married. —*adj.* engaged to be married.
bet·ter¹ (bet´ər) comparative of **good.** *adj.* **1.** of higher quality or excellence: *better service.* **2.** more advantageous, desirable, or appropriate: *Copper is a better conductor than iron.* **3.** improved in health: *My sister is much better today.* **4.** larger; greater: *the better part of her salary.* **5. to go (someone) one better.** *Informal.* to outdo; surpass. —*adv.,* comparative of **well¹. 1.** in a more excellent way; more advantageously or successfully: *The child was better behaved today than yesterday. Cactuses grow better in a hot, dry climate.* **2.** in or to a higher degree; to a fuller extent; more: *The trip took better than two hours. I like her better now.* **3. better off. a.** in a better condition or position: *We'd be better off staying here.* **b.** in an improved financial position; wealthier: *We are better off this year than we were last year.* **4. had better.** would be wise to; ought to. **5. to think better of.** to reconsider and reach a wiser or more favorable conclusion about. —*n.* **1.** that which is more desirable or of greater excellence: *the better of the two choices, the better of the two candidates.* **2.** also, **betters.** one's superior, as in rank, skill, or power. **3. to get (or have) the better of.** to gain or have an advantage over; outdo; defeat. —*v.t.* **1.** to make better; improve: *You can better yourself by taking this new job.* **2.** to outdo; surpass; excel: *The runner bettered his previous record.* [Old English *betera* of greater excellence, improved in health.]
bet·ter² (bet´ər) also, **bet·tor.** *n.* one who bets. [BET + -ER¹, or -OR.]
bet·ter·ment (bet´ər mənt) *n.* **1.** act of bettering; being bettered; improvement. **2.** improvement, other than by mere repairs, that enhances the value of real property.
be·tween (bi twēn´) *prep.* **1.** in the space separating (two points, places, or objects): *Troops bivouacked between the river and the hill.* **2.** in the period separating (two events or times): *no snacks between meals.* **3.** in the interval or range separating: *between one and two miles, between the rich and the poor.* **4.** from one to the other of; connecting: *a bridge between the island and mainland.* **5.** involving (two or more parties): *a discussion between draftees and career men in the army.* **6.** by the joint action of: *Between them they can finish in an hour.* **7.** in the joint possession of: *They had three dollars between them.* **8.** one or the other of: *to choose between peace and war.* **9. between you and me.** in confidence; confidentially. —*adv.* **1.** in the intermediate space, position, or relation; in an intervening time: *windows on either side of the wall with space between. Changes have been few and far between.* **2. in between. a.** in an undetermined or intermediate position: *He is neither a liberal nor a conservative; he's somewhere in between.* **b.** placed in the middle: *two rooms with a hall in between.* [Old English *betwēonum* among, in the middle of, from *be-* BY + *twēonum,* dative plural of *twēone* double.]
be·twixt (bi twikst´) *prep.* between. —*adv.* **1.** between. **2. betwixt and between.** in an intermediate position; neither one nor the other; undecided. [Old English *betweox.*]

Bev (bev) *also,* **bev, BeV.** *n.* billion electron volts. [From *B*(illion) *e*(lectron) *v*(olts).]

bev·a·tron (bev'ə tron') *n.* high-speed synchrotron that accelerates protons to energies in the billions of electron volts. [BEV + Greek *-tron* device.]

bev·el (bev'əl) *n.* **1.a.** slanting edge or surface formed by two lines or surfaces meeting at anything other than a right angle. **b.** angle formed by such an edge or surface. **2.** tool for plotting angles or for adjusting surfaces of work to a particular inclination. —*v.t.* **-eled, -el·ing;** *also, British,* **-elled, -el·ling.** to cut or shape to a bevel. —*v.i.* to incline or slope at a bevel. —*adj.* oblique; sloping. [Probably from an unrecorded Old French word; of uncertain origin.]

bevel gear, gear fitting into another so that the shafts would intersect if extended.

bev·er·age (bev'ər ij, bev'rij) *n.* a drink, hot or cold, usually consisting of something other than plain water. [Old French *bevrage,* from *bevre* to drink, from Latin *bibere*.]

bev·y (bev'ē) *pl.* **bev·ies.** *n.* **1.** group, esp. of girls or women. **2.** flock of birds, esp. of quail. [Middle English *bevey* group; possibly from an earlier meaning "a drinking company," from Old French *bevee* drink, going back to Latin *bibere* to drink.]

Bevel gears

be·wail (bi wāl') *v.t., v.i.* to complain; mourn; lament: *The unfortunate man bewailed his failure.*

be·ware (bi wār') *v.i.* to be wary or careful (of); look out (for): *Beware the ides of March. Beware of the dog.* [From *be ware* be wary; from *be,* imperative of *to* BE + WARE².]

be·wil·der (bi wil'dər) *v.t.* to confuse completely; perplex; confound. [BE- + archaic *wilder* to lead astray, perplex, possibly from WILDERNESS.] —**be·wil'dered·ly, be·wil'der·ing·ly,** *adv.* —**Syn.** *see* puzzle.

be·wil·der·ment (bi wil'dər mənt) *n.* **1.** state of being bewildered; utter confusion. **2.** confusing or perplexing tangle.

be·witch (bi wich') *v.t.* **1.** to affect by witchcraft or magic; cast a spell over. **2.** to charm; fascinate; enchant: *Her smile bewitched us all.*

be·witch·ing (bi wich'ing) *adj.* fascinating; enchanting; charming. —**be·witch'ing·ly,** *adv.*

bey (bā) *n.* **1.** governor of a minor Turkish province or district. ▲ used as a title of respect in Turkey. **2.** native ruler of Tunis. [Turkish *beg* prince, gentleman.]

be·yond (bē ond', bi yond') *prep.* **1.** on or to the farther side of; farther on than: *The camp is beyond those hills. We drove beyond the city limits.* **2.** later than: *The child was up well beyond his bedtime.* **3.** out of the reach, scope, or understanding of: *beyond belief. That concept is beyond me.* **4.** more than; over and above: *gems priced far beyond their worth. He's living beyond his means.* —*adv.* farther on or away. —*n.* **the (great) beyond.** that which occurs after death; life after death. [Old English *begeondan* farther away, farther on than.]

Bey·routh (bā rōōt') Beirut.

bez·ant (bez'ənt) *n.* gold coin widely circulated in Europe during medieval times; solidus. [Old French *besant,* from Latin *byzantius (nummus)* Byzantine (coin), from *Byzantium,* where it was first struck.]

bez·el (bez'əl) *n.* **1.** sloping edge of a cutting tool. **2.** oblique sides or faces of a cut jewel, esp. those on the upper portion. **3.** groove and flange by which a jewel or watch crystal is held in place. [Old French *bisel* sloping edge, possibly going back to Latin *bis* twice + *-el.*]

be·zique (bə zēk') *n.* card game, similar to pinochle, played with two or more decks of cards using only the cards above the six.

bf., boldface. Also, **b.f.**

bg. *pl.* **bgs.** bag.

Bha·ga·vad-Gi·ta (bug'ə vəd gē'tä) *n.* sacred Hindu text in the Sanskrit epic, *The Mahabharata,* consisting of a dialogue which relates the philosophy of Krishna. [Sanskrit *Bhagavadgītā* song of the Blessed One.]

bhang (bang) *n.* **1.** hemp plant of India. **2.** dried hemp leaves and flowers, used as a narcotic and intoxicant. It is related to marijuana and hashish. [Hindi *bhāng* hemp, from Sanskrit *bhangā.*]

Bhu·tan (bōō tän') *n.* country of south-central Asia, in the Himalayas, bounded by Tibet, India, and Sikkim. Capital, Thimbu. Area, 18,000 sq. mi. Pop. (1975 est.), 1,200,000.

bi- *prefix* **1.a.** having two; two: *bicameral, bicycle.* **b.** involving two: *bilateral.* **2.** twice; doubly: *biconvex.* **3.a.** coming or occurring every two: *bimonthly, biweekly.* **b.** coming or occurring twice each: *biannual.* **4.** *Chemistry.* **a.** having proportionally twice as much. For example, a molecule of sodium bicarbonate has proportionally twice as much carbonate as a molecule of sodium carbonate. **b.** indicating the doubling

and linkage of an organic radical or molecule: *bisulfate.* [Latin *bi-* twice, doubly, two.]

Bi, bismuth.

Bi·a·fra (bē äf'rə) *n.* eastern region of Nigeria, which seceded in 1967 but was defeated and reincorporated into the Nigerian federal government in 1970.

bi·a·ly (bē ä'lē) *n.* flat roll having an onion flavor, usually with a slight depression in the center of one side. [Short for Yiddish *Bialystoker kuchen* roll from *Bialystok,* Poland.]

Bia·ly·stok (byä'lē stok') *n.* city in northeastern Poland. Pop. (1968 est.), 158,500.

bi·an·nu·al (bī an'ū əl) *adj.* occurring twice a year; semiannual. —**bi·an'nu·al·ly,** *adv.*

bi·as (bī'əs) *n.* **1.** mental or emotional inclination or tendency; prejudice. **2.** slanting line cutting diagonally across the grain of a fabric. **3.a.** uneven shape of a ball used in bowls, which causes it to swerve when rolled. **b.** swerved course taken by such a ball. —*adj.* slanting across the grain of the fabric; diagonal; oblique. —*adv.* diagonally; obliquely. —*v.t.* **bi·ased, bi·as·ing;** *also, British,* **bi·assed, bi·as·sing.** to cause to have a bias; influence; prejudice [French *biais* slant, through Old Provençal, probably going back to Greek *epikarsios* slanting.]

bi·ax·i·al (bī ak'sē əl) *adj.* having two axes.

bib (bib) *n.* **1.** piece of cloth or plastic tied under the chin, esp. in the case of infants, to protect the clothing from spilled food or drink. **2.** upper front part of an apron or overalls. [From earlier *bib* to drink, from Latin *bibere;* possibly because a child's bib drinks or *bibs* what its wearer spills.]

Bib., Bible; Biblical.

bib and tucker *Informal.* clothes.

bib·cock (bib'kok') *n.* faucet with the nozzle bent downward.

bi·be·lot (bib'lō, bē blō') *n.* small decorative object valued for its beauty or rarity. [French *bibelot* trinket, going back to Old French *bel* beautiful, from Latin *bellus* handsome.]

Bi·ble (bī'bəl) *n.* **1.** sacred writings of the Christian religion, including the Old and New Testaments, and in Roman Catholicism, much of the Apocrypha. **2.** sacred writings of the Jewish religion, the Old Testament only. **3.** book or writings sacred to any religion: *The Koran is the Bible of the Muslims.* **4.** bible. any book used or accepted as an authority. [Old French *bible* the Bible, through Latin, going back to Greek *biblos* book, papyrus (from which paper for books was made), from the Phoenician city *Byblos,* export center for papyrus.]

Bible Belt, area, esp. in southern and midwestern United States, noted for its avid religious fundamentalism.

bib·li·cal (bib'li kəl) *also,* **Bib·li·cal.** *adj.* **1.** of, in, or relating to the Bible: *a biblical scholar, biblical names.* **2.** in accord with the Bible. —**bib'li·cal·ly;** *also,* **Bib'li·cal·ly,** *adv.*

bib·li·og·ra·pher (bib'lē og'rə fər) *n.* one who makes bibliographies; expert in bibliography

bib·li·og·ra·phy (bib'lē og'rə fē) *pl.,* **-phies.** *n.* **1.a.** list of books or other literature on a particular subject or person, including such information as the title of the work, author, publisher, and publication date. **b.** similar list of works of a particular author or publishing house. **2.** study dealing with the description, comparison, and history of books and other written material. [Greek *bibliographia* the writing of books, from *biblion* literally, little book + *graphein* to write.] —**bib'li·o·graph'ic;** *also,* **bib'li·o·graph'i·cal,** *adj.* —**bib'li·o·graph'i·cal·ly,** *adv.*

bib·li·o·ma·ni·a (bib'lē ō mā'nē ə) *n.* passion for collecting books. [Greek *biblion* literally, little book + *maniā* madness.] —**bib'li·o·ma'ni·ac,** *n., adj.* —**bib·li·o·ma·ni·a·cal** (bib'lē ō mə nī'ə kəl), *adj.*

bib·li·o·phile (bib'lē ə fīl') *n.* one who loves books, esp. one who enjoys collecting them. [French *bibliophile,* from Greek *biblion* literally, little book + *philos* friend.]

bib·u·lous (bib'yə ləs) *adj.* **1.** fond of or given to drinking alcoholic beverages. **2.** absorbent. [Latin *bibulus* drinking freely.]

bi·cam·er·al (bī kam'ər əl) *adj.* having or consisting of two legislative chambers, houses, or branches: *The United States Congress is a bicameral legislature.* Distinguished from **unicameral.** [BI- + Latin *camera* chamber, from Greek *kamarā* vault.]

bi·car·bo·nate (bī kär'bə nit, -nāt') *n.* any salt containing the radical HCO₃⁻, as sodium bicarbonate, NaHCO₃.

bicarbonate of soda, sodium bicarbonate.

bice (bīs) *n.* blue or green pigment made from carbonates of copper, used in painting. [Old French *bis* of dark color; of uncertain origin.]

bi·cen·te·nar·y (bī sen'tə ner'ē, bī'sen ten'ə rē) *pl.,* **-nar·ies.** *n., adj.* bicentennial.

bi·cen·ten·ni·al (bī'sen ten'ē əl) *adj.* **1.** occurring every 200 years. **2.** consisting of or lasting 200 years. —*n.* **1.** 200th anniversary. **2.** its celebration.

bi·ceps (bī'seps) *pl.,* **-ceps** or **-ceps·es.** *n.* **1.** large muscle in the front of the upper arm. **2.** large muscle in the back of the thigh. [Latin *biceps* two-headed; because these muscles have two heads or origins.]

at; āpe; cär; end; mē; it; īce; hot; ōld; fôrk; wood; fōōl; oil; out; up; ūse; turn; sing; thin; <u>th</u>is; zh in treasure; ə in ago, taken, pencil, lemon, circus.

bi·chlo·ride (bī klôr′īd) *n.* **1.** compound containing two atoms of chlorine; dichloride. **2.** bichloride of mercury.

bichloride of mercury, very poisonous white crystalline compound, used. esp. in photography, tanning, and metallurgy. Formula: $HgCl_2$

bi·chro·mate (bī krō′māt) *n.* dichromate.

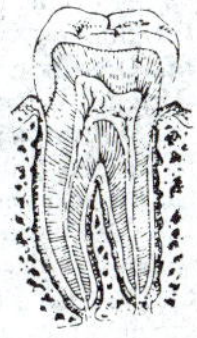

Bicuspid

bick·er (bik′ər) *v.i.* **1.** to quarrel peevishly; wrangle; squabble. **2.** *Archaic.* to babble; gurgle; patter. **3.** *Archaic.* to flicker; twinkle. —*n.* petty quarrel; dispute; altercation. [Middle English *bikeren* to skirmish; of uncertain origin.]

bi·con·cave (bī′kon kāv′, bī kon′kāv) *adj.* concave on both sides.

bi·con·vex (bī′kon veks′, bī kon′veks) *adj.* convex on both sides.

bi·cus·pid (bī kus′pid) *n.* any of eight human adult teeth with double-pointed crowns; premolar. —*adj.* having two cusps, or points. [BI- + Latin *cuspis* point.]

bicuspid valve, mitral valve.

bi·cy·cle (bī′sə kəl, -sik′əl) *n.* vehicle consisting of a frame suspended between two wheels, one behind the other, a saddle seat for the rider, handlebars for steering, and two foot pedals or a motor for propulsion. —*v.i.,* **-cled, -cling.** to ride a bicycle. [French *bicycle* this vehicle, from *bi-* two (from Latin *bi-*) + Greek *kyklos* wheel.] —**bi′cy·cler, bi′cy·clist,** *n.*

Bicycle

bid (bid) *(v.t. defs. 1,2,6, v.i. def. 2)* **bade** or **bid** or *(archaic)* **bad, bid·den** or **bid, bid·ding;** *(v.t. defs. 3,4,5, v.i. defs. 1,3,4)* **bid, bid·ding.** *v.t.* **1.** to command; order; ask: *The captain bids you to join him on deck.* **2.** to say or express, as a greeting: *The children bade their friends farewell.* **3.** to offer (an amount) as the price or terms (often with *for*): *The company that bids the lowest price will win the contract. We bid too little for the lamp.* **4.** to declare (the number of points or tricks) one will attempt to make or state (the suit) one will play in certain card games. **5.** *Informal.* to issue an invitation to join. **6.** *Archaic.* to ask to attend; invite. —*v.i.* **1.** to make a bid. **2. to bid fair.** to seem likely or probably: *His candidacy bids fair to succeed.* **3. to bid in.** to raise the price at an auction when the final price is considered too low, in order to retain ownership. **4. to bid up.** to raise the price by successively higher bids. —*n.* **1.** offer or proposal, as of a price for an object or fees for services: *We received three bids for the contract.* **2.** amount offered. **3.** attempt to win or achieve: *a bid for the presidency.* **4.a.** number of tricks or points one engages to make in certain card games. **b.** player's turn to bid. **5.** *Informal.* invitation. [Partly from Old English *biddan* to ask, order; partly from Old English *bēodan* to offer, command.] —**bid′der,** *n.*

bid·da·ble (bid′ə bəl) *adj.* **1.** worth enough or suitable to bid on: *biddable bridge hand.* **2.** *Archaic.* obedient; docile.

bid·den (bid′ən) a past participle of **bid.**

bid·ding (bid′ing) *n.* **1.** command; order; request: *We came at his bidding.* **2.** making of bid; bids collectively: *The bidding at the auction is slow. The bidding in this game is hard to follow.* **3. to do one's bidding.** to obey or carry out commands of another.

bid·dy[1] (bid′ē) *pl.,* **-dies.** *n.* chicken, esp. a hen. [Possibly imitative.]

bid·dy[2] (bid′ē) *pl.,* **-dies.** *n.* *Informal.* fussy old woman. [Familiar form of *Bridget* feminine proper name.]

bide (bīd) **bid·ed** or **bode, bid·ed, bid·ing.** *v.t.* **1. to bide one's time.** to wait patiently for a good opportunity. **2.** *Archaic.* to endure; suffer; withstand. —*v.i. Archaic.* to dwell; abide; stay. [Old English *bīdan* to wait.]

bi·den·tate (bī den′tāt) *adj.* having two teeth or toothlike projections.

bi·en·ni·al (bī en′ē əl) *adj.* **1.** occurring every two years: *biennial elections.* **2.** lasting or living two years. —*n.* **1.** plant that lives two years, usually producing flowers, fruit, and seeds in the second year. **2.** event that occurs once every two years. [Latin *biennālis* of two years; English spelling influenced by Latin *biennium* period of two years.] —**bi·en′ni·al·ly,** *adv.*

bier (bēr) *n.* **1.** movable stand on which a coffin or corpse is placed before burial. **2.** coffin. [Old English *bǣr* this stand.]

biest·ings (bē′stingz) beestings.

biff (bif) *Slang. n.* a blow; hit. —*v.t.* to strike; hit. [Imitative.]

bi·fid (bī′fid) *adj.* divided into two equal parts by a cleft; forked. [Latin *bifidus.*]

bi·fo·cal (bī fō′kəl) *adj.* having two focal lengths. —*n.* **1.** lens ground with two focal lengths, one for focusing on distant objects, the other for close ones. **2.** *also,* **bifocals.** pair of eyeglasses having bifocal lenses.

Bif·rost (biv′rost) *n.* *Norse Mythology.* the rainbow bridge between Asgard, home of the gods, and Midgard, the earth.

bi·fur·cate (bī′fər kāt′, bī fur′kāt; *adj.,also* bī′fər kit, bī fur′-) **-cat·ed, -cat·ing.** *v.i., v.t.* to divide into two branches. —*adj.* divided into two branches. [Medieval Latin *bifurcatus,* past participle of *bifurcari* to divide into two parts, from Latin *bifurcus* having two prongs.]

bi·fur·ca·tion (bī′fər kā′shən) *n.* **1.** act of bifurcating; state of being bifurcated; division into two parts. **2.** point at which the division occurs.

big (big) **big·ger, big·gest.** *adj.* **1.** of great size, amount, capacity, or extent; large: *a big city, a big dinner, a big car.* **2.** important; prominent: *his big moment, a big man in industry.* **3.** full grown; mature: *You're a big girl now.* **4.** loud: *a big voice.* **5.** pregnant (with *with*) *big with child.* **6.** full; brimming: *eyes big with tears.* **7.** boastful; haughty; pretentious: *a big talker.* **8.** magnanimous; generous: *a man with a big heart.* —*adv. Informal.* boastfully, extravagantly, or pompously: *He talks big.* [Middle English *big* large, strong, rich; of uncertain origin.] —**big′gish,** *adj.* —**big′ness,** *n.* —**Syn.** *adj.* **1.** see **great.**

big·a·mist (big′ə mist) *n.* one who commits bigamy.

big·a·mous (big′ə məs) *adj.* **1.** guilty of bigamy. **2.** involving bigamy. —**big′a·mous·ly,** *adv.*

big·a·my (big′ə mē) *n.* criminal offense of willfully marrying a second time while a first marriage is still legal. [Old French *bigamie,* from *bigame* bigamist, from Late Latin *bigamus* twice married, from Latin *bi-* twice + Greek *gamos* marriage.]

big-bang theory (big′bang′) theory that the universe began billions of years ago as the result of a huge cosmic explosion of a dense mass of material.

Big Ben (ben) **1.** bell in the clock tower of the House of Commons in London. **2.** the clock itself.

Big Dipper, group of seven stars in the constellation Ursa Major, which forms the outline of a dipper.

big game **1.** large animals sought by hunters or fishermen for sport. **2.** important objective, esp. one involving risk.

big-heart·ed (big′här′tid) *adj.* generous; kind; charitable.

Bighorn

big·horn (big′hôrn′) *pl.,* **-horn** or **-horns.** *n.* wild sheep, *Ovis canadensis,* of the Rocky Mountains, having a coarse, grayish-brown coat. The male has horns which are tightly curled and may be 50 inches long. It is the largest wild sheep in North America. Height: 3½ feet at the shoulder. Also, **Rocky Mountain sheep.**

bight (bīt) *n.* **1.** bend or curve, as in a river, coastline, or mountain chain. **2.** bay bounded by such a bend. **3.** part of a rope between the ends; loop of a rope. [Old English *byht* bending.]

big·no·ni·a (big nō′nē ə) *n.* climbing, woody vine, *Bignonia capreolata,* native to warm southern and eastern regions of the United States, having trumpet-shaped, brilliant scarlet flowers which grow in large clusters. [Modern Latin *bignonia,* from Abbé *Bignon,* 1662–1743, librarian at the court of Louis XV.]

big·ot (big′ət) *n.* one who intolerantly and obstinately adheres to his beliefs to the exclusion of all others; narrow-minded, prejudiced person. [French *bigot,* possibly from Old French *bigot,* term used by the medieval French to insult the Normans.]

big·ot·ed (big′ə tid) *adj.* characteristic of a bigot; narrow-minded; intolerant; prejudiced. —**big′ot·ed·ly,** *adv.*

big·ot·ry (big′ə trē) *pl.,* **-ries.** *n.* bigoted behavior or thinking.

big shot *Slang.* person of importance or influence. Also, **big wheel.**

big time *Slang.* highest or best level, as of a profession or occupation.

big top *Informal.* **1.** main tent of a circus. **2.** circus.

big·wig (big′wig′) *n.* *Informal.* person or importance or influence. [BIG + WIG; from the large wigs formerly worn by men of importance.]

bi·jou (bē′zhōō) *pl.,* **-joux** (-zhōōz). *n.* **1.** jewel. **2.** small, finely made object. [French *bijou,* from Breton *bizou* ring, from *biz* finger.]

bike (bīk) *Informal. n.* bicycle. —*v.i.* **biked, bik·ing.** to ride a bicycle.

Bi·ki·ni (bi kē′nē) *n.* **1.** atoll in the west-central Pacific, in the Marshall Islands, site of U.S. nuclear weapons tests. **2. bikini.** scanty bathing suit, esp. a two-piece suit for a woman or girl.

bi·la·bi·al (bī lā′bē əl) *adj.* **1.** (of a consonant) formed by both lips touching or almost touching. *B, p, m,* and *w* are bilabial consonants. **2.** having two lips; bilabiate. —*n.* bilabial speech sound.

bi·la·bi·ate (bī lā′bē it) *adj.* *Botany.* having two lips, as a corolla.

bi·lat·er·al (bī lat′ər əl) *adj.* **1.** affecting or influencing two sides or parties; reciprocal: *a bilateral agreement.* **2.** arranged on two sides, as of an axis: *bilateral symmetry.* **3.** having two sides. **4.** having bilateral symmetry. —**bi·lat′er·al·ly,** *adv.*

Bil·ba·o (bil bä′ō) *n.* port city in northern Spain, near the Bay of Biscay. Pop. (1968 est.), 360,429.

bil·ber·ry (bil′ber′ē) *pl.*, **-ries.** *n.* **1.** blue-black fruit of any of several low shrubs of the heath family, related to the blueberry, native to the northern hemisphere and growing as far north as the Arctic Circle. **2.** shrub bearing this fruit. [Probably of Scandinavian origin.]

bil·bo¹ (bil′bō) *pl.*, **-boes.** *also.* **bil·boes.** *n.* ankle fetters consisting of a long metal bar with a lock and sliding shackles, formerly used esp. on sailing ships for confining prisoners. [Of uncertain origin.]

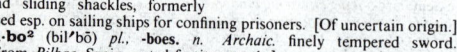
Bilbo¹

bil·bo² (bil′bō) *pl.*, **-boes.** *n. Archaic.* finely tempered sword. [From *Bilbao.* Spain, noted for its swords.]

bile (bīl) *n.* **1.** bitter yellow or greenish liquid secreted by the liver and poured into the duodenum where it aids in digestion, esp. in emulsifying fats. **2.** bad temper; nastiness. [French *bile,* from Latin *bīlis* the humor thought to cause anger. See HUMOR.]

bilge (bilj) *n.* **1.** bottom part of the hull of a boat or ship, esp. the lowest interior part. **2.** bilge water. **3.** bulging part of a cask or barrel. **4.** *Informal.* nonsense; foolishness. —*v.i., v.t.,* **bilged, bilg·ing.** to bulge; swell out. [Probably form of BULGE.]

bilge water, stagnant water that collects in the bilge of a ship.

bil·i·ary (bil′ē er′ē) *adj.* **1.** of or relating to bile. **2.** conveying bile. **3.** bilious (def. 3).

bi·lin·e·ar (bī lin′ē ər) *adj.* of, relating to, or having reference to two straight lines.

bi·lin·gual (bī ling′gwəl) *adj.* **1.** capable of speaking a foreign language as fluently or almost as fluently as one's native language. **2.** expressed in, using, or containing two languages: *bilingual translation.* [Latin *bilinguis* speaking two languages + -AL¹.] —**bi·lin′gual·ly,** *adv.*

bil·ious (bil′yəs) *adj.* **1.** bad-tempered; nasty; cross. **2.** of, relating to, or characteristic of bile. **3.** caused by or having some disorder of the liver, esp. an excess secretion of bile. [French *bilieux,* from Latin *bīliōsus,* from *bīlis.* See BILE.] —**bil′ious·ly,** *adv.* —**bil′ious·ness,** *n.*

-bility *suffix* (used to form nouns from adjectives ending in **-ble**) condition of being: *responsibility.*

bilk (bilk) *v.t.* **1.** to cheat; deceive; swindle. **2.** to thwart. —*n.* cheater; swindler. [Possibly a form of BALK.] —**bilk′er,** *n.*

bill¹ (bil) *n.* **1.** statement of money owed for goods supplied or services given: *telephone bill, grocery bill.* **2.** piece of paper money; bank note: *a dollar bill.* **3.** written or printed advertisement or public notice; poster or handbill: *Do not post bills here.* **4.a.** itemized statement or list of items. **b.** printed or written program, as of a theatrical performance or concert; playbill. **c.** bill of fare. **5.** entertainment offered, as in a theater or concert hall: *I liked the bill at the Bijou.* **6.** draft of a proposed law. **7.a.** bill of exchange. **b.** promissory note. **8.** formal, written statement of charges against a defendant, esp. a statement of complaint filed in court. **9. to fill the bill.** *Informal.* to satisfy or meet the requirements. **10. to foot the bill.** *Informal.* to pay. —*v.t.* **1.a.** to send or submit a statement of money owed or an itemized list to. **b.** to charge or enter, as to an account. **2.** to announce or advertise by bills or posters. **3.** to make arrangements for the appearance of; present: *She was billed as the main attraction.* [Medieval Latin *billa,* form of *bulla* seal, document with seal, from Latin *bulla* bubble, knob.]

bill² (bil) *n.* **1.** horny beak of a bird. **2.** mouth part shaped like a bird's bill: *the bill of a turtle.* **3.** anything resembling the shape of a bird's bill. —*v.i.* **1.** (of birds) to join or touch bills. **2.** *Archaic.* to caress or show affection. **3. to bill and coo.** to kiss, caress, and speak softly, as lovers do. [Old English *bile* beak.]

Syn. n. 1. Bill, beak refer to the horny parts of the mouth of a bird. **Bill** is more general, but specifically implies an elongated or a flattened shape: *The duck's bill is used to strain food from the bottom of lakes or ponds.* **Beak** suggests a more powerful shape, such as the hooked beak of the eagle: *The vulture's beak and claws rip the flesh from the bones of its prey.*

bill³ (bil) *n.* **1.** spear having a hook-shaped blade with a spike at the back, formerly used as a military weapon; halberd. **2.** billhook. **3.** point of an anchor's fluke. [Old English *bil* sword.]

bil·la·bong (bil′ə bong′) *n. Australian.* branch of a river flowing away from the main stream.

bill·board (bil′bôrd′) *n.* panel on which advertisements or announcements are posted, esp. one used outdoors.

bil·let¹ (bil′it) *n.* **1.** quarters officially assigned to a serviceman. **2.** official order to provide board and lodging for a serviceman. **3.** job; position; appointment. —*v.t.,* **bil·let·ed, bil·let·ing.** **1.** to lodge, as soldiers; quarter. **2.** to assign (soldiers) to lodging. [Old French *billette* letter of safe-conduct, going back to Medieval Latin *billa* document with seal. See BILL¹.]

bil·let² (bil′it) *n.* **1.** small thick stick of wood, esp. one used for fuel. **2.** small bar of steel. **3.** one of a series of log-shaped, ornamental inserts forming part of a molding. **4.** strap on a saddle. [French *billette* billet of wood, diminutive of *bille* log of wood; possibly of Celtic origin.]

bil·let-doux (bil′ā dōō′) *pl.,* **bil·lets-doux** (bil′ā dōōz′). *n.* love letter. [French *billet doux* literally, sweet letter, going back to Medieval Latin *billa* document + Latin *dulcis* sweet. See BILL¹.]

bill·fold (bil′fōld′) *n.* folding case for paper money; wallet.

bill·head (bil′hed′) *n.* **1.** sheet of paper with a business letterhead, used for billing. **2.** letterhead on such a sheet.

bill·hook (bil′hook′) *n.* hook-shaped tool used for pruning or cutting.

bil·liard (bil′yərd) *adj.* of or for billiards: *a billiard player, a billiard ball.* —*n.* carom.

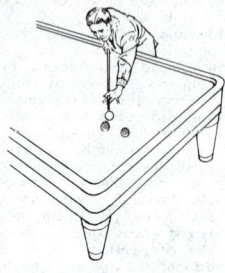
Billiards

bil·liards (bil′yərdz) *n.* **1.** game played with three hard balls and a cue on a cloth-covered rectangular table having cushions along the edges. **2.** any of several similar games, such as pool. ▲ construed as singular in both meanings. [French *billard* the game, billiard cue, from *bille* log. See BILLET².]

bil·ling (bil′ing) *n.* relative position that a performer or act occupies on an advertisement or program for a show: *The actor got top billing in his last show.*

Bil·lings (bil′ingz) *n.* city in south-central Montana, on the Yellowstone River. Pop. (1970), 61,581.

bil·lings·gate (bil′ingz gāt′) *n.* vulgar, abusive language. [From *Billingsgate* fish market at a London gate, notorious for vulgar language.]

bil·lion (bil′yən) *n.* **1.a.** in the U.S. and France, the cardinal number that is one thousand times one million. **b.** symbol representing this number; 1,000,000,000. **2.a.** in Great Britain and Germany, the cardinal number that is one million times one million. **b.** symbol representing this number; 1,000,000,000,000. —*adj.* numbering one billion. [French *billion,* from *bi-* BI- + *million* MILLION.]

bil·lion·aire (bil′yə nâr′) *n.* one who has a billion or more units of a particular currency, as of dollars, pounds, or francs.

bil·lionth (bil′yanth) *adj.* **1.** (the ordinal of billion) being last in a series of one billion. **2.** being one of a billion equal parts. —*n.* **1.** that which is last in a series of one billion. **2.** one of a billion equal parts.

bill of attainder, legislative act sentencing an accused person to death and attainder without a trial. Bills of attainder are prohibited in the United States by the Constitution.

bill of exchange, written order given by one person to another to pay to a designated person a certain sum of money at a specified time.

bill of fare, list of the foods served; menu.

bill of health 1. certificate given to the captain of a ship stating whether or not there are infectious diseases on a ship or in a port at the time of a ship's departure. **2. clean bill of health.** *Informal.* favorable recommendation or report.

bill of lading, written acknowledgment given by a carrier representing both a receipt and contract for goods being shipped.

bill of rights 1. Bill of Rights. first ten amendments to the Constitution of the United States guaranteeing fundamental rights and liberties. **2.** any formal declaration or summary of the fundamental rights and liberties guaranteed to, or felt to be essential to, a group of people.

bill of sale, written statement issued by a seller to a buyer transferring ownership of personal property.

bil·low (bil′ō) *n.* **1.** great wave or swell of a body of water. **2.** any great wave or surging mass: *Billows of smoke engulfed the men.* —*v.i.* **1.** to rise or roll in billows; surge; swell. **2.** to swell out: *The sail billowed in the wind.* —*v.t.* to cause to swell out: *The wind billowed the girl's skirt.* [Old Norse *bylgja* a wave.]

bil·low·y (bil′ō ē) *-low·i·er, -low·i·est. adj.* full of or characterized by billows; swelling; surging.

bill·post·er (bil′pōs′tər) *n.* one who is hired to post advertisements or notices.

bil·ly (bil′ē) *pl.,* **-lies.** *n.* nightstick. Also, **billy club.** [Probably from *Billy,* nickname of *William,* an example of the use of a nickname for a tool.]

billy goat *Informal.* male goat.

bi·me·tal·lic (bī′mi tal′ik) *adj.* **1.** made of, containing, or relating to two metals. **2.** relating to, based on, or using bimetallism.

at; āpe; cär; end; mē; it; īce; hot; ōld; fôrk; wood; fōōl; oil; out; up; ūse; turn; sing; thin; this; zh in treasure; ə in ago, taken, pencil, lemon, circus.

bi·met·al·lism (bī met′əl iz′əm) *n.* monetary system in which two metals, usually gold and silver, in a legally fixed ratio, are used as currency and the standard of currency. The relative value of the metals is fixed by law.

bi·month·ly (bī munth′lē) *adj.* **1.** occurring every two months. **2.** occurring twice a month; semimonthly. —*n. pl.,* **-lies.** bimonthly publication. —*adv.* **1.** every two months. **2.** twice a month.

bin (bin) *n.* receptacle or enclosed place for holding or storing something, as grain or coal. —*v.t.,* **binned, bin·ning.** to store in a bin. [Old English *binn* manger, crib.]

bin-, form of **bi-** before a vowel.

bi·na·ry (bī′nər ē) *adj.* **1.** consisting of, involving, or characterized by two things or parts. **2.** using or based on the binary system. —*n.* binary star. [Late Latin *bīnārius* consisting of two, from Latin *bīnī* two each.]

binary compound, compound composed of two elements: *Hydrochloric acid (HCL) is a binary compound.*

binary star, pair of stars revolving around a common center of gravity.

binary system, number system with a base of two, in which any number can be expressed by 0 or 1 or a combination of these.

bi·nate (bī′nāt) *adj. Botany.* growing in pairs; double: *a binate leaf.* [Latin *bīnī* two each + -ATE¹.]

bin·au·ral (bī nôr′əl) *adj.* **1.** relating to or involving the use of both ears. **2.** stereophonic: *binaural recording.* **3.** having two ears. [Latin *bīnī* two each + AURAL.]

bind (bīnd) **bound, bind·ing.** *v.t.* **1.** to tie, as with a rope; fasten together; secure: *to bind a sail to the mast, to bind wheat into bundles.* **2.** to fasten around or encircle; gird: *A headband bound her hair.* **3.** to bandage (often with *up*): *to bind up a wound.* **4.** to be under an obligation or compulsion (to do something): *We are bound to obey the laws.* **5.** to put under a definite legal obligation: *The dealer was bound by his contract.* **6.** to confine; restrain: *bound by superstition.* **7.** to cause to cohere or stick together: *Water binds particles of dirt to form mud.* **8.** to attach, as by ties of love, gratitude, or loyalty: *He was bound to his ideals.* **9.** to strengthen or ornament by a border or edge: *The seamstress bound the hem of the dress.* **10.** to fasten or enclose between covers: *to bind a book.* **11. to bind out.** to apprentice or indenture. **12.** *Law.* **to bind over.** to put (a person) under legal bond or recognizance to do some particular act, as to appear at court or pay a debt. —*v.i.* **1.** to be obligatory: *a rule that binds.* **2.** to stick together; cohere. —*n.* **1.** *Music.* tie or slur between notes. **2.** *Informal.* difficult situation. [Old English *bindan* to tie fast, tie together, cause to cohere.]

bind·er (bīn′dər) *n.* **1.** one who binds, esp. a bookbinder. **2.** anything that binds, as string or glue. **3.** removable cover for holding sheets of paper or other material together. **4.** machine that reaps grain and ties it in sheaves. **5.** temporary agreement binding parties pending the preparation of a formal contract, used esp. in real estate transactions.

bind·er·y (bīn′dər ē, -drē) *pl.,* **-er·ies.** *n.* place where books are bound.

bind·ing (bīn′ding) *n.* **1.** anything that binds. **2.** cloth tape used to protect or finish raw edges, as of a garment, carpet, or blanket. **3.** cover and backing holding together and enclosing the pages of a book. **4.** act of binding. —*adj.* **1.** having the power to obligate; obligatory: *He signed a binding agreement to pay back the loan in one year.* **2.** that binds in any way.

binding energy, quantity of energy required to break a particular atomic nucleus into its constituent parts.

bind·weed (bīnd′wēd′) *n.* any of various trailing or climbing herbaceous plants, genus *Convolvulus,* found in most temperate and tropical regions, bearing showy, trumpet-shaped flowers which usually open in the morning.

binge (binj) *n. Informal.* period of unrestrained or extreme indulgence, as in eating, drinking, or spending money; spree. [Possibly from dialectal English *binge* to soak; of uncertain origin.]

Bing·ham·ton (bing′əm tən) *n.* city in south-central New York. Pop. (1970), 64,123.

bin·go (bing′gō) *n.* form of lotto, usually played by large groups for prizes.

bin·na·cle (bin′ə kəl) *n.* case or stand containing a ship's compass, usually placed near the helm. [Modification of obsolete *bittacle,* from Spanish *bitácula,* from Latin *habitáculum* dwelling.]

bi·noc·u·lar (bə nok′yə lər, bī-) *adj.* using or for both eyes: *binocular vision; binocular microscope.* —*n.* binoculars. optical instrument for

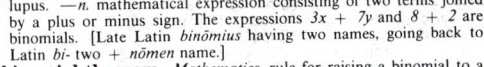

Binoculars

both eyes, using field glasses or opera glasses, used to magnify distant objects. [Latin *bīnī* two each + *oculus* eye.]

bi·no·mi·al (bī nō′mē əl) *adj.* **1.** consisting of two terms: *a binomial equation.* **2.** consisting of two names. Binomial nomenclature is used to classify plants and animals. The genus name is given first, followed by the species designation, as in the taxonomic name for the wolf, *Canis*

lupus. —*n.* mathematical expression consisting of two terms joined by a plus or minus sign. The expressions $3x + 7y$ and $8 + 2$ are binomials. [Late Latin *binōmius* having two names, going back to Latin *bi-* two + *nōmen* name.]

binomial theorem *Mathematics.* rule for raising a binomial to a power without writing out the actual multiplication.

bio- *combining form* of life or living things: *biology, biography.* [Greek *bios* life.]

bi·o·as·tro·nau·tics (bī′ō as′trə nô′tiks) *n.pl.* science that deals with the effects of space flight on living things. ▲ construed as singular.

bi·o·chem·is·try (bī′ō kem′is trē) *n.* science dealing with the chemical structure, products, and processes of living things. [BIO- + CHEMISTRY.] —**bi′o·chem′i·cal,** *adj.* —**bi′o·chem′ist,** *n.*

bi·o·feed·back (bī′ō fēd′bak) *n.* method of learning to control changes in one's own body, as in one's blood pressure or heart rate, by using electrocardiographs, electroencephalographs, and the like.

biog., biographer; biographical; biography.

bi·o·gen·e·sis (bī′ō jen′ə sis) *n.* **1.** theory that life develops only from living organisms. **2.** such development itself. [BIO- + GENESIS.]

bi·o·ge·og·ra·phy (bī′ō jē og′rə fē) *n.* science dealing with the geographical distribution of living organisms.

bi·og·ra·pher (bī og′rə fər, bē-) *n.* one who writes biographies.

bi·o·graph·i·cal (bī′ə graf′i kəl) *adj.* **1.** of or relating to a person's life: *biographical information.* **2.** of, relating to, or containing biography. Also, **bi′o·graph′ic.** —**bi′o·graph′i·cal·ly,** *adv.*

bi·og·ra·phy (bī og′rə fē, bē-) *pl.,* **-phies.** *n.* **1.** account of a person's life. **2.** such accounts collectively, considered as a form of literature or history. [Late Greek *biographiā* a writing of lives, from Greek *bios* life + *graphein* to write.]

bi·o·log·i·cal (bī′ə loj′i kəl) *adj.* **1.** of or relating to biology: *biological experiment.* **2.** used in or resulting from applied biology: *biological pest control.* Also, **bi′o·log′ic.** —**bi′o·log′i·cal·ly,** *adv.*

biological warfare, warfare using bacteria, viruses, and other toxic biological products.

bi·ol·o·gy (bī ol′ə jē) *n.* science of living organisms. Its two major divisions are botany, the science of plants, and zoology, the science of animals. [BIO- + -LOGY.] —**bi·ol′o·gist,** *n.*

bi·o·lu·mi·nes·cence (bī′ō lōō′mə nes′əns) *n.* emission of light from living organisms, as from fireflies and certain types of bacteria.

bi·om·e·try (bī om′ə trē) *n.* science that uses statistical methods in the study of biological problems. Also, **bi·o·met·rics** (bī′ə met′riks). [BIO- + -METRY.]

bi·on·ics (bī on′iks) *n.* the study of the mechanisms and systems of living things for the purpose of designing devices based on them. The design of electronic computers, based on knowledge of the nerves and the brain, is an example of bionics. ▲ construed as singular.

bi·o·nom·ics (bī′ə nom′iks) *n* ecology (def. 1). ▲ construed as singular. [BIO- + Greek *nomos* law + -ICS.] —**bi′o·nom′i·cal,** *adj.*

bi·o·phys·ics (bī′ō fiz′iks) *n.,pl.* science that applies the concepts and methods of physics to the study of biological organisms and processes. ▲ construed as singular.

bi·op·sy (bī′op′sē) *pl.,* **-sies.** *n.* surgical removal of living tissue for microscopic examination. [BI(O)- + Greek *opsis* sight.]

bi·o·sphere (bī′ə sfēr′) *n.* the part of the earth and its atmosphere where life is found.

bi·ot·ic (bī ot′ik) *adj.* of, relating to, or caused by living organisms. Also, **bi·ot′i·cal.** [Greek *biōtikos* relating to life, from *bios* life.]

bi·o·tin (bī′ə tin) *n.* crystalline acid which, as part of the vitamin B complex, is necessary for metabolism and growth. Formula: $C_{10}H_{16}N_2O_3S$ Also, **vitamin H.** [Greek *biotos* life, substance (from *bios* life) + -*in*¹.]

bi·o·tite (bī′ə tīt′) *n.* mica of a black, dark brown, or dark green variety, containing potassium, magnesium, and iron, and found chiefly in igneous rock. [From the French scientist Jean B. *Biot,* 1774–1862.]

bi·par·ti·san (bī pär′tə zən) *adj.* composed of, representing, or supported by two parties, esp. the Republicans and Democrats.

bi·par·tite (bī pär′tīt) *adj.* **1.** consisting of two parts, esp. two corresponding parts. **2.** *Botany.* divided into two parts, almost to the base, as in a leaf. [Latin *bipartītus,* past participle of *bipartīre* to divide into two parts.]

bi·ped (bī′ped′) *n.* animal having two feet. —*adj.* two-footed. [Latin *bipēs* two-footed.]

bi·pin·nate (bī pin′āt) *adj. (of a pinnate leaf)* having pinnate leaflets.

bi·plane (bī′plān′) *n.* airplane with two sets of wings, one above the other.

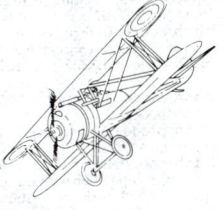

Biplane

at; āpe; cär; end; mē; it; īce; hot; ōld; fôrk; wood; fōōl; oil; out; up; ūse; turn; sing; thin; this; zh in treasure; ə in ago, taken, pencil, lemon, circus.

97

bi·po·lar (bī pō′lər) *adj.* **1.** having or relating to two poles. **2.** of, characteristic of, or found at both polar regions.

birch (burch) *n.* **1.** any of a group of shrubs or trees, genus *Betula*, found in temperate regions and bearing saw-toothed leaves. The pale or white bark of many trees is easily peeled in thin papery strips and was used by American Indians to make canoes. **2.** the hard, close-grained wood of any of these trees. **3.** birch rod or a bundle of birch twigs, used as a whip. —*v.t.* to beat with a birch; whip. [Old English *birce* birch tree.] —**birch′en**, *adj.*

bird (burd) *n.* **1.** any of a class, Aves, of warm-blooded, egg-laying vertebrates that have feathers and wings. **2.** game bird. **3.** shuttlecock. **4.** clay pigeon. **5.** *Informal.* person: *He was a queer bird.* **6.** *Informal.* sound of derision; hiss; jeer. ▲ usually used in the phrases *to give (some-one) the bird* and *to get the bird.* **7.** *Slang.* missile, rocket, or other flying object. **8. for the birds.** *Slang.* unappealing or worthless. —*v.i.* **1.** to observe or identify birds in their natural environments. **2.** to trap or shoot birds. [Old English *brídd* young bird.]

bird·bath (burd′bath′, -bäth′) *n.* decorative basin, frequently on a pedestal, placed outdoors as an ornament or for birds to bathe in and drink from.

bird·brain (burd′brān′) *n. Informal.* foolish, absent-minded person.

bird call 1. sound made by a bird; song of a bird. **2.a.** imitation of the sound made by a bird. **b.** instrument for imitating this sound.

bird dog, any of various dogs specially trained to hunt and retrieve game birds.

bird·house (burd′hous′) *n.* **1.** aviary. **2.** small box, usually resembling a house, in which birds may nest.

bird·ie (bur′dē) *n.* **1.** *Informal.* small bird; bird. **2.** golf score of one under par on a hole.

bird·lime (burd′līm′) *n.* sticky substance made from mistletoe which is smeared on twigs to catch small birds. —*v.t.*, **-limed, -lim·ing.** to smear or catch with or as with birdlime.

bird·man (burd′man′, -mən) *pl.* **-men** (-men′, -mən). *n.* **1.** *Informal.* aviator. **2.** one who deals with birds, such as an ornithologist.

bird of paradise, any of numerous songbirds, family Paradisaeidae, native to Australia, New Guinea, and neighboring islands. The male of the species is noted for its colorful, variegated plumage.

bird of passage 1. migratory bird. **2.** person who continuously wanders; one who does not stay in one locality for long; transient.

bird of prey, any of various flesh-eating birds, as eagles, hawks, owls, and vultures.

bird·seed (burd′sēd′) *n.* mixture of small seeds fed chiefly to caged birds.

bird's-eye (burdz′ī′) *adj.* **1.** seen from above: *a bird's-eye view of a town.* **2.** general; overall: *a bird's-eye view of the problem.* **3.** having markings resembling birds' eyes: *a desk of bird's-eye maple.* —*n.* **1.** fabric, usually cotton or linen, woven with a pattern resembling birds' eyes. **2.** any of various plants with small, bright-colored flowers.

bird shot, small-sized metal shot, used esp. for hunting game birds.

bi·reme (bī′rēm) *n.* galley with two rows or tiers of oars on each side, used in ancient times. [Latin *birēmis* having two rows of oars.]

bi·ret·ta (bə ret′ə) *n.* stiff, square cap with three or four projections on top, worn by Roman Catholic clergymen. Its color is black for priests, purple for bishops, and red for cardinals. [Italian *berretta,* from Late Latin *birrus* hooded cloak; possibly of Celtic origin.]

Biretta

Bir·ken·head (bur′kən hed′) *n.* port city in northwestern England, near Liverpool. Pop. (1968 est.), 142,500.

Bir·ming·ham (*def. 1* bur′ming əm; *def. 2* bur′ming ham′) *n.* **1.** largest city of Alabama, in the north-central part of the state. Pop. (1970), 300,910. **2.** city in west-central England. Pop. (1968 est.), 1,074,900.

birth (burth) *n.* **1.a.** act or fact of being born; nativity. **b.** act of bearing or bringing forth offspring; parturition. **2.** beginning of anything; origin. **3.a.** descent; lineage; extraction. **b.** noble lineage; good family. **4.** natural or inherited bent or ability: *an artist by birth.* **5.** *Archaic.* that which is born; offspring. **6. to give birth to. a.** to bring forth (offspring). **b.** to bring forth (anything); be the cause of. [Old Norse *byrth.*]

birth control, regulation of the number of births, esp. by the limiting or preventing of conception.

birth·day (burth′dā′) *n.* **1.** day of a person's birth. **2.** anniversary of this day.

birth·mark (burth′märk′) *n.* mark or blemish on the skin present at birth.

birth·place (burth′plās′) *n.* **1.** place of a person's birth. **2.** any place of origin.

birth·rate (burth′rāt′) *also,* **birth rate.** *n.* number of births occurring in a given population within a specific time, often expressed as live births per thousand of the population.

birth·right (burth′rīt′) *n.* right, privilege, or possession to which one is entitled by birth.

birth·stone (burth′stōn′) *n.* jewel associated with a particular month of the year.

bis-, form of **bi-** before *c* or *s,* as in *bissextile.*

Bi·sa·yan (bi sä′yən) *n.* Visayan.

Bi·sa·yas (bē sä′yäs) *n.* Visayan Islands.

Bis·cay, Bay of (bis′kā, -kē) broad inlet of the north Atlantic, between western France and northern Spain.

bis·cuit (bis′kit) *pl.* **-cuits** or **-cuit.** *n.* **1.** small, raised, baked cake made of a type of bread dough, usually with baking powder or soda as the leavening agent. **2.** *British.* cracker or thin cookie. **3.** pottery after the first firing and before painting or glazing. [French *biscuit,* from *bis* twice (from Latin *bis*) + *cuit* cooked, past participle of *cuire* to cook (from Latin *coquere*); from the practice of baking bread twice to preserve it for long sea voyages.]

bi·sect (bī sekt′) *v.t.* **1.** to divide (a geometrical figure) into two equal parts. **2.** to cut in two. —*v.i.* to divide in two; fork: *The road bisects soon.* [BI- + Latin *sectus,* past participle of *secāre* to cut.] —**bi·sec′tion,** *n.*

bi·sec·tor (bī sek′tər, bī′sek′-) *n.* line or plane that bisects.

bi·sex·u·al (bī sek′shōō əl) *adj.* **1.** having both male and female organs; hermaphroditic. **2.** of or relating to both sexes. —*n.* **1.** hermaphrodite. **2.** one who is sexually attracted by both sexes. —**bi·sex′u·al·ism, bi·sex·u·al·i·ty** (bī′sek shōō-al′ə tē), *n.* —**bi·sex′u·al·ly,** *adv.*

bish·op (bish′əp) *n.* **1.** high-ranking clergyman in any of various churches, usually the administrative head of a diocese and often having the spiritual duties of confirming and ordaining. **2.** one of the chess pieces that may be moved diagonally across any number of squares. [Old English *bisc(e)op* church bishop, going back to Church Latin *episcopus* overseer, church bishop, from Greek *episkopos.*]

Bishop *(def. 2)*

bish·op·ric (bish′ə prik) *n.* **1.** office, rank, or jurisdiction of a bishop. **2.** church district administered by a bishop; diocese. [Old English *bisceoprīce* diocese, from *bisc(e)op* BISHOP + *rīce* realm.]

Bis·marck (biz′märk) **1. Otto von.** 1815–98, German statesman. **2.** capital of North Dakota, in the south-central part of the state. Pop. (1970), 34,703.

Bismarck Archipelago, large island group in the western Pacific, just east of New Guinea, administered by Australia. Land area (approx.), 19,000 sq. mi. Pop. (1961 est.), 173,390.

bis·muth (biz′məth) *n.* brittle, crystalline, gray-white metallic element with a reddish tinge, used esp. in low-melting-point alloys and some drugs. Symbol: **Bi** See **element** for table. [German *Bismuth,* form of *Wismut;* of uncertain origin.]

bi·son (bī′sən, -zən) *pl.* **-son.** *n.* **1.** cud-chewing mammal, *Bison bison,* of North America, having a large head, short, permanent horns, humped shoulders, and a thick brown coat; buffalo. Height: 5½ feet at the shoulder. **2.** aurochs. [Latin *bison* wild ox; of Germanic origin.]

Bison

bisque¹ (bisk) *n.* **1.** thick, creamy soup made of fish or meat, esp. shellfish or game. **2.** any thick, creamy soup, esp. one made of vegetables. **3.** ice cream containing crushed macaroons or nuts. [French *bisque* soup made of shellfish or fish; of uncertain origin.]

bisque² (bisk) *n.* in ceramics, biscuit. [Short for BISCUIT *(def. 3).*]

bis·sex·tile (bi seks′til, -tīl) *n.* leap year. —*adj.* indicating or designating the extra day of a leap year. [Latin *bissextilis (annus)* leap (year), from *bis* twice + *sextus* sixth. The additional day in leap year was shown on the ancient Roman calendar by having the *sixth* day before March 1 occur twice, that is, be repeated the next day.]

bis·ter (bis′tər) *also,* **bis·tre.** *n.* **1.** orange-yellow to brown-black pigment, used esp. in drawings and watercolors. **2.** dark brown. [French *bistre;* of uncertain origin.]

bis·tro (bis′trō, bēs′-) *n.* small bar, nightclub, or cafe. [French *bistro* tavern, wineshop; possibly from Russian *bystro* hurry up; used by Russian troops in ordering drinks at taverns during their occupation of Paris after the defeat of Napoleon.]

bi·sul·fate (bī sul′fāt) *also,* **bi·sul·phate.** *n.* **1.** any salt containing the radical -HSO₄. **2.** radical with a negative valence of one that combines with sodium to form sodium bisulfate.

bi·sul·fide (bī sul′fīd) *also,* **bi·sul·phide.** *n.* disulfide.

at; āpe; cär; end; mē; it; īce; hot; ōld; fôrk; wood; fōōl; oil; out; up; ūse; turn; sing; thin; this; zh in treasure; ə in ago, taken, pencil, lemon, circus.

bi·sul·fite (bī sul′fīt) *also,* **bi·sul·phite.** *n.* salt of sulfurous acid containing the radical -HSO₃.

bit¹ (bit) *n.* **1.** metal mouthpiece of a bridle and the rings that attach it to bridle straps. **2.a.** boring or drilling part that fits into a brace, drill press, or similar tool. **b.** cutting or end part of a tool. **3.** part of a key that enters the lock and acts on the bolt and tumblers. —*v.t.,* **bit·ted, bit·ting. 1.** to put a bit in the mouth of (a riding animal); train to the bit. **2.** to curb or restrain with, or as with, a bit. [Old English *bite* bite.]

bit² (bit) *n.* **1.** small piece, part, or quantity: *The plate fell and broke into bits.* **2.** somewhat: *a bit of an actor.* ▲ commonly used adverbially in the phrase *a bit,* as in *a bit awkward, a bit too small.* **3.** short while: *This will only take a bit.* **4.** *Informal.* amount equivalent to twelve and a half cents, originally a Spanish or Mexican coin used as currency in the southwestern United States. ▲ now used only in multiples of two, as *two bits, four bits.* **5.** *Slang.* incident of action or behavior; act; routine: *the singing bit.* **6. bit by bit.** a little at a time; gradually: *Bit by bit, the group accepted the idea.* —*adj.* insignificant: *a bit part in a play.* [Old English *bita* morsel, small piece bitten off.]

Syn. 1. Bit, particle, speck mean a small piece. **Bit** is the most general term: *Bits of glass were all over the floor.* **Particle** suggests a piece just large enough to be distinguished: *Particles of soot collected on the window sills and soon discolored the white paint.* **Speck** implies a bit or particle distinguishable esp. because of its color: *grey sand with black specks.*

bit³ (bit) past tense and a past participle of **bite.**

bit⁴ (bit) *n.* **1.** unit of information recording the decision made by a computer between two alternatives. **2.** unit of information storage capacity in a computer. [BI(NARY) + (DIGI)T.]

bitch (bich) *n.* female of the dog or other canine. [Old English *bicce* female dog.]

bite (bīt) **bit, bit·ten** or **bit, bit·ing.** *v.t.* **1.** to cut, pierce, or seize with the teeth: *The girl bit her tongue while chewing gum. The dog bit the bone.* **2.** to remove with the teeth; cut or tear (with *off* or *out*): *He bit off a piece of the candy bar.* **3.** to pierce the skin of with teeth, fangs, or similar parts: *A snake bit the camper. I killed the mosquito as it was about to bite me.* **4.** to cut or pierce with or as with an instrument. **5.** to cause to smart or sting: *The winter wind bit our faces.* **6.** to eat into; corrode: *Acid bites metal.* **7.** to take a firm hold on; grip. **8. to bite off more than one can chew.** to undertake something beyond one's capabilities. —*v.i.* **1.** to cut, pierce, or seize something: *The surgeon's scalpel bit deeply. The dog's teeth bit through the skin.* **2.** to cause smarting or stinging. **3.** (of fish) to take or be caught by the bait. **4.** to accept anything deceptive; be tricked. —*n.* **1.** act of biting. **2.** wound made by biting or stinging. **3.** piece bitten off; mouthful; morsel. **4.** *Informal.* small meal; snack: *We stopped for a bite before the show.* **5.** effect or quality of biting; sting: *the bite of his sarcasm, the bite of the cold.* **6.** grip or hold on a surface: *the extra bite of snow tires.* **7.** manner in which the upper and lower teeth meet. [Old English *bītan* to cut into with the teeth.] —**bit′er,** *n.*

Bi·thyn·i·a (bi thin′ē ə) *n.* ancient kingdom and later a Roman province in northwestern Asia Minor, on the Black Sea.

bit·ing (bī′ting) *adj.* **1.** sharp; stinging: *biting cold.* **2.** sarcastic; cutting; caustic: *his biting wit.* —**bit′ing·ly,** *adv.*

bitt (bit) *n.* post on a ship's deck to which ropes are secured. —*v.t.* to put (a rope) around a bitt. [Possibly from Old Norse *biti* beam.]

bit·ten (bit′ən) a past participle of **bite.**

bit·ter (bit′ər) *adj.* **1.** having a sharp, biting, unpleasant taste. **2.** emotionally or intellectually unpleasant; hard to admit or bear: *the bitter truth.* **3.** harsh or biting; sarcastic: *bitter humor.* **4.** causing or showing pain, misery, or discomfort: *the bitter cold, bitter tears.* **5.** having or showing intense animosity: *a bitter quarrel, bitter enemies.* **6.** resentful; unforgiving: *He was still bitter about losing the job.* **7. to the bitter end. a.** until the very end, however painful or unpleasant. **b.** to death itself. —*n.* that which is bitter; bitterness. —*adv.* extremely: *a bitter cold morning.* [Old English *biter* severe, not sweet.] —**bit′ter·ly,** *adv.* —**bit′ter·ness,** *n.*

bit·tern (bit′ərn) *n.* any of several marsh birds, family Ardeidae, closely related to, but smaller than, the heron, found throughout the world. [Old French *butor,* going back to Latin *būtiō* bittern + *taurus* bull; possibly because it "bellows" like a bull).]

bit·ter·root (bit′ər rŏŏt′, -root′) *n.* low-growing plant, *Lewisia rediviva,* found in the northern Rocky Mountain region, bearing a circle of pink or rose-colored flowers at its base and a single white or rose-colored flower at the top. [So called because of its bitter taste.]

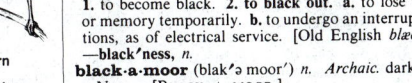

Bittern

bit·ters (bit′ərz) *n.pl.* liquid, usually alcoholic, prepared from bitter herbs and roots or angostura bark, used to flavor mixed drinks or as an ingredient in medicine.

bit·ter·sweet (bit′ər swēt′) *n.* **1.** climbing, woody plant, *Solanum dulcamara,* of the nightshade family, native to Europe, northern Africa, and Asia, bearing drooping clusters of violet flowers that ripen into poisonous, scarlet berries. **2.** climbing shrub, *Celastrus scandens,* that grows wild in North American woodlands, bearing clusters of small, greenish flowers. —*adj.* **1.** containing a small amount of sweetener; moderately sweet: *bittersweet chocolate.* **2.** both pleasant and painful: *bittersweet memories.*

bi·tu·men (bi tōō′mən, -tū′-, bi-) *n.* any of various dark brown or black flammable substances of variable hardness, such as asphalt, bituminous coal, or crude petroleum, composed chiefly of hydrocarbons. [Latin *bitūmen.*]

bi·tu·mi·nous (bi tōō′mə nəs, -tū′-, bi-) *adj.* made of, containing, or like bitumen.

bituminous coal, dull to shiny black coal with a low carbon content that burns with a smoky flame. Also, **soft coal.**

bi·va·lence (bī vā′ləns, biv′ə ləns) *n.* quality or state of being bivalent. Also, **bi·va′len·cy.**

bi·va·lent (bī vā′lənt, biv′ə lənt) *adj.* having a valence of plus or minus two. [BI- + Latin *valēns,* present participle of *valēre* to be strong.]

bi·valve (bī′valv′) *n.* mollusk whose shell consists of two parts, or valves, hinged together, as the oyster or clam. —*adj.* **1.** having two shells united by a hinge. **2.** having two valves, as a seedcase.

biv·ou·ac (biv′ōō ak′, biv′wak) *n.* temporary encampment, esp. one made by soldiers in the field, with or without shelter. —*v.i.,* **-acked, -ack·ing.** to camp out in a bivouac. [French *bivouac* temporary encampment, probably from dialectal German *Beiwacht* literally, additional watch or guard (with reference to a watch by citizens to aid the regular watch).]

bi·week·ly (bī wēk′lē) *adj.* **1.** occurring every two weeks. **2.** occurring twice a week; semiweekly. —*n. pl.,* **-lies.** biweekly publication. —*adv.* **1.** every two weeks. **2.** twice a week; semiweekly.

bi·year·ly (bī yēr′lē) *adj. and adv.* **1.** (occurring) twice a year; semiannually. **2.** (occurring) every two years.

bi·zarre (bi zär′) *adj.* strikingly odd, as in manner or style; eccentric; fantastic; grotesque. [French *bizarre* originally, brave, from Spanish *bizarro* brave; possibly from Basque *bizarra* beard (a bearded man being regarded as brave).] —**bi·zarre′ly,** *adv.* —**bi·zarre′ness,** *n.* —**Syn.** see grotesque.

Bi·zet, Georges (bē zā′; zhôrzh) 1838–75, French composer.

Bk, berkelium.

bk. 1. book. **2.** bank.

bkg., banking.

bkt. *pl.,* **bkts.** basket.

bl. 1. bale. **2.** barrel.

b.l., bill of lading. Also, **B/L.**

blab (blab) **blabbed, blab·bing.** *v.t.* to tell or reveal (secrets) thoughtlessly or indiscreetly. —*v.i.* **1.** to chatter idly; prattle. **2.** to reveal a secret; talk indiscreetly. —*n.* loose talk; idle chatter. [Imitative.] —**blab′ber,** *n.*

blab·ber (blab′ər) *v.i.* to chatter idly. —*n.* idle chatter. [Imitative.]

blab·ber·mouth (blab′ər mouth′) *n. Informal.* one who talks too much or indiscreetly.

black (blak) *adj.* **1.** absorbing all light. Opposed to **white. 2.** having no light; in darkness; dark: *the black depths of the ocean.* **3.a.** of, relating to, or belonging to a dark-skinned people, esp. of African descent. **b.** dark-skinned. **4.** gloomy or ominous: *black despair, black humor.* **5.** angry; sullen: *black looks.* **6.** dirty; soiled: *After the game his uniform was black.* **7.** evil; wicked: *black deeds.* **8.** indicating disgrace or discredit: *a black day for the family.* —*n.* **1.** total absorption of light. Although technically black is the complete absorption of light, it is perceived as a color and as the darkest of all colors. Opposed to **white. 2.** something that imparts black, as a dye or paint. **3.** something black, as a checker. **4.** member of a dark-skinned people, esp. of African descent. **5.** black clothes, esp. those worn for mourning. **6. in the black.** making a profit; prospering financially. Opposed to **in the red.** —*v.t.* **1.** to make black. **2.** to clean and polish with blacking. **3. to black out. a.** to turn off or cover lights, esp. as a precaution against enemy detection and attack. **b.** to obliterate with black, esp. to censor or delete. **c.** to interrupt normal operations of, as of electrical service. —*v.i.* **1.** to become black. **2. to black out. a.** to lose vision, consciousness, or memory temporarily. **b.** to undergo an interruption of normal operations, as of electrical service. [Old English *blæc* opposite of white.] —**black′ness,** *n.*

black·a·moor (blak′ə moor′) *n. Archaic.* dark-skinned person, esp. a Negro. [BLACK + MOOR.]

black-and-blue (blak′ən blōō′) *adj.* discolored as a result of ruptured blood vessels under the skin.

Black and Tan, member of the British recruits sent to Ireland in June 1920 to aid the royal Irish constabulary in putting down the Sinn

at; āpe; cär; end; mē; it; īce; hot; ōld; fôrk; wood; fōōl; oil; out; up; ūse; turn; sing; thin; this; zh in treasure; ə in ago, taken, pencil, lemon, circus.

99

Fein rebellion. [From the *black and tan* uniforms worn by these recruits.]

black and white 1. writing; print: *Give us in black and white your opinion of the matter.* 2. photograph or picture in which black, white, and gray are the only colors.

black art, witchcraft; magic.

black·ball (blak′bôl′) *v.t.* 1. to vote against. 2. to ostracize. —*n.* vote rejecting a person or thing. [From the ancient Greek method of indicating a negative vote by putting a small *black ball* in a container.]

black bass (bas) any of several freshwater game fish, genus *Micropterus,* found in eastern and central North America. Length: to 28 inches.

black bear, any of various bears, genus *Euarctos,* native to North America and Mexico, having fur ranging from black to cinnamon-colored.

Black Belt 1. area of rich, black farming soil in Alabama and Mississippi. 2. region in a city or state that has a predominantly Negro population.

black·ber·ry (blak′ber′ē) *pl.,* **-ries.** *n.* 1. sweet black fruit of any of several bramble bushes, genus *Rubus,* of the rose family, esp. *R. alleghemiensis,* of the northeastern United States and Canada. 2. thorny bush that bears this fruit.

Blackberries

black·bird (blak′burd′) *n.* 1. any of various New World birds, family Icteridae, that are all or mostly black or dark in color, as the red-winged blackbird, cowbird, and grackle. 2. black or dark-brown thrush, *Turdus merula,* native to Europe. Also, **merle.**

black·board (blak′bôrd′) *n.* hard, smooth surface of slate or other dark material for writing or drawing on with chalk.

black body, hypothetical surface or body capable of absorbing all radiation falling on it and reflecting none.

black book, book containing a blacklist. —**to be in one's black book,** to be out of favor with someone.

black bread, pumpernickel.

black·cap (blak′kap′) *n.* 1. black raspberry. 2. any of several birds having a black crown, as the European warbler, *Sylvia atricapilla,* or the chickadee.

black·damp (blak′damp′) *n.* suffocating gaseous mixture consisting mostly of carbon dioxide, produced esp. by explosions or fires in mines. Also, **choke′damp′.**

Black Death, epidemic of bubonic plague that spread through Europe, Africa, and Asia in the fourteenth century. By 1352 it had wiped out one-third of the total population of Europe. [From the *black* spots on the body caused by the disease.]

black diamond 1. black diamonds. mineral coal. 2. carbonado.

black·en (blak′ən) *v.t.* 1. to make black; darken. 2. to sully; defame. —*v.i.* to become black or dark. —**black′en·er,** *n.*

black eye 1. discoloration of the skin around the eye, usually caused by a blow. 2. *Informal.* disgrace; discredit; dishonor.

black-eyed pea (blak′īd′) cowpea.

black-eyed Su·san (sōō′zən) showy daisylike flower head of a plant, *Rudbeckia serotina,* of the composite family, having yellow petal-like rays surrounding a dark brown center, native to eastern Canada and the United States.

Black-eyed Susan

black·face (blak′fās′) *n.* 1. make-up used by performers playing Negro roles. 2. performer playing a Negro role in this make-up. 3. boldface.

black·fish (blak′fish′) *pl.,* **-fish** or **fish·es.** *n.* 1. any of various dark-colored saltwater fish, as the sea bass and the tautog. 2. either of two freshwater fish, genus *Dallia,* of the swamps and bogs of Alaska and Siberia, valued as a food fish.

black flag, Jolly Roger.

black·fly (blak′flī′) *n.* dark-colored biting fly, family Simuliidae, common to North American forests.

Black·foot (blak′foot′) *pl.,* **-feet** or **-foot.** *n.* 1. member of any of three tribes of Plains Indians of Algonquian linguistic stock who lived east of the Rocky Mountains in Saskatchewan and Montana. 2. the Algonquian language of the Blackfeet. [Translation of Blackfoot *Siksika;* said to refer to their custom of blackening their moccasins.]

Black Forest, mountainous forested district in southwestern West Germany. Also, *German,* **Schwarz′wald′.**

Black Friar, Dominican friar. [From the *black* color of his mantle.]

black grouse, grouse of Europe and northern Asia, *Lyrurus tetrix,* the male of which is black with white markings.

black·guard (blag′ärd, -ərd) *n.* low, unscrupulous character; scoundrel. —*v.t.* to revile contemptuously; villify. [Originally used contemptuously to refer to kitchen servants, who were soiled by their work. See BLACK, GUARD.] —**black′guard·ly,** *adj., adv.*

Black Hand, secret criminal society brought to the United States by Sicilian immigrants in the late nineteenth century. It is often identified with the Mafia.

black·head (blak′hed′) *n.* 1. small, black, oily plug formed in a pore in the skin, usually occurring on the face, shoulders, and back. 2. any of various birds whose heads are partially or totally black. 3. infectious protozoan disease of turkeys and certain other fowl.

black·heart (blak′härt′) *n.* disease of trees and other plants, such as the potato, characterized by a blackening and decay of the internal tissues.

Black Hills, mountain range in southwestern South Dakota and northeastern Wyoming.

black hole 1. hypothetical hole in outer space which forms when a huge star burns out, loses its ability to withstand gravitational forces, and begins to collapse. Its matter is compressed so densely that gravity prevents the escape of visible light rays. 2. see **Black Hole of Calcutta.**

Black Hole of Calcutta, small cell at Calcutta in which 146 British subjects were confined for a night in 1756, only 23 of whom survived.

black·ing (blak′ing) *n.* substance used to blacken or to give a polished black surface.

black·jack (blak′jak′) *n.* 1. small, flexible-handled bludgeon covered with leather. 2. pirate's black flag. 3. card game in which the players play against the dealer, the winner being the one whose cards bear numbers adding up to twenty-one or to the closest number below that. If both the dealer and another player have twenty-one, the dealer wins. Also, **twen′ty-one′.** 4. oak tree, *Quercus marilandica,* found in the eastern United States, having a heavy black bark. —*v.t.* to strike with a blackjack.

black lead, graphite.

black·leg (blak′leg′) *n.* 1. *Informal.* gambler who cheats, esp. at cards. 2. *British.* strikebreaker; scab. 3. bacterial disease of cattle and sheep that is usually fatal. 4. any of several bacterial or fungous diseases causing a blackening of the base of plant stems, esp. in cabbages or potatoes.

black letter, heavy, angular, elaborate form of Gothic type.

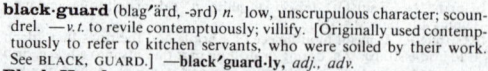

Black letters

black·list (blak′list′) *n.* list of persons or organizations to be regarded as suspect, boycotted, or punished in some way. —*v.t.* to place on a blacklist.

black lung, disease of the lungs that affects miners, caused by constant inhalation of coal dust.

black·ly (blak′lē) *adv.* 1. darkly; gloomily; dismally. 2. angrily; threateningly. 3. wickedly.

black magic, magic used for evil purposes; witchcraft.

black·mail (blak′māl′) *n.* 1. extortion, esp. of money, by threat of exposure or any form of intimidation. 2. payment so extorted. —*v.t.* to extort or attempt to extort blackmail from. [BLACK + Scottish *mail* rent, tribute, from Old English *māl* tribute, from Old Norse *māl* agreement, speech; from the tribute formerly extorted by bandits and freebooters from Scottish and English farmers for protection against pillage. *Black mail* was paid in such form as cattle and *white mail* in silver.] —**black′mail′er,** *n.*

Black Ma·ri·a (mə rī′ə) *Informal.* patrol wagon.

black mark, indication of something unfavorable or disgraceful.

black market, market or place where goods are sold in violation of official controls.

black nightshade, any of several varieties of the plant *Solanum nigrum,* found in temperate and tropical regions, bearing white flowers and black berries that are poisonous when unripe.

black oak 1. any of various oaks of North America, having dark leaves and bark, esp. *Quercus velutina,* whose inner bark is used in making dye. 2. the wood of any of these trees.

black·out (blak′out′) *n.* 1. temporary loss of vision, consciousness, or memory. 2. temporary stoppage or interruption of normal operation, as of electric service in a certain area. 3. turning out or covering of lights to prevent enemy detection and attack. 4. turning off of all stage lights, esp. to indicate a separation between scenes. 5. (of news) deliberate noncoverage or withholding of information.

black pepper, see **pepper.**

Black·pool (blak′pōōl′) *n.* seaside resort city in northwestern England. Pop. (1968 est.), 147,900.

Black Power, collective power of American Negroes to exert political, social, and economic pressure to achieve racial equality.

Black Prince, see **Edward the Black Prince.**

Black Sea, inland sea between Europe and Asia, bordered by the

Soviet Union, Turkey, Bulgaria, and Romania. In ancient times it was known as the Pontus Euxinus, or Euxine Sea.

black sheep, one who is regarded as a disgrace or discredit by the other members of his family or group.

Black Shirt, member of the Italian Fascist corps of armed guards or of the SS of Nazi Germany. [A *black shirt* was part of their uniform.]

black·smith (blak′smith′) *n.* **1.** one who makes horseshoes and shoes horses. **2.** one who works with iron, as with an anvil and forge. [From their working with iron, a *black* metal.]

black·snake (blak′snāk′) *n.* **1.** nonpoisonous snake, *Coluber constrictor,* of the eastern United States, having dull black scales. Length: 4–5 feet. **2.** any of various other snakes having black or dark-colored skins. **3.** heavy, flexible whip of braided leather or rawhide.

black spruce **1.** North American spruce tree, *Picea mariana,* noted for its dark foliage. **2.** the light, pliable wood of this tree.

Black·stone, Sir William (blak′stōn′, -stən) 1723–1780, English jurist, legal scholar, and author.

black tea, tea made from tea leaves that have withered and fermented before being subjected to the drying process.

black·thorn (blak′thôrn′) *n.* **1.** thorny shrub, *Prunus spinosa,* of the rose family, found in Europe and parts of Asia, bearing white flowers and deep blue, plumlike fruit. Also, *sloe.* **2.** walking stick made from the wood of this shrub. **3.** hawthorn of North America, *Crataegus calpodendron.*

black tie **1.** black bow tie, worn with a tuxedo. **2.** semiformal evening wear. Distinguished from *white tie.*

black·top (blak′top′) *n.* **1.** bituminous material, as asphalt, used to pave roads. **2.** road paved with such a material. —*v.t.,* **-topped, -top·ping.** to pave with blacktop.

black walnut **1.** strong, dark-brown wood of a North American tree, *Juglans nigra,* used chiefly for furniture and gun stocks. **2.** the tree itself. **3.** the oily, edible nut of this tree.

black widow, glossy black spider, *Latrodectus mactans,* commonly found in Central America and in southern and western parts of the United States. The female is poisonous, has a red hourglass-shaped marking on the underside of its abdomen, and is more than twice the size of the male. [From its color and its practice of eating its mate.]

Female   Male

Black widow

blad·der (blad′ər) *n.* **1.** elastic, membranous sac in the body that stores or receives a liquid or gas, esp. the bladder in the pelvic cavity that stores urine received from the kidneys. **2.** something resembling a bladder in shape, use, or inflatability, as the inflatable inner bag of a football. **3.** inflated sac in certain plants, esp. one that acts as a food trap or as a float on an aquatic plant. [Old English *blǣdre* membranous sac in the body.]

blad·der·wort (blad′ər wurt′) *n.* any of various plants growing in marshes or in water, genus *Utricularia,* found in temperate and tropical regions, having small bladders on their leaves.

blade (blād) *n.* **1.** sharp-edged part of anything that cuts: *That knife's blade is twice as long as its handle.* **2.** leaf, as of grass. **3.** broad part of a leaf or petal. See *leaf* for illustration. **4.** broad, flat part, as on certain implements or devices: *the blade of an oar, the blade of a shovel, the blades of a fan.* **5.** sword. **6.** sharp runner, as of an ice skate. **7.** broad, flat bone or part of a bone. **8.** dashing, rakish young man: *a gay blade.* [Old English *blæd* leaf, broad flat part of an implement.] —**blad′ed,** *adj.*

Blake, William (blāk) 1757–1827, English poet, artist, and philosopher.

blam·a·ble (blā′mə bəl) *also,* **blame·a·ble.** *adj.* deserving blame; reprehensible. —**blam′a·bly,** *also,* **blame·a·bly,** *adv.*

blame (blām) **blamed, blam·ing.** *v.t.* **1.** to find fault with; censure: *I can't blame you for trying.* **2.** to accuse or hold (someone or something) responsible: *I blame you for their lateness.* **3.** to fix responsibility for (something): *They blamed the breakage on the earthquake.* —*n.* **1.** responsibility for something wrong: *He took all the blame upon himself.* **2.** censure; condemnation: *They heaped blame upon him.* **3. to be to blame.** to be at fault; be blamable. [Old French *blasmer* to accuse, censure, going back to Latin *blasphēmāre* to speak ill of, from Greek *blasphēmein.* Doublet of BLASPHEME.]

Syn. *v.t.* **1.** Blame, censure, criticize, reproach mean to express an unfavorable or disapproving judgment or to find fault with. Blame implies that the one finding fault sets himself up as a judge of what is right or wrong: *He blames the accident on the other driver.* Censure strengthens the sense of competence in judgment and suggests a more public expression of disapproval: *The legislature voted to censure the senator for his misuse of public funds, but he was not expelled.* Criticize,

usually used in the sense of unfavorable judgment, emphasizes the position taken by the one finding fault as a competent critic or judge: *He criticized her taste in clothing.* Reproach suggests that the one finding fault is personally involved, at least emotionally, and implies hope for improvement: *Her failure to reproach him for his oversight made him feel even guiltier.* **2.** see *accuse.*

blame·less (blām′lis) *adj.* not deserving blame; innocent. —**blame′-less·ly,** *adv.* —**blame′less·ness,** *n.*

blame·wor·thy (blām′wur′the) *adj.* deserving of blame.

blanch (blanch) *v.i.* to become white; turn pale: *She blanched with fear.* —*v.t.* **1.** to remove color from; bleach. **2.** to make pale, as from fear or sickness. **3.a.** to remove the skin of, as almonds, by scalding. **b.** to scald, as vegetables, in order to whiten or make firm. **4.** to brighten (metals) by means of acid or by coating with tin. [Old French *blanchir* to whiten, from *blanc* white; of Germanic origin.]

blanc·mange (blə mänj′, -mänzh′) *n.* sweet gelatinous dessert, shaped in a mold, and made of milk that is thickened and flavored. [Old French *blancmanger* literally, white food, from *blanc* white (of Germanic origin) + *manger* food (going back to Latin *mandūcāre* to eat).]

bland (bland) *adj.* **1.** lacking individual flavor; uninteresting; vapid; dull: *bland reporting, a bland personality.* **2.** not stimulating or irritating; mild: *a bland diet, a bland climate.* **3.** unemotional; suave: *a bland reaction to a serious situation.* [Latin *blandus* soft.] —**bland′ly,** *adv.* —**bland′ness,** *n.*

blan·dish (blan′dish) *v.t.* to coax; flatter; cajole. [Old French *blandiss-,* a stem of *blandir* to flatter, from Latin *blandīrī.*]

blan·dish·ment (blan′dish mənt) *n.* flattering speech or action; coaxing; flattery.

blank (blangk) *adj.* **1.** not written or printed upon; unmarked: *a blank sheet of paper, a blank canvas.* **2.** having spaces to be filled out: *a blank ballot.* **3.** void of interest or thought; empty: *His mind is blank.* **4.** expressionless; vacant: *a blank gaze.* **5.** bewildered; disconcerted: *a blank look.* **6.** lacking some finishing feature or characteristic: *a blank cartridge, a blank key.* **7.** complete; utter; absolute: *blank dismay.* —*n.* **1.** empty space to be filled out, as in a printed form. **2.** form or document containing such spaces. **3.** empty space or time; void: *His future is a blank.* **4.** partially completed object, as a piece of metal, ready to be finished by a further operation. **5.** cartridge containing powder, but no bullet. **6. to draw a blank.** to be unsuccessful in an attempt, as to think of a solution or an answer. —*v.t.* **1.** to obscure or delete (often with *out*). **2.** to keep (an opponent) from scoring in a game. [French *blanc* white; of Germanic origin.] —**blank′ly,** *adv.* —**blank′ness,** *n.*

blank check **1.** signed check without the amount filled in. **2.** freedom to act without control; carte blanche.

blan·ket (blang′kit) *n.* **1.** covering made of wool or other woven fabric, used esp. for warmth, as in bed. **2.** anything that covers like a blanket: *a blanket of fog.* —*v.t.* to cover with or as with a blanket. —*adj.* applicable to or covering a wide range of conditions or items: *blanket approval.* [Old French *blankete* woolen covering; originally, white wool cloth, from *blanc* white; of Germanic origin.]

blank verse **1.** unrhymed verse written in iambic pentameter. Much of Shakespeare's work is in blank verse. **2.** unrhymed verse having any regular meter.

blare (blār) **blared, blar·ing.** *v.t., v.i.* **1.** to sound loudly and harshly: *Bugles blared the salute. The orchestra blared.* **2.** to proclaim noisily: *The radio blared the news.* —*n.* loud, harsh sound. [Imitative.]

blar·ney (blär′ne) *n.* smooth flattering talk; artful coaxing; cajolery. [From the BLARNEY STONE.]

Blarney Stone, stone block in a wall of a castle in Ireland, said to endow those who kiss it with skill in flattery and cajolery.

bla·sé (blä zā′, blä′zā) *adj.* indifferent; jaded; world-weary; bored. [French *blasé,* past participle of *blaser* to weary by indulgence; of uncertain origin.]

blas·pheme (blas fēm′, blas′fēm) **-phemed, -phem·ing.** *v.t.* to speak impiously or irreverently of (God or anything sacred). —*v.i.* to speak or utter blasphemy. [Old French *blasfemer,* from Latin *blasphēmāre* to speak ill of, from Greek *blasphemein.* Doublet of BLAME.] —**blas·phem′er,** *n.*

blas·phe·mous (blas′fə məs) *adj.* characterized by or using blasphemy; irreverent. [Late Latin *blasphēmus,* from Greek *blasphēmos.*] —**blas′phe·mous·ly,** *adv.*

blas·phe·my (blas′fə mē) *pl.,* **-mies.** *n.* **1.** expression of contempt or irreverence for God or anything sacred. **2.** act of claiming the attributes of God.

blast (blast) *n.* **1.** strong rush of wind; gust: *The chilling blasts swept over the lake.* **2.** loud, explosive sound, as that made by a horn: *the blast of the trumpets, the blast of the radio.* **3.** strong current of air produced artificially. **4.a.** explosion, as of dynamite; detonation and its effects. **b.** charge set off in such an explosion. **5.** current of compressed air

directed into a blast furnace to promote combustion during smelting. **6.** *Informal.* violent attack or denunciation. **7.** *Informal.* good time, esp. a wild party. **8.** destructive influence; blight. **9. (at) full blast,** at maximum speed, capacity, or volume. —*v.t.* **1.** to blow up or shatter with or as with an explosive. **2.** to bring damage or blight to; ruin; wither: *to blast one's hopes. Frost blasted the blossoms.* **3.** *Informal.* to upbraid or denounce vigorously. —*v.i.* **1.** to sound loudly or harshly: *The loudspeakers blasted.* **2. to blast off.** (of a rocket or missile) to take off; begin flight. [Old English *blǣst* gust of wind.] —**blast′er,** *n.*

blast·ed (blas′tid) *adj.* **1.** withered; destroyed; blighted. **2.** damned.

blast furnace, vertical smelting furnace in which the heat is maintained by a blast of preheated air, used esp. in the reduction of iron ore.

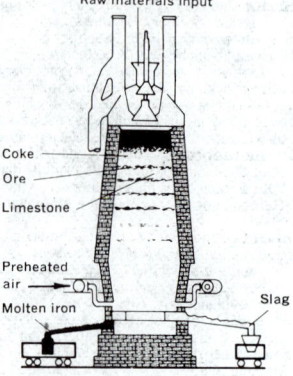

Raw materials input
Coke
Ore
Limestone
Preheated air
Molten iron
Slag

Blast furnace

blas·to·coele (blas′tə-sēl′) *also,* **blas·to·coel, blas·to·cele.** *n.* cavity of a blastula.

blas·to·derm (blas′tə-durm′) *n.* layer of germinal cells arising from the segmentation of the fertilized ovum and later forming the wall of the blastula. [Greek *blastos* germ + *derma* skin.] —**blas′to·der′mic,** *adj.*

blast-off (blast′ôf′) *n.* launching of a rocket or missile.

blas·to·mere (blas′tə-mēr′) *n.* one of the cells produced during the cleavage of the fertilized ovum. —**blas·to·mer·ic** (blas′tə-mer′ik), *adj.*

blas·to·pore (blas′tə-pôr′) *n.* opening or the archenteron on the surface of a gastrula.

blas·tu·la (blas′chə-lə) *pl.,* **-lae** (-lē′) *n.* early stage in development of an animal embryo, usually consisting of a single layer of cells forming a sphere around a central cavity. [Modern Latin *blastula,* diminutive of Greek *blastos* germ.] —**blas′tu·lar,** *adj.*

Blastula
exterior and cross section

blat (blat) **blat·ted, blat·ting.** *v.i., v.t.* to bleat —*n.* a bleat. [Imitative.]

bla·tant (blāt′ənt) *adj.* **1.** conspicuously evident; obtrusive: *blatant negligence.* **2.** obvious in a coarse or offensive manner. **3.** *Archaic.* bleating; bellowing; noisy: *blatant herds.* [Coined by Edmund Spenser to describe a noisy beast symbolizing slander; possibly from Latin *blatīre* to babble.] —**bla′tan·cy,** *n.* —**bla′tant·ly,** *adv.*

blath·er (blath′ər) *also,* **bleth·er.** *n.* foolish talk; nonsense. —*v.t., v.i.* to speak foolishly. [Old Norse *blathra* to talk foolishly.]

blath·er·skite (blath′ər-skīt′) *n.* talkative, foolish person.

blaze[1] (blāz) *n.* **1.** brilliant flame or fire. **2.** bright, intense light or glow: *the blaze of noon.* **3.** brilliant or striking display: *a blaze of color.* **4.** strong, sudden outburst: *a blaze of fury.* **5. blazes.** *Slang.* hell. —*v.i.,* **blazed, blaz·ing. 1.** to burn brightly. **2.** to shine brilliantly; be bright: *The city streets blazed with light.* **3.** to burn with or display strong feeling. **4. to blaze away. a.** to work at vigorously or enthusiastically. **b.** to keep on shooting a gun or guns. [Old English *blæse* flame, torch.]

blaze[2] (blāz) *n.* **1.** light-colored marking on the face of an animal. **2.** mark made on a tree, as by chipping off a piece of bark, to indicate a trail or boundary. —*v.t.,* **blazed, blaz·ing. 1.** to mark (a tree) with blazes. **2.** to indicate (a trail) by marking trees: *He blazed a path through the forest.* **3.** to open up or take the lead in; pioneer: *His work blazed the way for future negotiations.* [Probably from Middle Low German *bles* white spot.]

blaze[3] (blāz) **blazed, blaz·ing.** *v.t.* to make known; proclaim; publicize: *Blaze forth the news.* [Old Norse *blāsa* to blow.]

blaz·er (blā′zər) *n.* sports jacket, usually solid-colored or striped, with metal buttons, originally having the identifying insignia of a particular school, club, or other group on the breast pocket.

bla·zon (blā′zən) *v.t.* **1.** to decorate or embellish, as with blazonry; adorn. **2.** to describe or illustrate (armorial bearings) according to the rules of heraldry. **3.** *Archaic.* to make public; proclaim. —*n.* **1.** coat

of arms; heraldic shield or banner; armorial bearings. **2.** description or art of describing or illustrating armorial bearings. **3.** ostentatious display; show. [Middle French *blason* coat of arms, from Old French *blason* shield; of uncertain origin.]

bla·zon·ry (blā′zən-rē) *n.* **1.** art of describing or illustrating armorial bearings. **2.** coats of arms; armorial bearings. **3.** brilliant display; spectacle.

bldg. *pl.,* **bldgs.** building.

bleach (blēch) *v.t., v.i.* **1.** to make or become white, colorless, or pale. —*n.* **1.** substance used as a bleaching agent. **2.** act or process of bleaching: *These clothes need another bleach.* **3.** degree of whiteness or paleness obtained from bleaching. [Old English *blǣcan* to whiten, fade.]

bleach·er (blē′chər) *n.* **1.** one who or that which bleaches. **2. bleachers. a.** roofless part of the stands in a stadium, usually low-priced, unreserved, and, in baseball, past the outfield. **b.** any similar group of seats or tiered stand: *Wooden bleachers were set up for the parade.*

bleaching powder 1. powder that bleaches. **2.** chloride of lime.

bleak (blēk) *adj.* **1.** exposed, barren, and wind-swept; desolate: *bleak stretches of deserted farmland.* **2.** cold; chilling: *a bleak December.* **3.** dreary; cheerless; depressing: *a bleak outlook.* [Old Norse *bleikr* white, pale.] —**bleak′ly,** *adv.* —**bleak′ness,** *n.*

blear (blēr) *adj.* dim; blurred; indistinct. —*v.t.* **1.** to dim or blur (the eyes or vision). **2.** to make dim or indistinct; obscure. [Middle English *bleren* to dim the eyes; of uncertain origin.]

blear-eyed (blēr′īd′) *adj. Archaic.* bleary-eyed.

blear·y (blēr′ē) **blear·i·er, blear·i·est.** *adj.* **1.** (of the eyes or vision) dimmed or blurred. **2.** groggy from lack of sleep; exhausted. **3.** dim; indistinct. —**blear′i·ness,** *n.*

blear·y-eyed (blēr′ē-īd′) *adj.* **1.** having bleared eyes. **2.** groggy or dazed from exhaustion.

bleat (blēt) *n.* **1.** cry of a sheep, goat, or calf. **2.** any similar sound. —*v.i.* **1.** to utter the cry of a sheep, goat, or calf. **2.** to make a similar sound. **3.** to whine or complain. —*v.t.* **1.** to utter with or as with a bleat or a similar sound. [Old English *blǣtan* to cry, as a sheep, goat, or calf.] —**bleat′er,** *n.*

bleb (bleb) *n.* **1.** skin blister that is filled with fluid. **2.** air bubble, as in liquid or glass. [Probably imitative.]

bleed (blēd) **bled, bleed·ing.** *v.i.* **1.** to lose or shed blood: *His wounds bled.* **2.** to suffer wounds or die: *those who bled for the cause.* **3.** to feel anguish, sympathy, or pity: *My heart bled for her.* **4.** to ooze sap or other fluid. **5.** (of a dye or paint) to run or become diffuse. **6.** *Printing.* to extend to, or seem to run off, the edge or edges of a page. —*v.t.* **1.** to draw blood from, esp. as a remedy for illness. **2.** to lose or exude: *to bleed sap.* **3.** to drain or extract (liquid, sap, or other substance) from. **4.** *Informal.* to extort money or something valuable from. **5.** *Printing.* **a.** to permit (an illustration or ornamentation) to extend to the edge of the page. **b.** to trim (a book or sheet) so closely as to mutilate the text or illustration. —*n. Printing.* **1.** illustration that bleeds. **2.** page that has been bled. —*adj. Printing.* having printed matter that bleeds: *a bleed page.* [Old English *blēdan* to lose blood.]

bleed·er (blē′dər) *n.* **1.** one who bleeds excessively, esp. a hemophiliac. **2.** one who bleeds a patient as a remedy for his illness.

bleeding heart 1. any of several plants, genus *Dicentra,* esp. *D. spectabilis,* the common bleeding heart, widely cultivated for its drooping clusters of red or pink, heart-shaped flowers. **2.** *Informal.* one who displays excessive pity and concern for others.

Bleeding heart

blem·ish (blem′ish) *n.* **1.** physical flaw or defect, esp. a mark on the skin. **2.** any imperfection, flaw, or stain. **1.** to stain; mar; sully. [Old French *blemiss-,* a stem of *ble(s)mir* to stain; of Germanic origin.] **Syn.** **2. Blemish, defect, flaw**[1] mean an imperfection. **Blemish** suggests an external and superficial imperfection: *Mark's record as a police officer is without blemish.* **Defect** suggests a more serious irregularity or one that may cause a malfunction: *The boy's new eyeglasses corrected the defect in his vision.* **Flaw** suggests a defect in the continuity or cohesion that may mar or cause a weakness in something that is otherwise perfect: *Only the trained eye can detect a flaw in this diamond.*

blench[1] (blench) *v.i. Archaic.* to shrink away; flinch. [Old English *blencan* to deceive.]

blench[2] (blench) *v.t., v.i.* to make or become pale; whiten. [Form of BLANCH.]

blend (blend) **blend·ed** or **blent, blend·ing.** *v.t.* **1.** to mix together thoroughly; combine so as to make separate components indistinguishable: *She blended flour and milk to make pancake batter.* **2.** to mix (varieties) so as to produce a desired quality: *to blend tobacco.*

—*v.i.* **1.** to mix; mingle; unite: *with voices blended in song.* **2.a.** to pass or shade gradually or imperceptibly into each other: *Sea and sky seemed to blend.* **b.** to be or become indistinguishable from (with *into*): *His black coat blended into the surrounding darkness.* **3.** to fit together; harmonize: *The rug blends well with the decor.* —*n.* **1.** result or product of blending; mixture: *a new blend of coffee.* **2.** word formed by combining separate words or parts of separate words. *Telecast is a blend of television and broadcast.* [Probably from *blend-*, a stem of Old Norse *blanda* to mix.] —**Syn.** *v.t.* **1.** see **mix.**

blende (blend) *n.* **1.** sphalerite. **2.** any of several other minerals having a bright but nonmetallic luster. [German *Blende* sphalerite, from *blenden* to deceive; because sphalerite resembles an ore rich in lead, but contains none.]

blended whiskey, whiskey consisting of either a blend of whiskeys or a blend of whiskey and neutral spirits.

blend·er (blen'dər) *n.* **1.** machine with high-speed rotary blades for mixing drinks and soft foods and chopping or liquefying solid foods. **2.** one who or that which blends.

blen·ny (blen'ē) *pl.* **-nies.** *n.* any of various small, saltwater fish, family Blenniidae, having an elongated body and a dorsal fin. [Latin *blennius* a saltwater fish, from Greek *blennos* a type of fish.]

bless (bles) *blessed* or *blest*, **bless·ing.** *v.t.* **1.** to make or pronounce holy; consecrate: *And God blessed the seventh day* (Genesis 2:3). **2.** to invoke divine favor or protection for: *The minister blessed the congregation.* **3.** to endow or favor (with *with*): *He was blessed with good health.* **4.** to confer good or happiness upon (with *with*): *He blessed us with his presence.* **5.** to extol; praise; glorify: *Bless His holy name* (Psalms 103:1). **6.** to make the sign of the cross over. **7.** *Archaic.* to guard or protect (with *from*). [Old English *blētsian* originally, to consecrate with blood, later used as the equivalent of Latin *benedícere* to praise, consecrate.]

bless·ed (bles'id, blest) *also,* **blest.** *adj.* **1.** consecrated by a religious rite; holy: *blessed water.* **2.** worthy of adoration or worship: *the blessed Trinity.* **3.** enjoying great happiness; fortunate. **4.** bringing happiness or pleasure. **5.** enjoying the bliss of heaven; beatified. **6.** cursed; damned: *a blessed nuisance.* ▲ used as a euphemism. —*n.* **the blessed. a.** people who are blessed. **b.** in Roman Catholicism, the dead who are beatified. —**bless'ed·ly,** *adv.* —**bless'ed·ness,** *n.*

blessed event *Informal.* birth of a child.

Blessed Virgin, the Virgin Mary.

bless·ing (bles'ing) *n.* **1.** authoritative pronouncement of divine favor; benediction. **2.** invocation or appeal to divine favor. **3.** prayer of thanksgiving, usually made before or after a meal. **4.** words used in any of these: *He had soon memorized the blessing.* **5.** bestowal of divine favor: *Ask God's blessing.* **6.** something which provides happiness or prosperity; boon: *He enjoyed the blessings of a happy home.* **7.** approval: *He gave his blessing to the marriage.* **8.** wish for good fortune or success: *blessings for the New Year.*

blest (blest) *v.* a past tense and past participle of **bless.** —*adj.* blessed.

bleth·er (bleth'ər) *blather.*

blew (blōō) past tense of **blow**[2] and **blow**[3].

blight (blīt) *n.* **1.** any of several diseases that wither or kill plants. Mildew, rust, and smut are blights. **2.** bacteria or fungus that causes such a disease. **3.** something that damages, spoils, or frustrates. **4.** state of being blighted; ruined condition. —*v.t.* **1.** to cause to wither or decay; blast: *Rain blighted the corn.* **2.** to spoil; frustrate; ruin. [Of uncertain origin.]

blimp (blimp) *n.* *Informal.* small, nonrigid airship, used chiefly for observation. [Said to be from *B limp,* a type of limp or nonrigid airship.]

blind (blīnd) *adj.* **1.** unable to see; sightless. **2.** lacking in insight or perception: *He was blind to her needs.* **3.** independent of reason or intelligence: *blind faith.* **4.** without rational direction or control; random: *blind chance.* **5.** uncontrolled; heedless; reckless: *blind fury, blind tenacity.* **6.** not directed or governed by sight: *blind flying, blind groping in the dark.* **7.** closed at one end: *a blind roadway.* **8.** not easily seen; hidden: *a blind corner.* **9.** unconscious; insensible: *a blind stupor.* **10.** *Informal.* drunk. **11.** without openings for light or passage: *a blind wall, a blind hedge.* **12.** of, relating to, or for the sightless. **13.** *Archaic.* hard to make out; illegible: *blind writing.* —*n.* **1.** something that obstructs vision or keeps out light. **2.** Venetian blind. **3.** person, thing, or action used to mislead; pretext; decoy. **4.** place of concealment; ambush: *The hunter ducked into his blind.* —*v.t.* **1.** to make blind; render sightless. **2.** to deprive of sight temporarily; dazzle: *The glare blinded him.* **3.** to deprive of the power to discern or judge: *blinded by jealousy.* **4.** to darken; obscure; conceal: *a road blinded by snow.* —*adv.* **1.** without sight or the aid of vision: *to fly blind.* **2.** without guidance or reason: *He was working blind.* [Old English *blind* sightless, lacking in perception.] —**blind'ly,** *adv.* —**blind'ness,** *n.*

blind alley 1. passageway shut off at one end. **2.** any position or activity that leads nowhere.

blind date *Informal.* **1.** date between two persons of opposite sex who have never met, arranged by a third party. **2.** either of the two persons.

blind·er (blīn'dər) *n.* either of a pair of flaps attached to a horse's bridle to prevent him from seeing sideways. Also, **blink'er.**

blind·fold (blīnd'fōld') *v.t.* **1.** to cover the eyes of, esp. with a cloth. **2.** to obstruct the understanding or judgment of; mislead; deceive. —*n.* cover for the eyes, esp. one of cloth. [Middle English *blindfellen* to strike blind, from *blind* + *fellen* to strike down, FELL[2]; altered by confusion with FOLD[1].] —**blind'fold·ed,** *adj.*

blind·man's buff (blīnd'manz' buf') group game in which a blindfolded player tries to catch and identify another player.

blind spot 1. minute point on the retina which is not sensitive to light because the optic nerve enters the eye there. **2.** area or subject about which one is ignorant or incapable of exercising objective judgment; uninformed or prejudiced attitude. **3.** area in which radio or television reception is poor. **4.** area not covered by the usual means of perception or detection, as by a rear-view mirror or by a radar system.

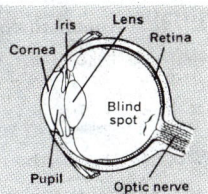

Blind spot
in the human eye

blind·worm (blīnd'wurm') *n.* small, limbless, snakelike lizard, *Anguis fragilis,* of Europe and Africa, having very tiny eyes. Length: 1 foot. Also, **slow'worm'.** [It was erroneously believed to have no eyes at all.]

blink (blingk) *v.i.* **1.** to wink rapidly, often involuntarily. **2.** to look with winking or half-shut eyes; squint. **3.** to flash on and off; glimmer; twinkle: *A star blinked in the sky.* **4. to blink at. a.** to deliberately overlook or ignore. **b.** to look at with surprise, dismay, or amazement: *He blinked at her angry accusations.* —*v.t.* **1.** to wink (one's eyes). **2.** to cause to wink: *He blinked his car lights as a signal.* —*n.* **1.** rapid closing and opening of the eye. **2.** twinkle; glimmer. **3.** *Archaic.* glance of the eye; glimpse. **4. on the blink.** *Slang.* not working properly; out of order: *The radio is on the blink.* [Of uncertain origin.]

blink·er (bling'kər) *n.* **1.** blinder. **2.a.** flashing light signal. **b.** device that flashes a light on and off. **3.** *Slang.* eye. **4. blinkers.** goggles.

blintz (blints) *also,* **blintze, blint'sa.** *n.* thin pancake dough rolled around a filling, as of cheese or fruit, and fried. [Yiddish *blintse,* from Russian *blinyets,* diminutive of *blin* pancake.]

blip (blip) *n.* image on a radar screen that indicates the presence of an object. [Imitative.]

bliss (blis) *n.* **1.** supreme happiness or joy; rapture. **2.** spiritual joy, esp. the joy of the blessed in heaven. [Old English *bliss, blīths* joy.]

bliss·ful (blis'fəl) *adj.* full of, characterized by, or causing bliss. —**bliss'ful·ly,** *adv.* —**bliss'ful·ness,** *n.*

blis·ter (blis'tər) *n.* **1.** bubblelike swelling of the skin, filled with watery matter and usually caused by rubbing or by a burn. **2.** similarly shaped swelling, as on a plant, painted surface, or molded plastic. **3.** domelike, transparent structure on the body of certain aircraft. —*v.t.* **1.** to raise blisters on: *The sun blistered his face.* **2.** to subject to harsh or scorching criticism. —*v.i.* to have or develop blisters. [Old French *blestre* a swelling; of Germanic origin.] —**blis'ter·y,** *adj.*

blister beetle, any of various beetles of the family Meloidae, many of which secrete a substance that can blister the skin.

blis·ter·ing (blis'tər ing) *adj.* **1.** causing blisters: *blistering heat.* **2.** harsh; withering; scathing: *a blistering reply.* **3.** severe; intense: *a blistering attack on the fort.* —**blis'ter·ing·ly,** *adv.*

B.Lit., Bachelor of Letters; Bachelor of Literature.

blithe (blīth, blith) *adj.* **1.** lighthearted; gay; cheerful. **2.** casual; unconcerned; heedless: *his blithe indifference to the problem.* [Old English *blīthe* joyous.] —**blithe'ly,** *adv.*

blith·er·ing (blith'ər ing) *adj.* talking foolishly; jabbering.

blithe·some (blīth'səm, blith'-) *adj.* lighthearted; gay; cheerful. —**blithe'some·ly,** *adv.* —**blithe'some·ness,** *n.*

blitz (blits) *n.* blitzkrieg. —*v.t.* to subject to or overwhelm with a blitz. [Short for BLITZKRIEG.]

blitz·krieg (blits'krēg') *n.* **1.a.** method of offensive warfare based on sudden, swift, and massive attacks designed to overwhelm the enemy quickly. **b.** attack or campaign using this method. **2.** any sudden, overwhelming attack. [German *Blitzkrieg* lightning war.]

bliz·zard (bliz'ərd) *n.* **1.** severe storm characterized by strong wind, wind-driven snow, and intense cold. **2.** any long, heavy snowstorm. [Of uncertain origin.]

B.LL., Bachelor of Laws. Also, **LL.B.**

bloat (blōt) *v.i.* to become swollen or puffed up; swell. —*v.t.* **1.** to cause to swell or expand; inflate. **2.** to cure (fish) by salting, smoking, and partial drying. [From Middle English *blote* soft, probably from Old Norse *blautr* soft, wet.]

bloat·er (blō′tər) n. **1.** herring or mackerel that has been bloated, or cured. **2.** deep-water cisco, *Leucichthys hoyi*, of the Great Lakes.
blob (blob) n. **1.** drop or lump of a thick, viscous substance: *a blob of paint.* **2.** *Informal.* shapeless thing. [Imitative.]
bloc (blok) n. group, often composed of members having diverse affiliations, formed to pursue a common purpose: *the farm bloc, the Asian bloc in the United Nations.* [French *bloc* the whole collection; of Germanic origin.]
block (blok) n. **1.** solid piece of matter, often having one or more flat surfaces: *a block of wood, a block of ice.* **2.** heavy slab of wood on which cutting or chopping is done: *a butcher's block.* **3.** obstacle; hindrance; stoppage. **4.a.** area or group of buildings, enclosed by streets: *Walk around the block.* **b.** length of a side of such an area: *I walked six blocks.* **5.** cubelike child's toy, used for building. **6.** piece of wood on which the head of a person about to be beheaded is placed. **7.** quantity or number of things dealt with as a unit: *a block of tickets, a block of stock shares.* **8.** hollow brick used for construction. **9.** platform or stand from which something is auctioned. **10.** mold or form upon which an object is shaped or displayed: *a hat block.* **11.** *Slang.* person's head. **12.** *Machinery.* pulley or system of pulleys mounted in a casing. **13.** *Sports.* action that hinders, interferes with, or stops an opponent's movement or play. **14.** piece of wood or other solid material used as a support: *a mounting block.* **15.** *Psychology.* interruption in thought or action produced by emotional rather than physical causes: *a mental block.* **16.** section of railroad track controlled by signals. **17.** *Medicine.* interruption or obstruction of normal physiological functioning. **18.** group of four or more attached stamps in the shape of a square or rectangle. **19.** *Printing.* piece of engraved wood from which impressions are printed. **20. to go to the block.** to be beheaded. —v.t. **1.** to obstruct passage through or to stop up (often with *up*): *Trees blocked our path.* **2.** to stand in the way of; be an obstacle to; hinder: *to block the enactment of a law.* **3.** to shape or stamp with or as with a block: *to block a sweater.* **4.** to strengthen, support, or fit with blocks. **5.** *Sports.* to hinder or interfere with (an opponent's or the ball's movement). **6.** *Psychology.* to interrupt or suppress (something) by the action of or as a result of emotional forces. **7.** *Medicine.* to prevent the transmission of impulses in (a nerve). **8. to block in** (or *out*). to plan or outline roughly; sketch. —v.i. *Sports.* to hinder an opponent's actions. [Old French *bloc* log, mass, the whole collection; of Germanic origin.] —**block′er,** n.

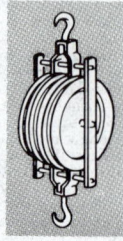

Block (def. 12)

block·ade (blo kād′) n. **1.** a shutting off of an area by troops or ships to prevent ingoing and outgoing movement. **2.** forces that carry on a blockade. **3.** something that shuts off or obstructs; obstacle. **4. to run the blockade.** to break through or elude a blockade. —v.t., **-ad·ed, -ad·ing.** to subject to a blockade. —**block·ad′er,** n.
block·ade-run·ner (blo kād′run′ər) n. person or ship that is engaged in slipping back and forth through a blockade.
block·age (blok′ij) n. obstruction.
block and tackle, arrangement of pulley blocks and ropes used for lifting or hauling.
block·bust·er (blok′bus′tər) n. *Informal.* **1.** aerial bomb weighing two or more tons and having great demolition power. **2.** person or thing that is remarkably impressive or successful.
block·head (blok′hed′) n. stupid or foolish person; dolt.
block·house (blok′hous′) n. **1.** fortified building having loopholes from which to fire, originally made of timber and having a projecting upper story, now made of concrete or other heavy material. **2.** heavily reinforced building serving as an observation and control center near a launching pad.

Blockhouse

block·ish (blok′ish) adj. stupid; dull.
block letter 1. letter or lettering without serifs. **2.** printing type that is cut from wood.
block plane, small plane used chiefly for smoothing ends of wood across the grain.
block printing, printing from engraved wood blocks or linoleum.
block signal, railway signal controlling the movement of trains into and within a block.
block system, control system in which a railroad track is divided into blocks, the movement of trains into each block being regulated by an automatic signal.

Bloem·fon·tein (bloom′fon tān′) n. judicial capital of the Republic of South Africa, in the central part of the country. Pop. (1960), 112,606.
bloke (blōk) n. *British. Slang.* fellow; guy.
blond (blond) adj. **1.** (of hair) having some shade of light yellow as its main color. **2.** *also,* **blonde.** (of a person) having such hair with light-colored skin and eyes. **3.** light-colored: *blond furniture, a blond complexion.* —n. *also,* **blonde.** blond person. ▲ Blonde is used for a female; **blond** is used for both sexes. [Old French *blond* fair, fair-haired; probably of Germanic origin.] —**blond′ness;** *also,* **blonde′ness,** n. —**blond′ish,** adj.
blood (blud) n. **1.** fluid circulated by the heart through the bodies of vertebrates and many invertebrates, consisting of semisolid corpuscles suspended in plasma, and functioning chiefly to convey materials from one part of the body to another. **2.** shedding of blood; murder: *He avenged the blood of his father.* **3.** descent from a common ancestor; kinship: *a cousin related by blood.* **4.** family; lineage, esp. noble lineage: *of noble blood.* **5.** national or racial extraction: *He is of Indian blood.* **6.** temperament; disposition; passion: *a man of hot blood.* **7.** good breed or pedigree; purebred stock. **8.** spirited young man; rake.
  bad blood. hatred; hostility: *There was bad blood between them.*
  fresh (or **new** or **young**) **blood.** people considered as a source of new vigor, energy, or ideas: *We need some new blood in the company.*
  in cold blood. without emotion or compassion; deliberately.
  to have (someone's) blood on one's head (or **hands**). to be responsible for (someone's) death or ruination.
  to make one's blood boil. to make one angry; infuriate.
  to make one's blood run cold. to make one frightened; terrify.
  to run (or **be**) **in one's blood. a.** to be hereditary. **b.** to be natural or important to.
  —v.t. to expose (a hunting dog) to the blood of the game it is to hunt. [Old English *blōd* the fluid circulated by the heart.]
blood bank 1. place where whole blood or plasma is collected, processed, and stored for future use. **2.** reserve of blood so stored.
blood bath, merciless slaughter of many people; massacre.
blood brother 1. person bound to another by a ceremonial intermingling of their blood. **2.** anyone with whom very close kinship or group loyalty is felt.
blood count, count of the number of red and white blood cells in a given sample of blood.
blood·cur·dling (blud′kurd′ling) adj. causing great horror or fear; terrifying.
blood·ed (blud′id) adj. **1.** (of horses and other livestock) of good blood or stock; thoroughbred. **2.** having (a specified kind of) blood. **3.** having or exhibiting (a specified) temperament or state of mind. ▲ used in combination in defs. 2 and 3, as in *a warm-blooded animal, a cold-blooded murder.*
blood group, one of the groups into which blood is classified according to the presence or absence of certain agglutinogens and antigens. Also, **blood type.**
blood-guilt·y (blud′gil′tē) adj. guilty of murder or bloodshed. —**blood′guilt′, blood′guilt′i·ness,** n.
blood·hound (blud′hound′) n. **1.** one of a breed of hunting dogs having a smooth, black-and-tan or red-and-tan coat, noted for its keen sense of smell and skill in tracking. Height: to 26 inches at the shoulder. **2.** *Informal.* keen pursuer; sleuth.
blood·less (blud′lis) adj. **1.** without bleeding or bloodshed: *a bloodless revolution, bloodless surgery.* **2.** lacking blood; pale: *bloodless lips.* **3.** lacking vitality; spiritless. **4.** lacking warmth; cold-hearted.
blood·let·ting (blud′let′ing) n. act or process of removing blood by opening a vein.
blood·line (blud′līn′) n. line of direct descent, esp. of animals; strain; pedigree.
blood·mo·bile (blud′mə bēl′) n. motor vehicle equipped for the collection of blood from donors.
blood money 1. money obtained at the cost of another's life or well-being. **2.** payment to a hired murderer. **3.** compensation paid to next of kin for the killing of a relative.
blood plasma, liquid part of the blood, without any of its corpuscles. Also, **plas′ma.**
blood platelet, one of the minute round, oval, or rod-shaped cell fragments in the blood of vertebrates essential to blood clotting. Also, **plate′let, throm′bo·cyte′.**
blood poisoning, diseased condition of the blood caused by the presence of toxic matter or toxic bacteria.
blood pressure, force exerted by the blood against the inner walls of the blood vessels, esp. the arteries, created by the pumping action of the heart.
blood relation one related by birth; kinsman. Also, **blood relative.**
blood·root (blud′rōōt′, -root′) n. North American plant, *Sanguinaria canadensis,* of the poppy family, having white or rose flowers and a red root which yields an acrid, red sap.

at; āpe; cär; end; mē; it; īce; hot; ōld; fôrk; wood; fōōl; oil; out; up; ūse; turn; sing; thin; this; zh in treasure; ə in ago, taken, pencil, lemon, circus.

blood·shed (blud′shed′) *n.* violence attended by loss of blood or life: *We won the battle without much bloodshed.*
blood·shot (blud′shot′) *adj.* (of an eye) suffused with reddish streaks from dilation of the blood vessels.
blood·stain (blud′stān′) *n.* discoloration produced by blood.
blood·stained (blud′stānd′) *adj.* 1. soiled or smeared with blood. 2. guilty of bloodshed or slaughter.
blood·stone (blud′stōn′) *n.* semiprecious stone consisting of chalcedony of a dark-green variety, flecked with spots of red jasper. Also, **he′li·o·trope′.**
blood stream, blood as it flows through a circulatory system.
blood·suck·er (blud′suk′ər) *n.* 1. animal that sucks blood, esp. a leech. 2. *Informal.* one who takes as much as he can from others; extortionist.
blood test, analysis of the blood for various factors, as blood type or presence of illness.
blood·thirst·y (blud′thurs′tē) *adj.* eager to shed blood; murderous; brutal. —**blood′thirst′i·ly,** *adv.* —**blood′thirst′i·ness,** *n.*
blood type, blood group.
blood vessel, any of the flexible tubes, as an artery, vein, or capillary, through which the blood flows.
blood·y (blud′ē) **blood·i·er, blood·i·est.** *adj.* 1. stained or covered with blood: *a bloody knife.* 2. losing blood; bleeding: *a bloody wound.* 3. of, like, containing, or composed of blood. 4. involving much bloodshed: *a bloody brawl.* 5. relishing bloodshed; bloodthirsty. 6. having the color of blood; blood-red. 7. *British Slang.* damned: *a bloody nuisance.* —*adv. British Slang.* very; exceedingly: *He's bloody drunk.* —*v.t.,* **blood·ied, blood·y·ing.** to stain or cover with blood. —**blood′i·ly,** *adv.* —**blood′i·ness,** *n.*
Bloody Mary 1. Mary I of England. 2. *also,* **bloody mary.** mixed drink made chiefly of vodka and tomato juice.
bloom¹ (bloom) *n.* 1. flower of a plant. 2. state or time of flowering: *roses in bloom.* 3. time or state of flourishing; peak: *the bloom of perfect manhood.* 4. rosy glow of the cheeks or skin suggesting health and freshness. 5. delicate, powdery coating on certain fruits and leaves: *the bloom on a peach.* 6. any similar surface coating, as the powder that appears on newly minted coins. —*v.i.* 1. to produce or yield blossoms; flower: *Cherry trees bloom in early April.* 2. to be at or come to one's peak; flourish: *Her true self has just begun to bloom.* 3. to glow with color, health, or beauty. [Old Norse *blōm* flower.] —**bloom′er,** *n.*
bloom² (bloom) *n.* 1. spongy mass of wrought iron intended to be further hammered or rolled into bars. 2. bar of iron or steel that is obtained from rolling or hammering an ingot. [Old English *blōma* lump of iron.]
bloom·ers (bloo′mərz) *n.* 1. loose, baggy pants gathered at the bottom, worn mid-thigh or knee length by women or girls chiefly as an athletic costume. 2. women's underpants resembling these. 3. *Slang.* any type of women's underpants. 4. bloomer. costume for women or girls consisting of a short skirt and loose pants gathered at the ankles. [From Amelia J. **Bloomer,** 1818–94, U.S. feminist who promoted the costume (*def. 4*).]
bloom·ing (bloo′ming) *adj.* 1. in flower; blossoming. 2. thriving; flourishing. 3. *Informal.* complete; utter; damned: *a blooming idiot.* —**bloom′ing·ly,** *adv.*
Bloom·ing·ton (bloo′ming tən) *n.* city in southeastern Minnesota, a residential suburb of Minneapolis. Pop. (1970), 81,970.
bloop·er (bloo′pər) *n.* 1. *Informal.* blunder, esp. one made in public. 2. *Baseball.* weakly hit fly ball.
blos·som (blos′əm) *n.* 1. flower, esp. one of a fruit-producing plant. 2. time or state of flowering; bloom: *a peach tree in blossom.* —*v.i.* 1. to put forth blossoms; bloom. 2. to start to flourish; develop; thrive (often with *out* or *into*). [Old English *blōstma* flower.] —**blos′som·y,** *adj.*
blot (blot) *n.* 1. spot or stain, esp. of ink. 2. blemish on character or reputation; disgrace. 3. something that detracts from or mars beauty. —*v.t.* **blot·ted, blot·ting.** 1. to spot or spatter with or as if with ink. 2. to blot out. a. to hide; obscure; darken: *The clouds blotted out the moon.* b. to wipe out completely; destroy: *to blot out a memory.* c. to cross out or erase: *to blot out a word.* 3. to dry or absorb with or as with blotting paper. —*v.i.* 1. to make blots: *The ink blotted.* 2. to become stained or marked with a blot: *This paper blots easily.* [Of uncertain origin.]
blotch (bloch) *n.* 1. spot or stain, esp. one that is large and irregular in shape. 2. blemished or discolored patch on the skin. —*v.t.* to mark or cover with blotches. [Probably a blend of BLOT and BOTCH.] —**blotch′i·ness,** *n.* —**blotch′y,** *adj.*
blot·ter (blot′ər) *n.* 1. piece or pad of blotting paper. 2. book in which transactions or events are recorded in the order of their occurrence: *a sales blotter, a police blotter.*
blotting paper, soft, porous paper used to absorb excess ink.
blouse (blous, blouz) *n.* 1. woman's or girl's shirtlike garment, worn tucked in at the waistline or outside the skirt or pants. 2. smocklike overgarment, often belted at the waist, varying from hip length to knee length, as worn by certain European peasants and workmen. 3. loose-fitting shirt of a sailor's uniform. 4. jacket or tunic worn as part of the U.S. Army uniform. —*v.t.* **bloused, blous·ing.** to hang in full, loose folds; drape. [French *blouse* the shirtlike garment; of uncertain origin.]
blow¹ (blō) *n.* 1. forceful, heavy stroke with the fist or a weapon: *a blow to the jaw.* 2. severe or painful misfortune; calamity; shock: *The news came as a blow.* 3. sudden, forceful attack, action, or effort: *Strike a blow for freedom.* 4. **at one blow,** by a single action or effort. 5. **blow-by-blow,** in exact detail and sequence; extremely thorough: *a blow-by-blow description.* 6. **to be at blows,** to be in conflict; be fighting. 7. **to come to blows,** to begin fighting. [Of uncertain origin.]
Syn. n. 1. Blow, hit, stroke¹ mean the impact of one thing on another. Blow suggests power and weight: *With blows of his ax the fireman battered down the door of the burning house.* Hit emphasizes the actual contact: *He made a hit on the bull's-eye with the first dart he threw.* Stroke emphasizes the manner of making the contact, generally at the end of a broad sweeping motion: *He urged his horse on with repeated strokes of his whip.*
blow² (blō) **blew, blown, blow·ing.** *v.i.* 1. (of wind or air) to be in motion; move with velocity or force: *The wind blows.* 2. to produce or send forth a current of air: *The fan was blowing.* 3. to move or be carried by a current of air or wind: *His hat blew off.* 4. to produce sound by a blast of air: *The whistle blows at noontime.* 5. to stop working properly; fail (often with *out*): *The tire blew out. The fuse blew.* 6. to be breathless or winded; pant. 7. to spout water and air: *The whale blew before submerging.* 8. *Slang.* to go away; depart. —*v.t.* 1. to direct a current of air upon. 2. to drive by a current of air: *The wind blew the leaves.* 3. to cause to sound by directing a blast of air: *to blow a horn, to blow taps on a bugle.* 4. to form or shape (something) by air pressure: *to blow glass, to blow bubbles.* 5. to expel from the mouth: *to blow smoke rings.* 6. to break or destroy, as by a rupture or explosion. 7. to clear or empty by forcing air into or through. 8. to melt (a fuse) by overloading. 9. *Slang.* to spend (money) quickly or recklessly; squander: *He blew his salary on five new suits.* 10. *Slang.* to spend money on; treat (someone) (with *to*): *I'll blow you to dinner.* 11. *Slang.* to handle awkwardly or unsuccessfully; bungle: *He blew his chances for that job.* 12. *Slang.* to go away from; leave, esp. hurriedly: *He blew town.* 13. to put (a horse) out of breath. 14. (of insects) to deposit eggs on or in. —*n.* 1. act or instance of producing or directing a current of air. 2. blast of wind or air: *A blow came in from the northeast.* 3. blast of wind or air: *A blow came in from the northeast.*
to blow hot and cold, to change one's mind; vacillate.
to blow in, to arrive; appear.
to blow off steam, to release pent-up emotions noisily or violently.
to blow one's stack (fuse, top, cork, or **gasket).** *Informal.* to become violently angry; lose self-control.
to blow out. a. to extinguish by a gust of air. **b.** to burst. **c.** to burn out; become useless.
to blow over. a. to pass by or over; subside: *The storm finally blew over.* **b.** to be forgotten: *The scandal blew over quickly.*
to blow the whistle on, to expose; inform upon.
to blow up. a. to explode. **b.** to fill with air or gas; inflate. **c.** *Informal.* to lose one's temper. **d.** to exaggerate; magnify. **e.** to arise and increase in intensity: *A storm blew up last night.* **f.** to enlarge (a photograph). [Old English *blāwan* to send forth air.]
blow³ (blō) **blew, blown, blow·ing.** *Archaic. v.t., v.i.* to blossom or cause to blossom. —*n.* 1. display of blossoms or flowers: *a blow of tulips.* 2. state of flowering; bloom: *a tree in full blow.* [Old English *blōwan* to bloom.]
blow·er (blō′ər) *n.* 1. machine or device for producing a current of air or forcing air into a specified area: *They cooled the mine shaft with blowers.* 2. one who or that which blows.
blow·fish (blō′fish′) *pl.* **-fish** or **-fish·es.** *n.* any of several fish that can swell their bodies, as the puffer and the walleye.
blow·fly (blō′flī′) *pl.,* **-flies.** *n.* any of various two-winged flies, family Calliphoridae, that deposit their larvae on the wounds, wastes, or flesh of animals.
blow·gun (blō′gun′) *n.* tube through which darts or other missiles may be blown by the pressure of the breath. Also, **blow′pipe′, blow′tube′.**
blow·hard (blō′härd′) *n. Slang.* braggart.
blow·hole (blō′hōl′) *n.* 1. breathing hole of certain whales and other

Blouse (def. 2)

cetaceans, often situated at the top of the head. **2.** escape vent for gas or air, as in mines. **3.** hole in the ice to which underwater animals, as whales or seals, come to breathe. **4.** defect in cast metal caused by an air or gas bubble.

blown¹ (blōn) v. past participle of **blow².** —*adj.* **1.** inflated; distended; swollen. **2.** made by using a blowpipe or similar device: *colored bottles of blown glass.* **3.** out of breath: *Their horses were blown from the race.* **4.** flyblown.

blown² (blōn) v. past participle of **blow³.** —*adj.* in full bloom. ▲ now chiefly found in the hyphenated term *full-blown.*

blow-out (blō′out′) n. **1.** sudden bursting of an automobile tire. **2.** *Informal.* big, lively partly or other social gathering; spree. **3.** the melting of an electric fuse caused by the input of excessive current.

blow-pipe (blō′pīp′) n. **1.** blowgun. **2.** tube for blowing air or gas into a flame to concentrate and increase its heat. **3.** blowtube (*def. 1*).

blow-torch (blō′tôrch′) n. small portable torch producing a gasoline flame intensified to great heat by a blast of air, used esp. in working on metals.

blow-tube (blō′tōōb′, -tūb′) n. **1.** tube used to shape molten glass. Also, **blow′-pipe′. 2.** blowgun.

Blowtorch

blow-up (blō′up′) n. **1.** explosion. **2.** *Informal.* outburst of temper; quarrel. **3.** enlargement, as of a snapshot.

blow-y (blō′ē) **blow·i·er, blow·i·est.** adj. windy.

blowz·y (bou′zē) **blowz·i·er, blowz·i·est.** adj. **1.** unkempt; slovenly; frowzy. **2.** red-faced, fat, and coarse-complexioned. [Dialectal English *blowze* wench, slattern (of uncertain origin) + -Y¹.]

bls. **1.** bales. **2.** barrels.

blub·ber (blub′ər) n. **1.** layer of fat in whales and other cetaceans, used as a source of oil. **2.** profuse, noisy weeping. **3.** *Informal.* fat, esp. in great quantity. —*v.i.* to weep and sob noisily. —*v.t.* to utter with copious tears and sobs. —*adj.* swollen; thick: *blubber lips.* [Imitative.] —**blub′ber·er,** n.

blub·ber·y (blub′ər ē) adj. of or like blubber; fat.

blu·cher (blōō′kər, -chər) n. **1.** heavy leather half boot or high shoe. **2.** shoe in which the tongue and vamp are of one piece, and the quarters extend forward to lace across the tongue. [From the Prussian field marshal, Gebhard von *Blücher,* 1742–1819.]

bludg·eon (bluj′ən) n. short club, often weighted or thicker at one end. —*v.t.* **1.** to strike with or as with a bludgeon. **2.** to bully; coerce. [Of uncertain origin.] —**bludg′eon·er,** n.

blue (blōō) n. **1.** color between green and violet in the spectrum. **2.** something that imparts blue color, as a dye or paint. **3.** member of a group whose uniform or representative color is blue, esp. a Union soldier in the U.S. Civil War. **4. blues.** *Informal.* blue uniform of a sailor. **5. the blue. a.** the sky. **b.** the sea. **6. out of the blue.** from an unknown source; suddenly and unexpectedly. —*adj.,* **blu·er, blu·est. 1.** having the color blue. **2.** depressed or depressing; melancholy: *a blue outlook. I've felt blue all day.* **3.** (of skin) of a bluish-purple color; discolored: *His face was blue from the cold.* **4.** exasperated; enraged; livid: *blue with rage, blue in the face.* **5.** *Music.* of or having the characteristics of blues; designating the notes characteristic of blues. **6.** *Slang.* profane; obscene. **7. once in a blue moon.** very seldom; rarely. **8. true blue.** staunchly loyal; steadfast. —*v.t.,* **blued, blu·ing** or **blue·ing. 1.** to make blue. **2.** to treat with bluing. [Old French *bleu* the color blue, having the color blue; of Germanic origin.] —**blue′ness,** n.

blue baby, newborn infant whose skin has a bluish color because its blood does not receive adequate oxygen from its lungs, usually caused by a congenital heart or lung defect.

blue·beard (blōō′bērd′) n. person who has murdered his wife or wives. [From *Bluebeard,* figure in folklore who murdered six of his seven wives.]

blue·bell (blōō′bel′) n. any of various plants with blue, bell-shaped flowers, such as the harebell of Scotland, *Campanula rotundifolia.*

blue·ber·ry (blōō′ber′ē) pl., **-ries.** n. **1.** small, dark-blue, edible berry with tiny seeds, grown on any of several shrubs, genus *Vaccinium,* widely cultivated in many parts of the world. **2.** any of the shrubs producing this berry.

blue·bird (blōō′bûrd′) n. any of several small songbirds, genus *Sialia,* of the thrush family, found in North America and having predominantly blue plumage. Length: 7 inches.

blue-black (blōō′blak′) adj. black with a bluish tint; almost black.

blue blood 1. aristocratic or royal descent. **2.** person of such descent; aristocrat. [Translation of Spanish *sangre azul.* Supposedly, the blood of Spanish aristocrats was thought to have a bluer tint than that of the common people.] —**blue′blood′ed,** adj.

blue·bon·net (blōō′bon′it) n. **1.** any of several plants, genus *Lupinus,* of the pea family, having clusters of blue, bonnet-shaped flowers, esp. *L. subcarnosus,* native to the prairies of the southwestern United States. **2.** any of various plants with blue flowers, such as a blue cornflower. **3.** broad, flat, blue-colored cap, often of wool, formerly worn in Scotland. **4.** one who wears such a cap; Scotsman.

blue book 1. directory or register of socially prominent persons. **2.** booklet with blue paper covers, used for writing college examination answers. **3.** publication providing listed information on a given topic: *blue book of government employees.*

blue·bot·tle (blōō′bot′al) n. **1.** large blowfly, genus *Calliphora,* with a steel-blue abdomen and hairy body. **2.** blue cornflower. **3.** any of various other plants having tubular blue flowers, as the grape hyacinth.

blue cheese, pungent cheese, similar to Roquefort, veined with blue mold.

blue-chip (blōō′chip′) adj. **1.** having a good record of earnings and price stability: *blue-chip securities.* **2.** most excellent or valuable; best: *blue-chip service.*

Bluebonnet

blue chip, stock that is well known and valued for its good record. [From the *blue chips* used in gambling, which have a high value.]

blue-col·lar (blōō′kol′ər) adj. of, designating, or relating to semiskilled or skilled manual labor. [From the *blue* shirts worn by many such workers.]

blue·fish (blōō′fish′) pl., **-fish** or **-fishes.** n. **1.** saltwater food and game fish, *Pomatomus saltatrix,* having a bluish and silver body, found in coastal waters in various parts of the world. **2.** any of various other fishes of a bluish color, as the cunner.

blue flag, iris with blue or purple flowers, esp. *Iris versicolor.*

blue·grass (blōō′gras′) n. any of various grasses, genus *Poa,* with bluish-green stems, widely raised as pasturage and lawn grass, esp. **Kentucky bluegrass,** *P. pratensis.*

blue gum, any of a group of eucalyptus trees, *Eucalyptus globulus,* bearing leaves that contain a strong-smelling oil used in medicine as an antiseptic and an expectorant.

blue·ing (blōō′ing) bluing.

blue·ish (blōō′ish) bluish.

blue·jack·et (blōō′jak′it) n. enlisted man in the British or U.S. navy; sailor.

blue jay, crested jay, *Cyanocitta cristata,* of eastern North America, predominantly blue in color with black-and-white markings. Length: 11–12½ inches.

blue jeans, pants or overalls, usually made of blue denim, originally designed as work clothes but now widely worn for general use.

Blue jay

blue law 1. one of numerous laws, originating in colonial New England, prohibiting recreation or business on Sunday. **2.** any strict law, esp. one regulating personal conduct.

Blue Nile, river flowing through northwestern Ethiopia and eastern Sudan, a tributary of the Nile.

blue note, flatted third or seventh note of a scale. It is a characteristic feature of blues and jazz.

blue-pen·cil (blōō′pen′səl) **-ciled, -cil·ing;** also, British. **-cilled, -cil·ling.** v.t. to correct or modify with or as with a blue-colored pencil; edit.

blue·point (blōō′point′) n. small oyster, usually eaten raw. [From *Blue Point,* Long Island, where beds of such oysters are located.]

blue·print (blōō′print′) n. **1.** photographic print, usually showing white lines on a blue background, used chiefly for architectural plans and mechanical drawings. **2.** detailed outline or plan of action: *a blueprint for democracy.* —*v.t.* to make a blueprint of.

blue racer, nonpoisonous snake, *Coluber constrictor flaviventris,* of the blacksnake family, that is blue green in color and is native to the central and south-central United States.

blue-rib·bon (blōō′rib′ən) adj. having some superior or special characteristic: *a blue-ribbon champion, a blue-ribbon jury.*

blue ribbon, highest honor or award; first prize.

Blue Ridge Mountains, eastern range of the Appalachian Mountains extending from northeastern West Virginia to northern Georgia. Also, **Blue Ridge.**

blues (blōōz) n. **1. the blues.** *Informal.* depression; melancholy. **2. also, the blues.** music expressive of melancholy, characterized by the frequent occurrence of blue notes and a syncopated, often slow, jazz

at; āpe; cär; end; mē; it; īce; hot; ōld; fôrk; wood; fōōl; oil; out; up; ūse; turn; sing; thin; this; zh in treasure; ə in ago, taken, pencil, lemon, circus.

rhythm. [Short for earlier *blue devils*, slang term for the hallucinations or depression often accompanying extreme intoxication.]

blue·stock·ing (blōō'stok'ing) *n.* woman having or affecting literary or intellectual interests. [From the unconventional blue stockings worn by one of the male guests at a series of literary-social gatherings sponsored by a group of women in mid-eighteenth century London. The derisive term *Blue Stocking Society* was then applied to both the gatherings and the women who held them.]

blue·stone (blōō'stōn') *n.* **1.** bluish, fine-grained sandstone. **2.** blue vitriol.

blue streak *Informal.* **1.** something moving with great speed: *He took off like a blue streak.* **2. to talk a blue streak.** to speak rapidly and at great length.

blu·et (blōō'it) *n.* **1.** delicate, low-growing plant, *Houstonia caerulea*, native to North America, bearing light-blue, white, or violet flowers with yellowish centers. Also, **in'no·cence, Quak'er·la'dies. 2.** any of various plants having blue flowers, as the cornflower. [French *bluet*, diminutive of *bleu* blue; of Germanic origin.]

blue vitriol, copper sulfate.

bluff¹ (bluf) *n.* bold, broad cliff or headland. —*adj.* **1.** rising with or having a flat, broad front: *bluff cliffs.* **2.** good-naturedly blunt; rough and hearty. [Possibly from Middle Dutch *blaf* broad, flat.] —**bluff'ly,** *adv.* —**bluff'ness,** *n.*

bluff² (bluf) *v.t.* **1.** to deceive (someone) by putting on a false front: *He bluffed them into thinking he was an expert.* **2.** to convince or frighten (someone) by using deception or idle threats. —*v.i.* to use pretense or deception; fake: *He bluffed all through the conference.* —*n.* **1.** act or instance of bluffing. **2. to call (someone's) bluff.** to challenge (someone's) threat; expose a deception. [Possibly from Dutch *bluffen* to boast.] —**bluff'er,** *n.*

blu·ing (blōō'ing) *also,* **blue·ing.** *n.* preparation used in laundering to whiten and brighten fabrics.

blu·ish (blōō'ish) *also,* **blue·ish.** *adj.* somewhat blue.

blun·der (blun'dər) *n.* careless or stupid mistake. —*v.i.* **1.** to move or act blindly or clumsily; stumble; flounder. **2.** to make a stupid, clumsy, or careless mistake. —*v.t.* to utter (something) thoughtlessly or confusedly (with *out*). [Possibly of Scandinavian origin.] —**blun'der·er,** *n.* —**Syn.** *see* **mistake.**

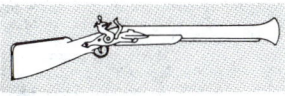

Blunderbuss

blun·der·buss (blun'dər bus') *n.* **1.** obsolete short gun with a flared muzzle for scattering shot at close range. **2.** stupid, blundering person. [Modification (influenced by BLUNDER) of Dutch *donderbus* this gun; literally, thunder box (possibly because of its random firing).]

blunt (blunt) *adj.* **1.** having a dull edge or point; not sharp. **2.** abrupt of speech or manner; outspoken; frank. —*v.t.* **1.** to make less sharp or keen; dull. —*v.i.* to become blunt or dull. [Of uncertain origin.] —**blunt'ly,** *adv.* —**blunt'ness,** *n.* —**Syn.** *adj.* **1.** *see* **dull. 2.** *see* **frank¹.**

blur (blûr) *blurred, blur·ring. v.t., v.i.* **1.** to make or become indistinct in form or outline: *Fog blurred the skyline.* **2.** to smudge or smear; stain: *He blurred the page. The ink blurred.* **3.** to dim: *Age blurred his eyesight. His eyes blurred with tears.* —*n.* **1.** something indistinct or dim; blurred appearance. **2.** smudge or smear; stain. [Of uncertain origin.] —**blur'ry,** *adj.*

blurb (blûrb) *n.* brief advertisement or description: *the blurb on a book jacket.* [Coined by the American humorist Gelett Burgess about 1914.]

blurt (blûrt) *v.t.* to utter suddenly, inadvertently, or impulsively (often with *out*): *He indiscreetly blurted out the truth.* [Imitative.]

blush (blush) *v.i.* **1.** to become red in the face from shame, embarrassment, or modesty: *to blush like a shy child.* **2.** to be ashamed or embarrassed (often with *at* or *for*): *I blushed at my ridiculous mistake.* **3.** to be or become rosy; bloom. —*n.* **1.** reddening of the face from shame, embarrassment, or modesty. **2.** red or rosy tint. **3. at first blush.** upon first glance. [Old English *blyscan* to redden.] —**blush'er,** *n.*

blus·ter (blus'tər) *v.i.* **1.** to blow with noise or stormy violence; be gusty: *The storm blustered outside.* **2.** to be noisy or swaggering; utter loud empty threats: *He blustered and raged.* —*v.t.* to utter noisily and violently (often with *out*). —*n.* **1.** noisy, stormy blowing, as of the wind. **2.** noisy, swaggering talk or manner. [Probably of Germanic origin.] —**blus'ter·er,** *n.* —**blus'ter·y,** *adj.*

blvd., boulevard.

B'nai B'rith (bə nā' brith') Jewish service organization that conducts various social, educational, cultural, and charitable programs. [Hebrew *b'nēy b'rīth* sons of the covenant.]

bo·a (bō'ə) *pl.* **bo·as.** *n.* **1.** any of various nonpoisonous, constrictor snakes, family Boidae, found in the tropical and temperate regions

having vestigial hind legs and noted for their great muscular strength. Length: 2–33 feet. **2.** long scarf of fur or feathers. [Modern Latin *Boa,* from Latin *boa* large serpent.]

boa constrictor, nonpoisonous, constrictor snake, *Boa constrictor*, of Mexico, Central and South America, having pale brown skin with dark brown marks on its back. Its loosely hinged jaws enable it to swallow animals much larger than its head. Average length: 10 feet.

Boa constrictor

boar (bôr) *pl.* **boars** or **boar.** *n.* **1.** uncastrated male swine. **2.** wild boar. [Old English *bār.*]

board (bôrd) *n.* **1.** thin piece of sawed wood longer than it is wide. **2.** piece of wood or other material used for some specific purpose: *a diving board.* **3.** group of persons who direct or supervise an activity; council: *board of trustees.* **4.a.** food or meals, esp. meals provided regularly for pay. **b.** *Archaic.* table on which meals are served. ▲ *def.* **4b** now chiefly restricted to the phrase *groaning board* to mean a table heavily laden, as at a feast. **5.** pasteboard or other stiff material used for the covers of books. **6.a.** *Nautical.* side of a ship. **b.** distance covered by a vessel in a single tack. **7. across the board. a.** (of betting) wagering equal amounts of money on several possibilities, as for a horse to win, place, and show. **b.** all-inclusive: *a 10 percent salary increase across the board.* **8. on board.** aboard a ship or other conveyance. **9. the boards.** the stage. **10. to go by the board.** to be forgotten, ruined, or ignored. **11. to tread the boards.** to act in the theater. —*v.t.* **1.** to cover or close up with boards (often with *up*). **2.** to provide with meals, or with lodging and meals, for pay. **3.** to place (someone) where meals and lodging are provided: *He boarded his son with that family.* **4.** to get on (a ship or other conveyance). **5.** *Nautical.* to come alongside of and go aboard (a vessel) as a member of a boarding party. —*v.i.* **1.** to receive meals, or lodging and meals, for pay. **2.** *Nautical.* to tack. [Old English *bord* plank, table, ship's side.]

board·er (bôr'dər) *n.* one who receives regular meals, or room and board, for a fixed price.

board foot *pl.* **board feet.** unit of measure for logs and lumber, equal to the volume of a board one foot square and one inch thick. See **weights and measures** for table.

board·ing (bôr'ding) *n.* wooden boards collectively.

boarding house, house at which regular meals, or lodging and meals, are furnished for a fixed price.

boarding party, group assigned to board a ship, esp. an enemy ship.

boarding school, school at which lodging and meals are provided for the pupils.

board measure, system of measure whose unit is the board foot.

board of trade, 1. association of businessmen to promote and protect business interests. **2. Board of Trade.** department of the British government supervising commerce and industry.

board·walk (bôrd'wôk') *n.* promenade, esp. of boards, along a beach.

boar·hound (bôr'hound') *n.* large dog used for hunting wild boars, esp. the Great Dane.

boast (bōst) *v.i.* **1.** to speak with vanity or exaggeration, esp. about oneself; brag. **2.** to be proud: *That's nothing to boast of.* —*v.t.* **1.** to assert with exaggeration; brag about. **2.** to possess with pride; take pride in: *The library boasts 500 new volumes.* —*n.* **1.** vain or exaggerated statement; bragging. **2.** something boasted of; cause for pride. [Anglo-Norman *bost* bragging; of uncertain origin.] —**boast'er,** *n.* **Syn.** *v.i.* **1. Boast, brag** mean to express self-praise. **Boast** implies an offensive statement, justified or not, of one's accomplishments, family, superiority, and so forth: *He boasts of having close connections with several influential politicians.* **Brag** suggests a cruder stretching or embroidery of the truth so as to magnify one's status, esp. as regards courage, strength, stamina, or a similar trait: *The fishermen bragged about the size of their catches.*

boast·ful (bōst'fəl) *adj.* characterized by or given to boasting; bragging. —**boast'ful·ly,** *adv.* —**boast'-ful·ness,** *n.*

boat (bōt) *n.* **1.** small vessel for use on water, propelled by oars, sails, or a motor. **2.** vessel of any size; ship: *His boat left the dock at noon.* ▲ *Def.* **2** is acceptable in common usage, but in nautical usage **boat** refers only to a vessel of small size. An ocean liner would be called a **ship**, not a **boat. 3.** open, boat-shaped dish, as for gravy. **4. in the same boat.** in

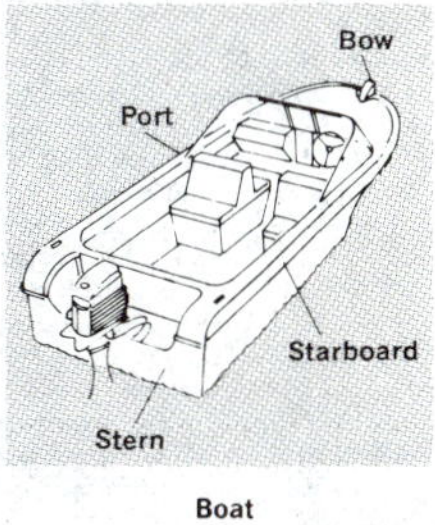

Boat

[labels: Bow, Port, Starboard, Stern]

the same situation or condition. **5. to miss the boat.** to fail to make use of an opportunity. —*v.i.* to travel in a boat. —*v.t.* to place or carry in a boat. [Old English *bāt* small vessel.]

boat hook, pole with a metal hook on one end, used for pulling or pushing a boat.

boat·house (bōt′hous′) *n.* building near the water's edge for sheltering or storing boats.

boat·ing (bō′ting) *n.* act or practice of using a boat, esp. for pleasure: *I enjoy boating on the lake.*

boat·load (bōt′lōd′) *n.* **1.** amount that a boat can hold or transport. **2.** load carried by a boat.

boat·man (bōt′mən) *pl.*, **-men.** *n.* one who operates, works on, or deals in selling, renting, or servicing boats.

boat·swain (bō′sən, bōt′swān′) *also*, **bo's'n, bo·sun.** *n.* ship's petty officer or warrant officer who has charge of certain gear, as the rigging or anchors, and whose duties include summoning the crew and directing their work.

Bo·az (bō′az) *n.* in the Old Testament, the husband of Ruth.

bob¹ (bob) **bobbed, bob·bing.** *v.i.* **1.** to move up and down, or to and fro, with a short, jerky motion: *The buoy bobbed in the water.* **2.** *Archaic.* to curtsy briefly. **3.** to try to snatch floating or dangling fruit with the teeth (with *for*): *to bob for apples.* **4. to bob up.** to appear suddenly and unexpectedly. —*v.t.* to move (something) up and down with a short, jerky motion: *He bobbed his head.* —*n.* short, jerking movement. [Probably imitative.]

bob² (bob) *n.* **1.** short haircut for a woman or child. **2.** docked tail, as of a horse. **3.** small, hanging weight, as at the end of a pendulum or plumb line. **4.** float or cork for a fishing line. **5.** bobsled. —*v.t.*, **bobbed, bob·bing.** to cut short, as hair or a tail. —*v.i.* to fish with a bob. [Middle English *bobbe*; of uncertain origin.]

bob³ (bob) *pl.*, **bob.** *n.* *British. Informal.* shilling. [Possibly from *Bob,* nickname of *Robert.*]

bob·bin (bob′in) *n.* **1.** spool around which thread or yarn is wound, used in weaving, machine sewing, or spinning. **2.** something resembling a bobbin in shape or function, as a reel around which wire is coiled, or a small, notched pin used in making lace. [French *bobine;* of uncertain origin.]

bob·bi·net (bob′i net′) *n.* machine-made net fabric having hexagonal meshes. [BOBBIN + NET¹.]

bobbin lace, lace made by hand on a pattern laid out on a pad or pillow, the thread or bobbins being wound around pins showing the pattern. Also, **pillow lace.**

bob·by (bob′ē) *pl.*, **-bies.** *n.* *British. Informal.* policeman. [From Sir *Robert* Peel, who, in 1828, reorganized the London police force.]

bobby pin, flat hairpin with prongs that press close together to hold hair tightly.

bobby socks *Informal.* ribbed, often heavy, socks, usually folded just above the ankle.

bob·by·sox·er (bob′ē sok′sər) *n.* *Slang.* teen-age girl, esp. one of the teen-agers who followed the fads and fashions popular in the 1940s.

bob·cat (bob′kat′) *n.* North American lynx, *Lynx rufus,* having a reddish-brown coat and white belly speckled with dark spots. Length: to 3 feet. Also, **wild′cat′.**

bob·o·link (bob′ə lingk′) *n.* songbird of North and South America, *Dolichonyx oryzivorus,* having predominantly buff-colored plumage. In early spring the male's plumage turns black with yellow and honey-colored markings. Also, **reed′bird′, rice′bird′.** [Imitative of the cry of this bird.]

bob·sled (bob′sled′) *n.* **1.** long racing sled with two sets of runners, a steering wheel, and a brake. **2.a.** long sled formed by attaching one short sled behind another. **b.** either of the short sleds so joined. —*v.i.*, **-sled·ded, -sled·ding.** to ride on a bobsled. Also, **bob′sleigh′.**

bob·stay (bob′stā′) *n.* *Nautical.* rope or chain connecting the bowsprit to the cutwater, used to counteract the pull of the forestays. See **bowsprit** for illustration.

bob·tail (bob′tāl′) *n.* **1.** tail cut short; short tail. **2.** animal having such a tail. —*v.t.* to cut the tail of. —*adj.* having a bobtail.

bob·white (bob′hwīt′, -wīt′) *n.* American game bird of the eastern and central United States, *Colinus virginianus,* of the quail family, having reddish-brown plumage with streakings of white, black, and buff. Length: 10 inches.

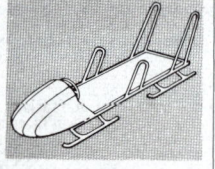

Bobsled

Bobwhite

Boc·cac·ci·o, Gio·van·ni (bō kä′chē ō′; jō vä′nē) 1313–75, Italian writer and humanist.

boc·cie (boch′ē) *n.* game similar to bowls, of Italian origin, played on a narrow court, usually of hard-packed earth and enclosed by low sides. [Italian *boccie* bowls, plural of *boccia* (wooden) ball; of uncertain origin.]

bock beer (bok) strong, dark beer, usually brewed in the cold months and sold in the spring. Also, **bock.** [German *Bock* for *Bockbier,* short for *Eimbockbier* beer from Eimbeck, a West German city.]

bode¹ (bōd) **bod·ed, bod·ing.** *v.t.* **1.** to be an omen or indication of; portend: *This bodes disaster.* **2.** *Archaic.* to foretell; predict. —*v.i.* **1. to bode ill.** to be a bad omen. **2. to bode well.** to be a good omen: *This bodes well for your success.* [Old English *bodian* to announce.]

bode² (bōd) a past tense of **bide.**

bod·ice (bod′is) *n.* **1.** that part of a woman's or girl's dress from the neckline to the waistline. **2.** vest worn over a woman's dress or blouse, that laces up the front. [Modification of *bodies,* plural of BODY. For a similar development, see PENCE.]

bod·ied (bod′ēd) *adj.* having a (specified kind of) body. ▲ used in combination, as in *able-bodied, full-bodied.*

bod·i·less (bod′ē lis) *adj.* having no body or material form; incorporeal: *bodiless phantoms.*

bod·i·ly (bod′ə lē) *adj.* of or relating to the body: *bodily harm.* —*adv.* in the flesh; in person: *They carried him bodily out of the room.*

bod·kin (bod′kin) *n.* **1.** small, pointed tool for making holes in cloth. **2.** long, ornamental pin for fastening hair. **3.** large, blunt needle for pulling tape or other material through a hem. **4.** *Archaic.* dagger. [Middle English *boydekyn* dagger; of uncertain origin.]

bod·y (bod′ē) *pl.*, **bod·ies.** *n.* **1.** the whole physical structure and material of a human being, animal, or plant. **2.a.** main portion of a human being or animal excluding the head and limbs; trunk. **b.** main stem or stalk of a plant or tree. **3.** main or central part of anything, as the nave of a church, fuselage of an airplane, or hull of a ship. **4.** dead person; corpse: *He found the body in the bushes.* **5.** part of a vehicle which carries the load: *the body of an automobile.* **6.** main part of a document, excluding introduction, appendices, and other supplementary material. **7.** group of persons or things considered as a whole: *a legislative body, a body of laws.* **8.** main portion of such a group; majority: *The body of the people voted against the measure.* **9.** distinct mass; portion of matter: *the force of a body in motion, a body of cold air.* **10.** person. **11.** strength; substance; density; consistency: *Wool has more body than organdy.* **12.** that part of a garment that covers the trunk, or the trunk above the waist. **13.** *Printing.* part of a piece of type on which the letter is cast. **14. to keep body and soul together.** to keep or remain alive. —*v.t.*, **bod·ied, bod·y·ing.** **1.** *Archaic.* to provide with or as with a body. **2. to body forth. a.** to put into real or tangible form. **b.** to represent; symbolize. [Old English *bodig* physical frame of a man or animal, trunk, main part of something.]

bod·y·guard (bod′ē gärd′) *n.* person or persons who protect someone from physical danger or attack.

body politic, people of a state, nation, or other political entity considered as a whole.

body snatcher, one who steals corpses from graves, esp. for dissection.

Boe·o·tia (bē ō′shə) *n.* ancient district in east-central Greece.

Boe·o·tian (bē ō′shən) *adj.* **1.** of or relating to Boeotia or its people. **2.** dull; provincial. —*n.* **1.** person of Boeotia. **2.** any dull or provincial person.

Boer (bôr) *n.* South African of Dutch descent. —*adj.* of or relating to the Boers. [Dutch *boer* farmer.]

Boer War, war between Great Britain and the Dutch republics of Transvaal and the Orange Free State, from 1899 to 1902, in which the Boers were defeated.

bog (bog, bôg) *n.* wet, spongy ground or area composed chiefly of decayed plant material; marsh; mire. —*v.t.*, *v.i.*, **bogged, bog·ging.** **1.** to sink or stick in a bog or soggy ground. **2. to bog down.** to cause to or become stuck as if in a bog. [Irish or Scottish Gaelic *bogach* marsh, from *bog* soft.] —**bog′gy,** *adj.*

bo·gey¹ (bō′gē) *n.* bogy¹.

bo·gey² (bō′gē) *pl.*, **-geys.** *n.* **1.** one stroke over par for a hole in golf. **2.** par in golf. —*v.t.*, *v.i.*, **-geyed, -gey·ing.** to use one stroke more than par for (a hole in golf). [Said to be from Colonel *Bogey,* an imaginary partner.]

bo·gey·man (bŏŏg′ē man′, bŏŏ′gē-, bō′-) *n.* frightful imaginary figure. esp. one described to threaten children.

bog·gle (bog′əl) **-gled, -gling.** *v.i.* **1.** to start with fright or astonishment. **2.** to hesitate or shrink from scruples or doubt (with *at*). —*v.t.* to astound; startle; overwhelm: *That boggles the imagination.* [Possibly from BOGLE.]

bo·gie¹ (bō′gē) bogy¹.

bo·gie² (bō′gē) *n.* **1.** four-wheeled support under a railroad car.

at; āpe; cär; end; mē; it; īce; hot; ōld; fôrk; wood; fōōl; oil; out; up; ūse; turn; sing; thin; this; zh in treasure; ə in ago, taken, pencil, lemon, circus.

2. one of the wheels supporting the tread of a tractor or tank. [Of uncertain origin.]

bo·gle (bō′gəl) *n.* hobgoblin; specter. [Scottish *bogle.*]

Bo·go·tá (bō′gə tä′) *n.* capital and largest city of Colombia, in the west-central part of the country. Pop. (1969 est.), 2,037,904.

bo·gus (bō′gəs) *adj.* not genuine; counterfeit; sham. [First found in 1827 as name of a machine coining counterfeit money; possibly related to BOGY¹.]

bo·gy¹ (bō′gē) *pl.,* **-gies.** *also,* **bo·gey, bo·gie.** *n.* **1.** evil spirit; goblin; specter. **2.** frightening or dreaded person or thing; bugbear. **3.** *Military. Slang.* unidentified enemy aircraft. [Possibly modification of BOGLE; possibly from Welsh *bwg* ghost.]

bo·gy² (bō′gē) *pl.,* **-gies.** *n.* bogie².

Bo·he·mi·a (bō hē′mē ə) *n.* historic region and ancient kingdom, in western Czechoslovakia. Area, approx. 20,000 sq. mi. Pop. (1961), 6,039,087.

Bo·he·mi·an (bō hē′mē ən) *n.* **1.** one of the people of Bohemia. **2.** the language spoken in Bohemia; Czech. **3.** *also,* **bohemian.** person who has little regard for conventionalities and leads a nonconformist life, esp. one connected with the arts. **4.** gypsy. —*adj.* **1.** of or relating to Bohemia, its people, or their language. **2.** *also,* **bohemian.** characteristic of or relating to a bohemian. —**Bo·he′mi·an·ism;** *also,* **bo·he′mi·an·ism,** *n.*

Bohr, Niels (bôr; nēls) 1885–1962, Danish physicist.

boil¹ (boil) *v.i.* **1.** (of a liquid) to form bubbles that escape as vapor due to the application of heat. **2.** to contain a boiling liquid: *The pot is boiling.* **3.** to reach the boiling point: *Turn off the flame as soon as the water boils.* **4.** to be stirred up or angry: *He boiled with rage.* **5.** to be agitated like boiling water; seethe. **6. to boil away.** to evaporate by boiling. **7. to boil over. a.** to overflow during boiling. **b.** to lose one's temper; show anger. —*v.t.* **1.** to bring to the boiling point: *The cook boiled the water.* **2.** to cook, cleanse, or prepare by boiling: *to boil potatoes.* **3.** to cause to undergo the action of a boiling liquid: *to boil dirty clothes.* **4.** to separate or collect by boiling: *to boil sugar.* **5. to boil down. a.** to reduce or lessen by boiling. **b.** to condense; abridge. —*n.* act or state of boiling. [Old French *boillir* to form bubbles, from Latin *bullire.*]

boil² (boil) *n.* painful, pus-filled swelling beneath the skin, formed around a hard core. It is caused by bacterial infection. [Old English *bȳl.*]

boil·er (boi′lər) *n.* **1.** large container with a system of tubes in which water or other liquid is transformed into steam or other vapor for heat or power. **2.** container in which something is heated or boiled. **3.** tank in which water is heated or hot water is stored.

boiling point **1.** temperature at which the transition of a liquid to its gaseous state begins. The boiling point of water at sea level is 212 degrees Fahrenheit, or 100 degrees centigrade. **2.** *Informal.* point at which a person loses his temper.

Boi·se (boi′sē) *n.* capital of Idaho, in the southwestern part of the state. Pop. (1970), 74,990.

bois·ter·ous (bois′tər əs, -trəs) *adj.* noisy and exuberant; unrestrained: *boisterous merriment.* [Of uncertain origin.] —**bois′ter·ous·ly,** *adv.* —**bois′ter·ous·ness,** *n.*

bo·la (bō′lə) *also,* **bo·las** (bō′ləs). *n.* weapon used chiefly in South America, consisting of heavy balls tied to the ends of a cord. It is thrown to entangle the victim. [Spanish and Portuguese *bola* ball, from Latin *bulla* bubble, knob.]

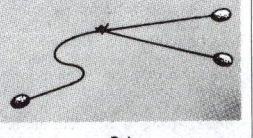

Bola

bold (bōld) *adj.* **1.** having courage; fearless; intrepid. **2.** showing or requiring spirit or courage; daring: *a bold enterprise.* **3.** forward; presumptuous; impudent. **4.** standing out prominently; distinct and striking: *bold handwriting.* **5.** steep; abrupt: *a bold cliff.* **6. to make bold.** to take the liberty; venture. [Old English *bald* courageous.] —**bold′ly,** *adv.* —**bold′ness,** *n.*

Syn. 3. Bold, brash, brazen denote impudent shamelessness. **Bold** implies lack of restraint and a rude disregard of other's feelings: *Her bold behavior scandalized the neighbors.* **Brash** implies being impetuous and self-assertive and disregarding the claims of others: *The lieutenant's brash action soon brought down the commander's wrath upon his head.* **Brazen** implies arrogant defiance: *The brazen raids on the treasury by the two executives seemed to pass unnoticed by their colleagues on the board of directors.*

bold·face (bōld′fās′) *n.* type with heavy, thick lines that stands out clearly. **This is printed in boldface.**

bole (bōl) *n.* trunk of a tree. [Old Norse *bolr.*]

bo·le·ro (bə lâr′ō) *pl.,* **-ros.** *n.* **1.** lively Spanish dance in ¾ time that is usually accompanied by castanets. **2.** music for this dance.

3. short, open jacket ending at or above the waistline. [Spanish *bolero,* possibly from *bola* ball¹, globe, from Latin *bulla* bubble, knob.]

Bol·eyn, Anne (bool′in, boo lin′) c.1507–36, queen of England and second wife of Henry VIII.

bol·i·var (bol′i vər, bō lē′vär) *pl.,* **bol·i·vars** or **bo·li·va·res** (bō′lē vär′ās). *n.* monetary unit of Venezuela equal to 100 centimos. [From Simón *Bolívar.*]

Bo·lí·var, Si·món (bol′i vər, bō lē′vär; sī′mən, sē mōn′) 1783–1830, South American revolutionary leader and statesman.

Bo·liv·i·a (bə liv′ē ə) *n.* country in west-central South America. Capitals, La Paz and Sucre. Area, 424,162 sq. mi. Pop. (1969 est.), 4,804,000.

bo·li·vi·a·no (bō liv′ē ä′nō, bə-) *pl.,* **-nos** (-nōz). *n.* monetary unit of Bolivia equal to 100 centavos. [Spanish *boliviano,* from BOLIVIA.]

boll (bōl) *n.* rounded seed pod or capsule of a plant, as of cotton or flax. [Form of BOWL¹.]

bol·lix (bol′əks) *also,* **bol·lox.** *v.t.* *Informal.* to make a mess of (often with *up*). [From earlier *ballocks* testicles, from old English *beallucas.*]

boll weevil, long-beaked beetle, *Anthonomus grandis,* of Central America and the southern United States, which damages cotton bolls.

boll·worm (bōl′wurm′) *n.* moth larva that feeds on cotton bolls and ears of corn.

Boll weevil

bo·lo (bō′lō) *pl.,* **-los.** *n.* long, single-edged knife, used in the Philippines. [Spanish *bolo,* from the native Philippine name.]

bo·lo·gna (bə lō′nə, -nē) *also,* **ba·lo·ney, bo·lo·ney.** *n.* highly seasoned, smoked sausage made of beef, veal, and pork. Also, **bologna sausage.** [From BOLOGNA.]

Cotton bud

Bo·lo·gna (bə lōn′yə) *n.* city in northern Italy. Pop. (1968 est.), 486,973.

Boll weevil

Bol·she·vik (bōl′shə vik, bol′-) *pl.,* **-viks** or **-vi·ki** (-vē′kē, -vik′ē). *also,* **bol·she·vik.** *n.* **1.** member of the left-wing majority faction of the Social Democratic Party in czarist Russia that, in 1917, led by Lenin and Trotsky, overthrew the provisional government of Kerensky and established the Soviet Union. In 1918 this group changed its name to the Russian Communist Party. **2.** any radical. —*adj.* of or relating to Bolsheviks or Bolshevism. [Russian *bolshevik* member of the majority, from *bolshe* greater.]

Bol·she·vism (bōl′shə viz′əm, bol′-) *also,* **bol·she·vism.** *n.* doctrines and policies of the Bolsheviks; revolutionary Marxism.

Bol·she·vist (bōl′shə vist, bol′-) *n., adj.* Bolshevik. —**Bol′she·vis′tic;** *also,* **bol′she·vis′tic,** *adj.*

bol·ster (bōl′stər) *n.* **1.** narrow, often cylindrical, pillow, as long as the width of a bed or couch. **2.** any cushion, pad, or pillow. **3.** something resembling a bolster in shape or use; support. —*v.t.* **1.** to uphold or reinforce: *to bolster someone's spirits.* **2.** to support or prop with a cushion: *to bolster a sick child with a pillow.* [Old English *bolster* cushion.]

bolt¹ (bōlt) *n.* **1.** pin or rod used for holding things together, usually with a head at one end and threads for a nut to be attached on the other end. **2.** sliding bar for fastening a door or gate. **3.** part of a lock that is moved out or withdrawn by turning the key. **4.** sudden spring or start: *He made a bolt for the door.* **5.** stroke of lightning; thunderbolt. **6.** roll of cloth or paper. **7.** withdrawal of support or breaking away (from a group or a set of ideas). **8.** short, stout arrow with a thick blunt head, used with a crossbow. **9. bolt from the blue.** sudden, unexpected occurrence. —*v.t.* **1.** to fasten or secure with or as with a bolt: *Bolt the door if you want privacy.* **2.** to swallow (food) quickly or without chewing; gulp: *He bolted his dinner and ran to the game.* **3.** to break away from (a group or set of ideas); abandon. —*v.i.* **1.** to spring or move suddenly (often with *out* or *from*): *He bolted up the stairs.* **2.** to break away from control; start and run off: *His horse bolted.* **3.** to break away from a group or their ideas: *The presidential candidate bolted and started a third party movement.* —*adv.* **bolt upright.** erect and straight. [Old English *bolt* arrow.] —**bolt′er,** *n.*

Bolt   Nut

Bolt¹ *(def. 1)*

bolt² (bōlt) *v.t.* to sift through a cloth or sieve. [Old French *buleter;* possibly of Germanic origin.] —**bolt′er,** *n.*

Bol·ton (bōlt′ən) *n.* city in northwestern England. Pop. (1968 est.), 153,700.

bolt·rope (bōlt′rōp′) *n.* rope sewn along the edge of a sail to strengthen it.

bo·lus (bō′ləs) *n.* **1.** small, rounded mass, esp. of chewed food. **2.** large pill. [Late Latin *bōlus,* from Greek *bōlos* lump.]

bomb (bom) *n.* **1.** projectile containing an explosive, incendiary, or

chemical substance, to be set off by contact or other means, usually dropped from aircraft. **2.** any similar explosive device: *a tear gas bomb, a dynamite bomb.* **3.** container whose contents are stored under pressure for later release as a fine spray or foam. **4.** *Slang.* total failure: *That play was a real bomb.* —*v.t.* to attack or destroy (something) with a bomb or bombs. —*v.i.* **1.** to drop or set off bombs. **2.** *Slang.* to fail completely. [French *bombe* the projectile, going back to Latin *bombus* a booming, from Greek *bombos* deep hollow sound; imitative.]

bom·bard (bom bärd′) *v.t.* **1.** to attack with or bombs. **2.** to subject to a vigorous or persistent attack: *He bombarded her with questions.* **3.** *Physics.* to subject (atomic nuclei) to a stream of high-speed subatomic particles. [French *bombarder,* from *bombarde* cannon, from Medieval Latin *bombarda* weapon for hurling stones, from Latin *bombus.* See BOMB.] —**bom·bard′ment,** *n.*

bom·bar·dier (bom′bar dēr′) *n.* **1.** crew member of a bomber who aims and discharges the bombs. **2.** noncommissioned artillery officer in the British army ranking next below a corporal.

bom·bast (bom′bast) *n.* pretentious, inflated language; pompous verbosity. [Old French *bombace* cotton padding, from Late Latin *bombax* cotton, modification of Latin *bombyx* cotton, silk, from Greek *bombyx* silk.]

bom·bas·tic (bom bas′tik) *adj.* given to or characterized by pretentious, inflated language; grandiloquent. —**bom·bas′ti·cal·ly,** *adv.*

Bom·bay (bom bā′) *n.* largest city and chief port of India, on the western coast of the country. Pop. (1969 est.), 5,534,358.

bom·ba·zine (bom′bə zēn′) *n.* twilled cloth with a silk warp and worsted filling. [French *bombasin,* from Italian *bambagino* cotton cloth, going back to Late Latin *bombax.* See BOMBAST.]

bomb bay, section in a bomber in which bombs are carried and from which they are dropped.

bomb·er (bom′ər) *n.* **1.** military airplane designed for dropping bombs. **2.** one who drops, plants, or throws bombs.

bomb·proof (bom′proof′) *adj.* safe from damage by bombs: *a bomb-proof shelter.*

bomb·shell (bom′shel′) *n.* **1.** bomb. **2.** one who or that which has a startling or overwhelming effect.

bomb shelter, place, usually underground, where people may take refuge from an air raid.

bomb·sight (bom′sīt′) *n.* instrument in a bomber used to sight the target and help the bombardier drop bombs accurately.

bo·na fide (bō′nə fīd′, bon′ə, bō′nə fī′dē) **1.** in good faith without fraud or deception. **2.** genuine; authentic. [Latin *bonā fidē* in good faith.]

bo·nan·za (bə nan′zə) *n.* **1.** rich mine or mass of ore. **2.** any source of great profit or wealth. [Spanish *bonanza* fair weather, prosperity, going back to Latin *bonus* good.]

Bo·na·parte (bō′nə pärt′) **1.** Napoleon. see **Napoleon I. 2.** Jerome. 1784–1860, brother of Napoleon; king of Westphalia from 1807 to 1813. **3.** Joseph. 1768–1844, brother of Napoleon; king of Naples from 1806 to 1808 and king of Spain from 1808 to 1813. **4.** Lou·is (loo′ē, lwē). 1778–1846, brother of Napoleon; king of Holland from 1806 to 1810. **5.** Lu·cien (loo′shən). 1775–1840, brother of Napoleon.

Bo·na·part·ist (bō′nə pär′tist) *n.* adherent of Napoleon Bonaparte, his policies, or his dynasty.

bon·bon (bon′bon′) *n.* piece of candy, esp. one with a fondant or chocolate coating and a fondant center. [French *bonbon* literally, good-good, repetition of *bon* good, from Latin *bonus* good.]

bond (bond) *n.* **1.** something that binds, fastens, or holds together: *The bonds were made of rope.* **2.** binding or uniting force or influence; tie: *bonds of friendship, bonds of affection.* **3.** *Finance.* interest-bearing certificate of indebtedness issued by a government or corporation and promising to repay a specified sum of money at a fixed future date. **4.** *Chemistry.* unit of combining capacity between the atoms of a molecule, equivalent to the power of one hydrogen atom. **5.** *Law.* **a.** obligation to pay or forfeit a specified sum of money if certain acts are or are not committed. **b.** amount of money so specified; surety; bail. **c.** person acting as surety or bail. **6.** *Insurance.* policy covering losses suffered through the acts of an employee or other unforeseeable circumstances. **7.** bond paper. **8.** substance that causes parts or particles to adhere together or unite. **9.** storage of imported goods in a warehouse until taxes upon them are paid. **10.** *Building.* method of arranging building units, as bricks or boards, by overlapping them to form a solid whole. —*v.t.* **1.** to place in or under bond; guarantee: *to bond an employee, to bond imported goods.* **2.** to provide or act as surety for; furnish bond for. **3.** to place a bonded debt upon; mortgage. **4.** to cause to adhere; unite. —*v.i.* to hold together; join; adhere. [Form of BAND².]
Syn. *n.* **1. Bond, tie** mean something that holds two or more things or people together. **Bond** implies something rigid, a restraint on the individual so that things or people thus held together may be considered one: *They entered into the bond of matrimony.* **Tie** implies a more flexible linking, connecting things or things but leaving them much individual

freedom: *His family ties were strong enough to keep him from joining the emigration westward.*

bond·age (bon′dij) *n.* **1.** involuntary servitude; slavery. **2.** subjection to any binding or dominating influence.

bond·ed (bon′did) *adj.* **1.** secured or guaranteed by a bond or bonds. **2.** placed in bond; stored in a bonded warehouse.

bonded fabric, fabric consisting of two layers of material held together by an adhesive medium.

bond·hold·er (bond′hōl′dər) *n.* owner of a bond or bonds issued by a government or corporation.

bond·maid (bond′mād′) *n.* female bond servant.

bond·man (bond′mən) *pl.,* **-men.** *n.* male slave or feudal serf. —**bond′wo′man,** *n.*

bond paper, strong, durable paper made chiefly from rag pulp.

bond servant 1. one bound to service without pay. **2.** slave.

bonds·man (bondz′mən) *pl.,* **-men.** *n.* **1.** person who assumes responsibility for another by furnishing a bond; surety. **2.** bondman.

bone (bōn) *n.* **1.** one of the parts of the skeleton of a vertebrate animal. **2.** hard porous tissue of which such parts are composed. **3.** substance resembling bone, as ivory or whalebone. **4.** strip of whalebone or other sturdy material used to shape a corset or other garment; stay. **5. bones. a.** skeleton; body. **b.** *Slang.* dice. **c.** clappers of bone or wood used as noisemakers or for musical accompaniment. **6. to feel (something) in one's bones.** to feel certain of (something) for no apparent reason; know (something) intuitively. **7. to have a bone to pick.** to have something to dispute or complain about. **8. to make no bones about.** to be direct or blunt about; make no attempt to conceal. —*v.t.,* **boned, bon·ing. 1.** to remove the bones from: *to bone chicken.* **2.** to stiffen (a garment) with whalebone or similar material. **3. to bone up on.** to review (a subject) by diligent study. [Old English *bān* one of the parts of a skeleton.]

bone ash, white, porous ash of bones, composed chiefly of calcium phosphate, made by roasting animal bones in open air, used esp. as a fertilizer or for bone china.

bone·black (bōn′blak′) *n.* black charcoal made by roasting animal bones in closed iron containers, used esp. as a pigment and for removing color from certain substances.

bone china, translucent white china made with bone ash.

bone-dry (bōn′drī′) *adj.* very dry.

bone·fish (bōn′fish′) *pl.,* **-fish** or **-fish·es.** *n.* any of various silvery fish, family Albulidae, found in warm, shallow ocean waters and having a skeleton made up of many small bones. Length: to 3½ feet.

bone meal, crushed or ground animal bones used as fertilizer or feed.

bone of contention, subject or cause of dispute or disagreement.

bon·er (bō′nər) *n. Informal.* foolish mistake.

bone·set (bōn′set′) *n.* North American plant, *Eupatorium perfoliatum,* of the family Compositae, bearing clusters of white or grayish flowers and having a strong smell, formerly used medicinally.

bon·fire (bon′fīr′) *n.* large fire built in the open air. [Earlier *bone fire;* referring to fires built out-of-doors for burning bones.]

bon·go drums (bong′gō) pair of small, connected drums to be played with the hands while being held between the knees. Also, **bon′gos.**

bon·ho·mie (bon′ə mē′, bō′nə-) *also,* **bon·hom·mie.** *n.* good nature; affability. [French *bonhomie,* from *bonhomme* good-natured man, going back to Latin *bonus* good + *homō* man.]

Bon·i·face, Saint (bon′ə fās′) c.680–754, Catholic martyr.

bo·ni·to (bə nē′tō) *pl.,* **-tos** or **-toes.** *n.* any of various edible saltwater fish, genera *Sarda* and *Euthynnus,* closely related to the tuna and mackerel. [Spanish *bonito,* going back to Latin *bonus* good.]

bon jour (bôN zhoor′) *French.* good morning; good day.

bon mot (bon′mō′; *French* bôN mō′) *pl.,* **bons mots** (bon′mōz′; *French* bôN mō′) clever saying or remark. [French *bon mot* literally, good word.]

Marrow cavity

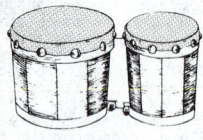

Bone cross section

Boneset

Bongo drums

Bonito

at; āpe; cär; end; mē; it; īce; hot; ōld; fôrk; wood; fōol; oil; out; up; ūse; turn; sing; thin; this; zh in treasure; ə in ago, taken, pencil, lemon, circus.

Bonn (bon) *n.* capital of West Germany, in the western part of the country. Pop. (1968 est.), 138,090.

bonne (bôn) *n.* nursemaid or housemaid. [French *bonne,* feminine of *bon* good, from Latin *bonus.*]

bon·net (bon′it) *n.* **1.** hat enclosing both the sides and the back of the head and tied under the chin, worn esp. by women and girls. **2.** any girl's or woman's hat. **3.** traditional cap worn by men and boys in Scotland. **4.** something resembling a bonnet in shape or function, as the protective hood or cowl of a chimney. **5.** *British.* automobile hood. —*v.t.* to put a bonnet on. [Old French *bonet* or *bonnet* such a hat; originally, material used for hats; of uncertain origin.]

bon·ny (bon′ē) **-ni·er, -ni·est.** *also,* **bon·nie.** *adj. Scottish.* **1.** good-looking; comely. **2.** fine; admirable. **3.** robust; healthy-looking. [Possibly from Old French *bon* good, from Latin *bonus.*] —**bon′ni·ly,** *adv.* —**bon′ni·ness,** *n.*

bon soir (bôn swär′) *French.* good evening; good night.

bo·nus (bō′nəs) *n.* something given in addition to what is usual or due; something extra: *a Christmas bonus.* [Latin *bonus* good.]

bon vi·vant (bôn vē vän′) *pl.,* **bons vi·vants** (bôn vē vän′). one who is given to luxurious living. [French *bon vivant* literally, good liver.]

bon vo·yage (bôn′voi äzh′; *French* bôn vwä yäzh′) pleasant trip; good-by. [French *bon voyage* literally, good trip.]

bon·y (bō′nē) **bon·i·er, bon·i·est.** *adj.* **1.** of, relating to, or like bone. **2.** having many bones: *a bony fish.* **3.** having prominent bones; thin; gaunt. —**bon′i·ness,** *n.*

boo (boo) *n., interj.* sound made to express dislike or disapproval or to frighten. —*v.t.,* **booed, boo·ing.** to express disapproval of by making this sound: *The audience booed the last speaker.* —*v.i.* to make this sound. [Imitative.]

boob (boob) *n. Slang.* stupid or foolish person; dunce. [From BOOBY.]

boo-boo (boo′boo′) *n.* **1.** bruise or other small hurt. ▲ said of a baby's bruise or in imitation of baby talk. **2.** *Slang.* mistake.

boo·by (boo′bē) *pl.,* **-bies.** *n.* **1.** stupid or foolish person; dunce. **2.** any of several web-footed sea birds, genus *Sula,* found in tropical and subtropical waters, having a long, straight bill, a heavy, streamlined body, and long, pointed wings. Length: 30 inches. [Spanish *bobo* fool, from Latin *balbus* stammering.]

booby prize, prize, often a funny one, given to the person who has done the worst in a competition.

booby trap **1.** bomb or other harmful device camouflaged to appear harmless and arranged so that the victim's own movements set it into action. **2.** any trick or device for causing someone harm unexpectedly or as a result of one's own action.

boo·dle (boo′dəl) *n. Slang.* money obtained illegally, esp. bribe money. [Dutch *boedel* property, possessions.]

boog·ie-woog·ie (boog′ē woog′ē, boo′gē woo′gē) *n.* form of jazz music, usually for piano, characterized by repeated bass figures in 8/8 time with melodic and harmonic variations in the treble. [Probably imitative.]

boo·hoo (boo′hoo′) **-hooed, -hoo·ing.** *v.i.* to weep noisily; blubber. —*n. pl.,* **-hoos.** noisy sob; loud weeping. [Imitative.]

book (book) *n.* **1.** written or printed work of some length, esp. one on sheets bound together between two protective covers. **2.** set of blank or ruled sheets of paper bound together: *an address book.* **3.** section of a literary work or treatise: *the fifth book of the Aeneid.* **4.** set of items bound together like a book: *a book of matches, a book of stamps.* **5.** words or text of an opera or musical play; libretto. **6.** script of a play. **7.** list or record of bets. **8.** number of cards or tricks which must be won before a score may be recorded in a card game. **9. books.** business accounts.

by the book. according to rule; in the prescribed way.

(one) for the books. (something) worthy of special note.

on the books. a. recorded. **b.** listed; enrolled.

the book. set of rules or ideas regarded as authoritative or definitive.

the Good Book. the Bible.

to bring to book. a. to demand an account from. **b.** to reprove sharply; reprimand.

to know like a book. to know completely and thoroughly.

to make book. *Informal.* to place a bet or accept bets.

—*v.t.* **1.** to arrange for; engage; reserve: *to book passage for two, to book a singer for a week's engagement.* **2.** to enter charges against (someone) in a police record. [Old English *bōc* beech tree, writing tablet. Tablets or sticks of beech wood, on which runic characters were inscribed, were the first "books" of the early English.]

book·bind·er (book′bīn′dər) *n.* one whose business or trade is the binding of books.

book·bind·er·y (book′bīn′dər ē) *pl.,* **-er·ies.** *n.* place where books are bound.

book·bind·ing (book′bīn′ding) *n.* art, trade, or process of binding books.

book·case (book′kās′) *n.* cabinet for holding books.

book club **1.** organization that sells its subscribers selected books, usually at a saving. **2.** club organized for the reading and discussion of books.

book·end (book′end′) *n.* support placed at the end of a row of books to hold them upright.

book·ie (book′ē) *n. Informal.* bookmaker (def. 1).

book·ish (book′ish) *adj.* **1.** fond of reading or study; scholarly. **2.** better acquainted with books than with practical experience. **3.** pedantic; stilted. —**book′ish·ly,** *adv.* —**book′ish·ness,** *n.*

book·keep·ing (book′kē′ping) *n.* art or work of keeping systematic records of business accounts or transactions. —**book′keep′er,** *n.*

book learning, knowledge derived from books, as distinguished from that gained from practical experience. —**book-learn·ed** (book′-lur′nid, -lurnd′) *adj.*

book·let (book′lit) *n.* small, thin book or pamphlet.

book·mak·er (book′mā′kər) *n.* **1.** one who makes a business of taking bets, as on horse races. **2.** one who composes, prints, or binds books.

book·mark (book′märk′) *n.* object inserted between the pages of a book to mark a place.

book·mo·bile (book′mə bēl′) *n.* motor vehicle equipped to carry books and serve as a traveling library.

Book of Common Prayer, official book of worship of the Church of England, also used in revised versions by other Anglican churches.

Book of Mormon, see Mormon.

book·plate (book′plāt′) *n.* printed label pasted in a book to indicate its ownership, often having a design.

book·rack (book′rak′) *n.* **1.** rack to hold an open book. **2.** rack or shelf for holding books.

book review, essay or talk offering a critical appraisal of a book.

book·sell·er (book′sel′ər) *n.* one whose business or trade is selling books.

book·stall (book′stôl′) *n.* **1.** stall or stand, often outdoors, where both new and secondhand books are sold. **2.** *British.* newstand.

book·stand (book′stand′) *n.* **1.** bookstall (def. 1). **2.** bookrack.

book·store (book′stôr′) *n.* store where books are sold. Also, **book shop.**

book value, value of a business or asset as it appears on the account books. Distinguished from **market value.**

book·worm (book′wurm′) *n.* **1.** one who devotes much time to reading and studying, often to the exclusion of other activities. **2.** any of various insect larvae that feed on the bindings or pages of books.

Bool·e·an algebra (boo′lē an) algebra that is based on laws of the relationships among sets, applied esp. to solving problems in logic and to designing electrical switching circuits and digital computers. [From George *Boole,* 1815–64, British mathematician and logician.]

boom[1] (boom) *n.* **1.** deep, hollow reverberating sound: *the boom of crashing waves.* **2.** period of rapid economic growth and prosperity: *the boom that followed the depression.* **3.** any great increase or favorable upturn: *a boom in building.* —*v.i.* **1.** to make a deep, hollow, reverberating sound: *The cannon boomed in the distance.* **2.** to increase or develop suddenly and rapidly; flourish: *Business has been booming.* —*v.t.* to give forth or utter with a booming sound (often with *out*): *The loudspeaker boomed out his name.* —*adj.* caused by a boom: *boom prices, boom town.* [Imitative.]

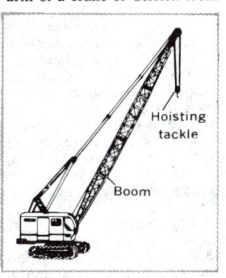

Boom² (def. 1)

boom[2] (boom) *n.* **1.** spar used to extend the foot of certain sails or to facilitate cargo handling. **2.** movable arm of a crane or derrick from which the object to be moved is suspended. **3.** long adjustable pole used to support a microphone. **4.a.** chain, cable, or connection of timbers in a waterway to prevent logs from floating away. **b.** mass of logs or area shut off or enclosed in this way. [Dutch *boom* tree, pole.]

boom·er·ang (boo′mə rang′) *n.* **1.** flat curved piece of wood, one type of which can be thrown so as to return to the thrower. It is used as a weapon by Australian aborigines and some Africans. **2.** something that recoils upon its originator; something that backfires. —*v.i.* to act as a boomerang: *That plan boomeranged.* [From the native Australian.]

Boom² (def. 2)

boon¹ (bōōn) *n.* **1.** greatly appreciated benefit; blessing: *Her thoughtful concern was a boon to me.* **2.** *Archaic.* favor sought; request. [Old Norse *bōn* petition.]

boon² (bōōn) *adj.* jolly; merry; convivial: *boon companion.* [Old French *bon* good, from Latin *bonus.*]

boon·docks (bōōn′doks′) *n. Informal.* poor, unsophisticated, backwoods area. [Tagalog *bundok* mountain; applied by U.S. Marines stationed in the Philippines to the backwoods.]

boon·dog·gle (bōōn′dog′əl) **-gled, -gling.** *Informal. v.i.* to do useless or unnecessary work; waste time. —*n.* useless, wasteful work. [Supposedly coined in 1925 by Robert H. Link, American Scoutmaster.] —**boon′dog′gler,** *n.*

Boone, Daniel (bōōn) 1734–1820, U.S. frontiersman.

boor (bōōr) *n.* crude, bad-mannered, or awkward person. [Dutch *boer* farmer, peasant.]

boor·ish (bōōr′ish) *adj.* crude; bad-mannered; awkward. —**boor′ish·ly,** *adv.* —**boor′ish·ness,** *n.*

boost (bōōst) *v.t.* **1.** upward shove or push: *a boost over the wall.* **2.** something that aids or advances (a person or thing): *a boost to morale.* **3.** increase or rise: *a tax boost.* —*v.t.* **1.** to lift by pushing from below. **2.** to advance by speaking well of; promote. **3.** to raise; increase: *to boost prices.* [Of uncertain origin.]

boost·er (bōōs′tər) *n.* **1.** enthusiastic supporter. **2.** something that increases or reinforces power or effectiveness, as a booster shot or an amplifier for a radio or television receiver. **3.** *Aeronautics.* **a.** first-stage engine of a rocket providing thrust for the launching and initial part of the flight. Also, **booster engine. b.** stage of a flight during which this engine operates. Also, **booster stage.**

booster shot, supplementary inoculation against a disease, given to prolong or reinforce immunity.

boot¹ (bōōt) *n.* **1.** covering for the foot and part or most of the leg. **2.** kick. **3.** something resembling a boot in shape or function, as a sheath on a saddle to hold a rifle or a protective covering for an open vehicle. **4.** protective covering for the foot and leg of a horse. **5.** *British.* baggage compartment of an automobile; trunk. **6.** thick patch for the inner surface of an automobile tire. **7. the boot.** *Informal.* abrupt dismissal or discharge. **8. to die in one's boots** or **to die in one's boots on.** to die while in action. **10. to lick the boots of.** to fawn on; flatter subserviently. —*v.t.* **1.** to kick. **2.** *Informal.* to dismiss or discharge abruptly. **3.** to put boots on. [Old French *bote* covering for the foot and leg; of uncertain origin.]

boot² (bōōt) *n.* **1. to boot.** in addition; besides. **2.** *Archaic.* remedy; profit; benefit. —*v.t., v.i. Archaic.* to be of use; be of avail: *It boots us little.* [Old English *bōt* advantage.]

boot·black (bōōt′blak′) *n.* one whose work is polishing shoes and boots.

boot camp *Informal.* military camp for basic training.

boot·ee (bōō′tē, bōō tē′) *n.* infant's soft, usually knitted or socklike, shoe.

Bo·ö·tes (bō ō′tēz) *n.* constellation in the northern sky containing the bright star Arcturus, conventionally depicted as a man holding a crook. [Latin *Boōtes,* from Greek *Boōtēs* literally, plowman.]

booth (bōōth) *pl.,* **booths** (bōōthz, bōōths). *n.* **1.** small compartment designed for a specific use: *a voting booth, a telephone booth, a ticket booth.* **2.** seating compartment, as in a restaurant, consisting of a table and a set of seats whose backs serve as partitions. **3.** stall for the display or sale of goods: *refreshment booth at a bazaar.* [Of Scandinavian origin.]

Booth (bōōth) **1. Edwin Thomas.** 1833–93, U.S. actor and theatrical producer. **2. John Wilkes** (wilks). brother of Edwin, 1838–65, U.S. actor and assassin of Abraham Lincoln. **3. William.** 1829–1912, English founder and first general of the Salvation Army.

boot·jack (bōōt′jak′) *n.* device to hold a boot while the foot is pulled out.

boot·leg (bōōt′leg′) **-legged, -leg·ging.** *v.t., v.i.* to make, sell, or transport (liquor or other goods) illegally. —*adj.* made, transported, or sold illegally: *bootleg whisky.* —*n.* bootlegged article, esp. alcoholic liquor. [From the practice of smuggling products, esp. liquor, in the legs of boots.] —**boot′leg′ger,** *n.*

boot·less (bōōt′lis) *adj.* unprofitable; useless. —**boot′less·ly,** *adv.*

boot·lick (bōōt′lik′) *v.t., v.i. Slang.* to flatter or seek favor servilely; fawn (on). —**boot′lick′er,** *n.*

boots (bōōts) *n. British.* servant at an inn or hotel who polishes shoes and boots.

boot tree, device for insertion into a boot or shoe to stretch it or keep it in shape.

boo·ty (bōō′tē) *pl.,* **-ties.** *n.* **1.** goods taken from an enemy in combat; spoils of war. **2.** goods seized by violence and robbery; plunder. **3.** any rich prize or gain. [Old French *butin,* from Middle Low German *būte* share, distribution; influenced by BOOT².]

booze (bōōz) *Informal. n.* **1.** alcoholic drink, esp. hard liquor.

2. drinking spree. —*v.i.,* **boozed, booz·ing.** to drink excessively. [Form of archaic *bouse* to booze, from Middle Dutch *būzen.*] —**booz′er,** *n.*

bop¹ (bop) **bopped, bop·ping.** *Slang. v.t.* to hit or punch. —*n.* blow or punch. [Imitative.]

bop² (bop) *n.* bebop.

bor., borough.

bo·rac·ic (bə ras′ik) *adj.* boric.

bor·age (bôr′ij) *n.* **1.** young leaves and flower tips of a plant, *Borago officinalis,* used esp. in salads or as a flavoring agent. **2.** the plant itself, native to Europe and North Africa, having hairy oblong or oval-shaped leaves and blue or purple flowers. [Old French *borrace* the plant, from Medieval Latin *borrago,* possibly from Late Latin *burra* rough hair (with reference to the plant's hairy leaves).]

bo·rate (bôr′āt) *n.* salt or ester of boric acid; any compound containing BO_3.

bo·rat·ed (bôr′ā′tid) *adj.* mixed or treated with borax or boric acid.

Borage

bo·rax (bôr′aks) *n.* compound of sodium, boron, and oxygen in the form of white or colorless translucent crystals, used esp. in soaps and cleansing powders. Formula: $Na_2B_4O_7 \cdot 10H_2O$ [Old French *boras,* from Arabic *būraq,* from Persian *būrah.*]

Bor·deaux (bôr dō′) *n.* **1.** port city in southwestern France. Pop. (1968). 266,662. **2.** any of several red or white wines originally produced in the region around Bordeaux.

Bordeaux mixture, light-blue liquid mixture of copper sulfate, slaked lime, and water, sprayed on trees and plants as a bactericide and fungicide.

bor·der (bôr′dər) *n.* **1.** boundary line of a territory, country, or state: *You must go through customs in order to pass across the border.* **2.** strip along an edge, esp. one that is ornamental: *a blue border on a dress, a border of tulips in a garden.* **3.** edge or the part near it; brink. —*v.t.* **1.** to lie on or form the edge of; bound: *The design bordered the page.* **2.** to put a border or edging on. —*v.i.* **to border on** (or **upon**). **a.** to lie on the border; be next to or adjoining: *His land borders on mine.* **b.** to approach closely; verge on: *Those ideas border on heresy.* [Old French *bordeüre* an edge, from *border* to edge, from *bord* an edge; of Germanic origin.] —**Syn.** *n.* **1.** see **boundary.** **2.** see **edge.**

bor·der·land (bôr′dər land′) *n.* **1.** land lying near or at a border. **2.** vague situation or region; borderline.

bor·der·line (bôr′dər līn′) *n.* **1.** dividing line; boundary. **2.** unclear situation or position: *the borderline between passing and failing.* —*adj.* uncertain; indefinite: *a borderline case.*

Border States, the five slave states that bordered on the North at the time of the Civil War, four of which (Delaware, Maryland, Kentucky, and Missouri) remained in the Union; the fifth (Virginia) seceded, but part of it remained in the Union and became West Virginia.

bore¹ (bôr) **bored, bor·ing.** *v.t.* **1.** to make (a hole or passage), as by drilling, digging, or pushing: *They bored a tunnel through the mountain.* **2.** to make a hole in or through, as with a rotating tool: *to bore a plank.* —*v.i.* **1.** to make a hole or passage: *The animal bored into the ground.* **2.** to be drilled or drillable by an instrument: *The wood bored easily.* —*n.* **1.** hole made by or as if by boring. **2.** long, hollow interior, as of a tube or gun barrel. **3.** diameter of a hole or the inside of a tube, as of a gun barrel. [Old English *borian* to make a hole.]

bore² (bôr) **bored, bor·ing.** *v.t.* to weary by being dull or monotonous. —*n.* one who or that which bores. [Of uncertain origin.]

bore³ (bôr) past tense of **bear¹.**

bore⁴ (bôr) *n.* tidal bore. [Possibly from Old Norse *bāra* wave.]

bo·re·al (bôr′ē əl) *adj.* of or characteristic of the North or the north wind.

Bo·re·as (bôr′ē əs) *n.* **1.** Greek god of the north wind. **2.** north wind.

bore·dom (bôr′dəm) *n.* state of being bored; tedium.

bor·er (bôr′ər) *n.* **1.** tool for boring holes. **2.** any of various insects or their wormlike larvae that do harm by boring into wood, fruit, or other parts of plants.

Bor·gia (bôr′jə) **1. Ce·sa·re** (chā′zä rā). c.1475–1507, Italian soldier and politician, notorious as a poisoner. **2. Lu·cre·zia** (lōō krē′zhə). 1480–1519, his sister; erroneously reputed to have been a poisoner.

bo·ric (bôr′ik) *adj.* of or containing boron. Also, **bo·rac·ic.**

boric acid, compound of hydrogen, boron, and oxygen in the form of odorless white granules or colorless crystals, used as an external antiseptic, esp. for the eyes, and in various manufacturing processes. Formula: H_3BO_3

born (bôrn) *adj.* **1.** brought into life or existence. **2.** by birth or nature; innate: *a born politician.* [Past participle of BEAR¹.]

borne (bôrn) past participle of **bear¹.**

Bor·ne·o (bôr′nē ō′) n. large island in the Malay Archipelago, made up of Sarawak, Sabah, and Brunei, which belong to Malaysia, and Kalimantan, which belongs to Indonesia. Area, 290,000 sq. mi.

Bo·ro·din, Alexander Por·fir·e·vich (bôr′ə dēn′; por fir′ə-vich′) 1833–87, Russian composer.

bo·ron (bôr′on) n. semimetallic element in the form of yellowish-brown crystals or dark brown powder, produced from borax and similar minerals. Symbol: **B** See **element** for table. [BOR(AX) + (CARB)ON.]

bor·ough (bur′ō) n. 1. in some states of the United States, an incorporated munic.,pality smaller than a city. 2. one of the administrative divisions of a city, as in New York City or London. 3. British. **a.** major city. It is one of the two principal units of local government. **b.** former political subdivision having the right to send representatives to Parliament and a royal charter guaranteeing self-government. 4. political subdivision, usually smaller than a county, as in Australia and New Zealand. [Old English burg, burh fortress, town.]

bor·row (bôr′ō, bor′ō) v.t. 1. to take or obtain (something) with the understanding that it or its equivalent will be returned: to borrow a book from the library. I borrowed ten dollars and repaid by check. 2. to adopt (from another source) and use as one's own: Many words in English have been borrowed from French. 3. **to borrow trouble.** to create unnecessary difficulties for oneself. 4. Mathematics. in subtraction, to take (a unit) from a position in the minuend and add it (as 10 in the decimal system) to the position of the next lower denomination. —v.i. to engage in borrowing, esp. money. [Old English borgian, from borg pledge.] —**bor′row·er,** n.

Bors (bôrs) n. in Arthurian legend, one of King Arthur's knights and the nephew of Lancelot.

borscht (bôrsht) also, **borsch** (bôrsh). n. beet soup of Russian origin, eaten hot or cold. [Russian borshch.]

bor·zoi (bôr′zoi) n. hound of a breed originally developed in Russia for hunting wolves, noted for its swiftness, having a narrow head, a long, curving tail, and a coat of long, silky hair. Height: 30 inches at the shoulder. Also, **Russian wolfhound.** [Russian borzoi swift.]

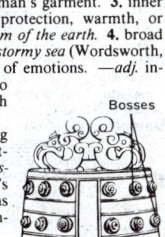

Borzoi

bos·cage (bos′kij) n. shrubbery or trees; thicket; grove. [Old French boscage, from bosc forest; of Germanic origin.]

Bosch, Hie·ro·ny·mus (bosh, bôsh; hē ron′ə məs) c.1450–1516, Flemish painter.

bosh (bosh) n., interj. Informal. foolish talk; nonsense. [Turkish bosh worthless.]

bosk (bosk) n. small wooded area; thicket; grove. [Variant of busk, dialectal form of BUSH.]

bosk·y (bos′kē) adj. 1. wooded; bushy. 2. shaded by trees or shrubs.

bo's'n (bō′sən) boatswain.

Bos·ni·a (boz′nē ə) n. historic region in western Yugoslavia. —Bos′ni·an, adj., n.

Bosnia and Her·ze·go·vi·na (hur′tsə gə vē′nə) also, **Bos·ni·a-Her·ze·go·vi·na.** political subdivision of Yugoslavia, in the west-central part of the country. Pop. (1968 est.), 3,595,000.

bos·om (booz′əm, boo′zəm) n. 1. upper front part of the human chest, esp. of a woman. 2. upper front part of a woman's garment. 3. inner or enclosed part, thought of as providing protection, warmth, or privacy: bosom of the family, lying in the bosom of the earth. 4. broad surface or expanse: tossed on the bosom of the stormy sea (Wordsworth, 1837). 5. human breast regarded as the seat of emotions. —adj. intimate; dear: a bosom friend. —v.t. Archaic. to take to or enclose in the bosom. [Old English bōsm breast.]

Bos·po·rus (bos′pər əs) n. strait connecting the Black Sea and the Sea of Marmara, separating European and Asiatic Turkey. [Latin Bosporus, going back to Greek boos poros cow's ford; according to Greek mythology, this was the strait crossed by the heroine Io while wandering in the form of a heifer.]

boss¹ (bôs) n. Informal. 1. one who directs or supervises others, esp. one who exercises authority over workers, as an employer or foreman. 2. party politician who controls a political organization, as in a certain locality. —v.t. 1. to order or command, esp. in a domineering fashion. 2. to direct or supervise. —adj. master; chief. [Dutch baas master.]

boss² (bôs) n. 1. raised ornamental portion

on a flat surface, as on silver, ivory, or leather. 2. protuberance or projection, as of rock, machine parts, or plants. —v.t. to ornament with bosses; emboss. [Old French boce protuberance; of uncertain origin.]

bos·sa no·va (bô′sə nō′və, bos′ə) 1. music of Brazilian origin, influenced by jazz and rhythmically similar to the samba. 2. slow, smooth dance performed to this music. [Portuguese bossa nova literally, new bump, from bossa bump (from Old French boce. See BOSS²) + nova new (going back to Latin novus.]

boss·y¹ (bô′sē) boss·i·er, boss·i·est. adj. inclined to order others; domineering. [BOSS¹ + -Y¹.]

boss·y² (bô′sē) adj. having or decorated with bosses. [BOSS² + -Y¹.]

Bos·ton (bôs′tən) n. capital of Massachusetts, in the eastern part of the state. Pop., metropolitan area (1970), 2,753,700.

Boston bull, Boston terrier.

Boston cream pie, rich cake with a creamy filling between its two layers, often topped with chocolate icing or confectioner's sugar.

Boston Tea Party, raid on British ships in Boston Harbor on December 16, 1773, in which American colonists, disguised as Indians, threw chests of tea overboard as a protest against British taxation on tea.

Boston terrier, any of a breed of short-haired dogs having a smooth black or brindled coat with white markings. Height: 16 inches at the shoulder.

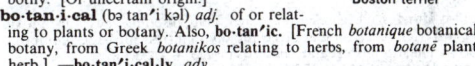

bo·sun (bō′sən) boatswain.

Bos·well, James (boz′wel′, ˌ_wəl) 1740–95, English diarist and biographer of Samuel Johnson, born in Scotland.

bot (bot) also, **bott.** n. parasitic larva of a botfly. [Of uncertain origin.]

Boston terrier

bo·tan·i·cal (bə tan′i kəl) adj. of or relating to plants or botany. Also, **bo·tan′ic.** [French botanique botanical, botany, from Greek botanikos relating to herbs, from botanē plant, herb.] —**bo·tan′i·cal·ly,** adv.

botanical garden, grounds containing gardens, greenhouses, and sometimes research facilities, for the study and display of plants.

bot·a·nize (bot′ən īz′) -nized, -niz·ing. v.i. Archaic. to study plant life or collect it for study.

bot·a·ny (bot′ən ē) pl., -nies. n. science or study of plants, including the origin, development, structure, function, and distribution of all forms of plant life. [French botanique. See BOTANICAL.] —**bot′an·ist,** n.

botch (boch) v.t. to do or make in a poor or inept way; bungle. —n. poor piece of work or inept performance. [Middle English bocchen to patch, mend; of uncertain origin.]

botch·y (boch′ē) botch·i·er, botch·i·est. adj. poorly made or performed; botched.

bot·fly (bot′flī′) pl., -flies. n. any of various flies whose larvae are parasites of certain mammals, esp. horses, cattle, and sheep.

both (bōth) adj., pron. the two; the one and the other: both dogs, both your houses. Both of them went. I followed both. —conj. alike; equally; as well (with and): both Molly and me. [Old Norse bāthir the two.]

both·er (both′ər) v.t. 1. to give trouble to; pester; annoy: The mischievous boy kept bothering his sister. 2. to make uneasy or anxious: Meeting new people bothers her. —v.i. to take trouble; concern oneself: Don't bother about it. —n. 1. one who or that which bothers. 2. state of worry or annoyance: She always gets into a bother. [Probably form of POTHER.]

both·er·a·tion (both′ə rā′shən) n., interj. Informal. bother.

both·er·some (both′ər səm) adj. troublesome; annoying.

Both·ni·a, Gulf of (both′nē ə) northern arm of the Baltic Sea, between Sweden and Finland.

Bot·swa·na (bot swä′nə) n. country in south-central Africa, formerly the British protectorate Bechuanaland. Capital, Gaborone. Area, 238,-605 sq. mi. Pop. (1969 est.), 629,000.

bott (bot) botch.

Bot·ti·cel·li, San·dro (bot′i chel′ē; san′drō) c.1444–1510, Florentine painter.

bot·tle (bot′əl) n. 1. container usually made of glass, and typically having a narrow neck that can be stopped, used esp. for holding liquids. 2. amount held by a bottle: We drank a whole bottle of soda. 3. milk in a bottle for a baby. 4. **to hit the bottle.** to drink an intoxicating beverage. —v.t. -tled, -tling. 1. to put into a bottle or bottles. 2. **to bottle up.** to hold in or back; restrain. [Old French boteille container having a narrow neck, from Medieval Latin butticula, diminutive of Late Latin buttis cask, from Greek pytinē flask.] —**bot′tler,** n.

bottle green, dark green.

bot·tle·neck (bot′əl nek′) n. 1. narrow opening or passageway. 2. situation or thing that hinders progress: The traffic was slowed by a

Bors (bôrs) ...

Bosses

Bosses on a Chinese bell

---

at; āpe; cär; end; mē; it; īce; hot; ōld; fôrk; wood; fo͞ol; oil; out; up; ūse; turn; sing; thin; this; zh in trˉsure; ə in ago, taken, pencil, lemon, circus.

113

bottleneck in the road. The astronaut's illness created a temporary bottleneck in the space program.

bot·tle·nose (bot′əl nōz′) *n.* any dolphin of the genus *Tursiops*, esp. *T. truncatus*, of the North Atlantic and Mediterranean, which may be trained to perform tricks. Length: 10–12 feet.

bot·tom (bot′əm) *n.* **1.** lowest part of anything: *She put the clothes at the bottom of the pile. Footnotes are usually found at the bottom of a page.* **2.** part on which an object rests or stands; underside: *the bottom of a plate.* **3.** ground beneath a body of water: *The boat capsized and sank to the bottom.* **4.** cause or source; basis; origin: *The detective tried to get to the bottom of the mystery.* **5.** *Informal.* buttocks. **6.** second half of a baseball inning: *He hit a home run in the bottom of the eighth.* **7.** seat, as of a chair. **8.a.** the part of a boat's or ship's hull which is below the waterline. **b.** *Archaic.* ship, esp. a cargo ship. **9.** low-lying land adjacent to a river, usually rich in alluvial deposits. Also, **bottoms, bottom land. 10. bottoms.** pants of a pair of pajamas. **11. at bottom.** in reality; fundamentally; essentially. **12. bottoms up.** *Informal.* drink up. —*adj.* on or at the bottom; lowest; undermost: *a bottom stair.* —*v.i.* **1.** to reach, rest on, or touch the bottom: *The submarine bottomed to observe the ocean floor.* **2.** *Archaic.* to be founded or based; rest. —*v.t.* **1.** to bring (a submarine) to the ocean bottom. **2.** *Archaic.* to found or base (with *on* or *upon*): *He bottomed his decision on legal precedent.* [Old English *botm* lowest part.] —**bot′tom·most′,** *adj.*

bottom dollar *Slang.* last dollar.

bottom land, bottom *(def. 9).*

bot·tom·less (bot′əm lis) *adj.* **1.** having an immeasurable depth: *a bottomless well.* **2.** having no bottom. **3. the bottomless pit.** hell.

bot·tom·ry (bot′əm rē) *pl.,* **-ries.** *n.* contract by which a shipowner borrows money for equipment, repairs, or a voyage, pledging his ship as security for the loan. If the ship is lost, the lender loses his claim. Dutch *bodemerij*, from *bodem* ship; English spelling influenced by BOTTOM.]

bot·u·lism (boch′ə liz′əm) *n.* often fatal poisoning caused by a toxin from certain bacteria that breed rapidly in airless media, esp. improperly canned foods. [Latin *botulus* sausage + -ISM.]

bou·clé (bōō klā′) *n.* **1.** woven or knitted fabric with an irregular surface of small twists and loops. **2.** yarn used in making this fabric. [French *bouclé* buckled, curled, going back to Old French *boucle* curl, metal ring. See BUCKLE.]

bou·doir (bōōd′wär, -wôr) *n.* lady's bedroom, dressing room, or private sitting room. [French *boudoir* lady's private room; literally, place for sulking, from *bouder* to sulk; imitative; with reference to the earlier practice of a lady's withdrawing to her *boudoir* when angry.]

bouf·fant (bōō fänt′) *adj.* puffed out: *a bouffant hairdo, a bouffant skirt.* [French *bouffant*, from *bouffer* to swell; imitative.]

bough (bou) *n.* branch of a tree, esp. a main one. [Old English *bōg* shoulder, arm.] —**Syn.** see **branch.**

bought (bôt) past tense and past participle of **buy.**

bouil·la·baisse (bōōl′yə bās′) *n.* chowder made of fish and shellfish, vegetables, wine, and seasonings such as garlic and saffron. [French *bouillabaisse*, from Provençal *bouiabaisso* literally, boil and settle, going back to Latin *bullire* to bubble + *ad* to + Late Latin *bassus* low.]

bouil·lon (bool′yon, -yän) *n.* clear, thin soup usually made from chicken or beef stock and having a strong flavor. [French *bouillon* broth, from *bouillir* to boil, from Latin *bullire* to bubble.]

bouillon cube, cube of dehydrated concentrate of bouillon.

boul·der (bōl′dər) *n.* large, rounded rock, esp. one lying on the surface of the ground. [Of Scandinavian origin.]

Boul·der (bōl′dər) *n.* city in north-central Colorado, near Denver. Pop. (1970), 66,870.

Boulder Dam, see Hoover Dam.

boul·e·vard (bool′ə värd′, bōō′lə-) *n.* broad city street, often having trees or other greenery. [French *boulevard* originally, rampart; of Germanic origin.]

boulle (bool) buhl.

bounce (bouns) *bounced, bounc·ing. v.i.* **1.** to spring back from a surface, as a ball; rebound: *The rubber doll bounced off the chair.* **2.** to move or walk in a springy or energetic manner: *The little girl bounced down the street.* **3.** *Informal.* (of a check) to be rejected for payment by a bank because of insufficient funds in the drawer's account. **4. to bounce back.** to recover, as from a physical or emotional blow: *After losing the game, they bounced back to win the tournament.* —*v.t.* **1.** to cause (something) to spring back or rebound: *She bounced the ball. He bounced the child on his knee.* **2.** *Slang.* to force (someone) to leave: *He was bounced from the restaurant.* **3.** *Slang.* to dismiss from a job or position. —*n.* **1.** a springing back; rebound: *She hit the ball on the second bounce.* **2.** capacity to spring back or rebound: *The ball has lost its bounce.* **3.** *British. Informal.* **4.** *British. Informal.* bluster; impudence. **5. to give (or get) the bounce.** *Slang.* to dismiss or be dismissed. [Middle English *bunsen* to beat; probably imitative.]

bounc·er (boun′sər) *n.* **1.** *Informal.* man employed, as by a night club

or bar, to make disorderly persons leave. **2.** that which bounces, esp. in a particular way: *The ball was a good bouncer.*

bounc·ing (boun′sing) *adj.* big or strong; healthy; strapping: *a bouncing baby boy.*

bouncing Bet, soapwort, *Saponaria officinalis,* having thick clusters of very light pink or sometimes white flowers. It grows wild in the United States. Also, **bouncing Bess.**

bounc·y (boun′sē) *bounc·i·er, bounc·i·est. adj.* **1.** tending to bounce; bouncing readily: *bouncy cushions, a bouncy ball.* **2.** lively; vivacious; exuberant: *a bouncy personality.* —**bounc′i·ly,** *adv.* —**bounc′i·ness,** *n.*

bound[1] (bound) *v.* past tense and past participle of **bind.** —*adj.* **1.** made fast by a bond; tied. **2.** certain; sure: *He's bound to fail if he doesn't study.* **3.** under legal or moral obligation; obliged. **4.** having a binding or cover, as a book. **5.** *Informal.* determined; resolved: *She is bound to have her way.* **6. bound up in (or with).** inseparably connected with; deeply devoted to. [Short for BOUNDEN.]

bound[2] (bound) *v.i.* **1.** to move by a series of leaps; spring; jump: *The children went bounding over the hill. He bounded onto the stage.* **2.** to spring back from a surface, as a ball; rebound: *The arrow bounded off the target.* —*n.* long or high leap: *With one great bound the dog cleared the stream.* [Old French *bondir* to rebound; originally, resound, going back to Latin *bombus* deep sound. See BOMB.]

bound[3] (bound) *n.* **1.** *also,* **bounds. a.** limiting line; boundary: *His love of money knows no bounds.* **b.** area near or within a boundary: *the outermost bounds of the realm.* **2. out of bounds.** beyond specified limits; not allowed; prohibited. —*v.t.* **1.** to form the boundary of. **2.** to have a boundary with; lie adjacent to. [Old French *bonde, bodne* boundary, from Late Latin *bodina* limit; of uncertain origin.]

bound[4] (bound) *adj.* going or intending to go; on the way (often with *for*): *I am bound for California. He's homeward bound.* [Old Norse *būinn* ready, past participle of *būa* to get ready.]

bound·a·ry (boun′dər ē, -drē) *pl.,* **-ries.** *n.* something that limits or marks a separation; border: *the boundary of a ball field, the boundary between illusion and reality.*

Syn. Boundary, border, frontier indicate a line of demarcation between two states or countries. **Boundary** is the most precise in meaning, suggesting the actual line as marked on a map: *He stood at the boundary between Texas and Oklahoma, with one foot on either side.* **Border** is often used of a territorial feature, such as a river or mountain range, between two countries: *The Rio Grande River forms the border between Texas and Mexico.* **Frontier** refers to the part of a nation's territory that fronts on its boundary with another country: *The population along the Texas frontier with Mexico is predominantly Latin American.*

bound·en (boun′dən) *adj.* obligatory or binding. ▲ used in the phrase *bounden duty.* [Past participle of BIND.]

bound·er (boun′dər) *n. British. Informal.* cad; rogue.

bound·less (bound′lis) *adj.* having no bounds or limits; vast: *His energy seems boundless.* —**bound′less·ly,** *adv.* —**bound′less·ness,** *n.*

boun·te·ous (boun′tē əs) *adj.* **1.** plentiful; abundant: *a bounteous crop.* **2.** giving freely; generous; beneficent: *a bounteous gentleman.* [Earlier *bountevous,* from Old French *bontif, bontive* kind, from *bonte.* See BOUNTY.] —**boun′te·ous·ly,** *adv.* —**boun′te·ous·ness,** *n.*

boun·ti·ful (boun′ti fəl) *adj.* **1.** plentiful; abundant: *a bountiful supply.* **2.** overflowing with generosity: *a bountiful nature.* —**boun′ti·ful·ly,** *adv.* —**boun′ti·ful·ness,** *n.*

boun·ty (boun′tē) *pl.,* **-ties.** *n.* **1.** reward or premium, esp. one given by a government for the killing of certain animals or the raising of certain crops. **2.** generosity in giving: *Many were dependent on his bounty.* **3.** *Archaic.* gift generously given: *nature's bounties.* [Old French *bonte* goodness, from Latin *bonitas.*]

bou·quet (bō kā′, bōō-) *n.* **1.** bunch of flowers, esp. one arranged and fastened together. **2.** fragrance or aroma, esp. of a wine. [French *bouquet* bunch, as of flowers; originally, thicket, diminutive of Old French *bosc* forest; of Germanic origin.]

bour·bon (bur′bən) *also,* **Bour·bon.** *n.* whiskey distilled from a mash of malt, rye, and not less than 51 percent corn. [From *Bourbon* County, Kentucky, where it was first made.]

Bour·bon (bōōr′bən, boor bōn′) *n.* **1.a.** royal family of France, 1589–1792, 1814–48, noted for its conservative policies. **b.** any of the branches of this family in Spain, Naples, or Sicily. **2.** an extreme conservative, esp. a U.S. Southern Democrat of such views. [From *Bourbon* a barony and castle in central France, said to be from *Borvo* a god of ancient Gaul.] —**Bour′bon·ism,** *n.*

bour·geois (boor zhwä′, boor′zhwä) *adj.* **1.** of, characteristic of, or belonging to the middle class or the bourgeoisie. **2.** conforming to narrow ideas of respectability and success; materialistic; conventional. —*n. pl.,* **-geois.** member of the propertied or middle class. [French *bourgeois,* from Old French *burgeis* citizen. See BURGESS.]

bour·geoi·sie (boor′zhwä zē′) *n.* **1.** the middle class. **2.** in Marxist theory, the capitalist class. [French *bourgeoisie,* from *bourgeois* middle-class person. See BOURGEOIS.]

at; āpe; cär; end; mē; it; īce; hot; ōld; fôrk; wood; fōol; oil; out; up; ūse; turn; sing; thin; this; zh in treasure; ə in ago, taken, pencil, lemon, circus.

Bour·gogne (boor gōn′yə) *n. French.* Burgundy *(def. 1).*

bourn¹ (bôrn) *also,* **bourne, burn.** *n. British.* small stream; brook. [Old English *burna.*]

bourn² (bôrn, boorn) *also,* **bourne.** *n. Archaic.* **1.** boundary; limit. **2.** goal; destination. [French *borne* limit, boundary, from Old French *bodne.* See BOUND³.]

Bourse (boors) *n.* **1.** stock exchange in Paris. **2.** any of various stock exchanges in principal cities of continental Europe. [French *bourse* stock exchange, purse, from Late Latin *bursa* purse, from Greek *bursā* skin. Doublet of BURSA and PURSE.]

bout (bout) *n.* **1.** trial of strength or skill; contest; match: *a boxing bout, a fencing bout.* **2.** spell or period: *a bout of influenza, a drinking bout.* [Form of obsolete *bought* turn, bend, possibly from Low German *bucht.*]

bou·tique (boo tēk′) *n.* small specialty shop or department, esp. one selling women's apparel. [French *boutique,* going back to Greek *apothēkē* storehouse.]

bou·ton·niere (boo′tən yâr′) *n.* flower worn in the buttonhole of a lapel. [French *boutonnière* buttonhole, from *bouton* bud, button, from Old French *bouter* to bud; of Germanic origin.]

bo·vine (bō′vīn, -vin, -vēn) *adj.* **1.** of, relating to, or characteristic of a cow or cattle. **2.** dull; sluggish; cowlike: *bovine mentality.* —*n.* any of various mammals that constitute the family Bovidae, including domestic cattle, sheep, goats, and antelopes. [Late Latin *bovīnus* of oxen or cows, from Latin *bōs* ox, cow.]

bow¹ (bou) *v.i.* **1.** to incline the head or upper part of the body forward, as in respect, submission, or greeting. **2.** to submit; yield; to bow to authority. **3.** to bend, as under a weight: *The trees bowed in the wind.* **4. to bow and scrape.** to be too polite or slavish. **5. to bow out.** to withdraw. —*v.t.* **1.** to cause to stoop or bend: *Age had bowed his once straight back.* **2.** to bend forward, as in respect, submission, or greeting: *to bow one's head.* **3.** to express by bowing: *to bow one's agreement.* **4.** to usher in or out with a bow or bows: *He bowed us out of the audience hall.* —*n.* forward inclination of the head or upper part of the body, as in respect, submission, or greeting. [Old English *būgan* to bend.] —**Syn.** *v.t.* **1.** see **bend.**

bow² (bō) *n.* **1.** implement for shooting arrows, consisting of a strip of wood or other stiffly flexible material. It is bent and held by a taut string connecting the two ends. **2.** knot with two or more loops extending from it. **3.** device for playing musical instruments of the violin family, consisting of a slender rod, having fibers, usually of horsehair, stretched tautly from one end to the other. See **violin** for illustration. **4.** curve; bend. **5.** something curved, esp. a rainbow. **6.a.** rim of a pair of eyeglasses. **b.** curved part of a pair of eyeglasses passing over the ear. —*v.t., v.i.* **1.** to curve. **2.** to play by means of a bow. [Old English *boga* this weapon, arch.]

Bow²

bow³ (bou) *n.* **1.** forward end of a boat, ship, or airship. Opposed to **stern.** See **boat** for illustration. **2.** rower nearest the bow of a boat. [Of Germanic or Scandinavian origin.]

bowd·ler·ize (boud′lə rīz′) *-ized, -iz·ing. v.t.* to edit a book by removing words and passages considered objectionable. [From Dr. Thomas *Bowdler,* who in 1818 published an expurgated edition of Shakespeare's plays suitable, from his point of view, "to be read aloud in the family."]

bow·el (bou′əl) *n.* **1.** intestine. **2.** *usually,* **bowels.** intestines; entrails. **3. bowels.** the inner part or deep recesses of something: *The well reached to the very bowels of the earth.* [Old French *boel* intestine, from Latin *botellus* sausage, intestine, diminutive of *botulus* sausage.]

bow·er¹ (bou′ər) *n.* **1.** shelter of leafy branches, often entwined; arbor. **2.** *Archaic.* rustic dwelling; cottage. **3.** *Archaic.* chamber; boudoir. [Old English *būr* dwelling, chamber.]

bow·er² (bou′ər) *n.* anchor carried at the bow of a ship. [BOW³ + -ER².]

bow·er·y (bou′ər ē) *adj.* like a bower; leafy; shady.

Bow·er·y (bou′ər ē, bour′ē) *n.* New York City street and surrounding area known as a haven for derelicts. [Dutch *bouwerij* farm; because it ran through the *bouwerij,* or farm, of Peter Stuyvesant.]

bow·fin (bō′fin′) *n.* mottled, green ganoid fish, *Amia calva,* found in fresh waters of the eastern United States. It is the only surviving species of the order Amiiformes. Length: 2½–3 feet.

Bowfin

bow·ie knife (bō′ē, boo′ē) single-edged knife, ten to fifteen inches long, with a hilt and crosspiece. The front part of the blunt edge curves concavely to meet the cutting edge in a sharp point. [From Colonel James *Bowie,* 1796–1836, U.S. frontiersman, who used this kind of knife.]

Bowie knife

bow·ing¹ (bou′ing) *n.* act of one who bows, as in respect or greeting. [BOW¹ + -ING.]

bow·ing² (bō′ing) *n.* act, art, or technique of using a bow in playing a stringed instrument, as a violin. [BOW² + -ING.]

bow·knot (bō′not′) *n.* slipknot having one or two loops, which can be untied by pulling the ends.

bowl¹ (bōl) *n.* **1.** hollow, rounded, concave vessel used as a container. **2.** amount a bowl can hold; contents of a bowl: *a bowl of soup.* **3.** a part shaped like a bowl: *the bowl of a pipe.* **4.** large drinking cup; goblet. **5.** convivial drinking. **6.** structure, esp. a stadium or theater, having the shape of a bowl. **7.** geological formation having a bowl-like shape. [Old English *bolla* hollow, rounded container.]

bowl² (bōl) *n.* **1.** ball with a bias used in the game of bowls. **2.** act of or turn at bowling. —*v.i.* **1.** to participate in a game of bowls, tenpins, duckpins, candlepins, or ninepins: *They bowled every Sunday.* **2.** to roll a ball or bowl: *Bowl fast, people are waiting.* —*v.t.* **1.** to roll (a ball or bowl). **2.** (in bowling) to make a score of: *She bowled 175.* **3.** to move with a rapid and easy motion, esp. on wheels. **4. to bowl over. a.** to knock over: *He was bowled over by the surging waves.* **b.** *Informal.* to confound or confuse; overwhelm: *She was bowled over by the bad news.* [French *boule* ball, from Latin *bulla* bubble, knob.] —**bowl′er,** *n.*

bow·leg (bō′leg′) *n.* **1.** leg curving outward. **2.** outward curvature of the legs.

bow·leg·ged (bō′leg′id, -legd′) *adj.* with legs curved outward; having bowlegs.

bowl·er (bō′lər) *n. British.* derby hat. [From John *Bowler,* nineteenth-century London maker of hats.]

bow·line (bō′lin, -līn′) *n.* **1.** knot used in making a secure loop. Also, **bowline knot.** *Nautical.* rope leading forward from the windward edge of a square sail, used to hold the sail taut when sailing into the wind.

bowl·ing (bō′ling) *n.* **1.** any of several games, esp. tenpins, duckpins, and candlepins, in which a number of wooden pins are set up at one end of a bowling alley and a player standing at the opposite end rolls a ball at the pins in an attempt to knock them all down. **2.** game of bowls. **3.** act of playing one of these games.

bowling alley 1. long, narrow course along which a ball or bowl is rolled in bowling or bowls. **2.** building or establishment containing one or more of these alleys.

bowling green, smooth, level lawn used for or as for the game of bowls.

bowls (bōlz) *n.* game played by making a ball or balls having a bias roll toward a ball that has come to rest at some distance from the player. The aim is to roll the biased ball as close as possible to the resting one. [Plural of BOWL².]

bow·man (bō′mən) *pl.,* **-men.** *n.* archer.

bow·shot (bō′shot′) *n.* distance covered by an arrow when shot from a bow.

bow·sprit (bou′sprit′, bō′-) *n.* large spar projecting forward from the bow of a ship. [Probably from Middle Low German *bōchsprēt,* from *bōch* bow¹ + *sprēt* pole.]

bow·string (bō′string′) *n.* strong cord connecting the two ends of a bow. —*v.t.* **-stringed** or **-strung, -string·ing.** to kill or execute by strangling.

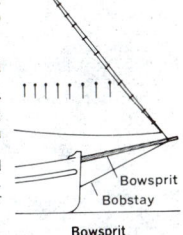

Bowsprit
Bobstay
Bowsprit

bow tie (bō) necktie tied in a bowknot.

bow window (bō) curved bay window.

box¹ (boks) *n.* **1.** any of several types of rigid containers of varying sizes, shapes, and materials, usually with a top or lid. **2.a.** such a container with its contents: *to buy a box of crayons.* **b.** quantity contained in a box: *He ate a box of crackers.* **3.** anything resembling a box in shape, function, or use, as a protective covering or enclosure for a mechanical part or a driver's seat on a carriage. **4.** compartment or space partitioned off to accommodate a limited number of people: *a jury box, a press box.* **5.** small booth for sheltering one or two persons: *a sentry box.* **6.** *Baseball.* any of several specified areas on the field for batter, pitcher, or coaches. **7.** stall for a horse. **8.** space on a printed page set off by borders, lines, or white spaces. **9.** small square or rectangular compartment: *a post-office box.* **10.** difficulty; predicament.

at; āpe; cär; end; mē; it; īce; hot; ōld; fôrk; wood; fōol; oil; out; up; ūse; turn; sing; thin; this; zh in treasure; ə in ago, taken, pencil, lemon, circus.

115

11. *British.* gift in a box, esp. a Christmas gift. —*v.t.* **1.** to place or pack in a box. **2. to box in. a.** in racing, to block (another racer) to prevent his getting ahead. **b.** to box up. **3. to box up.** to surround or confine in or as in a box. **4. to box the compass. a.** to name the thirty-two points of the compass in order. **b.** to make a complete turn. [Old English *box* container made of boxwood, from Latin *buxum* boxwood, something made of boxwood, from Latin *buxus* box tree. See BOX¹.]

box² (boks) *n.* blow struck with the open hand or the fist, esp. on the ear or side of the head. —*v.t.* **1.** to strike a blow with the hand or fist. **2.** to fight (someone) with the fists: *He boxed his opponent with great skill.* —*v.i.* to fight with the fists. [Possibly imitative.]

box³ (boks) *n.* **1.** any of various ornamental evergreen trees or shrubs, genus *Buxus*, most varieties of which have small, oval, leathery leaves and are planted as hedges. **2.** hard wood of this plant. Also, **box′wood′**. [Old English *box* box tree, from Latin *buxus*, from Greek *pyxos*.]

box·car (boks′kär′) *n.* roofed railroad freight car, completely closed, as by a sliding door in a side.

Box elder

box elder, rapidly growing North American tree, *Acer negundo*, of the maple family, having low, spreading branches and compound leaves.

box·er (bok′sər) *n.* **1.** one who engages in boxing; prize fighter; pugilist. **2.** any of a breed of short-haired dogs having a smooth, tan or brindled coat, often with white markings, and a square, black muzzle. Height: 22–24 inches at the shoulder.

Box·er (bok′sər) *n.* member of the Chinese secret society that fomented and led the Boxer Rebellion. [From a version of the society's name, *I Ho Ch'üan* literally, righteous harmonious fists, which Westerners changed to Boxers.]

Boxer

Boxer Rebellion, unsuccessful uprising in China in 1899–1900, aimed at expelling foreigners and foreign influence.

box·ing¹ (bok′sing) *n.* **1.** sport in which two contestants fight each other with their fists, esp. when wearing padded gloves. **2.** act of fighting with the fists: *a bout of boxing.* [BOX² + -ING¹.]

box·ing² (bok′sing) *n.* **1.** material used for making boxes. **2.** boxlike enclosure or casing, as for shutters of a window. **3.** act of placing within or providing with a box. [BOX¹ + -ING¹.]

Boxing Day, in England, a legal holiday observed on the first weekday after Christmas. [From the British practice of giving *boxes* containing presents to service workers on this day.]

boxing glove, padded mitten worn for boxing.

box kite, tail-less kite consisting of two or more open-ended paper boxes over a light framework.

box office 1. booth or window, as in a theater, where admission tickets are sold. **2.** receipts of a theatrical performance or sports event.

Box kite

box pleat, double pleat with the undersides folded toward each other: *a skirt with box pleats.*

box score, condensed record of each player's performance in an athletic contest, esp. a baseball game, arranged in the form of a columnar table.

box seat, seat in a box at a theater, stadium, or similar place of public assembly.

box spring, rectangular frame containing rows of coiled springs, used as a resilient support for a mattress.

box·wood (boks′wood′) *n.* **1.** hard, close-grained wood of the box tree or shrub. **2.** the tree or shrub itself. [BOX¹ + WOOD.]

boy (boi) *n.* **1.a.** male child from birth to physical maturity. **b.** son. **c.** immature youth, esp. one lacking emotional maturity: *Jim doesn't understand—he's just a boy.* **2.** man; fellow: *Let's go, boys.* **3.** male domestic servant, esp. a native attendant in such countries as India and China. **4.** man considered to be of inferior rank. ▲ usually considered offensive. [Middle English *boi, boy* young male child; of uncertain origin.]

bo·yar (bō yär′, boi′ər) *n.* member of a privileged aristocratic class in czarist Russia. [Russian *boyarin* lord.]

boy·cott (boi′kot) *v.t.* **1.** to combine in refusing to patronize, associate with, participate in, or have any dealings with: *to boycott a store, to*

boycott an election. **2.** to refuse to buy, sell, or use (a product): *The association agreed to boycott all imported meats.* —*n.* act of boycotting. [From Captain Charles *Boycott*, 1832–97, agent for an absentee Irish landlord, who was ostracized and harassed by Irish farmers for his harsh actions against them.]

boy·friend (boi′frend′) *n. Informal.* male friend, esp. a sweetheart.

boy·hood (boi′hood′) *n.* **1.** time or state of being a boy: *Tom spent his boyhood in Virginia.* **2.** boys collectively.

boy·ish (boi′ish) *adj.* **1.** of or pertaining to boys or boyhood. **2.** boylike; puerile. —**boy′ish·ly,** *adv.* —**boy′ish·ness,** *n.*

Boyle, Robert (boil) 1627–91, English physicist and chemist.

Boy Scouts, worldwide organization for boys and young men designed to teach them patriotism, courage, self-reliance, and good citizenship.

boy·sen·ber·ry (boi′zən ber′ē) *pl.*, **-ries.** *n.* soft purple fruit of the widely cultivated hybrid plant, *Rubus ursinus*, variety loganobaccus. [From the early twentieth-century American horticulturist Rudolph *Boysen*, its developer.]

Bp., Bishop.

B.P.O.E., Benevolent and Protective Order of Elks, a fraternal organization.

Br, bromine.

Br. 1. Britain. **2.** British.

bra (brä) *n.* brassiere.

Bra·bant (brə bant′, brä′bənt) *n.* historic region in northwestern Europe, including parts of northern Belgium and the southern Netherlands. Area, 4265 sq. mi.

brace (brās) *n.* **1.** something that supports or holds in place. **2.** pair; couple: *a brace of pheasants, a brace of pistols.* **3.** cranklike device to hold and rotate a boring tool. **4.** double-curved line,{ }, used in writing or printing to connect two or more items, as lines, words, figures, or musical staves. **5.** *pl.* **braces.** metal wire or wires used to straighten irregularly aligned teeth. **6. braces.** *British.* suspenders. —*v.t.*, **braced, brac·ing. 1.** to make strong, firm, or steady, with or as with a brace; support. **2.** to prepare to meet some form of shock: *Brace yourself for the news.* **3.** to make taut or increase the tension of: *He braced his muscles and lifted the weight.* **4.** to give stimulus to; invigorate: *The cold winter air braces one.* —*v.i.* to brace up. *Informal.* to rouse one's strength, courage, or resolution. [Old French *brace* the two arms, from Latin *bracchia*, plural of *bracchium* arm, from Greek *brachión*.]

Brace (def. 3)

brace and bit, tool for drilling or boring, consisting of a bit fitted into a brace.

brace·let (brās′lit) *n.* **1.** ornamental band or chain worn around the wrist, arm, or ankle. **2.** something resembling a bracelet, esp. a handcuff. [Old French *bracelet* little arm, diminutive of *bracel* armlet, going back to Latin *bracchium* arm. See BRACE.]

brac·er (brā′sər) *n.* **1.** one who or that which braces. **2.** *Informal.* drink of liquor taken as a stimulant.

brach·i·o·pod (brak′ē ə pod′, brā′kē-) *n.* any of the mollusklike sea animals constituting the phylum Brachiopoda, characterized by a shell with top and bottom halves and a pair of cilia-covered tentacles near the mouth, used in feeding. [Modern Latin *brachiopoda*, from Greek *brachión* arm + *pous* foot.]

brac·ing (brā′sing) *adj.* invigorating; refreshing; stimulating. —*n.* brace or system of braces. —**brac′ing·ly,** *adv.*

brack·en (brak′ən) *n.* brake³.

brack·et (brak′it) *n.* **1.** piece of wood, metal, or stone projecting from a wall and used as a support for a shelf or other object. **2.** support joined or bent at an angle, esp. a right angle. **3.** shelf supported by brackets. **4.** gas or electric fixture projecting from a wall. **5.** either of two symbols, [and], used to enclose words, letters, or figures, esp. to set them off from a context. **6.** grouping or classification based on a specific criterion, esp. that of taxable income: *the middle-income bracket.* —*v.t.* **1.** to supply or support with a bracket or brackets. **2.** to enclose within brackets, as words or phrases. **3.** to classify together; associate. **4.** to fire shots on both sides of (a target) to find the correct range. [French *braguette* front flap of breeches, diminutive of *brague* breeches, going back to Latin *brāca*; of Celtic origin.]

brack·ish (brak′ish) *adj.* **1.** having a somewhat salty taste; briny. **2.** distasteful; nauseating. [Obsolete *brack* salty from Dutch *brak*) + -ISH.] —**brack′ish·ness,** *n.*

bract (brakt) *n.* modified leaf, esp. one at or near the base of a flower or flower cluster.

Bracts

at; āpe; cär; end; mē; it; īce; hot; ōld; fôrk; wood; fōol; oil; out; up; ūse; turn; sing; thin; this; zh in treasure; ə in ago, taken, pencil, lemon, circus.

Some bracts are very prominent and showy and are frequently mistaken for flower petals. [Latin *bractea* thin plate of metal.]

brad (brad) *n.* small thin nail with a head only slightly wider than the nail's thickness. [Old Norse *broddr* spike.]

brad·awl (brad'ôl') *n.* awl with a chisel edge instead of a point, used to make holes for brads.

Brad·dock, Edward (brad'ək) 1695–1755, English general, known for his role in the French and Indian War.

Brad·ford (brad'fərd) **1. William.** c.1590–1657, Pilgrim leader and a governor of the Plymouth Colony. **2.** city in north-central England. Pop. (1968 est.), 294,400.

brae (brā) *n. Scottish.* slope; hillside. [Old Norse *brā* eyelash (suggesting "brow of a hill").]

brag (brag) **bragged, brag·ging.** *v.t., v.i.* to boast: *Henry bragged that his bicycle was the fastest.* —*n.* **1.** a boast; boastful talk. **2.** one who boasts; braggart. [Of uncertain origin.] —**brag'ger,** *n.* —**Syn.** *v.i.* see **boast.**

brag·ga·do·ci·o (brag'ə dō'shē ō') *pl.,* **-ci·os.** *n.* **1.** empty boasting or bragging. **2.** boaster; braggart. [From *Braggadocchio,* name created by the English poet Edmund Spenser for a boastful and cowardly character, from BRAG + *-occhio,* an Italian suffix signifying an increase.]

brag·gart (brag'ərt) *n.* one who brags a great deal; boaster. —*adj.* bragging; boastful. [Middle French *bragard,* from *braguer* to brag; of uncertain origin.]

Brahe, Ty·cho (brä, brä'hē; tē'kō) 1546–1601, Danish astronomer.

brah·ma (brä'mə, brā'-) *n.* any of an Asian breed of large domestic fowl, having feathered legs and small wings and tail. [Short for BRAHMAPUTRA; because first imported from a town on this river.]

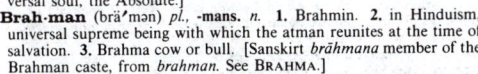

Brah·ma (brä'mə; *def.* 2. also, brä'mə) *n.* **1.** one of the three principal gods of Hinduism; the creator. **2.** any of a hardy breed of cattle native to India, now raised widely in hot or tropical regions. It has a prominent hump over the shoulder and a deep fold of drooping skin under the throat. [Sanskrit *brahman* prayer, the universal soul, the Absolute.]

Brahma

Brah·man (brä'mən) *pl.,* **-mans.** *n.* **1.** Brahmin. **2.** in Hinduism, universal supreme being with which the atman reunites at the time of salvation. **3.** Brahma cow or bull. [Sanskrit *brāhmana* member of the Brahman caste, from *brahman.* See BRAHMA.]

Brah·man·ism (brä'mə niz'əm) *n.* system of religious and social institutions derived from the Hinduism of pre-Buddhist India.

Brah·ma·pu·tra (brä'mə pōō'trə) *n.* large river in southern Asia, flowing from southwestern Tibet to the Bay of Bengal.

Brah·min (brä'min) *pl.,* **-min.** *also,* **Brah·man.** *n.* **1.** member of the Hindu priestly caste, the highest of the four main castes. **2.** cultivated intellectual member of the upper class, usually considered snobbish or conservative.

Brahms, Jo·han·nes (brämz; yō hä'nəs) 1833–97, German composer.

braid (brād) *n.* **1.** ropelike strip or band in which three or more strands of hair, straw, leather, or the like are woven together. **2.** band of material woven in this way that is used for trimming or binding. Also, **braid'ing.** —*v.t.* **1.a.** to weave or intertwine three or more strands of (hair, straw, leather, or the like). **b.** to form (something) by such weaving: *He braided a belt out of thongs.* **2.** to ornament or trim with braid. [Old English *bregdan* to weave.] —**braid'er,** *n.*

brail (brāl) *n.* one of the ropes fastened to the edge of a fore-and-aft sail, used to take in the sail. —*v.t.* to haul in (a sail) with brails (usually with *up*). [Old French *braiel* belt, from Late Latin *brācāle,* from Latin *brāca* breeches; of Celtic origin.]

braille (brāl) *also,* **Braille.** *n.* **1.** system of writing and printing for the blind, in which the characters are composed of raised dots in specific

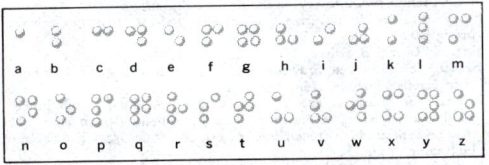

Braille alphabet

patterns that may be recognized and read by touch. **2.** the characters themselves. [From the blind Frenchman Louis *Braille,* 1809–52, who developed the system.]

brain (brān) *n.* **1.** main organ of the nervous system in man and other vertebrates, located in the cranium at the top of the spinal cord, composed of a complex mass of nerves and supporting tissue, and divided into several parts with varying functions. The brain controls and coordinates all voluntary actions and many involuntary functions; it receives and correlates sensory impulses, initiates responses, and is the seat of thought, understand, and the emotions. **2.** clump of nerve cells in some invertebrates corresponding to the brain of vertebrates. **3.** *Informal.* very intelligent person. **4.** *also,* **brains. a.** intelligence. **b.** one who formulates the plans of action for a group or organization. **5. to have (something) on the brain,** to be obsessed by (something). **6. to rack one's brains,** to strain to remember, understand, or solve. —*v.t.* **1.** to kill by smashing the skull of. **2.** to hit (someone) on the head. [Old English *brægen* main organ of the nervous system in vertebrates.]

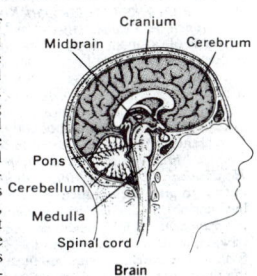

Brain

brain·child (brān'chīld') *n. Informal.* invention, discovery, or idea regarded as the product of someone's mental effort.

brain·less (brān'lis) *adj.* without intelligence; foolish. —**brain'less·ly,** *adv.* —**brain'less·ness,** *n.*

brain·pan (brān'pan') *n.* that part of the skull which encloses the brain; cranium.

brain·storm (brān'stôrm') *n.* **1.** *Informal.* sudden inspiration or idea. **2.** sudden, violent mental disturbance.

brain·storm·ing (brān'stôr'ming) *n.* spontaneous and unrestrained offering of ideas by participants in a group discussion.

brain trust, group of experts whose advice is sought by one who establishes policy.

brain·wash (brān'wôsh', -wosh') *v.t.* **1.** to change the beliefs or behavior patterns of (someone), esp. a prisoner, by using techniques of coercion and manipulation which have a psychological effect. **2.** to persuade (someone) by subtle or high-pressure techniques: *The salesman brainwashed Paul into buying that car.*

brain·wash·ing (brān'wô'shing, -wosh'ing) *n.* action or process by which a person is brainwashed.

brain·y (brā'nē) **brain·i·er, brain·i·est.** *adj. Informal.* intelligent; scholarly. —**brain'i·ness,** *n.*

braise (brāz) **braised, brais·ing.** *v.t.* to cook (meat or vegetables) by browning quickly on all sides, then simmering in a covered pot or pan with a little liquid. [French *braiser* to stew, from *braise* live coals; of Germanic origin.]

brake[1] (brāk) *n.* device for slowing or stopping the motion of a wheel or vehicle, esp. by means of friction. —*v.t.* **braked, brak·ing.** to cause to slow up or stop by applying a brake: *to brake a bicycle.* —*v.i.* to apply a brake: *He braked suddenly on seeing the child.* [Probably from Middle Dutch *braeke* device for breaking.]

brake[2] (brāk) *n.* clump or thicket, as of cane, brush, or briar. [Middle Low German *brake* thicket.]

brake[3] (brāk) *n.* coarse, hardy fern, *Pteridium aquilinum,* whose fronds are long, sturdy stalks topped by three fanlike blades. It may grow over 3 feet in height and is often used for thatch or fodder. Also, **brack'en.** [Probably short for *bracken;* possibly of Scandinavian origin.]

brake band, flexible band with friction lining, extending partially around a wheel or drum and exerting a braking force when tightened against the wheel or drum.

Brake band

brake·man (brāk'mən) *pl.,* **-men.** *n.* member of a train crew who assists the conductor.

bram·ble (bram'bəl) *n.* **1.** any of a large group of shrubs and plants of the rose family, having thorny stems and including the blackberry and raspberry. Many species are cultivated for their small, tasty fruits, and others are grown as ornamentals. **2.** any thorny shrub or stem; brier. [Old English *bræmbel.*]

bram·bly (bram'blē) **-bli·er, -bli·est.** *adj.* **1.** full of brambles. **2.** like a bramble; thorny.

bran (bran) *n.* ground husks of any of several cereal grains, separated from the flour by sifting. [Old French *bran;* possibly of Celtic origin.]

branch (branch) *n.* **1.** woody part of a tree or shrub growing out and

away from the main part. **2.a.** physical subdivision resembling a tree branch: *a branch of an antler, a branch of a railroad line.* **b.** tributary stream: *a branch of the Missouri River.* **c.** small stream, esp. a brook: *The branch went completely dry one summer.* **3.a.** subdivision, part, or offshoot of a main body: *Calculus is a branch of mathematics.* **b.** one of two or more lines of descent of a family sharing a common ancestor. **4.** unit of an organization located apart from the main establishment: *a neighborhood branch of a library, a suburban branch of a store.* —*v.i.* **1.** to put forth branches; spread in branches. **2.** to separate or diverge from a main route or body: *Turn left where the path branches.* **3. to branch off. a.** to separate into branches; go in different directions: *The trail branches off west of the pass.* **b.** to go in another direction: *He decided to branch off into building his own hi-fi sets.* **4. to branch out. a.** to give forth branches. **b.** to extend, enlarge upon, or vary, as business or other activities: *I'm going to branch out and learn computer programming.* [Old French *branche* bough, from Late Latin *branca* paw, claw; of uncertain origin.]
Syn. *n.* **1. Branch, bough, limb** mean one of the woody members growing out of the trunk of a tree or its ramifications. **Branch** may refer to any such outgrowth, large or small: *Many branches are still bare early in the spring.* **Bough**, a literary word, applies to a main branch and also to a branch in blossom or heavy with fruit: *My heart is like an apple-tree whose boughs are bent with thickset fruit* (Rosetti, 1890). **Limb** usually refers to a large branch, esp. one growing out from the trunk: *The lumberjack cut down the knotty limbs of the towering oak.*
brand (brand) *n.* **1.** kind, quality, or make of a product, as indicated by the manufacturer's identifying mark: *a good brand of chocolate.* **2.** the manufacturer's mark itself; trademark. **3.** mark of ownership applied to the skin of livestock by burning with a hot iron. **4.** iron for branding. **5.a.** mark of disgrace. **b.** mark burned onto the skin of criminals. **6.** burning or partly burned piece of wood. **7.** disease of plants causing the leaves to look burnt. **8.** *Archaic.* sword. —*v.t.* **1.** to mark with a brand. **2.** to put a mark of disgrace on; stigmatize. [Old English *brand* torch, burning, sword.] —**brand′er**, *n.*
Bran·deis, Louis Dem·bitz (brăn′dīs; dem′bĭts) 1856–1941, U.S. lawyer and associate justice of the U.S. Supreme Court from 1916 to 1939.
Bran·den·burg (brăn′dən bûrg′) *n.* historic region of northeastern Germany, now divided between East Germany and Poland.
bran·dish (brăn′dĭsh) *v.t.* to wave, shake, or swing threateningly, as a weapon; flourish: *The guard brandished his club at the intruders.* —*n.* threatening wave or shake; flourish. [Old French *brandiss-*, a stem of *brandir* to brandish, from Anglo-Norman *brand* sword, from Old Norse *brandr* torch, sword.]
brand-new (brand′nōō′, -nū′, brăn′-) *adj.* entirely new; newly acquired; unused.
bran·dy (brăn′dē) *pl.* **-dies.** *n.* **1.** alcoholic beverage distilled from wine. **2.** similar alcoholic beverage distilled from fermented fruit juice: *peach brandy.* —*v.t.* **-died, -dy·ing.** to treat, flavor, or preserve with brandy. [Earlier *brandywine*, from Dutch *brandewijn* the beverage, from *branden* to burn, distill + *wijn* wine (from Latin *vīnum*).]
brant (brant) *pl.* **brants** or **brant.** *n.* any of various wild geese, genus *Branta*, having black and brownish-gray feathers. Brants breed in the tundra of northern North America and Arctic Eurasia and migrate south in the autumn. Length: about 2 feet. [Possibly of Scandinavian origin.]
Braque, Georges (brăk; zhôrzh) 1882–1963, French painter, a founder of the Cubist school of art.

Brant

brash (brăsh) *adj.* **1.** impudent; disrespectful: *in a brash manner.* **2.** impetuous; rash. —**Syn.** 1. see **bold**.
bra·sier (brā′zhər) brazier.
Bra·si·lia (brä sēl′yä) *n.* capital of Brazil, in the east-central part of the country. Pop. (1968 est.), 379,699.
brass (brăs) *n.* **1.** alloy of copper, whose main added element is zinc. It is valued for durability, ductility, and beauty; with a high zinc proportion it resembles gold. **2.** object or objects made of brass, such as utensils or ornaments: *They polished all the brass in the kitchen.* **3.** *also,* **brasses.** musical wind instruments, of the trumpet, horn, or other related families, made of brass or other metal, these instruments collectively in an orchestra or band. **4.** *Informal.* extreme boldness or self-assurance; impudence. **5.** *Informal.* money. **6. the brass.** *Informal.* high-ranking officials, esp. military officers. —*adj.* made or composed of brass. [Old English *bræs* alloy of copper and tin.]
bras·sard (brăs′ärd, brə särd′) *n.* **1.** band worn above the elbow, bearing an insignia or identifying mark. **2.** armor for the upper arm.

[French *brassard* arm guard, armlet, from *bras* arm, from Latin *brucchium.* See BRACE.]
bras·sart (brăs′ərt) brassard *(def. 2).*
brass band, band in which most or all of the instruments are brasses.
brass hat *Slang.* high-ranking official, esp. a military officer.
brass·ie (brăs′ē) *pl.* **brass·ies.** *also,* **brass·y.** *n.* golf club having a wooden head, often with a metal plate on the sole, used for long low shots; number two wood.
bras·siere (brə zēr′) *n.* woman's undergarment which supports the breasts. [French *brassière*, from *bras* arm, from Latin *bracchium.* See BRACE.]
brass knuckles, metal bar or rings fitting over the knuckles, used in rough fighting.
brass tacks *Informal.* basic or essential facts.
brass·ware (brăs′wâr′) *n.* articles made of brass.
brass·y (brăs′ē) **brass·i·er, brass·i·est.** *adj.* **1.** of, like, or containing brass. **2.** harsh and loud in tone: *a brassy voice.* **3.** cheap and showy: *brassy taste in clothes.* **4.** *Informal.* brazen; impudent. —*n.* brassie. —**brass′i·ly**, *adv.* —**brass′i·ness**, *n.*
brat (brăt) *n.* child, esp. one who misbehaves or is ill-mannered. [Possibly from dialectal English *brat* rag, from Old English *bratt* cloak.]
Bra·ti·sla·va (brä′tyĭ slä′vä) *n.* city in southern Czechoslovakia, on the Danube. Pop. (1967 est.), 278,835.
Braun·schweig (broun′shvīk′) *n.* German. Brunswick.
bra·va·do (brə vä′dō) *n.* boldness or daring, esp. an ostentatious display of supposed fearlessness or confidence. [Spanish *bravada* boast, bravado, from *bravo* courageous, savage. See BRAVE.]
brave (brāv) **brav·er, brav·est.** *adj.* **1.** having or showing courage: *brave men.* **2.** *Archaic.* making a fine appearance; elegant; showy: *brave flags.* **3.** *Archaic.* fine; excellent. —*n.* American Indian warrior. —*v.t.*, **braved, brav·ing. 1.** to encounter or endure courageously: *The rescuers braved the storm.* **2.** to dare; defy; challenge: *He braved the might of the dragon.* [French *brave* courageous, from Italian and Spanish *bravo* courageous, bold, wild, possibly going back to Latin *barbarus.* See BARBAROUS.] —**brave′ly**, *adv.* —**brave′ness**, *n.*
Syn. *adj.* **1. Brave, courageous, valiant** mean willing to face danger, difficulty, or even death, when demanded by circumstances. **Brave** implies self-control in the face of danger, whether or not one experiences fear: *The brave captain left the burning ship after all the passengers were in lifeboats.* **Courageous** stresses the firmness of character underlying bravery and is often used when the danger or difficulty is not physical: *a courageous defense of an unpopular cause.* **Valiant** suggests heroic courage, as in a defense against hopeless odds: *The valiant defenders fought to the last man.*
brav·er·y (brā′vər ē) *n.* quality of being brave; courage.
bra·vo[1] (brä′vō) *interj.* well done; good; excellent. —*n. pl.*, **-vos.** shout of "bravo." [Italian *bravo* fine, brave. See BRAVE.]
bra·vo[2] (brä′vō, brä′-) *pl.*, **-voes** or **-vos.** *n.* reckless, daring fighter, esp. one for hire in sixteenth- or seventeenth-century Europe. [Italian *bravo* villain, bold. See BRAVE.]
bra·vu·ra (brə vyoor′ə) *n.* **1.** musical piece or passage requiring great skill and technical power on the part of the performer. **2.** display of daring; performance brilliantly executed. [Italian *bravura* bravery, spirit, from *bravo.* See BRAVE.]
braw (brô, brä) *adj.* Scottish. **1.** splendid in appearance. **2.** excellent; fine. [Scottish form of BRAVE.]
brawl (brôl) *n.* **1.** noisy, unruly fight or quarrel. **2.a.** noisy commotion. **b.** *Informal.* loud, uproarious party. —*v.i.* **1.** to fight or quarrel noisily and in an unruly fashion. **2.** to babble loudly, as a brook. [Of uncertain origin.] —**brawl′er**, *n.*
brawn (brôn) *n.* **1.a.** muscular strength: *He's all brawn and little brain.* **b.** muscle. **2.** flesh of a boar, esp. boiled and pickled. **3.** headcheese. [Old French *braon* fleshy part; of Germanic origin.]
brawn·y (brô′nē) **brawn·i·er, brawn·i·est.** *adj.* strong; muscular. —**brawn′i·ness**, *n.*
bray[1] (brā) *n.* **1.** loud, harsh cry made by a donkey or mule. **2.** any sound resembling such a cry: *the bray of trumpets.* —*v.i.* to make a loud, harsh cry or sound. —*v.t.* to make (as a cry or sound) in loud, harsh tones (often with *out*): *The orator brayed out his speech.* [Old French *braire* to cry; probably of Celtic origin.]
bray[2] (brā) *v.t.* to pulverize. [Old French *breier* to crush; of Germanic origin.]
Braz., Brazil; Brazilian.
braze[1] (brāz) *v.t.* **brazed, braz·ing.** *v.t.* to cover or ornament with brass. [Old English *bræsian*, from *bræs* brass.]
braze[2] (brāz) *v.t.* **brazed, braz·ing.** *v.t.* to join (metal parts) by a process similar to soldering, using an alloy with a melting point above 427 degrees centigrade. [French *braser* to solder, from *braise* live coals; of Germanic origin.]
bra·zen (brā′zən) *adj.* **1.** made of brass. **2.** loud; harsh; forthright: *the brazen bells.* **3.** shameless; impudent: *brazen behavior.* —*v.t.* to

behave defiantly or unashamedly about (with *out* or *through*): *He bra-zened out the accusation from the witness stand.* [Old English *bræsen* of brass, bold, from *bræs* bold.] **—bra′zen·ly,** *adv.* **—bra′zen·ness,** *n.* **—Syn.** *adj.* **3.** see **bold.**

bra·zier¹ (brā′zhər) *n.* metal container to hold burning charcoal or coal, formerly used for heating or lighting or, when furnished with a grill or rack, for cooking food. [French *brasier* brazier, furnace, from *braise* live coals; of Germanic origin.]

bra·zier² (brā′zhər) *also,* **bra·sier.** *n.* one who works in brass. [From BRASS. Compare GLAZIER and GLASS.]

Bra·zil (brə zil′) *n.* largest country in South America, in the northeast-ern part of the continent, on the Atlantic. Capital, Brasília. Area, 3,286,487 sq. mi. Pop. (1969 est.), 90,840,000.

Bra·zil·ian (brə zil′yən) *adj.* of or relating to Brazil, its people, or its culture. *—n.* na-tive or inhabitant of Brazil.

Brazil nut, large nut with a dark, rough shell and triangular, cream-colored kernel, seed of a tropical evergreen tree, *Bertholletia excelsa,* native to Brazil.

Brazil nut shell and nut

bra·zil·wood (brə zil′wood′) *n.* deep-red wood of any of several tropical trees of the pea family, esp. *Caesalpinia echinata,* native to Brazil, which yield red and purple dyes.

Braz·za·ville (braz′ə vil′) *n.* capital of the Republic of the Congo, in the southeastern part of the country. Pop. (1962), 136,200.

breach (brēch) *n.* **1.** gap or break made in something solid. **2.** violation of or failure to live up to a law, promise, or obligation: *a breach of duty, breach of contract.* **3.** rupture of friendly relations; quarrel. *—v.t.* to break through; make a gap in. [Partly from Old English *brice* breaking; partly from Old French *breche* fracture, from Old High German *brecha.*]

breach of promise, breaking of one's word, esp. a promise to marry.

breach of the peace, disturbance of the public peace, as by a riot.

bread (bred) *n.* **1.** food made by mixing flour or meal with liquid and usually a leavening agent, then kneading and baking. **2.** food in general; sustenance. **3.** livelihood: *He earns his bread by writing.* **4.** *Slang.* money. **5. to break bread. a.** to eat together; share a meal. **b.** to administer or partake of Communion. **6. to cast one's bread upon the waters.** to do good without seeking reward; be generous. **7. to know which side one's bread is buttered on.** to know what is to one's advan-tage or where that advantage lies. **8. to take the bread out of one's mouth.** to deprive someone of his livelihood. *—v.t.* to cover with or as with bread crumbs before cooking. [Old English *brēad* the food; origi-nally, fragment, morsel.]

bread-and-but·ter (bred′ən but′ər) *adj. Informal.* **1.** concerning one's livelihood: *Bread-and-butter issues worried the union members.* **2.** prosaic; commonplace. **3.** giving thanks for hospitality: *a bread-and-butter note.* **4.** *British.* youthful; immature.

bread and butter 1. bread spread with butter. **2.** *Informal.* liveli-hood.

bread·bas·ket (bred′bas′kit) *n.* **1.** basket for holding bread or rolls. **2.** chief grain-supplying region: *breadbasket of the nation.* **3.** *Slang.* stomach.

bread·board (bred′bôrd′) *n.* **1.** board on which dough may be rolled or shaped, bread sliced, or other food prepared. **2.** board, usually perforated, on which experimental electrical or electronic circuits may be set up quickly.

bread·fruit (bred′frōōt′) *n.* **1.** round, starchy fruit of a tropical tree, *Artocarpus altilis,* native to southern Asia and Polynesia. It may be cooked and eaten, or dried and ground into flour. **2.** tree bearing this fruit, having leathery, glossy green leaves and yellow flowers. [BREAD + FRUIT; because of the fruit's similarity to bread when baked.]

Breadfruit leaf and fruit

bread line, line of people waiting to receive food distributed as charity or relief.

bread·stuff (bred′stuf′) *n.* **1.** material for making bread; grain, flour, or meal. **2.** bread.

breadth (bredth, bretth) *n.* **1.** measure of a surface from side to side; width. **2.** something having a definite and regular width: *a breadth of silk.* **3.** spaciousness; extent; largeness: *They were overwhelmed by the breadth of the country.* **4.** freedom from narrowness; liberality; compre-hensiveness: *breadth of social vision, an article of great breadth.* [Earlier *bredethe,* from Middle English *brede* width, from Old English *brǣdu.*]

breadth·wise (bredth′wīz′, bretth′-) *also,* **breadth′ways′.** *adv., adj.* in the direction of the breadth.

bread·win·ner (bred′win′ər) *n.* one who provides support for him-self and his dependents.

break (brāk) **broke** or *(archaic)* **brake, bro·ken** or *(archaic)* **broke, break·ing.** *v.t.* **1.** to separate or fragment by force; reduce into pieces; shatter: *to break a window.* **2.** to pierce or lay open a surface; wound: *to break ground, to break the skin.* **3.** to destroy or disrupt the complete-ness, continuity, or order of: *to break formation, to break stride.* **4.a.** to render ineffective or unusable by smashing, crushing, or injuring; make inoperable. **b.** to fracture the bone of. **5.** to violate; transgress: *to break the law, to break one's word.* **6.** to force one's way through or into: *He broke the sound barrier.* **7.** to escape from; make one's way out of. **8.** to lessen or destroy the force, intensity, or effect of; weaken: *The matted leaves broke his fall. Jetties broke the waves.* **9.** to interrupt abruptly the uniformity or continuing state or quality of: *Her scream broke the silence.* **10.** to sever (a bond or something confining); dissolve; loosen: *to break the chains of slavery.* **11.** to put an end to; stop; over-come: *to break a strike.* **12.** to reduce in rank; demote: *to break a sergeant to corporal.* **13.** to train to obedience; tame: *to break a mustang to the saddle.* **14.** to crush, impair, or reduce the spirit of; discourage. **15.** to impair the health or strength of; exhaust; wear out. **16.** to surpass; excel: *to break the speed record.* **17.** to make known; disclose; inform: *to break the news.* **18.** to cause (someone) to discontinue a habit (with *of*): *to break a child of lying.* **19.** to make bankrupt; ruin financially. **20.** to open and stop the flow of electric current in that. **21.** to give or receive change for: *to break a dollar.* **22. to break camp.** to pack up equipment in preparation for departure. **23. to break ground.** to begin operations; start (something), esp. excavation for building. **24. to break the ice. a.** to begin something. **b.** to overcome the first awkward moments of a new acquaintance or endeavor. *—v.i.* **1.** to come apart; separate into pieces; burst; shatter. **2.** to become inoperable or unusable; weaken. **3.** to escape or part forcefully; move away suddenly: *The water broke from the bursting dam. The deer broke cover.* **4.** to divide up; disperse; scatter: *The clouds broke and the sun shone again.* **5.** to happen; de-velop: *He took advantage of the way things broke and managed to make a large profit.* **6.** to come into being; become evident; happen suddenly or violently: *The storm broke. The day is breaking.* **7.** to change or fall off suddenly or abruptly. **8.** to sever a connection, association, or rela-tionship abruptly (usually with *with*). **9.** to interrupt or end tem-porarily. **10.** to decline suddenly in price or value: *The pound broke, but the dollar and franc remained stable.* **11.** to become overwhelmed or crushed with sorrow: *His heart broke.*

to break away. a. to start before the starting signal is given. **b.** to escape suddenly; free oneself; get away. **c.** to sever connections with (usually with *from*).

to break down. a. to fail to function; stop working. **b.** to become ill through physical or mental collapse. **c.** to give way to emotion. **d.** to analyze or be analyzed or separated into distinct parts. **e.** to crush or overcome, as opposition. **f.** to decompose.

to break in. a. to adapt for particular use; train. **b.** to enter forcibly or suddenly. **c.** to interrupt.

to break in on (or **upon**). **a.** to intrude on. **b.** to interrupt.

to break into. a. to enter by force. **b.** to interrupt or interfere with. **c.** to burst forth suddenly, as with speech or an action.

to break off. a. to stop abruptly; discontinue suddenly. **b.** to sever connections or relations; stop being close to someone (with *with*).

to break out. a. to start suddenly and unexpectedly. **b.** to erupt or become covered with eruptions on the skin. **c.** to escape from re-straint or confinement.

to break up. a. to disperse; scatter; disintegrate. **b.** to dissolve; dis-band. **c.** to put an end to; stop. **d.** to make or become upset; become greatly distressed. **e.** to take apart; dismantle. **f.** to sever a relation-ship. **g.** to laugh or cause to laugh.

to break with. a. to sever relations or connections with. **b.** to cease conforming to.

—n. **1.** result of breaking; broken place; rupture; crack. **2.** act of breaking; fracture; shattering. **3.** sudden rush or dash, as in attempting to escape: *to make a break for it.* **4.** act of breaking in, out, or forth: *a prison break.* **5.** beginning; opening or start: *the break of day.* **6.a.** sudden or marked change or deviation: *a break in the cold spell.* **b.** sudden decline or lowering, as of prices or values. **7.** sudden interrup-tion of continuity or regularity; stoppage; suspension: *a break in diplo-matic relations.* **8.** *Slang.* fortunate chance or opportunity: *a lucky break.* **9.** brief rest period; pause: *a coffee break.* **10.** opening or inter-ruption in an electric circuit which renders it incomplete. **11.** *Music.* **a.** point in the scale where a voice or musical instrument changes from one register or quality to another. **b.** brief elaborate jazz phrase played during a pause between regular phrases of the melody. [Old English *brecan* to shatter, violate, burst.]

Syn. *v.t.* **1.** Break, smash, shatter mean to cause to come apart through force. **Break** means to split a rigid body into pieces and damage its wholeness: *The boy broke the pencil in two.* **Smash** means to reduce an

ăt; āpe; cär; end; mē; it; īce; hot; ōld; fôrk; wood; fōōl; oil; out; up; ūse; turn; sing; thin; this; zh in treasure; ə in ago, taken, pencil, lemon, circus.

119

object to fragments violently and noisily and destroy its shape: *The angry man smashed the vase against the floor.* **Shatter** means to break into many small pieces or shreds with a wide scattering of fragments: *The explosion shattered the windows.*

break·a·ble (brā′kə bəl) *adj.* capable of being broken. —*n.* object easily broken.

break·age (brā′kij) *n.* **1.** a breaking or break. **2.** that which is broken. **3.a.** damage caused by breaking. **b.** compensation allowed for such damage.

break·down (brāk′doun′) *n.* **1.** failure to operate, as of a machine, a system, or an organization. **2.** (of the body or emotions) collapse. **3.a.** fast, lively country dance. **b.** music for or as for such a dance, esp. played on a fiddle or banjo. **4.** analysis: *a breakdown of the data.*

break·er¹ (brā′kər) *n.* **1.** large wave that foams as it breaks on the rocks or shore. **2.** one who or that which breaks. [BREAK + -ER¹.]

break·er² (brā′kər) *n.* small keg or cask, used esp. on a boat or ship to carry water for an emergency. [Modification of Spanish *barrica* cask. See BARRICADE.]

break·fast (brek′fəst) *n.* first meal of the day, usually eaten in the morning. —*v.i.* to eat breakfast. [BREAK + FAST²; because it is the meal that breaks the night's fast.]

break·neck (brāk′nek′) *adj.* extremely dangerous: *The car raced by us at breakneck speed.*

break·through (brāk′thrōō′) *n.* **1.** military attack that penetrates through enemy lines to a rear area. **2.** major development or discovery helping to overcome hindrances to an undertaking: *a technological breakthrough.* **3.** turning point.

break·up (brāk′up′) *n.* **1.** separation into smaller parts: *the breakup of the large estates into small farms.* **2.** stopping or ending, as of a game or personal relationship. **3.** collapse; dissolution.

break·wa·ter (brāk′wô′tər, -wot′ər) *n.* wall or other structure that protects an area from the effects of waves.

bream¹ (brēm) *pl.*, **breams** or **bream.** *n.* **1.** any of various European freshwater fish, genus *Abramis,* of the carp family, having a deep, compressed body. **2.** any of various freshwater sunfish of the southeastern United States. **3.** sea bream. [French *brême;* of Germanic origin.]

bream² (brēm) *v.t.* to clean (the hull of a wooden ship) by burning and scraping. [Possibly from Dutch *brem* broom, furze.]

breast (brest) *n.* **1.** front part of the human body between the neck and the abdomen; chest. **2.** corresponding upper ventral part of an animal's body. **3.** upper, front part of a garment, esp. a coat or dress. **4.** something resembling or likened to the breast. **5.** either of the two mammary glands of the human female. **6.** center of the emotions. **7. to make a clean breast of.** to make complete confession of; disclose. —*v.t.* to struggle against; contend with. [Old English *brēost* chest.]

breast·bone (brest′bōn′) *n.* flat, narrow bone in the center of the breast to which the ribs are joined; sternum.

breast·pin (brest′pin′) *n.* ornamental pin worn on the breast or near the throat, esp. to keep a garment closed; brooch.

breast·plate (brest′plāt′) *n.* **1.** vestlike piece of armor worn to protect the chest. See **armor** for illustration. **2.** ornamental cloth worn over the chest by the Jewish high priests of ancient times. It was decorated with twelve jewels representing the twelve tribes of Israel.

breast stroke, stroke made while swimming face down, in which both arms go out in front of the head, then are swept in an arc to the sides and back, accompanied by a frog kick.

breast·work (brest′wurk′) *n.* low, hastily constructed defensive wall.

breath (breth) *n.* **1.** air inhaled and exhaled in breathing: *He drew in a breath of fresh country air. The fall knocked the breath out of me.* **2.** act or process of breathing; respiration: *He held his breath and dived.* **3.** single respiration: *with every breath I take.* **4.** ability to breathe freely and easily: *to be out of breath.* **5.** air exhaled from the lungs, esp. as made apparent by odor or vapor. **6.** air for breathing: *to gasp for breath.* **7.** slight current or whiff (of air): *to get a breath of fresh air. There's not a breath of air in this heat.* **8.** whisper or hint; suggestion. **9.** life; spirit. **10.** *Phonetics.* voiceless exhalation of air producing a hiss or similar sound, used in pronouncing such consonants as *h, s,* and *f.* **11.** *Archaic.* characteristic odor or fragrance.
in the same (or **next**) **breath.** almost simultaneously; immediately afterwards.
to catch one's breath. a. to rest between activities or after an activity; pause; relax. **b.** to check the breath suddenly, as in fear; gasp.
to hold one's breath. to wait in expectation or suspense.
to save one's breath. to remain silent when discussion would be useless.
to take one's breath away. to overwhelm or stun, as with astonishment or awe.
under one's breath. in a low or barely audible voice.
[Old English *brǣth* odor, exhaled air.]

breathe (brēth) breathed, breath·ing. *v.i.* **1.** to draw air into the lungs and force it out. **2.** to be alive; live. **3.** to pause and rest; relax. **4.** to emit a fragrance or aura: *The galley breathed of the sea.* **5.** *Archaic.* to blow softly, as wind. **6. to breathe again** (or **freely**). to feel relieved or reassured. —*v.t.* **1.** to inhale and expel from the lungs, as when breathing. **2.** to inject; infuse: *Margaret's enthusiasm breathed new life into the campaign.* **3.** to emit by or as by breathing: *to breathe a sigh of relief. The dragon breathed fire.* **4.** to express or manifest; display: *to breathe hatred, to breathe confidence.* **5.** to whisper or say confidentially: *She promised not to breathe a word about his secret.* **6.** to allow to rest or recover breath: *Breathe your horse.* **7.** *Phonetics.* to utter with the breath only, without the voice. **8. to breathe one's last.** to die. [From BREATH.]

breath·er (brē′thər) *n.* **1.** *Informal.* short rest period. **2.** one who breathes, esp. in a particular way.

breath·ing (brē′thing) *n.* **1.** respiration. **2.** *Linguistics.* aspiration.

breathing space, space or area in which one can breathe or move about freely.

breathing spell, pause in which to rest or think.

breath·less (breth′lis) *adj.* **1.** out of breath: *The climb left him breathless.* **2.** in a state of fear or excitement; tense: *The children were breathless as they watched the tightrope act.* —**breath′less·ly,** *adv.* —**breath′less·ness,** *n.*

breath·tak·ing (breth′tā′king) *adj.* causing extreme excitement or pleasure; thrilling; overwhelming: *breathtaking suspense, breathtaking beauty.*

brec·ci·a (brech′ē ə) *n.* sedimentary rock formed by angular fragments cemented together by some substance, as silt. [Italian *breccia,* from Old High German *brecha* breaking.]

Brecht, Ber·tolt (brekt; *Ger.* ber′tôlt) 1898–1956, German dramatist and poet.

Breck·in·ridge, John Cab·ell (brek′ən rij′; kab′əl) 1821–75, vice-president of the United States, from 1857 to 1861, who became a Confederate general.

bred (bred) past tense and past participle of **breed.**

breech (brēch) *n.* **1.** part of a firearm behind or at the rear of the barrel, that takes the projectile. **2.** lower or back part of something, as a pulley. **3.** lower, rear part of the body; buttocks. [Old English *brēc* breeches. See BREECHES.]

breech·cloth (brēch′klôth′) *also,* **breech·clout** (brēch′klout′). *n.* **1.** narrow length of cloth passing between the legs and having its ends held up at the waist, front and back, by a string or belt. **2.** loincloth.

breech·es (brich′iz) *n.,pl.* **1.** trousers reaching to or just below the knees. **2.** *Informal.* trousers. [Old English *brēc* breeches, plural of *brōc* buttocks, covering for the buttocks.]

breeches buoy, apparatus consisting of canvas shorts attached to a life preserver, hung from a pulley that slides along a rope strung between two ships or between a ship and a shore point. It is used to transfer personnel or rescue people.

breech·ing (brē′ching, brich′ing) *n.* part of a harness that passes around the rump of a horse or similar draft animal, enabling it to back up with or hold back its load. See **harness** for illustration.

breech·load·er (brēch′lō′dər) *n.* firearm that is loaded at the breech rather than at the muzzle. —**breech′load′ing,** *adj.*

breed (brēd) bred, breed·ing. *v.t.* **1.** to cause to reproduce, esp. in order to develop certain qualities; raise. **2.** to give rise to; produce; cause. **3.** to bring up; train; rear: *Henry was born and bred an aristocrat.* **4.** to mate: *They bred the stallion with the mare.* —*v.i.* **1.** to produce offspring: *Trout breed in this pond.* **2.** to be produced; develop: *Crime breeds in slums.* —*n.* **1.** variety·or strain of a species: *Beagles are a breed of dogs.* **2.** kind or sort of anything; type. [Old English *brēdan* to hatch, nourish.]

breed·er (brē′dər) *n.* **1.** one who breeds animals or plants. **2.** animal or plant that produces offspring, one kept for this purpose.

breeder reactor, nuclear reactor that produces at least as much fissionable material as it consumes. Also, **breeder pile.**

breed·ing (brē′ding) *n.* **1.** the bringing up or training of the young, esp. training in character or deportment. **2.** admirable character and social behavior; good manners. **3.** production of offspring. **4.** controlled reproduction of plants or animals, usually to bring about improvements in offspring. **5.** production by a nuclear reactor of at least as much fissionable material as is consumed.

Breed's Hill (brēdz) see **Bunker Hill.**

breeze (brēz) *n.* **1.** light current of air; soft, gentle wind. **2.** *Informal.* something easy to do. **3.** *British. Informal.* quarrel; disturbance. **4. to shoot the breeze.** *Slang.* to talk or gossip casually; chat. —*v.i.* breezed, breez·ing. *Informal.* **1.** to move in a relaxed or jaunty manner. **2. to breeze through.** to do or complete effortlessly and quickly. [French *brise* gentle wind; of uncertain origin.]

breeze·way (brēz′wā′) *n.* roofed passageway, open at the sides, between two structures, as a house and garage.

at; āpe; cär; end; mē; it; īce; hot; ōld; fôrk; wood; fōōl; oil; out; up; ūse; turn; sing; thin; this; zh in treasure; ə in ago, taken, pencil, lemon, circus.

breez·y (brē′zē) breez·i·er, breez·i·est. *adj.* **1.** swept by gentle winds: *breezy shores.* **2.** lively or carefree; sprightly. —**breez′i·ly,** *adv.* —**breez′i·ness,** *n.*

Brem·en (brem′ən, brā′mən) *n.* port city in northern West Germany. Pop. (1968 est.), 605,066.

Bren·ner (bren′ər) *n.* major mountain pass in the Alps, on the border between Austria and Italy.

br′er (brur, brer) *n.* brother. ▲ used in parts of the southern United States before a name or noun functioning as a name: *Br′er Rabbit.*

Bres·lau (bres′lou, brez′-) *n. German.* Wroclaw.

Brest (brest) *n.* **1.** port city in northwestern France, on the Atlantic. Pop. (1968), 154,023. **2.** city in the western Soviet Union, in Byelorussia. Pop. (1970), 122,000. Formerly, **Brest Li·tovsk** (li tofsk′).

breth·ren (breth′rən) plural of **brother.** ▲ used chiefly for fellow members of a religion or fraternal society.

Bret·on (bret′ən) *n.* **1.** native or inhabitant of Brittany. **2.** Celtic language spoken by Bretons. —*adj.* of or relating to Brittany, its people, or their language. [French *Breton,* from Latin *Brittō* a Breton, or a Briton.]

breve (brēv) *n.* **1.** mark (ˇ) placed over a vowel or syllable to show that it has a short sound. **2.a.** musical note equivalent to two whole notes. **b.** symbol for it. [Italian *breve,* from Latin *brevis* short.]

bre·vet (bra vet′) *n.* formerly, a commission promoting a military officer without a corresponding increase in pay, conferred esp. as an honor. —*v.t.,* **-vet·ted** or **-vet·ed, -vet·ting** or **-vet·ing.** to promote by brevet. [French *brevet* note, diminutive of *bref* document, letter, from Latin *breve* note, from *brevis* short.]

bre·vi·ar·y (brē′vē er′ē, brev′ē-) *pl.* **-ar·ies.** *n.* in the Roman Catholic and Orthodox churches, book or books of prayers and ceremonies arranged for each day of the calendar year, which certain clergymen are required to follow. [Latin *breviārium* summary.]

brev·i·ty (brev′ə tē) *n.* shortness, esp. in speech or writing: *Brevity is the soul of wit* (Shakespeare, *Hamlet*). [Latin *brevitās.*]

brew (broō) *v.t.* **1.** to produce (beer, ale, or a similar beverage) by steeping, boiling, and fermenting malt and hops. **2.** to prepare (a nonalcoholic beverage, as tea or coffee) by steeping, boiling, or mixing. **3.** to plan or devise; concoct: *to brew trouble.* —*v.i.* **1.** to be brewed: *The tea brewed for half an hour.* **2.** to be imminent: *There is a gale brewing in the west. Mischief is brewing.* —*n.* **1.** drink prepared by brewing: *a strong brew, a witches′ brew.* **2.** amount that is brewed at one time. [Old English *brēowan* to make beer or ale by boiling and fermenting.]

brew·er (broō′ər) *n.* one who brews, esp. one whose business or trade is the preparation of ale or other malt beverages.

brew·er·y (broō′ər ē) *pl.* **-er·ies.** *n.* place where beer or other malt beverages are brewed.

brew·ing (broō′ing) *n.* **1.** process by which beer or other malt beverages are produced. **2.** amount brewed at one time.

bri·ar¹ (brī′ər) *also,* **bri·er.** *n.* **1.** tree heath. **2.** its root, composed of a fine-grained wood which is used for making tobacco pipes. **3.** tobacco pipe made from this root. [French *bruyère* heath, heather; of Celtic origin.]

bri·ar² (brī′ər) **brier¹**.

Bri·a·re·us (brī ār′ē əs) *n. Greek Mythology.* monster with a hundred arms and fifty heads.

bri·ar·root (brī′ər roōt′, -root′) *also,* **bri·er·root.** *n.* briarwood.

bri·ar·wood (brī′ər wood′) *also,* **bri·er·wood.** *n.* **1.** wood of the root of the tree heath, used in making tobacco pipes. **2.** tobacco pipe made from this wood.

bribe (brīb) *n.* **1.** something given or offered to a person in a position of trust to induce him to act corruptly: *The judge rejected a bribe from the defendant′s family.* **2.** something that influences or persuades; inducement. —*v.t.,* **bribed, brib·ing. 1.** to give or offer a bribe to: *He bribed the reporter.* **2.** to influence or induce with a bribe: *The mother bribed her child with candy.* [Old French *bribe* gift, scrap of bread given to a beggar; of uncertain origin.] —**brib′a·ble,** *adj.* —**brib′er,** *n.*

brib·er·y (brī′bər ē) *pl.* **-er·ies.** *n.* act or practice of giving, offering, or accepting a bribe.

bric-a-brac (brik′ə brak′) *also,* **bric-à-brac.** *n.* small decorative objects; knickknacks. [French *bric-à-brac;* imitative.]

brick (brik) *n.* **1.** molded, usually rectangular, block of clay baked by fire, esp. in a kiln, or by the sun, used in building and paving. **2.** bricks collectively. **3.** something shaped like a brick: *a brick of gold.* **4.** *Informal.* good or admirable person. —*v.t.* **1.** to enclose, cover, or wall with bricks: *to brick up a doorway.* **2.** to build or pave with bricks. [French *brique* baked clay block, fragment, from Middle Dutch *bricke.*]

brick·bat (brik′bat′) *n.* **1.** piece of brick or other material, esp. when used as a missile. **2.** *Informal.* insulting or critical remark.

brick·lay·er (brik′lā′ər) *n.* one whose business or trade is building with bricks and other masonry materials. —**brick′lay′ing,** *n.*

brick red, any of various shades of a brownish-red color.

brick·work (brik′wurk′) *n.* work of or with bricks.

brick·yard (brik′yärd′) *n.* place where bricks are made or sold.

brid·al (brīd′əl) *adj.* of or relating to a bride or wedding: *a bridal bouquet, a bridal suite.* —*n. Archaic.* wedding. [Old English *brȳdealu* wedding feast, from *brȳd* bride + *ealu* ale; from the early English custom of drinking ale at a marriage ceremony.]

bridal wreath, any of various white-flowered shrubs, genus *Spiraea,* of the rose family, having oval-shaped, dark-green leaves.

bride (brīd) *n.* woman newly married or about to be married. [Old English *brȳd.*]

bride·groom (brīd′groōm′, -groōm′) *n.* man newly married or about to be married. [Old English *brȳdguma* literally, bride man, from *brȳd* bride + *guma* man; influenced in spelling by GROOM (*def. 1*).]

brides·maid (brīdz′mād′) *n.* woman, usually young and unmarried, who attends a bride at her wedding.

bridge¹ (brij) *n.* **1.** any structure built across a waterway, chasm, or other obstacle to afford passage. **2.** means of access, transition, or connection; intermediate phase: *The joint venture served as a bridge to full partnership.* **3.** firm connecting part in the body, esp. the upper, bony ridge of the nose. **4.** curved part of a pair of eyeglasses that joins the two lenses and rests on the bridge of the nose. **5.** one or more false teeth in a mounting supported by the adjacent natural teeth. **6.** raised structure on a deck of a ship, from which the ship is navigated and steered. **7.** in certain string instruments, thin piece of wood or other material over which the strings are stretched, raising them above the soundboard. **8.** anything resembling a bridge in shape, position, or function, as a notched piece of wood attached to a long handle, sometimes used in pool and billiards to support the cue in striking a ball. **9. to burn one′s bridges (behind one).** to cut off all means or opportunities for retreat. —*v.t.,* **bridged, bridg·ing. 1.** to build a bridge or bridges over: *to bridge a ravine.* **2.** to span: *An overpass bridged the highway.* **3.** to serve as or make a way of passing or overcoming: *to bridge the gap in understanding between different cultures.* [Old English *brycg* structure over a waterway.]

bridge² (brij) *n.* **1.** contract bridge. **2.** any of various similar card games for up to four hands. [Earlier *biritch,* possibly from Russian *birich* announcer.]

bridge crane, crane mounted on a horizontal bridge which runs along tracks supported by stationary uprights.

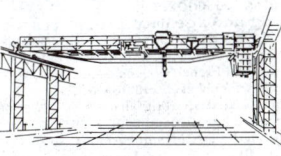

Bridge crane

bridge·head (brij′hed′) *n.* **1.** area secured on the enemy side of an obstacle into which men and supplies may be funneled so that further advance may be made. **2.** any position taken as a foothold from which to advance further.

Bridge·port (brij′pôrt′) *n.* city in southwestern Connecticut. Pop. (1970), 156,542.

Bridg·et, Saint (brij′it) *also,* **Brig·id.** c.450–c.525, one of the patron saints of Ireland. She was abbess of the first convent in Ireland.

bridge table, square table having folding legs, on which card games are played.

Bridge·town (brij′toun′) *n.* capital and largest city of Barbados, on the southwestern coast of the island. Pop. (1969 est.), 12,400.

bridge·work (brij′wurk′) *n.* mounting for false teeth.

bridg·ing (brij′ing) *n.* braces placed diagonally or at right angles between two adjacent beams to reinforce and separate them.

bri·dle (brīd′əl) *n.* **1.** head part of a riding or draft animal′s gear, used to guide or control the animal and usually consisting of a bit, reins, and headstall. **2.** anything that restrains; curb; control: *a bridle on one′s tongue.* —*v.t.,* **-dled, -dling. 1.** to put a bridle on. **2.** to restrain, as with a bridle; curb: *to bridle one′s anger.* —*v.i.* to show anger, indignation, or scorn, as by throwing back the head: *She bridled at his accusations.* [Old English *brīdel* head part of a harness.]

bridle hand, the left hand, in which the reins are usually held.

bridle path, path for horseback riding.

Brie (brē) *n.* variety of soft, creamy cheese with a strong aroma and a mild, rich flavor, ripened by mold or bacteria. [From *Brie,* district in France where it was first made.]

brief (brēf) *adj.* **1.** short in duration; quickly ending: *a brief interruption, a brief stay.* **2.** short in expression; using few words; concise; succinct: *I′ll be brief and to the point. Give a brief summary.* **3.** short in extent or length: *wearing the briefest petticoat* (Scott, 1824). **4.** curt; abrupt: *You very brief with him.* —*n.* **1.** *Law.* summary of the facts, the applicable points of law, and other material pertinent to a case, prepared by the counsel as the basis for arguing a case in court.

at; āpe; cär; end; mē; it; īce; hot; ōld; fôrk; wood; foōl; oil; out; up; ūse; turn; sing; thin; this; zh in treasure; ə in ago, taken, pencil, lemon, circus.

2. briefs. short, close-fitting underpants. **3. in brief.** in a few words; in short. —v.t. **1.** to instruct by a briefing: *The commander briefed his men.* **2.** *British.* to inform by a legal brief. [Old French *brief, bref* short, from Latin *brevis.*] —**brief′ly,** *adv.* —**brief′ness,** *n.* —**Syn.** *adj.* **1.** see short.

brief·case (brēf′kās′) *n.* flat or expansible case, frequently clamped or zippered and having a handle, used esp. for carrying papers and books.

brief·ing (brē′fing) *n.* **1.** meeting at which the important details of a military operation are outlined for the participants. **2.** the outline itself, esp. one given to the pilots or crew of combat planes before they take off. **3.** any similar discussion of procedure, instructions, or other essential information.

bri·er¹ (brī′ər) *also*, **bri·ar.** *n.* **1.** any thorny shrub or plant, esp. the wild rose; bramble. **2.** thorny stem or thorn on such a plant. [Old English *brēr, brēr* this shrub.]

bri·er² (brī′ər) *briar¹.*

bri·er·root (brī′ər rōōt′, -root′) *n.* briarroot.

bri·er·wood (brī′ər wood′) *n.* briarwood.

brig (brig) *n.* **1.** two-masted ship with both masts square-rigged. **2.** place on a ship for confining prisoners. **3.** naval prison. [Short for BRIGANTINE.]

Brig., Brigade; Brigadier.

Brig

bri·gade (bri gād′) *n.* **1.** military unit consisting of from two to five battalions and forming part of a division. **2.** formerly, military unit consisting of two regiments and forming part of a division. **3.** group of people organized for a particular purpose: *a fire brigade.* [French *brigade* troop, from Italian *brigata,* from *brigare* to fight, from *briga* strife; of Celtic origin.]

brig·a·dier (brig′ə dēr′) *n.* brigadier general. [French *brigadier* corporal, from *brigade* troop. See BRIGADE.]

brigadier general, commissioned officer in the U.S. Army, Air Force, or Marines, ranking above a colonel and below a major general.

brig·and (brig′ənd) *n.* robber or bandit, esp. one of a band of roving outlaws. [Old French *brigand,* from Italian *brigante,* from *brigare* to fight. See BRIGADE.]

brig·and·age (brig′ən dij) *n.* practices of brigands; robbery.

brig·an·dine (brig′ən dēn′) *n.* flexible body armor made of cloth, leather, or canvas, with overlapping metal plates sewed or riveted to it. [Old French *brigandine* armor used by *brigands,* from *brigand* foot soldier. See BRIGAND.]

brig·an·tine (brig′ən tēn′) *n.* two-masted ship with both masts square-rigged, except for a fore-and-aft mainsail. [French *brigantin,* from Italian *brigantino* pirate ship, from *brigante* robber. See BRIGAND.]

bright (brīt) *adj.* **1.** radiating or reflecting much light; filled with light; shining: *a bright, sunny day. The waxed floor had a bright finish.* **2.** of brilliant color; vivid: *a bright yellow dress.* **3.** having or showing much intelligence; quick-witted; clever: *a bright student, a bright idea.* **4.** favorable or hopeful; auspicious: *bright prospects, a bright future.* **5.** lively; cheerful: *Everything seemed bright and gay.* **6.** glorious; splendid: *the brightest period of the empire.* —*adv.* in a bright manner; brightly. [Old English *beorht, briht* shining.] —**bright′ly,** *adv.* —**bright′ness,** *n.*

Syn. 1. Bright, brilliant, radiant, luminous mean giving off light. **Bright** is the general word, applicable to anything that emits or reflects strong light or can be thought of as doing so: *a bright lamp, bright red, bright-eyed.* **Brilliant** means very bright: *whitewashed houses brilliant in the Mediterranean sun.* It is also used to mean sparkling: *a brilliant diamond.* **Radiant** stresses the emission of light, rather than the reflection of it, and is often used figuratively: *the radiant intelligence of a Darwin, countenance radiant with warmth.* **Luminous** suggests a soft glow: *The walls of the city were luminous in the moonlight.*

bright·en (brīt′ən) *v.t., v.i.* to make or become bright or brighter. —**bright′en·er,** *n.*

Brigh·ton (brīt′ən) *n.* city in southeastern England, on the English Channel. Pop. (1968 est.) 164,700.

Bright's disease (brīts) any of various forms of kidney disease characterized by a degeneration of the kidneys and the presence of albumin in the urine. [From Dr. Richard Bright, 1789–1858, English physician who studied and wrote about the disease.]

Brig·id, Saint (brij′id) see Bridget, Saint.

brill (bril) *n. pl.* brill *or* brills. *n.* European flatfish, *Scophthalmus rhombus.* [Possibly from Cornish *brilli* mackerel.]

bril·liance (bril′yəns) *n.* quality or state of being brilliant. Also, **bril·lian·cy.**

bril·liant (bril′yənt) *adj.* **1.** sparkling with light or luster; shining radiantly: *brilliant spotlights, brilliant stars.* **2.** splendid or outstanding;

magnificent: *a brilliant career.* **3.** having or showing great intelligence, ability, or talent: *a brilliant mathematician.* **4.** intensely rich in color; vivid: *a peacock's brilliant plumage, brilliant reds and blues.* —*n. gem,* esp. a diamond, cut in a particular form with many facets to increase its sparkle. [French *brillant* shining, present participle of *briller* to shine, possibly going back to Latin *bēryllus* beryl (noted for its glassy luster). See BERYL.] —**bril′liant·ly,** *adv.* —**Syn.** *adj.* **1.** see bright.

bril·lian·tine (bril′yən tēn′) *n.* **1.** oily preparation used to dress the hair. **2.** lightweight glossy fabric made of cotton and wool or mohair, used esp. for summer suits or dresses. [French *brillantine,* from *brillant* shining. See BRILLIANT.]

brim (brim) *n.* **1.** upper edge or rim of a cup, bowl, or similar object. **2.** projecting edge or rim: *the brim of a hat.* **3.** *Archaic.* edge or margin. —*v.i.* **brimmed, brim·ming. 1.** to be full to the brim; overflow: *Her eyes brimmed with tears. He brimmed with happiness.* **2. to brim over.** to overflow: *brimming over with joy.* —*v.t. Archaic.* to fill to the brim. [Old English *brymme* edge, border.]

brim·ful (brim′fool′) *adj.* full to the brim; completely full.

brim·mer (brim′ər) *n. Archaic.* cup, bowl, or similar object full to the brim.

brim·stone (brim′stōn′) *n.* sulfur: *the fire and brimstone of hell.* [Middle English *brinston* literally, burn stone, from *brinnen* to burn¹ + *ston* stone. See BURN¹, STONE.]

brind·ed (brin′did) *adj. Archaic.* brindled. [Middle English *brended,* from *brend,* past participle of *brennen* to burn¹. See BURN¹.]

brin·dle (brin′dəl) *adj.* brindled. —*n.* **1.** brindled color. **2.** brindled animal. [From BRINDLED.]

brin·dled (brin′dəld) *adj.* gray or tawny with irregular, darker streaks or spots. [Modification of BRINDED.]

brine (brīn) *n.* **1.** water full of or saturated with salt, esp. used for pickling or preserving food. **2.** sea water; ocean. —*v.t.* **brined, brin·ing.** to treat with or steep in brine. [Old English *brȳne* salt water.]

bring (bring) brought, bring·ing. *v.t.* **1.** to carry, convey, or cause (someone or something) to come with oneself: *Bring all your books home. He brought a message from her.* **2.** to cause to come; attract; draw: *What brings you here? The screams brought the police. The news brought tears to her eyes.* **3.** to cause to come into a particular state or condition: *to bring a fire under control. Bring the water to a boil.* **4.** to cause to come about or happen; result in; produce: *Floods bring disaster. The drug brought relief from pain.* **5.** to cause (someone or oneself) to adopt a course of action or belief; persuade; induce: *He couldn't bring himself to do it.* **6.** to sell for: *The car brought a high price.*

to bring about. to make happen; cause; accomplish: *The move brought about many changes in his life.*

to bring around (or **round**). **a.** to cause (someone) to adopt an opinion or viewpoint; convince; persuade. **b.** to restore to consciousness; revive.

to bring down. to fell by wounding or killing: *He brought down four ducks.*

to bring down the house. to elicit a burst of applause or laughter from an audience, as in a theater: *His impersonations brought down the house.*

to bring forth. a. to produce (offspring or fruit). **b.** to disclose or advance; introduce: *to bring forth a proposal. He brought forth new evidence.* **c.** to give rise to; cause: *His statements brought forth cries of protest.*

to bring forward. a. to introduce; present: *to bring arguments forward in support of a plan.* **b.** in bookkeeping, to carry (a figure) over from one page or column to another.

to bring in. a. to yield or produce, as profits. **b.** to give or submit (a verdict).

to bring off. to accomplish successfully.

to bring on. to lead to; cause: *The crisis brought on a full-scale war.*

to bring out. a. to cause to be evident; make clear: *That's not the point I want to bring out.* **b.** to introduce or present to the public: *to bring out the fall fashions.*

to bring suit. to start or institute legal proceedings.

to bring to. a. to restore to consciousness; revive. **b.** *Nautical.* to cause (a ship) to come to a standstill.

to bring up. a. to rear; educate. **b.** to introduce to notice or consideration: *to bring up a subject in conversation.* **c.** to cause to pause or stop: *The suggestion brought him up short.* **d.** to cough up; vomit.

[Old English *bringan* to cause to come.]

Syn. 1. Bring, fetch mean to convey toward the speaker. **Bring** means to convey from one place to another where the speaker is or will be: *Bring that over here. Bring her along tonight.* **Fetch,** an infrequent word nowadays, except in reference to retrieving by dogs, implies the actions of going, getting, and bringing back: *Fetch me those books from the next room.*

brink (bringk) *n.* **1.** edge or margin of a steep place, as of a precipice

at; āpe; cär; end; mē; it; īce; hot; ōld; fôrk; wood; fōōl; oil; out; up; ūse; turn; sing; thin; this; zh in treasure; ə in ago, taken, pencil, lemon, circus.

or the bank of a river. **2.** point at which something is likely to begin; verge: *on the brink of disaster. The little boy was on the brink of tears when his toy truck broke.* [Middle English *brink*; probably of Scandinavian origin.]

brink·man·ship (brĭngk′mən shĭp′) *n.* practice of manipulating a dangerous situation to the brink of disaster in order to secure some advantage, esp. when employed by a country in its foreign affairs.

brin·y (brī′nē) **brin·i·er, brin·i·est.** *adj.* of or like brine; salty: *briny taste.* —**brin′i·ness,** *n.*

bri·oche (brē ōsh′) *n.* soft, light roll rich in eggs and butter. [Dialectal French *brioche*, from *brier* to knead, form of French *broyer* to pound; of Germanic origin.]

bri·quette (brĭ ket′) *also,* **bri·quet.** *n.* molded block of compressed coal dust or other material, used for fuel. [French *briquette*, diminutive of *brique* brick. See BRICK.]

Bris·bane (brĭz′bān, -bən) *n.* port city in eastern Australia. Pop. (1968 est.), 680,000.

Bri·se·is (brī sē′ĭs) *n. Greek Legend.* beautiful woman captured by Achilles in the Trojan war but taken from him by the Greek king Agamemnon, causing Achilles to withdraw from battle.

brisk (brĭsk) *adj.* **1.** quick and lively; energetic; vigorous: *a brisk manner, a brisk pace.* **2.** keen; invigorating; bracing: *a brisk wind.* [Probably from French *brusque*. See BRUSQUE.] —**brisk′ly,** *adv.* —**brisk′-ness,** *n.*

bris·ket (brĭs′kĭt) *n.* **1.** cut of meat from the breast of an animal, esp. a beef animal. See *beef* for illustration. **2.** breast of an animal. [Middle English *brusket*; of uncertain origin.]

bris·tle (brĭs′əl) *n.* **1.** one of the coarse, short, stiff hairs of a hog, often used for making brushes. **2.** something resembling this: *The donkey had bristles on its ears and chin. My toothbrush has nylon bristles.* —*v.i.* **-tled, -tling. 1.** to raise the hairs on the back, as in fear, anger, or excitement: *The cat bristled at the sight of water.* **2.** to show anger or irritation: *I bristled at his accusations.* **3.** to become stiffly erect: *The cat's hair bristled as the dog approached.* **4.** to bristle with. to be thick with or full of: *The shores bristled with crabs. He bristled with excitement.* —*v.t.* **1.** to cause to be stiffly erect: *The porcupine bristled his quills. The rooster bristled his crest.* **2.** to furnish with bristles. [Middle English *brustel* hog's hair, stiff hair, diminutive of Old English *byrst* hog's hair.]

bris·tle·tail (brĭs′əl tāl′) *n.* any of the wingless insects of the order Thysanura, such as the silverfish, with long bristle-like appendages at the end of the abdomen.

Bristletail (silverfish)

Bris·tol (brĭs′təl) *n.* **1.** port city in southwestern England. Pop. (1968 est.), 427,800. **2.** city in central Connecticut, near Hartford. Pop. (1970), 55,487.

Bristol board, fine pasteboard having a smooth finish.

Bristol Channel, inlet of the Atlantic, between southern Wales and southwestern England.

Brit., British; British.

Brit·ain (brĭt′ən) *n.* Great Britain.

Bri·tan·ni·a (brĭ tan′ē ə, -tan′yə) *n.* **1.** Great Britain and Ireland. **2.** British Empire. **3.** female figure thought of as representing Great Britain or the British Empire. **4.** Britannia metal. [Latin *Brittannia, Brittānia* island of Britain, from *Brittō.* See BRITON.]

Britannia metal, pewterlike, white alloy of tin, whose main added element is antimony, with lesser amounts of copper. It is malleable and tarnish-resistant and is used esp. in making tableware.

Bri·tan·nic (brĭ tan′ĭk) *adj.* British.

Brit·i·cism (brĭt′i sĭz′əm) *n.* word, phrase, or idiom occurring only or mainly in British English. *Lorry* is a Briticism for *truck.*

Brit·ish (brĭt′ĭsh) *adj.* of, relating to, or characteristic of Great Britain or its people. —*n.* **1. the British.** the people of Great Britain. **2.** British English. [Old English *Brittisc* relating to the ancient Britons, from *Bret* a Briton; of Celtic origin.]

British Columbia, westernmost province of Canada, on the Pacific. Area, 366,255 sq. mi. Pop. (1970 est.), 2,070,000.

British Commonwealth of Nations, see **Commonwealth of Nations.**

British Empire, formerly, all the countries, colonies, dependencies, and protectorates that owed allegiance to the British crown. The term now has no official use.

British English, the English language as spoken and written predominantly in Great Britain. Distinguished esp. from **American English.**

Brit·ish·er (brĭt′i shər) *n.* native or subject of Great Britain, esp. of England.

British Guiana, Guyana.

British Honduras, former British possession on the northeastern coast of Central America, on the Caribbean, now Belize.

British Isles, island group off the western coast of continental Europe, including Great Britain, Ireland, and many smaller islands.

British thermal unit, unit for measuring the amount of heat needed to raise the temperature of one pound of water one degree Fahrenheit.

British West Indies, British island possessions in the West Indies, comprising the Bahamas, the Windward Islands, Leeward Islands, British Virgin Islands, and others.

Brit·on (brĭt′ən) *n.* **1.** Britisher. **2.** member of an ancient Celtic people inhabiting southern Britain at the time of the Roman invasion. [Old French *Breton* Breton, from Latin *Brittō* ancient Briton, Breton; probably of Celtic origin.]

Brit·ta·ny (brĭt′ə nē) *n.* historic region in northwestern France, between the English Channel and the Bay of Biscay.

brit·tle (brĭt′əl) *adj.* **1.** liable to break or snap; easily broken: *brittle fingernails.* **2.** curt; irritable: *a brittle manner, a brittle personality.* [Middle English *britel* easily broken, going back to Old English *brēotan* to break.] —**brit′tle·ness,** *n.* —**Syn. 1.** see **fragile.**

Br·no (bûr′nō) *n.* city in central Czechoslovakia. Pop. (1967 est.), 333,831. Also, *German,* **Brünn.**

bro., brother.

broach (brōch) *n.* **1.** cutting tool consisting of a tapered steel shaft with transverse cutting edges, driven or pulled through rough holes to enlarge or shape them. **2.** spit for roasting. —*v.t.* **1.** to mention or suggest for the first time; introduce: *I hesitated to broach the topic while he was angry.* **2.** to draw, as to draw out a liquid; tap: *to broach a keg of wine.* [Old French *broche* a roasting spit, clasp, from Late Latin *brocca* pointed stick, from Latin *broccus* projecting.]

broad (brôd) *adj.* **1.a.** of large extent from side to side; wide: *The broad boulevard had four traffic lanes.* **b.** large in size; spacious: *broad plains, a broad expanse of mountains.* **2.** tolerant; open-minded: *a broad outlook.* **3.** having a wide range or application; extensive: *broad interests, a broad rule.* **4.** concerning the main features; general: *a broad description.* **5.** clear; obvious: *a broad hint.* **6.** widely diffused; full: *broad daylight.* **7.** coarse; vulgar; earthy: *broad humor.* **8.** strongly marked or idealectal: *a broad accent.* **9.** (of vowel sounds) formed with the mouth open wide and the back portion of the tongue in a low, flat position. The *a* in *father* is broad. [Old English *brād* wide.] —**broad′ly,** *adv.* —**broad′ness,** *n.*

broad·ax (brôd′aks′) *pl.,* **ax·es.** *also,* **broad·axe.** *n.* **1.** wide-bladed ax, used esp. to cut logs or to make incisions in trees to obtain turpentine. **2.** battle-ax *(def.1).*

broad·brim (brôd′brĭm′) *n.* **1.** hat with a wide brim. **2.** *also,* **Broad-brim.** *Informal.* Quaker.

broad·cast (brôd′kast′) **-cast** *or* **-cast·ed, -cast·ing.** *v.t.* **1.** to transmit (information or entertainment) by radio or television. **2.** to make widely known or spread: *He broadcast the secret to the whole school.* **3.** to scatter over a wide area, as seed. —*v.i.* to transmit by radio or television: *The major stations are not broadcasting today.* —*n.* **1.** that which is broadcast by radio or television, esp. a program: *He will appear on tomorrow's broadcast.* **2.** act of broadcasting, esp. transmission by radio or television. —*adj.* **1.** of, relating to, or transmitted by radio or television broadcasts. **2.** scattered over a wide area: *broadcast seed.* —*adv.* by scattering over a large area. [BROAD + CAST.] —**broad′cast′er,** *n.*

broad·cloth (brôd′klôth′) *n.* **1.** smooth, closely woven cotton or cotton polyester fabric, used esp. in making shirts, pajamas, and dresses. **2.** fabric similar to cotton broadcloth but made of rayon or silk. **3.** woolen fabric of compact weave, often a twill, used esp. in suits and coats.

broad·en (brôd′ən) *v.t., v.i.* to make or become broad or broader: *The workmen broadened the road. One's views broaden at college.*

broad-gauge (brôd′gāj′) *adj.* (of railroad tracks) having a width between rails greater than the standard gauge of 56½ inches.

broad jump 1. field event in which the contestant jumps for distance either from a standing position or from a running start. **2.** such a jump.

broad·loom (brôd′lōōm′) *n.* carpet woven on a wide loom, usually in widths ranging from six to eighteen feet. Also, **broadloom carpet.**

broad-mind·ed (brôd′mīn′dĭd) *adj.* tolerant of views and behavior different from one's own; liberal. —**broad-′mind′ed·ly,** *adv.* —**broad-′mind′ed·ness,** *n.*

broad·side (brôd′sīd′) *n.* **1.** whole side of a boat or ship above the water line. **2.a.** simultaneous discharge of all the guns on one side of a ship. **b.** all the guns on one side of a ship. **3.** condemning or abusive attack. **4.** broad surface or side, esp. of a large structure. **5.** *Archaic.* large sheet of paper printed on one side only, as with advertisements. —*adv.* with the side turned; on the side; sideward: *The wave caught the boat broadside, almost capsizing it.*

broad-spec·trum (brôd′spek′trəm) *adj.* (of drugs) effective against a wide range of microorganisms: *a broad-spectrum antibiotic.*

---

broad·sword (brôd′sôrd′) *n.* sword with a broad, flat blade, made for cutting rather than thrusting.

broad·tail (brôd′tāl′) *n.* fur from prematurely born karakul lambs, having a wavy surface instead of the tight curls of Persian lamb.

Broad·way (brôd′wā′) *n.* street running through New York City, noted for its entertainment section and as the center of the country's theater industry.

Brob·ding·nag (brob′ding nag′) *also,* **Brob·dig·nag.** *n.* the land of giants in Jonathan Swift's *Gulliver's Travels.*

Brob·ding·nag·i·an (brob′ding nag′ē ən) *also,* **Brob·dig·nag·i·an.** *adj.* of or like Brobdingnag or its inhabitants; of enormous size; gigantic. —*n.* person of enormous size; giant.

bro·cade (brō kād′) *n.* elegant, heavy fabric woven with raised designs. —*v.t.,* **-cad·ed, -cad·ing.** to weave (fabric) with a raised design. [Spanish *brocado* this fabric, from *broca* reel for weaving, spindle, going back to Latin *broccus* projecting (like teeth).]

broc·co·li (brok′ə lē) *n.* **1.** thick branching green stems and unripened flower buds of a plant, *Brassica oleracea,* variety *italica,* cooked and eaten as a vegetable. **2.** the plant itself, related to the cabbage. [Italian *broccoli* sprouts, going back to Latin *broccus* projecting (like teeth).]

Broccoli

bro·chure (brō shoor′) *n.* pamphlet. [French *brochure* literally, stitching (of the pages), from *brocher* to stitch, from *broche* spindle, spit, going back to Latin *broccus* projecting (like teeth).]

Brock·ton (brok′tən) *n.* city in southeastern Massachusetts. Pop. (1970), 89,040.

bro·gan (brō′gən) *n.* coarse, sturdy shoe, esp. one that reaches to the ankle. [Irish and Scottish Gaelic *brōgan,* diminutive of *brōg* shoe. See BROGUE².]

brogue¹ (brōg) *n.* thick or rough Irish or Scottish accent in the pronunciation of English. [Possibly from Irish *barrōg* hold, grip, in the sense of a hold on the tongue; possibly from an association of the BROGUES² worn by the Irish and the Scottish with their pronunciation of English.]

brogue² (brōg) *n.* **1.** coarsely made shoe of untanned hide, formerly worn in Ireland and Scotland. **2.** any heavy, clumsy shoe. [Irish and Scottish Gaelic *brōg* shoe, from Old Norse *brōk* hose.]

broil¹ (broil) *v.t.* **1.** to cook by exposing to fire or direct heat; grill. **2.** to make very hot; scorch. —*v.i.* **1.** to be cooked by exposure to direct heat. **2.** to be subjected to great heat; become very hot: *to broil under the hot sun at the beach.* **3.** to become very angry. —*n.* anything broiled, esp. meat. [Anglo-Norman *broiller* to boil, roast; of uncertain origin.]

broil² (broil) *n.* angry quarrel; tumult; brawl. —*v.i.* to raise or engage in a broil; quarrel. [French *brouiller* to confuse; of uncertain origin.]

broil·er (broi′lər) *n.* **1.** any device for broiling food. **2.** a chicken, usually young and tender, suitable for broiling.

broke (brōk) *v.* past tense of **break.** —*adj.* **1.** *Informal.* having little or no money. **2. to go broke.** *Informal.* to lose all one's money; become bankrupt. **3. to go for broke.** *Slang.* to risk everything in an attempt to win or achieve something.

bro·ken (brō′kən) *v.* past participle of **break.** —*adj.* **1.** separated forcibly into fragments; fractured: *a broken window, a broken arm.* **2.** having continuity interrupted as if by breaking: *broken home, broken circuit, broken ground.* **3.** transgressed; violated: *a broken promise.* **4.** lacking morale; depressed; humbled: *a broken man.* **5.** reduced to obedience or discipline; tamed: *a broken horse.* **6.** weakened; exhausted: *broken health.* **7.** imperfectly spoken: *The tourists spoke broken English.* **8.** financially ruined; bankrupt. **9.** incomplete; fragmentary: *broken set.* **10.** uttered disjointedly or haltingly: *broken sobs.* —**bro′ken·ly,** *adv.* —**bro′ken·ness,** *n.*

bro·ken-down (brō′kən doun′) *adj.* **1.** in poor condition; dilapidated: *a broken-down house.* **2.** not functioning: *a broken-down car.*

bro·ken-heart·ed (brō′kən här′tid) *adj.* crushed by despair or grief; heartbroken.

broken wind, heaves. —**bro′ken-wind′ed,** *adj.*

bro·ker (brō′kər) *n.* agent who arranges for the purchase or sale of stocks, bonds, commodities, or other property, negotiates contracts, or handles other business affairs for a client, receiving a commission or fee for his services: *insurance broker, real estate broker, ticket broker.* [Anglo-Norman *brocour* agent, originally, seller of wine, one who broached wine barrels, from Old French *broche.* See BROACH.]

bro·ker·age (brō′kər ij) *n.* **1.** business of a broker; broker's trade. **2.** fee or commission charged by a broker.

brokerage house, business establishment that deals in the purchase or sale of commodities and securities for other people.

bro·mide (brō′mīd) *n.* **1.** compound consisting of bromine and another element or radical. **2.** bromine compound used as a sedative or analgesic, esp. potassium bromide. **3.** *Informal.* **a.** trite or commonplace statement; platitude. **b.** one who makes such statements. [BROM(INE) + -IDE.]

bro·mid·ic (brō mid′ik) *adj. Informal.* commonplace; trite.

bro·mine (brō′mēn) *n.* reddish-brown nonmetallic liquid element of the halogen group having a disagreeable odor and irritating fumes and causing chemical burns on contact. It is used esp. in gasoline, drugs, dyes, and photographic chemicals. Symbol: **Br** See **element** for table. [Greek *brōmos* stink + -INE², so called because of its bad odor.]

bronch-, form of broncho- before vowels.

bron·chi (brong′kī, -kē) plural of **bronchus.**

bron·chi·a (brong′kē ə) *n. pl.* bronchial tubes that are branches or subdivisions of the bronchi but are larger than the bronchioles.

bron·chi·al (brong′kē əl) *adj.* of or relating to the bronchi, bronchia, or bronchioles.

bronchial tubes, the passages through which air flows to and from the lungs, consisting of the bronchi and their branching tubes.

bron·chi·ole (brong′kē ōl′) *n.* smallest subdivision of a bronchus.

bron·chi·tis (brong kī′tis) *n.* inflammation of the bronchial tubes. [Modern Latin *bronchitis,* from Greek *bronchos* windpipe + -ITIS.] —**bron·chit·ic** (brong kit′ik) *adj.*

bron·cho (brong′kō) *pl.,* **-chos.** *n.* bronco.

broncho- *combining form* of or relating to a bronchus or the bronchi: *bronchopneumonia.* [Greek *bronchos* windpipe.]

bron·cho·pneu·mo·nia (brong′kō nŏō mōn′yə, -nū-) *n.* inflammation of the lungs in which the bronchioles become clogged. Also, **bronchial pneumonia.**

bron·chus (brong′kəs) *pl.,* **-chi.** *n.* either of the two main divisions of the windpipe that allow the passage of air into the lungs. [Modern Latin *bronchus,* from Greek *bronchos* windpipe.]

bron·co (brong′kō) *pl.,* **-cos.** *also,* **bron·cho.** *n.* small, untamed or partially tamed horse of the western United States. [Spanish *bronco* rough, rude (applied to a wild pony); of uncertain origin.]

bron·co·bust·er (brong′kō bus′tər) *n.* in the western United States, one who breaks broncos to the saddle.

Bron·të (bron′tē) **1. Anne.** 1820–49, English novelist. **2. Charlotte.** 1816–55, her sister; English novelist. **3. Emily.** 1818–48, her sister; English novelist.

bron·to·sau·rus (bron′tə sôr′əs) *n.* any of various plant-eating dinosaurs, genus *Apatosaurus,* order Saurischia, which lived during the Jurassic period. It was one of the largest land animals, growing to as long as eighty feet and weighing up to thirty-five tons. Also, **bron·to·saur** (bron′tə sôr′). [Modern Latin *Brontosaurus,* from Greek *brontē* thunder + *sauros* lizard. The scientific name *Brontosaurus* has been replaced by *Apatosaurus.*]

Brontosaurus

Bronx, The (brongks) *n.* borough of New York City, northeast of Manhattan. Area, 43.1 sq. mi. Pop. (1970), 1,472,216.

bronze (bronz) *n.* **1.** alloy of copper and tin, which is hard and malleable and resists corrosion. **2.** alloy of copper and a metal other than tin, such as manganese, silicon, or aluminum. ▲ In commercial usage some copper-base alloys may be called *bronze* since they are higher in quality than *brass.* **3.** work of art, as a statue, made of bronze. **4.** reddish-brown color similar to that of bronze. —*adj.* **1.** made of bronze. **2.** of the color of bronze. —*v.t.,* **bronzed, bronz·ing.** to give a bronzelike color or appearance to; brown. —*v.i.* to become bronze in color; turn brown; tan. [French *bronze* alloy of copper and tin, from Italian *bronzo;* of uncertain origin.] —**bronz′y,** *adj.*

Bronze Age, stage in the development of civilization, from the end of the Stone Age to the Iron Age, characterized by the widespread use of bronze, as in making tools and weapons.

brooch (brōch, brōōch) *n.* ornamental pin usually worn at the neck or breast, fastened by a clasp. [Form of BROACH.]

brood (brōōd) *n.* **1.** the young of an animal, esp. of a bird, produced or cared for at the same time. **2.** all of the children in one family. **3.** breed; kind; species. —*v.i.* **1.** to meditate moodily and persistently: *He brooded over his failure.* **2.** to sit on eggs in order to hatch them; incubate. —*v.t.* to sit on (eggs) until they hatch; incubate. —*adj.* **1.** *also,* **brooding.** (of a hen) that hatches eggs and cares for newly

at; āpe; cär; end; mē; it; īce; hot; ōld; fôrk; wood; fōōl; oil; out; up; ūse; turn; sing; thin; this; zh in treasure; ə in ago, taken, pencil, lemon, circus.

hatched chicks. **2.** of or relating to a female animal kept for breeding: *a brood mare, a brood cow.* [Old English *brōd* the young of an animal.]

brood·er (brōō′dər) *n.* **1.** structure for keeping newly hatched chicks in a heated, controlled environment, usually for six to eight weeks. **2.** hen that hatches eggs and cares for newly hatched chicks. **3.** person who broods.

brook¹ (brook) *n.* small, natural stream. [Old English *brōc.*]

brook² (brook) *v.t.* to put up with; endure; tolerate: *The teacher brooks no nonsense.* ▲ usually used with a negative construction. [Old English *brūcan* to use.]

brook·let (brook′lit) *n.* small brook.

Brook·line (brook′līn) *n.* town in eastern Massachusetts, a residential suburb of Boston. Pop. (1970), 58,886.

Brook·lyn (brook′lin) *n.* borough of New York City, southeast of Manhattan. Area, 78.5 sq. mi. Pop. (1970), 2,601,852.

brook trout, olive-brown game fish of eastern North America, *Salvelinus fontinalis,* having wormlike markings or speckles on its back. Also, **speckled trout.**

broom (brōom, broom) *n.* **1.** brush with a long handle, used for sweeping. **2.** any of several trees and shrubs of the pea family, esp. of the genera *Cytisus* and *Genista.* **3.** any of various other plants, as butcher's-broom. [Old English *brōm* broom shrub.]

broom·corn (brōom′kôrn′, broom′-) *n.* any of a group of grassy plants, genus *Sorghum,* whose grain grows on long, strawlike stems which are used in some regions for making brooms.

broom·stick (brōom′stik′, broom′-) *n.* handle of a broom.

bros., brothers.

broth (brôth) *pl.,* **broths** (brôths, brôthz). *n.* thin soup. [Old English *broth.*]

broth·el (broth′əl, brô′thəl) *n.* house of prostitution. [From Middle English *brothel* prostitute, scoundrel, going back to Old English *brothen* ruined.]

broth·er (bruth′ər) *pl.,* **brothers** or *(defs. 4, 5)* **breth·ren.** *n.* **1.** male person having the same parents as another person of either sex. **2.** male person having one parent in common with another person of either sex; half brother. **3.** stepbrother. **4.** person to whom one feels closely associated, as through affection; fellow human being. **5.** fellow member, as of a church, profession, or fraternal order. **6.** male member of a religious order who is not a priest. [Old English *brōthor* male child having the same parents as another child, fellow man, member of a Christian order.]

broth·er·hood (bruth′ər hood′) *n.* **1.** state or quality of being a brother or brothers; brotherly relationship. **2.** all the members of an association of men, as of a fraternal order.

broth·er-in-law (bruth′ər in lô′) *pl.,* **broth·ers-in-law.** *n.* **1.** brother of one's husband or wife. **2.** husband of one's sister. **3.** husband of one's wife's sister.

Brother Jonathan *Archaic.* the United States government or any of its people. Formerly contrasted with **John Bull.** [Term used by British soldiers and Americans loyal to England at the time of the Revolutionary War to denote American patriots.]

broth·er·ly (bruth′ər lē) *adj.* relating to, characteristic of, or befitting a brother; kind; affectionate. —*adv.* in the manner of a brother. —**broth′er·li·ness,** *n.*

brougham (brōom, brōō′əm, brō′-) *n.* **1.** closed, four-wheeled, horse-drawn carriage having seating capacity for two or four passengers and an uncovered

Brougham

raised seat for the driver. **2.** automobile having an enclosed passenger compartment and an exposed driver's seat. **3.** early electric automobile resembling a coupe. [From the British statesman Lord *Brougham,* 1778–1868.]

brought (brôt) past tense and past participle of **bring.**

brow (brou) *n.* **1.** forehead. **2.** *also,* **brows.** eyebrow. **3.** general expression; countenance. **4.** edge of a steep place; upper portion of a slope. [Old English *brū* eyebrow.]

brow·beat (brou′bēt′) -**beat,** -**beat·en,** -**beat·ing.** *v.t.* to intimidate with stern, overbearing looks or words; bully: *The leader browbeat us until we agreed to go with him.*

brown (broun) *n.* dark color combining red, yellow, and black. —*adj.* **1.** of the color brown. **2.** dark-complexioned; tanned. —*v.t.* to make brown. —*v.i.* to become brown. [Old English *brūn* dusky, dark.] —**brown′ish,** *adj.* —**brown′ness,** *n.*

Brown, John (broun) 1800–59, U.S. abolitionist who in 1859 led the Harper's Ferry raid.

brown bear, any of various bears, genus *Ursus,* native to North

America, Europe, and Asia, and having fur that ranges from yellowish-brown to very dark brown. Height: to 9 feet.

brown bet·ty (bet′ē) baked pudding of bread crumbs, sugar, spices, butter, and fruit, esp. apples.

brown bread, any bread made of dark flour, as rye bread or whole wheat bread.

brown coal, lignite.

Browne, Sir Thomas (broun) 1605–82, English author and physician.

Brown·i·an movement (brou′nē ən) rapid erratic movements of small particles suspended in gas or liquid, caused by impact with molecules of the gas or liquid. Also, **Brownian motion.** [From the British botanist Robert *Brown,* 1773–1858, its discoverer.]

brown·ie (brou′nē) *n.* **1.** good-natured elf or goblin that does good deeds. **2.** flat, sweet cake, usually chocolate, sometimes made with nuts or topped with frosting. **3. Brownie,** girl between the ages of seven and nine who belongs to the junior division of the Girl Scouts. [BROWN + -IE.]

Brown·ing (brou′ning) **1. Robert.** 1812–89, English poet. **2. Elizabeth Bar·rett** (bar′it). 1806–61, his wife; English poet.

brown rice, rice with the hulls removed, but with the layers of bran still intact.

brown shirt 1. also, **Brown Shirt.** storm trooper. **2.** any Nazi.

brown·stone (broun′stōn′) *n.* **1.** reddish-brown sandstone, used as a building material. **2.** house with a brownstone façade.

brown study, state of being absorbed in serious thought; meditation.

brown sugar, partially refined sugar retaining traces of molasses, which gives it a dark or golden-brown color.

Browns·ville (brounz′vil′) *n.* city in southernmost Texas. Pop. (1970), 52,522.

brown thrasher, reddish-brown songbird, *Toxostoma rufum,* of eastern North America, closely related to the mockingbird, having a slender, curved beak, long tail, and black and white markings. Length: 11 inches.

browse (brouz) **browsed, brows·ing.** *v.i.* **1.** to glance through or look at leisurely or casually, as a book, store, or merchandise: *We browse through the antique shop.* **2.** to feed, as on leaves or twigs: *The deer browsed in the field.* —*v.t.* **1.** to cause to feed on browse: *The farmer browsed his cattle.* **2.** to feed on (browse): *The cows browsed the hillside.* —*n.* tender parts of shrubs or trees on which certain animals, as cattle or deer, feed. [Middle French *broust* bud, shoot; of Germanic origin.] —**brows′er,** *n.*

Bruce, Robert the (brōōs) 1274–1329, king of Scotland from 1306 to 1329. Also, **Robert I.**

bru·cel·lo·sis (brōō′sə lō′sis) *n.* undulant fever. [Modern Latin *Brucella* (from David *Bruce,* 1855–1931, British doctor) + -OSIS.]

Bruck·ner, Anton (brook′nər) 1824–96, Austrian composer.

Brue·ghel, Pieter (broi′gəl, brōō′-) c.1525–69, Flemish painter.

Bru·ges (brōō′jiz, brōōzh) *n.* historic city in northwestern Belgium. Pop. (1968 est.), 51,274. Also, *Flemish,* **Brug·ge** (brœKH′ə).

bru·in (brōō′in) *n.* bear, esp. a brown bear. [Dutch *bruin* brown, name (and color) of the bear in a medieval bestiary.]

bruise (brōōz) *n.* **1.** injury, as from a fall or blow, that discolors but does not break the surface of the skin. **2.** discoloration on the outer surface of a fruit, vegetable, or plant caused by such an injury. —*v.t.* **bruised, bruis·ing.** **1.** to cause a bruise on the surface of: *to bruise one's leg, to bruise a banana.* **2.** to injure or hurt slightly: *The critic's comments bruised the actor's feelings.* **3.** to pound, crush, or grind (drugs or food). —*v.i.* to become bruised. [Partly from Old English *brȳsan* to crush; partly from Old French *bruisier* to break; of uncertain origin.]

bruis·er (brōō′zər) *n. Informal.* **1.** bully. **2.** tough, husky person.

bruit (brōōt) *v.t.* to spread a rumor of; announce; report: *Reports of victory were bruited about.* —*n. Archaic.* **1.** report; rumor. **2.** noise; din; clamor. [Old French *bruit* loud noise, from *bruire* to roar, possibly going back to Latin *rugīre* to roar.]

brum·ma·gem (brum′ə jəm) *Informal. adj.* showy but worthless; sham. —*n.* something showy but worthless or of inferior quality. [Modification of *Birmingham,* English city at one time noted for cheap, showy products and counterfeit coins.]

brunch (brunch) *n.* meal eaten late in the morning in lieu of breakfast and lunch. —*v.i.* to eat brunch. [Blend of BR(EAKFAST) and (L)UNCH.]

Bru·nei (broo nī′) *n.* British protectorate on the northern coast of Borneo. Area, 2226 sq. mi. Pop. (1969 est.), 116,000.

Bru·nel·les·chi, Fi·lip·po (brōō′nə les′kē; fi lip′ō) 1377–1446, Florentine architect.

bru·nette (brōō net′) *also,* **bru·net.** *adj.* **1.** (of hair) having some shade of brown or brownish-black as its color. **2.** (of a person) having such hair. **3.** dark-colored: *brunet complexion.* —*n.* person with brunet hair. ▲ **brunette** is used for the feminine and is the more common form; **brunet** is used for both the masculine and the neuter: *a brunette (girl),*

a brunet (man), brunet (color). [French *brunette,* feminine of *brunet* brownish, diminutive of *brun* brown; of Germanic origin.]

Brun·hild (brōōn'hild', broon'hilt') *n.* in the *Nibelungenlied,* legendary queen of Iceland, whom Siegfried won as a wife for Gunther.

Brünn (broon) *n. German.* Brno.

Brünn·hil·de (broon hil'də) *n.* heroine of Richard Wagner's operatic cycle based on the *Nibelungenlied.*

Bruns·wick (brunz'wik) *n.* **1.** city in northeastern West Germany. Pop. (1968 est.), 227,319. **2.** historic state in northern Germany. Also, *German,* **Braun'schweig'.**

brunt (brunt) *n.* main stress or violence: *Foot soldiers bore the brunt of the attack.* [Of uncertain origin.]

brush¹ (brush) *n.* **1.** implement consisting of bristles, hairs, wires, or similar material, set into a stiff back and often having a handle: *a hair brush, a paint brush, a clothes brush.* **2.** act of brushing. **3.** light, momentary touch. **4.** slight encounter; skirmish. **5.** anything resembling a brush, as the bushy tail of an animal. **6.** brushwork. **7.** electrical conductor that serves to make contact between stationary and moving parts, as of a motor or generator. —*v.t.* **1.** to use a brush on, as in painting, cleaning, or smoothing: *He brushed his hair.* **2.** to remove with or as with a brush: *He brushed the ashes from his coat.* **3.** to graze lightly in passing. **4. to brush aside** (or **away**). to regard as unworthy of consideration; disregard. **5. to brush off.** to dismiss or reject curtly. **6. to brush up. a.** to refresh one's acquaintance with. **b.** to improve in any way; renovate. —*v.i.* to graze lightly and quickly, as in passing: *She brushed against a chair as she rushed to answer the telephone.* [Old French *broisse* brushwood, possibly going back to Latin *bruscum* outgrowth on the maple.] —**brush'y,** *adj.*

brush² (brush) *n.* **1.** growth of shrubs and bushes; thicket. **2.** cut or broken twigs or branches. **3.** thinly settled country; backwoods. [Old French *broche* brushwood, possibly going back to Latin *bruscum* outgrowth on the maple.] —**brush'y,** *adj.*

brush-off (brush'ôf') *n. Informal.* curt dismissal or rejection.

brush·wood (brush'wood') *n.* **1.** broken or cut-off twigs or branches. **2.** dense growth of small trees, shrubs, or bushes.

brush·work (brush'wurk') *n.* **1.** characteristic manner of applying paint with a brush: *Van Gogh's brushwork.* **2.** quality of the marks made on the surface of a painting by a brush as paint is applied.

brusque (brusk) *adj.* rude in manner or speech; blunt. [French *brusque* harsh, from Italian *brusco* rough, sour, possibly a blend of Late Latin *brūcus* heather, and Latin *rūscum* broom (shrub).] —**brusque'ly,** *adv.* —**brusque'ness,** *n.* —**Syn.** see **abrupt.**

Brus·sels (brus'əlz) *n.* capital of Belgium, in the central part of the country. Pop. (1968 est.), 166,920.

Brussels carpet, wool carpet having a patterned pile formed from loops of several colors, attached to a strongly woven back of heavy linen, cotton, jute, or woolen yarn.

Brussels lace, fine lace with elaborate appliqued motifs, formerly handmade.

Brussels sprouts 1. buds resembling small cabbages that grow on the stem of a plant, *Brassica oleracea,* variety *gemmifera,* which are cooked and eaten as a vegetable. **2.** the leafy plant itself, widely cultivated in temperate regions.

bru·tal (brōōt'əl) *adj.* characteristic of or like a brute; inhuman; cruel; savage. —**bru'tal·ly,** *adv.*

bru·tal·i·ty (brōō tal'ə tē) *pl.* **-ties.** *n.* **1.** quality of being brutal; cruelty; inhumanity. **2.** brutal act.

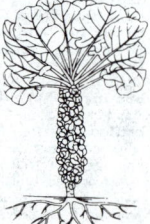

Brussels sprouts

bru·tal·ize (brōōt'əl īz') **-ized, -iz·ing.** *v.t., v.i.* to make or become brutal. —**bru'tal·i·za'tion,** *n.*

brute (brōōt) *n.* **1.** any animal except man. **2.** brutal person. **3.** animal nature in man. —*adj.* **1.** without the ability to reason; not human. **2.** of brutal character or quality; characteristic of animals: *brute strength.* **3.** without reason; unconscious; irrational: *The land has been changed by the brute forces of nature* (Kingsley, 1866). [French *brut* raw, rude, from Latin *brūtus* heavy, stupid.] —**Syn.** *n.* **1.** see **animal.**

brut·ish (brōō'tish) *adj.* relating to, like, or characteristic of a brute; stupid; savage. —**brut'ish·ly,** *adv.* —**brut'ish·ness,** *n.*

Bru·tus, Marcus Jun·ius (brōō'təs; jōōn'yəs) c.85–42 B.C., Roman scholar, soldier, and politician, assassin of Julius Caesar.

Bry·an, William Jen·nings (brī'ən; jen'ingz) 1860–1925, U.S. politician, a leader of the Democratic Party.

Bry·ant, William Cul·len (brī'ənt; kul'ən) 1794–1878, U.S. poet and editor.

Bryn·hild (brin'hild') *n. Norse Legend.* Valkyrie whom Sigurd tricked into marrying Gunnar.

bry·ol·o·gy (brī ol'ə jē) *n.* branch of botany that deals with the study of bryophytes. [Greek *bryon* moss + -LOGY.]

bry·o·ny (brī'ə nē) *pl.,* **-nies.** *n.* any of the climbing plants in the genus *Bryonia,* of the gourd family, native to temperate regions of Europe and western Asia, having five-lobed leaves, greenish-white flowers, and red berries. [Latin *bryōnia,* from Greek *bryōniā.*]

bry·o·phyte (brī'ə fīt') *n.* any of the mosses or liverworts, two classes of small green plants which constitute a division, Bryophyta, of the plant kingdom. [Modern Latin *Bryophyta,* from Greek *bryon* moss + *phyton* plant.] —**bry'o·phyt'ic** (brī'ə fit'ik), *adj.*

b.s. **1.** bill of sale. **2.** balance sheet.

B.S. Bachelor of Science. Also, **B.Sc.**

btl. bottle.

btry. battery.

BTU, British thermal unit or units.

bu., bushel; bushels.

bub·ble (bub'əl) *n.* **1.** thin globular film of liquid filled with air or other gas: *The children blew bubbles with a bubble pipe.* **2.** small globule of air or other gas in a solid or liquid: *There are bubbles in carbonated soda.* **3.** act, process, or sound of bubbling: *the bubble of boiling water.* **4.** something unsubstantial or worthless, esp. an unsuccessful or fraudulent financial scheme. —*v.i.* **-bled, -bling. 1.** to form or rise in bubbles: *The boiling soup bubbled rapidly.* **2.** to flow with or make a gurgling sound. **3.** to show an emotion, as happiness, glee, or enthusiasm, in an effervescent manner: *She bubbled with joy.* **4. to bubble over. a.** to overflow. **b.** to effervesce, as with great happiness, glee, or enthusiasm. —*v.t.* to cause to bubble; form bubbles in. [Imitative.] —**bub'bly,** *adj.*

bubble chamber, device filled with a superheated liquid through which accelerated subatomic particles pass, leaving trails of bubbles by which the particles can be identified.

bubble gum, chewing gum that can be blown into large bubbles.

bub·bler (bub'lər) *n.* drinking fountain from which bubbling water enables one to drink without using a cup.

Bu·ber, Martin (bōō'bər) 1878–1965, philosopher and Jewish religious scholar.

bu·bo (bū'bō) *pl.,* **bu·boes.** *n.* inflammation and swelling of a lymph node, esp. in the groin or armpit. [Late Latin *bubo* swelling, from Greek *boubōn* groin, swollen gland.]

bu·bon·ic (bū bon'ik, bōō-) *adj.* relating to or characterized by buboes.

bubonic plague, serious disease characterized by the formation of buboes and a high fever, carried to humans by fleas from infected rodents.

buc·cal (buk'əl) *adj.* **1.** of or relating to the cheek. **2.** relating to the sides of the mouth or to the mouth; oral. [Latin *bucca* cheek, mouth + -AL.]

buc·ca·neer (buk'ə nēr') *n.* **1.** pirate. **2.** any of certain pirates of the seventeenth and eighteenth centuries who attacked and robbed Spanish ships and settlements in America. [French *boucanier,* originally, one who smokes meat, from *boucan* frame for smoking meat, from Tupi-Guarani *mccaem;* adopted by seventeenth-century French settlers in the West Indies, many of whom became pirates.]

Bu·ceph·a·lus (bū sef'ə ləs) *n.* the war horse of Alexander the Great. [Latin *Būcephalus,* from Greek *Boukephalos* literally, ox head, from *bous* ox + *kephalē* head.]

Bu·chan·an, James (bū kan'ən, bə-) 1791–1868, fifteenth president of the United States from 1857 to 1861.

Bu·cha·rest (bōō'kə rest', bū'-) *n.* capital and largest city of Romania, in the southern part of the country. Pop. (1968 est.), 1,431,993.

Buch·en·wald (book'ən wôld') *n.* Nazi concentration camp built in 1933 near Weimar, Germany.

buck¹ (buk) *n.* **1.** male of certain animals, esp. of deer or antelope. **2.a.** man. **b.** fop; dandy. **3.** act of bucking. —*v.i.* **1.** (of certain riding animals) to jump, kick, arch the back, or otherwise contort the body, in order to throw off the rider or load. **2.** *Informal.* to resist obstinately; balk (with *at): to buck at authority.* **3. to buck up.** *Informal.* to become more confident or courageous; cheer up. —*v.t.* **1.** to throw by bucking. **2.** *Informal.* to resist; oppose. **3.** to charge at and strike with the head; butt. **4.** in football, to make a quick charge into (the opposing line) while carrying the ball. **5. to buck for.** *Informal.* to strive for (a better position, raise, or other gain). —*adj. Slang.* of the lowest grade of a specific military rank: *buck private, buck sergeant.* [Old English *buc* male deer, and *bucca* male goat.]

buck² (buk) *n. Slang.* dollar. **2. to pass the buck.** *Informal.* to shift the responsibility, duty, or blame to someone else. [Possibly from the use of silver dollars as *bucks,* or markers, passed from one player to another to indicate the dealer's turn in poker.]

buck³ (buk) *n.* **1.** sawhorse. **2.** padded block on a frame resembling a sawhorse, used in gymnastics. [Short for SAWBUCK.]

buck·a·roo (buk'ə rōō') *pl.,* **-roos.** *also,* **buck·er·oo.** *n.* cowboy. [Modification of VAQUERO.]

buck·board (buk′bôrd′) *n.* open, four-wheeled carriage which has a platform of long, flexible boards in place of body and springs upon which the seat rests.

buck·er (buk′ər) *n.* horse that bucks.

buck·er·oo (buk′ə rōō′) *pl.*, **-oos.** *n.* buckaroo.

buck·et (buk′it) *n.* **1.** round, hollow container with a flat bottom and usually a curved handle, used for carrying or holding water, sand, or other substances; pail. **2.** anything resembling this, as any of various scooplike devices mounted on or attached to machines such as dredges and steam shovels; dipper; scoop. **3.** amount that a bucket can hold; bucketful. **4.** *Informal.* great amount: *The rain came down in buckets.* **5. to kick the bucket.** *Slang.* to die. —*v.t.*, **-et·ed, -et·ing.** to lift, draw, or carry in a bucket. [Anglo-Norman *buket* pail, possibly from Old English *būc* pitcher.]

Buckboard

bucket brigade, row of people who pass buckets of water from person to person in order to put out a fire.

buck·et·ful (buk′it fool′) *n.* as much as a bucket can hold.

bucket seat, low single seat, usually with a rounded back, used esp. in automobiles.

bucket shop **1.** places where highly speculative, worthless, or illegal stocks are sold, frequently by high-pressure or unethical tactics. **2.** formerly, an establishment which purported to be a brokerage house but did not execute the customer's orders, took an opposing position in the market, and thereby gained from the customer's losses.

buck·eye (buk′ī′) *n.* **1.** any of several North American shrubs or small trees, genus *Aesculus*, of the horse chestnut family, bearing showy clusters of yellow, white, or red flowers and inedible round fruits with one or two seeds in each. **2.** shiny brown nutlike seed of this tree. [BUCK + EYE; because the seed resembles the eye of a deer.]

Buck·ing·ham Palace (buk′ing əm, -ham′) palace in Westminster, London, the official residence of British monarchs.

buck·le (buk′əl) *n.* **1.** clasp, often with a movable tongue, used to fasten two loose ends, as of a belt or strap. **2.** ornament that resembles this, as on a shoe. **3.** bulge, bend, or other distortion: *a buckle in the road surface.* —*v.t.*, **-led, -ling.** **1.** to fasten with a buckle. **2.** to cause (something) to bulge, bend, or kink, as under heat or pressure. —*v.i.* **1.** to be fastened or joined by a buckle. **2.** to bulge, bend, or kink. **3.** to give way, as by bending or folding: *A beam supporting the building buckled.* **4. to buckle down (to).** to apply oneself with vigor (to). [Old French *boucle* metal ring, boss on a shield, from Latin *buccula* cheek strap of a helmet, diminutive of *bucca* cheek.]

buck·ler (buk′lər) *n.* **1.** small, round shield. **2.** means of defense; protection. [Old French *bocler* shield with a boss, from *boucle* boss on a shield. See BUCKLE.]

buck·ram (buk′rəm) *n.* coarse cloth which has been stiffened with size, used esp. in bookbinding or as interlining in garments. [Old French *boquerant* fine linen, going back to *Bokhara*, central Asian city that was the original source of this linen.]

buck·saw (buk′sô′) *n.* saw set in an H-shaped frame with one side of the frame extended to form a handle.

buck·shot (buk′shot′) *n.* large, round metal pellets for shotgun shells.

Bucksaw

buck·skin (buk′skin′) *n.* **1.** strong, soft, yellowish-tan leather, made from the skins of deer or sheep. **2.** buckskins. breeches or clothing made of buckskin. **3.** horse the color of buckskin.

buck·thorn (buk′thôrn′) *n.* **1.** any of a large group of usually thorny trees or shrubs, genus *Rhamnus*, found generally in temperate regions, bearing pale-green clustered flowers and black berries. **2.** tree or shrub, genus *Bumelia*, having thorny branches, found esp. in the southern United States. [BUCK + THORN, translation of Modern Latin *cervi spina* stag's thorn.]

buck·tooth (buk′tooth′) *pl.*, **-teeth.** *n.* projecting upper front tooth. [BUCK + TOOTH.] —**buck′toothed′,** *adj.*

buck·wheat (buk′hwēt, -wēt′) *n.* **1.** grain of any of a group of cereal plants, genus *Fagopyrum*, used for animal feed or ground into flour, esp. for pancakes. **2.** flour made from this grain. **3.** any of the plants that bear this grain, widely cultivated throughout the world, having heart-shaped leaves and clusters of small white flowers. [Dialectal English *buck* beech (from Old English *bōc*) + WHEAT; its seeds are shaped like the nuts of the beech.]

buckwheat cake, pancake made of buckwheat flour.

bu·col·ic (bū kol′ik) *adj.* **1.** of or relating to shepherds; pastoral. **2.** relating to country life; rustic; rural. —*n.* pastoral poem. [Latin *būcolicus* pastoral, from Greek *boukolikós*, from *boukolos* herdsman.] —**Syn.** *adj.* **2.** see **rural.**

bud (bud) *n.* **1.** small swelling on a plant containing a rudimentary branch, stem, leaf, or flower. **2.** flower that has not completely blossomed: *a bouquet of rose buds.* **3.** act or time of budding: *The trees are in bud.* **4.** budlike protuberance on certain lower organisms, as the yeast or hydra, which develops into a new individual. **5. to nip in the bud.** to stop or destroy in the initial or early stage of development. —*v.i.* **bud·ded, bud·ding.** **1.** to put forth buds. **2.a.** to begin to grow or develop. **b.** to be at an early or promising stage of development. —*v.t.* **1.** to cause to bud. **2.** to bring or put forth as a bud or buds. **3.** to insert (a bud) from one kind of plant into the stem or bark of another kind. [Of uncertain origin.]

Bu·da·pest (bōō′də pest′) *n.* capital and largest city of Hungary, in the north-central part of the country. Pop. (1968 est.), 2,000,000.

Bud·dha (bōō′də, bood′ə) c.563–483 B.C., founder of Buddhism. Also, **Gau′ta·ma.** [Sanskrit *buddha* enlightened.]

Bud·dhism (bood′iz′əm, boo′diz′-) *n.* religion, based on the teachings of Buddha, that originated in India and has spread over much of Asia. It teaches that pain and evil are caused by desire and that to conquer desire is to attain Nirvana. —**Bud′dhist,** *adj., n.*

bud·dy (bud′ē) *pl.*, **-dies.** *n. Informal.* pal; companion; comrade.

budge (buj) **budged, budg·ing.** —*v.i.* to move or stir slightly; give way: *She would not budge an inch.* —*v.t.* to cause to move or stir slightly; give way. ▲ usually used with a negative construction. [French *bouger* to stir, going back to Latin *bullīre* to boil.]

budg·et (buj′it) *n.* **1.** estimate or statement of expected income and expenditures for a given period. **2.** amount of money allotted for a particular purpose or given period of time: *My budget for this week includes new shoes.* —*v.t.*, **-et·ed, -et·ing.** **1.** to plan or allot for the use or expenditure of. **2.** to plan for in a budget; plan according to a budget. [Old French *bougette* little bag, diminutive of *bouge* leather bag, from Latin *bulga* of Celtic origin.] —**budg·et·ar·y** (buj′ə ter′ē), *adj.*

bud scale, any of the small, thick leaves that protect developing leaf buds, as from cold or injury.

Bue·nos Ai·res (bwā′nəs âr′ez, ī′rēz, bō′nəs) capital, chief port, and largest city of Argentina, on the eastern coast of the country. Pop. (1969 est.), 3,549,000.

buff¹ (buf) *n.* **1.** soft, sturdy, yellowish-brown or tan leather with a napped surface, usually made from the hide of buffalo or oxen. **2.** formerly, military jacket made of buff leather. **3.** medium tan color; yellowish-brown. **4.** buffer² (*def.* 2). **5.** *Informal.* bare skin. —*adj.* **1.** made of buff leather. **2.** medium tan; yellowish-brown. —*v.t.* to polish or clean with or as with a buff or buffer. [French *buffle* buffalo, from Italian *bufalo*. See BUFFALO.]

buff² (buf) *n.* enthusiast; devotee; fan: *an opera buff.* [Short for *buffalo robe,* winter clothing often worn by the nineteenth-century American volunteer firemen.]

buf·fa·lo (buf′ə lō′) *pl.*, **-loes** or **-los** or **-lo.** *n.* **1.** North American bison. **2.** any of various wild or domesticated oxen, subfamily Bovinae, of India, southeastern Asia, and parts of Africa, as the water buffalo. —*v.t.*, **-loed, -lo·ing.** *Slang.* **1.** to fool; bewilder. **2.** to intimidate. [Italian *bufalo* ox, going back to Greek *boubalos* antelope, wild ox.]

Water buffalo

Buf·fa·lo (buf′ə lō′) *n.* port city in western New York, on Lake Erie. Pop. (1970), 462,768.

Buffalo Bill, 1846–1917, U.S. scout and showman; born William F. Cody.

buffalo grass, short, hardy grass, *Buchloë dactyloides,* of central and western North America, having creeping stems, narrow, flat leaves, and short flower spikes. It forms a thick gray-green turf that provides a valuable forage for cattle.

buff·er¹ (buf′ər) *n.* **1.** person or thing that softens or neutralizes impact, as from a collision or the clash of opposing forces. **2.** chemical substance that, in solution, tends to resist changes in acidity or alkalinity. [Dialectal English *buff* to strike (from Old French *bu(f)fer* to strike, ultimately imitative) + -ER¹.]

buff·er² (buf′ər) *n.* **1.** person who buffs. **2.** wheel, stick, or other device covered with a soft material, as chamois, used for polishing. [BUFF² (verb) + -ER¹.]

buffer state, small country lying between two larger ones and regarded as reducing the chance of conflict between them.

buf·fet¹ (buf′it) **-fet·ed, -fet·ing.** *v.t.* **1.** to beat or strike with the hand or fist. **2.** to strike repeatedly; knock about: *The rough water buffeted*

the buoy. **3.** to fight against; contend with: *The ship buffeted the waves.*
—*n.* **1.** blow with the hand or fist. **2.** something that hits with the force of a blow; violent shock: *the buffet of a hurricane.* [Old French *buffet* blow, diminutive of *buffe;* imitative.]

buf·fet² (bə fā′, boo-) *n.* **1.** piece of furniture with a flat surface for serving and with cabinets for the storage and display of such items as dishes, silver, glassware, and table linen; sideboard. **2.** meal laid out on a buffet or similar surface, as a table or tables, so that those partaking may serve themselves. ▲ often used in combinations such as *buffet supper* and *buffet luncheon.* **3.** counter where refreshments or light meals are served. [French *buffet;* of uncertain origin.]

buf·foon (bə fōōn′) *n.* one who amuses others with pranks and jokes; clown. [French *bouffon,* from Italian *buffone,* from *buffare* to joke, puff; with reference to the medieval jesters' making noise by puffing out their cheeks and blowing the air out; imitative.] —**buf·foon′er·y,** *n.*

bug (bug) *n.* **1.** any of the insects of the order Hemiptera, such as stinkbugs and squash bugs, having beaklike sucking mouth parts. Most have membranous hind wings, with fore wings thick at the base and membranous at the tip, though some, such as bedbugs, are wingless and others have vestigial wings. **2.** any insect or similar animal. **3.** *Informal.* disease-causing germ. **4.** *Informal.* defect or difficulty, as in a machine: *a bug in the television set.* **5.** *Informal.* fan or hobbyist; buff. **6.** *Slang.* small hidden microphone used to overhear conversations. —*v.t.* **bugged, bug·ging. 1.** *Slang.* to place a hidden microphone in. **2.** *Slang.* to annoy, bother, or worry (someone). [Of uncertain origin.]

bug·a·boo (bug′ə bōō′) *pl.,* **-boos.** *n.* real or imaginary object of fear. [Obsolete *bug* bogy¹ (possibly from Welsh *bwg* ghost) + BOO.]

bug·bear (bug′bâr′) *n.* bugaboo. [Obsolete *bug* bogy¹ (possibly from Welsh *bwg* ghost) + BEAR².]

bug·gy¹ (bug′ē) *pl.* **-gies.** *n.* **1.** light, four-wheeled carriage with one seat, and either with or without a hood to cover it. **2.** baby carriage; perambulator. [Of uncertain origin.]

bug·gy² (bug′ē) **-gi·er, -gi·est.** *adj.* **1.** infested or swarming with bugs. **2.** *Slang.* crazy. [BUG + -Y¹.]

bu·gle¹ (bū′gəl) *n.* brass wind instrument resembling, but smaller than, a trumpet, usually without keys or valves, used esp. for giving military signals and calls. —*v.i.* **-gled, -gling.** to sound or play a bugle. —*v.t.* to summon by blowing on a bugle. [Short for earlier *bugle horn* musical instrument made from the horn of an ox or buffalo, from Old French *bugle* wild ox, buffalo, from Latin *būculus* steer.] —**bu′-gler,** *n.*

bu·gle² (bū′gəl) *n.* tubular bead used to ornament women's clothing. Also, **bugle bead.** [Possibly from BUGLE¹; because of its resemblance to a horn.]

buhl (bōōl) *n.* furniture decoration of an elaborate type, consisting of wood inlaid with such materials as tortoise shell, mother of pearl, and metals. [German *Buhl,* from French *boulle;* from the French cabinetmaker Charles André *Boulle,* 1642–1732.]

build (bild) **built, build·ing.** *v.t.* **1.** to construct, erect, or make by assembling materials or parts. **2.** to establish and strengthen: *to build a good reputation.* **3.** to form a basis for: *to build an argument on logic.* **4.** to build up. **a.** to construct by degrees; develop or form gradually: *to build up a large clientele.* **b.** to strengthen: *Exercise builds up the muscles.* **c.** to fill (an area) with buildings or houses. —*v.i.* **1.** to construct a building or have a building erected. **2.** to use as a basis or foundation for development (with *on* or *upon*): *Let's build on your idea.* **3.** to increase, as in intensity, speed, or size: *The story built to a surprising climax.* **4.** to form groups of cards by denomination or suit. —*n.* manner of construction; physique: *The football player has a solid build.* [Old English *byldan* to construct (a house), from *bold* dwelling.] —**Syn.** *v.t.* **1.** see **make.**

build·er (bild′ər) *n.* **1.** one who builds. **2.** one whose occupation or profession is building houses or other structures.

build·ing (bil′ding) *n.* **1.** that which is built; structure; edifice. **2.** act, process, or business of constructing.

building block 1. one of a set of children's toy blocks. **2.** fundamental or elementary principle or part: *The right to vote is a building block of democracy.*

build·up (bild′up′) *also,* **build-up.** *n.* **1.** increase, as in number or strength: *armament buildup, troop buildup.* **2.** *Informal.* publicity or praise used to make someone or something famous or interesting.

built (bilt) past tense and past participle of **build.**

built-in (bilt′in′) *adj.* **1.** built as an integral, permanent part of something: *a built-in bureau.* **2.** inherent in the nature of someone or something: *built-in reflexes.* **3.** created as an essential part of something: *a system of government with built-in checks and balances.*

Bu·jum·bu·ra (bōō′zhoom boor′ä) *n.* capital and chief port of Burundi, in the western part of the country. Pop. (1966 est.), 70,000.

bulb (bulb) *n.* **1.** enlarged, rounded budlike part below the ground on some plants, as the onion, consisting of a short stem surrounded by scalelike leaves which provide nourishment for the growing plant.

2. underground stem resembling a bulb, as a tuber. **3.** any plant that develops from a bulb, such as a tulip or daffodil. **4.** any enlarged, rounded object or part: *electric light bulbs, a thermometer bulb.* [Latin *bulbus* bulbous root, onion, from Greek *bolbos.*]

bulb·ar (bul′bər) *adj.* of or relating to a bulb-shaped organ, esp. the bulb of the spinal cord, the medulla oblongata: *bulbar paralysis.*

bulb·ous (bul′bəs) *adj.* **1.** of, having, or growing from bulbs. **2.** bulb-shaped; round; swollen.

bul·bul (bōōl′bōōl′) *n.* **1.** any of various thrushlike songbirds, family Pycnonotidae, native to tropical and subtropical forests of Africa and southern Asia. Length: 6–11 inches. **2.** songbird mentioned in Persian poetry, believed to have been a nightingale. [Persian *bulbul* Persian songbird; imitative.]

Cross section of a hyacinth bulb

[Labels on illustration: Sprouts, Leaves, Stem, Roots]

Bul·gar (bul′gär, bōōl′-) *n.* Bulgarian.

Bul·gar·i·a (bul gâr′ē ə, bōōl-) *n.* country in southeastern Europe, in the east-central part of the Balkan Peninsula. Capital, Sofia. Area, 42,823 sq. mi. Pop. (1969 est.), 8,436,000.

Bul·gar·i·an (bul gâr′ē ən, bōōl-) *adj.* of or relating to Bulgaria, its people, or their language. —*n.* **1.** member or close descendant of the people of Bulgaria. **2.** Slavic language of the Bulgarians.

bulge (bulj) *n.* rounded protuberance; swelling; hump. —*v.i.* **bulged, bulg·ing.** to swell out; be protuberant: *The bag bulged with groceries.* —*v.t.* to cause to swell out. [Old French *bouge, boulge* leath ... bag, swelling. See BUDGET.] —**bulg′y,** *adj.*

Bulge, Battle of the (bulj) last major German counteroffensive of World War II, begun on December 16, 1944, against the Allies in Belgium and repulsed in January 1945.

bulk (bulk) *n.* **1.** size, esp. large size; magnitude; volume: *a package of great bulk.* **2.** main or greater part: *The bulk of the people voted.* **3. in bulk. a.** not packaged; loose. **b.** in large quantities. —*v.i.* **1.** to have bulk; appear important; loom. **2.** to increase in bulk; swell; grow. —*v.t.* to cause to swell or grow in size. [Probably blend of Old Norse *bulki* heap and Old English *būc* belly.] —**Syn.** *n.* see **mass.**

bulk·head (bulk′hed′) *n.* **1.** major vertical partition or wall, esp. in a ship or airplane, used to form compartments and to isolate the effects of fire, flooding, or other damage. **2.** retaining wall or partition, designed to protect embankments of earth in a tunnel or along a shore, or to prevent the passage of water or gases, as in a mine. **3.** boxlike structure built on a roof to cover the top of a staircase or other opening. **4.** horizontal or inclined door giving access from the outside of a house to the cellar. —*v.t.* to construct (a bulkhead or similar retaining wall) against an earth embankment.

bulk·y (bul′kē) **bulk·i·er, bulk·i·est.** *adj.* **1.** of great bulk; large. **2.** unwieldy; clumsy. —**bulk′i·ly,** *adv.* —**bulk′i·ness,** *n.*

bull¹ (bool) *n.* **1.** mature male of any animal of the cattle family. **2.** male of certain other large animals, as the elephant, moose, whale, or seal. **3.** speculator, esp. one in the stock market, who attempts to raise prices or who anticipates a rise in prices and buys so that he may sell at a higher rate. Opposed to **bear. 4.** *Slang.* policeman; detective. **5.** *Slang.* foolish, empty talk; nonsense. **6. to take the bull by the horns.** to face and deal courageously with some danger or difficulty. **7. bull in a china shop.** one who is clumsy and causes destruction. —*v.t. Slang.* to achieve by pretended knowledge; bluff: *He bulled his way through the exam.* —*adj.* **1.** male. **2.** resembling a bull, as in size or strength. **3.** characterized by rising prices on a stock, bond, or commodity exchange: *a bull market in aerospace stocks.* [Old English *bula* male of the cattle family, from Old Norse *boli.*]

bull² (bool) *n.* papal document issued only for pronouncements on matters of great importance, presented according to a prescribed form on parchment with a lead seal attached. [Medieval Latin *bulla* seal, document, from Latin *bulla* knob, bubble.]

bull³ (bool) *n.* absurd and ludicrous inconsistency in language involving a contradiction in terms. The statement *We wintered in Florida one summer* is a bull. [Of uncertain origin.]

bul·la (bool′ə) *pl.,* **bul·lae** (bool′ē, bool′ī). *n.* round lead seal attached to a papal bull. [Medieval Latin *bulla* lead seal attached to an edict. See BULL².]

bull·dog (bool′dôg′) *n.* heavily built

Bulldog

at; āpe; cär; end; mē; it; īce; hot; ōld; fôrk; wood; fōōl; out; up; ūse; turn; sing; thin; this; zh in treasure; ə in ago, taken, pencil, lemon, circus.

dog, originally bred in England, having a large head, square jaw, short bowed legs, and a smooth coat. It is noted for its courage. Height: 15 inches at the shoulder. —*v.t.* **-dogged, -dog·ging.** to wrestle (a steer) to the ground by taking hold of its horns and twisting its neck. —*adj.* resembling or characteristic of a bulldog; courageous; obstinate. [BULL[1] + DOG; possibly because such dogs were once used to bait bulls.]

bull·doze (bool′dōz′) **-dozed, -doz·ing.** *v.t.* **1.** to use a bulldozer on, as for moving earth or clearing land. **2.** *Informal.* to intimidate by violence or threats; bully. [Possibly from BULL[1] + modification of DOSE; with the sense of a dose of medicine enough for a bull.]

bull·doz·er (bool′dō′zər) *n.* **1.** vehicle with a powerful motor that moves on tanklike treads and carries a wide, heavy metal blade mounted in front, used for such work as road grading, building demolition, and land clearing. **2.** *Informal.* one who intimidates others with threats or violence.

Bulldozer

bul·let (bool′it) *n.* **1.** small, cylindrical piece of metal with a rounded or tapered point, set in a cartridge filled with gunpowder, used as ammunition in various types of guns. See **cartridge** for illustration. **2.** cartridge. **3.** anything resembling a bullet in shape or speed: *The car shot through the intersection like a bullet.* [French *boulet,* diminutive of *boule* ball, from Latin *bulla* bubble, knob.]

bul·le·tin (bool′it ən) *n.* **1.** brief official public report or statement on the current condition of something: *an official bulletin on the progress of the war.* **2.** short account, statement, or report of news or other matters of public interest: *a television bulletin about an airplane crash.* **3.** periodical publication, as of a society, church, or other organization. —*v.t.* to make known by a bulletin. [French *bulletin* from Italian *bulletino* pass, going back to Medieval Latin *bulla.* See BULL[2].]

bulletin board, board for posting such items as notices, announcements, and pictures.

bul·let·proof (bool′it proof′) *adj.* capable of resisting the penetration of a bullet: *bulletproof vest, bulletproof glass.*

bull·fight (bool′fīt′) *n.* exhibition in an arena, esp. in Spain, Portugal, or Latin America, in which a bull is repeatedly provoked by one or more men, until it is exhausted, when it is killed ceremoniously by the matador. In the Portuguese version the bull is not killed. —**bull′·fight′er, bul′fight′ing,** *n.*

bull·finch (bool′finch′) *n.* Eurasian songbird, *Pyrrhula pyrrhula,* related to the cardinal and grosbeak, the male of which has a gray back, black cap, wings, and tail, and a rose-colored breast.

bull·frog (bool′frôg′, -frog′) *n.* brownish-green frog, *Rana catesbeiana,* the male of which has a loud, bellowing call. The largest frog in the United States, it may grow to eight inches in length.

Bullhead

bull·head (bool′hed′) *n.* any of a group of freshwater catfish, genus *Ictalurus,* native to eastern North America, having a large flat head with four pairs of sensitive feelers around the mouth and no scales. Length: up to 16 inches.

bull·head·ed (bool′hed′id) *adj.* foolishly stubborn; obstinate; headstrong. —**bull′head′ed·ness,** *n.*

bul·lion (bool′yən) *n.* gold, silver, or other precious metal, esp. such metal in the form of bars or ingots. [Anglo-Norman *bullion* mint, apparently from Old French *boillir* to boil (suggesting melted metal), from Latin *bullīre* to bubble.]

bull·ish (bool′ish) *adj.* **1.** of, relating to, or resembling a bull. **2.** tending toward, marked by, or causing rising prices on a stock, bond, or commodity exchange. —**bull′ish·ly,** *adv.* —**bull′ish·ness,** *n.*

bull mastiff, heavily built dog of a breed originally developed by crossing a bulldog and a mastiff. It has a blunt, wrinkled muzzle and a tan or brown coat, often marked with white. Height: 26 inches at the shoulder.

Bull mastiff

Bull Moose, member or supporter of the Progressive Party led by Theodore Roosevelt in the presidential campaign of 1912. [Term first

used on several occasions by Theodore Roosevelt to denote either a forceful person or himself; later applied to the Progressive Party, whose symbol it became.]

bull·necked (bool′nekt′) *adj.* having a short, thick neck.

bull·ock (bool′ək) *n.* castrated bull; ox or steer. [Old English *bulluc* bull calf.]

bull·pen (bool′pen′) *n.* **1.** area set apart, esp. by a fence, from the playing field in baseball, where relief pitchers may warm up without interfering with a game in progress. **2.** *Slang.* room within a jail for the temporary detention of prisoners.

bull·ring (bool′ring′) *n.* arena for bullfights.

Bull Run, stream in northeastern Virginia, site of two Civil War battles, in 1861 and 1862, in which the Union forces were defeated.

bull session *Informal.* informal group discussion, usually among close friends.

bull's-eye (boolz′ī′) *n.* **1.** central circle of a target. **2.** shot that hits the bull's-eye. **3.** round piece of thick glass set in a ship's deck or similar structure to admit light. **4.** convex lens shaped like a half-sphere. **5.** lantern having such a lens. **6.** small, circular opening or window.

bull terrier, strong, agile dog, originally bred in England by crossing a bulldog with the now extinct white terrier, having a strong build, broad pointed jaw, and a white or brindled coat. Height: 20 inches at the shoulder.

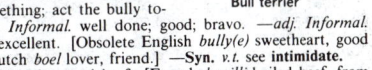
Bull terrier

bul·ly (bool′ē) *pl.,* **-lies.** *n.* quarrelsome person who browbeats, frightens, or hurts smaller or weaker people. —*v.t.,* **-lied, -ly·ing.** to threaten or intimidate into doing something; act the bully toward. —*interj. Informal.* well done; good; bravo. —*adj. Informal.* first-rate; fine; excellent. [Obsolete English *bully(e)* sweetheart, good fellow, from Dutch *boel* lover, friend.] —**Syn.** *v.t.* see **intimidate.**

bully beef, canned corned beef. [French *bouilli* boiled beef, from *bouillir* to boil, from Latin *bullīre* to bubble.]

bul·ly·rag (bool′ē rag′) **-ragged, -rag·ging.** *v.t. Archaic.* to bully; intimidate; abuse.

bul·rush (bool′rush′) *n.* **1.** any of a large group of coarse plants, genus *Scirpus,* having grasslike leaves and small flower-bearing spikelets and growing in wet ground or shallow water. The sturdy stems of one species, *S. lacustris,* are used to weave mats, baskets, and chair seats. **2.** in the Bible, the papyrus plant of Egypt. **3.** *British.* cattail. [Possibly from BULL[1] large (adjective) + RUSH[2].]

bul·wark (bool′wərk) *n.* **1.** defensive earthwork; rampart; fortification. **2.** any means of defense or protection; safeguard: *A mighty fortress is our God, a bulwark never failing* (Luther, 1524). **3.** breakwater. **4.** *also,* **bulwarks.** the part of a ship's side above the deck. —*v.t.* to furnish with a bulwark or bulwarks; defend; protect. [Probably from Middle High German *bolwerc* fortification, from *bole* plank + *werc* work.]

Bul·wer-Lyt·ton (bool′wər lit′ən) **1. Edward George.** 1803–73, English novelist, dramatist, and politician. **2. Edward Robert.** 1831–91, his son; English diplomat and poet who wrote under the pseudonym Owen Meredith.

bum (bum) *n. Informal.* **1.** idle or worthless person; loafer; tramp; vagrant. **2. on the bum. a.** living the life of a bum. **b.** out of order; broken. **3. the bum's rush.** *Slang.* forcible ejection. —*v.i.* **bummed, bum·ming. 1.** to live or be like a bum; be idle; loaf. **2.** to live off others. —*v.t.* to get (something) by begging: *to bum a cigarette, to bum a ride.* —*adj.,* **bum·mer, bum·mest. 1.** of inferior or poor quality; bad. **2.** in poor physical condition: *a bum leg.* [Short for earlier *bummer* loafer, from German *Bummler* tramp.] —**bum′mer,** *n.*

bum·ble (bum′bəl) **-bled, -bling.** *v.i.* to act or work in an awkward or clumsy manner. —*v.t.* to handle (something) in an awkward or clumsy manner; bungle. [Form of BUNGLE.] —**bum′·bler,** *n.*

bum·ble·bee (bum′bəl bē′) *n.* any of several species of thick-bodied, hairy, black-and-yellow bees, genus *Bombus,* which are closely related to honeybees but live in smaller, more primitive colonies. [From obsolete *bumble* to buzz (imitative) + BEE.]

Bumblebee

bump (bump) *v.i.* **1.** to strike suddenly; collide. **2.** to move with a bump or succession of bumps. —*v.t.* **1.** to hit suddenly; knock against. **2.** to cause to strike or knock: *to bump one's head against the wall.* **3. to bump into.** to meet by or as if by accident. **4. to bump off.** *Slang.*

to kill; murder. —*n.* **1.** heavy jolt; thump. **2.** swelling or lump caused by a collision or blow. **3.** any uneven swelling or protuberance: *a bump in the road.* [Imitative.]

bump·er (bum′pər) *n.* **1.** protective device, usually in the shape of a horizontal bar, attached to the front and rear ends of a vehicle to absorb the shock of collision. **2.** cup or glass filled to the brim, esp. when drunk as a toast. —*adj.* unusually large or abundant, as a crop or harvest. [BUMP + -ER¹.]

bump·kin (bump′kin) *n.* awkward country fellow; clumsy yokel. [Possibly from Dutch *boomken* little tree; hence, blockhead.]

bump·tious (bump′shəs) *adj.* offensively self-assertive or conceited; domineering. [From BUMP; modeled upon FRACTIOUS.] —**bump′-tious·ly,** *adv.* —**bump′tious·ness,** *n.*

bump·y (bump′pē) **bump·i·er, bump·i·est.** *adj.* **1.** having an uneven surface; full of bumps: *a bumpy piece of wood.* **2.** causing bumps or jolts: *a bumpy train ride.* —**bump′i·ness,** *n.*

bun (bun) *n.* **1.** bread roll, variously shaped, sometimes sweetened or containing small pieces of fruit, such as raisins: *hamburger bun, a breakfast bun.* **2.** knot or roll of hair arranged in the shape of a bun. [Of uncertain origin.]

bu·na (bōō′nə, bū′-) *n.* synthetic rubber made from butadiene and styrene or some similar compound; the most widely used synthetic rubber. [BU(TADIENE) + NA, symbol for *sodium*.]

bunch (bunch) *n.* **1.** number of things of the same kind growing, fastened, grouped, or classified together; collection: *a bunch of bananas, a bunch of letters.* **2.** *Informal.* group of people: *A bunch of us went to the movies.* —*v.i.* to place into or form a bunch or bunches; gather together. —*v.t.* to group or make into a bunch or bunches; gather. [Of uncertain origin.] —**bunch′y,** *adj.*

bunch·ber·ry (bunch′ber′ē) *pl.,* **-ries.** *n.* shrublike plant, *Cornus canadensis,* of the dogwood family, found in eastern Asia and North America, bearing clusters of white petal-like leaves in the spring and clusters of small bright-red berries in the fall.

Bunche, Ralph Johnson (bunch) 1904–71, American statesman, educator, and United Nations official.

bunch grass, any of various grasses that grow in clumps or large tufts and are native to the dry soils and prairies of the western United States.

bun·co (bung′kō) *pl.,* **-cos.** *n.* bunko. —*v.,* **-coed, -co·ing.** to bunko.

bun·combe (bung′kəm) *n.* bunk².

bun·dle (bund′əl) *n.* **1.** number of things tied, wrapped, or otherwise bound together; parcel; package. **2.** group; bunch; collection: *a bundle of energy, a bundle of money.* **3.** vascular bundle. **4.** *Physiology.* number of fibers, as nerve or muscle fibers, grouped together and running in the same direction. —*v.t.,* **-dled, -dling. 1.** to wrap or bind together; make into a bundle. **2.** *Informal.* to send or remove hastily and unceremoniously: *Her mother bundled her off to school.* —*v.i.* **1.** to go hastily; hurry. **2.** in an early New England courting custom, to lie or sleep without undressing in the same bed with one's sweetheart, separated by a board. **3. to bundle up.** to dress warmly. [Middle Dutch *bundel* sheaf.] —**bun′dler,** *n.*

Syn. *n.* **1. Bundle, package, parcel** refer to something bound or wrapped up for convenience in carrying, storing, or shipping. **Bundle** suggests a collection of objects of the same or different sizes put together in a makeshift way: *a bundle of laundry.* **Package** and **parcel** suggest care in wrapping or boxing, as for the purpose of safe transport or decoration: *The package (or parcel) of fruit was delivered this afternoon.* Of the two, **parcel** is the more formal word.

bung (bung) *n.* **1.** stopper, esp. a large cork, for closing the hole that is used for filling or emptying a barrel, cask, or similar container. **2.** bunghole. —*v.t.* **1.** to close (a bunghole) with a bung (often with *up* or *down*). **2.** to stop up; shut. [Middle Dutch *bonghe* stopper, possibly going back to Latin *puncta* hole.]

bun·ga·low (bung′gə lō′) *n.* small house or cottage, usually of one or one-and-a-half stories. [Hindi *banglā* relating to Bengal; hence, a Bengalese type of house.]

bung·hole (bung′hōl′) *n.* hole in a barrel, cask, or similar container through which it is filled or emptied.

bun·gle (bung′gəl) **-gled, -gling.** *v.i.* to work or act in a clumsy, unskillful way. —*v.t.* to do or make (something) in a clumsy, unskillful manner; botch. —*n.* clumsy, unskillful performance, job, or piece of work. [Possibly of Scandinavian origin.] —**bun′gler,** *n.* —**bun′gling·ly,** *adv.*

bun·ion (bun′yən) *n.* inflamed and often painful swelling on the foot, at the base of the big toe. [Of uncertain origin.]

bunk¹ (bungk) *n.* **1.** shelflike, narrow bed or sleeping berth built in or against a wall. **2.** *Informal.* any bed. **3.** *Informal.* bunkhouse; cabin.

—*v.i. Informal.* **1.** to sleep in a bunk. **2.** to sleep, esp. in rough quarters: *We bunked at the campsite.* [Possibly from BUNKER.]

bunk² (bungk) *n. Informal.* empty, insincere, or untrue talk or speech-making; nonsense; humbug. Also, **bun′combe, bun′kum.** [Shortened from BUNKUM, phonetic spelling of BUNCOMBE, from *Buncombe* county, North Carolina, whose congressman in 1820 explained that a long, irrelevant speech he had made was meant not for Congress but for Buncombe.]

bunk·bed (bungk′bed′) *n.* piece of furniture consisting of two or more single beds, one above the other.

bunk·er (bung′kər) *n.* **1.** military fortification consisting of a chamber built largely below ground, protected by earth or steel and concrete. **2.** obstacle in or along a golf fairway or close to the green, as a sand trap or barrier of earth. **3.** storage compartment or bin, as for coal on a ship. [Of uncertain origin.]

Bunker Hill, hill in eastern Massachusetts, near Boston. The Battle of Bunker Hill, in 1775, the first major battle of the American Revolution, was actually fought on nearby Breed's Hill.

bunk·house (bungk′hous′) *n.* rough building with sleeping quarters or bunks, as for workers or campers.

bun·ko (bung′kō) *pl.,* **-kos.** *also,* **bun·co** *n. Informal.* swindle; confidence game. —*v.t.,* **-koed, -ko·ing.** *Informal.* to swindle. [Possibly from Spanish *banca* name of a card game, bank, from Italian *banca* bank, bench. See BANK².]

bun·kum (bung′kəm) *n.* bunk².

bun·ny (bun′ē) *pl.,* **-nies.** *n. Informal.* rabbit, esp. a young rabbit. [Dialectal English *bun* rabbit (of uncertain origin) + -Y².]

Bun·sen burner (bun′sən) gas burner, used esp. in science laboratories, consisting of a short metal tube into which gas is fed. Openings at the base allow air to enter and mix with the gas which, when lighted, burns with a very hot, blue flame. [From the German chemist, Robert W. Bunsen, 1811–99, who invented it.]

Bunsen burner

bunt (bunt) *v.t., v.i.* **1.** to tap (a pitched baseball) so that it goes only a short distance into the infield. **2.** to strike or push with or as with the head or horns; butt. —*n.* **1.a.** act of bunting. **b.** hit made by bunting. **c.** ball hit by bunting. **2.** to push or shove; butt. [Modification of BUTT¹.] —**bunt′er,** *n.*

bunt·ing¹ (bun′ting) *n.* **1.** sacklike blanket or wrapper for babies, made of wool, cotton, or other soft material. **2.** worsted cloth used in making flags. **3.** decorative banners or drapes of cloth printed with the colors or symbols of a national flag. [Of uncertain origin.]

bunt·ing² (bun′ting) *n.* any of various colorful songbirds, family Fringillidae, of North America and Eurasia, related to and resembling the sparrow in every respect except color, having a short, stout, pointed bill. Length: 5½ inches. [Of uncertain origin.]

bunt·line (bunt′lin, -līn′) *n.* any of the ropes used to haul up a square sail for furling. [*Bunt* middle part of a sail (of uncertain origin) + LINE¹.]

Bun·yan, John (bun′yən) 1628–86, English author and preacher.

bu·oy (bōō′ē, boi) *n.* **1.** floating marker anchored to the bottom of a waterway, used to warn of an underwater hazard or indicate a channel. **2.** life buoy. —*v.t.* **1.** to furnish or mark with a buoy or buoys. **2.** to prevent from sinking; keep afloat (often with *up*). **3.** to hold up or sustain, as spirit or hope (often with *up*): *The victory buoyed up the morale of the troops.* [Middle Dutch *boeie* anchored floating marker, fetter, going back to Latin *boia* fetter; because it was fastened in place.]

Lighted buoy   Spar buoy

Can buoy   Nun buoy

Buoys

buoy·an·cy (boi′ən sē, bōō′yən-) *n.* **1.** power or tendency to float or rise in a liquid or gas: *Cork has great buoyancy.* **2.** power of a liquid or gas to keep something afloat. **3.** ability to recover from depression or sadness; light-heartedness; cheerfulness.

buoy·ant (boi′ənt, bōō′yənt) *adj.* having or marked by buoyancy. —**buoy′ant·ly,** *adv.*

bur (bur) *n.* burr¹ (*defs. 1–3*).

Bur·bank (bur′bangk′) *n.* **1.** Luther. 1849–1926, U.S. nurseryman and plant breeder. **2.** city in southern California, a residential suburb of Los Angeles. Pop. (1970), 88,871.

bur·ble (bur′bəl) **-bled, -bling.** *v.i., v.t.* to make a bubbling sound or utter with such a sound; gurgle. [Imitative.]

bur·bot (bur′bət) *pl.,* **-bots** or **-bot.** *n.* freshwater fish, *Lota lota,* of

at; āpe; cär; end; mē; it; īce; hot; ōld; fôrk; wood; fōōl; oil; out; up; ūse; turn; sing; thin; this; zh in treasure; ə in ago, taken, pencil, lemon, circus.

the cod family, native to North America, Europe, and Siberia, having a long, slender body and barbels on its chin and snout. Length: 2½–5 feet. [French *bourbotte,* from *bourbe* mud; of Celtic origin.]

Burck·hardt, Jacob (bûrk′härt′) 1818–97, Swiss historian.

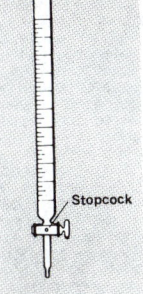

Burbot

bur·den¹ (bûrd′ən) *n.* **1.** something that is carried or borne; load. **2.** something wearisome, oppressive, or difficult to bear. **3.** cargo capacity of a ship; weight of a ship's cargo. —*v.t.* to put a heavy load on; overload; oppress: *The government burdened the nation with many kinds of taxes.* [Old English *byrthen* load.] —**Syn. 2.** see encumbrance.

bur·den² (bûrd′ən) *n.* **1.** chief topic, theme, idea, or sentiment: *the burden of an essay.* **2.** refrain or recurring chorus at the end of the stanzas of a song or ballad. [Old French *bourdon* humming, drone bee, from Late Latin *burdo* drone bee; imitative.]

burden of proof, obligation of proving a disputed or controversial statement or charge.

bur·den·some (bûrd′ən səm) *adj.* hard to bear; very heavy; oppressive.

bur·dock (bûr′dok) *n.* any of a small group of coarse, burr-bearing plants constituting the genus *Arctium,* of the composite family, esp. the **common burdock,** *A. minus,* and the **great burdock,** *A. lappa,* which are widely distributed as weeds in the eastern United States and Canada. [BUR + DOCK⁴.]

bu·reau (byoor′ō) *pl.* **bu·reaus** or **bu·reaux** (byoor′ōz) *n.* **1.** chest of drawers, esp. for clothes, sometimes with a mirror. **2.** government division, department, or agency: *the bureau for Far Eastern affairs.* **3.** office or agency, esp. one where business is transacted or information is given: *credit bureau.* **4.** *Archaic.* desk or writing table with drawers. [French *bureau* desk, office; originally, coarse russet cloth used to cover desks, from Old French *burel* coarse russet cloth, going back either to Latin *burrus* red, from Greek *pyrrhos* red, or to Late Latin *burra* tuft of wool, rough cloth.]

bu·reauc·ra·cy (byoo rok′rə sē) *pl.* **-cies.** *n.* **1.** government by bureaus and numerous officials. **2.** government officials collectively. **3.** excessive multiplication of, and concentration of power in, administrative bureaus. **4.** governmental red tape, officialism, and strict adherence to routine. [French *bureaucratie,* from *bureau* desk, office + Greek *-kratiā* power, rule. See BUREAU.]

bu·reau·crat (byoor′ə krat′) *n.* **1.** official in a bureaucracy. **2.** official who follows and insists on rigid routine and formality. —**bu′reau·crat′ic,** *adj.* —**bu′reau·crat′i·cal·ly,** *adv.*

bu·rette (byoo ret′) *also,* **bu·ret.** *n.* glass tube marked to measure volume, with a stopcock at the bottom, used for accurately controlling the flow of small amounts of liquid. [French *burette,* diminutive of *buire* bottle, pitcher; of Germanic origin.]

burg (bûrg) *n.* **1.** *Informal.* small town or city. **2.** *Archaic.* fortified or walled town. [Old English *burg, burh.*]

bur·geon (bûr′jən) *v.i.* **1.** to grow rapidly; flourish. **2.** to bud; sprout. —*v.t.* to sprout or put forth, as leaves, buds, or shoots. —*n.* bud; sprout. [Old French *burjon* bud, going back to Late Latin *burra* tuft of wool; because of the hairiness of many buds.]

Stopcock

Burette

burg·er (bûrg′ər) *n. Informal.* hamburger.

bur·gess (bûr′jis) *n.* **1.** inhabitant, esp. a citizen or officer, of a British borough of earlier times. **2.** member of the popularly elected house of the legislature in colonial Virginia, the House of Burgesses. **3.** in Pennsylvania, mayor of a borough. [Old French *burgeis* citizen, from Late Latin *burgēnsis* relating to a city, from *burgus* fortress; of Germanic origin.]

burgh (bûrg) *n.* chartered town in Scotland. [Form of BOROUGH.]

burgh·er (bûr′gər) *n.* inhabitant of a city, esp. a merchant city in feudal times.

bur·glar (bûr′glər) *n.* one who commits burglary. [Medieval Latin *burglator,* going back to Late Latin *burgus.* See BURGESS.]

bur·glar·i·ous (bər glâr′ē əs) *adj.* of, relating to, or involving burglary. —**bur·glar′i·ous·ly,** *adv.*

bur·glar·ize (bûr′glə rīz′) **-ized, -iz·ing.** *v.t.* to subject to burglary; break into and steal from.

bur·glar·y (bûr′glə rē) *pl.,* **-glar·ies.** *n.* the breaking into and entering of a dwelling of another at night with the intent to commit some

other felony; extended by statute in some states to include breaking into and entering any kind of building, by night or day, with the intent to commit some offense.

bur·gle (bûr′gəl) **-gled, -gling.** *v.t., v.i. Informal.* to burglarize. [From BURGLAR.]

bur·go·mas·ter (bûr′gə mas′tər) *n.* mayor or chief magistrate of a town in the Netherlands, Flanders, Germany, or Austria. [Dutch *burgemeester,* from *burg* town + *meester* master, from Latin *magister.*]

Bur·goyne, John (bər goin′) 1722–92, British general.

Bur·gun·di·an (bər gun′dē ən) *adj.* of or relating to Burgundy or its people. —*n.* native or inhabitant of Burgundy.

Bur·gun·dy (bûr′gən dē) *pl.,* **-dies.** *n.* **1.** historic region in east-central France, formerly an independent kingdom, a duchy, and later a province of France. Also, *French,* **Bour·gogne′.** **2.** red or white wine of a type originally produced in Burgundy, France.

bur·i·al (ber′ē əl) *n.* act of burying, esp. the interment of a dead body. —*adj.* of or relating to burying: *a burial mound.* [Old English *byrgels* tomb.]

burial ground, graveyard; cemetery.

bur·ied (ber′ēd) past tense of **bury.**

bu·rin (byoor′in) *n.* steel cutting tool used by engravers for incising lines in a metal plate. [French *burin,* probably from Italian *burino* (now *bulino*); of Germanic origin.]

Burke, Edmund (bûrk) 1729–97, English statesman and writer.

burl (bûrl) *n.* **1.** small knot or lump, as in wool, thread, or cloth. **2.** knot, lump, or other growth on certain tree trunks, used for ornamental veneering. —*v.t.* to finish (cloth), as by removing burls or loose threads. [Old French *bourle* tuft of wool, going back to Late Latin *burra.*]

bur·lap (bûr′lap) *n.* coarse fabric, usually made from jute or hemp, used in making such items as sacks, curtains, and wall coverings. [Of uncertain origin.]

bur·lesque (bər lesk′) *n.* **1.** literary or dramatic composition that presents a comical treatment of a serious subject or a mock-serious treatment of an unimportant subject; parody; caricature: *"Don Quixote" is, in part, a burlesque of medieval chivalry and romance.* **2.** coarse theatrical entertainment consisting of earthy comedy skits and musical numbers featuring striptease. **3.** striptease. —*v.t.* **-lesqued, -lesquing.** to make ridiculous, as by grotesque parody, imitation, or caricature. —*adj.* **1.** derisively comic; humorously mocking. **2.** of or relating to theatrical burlesque. [French *burlesque* ludicrous, a parody, from Italian *burlesco* comical, from *burla* joke; of uncertain origin.] —**bur·les′quer,** *n.* **3.** see caricature.

bur·ley (bûr′lē) *pl.,* **-leys.** *also,* **Bur·ley.** *n.* light-brown American tobacco raised mainly in Kentucky, used esp. in pipe tobaccos.

Bur·ling·ton (bûr′ling tən) *n.* **1.** largest city in Vermont, in the northwestern part of the state. Pop. (1970), 38,633. **2.** city in southeastern Iowa. Pop. (1970), 32,366. **3.** city in north-central North Carolina. Pop. (1970), 35,930.

bur·ly (bûr′lē) **-li·er, -li·est.** *adj.* large in bodily size; strongly built; sturdy. [Probably going back to Old English *borlīce* excellently.] —**bur′li·ness,** *n.*

Bur·ma (bûr′mə) *n.* Asian country between India and Thailand, south of China. Capital, Rangoon. Area, 261,790 sq. mi. Pop. (1969 est.), 26,980,000.

Burma Road, road connecting eastern Burma with southern China, built by the Allies during World War II as a supply route.

Bur·mese (bər mēz′, -mēs′) *pl.,* **-mese.** *n.* **1.** member or close descendant of the people of Burma. **2.** the language predominantly spoken in Burma, belonging to the Sino-Tibetan family of languages. —*adj.* of or relating to Burma, its people, culture, or language.

burn¹ (bûrn) **burned** or **burnt, burn·ing.** *v.t.* **1.** to cause to be destroyed or consumed by fire; subject to the action of fire. **2.a.** to injure or damage by fire or anything resembling fire in its effect, as heat, acid, or friction: *to burn one's finger.* **b.** to alter in appearance or texture, as to discolor, sear, or spoil. **c.** to sunburn. **3.** to cause by or as by fire: *An ash burned a hole in the dress.* **4.** to cause or produce a sensation of heat in: *The chili burned his mouth.* **5.a.** to consume for a purpose, as for heat or light: *to burn wood, to burn gas.* **b.** to use or expend (energy): *Jimmy burns a lot of energy playing football.* **6.** *Informal.* to anger; gall: *That comment really burns me.* **7.** to put to death by fire. **8.** to finish, harden, or glaze by fire or heat; fire: *to burn clay.* **9.** to produce by or as if by burning: *He burned the image of a cross into the wood.* **10.** to cauterize; brand. **11.** *Chemistry.* to cause to undergo combustion. **12.** *Physics.* to cause the nuclei of (uranium, plutonium, hydrogen, or other nuclear fuels) to undergo fission or fusion. **13.** *Slang.* to electrocute. —*v.i.* **1.** to be on fire; flame. **2.** to be destroyed, changed, or injured by or as if by fire: *The steak burned on the outside. The material burned when acid spilled on it.* **3.** to give off light or heat; shine; glow: *The street lights burned all night.* **4.** to feel or seem to be hot: *The child burned with a fever.* **5.** to be consumed by strong emotion,

at; āpe; cär; end; mē; it; īce; hot; ōld; fôrk; wood; fōōl; oil; out; up; ūse; turn; sing; thin; this; zh in treasure; ə in ago, taken, pencil, lemon, circus.

131

as love or anger. **6.** *Chemistry.* to undergo combustion; oxidize. **7.** to be produced by or as if by burning: *His words burned in my mind.* **8.** to die by fire. **9.** *Slang.* to be electrocuted.
  to burn down. to destroy or be destroyed by fire.
  to burn up. a. to make or become angry, irritated, or annoyed. **b.** to consume or be consumed by or as if by fire.
  to burn out. a. to stop burning or die out through lack of fuel. **b.** to destroy or wear out, as by heat or friction: *We burned out the car's transmission.* **c.** to drive or be driven out by means of fire or heat. **d.** to burn up or destroy the house, place of business, or property of.
  to burn off. to remove paint from (a surface) by subjecting it to fire, as from a blowtorch.
—*n.* **1.** injury, damage, or effect caused by or as if by burning: *a burn from exposure to wind and sun, a burn on one's fingers.* **2.** firing of one or more rocket engines of a spacecraft while in flight. [Partly from Old English *beornan* to be on fire; partly from Old English *bærnan* to set on fire.] —**burn'a·ble,** *adj.*

burn² (burn) *n.* burn¹.

burn·er (bur'nər) *n.* **1.** one who or that which burns. **2.** that part of a stove, furnace, or similar device from which the flame issues or is produced.

burn·ing (bur'ning) *adj.* **1.** on fire; in flames. **2.** glowing; scorching; hot. **3.** causing intense emotion or controversy; of the utmost importance: *a burning question.* **4.** ardent; vehement; excited: *burning desire.*

burning glass, convex lens used to heat or cause something to ignite by focusing the sun's rays upon it.

bur·nish (bur'nish) *v.t.* to polish by friction; make smooth and shiny: *to burnish metal.* —*n.* polish; luster; gloss. [Old French *burniss-,* a stem of *burnir* to polish, make brown, from *brun* brown; of Germanic origin.] —**bur·nish·er** (bur'ni shər) *n.* **1.** tool, usually with a smooth, rounded head, used for burnishing. **2.** one who burnishes.

bur·noose (bər nōōs', bər'nōōs) *also,* **bur·nous,** *n.* cloak with a hood, as that worn by Moors and Arabs. [French *burnous,* from Arabic *burnus,* from Greek *birros.*]

Burns, Robert (burnz) 1759–96, Scottish poet.

burn·sides (burn'sīdz') *n.* side whiskers, often with a mustache; muttonchops. [From the American Civil War general Ambrose E. Burnside, 1824–81, who wore whiskers of this style.]

burnt (burnt) a past tense and past participle of **burn**¹.

burnt orange, brownish-orange color.

burnt sienna, see **sienna.**

burnt umber, see **umber.**

burp (burp) *Informal. n.* belch. —*v.i.* to belch. —*v.t.* to cause (a baby) to belch. [Imitative.]

burr¹ (bur) *n. also (defs. 1–3),* **bur. 1.** prickly seed case covered with tiny barbs that sticks to clothing or fur. **2.** any plant bearing burrs, esp. a weed. **3.** one who or that which clings like a burr. **4.** rough or sharp edge left on metal by a cutting or drilling tool. **5.** any of several small cutting heads used on dentists' drills. **6.** any of various other tools used for cutting or drilling. —*v.t.,* **burred, bur·ring. 1.** *also,* **bur.** to remove burrs from. **2.** to form a rough edge on. [Possibly of Scandinavian origin.]

burr² (bur) *n.* **1.** rough, trilled pronunciation of *r,* as heard in Scotland and northern England. **2.** any rough or guttural pronunciation. **3.** humming or whirring sound. —*v.t.* to pronounce (something) with a burr. —*v.i.* **1.** to speak with a burr. **2.** to make a humming or whirring sound. [Possibly imitative.]

Burr, Aaron (bur) 1756–1836, U.S. politician and lawyer, vice-president of the United States, from 1801 to 1805.

bur·ro (bur'ō, boor'ō) *pl.,* **-ros.** *n.* small donkey. [Spanish *burro,* from *borrico,* from Late Latin *burricus* small horse; of uncertain origin.]

Bur·roughs, Edgar Rice (bur'ōz) 1875–1950, U.S. novelist.

bur·row (bur'ō) *n.* **1.** hole dug in the ground, as by a rabbit or fox, for refuge or habitation. **2.** any similar passage for shelter, retreat, or refuge. —*v.i.* **1.** to live or hide in a burrow. **2.** to dig a burrow or burrows. **3.** to penetrate or dig. **4.** to hunt; search: *The woman burrowed into her purse for change.* —*v.t.* **1.** to construct by burrowing. **2.** to dig a burrow or burrows in. [Form of BOROUGH.] —**bur'row·er,** *n.*

bur·sa (bur'sə) *pl.,* **-sae** (-sē) or **-sas.** *n.* closed, fluid-filled sac that helps prevent friction in certain parts of the body, as at a joint or where a tendon passes over a bone. [Late Latin *bursa* purse, from Greek *byrsā* skin. Doublet of BOURSE, PURSE.]

bur·sar (bur'sər, -sär) *n.* treasurer, as of a college. [Medieval Latin *bursarius,* from Late Latin *bursa* purse. See BURSA.]

bur·sa·ry (bur'sə rē) *pl.,* **-ries.** *n.* treasury, as of a college.

bur·si·tis (bər sī'tis) *n.* severely painful condition resulting from inflammation of a bursa, the most commonly affected areas being the shoulder, elbow, and hip joints. [BURSA + -ITIS.]

burst (burst) **burst, burst·ing.** *v.i.* **1.** to break open or fly apart suddenly

and violently from or as from internal pressure; explode. **2.** to be full to the point of overflowing: *to burst with pride. The closet was bursting with junk.* **3.** to come, appear, or issue forth suddenly or violently. **4.** to give vent suddenly to an action or emotional expression: *to burst into bloom, to burst into tears.* —*v.t.* **1.** to cause to break open or explode suddenly and violently; shatter: *to burst a balloon.* **2.** to fill or cause (something) to bulge to the breaking point. —*n.* **1.** sudden issuing forth or eruption; outbreak: *a burst of gunfire, a burst of enthusiasm.* **2.** sudden display of activity or energy; spurt: *a burst of speed.* **3.** result of bursting; crack; break. **4.a.** series of shots fired by one continued pressing on the trigger of an automatic weapon. **b.** explosion of a shell or bomb. [Old English *berstan* to break.]

bur·then (bur'thən) *Archaic.* burden¹.

Bur·ton, Sir Richard Francis (burt'ən) 1821–90, English explorer and author.

Bu·run·di (bə run'dē, boo rōōn'dē) *n.* country in east-central Africa. Capital, Bujumbura. Area, 10,747 sq. mi. Pop. (1969 est.), 3,475,000.

bur·y (ber'ē) **bur·ied, bur·y·ing.** *v.t.* **1.** to put (a dead body) in the earth, a tomb, or the sea, usually with funeral rites; inter. **2.** to cover up or hide; conceal: *The pirates buried their treasure.* **3.** to cause to sink, plunge, or lodge (*in* something): *He buried the axe in the tree trunk.* **4.** to interest (oneself) in; engross: *He buried himself in the newspaper.* **5.** to put out of one's mind; forget; abandon: *He buried his anger.* [Old English *byrgan* to inter.]

bus (bus) *pl.,* **bus·es** or **bus·ses.** *n.* motor vehicle with rows of seats to accommodate many passengers, used esp. on a fixed, regular route. —*v.t.,* **bused** or **bussed, bus·ing** or **bus·sing.** to transport by bus: *They bused the orchestra from city to city.* —*v.i.* to travel by bus: *He bused to the city.* [Short for OMNIBUS.]

bus., business.

bus·boy (bus'boi') *also,* **bus boy.** *n.* waiter's assistant who performs various duties, as clearing and resetting the tables.

bus·by (buz'bē) *pl.,* **-bies.** *n.* fur hat with a bag hanging from the top over the right side, worn by hussars, artillerymen, and engineers in the British army. [Apparently from the proper name *Busby,* possibly the name of the manufacturer or a wearer.]

bush (boosh) *n.* **1.** shrub, esp. a thick shrub without a distinct trunk. **2.** clump of shrubs or trees; thicket; undergrowth. **3.** wild, uncultivated tract of country covered with scrub: *the Australian bush.* **4. to beat the bushes.** to search all over for someone or something. —*v.i.* to be or become thick or bushy; resemble a bush. —*v.t.* to protect (plants, crops, or trees) with bushes set around them; cover or support with bushes. [Middle English *busk* shrub, thicket, from Old Norse *buskr.*]

Busby

bush·el¹ (boosh'əl) *n.* **1.** dry measure equal to four pecks or thirty-two quarts. See **weights and measures** for table. **2.** container holding a bushel. [Old French *boissel* the measure, probably from *boisse* sixth of a bushel; possibly of Celtic origin.]

bush·el² (boosh'əl) **-eled** or **-elled, -el·ing** or **-el·ling.** *v.t., v.i.* to repair or alter (clothing). [Possibly from German *bosseln* to patch.] —**bush'el·er;** *also,* **bush'el·ler,** *n.*

bu·shi·do (bōō'shē dō') *also,* **Bu·shi·do.** *n.* unwritten code of honor of the Samurai warriors of feudal Japan, which prescribed loyalty, courage, self-sacrifice, and death before dishonor, usually by hara-kiri. [Japanese *bushidō* literally, warrior's way.]

bush·ing (boosh'ing) *n.* **1.** replaceable metal lining, as for a machine part, used to lessen abrasion and wear or to decrease the internal diameter of either a pipe or a part into which another part fits. **2.** lining that insulates and prevents abrasion of electric conductors. [From earlier *bush* metal lining, from Middle Dutch *busse* box, from Late Latin *buxis,* from Greek *pyxis.*]

bush·man (boosh'mən) *pl.,* **-men.** *n.* **1.** settler or farmer in the Australian bush. **2. Bushman.** one of a group of south African people who speak a Khoisan language and live in the region of the Kalahari Desert, in Botswana, and in southern Angola. **3. Bushman.** language of the Bushmen, forming with Hottentot the Khoisan family of African languages. [BUSH + MAN; influenced by Afrikaans *boschjesman* literally, man of the bush.]

bush·mas·ter (boosh'mas'tər) *n.* deadly tropical pit viper, *Lachesis mutus,* found in Central and South America. It is the longest poisonous snake in the Western Hemisphere, occasionally growing to twelve feet.

bush pilot, pilot who flies a small plane to and from areas that are usually inaccessible to larger aircraft or other conventional means of transportation, as automobiles or trains.

bush·whack (boosh'hwak', -wak') *v.t.* to attack from ambush. [From BUSHWHACKER.]

bush·whack·er (boosh'hwak'ər, -wak'ər) *n.* **1.** one who attacks

    at; āpe; cär; end; mē; it; īce; hot; ōld; fôrk; wood; fōōl; oil; out; up; ūse; turn; sing; thin; this; zh in treasure; ə in ago, taken, pencil, lemon, circus.

from ambush. **2.** Confederate guerrilla. **3.** woodsman. [Originally from the idea of one who "whacks" through the bushes.]

bush·y (boosh′ē) **bush·i·er, bush·i·est.** *adj.* **1.** resembling a bush; thick and spreading. **2.** full of or overgrown with bushes. —**bush′i·ness,** *n.*

bus·i·ly (biz′ə lē) *adv.* in a busy manner; actively; industriously.

busi·ness (biz′nis) *n.* **1.** one's occupation, trade, or profession. **2.** commercial or industrial enterprise, as a store or factory. **3.** volume of buying and selling; commercial transactions; trade: *Business was bad at the store.* **4.** matter; affair: *He was tired of the whole silly business.* **5.** commercial policy or custom: *It's bad business not to advertise.* **6.** rightful interest or concern; responsibility: *What business is it of yours? He made it his business to be on time.* **7.** any action or gesture by an actor or entertainer. Distinguished from **dialogue** or **lyrics.** **8. to get down to business.** *Informal.* to settle down and work seriously. **9. to give (someone) the business.** *Slang.* to treat harshly. **10. to go about one's business.** to do unceremoniously what one has set out to do. **11. to have no business.** to have no right (to do or say something). **12. to mean business.** *Informal.* to be in earnest. **13. to mind one's own business.** to refrain from meddling in what does not concern one; attend to one's own affairs. —*adj.* of, relating to, connected with, or engaged in business: *business hours, a business card.* [BUSY + NESS.]

business college, school that gives training in clerical or secretarial skills, as typing and shorthand, or in any of various technical areas, as bookkeeping or operation of business machines, in preparation for a career in business or commerce.

busi·ness·like (biz′nis līk′) *adj.* having qualities suitable to business; methodical.

busi·ness·man (biz′nis man′) *pl.,* **-men.** *n.* one who owns, operates, or works in a business. —**busi′ness·wom′an,** *n.*

business school 1. school, usually part of a university, which teaches techniques of management, finance, and commerce. **2.** business college.

bus·kin (bus′kin) *n.* **1.** laced half boot usually reaching the middle of the calf. **2.** thick-soled boot worn by actors in tragedies during the Hellenistic and Roman periods. Also, **co·thur′nus. 3.** tragic drama; tragedy. [Old French *brousequin* the boot; of uncertain origin.]

bus·man's holiday (bus′mənz) holiday spent by choice in doing something similar to one's regular work.

Bus·ra, (bus′rə) *also,* **Bus·rah.** *n.* Basra.

buss (bus) *Archaic. n.* kiss; smack. —*v.t.* to kiss (someone). [Probably imitative.]

bust¹ (bust) *n.* **1.** piece of sculpture representing the head, shoulders, and breast of an individual. **2.** the bosom of a woman. [French *buste,* from Italian *busto,* perhaps from Latin *bustum* tomb; possibly because tombs were often decorated with a bust of the deceased.]

bust² (bust) *Slang. v.t.* **1.** to burst; break. **2.** to cause to go bankrupt. **3.** to hit; thump; sock. **4.** to reduce in rank; demote. **5.** to arrest (someone). **6.** to tame; break: *The cowboy busted the mustang.* —*v.i.* **1.** to burst; break. **2.** to become bankrupt. —*n.* **1.** utter failure; flop. **2.** spree. **3.** blow; hit. **4.** bankruptcy or economic depression: *a period of boom and bust.* [Form of BURST.]

bus·tard (bus′tərd) *n.* any of various game birds, family Otididae, native to Eurasia, Africa, and Australia, having long legs, a large, heavy body, and a long neck. Height: 4 feet. [Blend of Old French *bistarde* and *oustarde,* both from Latin *avis tarda* slow bird.]

bus·tle¹ (bus′əl) **-tled, -tling.** *v.i.* to move quickly and energetically; commotion; stir: *the bustle of a city.* [Possibly a modification of obsolete *buskle* to prepare, going back to Old Norse *būask* to get ready.]

bus·tle² (bus′əl) *n.* **1.** large amount of gathered material worn over the back of a skirt just below the waist. **2.** pad or frame formerly worn by women to add fullness to the back part of a skirt. [Of uncertain origin.]

bus·y (biz′ē) **bus·i·er, bus·i·est.** *adj.* **1.** actively and attentively engaged in something: *I am busy making plans for the wedding.* **2.** full of or marked by activity: *Tomorrow is going to be a busy day.* **3.** in use: *When we phoned, the line was busy.* **4.** meddling; prying; officious. **5.** cluttered with many small, complex details and parts; excessively ornamented; fussy: *busy wallpaper.* —*v.t.* **bus·ied, bus·y·ing.** to make or keep busy; occupy (oneself): *Robin busied herself cleaning the house.* [Old English *bisig* occupied.]

bus·y·bod·y (biz′ē bod′ē) *pl.,* **-bod·ies.** *n.* one who pries into other people's affairs; meddler.

but (but; *unstressed* bət) *conj.* **1.** on the other hand; in contrast: *They behave not like men but like children. He has nothing for you, but I have.* **2.** contrary to expectation; yet; nevertheless: *It is early November, but it has begun snowing. I was not invited, but I plan to go anyway.* **3.** other than; except: *There was no direct route but through the center of town. We have no choice but to arrive late.* **4.** that: *There is no doubt but he will recover.* **5.** without the result that; unless: *It never rains but it pours.* **6.** that . . . not: *Who knows but we may make a fortune?* —*prep.* **1.** other than; except: *Everyone has signed but you.* **2. but for.** if it were not for; except for: *We would have no money but for their aid.* —*adv.* **1.** only; merely; just: *I have but a day. I saw him but a few minutes ago.* **2. all but.** nearly; almost: *The food was all but gone.* —*n.* objection or limitation; exception: *No ifs, ands, or buts about it.* [Old English *būtan* except, without, unless.]

Syn. conj. 1. But, however, yet express varying degrees of opposition to what has gone before. **But** states the opposition simply and without special emphasis: *He is poor but generous.* **However,** a formal word, weakens the opposition by stating it almost as an afterthought: *This book is not for loan; however, you may read it here.* **Yet,** the strongest of these words, implies opposition despite what has gone before: *His story sounded unbelievable, yet we knew it was true.*

bu·ta·di·ene (bū′tə dī′ēn, -dī ēn′) *n.* flammable, colorless gas obtained from butanes and butenes or as a by-product of ethylene production, used esp. in making synthetic rubber, nylon, and rocket fuels. Formula: C_4H_6 [BUTA(NE) + DI-¹ + -ENE.]

bu·tane (bū′tān) *n.* either of two colorless, flammable gases, used to make such products as liquefied petroleum gas, high-octane gasoline, and synthetic rubber. Formula: C_4H_{10} [Latin *būt(yrum)* butter + -ANE. See BUTTER.]

butch·er (booch′ər) *n.* **1.** one who slaughters animals or dresses their flesh for market. **2.** one who deals in meat. **3.** one guilty of cruel, bloody, or indiscriminate slaughter. **4.** one who is clumsy and unskillful; bungler. —*v.t.* **1.** to slaughter or dress (animals) for market or for food. **2.** to slaughter in a cruel, bloody, or indiscriminate manner. **3.** to spoil by bad work; botch: *The pianist butchered the concerto.* [Old French *bochier* originally, killer of male goats, seller of goat meat, from *boc* male goat; possibly of Celtic origin.] —**butch′er·er,** *n.*

butch·er·bird (booch′ər burd′) *n.* shrike.

butch·er's-broom (booch′ərz brōōm′, -broom′) *n.* evergreen shrub, *Ruscus aculeatus,* of the lily family, having small greenish flowers and red or yellow berrylike fruit.

butch·er·y (booch′ər ē) *pl.,* **-er·ies.** *n.* **1.** cruel or wholesale slaughter; carnage. **2.** slaughterhouse. **3.** trade or business of a butcher.

bu·tene (bū′tēn) *n.* any of three colorless, flammable hydrocarbons in the form of a gas, used esp. in making such products as butadiene and gasoline. Formula: C_4H_8 [Latin *būt(yrum)* butter + -ENE. See BUTTER.]

but·ler (but′lər) *n.* male servant, usually the head servant in a household, who supervises the other workers, oversees the preparation and serving of food and drinks, and may perform other household services. [Anglo-Norman *buteler,* corresponding to Old French *botillier* one who carries bottles, from *boteille.* See BOTTLE.]

But·ler, Samuel (but′lər) 1835–1902, English novelist.

butler's pantry, serving pantry, esp. between the kitchen and dining room.

butt¹ (but) *n.* **1.** end of something, esp. the thicker or larger end: *a rifle butt, the butt of a spear.* **2.** leftover end, esp. the part of a cigar or cigarette which remains after smoking; stub. **3.** *Informal.* buttocks. **4.** *Slang.* cigarette. [Of uncertain origin.]

butt² (but) *n.* **1.** person or thing that is the object of ridicule, scorn, criticism, or sarcasm: *The king was the butt of the satire.* **2.** target. **3.** embankment, ditch, or structure on a range in front of which the target is placed, designed to protect the marker or stop the projectile. **4. the butts.** *Archaic.* target range. [Probably from Old French *but* goal; of uncertain origin.]

butt³ (but) *v.i.* **1.** to push or strike with or as with the head or horns. **2. to butt in.** *Informal.* to meddle, interfere, or intrude. —*v.t.* **1.** to strike or push (something) with or as with the head or horns. **2. to butt into.** *Informal.* to interfere, intrude, or meddle in. —*n.* push, thrust, or blow with or as with the head or horns. [Anglo-Norman *buter* to push; of Germanic origin.]

butt⁴ (but) *v.t.* to join or meet the edge or end of (something); abut. —*v.i.* to be joined at the edges or ends; abut. [Partly from BUTT¹; partly from BUTT².]

butt⁵ (but) *n.* **1.** large cask, as for wine, ale, or beer. **2.** liquid measure for wine, equal to 126 U.S. gallons. [Old French *bout* cask, from Late Latin *buttis.* See BOTTLE.]

butte (būt) *n.* isolated, usually flat-topped mountain, hill, or pinnacle, formed by the erosion of all but a portion of a mesa, plateau, or other

Buskin

Bustard

at; āpe; cär; end; mē; it; īce; hot; ōld; fôrk; wood; fōōl; out; up; ūse; turn; sing; thin; <u>th</u>is; zh in treasure; ə in ago, taken, pencil, lemon, circus.

133

level surface. [French *butte* rising ground, from Old French *but* goal; of uncertain origin.]

but·ter (but′ər) *n.* **1.** yellow or white, semisolid fatty substance, derived from cream by churning, used esp. as a spread or in cooking. **2.a.** any of several food preparations used as spreads. **b.** any of various vegetable oils which have a solid consistency at ordinary temperatures: *cocoa butter.* **3.** chlorides of some metals: *butter of bismuth, butter of zinc.* **4. to look as if butter wouldn't melt in one's mouth.** to look innocent and coy. —*v.t.* **1.** to spread with butter. **2.** *Informal.* to flatter (usually with *up*): *We buttered him up.* **3. to know which side one's bread is buttered on.** to know where one's advantage or security lies. [Old English *butere* the substance derived from cream by churning, from Latin *būtȳrum*, from Greek *boutȳron*, from *bous* cow + *tȳros* cheese.]

but·ter·cup (but′ər kup′) *n.* **1.** cup-shaped flower, usually bright yellow, of any of a large group of plants, genus *Ranunculus,* of the crowfoot family, found throughout the world. **2.** plant bearing this flower, often having deeply divided leaves resembling a three-toed crow's foot.

but·ter·fat (but′ər fat′) *n.* yellow or white fat cells in milk, consisting of a mixture of glycerides of fatty acids, from which butter is made.

but·ter·fin·gers (but′ər fing′gərz) *n. Informal.* one who drops things easily or frequently.

but·ter·fish (but′ər fish′) *pl.,* **-fish** or **-fish·es.** *n.* saltwater fish, *Poronotus triacanthus,* of the Atlantic coast of North America, which has a silvery-blue body and a deeply forked tail, valued as a food fish. Length: 8–12 inches.

but·ter·fly (but′ər flī′) *pl.,* **-flies.** *n.* **1.** any of various insects, order Lepidoptera, characterized by slender bodies and four large, usually bright-colored wings. **2.** stroke in swimming face down, similar to the breast stroke, in which both arms are brought forward simultaneously over the water, causing the shoulders to lunge out of the water. The arms are then drawn down and back, accompanied by either a dolphin kick or frog kick. **3.** person, esp. a woman, who is giddy, capricious, vain, or showily dressed. [Old English *butterflēge* this insect; possibly so called because it was once believed that witches took the form of butterflies to steal dairy products.]

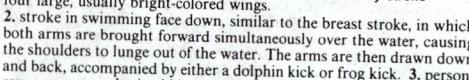

Butterfly stroke

butterfly fish 1. brightly colored flatbodied saltwater fish, family Chaetodontidae, commonly found in warm coralreef pools. Length: to 2 feet. **2.** silvery freshwater fish, family Pantodontidae, found in the swamps of tropical western Africa, having an enormous mouth and large pectoral fins.

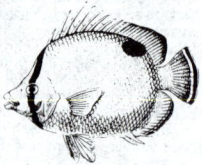

Butterfly fish

butterfly weed, wild flowers, *Asclepias tuberosa,* of the milkweed family, widely distributed thoughout the United States, having lance-shaped, hairy leaves and small, loosely clustered orange or orange-and-yellow flowers.

but·ter·milk (but′ər milk′) *n.* **1.** curdled, sour beverage, similar to yogurt, made from skim milk to which certain bacteria cultures have been added. **2.** liquid remaining after cream has been churned into butter.

but·ter·nut (but′ər nut′) *n.* **1.** edible, oily nut of the tree *Juglans cinerea,* of the walnut family, found in eastern and central North America. **2.** tree bearing this nut, having coarse-grained, soft wood that is used for furniture and interiors.

butternut squash, small, pear-shaped winter squash with a smooth skin and tan flesh.

but·ter·scotch (but′ər skoch′) *n.* **1.** somewhat hard, sticky candy made from brown sugar, butter, and corn syrup. **2.** flavoring made from similar ingredients. —*adj.* made or flavored with butterscotch.

but·ter·y¹ (but′ər ē) *adj.* **1.** having the quality, consistency, taste, or appearance of butter. **2.** containing or spread with butter. [BUTTER + -Y¹.]

but·ter·y² (but′ər ē, but′rē) *pl.,* **-ter·ies.** *n. British.* pantry. [Old French *boterie* place to store bottles and casks, from *bout* butt (cask). See BUTT³, BOTTLE.]

but·tock (but′ək) *n.* **1.** either of the two fleshy parts of the body behind the hips. **2.** buttocks. rump. [From BUTT¹ + English diminutive suffix -ock.]

but·ton (but′ən) *n.* **1.** knob, disk, or other object sewn or otherwise attached to clothing or other material, serving as a fastening when passed through a hole, slit, or loop, or used for ornament. **2.** anything resembling a button: *a campaign button. Press the elevator button.*

3. head of a young mushroom. **4. on the button.** completely right or precise; exactly. —*v.t.* to fasten with or as with a button or buttons. —*v.i.* to be capable of being fastened with a button or buttons. [Old French *boton* knob sewn to clothing; originally, bud, from *boter* to bud; of Germanic origin.] —**but′ton·er,** *n.*

but·ton·hole (but′ən hōl′) *n.* hole or slit through which a button passes. —*v.t.,* **-holed, -hol·ing. 1.** to make buttonholes in. **2.** to sew with a buttonhole stitch. **3.** to detain (a person) in conversation by or as if by seizing the buttonhole at the top of the shirt: *The reporters buttonholed the senator.*

but·ton·hook (but′ən hook′) *n.* small, metal hook used for pulling small buttons through buttonholes, esp. in shoes or gloves.

but·ton·wood (but′ən wood′) *n.* plane tree of North America; sycamore.

but·tress (but′ris) *n.* **1.** strong or heavy structure, usually of brick or stone, built against a wall or building to strengthen or support it. **2.** any support or prop. —*v.t.* **1.** to support or strengthen with a buttress. **2.** to prop up; support. [Old French *bouterez* (plural) supports, from Old French *bo(u)ter* to push; of Germanic origin.]

Buttress

bu·tyr·ic acid (bū tir′ik) colorless liquid compound with a bad odor that occurs in rancid milk fats and is a by-product of hydrocarbon synthesis, used esp. in perfume and flavor ingredients and in solvents. Formula: $C_4H_8O_2$ [Latin *būtȳr(um)* butter + -IC; because found in butter. See BUTTER.]

bux·om (buk′səm) *adj.* (of women) plump and healthy; full-bosomed. [Middle English *buhsum* pliable, obedient, going back to Old English *būgan* to bend; development of meaning from "pliable" to "plump" in Modern English.]

buy (bī) *v.t.* **bought, buy·ing. 1.** to acquire possession of by giving an equivalent, usually in money; purchase: *We bought a house. The candidate bought time on television during the campaign.* **2.** to be a means of purchasing or an equivalent price for; obtain: *Money cannot buy health.* **3.** to obtain by exchange or sacrifice: *to buy approval with good deeds.* **4.** to bribe: *That policeman cannot be bought.* **5.** *Informal.* to accept as true; believe: *They wouldn't buy our excuse.* **6. to buy off.** to get rid of (a person, opposition, or interference) by payment; bribe: *He bought off his critics.* **7. to buy out.** to purchase all the shares, rights, or interests of (a person), as in a partnership or business. **8. to buy up.** to purchase the whole of or the whole available supply of. **9. to buy into.** to purchase shares, stock, or interest in. —*v.i.* to make a purchase; be or become a purchaser. —*n. Informal.* **1.** bargain. **2.** something bought; purchase. [Old English *bycgan* to purchase.]
Syn. *v.t.* **1. Buy, purchase** mean to acquire something by paying a price. **Buy** is the usual word for any such transaction: *to buy a new car.* **Purchase** may be merely formal for **buy,** but it is often used of a large or important transaction: *The financier purchased a controlling interest in the company.*

buy·er (bī′ər) *n.* **1.** one who buys; purchaser. **2.** one who is employed to purchase merchandise for a business, esp. for a particular department of a retail store or chain of stores.

buyer's market, economic situation in which the supply of a commodity is greater than the immediate demand for it, thus giving the buyer greater freedom to pick and choose and to negotiate a lower price.

buzz (buz) *n.* **1.** continuous humming or sharp rasping sound resembling that made by some insects. **2.** confused sound, as that made by many people engaged in conversation. **3.** rumor; report. **4.** *Informal.* telephone call: *Give me a buzz when you get home.* —*v.i.* **1.** to make a continuous humming or sharp rasping sound.
2. to talk or gossip excitedly and continuously, esp. in low tones. **3.** to signal by using a buzzer: *He buzzed, but no one answered.* **4.** to move busily or hastily; scurry: *She buzzed around town doing her shopping.* —*v.t.* **1.** to utter or express something, as gossip or rumors, by buzzing. **2.** to signal with a buzzer. **3.** to produce a buzzing sound with; cause to buzz. **4.** to fly an airplane fast and low over. **5.** *Informal.* to telephone (someone). [Imitative.]

buz·zard (buz′ərd) *n.* **1.** any of various soaring birds of prey, esp. the genus *Buteo,* native to all temperate regions of the world except the South Pacific, having sharp, hooked beaks and long, sharp talons. Height: 20–32 inches. **2.** any of various other birds, as the turkey buzzard, vulture, or condor. [Old French *busart* hawk, going back to Latin *būteō.*]

Buzzard

buzz bomb, ballistic missile used by the Germans against England during World War II. Also, **robot bomb.**

at; āpe; cär; end; mē; it; īce; hot; ōld; fôrk; wood; fōol; oil; out; up; ūse; turn; sing; thin; this; zh in treasure; ə in ago, taken, pencil, lemon, circus.

buzz·er (buz′ər) *n.* device that produces a buzzing sound, esp. an electrical device used as a signal.
buzz saw, power saw that has a rotating circular blade.
bx. *pl.,* **bxs.** box.
by (bī) *prep.* **1.** close to; near; beside: *A river runs by the house.* **2.** up to and beyond; past: *The bus sped by us.* **3.** through the action, means, agency, or use of: *to take by force. The city was destroyed by fire. The book was written by Voltaire.* **4.** on the evidence or authority of; according to: *to go by the rules.* **5.** on the part of: *The accident was regretted by all concerned.* **6.** by way of; through: *We came by the northern route.* **7.** during the course of: *by day.* **8.** not later than: *Be here by eight o'clock.* **9.** in the direction of; toward: *north by northwest.* **10.** in the presence of; before: *I swear by all that is holy.* **11.** according to (a fixed standard); in terms of: *We buy milk by the gallon. She measured the cloth by the yard.* **12.** in relation to; with respect to; regarding: *He did well by his family.* **13.** in immediate succession to: *piece by piece, one by one.* **14.** in or to the extent or amount of: *older by five years, smaller by a third.* **15.** combined in multiplication or measurement with: *to multiply 3 by 4. The rug measures nine by twelve feet.* **16. by the way.** incidentally. —*adv.* **1.** close at hand; near: *close by.* **2.** past and beyond: *He ran by.* **3.** past; over: *in years gone by.* **4.** *Informal.* at or in another's house: *I'll stop by on my way to the store.* **5. by and by.** at some future time; before long. **6. by and large.** on the whole; everything considered; generally. —*n.* **by the by** (or **bye**). incidentally. —*adj.* bye. [Old English *bī* near, according to, through.]
by- *prefix* **1.** of less importance; secondary: *by-product, by-election.* **2.** near by: *bystander.* **3.** aside: *byway, by-street.* [From BY (adverb).]
by-and-by (bī′ən bī′) *n.* future time: *in the sweet by-and-by.*
bye (bī) *n.* **1.** right, usually gained by draw, to enter subsequent rounds in an elimination tournament without competing in one or more earlier rounds. **2.** hole or holes left unplayed after a match-play golf tournament has been won. —*adj. Archaic.* **1.** *also,* **by.** of secondary importance; incidental. **2.** situated to one side. [Form of BY (preposition).]
bye-bye (bī′bī′) *interj. Informal.* good-by.
by-e·lec·tion (bī′i lek′shən) *n. British.* special election held to fill a vacancy in office.
Bye·lo·rus·sia (byel′ō rush′ə) *n.* republic of the Soviet Union, in the westernmost part of the country, bordering Poland. Official name: **Byelorussian Soviet Socialist Republic.** Area, 80,150 sq. mi. Pop. (1970), 9,003,000. Also, **White Russia.**
Bye·lo·rus·sian (byel′ō rush′ən) *n.* **1.** member or close descendant of the people of Byelorussia. **2.** Slavic language of these people, closely related to Russian and Ukrainian. —*adj.* of or relating to these people, their language, or their culture. Also, **White Russian.**
by·gone (bī′gôn′, -gon′) *adj.* gone by; past; former. —*n.* **1.** *also,* **bygones.** something gone by or past. **2. to let bygones be bygones.** to let past disagreements, conflicts, or enmity be forgotten.
by·law (bī′lô′) *n.* law or rule regulating the internal affairs of a government body, a corporation, or an organization, supplementary to its charter or constitution. [Middle English *bilawe* literally, town law, going back to Old Norse *bȳr* town + *lög* law.]
by·line (bī′līn′) *n.* the name of the writer of a newspaper or magazine article printed at the beginning or end of the article.
by·name (bī′nām′) *n.* **1.** secondary name; surname. **2.** nickname.
by·pass (bī′pas′) *n.* **1.** secondary road between two points that avoids a main route, urban center, or other heavily traveled place. **2.** pipe or channel for temporarily diverting the flow of a liquid or gas from a main pipe. **3.** *Electricity.* a shunt. —*v.t.* **1.** to go around or avoid by or as if by a bypass. **2.** to cause (a liquid or gas) to follow a bypass. **3.** to furnish with a bypass.
by·path (bī′path′) *n.* private or side path.
by·play (bī′plā′) *n.* actions or conversations that take place apart from the main action or conversation, esp. in a theatrical production.
by·prod·uct (bī′prod′əkt) *n.* secondary or incidental product or result, esp. in a manufacturing process.
Byrd, Richard Evelyn (burd) 1888–1957, U.S. Antarctic explorer, pioneer aviator, and author.
by·road (bī′rōd′) *n.* side road.
By·ron, Lord (bī′rən) 1788–1824, English poet, born George Gordon.
By·ron·ic (bī ron′ik) *adj.* **1.** of or relating to Byron or his works. **2.** like or characteristic of Byron or his works, esp. romantic, heroic, cynical, satiric, and melancholic.
by·stand·er (bī′stan′dər) *n.* one who is present but does not take an active part; chance onlooker.
by·street (bī′strēt′) *n.* side street.
by·way (bī′wā′) *n.* **1.** secluded or rarely traveled road; side road. **2.** subordinate, minor, or obscure aspect of an area of interest.
by·word (bī′wurd′) *n.* **1.** proverbial or common saying. **2.** word or phrase that typifies certain characteristics of a person or thing: *The name "Genghis Khan" became a byword for cruelty and destruction.* **3.** nickname, esp. a scornful or derisive one. **4.** person or thing that is typical or proverbial or is the object of contempt or scorn. [Old English *bīword* proverb.]
Byz·an·tine (biz′ən tēn′, -tīn′, bi zan′tin) *adj.* **1.** of or relating to Byzantium, the Byzantine Empire, or its art or culture. **2.** of, relating to, or having the characteristics of a style of architecture developed in the Byzantine Empire during the fifth and sixth centuries. Byzantine architecture is characterized by the use of round arches, domes, rich mosaic decorations, and centralized plans. —*n.* member of the people inhabiting ancient Byzantium.
Byzantine Empire, eastern part of the later Roman Empire, usually dated from A.D. 330, when Constantine the Great moved the imperial capital from Rome to Byzantium and renamed it Constantinople. It lasted after the fall of the western part, ending in 1453, when the capital fell to the Ottoman Turks. Also, **Eastern Roman Empire.**
By·zan·ti·um (bi zan′shē əm, -tē əm) *n.* ancient Greek city which became the capital of the Roman Empire and was renamed Constantinople.

at; āpe; cär; end; mē; it; īce; hot; ōld; fôrk; wood; fōōl; oil; out; up; ūse; turn; sing; thin; this; zh in treasure; ə in ago, taken, pencil, lemon, circus.

c, C (sē) *pl.,* **c's, C's.** *n.* **1.** third letter of the English alphabet. **2.** shape of this letter or something having this shape. **3.** third item in a series or group. **4.** *Music.* **a.** first note or tone of the diatonic scale of C major. See **do²** for illustration. **b.** scale or key that has this note or tone as its tonic.

C 1. Roman numeral for 100. **2.** carbon.

c. 1. cent; cents. **2.** circa. **3.** centimeter. **4.** centigrade. **5.** cubic. **6.** century. **7.** copyright. **8.** *Baseball.* catcher. **9.** center.

C. 1. Centigrade. **2.** Catholic. **3.** Conservative. **4.** Celtic. **5.** Court. **6.** Corps. **7.** Cape.

Ca, calcium.

ca., circa.

C.A., Central America.

Caa·ba (kä′bə) Kaaba.

cab (kab) *n.* **1.** taxicab. **2.** any of various carriages for hire with a driver, such as a hansom, brougham, or cabriolet. **3.** the enclosed or covered part, as of a truck, locomotive, steam shovel, or crane, where the controls and operator are housed. [Short for CABRIOLET.]

ca·bal (kə bal′) *n.* **1.** small group of people secretly united to advance themselves or their aims by scheming and intrigue. **2.** scheme or intrigue developed by such a group; plot. —*v.i.,* **-balled, -bal·ling.** to form or join in a cabal; conspire. [French *cabale* intrigue, cabala, from Medieval Latin *cab(b)ala* (the cabala having been associated with secrecy and magic in the Middle Ages). See CABALA.]

cab·a·la (kab′ə lə, kə bä′-) *also,* **cab·ba·la, kab·a·la, kab·ba·la.** *n.* **1.** occult system of religious philosophy developed in the Middle Ages by Jewish rabbis, based on a mystical interpretation of the Scriptures. **2.** any esoteric or occult doctrine. [Medieval Latin *cab(b)ala,* transliteration of Hebrew *qabbālāh* tradition.] —**cab′a·list,** *n.*

cab·al·le·ro (kab′əl yār′ō, kab′ə lâr′ō) *pl.,* **-ros.** *n.* **1.** Spanish gentleman, knight, or cavalier. **2.a.** horseman. **b.** lady's escort or admirer. [Spanish *caballero,* from Late Latin *caballārius.* See CAVALIER.]

ca·ba·na (kə ban′ə, -ban′yə) *n.* **1.** small shelter at a swimming area, used as a bathhouse. **2.** summer cottage; cabin. [Spanish *cabaña* hut, from Late Latin *capanna;* of uncertain origin.]

cab·a·ret (kab′ə rā′) *n.* restaurant or cafe providing food and drink, dancing, and entertainment; nightclub. [French *cabaret* tavern, possibly going back to Late Latin *camera.* See CHAMBER.]

cab·bage (kab′ij) *n.* **1.** leafy head of a plant, *Brassica oleracea,* variety capitata, of the mustard family, having thick, coarsely veined, green or reddish-purple leaves, eaten as a vegetable either raw or cooked. **2.** the plant itself, widely cultivated in temperate regions. [Dialectal Old French *caboche* head, probably going back to Latin *caput;* referring to its shape.]

cabbage palm 1. any of several palm trees of the southeastern United States and northern Latin America, bearing large fan-shaped leaves and edible leaf buds. **2.** any tree of several species of the royal palm, esp. *Roystonea oleracea,* of southern Florida and the West Indies, bearing large feather-like leaves in a crown at the top of the trunk.

cab·ba·la (kab′ə lə, kə bä′-) cabala.

cab·by (kab′ē) *pl.,* **-bies.** *also,* **cab·bie.** *n. Informal.* cabdriver.

cab·driv·er (kab′drī′vər) *n.* driver of a cab, esp. of a taxicab.

cab·in (kab′in) *n.* **1.** small, simply constructed house, usually having only one story; cottage. **2.a.** room or compartment serving as living or working quarters on a ship. **b.** compartment below the deck of a small boat, providing living quarters or shelter. **3.** enclosed space for passengers, crew, or cargo in an aircraft. —*v.i.* to live in a cabin. —*v.t.* to confine; cramp. [French *cabane* hut, going back to Late Latin *capanna;* of uncertain origin.]

cabin boy, boy who waits on the officers and passengers of a ship.

cabin class, class of accommodations on a passenger ship, below first class and above tourist class.

cabin cruiser, powerboat equipped with living facilities.

cab·i·net (kab′ə nit) *n.* **1.** piece of furniture fitted with shelves or drawers and often having doors, for storing or displaying objects; cupboard: *a kitchen cabinet, a china cabinet.* **2.** *also,* **Cabinet.** council which advises the chief executive or sovereign of a nation, usually composed of the heads of various departments of the government: *a policy set by a cabinet.* **3.** small, private room. —*adj.* **1.** of or relating to a political cabinet. **2.** of such value, size, or beauty as to be kept or displayed in a cabinet. **3.** *Archaic.* private; confidential; secret. [Middle French *cabinet* small room, piece of furniture, diminutive of dialectal Old French *cabine* gambling house; of uncertain origin.]

cab·i·net·mak·er (kab′ə nit mā′kər) *n.* one who makes or repairs fine furniture and woodwork.

cab·i·net·work (kab′ə nit wurk′) *n.* any fine furniture or woodwork.

ca·ble (kā′bəl) *n.* **1.** strong, thick rope, esp. one made of wires twisted together. **2.** *Nautical.* **a.** heavy rope or chain used to moor a vessel. **b.** cable's length. **3.** electrical transmission line consisting of one or more conductors enclosed in a protective covering. **4.** cablegram. —*v.t.,* **-bled, -bling. 1.** to fasten with or as with a cable. **2.** to furnish with a cable or cables. **3.** to transmit (a message) by submarine cable. **4.** to send a cablegram to. —*v.i.* to transmit a message by submarine cable. [Old French *cable* thick rope, from Late Latin *capulum* halter, from Latin *capere* to hold.]

Protective covering
Conductors
Rubber insulation
Cable

cable car, car drawn by an overhead cable or pulled along rails by an underground cable, used to carry passengers or cargo up and down.

ca·ble·cast·ing (kā′bəl kas′ting) *n.* broadcasting by cable TV.

ca·ble·gram (kā′bəl gram′) *n.* message sent by submarine telegraph cable. [CABLE + -GRAM¹.]

cable's length, unit of measurement equal to 720 feet, or 120 fathoms, in U.S. usage, or 608 feet, 1/10 of a nautical mile, in British usage.

cable TV, a system for transmitting television programs by cable to the individual sets of subscribers who pay for such a service. Also, **cable television.**

cab·man (kab′mən) *pl.,* **-men.** *n.* cabdriver.

cab·o·chon (kab′ə shon′) *n.* precious stone having a convex shape, which has been highly polished but not faceted. [Old French *cabochon,* from *caboche* head. See CABBAGE.]

ca·boo·dle (kə bood′əl) *n. Slang.* collection; lot; group. [Possibly contraction of the phrase *whole kit and boodle.* See KIT, BOODLE.]

ca·boose (kə boos′) *n.* **1.** railroad car, usually at the rear of a freight train, used by the trainmen and workmen. **2.** small deckhouse used for cooking on a ship; galley. [Middle Dutch *kabuys* ship's kitchen or galley, probably contraction of *kaban huys* cabin house.]

Cab·ot (kab′ət) **1. John.** c.1450–98, Italian explorer of North America for England. **2. Sebastian.** c.1476–1557, his son; explorer of North America for England.

Ca·bri·ni, Saint Frances Xavier (kə brē′nē) 1850–1917, Roman Catholic nun who was the first American to be canonized.

cab·ri·o·let (kab′rē ə lā′) *n.* **1.** light, one-horse carriage, usually two-wheeled, with a folding top. **2.** early automobile of the coupe type, with a convertible top. [French *cabriolet* one-horse carriage, diminutive of *cabriole* leap, from Italian *capriola* leap (like that of a goat), going back to Latin *caper* goat; because the light carriage bounced, from *caper* goat's leaping.]

Cabriolet

ca·ca·o (kə kä′ō, -kā′ō) *pl.,* **-ca·os.** *n.* **1.** nutlike seed of an evergreen tree, genus *Theobroma,* cultivated in tropical regions and valued as the source of cocoa, chocolate, and cocoa butter. **2.** wide, branching tree

at; āpe; cär; end; mē; it; īce; hot; ōld; fôrk; wood; fōōl; oil; out; up; ūse; turn; sing; thin; this; zh in treasure; ə in ago, taken, pencil, lemon, circus.

that produces this seed. [Spanish *cacao*, from Nahuatl *cacauatl* this tree.]

cach·a·lot (kash′ə lot′, -lō′) *n.* sperm whale. [French *cachalot*, from Portuguese *cachalote;* of uncertain origin.]

cache (kash) *n.* **1.** hiding place for storing things, as provisions or treasure. **2.** something hidden or stored in such a place. —*v.t.,* **cached, cach·ing.** to hide or store in a cache. [French *cache* hiding place, from *cacher* to hide, going back to Latin *coāctāre* to force.]

ca·chet (ka shā′) *n.* **1.** seal or stamp, as on an official letter or document. **2.** distinguishing mark or feature, esp. one establishing authenticity. **3.** design or slogan stamped or printed on mail. **4.** hollow wafer forming a capsule in which bad-tasting medicine is enclosed. [French *cachet* seal, from *cacher* to press, hide. See CACHE.]

cach·in·nate (kak′ə nāt′) *v.i.* to laugh loudly or immoderately. [Latin *cachinnātus,* past participle of *cachinnāre.*] —**cach′in·na′tion,** *n.*

ca·cique (kə sēk′) *n.* native chief among the Indians of the West Indies, Mexico, and other parts of Latin America. [Spanish *cacique;* of Carib origin.]

cack·le (kak′əl) **-led, -ling.** *v.i.* **1.** to utter a shrill, broken cry, as a hen makes after laying an egg. **2.** to laugh or talk with such a sound: *The children cackled at the funny story.* —*n.* **1.** act or sound of cackling. **2.** idle talk; chatter. [Imitative.] —**cack′ler,** *n.*

cac·o·mis·tle (kak′ə mis′əl) *n.* raccoonlike mammal, *Bassariscus astutus,* native to woods and rocky hillsides from Oregon to Mexico, having a pointed muzzle, large eyes, pale yellowish-gray fur, and a long tail ringed with black and white bands. Length: 32 inches including tail. [Spanish *cacomiztle,* from Nahuatl *claco* half + *miztli* lion.]

ca·coph·o·ny (kə kof′ə nē) *pl.,* **-nies.** *n.* harsh or unpleasant sound; dissonance; discord. [Greek *kakophōniā* harsh sound.] —**ca·coph′o·nous,** *adj.*

cac·tus (kak′təs) *pl.,* **-tus·es** or **-ti** (-tī). *n.* any of a large group of plants, including vines, shrubs, and trees, found chiefly in desert regions of North and South America and differing from all other plants in having growth centers in their surface tissue. Cactuses usually have a central, woody stem surrounded by thick, pulpy tissue in which water is stored, a leathery skin, and spines or scales. Many species bear beautiful flowers and edible fruits. [Latin *cactus* a prickly plant found in Sicily, from Greek *kaktos.*]

Barrel cactus   Prickly pear cactus

Cactuses

cad (kad) *n.* one who does not behave like a gentleman; ill-bred or ill-mannered person. [Short for CADDIE.] —**cad′dish,** *adj.*

ca·dav·er (kə dav′ər) *n.* dead body, esp. a corpse prepared or used for dissection. [Latin *cadāver.*]

ca·dav·er·ous (kə dav′ər əs) *adj.* of, relating to, or like a corpse; pale; ghastly; gaunt.

cad·die (kad′ē) *also,* **caddy.** *n.* one who assists a golfer, as by carrying his golf clubs. —*v.i.,* **-died, dy·ing.** to act as a caddy. [French *cadet* younger son, young officer. See CADET.]

cad·dis fly (kad′is) small, mothlike insect, order Trichoptera, whose larva lives in fresh water. [Of uncertain origin.]

caddis worm, larva of a caddis fly, used as bait by anglers.

Cad·do·an (kad′ō ən) *n.* North American Indian language family spoken predominantly in parts of North and South Dakota, Kansas, Nebraska, Oklahoma, and other parts of the Great Plains.

cad·dy¹ (kad′ē) *pl.,* **-dies.** *n.* small box, can, or chest, esp. one used to hold tea. [Malay *kātī* a weight of 1⅓ lbs.]

cad·dy² (kad′ē) caddie.

ca·dence (kād′əns) *n.* **1.** rhythmic flow, as in poetry, speech, or natural sounds; rhythm. **2.** measure or beat of any rhythmical movement, as dancing or marching. **3.** fall of the voice, as at the end of a sentence. **4.** rising and falling of sound, esp. modulation of the voice. **5.** *Music.* **a.** melodic or harmonic sequence that concludes a phrase, passage, movement, or composition. **b.** cadenza. [French *cadence,* from Italian *cadenza,* from Late Latin *cadentia* falling (as of dice), from Latin *cadere* to fall. Doublet of CADENZA, CHANCE.]

ca·den·za (kə den′zə) *n. Music.* elaborate and technically difficult passage for solo voice or instrument, usually occurring near the end of an aria, a movement of a concerto, or other musical composition. [Italian *cadenza,* from Late Latin *cadentia* falling (as of dice), from Latin *cadere* to fall. Doublet of CADENCE, CHANCE.]

ca·det (kə det′) *n.* **1.** student in a military academy in training for service as an officer. **2.** younger son or brother. [French *cadet,* from Gascon dialect *capdet* chief, going back to Late Latin *capitellum* small head, diminutive of Latin *caput* head.] —**ca·det′ship,** *n.*

cadge (kaj) **cadged, cadg·ing.** *Informal. v.t.* to get by begging. —*v.i.* to beg; sponge. [Of uncertain origin.] —**cadg′er,** *n.*

ca·di (kä′dē, kā′-) *pl.,* **-dis.** *n.* minor Muslim magistrate or judge, usually of a town or village. [Arabic *qādī* judge.]

Cá·diz (kə diz′, kā′diz, kā′diz) *n.* port city in southwestern Spain. Pop. (1968), 132,310.

Cad·me·an (kad mē′ən) *adj.* of or relating to Cadmus.

cad·mi·um (kad′mē əm) *n.* soft, malleable, ductile, metallic element, with a bluish-white luster, obtained as a by-product of zinc refining. Cadmium resembles zinc in appearance and behavior and is used esp. to plate steel and other metals for corrosion resistance. Symbol: Cd See **element** for table. [Modern Latin *cadmium,* from Latin *cadmīa* calamine (cadmium being found with calamine in zinc ore), from Greek *kadmeiā* (*gē*) Cadmean (earth), calamine, from *Kadmos* Cadmus, founder of Thebes, where calamine supposedly was first found.]

Cad·mus (kad′məs) *n. Greek Mythology.* brother of Europa who, while searching for her, founded the Greek city of Thebes.

cad·re (kä′drə, kad′rē) *n.* **1.** framework; frame. **2.** nucleus of military personnel necessary for the establishing and training of a new unit. **3.** personnel forming the nucleus of a larger group or organization. [French *cadre,* from Italian *quadro* framework, square, painting, from Latin *quādrus* square.]

ca·du·ce·us (kə dōō′sē əs, -dū′-) *pl.,* **-ce·i** (sē ī′). *n.* **1.** wand or staff carried by an ancient Greek or Roman herald, esp. the winged staff with two snakes twined around it carried by Mercury, or Hermes, as the herald of the gods. **2.** similar staff used as the emblem of the medical profession. [Latin *cādūceus* herald's staff, from dialectal Greek *kārykeion.*]

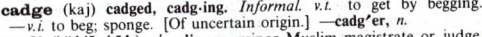

Caduceus

cae·cil·i·an (sē sil′ē ən) *n.* any of a group of limbless, burrowing tropical amphibians, order Apoda, resembling earthworms. [Latin *caecilia* lizard + -AN.]

cae·cum (sē′kəm) cecum.

Caed·mon (kad′mən) died A.D. c.670, early English poet.

Caen (kän) *n.* port city in northwestern France. Pop. (1968), 110,262.

Cae·sar (sē′zər) *n.* **1.** Ga·ius Jul·ius (gā′əs jōōl′yəs). c.100–44 B.C., Roman statesman and general. ▲ The name *Caesar* was used as a title by the Roman emperors from Augustus to Hadrian and also by certain later rulers, as the Holy Roman and Byzantine emperors. **2.** any emperor. **3.** dictator; tyrant.

Cae·sar·e·an (si zâr′ē ən) *also,* **Cae·sar·i·an, Ce·sar·e·an, Ce·sar·i·an.** *adj.* of or relating to Julius Caesar or the Caesars. —*n.* Cesarean section.

Caesarean section, Cesarean section.

cae·sar·ism (sē′zə riz′əm) *n.* imperial or military absolutism.

cae·si·um (sē′zē əm) cesium.

cae·su·ra (si zhoor′ə, -zoor′ə) *pl.,* **-su·ras, -su·rae** (zhoor′ē, -zoor′ē). *also,* **ce·su·ra.** *n.* pause or break in a line of verse. In Greek and Latin prosody the caesura occurs with the ending of a word within a metrical foot. In English prosody it usually agrees with the sense of the line and falls near the middle of it. [Latin *caesūra* literally, a cutting off.]

ca·fé (ka fā′, ka·) *n.* **1.** coffee house; restaurant. **2.** barroom, cabaret, or night club. **3.** *French.* coffee. [French *café* coffee, coffee house, Italian *caffè,* from Turkish *kahveh.* See COFFEE.]

ca·fé au lait (kaf′ə ō lā′, ka fā ō lā′) *French.* **1.** coffee with milk or cream, esp. strong coffee with an equal quantity of scalded milk. **2.** soft, pale brown.

caf·e·te·ri·a (kaf′ə tēr′ē ə) *n.* restaurant in which a customer buys food at a counter and carries it to his table himself. [Spanish *cafetería* coffee shop, from *café* coffee, from Italian *caffè,* from Turkish *kahveh.* See COFFEE.]

caf·feine (ka fēn′, kaf′ē in) *also,* **caf·fein.** *n.* odorless, bitter white alkaloid, found esp. in coffee, tea, and cola, and used medicinally as a stimulant and diuretic. Formula: $C_8H_{10}N_4O_2·H_2O$ [French *caféine,* from *café* coffee. See CAFÉ.]

caf·tan (kaf′tən, käf tän′) *also,* **kaf·tan.** *n.* long, sacked robe which is worn as an outer garment, usually over a shirt and trousers and under a coat, esp. in certain Middle Eastern countries. [Turkish *qaftān* dress.]

Caftan

cage (kāj) *n.* **1.** boxlike structure or enclosure for confining birds or animals, usually having open-work of wires or bars. **2.** anything like a cage in form or function, as the enclosed platform of certain elevators or a cashier's window. **3.** anything that confines or imprisons; prison. **4.** *Baseball.* screen placed behind home plate during batting practice. **5.** *Hockey.* framed net structure serving as a goal. **6.** *Basketball.* basket. —*v.t.,*

caged, cag·ing. to put or confine in or as in a cage. [Old French *cage* enclosure for animals, from Latin *cavea*.]

cage·ling (kāj′ling) *n.* caged bird.

cage·y (kā′jē) **cag·i·er, cag·i·est.** *also,* **cag·y.** *adj. Informal.* wary of being tricked; shrewd; cautious. [Of unknown origin.] —**cag′i·ly,** *adv.* —**cag′i·ness,** *n.*

ca·hoot (kə hōōt′) *Slang. n.* **1. to be in cahoots** (or **cahoot**). to be in partnership, league, or collusion. **2. to go cahoots.** to be partners; share equally. [Possibly from French *cahute* hut, blend of *cabane* hut (see CABIN) and *hutte* hut (of Germanic origin).]

Cai·a·phas (kā′ə fəs, kī′-) *n.* in the New Testament, the Jewish high priest who presided at the council that condemned Jesus to death.

cai·man (kā′mən) *pl.,* **-mans.** *also,* **cay·man.** *n.* any of several aquatic reptiles, order Crocodilia, of Central and South America, closely related to and resembling the alligator. Length: to 15 feet. [Spanish *caimán;* of Carib origin.]

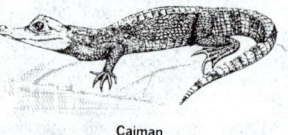

Caiman

Cain (kān) *n.* **1.** in the Old Testament, the oldest son of Adam and Eve who murdered his brother Abel. **2. to raise Cain.** *Slang.* to make a great disturbance; cause a commotion; make trouble.

ca·ique (kä ēk′) *n.* **1.** long, narrow rowboat, popular in Turkey. **2.** sailboat popular in the eastern Mediterranean. [French *caïque,* from Italian *caicco,* from Turkish *qāïq* boat.]

cairn (kârn) *n.* mound of stones piled up as a memorial or landmark. [Gaelic *carn* heap of stones.]

cairn terrier, small terrier of a breed originally developed on the Isle of Skye, having a short, wide head, short, pointed ears, and a shaggy coat. Height: 10 inches at the shoulder. [Supposedly because it hunts among *cairns.*]

Cai·ro (kī′rō) *n.* capital of the United Arab Republic, in the northeastern part of the country. It is the largest city in Africa. Pop. (1966 est.), 4,225,700.

cais·son (kā′sən, -son) *n.* **1.a.** large, boxlike or cylindrical structure used for laying underwater foundations, as for a bridge. In a **pneumatic caisson** there is an airtight

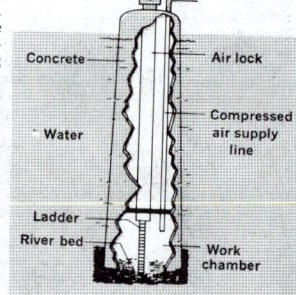

Pneumatic caisson

work chamber at the bottom into which compressed air is pumped to force out the water and which workers enter through an air lock. **b.** similar structure sunk into the ground so that soil can be removed and replaced by concrete to form part of a foundation. **2.** watertight container which is attached to a sunken ship and filled with air. The buoyancy of the caisson helps to raise the ship to the surface. **3.** box for ammunition. **4.** *Artillery.* ammunition wagon composed of a limber and detachable two-wheeled vehicle. [French *caisson* ammunition wagon, coffer, from *caisse* chest, going back to Latin *capsa* box.]

caisson disease, the bends.

cai·tiff (kā′tif) *n.* base, despicable, or cowardly person; scoundrel. —*adj.* base; despicable; cowardly. [Dialectal Old French *caitif* captive, wretched man, going back to Latin *captīvus* captive. Doublet of CAPTIVE.]

ca·jole (kə jōl′) **-joled, -jol·ing.** *v.t., v.i.* to coax or persuade by flattery, soothing words, or false promises; wheedle: *The salesman tried to cajole the couple into buying a new vacuum cleaner.* [French *cajoler* to coax, originally, to chatter like a bird in a cage, probably modification (influenced by French *cage* CAGE) of Middle French *gaioler* to chatter like a bird in a cage, from dialectal Old French *gaiole* cage, going back to Latin *cavea.*] —**ca·jol′er, ca·jol′ment,** *n.* —**Syn.** see **coax.**

ca·jol·er·y (kə jō′lər ē) *pl.,* **-er·ies.** *n.* act or practice of cajoling.

Ca·jun (kā′jən) *n.* descendant of the French who formerly lived in Acadia and settled in Louisiana in the eighteenth century. [Modification of ACADIAN.]

cake (kāk) *n.* **1.** baked mixture of various ingredients, as flour, sugar, eggs, and flavoring, often covered with icing: *a chocolate cake.* **2.** flat, thin portion of dough or batter which is baked or fried, as a

pancake. **3.** any flat mass of food. **4.** shaped, flattened, or compressed mass: *a cake of soap.* **5. to take the cake.** *Slang.* **a.** to win the prize. **b.** to excel in some negative quality, as stupidity. —*v.t., v.i.,* **caked, caking.** to form into a hardened mass: *The wax caked where it had been applied too thickly.* [Old Norse *kaka* small mass of baked dough.]

cakes and ale, the good things of life; material pleasures.

cake·walk (kāk′wôk′) *n.* **1.** march or promenade, of American Negro origin, in which a cake was awarded to the one who performed the most original and intricate steps. **2.** dance developed from the promenade. **3.** music for this dance. —*v.i.* to participate in a cakewalk.

cal. **1.** calendar. **2.** caliber.

Cal., California.

cal·a·bash (kal′ə bash′) *n.* **1.** gourd. **2.** dried fruit of a tropical American tree, *Crescentia cujete,* used for bowls, dippers, and water jugs. **3.** tree bearing this fruit, having large horizontal branches that bear clusters of leaves at intervals. [French *calebasse* gourd, from Spanish *calabaza,* possibly from Persian *kharbuz* melon, or from Arabic *qar′* gourd + *yābis* dry.]

cal·a·boose (kal′ə bōōs′) *n. Informal.* jail; lockup. [Spanish *calabozo* prison, possibly from Arabic *qal′a* castle + *būs* hidden.]

ca·la·di·um (kə lā′dē əm) *n.* any of a group of small tropical plants, genus *Caladium,* of the arum family, having heart-shaped or spade-shaped leaves with red, pink, violet, or yellow patterns, popular as a house plant. [Modern Latin *Caladium,* from Malay *keladi* a plant of this genus.]

Cal·ais (kal′ā, kal′is) *n.* seaport on the northern coast of France, the continental European city closest to England. Pop. (1963), 70,372.

cal·a·man·co (kal′ə mang′kō) *n.* glossy woolen fabric having a pattern on one side only, popular in the eighteenth century. [Of uncertain origin.]

cal·a·mine (kal′ə mīn′, -min) *n.* **1.** hemimorphite. **2.** odorless pink powder made from a mixture of zinc oxide and ferric oxide, used medicinally in skin lotions and ointments. [French *calamine,* from Medieval Latin *calamina,* modification of Latin *cadmīa,* from Greek *kadmeiā.* See CADMIUM.]

ca·lam·i·tous (kə lam′ə təs) *adj.* marked by or causing calamity; disastrous. —**ca·lam′i·tous·ly,** *adv.*

ca·lam·i·ty (kə lam′ə tē) *pl.,* **-ties.** *n.* **1.** great misfortune; disaster. **2.** state of affliction or adversity; distress; misery. [Latin *calāmitās* misfortune.] —**Syn. 1.** see **disaster.**

cal·a·mus (kal′ə məs) *pl.,* **-mi** (-mī′). *n.* **1.** sweet flag. **2.** any tropical climbing palm, genus *Calamus,* yielding rattan. **3.** lower part of the shaft of a feather; quill. [Latin *calamus* reed, from Greek *kalamos.*]

ca·lash (kə lash′) *also,* **ca·lèche.** *n.* **1.** light, low-wheeled carriage, usually having a folding top. **2.** folding hood or top of a carriage. **3.** woman's bonnet that folded back like a carriage top, worn esp. in the eighteenth and nineteenth centuries. [French *calèche,* from German *Kalesche* light carriage, from Polish *kolaska* small carriage, from *kolo* wheel.]

Calash

cal·car·e·ous (kal kâr′ē əs) *adj.* consisting of or containing calcium, calcium carbonate, or lime; chalky. [Latin *calcārius* relating to lime, from *calx* lime. See CALX.]

cal·ces (kal′sēz) plural of **calx.**

cal·cic (kal′sik) *adj.* of, derived from, or containing calcium or lime.

cal·cif·er·ous (kal sif′ər əs) *adj.* yielding or containing calcite. [Latin *calc-,* stem of *calx* lime + -FEROUS. See CALX.]

cal·ci·fi·ca·tion (kal′sə fi kā′shən) *n.* **1.** process of calcifying, esp. the depositing of lime salts in organic tissue. **2.** calcified formation or structure.

cal·ci·fy (kal′sə fī′) **-fied, -fy·ing.** *v.t., v.i.* to harden or become hard or stony by the deposit of lime salts.

cal·ci·mine (kal′sə mīn′) **-mined, -min·ing.** *also,* **kal·so·mine.** *n.* white or colored wash consisting of whiting or zinc white, water, and glue, used esp. on plastered ceilings and walls. —*v.t.* to cover with calcimine.

cal·ci·na·tion (kal sə nā′shən) *n.* act or process of calcining.

cal·cine (kal′sīn) **-cined, -cin·ing.** *v.t.* to cause (a substance) to lose moisture or impurities or to be oxidized or reduced by heating it to a high temperature. Limestone is calcined to make lime. —*v.i.* to undergo calcination. [French *calciner,* going back to Latin *calx* lime. See CALX.]

cal·cite (kal′sīt) *n.* translucent white or transparent mineral, calcium carbonate, the chief constituent of limestone, chalk, and marble. It is one of the most common minerals.

cal·ci·um (kal′sē əm) *n.* malleable, ductile, silvery-white metallic ele-

ment that is essential for the growth of bones and teeth, as well as for plant growth. Symbol: **Ca** See **element** for table. [Modern Latin *calcium,* from Latin *calx* lime; because it is found in lime. See CALX.]

cal·ci·um car·bide, lumpy, grayish-black compound produced in an electric furnace from the reaction of coke or anthracite coal with crushed limestone, used to form acetylene gas and calcium cyanamide. Formula: CaC_2

cal·ci·um car·bon·ate, compound of calcium, carbon, and oxygen which occurs as a white powder or as colorless crystals in its pure state and, in nature, as chalk, limestone, marble, and several other mineral forms. It is used in medicine as an antacid and is used in baking powder, tooth powders, and cement. Formula: $CaCO_3$

cal·ci·um chlo·ride, water-absorbing compound of calcium and chlorine in the form of colorless crystals, used esp. as a drying agent and antifreeze. Formula: $CaCl_2$

cal·ci·um cy·an·a·mide, grayish-black lumpy or powdered compound that decomposes in water to yield ammonia and acetylene, used in fertilizers, weed killers. Formula: $CaCN_2$

cal·ci·um cy·a·nide, poisonous, gray compound, used esp. as a fumigating agent and pesticide. Formula: $Ca(CN)_2$

cal·ci·um hy·drox·ide, slaked lime.

cal·ci·um phos·phate, any of several phosphates of calcium found in some rocks and in various animal tissue, used in various products, as medicines, cleaning agents, and fertilizers.

cal·cu·la·ble (kal′kyə lə bəl) *adj.* **1.** capable of being calculated. **2.** that can be relied on; dependable. —**cal′cu·la·bly,** *adv.*

cal·cu·late (kal′kyə lāt′) **-lat·ed, -lat·ing.** *v.t.* **1.** to determine by arithmetical methods; compute. **2.** to ascertain beforehand by reasoning; estimate: *to calculate the time needed to make the trip.* **3.** *Informal.* to plan; intend: *The speech was calculated to win votes.* **4.** *Informal.* to think; suppose; guess. —*v.i.* **1.** to perform an arithmetical process; compute. **2.** to rely or count (with *on* or *upon*). [Late Latin *calculātus,* past participle of *calculāre* to compute, reckon, from Latin *calculus* small stone, diminutive of *calx* limestone; reckoning was often done in ancient times with the aid of stones used as counters. See CALX.]
Syn. *v.t.* **1. Calculate, compute, reckon** mean to ascertain by mathematical operations. **Calculate** can be used as the general word but specifically applies to intricate operations which often do not admit of an exact or readily confirmable result: *The scientist calculated the number of atoms in a cubic centimeter of oxygen.* **Compute** implies known figures and standard formulas and, therefore, an exact result: *The bank clerk computed the interest due on a savings account.* **Reckon** suggests simple arithmetical processes and may or may not imply an approximate result: *The waitress reckoned my bill.*

cal·cu·lat·ed (kal′kyə lā′tid) *adj.* **1.** done or attempted after estimating the probable results: *a calculated risk.* **2.** done or ascertained by mathematical calculation.

cal·cu·lat·ing (kal′kyə lā′ting) *adj.* **1.** given to or characterized by careful or shrewd consideration of self-interest; selfish; scheming. **2.** that calculates: *a calculating machine.*

cal·cu·la·tion (kal′kyə lā′shən) *n.* **1.** act or process of calculating. **2.** product or result of calculating. **3.** careful or shrewd planning: *His actions were spontaneous and without calculation.* —**cal′cu·la′tive,** *adj.*

cal·cu·la·tor (kal′kyə lā′tər) *n.* **1.** one who calculates. **2.** machine for performing mathematical operations mechanically.

cal·cu·lus (kal′kyə ləs) *pl.,* **-li** (-lī′) *or* **-lus·es.** *n.* **1.** any method or system of calculation in higher mathematics, using a special system of algebraic notation. **Differential calculus** deals with the rates at which quantities change. **Integral calculus** develops methods for finding the areas enclosed by curved boundaries. **2.** abnormal stonelike mass of mineral matter formed in a duct or organ of the body. Kidney stones are calculi. [Latin *calculus* small stone, calculation. See CALCULATE.]

Cal·cut·ta (kal kut′ə) *n.* port city in northeastern India. Pop. (1969), 3,134,161.

cal·dron (kôl′drən) cauldron.

Ca·leb (kā′ləb) *n.* in the Old Testament, a Hebrew leader who was permitted to enter Canaan with Joshua as a reward for his faithfulness during the forty-year wanderings of the Israelites.

ca·lèche (kə lesh′) *n.* calash.

Cal·e·do·ni·a (kal′ə dō′nē ə) *n.* Scotland. ▲ used primarily in literature. —**Cal′e·do′ni·an,** *adj., n.*

cal·en·dar (kal′ən dər) *n.* **1.** table showing the days, weeks, and months of a given year. **2.** method of dividing time into fixed intervals, esp. with reference to the beginning, length, and division of the year. **3.** list, register, or schedule, esp. one arranged in chronological order, as a list of cases to be tried in court or of bills to be considered by a legislature. —*v.t.* to enter in a calendar; list. [Latin *calendārium* account book, from *calendae* calends, the day on which accounts were due for payment in ancient Rome.]

calendar month, month (*def. 1*).
calendar year, year (*def. 1*).

cal·en·der (kal′ən dər) *n.* machine consisting of a number of rollers through which cloth, paper, or other material is passed in order to produce a desired finish or a uniform thickness. —*v.t.* to press in a calender. [French *calandre* this machine, probably going back to Greek *kylindros* cylinder, roller.]

cal·ends (kal′əndz) *also,* **kal·ends.** *n.,pl.* first day of the month in the ancient Roman calendar. ▲ construed as singular or plural. [Latin *calendae.*]

ca·len·du·la (kə len′jə lə) *n.* any of a group of plants, genus *Calendula,* of the composite family, bearing bright yellow or orange flowers. [Modern Latin *Calendula,* diminutive of Latin *calendae* calends. It supposedly bloomed on the first day of the month.]

cal·en·ture (kal′ən chər) *n.* tropical fever accompanied by delirium and hallucinations, thought to be caused by excessive heat. [Spanish *calentura* fever, going back to Latin *calēre* to be hot.]

calf[1] (kaf) *pl.,* **calves.** *n.* **1.** young of various bovine animals, esp. of the domestic cow. **2.** young of various other mammals, as the elephant, whale, and seal. **3.** calfskin. **4. to kill the fatted calf.** to prepare a great feast, celebration, or welcome. [Old English *cealf* young of bovine animals.]

calf[2] (kaf) *pl.,* **calves.** *n.* fleshy part of the back of the leg between the knee and ankle. [Old Norse *kálfi.*]

calf·skin (kaf′skin′) *n.* **1.** skin or hide of a calf. **2.** leather made from it.

Cal·ga·ry (kal′gər ē) *n.* city in southwestern Canada, in the province of Alberta. Pop. (1968), 361,000.

Cal·houn, John Cald·well (kal hōōn′; käld′wel′, -wəl) 1782–1850, political leader of the pre-Civil War South and vice-president of the United States from 1825 to 1832.

Ca·li (kä′lē) *n.* city in western Colombia. Pop. (1969 est.), 820,809.

cal·i·ber (kal′ə bər) *also,* **cal·i·bre.** *n.* **1.** diameter of a round body, esp. the internal diameter of a hollow tube. **2.a.** diameter of the bore of a gun. **b.** diameter of a bullet or shell. **3.** degree of merit, ability, or importance; quality: *The job requires a man of high caliber.* [French *calibre* sort, bore of a gun, through Italian *calibro,* from Arabic *qālib* mold¹, model, probably from Greek *kālopous* shoemaker's last; literally, wooden foot.]

cal·i·brate (kal′ə brāt′) **-brat·ed, -brat·ing.** *v.t.* **1.** to determine, check, or correct the graduations of (a thermometer or similar measuring instrument). **2.** to determine the caliber of, as the interior of a thermometer tube. —**cal′i·bra′tion, cal′i·bra′tor,** *n.*

cal·i·co (kal′ə kō′) *pl.,* **-coes** *or* **-cos.** *n.* cotton fabric printed with small, usually brightly colored motifs. —*adj.* **1.** made of calico. **2.** resembling calico; spotted: *a calico cat.* [From *Calicut,* port of India, from which this fabric was first imported.]

cal·i·co·back (kal′ə kō bak′) harlequin bug.

Cal·i·cut (kal′ə kut′) see Kozhikode.

ca·lif (kā′lif, kal′if) caliph.

Calif., California.

ca·lif·ate (kal′ə fāt′, -fit, kal′ə-) caliphate.

Cal·i·for·nia (kal′ə fôrn′yə, -fôr′nē ə) *n.* **1.** most populous state of the United States, on the Pacific coast. Capital, Sacramento. Area, 158,693 sq. mi. Pop. (1970), 19,953,134. Abbreviation, **Calif., Cal.** **2. Gulf of.** long inlet of the Pacific, just south of California, separating Lower California from the Mexican mainland. —**Cal′i·for′nian,** *adj., n.*

California poppy **1.** saucer-shaped flower of a plant, *Eschscholzia californica,* of the poppy family, bearing four satiny petals ranging in color from pale yellow to orange. **2.** the plant itself.

cal·i·for·ni·um (kal′ə fôr′nē əm) *n.* synthetic radioactive element first produced in 1950 at the University of California. Symbol: **Cf** See **element** for table.

Ca·lig·u·la (kə lig′yə lə) *n.* A.D. 12–41, Roman emperor from 37 to 41.

cal·i·per (kal′ə pər) *also,* **cal·li·per.** *n.* **1.** *also,* **calipers.** hinged instrument resembling a pair of tongs, used esp. to measure the internal or external dimensions of a small object. **2.** caliper rule. [Form of CALIPER.]

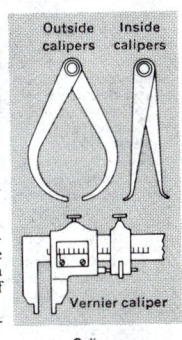

Outside Inside calipers calipers

Vernier caliper

Calipers

caliper rule, graduated rule with one stationary jaw and one sliding jaw.

ca·liph (kā′lif, kal′if) *also,* **ca·lif, ka·lif, ka·liph,** *n.* formerly, successor of Muhammad as the religious and secular head of Islam. [Old French *calife,* from Arabic *khalifa* successor.]

ca·liph·ate (kal′ə fāt′, -fit, kal′ə-) *also,* **ca·li·fate.** *n.* office, reign, government, or dominion of a caliph.

cal·is·then·ics (kal′is then′iks) *also,* **cal·lis·then·ics.** *n.* **1.** light gym-

at; āpe; cär; end; mē; it; īce; hot; ōld; fôrk; wood; fōōl; oil; out; up; ūse; turn; sing; thin; this; zh in treasure; ə in ago, taken, pencil, lemon, circus.

139

nastic exercises designed to develop strength and grace and to promote good health. **2.** science or practice of such exercises. ▲ construed as plural in def. 1, as singular in def. 2. [Greek *kallos* beauty + *sthenos* strength + -ICS.] **—cal'is·then'ic,** *adj.*
calk¹ (kôk) caulk.
calk² (kôk) *n.* **1.** one of the projecting pieces of a horseshoe that grips the ground and prevents the horse from slipping. **2.** sharp, projecting piece of metal on the bottom of the heel or toe of a shoe or boot to prevent slipping. *—v.t.* to furnish with calks. [Short for earlier *calkin,* from Old French *calcain* heel, from Latin *calcāneum.*]
calk·er (cô'kər) caulker.
call (kôl) *v.t.* **1.** to utter in a loud voice; read over loudly; proclaim; announce: *The teacher called the roll.* **2.** to command or request the presence or attendance of; summon: *He was called to testify in the case. The doorman called a cab.* **3.** to convoke; convene: *to call a meeting.* **4.** to summon to a special duty, office, or activity: *He was called to the army.* **5.** to arouse from sleep; waken: *Call me for breakfast at seven o'clock.* **6.** to make a telephone call to: *Call me from the airport when you get there.* **7.** to attract or lure (birds or animals) by imitating their characteristic sound. **8.** to give a name to; name: *She called the puppy Rover.* **9.** to characterize or designate in some way: *I call him an honest man.* **10.** to consider or estimate to be: *Although all the votes were not counted, they called it a Republican victory.* **11.** *Baseball.* **a.** to stop or suspend (a game): *The game was called on account of darkness.* **b.** to rule on, as a pitch or player's action: *The umpire called the ball a strike.* *Poker.* to demand a show of hands by equaling the bet of (another). **13.** to demand payment of: *to call a loan.* **14.** to demand for payment or redemption: *The company will call its bonds April first.* *—v.i.* **1.** to speak loudly; cry; shout: *Did you hear her call?* **2.** to make a short visit or stop: *We called at your house yesterday.* **3.** to make a telephone call.
to call back. a. to summon (a person) to return; bring back. **b.** to telephone again or in return.
to call down. a. to invoke from above: *to call down the wrath of God.* **b.** *Informal.* to scold; rebuke; reprimand.
to call for. a. to go and get; stop to obtain (something or someone): *We called for the packages at the post office.* **b.** to need; require; demand.
to call forth. to summon into action; elicit; cause to appear.
to call in. a. to collect, as money or debts. **b.** to withdraw from circulation, as currency. **c.** to summon or invite, as for assistance or consultation.
to call off. a. to cancel, as something previously scheduled. **b.** to summon away; divert. **c.** to read aloud: *He called off the names of the winners.*
to call on (or **upon**). **a.** to make a brief visit to. **b.** to appeal to or demand from (a person).
to call out. a. to utter or cry out in a loud voice. **b.** to summon into service; order into action: *Call out the national guard.*
to call up. a. to telephone. **b.** to bring or summon into action or discussion: *He was called up for military duty.* **c.** to bring to mind; remember.
—n. **1.** act of calling; shout; cry. **2.a.** characteristic sound or cry of a bird or animal. **b.** device which produces an imitation of such a sound, in order to attract or lure birds or animals. **3.** invitation; summons. **4.** signal or summons as played on a drum or bugle: *Reveille is the first call of the day.* **5.** claim; demand: *A busy person has many calls on his time.* **6.** need; occasion; cause: *There was no call for her to punish the child in public.* **7.** short, usually formal, visit or stop. **8.** act or instance of communicating by telephone. **9.** roll call. **10.** demand for payment or redemption of money. **11.** calling (*def. 2*). **12.** *Poker.* act or instance of demanding a show of hands by equaling the bet of another. **13.** *Sports.* ruling by a game official. **14. on call. a.** available when summoned; ready. **b.** subject to payment or return on demand. **15. within call.** within hearing distance; nearby. [Old English *ceallian* to cry out, shout, from Old Norse *kalla.*]
Syn. *v.t.* **Call, summon** mean to request that someone come. **Call** is the general word meaning to request the presence or appearance of someone at a particular place: *Call the next witness. He called his waiter to the table.* **Summon** usually applies to an official or formal request: *The president summoned his cabinet.*
cal·la (kal'ə) *n.* **1.** any of a group of plants, genus *Zantedeschia,* found in southern Africa, bearing tiny flowers on a spike inside a showy white or yellow spathe. Also, **calla lily. 2.** marsh plant, *Calla palustris,* in North America, Europe, and Asia, bearing heart-shaped leaves and tiny flowers in a spike inside a showy white spathe. [Modern Latin *Calla,* from Latin *calla* name of a plant.]
Cal·la·o (kä yä'ō) *n.* city on the west coast of central Peru and the major seaport of the country. Pop. (1969), 321,700.
call·boy (kôl'boi') *n.* **1.** boy or man who summons actors or other performers when it is time for them to appear on stage. **2.** bellboy.

call·er (kô'lər) *n.* **1.** one who makes a short visit. **2.** one who or that which calls. **3.** one who calls directions to dancers in a square dance.
cal·lig·ra·phy (kə lig'rə fē) *n.* **1.** beautiful or elegant handwriting. **2.** handwriting; penmanship. [Greek *kalligraphiā* beautiful writing, going back to *kallos* beauty + *graphein* to write.] **—cal·lig'ra·pher, cal·lig'ra·phist,** *n.* **—cal·li·graph·ic** (kal'ə graf'ik), *adj.*
call·ing (kô'ling) *n.* **1.** vocation; profession. **2.** strong impulse toward a course of action, esp. of a religious nature: *He felt a calling to join the ministry.* **3.** act of one who or that which calls, esp. crying or shouting aloud.
calling card, small card with one's name on it, used for social purposes. Also, **visiting card.**
cal·li·o·pe (kə lī'ə pē'; *def. 1 also* kal'ē ōp') *n.* **1.** musical instrument consisting of a series of steam whistles, played by means of a keyboard. **2. Calliope.** Greek Muse of eloquence and epic poetry. [Latin *Calliopē* the Muse, from *Kalliopē* literally, beautiful-voiced, from *kallos* beauty + *ops* voice.]
cal·li·op·sis (kal'ē op'sis) *n.* coreopsis.
cal·li·per (kal'ə pər) caliper.
cal·lis·then·ics (kal'is then'iks) calisthenics.
Cal·lis·to (kə lis'tō) *n.* *Greek Mythology.* nymph loved by Zeus, changed into a bear by the jealous Hera and set among the constellations as Ursa Major by Zeus.
call letters, letters that identify a radio or television transmitting station.
call loan, loan that must be repaid on demand.
call money, money loaned that is subject to repayment on demand.
cal·los·i·ty (kə los'ə tē) *pl.,* **-ties.** *n.* **1.** callus (*defs. 1, 3*). **2.** quality or state of being hardened in mind or feelings; insensitivity.
cal·lous (kal'əs) *adj.* **1.** thickened and hardened, as a callus on the skin. **2.** hardened in mind or feelings; unfeeling; insensitive. *—v.t., v.i.* to make or become callous. [Latin *callōsus* hard-skinned.] **—cal'lous·ly,** *adv.* **—cal'lous·ness,** *n.*
cal·low (kal'ō) *adj.* **1.** inexperienced; immature: *a callow youth.* **2.** (of birds) lacking sufficient feathers for flight; unfledged. [Old English *calu* bald.] **—cal'low·ness,** *n.*
call-up (kôl'up') *n.* **1.** order to report for active military service, usually issued to reserves. **2.** total number of men included in such an order.
cal·lus (kal'əs) *pl.,* **-lus·es.** *n.* **1.** hardened and thickened area of the skin. **2.** new growth of bony tissue that forms between and around the ends of a fractured bone and reunites them. **3.** hardened, thickened layer of tissue that forms over a wound of a plant. [Latin *callus* hardened skin.]
calm (käm) *adj.* **1.** without or nearly without wind or motion; not stormy. **2.** free from agitation or excitement; undisturbed by passion; quiet; serene: *The policeman remained calm during the disturbance.* *—n.* **1.** condition of being without motion or wind; stillness. **2.** *Meteorology.* state in which the wind velocity is less than one mile per hour or in which there is no wind at all. **3.** freedom from agitation or passion; tranquility; serenity. *—v.t., v.i.* to make or become calm or quiet (often with *down*): *The mother calmed her child. He calmed down after the fight.* [French *calme* quiet, from Italian *calma* rest, going back to Greek *kauma* heat of the sun or the day (at which time flocks and people rested in the shade).] **—calm'ly,** *adv.* **—calm'ness,** *n.*
Syn. *adj.* **2. Calm, tranquil, serene** mean free from agitation or excitement. **Calm** is applicable to persons and things and suggests the weathering of a crisis or storm: *He was the only one who remained calm when the extent of the damage became known. The high wind passed and the sea became calm again.* **Tranquil** is used mostly of persons and implies greater depth than **calm:** *Hers was a tranquil temperament, and she was much given to meditation.* **Serene** suggests a sublime tranquility, inspired by stoical or religious acceptance: *The hermit had the serene face of a mystic.*
cal·o·mel (kal'ə mel', -məl) *n.* mercurous chloride, a compound of mercury and chlorine in the form of a white, tasteless, crystalline powder, used esp. as an insecticide, antiseptic, or laxative. Formula: Hg_2Cl_2 [French *calomel,* from Greek *kalos* beautiful + *melās* black.]
ca·lor·ic (kə lôr'ik, -lor'-) *n.* **1.** heat. **2.** supposed substance to which the sensation and phenomena of heat were formerly attributed. *—adj.* of or relating to heat or calories.
cal·o·rie (kal'ər ē) *pl.,* **-ries.** *also,* **cal·o·ry.** *n.* **1.** unit of heat. **a. small** (or **gram**) **calorie.** quantity of heat required to raise the temperature of one gram of water one degree centigrade. **b. large** (or **kilogram**) **calorie.** quantity of heat equal to 1000 gram calories, required to raise the temperature of one kilogram of water one degree centigrade. **2.** unit equivalent to the large calorie, used to measure the heat output of organisms or the energy-producing value of food. **3.** quantity of food having such an energy-producing value. [French *calorie* small calorie, from Latin *calor* heat.]
cal·o·rif·ic (kal'ə rif'ik) *adj.* relating to or producing heat.

at; āpe; cär; end; mē; it; īce; hot; ōld; fôrk; wood; fōol; oil; out; up; ūse; turn; sing; thin; this; zh in treasure; ə in ago, taken, pencil, lemon, circus.

cal·o·rim·e·ter (kal′ə rim′ə tər) *n.* apparatus for measuring the amount of heat emitted or absorbed by a substance for determining the specific heat of a substance.

cal·u·met (kal′yə met′, kal′yə met′) *n.* peace pipe. [Dialectal French *calumet* herb stem, pipe, going back to Latin *calamus* reed, from Greek *kalamos.*]

ca·lum·ni·ate (kə lum′nē āt′) -at·ed, -at·ing. *v.t.* to utter false and malicious statements or accusations about; slander. [Latin *calumniātus,* past participle of *calumniārī* to slander.] —**ca·lum·ni·a′tion, ca·lum·ni·a′tor,** *n.*

ca·lum·ni·ous (kə lum′nē əs) *adj.* containing or characterized by calumny; slanderous. Also, **ca·lum·ni·a·to·ry** (kə lum′nē ə tôr′ē). —**ca·lum′ni·ous·ly,** *adv.*

Calumet

cal·um·ny (kal′əm nē) *pl.,* **-nies.** *n.* false and malicious statement or accusation intended to damage another's reputation; slander. [French *calomnie,* from Latin *calumnia* false accusation. Doublet of CHALLENGE.]

Cal·va·ry (kal′vər ē) *n.* hill near ancient Jerusalem where Jesus was crucified. [Latin *calvāria* skull, translation in the Vulgate of Aramaic *gogolthā:* the hill was skull-shaped.]

calve (kav) **calved, calv·ing.** *v.t., v.i.* to give birth to (a calf). [Old English *cealfian,* from *cealf.* See CALF.]

Cal·vert (kal′vərt) **1. Sir George.** c.1580–1632, English statesman who founded the colony of Maryland and became the first Baron Baltimore. **2. Leonard.** c.1606–47, his son, first governor of the colony of Maryland.

calves (kavz) plural of **calf.**

Cal·vin, John (kal′vin) 1509–64, French theologian and leader of the Protestant Reformation at Geneva.

Cal·vin·ism (kal′vin iz′əm) *n.* religious teachings of John Calvin, which emphasize the omnipotence of God, the doctrine of predestination, and an austere moral code. —**Cal′vin·ist,** *n.* —**Cal′vin·ist′ic,** *adj.*

calx (kalks) *pl.,* **calx·es** or **cal·ces.** *n.* ashy powder left after a mineral substance has been calcined. [Latin *calx* lime, limestone, stone, probably from Greek *chalix* pebble.]

cal·y·ces (kal′ə sēz, kā′lə-) plural of **calyx.**

ca·lyp·so (kə lip′sō) *n.* improvised song, originally from the British West Indies, usually dealing with topical or humorous themes. [Possibly from CALYPSO.]

Ca·lyp·so (kə lip′sō) *n. Greek Legend.* sea nymph who detained the shipwrecked Odysseus on an island for seven years.

ca·lyx (kā′liks, kal′iks) *pl.,* **ca·lyx·es** or **ca·ly·ces.** *n.* outer circle of floral leaves which surround an unopened flower and usually fold back beneath the petals when the bud opens. [Latin *calyx* covering, calyx, from Greek *kalyx* shell, calyx.]

Shaft

Cam

Cam

cam (kam) *n.* projection on a revolving shaft that changes a rotating motion into a back-and-forth linear motion. [Dutch *kam* cog, comb.]

Ca·ma·güey (käm′ə gwā′) *n.* city in east-central Cuba. Pop. (1966 est.), 170,000.

ca·ma·ra·de·rie (käm′ə rad′ər ē, käm′ə rä′dər ē) *n.* friendliness and loyalty among comrades; fellowship; comradeship. [French *camaraderie,* from *camarade.* See COMRADE.]

cam·a·ril·la (kam′ə ril′ə) *n.* group of secret or unofficial advisers; cabal; clique. [Spanish *camarilla,* diminutive of *camara* chamber, from Late Latin *camera.* See CAMERA.]

cam·ass (kam′əs) also, **cam·as.** *n.* any of a group of ornamental plants, genus *Camassia,* of the lily family, esp. *C. quamash,* of the northwestern United States, bearing sword-shaped leaves and clusters of blue or white flowers. [Chinook jargon *kamass.*]

cam·ber (kam′bər) *v.t., v.i.* to bend or curve upward in the middle; arch slightly. —*n.* **1.** slight arch or convexity of a surface, as of a beam or road. **2.** *Aeronautics.* curvature of a line midway between the curving upper and lower surfaces of an airfoil. [Old French *cambre* bent, from Latin *camur* crooked.]

cam·bi·um (kam′bē əm) *n.* layer of growth tissue between the bark and the wood of trees and woody plants that gives rise to cells for both new bark and new wood. [Late Latin *cambium* exchange, from Latin *cambiāre* to exchange.]

Cam·bo·di·a (kam bō′dē ə) *n.* country in southeastern Asia. It is officially known as the **Khmer Republic.** Capital, Phnom Penh. Area, 69,898 sq. mi. Pop. (1975 est.), 8,100,000.

Cam·brai (kän brā′) *n.* city in northern France. Pop. (1962), 32,897.

Cam·bri·a (kam′brē ə) *n.* Wales. ▲ used primarily in literature.

Cam·bri·an (kam′brē ən) *n.* **1.** first geological period of the Paleozoic era during which marine shelled invertebrate animals were common. See geology for table. **2.** Welshman. —*adj.* **1.** of, relating to, or characteristic of this period. **2.** of or relating to Cambria; Welsh.

cam·bric (kām′brik) *n.* soft, lightweight linen or cotton fabric, used esp. for handkerchiefs, children's dresses, and nightgowns. [From the former Flemish town *Kamerijk* (now *Cambrai,* in France), where this fabric was first made.]

cambric tea, drink made with water, milk, sugar, and usually, a little tea.

Cam·bridge (kām′brij) *n.* **1.** city in eastern Massachusetts. Pop. (1970), 100,361. **2.** city in eastern England. Pop. (1968), 100,500. **3.** university in Cambridge, England.

Cam·by·ses (kam bī′sēz) died c.521 B.C., king of Persia from 529 to 522 B.C., son of Cyrus the Great.

Cam·den (kam′dən) *n.* city in southwestern New Jersey, on the Delaware River. Pop. (1970), 102,551.

came (kām) past tense of **come.**

cam·el (kam′əl) *n.* **1.** any of various cud-chewing mammals, genus *Camelus,* of the desert regions of Africa, Asia, Asia Minor, and Arabia, having a humped back, a sandy-white to deep brown coat, and cloven hoofs, valued for riding, as a beast of burden, and as a source of meat, milk, and leather. There are two species of camels: the dromedary, having one hump, and the Bactrian camel, having two humps. Height: 7 feet at the hump. **2.** medium tan color. [Old English *camel,* from Latin *camēlus,* from Greek *kamēlos,* from Hebrew *gāmāl.*]

Camel

cam·el·eer (kam′ə lēr′) *n.* camel driver.

ca·mel·lia (kə mēl′yə, -mē′lē ə) *n.* **1.** fragrant flower of any of a group of shrubs and trees, genus *Camellia,* of the tea family, widely cultivated in warm, damp regions and having white, red, or pink petals. **2.** woody plant bearing this flower. [From the seventeenth-century Jesuit missionary G. J. *Kamel* (Latinized form of his name: *Camellus*), who introduced it to Europe from the East.]

cam·el·o·pard (kə mel′ə pärd′) *n. Archaic.* giraffe. [Latin *camēlopardālis,* from Greek *kamēlopardalis,* from *kamēlos* camel + *pardalis* leopard; because its head resembles a camel's; and its spots, a leopard's. See CAMEL.]

Cam·e·lot (kam′ə lot′) *n.* legendary site of King Arthur's court.

camel's hair 1. hair of a camel. **2.** soft fabric made of this hair alone or in combination with wool. It usually has a distinctive tan color and is used for coats, suits, and sweaters.

Cam·em·bert (kam′əm bār′) *n.* rich, creamy soft cheese with a pungent flavor. [From the French village *Camembert,* where it was first made.]

cam·e·o (kam′ē ō′) *pl.,* **-e·os.** *n.* piece of jewelry made from a precious or semiprecious stone or a shell, carved in relief. The stone often consists of different colored layers, as onyx, so that the darker layer can serve as a background for a figure, usually the head of a woman, carved in relief from the lighter part. [Italian *cammeo;* of uncertain origin.]

cam·er·a (kam′ər ə, kam′rə) *pl.,* (defs. 1, 2) **-er·as** or (def. 3) **-er·ae** (-ər ē). *n.* **1.** device for taking photographs which consists of a light-proof box with a lens and shutter through which light is admitted and the image focused on a light-sensitive film or plate. **2.** *Television.* device that transforms an image into electrical impulses for transmission. **3.** judge's chambers. **4. in camera. a.** in a judge's chambers. **b.** privately. [Late Latin *camera* room, chamber, from Latin *camera* arch, vault, from Greek *kamarā* vault. Doublet of CHAMBER.]

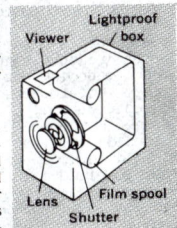

Lightproof box
Viewer
Lens
Film spool
Shutter

Camera

cam·er·al (kam′ər əl) *adj.* of or relating to a legislature or a judge's chambers.

cam·er·a lu·ci·da (kam′ər ə lōō′si də) instrument consisting of a glass prism mounted on a stand in such a manner that the image of an object appears as if projected on a flat surface, upon which it can be traced. [Modern Latin *camera lucida* literally, light chamber. See CAMERA, LUCID.]

at; āpe; cär; end; mē; it; īce; hot; ōld; fôrk; wood; fōōl; oil; out; up; ūse; turn; sing; thin; **this**; zh in treasure; ə in ago, taken, pencil, lemon, circus.

cam·er·a·man (kam′ər ə man′, -mən, -kam′rə-) *pl.*, **-men.** *n.* one whose job is operating a motion-picture or television camera.

cam·e·ra ob·scu·ra (kam′ər ə ob skyoor′ə, kam′rə) device consisting of a darkened box into which light enters through a small opening or lens in one side and the image is formed on the opposite side and reflected by a mirror onto a wall or screen. It was the forerunner of the modern camera. [Modern Latin *camera obscura* literally, dark chamber. See CAMERA, OBSCURE.]

Cam·er·oon (kam′ə roon′) *also*, **Cameroun,** *n.* country in west-central Africa consisting of most of the territory of the former Cameroons. Capital, Yaoundé. Area, 183,569 sq. mi. Pop. (1969 est.), 5,680,000.

Cam·er·oons (kam′ə roonz′) *n.* two former United Nations trust territories: one under French administration, now Cameroon; and one under British administration, now divided between Cameroon and Nigeria.

Cam·er·oun (kam′ə roon′) *n.* **1.** Cameroon. **2.** former United Nations trust territory under French administration, now included in Cameroon.

cam·i·on (kam′ē ən) *n.* **1.** heavy wagon or cart; dray. **2.** truck, esp. one used for carrying military supplies or artillery. [French *camion;* of uncertain origin.]

cam·i·sole (kam′ə sōl′) *n.* **1.** woman's undergarment, resembling the top of a slip, often trimmed with lace or ribbons. **2.** bed jacket. [French *camisole* woman's jacket, going back to Late Latin *camīsia* shirt; of uncertain origin.]

cam·let (kam′lit) *n.* **1.** a fine, costly, worsted fabric, originally made in Asia of camel's hair or angora wool, used for clothing from the twelfth to the seventeenth centuries. **2.** any of several other fine fabrics of silk and wool or hair made in imitation of this. Some types were waterproof and used for such items as cloaks. [French *camelot,* from Arabic *khamlat* plush.]

Cam·ões, Lu·ís de (kə moinsh′; loo ēsh′ də) c.1524–80, Portuguese poet.

cam·o·mile (kam′ə mīl′, -mēl′) *also*, **cham·o·mile.** *n.* any of several strongly scented plants of the composite family, found in temperate regions, bearing daisylike flower heads, which in certain species are dried and used to make an herb tea. [Late Latin *c(h)amomilla,* going back to Greek *chamaimēlon* literally, earth apple; because its flowers smell like apples.]

Ca·mor·ra (kə môr′ə, -mor′ə) *n.* **1.** secret society formed in Naples, Italy, about 1820, that became politically powerful and later was associated with violence, blackmail, and robbery. **2. camorra.** any secret society similar to this.

cam·ou·flage (kam′ə fläzh′) *n.* **1.** *Military.* act or process of disguising or changing the appearance of men, equipment, or installations in order to conceal them from the enemy, as by paint, nets, or foliage. **2.** any disguise or behavior that serves to conceal or deceive, as the protective coloration of an animal. —*v.t.*, **-flaged, -flag·ing.** to disguise or conceal by means of camouflage. [French *camouflage* disguise, from *camoufler* to disguise, from Italian *camuffare;* of uncertain origin.]

camp (kamp) *n.* **1.** outdoor site, often with tents, huts, or other structures, where people live or sleep temporarily, esp. while traveling or marching; encampment: *The scouts made camp by the river. Company A had its base camp near the border for two months.* **2.** place, usually in the country, that provides supervised recreational activities esp. for children and is attended for a fixed period of time: *day camp, YMCA camp.* **3.** group of permanent structures in which a number of persons may be sheltered or confined: *an army camp, a prisoner-of-war camp, a labor camp.* **4.** area employed for or occupied by a camp. **5.** people occupying a camp. **6.** group of people who support a common theory, policy, or doctrine: *The controversy divided the townspeople into two camps.* —*v.i.* **1.** to set up or live in a temporary camp. **2.** to maintain a position stubbornly: *Student protestors camped in front of the dean's office.* **3. to camp out.** to live or sleep outdoors overnight or temporarily, as in a tent. [Old French *camp* field, field of battle, from Italian *campo* field, from Latin *campus.* Doublet of CAMPUS.]

Cam·pa·gna (käm pän′yə) *n.* low coastal plain surrounding Rome.

cam·paign (kam pān′) *n.* **1.** series of related military operations for accomplishing a common objective, usually conducted in a particular region or period of time and constituting a distinct part of a war. **2.** organized series of actions conducted to accomplish a particular goal: *an election campaign, a fund-raising campaign.* —*v.i.* to conduct or serve in a campaign. [French *campagne* open country, military campaign, from Italian *campagna,* from Late Latin *campānia* open country, from Latin *campus* field.] —**cam·paign′er,** *n.*

Cam·pa·nia (kam pän′yə, -pä′nē ə) *n.* region in southwestern Italy bordering the Tyrrhenian Sea. Area, 5249 sq. mi. Pop. (1965 est.), 5,010,000.

cam·pa·ni·le (kam′pə nē′lē) *pl.*, **-ni·les** or **-ni·li** (-nē′lē). *n.* bell tower, esp. one that is freestanding. [Italian *campanile,* from *campana* bell, from Late Latin *campāna.*]

cam·pan·u·la (kam pan′yə lə) *n.* **1.** bell-shaped flower of any of a large group of plants, genus *Campanula.* **2.** plant bearing this flower. [Modern Latin *campanula* little bell, diminutive of Late Latin *campāna* bell.]

camp chair, light, portable folding chair.

camp·er (kam′pər) *n.* **1.** one who camps. **2.** vehicle or trailer built or adapted for camping.

camp·fire (kamp′fīr′) *n.* **1.** outdoor fire in a camp, used for warmth or cooking. **2.** social gathering or meeting, as around a campfire.

Camp Fire Girls, national organization for girls from the age of seven through eighteen, that encourages participation in outdoor activities, sports, creative arts, and community service.

camp·ground (kamp′ground′) *n.* place for a camp or a camp meeting.

cam·phor (kam′fər) *n.* white, aromatic, flammable, crystalline compound obtained from the wood of a variety of evergreen tree or made synthetically, used as a mothproofing agent, in some medicines, and in the manufacture of plastics. Formula: $C_{10}H_{16}O$ [Medieval Latin *camphora,* from Arabic *kāfūr,* either from Sanskrit *karpūra* or from Malay *kāpūr* chalk.] —**cam·phor·ic** (kam fôr′ik, -for′-), *adj.*

cam·phor·ate (kam′fə rāt′) **-at·ed, -at·ing.** *v.t.* to impregnate or treat with camphor.

camphor ball, moth ball.

camphor ice, ointment made from camphor, white wax, spermaceti, and castor oil, used for chapped skin.

cam·pi·on (kam′pē ən) *n.* any plant of either of the genera, *Silene* or *Lychnis,* of the pink family, bearing white, pink, or red flowers. The stems or other parts are sticky, serving to trap insects. [Probably from Latin *campus* field (with the sense of field flower).]

camp meeting, religious gathering, usually lasting several days, held outdoors or in a tent.

camp·site (kamp′sīt′) *n.* area reserved for camping, usually having cooking, eating, sanitary, and other facilities.

camp·stool (kamp′stool′) *n.* light, portable folding seat.

cam·pus (kam′pəs) *n.* grounds, including buildings, of a school, college, or university. —*adj.* of or relating to a school, college, or university or to its students: *She was active in campus politics.* [Latin *campus* field; possibly because college grounds were originally located in open country. Doublet of CAMP.]

Ca·mus, Albert (ka moo′) 1913–60, French philosopher, author, playwright, and critic.

can¹ (kan; *unstressed* kən) Present: *sing.,* first person, **can;** second, **can** or *(archaic)* **canst;** third, **can;** *pl.,* **can.** Past: **could** or *(archaic)* **could·est** or **couldst.** *auxiliary verb* (followed by an infinitive without *to*) **1.** to be able to: *I can run faster than you. The car can hold five passengers.* **2.** to know how to: *He can speak French. Can you dance the waltz?* **3.** to have the right to: *The general can give orders which must be obeyed.* **4.** *Informal.* to be permitted to; may: *Mother says we can go to the movies.* ▲ In informal usage *can,* implying ability, is generally used in the sense of *may,* implying permission: *Can I see you tomorrow?* In formal speech and writing the distinction is still observed. [Old English *cunnan* to know, know how, be able.]

can² (kan) *n.* **1.** metal container or receptacle: *a garbage can, a water can.* **2.** container of iron coated with tin, in which food or other perishable products are sealed for preservation. **3.** contents of a can: *He drank a can of root beer.* **4.** *Slang.* jail. —*v.t.*, **canned, can·ning. 1.** to put or preserve in a can or jar. **2.** *Slang.* to fire from a job; discharge: *The boss canned him for being late too often.* **3.** *Slang.* to put an end to; stop: *Can it!* [Old English *canne* container for liquids, cup.]

Can. 1. Canada. **2.** Canadian.

Ca·naan (kā′nən) *n.* region in Palestine between the Jordan River and the Mediterranean; the Promised Land.

Ca·naan·ite (kā′nə nīt′) *n.* member of the Semitic people inhabiting the land of Canaan prior to its conquest by the Hebrews.

Can·a·da (kan′ə də) *n.* country in northern North America, bordering the United States. Capital, Ottawa. Area, 3,851,809 sq. mi. Pop. (1969 est.), 21,089,000. [Huron *kanáda* village; applied to the territory of Canada by early explorers because they mistakenly thought it was a place name.] —**Ca·na·di·an** (kə nā′dē ən), *adj.*, *n.*

Canada balsam, yellow oleoresin obtained from the bark of the balsam fir, used as a transparent cement for mounting microscopic specimens on slides and in the manufacture of fine lacquers.

Canada goose, wild goose, *Branta canadensis,* native to Arctic and temperate regions of North America, having a black head and neck, white patches on the face, and a brownish-gray body. Length: 22–38 inches.

ca·naille (kə näl′, ka nī′) *n.* rabble; riffraff. [French *canaille,* from Italian *canaglia,* from *cane* dog, from Latin *canis.*]

ca·nal (kə nal′) *n.* **1.** man-made inland waterway built to carry water for navigation, irrigation, drainage, or power. **2.** tubular passage or duct in a plant or in the body of an animal. **3.** long narrow arm of the sea;

at; āpe; cär; end; mē; it; īce; hot; ōld; fôrk; wood; fōol; oil; out; up; ūse; turn; sing; thin; <u>th</u>is; zh in treasure; ə in ago, taken, pencil, lemon, circus.

channel. **4.** any of the long, faint, narrow markings on the planet Mars, as seen through a telescope. [Latin *canālis* pipe, channel, from *canna* reed, from Greek *kanna;* of Semitic origin. Doublet of CHANNEL[1].]

canal boat, long, narrow boat, as a barge, used on canals.

ca·nal·ize (kə nal′īz, kan′əl īz′) *-ized, -iz·ing. v.t.* **1.** to provide with an outlet; direct into certain channels: *to canalize one's energy.* **2.** to convert into or make like a canal: *to canalize a river.* **3.** to furnish with a canal or series of canals. —**ca·nal′i·za′tion,** *n.*

Canal Zone, strip of territory across the Isthmus of Panama, extending approximately five miles on each side of the Panama Canal. It is administered by the United States. Area, approx. 553 sq. mi. Pop. (1969 est.), 57,000. Also, **Panama Canal Zone.**

can·a·pé (kan′ə pē, -pā′) *n.* cracker or thin piece of bread, topped with cheese, meat, or fish or spread with a seasoned mixture and served hot or cold as an appetizer. [French *canapé* appetizer, couch, from Medieval Latin *canapeum* mosquito net, going back to Greek *kōnōpeion;* possibly because the spread on a canapé is like a canopy.]

ca·nard (kə närd′) *n.* false or exaggerated story, report, or rumor; hoax. [French *canard* duck, hoax, from phrase *vendre des canards à moitié* to deceive; literally, to sell ducks by halves, from Old French *caner* to cackle; imitative.]

ca·nar·y (kə när′ē) *pl.,* **-nar·ies.** *n.* **1.** small yellow songbird, *Serinus canarius,* of the finch family, widely kept as a pet. **2.** canary yellow. **3.** sweet white wine from the Canary Islands. [French *canari,* from Spanish *canario,* bird from the Canary Islands, its original habitat.]

Canary Islands, Spanish island group in the North Atlantic, off the northwest coast of Africa. Land area, 2807 sq. mi. Pop. (1960), 944,445. Also, **Ca·nar′ies.** [Latin *Canāriae (insulae)* literally, (islands) of dogs, from *canis* dog; because the ancient Romans found many large dogs there.]

canary yellow, light, bright yellow.

ca·nas·ta (kə nas′tə) *n.* **1.** form of rummy for two to six players, usually using two decks of 52 cards and four jokers. **2.** meld of seven or more cards of a kind. [Spanish *canasta* basket (because many, or a "basketful" of, cards are used), going back to Latin *canistrum.* See CANISTER.]

Ca·nav·er·al, Cape (kə nav′ər əl) site of the principal U.S. launching and testing center for missiles and spacecraft.

Can·ber·ra (kan′ber·ə, -bər ə) *n.* capital of Australia, in the southeastern part of the nation. Pop. (1969), 119,235.

can·can (kan′kan′) *n.* form of quadrille which originated in Paris in the early nineteenth century, characterized by exaggerated, high kicking and leaping. [French *cancan* originally, a word for the duck *(canard)* in baby talk; because the dance resembles the waddle of a duck.]

can·cel (kan′səl) *-celed, -cel·ing; also, British,* **-celled, -cel·ling.** *v.t.* **1.** to cross out with a line or mark; delete. **2.** to do away with, withdraw, or stop (something which has been planned or expected), esp. without the intention of scheduling it again. **3.** to make null and void; annul. **4.** to deface, esp. a postage stamp, so that it cannot be used again. **5.** to make up for; neutralize; offset. **6.** *Mathematics.* to eliminate (a common factor) from the numerator and denominator of a fraction or from both sides of an equation. —*v.i.* to offset each other (with *out*). —*n.* **1.** deletion or omission of printed matter. **2.** matter deleted or omitted. [Latin *cancellāre* to cross out with latticelike lines, from *cancellī* lattice, crossbars, diminutive of *cancer* crab; possibly with reference to the resemblance of a crab's shape (with its ten legs) to that of a lattice.]

can·cel·la·tion (kan′sə lā′shən) *n.* **1.** act of canceling; being canceled. **2.** marks used in canceling. **3.** that which is canceled.

can·cer (kan′sər) *n.* **1.** any of a group of frequently fatal diseases, including carcinoma, sarcoma, and leukemia, characterized by abnormal cellular growth that destroys healthy tissues and organs. **2.** any malignant tumor. **3.** any destructive or spreading evil. **4. Cancer. a.** constellation in the northern sky, conventionally depicted as a crab. **b.** fourth sign of the zodiac. See **zodiac** for illustration. [Latin *cancer* crab, malignant tumor. Doublet of CANKER, CHANCRE.] —**can′cer·ous,** *adj.*

can·de·la (kan dē′lə) *n.* unit of luminous intensity equal to 1/60 of the light emitted by one square centimeter of the surface of a black object at the solidification temperature of platinum (1773.5° centigrade). Also, **can′dle.**

can·de·la·brum (kand′əl ä′brəm, -ā′brəm) *pl.,* **-bra** (-brə) or **-brums.** *also,* **can·de·la·bra.** *n.* large ornamental branched candlestick. [Latin *candēlābrum* candlestick, from *candēla* candle.]

can·des·cent (kan des′ənt) *adj.* glowing, esp. with heat; incandescent. [Latin *candēscēns,* present participle of *candēscere* to begin to glow.] —**can·des′cence,** *n.*

can·did (kan′did) *adj.* **1.** honest and straightforward; frank; sincere: *a candid opinion.* **2.** free from bias; fair; impartial. [Latin *candidus* white, shining, pure.] —**can′did·ly,** *adv.* —**can′did·ness,** *n.* —**Syn. 1.** see **frank**[1].

can·di·da·cy (kan′di də sē) *pl.,* **-cies.** *n.* state or position of being a candidate.

can·di·date (kan′də dāt′, -dit) *n.* one who seeks, or is put forward by others for, an office or honor. [Latin *candidātus* a person dressed in white, candidate for office, from *candidus* white; in ancient Rome, those seeking political office would wear spotless white togas to symbolize integrity.]

Syn. Candidate, aspirant, nominee, applicant mean someone who offers himself, or is offered, as a seeker for a post, honor, or the like. **Candidate** is the most widely applicable word: *a presidential candidate, a Ph.D. candidate, a candidate for the priesthood.* **Aspirant** emphasizes ambitiousness for great accomplishment: *aspirants to high political office.* **Nominee** is used mostly in politics and stresses the actual naming for a particular office: *There were several candidates for legislative nomination, but that man ended up as the nominee.* **Applicant** means someone who submits a formal request for employment, admission, or the like. Unlike the preceding words, it carries no suggestion that the person is actually under consideration: *Going through the list of applicants, he winnowed out those who obviously were not qualified.*

can·di·da·ture (kan′di də chər) *n. British.* candidacy.

candid camera, small camera with a fast lens for taking unposed, informal pictures.

can·died (kan′dēd) *adj.* **1.** cooked in or coated with sugar: *candied yams.* **2.** wholly or partially crystallized into sugar.

can·dle (kand′əl) *n.* **1.** mass of wax, tallow, or other solid fat, usually cylindrical, formed around a wick, which is burned to give light or low heat. **2.** anything like a candle in shape or use. **3.** candela. **4.** International candle. **5. to burn the candle at both ends.** to expend one's energy by working or playing too hard; live recklessly. **6. to hold a candle to.** to compare favorably with; be as good as: *As a musician he can't hold a candle to his more talented brother.* —*v.t.,* **-dled, -dling.** to examine (eggs) for signs of fertilization and for freshness and quality, by holding them in front of a light. [Old English *candel* light made of wax or tallow around a wick, from Latin *candēla.*]

can·dle·hold·er (kand′əl hōl′dər) *n.* candlestick.

can·dle·light (kand′əl līt′) *n.* **1.** light given by a candle or candles. **2.** twilight; dusk; nightfall.

Can·dle·mas (kand′əl məs) *n.* church festival celebrating the purification of the Virgin Mary and the presentation of the infant Jesus in the Temple, during which candles for sacred use are blessed. February 2. [Old English *candelmæsse.*]

can·dle·pin (kand′əl pin′) *n.* **1.** cylindrical wooden pin, tapering slightly toward top and bottom, used in the game of candlepins. **2. candlepins.** bowling game using ten of these pins, in which three balls are bowled in each frame and the pins that are knocked down are not removed until the completion of the frame. ▲ construed as singular.

can·dle·pow·er (kand′əl pou′ər) *n.* measure of the intensity of a source of light based on the light emitted in a particular direction from that source and expressed in candles.

can·dle·stick (kand′əl stik′) *n.* holder with a cup or spike for a candle.

can·dle·wick (kand′əl wik′) *n.* wick of a candle.

can·dor (kan′dər) *also, British,* **can·dour.** *n.* **1.** frankness, as of speech; honesty; openness. **2.** freedom from prejudice; fairness; impartiality. [Latin *candor* brightness, whiteness, purity.]

can·dy (kan′dē) *pl.,* **-dies.** *n.* **1.** solid confection made chiefly of sugar or syrup combined with other ingredients, as chocolate, milk, nuts, and fruits. **2.** piece of such a confection. —*v.t.,* **-died, -dy·ing.** **1.** to cause to form into crystals. **2.** to preserve by cooking or coating with sugar. **3.** to cover or encrust with or as with sugar crystals. —*v.i.* to become crystallized into or covered with sugar. [French *(sucre) candi* (sugar) candy, through Italian, from Arabic *qand* sugar, going back to Sanskrit *khanda* pieces of sugar; originally, fragment.]

can·dy·tuft (kan′dē tuft′) *n.* any of a group of plants, genus *Iberis,* of the mustard family, bearing narrow leaves and clusters of small white, purple, or pink flowers. [From *Candia* earlier name of Crete + TUFT; because it came from Crete.]

cane (kān) *n.* **1.** stick or staff, usually made of wood, esp. one used to help a person in walking; walking stick. **2.** stick or rod, esp. one used for beating or flogging. **3.** slender, woody, jointed stem of certain tall grasses, as bamboo, reed, and rattan. **4.** any plant having such a stem. **5.** material made of such stems, as rattan, used in making furniture and wickerwork. **6.** sugarcane. —*v.t.,* **caned, can·ing.** **1.** to beat or flog with a cane. **2.** to make or furnish with cane, as furniture. [Old French *can(n)e* reed, from Latin *canna,* from Greek *kanna;* of Semitic origin. Doublet of CANNA.]

cane·brake (kān′brāk′) *n.* thicket of cane.

ca·nel·la (kə nel′ə) *n.* **1.** inner bark of a tree, *Canella alba,* having a smell resembling cinnamon and a pungent taste, yielding an oil used as a spice and in making perfume. **2.** evergreen tree from which this bark is obtained, found in the West Indies and the Florida Keys.

at; āpe; cär; end; mē; it; īce; hot; ōld; fôrk; wood; fōōl; oil; out; up; ūse; turn; sing; thin; this; zh in treasure; ə in ago, taken, pencil, lemon, circus.

[Medieval Latin *canella* cinnamon, diminutive of Latin *canna* reed. See CANE.]

cane sugar, sugar obtained from sugarcane.

ca·nine (kā′nīn) *adj.* **1.** of, resembling, or relating to a dog. **2.** of or relating to the dog family, Canidae, which includes dogs, foxes, wolves, and jackals. —*n.* **1.** domestic dog. **2.** any member of the dog family. **3.** canine tooth. [Latin *canīnus* relating to a dog, from *canis* dog.]

canine tooth, one of the four sharp-pointed teeth situated between the incisors and the bicuspids in the upper and lower jaw.

Ca·nis Ma·jor (kā′nis mā′jər) constellation in the southern sky, near the celestial equator, containing the bright star Sirius, conventionally depicted as a dog. [Latin *Canis Mājor* the Greater Dog.]

Ca·nis Mi·nor (kā′nis mī′nər) constellation in the northern sky, near the celestial equator, containing the bright star Procyon, conventionally depicted as a dog. [Latin *Canis Minor* the Lesser Dog.]

can·is·ter (kan′is tər) *n.* **1.** small box, can, or other container, usually made of metal, for holding coffee, sugar, flour, or other dry foods. **2.** can filled with musket balls or scrap metal which scattered its contents when fired from a cannon; case shot. Also (*def. 2*), **canister shot.** [Latin *canistrum* basket made of reeds, from Greek *kanastron* wicker basket, from *kanna* reed. See CANE.]

can·ker (kang′kər) *n.* **1.** ulceration, esp. of the mouth or lip. Also, **canker sore. 2.a.** any of various diseases of trees, that cause decay of the bark and underlying tissue. **b.** lesion caused by such a disease. **3.** anything that corrodes, corrupts, or destroys: *Banish the canker of ambitious thoughts* (Shakespeare, *Henry VI, Part II*). **4.** cankerworm. —*v.t.* **1.** to affect with canker. **2.** to corrode, corrupt, or destroy. —*v.i.* to become infected with or as with canker. [Old English *cancer* and dialectal Old French *cancre* ulcer, both from Latin *cancer* malignant tumor. Doublet of CANCER, CHANCRE.]

can·ker·ous (kang′kər əs) *adj.* **1.** of the nature of canker. **2.** causing canker.

can·ker·worm (kang′kər wurm′) *n.* larva of any of several moths, family Geometridae, that is very destructive to shade and fruit trees.

can·na (kan′ə) *n.* **1.** red or yellow flower of any of a group of plants, genus Canna. The stamens are broad and petal-like and form the showy part of the flower. **2.** plant bearing this flower, having large, oblong leaves. [Latin *canna* reed, from Greek *kannā;* of Semitic origin. Doublet of CANE.]

Can·nae (kan′ē) *n.* ancient town in southeastern Italy, site of Hannibal's decisive victory over the Romans in 216 B.C.

canned (kand) *adj.* **1.** preserved in a can or jar. **2.** *Informal.* recorded: *The television comedy was broadcast with canned laughter.*

can·nel coal (kan′əl) black bituminous coal having a uniform and fine-grained compact texture, which is easily ignited and burns with a bright flame. Also, **cannel.** [Form of CANDLE + COAL; because, like a candle, it does not smoke when burning.]

can·ner (kan′ər) *n.* person or business that cans food.

can·ner·y (kan′ər ē) *pl.,* **-ner·ies.** *n.* factory where foods are canned.

Cannes (kan, kanz) *n.* resort and port city in southeastern France, on the Mediterranean. Pop. (1968), 67,152.

can·ni·bal (kan′ə bəl) *n.* **1.** human being who eats human flesh. **2.** animal that eats its own kind. —*adj.* of or relating to cannibals; given to cannibalism. [Spanish *canibal,* form of *caríbal* human cannibal, Carib; of Carib origin; Modern English meaning from the Carib practice of eating human flesh.]

can·ni·bal·ism (kan′ə bə liz′əm) *n.* act or practice of eating the flesh of one's own kind. —**can′ni·bal·is′tic,** *adj.*

can·ni·bal·ize (kan′ə bə līz′) **-ized, -iz·ing.** *v.t.* to take parts from (something) to build, repair, or strengthen one or more other things: *The boys built their hot rod by cannibalizing abandoned cars.*

can·ni·kin (kan′ə kin) *n.* small can or cup. [CAN² + -KIN.]

can·ning (kan′ing) *n.* act, process, or business of preserving food by sealing it in airtight containers.

can·non (kan′ən) *pl.,* **-nons** or **-non.** *n.* **1.** large, mounted firearm, as a gun, howitzer, or mortar. See **tank** for illustration. **2.** cannon bone. [French *canon* gun, gun barrel, going back to Latin *canna* reed, tube. See CANE.]

can·non·ade (kan′ə nād′) *n.* **1.** very heavy or continuous firing of artillery. **2.** attack with artillery. —*v.t.* **-ad·ed, -ad·ing.** to attack with artillery. —*v.i.* to fire artillery continuously. [French *canonnade* cannon shot, from Italian *cannonata* firing of a cannon, from *cannone* cannon, large tube, going back to Latin *canna* reed, tube. See CANE.]

cannon ball, heavy ball, made of iron or other metal, designed to be fired from a cannon.

cannon bone, long bone between the hock or knee and the fetlock, in hoofed animals, esp. the horse. See **horse** for illustration.

can·non·eer (kan′ə nēr′) *n.* artilleryman; gunner.

can·non·ry (kan′ən rē) *pl.,* **-ries.** *n.* **1.** artillery. **2.** continuous cannon fire.

cannon shot. 1. cannon balls or other projectiles for a cannon. **2.** shot fired from a cannon. **3.** range of a cannon.

can·not (kan′ot, ka not′) **1.** can not. **2. cannot but.** have no choice except to; must: *We cannot but admire his bravery.*

can·ny (kan′ē) **-ni·er, -ni·est.** *adj.* **1.** cautiously shrewd; prudent; wary. **2.** frugal; thrifty. **3.** clever; skillful. —**can′ni·ly,** *adv.* —**can′ni·ness,** *n.* [CAN¹ + -Y¹.]

ca·noe (kə nōō′) *n.* light, narrow boat, usually pointed at both ends, propelled by hand with a paddle. —*v.i.* **ca·noed, ca·noe·ing.** to paddle or go in a canoe. —*v.t.* to transport by canoe. [Spanish *canoa* Indian boat; of Carib origin; Modern English spelling influenced by French *canoē* Canadian canoe.] —**ca·noe′ist,** *n.*

can·on¹ (kan′ən) *n.* **1.** law, rule, or decree of a church, usually enacted by a church council. **2.** general rule, fundamental principle, or standard: *canons of good behavior.* **3.** collection or list of the books of the Bible accepted by the church as genuine and divinely inspired. **4.** list of saints officially recognized by the Roman Catholic Church and certain other churches. **5.** list or catalogue, as of the works of a particular author. **6.** *also,* **Canon.** portion of the Mass following the Sanctus. **7.** *Music.* form of contrapuntal composition in which the different vocal or instrumental parts take up the melody successively at the same or at a different pitch. [Old English *canon* rule, from Latin *canōn,* from Greek *kanōn* rod, carpenter's rule, rule, standard.]

can·on² (kan′ən) *n.* **1.** in the Church of England, one of the clergymen serving in a cathedral or collegiate church. **2.** in the Middle Ages, one of a group of Roman Catholic clergymen living according to certain rules, or canons, of the church. [Dialectal Old French *canonie* priest, from Church Latin *canōnicus* clergyman, one belonging to the canon or rule, from Latin *canōn.* See CANON¹.]

ca·non·i·cal (kə non′i kəl) *adj.* **1.** relating to, prescribed by, or conforming to canon law. **2.** of or contained in the canon of the Bible. **3.** authoritative; recognized; accepted: *a canonical source of knowledge.* —*n.* **canonicals.** vestments prescribed by canon to be worn by clergymen when officiating. —**ca·non′i·cal·ly,** *adv.*

canonical hours, seven periods of the day fixed by canon for prayer and devotion.

can·on·ize (kan′ə nīz′) **-ized, -iz·ing.** *v.t.* **1.** to declare (a deceased person) a saint; place in the canon of saints: *Sir Thomas More was canonized in 1935.* **2.** to glorify. **3.** to admit into the canon of the Bible. **4.** to sanction by the authority of the church. —**can′on·i·za′tion,** *n.*

canon law, in a Christian church, the body of law governing matters of faith and discipline.

Ca·no·pus (kə nō′pəs) *n.* second brightest star in the sky and the brightest in the constellation Carina.

can·o·py (kan′ə pē) *pl.,* **-pies.** *n.* **1.** awning, drapery, or similar covering, often suspended over a bed, throne, or entrance of a building, or supported on poles over a person or sacred object. **2.** overhanging shelter or covering: *the canopy of heaven.* **3.** sliding, transparent covering of an airplane cockpit. **4.** umbrellalike lifting surface of a parachute. —*v.t.* **-pied, -py·ing.** to cover with or as with a canopy. [Medieval Latin *canapeum* mosquito net, going back to Greek *kōnōpion* mosquito net, bed with a mosquito net, from *kōnōps* mosquito. Doublet of CANAPÉ.]

Ca·nos·sa (kə nos′ə) *n.* ancient town in northern Italy where Henry IV of the Holy Roman Empire did penance before Pope Gregory VII in 1077.

canst (kanst) *Archaic.* present indicative, second person singular of can.

cant¹ (kant) *n.* **1.** trite, pretentious, or insincere talk, esp. the hypocritical expression of religious or moralistic sentiments. **2.** words or phraseology peculiar to a particular class, profession, sect, or other group; jargon. **3.** whining, singsong speech. —*v.i.* to speak in cant; use cant. [Latin *cantus* song and *cantāre* to sing; originally applied to the whining of beggars and probably to the chanting in Christian religious services.]

cant² (kant) *n.* **1.** inclination from a line or surface; slope; tilt. **2.** sudden movement that tilts or overturns something. **3.** corner or external angle, as of a building. **4.** slanting or sloping surface, as one produced by cutting off a corner or edge. —*v.t.* **1.** to put or set at an angle; tilt; slant. **2.** to give a sloping edge to; bevel. **3.** to throw with a sudden jerk; pitch; toss. —*v.i.* to tilt, slant, or slope. [Middle Dutch *cant* border, edge, corner, going back to Late Latin *cantus* corner, from Latin *cant(h)us* tire², wheel; of Celtic origin.]

at; āpe; cär; end; mē; it; īce; hot; ōld; fôrk; wood; fōol; oil; out; up; ūse; turn; sing; thin; this; zh in treasure; ə in ago, taken, pencil, lemon, circus.

Canine tooth

Canoe

can't (kant) cannot.

can·ta·bi·le (kän tä′bə lā′, kan tab′ə lē) *Music. adj., adv.* in a smooth and flowing style. —*n.* cantabile passage, piece, or style. [Italian *cantabile* singable, from *cantare* to sing, from Latin *cantāre*.]

Can·ta·brig·i·an (kan′tə brij′ē ən) *adj.* of or relating to Cambridge, England, or Cambridge University. —*n.* **1.** student or graduate of Cambridge University. **2.** native or inhabitant of Cambridge, England. [Medieval Latin *Cantabrigia* Cambridge + -AN.]

can·ta·loupe (kan′tə lōp′) *also,* **can·ta·loup.** *n.* variety of muskmelon, Cucumis melo cantalupensis, having a coarse, pale-green or yellow rind and sweet, usually yellowish-orange flesh. [French *cantaloup,* from Italian *Cantalupo,* name of a former papal residence, where it was first grown in Europe.]

can·tan·ker·ous (kan tang′kər əs) *adj.* characterized by ill-tempered contradiction or opposition; contradictory; contentious; stubborn. [Probably modification of Middle English *contek* strife; influenced by words like *cankerous, rancorous.*] —**can·tan′ker·ous·ly,** *adv.* —**can·tan′ker·ous·ness,** *n.*

can·ta·ta (kən tä′tə) *n.* sacred or secular choral work, consisting of arias, recitatives, duets, choruses, and instrumental interludes, resembling a short oratorio or a lyric drama set to music but not acted. [Italian *cantata,* from Italian *cantare* to sing, from Latin *cantāre.*]

can·teen (kan tēn′) *n.* **1.** small metal container for carrying water or other liquids. **2.a.** place run by civilian volunteers where free food, beverages, and, usually, entertainment are provided for servicemen. **b.** post exchange. **3.** place providing food and beverages, as a snack bar at a factory. [French *cantine,* from Italian *cantina* cellar (formerly often used as a shop), going back to Late Latin *cantus* corner. See CANT².]

can·ter (kan′tər) *n.* slow, easy gallop. —*v.i.* to move or ride at a canter. —*v.t.* to cause to move at a canter. [Short for *Canterbury gallop,* the pace of pilgrims riding on horseback to the shrine at Canterbury.]

Can·ter·bur·y (kan′tər ber′ē, -bər ē) *n.* city in southeastern England, the religious center of England, and site of a famous cathedral. Pop. (1961), 30,415.

Canterbury bell **1.** tall stalk of bell-shaped flowers borne by a plant, *Campanula medium,* of the bellflower family, having white, pink, or blue-violet petals. **2.** plant bearing this flower, widely cultivated as a garden plant, having hairy leaves and stems. [Because of its resemblance to the bells on the horses of pilgrims riding to the shrine at *Canterbury.*]

cant hook, pole with a movable hooked arm at or near one end, used by loggers and linemen to grip and turn over logs or poles.

Cant hook

can·ti·cle (kan′ti kəl) *n.* nonmetrical hymn whose text is usually taken directly from the Bible. [Latin *canticulum* little song, diminutive of *canticum* song.]

Canticle of Canticles, in the Douay Bible, the Song of Solomon.

Can·ti·cles (kan′ti kəlz) *n.,pl.* Song of Solomon. ▲ construed as singular.

can·ti·le·ver (kant′əl ē′vər, -ev′ər) *n.* projecting bracket, beam, or slab that is supported at one end only. [Possibly CANT² + LEVER.]

cantilever bridge, bridge formed by two cantilevers whose projecting ends meet but do not support each other.

can·tle (kan′təl) *n.* part of the seat of certain saddles that curves up at the back. See saddle for illustration. [Anglo-Norman *cantel* piece, corner, going back to Late Latin *cantus* corner. See CANT².]

Cantle

can·to (kan′tō) *pl.* **-tos.** *n.* one of the main divisions of a long poem. [Italian *canto,* from Latin *cantus* song.]

can·ton (kan′tən, -ton) *n.* small territorial district or political division of a country, esp. one of the states of the Swiss confederation. —*v.t.* **1.** to divide into cantons or districts. **2.** to quarter (troops). [Old French *canton* corner, portion, going back to Late Latin *cantus* corner. See CANT².] —**can′ton·al,** *adj.*

Can·ton (def. 1 kan tōn′, kan′ton′; def. 2 kan′tən) *n.* **1.** city in southeastern China. Pop. (1965 est.), 3,000,000. **2.** city in northeastern Ohio. Pop. (1970), 110,053.

Canton crepe (kan′ton′) heaviest of all silk or rayon crepe fabrics, used esp. for linings, nightgowns, and scarves.

Can·ton·ese (kan′tə nēz′, -nēs′) *pl.* **-ese.** *n.* **1.** native or inhabitant of Canton, China. **2.** Chinese dialect spoken in and around Canton. —*adj.* of or relating to the region around Canton, China, its people, or their dialect or culture.

Can·ton flannel (kan′ton′) heavy, absorbent cotton cloth that has a soft nap, used esp. for sleepwear and shirts. Also, **cotton flannel.**

can·ton·ment (kan tōn′mənt, -ton′-) *n.* **1.** military installation which includes quarters for servicemen and their families. **2.** temporary housing for troops. **3.** assignment of troops to such quarters. [French *cantonnement* housing for troops, from *cantonner* to quarter, from *canton* corner, portion. See CANTON.]

can·tor (kan′tər) *n.* **1.** singer who leads a choir or congregation; precentor. **2.** in a synagogue, one who sings the liturgy. [Latin *cantor* singer.]

Can·tor, Ge·org (kan′tər; gä′ôrk) 1845–1918, German mathematician, founder of the theory of sets.

Ca·nuck (kə nuk′) *n.* *Slang.* **1.** Canadian. **2.** French Canadian. ▲ usually considered offensive. [Modification of CANADIAN.]

Ca·nute (kə nōōt′, -nūt′) c.994–1035, king of England, from 1016 to 1035; of Denmark, from 1018 to 1035; and of Norway, from 1028 to 1035. Also, **Cnut.**

can·vas (kan′vəs) *n.* **1.** heavy cloth made of cotton, flax, or hemp, used to make items which must be strong and durable, as tents, sails, boat and truck covers, or awnings. **2.** piece of canvas on which a painting, esp. an oil painting, is made. **3.** oil painting done on canvas. **4.** *Nautical.* sail or sails. **5.** tent, esp. a circus tent. **6. under canvas. a.** in tents. **b.** with sails spread. [Dialectal Old French *canevas* made of hemp, going back to Latin *cannabis* hemp, from Greek *kannabis.*]

can·vas·back (kan′vəs bak′) *n.* wild duck, *Aythya valisineria,* of North America, the male of which has black and brown plumage and white feathers on its back. It is valued as a game bird and for its savory flesh. Length: 24 inches. [Because the markings on its back recall the doublets of certain economical gentlemen of the seventeenth century, that had fine, expensive cloth fronts, but cheap canvas on the backs.]

can·vass (kan′vəs) *v.t.* **1.** to go through (a place) or among (people) to solicit votes, opinions, orders, or contributions. **2.** to examine carefully; scrutinize. —*v.i.* to go about soliciting votes, opinions, orders, or contributions. —*n.* act or process of soliciting, as of votes, opinions, orders, or contributions. [From CANVAS, with the idea, originally, of sifting something through canvas; hence, to investigate, discuss, i.e., to "sift" opinions or responses.] —**can′vass·er,** *n.*

can·yon (kan′yən) *n.* deep valley with steep sides, usually with a stream running through it. [Spanish *cañón* tube, gorge, going back to Latin *canna* reed, cane. See CANE.]

can·zo·net (kan′zə net′) *n.* short, light song or air. [Italian *canzonetta* little song, going back to Latin *cantiō* song.]

caou·tchouc (kou chōōk′, -chook′) *n.* latex. [French *caoutchouc* rubber, from Carib *cahuchu* sap of a tree.]

cap (kap) *n.* **1.** soft, close-fitting head covering, usually brimless or with a visor. **2.** special head covering worn to show rank, membership, or occupation: *a nurse's cap.* **3.** something resembling a cap in shape, position, or use: *a mushroom cap, a bottle cap.* **4.** paper wrapping or covering containing a small quantity of explosive, used in toy guns. **5. to set one's cap for.** *Informal.* to try to win for a suitor or husband. —*v.t.,* **capped, cap·ping. 1.** to put a cap on; cover. **2.** to serve as a cap, cover, or top for; lie on top of: *Clouds capped the mountains.* **3.** to follow with something equal to or better than; match; surpass: *He capped his friend's story with an even more exciting one.* **4.** to finish; complete. **5. to cap the climax.** to exceed the limit; surpass expectation or belief. [Old English *cæppe* hood, close head covering, from Late Latin *cappa* hood, cloak; of uncertain origin.]

cap. **1.** *pl.,* **caps.** capital letter. **2.** capitalize. **3.** capacity. **4.** capital.

ca·pa·bil·i·ty (kā′pə bil′ə tē) *pl.,* **-ties.** *n.* **1.** quality of being capable; ability; capacity. **2.** quality or ability that may be used or developed; potentiality.

ca·pa·ble (kā′pə bəl) *adj.* **1.** having or showing ability; efficient; competent: *a capable doctor, a capable performance.* **2. capable of. a.** having the capacity, ability, or quality needed for: *He is capable of accomplishing great deeds.* **b.** open to the influence or affect of; susceptible to: *The politician made a statement capable of misunderstanding.* [Late Latin *capābilis* able, from Latin *capere* to take, hold.] —**ca′pa·ble·ness,** *n.* —**ca′pa·bly,** *adv.* —**Syn. 1.** see **able.**

ca·pa·cious (kə pā′shəs) *adj.* able to hold or contain much; roomy; spacious: *a capacious auditorium.* —**ca·pa′cious·ly,** *adv.* —**ca·pa′cious·ness,** *n.*

ca·pac·i·tance (kə pas′ət əns) *n.* ratio of the amount of electric charge stored in a capacitor to the voltage across its terminals; capacity.

ca·pac·i·tor (kə pas′ə tər) *n.* device for receiving and storing an electric charge, consisting usually of two metallic plates or foils separated by a nonconductor. Also, **con·dens′er.**

ca·pac·i·ty (kə pas′ə tē) *n.* **1.** ability to receive or contain: *The auditorium has a seating*

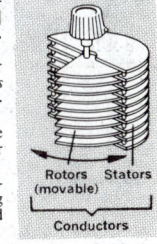

Rotors Stators
(movable)

Conductors

Capacitor

at; āpe; cär; end; mē; it; īce; hot; ōld; fôrk; wood; fōōl; oil; out; up; ūse; turn; sing; thin; this; zh in treasure; ə in ago, taken, pencil, lemon, circus.

145

capacity of 200. **2.** maximum amount that can be held or contained in a space; content; volume: *The room is filled to capacity.* **3.** power of grasping or taking in impressions, ideas, or knowledge; mental ability: *a scholar of great capacity.* **4.** ability, power, or faculty to do something. **5.** specific position, occupation, or function: *He is representing the company in the capacity of salesman.* **6.** *Law.* legal qualification or competency. **7.** capacitance. [Latin *capácitás* ability to hold much.]

cap and bells, cap trimmed with bells, worn by a court jester.

cap and gown, mortarboard and loose gown, worn by teachers, students, and other participants at academic functions, esp. at graduation.

cap·a·pie (kap'ə pē') *adv.* from head to foot; all over. [Old French *cap a pie,* going back to Latin *caput* head + *ad* to + *pēs* foot.]

ca·par·i·son (kə par'ə sən) *n.* **1.** ornamental covering for a horse. **2.** rich dress, equipment, or trappings. —*v.t.* **1.** to cover (a horse) with a caparison. **2.** to dress or adorn sumptuously. [Middle French *caparasson* trappings for a horse, going back to Late Latin *cap(p)a* hood, cape; of uncertain origin.]

Caparison (def. 1)

cape¹ (kāp) *n.* outer garment without sleeves, which falls loosely over the shoulders and is worn in place of, or attached to, a jacket or coat. [French *cape,* from Spanish *capa,* from Late Latin *cap(p)a* hood, cloak; of uncertain origin.]

cape² (kāp) *n.* point of land extending out from the coastline into the sea or a lake. [French *cap* head, cape², from Italian *capo,* from Latin *caput* head.]

cap·e·lin (kap'ə lin) *n.* small fish, *Mallotus villosus,* similar to a smelt, found in the North Atlantic and used commercially as bait for cod. [French *capelan* codfish, from Provençal *capelan* codfish, chaplain, from Medieval Latin *cappellanus.* See CHAPLAIN.]

Ca·pel·la (kə pel'ə) *n.* yellow double star, the brightest star in the constellation Auriga. [Latin *capella* female goat.]

Cape Province, Cape of Good Hope province. Also, **Cape Colony.**

ca·per¹ (kā'pər) *v.i.* to leap or jump about in a frolicsome manner; prance. —*n.* **1.** frolicsome leap, skip, or jump. **2.** capricious action; prank; antic. **3.** *Slang.* illegal act, as a robbery or burglary. [Short for CAPRIOLE.] —**Syn.** 2. see **prank¹.**

ca·per² (kā'pər) *n.* **1.** the pickled green flower bud of a shrub, *Capparis spinosa,* used as a condiment. **2.** the spiny, vinelike shrub itself, which grows wild in rocky regions of the Mediterranean. [Latin *capparis,* from Greek *kapparis.*]

cap·er·cail·lie (kap'ər kāl'yē) *n.* large grouse, *Tetrao urogallus,* native to the evergreen forests of Eurasia. The male, which is black, is the largest of all grouse. Length: 2–3 feet. [Gaelic *capullcoille* great cock of the wood, from *capull* horse (from Latin *caballus* inferior horse) + *coille* forest.]

Ca·per·na·um (kə pur'nā əm, -nē əm) *n.* ancient town in northeastern Palestine, on the northern shore of the Sea of Galilee.

Ca·pet, Hugh (kā'pit, kap'it) A.D. c.938–996, king of France from 987 to 996 and founder of the Capetian dynasty of French kings.

Ca·pe·tian (kə pē'shən) *adj.* having to do with the French dynasty (987–1328) founded by Hugh Capet.

Cape Town (kāp'toun') *also,* **Cape·town.** legislative capital and port city of the Republic of South Africa, on the southwestern coast of the country. Pop. (1960), 508,341.

Cape Verde (kāp'vurd') see **Verde, Cape.**

Cape Verde Islands, island country in the North Atlantic, west of Cape Verde. Land area, 1557 sq. mi. Pop. (1975 est.), 300,000.

ca·pi·as (kā'pē əs) *n.* writ requiring an officer to take into custody the person named in it. [Latin *capias* you may take (second person singular of present subjective of *capere* to take).]

cap·il·lar·i·ty (kap'ə ler'ē tē) capillary action.

cap·il·lar·y (kap'ə ler'ē) *pl.,* **-lar·ies.** *n.* **1.** any of the smallest blood vessels of the circulatory system, connecting the arteries and veins. **2.** tube with a small, hairlike opening. —*adj.* **1.** of, relating to, or resembling hair; fine; slender. **2.** having a very small opening, as a tube or vessel. **3.** of, relating to, or taking place in a capillary or capillaries. [Latin *capillāris* relating to hair, from *capillus* hair.]

capillary action, rising or falling of a liquid where it touches a solid, due to the forces of adhesion, cohesion, and surface tension. Also, **cap'il·lar'i·ty.**

cap·i·tal¹ (kap'it əl) *n.* **1.** city or town in which is located the official seat of government of a country, state, or other political division. **2.** capital letter. **3.** total amount of money or property owned or used by a corporation or individual. **4.** wealth in any form used or available for use in the production of more wealth. **5.** capitalists as a group or class. **6.** any source of profit, power, or advantage; assets. **7. to make capital of.** to turn or use to one's own advantage; exploit. —*adj.* **1.** main, principal, or chief, esp. in being the offical seat of government: *a capital city.* **2.** of or relating to capital. **3.** excellent; first-rate: *He is a capital fellow.* **4.** punishable by or involving the death penalty: *a capital offense.* **5.** most serious; grave; fatal: *He has made a capital error.* [Old French *capital* chief, from Latin *capitālis* chief, relating to the head, from *caput* head.]

cap·i·tal² (kap'it əl) *n.* head or top part of a column, pilaster, or pillar. [Late Latin *capitellum,* diminutive of Latin *caput* head.]

capital gain, profit realized from the sale of capital investments, as stocks, bonds, or real estate.

capital goods, goods used in the production of other goods, as raw materials, buildings, or machinery, usually not including land or money. Distinguished from **consumer goods.**

cap·i·tal·ism (kap'it əl iz'əm) *n.* **1.** economic system in which capital goods and the means of production and distribution are privately owned, and the wealth and goods passing freely between producers and consumers, with the competition between producers determining the price. **2.** concentration of wealth in the hands of a few individuals or corporations, and the power and influence that result from such concentration.

cap·i·tal·ist (kap'it əl ist) *n.* **1.** person who has capital, particularly capital which is available for, or in use in, some economic enterprise. **2.** supporter of capitalism. **3.** any affluent person. —**cap'i·tal·is'tic,** *adj.*

cap·i·tal·i·za·tion (kap'it əl i zā'shən) *n.* **1.** act or process of capitalizing. **2.** amount resulting from capitalizing. **3.** total value of the authorized stocks and bonds of a corporation. **4.** present value of a business or property.

cap·i·tal·ize (kap'it əl īz') -ized, -iz·ing. *v.t.* **1.** to write or print with a capital letter or letters, or begin with a capital letter. **2.** to convert into capital. **3.** to provide capital for; finance. **4.** to calculate the present value of (a business or property) on the basis of future earnings or worth. —*v.i.* to use to one's advantage; profit (often with *on*): *He should capitalize on this opportunity.*

capital letter, form of a letter of the alphabet, usually the largest form, used esp. as the initial letter of a sentence or proper noun.

cap·i·tal·ly (kap'it əl ē) *adv.* in a capital manner; excellently; admirably.

capital punishment, death penalty for a crime.

capital ship, large warship, formerly a heavily armed sailing ship, now usually a battleship or aircraft carrier.

capital stock **1.** total number of shares that a company is authorized to issue. **2.** total of the par values of the shares that a company is authorized to issue.

cap·i·ta·tion (kap'i tā'shən) *n.* **1.** tax or fee imposed uniformly on each individual; poll tax. **2.** counting or assessing of individuals. [Late Latin *capitātiō* poll tax, from Latin *caput* head.]

Cap·i·tol (kap'it əl) *n.* **1.** building in which the U.S. Congress meets, in Washington, D.C. **2.** *also,* **capitol.** building in which a state legislature meets; statehouse. **3.** temple of Jupiter on the Capitoline hill in ancient Rome. **4.** Capitoline. [Latin *Capitōlium* ancient temple of Jupiter in Rome, from *caput* head; possibly because a *caput* or man's head was uncovered when the foundation of this Roman temple was laid.]

Cap·i·to·line (kap'it əl īn') *n.* one of the seven hills on which ancient Rome was built.

ca·pit·u·late (kə pich'ə lāt') -lat·ed, -lat·ing. *v.i.* **1.** to surrender or yield on stipulated terms or conditions: *The rebels capitulated with the understanding that they would be granted amnesty.* **2.** to give up; cease resisting. [Medieval Latin *capitulatus,* past participle of *capitulare* to arrange under separate headings, to arrange terms, going back to Latin *caput* head.] —**ca·pit'u·la'tor,** *n.*

ca·pit·u·la·tion (kə pich'ə lā'shən) *n.* **1.** act of capitulating. **2.** treaty or document containing the conditions of surrender. **3.** statement of the main points of a subject; summary. —**Syn.** 1. see **surrender.**

ca·pon (kā'pon, -pən) *n.* young rooster that has been castrated to promote fattening and to improve the flesh for eating. [Old English *capūn,* from Latin *capō.*]

ca·pote (kə pōt') *n.* **1.** long cloak with a hood. **2.** close-fitting bonnet. [French *capote* hooded cloak, diminutive of *cape.* See CAPE¹.]

Cap·pa·do·cia (kap'ə dō'shə) *n.* ancient region and former kingdom in Asia Minor, later annexed by Rome.

Ca·pri (käp'rē, kap'-, kə prē') *n.* small Italian island off the southwestern coast of the country, at the entrance to the Bay of Naples. Area, approx. 5 sq. mi. Pop. (1961), 10,872.

ca·pric·cio (kə prē'chē ō', -chō) *pl.,* **-ci·os.** *n.* **1.** caprice; prank. **2.** musical composition written in a free, irregular form and usually in a spirited, whimsical style. [Italian *capriccio* whim, shudder (suggesting "head with hair standing on end"), from *capo*

at; āpe; cär; end; mē; it; īce; hot; ōld; fôrk; wood; fōol; oil; out; up; ūse; turn; sing; thin; this; zh in treasure; ə in ago, taken, pencil, lemon, circus.

head (from Latin *caput*) + *riccio* hedgehog (from Latin *ērīcius*); sense influenced by Italian *capro* goat (with its friskiness).]

ca·price (kə prēs′) *n.* **1.** sudden change of mind without adequate or apparent motivation; whim. **2.** inclination to change one's mind in this manner; capriciousness. **3.** *Music.* capriccio. [French *caprice,* from Italian *capriccio* shudder, whim. See CAPRICCIO.]

Syn. 1. Caprice, whim, vagary denote an arbitrary, seemingly inexplicable, notion or desire. **Caprice** connotes willfulness, an impulse to have one's way: *It was her caprice to make him wait while she fussed with her hair.* **Whim** suggests a notion that occurs and passes quickly: *He was a tyrant who had men executed simply on a whim.* **Vagary** implies a wayward or erratic notion: *He had the political vagaries of a money-sheltered intellectual without actual experience of politics.*

ca·pri·cious (kə prish′əs, -prē′shəs) *adj.* subject to or characterized by caprice; guided by whim or fancy; changeable; fickle. —**ca·pri′·cious·ly,** *adv.* —**ca·pri′cious·ness,** *n.* —**Syn.** see fickle.

Cap·ri·corn (kap′rə kôrn) *n.* **1.** Tropic of Capricorn. **2.** constellation in the southern sky, conventionally depicted as a goat. **3.** tenth sign of the zodiac. See **zodiac** for illustration. [Latin *Capricornus* a sign of the zodiac; literally, goat-horned, from *caper* goat + *cornu* horn.]

cap·ri·ole (kap′rē ōl′) *n.* **1.** vertical leap made by a horse, with a backward kick of the hind legs at the top of the jump. **2.** leap, spring, or caper. —*v.i.* **-oled, -ol·ing.** to perform a capriole. [Middle French *capriole* leap, caper[1], from Italian *capriola* leap (like that of a goat), going back to Latin *caper* goat.]

caps 1. capital letters. **2.** capitalize.

cap·si·cum (kap′si kəm) *n.* any of a group of plants, genus *Capsicum,* of the nightshade family, widely cultivated for their red or green pods containing seeds that are usually sharp-tasting. Peppers, pimientos, and chilies are kinds of capsicum. [Modern Latin *capsicum,* probably from Latin *capsa* box; because of its pods.]

cap·size (kap′sīz, kap sīz′) **-sized, -siz·ing.** *v.t., v.i.* to overturn: *The rough waves capsized the boat. The boat capsized in the storm.* [Of uncertain origin.]

cap·stan (kap′stən) *n.* **1.** device with a vertical spindle which is rotated manually or by motor to wind up rope or cable, as in hoisting an anchor. **2.** *Electronics.* rotating axle on a tape recorder, which turns the reels of tape at a carefully controlled speed. [Provençal *cabestan* device for winding up rope, from *cabestre* halter, from Latin *capistrum.*]

Capstan

capstan bar, one of the levers by which a capstan is turned.

cap·stone (kap′stōn′) *n.* **1.** top or finishing stone of a wall or other structure. **2.** highest point or greatest achievement: *Performing for the queen was the capstone of the actor's career.*

cap·su·lar (kap′sə lər) *adj.* of, in, or resembling a capsule.

cap·sule (kap′səl) *n.* **1.** small soluble case enclosing a dose of medicine. **2.** sealed, pressurized cabin in a spacecraft, designed to support life during flight and to be recovered after flight. **3.** dry seedcase that develops from a compound pistil and opens when ripe. The seeds of the iris, azalea, and poppy develop in capsules. **4.** any membrane or membranous sac enclosing an organ or body part. —*adj.* in a concise form; very brief: *a capsule commentary.* [French *capsule,* small container, from Latin *capsula,* diminutive of *capsa* box.]

Capt., Captain.

cap·tain (kap′tən) *n.* **1.** one who is at the head of or has authority over others; leader; chief. **2.** person in command of a boat or ship. **3.** in the U.S. Navy and Coast Guard, officer ranking below a commodore or a rear admiral and above a commander. **4.** in the U.S. Army, Air Force, and Marine Corps, officer ranking below a major and above a first lieutenant. **5.** leader of a side or team, as in a sport. **6.** headwaiter. —*v.t.* to act as captain of; lead: *John will captain the basketball team this year.* [Old French *capitaine* commander of a body of troops, from Late Latin *capitāneus* chief, from Latin *caput* head. Doublet of CHIEFTAIN.] —**cap′tain·cy, cap′tain·ship′,** *n.*

cap·tion (kap′shən) *n.* **1.** title or descriptive material for a picture. **2.** title or heading, as at the head of a chapter, page, or article. —*v.t.* to furnish with a caption; entitle. [Latin *captiō* a seizing.]

cap·tious (kap′shəs) *adj.* **1.** apt to make much of unimportant faults or defects; difficult to please: *a captious critic.* **2.** designed to entrap or entangle in argument by subtlety: *a captious question.* [Latin *captiōsus* deceptive, sophistical.] —**cap′tious·ly,** *adv.* —**cap′tious·ness,** *n.* —**Syn.** see critical.

cap·ti·vate (kap′tə vāt′) **-vat·ed, -vat·ing.** *v.t.* **1.** to capture and hold the attention or affection of, as by beauty or excellence; charm; fasci-

nate; enchant: *The audience was captivated by his singing.* **2.** Archaic. to capture; seize; subdue. —**cap′ti·va′tion, cap′ti·va′tor,** *n.*

cap·tive (kap′tiv) *n.* **1.** one taken and held in confinement; prisoner: *The enemy captives were brought to the commanding officer for questioning.* **2.** one captivated or enthralled, as by beauty, love, or passion. —*adj.* **1.** taken or kept prisoner, as in war: *The captive soldiers were not harmed.* **2.** enthralled, as by beauty, love, or passion; captivated. **3.** confined; restrained: *a captive balloon.* [Latin *captīvus* prisoner, from *capere* to take.] Doublet of CAITIFF.] —**Syn.** see **prisoner.**

captive audience, any group of people compelled by circumstances to listen to something.

cap·tiv·i·ty (kap tiv′ə tē) *pl.,* **-ties.** *n.* state or condition of being captive: *Some zoo animals thrive in captivity.*

cap·tor (kap′tər) *n.* one who captures.

cap·ture (kap′chər) **-tured, -tur·ing.** *v.t.* to take or seize by force, surprise, or stratagem: *to capture an enemy stronghold, to capture an opponent's chess piece.* —*n.* **1.** act of capturing. **2.** one who or that which is captured. [French *capture* act of capturing, what is captured, from Latin *captūra.*] —**Syn.** *v.t.* see **catch.**

Capuchin

cap·u·chin (kap′yə chin, -shin) *n.* **1.** any of various tree-dwelling monkeys, genus *Cebus,* having a long, prehensile tail, black or brown fur, and, in some species, black hair on the head that resembles a monk's cowl. Length: 14–24 inches without tail. **2.** Capuchin. member of one of the branches of the Franciscan Order. A Capuchin monk is usually bearded and wears a coarse brown habit with a distinctive long, pointed hood and sandals. [Middle French *capuchin* Capuchin monk, from Italian *cappuccino* Capuchin monk, small hood (as worn by the Capuchins), diminutive of *cappuccio* hood, going back to Late Latin *cappa.* See CAPE[1].]

Cap·u·let (kap′yə lət) *n.* family of Juliet in Shakespeare's *Romeo and Juliet.*

cap·y·ba·ra (kap′ə bär′ə) *n.* rodent, *Hydrochoerus hydrochoerus,* native to banks of rivers and streams in South America, resembling a large guinea pig, and having a coarse coat of brownish, bristly hair. It is the largest living rodent. Height: 21 inches at the shoulder. [Of Tupi-Guarani origin.]

car (kär) *n.* **1.** automobile. **2.** vehicle designed to move on rails: *a railroad car.* **3.** any wheeled vehicle. **4.** cage of an elevator, which carries the passengers or cargo. **5.** Archaic. chariot. [Anglo-Norman *carre* wagon, from Late Latin *carra;* of Celtic origin.]

car·a·bao (kar′ə bä′ō, kär′-) *pl.,* **-ba·os.** *n.* Philippine water buffalo that is often domesticated as a draft animal. [Spanish *carabao;* from native Philippine word.]

car·a·bi·neer (kar′ə bə nēr′) *also,* **car·a·bi·nier.** *n.* formerly, a soldier in the cavalry armed with a carbine.

Car·a·cal·la (kar′ə kal′ə) A.D. 188–217, Roman emperor from 211 to 217.

Ca·ra·cas (kə rä′kəs) *n.* capital and largest city of Venezuela, in the northern part of the country. Pop. (1969), 786,710.

car·a·cole (kar′ə kōl′) *n.* half turn executed by a horse and rider. —*v.i.* **-coled, -col·ing.** to make a caracole or move in a series of caracoles. [French *caracole* gambol, a caracole, from Spanish *caracol* snail, spiral shell, a caracole; of uncertain origin; from the comparison of the movements of a horse to the spirals on a snail shell.]

car·a·cul (kar′ə kəl) *also,* **kar·a·kul.** *n.* loosely curled wool of young karakul lambs. [Form of KARAKUL.]

ca·rafe (kə raf′) *n.* glass bottle for water or other beverages; decanter. [French *carafe,* from Italian *caraffa,* from Spanish *garrafa,* from Arabic *gharrāf* drinking vessel.]

car·a·mel (kar′ə məl, -mel′, kär′məl) *n.* **1.** burnt sugar used as a coloring or flavoring agent. **2.** chewy candy made mainly from sugar, cream, and corn syrup, usually in the form of small squares. [French *caramel,* from Spanish *caramelo;* of uncertain origin.]

car·a·pace (kar′ə pās′) *n.* hard or bony covering on the back of some animals, as turtles or lobsters. [French *carapace,* from Spanish *carapacho;* of uncertain origin.]

car·at (kar′ət) *n.* **1.** unit of weight equal to ⅕ of a gram, used chiefly in measuring the weight of gems. **2.** karat. [French *carat,* through Italian and Arabic, from Greek *keration* small weight, seed of the carob tree; literally, small horn. The seeds were used as a unit of weight in ancient times because of their uniform size and weight.]

car·a·van (kar′ə van′) *n.* **1.** company of travelers, merchants, or pilgrims traveling together for safety and security, esp. through deserts or dangerous regions. **2.** number of vehicles traveling together: *The*

at; āpe; cär; end; mē; it; īce; hot; ōld; fôrk; wood; fōōl; oil; out; up; ūse; turn; sing; thin; this; zh in treasure; ə in ago, taken, pencil, lemon, circus.

147

caravan of army trucks stopped to refuel. **3.** *British.* house on wheels; trailer; van. [French *caravane* convoy, from Persian *kārwān* company of travelers.]

car·a·van·sa·ry (kar'ə van'sər ē) *pl.,* **-ries.** *also,* **car·a·van·se·rai** (kar'ə van'sə rī'). *n.* **1.** in certain Oriental countries, inn with a central court, for accommodating caravans. **2.** any large inn or hotel. [Persian *kārwānsarāi* caravan inn, from *kārwān* caravan + *sarāi* inn.]

car·a·vel (kar'ə vel') *n.* any of several types of sailing ships developed in Portugal and Spain in the fifteenth century. Two of Columbus' ships were caravels. [French *caravelle,* from Portuguese *caravela,* going back to Greek *karabos* light ship.]

car·a·way (kar'ə wā') *n.* **1.** pungent seeds of a plant, *Carum carvi,* of the parsley family, used as a spice. **2.** the plant itself. [Spanish *alcaravea,* from Arabic *al-karawiyā',* possibly going back to Greek *kareon* cumin.]

car·bide (kär'bīd) *n.* **1.** any of a large group of compounds that contain carbon and one other element. **2.** calcium carbide.

car·bine (kär'bīn, -bēn) *n.* **1.** lightweight automatic or semiautomatic .30 caliber weapon, shorter and less powerful than a rifle, but more easily handled and with a greater range than a pistol. **2.** formerly, a short rifle or musket used by the cavalry. [French *carabine* short rifle, from *carabin* carabineer; of uncertain origin.]

car·bi·neer (kär'bə nēr') carabineer.

car·bo·hy·drate (kär'bō hī'drāt, -bə-) *n.* compound of carbon, hydrogen, and oxygen produced by green plants in the process of photosynthesis. Cellulose, sugars, and starches are carbohydrates. [CARBO(N) + HYDRATE.]

car·bo·lat·ed (kär'bə lā'tid) *adj.* containing or impregnated with carbolic acid.

car·bol·ic acid (kär bol'ik) *n.* phenol.

car·bo·lize (kär'bə līz') **-lized, -liz·ing.** *v.t.* to treat or impregnate with carbolic acid.

car·bon (kär'bən) *n.* **1.** common nonmetallic element occurring in crystalline forms, such as diamond and graphite, and in amorphous forms, such as charcoal. Carbon is present in all organic compounds and in many inorganic compounds. Symbol: C See **element** for table. **2.** carbon copy (*def. 1*). **3.** piece of carbon paper. [French *carbone* the element, from Latin *carbō* coal.]

carbon 12, most common isotope of carbon, now used instead of oxygen as the standard for determining the atomic weight of chemical elements.

carbon 14, radioactive isotope of carbon, widely used as a tracer element and in radiocarbon dating.

car·bo·na·ceous (kär'bə nā'shəs) *adj.* of, relating to, or containing carbon.

car·bo·na·do (kär'bə nā'dō) *pl.,* **-does.** *n.* very hard crystalline carbon, related to diamond, used in industry for cutting and grinding. [Portuguese *carbonado* literally, carbonated, from *carbone* the element, from French *carbone.* See CARBON.]

carbon arc, arc or discharge of electricity produced in a gap between electrically charged rods of carbon, employed in welding and as a very bright light source for spotlights and movie projectors.

car·bon·ate (*n.,* kär'bə nāt', -nit; *v.,* kär'bə nāt') *n.* salt or ester containing the radical -CO₃. —*v.t.* **-at·ed, -at·ing.** to charge or impregnate (a substance) with carbon dioxide, esp. to dissolve carbon dioxide in (a liquid) to make effervescent.

car·bon·a·tion (kär'bə nā'shən) *n.* **1.** impregnation or saturation with carbon dioxide, esp. in manufacturing soda water. **2.** removal of lime, as in sugar refining, by precipitating it with carbon dioxide.

carbon copy **1.** copy, as of a letter, made by using carbon paper. **2.** close or exact replica; duplicate: *The child's a carbon copy of his father.*

carbon cycle **1.** *Biology.* continual exchange of carbon between living organisms and the earth's atmosphere and water, during which carbon is extracted from the water or air for use by plants and animals and is eventually returned to the water or air through respiration or decomposition. **2.** *Physics.* series of thermonuclear reactions by which hydrogen is transformed into helium through the catalytic action of carbon and nitrogen, releasing great amounts of energy. It is one of the sources of the energy of the sun and other stars.

carbon dioxide, colorless, odorless gas, composed of carbon and oxygen, that is present in the atmosphere and used commercially in soft drinks, fire extinguishers, and, in solid form, as a refrigerating agent. It is exhaled by plants and animals as a waste product and is absorbed by green plants as part of photosynthesis. Formula: CO₂.

carbon disulfide, colorless, flammable, poisonous liquid that is explosive when mixed with air and ignited, used as a solvent and disinfectant. Formula: CS₂.

car·bon·ic (kär bon'ik) *adj.* of, containing, or obtained from carbon.

carbonic acid, weak acid formed when carbon dioxide is dissolved in water. Formula: H₂CO₃.

Car·bon·if·er·ous (kär'bə nif'ər əs) *n.* period of the Paleozoic era during which most of the coal-forming tropical forests flourished. It consists of two subdivisions: Mississippian and Pennsylvanian. See **geology** for table. —*adj.* **1.** of, relating to, or characteristic of this period. **2. carboniferous.** containing carbon or coal. [CARBON + -FEROUS.]

car·bon·i·za·tion (kär'bə ni zā'shən) *n.* act of carbonizing; being carbonized, esp. the conversion of organic matter, as wood, into coal or charcoal.

car·bon·ize (kär'bə nīz') **-ized, iz·ing.** *v.t.* **1.** to change (a substance) into carbon, as by burning. **2.** to cover, treat, or combine (something) with carbon.

carbon monoxide, colorless, odorless, very poisonous gas, formed when carbon burns in an atmosphere lacking sufficient oxygen for complete combustion. Formula: CO

carbon paper, thin paper coated on one side with a preparation of carbon or other inky or coloring substance, that is placed between two sheets of paper to reproduce on the lower sheet any marks made by pressure, as of writing or typing, on the top sheet.

carbon tet·ra·chlo·ride (tet'rə klôr'īd) colorless, poisonous, nonflammable liquid, made from carbon and chlorine, used in refrigerants and propellants, as a cleaning fluid, and in fire extinguishers. Formula: CCl₄

car·bon·yl (kär'bə nil) *n. Chemistry.* radical consisting of a carbon atom joined to an oxygen atom by a double bond, occurring in aldehydes, ketones, and many other classes of compounds.

Car·bo·run·dum (kär'bə run'dəm) *n. Trademark.* any of various abrasives of silicon carbide. [CARBO(N) + (CO)RUNDUM.]

car·box·yl group (kär bok'sil) the radical —COOH, characteristic of organic acids.

car·boy (kär'boi') *n.* large bottle, usually of glass, enclosed in basketwork or a wooden box or crate for protection, used esp. for containing acids and other corrosive liquids: *a ten-gallon carboy.* [Persian *qarābah* large flagon.]

car·bun·cle (kär'bung'kəl) *n.* **1.** hard, painful, pus-filled inflammation under the skin, resembling a boil, but larger and more severe, often accompanied by fever, headache, and loss of appetite. **2.** smooth, deepred garnet cut without facets. [Dialectal Old French *carbuncle* the gem, from Latin *carbunculus* small coal, red gem, tumor, diminutive of *carbō* coal.]

car·bu·ret (kär'bə rāt', -byə rāt', -byə ret') **-ret·ed, ret·ing;** *also, British.* **-ret·ted, -ret·ting.** *v.t.* **1.** to mix (air or gas) with volatile carbon compounds, such as gasoline or benzine. **2.** to combine (a substance) chemically with carbon. [From CARBON.]

car·bu·re·tion (kär'bə rā'shən, -byə-) *n.*

car·bu·re·tor (kär'bə rā'tər, -byə-) *also, British,* **car·bu·ret·tor.** *n.* device in an internal combustion engine which mixes a fine spray of gasoline with air to form a combustible mixture that can be burned in the cylinders of the engine.

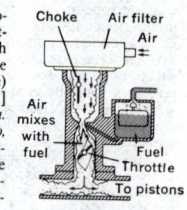

Carburetor

car·cass (kär'kəs) *n.* **1.** dead body of an animal. **2.** body, esp. of a human being. **3.** something from which life, essence, or power is gone; decaying or worthless remains, as the ruined framework of a structure: *The carcass of an old barn stood on the hill.* [French *carcasse;* of uncertain origin.]

car·cin·o·gen (kär sin'ə jən) *n.* substance or agent capable of inducing cancer. —**car·cin·o·gen·ic** (kär sin'ə jen'ik), *adj.*

car·ci·no·ma (kär'sə nō'mə) *pl.,* **-mas** or **-ma·ta** (-mə tə). *n.* any of several types of malignant growths, originating in epithelial tissue, as in the skin, stomach, or breast. [Latin *carcinōma* cancerous ulcer, from Greek *karkinōma.*]

card¹ (kärd) *n.* **1.** flat, usually rectangular piece of stiff paper or thin cardboard, used for various purposes, as for writing down information: *a business card, a membership card. The card was misfiled in the index.* **2.** one of a pack of such pieces, marked with pictures, numbers, or symbols, used in fortunetelling and in playing various games; playing card. **3. cards. a.** games played with such cards, as bridge or poker. **b.** playing of such a game: *I beat him at cards.* **4.** something, as a further resource, useful in attaining an objective; something comparable to a high playing card held during a game. **5.** piece of stiff paper or cardboard, usually ornamented, bearing a message or greeting, as for a particular occasion; greeting card: *an anniversary card, a graduation card. I sent him a card on his birthday.* **6.** post card. **7.** number of articles attached to a piece of cardboard and to be sold as a unit: *a card of buttons.* **8.** program or listing of events or participants, as in racing or boxing. **9.** large, usually rectangular piece of cardboard on which an advertisement or announcement is printed, as for placing in a window. **10.** compass card. **11.** *Informal.* one who is amusing or facetious;

at; āpe; cär; end; mē; it; īce; hot; ōld; fôrk; wood; fool; oil; out; up; ūse; turn; sing; thin; this; zh in treasure; ə in ago, taken, pencil, lemon, circus.

wag. **12. in** (or **on**) **the cards.** likely to happen; possible; impending. **13. to put** (or **lay**) **one's cards on the table.** to reveal something frankly and openly, as one's intentions or resources; be completely straightforward. —*v.t.* to put on a card. [French *carte* piece of stiff paper, playing card, from Latin *charta* paper, leaf of papyrus, from Greek *chartēs* leaf of papyrus, writing. Doublet of CHART.]

card² (kärd) *n.* **1.** textile machine having wire teeth, for combing or brushing matted or loose fibers, removing short fibers, and producing a sliver. **2.** tool or comb having metal or wire teeth, used to separate, comb, or straighten hairs or fibers. —*v.t.* to use a card on, as in preparing wool for spinning. [French *carde* the implement, going back to Latin *cardu(u)s* thistle (used to make a card).] —**card′er,** *n.*

car·da·mom (kär′də məm) *also,* **car·da·mon** (kär′də mən), **car·da·mum.** *n.* **1.** dark-brown, aromatic seed of a plant, *Elettaria cardamomum,* of the ginger family, used whole or ground as a spice in foods and beverages, as in curries and spicy wines. **2.** the plant itself, bearing these seeds in a small greenish-brown capsule. [Latin *cardamōmum* the spice, from Greek *kardamōmon.*]

card·board (kärd′bôrd′) *n.* thin pasteboard or other stiff material made of paper pulp, used to make such items as cartons and boxes.

card catalog, alphabetical file of cards indicating the books and other items in a library collection, each card usually identifying a single item by author, title, or subject.

card file, card index.

cardi-, form of **cardio-** before vowels, as in *cardiac.*

car·di·ac (kär′dē ak′) *adj.* **1.** of, relating to, situated near, or affecting the heart: *a cardiac patient, a cardiac massage.* **2.** of or relating to the esophageal opening of the stomach. —*n.* one who has heart disease. [Latin *cardiacus* relating to the heart, from Greek *kardiakos,* from *kardia* heart.]

cardiac arrest, sudden stoppage of the heart, as from shock, most commonly suffered by patients while undergoing surgery.

cardiac muscle, striated muscle found in the outer wall of the heart. See **muscle** for illustration.

Car·diff (kär′dif) *n.* capital, port, and largest city of Wales. Pop. (1968 est.), 287,500.

car·di·gan (kär′di gən) *n.* sweater that opens down the front like a jacket. [From the Earl of *Cardigan,* 1797–1868, English army officer who popularized it.]

car·di·nal (kär′dən əl) *n.* **1.** in the Roman Catholic Church, one of a number of prelates forming the chief advisory body of the pope, typically wearing rich red robes. Cardinals rank immediately below the pope; at his death, they meet to elect a new one. **2.** crested finch, *Richmondena cardinalis,* native to various parts of North, Central, and South America, the male of which has bright red plumage with a black patch around the bill. **3.** deep, rich red color. **4.** cardinal number. —*adj.* **1.** of primary or fundamental importance; chief; principal. **2.** of the color cardinal. [Latin *cardinālis* chief, that on which something hinges, from *cardō* hinge.]

Cardinal (def. 2)

car·di·nal·ate (kär′dən əl āt′) *n.* **1.** rank, dignity, or term of office of a cardinal. **2.** Sacred College of Cardinals.

cardinal flower 1. trumpet-shaped, bright red flower of any of a group of plants, *Lobelia cardinalis,* that grow wild in damp regions of eastern and central North America. **2.** plant bearing this flower, having lance-shaped leaves.

cardinal number, number that indicates a total or how many, as zero, one, two, and so forth. ▲ **Cardinal** numbers express the result of counting or of operations that depend on counting: *Six times two is twelve. There are three kittens in the box.* **Ordinal** numbers express the order or sequence of counting or of any other way of breaking down a set or collection one by one rather than dealing with its members all at once: *The first kitten is black, the second buff, the third gray.*

cardinal points, four principal directions of the compass: north, south, east, and west.

cardinal sins, seven deadly sins.

cardinal virtues, justice, temperance, prudence (or wisdom), and fortitude (or courage), classified by Plato and considered by ancient philosophers and theologians as the qualities essential to moral excellence. Often distinguished from **theological virtues.**

card index, file or other systematic arrangement of cards on which records or other data, as a listing, are entered. Also, **card file.**

card·ing (kär′ding) *n.* process of preparing textile fibers, as wool, cotton, or flax, for spinning, during which the raw material is passed through rollers and brushes to clean, untangle, and align the fibers.

cardio- *combining form* heart: *cardiogram.* [Greek *kardiā* heart.]

car·di·o·gram (kär′dē ə gram′) *n.* electrocardiogram.

car·di·o·graph (kär′dē ə graf′) *n.* electrocardiograph.

car·di·ol·o·gy (kär′dē ol′ə jē) *n.* study of the heart, its functions, and its diseases. —**car′di·ol′o·gist,** *n.*

car·di·o·vas·cu·lar (kär′dē ō vas′kyə lər) *adj.* of or relating to the heart or blood vessels.

card·sharp (kärd′shärp′) *n.* person, esp. a professional gambler, who cheats at cards. Also, **card′sharp′er, card′shark′** (kärd′shärk′).

care (kãr) *n.* **1.** troubled state of mind, as that arising from anxiety, doubt, or concern; worry; distress. **2.** cause of this: *She acts as though she hasn't a care in the world.* **3.** close and serious attention: *He took great care in compiling the report.* **4.** temporary keeping or charge; supervision; custody: *She was under a doctor's care.* Address the letter *in care of my sister.* **5.** object of concern or attention. —*v.i.,* **cared, caring. 1.** to have or show interest or solicitude; be anxious or concerned: *He cares about his personal appearance. I care about what happens to you.* **2.** to have a liking, fondness, or affection (often with *about*): *I don't care for beets. He cares very much about her.* **3.** to have an inclination; wish; desire: *If you care to, go with them. Would you care to dance?* **4.** to have an objection; mind. ▲ used chiefly in conditional or negative expressions: *He doesn't care if the appointment is canceled.* **5.** to make provision or look out; look after (with *for*): *to care for the aged.* —*v.t.* to have an objection or pay attention to; feel interest, concern, or distress about: *I don't care what people say.* [Old English *caru* grief, trouble, interest.] —**car′er,** *n.*

Syn. *n.* **1. Care, concern, solicitude** indicate a troubled state of mind arising esp. from involvement with the interests of others. **Care** suggests distress because of heavy responsibility or, less often, anxious attention: *a mother's face worn with care for her sickly child.* **Concern** stresses involvement or interest: *concern for the country's future, his concern for the underprivileged.* **Solicitude** suggests sympathetic attentiveness: *the solicitude with which she attended to her needs after she left the hospital.*

CARE, Cooperative for American Relief Everywhere, Inc., nonprofit, voluntary American agency that distributes food, funds, and goods to the needy in other countries, founded after World War II as the Cooperative for American Remittances to Europe.

ca·reen (kə rēn′) *v.i.* **1.** to sway from side to side while moving, as if out of control; lurch: *The car careened around the corner.* **2.** to list or lean to one side: *The schooner careened as her sails caught the wind.* —*v.t.* **1.** to turn (a ship) over on one side in order to clean, caulk, or repair the bottom. **2.** to cause to list or lean to one side. [Middle French *carène* keel of a ship, going back to Latin *carīna.*]

ca·reer (kə rēr′) *n.* **1.** occupation or profession, esp. as followed by one's lifework; calling; vocation: *a career in medicine. She chose acting as her career.* **2.** course of action or progress through life, or some portion of it, esp. as related to some remarkable activity or pursuit. **3.** rushing course or speed: *The horse stumbled in full career.* —*v.i.* to move or run with a swift, headlong motion; rush or dash along. [French *carrière* racecourse, course, profession, going back to Late Latin *carrāria (via)* (road) for carriages, from Latin *carrus* wagon.]

care·free (kãr′frē′) *adj.* free from care or worry; untroubled; happy-go-lucky; lighthearted.

care·ful (kãr′fəl) *adj.* **1.** marked by thoughtful prudence and attention; watchfully cautious; mindful; wary: *Be careful not to trip. He was careful not to reveal the secret.* **2.** done or made with thought, thoroughness, or attention to detail; painstaking: *careful research, a careful analysis of the problem.* **3.** taking pains with or attentive to one's work; thorough. **4.** *Archaic.* anxious; worried. —**care′ful·ly,** *adv.* —**care′-ful·ness,** *n.*

Syn. 1. Careful, meticulous, punctilious mean showing close attention to details in one's performance. **Careful** stresses the exercise of caution to avoid errors or sloppiness: *She was a careful typist who checked her work before sending it out.* **Meticulous** suggests finicky attention stemming from fear of making an error: *a meticulous researcher who verified every date twice.* **Punctilious** suggests extreme attention to small details: *punctilious handwriting in which every "t" is crossed, every "i" dotted.*

care·less (kãr′lis) *adj.* **1.** not paying enough attention or exercising enough caution; not watchful: *to be careless in crossing the street.* **2.** resulting from or done with a lack of care, attentiveness, or thoughtfulness: *a careless mistake.* **3.** not caring or troubling; unconcerned; indifferent: *He's careless about his appearance.* **4.** artless; unstudied; effortless: *careless grace.* **5.** carefree: *a careless existence.* —**care′-less·ly,** *adv.* —**care′less·ness,** *n.*

ca·ress (kə res′) *v.t.* **1.** to touch or stroke gently and lovingly; fondle; pet: *The child caressed her kitten.* **2.** to touch soothingly, as if with affection: *The music caressed her ears.* —*n.* **1.** gentle, loving touch or stroke: *He gave the pony a caress.* **2.** light, soothing touch: *the soft caress of the breeze.* [French *caresse* stroking, fondling, from Italian *carezza,* going back to Latin *carus* dear.]

car·et (kar′it) *n.* mark (∧) used, as in editing, to indicate where something should be inserted, as in *the boy ∧ away.* [Latin *caret* it is lacking.]

the boy ∧ away. (*ran* shown above the caret)

care·tak·er (kâr′tā′kər) *n.* one who takes care of a person, place, or thing; custodian, esp. of a building, property, or estate.

care·worn (kâr′wôrn′) *adj.* showing signs of having undergone anxiety, worry, or distress: *a careworn face.*

car·fare (kär′fâr′) *n.* passenger fare, as on a streetcar or bus.

car·go (kär′gō) *pl.,* **-goes** or **-gos.** *n.* **1.** goods and merchandise carried by a ship, plane, or vehicle; freight. **2.** load. [Spanish *cargo* load, burden, from *cargar* to load, from Late Latin *carricāre,* from Latin *carrus* two-wheeled wagon; of Celtic origin.] —**Syn. 2.** see **load.**

car·hop (kär′hop′) *n.* waitress or waiter at a drive-in restaurant.

Car·ib (kar′ib) *n.* **1.** member of one of several Indian tribes who live in the West Indies and northeastern South America. **2.** family of South American Indian languages that are spoken predominantly in the West Indies and northeastern South America. [Spanish *caribe;* of Carib origin.]

Car·ib·be·an (kar′ə bē′ən, kə rib′ē-) *n.* **1.** sea bounded on the north and east by the West Indies, on the west by Central America, and on the south by South America. Also, **Caribbean Sea. 2. the Caribbean.** region consisting of this sea and those lands in and around it. —*adj.* **1.** of or relating to the Caribbean. **2.** of or relating to the Caribs, their language, or their culture.

car·i·bou (kar′ə bōō′) *pl.,* **-bous** or **-bou.** *n.* any of a group of large deer, genus *Rangifer,* native to the northern regions of the world, having a coarse, heavy coat and large antlers. The doe, unlike all other female deer, bears antlers. The Eurasian caribou, *R. tarandus,* is commonly called the reindeer. Caribou are valued for their hide, meat, and milk and as draft animals. [French *caribou;* of Algonquian origin.]

car·i·ca·ture (kar′ə bē′ən, kə rib′ē-) *n.* **1.** pictorial or descriptive representation that ridiculously exaggerates or distorts the characteristics or striking features of a person or thing. **2.** art or process of making such representations. **3.** something so distorted or inferior as to seem a ludicrous imitation; poor or inept likeness or copy. —*v.t.,* **-tured, tur·ing.** to make a caricature of; represent so as to make ridiculous. [French *caricature* satirical picture, from Italian *caricatura* literally, a loading, from *caricare* to load, going back to Latin *carrus* two-wheeled wagon; of Celtic origin; because such a picture was loaded to excess or exaggerated.] —**car′i·ca·tur·ist,** *n.*

Syn. *n.* **1.** Caricature, burlesque, parody refer to renderings of a work of art, public figure, or the like that are intended to poke fun or to satirize. **Caricature** implies exaggeration of the salient features of the subject: *His caricatures of the candidates seemed to catch the essence of the man in every case.* **Burlesque** suggests an attempt to deflate by broad or riotous humor: *The best skit was a burlesque of a solemn business convention.* In precise use, **parody** refers to a satirical imitation of a writer's style or other mannerisms, esp. when the subject is changed so as to make it absurd. Ordinarily, however, the word applies to any written or spoken imitation whose object is to ridicule: *a clever parody of the typical television commercial.*

car·ies (kâr′ēz, -ē ēz) *n.,pl.* decay of the teeth, often resulting in inflammation of the dental pulp if left untreated. Also, **dental caries.** [Latin *cariēs* rottenness.]

car·il·lon (kar′ə lon′, -lən) *n.* **1.** set of stationary bells sounded by means of a keyboard or by machinery. **2.** melody played on a carillon. **3.** organ stop that produces a sound like that of a carillon. [French *carillon* chime, musical bells, going back to Late Latin *quaterniō* group of four, originally, a group of four bells.]

car·il·lon·neur (kar′ə lə noor′) *n.* one who plays a carillon.

car·i·ole (kar′ē ōl′) *also,* **car·ri·ole.** *n.* **1.** small, open carriage designed to be drawn by one horse. **2.** light, covered cart. [French *cariole,* from Italian *carriuola* wheelbarrow, from *carro* cart, from Latin *carrus* two-wheeled wagon; of Celtic origin.]

car·i·ous (kâr′ē əs) *adj.* having caries; decayed. [Latin *cariōsus* rotten.]

cark·ing (kär′king) *adj.* Archaic. troublesome; annoying; distressing. [From obsolete *cark* burden, distress (from Anglo-Norman *kark* burden, weight, going back to Late Latin *carricāre* to load, from Latin *carrus* two-wheeled wagon; of Celtic origin) + -ING[1].]

carl (kärl) *also,* **carle.** *n.* Archaic. **1.** peasant; rustic. **2.** boor; churl. [Old Norse *karl* man.]

car·load (kär′lōd′) *n.* amount that a car, as a railroad freight car, can hold or carry.

Car·lo·vin·gi·an (kär′lə vin′jē ən) Carolingian.

Carls·bad (kärlz′bad′) *n.* Karlovy Vary.

Carlsbad Caverns, largest-known network of underground caverns in the world, in southeastern New Mexico.

Carls·ruh·e (kärlz′rōō′ə) Karlsruhe.

Car·lyle, Thomas (kär līl′) 1795–1881, Scottish essayist, historian, and social philosopher.

car·ma·gnole (kär′mən yōl′) *n.* **1.** lively dance and song popular during the French Revolution of 1789. **2.** costume worn by French revolutionists, consisting of a short jacket with wide lapels and metal buttons, a red cap, black pantaloons, and a tricolored girdle. [French *carmagnole,* from *Carmagnola,* town in Piedmont, Italy, where the jacket of the costume originated.]

Car·mel, Mount (kär mel′, kär′məl) short, mountainous ridge in northern Israel, meeting the Mediterranean near Haifa.

Car·mel·ite (kär′mə līt′) *n.* member of a religious order of friars and nuns founded in Palestine in the twelfth century. —*adj.* of or relating to the Carmelites or their order.

car·min·a·tive (kär min′ə tiv, kär′mə nā′tiv) *n.* any agent that expels gas from the stomach and intestines. —*adj.* having the power to expel gas from the stomach and intestines. [Latin *carminātus,* past participle of *carmināre* to card wool, purify + -IVE.]

car·mine (kär′mən, -mīn) *n.* **1.** deep-red or purplish-red color; crimson. **2.** crimson pigment obtained from the dye cochineal. [French *carmin,* from Medieval Latin *carminium* the crimson pigment, from blend of Arabic *qirmizī* crimson, and Latin *minium* red lead. See CRIMSON, MINIUM.]

car·nage (kär′nij) *n.* **1.** extensive and bloody slaughter, as in battle; massacre. **2.** Archaic. dead bodies, as of soldiers. [French *carnage* slaughter, going back to Latin *carō* flesh, meat.]

car·nal (kärn′əl) *adj.* **1.** relating to or characterized by bodily passions and appetites; sensual: *carnal pleasures.* **2.** sexual: *carnal knowledge.* **3.** not spiritual; worldly. [Latin *carnālis,* from *carō* flesh.] —**car·nal·i·ty** (kär nal′ə tē), *n.* —**car′nal·ly,** *adv.*

car·na·tion (kär nā′shən) *n.* **1.** fragrant flower of any of a large group of plants, *Dianthus caryophyllus,* cultivated commercially and as a garden flower. The varieties differ greatly in size, shape, and color. **2.** plant bearing this flower, having grayish-green grasslike leaves. **3.** light red color. [French *carnation,* from Italian *carnagione* flesh, flesh color, going back to Latin *carō* flesh; because the flower was originally flesh-colored.]

Car·ne·gie, Andrew (kär nā′gē, kär′nə-) 1835–1919, U.S. steel manufacturer and philanthropist.

Carnation

car·nel·ian (kär nēl′yən) *also,* **cor·nel·ian.** *n.* semiprecious stone made of chalcedony of a red to reddish-orange variety. [Modification (influenced by Latin *carō* flesh) of CORNELIAN, from Old French *corneline,* from *corne* a kind of cherry, going back to Latin *cornum;* because of the stone's color.]

car·ni·val (kär′nə vəl) *n.* **1.** amusement show, usually one that travels, having rides, side shows, games, and refreshments. **2.** any merrymaking, revelry, or festival, as a program of entertainment or sports: *the winter carnival.* **3.** *also,* **Carnival.** period of feasting and merrymaking immediately preceding Lent, varying from three days to a few weeks and observed esp. in countries with large Roman Catholic populations. [Italian *carnevale* Shrovetide, from Medieval Latin *carnelevarium* Shrovetide, removal of meat (during Lent), from Latin *carō* flesh + *levāre* to raise, take away.]

car·ni·vore (kär′nə vôr′) *n.* any of numerous mammals constituting the order Carnivora, including dogs, lions, bears, and weasels, having long, daggerlike canine teeth and sharp claws. Although most carnivores feed chiefly on flesh, many also eat other things and some are omnivorous. Many flesh-eating animals, as birds of prey, sharks, and human beings, are not carnivores.

car·niv·o·rous (kär niv′ər əs) *adj.* **1.** flesh-eating. **2.** of or relating to carnivores. [Latin *carnivorus* feeding on flesh.] —**car·niv′o·rous·ly,** *adv.* —**car·niv′o·rous·ness,** *n.*

car·no·tite (kär′nə tīt′) *n.* yellowish, radioactive mineral found predominantly in southwestern Colorado. It is a source of uranium. [From Adolphe Carnot, 1839–1920, French mining engineer.]

car·ob (kar′əb) *n.* **1.** evergreen tree, *Ceratonia siliqua,* native to the eastern Mediterranean, but cultivated in many warm regions for its edible pod. **2.** St. John's bread. [Middle French *carobe* this evergreen tree, going back to Arabic *kharrūb* bean pod.]

car·ol (kar′əl) *n.* song of joy or praise, esp. a Christmas song or hymn. —*v.i.,* **-oled, -ol·ing;** *also, British,* **-olled, -ol·ling. 1.** to sing Christmas carols in a group. **2.** to sing, esp. in a lively, joyous manner; warble. —*v.t.* **1.** to sing (something) joyously. **2.** to celebrate or praise in song. [Old French *carole* round dance, through Latin, from Greek *choraulēs* flute player who accompanied a choral dance.] —**car′ol·er;** *also, British,* **car′ol·ler,** *n.*

Car·o·li·na (kar′ə lī′nə) *n.* **1.** former British colony on the southern Atlantic coast of America, divided into North Carolina and South Carolina in 1729. **2. the Carolinas.** North Carolina and South Carolina.

Car·o·line Islands (kar′ə līn′, -lin) archipelago in the western Pacific, north of New Guinea, administered by the United States. Land area, approx. 460 sq. mi. Pop. (1963), 57,452.

Car·o·lin·gi·an (kar′ə lin′jē ən) *adj.* of or relating to the dynasty

at; āpe; cär; end; mē; it; īce; hot; ōld; fôrk; wood; fōōl; oil; out; up; ūse; turn; sing; thin; this; zh in treasure; ə in ago, taken, pencil, lemon, circus.

that ruled in France from A.D. 751 to 987, in Germany from A.D. 751 to 911, in Italy from A.D. 751 to 887, and that reached its greatest prominence under Charlemagne. —*n.* sovereign or member of Carolingian family or dynasty. Also, **Car′lo·vin′gi·an.**

Car·o·lin·i·an (kar′ə lin′ē ən) *adj.* of or relating to North Carolina or South Carolina or both. —*n.* native or inhabitant of North Carolina or South Carolina.

car·om (kar′əm) *also,* **car·rom.** *n.* **1.** *Billiards.* shot in which the cue ball strikes two other balls in succession. **2.** any strike and rebound. —*v.i.* **1.** to make a carom. **2.** to strike and rebound. [French *carambole* 'red ball in billiards, from Spanish *carambola* a round and orange-colored fruit, red ball in billiards; of uncertain origin.]

car·o·tene (kar′ə tēn′) *n.* orange-yellow hydrocarbon out of which the liver manufactures vitamin A, occurring as a pigment in eggs, butter, and certain vegetables, such as carrots and sweet potatoes; provitamin A. [Latin *carōt(a)* carrot + -ENE. See CARROT.]

ca·rot·id (kə rot′id) *n.* either of two large arteries, one on each side of the neck, that carry blood to the head. Also, **carotid artery.** —*adj.* of, relating to, or near these arteries. [Greek *karōtides* carotid arteries, from *karoun* to stupefy; because compressing them was formerly thought to cause stupor.]

ca·rous·al (kə rou′zəl) *n.* boisterous or uproarious drinking party; noisy, drunken, jovial banquet or revel.

ca·rouse (kə rouz′) **-roused, -rous·ing.** *v.i.* to drink freely and heavily; take part in a carousal. —*n.* carousal. [Old French *carous* all out, from German *garaus (trinken)* (to drink) completely out, all out (in the sense of "emptying one's cup").] —**ca·rous′er,** *n.*

car·ou·sel (kar′ə sel′, -zel′) *also,* **car·rou·sel.** *n.* merry-go-round *(def. 1).* [French *carrousel,* Italian *carosello;* of uncertain origin.]

carp[1] (kärp) *v.i.* to find fault or complain, esp. petulantly or unreasonably (often with *at*): *A boss who carps at small errors.* [Old Norse *karpa* to brag; meaning probably influenced by Latin *carpere* to pluck.] —**carp′er,** *n.*

carp[2] (kärp) *pl.,* **carps** or **carp.** *n.* **1.** freshwater fish, *Cyprinus carpio,* popular as a food fish, esp. in the Far East and in Europe where it is bred and raised as a delicacy. Length: 2 feet. **2.** any of a group of similar or related fish, including goldfish, minnows, chub, and dace. [Old French *carpe,* from Late Latin *carpa;* possibly of Germanic origin.]

car·pal (kär′pəl) *adj.* of, relating to, or near the wrist. —*n.* bone of the wrist. See **hand** for illustration. [Modern Latin *carpalis,* from Greek *karpos* wrist.]

Car·pa·thi·an Mountains (kär pā′thē ən) mountain system in central and eastern Europe, extending in an arc from southwestern Czechoslovakia to central Romania. Also, **Car·pa′thi·ans.**

car·pe di·em (kär′pē dī′em) *Latin.* take advantage of or make the most of the present; enjoy today.

car·pel (kär′pəl) *n.* pistil or a component of a compound pistil. [French *carpelle,* from Greek *karpos* fruit.]

car·pen·ter (kär′pən tər) *n.* one who builds and repairs wooden parts and structures, as a house or its framework. —*v.i.* to do a carpenter's work; work as a carpenter. —*v.t.* to make or repair by or as if by carpentry. [Old French *carpentier* worker in wood, from Late Latin *carpentārius* carriage maker, going back to Latin *carpentum* carriage; of Celtic origin.]

car·pen·try (kär′pən trē) *n.* **1.** business, trade, or work of a carpenter. **2.** work produced by a carpenter.

car·pet (kär′pit) *n.* **1.** floor covering made of heavy, often woven or felted, fabric. **2.** fabric used for it. **3.** any covering, surface, or expanse resembling a carpet: *a carpet of leaves, a carpet of flowers.* **4. on the carpet.** before an authority for a reproof or reprimand: *He was called on the carpet for his negligence.* —*v.t.* to cover or furnish with or as with a carpet: *to carpet a room.* [Medieval Latin *carpita* a thick cloth, probably from Latin *carpere* to pluck, spin (wool).]

car·pet·bag (kär′pit bag′) *n.* formerly, satchel or bag for traveling, esp. one made of carpeting. —*v.i.* **-bagged, -bag·ging.** to act as a carpetbagger.

car·pet·bag·ger (kär′pit bag′ər) *n.* **1.** any Northerner who went to the South immediately after the Civil War, esp. one who sought to gain political or other advantages from the disorganized conditions then prevailing in the Southern states. **2.** person taking up residence in a place seeking to gain advantages for himself, esp. one who interferes with the politics of a locality with which he is thought to have no permanent or genuine connection. [CARPETBAG + -ER[1]; because many of these Northerners came South carrying clothes in carpetbags.]

carpet beetle, any of a group of small beetles, order Coleoptera, whose larvae destroy carpets, fur, and woolen goods.

car·pet·ing (kär′pi ting) *n.* **1.** fabric used for carpets. **2.** carpets collectively.

carpet sweeper, mechanical device for cleaning carpets and rugs that, when pushed, rotates a brush that sweeps dirt from the surface into an attached dustpan.

carp·ing (kär′ping) *adj.* tending to carp; overly critical; faultfinding. —**carp′ing·ly,** *adv.*

car·port (kär′pôrt′) *n.* shelter for an automobile, usually a roof projecting from the side of a building.

car·pus (kär′pəs) *pl.,* **-pi** (-pī). *n.* bones of the wrist collectively; wrist. [Modern Latin *carpus* wrist, from Greek *karpos.*]

car·rack (kar′ək) *n.* large three-masted ship developed in the fourteenth century. [Old French *carraque* small ship, going back to Arabic *qarārqīr* merchant ships.]

Car·ra·ra (kə rär′ə) *n.* city in northwestern Italy, noted for its white marble. Pop. (1961), 64,901.

car·rel (kar′əl) *also,* **car·rell.** *n.* small enclosure or partitioned area for individual study, near the stacks in a library. [Modification of Middle English *carole* round dance, ring, enclosed place, from Old French *carole* round dance. See CAROL.]

car·riage (kar′ij) *n.* **1.** wheeled, usually horse-drawn vehicle designed to carry persons. **2.** light, wheeled vehicle for a baby, designed to be pushed by a person on foot; perambulator. **3.** manner of carrying or holding the head and body: *He has a stately carriage.* **4.** movable part of a machine that carries or supports some other part: *the carriage of a typewriter.* **5.** act of carrying or transporting; conveyance. **6.** cost or price of transportation. [Dialectal Old French *cariage* something carried, from *carier* to carry. See CARRY.] —**Syn. 3.** see **bearing.**

carriage trade, wealthy or upper-class patrons, as of a theater, restaurant, or other establishment. [Because they formerly drove up in private carriages.]

car·ri·er (kar′ē ər) *n.* **1.** person or organization whose business it is to carry or transport something. Railroad and trucking companies and shipping lines are carriers. **2.** commercial or military vehicle used to carry or transport something: *a troop carrier.* **3.** that which acts as a medium or device in or on which something is carried: *The blood serves as a carrier of oxygen to the cells.* **4.** any organism that carries or transmits an infectious disease, often without contracting it. **5.** carrier wave. **6.** aircraft carrier.

carrier pigeon 1. homing pigeon used to carry messages. **2.** pigeon of a variety developed in England, having a straight thick beak, long wattles, and plumage that is usually dark or grayish-brown. Originally bred for its homing instinct. The carrier pigeon is now used only for show purposes.

carrier wave, wave which can be modulated and carries signals to be transmitted, as through a radio system.

car·ri·ole (kar′ē ōl′) *n.* cariole.

car·ri·on (kar′ē ən) *n.* dead and putrifying flesh. [Anglo-Norman *caroine* carcass, going back to Latin *carō* flesh.]

carrion crow 1. black crow, *Corvus corone,* of Europe. **2.** black vulture, *Coragyps atratus,* of the southern United States.

Car·roll, Lewis (kar′əl) 1832–98, English author; born Charles L. Dodgson.

car·rom (kar′əm) *n.* carom.

car·rot (kar′ət) *n.* **1.** fleshy root of a plant, *Daucus carota,* of the parsley family, eaten as a vegetable. **2.** the plant itself. [Middle French *carote,* from Latin *carōta,* from Greek *karōton.*]

car·rot·y (kar′ə tē) *adj.* resembling a carrot in color; orange-red.

car·rou·sel (kar′ə sel′, -zel′) *n.* carousel.

car·ry (kar′ē) **-ried, -ry·ing.** *v.t.* **1.** to move while bearing the weight of; transport: *She carried the child upstairs.* **2.** to serve as a means of conveyance or transmission for: *Air carries sound waves. The messenger carried the messages.* **3.** to have on one's person: *He always carries a pen.* **4.** to have as an attribute, property, or mark: *His opinion carried great weight.* **5.** to bear the weight or burden of; sustain: *Pillars carried the upper floor.* **6.** to continue or extend (something) in a particular direction or to a certain point: *The engineers carried the highway across the marshland. He carried his political opinions into his business life.* **7.** to keep in stock, as for sale; deal in: *That store carries stationery supplies.* **8.** to pass or adopt (a motion or bill): *The motion was carried on the first vote.* **9.** to be successful or victorious in; win or capture: *He carried all of the Southern states in the election.* **10.** to transfer and add, as a number or total from one column or page to another. **11.** to cause to go or come; impel: *The hurricane carried the ship off course.* **12.** to sing (a melody or part) correctly: *to carry a tune.* **13.** to hold (one's body or a part of it) in a certain way: *The queen carried herself regally.* **14.** to have as a consequence or result: *The crime carries a three-year prison term.* **15.** to be pregnant with: *The mare is carrying a foal.* **16.** to extend credit to and maintain on one's account books in hope of future payment. —*v.i.* **1.** to exert projecting or propelling force for a distance: *The arrow carried for twenty yards. The actress′ voice carried well.* **2.** to be approved by vote: *The civil rights bill carried by a large majority.* **3.** to act as a bearer or carrier.

to carry away. to arouse great emotional reaction in; enthuse.

to carry forward. a. to transfer, as a total or item, to another column or page. **b.** to make progress or proceed with.

at; āpe; cär; end; mē; it; īce; hot; ōld; fôrk; wood; fōōl; oil; out; up; ūse; turn; sing; thin; this; zh in treasure; ə in ago, taken, pencil, lemon, circus.

151

to carry off. a. to win, as a prize or honor. **b.** to accomplish or do (something): *The thieves succeeded in carrying off the robbery.* **c.** to cause to die; kill.

to carry on. a. to keep up; keep going; continue. **b.** to engage in; manage; conduct. **c.** *Informal.* to behave in a wild, foolish, or silly manner.

to carry out. a. to obey; execute: *The soldier carried out his orders promptly.* **b.** to bring to completion; accomplish.

to carry over. a. to transfer, as an item or total, to another column or page. **b.** to set aside; postpone.

to carry through. a. to accomplish; complete. **b.** to bring through difficulties or trouble; sustain.

—*n. pl.* **-ries. 1.** range or distance covered or traveled by something, as by a gun or projectile. **2.** portage, as between navigable bodies of water. [Dialectal Old French *carier* to convey in a vehicle, from Late Latin *carricāre* to load (as a wagon), from Latin *carrus* two-wheeled wagon. Doublet of CHARGE.]

Syn. *v.t.* **1. Carry, bear¹, convey, transport** mean to move objects or people from one place to another. **Carry** is the general word: *She carried the suitcase into the house.* **Bear** stresses the importance or dignity of what is carried: *The carriage bore the royal couple to church.* **Convey** is used to suggest continuous movement through a medium: *Pipelines convey natural gas to the city.* **Transport** applies to the movement of persons or goods in bulk and strongly implies a destination: *The airliner transported his platoon to Vietnam. Trucks transported eggs to market.*

car·ry·all¹ (kar′ē ôl′) *n.* covered, lightweight, one-horse carriage for several persons. [Modification of CARIOLE.]

car·ry·all² (kar′ē ôl′) *n.* large handbag or basket. [CARRY + ALL.]

carrying charge, interest or other charge added to the cost of an item bought on an installment plan.

car·ry·o·ver (kar′ē ō′vər) *n.* **1.** something retained or remaining: *His interest in stamps is a carry-over from his childhood.* **2.** amount carried forward in an account book.

car·sick (kär′sik′) *adj.* nauseated from riding in a car, train, or bus. —**car′sick′ness,** *n.*

Car·son, Kit (kär′sən; kit) 1809–68, U.S. frontiersman and scout.

Carson City, capital of Nevada, in the western part of the state. Pop. (1970), 15,468.

cart (kärt) *n.* **1.** sturdy two-wheeled vehicle, usually drawn by horses or mules, for conveying heavy loads. **2.** small, wheeled vehicle moved manually; pushcart. **3.** light two-wheeled carriage. **4. to put the cart before the horse,** to reverse the proper order; do or say something backwards. —*v.t.* to carry in or as in a cart. [Partly from Old English *cræt* chariot; partly from Old Norse *kartr* a two-wheeled vehicle.]

cart·age (kär′tij) *n.* **1.** act of carting. **2.** rate charged for this.

Car·ta·ge·na (kär′tə jē′nə) *n.* **1.** port city in northwestern Colombia. Pop. (1969), 229,040. **2.** port city in southeastern Spain. Pop. (1970), 144,316.

carte blanche (kärt′ blänch′, bläNsh′) *pl.,* **cartes blanches** (kärt′ blän′chiz, bläNsh′). *n.* complete authority or freedom of action or judgment. [French *carte blanche* literally, white card (with a signature above which anything may be written). See CARD¹, BLANK.]

car·tel (kär tel′, kär′təl) *n.* **1.** international syndicate or trust of commercial enterprises formed to establish a monopoly by controlling prices and production. **2.** written agreement between warring nations, as for the exchange of prisoners. **3.** written challenge to a duel. [French *cartel,* from Italian *cartello* written challenge, placard, diminutive of *carta* sheet of paper, from *c(h)arta* paper. See CARD¹.]

Car·ter, Jimmy (kär′tər) 1924– , thirty-ninth president of the United States, since 1977. His full name is **James Earl Carter.**

Car·te·sian (kär tē′zhən) *adj.* of or relating to Descartes, or to his philosophy or mathematical methods. —*n.* follower of Descartes, or of his philosophy or mathematical methods. [From *Cartesius.* Latinized form of *Descartes* + -AN.]

Cartesian coordinate system, system of coordinates that locates a point in a plane by its distance from each of two perpendicular lines at right angles to each other.

Car·thage (kär′thij) *n.* ancient city and state in North Africa, on the site of modern Tunisia, founded by the Phoenicians and destroyed by the Romans in 146 B.C.

Car·tha·gin·i·an (kär′thə jin′ē ən) *adj.* of or relating to Carthage, its people, or its civilization. —*n.* member of the people inhabiting ancient Carthage.

Car·thu·sian (kär thoo′zhən) *n.* member of a religious order of monks and nuns, founded in France in 1084. —*adj.* relating to this order. [From *Carthusia,* Latinized form of *Chartreuse,* French town where the first monastery of this order was located + -AN.]

Car·ti·er, Jacques (kär′tē ā′; zhäk) 1491–1557, French navigator who discovered the St. Lawrence River.

car·ti·lage (kär′təl ij) *n.* **1.** tough, flexible connective tissue in the skeletal structure of man and other vertebrates; gristle. **2.** part or struc-

ture formed of cartilage. See **nose** for illustration. [French *cartilage,* gristle, from Latin *cartilāgō.*]

car·ti·lag·i·nous (kär′əl aj′ə nəs) *adj.* **1.** of or resembling cartilage. **2.** having a skeleton consisting mostly of cartilage.

cart·load (kärt′lōd′) *n.* amount that a cart holds or can hold.

car·tog·ra·pher (kär tog′rə fər) *n.* one who makes or compiles maps or charts.

car·tog·ra·phy (kär tog′rə fē) *n.* art and science of making or compiling maps or charts. [French *carte* map, card¹ + -GRAPHY. See CARD¹.]

car·ton (kärt′ən) *n.* **1.** container made of any of several materials, as cardboard or plastic: *an egg carton, a carton of groceries.* **2.** amount that a carton holds or can hold: *a carton of milk.* [French *carton* pasteboard, from Italian *cartone,* from *carta* paper, from Latin *charta.* See CARD¹.]

car·toon (kär tōōn′) *n.* **1.** sketch or drawing, as in a magazine or periodical, depicting a humorous situation or satirizing some person or subject of public interest. **2.** animated cartoon. **3.** comic strip. **4.** full-size preliminary drawing of a design or picture, to be copied in or transferred to a fresco, mosaic, tapestry, mural painting, or stained glass. [French *carton* pasteboard. See CARTON.] —**car·toon′ist,** *n.*

car·tridge (kär′trij) *n.* **1.** cylindrical case, as of metal or paper, usually containing a percussion cap, a propelling charge of gunpowder, and a bullet. **2.** roll of camera film enclosed in a protective case which fits into a camera as a unit. **3.** device that holds a phonograph needle and transforms its vibrations into an electric current as the needle follows the groove of a record. **4.** small container, designed for easy replacement as a unit, as in a pen or tube. **5.** case designed to hold magnetic tape for easy insertion into a tape player. [Modification of French *cartouche* roll of paper, the cylindrical case for firearms, from Italian *cartoccio,* from *carta* paper, from Latin *charta.* See CARD¹.]

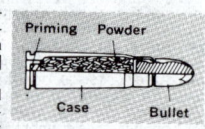

Priming Powder

Case Bullet

Cartridge

cart·wheel (kärt′hwēl′, -wēl′) *n.* sideways handspring.

Cart·wright, Ed·mund (kärt′rīt′) 1743–1823, English clergyman who invented the power-driven loom.

Ca·ru·so, En·ri·co (kə rōō′sō; en rē′kō) 1873–1921, Italian operatic tenor.

carve (kärv) **carved, carv·ing.** *v.t.* **1.** to cut, esp. meat, into slices or pieces: *Father carved the turkey.* **2.** to make or shape by or as by cutting (often with *out*): *He carved a doll from a block of wood. They carved a new nation out of the wilderness. He carved out a career for himself.* **3.** to adorn, as with figures or designs; decorate by cutting: *The chest was carved with many figures.* —*v.i.* to cut meat into slices or pieces. [Old English *ceorfan* to cut.]

car·ven (kär′vən) *adj. Archaic.* carved.

carv·er (kär′vər) *n.* **1.** one who carves. **2.** knife used for carving.

Car·ver, George Washington (kär′vər) 1864–1943, American botanist and educator.

carv·ing (kär′ving) *n.* **1.** carved work, as a figure or design. **2.** act or art of one who carves.

carving knife, knife used for carving.

car·y·at·id (kar′ē at′id) *pl.,* **-ids** or **-i·des** (-ə dēz). *n.* statue of a draped female figure serving as a column. [Latin *caryātidēs* (plural), from Greek *Karyátides* (plural).]

ca·sa·ba (kə sä′bə) *also,* **cas·sa·ba.** *n.* muskmelon having a creamy white pulp. Also, **casaba melon.** [From *Kasaba,* Turkey, famous for this kind of melon.]

Cas·a·blan·ca (kas′ə blang′kə, kä′sə bläng′kə) *n.* largest city and chief port of Morocco, in the northwestern part of the country. Pop. (1969), 1,320,000.

cas·cade (kas kād′) *n.* **1.** small waterfall; series of such waterfalls. **2.** anything resembling this: *a cascade of ruffles.* —*v.i.* **-cad·ed, -cad·ing.** to fall or flow in or as in a cascade. [French *cascade* waterfall, from Italian *cascata,* going back to Latin *cāsus* a falling.]

Cascade Range, mountain range in the northwestern United States and southwestern Canada. Also, **Cas·cades′.**

cas·car·a sa·gra·da (kas kär′ə sə grä′də) *n.* **1.** North American tree, *Rhamnus purshiana,* of the buckthorn family, bearing black, berry-like fruits, and having reddish-brown bark, used for making a laxative. **2.** the laxative itself, an extract prepared from dried strips of bark of this tree. Also, **cas·car′a.**

case¹ (kās) *n.* **1.** specific example or occurrence: *We are dealing with a case of negligence.* **2.** actual state of affairs or circumstances: *If that's the case, then we must go.* **3.** instance of a disease or injury: *The doctor treated many cases of the flu.* **4.** one who has a disease or injury; patient. **5.** statement, as of arguments or reasons: *He presented his case for the*

at; āpe; cär; end; mē; it; īce; hot; ōld; fôrk; wood; fōōl; oil; out; up; ūse; turn; sing; thin; this; zh in treasure; ə in ago, taken, pencil, lemon, circus.

proposed legislation. **6.** matter or problem: *His is a difficult case to handle.* **7.a.** action or suit brought before a court of law for decision. **b.** statement of facts or circumstances presented for consideration by a court of law. **8.a.** one of the various inflectional forms of a noun, pronoun, or adjective, used to indicate its syntactical relation to other words in a sentence through word ending or position. **b.** any such relation shown by inflection or other means. **c.** such relationships or forms collectively. **9.** *Informal.* peculiar or remarkable person. **10. in any case.** no matter what happens; anyhow; regardless. **11. in case.** in the event that; if: *In case anything happens, call me immediately.* **12. in case of.** in the event of: *In case of emergency, use the back exit to get out.* —*v.t.,* **cased, cas·ing.** *Informal.* to look over carefully, esp. with criminal intent: *He cased the store before robbing it.* [Old French *cas* chance, event, from Latin *cāsus* a falling, chance.]

case² (kās) *n.* **1.** something designed to contain, enclose, or protect: *a camera case.* **2.** box and its contents; amount contained in a case: *We ordered three cases of soda for the party.* **3.** frame, as of a window. **4.** *Printing.* shallow tray divided into compartments, used for holding type. —*v.t.,* **cased, cas·ing.** to put in or cover with a case; encase. [Dialectal Old French *casse* box, chest, from Latin *capsa*.]

case·hard·en (kās′härd′ən) *v.t.* **1.** to harden (iron or steel) on the surface, allowing the interior to remain ductile. **2.** to make (someone) callous or unfeeling.

case history, record of or report on a person or group. It is prepared for the purposes of study, diagnosis, or treatment of some physical, mental, or social problem or disorder. Also, **case study.**

ca·sein (kā′sēn, -sē in) *n.* **1.** chief protein present in milk, which forms, when coagulated by rennet, the basis of cheese, and, when precipitated, is used in the manufacture of paints, plastics, and adhesives. **2.** paint made from the curd of sour milk, producing a dull finish. [Latin *cāseus* cheese + -IN¹.]

case knife **1.** knife kept in a sheath. **2.** table knife.

case·mate (kās′māt′) *n.* vaulted chamber in a fortification, or an armored enclosure on a ship, having openings through which guns may be fired. [French *casemate,* from Italian *casamatta,* going back to Greek *chasmata* gaps, chasms.]

case·ment (kās′mənt) *n.* **1.** frame of a window that opens on hinges on one side. **2.** window having such a frame.

ca·se·ous (kā′sē əs) *adj.* of or like cheese. [Latin *cāseus* cheese.]

ca·sern (kə zurn′) *also,* **ca·serne.** *n.* building for housing soldiers in a fortified town; barracks. [French *caserne,* from Provençal *cazerna* literally, place for four persons, possibly from Latin *quaterni* four each.]

case shot, canister.

case·work·er (kās′wur′kər) *n.* social worker who is assigned to interview and give guidance and advice to an individual or family with social, psychological, or economic difficulties. —**case′work′,** *n.*

cash (kash) *n.* **1.** money in the form of coins or bills. **2.** money or its equivalent, as a check, paid at the time of buying something. —*v.t.* **1.** to give or obtain cash for: *to cash a check.* **2. to cash in. a.** in gambling, to exchange for cash: *to cash in one's chips.* **b.** *Slang.* to die. **3. to cash in on.** *Informal.* **a.** to make a profit from. **b.** to turn to, or use to, one's advantage. [Old French *casse* money; originally, money box, from Italian *cassa,* from Latin *capsa* box, chest.]

cash·book (kash′book′) *n.* book in which a record is kept of money received and paid out.

cash·ew (kash′ōō, kə shōō′) *n.* **1.** kidney-shaped edible nut of a tropical evergreen tree, *Anacardium occidentale.* **2.** the tree producing this nut. [Portuguese *caju, acajú,* from Tupi-Guarani *acajú.*]

cash·ier¹ (ka shēr′) *n.* one who is in charge of cash intake and outflow and other monetary transactions, as in a bank or business. [French *caissier* treasurer, from *caisse* money, box, going back to Latin *capsa* box, chest.]

cash·ier² (ka shēr′) *v.t.* to dismiss from service in disgrace, as a military man. [Dutch *casseren,* from French *casser* to break, revoke, discharge, from Latin *quassāre* to shake violently (influenced by Late Latin *cassāre* to annul).]

cashier's check, check drawn by a bank on its own funds and signed by its cashier.

cash·mere (kazh′mēr, kash′-) *n.* **1.** fine, soft woolen fabric, woven of a mixture of sheep's wool and the hair of the Kashmir goat, used for such items as coats, suits, or sweaters. **2.** fine, silken hair of the Kashmir goat. **3.** rare and expensive cloth made solely of this hair, used esp. for shawls. [From KASHMIR, noted for its goats and their fine wool.]

Cash·mere (kash mēr′) Kashmir.

Cashmere goat, Kashmir goat.

cash on delivery, immediate payment in cash upon delivery of merchandise.

cash register, machine, usually with a money drawer, which automatically shows and records the amount of a sale.

cas·ing (kā′sing) *n.* **1.** something that contains, encloses, or protects. **2.** shoe of a pneumatic tire. **3.** frame, as of a door or window.

ca·si·no (kə sē′nō) *pl.,* **-nos.** *n.* **1.** building or room for public entertainment, esp. for gambling. **2.** *also,* **cas·si·no.** card game for two, three, or four players using a regular 52-card deck, with the highest point count for cards taken determining the winner. [Italian *casino* house, gaming house, diminutive of *casa* house, from Latin *casa* cottage.]

cask (kask) *n.* **1.** large wooden barrel, usually used to hold liquids. **2.** amount contained in a cask. [Spanish *casco* vat, helmet, from *cascar* to crack, going back to Latin *quassāre* to shake violently.]

cas·ket (kas′kit) *n.* **1.** wood or metal rectangular box, usually ornamented, in which a corpse is placed for interment; coffin. **2.** small box or chest, as for jewels. [Modification of French *cassette* small box, from *casse* box, chest, from Latin *capsa.*]

Cas·pi·an Sea (kas′pē ən) inland sea in the southern Soviet Union, bordering northern Iran. It is the largest inland body of water in the world.

casque (kask) *n.* helmet. [French *casque,* from Spanish *casco* skull, helmet, from *cascar* to crack, going back to Latin *quassāre* to shake violently.]

cas·sa·ba (kə sä′bə) casaba.

Cas·san·dra (kə san′drə) *n.* **1.** *Greek Legend.* a daughter of King Priam of Troy. Apollo, who was in love with her, gave her the gift of prophecy, but when she refused to love him in return, he decreed that no one should believe her prophecies. **2.** one who prophesies misfortune and disaster, but is not believed.

cas·sa·va (kə sä′və) *n.* **1.** bushy shrub, *Manihot esculenta,* widely cultivated in tropical regions for its edible roots. **2.** nutritious starch obtained from its roots from which tapioca and bread are made. Also, **man′i·oc′.** [French *cassave* the shrub, from Spanish *casabe* manioc bread; of Taino origin.]

cas·se·role (kas′ə rōl′) *n.* **1.** deep baking dish, often of glass or earthenware, in which food can be cooked and served. **2.** any food prepared and served in a casserole. **3.** small, deep dish with a handle, used in chemical laboratories for heating substances. [French *casserole* saucepan, from Middle French *casse* pan, ladle, from Late Latin *cattia* ladle, from Greek *kyathion* small ladle.]

cas·sette (kə set′) *n.* **1.** cartridge *(def. 2).* **2.** small case designed to hold magnetic tape for easy insertion in a tape player.

cas·sia (kash′ə, kas′ē ə) *n.* **1.** aromatic bark of a tree, *Cinnamomum cassia,* of the laurel family, used as a substitute for cinnamon. **2.** evergreen tree bearing this bark, having glossy oblong leaves and found mainly in China. **3.** any of a large group of plants, shrubs, and trees, genus *Cassia,* of the pea family, found in both tropical and temperate regions. **4.** sweet edible pulp from the pods of the tree, *Cassia fistula,* that is mildly laxative. [Latin *cassia* tree like cinnamon, from Greek *kasiā* spice like cinnamon, from Hebrew *q'tsī'āh* bark like that of cinnamon.]

cas·si·mere (kas′ə mēr′) *n.* light- to medium-weight wool fabric, often a serge, used chiefly for men's suits. [Form of CASHMERE.]

cas·si·no (kə sē′nō) casino *(def. 2).*

Cas·si·no (kə sē′nō) town in central Italy, site of a famous monastery. Pop. (1961), 8,000.

Cas·si·o·pe·ia (kas′ē ə pē′ə) *n.* **1.** *Greek Legend.* wife of Cepheus and mother of Andromeda. **2.** constellation in the northern sky, which daily orbits the celestial pole, conventionally depicted as the seated figure of Cassiopeia.

cas·sit·e·rite (kə sit′ə rīt′) *n.* brown or black translucent mineral that is the world's major source of tin, found esp. in China and Malaya. Formula: SnO₂ Also, **tin stone.** [Greek *kassiteros* tin + -ITE¹.]

Cas·sius Lon·gi·nus, Ga·ius (kash′əs lon jī′nəs; gā′əs) died 42 B.C., Roman general and politician.

cas·sock (kas′ək) *n.* ankle-length garment worn by the clergy and certain laymen assisting at services in the Roman Catholic, Anglican, and other churches. In the Roman Catholic Church the cassocks of the priests are black, those of bishops violet, those of cardinals red, and that of the pope white. [French *casaque* long coat, from Persian *kazagand* type of jacket.] —**cas′socked,** *adj.*

Cassock

cas·so·war·y (kas′ə wer′ē) *pl.,* **-war·ies.** *n.* any of several flightless birds, genus *Casuarius,* of Australia and New Guinea, related to and resembling the ostrich and having black, bristlelike feathers and a bril-

Cassowary

---

at; āpe; cär; end; mē; it; īce; hot; ōld; fôrk; wood; fōōl; oil; out; up; ūse; turn; sing; thin; this; zh in treasure; ə in ago, taken, pencil, lemon, circus.

liantly colored bare head and neck. Height: 5 feet. [Malay *kasuārī*.]
cast (kast) **cast, cast·ing.** *v.t.* **1.** to impel through the air; throw: *He cast a stone against the window.* **2.** to cause to fall over or upon or in a particular direction; project: *His figure cast a shadow on the ground.* **3.** to direct or turn: *She cast an eye in his direction.* **4.** to put or place, as if by throwing: *He always tried to cast the blame on others.* **5.** to discard, dismiss, or ignore: *He cast all caution aside.* **6.** to deposit or register, as a ballot or vote. **7.a.** to assign the parts, as of a play or motion picture, to the actors: *They have cast the movie.* **b.** to select (an actor) for a particular part: *John was cast as Hamlet.* **8.** to compute astrologically: *to cast one's horoscope.* **9.a.** to shape (a substance) by pouring into a mold to harden. **b.** to make by this process. **10.** to shed; molt. **11.** to lose or throw away: *The horse cast its shoe.* **12.** to arrange or devise: *He cast his plan to hurt his enemies.* **13.** to cast out. to put or drive out; expel. **14. to cast away.** to shipwreck. **15. to cast up.** to cause to appear; turn up. —*v.i.* **1.** to throw something, esp. a fishing line. **2.** to take shape in a mold. **3. to cast about for.** to search; look: *He cast about for an explanation.* **4. to cast off. a.** to let loose; free: *to cast off a boat from its mooring.* **b.** in knitting, to make the last row of stitches. **5. to cast on.** in knitting, to make the first row of stitches. —*n.* **1.** act or manner of throwing. **2.** distance to which something is thrown. **3.** that which is formed or shaped in a mold. **4.** group of actors, as in a play or motion picture. **5.** rigid form, usually made from plaster of Paris, used to immobilize a broken bone or badly sprained muscle. **6.** impression; mold: *The police made a cast of the footprints.* **7.** tinge of color: *The sky had a bluish cast.* **8.** form, appearance, or shape of something, as facial features. **9.** throw of dice; the number thrown. **10.** kind; sort. **11.** a twist or turn to one side: *to have a cast in one eye.* [Old Norse *kasta* to throw.] —**Syn.** *v.t.* see **toss.**

cas·ta·net (kas'tə net') *n.* one of a pair of small concave pieces, as of hard plastic or ivory, held in the hand and clicked together rhythmically, esp. as an accompaniment to certain Spanish music and dancing. [Spanish *castañeta,* diminutive of *castaña* chestnut, from Latin *castanea* chestnut tree, from Greek *kastanon* chestnut; because it resembles a chestnut shell.]

cast·a·way (kast'ə wā') *n.* one who is shipwrecked or set adrift at sea. —*adj.* thrown away; discarded.

caste (kast) *n.* **1.** one of the hereditary social classes into which Hindus are traditionally divided. **2.** any social system or set of principles that divides a society according to class distinctions based on heredity, wealth, position, or religion. **3.** exclusive social or professional group: *a priestly caste.* **4. to lose caste.** to lose social standing or prestige. [Portuguese *casta;* originally, a pure stock, from *casto* pure, from Latin *castus.* Doublet of CHASTE.]

cas·tel·lat·ed (kast'ə lā'tid) *adj.* built with turrets and battlements; resembling a castle.

cast·er (kas'tər) *n.* **1.** one who or that which casts. **2.** *also,* **castor. a.** one of a set of swiveling wheels or rollers placed or fitted under furniture or other large, heavy articles to facilitate moving. **b.** bottle for holding condiments, as salt, mustard, or vinegar; cruet. **c.** stand for such bottles. [CAST + -ER¹.]

cas·ti·gate (kas'tə gāt') **-gat·ed, -gat·ing.** *v.t.* to criticize or rebuke severely. [Latin *castigātus,* past participle of *castigāre* to correct (in the sense of making pure), from *castus* pure.] —**cas'ti·ga'tion, cas'ti·ga'tor,** *n.*

Cas·tile (kas tēl') *n.* region and former kingdom in north-central and central Spain.

Castile soap *also,* **castile soap.** fine, hard soap made from olive oil and caustic soda.

Cas·til·ian (kas til'yən) *adj.* of, relating to, or characteristic of Castile, its people, or their language. —*n.* **1.** standard form of Spanish based on the dialect of Castile. **2.** native or inhabitant of Castile.

cast·ing (kas'ting) *n.* **1.** that which is shaped in a mold; cast. **2.** act of one who or that which casts: *The casting for the play has been completed.*

cast-i·ron (kast'ī'ərn) *adj.* **1.** made of cast iron. **2.** unyielding; inflexible: *cast-iron rules.* **3.** hardy; strong: *a cast-iron stomach.*

cast iron, hard, brittle form of pig iron, having a high carbon content, made by casting.

cas·tle (kas'əl) *n.* **1.** large fortified building or group of buildings serving as a stronghold or residence, as of a feudal prince or noble. **2.** any large, imposing house. **3.** rook² *n.* —*v.t.,* **-tled, -tling.** *Chess.* to move (the king) two squares to the right or left

Castle

and move the rook to the square passed over by the king. —*v.i. Chess.* to castle the king. [Anglo-Norman *castel* fortress, from Latin *castellum,* diminutive of *castrum* fortified place.]

castle in Spain, castle in the sky.

castle in the sky, something imagined and wished for but not likely to come true; daydream. Also, **castle in the air.**

cast-off (kast'ôf') *adj.* discarded or abandoned. —*n.* one who or that which has been discarded or abandoned.

cas·tor¹ (kas'tər) caster (*def. 2*).

cas·tor² (kas'tər) *n.* oily, strong-smelling substance, secreted by certain glands in beavers, used in perfumery and, formerly, in making medicines. [Latin *castor* beaver, from Greek *kastōr.*]

Cas·tor and Pol·lux (kas'tər; pol'əks) **1.** *Classical Mythology.* twin brothers whose mother was Leda and whose father was usually regarded as being Zeus. Castor was traditionally thought to be the mortal twin of the pair and Pollux to be the immortal. **2.** two bright stars in the constellation Gemini. Pollux is the brightest star in the constellation; Castor, a system of six stars, appears as one star to the naked eye.

castor bean, oval bean of the castor-oil plant.

castor oil, pale yellow or colorless oil obtained from castor beans, used as a strong laxative, a low-temperature lubricant, and in the preparation of such products as paints and soaps.

castor-oil plant, the wide-leaved plant, *Ricinus communis,* whose beans yield castor oil.

cas·trate (kas'trāt) **-trat·ed, -trat·ing.** *v.t.* **1.** to remove the testicles of; emasculate. **2.** to deprive of vitality or strength; make ineffectual. [Latin *castrātus,* past participle of *castrāre.*] —**cas·tra'tion,** *n.*

cast steel, steel which has been formed by casting.

cas·u·al (kazh'ōō əl) *adj.* **1.** without intention or design; offhand: *a casual remark.* **2.** occurring by chance; unexpected; accidental: *a casual meeting.* **3.** (of clothes) designed for informal wear: *Casual dress was suggested for the party.* **4.** unconcerned or indifferent; nonchalant: *a casual attitude.* **5.** temporary or irregular. —*n.* **1.** one who is employed irregularly or temporarily. **2.** soldier temporarily assigned to a post or unit while awaiting a permanent assignment. [Late Latin *cāsuālis* accidental, occurring by chance, from Latin *cāsus* a falling, chance.] —**cas'u·al·ly,** *adv.* —**cas'u·al·ness,** *n.*

cas·u·al·ty (kazh'ōō əl tē) *pl.,* **-ties.** *n.* **1.** serviceman who has been lost to his unit as a result of having been wounded, killed, captured, or missing in action. **2.** one who is injured or killed in an accident. **3.** one who or that which is ruined or destroyed: *He was fired and became the second casualty in the office that week.* **4.** accident, esp. one involving a death.

cas·u·ist (kazh'ōō ist) *n.* **1.** one who studies or resolves cases of conscience or problems concerning conduct and duty. **2.** one who reasons cleverly but equivocally about such matters. [French *casuiste,* going back to Medieval Latin *cāsus* case of conscience, from Latin *cāsus* a falling, chance.]

cas·u·is·tic (kazh'ōō is'tik) *adj.* **1.** of or relating to casuists or casuistry. **2.** specious; sophistical. Also, **cas'u·is'ti·cal.** —**cas'u·is'ti·cal·ly,** *adv.*

cas·u·ist·ry (kazh'ōō is trē) *pl.,* **-ries.** *n.* **1.** the method or practice of applying moral principles to concrete situations. **2.** clever but false or misleading reasoning; sophistry.

ca·sus bel·li (kā'səs bel'ī) *Latin.* cause or reason for declaring war.

cat (kat) *n.* **1.** carnivorous mammal, *Felis catus,* domesticated, and commonly kept as a pet or for catching mice. **2.** any animal of the cat family, Felidae, as the domestic cat, lion, tiger, leopard, or lynx. **3.** spiteful or backbiting woman. **4.** catfish. **5.** tackle for hoisting an anchor to the cathead. **6. to let the cat out of the bag.** to inadvertently reveal a secret. —*v.t.* to hoist (an anchor) to the cathead. [Old English *cat(t)* the domesticated animal, possibly going back to Late Latin *cattus;* possibly of Hamitic origin.]

cata- *prefix* down or against: *catacomb, catalyst, catastrophe.* [Greek *kata* down, against, in accordance with.]

ca·tab·o·lism (kə tab'ə liz'əm) *n.* chemical process by which living tissue is broken down into simpler substances or waste matter, often accompanied by a liberation of energy; destructive metabolism. Distinguished from **anabolism.** [Greek *katabolē* a throwing down + -ISM.]

cat·a·chre·sis (kat'ə krē'sis) *pl.,* **-ses** (-sēz). *n.* any misuse of words, esp. of figures of speech. [Latin *catachrēsis,* from Greek *katachrēsis* misuse.]

cat·a·clysm (kat'ə kliz'əm) *n.* **1.** violent and extensive change in the ordinary processes of nature, as a flood or earthquake. **2.** any violent change or sudden upheaval, as a revolution or war. [French *cataclysme,* from Latin *cataclysmos* flood, from Greek *kataklysmos.*]

cat·a·clys·mic (kat'ə kliz'mik) *adj.* of, relating to, or resembling a cataclysm. Also, **cat'a·clys'mal.**

cat·a·combs (kat'ə kōmz') *n.,pl.* underground cemetery consisting of rooms and passages with recesses excavated in the walls for tombs. [French *catacombe,* from Late Latin *catacumba;* of uncertain

origin, but possibly from Latin *cata* by (from Greek *kata* against, down) + Late Latin *tumba* tomb (from Greek *tymbos* tomb).]

ca·tad·ro·mous (kə tad′rə məs) *adj.* of or relating to fish which live in fresh water but go down river to spawn in the sea. Opposed to **anadromous.** [CATA- + Greek *dromos* running, course + -OUS.]

cat·a·falque (kat′ə falk′, -fôk′) *n.* stand or frame on which a casket rests while a body lies in state or during a funeral service. [French *catafalque,* from Italian *catafalco;* of uncertain origin, but possibly going back to Latin *cata* by (from Greek *kata* down, against) + *fala* scaffold (of Etruscan origin).]

Cat·a·lan (kat′əl an′, kat′əl an′) *adj.* of or relating to Catalonia, its people, or their language. —*n.* **1.** native or inhabitant of Catalonia. **2.** Romance language of Catalonia, Valencia, Andorra, the Balearic Islands, and some parts of southern France.

cat·a·lep·sy (kat′əl ep′sē) *n.* condition associated with mental disorders in which the muscles become extremely rigid and the limbs remain in any position in which they are placed. [Greek *katalēpsis* seizure.]

cat·a·lep·tic (kat′əl ep′tik) *adj.* of, relating to, or having catalepsy. —*n.* one who has catalepsy.

Cat·a·li·na (kat′əl ē′nə) *n.* Santa Catalina. Also, **Catalina Island.**

cat·a·log (kat′əl ôg′, -og′) *n.* **1.** listing, usually in alphabetical order, which identifies and often describes items, as in a collection. **2.** publication containing such a listing: *The store sent us a catalog of their merchandise.* **3.** book or booklet issued by a college or university listing information, as rules, courses to be offered, or fees. **4.** card catalog. —*v.t.* to make a catalog of or enter in a catalog: *to catalog the paintings in a museum.* [French *catalogue* list, enumeration, from Late Latin *catalogus,* from Greek *katalogos* enrollment, register.] —**cat′a·log′er,** *n.* —**Syn.** *v.* **1.** see **list[1].**

cat·a·logue (kat′əl ôg′, -og′) *n.* catalog. —*v.t.* **-logued, -logu·ing.** to catalog. —**cat′a·logu′er,** *n.*

Cat·a·lo·ni·a (kat′əl ō′nē ə) *n.* historic region and former principality in the northeastern corner of Spain.

ca·tal·pa (kə tal′pə) *n.* **1.** any of a group of softwood trees, genus *Catalpa,* found in North America and Asia, having large, heart-shaped leaves, showy white, pink, or yellow flowers, and beanlike pods. **2.** the coarse-grained, durable wood of this tree. [Modern Latin *Catalpa,* said to be from Creek *kutuhlpa* head having wings; because of the shape of its flowers.]

ca·tal·y·sis (kə tal′ə sis) *pl.,* **-ses** (-sēz′) *n.* acceleration of a chemical reaction by the presence of a substance that remains unchanged by the reaction. [Greek *katalysis* dissolution.]

cat·a·lyst (kat′əl ist) *n.* **1.** substance that causes catalysis. **2.** one who or that which stirs to action: *His petition was the catalyst for reform.*

cat·a·lyt·ic (kat′əl it′ik) *adj.* of, relating to, or causing catalysis.

cat·a·lyze (kat′əl īz′) *v.t.* **-lyzed, -lyz·ing.** to submit to, or act upon, by catalysis. —**cat′a·lyz′er,** *n.*

cat·a·ma·ran (kat′ə mə ran′) *n.* **1.** any of various boats having two hulls connected by poles or by a platform which serves as a deck. Most catamarans are sailboats. **2.** raft made of logs lashed together in the shape of a boat hull. [Tamil *kattumaram* bound wood.]

Catamaran

cat·a·mount (kat′ə mount′) *n.* any of several wild animals of the cat family, as the cougar, lynx, or mountain lion. Also, **cat·a·moun·tain, cat-o′-moun′tain** (kat′ə mount′ən). [Short for *cat of the mountain.*]

Ca·ta·nia (kə tän′yə) *n.* port city on the eastern coast of Sicily. Pop. (1961). 363,928.

cat·a·pult (kat′ə pult′, -poolt′) *n.* **1.** war machine, similar to a ballista, used to shoot or hurl projectiles. **2.** track-mounted device used to launch an airplane from the deck of a ship. **3.** *British.* slingshot. —*v.t.* to hurl or shoot (something) from or as from a catapult. —*v.i.* to leap or be ejected. [Late Latin *catapulta* this war machine, from Greek *katapaltēs.*]

Catapult

cat·a·ract (kat′ə rakt′) *n.* **1.** large, steep waterfall. **2.** steep rapids in a river. **3.** violent flood or downpour of water. **4.** cloudy or opaque condition in the lens of the eye, or its capsule, resulting in impairment of vision. Many cataracts can be treated surgically. [Latin *cataracta* waterfall, portcullis, from Greek *katarraktēs.*]

ca·tarrh (kə tär′) *n.* inflammation of a mucous membrane, esp. that of the nose or throat, causing excessive secretion of mucus. [French *catarrhe,* from Late Latin *catarrhus,* from Greek *katarrhous* literally, a flowing down.] —**ca·tarrh′al,** *adj.*

ca·tas·tro·phe (kə tas′trə fē′) *n.* great and sudden disaster or misfortune: *The plane crash was the worst catastrophe of the year.* [Greek *katastrophē* overturning.] —**Syn.** see **disaster.**

cat·a·stroph·ic (kat′əs trof′ik) *adj.* of, resulting from, or resembling a catastrophe.

Ca·taw·ba (kə tô′bə) *pl.,* **-bas.** *n.* **1.** sweet, purplish-red variety of grape, grown in the eastern United States. **2.** dry, white wine made from it. [From the *Catawba* River in South Carolina.]

cat·bird (kat′burd′) *n.* slate-gray songbird, *Dumetella carolinensis,* of North and Central America, related to the mockingbird and having a black cap and tail.

cat·boat (kat′bōt′) *n.* sailboat with a single, usually gaff-rigged, mast set well forward.

cat·call (kat′kôl′) *n.* shrill cry or whistle expressing disapproval, derision, or impatience. —*v.i.* to make catcalls. —*v.t.* to express disapproval, derision, or impatience of with catcalls.

catch (kach) *caught, catch·ing. v.t.* **1.** to take hold of or seize (something), as after a chase or search: *to catch a thief. He caught my arm as I was leaving.* **2.** to stop or intercept the motion or passage of: *to catch a ball. He caught the water from the leaking roof in a pail.* **3.** to take (animals), as by trapping, netting, or shooting: *to catch salmon, to catch butterflies.* **4.** to be in time for boarding; get aboard: *to catch a train.* **5.** to cause to become stuck, entangled, or hooked: *She caught her sweater on a nail.* **6.** to overtake or detain: *The storm caught us as we left the house. We caught him just as he was leaving.* **7.** to hit; strike: *The blow caught him in the stomach.* **8.** to come upon suddenly or unexpectedly; surprise or discover: *The police caught him in the act.* **9.** to check (oneself) suddenly or momentarily, esp. in speaking: *He caught himself before he divulged the secret.* **10.** to take, get, or perceive suddenly or momentarily: *to catch a glimpse of a person.* **11.** to ensnare or deceive. **12.** to become affected or infected with: *to catch a cold.* **13.** to attract suddenly or momentarily, as the senses: *The brightly colored dress caught my eye.* **14.** to grasp with the senses or intellect: *I finally caught the gist of the conversation.* **15.** to portray or reproduce accurately: *The artist caught her mood in the portrait.* **16.** *Informal.* to see, as a motion picture. **17. to catch it.** *Informal.* to receive a scolding or punishment. **18. to catch (someone) up on.** to bring (someone) up to date on. —*v.i.* **1.** to grasp or seize. **2.** to become lighted; ignite. **3.** to become entangled or hooked: *The fabric caught in the zipper.* **4.** to become fastened or take hold: *The bolt didn't catch.* **5.** to spread by or as by infection. **6.** to act as catcher in baseball. **7. to catch on.** *Informal.* **a.** to understand. **b.** to become popular or fashionable. **8. to catch up with. a.** to come up to or overtake: *He caught up with his friends even though he left late.* **b.** to bring or get up to date: *She caught up with her correspondence.* **c.** to raise up or fasten in loops with: *The skirt was caught up with bows.* **9. to catch up to.** to come up to or overtake: *He caught up to his opponent near the end of the race.* **10. to catch up in. a.** to bring or get up to date: *She must catch up in her work.* **b.** to become absorbed or entangled in: *He was caught up in his book.* **11. to catch up on.** to bring or get up to date. **12. to catch up.** to grab or pick up suddenly or quickly: *The thief caught up the jewels and ran.* —*n.* **1.** act of catching: *The outfielder made a great catch.* **2.** that which catches; fastening: *He fixed the catch on the door.* **3.** that which is caught; quantity caught: *The fisherman had a good catch.* **4.** small part; fragment: *catches of song.* **5.** a round for three or more voices. **6.** game in which an object, esp. a ball, is thrown and caught. **7.** break in the voice, esp. as a result of emotion. **8.** *Informal.* someone who is desirable as a prospect for marriage. **9.** *Informal.* hidden condition; trick or trap: *The plan seems too good; there must be a catch somewhere.* —*adj.* **1.** attracting or intended to attract attention or interest: *a catch phrase.* **2.** tricky; deceptive: *a catch question.* [Anglo-Norman *cachier* to hunt, going back to Latin *captāre* to try to catch, chase. Doublet of CHASE[1].]

Syn. *v.t.* **1.** *Catch, capture, seize* mean to take captive. **Catch** suggests entrapment or taking by surprise, esp. while in motion: *The prowler was caught as he left the grounds.* **Capture** suggests the overwhelming of resistance: *The fugitive was captured after a fierce gun battle.* **Seize** stresses the actual laying hold or taking possession of, without suggesting that the action was more than temporary: *The rebels seized the radio station but were forced to abandon it after a counterattack.*

catch·all (kach′ôl′) *n.* **1.** anything which serves as a receptacle for odds and ends: *The closet was a catchall.* **2.** word or phrase used to cover various conditions or situations.

catch·er (kach′ər) *n.* **1.** one who or that which catches. **2.** baseball

---

at; āpe; cär; end; mē; it; īce; hot; ōld; fôrk; wood; fool; oil; out; up; ūse; turn; sing; thin; this; zh in treasure; ə in ago, taken, pencil, lemon, circus.

player who is positioned behind home plate to catch pitched balls not hit by the batter and to guard the plate from runners advancing from third base.

catch·fly (kach′flī′) pl. **-flies.** n. campion.

catch·ing (kach′ing) adj. **1.** contagious; infectious: *Some diseases are catching.* **2.** attractive; fascinating.

catch·pen·ny (kach′pen′ē) adj. made to be sold quickly; cheap and showy. —n. pl., **-nies.** catchpenny article.

catch·pole (kach′pōl′) also, **catch·poll.** n. Archaic. sheriff's deputy or bailiff who makes arrests, esp. for debt.

catch·up (kech′əp, kach′-) ketchup.

catch·word (kach′wurd′) n. **1.** word or phrase which is used repeatedly for effect; slogan. **2.** word placed so as to attract attention, as a word placed at the top of a page in a dictionary.

catch·y (kach′ē) **catch·i·er, catch·i·est.** adj. **1.** catching the attention and easy to remember: *a catchy title.* **2.** tricky; deceptive: *a catchy question.*

cate (kāt) n. Archaic. choice food; delicacy. [Short for Middle English *acate* purchase, from Anglo-Norman *acat,* from *acater* to buy, going back to Latin *ad* to + *capere* to take.]

cat·e·chet·i·cal (kat′ə ket′i kəl) adj. relating to oral instruction by questions and answers. Also, **cat′e·chet′ic.**

cat·e·chism (kat′ə kiz′əm) n. **1.** small book or manual in which the precepts of a religion, esp. a Christian denomination, are set forth in question and answer form. **2.** similar book or manual about any subject. **3.** series of long or formal questions used as an examination, as of a political candidate.

cat·e·chist (kat′ə kist′) n. one who catechizes.

cat·e·chize (kat′ə kīz′) **-chized, -chiz·ing.** also, **cat·e·chise.** v.t. **1.** to instruct by questions and answers, esp. in Christian belief. **2.** to question closely and systematically. [Church Latin *catēchizāre* to instruct in religion, going back to Greek *katēchein* to instruct orally, din (something) in.] —**cat′e·chiz′er,** also, **cat·e·chis′er,** n.

cat·e·chu (kat′ə chōō′, -kū′) n. gummy, dark brown substance, most of which is obtained from certain acacia trees. It is used as an ingredient in dyes and certain medicines and as a tanning extract. [Modern Latin *catechu,* from Malay *kāchū.*]

cat·e·chu·men (kat′ə kū′mən) n. in the early Christian Church, one being instructed in the faith prior to baptism. [Church Latin *catēchūmenus,* from Greek *katēchoumenos* one being instructed orally, present participle of *katēchein* to instruct orally.]

cat·e·gor·i·cal (kat′ə gôr′i kəl, -gor′-) adj. **1.** without conditions or qualifications; absolute. **2.** of, relating to, or in a category. —**cat′e·gor′i·cal·ly,** adv.

cat·e·go·rize (kat′ə gə rīz′) **-rized, -riz·ing.** v.t. to put into a category; classify.

cat·e·go·ry (kat′ə gôr′ē) pl., **-ries.** n. group or division in any system of classification; class. [Late Latin *catēgoria* accusation, class (in logic), from Greek *katēgoria.*]

cat·e·nate (kat′ən āt′) **-nat·ed, -nat·ing.** v.t. to link together like a chain; form into a chain. [Latin *catēnātus,* past participle of *catēnāre* to chain together.] —**cat′e·na′tion,** n.

ca·ter (kā′tər) v.i. **1.** to provide food, supplies, or other services, or entertainment: *a restaurant that caters for large private parties.* **2.** to provide with what is needed or desired (with *to* or *for*): *The shop caters to a small, wealthy clientele.* —v.t. to provide with food, supplies, or other services, as entertainment: *to cater a wedding.* [From obsolete *cater* buyer, short for Middle English *acatour* buyer of provisions, from Anglo-Norman *acatour* buyer, from *acater* to buy. See CATE.]

cat·er·cor·ner (kat′ər kôr′nər, kat′ə-) also, **cat·ty·cor·ner, kit·ty·cor·ner,** adv. in a diagonal position, usually in a corner. [Obsolete *cater* four (from French *quatre,* from Latin *quattuor*) + CORNER.]

ca·ter·er (kā′tər ər) n. one who caters, esp. one who provides food, supplies, or other services, as for a party.

cat·er·pil·lar (kat′ər pil′ər) n. **1.** worm-like larva, esp. of a butterfly or moth. **2.** crawler tractor. Trademark: Caterpillar. [Dialectal Old French *catepelose* literally, hairy cat, from Late Latin *catta pilōsa* hairy female cat; influenced by obsolete English *piller* robber. See CAT, PILOSE.]

Caterpillar

cat·er·waul (kat′ər wôl′) v.i. to howl or screech like a cat. —n. such a howl or screech. [Middle English *caterwawen* to howl like a cat, from CAT + WAW to howl like a cat (imitative).]

cat·fish (kat′fish′) pl., **-fish** or **-fish·es.** n. any of various, usually scaleless, fish, suborder Siluroidea, found in rivers or tropical lakes in Europe and America, having a large head, sensitive barbels around the mouth, and a characteristic small, fleshy fin on its back.

cat·gut (kat′gut′) n. tough string or cord processed from the dried and twisted intestines of sheep and certain other animals, used for surgical sutures and for stringing musical instruments and tennis rackets.

cath-, form of cata- before *h,* as in *cathode.*

Cath., Catholic.

ca·thar·sis (kə thär′sis) n. purifying or purging of the emotions, esp. through an art medium, as drama. [Modern Latin *catharsis,* from Greek *katharsis* purification.]

ca·thar·tic (kə thär′tik) n. medicine causing movement of the bowels; laxative. —adj. purgative or purifying.

Ca·thay (ka thā′) n. Archaic. China.

cat·head (kat′hed′) n. beam which projects from a ship's side at the bow. The anchor is hoisted and secured to it.

ca·the·dra (kə thē′drə, kath′ə-) n. **1.** bishop's throne in the cathedral of his diocese. **2.** official chair, as of a professor. [Latin *cathedra* chair, from Greek *kathedrā.* Doublet of CHAIR.]

ca·the·dral (kə thē′drəl) n. **1.** official church of a bishop, containing his throne. **2.** any large or important church. —adj. **1.** relating to or possessing a bishop's throne. **2.** authoritative. **3.** of, relating to, or suggestive of a cathedral. [Medieval Latin *(ecclesia) cathedralis* (church) having a cathedra, or bishop's throne, from Latin *cathedra* chair. See CATHEDRA.]

Cath·er, Wil·la Si·bert (kath′ər; wil′ə sē′bərt) 1873-1947, U.S. novelist.

Cath·er·ine I (kath′ər in, kath′rin) c.1684-1727, empress of Russia from 1725 to 1727, and wife of Peter the Great.

Catherine II, Catherine the Great.

Catherine de' Medici c.1519-89, queen of France from 1547 to 1559.

Catherine of Aragon, 1485-1536, first wife of Henry VIII of England.

Catherine of Siena, Saint, 1347-80, Italian mystic and lay member of the Dominican order.

Catherine the Great, 1729-96, empress of Russia from 1762 to 1796.

cath·e·ter (kath′ə tər) n. slender, flexible tube for inserting into a cavity of the body to keep a passage open or to drain fluids, esp. one used to remove urine from the bladder. [Late Latin *cathetēr,* from Greek *kathetēr.*]

cath·ode (kath′ōd) n. **1.** electrode through which electrons enter an electrical device or medium. When electricity is used to produce a chemical reaction, the negative electrode is the cathode, but when a chemical reaction is used to produce electricity the positive electrode is the cathode. **2.** in electrolysis, electrode that has an excess of electrons and is negatively charged. Positively charged ions are reduced at the cathode. See **electrolysis** for illustration. **3.** electrode from which electrons are emitted. Opposed to **anode** in all definitions. [Greek *kathodos* a way down, from *kata* down + *hodos* way.]

cathode ray, stream of electrons emitted from the cathode in a vacuum tube.

cathode-ray tube, vacuum tube in which a visible glowing pattern is produced on a luminescent screen by a cathode ray emitted from an electron gun at the back of the tube. It is used in television sets, oscilloscopes, and radar sets.

cath·o·lic (kath′ə lik, kath′lik) adj. **1.** of universal interest or use. **2.** having sympathies with, or embracing, all; broad. **3. Catholic. a.** of or relating to the Christian church under the authority of the pope; Roman Catholic. **b.** of or relating to the ancient undivided Christian church, or to those churches claiming unbroken descent from it, as the Roman, Orthodox, Eastern, and Anglican. —n. **Catholic.** member of a Catholic Church, esp. the Roman Catholic Church. [Church Latin *catholicus* universal, orthodox, from Greek *katholikos* universal, general.]

Ca·thol·i·cism (kə thol′ə siz′əm) n. **1.** beliefs, practices, and government of the Roman Catholic Church. **2.** catholicity.

cath·o·lic·i·ty (kath′ə lis′ə tē) n. state or quality of being catholic.

ca·thol·i·cize (kə thol′ə sīz′) **-cized, -ciz·ing.** v.i., v.t. **1.** to make or become catholic. **2.** Catholicize. to make or become Catholic.

Cat·i·line (kat′ol īn′) c.108-62 B.C., Roman soldier and politician, leader of a conspiracy in 62 B.C. against the Roman republic.

cat·i·on (kat′ī′ən) n. positively charged ion of an electrolyte, attracted to the cathode in electrolysis. [Greek *kation* a going down, noun use of neuter present participle of *katienai* to go down.]

cat·kin (kat′kin) n. fuzzy spike of tiny flowers that grow on certain trees, as willows or birches. Also, **am′ent.** [Obsolete Dutch *katteken* literally, little cat; because it resembles a cat's tail.]

cat·nap (kat′nap′) n. short nap. —v.i., **-napped, -nap·ping.** to take a short nap.

cat·nip (kat′nip′) n. **1.** dried leaves and stems of a plant, *Nepeta cataria,* of the mint family, used as a stuffing for cats' toys because cats

are stimulated by its strong aroma. **2.** the strongly aromatic plant itself, that grows wild in North America. [CAT + dialectal English *nip* catnip, form of dialectal English *nep*, going back to Latin *nepeta*.]

Ca·to (kā′tō) **1. Marcus Por·cius** (pôr′shəs). 234–149 B.C., Roman statesman. Also, **Cato the Elder. 2. Marcus Porcius.** 95–46 B.C., great-grandson of Cato the Elder; Roman statesman.

cat-o'-moun·tain (kat′ə mount′ən) catamount.

cat-o'-nine-tails (kat′ə nīn′tālz′) *pl.*, **-tails.** *n.* whip usually consisting of nine knotted cords fastened to a handle.

cat-rig (kat′rig′) *n.* rig having one sail and a single mast set well forward. —**cat′-rigged′,** *adj.*

cat's cradle, children's game in which a loop of string is intertwined over the fingers of both hands in such a way as to form different patterns.

cat's-eye (kats′ī′) *n.* gem which reflects light in a manner suggestive of a cat's eye.

Cats·kill Mountains (kats′kil′) mountain range in southeastern New York. It is part of the Appalachian mountain system. Also, **Cats′kills′.**

cat's-paw (kats′pô′) *also,* **cats-paw.** *n.* **1.** one used as a pawn by another; dupe. **2.** light breeze that ruffles the surface of calm water. **3.** *Nautical.* double loop made by twisting two bights of a line and securing it to a hook.

cat-sup (kat′səp, kech′əp, kach′-) ketchup.

Catt, Carrie Chap·man (kat; chap′mən) 1859–1947, U.S. woman suffragist leader.

cat-tail (kat′tāl′) *n.* any of various tall marsh plants, genus *Typha,* bearing long, narrow leaves and flowers clustered in spikes which turn velvety brown when mature.

Cat·te·gat (kat′ə gat′) Kattegat.

cat·tle (kat′əl) *n.* domesticated bovine animals, as cows, bulls, and steers, raised primarily for meat and dairy products. [Anglo-Norman *catel* property (cattle being an important early form of property), from Late Latin *capitāle,* from Latin *capitālis* chief, relating to the head, from *caput* head. Doublet of CHATTEL.]

cat·tle·man (kat′əl mən) *pl.,* **-men.** *n.* man who owns, raises, or deals in cattle.

cat·ty (kat′ē) **-ti·er, -ti·est.** *adj.* **1.** slyly malicious; spiteful. **2.** of, relating to, or resembling cats. —**cat′ti·ly,** *adv.* —**cat′ti·ness,** *n.*

cat·ty-cor·ner (kat′ē kôr′nər) catercorner.

Ca·tul·lus, Ga·ius Va·le·ri·us (kə tul′əs; gā′əs və lēr′ē əs) c.87–c.54 B.C., Roman lyric poet.

cat·walk (kat′wôk′) *n.* narrow walking space or platform, as along a bridge.

Cau·ca·sia (kô kā′zhə, -shə) *n.* region in the southern Soviet Union between the Black and Caspian seas. Also, **Cau′ca·sus.**

Cau·ca·sian (kô kā′zhən, -shən, -kazh′ən) *n.* **1.** Caucasoid. **2.** native or inhabitant of the Caucasus. —*adj.* **2.** of or relating to the Caucasus, its inhabitants, or their languages. [Latin *Caucasus* Caucasus, from Greek *Kaukasos* + -IAN; first applied to the white race by the German anthropologist Johann Blumenbach, 1752–1840, because he thought it had originated in the Caucasus.]

Cau·ca·soid (kô′kə soid′) *n.* member of one of the major ethnic divisions of the human race whose physical characteristics vary greatly, with skin color ranging from pale pink to dark brown, hair color from blond to dark brown, and body size from slender to stocky. Caucasoids inhabit Europe, parts of Asia, Africa, and Australia, and the Western Hemisphere. —*adj.* of, relating to, characteristic of, or resembling Caucasoids. [CAUCAS(IAN) + -OID.]

Cau·ca·sus (kô′kə səs) *n.* **1.** mountain range in the southern Soviet Union between the Black and Caspian seas, conventionally regarded as part of the boundary between Europe and Asia. **2.** Caucasia.

cau·cus (kô′kəs) *n.* meeting of all the members of a particular political party or faction to choose party leaders, nominate candidates, and determine the general policies which their parties will advocate. —*v.i.* to meet in or hold a caucus. [Possibly from Algonquian *cau-cau-as-u* meeting, adviser, counselor.]

cau·dal (kôd′əl) *adj.* **1.** of, relating to, or near the tail: *the caudal fin of a fish.* **2.** tail-like. [Modern Latin *caudalis,* from Latin *cauda* tail.] —**cau′dal·ly,** *adv.*

cau·date (kô′dāt) *adj.* having a tail or tail-like appendage.

cau·dle (kôd′əl) *n.* warm drink made of gruel mixed with wine, ale, spices, and eggs, usually given to invalids. [Dialectal Old French *caudel* going back to Latin *cal(i)dum.*]

caught (kôt) past tense and past participle of **catch.**

caul (kôl) *n.* membrane that encloses a fetus before birth, or a portion of it that sometimes envelops the head of a child at birth, formerly believed to bring good luck. [Old French *cale* cap, from *calotte* skull-cap, possibly going back to Latin *calautica* type of woman's head-covering.]

caul·dron (kôl′drən) *also,* **cal·dron.** *n.* large kettle or boiler.

[Anglo-Norman *caudron,* from Late Latin *caldāria,* going back to Latin *cal(i)dus* hot.]

cau·li·flow·er (kô′li flou′ər, kol′ē-) *n.* **1.** white head of a plant, *Brassica oleracea,* variety *botrytis,* of the mustard family, eaten as a vegetable either raw or cooked. **2.** the low-growing plant itself, probably developed from the wild cabbage of western Europe. [Modification (influenced by Latin *caulis* cabbage + English FLOWER) of earlier *colyflory,* from obsolete French *chou fleuri* literally, flowered cabbage, going back to Latin *caulis* + *flōs* flower.]

cauliflower ear, ear that has been misshapen by repeated blows or injuries usually received in boxing.

caulk (kôk) *also,* **calk.** *v.t.* to fill up (a seam, crack, or joint) with a substance, as tar or oakum, so that it will not leak; make watertight or airtight. [Dialectal Old French *cauquer* to tread, press, from Latin *calcāre.*]

caulk·er (kô′kər) *also,* **calk·er.** *n.* **1.** one who caulks. **2.** tool used for caulking.

caus·al (kô′zəl) *adj.* **1.** of, indicating, or acting as a cause. **2.** *Grammar.* expressing or implying cause or reason. In the sentence *Some men are sportsmen because they have energy,* the word *because* is a causal conjunction. —**caus′al·ly,** *adv.*

cau·sal·i·ty (kô zal′ə tē) *pl.,* **-ties.** *n.* **1.** principle that every effect requires a cause for its existence; relationship between cause and effect. **2.** causal quality or agency.

cau·sa·tion (kô zā′shən) *n.* **1.** act of causing. **2.** that which produces an effect; cause. **3.** relation of cause and effect; causality.

caus·a·tive (kô′zə tiv) *adj.* **1.** effective as or producing a cause. **2.** *Grammar.* expressing or indicating causation. In *ennoble, en-* is a causative prefix.

cause (kôz) *n.* **1.** that which produces an effect or makes something happen: *The hurricane was the cause of great damage along the coast.* **2.** ground, as for action; reason; motive: *He had no cause for alarm.* **3.** subject, object, or principle of concern or interest to an individual or group and to which they give their support: *Helping the poor is a worthy cause.* **4.a.** matter or question to be decided by a court of law; ground of action. **b.** judicial proceeding; suit. —*v.t.,* **caused, caus·ing.** to result in or make happen; produce or make: *The traffic jam caused him to be late. Negligence causes many accidents.* [Old French *cause* motive, from Latin *causa* reason, lawsuit.] —**caus′a·ble, cause′less,** *adj.*

Syn. *n.* **1.** Cause, determinant, antecedent denote what produces or helps to produce an effect or result. **Cause,** the most general and most forceful of these words, suggests a necessary connection, whether immediate or not, in bringing on the result: *One of the causes of revolution is social discontent. The cause of his death was a heart attack.* **Determinant** suggests something that, usually in combination with other factors, shapes the character of a result rather than directly bringing it on: *Upbringing is a determinant of adult behavior.* An **antecedent** is an event or the like that comes before another and is regarded as influencing it: *the antecedents of World War II.*

cause cé·lè·bre (kôz′ sə leb′rə, kôz′) any controversy or issue, esp. one of a legal nature, that becomes famous. [French *cause célèbre* famous legal case, going back to Latin *causa* lawsuit + *celeber* famous.]

cau·se·rie (kō′zə rē′) *n.* **1.** informal conversation or discussion; chat. **2.** short article, essay, or other composition written in an informal, conversational style. [French *causerie,* from *causer* to talk, from Latin *causāri* to converse, plead, discuss.]

cause·way (kôz′wā′) *n.* **1.** raised road or path, as across a body of water. **2.** highway. [Earlier *causey way,* from dialectal Old French *cauciee* (Modern French *chaussée*) paved road, going back to Latin *calx* limestone) + English WAY. See CALX.]

caus·tic (kôs′tik) *adj.* **1.** capable of corroding or destroying animal tissue; corrosive. **2.** sarcastic; cutting; biting: *a caustic remark.* —*n.* substance which is destructive or corrosive to animal tissue. [Latin *causticus* corrosive, from Greek *kaustikos.*]

caus·ti·cal·ly (kôs′tik lē) *adv.* in a caustic manner; sarcastically.

caustic soda, sodium hydroxide.

cau·ter·ize (kô′tə rīz′) **-zed, -iz·ing.** *v.t.* to sear with a hot iron or a caustic substance, esp. to destroy dead tissue or prevent infection. —**cau′ter·i·za′tion,** *n.*

cau·tion (kô′shən) *n.* **1.** care with regard to danger or risk; prudence; wariness: *He exercised extreme caution in working with the chemicals.* **2.** warning. **3.** *Informal.* very odd or unusual person. —*v.t.* to urge (someone) to be careful; warn. —*v.i.* to warn. [Latin *cautiō* carefulness, wariness.]

cau·tion·ar·y (kô′shə ner′ē) *adj.* of the nature of or conveying a warning.

cau·tious (kô′shəs) *adj.* characterized by or exhibiting caution; careful. —**cau′tious·ly,** *adv.* —**cau′tious·ness,** *n.*

Syn. Cautious, guarded, wary mean watchful and prudent in speech and conduct. **Cautious,** the most general of these words, suggests pro-

---

ceeding with care: *He was a cautious investor who studied the market before buying.* **Guarded** suggests watchful restraint, esp. in qualifying what one says: *He gave a guarded answer about his political plans.* **Wary** suggests alertness in watching out for dangers or extreme caution in avoiding them: *She was wary of walking alone at night.*

cav., cavalry.

cav·al·cade (kav′əl kād′, kav′əl kād′) *n.* **1.** procession, esp. of people on horseback or in vehicles. **2.** large impressive group or gathering: *a cavalcade of movie stars.* [Middle French *cavalcade* riding on a horse, from Italian *cavalcata* band of horsemen, going back to Latin *caballus* nag, inferior horse.]

cav·a·lier (kav′ə lēr′) *n.* **1.** horseman, esp. one who is armed; knight. **2.** gallant or courteous gentleman; one serving as the escort of a lady. **3.** Cavalier. supporter of Charles I of England in his struggles with Parliament from 1641 to 1649. —*adj.* **1.** free and easy; offhand. **2.** haughty; disdainful. **3.** Cavalier. of or relating to the Cavaliers. —*v.i.* to behave in a cavalier manner; be haughty. [French *cavalier* knight who rides a horse, gentleman, from Italian *cavaliere,* from Late Latin *caballārius* horseman, from Latin *caballus* inferior horse, nag. In Latin the elegant word for horse was *equus,* yet aristocratic English words concerning horses come from *caballus,* a working class word for the animal. Doublet of CHEVALIER.] —**cav′a·lier′ly,** *adv.*

cav·al·ry (kav′əl rē) *pl.,* **-ries.** *n.* **1.** military unit trained to fight on horseback. **2.** in some countries, a military unit composed of armored vehicles, as tanks. [Middle French *cavallerie* horsemen, from Italian *cavalleria* knighthood, troop of horse, from *cavaliere* knight. See CAVALIER.]

cav·al·ry·man (kav′əl rē mən, -man′) *pl.,* **-men.** *n.* member of the cavalry.

cav·a·ti·na (kav′ə tē′nə) *n.* **1.** short, simple song or melody, usually without a second part or repeat, often found in a larger work, as an oratorio or opera. **2.** short, lyric, instrumental composition or passage. [Italian *cavatina* melodious air, from *cavata* production of sound, from *cavare* to extract, from Latin *cavāre* to make hollow.]

cave (kāv) *n.* natural hollow chamber or cavity beneath the earth's surface or in the side of a mountain. —*v.i.,* **caved, cav·ing. 1.** to fall in or down; collapse. **2. to cave in. a.** to fall in or down; collapse. **b.** *Informal.* to give in; surrender. —*v.t.* to hollow out: *The boys caved out a fort in the hill.* **2. to cave in.** to cause (something) to fall in or down. [Old French *cave* den, cavity, going back to Latin *cavus* hollow.]

ca·ve·at (kā′vē at′) *n.* **1.** formal notice to a legal authority to prevent some specific action until the notifier can be heard. **2.** warning. [Latin *caveat* let him beware; with reference to the first word of certain legal texts.]

ca·ve·at emp·tor (kā′vē at′ emp′tôr) *Latin.* let the buyer beware.

cave dweller, one who lives in a cave, esp. one who did so during prehistoric times.

cave-in (kāv′in′) *n.* **1.** collapse or falling in, as of a mine. **2.** site of such a collapse.

cave man 1. cave dweller of the Paleolithic period. **2.** *Informal.* man who behaves in a rough, crude manner, esp. toward women.

cav·ern (kav′ərn) *n.* underground cave, esp. one of very great size or extent. [French *caverne,* from Latin *caverna,* from *cavus* hollow.]

cav·ern·ous (kav′ər nəs) *adj.* **1.** full of or containing caverns or cavities. **2.** characteristic of a cavern; hollow and deep. **3.** deep-set: *cavernous eyes.* **4.** deep-sounding: *a cavernous voice.*

cav·i·ar (kav′ē är′) *also,* **cav·i·are.** *n.* salty processed roe of sturgeon and certain other large fish, served as an appetizer. [French *caviar,* from Italian *caviaro,* going back to Turkish *khāvyār.*]

cav·il (kav′əl) —**iled, -il·ing;** *also, British,* **-illed, -il·ling.** *v.i.* to find fault unnecessarily; raise trivial objections; quibble (often with *at* or *about*). —*v.t.* to find fault with unnecessarily. —*n.* captious, quibbling objection; trivial criticism. [Old French *caviller* to wrangle, mock, from Latin *cavillārī* to jeer.] —**cav′il·er;** *also, British,* **cav′il·ler,** *n.*

cav·i·ty (kav′ə tē) *pl.,* **-ties.** *n.* **1.** hollow place; hole. **2.** hollow space in a tooth caused by decay. **3.** space within the body or an organ. [Late Latin *cavitas* hollowness, from Latin *cavus* hollow.] —**Syn. 1.** see **hole.**

ca·vort (kə vôrt′) *v.i.* *Informal.* to run and jump around playfully; frisk. [Possibly modification of CURVET.]

ca·vy (kā′vē) *pl.,* **-vies.** *n.* any of various rodents, family Caviidae, of South America, having short legs, small ears, and a rounded body, the best known of which is the guinea pig. [Modern Latin *Cavia;* of Carib origin.]

caw (kô) *n.* harsh cry or call, as of a crow or raven. —*v.i.* to make this cry or call. [Imitative.]

Cawn·pore (kôn′pôr′) see **Kanpur.**

Cax·ton, William (kaks′tən) c.1422–91, first English printer.

cay (kā, kē) *n.* low mound or island of sand and, often, coral fragments, built up on a reef slightly above high tide level; key. [Spanish *cayo* rock, shoal, from Taino *cayo* small island.]

cay·enne (kī en′, kā-) *n.* hot, biting spice made from the ground seeds and pods of any of several hot red peppers, esp. *Capsicum frutescens,* variety longum. [Modification (influenced by CAYENNE) of Tupi-Guarani *kyinha* this spice.]

Cay·enne (kī en′, kā-) *n.* capital, port, and largest city of French Guiana, on the northern coast of the territory. Pop. (1961), 18,615.

cay·man (kā′mən) caiman.

Cay·man Islands (kā′mən, kī män′) three British islands in the Greater Antilles, northwest of Jamaica. Land area, 100 sq. mi. Pop. (1965 est.), 9,000.

Ca·yu·ga (kā ū′gə, kī-) *pl.,* **-ga** or **-gas.** *n.* member of a tribe of Iroquois Indians formerly living in what is now the state of New York.

cay·use (kī ūs′, -ōōs′) *n.* Indian pony of the western United States.

Cb, columbium.

CB, citizen's band (radio).

cc., cubic centimeter; cubic centimeters.

CCC, Civilian Conservation Corps.

C clef, movable clef indicating that the line of the staff on which it is placed represents middle C. There are three C clefs: the **alto clef,** having the symbol on the third line of the staff, the **tenor clef,** having the symbol on the fourth line, and the **soprano clef** having the symbol on the first line of the staff. See **clef** for illustration.

Cd, cadmium.

cd., cord; cords.

CD, civil defense.

cd. ft., cord foot; cord feet.

Cdr, Commander.

Ce, cerium.

C.E., Civil Engineer.

cease (sēs) **ceased, ceas·ing.** *v.i.* to come to an end; stop. —*v.t.* to put an end to; discontinue: *The factory will cease operations next week.* [Old French *cesser* to yield, stop, from Latin *cessāre* to stop, delay.] —**Syn.** *v.i.* see **stop.**

cease-fire (sēs′fīr′) *n.* temporary cessation of hostilities by mutual agreement of the combatants.

cease·less (sēs′lis) *adj.* continual; incessant. —**cease′less·ly,** *adv.* —**cease′less·ness,** *n.*

Ce·bu (sā bōō′) *n.* **1.** island in the south-central Philippines. Area, 1703 sq. mi. **2.** eastern port of this island. Pop. (1968), 332,100.

Ce·cil·ia, Saint (si sēl′yə) died c.230, virgin martyr of the second or third century.

ce·cro·pi·a moth (si krō′pē ə) large silkworm moth native to the eastern United States, having colorful markings.

ce·cum (sē′kəm) *pl.,* **-ca** (sē′kə). *also,* **cae·cum.** *n.* pouch or cavity that is open at one end, esp. the blind pouch which is the beginning of the large intestine and to which the vermiform appendix is attached. See **alimentary canal** for illustration. [Short for Latin *intestīnum caecum* blind intestine.] —**ce′cal,** *adj.*

ce·dar (sē′dər) *n.* **1.** any of several evergreen trees, genus *Cedrus,* of the pine family, having rough dark-gray bark and numerous branches that bear needle-shaped leaves. One of the best-known species is the **cedar of Lebanon,** *C. libani.* **2.** any of various other trees that have fragrant wood or needle-shaped leaves but are not true cedars, as the **red cedar,** *Juniperus virginiana.* **3.** durable fragrant wood of the true cedar, used for making chests and cabinets. [Latin *cedrus* cedar tree, from Greek *kedros.*]

ce·dar·bird (sē′dər burd′) *n.* cedar waxwing.

Cedar Rapids, city in eastern Iowa. Pop. (1970), 110,642.

cedar waxwing, crested waxwing, *Bombycilla cedrorum,* native to North America, having brownish-gray plumage with yellow, black, and red markings. Also, **ce′dar·bird′.**

cede (sēd) **ced·ed, ced·ing.** *v.t.* to give up, as title or possession; surrender; relinquish: *to cede territory.* [Latin *cēdere* to yield, go.]

ce·dil·la (si dil′ə) *n.* mark (,) placed under certain letters to indicate pronunciation. It is used esp. under *c* coming before a hard vowel to indicate the sound *s,* as in *façade.* [Spanish *cedilla,* diminutive of *ceda* the letter *z,* through Latin, from Greek *zēta* the letter *z;* because a *z* used to be added to *c* to indicate a soft pronunciation of *c,* as in French or Spanish.]

ceil (sēl) *v.t.* to furnish with a ceiling. [Possibly from Middle French *ciel* canopy, ceiling, sky, from Latin *caelum* heaven.]

ceil·ing (sē′ling) *n.* **1.** interior, overhead covering or surface of a room. **2.** maximum height above sea level at which a given aircraft can maintain horizontal flight under standard air conditions. **3.** vertical visibility measured from sea level to the bottom of the lowest cloud bank. **4.** maximum or upper limit set on anything: *a ceiling on prices.* **5. to hit the ceiling.** *Informal.* to lose one's temper; become very angry. [CEIL + -ING¹.]

cel·an·dine (sel′ən dīn′, -dēn) *n.* a plant of the poppy family that grows wild as a weed but is sometimes cultivated as a garden plant because of its clusters of yellow flowers. [Old French *celidoine,* from

Late Latin *chelidonium,* from Greek *chelidonion,* from *chelidōn* swallow.]

Cel·a·nese (sel′ə nēz′, sel′ə nēz′) *Trademark. n.* an acetate fabric.

Cel·e·bes (sel′ə bēz′) *n.* large island in Indonesia, east of Borneo. Area, approx. 70,000 sq. mi. Pop. (1961), 6,571,000.

cel·e·brant (sel′ə brənt) *n.* **1.** one who participates in a celebration. **2.** priest who officiates at a Mass or other liturgical service.

cel·e·brate (sel′ə brāt′) -brat·ed, -brat·ing. *v.t.* **1.** to commemorate (an event) with ceremonies, festivities, or other observances: *We celebrated his birthday.* **2.** to perform, as a ritual, publicly with the proper ceremonies; solemnize: *The priest celebrated the Mass.* **3.** to honor or make known publicly, esp. with praise; extol: *Their courage was celebrated in all the newspapers.* —*v.i.* **1.** to commemorate an event with ceremonies, festivities, or other observances. **2.** *Informal.* to have a merry time. [Latin *celebrātus,* past participle of *celebrāre* to honor, frequent.] —**cel′e·bra′tor,** *n.*

cel·e·brat·ed (sel′ə brā′tid) *adj.* well-known; famous. —**Syn.** see **famous.**

cel·e·bra·tion (sel′ə brā′shən) *n.* **1.** act of celebrating. **2.** that which is done to celebrate something.

ce·leb·ri·ty (sə leb′rə tē) *pl.,* -ties. *n.* one who is well-known or much publicized.

ce·ler·i·ty (sə ler′ə tē) *n.* swiftness; speed. [Latin *celeritās.*]

cel·er·y (sel′ər ē) *n.* **1.** thick crisp green or creamy-white leafstalks of a plant, *Apium graveolens,* variety *dulce,* of the parsley family. **2.** the plant itself. [French *céleri* the plant, from dialectal Italian *selleri* (plural), from Latin *selīnon* parsley, from Greek *selīnon.*]

ce·les·ta (sə les′tə) *n.* musical keyboard instrument having steel plates which, when struck by hammers, produce a tone similar to that of the glockenspiel. [French *célesta,* from *céleste* heavenly, from Latin *caelestis.*]

ce·les·tial (sə les′chəl) *adj.* **1.** of or relating to the sky or heavens: *a celestial body.* **2.** heavenly; divine: *celestial beauty.* [Old French *celestiel* heavenly, from Latin *caelestis.*] —**ce·les′tial·ly,** *adv.*

celestial equator, the great circle formed by the intersection of the plane of the earth's equator and the celestial sphere. See **declination** for illustration.

celestial mechanics, science that deals with the motion of celestial bodies, esp. those under the influence of gravitational fields.

celestial navigation, method of navigation in which position is determined by the observation of celestial bodies with respect to points on the earth which lie beneath those bodies.

celestial pole, either of the two intersections of the earth's axis with the celestial sphere.

celestial sphere, imaginary sphere surrounding the earth and representing the entire sky and to whose inner surface the stars are apparently attached.

ce·li·ac (sē′lē ak′) *also,* **coe·li·ac.** *adj.* of, relating to, or situated within the abdominal cavity. [Latin *coeliacus,* from Greek *koiliakos,* from *koiliā* abdomen.]

cel·i·ba·cy (sel′ə bə sē) *n.* state of being unmarried, esp. in accordance with religious vows.

cel·i·bate (sel′ə bit) *n.* one who remains unmarried, esp. in accordance with religious vows. —*adj.* unmarried. [Latin *caelibatus* single life, from *caelebs* unmarried.]

cell (sel) *n.* **1.** small, usually austere, room, as in a prison, convent, or monastery. **2.** basic unit of all living organisms, consisting of a mass of protoplasm with a nucleus near the center and surrounded by a cell membrane or wall. **3.** device that transforms chemical, solar, or light energy into electrical energy. **4.** local, underground unit of a political organization, esp. of a Communist party. **5.** small cavity or compartment, as in a honeycomb. [Latin *cella* small room, storeroom.]

cel·lar (sel′ər) *n.* **1.** room or group of rooms, either wholly or partly underground, usually under a building and often used as a place for storage. **2.** wine cellar *(def. 1).* **3.** stock of wines. [Anglo-Norman *celer* storeroom, from Late Latin *cellārium* pantry, from Latin *cella* small room, storeroom.]

cel·lar·er (sel′ər ər) *n.* one who is in charge of a cellar and the wines or provisions in it, esp. in a monastery.

Cel·li·ni, Ben·ve·nu·to (cha lē′nē; ben′və noo̅′tō) 1500–71, Florentine author, sculptor, and goldsmith.

cel·list (chel′ist) *also,* **'cel·list.** *n.* one who plays the cello. Also, **vi′olon·cel′list.**

cell membrane, very thin membrane that covers the entire surface of a cell. See **cell** for illustration.

cel·lo (chel′ō) *pl.,* -los. *also,* **'cel·lo.** *n.* tenor instrument of the violin family, intermediate between the viola and double bass in size and pitch. Also, **vi′o·lon·cel′lo.**

cel·lo·phane (sel′ə fān′) *n.* thin, flexible, usually transparent, material made from cellulose, used esp. as a wrapping material. [CELLULOSE + Greek *phainein* to show.]

cel·lu·lar (sel′yə lər) *adj.* **1.** of, relating to, or resembling a cell or cells. **2.** consisting of cells. —**cel·lu·lar·i·ty** (sel′yə lar′ə tē), *n.*

Cel·lu·loid (sel′yə loid′) *n. Trademark.* strong, transparent, flammable plastic made from nitrocellulose, alcohol, and camphor.

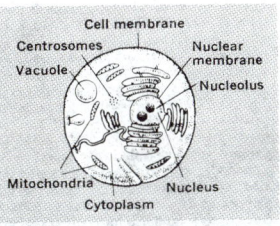

Cello

cel·lu·lose (sel′yə lōs′) *n.* compound of carbon, hydrogen, and oxygen in the form of a white solid that is insoluble in water. It is the major component of the walls of plant cells and thus makes up the woody part of trees and plants. It is used esp. to make paper, rayon, and other products. Formula: $(C_6H_{10}O_5)$ [French *cellulose,* from Latin *cellula* small storeroom, diminutive of *cella* small room, storeroom.]

cellulose acetate, thermoplastic resin made by treating cellulose with acetic acid and other compounds, used to make synthetic acetate fibers and membranes for removing salt from seawater.

cellulose nitrate, nitrocellulose.

cel·lu·lous (sel′yə ləs) *adj.* consisting or full of cells.

cell wall, in plants, hard outer layer of cellulose that covers the cell membrane.

Cel·si·us (sel′sē əs, -shē-) *adj.* centigrade. [From Anders *Celsius,* 1701–44, Swedish astronomer who established the centigrade scale.]

Celt (selt, kelt) *also,* **Kelt.** *n.* **1.** member of a Celtic-speaking people to which the Irish, Highland Scots, Welsh, Cornish, and Bretons belong. **2.** member of an ancient people of central and western Europe, including the Gauls and Britons. [French *Celte,* from Latin *Celtae* (plural), from Greek *Keltoi* (plural).]

Celt·ic (sel′tik, kel′tik) *also,* **Kelt·ic.** *adj.* of or relating to the Celts, their languages, or their culture. —*n.* group of languages belonging to the Indo-European language family, including Irish, Scots Gaelic, Breton, Welsh, and Cornish.

Celtic cross, Latin cross having a circle behind the intersection of the crosspiece. See **cross** for illustration.

cel·tuce (sel′təs) *n.* **1.** leaves and leaf stalks of a plant, *Lactuca sativa,* variety *asparagina,* of the composite family, eaten as a vegetable either raw or cooked and tasting like a mixture of celery and lettuce. **2.** the plant itself. [CEL(ERY) + (LET)TUCE.]

ce·ment (sə ment′) *n.* **1.** construction material made by burning a mixture of limestone, clay or shale, silica, gypsum, and other substances to form a powder that, when it is mixed with water, forms a slow-hardening paste. **2.** concrete. **3.** any soft substance, as glue, that hardens and acts as an adhesive. **4.** anything that joins together or unites; bond. —*v.t.* **1.** to cause to adhere or fasten together with cement: *to cement bricks. John cemented the wing to the model airplane.* **2.** to coat or cover with cement: *to cement a driveway.* **3.** to join together or unite; bind. —*v.i.* to become joined or fastened together. [Old French *ciment* mixture of limestone and crushed bricks, from Latin *caementum* rough stone, stone chips used to make mortar.] —**ce·ment′er,** *n.*

ce·men·tum (sə men′təm) *n.* substance that covers the root of a tooth, protecting the dentin and helping to anchor the tooth in the jawbone. [Modern Latin *cementum,* from Latin *c(a)ementum* rough stone.]

cem·e·ter·y (sem′ə ter′ē) *pl.,* -ter·ies. *n.* place for burying the dead; graveyard. [Late Latin *coemētērium,* from Greek *koimētērion* literally, sleeping place, from *koimān* to put to sleep.]

cen. 1. central. **2.** century.

cen·o·bite (sen′ə bīt′, sē′nə-) *also,* **coe·no·bite.** *n.* member of a religious order living in a monastery or convent. [Late Latin *coenobita* monk, from *coenobium* monastery, convent, from Greek *koinobion* convent, community life, from *koinos* common + *bios* life.]

cen·o·taph (sen′ə taf′) *n.* empty tomb or monument erected in memory of a deceased person whose body is buried elsewhere. [French *cénotaphe,* from Late Latin *cenotaphium,* from Greek *kenotaphion.*]

Ce·no·zo·ic (sē′nə zō′ik, sen′ə-) *n.* most recent geological era, comprising the Tertiary and Quaternary periods; age of mammals.

Labels on cell diagram:
Cell membrane · Centrosomes · Vacuole · Nuclear membrane · Nucleolus · Mitochondria · Cytoplasm · Nucleus

Cell

—*adj.* of, relating to, or characteristic of this era. [Greek *kainos* recent, new + *zōē* life + -IC.]

cen·ser (sen′sər) *n.* container in which incense is burned. Also, **thur′i·ble.** [Old French *censier,* going back to Latin *incēnsum* incense.]

cen·sor (sen′sər) *n.* **1.** one who examines and appraises material, as literature, plays, or motion pictures, for the purpose of deleting or suppressing that which is considered objectionable by the government or organization that employs him. **2.** official, usually employed by a government, esp. during wartime, to examine material, as letters, dispatches, or literature, for the purpose of deleting or suppressing information considered vital or dangerous to national security. **3.** one of two magistrates of ancient Rome who were in charge of taking the census and of supervising public morals. **4.** anyone who censures, denounces, or otherwise criticizes the behavior or morality of others. —*v.t.* to act as censor of: *Some governments censor books.* [Latin *cēnsor* assessor, critic.] —**cen·so′ri·al,** *adj.*

cen·so·ri·ous (sen sôr′ē əs) *adj.* tending to or containing censure; severely critical: *His censorious manner kept people away from him.* —**cen·so′ri·ous·ly,** *adv.* —**cen·so′ri·ous·ness,** *n.*

cen·sor·ship (sen′sər ship′) *n.* **1.** act or system of censoring. **2.** office or power held by a censor.

cen·sur·a·ble (sen′shər ə bəl) *adj.* worthy of censure.

cen·sure (sen′shər) *-sured, -sur·ing. v.t.* to express disapproval of or find fault with; blame; condemn. —*n.* expression of disapproval or blame; condemnation. [Latin *cēnsūra* opinion, judgment.] —**cen′sur·er,** *n.* —**Syn.** *v.t.* see **blame.**

cen·sus (sen′səs) *n.* official count of the population of a country or district, made in order to obtain certain statistics, such as age, sex, occupation, or economic status. [Latin *cēnsus* registration of citizens and their property.]

cent (sent) *n.* **1.** coin of the United States equal to one-hundredth of a dollar. **2.** one-hundredth of various other monetary units, as of the rand or the guilder. [Contraction of Latin *centēsimus* hundredth, from *centum* hundred.]

cent. **1.** central. **2.** century. **3.** centigrade.

cen·tare (sen′tār) *n.* centiare.

cen·taur (sen′tôr) *n.* Greek Mythology. one of a race of creatures having a human head, arms, and torso attached to the body and legs of a horse. [Latin *Centaurus,* from Greek *Kentauros.*]

Cen·tau·rus (sen tôr′əs) *n.* constellation south of the celestial equator containing the bright star Alpha Centauri.

cen·ta·vo (sen tä′vō) *pl.,* **-vos.** *n.* one-hundredth of various monetary units, as of the peso in certain Latin American countries. [Spanish *centavo* hundredth part, from Latin *centum* hundred.]

Centaur

cen·te·nar·i·an (sen′tə nār′ē ən) *n.* one who is one hundred years old or older. —*adj.* **1.** of the age of one hundred years. **2.** of or relating to a period of one hundred years.

cen·te·nar·y (sen′tə ner′ē, sen ten′ər ē) *pl.,* **-nar·ies.** *n.* **1.** centennial. **2.** period of one hundred years. —*adj.* **1.** of or relating to a period of one hundred years. **2.** recurring once in every one hundred years. [Latin *centēnārius* relating to a hundred, going back to Latin *centum* hundred.]

cen·ten·ni·al (sen ten′ē əl) *n.* hundredth anniversary or its celebration. —*adj.* **1.** of, relating to, or marking a period of one hundred years or its completion. **2.** of or relating to a hundredth anniversary. **3.** one hundred years old; enduring one hundred years. [Latin *centum* hundred + BIENNIAL.] —**cen·ten′ni·al·ly,** *adv.*

cen·ter (sen′tər) *also, British,* **cen·tre.** *n.* **1.** point or place equally distant from the sides, extremities, or exterior points of anything; middle part or point: *the center of the page, candies with chocolate centers.* **2.** place or point around which something, as interest or activity, revolves, converges, or is concentrated; pivotal or focal point: *a tourist center, the center of attention.* **3.** point, line, or axis around which anything, as a wheel, revolves. **4.** Geometry. point within a circle or sphere equally distant from all points on the circumference or surface. **5.** *also,* **Center.** group holding moderate political views, as between those of conservatives and liberals or radicals. **6.** *Sports.* **a.** football player who lines up in the middle of the offensive line and snaps the ball back to the quarterback. **b.** in basketball, hockey, and lacrosse, player who begins play. **7.** group or cluster of nerve cells governing a specific function or activity. —*v.t.,* **-tered, -ter·ing. 1.** to place or fix

in or at the center: *We centered the mirror on the wall.* **2.** to draw or gather toward one point; collect around a focal point; concentrate: *She centered her attention on the problem.* —*v.i.* to be centered or concentrated: *The main action of the story centered around the child.* [Latin *centrum* middle point (of a circle), from Greek *kentron* spike, goad, point around which a compass draws a circle.]

cen·ter·board (sen′tər bôrd′) *n.* fin-shaped board or plate lowered through a slot in the bottom of a sailboat to prevent drifting.

center field *Baseball.* **1.** middle section of the outfield behind second base, when viewed from home plate. **2.** position of the player stationed in this area.

center of gravity, center of mass, esp. of a body that is acted upon by gravity.

center of mass, point at which the mass of a body or system of bodies is theoretically concentrated.

cen·ter·piece (sen′tər pēs′) *n.* ornamental object, as a vase of flowers or a bowl, to be placed in the center of a table.

cen·tes·i·mal (sen tes′ə məl) *adj.* **1.** hundredth. **2.** relating to or divided into hundredths. [Latin *centēsimus* hundredth (from *centum* hundred) + -AL¹.] —**cen·tes′i·mal·ly,** *adv.*

cen·tes·i·mo (sen tes′ə mō′; *Italian* chen te′zē mō′; *Spanish* sen te′sē mō′) *pl., (Italian)* **-mi** (-mē′) or **-mos** (-mōz′; *Spanish* -mōs′). *n.* one-hundredth of various monetary units, as of the lira, escudo, and balboa. [Italian *centesimo* hundredth, from Latin *centēsimus.* See CENT.]

centi- *combining form* **1.** hundredth: *centipede.* **2.** hundredth part of: *centigram, centimeter.* [Latin *centum* hundred.]

cen·ti·are (sen′tē är′) *n.* unit of measure equal to one square meter. Also, **cen′tare.** See **weights and measures** for table. [French *centiare,* from Latin *centum* hundred + French *are.* See ARE².]

cen·ti·grade (sen′tə grād′) *adj.* of, according to, or designating the temperature scale on which the freezing point of water is at 0 degrees and the boiling point is at 100 degrees under standard atmospheric pressure. A temperature change of 5 degrees on the centigrade scale is equal to a change of 9 degrees on the Fahrenheit scale. Also, **Cel′si·us.** [CENTI- + Latin *gradus* step, degree.]

cen·ti·gram (sen′tə gram′) *also, British,* **cen·ti·gramme.** *n.* unit of metric weight equal to one-hundredth of a gram. [French *centigramme,* going back to Latin *centum* hundred + Greek *gramma* small weight.]

cen·til·lion (sen til′yən) *n.* **1.** in the United States and France, the cardinal number that is represented by 1 followed by 303 zeros. **2.** in Great Britain and Germany, the cardinal number that is represented by 1 followed by 600 zeros. —*adj.* numbering one centillion. [Latin *centum* one hundred; formed on the model of MILLION.] —**cen·til′lionth,** *adj., n.*

cen·time (sän′tēm) *n.* one-hundredth of any of various monetary units, as of the franc. [French *centime,* going back to Latin *centēsimus* hundredth.]

cen·ti·me·ter (sen′tə mē′tər) *also, British,* **cen·ti·me·tre.** *n.* unit of metric measure equal to one-hundredth of a meter. [French *centimètre,* going back to Latin *centum* hundred + Greek *metron* measure.]

cen·ti·me·ter-gram-sec·ond (sen′tə mē′tər gram′sek′ənd) *adj.* of, relating to, or being a system of measurement in which the centimeter is the unit of length, the gram is the unit of mass, and the second is the unit of time.

cen·ti·mo (sen′tə mō′) *pl.,* **-mos.** *n.* one-hundredth of various monetary units, as of the peseta, the bolivar, and the colon. [Spanish *céntimo,* from French *centime.* See CENTIME.]

cen·ti·pede (sen′tə pēd′) *n.* any of a group of small wormlike invertebrates, class Chilopoda, with a flattened, elongated body made up of many segments, each bearing a pair of legs. In some centipedes the foremost pair of legs is modified into poisonous claws. [Latin *centipeda,* from *centum* hundred + *pēs* foot.]

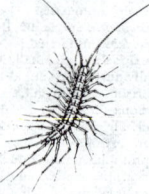

Centipede

cen·tral (sen′trəl) *adj.* **1.** in, at, or near the center or middle: *The railroad station has a central location in town.* **2.** of or forming the center. **3.** constituting that from which other things proceed or upon which they depend or pivot; essential; principal: *the central character of a book.* **4.** that exercises a controlling or directing influence, as over local activities or divisions: *a central agency.* —*n.* **1.** main telephone exchange of an area, as a town or city. **2.** telephone operator at such an exchange. [Latin *centrālis* relating to a center, from *centrum* middle point. See CENTER.] —**cen′tral·ly,** *adv.*

Central African Republic, country in central Africa. Capital, Bangui. Area, 240,535 sq. mi. Pop. (1969 est.), 1,518,000.

Central America, region between the Pacific and the Caribbean,

at; āpe; cär; end; mē; it; īce; hot; ōld; fôrk; wood; fōol; oil; out; up; ūse; turn; sing; thin; this; zh in treasure; ə in ago, taken, pencil, lemon, circus.

occupying the long isthmus of North America that links that continent with South America. Area, 205,087 sq. mi. —**Central American.**

Central Intelligence Agency, U.S. government organization, established in 1947 to coordinate intelligence activities and to give advice on policy matters.

cen·tral·i·ty (sen tral′ə tē) *pl.,* **-ties.** *n.* **1.** state or quality of being central. **2.** central position or situation.

cen·tral·i·za·tion (sen′trə li zā′shən) *n.* **1.** act of centralizing; being centralized. **2.** concentration of power in a central group or institution.

cen·tral·ize (sen′trə līz′) **-ized, -iz·ing.** *v.t.* to bring or organize under one control or a central authority. —*v.i.* to come together at a center.

central nervous system, that part of the nervous system composed of the brain and the spinal cord.

Central Powers, countries that fought against the Allies in World War I: Germany and Austria-Hungary, and their allies, Turkey and Bulgaria.

Central Standard Time, the local time of the ninetieth meridian west of Greenwich, England, used in the east-central United States. It is six hours earlier than Greenwich Time.

cen·tre (sen′tər) *British. n.* center. —*v.t., v.i.,* **-tred, -tring.** to center.

centri-, form of **centro,** as in *centrifugal.*

cen·tric (sen′trik) *adj.* in or at a center; central. Also, **cen′tri·cal.** —**cen′tri·cal·ly,** *adv.* —**cen·tric·i·ty** (sen tris′ə tē), *n.*

cen·trif·u·gal (sen trif′yə gəl, -ə gəl) *adj.* **1.** moving or directed away from a center. Opposed to **centripetal. 2.** using or operating by centrifugal force: *a centrifugal pump.* [Modern Latin *centrifugus* fleeing from the center (from Latin *centrum* middle point + *fugere* to flee). See CENTER.] —**cen·trif′u·gal·ly,** *adv.*

centrifugal force, force generated when a body is moving in a curved path, tending to move the body away from the center of curvature.

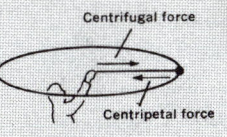

Centrifugal force

cen·tri·fuge (sen′trə fūj′) *n.* **1.** device using centrifugal force to separate substances of different densities by spinning them at high speeds. **2.** large machine that simulates gravitational effects, usually consisting of a capsule or chair spun in a circle at the end of a long support, used chiefly in training astronauts to withstand gravitational pull. —*v.t.,* **-fuged, -fug·ing.** to subject to the action of a centrifuge. [French *centrifuge* centrifugal, from Latin *centrum* middle point + *fugere* to flee. See CENTER.]

cen·tri·ole (sen′trē ōl′) *n.* tiny cylindrical body in all animal cells and many plant cells, usually paired. Centrioles duplicate themselves just before mitosis and move to opposite ends of the cell during mitosis, where they form the poles of the spindle to which the chromosomes move. [Latin *centrum* middle point + Latin *-olus,* diminutive suffix. See CENTER.]

cen·trip·e·tal (sen trip′ət əl) *adj.* **1.** moving or directed toward a center. Opposed to **centrifugal. 2.** using or operating by centripetal force. [Modern Latin *centripetus* seeking the center (from Latin *centrum* middle point + *petere* to seek) + -AL¹. See CENTER.] —**cen·trip′e·tal·ly,** *adv.*

centripetal force, force that causes a body to move in a curved rather than straight path, acting toward the center of curvature. See **centrifugal force** for illustration.

cen·trist (sen′trist) *n.* one whose political views are moderate, esp. in certain European countries; member of a center party.

centro-, combining form center: *centrosome.* [Latin *centrum* middle point. See CENTER.]

cen·tro·some (sen′trə sōm′) *n.* area, in the cytoplasm of a cell, that contains the centrioles. See **cell** for illustration. [Greek *kentron* spike, central point + *sōma* body.]

cen·tro·sphere (sen′trə sfēr′) *n.* protoplasm surrounding the centrosome. [Greek *kentron* spike, central point + *sphaira* ball, globe.]

cen·tu·ple (sen′tōō′pəl, -tū′-, sen′tə pəl, -tyə-) *adj.* multiplied by a hundred; hundredfold. —*v.t.,* **-pled, -pling.** to multiply by a hundred; increase a hundredfold. [French *centuple* hundredfold, from Late Latin *centuplus,* from Latin *centum* hundred.]

cen·tu·ri·on (sen toor′ē ən, -tyoor′-) *n.* commander of a century in the ancient Roman army. [Latin *centuriō,* going back to *centum* hundred.]

cen·tu·ry (sen′chər ē) *pl.,* **-ries.** *n.* **1.** period of one hundred years. **2.** period of one hundred years reckoned forward or backward from some fixed date, esp. from the birth of Christ: *The U.S. Civil War took place in the nineteenth century.* **3.** in the ancient Roman army, infantry division originally consisting of one hundred men. **4.** one of 193 political divisions of the ancient Roman people, each division having one

vote. [Latin *centuria* division of a hundred units, from *centum* hundred.]

century plant, desert plant, *Agave americana,* found in Mexico and the southwestern United States, having thick, spiny-edged leaves and a flower stalk that grows to a height of twenty to forty feet. [It was formerly believed to bloom only once every century.]

ce·phal·ic (si fal′ik) *adj.* **1.** of or relating to the head. **2.** near, on, in, or toward the head. [Latin *cephalicus* relating to the head, from Greek *kephalikos,* from *kephalē* head.]

ceph·a·lo·pod (sef′ə lə pod′) *n.* any of a group of highly developed mollusks, class Cephalopoda, including the octopus, squid, and cuttlefish, having a clearly defined head with large, well-developed eyes, a sharp beak, and muscular tentacles around the mouth that bear suckers. [Modern Latin *Cephalopoda,* from Greek *kephalē* head + *pous* foot.]

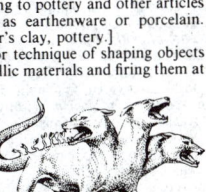

Century plant

ceph·a·lo·tho·rax (sef′ə lō thôr′aks) *n.* anterior portion of the body in crustaceans, arachnids, and certain animals, consisting of the united head and thorax. [Greek *kephalē* head + *thōrax* chest.]

Ce·phe·us (sē′fē əs, sē′fūs) *n.* **1.** *Greek Legend.* Ethiopian king who was the father of Andromeda and husband of Cassiopeia. **2.** constellation near the northern sky.

ce·ram·ic (si ram′ik) *adj.* of or relating to pottery and other articles made of fired and baked clay, such as earthenware or porcelain. [Greek *keramikos,* from *keramos* potter's clay, pottery.]

ce·ram·ics (si ram′iks) *n.,pl.* **1.** art or technique of shaping objects from clay and other inorganic, nonmetallic materials and firing them at high temperatures. **2.** articles made by this technique, as pottery, glass, abrasives, bricks, and tiles. ▲ construed as singular in def. 1, as plural in def. 2. —**ce·ra·mist** (ser′ə mist′, si ram′ist), **ce·ram′i·cist,** *n.*

Cer·ber·us (sur′bər əs) *n. Classical Mythology.* monstrous three-headed dog having a mane and tail of serpents and guarding the entrance to Hades.

Cerberus

cere (sēr) *n.* fleshy, waxy-looking membrane above the upper portion of the beak of certain birds, as parrots, parakeets, and birds of prey, that contains the nostrils. [French *cire* wax, from Latin *cēra.*]

ce·re·al (sēr′ē əl) *n.* **1.** any of a number of foods, as cornflakes or oatmeal, made from the seeds or seedlike fruits of cereal grains. **2.** seed or seedlike fruit itself. **3.** any one of a number of plants of the grass family that bears such seeds or seedlike fruits, as wheat or barley. —*adj.* of or relating to edible grain or the plants producing it. [Latin *cereālis* relating to grain, relating to CERES.]

cer·e·bel·lum (ser′ə bel′əm) *pl.,* **-bel·lums** or **-bel·la** (-bel′ə). *n.* the part of the brain that coordinates muscular activity and is involved with the maintenance of posture and balance. See **brain** for illustration. [Latin *cerebellum* small brain, diminutive of *cerebrum* brain.]

cer·e·bral (ser′ə brəl, sə rē′-) *adj.* **1.** of or relating to the cerebrum. **2.** relating to, involving, or appealing to the intellect; intellectual.

cerebral palsy, condition characterized by lack of control over the muscles, esp. those involved in the performance of voluntary actions, resulting from damage to the brain before or during birth.

cer·e·brate (ser′ə brāt′) **-brat·ed, -brat·ing.** *v.i.* to use the brain; think. —**cer′e·bra′tion,** *n.*

cer·e·bro·spi·nal (ser′ə brō spīn′əl) *adj.* of or relating to the brain and spinal cord.

cer·e·brum (ser′ə brəm, sə rē′-) *pl.,* **-brums** or **-bra** (-brə). *n.* the largest part of the human brain, occupying the whole upper portion of the cranium. The cerebrum interprets sensation, controls voluntary muscles, and coordinates mental processes. See **brain** for illustration. [Latin *cerebrum* brain.]

cere·cloth (sēr′klôth′) *n.* cloth treated with wax or a similar substance, used esp. to wrap the dead. [Originally *cered cloth,* from obsolete *cere* to wax, from Latin *cērāre.*]

cere·ment (sēr′mənt) *also,* **cere·ments.** *n.* **1.** cerecloth. **2.** any burial clothes; shroud. [French *cirement* a waxing, from *cirer* to wax, from Latin *cērāre.*]

cer·e·mo·ni·al (ser′ə mō′nē əl) *adj.* **1.** of, relating to, or characterized by ceremony or ceremonies; ritual: *a ceremonial dinner.* **2.** used in or in connection with a ceremony: *ceremonial robes.* —*n.* prescribed set of rites or formalities observed on or for some particular occasion; ritual: *the ceremonial of graduation.* —**cer′e·mo′ni·al·ly,** *adv.*

at; āpe; cär; end; mē; it; īce; hot; ōld; fôrk; wood; fōōl; oil; out; up; ūse; turn; sing; thin; this; zh in treasure; ə in ago, taken, pencil, lemon, circus.

161

cer·e·mo·ni·ous (ser′ə mō′nē əs) *adj.* **1.** given to or carefully observant of ceremony or formality; elaborately or studiously polite: *a ceremonious bow.* **2.** characterized by or conducted with ceremony; formal: *a ceremonious occasion.* —**cer′e·mo′ni·ous·ly,** *adv.* —**cer′e·mo′ni·ous·ness,** *n.*

cer·e·mo·ny (ser′ə mō′nē) *pl.,* **-nies.** *n.* **1.** formal act or set of acts prescribed by ritual, etiquette, or convention and performed in a prescribed manner: *a wedding ceremony, a graduation ceremony, an inaugural ceremony.* **2.** conventional act or observance of courtesy, civility, or politeness: *Having completed the ceremony of introductions, the speaker began.* **3.** strict adherence to conventional forms of social behavior: *The greeting of the dignitaries was conducted with much ceremony. They got up and left without ceremony.* **4.** routine faithfully followed with a great deal of pomp, pretentiousness, or elaborateness: *She made a nightly ceremony of doing her hair.* **5.** rite that has lost its significance or meaning; empty ritual or formality. **6. to stand on** (or **upon**) **ceremony.** to behave with or insist on strict adherence to formalities: *You needn't stand on ceremony with us.* [Old French *ceremonie* rite, from Latin *caerimōnia* sacred rite, sanctity.]
Syn. 1. Ceremony, rite, ritual denote a set of observances followed on special and solemn occasions. **Ceremony** suggests an elaborate and formal act or set of procedures performed as required by religion, custom, or law: *The Independence Day was celebrated with appropriate ceremonies.* **Rite** stresses the symbolic significance of an act or series of acts established by tradition or religious prescription: *Baptism is one of the most important rites in the Catholic Church.* **Ritual** tends to emphasize the customary or established character of procedures followed on religious or public occasions: *John was initiated as a member of the club after the usual rituals.*

Ce·res (sēr′ēz) *n.* **1.** Roman goddess of grain and agriculture. Her Greek counterpart is Demeter. **2.** largest of the asteroids and the first to be discovered, first sighted in 1801.

ce·re·us (sēr′ē əs) *n.* **1.** any of a group of large, columnar, usually treelike cactuses, genus *Cereus,* found in South America. **2.** any of various other cactuses, as the night-blooming cereus, genus *Hylocereus.* [Latin *cēreus* wax candle, from *cēra* wax; because its shape suggests a wax candle.]

ce·rise (sə rēs′, -rēz′) *n.* bright, red color; cherry. [French *cerise* cherry, going back to Latin *cerasus* cherry tree, from Greek *kerasos.*]

ce·ri·um (sēr′ē əm) *n.* malleable, grayish metallic element, used esp. in refining processes and alloys. It is the most abundant of the rare-earth elements. Symbol: **Ce** See element for table. [Modern Latin *cerium,* from the asteroid Ceres, from Latin *Cerēs* Roman goddess of grain.]

cer·tain (surt′ən) *adj.* **1.** free from doubt or reservation; fully confident; positive; assured: *I am certain of his loyalty. They're certain she wasn't there.* **2.** established as true; beyond doubt or question; indisputable: *It is now certain that he won the election.* **3.** bound to happen; destined; inevitable; sure: *Capture means certain death.* **4.** agreed upon; settled; determined: *They plan to meet at a certain time.* **5.** that may be depended on; reliable; trustworthy; unfailing: *It's a certain cure for a headache.* **6.** definite, but not named or specified; particular: *The room has a certain charm about it.* **7.** appreciable: *There has been a certain amount of improvement in his health.* **8. for certain.** without doubt; surely. [Old French *certain* assured, definite, going back to Latin *certus* sure.] —**Syn. 1.** see **sure.**

cer·tain·ly (surt′ən lē) *adv.* definitely; surely: *You certainly is sloppy. There is certainly one in our car.*

cer·tain·ty (surt′ən tē) *pl.,* **-ties.** *n.* **1.** quality, state, or fact of being certain: *a feeling of certainty. In view of the facts, his certainty was appalling.* **2.** something certain; established fact: *After three days, our victory became a certainty.*

cer·tes (sur′tēz) *adv.* Archaic. truly; certainly. [Old French *certes,* going back to Latin *certus* sure.]

cer·tif·i·cate (*n.,* sər tif′ə kit; *v.,* sər tif′ə kāt′) *n.* **1.** official document attesting to the truth of the facts contained therein: *a death certificate, a birth certificate, a marriage certificate.* **2.** official document certifying that an individual has met all the qualifications necessary for a particular profession and authorizing professional practice: *a teaching certificate.* **3.** official document certifying to the completion of an educational course. —*v.t.* **-cat·ed, -cat·ing.** to furnish with or attest to by a certificate. [Medieval Latin *certificatum* thing certified, from *certificare* to certify. See CERTIFY.]

cer·ti·fi·ca·tion (sur′tə fi kā′shən) *n.* **1.** act of certifying; being certified. **2.** a certified statement; certificate.

cer·ti·fied (sur′tə fīd′) *adj.* **1.** reliably or authoritatively endorsed or guaranteed, as by a certificate. **2.** furnished with or having a certificate: *a certified representative.*

certified check, check whose payment is guaranteed by the bank upon which it is drawn.

certified mail, uninsured first-class mail requiring a signed receipt for the sender as proof of delivery.

certified milk, raw or pasteurized milk produced according to rules and regulations of an authorized medical milk commission.

certified public accountant, person who has received a certificate from a state verifying that he has satisfactorily met requirements of the state law to act in the capacity of public accountant.

cer·ti·fy (sur′tə fī′) **-fied, -fy·ing.** *v.t.* **1.** to make a declaration of or vouch for (something), often by a signed statement or official document; testify or attest to: *to certify one's date of birth.* **2.** to give reliable information of; guarantee as certain; confirm: *He cited examples in order to certify his statement.* **3.** to endorse as having met particular standards or requirements; guarantee the quality or value of. **4.** to guarantee in writing on the face of (a check) that the account drawn on has sufficient funds for payment. **5.** *Archaic.* to assure or inform with certainty. —*v.i.* to vouch or testify (with *to*). [Old French *certifier* to secure, make sure, guarantee, from Medieval Latin *certificare* to make sure, from Latin *certus* sure + *facere* to make.] —**cer′ti·fi′a·ble,** *adj.* —**cer′ti·fi′er,** *n.*
Syn. 1. Certify, attest mean to testify to the truth or authenticity of something. **Certify** means to declare formally that something is true or as represented: *The doctor certified his findings to the commission.* **Attest** means to witness or authenticate in one's official capacity and to affirm the evidence presented as indisputable to one's knowledge: *The notary public attested the document.*

cer·ti·o·rar·i (sur′shē ə rār′ē) *n.* *Law.* **1.** writ issued from a higher court, calling for the record of a proceeding from a lower court or an official or quasi-judicial body for review or inspection. **2.** permission to present a case for review or inspection. [Late Latin *certiōrārī* to be informed, from Latin *certior,* comparative of *certus* sure; because *certiōrārī* is used in the Latin text of the writ.]

cer·ti·tude (sur′tə tōod′, -tūd′) *n.* complete assurance or confidence; certainty. [Late Latin *certitūdō,* from Latin *certus* sure.]

ce·ru·le·an (sə rōō′lē ən) *n.* sky-blue color; azure. [Latin *caeruleus* dark blue + -AN.]

ce·ru·men (sə rōō′mən) *n.* earwax. [Modern Latin *cerumen,* from Latin *cera* wax.]

Cer·van·tes, Mi·guel de (sər van′tēz, -tās, -vän′-; mē gel′ dā) 1547–1616, Spanish author.

cer·vi·cal (sur′vi kəl) *adj.* of, relating to, or situated in or near a cervix.

cer·vine (sur′vīn) *adj.* of, relating to, or resembling deer. [Latin *cervīnus* relating to deer, from *cervus* deer.]

cer·vix (sur′viks) *pl.,* **-vix·es** or **-vi·ces** (-və sēz). *n.* **1.** the neck, esp. the back of the neck, connecting the head and the trunk of the body. **2.** lower, necklike part of the uterus, connecting with the vagina. **3.** any necklike part of an organ, as in the bladder. [Latin *cervix* neck.]

Ce·sar·e·an (si zâr′ē ən) *also,* **Ce·sar·i·an.** Caesarean.

Cesarean section *also,* **Caesarean section.** delivery of a baby from its mother's uterus by a surgical incision made through the abdomen into the uterus. It is performed when normal delivery is impossible or dangerous. Also, **Cesarean birth, Cesarean operation.** [Because Julius Caesar supposedly was delivered in this way.]

ce·si·um (sē′zē əm) *also,* **cae·si·um.** *n.* soft, silvery metallic element used esp. in photoelectric cells, infrared devices, spectrometers, and other optical instruments. It is the most reactive and one of the rarest of metals. Symbol: **Cs** See element for table. [Modern Latin *caesium,* from Latin *caesius* bluish gray; because its spectrum has two blue lines.]

ces·sa·tion (se sā′shən) *n.* a ceasing or halting; discontinuance; stop: *a cessation of hostilities.* [Latin *cessātiō.*]

ces·sion (se′shən) *n.* **1.** act of ceding; a giving up or surrendering, as of rights or territory, to another. **2.** that which is ceded, as territory. [Latin *cessiō* a giving up.]

cess·pool (ses′pōol′) *n.* **1.** pit, well, or other underground container, often brick-lined, that is connected to plumbing as a receptacle for sewage. **2.** any foul or filthy receptacle or place. [Of uncertain origin.]

c'est la vie (sā lä vē′) *French.* such is life; that's life.

ces·tode (ses′tōd) *n.* tapeworm. [Greek *kestos* band.]

ces·toid (ses′toid) *adj.* ribbonlike, as the tapeworm.

ces·tus (ses′təs) *also,* **caes·tus.** *n.* device consisting of leather thongs wound around the fingers and forearms, often with metal studs or spikes attached, used by boxers of ancient Greece and Rome. [Latin *caestus,* from *caedere* to strike.]

Cestus

ce·su·ra (si zhoor′ə, -zoor′ə) caesura.

ce·ta·cean (si tā′shən) *adj.* of, relating to, or belonging to an order, Cetacea, of aquatic, fishlike mammals, including whales, dolphins, and porpoises. —*n.* cetacean mammal. [Modern Latin *Cetacea* (from Latin *cētus* whale, from Greek *kētos*) + -AN.] —**ce·ta′ceous,** *adj.*

at; āpe; cär; end; mē; it; īce; hot; ōld; fôrk; wood; fōol; oil; out; up; ūse; turn; sing; thin; this; zh in treasure; ə in ago, taken, pencil, lemon, circus.

Cey·lon (si lon′) n. see **Sri Lanka.** —**Cey·lo·nese** (sē′lə nēz′, -nēs′), adj., n.

Cé·zanne, Paul (sā zan′) 1839–1906, French painter.

Cf, californium.

cf., compare. [Abbreviation of Latin *confer*.]

C.F.I., cost, freight, and insurance.

cg., centigram; centigrams. Also, **cg, cgm.**

CGS, centimeter-gram-second.

ch. 1. chapter. **2.** church. Also, **Ch.**

Cha·blis (shab′lē, sha blē′) n. dry, white, Burgundy wine. [From *Chablis,* French town where it is made.]

cha-cha (chä′chä′) n. **1.** ballroom dance of Latin-American origin, similar to the mambo. Also, **cha′-cha′-cha′. 2.** music for this dance. [Spanish *cha-cha-cha* this dance; probably imitative of the beat of this music.]

cha·conne (shȧ kôn′, -kon′) n. musical composition in slow triple time, having a melodic or harmonic motif that is usually played by the bass and repeated over and over. [French *chaconne,* from Spanish *chacona* slow dance in triple time and its music; of uncertain origin.]

Chad (chad) n. **1.** country in north-central Africa, formerly a French colony. Capital, Fort-Lamy. Area, 495,800 sq. mi. Pop. (1969 est.), 3,510,000. **2.** Lake. large lake at the southern edge of the Sahara Desert in north-central Africa.

Chaer·o·ne·a (ker′ə nē′ə) n. ancient town in Boeotia, Greece, where the Macedonians under Philip II and his son Alexander defeated the united Greeks in 338 B.C.

chafe (chāf) *chafed, chaf·ing. v.t.* **1.** to wear away or make sore by friction or rubbing; abrade: *The diaper chafed the baby's skin. The pulley had chafed the cable.* **2.** to make angry; irritate; annoy: *His rude behavior chafed her.* **3.** to restore warmth or sensation to by rubbing: *We chafed her numb hands.* —*v.i.* **1.** to be worn away or made sore by friction. **2.** to be irritated or annoyed; fret; fume: *He chafed under the constant criticism.* —*n.* soreness or wear caused by friction or rubbing. [Old French *chaufer* to warm, going back to Latin *calefacere* to make warm.]

chaf·er (chā′fər) n. any of a group of destructive beetles, family Scarabaeidae, including the June bug and cockchafer. [Old English *ceafor* beetle.]

chaff[1] (chaf) n. **1.** husks of wheat, oats, rye, and other grains, separated from the seed by threshing and winnowing. **2.** finely cut hay or straw used as feed for livestock. **3.** any worthless matter; refuse. [Old English *ceaf* husks of grain.]

chaff[2] (chaf) *v.t., v.i.* to tease or make fun (of) in a good-natured way. —*n.* good-natured teasing; raillery. [Possibly a form of CHAFE.]

chaf·fer (chaf′ər) *v.i.* to haggle about price; bargain. [Middle English *chaffare* trade, wares, from Old English *cēap* bargain + *faru* journey, business.] —**chaf′fer·er,** *n.*

chaf·finch (chaf′inch) n. European finch, *Fringilla coelebs,* having a pleasant, short song, popular as a cage bird. [Old English *ceaffinc,* from *ceaf* chaff + *finc* finch; referring to its fondness for chaff.]

chafing dish, pan or dish with a heating device underneath it, for cooking or keeping food warm at the table.

Chafing dish

Cha·gall, Marc (shȧ gäl′) 1887—, Russian artist who has lived and worked chiefly in France.

Cha·gres (chä′gres) n. river in Panama and the Canal Zone, the principal source of water for the Panama Canal.

cha·grin (shə grin′) n. feeling of vexation or distress arising from disappointment, failure, or humiliation. —*v.t.* to vex or distress by disappointment or humiliation: *She was deeply chagrined by the failure of her plan.* [French *chagrin* grief; of uncertain origin.]

chain (chān) n. **1.** series of connected or interlocking links or rings, usually of metal, used chiefly to bind, drag, hold, or ornament. **2.** series connected or following in succession; sequence: *a chain of events, a mountain chain.* **3. a.** shackles; fetters: *The prisoners were led off the boat in chains.* **b.** imprisonment; bondage; confinement: *Moses helped the Hebrews throw off their chains and led them out of Egypt.* **4.** anything that binds or restrains. **5.** number of similar business establishments under the same ownership or management: *a chain of movie theaters, a chain of drugstores.* **6.** series of atoms of the same element linked together. **7.a.** measuring instrument consisting of links of equal length, used in surveying and engineering. **b.** unit of length, as measured by such an instrument, equal to 100 or 66 feet. —*v.t.* **1.** to fasten, secure, or connect with a chain: *He chained his bicycle to the post. She chained the door.* **2.** to restrain or confine; bind; fetter: *All that work chained him to his desk.* [Old French *chaeine* fetter, from Latin *catēna* fetter, series.]

chain gang, group of convicts chained together, usually while at hard labor or outdoors.

chain letter, letter sent to a number of people, asking each to send a copy in turn to a specific number of other persons.

chain mail, flexible body armor made of interlaced metal rings or links.

chain reaction 1. any series of events so related to one another that each is caused by the preceding one and initiates a succeeding one. **2.** series of self-sustaining nuclear reactions in which the nuclei of radioactive atoms split and release neutrons. Some of these then split other nuclei, releasing more neutrons and continuing the process.

chain saw, portable power saw with teeth on an endless chain.

chain-smoke (chān′smōk′) **-smoked, -smok·ing.** *v.i.* to smoke one cigarette or cigar after another in almost continuous succession. —*v.t.* to smoke, as one cigarette after another, in almost continuous succession.

chain smoker, person who smokes one cigarette or cigar after another in almost continuous succession.

chain-stitch (chān′stich′) *v.t.* to sew or crochet with chain stitches.

chain stitch, stitching made by looping each stitch and connecting it to the next one, forming links as in a chain.

Chain mail

chain store, one of a group of retail stores owned and operated by one company and retailing similar merchandise.

chair (chār) n. **1.** piece of furniture that has a seat, legs, a backrest, and sometimes, arms, usually designed to seat one person. **2.** seat of office, dignity, or authority. **3.** office or position of authority or dignity, esp. of a professor: *He holds the chair of medieval literature at the university.* **4.** presiding officer; chairman: *The speaker rose to address the chair.* **5.** sedan chair. **6.** *Slang.* the electric chair. **7. to take the chair.** to assume the position of chairman; preside at or open a meeting. —*v.t.* to preside over; act as chairman of: *to chair a panel discussion.* [Old French *chaiere* seat, from Latin *cathedra,* from Greek *kathedrā.* Doublet of CATHEDRA.]

chair·man (chār′mən) pl., **-men.** n. presiding officer of a meeting, committee, board, or organization. —**chair′wom′an,** n.

chair·man·ship (chār′mən ship′) n. position, duties, or term of office of chairman.

chaise (shāz) n. **1.** light, two-wheeled carriage, often with a hood or folding top, usually seating one or two passengers. **2.** similar vehicle having four wheels. [French *chaise* seat, form of *chaire* seat, from Old French *chaiere.* See CHAIR.]

chaise longue (shāz′lông′, chāz′-) chair with a seat long enough to support the legs when outstretched. Also, **chaise lounge.** [French *chaise longue* lounging chair; *longue* long. See CHAISE.]

Chal·ce·don (kal′sə don′, kal sēd′ən) n. ancient city in northwestern Asia Minor.

chal·ced·o·ny (kal sed′ən ē, kal′sə dō′nē) pl., **-nies.** n. any of several fine-grained translucent varieties of quartz having a waxy luster and occurring in various colors. Agate, carnelian, and onyx are chalcedony. [Latin *chalcēdonius* a precious stone mentioned only in the New Testament, from Greek *chalkēdōn.*]

chal·cid (kal′sid) n. any of a group of very small four-winged or wingless insects, family Chalcididae, whose larvae are parasitic on the eggs, larvae, or pupae of other insects. [Greek *chalkos* copper; referring to its color.]

chal·co·cite (kal′kə sīt′) n. gray mineral with a metallic luster, an important ore of copper; cuprous sulfide. Formula: Cu₂S [Modification of French *chalcosine,* from Greek *chalkos* copper.]

chal·co·py·rite (kal′kə pī′rīt) n. yellowish, opaque mineral with a metallic luster, one of the most important sources of copper. Formula: CuFeS₂ [Modern Latin *chalcopyrites,* from Greek *chalkos* copper + Latin *pyritēs* flint. See PYRITES.]

Chal·de·a (kal dē′ə) n. ancient region in southernmost Babylonia, now in southern Iraq. In Biblical times it included all of Babylonia.

Chal·de·an (kal dē′ən) n. **1.** one of an ancient Semitic people of Chaldea who became dominant in and ruled Babylonia. **2.** Semitic language of the Chaldeans, a dialect of Aramaic. **3.** one versed in occult learning, as that of the Chaldeans; astrologer; soothsayer. —*adj.* **1.** of or relating to Chaldea, its people, their language, or their culture. **2.** of or relating to astrology or occultism, esp. as first practiced by the Chaldeans. Also, **Chal·da·ic** (kal dā′ik). [Latin *Chaldaeus* (from Greek *Chaldaios*) of Semitic origin) + -AN.]

cha·let (sha lā′) n. **1.** house characterized by wide, sloping roofs with overhanging eaves, commonly found in Switzerland and other Alpine regions of Europe. **2.** any cottage, house, or villa built in this style. **3.** any herdsman's hut or simple cottage in the Alpine regions of Europe, esp. in Switzerland. [Swiss French *chalet* cottage, from a pre-Latin word for "shelter."]

chal·ice (chal′ĭs) n. 1. drinking cup or goblet. 2. cup or vessel containing the wine consecrated at Holy Communion. 3. cup-shaped flower. [Old French c(h)alice cup, from Latin calix.]

chalk (chôk) n. 1. soft, porous limestone composed chiefly of calcite, used esp. to make lime and portland cement, and, sometimes, as a fertilizer. 2. synthetic substance similar to this, usually in the form of a crayon, used esp. for writing or drawing, as on a blackboard. —v.t. 1. to mark, write, or draw with chalk: Numbers were chalked in front of each line of runners. He chalked off part of the floor for dancing. 2. to rub, treat, or prepare with chalk: to chalk the tip of a billiard cue. 3. to whiten with chalk: The children chalked their faces on Halloween. 4. to chalk up. a. to score or earn: He chalked up thirty points for his team. b. to credit or attribute; ascribe: You can chalk up his mistake to ignorance. c. to set down as being a part of: Chalk it up to experience. [Old English cealc limestone, plaster, from Latin calx limestone. See CALX.]

Chalice

chalk·y (chô′kē) chalk·i·er, chalk·i·est. adj. 1. resembling chalk: a chalky taste. The medicine had a chalky consistency. 2. of or containing chalk. —chalk′i·ness, n.

chal·lenge (chal′ĭnj) -lenged, -leng·ing. v.t. 1. to invite or summon defiantly or provocatively, as to combat or to a contest. 2. to bid or call upon boldly or defiantly: I challenge you to show your proof. 3. to call into question; take exception to (something), esp. as being invalid: I challenge that interpretation. 4. to excite or make demands upon the talents or interests of; arouse; stimulate: a science project that challenged the entire class. 5. to stop and demand a countersign or form of identification from: The sentry challenged anyone approaching the tent. 6. to claim as due; demand; require. 7. Law. to object or take formal exception to, as a juror. —v.i. to make or present a challenge. —n. 1. invitation or summons, as to combat or to a contest. 2. a calling to account; demand, as for an explanation. 3. a calling into question, esp. of something's validity. 4. something that excites or makes demands upon one's talents and interests. 5. demand, as of a sentry, for a countersign or identification. 6. Law. formal objection made by counsel as to the seating of a juror. [Anglo-Norman chalenge accusation, claim, from Latin calumnia false accusation. Doublet of CALUMNY.] —chal′lenge·a·ble, adj. —chal′leng·er, n.

chal·lis (shal′ē) also, chal·lie. n. lightweight woolen, cotton, or rayon fabric, used esp. for blouses, robes, and scarves. [Of uncertain origin.]

cha·lyb·e·ate (kə lĭb′ē ĭt) adj. 1. containing or impregnated with salts of iron, as a medicine or mineral spring. 2. having a taste of iron. —n. water or medicine containing dissolved iron or iron salts. [Latin chalybs steel (from Greek chalyps, from Chalybes the Chalybes, an ancient people of Asia Minor noted for their work in iron and steel) + -ATE².]

cham (kam) Archaic. khan¹.

cham·ber (chām′bər) n. 1. room, esp. a bedroom. 2. also, chambers. room where a judge conducts business when not holding a court session, esp. his private office. 3. deliberative body, council, or assembly habitually meeting together, esp. one of the divisions of a legislative assembly: chamber of deputies. The Senate is the upper chamber of Congress. 4. hall where such a body meets. 5. reception room, as in a palace, of a person of authority or rank. 6. cavity or enclosed space in the body of an animal or plant: the four chambers of the heart. 7. rear portion of the barrel of a firearm, into which the ammunition, as a cartridge or shell, is inserted. 8. any enclosed compartment, as the spaces between the gates of a canal lock. 9. chambers. British. suite of rooms; apartment. —adj. of or relating to chamber music: a chamber concert, a chamber orchestra. —v.t. 1. to provide with a chamber. 2. to put in or as in a chamber. [Old French chambre bedroom, dwelling, from Late Latin camera room, from Latin camera arch, vault, from Greek kamarā vault. See CAMERA.]

cham·bered nautilus (chām′bərd) salt-water cephalopod, Nautilus macromphalus, having a creamy or brown spiral shell that is divided into chambers and may grow from eight to ten inches. Also, pearly nautilus.

cham·ber·lain (chām′bər lĭn) n. 1. officer in charge of the management of the household of a monarch or nobleman; steward. 2. one who receives or keeps funds and revenues; treasurer. 3. high official of certain royal courts. [Old French chamberlenc high official in a king's service; literally, one who takes care of bedchambers, through German, going back to Late Latin camera room (see CHAMBER) + German -ling (see -LING¹).]

Cham·ber·lain, (Arthur) Nev·ille (chām′bər lĭn; nev′əl) 1869–1940, British statesman; prime minister of England from 1937 to 1940.

cham·ber·maid (chām′bər mād′) n. maid who makes the beds and cleans the rooms, esp. in a hotel or motel.

chamber music, music written for a small instrumental ensemble,

suitable for performance in a room or small hall. The string quartets of Haydn and Mozart are chamber music.

chamber of commerce, association organized to regulate and promote industrial and commercial interests of a particular locality.

chamber pot, portable vessel used as a toilet, usually kept in a bedroom.

cham·bray (sham′brā) n. cotton fabric woven with a colored warp and white filling, used esp. for dresses, shirts, and pajamas. [From Cambrai, France.]

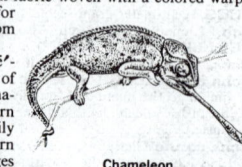

Chameleon

cha·me·leon (kə mēl′yən, -mē′lē ən) n. 1. any lizard of either of two groups, the family Chamaeleonidae, of Africa and southern Europe and Asia, or the family Iguanidae, found in the southeastern United States, whose skin changes color according to variations in temperature, emotion, and other factors, often serving to camouflage it from its enemies. 2. person of quickly changeable disposition or opinions; fickle person. [Latin chamaeleōn the Old World chameleon, from Greek chamailéōn, from chamai on the ground, dwarf + léōn lion.]

cham·fer (cham′fər) n. slanting surface produced by beveling an edge or corner. —v.t. 1. to cut so as to form a slanting surface; bevel. 2. to cut a furrow in; flute; channel. [Middle French chanfrain beveled edge, going back to Old French chant edge, from Late Latin cantus (see CANT²) + fraindre to break, from Latin frangere.]

cham·ois (sham′ē) pl., -ois (-ēz). n. 1. goatlike antelope, Rupicapra rupicapra, native to the mountains of Europe, the Caucasus, and western Asia, having a long, reddish-brown coat that turns dark brown in the winter. Height: 2½ feet at the shoulder. 2. also, chammy, shammy. soft, pliable leather, originally made from the skin of the chamois, now made from the skins of various animals. [French chamois, from Late Latin camox the antelope; probably of pre-Roman origin.]

Chamois

cham·o·mile (kam′ə mīl′, -mēl′) camomile.

champ¹ (champ) v.t. 1. to crush and chew vigorously and noisily; munch. 2. to bite upon restlessly or impatiently: The horse was champing the bit. —v.i. 1. to make biting or chewing movements with the jaws and teeth: The burro champed loudly. 2. to champ at the bit. to show signs of restlessness or be impatient, as to begin some action. —n. act of champing. [Probably imitative.]

champ² (champ) n. Informal. champion. [Short for CHAMPION.]

cham·pagne (sham pān′) n. 1. sparkling, effervescent white or light-pink wine, originally from Champagne, France. 2. still white wine produced in this region. 3. pale, brownish-yellow color.

Cham·pagne (sham pān′) n. region in northeastern France, formerly a province.

cham·paign (sham pān′) n. flat, open country; plain. —adj. flat and open. [Old French champaigne open country, from Late Latin campania, from Latin campus field.]

Cham·paign (sham pān′) n. city in east-central Illinois. Pop. (1970), 56,532.

cham·pi·on (cham′pē ən) n. 1. winner of first place or first prize in a competition: the heavyweight boxing champion. 2. one who fights for or defends a person or cause. 3. brave fighter or warrior; hero. —adj. having won or capable of winning first place or first prize; superior to all others: a champion wrestler. —v.t. to fight in behalf of; defend; support: He always champions the underdog. [Old French champion combatant, from Medieval Latin campio fighter (in the field), from Latin campus field (of combat).]

cham·pi·on·ship (cham′pē ən ship′) n. 1. position or honor of being a champion: He won the championship last year. 2. act of championing; advocacy; defense; support: their championship of civil liberties. 3. competition held in order to determine a champion.

Cham·plain (sham plān′) n. 1. Lake. lake on the border between New York and Vermont, extending into southwestern Quebec. 2. Samuel de. 1567–1635, French explorer who founded Quebec.

Champs É·ly·sées (shän′zā lē zā′) fashionable, tree-lined avenue in Paris. [French Champs Élysées literally, Elysian fields.]

chance (chans) n. 1. favorable or suitable time or occasion; opportunity: the chance of a lifetime. 2. likelihood or probability (of anything happening); possibility: There is little chance of winning. 3. good possi-

bility of being successful: *He doesn't stand a chance with her.* **4.** risk; hazard; gamble: *Don't take any chances.* **5.** absence of any understandable, predictable, or logical cause or causes of events, often thought of as an impersonal force that determines events in a random and unaccountable way: *Everything is subject to chance.* **6.** unusual or unexpected occurrence; accident: *By some strange chance we discovered the error.* **7.** ticket in a lottery, raffle, sweepstakes, or similar contest. —*v.i.* **chanced, chanc·ing. 1.** to happen by chance: *If an argument should chance to arise, try to settle it amicably.* **2. to chance on** (or **upon**). to meet unexpectedly or accidentally: *We chanced upon them at the park.* —*v.t. Informal.* to take the chance of; hazard; risk: *Do you dare chance the possibility of being caught?* —*adj.* happening by chance; unplanned; accidental: *a chance meeting, a chance remark.* [Old French *cheance* a falling (as of dice), hazard, luck, from Late Latin *cadentia* a falling (as of dice), from Latin *cadere* to fall. Doublet of CADENCE, CADENZA.]

Syn. *n.* **1.** see opportunity. **5.** Chance, fortune, luck denote the quality of events that happen without predictable or apparent cause. **Chance** refers to the impersonal, uncontrolled, and unpredictable force that determines blindly the outcome of problematical events: *Dice is a game of chance.* **Fortune** stresses the arbitrary and capricious distribution of the lots of life uninfluenced by human choice: *The vicissitudes of fortune made Harry a rich man once again.* **Luck** indicates a force or combination of forces that brings good or evil in a random or irrational way: *It was the batter's luck that the catcher dropped the ball.*

chan·cel (chan′səl) *n.* space around the altar of a church, used by the clergy and the choir, often set off by a railing, lattice, or screen. [Old French *chancel* enclosure, from Latin *cancelli* lattice; because it was closed off by a lattice. See CANCEL.]

chan·cel·ler·y (chan′sə lər ē, -slər ē) *pl.* **-ler·ies.** also, **chan·cel·lor·y.** *n.* **1.** position of a chancellor. **2.** office of a chancellor or the building that houses it. **3.** office of an embassy, legation, or consulate or the building that houses it. [Old French *chancelerie* the position, court of chancery, from *chancelier.* See CHANCELLOR.]

chan·cel·lor (chan′sə lər, -slər) *n.* **1.** prime minister in certain European countries, as West Germany and Austria. **2.** chief administrative officer or president at certain American universities. **3.** judge or presiding judge of a court of equity in some states of the United States. **4.** high official who serves as the chief secretary of a sovereign or embassy. [Old French *chancelier* high official of a king, from Late Latin *cancellārius* secretary; originally, officer in a law court standing near the *cancellī,* or lattice, in front of the judge's seat. See CHANCEL.] —*chan′cel·lor·ship′, n.*

Chancellor of the Exchequer, the minister of finance in the British government. He is a member of the Cabinet.

chan·cer·y (chan′sər ē) *pl.* **-cer·ies.** *n.* **1.** court of equity. Also, **court of chancery. 2.** equity (*defs.* 3a, 3b). **3.** chancellery. **4.** court or office where public records are kept; archives. **5.** in chancery. **a.** in a court of equity; in litigation. **b.** in wrestling or boxing, with the head encircled by the opponent's arm; in a headlock. **c.** in an embarrassing or helpless situation. [Short for CHANCELLERY.]

chan·cre (shang′kər) *n.* ulcer or sore having a hard base and formed at the primary site of infection, esp. the initial lesion of syphilis. [French *chancre,* from Latin *cancer* crab, cancer. Doublet of CANCER, CANKER.] —*chan′crous, adj.*

chanc·y (chan′sē) **chanc·i·er, chanc·i·est.** *adj. Informal.* subject to chance; uncertain; risky.

chan·de·lier (shan′də lēr′) *n.* lighting fixture designed to be suspended from the ceiling, usually having several lights arranged on projecting arms or branches. [French *chandelier* candlestick, going back to Latin *candēlābrum,* from *candēla* candle.]

chan·dler (chand′lər) *n.* **1.** one who makes or sells candles. **2.** dealer or merchant, esp. one who deals in groceries or ship's supplies. [Old French *chandelier* maker or seller of candles, from Late Latin *candēlārius,* from Latin *candēla* candle.]

chan·dler·y (chand′lər ē) *pl.* **-dler·ies.** *n.* **1.** place for storing candles. **2.** business, goods, or shop of a chandler.

change (chānj) **changed, chang·ing.** *v.t.* **1.** to make different; alter; modify: *to change one's attitude. She changed the arrangement of flowers in the vase.* **2.** to cause to pass from one form, composition, or state to another; transform (often with *into*): *a movement to change the monarchy into a republic. The magician changed the scarf into a pigeon.* **3.** to substitute another or others for; replace with or switch to another or others: *to change one's shirt, to change jobs, to change sides during an argument.* **4.** to give and receive reciprocally; exchange: *Change*

seats with the person sitting next to you. **5.** to give or receive the equivalent of (money), as in smaller units or foreign currency: *He changed a five-dollar bill for five singles. He changed his dollars into francs.* **6.** to remove and replace the covering or coverings on: *to change a bed. to change a baby.* —*v.i.* **1.** to become different, altered, or modified: *The scenery changed as the train went further south. His voice changed as he became older.* **2.** to become transformed (often with *into*): *The pumpkin changed into a coach.* **3.** to put on other clothes (often with *into*): *The actors changed between acts. He changed into a dinner jacket.* **4.** to make an exchange: *If you're not comfortable in that chair, I'll change with you.* **5.** to transfer from one means of conveyance to another: *We have to change here for an express.* **6.** (of the moon) to pass from one phase to another. —*n.* **1.** act or fact of changing: *The schedule is subject to change. This represents a change in our policy. We have to make a change at the next stop.* **2.** that which is or may be substituted for another: *We've left a change of towels for you in the guest room.* **3.** something different from the usual; variety; novelty; diversity: *Leave him alone for a change. It would be a nice change to go south in the winter.* **4.** coins as distinguished from paper currency: *I've got lots of change in my pocket.* **5.** amount returned when money given in payment exceeds the sum due: *The waitress gave him his change.* **6.** money of lower denomination given in exchange for higher: *He asked for change of one dollar in dimes.* **7.** clean, fresh, or different set of clothes. [Old French *changier* to alter, from Late Latin *cambiāre* to exchange; probably of Celtic origin.] —*chang′er, n.*

Syn. *v.t.* **1.** Change, alter, modify mean to make different. **Change** is the most informal of these words and also the most general in meaning, for it can refer to almost any difference: *She changed the decor of the room. She changed her mind about going at the last minute.* **Alter** suggests difference in details, as opposed to substantial change: *They altered their course to avoid the storm.* **Modify** sometimes suggests an alteration intended to bring into accordance with something, esp. with a standard: *He modified his beliefs to fit the facts.*

change·a·ble (chān′jə bəl) *adj.* **1.** liable or likely to change; inconstant; variable: *a changeable personality, a changeable mood.* **2.** that can be changed; alterable: *a changeable policy.* **3.** changing in color or appearance when looked at from different points of view. —*change′-a·bil′i·ty, change′a·ble·ness, n.* —*change′a·bly, adv.*

change·ful (chānj′fəl) *adj.* full of change; given to change; variable; inconstant. —*change′ful·ly, adv.* —*change′ful·ness, n.*

change·less (chānj′lis) *adj.* unchanging; constant; enduring. —*change′less·ly, adv.* —*change′less·ness, n.*

change·ling (chānj′ling) *n.* **1.** child secretly substituted for another, esp. in infancy. **2.** in folklore, child, usually strange, stupid, or ugly, left by fairies in place of a child they have stolen.

change of life, menopause.

change·o·ver (chānj′ō′vər) *n.* shift, transition, or transfer, as in activities, methods of production, or management.

chan·nel¹ (chan′əl) *n.* **1.** deepest part of a river, harbor, or other waterway, often dredged and maintained as a passage for boats and ships. **2.** bed of a stream, river, or other waterway. **3.** wide strait. **4.** means by which something is directed or conveyed; course through which something passes: *He directed his efforts into other channels.* **5.** channels. proper or official route or means, esp. of communication: *His request for new typewriters had to go through channels.* **6.** furrow or groove. **7.** tube or tubular passage, as for liquids. **8.** band of electromagnetic frequencies assigned to a broadcasting station for the transmission and reception of electronic signals. —*v.t.* **-neled, -nel·ing;** *esp. British,* **-nelled, -nel·ling. 1.** to make or form by or as by erosion; cut out as a channel: *The stream channeled its way over the mountains.* **2.** to direct or convey through or as through a channel: *He channeled his thoughts toward one phase of the problem. They channeled the stream onto the neighboring property.* **3.** to form or cut a channel in. [Old French *chanel* canal, from Latin *canālis* pipe, canal. Doublet of CANAL.]

chan·nel² (chan′əl) *n.* ledge, as a wooden plank, projecting from the side of a ship, used esp. to extend the shrouds. [Earlier *chain wale,* from CHAIN + WALE.]

Channel Islands, British island group in the English Channel, including Jersey, Guernsey, and Alderney. Land area, 75 sq. mi. Pop. (1969 est.), 117,000.

chan·nel·ize (chan′əl īz′) **-ized, -iz·ing.** *v.t.* to channel. —*chan′-nel·i·za′tion, n.*

chan·son (shan sōn′; *French* shäN sôN′) *n. French.* song.

chant (chant) *n.* **1.** repetitive, monotonous, usually rhythmic, utterance or song: *an Indian war chant. The crowd broke into a chant when the candidate appeared.* **2.** simple liturgical melody, usually unaccompanied, in which a number of syllables or words are sung or intoned on one note. **3.** psalm, canticle, or other nonmetrical sacred text sung or intoned. **4.** *Archaic.* song; melody. —*v.t.* **1.** to recite or shout in a repetitive or rhythmic tone: *She led the group in chanting their slogan.*

---

at; āpe; cär; end; mē; it; īce; hot; ōld; fôrk; wood; fōōl; oil; out; up; ūse; turn; sing; thin; this; zh in treasure; ə in ago, taken, pencil, lemon, circus.

2. to sing, as a psalm, to a chant; intone, as in a church service: *to chant the litany.* **3.** *Archaic.* to sing. —*v.i.* **1.** to recite or shout a chant: *The protesters chanted in the street below.* **2.** to sing or intone a chant or chants: *The choir chanted in the background.* [Old French *chanter* to sing, from Latin *cantāre.*]

chant·er (chan′tər) *n.* **1.** one who chants, as a cantor. **2.** pipe of a bagpipe on which the melody is played. [Old French *chanteor* singer, from Latin *cantātor.*]

chan·teuse (shan tōōs′; *French* shäN tœz′) *n.* *French.* female singer, esp. one who sings in a night club or cabaret.

chan·tey (shan′tē, chan′-) *pl.*, **-teys.** *also,* **chan·ty, shan·tey, shan·ty.** *n.* sailors' song, originally sung in rhythm with their work. [Modification of French *chanter* to sing, from Latin *cantāre.*]

chan·ti·cleer (chan′tə klēr′) *n.* rooster. ♣ used as a proper name in medieval fables about Reynard the Fox and in other literature. [Old French *Chantecler* the cock in these fables, from *chanter* to sing (from Latin *cantāre*) + *cler* clear (from Latin *clārus*).]

Chan·til·ly (shan til′ē) *n.* delicate bobbin lace made of silk or other fibers, used chiefly for evening and bridal gowns. Also, **Chantilly lace.** [From *Chantilly,* town in northern France where it was originally made.]

chan·try (chan′trē) *pl.*, **-tries.** *n.* **1.** endowment for the singing or saying of Masses for the soul of the donor, or for the souls of those specified by the donor. **2.** chapel or altar so endowed. [Old French *chanterie* singing, from *chanter.* See CHANT.]

chan·ty (shan′tē, chan′-) *pl.*, **-ties.** *n.* chantey.

Cha·nu·kah (hä′nə kə; *Hebrew* κHä nōō kä′) Hanukkah.

cha·os (kā′os) *n.* **1.** utter confusion and disorder. **2.** *also,* **Chaos.** infinite space or formless matter out of which the cosmos or ordered universe supposedly evolved. [Latin *chaos* empty space, from Greek *chaos* vast chasm, space.]

cha·ot·ic (kā ot′ik) *adj.* in utter confusion and disorder: *The candidate's headquarters was chaotic on the night of the election.* Also, **cha·ot′i·cal.** —**cha·ot′i·cal·ly,** *adv.*

chap¹ (chap) chapped, chap·ping. *v.t.* to cause to split, crack, or become rough: *My hands are chapped from washing all those dishes.* —*v.i.* to become split, cracked, or roughened: *My lips always chap in the winter.* [Middle English *chappen* to cut; of uncertain origin.]

chap² (chap) *n.* *Informal.* man or boy; fellow. [Short for CHAPMAN.]

chap³ (chap) *n.* chop¹. [Of uncertain origin.]

chap., chapter.

cha·pa·ra·jos (shap′ə rä′ōs) *also,* **cha·pe·re·jos.** *n.,pl.* chaps. [Spanish *chaparajos* (because worn as a protection against the thorns of the chaparral), from *chaparral.* See CHAPARRAL.]

chap·ar·ral (shap′ə ral′) *n.* dense thicket of low or shrubby trees or thorny, stiff-branched shrubs, usually found in dry, sunny regions. [Spanish *chaparral* plantation of evergreen oaks, from *chaparro* evergreen oak, from Basque *txapar,* diminutive of *saphar* thicket.]

chap·book (chap′book′) *n.* small book or pamphlet containing popular tales, poems, ballads, and similar literature, formerly peddled by chapmen.

cha·peau (sha pō′) *pl.*, **-peaux** (-pō′, -pōz′) or **-peaus.** *n.* hat. [French *chapeau,* going back to Late Latin *cappa* hood. See CHAPEL.]

chap·el (chap′əl) *n.* **1.** building used for worship, as one connected with a university or other institution, that does not have the ecclesiastical privileges or status of a church. **2.** room or recess within a church or other public or private building, usually containing an altar, used for religious services. **3.** religious service conducted in such a building or room. **4.** *British.* place for worship for Roman Catholics or Protestant Nonconformists. **5.** choir or orchestra attached to a chapel, esp. one belonging to a sovereign. **6.** association of printers working in a printing house. [Old French *chapele* holy place for worship, place for keeping sacred things, from Late Latin *cappella* cloak, shrine where the cloak (or *cappella*) of St. Martin of Tours was preserved as a sacred relic, diminutive of *cappa* cape, hood; of uncertain origin.]

chap·er·on (shap′ə rōn′) *n.* **1.** mature person who attends and supervises social gatherings of young unmarried people. **2.** mature woman who, for the sake of propriety, accompanies a young unmarried woman in public. —*v.t.* to act as chaperon to. [French *chaperon* protector (compared jokingly to a hood); originally, hood, from Old French *chape* cape, from Late Latin *cappa* hood, cape; of uncertain origin.] —**chap′er·on′age,** *n.*

chap·er·one (shap′ə rōn′) *n.* chaperon. —*v.t.,* **-oned, -on·ing.** to chaperon.

chap·fall·en (chap′fô′lən, chop′-) *also,* **chop·fall·en** (chop′fô′lən). *adj.* dejected; dispirited; crestfallen.

chap·lain (chap′lin) *n.* clergyman who performs religious functions for any of various groups or organizations, as a regiment in the armed forces, a college, or a court. [Old French *chapelain* priest of a chapel, from Medieval Latin *cappellanus* originally, guardian of the cloak (or

capella) of St. Martin of Tours, from Late Latin *cappella.* See CHAPEL.] —**chap′lain·cy, chap′lain·ship′,** *n.*

chap·let (chap′lit) *n.* **1.** wreath or garland to be worn on the head. **2.** string of beads used to keep count when saying the prayers of the rosary. A chaplet is equal to one third of a complete rosary. **3.** prayers said with such beads. **4.** *Archaic.* string of beads; necklace. [Old French *chapelet* wreath, little hat, from *chapel* hat, wreath, going back to Late Latin *cappa.* See CHAPEL.]

chap·man (chap′mən) *pl.*, **-men.** *n.* *British.* peddler; hawker. [Old English *cēapman* merchant, from *cēap* trade + *mann* man. See CHEAP.]

chaps (chaps, shaps) *n.,pl.* strong leather leggings worn over trousers, esp. by cowboys to protect their legs while riding horseback. [Short for CHAPARAJOS.]

chap·ter (chap′tər) *n.* **1.** any of several main divisions of a book, treatise, or the like. **2.** major division, as a period, episode, or part: *a new chapter in one's life.* **3.** local branch or division of an organization, as of a club, fraternity, or society. **4.** group of clergymen who serve the needs of a cathedral. **5.** meeting of such a group. —*v.t.* to arrange or divide into chapters. [Old French *chapitre* section of a book, assembly of clerics, from Late Latin *capitulum* meeting of clerics (at which a *chapter* of the Bible was often read), from Latin *capitulum* section of a book, small head, diminutive of Latin *caput* head.]

Chaps

chapter house **1.** building used for the assembly of the chapter of a cathedral. **2.** house or meeting room of a college fraternity or sorority.

Cha·pul·te·pec (chə pool′tə pek′) *n.* rocky hill in Mexico City, Mexico, captured by U.S. forces in 1847 in the last major battle of the Mexican War.

char¹ (chär) charred, char·ring. *v.t.* **1.** to burn slightly or partially; scorch: *The fire charred and blackened many of the trees in the park.* **2.** to reduce to charcoal by burning. —*v.i.* to become charred. —*n.* charred substance; charcoal. [Probably from CHARCOAL.]

char² (chär) *British.* *n.* **1.** chore, esp. a household chore. **2.** charwoman. —*v.i.,* charred, char·ring. to do chores, esp. housework; work as a charwoman. [Old English *cierr, cerr* turn of work.]

char·a·banc (shar′ə bang′, -bangk′) *pl.*, **-bancs.** *also,* **char·à·banc.** *n.* *British.* long vehicle with rows of transverse seats facing forward, esp. a sightseeing bus. [French *charàbancs* literally, car with benches, going back to Latin *carrus* wagon (see CARGO) + *ad* to + an unrecorded Germanic word meaning "bench."]

char·ac·ter (kar′ik tər) *n.* **1.** moral qualities strongly developed or strikingly displayed; moral force or excellence; integrity: *to call someone's character into question.* **2.** pattern of behavior or sum of the qualities or features marking a person or persons; mental or moral constitution; personality: *Selfishness formed the basis of his character.* **3.** qualities or features that are typical of or together define the identity of something; all qualities or features possessed; nature: *Editing those two scenes changed the whole character of the play.* **4.** person delineated or represented in a play, novel, or the like: *The story's plot is exciting, and it contains some interesting characters.* **5.** personality that an actor portrays, as in a play or motion picture; role or part: *He plays the character of the old hermit.* **6.** person; individual: *That man is the meanest looking character I've ever seen.* **7.** position or function, either actual or assumed; capacity; status: *in his character as president.* **8.** mark or sign, as a letter or hieroglyphic, used as a symbol in writing or printing or as one of the components of an alphabet. **9.** style of writing or printing: *This is not my writing, though, I confess, much like the character* (Shakespeare, *Twelfth Night*). **10.** account, statement, or description of the qualities of a person or thing. **11.** *Informal.* person who is eccentric, amusing, or otherwise remarkable in behavior or personality: *He's quite a character.* **12.** *Biology.* characteristic. **13. in character.** appropriate to or consistent with one's disposition or usual or expected behavior. **14. out of character.** inappropriate to or inconsistent with one's disposition or usual or expected behavior. [Latin *character* tool for marking, mark, characteristic, from Greek *charaktēr.*] —**Syn. 2.** see disposition.

character actor, actor who is capable of portraying a wide variety of characters or who specializes in portraying individuals of a certain type.

char·ac·ter·is·tic (kar′ik tə ris′tik) *n.* **1.** that which is typical of, helps to define the identity of, or is thought of as belonging to a person or thing; distinguishing or essential element, property, or trait: *Her kindness is her most outstanding characteristic. The specimen can be identified by checking for the following characteristics.* **2.** *Biology.* distinctive trait, feature, or property, as size or color, that is determined by the genes and is common to all members of a group. **3.** *Mathematics.* the integral part of a logarithm. —*adj.* relating to, constituting, or indicating the character or particular qualities of a person or thing;

at; āpe; cär; end; mē; it; īce; hot; ōld; fôrk; wood; fōōl; oil; out; up; ūse; turn; sing; thin; this; zh in treasure; ə in ago, taken, pencil, lemon, circus.

distinctive; typical: *a characteristic gesture, a characteristic taste, formations characteristic of a geological period.* —**char·ac·ter·is'ti·cal·ly,** *adv.*

Syn. *n.* **1. Characteristic, trait, feature** designate an essential attribute or a distinguishing quality. **Characteristic** is the typical and intrinsic property that reveals the character of something and marks it apart from others: *Heavily accented rhythm is a characteristic of jazz music.* **Trait** is a particularly distinctive quality or notable aspect: *Generosity is Dick's most endearing trait.* **Feature** is a part or detail that is prominent enough to demand and hold attention: *Romanticism is a feature of Victorian poetry.*

char·ac·ter·i·za·tion (kar'ik tər i zā'shən) *n.* **1.** result of characterizing; description; portrayal. **2.** act of characterizing. **3.** creation or representation of characters in an art form, as in a play or novel.

char·ac·ter·ize (kar'ik tə rīz') **-ized, -iz·ing,** *v.t.* **1.** to be a characteristic of; distinguish: *an illness that is characterized by high fever, the metaphors that characterize his poetry.* **2.** to describe or delineate the character or qualities of (a person or thing); depict; portray: *The author characterizes the central figure as a weakling.* **3.** to ascribe or attribute character to.

character sketch 1. short description, esp. in essay form, of a person or particular type of person. **2.** in the theater, brief portrayal of an individual; short impersonation.

character witness, one who attests to the moral character and integrity of someone before a court of law.

cha·rade (shə rād') *n.* **1. charades.** game in which the participants, usually divided into two teams, attempt to guess words or phrases pantomimed, often syllable by syllable, by one of the players. ▲ construed as singular. **2.** word or phrase pantomimed in this game. **3.** something thought of as resembling such a game; false show or pretense: *Their friendliness toward each other was a mere charade.* [French *charade* this game, from Provençal *charrado* talk, chat, from *charra* to chatter; of imitative origin.]

char·coal (chär'kōl') *n.* **1.** black, brittle, porous solid produced by heating or charring animal or vegetable matter that contains carbon. It is used as fuel and in the manufacture of food and chemicals. **2.** pencil or crayon made of charcoal. **3.** drawing made with such a pencil or crayon. —*v.t.* to mark, write, or blacken with charcoal. [Middle English *charcole* the black, porous solid, possibly from *char* turn (from Old English *cierr*) + *cole* coal; in the sense of "turned to coal." See COAL.]

chard (chärd) Swiss chard.

chare (chār) *British.* char² (*n., def.* 1; *v.*).

charge (chärj) **charged, charg·ing,** *v.t.* **1.** to fix or ask as a price: *They charged ten dollars to repair the radio.* **2.** to require payment from; make financially liable: *They charged him for the broken window.* **3.** to defer payment for (something) until a bill is rendered; cause the purchase of to be recorded as a debt: *She charged the new dress.* **4.** to lay the liability of payment for (something); record or enter as a debt: *They charged the bill to petty cash. She charged the purchase to her account.* **5.** to rush violently upon or toward in an attack: *The infuriated bull charged one of the horses. The troops charged the fortress. The agitators charged the picket line.* **6.** to bring an accusation or lay blame upon; blame; accuse: *He was charged with the theft.* **7.** to assert as an accusation: *The senator charged that irregularities had been found in the records.* **8.** to impose a task, duty, or responsibility upon; burden, as with care; entrust: *She was charged with the supervision of the children.* **9.** to fill or supply (something) with the quantity it is fitted to receive: *to charge a furnace with ore. They charged the cannon with shot.* **10.** to supply with a quantity of electricity or electrical energy: *to charge a storage battery.* **11.** to diffuse or distribute throughout; saturate: *to charge water with carbon dioxide. The air was charged with vapor.* **12.** to fill full as if with electricity; make pulsating; suffuse: *The air was charged with excitement. Her reply was charged with emotion. These events are charged with significance.* **13.** to command or order; enjoin: *Satan, avoid! I charge thee, tempt me not!* (Shakespeare, *Comedy of Errors*). **14.** to exhort or instruct officially or authoritatively, as on matters or points of law: *The judge charged the jury.* **15.** to ascribe the responsibility for: *He charged the accident to his carelessness.* —*v.i.* **1.** to rush violently or go quickly and energetically, as in an attack: *The elephant charged at the hunter. He charged off to look for her. I charged up the stairs after my little brother.* **2.** to fix or ask a price: *They always charge for that service.* —*n.* **1.** required payment; price asked: *There was an hourly charge of $5.00 for cleaning services. The charge for admission was $1.50.* **2.** charged purchase or liability to pay; debt. **3.** care or custody; management; superintendence: *She had charge of her brother while their mother went out. He took charge of the situation when he arrived. We were in charge of handing out the books.* **4.** violent or rushing attack: *The charge was repulsed by the enemy.* **5.** signal or order for such an attack: *The bugler sounded the charge.* **6.** accusation; allegation: *He was faced with the charge of misconduct. They were*

arrested on the charge of robbery. He made startling charges during the hearings of the committee.* **7.** person or thing entrusted to the care, custody, or management of another: *Parentless children are the charges of an orphanage.* **8.** that with which one is entrusted; task; duty; responsibility: *A child's education is the charge of his parents.* **9.** command; order. **10.** quantity that an apparatus or receptacle is fitted to receive and hold: *The charge for the furnace is two tons.* **11.** electric charge. **12.** amount of powder or other explosive to be detonated at one time, as in a cartridge or shell. **13.** official or authoritative instruction concerning points of law given by a judge to a jury before it retires to deliberate. **14.** *Heraldry.* geometric design or other figure, as a lion or bird, used on an escutcheon; bearing. **15.** *Slang.* thrill; kick: *He got a big charge out of seeing her again.* **16. in charge.** in the position of authority or responsibility; having supervisory power; in command: *Who's in charge here?* [Old French *charger* to load, from Late Latin *carricāre* to load (a wagon), from Latin *carrus* two-wheeled wagon; of Celtic origin. Doublet of CARRY.] —**charge'a·ble;** *also,* **charg'a·ble.** *adj.* —**Syn.** *v.t.* **6.** see accuse. *n.* **1.** see price.

charge account, credit arrangement, esp. with a retail store, by which an individual may make purchases to be paid for at some specified future date.

char·gé d'af·faires (shär zhā' də fâr') *pl.,* **char·gés d'af·faires** (shär shāz' də fâr'). **1.** official who serves as the administrative assistant to the chief of a mission, as an ambassador or minister. **2.** formerly, diplomatic representative sent by his country to a government to which a diplomat of higher standing, as an ambassador, is not sent. [French *chargé d'affaires* literally, one charged with affairs.]

charg·er¹ (chär'jər) *n.* **1.** horse trained or suitable for use in battle. **2.** one who or that which charges. **3.** electrical device used to recharge storage batteries. [CHARGE + -ER¹.]

charg·er² ((chär'jər) *n.* *Archaic.* large, flat dish; platter. [Middle English *chargeour;* of uncertain origin.]

char·i·ly (châr'ə lē) *adv.* in a chary manner; carefully; sparingly.

char·i·ness (châr'ē nis) *n.* quality of being chary; caution; sparingness.

char·i·ot (char'ē ət) *n.* **1.** two-wheeled vehicle, usually drawn by two, three, or four horses, all abreast, and driven from a standing position, used chiefly in warfare, processions, and races in ancient times. **2.** light, stately, four-wheeled coach or pleasure carriage. [Old French *chariot* wagon, from *char* cart, wagon, from Latin *carrus* two-wheeled wagon; of Celtic origin.]

Etruscan war chariot

char·i·ot·eer (char'ē ə tēr') *n.* driver of a chariot, as in ancient Greece or Rome.

cha·ris·ma (kə riz'mə) *n.* **1.** unique and magnetic personal quality, as of a politician, leader, or celebrity, that enables an individual to inspire and capture the loyalty and devotion of a large following of people. **2.** extraordinary spiritual power, as for healing or prophesying, given by the Holy Spirit. [Greek *charisma* favor, grace, gift.] —**char·is·mat·ic** ((kar'iz mat'ik), *adj.*

char·i·ta·ble (char'ə tə bəl) *adj.* **1.** of or for charity; providing assistance to the poor or needy: *à charitable institution.* **2.** merciful, lenient, or forgiving, esp. in judging others; kindly; tolerant: *It was charitable of you to overlook his thoughtlessness.* **3.** generous in giving help to the poor or needy; beneficent. —**char'i·ta·ble·ness,** *n.* —**char'i·ta·bly,** *adv.*

char·i·ty (char'ə tē) *pl.,* **-ties.** *n.* **1.** the providing of assistance to the poor or needy, esp. on a widespread or organized basis; charitable actions considered collectively. **2.** that which is given to help the poor or needy: *The old woman refused to accept charity when her husband died.* **3.** fund, institution, or organization for assisting the poor or needy: *Give generously to your favorite charity.* **4.** disposition to assist the poor or needy; feeling of good will or benevolence: *She cared for the orphans out of charity.* **5.** mercy, leniency, or forgiveness, esp. in judging others; kindness; tolerance: *With malice toward none; with charity for all* (Lincoln, 1865). **6.** Christian love for one's fellow men; brotherly love: *And now abideth faith, hope, charity, these three; but the greatest of these is charity* (I Corinthians 13:2). [Old French *charite,* from Latin *cāritās* love, dearness.]

Syn. 1. Charity, philanthropy denote voluntary help extended to the needy. **Charity** suggests a kindly desire to lighten the load of the poor or helpless by providing them with relief: *charity for orphans, charity to beggars.* **Philanthropy,** on the other hand, suggests a humanitarian desire to help develop the abilities or further the skill of the recipients. It usually implies an organized intermediary and large sums of money: *His favorite philanthropy was a scholarship program he had endowed at the university.*

cha·riv·a·ri (shiv'ə rē', shiv'ər ē) *pl.,* **-ris.** *also,* **chiv·a·ree, shiv·a·ree.** *n.* mock serenade, as for a newly married couple, made by beating on

kettles or other household utensils or by playing musical instruments out of tune. [French *charivari*, from Late Latin *caribaria* headache, from Greek *karēbariā*; referring to the effect of such a serenade on the hearer.]

char·la·tan (shär′lə tən) *n.* one who professes to have knowledge or skill which he does not possess; quack; impostor. [French *charlatan*, from Italian *ciarlatano* mountebank, babbler; modification (influenced by Italian *ciarlare* to chat) of *cerretano* mountebank; literally, inhabitant of *Cerreto*, Italian town supposedly once regarded as being inhabited by cheats and impostors.] —**char′la·tan·ism, char′la·tan·ry,** *n.*

Char·le·magne (shär′lə mān′) *n.* A.D. c.742–814, king of the Franks from 768 to 814 and, as Charles I, emperor of the Holy Roman Empire from 800 to 814. Also, **Charles the Great.**

Charles (chärlz) *n.* river in eastern Massachusetts.

Charles, Prince, 1948–, Prince of Wales, eldest son of Elizabeth II, and heir apparent to the throne of Great Britain.

Charles I, 1600–49, king of England, Scotland, and Ireland from 1625 until his execution in 1649; born Charles Stuart.

Charles II, 1630–85, king of England, Scotland, and Ireland from 1660 to 1685; born Charles Stuart.

Charles V, 1500–58, emperor of the Holy Roman Empire from 1519 to 1558 and, as Charles I, king of Spain from 1516 to 1556.

Charles Edward Stuart, see **Stuart, Charles Edward.**

Charles Mar·tel (mär tel′) A.D. c.688–741, ruler of the Franks and grandfather of Charlemagne.

Charles the Great. Charlemagne.

Charles·ton¹ (chärl′stən) *n.* **1.** capital of West Virginia, in the western part of the state. Pop. (1970), 71,505. **2.** port city in southeastern South Carolina. Pop. (1970), 66,945.

Charles·ton² (chärl′stən) *n.* lively dance in 4/4 time, popular esp. in the 1920s. —*v.i.* to do this dance. [From *Charleston*, South Carolina.]

char·ley horse (chär′lē) severe muscular stiffness or soreness, caused by strain. [Possibly from the use of *Charley* as a name for a lame horse.]

char·lock (chär′lək) *n.* weed, *Brassica arvensis*, of the mustard family, bearing yellow flowers and found in grainfields. If it becomes mixed with animal feed and is eaten, it can cause colic and other illnesses. [Old English *cerlic*.]

char·lotte (shär′lət) *n.* sweet dish consisting of whipped cream, custard, gelatin, or fruit enclosed in a mold of bread, cake, or crumbs. [French *charlotte*, possibly from the feminine proper name *Charlotte*.]

Char·lotte (shär′lət) *n.* largest city of North Carolina, in the southern part of the state. Pop. (1970), 241,178.

Char·lotte A·ma·lie (shär′lət ä′mə lē, ə mä′lē ə) capital, largest city, and chief port of the U.S. Virgin Islands, on the southern coast of St. Thomas. Pop. (1970), 12,372. Formerly, **St. Thomas.**

char·lotte russe (shär′lət rōōs′) dessert made of a sponge cake mold with a filling or topping of whipped cream or custard. [French *charlotte russe* literally, Russian charlotte. See CHARLOTTE.]

Char·lottes·ville (shär′ləts vil′) *n.* city in central Virginia. Pop. (1970), 38,880.

charm (chärm) *n.* **1.** power to fascinate, attract, or delight greatly: *a woman of great charm. A fireplace holds much charm on cold winter nights.* **2.** any fascinating, attractive, or delightful quality or feature: *Her beautiful eyes were among her greatest charms.* **3.** small ornament or trinket, often worn on a chain bracelet. **4.** something worn to ward off evil or ensure good luck; amulet: *He carries a rabbit's foot as a good luck charm.* **5.a.** any action or formula supposed to have magic power. **b.** the chanting or recitation of such a formula. —*v.t.* **1.** to fascinate, attract, or delight greatly; captivate: *We were charmed by the child's story. Her graciousness charmed everyone at the party.* **2.** to affect by or as if by magic; bewitch: *The playing of the flute charmed the cobra.* **3.** to endow with or protect by, or as by, magic power. —*v.i.* **1.** to be greatly fascinating, attractive, or delightful. **2.** to use spells or enchantments; practice magic. [Old French *charme* magical formula, incantation, from Latin *carmen* song, incantation.] —**charm′er,** *n.*

Syn. *n.* **4. Charm, talisman, amulet** denote an object believed to be endowed with supernatural or magical powers. **Charm** is an object or incantation believed to work a spell averting evil spirits and ensuring good fortune: *The primitive houses were decorated with charms against the evil god.* **Talisman** is an object supposed to be invested with occult powers that confer supernatural protection on its wearer: *The king carried a talisman with him to battle.* **Amulet** is an object worn on a person because of its supposedly magical powers to preserve one from danger or illness: *The hair of an elephant's tail is sometimes used as an amulet.*

char·meuse (shär mœz′) *n.* soft lightweight fabric, usually of silk, having a satin finish and used chiefly for evening dresses. [French *charmeuse* literally, female charmer, from *charmer* to enchant, going back to Latin *carmen* song, incantation.]

charm·ing (chär′ming) *adj.* that charms or is full of charm; enchanting; captivating. —**charm′ing·ly,** *adv.*

char·nel (chär′nəl) *n.* charnel house. —*adj.* of, like, or fit for a charnel house; sepulchral; ghastly. [Old French *charnel* (as noun) cemetery, (as adjective) fleshly, from Late Latin *carnāle* cemetery, noun use of neuter of Latin *carnālis* fleshly.]

charnel house, vault or place in which the bones or bodies of the dead are placed.

Char·on (kār′ən, kar′-) *n. Greek Mythology.* the boatman who ferried the souls of the dead across the river Styx to the entrance of Hades.

chart (chärt) *n.* **1.** sheet showing information in the form of lists, diagrams, tables, or the like: *a chart of geological periods, a chart of the foods in a balanced diet.* **2.** graphic representation, as by curves, of the fluctuations of any variable, as population, prices, or barometric pressure. **3.a.** map, esp. an aeronautical or marine map, containing information necessary for navigation, as the location and depth of channels and harbors, or the location of air lanes and airports. **b.** outline map used to show special conditions or facts: *a chart of the topography of the region, a weather chart.* —*v.t.* **1.** to make a map or chart of: *to chart a coastline.* **2.** to plan or map out: *to chart a course of action.* [Old French *charte* card¹, map, from Latin *charta* paper, leaf of papyrus, from Greek *chartēs* leaf of papyrus, writing. Doublet of CARD¹.] —**Syn.** *v.t.* **1.** see **map.**

char·ter (chär′tər) *n.* **1.** formal written document issued by a national or state government or a sovereign to a group of citizens, or a corporation, granting the right to organize for carrying on some specified activity and imposing certain obligations. **2.** *also,* **Charter.** document defining the functions or form of organization of a body, or setting forth its aims and principles; constitution. **3.** written permission or authorization from a society or organization to establish a new local chapter or branch. **4.a.** contract or agreement to lease all or part of a carrier, as a ship or airplane, for transporting goods or persons. **b.** a leasing under such a contract: *Those planes are available for charter.* —*v.t.* **1.** to lease or hire by charter: *Our school chartered three buses for the trip.* **2.** to grant a charter to; establish by charter: *to charter a bank.* [Old French *chartre* letter, edict registering property, granted privileges, from Latin *chartula* a little paper, diminutive of *charta* paper. See CHART.] —**Syn.** *v.t.* **1.** see **lease.**

charter member, any of the original members of an organization, such as a club, society, or company.

Chart·ist (chär′tist) *n.* member of a political movement of British workers, active from 1838 to 1849, who advocated and demonstrated for universal suffrage for men, secret ballots, the elimination of property qualifications for members of Parliament, and other reform measures. [From the *charter* of this movement, which presented its ideas and aims.] —**Chart′ism,** *n.*

Char·tres (shär′trə) *n.* city in north-central France, noted for its cathedral. Pop. (1962), 31,495.

char·treuse (shär trōōz′, -trōōs′) *n.* **1.** pale yellowish-green color. **2.** pale-green, yellow, or white liqueur originally made by Carthusian monks. [French *chartreuse* Carthusian monastery, this liqueur, from *Grande Chartreuse*, mountainous region in southeastern France where the first Carthusian monastery was built.]

char·wom·an (chär′wōom′ən) *pl.* **-wom·en.** *n.* woman hired to clean, as in homes, offices, or public buildings. [CHAR² + WOMAN.]

char·y (chär′ē) *adj.* **char·i·er, char·i·est.** *adj.* **1.** hesitant and circumspect about dangers or risks; careful; cautious; wary: *a chary suitor, to be chary of strangers.* **2.** reluctant in granting or giving; not lavish; sparing; frugal (often with *of*): *He is chary of his favors. She was chary of complimenting others.* [Old English *cearig* careful, sorrowful.]

Cha·ryb·dis (kə rib′dis) *n. Greek Mythology.* hideous monster having the form of a raging whirlpool, dwelling in the Strait of Messina opposite the cave of the monster Scylla. Most sailors who were not devoured by Scylla were drowned by Charybdis.

chase¹ (chās) chased, chas·ing. *v.t.* **1.** to go after and try to catch; pursue, as for the purpose of capturing, seizing, or overtaking: *The cat chased the birds. The police chased the thief down the alley. The children chased the hoop in the park.* **2.** to cause to depart or flee; drive: *He chased the children out of his yard. Her continual gossiping chased her friends away.* **3.** to devote one's attention to in order to win or gain; follow hopefully and persistently: *to chase girls, to chase a dream.* **4.** to investigate or try to verify; seek out (often with *down*): *to chase down a rumor, to chase a lead.* —*v.i.* **1.** to follow in pursuit: *The boy chased after the ball that had rolled into the street.* **2.** *Informal.* to rush about; hurry: *She chased all over town looking for a new dress.* —*n.* **1.** act of chasing; pursuit: *to join in a chase. They caught the prey after a long chase.* **2. the chase.** the sport of hunting. **3.** that which is chased or hunted; quarry. **4.** *British.* tract of unenclosed land used as a private game preserve. **5. to give chase.** to pursue. [Old French *chacier* to hunt, pursue, going back to Latin *captāre* to try to catch, pursue. Doublet of CATCH.] —**Syn.** *v.t.* **1.** see **hunt.**

at; āpe; cär; end; mē; it; īce; hot; ōld; fôrk; wood; fōōl; oil; out; up; ūse; turn; sing; thin; this; zh in treasure; ə in ago, taken, pencil, lemon, circus.

chase² (chās) *chased, chas·ing. v.t.* to decorate (a metal surface) by embossing or engraving. [Short for ENCHASE.]

chase³ (chās) *n.* **1.** furrow, as one in a wall to receive a pipe; groove or trench. **2.** rectangular metal frame into which pages of type or plates are locked for printing or plate making. *—v.t.* to groove; indent. [French *châsse* setting, frame, from Latin *capsa* box, chest.]

chase gun, gun located on the bow or stern of a ship, used when pursuing or being pursued.

chas·er (chā′sər) *n.* **1.** one who or that which chases. **2.** small, fast ship designed for pursuit. **3.** chase gun. **4.** *Informal.* drink, as of water or beer, taken after a drink of hard liquor.

chasm (kaz′əm) *n.* **1.** deep, yawning crack or fissure in the earth's surface, or in a mountain, rock, glacier, or the like; gorge. **2.** break marking a divergence, as in opinion; profound difference, as of feelings or beliefs: *The chasm between the two political parties was widening.* **3.** marked interruption of or gap in continuity; hiatus. [Latin *chasma* opening, abyss, from Greek *chasma* opening, gulf.] *—chas′mal, adj.*

chas·sé (sha sā′) *n.* gliding dance step in which the same foot always takes the lead. *—v.i.* to execute this step. [French *chassé* this dance step, from *chasser* to pursue, from Old French *chacier.* See CHASE¹.]

chas·seur (sha sur′) *n.* **1.** member of a military unit, esp. a member of a French infantry unit, trained and equipped for rapid movement. **2.** huntsman; hunter. **3.** liveried attendant or servant. [French *chasseur* hunter, from Old French *chaceor,* from *chacier* to hunt. See CHASE¹.]

chas·sis (shas′tē, chas′ē) *pl.* **chas·sis** (shas′ēz, chas′ēz). *n.* **1.** skeleton of a motor vehicle, including the wheels, frame, and mechanical parts, on which the body is supported. **2.** framework on which the parts of a radio or television set are mounted. **3.** rails or frame on which a gun carriage moves backward and forward. [French *châssis* frame, from *châsse,* from Latin *capsa* box, chest.]

chaste (chāst) *adj.* **1.** not having engaged in unlawful sexual intercourse; virtuous. **2.** free from indecency or offensiveness; modest. **3.** restrained or simple in style. [Old French *chaste* pure, from Latin *castus.* Doublet of CASTE.] *—chaste′ly, adv. —chaste′ness, n.*

chas·ten (chā′sən) *v.t.* **1.** to punish or reprimand for the purpose of correcting or improving. **2.** to restrain from excess; temper; subdue. **3.** to make chaste in style; purify. [From obsolete *chaste* to correct, from Old French *chastier* to punish, from Latin *castīgāre* to make pure, correct, from *castus* pure.] *—chas′ten·er, n.*

chas·tise (chas tīz′, chas′tīz) *-tised, -tis·ing. v.t.* to punish, reprimand, or discipline severely. [Probably from obsolete *chaste* to correct. See CHASTEN.] *—chas′tise·ment, chas·tis′er, n.*

chas·ti·ty (chas′tə tē) *n.* **1.** state or quality of being chaste. **2.** abstinence from all sexual intercourse.

chastity belt, beltlike device, worn by women, esp. in the Middle Ages, designed to prevent sexual intercourse.

chas·u·ble (chaz′yə bəl, -ə bəl, chas′-) *n.* sleeveless outer vestment worn over the alb by a priest officiating at Mass. [Old French *chasuble,* from Late Latin *casubula,* going back to Latin *casa* house. It was originally a hooded mantle, resembling a small house.]

Chasuble

chat (chat) *chat·ted, chat·ting. v.i.* to converse in a light, familiar, or informal manner. *—n.* **1.** informal, friendly talk or conversation. **2.** any of several songbirds, as the stonechat or wheatear, having a chattering cry. [Short for CHATTER.]

cha·teau (sha tō′) *pl.* **-teaux** (-tōz′). *n.* **1.** castle in a French-speaking country or region. **2.** any large and elaborate country house, esp. one resembling a castle. [French *château,* from Old French *chastel* castle, from Latin *castellum* castle.]

cha·teau·bri·and (shä tō brē äN′) *n.* tender, boneless steak cut from the tenderloin of beef, usually served in a wine sauce with mushrooms. [From CHATEAUBRIAND.]

Cha·teau·bri·and, Fran·çois Re·né (shä tō brē äN′; frän swä′ rə nā′) 1768–1848, French author and statesman.

Châ·teau-Thier·ry (shä tō tye rē′, -tē′ə rē) *n.* town in northern France where American and French troops halted the German advance on Paris in 1918 during World War I. Pop. (1962) 10,006.

chat·e·lain (shat′əl ān′) *n.* keeper of a castle. [French *châtelain* lord of a castle, from Latin *castellānus* occupant of a castle, from *castellum* fortress, castle. See CASTLE.]

chat·e·laine (shat′əl ān′) *n.* **1.** mistress or lady of a castle, chateau, or fashionable household. **2.** ornamental chain or clasp, usually worn at a woman's waist, to which keys, a purse, or other articles may be attached. [French *châtelaine,* feminine of *châtelain.* See CHATELAIN.]

Chat·ta·noo·ga (chat′ə nōō′gə) *n.* city in southern Tennessee, on the Tennessee River. Pop. (1970), 119,082.

chat·tel (chat′əl) *n.* article of personal property, as furniture or live-

stock, as distinguished from real property, as lands or buildings; any movable possession. [Old French *chatel* property, from Late Latin *capitāle,* noun use of neuter of Latin *capitālis* chief, relating to the *caput* or head. Doublet of CATTLE.]

chat·ter (chat′ər) *v.i.* **1.** to talk rapidly and incessantly, usually about matters of little consequence; jabber: *She chattered on and on about her new wardrobe.* **2.** to click together rapidly or uncontrollably: *My teeth chattered from the cold.* **3.** to utter a rapid succession or series of short sounds: *The magpies chattered in the trees.* **4.** to rattle or vibrate during cutting, as an electric saw, so as to produce surface marks or an uneven finish. *—v.t.* to utter incessantly, rapidly, or foolishly: *to chatter nonsense. —n.* **1.** foolish or inconsequential talk. **2.** act or sound of chattering. [Imitative.] *—chat′ter·er, n.*

chat·ter·box (chat′ər boks′) *n.* one who talks incessantly.

chatter mark 1. mark caused by the chattering of a tool or machine. **2.** one of a series of small, curved abrasions on the surface of a glaciated rock.

Chat·ter·ton, Thomas (chat′ər tən) 1752–70, English poet.

chat·ty (chat′ē) *-ti·er, -ti·est. adj.* **1.** given to chatting; talkative. **2.** full of chat; light, familiar, and informal: *a chatty letter. —chat′ti·ly, adv. —chat′ti·ness, n.*

Chau·cer, Geof·frey (chô′sər; jef′rē) c.1344–1400, English poet.

Chau·ce·ri·an (chô sēr′ē ən) *adj.* of, relating to, or characteristic of Chaucer or his works. *—n.* scholar specializing in the study of Chaucer and his works.

chauf·feur (shō′fər, shō fur′) *n.* person employed as the driver of an automobile, esp. a limousine. *—v.t., v.i.* to act or work as a chauffeur (for); drive: *He chauffeured us to the airport. He chauffeurs for a company in New York City.* [French *chauffeur* stoker, heater, from *chauffer* to heat, going back to Latin *calefacere* to make warm; because the first automobiles were often powered by steam, the French humorously referred to drivers as "stokers" or *chauffeurs.*]

chau·tau·qua (shə tô′kwə) *also,* **Chau·tau·qua** *n.* **1.** educational movement begun in 1874 at Chautauqua, New York, establishing summer programs of instruction in education, religion, and the arts. Also, **Chautauqua movement. 2.** any of various similar programs, esp. those formerly offered by a number of traveling groups that brought information, religious inspiration, and professional entertainment to the small towns and cities of the rural United States. [From *Chautauqua,* New York.]

chau·vin·ism (shō′və niz′əm) *n.* **1.** overzealous, uncritical, or militant enthusiasm for one's country or its military glory; exaggerated or fanatical patriotism. **2.** exaggerated, unreasoning pride in or attachment to one's own group, race, or sex. [French *chauvinisme,* from Nicolas *Chauvin,* French soldier noted for his blind patriotism and devotion to Napoleon I.] *—chau′vin·ist, adj.,n. —chau·vin·is′tic, adj. —chau′vin·is′ti·cal·ly, adv.*

Ch. E., Chemical Engineer.

cheap (chēp) *adj.* **1.** low in price; inexpensive, esp. as compared with its value or going price: *It was a good dinner and very cheap, too.* **2.** charging low prices: *a cheap dress shop.* **3.** of little value or worth; inferior in quality; shoddy: *a novel printed on cheap paper.* **4.** unwilling to spend money; ungenerous; stingy; miserly. **5.** worthy of contempt; not esteemed; vulgar, common, or immoral: *All her makeup made her seem cheap.* **6.** costing little effort or trouble; easily obtained: *Talk is cheap.* **7.** (of money) **a.** obtainable at a low rate of interest. **b.** depreciated in exchange value or buying power: *Cheap dollars are often the result of an inflation. —adv.* at a low price; cheaply: *He went to a wholesaler and got the radio cheap.* [Old English *cēap* bargain, price, trade, going back to Latin *caupō* tradesman.] *—cheap′ly, adv. —cheap′ness, n.*

cheap·en (chē′pən) *v.t.* to lower the price or value of; bring into contempt; make cheap: *Her gaudy dress cheapened her. —v.i.* to become cheap.

cheap·skate (chēp′skāt′) *n. Informal.* stingy or miserly person. [CHEAP + SKATE².]

cheat (chēt) *v.t.* **1.** to defraud or swindle; trick: *They cheated us out of our share of the money.* **2.** to deprive, esp. of something expected, by or as by trickery: *The rain cheated us of our picnic. —v.i.* **1.** to practice fraud or act dishonestly: *They were accused of cheating on an exam. He cheats at cards.* **2.** *Slang.* to be unfaithful in a sexual or romantic relationship (often with *on). —n.* **1.** one who is dishonest or unfaithful. **2.** dishonest act or practice; fraud; trick. [Short for ESCHEAT; from the dishonest practice of those who took care of the *escheats* in feudal times. See ESCHEAT.] *—cheat′er, n.*

Syn. *v.t.* **1.** Cheat, defraud, swindle mean to gain an advantage or profit by culpably dishonest means. To **cheat** is to trick and deceive by the use of wiles and stratagems: *Henry won the last game by cheating his opponent.* **Defraud** involves misrepresentation to gain something rightfully belonging to another: *The trustee was accused of defrauding his ward of the property.* **Swindle** suggests a particularly

ruthless or flagrant action, often by imposture or abuse of confidence: *The salesman swindled his customers by selling them shares in a bogus company.*

check (chek) *n.* **1.** one who or that which stops, controls, or limits: *an economist who felt that higher taxes would act as a check on inflation.* **2.** test, examination, or inspection: *They ran a check on the computer.* **3.** search, inquiry, or investigation: *We made a quick check for the missing files.* **4.** mark, usually √, used to indicate that something has been approved, noted, or otherwise examined. **5.** control or supervision, as by which accuracy or correctness is maintained: *The head operator kept a check on his workers.* **6.** *also, British,* **cheque.** written order directing a bank to pay a specified sum. **7.** slip of paper listing an amount owed, esp. in payment for a meal. **8.** ticket, tag, or other token showing ownership or used for identification, as in reclaiming something left for temporary safekeeping: *a baggage check.* **9.** sudden stoppage; abrupt halt. **10.** square in a checkered surface or pattern. **11.** checkered pattern. **12.** fabric having such a pattern. **13.** *Chess.* position of a king when it is under direct attack from one of the opposing pieces and is subject to being taken on the next opposing move. **14.** *Hockey.* defensive blocking of the opponent in possession of the puck by use of one's body or stick. **15. in check.** under control or restraint: *He held his anger in check.* —*v.t.* **1.** to halt the course or progress of sharply or forcefully; bring to a sudden stop: *to check the spread of a disease. They checked the advancing enemy army.* **2.** to hold in control or restraint; restrain; curb: *to check one's temper. He checked the impulse to laugh at her mistake.* **3.** to compare, as with an authority or source of information, for accuracy: *Check the copy against the original. He checked his answers with those in the back of the book.* **4.** to test, investigate, or verify as to correctness (often with *out*): *to check someone's references. The reporter checked the story out. My professor checked the sources I mentioned in my footnotes.* **5.** to inspect and ascertain the condition of; examine: *The medic checked him for broken bones after he'd been tackled by the quarterback.* **6.** to mark with or as with a check (often with *off*): *Please check the correct answer. I checked each item off as he dictated the list.* **7.** to leave (something) for temporary safekeeping or custody, as in a checkroom: *He checked his coat as he came in.* **8.** to deposit (baggage), as with an airline, so as to send to a particular destination, usually aboard the same carrier on which one is traveling (often with *in*): *I haven't checked my bags yet. We're supposed to check our luggage in before 8:00.* **9.** to tally the price of purchases made and collect the total for (often with *out*): *The cashier checked out the groceries.* **10.** to mark in or with a pattern of small squares; checker. **11.** *Chess.* to place (an opponent's king) in check. **12.** *Hockey.* to block the progress of (the opponent in possession of the puck by use of one's body or stick. —*v.i.* **1.** to make an inquiry or investigation, as for verification (often with *on* or *up*): *I checked up to see if they'd left. Check on the time the train leaves.* **2.** to agree on every point; correspond accurately: *My totals check with yours.* **3.** *Chess.* to place the opponent's king in check. **4.** *Hockey.* to block the opponent in possession of the puck by use of one's body or stick. **5. to check in.** to register as a guest, as at a hotel. **6. to check out. a.** to pay one's bill at and depart from a hotel or motel. **b.** to prove to be true or correct after examination or investigation: *The suspect's story checked out and he was freed on bail.* —*interj. Chess.* call telling an opponent that his king is in check and must be moved. [Old French *eschec* check at chess, repulse, loss, through Arabic, from Persian *shāh* king (the most important chesspiece).]

check·book (chek′book′) *n.* book of blank checks issued by a bank to a depositor.

checked (chekt) *adj.* marked with squares; checkered: *a checked tablecloth.*

check·er[1] (chek′ər) *n.* **1.** cashier, esp. in a supermarket. **2.** one who or that which checks. [CHECK + -ER[1].]

check·er[2] (chek′ər) *also, British,* **cheq·uer.** *n.* **1.** one of the flat, circular, usually red or black pieces used in the game of checkers. **2.** pattern of squares of alternating colors or shades. **3.** one of the squares of such a pattern. —*v.t.* **1.** to mark with squares of alternating colors or shades, as a checkerboard. **2.** to vary or mottle with patches of different colors or shades; variegate: *The sky was checkered with clouds.* **3.** to vary with contrasting elements or situations; fill with variations. [Old French *eschekier* chessboard, from *eschec* check at chess. See CHECK.]

check·er·ber·ry (chek′ər ber′ē) *pl.,* **-ries.** *n.* **1.** wintergreen (*def.* 1). **2.** partridgeberry.

check·er·board (chek′ər bôrd′) *n.* square board marked off into sixty-four alternately colored squares, used in playing checkers and chess.

check·ered (chek′ərd) *adj.* **1.** marked with squares of alternating colors or shades: *a checkered scarf.* **2.** marked with patches of different colors or shades: *a landscape checkered by shadows.* **3.** filled with changes of fortune or contrasting elements or situations; varied.

check·ers (chek′ərz) *also, British,* **cheq·uers.** *n.,pl.* game for two

played on a checkerboard, each player having twelve pieces. The game is won when one of the players cannot make a move because his pieces have been captured or blocked. Also, *British,* **draughts.** ▲ construed as singular. [Plural of CHECKER.]

checking account, bank account against which checks may be drawn by the depositor.

check list, list used for reference, verification, or comparison.

check·mate (chek′māt′) *-mat·ed, -mat·ing. v.t.* **1.** *Chess.* to put (the opponent's king) in check from which no escape is possible, thus winning the game. **2.** to defeat, thwart, or arrest completely, esp. by a shrewd or skillful maneuver. —*n.* **1.** *Chess.* situation or position of a king when it has been checkmated. **2.** complete or utter defeat or arrest. —*interj. Chess.* exclamation by a player announcing that his opponent's king is checkmated. [Old French *esche et mat* checkmate (in chess); literally, check and conquered, through Arabic, from Persian *shāh-māt* literally, the king is dead.]

check·off (chek′ôf′) *n.* practice whereby an employer deducts union dues from employees' wages and turns these deductions over to the union.

check·out (chek′out′) *n.* **1.** process of examining and testing the readiness of something, as a machine part, for performance. **2.** process of itemizing and charging for purchases, as in a supermarket. **3.** time by which one must vacate a hotel or motel room or be charged for remaining in it.

check·point (chek′point′) *n.* place, as at a border, where vehicles or travelers are stopped for inspection or clearance.

check·rein (chek′rān′) *n.* **1.** short rein fastened from the bit to the harness to keep a horse from lowering its head. **2.** short rein connecting the bit of one horse in a team to the driving rein of the other.

check·room (chek′room′, -room′) *n.* room in which personal property, as hats, coats, or packages, may be left temporarily.

checks and balances, system, as among legislative, executive, and judiciary branches, in which the actions of each branch or part of a government are subject to restraints or vetoes from the others, so that no one branch becomes supreme.

check·up (chek′up′) *n.* **1.** complete physical examination. **2.** examination or inspection: *We took the car for its thousand-mile checkup.*

Ched·dar (ched′ər) *also,* **ched·dar.** *n.* any of several types of hard, smooth cheese, ranging in color from white to dark yellow and in taste from strong and sharp to mild. Also, **Cheddar cheese.** [From the village of *Cheddar,* England, where it was first made.]

cheek (chēk) *n.* **1.** either side of the face below the eye, esp. that part above the level of the mouth. **2.** something resembling this part of the face in shape or position: *the cheek of a vise.* **3.** saucy or brazen insolence; impudence; effrontery. **4.** buttock. **5. cheek by jowl.** side by side; in close intimacy. [Old English *cēce* side of the face below the eye.]

cheek·bone (chēk′bōn′) *n.* either of two bony prominences at the upper part of the cheek, just below the eye.

cheek pouch, pouch or bag in the cheek of any of various animals, as the squirrel or monkey, used for holding food.

cheek·y (chē′kē) **cheek·i·er, cheek·i·est.** *adj. Informal.* saucily or brazenly insolent; impudent. —**cheek′i·ly,** *adv.* —**cheek′i·ness,** *n.*

cheep (chēp) *v.t., v.i.* to make or utter with a faint, shrill sound, as a young bird; chirp; peep. —*n.* faint, shrill, chirping sound. [Imitative.]

cheer (chēr) *n.* **1.** lively shout of acclamation, encouragement, or joy: *A cheer arose from the crowd when the president appeared.* **2.** traditional set of words or sounds used by spectators to encourage or show enthusiasm, as for a contestant or athletic team: *a school cheer, our class cheer.* **3.** gladness, gaiety, or animation: *There is a general feeling of cheer as the holiday season nears.* **4.** that which gives joy or gladness; comfort; encouragement: *The doctor spoke words of cheer to the sick child.* **5.** state of mind or spirits; mood: *to be of good cheer.* **6.** food and drink, as for a feast; provisions; fare. —*v.t.* **1.** to salute or acclaim with cheers: *The audience cheered him as he walked on stage.* **2.** to make hopeful or glad; restore cheer to; comfort or gladden (often with *up*): *The mourners were cheered by the kind words. The news cheered him up.* **3.** to incite or urge on, with or as with cheers; encourage (often with *on*): *to cheer on a team.* —*v.i.* **1.** to utter cheers: *The crowd cheered wildly. We cheered as he neared the finish line.* **2.** to become hopeful or glad (often with *up*): *He cheered up at the thought of seeing her again.* [Old French *chere* face (suggesting a glad expression on the face, hence, gladness), from Late Latin *cara,* from Greek *karā* head, face.]

cheer·ful (chēr′fəl) *adj.* **1.** showing or feeling cheer; full of good spirits; happy; joyous: *a cheerful personality, a cheerful smile.* **2.** bringing cheer: *a cheerful fire, cheerful surroundings.* **3.** ungrudging; willing: *a cheerful worker.* —**cheer′ful·ly,** *adv.* —**cheer′ful·ness,** *n.*

cheer·i·o (chēr′ē ō′) *pl.,* **-i·os.** *interj. British. Informal.* **1.** hello. **2.a.** good-by. **b.** good luck. ▲ often used as a toast to drinking companions.

cheer·lead·er (chēr′lē′dər) *n.* one who leads organized or traditional cheering, esp. at a sports event.

---

at; āpe; cär; end; mē; it; īce; hot; ōld; fôrk; wood; fōōl; oil; out; up; ūse; turn; sing; thin; <u>th</u>is; zh in treasure; ə in ago, taken, pencil, lemon, circus.

cheer·less (chēr′lis) *adj.* devoid of cheer; joyless; gloomy. —**cheer′less·ly,** *adv.* —**cheer′less·ness,** *n.*

cheer·y (chēr′ē) *adj.*, **cheer·i·er, cheer·i·est.** *adj.* bringing or full of cheerfulness; gay: *a cheery hello.* —**cheer′i·ly,** *adv.*

cheese¹ (chēz) *n.* **1.** any of a group of dairy products, variously prepared and flavored, usually ripened and made from the pressed curd of milk. **2.** mass or cake of cheese. **3.** something resembling cheese in shape or consistency. [Old English *cēse* the dairy product, going back to Latin *cāseus.*]

cheese² (chēz) *n.* Slang. important person: *He's the big cheese around the office.* [Possibly from Urdu *chīz* thing, from Persian *chīz.*]

cheese·burg·er (chēz′bûr′gər) *n.* hamburger with cheese, usually melted on top of the meat.

cheese·cake (chēz′kāk′) *n.* **1.** rich, creamy cake made of cream cheese or cottage cheese, eggs, sugar, milk, and various flavorings, often having a bottom crust. **2.a.** *Informal.* photograph of a woman posed to display her figure and face. **b.** such photographs collectively.

cheese·cloth (chēz′klôth′) *n.* thin, loosely woven cotton cloth. [Because first used for wrapping cheese.]

chees·y (chē′zē) **chees·i·er, chees·i·est.** *adj.* **1.** of or like cheese. **2.** *Slang.* of inferior quality; poorly made; cheap. —**chees′i·ness,** *n.*

chee·tah (chē′tə) *also,* **che·tah.** *n.* leopardlike wild mammal, genus *Acinonyx,* of the cat family, native to Africa and southern Asia, having a tawny coat with black spots or blotches, long legs, and claws that are permanently extended. It is capable of attaining speeds up to seventy miles per hour for short distances. Height: 2 feet at the shoulder. [Hindi *chītā* leopard, panther, going back to Sanskrit *chitra* spotted.]

Cheetah

chef (shef) *n.* **1.** head cook of a restaurant, household, or other establishment. **2.** cook. [French *chef* chief, master, head (short for *chef de cuisine* head cook), going back to Latin *caput* head. Doublet of CHIEF.]

chef-d'oeu·vre (shā dœ′vrə) *pl.,* **chefs-d'oeuvre** (shā dœ′vrə). *n.* masterpiece, esp. in art or literature. [French *chef d'oeuvre* literally, chief piece of work, going back to Latin *caput* head + *dē* from + *opus* work.]

Che·ka (che′kä) *n.* commission in the Soviet Union that acted as a secret police force against counterrevolutionary activities from 1917 to 1922. [Russian *che* and *ka,* the first letters of *Chrezvychainaya Kommissiya* Extraordinary Commission.]

Che·khov, An·ton (chek′ôf, -of; än tôn′) 1860–1904, Russian author.

che·la (kē′lə) *pl.,* **-lae** (-lē). *n.* pincerlike claw of certain crustaceans, as the lobster or crab, and of certain arachnids, as the scorpion. [Modern Latin *chela,* from Greek *chēlē* claw.]

Lobster chela

che·lo·ni·an (ki lō′nē ən) *adj.* of or relating to turtles. —*n.* turtle. [Modern Latin *Chelonia* (from Greek *chelōnē* tortoise) + -AN.]

Chel·sea (chel′sē) *n.* area in central London, traditionally the artists' quarter of the city.

chem-, form of **chemo-** before vowels, as in *chemist.*

chem., chemistry; chemical; chemist.

chemi-, form of **chemo-.**

chem·ic (kem′ik) *adj. Archaic.* **1.** of or relating to alchemy. **2.** chemical.

Chela

chem·i·cal (kem′i kəl) *adj.* of, relating to, or produced by chemistry or its phenomena, laws, or operations: *a chemical formula, a chemical reaction, the chemical composition of a substance.* —*n.* substance obtained by or used in a chemical process. —**chem′i·cal·ly,** *adv.*

chemical bond, electrical force of attraction that holds together the atoms of a molecule or the ions in a crystal.

chemical engineering 1. application of chemical knowledge and principles to industrial processes. **2.** science dealing with or profession practicing this application.

Chemical Mace *Trademark.* mace³.

chemical warfare, use of chemical products, as gases, incendiaries, or smoke-producing substances, as weapons.

che·mise (shə mēz′) *n.* **1.** loose, shirtlike undergarment worn as a slip. **2.** shift (*def. 5*). [Old French *chemise* shirt, from Late Latin *camīsia;* of uncertain origin.]

chem·ist (kem′ist) *n.* **1.** one versed or trained in the science of chemistry; one professionally engaged in making chemical investigations. **2.** *British.* druggist. [Short for ALCHEMIST. See ALCHEMY.]

chem·is·try (kem′is trē) *pl.,* **-tries.** *n.* **1.** science that deals with the composition and properties of substances and the changes that take place when they react with other substances. **2.** chemical composition, properties, or processes: *the chemistry of carbon, body chemistry.* **3.** any process or reaction similar to those dealt with by the science of chemistry; causal or characteristic quality or factor: *the chemistry of love.* [From CHEMIST. See ALCHEMY.]

Chem·nitz (kem′nits) *n.* see **Karl-Marx-Stadt.**

chemo- *combining form of or relating to chemistry, chemicals, or chemical reactions: chemotherapy.* [Going back to Late Greek *chēmiā* alchemy, chemistry; of uncertain origin.]

chem·o·ther·a·py (kem′ō ther′ə pē, kē′mō-) *n.* **1.** use of chemical substances to treat diseases caused by bacteria, viruses, or other parasites. **2.** use of tranquilizers, stimulants, and other drugs to treat mental illness.

chem·ur·gy (kem′ər jē) *n.* branch of chemistry that deals with the development of new industrial uses for plant and animal products. [CHEM(O)- + Greek *ergon* work.]

che·nille (shə nēl′) *n.* **1.** yarn, often of cotton, silk, or worsted, with a velvety, fuzzy pile, used for embroidery, tassels, and fringes. **2.** fabric woven from this yarn, used for such items as rugs and bedspreads. [French *chenille* caterpillar, from Latin *canīcula* little dog, diminutive of *canis* dog; because of its furry appearance.]

Che·ops (kē′ops) *n.* c.2900 B.C., pharaoh of ancient Egypt during the fourth dynasty, best known for building the Great Pyramid near Giza as his tomb. Also, **Khu′fu.**

cheque (chek) *n. British.* check (*def. 6*).

cheq·uer (chek′ər) *British.* checker².

cheq·uers (chek′ərz) *British.* checkers.

Cher·bourg (shâr′boorg′) *n.* seaport, naval base, and resort in northwestern France, on the English Channel. Pop. (1962), 37,486.

cher·ish (cher′ish) *v.t.* **1.** to treat with affection; care for tenderly; hold dear: *The governess cherished the child as though he were her own.* **2.** to hold or entertain in the mind; cling fondly or steadfastly to: *She cherished the memory of her father. He cherished the hope of being a great ball player someday.* [Old French *cheriss-,* a stem of *cherir* to hold dear, from *cher* dear, from Latin *cārus.*]

Syn. 1. Cherish, treasure mean to value highly. **Cherish** implies great or considerable love, affection, or attachment: *Most Americans cherish freedom and independence.* **Treasure** stresses the preserving and guarding of what one regards as precious to keep it from being diminished, forgotten, lost, or injured: *The old woman treasured the mementos of her youth.*

Cher·o·kee (cher′ə kē, cher′ə kē′) *pl.,* **-kees** or **-kee.** *n.* **1.** member of a tribe of North American Indians, formerly the largest tribe that lived in the southeastern United States, now living mostly in Oklahoma. **2.** their language, belonging to the Iroquoian language family. [Modification of *Tsálagi* or *Tsaragi,* Cherokee name for themselves, possibly from Choctaw *chiluk-ki* cave people; because of the many caves in Cherokee territory.]

Cherokee rose 1. fragrant white flower of a climbing evergreen plant, *Rosa laevigata,* native to China, Japan, and the southern United States and usually having three sharply toothed leaflets. **2.** the plant itself.

che·root (shə root′) *n.* cigar cut square at both ends. [Tamil *shuruttu* roll of tobacco.]

cher·ry (cher′ē) *pl.,* **-ries.** *n.* **1.** small, round, or heart-shaped fruit of any of several shrubs or trees, genus *Prunus,* of the rose family, cultivated in temperate regions of the world, having a smooth skin and a fleshy pulp enclosing a pit. **2.** tree or shrub bearing this fruit, having clusters of white or pink flowers. **3.** its wood. **4.** bright red color. —*adj.* **1.** made of or consisting of cherries. **2.** bright red. **3.** made of cherry wood. [Dialectal Old French *cherise* fruit of the cherry tree, going back to Latin *cerasus* cherry tree, from Greek *kerasos.*]

cher·ry·stone (cher′ē stōn′) *n.* **1.** quahog. Also, **cherrystone clam. 2.** pit of a cherry.

cher·ub (cher′əb) *pl.,* **cher·ubs** or (*defs. 1, 2*) **cher·u·bim** (cher′ə bim′). *n.* **1.** member of the second of the nine orders of angels. **2.** conventional representation of a cherub, often a chubby, winged child. **3.** beautiful, innocent, or sweet child. [Hebrew *k'rūb* winged angel.] —**che·ru·bic** (chə roo′bik); *also,* **che·ru′bi·cal,** *adj.* —**che·ru′bi·cal·ly,** *adv.*

cher·vil (chur′vəl) *n.* **1.** aromatic leaves of a plant, *Anthriscus cerefolium,* of the parsley family, used as a garnish and in salads and soups. **2.** carrot-shaped root of a plant, *Chaerophyllum bulbosum,* of the parsley family, eaten as a vegetable, either raw or cooked. **3.** either of these plants. **4.** any of several related plants. [Old English *cærfille* the plant *Anthriscus cerefolium,* through Latin, from Greek *chairephyllon.*]

cher·vo·nets (cher vô′nets) *pl.,* **-von·tsi** (-vôn′tsē) *n.* former monetary unit and coin of the USSR, worth ten rubles. [Russian *chervonets.*]

Ches·a·peake (ches'ə pēk') *n.* city in southeastern Virginia, a residential suburb of Norfolk. Pop. (1970), 89,580.

Chesapeake Bay, long arm of the Atlantic, on the eastern coast of the United States, in Virginia and Maryland.

Chesh·ire cat (chesh'ər, -ēr) grinning cat in Lewis Carroll's *Alice's Adventures in Wonderland,* which gradually faded away until only a grin remained.

chess (ches) *n.* game for two played on a chessboard, each player having sixteen chessmen. The players take turns moving their pieces, each with the aim of checkmating his opponent's king. [Old French *esches,* plural of *eschec* check (at chess). See CHECK.]

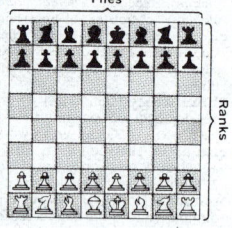

Files / Ranks

Chessboard

chess·board (ches'bôrd') *n.* square board marked off into sixty-four alternately colored squares, used in playing chess or checkers.

chess·man (ches'man', -mən) *pl.,* **-men** (-men, -mən). *n.* any of the pieces used in playing chess. Each player has a king, queen, eight pawns, two bishops, two knights, and two rooks. Also, **chess·piece** (ches'pēs').

chest (chest) *n.* **1.** that part of the body extending from the base of the neck to the diaphragm. Also, **tho'rax.** **2.** this part considered as the seat of the emotions or conscience: *If something's bothering you, get it off your chest.* **3.** chest of drawers. **4.a.** box or boxlike container, usually with a hinged lid, for the storage or safekeeping of articles: *a tool chest.* **b.** box or case in which a commodity, esp. tea, is packed for shipping. **5.** quantity contained in such a chest. [Old English *cest, cist* box, basket, going back to Latin *cista,* from Greek *kistē.*]

Ches·ter (ches'tər) *n.* **1.** city in southeastern Pennsylvania, on the Delaware River, an industrial suburb of Philadelphia. Pop. (1970), 56,331. **2.** city in western England. Pop. (1961), 59,268.

ches·ter·field (ches'tər fēld') *n.* **1.** overcoat, usually single-breasted, having concealed buttons and a velvet collar. **2.** over-stuffed davenport or sofa, usually having upright, upholstered arms. [From one of the Earls of *Chesterfield.*]

Ches·ter·field, Earl of (ches'tər fēld') 1694–1773, British statesman and author famous for his letters to his son and godson instructing them in conduct and manners.

Ches·ter·ton, Gilbert Keith (ches'tər tən) 1874–1936, English author and critic.

Chester White, large, white hog of a breed that originated in Chester county, Pennsylvania.

chest·nut (ches'nut', -nət) *n.* **1.** edible nut of a tree, genus *Castanea,* of the beech family, cultivated in North America, southern Europe, and Japan, having a shiny, usually mahogany-colored shell. **2.** tree producing this nut, having leathery, oblong leaves and fragrant flowers. **3.** wood of this tree. **4.** any of several similar trees, as the horse chestnut or water chestnut. **5.** reddish-brown color. Also, **chestnut brown. 6.** reddish-brown horse having mane and tail of the same or a lighter color. **7.** *Informal.* anything, as an anecdote, phrase, or expression, repeated or used to the point of staleness, esp. an old joke. [From obsolete *chesten* chestnut (tree and nut), from Old French *chastaigne,* from Latin *castanea,* from Greek *kastanon* + NUT.]

chest of drawers, piece of furniture consisting of a frame containing a set of drawers for holding clothing, linens, or other articles.

che·tah (chē'tə) cheetah.

che·val-de-frise (shə val'də frēz') *pl.,* **che·vaux-de-frise** (shə vō'də frēz'). *n.* **1.** obstacle consisting of a timber or sawhorse covered with projecting spikes or barbed wire, used to close a gap in a defensive position. **2.** protecting line, as a row of spikes or broken glass, on top of a wall. [French *cheval de Frise* literally, horse of Friesland; because first used by the Frisians to offset their lack of cavalry. See CHEVAL GLASS.]

che·val glass (shə val') full-length mirror mounted and standing on swivels in a frame. [French *cheval* horse, support, from Latin *caballus* inferior horse, nag + GLASS.]

chev·a·lier (shev'ə lēr') *n.* **1.** member, usually holding the lowest rank, in certain orders of knighthood or honor, as in the French Legion of Honor. **2.** knight or cavalier. [Old French *chevalier* knight, horseman, from Late Latin *caballārius* horseman, from Latin *caballus* inferior horse, nag. Doublet of CAVALIER.]

Chev·i·ot (shev'ē ət, chev'-) *n.* **1.** sheep of a breed that originated in the Cheviot Hills, valued as meat and for their thick wool. **2.** lustrous, wiry, white wool obtained from these sheep. **3.** cheviot, rough fabric, the better grades of which are made from this wool, woven with a twill and used for such items as suits and overcoats.

Cheviot Hills, mountain range forming part of the boundary between England and Scotland.

chev·ron (shev'rən) *n.* **1.** emblem or insignia, often consisting of stripes meeting at an angle, worn on the sleeve, as by police or servicemen, to indicate rank, length of service, or some other distinction. **2.** ornamental molding in the shape of an inverted V or zigzag pattern, used esp. in Norman and other Romanesque architecture. **3.** *Heraldry.* charge or bearing formed by two stripes that meet at an angle, like an inverted V. [Old French *chevron* rafter, kid', going back to Latin *caper* goat; possibly referring to the resemblance of rafters meeting at an angle to the horns of butting goats.]

Chevrons

chew (chōō) *v.t.* **1.** to crush or grind with the teeth: *Chew your food thoroughly.* **2.** to damage or tear, as if by chewing (often with *up*): *The broken computer chewed up the edges of the cards.* **3.** to make by or as by chewing: *The puppy chewed a hole in the slipper.* **4.** to consider or examine carefully; meditate on (often with *over*): *He wanted to chew over the problem for a day before making his decision.* —*v.i.* **1.** to perform the action of crushing or grinding with the teeth; work the jaws and teeth: *The dog lay by the fireplace and chewed on his bone.* **2.** to tear with or as with the teeth: *The goat chewed through the fence.* **3.** *Informal.* to chew tobacco. **Informal. to chew out.** *Informal.* to scold or censure severely; upbraid. —*n.* **1.** act of chewing. **2.** that which is chewed or for chewing: *a chew of tobacco.* [Old English *cēowan* to grind with the teeth.]

chewing gum, preparation, usually of chicle, sweetened and flavored for chewing.

che·wink (chi wingk') *n.* towhee. [Imitative.]

chew·y (chōō'ē) **chew·i·er, chew·i·est.** *adj.* soft or sticky and needing much chewing to be eaten: *chewy caramels.*

Chey·enne¹ (shī en', -an') *n.* capital and largest city of Wyoming, in the southeastern part of the state. Pop. (1970), 40,914. [From the *Cheyenne* Indians. See CHEYENNE².]

Chey·enne² (shī en', -an') *pl.,* **-enne** or **-ennes.** *n.* member of a tribe of North American Indians, speaking an Algonquian language, formerly living in the Great Plains, now living mainly in Montana and Oklahoma. [Sioux *Shaiyena* people who speak a strange language.]

chez (shā) *prep.* *French.* at or in the home of; by; with.

chg., charge.

chi (kī) *n.* twenty-second letter (X, χ) of the Greek alphabet, represented in English by *ch (k).*

Chiang Kai-shek (jyäng' kī'shek', chang') 1886–1975, Chinese general and political leader.

Chi·an·ti (kē än'tē, -an'-) *n.* **1.** dry, red Italian wine. **2.** any similar wine, esp. a red one.

chi·a·ro·scu·ro (kē är'ə skoor'ō, -skyoor'ō) *pl.,* **-ros.** *n.* **1.** treatment and distribution of light and shade in a painting or drawing. **2.** manner in which an artist uses or treats light and shade. **3.** painting or drawing in which only light and shade are represented. [Italian *chiaroscuro* light and shade; literally, clear dark; from *chiaro* clear (from Latin *clārus*) + *oscuro* dark (from Latin *obscūrus*).] —**chi·a'ro·scu'rist,** *n.*

chi·as·mus (kī az'məs) *pl.,* **-ma·ta** (-mə tə). *n.* *Rhetoric.* reversal in the order of words in one of two otherwise parallel phrases, for example: *Do not live to eat, but eat to live.* [Greek *chīasmos* a placing crosswise, going back to *chi* the Greek letter; with reference to the shape (X) of the letter's symbol.]

Chib·cha (chib'chä) *pl.,* **-chas** or **-cha.** *n.* member of a South American Indian tribe, formerly living in parts of what is now Colombia and Ecuador, whose highly advanced culture was destroyed by the Spanish conquistadors.

chic (shēk) *adj.* attractive, tasteful, and fashionable in style; stylish; smart. —*n.* tasteful elegance, sophistication, and fashionableness, esp. in dress; style. [French *chic,* possibly from German *Schick* fitness, taste.]

Chi·ca·go (shi kä'gō, -kô'-) *n.* largest city of Illinois, a port in the northeastern part of the state, located on Lake Michigan. Pop. (1970), 3,366,957.

Chicago Heights, city in northeastern Illinois. Pop. (1970), 40,900.

chi·cane (shi kān') **-caned, -can·ing.** *v.t., v.i.* to deceive by chicanery; trick. —*n.* chicanery. [French *chicane* a quibble, from *chicaner* to quibble, wrangle; of uncertain origin.]

chi·can·er·y (shi kā'nər ē) *pl.,* **-er·ies.** *n.* **1.** use of unfair or deceitful methods; trickery; subterfuge: *In spite of all his lawyer's chicanery, he was found guilty of the crime.* **2.** unfair or deceitful method; trick; subterfuge.

Chi·chén It·zá (chē chen' ēt sä', ēt'sə) ancient Mayan city in southeastern Mexico, on the Yucatan peninsula. It is one of the principal archaeological sites of the New World.

at; āpe; cär; end; mē; it; īce; hot; ōld; fôrk; wood; fōōl; oil; out; up; ūse; turn; sing; thin; this; zh in treasure; ə in ago, taken, pencil, lemon, circus.

chick (chik) *n.* **1.** young chicken. **2.** young of certain birds. **3.** *Slang.* young woman. [Short for CHICKEN.]

chick·a·dee (chik′ə dē′) *n.* any of various small North American birds, family Paridae, having a stout body and gray or brown plumage with black, white, or chestnut markings. The most common species is the black-capped chickadee, *Parus atricapillus,* having a gray body and a black cap and throat. [Imitative.]

Chickadee

Chick·a·mau·ga (chik′ə mô′gə) *n.* creek flowing from northwestern Georgia into the Tennessee River, site of a Confederate victory in 1863 during the Civil War.

chick·a·ree (chik′ə rē) *n.* the red squirrel. [Imitative.]

Chick·a·saw (chik′ə sô′) *pl.,* **-saws** or **-saw.** *n.* member of a Muskogean tribe of North American Indians formerly living in what is now Tennessee and northern Mississippi, now living in Oklahoma.

chick·en (chik′ən) *n.* **1.** common domestic fowl, *Gallus gallus.* **2.** hen or rooster of any age. **3.** flesh of a chicken, esp. when prepared for food. **4.** *Slang.* one who is cowardly. **5.** *Slang.* young person. —*adj.* **1.** immature: *a chicken lobster.* **2.** *Slang.* chicken-hearted; cowardly. —*v.i. Slang.* to lose one's courage; become cowardly (with *out*). [Old English *cīcen* young fowl.]

chick·en-heart·ed (chik′ən här′tid) *adj.* cowardly.

chicken pox, mild but highly contagious virus disease, generally occurring in children and characterized by a blotchy red rash which develops into blisters and, finally, scabs. Also, **var′i·cel′la.**

chick·pea (chik′pē′) *n.* **1.** oval or oblong fruit of a plant, *Cicer arietinum,* of the pea family, cooked and eaten as a vegetable. **2.** plant bearing this fruit, usually having white leaves. [French *chiche* (going back to Latin *cicer*) + PEA.]

chick·weed (chik′wēd′) *n.* common weed, *Stellaria media,* of the pink family, found throughout the world, having a creeping root, small oval leaves, and tiny white flowers. [Because eaten by chickens.]

chic·le (chik′əl) *n.* gum obtained from the milky juice of the sapodilla tree, used chiefly for making chewing gum. [Spanish *chicle,* from Nahuatl *chictli.*]

Chic·o·pee (chik′ə pē′) *n.* city in southwestern Massachusetts. Pop. (1970), 66,676.

chic·o·ry (chik′ər ē) *pl.,* **-ries.** *n.* **1.** leaves of a plant, *Cichorium intybus,* of the composite family, eaten as a vegetable, either raw or cooked. **2.** dried, roasted, and ground root of this plant, mixed with or substituted for coffee. **3.** the plant itself. [French *chicorée* the plant, from Latin *cichoreum,* from Greek *kichorion.*]

chide (chīd) **chid·ed** or **chid** (chid); **chid·ed** or **chid** or **chid·den** (chid′ən); **chid·ing.** *v.t.* to find fault with; reproach. [Old English *cīdan* to rebuke, quarrel.] —**chid′ing·ly,** *adv.* —**chid′er,** *n.*

chief (chēf) *n.* **1.** one who is highest in rank or authority, as the leader of a group or tribe. **2.** upper third of an escutcheon. —*adj.* **1.** highest in rank or authority: *chief cook.* **2.** most important; principal; main: *chief problem.* **3.** **in chief.** of the highest title, rank, or authority. [Old French *ch(i)ef* head, going back to Latin *caput.* Doublet of CHEF.]
Syn. *n.* **1. Chief, chieftain** indicate a person with rank which gives him authority. **Chief** implies authority over a distinguishable group: *That lawyer is chief of the defense counsel.* **Chieftain** is generally limited to the principal man of a tribe, clan, or primitive group: *The chieftain led his warriors in a war dance.* —*adj.* **1.** see **main.**

Chief Executive, president of the United States.

chief justice. 1. presiding or head judge of a court having several judges. **2. Chief Justice.** head of the U.S. Supreme Court and chief judicial officer of the United States.

chief·ly (chēf′lē) *adv.* **1.** mainly but not exclusively: *The dish consisted chiefly of meat.* **2.** above all; especially.

chief of staff. 1. *Military.* senior officer or head of a staff; principal assistant to a commander. **2. Chief of Staff.** top military officer of the U.S. Army or Air Force.

chief·tain (chēf′tən) *n.* head, esp. of a tribe or clan. [Modification (influenced by CHIEF) of Old French *chevetaine,* from Late Latin *capitaneus* chief, from Latin *caput* head. Doublet of CAPTAIN.] —**chief′tain·cy, chief′tain·ship′,** *n.* —Syn. see **chief.**

chif·fon (shi fon′, shif′on) *n.* sheer, lightweight fabric, usually of silk or rayon, used for such items as scarves and dresses. —*adj.* **1.** made of or resembling chiffon. **2.** made partially of vigorously beaten egg whites or gelatin, giving a light, airy consistency: *lemon chiffon pie.* [French *chiffon,* from *chiffe;* of uncertain origin.]

chif·fo·nier (shif′ə nēr′) *n.* high bureau or chest of drawers, often having a mirror at the top. [French *chiffonnier* literally, place for pieces of cloth, from *chiffon* rag. See CHIFFON.]

chig·ger (chig′ər) *also,* **jig·ger.** *n.* **1.** larva of any of various mites, family Trombidiidae. It pierces the skin of man and other animals and sucks tissue fluids, leaving red spots and causing severe itching. **2.** chigoe *(def. 1).* [Modification of CHIGOE.]

chi·gnon (shēn′yon, shēn yon′) *n.* twist or knot of hair usually worn at the nape of the neck. [French *chignon* coil of hair; earlier, nape of the neck; literally, little chain (referring to the chain of vertebrae then), going back to Latin *catēna* chain.]

chig·oe (chig′ō) *n.* **1.** small, bloodsucking sand flea, *Tunga penetrans,* found in tropical America and Africa, the female of which burrows under the skin, esp. between the toes and under the toenails, causing painful sores and itching. **2.** chigger *(def. 1).* [Of Carib origin.]

Chi·hua·hua (chi wä′wə, -wä′wä) *n.* **1.** city in northern Mexico. Pop. (1969), 247,082. **2. chihuahua.** dog of a breed originally native to Mexico having large, pointed ears and a smooth or wavy coat that is usually tan. It is the smallest breed of dog. Height: 5 inches at the shoulder.

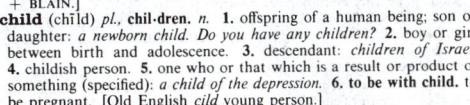

Chihuahua

chil·blain (chil′blān′) *n.* mild form of frostbite affecting the hands and feet and characterized by an itching inflammation of the skin. [CHILL + BLAIN.]

child (chīld) *pl.,* **chil·dren.** *n.* **1.** offspring of a human being; son or daughter: *a newborn child. Do you have any children?* **2.** boy or girl between birth and adolescence. **3.** descendant: *children of Israel.* **4.** childish person. **5.** one who or that which is a result or product of something (specified): *a child of the depression.* **6. to be with child.** to be pregnant. [Old English *cild* young person.]

child·bear·ing (chīld′bâr′ing) *n.* act of giving birth to a child or children.

child·birth (chīld′burth′) *n.* act of giving birth to a child or children.

child·hood (chīld′hood′) *n.* age span ranging from birth to adolescence.

child·ish (chīl′dish) *adj.* **1.** of, like, or befitting a child: *a childish dress.* **2.** immature; silly: *childish fears, a childish waste of time.* —**child′ish·ly,** *adv.* —**child′ish·ness,** *n.*
Syn. **2. Childish, childlike, childlike** indicate having the qualities of a child. **Childish** tends to be derogatory, hinting at such traits, esp. in adults, as petulance or emotional immaturity: *His big manly voice, turning again toward childish treble, pipes and whistles in his sound* (Shakespeare, *As You Like It*). **Childlike** usually indicates approbation, suggesting those traits adults admire or find charming in children: *She has a childlike enthusiasm for the circus.* **Infantile** intensifies the derogatory connotations of childish when used of adults: *He looked upon sport as an infantile pastime.*

child labor, employment of children at regular and sustained labor.

child·like (chīld′līk′) *adj.* like or befitting a child; innocent: *childlike simplicity.* —Syn. see **childish.**

chil·dren (chil′drən) plural of **child.**

Children's Crusade, unsuccessful crusade to recover the Holy Land from the Muslims, undertaken by thousands of French and German children in 1212.

child's play, anything easily done or accomplished.

Chil·e (chil′ē; *Spanish* chē′lā) *n.* country on the southwestern coast of South America. Capital, Santiago. Area, 292,258 sq. mi. Pop. (1969 est.), 9,566,000. —**Chil′e·an,** *adj, n.*

Chile saltpeter, sodium nitrate.

chil·i (chil′ē) *pl.,* **chil·ies.** *also,* **chil·e, chil·li.** *n.* **1.** pod of the red pepper, esp. variety *longum,* used to make a hot spice. **2.** the plant itself. **3.** chili con carne. [Spanish *chile* red pepper, from Nahuatl *chilli.*]

chili con car·ne (kon kär′nē) *also,* **chile con car·ne.** highly seasoned dish made of meat, red peppers, tomato sauce, and, usually, beans. [Spanish *chile con carne* literally, chili with meat.]

chili powder, powdered spice consisting of a blend of dried and ground chili pods, and other herbs and spices, as oregano, garlic, cloves, and allspice.

chili sauce, highly spiced sauce used as a condiment, made of red peppers, tomatoes, vinegar, sugar, and onions.

chill (chil) *n.* **1.** coldness, esp. when moderate but penetrating: *There was a slight chill in the air. She heated the cold milk to take off the chill.* **2.** sensation of cold, esp. when accompanied by shivering and fever: *to get a chill.* **3.a.** lack of warmth or friendliness; icy manner: *a chill in one's voice.* **b.** depressing or discouraging influence or effect: *She cast a chill over the festivities.* **4.** disquieting feeling, as of fear or anxiety: *The macabre sight sent a chill through her.* —*v.t.* **1.** to make cold: *to chill wine.* **2.** to cause a sensation of cold in: *The night air chilled his bones.* **3.** to check, as enthusiasm; depress or discourage. **4.** to harden the surface (of a metal) by sudden cooling. —*v.i.* **1.** to become cold. **2.** to have the sensation of or be affected by cold. **3.** to become hardened on the surface by sudden cooling, as metal. —*adj.* chilly. [Old English *c(ie)le* coldness.] —**chill′ness,** *n.*

chill·y (chil′ē) chill·i·er, chill·i·est. *adj.* **1.** cold: *chilly night air.* **2.** affected by, sensitive to, or feeling cold: *to be chilly.* **3.** lacking warmth; unfriendly: *a chilly reception.* —**chill′i·ness,** *n.* —**Syn. 1.** see **cold.**

chime (chīm) *also (defs. 1, 2, 4),* **chimes.** *n.* **1.** set of large bells, tuned to a musical scale, which produce tones when swung or struck. **2.** orchestral percussion instrument which consists of a series of vertical metal tubes sounded with a mallet. **3.** single bell, as in a clock. **4.** sound or series of musical sounds made by a chime. **5.** accord; harmony. —*v.t.,* **chimed, chim·ing. 1.** to produce a musical sound by striking; ring: *to chime bells.* **2.** to give or announce by ringing: *The clock chimed the hour.* **3.** to recite or repeat mechanically or in cadence. —*v.i.* **1.** to ring: *The clock chimed every hour.* **2.** to be in accord; harmonize (with *with*). **3. to chime in. a.** to be in accord; harmonize. **b.** *Informal.* to join in or interrupt a conversation. [Old French *chimbe, cymbe* cymbal, from Latin *cymbalum,* from Greek *kymbalon.*]

Chi·me·ra (ki mēr′ə, kī-) *pl.,* **-ras.** *also,* **Chi·mae·ra.** *n.* **1.** *Greek Mythology.* a fire-breathing monster with a lion's head, a goat's body, and a serpent's tail. It was finally destroyed by Bellerophon. **2. chimera. a.** any imaginary monster. **b.** fantastic or unfounded idea; silly fancy. [Latin *chimaera* this mythological monster, from Greek *chimaira* female goat, this mythological monster.]

chi·mer·i·cal (ki mer′i kəl, -mēr′-, kī-) *adj.* **1.** unreal; imaginary. **2.** filled with wild ideas; whimsical; fanciful: *a chimerical mind.* Also, **chi·mer′ic.**

chim·ney (chim′nē) *pl.,* **-neys.** *n.* **1.** vertical structure containing a flue by which smoke or vapor from a fireplace or furnace ascends and escapes. **2.** part of such a structure rising above a roof. **3.** smokestack. **4.** cylinder, usually of glass, surrounding the flame of a lamp to protect the flame and promote combustion. [Old French *cheminee* fireplace, from Late Latin *camīnāta,* from Latin *camīnus* furnace, from Greek *kamīnos.*]

chimney piece, mantel *(def. 2).*

chimney pot, cylindrical pipe, as of earthenware or metal, placed on top of a chimney to increase the draft and prevent smoking.

chimney sweep, one whose business is cleaning out soot from chimneys.

chimney swift, North American swift, *Chaetura pelagica,* having narrow, crescent-shaped wings and dull plumage. It often builds its nest in unused chimneys and is capable of rapid and sustained flight.

chim·pan·zee (chim′pan zē′, chim-pan′zē) *n.* tree-dwelling anthropoid ape, genus *Pan,* native to western and central Africa, having brownish-black hair and protruding ears. It is smaller and more intelligent than a gorilla. [From the native West African name of the ape.]

chin (chin) *n.* **1.** part of the face below the mouth and above the neck. **2.** central, front part of the lower jaw. —*v.t.,* **chinned, chin·ning.** to lift (oneself), from or as from an overhead horizontal bar, by pulling with the arms until the chin is level with or above the hands. [Old English *cin(n)* part of the lower jaw.]

chi·na (chī′nə) *n.* **1.** fine, vitreous pottery composed principally of clay, feldspar, and flint, believed to have originated in China. China differs from porcelain in that it requires two firings. **2.** objects, esp. dishes, made of this material.

Chi·na (chī′nə) *n.* **1. People's Republic of.** country in eastern Asia under Communist control since 1949. It is the most populous country in the world. Capital, Peking. Area, 3,691,500 sq. mi. Pop. (1966 est.) 710,000,000. Also, **Communist China, Red China. 2. Republic of.** country comprising the island of Taiwan and nearby islands. The Chinese Nationalist government took refuge on Taiwan in 1949 when mainland China fell under Communist control. Capital, Taipei. Area, 13,885 sq. mi. Pop. (1970 census), 14,501,000. Also, **Nationalist China, Taiwan.**

Chi·na·man (chī′nə mən) *pl.,* **-men.** *n.* Chinese. ▲ It has a derogatory or contemptuous connotation.

China Sea, part of the Pacific Ocean which borders on China. It consists of the East China Sea and the South China Sea.

Chi·na·town (chī′nə toun′) *n.* Chinese section of any city outside China, esp. of San Francisco and New York City.

chi·na·ware (chī′nə wâr′) *n.* **1.** china *(def. 2).* **2.** dishes of any kind.

chinch (chinch) *n.* **1.** chinch bug. **2.** any bedbug. [Spanish *chinche* bedbug, from Latin *cīmex* bug.]

chinch bug, small black-and-white insect pest, *Blissus leucopterus,*

common in the middle and southwestern United States, very destructive to wheat, corn, and other cereal grasses, esp. in dry weather.

chin·chil·la (chin chil′ə) *n.* **1.** valuable, very fine, silver or bluish-gray fur of any of a group of South American rodents, genus *Chinchilla,* used to make women's coats and jackets, and to trim other apparel. **2.** the squirrel-like animal that bears this fur. It has large dark eyes and broad ears rounded at the tip. Some species are raised commercially. **3.** heavy fabric, usually made partially or entirely of wool, characterized by a nubby finish, used for such items as coats and women's suits. [Spanish *chinchilla* South American rodent; probably of Quechua origin.]

Chinchilla

chine (chīn) *n.* **1.** backbone; spine. **2.** cut of meat including the whole or part of an animal's backbone with the adjoining flesh. [Old French *eschine* spine; of Germanic origin.]

Chi·nese (chī nēz′, -nēs′) *pl.,* **-nese.** *n.* **1.** member or close descendant of the people of China. ▲ see **Chinaman** for usage note. **2.** language belonging to the Sino-Tibetan language family, consisting of many dialects. Mandarin, the dialect spoken in Peking, is standard Chinese. —*adj.* of or relating to China, or to the Chinese, their language, or their culture.

Chinese checkers, game for two to six players, using marbles on a board shaped like a six-pointed star and containing holes in each triangle of the star. The object is to move the marbles filling one triangle to the opposite triangle.

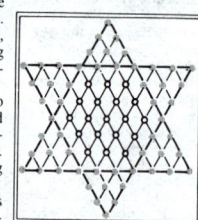

Chinese checkers board

Chinese Empire, China from its founding, through rule by various imperial dynasties, until it became a republic in 1912.

Chinese lantern 1. collapsible lantern of thin paper, usually decorated. **2.** garden plant, *Physalis alkekengi,* of the nightshade family, bearing a large, bright orange-red, bladderlike calyx which encloses a small berry.

Chinese puzzle 1. complicated or ingenious puzzle. **2.** anything complicated and hard to solve.

Chinese Wall, Great Wall of China.

chink[1] (chingk) *n.* crack; fissure: *The chinks in the wall admitted light.* —*v.t.* to fill the chinks in; plug. [Old English *cinu* fissure.]

chink[2] (chingk) *n.* short, sharp sound, as of metal or glass striking together. —*v.t., v.i.* to make or cause to make a short, sharp sound. [Imitative.]

Chi·nook (shi nook′, -nōōk′, chi-) *pl.,* **-nooks** or **-nook.** *n.* **1.** member of a former tribe of North American Indians who lived near the mouth of the Columbia River in what is now the state of Washington. **2.** language spoken by these people. **3. chinook.** king salmon. **4. chinook. a.** warm, moist, southwest wind that blows from the sea along the coasts of Washington and Oregon. **b.** warm, dry wind that descends from the Rocky Mountains to the neighboring plains of the western United States and Canada. [From an American Indian name of the tribe, *Tsinūk.*]

Chinook jargon, language based on Chinook incorporating elements of other Indian languages, French, and English, formerly used as a lingua franca in the Pacific Northwest.

chin·qua·pin (ching′kə pin′) *n.* **1.** shrub or small tree, *Castanea pumila,* of the beech family, closely related to the chestnut, found in North America. **2.** evergreen tree, *Castanopsis chrysophylla,* found in California and Oregon and distinguished by yellow scales on the underside of its leathery leaves. **3.** edible nut of either of these trees. [Of Algonquian origin.]

chintz (chints) *n.* cotton fabric, usually glazed and printed with a colorful pattern, used for such items as curtains and slipcovers. [Earlier *chints,* plural of *chint* used as singular, from Hindi *chīnt* spotted cotton cloth, from Sanskrit *chitra* spotted.]

chintz·y (chint′sē) *adj. Informal.* cheap; tawdry.

chin-up (chin′up′) *n.* exercise of chinning.

Chi·os (kī′os, -ōs, kē′-) *n.* Greek island in the eastern Aegean, off the western coast of Turkey. Area, 321 sq. mi. Pop. (1961), 62,223.

chip (chip) *n.* **1.** small, usually thin, fragment that has been cut or broken off: *a wood chip, a diamond chip.* **2.** place where such a fragment has been cut or broken off: *a chip on the edge of a glass.* **3.** small, usually thin, slice of food: *chocolate chip.* **4.** French-fried potato: *fish and chips.* **5.** disk or counter used in certain games, as poker. **6.** thin strip, as of wood or straw, used in weaving. **7.** *also,* **chips.** dried dung used for fuel. **8. a chip off the old block.** *Informal.* child who resembles either parent, esp. the father. **9. a chip on one's shoulder.** *Informal.* belligerent atti-

at; āpe; cär; end; mē; it; īce; hot; ōld; fôrk; wood; fōōl; oil; out; up; ūse; turn; sing; thin; this; zh in treasure; ə in ago, taken, pencil, lemon, circus.

Chimpanzee

tude or haughty manner. **10. in the chips.** *Informal.* having money; affluent. —*v.t.,* **chipped, chip·ping. 1.** to cut or break off a fragment or fragments from: *to chip a bone, to chip one's tooth.* **2.** to shape or produce by cutting off small fragments: *The stonecutter chipped the name on the gravestone.* —*v.i.* **1.** to break off in small pieces: *The paint chipped.* **2. to chip in.** *Informal.* to give one's share; contribute. [Old English *cipp* log, piece cut off a log.]

chip·munk (chip'mungk') *n.* any of various rodents of the squirrel family, native to North America and Asia, having brown or gray fur with black and white or buff stripes on the back and tail, round ears, large cheek pouches, and a slender, flattened tail. Length: 10 inches including tail. [Modification of Ojibwa *atchitamon* the red squirrel; literally, head first; with reference to its habit of climbing down trees head first.]

Chipmunk

chipped beef, beef which is sliced thinly and smoked or dried, sometimes served with a cream sauce.

Chip·pen·dale (chip'ən dāl') *adj.* designating a style of furniture designed by or resembling that of Chippendale, characterized by elegance, intricate carving, and fine proportions. [From Thomas *Chippendale,* c.1718–79, English furniture designer.]

chip·per (chip'ər) *adj.* lively or happy. [Possibly form of dialectal English *kipper* frisky, lively; of uncertain origin.]

Chip·pe·wa (chip'ə wä', -wā', -wə) *pl.,* **-wa** or **-was.** *n.* Ojibwa.

chipping sparrow, sparrow, *Spizella passerina,* of eastern and central North America, having a reddish-brown crown.

Chippendale chair

chi·rog·ra·phy (kī rog'rə fē) *n.* art or individual style of handwriting. [Greek *cheirographos* written with the hand (from *cheir* hand + *-graphos* written) + -Y³.] —**chi·rog'ra·pher,** *n.* —**chi·ro·graph·ic** (kī'rə-graf'ik), *adj.*

Chi·ron (kī'ron) *n. Greek Mythology.* a wise centaur, skilled in the arts, medicine, and prophecy. He was the teacher of many Greek heroes, including Jason, Achilles, and Hercules.

chi·rop·o·dist (kə rop'ə dist, kī-, shə rop'-) *n.* podiatrist.

chi·rop·o·dy (kə rop'ə de, kī-, sha rop'-) *n.* podiatry.

chi·ro·prac·tic (kī'rə prak'tik) *n.* system of manual and mechanical therapy based on the theory that disease results from interference with the normal functioning of the nervous system. Treatment includes massage and manipulation, esp. of the vertebrae, and the use of heat, water, electric, and other forms of therapy. [Greek *cheir* hand + *praktikos* concerned with action, effective, practical.] —**chi'ro·prac'tor,** *n.*

chi·rop·ter (kī rop'tər) *n.* any mammal of the order Chiroptera, consisting of the bats. [Greek *cheir* hand + *pteron* wing.]

chi·rop·ter·an (kī rop'tər ən) *n.* chiropter. —*adj.* of or relating to a chiropter.

chirp (churp) *v.i.* to make a short, sharp sound, as that made by a bird. —*v.t.* to utter by or as by chirping. —*n.* short, sharp sound, as that made by a bird. [Imitative.] —**chirp'er,** *n.*

chirr (chur) *also,* **churr.** *v.i.* sharp, trilling sound, as that made by a grasshopper. —*v.i.* to make such a sound. [Imitative.]

chi·rur·geon (kī rur'jən) *n. Archaic.* surgeon. [Old French *cirurgien.* See SURGEON.] —**chi·rur'ger·y,** *n.*

chis·el (chiz'əl) *n.* metal tool with a sharp cutting edge at the end of a blade, used to shape stone, wood, or metal. —*v.t.,* **-eled, -el·ing;** *also, British,* **-elled, -el·ling. 1.** to cut or shape with or as with a chisel. **2.** *Slang.* **a.** to cheat; swindle: *They chiseled him out of ten dollars.* **b.** to obtain in such a way. —*v.i.* to work with a chisel. [Dialectal Old French *chisel* this tool, from Late Latin *cisellus* forceps; literally, cutting tool, from Latin *caesus,* past participle of *caedere* to cut.] —**chis'el·er;** *also, British,* **chis'el·ler,** *n.*

Chisel

Chis·holm Trail (chiz'əm) cattle trail running from San Antonio, Texas, to Abilene, Kansas. [From the nineteenth-century American guide and trader Jesse Chisholm.]

chit (chit) *n.* pert young person, esp. a girl. [Probably a form of *kit*³, short for KITTEN.]

chit-chat (chit'chat') *n.* **1.** light informal conversation. **2.** gossip. —*v.i.,* **-chat·ted, -chat·ting.** to converse informally. [Repetition of CHAT with vowel change.]

chi·tin (kī'tin) *n.* horny substance forming the hard outer covering

in insects and crustaceans. [French *chitine,* from Greek *chitōn* tunic, covering; of Semitic origin.] —**chi'tin·ous,** *adj.*

chi·ton (kīt'ən, kī'ton) *n.* tuniclike garment worn by men and women in ancient Greece. [Greek *chitōn;* of Semitic origin.]

chit·ter·lings (chit'linz) *also,* **chit·lings, chit·lins.** *n.* small intestines of pigs, prepared as food. [Of uncertain origin.]

chiv·al·ric (shiv'əl rik) *adj.* **1.** of or relating to chivalry. **2.** chivalrous.

chiv·al·rous (shiv'əl rəs) *adj.* **1.** having or exhibiting the qualities characteristic of chivalry, as gallantry, honor, and courtesy. **2.** of or relating to chivalry. —**chiv'al·rous·ly,** *adv.* —**chiv'al·rous·ness,** *n.*

chiv·al·ry (shiv'əl rē) *n.* **1.** qualities of an ideal knight, such as honor, courtesy, generosity, valor, respect for women, protection of the weak, and skill in battle. **2.** feudal system which embodied these ideals and formed them into a code of behavior. **3.a.** body of knights. **b.** gallant gentlemen. [Old French *chevalerie* knighthood, from *chevalier* knight, warrior with a horse, from Late Latin *caballārius* horseman, from Latin *caballus* inferior horse, nag. See CAVALIER.]

Chiton

chiv·a·ree (shiv'ə rē') charivari.

chive (chīv) *n.* **1.** long, slender leaves of a plant, *Allium schoenoprasum,* related to the onion, used as a garnish for seasoning. **2.** the plant itself. [Dialectal Old French *chive* this plant, from Latin *cēpa* onion.]

Ch. J., Chief Justice.

chla·mys (klā'mis, klam'is) *n.* short cloak, usually fastened over the shoulder, worn by men in ancient Greece. [Latin *chlamys,* from Greek *chlamys.*]

chlo·ral hydrate (klôr'əl) white, crystalline compound prepared from chlorine, ethyl alcohol, and water, used as a hypnotic. Formula: $CCL_3CH(OH)_2$.

chlor·am·phen·i·col (klôr'am fen'i kôl') *n.* Chloromycetin.

chlo·rate (klôr'āt) *n.* salt of chloric acid.

chlo·ric acid (klôr'ik) strong acid that reacts violently with organic compounds. It exists only in solution. Formula: $HClO_3$.

chlo·ride (klôr'īd) *n.* compound of chlorine with another element or radical, esp. a salt of hydrochloric acid.

chloride of lime, white powder used as a bleaching agent and disinfectant, prepared by treating slaked lime with chlorine; bleaching powder. Formula: $CaCl(ClO)$ Also, **chlorinated lime.**

Chlamys

chlo·rin·ate (klôr'ə nāt') *-at·ed, -at·ing. v.t.* to combine or treat with chlorine. —**chlo'rin·a'tion,** *n.*

chlo·rine (klôr'ēn, -in) *n.* nonmetallic element occurring naturally as a poisonous, greenish-yellow gas with an irritating, pungent odor. Chlorine and its compounds are used in bleaching and disinfecting. The most familiar chlorine compound is sodium chloride. Symbol: **Cl** See **element** for table. [Greek *chlōros* greenish yellow + -INE²; because of its color.]

chlo·rite¹ (klôr'īt) *n.* common mineral, formed by alteration of magnesium and iron silicates, usually green in color with a vitreous to pearly luster and often occurring in clusters of thin, flexible scales. [Latin *chlōrītis* a green precious stone, from Greek *chlōrītis.*]

chlo·rite² (klôr'īt) *n.* a salt of chlorous acid. [Greek *chlōros* greenish yellow + -ITE².]

chlo·ro·form (klôr'ə fôrm') *n.* compound of carbon, hydrogen, and chlorine in the form of a colorless nonflammable liquid with a sweetish smell. Formerly used as an anesthetic, it is now used esp. to extract and purify antibiotics and to dissolve rubber, fats, and other substances. Formula: $CHCl_3$. —*v.t.* to cause anesthesia or death by means of chloroform. [CHLOR(INE) + FORM(IC ACID); because it is able to form potassium *chloride* and *formic* acid.]

Chlo·ro·my·ce·tin (klôr'ə mī sē'tin) *n. Trademark.* chloramphenicol, an antibiotic drug which is very effective in the treatment of certain diseases, esp. typhoid fever, but must be used with care. [Greek *chlōros* greenish yellow + *mykēs* fungus + -IN¹.]

chlo·ro·phyll (klôr'ə fil') *also,* **chlo·ro·phyl.** *n.* organic compound of carbon, hydrogen, nitrogen, oxygen, and magnesium that is the green coloring matter of plants and is required for the process of photosynthesis by which plants manufacture food materials. [French *chlorophylle,* from Greek *chlōros* greenish yellow + *phyllon* leaf.]

chlo·ro·plast (klôr'ə plast') *n.* any of the small bodies in a plant cell which contain chlorophyll. [Greek *chlōros* greenish yellow + *plastos* formed.]

at; āpe; cär; end; mē; it; īce; hot; ōld; fôrk; wood; fŏŏl; oil; out; up; ūse; turn; sing; thin; this; zh in treasure; ə in ago, taken, pencil, lemon, circus.

175

chlo·ro·prene (klôr′ə prēn′) n. colorless liquid used in making synthetic rubber. Formula: C₄H₅Cl

chlo·ro·quine (klôr′ə kwīn′) n. synthetic organic compound used in the treatment of malaria.

chlo·rous (klôr′əs) adj. of, relating to, or containing trivalent chlorine.

chlor·tet·ra·cy·cline (klôr′tet rə-sī′klin) n. Aureomycin.

chm., chmn., chairman.

chock (chok) n. 1. block or wedge put under or in front of something to keep it from moving, as in front of the wheels of an airplane on the ground. 2. metal fitting, as on a boat or ship, having projections at both ends which are curved toward the center and through which cable or rope may pass. —v.t. 1. to furnish or secure with a chock or chocks. 2. to place, as a boat, on chocks. [Dialectal Old French *chouque* log; possibly of Celtic origin.]

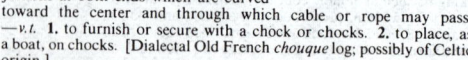

Chocks

chock·a·block (chok′ə blok′) adj. 1. (of a boat or ship's tackle) having the blocks touching. 2. very crowded; crammed.

chock·full (chok′fool′) also, **chuck·full.** adj. as full as can be; crammed.

choc·o·late (chô′kə lit, chok′ə-, chôk′lit, chok′-) n. 1. food product prepared from ground and roasted cacao beans which still retain the fat. 2. beverage made by dissolving chocolate or cocoa in hot milk or water and adding sugar. 3. candy made of or coated with chocolate: *a box of chocolates.* 4. dark-brown color. —adj. 1. made of or flavored with chocolate. 2. dark-brown. [Spanish *chocolate*, from Nahuatl *chocolatl* food made from cacao seeds.]

Choc·taw (chok′tô) pl. **-taws** or **-taw.** n. 1. member of a Muskogean tribe of North American Indians, formerly living in parts of what are now Mississippi, Alabama, and Louisiana, now living in Oklahoma. 2. Muskogean language spoken by these people. [Possibly modification of Spanish *chato* flat, going back to Greek *platys*; with reference to the Choctaw practice of flattening the head.]

choice (chois) n. 1. act or instance of choosing: *It was a wise choice.* 2. power or opportunity to choose: *We were given a choice between the two.* 3. one who or that which is chosen. 4. variety from which to choose: *a menu with a wide choice of dishes.* 5. alternative: *Our only choice was to go.* 6. preferable part of anything; select portion. —adj. **choic·er, choic·est.** 1. worthy of being chosen; select; excellent: *a choice spot for a picnic.* 2. carefully selected. 3. indicating a U.S. government grade of meat less tender than prime. [Old French *chois* act of choosing, preference, from *choisir* to choose; of Germanic origin.] **—choice′ly,** adv. **—choice′ness,** n.

Syn. n. 2. Choice, alternative, option indicate an opportunity to select. **Choice** implies an absence of limitations imposed on the method of selection or on the possible selections: *The voters will have their choice among candidates of the whole political spectrum.* **Alternative** implies, strictly, two possibilities, but commonly is extended to a small number: *The circumstances were such that he had no alternative to choosing the desperate course he did take.* **Option** implies a granting of the power to select by someone who possesses it and emphasizes that power: *The legislature granted to municipalities the option of controlling traffic on state roads within their boundaries.*

choir (kwīr) n. 1. organized group of singers, esp. one used in a religious service. 2. that part of a church set apart for the use of such singers. 3. organized company or chorus, as of a particular group of instruments: *the brass choir.* [Old French *cuer* group of singers, the choir of a church, from Latin *chorus* band of singers and dancers, from Greek *choros.* Doublet of CHORUS.]

choir·boy (kwīr′boi′) n. boy who is a member of and sings in a church choir.

choir master, leader or director of a choir.

choke (chōk) v. **choked, chok·ing.** v.t. 1. to prevent or hinder the breathing of by or as by squeezing the throat or blocking the windpipe. 2.a. to obstruct by or as by filling; block; clog: *Dirt choked the drain.* b. to fill completely. 3. to check the growth, progress, or action of. 4. to regulate the amount of air that enters the carburetor in order to enrich the fuel mixture of a (gasoline engine). 5. to suppress; check; repress, as a feeling; stifle. 6. **to choke off.** to put a stop to; end: *to choke off further discussion.* —v.i. 1. to be prevented or hindered from breathing. 2. to become obstructed, blocked, or clogged. 3. **to choke up.** a. to become speechless, as from sorrow or anger. b. to give a poor performance because of tension or nervousness. 4. **to choke up on.** to grip (a baseball bat) nearer the striking surface. —n. 1. act or sound of choking. 2. valve that regulates the amount of air that enters the carburetor of an internal combustion engine. See **carburetor** for illustration. 3. choke coil. [Possibly short for obsolete *achoke* to suffocate, from Old English *ācēocian.*]

choke·bore (chōk′bôr′) n. 1. bore of a shotgun that is made to narrow toward the muzzle in order to limit the scattering of the shot and to gain longer range. 2. shotgun with such a bore.

choke·cher·ry (chōk′cher′ē) pl. **-ries.** n. 1. bitter edible cherrylike fruit of a tree or shrub, genus *Aronia*, of the rose family, used to make jams and jellies. 2. the tree or shrub itself.

choke coil, coil of wire that allows direct current to flow while limiting the flow of alternating current.

choke·damp (chōk′damp′) n. blackdamp.

chok·er (chō′kər) n. 1. one who or that which chokes. 2. necklace fitting tightly around the throat.

chol·er (kol′ər) n. irritability or anger. [Old French *colere*, going back to Greek *cholerā* cholera, from *cholē* bile, the humor thought to cause anger. See HUMOR.]

chol·er·a (kol′ər ə) n. infectious disease of the intestines, characterized by severe vomiting and diarrhea. Also, **Asiatic cholera.** [Latin *cholera* bile, cholera, from Greek *cholerā* cholera, from *cholē* bile.]

chol·er·ic (kol′ər ik) adj. 1. easily irritated or angered; irascible. 2. indicating or expressing anger: *a choleric speech.*

cho·les·ter·ol (kə les′tə rôl′) n. fatty material present in all body tissues, required for the digestion of fats, the production of certain hormones, and the manufacture of vitamin D. Some authorities believe that large amounts of this substance in the blood increase the possibility of hardening of the arteries. Formula: C₂₇H₄₅OH [Greek *cholē* bile, gall¹ + *stereos* solid + -OL; referring to its originally having been found in gallstones.]

chomp (chomp) v.i. Informal. to bite and chew noisily. [Form of CHAMP¹.]

choose (chooz) v. **chose, cho·sen, choos·ing.** v.t. 1. to select, esp. by preference, from all that are available: *He chose the largest apples.* 2. to prefer and decide; think fit (to do something): *to choose to stay.* —v.i. 1. to select. 2. to think fit: *You can go if you choose.* [Old English *cēosan* to select.] **—choos′er,** n.

Syn. v.t. 1. Choose, pick¹, select indicate taking one or more of several alternatives. **Choose** suggests that deliberation precedes the choice: *She has a right to choose the course that seems best for her.* **Pick** suggests that personal inclination is a principal factor: *He picked the tallest boys for his starting team.* **Select** suggests a weighing of the worth and importance of the several alternatives: *The members of the jury were carefully selected from the panel.*

choos·y (choo′zē) **choos·i·er, choos·i·est.** also, **choos·ey.** adj. Informal. inclined to be selective; fussy.

chop¹ (chop) **chopped, chop·ping.** v.t. 1.a. to cut or sever by a quick blow or blows, with a sharp instrument, as an ax: *to chop a tree down.* b. to make or form in this way: *The fireman chopped a hole in the wall.* 2. to cut into pieces: *to chop onions.* 3. to cut short: *He chopped the story by three paragraphs.* 4. to hit (a ball) with a short, quick, downward stroke, as in tennis. —v.i. to make cutting strokes. —n. 1. act of chopping. 2. short, quick, downward stroke: *to give a chop to the ball.* 3. small cut of meat, as of lamb, pork, or veal, which usually includes a piece of the rib. [Form of CHAP¹.]

chop² (chop) **chopped, chop·ping.** v.i. to change or shift suddenly, as the wind. [Form of obsolete *chap* to exchange, change constantly, going back to Old English *cēapian* to trade.]

chop³ (chop) also, **chops, chap.** n. 1. jaw or cheek. 2. mouth. [Of uncertain origin.]

chop·fall·en (chop′fô′lən) chapfallen.

chop·house (chop′hous′) n. restaurant which specializes in chops and steaks.

Cho·pin, Fré·dé·ric Fran·çois (shō′pan, shō pan′; fred′ər ik fran swä′) 1810–49, Polish pianist and composer in France.

cho·pine (chō pēn′, chop′in) n. woman's shoe popular in the sixteenth and seventeenth centuries, having a high, thick platform which served as both a heel and sole. [Middle French *chappin*, from Spanish *chapín* shoe with high cork sole, from *chapa* leather or metal covering; of uncertain origin.]

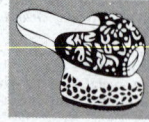

Chopine

chop·per (chop′ər) n. 1. one who or that which chops. 2. Slang. helicopter. 3. **choppers.** Slang. teeth, esp. false teeth.

chop·py¹ (chop′ē) **-pi·er, -pi·est.** adj. 1. rough with short, irregular, broken waves: *a choppy sea.* 2. not continuous; jerky; broken. [CHOP¹ + -Y¹.] **—chop′pi·ly,** adv. **—chop′pi·ness,** n.

chop·py² (chop′ē) **-pi·er, -pi·est.** adj. changing or shifting suddenly, as the wind. [CHOP² + -Y¹.]

chop·sticks (chop′stiks′) n.,pl. pair of eating utensils first developed in China, consisting of long, slender sticks, usually wood or ivory, which are held between the thumb and fingers. [Pidgin English *chop* quick + STICK¹, translation of Chinese (Mandarin) *k'uai tze* chopsticks; literally, quick ones.]

at; āpe; cär; end; mē; it; īce; hot; ōld; fôrk; wood; fōol; oil; out; up; ūse; turn; sing; thin; this; zh in treasure; ə in ago, taken, pencil, lemon, circus.

chop su·ey (chop′ sōō′ē) dish of Chinese-American origin consisting of vegetables, such as bamboo shoots, mushrooms, and onions, cooked with small pieces of meat, fish, or chicken, usually served with rice. [Chinese (Cantonese) *shap sui* odds and ends.]

cho·ral (adj., kôr′əl; n., kə ral′, käl′, kô-, kôr′əl) adj. **1.** of or relating to a choir or chorus. **2.** performed by or written for a choir or chorus. —n. chorale.

cho·rale (kə ral′, -räl′, kôr′əl) also, **cho·ral.** n. **1.** hymn having a plain melody and stately rhythm, usually sung in unison. **2.** group of people singing such music; chorus.

chord¹ (kôrd) n. combination of three or more musical tones or notes sounded simultaneously to produce a harmony. [Earlier *cord*, short for AC-CORD.]

chord² (kôrd) n. **1.** line segment joining any two points on a curve. **2.** feeling: *to strike a chord of compassion.* **3.** top or bottom member of a truss, as on a bridge. **4.** *Archaic.* string of a musical instrument. [Latin *chorda* gut, string of a musical instrument, from Greek *chordē.* Doublet of CORD.]

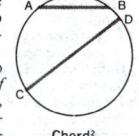

Chord²
AB, CD are chords

chor·date (kôr′dāt) n. any animal of the phylum Chordata, that includes all animals with backbones or notochords. [Modern Latin *Chordata*, from Latin *chorda.* See CHORD².]

chore (chôr) n. **1.** small or minor job: *She had several chores to do before noon.* **2.** pl. chores. routine duties, esp. those of a domestic nature. **3.** difficult or unpleasant task: *It's a real chore to call every day.* [Form of CHAR².]

cho·re·a (kôr′ē ə) n. Saint Vitus dance. [Modern Latin *chorea* (Sancti Viti) dance (of Saint Vitus), from Greek *choreiā* dance.]

cho·re·o·graph (kôr′ē ə graf′) v.t., v.i. to create, arrange, or direct (dance movement) as for ballet or modern dance. —**cho·re·og·ra·pher** (kôr′ē og′rə fər) n.

cho·re·og·ra·phy (kôr′ē og′rə fē) n. **1.** art of creating, arranging, or directing dance movement, as in ballet or modern dance. **2.** dance movement so created. [Greek *choreiā* dance + -GRAPHY.]

cho·ric (kôr′ik) adj. of, relating to, or suitable for the chorus, esp. in ancient Greek drama.

chor·is·ter (kôr′is tər, kor′-) n. **1.** one who sings in a choir. **2.** choirboy. **3.** one who leads a choir. [Medieval Latin *chorista* singer in a choir (from Latin *chorus* band of singers and dancers) + -ER¹. See CHOIR.]

cho·roid (kôr′oid) n. membrane forming the middle coat of the eyeball and lying between the sclerotic coat and the retina. The choroid, in the front of the eye, forms the iris. Also, **choroid coat.** —adj. of or relating to the choroid. [Greek *choroeidēs* like a membrane, from *chorion* membrane.]

chor·tle (chôrt′əl) -tled, -tling. v.t., v.i. to utter or utter with a low, sonorous chuckle. —n. such a chuckle. [Blend of CHUCKLE and SNORT, coined by Lewis Carroll.] —**chor′tler,** n.

cho·rus (kôr′əs) pl. **-rus·es.** n. **1.** large, organized group of people who sing together. **2.** group of people who sing, dance, and often play minor parts, as in a musical comedy. **3.** vocal composition, usually written for four or more parts, to be sung by a large group. **4.** recurring refrain, esp. of a song. **5.** group of people who recite or speak simultaneously. **6.a.** a simultaneous utterance: *a chorus of loud laughter.* **b.** that which is so uttered: *The chorus was loud.* **7.** in Greek drama, group of actors who comment upon and often take part in the main action. **8.** in Elizabethan drama, single actor, who recites the prologue and epilogue and explains or comments upon the action. **9. in chorus,** in unison; simultaneously. —v.t.,v.i., **-rused, -rus·ing.** to sing or speak simultaneously. [Latin *chorus* band of singers and dancers, dance in a ring, from Greek *choros.* Doublet of CHOIR.]

chose (chōz) past tense of **choose.**

cho·sen (chō′zən) v. past participle of **choose.** —adj. **1.** taken by preference; select. **2.** elect, as in the sight of God.

Cho·sen (chō′sen′) Korea.

Chou dynasty (jō) dynasty that ruled eastern China from about 1028 B.C. to 256 B.C. during the classical age of Chinese history. Lao-tse and Confucius lived during this time.

Chou En-lai (jō′ en lī′) 1898-1976, Chinese Communist political leader.

chough (chuf) n. glossy, blue-black bird, genus *Pyrrhocorax*, of the crow family, native to Europe. It has red feet and a red or yellow beak. [Middle English *choughe* crow; possibly imitative.]

chow¹ (chou) n. *Slang.* food. [Short for CHOW-CHOW.]

chow² (chou) n. dog of a breed originally developed in China, having a compact body, large head, thick, usually brown or black

Chow

coat, and a bluish-black tongue. Also, **chow chow.** [From a word in a Chinese dialect akin to Cantonese *kaú* dog.]

chow-chow (chou′chou′) n. **1.** relish of mixed chopped vegetables, esp. pickles, cooked in a highly spiced mustard sauce. **2.** Chinese dish of mixed fruits preserved in a rich syrup. [Possibly from pidgin English *chow-chow* literally, mixed; of uncertain origin.]

chow·der (chou′dər) n. thick soup usually made of fish or shellfish, esp. clams, with vegetables and, sometimes, milk. [French *chaudière* pot (from Late Latin *caldāria* pot for boiling, going back to Latin *calidus* hot); from the phrase *faire la chaudière* to contribute to a community pot in which a dish of fish and biscuits is prepared.]

chow mein (chou′ mān′) dish of Chinese-American origin made of shredded fish or meat and vegetables, as celery, onions, and bean sprouts, usually served with rice and fried noodles. [Chinese (Mandarin) *ch'ao mien* literally, fried noodles.]

Chr., Christian.

chres·tom·a·thy (kres tom′ə thē) pl., **-thies.** n. collection of choice literary passages, used esp. as an aid in learning a foreign language. [Greek *chrēstomatheia* desire of learning, book of choice passages.]

chrism (kriz′əm) n. consecrated oil, used by some churches in certain sacred rites, as baptism and confirmation. [Old English *crisma*, from Late Latin *chrīsma*, from Greek *chrīsma* unguent.] —**chris·mal** (kriz′məl), adj.

Christ (krīst) n. Jesus. [Old English *Crīst*, from Latin *Christus*, from Greek *Christos* literally, anointed, translation of Hebrew *māshīah* anointed, Messiah.]

Christ·church (krīst′church′) n. largest city in New Zealand, on the eastern coast of South Island. Pop. (1969), 165,700.

chris·ten (kris′ən) v.t. **1.** to receive into a Christian church by baptism; baptize. **2.** to give a name to at baptism. **3.** to give a name to, as a ship. **4.** *Informal.* to use for the first time. [Old English *cristnian* to make Christian, from *crīsten* Christian, from Latin *Christiānus*, from Greek *Christiānos*, from *Christos.* See CHRIST.]

Chris·ten·dom (kris′ən dəm) n. **1.** countries of the world, collectively, in which Christianity is the predominant religion. **2.** Christians collectively. [Old English *crīstendom*, from *crīsten* Christian + *dōm* authority, dominion. See CHRISTEN.]

chris·ten·ing (kris′ə ning, kris′ning) n. **1.** act or ceremony of baptizing and naming an infant; baptism. **2.** ceremony at which something is given a name or used for the first time.

Chris·tian (kris′chən) n. **1.** one who believes in and follows the teachings of Jesus; member of the religion based on those teachings. **2.** *Informal.* decent, respectable, or civilized person. —adj. **1.** of or relating to Jesus or His teachings. **2.** believing in the divine nature of Jesus and following His teachings or belonging to the religion based on them. **3.** of or relating to Christians or Christianity. **4.** showing character and conduct consistent with discipleship to Jesus. **5.** *Informal.* decent, respectable, or civilized.

Christian Church, Protestant denomination founded in the United States in the early nineteenth century. Also, **Disciples of Christ.**

Christian Era, era reckoned from the date formerly thought to be that of the birth of Christ. Dates in this era are denoted A.D., those before it, B.C.

Chris·tia·ni·a (kris tyä′nē ə) n. see Oslo.

Chris·ti·an·i·ty (kris′chē an′ə tē) n. **1.** religion based on the teachings of Jesus; Christian religion. **2.** Christians collectively; Christendom.

Chris·tian·ize (kris′chə nīz′) -ized, -iz·ing. v.t. **1.** to convert to Christianity. **2.** to imbue with Christian principles. —**Chris′tian·i·za′tion, Chris′tian·iz′er,** n.

Christian name, name given at baptism; first name.

Christian Science, religion founded by Mary Baker Eddy in 1866 that believes in the mind as a reality and matter as an illusion. It stresses healing of disease by spiritual means.

Christ·like (krīst′līk′) adj. like Jesus; exhibiting the spirit of Jesus.

Christ·mas (kris′məs) n. yearly celebration commemorating the birth of Jesus. December 25. Also, **Christmas Day.** [Old English *Crīstes mæsse* Christ's Mass. See CHRIST, MASS.]

Christmas Eve, day before Christmas.

Christmas Island 1. island in the Indian Ocean, south of Java, administered by Australia. Area, approx. 55 sq. mi. **2.** large atoll in the north-central Pacific Ocean, administered by Great Britain. Area, 222 sq. mi.

Christ·mas·tide (kris′məs tīd′) n. season of Christmas.

Christmas tree, tree, esp. an evergreen, decorated at Christmas time.

Chris·to·pher, Saint (kris′tə fər) died c.250, Christian martyr.

chro·mate (krō′māt) n. salt of chromic acid.

chro·mat·ic (krō mat′ik, krə-) adj. **1.** of, relating to, or containing color or colors. **2.** of, relating to, or designating the use of all the notes of the chromatic scale. Distinguished from **diatonic.** [Greek

chrōmatikos, from *chrōma* color, chromatic scale.] —**chro·mat′i·cal·ly,** *adv.*

chro·mat·ics (krō mat′iks, krə-) *n.,pl.* science of colors. ▲ construed as singular.

chromatic scale, twelve-tone musical scale progressing entirely by half tones.

chro·ma·tin (krō′mə tin) *n.* network of material in a cell nucleus that makes up the chromosomes during cell division. It absorbs stains readily. [Greek *chrōmat-,* stem of *chrōma* color + -IN¹.]

chrome (krōm) *n.* **1.** chromium. **2.** chrome yellow. [French *chrome* chromium, from Greek *chrōma* color; from the striking colors of its compounds.]

chrome steel, tough steel alloy containing chromium. Also, **chromium steel.**

chrome yellow, any of various shades of yellow pigment, ranging from lemon to deep orange and composed of lead chromate.

chro·mic (krō′mik) *adj.* of, relating to, or containing chromium.

chro·mite (krō′mīt) *n.* mineral, chromic iron oxide, the chief source of chromium. Formula: FeCr₂O₄.

chro·mi·um (krō′mē əm) *n.* hard, brittle, silver-white metallic element that does not tarnish in air. It is used for electroplating and in many alloys to provide strength as well as resistance to corrosion and heat. Symbol: **Cr** See **element** for table. [Modern Latin *chromium,* from Greek *chrōma* color; from the striking colors of its compounds.]

chro·mo (krō′mō) *pl.* **-mos.** *n.* chromolithograph.

chro·mo·lith·o·graph (krō′mō lith′ə graf′) *n.* color print produced from a series of metal plates or specially prepared stones. [Greek *chrōma* color + LITHOGRAPH.]

chro·mo·some (krō′mə sōm′) *n.* tiny structure in the nuclei of plant and animal cells, composed chiefly of proteins and DNA. Chromosomes carry the genetic material that determines sex, size, color, and many other characteristics. [Greek *chrōma* color + *sōma* body.]

chro·mo·sphere (krō′mə sfēr′) *n.* **1.** gaseous layer several thousand miles thick, consisting largely of hydrogen, helium, and calcium, which surrounds the sun. **2.** similar gaseous layer around a star. [Greek *chrōma* color + SPHERE.]

chron. **1.** chronological. **2.** chronology.

Chron., Chronicles.

chron·ic (kron′ik) *adj.* **1.** (of an illness) lasting a long time or recurring: *chronic bronchitis.* Distinguished from **acute. 2.** habitual; constant: *a chronic complainer.* **3.** having had an illness or habit for a long time: *a chronic invalid.* [Latin *chronicus* relating to time, from Greek *chronikos,* from *chronos* time.] —**chron′i·cal·ly,** *adv.*

Syn. 2. Chronic, habitual, inveterate mean that something is long-lasting and firmly established. **Chronic,** used usually of habits, suggests recurrence and resistance to change or amelioration: *The economy flourishes despite a fairly high rate of chronic unemployment.* **Habitual** implies a trait so ingrained as to be characteristic: *His habitual reserve keeps him from enjoying a full social life.* **Inveterate** suggests something of long standing and often is used to carry a negative impression: *An inveterate gambler, he would bet on the number of apples in a basket.*

chron·i·cle (kron′i kəl) *n.* detailed and continuous register of events in order of time or occurrence; history. —*v.t.,* **-cled, -cling.** to record in or as in a chronicle. [Anglo-Norman *cronicle* annals, from Medieval Latin *chronica,* from Greek *chronika,* going back to *chronos* time.] —**chron′i·cler,** *n.*

Chron·i·cles (kron′i kəlz) *n.,pl.* either of two books, I Chronicles and II Chronicles, of the Old Testament. ▲ construed as singular.

chron·o·graph (kron′ə graf′) *n.* **1.** instrument that measures time intervals and records them, usually by means of a stylus on a graph carried by a rotating drum. **2.** stop watch. [Greek *chronos* time + -GRAPH.]

chron·o·log·i·cal (kron′ə loj′i kəl) *adj.* **1.** arranged according to the order of time or occurrence. **2.** relating to or containing chronology. Also, **chron′o·log′ic.** —**chron′o·log′i·cal·ly,** *adv.*

chro·nol·o·gy (krə nol′ə jē) *pl.,* **-gies.** *n.* **1.** arrangement according to the order of time or occurrence. **2.** table or list arranged in this way. **3.** science of computing periods of time and of arranging and recording the dates and historical order of past events. [Greek *chronos* time + -LOGY.] —**chro·nol′o·ger, chro·nol′o·gist,** *n.*

chro·nom·e·ter (krə nom′ə tər) *n.* clock, specially designed for precise timekeeping at sea, set on Greenwich mean time and used to determine longitude. [Greek *chronos* time + -METER.]

chron·o·scope (kron′ə skōp′) *n.* instrument that measures short time intervals. [Greek *chronos* time + -SCOPE.]

chrys·a·lid (kris′ə lid) *pl.,* **chrys·al·i·des** (kri sal′ə dēz′). *n.* chrysalis. —*adj.* of or relating to a chrysalis.

chrys·a·lis (kris′ə lis) *pl.,* **-lis·es.** *n.* **1.** pupal stage during which a butterfly or moth undergoes stuctural changes while enclosed in a cocoon and before emerging as a winged adult. **2.** cocoon. **3.** anything in a stage of development or transition. [Latin *chrȳsallis* gold-colored

pupa of the butterfly, from Greek *chrȳsallis,* from *chrȳsos* gold; Semitic origin.]

chry·san·the·mum (krə san′thə məm) *n.* **1.** globe-shaped or daisy-like flower head of any of a large group of plants, genus *Chrysanthemum,* of the composite family, growing in all colors except blue and purple. **2.** leafy plant bearing this flower head, widely cultivated as a garden plant. [Latin *chrȳsanthemum* marigold, from Greek *chrȳsanthemon,* from *chrȳsos* gold (of Semitic origin) + *anthemon* flower.]

Chry·se·is (krī sē′is) *n. Greek Legend.* a beautiful young woman captured by the Greeks in a raid near Troy. The Greeks held her captive until Apollo, in answer to her father's prayers, sent a plague upon their camp.

chrys·o·ber·yl (kris′ə ber′əl) *n.* semiprecious stone that consists of yellowish or pale-green beryllium aluminate. [Latin *chrȳsobēryllus,* from Greek *chrȳsobēryllos* gold-colored beryl, from *chrȳsos* gold (of Semitic origin) + *bēryllos* beryl. See BERYL.]

chrys·o·lite (kris′ə līt′) *n.* semiprecious stone that is a green or yellow silicate of magnesium and iron. Also, **ol′i·vine′.** [Old French *crisolite,* from Latin *chrȳsolithus* topaz, from Greek *chrȳsolithos,* from *chrȳsos* gold (of Semitic origin) + LITHOS stone.]

chrys·o·prase (kris′ə prāz′) *n.* semiprecious stone that is an apple-green variety of chalcedony. [Latin *chrȳsoprasos* golden-green gem, from Greek *chrȳsoprasos,* from Greek *chrȳsos* gold (of Semitic origin) + *prason* leek.]

Chrys·os·tom, Saint John (kris′əs təm, kris os′təm) A.D. c.345-407, bishop and theologian of the early Christian Church.

chrys·o·tile (kris′ə til) *n.* light-green or yellow fibrous variety of the mineral serpentine. It is the principal type of asbestos. [Greek *chrȳsos* gold (of Semitic origin) + *tilos* something plucked (as fiber).]

chub (chub) *pl.,* **chubs** or **chub.** *n.* any of several freshwater and saltwater fish, as the **freshwar chub,** or minnow, of the order Cypriniformes, and the **Bermuda chub,** order Perciformes. [Of uncertain origin.]

chub·by (chub′ē) **-bi·er, -bi·est.** *adj.* round and plump. —**chub′bi·ness,** *n.*

chuck¹ (chuk) *n.* **1.** gentle or playful pat or tap, esp. under the chin. **2.** throw; toss. —*v.t.* **1.** to pat or tap gently or playfully, esp. under the chin. **2.** *Informal.* to throw; toss; pitch: *He chucked the ball over the fence.* **3.** *Informal.* to throw away; discard: *We chucked the idea.* [Possibly from Old French *choquer* to knock; of uncertain origin.]

chuck² (chuk) *n.* **1.** device for holding a piece of work or a tool in a machine, as in a lathe or drilling machine. **2.** cut of beef including parts between the neck and the shoulder blade and first three ribs. See **beef** for diagram. [Form of CHOCK.]

Chuck of a drill

chuck-full (chuk′fool′) chock-full.

chuck·le (chuk′əl) **-led, -ling.** *v.i.* to laugh in a soft manner, esp. to oneself, as in expressing mild amusement or satisfaction: *John chuckled when he heard of our predicament.* —*n.* soft laugh, as expressive of mild amusement or satisfaction. [Imitative.] —**chuck′ler,** *n.*

chuck·le·head (chuk′əl hed′) *n. Informal.* stupid person.

chuck wagon, wagon that carries cooking equipment and provisions, as for lumbermen or harvest hands, esp. in the western United States.

chuck·wal·la (chuk′wä′lə) *n.* lizard, genus *Sauromalus,* related to the iguana, found in the southwestern United States and northwestern Mexico. When frightened it can inflate its lungs, increasing its size by more than half. Length: to 16 inches. [Modification of Spanish *chacahuala;* of Shoshonean origin.]

chug (chug) *n.* short, dull, explosive sound, as that made by the exhaust of an engine. —*v.i.* **chugged, chug·ging.** to move with or make such sounds: *The old car chugged along.* [Imitative.]

chuk·ker (chuk′ər) *also,* **chuk·kar.** *n.* any of the eight periods in polo, lasting 7½ minutes each. [Hindi *chakar* a period (of play), from Sanskrit *cakrāh* wheel, circle.]

Chu·la Vis·ta (chōō′lə vis′tə) city at the southwestern tip of California, near San Diego. Pop. (1970), 67,901.

chum (chum) *n.* close friend. —*v.i.* **chummed, chum·ming.** to be close friends. [Possibly short for earlier *chamberfellow* roommate; said to be first used as slang at Oxford University in England.]

chum·my (chum′ē) **-mi·er, -mi·est.** *adj. Informal.* friendly; intimate. —**chum′mi·ly,** *adv.*

chump (chump) *n.* **1.** *Informal.* one who is easily fooled or deceived; dupe. **2.** short, heavy chunk of wood. [Possibly blend of CHUNK and LUMP.]

Chung·king (choong′king′) *n.* port city in west-central China, on the Yangtze River. Pop. (1957), 2,121,000.

chunk (chungk) *n. Informal.* **1.** thick piece or lump, as of wood, bread, or cheese. **2.** amount; quantity: *A large chunk of his salary was spent on entertainment.* [Form of CHUCK².]

chunk·y (chung′kē) chunk·i·er, chunk·i·est. *adj. Informal.* **1.** stocky. **2.** like a chunk. —**chunk′i·ness,** *n.*

church (church) *n.* **1.** building for public worship, esp. that of a Christian denomination. **2.** public worship; religious services: *to go to church every Sunday.* **3.** Christians collectively. **4.** *also,* **Church.** particular group of Christians united by similar doctrines, beliefs, and disciplines; denomination. **5.** locally organized congregation of Christians. **6.** ecclesiastical authority, power, or organization: *the separation of church and state.* **7.** clerical profession. [Old English *cirice* building for Christian worship, going back to Greek *kȳriakon* (*dōma*) (house) of the Lord, from *kȳrios* master, lord.]

church·go·er (church′gō′ər) *n.* one who goes to church regularly. —**church′go′ing,** *n., adj.*

Church·ill (chur′chil, -chəl) **1. John.** 1650–1722, Duke of Marlborough who in 1704 defeated the French at Blenheim. **2. Sir Winston L. S.** 1874–1965, British statesman and writer, prime minister of England, from 1940 to 1945 and from 1951 to 1955.

Churchill Downs, race track for thoroughbred horse races located at Louisville, Kentucky, site of the Kentucky Derby.

Church Latin, form of Latin used by the Roman Catholic Church.

church·ly (church′lē) *adj.* **1.** of, relating to, or suitable for a church. **2.** belonging or devoted to a church.

church·man (church′mən) *pl.,* **-men.** *n.* **1.** clergyman. **2.** member or supporter of a church.

Church of Christ, Scientist, official name of the Christian Science Church.

Church of England, established church in England, headed by the British sovereign and having an episcopal hierarchy. Established by Henry VIII, the Church of England is the mother church of the U.S. Protestant Episcopal Church.

Church of Jesus Christ of Latter-day Saints, official name of the Mormon Church.

church·war·den (church′wôrd′ən) *n.* in the Church of England and the Protestant Episcopal Church, an elected lay official whose duty is the management of secular affairs.

church·wom·an (church′woom′ən) *pl.,* **-wom·en.** *n.* woman member or supporter of a church.

church·yard (church′yärd′) *n.* ground around or adjoining a church, often used as a cemetery.

churl (churl) *n.* **1.** surly, ill-bred person. **2.** rustic; peasant. [Old English *ceorl* freeman of the lowest rank, man.]

churl·ish (chur′lish) *adj.* of, like, or characteristic of a churl. —**churl′ish·ly,** *adv.* —**churl′ish·ness,** *n.*

churn (churn) *n.* vessel in which cream or milk is agitated to separate the fat globules in order to make butter. —*v.t.* **1.** to stir or agitate (cream or milk) in a churn. **2.** to make (butter) in a churn. **3.** to stir or agitate with violent or continued motion: *The plow churned up the soil.* —*v.i.* **1.** to work a churn. **2.** to move with violent agitation: *The water churned at the bottom of the waterfall.* [Old English *cyrin* vessel for making butter.] —**churn′er,** *n.*

churr (chur) chirr.

chute (shoot) *n.* **1.** inclined or vertical trough or passage, usually having a slanted opening, down or through which various things may be passed or conveyed: *a mail chute, a coal chute.* **2.** rapids in a river. **3.** steep or curving slope, as for toboggans. **4.** *Informal.* parachute. [French *chute* fall, going back to Latin *cadere* to fall; influenced by English SHOOT in meaning.]

chut·ney (chut′nē) *pl.,* **-neys.** *n.* condiment or relish made of fruits, herbs, and spices. [Hindi *chatni* relish.]

chutz·pah (KHOOTS′pə) *n. Informal.* nerve; gall. [Of Yiddish origin.]

chyle (kīl) *n.* milky fluid consisting of emulsified fat and lymph, formed from digested food in the small intestine and passed into the veins. [Late Latin *chylus* juice, from Greek *chylos*.] —**chy′lous,** *adj.*

chyme (kīm) *n.* pulpy, semiliquid mass of partly digested food which passes from the stomach into the small intestine. [Late Latin *chymos* fluid of the stomach, from Greek *chymos* juice of a plant or animal.] —**chy′mous,** *adj.*

CIA, Central Intelligence Agency.

ci·bo·ri·um (si bôr′ē əm) *pl.,* **-bo·ri·a** (-bôr′ē ə). *n.* **1.** covered container which holds the bread of the Eucharist. **2.** canopy over an altar, esp. one that is permanent. [Medieval Latin *ciborium* vessel for the sacrament, from Latin *cibōrium* drinking cup, from Greek *kibōrion* seed vessel of the Egyptian bean, cup from or resembling it.]

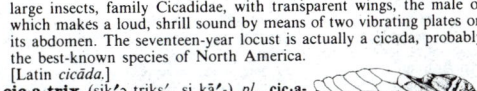
Cicada

ci·ca·da (si kā′də, -kä′-) *pl.,* **-das** or **-dae** (-dē). *n.* any of a group of large insects, family Cicadidae, with transparent wings, the male of which makes a loud, shrill sound by means of two vibrating plates on its abdomen. The seventeen-year locust is actually a cicada, probably the best-known species of North America. [Latin *cicāda*.]

cic·a·trix (sik′ə triks′, si kā′-) *pl.,* **cic·a·tri·ces** (sik′ə trī′sēz). *also,* **cic·a·trice** (sik′ə tris). *n.* **1.** scar consisting of fibrous connective tissue formed when a wound heals. **2.** scar left on a tree or plant, as one left when a leaf falls. **3.** hilum. [Latin *cicātrix* scar.]

cic·a·trize (sik′ə trīz′) **-trized, -triz·ing.** *v.t., v.i.* to heal or become healed by the formation of a scar.

Cic·e·ro (sis′ə rō′) *n.* **1. Marcus Tul·li·us** (tul′ē əs). 106–43 B.C., Roman orator, writer, and statesman. Also, **Tul′ly. 2.** city in northeastern Illinois, an industrial suburb of Chicago. Pop. (1970), 67,058.

cic·e·ro·ne (sis′ə rō′nē) *pl.,* **-nes.** *n.* one who shows and explains points of interest, curiosities, and antiquities to sightseers; guide. [Italian *cicerone*, from CICERO; probably with reference to the oratorical habits of guides.]

Cic·e·ro·ni·an (sis′ə rō′nē ən) *adj.* of, relating to, or characteristic of Cicero or his orations and writings.

cich·lid (sik′lid) *n.* any of a group of freshwater fish, family Cichlidae, found in North and South America, including the angelfish and other popular home aquarium fish. [Modern Latin *Cichlidae*, from Greek *kichlē* thrush, wrasse.]

Cid, The (sid) c.1040–99, Spanish soldier who fought against the Moors and became a national hero; born Rodrigo Diaz de Bivar. [Spanish (*el*) *cid* (the) chief, from Arabic *sayyid* lord.]

-cide[1] *combining form* killing of: *homicide.* [Latin *-cīdium*, from *caedere* to kill.]

-cide[2] *combining form* killer of: *matricide.* [Latin *-cīda*, from *caedere* to kill.]

ci·der (sī′dər) *n.* juice pressed from apples or, formerly, from other fruits, used as a beverage and in making certain products, as vinegar or applejack. [Old French *sidre*, from Late Latin *sīcera* strong drink, from Late Greek *sīkera*, from Hebrew *shēkār*.]

cider press, machine used to crush and to extract juice from the pulp of apples for making cider.

ci·de·vant (sēd ə vän′) *adj.* former: *a ci-devant premier.* [French *ci-devant* formerly, from *ci-* here (from Latin *ecce hīc* behold here) + *devant* before (going back to Latin *dē* from + *ab ante* from before).]

c.i.f., cost, insurance, and freight.

ci·gar (si gär′) *n.* compact roll of tobacco leaves prepared for smoking. [Spanish *cigarro*, possibly going back to Mayan *siq* tobacco.]

cig·a·rette (sig′ə ret′, sig′ə ret′) *n.* small roll of finely shredded tobacco leaves, enclosed in thin paper, used for smoking. [French *cigarette*, diminutive of *cigare* cigar, from Spanish *cigarro*. See CIGAR.]

cil·i·a (sil′ē ə) *sing.,* **-i·um** (-ē əm). *n.,pl.* **1.** eyelashes. **2.a.** minute hairlike projections which line the trachea, bronchi, and bronchioles, and are constantly in motion, thus filtering the air entering and leaving the lungs. **b.** similar hairlike projections on certain cells, as paramecia, which move to and fro propelling the cell through the water. See **paramecium** for illustration. [Latin *cilia*, plural of *cilium* eyelid.]

cil·i·ar·y (sil′ē er′ē) *adj.* **1.** of, relating to, or resembling cilia; hairlike. **2.** of or relating to the ciliary body.

ciliary body, portion of the choroid whose ligaments and muscles support and adjust the shape of the lens of the eyeball.

cil·i·ate (sil′ē it, -āt′) *adj.* having cilia. Also, **cil·i·at·ed** (sil′ē ā′tid). —*n.* any of a class of one-celled organisms having cilia with which to move about and obtain food.

Cim·me·ri·an (si mēr′ē ən) *n. Greek Legend.* any of a group of people who lived in eternal darkness and gloom. —*adj.* very dark and gloomy.

cinch (sinch) *n.* **1.** girth for fastening a saddle or pack on a horse. **2.** *Informal.* firm or tight grip. **3.** *Slang.* something sure or easy. **4.** *Slang.* one who or that which is certain to succeed: *He is a cinch to win the contest.* —*v.t.* **1.** to fasten with or as with a cinch; bind firmly. **2.** *Informal.* to get a firm or tight grip on. **3.** *Slang.* to make sure of: *His touchdown cinched the victory for his team.* [Spanish *cincha* saddle girth, from Latin *cingula* belt.]

cin·cho·na (sin kō′nə) *n.* **1.** any of a group of trees, genus *Cinchona*, found in South America, Asia, and Jamaica. Two species widely cultivated for their bark are the **yellow-barked cinchona,** *C. calisaya,* and the **red-barked cinchona,** *C. succirubra.* **2.** bark of this tree, from which quinine and other similar drugs are derived. Also (*def. 2*), **Peruvian bark.** [Modern Latin *cinchona*; named in honor of the Spanish Countess *Chinchón,* c.1576–1641.]

Cin·cin·nat·i (sin′sə nat′ē, -nat′ə) *n.* port city in southwestern Ohio, on the Ohio River. Pop. (1970), 452,524.

at; āpe; cär; end; mē; īce; hot; ōld; fôrk; wood; fōōl; oil; out; up; ūse; turn; sing; thin; this; zh in treasure; ə in ago, taken, pencil, lemon, circus.

179

Cin·cin·na·tus, Lu·cius Quinc·ti·us (sin′sə nā′təs; lōō′shəs kwingk′tē əs) c.519–c.439 B.C., Roman patriot.

cinc·ture (singk′chər) *n.* **1.** belt; girdle. **2.** anything that encompasses; enclosure; border. —*v.t.*, **-tured, -tur·ing.** to encompass with or as with a cincture; gird. [Latin *cinctūra* girdle.]

cin·der (sin′dər) *n.* **1.** combustible substance, esp. coal, that is burning but has ceased to flame. **2.** combustible substance, as wood or coal, burned but not reduced to ashes. **3.** cinders. ashes. **4.** speck, as of dirt or ash: *to have a cinder in one's eye.* **5.** volcanic scoria. [Old English *sinder* dross, slag.]

cinder block, building brick that is partially hollow, made from cinders and cement.

Cin·der·el·la (sin′də rel′ə) *n.* **1.** heroine in a fairy tale who was forced by her cruel stepmother and stepsisters to work very hard. With the help of her fairy godmother she eventually married a prince. **2.** any girl whose worth, beauty, or talent goes for a time unrecognized.

cin·e·ma (sin′ə mə) *n.* **1.** motion picture. **2.** motion-picture theater. **3. the cinema.** motion pictures collectively; art or business of making motion pictures. [Short for earlier *cinematograph* motion picture camera or projector, from Greek *kīnēmat-*, stem of *kīnēma* motion + -GRAPH.]

Cin·e·ma·Scope (sin′ə mə skōp′) *n. Trademark.* method of making and projecting motion pictures using stereophonic sound and two special lenses, one of which squeezes the image horizontally as it is photographed, the other of which reexpands it as it is projected onto a wide screen.

cin·e·ma·tog·ra·phy (sin′ə mə tog′rə fē) *n.* art and process of photographing motion pictures: *He received an award for cinematography.* —**cin′e·ma·tog′ra·pher,** *n.* —**cin·e·mat·o·graph·ic** (sin′ə mat′ə graf′ik), *adj.*

Cin·e·ram·a (sin′ə ram′ə, -rä′mə) *n. Trademark.* method of making and projecting motion pictures which, in combination with stereophonic sound, gives an illusion of depth and produces a feeling of audience participation. Three cameras mounted in one unit take photographs and three projectors set at the same angle as the cameras project the film onto a deeply curved screen. [From Greek *kīnein* to move, on the model of PANORAMA.]

cin·e·rar·i·a (sin′ə rãr′ē ə) *n.* ornamental plant, *Senecio cruentus,* of the composite family, having heart-shaped woolly leaves and bearing daisylike flower heads which may be white, blue, pink, or purplish-red. [Modern Latin *cineraria,* from Latin *cinerāris* relating to ashes; from *cinis* ashes; from the color of the down on its leaves.]

cin·e·rar·i·um (sin′ə rãr′ē əm) *pl.,* **-rar·i·a.** *n.* place for keeping the ashes of a cremated body. [Latin *cinerārium,* from *cinis* ashes.] —**cin′e·rar′y,** *adj.*

cin·na·bar (sin′ə bär′) *n.* **1.** red, crystallized mineral, mercuric sulfide, the chief source of mercury. Formula: HgS **2.** artificial mercuric sulfide, prepared commercially for use as a red paint pigment. **3.** bright red color; vermilion. [Late Latin *cinnābaris* this mineral, from color, from Greek *kinnabari;* of Oriental origin.]

cin·na·mon (sin′ə mən) *n.* **1.** reddish-brown spice made from the dried, highly aromatic, inner bark of a tree, *Cinnamomum zeylanicum,* of the laurel family. **2.** the inner bark itself, either ground or rolled into sheets. **3.** the tree yielding this bark, cultivated in tropical regions. **4.** bark of the cassia tree, used as a substitute for cinnamon. **5.** light, reddish-brown color. [Latin *cinnamomum* this spice, from Greek *kinnamōmon,* from Hebrew *qinnāmōn.*]

cinque·foil (singk′foil′) *n.* **1.** any of a group of hardy plants and shrubs, genus *Potentilla,* of the rose family, found in northern temperate or frigid climates throughout the world, having compound leaves, and bearing flat white or yellow flowers consisting of fine broad petals. **2.** ornament, used esp. in architecture, consisting of five foils or arcs joined by pointed projections. [Latin *quinquefolium* this plant, from *quinque* five + *folium* leaf.]

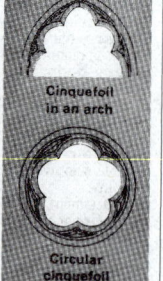

Cinquefoil in an arch

Circular cinquefoil

Cinquefoils

CIO, Congress of Industrial Organizations.

ci·on (sī′ən) scion (*def.* 1).

ci·pher (sī′fər) *also,* **cy·pher.** *n.* **1.** zero. **2.** the symbol representing this; 0. **3.** one who or that which is of no value or importance; nonentity. **4.** system of writing which renders a message or text unintelligible to those who do not have the prearranged key or pattern; code. **5.** message written· in cipher; cryptogram. **6.** key or pattern to a cipher. **7.** any Arabic numeral. **8.** combination of letters, esp. the initials of a name. —*v.t.* **1.** to work (something) out arithmetically. **2.** to write in cipher. —*v.i.* to figure arithmetically. [Old French *cifre* zero, through Spanish, from Arabic *çifr,* noun

use of adjective *çifr* empty; applied to code writing because of the earlier use of numbers in devising codes. Doublet of ZERO.]

cir·ca (sur′kə) *prep. Latin.* around; about. ▲ used esp. to indicate an approximate date.

Cir·ce (sur′sē) *n. Greek Mythology.* a beautiful enchantress who lived on an island and changed half of Odysseus's men into swine. After rescuing them, he escaped from her. —**Cir·ce′an,** *adj.*

cir·ci·nate (sur′sə nāt′) *adj.* **1.** circular; coiled. **2.** curled up from the tip toward the base, as the fronds of certain ferns. [Latin *circinātus,* past participle of *circināre* to make round.] —**cir′ci·nate′ly,** *adv.*

cir·cle (sur′kəl) *n.* **1.** continuous curved line, lying in a plane, every point of which is equally distant from the center. **2.** plane figure bounded by such a line. **3.** anything shaped like a circle, as a halo, crown, or ring. **4.** group of people united by common interests: *a circle of friends.* **5.** gallery or tier of seats in a theater. **6.** complete series or course ending at the point where it began and perpetually repeated: *the circle of the seasons.* **7.** area or sphere in which influence, action, or interest is exerted; realm. **8.** *Logic.* fallacious form of argument in which the conclusion and premise are used to prove one another. Also, **vicious circle.** —*v.t.,* **-cled, -cling.** **1.** to surround with or as with a circle; encompass: *The enemy circled the camp.* **2.** to move around in or as in a circle: *The animal circled his prey before attacking.* —*v.i.* **1.** to move around in a circle: *The airplane circled for an hour before it could land.* [Latin *circulus* circular figure, small ring, diminutive of *circus* ring.] —**cir′cler,** *n.*

cir·clet (sur′klit) *n.* **1.** small circle. **2.** ornamental ring or band worn about the head, neck, arm, or finger.

cir·cuit (sur′kit) *n.* **1.** act of going around; circular course; revolution. **2.** periodic journey from one place to another, as by a judge or preacher. **3.** district traveled through, or included in, such a journey, esp. the district assigned to a judge for holding court. **4.** distance around an area; area enclosed. **5.** system or part of a system of electric or electronic components through which an electric current flows. **6.** group of associated theaters under one management at which productions, as movies or plays, are presented simultaneously or in turn. —*v.t.* to make a circuit of. —*v.i.* to go in a circuit. [Latin *circuitus* a going about.] —**cir′cuit·al,** *adj.*

circuit breaker, safety switch that automatically interrupts the flow of current through an electric circuit when the current becomes dangerously strong.

circuit court, court which sits at intervals in various places within the territory over which it has jurisdiction.

cir·cu·i·tous (sər kū′ə təs) *adj.* roundabout; indirect. —**cir·cu′i·tous·ly,** *adv.* —**cir·cu′i·ty,** —**cir·cu′i·tous·ness,** *n.*

circuit rider, formerly, a Methodist minister who traveled over a circuit to preach.

cir·cu·lar (sur′kyə lər) *adj.* **1.** having the form of a circle; round: *a circular desk.* **2.** moving in or forming a circle: *the circular motion of a phonograph record.* **3.** of or relating to a circle or its mathematical properties. **4.** roundabout; indirect: *a circular way of approaching a subject.* **5.** sent to several persons or intended for general circulation. —*n.* printed material, as a letter or advertisement, printed in large quantities for general circulation. [Late Latin *circulāris* round, from Latin *circulus* See CIRCLE.] —**cir·cu·lar·i·ty** (sur′kyə lar′ə tē), **cir′cu·lar·ness,** *n.* —**cir′cu·lar·ly,** *adv.*

cir·cu·lar·ize (sur′kyə lə rīz′) **-ized, -iz·ing.** *v.t.* **1.** to send circulars to. **2.** to make circular.

circular measure, system for measuring circles.

circular saw, power saw having a thin, metal disk with a toothed edge mounted in a framework and rotated at high speed.

cir·cu·late (sur′kyə lāt′) **-lat·ed, -lat·ing.** *v.i.* **1.** to move in a circular course back to the starting point: *Blood circulates in the body.* **2.** to pass from place to place or person to person; move freely: *to circulate among one's guests. The rumor circulated throughout the office. Air circulates in a room.* —*v.t.* to cause to pass from place to place or person to person; put into circulation: *to circulate money.* [Latin *circulātus,* past participle of *circulāri* to gather in a circle, from *circulus.* See CIRCLE.] —**cir′cu·la′tor,** *n.* —**Syn.** *v.t.* see spread.

circulating library, library from which books may be borrowed or rented. Also, **lending library.**

circulating medium, currency.

cir·cu·la·tion (sur′kyə lā′shən) *n.* **1.** act of circulating. **2.** movement of the blood to and from the heart through the blood vessels of the body. **3.a.** extent or amount of distribution and sales of a publication, as a newspaper. **b.** number of copies of a newspaper or magazine that are distributed and sold. **c.** number of items lent by a library.

Circular saw

at; āpe; cär; end; mē; it; īce; hot; ōld; fôrk; wood; fōōl; oil; out; up; ūse; turn; sing; thin; *this*; zh in treasure; ə in ago, taken, pencil, lemon, circus.

cir·cu·la·to·ry (sur′kyə lə tôr′ē) *adj.* of or relating to circulation, esp. of the blood.

circulatory system, network of tissues that transport fluids throughout an organism. In animals, the circulatory system usually consists of blood, lymphatic vessels, and the heart.

circum- *prefix* around; about: *circumnavigate.* [Latin *circum.*]

cir·cum·am·bi·ent (sur′kəm am′bē ənt) *adj.* surrounding; encompassing.

cir·cum·cise (sur′kəm sīz′) *-cised, -cis·ing. v.t.* to remove all or part of the foreskin of. [Latin *circumcīsus,* past participle of *circumcīdere* to cut around.]

cir·cum·ci·sion (sur′kəm sizh′ən) *n.* 1. act or rite of circumcising. 2. **Circumcision.** feast day commemorating the circumcision of the infant Jesus. January 1.

cir·cum·fer·ence (sər kum′fər əns) *n.* 1. line bounding any rounded plane figure, esp. a circle. 2. measurement of this line; distance around. [Latin *circumferentia* boundary of a circle.] —**cir·cum·fer·en·tial** (sər kum′fə ren′chəl), *adj.*

cir·cum·flex (sur′kəm fleks′) *n.* any of various marks, as ^ or ˉ, placed over a letter to indicate pronunciation in certain languages or in phonetic transcriptions. Also, **circumflex accent.** —*adj.* 1. pronounced or marked with a circumflex. 2. bending or winding around. —*v.t.* 1. to pronounce or mark with a circumflex. 2. to bend or wind around. [Latin *circumflexus,* past participle of *circumflectere* to bend around.]

cir·cum·flu·ent (sər kum′flōō ənt) *adj.* flowing around; surrounding. [Latin *circumfluēns,* present participle of *circumfluere* to flow round.]

cir·cum·flu·ous (sər kum′flōō əs) *adj.* 1. circumfluent. 2. surrounded by or as by water. [Latin *circumfluus.*]

cir·cum·fuse (sur′kəm fūz′) *-fused, -fus·ing. v.t.* 1. to pour or spread about. 2. to surround, as with a liquid; suffuse. [Latin *circumfūsus,* past participle of *circumfundere* to pour around.] —**cir′cum·fu′sion,** *n.*

cir·cum·lo·cu·tion (sur′kəm lō kū′shən) *n.* 1. roundabout or indirect way of speaking; use of too many words. 2. instance of this; roundabout expression. [Latin *circumlocūtiō.*]

cir·cum·nav·i·gate (sur′kəm nav′ə gāt′) *-gat·ed, -gat·ing. v.t.* to sail completely around, esp. the earth. —**cir′cum·nav′i·ga′tion, cir′cum·nav′i·ga′tor,** *n.*

cir·cum·po·lar (sur′kəm pō′lər) *adj.* 1. near or around either of the terrestrial poles. 2. near or revolving around either of the celestial poles.

cir·cum·scribe (sur′kəm skrīb′) *-scribed, -scrib·ing. v.t.* 1. to draw a line around; form the boundaries of; encircle. 2. to restrict; confine: *to circumscribe one's activities.* 3.a. to draw (a geometric figure) around another geometric figure so that the outer touches the inner at as many points as possible. b. to enclose (a geometric figure) in this way: *The circle circumscribes the pentagon.* [Latin *circumscrībere* to draw around, limit.]

cir·cum·scrip·tion (sur′kəm skrip′shən) *n.* 1. act of circumscribing; being circumscribed. 2. that which circumscribes. 3. that which is circumscribed. 4. inscription around something, as a coin, medal, or seal. [Latin *circumscrīptiō* boundary, limit.]

cir·cum·spect (sur′kəm spekt′) *adj.* examining carefully all the circumstances that may affect an action or decision; cautious; prudent. [Latin *circumspectus.*] —**cir′cum·spect′ly,** *adv.* —**cir′cum·spect′ness,** *n.*

cir·cum·spec·tion (sur′kəm spek′shən) *n.* circumspect observation or action; caution; prudence.

cir·cum·stance (sur′kəm stans′) *n.* 1. condition, fact, or event accompanying and often affecting another condition, act, or event: *Good weather and other circumstances made our picnic a success.* 2. *also,* **circumstances.** existing state of affairs surrounding and affecting a person or action; external factors considered as helping or hindering: *Due to circumstances beyond our control the lecture was canceled.* 3. event; occurrence. 4. **circumstances.** condition of wealth or poverty; means. 5. detail, esp. full detail, as in a narrative. 6. **under no circumstances.** under no conditions; never. [Latin *circumstāntia* a surrounding, attribute, condition.]

Syn. 2. Circumstance, situation, condition indicate an existing state of affairs. **Circumstance** suggests the surrounding environment, events, pressures, or the like within or among which something occurs: *The people who get on in this world are the people who get up and look for the circumstances they want* (G. B. Shaw, 1893). **Situation** implies a unique grouping of circumstances that gives a state of affairs its individual character: *In my present situation, a bank loan would be helpful.* **Condition** suggests that a certain state of affairs exists: *Weather conditions make it improbable that the teams will play tomorrow.*

cir·cum·stan·tial (sur′kəm stan′shəl) *adj.* 1. relating to, affected by, or depending on circumstances. 2. incidental; unessential; secondary. 3. full of details; particular: *He gave a circumstantial account of what happened.* —**cir′cum·stan′tial·ly,** *adv.*

circumstantial evidence, evidence of facts or circumstances from which other facts in question can be inferred.

cir·cum·stan·ti·ate (sur′kəm stan′shē āt′) *-at·ed, -at·ing. v.t.* to confirm or support with facts or particulars. —**cir′cum·stan′ti·a′tion,** *n.*

cir·cum·vent (sur′kəm vent′) *v.t.* 1. to go around: *to circumvent the town to avoid traffic.* 2. to avoid; evade: *He circumvented the issue.* 3. to entrap or get the better of, as by craft or fraud. [Latin *circumventus,* past participle of *circumvenīre* to surround, deceive, from *circum* around + *venīre* to come.] —**cir′cum·ven′tion,** *n.*

cir·cus (sur′kəs) *n.* 1.a. traveling show, usually featuring acrobats, clowns, and both trained and wild animals. b. all the persons, animals, and equipment associated with such a show. c. performance given by such a show. 2.a. in ancient Rome, oval or oblong structure, open at one end, with tiers of seats surrounding an open space, used esp. for horse and chariot races. b. entertainment given in such a structure. [Latin *circus* ring, round place for games. Doublet of CIRQUE.]

Cir·cus Max·i·mus (sur′kəs mak′sə məs) largest circus in ancient Rome.

cirque (surk) *n.* 1. circular space, esp. a bowl-shaped depression, located at the head of a valley and having steep walls. 2. *Archaic.* circlet; ring. [French *cirque* circus, geological cirque, from Latin *circus* ring. Doublet of CIRCUS.]

cir·rate (sir′āt) *adj.* *Biology.* characteristic of or having a cirrus or cirri. Also, **cir·rose** (sir′ōs), **cir·rous** (sir′əs).

cir·rho·sis (si rō′sis) *n.* chronic disease of the liver marked by the growth of scar tissue, the destruction of normal liver cells, and a distortion in shape. [Modern Latin *cirrhosis,* from Greek *kirrhos* orange, tawny; from the color of the affected liver.]

cir·ri·ped (sir′ə ped′) *n.* any of a group of parasitic crustaceans, order Cirripedia, as the barnacle, having threadlike appendages, which are free-swimming in the larval stage and become attached to rocks or other organisms in adulthood. [Modern Latin *Cirripedia,* from Latin *cirrus* curl + *ped-,* stem of *pēs* foot.]

cir·ro·cu·mu·lus (sir′ō kū′myə ləs) *n.* cloud made up of ice crystals appearing in thin layers of ripples or small puffs, formed at an altitude of about 20,000 to 25,000 feet. [CIRRUS + CUMULUS.]

cir·ro·stra·tus (sir′ō strā′təs, -strat′əs) *n.* thin, veil-like cloud of ice crystals formed at about 20,00 to 25,000 feet. The sun or moon appears to have a halo around it when it shines through such clouds. [CIRRUS + STRATUS.]

cir·rus (sir′əs) *pl.* **cir·ri** (sir′ī). *n.* 1. white, thin, fibrous cloud composed of ice crystals in small patches or bands, found at altitudes above 20,000 feet. 2. *Biology.* a. threadlike part of a plant. b. threadlike, flexible appendage of an animal, as a feeler or tentacle. [Latin *cirrus* curl.]

cis·al·pine (sis al′pīn, -pin) *adj.* situated on the southern side of the Alps, toward Rome. [Latin *Cisalpīnus,* going back to *cis* side of + *Alpēs* Alps.]

cis·co (sis′kō) *pl.,* **-coes** *or* **-cos.** *n.* any of several whitefish or herring found in the Great Lakes. [Shortened from French *ciscoette,* modification of Ojibwa *pemitewiskawet* fish having oily flesh.]

cis·lu·nar (sis lōō′nər) *adj.* of, relating to, or designating the area between the earth and the moon.

Cis·ter·cian (sis tur′shən) *n.* member of an order of monks and nuns who live by the Benedictine rule, founded in France in 1098. —*adj.* of or relating to this order. [Medieval Latin *Cistercium* Citeaux (French village where this order was founded) + -AN.]

cis·tern (sis′tərn) *n.* 1. artificial or natural reservoir or tank for storing liquids, esp. rain water. 2. cavity in the body containing some natural fluid. [Old French *cisterne* reservoir, from Latin *cisterna,* from *cista* box. See CHEST.]

cit·a·del (sit′əd əl, -ə del′) *n.* 1. fortress commanding a city. 2. any strongly fortified place. [Italian *cittadella* small town, diminutive of earlier Italian *cittade* city, from Latin *cīvitās* city, state.] —**Syn.** 1. see stronghold.

ci·ta·tion (sī tā′shən) *n.* 1. act of citing or quoting. 2. passage or words cited; quotation. 3. public commendation or award, as for bravery or outstanding achievement. 4. summons to appear before a court of law. 5.a. specific mention of a soldier or unit, in an official dispatch, for bravery or meritorious service. b. medal or award given for this.

cite (sīt) *cit·ed, cit·ing. v.t.* 1. to quote, as a passage or author, esp. as an authority. 2. to refer to as support, proof, or confirmation. 3. to give a public commendation to, as for bravery or outstanding achievement. 4. to summon to appear before a court of law. 5. *Military.* to mention in a citation. [French *citer* to summon, quote, from Latin *citāre.*] —**cit′a·ble;** *also,* **cite′a·ble,** *adj.*

cith·a·ra (sith′ər ə, kith′-) *n.* ancient Greek stringed instrument

Cithara

somewhat resembling the lyre. [Latin *cithara,* from Greek *kithárā.* Doublet of GUITAR, ZITHER.]

cith·ern (sith′ərn, sith′-) cithern.

cit·ied (sit′ēd) *adj.* **1.** occupied by a city or cities. **2.** made into or resembling a city.

cit·i·fied (sit′i fīd′) *adj.* having the manners or fashions characteristic of urban life.

cit·i·zen (sit′ə zən, -sən) *n.* **1.** native or naturalized member of a country who owes allegiance to and is entitled to protection from its government. **2.** permanent resident, esp. of a city or town. [Anglo-Norman *citezein,* modification of Old French *citeain* townsman, from *cite* city, from Latin *cīvitās* city, state.]
Syn. 1. Citizen, subject, national refer to a person acknowledged to be a member of a country. **Citizen** implies the rights and privileges of a member of a republican government, that is, a nation whose power in theory derives from its people, of whom he is one: *All person born or naturalized in the United States, and subject to the jurisdiction thereof, are citizens of the United States and of the state wherein they reside* (*U.S. Constitution,* Amendment XIV). **Subject** suggests domination by another person, in this context a sovereign or ruler in whose person political power resides: *British subjects are limited in the amoun of money they may take abroad.* **National** implies residence in a country other than the one to which allegiance is owed and connotes a degree of protection by the home government: *American nationals were askea to report to the nearest consular office.*

cit·i·zen·ry (sit′ə zən rē, -sən rē) *pl.,* **-ries.** *n.* citizens collectively.

citizen's band radio, radio communication on a designated frequency, intended for the use of the public for short-distance radio signaling by licensees.

cit·i·zen·ship (sit′ə zən ship′, -sən-) *n.* status or position of being a citizen, including its rights, duties, and privileges.

cit·rate (sit′rāt) *n.* salt or ester of citric acid.

cit·ric (sit′rik) *adj.* of or derived from citrus fruits.

citric acid, organic acid, composed of carbon, hydrogen, and oxygen, found in almost all plants but esp. in lemons, limes, and other citrus fruits. It is used as a flavoring and in medicine. Formula: $C_6H_8O_7$.

cit·rine (sit′rin) *n.* lemon yellow color. [French *citrin* pale yellow, from Latin *citrus* citron tree.]

cit·ron (sit′rən) *n.* **1.** large lemonlike fruit of a shrub or small tree, *Citrus medica,* grown in Asia, the Mediterranean regions, and the West Indies, valued mainly for its thick, warty, yellow-green rind which is used in desserts and in making liqueurs and perfumes. **2.** the shrub or tree bearing this fruit. **3.** preserved or candied rind of this fruit, used in confections, esp. in fruit cakes. **4.** citron melon. [French *citron* citron fruit, lemon, from Latin *citrus* citron tree.]

cit·ron·el·la (sit′rə nel′ə) *n.* **1.** pale-yellow oil distilled from the leaves of a plant, *Cymbopogon nardus,* of the grass family, having a lemon fragrance and used to make insect repellent and to scent soaps and cosmetics. **2.** the plant itself, grown chiefly in Java, Ceylon, India, and Central America. [Modern Latin *citronella,* going back to French *citron;* from its scent resembling the citron. See CITRON.]

citron melon, small round watermelon, *Citrullus vulgaris,* variety *citroides,* grown in warm temperate regions. Its hard white flesh is inedible, but its rind is used for making preserves.

cit·rus (sit′rəs) *n.* **1.** any of a group of shrubs and small trees, genus *Citrus,* valued esp. for its fruit, grown in warm regions throughout the world. **2.** citrus fruit. —*adj. also,* **cit·rous.** of or relating to such trees or their fruit. [Latin *citrus* citron tree, citrus tree.]

citrus fruit, fleshy, juicy fruit of any of a group of shrubs and small trees, genus *Citrus,* as the orange, lemon, lime, or grapefruit.

cit·tern (sit′ərn) *also,* **cith·ern.** *n.* musical instrument of the guitar family, having wire strings. [Blend of Latin *cithara* type of guitar or lute and GITTERN. See CITHARA.]

cit·y (sit′ē) *pl.,* **cit·ies.** *n.* **1.** any densely populated center, where people live and engage in commerce and industry. **2.** in the United States, any incorporated municipality, chartered by a state. **3.** in Canada, any municipality of the highest class. **4.** inhabitants of a city collectively. **5.** city-state. **6. the City.** City of London. See **London** *(def. 2).* —*adj.* of or relating to a city; urban. [Old French *cite* large town, body of citizens, from Latin *cīvitās* community, state, citizenship, from *cīvis* citizen.]
Syn. n. 1. City, town are used of large, urban population centers. **City** denotes an incorporated entity with a charter and a government quite autonomous in most respects: *The city refused to permit its fire department to fight fires in nearby unincorporated areas.* **Town,** as an urban area, may have as many inhabitants as a city but generally has fewer; it is not incorporated, although it exists as a separate entity within the

Cittern

state: *We attended the weekly meeting of the town's council to support the proposal for a new school.*

city desk, department of a newspaper office which receives and edits local news.

city editor, newspaper editor who has charge of collecting and editing local news and of distributing assignments to reporters.

city fathers, officials of a city, as councilmen or magistrates.

city hall. 1. building serving as the administrative headquarters of a city government. **2.** administrative body of a city.

city manager, administrator not publicly elected but appointed by a city council to manage the government of a city.

city of David 1. Bethlehem. **2.** Jerusalem.

City of God, heaven.

City of Seven Hills, Rome.

city planning, organized efforts to physically improve cities.

cit·y-state (sit′ē stāt′) *n.* self-governing political unit which consisted of a city and sometimes the surrounding territory which it controlled.

Ciu·dad Juá·rez (sū thäth′ hwä′rez, sē′oo däd′ wär′əz) city at the northern border of Mexico, on the Rio Grande, opposite El Paso, Texas. Pop. (1960), 262,119. Also, **Juá′rez.**

Ciu·dad Tru·jil·lo (sū thäth′ trōō hē′yō) see Santo Domingo.

civ·et (siv′it) *n.* **1.** any of various catlike animals related to the mongoose, native to the warmer regions of Africa, Europe, and Asia; having a narrow head, a pointed muzzle, and a slender body. Also, **civet cat.** **2.** fur of any of these animals. **3.** thick, yellowish substance, having a strong musklike odor, secreted by the anal glands of the civet, used in perfumes. [French *civette* civet perfume, civet cat, through Italian, from Arabic *zabād* civet perfume.]

Civet

civ·ic (siv′ik) *adj.* of or relating to a city or citizenship. [Latin *cīvicus* relating to a citizen, from *cīvis* citizen.]

civ·ics (siv′iks) *n.* study of the function, services, and purpose of a government and of the duties, rights, and privileges of citizenship. ▲ construed as singular.

civ·il (siv′əl) *adj.* **1.** of or relating to a citizen or citizens. **2.** of or relating to the relations between a government and its citizens: *civil affairs.* **3.** occurring within the boundaries of a nation or among its citizens; domestic; internal: *civil strife.* **4.** not military or ecclesiastical: *a civil wedding ceremony.* **5.** coolly polite; courteous. **6.** having social order and organized government; civilized. **7.a.** of or in accordance with civil law: *civil court, civil proceedings.* Distinguished from **criminal.** **b.** relating to an individual's rights and to the legal proceedings involving such rights. **8.** of or relating to those divisions of time which are recognized as legal standards: *The civil week goes from Sunday to Saturday.* [Latin *cīvīlis* relating to a citizen, polite, from *cīvis* citizen.]

civil defense, organized plans for defense to be carried out by civilians in case of enemy attack.

civil disobedience, refusal to obey a governmental law or laws as a means of passive resistance because of one's moral conviction.

civil engineering, profession of designing and supervising the construction of roads, bridges, and other public works.

ci·vil·ian (si vil′yən) *n.* **1.** one who is not a member of the military. **2.** one who does not belong to a police force, fire-fighting unit, or similar organization. —*adj.* of or relating to civilians.

ci·vil·i·ty (si vil′ə tē) *pl.,* **-ties.** *n.* **1.** cool politeness. **2.** act or expression of politeness or courtesy.

civ·i·li·za·tion (siv′ə li zā′shən) *n.* **1.** state or stage of human society characterized by a highly organized and complex level of social, economic, cultural, political, and intellectual development. **2.** countries and peoples that have attained such a stage of development. **3.** way of life of a particular people, place, or time: *Medieval civilization, Greek civilization.* **4.** act or process of civilizing or of becoming civilized. **5.** *Informal.* style or way of life which includes those comforts to which one is accustomed: *After camping, it was good to be back in civilization.*

civ·i·lize (siv′ə līz′) **-lized, -liz·ing.** *v.t.* **1.** to bring out of a primitive or savage state. **2.** to bring to a socially accepted level of good breeding or culture; refine. [French *civiliser,* going back to Latin *cīvīlis.* See CIVIL.] —**civ′i·liz′er,** *n.*

civ·i·lized (siv′ə līzed′) *adj.* **1.** advanced beyond that which is primitive or savage: *civilized society.* **2.** of or relating to countries or people so advanced: *civilized way of life.* **3.** cultured; polite.

civil law. 1. body of law of a state or country that controls and regulates private rights. **2.** in European legal systems, codified law. Opposed to **common law.**

civil liberties, rights which guarantee an individual freedom from arbitrary interference by a government.

civ·il·ly (siv'ə lē) *adv.* **1.** coolly polite. **2.** in accordance with the civil law.

civil marriage, marriage performed by a government official instead of by a clergyman.

civil rights, individual rights, esp. those of personal liberty guaranteed to all citizens.

civil servant, one who is employed in the civil service.

civil service 1. branch of governmental service in which individuals are hired on the basis of merit which is proven by the use of competitive examinations. **2.** body of employees in any government agency, except the military.

civil war 1. war between two sections or groups within a country. **2. Civil War.** in the United States, the war between the North and the South from 1861 to 1865.

civil year, calendar year.

Cl, chlorine.

cl. 1. centiliter. **2.** class. **3.** clause. **4.** clearance. **5.** claim.

clab·ber (klab'ər) *n.* milk which has curdled in the process of souring. —*v.t., v.i.* to curdle, as milk. [Short for earlier *bonnyclabber* sour curdled milk, from Irish *bainne clabair*.]

clack (klak) *v.i.* **1.** to make a short, sharp sound, as by striking two pieces of wood together. **2.** to talk rapidly and continually; chatter. **3.** to cluck or cackle, as a hen does. —*v.t.* **1.** to cause to make a short, sharp sound. **2.** to babble; chatter. —*n.* **1.** short, sharp sound: *the clack of knitting needles.* **2.** rapid, continuous talk; chatter. [Imitative.] —**clack'er,** *n.*

clad (klad) past tense and past participle of **clothe.**

claim (klām) *v.t.* **1.** to assert or demand possession of or recognition of one's right to: *The old man claimed the land. None of the passengers claimed the suitcase. Both teams claimed a victory.* **2.** to declare as a fact or as true; maintain; contend: *He claimed that he saw the accident.* **3.** to call for; require: *His work claimed the better part of his waking hours.* —*n.* **1.** right or title to something: *Her claim to the inheritance was questioned. Her only claim to fame was her voice.* **2.** declaration of something as a fact or as true; contention: *His claim of innocence was disproved. We could not refute his claims without additional evidence.* **3.** demand for that which is due: *They filed a claim with the insurance company.* **4.** that which is claimed, as a piece of land. [Old French *cla(i)mer* to call, cry out, lay claim to, from Latin *clāmāre* to call, proclaim.] —**claim'a·ble,** *adj.* —**Syn.** *v.t.* **1.** see **demand.**

claim·ant (klā'mənt) *n.* one who makes a claim.

clair·voy·ance (klâr voi'əns) *n.* alleged ability to perceive objects or events that are beyond the recognized range of the sense organs. [French *clairvoyance* clear-sightedness, from *clairvoyant.* See CLAIR-VOYANT.]

clair·voy·ant (klâr voi'ənt) *adj.* of, relating to, or having clairvoyance. —*n.* one who is clairvoyant. [French *clairvoyant* clear-sighted, going back to Latin *clārus* clear, bright + *vidēre* to see.]

clam (klam) *n.* **1.** any of a group of bivalve mollusks, found in both salt and fresh water, many of which are highly valued as seafood, the quahog and mussel. **2.** edible part of such a mollusk. —*v.i.* **clammed, clam·ming.** **1.** to dig for clams. **2. to clam up.** *Slang.* to become or remain silent, esp. in an effort to withhold something; stop talking. [Old English *clamm* fetter; with reference to the firm way a clam's shell closes up.]

clam·bake (klam'bāk') *n.* **1.** outdoor party at which seafood, esp. clams, is served. **2.** *Informal.* social gathering, esp. one that is large and noisy.

clam·ber (klam'bər, klam'ər) *v.i., v.t.* to climb by using both the hands and feet, esp. hastily or awkwardly. —*n.* act or instance of clambering. [From *clamb,* obsolete past tense of CLIMB + -ER[2].]

clam·my (klam'ē) *-mi·er, -mi·est. adj.* cold and damp. —**clam'mi·ly,** *adv.* —**clam'mi·ness,** *n.*

clam·or (klam'ər) *British.* **clam·our.** *n.* **1.** loud, noisy outcry; uproar: *A clamor went up from the angry crowd.* **2.** vehement expression, as of protest or dissatisfaction: *They made a clamor for reform.* **3.** any loud and continuous noise: *the clamor of the trumpets.* —*v.i.* to make or utter loud continuous cries. —*v.t.* to utter loudly or noisily. [Old French *clamor* cry, appeal, from Latin *clāmor* loud cry.]

clam·or·ous (klam'ər əs) *adj.* **1.** loud and noisy; vociferous. **2.** uttering vehement expressions, as of protest or dissatisfaction. —**clam'or·ous·ly,** *adv.* —**clam'or·ous·ness,** *n.*

clamp (klamp) *n.* any of several devices that operate on the principle of a vise, having two jaws that can be tightened to hold two

things firmly together. —*v.t.* **1.** to fasten with or place in a clamp or clamps. **2. to clamp down on.** *Informal.* to become more strict with. [Of Germanic origin.]

clan (klan) *n.* **1.** group of families in a community who claim descent from a remote common ancestor. **2.** group of people closely united by a common interest; clique. **3.** *Informal.* family. [Gaelic *clann* family, offspring, from Latin *planta* sprout, scion.]

clan·des·tine (klan des'tin) *adj.* secret, esp. for an illicit purpose; surreptitious; furtive. [Latin *clandestīnus.*] —**clan·des'tine·ly,** *adv.* —**clan·des'tine·ness,** *n.*

clang (klang) *n.* loud, reverberating, ringing sound, as of metal striking metal. —*v.t.* to cause to make a clang: *He clanged the bell at noon.* —*v.i.* to make a clang: *The bells clanged.* [Latin *clangere* to resound; partly imitative.]

clan·gor (klang'gər, klang'ər) *also, British,* **clang·our.** *n.* continuous clanging. —*v.i.* to make a clangor. [Latin *clangor* sound.] —**clan'gor·ous,** *adj.*

clank (klangk) *n.* sharp, abrupt, metallic sound, as the rattling of chains. —*v.i.* to make a clank or a series of clanks. —*v.t.* to cause to clank. [Imitative.]

clan·nish (klan'ish) *adj.* **1.** of, relating to, or characteristic of a clan. **2.** tending to stick closely together in a group; cliquish. —**clan'nish·ly,** *adv.* —**clan'nish·ness,** *n.*

clans·man (klanz'mən) *pl.,* **-men.** *n.* member of a clan.

clap (klap) *n.* **1.** short, sharp sound, as that produced by two surfaces or forces coming together suddenly: *a clap of thunder, a clap of the hands.* **2.** friendly slap: *a clap on the back.* —*v.t.,* **clapped, clap·ping. 1.** to strike (one's hands) together. **2.** to strike with a clap: *The child clapped the blocks together.* **3.** to strike with the palm of the hand, as in friendship. **4.** to put or place, esp. with a sudden or forceful motion: *She clapped her hands to her face. They clapped the prisoner in a cell.* —*v.i.* **1.** to strike one's hands together, esp. as an expression of approval or enjoyment; applaud. **2.** to make a short, sharp sound, or by as by suddenly striking two surfaces together: *The shutters clapped in the breeze.* [Old English *clæppan* to beat.]

clap·board (klab'ərd, klap'bôrd') *n.* thin, narrow board, having one thick edge, used as siding by being nailed horizontally in an overlapping manner. —*v.t.* to cover with clapboards. [Partial translation of Low German *klappholt* stave wood, from *klappen* to clap, fit together + *holt* wood.]

clap·per (klap'ər) *n.* **1.** the tongue of a bell. **2.** one who or that which makes a clapping sound.

clap·trap (klap'trap') *n.* hokum; nonsense. [CLAP + TRAP[1]; originally referring to any device, or *trap,* used by actors to obtain applause, or a *clap.*]

claque (klak) *n.* **1.** individual or organized group hired to applaud a performance, as in a theater. **2.** group of fawners or sycophants. [French *claque* paid applauders in a theater, from *claquer* to clap; imitative.]

Clar·en·don, Earl of (klar'ən dən) 1609–74, English statesman and historian; born Edward Hyde.

clar·et (klar'it) *n.* **1.** dry red wine, esp. red Bordeaux wine. **2.** deep purplish-red color. [Old French *claret* wine clarified with honey, diminutive of *cler* clear, bright, from Latin *clārus.*]

clar·i·fy (klar'ə fī') *-fied, -fy·ing. v.t.* **1.** to show more intelligibly; explain: *He clarified his stand on the issue.* **2.** to make pure and clear: *to clarify butter.* —*v.i.* to become intelligible. [Old French *clarifier* to make bright or clear, from Late Latin *clārificāre,* from Latin *clārus* clear, bright + *facere* to make.] —**clar'i·fi·ca'tion, clar'i·fi'er,** *n.*

clar·i·net (klar'ə net') *n.* musical instrument of the woodwind family, having a single-reed mouthpiece and played by means of finger holes and keys. [French *clarinette,* diminutive of *clarine* bell, going back to Latin *clārus* clear.] —**clar'i·net'ist;** *also, British,* **clar'i·net'tist,** *n.*

Clarinet

clar·i·on (klar'ē ən) *adj.* loud and clear. —*n.* **1.** trumpet having a clear, shrill tone, popular in the seventeenth and eighteenth centuries. **2.** *Archaic.* **a.** sound of a clarion. **b.** sound resembling this. [Medieval Latin *clario* type of trumpet, from Latin *clārus* clear.]

clar·i·ty (klar'ə tē) *n.* quality of being clear; lucidity. [Latin *clāritās.*]

Clark (klärk) **1. George Rogers.** 1752–1818, U.S. general and frontiersman. **2. William.** 1770–1838, brother of George; U.S. soldier and co-leader of the Lewis and Clark expedition.

clash (klash) *n.* **1.** loud, harsh, resounding noise, as of the collision of two metal objects: *the clash of cymbals.* **2.** noisy collision: *He heard the clash of swords.* **3.** strong disagreement or conflict, esp. of conflicting

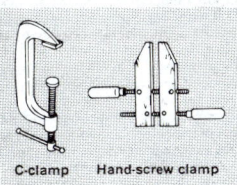

C-clamp   Hand-screw clamp

Clamps

at; āpe; cär; end; mē; it; īce; hot; ōld; fôrk; wood; fōōl; oil; out; up; ūse; turn; sing; thin; this; zh in treasure; ə in ago, taken, pencil, lemon, circus.

183

interests or opinions —*v.i.* **1.** to come together with a clash. **2.** to be at variance; conflict; disagree. —*v.t.* to cause to strike together with a clash. [Imitative.] —**Syn.** *v.i.* **2.** see **conflict.**

clasp (klasp) *n.* **1.** fastening, as a hook, used to hold two objects or parts together. **2.** grasp or embrace. —*v.t.* **1.** to fasten together or secure with or as with a clasp. **2.** to encompass and hold closely with the arms and hands; embrace. **3.** to take firm hold of; grip with the hand. [Of uncertain origin.] —**clasp′er,** *n.*

clasp knife, large pocket knife with one or more blades which fold into the handle.

class (klas) *n.* **1.** number of persons or things grouped together because they are similar in some way; category: *a new class of artists, a class of firearms.* **2.** group of students taught or studying together: *The biology class took a field trip to the aquarium.* **3.** meeting of such a group: *She had a nine o'clock history class.* **4.** group of students in school or college who are ranked together or graduate in the same year: *She was a member of the class of 1969. He was in the freshman class.* **5.** rank, section, or division of society, regarded as a unit due to common economic, occupational, or other social characteristics: *the upper classes, the working class.* **6.** one of the levels of accommodation available on public transportation. **7.** group of animals or plants classified below a phylum or division and above an order: *Man belongs to order primates and tigers belong to order carnivora, but they both belong to class mammalia.* **8.** *Slang.* excellence, esp. of style; elegance. —*v.t.* to place or group in a class; classify. —*v.i.* to be in a class; rank. [Latin *classis* a division of the Roman people, fleet].]

class action, legal action taken by one or more persons on their own behalf and on behalf of all other persons whom the case affects: *to bring a class action against an industry that is polluting the atmosphere.*

clas·sic (klas′ik) *adj.* **1.** serving as a standard, model, or guide: *That cathedral has been considered an example of classic design for over a century.* **2.** simple, regular, and restrained, as in style or lines: *The suit was a classic style.* **3.** typical: *a classic case of mistaken identity.* **4.** worthy of setting a standard; unique: *The expression on your face is classic.* **5.** classical. —*n.* **1.** author, artist, or artistic work of acknowledged excellence and endurance. **2. the classics.** literature of ancient Greece and Rome. **3.** style, or item executed in such a style, that is simple, restrained, and enduring. **4.** any event which is considered typical or traditional: *The world series is the classic of baseball.* [Latin *classicus* of the first rank, from *classis* a class of the Roman people; referring first to people, then to works of literature.]

clas·si·cal (klas′i kəl) *adj.* **1.** of or relating to ancient Greece or Rome, their art, literature, or culture. **2.** learned in or based on the classics: *a classical scholar, classical studies.* **3.** *Music.* **a.** of or relating to music that conforms to certain established standards of form and style and is of enduring interest and value. Bach's cantatas, Beethoven's sonatas, and Brahms' symphonies are examples of classical music. **b.** of, relating to, or adhering to a musical style of the middle eighteenth through the early nineteenth centuries, characterized by homophony, symmetry, simplicity, formal structure, and emotional restraint. Mozart and Haydn are the most famous classical composers. **4.** thought of as standard and authoritative: *classical economics.* **5.** relating to a course of study based upon the humanities, fine arts, and general sciences, as opposed to the technical fields. **6.** classic. —**clas′si·cal·ly,** *adv.*

clas·si·cism (klas′ə siz′əm) *n.* **1.** aesthetic principles derived from the literature and art of ancient Greece and Rome but found as ideals in all ages. Classicism strives for perfect order, harmony, and clarity in form achieved by an emphasis on such elements as symmetry, proportion, technical perfection, simplicity, and restraint. **2.** adherence to these principles.

clas·si·cist (klas′ə sist) *n.* **1.** one who adheres to the principles of classicism. **2.** one who is versed or expert in the classics. **3.** one who strongly advocates the study of the classics.

clas·si·fi·ca·tion (klas′ə fi kā′shən) *n.* **1.** act of classifying. **2.** result of classifying or being classified. **3.** *Biology.* grouping of plants and animals in categories, as genus or species, on the basis of their structural and evolutionary relationships.

clas·si·fied (klas′ə fīd′) *adj.* not available for public knowledge, esp. for reasons of national security; secret.

classified ad, condensed advertisement, usually one arranged in a special section of a newspaper or magazine, as for help wanted or real estate. Also, **classified advertisement.**

clas·si·fy (klas′ə fī′) **-fied, -fy·ing.** *v.t.* **1.** to arrange or group in classes according to a given criterion or criteria. **2.** to designate or label something as secret in order to restrict or limit knowledge of its contents. [Latin *classis* class + -FY. See CLASS.] —**clas′si·fi′a·ble,** *adj.* —**clas′si·fi′er,** *n.*

class·mate (klas′māt′) *n.* member of the same class in school or college.

class·room (klas′rōōm′, -rŏŏm′) *n.* room in which classes are held.

class struggle 1. in Marxist theory, the economic and political struggle for power between capitalists and workers. **2.** any conflict between the social classes of a society.

clat·ter (klat′ər) *n.* **1.** rattling noise, as of hard objects striking against one another: *the clatter of dishes.* **2.** noisy disorder; commotion: *the clatter of a mob in the streets.* **3.** noisy or idle talk; chatter: *the clatter at a large party.* —*v.i.* **1.** to make a rattling noise: *The pots and pans clattered as she put them away.* **2.** to move rapidly with such a noise: *The wagon clattered over the wooden bridge.* **3.** to talk noisily or idly; chatter: *The children clattered after school.* —*v.t.* to cause to clatter. [Probably from an unrecorded Old English word.]

Clau·di·us I (klô′dē əs) 10 B.C.–A.D. 54, Roman emperor from A.D. 41 to 54.

clause (klôz) *n.* **1.** group of words containing a subject and predicate, forming part of a complex or compound sentence. The two kinds of clauses are the independent clause and the dependent clause. **2.** subdivision, as an article, stipulation, or provision, of a formal or legal document. [Old French *clause,* from Medieval Latin *clausa* close of a periodic sentence, section of a law, going back to Latin *claudere* to close.]

claus·tro·pho·bi·a (klôs′trə fō′bē ə) *n.* abnormal fear of being in small, crowded, or enclosed spaces. [Modern Latin *claustrophobia,* from Latin *claustrum* bolt, enclosure + Greek *-phobia.* See PHOBIA.]

cla·vate (klā′vāt) *adj.* shaped like a club. [Modern Latin *clavatus,* from Latin *clāva* club.]

clave (klāv) *Archaic.* past tense of **cleave².**

clav·i·chord (klav′ə kôrd′) *n.* keyboard instrument whose tones are produced by the striking of brass wedges against metal strings. It was a forerunner of the piano. [Medieval Latin *clavichordium* key string, from Latin *clāvis* key + *chorda* string. See CHORD².]

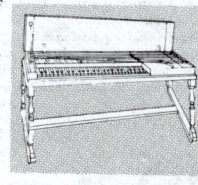

Clavichord

clav·i·cle (klav′i kəl) *n.* either of two long slender bones connecting the breastbone and the shoulder blade; collarbone. [Modern Latin *clavicula,* from Latin *clāvicula* bolt, small key, diminutive of *clāvis* key; referring to its shape.]

cla·vier (klə vēr′, klā′vē ər, klav′ē ər) *n.* **1.** any stringed keyboard instrument, as the clavichord, harpsichord, or piano. **2.** keyboard of a musical instrument, esp. of a stringed instrument. [French *clavier,* going back to Latin *clāvis* key.]

claw (klô) *n.* **1.a.** sharp, usually curved nail on the foot of a bird or animal. **b.** foot with such a nail or nails. **2.** one of the pincers or pincerlike appendages of certain crustaceans or insects, as of a lobster or scorpion. **3.** anything resembling a claw, as the forked end of the head of a hammer. —*v.t., v.i.* to scratch or tear with or as with claws. [Old English *clawu* nail, foot with such nails, a pincer of a shellfish.]

Bird   Cat   Lobster

Claws

claw hammer 1. hammer having one end of the head forked and curved for pulling out nails. **2.** *Informal.* swallowtail coat.

clay (klā) *n.* **1.a.** a fine-grained earth, consisting mostly of aluminum silicates, that can be molded when wet but hardens permanently when fired, as in the making of pottery, sculptured models, bricks, and porcelain. **b.** synthetic substance similar to this, used esp. for modeling, that does not harden permanently and cannot be fired. Also, **modeling clay. 2.** someone or something that can be shaped, manipulated, or easily influenced: *The mother was clay in the hands of her son.* **3.** the human body, esp. as distinguished from the soul. **4.** earth; soil. **5.** feet of clay. personal weakness or flaw in one considered a hero or model. [Old English *clæg* sticky earth.] —**clay′ey,** *adj.*

Clay, Henry (klā) 1777–1852, U.S. statesman.

clay·more (klā′môr′) *n.* broadsword used by Scottish Highland warriors. [Gaelic *claidheamh mór* broadsword, from *claidheamh* sword + *mór* great.]

clay pigeon 1. saucer-shaped clay disk tossed into the air as a target in trapshooting. **2.** *Slang.* person who can be taken advantage of easily.

-cle *suffix* used to form the diminutive of nouns: *corpuscle.* [French *-cle,* from Latin *-culus.*]

clean (klēn) *adj.* **1.** free from dirt or filth; unsoiled; unstained. **2.** free from foreign or extraneous matter; unadulterated; pure: *clean and wholesome air.* **3.** characterized by or having moral integrity; honorable: *clean living, a clean record.* **4.** fair or within the rules, as in

sports: *a clean fighter, a clean basketball game.* **5.** not obscene or indecent: *a clean joke.* **6.** free from embellishments or irregularities; even: *a clean incision, the clean lines of some modern sculpture.* **7.** complete; entire; thorough: *to make a clean break with the past.* **8.** trim; well-proportioned: *the clean limbs of a thoroughbred horse.* **9.** neat or clean in habits: *a clean housewife. The cat is a clean animal.* **10.** skillful; adroit; deft: *a clean golf swing.* **11.** empty or blank; bare: *a clean sheet of paper.* **12.** free from obstructions or restrictions: *a clean getaway.* **13.** having few corrections or alterations; legible: *clean copy for the printer.* **14.** (of nuclear devices) producing relatively little or no radioactive fallout. —*adv.* **1.** in a clean manner. **2.** completely; entirely; wholly: *The arrow passed clean through his body.* **3. to come clean.** *Slang.* to tell the truth; confess. —*v.t.* **1.** to make free of dirt, impurities, or extraneous matter: *to clean a car, to clean the dishes off a table.* **2.** to prepare food, as fowl, for cooking. **3. to clean out. a.** to remove dirt or trash from. **b.** to empty; exhaust: *to clean out a supply cabinet. Our customers cleaned out our stock during the last sale.* **c.** to take away the money or resources from: *His last business venture cleaned him out.* **4. to clean up. a.** to clear of dirt, trash, disorder, or other undesirable matter. **b.** *Informal.* to finish; complete: *We'll clean up this project before starting the next.* —*v.i.* **1.** to undergo or perform cleaning: *The maid cleaned thoroughly.* **2. to clean up. a.** to make oneself fresh or clean: *Let's clean up before we eat.* **b.** to finish one's work or assignment. **c.** *Slang.* to make a large profit. [Old English *clǣne* clear, pure.] —**clean′ness**, *n.* **Syn.** *v.t.* **1. Clean, cleanse** mean to rid of dirt or other impure substances. **Clean,** the general term, suggests methods, as brushing, sweeping, or scrubbing: *The crew cleaned the yard rapidly.* **Cleanse** suggests purification by technical, sometimes subtle, methods: *It is important to cleanse wounds.*
clean-cut (klēn′kut′) *adj.* **1.** sharply defined, as in outline or meaning; clear; definite: *a clean-cut statement of the facts.* **2.** having a wholesome appearance or personality: *a clean-cut young man.*
clean·er (klē′nər) *n.* **1.** one whose work or business is cleaning, esp. dry cleaning. **2.** that which cleans, as a machine or chemical substance.
clean-limbed (klēn′limd′) *adj.* having shapely or well-proportioned limbs.
clean·li·ness (klen′lē nis) *n.* state of being clean, esp. habitually clean.
clean·ly¹ (klen′lē) -li·er, -li·est. *adj.* carefully and habitually clean or kept clean. [Old English *clǣnlīc.*]
clean·ly² (klēn′lē) *adv.* in a clean manner. [Old English *clǣnlīce* purely, entirely.]
cleanse (klenz) **cleansed, cleans·ing.** *v.t.* **1.** to free from dirt, filth, or other undesirable matter: *to cleanse a wound.* **2.** to free from moral taint or guilt; purge: *to cleanse one's soul.* [Old English *clǣensian* to clean, purify.] —**Syn. 1.** see **clean.**
cleans·er (klen′zər) *n.* substance, as soap or detergent, that removes dirt or other undesirable matter.
clean-shav·en (klēn′shā′vən) *adj.* having all the hair, esp. the facial hair, shaved off.
clean-up (klēn′up′) *n.* **1.** thorough removal of dirt or disorder, esp. an elimination of vice or corruption. **2.** *Slang.* exceptionally large profit. —*adj.* designating the fourth position or batter in a baseball batting order.
clear (klēr) *adj.* **1.** free from anything that darkens, dims, or clouds; bright: *a clear morning, a clear sky.* **2.** free from anything impairing transparency or purity of color; not murky: *a clear yellow, clear water.* **3.** free from blemishes: *a clear complexion.* **4.** free from obstructions or hindrances; not blocked; open: *The road into town is now clear.* **5.** sharply defined and easily seen; not blurred; distinct: *a clear photograph, clear fingerprints.* **6.** easily understood; fully intelligible: *He gave a clear description of what happened.* **7.** not to be doubted; unmistakable: *It soon became clear he was lying.* **8.** free from confusion, uncertainty, or doubt; not vague: *clear thinking.* **9.** free from entanglement or connection; out of reach or touch; not in contact (often with *of*): *Stand clear of the falling tree. We kept clear of them after the quarrel.* **10.** undisturbed or untroubled; serene: *a clear brow, a clear conscience.* **11.** that discerns, reasons, or judges sharply and without confusion; perceptive: *a clear head, a clear mind, a clear thinker.* **12.** without limitation or qualification; complete; absolute: *a clear defeat.* **13.** without diminution or further cost to be deducted; net: *a clear profit. He made a clear $500 on the sale.* **14.** free from hoarse or rasping qualities; sounding distinctly or purely; plainly audible: *a clear voice, a clear tone.* **15.** free from knots, roughness, or protrusions: *a clear pine board.* —*adv.* **1.** in a clear manner; plainly; distinctly: *She shouted it loud and clear.* **2.** completely; entirely: *He climbed clear to the top.* —*v.t.* **1.** to free from that which occupies, obstructs, or impedes use or passage (often with *off, of,* or *out*): *Please clear the aisle. He cleared off the counter. They cleared the street of traffic.* **2.** to remove, as that which occupies, obstructs, or encumbers (often with *away, off,* or

out): *They cleared the spectators from the courtroom. The men cleared away the debris. Clear the dishes off the table. We cleared the snow out of the driveway.* **3.** to free from blemishes, impurities, or foreign matter (often with *up*): *This ointment should clear up your skin in a few days.* **4.** to pass by, over, or through without touching: *The runner cleared the hurdle. The plane barely cleared the trees.* **5.** to free of accusations or suspicions of guilt, blame, or responsibility; acquit; vindicate: *Her testimony cleared him of the charges. They struggled to clear their father's name.* **6.** to go through or away from, esp. without difficulty or entanglement; pass: *The bill cleared the Senate.* **7.** to submit for approval and receive authorization or clearance for: *We cleared the budgetary request with the accountant.* **8.** to give approval or clearance to or for; authorize: *The manager cleared them for top security research projects. The mechanics cleared the plane for take-off.* **9.** to remove cloudiness from; brighten: *to clear a mirror.* **10.** to free of confusion, uncertainty, or vagueness: *The cold shower cleared his head.* **11.** to remove accumulated totals or information or previously made settings from: *to clear an adding machine, to clear a cash register.* **12.** to gain as profit beyond expenses or charges; net: *He clears $20,000 annually.* **13.** to charge (a check) to an account having sufficient funds to cover the amount: *The bank cleared the check I wrote for the groceries.* **14.** to pass (checks, notes, or bills) through a clearinghouse in order to settle accounts between different banks. **15. to clear the air.** to dispel ambiguities or emotional tensions; settle misunderstandings or differences. —*v.i.* **1.** to become free of cloudiness, fog, or obscurity; grow bright or become fair, as the weather (often with *up*): *The sky cleared around noon. It finally cleared up after two days of rain.* **2.** to pass away or vanish; disperse; disappear (often with *away* or *up*): *When the smoke cleared away, we could see the rubble. The morning mist cleared before we left. His rash cleared up in a week.* **3.** to become free of confusion, uncertainty, or vagueness: *His head cleared after he'd eaten some breakfast. My vision cleared after I'd been up for a while.* **4.** to become free of murkiness: *We watched the solution clear in the test tube.* **5.** to obtain clearance. **6.** (of a check) to be charged to an account having sufficient funds to cover the amount. **7.** to pass checks, notes, or bills through a clearinghouse in order to settle accounts between different banks. **8.** *Informal.* to go away; depart; leave (often with *off* or *out*): *He told them to clear off or he'd call the police. The spy cleared out of the country.* **9. to clear up.** to clarify or solve: *to clear up a mystery, to clear up a misunderstanding.* —*n.* **in the clear.** *Informal.* free or absolved of guilt; not under suspicion. [Old French *cler* pure, bright, from Latin *clārus* bright, manifest.] —**clear′ly,** *adv.* —**clear′ness,** *n.*
Syn. *adj.* **2. Clear, transparent, translucent** refer to being able to see through something. **Clear** suggests that nothing interferes with vision: *Through the clear water, we could see fish on the bottom.* **Transparent** implies clarity that permits one to see right through something: *He covered the album page with transparent plastic to protect the stamps.* **Translucent** suggests enough light passing through to permit shapes, but not details, to be made out: *If it is cut into thin slabs, the marble is translucent.*
clear·ance (klēr′əns) *n.* **1.** act of clearing: *the slum clearance, the ship's narrow clearance of the harbor, the clearance of the trees for new construction.* **2.** approval or certification as free from objection, prohibition, or suspicion: *budgetary clearance for additional expenses. The scientist was given clearance to examine the secret plans.* **3.** disposal of merchandise, esp. discontinued stock, at reduced prices to make room for new goods. Also, **clearance sale.** **4.** permission to proceed, as after having satisfied certain requirements: *The plane received clearance from the control tower. The ship and its cargo received clearance at port.* **5.** official certificate granting such permission. Also, **clearance papers.** **6.** amount of clear space between two things, as between an overpass and the road underneath it: *This tunnel has a clearance of ten feet.* **7.** distance by which a moving object clears something: *a clearance of two feet between the truck and the walls of the tunnel.* **8.** process of clearing checks, notes, or bills through a clearinghouse.
clear-cut (klēr′kut′) *adj.* **1.** having a distinct outline: *the clear-cut features of his face, a clear-cut profile.* **2.** completely evident or clear; direct; definite: *His clear-cut explanation disposed of all possible doubt.*
clear-head·ed (klēr′hed′id) *adj.* not muddled or mentally confused; alert; sensible: *Although everyone was bewildered, he remained clear-headed enough to give instructions. They suggested a clear-headed approach to the problem.* —**clear′-head·ed·ly,** *adv.* —**clear′-head′-ed·ness,** *n.*
clear·ing (klēr′ing) *n.* **1.** tract of land, esp. within a densely wooded area, free of trees, brush, or other obstructions. **2.** exchange between banks of checks, notes, or bills in a clearinghouse to settle differences in accounts.
clear·ing·house (klēr′ing hous′) also, **clearing house.** *n.* **1.** office maintained by a voluntary association, as of bankers or brokers, where accounts among its members are settled by the mutual exchange of checks, notes, bills, or stocks. **2.** any central source or headquarters

at; āpe; cär; end; mē; it; īce; hot; ōld; fôrk; wood; fōol; oil; out; up; ūse; turn; sing; thin; this; zh in treasure; ə in ago, taken, pencil, lemon, circus.

185

for assignment, collection, or distribution, as of funds or information.
clear-sight-ed (klēr′sī′tid) adj. **1.** having or showing acute and ac-curate perception and sound judgment; discerning. **2.** having keen vision. —**clear′-sight′ed-ly,** adv. —**clear′-sight′ed-ness,** n.

clear-sto-ry (klēr′stôr′ē) clere-story.

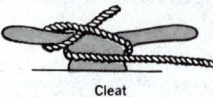
Cleat

cleat (klēt) n. **1.a.** protruding piece of rubber or metal attached to the sole of a shoe to increase traction. **b. cleats.** sports shoes that grip the ground by means of cleats on the sole, used chiefly in football, baseball, and track. **2.** wedgelike metal or wood block with projections at both ends, used for controlling or securing ropes, esp. on the spar or rail of a boat. **3.** piece of wood or iron fastened across a surface as a support or to prevent slipping, as on a ramp. —v.t. **1.** to furnish with a cleat or cleats. **2.** to fasten to or with a cleat. [Middle English clete wedge, from an unrecorded Old English word.]

cleav-a-ble (klē′və bəl) adj. capable of being cleft or split.

cleav-age (klē′vij) n. **1.** process or state of being cleft; fissure; rift: cleavage of opinion, the cleavage between social classes. **2.a.** series of cell divisions by which a fertilized egg splits into a number of smaller cells without increasing in overall size. This process changes the egg into an embryo. **b.** any one of these cell divisions. **3.** tendency of certain crystals and rocks to split in a way that produces smooth plane surfaces. **4.** Informal. space between a woman's breasts, esp. as emphasized by a low neckline.

cleave¹ (klēv) cleft or cleaved or clove, cleft or cleaved or clo-ven, cleav-ing. v.t. **1.** to split or part by force; rend apart; divide: The lightning cleft the tree. **2.** to pass through; pierce: The ship's prow clove the choppy waters. **3.** to form by or as by cutting: to cleave a trail through the forest. —v.i. **1.** to come apart; split. **2.** to advance or penetrate (with through): The ship cleaves through the waves. [Old English clēofan to split.]

Cleaver

cleave² (klēv) cleaved or (archaic) clave, cleaved, cleav-ing. v.i. **1.** to stick fast; adhere (with to): Mud cleaved to his shoes. **2.** to remain attached, devoted, or faithful (with to): to cleave to a principle. [Old English cleofian, clifian to stick, adhere.]

cleav-er (klē′vər) n. heavy, short-handled, broadbladed implement for chopping meat, used esp. by butchers.

cleek (klēk) n. a golf club having a wooden head, used chiefly for long-distance shots. [Middle English cleke hook, from cleken to seize (with the hand or a hook), from an unrecorded Old English word.]

clef (klef) n. Music. symbol placed on a given line of a staff to indicate the name and pitch of the notes on the various lines and spaces. [French clef key, key in music, from Latin clāvis key.]

Treble clef / Bass clef / Alto / Tenor

C clefs

Clef

cleft¹ (kleft) n. **1.** space or opening made by splitting; crack; fissure: a cleft in a rock. **2.** indentation made by separation of parts: the cleft in a horse's hoof. [Modification of earlier clift crack, split, from Old English (ge)clyft.]

cleft² (kleft) v. a past tense and past participle of cleave¹. —adj. **1.** appearing to be split; partially or completely divided: a cleft chin. **2.** Botany. having deep narrow divisions, as a leaf.

cleft palate. complete or partial split along the length of the palate of the mouth, resulting from faulty embryonic development.

cleis-tog-a-mous (klīs tog′ə məs) adj. (of flowers) small, closed, and self-pollinated. [Greek kleistos shut + gamos marriage.]

clem-a-tis (klem′ə tis) n. any of a group of climbing plants, genus Clematis, widely distributed in temperate regions and cultivated for their showy white, red, blue, or purple flowers. [Latin clēmatis, from Greek klēmatis, from klēma vine branch; referring to its long, twining branches.]

Clem-en-ceau, Georges (klem′ən sō′; zhôrzh) 1841–1929, French statesman and author, premier of France from 1906 to 1909 and from 1917 to 1920.

clem-en-cy (klem′ən sē) n. **1.** disposition to be forbearing, forgiving, or merciful in punishing or judging; leniency: The man showed clemency in his refusal to prosecute the thief. **2.** (of weather or climate) temperateness; mildness. [Latin clēmentia.] —Syn. **1.** see mercy.

Clem-ens, Samuel Lang-horne (klem′ənz; lang′hôrn′) see Twain, Mark.

clem-ent (klem′ənt) adj. **1.** forbearing, forgiving, or merciful in disposition or character; lenient: a clement judge, a clement use of authority.

2. (of weather or climate) temperate; mild. [Latin clēmēns.] —**clem′-ent-ly,** adv.

clench (klench) v.t. **1.** to close or press together tensely or tightly: to clench one's fists, to clench one's teeth. **2.** to grasp or grip firmly or tensely; clutch: She clenched her mother's hand as they headed for the doctor's office. **3.** to clinch (defs. 2, 3). —n. **1.** act or instance of clenching; firm or tense grasp or grip. **2.** that which clenches or grips. [Old English (be)clencan to hold fast.]

Cle-o-pat-ra (klē′ə pat′rə, -pät′-) 69–30 B.C., queen of Egypt from 51 to 49 B.C. and from 48 to 30 B.C.

clep-sy-dra (klep′si drə) pl., -dras or -drae (-drē). n. water clock. [Latin clepsydra, from Greek klep-sydrā, from kleptein to steal + hydōr water; referring to the water's stealing out of the vessel.]

clere-sto-ry (klēr′stôr′ē) pl., -ries. also, clear-sto-ry. n. highest story or uppermost portion of a wall of a building, esp. a church, having a series of windows for lighting and airing the interior. [Earlier clere light, clear + STORY²; referring to its windows. See CLEAR.]

Clerestory

cler-gy (klur′jē) pl., -gies. n. body of persons ordained for religious service, as ministers, priests, or rabbis, collectively. Distinguished from laity. [Old French clergie clerkship, body of clergymen, from clerc clergyman, from Latin clēricus. See CLERIC.]

cler-gy-man (klur′jē mən) pl., -men. n. one ordained as a minister, priest, or rabbi; member of the clergy.

cler-ic (kler′ik) n. clergyman. —adj. clerical (def. 2). [Latin clēricus clergyman, from Greek klērikos clergyman, relating to the clergy, from klēros clergy; originally, lot; because their lot is the service of God.]

cler-i-cal (kler′i kəl) adj. **1.** of or relating to clerks or office workers or their work: clerical errors, clerical duties. **2.** of, relating to, or characteristic of a clergyman or the clergy: clerical robes. **3.** advocating clericalism. —n. **1.** clergyman. **2. clericals.** clerical attire, as a cassock, worn by certain clergymen when not officiating at religious services. [Late Middle English clericalis relating to the clergy, from Latin clēricus clergyman. See CLERIC.] —**cler′i-cal-ly,** adv.

clerical collar. stiff, white, bandlike collar fastened at the back of the neck and worn without a tie by certain clergymen.

cler-i-cal-ism (kler′i kə liz′əm) n. **1.** excessive power or influence of the clergy in politics or secular affairs. **2.** belief in the desirability of such power or influence. —**cler′i-cal-ist,** n.

clerk (klurk; British klärk) n. **1.** one employed, as in a commercial establishment, to handle correspondence, keep records, accounts, or files, and do other general office work, as typing. **2.** salesclerk. **3.** one whose job involves direct dealing with, or service to, customers or clients: a room clerk in a hotel, a reservations clerk for an airline. **4.** official who keeps records and correspondence and performs routine business, as in a court of law or legislature: a county clerk, a town clerk. **5.** attorney who works as an assistant to a judge after having been admitted to the bar. **6.** layman or student of the ministry who assists the parish priest. **7.** Archaic. literate person; scholar. **8.** Archaic. clergyman. —v.i. **1.** to work or act as a clerk: He clerks behind the glove counter. **2.** (of an attorney) to work as an assistant to a judge after having been admitted to the bar. [Partly from Old English cler(i)c clergyman, partly from Old French clerc clergyman, official in charge of records and correspondence, both from Latin clēricus clergyman. Since education and, therefore, writing duties in the Middle Ages were done largely by the clergy, clerk came to denote notaries and literate persons as well as priests. See CLERIC.] —**clerk′ship,** n.

clerk-ly (klurk′lē) -li-er, -li-est. adj. **1.** of, relating to, or characteristic of a clerk. **2.** Archaic. learned; scholarly.

Cler-mont-Fer-rand (kler môn′ fe räN′) n. city in south-central France. Pop. (1968), 148,896.

Cleve-land (klēv′lənd) n. **1.** largest city in Ohio, a port in the northeastern part of the state, on Lake Erie. Pop. (1970), 750,903. **2. (Stephen) Grover.** 1837–1908, twenty-second and twenty-fourth president of the United States, from 1885 to 1889 and from 1893 to 1897.

Cleveland Heights, city in northeastern Ohio, a residential suburb of Cleveland. Pop. (1970), 60,767.

clev-er (klev′ər) adj. **1.** mentally keen and alert; shrewd; quick-witted: a clever young man, a clever liar. **2.** showing skill or mental keenness; shrewd; ingenious: a clever scheme, a clever remark. **3.** having or showing skill in performing a physical act, esp. with the hands; adroit. [Of uncertain origin.] —**clev′er-ly,** adv. —**clev′er-ness,** n.

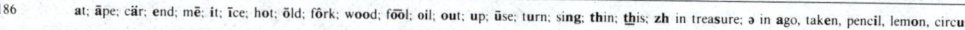

at; āpe; cär; end; mē; it; īce; hot; ōld; fôrk; wood; fo͞ol; out; up; ūse; turn; sing; thin; this; zh in treasure; ə in ago, taken, pencil, lemon, circus.

Syn. 1. Clever, adroit, ingenious point to a resourceful mind. **Clever** indicates facility and intelligence: *He is a clever card player who almost always wins.* **Adroit** adds cunning and flexibility: *Trapping so adroit a witness in a lie proved to be impossible.* **Ingenious** suggests intellectual brilliance and inventive skill: *He developed an ingenious machine for garbage disposal.*

clev·is (klev′is) *n.* fastening device consisting of a U-shaped piece of metal into which something, as a shaft, hook, or lever, can be bolted. [Possibly of Scandinavian origin.]

clew (kloō) *n.* **1.** *British.* clue (def. 1). **2.** ball of thread, yarn, or cord. **3.** either lower corner of a square sail or the lower aft corner of a fore-and-aft sail. —*v.t. also,* **clue. 1.** to coil or roll into a ball. **2.** to raise or lower (a sail) by the clews. [Old English *cleowen, cliwen* ball of thread. In certain legends, as that of Theseus, a ball of thread served as a means of solving a problem (or *clue*), for it was used in escaping from a labyrinth.]

clew-line (kloō′līn′) *n.* rope attached to the clew of a square sail, used to raise and lower the sail.

cli·ché (klē shā′) *n.* **1.** expression, phrase, or idea made trite by overuse, as *pretty as a picture.* **2.** trite or hackneyed plot, theme, or motif, as in art or literature. [French *cliché* stereotype plate, trite expression, from *clicher* to stereotype, imitative of the sound of the die hitting the metal; referring to the repetition of an expression or phrase over and over again in the same way.] —**Syn. 1.** see **truism.**

click (klik) *n.* **1.** light, sharp, often metallic sound: *the click of her fingernails on the typewriter keys, the click of his key in the lock.* **2.** pawl. **3.** speech sound, esp. characteristic of certain South African languages, produced by pressing the tongue against some part of the mouth and quickly withdrawing it with a sucking action. Also, **suction stop.** —*v.t.* to move (something) with a click; cause to make a click or clicks: *to click one's heels together. He sat there clicking the top of his pen.* —*v.i.* **1.** to move with a click; produce a click or clicks: *Her high heels clicked on the sidewalk.* **2.** *Informal.* **a.** to fit or function harmoniously; agree: *The dress clicked with the rest of her wardrobe.* **b.** to become comprehensible or intelligible; make sense. **3.** *Slang.* to be a success; do or go well: *The show clicked.* [Imitative.]

click beetle, any of a group of beetles, family Elateridae, that when placed on their backs throw themselves into the air and right themselves while making a loud snapping noise. Also, **snapping beetle.**

cli·ent (klī′ənt) *n.* **1.** one who or that which engages the professional advice or services of another: *an advertising agency with many clients, a lawyer who had many corporations for clients.* **2.** customer (def. 1). **3.** one who receives benefits or services from a government bureau or social service agency. **4.** in ancient Rome, one, esp. a plebian, under the guardianship and protection of a patrician. [Latin *cliēns* retainer[1], dependent.] —**Syn. 2.** see **customer.**

cli·en·tele (klī′ən tel′) *n.* clients or customers collectively. [French *clientèle,* from Latin *clientēla.*]

cliff (klif) *n.* high, steep, often perpendicular or overhanging face of rock, earth, or glacial ice. [Old English *clif* rock, steep descent.]

cliff dweller 1. *also,* **Cliff Dweller.** member of a tribe of prehistoric Indians, the ancestors of the Pueblo Indians of the southwestern United States, who built their houses in ledges of cliff walls. **2.** *Informal.* one who lives in an apartment house, esp. in a large city.

cliff-hang·er (klif′hang′ər) *also,* **cliff-hang·er** *n.* **1.** exciting adventure serial or melodrama, esp. one presented in installments each of which ends in suspense. **2.** any contest or situation having an uncertain and anxiously awaited outcome: *The election was a real cliff-hanger.*

cliff swallow, migratory swallow, *Petrochelidon pyrrhonota,* that lives in colonies in bottle-shaped mud nests under the eaves of buildings or against cliffs.

Clif·ton (klif′tən) *n.* city in northeastern New Jersey. Pop. (1970), 82,437.

cli·mac·ter·ic (klī mak′tər ik, klī′mak ter′ik) *n.* **1.** critical or crucial period or stage, as a major turning point in a person's life. **2.** any period of life in which major physiological changes, esp. the menopause, are supposed to occur. —*adj. also,* **cli·mac·ter′i·cal.** of or relating to a critical period. [Latin *climactēricus* relating to a critical period, from Greek *klīmaktērikos,* from *klīmaktēr* critical period, rung of a ladder.]

cli·mac·tic (klī mak′tik) *adj.* of, relating to, or constituting a climax: *The third scene was a climactic one.*

cli·mate (klī′mit) *n.* **1.** weather characteristic of or prevailing in an area over an extended period of time, usually considered in terms of average temperature, humidity, precipitation, and wind conditions. **2.** area or region considered with regard to its characteristic or prevailing weather: *He liked living in cooler climates.* **3.** prevailing temper, trend, or conditions: *the climate of opinion. The climate on campus was one of unrest.* [Late Latin *climat-,* stem of *clima* region, weather of a region, from Greek *klīma.*] —**cli·mat·ic** (klī mat′ik); *also,* **cli·mat′i·cal,** *adj.* —**cli·mat′i·cal·ly,** *adv.*

cli·ma·tol·o·gy (klī′mə tol′ə jē) *n.* science dealing with the study of climate. —**cli·ma·to·log·ic** (klī′mə tə loj′ik); *also,* **cli′ma·to·log′i·cal,** *adj.* —**cli′ma·to·log′i·cal·ly,** *adv.* —**cli′ma·tol′o·gist,** *n.*

cli·max (klī′maks) *n.* **1.** highest point, as of development, intensity, interest, or excitement; culmination: *His election to the presidency was the climax of his career.* **2.** turning point or point of highest dramatic tension in the action or theme of a play, book, or the like. **3.** final stage in the ecological development of a given community in which plant and animal life is stable and self-perpetuating and will remain so unless disturbed by some natural disaster. —*v.i., v.t.* to reach or bring to a climax: *The play climaxed in the third act. The evening was climaxed by his memorable speech.* [Late Latin *climax* ascending series of expressions, from Greek *klīmax* ladder, ascending series of expressions.]

climb (klīm) climbed *or (archaic)* clomb, climb·ing. *v.i.* **1.** to move upward or toward the top of something by using the hands or feet: *We climbed for an hour before we reached a ledge on the mountain. He climbed clear to the top of the tree.* **2.** to move or proceed by using the hands or feet: *to climb through a window, to climb into bed.* **3.** to move upward or move higher, as if by climbing; rise: *a country that climbed to a pinnacle of power. The plane climbed to an altitude of 12,000 feet. Prices climbed last summer.* **4.** to have height or elevation; extend upward: *The building climbs to a height of 20 stories.* **5.** to grow in an upward direction, as certain plants, by twining around or clinging to another object for support: *The vines climbed up the latticework along the door.* —*v.t.* to move toward the top of or up (something), esp. by using the hands or feet: *He climbed the ladder. The car climbed the hill with difficulty.* —*n.* **1.** act or process of climbing; ascent: *his climb to fame and fortune. Their climb up the hill took an hour.* **2.** distance to be climbed: *It's only a short climb to the top from here.* **3.** place or thing to be climbed: *That mountain is quite a treacherous climb.* [Old English *climban* to move upward by using the hands or feet.]

Syn. *v.t.* **Climb, ascend, mount[1], scale[3]** mean to move up something high or steep. **Climb** suggests extra effort or help: *It took them several hours to climb the bluff.* **Ascend** implies less effort, simply suggesting upward movement: *They ascended the slope by using the newly installed ski lift.* **Mount** stresses reaching a higher level, esp. the top of something: *He mounted the steps to the fountain.* **Scale** suggests effort and motion upward in stages: *They scaled the rock face and moved toward the snow field.*

climb·er (klī′mər) *n.* **1.** one who or that which climbs. **2.** climbing plant, as ivy. **3.** climbing iron. **4.** *Informal.* social climber.

climbing iron, one of a pair of frames with metal spikes or spurs attached, for strapping to the legs or shoes to aid in climbing trees, telephone poles, or the like.

clime (klīm) *n. Archaic.* country; region; climate. [Late Latin *clīmu.* See CLIMATE.]

Clinch (def. 3)

clinch (klinch) *v.t.* **1.** to make final and definite; settle conclusively: *to clinch a deal.* **2.** to fasten or secure firmly, as a driven nail or bolt, by bending over or flattening the protruding point. **3.** to fasten (objects) together by using nails, bolts, or the like secured in this way. Also *(defs. 2, 3),* **clench.** —*v.i.* **1.** to engage in a clinch, esp. in boxing. **2.** *Slang.* to embrace passionately. —*n.* **1.** act of clinching. **2.** a grasping or holding of an opponent's arms or body by one or both fighters, esp. in boxing, to prevent or hinder punching. **3.** *Nautical.* half hitch in which the loose end of the rope is lashed back on the knot it has formed. **4.** *Slang.* close or passionate embrace. [Form of CLENCH.]

clinch·er (klin′chər) *n.* **1.** one who or that which clinches, esp. a nail made for clinching. **2.** *Informal.* that which is deciding or conclusive, as a point made in an argument: *Of all the reasons for not moving there, the high cost of living is the clincher.*

cling (kling) clung, cling·ing. *v.i.* **1.** to adhere closely, as if glued; stick: *The wet shirt clung to his back.* **2.** to hold tightly, as by grasping or embracing: *The shivering children clung to each other in fear.* **3.** to remain close or in contact; be or stay near, as if attached: *She clung to his side. The car clung to the road as it took the curves.* **4.** to remain emotionally attached; abide faithfully by; refuse to part with (with *to*): *He clings to his routine. They still cling to their cherished, outdated ideas.* —*n.* clingstone. [Old English *clingan* to shrink, contract.]

clinging vine, *Informal.* woman who displays helpless or excessive dependence on a man.

cling·stone (kling′stōn′) *n.* fruit, esp. a peach, in which the flesh adheres to the stone. Distinguished from *freestone.* Also, **cling.**

clin·ic (klin′ik) *n.* **1.** institution or building, often connected with a hospital or medical school, where outpatients are treated, often for a reduced fee. **2.** institution or part of an institution where specialists cooperate in the study, diagnosis, and treatment of certain types of

patients or certain diseases: *a cancer clinic, a maternity clinic.* **3.** organization or institution offering advice, remedial work, repair, or instruction in some specific field: *a marriage clinic, a reading clinic, a doll clinic.* **4.** instruction given by doctors to medical students in the presence of a patient in which the patient is examined, his illness discussed, and treatment recommended. **5.** meeting in which such instruction takes place. [Latin *clīnicus* doctor treating patients in bed, from Greek *klīnikos* relating to a bed, doctor treating patients in bed, from *klīnē* bed.]

clin·i·cal (klin′i kəl) *adj.* **1.** of or relating to a clinic. **2.** based on or dealing with the direct observation and treatment of patients rather than laboratory experimentation. **3.** coolly scientific or analytical; unemotional; detached. **4.** relating to the course of a disease or the care of a patient. **5.** (of a sacrament) administered on a sickbed or deathbed: *clinical baptism, clinical conversion.* —**clin′i·cal·ly,** *adv.*

clinical thermometer, thermometer used to measure body temperature.

clink¹ (klingk) *v.t., v.i.* to make or cause to make a light, sharp, ringing sound: *They clinked their glasses together in a toast. The coins clinked in his pocket.* —*n.* light, sharp, ringing or tinkling sound. [Possibly from Middle Dutch *clinken* to sound; imitative.]

clink² (klingk) *n. Slang.* jail; prison. [Possibly from *Clink*, an English prison in London; possibly referring to the *clinking* of chains in a prison.]

clink·er (kling′kər) *n.* **1.** hard residue consisting of impurities that remain after coal is burned. **2.** very hard brick. **3.** slag. **4.** *Slang.* **a.** mistake; error. **b.** any utter failure, esp. an inferior product. [Earlier *klincard*, from obsolete Dutch *klinkaard* brick that rings when struck; literally, that which clinks, from *klinken* to sound.]

clink·er-built (kling′kər bilt′) *adj.* built or faced with overlapping planks, boards, or plates, as a ship.

cli·nom·e·ter (klī nom′ə tər, kli-) *n.* instrument for measuring angles of inclination or slope. [Greek *klinein* to slope + -METER.]

Clin·ton, De Witt (klin′tən; di wit′) 1769–1828, U.S. statesman.

Cli·o (klī′ō) *n. Greek Mythology.* Muse of history. [Latin *Clīo,* from Greek *Kleiō* literally, the proclaimer, from *kleiein* to tell of, make famous.]

clip¹ (klip) *clipped, clip·ping. v.t.* **1.** to cut, as with shears or scissors; remove or detach by severing: *to clip wool from sheep. She clipped off the loose strands of thread. He clipped the article out of the paper.* **2.** to make shorter by cutting; trim: *to clip one's nails, to clip a hedge.* **3.** to trim or cut the hair or fleece of: *to clip a poodle, to clip sheep.* **4.** to cut short; curtail; abridge. **5.** to pronounce rapidly, crisply, and distinctly, often omitting certain sounds: *She clipped her words angrily.* **6.** to pare the edge of (a coin). **7.** *Informal.* to hit with a quick, sharp blow: *to clip someone on the chin.* **8.** *Slang.* to cheat or swindle, esp. by overcharging: *The salesman clipped him by overcharging five dollars.* —*v.i.* **1.** to cut or trim. **2.** *Informal.* to move rapidly: *He clipped along at 70 m.p.h.* —*n.* **1.** act of clipping. **2.** quantity of wool obtained from sheep at one shearing or during one season. **3.** *clips.* clippers or shears. **4.** *Informal.* **a.** rate or pace: *He moved along at a good clip.* **b.** quick, sharp blow or punch. **c.** single instance or occasion: *He corrected twenty exams at a clip.* [Old Norse *klippa* to cut; imitative.]

clip² (klip) *n.* **1.** device that grips or holds articles together, as a paper clip or a clasp for the hair: *a money clip, a tie clip.* **2.** holder for ammunition for certain firearms that fits into the magazine. —*v.t., clipped, clip·ping.* **1.** to fasten with or as with a clip: *He clipped the sheets together.* **2.** *Football.* to block (an opposing player not carrying the ball), usually from behind, by illegally throwing the body across the lower part of the player's legs. [Old English *clyppan* to embrace.]

clip·board (klip′bôrd′) *n.* board with a spring clip at one end for holding paper, a pad, or the like, used as a portable writing surface.

clip joint *Slang.* nightclub, store, or other establishment that cheats or overcharges customers.

clip·per (klip′ər) *n.* **1.** *also,* **clip·pers.** tool or instrument for clipping, cutting, or shearing: *a barber's clippers.* **2.** fast-sailing cargo ship developed in the

Clipper

United States in the nineteenth century, having a narrow beam and, usually, three square-rigged masts. **3.** one who clips.

clip·ping (klip′ing) *n.* that which is cut off or out, esp. an item cut from a newspaper or magazine.

clique (klēk, klik) *n.* small, exclusive group of people, often snobbish or having some aim or intrigue in common. [French *clique,* possibly from Middle French *clique* latch (in the sense of a secretive group

closed, or latched in, together), from *cliquer* to click; imitative.] —**cli′quey;** *also,* **cli′quy,** *adj.*

cli·quish (klē′kish, klik′ish) *adj.* **1.** disposed to form or adhere to a clique. **2.** having the characteristics of a clique; exclusive. —**cli′quish·ly,** *adv.* —**cli′quish·ness,** *n.*

clit·o·ris (klit′ər is, klī′tər-) *n. Anatomy.* small erectile organ at the upper end of the vulva, homologous to the penis. [Greek *kleitoris.*]

Clive, Robert (klīv) 1725–74, English general and statesman in India.

clo·a·ca (klō ā′kə) *pl.,* **-cae** (-sē). *n.* **1.** chamber found in birds, fish, reptiles, amphibians, and some primitive mammals, into which the intestinal, urinary, and genital tracts open. **2.** sewer. [Latin *cloāca* sewer, drain.]

cloak (klōk) *n.* **1.** loose outer garment, with or without sleeves. **2.** something that covers or conceals; disguise; pretense: *under a cloak of secrecy.* —*v.t.* **1.** to cover with or as with a cloak. **2.** to cover; conceal; disguise: *The meeting was cloaked in mystery.* [Old French *cloque, cloche* cape¹, bell, from Late Latin *clocca;* of Celtic origin; referring to the bell-like shape of a cape. Doublet of CLOCHE, CLOCK¹.] —**Syn.** *v.t.* **2.** see **mask.**

cloak-and-dag·ger (klōk′ən dag′ər) *adj.* characterized by exaggerated intrigue, as tales of spies and secret agents: *a cloak-and-dagger movie.*

cloak·room (klōk′rōōm′, -rōom′) *n.* room where wearing apparel, as coats and hats, or articles, as umbrellas, may be left temporarily.

clob·ber (klob′ər) *v.t. Slang.* **1.** to hit with overwhelming force. **2.** to defeat utterly. [Of uncertain origin.]

cloche (klōsh) *n.* close-fitting, helmet-shaped hat for women, usually having a deep, rounded crown and brim. [French *cloche* bell, from Late Latin *clocca;* of Celtic origin. Doublet of CLOAK, CLOCK¹.]

clock¹ (klok) *n.* **1.** any of various instruments for measuring and indicating the passage of time, usually with hands that pass over a dial marked to show hours or minutes. Distinguished from **watch. 2.** time clock: *I couldn't stand a job where I'd have to punch a clock.* —*v.t.* to determine or record the performance or speed of; time, as with a stopwatch: *to clock a race, to clock a runner.* [Middle Dutch *clocke* clock (the instrument), bell, from Late Latin *clocca* bell; of Celtic origin; possibly because many clocks had bells with which to strike the hour. Doublet of CLOAK, CLOCHE.] —**clock′er,** *n.*

clock² (klok) *n.* decorative pattern woven or embroidered on the side of a stocking. [Probably from CLOCK¹; because originally a bell-shaped ornament.]

clock·ra·di·o (klok′rā′dē ō′) *n.* radio equipped with a clock and alarm mechanism and designed so that the clock can be set to turn on the radio, with or without the alarm, at any chosen time.

clock·wise (klok′wīz′) *adv., adj.* in the direction in which the hands of a clock rotate.

clock·work (klok′wurk′) *n.* **1.** mechanism consisting of gears, wheels, and springs, as that which runs mechanical devices. **2.** like clockwork. with regularity, precision, and smoothness; perfectly.

clod (klod) *n.* **1.** lump or mass, esp. of earth or clay. **2.** dull, awkward, or stupid person; dolt. [Modification of Middle English *clot* lump, clot. See CLOT.]

clod·hop·per (klod′hop′ər) *n.* **1.** *Informal.* clumsy, awkward boor; bumpkin. **2.** any large, heavy, clumsy-looking shoe or boot.

clog (klog) *clogged, clog·ging. v.t.* **1.** to stuff or stop up, as with thick or sticky matter; block; obstruct: *to clog a drain, to clog the pores of the skin.* **2.** to impede or encumber the progress or action of. —*v.i.* to become obstructed, stopped up, or impeded. —*n.* **1.** shoe or sandal with a thick sole of wood or cork. **2.** block of wood or other weight fastened, as to a horse, to hinder movement or prevent escape. **3.** anything that impedes or encumbers. [Of uncertain origin.]

clog dance, dance, as any of several folk dances of France or Holland, in which clogs are worn to beat out the rhythm.

cloi·son·né (kloi′zə nā′) *n.* technique or process of decorating metal objects by applying thin strips of metal in a pattern and filling the spaces with colored enamel. —*adj.* relating to or formed or decorated by this technique. [French *cloisonné* partitioned, past participle of *cloisonner* to partition, from *cloison* partition, going back to Latin *clausus,* past participle of *claudere* to close.]

clois·ter (klois′tər) *n.* **1.** place of religious seclusion, as a convent or monastery. **2.** seclusion of a cloister; monastic life. **3.a.** covered walk or arcade along the wall or walls of a

Cloister

at; āpe; cär; end; mē; it; īce; hot; ōld; fôrk; wood; fōōl; oil; out; up; ūse; turn; sing; thin; this; zh in treasure; ə in ago, taken, pencil, lemon, circus.

building, having a row of columns on one side and usually built around the courtyard of a monastery, church, or college building. **b.** open courtyard surrounded by such walks, usually square or rectangular in shape. **4.** any place of quiet seclusion. —*v.t.* to confine in or as if in a cloister; seclude. [Old French *cloistre, clostre* place of religious seclusion, going back to Latin *claustrum* enclosed place, bar.]

Syn. *n.* **1. Cloister, convent, monastery** refer to places where members of a religious community may retire from the everyday world. **Cloister** emphasizes isolation: *The orthodox saying was that a monk out of his cloister was like a fish out of water* (Power, 1924). **Convent** stresses the idea of community and has become limited to a house of nuns: *Most of the records which survived were found in the archives of convents of Franciscan nuns* (Heer, 1966). **Monastery** is a cloister for men: *The monasteries took no small pride in their distinguished members and there is a good deal of jealousy among them* (Waddell, 1927).

clois·tered (klois'tərd) *adj.* **1.** retired or secluded from the world; sheltered: *a cloistered academic life.* **2.** living in a cloister or cloisters: *cloistered nuns.*

clone (klōn) *n.* any group of genetically identical individuals reproduced asexually from a single ancestor. —*v.i., v.t.* to reproduce asexually. [Greek *klōn* twig.]

clo·nus (klō'nəs) *n.* series of muscular spasms in which rigidity and relaxation alternate rapidly. [Modern Latin *clonus,* from Greek *klonos* violent motion, turmoil.] —**clo·nic** (klō'nik, klon'ik), *adj.*

close (*v., n. defs. 1, 3,* klōz; *adj. adv., n. def. 2,* klōs) **closed, clos·ing.** *v.t.* **1.** to move (something) into a position so as to obstruct or eliminate an entrance, passage, or opening; shut: *to close a window, to close a drawer, to close one's mouth.* **2.** to bring together the parts of so as to eliminate openings or gaps or form a whole (often with *up*): *to close a penknife, to close a book, to close one's fist, to close up the ranks.* **3.** to fill or obstruct; stop up: *Rocks from the landslide closed the mountain pass.* **4.** to suspend or stop the operations of (often with *up* or *down*): *to close an account. They closed the schools because of the blizzard.* **5.** to prevent or restrict access to or passage across (often with *off*): *Officials closed the western border to tourists. The workmen closed off the street for repairs.* **6.** to bring to a conclusion; end; finish: *to close a deal. He closed his lecture with a humorous anecdote.* **7.** to shut in; enclose; confine: *They closed him in the room as a punishment.* **8.** to shut off, as from suggestion or change; make unresponsive or impervious: *She closed her mind to opposing arguments.* —*v.i.* **1.** to become shut: *The door closed with a bang.* **2.** to suspend or stop operation: *Banks close on legal holidays.* **3.** to come to a conclusion; end; finish: *His essay closes with a dramatic accusation.* **4.** to come together, as parts of a whole (often with *up*): *The wound closed up after a week. The waters closed over his head.* **5.** to engage in hand-to-hand fighting; come near or up to so as to attack; grapple (often with *with*): *We closed with the enemy before dark.* **6.** to draw near (often with *on*): *His pursuers closed in on him rapidly.* **7.** to be at a certain point or worth a certain amount at the end of a business day: *The market closed at 4.75. That stock closed two points higher today.* **8.** to sign final papers for the sale of real estate. **9. to close in (on). a.** to advance upon or surround (something or someone) so as to prevent escape: *The police closed in on the hide-out.* **b.** to envelop or approach (something or someone) from all sides, as if to shut in or entrap: *The walls seemed to close in on him. We were still lost as night was closing in.* **10. to close out.** to dispose of (all or particular merchandise), usually at greatly reduced prices, so as to make room for new stock or to liquidate a business: *The merchant closed out his summer stock.* —*adj.* **clos·er, clos·est.** **1.** being in or having proximity in time or space; with little or no intervening distance: *He fired at close range. Those holidays follow in close succession.* **2.** being in or having proximity in relation, degree, effect, or condition: *a close cousin. She's close to tears. Spanish is close to Italian.* **3.** having component parts or elements near each other; compact; dense: *a close weave, a close formation of troops.* **4.** attached or characterized by strong affection, intimacy, or loyalty: *a close friend, a close friendship. My sister and I are very close.* **5.** conforming to or approximating a model or original: *a close translation, a close copy, a close resemblance.* **6.** directed or maintained strictly and undeviatingly; thorough; rigorous: *under close surveillance, a close examination of his motives.* **7.** near to the ground, skin, or other surface: *a close haircut.* **8.** established or decided by a narrow margin: *a close race.* **9.** fitting snugly or tightly: *a close cap.* **10.** confined in space; cramped; crowded. **11.** lacking freely circulating air; oppressive, stifling, or stuffy: *It's very close outside today. It's very close in this room.* **12.** in strict confinement; carefully guarded: *a close secret.* **13.** marked by a narrow escape; barely avoiding disaster: *That was close—next time they'll catch us.* **14.** secretive in manner; uncommunicative; reticent. **15.** stingy; miserly. **16.** difficult to obtain; scarce, as money or credit. **17.** shut or shut in; not open: *close hatches.* **18.** strictly ordered and logical: *close reasoning.* **19.** Phonetics. (of a vowel) articulated with the tongue close to or touching the palate, as the vowels in *feet.* —*adv.* in a close manner;

closely: *He held her close in his arms. You're not parked close enough to the curb.* —*n.* **1.** conclusion; end; finish: *the close of day, to bring the case to a close.* **2.** enclosed place, esp. enclosed land surrounding or beside a cathedral or other building. **3.** act of closing. [Old French *clos,* past participle of *clore* to shut, enclose, end, from Latin *claudere.*] —**close·ly** (klōs'lē), *adv.* —**close·ness** (klōs'nis), **clos·er** (klō'zər), *n.*

Syn. *adj.* **1.** see **near.** **3. Close, compact¹, crowded, dense** denote having parts very near each other. **Close** implies small space between parts, which usually remain individually distinguishable: *The houses seem to be built as close as possible to each other.* **Compact** suggests a squeezing together into minimum space, often with the connotation of efficient grouping of the parts: *An experienced camper knows how to arrange his supplies and equipment in a compact bundle.* **Crowded** implies a squeezing tightly together, but with a suggestion that the parts interfere with each other rather than being efficiently arranged: *Going to work downtown meant boarding a crowded bus every morning.* **Dense** implies a mass of similar things with very little space separating them: *The dense outer layer keeps moisture from reaching the animal's skin.* **4.** see **familiar.** —*v.t.* **6.** see **end.**

close call *Informal.* narrow escape.

close circuit **1.** electric circuit through which current can flow without interruption. **2.** television system in which signals are transmitted, usually by a cable, to a limited and predetermined number of receivers. Also (*def.* 2), **closed-circuit television.** —**closed'-cir'cuit,** *adj.*

closed corporation, corporation in which all or most of the stock is owned by a small number of people and whose stock is not for sale on the open market.

closed-end investment company (klōzd'end') investment company selling a fixed number of shares to the public and not obligated to redeem the holders' shares upon request. Distinguished from **mutual fund.**

closed primary, direct primary election in which only members of a given political party may vote.

closed shop, establishment in which only union members in good standing are hired and employed. Distinguished from **open shop** and **union shop.**

closed syllable, syllable ending in a consonant or consonant cluster, as *hat* and *hatch.*

close·fist·ed (klōs'fis'tid) *adj.* stingy; miserly.

close-grained (klōs'grānd') *adj.* having fine and closely arranged fibers, crystals, or particles; compact and dense in structure or texture, as wood.

close-hauled (klōs'hôld') *adj., adv.* with sails pulled in tight so as to sail as nearly as possible in the direction from which the wind is blowing.

close-mouthed (klōs'mouthd', -moutht') *adj.* not given to talking or disclosing information; secretive. Also, **close'-lipped'.**

close-or·der drill (klōs'ôr'dər) systematic practice in formation marching and the formal handling of arms in which the participants are arranged at close intervals.

close-out (klōz'out') *also,* **close-out.** *n.* sale in which all or particular merchandise is to be disposed of, usually at greatly reduced prices.

close quarters **1.** small, cramped place or position: *to live in close quarters.* **2.** immediate contact or close range: *to fight at close quarters.*

close shave *Informal.* narrow escape.

clos·et (kloz'it) *n.* **1.** small room or recess, usually enclosed, for storing clothing. **2.** cabinet, enclosed recess, or small room for storing household utensils, food, or other articles: *a china closet.* **3.** small, private room, esp. one for prayer, study, or consultation. **4.** water closet. —*v.t.* to confine or shut up in or as in a closet, as for a consultation or study: *He closeted himself in with his books for several hours.* [Old French *closet* small enclosure, diminutive of *close* enclosure, from *clore.* See CLOSE.]

close-up (klōs'up') *n.* **1.** photograph or television or motion-picture shot taken at close range or with a telescopic lens. **2.** detailed or intimate examination, as of an issue or person.

clos·ing (klō'zing) *n.* proceeding in which real estate is sold.

clo·sure (klō'zhər) *n.* **1.** act of closing; being closed. **2.** that which closes or shuts. **3.** a bringing to a conclusion; end. **4.** cloture. [Old French *closure* barrier, from Late Latin *clausūra* bar, bolt, from Latin *clausus,* past participle of *claudere* to close, shut.]

clot (klot) *n.* semi-solid or thickened mass, formed esp. by coagulation: *a clot of blood.* —*v.t., v.i.,* **clot·ted, clot·ting.** to form or cause to form into clots. [Old English *clot,* clott mass, lump.]

cloth (klôth) *pl.* **cloths** (klôthz, klôths). *n.* **1.** something made by weaving, knitting, braiding, or felting textile fibers; fabric. **2. the cloth.** the clergy: *a man of the cloth.* [Old English *clāth* fabric, garment.]

clothe (klōth) **clothed** *or* **clad, cloth·ing.** *v.t.* **1.** to put clothes on; dress. **2.** to provide with clothes. **3.** to cover as with clothing: *Snow clothed the field.* **4.** to endow; invest: *The judge was clothed with dignity.* [Old English *clāthian* to dress.]

at; āpe; cär; end; mē; it; īce; hot; ōld; fôrk; wood; fōōl; oil; out; up; ūse; turn; sing; thin; this; zh in treasure; ə in ago, taken, pencil, lemon, circus. 189

clothes (klōz, klō<u>th</u>z) n., pl. **1.** articles of clothing for the human body; attire. **2.** bedclothes.

clothes·horse (klōz′hôrs′, klō<u>th</u>z′-) n. **1.** frame on which clothes are hung to dry or air. **2.** Informal. one, esp. a woman, who is overly concerned with or interested in clothes.

clothes·line (klōz′līn′, klō<u>th</u>z′-) n. rope or wire on which articles, esp. clothes, are hung to dry or air.

clothes moth, any of various small moths, family Tineidae, whose larvae feed on wool, fur, and other materials made from, or soiled with, animal products.

clothes·pin (klōz′pin′, klō<u>th</u>z′-) n. clamp or forked piece of wood or plastic used to fasten clothes on a line.

clothes pole, pole used to support a clothesline.

clothes·press (klōz′pres′) n. place for keeping clothes; wardrobe.

clothes tree, upright pole with hooks or pegs near the top on which to hang clothes.

cloth·ier (klō<u>th</u>′yər, klō′<u>th</u>ē ər) n. one who sells or makes cloth or clothing.

cloth·ing (klō′<u>th</u>ing) n. **1.** articles worn to protect, cover, or adorn the body; clothes; attire; garments. **2.** covering.

Clo·tho (klō′thō) n. Greek Mythology. one of the three Fates, the spinner of the thread of life.

cloth yard, unit for measuring cloth, equal to the standard yard.

clo·ture (klō′chər) also, **clo·sure.** n. method of ending debate in a legislative body in order to bring a question to a vote. [French clôture closing, going back to Latin clausus, past participle of claudere to close.]

cloud (kloud) n. **1.** visible mass of water vapor or ice particles suspended in the atmosphere, usually at a considerable altitude. **2.** any similar mass, as of smoke, dust, or steam. **3.** great number or mass of persons or things in motion: a cloud of locusts, a cloud of arrows. **4.** something that obscures, darkens, or dims: a cloud of suspicion. **5.** dimness or murkiness in something otherwise clear or transparent: a cloud in the water. **6.** streak or spot of different, usually darker, color, as in marble. **7. in the clouds.** daydreaming. **8. under a cloud.** under suspicion; distrusted: His reputation was under a cloud. —v.t. **1.** to cover with or as with a cloud or clouds. **2.** to obscure, darken, or dim: to cloud the truth. His judgment was clouded by selfishness. **3.** to make gloomy or troubled: a face clouded with anxiety. **4.** to place under suspicion, as a reputation; sully. —v.i. to become overcast (often with up or over). [Old English clūd hill, rock; originally, mass.]

cloud·ber·ry (kloud′ber′ē) pl., **-ries.** n. **1.** edible, orange-yellow fruit of a plant, Rubus chamaemorus, a species of raspberry. **2.** the plant itself, found in cold regions of the Northern Hemisphere, bearing rounded, lobed leaves and large white flowers.

cloud·burst (kloud′bûrst′) n. sudden, heavy rainfall.

cloud chamber, apparatus used to detect the paths of elementary particles by means of a gas supersaturated with water vapor which condenses as the particles move through, creating a cloudlike trail by which the particles can be studied and identified.

cloud·less (kloud′lis) adj. without clouds; clear; bright. —**cloud′·less·ly,** adv. —**cloud′less·ness,** n.

cloud seeding, any of various techniques used to produce rain artificially by scattering particles, usually of dry ice or silver iodide, into clouds.

cloud·y (kloud′ē) cloud·i·er, cloud·i·est. adj. **1.** covered with or obscured by clouds; overcast: a cloudy sky. **2.** having little sunshine: a cloudy day. **3.** of or resembling clouds. **4.** not clear or transparent: a cloudy liquid. **5.** confused or not easily understood; vague: cloudy ideas. **6.** gloomy or troubled: cloudy looks. **7.** having cloudlike markings; streaked or spotted: cloudy marble. —**cloud′i·ness,** n.

clough (kluf, klou) n. narrow valley; ravine. [Middle English clough, from an unrecorded Old English word.]

clout (klout) n. **1.** Informal. heavy blow, esp. with the hand; cuff. **2.** Informal. influence, force, or power. **3.** Baseball. long, powerful hit. **4.** white object, as cloth, used as a target in long-distance archery. **5.** Archaic. small piece of cloth, esp. a rag. —v.t. Informal. to hit, esp. with the hand. [Old English clūt piece of cloth or metal.]

clove¹ (klōv) n. **1.** dried, unopened flower bud of a tree, Syzygium aromaticum, of the myrtle family, used as a spice either whole or ground. **2.** the tropical, evergreen tree itself, bearing oval, oblong leaves and clusters of small, pale-purple flowers. [Old French clou (de girofle) literally, nail (of clove tree), from Latin clāvus nail; because the bud resembles a nail.]

clove² (klōv) n. one of the separable sections of a compound bulb, as garlic. [Old English clufu.]

clove³ (klōv) past tense of **cleave¹**.

clove hitch, type of knot used to tie a line, esp. a rope, around something, as a spar. See **hitch** for illustration.

clo·ven (klō′vən) v. a past participle of **cleave¹**. —adj. split; divided.

cloven hoof 1. divided hoof, as of cows, oxen, or deer. **2.** such a hoof

considered as the symbol of Satan, who was supposed to have such hoofs. Also, **cloven foot.**

clo·ven-hoofed (klō′vən hooft′, -hoōft′) adj. **1.** having divided hoofs. **2.** satanic; devilish. Also, **clo′ven-foot′ed.**

clo·ver (klō′vər) n. **1.** any of a group of plants, genus Trifolium, of the pea family, bearing compound leaves, usually composed of three leaflets, and dense, rounded heads or spikes of small red, white, yellow, or purple flowers. Clovers are among the most widely cultivated and important cover and forage crops. **2.** any of various plants of the pea family, as **sweet clover,** genus Melilotus, and **bush clover,** genus Lespedeza. **3. in clover.** living in a prosperous or luxurious manner or situation. [Old English clāfre, clæfre plant of the genus Trifolium.]

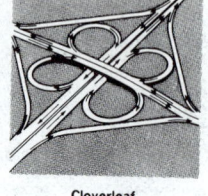

clo·ver·leaf (klō′vər lēf′) pl., **-leaves.** n. complex intersection of curving ramps that connect highways crossing each other on different levels.

Clovis I (klō′vis) c.465–511, king of the Franks from 481 to 511 and founder of the Merovingian dynasty.

Cloverleaf

clown (kloun) n. **1.** professional entertainer, esp. in a circus, who amuses the audience, as by performing tricks or exaggerated pantomiming, and is usually dressed in a ridiculous costume with bizarre makeup. **2.** ill-mannered, clumsy person; boor. —v.i. to behave like a clown. [Of uncertain origin.]

clown·ish (klou′nish) adj. of or resembling a clown: clownish behavior. —**clown′ish·ly,** adv. —**clown′ish·ness,** n.

cloy (kloi) v.t. to weary with an excess of anything pleasant, as sweet or rich food; satiate. —v.i. to cause to feel or become satiated. [Earlier accloy to drive a nail into, fill up, from Middle French encloer to drive a nail into, going back to Latin in in + clāvāre to nail.] —**cloy′ing·ly,** adv.

club (klub) n. **1.** thick, heavy stick, usually tapered at one end, used esp. as a weapon. **2.** any of various sticks or bats used to hit a ball in certain games, as golf. **3.** group of people organized for some special purpose: an athletic club. **4.** building or room used or occupied by such a group. **5.** organization that is usually joined by payment of a membership fee, which offers its members certain puchasing advantages: a theater club. **6.a.** playing card bearing one or more black marks in the shape of a trefoil. **b. clubs.** suit of such cards. —v.t. **clubbed, club·bing. 1.** to beat or strike with or as with a club. **2.** to unite, contribute, or combine for a common purpose. —v.i. to unite, contribute, or combine for a common purpose (often with together): The golf enthusiasts clubbed together. [Old Norse clubba thick stick.]

club car, railroad passenger car equipped with lounge chairs, card tables, and usually a bar or buffet.

club·foot (klub′foot′) pl., **-feet.** n. **1.** condition in which the foot is deformed or twisted out of position, caused by abnormal development before birth. Also, **tal′i·pes. 2.** foot so deformed. —**club′foot′ed,** adj.

club·house (klub′hous′) n. building used or occupied by a club.

club moss, any of two groups of small evergreen plants, genera Lycopodium and Selaginella, found in tropical and temperate regions growing along the ground and bearing small, upright branches covered with tiny, dark-green leaves that look like pine needles.

club sandwich, sandwich made with three slices of bread, usually toasted, and a filling of cold meats, lettuce, tomato, and a dressing.

club soda, soda water.

club steak, small, boneless cut of beef from the loin tip.

cluck (kluk) n. **1.** low, guttural sound made by a hen when brooding or calling her chicks. **2.** any similar sound. —v.i. **1.** to make the low, guttural sound of a hen brooding or calling her chicks. **2.** to utter any similar sound: The driver clucked to his horse to urge it on. —v.t. to call or express by clucking. [Imitative.]

clue (kloō) n. **1.** guide or key which aids in finding the solution to a problem or mystery. **2.** clew (defs. 2,3). —v.t., **clued, clu·ing. 1.** to clew (defs. 1,2). **2. to clue (someone) in.** Slang. to make aware of the facts. [Form of CLEW.]

clum·ber spaniel (klum′bər) spaniel having a long, heavy-boned body, short legs, a very large head, and a thick coat of silky, straight white hair with lemon or orange markings, used as a hunting dog. Height: 17 inches at the shoulder. Also, **clum′ber.** [From Clumber, an estate of the Duke of Newcastle in England.]

Clumber spaniel

clump (klump) n. **1.** small, closely gathered group; cluster: a clump of trees. **2.** irregular mass; lump: a clump of clay. **3.** heavy, dull sound,

as of footsteps. —v.t. to gather or form into a clump. —v.i. to walk heavily and clumsily. [Middle Low German *klumpe* shoe made of a lump of wood.] —**clump′y,** *adj.*

clum·sy (klum′zē) **-si·er, -si·est.** *adj.* **1.** lacking dexterity, grace, or skill; awkward: *a clumsy dancer.* **2.** ungracefully or awkwardly made or made; unwieldy: *clumsy boots.* **3.** awkwardly or unskillfully said or done, ill-contrived: *clumsy sentences.* [From obsolete *clumse* to be numb with cold (hence, awkward); probably of Scandinavian origin.] —**clum′si·ly,** *adv.* —**clum′si·ness,** *n.* —**Syn. 1.** see **awkward.**

clung (klung) past tense and past participle of **cling.**

Clu·ny (kloo′nē) *n.* town in east-central France, one of the principal religious and cultural centers of medieval Europe and site of the remains of a famous Benedictine abbey. Pop. (1962), 3711.

Cluny lace, bobbin lace made of heavy linen or cotton thread, usually with an open design, used for trimming.

clus·ter (klus′tər) *n.* **1.** group of things of the same kind growing naturally together; bunch: *Grapes grow in a cluster.* **2.** group of similar persons or things situated or grouped close together: *She arranged the spring flowers in a cluster. The ring had a cluster of pearls.* **3.** oak-leaf cluster. —v.i. to group or form into a cluster or clusters: *The children clustered around the Christmas tree.* —v.t. **1.** to group or form (something) into a cluster or clusters. **2.** to furnish or cover with clusters: *The hills are clustered with flowers.* [Old English *clyster* bunch.]

clutch[1] (kluch) *v.t.* **1.** to grasp or hold tightly or firmly: *He clutched the money in his hand.* **2.** to seize eagerly with or as with the hand or claws; snatch. —v.i. to attempt to grasp or seize (with *at*). —n. **1.** strong hold; grip. **2.** claw, paw, or hand that clutches. **3.** clutches. control; power: *He fell into the clutches of the enemy.* **4.** act of clutching. **5.** device in a machine that engages or disengages the engine. **6.** lever or pedal which operates such a device. **7.** *Informal.* serious or difficult situation or circumstance. [Old English *clyccan* to bend, clench.]

clutch[2] (kluch) *n.* **1.** number of eggs laid at one time. **2.** brood of chickens. [Earlier *cletch* brood, from *cleck* to hatch, from Old Norse *klekja.*]

clut·ter (klut′ər) *n.* confused or disorderly state or collection; litter. —v.t. to crowd or litter with a disorderly or confused collection of things: *She cluttered the kitchen with her grocery bags.* [From CLOT.]

Clyde (klīd) *n.* **1.** river in southwestern Scotland. **2.** Firth of, large estuary of the Clyde in southwestern Scotland.

Clydes·dale (klīdz′dāl′) *n.* one of a breed of strong, heavy draft horses. [From *Clydesdale,* the valley of the Clyde River, where this breed was originally developed.]

Cly·tem·nes·tra (klī′eeəm nes′trə) *n. Greek Legend.* the wife of Agamemnon, who was killed along with her lover Aegisthus by Orestes.

Cm, curium.

cm, centimeter; centimeters. Also, **cm.**

cml., commercial.

Cnos·sus (nos′əs, knos′-) Knossos.

Cnut (kə noot′, -nūt′) Canute.

Co, cobalt.

co- *prefix* **1.** with; together: *coexist.* **2.** fellow: *copilot.* **3.** equally: *coextend, coeval.* **4.** complement of: *cosine, cosecant.* [Latin *co-,* form of *com-* with. See COM-.]

co. **1.** Company. **2.** County. Also, **Co.**

c.o. **1.** in care of. **2.** carried over. Also, **c/o**

CO **1.** Commanding Officer. **2.** conscientious objector.

coach (kōch) *n.* **1.** large, four-wheeled closed carriage with seats inside for passengers and a raised seat outside for the driver. **2.** railroad passenger car, esp. one offering low rates. **3.** class of passenger travel offering the lowest rates for traveling, as on trains or airplanes. **4.** bus. **5.** one who trains or teaches an athlete or athletic team. **6.** one who trains and teaches in speech, dramatics, or voice. **7.** member of a baseball organization, positioned in either of two coaches' boxes, who gives instructions to batters and base runners. **8.** formerly, a closed two-door automobile like a sedan. —v.t. to act as a coach to; train or teach. —v.i. **1.** to study with or be trained by a coach. **2.** to act as a coach: *He coaches for the baseball team.* [French *coche* this carriage, going back to Hungarian *kocsi* literally, of Kocs, Hungarian town where these carriages are said to have originated.]

Coach

coach-and-four (kōch′ən fôr′) *n.* coach drawn by four horses.

coach dog, Dalmatian.

coach·man (kōch′mən) *pl.* **-men.** *n.* one who drives a coach or carriage.

co·ad·ju·tor (kō aj′ə tər, kō′ə joo′tər) *n.* **1.** assistant; helper. **2.** bishop appointed to assist a diocesan bishop or archbishop with the

right to succeed him. [Old French *coadjuteur,* going back to Latin *co-* with + *adjūtor* helper.]

co·ag·u·la·ble (kō ag′yə lə bəl) *adj.* that can be coagulated. —**co·ag′u·la·bil′i·ty,** *n.*

co·ag·u·lant (kō ag′yə lənt) *n.* substance that produces coagulation.

co·ag·u·late (kō ag′yə lāt′) **-lat·ed, -lat·ing.** *v.t., v.i.* to change or become changed from a liquid into a thickened mass; clot; congeal. [Latin *coāgulātus,* past participle of *coāgulāre* to cause to curdle.] —**co·ag′u·la′tor,** *n.* —**co·ag·u·la·to·ry** (kō ag′yə lə tôr′ē), *adj.*

co·ag·u·la·tion (kō ag′yə lā′shən) *n.* **1.** act of coagulating; being coagulated. **2.** coagulated mass.

coal (kōl) *n.* **1.** black or dark-brown combustible substance widely used as a fuel, formed mostly of vegetable matter which had been covered over by geologic layers for centuries and carbonized under pressure. There are three main types: anthracite and bituminous coal and lignite. **2.** piece of this substance. **3.** any piece of fuel, as wood or coal, that is glowing, charred, or burned. **4.** charcoal. **5.** **to rake (haul, drag, or call) over the coals.** to scold; reprimand. —v.t. **1.** to provide with coal. **2.** to convert or reduce to charcoal by burning; char. —v.i. to take in a supply of coal. [Old English *col* piece of carbon or partly burnt wood.]

coal·er (kō′lər) *n.* something, as a ship or railroad, used for carrying or supplying coal. **2.** one who sells or supplies coal.

co·a·lesce (kō′ə les′) **-lesced, -lesc·ing.** *v.i.* **1.** to grow together so as to form one body; fuse: *The two parts of the broken bone coalesced.* **2.** to unite, as into one unit or organization; combine. [Latin *coalēscere.*] —**co′a·les′cence,** —**co′a·les′cent,** *adj.*

coal·field (kōl′fēld′) *n.* region where deposits of coal are found.

coal gas **1.** mixture of gases, consisting primarily of hydrogen and methane, produced by heating bituminous coal in the absence of oxygen, used esp. in open hearth furnaces and as a source of such compounds as ammonia and benzene. **2.** gas given off by burning coal.

coaling station, place where coal is supplied to ships or trains.

co·a·li·tion (kō′ə lish′ən) *n.* **1.** alliance of statesmen, political parties, or nations for some special purpose. **2.** union into one mass or body; combination. [Medieval Latin *coalitio* society, meeting, corporation, from Latin *coalēscere* to grow together.] —**Syn. 1.** see **alliance.**

coal measures, strata, esp. of the Carboniferous period, containing beds of coal.

coal oil, kerosene.

coal scuttle, pail or other bucketlike container, often with a wide, projecting lip, for carrying or holding coal. Also, **coal hod.**

coal tar, black, sticky residue left after heating bituminous coal in the absence of oxygen, used as a basis for many synthetic products, as dyes, nylon, aspirin, and plastics.

coam·ing (kō′ming) *n.* raised edge, as around a hatch on a ship, used to keep out water. [Of uncertain origin.]

coarse (kôrs) **coars·er, coars·est.** *adj.* **1.** lacking refinement or delicacy; crude; vulgar: *coarse behavior, coarse language.* **2.** lacking fineness of texture or structure; thick or rough: *coarse cloth, coarse skin, coarse hair.* **3.** composed of large parts or particles: *coarse sand.* **4.** of inferior or poor quality or worth; common; base. [Earlier *corse, course;* of uncertain origin.] —**coarse′ly,** *adv.* —**coarse′ness,** *n.*

Syn. 1. Coarse, gross, vulgar suggest lack of refinement in taste, behavior, language, or the like. **Coarse** stresses the lack of fine feeling or social polish: *His coarse manners shocked everyone.* **Gross** stresses lack of delicacy and accents the physical rather than the spiritual nature of man: *Her gross eating habits offended her dinner companions.* **Vulgar** stresses offensiveness and suggests lack of breeding as well as indelicacy and crudeness: *His language, though plain, never becomes vulgar.*

coarse-grained (kôrs′grānd′) *adj.* **1.** having a coarse texture or grain. **2.** lacking refinement or delicacy; crude.

coars·en (kôr′sən) *v.t., v.i.* to make or become coarse.

coast (kōst) *n.* **1.** land next to the sea. **2.** **the Coast.** region of the United States bordering the Pacific. **3. a.** a ride or slide down a hill or similar incline, as on a sled. **b.** incline, as a hill, down which one may slide. **4. the coast is clear.** there is no danger or hindrance present. —v.i. **1.** to ride or slide down an incline by the force of gravity, as on a sled. **2.** to continue to move on acquired momentum after power has been shut off: *The car coasted after we turned off the engine.* **3.** to advance or move along without making any effort: *He coasted through his senior year in college.* **4.** to sail along or near a coast. —v.t. to sail along or near the coast of. [Old French *coste* rib, shore, slope of a hill, from Latin *costa* rib, side.] —**Syn.** n. **1.** see **beach.**

coast·al (kōst′əl) *adj.* of, at, near, or along a coast.

coastal plain, low, usually flat land area along a coast.

coast·er (kōs′tər) *n.* **1.** small mat, as of cork or paper, or shallow tray, as of glass, silver, or plastic, placed under a glass or bottle to protect the surface beneath. **2.** ship that engages in trade along a coast. **3.** sled or toboggan. **4.** roller coaster. **5.** one who or that which coasts.

coaster brake, brake on the rear wheel of a bicycle, operated by pushing the pedals backwards.

at; āpe; cär; end; mē; it; īce; hot; ōld; fôrk; wood; fōōl; oil; out; up; ūse; turn; sing; thin; this; zh in treasure; ə in ago, taken, pencil, lemon, circus.

191

Coast Guard **1.** military service responsible for preserving safety and order along the coasts and inland waterways of the United States. **2. coast guard. a.** any similar military service. **b.** member of any such service. **—coast′guards′man,** *n.*

coast-line (kōst′līn′) *n.* outline or contour of a coast.

coast-ward (kōst′wərd) *also,* **coast-wards.** *adj.* directed toward the coast. *—adv.* toward the coast.

coast-wise (kōst′wīz′) *also,* **coast-ways.** *adj.* following, or carried on, along the coast. *—adv.* by way of or along the coast.

coat (kōt) *n.* **1.** outer garment with sleeves, usually designed to be worn outdoors over other clothing. **2.** natural, external covering, as the fur of an animal. **3.** any outer layer which covers a surface. *—v.t.* **1.** to cover with a layer, as of paint: *The stove was coated with grease.* **2.** to provide or cover with a coat. [Old French *cote* tunic; of Germanic origin.]

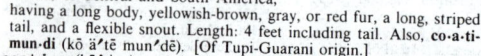

co-a-ti (kō ä′tē) *pl.,* **-tis.** *n.* any of various raccoonlike mammals, genus *Nasua,* of Central and South America, having a long body, yellowish-brown, gray, or red fur, a long, striped tail, and a flexible snout. Length: 4 feet including tail. Also, **co-a-ti-mun-di** (kō ä′tē mun′dē). [Of Tupi-Guarani origin.]

Coati

coat-ing (kō′ting) *n.* **1.** layer covering a surface. **2.** cloth for making coats.

coat of arms *pl.,* **coats of arms. 1.** shield, or representation of a shield, bearing heraldic devices; escutcheon. **2.** heraldic devices collectively, esp. of a person or family, usually including an escutcheon, a crest, supporters, if any, and a motto. Originally worn as identification, it often contains symbols of the history or tradition of the bearer. [Translation of French *cotte d'armes* surcoat decorated with heraldic devices worn by medieval knights over their armor.]

coat of mail *pl.,* **coats of mail.** shirt or coat made of chainmail, formerly worn as armor.

co-au-thor (kō ô′thər) *n.* joint author. *—v.t.* to write as a joint author with another or others.

Coat of arms

coax (kōks) *v.t.* **1.** to persuade or try to persuade, as by flattery, pleasant manners, or soft, gentle speech; wheedle. **2.** to obtain by coaxing: *He coaxed extra money from his father.* [From earlier *cokes* a fool; of uncertain origin.] **—coax′er,** *n.*

Syn. 1. Coax, cajole, wheedle mean to persuade by ingratiating talk. **Coax** suggests a gentle wooing, an appeal to a feeling of closeness: *He refused to be bullied or coaxed into a decision.* **Cajole** implies that use of flattery or other seductive wiles: *At first they threatened him, then they cajoled, but to no avail.* **Wheedle** suggests more obvious, almost obsequious wiles and more blatant flattery: *He has a tongue that could wheedle a bird out of a tree.* (H.B. Stowe, 1869).

co-ax-i-al (kō ak′sē əl) *adj.* **1.** having a common axis. Also, **co-ax′al.** **2.** (of a loudspeaker) with two or more speaker elements mounted one inside the other on the same axis, each receiving only the frequencies for which it is designed. [CO- + AXIS + -AL¹.]

coaxial cable, high-frequency telephone, telegraph, and television cable capable of transmitting thousands of electronic signals simultaneously, composed of a number of parallel wires, each surrounded by insulating material that is encased in a thin sheath of conducting material.

cob (kob) *n.* **1.** corncob (*def. 1*). **2.** thick-set horse with short legs.

co-balt (kō′bôlt) *n.* hard silver-white or pinkish metallic element, used esp. in alloys and as a coloring agent. Symbol: Co See element for table. [German *Kobalt,* form of *Kobold* goblin; so called by German miners because cobalt ore, which contains arsenic and sulfur, was harmful to their health.]

cobalt 60, radioactive isotope of cobalt, used in medicine for radiotherapy.

cobalt blue 1. deep blue pigment made from cobalt. **2.** deep blue color.

cob-ble¹ (kob′əl) **-bled, -bling.** *v.t.* **1.** to mend or make, as shoes or boots. **2.** to mend or put together clumsily or roughly. [Possibly from COBBLER.]

cob-ble² (kob′əl) *n.* cobblestone. *—v.t.,* **-bled, -bling.** to pave with cobblestones. [From dialectal *cob* lump (of uncertain origin).]

cob-bler (kob′lər) *n.* **1.** one whose work is making or mending shoes. **2.** deep-dish fruit pie having no bottom crust and a thick top crust. **3.** iced, sweetened fruit drink made with wine or liquor and usually served with a garnish, as lemon or mint. **4.** *Archaic.* clumsy workman. [Of uncertain origin.]

cob-ble-stone (kob′əl stōn′) *n.* naturally rounded stone, formerly used in paving.

co-bel-lig-er-ent (kō′bi lij′ər ənt) *n.* nation that aids or cooperates with another or others in waging war, but is not bound by a formal alliance.

COBOL (kō′bôl′) *n.* computer coding system oriented toward business applications. [Short for *co(mmon) b(usiness) o(riented) l(anguage)*.]

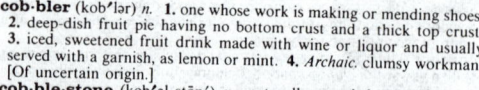

co-bra (kō′brə) *n.* any of several large, usually hooded, venomous snakes, family Elapidae, found in Africa and Asia. The **king cobra,** *Naja hannah,* is the world's longest venomous snake. Length: to 18½ feet. [Short for Portuguese *cobra (de capello)* snake (with a hood); *cobra* from Latin *colubra.*]

Cobra

cob-web (kob′web′) *n.* **1.** network of fine thread spun by a spider. **2.** single thread of this, or the material of which it is made. **3.** anything resembling this, as in use or construction. [Short for Old English *āttorcoppe* spider; literally, poison head + WEB.] **—cob′web′by,** *adj.*

co-ca (kō′kə) *n.* **1.** any of a group of tropical shrubs or small trees, genus *Erythroxylon,* of South America. **2.** dried leaves of one of these shrubs, *E. coca,* which yield alkaloids, as cocaine. [Spanish *coca;* of Quechua origin.]

co-caine (kō kān′, kō′kān) *also,* **co-cain.** *n.* white, crystalline alkaloid obtained from coca leaves, used esp. as a local anesthetic. Formula: $C_{17}H_{21}NO_4$. [COCA + -INE².]

coc-cus (kok′əs) *pl.,* **coc-ci** (kok′sī). *n.* any bacterium characterized by a spherical or oval shape. See bacteria for illustration. [Modern Latin *coccus,* from Greek *kokkos* seed, berry.]

coc-cyx (kok′siks) *pl.,* **coc-cy-ges** (kok′si jēz, kok sī′-). *n.* small triangular bone at the lower end of the spinal column consisting of four rudimentary vertebrae. [Latin *coccyx* cuckoo, from Greek *kókkyx;* because supposedly shaped like a cuckoo's beak.]

co-chin (kō′chin, koch′in) *also,* **Co-chin.** *n.* any of a variety of large domestic fowl having heavily feathered legs. [From COCHIN CHINA, where it originated.]

Co-chin China (kō′chin, koch′in) former French colony in southern Indochina, now part of South Vietnam.

coch-i-neal (koch′ə nēl′) *n.* dark-red dye prepared from the dried bodies of a female scale insect, *Coccus cacti,* of Mexico and Central America, used chiefly as a coloring in foods, inks, and cosmetics. [Spanish *cochinilla,* from Latin *coccinus* scarlet, going back to Greek *kokkos* variety of berry or gall³ used to dye scarlet.]

coch-le-a (kok′lē ə) *pl.,* **-le-ae** (-lē ē′). *n.* tube of the inner ear, shaped somewhat like a snail shell, containing the sensory ends of the auditory nerve. [Latin *cochlea* snail, snail shell, from Greek *kochliās* snail with a spiral shell.] **—coch′le-ar,** *adj.*

cock¹ (kok) *n.* **1.** male chicken; rooster. **2.** male of various other birds. **3.a.** hammer of a firearm. **b.** position into which this hammer is brought when pulled back in preparation for firing. **4.** device, as a faucet or valve, used to control the flow of a liquid or gas. *—v.t.* to pull back the hammer of (a firearm) to a firing position. [Old English *cocc* male bird.]

cock² (kok) *v.t.* to turn up or upward or tilt to one side, esp. in a jaunty, pert, or inquisitive manner: *to cock one's head. The dog cocked his ears.* *—n.* upward turn or tilt to one side, as of the head, ear, or eye. [From COCK¹; with reference to the movement of a cock's head and chest when he crows.]

cock³ (kok) *n.* small, cone-shaped stack of hay. *—v.t.* to arrange in such stacks. [Possibly of Scandinavian origin.]

cock-ade (ko kād′) *n.* knot of ribbon, rosette, or similar ornament worn, esp. on a hat, as a badge, insignia, or indication of rank. [French *cocarde* rosette on a cap, from Old French *coquard* vain, from *coq* cock¹; imitative.]

Cock-aigne (ko kān′) *n.* imaginary country of idleness and luxury. [Middle French *(pais de) cocaigne* land (of) plenty, possibly from Middle Low German *kōkenje* small sweet cake.]

cock-and-bull story (kok′ən bool′) absurd, improbable story or account.

cock-a-too (kok′ə too′) *pl.,* **-toos.** *n.* any of various crested parrots, family Psittacidae, native to Australia, the East Indies, and southwestern Asia, having white plumage that may be tinged with pink or yellow.

at; āpe; cär; end; mē; it; īce; hot; ōld; fôrk; wood; fōōl; oil; out; up; ūse; turn; sing; thin; this; zh in treasure; ə in ago, taken, pencil, lemon, circus.

[Dutch *kaketoe*, from Malay *kakatua*; spelling influenced by COCK[1].]

cock·a·trice (kok′ə tris′) *n.* fabled serpent, hatched from a cock's egg, whose glance was supposed to cause death. [Old French *cocatris* crocodile, fabled serpent, modification of Late Latin *calcātrix* literally, treader, from Latin *calcāre* to tread.]

cock·boat (kok′bōt′) *n.* ship's small rowboat. Also, **cock′le·boat′.**

cock·chaf·er (kok′chā′fər) *n.* black-and-brown beetle, family Scarabaeidae, common in Europe, the destructive larvae of which eat the roots of many kinds of plants.

cock·crow (kok′krō′) *n.* time when roosters begin to crow; dawn.

cocked hat, hat with the brim turned up so as to form two or more points; tricorne.

cock·er (kok′ər) *n.* cocker spaniel.

cock·er·el (kok′ər əl, kok′rəl) *n.* young rooster, less than one year old.

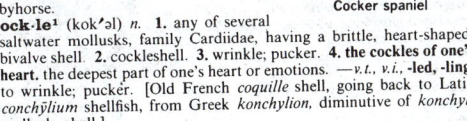

Cocked hat

cocker spaniel, spaniel having a short, compact body, long, silky hair, and drooping ears, kept as a bird dog or house pet. Height: 14 inches at the shoulder. [From WOODCOCK + SPANIEL; with reference to its skill in hunting woodcocks and other game birds.]

cock·eyed (kok′īd′) *adj.* **1.** cross-eyed. **2.** *Slang.* tilted to one side; off-center. **3.** *Slang.* absurd; foolish.

cock·fight (kok′fīt′) *n.* fight between gamecocks that are usually fitted with steel spurs on their legs. —**cock′fight′·ing,** *n.*

cock·horse (kok′hôrs′) *n.* hobbyhorse.

Cocker spaniel

cock·le[1] (kok′əl) *n.* **1.** any of several saltwater mollusks, family Cardiidae, having a brittle, heart-shaped, bivalve shell. **2.** cockleshell. **3.** wrinkle; pucker. **4. the cockles of one's heart,** the deepest part of one's heart or emotions. —*v.t., v.i.,* **-led, -ling.** to wrinkle; pucker. [Old French *coquille* shell, going back to Latin *conchylium* shellfish, from Greek *konchylion,* diminutive of *konchylē* mollusk, shell.]

cock·le[2] (kok′əl) *n.* any of several weeds that grow in grain fields. [Old English *coccel.*]

cock·le·boat (kok′əl bōt′) *n.* cockboat.

cock·le·bur (kok′əl bur′) *n.* any of a group of weeds, genus *Xanthium,* widely distributed in North America and Mexico and bearing spiny burs.

cock·le·shell (kok′əl shel′) *n.* **1.** shell of a cockle. **2.** small, light, shallow boat.

cock·loft (kok′lôft′) *n.* small loft or attic; garret.

cock·ney (kok′nē) *pl.,* **-neys.** *n.* **1.** native or resident of the East End of London, England. **2.** accent peculiar to this district. —*adj.* of, relating to, or resembling cockneys or their accent. [Middle English *cokeney* cook's egg, spoiled child, city dweller, going back to Old English *cocc* cock[1] + *æg* egg.]

cock·pit (kok′pit′) *n.* **1.** open or enclosed compartment in an airplane where the pilot and copilot sit. **2.** pit or enclosed area for cockfights. **3.** place where many contests or battles are or have been fought. **4.** formerly, quarters below the deck of warships, used for treating the wounded during battle.

cock·roach (kok′rōch′) *n.* any of a group of brown or black insects, family Blattidae, with oval, flattened, leathery bodies, bristly legs, and long antennae. Some species are common household pests. [Modification of Spanish *cucaracha,* from *cuca* caterpillar; of uncertain origin.]

cocks·comb (koks′kōm′) *n.* **1.** comb or fleshy red crest on the head of a rooster. **2.** jester's cap resembling this in shape. **3.** any of a group of plants, genus *Celosia,* having showy red, purple, or yellow flower spikes that resemble a rooster's comb or a feathery plume.

cock·sure (kok′shoor′) *adj.* **1.** overly confident or sure. **2.** absolutely certain. —**cock′sure′·ly,** *adv.* —**cock′sure′·ness,** *n.*

cock·swain (kok′sən, -swān′) coxswain.

cock·tail (kok′tāl′) *n.* **1.** any of various, usually iced, alcoholic drinks made by mixing liquor with flavoring ingredients, as bitters, liqueurs, or fruit juices. **2.** any of various appetizers, as fruit juice, a mixture of diced fruits, or seafood.

Cockscomb

cock·y (kok′ē) **cock·i·er, cock·i·est.** *adj. Informal.* arrogantly self-confident. —**cock′i·ly,** *adv.* —**cock′i·ness,** *n.*

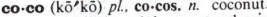

co·co (kō′kō) *pl.,* **co·cos.** *n.* coconut.

co·coa (kō′kō) *n.* **1.** brown powder made by drying, fermenting, roasting, and grinding cacao seeds and removing the cocoa butter. It is used esp. in making various chocolate drinks. **2.** chocolate beverage made by mixing this powder with hot milk or water and, sometimes, sugar. **3.** light, dull-brown color. [Form of CACAO.]

cocoa butter, yellowish-white fat obtained from cacao seeds, used in making such items as chocolate, soap, and cosmetics.

co·co·nut (kō′kə nut′, -nət) *also,* **co·coa·nut.** *n.* **1.** large, oval fruit of the coconut palm, having a smooth outer rind, a reddish-brown fibrous husk, and a hard inner shell lined with edible white meat and containing a milky fluid called **coconut milk. 2.** coconut palm.

coconut oil, oil extracted from the dried fruit of coconuts.

coconut palm, tall palm tree, *Cocos nucifera,* that bears coconuts and has huge feathery leaves.

co·coon (kə kōōn′) *n.* **1.** protective case consisting of silk, leaves, or other materials that encloses the pupa of certain insects, as the silkworm, during the pupal stage. **2.** any similar protective covering, as the egg containers of certain spiders. [French *cocon* the protective case for the silkworm, from Provençal *coucoun,* from *coco* shell, from Latin *coccum* berry, from Greek *kokkos* berry, seed.]

cod (kod) *pl.,* **cods** or **cod.** *n.* any of a group of commercially important food fish, family Gadidae, found in the colder northern waters of the Atlantic and Pacific oceans. [Possibly from obsolete *cod* bag, from Old English *cod,* with reference to its shape.]

Atlantic cod

c.o.d., collect on delivery. Also, **C.O.D.**

co·da (kō′də) *n.* passage at the end of a musical composition or movement, more or less independent of it and bringing it to a formal, satisfactory close. [Italian *coda,* from Latin *cauda* tail.]

cod·dle (kod′əl) **-dled, -dling.** *v.t.* **1.** to treat tenderly or overindulgently; pamper. **2.** to cook gently in a liquid at or just below the boiling point; simmer: *to coddle eggs.* [Possibly a form of CAUDLE.]

code (kōd) *n.* **1.** systematic collection of an existing body of law: *a penal code.* **2.** any system or collection of principles and rules of conduct: *a moral code, a code of ethics.* **3.a.** system of communication in which sounds, light flashes, flags, or other signals represent numbers, letters, or words, used to send messages, as by telegraph or heliograph. **b.** system of writing using letters, words, numbers, or other symbols which are arbitrarily given certain meanings, used for secrecy or brevity in communication: *The message was written in code.* **4.** message in code. **5.** key or pattern to a code. —*v.t.,* **cod·ed, cod·ing.** to put into the form of a code. [Old French *code* code of laws, from Latin *cōdex* wooden tablet for writing, book, code of laws. Doublet of CODEX.]

co·deine (kō′dēn) *also,* **co·dein.** *n.* habit-forming drug derived from opium, used to relieve pain and cough and to induce sleep. [Greek *kōdeia* poppy head + -INE[2].]

co·dex (kō′deks) *pl.,* **co·di·ces** (kō′də sēz′, kod′ə-). *n.* ancient manuscript, esp. of the Scriptures or classics. [Latin *cōdex* wooden tablet for writing, book. Doublet of CODE.]

cod·fish (kod′fish′) *pl.,* **-fish** or **-fish·es.** *n.* cod.

codg·er (koj′ər) *n. Informal.* odd, eccentric, or testy man, esp. one who is old. [Possibly form of CADGER.]

cod·i·cil (kod′ə sil) *n.* **1.** supplement to a will to add to, change, or explain something in it. **2.** supplement; appendix. [Latin *cōdicillus* a writing, addition to a will, diminutive of *cōdex* book. See CODEX.]

cod·i·cil·la·ry (kod′ə sil′ər ē) *adj.* relating to, or of the nature of, a codicil.

cod·i·fy (kod′ə fī′, kō′də-) **-fied, -fy·ing.** *v.t.* to reduce to a system or code, as laws. [CODE + -FY.] —**cod′i·fi·ca′tion,** **cod′i·fi′er,** *n.*

cod·ling (kod′ling) *also,* **cod·lin** (kod′lin). *n.* **1.** variety of apple having an elongated shape, used for cooking. **2.** unripe apple. [Middle English *quere(e)lynge* hard apple, possibly from Anglo-Norman *quere de lion* heart of lion (with reference to its shape), going back to Latin *cor* heart + *dē* + *leō* lion; influenced in spelling by English *coddle* to cook.]

codling moth, moth, *Carpocapsa pomonella,* whose larvae are destructive to apples, pears, and other fruits.

cod-liv·er oil (kod′liv′ər) oil extracted from the livers of cod and certain other fish, used as a source of vitamins A and D.

Co·dy, William Frederick (kō′dē) Buffalo Bill.

co·ed (kō′ed) *also,* **co-ed.** *n. Informal.* female student at a coeducational college or school. —*adj.* (of an educational institution) having both male and female students in attendance. [Short for COEDUCATION.]

co·ed·u·ca·tion (kō′ej ə kā′shən) *n.* education of students of both sexes in the same school or college. [Co- + EDUCATION.] —**co′·ed·u·ca′tion·al,** *adj.* —**co′·ed·u·ca′tion·al·ly,** *adv.*

co·ef·fi·cient (kō′i fish′ənt) *n.* **1.** *Mathematics.* number or algebraic expression put before and multiplying an algebraic expression. In $3x^2y$, 3 is the numerical coefficient of x^2y; in $3x^2(y + z)$, $3x^2$ is the coefficient of $(y + z)$. **2.** *Physics.* numerical constant determined for a property of a given substance under certain conditions and used to measure or calculate change in that property or substance under other conditions. —*adj.* cooperating. [Co- + EFFICIENT.]

coe·la·canth (sē′lə kanth′) *n.* primitive, paddle-finned, bony fish, *Latimeria chalumnae,* long thought to be extinct. First caught in 1938 off the coast of South Africa, it is believed important in the evolutionary sequence from primitive sea vertebrates to land vertebrates. [Modern Latin *coelacanthus* literally, having a hollow spine, from Greek *koilos* hollow + *akantha* thorn, spine.]

coe·len·ter·ate (si len′tə rāt′, -tər it) *n.* any of a group of invertebrates, phylum Coelenterata, including coral, jellyfish, and hydras, usually found in salt water and having a saclike body with numerous tentacles around a single mouth opening. —*adj.* relating to, belonging to, or characteristic of this group. [Modern Latin *coelenterata* (plural) literally, having empty intestines, from Greek *koilos* hollow + *enteron* intestine.]

coe·li·ac (sē′lē ak′) celiac.

coe·no·bite (sē′nə bīt′, sen′ə-) cenobite.

co·e·qual (kō ēk′wəl) *adj.* same, as in rank, ability, value, or size. —*n.* one who or that which is coequal with another or others. —**co·e·qual·i·ty** (kō′i kwol′ə tē), *n.* —**co·e′qual·ly,** *adv.*

co·erce (kō urs′) **co·erced, co·erc·ing.** *v.t.* **1.** to force, as by physical violence, threats, or authority. **2.** to bring about by force. **3.** to control or restrain by force. [Latin *coercēre* to shut in, restrain.] —**co·erc′er,** *n.* —**co·erc′i·ble,** *adj.*

co·er·cion (kō ur′shən) *n.* **1.** use of force to compel or control; constraint. **2.** government by force.

co·er·cive (kō ur′siv) *adj.* tending or serving to coerce. —**co·er′cive·ly,** *adv.* —**co·er′cive·ness,** *n.*

co·e·val (kō ē′vəl) *adj.* of, belonging to, or living in the same age, date, time, or duration; contemporary. —*n.* contemporary. [Late Latin *coaevus* of the same age (from Latin *co-* with + *aevum* age) + -AL[1].]

co·ex·ist (kō′ig zist′) *v.i.* **1.** to exist in or at the same place or time as another. **2.** to live together peacefully, despite differences in policy or principle, as countries. —**co′ex·ist′ence,** *n.* —**co′ex·ist′ent,** *adj.*

co·ex·tend (kō′iks tend′) *v.t., v.i.* to extend to or through the same space or time. —**co′ex·ten′sion,** *n.*

co·ex·ten·sive (kō′iks ten′siv) *adj.* extending to or through the same space or time; extending equally. —**co′ex·ten′sive·ly,** *adv.*

cof·fee (kô′fē) *n.* **1.** aromatic, dark-brown beverage prepared from ground or crushed coffee beans and hot or boiling water. **2.** coffee beans collectively, whether whole or ground. **3.** any of a group of tropical evergreen shrubs and small trees, genus *Coffea,* which bear coffee beans. **4.** rich, dark-brown color. [Turkish *kahveh* the beverage, from Arabic *qahwah;* said to be from *Kaffa,* region in Ethiopia, where the coffee plant originated.]

coffee bean, seed of the coffee plant, dried, roasted, and ground to make the beverage coffee.

cof·fee·house (kô′fē hous′) *n.* place where coffee and other refreshments are sold.

cof·fee·pot (kô′fē pot′) *n.* container, usually with a cover, for preparing or serving coffee.

coffee shop, informal restaurant where coffee and food are served.

coffee table, low table, usually placed in front of a sofa.

cof·fer (kô′fər, kof′ər) *n.* **1.** box or chest, esp. one used for holding money or other valuables; strongbox. **2.** coffers. monetary resources; treasury. **3.** recessed ornamental panel, usually in a series, in a ceiling, vault, or dome. **4.** cofferdam. [Old French *cofre* chest, from Latin *cophinus* basket, from Greek *kophinos.* Doublet of COFFER.]

cof·fer·dam (kô′fər dam′, kof′ər-) *n.* **1.** temporary watertight enclosure built in water and pumped dry to permit construction of foundations, bridge piers, or similar structures on the enclosed area. **2.** any of certain similar, usually watertight, structures.

cof·fin (kô′fin) *n.* box or case into which a corpse is placed for burial. —*v.t.* to put into or as in a coffin. [Old French *cofin* chest, case, from Latin *cophinus* basket, from Greek *kophinos.* Doublet of COFFER.]

Cogwheels

cog (kog) *n.* **1.** one of a series of teeth on the circumference of a wheel that transmits or receives motion by locking into similar teeth on another wheel or on a track. **2.** cogwheel. **3.** projection or tenon on the end of a piece of wood that fits into a notch on another piece to form a joint. **4.** *Informal.* one who plays a minor, but often necessary, part in a large process or organization. [Of Scandinavian origin.]

co·gen·cy (kō′jən sē) *n.* state or quality of being cogent.

co·gent (kō′jənt) *adj.* having the power to be persuasive; forcible; convincing: *a cogent reason.* [Latin *cōgēns,* present participle of *cōgere* to drive together, compel.] —**co′gent·ly,** *adv.*

cog·i·tate (koj′ə tāt′) -**tat·ed, -tat·ing.** *v.i.* to think or consider earnestly and carefully; meditate; ponder. [Latin *cōgitātus,* past participle of *cōgitāre* to think.] —**cog′i·ta′tor,** *n.*

cog·i·ta·tion (koj′ə tā′shən) *n.* careful and earnest thought or consideration; meditation; reflection.

cog·i·ta·tive (koj′ə tā′tiv) *adj.* capable of or given to cogitation.

co·gnac (kōn′yak, kon′-) *n.* brandy originally made in the French town of Cognac.

cog·nate (kog′nāt) *adj.* **1.** related through a common origin; derived from the same source: *cognate words, cognate languages.* **2.** having the same ancestor or parentage; related by birth. **3.** allied in nature, quality, or characteristics. —*n.* one who or that which is cognate. [Latin *cōgnātus* related by blood, kindred.]

cog·ni·tion (kog nish′ən) *n.* **1.** act or faculty of knowing or perceiving. **2.** that which is known or perceived. [Latin *cognitiō.*]

cog·ni·za·ble (kog′nə zə bəl, kon′ə-) *adj.* **1.** capable of being known or perceived. **2.** within the jurisdiction of a court of law.

cog·ni·zance (kog′nə zəns, kon′-) *n.* **1.** knowledge or perception; notice: *to take cognizance of a fact.* **2.a.** right or power of a court of law to try and settle cases; jurisdiction. **b.** exercise of jurisdiction. [Old French *conoissance* knowledge, from *conoistre* to know, from Latin *cognōscere.*]

cog·ni·zant (kog′nə zənt, kon′ə-) *adj.* having cognizance; aware. —**Syn.** See aware.

cog·no·men (kog nō′mən) *n.* **1.** family name; surname. **2.** any name, esp. a nickname. [Latin *cognōmen* family name.]

cog·wheel (kog′hwēl′, -wēl′) *n.* wheel with cogs.

co·hab·it (kō hab′it) *v.i.* to live together as man and wife. [Late Latin *cohabitāre* to dwell together, from Latin *co-* together + *habitāre* to inhabit.] —**co·hab′i·ta′tion,** *n.*

co·here (kō hēr′) -**hered, -her·ing.** *v.i.* **1.** to stick or hold together, as parts of a mass. **2.** to be logically connected or related; be consistent. [Latin *cohaerēre* to stick together.]

co·her·ence (kō hēr′əns, -her′-) *n.* **1.** logical connection; consistency. **2.** sticking or holding together; cohesion. Also, **co·her′en·cy.**

co·her·ent (kō hēr′ənt, -her′-) *adj.* **1.** logically connected; consistent. **2.** sticking or holding together. **3.** intelligible or articulate. —**co·her′ent·ly,** *adv.*

co·he·sion (kō hē′zhən) *n.* **1.** act or state of cohering. **2.** attraction between molecules of a substance which holds the substance together. [French *cohésion,* going back to Latin *cohaesus,* past participle of *cohaerēre* to stick together.]

co·he·sive (kō hē′siv) *adj.* capable of, having, or causing cohesion. —**co·he′sive·ly,** *adv.* —**co·he′sive·ness,** *n.*

co·hort (kō′hôrt′) *n.* **1.** companion, associate, or follower. **2.** any one of ten divisions constituting a legion in the ancient Roman army. **3.** any band, company, or group, esp. of soldiers. [Latin *cohors* enclosure, company of soldiers. Doublet of COURT.]

coif (koif) *n.* **1.** any of various close-fitting caps that conform to the shape of the head. Nuns wear coifs under their veils. Knights wore leather coifs under their helmets. **2.** coiffure. —*v.t.* **1.** to cover with or as with a coif. **2.** to dress or arrange (the hair). [Old French *coif(f)e* headdress, from Late Latin *cofia* helmet, cap; possibly of Germanic origin.]

coif·feur (kwä fœr′) *n.* *French.* male hairdresser. [French *coiffeur,* from *coiffer* to arrange the hair, from *coiffe.* See COIF.]

coif·fure (kwä fyoor′) *n.* **1.** hair style. **2.** headdress. [French *coiffure,* from *coiffer.* See COIF, COIFFEUR.]

coign (koin) *n.* projecting corner. [Form of COIN corner (obsolete meaning).]

coign of vantage, advantageous position for observing or acting.

coil[1] (koil) *n.* **1.** anything made up of a series of concentric spirals or rings: *a coil of wire.* **2.** one of the spirals or rings of such a series. **3.** spiral pipe or series of connected pipes arranged in rows to conduct heat or liquids, as in a radiator. **4.** spiral wire for conducting electricity. —*v.i.* **1.** to form coils; wind around. **2.** to move in a winding course: *The road coiled around the mountain.* —*v.t.* to wind in coils: *The sailor*

coiled the rope around the anchor. [Old French *coillir* to collect, from Latin *colligere*.]

coil² (koil) *n.* *Archaic.* disturbance; trouble. [Of uncertain origin.]

coin (koin) *n.* **1.** piece of metal stamped with official government markings and of fixed weight and value, used as money. **2.** metal money collectively. —*v.t.* **1.** to make (money) by stamping metal. **2.** to make (metal) into coins. **3.** to make up; devise: *to coin a phrase.* [Old French *coin* corner, wedge, die to stamp money, a coin (so called because stamped by a wedge), from Latin *cuneus* wedge.] —**coin'er,** *n.*

coin·age (koi'nij) *n.* **1.** act, process, or right of making coins. **2.** that which is coined; metal money. **3.** coins collectively. **4.** act or process of making up or devising. **5.** that which is made up or devised.

co·in·cide (kō'in sīd') **-cid·ed, -cid·ing.** *v.i.* **1.** to occur at the same time: *The football practice coincided with his classes.* **2.** to occupy the same area or place in space: *The two roads coincide after fifty miles.* **3.** to agree exactly; correspond: *Their views coincided.* [Medieval Latin *coincidere* literally, to fall upon together, from Latin *co-* together + *incidere* to fall upon.]

co·in·ci·dence (kō in'si dəns) *n.* **1.** notable and remarkable concurrence, as of events, ideas, or circumstances, apparently by mere chance: *By coincidence we both arrived at the same time.* **2.** fact or condition of coinciding.

co·in·ci·dent (kō in'si dənt) *adj.* **1.** occurring at the same time. **2.** occupying the same area or place in space. **3.** in exact agreement; corresponding: *An account coincident with the facts.* —**co·in'ci·dent·ly,** *adv.*

co·in·ci·den·tal (kō in'si dent'əl) *adj.* characterized by, resulting from, or involving coincidence. —**co·in'ci·den'tal·ly,** *adv.*

co·in·sur·ance (kō'in shoor'əns) *n.* insurance shared jointly, as between the insurer and the insured.

co·in·sure (kō'in shoor') **-sured, -sur·ing.** *v.t.* to insure with coinsurance. —*v.i.* to take out coinsurance.

coir (koir) *n.* fiber obtained from the husks of coconuts, used to make such items as rope, mats, and brushes. [Malayalam *kāyar* cord.]

co·i·tus (kō'i təs) *n.* sexual intercourse. [Latin *coitus* a coming together.] —**co'i·tal,** *adj.*

coke (kōk) *n.* gray-black solid fuel, obtained by heating bituminous coal in the absence of oxygen, that burns with much heat and little smoke or ash, used esp. in blast furnaces. —*v.t., v.i.,* **coked, cok·ing.** to convert into or become coke. [Of uncertain origin.]

col-, form of **com-** before *l,* as in *collateral.*

col. 1. column. **2.** color; colored. **3.** colony.

Col. 1. Colonel. **2.** Colossians.

col·an·der (kul'ən dər, kol'-) *n.* kitchen utensil with perforations, used to rinse food or to drain excess liquid from food. [Going back to Medieval Latin *colatorium* strainer, from Latin *cōlāre* to strain.]

Col·bert, Jean Bap·tiste (kôl bâr'; zhän bä tēst') 1619–83, French statesman and financier.

col·chi·cum (kol'chə kəm) *n.* **1.** any of a group of plants, genus *Colchicum,* of the lily family, found in Europe and Asia and bearing flowers. **2.** dried seeds and corm of *C. autumnale.* **3.** drug made from them, used in the treatment of gout. [Latin *colchicum* plant with a poisonous root, from Greek *Kolchikos* of Colchis, from *Kolchis* Colchis; with reference to Medea, a princess of Colchis noted for her skill in poisoning.]

Col·chis (kol'kis) *n.* ancient country on the eastern shore of the Black Sea. The legendary Golden Fleece was located there.

cold (kōld) *adj.* **1.** having a lower temperature than that of the normal human body. **2.** having a relatively low temperature; with little or no warmth: *cold air; My dinner is cold.* **3.** feeling a lack of warmth; chilly: *The children were cold after playing outside.* **4.** not influenced by emotion; objective: *a cold, calculating move.* **5.** lacking in enthusiasm or intensity of feeling; indifferent; apathetic: *a cold audience.* **6.** not friendly or cordial: *a cold reception.* **7.** dispiriting; depressing. **8.** not fresh; stale or weak: *a cold scent.* **9.** dead. **10.** lacking warmth of color; of a bluish tone. **11.** *Informal.* unconscious: *He was out cold.* **12.** *Informal.* far from the person or object sought, as in certain children's games. **13. cold feet.** lack or loss of courage; timidity. **14. to throw cold water on.** to discourage. —*n.* **1.** absence of warmth or heat. **2.** sensation produced by the loss or absence of heat. **3.** acute inflammation of the mucous membranes of the upper respiratory organs, characterized by coughing and sneezing. **4. in the cold.** ignored or neglected. **5. to catch** (or **take**) **cold.** to become affected with a cold. —*adv. Informal.* **1.** thoroughly; completely: *to know something cold.* **2.** without any former knowledge or preparation. [Old English *cald, ceald* of cool temperature.] —**cold'ly,** *adv.* —**cold'ness,** *n.*

Syn. *adj.* **2.** *Cold, chilly, cool* indicate a temperature lower than normal. *Cold* is the most general word and suggests that the temperature may be low enough to cause suffering: *He shuddered in the cold wind. Chilly* suggests a temperature that may cause minor discomfort: *It's too chilly for a dip in the lake this morning.* *Cool* suggests a temperature just below

the mean, often indicating a lack of expected warmth that is not disagreeable but may be refreshing: *It was cool in the shadow of the tree.*

cold-blood·ed (kōld'blud'id) *adj.* **1.** having blood, as fish and reptiles, which varies in temperature with that of the surrounding air, water, or land. **2.** lacking feeling, sensitivity, or sympathy; cruel. **3.** sensitive to cold. —**cold-'blood'ed·ly,** *adv.* —**cold-'blood'ed·ness,** *n.*

cold chisel, chisel of tempered steel, used for cutting cold metal.

cold cream, creamy preparation used for cleansing and soothing the skin.

cold cuts, cooked meat or fowl, as roast beef, turkey, pastrami, and bologna, which has been sliced and is served cold.

cold frame, boxlike structure having a transparent cover and no bottom, used to protect plants against cold and wind.

cold front, forward edge of a mass of cold air advancing into an area of warmer air.

cold-heart·ed (kōld'här'tid) *adj.* without feeling or sympathy; unkind. —**cold'-heart'ed·ly,** *adv.*

cold light, light produced by luminescence, as fluorescent light.

cold pack, cold, wet wrapping, as a towel or an ice pack, used to relieve swelling or reduce pain.

cold-shoul·der (kōld'shōl'dər) *v.t. Informal.* to show deliberate unfriendliness or indifference toward.

cold shoulder *Informal.* deliberate unfriendliness or indifference; slight.

cold sore, blister in or near the mouth caused by a virus and often accompanying a cold.

cold storage, storage of perishable objects in an artificially cooled chamber.

cold sweat, perspiration accompanied by chill, usually caused by fear or shock.

cold war 1. also, **Cold War.** state of rivalry and hostility in international relations after World War II, involving the United States and its allies on one side and the Soviet Union and its allies on the other, and generally stopping short of military conflict. **2.** any state of intense political, economic, or ideological rivalry between nations, stopping short of actual warfare.

cold wave 1. period of sudden, unusually cold weather. **2.** permanent wave using a cold liquid solution instead of heat.

cole (kōl) *n.* any of various plants belonging to the same genus as the cabbage, esp. rape. Also, **cole'wort'.** [Old English *cāl, cawel* cabbage, from Latin *caulis.*]

co·le·op·ter·ous (kō'lē op'tər əs, kol'ē-) *adj.* of or relating to the most numerous order of insects, Coleoptera, including the boll weevil and the Japanese beetle, characterized by chewing mouthparts and hardened forewings which sheathe the delicate hind wings. [Modern Latin *Coleoptera* (plural), from Greek *koleos* sheath + *pteron* wing + -OUS.]

Cole·ridge, Samuel Taylor (kōl'rij) 1772–1834, English poet and critic.

cole·slaw (kōl'slô') *n.* salad made of sliced, shredded, or grated raw cabbage, mixed with a dressing. Also, **slaw.** [Dutch *koolsla,* from *kool* cabbage (from Latin *caulis*) + *sla,* short for *salade* salad (from French *salade*). See SALAD.]

Coleus

co·le·us (kō'lē əs) *n.* any of a group of tropical plants or shrubs, genus *Coleus,* of the mint family, several species of which are cultivated as house plants because of their showy leaves, which are outlined or patterned in yellow, red, orange, or purple. [Modern Latin *Coleus,* from Greek *koleos* sheath; because of the way its stamens are joined.]

cole·wort (kōl'wurt') *n.* **1.** cole. **2.** cabbage with a loosely packed head.

col·ic (kol'ik) *n.* sudden attack of severe pain in the abdomen, esp. in infants. [French *colique,* from Late Latin *cōlicus* sick with colic, from Greek *kōlikos.*]

col·ick·y (kol'i kē) *adj.* **1.** having or subject to colic. **2.** relating to, producing, or resembling colic.

col·i·se·um (kol'ə sē'əm) *n.* large, usually oval, building or stadium in which athletic contests and other entertainments are presented. **2. Coliseum.** Colosseum. [Form of COLOSSEUM.]

co·li·tis (kə lī'tis) *n.* inflammatory disease of the colon, often characterized by abdominal cramps and diarrhea containing blood and mucus. [Modern Latin *colitis,* from Greek *kolon* large intestine + -ITIS.]

coll. 1. college. **2.** colleague. **3.** colloquial. **4.** collection. **5.** collector.

col·lab·o·rate (kə lab'ə rāt') **-rat·ed, -rat·ing.** *v.i.* **1.** to work or cooperate with another or others, esp. in connection with literary or scientific endeavors. **2.** to aid or cooperate traitorously; be a collaborationist. [Latin *collabōrātus,* past participle of *collabōrāre* to work together.] —**col·lab'o·ra'tion, col·lab'o·ra'tor,** *n.*

col·lab·o·ra·tion·ist (kə lab'ə rā'shə nist) *n.* one who practices or

at; āpe; cär; end; mē; it; īce; hot; ōld; fôrk; wood; fōōl; oil; out; up; ūse; turn; sing; thin; this; zh in treasure; ə in ago, taken, pencil, lemon, circus.

195

advocates cooperation with an enemy invader or occupier of his country.

col·lage (kə läzh′) *n.* **1.** artistic composition with an emphasis on texture and pattern, made by pasting objects and paper, cloth, or other materials together on a surface. **2.** art or technique of producing such compositions. [French *collage*, from *colle* glue, paste, from Greek *kolla.*]

col·lapse (kə laps′) -lapsed, -laps·ing. *v.i.* **1.** to fall in or together; cave in: *The roof collapsed when the beams gave way.* **2.** to become more compact by being folded or pushed together: *The cot collapses for easy storage.* **3.** to fail completely or suddenly; come to nothing: *His plans collapsed when he lost financial backing.* **4.** to lose strength or health, as from fatigue or disease. **5.** to fall down, as from a blow or exhaustion. —*v.t.* to cause to collapse. —*n.* **1.** falling in or together; cave-in. **2.** any sudden or complete failure. **3.** breakdown, as from exhaustion or a loss of health. [Latin *collapsus,* past participle of *collābī* to fall together, fall in ruins.]

col·laps·i·ble (kə lap′sə bəl) *also,* **col·laps·a·ble.** *adj.* capable of being folded or pushed together: *a collapsible chair.*

col·lar (kol′ər) *n.* **1.** part of a garment at the neckline, usually sewed on as a separate piece. **2.** separate band of jewels, cloth, fur, or other material worn to ornament the neckline. **3.** band, as of leather or metal, placed around the neck of an animal, esp. a dog. **4.** cushioned band that fits over the base of a horse's neck to bear the strain of the load he pulls. See **harness** for illustration. **5.** any of various devices, as a ring or flange on a rod or shaft, that prevent or limit sideward motion. —*v.t.* **1.** to put a collar on. **2.** to seize by the neck or collar. **3.** *Informal.* to lay hold of; seize. [Old French *colier* necklace, collar, from Latin *collāre,* from *collum* neck.]

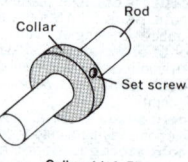

Collar (def. 5)

col·lar·bone (kol′ər bōn′) *n.* either of two bones connecting the breastbone and the shoulder blade; clavicle.

col·late (kə lāt′, kol′āt, kō′lāt) -lat·ed, -lat·ing. *v.t.* **1.** to arrange in proper order: *She collated the pages of the report.* **2.** to compare critically and carefully, as texts or facts. [Latin *collātus* brought together, past participle of *conferre* to bring together.] —**col·la′tor,** *n.*

col·lat·er·al (kə lat′ər əl) *adj.* **1.** situated or placed side by side; parallel. **2.** connected but occupying a subordinate position; secondary: *collateral causes.* **3.** accompanying; attendant. **4.** additional; confirming: *collateral evidence.* **5.** guaranteed or secured by collateral: *a collateral loan.* **6.** descended from common ancestors, but in a different line: *Children of brothers are collateral cousins.* —*n.* **1.** property, usually something for which there is a stable and immediately available market, as stocks or bonds, pledged as security for a loan. **2.** one who is related by blood, other than in the direct line of descent, as a nephew. [Medieval Latin *collateralis* alongside of, from Latin *col-* + *laterālis* lateral. See COL-.] —**col·lat′er·al·ly,** *adv.*

col·la·tion (kə lā′shən, kō-) *n.* **1.** act, process, or result of collating. **2.** light, informal, usually cold meal.

col·league (kol′ēg) *n.* fellow member, as of a profession; associate. [Middle French *collègue,* from Latin *collēga* partner in office.] —**Syn.** see **associate.**

col·lect (*v., adj., adv.,* kə lekt′; *n.,* kol′ekt) *v.t.* **1.** to gather together; assemble: *She collected old clothes for the rummage sale.* **2.** to make a collection of as a hobby or study: *to collect books.* **3.** to request and receive (payments or contributions): *to collect tolls.* **4.** to call for and remove: *He collected the garbage at five o'clock.* **5.** to regain control of or summon up: *to collect one's thoughts.* —*v.i.* **1.** to assemble: *A great crowd collected to hear the speaker.* **2.** to accumulate: *Old newspapers collected in front of the deserted house.* **3.** to request and receive payments or contributions: *She collects for charities.* —*n.* short prayer which varies according to feast day or season, used in certain liturgies, esp. the Roman Catholic and Anglican. —*adj., adv.* to be paid for at the time or place of delivery: *a collect phone call, to call collect.* [Latin *collēctus,* past participle of *colligere* to gather, bring together.] —**col·lect′a·ble;** *also,* **col·lect′i·ble,** *adj.* —**Syn.** *v.t.* **1.** see **gather.**

col·lect·ed (kə lek′tid) *adj.* in control of oneself; composed. —**col·lect′ed·ly,** *adv.* —**col·lect′ed·ness,** *n.*

col·lec·tion (kə lek′shən) *n.* **1.** act or process of collecting. **2.** that which is gathered together, esp. as a hobby or for study. **3.** act of soliciting and collecting money; money collected. **4.** that which has accumulated; mass.

col·lec·tive (kə lek′tiv) *adj.* **1.** of, relating to, characteristic of, or deriving from a group of persons or things; common; united. **2.** formed by collecting. **3.** constituting or representing a whole or collection. **4.** characterized by collectivism: *a collective farm.* —*n.* **1.** collective noun. **2.** organization or enterprise characterized by collectivism.

3. group of individuals who make up and work in such an organization or enterprise. —**col·lec′tive·ly,** *adv.*

collective bargaining, negotiation between union representatives and employers for reaching an agreement on terms of employment, as wages, hours, or working conditions.

collective noun, singular noun denoting a group of persons or things. It takes a singular verb if the group acts as a single unit, as in *The jury was locked in for the night;* it takes a plural verb if the group acts as individuals, as in *The jury were divided in their opinions.*

col·lec·tiv·ism (kə lek′ti viz′əm) *n.* economic and political system in which the people as a community or the government owns and controls the means of production and distribution. —**col·lec′tiv·ist,** *adj., n.* —**col·lec′tiv·is′tic,** *adj.*

col·lec·tor (kə lek′tər) *n.* **1.** one who collects objects of interest or value: *rare book collector, coin collector.* **2.** one who is employed to collect money due: *a tax collector, a toll collector.* **3.** any thing or person that collects. —**col·lec′tor·ship′,** *n.*

col·leen (kol′ēn, ko lēn′) *n.* girl, esp. an Irish girl. [Irish Gaelic *cailín,* diminutive of *caile* girl.]

col·lege (kol′ij) *n.* **1.** institution of higher education that grants degrees upon completion of courses of general study in liberal arts and sciences. **2.** a major division in a university that offers a four-year course of general or specialized study leading to a bachelor's degree, as distinguished from the professional, graduate, or technical schools. **3.** independent institution for vocational or technical instruction that grants no academic degrees: *a barber's college.* **4.** higher education in general: *to go to college.* **5.** group of individuals engaged in a common pursuit and having certain rights, duties, and powers. **6.** building or buildings and grounds occupied by a college. [Latin *collēgium* association, society of persons.]

College of Cardinals, cardinals of the Roman Catholic Church, collectively, who elect and advise the pope. Also, **Sacred College, Sacred College of Cardinals.**

col·le·gian (kə lē′jən, -jē ən) *n.* **1.** college student. **2.** member of a college.

col·le·giate (kə lē′jit, -jē it) *adj.* **1.** of, for, or characteristic of college students: *a collegiate program of study.* **2.** of or like a college.

col·lide (kə līd′) -lid·ed, -lid·ing. *v.i.* **1.** to come together with force; crash: *The two cars collided.* **2.** to clash; conflict. [Latin *collīdere* to clash together.]

col·lie (kol′ē) *n.* dog originally bred for tending sheep, having a long, narrow head, slender body, and typically, a long-haired coat of white and tan or white, tan, and black. Height: to 2 feet at the shoulder. [Of uncertain origin.]

Collie

col·lier (kol′yər) *n. British.* **1.** coal miner. **2.a.** ship for transporting coal. **b.** one of its crew. [Middle English *colier* charcoal burner, from *col.* See COAL.]

col·lier·y (kol′yər ē) *pl.,* -lier·ies. *n.* a coal mine with its buildings and equipment.

col·li·mate (kol′ə māt′) -mat·ed, -mat·ing. *v.t.* **1.** to bring into line; make parallel; to collimate diverging rays of light. **2.** to adjust the line of sight of (an instrument): *to collimate a telescope.* [Latin *collimātus,* past participle of *collimāre,* incorrect reading for *collīneāre* to aim, going back to *co-* together + *līnea* line.] —**col′li·ma′tion,** *n.*

col·lin·e·ar (kə lin′ē ər, kō-) *adj.* (of points) contained in the same straight line.

col·li·sion (kə lizh′ən) *n.* **1.** a coming together with force; act of colliding. **2.** opposition; conflict: *a collision of interests.* [Late Latin *collīsiō* a dashing together, from Latin *collīdere* to clash together.]

col·lo·cate (kol′ə kāt′) -cat·ed, -cat·ing. *v.t.* to place or arrange side by side or in relation to one another: *to collocate ideas.* [Latin *collocātus,* past participle of *collocāre* to place together.] —**col′lo·ca′tion,** *n.*

col·lo·di·on (kə lō′dē ən) *n.* flammable, gluelike solution of pyroxylin in a mixture of alcohol and ether, which leaves a transparent, plastic film upon evaporating, chiefly used to coat minor wounds and to make such items as patent leather and artificial pearls. [Greek *kollōdēs* like glue, from *kolla* glue.]

col·loid (kol′oid) *n.* **1.** substance evenly dispersed through another substance in particles that are larger than ordinary molecules but too small to be visible to the naked eye. Both the particles and the medium in which they are dispersed may be a gas, liquid, or solid. **2.** colloidal system. [Greek *kolla* glue + -OID.] —**col·loi·dal** (kə loid′əl), *adj.* —**col·loi′dal·ly,** *adv.*

colloidal system, combination of a colloid and the substance in which it is dispersed. If left undisturbed, the particles of a colloidal system will not precipitate but will remain dispersed. Sols, emulsions, and aerosols are colloidal systems. Also, **colloidal dispersion.**

at; āpe; cär; end; mē; it; īce; hot; ōld; fôrk; wood; fōōl; oil; out; up; ūse; turn; sing; thin; this; zh in treasure; ə in ago, taken, pencil, lemon, circus.

colloq., colloquial; colloquialism.

col·lo·qui·al (kə lōʹkwē əl) *adj.* (of language) used in, characteristic of, or appropriate for ordinary or familiar conversation: *"Movie" is a colloquial term for "motion picture".* —**col·loʹqui·al·ly,** *adv.* —**col·loʹqui·al·ness,** *n.*

col·lo·qui·al·ism (kə lōʹkwē ə lizʹəm) *n.* **1.** colloquial word, phrase, or expression. **2.** the use of these; colloquial style or usage.

col·lo·qui·um (kə lōʹkwē əm) *n.* group discussion or conference. [Latin *colloquium.*]

col·lo·quy (kolʹə kwē) *pl.* **-quies.** *n.* **1.** conversation, discussion, or conference, esp. one that is formally arranged. **2.** literary work written in the form of a dialogue or conversation. [Latin *colloquium* conversation, conference.]

col·lude (kə lōōdʹ) **-lud·ed, -lud·ing.** *v.i.* to act in collusion; cooperate secretly; conspire; plot. [Latin *collūdere* to play with, act secretly and deceptively.]

col·lu·sion (kə lōōʹzhən) *n.* secret agreement or cooperation between two or more persons for a fraudulent or deceitful purpose, esp. one arranged to defraud another or to circumvent the law. [Latin *collūsiō.*] —**Syn.** see **conspiracy.**

col·lu·sive (kə lōōʹsiv) *adj.* characterized by or involving collusion. —**col·luʹsive·ly,** *adv.* —**col·luʹsive·ness,** *n.*

Colo., Colorado.

co·logne (kə lōnʹ) *n.* fragrant liquid made from alcohol and scented oils and used as perfume. Also, **eau de Cologne.** [It was first manufactured in COLOGNE.]

Co·logne (kə lōnʹ) *n.* city in the western part of West Germany, near Bonn. Pop. (1968 est.), 853,864. Also, German, **Köln.**

Co·lom·bi·a (kə lumʹbē ə) *n.* nation in northwestern South America, on the Pacific and the Caribbean. Capital, Bogotá. Area, 439,513 sq. mi. Pop. (1970 est.), 21,117,000. [From Christopher COLUMBUS.] —**Co·lomʹbi·an,** *adj., n.*

Co·lom·bo (kə lumʹbō) *n.* capital and chief port of Ceylon, on the west coast of the island. Pop. (1967 est.), 551,200.

co·lon¹ (kōʹlən) *n.* mark of punctuation (:) used chiefly to introduce, set apart, or direct attention to that which follows, as a list or series, a quotation, or an explanation. [Greek *kōlon* limb, clause; because it often separates a clause.]

co·lon² (kōʹlən) *pl.* **co·lons** or **co·la** (kōʹlə). *n.* lower part of the large intestine, extending from the cecum to the rectum. [Latin *colon* large intestine, from Greek *kolon.*]

co·lon³ (kō lōnʹ) *pl.* **co·lons** or **co·lo·nes** (kō lōʹnäs). *n.* monetary unit of Costa Rica and El Salvador, equal to 100 centimos. [Spanish *colón,* from Cristóbal *Colón,* Spanish for Christopher COLUMBUS.]

colo·nel (kurʹnəl) *n.* military officer usually ranking above a lieutenant colonel and below a brigadier general. [French *colonel,* from Italian *colonnello* literally, little column (of soldiers led by him), from *colonna* column, from Latin *columna.*] —**coloʹnel·cy, coloʹnel·ship,** *n.*

co·lo·ni·al (kə lōʹnē əl) *adj.* **1.** of or relating to a colony or colonies: *colonial government, the disintegration of colonial empires.* **2.a.** also, **Colonial.** of, relating to, or characteristic of the thirteen British colonies that became the United States of America. **b.** of, relating to, or characteristic of the period of these colonies. —*n.* member or inhabitant of a colony. —**co·loʹni·al·ly,** *adv.*

co·lo·ni·al·ism (kə lōʹnē ə lizʹəm) *n.* **1.** policy of a nation seeking to acquire, extend, or retain its political, economic, and cultural control over other peoples or territories. **2.** state of being a colony.

col·o·nist (kolʹə nist) *n.* **1.** member or inhabitant of a colony. **2.** one who helps to found or settle a colony.

col·o·nize (kolʹə nīzʹ) **-nized, -niz·ing.** *v.t.* **1.** to establish a colony or colonies in; send colonists to: *Spain colonized parts of South America.* **2.** to migrate to and settle in; occupy as a colony: *The Puritans colonized Plymouth.* —*v.i.* to form or establish a colony or colonies. —**col·o·ni·zaʹtion, colʹo·nizʹer,** *n.*

col·on·nade (kolʹə nādʹ) *n.* series of columns, placed at regular intervals, usually supporting an entablature. [French *colonnade,* from Italian *colonnato,* from *colonna* column, from Latin *columna.*]

col·o·ny (kolʹə nē) *pl.* **-nies.** *n.* **1.** any territory politically, economically, and culturally subject to another, usually distant, country. **2.a.** body of emigrants or their descendants living in an area or land apart from, but under the control of, the parent country: *A colony of Puritans settled in Plymouth.* **b.** area or land so inhabited: *Plymouth was an English colony.* **3. the Colonies.** the thirteen British col-

Colonnade

onies that became the first states of the United States: New Hampshire, Massachusetts, Rhode Island, Connecticut, New York, New Jersey, Pennsylvania, Delaware, Maryland, Virginia, North Carolina, South Carolina, and Georgia. **4.a.** group of people living or drawn together in a locality because of common nationality, religion, or interests: *the American colony in Paris.* **b.** area or district inhabited or occupied by such a group. **5.** group of animals or plants of the same kind, living or growing together in the same place: *a colony of bees.* [Latin *colōnia* farm, settlement, going back to *colere* to cultivate.]

col·o·phon (kolʹə fonʹ, -fən) *n.* **1.** identifying device, as a distinctive emblem or trademark, of a publisher or printer. **2.** inscription formerly placed at the end of a book, giving the publisher and other information relative to its publication. [Greek *kolophōn* summit, finishing touch.]

col·or (kulʹər) *also, British,* **col·our.** *n.* **1.** quality of an object or substance, perceived as a visual sensation, resulting from its transmission or reflection of light of any or all of the various parts of the spectrum. **2.** one of the constituents of the spectrum, sometimes including black and white; particular hue, tint, or shade. **3.** two or more of these used as or in a medium of presentation: *That television show is in color. We've got a picture of her in color.* **4.** that which is used for coloring, as paint, dye, or pigment. **5.** rosiness of the skin, esp. of the face, characteristic of good health. **6.** ruddiness or redness of or as if of a blush. **7.** skin pigmentation or complexion, esp. as regarded as a racial feature: *without regard to race, creed, or color.* **8.** vivid, lively, or picturesque quality or character; vitality; interest: *Her anecdotes added color to her lecture.* **9.** general character or variety; nature: *a development that changed the whole color of the political situation.* **10.** outward show or appearance, often concealing an underlying true character; semblance; aspect: *The nonsense he was speaking had the color of reason.* **11.** false appearance or pretense; pretext; disguise: *a tyrant who carried out crimes against the people under the color of justice.* **12. colors. a.** any distinctive color or pattern of colors, as of a badge or uniform, worn or used as a symbol or for identification: *my school colors, party colors, a jockey's colors.* **b.** flag, ensign, or standard, as of a regiment or school, esp. the national flag: *They raised the colors over the captured fort.* **c.** personality; characteristics; attitude: *to show one's true colors.* **13.** *Music.* timbre or distinguishing quality of tone. **14.** particle of metal, esp. gold, found in soil, rock, or other material, usually indicating the quality of the ore in which it is contained. —*v.t.* **1.** to give or apply color to, as by painting, dyeing, or staining: *He colored the pictures with a yellow crayon. She colors her hair.* **2.** to cause to appear different from the reality; misrepresent, as by distorting or exaggerating: *to color one's account of an incident. The witness colored his testimony.* **3.** to modify or change in character or nature; affect; influence: *Your judgment is being colored by your emotions.* —*v.i.* **1.** to become red in the face; blush; flush. **2.** to take on or change color. [Old French *color* complexion, hue, appearance, from Latin *color.*] —**colʹor·er,** *n.*

Col·o·rad·o (kolʹə radʹō, -räʹdō) *n.* **1.** state in the western United States. Capital, Denver. Area, 104,247 sq. mi. Pop. (1970), 2,207,259. Abbreviation, **Colo. 2.** river flowing from northern Colorado into the Gulf of California. **3.** desert in southeastern California and northwestern Mexico. —**Col·o·radʹan,** *adj., n.*

Colorado potato beetle, small, oval yellow beetle with black stripes, *Leptinotarsa decemlineata,* found throughout North America and Europe, which feeds on the leaves of potato plants and attacks such plants as tomatoes and eggplants. Also, **potato beetle, potato bug.**

Colorado Springs, city in central Colorado, site of the U.S. Air Force Academy. Pop. (1970), 135,060.

col·or·a·tion (kulʹə rāʹshən) *n.* arrangement of colors; appearance as to color; coloring.

col·or·a·tu·ra (kulʹər ə toorʹə, -tyoorʹə) *n.* **1.** coloratura soprano. **2.** florid ornamentations, such as trills or runs, in vocal music. **3.** music characterized by such ornamentation. —*adj.* characterized by or suitable for coloratura. [Italian *coloratura* ornamental musical passages; literally, coloring, from *colorare* to color, from Latin *colōrāre.*]

coloratura soprano 1. high soprano voice having a wide range and great flexibility, trained for performing coloratura. **2.** singer with such a voice.

col·or·bear·er (kulʹər bârʹər) *n.* one who carries the colors or flag, as in a ceremony or parade.

col·or·blind (kulʹər blīndʹ) *adj.* affected with color blindness.

color blindness, impairment in the ability to perceive colors. It is most often a difficulty in distinguishing between certain colors, as between red and green, but sometimes it is a total inability to distinguish any colors except black, white, and gray.

col·or·cast (kulʹər kastʹ) *n.* television program broadcast in color. —*v.t., v.i.* to broadcast (a television program) in color.

col·ored (kulʹərd) *adj.* **1.** having color, esp. other than solid black or white. **2.** of a race other than the Caucasoid, esp. of the Negro race. **3.** influenced, as by prejudice or emotion; distorted; slanted: *a highly colored account of what had occurred.*

col·or·fast (kul′ər fast′) *adj.* (of fabrics) having color that is resistant to fading or running.

color film, film for taking color photographs and slides.

col·or·ful (kul′ər fəl) *adj.* **1.** abounding or rich in color. **2.** vivid, lively, or picturesque. —**col′or·ful·ly,** *adv.* —**col′or·ful·ness,** *n.*

color guard, persons who carry and escort the colors, as in a ceremony.

col·or·im·e·ter (kul′ə rim′ə tər) *n.* instrument used to measure the hue, purity, and brightness of a color. —**col·or·i·met·ric** (kul′ər ə met′rik) *adj.; also,* **col′or·i·met′ri·cal** (kul′ər ə met′ri kəl), *adj.* —**col′or·im′e·try,** *n.*

col·or·ing (kul′ər ing) *n.* **1.** way in which anything is colored; complexion or appearance as to color: *the coloring of the autumn landscape, a fawn's mottled coloring.* **2.** substance used to impart color: *food coloring.* **3.** act or technique of applying color. **4.** false appearance or semblance.

coloring book, book of outline drawings for coloring with crayons or other materials.

col·or·ist (kul′ər ist) *n.* one who uses or works with color, esp. an artist who uses colors skillfully or a hairdresser who specializes in dyeing women's hair.

col·or·less (kul′ər lis) *adj.* **1.** lacking liveliness or distinctive character; not vivid or interesting; dull: *a colorless personality.* **2.** without color: *a colorless liquid.* **3.** dull in or empty of color; pallid: *His face was white and colorless.* —**col′or·less·ly,** *adv.* —**col′or·less·ness,** *n.*

co·los·sal (kə los′əl) *adj.* **1.** extraordinarily or awesomely large; immense; gigantic; vast. **2.** *Informal.* of an extraordinary or astonishing degree: *The show was a colossal success.* —**co·los′sal·ly,** *adv.*

Col·os·se·um (kol′ə sē′əm) *n.* **1.** oval-shaped amphitheater in Rome, built between A.D. 72 and 82, that was the site of games and gladiatorial fights in ancient times. Also, **Col′i·se′um. 2. colosseum.** coliseum (*def. !*). [Late Latin *colossēum,* noun use of neuter of Latin *colossēus* gigantic, from *colossus.* See COLOSSUS.]

Co·los·sians (kə losh′əns) *n.,pl.* book of the New Testament, consisting of a letter written by Saint Paul to a Christian community in Asia Minor. ▲ construed as singular.

co·los·sus (kə los′əs) *pl.* **-los·si** (-los′ī) or **-los·sus·es.** *n.* **1.** gigantic statue. **2.** person or thing of awesome or immense size or power. [Latin *colossus* gigantic statue, from Greek *kolossos.*]

Colossus of Rhodes, bronze statue of the sun god Helios that stood at the entrance to the harbor of Rhodes. It was built about 280 B.C. and was more than a hundred feet high.

co·los·trum (kə los′trəm) *n.* milky fluid secreted after parturition by the female mammary gland. [Latin *colostrum.*]

col·our (kul′ər) *British.* color.

col·por·teur (kol′pôr′tər) *n.* person who travels about selling or distributing Bibles and religious literature. [French *colporteur* peddler, from *colporter* to peddle; literally, to carry on the neck; modification (influenced by French *col* neck) of Old French *comporter* to transport, from Latin *comportāre* to bring together.]

colt (kōlt) *n.* **1.** male horse, or other male member of the horse family, under four years old. **2.** *Informal.* foal. **3.** young or inexperienced person. [Old English *colt* young camel, young ass.]

col·ter (kōl′tər) *also,* **coul·ter.** *n.* sharp blade or disk attached to a plow to cut the earth ahead of the plowshare. [Old English *culter,* from Latin *culter* knife, plowshare.]

colt·ish (kōl′tish) *adj.* **1.** not trained or disciplined; awkward; unruly. **2.** having the liveliness of a colt; frisky; playful. **3.** of, relating to, or resembling a colt.

colts·foot (kōlts′foot′) *pl.* **-foots.** *n.* plant bearing yellow flower heads, *Tussilago farfara,* of the composite family, having large leaves whose shape suggests a horse's hoofprint.

Co·lum·bi·a (kə lum′bē ə) *n.* **1.** river flowing into the Pacific that forms most of the border between Washington and Oregon. **2.** capital of South Carolina, in the central part of the state. Pop. (1970), 113,542. **3.** city in central Missouri. Pop. (1970), 58,804. **4.** the United States of America. **5.** university in New York City. [From Christopher COLUMBUS.]

Co·lum·bi·an (kə lum′bē ən) *adj.* **1.** of or relating to Columbia (*defs. 2, 3*). **2.** of or relating to Christopher Columbus.

col·um·bine (kol′əm bīn′) *n.* **1.** showy, drooping flower of any of a group of plants, genus *Aquilegia,* growing in a variety of colors and having five petals that extend backward to form hollow, tubelike projections. **2.** plant bearing this flower. [Late Latin *columbīna* the plant, from Latin *columbīnus* like a dove, from *columba* dove; because its flower was thought to resemble a group of doves.]

Columbine

Col·um·bine (kol′əm bīn′) *n.* stock character from commedia dell'-

arte, sweetheart of Harlequin, usually costumed in a tutu. [Italian *Colombina,* diminutive of *colomba* dove, from Latin *columba.*]

co·lum·bi·um (kə lum′bē əm) *n.* niobium. [Modern Latin *columbium,* from *Columbia* the United States, where it was first found. See COLUMBIA.]

Co·lum·bus (kə lum′bəs) **1. Christopher.** c.1451–1506, Italian explorer who discovered America for Spain in 1492. **2.** capital of Ohio, in the central part of the state. Pop. (1970), 539,677. **3.** city in western Georgia. Pop. (1970), 154,168.

Columbus Day, legal holiday commemorating the discovery of America by Christopher Columbus. October 12.

col·umn (kol′əm) *n.* **1.** written or printed group of items arranged one above the others; vertical row: *a column of figures.* **2.** one of two or more vertical sections of printed or written matter on a sheet or page, separated by lines or by blank spaces. **3.** feature article that appears regularly or at intervals in a newspaper, magazine, or periodical, written by a single editor or special writer or devoted to a particular subject: *a gossip column.* **4.** upright structure, usually cylindrical and longer than it is wide, consisting of a base, shaft, and capital, and serving as a support or ornament, as for part of a building, or standing alone as a monument. **5.** something resembling such a structure: *the white column of her throat. A column of smoke appeared above the hill.* **6.** military formation in which the units, as men, vehicles, or ships, are arranged one behind the other in one or more rows. Distinguished from **line. 7.** something resembling such a formation: *a column of ants.* [Latin *columna* pillar.]

Capital
Shaft
Base

Column

co·lum·nar (kə lum′nər) *adj.* **1.** relating to or resembling a column. **2.** made of, with, or arranged in columns.

co·lum·ni·a·tion (kə lum′nē ā′shən) *n.* use or arrangement of columns in a structure.

col·um·nist (kol′əm nist, -ə mist) *n.* writer or editor of a column in a newspaper, magazine, or periodical.

col·za (kol′zə) *n.* **1.** rapeseed. **2.** rapeoil. [French *colza* rapeseed, going back to Dutch *kool* cabbage (from Latin *caulis*) + *zaad* seed.]

com- *prefix* in association with; together: *combine.* [Latin *com-,* form of *cum* with, together.]

com. 1. comedy. **2.** commerce. **3.** common; commonly.

Com. 1. Commissioner. **2.** Commission. **3.** Committee.

co·ma¹ (kō′mə) *pl.* **co·mas.** *n.* **1.** state of unconsciousness from which a person cannot be aroused by an external stimulus, caused by disease, injury, or poison. It may last for hours, days, or months, or, in rare cases, for years. **2.** *Informal.* state of mental distraction or apathy; stupor. [Modern Latin *coma,* from Greek *kōma* deep sleep.]

co·ma² (kō′mə) *pl.* **co·mae** (kō′mē). *n.* **1.** gaseous, luminous envelope surrounding the nucleus of a comet. **2.** tuft of long silky hairs or bristles at the end of certain seeds. [Latin *coma* hair (of the head), from Greek *komē.*]

Co·man·che (kə man′chē) *pl.* **-ches** or **-che.** *n.* **1.** member of a tribe of North American Indians formerly of the southern part of the Great Plains, now living in Oklahoma. **2.** language of this tribe, belonging to the Uto-Aztecan language family. [Spanish *Comanche* member of this tribe, probably from Ute *komanci* stranger.]

com·a·tose (kom′ə tōs′, kō′mə-) *adj.* **1.** relating to, characterized by, or in a coma. **2.** *Informal.* apathetic; lethargic; torpid. [Greek *kōma* deep sleep + -OSE¹.]

comb (kōm) *n.* **1.** toothed implement of plastic, bone, metal, or other sturdy material, for smoothing, arranging, or fastening the hair. **2.** something resembling a comb in shape or function, as a card for dressing fibers. **3.** thick, usually reddish, fleshy growth on the head of domestic fowl and certain other birds, most fully developed in the male. **4.** something resembling this, as the crest of a wave. **5.** honeycomb. **6.** currycomb. —*v.t.* **1.** to smooth or arrange (the hair) with or as with the comb. **2.** to remove with or as with a comb. **3.** to search (something) extensively and with care; look everywhere in: *They combed the woods looking for the child.* **4.** to card, as fibers. —*v.i.* **1.** to search extensively and with care (usually with *through*). **2.** (of waves) to roll over or break at the crest. [Old English *camb* implement for arranging the hair, cock's crest.]

com·bat (*n.,* kom′bat; *v.,* kəm bat′, kom′bat) *n.* **1.** military engagement with an enemy: *a soldier wounded in combat.* **2.** fight, contest, or struggle, esp. a direct physical struggle between two persons. —*v.t.* **-bat·ed, -bat·ing;** *also, British.* **-bat·ted, -bat·ting. 1.** to take measures or struggle against; oppose vigorously; resist: *to combat inflation.* **2.** to engage in battle. —*v.i.* **1.** to fight; struggle. [Old French *combatre* to fight, going back to Latin *com-* with + *battuere* to beat, strike.] —**com·bat′er,** *n.* —**Syn.** *n.* **2.** see **fight.**

at; āpe; cär; end; mē; it; īce; hot; ōld; fôrk; wood; fōol; oil; out; up; ūse; turn; sing; thin; this; zh in treasure; ə in ago, taken, pencil, lemon, circus.

com·bat·ant (kəm bat′ənt, kom′bət ənt) *n.* one who or that which is engaged in or ready for combat or hostilities; fighter. —*adj.* **1.** ready or disposed to fight. **2.** fighting.

combat boot, heavy, laced leather boot designed to be worn by military personnel.

combat fatigue, battle fatigue.

com·bat·ive (kəm bat′iv, kom′bə tiv) *adj.* ready or eager to fight; quarrelsome; pugnacious. —**com·bat′ive·ly,** *adv.* —**com·bat′ive·ness,** *n.*

combe (kōōm, kōm) *also.* **coomb, comb.** *n. British.* deep narrow valley or deep hollow. [Old English *cumb;* of Celtic origin.]

comb·er (kō′mər) *n.* **1.** long, rolling wave that curls over or breaks at the crest. **2.** one who or that which combs, as a carder.

com·bi·na·tion (kom′bə nā′shen) *n.* **1.** that which is formed by combining; mixture; union: *Green is a combination of yellow and blue.* **2.a.** series of numbers or letters dialed in a set sequence or direction to open a combination lock. **b.** mechanism of a combination lock. **3.** act of combining; being combined. **4.** alliance or association of persons or groups to further some common purpose. **5.** one-piece undergarment consisting of an undershirt or chemise and drawers. **6.** any of the possible arrangements of a certain number of or all the elements of a set, in which the order is immaterial. Some possible combinations of *x, y,* and *z* are *xy, xz,* and *yz.*

combination lock, lock opened by turning one or more dials to a series of numbers or letters in a set sequence or direction.

com·bine (*v.,* kəm bīn′; *n.,* kom′bīn) **-bined, -bin·ing.** *v.t.* **1.** to bring into close relationship; join together; unite: *to combine forces.* **2.** to cause to mix together; mingle; blend. **3.** to possess or exhibit simultaneously or in union. —*v.i.* **1.** to become one; constitute a whole; merge: *The colonies combined to form the United States.* **2.** to associate or unite for a common purpose; form an alliance; act together. **3.** to unite to form a chemical compound. One atom of carbon combines with two atoms of oxygen to form a molecule of carbon dioxide, CO_2. —*n.* **1.** alliance of persons or groups for business or political purposes or to further personal interests. **2.** farm machine, either tractor-drawn or self-propelled, that combines the functions of a harvester and a thresher by cutting, threshing, and cleaning grains and other field crops. [Late Latin *combīnāre* to unite, from Latin *com-* together + *bīnī* two each, two at a time.] —**com·bin′a·ble,** *adj.* —**com·bin′er,** *n.* —**Syn.** *v.t.* see **join.**

comb·ings (kō′mingz) *n.,pl.* hairs, wool, or other material removed by or from a comb.

combining form, linguistic form, usually a stem of a word, often of Greek or Latin origin, used only to form compound words and never independently, as *psycho-* in *psychoanalysis.*

comb jelly, any of a group of saltwater invertebrates, phylum Ctenophora, that move by means of cilia extending lengthwise along the body and that often have two trailing tentacles with sticky cells for capturing food. Length: from ¾ inch to 3 feet. Also, **cten′o·phore′.**

Comb jelly

com·bo (kom′bō) *n.* **1.** small jazz or dance band, usually three or four musicians. **2.** *Informal.* combination (def. 1). [Modification and shortening of COMBINATION.]

com·bus·ti·ble (kəm bus′tə bəl) *adj.* **1.** capable of catching fire and burning. **2.** easily aroused or excited; fiery. —*n.* substance capable of catching fire and burning. —**com·bus′ti·bil′i·ty,** *n.* —**com·bus′ti·bly,** *adv.*

com·bus·tion (kəm bus′chən) *n.* **1.** act or process of burning. **2.a.** rapid oxidation of a substance accompanied by the release of heat and sometimes light. **b.** any chemical reaction attended by the release of heat or light. **c.** slow oxidation accompanied by little heat and no light, as of food in the body. **3.** violent agitation or disturbance. [Late Latin *combustiō* a burning, from Latin *combustus,* past participle of *combūrere* to burn up.]

Comdr., Commander.

Comdt., Commandant.

come (kum) **came, come, com·ing.** *v.i.* **1.** to move or advance to or toward the speaker or a particular place; draw near; approach: *Will you please come here? He's coming down the street now.* **2.** to advance or arrive as the result of motion or progress: *He came to the first barrier and jumped over it. They came home for the holidays. Now we come to Chapter three.* **3.** to arrive or occur in time, in due course, or in orderly progression: *Easter comes late this year. Wait till your turn comes.* **4.** to move, pass, or be brought into a particular state, condition, or position: *to come into prominence, to come into play, to come to a boil. We came to a sudden stop. It came to my attention.* **5.** to exist or occur in a particular place or position or at a particular point: *Five comes before six.* **6.** to reach; extend: *Her hair comes to her shoulders. She barely comes up to his chin.* **7.** to be derived; originate; emanate: *Paper pulp comes from trees. I can't believe those words came from his mouth.* **8.** to be or have been a native or resident (with *from*): *They come from California.* **9.** to make progress; manage; fare (often with *on*): *The plants are coming on nicely. The project's coming along well. He's coming along rapidly with his studies.* **10.** to be born or issue; descend: *They come from a well-known family.* **11.** to be classified or be included: *Budget control comes under managerial duties. This case comes under the jurisdiction of a lower court.* **12.** to take place; befall; occur: *They said no harm would come to us. Come what may. I'll be there.* **13.** to exist or happen as a result: *This comes of your carelessness. No good will come of it.* **14.** to be available, offered, sold, or produced: *This dress comes in several colors. This car comes with or without a convertible top. Gasoline came high during the war.* **15.** to prove or turn out to be: *The prediction came true.* **16.** to be passed along, as by tradition or inheritance (often with *down*): *customs that have come down to us through many generations.* **17.** to occur to the mind: *The idea just came to me.* **18.** to be within one's range of possible activities or talents: *Skiing comes easily to her. Math doesn't come easily to him.* **19.** to relate; concern; involve: *When it comes to details, he's very sloppy.* **20.** *Informal.* **a.** to chance; happen: *How'd you come to know that? How'd they come to meet her?* **b.** to exist: *He's as mean as they come.*

to come about. a. to take place; occur; happen. **b.** *Nautical.* to shift to another tack.

to come across. a. to find or meet with by chance. **b.** to be clear, convincing, or understandable; be communicated, as to an audience. **c.** *Slang.* to do or give what is demanded or expected of one, esp. to pay over money; make good one's promise.

to come around (or **round**). **a.** to recover consciousness; revive. **b.** to change one's opinion, attitude, or stance so as to agree with another's; be persuaded.

to come at. to rush toward; attack.

to come back. to occur to the mind again: *It all comes back to me now.*

to come back (at). *Informal.* to retort or answer (someone) sharply: *He came back at her with a nasty remark. She came back with a question just as cutting.*

to come between. to cause bad feeling; estrange; separate: *Don't let a little thing like that come between you two.*

to come by. to gain; obtain; acquire: *This jewel is honestly come by. How did you come by such wealth?*

to come down on (or **upon**). *Informal.* to take to task; upbraid; scold: *The principal came down hard on him.*

to come down with. *Informal.* to become ill with: *She came down with the flu.*

to come forward. to offer or present oneself, as for work or duty; volunteer.

to come in. to be brought into use or fashion.

to come in for. to be eligible to receive or be subjected to; get; acquire: *He came in for a share of the blame.*

to come into. a. to inherit. **b.** to get; obtain; acquire.

to come off. to take place; occur; happen: *The party came off successfully.*

to come on. *Informal.* to give the impression of being; appear to be: *He comes on like a big executive.*

to come out. a. to become known or evident; be disclosed or revealed: *The truth has come out at last.* **b.** to declare oneself; express or reveal one's opinions: *He came out for community control of schools.* **c.** to be published or released; be presented to the public: *The magazine comes out once a month. That movie came out last year.* **d.** to emerge; end; result: *Everything will come out all right.* **e.** to make a formal social debut.

to come out with. a. to give vent to; declare openly; utter: *He came out with a derogatory remark.* **b.** to make available or offer to the public: *The company came out with three new models.*

to come over. to take possession of; happen to; seize: *A strange feeling came over me. What's come over you?*

to come through. a. to endure or finish successfully; survive. **b.** *Informal.* to perform or do what is expected or anticipated.

to come to. a. to recover consciousness; revive. **b.** to be equal or equivalent to; amount to: *The bill comes to $5. It all comes to the same thing.* **c.** *Nautical.* to anchor.

to come up. to be presented as the subject of attention; arise: *The bill came up for debate. The question came up during our discussion.*

to come upon (or **on**). **a.** to find or meet with by chance. **b.** to attack, esp. suddenly.

to come up to. to compare with, as to excellence or quantity; rival, as a standard; equal: *His work didn't come up to that of his brother. The results did not come up to his anticipation.*

to come up with. to think of or produce; present; propose: *He came up with a new suggestion. They came up with the answer.*

[Old English *cuman* to go toward, happen.]

at; āpe; cär; end; mē; it; īce; hot; ōld; fôrk; wood; fōōl; oil; out; up; ūse; turn; sing; thin; this; zh in treasure; ə in ago, taken, pencil, lemon, circus.

199

come·back (kum′bak′) *n.* **1.** return to or recovery of a former prosperity, condition, or position: *a boxer who made a remarkable comeback.* **2.** *Informal.* clever or effective retort.

co·me·di·an (kə mē′dē ən) *n.* **1.** professional entertainer, as in a nightclub or on a television show, who tells jokes, does amusing impersonations, or performs comic routines. **2.** actor who specializes in comic roles. **3.** *Informal.* one who continually amuses or attempts to amuse others. [French *comédien* actor, from *comédie.* See COMEDY.]

co·me·di·enne (kə mē′dē en′) *n.* **1.** female who is a professional comic entertainer. **2.** actress who specializes in comic roles.

come·down (kum′doun′) *n.* change for the worse in one's circumstances; descent in position or status, esp. a humiliating one.

com·e·dy (kom′ə dē) *pl.,* **-dies.** *n.* **1.** drama in which life is viewed or treated humorously and which usually has a happy ending. **2.** branch of drama composed of such plays. Distinguished from **tragedy.** **3.** any piece of literature or presentation on stage, screen, television, or radio of a humorous nature. **4.** art of writing, acting, or producing a comedy or comedies. **5.** situation or series of events having humorous or comic qualities. **6.** humorous or comic state, quality, or effect. [Old French *comedie* play, humorous play, from Latin *cōmoedia* humorous play, from Greek *kōmōidia,* going back to *kōmos* revel + *aeidein* to sing; because comedies in ancient Greece were originally festive performances with singing.] —**co·me·dic** (kə mē′dik, -med′ik); *also,* **co·me′di·cal,** *adj.*

come-hith·er (kum′hith′ər) *adj.* inviting or alluring; seductive.

come·ly (kum′lē) **-li·er, -li·est.** *adj.* **1.** pleasing in appearance; good-looking; attractive. **2.** suitable; proper; becoming. [Old English *cȳmlīc* beautiful.] —**come′li·ness,** *n.*

come-on (kum′ôn′, -on′) *n.* *Slang.* something or someone offered to allure or attract; lure; inducement.

com·er (kum′ər) *n.* **1.** one who comes or arrives: *The challenger was willing to take on all comers.* **2.** *Informal.* one who or that which shows great promise or potential.

co·mes·ti·ble (kə mes′tə bəl) *n.* *also,* **comestibles.** food. —*adj.* edible; eatable. [Late Latin *comestibilis,* from Latin *comestus,* past participle of *comedere* to eat up.]

com·et (kom′it) *n.* bright celestial body, traveling in a long elliptical orbit around the sun, consisting largely of ice, frozen gases, and dust particles, and having one or more long, gaseous, visible tails that point away from the sun. [Old French *comete,* from Latin *comēta,* from Greek *komētēs (astēr)* literally, long-haired (star); referring to its tail.]

come-up·pance (kum′up′əns) *also,* **come-up·ance.** *n.* *Informal.* punishment or retribution one deserves; just deserts.

com·fit (kum′fit, kom′-) *n.* piece of candy or sweetmeat; confection. [Old French *confit* literally, preserved, past participle of *confire* to candy, preserve, from Late Latin *conficere* to prepare.]

com·fort (kum′fərt) *n.* **1.** state of ease, well-being, and satisfaction of bodily wants, with freedom from pain or anxiety: *With that income you'll be able to live in comfort.* **2.** relief or support in affliction or sorrow; consolation; solace: *to bring comfort to the sick.* **3.** one who or that which gives or provides this: *Jack was a comfort to his father after his mother's death.* **4.** *also,* **comforts.** that which gives physical ease, well-being, or cheer. **5.** ability to give physical ease and well-being. **6.** cause or matter of satisfaction or relief: *It's no comfort to me that the exam was postponed for only one day.* **7.** assistance; support; encouragement: *to give aid and comfort to the enemy.* —*v.t.* to ease the grief or sorrow; bring solace or cheer to; console. [Old French *conforter* to console, urge, from Late Latin *confortāre* to strengthen, from Latin *con-* together + *fortis* strong.]

Syn. *v.t.* **Comfort, console¹, solace** mean to ease distress caused by pain or sorrow. **Comfort** implies bringing cheer to someone and thus lessening his trouble: *They comforted the child with promises of toys.* **Console** stresses the soothing of grief or sorrow: *They tried to console young Richard, who was in misery over the loss of his puppy.* **Solace** implies some particular thing that raises low spirits or eases melancholy: *Music solaced his darker moments.* —*n.* **1.** see **ease.**

com·fort·a·ble (kumf′tə bəl, kum′fər tə-) *adj.* **1.** providing physical ease or comfort. **2.** free from mental or physical distress; at ease. **3.** adequate or more than adequate: *a comfortable salary.* **4.** *Informal.* well-off; well-to-do. —**com′fort·a·ble·ness,** *n.* —**com′fort·a·bly,** *adv.*

com·fort·er (kum′fər tər) *n.* **1.** one who or that which comforts. **2.** quilted blanket or covering for a bed. **3. the Comforter.** the Holy Spirit.

com·fort·ing (kum′fər ting) *adj.* that comforts; consoling; reassuring; cheering: *comforting words.* —**com′fort·ing·ly,** *adv.*

comfort station, public toilet or rest room.

com·ic (kom′ik) *adj.* **1.** of, relating to, or connected with comedy. **2.** causing laughter or mirth; amusing; funny. —*n.* **1.** comedian. **2. comics.** comic strips or a section of a newspaper in which they appear. **3.** comic book. [Latin *cōmicus* relating to comedy, from Greek *kōmikos,* from *kōmos* revel. See COMEDY.]

com·i·cal (kom′i kəl) *adj.* causing laughter or mirth; amusing; funny; ludicrous. —**com·i·cal·i·ty** (kom′i kal′ə tē), **com′i·cal·ness,** *n.* —**com′i·cal·ly,** *adv.* —**Syn.** see **funny.**

comic book, booklet or small magazine consisting of comic strips.

comic opera, opera or operetta of a light or humorous character, usually having a happy ending, and often having some spoken dialogue.

comic strip, sequence of cartoon drawings relating a story or presenting a situation, usually having captions or dialogue enclosed in balloons pointing to the speaker, esp. when printed in a newspaper or similar publication on a regular or serialized basis.

Com·in·form (kom′in fôrm′) *n.* organization of the Communist parties of the Soviet Union, eastern Europe, France, and Italy, established in 1947 to coordinate Communist policies, activities, and information among its members and dissolved in 1956. [Short for *Com(munist) Inform(ation Bureau).*]

com·ing (kum′ing) *adj.* **1.** approaching, esp. in time: *this coming Monday.* **2.** *Informal.* **a.** deserving; due: *You'll get what's coming to you.* **b.** showing promise or on the way to importance or popularity: *the coming thing.* —*n.* approach; arrival.

com·ing-out (kum′ing out′) *n.* *Informal.* formal social debut.

Com·in·tern (kom′in turn′) *n.* international organization of Communist parties, created at Moscow in 1919 to establish Communism as a worldwide force, dissolved in 1943. [Short for *Com(munist) Intern(ational).*]

co·mi·ti·a (kə mish′ē ə) *n.,pl.* in ancient Rome, an assembly of the people for the exercise of legislative, electoral, or judicial functions. [Latin *comitia,* plural of *comitium* place of assembly.]

com·i·ty (kom′ə tē) *pl.,* **-ties.** *n.* mutual respect or courtesy; civility; politeness. [Latin *cōmitās.*]

com·ma (kom′ə) *n.* punctuation mark (,) chiefly used to indicate a slight separation of ideas, to separate items in a series, and to set off certain grammatical constructions, as a main clause. [Late Latin *comma,* from Latin *comma* clause of a sentence, from Greek *komma* piece cut off, clause.]

comma bacillus, the bacterium, *Vibrio comma* or *cholerae,* that causes cholera.

com·mand (kə mand′) *v.t.* **1.** to order, esp. with authority: *The general commanded his troops to retreat.* **2.** to have authority, power, or influence over; control: *The British once commanded the seas.* **3.** to be worthy of and get: *He commanded our respect and admiration.* **4.** to dominate by reason of position or location; overlook: *The tower commanded the small town.* **5.** to have at one's disposal or use: *He commands a large vocabulary.* —*v.i.* to be in a position of authority, power, or influence; be in control: *He was born to command.* —*n.* **1.** act of ordering; bidding. **2.** that which is commanded; order. **3.** possession or exercise of authority or power to command: *He assumed complete command of the project.* **4.** control or mastery: *She has a good command of Italian.* **5.** power to dominate by reason of position or location: *The guns had a command of the enemy position.* **6.** range of vision; outlook: *The telescope provided a command of the valley.* **7.** troops, equipment, or an area under a commander. **8.** officer or officers in command. [Old French *comander* to order, entrust, from Late Latin *commandāre* to order, commit to another, from Latin *com-* together + *mandāre* to order, entrust.]

Syn. *v.t.* **1. Command, direct, order** mean to say to someone that he must do something. **Command** implies authority and is formal: *The admiral commanded the fleet to seek out the enemy.* **Direct** suggests guidance rather than imperious insistence: *He directed the staff to urge customers to buy the larger television sets.* **Order** indicates power rather than authority: *The troops ordered the inhabitants to leave their houses.*

com·man·dant (kom′ən dant′, -dänt′) *n.* officer in command of a military or naval installation or district. [French *commandant,* noun use of present participle of *commander.* See COMMAND.]

com·man·deer (kom′ən dēr′) *v.t.* **1.** to seize (private property), esp. for military use. **2.** *Informal.* to take by force or coercion. **3.** *Archaic.* to force (someone) into military service. [Afrikaans *kommandeeren* to command, requisition, from French *commander.* See COMMAND.]

com·mand·er (kə man′dər) *n.* **1.** officer in command of a military unit. **2.** in the U.S. Navy or Coast Guard, officer ranking above a lieutenant commander and below a captain. **3.** one who is officially in command. **4.** member of high rank or merit, as in certain orders of knighthood or fraternal societies.

commander in chief *pl.,* **commanders in chief. 1.** *also,* **Commander in Chief.** supreme commander of the armed forces of a country. **2.** officer commanding armed forces in a particular theater of operations.

com·mand·ing (kə man′ding) *adj.* **1.** demanding attention or respect; arresting. **2.** (of a view or position) unobstructed, overlooking, or dominating. **3.** exercising command; controlling.

commanding officer, officer having command of a unit of the armed forces or of the police.

at; āpe; cär; end; mē; it; īce; hot; ōld; fôrk; wood; fōōl; oil; out; up; ūse; turn; sing; thin; this; zh in treasure; ə in ago, taken, pencil, lemon, circus.

com·mand·ment (kə mand′mənt) *n.* **1.** order; dictate. **2.** *also,* Commandment. law, esp. one of the Ten Commandments.

com·man·do (kə man′dō) *pl.,* **-dos** or **-does.** *n.* **1.** member of a military unit specially trained for scouting, sabotage, and hit-and-run raids. **2.** unit made up of such personnel. [Afrikaans *kommando* party of militia, from Portuguese *commando* party commanded, from *commandar* to command, going back to Latin *com-* together + *mandāre* to command, entrust.]

command performance, performance of a play, film, ballet, or other entertainment given before royalty by order or request.

com·me·dia dell'ar·te (kə mä′dē ə del är′tē) comedy based upon improvisation of dialogue and action revolving around various stock characters, such as Harlequin and Columbine. It originated in Italy in the sixteenth century. [Italian *commedia dell'arte* literally, comedy of art.]

comme il faut (kô mēl fō′) *French.* as it should or must be; proper.

com·mem·o·rate (kə mem′ə rāt′) **-rat·ed, -rat·ing.** *v.t.* **1.** to preserve the memory of; memorialize: *The town commissioned a statue to commemorate the battle.* **2.** to honor the memory of; celebrate: *They commemorated the revolution with a parade.* [Latin *commemorātus* past participle of *commemorāre* to call to mind.]

com·mem·o·ra·tion (kə mem′ə rā′shən) *n.* **1.** act of commemorating. **2.** that which serves to commemorate, as a memorial or ceremony.

com·mem·o·ra·tive (kə mem′ə rā′tiv, -ər ə tiv) *adj.* serving to commemorate.

com·mence (kə mens′) **-menced, -menc·ing.** *v.i., v.t.* to begin; start. [Old French *com(m)encier,* going back to Latin *com-* together + *initiāre* to initiate.] —**Syn.** see **begin.**

com·mence·ment (kə mens′mənt) *n.* **1.** act or fact of commencing; beginning; start; inception. **2.a.** day on which a college, university, or other school confers degrees upon, and gives diplomas to, qualified students. **b.** ceremonies that are conducted on this day; graduation exercises.

com·mend (kə mend′) *v.t.* **1.** to express admiration for a very favorable opinion of; praise: *The general commended the sergeant for his bravery.* **2.** to present as worthy of attention or regard; recommend. **3.** to deliver to one's care or keeping; commit; entrust. [Latin *commendāre* to entrust, recommend.]

com·mend·a·ble (kə men′də bəl) *adj.* worthy of praise; laudable.

com·men·da·tion (kom′ən dā′shən) *n.* **1.** act of commending; praise; recommendation. **2.** that which expresses approval or praise; citation. —**com·men·da·to·ry** (kə men′də tôr′ē), *adj.*

com·men·sal (kə men′səl) *adj.* of, relating to, or participating in commensalism.

com·men·sal·ism (kə men′səl liz′əm) *n.* relationship between two organisms in which one is benefited and the other, the host, is neither benefited nor harmed.

com·men·su·ra·ble (kə men′sər ə bəl, -shər-) *adj.* **1.** measurable by the same standards, values, or units; having a common divisor. **2.** proportionate; commensurate. —**com·men′su·ra·bly,** *adv.*

com·men·su·rate (kə men′sər it, -shər-) *adj.* **1.** corresponding in measure or degree; proportionate: *The increase in price was commensurate with the increase in demand.* **2.** having the same measure; of equal size; coextensive: *His losses were commensurate with his winnings.* **3.** measurable by the same standards, values, or units; commensurable. [Late Latin *commēnsūrātus* equal in measure, going back to Latin *com-* together + *mēnsūra* a measure.] —**com·men′su·rate·ly,** *adv.*

com·ment (kom′ent) *n.* **1.** brief statement that explains, criticizes, or expands on something. **2.** remark: *She angered him with her sarcastic comments.* **3.** gossip; discussion: *the subject of much comment.* **4.** observation or revelation about; commentary: *His new film provides an interesting comment on our times.* —*v.i.* to make a comment or comments. [Late Latin *commentum* interpretation, from Latin *commentum* invention.]

com·men·ta·ry (kom′ən ter′ē) *pl.,* **-tar·ies.** *n.* **1.** series of notes or remarks explaining, describing, or expanding on material presented: *a commentary at the back of a book. He accompanied his slides with a commentary.* **2.** anything that reveals, points out, or serves to illustrate: *The need for tanks to keep order was a frightening commentary on conditions in the city.* **3.** *also,* **commentaries.** historical narrative or record; memoirs.

com·men·tate (kom′ən tāt′) **-tat·ed, -tat·ing.** *v.t.* to gave a commentary on. —*v.i.* to serve as a commentator. [from COMMENTATOR.]

com·men·ta·tor (kom′ən tā′tər) *n.* **1.** radio or television reporter; newscaster. **2.** anyone who describes, reports, or comments, esp. on social mores or history. [Latin *commentātor* inventor, interpreter.]

com·merce (kom′ərs) *n.* business transaction involving the exchanging or buying and selling of commodities or services, esp. on a large scale; trade. [Latin *commercium* trade, intercourse.]

com·mer·cial (kə mur′shəl) *adj.* **1.** of, relating to, or engaged in commerce. **2.** designed for or oriented toward monetary gain.

—*n.* short advertising message on radio or television. —**com·mer′cial·ly,** *adv.*

com·mer·cial·ism (kə mur′shə liz′əm) *n.* **1.** emphasis on or concern with monetary gain. **2.** methods, principles, and spirit of commerce.

com·mer·cial·ize (kə mur′shə līz′) **-ized, -iz·ing.** *v.t.* to put on a commercial basis; emphasize the profitable aspects of. —**com·mer′·cial·i·za′tion,** *n.*

commercial traveler, traveling salesman.

com·mi·na·tion (kom′ə nā′shən) *n.* **1.** in the Church of England, recital of divine threats against sinners, used esp. after the Litany on Ash Wednesday. **2.** threat or denunciation. [Latin *comminātiō* threatening.]

com·min·gle (kə ming′gəl) **-gled, -gling.** *v.t., v.i.* to mix together; mingle.

com·mi·nute (kom′ə nōōt′, -nūt′) **-nut·ed, -nut·ing.** *v.t.* to break down into minute particles; pulverize. [Latin *comminūtus,* past participle of *comminuere.*] —**com′mi·nu′tion,** *n.*

com·mis·er·ate (kə miz′ə rāt′) **-at·ed, -at·ing.** *v.i.* to feel or express sympathy: *He commiserated with her over her loss.* —*v.t.* to feel or express sympathy for; pity. [Latin *commiserātus,* past participle of *commiserāri,* going back to *com-* with + *miser* wretched.] —**com·mis′er·a′tive,** *adj.*

com·mis·er·a·tion (kə miz′ə rā′shən) *n.* feeling or expression of sympathy; compassion.

com·mis·sar (kom′ə sär′) *n.* **1.** formerly, head of a government department in the Soviet Union. **2.** official of the Communist Party whose duties are political indoctrination and the enforcement of party loyalty. [Russian *komissar,* from German *Kommissar* commissioner, from Medieval Latin *commissarius.* See COMMISSARY.]

com·mis·sar·i·at (kom′ə sâr′ē ət) *n.* formerly, any government department in the Soviet Union. [Russian *kommissariat* and Modern Latin *commissariatus,* both from Medieval Latin *commissarius.* See COMMISSARY.]

com·mis·sar·y (kom′ə ser′ē) *pl.,* **-sar·ies.** *n.* **1.** store that sells food and supplies, esp. in a military camp. **2.** place to eat, as a cafeteria. **3.** one who is entrusted with a special duty or commission by a higher authority; deputy; representative. **4.** formerly, military officer in charge of supplying provisions. [Medieval Latin *commissarius* person in charge, commissioner, from Latin *commissus,* past participle of *committere* to put together, entrust.]

com·mis·sion (kə mish′ən) *n.* **1.** group of persons who have been appointed or elected to perform certain duties: *He was a member of the commission investigating crime.* **2.** fee paid for services or work done, often based on a percentage of the total amount of business transacted: *The salesman received a $10.00 commission on the sale.* **3.a.** in the United States, document issued by the president, giving military rank and authority. **b.** rank and authority granted by such a document. **4.a.** act of committing; performance; perpetration. **b.** that which is committed, as a crime. **5.** assignment or appointment to do something, as a work of art. **6.a.** a giving of authority to act for, or in behalf of, another. **b.** authority given. **c.** that for which authority is given. **7.** order; command. **8.** written warrant or document granting certain powers, privileges, and duties. **9. out of commission.** not in service or use; not in working order. **10. in commission.** ready for service or use: *The battleship was in commission in the Pacific.* —*v.t.* **1.** to give military rank and authority to, as an officer. **2.** to give authority to; empower. **3.** to hire or appoint (someone) to do something: *We commissioned the sculptor to do a bust.* **4.** to put (a ship) in commission. [French *commission* mandate, charge, from Late Latin *commissiō,* from Latin *commissiō* a bringing together in contest.]

commissioned officer, in the United States, officer of the armed forces who receives his commission from the president.

com·mis·sion·er (kə mish′ə nər) *n.* **1.** member of a commission. **2.** official appointed as the head of a government department: *a parks commissioner, a highway commissioner.* **3.** member of a group of individuals elected or appointed to the governing body of a city or county. **4.** official appointed by a sports league to act as an administrator and arbitrator: *a baseball commissioner.*

commission merchant, one who buys or sells goods on a commission.

com·mit (kə mit′) **-mit·ted, -mit·ting.** *v.t.* **1.** to perpetrate; do: *to commit murder.* **2.** to put into the charge or keeping of another; entrust. **3.** to put into official custody, as of a prison or mental institution. **4.** to devote or pledge; bind (with *to*): *He was fully committed to the plan.* **5.** to state the position of: *He wouldn't commit himself on an issue.* **6.** to refer, as a legislative bill or report, to a committee for consideration. **7. to commit to memory.** to learn by heart; memorize. **8. to commit to writing** (or **paper**). to record in writing; write down. [Latin *committere* to put together, entrust, perpetrate wrong.] —**com·mit′ta·ble,** *adj.*

at; āpe; cär; end; mē; it; īce; hot; ōld; fôrk; wood; fōol; oil; out; up; ūse; turn; sing; thin; this; zh in treasure; ə in ago, taken, pencil, lemon, circus.

201

com·mit·ment (kə mit′mənt) *n.* **1.** act of committing; being committed. **2.** obligation; pledge. **3.** court order directing that a person be confined, as in a prison or mental institution. Also, **com·mit′tal.**

com·mit·tee (kə mit′ē) *n.* group of persons appointed or elected to perform certain duties or to investigate, report, or act on a particular matter. [COMMIT + -EE.]

com·mit·tee·man (kə mit′ē mən, -man′) *pl.,* **-men** (-mən, -men′). *n.* member of a committee. —**com·mit′tee·wom′an,** *n.*

committee of the whole, all the attending members of a legislative assembly, who have constituted themselves as a group to consider proposals under modified, usually less formal, rules of debate.

com·mode (kə mōd′) *n.* **1.** toilet *(def. 2).* **2.** small piece of furniture, as a cabinet or chair, containing a chamber pot. **3.** movable, usually covered, washstand. **4.** chest or cabinet of drawers. [French *commode* convenient, from Latin *commodus.*]

com·mo·di·ous (kə mō′dē əs) *adj.* having or containing ample room; roomy; spacious. [Medieval Latin *commodiosus* useful, from Latin *commodus* convenient.] —**com·mo′di·ous·ly,** *adv.* —**com·mo′di·ous·ness,** *n.*

com·mod·i·ty (kə mod′ə tē) *pl.,* **-ties.** *n.* **1.** article of trade or commerce; ware or product. **2.** something whose usefulness is exploited or turned to advantage or profit; something bought or sold. [Latin *commoditās* advantage, convenience.]

com·mo·dore (kom′ə dôr′) *n.* **1.** in the U.S. Navy, officer ranking above a captain and below a rear admiral. ▲ used as a rank only in time of war. **2.** formerly, captain who holds a temporary command of a squadron in the U.S. Navy or Merchant Marine. **3.** president or head of a yacht club. [Earlier *commandore,* from Dutch *commandeur* commander of a town, from French *commandeur* commander, from *commander.* See COMMAND.]

com·mon (kom′ən) *adj.* **1.** of frequent or habitual occurrence; appearing frequently; usual: *a common mistake.* **2.** general; widespread: *common knowledge, a word in common use.* **3.** belonging equally to two or more; shared by all alike: *common property, common interests.* **4.** relating or belonging to the community as a whole; public: *the common good.* **5.** undistinguished by special or superior characteristics; average; standard: *common courtesy.* **6.** not distinguished by rank, station, or special status: *the common people.* **7.** of the most familiar, widely known, or frequently occurring kind of species: *the common bluebird, the common pea.* **8.** of mediocre or inferior quality; not rare or costly. **9.** coarse; unrefined; vulgar: *He has rather common manners.* —*n.* **1.** *also,* **commons.** tract of land, as a pasture or park, owned or used by the public. **2. in common.** in joint use or possession; shared equally: *a couple who have much in common.* [Old French *comun* general, mutual, from Latin *commūnis* general, universal.] —**com′mon·ness,** *n.*

Syn. *adj.* **1. Common, familiar, ordinary** mean occurring or encountered frequently. **Common** suggests that the thing encountered is usual, widespread, undistinguished, and unexceptional: *Failure to signal a turn is probably the most common driving error.* **Familiar** implies repetition of occurrence: *That's a very familiar tune.* **Ordinary** indicates approximation to the average in frequency or quality: *He followed his ordinary routine and went to bed early.* **2.** see **general.**

com·mon·age (kom′ə nij) *n.* **1.** formerly, right to pasture animals on a common, as during feudal times in England. **2.** land on which this right was held.

com·mon·al·ty (kom′ən əl tē) *pl.,* **-ties.** *n.* the common people, as opposed to royalty or the nobility or upper classes. Also, **com·mon·al·i·ty** (kom′ə nal′ə tē).

common carrier, individual or company, as a railroad or steamship line, engaged in transporting goods or people for a fee.

common cold, cold *(n., def. 3).*

common denominator, any number that can be divided by each of the denominators of a given group of fractions without leaving a remainder. The number 18 is a common denominator of ¹/₃, ⁵/₆, and ⁷/₉.

common divisor, any number or algebraic expression that divides two or more other numbers or algebraic expressions without leaving a remainder. The number 3 is a common divisor of $6x$, $9x^2y$, and 21. Also, **common factor.**

com·mon·er (kom′ə nər) *n.* **1.** one of the common people, esp. one not of noble rank. **2.** student at certain British universities who receives no financial aid from his college or university.

common fraction, fraction whose numerator and denominator are integers.

common law, body or system of law based on custom, usage, and court decisions, as distinct from statutory law.

common-law marriage, marriage in which the parties agree to live together as man and wife without having undergone a religious or civil ceremony.

common logarithm, logarithm to the base 10.

com·mon·ly (kom′ən lē) *adv.* **1.** usually; generally; ordinarily. **2.** in a common manner.

Common Market, economic association formed in 1958 by France, West Germany, Italy, Belgium, the Netherlands, and Luxembourg to abolish barriers to free trade among members by allowing goods, workers, capital, and services to move freely across national boundaries.

common multiple, any number or algebraic expression that is divisible by two or more other numbers or algebraic expressions without leaving a remainder. The number 20 is a common multiple of 2, 4, 5, and 10.

common noun, noun that names any one or all of the members of a class, as *dog, dogs, street, streets.* Distinguished from **proper noun.**

com·mon·place (kom′ən plās′) *adj.* not original, remarkable, or interesting; ordinary. —*n.* **1.** customary or obvious remark; platitude. **2.** anything ordinary, uninteresting, or generally accepted and taken for granted. —**com′mon·place′ness,** *n.* —**Syn.** *adj.* see **ordinary.**

com·mons (kom′ənz) *n.,pl.* **1.** hall or building for dining, esp. at a college or university. **2.** food served in such a hall or building. **3. Commons.** House of Commons. ▲ construed as singular in defs. 1, 2, and 3. **4.** the common people; commonalty.

common sense, understanding independent of specialized knowledge; native sound or prudent judgment.

common stock, stock representing the basic ownership of a corporation, carrying voting rights with it, and receiving dividends only after those due the holders of preferred stock have been paid. Distinguished from **preferred stock.**

com·mon·weal (kom′ən wēl′) *also,* **common weal.** *n.* **1.** general or public welfare; common good. **2.** *Archaic.* commonwealth.

com·mon·wealth (kom′ən welth′) *n.* **1.** whole body of people of a nation or state; body politic. **2.** state in which supreme power is held by the people; republic or democratic state or country. **3.** any of certain states of the United States: Kentucky, Massachusetts, Pennsylvania, and Virginia. ▲ used rather than *state* as an official designation. **4. the Commonwealth.** Commonwealth of Nations. **5. Commonwealth.** government established in England by Oliver Cromwell, lasting from 1649 to 1653 or, in some views, to 1660. [COMMON + WEALTH.]

Commonwealth of Nations, worldwide association of nations and their dependent territories, consisting of those states that formerly constituted the British Empire. All members are equal but recognize the British monarch as titular head of the association. Formerly known as the British Commonwealth of Nations. Also, **the Commonwealth.**

com·mo·tion (kə mō′shən) *n.* noisy or turbulent disturbance, excitement, or disorder; agitation; turmoil.

com·mu·nal (kə mūn′əl, kom′yən əl) *adj.* **1.** of, relating to, or characteristic of a commune or community. **2.** belonging to the people of a community; public. —**com·mu′nal·ly,** *adv.*

com·mu·nal·ism (kə mūn′əl iz′əm, kom′yən əl-) *n.* **1.** theory or system of government in which each commune is virtually an independent state, and the nation is merely a federation of such states. **2.** belief in or practice of communal ownership of goods and property. —**com·mu′nal·ist,** *n., adj.* —**com·mu′nal·is′tic,** *adj.*

com·mu·nal·ize (kə mūn′ə līz′, kom′yə nə-) **-ized, -iz·ing.** *v.t.* to make communal; make community property. —**com·mu′nal·i·za′tion,** *n.*

com·mune¹ (kə mūn′) **-muned, -mun·ing.** *v.i.* to confer or converse intimately; experience a profound feeling of unity and receptivity (with *with*): *to commune with nature.* [Old French *comuner* to share, have in common, from *comun.* See COMMON.]

com·mune² (kom′ūn) *n.* **1.** society or community, often rural, in which property is owned and used in common and work and facilities, as living quarters or nurseries, are usually shared. **2. the Commune. a.** revolutionary committee in Paris that governed France from July 1792 to 1794. **b.** radical coalition that governed Paris from March 18 to May 28, 1871. **3.** smallest unit of local government in France, Italy, Belgium, and other European countries. [French *commune* township, parish, from Medieval Latin *communia* group sharing a common life, from Latin *commūnis* general, universal.]

com·mu·ni·ca·ble (kə mū′ni kə bəl) *adj.* capable of being communicated or transmitted: *a communicable disease.*

com·mu·ni·cant (kə mū′ni kənt) *n.* **1.** one who receives Holy Communion. **2.** one who communicates. —*adj.* communicating.

com·mu·ni·cate (kə mū′ni kāt′) **-cat·ed, -cat·ing.** *v.t.* **1.** to make known or understood; impart or transfer knowledge or information of: *You don't communicate your ideas very well in this essay.* **2.** to pass on or along; transmit, as a disease. —*v.i.* **1.** to transfer information, as facts or emotions, from a source to a receiver; exchange or share feelings, thoughts, or information: *The couple communicated without words. We've been communicating by mail.* **2.** to be connected or form a connecting passage. **3.** to receive Holy Communion. [Latin *commūnicātus,* past participle of *commūnicāre* to impart, share.] —**com·mu′ni·ca′tor,** *n.*

at; āpe; cär; end; mē; it; īce; hot; ōld; fôrk; wood; fōol; oil; out; up; ūse; turn; sing; thin; **this;** zh in treasure; ə in ago, taken, pencil, lemon, circus.

Syn. *v.t.* **1. Communicate, impart** mean to transfer something such as feelings or information. **Communicate** emphasizes that whatever is transferred is then shared: *The infant communicated his joy to his parents.* **Impart** also suggests sharing, but with the implication that what is shared remains essentially the giver's: *He made every effort to impart his skill in working metal to his apprentices.*

com·mu·ni·ca·tion (kə mū′ni kā′shən) *n.* **1.** transfer of information, as facts, wishes, or emotions, from a source to a receiver. **2.** that which is communicated or communicates; message. **3.** act or process of communicating. **4. communications.** **a.** system or systems for communicating, esp. involving telephone, telegram, radio, television, and similar advanced technology. **b.** science, study, or technology of communicating. **5.** connecting passage or opening; channel.

communications satellite, man-made satellite that relays radio or other electromagnetic signals between ground stations on earth.

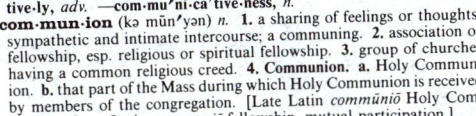
Communications satellite

com·mu·ni·ca·tive (kə mū′ni kā′-tiv, -kə tiv) *adj.* inclined to communicate or disclose information readily; talkative. —**com·mu′ni·ca·tive·ly,** *adv.* —**com·mu′ni·ca′tive·ness,** *n.*

com·mun·ion (kə mūn′yən) *n.* **1.** a sharing of feelings or thoughts; sympathetic and intimate intercourse; a communing. **2.** association or fellowship, esp. religious or spiritual fellowship. **3.** group of churches having a common religious creed. **4. Communion.** **a.** Holy Communion. **b.** that part of the Mass during which Holy Communion is received by members of the congregation. [Late Latin *commūniō* Holy Communion, from Latin *commūniō* fellowship, mutual participation.]

com·mu·ni·qué (kə mū′ni kā′, kə mū′ni kā′) *n.* official communication, announcement, or bulletin. [French *communiqué,* from *communiquer* to communicate, from Latin *commūnicāre* to impart, share.]

com·mu·nism (kom′yə niz′əm) *n.* **1.** theory of social and economic organization, advanced chiefly by Karl Marx, advocating public ownership of the means of production, as factories and resources, the sharing of the products of labor, and the establishment of a society in which hostile, competitive social classes disappear. **2.** *also,* **Communism.** **a.** revolutionary political movement advocating this theory and seeking to establish an international classless society in which productive resources are owned in common and used for the benefit of all. **b.** system of government based on this theory, as in the Soviet Union. **3.** social system characterized by the communal sharing of goods and services. [French *communisme,* from *commun* general, universal, from Latin *commūnis.*]

com·mu·nist (kom′yə nist) *also,* **Com·mu·nist.** *n.* **1.** member of a Communist Party. **2.** person who advocates or supports communism. —*adj.* relating to, characteristic of, or resembling communism, communists, or a Communist Party. —**com′mu·nis′tic,** *adj.*

Communist China, China (def. 1).

Communist Party **1.** official state party of the Soviet Union since 1918. **2.** any political party that supports communism, esp. one affiliated with the Soviet Communist Party.

com·mu·ni·ty (kə mū′nə tē) *pl.,* **-ties.** *n.* **1.** number of people living in the same locality, as a district or town, and under the same government. **2.** the locality itself. **3.** number of people considered as a group or unit because of some similarity or commonly held characteristic, as identical religion, occupation, or interests. **4.** society as a whole or in general; the public. **5.** holding in common; joint possession; sharing. **6.** similar character; agreement; identity. **7.** group of animals and plants living together in the same area. [Old French *comunete* society of people, from Latin *commūnitās* fellowship.]

community center, meeting place used by a community for recreational, social, and cultural activities.

community chest, fund formed by voluntary contributions from the people of a community and drawn upon by various charitable organizations for local welfare activities.

community college, junior college, esp. one partially supported by the community it serves.

com·mu·nize (kom′yə nīz′) **-nized, -niz·ing** *v.t.* **1.** to place under community control or ownership. **2.** to make communist.

com·mu·ta·tion (kom′yə tā′shən) *n.* **1.** substitution, as of one type of payment for another. **2.** reduction or change, as of a prison sentence or penalty. **3.** regular travel, esp. over a considerable distance, to and from work.

commutation ticket, transportation ticket, sold at a reduced rate, which entitles the holder to travel over a given route a given number of times or during a specified period.

com·mu·ta·tive (kə mū′tə tiv, kom′yə tā′tiv) *adj.* of, relating to, or characterized by substitution or interchange.

com·mu·ta·tor (kom′yə tā′tər) *n.* split ring that revolves with the armature of an electric generator or motor and causes a periodic reversal of the generated or supplied current.

com·mute (kə mūt′) **-mut·ed, -mut·ing.** *v.t.* **1.** to substitute, as one type of payment for another; interchange. **2.** to reduce or change, as a prison sentence or penalty. —*v.i.* to travel regularly, esp. over a considerable distance, between one's place of business and one's home. [Latin *commūtāre* to exchange.] —**com·mut′er,** *n.*

Co·mo, Lake (kō′mō) lake in northern Italy.

Com·o·ro Islands (käm′ə rō′) island country off the southeastern coast of Africa. Land area, 838 sq. mi. Pop. (1972 est.), 275,000.

comp. **1.** compound. **2.** companion. **3.** compare. **4.** comparative. **5.** composer. **6.** composition. **7.** compositor.

com·pact[1] (*adj., v.,* kəm pakt′; *n.,* kom′pakt) *adj.* **1.** closely and firmly united; tightly packed together. **2.** occupying a relatively small space or area. **3.** expressed succinctly; concise; terse. **4.** (of an automobile) smaller and more economical to operate than the standard size. **5.** solid and firm: *He has a compact build.* **6.** *Archaic.* composed; made (with *of*). —*v.t.* to press together closely and firmly; pack. —*n.* **1.** small case containing face powder and a mirror, designed to be carried in a purse. **2.** compact car. [Latin *compactus* joined together, past participle of *compingere* to join or put together.] —**com·pact′ly,** *adv.* —**com·pact′ness,** *n.* —**Syn.** *adj.* **1.** see **close.**

com·pact[2] (kom′pakt) *n.* agreement or contract. [Latin *compactum,* from *compacīscī* to make an agreement.]

com·pan·ion (kəm pan′yən) *n.* **1.** one who associates with or accompanies another or others. **2.** one employed to live with, accompany, or assist another. **3.** anything that matches, or forms a pair with, another. **4.** member of the lowest rank in orders of knighthood. [Old French *compaignon* comrade, from Late Latin *compāniō* literally, bread-sharer, from Latin *com-* with + *pānis* bread.] —**Syn.** **1.** see **associate.**

com·pan·ion·a·ble (kəm pan′yən ə bəl) *adj.* suitable as a companion; sociable. —**com·pan′ion·a·bil′i·ty,** *n.* —**com·pan′ion·a·bly,** *adv.*

com·pan·ion·ship (kəm pan′yən ship′) *n.* fellowship.

com·pan·ion·way (kəm pan′yən wā′) *n.* **1.** stairway leading from the deck of a ship to the cabin or deck below. **2.** space where such a stairway is located.

com·pa·ny (kum′pə nē) *pl.,* **-nies.** *n.* **1.** guest or guests: *We had company for dinner.* **2.** business establishment: *an oil company.* **3.** group of entertainers or all those associated with a theatrical presentation; troupe: *a dance company, a repertory company.* **4.** companionship; fellowship: *He was lonesome for the company of others.* **5.** person or persons with whom one habitually associates: *He judges people by the company they keep.* **6.** group or gathering of persons, as for social purposes. **7.** *also,* **Company.** partner or partners not named, as in the title of a firm: *H. Bradley Wells and Company.* **8.** military unit composed of a headquarters and two or more platoons, forming part of a battalion. **9.** ship's crew, including the officers. **10. to keep (someone) company.** to be with (someone). **11. to keep company.** to date; court (often *with*). **12. to part company. a.** to separate and go in different directions. **b.** to end an association or friendship. [Old French *compagnie* association, body of troops, from Late Latin *compāniēs* body of soldiers dwelling together, army mess, from Latin *com-* with + *pānis* bread.]

Syn. **6. Company, band[1], party, group** mean a number of people gathered together or acting toward some common goal. **Company** stresses fellow feeling or the existence of something in common, regardless of whether the grouping is temporary or established on a more enduring basis: *He conducted a company of tourists.* **Band** suggests not only a common aim but also some form of organization: *The band of exiles landed their ship on the unfamiliar shore.* **Party** implies people meeting once and stresses the purpose for such a gathering: *He was asked by his boss to join the hunting party.* **Group** often suggests a common interest or characteristic: *He was a member of a small group that met Friday evenings to play chamber music.*

company union, labor union with membership limited to workers in one company, usually organized and dominated by the employer.

compar., comparative.

com·pa·ra·ble (kom′pər ə bəl) *adj.* **1.** capable of being compared. **2.** worthy of comparison. —**com′pa·ra·bly,** *adv.* —**Syn.** **1.** see **like[1].**

com·par·a·tive (kəm par′ə tiv) *adj.* **1.** that compares or involves comparison: *a comparative study of the anatomies of man and apes.* **2.** estimated by comparison; not absolute; relative: *He was a comparative stranger to them.* **3.** denoting the second of the three degrees of quantity, quality, or relation that can be expressed by an adjective or adverb. *Faster* is the comparative degree of the adjective *fast.* Distinguished from **positive** and **superlative.** —*n.* **1.** comparative degree. **2.** word or group of words that expresses this degree. —**com·par′a·tive·ly,** *adv.* **Syn.** *adj.* **2. Comparative, relative** indicate a matching against something else. **Comparative** implies direct and explicit contrast with some thing or things similar: *They are comparative strangers.* **Relative** sug-

at; āpe; cär; end; mē; it; īce; hot; ōld; fôrk; wood; fŏŏl; oil; out; up; ūse; turn; sing; thin; this; zh in treasure; ə in ago, taken, pencil, lemon, circus.

203

gests direct contrast but with something not necessarily directly mentioned: *the relative speeds of a car and a bicycle.*

com·pare (kəm pãr′) **-pared, -par·ing.** *v.t.* **1.** to examine in order to find or show similarities and differences: *The police compared the fingerprints on the gun with those on the door.* **2.** to represent or speak of as similar, analogous, or alike; parallel; liken (with *to*): *The blue of her eyes has often been compared to the blue of violets.* **3.** to form the comparative and superlative degrees of (an adjective or adverb). —*v.i.* to be worthy of being compared; be considered as alike or similar (with *with*): *Does his latest book compare with his first?* —*n.* **beyond** (or **without**) **compare.** beyond comparison; without an equal. [Old French *comparer* to put persons or things in comparison, from Latin *comparāre* to match, pair together.]

com·par·i·son (kəm par′ə sən) *n.* **1.** act of comparing; being compared. **2.** comparable quality or character; likeness; similarity. **3.** change in form of an adjective or adverb to indicate the positive, comparative, or superlative degrees. [Old French *comparaison* a comparing, from Latin *comparātiō.*]

Syn. 1. Comparison, contrast indicate a matching of things to disclose in what ways they are alike or different. **Comparison** implies matching things obviously different, which suggests that similarities will be noted: *A comparison of the two teams indicates that Saturday's game will probably be close.* **Contrast** suggests that the things matched have obvious similarities, but that the ways in which they are different will be noted: *The contrast between the two approaches to the problem proved to be rather striking.*

com·part·ment (kəm pärt′mənt) *n.* **1.** any of the divisions or separate sections into which an enclosed space is divided: *The handbag has a separate compartment for change. The dresser drawer was partitioned into four compartments.* **2.** separate room, chamber, or similarly enclosed space: *There were ten compartments in each car of the train.* [French *compartiment* partition, from Italian *compartimento,* from *compartire* to divide, share, going back to Latin *com-* together + *partīre* to divide.]

com·part·men·tal·ize (kəm pärt′ment′əl īz′) **-ized, -iz·ing.** *v.t.* to divide into separate compartments or categories.

com·pass (kum′pəs, kom′-) *n.* **1.** instrument for determining and showing directions, consisting of a magnetized needle which is freely suspended on a pivot and points to the North Magnetic Pole. **2.** circumference or boundary of an enclosed area. **3.** range or extent within limits; reach; scope: *within the compass of his capabilities.* **4.** range of tones of a voice or musical instrument. **5.** *Usually,* **compasses.** instrument for drawing circles and measuring distances, consisting of two straight and equal legs connected at one end. **6.** *Archaic.* circular course; circuit. —*v.t.* **1.** to make a circuit of; go around: *a voyage that compassed the globe.* **2.** to encircle; surround; encompass: *The mountains compassed the valley.* **3.** to grasp mentally; comprehend: *He could not compass such a difficult idea.* **4.** to accomplish or gain; achieve; obtain: *men who would unscrupulously employ corruption to compass their ends* (Macaulay, 1840). **5.** to plot; scheme; contrive. [Old French *compas* pair of compasses, circle, measure, from *compasser* to measure, go round, going back to Latin *com-* together + *passus* step.] —**Syn.** *n.* **3.** see **scope.**

compass card. dial on a mariner's compass marked for every two degrees between 0° and 360°, and for the thirty-two geographical points.

com·pas·sion (kəm pash′ən) *n.* sympathy for another's suffering or misfortune combined with a desire to help. [Old French *compassion,* from Late Latin *compassiō,* going back to Latin *com-* with + *patī* to suffer.] —**Syn.** see **pity.**

com·pas·sion·ate (kəm pash′ə nit) *adj.* feeling or expressing compassion; sympathetic. —**com·pas′sion·ate·ly,** *adv.*

compass saw. tool with a small, tapering blade for sawing in circles, or cutting wood in patterns. Also, **fret saw, keyhole saw.**

com·pat·i·ble (kəm pat′ə bəl) *adj.* **1.** capable of existing or functioning together in harmony; congenial; consistent: *She and her roommate were not compatible. His testimony was not compatible with that of the first witness.* **2.** in television, capable of receiving or being received in both black and white and in color. [French *compatible,* going back to Latin *compatī* to suffer with.] —**com·pat′i·bil′i·ty,** *n.* —**com·pat′i·bly,** *adv.*

com·pa·tri·ot (kəm pā′trē ət, -pat′rē-) *n.* fellow countryman. [Middle French *compatriote,* going back to Latin *com-* with + *patriōta* countryman (from Greek *patriōtēs* fellow countryman).]

com·peer (kəm pēr′, kom′pēr) *n.* **1.** one of equal rank or standing; equal; peer. **2.** comrade; associate; companion. [Old French *comper* equal, from Latin *compār* equal, comrade.]

com·pel (kəm pel′) **-pelled, -pel·ling.** *v.t.* **1.** to drive or urge irresistibly; constrain; oblige: *The transit strike compelled many people to drive to work.* **2.** to obtain or bring about by force; exact; command.

Compass
(def. 5)

[Latin *compellere* to drive together, force.] —**com·pel′la·ble,** *adj.* —**com·pel′ler,** *n.* —**Syn.** **2.** see **force.**

com·pend (kom′pend) *n.* compendium.

com·pen·di·ous (kəm pen′dē əs) *adj.* brief but comprehensive; concise. [Latin *compendiōsus* abridged, short.] —**com·pen′di·ous·ly,** *adv.* —**com·pen′di·ous·ness,** *n.*

com·pen·di·um (kəm pen′dē əm) *pl.,* **-di·ums** or **-di·a** (-dē ə). *n.* summary covering a subject comprehensively. [Latin *compendium* saving, abridgement; literally, that which is weighed together.]

com·pen·sate (kom′pən sāt′) **-sat·ed, -sat·ing.** *v.t.* **1.** to make suitable or equal return or payment to; recompense; remunerate: *The company compensated her for the extra hours she worked.* **2.** to make up for; counterbalance; offset. —*v.i.* to provide with or be an equivalent; make up: *The football player's speed compensated for his small size.* [Latin *compēnsātus,* past participle of *compēnsāre* to weigh one thing against another.] —**com′pen·sa′tor,** *n.* —**com′pen·sa′tive,** **com·pen·sa·to·ry** (kəm pen′sə tôr′ē), *adj.*

com·pen·sa·tion (kom′pən sā′shən) *n.* **1.** act of compensating. **2.** that which compensates, as payment given or received as an equivalent for services, loss, or damage. **3.** increased activity or development of an organ or function to make up for loss or weakness of another.

com·pete (kəm pēt′) **-pet·ed, -pet·ing.** *v.i.* to contend with another or others for or as if for a prize; vie: *The two girls competed with each other for the highest mark.* [Latin *competere* to strive for (in competition) with another, be suitable.]

Syn. Compete, vie, contend refer to a striving against a rival or rivals. **Compete** suggests a reward or prize: *He was clever enough to compete for the mathematics scholarship.* **Vie** focuses on the contention rather than its outcome: *Both children vied for her attention.* **Contend** implies an effort to overcome a rival, a physical obstacle, a disease, or the like: *The two companies contended for the film rights to the popular novel.*

com·pe·tence (kom′pət əns) *n.* **1.** state of being competent; ability; fitness. **2.** sufficient income or other means to provide a comfortable living. **3.** condition of being legally qualified or admissible. Also, **com′pe·ten·cy.**

com·pe·tent (kom′pət ənt) *adj.* **1.** having sufficient ability; capable. **2.** sufficient or adequate for the purpose: *Although they were inexperienced, they did a competent job.* **3.** legally qualified or admissible. [Latin *competēns,* present participle of *competere* to be suitable, compete.] —**com′pe·tent·ly,** *adv.* —**Syn.** **1.** see **able.**

com·pe·ti·tion (kom′pə tish′ən) *n.* **1.** act of competing; rivalry. **2.** trial or match for determining relative skill or ability; contest. **3.** business rivalry between two or more persons or firms competing for the same customers or market. **4. the competition.** one's competitors or rivals. —**Syn.** **1.** see **emulation.**

com·pet·i·tive (kəm pet′ə tiv) *adj.* of, involving, or characterized by competition: *a competitive examination, competitive prices, a competitive spirit.* —**com·pet′i·tive·ly,** *adv.* —**com·pet′i·tive·ness,** *n.*

com·pet·i·tor (kəm pet′ə tər) *n.* one who competes.

com·pi·la·tion (kom′pə lā′shən) *n.* **1.** act of compiling. **2.** that which is compiled, as an anthology, list, or report.

com·pile (kəm pīl′) **-piled, -pil·ing.** *v.t.* **1.** to collect and put together (various material or data): *to compile statistics.* **2.** to make or form, as a book or report, by organizing material or data collected from various sources: *to compile an anthology of poems.* **3.** to pile up or amass: *Their team compiled over 100 points in three games.* [Old French *compiler* to put together, collect, from Latin *compilāre* to gather together, rob.] —**com·pil′er,** *n.*

com·pla·cence (kəm plā′səns) *n.* complacency.

com·pla·cen·cy (kəm plā′sən sē) *n.* feeling of contentment or satisfaction, esp. self-satisfaction.

com·pla·cent (kəm plā′sənt) *adj.* feeling or showing satisfaction, esp. self-satisfaction. [Latin *complacēns,* present participle of *com-placēre* to please.] —**com·pla′cent·ly,** *adv.*

com·plain (kəm plān′) *v.i.* **1.** to express dissatisfaction: *She complained that the exam was too hard.* **2.** to talk about one's pains or ills. **3.** to make a formal accusation or charge. [Old French *complaindre* to lament, going back to Latin *com-* with + *plangere* to lament.] —**com·plain′er,** *n.*

com·plain·ant (kəm plā′nənt) *n.* one who files a complaint in a legal action or proceeding.

com·plaint (kəm plānt′) *n.* **1.** expression of dissatisfaction. **2.** cause for complaining; grievance. **3.** illness; ailment. **4.** formal charge or accusation in a legal action or proceeding.

com·plai·sance (kəm plā′səns, -zəns, kom′plə zəns′) *n.* disposition to please or oblige others; agreeableness; graciousness.

com·plai·sant (kəm plā′sənt, -zənt, kom′plə zant′) *adj.* characterized by complaisance; obliging; agreeable; courteous. [French *complaisant,* present participle of *complaire* to please, from Latin *complacēre.*] —**com·plai′sant·ly,** *adv.*

com·ple·ment (*n.,* kom′plə mənt; *v.,* kom′plə ment′) *n.* **1.** that

at; āpe; cär; end; mē; it; īce; hot; ōld; fôrk; wood; fōōl; oil; out; up; ūse; turn; sing; thin; this; zh in treasure; ə in ago, taken, pencil, lemon, circus.

which completes or makes perfect. **2.** quantity or amount that completes or is required to complete. **3.** total number of officers and men constituting the crew of a ship. **4.** either of two parts which together form a whole. **5.** *Geometry.* measure of an angle or arc that must be added to the measure of a given angle or arc to produce a sum equal to 90 degrees. **6.** *Grammar.* word or phrase used to complete a construction, esp. in the predicate. There are two kinds of complement: the **subjective complement**, which describes or identifies the subject, and the **objective complement**, which describes or identifies the object. —*v.t.* to add or be a complement to; complete. [Latin *complēmentum* that which completes, from *complēre* to fill up, complete. Doublet of COMPLIMENT.]

Syn. *v.t.* **Complement, supplement** indicate the making up of a deficiency. **Complement** suggests completion, a combining of two things so that together they make a whole: *All he needed were those two pieces to complement his collection of ancient Peloponnesian coins.* **Supplement** suggests enhancement by the addition of something: *He supplemented his diet with a daily dosage of vitamins and minerals.*

com·ple·men·tal (kom′plə men′təl) *adj.* complementary.

com·ple·men·ta·ry (kom plə men′tər ē, -trē) *adj.* **1.** serving as a complement; completing. **2.** mutually supplying each other's needs.

complementary angle, angle that is the complement of a given angle.

complementary colors, two colors of the spectrum which, when combined, produce white or gray. Yellow and blue are complementary colors.

com·plete (kəm plēt′) *adj.* **1.** having all its parts or elements; whole; entire. **2.** ended; finished. **3.** realized to the fullest extent; total; thorough. **4.** *Archaic.* expert; accomplished; skilled. —*v.t.*, **-plet·ed, -plet·ing. 1.** to make whole; include all parts of. **2.** to bring to an end; finish. [Latin *complētus,* past participle of *complēre* to fill up, finish.] —**com·plete′ly,** *adv.* —**com·plete′ness,** *n.*

Syn. *adj.* **1. Complete, entire, total, whole** indicate that no parts are lacking. **Complete** suggests the presence of the full number of necessary parts: *The puzzle was not complete without the missing pieces.* **Entire** implies that no part has been omitted and that nothing can be added: *I intend to devote the entire summer to finishing the job.* **Total** suggests that everything has been taken into account, that there are no exceptions: *The car was smashed beyond repair, a total wreck.* **Whole** implies that nothing is missing and that no omission can be envisaged: *The whole plan, when it was revealed, startled those who had until then seen only parts.*

com·ple·tion (kəm plē′shən) *n.* act of completing; being completed.

com·plex (*adj.,* kəm pleks′, kom′pleks; *n.,* kom′pleks) *adj.* **1.** difficult to understand, analyze, or execute; intricate; complicated: *a complex theory.* **2.** consisting of a combination of related elements or parts. —*n.* **1.** whole made up of a combination of related parts: *an industrial complex consisting of ten manufacturing plants.* **2.** group of related ideas, emotions, memories, or desires that have been partially or totally repressed in the unconscious mind, but can influence a person's thoughts and actions to an abnormal degree. **3.** *Informal.* excessive or unreasonable concern or fear; obsession: *She has a complex about being late.* [Latin *complexus* entwined around; hence, complicated, past participle of *complectī* to embrace, entwine around.] —**com·plex′ly,** *adv.* —**com·plex′ness,** *n.*

Syn. *adj.* **1. Complex, complicated, intricate** indicate having many differing parts not easily distinguished. **Complex** implies that examination and study are necessary to clarify the relationship of the numerous parts: *It is best for the amateur mechanic not to tinker with the complex mechanism of the carburetor.* **Complicated** suggests an interrelationship of parts that is difficult to understand: *To an outsider, the political situation there seems impossibly complicated.* **Intricate** suggests an elaboration and interweaving that is difficult to trace: *The intricate ecology of the region needs a large diagram to explain it.*

complex fraction, any fraction with a common fraction, mixed number, or algebraic expression in the numerator, in the denominator, or in both. The fractions $\frac{1}{2}/2\frac{1}{8}$ and $\frac{3}{4}/1\frac{3}{4}$ are complex fractions. Also, **compound fraction.**

com·plex·ion (kəm plek′shən) *n.* **1.** natural color, texture, and general appearance of the skin, esp. of the face. **2.** general appearance or character; aspect: *The testimony of the witness gave a new complexion to the case.* [Old French *complexion* appearance, nature, from Late Latin *complexiō* physical constitution, temperament, from Latin *complexiō* combination, association.]

com·plex·ioned (kəm plek′shənd) *adj.* having a (specified kind of) complexion. ▲ used in combination, as in *fair-complexioned.*

com·plex·i·ty (kəm plek′sə tē) *pl.,* **-ties.** *n.* **1.** state or quality of being complex. **2.** that which is complex.

complex number, any number written $a + bi$ in which i is the positive square root of negative one and a and b are real numbers.

complex sentence, sentence that consists of one independent clause

and one or more dependent clauses, for example: *After the girls played tennis for an hour, they decided to go for a swim.*

com·pli·ance (kəm plī′əns) *n.* **1.** act of complying or yielding; acquiescence. **2.** tendency to yield to others. **3. in compliance with.** in accordance with: *She acted in compliance with our request.*

com·pli·an·cy (kəm plī′ən sē) *n.* compliance.

com·pli·ant (kəm plī′ənt) *adj.* complying or tending to comply; yielding; submissive. —**com·pli′ant·ly,** *adv.* —**Syn.** see **obedient.**

com·pli·cate (kom′plə kāt′) **-cat·ed, -cat·ing.** *v.t.* to make complex, difficult, or intricate. [Latin *complicātus,* past participle of *complicāre* to fold together.]

com·pli·cat·ed (kom′plə kā′tid) *adj.* difficult to understand, analyze, or do; intricate. —**Syn.** see **complex.**

com·pli·ca·tion (kom′plə kā′shən) *n.* **1.** act or process of complicating. **2.** complicated state or condition; complexity. **3.** that which complicates, as an element, detail, or condition. **4.** secondary disease or condition that occurs with and aggravates the primary disease.

com·plic·i·ty (kəm plis′ə tē) *n.* state of being an accomplice, esp. in wrongdoing: *He was proven guilty of complicity in the fraud.* [French *complicité* conspiracy, participation, going back to Latin *complex* confederate, participant.]

com·pli·ment (*n.,* kom′plə mənt; *v.,* kom′plə ment′) *n.* **1.** expression of admiration or praise; flattering comment: *She received many compliments on her cooking.* **2. compliments.** expression of regard, greeting, or good wishes: *Extend my compliments to your mother.* **3. compliments of.** as a gift from: *compliments of the management.* —*v.t.* **1.** to pay a compliment to. **2.** to present with something as a mark of courtesy. [French *compliment* commendation, through Italian and Spanish, going back to Latin *complēmentum* that which completes. Doublet of COMPLEMENT.] —**Syn.** *n.* see **praise.**

com·pli·men·ta·ry (kom′plə men′tər ē, -trē) *adj.* **1.** containing, expressing, or of the nature of a compliment. **2.** free: *a complimentary ticket to the football game.*

com·plin (kom′plin) *also,* **com·pline.** *n.* last of the seven canonical hours or the service for it. [Old French *complie* this hour, from Late Latin *complēta (hōra)* literally, completed (hour) (because it completed the hours of the service), feminine of Latin *complētus* complete.]

com·ply (kəm plī′) **-plied, -ply·ing.** *v.i.* to act in accordance, as with a request, wish, rule, or command. [Italian *complire* to fulfill, suit, from Spanish *cumplir* to accomplish, from Latin *complēre* to fill up, finish.] —**com·pli′er,** *n.*

com·po·nent (kəm pō′nənt) *n.* constituent or element; ingredient: *the components of a chemical, the components of her personality.* —*adj.* serving to constitute: *component parts.* [Latin *compōnēns,* present participle of *compōnere* to put together, arrange.] —**Syn.** *n.* see **ingredient.**

com·port (kəm pôrt′) *v.t.* to behave or conduct (oneself). —*v.i.* to suit, befit, or agree (with *with*): *His flippant attitude does not comport with the responsibility of his position.* [Late Latin *comportāre* to behave, from Latin *comportāre* to carry together.]

com·port·ment (kəm pôrt′mənt) *n.* behavior; deportment; conduct.

com·pose (kəm pōz′) **-posed, -pos·ing.** *v.t.* **1.** to make up; constitute: *Twelve men compose a jury. The fabric was composed of synthetic fibers.* **2.** to make or form from parts or elements; fashion: *He composed his argument from four logical statements.* **3.** to create (a musical or literary work). **4.** to make tranquil or quiet; calm: *It was hard for her to compose herself after such a shock.* **5.** to arrange artistically, as the elements in a painting. **6.** *Printing.* **a.** to set (type). **b.** to set the type for: *The printer composed the page.* —*v.i.* to compose music. [French *composer* to make

up, form, fashion, alteration (influenced by French *poser* to place, put) of Latin *compōnere* to put together, arrange.]

com·posed (kəm pōzd′) *adj.* self-controlled; calm; tranquil. —**com·pos·ed·ly** (kəm pō′zid lē) *adv.*

com·pos·er (kəm pō′-zər) *n.* one who composes, esp. music.

composing stick, small adjustable tray used by compositors to gather and assemble type.

com·pos·ite (kəm-pos′it) *adj.* **1.** made up of various parts or elements. **2.** belonging to the family Compositae, the largest and most highly evolved group of flowering plants, found throughout the world. They bear tiny florets clustered into

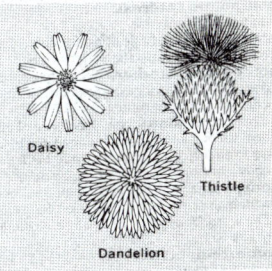

Daisy

Thistle

Dandelion

Composite flowers

at; āpe; cär; end; mē; it; īce; hot; ōld; fôrk; wood; fōōl; oil; out; up; ūse; turn; sing; thin; this; zh in treasure; ə in ago, taken, pencil, lemon, circus.

205

dense flower heads. Daisies and chrysanthemums are composite flowers. —n. **1.** that which is composed of various parts or elements. **2.** composite plant. **3.** composite photograph. [Latin *compositus*, past participle of *compōnere* to put together, arrange. Doublet of COMPOST.] —**com·pos′ite·ly,** *adv.*

composite photograph, photograph made by combining two or more photographs.

com·po·si·tion (kom′pə zish′ən) *n.* **1.** act of combining parts or elements in order to form a whole. **2.** manner in which something is composed; make-up; ingredients: *The chemist analyzed the substance to determine its composition.* **3.** substance formed by a mixture of various ingredients. **4.** act, process, or art of creating a musical, literary, or artistic work. **5.** musical, literary, or artistic work. **6.** short essay, esp. one written as an exercise for school. **7.** *Printing.* setting of type. [Old French *composition* a making, framing, from Latin *compositiō* a putting together, connection.] —**Syn. 6.** see **essay.**

com·pos·i·tor (kəm poz′ə tər) *n.* typesetter *(def. 1).*

com·post (kom′pōst) *n.* **1.** mixture of decaying vegetable matter and manure used to fertilize and condition soil. **2.** mixture; compound. [Old French *compost* a composition, and *compost* mixture, both going back to Latin *compositus* mixed, past participle of *compōnere* to put together. Doublet of COMPOSITE.]

com·po·sure (kəm pō′zhər) *n.* self-control; tranquility; calmness.

com·pote (kom′pōt) *n.* **1.** fruit that is stewed or preserved in syrup. **2.** shallow bowl or dish having a stem, usually used for fruit or candy. [French *compote* stewed fruit, going back to Latin *composita*, feminine past participle of *compōnere* to put together.]

com·pound¹ *(adj.,* kom′pound′, kom pound′*; v.,* kəm pound′*; n.,* kom′pound′) *adj.* composed of or produced by the union of two or more parts or elements. —*v.t.* **1.** to mix (parts, elements, or ingredients) to form a compound substance: *He compounded water, sand, and soil and formed bricks.* **2.** to make by combining various parts, elements, or ingredients: *A pharmacist compounds drugs from prescribed ingredients.* **3.** to compute (interest) on the sum of the principal and the accrued interest. **4.** to add to; intensify: *She compounded the insult by walking away as he started to speak.* **5. to compound a felony** (or **crime**). to agree not to prosecute or disclose a crime, in return for payment or other consideration. —*n.* **1.** combination of two or more parts, elements, or ingredients; mixture. **2.** substance formed by chemical combination of two or more elements in a fixed proportion. A compound has properties different from the elements of which it is made, is held together by chemical bonds, and can be separated into its component parts by chemical processes only. **3.** compound word. [Middle French *compondre* to put together, arrange, from Latin *compōnere.*] —**com·pound′a·ble,** *adj.* —**com·pound′er,** *n.*

com·pound² (kom′pound′) *n.* **1.** in the Orient, an enclosed area containing a residence, factory, or other buildings, esp. when owned by Europeans. **2.** any similar enclosed area: *a prison compound.* [Malay *kampong* enclosure.]

com·pound-com·plex sentence (kom′pound kom pleks′) sentence that consists of two or more independent clauses and one or more dependent clauses, for example: *One afternoon the vacationing group divided up, and Jack, Molly, and Tom, who love archaeology, went to the museum.*

compound eye, eye, as in many insects, consisting of numerous units, each of which has a lens system and nerve fibers connecting it to the central nervous system. See **housefly** for illustration.

compound fraction, complex fraction.

compound fracture, fracture in which the broken bone pierces the flesh and projects through the wound.

compound interest, interest computed on the sum of the principal and accrued interest.

compound leaf, leaf, as a pinnate leaf, having two or more leaflets on a common leafstalk.

compound number, quantity expressed in two or more units or denominations, for example: 5 feet, 10 inches; 7 pounds, 10 ounces; and 4 hours and 17 minutes.

compound sentence, sentence that consists of two or more independent clauses, usually connected by a conjunction or conjunctions, for example: *The secretary wrote the letters in shorthand Monday afternoon, and she typed them on Tuesday.*

compound word, word composed of two or more words which are written as one word, joined together by a hyphen, or written separately. The words *blueberry, fair-haired,* and *elementary school* are compound words.

com·pre·hend (kom′pri hend′) *v.t.* **1.** to grasp mentally; understand fully. **2.** to take in or contain; include; embrace: *The topic he was assigned comprehended all of the major political developments of 1968.* [Latin *comprehendere* to grasp, perceive.]

Syn. 1. Comprehend, apprehend mean to perceive mentally. **Comprehend** implies the taking in of the meaning and implications of some-

thing: *He comprehends the subtleties of the poem.* **Apprehend** implies taking hold of a meaning without absorbing its implications: *He was quick to apprehend the danger involved but didn't know how to avert it.*

com·pre·hen·si·ble (kom′pri hen′sə bəl) *adj.* capable of being comprehended; understandable. Also, **com·pre·hen·di·ble** (kom′pri·hen′də bəl). —**com′pre·hen′si·bil′i·ty,** *n.* —**com′pre·hen′si·bly,** *adv.*

com·pre·hen·sion (kom′pri hen′shən) *n.* **1.** act, fact, or power of grasping mentally; understanding. **2.** act or fact of containing or including; inclusion. [Latin *comprehēnsiō* a seizing, perception.]

com·pre·hen·sive (kom′pri hen′siv) *adj.* large in scope or content; including much; extensive: *a comprehensive study of the animal life in a region.* —**com′pre·hen′sive·ly,** *adv.* —**com′pre·hen′sive·ness,** *n.*

com·press (*v.,* kəm pres′*; n.,* kom′pres′) *v.t.* to press or squeeze together so as to make more compact; condense. —*n.* **1.** pad or cloth used to apply cold, heat, moisture, medication, or pressure to some part of the body. **2.** apparatus for pressing cotton into bales. [Late Latin *compressāre* to press, oppress, from Latin *comprimere* to press together.] —**com·press′i·bil′i·ty,** *n.* —**com·press′i·ble,** *adj.* —**Syn. v.t.** see **condense.**

com·pressed (kəm prest′) *adj.* **1.** pressed or squeezed together; made more compact. **2.** narrow or flattened laterally or lengthwise, as the body of certain fish or parts of certain plants.

compressed air, air that has been compressed within some type of chamber or container so that it can exert expansive force. It is used to provide energy to move the pistons in internal combustion engines and to support the outer walls or caissons used in underwater construction.

com·pres·sion (kəm presh′ən) *n.* **1.** act or process of compressing; being compressed. **2.** process by which the volume of a confined gas is reduced by the application of pressure, as in an internal combustion engine.

com·pres·sive (kəm pres′iv) *adj.* compressing or tending to compress.

com·pres·sor (kəm pres′ər) *n.* **1.** machine that compresses a gas so that its expansion may be used as a source of power. **2.** one who or that which compresses. **3.** surgical instrument for applying pressure to a part of the body, as to an artery. [Latin *compressor* one who compresses.]

com·prise (kəm prīz′) **-prised, -pris·ing.** also, **com·prize.** *v.t.* to consist of; be composed of; include; contain: *These two books comprise all of his published poetry.* [French *compris,* past participle of *comprendre* to include, understand, from Latin *comprehendere* to grasp, perceive.]

com·pro·mise (kom′prə mīz′) *n.* **1.** settlement of a dispute by the partial surrender by each side of claims or demands; adjustment of differences by mutual concessions. **2.** result of such a settlement. **3.** something intermediate between or combining the characteristics of two different things. —*v.i.* **1.** to settle or adjust (a dispute or differences) by mutual concessions. **2.** to expose to disrepute, suspicion, or danger; endanger the reputation or interests of: *He compromised himself as their leader by yielding to public pressure.* [French *compromis* mutual agreement, from Latin *comprōmissum* mutual promise to accept arbitration.] —**com′·pro·mis′er,** *n.*

comp·tom·e·ter (komp tom′ə tər) *n.* machine on which numbers can be added, subtracted, multiplied, and divided.

Comp·ton (komp′tən) *n.* city in southwestern California, near Los Angeles. Pop. (1970), 78,611.

comp·trol·ler (kən trō′lər) *n.* controller *(def. 1).* —**comp·trol′·ler·ship′,** *n.*

com·pul·sion (kəm pul′shən) *n.* **1.** act of compelling; coercion. **2.** state of being compelled. **3.** irresistible or irrational impulse to perform a particular act. [Late Latin *compulsiō* a driving, urging, from Latin *compellere* to drive together, compel.]

com·pul·sive (kəm pul′siv) *adj.* **1.** of, relating to, or caused or characterized by compulsion: *a compulsive liar, compulsive gambling.* **2.** compulsory. —**com·pul′sive·ly,** *adv.* —**com·pul′sive·ness,** *n.*

com·pul·so·ry (kəm pul′sər ē) *adj.* **1.** required; obligatory; mandatory. **2.** involving compulsion; coercive. —**com·pul′so·ri·ly,** *adv.*

com·punc·tion (kəm pungk′shən) *n.* uneasiness of mind due to feelings of remorse or guilt; twinge of conscience; qualm. [Late Latin *compūnctiō* pricking (of conscience), remorse, from Latin *compungere* to prick sharply.] —**Syn.** see **regret.**

com·pu·ta·tion (kom′pyə tā′shən) *n.* **1.** act, process, or method of computing. **2.** result of computing; amount computed.

com·pute (kəm pūt′) **-put·ed, -put·ing.** *v.t.* to determine, as an amount or number, by mathematical calculation; calculate. —*v.i.* to make a computation; reckon. [Latin *computāre.* Doublet of COUNT¹.] —**com·put′a·bil′i·ty,** *n.* —**com·put′a·ble,** *adj.* —**Syn. v.t.** see **calculate.**

com·put·er (kəm pū′tər) *n.* **1.** automatic electronic device that rapidly performs complex mathematical and logical operations using infor-

mation and instructions it receives and stores. **2.** any device or person that computes.

com·put·er·ize (kəm pū′tə rīz′) **-ized, -iz·ing.** *v.t.* **1.** to adapt to, control by, or store in an electronic computer. **2.** to equip with electronic computers: *The company computerized its sales division.*

com·rade (kom′rad, -rəd) *n.* **1.** close friend or companion. **2.** one who participates with another or others in a common interest, activity, occupation, or other concern; associate. **3.** fellow member, as of a political party, esp. the Communist Party. [French *camarade* roommate, companion, from Spanish *camarada,* from *camara* room, from Late Latin *camera.* See CAMERA.] **—com′rade·ship,** *n.* **—Syn. 2.** see **associate.**

comte (kônt) *French.* count².

Co·mus (kō′məs) *n.* youthful Greek and Roman god of drunken revelry and entertainment.

con¹ (kon) *adv.* against: *The senator weighed the arguments pro and con before voting.* **—***n.* reason, argument, or person against. [Short for Latin *contrā* against.]

con² (kon) **conned, con·ning.** *v.t.* to peruse, examine, or study carefully: *patiently conning the page again and again* (Dickens, 1838). [Old English *cunnian* to try (to know), test.]

con³ (kon) **conned, con·ning.** *also,* **conn.** *Nautical. v.t.* to direct the steering of (a vessel). **—***n.* action or post of one who cons. [Short for obsolete *cond, condue* to conduct, from Old French *conduire* to lead, from Latin *condūcere* to lead to.]

con⁴ (kon) **conned, con·ning.** *Slang. v.t.* to cheat, swindle, or deceive: *The swindler conned $100 from him.* **—***adj.* confidence: *a con man, a con game.* [From CONFIDENCE.]

con- *prefix* form of **com-** before all consonants except *b, h, l, m, p, r,* and *w,* as in *concentrate, connote, congenial.*

con. **1.** conclusion. **2.** against.

Con·a·kry (kon′ə krē) *n.* capital and chief port of Guinea, in the western part of the country. Pop. (1967 est.), 197,267.

con a·mo·re (kôn ä môr′ā) *Italian.* **1.** *Music.* with love; tenderly. **2.** with enthusiasm or zeal.

con·cat·e·nate (kon kat′ən āt′) **-nat·ed, -nat·ing.** *v.t.* to link or join together; connect in a series or chain. **—***adj.* joined or linked together. [Late Latin *concatēnātus,* past participle of *concatēnāre* to link together, connect, from Latin *con-* together + *catēna* chain.]

con·cat·e·na·tion (kon kat′ən ā′shən) *n.* **1.** series of interconnected or interdependent things or events: *taking in the whole concatenation of causes and effects* (Johnson, 1753). **2.** act of concatenating; being concatenated.

con·cave (*adj.,* kon kāv′, kon′kāv; *n.,* kon′kāv) *adj.* hollow and curving inward like the inside of a circle or bowl. Opposed to **convex.** **—***n.* concave surface. [Latin *concavus* hollow, curved.] **—con·cave′ly,** *adv.* **—con·cave′ness,** *n.*

con·cav·i·ty (kon kav′ə tē) *pl.* **-ties.** *n.* **1.** state of being concave. **2.** concave surface or space.

con·ca·vo-con·vex (kon kā′vō kon veks′) *adj.* **1.** concave on one side and convex on the other. **2.** of or designating a lens in which the concave face has a greater degree of curvature than the convex face, making the lens thinnest in the middle.

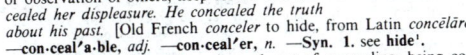

Flat

Concave

Concave lens

Convex

Concave

Concavo-convex lens

con·ceal (kon sēl′) *v.t.* **1.** to put or keep out of sight; hide: *He concealed the car key under the dashboard.* **2.** to keep from the knowledge or observation of others; keep secret: *She concealed her displeasure. He concealed the truth about his past.* [Old French *conceler* to hide, from Latin *concēlāre.*] **—con·ceal′a·ble,** *adj.* **—con·ceal′er,** *n.* **—Syn. 1.** see **hide¹.**

con·ceal·ment (kon sēl′mənt) *n.* **1.** act of concealing; being concealed. **2.** means or place for hiding.

con·cede (kon sēd′) **-ced·ed, -ced·ing.** *v.t.* **1.** to acknowledge as true, just, or proper; admit: *The losers were forced to concede defeat.* **2.** to acknowledge as won by an opponent before the results have been determined. **3.** to grant or yield, as a right or privilege. **—***v.i.* to make a concession; yield. [Latin *concēdere* to retire, yield.] **—Syn.** *v.t.* **1.** see **grant.**

con·ceit (kon sēt′) *n.* **1.** very high opinion of oneself or of one's accomplishments; personal vanity or pride. **2.** fanciful, ingenious, or witty thought or expression. **3.** elaborate or extended poetic device, esp. a metaphor. [From CONCEIVE, on the model of the pair *deceit, deceive.*] **—Syn. 1.** see **egotism.**

con·ceit·ed (kon sē′tid) *adj.* having an excessively high opinion of oneself or of one's accomplishments; vain. **—con·ceit′ed·ly,** *adv.* **—con·ceit′ed·ness,** *n.*

con·ceiv·a·ble (kon sē′və bəl) *adj.* that can be conceived; imaginable. **—con·ceiv′a·bil′i·ty,** *n.* **—con·ceiv′a·bly,** *adv.*

con·ceive (kən sēv′) **-ceived, -ceiv·ing.** *v.t.* **1.** to form or develop mentally; plan; devise: *The coach conceived the strategy that won the game for us.* **2.** to have or form a mental image or idea of; imagine: *We could not conceive that they would do such a silly thing.* **3.** to become pregnant with. **—***v.i.* **1.** to form a mental image or idea; think (with *of*): *They could not conceive of the possibility of failure.* **2.** to become pregnant. [Old French *conceveir* to become pregnant, perceive, from Latin *concipere.*]

con·cen·trate (kon′sən trāt′) **-trat·ed, -trat·ing.** *v.t.* **1.** to bring, draw, or direct to a common center or objective; focus: *They concentrated their guns on the weakened section of the wall. He concentrated his efforts on winning.* **2.** to increase the strength, density, or purity of by reducing the amount of or removing that which is undesirable or unnecessary. **—***v.i.* **1.** to direct all of one's efforts or attention: *He could not concentrate because the room was noisy. She concentrated on studying for her exam.* **2.** to come to or toward a common center; converge. **3.** to become stronger, denser, or purer. **—***n.* substance, as a chemical solution, that has been concentrated. [CON- + Latin *centrum* center + -ATE¹.] **—con′cen·tra′tor,** *n.*

con·cen·tra·tion (kon′sən trā′shən) *n.* **1.** act of concentrating; being concentrated. **2.** close or complete attention fixed on a particular subject or goal: *The successful solution of the problem required patience and concentration.* **3.** that which is concentrated. **4.** relative strength or amount of a substance, as a solute, per unit volume.

concentration camp, prison camp used to confine persons considered dangerous by a government or military ruler. They have been used in times of war to detain, punish, or, as in Nazi Germany, kill large numbers of people.

con·cen·tric (kən sen′trik) *adj.* having a common center. Also, **con·cen′tri·cal.** **—con·cen′tri·cal·ly,** *adv.* **—con·cen·tric·i·ty** (kon′-sen tris′ə tē), *n.*

Con·cep·ción (kôn′sep syōn′) *n.* city in central Chile. Pop. (1968 est.), 187,251.

con·cept (kon′sept) *n.* thought or notion, esp. a generalized idea or mental image formed on the basis of knowledge or experience: *He has no concept of fair play. Do you have any concept of what the room will look like with those colors?* [Late Latin *conceptus* thought, from Latin *conceptus* a collecting, conceiving.]

con·cep·tion (kən sep′shən) *n.* **1.** act or power of forming concepts. **2.** mental image or idea; concept. **3.** design; plan. **4.** act of conceiving or being conceived, as in the womb. **5.** that which is so conceived; embryo; fetus. **—Syn. 2.** see **idea.**

con·cep·tu·al (kən sep′chōō əl) *adj.* of or relating to conception or concepts. **—con·cep′tu·al·ly,** *adv.*

con·cep·tu·al·ize (kən sep′chōō ə līz′) **-ized, -iz·ing.** *v.t.* to form a concept or conception of.

con·cern (kən surn′) *v.t.* **1.** to relate to; be of interest or importance to: *Conservation concerns us all.* **2.** to cause to worry; trouble or distress: *Her illness concerns me very much.* **3.** to involve or occupy: *Don't concern yourself about other people's affairs.* ▲ used reflexively or in the passive. **—***n.* **1.** that which relates to or affects someone; affair: *International sales are his special concern.* **2.** solicitude; worry; anxiety: *Concern for the victims was evident in his voice.* **3.** business organization or establishment; company; firm: *He heads the largest clothing concern in the area.* **4.** relation; interest: *He has little concern with sports.* [Medieval Latin *concernere* to relate to, from Late Latin *concernere* to mix, from Latin *con-* together + *cernere* to sift, see.] **—Syn.** *n.* **2.** see **care.**

con·cerned (kən surnd′) *adj.* **1.** interested; involved; occupied. **2.** troubled; anxious.

con·cern·ing (kən sur′ning) *prep.* having to do with; relating to; regarding.

con·cert (*n., adj.,* kon′sərt; *v.,* kən surt′) *n.* **1.** public performance of vocal or instrumental music: *a jazz concert, a folk concert.* **2.** accord or harmony, as in plan or action. **3. in concert.** all together; in agreement or accord. **—***adj.* of, relating to, or intended for concerts: *a concert pianist, a concert hall.* **—***v.t.* **1.** to plan or arrange (something) by mutual agreement. **2.** to contrive; devise. **—***v.i.* to plan or arrange by mutual agreement. [French *concert* musical performance, harmony, from Italian *concerto,* from *concertare* to bring into harmony, of uncertain origin.]

con·cert·ed (kən sur′tid) *adj.* **1.** planned or carried out by mutual agreement: *a concerted attack.* **2.** utilizing all resources: *He made a concerted effort to solve the problem.* **3.** *Music.* arranged in parts for voices or instruments.

con·cer·ti·na (kon′sər tē′nə) *n.* musical instrument resembling an accordian, having a bellows and buttonlike keys. [From CONCERT.]

con·cert·mas·ter (kon′sərt mas′tər) *n.* leader of the first violin section of an orchestra, who serves as assistant to the conductor.

Concertina

con·cer·to (kən cher′tō) *pl.*, **-tos** or **-ti** (tē). *n.* musical composition for a solo instrument or instruments accompanied by an orchestra, usually in three movements. [Italian *concerto* concert, harmony. See CONCERT.]

concerto gros·so (grō′sō) *pl.*, **concerti gros·si** (grō′sē). musical composition for a small group of solo instruments and an orchestra.

con·ces·sion (kən sesh′ən) *n.* **1.** act of granting or conceding: *the concession of a wage increase.* **2.** something granted or conceded: *to demand a number of concessions.* **3.** something, as a grant of land or a franchise, conceded by a government or other authority. **4.a.** privilege of operating a business within certain premises. **b.** the business itself. [Latin *concessiō* granting, yielding.]

con·ces·sion·aire (kən sesh′ə nâr′) *n.* one who owns or operates a concession or who has been granted a concession.

con·ces·sive (kən ses′iv) *adj.* **1.** characteristic of or tending to concede. **2.** *Grammar.* expressing concession. The word *although* is a concessive conjunction.

conch (kongk, konch) *pl.* **conchs** (kongks) or **conch·es** (kon′chiz). *n.* **1.** any of various tropical saltwater mollusks, having large spiral shells, esp. *Strombus gigas* of the Florida Keys and the West Indies. **2.** shell of this animal, esp. when used as a horn or to make buttons or cameos. [Latin *concha* shell, mussel, from Greek *konchē*.]

Conch

con·chol·o·gy (kong kol′ə jē) *n.* branch of zoology comprising the study of mollusk shells. [Greek *konchē* shell + -LOGY.] **—con·cho·log·i·cal** (kong′kə loj′i kəl), *adj.*

con·ci·erge (kon′sē urzh′; *French* kôN syerzh′) *n.* caretaker of a building, esp. in France, who checks people entering or leaving. [French *concierge*, going back to Latin *conservus* fellow servant.]

con·cil·i·ate (kən sil′ē āt′) **-at·ed, -at·ing.** *v.t.* **1.** to overcome the hostility or mistrust of; win over; placate: *The only thing that will conciliate the strikers is a raise in salary.* **2.** to gain (good will or favor) by friendly or pleasing acts. **3.** to reconcile; make compatible. [Latin *conciliātus*, past participle of *conciliāre* to combine, bring together.] **—con·cil′i·a′tion, con·cil′i·a′tor,** *n.* **—con·cil′i·a′tive, con·cil·i·a·to·ry** (kən sil′ē ə tôr′ē), *adj.*

con·cise (kən sīs′) *adj.* expressing much in few words; terse; compact. [Latin *concīsus* divided, short, past participle of *concīdere* to cut to pieces.] **—con·cise′ly,** *adv.* **—con·cise′ness,** *n.*

Syn. **Concise, succinct, terse** mean brevity in expression. **Concise** suggests cutting to essentials: *His letter was concise, omitting everything not pertinent to the job for which he was applying.* **Succinct** suggests compression in a very small space: *From his years as a reporter he developed a succinct style of writing.* **Terse** means brief but polished, very simple, and direct: *His terse summing of the trial is famous.*

con·clave (kon′klāv, kong′-) *n.* **1.** private meeting. **2.a.** meeting of the cardinals of the Roman Catholic Church to elect a pope. **b.** private chamber where the cardinals meet for this purpose. [Medieval Latin *conclave* assembly of cardinals, from Latin *conclāve* room that can be locked, from *con-* together + *clāvis* key.]

con·clude (kən klōōd′) **-clud·ed, -clud·ing.** *v.t.* **1.** to bring to an end; finish: *He concluded his speech.* **2.** to arrange or settle finally: *Preparations for the meeting were concluded on Tuesday.* **3.** to reach a decision or come to an opinion about: *What do you conclude from the facts?* **—***v.i.* **1.** to end; close; terminate: *The election campaign concluded with a mass meeting.* **2.** to reach a decision; come to an opinion. [Latin *conclūdere* to shut up, close.] **—con·clud′er,** *n.*

Syn. *v.t.* **1.** see **end.** **3. Conclude, deduce** mean taking a logical approach in making up one's mind. **Conclude** indicates a sound or probable answer arrived at by reasoning from given facts or opinions: *After much study, he concluded that the stock would rise in value.* **Deduce** indicates a solid basis in fact or principle for the specific answer reached: *From the readings of their instruments they deduced that a hurricane was approaching.*

con·clu·sion (kən klōō′zhən) *n.* **1.** end; termination: *The audience cheered at the conclusion of the speech.* **2.** closing portion of a discourse, usually containing a summary and opinion of what preceded. **3.** result; outcome. **4.** final arrangement; settlement: *The conclusion of the sale took place in the lawyer's office.* **5.** final decision or opinion: *Our conclusion is that the problem is insoluble.* **6.** *Logic.* proposition that necessarily follows from the major and minor premises of a syllogism. See **syllogism. 7. in conclusion.** as a final statement; to sum up. [Latin *conclūsiō* a shutting up, end.]

con·clu·sive (kən klōō′siv) *adj.* decisive; definitive; final. **—con·clu′sive·ly,** *adv.* **—con·clu′sive·ness,** *n.*

con·coct (kon kokt′, kən-) *v.t.* **1.** to prepare by mixing several ingredients: *The witches concocted an evil brew.* **2.** to put together; devise: *The thieves concocted a plan.* [Latin *concoctus*, past participle of *concoquere* to devise; literally, to cook together.] **—con·coc′tion, con·coc′tor,** *n.*

con·com·i·tance (kon kom′ə təns, kən-) *n.* accompaniment; coexistence.

con·com·i·tant (kon kom′ə tənt, kən-) *adj.* happening together; accompanying; attendant: *concomitant circumstances.* **—***n.* accompanying or attendant state, quality, or circumstance. [Late Latin *concomitāns*, present participle of *concomitārī* to accompany, from Latin *con-* together + *comitārī* to accompany.] **—con·com′i·tant·ly,** *adv.*

con·cord (kon′kôrd, kong′-) *n.* **1.** agreement between persons, nations, or things; accord. **2.** treaty establishing a state of peace and harmony. **3.** *Music.* harmonious combination of tones; consonance. Opposed to **discord. 4.** *Grammar.* agreement in number, person, gender, or case. [Old French *concorde* agreement, from Latin *concordia* agreement, harmony, going back to *con-* together + *cor* heart.]

Con·cord (kong′kərd) *n.* **1.** town in eastern Massachusetts, site of one of the first battles of the American Revolution, on April 19, 1775. Pop. (1970), 16,148. **2.** capital of New Hampshire, in the southern part of the state. Pop. (1970), 30,022. **3.** city in western California, northeast of Oakland. Pop. (1970), 85,164.

con·cord·ance (kon kôrd′əns, kən-) *n.* **1.** agreement; harmony. **2.** alphabetical index of the important words of a book or an author's works, indicating the passages in which the words occur.

con·cord·ant (kon kôrd′ənt, kən-) *adj.* agreeing; harmonious. **—con·cord′ant·ly,** *adv.*

con·cor·dat (kon kôr′dat) *n.* **1.** formal agreement; compact; covenant. **2.** treaty between the Vatican and a secular government concerning the regulation of church affairs. [Medieval Latin *concordatum* agreement, from Latin *concordāre* to agree.]

Concord grape, North American grape, having a blue-black color. [From *Concord*, Massachusetts, where is was found.]

con·course (kon′kôrs, kong′-) *n.* **1.** moving or coming together: *a concourse of ideas.* **2.** large gathering; crowd. **3.** large, open place where crowds gather, as in a park. **4.** wide street; boulevard. [Old French *concours* meeting, from Latin *concursus* a running together, meeting.]

con·cres·cence (kən kres′əns, kon-) *n.* growing together of parts, esp. the growing together of cells of an embryo. [Latin *concrēscentia* a growing together.]

con·crete (*adj., n., v.t., def. 1* kon′krēt, kong′-, kon krēt′; *v.t., def. 2* kon krēt′) *adj.* **1.** of or relating to things or events that can be perceived or experienced: *A chair is a concrete object.* **2.** specific; particular: *The teacher asked for concrete facts explaining the fall of the Roman Empire.* **3.** naming something perceptible or tangible: *"Soap" is a concrete noun.* **4.** made of concrete: *a concrete driveway.* **5.** formed by the union of particles into a mass; solid. **—***n.* mixture of such substances as crushed stone, gravel, sand, or pebbles cemented together and used for building or paving. **—***v.t.* **-cret·ed, -cret·ing. 1.** to make of, treat, or cover with concrete. **2.** to form (something) into a mass; harden. **—***v.i.* to form into a mass; harden. [Latin *concrētus*, past participle of *concrēscere* to grow together, harden.] **—con·crete′ly,** *adv.* **—con·crete′ness,** *n.*

con·cre·tion (kon krē′shən) *n.* **1.** act or process of growing together or forming into a mass. **2.** solidified mass. **3.** *Geology.* rounded mass of mineral matter formed around a fossil or other nucleus, found in sedimentary rock. **4.** mass of inorganic matter found in a tissue or cavity of the human body.

con·cu·bi·nage (kon kū′bə nij) *n.* **1.** cohabitation out of wedlock. **2.** state of being a concubine.

con·cu·bine (kong′kyə bīn′, kon′-) *n.* **1.** woman who cohabits with a man out of wedlock. **2.** in certain polygamous societies, a wife of secondary or inferior rank. [Old French *concubine* woman who lives in concubinage, from Latin *concubīna*, from *con-* with + *cubāre* to lie.]

con·cu·pis·cence (kon kū′pə səns) *n.* abnormally strong desire, esp. sexual desire. [Late Latin *concupīscentia* great longing, from Latin *concupīscere* to desire greatly.] **—con·cu′pis·cent,** *adj.*

con·cur (kən kur′) **-curred, -cur·ring.** *v.i.* **1.** to hold the same opinion; agree: *The brothers rarely concur on any issue.* **2.** to act together or cooperate toward the same end: *Scientists from two countries concurred in developing the vaccine.* **3.** to happen at the same time or place; coincide. [Latin *concurrere* to run together, join.]

con·cur·rence (kən kur′əns) *n.* **1.** sharing of an opinion; agreement; accord. **2.** acting together toward the same end; cooperation. **3.** simultaneous happening; coincidence. **4.** *Geometry.* point where three or more lines meet.

con·cur·rent (kən kur′ənt) *adj.* **1.** existing together; happening simultaneously. **2.** acting in cooperation. **3.** *Law.* being equally able or authorized to deal with the same matter. **4.** in agreement; harmonious. **5.** coming toward or meeting at the same point. **—***n.* something that concurs. **—con·cur′rent·ly,** *adv.*

con·cus·sion (kən kush′ən) *n.* **1.** violent shaking or shock. **2.** injury produced by a blow to an organ, esp. the brain. [Latin *concussiō* a shaking] **—con·cus·sive** (kən kus′iv), *adj.*

con·demn (kən dem′) *v.t.* **1.** to express strong disapproval of; censure. **2.** to show or declare the guilt of; convict. **3.** to pronounce the punish-

at; āpe; cär; end; mē; it; īce; hot; ōld; fôrk; wood; fōōl; oil; out; up; ūse; turn; sing; thin; this; zh in treasure; ə in ago, taken, pencil, lemon, circus.

ment of; sentence: *The judge condemned the criminal to ten years in jail.*
4. to declare unfit for use: *The building was condemned and is to be torn down.* **5.** *Law.* to appropriate (private property) for public use under the right of eminent domain. [Latin *condemnāre* to sentence, censure.] —**con·dem′na·ble** (kən dem′nə bəl, -dem′ə-), *adj.*

con·dem·na·tion (kon′dem nā′shən, -dəm-) *n.* **1.** act of condemning; being condemned. **2.** strong disapproval or censure. **3.** cause or reason for condemning. —**con·dem·na·to·ry** (kən dem′nə tôr′ē), *adj.*

con·den·sa·tion (kon′den sā′shən, -dən-) *n.* **1.** act or process of condensing; being condensed. **2.** product of condensing. **3.** reduction of a gas or vapor to a liquid or solid form: *condensation of steam into water.* **4.** *Chemistry.* reaction between two or more molecules, in which a larger molecule is formed, often with the elimination of a simple molecule, as water.

con·dense (kən dens′) -**densed, -dens·ing.** *v.t.* **1.** to make denser or more compact; reduce the volume of. **2.** to make more concise; abridge: *He condensed his report into a series of recommendations.* **3.** to reduce (a gas or vapor) to a liquid or solid form. **4.** to make (light rays) more intense; concentrate. —*v.i.* to become condensed. [Latin *condēnsāre* to make very dense.] —**con·den′sa·bil′i·ty;** *also,* **con·den·si·bil′i·ty,** *n.* —**con·den′sa·ble;** *also,* **con·den′si·ble,** *adj.*

Syn. *v.t.* **1. Condense, compress** mean to make smaller in bulk. **Condense** suggests elimination of nonessential elements while maintaining the character of the thing condensed: *He managed to condense his letter of application to one page.* **Compress** suggests squeezing everything into a smaller space, lessening the bulk, but maintaining the entire mass of a thing: *They compressed the cotton into bales before shipping it.*

condensed milk, cow's milk, thickened by evaporating part of the water content and sweetened with sugar.

con·dens·er (kən den′sər) *n.* **1.** one who or that which condenses. **2.** capacitor. **3.** apparatus for changing a gas or vapor into a liquid. **4.** lens or series of lenses for concentrating light upon a small area.

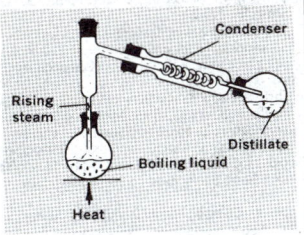

Rising steam

Condenser

Distillate

Boiling liquid

Heat

Condenser *(def. 3)*

con·de·scend (kon′di send′) *v.i.* **1.** to come down to the level of one's inferiors; lower oneself to do something; deign: *The physicist condescended to explain the theory in simple language.* **2.** to assume a superior manner. [French *condescendre* to yield, grant, from Late Latin *condēscendere* to grant, stoop, from Latin *con-* together + *dēscendere* to come down.]

con·de·scend·ing (kon′di sen′ding) *adj.* characterized by condescension. —**con′de·scend′ing·ly,** *adv.*

con·de·scen·sion (kon′di sen′shən) *n.* **1.** a coming down to the level of one's inferiors. **2.** superior attitude or manner. [Late Latin *condēscēnsiō,* from *condēscendere.* See CONDESCEND.]

con·dign (kən dīn′) *adj.* (esp. of punishment) deserved; adequate; fitting. [Old French *condigne* very worthy, from Latin *condignus.*]

con·di·ment (kon′də mənt) *n.* something used to make food more flavorful, as a seasoning, spice, or sauce. [Latin *condīmentum.*]

con·di·tion (kən dish′ən) *n.* **1.** particular manner of existence of a person or thing; state of being: *The condition of the land is poor for planting. His clothes were in shabby condition.* **2.** state of health: *His condition was described as serious.* **3.** state of physical fitness: *Athletes must be in top condition at all times.* **4.** social position or status; rank. **5.** something essential to the existence of something else; prerequisite: *Trust and respect are conditions of a happy marriage.* **6.** something that restricts, limits, or modifies something else; qualification: *You may go only under certain conditions.* **7. conditions.** circumstances that affect or influence one's mode of existence or activities: *living conditions.* **8.** something required prior to fulfillment or effectiveness of an agreement; provision; stipulation: *A halt in bombing was a condition for peace negotiations.* **9.** *Grammar.* dependent clause of a conditional sentence. **10.** requirement that a student with an unsatisfactory grade do special work to receive credit for a course. **11.** *Informal.* disease; ailment: *a heart condition.* **12. on condition that.** provided that; if. —*v.t.* **1.** to put in a fit or proper state: *Regular exercise conditions the body for strenuous activity.* **2.** to be a condition or prerequisite of. **3.** to make conditional; determine; limit (with *on* or *upon*): *She conditioned her acceptance of the favor on his coming to dinner next evening.* **4.** *Psychology.* to develop behavior patterns in, by recurring exposure to certain conditions or stimuli with which responses have become associated. **5.** to accustom (someone) to: *He soon conditioned the boys to the cold*

weather. **6.** to give a condition to (a student): *His teacher conditioned him in geometry.* [Old French *condicion* physical or moral state, Latin *condiciō, conditiō* agreement, situation.] —**con·di′tion·er,** *n.* —**Syn.** *n.* **7.** see **circumstance.**

con·di·tion·al (kən dish′ən əl) *adj.* **1.** depending on, subject to, or implying a condition or conditions; not absolute: *The sale of the painting was conditional on the expert's agreement that it was an original Rembrandt.* **2.** expressing a condition, as the clause *If he came.* —*n.* tense, word, clause, or mood expressing a condition. —**con·di′tion·al·ly,** *adv.*

con·di·tioned (kən dish′ənd) *adj.* **1.** having or subject to condition or conditions: *His answer to the reporter's question was both tentative and conditioned.* **2.** in good physical condition; fit. **3.** *Psychology.* having developed specific responses or reflexes through conditioning.

con·dole (kən dōl′) -**doled, -dol·ing.** *v.i.* to express sympathy; mourn (with *with*). [Late Latin *condolēre* to suffer with, from Latin *con-* with + *dolēre* to grieve.]

con·do·lence (kən dō′ləns) *n.* **1.** sympathy with someone suffering grief or sorrow. **2.** expression of sympathy: *He sent his condolences when her father died.*

con·do·min·i·um (kon′də min′ē əm) *n.* **1.** joint control or sovereignty, esp. by two or more countries. **2.** dominion or territory governed jointly. **3.a.** apartment house in which apartments are owned by the individual tenants. **b.** apartment in such a building. [Modern Latin *condominium,* from Latin *con-* with + *dominium* lordship, rule.]

con·done (kən dōn′) -**doned, -don·ing.** *v.t.* to allow (something) to occur without approving of it, but without offering reproof; overlook: *I can't condone his behavior.* [Latin *condōnāre* to give up, forgive.] —**con·do·na·tion** (kon′dō nā′shən, -də-), **con·don′er,** *n.* —**Syn.** see **excuse.**

con·dor (kon′dər, -dôr) *n.* **1.** South American vulture that is the largest extant flying bird, *Vultur gryphus,* native to the Andes and having black-and-white plumage, a white ruff, and a bare, dark-gray head and neck. Wingspan: 10 feet. **2.** slightly smaller but similar vulture, *Gymnogyps californianus,* that is native to the Pacific Coast of North America and is nearly extinct. [Spanish *cóndor,* from Quechua *cuntur.*]

Condor

con·duce (kən dōōs′, -dūs′) -**duced, -duc·ing.** *v.i.* to help bring about; lead (with *to* or *toward*): *His affability conduces to success as a salesman.* [Latin *condūcere* to lead to, bring together.]

con·du·cive (kən dōō′siv, -dū′-) *adj.* contributive; leading (with *to*): *A brisk walk is conducive to good appetite.* —**con·du′cive·ness,** *n.*

con·duct (*n.* kon′dukt; *v.* kən dukt′) *n.* **1.** way of acting; personal behavior; deportment: *The boy's conduct at the party was admirable.* **2.** administration or management, esp. of a business. **3.** act of leading; guidance. —*v.t.* **1.** to take charge of; manage: *He alone conducted the affairs of the company.* **2.** to direct or lead, esp. an orchestra: *Who will conduct the Philharmonic next season?* **3.** to behave or comport (oneself): *He conducted himself in a most gracious manner.* **4.** to act as an escort; lead; guide: *My cousin conducted us safely to the station.* **5.** to serve as a medium for; transmit, as heat, electricity, or sound: *The drainpipe conducts excess water from the well.* [Latin *conductus,* past participle of *condūcere* to lead to, bring together.] —**con·duct′i·bil′i·ty,** *n.* —**con·duct′i·ble,** *adj.* —**Syn.** *n.* **1.** see **behavior.**

con·duct·ance (kən duk′təns) *n.* property which allows a material to conduct electrical current; the reciprocal of resistance, expressed in mhos.

con·duc·tion (kən duk′shən) *n.* **1.** flow, as of heat, electricity, or sound, in a medium by the transmission of energy from one particle of the medium to another particle. **2.** act of conveying; transmission.

con·duc·tive (kən duk′tiv) *adj.* having conductivity. **2.** characteristic of or resulting from conduction.

con·duc·tiv·i·ty (kon′duk tiv′i tē) *n.* **1.** ability of a material to conduct heat, electricity, or sound. **2.** measure of the conductance of a given material.

con·duc·tor (kən duk′tər) *n.* **1.** one who conducts; director; guide; leader. **2.** director of an orchestra, chorus, or other musical group, who is responsible for interpreting the music, rehearsing the musicians, and leading the performance. **3.** person on a railroad train, streetcar, or bus, who collects the tickets or fares and announces stops. **4.** material or object that conducts or can conduct a form of energy, as electricity, heat, or sound.

con·duit (kon′dit, -dōō it, -dū-) *n.* **1.** channel, pipe, or tube used to convey liquids. **2.** tube or similar structure that serves as a protective passage for electrical wires or cables. [Old French *conduit* thing that

at; āpe; cär; end; mē; it; īce; hot; ōld; fôrk; wood; fōōl; oil; out; up; ūse; turn; sing; thin; this; zh in treasure; ə in ago, taken, pencil, lemon, circus.

209

conducts, escort, from Medieval Latin *conductus* escort, canal, from Latin *condūcere* to lead to.]

cone (kōn) *n.* **1.** *Geometry.* **a.** solid whose base is a circle, whose vertex is a point in another plane, and whose surface consists of all the straight lines between the vertex and the circumference of the base. **b.** surface generated by a straight line passing through the vertex and traced along any simple closed curve in another plane. **c.** any solid with such a surface and a base formed by the intersection of the surface and a plane. **2.** object or mass shaped like a cone: *an ice-cream cone.* **3.** fruit of an evergreen tree consisting of a mass of symmetrically arranged scales bearing seeds. **4.** cell in the retina of the eye that is sensitive to color and bright light. [French *cône,* from Latin *cōnus,* from Greek *kōnos.*]

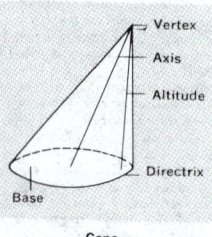

Vertex
Axis
Altitude
Directrix
Base

Cone

Con·el·rad (kŏn′əl rad′) *n.* system of radio broadcasting established for use in the United States in the event of enemy air attack or threat of attack and intended to maintain communication with the public in such a way that the enemy could not use the air waves for navigation. [Short for *con(trol of) el(ectromagnetic) rad(iation).*]

Con·es·to·ga wagon (kŏn′is-tō′gə) covered wagon with arched canvas top and broad wheels, formerly used for transportation across the prairies. [From *Conestoga,* Pennsylvania, where it was first made.]

Conestoga wagon

co·ney (kō′nē) *pl.,* **co·neys.** *n.* cony.

con·fab (kŏn′făb′) *Informal.* *n.* chat. —*v.i.,* **-fabbed, -fab·bing.** to chat; confabulate.

con·fab·u·late (kən fab′yə lāt′) **-lat·ed, -lat·ing.** *v.i.* to talk together casually and familiarly; chat. [Latin *confābulātus,* past participle of *confābulārī,* from *con-* together + *fābula* story.] —**con·fab′u·la′tion, con·fab′u·la′tor,** *n.* —**con·fab·u·la·to·ry** (kən fab′yə lə tôr′ē), *adj.*

con·fec·tion (kən fek′shən) *n.* **1.** any sweet mixture or delicacy, as a pastry or preserve. **2.** sweetened drug or medicine. **3.** frilly or stylish article of women's clothing. [Latin *confectiō* preparation.]

con·fec·tion·er (kən fek′shə nər) *n.* one who makes or sells confections, as candy or sweet pastry.

con·fec·tion·er·y (kən fek′shə ner′ē) *pl.,* **-er·ies.** *n.* **1.** place where confections are made or sold, esp. an ice-cream or candy shop. **2.** candies or sweets; confections collectively. **3.** work of a confectioner.

con·fed·er·a·cy (kən fed′ər ə sē) *pl.,* **-cies.** *n.* **1.** union of countries, states, or persons joined to further a mutual aim; league; alliance. **2. the Confederacy,** the Confederate States of America. **3.** group joined together for evil or unlawful purpose; conspiracy.

con·fed·er·ate (*n., adj.* kən fed′ər it; *v.,* kən fed′ə rāt′) *n.* **1.** individual or group associated with another for a mutual purpose; ally. **2. Confederate.** citizen or supporter of the Confederate States of America. **3.** one in league with another in a plot; accomplice. —*v.t., v.i.,* **-at·ed, -at·ing.** to unite in a confederacy. —*adj.* **1.** united in a league or alliance. **2. Confederate.** having to do with the Confederate States of America. [Latin *confoederātus,* past participle of *confoederāre* to unite in a league.]

Syn. *n.* **3. Confederate, accomplice** denote a person who participates in committing an unlawful act. **Confederate** is used of one who is an intentional colleague in a criminal or civil wrong: *He and three confederates were brought to trial for the robbery.* **Accomplice** is used of anyone who aids in the commission of a crime at any time or in any way: *Her silence clearly made her an accomplice in the plot.*

Confederate States of America, political union formed by the eleven Southern states that seceded from the United States in 1860–1861.

con·fed·er·a·tion (kən fed′ə rā′shən) *n.* **1.** act of confederating; being confederated. **2.** association for a mutual purpose, esp. a group of states joined in a relatively permanent alliance. **3. the Confederation.** union of the thirteen American states from 1781 to 1789, under the Articles of Confederation.

con·fer (kən fûr′) **-ferred, -fer·ring.** *v.i.* to consult together; deliberate: *The committee conferred for three hours before taking a vote.* —*v.t.* to grant; bestow (with *on* or *upon*): *The university conferred its highest degree upon the statesman.* [Latin *conferre.*] —**con·fer′ment, con·fer′ral,** *n.* —**Syn.** *v.i.* see **consult.** *v.t.* see **give.**

con·fer·ee (kŏn′fə rē′) *n.* **1.** one who takes part in a conference. **2.** one on whom something is conferred.

con·fer·ence (*defs. 1–3* kŏn′fər əns, -frəns; *def. 4* kən fûr′əns) *n.* **1.** meeting of persons for the purpose of deliberating or discussing something: *The conference on international economic problems met in Geneva.* **2.** meeting of members from the two houses of a legislature to resolve differences, as between similar bills from each house. **3.** association of organized groups, as of schools, churches, or athletic teams. **4.** act of conferring; bestowal.

con·fess (kən fes′) *v.t.* **1.** to disclose, esp. something personal that has been kept unknown. **2.** to concede; admit: *I must confess my error.* **3.** to declare (one's faith or belief). **4.a.** to disclose (one's sins) to a priest so as to be absolved. **b.** (of a priest) to hear the confession of (someone wishing to be absolved of his sins); act as a confessor to. —*v.i.* **1.** to admit or disclose one's guilt. **2.** to disclose one's sins to a priest. [Old French *confesser* to acknowledge, confess sins, from Late Latin *confessāre,* from Latin *confitērī.*] —**Syn.** *v.t.* **2.** see **admit.**

con·fess·ed·ly (kən fes′id lē) *adv.* admittedly; avowedly.

con·fes·sion (kən fesh′ən) *n.* **1.** act of confessing; acknowledgment, esp. of guilt. **2.** that which is confessed, esp. a written statement of what is confessed. **3.** act of telling one's sins to a priest so as to be absolved of them. **4.a.** confession of faith. **b.** religious group adhering to a common confession of faith; denomination.

con·fes·sion·al (kən fesh′ən əl) *n.* small compartment in a church where a priest hears confessions. —*adj.* of or relating to confession.

confession of faith **1.** affirmation of religious belief, esp. as accompanying or preceding a sacrament. **2.** declaration of the beliefs of a church; creed.

con·fes·sor (kən fes′ər) *n.* **1.** priest who hears confessions and grants absolution. **2.** one who confesses. **3.** one persecuted but not martyred for professing adherence to Christianity.

con·fet·ti (kən fet′ē) *n.* small bits or strips of paper that may be thrown about as a sign of celebration. [Italian *confetti,* plural of *confetto* confection, candy, from Medieval Latin *confectum,* going back to Latin *conficere* to prepare. Originally at carnival time in Italy confections, or small candies, were tossed about; later applied to bits of colored paper.]

con·fi·dant (kŏn′fə dant′, -dänt′, kŏn′fə dant′, -dänt′) *n.* someone to whom one's most private affairs or secrets are disclosed and entrusted.

con·fi·dante (kŏn′fə dant′, -dänt′, kŏn′fə dant′, -dänt′) *n.* woman confidant.

con·fide (kən fīd′) **-fid·ed, -fid·ing.** *v.t.* **1.** to disclose with the expectation of secrecy: *She confided her fears to her friend.* **2.** to entrust or give (something to someone) so that it will be kept safe. —*v.i.* **1.** to disclose private affairs or secrets (with *in*): *to confide in a friend.* **2.** to put trust or have faith (with *in*): *They confide in your good judgment.* [Latin *confīdere* to trust in, rely on.] —**con·fid′er,** *n.*

con·fi·dence (kŏn′fə dəns) *n.* **1.** firm trust or reliance. **2.** feeling of certainty; assurance. **3.** faith in one's own competence; self-assurance. **4.** excessive self-assurance; boldness. **5.** something disclosed in trust; secret. **6. in confidence.** privately and with reliance on another's good faith in keeping one's secrets. [Latin *confīdentia* firm trust in something.]

Syn. **1.** see **trust.** **3. Confidence, assurance** indicate certainty about one's own abilities. **Confidence** implies strong belief that one can cope with things: *His eagerness to experiment was an indication of his confidence in himself.* **Assurance** suggests no doubt at all about one's ability: *The potter handled the clay and wheel with assurance.*

confidence game, swindle brought about by gaining the confidence of the victim.

confidence man, one who swindles by means of a confidence game.

con·fi·dent (kŏn′fə dənt) *adj.* **1.** firmly assured; certain; sure. **2.** having faith in one's own competence; self-assured. **3.** excessively self-assured; bold. —*n.* confidant. —**con′fi·dent·ly,** *adv.*

con·fi·den·tial (kŏn′fə den′shəl) *adj.* **1.** originated or maintained in strict secrecy or privacy: *confidential files.* **2.** indicating intimacy or readiness to disclose matters of a secret nature: *a confidential tone.* **3.** entrusted with secret or private matters: *a confidential secretary.* —**con′fi·den′tial·ly,** *adv.*

con·fid·ing (kən fī′ding) *adj.* tending to confide; trusting. —**con·fid′ing·ly,** *adv.*

con·fig·u·ra·tion (kən fig′yə rā′shən) *n.* **1.** relative arrangement of parts. **2.** form or shape resulting from such an arrangement: *They were interested in the configuration of the southern plateau.* [Late Latin *configūrātiō* conformation, from Latin *configūrāre* to fashion after something.]

con·fine (*v.,* kən fīn′; *n.,* kŏn′fīn) **-fined, -fin·ing.** *v.t.* **1.** to keep within limits; restrict: *Please confine your discussion to the subject of the book.* **2.** to restrict to a particular place; keep or shut in: *Her illness confined her to bed. He was confined to prison for six years.* —*n. usually,* **confines.** limit; boundary; border: *The dog was not permitted within the*

at; āpe; cär; end; mē; it; īce; hot; ōld; fôrk; wood; fōōl; oil; out; up; ūse; turn; sing; thin; this; zh in treasure; ə in ago, taken, pencil, lemon, circus.

confines of the house. [French *confiner* to border on, imprison, from *confin* border, going back to Latin *confíne.*] —**con·fin′er,** *n.*

con·fine·ment (kən fīn′mənt) *n.* **1.** act of confining; being confined. **2.** imprisonment. **3.** childbirth.

con·firm (kən furm′) *v.t.* **1.** to affirm the validity of; verify: *to confirm a statement to the press.* **2.** to make binding by formal or authoritative approval; ratify: *The agency confirmed the contract.* **3.** to make firm or firmer; strengthen, as a belief, resolution, or desire: *The experiment confirmed his theory.* **4.** to admit to full membership in a church by administering the ceremony of confirmation to. [Old French *confermer* to make firm, from Latin *confirmāre.*] —**con·firm′a·ble,** *adj.*
Syn. 1. Confirm, corroborate, substantiate, authenticate mean to establish the truth of something. **Confirm** suggests removal of all doubts by some conclusive evidence or statement: *Their marriage license confirmed that they had been married earlier that month.* **Corroborate** suggests a strengthening of evidence by some new evidence or statement: *The new find corroborates the theory that a settlement existed here a thousand years ago.* **Substantiate** suggests evidence strongly supporting a theory, belief, or statement: *They substantiated their claim by producing dated receipts.* **Authenticate** suggests establishing that something dubious is true or genuine by bringing an expert's evidence to bear: *The curator of the silver collection authenticated the piece as being one of Revere's.*

con·fir·ma·tion (kon′fər mā′shən) *n.* **1.** act of confirming. **2.** that which confirms; proof. **3.a.** Christian rite whereby a baptized person, usually at a specified age, is admitted to full membership in a church. **b.** ceremony formally admitting a person to membership in the Jewish community, performed esp. among Reform Jews.

con·fir·ma·to·ry (kən fur′mə tôr′ē) *adj.* serving to confirm; confirming. Also, **con·firm′a·tive.**

con·firmed (kən furmd′) *adj.* **1.** firmly established; verified; proved: *a confirmed reservation on an airplane.* **2.** habitual; steadfast: *a confirmed bachelor.* **3.** having undergone the religious rite of confirmation. —**con·firm′ed·ly,** *adv.*

con·fis·cate (kon′fis kāt′) **-cat·ed, -cat·ing.** *v. t.* **1.** to seize for the public use or treasury, esp. as a penalty: *The authorities confiscated the smuggled perfumes and later sold them at auction.* **2.** to seize by or as by authority; appropriate: *The teacher confiscated the comic books.* —*adj.* **1.** seized by or as by authority; appropriated. **2.** deprived of property by confiscation. [Latin *confiscātus,* past participle of *confiscāre* to put in a chest, place in the treasury, appropriate, from *con-* together + *fiscus* chest, treasury.] —**con′fis·ca′tion, con′fis·ca′tor,** *n.*

con·fis·ca·to·ry (kən fis′kə tôr′ē) *adj.* having to do with or characterized by confiscation: *a confiscatory tax.*

con·fla·gra·tion (kon′flə grā′shən) *n.* very large and destructive fire. [Latin *conflagrātiō.*]

con·flict (*n.,* kon′flikt; *v.,* kən flikt′) *n.* **1.** struggle between two forces; battle; war. **2.** clash; opposition; disagreement: *a conflict between two accounts of a car accident.* **3.** emotional struggle of opposing impulses or desires within an individual: *She suffered from a conflict of feelings about her career.* —*v.i.* **1.** to be directly opposed or incompatible; clash. **2.** *Archaic.* to struggle; battle; contend. [Latin *conflíctus* a striking together, fight.]
Syn. *v.i.* **1. Conflict, clash** indicate opposition. **Conflict** suggests active disagreement that must be settled if matters are to proceed: *The hours of those two exams conflict.* **Clash** implies discord and lack of harmony that may lead to dissension and conflict unless modification takes place: *The two countries' interests clashed in the Middle East.* —*n.* **2.** see **fight.**

con·flu·ence (kon′floō əns) *n.* **1.a.** the flowing together of two or more bodies of water: *confluence of streams.* **b.** point at which this occurs. **c.** body of water resulting from this flowing together. **2.** a thronging of people or things; crowd.

Confluence at Pittsburgh, Pa.

con·flu·ent (kon′floō ənt) *adj.* flowing or running together; blending into one: *confluent rivers.* —*n.* confluent stream. [Latin *confluēns,* present participle of *confluere* to flow together.]

con·flux (kon′fluks′) *n.* confluence.

con·form (kən fôrm′) *v.i.* **1.** to act in accordance with an established rule or standard. **2.** to be the same or very similar. **3.** to be in accord; agree (with *to*). **4.** in English history, to comply with the principles and requirements of the Church of England. —*v.t.* **1.** to bring into agreement; make the same: *to conform a copy with the original.* [Old French *conformer* to fit with, comply with, from Latin *conformāre* to fashion, form.] —**con·form′er,** *n.*

con·form·a·ble (kən fôr′mə bəl) *adj.* **1.** corresponding; similar. **2.** in agreement; harmonious. **3.** obedient; submissive. —**con·form′-a·ble·ness,** *n.* —**con·form′a·bly,** *adv.*

con·form·ance (kən fôr′məns) *n.* conformity.

con·for·ma·tion (kon′fôr mā′shən) *n.* **1.** way in which the parts of something are arranged; shape or structure. **2.** symmetrical arrangement of the parts of something. **3.** act of conforming; being conformed.

con·form·ism (kən fôr′miz′əm) *n.* belief or practice of a conformist.

con·form·ist (kən fôr′mist) *n.* **1.** one who conforms. **2.** in English history, one who complies with the principles and requirements of the Church of England.

con·form·i·ty (kən fôr′mə tē) *pl.,* **-ties.** *n.* **1.** correspondence in form or manner; agreement. **2.** action or thought in accordance with an established standard. **3.** in English history, compliance with the usages of the Church of England.

con·found (kon found′, kon-) *v.t.* **1.** to put in a state of confusion; bewilder; disconcert: *The noise of the big city confounded him.* **2.** to fail to distinguish between; confuse. **3.** to mix so that the parts are indistinguishable. **4.** to damn. ▲ used as a mild oath. **5.** *Archaic.* to put to shame; abash. **6.** *Archaic.* to defeat or overthrow; destroy. [Old French *confondre* to overturn, destroy, from Latin *confundere* to pour together, mix, overwhelm.]

con·found·ed (kon foun′did, kon-) *adj.* **1.** confused; bewildered. **2.** damned. ▲ used as a mild oath. —**con·found′ed·ly,** *adv.*

con·fra·ter·ni·ty (kon′frə tur′nə tē) *pl.,* **-ties.** *n.* **1.** group of men united for a common purpose or in a common profession. **2.** lay brotherhood united for some religious or charitable purpose. [Medieval Latin *confraternitas* brotherhood, going back to Latin *con-* together + *frāter* brother.]

con·frere (kon′frār) *n.* fellow member; colleague. [Old French *frere* member of the same society or association, from Medieval Latin *confrater,* from Latin *con-* together + *frāter* brother.]

con·front (kən frunt′) *v.t.* **1.** to come face to face with; stand facing: *He confronted his accuser in court.* **2.** to face boldly or with defiance: *Escape being impossible, the stag turned to confront the hunters.* **3.** to bring face to face with; put before: *The policeman confronted the driver with a summons.* **4.** to place together for comparison. [French *confronter,* going back to Latin *con-* together + *frōns* forehead.] —**Syn. 1.** see **meet¹.**

Con·fu·cian (kən fū′shən) *adj.* of or having to do with Confucius, his teachings, or his followers. —*n.* adherent of Confucianism.

Con·fu·cian·ism (kən fū′shə niz′əm) *n.* ethical system based on the teachings of Confucius and his followers, emphasizing maintenance of peace, harmony, and justice through an elaborate social etiquette and duties to the ruler, ancestors, family, and friends. —**Con·fu′cian·ist,** *n., adj.*

Con·fu·cius (kən fū′shəs) *n.* c.551–c.479 B.C., Chinese philosopher and founder of Confucianism.

con·fuse (kən fūz′) **-fused, -fus·ing.** *v.t.* **1.** to bewilder; perplex: *The maze of highways confused him and he took the wrong road.* **2.** to throw into disorder; mix; jumble: *to confuse the issues of an argument.* **3.** to mistake one thing or person for another: *Even the family confused the twins.* **4.** to disconcert; embarrass: *The policeman so confused her that she couldn't find her license.* [Middle English *confusen* to perplex, from *confus* perplexed, from Latin *confūsus,* past participle of *confundere* to pour together, mix, overwhelm.] —**con·fus·ed·ly** (kən fū′zid lē), **con·fus′ing·ly,** *adv.*

con·fu·sion (kən fū′zhən) *n.* **1.** state of being confused; disorder; disarray. **2.** act of confusing. **3.** bewilderment. **4.** embarrassment.
Syn. n. 1. Confusion, disorder, disarray mean lack of order in arrangement. **Confusion** suggests such mixing of things that the parts cannot be clearly distinguished: *The discotheque was a confusion of loud noises.* **Disorder** implies a disturbing of something in proper order: *Lack of traffic signs caused disorder in the flow of traffic in the construction area.* **Disarray** suggests a breaking up and a mixing up of something well-arranged: *Obviously someone has been there, for the drawer was open and the papers were in disarray.*

con·fu·ta·tion (kon′fyoo tā′shən) *n.* **1.** act of confuting. **2.** that which confutes. —**con·fu·ta·tive** (kən fū′tə tiv), *adj.*

con·fute (kən fūt′) **-fut·ed, -fut·ing.** *v.t.* **1.** to prove to be incorrect; refute; disprove: *The doctors soundly confuted the diagnosis on the basis of the x-rays.* [Latin *confūtāre* to check, refute.] —**con·fut′a·ble,** *adj.* —**con·fut′er,** *n.*

Cong. 1. Congress; Congressional. **2.** Congregational; Congregationalist.

con·ga (kong′gə) *n.* **1.** dance of Cuban origin in which dancers form a single line, characterized by an exaggerated kick. **2.** the fast music for this dance, played in ⁴/₄ time, with the last beat strongly syncopated. —*v.i.,* **-gaed, -ga·ing.** to dance the conga. [Spanish *conga* this dance, from *congo* of the Congo.]

con game *Informal.* confidence game.

con·gé (kon′zhā, -jā; *French* kôN zhā′) *also,* **con·gee** (kon′jē). *n.* **1.** formal permission to leave. **2.** dismissal. [French *congé,* going back to Latin *commeātus* going to and fro, leave of absence.]

con·geal (kən jēl′) *v.t., v.i.* **1.** to change from a fluid to a solid state by or as by cooling or freezing. **2.** to thicken; coagulate. [Old French *congeler* to cause to freeze, from Latin *congelāre.*] —**con·geal′a·ble,** *adj.* —**con·geal′er, con·geal′ment,** *n.*

con·ge·ner (kon′jə nər) *n.* member of the same kind, class, or genus. [Latin *congener* of the same kind.] —**con·ge·ner·ic** (kon′jə ner′ik), **con·gen·er·ous** (kə jen′ər əs), *adj.*

con·gen·ial (kən jēn′yəl) *adj.* **1.** having similar tastes; compatible. **2.** agreeable; pleasant: *congenial work, a congenial host.* [CON- + GENIAL.] —**con·ge·ni·al·i·ty** (kən jē′nē al′ə tē), *n.* —**con·gen′ial·ly,** *adv.*

con·gen·i·tal (kən jen′ət əl) *adj.* existing from the time of birth; occurring before birth but not hereditary: *a congenital heart defect, a congenital birth defect.* [Latin *congenitus* born with + -AL¹.] —**con·gen′i·tal·ly,** *adv.*

con·ger (kong′gər) *n.* any of a group of saltwater eels, family Congridae, found in warm waters, esp. *Conger conger,* of European coastal waters, that is valued as food. Length: up to 6 feet. Also, **conger eel.** [Old French *congre,* from Latin *congrus, conger,* from Greek *gongros.*]

con·ge·ries (kən jēr′ēz) *n.,pl.* aggregate; heap; mass. ▲ construed as singular or plural. [Latin *congeriēs* heap.]

con·gest (kən jest′) *v.t.* **1.** to fill beyond capacity; overcrowd: *Weekends the automobiles congest all the roads near the city.* **2.** to cause an abnormal amount of blood, mucus, or other matter to collect in (an organ or part of the body). —*v.i.* to become congested. [Latin *congestus,* past participle of *congerere* to bring together.]

con·ges·tion (kən jes′chən) *n.* **1.** overcrowding: *traffic congestion.* **2.** excessive or abnormal amount of blood, mucus, or other matter in an organ or part of the body. —**con·ges·tive** (kən jes′tiv), *adj.*

con·glom·er·ate (*v.,* kən glom′ə rāt′; *adj., n.,* kən glom′ər it) -**at·ed, -at·ing.** *v.t., v.i.* **1.** to collect together into a mass or heap. —*adj.* **1.** massed together, esp. irregularly; made up of unlike parts. **2.** clustered into or

Conglomerate (def. 2)

forming a dense, irregular mass. —*n.* **1.** mass formed of diverse parts. **2.** sedimentary rock composed of rounded, worn fragments of rocks cemented together by a substance such as clay. **3.** corporation composed of many different companies. [Latin *conglomerātus,* past participle of *conglomerāre* to roll together, heap together, going back to *con-* together + *glomus* ball.]

con·glom·er·a·tion (kən glom′ə rā′shən) *n.* **1.** cohesive mass, esp. of unlike parts. **2.** act of conglomerating.

Con·go (kong′gō) *n.* **1.** long river in central Africa, flowing from the southeastern Republic of Congo into the Atlantic. **2. Democratic Republic of the.** country in central Africa, formerly the Belgian Congo. Capital, Kinshasa. Its official name is now Zaire. **3. Republic of.** country in west-central Africa. It was formerly a French territory. Capital, Brazzaville. Area, 132,000 sq. mi. Pop. (1969 est.), 880,000.

Congo Free State, see Belgian Congo.

Con·go·lese (kong′gə lēz′, -lēs′) *pl.* -**lese.** *n.* member or close descendant of the people of either of the Congo countries. —*adj.* of or relating to either of the Congo countries, their people, or culture.

Congo snake

con·go snake (kong′gō) eel-like salamander, *Amphiuma means,* common in swampy regions of the southeastern United States, having two pairs of weak, rudimentary legs. Length: to 40 inches. Also, **congo eel.**

con·grat·u·late (kən grach′ə lāt′) -**lat·ed, -lat·ing.** *v.t.* to express one's good wishes to (someone) on account of his success or good fortune. [Latin *congrātulātus,* past participle of *congrātulārī* to wish joy.] —**con·grat·u·la·to·ry** (kən grach′ə lə tôr′ē), *adj.*

Syn. Congratulate, felicitate mean to express gladness for someone else's success, joy, or the like. Congratulate implies warm, sympathetic feeling: *We all congratulated him on his narrow escape.* Felicitate suggests a more impersonal, formal message: *After the election, the winner was felicitated by his defeated opponents as well as by the members of his own party.*

con·grat·u·la·tion (kən grach′ə lā′shən) *n.* **1.** act of congratulating. **2. congratulations.** expression of good wishes for another's happiness, good fortune, or success.

con·gre·gate (*v.,* kong′grə gāt′; *adj.,* kong′grə git) *v.t., v.i.* -**gat·ed, -gat·ing.** **1.** to bring or come together in a crowd or mass: assemble. —*adj.* gathered together; assembled. [Latin *congregātus,* past participle of *congregāre* to assemble, going back to *con-* together + *grex* flock.]

con·gre·ga·tion (kong′grə gā′shən) *n.* **1.** act of assembling in a crowd or mass. **2.** gathering of people or things; assemblage. **3.a.** assembly of people for religious worship or instruction. **b.** group of people who regularly worship together. **4.** *Roman Catholic Church.* **a.** religious community under a common rule or simple vows. **b.** permanent committee of cardinals and other officials charged with administering a department of church affairs. **5.** in the Old Testament, the entire body of Hebrews.

con·gre·ga·tion·al (kong′grə gā′shən əl) *adj.* **1.** of or relating to a congregation. **2. Congregational.** of or relating to Congregationalism or Congregationalists.

Con·gre·ga·tion·al·ism (kong′grə gā′shən əl iz′əm) *n.* **1.** Protestant denomination holding that the Bible is the only authoritative guide to doctrine and worship and that each local congregation is responsible only to Christ. **2. congregationalism.** form of church government in which each local church is independent and autonomous. —**Con′gre·ga′tion·al·ist,** *n.*

con·gress (kong′gris) *n.* **1.** legislative body of any of various countries, esp. of a republic. **2. Congress. a.** federal legislature of the United States, consisting of the Senate and the House of Representatives. **b.** specific group of legislators making up Congress during one two-year term between elections to the House of Representatives. **3.** formal meeting of representatives, as of several nations or interested groups, gathered to discuss a subject of common concern. **4.** act of coming together. **5.** sexual intercourse. [Latin *congressus* meeting together, coming together.]

con·gres·sion·al (kən gresh′ən əl) *adj.* **1.** of or relating to a congress. **2. Congressional.** of or relating to Congress.

Congressional Medal of Honor, Medal of Honor.

con·gress·man (kong′gris mən) *pl.* -**men.** *also,* **Con·gress·man.** *n.* member of Congress, esp. of the House of Representatives.

Congress of Industrial Organizations, federation of labor unions organized according to industry rather than craft, formally established in 1938 as an offshoot of the American Federation of Labor. The two organizations merged in 1955 as the AFL-CIO.

con·gru·ence (kong′grōō əns) *n.* agreement; harmony. Also, **con′gru·en·cy.**

con·gru·ent (kong′grōō ənt) *adj.* **1.** agreeing; harmonious; coinciding: *His thoughts on the subject are congruent with your own.* **2.** *Geometry.* exactly alike in shape and size; coinciding exactly if placed one on the other. Symbol: ≅ **3.** (of numbers) leaving the same remainder when divided by a given quantity. [Latin *congruēns,* present participle of *congruere* to agree, correspond.] —**con′gru·ent·ly,** *adv.*

con·gru·i·ty (kong grōō′ə tē, kon-) *n., pl.* -**ties.** **1.** state of being congruous; agreement; harmony. **2.** *Geometry.* exact similarity in size and shape. **3.** point of agreement: *There is a definite congruity in the candidates' approach to the tax problem.*

con·gru·ous (kong′grōō əs) *adj.* **1.** harmonious; concordant. **2.** fitting; appropriate. **3.** congruent *(def. 2).* [French *congruus* suitable.] —**con′gru·ous·ly,** *adv.* —**con′gru·ous·ness,** *n.*

con·i·cal (kon′i kəl) *adj.* **1.** shaped like a cone. **2.** of or relating to a cone. Also, **con′ic.** —**con′i·cal·ly,** *adv.*

conic section *Geometry.* curve formed by the intersection of a plane with a right circular cone, or the plane section described by such a curve. Circles, ellipses, parabolas, and hyperbolas are conic sections.

conic sections, branch of geometry dealing with ellipses, parabolas, and hyperbolas. Also, **con′ics.**

co·ni·fer (kon′ə fər, kō′nə-) *n.* any of a large group of trees and shrubs that bear cones. Most conifers, such as the pines, spruces, and cedars, are evergreen and bear needle-shaped leaves. [Latin *cōnifer* bearing cones, from *cōnus* cone (from Greek *kōnos*), + *ferre* to bear¹.]

Circle   Ellipse   Parabola   Hyperbola
Conic sections

co·nif·er·ous (kō nif′ər əs) *adj.* **1.** bearing cones. **2.** of or relating to the conifers.

conj., 1. conjunction. **2.** conjugation.

con·jec·tur·al (kən jek′chər əl) *adj.* **1.** based on or involving conjecture. **2.** inclined to conjecture. —**con·jec′tur·al·ly,** *adv.*

con·jec·ture (kən jek′chər) *n.* **1.** act of forming an opinion not based on definite evidence or proof; guessing. **2.** opinion or conclusion so

formed. —*v.t., v.i.,* **-tured, -tur·ing.** to form an opinion not based on definite evidence or proof; guess. [Latin *conjectūra* guess, conclusion.] —**con·jec′tur·a·ble,** *adj.* —**con·jec′tur·er,** *n.* —**Syn.** *v.t.* see **guess.**

con·join (kən join′) *v.t., v.i.* to join together; unite; combine. [Old French *conjoindre,* from Latin *conjungere.*] —**con·join′er,** *n.*

con·joint (kən joint′) *adj.* **1.** joined together; united; combined. **2.** being made by, or involving, two or more in combination; joint. [French *conjoint,* past participle of *conjoindre.* See CONJOIN.] —**con·joint′ly,** *adv.*

con·ju·gal (kon′jə gəl) *adj.* having to do with marriage or marital relations. [Latin *conjugālis,* going back to *con-* together + *jugum* yoke; with reference to marriage as a yoking together as a team.] —**con′ju·gal·ly,** *adv.*

con·ju·gate (*v.,* kon′jə gāt′; *adj., n.,* kon′jə git, -gāt′) **-gat·ed, -gat·ing.** *v.t.* to give the inflections of (a verb). —*v.i.* Biology. to fuse in conjugation. —*adj.* **1.** joined together, esp. in pairs; coupled. **2.** (of words) derived from a common root. —*n.* conjugate word. [Latin *conjugātus,* past participle of *conjugāre* to join together, marry.]

con·ju·ga·tion (kon′jə gā′shən) *n.* **1.** act of conjugating; being conjugated. **2.** Grammar. **a.** inflections of a verb to indicate tense, person, number, and mood. **b.** arrangement of the inflections of a verb. **c.** group of verbs having the same inflections. **3.** Biology. temporary fusion of two similar cells with an accompanying transfer of hereditary material, occurring among some protozoans and algae. Contrasted with fission, or asexual division, it is sometimes considered a primitive sexual process.

con·junct (kən jungkt′, kon-) *adj.* joined together; associated; combined. [Latin *conjūnctus,* past participle of *conjungere* to join together.]

con·junc·tion (kən jungk′shən) *n.* **1.** act of joining; being joined together. **2.** simultaneous occurrence; combination: *Dieting in conjunction with exercise is a good way to lose weight.* **3.** word used to connect words, phrases, clauses, or sentences. **4.** Astronomy. **a.** apparent meeting of two or more planets or other heavenly bodies at the same celestial longitude. **b.** position or condition of such bodies.

con·junc·ti·va (kon′jungk tī′və) *pl.,* **-vas** or **-vae** (-vē). *n.* mucous membrane that covers the front of the eyeball and lines the inner surface of the eyelids. [Modern Latin *(membrana) conjunctiva* connective (membrane), feminine of Late Latin *conjūnctīvus.* See CONJUNCTIVE.]

con·junc·tive (kən jungk′tiv) *adj.* **1.** joining together; connecting; uniting: *conjunctive tissue.* **2.** joint; united: *conjunctive effort.* **3.** like or functioning like a conjunction: *a conjunctive pronoun.* **4.** uniting parts of a sentence in both meaning and construction. —*n.* conjunctive word; conjunction. [Late Latin *conjūnctīvus* connective, from Latin *conjūnctus.* See CONJUNCT.] —**con·junc′tive·ly,** *adv.*

con·junc·ti·vi·tis (kən jungk′tə vī′tis) *n.* inflammation of the conjunctiva. [CONJUNCTIVA + -ITIS.]

con·junc·ture (kən jungk′chər) *n.* combination of events or circumstances, esp. as related to a critical situation.

con·ju·ra·tion (kon′jə rā′shən, kun′-) *n.* **1.** magical form of words used in conjuring; spell; incantation. **2.** practice or performance of magic. **3.** invocation using a sacred or demonic name. **4.** Archaic. solemn appeal or entreaty, esp. to a deity.

con·jure (kon′jər, kun′-; *v.t. def. 4,* kən joor′) **-jured, -jur·ing.** *v.t.* **1.** to summon or cause to appear by magic words, as a devil or spirit. **2.** to bring about by or as by magic. **3.** to cause to appear or bring into existence in or as in a supernatural way (with *up*): *to conjure up a delicious sauce.* **4.** Archaic. to make a solemn appeal to. —*v.i.* **1.** to summon demons or spirits by means of spells; practice sorcery. **2.** to perform tricks by illusion or sleight of hand. [Old French *conjurer* to adjure, exorcise, from Latin *conjūrāre* to swear together.]

con·jur·er (kon′jər ər, kun′-) *also,* **con·ju·ror** (-) *n.* **1.** wizard; sorcerer. **2.** one who practices tricks involving sleight of hand; magician.

conn (kon) *n.*

Conn., Connecticut.

con·nate (kon′āt) *adj.* **1.** existing from birth; congenital; inborn. **2.** allied in origin or nature; cognate. **3.** Biology. congenitally or firmly united. [Late Latin *connātus,* past participle of *connāsci* to be born with, from Latin *con-* with + *nāscī* to be born.]

con·nect (kə nekt′) *v.t.* **1.** to join or fasten together; unite; link: *They connected the boxcar to the freight train.* **2.** to think of as having a close relationship; associate mentally: *The color black is often connected with death.* **3.** to put on the same telephone line (with *with*): *The operator will connect you with our sales department.* **4.** to link in an electric circuit: *Would you connect the iron?* —*v.i.* **1.** to be or become joined; meet: *This wire connects with that one.* **2.** to be scheduled so that passengers can transfer from one route to another, as on trains, buses, or airplanes. **3.** to hit or meet what is aimed at with success: *to connect for a home run, to connect with the opponent's jaw.* [Latin *connectere* to tie together.] —**con·nect′er,** *also,* **con·nec′tor,** *n.* —**con·nect′i·ble,** *also,* **con·nect′a·ble,** *adj.* —**Syn.** *v.t.* **1.** see **join.**

con·nect·ed (kə nek′tid) *adj.* **1.** joined or fastened together; linked:

connected by a tow rope. **2.** joined or linked in sequence: *connected thoughts.* **3.** related by ancestry or interests: *That man is connected with the governor's family.* —**con·nect′ed·ly,** *adv.* —**con·nect′ed·ness,** *n.*

Con·nect·i·cut (kə net′i kit) *n.* **1.** state in the northeastern United States, the southernmost of the New England states. Capital, Hartford. Area, 5009 sq. mi. Pop. (1970), 3,032,217. Abbreviation, **Conn. 2.** longest river in New England, flowing from northern New Hampshire into the Long Island Sound.

connecting rod, rod that connects two or more rotating parts of a machine in reciprocating motion, esp. one that connects a piston to the crankshaft in an automobile.

con·nec·tion (kə nek′shən) *also, British,* **con·nex·ion.** *n.* **1.** act of connecting; linking up. **2.** state or condition of being joined or linked: *the connection of church with state.* **3.** something that unites, relates, or joins; connecting part; link: *a pipe connection.* **4.a.** logical relationship between words or ideas; coherence: *the connection between cause and effect.* **b.** relation or association of a word or idea with the surrounding text: *It is interesting to note the connection in which this word is used.* **c.** relation with something else due to or based on sequence, cause, or involvement: *What is his connection with the case?* **5.** person with whom one has a useful association, esp. in business or politics: *The senator has many important connections.* **6.a.** family relationship, esp. by marriage or distant kinship. **b.** distant relative. **7.** scheduling of public transportation, as of trains, buses, or airplanes, that permits the passenger to transfer from one route to another without undue delay. **8.** religious denomination or sect. **9.** electrical circuit. **10.** line of communication between two points: *a bad telephone connection.* **11. in connection with. a.** together with. **b.** with reference or regard to.

con·nec·tive (kə nek′tiv) *adj.* tending or serving to connect. —*n.* **1.** that which connects. **2.** word used to connect words, phrases, and clauses. Conjunctions and relative pronouns are connectives.

connective tissue, any of several kinds of fibrous tissue found throughout the body that serves to unite and support other tissues and organs.

Conning tower

conn·ing tower (kon′-ing) **1.** armored pilot-house on the deck of a battleship. **2.** structure on the deck of a submarine in which the housing for the periscope and other equipment is located and which serves as a bridge and as an entrance when the submarine is surfaced. [*Conning,* present participle of CON.]

con·nip·tion (kə nip′shən) *n. Informal.* fit of rage or hysteria. [Of uncertain origin.]

con·niv·ance (kə nī′vəns) *n.* act or instance of conniving. —**Syn.** see **conspiracy.**

con·nive (kə nīv′) **-nived, -niv·ing.** *v.i.* **1.** to give tacit consent or assent to wrongdoing by overlooking or pretending ignorance (with *at*): *Some government officials connive at graft.* **2.** to cooperate secretly; conspire (with *with*). —*v.t. Informal.* to plan (something) in a sneaky manner: *They connived a plot to unseat the chairman.* [Latin *connīvēre* to shut the eyes, wink at.] —**con·niv′er,** *n.*

con·nois·seur (kon′ə sur′) *n.* one who is qualified because of his expert knowledge and discriminating taste to pass critical judgment on something, esp. the fine arts, wine, or food. [Obsolete French *connoisseur* literally, one who knows, from Old French *connoistre* to know, from Latin *cognōscere* to know, understand.]

con·no·ta·tion (kon′ə tā′shən) *n.* implied meaning or association of a word or expression in addition to the literal meaning. Distinguished from **denotation.** —**con·no·ta′tive,** *adj.*

con·note (kə nōt′) **-not·ed, -not·ing.** *v.t.* **1.** to imply or suggest a meaning in addition to the literal meaning: *"White" denotes a color, but it connotes purity.* **2.** to involve in direct association: *Smoke connotes fire.* [Medieval Latin *connotare* to mark in addition, from Latin *con-* together + *notāre* to mark.]

con·nu·bi·al (kə nōō′bē əl, -nū′-) *adj.* relating to or characteristic of marriage; matrimonial. [Latin *connūbiālis,* from *connūbium* marriage.]

co·noid (kō′noid) *adj.* resembling a cone in shape. Also, **co·noi·dal** (kō noid′əl). —*n.* **1.** something cone-shaped. **2.** Geometry. surface or solid formed by a conic section revolving about its axis. [Greek *kōnoeidēs* cone-shaped, from *kōnos* cone + *eidos* form.]

con·quer (kong′kər) *v.t.* **1.** to acquire or secure by force, as in a war: *to conquer a country.* **2.** to overcome by force; vanquish: *to conquer an enemy.* **3.** to overcome a mental, emotional, or moral obstacle by or as by inner effort: *to conquer a habit, to conquer shyness.* —*v.i.* to be

victorious. [Old French *conquerre* to win, achieve, going back to Latin *conquīrere* to seek together, win.] —**con'quer·a·ble,** *adj.* —**Syn.** *v.t.* **2.** see **defeat.**

con·quer·or (kong'kər ər) *n.* **1.** one who conquers. **2.** the Conqueror. William I of England.

con·quest (kon'kwest, kong'-) *n.* **1.** act of conquering. **2.** that which is conquered, esp. something acquired or subdued by force. **3.a.** person whose love or favor has been won. **b.** the winning of that person's love or favor. **4. the Conquest.** Norman Conquest. [Old French *conqueste* acquisition, from *conquerre*. See CONQUER.]

con·quis·ta·dor (kon kēs'tə dôr', -kwis'-) *pl.,* **-dors** or **-do·res** (-dôr'ās, -ēz). *n.* any of the Spanish conquerors in the Americas, esp. in Mexico and Peru during the sixteenth century. [Spanish *conquistador* conqueror, from *conquistar* to conquer, going back to Latin *conquīrere* to seek together, win.]

Con·rad, Joseph (kon'rad) 1857–1924, English novelist; born in Poland.

con·san·guin·e·ous (kon'sang gwin'ē əs) *adj.* of the same ancestor; akin. Also, **con·san'guine.** [Latin *consanguineus,* going back to *con-* together + *sanguis* blood.] —**con'san·guin'e·ous·ly,** *adv.*

con·san·guin·i·ty (kon'sang gwin'ə tē) *n.* kinship by descent from the same ancestor; relationship by blood.

con·science (kon'shəns) *n.* **1.** mental or emotional faculty that prompts one to do right and by which right and wrong are distinguished, esp. with regard to one's own behavior or motives. **2.** conformity to one's own moral principles; conscientiousness. **3. in all conscience, a.** in all reason or honesty; in truth. **b.** surely; certainly. [Old French *conscience* consciousness of good and evil, from Latin *conscientia* consciousness, knowledge.] —**con'science·less,** *adj.*

conscience money, money paid to relieve one's conscience for some wrongdoing.

con·science-strick·en (kon'shəns strik'ən) *adj.* remorseful for real or imaginary wrongdoing.

con·sci·en·tious (kon'shē en'shəs) *adj.* **1.** guided by one's conscience; scrupulous. **2.** done with much thought and care: *a conscientious effort.* —**con'sci·en'tious·ly,** *adv.* —**con'sci·en'tious·ness,** *n.*

conscientious objector, one whose religious or moral convictions will not allow him to participate in warfare.

con·scious (kon'shəs) *adj.* **1.** perceiving or knowing; aware (with *of* or *that*): *He was conscious of the man staring at him.* **2.** aware of the external world; physically and mentally awake: *Despite the blow on the head, he remained conscious.* **3.** felt by or known to oneself: *conscious anger.* **4.** deliberate; intentional: *a conscious insult.* **5.** self-conscious. [Latin *conscius* aware.] —**con'scious·ly,** *adv.* —**Syn. 1.** see **aware.**

con·scious·ness (kon'shəs nis) *n.* **1.** state of being conscious; awareness. **2.** totality of thoughts and feelings of a person or group.

con·script (*v.,* kən skript'; *adj., n.,* kon'skript) *v.t.* to compel (someone) to serve in the armed forces. —*adj.* conscripted; drafted. —*n.* one compelled to serve in the armed forces; draftee. [Latin *conscrīptus* enrolled, chosen, past participle of *conscrībere* to enroll, write together.]

conscript fathers (kon'skript) **1.** senators of ancient Rome. **2.** any legislators.

con·scrip·tion (kən skrip'shən) *n.* **1.** compulsory enrollment of men in a nation's armed services by an act of law; draft. **2.** forced enrollment in any organization or group under government control: *conscription for labor battalions.*

con·se·crate (kon'sə krāt') **-crat·ed, -crat·ing.** *v.t.* **1.** to set apart as sacred; make or declare holy: *They consecrated the shrine.* **2.** to dedicate or devote, as to a particular purpose: *She consecrated her life to the dance.* **3.** to elevate and hallow in a sacred or exalted office, esp. to crown a king or ordain a bishop. **4.** to impart the sacramental quality to the elements of the Eucharist. —*adj. Archaic.* consecrated. [Latin *consecrātus,* past participle of *consecrāre* to dedicate, make sacred.] —**con·se·cra'tion,** *n.* —**con'se·cra'tor,** *n.*

con·sec·u·tive (kən sek'yə tiv) *adj.* **1.** following one after another in an uninterrupted sequence; successive: *1, 2, 3, and 4, are consecutive numbers.* **2.** following in a logical order: *He appeared to be incapable of telling a consecutive story.* [French *consécutif,* going back to Latin *consequī* to follow.] —**con·sec'u·tive·ly,** *adv.* —**con·sec'u·tive·ness,** *n.* —**Syn. 2.** see **successive.**

con·sen·sus (kən sen'səs) *n.* **1.** general agreement. **2.** collective opinion. [Latin *consensus,* from *consentīre.* See CONSENT.]

con·sent (kən sent') *v.i.* **1.** to agree as to a proposal; approve or permit (often with *to*): *The man consented to the operation.* —*n.* **1.** agreement, as to a proposal; acquiescence; permission: *The delegation had to obtain the committee's consent.* **2.** agreement in opinion or sentiment: *consent of the governed.* [Old French *consentir* to agree, approve, from Latin *consentīre* to agree, from *con-* together + *sentīre* to feel.]

Syn. *v.i.* **Consent, accede, assent, acquiesce** mean to reach an agreement. **Consent** suggests agreement by a person having the authority to

make a final decision: *He would do nothing, he said, unless his father consented.* **Accede** suggests a giving in: *They acceded to the request of the other side for a delay in the trial.* **Assent** suggests agreeing without hesitation: *Although they assented to the first two amendments to the bill, they balked when it came to the next.* **Acquiesce** suggests agreement that is not quite wholehearted and in which there may be unexpressed reservations: *She acquiesced to their vacationing in the mountains.*

con·se·quence (kon'sə kwens', -kwəns) *n.* **1.** that which results from an earlier action or condition; effect. **2.a.** importance; significance: *a subject of no consequence.* **b.** social distinction, as in rank or position: *He comes from a family of great consequence.* **4.** logical conclusion arrived at through the process of reasoning. **5. in consequence.** as a result; therefore. **6. in consequence of.** as a result of; because of. —**Syn. 1.** see **effect.**

con·se·quent (kon'sə kwent', -kwənt) *adj.* **1.** following as a result or effect: *The experiment and consequent explosion wrecked the laboratory.* **2.** following as a logical conclusion: *The consequent answer must definitely be negative.* **3.** characterized by logic. [Latin *consequēns,* present participle of *consequī* to follow.]

con·se·quen·tial (kon'sə kwen'shəl) *adj.* **1.** following as an effect or conclusion; resultant. **2.** of consequence; important. **3.** self-important. —**con'se·quen'tial·ly,** *adv.* —**con'se·quen'tial·ness,** *n.*

con·se·quent·ly (kon'sə kwent'lē, -kwənt-) *adv.* as a result; therefore.

con·ser·va·tion (kon'sər vā'shən) *n.* **1.** act of preserving or protecting, as from loss, harm, or waste. **2.** public protection and care of natural resources such as forests, rivers, and wildlife.

con·ser·va·tion·ist (kon'sər vā'shə nist) *n.* one who advocates and works toward the conservation of natural resources.

conservation of energy, law of physics stating that energy can neither be created nor destroyed, but can only be changed from one form to another.

conservation of mass and energy, law of physics stating that the total amount of mass and energy in a closed system remains constant, although mass may be converted into energy and energy converted into mass within the system.

con·ser·va·tism (kən sur'və tiz'əm) *n.* **1.a.** disposition to have things continue as they are; opposition to change. **b.** principles and practices of people or groups opposing change. **2.** *also,* **Conservatism.** political philosophy based on tradition and supporting existing social, political, and economic institutions, opposing change except when absolutely necessary and favoring gradual change in such cases rather then a radical break with older practices.

con·ser·va·tive (kən sur'və tiv) *adj.* **1.** disposed to have things continue as they are; opposing change. **2.** *also,* **Conservative.** of or relating to a person or party adhering to the principles of conservatism. **3.** cautious; moderate: *a conservative estimate.* **4.** avoiding novelties and fads; traditional: *conservative taste.* **5. Conservative.** of, relating to, or designating the branch of Judaism that adheres to ancient Hebrew law as expressed in the Torah but also permits modification of tradition in the light of modern history. —*n.* **1.** conservative person. **2.a.** one who adheres to principles of conservatism. **b. Conservative.** member of a conservative political party, esp. the Conservative Party in Great Britain. **3.** a preservative. —**con·serv'a·tive·ly,** *adv.* —**con·serv'a·tive·ness,** *n.*

Conservative Party 1. one of the two major political parties in Great Britain. Traditionally it is opposed to radical change in existing social, political, and economic institutions. **2.** any of several similar political parties in other countries.

con·ser·va·toire (kən sur'və twär') *n.* conservatory (def. 1).

con·ser·va·tor (kən sur'və vā'tər, kən sur'və-) *n.* protector; guardian.

con·serv·a·to·ry (kən sur'və tôr'ē) *pl.,* **-ries.** *n.* **1.** school for instruction in music or the fine arts. **2.** small greenhouse or glass-enclosed room for growing and displaying plants. [Medieval Latin *conservatorium* place for preserving, from Latin *conservāre* to save, protect.]

con·serve (*v.,* kən surv'; *n.,* kon'surv', kən surv') **-served, -serv·ing.** *v.t.* **1.** to protect from loss, harm, or waste; keep safe. **2.** to preserve, as fruit, with sugar. —*n.* *also,* **conserves.** preserves, esp. a type made of two or more fruits stewed in sugar, often with raisins and nuts added. [Old French *conserver* to preserve, from Latin *conservāre* to preserve, protect.] —**Syn.** *v.t.* **1.** see **preserve.**

con·sid·er (kən sid'ər) *v.t.* **1.** to think about carefully; deliberate upon: *The company gave him three days to consider the offer.* **2.** to think to be; believe; regard: *The girls consider him very handsome.* **3.** to allow for; take into account; keep in mind: *You must consider his physical condition.* **4.** to think of; have regard for (others and their feelings): *He never considers anyone when he acts.* **5.** to think of as possible or acceptable: *Would you consider selling your car?* **6.** to examine carefully; scrutinize. —*v.i.* to think carefully; deliberate: *Take time to consider before you rush into anything.* [Old French *considerer* to observe closely, from Latin *considerāre* originally, to observe the stars, from

con- with + *sīdus* star; from the ancient astrological practice of consulting the stars when trying to make a decision.]

Syn. *v.t.* **1. Consider, contemplate, study, weigh** mean to examine something mentally, either to make a decision about it or to learn more about it. **Consider** implies bringing many ideas to bear on the problem: *He considered the new evidence in the light of what the previous witnesses had said.* **Contemplate** implies close attention to a limited subject: *Much may be learned of nature's ways by contemplating a blade of grass or a simple flower.* **Study** implies examination in detail: *He studied the action of certain industrial stocks in relation to the market as a whole.* **Weigh** implies measuring and comparing several things to reach a conclusion: *He weighed the advantages and disadvantages before deciding.*

con·sid·er·a·ble (kən sid′ər ə bəl) *adj.* **1.** worth considering; important: *He is a man of considerable stature in the community.* **2.** great in amount or extent: *He amassed a considerable fortune.* —*n. Informal.* a great deal; much. —**con·sid′er·a·bly,** *adv.*

con·sid·er·ate (kən sid′ər it) *adj.* **1.** characterized by a regard for others and their feelings. **2.** characterized by careful thought. —**con·sid′er·ate·ly,** *adv.* —**con·sid′er·ate·ness,** *n.*

con·sid·er·a·tion (kən sid′ə rā′shən) *n.* **1.** act of considering or taking into account; careful thought: *I will give consideration to your objections in making my decision.* **2.** that which is or should be taken into account; reason. **3.** opinion or thought; reflection: *After a moment's consideration he made his decision.* **4.** thoughtful or appreciative regard for others; respect: *The consideration with which he acted showed him to be a kind man.* **5.** claim to notice or regard; importance; consequence: *He was a man of some consideration in the community.* **6.** something given in payment; recompense; fee: *He refuses to do any extra work except for some consideration.* **7. in consideration of.** **a.** because of; in view of: *He received five dollars in consideration of his age.* **b.** in return for: *He received five hundred dollars in consideration of his services.* **8. under consideration.** being thought about or discussed. —**Syn.** see **respect.**

con·sid·ered (kən sid′ərd) *adj.* **1.** carefully thought out: *a considered reply.* **2.** highly regarded; respected.

con·sid·er·ing (kən sid′ər ing) *prep.* taking into account; in view of: *Considering his strength, he's very gentle.* —*adv. Informal.* keeping all things in mind: *She seems very bright, considering.*

con·sign (kən sīn′) *v.t.* **1.** to hand over; transfer: *He consigned the securities to his son.* **2.** to put into the care or charge of; entrust: *He consigned his dog to the animal shelter.* **3.** to send or deliver, esp. merchandise to be sold or disposed of: *The dealer consigned the books to his London agent.* **4.** to set apart; assign: *They consigned the funds to the anti-poverty program.* [French *consigner* to present, deliver, from Latin *consignāre* to seal, record.] —**con·sign′a·ble,** *adj.*

con·sign·ee (kon′sī nē′) *n.* one to whom merchandise is consigned.

con·sign·ment (kən sīn′mənt) *n.* **1.** act of consigning; being consigned. **2.** shipment of goods sent to a company or individual for safekeeping or sale: *a large consignment of Japanese silks.* **3. on consignment.** (of goods) sent to a retailer with the understanding that the goods will not be paid for until sold.

con·sign·or (kən sī′nər, kon′sī nôr′) *also,* **con·sign·er** (kən sī′nər). *n.* one who consigns merchandise to another.

con·sist (kən sist′) *v.i.* **1.** to be made up or composed (with *of*): *This Union consists of fifty states.* **2.** to be inherent; exist (with *in*): *Happiness consists in fulfillment.* [Latin *consistere* to stand still, exist.]

con·sist·en·cy (kən sis′tən sē) *pl.,* **-cies.** *n.* **1.** state of holding together; firmness; density; body: *That paint has a jellylike consistency.* **2.** degree of firmness or density: *Flour will give the dough a thicker consistency.* **3.** agreement between current thoughts or courses of action and ones preceding them: *There has been much consistency in his political views over the years.* **4.** agreement or conformity between things: *There is no consistency between the movie and the book.* Also, **con·sist′ence.**

con·sist·ent (kən sis′tənt) *adj.* **1.** characterized by adherence to the same thoughts or courses of action: *He remained consistent in his opposition to anything new.* **2.** in agreement or conformity; compatible: *The story is not consistent with the facts.* —**con·sist′ent·ly,** *adv.*

con·sis·to·ry (kən sis′tər ē) *pl.,* **-ries.** *n.* **1.** *Roman Catholic Church.* **a.** meeting of the College of Cardinals presided over by the pope for the transaction of church business, esp. for the naming of new cardinals. **b.** the cardinals who meet thus. **c.** place where the meeting occurs. **2.** *Church of England.* spiritual court of a diocesan bishop presided over by the chancellor. Also, **consistory court.** **3.** lowest court in various reformed churches, consisting primarily of the ministers and elders of an individual church. [Late Latin *consistōrium* place of assembly, from Latin *consistere* to stand still, exist.]

con·so·la·tion (kon sə lā′shən) *n.* **1.** act of consoling. **2.** one who or that which consoles. —**con·sol·a·to·ry** (kən sō′lə tôr′ē), *adj.*

consolation prize, award given to one who does admirably but does not win in a contest.

con·sole¹ (kən sōl′) **-soled, -sol·ing.** *v.t.* to comfort or cheer (someone) in sorrow or disappointment; solace. [French *consoler,* from Latin *consōlārī.*] —**con·sol′a·ble,** *adj.* —**con·sol′er,** *n.* —**Syn.** see **comfort.**

con·sole² (kon′sōl) *n.* **1.** cabinet of a radio, television set, or phonograph that rests on the floor. **2.** desklike case or frame of an organ, containing the keyboard, stops, and pedals. **3.** control panel for an electronic or mechanical device or system, as on a computer or in a television studio. **4.** ornamental bracket that supports a cornice or other structure. **5.** bracketlike leg, usually elaborately carved or decorated, used to support a table. **6.** console table. [French *console* bracket, console table, possibly blend of *consoler* to comfort and *consolider* to strengthen (from Latin *consolidāre*). See CONSOLE¹, CONSOLIDATE.]

Console² *(def. 4)*

con·sole table (kon′sōl) table supported by consoles, esp. one placed against a wall.

con·sol·i·date (kən sol′ə dāt′) **-dat·ed, -dat·ing.** *v.t.* **1.** to make united; combine: *They consolidated their earnings.* **2.** to make secure or strong: *They consolidated their gains by reinvesting in government bonds.* **3.** to make firm; solidify. **4.** *Military.* to organize and strengthen (a newly captured position) so that it can be used against the enemy. —*v.i.* to become consolidated. [Latin *consolidātus,* present participle of *consolidāre* to strengthen, make solid.]

consolidated school, school, usually rural, formed by uniting several smaller schools, attended by students from several school districts.

con·sol·i·da·tion (kən sol′ə dā′shən) *n.* **1.** act of consolidating; being consolidated. **2.** something that has been consolidated.

con·sols (kon′solz, kən solz′) *n.,pl.* government securities of Great Britain. [Short for *consol(idated annuities).*]

con·som·mé (kon′sə mā′) *n.* strong clear soup made of meat, poultry, or vegetable stock. [French *consommé,* from *consommer* to finish, from Latin *consummare;* because its making used to require a very long time.]

con·so·nance (kon′sə nəns) *n.* **1.** harmony; agreement; accordance. **2.** *Music.* simultaneous sounding of tones in harmony. Distinguished from **dissonance.** **3.** in prosody, correspondence or agreement of the final consonants but not vowels of stressed syllables, as *bill* and *wall,* and *furnished* and *varnished.* Also, **con′so·nan·cy.**

con·so·nant (kon′sə nənt) *n.* **1.** speech sound produced by the obstruction of the passage of air through the oral cavity. Distinguished from **vowel. 2.** any letter of the alphabet representing such a sound, as *f, m,* or *p.* —*adj.* **1.** in agreement; in accord. **2.** harmonious in sound. **3.** consonantal. [Latin *consonāns (littera)* this sound or letter; literally, (letter) sounding with (a vowel), from *consonāre* to sound together, harmonize; because it normally has to be *sounded with* a vowel.] —**con′so·nant·ly,** *adv.*

con·so·nan·tal (kon′sə nant′əl) *adj.* relating to or having one or more consonants.

con·sort (*n.,* kon′sort; *v.,* kən sôrt′) *n.* **1.** husband or wife; spouse. **2.** constant companion; partner. **3.** ship accompanying another. —*v.i.* **1.** to keep company; associate (with *with*): *They don't want him to consort with people like that.* **2.** to be in accord; agree (with *with*). [Latin *consort-,* stem of *consors* sharer, partner.]

con·sor·ti·um (kən sôr′shē əm) *pl.,* **-ti·a** (-shē ə). *n.* **1.** fellowship; association; partnership. **2.** international agreement or coalition of banks, businesses, or individuals to raise and invest large sums of money for a specific purpose: *The consortium was formed to develop African oil fields.* [Latin *consortium* partnership.]

con·spec·tus (kən spek′təs) *n.* **1.** general or overall view. **2.** short summary; digest; résumé. [Latin *conspectus* a looking at, sight.]

con·spic·u·ous (kən spik′ū əs) *adj.* **1.** easily seen or comprehended; obvious: *Her lies are so conspicuous no one ever believes her.* **2.** attracting attention; striking: *His red plaid jacket was very conspicuous in the crowd.* **3.** worthy of notice; outstanding. [Latin *conspicuus* visible.] —**con·spic′u·ous·ly,** *adv.* —**con·spic′u·ous·ness,** *n.*

con·spir·a·cy (kən spir′ə sē) *pl.,* **-cies.** *n.* **1.** act of secretly planning together to perform some evil or illegal act. **2.** plan so devised; plot. **3.** group devising such a plan. —**con·spir′a·tor,** *n.* —**con·spir·a·to·ri·al** (kən spir′ə tôr′ē əl), *adj.*

Syn. 2. Conspiracy, connivance, collusion mean an understanding reached secretly. **Conspiracy** suggests an agreement between two or more parties to act together for some wicked purpose: *The conspiracy to destroy the generating plants soon became known to the police.* **Connivance** suggests failure to make known something discreditable of which one is aware: *With the connivance of some city inspectors, the company was able to erect its warehouse in direct violation of the building code.* **Collusion** implies a dishonest acting in concert to achieve a result that

at; āpe; cär; end; mē; it; īce; hot; ōld; fôrk; wood; fōōl; oil; out; up; ūse; turn; sing; thin; this; zh in treasure; ə in ago, taken, pencil, lemon, circus.

215

would otherwise be out of the question: *Collusion among those controlling the sources of the metal caused a price rise that doubled profits in a few months.* See also **plot**.

con·spire (kən spīr′) **-spired, -spir·ing.** *v. i.* **1.** to plan a conspiracy; plot. **2.** to work or act together to effect something: *They conspired to bring about the meeting of the two people. All nature conspired to make the day unforgettably beautiful.* [Latin *conspīrāre* to breathe together, agree, plot.] **—con·spir′er,** *n.*

con·sta·ble (kon′stə bəl, kun′-) *n.* **1.** peace officer, esp. in a small, local jurisdiction. **2.** chief officer of the household, court, or military forces of a medieval ruler. **3.** keeper or warden of a royal fortress or castle. **4.** *British.* policeman. [Old French *conestable* officer of the Frankish kings in charge of the stable, from Late Latin *comes stabulī* literally, count of the stable. See COUNT², STABLE¹.]

con·stab·u·lar·y (kən stab′yə ler′ē) *pl.,* **-lar·ies.** *n.* **1.** collective body of constables of a district. **2.** district under the jurisdiction of a particular constable. **3.** police force organized along military lines. *—adj.* of or relating to constables or constabularies.

con·stan·cy (kon′stən sē) *n.* **1.** quality of being steadfast or unwavering; unchangeability. **2.** faithfulness; loyalty.

con·stant (kon′stənt) *adj.* **1.** invariable; unchanging: *Careful control insures that the quality of the product remains constant.* **2.** continuing with little or no intermission; happening over and over again; persistent: *constant chatter.* **3.** loyal; steadfast; faithful. *—n.* **1.** something that does not change: *The distortion of forms is a constant in his painting.* **2.** value that remains unchanged, such as pi, or a value that is believed never to change, as the speed of light. **3.** value that remains or is held unchanged under the specific circumstances of an investigation or within the limits of an experiment. [Old French *constant* lasting, continuous, from Latin *constāns,* present participle of *constāre* to stand firm.] **—con′stant·ly,** *adv.*

Con·stan·ta (kôn stän′tsä) *n.* chief port of Romania, in the southeastern part of the country on the Black Sea. Pop. (1968 est.), 165,245.

Con·stan·tine (kon′stən tēn′) *n.* historic city in northeastern Algeria. Pop. (1966), 243,558.

Con·stan·tine the Great (kon′stən tīn′, -tēn′) A.D. c.274–337, Roman emperor, from A.D. 324 to 337, founder of Constantinople, and first emperor to sanction and support the Christian Church.

Con·stan·ti·no·ple (kon′stan tə nō′pəl) *n.* capital of the Byzantine and Ottoman empires, now the city of Istanbul.

con·stel·la·tion (kon′stə lā′shən) *n.* **1.** any of eighty-eight groups of stars, many of which traditionally represent characters and objects in ancient mythology. **2.** area or division of the heavens occupied by such a group. **3.** *Astrology.* relative grouping of the planets and stars, esp. at the time of one's birth, as said to influence one's character and fate, or world events. **4.** brilliant or distinguished grouping of persons or things. [Late Latin *constellātiō* collection of stars, going back to Latin *con-* together + *stella* star.]

con·ster·na·tion (kon′stər nā′shən) *n.* dismay or amazement leading to confusion or fear: *We noted with consternation that the barometer was falling rapidly.* [Latin *consternātiō.*]

con·sti·pate (kon′stə pāt′) **-pat·ed, -pat·ing.** *v. t.* to cause constipation in. [Latin *constipātus,* past participle of *constipāre* to press together.]

con·sti·pa·tion (kon′stə pā′shən) *n.* condition of the bowels marked by infrequent or difficult evacuation.

con·stit·u·en·cy (kən stich′ōō ən sē) *pl.,* **-cies.** *n.* **1.** body of voters in a district who elect a legislator and are represented by him. **2.** district represented. **3.** any group of supporters.

con·stit·u·ent (kən stich′ōō ənt) *adj.* **1.** serving to form or make up; component: *Hydrogen and oxygen are the constituent parts of water.* **2.** having the authority of appointing or electing a representative. **3.** empowered to create or amend a constitution: *a constituent assembly.* *—n.* **1.** necessary part; element; component. **2.** one who elects another as a representative in public office; resident of a constituency: *The congressman voted for the bill most favorable to his constituents.* **3.** *Grammar.* any of the forms in a construction. [Latin *constituēns,* present participle of *constituere* to cause to stand, establish.] **—Syn. 1.** see **ingredient.**

con·sti·tute (kon′stə tōōt′, -tūt′) **-tut·ed, -tut·ing.** *v. t.* **1.** to make up; compose; form: *Four quarts constitute a gallon.* **2.** to appoint to an office or function; empower: *The court constituted him legal guardian of the child.* **3.** to set up; establish; found: *to constitute new traffic regulations.* **4.** to give legal form to: *There is a definite procedure by which the legislature constitutes itself.* [Latin *constitūtus,* past participle of *constituere* to cause to stand, establish.]

con·sti·tu·tion (kon′stə tōō′shən, -tū′-) *n.* **1.** way in which something is made up or put together: *The constitution of a primitive society is not necessarily simple.* **2.** physical makeup of the human body, esp. as to strength or resistance to disease. **3.a.** system of fundamental principles according to which a body, as a nation, state, or club, is

governed. **b.** written document containing these principles. **c. the Constitution.** supreme law and plan of government of the United States, in effect since 1789. **4.** act of constituting or appointing; establishment.

con·sti·tu·tion·al (kon′stə tōō′shən əl, -tū′-) *adj.* **1.** of, relating to, or inherent in the constitution of a person or thing: *a constitutional weakness.* **2.** beneficial to one's bodily health. **3.** of, in, or in conformity with a constitution, esp. of a nation, state, or private organization. *—n.* exercise, esp. a walk, taken for one's health. **—con′sti·tu′tion·al·ly,** *adv.*

con·sti·tu·tion·al·i·ty (kon′stə tōō′shə nal′ə tē, -tū′-) *n.* conformity with a constitution, esp. a political constitution: *The constitutionality of the act was questioned.*

constitutional monarchy, monarchy in which the powers of the monarch are defined and limited by a constitution.

con·sti·tu·tive (kon′stə tōō′tiv, -tū′-) *adj.* **1.** forming a constituent part; essential. **2.** having the power to enact or establish. **—con′sti·tu′tive·ly,** *adv.*

con·strain (kən strān′) *v. t.* **1.** to compel, force, or coerce. **2.** to confine, as by holding in or binding. **3.** to repress; restrain. [Old French *constreindre,* from Latin *constringere* to draw together, restrain.] **—con·strain·ed·ly** (kən strā′nid lē, -strānd′-), *adv.* **—con·strain′er,** *n.* **—Syn. 1.** see **force.**

con·straint (kən strānt′) *n.* **1.** confinement; restriction. **2.** a holding back or restraining of natural feelings; forced or unnatural manner. **3.** compulsion; coercion. **4.** something that constrains. [Old French *constreinte* binding, coercion, from *constreindre.* See CONSTRAIN.]

con·strict (kən strikt′) *v. t.* **1.** to make narrower; contract. **2.** to compress; squeeze; bind. *—v. i.* to become constricted. [Latin *constrictus,* past participle of *constringere* to draw together, restrain.]

con·stric·tion (kən strik′shən) *n.* **1.** act of constricting; being constricted. **2.** tightness or a feeling of tightness: *The sudden drop caused a constriction in his chest.* **3.** something that constricts or is constricted. **—con·stric′tive,** *adj.*

con·stric·tor (kən strik′tər) *n.* **1.** any of various snakes, as the python, boa, and anaconda, that kills by squeezing its prey in its coils. **2.** muscle that causes a cavity or organ of the body to contract.

con·struct (*v.,* kən strukt′; *n.,* kon′strukt) *v. t.* **1.** to put together; build. **2.** *Geometry.* to draw a geometrical figure according to given conditions. *—n.* something put together or formulated: *a mathematical construct.* [Latin *constructus,* past participle of *construere* to pile up, build, make.] **—con·struc′tor,** *n.* **—Syn.** *v. t.* **1.** see **make.**

con·struc·tion (kən struk′shən) *n.* **1.** act of constructing. **2.** way in which something is constructed. **3.** that which is constructed; structure. **4.** explanation; interpretation. **5.** *Grammar.* arrangement or relation of words to form a sentence, clause, or phrase. **—con·struc′tion·al,** *adj.*

con·struc·tion·ist (kən struk′shə nist) *n.* one who interprets in a particular way such things as laws or documents: *A strict constructionist emphasizes the literal wording.*

con·struc·tive (kən struk′tiv) *adj.* **1.** serving to improve, aid, or build: *constructive criticism.* **2.** of or relating to construction; structural. **3.** indirectly stated but inferred by interpretation. **—con·struc′tive·ly,** *adv.* **—con·struc′tive·ness,** *n.*

con·strue (kən strōō′) **-strued, -stru·ing.** *v. t.* **1.** to explain or understand the meaning of; interpret: *She does not construe the meaning of his words.* **2.** to translate. **3.** to analyze (a sentence, clause, or phrase) for its grammatical structure. **4.** to use syntactically: *Is "group" construed as a singular or plural?* *—v. i.* to be capable of analysis, translation, or understanding. [Latin *construere* to pile up, build, make.] **—con·stru′a·ble,** *adj.*

con·sub·stan·tial (kon′səb stan′shəl) *adj.* of or having the same substance or essence.

con·sub·stan·ti·a·tion (kon′səb stan′shē ā′shən) *n.* doctrine that the body and blood of Christ are present in the consecrated bread and wine of the Eucharist. Distinguished from **transubstantiation.**

con·sul (kon′səl) *n.* **1.** official appointed by his government to live in a foreign city to protect and promote his country's commercial interests and to protect citizens of his country traveling or living there. **2.** either of the two annually elected magistrates who jointly exercised supreme authority in the Roman republic. **3.** any of the three chief magistrates of the French republic from 1799 to 1804, one of which was Napoleon Bonaparte. [Latin *consul* the Roman magistrate.] **—con′su·lar,** *adj.* **—con′sul·ship′,** *n.*

con·su·late (kon′sə lit) *n.* **1.** official residence or headquarters of a consul. **2.** office, term of office, or authority of a consul. **3.a.** government by consuls. **b. Consulate.** government of France from 1799 to 1804.

consul general *pl.,* **consuls general.** highest ranking consular official, stationed in an important city and often supervising other consuls.

con·sult (kən sult′) *v. t.* **1.** to refer to for information or advice: *to consult a physician, to consult an encyclopedia.* **2.** to have consideration

at; āpe; cär; end; mē; it; īce; hot; ōld; fôrk; wood; fōōl; oil; out; up; ūse; turn; sing; thin; this; zh in treasure; ə in ago, taken, pencil, lemon, circus.

or regard for. —*v.i.* **1.** to ask advice. **2.** to confer together (with *with*): *The general practitioner consulted with the specialists.* **3.** to give advice as an authority. [Latin *consultāre* to take counsel, reflect.]
Syn. *v.i.* **2. Consult, confer, advise** indicate discussion to resolve something. **Consult** implies discussion with those competent to counsel wisely: *The designer consulted with the editor before sending the manuscript to the typesetter.* **Confer** implies a discussion among equals, each matching his opinions against the others: *Their position having been stated, they refused to confer with the other side.* **Advise** implies personal aims or plans: *After the quarrel with his brother, he advised with several distant relatives about how best to handle the estate.*

con·sult·ant (kən sul′tənt) *n.* **1.** one who gives professional or technical advice. **2.** one who seeks advice or information, as from another person or a reference work.

con·sul·ta·tion (kon′səl tā′shən) *n.* **1.** act of consulting. **2.** meeting to confer about something: *The doctors held a consultation before the operation.*

con·sume (kən sōōm′) -**sumed,** -**sum·ing.** *v.t.* **1.** to use up: *An automobile consumes gasoline.* **2.** to eat or drink up. **3.** to destroy, esp. by fire. **4.** to squander or waste, as time or money. **5.** to engross or absorb: *He was consumed with curiosity.* —*v.i.* to waste away. [Latin *consūmere* to take completely, devour, destroy.] —**con·sum′a·ble,** *adj.*

con·sum·ed·ly (kən sōō′mid lē) *adv.* extremely; excessively.

con·sum·er (kən sōō′mər) *n.* **1.** someone who uses up an article of production, as contrasted with its producer or seller. **2.** someone or something that uses up, wastes, or destroys.

consumer goods, goods for directly satisfying people's wants, as food or clothing, rather than for use in further production. Distinguished from **capital goods.**

con·sum·er·ism (kən sōō′mər iz′əm) *n.* movement to protect the consumer against unsafe or defective goods or false advertising claims. —**con·sum′er·ist,** *n.*

consumer price index, index which indicates any rise or fall in the prices of a number of basic items in a typical family budget.

con·sum·mate (*v.,* kon′sə māt′; *adj.,* kən sum′it, kon′sə mit) -**mat·ed,** -**mat·ing.** *v.t.* **1.** to bring to completion; fulfill: *The artist consummated his life's work in a magnificent fresco.* **2.** to complete or fulfill (a marriage) by sexual intercourse. —*adj.* **1.** complete; perfect. **2.** of the highest degree; excellent: *consummate skill.* **3.** skilled or accomplished: *a consummate liar.* [Latin *consummātus,* past participle of *consummāre* to complete, perfect, from *con-* together + *summus* highest.] —**con·sum′mate·ly,** *adv.*

con·sum·ma·tion (kon′sə mā′shən) *n.* act of consummating; being consummated.

con·sump·tion (kən sump′shən) *n.* **1.** act of consuming; being consumed. **2.** amount consumed: *The consumption of gasoline is greater in some cars than in others.* **3.** a wasting disease, esp. tuberculosis of the lungs. [Latin *consūmptiō* a consuming, wasting.]

con·sump·tive (kən sump′tiv) *adj.* **1.** of, relating to, or having consumption, esp. tuberculosis of the lungs. **2.** tending to consume; destructive; wasteful. —*n.* one affected with consumption.

cont. **1.** continued; continue. **2.** continent; continental. **3.** contents. **4.** containing.

Cont. Continental.

con·tact (kon′takt) *n.* **1.** act or instance of touching; coming together. **2.** state of being in communication: *The expedition was completely out of contact with civilization for months.* **3.** potentially useful connection or association: *Their close contact with congressmen was advantageous.* **4.a.** junction of conductors which permits an electrical current to pass. **b.** device creating such a connection. —*v.t.* **1.** to bring into contact; touch. **2.** *Informal.* to communicate with: *Try and contact him tomorrow.* —*v.i.* to be in contact; come into contact. [Latin *contāctus* a touching.]

contact flying, flying of an aircraft at an altitude that enables the pilot to navigate by watching the ground or water below.

contact lens, thin plastic lens worn to correct a defect in vision, individually ground to a prescription and fitted to the cornea.

con·ta·gion (kən tā′jən) *n.* **1.** communication of disease by direct or indirect contact. **2.** disease communicated in this manner; contagious disease. **3.** agent or substance by which disease is communicated. **4.** spreading of any idea or state of mind or emotion: *No one remained untouched by the contagion of hysteria.* **5.** influence that spreads rapidly, esp. an evil or corrupting one. [Latin *contāgiō* a touching, contact, infection.]

con·ta·gious (kən tā′jəs) *adj.* **1.** communicated by contact, as a disease. ▲ see usage note under **infectious.** **2.** carrying or capable of communicating disease. **3.** readily communicated from one person to another; catching: *Fear can be contagious.* —**con·ta′gious·ly,** *adv.* —**con·ta′gious·ness,** *n.*

con·tain (kən tān′) *v.t.* **1.** to have in it; hold: *The jar contains coffee.* **2.** to have the capacity to hold: *That car will comfortably contain six*

passengers. **3.** to consist of; comprise: *The puzzle contains twenty pieces.* **4.** to keep under control or within limits; restrain: *By occupying the hill, the troops managed to contain the hostile forces. He contained his fear.* **5.** to be divisible by without a remainder: *The number 12 contains 3, 4, 2, and 6.* [Old French *contenir* to confine, subdue, going back to Latin *continēre* to hold together, restrain.] —**con·tain′a·ble,** *adj.*
Syn. **2. Contain, accommodate, hold**¹ denote to be capable of retaining inside. **Contain** stresses actually retaining something: *The book contains twelve chapters. The auditorium was built to contain 200 people.* **Accommodate** suggests retaining easily: *The dining room could always accommodate a few more guests.* **Hold** implies capability rather than actual retention: *That bottle will hold one quart.*

con·tain·er (kən tā′nər) *n.* something that contains or may contain; receptacle.

con·tain·ment (kən tān′mənt) *n.* prevention of the expansion of a hostile political, military, or economic power.

con·tam·i·nate (kən tam′ə nāt′) -**nat·ed,** -**nat·ing.** *v.t.* to make impure by contact; defile; pollute. [Latin *contāminātus,* past participle of *contāmināre* to bring into contact, defile.] —**con·tam′i·na·tive,** *adj.* —**con·tam′i·na·tor,** *n.* —**Syn.** see **pollute.**

con·tam·i·na·tion (kən tam′ə nā′shən) *n.* **1.** act of contaminating; being contaminated; pollution: *Food should be kept covered to avoid contamination.* **2.** something that contaminates; impurity.

contd., continued.

con·temn (kən tem′) *v.t.* to treat or view with contempt; despise; scorn. [Latin *contemnere.*] —**con·tem·ner** (kən tem′ər, -tem′nər), *n.*

con·tem·plate (kon′təm plāt′) -**plat·ed,** -**plat·ing.** *v.t.* **1.** to give prolonged or intense attention to; consider carefully. **2.** to have in mind, as a plan of action; intend: *He goes to the park every day to sit and contemplate.* [Latin *contemplātus,* past participle of *contemplārī* to observe, from *con-* with + *templum* space marked out in the sky for observation, temple¹; with reference to the practice of ancient Roman priests of observing a *templum* for omens.] —**Syn.** *v.t.* **1.** see **consider.**

con·tem·pla·tion (kon′təm plā′shən) *n.* **1.** act of looking at or thinking about something long and intensely. **2.** meditation, esp. spiritual or religious meditation. **3.** expectation or intention: *She bought three dresses in contemplation of her trip.*

con·tem·pla·tive (kon′təm plā′tiv, kən tem′plə-) *adj.* of, relating to, or characterized by contemplation.

con·tem·po·ra·ne·ous (kən tem′pə rā′nē əs) *adj.* belonging to or occurring during the same period of time. [Latin *contemporaneus.*] —**con·tem′po·ra′ne·ous·ly,** *adv.* —**con·tem′po·ra′ne·ous·ness,** *n.* —**Syn.** see **contemporary.**

con·tem·po·rar·y (kən tem′pə rer′ē) *adj.* **1.** belonging to or living at the same time. **2.** of the same age or date. **3.** current; modern: *contemporary art, contemporary furniture.* —*n., pl.* -**rar·ies.** **1.** one who belongs to or lives at the same time as another or others. **2.** someone or something that is of the same age or date. [Latin *con-* together + *temporarius* relating to time.]
Syn. *adj.* **1. Contemporary, contemporaneous** refer to occurrence or existence at the same time. **Contemporary,** used esp. of people or their works, suggests existence at the same time and may apply to the past or the present: *Marlowe and Jonson were contemporary with Shakespeare.* **Contemporaneous** is used primarily of events, and never of the present: *Noah's flood appears to be contemporaneous with the one described in Sumerian literature.* **3.** see **modern.**

con·tempt (kən tempt′) *n.* **1.** feeling of a person toward someone or something he considers low, mean, or worthless; scorn; disdain. **2.** state of being scorned or despised; disgrace. **3.** willful disobedience to or open disrespect for the authority and dignity of a law court or lawmaking body: *contempt of court, contempt of Congress.* [Latin *contemptus* scorn.]

con·tempt·i·ble (kən temp′tə bəl) *adj.* deserving of or held in contempt or scorn; despicable. —**con·tempt′i·ble·ness,** *n.* —**con·tempt′i·bly,** *adv.*

con·temp·tu·ous (kən temp′chōō əs) *adj.* showing contempt; scornful: *a contemptuous remark.* —**con·temp′tu·ous·ly,** *adv.* —**con·temp′tu·ous·ness,** *n.*

con·tend (kən tend′) *v.i.* **1.** to vie in a contest; compete: *They contended for the blue ribbon.* **2.** to argue; dispute. **3. to contend with.** to deal with in or as in struggle: *The man had to contend with his wife's ill health.* —*v.t.* to assert or maintain as a fact: *The boy contended that he saw a ghost.* [Latin *contendere* to stretch out, fight.] —**con·tend′er,** *n.* —**Syn.** *v.i.* **1.** see **compete.**

con·tent¹ (kon′tent) *n.* **1.a.** *usually,* **contents.** all which is contained inside: *the contents of a box.* **b.** facts or topics dealt with; subject matter: *the content of an essay, a table of contents for a book.* **2.** ability to hold; capacity: *a barrel of more than usual content.* **3.** amount contained. [Latin *contentum* that which is contained, originally neuter of *contentus,* past participle of *continēre* to hold together, contain.]

con·tent² (kən tent′) *adj.* free of desire for more than one has; satisfied: *He was content to eat the leftovers.* —*v.t.* to make content; satisfy; please: *Simple praise is enough to content him. He contented himself with a subordinate job.* —*n.* contentment; satisfaction. [Latin *contentus* restrained, satisfied, past participle of *continēre* to hold together, contain.]

con·tent·ed (kən ten′tid) *adj.* enjoying contentment; satisfied. —**con·tent′ed·ly,** *adv.* —**con·tent′ed·ness,** *n.*

con·ten·tion (kən ten′shən) *n.* **1.** verbal argument; quarrel. **2.** point maintained in an argument: *He stood by his contention that the action was immoral.* **3.** struggle; contest. [Old French *contention* strife, dispute, from Latin *contentiō* a stretching, strife.]

con·ten·tious (kən ten′shəs) *adj.* **1.** quarrelsome; argumentative: *People often try to avoid a contentious person.* **2.** apt to cause contention; characterized by contention: *a contentious act.* —**con·ten′tious·ly,** *adv.* —**con·ten′tious·ness,** *n.*

con·tent·ment (kən tent′mənt) *n.* state of being contented; satisfaction. —**Syn.** see **satisfaction.**

con·ter·mi·nous (kən tur′mə nəs) *adj.* **1.** having a common boundary. **2.** contained within the same boundaries; coextensive. Also, **co·ter′mi·nous.** [Latin *conterminus* bordering on.] —**con·ter′mi·nous·ly,** *adv.*

con·test (*n.,* kon′test; *v.,* kən test′) *n.* **1.** competition, such as a race or a game, in which a prize or an honor is the ultimate goal. **2.** struggle; conflict. **3.** argument; dispute. —*v.t.* **1.** to struggle in order to win (something); fight for. **2.** to challenge the validity of; dispute: *to contest the decision of the umpire.* —*v.i.* to enter into competition; vie (with *with* or *against*): *Only a fool would contest against those odds.* [Latin *contestārī* to call to witness, introduce a lawsuit.] —**con·test′a·ble,** *adj.*

con·test·ant (kən tes′tənt) *n.* **1.** one who takes part in a contest. **2.** one who contests the legality or validity, as of an election or decision: *He was the chief contestant of the will.*

con·text (kon′tekst) *n.* **1.** parts surrounding a word, sentence, or passage which help determine the meaning: *to quote a passage out of context.* **2.** surroundings; environment. [Latin *contextus* a joining together, connection, going back to *con-* together + *texere* to weave.]

con·tex·tu·al (kən teks′chŏŏ əl) *adj.* relating to or depending on the context. —**con·tex′tu·al·ly,** *adv.*

con·ti·gu·i·ty (kon′tə gū′ə tē) *pl.,* **-ties.** *n.* **1.** state of being contiguous; proximity; contact. **2.** continuous extent; unbroken series.

con·tig·u·ous (kən tig′ū əs) *adj.* **1.** in actual contact; touching: *The warring countries are nowhere contiguous.* **2.** adjoining; near. [Latin *contiguus* bordering on, touching.] —**con·tig′u·ous·ly,** *adv.* —**con·tig′u·ous·ness,** *n.* —**Syn.** **2.** see **adjacent.**

con·ti·nence (kont′ən əns) *n.* self-restraint or moderation, esp. with regard to sexual desires.

con·ti·nen·cy (kont′ən ən sē) *pl.,* **-cies.** *n.* continence.

con·ti·nent¹ (kont′ən ənt) *n.* **1.** one of the seven great land areas of the earth, traditionally including Asia, Africa, North America, South America, Antarctica, Europe, and Australia. **2. the Continent.** mainland of Europe, as distinguished from the British Isles. **3.** *Archaic.* mainland. [Latin *(terra) continēns* mainland, literally, (land) holding together.]

con·ti·nent² (kont′ən ənt) *adj.* practicing self-restraint or moderation, esp. with regard to sexual desires. [Latin *continēns,* present participle of *continēre* to hold together, restrain.]

con·ti·nen·tal (kont′ə nent′əl) *adj.* **1.** *also,* **Continental,** of, on, or characteristic of the Continent; European: *continental cuisine.* **2. Continental.** of or relating to the American colonies during and immediately after the American Revolution. **3.** of, characteristic of, or resembling a continent: *a continental climate.* —*n.* *also,* **Continental.** inhabitant of the Continent; European. **2.** currency note issued by the Continental Congress during the American Revolution, which became worthless after the war. **3. Continental.** soldier in the American Army established by the Continental Congress on June 14, 1775. **4. not worth a continental.** worthless.

Continental Congress, either of two assemblies of delegates from the American colonies which met from 1774 to 1781. The Second Continental Congress convened in 1775, issued the Declaration of Independence in 1776, and governed the colonies until the Articles of Confederation were ratified in 1781.

continental divide **1.** elevation of land that separates river systems flowing toward one side of a continent from those flowing toward the other side. **2. Continental Divide.** such an elevation in North America formed by the various peaks of the Rocky Mountains, separating rivers flowing eastward from those flowing westward.

continental drift, slow movement of the continental land masses over centuries, resulting in slight changes of their positions with respect to one another.

con·tin·gen·cy (kən tin′jən sē) *pl.,* **-cies.** *n.* **1.** event or occurrence that is contingent; that which can possibly happen or may happen by chance if something else occurs: *A soldier in battle tries to prepare for any contingency.* **2.** quality or condition of being contingent or subject to chance: *the contingency of events.*

con·tin·gent (kən tin′jənt) *adj.* **1.** dependent, as upon an uncertain condition or occurrence; conditional: *Tom's visit is contingent upon his getting a ride.* **2.** likely to happen, but not certain; possible: *The conviction of the entire gang may be a contingent result of the trial.* **3.** happening by chance or by an unknown or unforeseen cause; accidental. Opposed to **necessary.** **4.** (of a proposition) possibly true; logically possible. —*n.* group, as of troops or delegates, contributed by another group as a part or share of a larger body. [Latin *contingēns,* present participle of *contingere* to happen.] —**con·tin′gent·ly,** *adv.*

con·tin·u·al (kən tin′ū əl) *adj.* **1.** going on without interruption; continuous: *The thief had a continual fear of being caught.* **2.** occurring over and over again; repeated frequently and regularly: *The continual chiming of the bells kept me awake all night.* —**con·tin′u·al·ly,** *adv.* **Syn.** *adj.* **2.** Continual, continuous, incessant, indicate repetition during a considerable period of time. **Continual** implies little time interval between occurrences: *The nights were made hideous by the continual howling of the coyotes.* **Continuous** implies no perceptible pause either in time or array: *A continuous line of telephone poles stretched off to the horizon.* **Incessant** suggests unbroken repetition of occurrence: *I knew that summer had come and the children were home from the incessant slamming of the screen door.*

con·tin·u·ance (kən tin′ū əns) *n.* **1.** act of continuing; being continued. **2.** duration: *a famine of long continuance.* **3.** sequel, as to a literary work. **4.** *Law.* adjournment or postponement of a pending court action to a future date.

con·tin·u·a·tion (kən tin′ū ā′shən) *n.* **1.** a going on, remaining, or extending without interruption: *The voters supported a continuation of the present city administration.* **2.** a going on (after an interruption); resumption: *the continuation of telephone service after the flood.* **3.** extension in space, time, or development: *The children hoped that the continuation of the serial would be more interesting.*

continuation school, part-time school intended mainly for young people who have not completed school, usually held in the evening.

con·tin·ue (kən tin′ū) **-tin·ued, -tin·u·ing.** *v.i.* **1.** to keep on in a condition or course of action; go on; persist: *Continue until you reach the stop sign, then turn left.* **2.** to remain in effect or existence; last; endure: *The snowfall continued for two days.* **3.** to remain in a place or position: *She chose to continue as head nurse.* **4.** to proceed, as after an interruption; resume: *The meeting will continue after lunch.* —*v.t.* **1.** to go on with; keep on with; persist in: *He continued his work despite his illness.* **2.** to go on with (after an interruption); resume: *The professor will continue the lecture tomorrow.* **3.** to extend or prolong (something) in space, time, or development: *He continued his magazine subscription for another year.* **4.** to cause to remain in a place or position; retain: *The team continued him as manager.* **5.** *Law.* to adjourn or postpone (a pending court action) to a future date. [Old French *continuer* to proceed, go on, from Latin *continuāre* to make continuous, connect.] —**con·tin′u·a·ble,** *adj.*

Syn. *v.i.* **2.** Continue, endure, last² mean to keep on indefinitely. **Continue** suggests endlessness with no gaps: *They continued to ignore the demands of the radicals.* **Endure** implies withstanding wear or abrasion: *The plastic finish will endure despite months of hard wear.* **Last** stresses the length of time: *How long will that candle last?*

con·ti·nu·i·ty (kon′tə nōō′ə tē, -nū′-) *pl.,* **-ties.** *n.* **1.** state or quality of being continuous: *the continuity of time.* **2.** connected whole; coherence: *The jury appreciated the continuity of the lawyer's argument.* **3.** detailed plan giving the events, sequence of scenes, or script, as of a motion picture or television program. **4.** transitional comments or announcements, as during a television program.

con·tin·u·ous (kən tin′ū əs) *adj.* extending or going on without interruption in space, time, or development; unbroken: *a continuous curve, a continuous movie.* —**con·tin′u·ous·ly,** *adv.* —**con·tin′u·ous·ness,** *n.* —**Syn.** see **continual.**

con·tin·u·um (kən tin′ū əm) *pl.,* **-tin·u·a** (-tin′ū ə). *n.* continuous whole, having no discernible segments. [Latin *continuum,* neuter of *continuus* continuous.]

con·tort (kən tôrt′) *v.t.* to twist or bend out of the normal shape; distort: *The patient's face was contorted with pain.* [Latin *contortus,* past participle of *contorquēre* to twist together.]

con·tor·tion (kən tôr′shən) *n.* **1.** act of contorting; being contorted. **2.** twisted or bent shape: *the amazing contortions of the acrobat's body.*

con·tor·tion·ist (kən tôr′shə nist) *n.* one who contorts, esp. a performer who twists and bends his body into unnatural positions.

con·tour (kon′toor) *n.* **1.** shape of the surface, as of a figure or mass, or the line representing this: *The contour of the earth can be seen from an orbiting spacecraft.* —*adj.* **1.** following contour lines of hilly land when plowing and planting, thereby creating terraces which help prevent erosion. **2.** made to fit the shape of the surface of something: *contour sheets.* —*v.t.* to shape or construct (something) to fit the con-

at; āpe; cär; end; mē; it; īce; hot; ōld; fôrk; wood; fōōl; oil; out; up; ūse; turn; sing; thin; this; zh in treasure; ə in ago, taken, pencil, lemon, circus.

tour (of something else), as a road around a mountain. [French *contour* circuit, outline, from Italian *contorno*, going back to Latin *con-* together + *tornāre* to turn. See TURN.] —**Syn.** *n.* see **profile.**

contour line, line, as on a map, connecting points of equal elevation.

contour map, map that shows the relative elevations of a surface by means of contour lines.

contr., contract; contracted; contraction.

contra- *prefix* against; opposite: *contravene, contradiction.* [Latin *contrā.*]

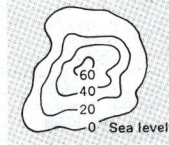

Contour map
of a 60-foot hill

con·tra·band (kon′trə band′) *n.* **1.** goods prohibited by law from being imported or exported; smuggled goods: *The man was arrested for dealing in contraband.* **2.** unlawful commerce in such goods; smuggling: *The government tried to prevent the contraband in drugs.* **3.** goods, usually arms and ammunition, which, according to international law, when furnished by a neutral country to a belligerent, may be rightfully seized by an opposing belligerent. Also, **contraband of war.** —*adj.* prohibited by law from being imported or exported: *contraband goods.* [Spanish *contrabando,* from Italian *contrabbando,* from *contra* against (from Latin *contrā*) + *bando* ban (of Germanic origin).]

con·tra·bass (kon′trə bās′) *n.* any of a family of musical instruments having a range below the bass, esp. the double bass of the viol family. —*adj.* pitched an octave lower than the normal bass.

con·tra·cep·tion (kon′trə sep′shən) *n.* prevention of conception, esp. by chemical or mechanical means. [CONTRA- + (CON)CEPTION.]

con·tra·cep·tive (kon′trə sep′tiv) *adj.* relating to or used for contraception: *a contraceptive device.* —*n.* chemical substance or mechanical device for preventing conception.

con·tract (*v.,* kən trakt′; *v.t. def. 3, v.i. def. 2 also* kon′trakt; *n.,* kon′trakt) *v.t.* **1.** to draw together (the parts of a thing) so as to shorten or make smaller: *A frightened hedgehog contracts its body into a ball.* **2.** to get or acquire; incur: *to contract pneumonia, to contract a debt.* **3.** to establish by agreement: *The two businesses contracted a merger.* **4.** to shorten (a word, syllable, or phrase) by omitting or combining sounds or letters. *Are not can be contracted to aren't, over to o'er.* —*v.i.* **1.** to draw together so as to become shorter or smaller: *The muscle contracted.* **2.** to make or enter into an agreement: *The farmer contracted to lease his land.* —*n.* **1.** agreement between two or more parties to do or not to do something; bargain; compact: *a social contract between the people and the state.* **2.** *Law.* **a.** agreement that is legally binding. **b.** document containing the terms of this agreement. **3.** *Bridge.* **a.** undertaking by the declarer to take the number of tricks in the final bid plus six tricks. **b.** the final bid itself. **c.** number of tricks specified in the bid. [Latin *contractus,* past participle of *contrahere* to draw together, make smaller, make an agreement.] —**con·tract′i·ble,** *adj.* **Syn.** *v.i.* **1.** Contract, shrink indicate a lessening of size. **Contract** emphasizes the loss of overall dimension: *The pupils contract when strong light enters the eye.* **Shrink** stresses loss of original dimension: *The sweater shrank from being washed in hot water.*

contract bridge, card game played by four players in teams of two with a fifty-two-card deck, in which only the number of tricks bid count toward game. Distinguished from **auction bridge.**

con·tract·ed (kən trak′tid) *adj.* drawn together; shortened or made smaller: *a contracted muscle.*

con·trac·tile (kən trak′təl) *adj.* having the ability to contract or draw together; producing contraction: *contractile tissue, the contractile force of cold.* —**con·trac·til·i·ty** (kon′trak til′ə tē), *n.*

con·trac·tion (kən trak′shən) *n.* **1.** act or process of contracting; being contracted: *the contraction of a disease.* **2.** a shortening of muscle tissue. **3.** shortened form of a word, syllable, or phrase made by an omission or combination of letters. *Wouldn't is a contraction of would not.*

con·trac·tive (kən trak′tiv) *adj.* contractile.

con·trac·tor (kon′trak′tər, kən trak′-) *n.* **1.** one who agrees to supply goods or do a job for a fixed price. **2.** one of the parties that makes a contract.

con·trac·tu·al (kən trak′chōō əl) *adj.* of, arising from, or having the force of a contract: *contractual agreements.*

con·tra·dict (kon′trə dikt′) *v.t.* **1.** to assert the opposite of or deny (a statement); declare to be untrue: *The eyewitness contradicted earlier testimony.* **2.** to assert the opposite of or deny what is stated by (someone): *She does not like to contradict her husband in public.* **3.** to be opposed to or inconsistent with: *Her words contradicted her deeds.* —*v.i.* to speak in opposition; oppose: *The shy girl was afraid to contradict.* [Latin *contrādictus,* past participle of *contrādīcere* to speak against.] —**Syn.** *v.t.* **1.** see **deny.**

con·tra·dic·tion (kon′trə dik′shən) *n.* **1.** statement that contradicts another: *That speech contains many contradictions.* **2.** act of denying

or asserting the opposite. **3.** opposition or disagreement; inconsistency: *There seems to be a contradiction between her words and actions.* **4.** one who or that which contains inconsistent elements, esp. a self-contradictory statement. The statement *A circle is square* is a contradiction.

con·tra·dic·to·ry (kon′trə dik′tər ē) *adj.* **1.** involving or constituting a contradiction; inconsistent: *contradictory accounts of the accident.* **2.** inclined to contradict: *a contradictory person.* —**con·tra·dic′to·ri·ly,** *adv.* —**con′tra·dic′to·ri·ness,** *n.*

con·tra·dis·tinc·tion (kon′trə dis tingk′shən) *n.* distinction by contrast or opposition. —**con′tra·dis·tinc′tive,** *adj.* —**con′tra·dis·tinc′tive·ly,** *adv.*

con·trail (kon′trāl′) *n.* trail of vapor which forms behind an airplane or rocket flying at a high altitude. Also, **vapor trail.** [CON(DENSATION) + TRAIL.]

con·tral·to (kən tral′tō) *pl.,* **-tos.** *n.* **1.** lowest female voice, intermediate between soprano and tenor; alto. **2.** part sung by a contralto. **3.** singer having a contralto voice. —*adj.* of or relating to a contralto: *a contralto voice.* [Italian *contralto* lowest female voice, singer having a contralto voice, going back to Latin *contrā* against + *altus* high.]

con·trap·tion (kən trap′shən) *n. Informal.* mechanical device; contrivance; gadget. [Possibly blend of CONTRIVE, APT, and -ION.]

con·tra·pun·tal (kon′trə punt′əl) *adj.* **1.** of or pertaining to counterpoint: *contrapuntal theory.* **2.** composed according to the rules of, or characterized by, counterpoint: *contrapuntal music.* [Italian *contrappunto* counterpoint (going back to Latin *contrā* against + *pūnctus* point) + -AL[1].]

con·tra·pun·tist (kon′trə pun′tist) *n.* one skilled in the composing of counterpoint.

con·tra·ri·e·ty (kon′trə rī′ə tē) *pl.,* **-ties.** *n.* **1.** state or quality of being contrary: *contrariety of opinion.* **2.** that which is contrary: *the many contrarieties of human nature.*

con·trar·i·wise (kon′trer ē wīz′, kən trār′ē-) *adv.* **1.** in the opposite direction or order. **2.** on the contrary: *Contrariwise, it is a very dangerous place.* **3.** perversely.

con·trar·y (kon′trer ē; *adj. def. 3 also* kən trār′ē) *adj.* **1.** opposite in nature or tendency; entirely different; mutually opposed: *contrary needs, contrary ideas.* **2.** opposite in position or direction: *contrary motion.* **3.** habitually tending to oppose or contradict; unaccommodating. **4.** unfavorable; adverse: *Contrary winds put us off our course.* —*n. pl.,* **-trar·ies.** **1.** fact, quality, or condition that is the opposite of something else; the opposite: *I believe the contrary to be the case.* **2.** one of a pair of opposites: *Hot and cold are contraries.* **3. on the contrary.** just the opposite: *On the contrary, we are not going to go.* **4. to the contrary.** to the opposite effect: *Did you hear any rumors to the contrary?* —*adv.* in opposition; contrarily: *Many people act contrary to what they think.* [Anglo-Norman *contrarie* directly opposed, from Latin *contrārius* opposite, opposed.] —**con′trar·i·ly,** *adv.* —**con′trar·i·ness,** *n.*

con·trast (*v.,* kən trast′; *n.,* kon′trast) *v.t.* to compare or set in opposition in order to reveal unlikeness or striking differences: *The anthropologist contrasted two cultures in his lecture.* —*v.i.* to reveal unlikeness or differences when compared: *The hat contrasted sharply with her dress. The colors in that painting contrast nicely.* —*n.* **1.** act of contrasting; being contrasted: *The student is now fairly conservative, in contrast to his earlier position.* **2.** unlikeness or striking difference revealed by contrasting: *the contrast between darkness and light.* **3.** one who or that which exhibits unlikeness or striking differences: *Her new hairdo was quite a contrast to her old drab one.* [French *contraster* to be or to put in contrast, from Italian *contrastare* to stand out against, going back to Latin *contrā* against + *stāre* to stand.] —**con·trast′a·ble,** *adj.* —**Syn.** *n.* **2.** see **comparison.**

con·tra·vene (kon′trə vēn′) **-vened, -ven·ing.** *v.t.* **1.** to go against; come in conflict with; violate; transgress: *to contravene a law. Slavery contravenes the principles of justice.* **2.** to oppose in argument; contradict: *to contravene the truth.* [Late Latin *contrāvenīre,* from Latin *contrā* against + *venīre* to come.]

con·tra·ven·tion (kon′trə ven′shən) *n.* act of contravening; opposition; violation.

con·tre·danse (kon′trə dans′, -däns′; *French* kôN trə däNs′) *also,* **con·tre·dance.** *n.* **1.** country dance in which the dancers face each other in two opposing lines. **2.** piece of music written for such a dance. [French *contredanse* quadrille, from English COUNTRY-DANCE; influenced by French *contre* against, opposite (with reference to the two opposing lines of dancers).]

con·tre·temps (*French* kôN trə täN′) *pl.,* **-temps** (-täNz′). *n.* embarrassing or awkward incident; mishap. [French *contre-temps* mishap, out of time (in music), going back to Latin *contrā* against + *tempus* time.]

con·trib·ute (kən trib′ūt) **-ut·ed, -ut·ing.** *v.t., v.i.* **1.** to give or furnish along with others to a common fund or for a common purpose: *He contributed $5 to the charity every payday. She never contributes to the discussion.* **2.** to furnish to a newspaper or magazine, as an article or

at; āpe; cär; end; mē; it; īce; hot; ōld; fôrk; wood; fōōl; oil; out; up; ūse; turn; sing; thin; this; zh in treasure; ə in ago, taken, pencil, lemon, circus.

219

story: *The professor often contributes to a literary journal.* **3. to contribute to.** to have a part in bringing about (a result): *actions which contributed to the king's downfall.* [Latin *contribūtus,* past participle of *contribuere* to bring together, add, collect, going back to *con-* together + *tribus* tribe; originally with reference to payments made by the ancient Roman *tribes.*] —**con·trib′u·tive,** *adj.* —**con·trib′u·tive·ly,** *adv.* —**Syn.** *v.t.* **1.** see **donate.**

con·tri·bu·tion (kon′trə bū′shən) *n.* **1.** act of contributing: *a contribution of money to help retarded children.* **2.** that which is contributed: *The invention of the typewriter was a great contribution to communication and printing.*

con·trib·u·tor (kən trib′yə tər) *n.* **1.** one who contributes: *All contributors to the fund drive will meet today.* **2.** one who furnishes his writings to a newspaper or magazine.

con·trib·u·to·ry (kən trib′yə tôr′ē) *adj.* having a part in bringing about a result; contributing.

con·trite (kən trīt′, kon′trīt) *adj.* **1.** deeply sorry or remorseful for one's sins or wrongdoings; penitent: *a contrite and humble spirit.* **2.** showing or arising from sorrow or remorse. [Old French *contrit* repentant, from Late Latin *contrītus,* from Latin *contrītus,* ground up, bruised, past participle of *conterere* to grind, bruise.] —**con·trite′ly,** *adv.* —**con·trite′ness,** *n.*

con·tri·tion (kən trish′ən) *n.* sorrow or remorse for one's sins or wrongdoings; penitence. —**Syn.** see **penitence.**

con·triv·ance (kən trī′vəns) *n.* **1.** that which is contrived, as a scheme or mechanical device. **2.** act of contriving or ability to contrive: *beyond the reach of human contrivance.*

con·trive (kən trīv′) -**trived,** -**triv·ing.** *v.t.* **1.** to devise or plan in a clever or ingenious way; scheme; plot: *The prisoners of war contrived an escape route.* **2.** to bring about, esp. with difficulty: *They contrived the plan in secret.* **3.** to create in a clever or ingenious way; invent; design: *to contrive a new lock, to contrive a new accounting system.* —*v.i.* to form schemes or plots: *The sneaky boy was always contriving.* [Old French *controver* to imagine, invent, going back to Latin *con-* with + *tropus* figure of speech. See **TROPE.**] —**con·triv′a·ble,** *adj.* —**con·triv′er,** *n.* —**Syn.** *v.t.* see **devise.**

con·trived (kən trīvd′) *adj.* obviously planned; forced; artificial.

con·trol (kən trōl′) *n.* **1.** power to direct or regulate; authority: *absolute control over a country.* **2.** a holding in check; restraint: *Control of the emotions during a crisis is difficult.* **3.** method or means of restraint: *controls over inflation.* **4.** *also,* **controls.** device or system for operating, regulating, or guiding a mechanism, as an airplane. **5.** standard of comparison, esp. one used to measure or verify the results of an experiment. **6.** *Spiritualism.* spirit that acts as an intermediary between a medium and the spirit to be contacted. —*v.t.,* -**trolled,** -**trol·ling.** **1.** to have power to direct or regulate; exercise authority over: *The federal government controls interstate commerce.* **2.** to hold in check; curb; restrain: *to control one's temper.* **3.** to use a control in (an experiment), esp. for verifying the results. [Old French *contrerolle* duplicate register kept as a check on the original, going back to Latin *contrā* against + Medieval Latin *rotulus* roll of paper, from Latin *rotulus* little wheel.] —**con·trol′la·bil′i·ty,** *n.* —**con·trol′la·ble,** *adj.* —**Syn.** *n.* **1.** see **authority.**

con·trol·ler (kən trō′lər) *n.* **1.** *also,* **comptroller.** officer, as in a bank or corporation, in charge of the bookkeeping, accounting, and auditing procedures and reports. **2.** one who or that which controls. —**con·trol′ler·ship′,** *n.*

control stick, lever by which the pilot of an airplane controls the movement of the ailerons and elevators and thereby controls the direction of flight. Also, **control column.**

control tower, structure on an airfield which controls communication with aircraft and air traffic.

con·tro·ver·sial (kon′trə vur′shəl) *adj.* **1.** causing or characterized by controversy: *a controversial issue. He has always been a controversial figure.* **2.** given to controversy; disputatious. —**con′tro·ver′sial·ly,** *adv.*

con·tro·ver·sial·ist (kon′trə vur′shə list) *n.* one who engages in or enjoys controversy.

con·tro·ver·sy (kon′trə vur′sē) *pl.,* -**sies.** *n.* dispute, debate, or disagreement, esp. one involving a difference of opinion: *the controversy over the authorship of Shakespeare's plays.* [Latin *contrōversia.*] —**Syn.** see **argument.**

con·tro·vert (kon′trə vurt′, kon′trə vurt′) *v.t.* **1.** to argue against; oppose; deny; contradict: *It is now difficult to controvert the idea that*

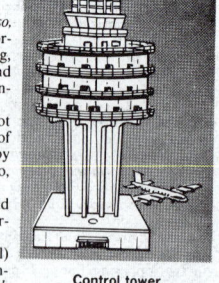

Control tower

the earth is round. **2.** to engage in controversy; argue about; dispute; debate. [From **CONTROVERSY.**] —**con′tro·vert′i·ble,** *adj.*

con·tu·ma·cious (kon′tə mā′shəs, kon′tyə-) *adj.* obstinately and willfully disobedient; insubordinate; rebellious.

con·tu·ma·cy (kon′too mə sē, kon′tyoo-) *pl.,* -**cies.** *n.* obstinate and willful disobedience of, or resistance to, authority; insubordination. [Latin *contumācia* obstinacy.]

con·tu·me·ly (kon′too mə lē, kon′tyoo-) *pl.,* -**lies.** *n.* **1.** rudeness in manner or speech; scornful or haughty insolence. **2.** instance of such insolence; humiliating insult. [Latin *contumēlia* reproach, insult.] —**con·tu·me·li·ous** (kon′too mē′lē əs, -tyoo-), *adj.* —**con′tu·me′li·ous·ly,** *adv.*

con·tuse (kən tōōz′, -tūz′) -**tused,** -**tus·ing.** *v.t.* to injure without breaking the skin; bruise. [Latin *contūsus,* past participle of *contundere* to bruise.]

con·tu·sion (kən tōō′zhən, -tū′-) *n.* injury in which the skin is not broken; bruise.

co·nun·drum (kə nun′drəm) *n.* **1.** riddle whose answer involves a pun. The riddle *What would make a gambler happy? A pair o' dice (paradise)* is a conundrum. **2.** any puzzling or difficult problem. [Of uncertain origin.]

con·va·lesce (kon′və les′) -**lesced,** -**lesc·ing.** *v.i.* to regain health and strength gradually after illness; recover. [Latin *convalēscere.*]

con·va·les·cence (kon′və les′əns) *n.* **1.** gradual recovery of health and strength after illness. **2.** period of this recovery.

con·va·les·cent (kon′və les′ənt) *adj.* **1.** recovering from illness: *a convalescent patient.* **2.** for or related to convalescence: *a convalescent home.* —*n.* one who is convalescing.

con·vec·tion (kən vek′shən) *n.* **1.** transfer of heat from one part of a gas or liquid to another by heated currents of the gas or liquid. **2.** act of conveying. [Late Latin *convectiō* a carrying together, from Latin *convehere* to carry together.]

con·vene (kən vēn′) -**vened,** -**ven·ing.** *v.i.* to come together, esp. for a meeting; assemble: *Congress will convene again in the fall.* —*v.t.* to cause to assemble; convoke. [Latin *convenīre* to come together.] —**con·ven′er,** *n.*

con·ven·ience (kən vēn′yəns) *n.* **1.** quality of being convenient; serviceability: *the convenience of frozen foods.* **2.** ease; comfort: *an information service for the convenience of visitors.* **3.** that which affords comfort or ease; something convenient: *A washing machine is one of the many modern conveniences.* **4. at one's convenience.** at a time or place, or under conditions, suitable to one's needs or wishes: *We will meet at your convenience.*

con·ven·ien·cy (kən vēn′yən sē) *pl.,* -**cies.** *n. Archaic.* convenience.

con·ven·ient (kən vēn′yənt) *adj.* **1.** easy to do, use, or reach; affording comfort or ease; favorable to one's needs or purposes: *a convenient location.* **2. convenient to.** near to one's needs or ease: *a home convenient to all transportation.* [Latin *conveniēns,* present participle of *convenīre* to come together, suit.] —**con·ven′ient·ly,** *adv.*

con·vent (kon′vent, -vənt) *n.* **1.** society of nuns. **2.** formerly, any group of persons living together under strict religious discipline. **3.** building or buildings occupied by such a society, esp. a nunnery. [Latin *conventus* assembly; literally, a coming together.] —**Syn.** **1.** see **cloister.**

con·ven·ti·cle (kən ven′ti kəl) *n.* **1.** secret meeting, esp. for religious worship, as that of the dissenters from the Church of England in the sixteenth and seventeenth centuries. **2.** place of such a meeting. [Latin *conventiculum* small assembly, diminutive of *conventus* assembly.]

con·ven·tion (kən ven′shən) *n.* **1.** formal meeting of delegates or members, as of a political, professional, or fraternal organization. **2.** delegates or members at such a meeting: *The convention voted on a new constitution.* **3.** general agreement or acceptance, esp. as the basis for a rule, practice, or custom: *to adhere to the dictates of convention.* **4.** generally accepted rule, practice, or custom: *Tipping one's hat is a convention.* **5.** international agreement, usually covering specific matters of less political importance than those in a treaty. [Latin *conventiō* meeting, agreement.]

con·ven·tion·al (kən ven′shən əl) *adj.* **1.** conforming to traditional or generally accepted practices or standards; not original or new: *a conventional approach to a problem.* **2.** established by, or in accordance with, accepted custom or usage; customary: *conventional rules of etiquette.* **3.** not involving or using nuclear weapons or energy: *conventional warfare.* **4.** following accepted models, standards, or traditions in art. —**con·ven′tion·al·ly,** *adv.*

con·ven·tion·al·ism (kən ven′shən əl iz′əm) *n.* **1.** adherence to, or regard for, that which is conventional. **2.** that which is conventional, as an idea, custom, or practice.

con·ven·tion·al·i·ty (kən ven′shə nal′ə tē) *pl.,* -**ties.** *n.* **1.** quality or character of being conventional: *the conventionality of his opinions.* **2.** conventional behavior or opinion; adherence to convention. **3.** con-

at; āpe; cär; end; mē; it; īce; hot; ōld; fôrk; wood; fōōl; oil; out; up; ūse; turn; sing; thin; **th**is; zh in treasure; ə in ago, taken, pencil, lemon, circus.

ventional rule, practice, or custom: *the conventionalities of polite society.*

con·ven·tion·al·ize (kən ven′shən əl īz′) **-ized, -iz·ing.** *v.t.*
1. to make conventional. **2.** to represent in a conventional manner.

con·ven·tu·al (kən ven′chŏō əl) *adj.* of, relating to, or belonging to a convent. —*n.* member of a convent.

con·verge (kən vurj′) **-verged, -verg·ing.** *v.i.* **1.** to come together or tend to come together at a place or point: *The roads converged at the stadium.* **2.** to come together, as in a common interest or conclusion; focus or center: *All attention converged on the center ring at the circus.* —*v.t.* to cause to converge. [Late Latin *convergere* to incline together, from Latin *con-* together + *vergere* to incline.]

con·ver·gence (kən vur′jəns) *n.* **1.** act or process of converging; being converged. **2.** degree or point of converging. —**con·ver′gent,** *adj.*

con·ver·gen·cy (kən vur′jən sē) *pl.,* **-cies.** *n.* convergence.

converging lens, lens that is thicker in the middle than at the edges, causing light rays to converge and focus on a point.

con·vers·a·ble (kən vur′sə bəl) *adj.* **1.** easy or pleasant to converse with; affable. **2.** inclined to converse; fond of talking. **3.** relating to or proper for conversation. —**con·vers′a·bly,** *adv.*

con·ver·sant (kən vur′sənt, kon′vər-) *adj.* familiar or acquainted, esp. by study: *to become conversant with the law.* —**con·ver′sant·ly,** *adv.*

con·ver·sa·tion (kon′vər sā′shən) *n.* informal or familiar talk between people.

con·ver·sa·tion·al (kon′vər sā′shən əl) *adj.* **1.** of or characteristic of conversation: *a conversational tone.* **2.** given to or adept at conversation. —**con′ver·sa′tion·al·ly,** *adv.*

con·ver·sa·tion·al·ist (kon′vər sā′shən əl ist) *n.* one who is given to or adept at conversation.

con·verse¹ (*v.,* kən vurs′; *n.,* kon′vurs′) **-versed, -vers·ing.** *v.i.* to talk informally or familiarly; engage in or hold a conversation: *Although they were strangers, they conversed with ease.* —*n.* informal or familiar talk; conversation. [Old French *converser* to associate with, from Latin *conversārī* to live with.] —**con·vers′er,** *n.*

con·verse² (*adj.,* kən vurs′, kon′vurs; *n.,* kon′vurs) *adj.* turned about in order or action; reversed; opposite; contrary. —*n.* **1.** that which is opposite or contrary to something else. **2.** proposition in logic which is derived from another by conversion. The statement *Health is not wealth* is the converse of the statement *Wealth is not health.* [Latin *conversus,* past participle of *convertere* to turn about.] —**con·verse′ly,** *adv.*

con·ver·sion (kən vur′zhən, -shən) *n.* **1.** act or process of converting or being converted; change in character, condition, or function; transformation. **2.a.** change by which one adopts a different belief, opinion, or course of action. **b.** adoption of a religion or religious way of life. **3.** unlawful appropriation and use of another person's property. **4.** interchange of the subject and predicate terms of a proposition in logic. **5.** play in football by which a team that has just scored a touchdown makes an extra point or points if the ball is kicked between the goal posts or carried or passed into the end zone.

con·vert (*v.,* kən vurt′; *n.,* kon′vurt) *v.t.* **1.** to change in character, condition, or function; transform: *to convert salt water to fresh water.* **2.a.** to cause (someone) to change a belief, opinion, or course of action: *We'll soon convert him to our way of thinking.* **b.** to cause (someone) to adopt a religion or religious way of life: *to convert a classmate to Christianity.* **3.** to exchange for an equivalent: *He converted his francs into dollars.* **4.** to appropriate and use (another person's property) unlawfully. **5.** to transpose the subject and predicate terms of (a proposition) in logic. —*v.i.* to change one's beliefs, course of action, or conduct. —*n.* one who has been converted, as from one religious belief to another. [Old French *convertir* to turn, going back to Latin *convertere* to turn about, change.]

con·vert·er (kən vur′tər) *n.* **1.** one who or that which converts. **2.** machine for changing alternating electric current to direct current or vice versa. **3.** any of various other machines or devices used to change the form of energy. **4.** Bessemer converter.

con·vert·i·ble (kən vur′tə bəl) *adj.* **1.** that can be converted. **2.** (of an automobile) having a roof that may be folded back or removed. —*n.* automobile with a roof that is convertible. —**con·vert′i·bil′i·ty,** *n.* —**con·vert′i·bly,** *adv.*

con·vex (kon veks′, kən-, kon′veks) *adj.* curved outward, as the outside of a circle or sphere. Opposed to **concave.** [Latin *convexus* vaulted, arched.]

Convex   Concave

Convex and concave surfaces

con·vex·i·ty (kon vek′sə tē) *pl.,* **-ties.** *n.* **1.** quality or condition of being convex. **2.** a convex surface or thing.

con·vex·o·con·cave (kon vek′sō kon kāv′) *adj.* convex on one side and concave on the other, with the convex side having a greater degree of curvature.

con·vey (kən vā′) *v.t.* **1.a.** to take or carry from one place to another;

transport: *The train conveyed the supplies to the warehouse.* **b.** to serve as the medium or path for; conduct: *pipes that convey water from a reservoir to a city.* **2.** to express; impart; communicate: *to convey the impression of being calm, to convey an idea through a painting.* **3.** to transfer the ownership of, as property or title to real property, from one person to another. [Anglo-Norman *conveier* to conduct, going back to Latin *cum* with + *via* road, way.] —**con·vey′a·ble,** *adj.* —**Syn. 1.** see **carry.**

con·vey·ance (kən vā′əns) *n.* **1.** act of conveying; communication; transport. **2.** that which transports or carries, esp. a vehicle: *buses and other public conveyances.* **3.a.** transfer of the ownership of real property from one person to another. **b.** document by which such a transfer is made.

con·vey·anc·er (kən vā′ən sər) *n.* one who is engaged in conveyancing.

con·vey·anc·ing (kən vā′ən sing) *n.* business dealing with the transfer of ownership of real property, including the preparation of documents and the investigation of titles to land.

con·vey·er (kən vā′ər) *also,* **con·vey·or.** *n.* **1.** one who or that which conveys. **2.** conveyor belt.

conveyor belt *also,* **conveyer belt.** mechanical device for transporting objects over relatively short distances, usually designed as a continuous belt or series of rollers.

con·vict (*v.,* kən vikt′; *n.,* kon′vikt) *v.t.* **1.** to find (someone) guilty of a criminal charge; prove (someone) guilty: *She was convicted of murder. The fingerprints found on the gun were used to convict her.* **2.** to arouse a sense of guilt in (someone): *convicted by his own conscience.* —*n.* **1.** one serving a prison sentence, esp. for an extended period of time. **2.** one who has been convicted by a court of law. [Latin *convictus,* past participle of *convincere* to prove clearly, refute, overcome.]

con·vic·tion (kən vik′shən) *n.* **1.a.** act of finding or pronouncing (someone) guilty of a criminal charge. **b.** state of being found or pronounced guilty. **2.** firmly established opinion or belief: *the courage of his convictions.* **3.** state of being convinced: *his conviction of the seriousness of the matter.*

con·vince (kən vins′) **-vinced, -vinc·ing.** *v.t.* to cause (someone) to believe or feel certain; cause to believe; persuade by argument or evidence: *We convinced her that it was her duty to stay.* [Latin *convincere* to prove clearly.] —**con·vin′ci·ble,** *adj.* —**Syn.** see **persuade.**

con·vinc·ing (kən vin′sing) *adj.* having power to convince; able to be believed; persuasive: *a convincing speech, her convincing performance.* —**con·vinc′ing·ly,** *adv.* —**con·vinc′ing·ness,** *n.*

con·viv·i·al (kən viv′ē əl) *adj.* **1.** fond of merriment and parties with good company; jovial; sociable. **2.** relating to or characteristic of a feast or jovial party; festive: *a convivial atmosphere.* —**con·viv′i·al′i·ty** (kən viv′ē al′ə tē), *n.* —**con·viv′i·al·ly,** *adv.*

con·vo·ca·tion (kon′və kā′shən) *n.* **1.** group of persons assembled by summons; assembly: *There was a convocation before the graduation exercises.* **2.** a calling together of such a group; summons to assemble.

con·voke (kən vōk′) **-voked, -vok·ing.** *v.t.* to call together; summon to meet or assemble. [Latin *convocāre.*] —**con·vok′er,** *n.*

con·vo·lute (kon′və lōōt′) **-lut·ed, -lut·ing.** *v.t., v.i.* to coil up or twist intricately; wind in and out. —*adj.* convoluted. [Latin *convolūtus,* past participle of *convolvere* to roll together.]

con·vo·lut·ed (kon′və lōō′tid) *adj.* turned in or wound up upon itself; intricately twisted, wound, or coiled.

con·vo·lu·tion (kon′və lōō′shən) *n.* **1.** one of the windings, twists, or coils of something convoluted. **2.** any of the irregular folds on the surface of the brain. **3.** act of convoluting; being convoluted.

con·vol·vu·lus (kən vol′vyə ləs) *pl.,* **-lus·es** or **-li** (-lī′). *n.* bindweed. [Latin *convolvulus,* from *convolvere* to roll together; with reference to its twining runners.]

con·voy (*n.,* kon′voi; *v.,* also kən voi′) *n.* **1.** group, as of ships or vehicles, traveling with a protective escort: *The convoy consisted of an aircraft carrier, two battleships, and five troop carriers.* **2.** group, as of warships, troops, or aircraft, that acts as a protective escort: *A convoy of ships escorted the submarine out of harbor.* **3.** any group of persons or vehicles traveling together: *A convoy of oil trucks passed us on the highway.* **4.** protection afforded by an escort: *to sail under the convoy of a large fleet.* —*v.t.* to accompany or escort in order to afford protection. [Old French *convoier* to accompany on the way, going back to Latin *cum* with + *via* road, way.]

con·vulse (kən vuls′) **-vulsed, -vuls·ing.** *v.t.* **1.** to cause violent shaking, agitation, or disturbance in: *a revolution that convulsed the nation.* **2.** to cause to shake with strong emotion or violent fits of laughter: *He stood convulsed in rage. His antics had the children convulsed in laughter.* **3.** to throw into muscular convulsions. [Latin *convulsus,* past participle of *convellere* to tear up, wrench.]

con·vul·sion (kən vul′shən) *n.* **1.** violent, involuntary contraction or

at; āpe; cär; end; mē; it; īce; hot; ōld; fôrk; wood; fōōl; oil; out; up; ūse; turn; sing; thin; this; zh in treasure; ə in ago, taken, pencil, lemon, circus.

221

series of contractions of the muscles; spasm. **2.** violent fit of laughter. **3.** violent disturbance or agitation; upheaval.

con·vul·sive (kən vul′siv) *adj.* **1.** of, like, or producing a convulsion or convulsions: *a convulsive shock.* **2.** having or characterized by convulsions: *convulsive disorders, convulsive laughter.*

co·ny (kō′nē) *pl.,* **-nies.** *also,* **co·ney.** *n.* **1.** rabbit fur. **2.** rabbit. **3.** pika. **4.** in the Old Testament, a small rabbitlike animal, probably a hyrax. [Anglo-Norman *conil, conin* rabbit, from Latin *cunīculus;* possibly of Iberian origin.]

coo (kōō) *n.* soft, murmuring sound, as that made by a pigeon or dove. —*v.i.* **cooed, coo·ing. 1.** to make a soft, murmuring sound, as that made by a pigeon or dove. **2.** to speak softly and lovingly; murmur in gentle, loving tones. —*v.t.* to express or utter with a coo: *He cooed his answer to her.* [Imitative.] —**coo′er,** *n.*

cook (kook) *v.t.* **1.** to prepare (food) for eating by the application of heat, as by roasting, boiling, baking, or frying. **2.** to prepare (something) by the application of heat. **3. to cook up.** *Informal.* **a.** to prepare; concoct: *to cook up trouble.* **b.** to devise or invent, esp. in order to deceive: *to cook up a good excuse.* —*v.i.* **1.** (of food) to undergo cooking; be cooked. **2.** to prepare food for eating; act as a cook. **3.** *Informal.* to undergo preparation: *How long has that plan been cooking?* **4.** *Informal.* to take place; occur; happen: *What's cooking?* —*n.* one who prepares food for table. [Old English *cōc* a cook, from Late Latin *cocus,* from Latin *coquus.*]

Cook, James (kook) 1728–79, English navigator.

cook·book (kook′book′) *n.* book containing recipes and other information about food and its preparation.

cook·er·y (kook′ər ē) *pl.,* **-er·ies.** *n.* **1.** art or practice of preparing and cooking food. **2.** place for cooking and serving food.

cook·ie (kook′ē) *also,* **cook·y** *n.* small, usually flat cake baked from sweetened dough, often with nuts, candy bits, or filling. [Dutch *koekje* small cake.]

Cook Islands, group of islands in the western part of the South Pacific, east of Australia, a possession of New Zealand. Land area, approx. 93 sq. mi. Pop. (1969 est.), 20,000.

cook·out (kook′out′) *n.* gathering at which food is cooked and eaten outdoors.

Cook Strait, body of water in New Zealand, separating North Island and South Island.

cook·y (kook′ē) *pl.,* **cook·ies.** *n.* cookie.

cool (kōōl) *adj.* **1.** moderately cold; providing warmth but not extremely cold: *a cool breeze.* **2.** not excited; calm; rational; composed: *to be cool in the face of danger.* **3.** lacking enthusiasm or warmth; not cordial: *His play received a cool response from the critics.* **4.** having or showing a detached audacity or impudence: *a cool lie, a cool maneuver.* **5.** giving protection or relief from heat: *a cool summer dress.* **6.** *Slang.* excellent; fabulous; great. **7.** *Informal.* without exaggeration; actual: *a cool million dollars.* **8.** (of color) suggesting coolness or serenity: *Blue and green are usually considered cool colors.* —*adv. Informal.* in a cool manner; with coolness: *to play it cool.* —*n.* **1.** that which is cool: *the cool of the day.* **2.** *Informal.* composure; rationality; calmness: *to keep one's cool.* —*v.t.* **1.** to make less warm. **2.** to lessen the intensity of; moderate; calm. **3. to cool one's heels.** *Informal.* to wait or be kept waiting at great length. —*v.i.* **1.** to become less warm. **2.** to lessen in intensity or excitement; become calmer. [Old English *cōl* moderately cold.] —**cool′ly,** *adv.* —**cool′ness,** *n.* —**Syn.** *adj.* 1. see **cold.**

cool·ant (kōō′lənt) *n.* substance, usually a liquid, used to cool machinery, as in an automobile engine or a dentist's drill.

cool·er (kōō′lər) *n.* **1.** container or apparatus for keeping or making something cool. **2.** that which cools, as an iced drink. **3.** *Slang.* jail.

cool·head·ed (kōōl′hed′id) *adj.* not easily excited or disturbed; calm.

Cool·idge, Calvin (kōō′lij) 1872–1933, thirtieth president of the United States, from 1923 to 1929.

coo·lie (kōō′lē) *n.* unskilled Oriental laborer, esp. one working for low wages. —*adj.* of or characteristic of a coolie: *coolie wages.* [Hindi *kūli* laborer; of uncertain origin.]

coomb (kōōm, kōm) combe.

coon (kōōn) *n.* raccoon.

coop (kōōp, koop) *n.* **1.** cage, pen, or enclosure for fowl or small animals. **2.** any place of confinement; jail. **3. to fly the coop.** *Slang.* to escape, as from jail or confinement. —*v.t.* to confine in or as in a coop (often with *in* or *up*): *They cooped the dog in the kitchen until the guests had gone.* [Latin *cūpa* cask.]

coop., cooperative.

coop·er (kōō′pər, koop′ər) *n.* one who makes or repairs barrels, casks, and similar containers. —*v.t.,* *v.i.* to make or repair (barrels, casks, and similar containers). [Middle Dutch *cūper* a cooper, from *cūpe* cask, from Latin *cūpa.*]

Coo·per (kōō′pər, koop′ər) **1. James Fen·i·more** (fen′ə môr′). 1789–1851, U.S. novelist and social critic. **2. Peter.** 1791–1883, U.S. industrialist and philanthropist.

coop·er·age (kōō′pər ij, koop′ər-) *n.* **1.** work or business of a cooper. **2.** place where a cooper works. **3.** fee charged for a cooper's work.

co·op·er·ate (kō op′ə rāt′) *-at·ed, -at·ing. also,* **co·op·er·ate.** *v.i.* to work or act with another or others for a common purpose; unite in action: *The three clubs cooperated in planning a party.* [Late Latin *cooperātus,* past participle of *cooperārī* to work together, from Latin *co-* together + *operārī* to work.] —**co·op′er·a′tor,** *n.*

co·op·er·a·tion (kō op′ə rā′shən) *also,* **co·op·er·a·tion.** *n.* act or process of cooperating; working with another for a common purpose.

co·op·er·a·tive (kō op′ər ə tiv, kō op′rə-, kō op′ə rā′-) *also,* **co·op·er·a·tive.** *adj.* **1.** willing to work together with others: *a cooperative child.* **2.** of or characterized by cooperation: *a cooperative effort to paint the kitchen.* **3.** of, relating to, or designating a cooperative. —*n.* business enterprise, as a store or apartment house, that is owned and operated by its members, who share its profits or benefits. —**co·op′er·a·tive·ly,** *adv.* —**co·op′er·a·tive·ness,** *n.*

co·or·di·nate (*v.,* kō ôr′də nāt′; *adj.,n.,* kō ôr′də nit, -nāt′) *-nat·ed, -nat·ing. also,* **co·or·di·nate.** *v.t.* **1.** to bring into proper order, esp. for harmonious and integrated action; adjust: *to coordinate the functions of government agencies, to coordinate eye movements.* —*v.i.* to work in harmony or in an integrated way. —*adj.* **1.** of equal rank or importance; of the same order. **2.** of, relating to, or using coordination or coordinates. —*n.* **1.** one who or that which is equal in rank or importance (to someone or something). **2.** *Mathematics.* one of a set of numbers that define the position of a point in a line, in a plane, or in three-dimensional space. [From COORDINATION.] —**co·or′di·nate·ly,** *adv.* —**co·or′di·nate·ness,** *n.* —**co·or′di·na·tive,** *adj.*

co·or·di·na·tion (kō ôr′də nā′shən) *also,* **co·or·di·na·tion.** *n.* **1.** act of coordinating; being coordinated. **2.** harmonious, integrated action or functioning: *good muscular coordination.* [Late Latin *coōrdinātiō* arrangement in the same order, from Latin *co-* with + *ōrdinātiō* arrangement.]

coot (kōōt) *n.* **1.** any of various water birds, genus *Fulica,* of temperate and tropical marsh lands, resembling small, plump ducks and having short wings, lobed toes, and usually black or gray plumage, esp. the **American coot,** *F. americana* or **mud hen.** Length: 16 inches. **2.** scoter. **3.** *Informal.* fool; simpleton. [Possibly of Low German origin.]

Coot

coot·ie (kōō′tē) *n. Slang.* louse.

cop (kop) *n. Informal.* policeman. —*v.t.* **copped, cop·ping.** *Slang.* to steal. [Possibly from Dutch *kapen* to steal, from Frisian *kāpia* to take away, buy, going back to Latin *caupō* tradesman.]

co·pa·cet·ic (kō′pə set′ik) copesetic.

co·pal (kō′pəl, -pal) *n.* any of a group of hard resins obtained from various tropical trees or from their fossil remains. Copals have a high melting point and are used chiefly in making varnish. [Spanish *copal,* from Nahuatl *copalli* resin.]

co·part·ner (kō pärt′nər, kō′pärt′nər) *n.* partner. —**co·part′ner·ship′,** *n.*

cope¹ (kōp) **coped, cop·ing.** *v.i.* to contend or deal, esp. with success; be able to handle (with *with*): *to cope with one's problems. We don't have enough help to cope with all the work.* [Old French *co(l)per* to strike, from *co(l)p* a blow, going back to Latin *colaphus,* from Greek *kolaphos.*]

cope² (kōp) *n.* **1.** long cape worn over the alb by bishops, priests, and other clergymen during processions and certain religious services. **2.** something resembling a cope in shape or function, as a canopy, a vaulted roof, or the sky. **3.** coping. —*v.t.* **coped, cop·ing.** to cover or furnish with a cope or coping. [Late Latin *cap(p)a* hood, cape; of uncertain origin.]

co·peck (kō′pek′) kopeck.

Co·pen·ha·gen (kō′pən hā′gən, -hä′-) *n.* capital of Denmark, on the island of Zealand. It is the largest city in Scandinavia and a major port of northern Europe. Pop. (1966 est.), 863,691.

Co·per·ni·can (kə pur′ni kən) *adj.* of or relating to Copernicus or to his theory that the earth, like the other planets, revolves around the sun and that the apparent movement of the stars is due to the earth's rotation on its axis.

Co·per·ni·cus, Nik·o·la·us (kə pur′ni kəs; nik′ə lā′əs) 1473–1543, Polish astronomer.

co·pe·set·ic (kō′pə set′ik) *also,* **co·pa·cet·ic, co·pe·set·tic.** *adj. Slang.* fine; in good shape. [Of uncertain origin.]

Cope²

cope·stone (kōp'stōn') *n.* **1.** top stone of a wall or building; stone used for or in a coping. **2.** finishing touch; crowning point; completion. [COPE² + STONE.]

cop·i·er (kop'ē ər) *n.* **1.** one who or that which makes copies, esp. a machine that makes copies of letters, documents, or other materials. **2.** one who imitates.

co·pi·lot (kō'pī'lət) *n.* second pilot in an aircraft who assists and relieves the pilot.

cop·ing (kō'ping) *n.* layer of brick or stone on the top of a wall, usually with a slope for shedding water. [COPE² + -ING¹.]

coping saw, narrow-bladed saw in a U-shaped frame, used for very fine work, such as cutting sharp angles or curves.

Coping saw

co·pi·ous (kō'pē əs) *adj.* large in quantity; plentiful; abundant: *copious notes, copious tears.* [Latin *cōpiōsus*, from *cōpia* abundance.] —**co'pi·ous·ly,** *adv.* —**co'pi·ous·ness,** *n.* —**Syn.** see **abundant.**

co·pla·nar (kō plā'nər) *adj. Geometry.* contained in the same plane.

Cop·land, Aaron (kōp'lənd) 1900—, U.S. composer.

co·pol·y·mer (kō pol'ə mər) *n.* compound formed by the polymerization of two or more dissimilar molecules, used in making plastics and synthetic rubber. —*v.t.* to make into a copolymer.

co·pol·y·mer·ize (kō pol'ə mə rīz') -ized, -iz·ing. *v.i.* to change into a copolymer. —**co·pol'y·mer·i·za'tion,** *n.*

cop·per (kop'ər) *n.* **1.** lustrous, yellow-red metallic element that is highly ductile and malleable and an excellent conductor of heat and electricity. The widespread use of copper in alloys makes it the most useful nonferrous metal. Symbol: **Cu** See **element** for table. **2.** lustrous reddish-brown color. **3.** coin made of copper or bronze, as a penny. **4.** large boiler or cauldron, used esp. on ships. **5.** *Slang.* policeman. —*adj.* **1.** made of copper. **2.** reddish-brown. —*v.t.* to cover or coat with copper. [Old English *copor* this metal, going back to Late Latin *cuprum*, from Latin *(aes) Cyprium* (metal) of Cyprus, going back to Greek *Kypros* Cyprus, one of the main sources of copper in ancient times.] —**cop'per·y,** *adj.*

cop·per·as (kop'ər əs) *n.* greenish crystalline sulfate of iron, used in medicine, in photography, and in making inks and dyes. Formula: FeSO₄·7H₂O [Old French *cop(u)perose,* from Late Latin *cuprī rosa* rose of copper. See COPPER, ROSE¹.]

cop·per·head (kop'ər hed') *n.* **1.** poisonous snake, *Agkistrodon contortrix,* usually inhabiting rocky and overgrown areas of the United States, having a copper-colored head and a light brown body with dark brown markings. Length: to 4½ feet. **2. Copperhead.** Northerner who sympathized with the Confederacy during the American Civil War.

cop·per·plate (kop'ər plāt') *n.* **1.** thin piece of copper etched or engraved with a picture, design, or writing. **2.** print made from such a plate. **3.** printing process using such plates.

cop·per·smith (kop'ər smith') *n.* one who works with copper, esp. one who makes objects from copper.

copper sulfate, chemical compound of copper, sulfur, oxygen, and water, occurring in the form of blue powder or efflorescent crystals. When dehydrated, it becomes white. Formula: CuSO₄·5H₂O Also, **blue vitriol.**

cop·pice (kop'is) *n.* copse.

cop·ra (kop'rə) *n.* dried meat of the coconut, the source of coconut oil. [Portuguese *copra,* from Malayalam *koppara* coconut, possibly going back to Sanskrit *kharparah* skull.]

copse (kops) *n.* thicket or grove of small trees or bushes. [Old French *copeiz* cut wood, from *col(l)per* to strike. See COPE¹.]

Copt (kopt) *n.* **1.** native Egyptian descended from the ancient Egyptians. **2.** member of the Coptic Church. [Modern Latin *Coptus,* through Arabic and Coptic, from Greek *Aigyptios* Egyptian.]

cop·ter (kop'tər) *n. Informal.* helicopter.

Cop·tic (kop'tik) *adj.* of or relating to the Copts, their language, or their culture. —*n.* ancient language of the Hamitic family, descended from Egyptian, and formerly spoken by the Copts. It is now used only as the liturgical language of the Coptic Church.

Coptic Church, Christian church of Egypt and formerly of Ethiopia, adhering to the doctrine of Monophysitism and governed by a patriarch.

cop·u·la (kop'yə lə) *pl.* **-las** or **-lae** (-lē). *n.* word that links the subject and the predicate, usually some form of the verb *to be* or such verbs as *seem, feel,* and *smell.* [Latin *cōpula* bond, connection.]

cop·u·late (kop'yə lāt') -lat·ed, -lat·ing. *v.i.* to unite in sexual intercourse. —*adj.* past participle of *cōpulāre* to bind together.]

cop·u·la·tion (kop'yə lā'shən) *n.* **1.** sexual intercourse. **2.** *Archaic.* act of coupling; joining; union.

cop·u·la·tive (kop'yə lā'tiv, -lə tiv) *adj.* **1.** acting as a copula; linking subject and predicate words or phrases. In the sentence *The cousins were also friends, were* is a copulative verb. **2.** joining coordinate words,

phrases, or clauses. The word *or* is a copulative conjunction. —*n.* copulative word. —**cop'u·la'tive·ly,** *adv.*

cop·y (kop'ē) *pl.* **cop·ies.** *n.* **1.** reproduction of an original; duplicate; imitation. **2.** one of a number of reproductions of the same work: *The poet gave me an autographed copy of his new book.* **3.a.** written, illustrative, or other material to be set for reproduction in a newspaper, book, or the like. **b.** written or printed matter for use in a book, advertisement, or the like, as distinguished from illustrative material. **c.** subject of an article, story, or book: *Election campaigns always make good copy.* **4.** *Archaic.* that which is to be imitated or reproduced; model; pattern. —*v.t., v.i.* **cop·ied, cop·y·ing. 1.** to make a copy of (something); reproduce. **2.** to make or do something in imitation of (something or somebody else); imitate. [Old French *copie* transcript, plenty, going back to Latin *cōpia* plenty; the meaning "transcript" developed from the sense of a plentiful supply of copies.] —**Syn.** *n.* **1.** see **duplicate.** *v.t.* **1.** see **imitate.**

cop·y·book (kop'ē book') *n.* book containing examples of handwriting for students to copy. —*adj.* commonplace; conventional; trite: *copybook phrases, copybook morality.*

cop·y·cat (kop'ē kat') *n. Informal.* one who constantly imitates others.

cop·y·hold (kop'ē hōld') *n.* tenure of land in England granted at the will of the lord of a manor and confirmed only by being recorded in the court roll of the manor.

cop·y·hold·er (kop'ē hōl'dər) *n.* **1.** one who reads copy to a proofreader. **2.** device for holding copy, as for a typist or typesetter. **3.** one who owns land by copyhold.

cop·y·ist (kop'ē ist) *n.* **1.** one who makes copies, esp. of documents or manuscripts. **2.** one who imitates.

cop·y·right (kop'ē rīt') *n.* exclusive right to produce, publish, or sell a literary or artistic work, granted by law for a certain number of years. —*v.t.* to obtain copyright for. —*adj.* relating to or protected by copyright.

cop·y·writ·er (kop'ē rī'tər) *n.* one who writes copy, esp. for advertisements.

co·quet (kō ket') -quet·ted, -quet·ting. *also,* **co·quette.** *v.i.* **1.** to coquette; flirt. **2.** to deal with something without seriousness; trifle; toy. [French *coqueter* to flirt; literally, to act like a cock, from *coquet* little cock, flirt, diminutive of *coq* cock¹; of imitative origin.]

co·quet·ry (kō'kə trē, kō ket'rē) *pl.* **-ries.** *n.* behavior or act of a coquette; flirtation.

co·quette (kō ket') *n.* woman who tries to interest men by pretending affection or attraction; flirt. —*v.i.,* **-quet·ted, -quet·ting.** to coquet. [French *coquette,* feminine of *coquet.* See COQUET.] —**co·quet'tish,** *adj.* —**co·quet'tish·ly,** *adv.* —**co·quet'tish·ness,** *n.*

co·qui·na (kō kē'nə) *n.* soft, whitish limestone made up of fragments of sea shells and corals, used for building. [Spanish *coquina* shellfish, probably going back to Latin *concha* shell, mussel.]

cor-, form of **com-** before *r,* as in *corrupt.*

cor. 1. corner. **2.** correction; corrected. **3.** corresponding. **4.** coroner.

Cor. 1. Corinthians. **2.** Coroner.

cor·a·cle (kôr'ə kəl, kor'-) *n.* small, light boat made by stretching animal skins or other waterproof material over a basketlike framework. [Welsh *corwgl.*]

cor·a·coid (kôr'ə koid, kor'-) *n.* **1.** bone extending from the shoulder blade to the breastbone in birds and reptiles. **2.** rudimentary bone projecting from the shoulder blade toward the breastbone in mammals. —*adj.* of, relating to, or designating either of these bones. [Modern Latin *coracoides,* from Greek *korakoeidēs* like a crow; because its shape resembles a crow's beak.]

cor·al (kôr'əl, kor'-) *n.* **1.** hard, skeletal substance resembling limestone secreted by certain polyps, usually found in tropical waters. **2.** any of the polyps that secrete this substance. **3.** mass or structure formed by the skeletons of these animals, such as a reef. **4.** pinkish-red color. —*adj.* **1.** made of coral. **2.** deep pink; pinkish-red. [Old French *coral* the substance, from Latin *corallum,* from Greek *korallion;* probably of Semitic origin.]

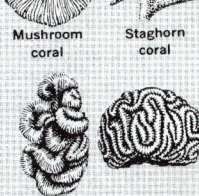

Mushroom coral · Staghorn coral · Rose coral · Brain coral

Types of coral

Coral Gables, city in southern Florida. Pop. (1970), 42,494.

coral reef, reef formed chiefly by the gradual build-up into a large mass of the limestone skeletons of certain species of coral.

Coral Sea, southwestern arm of the Pacific, off the coast of northeast-

at; āpe; cär; end; mē; it; īce; hot; ōld; fôrk; wood; fōol; oil; out; up; ūse; turn; sing; thin; this; zh in treasure; ə in ago, taken, pencil, lemon, circus.

223

ern Australia. It was the site of an American victory over the Japanese in 1942, during World War II.

coral snake, any of several narrow-headed, venomous snakes, family Elapidae, found in many parts of the world. Only two species are found in the United States: *Micrurus fulvius,* the common or eastern coral snake, having wide red and black bands, and *M. euryxanthus,* a rare species of Arizona and New Mexico. Length: to 3 feet.

Coral snake

cor·bel (kôr′bəl) *n.* bracketlike architectural feature, usually of stone, projecting from the side of a wall and supporting an overhanging structure; ancon; console. See **console** for illustration. —*v.t.* **-beled** or **-belled, -bel·ing** or **-bel·ling.** to provide with or support by a corbel or corbels. [Old French *corbel* corbel, raven, going back to Latin *corvus* raven; because of its resemblance to a raven's beak.]

Cor·cy·ra (kôr sī′rə) *n.* see Corfu.

cord (kôrd) *n.* **1.** string or small rope made of several strands twisted or woven together. **2.** electric wires encased in rubber or other insulating material, used to connect an appliance to an outlet or to make other electrical connections. **3.** anatomical structure resembling a cord. **4.a.** rib or ridge on the surface of a fabric. **b.** fabric having such ribs

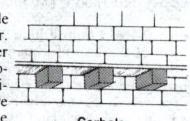

Corbels

or ridges, as corduroy. **5.** quantity of wood, usually sawed, equaling 128 cubic feet, usually arranged in a pile 4 feet wide, 4 feet high, and 8 feet long. See **weights and measures** for table. —*v.t.* **1.** to bind or fasten with cord; furnish with a cord. **2.** to pile (wood) in cords. [Old French *corde* rope, string, from Latin *chorda* gut, string of a musical instrument, from Greek *chordē.* Doublet of CHORD².]

cord·age (kôr′dij) *n.* **1.** cords or ropes collectively, esp. those in a ship's rigging. **2.** quantity of cut wood, measured in cords, in a given area.

cor·date (kôr′dāt) *adj.* heart-shaped: *a cordate shell, a cordate leaf.* [Modern Latin *cordatus,* from Latin *cor* heart.]

cord·ed (kôr′did) *adj.* **1.** fastened with cord. **2.** having ridges or twills; ribbed. **3.** (of timber) piled in cords.

cor·dial (kôr′jəl) *adj.* genuinely warm and friendly; hearty: *a cordial greeting.* —*n.* **1.** liqueur. **2.** stimulant such as a drink or medicine. [Medieval Latin *cordialis* relating to the heart, from Latin *cor* heart.] —**cor′dial·ly,** *adv.* —**cor′dial·ness,** *n.*

cor·di·al·i·ty (kôr jal′ə tē, kôr′jē al′-) *pl.* **-ties.** *n.* genuine warmth or friendliness; heartiness.

cor·dil·le·ra (kôrd′əl yãr′ə, kôr dil′ər ə) *n.* extensive series of mountain ranges, usually constituting the main mountain chain of a large land area. [Spanish *cordillera,* from *cordilla,* diminutive of *cuerda* string, chain, from Latin *chorda* cord.]

Cor·dil·le·ras (kôr′dəl yãr′əz, kôr dil′ər əz) *n.pl.* **1.** mountain system extending from Alaska to Cape Horn, including the Rocky Mountain system of North America and the Andes range in South America. **2.** that part of this system located in South America; the Andes. **3.** that part of this system located in North America. —**Cor′dil·le′ran,** *adj.*

cord·ite (kôr′dīt) *n.* smokeless gunpowder consisting of nitroglycerin, nitrocellulose, and petroleum jelly. [CORD + -ITE¹; because of its resemblance to cord.]

cor·do·ba (kôr′də bə) *n.* monetary unit of Nicaragua equal to 100 centavos.

Cór·do·ba (kôr′də bə; *Spanish* kôr′dô vä) *also,* **Cor·do·va** (kôr dō′-və, kôr′də-) *n.* **1.** city in southwestern Spain. Pop. (1968 est.), 225,562. **2.** city in north-central Argentina. Pop. (1960), 586,015.

cor·don (kôr′dən) *n.* **1.** line, as of men, ships, or barricades, set up to guard or close off an area. **2.a.** cord or ribbon worn, usually diagonally across the chest, as a badge of honor or rank. **b.** cord or ribbon worn as an ornament. —*v.t.* **1.** to form or place a cordon around (with *off*): *to cordon off an area for a parade.* **2.** to separate from contact with or prevent communication with from the outside (with *off*): *to cordon off a village to search for snipers.* [French *cordon* ribbon, from *corde.* See CORD.]

Cor·do·van (kôr′də vən) *adj.* **1.** of or relating to Córdoba. **2.** **cordovan,** of, relating to, or made of cordovan. —*n.* **1.** native or inhabitant of Córdoba. **2.** **cordovan. a.** soft, fine-grained leather usually made of split horsehide, originally made of goatskin in Córdoba, Spain. **b.** shoe made of this leather. [Spanish *cordobán* this leather, from *Córdoba* Córdoba.]

cor·du·roy (kôr′də roi′, kôr′də roi′) *n.* **1.** fabric, usually made of cotton with a ribbed pile surface, used for clothing and upholstery. The

ribs, or wales, in corduroy vary in width and in weight. **2. corduroys.** slacks made of corduroy. —*adj.* made of corduroy. [Possibly from French *corde du roi* literally, cord of the king, said to have been made originally of silk and used for hunting clothes by French kings.]

corduroy road, road constructed of logs laid side by side transversely, as over low, marshy ground.

cord·wain·er (kôrd′wā′nər) *n.* *Archaic.* one who works in cordovan leather, esp. a shoemaker. [Old French *cordoanier,* from *cordoan* cordovan leather, going back to Spanish *cordobán.* See CORDOVAN.]

cord·wood (kôrd′wood′) *n.* wood sold by the cord or cut for piling in cords.

core (kôr) *n.* **1.** hard or papery central part of certain fruits, such as apples and pears, containing the seeds. **2.** central or essential part: *an argument built around a core of fact, to get to the core of the matter.* **3.** innermost part of anything, as a piece of wood to which veneer is glued or a central strand of wire around which other strands are twisted. **4.** ferromagnetic material forming the central part of an electromagnet, induction coil, or armature. —*v.t.* **cored, cor·ing.** to remove the core of: *to core an apple.* [Of uncertain origin.] —**cor′er,** *n.* —**Syn.** *n.* **2.** see heart.

CORE (kôr) Congress of Racial Equality.

co·re·op·sis (kôr′ē op′sis) *n.* **1.** daisylike flower head of any of a group of plants, genus *Coreopsis,* of the composite family, usually yellow, orange, or red in color. **2.** plant bearing this flower head, having lobed or blade-shaped leaves and small, dry fruit. Also, **tick′seed, cal′li·op·sis.** [Modern Latin *coreopsis,* from Greek *koris* bedbug + *opsis* appearance; because of the resemblance of its seed to an insect.]

co·re·spond·ent (kō′ri spon′dənt) *n.* joint defendant, esp. one charged in a divorce suit with having committed adultery with the defendant.

Cor·fu (kôr′fū, -fōo) *n.* Greek island in the Ionian Sea, off the west coast of Greece. In ancient times it was known as Corcyra. Land area, 246 sq. mi. Pop. (1961), 101,770.

co·ri·an·der (kôr′ē an′dər) *n.* **1.** sweet, aromatic seed of a plant, *Coriandrum sativum,* of the parsley family, used mainly as a seasoning and an ingredient for anisette. **2.** plant bearing these seeds, having lacy, threadlike leaves and small white or pink flowers. [Old French *coriandre,* from Latin *coriandrum,* from Greek *koriannon.*]

Cor·inth (kôr′inth) *n.* port city in southern Greece, in the northeastern corner of the Peloponnesus. It was a major commercial and artistic center in ancient times. Pop. (1961), 15,892.

Co·rin·thi·an (kə rin′thē ən) *adj.* **1.** of, relating to, or characteristic of Corinth, its people, or their culture. **2.** of or relating to the most elaborate of the three orders of classical Greek architecture, characterized by columns having bell-shaped capitals decorated with carved acanthus leaves and small volutes. —*n.* **1.** native or inhabitant of Corinth. **2. Corinthians.** either of the two books of the New Testament composed of epistles written by the Apostle Paul to the Christians of Corinth.

Corinthian capital

Co·ri·o·lis effect (kôr′ē ō′lis) apparent deflection of a moving object owing to the rotation of the earth. The object, as a water current, appears to be deflected to the right in the Northern Hemisphere and to the left in the Southern Hemisphere. [From G. G. de *Coriolis,* 1792–1843, French mathematician who explained it in 1835.]

co·ri·um (kôr′ē əm) *pl.* **co·ri·a** (kôr′ē ə). *n.* dermis. [Latin *corium* skin.]

cork (kôrk) *n.* **1.** light, thick, porous outer bark of the cork oak, used esp. as insulating material and for floats. **2.a.** something made of cork, esp. a stopper for a bottle or other container. **b.** stopper, as for a bottle, made of another material. **3.** tissue forming the outer bark of woody plants, acting as a protective covering. —*v.t.* **1.** to stop or furnish with cork or a cork. **2.** to blacken with burnt cork. **3.** to restrain; check. [Spanish *alcorque* cork shoe, through Arabic, probably going back to Latin *cortex* rind, bark of the cork oak.]

corked (kôrkt) *adj.* **1.** stopped with a cork. **2.** corky *(def. 2).* **3.** blackened with burnt cork.

cork·er (kôr′kər) *n.* *Slang.* one who or that which is outstanding or remarkable.

cork oak, evergreen oak tree, *Quercus suber,* found widely throughout the Mediterranean region, from whose bark cork is obtained.

cork·screw (kôrk′skrōo′) *n.* device for removing corks from bottles, usually consisting of a pointed, metal spiral set in a handle. —*adj.* shaped like a corkscrew; spiral; winding. —*v.t., v.i.* to move in a spiral or zigzag course; wind; twist.

Corkscrew

cork·y (kôr′kē) **cork·i·er, cork·i·est.** *adj.* **1.** of or like cork. **2.** (of

wine) tasting of cork; spoiled, esp. by poor corking. Also, **corked.**

corm (kôrm) *n.* thick, fleshy underground stem that functions like a bulb but differs from it in structure, consisting mainly of stem rather than leafy tissue. The crocus and gladiolus are two common plants that develop from corms. [Modern Latin *cor-mus,* from Greek *kormos* trimmed tree trunk.]

cor·mo·rant (kôr′mər ənt) *n.* **1.** any of various swimming and diving birds, family Phalacrocoracidae, having webbed feet, a hooked bill, and a pouch under the beak for holding fish. Usually its plumage is black tinged with bronze or green. Length: to 3 feet. **2.** greedy or rapacious person. [Old French *cor-maren* this bird, from *corp* raven (from Latin *corvus*) + *marenc* of the sea (from Latin *marīnus*).]

Cormorant

corn[1] (kôrn) *n.* **1.** kernel or grain that grows in rows on the large spikes or ears of a tall, coarse grass, *Zea mays,* used for food. **2.** the plant itself, having a jointed stalk and broad, lance-shaped leaves and bearing both male and female flowers on the same plant. Also *(defs. 1, 2),* **maize, Indian corn. 3.** ear of this plant. **4.a.** major edible grain crop of a particular region, as wheat in England and oats in Scotland and Ireland. **b.** *British.* any food grain or the plant or plants it grows on. **5.** *Informal.* trite humor. —*v.t.* to preserve or season (beef) in strong brine or with coarse, dry salt. [Old English *corn* seed, grain.]

corn[2] (kôrn) *n.* small, conical hardening and thickening of the skin caused by friction or pressure, occurring esp. on a toe. [Old French *corn* horn, horny swelling, from Latin *cornū* horn.]

Corn Belt, region in the Middle West of the United States, consisting of the chief corn-growing states, extending from Ohio to Kansas and Nebraska.

corn borer, any of several moth larvae, family Pyraustidae or Pyralididae, that destroy corn and other crops.

corn bread, bread made from cornmeal.

corn·cob (kôrn′kob′) *n.* **1.** woody core of an ear of corn, on which the kernels grow in rows. **2.** tobacco pipe with a bowl made from a hollowed-out, dried corncob. Also *(def. 2),* **corncob pipe.**

corn cockle, whitish, hairy weed, *Agrostemma githago,* commonly found in wheat fields. Its red-purple flowers bear poisonous seeds.

corn crake, short-billed bird, *Crex crex,* of the rail family, common in the grain fields of Europe.

corn·crib (kôrn′krib′) *n.* structure for storing husked cobs of corn, built with slats that are spaced for ventilation.

cor·ne·a (kôr′nē ə) *n.* transparent outer covering or wall of the front of the eyeball, lying over the iris and the pupil. See **eye** for illustration. [Latin *cornea (tēla)* horny (web), going back to Latin *cornū* horn.] —**cor′ne·al,** *adj.*

corned (kôrnd) *adj.* (of beef) preserved or seasoned in strong brine or with coarse, dry salt.

Cor·neille, Pierre (kôr nā′; *pyär)* 1606–84, French dramatist.

cor·nel (kôr′nəl) *n.* any of a group of hardwood trees or shrubs, genus *Cornus,* of the dogwood family. [Middle Dutch *kornelle* fruit of the cornel, going back to Latin *cornus* the cornel.]

cor·nel·ian (kôr nēl′yən) carnelian.

cor·ne·ous (kôr′nē əs) *adj.* of, like, or consisting of horn; horny. [Latin *corneus,* from *cornū* horn.]

cor·ner (kôr′nər) *n.* **1.a.** point or place where converging lines or surfaces meet; angle: *the sharp corners of a table.* **b.** place where two streets meet. **2.** space between converging lines or surfaces near their meeting place: *The table stood in the far corner of the room.* **3.** place that is secluded, private, or secret: *The little boy sulked in his own little corner.* **4.** region; part; quarter: *The politician campaigned in every corner of our state.* **5.** place or position that is awkward or threatening, esp. one from which escape is difficult: *The student was driven into a corner by his friend's arguments.* **6.** purchase or control of enough of a particular stock or commodity to raise the price. **7.** piece used to protect, ornament, or form a corner: *These corners will hold that photograph in your scrapbook.* **8. to cut corners.** to reduce time, effort, or expenses in doing something; economize. **9. to turn the corner.** to pass the critical point. —*adj.* **1.** at or near a corner: *a corner store.* **2.** designed for or used in a corner: *a corner cabinet.* —*v.t.* **1.** to force or drive into an awkward or threatening place or position, esp. one from which escape is difficult. **2.** to form or get a corner on (a stock or commodity): *to corner the bubble-gum market.* **3.** to place in a corner. —*v.i.* **1.** to meet or be situated on or at a corner of angle. **2.** *Informal.* to make a turn at a corner: *Our new sports car corners beautifully.* [Anglo-Norman *cornere* angle[1], recess, nook, from Late Latin *cornēria* angle[1], going back to Latin *cornū* horn, point, end.]

cor·ner·stone (kôr′nər stōn′) *n.* **1.** stone that lies at the corner of a building, serving to unite two walls. **2.** any such stone, used to mark the actual or nominal starting point in building. It is often inscribed and made a repository of historical documents or objects. **3.** fundamental principle or part; foundation; basis.

cor·ner·wise (kôr′nər wīz′) *also,* **cor·ner·ways.** *adv.* from corner to corner; diagonally.

cor·net (*def. 1* kôr net′; *defs. 2, 3* kôr′nit, kôr net′) *n.* **1.** brass musical instrument of the trumpet family. See **trumpet** for illustration. **2.** paper cone twisted at one end, used as a holder for candy, nuts, or other small items. **3.** formerly, British cavalry officer who carried the troop flag. [Old French *cornet* little horn, diminutive of *corn* horn, going back to Latin *cornū.*]

cor·net·ist (kôr net′ist) *also,* **cor·net·ist.** *n.* one who plays a cornet.

corn·fed (kôrn′fed′) *adj.* **1.** fed on corn. **2.** healthy and robust, but unsophisticated.

corn·flakes (kôrn′flāks′) *n.,pl.* small toasted flakes made from corn, served cold, usually with milk, as a breakfast cereal.

corn·flow·er (kôrn′flou′ər) *n.* **1.** daisylike blue, purple, pink, or white flower of a plant, *Centaurea cyanus,* of the composite family, native to the Old World but now widely cultivated in North America. **2.** the plant itself. Also, **bachelor's button.** [Because it is commonly found growing in grain fields.]

corn·husk (kôrn′husk′) *n.* coarse leaves or husk enclosing an ear of corn.

cor·nice (kôr′nis) *n.* **1.** uppermost projecting part of an entablature. See **entablature** for illustration. **2.** any projecting horizontal molding, as along the top of a building or along the walls of a room just below the ceiling. **3.** ornamental frame or molding used to conceal curtain rods and other fixtures. —*v.t.,* **-niced, -nic·ing.** to furnish or decorate with a cornice. [Middle French *cornice* pillar, part of a wall, from Italian *cornice* part of a wall, ledge, possibly going back to Greek *korōnis* wreath, something curved.]

Cor·nish (kôr′nish) *adj.* of or relating to Cornwall, its people, or their now extinct language. —*n.* a Celtic language formerly spoken in Cornwall but extinct since the early eighteenth century.

Cor·nish·man (kôr′nish mən) *pl.,* **-men.** *n.* member or recent descendant of the people of Cornwall.

Corn Laws, series of laws severely limiting the import and export of wheat and other grains to and from Great Britain between 1436 and 1846.

corn·meal (kôrn′mēl′) *also,* **corn meal.** *n.* meal made from coarsely ground corn.

corn pone, simple corn bread that is baked or fried, usually made without milk or eggs. Also, **pone.**

corn shock, stack of cornstalks tied together and set upright in a field to dry out.

corn silk 1. long, silky, brown fibers projecting from the top of the husk on an ear of corn. **2.** any one of these fibers.

corn·stalk (kôrn′stôk′) *n.* stalk of corn.

corn·starch (kôrn′stärch′) *n.* white, powdery starch extracted from corn kernels, used in cooking as a thickening agent.

corn sugar, dextrose made from cornstarch.

corn syrup, syrup made from cornstarch, used as a sweetener and in making candies and jellies.

cor·nu·co·pi·a (kôr′nə kō′pē ə, kôrn′yə-) *n.*
1. curved, twisted horn overflowing with fruit, grain, and vegetables, a symbol of abundance and prosperity. **2.** any container or ornament shaped like a horn or cone. **3.** great store or supply; abundance. [Late Latin *cornūcōpia* horn of plenty, from Latin *cornū cōpiae;* in Greek mythology, the horn of the goat Amalthea, which nourished the infant Zeus.]

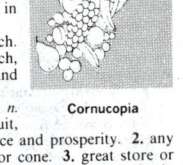
Cornucopia

Corn·wall (kôrn′wôl′) *n.* county in southwestern England. Pop. (1965 est.) 349,100.

Corn·wal·lis, Charles (kôrn wô′lis, -wol′is) 1738–1805, British general in the American Revolution who surrendered to Washington at Yorktown, Virginia in 1781.

corn·y (kôr′nē) *also,* **corn·i·er, corn·i·est.** *adj.* **1.** *Informal.* old-fashioned and overly sentimental; trite. **2.** of or abounding in corn. [CORN[1] + -Y[1]; said to refer to the supposedly unsophisticated taste of the CORN BELT.]

co·rol·la (kə rol′ə) *n.* petals of a flower, considered collectively as a flower part. [Latin *corolla* garland, diminutive of *corōna.* See CROWN.]

Corolla

cor·ol·lar·y (kôr′ə ler′ē, kor′-) *pl.,* **-lar·ies.** *n.* **1.** proposition that

at; āpe; cär; end; mē; it; īce; hot; ōld; fôrk; wood; fōōl; oil; out; up; ūse; turn; sing; thin; this; zh in treasure; ə in ago, taken, pencil, lemon, circus.

225

follows obviously from an already proven proposition and therefore requires no separate proof. **2.** easily drawn inference or deduction. **3.** anything that follows naturally; natural consequence or adjunct. [Late Latin *corollārium* deduction, from Latin *corollārium* garland given as a gift, additional gift, from *corolla*. See COROLLA.]

co·ro·na (kə rō′nə) *pl.*, **-nas** or **-nae** (-nē). *n.* **1.a.** luminous region seen closely surrounding a heavenly body, esp. the sun or moon, caused by the diffraction of light through mist or clouds. **b.** outer atmosphere of the sun, made up of free electrons, protons, and fine dust particles, usually seen during an eclipse. **2.** crown-like part, as the top of the head or the structure on the inner side of the corolla in such flowers as the daffodil. [Latin *corōna* crown, garland, from Greek *korōnē* something bent. Doublet of CROWN.]

Corona

Corona Aus·tra·lis (ôs trā′lis) constellation in the southern sky.
Corona Bo·re·al·is (bôr′ē al′is) constellation in the northern sky.
cor·o·nach (kŏr′ə nəкн, kŏr′-) *n.* in Scotland or Ireland, a lamentation for the dead; dirge.
Cor·o·na·do, Fran·cis·co Vás·quez de (kôr′ə nä′dō, kŏr′-; fran sis′kō väs′kes dā) c.1500–44, Spanish explorer of the American Southwest.
cor·o·nal (*n.*, kôr′ə nəl, kor′-; *adj.*, kə rō′nəl, kôr′ō nəl, kor′-) *n.* circlet for the head; crown or garland. —*adj.* of or relating to a crown or corona.
cor·o·nar·y (kôr′ə ner′ē, kor′-) *adj.* **1.a.** of, relating to, or designating either of two arteries that branch from the aorta and supply blood to the muscular tissue of the heart. **b.** encircling like a crown, as certain vessels or nerves. **2.** relating to or resembling a crown. —*n. pl.*, **-nar·ies.** coronary occlusion or coronary thrombosis. [Latin *corōnārius* relating to a crown, from *corōna*. See CORONA.]
coronary occlusion, blockage of one of the arteries that supplies blood to the heart.
coronary thrombosis, blockage in either of the coronary arteries caused by formation of a blood clot.
cor·o·na·tion (kôr′ə nā′shən, kor′-) *n.* act or ceremony of crowning a sovereign or the consort of a sovereign.
cor·o·ner (kôr′ə nər, kor′-) *n.* local official whose chief duty is to determine by an inquest the cause of any suspicious or violent death. [Anglo-Norman *cor(o)uner* English officer of justice (originally charged with watching over property belonging to the crown), from *coro(u)ne* crown, from Latin *corōna*. See CORONA.]
coroner's inquest, legal investigation into the cause of a death that has occurred suddenly or under suspicious or violent circumstances.
cor·o·net (kôr′ə net, kor′-) *n.* **1.** small crown denoting a noble rank lower than that of sovereign. **2.** crownlike head ornament, as one made with precious metals, jewels, or flowers. [Old French *coronete*, diminutive of *corone* crown, from Latin *corōna*. See CORONA.]
Co·rot, Jean Bap·tiste Ca·mille (kō rō′, zhän bä tēst′ kä mē′yə) 1796–1875, French landscape painter.
Corp. **1.** Corporation. **2.** Corporal. Also, **corp.**
cor·po·ral[1] (kôr′pər əl, -prəl) *adj.* of or relating to the human body; physical: *corporal punishment*. [Old French *corporal*, from Latin *corporālis*, from *corpus* body.] —**cor′po·ral·ly,** *adv.*
cor·po·ral[2] (kôr′pər əl, -prəl) *n.* lowest noncommissioned officer in the U.S. Army or Marine Corps, ranking below a sergeant and above a lance corporal. [Obsolete French *corporal*, form of *caporal*, from Italian *caporale*, from *capo* head, chief, from Latin *caput* head.]
cor·po·rate (kôr′pər it, -prit) *adj.* **1.** of, relating to, or forming a corporation: *corporate holdings, a corporate image.* **2.** of or relating to a united group of individuals; joint; collective. **3.** united or combined into a whole. [Latin *corporātus*, past participle of *corporāre* to make into a body, from *corpus* body.] —**cor′po·rate·ly,** *adv.*
cor·po·ra·tion (kôr′pə rā′shən) *n.* **1.** business organization that exists as a legal entity independent of the individuals that establish, own, or manage it. A corporation is created by a government charter and, within the limits imposed by the charter and the law, has the rights and liabilities of an individual, including the right to buy and sell property and to enter into contracts. **2.** any group of persons authorized to act as a single body. **3.** *Informal.* protruding abdomen; paunch.
cor·po·re·al (kôr pôr′ē əl) *adj.* **1.** of the body or of the nature of the body; not spiritual; mortal. **2.** having substance; material; tangible. [Latin *corporeus* of the body (from *corpus* body) + -AL[1].] —**cor·po·re·al·i·ty** (kôr pôr′ē al′ə tē), **cor·po′re·al·ness,** *n.* —**cor·po′re·al·ly,** *adv.* —**Syn.** see **physical.**
corps (kôr) *pl.*, **corps** (kôrz). *n.* **1.a.** unit of a military service with a specialized function. **b.** tactical military unit consisting of a headquarters, two or more divisions, and additional support units and forming

part of a field army. **2.** group of persons acting or working together. [French *corps* body, from Latin *corpus.* Doublet of CORPSE, CORPUS.]
corps de bal·let (kôr′də ba lā′) dancers in a ballet company who generally perform as a group rather than as soloists.
corpse (kôrps) *n.* dead body, esp. of a human being. [Old French *cor(p)s* body, from Latin *corpus.* Doublet of CORPS, CORPUS.]
corps·man (kôr′mən) *n.* enlisted man trained to give medical assistance.
cor·pu·lence (kôr′pyə ləns) *n.* fatness or fleshiness of the body; obesity. Also, **cor′pu·len·cy.**
cor·pu·lent (kôr′pyə lənt) *adj.* fat or fleshy; obese. [Latin *corpulentus,* from *corpus* body.]
cor·pus (kôr′pəs) *pl.*, **-po·ra** (-pər ə). *n.* **1.** complete collection of writings of a particular kind or on a particular subject. **2.** *Archaic.* body, esp. a dead one. **3.** main part or body of an anatomical organ. [Latin *corpus* body. Doublet of CORPS, CORPSE.]
Cor·pus Chris·ti (kôr′pəs kris′tē) **1.** in the Roman Catholic Church, a feast in honor of the Eucharist, held on the first Thursday after Trinity Sunday. **2.** port city in southern Texas. Pop. (1970), 204,-525. [Medieval Latin *corpus Christi* literally, body of Christ. See CORPUS, CHRIST.]
cor·pus·cle (kôr′pus əl, -pə səl) *n.* **1.** particle in the blood or lymph of vertebrates, esp. a red or white blood cell. **2.** any minute particle. [Latin *corpusculum* little body, atom, diminutive of *corpus* body.] —**cor·pus·cu·lar** (kôr pus′kyə lər) *adj.*
cor·pus de·lic·ti (kôr′pəs di lik′tī) **1.** physical object upon which a crime has been committed, esp. the victim's body in a murder case. **2.** essential fact or facts proving that a crime has been committed. [Modern Latin *corpus delicti* literally, body of the crime, from Latin *corpus* body + *dēlictum* crime.]
cor·pus ju·ris (kôr′pəs joor′is) complete collection of laws. [Late Latin *corpus jūris* literally, body of law.]
Corpus Juris Civilis, body of civil law compiled between A.D. 528 and 534, during the reign of Justinian I.
corr., correspondence; correspondent; corresponding.
cor·ral (kə ral′) *n.* **1.** fenced enclosure for cattle, horses, or other livestock. **2.** circular enclosure formed by wagons for defense against attack. —*v.t.*, **-ralled, -ral·ling. 1.** to drive into or enclose in a corral. **2.** to capture by surrounding or gathering together: *They corralled the entire gang.* **3.** to arrange (wagons) into a corral. [Spanish *corral* enclosure, from *corro* ring, from *correr* to run, from Latin *currere.*]
cor·rect (kə rekt′) *adj.* **1.** agreeing with fact or truth; free from error; accurate: *the correct address, the correct spelling.* **2.** conforming to an acknowledged or approved standard; proper: *correct dress for the banquet, correct behavior.* —*v.t.* **1.** to bring into agreement with fact or truth; remove error from; set right: *to correct the fallacies in his argument.* **2.** to note or mark the errors in: *I corrected the spelling mistakes in my letter and then mailed it.* **3.** to counteract or remove (something harmful or undesirable); rectify. **4.** to punish or rebuke so as to correct faults or improve; discipline: *to correct an unruly child.* **5.** to adjust to or bring into conformity with a standard; remove a fault from: *to correct one's eyesight with glasses.* [Latin *corrēctus,* past participle of *corrigere* to make straight, reform.] —**cor·rect′a·ble,** *adj.* —**cor·rect′ly,** *adv.* —**cor·rect′ness,** **cor·rec′tor,** *n.*
Syn. *adj.* **1.** Correct, precise, accurate, exact mean free from error or flaw. **Correct** is the general word: *His behavior toward the prisoners was correct, nothing more.* **Precise** implies meticulous accuracy: *He kept precise records of income and expenditures.* **Accurate** suggests care in avoiding error or deviation from an ideal pattern: *He drew an accurate picture of what it meant to live in the midst of a revolution.* **Exact** stresses a point-by-point matching of what is wanted: *Please have the exact change ready.*
cor·rec·tion (kə rek′shən) *n.* **1.a.** act of correcting; being corrected: *a correction in his thinking.* **b.** that which is substituted for an error; emendation: *spelling corrections on a paper.* **2.** act or process of punishing or rebuking; corrective discipline: *Ideally, correction should rehabilitate the criminal.* **3.** quantity added or subtracted in order to ensure accuracy: *correction for the thickness of a lens.* —**cor·rec′tion·al,** *adj.*
cor·rec·tive (kə rek′tiv) *adj.* tending or intended to correct or improve: *corrective lenses, corrective eye exercises.* —*n.* that which corrects or tends to correct. —**cor·rec′tive·ly,** *adv.*
Cor·reg·i·dor (kə reg′ə dôr′) *n.* fortified island in the Philippines, site of a surrender by U.S. forces to the Japanese in 1942, during World War II.
cor·re·late (kôr′ə lāt′, kor′-) **-lat·ed, -lat·ing.** *v.t.* to place in a mutual or reciprocal relation; show a meaningful connection between: *to correlate fact with theory.* —*v.i.* to be mutually or reciprocally related: *These data seem to correlate.* —*n.* either of two things mutually or reciprocally related, esp. so that one necessarily implies the other: *Good is the correlate of evil.* —*adj.* correlated. [From CORRELATION.]
cor·re·la·tion (kôr′ə lā′shən, kor′-) *n.* **1.** mutual or reciprocal rela-

tion: *the correlation between poor sanitation and disease.* **2.** act of correlating. [Medieval Latin *correlatio* mutual relation, from Latin *cum* with + *relātiō* a carrying back, report, reference.]

cor·rel·a·tive (kə rel′ə tiv) *adj.* **1.** having or involving a mutual or reciprocal relation, esp. so that one thing necessarily implies the other. **2.** *Grammar.* complementing one another and commonly used together. *Either* and *or* are correlative conjunctions. —*n.* **1.** either of two correlative things; correlate. **2.** correlative word or term. —**cor·rel′a·tive·ly** *adv.* —**cor·rel′a·tive·ness, cor·rel′a·tiv′i·ty,** *n.*

cor·re·spond (kôr′ə spond′, kor′-) *v.i.* **1.** to be in agreement or conformity; match (often with *with* or *to*): *Her words do not correspond with her actions. Her answer corresponds to mine.* **2.** to be similar, analogous, or equivalent, as in character or function (with *to*): *Our state assembly corresponds to the U.S. House of Representatives.* **3.** to communicate by exchanging letters. [Medieval Latin *correspondere* to answer to each other, from Latin *cum* together + *respondēre* to answer.] —**Syn. 1.** see **agree.**

cor·re·spon·dence (kôr′ə spon′dəns, kor′-) *n.* **1.a.** communication by exchange of letters: *The girls continued their correspondence throughout the summer.* **b.** letters written or exchanged: *The congressman found it difficult to read all his correspondence.* **2.** a corresponding or being correspondent; agreement or similarity: *the correspondence of a theory with the facts, a close correspondence between Greek and Roman gods.* Also (*def. 2*), **cor′res·pon′den·cy.**

correspondence course, course of instruction offered by a correspondence school.

correspondence school, any of various schools offering courses of study by mail in vocational, professional, or academic subjects.

cor·re·spon·dent (kôr′ə spon′dənt, kor′-) *n.* **1.** one who communicates with another by letter. **2.** one employed, as by a newspaper, to report news and commentary from the area to which he has been assigned. **3.** person or firm, esp. one located in a distant place, having regular business dealings with another. **4.** that which corresponds to something else. —*adj.* corresponding.

cor·re·spond·ing (kôr′ə spon′ding, kor′-) *adj.* **1.** that corresponds; agreeing or similar: *corresponding angles.* **2.** exchanging or handling written correspondence: *a corresponding secretary.* —**cor′re·spond′ing·ly,** *adv.*

cor·ri·dor (kôr′ə dər, -dôr′, kor′-) *n.* **1.** long hallway or passageway in a building, often having rooms opening onto it. **2.** narrow strip of land used as a passageway, esp. through foreign territory, and often providing access to the sea. **3.** air corridor. [French *corridor* passage, from Italian *corridore* long passage; literally, runner, going back to Latin *currere.*] —**Syn.** 1. see **passage.**

cor·ri·gen·dum (kôr′ə jen′dəm, kor′-) *pl.,* **-da** (-də). *n.* **1.** error to be corrected, esp. in a book after it has been printed; erratum. **2.** corrigenda, list of such errors in printed matter and their corrections; errata. [Latin *corrigendum* literally, (thing) to be corrected, from *corrigere* to make straight, reform.]

cor·ri·gi·ble (kôr′ə jə bəl, kor′-) *adj.* **1.** capable of being corrected, improved, or reformed. **2.** open to correction or reform. [Medieval Latin *corrigibilis*, from Latin *corrigere* to make straight, reform.] —**cor′ri·gi·bil′i·ty,** *n.* —**cor′ri·gi·bly,** *adv.*

cor·rob·o·rate (kə rob′ə rāt′) **-rat·ed, -rat·ing.** *v.t.* to strengthen or support, as by giving additional proof or evidence; confirm: *The evidence given by several witnesses corroborated the defendant's story.* [Latin *corrōborātus*, past participle of *corrōborāre* to strengthen, going back to *cum* together + *rōbur* oak, strength.] —**cor·rob′o·ra′tive,** **cor·rob·o·ra·to·ry** (kə rob′ər ə tôr′ē), *adj.* —**cor·rob′o·ra′tor,** *n.* —**Syn.** see **confirm.**

cor·rob·o·ra·tion (kə rob′ə rā′shən) *n.* **1.** act of corroborating; being corroborated. **2.** that which corroborates.

cor·rode (kə rōd′) **-rod·ed, -rod·ing.** *v.t.* **1.** to eat or wear away gradually, esp. by chemical action: *That acid corrodes metal.* **2.** to weaken or destroy: *Frequent criticism corrodes one's self-confidence.* —*v.i.* to become corroded: *Some substances corrode easily.* [Latin *corrōdere* to gnaw to pieces.] —**cor·rod′i·ble,** *adj.*

cor·ro·sion (kə rō′zhən) *n.* **1.** act or process of corroding; being corroded. **2.** product or result of corroding. [Late Latin *corrōsiō* a gnawing to pieces, from Latin *corrōdere* to gnaw to pieces.]

cor·ro·sive (kə rō′siv) *adj.* **1.** capable of producing corrosion: *a corrosive acid.* **2.** tending to weaken; destructive: *a corrosive effect.* **3.** tending to be biting or cutting. —*n.* that which corrodes, esp. a chemical agent. —**cor·ro′sive·ly,** *adv.* —**cor·ro′sive·ness,** *n.*

cor·ru·gate (kôr′ə gāt′, kor′-) **-gat·ed, -gat·ing.** *v.t.* to shape or contract (something), as a sheet of metal) into parallel ridges or folds; wrinkle. —*v.i.* to become corrugated: *materials which corrugate easily.* —*adj.* corrugated. [Latin *corrūgātus*, past participle of *corrūgāre* to wrinkle.]

cor·ru·gat·ed (kôr′ə gā′tid, kor′-) *adj.* shaped or contracted into parallel ridges or folds; wrinkled.

corrugated iron, sheet of iron or steel, usually galvanized, shaped into parallel ridges and troughs and used chiefly in making roofs and walls.

corrugated paper, heavy paper or cardboard shaped into parallel ridges and used for packaging.

cor·ru·ga·tion (kôr′ə gā′shən, kor′-) *n.* **1.** act of corrugating; being corrugated. **2.** one of a series of parallel ridges or folds; wrinkle.

cor·rupt (kə rupt′) *adj.* **1.** deviating from honesty; influenced by bribery; crooked: *corrupt practices at election time.* **2.** immoral or debased; depraved. **3.** made inferior to the original or correct form or version, as by additions or errors: *a corrupt form of German, a corrupt translation.* **4.** *Archaic.* rotten; decayed. —*v.t.* **1.** to induce to act dishonestly; destroy the integrity of; bribe: *It is easy to corrupt some politicians.* **2.** to pervert the morality of; debase: *Socrates was accused of corrupting the youth of his time.* **3.** to make inferior to an original or correct form or version. **4.** to make rotten; decay. —*v.i.* to become corrupt. [Latin *corruptus*, past participle of *corrumpere* to ruin, seduce, bribe; literally, to break to pieces.] —**cor·rupt′er;** also, **cor·rup′tor, cor·rupt′ness,** *n.* —**cor·rupt′ly,** *adv.*

Syn. *adj.* **2. Corrupt, depraved** indicate lowered quality or moral impairment. **Corrupt** suggests a moral breakdown, a disintegration of something once good and pure: *The city's licensing system became corrupt.* **Depraved** implies an extreme, often twisted, departure from what is normal and good: *His depraved tastes brought him into contact with the dregs of the underworld.*

cor·rupt·i·ble (kə rup′tə bəl) *adj.* that can be corrupted. —**cor·rupt′i·bil′i·ty, cor·rupt′i·ble·ness,** *n.* —**cor·rupt′i·bly,** *adv.*

cor·rup·tion (kə rup′shən) *n.* **1.** act of corrupting; being corrupted. **2.** lack of integrity; dishonesty. **3.** debased morality; depravity. **4.** corrupted form or incorrect version, as of a text or language. **5.** that which corrupts. **6.** rot; decay.

cor·rup·tive (kə rup′tiv) *adj.* tending to corrupt; causing corruption: *a corruptive influence.*

cor·sage (kôr säzh′) *n.* flower or small bouquet of flowers to be worn by a woman, usually at the shoulder or on the wrist. [Old French *corsage* bodice, chest, from *cors* body, from Latin *corpus.*]

cor·sair (kôr′sâr′) *n.* **1.** privateer or pirate, esp. of the Barbary Coast. **2.** privateering vessel or pirate ship. [French *corsaire* pirate, going back to Late Latin *cursārius*, from *cursus* plunder, from Latin *cursus* course. Doublet of HUSSAR.]

corse (kôrs) *n. Archaic.* corpse. [Form of CORPSE.]

cor·se·let (*def. 1* kôr′sə let′; *def. 2* kôrs′lit) *n.* **1.** woman's foundation garment similar to a corset but made with less reinforcing material. **2.** *also,* **cors·let.** plate armor, esp. the breastplate and back plate considered as one part. [French *corselet* literally, little body, diminutive of Old French *cors.* See CORSET.]

cor·set (kôr′sit) *n.* **1.** foundation garment reinforced with stitching and stiffening material, worn chiefly by women to shape and support the body, and usually extending from the midriff to below the hips. **2.** similar garment worn to support the muscles of the back or abdomen, esp. for medical reasons. [French *corset* little body, stays, diminutive of Old French *cors* body, from Latin *corpus.*]

Cor·si·ca (kôr′si kə) *n.* French island in the Mediterranean, southeast of France. Area, approx. 3345 sq. mi. Pop. (1968), 269,831. —**Cor′si·can,** *adj, n.*

cor·tege (kôr tezh′, -tāzh′) *also,* **cor·tège.** *n.* **1.** ceremonial procession, esp. a funeral procession. **2.** train of followers or attendants; retinue. [French *cortège* procession, from Italian *corteggio*, from *corte* court, from Latin *cohors.* See COHORT.]

Cor·tes (kôr′tiz, -tes) *n.* national legislature of Spain or Portugal.

cor·tex (kôr′teks) *pl.,* **-ti·ces** (-tə sēz′). *n.* **1.** outer portion of an internal organ, esp. the wrinkled gray matter covering most of the brain: *cerebral cortex.* **2.** zone of tissue in a tree beneath the epidermis of the bark, whose outer layers manufacture sugar, contain chlorophyll, and store nutrients. [Latin *cortex* rind, bark.]

Cor·tez, Her·nan·do (kôr tez′; *or* nän′dō) *also,* **Cor·tés** (kôr tes′). 1485–1547, Spanish conquistador of Mexico.

cor·ti·cal (kôr′ti kəl) *adj.* **1.** of, relating to, or consisting of a cortex. **2.** of or involving the cortex of the brain. —**cor′ti·cal·ly,** *adv.*

cor·ti·cat·ed (kôr′ti kit, -kāt′) *adj.* having a cortex. Also, **cor′ti·cat′ed.** [Latin *corticātus* covered with bark, from *cortex* bark.]

cor·ti·sone (kôr′tə sōn′, -zōn′) *n.* hormone produced by the cortex of the adrenal gland which affects the metabolism of carbohydrates, proteins, and fats. It is also made synthetically and used to treat rheumatoid arthritis and various allergic and inflammatory conditions.

co·run·dum (kə run′dəm) *n.* mineral consisting of aluminum oxide, second to the diamond in hardness. The dark-colored variety is used for polishing and grinding; transparent varieties include such gems as sapphires and rubies. Formula: Al$_2$O$_3$. [Tamil *kurundam*, possibly going back to Sanskrit *kuruvinda* ruby.]

cor·us·cate (kôr′əs kāt′, kor′-) **-cat·ed, -cat·ing.** *v.i.* to sparkle; glit-

at; āpe; cär; end; mē; it; īce; hot; ōld; fôrk; wood; fōol; oil; out; up; ūse; turn; sing; thin; this; zh in treasure; ə in ago, taken, pencil, lemon, circus.

227

ter. [Latin *coruscātus*, past participle of *coruscāre* to vibrate, glitter.]

cor·us·ca·tion (kôr′əs kā′shən, kor′-) *n.* **1.** sparkle; glitter: *the coruscations of a star.* **2.** flash of intellectual brilliance.

cor·vée (kôr vā′) *n.* **1.** unpaid work owed by a vassal to his feudal lord and usually performed by the vassal's serfs. **2.** forced, unpaid labor exacted by a government, esp. for the construction and repair of public works. [French *corvée*, from Late Latin *corrogāta (opera)* requisitioned (work), from Latin *corrogāre* to collect.]

cor·vette (kôr vet′) *also,* **cor·vet.** *n.* **1.** fast ship, smaller than a destroyer, armed with antisubmarine and antiaircraft guns and depth charges, used esp. to escort convoys. **2.** sailing warship smaller than a frigate and having one tier of guns. [French *corvette* sloop of war, from Middle Dutch *dorf* small ship, basket, from Latin *corbis* basket.]

cor·vine (kôr′vīn, -vin) *adj.* of or like a crow. [Latin *corvīnus*, relating to the raven, from *corvus* raven.]

Cor·vus (kôr′vəs) *n.* constellation in the southern sky, conventionally depicted as a crow. [Latin *corvus* raven.]

Cor·y·bant (kôr′ə bant, kor′-) *pl.,* **Cor·y·ban·tes** (kôr′ə ban′tēz, kor′-) *or* **Cor·y·bants.** *n.* one of the attendants or priests of the ancient Phrygian goddess Cybele. He accompanied her in her nightly wanderings in the mountains, worshiping her with wild, frenzied music and dancing. —**Cor′y·ban′tic,** *adj.*

cor·ymb (kôr′imb, -im, kor′-) *n.* form of inflorescence in which each small stemmed flower grows individually at different levels on a main stem, but develops so that the flowers reach approximately the same height forming a flat-topped cluster, as in cherry blossoms. See **inflorescence** for illustration. [Latin *corymbus* cluster of fruit or flowers, from Greek *korymbos* top, head, cluster.] —**co·rymb′ose,** *adj.*

cor·y·phée (kôr′ə fā′, kor′-) *n.* ballet dancer who ranks above the corps de ballet but is not a lead dancer. [French *coryphée*, through Latin, from Greek *koryphaios* leader.]

cos¹ (kôs, kos) *n.* romaine lettuce. [From the name of the Greek island from which it first came.]

cos², cosine.

cosec, cosecant.

co·se·cant (kō sē′kənt, -kant) *n.* (of an acute angle in a right triangle) the ratio of the hypotenuse to the side opposite the angle.

Cosecant of angle *A* = *AB/BC*

co·sig·na·to·ry (kō sig′nə tôr′ē) *adj.* signing jointly with another or others. —*n. pl.,* **-ries.** one who signs something jointly with another or others: *the cosignatories of the peace treaty.*

co·sine (kō′sīn) *n.* (of an acute angle in a right triangle) the ratio of the angle's adjacent side to the hypotenuse.

Cosine of angle *A* = *AC/AB*

cos·met·ic (koz met′ik) *n.* preparation designed chiefly to beautify various parts of the human body, as the face or hair. —*adj.* designed to beautify the appearance of the body, esp. the face and complexion: *a cosmetic soap, cosmetic surgery.* [Greek *kosmētikos* relating to adornment, going back to *kosmos* order, ornament.]

cos·mic (koz′mik) *adj.* **1.** of or relating to the cosmos as a whole: *cosmic law, cosmic order.* **2.** extending immeasurably; vast; endless: *cosmic proportions.* **3.** of or from outer space. [Greek *kosmikos* relating to the world, from *kosmos* order, world.] —**cos′mi·cal·ly,** *adv.*

cosmic dust, matter in fine particles falling on the earth from outer space.

cosmic rays, high-frequency radiation of great penetration, consisting mainly of positively charged high-energy particles that come to the earth from all directions in outer space.

cos·mog·o·ny (koz mog′ə nē) *pl.,* **-nies.** *n.* description or account of the origin of the universe. [Greek *kosmogoniā* origin of the world, from *kosmos* world, order + *gonos* offspring.]

cos·mog·ra·phy (koz mog′rə fē) *n.* **1.** science dealing with the description of the general physical features and structure of the universe, embracing astronomy, geography, and geology. **2.** description of the general physical features of the universe. [Greek *kosmographiā* description of the world, from *kosmos* world, order + *graphein* to write.]

cos·mol·o·gy (koz mol′ə jē) *n.* **1.** theory of the origin and nature of the universe: *the cosmologies of early philosophers.* **2.** branch of philosophy dealing with such theories. **3.** branch of astronomy dealing with such theories. [Greek *kosmos* world, order + -LOGY.] —**cos·mo·log·i·cal** (koz′mə loj′i kəl), —**cos·mol′o·gist,** *n.*

cos·mo·naut (koz′mə nôt′) *n.* astronaut, esp. a Soviet astronaut. [Greek *kosmos* world + *nautēs* sailor.]

cos·mo·pol·i·tan (koz′mə pol′ə tən) *adj.* **1.** composed of or having

elements, characteristics, or people from many different countries: *New York is a cosmopolitan city.* **2.** free from national or provincial attitudes or attachments: *a cosmopolitan outlook.* **3.** marked by or exhibiting sophistication; worldly: *cosmopolitan tastes, cosmopolitan manners.* **4.** (of a plant or animal) distributed widely throughout the world. —*n.* cosmopolitan person; cosmopolite. —**cos′mo·pol′i·tan·ism,** *n.*

cos·mo·o·lite (koz mop′ə lit′) *n.* one who is worldly or cosmopolitan in attitude or outlook. [Greek *kosmopolitēs* citizen of the world.]

cos·mos (koz′məs, -mōs) *n.* **1.** the universe considered as an ordered and harmonious system. **2.** any ordered and harmonious system. **3.a.** large daisylike flower head of any of a group of plants, genus *Cosmos,* of the composite family, widely cultivated in temperate regions and found in a variety of colors. **b.** plant bearing this flower head, having slender stems and feathery leaves. [Greek *kosmos* order, world.]

Cos·sack (kos′ak -ək) *n.* member of a people living mainly in the southeastern border regions of Russia, noted as horsemen and cavalrymen. [Russian *kazak,* from Turkic *quzzak* nomad, adventurer.]

cos·set (kos′it) *v.t.* to treat as a pet; pamper; fondle. —*n.* pet, esp. a pet lamb. [Possibly from Old English *cot-sǣta* cottage dweller; referring to a pet kept in the house.]

cost (kôst) *n.* **1.** amount of money, or its equivalent, paid or charged for something; price; expense: *the cost of education.* **2.** loss or sacrifice; detriment: *The war was won at great cost.* **3. costs.** money for legal expenses awarded at the discretion of the court to the winning party in a lawsuit, usually based on statutory limits. **4. at all costs,** regardless of the cost. Also, **at any cost.** —*v.t.,* **cost, cost·ing. 1.** to be acquired at the price of; require the expenditure of: *This book cost me ten dollars.* **2.** to involve the loss or sacrifice of: *That mistake cost him his life.* —*v.i. Informal.* requiring great expediture: *That sofa really costs.* [Old French *couster* to be of a certain price, cause pain, from Latin *cōnstāre* to stand together, consist.] —**Syn.** *n.* **1.** see **price.**

cos·tal (kôst′əl, kost′-) *adj.* of, relating to, or near a rib or the ribs. [Modern Latin *costalis,* from Latin *costa* rib.]

Cos·ta Me·sa (kos′tə mā′sə) city on the southern coast of California, near Los Angeles. Pop. (1970), 72,660.

co-star (*n.,* kō′stär′; *v.,* kō′stär′) *n.* **1.** actor or actress sharing star billing with another or others. **2.** actor or actress having less prominent billing than the star or stars. —*v.t., v.i.* **-starred, -star·ring. 1.** to be or cause to be a costar. **2.** to feature as costars.

cos·tard (kos′tərd) *n.* large English apple. [Modification of Old French *coste* rib, from Latin *costa;* with reference to its riblike markings.]

Cos·ta Ri·ca (kos′tə rē′kə) country in Central America, between Nicaragua and Panama. Capital, San José. Area, 19,575 sq. mi. Pop. (1969 est.), 1,685,000. —**Costa Rican.**

cos·ter·mon·ger (kôs′tər mung′gər, -mong′gər) *n. British.* one who sells food, as fruit, vegetables, or fish, in the street. Also, **cos′ter.** [Earlier *costardmonger,* from COSTARD + MONGER.]

cos·tive (kôs′tiv) *adj.* constipated. [Middle French *costivé,* from Latin *cōnstīpātus,* past participle of *cōnstīpāre* to press together.]

cost·ly (kôst′lē) **-li·er, -li·est.** *adj.* **1.** requiring or involving great expenditure; costing much: *a costly expedition, a costly habit.* **2.** of great value; splendid; sumptuous. —**cost′li·ness,** *n.*

cost of living, average cost of goods and services in a typical family budget in a given area during a given period of time.

cos·tume (*n.,* kos′tōōm, -tūm; *v.,* kos tōōm′, -tūm′) *n.* **1.** outfit worn to portray oneself as someone else, as by an actor or someone at a masquerade: *Halloween costume, costumes for a play.* **2.** style of dress, including accessories and hair style, belonging to a particular region, time, or class: *Roman costume, peasant costume.* **3.** special clothing or outfit worn for a particular occasion or activity: *a riding costume.* —*v.t.,* **-tumed, -tum·ing.** to provide with a costume. [French *costume* style of dress, from Italian *costume* dress, fashion; originally, custom, going back to Latin *cōnsuētūdō* custom. Doublet of CUSTOM.]

cos·tum·er (kos tōō′mər, -tū′-) *also,* **cos·tum·i·er** (kos tōō′mē ər, -tū′-, kos′tōō myā′). *n.* one who makes or deals in costumes.

co·sy (kō′zē) cozy.

cot¹ (kot) *n.* narrow, usually collapsible, bed, esp. one made of canvas stretched on a folding frame. [Hindi *khat* bed, couch, going back to Sanskrit *khatvā*.]

cot² (kot) *n.* **1.** small house; cottage. **2.** small structure for shelter or protection, esp. one for animals. **3.** protective covering or sheath, as for a sore finger. [Old English *cot* cottage, dwelling.]

cot³, cotangent.

co·tan·gent (kō tan′jənt, kō′tan′-) *n.* (of an acute angle in a right triangle) the ratio of the angle's adjacent side to the side opposite.

Cotangent of angle *A* = *AC/BC*

cote (kōt) *n.* small shelter for animals or birds. [Old English *cote* dwelling.]

at; āpe; cär; end; mē; it; īce; hot; ōld; fôrk; wood; fōōl; oil; out; up; ūse; turn; sing; thin; this; zh in treasure; ə in ago, taken, pencil, lemon, circus.

Côte d'A·zur (kōt dä zoor′) *n.* French part of the Riviera.

co·ten·ant (kō ten′ənt) *n.* **1.** one of two or more persons renting or owning the same land or dwelling place. **2.** one of two or more persons possessing any property together. —**co·ten′an·cy,** *n.*

co·te·rie (kō′tər ē) *n.* small, exclusive group of people who share a particular interest and often meet socially. [French *coterie* clique, circle, from Old French *coterie* an association of tenants holding land together; of Germanic origin.]

co·ter·mi·nous (kō tur′mə nəs) *adj.* conterminous.

co·thur·nus (kō thur′nəs) *pl.*, **-ni** (-nī). *n.* **1.** buskin (*def.* 2). **2.** tragic style in drama. Also, **co·thurn′.**

co·tid·al (kō tīd′əl) *adj.* of or relating to a coincidence in time of tides: *a cotidal line on a map.*

co·til·lion (kə til′yən) *n.* **1.** elaborate ballroom dance popular in the nineteenth century, usually led by one couple, and characterized by great complexity of steps and figures and frequent changing of partners. **2.** music for such a dance. **3.** any of various dances resembling the quadrille. **4.** formal ball, esp. one at which debutantes are presented. [French *cotillon* dance accompanied by games; literally, petticoat, diminutive of *cotte* coat; of Germanic origin.]

Co·to·pax·i (kō′tō päk′sē, -pä′hē) *n.* volcano in the Andes in north-central Ecuador. It is one of the highest active volcanos in the world.

Cots·wold (kots′wōld, -wəld) *n.* sheep of a breed having long, coarse hair, originally from the Cotswold Hills.

Cotswold Hills, range of hills in southwestern England.

cot·tage (kot′ij) *n.* **1.** small house, usually in a suburban or rural area. **2.** small house, as in a resort area, used for vacationing or as a summer house. [COT² + -AGE.]

cottage cheese, unripened, soft, white cheese made of strained and seasoned curds of sour skim milk. Also, **pot cheese.**

cottage pudding, plain cake covered with a hot, sweet sauce, esp. fruit sauce.

cot·tag·er (kot′i jər) *n.* **1.** one who lives or vacations in a cottage. **2.** British rural laborer.

cot·ter¹ (kot′ər) *n.* **1.** pin, bolt, wedge, or other mechanical part fitting into a hole or slot and holding other parts together. **2.** cotter pin. [Of uncertain origin.]

cot·ter² (kot′ər) *also,* **cot·tar.** *n.* **1.** *Scottish.* tenant farmer. **2.** cottager (*def.* 2). [COT² + -ER¹.]

cotter pin, pin-shaped cotter split lengthwise so that the ends may be bent to keep it in place.

cot·ton (kot′ən) *n.* **1.** soft white, gray, or brown fibers that grow in a fluffy mass in large seed pods, or balls, of certain plants, used in making textiles and other products. **2.** any of the woody, branching shrubs bearing these fibers, constituting the genus *Gossypium*, certain species of which are widely cultivated in warm areas. **3.** cotton plants collectively. **4.** crop of such plants. **5.** thread made of cotton fibers. **6.** any fabric woven of cotton. **7.** any downy substance resembling cotton fibers, growing around the seeds on other plants. —*adj.* having to do with or made of cotton. —*v.i.* **to cotton to. a.** to take a liking to; become friendly with: *That dog doesn't cotton to strangers.* **b.** to agree with; approve of: *to cotton to an idea.* [Old French *coton* cotton fiber, cotton cloth, from Arabic *qutn* cotton fiber.]

Cotton boll

cotton batting, thin layers of pressed cotton.

Cotton Belt, region of the southern United States where much cotton is grown.

cotton candy, light, fluffy candy consisting of threadlike fibers of melted sugar spun or wound around a cone or stick.

cotton gin, machine that separates the fibers of cotton from the seeds.

cot·ton·mouth (kot′ən mouth′) *n.* water moccasin.

cot·ton·seed (kot′ən sēd′) *pl.*, **-seeds** or **-seed.** *n.* seed of cotton, from which cottonseed oil is extracted. The residue, a protein-rich meal, is chiefly used as a fertilizer or as livestock feed.

cottonseed oil, oil extracted from cottonseed, refined for use as a cooking and salad oil and in the manufacture of lard substitutes, margarine, and various other products.

cot·ton·tail (kot′ən tāl′) *n.* any of various rabbits, genus *Sylvilagus*, of North America, having brown or grayish fur and a short, fluffy tail that is white underneath. Length: 12–17 inches.

cot·ton·wood (kot′ən wood′) *n.* **1.** any of several fast-growing trees, genus *Populus*, of the willow family, found in moist regions of North America, having leathery, triangular leaves with toothed edges and tiny brown seeds covered with silky white hairs. **2.** light soft wood of this tree.

cotton wool, raw cotton, before either picking or baling.

cot·ton·y (kot′ən ē) *adj.* resembling cotton in texture or color; soft; downy; white.

cot·y·le·don (kot′əl ēd′ən) *n.* rudimentary leaf that forms part of a plant embryo. In many plants the cotyledon develops into the first leaf or one of the first pair of leaves to grow above the ground. [Greek *kotylēdōn* cup-shaped hollow, from *kotylē* hollow, small cup.] —**cot′y·le′don·ous,** *adj.*

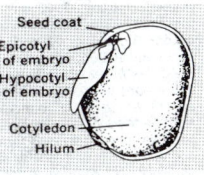
Cotyledon

couch (kouch) *n.* **1.** piece of furniture, usually upholstered, designed for several people to sit on or for one person to recline on; sofa; divan. **2.** any place for sleeping or resting. —*v.t.* **1.** to put into words; express: *His argument was couched in careful phrases.* **2.** to lower or bring down, esp. lower (a spear, gun, or other weapon) to the position of attack. **3.** to lay down on or as if on a bed or couch. —*v.i.* **1.** to lie in a resting place. **2.** to lie in ambush; be hidden; lurk. [Old French *couche* a lying down, place for lying down, from *coucher* to lay down, put to bed, from Latin *collocāre* to place together, lay in its place.]

couch·ant (kou′chənt) *adj.* **1.** lying down. **2.** *Heraldry.* lying down with the head raised. [French *couchant,* present participle of *coucher* to lay down, put to bed. See COUCH.]

cou·chée (kōō shā′) *n.* reception held by a person of high rank, esp. a sovereign, before retiring.

Couchant
A lion couchant

couch grass, quack grass.

cou·gar (kōō′gər) *n.* tawny or grayish-brown wild cat, *Felis concolor,* of North, Central, and South America, having a small round head, long limbs, and a slender, muscular body. Length: 6–8 feet including tail. Also, **pu′ma, mountain lion, cat′a·mount′.** [French *couguar,* going back to Tupi-Guarani *suasuarana* literally, false deer.]

cough (kôf) *v.i.* to expel air from the lungs suddenly with effort and noise. —*v.t.* **1.** to expel by coughing: *to cough blood.* **2. to cough up. a.** to expel from the lungs or throat by coughing. **b.** *Slang.* to hand over; give: *He coughed up the money he owed us.* —*n.* **1.** act or sound of coughing. **2.** illness or condition that causes frequent coughing. [From an unrecorded Old English word.]

cough drop, small medicated lozenge, usually flavored and sweetened, for relieving coughs, hoarseness, sore throat, and the like.

could (kood) past tense of **can¹.**

could·n't (kood′ənt) could not.

couldst (koodst) *Archaic.* second person singular past tense of **can¹.**

cou·lee (kōō′lē) *n.* **1.** in the western United States, a deep gulch or ravine, often dry, that has been formed by running water. **2.** stream of lava, either flowing or solidified. [French *coulée* a flow, from *couler* to flow, from Latin *cōlāre* to strain.]

cou·lomb (kōō′lom, -lōm, kōō lom′, -lōm′) *n.* unit used as a measure of the quantity of electric charge. It is the amount of charge that in one second passes a given point in a wire carrying a current of one ampere. [From the French physicist Charles A. de *Coulomb,* 1736–1806.]

coul·ter (kōl′tər) colter.

coun·cil (koun′səl) *n.* **1.** assembly or meeting convened for consultation, deliberation, or advice: *a council of physicians, a family council.* **2.** body of persons elected or appointed to serve in an administrative, legislative, or advisory capacity, as in a city, town, or borough. **3.** deliberation or discussion that takes place in a council. [Old French *concile* council, from Latin *concilium* assembly, gathering.]

Council Bluffs, city in southwestern Iowa. Pop. (1970), 60,348.

coun·cil·man (koun′səl mən) *pl.*, **-men.** *n.* member of a council.

Council of Trent, ecumenical council of the Roman Catholic Church held at Trent, Italy in three sessions between 1545 and 1563 to meet the challenge of the Protestant Reformation.

coun·ci·lor (koun′sə lər, -slər) *also, British,* **coun·cil·lor.** *n.* member of a council; councilman. —**coun′ci·lor·ship′,** *n.*

coun·sel (koun′səl) *n.* **1.** mutual exchange of ideas, opinions, or advice; consultation; deliberation: *The leaders met for counsel before proceeding with the rebellion.* **2.** advice, direction, or opinion given as the result of consultation: *In time of stress, people often fail to heed moderate counsel.* **3.** lawyer or lawyers engaged in giving legal advice or in preparing or conducting a case in court: *He refused to testify on advice of counsel.* **4.** deliberate purpose or plan; intent. **5.** *Archaic.* wise judgment; prudence. **6. to keep one's own counsel.** to keep one's opinions, intentions, or plans secret. **7. to take counsel.** to seek or exchange ideas, advice, or opinions; consult; deliberate. —*v.t.* **1.** to advise to; advise: *He counseled the boys to take greater care.* **2.** to urge the adoption of; recommend. —*v.i.* to give or take counsel or advice. [Old French *conseil* advice, plan, from Latin *cōnsilium* deliberation, advice.]

at; āpe; cär; end; mē; it; īce; hot; ōld; fôrk; wood; fōōl; oil; out; up; ūse; turn; sing; thin; this; zh in treasure; ə in ago, taken, pencil, lemon, circus.

229

coun·se·lor (koun′sə lər, -slər) *also, British,* **coun·sel·lor.** *n.* **1.** one who gives counsel or advice; adviser: *a guidance counselor in a high school.* **2.** lawyer, esp. one who conducts cases in court. Also, **counselor-at-law.** **3.** person employed to supervise activities and care for children at a camp. —**coun′se·lor·ship′,** *n.* —**Syn. 2. see lawyer.**

count¹ (kount) *v.t.* **1.** to list or recite numbers by name in sequence up to and including (a certain number): *By three he counted ten over the fallen boxer.* **2.** to list or check, one by one, all (people or things in a group) to ascertain the total number; enumerate: *She counted the eggs in the carton.* **3.** to include in reckoning; take into account: *There were forty people in the bus, counting the driver.* **4.** to believe to be; consider: *to count oneself fortunate. Great Britain counts France among her allies.* —*v.i.* **1.** to list or recite numbers in units or groups in sequence: *He counted to five.* **2.** to be of value; have importance or significance; matter: *Good manners count with some people. Every moment counts.* **3.** to be included in counting; be taken into account: *Your loyalty will count when appointments to office are made.* **4. to count for.** to be worth; be important: *His pompous words counted for little.* **5. to count in.** to include: *Count me in!* **6. to count off.** to divide into equal groups by counting: *The sergeant ordered his men to count off by fours.* **7. to count on** (or **upon**). to rely or depend on: *He counted on their support to win.* **8. to count out. a.** to exclude; omit: *We'll have to count out Frank for next Sunday's trip.* **b.** to declare (a fallen boxer) defeated when he cannot rise before a count of ten seconds is completed. —*n.* **1.** act of counting; reckoning; numbering: *He made a rapid count of those present.* **2.** number obtained by counting; total. **3.** *Law.* each distinct charge in an accusation: *He pleaded innocent to the first two counts.* **4.** *Boxing.* **a.** a counting of the seconds over a fallen boxer: *The count had reached five before he moved.* **b.** ten seconds, the maximum number of seconds a referee may allow a fallen boxer to regain his feet before he is declared the loser. [Old French *co(u)nter* to reckon, tell, from Latin *computāre* to reckon, calculate. Doublet of COMPUTE.] —**count′a·ble,** *adj.*

count² (kount) *n.* nobleman of certain European countries having a rank corresponding to that of a British earl. [Old French *conte,* from Late Latin *comes* member of the emperor's court, from Latin *comes* companion.]

count·down (kount′doun′) *n.* **1.a.** process of steps leading to a launching, as of a space vehicle or missile, marked by a count in reverse numerical order from a given time to zero, at which time the launching takes place. **b.** any similar process, as before the real or mock test of a nuclear weapon or other device. **2.** act of counting in reverse numerical order, esp. in the last stage of such a process.

coun·te·nance (koun′tə nəns) *n.* **1.** face; features; visage: *a handsome countenance.* **2.** expression of the face; look: *an unhappy countenance.* **3.** approval; support; encouragement: *We could not give countenance to such an illegal act.* **4.** calmness; composure. **5. out of countenance.** embarrassed, disconcerted, or confused. —*v.t.,* **-nanced, -nanc·ing.** to give countenance to; approve; support; encourage: *We countenanced their appeal for justice.* [Old French *contenance* look, visage, behavior, from Late Latin *continentia* demeanor, from Latin *continentia* a holding back, moderation.]

count·er¹ (koun′tər) *n.* **1.a.** long table or case across which sales are made, as in a store or restaurant. **b.** any long shelf or similar flat working area, as in a kitchen. **2.** thing used in counting, esp. a piece of metal, ivory, or other material used for keeping score in certain games. **3.** imitation coin; token. [Anglo-Norman *counteour* counting table, counting house, from Medieval Latin *computatorium* literally, place for counting, from Latin *computāre* to reckon, calculate.]

count·er² (koun′tər) *n.* one who or that which counts, esp. a mechanical device for counting. [COUNT¹ + -ER¹.]

coun·ter³ (koun′tər) *adv.* in an opposite direction or manner; in opposition; contrary: *The new rules ran counter to tradition.* —*adj.* opposite; opposing; contrary. —*v.t.* **1.** to go or act counter to; oppose; controvert: *Our theory countered his.* **2.** to deal a blow in boxing in return for (an opponent's blow). —*v.i.* **1.** to make an opposing move: *The debater countered with another argument.* **2.** to deal a blow in boxing while parrying or receiving one: *He countered with a left to the head.* —*n.* **1.** that which is opposite or contrary. **2.** boxing blow in return for an opponent's blow. **3.** stiff piece on the inside of the heel of a shoe. **4.** sloping underside of a ship's stern above the waterline. [Old French *contre* against, from Latin *contrā* against, opposite.]

counter- combining form **1.** in opposition to; against: *countermeasure.* **2.** in return; reciprocal: *counterattack.* **3.** corresponding: *counterpart.* [Old French *contre-, contre* against, towards, from Latin *contrā* against, opposite, in return.]

coun·ter·act (koun′tər akt′) *v.t.* to neutralize the action or force of; act in opposition to; check: *This drug will counteract the effects of poison.* —**coun′ter·ac′tion,** *n.* —**coun′ter·ac′tive,** *adj.*

coun·ter·at·tack (koun′tər ə tak′) *n.* attack made to counter another attack: *a counterattack against an invading force, a counterattack*

against persistent critics. —*v.t.* to make a counterattack against.

coun·ter·bal·ance (*n.,* koun′tər bal′əns; *v.,* koun′tər bal′əns) *n.* **1.** weight used to balance another weight; counterpoise. **2.** power or influence that balances or offsets a contrary force: *His easygoing nature is a counterbalance to his partner's quick temper.* —*v.t.,* **-anced, -anc·ing.** to act as a counterbalance to; offset.

coun·ter·check (koun′tər chek′) *n.* **1.** something that stops, restrains, or opposes something else. **2.** check made to confirm an earlier check; double check. —*v.t.* **1.** to stop, restrain, or oppose by a counteraction; check. **2.** to confirm by a second check; double-check.

coun·ter·claim (koun′tər klām′) *n.* opposing claim, esp. an action by the defendant against the plaintiff in a lawsuit. —*v.i.* to put in a counterclaim. —*v.t.* to make a counterclaim against (the plaintiff or a prior claim). —**coun′ter·claim′ant,** *n.*

coun·ter·clock·wise (koun′tər klok′wiz′) *adv., adj.* in the direction opposite to the movement of a clock's hands.

coun·ter·cul·ture (koun′tər cul′chər) *n.* culture, esp. of young people, that is opposed to the standards and traditions of their society.

coun·ter·cur·rent (koun′tər kur′ənt) *n.* current in the opposite direction; opposing current.

coun·ter·es·pi·o·nage (koun′tər es′pē ə näzh′, -nij) *n.* operations and measures designed to prevent and counteract espionage.

coun·ter·feit (koun′tər fit′) *v.t.* **1.** to make an unauthorized copy of, as money, documents, or handwriting, with intent to deceive or defraud: *It is a crime to counterfeit money.* **2.** to be an imitation of; resemble closely. **3.** to make a pretense of; pretend; feign: *to counterfeit sympathy.* —*v.i.* **1.** to make counterfeits. **2.** to practice deceit; pretend; feign. —*n.* copy or imitation of something genuine made with intent to deceive or defraud; forgery. —*adj.* **1.** made in imitation of an original, with intent to deceive or defraud; not genuine: *counterfeit postage stamps.* **2.** pretended; feigned. [Old French *contrefait,* past participle of *contrefaire* to copy, imitate, going back to Latin *contrā* against, opposite + *facere* to make.] —**coun′ter·feit′er,** *n.* —**Syn. adj. 1. see false.**

coun·ter·foil (koun′tər foil′) *n.* part of a check, money order, ticket, or similar document kept by the issuer as a record or receipt; stub. [COUNTER- + FOIL².]

coun·ter·in·tel·li·gence (koun′tər in tel′ə jəns) *n.* actions to counteract enemy intelligence, espionage, and sabotage activities.

coun·ter·ir·ri·tant (koun′tər ir′ə tənt) *n.* agent used to produce mild inflammation, esp. of the skin, in order to reduce a more deep-seated inflammation.

coun·ter·man (koun′tər man′) *n.* man who waits on customers at a counter, esp. in a cafeteria or other eating place.

coun·ter·mand (*v.,* koun′tər mand′; *n.,* koun′tər mand′) *v.t.* **1.** to revoke or reverse (an order or command.) **2.** to recall or order back by a contrary order. —*n.* contrary order or command revoking or reversing a previous one. [Old French *contremander* to contradict an earlier command, going back to Latin *contrā* against + *mandāre* to command.]

coun·ter·march (koun′tər märch′) *n.* **1.** a march back or in the opposite direction; return march. **2.** drill maneuver in which marchers reverse direction but retain their original order and positions. —*v.i., v.t.* to perform or cause to perform a countermarch.

coun·ter·meas·ure (koun′tər mezh′ər) *n.* action taken to counteract another.

coun·ter·mine (koun′tər mīn′) *n.* **1.** mine placed in the ground near, usually beneath, an enemy mine and intended to blow it up. **2.** counterplot. —*v.t.,* **-mined, -min·ing.** **1.** to make countermines against (an enemy or enemy mines). **2.** to lay down countermines in (a given area). **2.** to defeat (a plot) with a counterplot. —*v.i.* to make countermines.

coun·ter·of·fen·sive (koun′tər ə fen′siv) *n.* offensive undertaken by a military force to turn back the enemy's offensive and seize the initiative.

coun·ter·pane (koun′tər pān′) *n.* quilt or coverlet for a bed; bedspread. [Modification of obsolete *counterpoint* quilt, from Middle French *contrepointe,* going back to Latin *culcita pūncta* literally, stitched quilt.]

coun·ter·part (koun′tər pärt′) *n.* **1.** person or thing corresponding to or closely resembling another: *The U.S. Congress is the counterpart of the British Parliament.* **2.** person or thing that completes or complements another.

coun·ter·plot (koun′tər plot′) *n.* plot designed to defeat another plot. —*v.i.,* **-plot·ted, -plot·ting.** to devise a counterplot; plot in opposition. —*v.t.* to plot against (a plot or plotter); defeat by a counterplot.

coun·ter·point (koun′tər point′) *n. Music.* **1.** art or practice of having one or more distinct melodies occur simultaneously with a given basic melody according to certain rules of harmony. **2.** one or more melodies added to a principal melody in this way. [Old French *contrepoint* music arranged in counterpoint, from Medieval Latin *(cantus) contrapunctus* literally, (song) pointed against, from Latin *contrā*

at; āpe; cär; end; mē; it; īce; hot; ōld; fôrk; wood; fōōl; oil; out; up; ūse; turn; sing; thin; this; zh in treasure; ə in ago, taken, pencil, lemon, circus.

against, opposite + *pŭnctus* point; because the notes of the additional melody (originally represented by *points*) were formerly marked *opposite* (or *against*) the corresponding notes in the basic melody.]

coun·ter·poise (koun'tər poiz') *n.* **1.** weight used to balance another weight; counterbalance. **2.** any influence or power that balances or offsets a contrary force. **3.** state of being in balance. —*v.t.*, **-poised, -pois·ing.** to act in opposition to with equal weight, power, or effect; counterbalance. [Old French *contrepois* equal weight, going back to Latin *contrā* against, opposite + *pēnsum* something weighed.]

coun·ter·ref·or·ma·tion (koun'tər ref'ər mā'shən) *n.* **1.** reform movement opposed to or counteracting a previous one. **2. Counter Reformation.** reform movement in the Roman Catholic Church during the sixteenth century, aimed at revitalizing Catholicism in Europe and meeting the political and religious challenge of Protestantism. Also *(def. 2),* **Catholic Reformation.**

coun·ter·rev·o·lu·tion (koun'tər rev'ə loo'shən) *n.* **1.** revolution opposed to a previous one and seeking to reverse its effects. **2.** political activity opposed to combat a revolutionary movement. —**coun'·ter·rev'o·lu'tion·ist,** *n.*

coun·ter·rev·o·lu·tion·ar·y (koun'tər rev'ə loo'shə ner'ē) *adj.* relating to or of the nature of a counterrevolution. —*n. pl.* **-ar·ies.** one who takes part in or advocates a counterrevolution.

coun·ter·scarp (koun'tər skärp') *n.* outer slope or wall of a moat or ditch in a fortification. Distinguished from **escarp.** [French *contrescarpe,* going back to Italian *contra* against (from Latin *contrā*) + *scarpa.* See SCARP.]

coun·ter·shaft (koun'tər shaft') *n.* shaft receiving motion from the main shaft and transmitting it to a working part.

coun·ter·sign (koun'tər sīn') *n.* **1.** secret sign or signal given in answer to another, esp. a military password given in answer to the challenge of a guard or sentry. **2.** signature added to a previously signed check or other document to confirm or authenticate it. Also *(def. 2),* **coun·ter·sig·na·ture** (koun'tər sig'nə chər). —*v.t.* to sign a document (already signed by another) in order to confirm or authenticate it: *The treasurer of the company countersigned the checks.* [French *contresigner* to sign in addition, attest, going back to Latin *contrā* against + *signāre* to mark, sign.]

coun·ter·sink (koun'tər singk') **-sunk, -sink·ing.** *v.t.* **1.** to enlarge the upper part of (a hole or cavity) to receive the head of a screw, bolt, or similar bonding device. **2.** to set (a screw, bolt, or rivet) in a counter-sunk hole. —*n.* **1.** countersunk hole. **2.** tool, esp. a bit, for enlarging the upper end of a drilled hole.

coun·ter·spy (koun'tər spī') *pl.* **-spies.** *n.* spy who is employed to detect and counteract the activities of enemy spies.

coun·ter·ten·or (koun'tər ten'ər) *Music. n.* **1.** highest adult male voice. **2.** singer who has a countertenor voice. **3.** musical part for a countertenor voice. —*adj.* **1.** able to sing countertenor. **2.** for countertenor: *The countertenor part was difficult to sing.*

coun·ter·vail (koun'tər vāl') *v.t.* **1.** to act against with equal force, power, or effect; counteract. **2.** to compensate or make up for; offset. —*v.i.* to be of equal force in opposition (with *against*). [Old French *contrevaloir* to be effective against, going back to Latin *contrā* against + *valēre* to be worth.]

coun·ter·weigh (koun'tər wā') *v.t.* to counterbalance.

coun·ter·weight (koun'tər wāt') *n.* weight balancing another weight; counterpoise. —*v.t.* to counterweigh; counterbalance.

count·ess (koun'tis) *n.* **1.** wife or widow of a count or, in Great Britain, an earl. **2.** woman holding in her own right a rank equal to that of an earl or count. [Old French *contesse,* feminine of *conte.* See COUNT[2].]

counting house, building, office, or room used for such purposes as bookkeeping, correspondence, or business transactions. Also, **count·ing room.**

count·less (kount'lis) *adj.* too many to be counted; innumerable: *There were countless trees in the forest.*

coun·tri·fied (kun'tri fīd') *adj.* having the appearance, manner, or characteristics associated with the country or country life; rural; rustic.

coun·try (kun'trē) *pl.* **-tries.** *n.* **1.a.** tract or expanse of land; territory: *This is lovely country.* **b.** any district or region, esp. one considered as having a distinguishing characteristic: *We went camping in the hill country.* **2.a.** nation or independent state: *Fifty-one countries signed the United Nations Charter.* **b.** territory of a nation. **c.** people of a nation or independent state: *Half the country voted in the last election.* **3.** land of one's birth, residence, or citizenship. **4.** region outside of cities or towns; rural area. —*adj.* of or relating to rural areas: *the country gentry, a country bumpkin.* [Old French *contree* region, district, from Medieval Latin *contrata* land lying opposite, landscape, from Latin *contrā* against, opposite.]

country club, private social club usually located in a suburb, equipped with a clubhouse and various recreational facilities, as a golf course, swimming pool, or tennis courts.

country cousin, person from the country who finds city life bewildering and confusing.

coun·try-dance (kun'trē dans') *n.* folk dance of English origin in which partners form two lines facing each other.

coun·try-folk (kun'trē fōk') *n.* people who live in rural areas.

country gentleman, man of wealth or position who lives on his country estate.

coun·try·man (kun'trē mən) *pl.* **-men.** *n.* **1.** native or inhabitant of one's own country; compatriot. **2.** native or inhabitant of a particular country. **3.** man who lives in the country; rustic. —**coun'try·wom'an,** *n.*

coun·try-seat (kun'trē sēt') *n.* mansion or estate in the country, esp. one belonging to a country gentleman or nobleman.

coun·try·side (kun'trē sīd') *n.* **1.** rural region or district. **2.** its inhabitants.

coun·ty (koun'tē) *pl.* **-ties.** *n.* **1.** the political division next below a state in the United States. It is the largest unit for local government within a state. **2.** the most important territorial division for administrative, judicial, and political purposes in Great Britain and Ireland; shire. **3.** the people of a county. [Old French *conté* territory ruled by a count, from Late Latin *comitātus,* from *comes.* See COUNT[2].]

county agent, government official employed chiefly to advise and assist farmers and rural people, esp. in matters of agriculture and home economics.

county seat, town or city which is the center of county government.

coup (koo) *pl.* **coups** (kooz). *n.* **1.** sudden, brilliant action; unexpected, clever stratagem; master stroke. **2.** coup d'etat. [French *coup* stroke, blow, going back to Latin *colaphus* blow, from Greek *kolaphos.*]

coup de grâce (koo'də gräs') **1.** death blow, a shot to make sure that an executed man or mortally wounded animal is dead. **2.** decisive or finishing stroke. [French *coup de grâce* finishing stroke; literally, stroke of grace.]

coup d'e·tat (koo'dā tä') sudden seizure, usually forcible, of government control by a person or group, esp. one previously holding some official authority. [French *coup d'état* literally, stroke of state.]

coupe (koop, koo pā') *also,* **cou·pé** (koo pā'). *n.* **1.** two-door automobile seating two to six people. **2.** short, four-wheeled closed carriage with an inner seating capacity

Coupe (def. 2)

for two people and a seat outside for the driver. [French *coupé,* short for *(carrosse) coupé* literally, carriage cut off, noun use of the past participle of *couper* to cut, from *coup.* See COUP.]

Cou·pe·rin, Fran·çois (koo pə ran'; frän swä') 1668–1733, French composer.

cou·ple (kup'əl) *n.* **1.** two things of the same kind joined or considered together; pair. **2.** man and woman who are married, engaged, or are otherwise paired, as in a dance or game. **3.** *Informal.* small number; several; few: *We walked a couple of miles.* **4.** something joining two things together; link; coupler. —*v.t.,* **-pled, -pling.** to join, link, or fasten together in a pair or pairs. —*v.i.* to join or unite in a pair or pairs. [Old French *co(u)ple* a pair, from Latin *cōpula* bond, connection.]

cou·pler (kup'lər) *n.* **1.** one who or that which couples. **2.** device in a pipe organ for connecting two or more keys or keyboards so they can be played together. **3.** interlocking device used to connect two railroad cars.

cou·plet (kup'lit) *n.* two successive lines of verse, usually rhyming and in the same meter, that form a unit, for example: *Know then thyself, presume not God to scan; /The proper study of mankind is man.* (Pope, 1733–34) [Old French *couplet,* diminutive of *couple* a pair. See COUPLE.]

cou·pling (kup'ling) *n.* **1.** act of one who or that which couples. **2.** any of various devices for joining parts of machinery. **3.** coupler *(def. 3).* **4.** arrangement for transferring electrical energy from one circuit to another, in one or both directions.

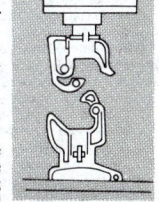

cou·pon (koo'pon, kū'-) *n.* **1.** detachable printed statement on a bond representing the amount of interest accrued on the bond during a specific period which the bondholder clips and presents for payment on the due date. **2.** detachable part of a ticket, certificate, or printed advertisement which entitles the holder to something. [French *coupon* literally, piece cut off, from *couper* to cut, from *coup.* See COUP.]

Coupling (top view)

cour·age (kur'ij) *n.* **1.** quality enabling one to face danger or difficulties without fear; bravery; boldness. **2. to have the courage of one's**

convictions. **to have the courage** to do what one believes is right. [Old French *corage* state of mind, feelings, going back to Latin *cor* heart.]

cou·ra·geous (kə rā′jəs) *adj.* having or marked by courage; brave; fearless. —**cou·ra′geous·ly,** *adv.* —**cou·ra′geous·ness,** *n.* —Syn. see **brave.**

Cour·bet, Gus·tave (kŏŏr bā′; goo stäv′) 1819–77, French painter.

cou·ri·er (kur′ē ər, koor′-) *n.* one carrying an important or urgent message. [Middle French *courier,* from Italian *corriere,* from *correre* to run, from Latin *currere.*] —Syn. see **messenger.**

course (kôrs) *n.* **1.** a moving from one point to the next; onward movement; progress; advance: *the course of history, in the course of human events.* **2.** line in which anything moves; direction taken: *a westward course.* **3.** continuous passage in time; duration: *in the course of a year.* **4.** sequential advance through progressive stages or conditions: *the course of the seasons.* **5.** natural or regular advance, order, or development: *the course of a disease.* **6.** normal line of conduct or action; way of acting or doing: *He made up his mind to take a conciliatory course.* **7.a.** way, path, or channel over which something moves: *the course of a river.* **b.** area arranged for certain sports or games: *a golf course, a race course.* **8.** ordered sequence or group of similar things: *a course of lectures, a course of treatment.* **9.** complete prescribed series of studies in a school, college, or university; curriculum: *a liberal arts course.* **10.** one unit of study in such a curriculum: *a course in biology, a psychology course.* **11.** part of a meal served at one time: *The main course was chicken.* **12.** single continuous row or layer of building materials, as bricks, stones, or wood, on the face or wall of a structure. **13.a.** lowest square sail on any mast of a square-rigged ship. **b.** point of the compass toward which a ship proceeds. **14. in due course.** at the proper time (in a sequence). **15. of course. a.** certainly; undoubtedly. **b.** as is or might be expected; naturally: *Of course, he was fired on the spot.* —*v.t.,* **coursed, cours·ing. 1.** to run or move through or over: *The deer coursed the open field.* **2.** to chase; pursue: *The cavalry coursed the fleeing troops.* **3.** to hunt (game) with dogs: *to course rabbits.* **4.** to cause (dogs) to run in a hunt: *The hunters coursed their hounds after the fox.* —*v.i.* **1.** to move swiftly; run; flow: *The tears coursed down her cheek.* **2.** to take or follow a particular course: *The boats coursed along the east bank of the river.* **3.** to hunt game with dogs. [Old French *cours* a running, from Latin *cursus* a running, place for running.] —Syn. *n.* **5.** see **direction. 7.a.** see **route.**

cours·er (kôr′sər) *n.* swift or spirited horse. [Old French *corsier* race horse, from *cours* a running, course. See COURSE.]

court (kôrt) *n.* **1.** open space partially or wholly enclosed by walls or buildings; courtyard. **2.** short street or wide alley. **3.** special section of a large building, as a hotel or museum, usually roofed with glass. **4.a.** level space or area marked off for certain games: *a basketball court, a tennis court.* **b.** division or part of such an area. **5.** residence of a sovereign or other high dignitary; royal palace. **6.** family, councilors, and retinue of a sovereign, collectively: *the court of the Medici.* **7.** sovereign and his officers and advisers as a ruling power: *He served as U.S. ambassador at the court in Oslo.* **8.** any formal assembly held by a sovereign: *He was presented at court.* **9.** place where justice is judicially administered; courtroom; courthouse. **10.** one or several persons appointed to act as a tribunal possessing the legal right to hear, investigate, and determine cases and administer justice; judge or judges: *criminal court, court of appeals.* **11.** judicial assembly of such persons. **12.** regular session of a judicial assembly: *Court is held every day at ten.* **13.** flattering attention paid to win favor. **14.** courtship; wooing. **15. out of court. a.** without a trial: *They settled the claim out of court.* **b.** without claim to consideration. **16. to pay court to. a.** to try to win the love of; woo. **b.** to pay attention to (a person) to win his favor. —*v.t.* **1.** to seek the love or affection of; woo. **2.** to pay flattering attention to (a person) to win his favor. **3.** to attempt to get or gain; seek: *to court flattery, to court favor.* **4.** to tempt; invite; entice: *to court defeat, to court danger.* —*v.i.* to keep company: *They courted for a year.* [Old French *cort* yard', royal court, court of justice, from Latin *cohors* enclosure, company of soldiers. Doublet of COHORT.]

cour·te·ous (kur′tē əs) *adj.* having or marked by good manners; polite. [Old French *corteis* courtly, well-bred, from *cort.* See COURT.] —**cour′te·ous·ly,** *adv.* —**cour′te·ous·ness,** *n.* —Syn. see **polite.**

cour·te·san (kôr′tə zən, kur′-) *n.* prostitute, esp. one who associates with men of wealth and rank. [French *courtisane* strumpet; earlier, lady of the court, court mistress, from Italian *cortigiana,* from *corte* court, from Latin *cohors* enclosure.]

cour·te·sy (kur′tə sē) *pl.,* **-sies.** *n.* **1.** courteous behavior; politeness. **2.** courteous act; favor. **3.** curtsy. **4. by courtesy.** as a favor or indulgence or by common consent as distinguished from legal right: *a title by courtesy.* [Old French *cortoisie* polite behavior, from *corteis.* See COURTEOUS.]

court·house (kôrt′hous′) *n.* **1.** building in which courts of law are held. **2.** building housing the principal offices of a county government.

cour·ti·er (kôr′tē ər) *n.* **1.** one who frequents or attends the court of a sovereign. **2.** one who seeks favor by flattery.

court·ly (kôrt′lē) **-li·er, -li·est.** *adj.* **1.** suitable for a king's court; refined; elegant; polished. **2.** flattering; obsequious. —**court′li·ness,** *n.*

court-mar·tial (kôrt′mär′shəl) *pl.,* **courts-mar·tial.** *n.* **1.** military court that tries persons subject to military law. **2.** trial by such a court. —*v.t.,* **-tialed, -tial·ing;** *also, British,* **-tialled, -tial·ling.** to try by court-martial.

court of chancery, court having jurisdiction in equity.

Court of St. James, royal court of Great Britain.

court plaster, cloth with an adhesive substance on one side, used for covering slight wounds; adhesive tape. [Because ladies of royal *courts* used to wear black patches of this material on their faces and shoulders as beauty spots.]

court·room (kôrt′rōōm′, -room′) *n.* room in which a court of law is regularly held.

court·ship (kôrt′ship′) *n.* act, process, or period of courting or wooing.

court tennis, form of tennis played on an indoor court having high cement walls off which the ball may be played.

court·yard (kôrt′yärd′) *n.* open area surrounded by walls or buildings, in or adjoining a large building.

cou·sin (kuz′in) *n.* **1.** son or daughter of one's uncle or aunt; first cousin. **2.** any kinsman or kinswoman; specifically, a relative with whom one shares a common ancestor. First cousins are descended from the same pair of grandparents; second cousins have great-grandparents in common. The children of one's first (or second) cousins are first (or second) cousins once removed; grandchildren of one's first cousins are first cousins twice removed. **3.** person of a kindred race or nation. **4.** title of address used by a sovereign to a fellow sovereign or to a nobleman. [Old French *cousin* son of an uncle or aunt, going back to Latin *consōbrīnus* child of a mother's sister.] —**cous′in·ly,** *adj.*

cous·in-ger·man (kuz′in jur′mən) *pl.,* **cous·ins-ger·man** *n.* first cousin. [Old French *cousin-germain.* See COUSIN, GERMAN.]

Cous·teau, Jacques-Yves (kōōs tō′; zhäk ēv) 1911—, French underwater explorer.

couth (kōōth) *n.* good manners; refinement; polish: *He has no couth.* —*adj.* well-mannered; refined; polished. ▲ used humorously. [Old English *cūth* familiar.]

cou·ture (kōō tōōr′) *n.* work of a couturier; dressmaking or fashion designing. [French *couture* sewing, going back to Latin *consuere* to sew together.]

cou·tu·ri·er (kōō tōōr′ē ā′, -ē ər, -tōōr′yā) *n.* male dressmaker or fashion designer. [French *couturier,* from *couture.* See COUTURE.]

cou·tu·ri·ere (kōō tōōr′ē ər, -ē er′) *n.* female dressmaker or fashion designer. [French *couturière,* feminine of *couturier.* See COUTURIER.]

co·va·lent bond (kō vā′lənt) chemical bond formed by the sharing of pairs of electrons by adjacent atoms.

cove (kōv) *n.* **1.** small, sheltered recess in a shoreline. **2.** sheltered hollow, as in hills, mountains, or a wood. [Old English *cofa* chamber.]

cov·en (kuv′ən) *n.* gathering of witches. [Old French *covine* band, going back to Latin *convenīre* to come together.]

cov·e·nant (kuv′ə nənt) *n.* **1.** agreement, usually formal, between two or more persons or parties; compact. **2. Covenant. a.** agreement between Scottish Presbyterians and members of the English Parliament in 1643, attempting to establish the Presbyterian Church as the state church of England, Scotland, and Ireland. Also, **Solemn League and Covenant. b.** agreement signed by Scottish Presbyterians in 1638 as a testament of their faith. Also, **National Covenant. 3.** in the Bible, compact between God and man including the solemn promises of God to man. **4.** *Law.* written agreement, usually under seal, as a contract. —*v.i.* to enter into a covenant. —*v.t.* to promise by or in a covenant. [Old French *covenant* a coming together, promise, from *covenir* to agree, meet together, from Latin *convenīre* to come together.]

cov·e·nant·er (kuv′ə nən tər; *def. 2 also* kuv′ə nan′tər) *n.* **1.** one who makes a covenant. **2. Covenanter.** one who signed or supported either of the Scottish Presbyterian Covenants.

Cov·en·try (kuv′ən trē, kov′-) *n.* **1.** city in south-central England. During the English civil war Royalists were sent there to be imprisoned. Pop. (1968), 335,400. **2.** state of banishment or exclusion from society; ostracism. ▲ used esp. in the phrase *to send to Coventry.*

cov·er (kuv′ər) *v.t.* **1.** to put something over or upon, as to protect, conceal, or enclose; overlay: *to cover a table with a tablecloth, to cover a wall with paint, to cover an injured man with a blanket.* **2.** to extend over the surface of; spread over: *Snow covered the ground. The dog was covered with mud.* **3.** to wrap up; clothe: *She covered the children with heavy clothing.* **4.** to conceal from view or knowledge; hide; screen (often with *up*): *to cover up a crime, to cover up the facts in a case. Darkness covered their flight.* **5.** to protect; shelter; shield: *The thick woods covered the fugitive.* **6.** to travel or pass over: *He covered the distance in fifteen minutes.* **7.** to treat of; include; encompass: *His*

---

at; āpe; cär; end; mē; it; īce; hot; ōld; fôrk; wood; fōōl; oil; out; up; ūse; turn; sing; thin; this; zh in treasure; ə in ago, taken, pencil, lemon, circus.

memorandum covers the subject almost completely. **8.** to be sufficient to pay for or provide security or protection against: *His insurance covered the cost of the damages.* **9.** to aim directly at, as with a firearm: *He covered the thief with a pistol.* **10.** to put or hold within range; command: *The fortress on the hill covered the harbor area beneath.* **11.** to act as a reporter for; get the details of: *She will cover the trial for the paper. This paper covers sports thoroughly.* **12.** to equal the bet of (an opponent); accept the conditions of (a bet). **13.** *Sports.* **a.** to guard or defend against (an opposing player): *to cover a pass receiver.* **b.** to be responsible for defending (an area or position): *to cover a base in baseball.* **14.** to brood or sit on (eggs or chicks); incubate. **15.** to put or wear a hat or cap on (one's head): *You may cover your head after the flag passes.* —*v.i.* **1.** to envelop or spread over in order to overlay or conceal something: *This paint covers in one coat.* **2.** to act as a substitute or replacement for another. **3.** to provide an excuse or alibi (often with *up*): *to cover up for a friend.* —*n.* **1.** that which covers: *the cover of a box, the cover of a book.* **2.** that which shelters or protects, esp. from attack: *The troops fought under the cover of the airplanes.* **3.** that which shelters or conceals game or wild animals. **4.** table setting, esp. for one person, including utensils and linens. **5.** something that disguises or conceals; pretense: *He obtained their confidence under the cover of friendship.* **6.** cover charge. **7.** amount held in reserve to meet or back liabilities: *The legislature voted to remove the gold cover.* **8. to break cover,** to come out from hiding. **9. under cover,** secret or secretly: *He kept the important information under cover. Plans for the attack were made under cover.* [Old French *covrir* to hide, put something over something, from Latin *cooperīre* to cover entirely.] —**cov′er·er,** *n.* —**cov′er·less,** *adj.*

cov·er·age (kuv′ ɘr ij) *n.* **1.** degree to which something covers or is covered. **2.** all the risks covered by the terms of an insurance policy. **3.** act or manner of gathering and reporting news: *comprehensive coverage of an election.*

cov·er·all (kuv′ ɘr ôl′) *n.* *also,* **cov·er·alls.** one-piece work garment, usually combining a long-sleeved shirt and trousers, designed to be worn over regular clothing.

cover charge, stated amount regularly added to the check in a restaurant or night club, esp. as a charge for entertainment.

cover crop, crop, such as clover or rye, sown in a field or orchard to protect the soil, as from erosion, or to enrich it between plantings of other crops.

covered wagon, large wagon with a canvas cover that can be removed or spread over the wagon on hoops or similar supports.

cov·er·ing (kuv′ ɘr ing) *n.* something that covers.

cov·er·let (kuv′ ɘr lit) *n.* outer covering for a bed; bedspread; counterpane. [Anglo-Norman *covrelit* from Old French *covrir* to cover + *lit* bed (from Latin *lectus*). See COVER.]

cov·ert (kuv′ɘrt, kō′vɘrt) *adj.* **1.** secret; concealed; hidden: *a covert glance, a covert attempt to communicate with the prisoner.* **2.** covered over; sheltered. —*n.* **1.** hiding place; shelter. **2.** thicket that gives shelter to wild animals or game. [Old French *covert*, past participle of *covrir* to cover. See COVER.] —**cov′ert·ly,** *adv.* —**cov′ert·ness,** *n.* —**Syn.** *adj.* **1.** see secret.

covert cloth, twilled fabric, usually of wool and woven with two colors of yarn in the warp.

cov·er·ture (kuv′ɘr choor′, -chɘr) *n.* covering, esp. shelter, disguise, or concealment.

cov·er·up (kuv′ɘr up′) *n.* way of concealing something, esp. something dishonest or illegal.

cov·et (kuv′it) *v.t.* to desire eagerly or inordinately (something belonging to another). —*v.i.* to feel eager or inordinate desire for something belonging to another. [Old French *coveitier* to desire, going back to Latin *cupiditās* desire.] —**cov′et·er,** *n.*

cov·et·ous (kuv′it ɘs) *adj.* eagerly or inordinately desirous. —**cov′et·ous·ly,** *adv.* —**cov′et·ous·ness,** *n.* —**Syn.** see greedy.

cov·ey (kuv′ē) *pl.,* **-eys.** *n.* **1.** small flock of birds, esp. partridge or grouse. **2.** any small group; bevy; company. [Old French *covee* flock of birds, especially of partridges, from *cover* to hatch, sit on, from Latin *cubāre* to lie down.]

cow[1] (kou) *pl.,* **cows** or *(archaic)* **kine.** *n.* **1.** mature female of any bovine animal, genus *Bos,* esp. the domestic bovine. **2.** mature female of various other large mammals, as the elephant, whale, or seal. [Old English *cū* female of the bovine family.]

cow[2] (kou) *v.t.* to intimidate with threats; frighten; overawe. [Old Norse *kūga* to tyrannize over.] —**Syn.** see intimidate.

cow·ard (kou′ɘrd) *n.* one who lacks courage; one who flees from danger, difficulty, or pain. —*adj.* cowardly. [Old French *coart* (also *Coart* the timid hare in the medieval tales about Reynard the Fox), from *coe, coue* tail, from Latin *cauda;* because a frightened animal turns tail or has his tail between his legs.]

cow·ard·ice (kou′ɘr dis) *n.* lack of courage.

cow·ard·ly (kou′ɘr lē) *adj.* **1.** lacking courage; timorous; fearful.

2. of, characteristic of, or befitting a coward. —*adv.* like a coward. —**cow′ard·li·ness,** *n.*

cow·bell (kou′bel′) *n.* small bell hung around a cow's neck to ring when she moves and thus indicate her whereabouts.

cow·bird (kou′burd′) *n.* any of several songbirds of the family Icteridae, native to North and South America, often found with cattle. Length: 7–8 inches.

cow·boy (kou′boi′) *n.* man who herds and tends cattle on a ranch, usually riding on horseback to perform his work.

cow·catch·er (kou′kach′ɘr) *n.* metal frame on the front of a locomotive or streetcar for clearing the tracks of obstructions.

cow·er (kou′ɘr) *v.i.* to crouch or cringe, as in fear or shame. [Of Scandinavian origin.]

cow·fish (kou′fish′) *pl.,* **-fish** or **-fishes.** *n.* **1.** any of several species of trunkfish having long, bony, hornlike projections over the eyes. **2.** any of various marine mammals, as the dugong, manatee, or dolphin.

Cowfish

cow·girl (kou′gurl′) *n.* woman whose work is like a cowboy's.

cow·hand (kou′hand′) *n.* cowboy.

cow·herd (kou′hurd′) *n.* one who herds or tends cattle.

cow·hide (kou′hīd′) *n.* **1.** hide of a cow or leather made from it. **2.** strong, flexible whip made of braided leather or rawhide. —*v.t.* **-hid·ed, -hid·ing** to whip with a cowhide; flog.

cowl (koul) *n.* **1.** hood attached to a monk's robe. **2.** monk's robe with a hood. **3.** top front part of an automobile body to which the windshield, the instrument board, and the rear end of the hood are attached. **4.** cowling. **5.** covering, usually shaped like a hood, placed on the top of a chimney or vent to increase the draft. —*v.t.* **1.** to cover with or as with a cowl. **2.** to put a monk's cowl on; make a monk of. [Old English *cūle, cug(e)le* monk's hood, going back to Latin *cucullus* hood.]

Cow·ley, Abraham (kou′lē) 1618–67, English poet.

cow·lick (kou′lik′) *n.* tuft of hair that grows in a different direction from the rest of the hair and will not lie flat.

cowl·ing (kou′ling) *n.* streamlined metal covering for a section of an airplane, esp. one designed to cover an engine.

cow·man (kou′mɘn) *pl.,* **-men.** *n.* one who owns cattle; rancher.

co·work·er (kō′wur′kɘr, kō wur′-) *n.* fellow worker.

cow·pea (kou′pē′) *n.* **1.** bushy or trailing vine, *Vigna sinensis,* widely planted as a forage or cover crop, bearing long pods which contain edible kidney-shaped seeds. **2.** seed of this plant. Also (def. 2), **black-eyed pea.**

Cow·per, William (kōō′pɘr, kou′-) 1731–1800, English poet.

cow·poke (kou′pōk′) *n.* *Informal.* cowboy.

cow pony, pony used in herding cattle.

cow·pox (kou′poks′) *n.* mild but very contagious eruptive disease of cows caused by a strain of the virus that causes smallpox in man. Smallpox vaccine is prepared from the cowpox virus.

cow·punch·er (kou′pun′chɘr) *n.* *Informal.* cowboy.

cow·rie (kour′ē) *pl.,* **-ries.** *also,* **cow·ry.** *n.* **1.** small glossy shell of any of various sea snails, family Cypraeidae, commonly found in warm shallow waters of the Pacific and Indian oceans. The shell of the **money cowrie,** *Cypraea moneta,* is used as money by certain tribes of Africa and southern Asia. **2.** one of these snails. [Hindi *kaurī* small shell used as money, from Sanskrit *kaparda;* of Dravidian origin.]

cow·skin (kou′skin′) *n.* cowhide.

cow·slip (kou′slip′) *n.* **1.** wild plant, *Primula veris,* of the primrose family, having fragrant yellow flowers. **2.** a common marsh marigold, *Caltha palustris,* having deep-yellow flowers. **3.** flower of either of these plants. [Old English *cūslyppe* the plant *Primula veris,* from *cū* cow[1] + *slyppe* slime; probably because the flower grows profusely in well-manured cow pastures.]

cox (koks) *n.* *Informal.* coxswain. —*v.t.* to act as coxswain to (a boat). —*v.i.* to be coxswain.

cox·comb (koks′kōm′) *n.* **1.** vain and pretentious fop; conceited dandy. **2.** cockscomb. [Earlier *cockscombe* jester's cap resembling a rooster's crest; hence, fool, fop. See COCK[1], COMB.]

cox·comb·ry (koks′kōm′rē) *pl.,* **-ries.** *n.* action, behavior, or manner characteristic of a coxcomb; foppery; vanity.

cox·swain (kok′sɘn, -swān′) *also,* **cock·swain.** *n.* person who steers a boat and has charge of the crew, esp. the crew member who steers and gives directions to oarsmen in a racing shell. [Earlier *cockswain,* from obsolete *cock* cockboat (from Old French *coque,* from Late Latin *caudica* canoe; literally, boat made from the trunk of a tree, from Latin *caudex* trunk of a tree) + SWAIN.]

coy (koi) *adj.* **1.** shy; modest; bashful. **2.** pretending to be shy; coquet-

tishly modest or bashful. [Old French *coi,* earlier *quei* calm, quiet, going back to Latin *quiētus.* Doublet of QUIET.] **—coy'ly,** *adv.* **—coy'-ness,** *n.*

coy·o·te (kī o'tē, kī'ōt) *pl.,* **-tes** or **-te.** *n.* wolflike mammal, *Canis latrans,* native to the prairies of central and western North America, known for its howling at night. Height: 21 inches at the shoulder. Also, **prairie wolf.** [Spanish *coyote,* from Nahuatl *coyotl.*]

coy·pu (koi'pōō') *pl.,* **-pus** or **-pu.** *n.* aquatic rodent, *Myocastor coypus,* native to South America, closely resembling the muskrat and valued for its thick, light-brown to black fur. Length: 3 feet including tail. Also, **nu'tri·a.** [Spanish *coipú,* from Araucanian *kóypu.*]

Coyote

coz·en (kuz'ən) *v.t.* to cheat; dupe; deceive. *—v.i.* to act dishonestly or deceitfully; cheat. [Possibly from obsolete Italian *cozzonare* to act like a horse trader, cheat, from *cozzone* horse trader, from Latin *coctiō* broker.]

coz·en·age (kuz'ə nij) *n.* act or practice of cozening; fraud.

co·zy (kō'zē) **co·zi·er, co·zi·est.** *also, **co·sy.** adj.* comfortable; snug. *—n. pl.* **co·zies.** padded cloth or knitted cover for keeping the contents of a teapot warm. [Possibly from Norwegian *koselig* snug.] **—co'zi·ly,** *adv.* **—co'zi·ness,** *n.*

cp., compare.
c.p. 1. candle power. 2. chemically pure.
C.P. 1. Common Prayer. 2. Communist Party.
C.P.A., Certified Public Accountant.
cpd., compound.
Cpl., Corporal. Also, **cpl.**
Cr, chromium.
cr., credit; creditor.

crab[1] (krab) *n.* 1. any of a widespread group of usually saltwater crustaceans, suborder Brachyura, having a broad, flat body with the abdomen tightly curled under the body, four pairs of legs, and a pair of pincer claws. Many kinds of crabs are highly valued as food. 2. any of various similar arthropods, such as the horseshoe crab. 3. machine or apparatus for hoisting or hauling heavy weights. 4. cross, ill-tempered person. 5. **to catch a crab.** to make a faulty stroke in rowing either by dipping the oar into the water on the recovery or missing the water on the stroke. *—v.i.* **crabbed, crab·bing.** 1. to fish for or catch crabs. 2. *Informal.* to find fault; complain. *—v.t.* 1. to find fault with; criticize. 2. *Informal.* to spoil; ruin. [Old English *crabba* the crustacean.] **—crab'ber,** *n.*

crab[2] (krab) *n.* crab apple. [Of uncertain origin.]

Coypu

Crab

crab apple 1. small, hard, sour apple of any of several trees, genus *Malus,* of the rose family, growing wild or cultivated. Some varieties are pickled or used for making jelly. 2. tree bearing this fruit, having oval leaves and small, fragrant pink, white, or red flowers.

crab·bed (krab'id) *adj.* 1. cross; peevish; crabby. 2. hard to understand; involved; perplexing. 3. (of handwriting) hard to read or decipher; cramped. [CRAB[1] + -ED[2].] **—crab'bed·ly,** *adv.* **—crab'bed·ness,** *n.*

crab·by (krab'ē) **-bi·er, -bi·est.** *adj.* ill-tempered; peevish; cross. **—crab'bi·ly,** *adv.* **—crab'bi·ness,** *n.*

crab grass, any of several hardy, creeping grasses, genus *Digitaria,* having fuzzy, sword-shaped leaves, and bearing spikes of purple flowers. Crab grass spreads rapidly and is a common lawn and agricultural weed pest.

crab tree, any of various species of trees that bear crab apples.

crack (krak) *n.* 1. a break that does not cause separation into parts: *a crack in a mirror.* 2. sudden, sharp noise: *the crack of a rifle.* 3. *Informal.* sharp, heavy, resounding blow: *He gave him a crack on the head.* 4. narrow opening; fissure: *Open the window a crack.* 5. *Informal.* instant; moment: *He gets up at the crack of dawn.* 6. *Slang.* try; attempt: *Let me have a crack at opening that jar.* 7. *Slang.* witty remark; sarcastic comment: *I've had enough of his cracks.* *—v.i.* 1. to break without completely separating into parts; become split or fissured: *The glaze on the pottery cracked.* 2. to break with a sudden sharp noise: *The branch cracked off the trunk.* 3. to become harsh, shrill, or dissonant; change tone or register: *His voice cracked.* 4. *Informal.* to break down; fail: *The men cracked under the pressure of work.* 5. **to crack down on.** *Slang.* to become strict with; take severe

measures against. 6. **to crack up.** *Informal.* **a.** to suffer a physical or mental breakdown. **b.** to be in an accident: *They cracked up at the intersection.* **c.** to become overwhelmed by laughter: *I cracked up over his jokes.* *—v.t.* 1. to cause to make a sudden, sharp noise; snap: *He cracked the whip above the horse's head.* 2. to break partially; cause to split or fissure: *to crack the ice on a pond.* 3. to break, as into pieces, with a sudden, sharp noise: *He cracked the coconut on the pavement.* 4. *Informal.* to hit or strike with a sharp, resounding noise: *The teacher cracked him on the hand with a ruler.* 5. *Informal.* to open; enter: *to crack a safe.* 6. *Informal.* to find the solution to; puzzle out: *He cracked the code.* 7. to cause (the voice) to become harsh, shrill, or dissonant. 8. to damage; destroy: *to crack a tradition.* 9. to subject, as petroleum or coal tar, to the process of cracking. 10. **to crack a book.** to open a book, esp. a textbook, to read or study. 11. **to crack a joke.** to tell a joke; make a witty remark. 12. **to crack a smile.** to begin to smile. 13. **to crack up.** *Informal.* **a.** to crash; destroy; wreck: *He cracked up the car.* **b.** to praise; extol. **c.** to cause to become overwhelmed by laughter. 14. **cracked up to be.** *Informal.* claimed or believed to be. *—adj. Informal.* excellent; first-rate: *He was a crack shot.* [Old English *cracian* to make a sharp noise in breaking, resound.]

Syn. *v.t.* 1. **Crack, fracture** mean to break. **Crack** implies that something brittle, hollow, or hard breaks with a sharp, snapping sound without causing it to come apart: *The boiling water cracked the glass.* **Fracture** means to break through the entire thickness of the material: *The skier fractured a bone in his right leg when he fell down the slope.*

crack-brained (krak'brānd') *adj.* crazy; insane.

crack·down (krak'doun') *n.* sudden, strict enforcement of laws or rules: *a crackdown on illegal gambling.*

cracked (krakt) *adj.* 1. having a crack or cracks; broken without a separation of parts; fractured. 2. broken into small pieces; crushed: *We put cracked ice in the punch bowl.* 3. (of the voice) harsh, shrill, or dissonant; changing in tone. 4. *Informal.* crazy; deranged.

crack·er (krak'ər) *n.* 1. thin, crisp biscuit. 2. one who or that which cracks. 3. firecracker. 4. small paper roll used as a party favor, containing candy, a toy, or another surprise, in which an explosion occurs when it is pulled sharply at both ends. 5. *Informal.* impoverished white person in parts of the southeastern United States, esp. rural areas of Georgia and Florida.

crack·er·jack (krak'ər jak') *Slang. n.* person or thing of exceptional ability or quality. *—adj.* of exceptional ability or quality.

crack·ing (krak'ing) *n.* process of decomposing complex hydrocarbons, esp. those in petroleum, into simpler hydrocarbons with lower boiling points by heat, pressure, and catalysis. Greater amounts of gasoline are obtained by cracking.

crack·le (krak'əl) **-led, -ling.** *v.i.* to make a succession of slight sharp sounds: *The dry leaves crackled when we walked on them.* *—v.t.* to crush or break with such sounds. *—n.* 1. one of a series of slight, sharp sounds. 2. network of minute cracks in the glazed surface of certain types of ceramics, glassware, and painted finishes. 3. ceramics or glassware having such a surface. Also (*def. 3*). **crack'le·ware'.** [CRACK + -LE.]

crack·ling (krak'ling) *n.* 1. rapid succession of slight, sharp sounds. 2. crisp, browned skin of roasted pork. 3. **cracklings.** *Informal.* crisp residues left after lard has been rendered from hog's fat.

crack·ly (krak'lē) *adj.* tending to crackle; making a crackling sound.

crack·nel (krak'nəl) *n.* 1. small, hard, brittle biscuit. 2. **cracknels.** **a.** small pieces of crisply fried fat pork. **b.** cracklings. [Modification of French *craquelin* a crisp biscuit, from Middle Dutch *krākelinc,* from *krāken* to crack.]

crack of doom 1. signal announcing Judgment Day. 2. the end of the world; doomsday.

crack·pot (krak'pot') *n. Slang.* eccentric or deranged person. *—adj.* eccentric; crazy; foolish.

cracks·man (kraks'mən) *pl.,* **-men.** *n. Slang.* burglar; safecracker.

crack-up (krak'up') *n.* 1. crash, as of a car or airplane. 2. *Informal.* mental or physical breakdown.

Crac·ow (krak'ou, krä'kō) Kraków.

cra·dle (krād'əl) *n.* 1. little bed for an infant, usually on rockers. 2. place or region where something starts or begins to develop: *a cradle of liberty, the cradle of civilization.* 3. framework supporting something large, as a ship, while it is being constructed or repaired. 4. frame used to protect a broken limb. 5. low frame set on rollers or casters, used by mechanics while working under an automobile. 6. part of a telephone which is electrically connected to the wall outlet and holds the handset. 7. box on rockers used to wash gold from gold-bearing earth. 8.a. frame with several long curved prongs, attached to a scythe for laying the cut grain evenly. **b.** scythe equipped with such a frame. Also, **cradle scythe.** 9. **to rob the cradle.** to take as one's spouse or sweetheart someone much younger than oneself. *—v.t.* **-dled, -dling.** 1. to put, rock, or hold in or as in a cradle: *She cradled the child in her arms.*

at; āpe; cär; end; mē; it; īce; hot; ōld; fôrk; wood; fōōl; oil; out; up; ūse; turn; sing; thin; this; zh in treasure; ə in ago, taken, pencil, lemon, circus.

2. to nurture, shelter, or train in infancy or the earliest stages of development: *Civilization was cradled somewhere in Asia.* 3. to support in or on a cradle, as a ship. 4. to wash (earth containing gold) in a cradle. 5. to cut (grain) using a cradle. [Old English *cradol* baby's bed.]

cra·dle·song (krād′əl sông′) *n.* lullaby.

craft (kraft) *n.* 1. special skill, dexterity, or ability: *The cabinetmaker worked with precision and craft.* 2. skill in deceiving; deceit; guile; cunning. 3. trade or occupation requiring special skill, dexterity, or ability, esp. manual dexterity. 4. members of a trade collectively. 5. boat, ship, or aircraft. 6. boats, ships, or aircraft collectively. [Old English *craft* strength, skill, trade.]

crafts·man (krafts′mən) *pl.,* **-men.** *n.* 1. skilled workman; artisan. 2. artist, esp. one who is technically excellent. —**crafts′man·ship′,** *n.*

craft union, labor union that limits membership to workers in a single craft or occupation or a few very closely related ones. Distinguished from **industrial union.**

craft·y (kraf′tē) **craft·i·er, craft·i·est.** *adj.* skillful in deceiving; wily; cunning. —**craft′i·ly,** *adv.* —**craft′i·ness,** *n.* —**Syn.** see **sly.**

crag (krag) *n.* steep, rugged, or projecting rock or cliff. [Of Celtic origin.] —**crag·ged** (krag′id) **crag′gy,** *adj.* —**crag′gi·ness,** *n.*

crake (krāk) *n.* any of various birds of the rail family, esp. those having short bills and long legs. [Old Norse *krāka*; of imitative origin.]

cram (kram) **crammed, cram·ming.** *v.t.* 1. to fill (a space or receptacle) with more than it normally or conveniently holds: *She crammed her closet with clothes.* 2. to force or crowd (something) into a space or receptacle: *We crammed more than a hundred books into the small bookcase.* 3. to fill to excess with food; stuff. 4. *Informal.* to prepare (a person) or study (a subject) for an examination or the like, hastily and intensely. —*v.i.* 1. to eat greedily or to excess; stuff. 2. to study hastily and intensely for an examination or similar purpose: *She crammed for her history exam.* [Old English *crammian* to stuff.] —**cram′mer,** *n.*

cramp¹ (kramp) *n.* 1. painful contraction occurring suddenly in a muscle or group of muscles. 2. spasm or temporary paralysis of particular muscles as a result of excessive use. 3. **cramps,** sharp abdominal pains. —*v.t.* to affect with or as with a cramp. [Old French *crampe* painful contraction; of Germanic origin.]

cramp² (kramp) *n.* 1. metal bar bent at the ends, for holding together pieces of stone, timber, or masonry. 2. clamp. 3. anything that confines or hinders. 4. confined or hindered condition or part. —*v.t.* 1. to fasten or hold with a cramp. 2. to confine; restrain; hamper. 3. **to cramp (someone's) style.** *Slang.* to hamper (someone's) normal efforts, skill, or confidence. —*adj.* cramped. [Middle Dutch *crampe* hook.]

cram·pon (kram′pon) *n.* 1. iron bar bent in the form of a hook, used esp. in hinged pairs to lift heavy objects. 2. **crampons,** spiked, iron plates attached to the soles of the shoes or boots of mountain climbers to prevent slipping. [French *crampon* grappling iron, calk²; of Germanic origin.]

cran·ber·ry (kran′ber′ē) *pl.,* **-ries.** *n.* 1. red, sour-tasting berry of any of several low, creeping shrubs, genus *Vaccinium,* of the heath family, grown in bogs and widely used for sauce, juice, and other things. 2. shrub bearing this fruit. [Low German *kraanbere* literally, crane berry; because its stamens are shaped like beaks.]

crane (krān) *n.* 1. any of various mobile machines having a long boom equipped with hoisting tackle for lifting and moving heavy loads. 2. metal arm pivoted on the wall of a fireplace and used to swing a kettle or a pot over the fire. 3. any of a group of large wading birds, family Gruidae, having very long legs, a long neck, a short, wide tail, long, broad wings, and gray, brown, or white plumage. 4. any of various similar birds. —*v.t.* 1. to stretch out (the neck). 2. to hoist, lower, or move by, or as if by, a crane. —*v.i.* to stretch out one's neck: *The people in the back row had to crane to see the stage.* [Old English *cran* the bird; with reference to the resemblance of the machine's boom to the long neck of the bird.]

Crane (def. 3)

Crane (krān) 1. **Hart.** 1899–1932, U.S. poet. 2. **Stephen.** 1871–1900, U.S. novelist and short-story writer.

cranes·bill (krānz′bil′) *also,* **crane's-bill.** *n.* any geranium, esp. the common wild American geranium.

cra·ni·al (krā′nē əl) *adj.* of, from, or relating to the cranium or skull: *a cranial nerve.* —**cra′ni·al·ly,** *adv.*

cra·ni·ol·o·gy (krā′nē ol′ə jē) *n.* science dealing with the variations in size, shape, and other characteristics of skulls, esp. human skulls. [Greek *krānion* skull + -LOGY.]

cra·ni·om·e·try (krā′nē om′ə trē) *n.* science of measuring skulls;

measurement of skulls and the relations between their parts. [Greek *krānion* skull + -METRY.]

cra·ni·um (krā′nē əm) *pl.,* **-ni·ums** or **-ni·a** (-nē ə). *n.* 1. skull of a vertebrate. 2. the part of the skull which encloses the brain; brain pan. [Medieval Latin *cranium* skull, from Greek *krānion.*]

crank (krangk) *n.* 1. device that transmits motion, esp. an arm attached at right angles to a shaft for transmitting rotary motion. 2. *Informal.* person given to peculiar ideas or behavior; eccentric. 3. *Informal.* grouchy, ill-tempered person. 4. eccentric notion or action; caprice; whim. 5. fanciful turn of speech. —*v.t.* 1. to start or operate with a crank: *It was necessary to crank the Model T Ford by hand.* 2. to bend into the shape of a crank. —*v.i.* to turn a crank. —*adj.* characteristic of the behavior of a crank; eccentric: *a crank telephone call.* [Old English *cranc,* as in *crancstæf* weaver's instrument.]

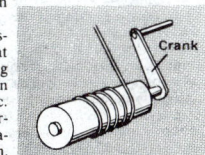
Crank

crank·case (krangk′kās′) *n.* metal case enclosing the crankshaft of an engine.

crank pin, pin or cylinder by which a connecting rod is attached to a crank.

crank·shaft (krangk′shaft′) *n.* shaft driven by or driving a crank.

crank·y (krang′kē) **crank·i·er, crank·i·est.** *adj.* 1. ill-tempered; irritable. 2. peculiar; eccentric. —**crank′i·ly,** *adv.* —**crank′i·ness,** *n.*

cran·ny (kran′ē) *pl.,* **-nies.** *n.* small, narrow opening; crack; crevice; fissure. [Old French *cran* notch, from *crener* to notch; of Celtic origin.] —**cran′nied,** *adj.*

Cran·ston (kran′stən) *n.* city in east-central Rhode Island. Pop. (1970), 73,037.

crap (krap) *n.* 1. craps. 2. losing throw in a game of craps. —*v.i.* 1. to make a losing throw in a game of craps: *He crapped on the first throw.* 2. **to crap out.** **a.** in craps, to roll a seven when trying to make a point. **b.** *Slang.* to run out of power or energy; come to a halt; fail.

crape (krāp) *n.* 1. crepe. 2. band of black crepe worn or hung as a sign of mourning.

crap·pie (krap′ē) *n.* North American sunfish of either of two species, the **black crappie,** *Pomoxis nigromaculatus,* found in clear quiet lakes and ponds, or the **white crappie,** *P. annularis,* found in swiftly running waters. Both are valued as food fish. [French *crapet* a freshwater fish; of uncertain origin.]

craps (kraps) *n.* gambling game played with two dice. On the first throw, a roll of 2, 3, or 12 loses; a 7 or 11 wins. If a 4, 5, 6, 8, 9 or 10 is rolled, the same number must be rolled again before a 7 in order to win the bet.

crap·shoot·er (krap′shōō′tər) *n.* one who plays craps.

crash¹ (krash) *n.* 1. sudden, loud noise, as of something shattering or breaking: *There was a crash when the ball went through the window.* 2. heavy fall or breaking with force, as of something solid: *the crash of a falling tree.* 3.a. sudden decline, collapse, or ruin, esp. of a commercial enterprise: *The crash of the great railroad empire was unexpected.* b. sudden general financial or business crisis and decline of values: *a stock-market crash.* 4. act of crashing, as of a car or airplane. —*v.i.* 1. to make a sudden, loud noise: *The thunder crashed overhead.* 2. to fall, strike, or break into pieces forcefully with a loud noise; smash: *The cups crashed to the floor.* 3. to move, strike, or go with such violence and noise: *to crash into a wall.* 4. to suffer sudden decline, collapse, or ruin: *His business crashed last year.* 5. to land, fall, or be driven abnormally so as to be damaged or destroyed: *The plane crashed during the night.* —*v.t.* 1. to break noisily and violently; smash; shatter: *He crashed the glass against the table.* 2. to force or drive with violence and noise. 3. to cause to be damaged or destroyed, as an automobile or airplane. 4. *Informal.* to enter, as a party or theater, either without paying admission or without an invitation. —*adj.* characterized by or carried out with extreme speed, intense effort, and assignment of all necessary resources: *a crash program.* [Imitative.] —**crash′er,** *n.*

crash² (krash) *n.* cotton or linen cloth, made from uneven and irregular yarns used for towels, tablecloths, curtains, and the like. [Short for Russian *krashenina* colored linen, from *krashenie* coloring.]

crash-dive (krash′dīv′) **-dived, -div·ing.** *v.i., v.t.* to make or cause to make a crash dive.

crash dive, sudden rapid dive made by a submarine, esp. to avoid attack by an enemy aircraft or surface vessel.

crash helmet, padded helmet for protection against head injury, worn esp. by motorcyclists, automobile racers, and aviators.

crash-land (krash′land′) *v.t.* to land (an aircraft), esp. with damage to the craft, under conditions that make normal landing impossible. —*v.i.* to crash-land an aircraft.

crash landing, landing of an aircraft, esp. with damage to the craft, under conditions that make normal landing impossible.

crass (kras) *adj.* **1.** grossly dull or stupid; insensitive. **2.** thick; coarse. [Latin *crassus* gross, thick, fat.] —**crass′ly**, *adv.* —**crass′ness**, *n.*

crate (krāt) *n.* **1.** box, case, or framework, usually of wooden slats, for protecting things during shipping or storage: *an orange crate, a furniture crate.* **2.** *Slang.* battered or decrepit automobile or airplane. —*v.t.,* **crat·ed, crat·ing.** to pack in a crate or crates. [Latin *crātis* wickerwork, hurdle.]

cra·ter (krā′tər) *n.* **1.** bowl-shaped depression at the mouth of a volcano. **2.** any depression resembling this, as one caused by the explosion of a bomb or by the impact of a meteorite. **3.** vessel or bowl used in ancient Greece for mixing wine and water. [Latin *crātēr* bowl, mouth of a volcano, from Greek *krātēr.*]

Crater Lake, lake in a crater on the site of a prehistoric volcano, in southwestern Oregon. It is the deepest lake in North America.

cra·vat (krə vat′) *n.* **1.** necktie. **2.** man's scarf of silk or other fine material worn as a neckcloth. [French *cravate* necktie, from *Cravate* Croatian, going back to Serbo-Croatian *Hrvat;* with reference to the linen scarf worn around the neck by Croatians in French service in the seventeenth century.]

crave (krāv) **craved, crav·ing.** *v.t.* **1.** to long for or yearn for; eagerly desire: *The artist craved recognition of his talents.* **2.** to need greatly; require: *The wound craved attention.* **3.** to ask for earnestly; beg: *The cavalier . . . knelt and craved a benediction* (Irving, 1804). —*v.i.* to long, yearn, or desire (with *for* or *after*): *to crave after the unknown.* [Old English *crafian* to demand.]

cra·ven (krā′vən) *adj.* cowardly. —*n.* coward. [Middle English *cravant* vanquished, from Old French *cravant,* present participle of *craver, crever* to burst, break, from Latin *crepāre* to burst.] —**cra′ven·ly**, *adv.* —**cra′ven·ness**, *n.*

crav·ing (krā′ving) *n.* intense or eager desire; longing; yearning.

craw (krô) *n.* **1.** crop of a bird or insect. **2.** stomach of any animal. [Probably from an unrecorded Old English word.]

craw·fish (krô′fish′) *pl.* **-fish** or **-fish·es.** —*n.* crayfish. —*v.i. Informal.* to retreat from a position, opinion, or plan; back out; back down. [Form of CRAYFISH.]

crawl[1] (krôl) *v.i.* **1.** to move slowly by dragging the body along the ground. **2.** to move slowly on hands and knees: *The baby crawled across the room.* **3.** to move slowly: *Traffic crawled through the city.* **4.** to move stealthily or abjectly: *Once he had discovered the bookkeeper's secret, he made him crawl. He crawled into the king's confidence.* **5.** to swarm or be alive with, or as with, crawling things: *The resort crawled with tourists.* **6.** to feel as if covered with crawling things: *The ghost story made my skin crawl.* —*n.* **1.** act of crawling; slow crawling motion: *Traffic was slowed to a crawl.* **2.** any of several swimming strokes combining an overarm motion with a flutter kick. The **American crawl** consists of six flutter kicks to each overarm cycle. The **Australian crawl** consists of eight flutter kicks to each overarm cycle. [Old Norse *krafla* to paw, creep.] —**crawl′er**, *n.*

crawl[2] (krôl) *n.* enclosure of stakes set upright in shallow water, used esp. to hold turtles, fish, or shellfish. [Afrikaans *kraal* enclosure, village, from Portuguese *curral* cattle pen, enclosure. See KRAAL.]

crawl·ers (krô′lərz) *n.* one-piece garment, combining waist and pants, worn by infants.

crawler tractor, tractor with two continuous tracks or belts rather than wheels.

crawl·y (krô′lē) **crawl·i·er, crawl·i·est.** *adj. Informal.* having the sensation of things crawling over one's skin; creepy.

cray·fish (krā′fish′) *pl.* **-fish** or **-fish·es.** *n.* any of several lobsterlike crustaceans found in fresh water in most parts of the world, valued as a food source, esp. in Europe and the southeastern United States. Also, **craw′fish′.** [Earlier *crevis,* from Old French *crevice,* from Old High German *krebiz;* influenced by FISH.]

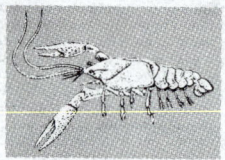

Crayfish

cray·on (krā′on, -ən) *n.* **1.a.** stick of a colored waxlike substance used for drawing. **b.** stick of chalk, charcoal, or clay, sometimes mixed with pigment, used as an artist's drawing implement. **2.** drawing made with a crayon or crayons. —*v.t., v.i.* to draw with a crayon or crayons. [French *crayon* pencil, drawing made with a crayon, from *craie* chalk, from Latin *crēta.*]

craze (krāz) *n.* **1.** something suddenly and temporarily very popular; fad; rage. **2.** minute crack in the glazed surface of ceramics or glassware. —*v.t.,* **crazed, craz·ing. 1.** to make insane; derange: *The sudden tragedy crazed him almost beyond recovery.* **2.** to make or cause minute cracks in the glazed surface of (ceramics or glassware). —*v.i.* **1.** to become insane. **2.** to become minutely cracked, as the glaze in the surface of pottery. [Of Scandinavian origin.]

cra·zy (krā′zē) **-zi·er, -zi·est.** *adj.* **1.** of unsound or deranged mind; insane; demented. **2.** caused by, marked by, or showing mental derangement. **3.** *Informal.* irrationally or extremely enthusiastic or excited: *The boy was crazy about cars.* **4.** out of balance; likely to come apart; unsound; shaky: *The hut stood at a crazy angle.* —**cra′zi·ly**, *adv.* —**cra′zi·ness**, *n.*

crazy bone, funny bone.

Crazy Horse, c.1849–77, Sioux chief who led the Indian forces at the battle of Little Bighorn.

crazy quilt, quilt made of pieces of cloth of various materials, shapes, colors, and sizes, which are sewed together without any regular pattern.

creak (krēk) *v.i.* **1.** to make a sharp, grating, or squeaking sound: *My new shoes creak when I walk.* **2.** to move with such a sound: *The gate creaked open.* —*v.t.* to cause to creak. —*n.* sharp, grating, or squeaking sound. [Imitative.]

creak·y (krē′kē) **creak·i·er, creak·i·est.** *adj.* likely to creak; creaking. —**creak′i·ly**, *adv.* —**creak′i·ness**, *n.*

cream (krēm) *n.* **1.** fatty, yellowish part of milk, which contains butterfat and rises to the top of milk that is not homogenized. **2.** food made from, containing, or resembling this substance: *chocolate creams.* **3.** soft preparation used to cleanse or protect: *shaving cream.* **4.** the choicest part of anything: *the cream of the crop.* **5.** yellowish white color of cream. —*v.t.* **1.** to add cream to: *She creamed and sugared her coffee.* **2.** to remove the cream from; skim: *to cream milk.* **3.** to take the best or choicest part from. **4.** to cook with cream, milk, or a cream sauce. **5.** to blend into a creamy consistency: *to cream butter and sugar.* **6.** to allow or cause (milk) to form cream. **7.** *Slang.* to defeat soundly; beat decisively. —*v.i.* **1.** to form cream or a creamy substance on the top. **2.** to foam; froth. —*adj.* **1.** containing or made of cream or milk. **2.** of the color of cream: *The bride wore a dress of cream velvet.* [Old French *cresme* holy oil, fatty part of milk, from blend of Late Latin *crāmum* fatty part of milk (of Celtic origin) and Latin *chrīsma* holy oil (from Greek *chrīsma* unguent).]

cream cheese, soft, smooth, unripened cheese made from a mixture of milk and cream.

cream·er (krē′mər) *n.* small pitcher used for serving cream.

cream·er·y (krē′mər ē) *pl.* **-er·ies.** *n.* **1.** place where butter, cheese, and other dairy products are made. **2.** place where milk, cream, and dairy products are sold.

cream of tar·tar (tär′tər) white crystalline or powdery compound containing potassium, hydrogen, carbon, and oxygen, used esp. in baking powder, and also in medicine and the tinning of metals. Also, **potassium bitartrate.** Formula: $KHC_4H_4O_6$

cream·puff (krēm′puf′) *n.* very light pastry shell filled with custard or whipped cream.

cream sauce, sauce made of cream or milk cooked with flour and butter.

cream·y (krē′mē) *adj.* **1.** containing cream. **2.** resembling cream in appearance, color, or consistency: *creamy skin.* —**cream′i·ly**, *adv.* —**cream′i·ness**, *n.*

crease[1] (krēs) *n.* line or mark produced by or as by a fold; wrinkle; ridge, as in pressed cloth. —*v.t.,* **creased, creas·ing. 1.** to make a crease or creases on or in. **2.** to graze with a bullet. —*v.i.* to become creased. [Earlier *creast* ridge, form of CREST.] —**creas′er**, *n.*

crease[2] (krēs) *knis.*

cre·ate (krē āt′) **-at·ed, -at·ing.** *v.t.* **1.** to bring into being; cause to exist: *In the beginning God created the heaven and the earth* (Genesis 1:1). **2.** to give rise to; cause; occasion: *His attitude created much ill will.* **3.** to produce by one's own thought or imagination: *Shakespeare created many comic characters.* **4.** to invest with new office, rank, or function: *The queen created him a peer.* **5.** (of an actor) to be the first to portray (a character or role). [Latin *creātus,* past participle of *creāre* to make, produce.]

cre·a·tion (krē ā′shən) *n.* **1.** act of creating; being created. **2.** that which is created, esp. something that is a product of human intelligence, imagination, or power. **3.** everything created; the world and everything in it; universe. **4. the Creation,** God's act of creating the universe.

cre·a·tive (krē ā′tiv) *adj.* **1.** having the power or quality of creating: *creative imagination.* **2.** marked by originality of thought, presentation, or performance: *creative writing.* **3.** originative; productive (with *of*): *Laws and customs cannot be creative of virtue* (Martineau, 1837). —**cre·a′tive·ly**, *adv.* —**cre·a′tive·ness**, **cre′a·tiv′i·ty**, *n.*

cre·a·tor (krē ā′tər) *n.* **1.** one who or that which creates: *A. Conan Doyle is the creator of Sherlock Holmes.* **2. the Creator,** God.

crea·ture (krē′chər) *n.* **1.** living being, esp. an animal as distinct from man: *the small creatures of the wood.* **2.** human being: *She's a beautiful creature.* **3.** one who is completely dependent upon or under the influence of someone or something; puppet; tool: *Man is a creature of habit.* **4.** anything created; creation. [Old French *creature* animal, person, from Late Latin *creātūra* thing created, creation, from Latin *creāre* to make, produce.]

at; āpe; cär; end; mē; it; īce; hot; ōld; fôrk; wood; fool; oil; out; up; use; turn; sing; thin; this; zh in treasure; ə in ago, taken, pencil, lemon, circus.

creature comforts. physical comforts, esp. food, clothing, and shelter.

crèche (kresh, krāsh) *n.* **1.** representation of the Nativity scene, usually including figures of the Christ child, Mary, Joseph, the shepherds, the Three Wise Men, and the animals at the manger, often displayed at Christmas. **2.** *British.* day nursery. [French *crèche* manger, crib, day nursery; of Germanic origin.]

Cré·cy (kres′ē, krā sē′) *also,* **Cres·sy.** *n.* town in northern France, site of an English victory over the French, in 1346.

cre·dence (krēd′əns) *n.* belief, esp. in the reports or statements of others: *He doesn't give credence to rumors.* [Old French *credence,* from Medieval Latin *credentia,* from Latin *crēdere* to believe.]

cre·den·tials (kri den′shəlz) *n.pl.* **1.** document or letter establishing the identity, authority, or the right to confidence or accreditation of the bearer. **2.** anything that entitles a person to status, confidence, authority, or credit.

cre·den·za (kri den′zə) *n.* buffet or sideboard, esp. one without legs. [Italian *credenza* literally, belief, trust, from Medieval Latin *credentia,* from Latin *crēdere* to believe; because in earlier times a nobleman's food was placed on such a sideboard to be tested for poison before the meal.]

cred·i·ble (kred′ə bəl) *adj.* that can be believed; believable; reliable: *There was only one credible account of the incident.* [Latin *crēdibilis,* from *crēdere* to believe.] —**cred′i·bil′i·ty, cred′i·ble·ness,** *n.* —**cred′i·bly,** *adv.*

cred·it (kred′it) *n.* **1.** belief in or reliance on the truth of something; faith; trust: *We gave credit to his story.* **2.** influence or authority derived from one's reputation or character. **3.** quality or state of being worthy of belief or trust. **4.** favorable estimation of one's character; good reputation; esteem: *Civic service brings credit to a man.* **5.** honor or commendation due for some action or quality; praise: *She deserves credit for the success of the party.* **6.** person or thing that brings honor, approval, or praise: *He is a credit to his school.* **7. credits.** acknowledgments for work done or assistance given, as in a motion picture: *His name appeared in the credits.* **8.** trust or confidence in a person's or firm's ability and intention to meet financial obligations: *to sell or buy on credit.* **9.** reputation in financial matters: *His credit was no longer good at the store.* **10.** amount of money against which a person or firm may draw: *The new arrangement more than doubles their credit.* **11.a.** entry of an amount in an account in payment of an existing or future debt: *Carry that payment as a credit against next month's billing.* **b.** the right-hand side of an account where such entries are made. **c.** the sum of the entries, or any one entry, on this side of the account. **12.** balance in one's favor in an account. **13.** time allowed for payment of a debt. **14.a.** official entry on a student's record certifying satisfactory completion of a course of study: *He received credit for the course.* **b.** unit of such study: *He took three credits of math.* **15. to do credit to.** to bring honor, approval, or praise to. **16. to give someone credit for. a.** to believe that one has: *Give him credit for sincerity.* **b.** to praise someone for: *He gave her credit for her contribution to the project's success.* **17. to give credit to.** to accept or believe as true; have faith in; trust. **18. on credit.** with the understanding that one will pay at a future time. —*v. t.* **1.** to give financial credit to: *He credited the checks to his account.* **2.** to enter on the credit side of an account. **3.** to give educational credits to (a student). **4.** to believe; trust: *Do you expect me to credit that absurd tale?* **5. to credit (someone) with.** to attribute or ascribe to someone; consider or believe someone to have. **6. to credit (something) to.** to ascribe to; attribute to: *They credit the defeat to poor planning by the general.* [French *crédit* trust, reputation, from Latin *crēditum* thing entrusted, loan, from *crēdere* to believe.]

cred·it·a·ble (kred′i tə bəl) *adj.* bringing honor or approval; praiseworthy: *a creditable performance.* —**cred′it·a·ble·ness,** *n.* —**cred′it·a·bly,** *adv.*

credit card, card entitling its holder to make purchases or obtain services on credit from commercial establishments recognizing the validity of the card.

cred·i·tor (kred′i tər) *n.* person or firm that gives credit; one to whom something, esp. a loan, is owed.

credit union, cooperative association able to make loans to its members at low interest rates by common pooling of the members' savings.

cre·do (krē′dō, krā′-) *n., pl.* **-dos.** *n.* **1.** creed. **2.** Credo. Apostles' Creed or Nicene Creed. **3.** musical setting for either of these Creeds. **4.** portion of the Mass at which the Nicene Creed is said or sung. [Latin *crēdō* I believe; first word in the Latin texts of the Apostles' Creed and the Nicene Creed.]

cre·du·li·ty (kri dōō′li tē, -dū′-) *n.* readiness to believe, trust, or accept on weak or insufficient evidence; gullibility.

cred·u·lous (krej′ə ləs) *adj.* **1.** tending to believe readily; gullible. **2.** characterized by or arising from credulity: *credulous superstitions.* [Latin *crēdulus* easy of belief, from *crēdere* to believe.] —**cred′u·lous·ly,** *adv.* —**cred′u·lous·ness,** *n.*

Cree (krē) *n., pl.* **Crees** or **Cree.** *n.* member of an Algonquian tribe of North American Indians, formerly living in eastern and central Canada, now living mainly in Manitoba.

creed (krēd) *n.* **1.** formal and authoritative statement of religious belief; confession of faith. **2.** any formal statement of belief, principles, or opinions: *a political creed, Shelley's poetic creed.* **3.** Creed. Apostles' Creed or Nicene Creed. [Old English *crēda* belief, from Latin *crēdō* I believe. See CREDO.]

creek (krēk, krik) *n.* **1.** small stream, usually larger than a brook and smaller than a river. **2.** *British.* narrow inlet, going further inland than a cove. [Old Norse *kriki* bay, nook.]

Creek (krēk) *pl.,* **Creeks** or **Creek.** *n.* **1.** member of a confederation of North American Indian tribes of the Muskhogean linguistic family, formerly living in Alabama, Georgia, and northern Florida, now living in Oklahoma. **2.** Muskhogean language of these tribes.

creel (krēl) *n.* **1.** angler's basket for holding fish. **2.** basketlike wickerwork trap for catching fish, crabs, lobsters, or the like. [Possibly from French *creil* wickerwork, going back to Latin *crātis.*]

creep (krēp) *crept,* **creep·ing.** *v. i.* **1.** to move with the body prone or close to the ground, esp. on hands and knees; crawl: *The child crept across the room.* **2.** to move slowly, imperceptibly, timidly, or stealthily. **3.** to move or behave in a humble or servile manner: *He crept from the room, abashed.* **4.** to have a sensation as of things crawling over the skin; shiver in fear or repugnance: *The howling of the wolves made my flesh creep.* **5.** (of a plant) to grow along a surface by sending out small tendrils or roots along the length of the stem. **6.** to slip gradually out of position. —*n.* **1.** act of creeping; slow movement. **2.** slow but continuous deformation of metal, concrete, or other materials under prolonged stress or steady load. **3.** *Slang.* repugnant or stupid person. **4. the creeps.** *Informal.* sensation as of things crawling over one's skin; aversion; uneasiness. [Old English *crēopan* to crawl.]

creep·er (krē′pər) *n.* **1.** one who or that which creeps. **2.** any plant that grows along a surface by sending out small tendrils or roots along the length of the stem; climber. **3.** any small tendrils or roots along the length of the stem; climber. **4.** any small, brown bird, family Certhiidae, of wooded regions of the Northern Hemisphere, that climbs tree trunks to find the insects on which it feeds. **5.** creepers. **a.** one-piece garment, combining shirt and pants, worn by infants. **b.** set of spiked attachments worn on the legs or shoes to prevent slipping, as in climbing a pole.

creep·y (krē′pē) **creep·i·er, creep·i·est.** *adj.* **1.** having or causing a sensation of aversion or uneasiness, as of things crawling over one's skin. **2.** moving slowly; creeping. —**creep′i·ness,** *n.*

creese (krēs) *kris.*

cre·mate (krē′māt, kri māt′) **-mat·ed,** **-mat·ing.** *v. t.* **1.** to reduce (a dead body) to ashes by burning, esp. as a funeral rite. **2.** to consume by fire; burn up. [Latin *cremātus,* past participle of *cremāre* to burn.] —**cre·ma′tion,** *n.*

cre·ma·tor (krē′mā′tər, kri mā′-) *n.* **1.** one who cremates. **2.** crematory furnace. [Late Latin *cremātor* burner, from Latin *cremāre* to burn.]

cre·ma·to·ri·um (krē′mə tôr′ē əm, krem′ə-) *n.* crematory.

cre·ma·to·ry (krē′mə tôr′ē, krem′ə-) *pl.,* **-ries.** *n.* furnace or establishment for cremating. —*adj.* of or relating to cremation.

crème (krem, krēm) *n.* French. **1.** cream. **2.** thick, sweet liqueur.

crème de ca·ca·o (krem′ də kä kā′ō, krēm′də kō′kō) sweet brown or white liqueur flavored with cacao and vanilla. [French *crème de cacao* literally, cream of cacao.]

crème de menthe (krem′ də menth′, krēm′ də mint′) sweet green or white liqueur flavored with mint. [French *crème de menthe* literally, cream of mint.]

Cre·mo·na (kri mō′nə) *n.* city in northern Italy, noted for the violins and other stringed instruments made there by the Stradivari, Guarneri, and Amati families. Pop. (1965 est.), 79,100.

cre·nate (krē′nāt) *adj.* having a notched or scalloped margin or edge, as a leaf. [Modern Latin *crenatus,* from Late Latin *crēna* notch; of uncertain origin.]

cre·na·tion (kri nā′shən) *n.* **1.** crenate formation. **2.** state of being crenate.

cren·el (kren′əl) *also,* **cre·nelle** (krə nel′). *n.* indentation in a battlement through which defenders may fire on attackers. See **battlement** for illustration. [Old French *crenel* battlement. See CRENELATE.]

cren·el·ate (kren′əl āt′) **-at·ed, -at·ing.** *also, British,* **cren·el·late.** *v. t.* to furnish with crenels. [French *créneler* to embattle[2], notch, from Old French *crenel* battlement, going back to Late Latin *crēna* notch; of uncertain origin.]

Cre·ole (krē′ōl) *n.* **1.a.** direct descendant of the original French and Spanish settlers of the Gulf Coast, esp. Louisiana. **b.** white person of European descent, esp. Spanish or French, in the West Indies or Latin America. **2.a.** dialect of French spoken by Creoles in Louisiana. **b.** dialect of French spoken in Haiti or Martinique. **3. creole.** one who has both Negro and Creole ancestors. —*adj.* **1.** of, relating to, or characteristic of Creoles. **2. creole.** (of food) prepared with sweet pep-

at; āpe; cär; end; mē; it; īce; hot; ōld; fôrk; wood; fōōl; oil; out; up; ūse; turn; sing; thin; this; zh in treasure; ə in ago, taken, pencil, lemon, circus.   237

pers and onions and highly seasoned, usually served with rice. [French *créole* white person of European origin born in the West Indies, from Spanish *criollo* one born in America or the West Indies, from Portuguese *crioulo* one born in the colonies; literally, one brought up, from *criar* to bring up, nourish, from Latin *creāre* to make, produce.]

Cre·on (krē′on) *n. Greek Legend.* a king of Thebes, the successor to Oedipus.

cre·o·sol (krē′ə sōl′) *n.* colorless, oily, aromatic liquid used as an antiseptic. Formula: $C_8H_{10}O_2$ [CREOS(OTE) + -OL.]

cre·o·sote (krē′ə sōt′) *n.* **1.** colorless or yellowish oily liquid obtained by distilling wood tar and used in medicines and antiseptics. **2.** similar liquid obtained from coal tar and used as a wood preservative. —*v.t.,* **-sot·ed, -sot·ing.** to treat with creosote. [German *Kreosot* the liquid distilled from wood tar, from Greek *kreas* flesh + *sōtēr* savior, preserver; because it preserves flesh owing to its antiseptic qualities.]

creosote bush, evergreen shrub, *Larrea tridentata*, found in hot, dry regions in the southwestern United States and Mexico, whose small, olive-green leaves have a strong, tarlike odor.

crepe (krāp) *n.* **1.** *also,* **crêpe. a.** any of various fabrics, made of silk, cotton, rayon, and wool, characterized by a crinkled surface. **b.** band of black crepe worn or hung as a sign of mourning; crape. **2.** crepe paper. **3.** crepe rubber. **4.** *also,* **crêpe.** thin, light pancake, usually spread or rolled up with a filling and served as an hors d'oeuvre or dessert. [French *crêpe* the fabric, pancake, from Old French *crespe* curly, from Latin *crispus.*]

crepe de Chine (krāp′ də shēn′) soft, medium-weight, silk crepe. [French *crêpe de Chine* literally, crepe of China.]

crepe paper, thin paper with a crinkled surface like crepe.

crepe rubber, crude or synthetic rubber with a crinkled texture, used esp. for the soles of shoes.

crepes su·zette (krāps′soō zet′) very thin dessert pancakes rolled and heated in a sweet sauce flavored with orange or lemon juice and a liqueur, often served in flaming cognac. [French *crêpes* pancakes + *Suzette* female proper name. See CREPE.]

crep·i·tate (krep′ə tāt′) *-tat·ed, -tat·ing. v.i.* to make repeated sounds; crackle; rattle. [Latin *crepitātus,* past participle of *crepitāre* to crackle, rattle.] —**crep′i·tant,** *adj.* —**crep′i·ta′tion,** *n.*

crept (krept) past tense and past participle of **creep.**

cre·pus·cu·lar (kri pus′kyə lər) *adj.* **1.** of, relating to, or resembling twilight; dim; obscure. **2.** (of animals) appearing, active, or flying at twilight. [Latin *crepusculum* twilight + -AR¹.]

cresc., crescendo.

cre·scen·do (kri shen′dō) *adj., adv.* with a gradual increase in loudness or force. —*n. pl.,* **-dos. 1.** gradual increase in loudness or force. **2.** *Music.* a crescendo passage. [Italian *crescendo,* present participle of *crescere* to increase, grow, from Latin *crescere.*]

cres·cent (kres′ənt) *n.* **1.** shape of the visible part of the moon in its first or last quarter, having one convex edge and one concave edge. See **moon** for illustration. **2.** anything crescent-shaped: *The houses were built in a crescent.* **3.a.** emblem appearing on the flags of Turkey and other Muslim countries. **b. the Crescent.** Muslim power or religion. —*adj.* **1.** increasing; growing. **2.** shaped like the moon in its first or last quarter. [Old French *creissant* crescent of the moon, originally present participle of *creistre* to grow, from Latin *crēscere.*]

cre·sol (krē′sôl) *n.* any of three isomeric liquid or crystalline organic compounds derived principally from coal tar and used esp. as an antiseptic. Formula: $CH_3C_6H_4OH$ from *of* CREOSOL.]

cress (kres) *n.* **1.** pungent leaves of any of several plants of the mustard family, esp. watercress, used as a garnish or in salads. **2.** any of these plants. [Old English *cresse, cærse* watercress.]

cres·set (kres′it) *n.* metal container mounted on a pole or suspended from above, containing burning pitch-covered rope, oil, grease, wood, or other fuel for illumination. [Old French *cresset, craisset,* from *craisse* oil, grease (with which a cresset was filled), going back to Latin *crassus* thick, fat.]

Cres·si·da (kres′i də) *n. Medieval Legend.* a Trojan woman who is unfaithful to her lover, Troilus.

Cres·sy (kres′ē) Crécy.

crest (krest) *n.* **1.** comb, tuft, ridge, or other natural growth on the head, neck, or back of a bird or other animal. **2.** plume or similar ornament on the top of a helmet. **3.** heraldic device placed above the escutcheon in a coat of arms. It is sometimes used separately and put on such personal articles as dishes or writing paper. **4.** highest point or stage; summit, head, or apex of anything: *the crest of a hill, the crest of a wave, the crest of a politician's popularity.* —*v.i.* to reach the highest point or stage: *The flood crested late Sunday night. The waves crest far from the beach.* [Old French *creste* tuft, from Latin *crista.*]

crest·ed (kres′tid) *adj.* having a crest.

crest·fall·en (krest′fô′lən) *adj.* dejected; discouraged; disheartened.

Cre·ta·ceous (kri tā′shəs) *n.* last geological period of the Mesozoic era, during which sandstone, limestone, and chalk deposits were formed. See **geology** for chart. —*adj.* **1.** of, relating to, or characteristic of this period. **2. cretaceous.** containing, abounding in, or resembling chalk; chalky. [Latin *crētāceus* chalky, from *crēta* chalk.]

Cre·tan (krēt′ən) *adj.* of or relating to Crete or its people. —*n.* native or inhabitant of Crete.

Crete (krēt) *n.* Greek island in the eastern Mediterranean, southeast of Greece. Area, 3235 sq. mi. Pop. (1961), 483,258.

cre·tin (krēt′ən, krē′tin) *n.* one afflicted with cretinism. [French *crétin,* from Swiss French *crestin* deformed idiot, human being, Christian (with reference to the humanity even of a deformed person), from Latin *Chrīstiānus* Christian, from Greek *Chrīstiānos,* from *Chrīstos.* See CHRIST.]

cre·tin·ism (krēt′ən iz′əm, krē′tin-) *n.* condition present at birth or developing in infancy characterized by stunted physical and mental development, caused by a severe deficiency of thyroxin.

cre·tonne (krē′ton, kri ton′) *n.* strong, medium-weight cotton fabric in bold print patterns, used for curtains, draperies, and slipcovers. [French *cretonne,* from *Creton,* Norman village where the fabric was first made.]

cre·vasse (kri vas′) *n.* deep fissure or crevice, esp. in a glacier. [French *crevasse,* from Old French *crevace.* See CREVICE.]

crev·ice (krev′is) *n.* narrow crack into or through something; fissure; chink. [Old French *crevace* fissure, ravine, from *crever* to split, from Latin *crepāre* to rattle, crack.]

crew¹ (kroō) *n.* **1.a.** all those who man a ship or aircraft. **b.** all of these except the officers. **2.** group of people assigned to or working together on a specific job, usually under a foreman or overseer: *a road crew, a wrecking crew.* **3.** any group of people; crowd; company; gang. **4.a.** sport of competitive rowing, esp. in eight-oared shells. **b.** the oarsmen and coxswain who man a shell in this sport. [Old French *creue* increase, reinforcement, from *croistre* to grow, from Latin *crēscere.*]

crew² (kroō) a past tense of **crow¹.**

crew cut, style of man's haircut in which the hair is closely cropped.

crew·el (kroō′əl) *n.* loosely twisted, worsted yarn, used for embroidery. [Of uncertain origin.]

crew·el·work (kroō′əl wurk′) *n.* embroidery done with wool yarn on linen or other fabric.

crib (krib) *n.* **1.** baby's small bed with high sides, usually slatted. **2.** manger or rack for fodder. **3.** small building or bin for storing commodities, as grain or salt: *a corn crib.* **4.** stall or pen for cattle. **5.** small room or house; shack. **6.** framework of wood or metal used to strengthen or support, as in a mine shaft. **7.** *Informal.* petty theft, esp. taking as one's own another's words or ideas. **8.** *Informal.* **a.** literal translation of a text in a foreign language, often used dishonestly by students; pony. **b.** unauthorized aid, as certain notes, used dishonestly by students, esp. during examinations. —*v.t.,* **cribbed, crib·bing. 1.** to enclose in, or as in, a crib; confine. **2.** to provide with a crib or cribs. **3.** *Informal.* to plagiarize (another's words or ideas). **4.** *Informal.* to steal; pilfer: *The pickpocket cribbed the wallet.* —*v.i. Informal.* to use unauthorized notes or aids; employ a crib: *He cribbed on the history examination.* [Old English *cribb* manger, rack for fodder.]

crib·bage (krib′ij) *n.* card game, usually for two players, in which points are counted during the play of the hand and then for cards held. Score is kept on a small board by advancing pegs along the length of a series of holes.

crick (krik) *n.* painful spasm of the muscles, esp. of the neck or back, limiting movement of the part affected. —*v.t.* to cause a spasm in (a muscle or part). [Of uncertain origin.]

crick·et¹ (krik′it) *n.* hopping insect, family Gryllidae, related to the grasshopper, having strong hind legs and long slender antennae. The male of the species makes a chirping noise by rubbing the bases or edges of the forewings together. [Old French *criquet,* from *criquer* to rattle, crackle; imitative.]

Cricket

crick·et² (krik′it) *n.* **1.** game played on a grass field with a ball, bats, and wickets by two teams of eleven players each. The batsman defends his wicket against the ball bowled by an opposing player. **2.** *Informal.* fair play; good sportsmanship. —*v.i.* to play cricket. [Old French *criquet* wicket, stick, from Middle Dutch *cricke* crutch, stick.] —**crick′et·er,** *n.*

crick·et³ (krik′it) *n.* low, wooden stool; footstool. [Of uncertain origin.]

cried (krīd) past tense and past participle of **cry.**

cri·er (krī′ər) *n.* **1.** one who cries. **2.** official who makes public announcements. **3.** one who shouts out announcements about wares for sale; hawker.

crime (krīm) *n.* **1.** act forbidden by law, or the omission of a duty prescribed by law, for which the offender is liable to punishment by the state. **2.** any grave offense against morality; iniquity; sin: *Religious*

at; āpe; cär; end; mē; it; īce; hot; ōld; fôrk; wood; fool; oil; out; up; ūse; turn; sing; thin; this; zh in treasure; ə in ago, taken, pencil, lemon, circus.

persecution is a crime. **3.** criminal activity; violation of law: *There was much crime in the cities.* **4.** *Informal.* unfortunate, regrettable, or shameful act; shame: *It's a crime to stay inside on such a beautiful day.* [Old French *crime* offense, fault, from Latin *crīmen* accusation, offense.]

Cri·me·a (krī mē′ə) *n.* peninsula in the southern part of the Soviet Union, on the northern coast of the Black Sea. Area, 10,000 sq. mi. Pop. (1967 est.), 1,565,000.

crim·i·nal (krim′ən əl) *n.* person guilty or convicted of a crime. —*adj.* **1.** of the nature of or involving crime: *criminal negligence.* **2.** relating to crime or its punishment: *criminal law.* **3.** guilty of crime: *the criminal element of society.* [Late Latin *crīminālis* relating to crime, from Latin *crīmen* accusation, offense.] —**crim′i·nal·ly,** *adv.*

crim·i·nal·i·ty (krim′ə nal′ə tē) *pl.,* **-ties.** *n.* **1.** quality or state of being criminal. **2.** criminal act or practice.

crim·i·nate (krim′ə nāt′) **-nat·ed, -nat·ing.** *v.t.* to incriminate. —**crim·i·na·to·ry** (krim′ə nə tôr′ē) *adj.*

crim·i·nol·o·gy (krim′ə nol′ə jē) *n.* scientific study and investigation of crime and criminals. [Latin *crīmen* accusation, offense + -LOGY.] —**crim′i·nol′o·gist,** *n.*

crimp¹ (krimp) *v.t.* to press into small, regular ridges, folds, pleats, or waves: *She crimped her hair with a curling iron.* —*n.* **1.** something that has been or appears to have been crimped; ridge; fold. **2.** *usually,* **crimps.** waved or curled hair. **3. to put a crimp in.** *Slang.* to prevent the smooth development of; hinder; obstruct. [Middle Low German *krimpen* to wrinkle, shrink.] —**crimp′er,** *n.*

crimp² (krimp) *n.* person who procures men to serve as soldiers or sailors by decoying or entrapping them. —*v.t.* to decoy or entrap (men) to serve as soldiers or sailors. [Of uncertain origin.]

crim·ple (krim′pəl) **-pled, -pling.** *v.i., v.t.* *Informal.* to wrinkle, crumple, or curl. [CRIMP¹ + -LE.]

crimp·y (krim′pē) **crimp·i·er, crimp·i·est.** *adj.* having a crimped appearance; ridged; pleated; wavy.

crim·son (krim′zən) *n.* deep-red color. —*adj.* **1.** deep-red. **2.** bloody. —*v.t., v.i.* to make or become crimson. [Obsolete Spanish *cremesin* deep-red color, from Arabic *qirmizī,* from *qirmiz* insect from which a red dye was obtained, going back to Sanskrit *krmi* insect, worm.]

cringe (krinj) **cringed, cring·ing.** *v.i.* **1.** to shrink, flinch, or crouch, as in fear, pain, repugnance, or servility. **2.** to behave in an obsequious, servile manner; fawn. [Old English *cringan* to fall in battle, yield.] —**cring′er,** *n.*

crin·gle (kring′gəl) *n.* one of a set of small loops or eyes of rope or metal along the edge of a sail. The sail can be fastened to the boom or yard by ropes running through the cringles. [Low German *kringel* ring, diminutive of *kring* ring, circle.]

crin·kle (kring′kəl) **-kled, -kling.** *v.i.* **1.** to form numerous wrinkles or ripples; wrinkle. **2.** to make a rustling or crackling sound; crackle. —*v.t.* **1.** to cause to form numerous wrinkles or ripples; crumple. **2.** to cause to rustle or crackle. —*n.* wrinkle; ripple. [Old English *crincan* to yield, bend + -LE.] —**crin′kly,** *adj.*

cri·noid (krī′noid, krin′oid) *n.* any of a group of colorful, flower-shaped saltwater animals, having branched, radiating arms around a single mouth opening and found anchored to the bottom by a slender, segmented stalk, usually in deeper tropical waters. Also, **sea lily, feather star.** —*adj.* **1.** of or relating to crinoids. [Greek *krinoeidēs* like a lily, from *krinon* lily.]

crin·o·line (krin′ə lin, -lēn′) *n.* **1.** stiff petticoat worn to give fullness to a skirt or dress. **2.** stiff fabric, originally made with horsehair, used as a lining for skirts, millinery, or the like. **3.** hoop skirt. [French *crinoline* haircloth, stiff petticoat once made of haircloth, going back to Latin *crīnis* hair + *līnum* flax.]

Crinoid

crip·ple (krip′əl) *n.* **1.** one who is lame or otherwise physically disabled. **2.** one who is disabled or deficient in any way: *an emotional cripple.* —*v.t.,* **-pled, -pling. 1.** to make a cripple of. **2.** to impair the power or efficiency of; disable; weaken: *The attack on Pearl Harbor crippled the U.S. Pacific fleet.* [Old English *crypel* disabled or lame person.] —**crip′pler,** *n.*

cri·sis (krī′sis) *pl.,* **-ses** (-sēz). *n.* **1.** decisive or important turning point. **2.** condition or period of difficulty, insecurity, or suspense: *an economic crisis, a crisis in the nation's domestic affairs.* **3.** turning point in an acute disease, toward recovery or death. [Latin *crisis* decision, from Greek *krisis* decision, turning point of a disease.] —**Syn. 2.** see **emergency.**

crisp (krisp) *adj.* **1.** easily crumbled or crushed; brittle: *crisp potato chips.* **2.** firm; fresh: *crisp lettuce.* **3.** brisk; bracing; invigorating: *a cold, crisp autumn day.* **4.** clear and terse: *What he said was crisp and decided.*

5. lively; pithy; sparkling: *crisp epigrams, crisp repartee.* **6.** (of hair) curly, wavy, or wiry. —*v.t., v.i.* to make or become crisp. [Old English *crisp* curly, from Latin *crispus.*] —**crisp′ly,** *adv.* —**crisp′ness,** *n.*

crisp·y (kris′pē) **crisp·i·er, crisp·i·est.** *adj.* crisp. —**crisp′i·ness,** *n.*

criss·cross (kris′krôs′) *adj.* arranged in or marked with crossed lines; crossed; crossing. —*adv.* crosswise. —*n.* **1.** intersecting lines. **2.** mark or pattern made by intersecting lines. —*v.t.* **1.** to mark with intersecting lines. **2.** to cross repeatedly: *He crisscrossed the neighborhood looking for his dog.* —*v.i.* to form a crisscross; intersect frequently: *The paths crisscrossed in the snow.* [Modification of archaic *christcross* a symbol of the cross placed in front of the alphabet in a hornbook. See CHRIST, CROSS.]

cri·te·ri·on (krī tēr′ē ən) *pl.,* **-te·ri·a** (-tēr′ē ə) or **-te·ri·ons.** *n.* rule, standard, or test by which something can be judged or measured: *In ancient Greece, symmetry and balance were the criteria of artistic beauty.* [Greek *kritērion* means for judging, from *kritēs* judge.] —**Syn.** see **standard.**

crit·ic (krit′ik) *n.* **1.** one who judges works of the fine arts or the performing arts, reviewing them for their merits and faults, esp. one who reports professionally for publication or broadcast. **2.** one who analyzes or evaluates anything: *an astute critic of the social scene.* **3.** one who judges severely or unfavorably; faultfinder. [Latin *criticus* able to judge, from Greek *kritikos* able to judge, literary critic, from *kritēs* judge.]

crit·i·cal (krit′i kəl) *adj.* **1.** inclined to find fault or judge with severity. **2.** exercising, involving, or marked by careful analysis, judgment, and evaluation; judicial: *highly developed critical faculties.* **3.** of or relating to critics or criticism. **4.** of, relating to, or of the nature of a crisis or turning point, esp. of a disease; crucial: *The patient's condition is now critical.* **5.** involving suspense, fear, uncertainty, risk, or danger. **6.** (of supplies or manpower) of vital importance but in current or anticipated short supply: *The availability of teachers in this area has become critical.* —**crit′i·cal·ly,** *adv.* —**crit′i·cal·ness,** *n.*

critical angle, angle of incidence beyond which total reflection of a light ray takes place.

crit·i·cism (krit′ə siz′əm) *n.* **1.** act of criticizing, esp. unfavorably. **2.** disapproval; faultfinding; censure. **3.** art or profession of judging the quality of something, esp. of an artistic work. **4.** critical comment, article, or review; critique. **5.** detailed investigation of the origin, history, accuracy, or the like of a document, esp. an effort to determine the original text of a literary work or, specifically, of the Bible or its parts.

Syn. 4. Criticism, critique, review indicate a written or spoken summary of one's conclusions about a work, performance, or production, esp. in the fine arts. **Criticism** suggests analysis of some depth and the use of criteria: *His criticism of the structure of the play was well-informed.* **Critique** is a formal, analytical discourse on the matter and treatment of a work: *His critique was the feature article in the journal.* **Review** applies to a short analysis of the content of a work, esp. a book, motion picture, or recording, meant to inform a possible purchaser: *Her review of the book was unfairly based on the author's private life.*

crit·i·cize (krit′ə sīz′) **-cized, -ciz·ing.** *v.i.* **1.** to judge disapprovingly; censure. **2.** to act as a critic; pass judgment. —*v.t.* **1.** to find fault with: *They criticized her behavior.* **2.** to discuss, judge, or examine critically: *to criticize a poem.* —**crit′i·ciz′er,** *n.* —**Syn.** *v.t.* **1.** see **blame.**

cri·tique (kri tēk′) *n.* **1.** critical comment, article, or review. **2.** art or practice of criticism. [French *critique,* from Greek *kritikē* the critical art.] —**Syn.** **1.** see **criticism.**

crit·ter (krit′ər) *n.* *Informal.* creature.

croak (krōk) *n.* deep, hoarse sound like that made by a frog or raven. —*v.i.* **1.** to make a deep, hoarse sound. **2.** to speak in a deep, hoarse voice. **3.** to prophesy evil or misfortune; grumble. **4.** *Slang.* to die. —*v.t.* to utter with a croak. [Imitative.]

croak·er (krō′kər) *n.* **1.** any of a group of saltwater fish, family Sciaenidae, which are found in warm, coastal waters and which characteristically produce a loud, croaking sound. **2.** one who or that which croaks.

Cro·at (krō′at) *n.* **1.** native or inhabitant of Croatia; a Croatian. **2.** language of the Croats; Serbo-Croatian.

Cro·a·tia (krō ā′shə) *n.* historic region that is now a political subdivision of Yugoslavia, in the northwestern part of the country. Area, 21,714 sq. mi. Pop. (1961), 4,159,696.

Cro·a·tian (krō ā′shən) *adj.* of or relating to Croatia, the Croats, or their language. —*n.* **1.** a Croat. **2.** Serbo-Croatian.

Cro·ce, Be·ne·det·to (krō′chä; ben′ə det′ō) 1866–1952, Italian philosopher.

cro·chet (krō shā′) **-cheted** (-shād′), **-chet·ing** (-shā′ing). *v.i., v.t.* to make interlocking loops or stitches using a single needle with a hook at one end. —*n.* needlework done or produced by crocheting; crocheting. [French *crochet* little hook, diminutive of *croc* hook; of Scandinavian origin.]

at; āpe; cär; end; mē; it; īce; hot; ōld; fôrk; wood; fōōl; oil; out; up; ūse; turn; sing; thin; this; zh in treasure; ə in ago, taken, pencil, lemon, circus.

cro·chet·ing (krō shā´ing) n. **1.** piece of crocheted work. **2.** action of one who or that which crochets.

crock (krok) n. earthenware pot, jar, or other small vessel. [Old English *crocca* earthenware pot, pitcher.]

crock·er·y (krok´ər ē) n. earthenware.

crock·et (krok´it) n. projecting, carved ornament, usually in the form of curved foliage, used to decorate the sloping angles of spires, pinnacles, or other structures in Gothic architecture. [Anglo-Norman *croket*, form of Old French *crochet* little hook. See CROCHET.]

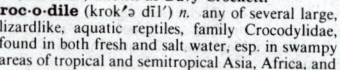

Crockets

Crock·ett, David (krok´it) 1786–1836, U.S. frontiersman, known as **Davy Crockett**.

croc·o·dile (krok´ə dīl´) n. any of several large, lizardlike, aquatic reptiles, family Crocodylidae, found in both fresh and salt water, esp. in swampy areas of tropical and semitropical Asia, Africa, and America, including southern Florida. They are covered with bony protective plates, have strong jaws with long rows of teeth, and usually grow 6–10 feet in length. See **alligator** for illustration. [Latin *crocodilus*, from Greek *krokodeilos* lizard, alligator, possibly from *kroke* pebble + *drilos* worm; with reference to the habit of reptiles of lying on stones in the sun.]

crocodile tears, pretended or insincere tears; hypocritical show of grief.

croc·o·dil·i·an (krok´ə dil´ē ən) adj. of, relating to, or like a crocodile. —n. any reptile of the order Crocodilia, including crocodiles, alligators, caymans, and gavials.

cro·cus (krō´kəs) pl. **cro·cus·es** or **cro·ci** (-sī). n. **1.** cup-shaped flower of any of a group of plants, genus *Crocus*, of the iris family, widely cultivated as a garden flower of various colors. Most crocuses bloom in early spring, but some bloom in autumn, as the saffron. **2.** plant bearing this flower, having a single flower stalk and grasslike leaves, growing directly from an underground bulblike stem. [Latin *crocus* saffron, from Greek *krokos* of Semitic origin.]

Croe·sus (krē´səs) n. **1.** died c.546 B.C., king of Lydia from 560 to 546 B.C., noted for his great wealth. **2.** any very rich man.

croft (krôft) n. British. **1.** small field for farming, esp. one next to a house. **2.** small rented farm. [Old English *croft* field.]

croft·er (krôf´tər) n. British. tenant farmer working a croft, esp. in Scotland or northern England.

croix de guerre (krwä də gâr´) French military decoration awarded for distinguished service in war. [French *croix de guerre* literally, cross of war.]

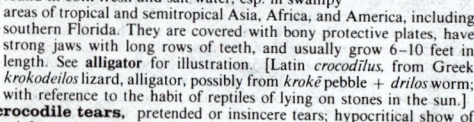

Croix de guerre

Cro·Mag·non (krō mag´non, -man´yən) n. member of a prehistoric group of men living in Europe and distinguished by a well-developed brain, tall, erect stature, and the use of stone and bone implements. Cro-Magnon is one of the earliest forms of *Homo sapiens* yet found. —adj. relating or belonging to this group. [Because bones of this form of man were found in the *Cro-Magnon* cave in southern France.]

crom·lech (krom´lek) n. **1.** prehistoric monument of upright stones or monoliths arranged in a circle. Stonehenge is the best-known example of a cromlech. **2.** dolmen. [Welsh *cromlech* incumbent flagstone, from *crom* bowed + *llech* flat stone.]

Cromp·ton, Samuel (kromp´tən) 1753–1827, English inventor.

Crom·well (krom´wel, -wəl) **1. Oliver.** 1599–1658, English statesman and soldier and lord protector of England. **2. Richard.** 1626–1712, his son; English soldier and politician. **3. Thomas.** c.1485–1540, Earl of Essex, English statesman.

crone (krōn) n. withered old woman. [Middle Dutch *croonje* carcass, old sheep, from dialectal Old French *carogne* carcass, going back to Latin *caro* flesh.]

Cro·nus (krō´nəs) also, **Kro·nos.** n. Greek Mythology. youngest of the Titans, who overthrew his father, Uranus, to become ruler of the universe and was in turn overthrown by his son Zeus. His Roman counterpart is Saturn.

cro·ny (krō´nē) pl., **-nies.** n. close friend; pal. [Greek *chronios* lasting.]

crook (krook) n. **1.** shepherd's staff with a hooklike curve at one end. **2.** crosier. **3.** any bend, curved, or angular thing or part: *the crook of the arm.* **4.** any bend, curve, or turn: *The captain knew the crooks of the river by heart.* **5.** Informal. person not to be trusted; thief; swindler. —v.t. to bend into an angular or curved form: *She motioned to us to come by crooking her finger.* —v.i. to be or become crooked; bent; curve. [Old Norse *krōkr* hook, curve.] —Syn. v.t. see **bend**[1].

crook·ed (krook´id) adj. **1.** not straight; bent; twisted. **2.** dishonest. —**crook´ed·ly,** adv. —**crook´ed·ness,** n.

Crookes, Sir William (krooks) 1832–1919, English chemist and physicist.

crook·neck (krook´nek´) n. any of several varieties of squash having a long curved neck.

croon (kroon) v.i. **1.** to sing or hum in a soft, low tone. **2.** to sing in a soft and sentimental manner. —v.t. **1.** to sing or hum (a song or melody) in a soft, low tone. **2.** to sing (a popular song) in a soft and sentimental manner. —n. soft, low singing or humming. [Middle Low German *krōnen* to mourn, groan; imitative.] —**croon´,** n.

crop (krop) n. **1.** any agricultural product growing or gathered for use, as wheat, corn, or cotton. **2.** the entire yield (of any product) in one place or season: *The winter wheat crop was not large this year.* **3.** group or collection of anything appearing or produced together: *a crop of recruits, a crop of memos.* **4.** act or result of cropping. **5.a.** a short haircut. **b.** style of cutting the hair in this way. **6.** mark made in clipping the ear of an animal. **7.** pouchlike enlargement of a bird's gullet in front of the stomach in which preliminary preparation for digestion occurs; craw. **8.** short whip with a leather loop in place of a lash. **9.** handle of a whip. —v.t., **cropped, crop·ping.** **1.** to cut or bite off the top end of: *Sheep crop grass very short. The gardener cropped the hedges.* **2.** to reap; harvest. **3.** to cut short; trim; clip: *The pages in this book have all been cropped.* **4.** to cause to bear a crop; raise crops on: *He cropped several acres with barley.* —v.i. to **crop up** (or **out**). **a.** to come up or appear unexpectedly: *Something cropped up and John had to cancel his plans.* **b.** to come to or appear on the surface; sprout: *The veins of coal cropped out along the side of the mountain.* [Old English *cropp* bird's craw, sprout, ear of corn.]

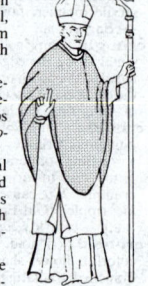

Crop (def. 7)

crop·per (krop´ər) n. **1.** one who or that which crops. **2.** Informal. heavy fall, as from a horse: *He took a cropper at the water jump.* **3.** Informal. failure in an undertaking; collapse. **4. to come a cropper.** Informal. **a.** to fall heavily or headlong. **b.** to fail miserably; collapse.

cro·quet (krō kā´) n. outdoor game in which each player uses a mallet to drive a ball through small, bent wickets arranged in a particular order to form a course. [Dialectal French *croquet*, form of French *crochet* little hook. See CROCHET.]

cro·quette (krō ket´) n. small rounded or cone-shaped mass of chopped food, as meat, fish, or vegetables, coated with beaten egg and bread crumbs and fried in deep oil. [French *croquette*, from *croquer* to crunch; imitative.]

cro·sier (krō´zhər) also, **cro·zier.** n. ornamental staff carried by or before bishops, archbishops, and certain abbots and abbesses, during religious ceremonies as a symbol of office. [Old French *crossier* bearer of a bishop's staff, from *crosse* bishop's staff; of Germanic origin.]

Crosier

cross (krôs) n. **1.** upright stake with a transverse bar, used esp. by the ancient Romans as an instrument of torture and execution. **2. the Cross.** cross on which Christ was crucified. **3.a.** representation of the cross upon which Christ died, considered as the symbol of Christianity. **b.** this representation mounted with the figure of Christ; crucifix. **c.** also, **the Cross.** Christianity; Christendom. **4.** any of various similar representations, conventionally used as a symbol, badge, or ornament. **5.** any object, figure, or mark formed by the intersection of two lines. **6.** sign of the cross. **7.** any obstruction, misfortune, or affliction that tries one's patience or virtue. **8.** person or thing that combines the characteristics of two or more individuals or things: *He is a cross between a businessman and a scholar. That show is a cross between burlesque and slapstick.* **9.a.** a cross-breeding. **b.** product of crossbreeding; hybrid. **10. to take (up) the cross.** to join a crusade; became a crusader. —v.t. **1.** to move or pass from one to the other side of; go across: *to cross a room. The ship crossed the ocean in seven days.* **2.** to place or lay one thing or part over another: *Cross one lace over the other, then tie them.* **3.** to pass (each other) so as to intersect: *That street crosses the railroad tracks.* **4.** to draw a line or lines through or across: *Cross all your t's neatly.* **5.** to extend across; span: *The bridge crosses the river.* **6.** to pass while going in

Latin Papal

Maltese Celtic

Crosses

at; āpe; cär; end; mē; it; īce; hot; ōld; fôrk; wood; fōol; oil; out; up; ūse; turn; sing; thin; this; zh in treasure; ə in ago, taken, pencil, lemon, circus.

different directions; meet (each other) in passing: *Your letter must have crossed mine in the mail.* **7.** to interfere with; oppose; thwart: *Cross me and you'll regret it.* **8.** to make the sign of the cross upon or over: *The girl crossed herself as she entered the church.* **9.** to crossbreed (animals or plants). **10. to cross one's fingers.** to hope for luck or success, as by placing one's middle finger over the index finger. **11. to cross one's heart.** to make a promise or affirm the truth of a statement, as by making the sign of the cross over one's heart. **12. to cross one's mind.** to occur to one suddenly or momentarily. **13. to cross one's palm.** to give (someone) money or a bribe. **14. to cross off** (or **out**). to mark out or over, as by drawing a line across; cancel: *Cross your name off the list.* —*v.i.* **1.** to move, pass, or extend across: *The dog crossed at the corner. The trail crosses through the woods.* **2.** to pass so as to intersect; lie or be crosswise: *The friends met where the two roads crossed.* **3.** to meet in passing: *Our paths may not yet crossed.* **4.** to crossbreed. —*adj.* **1.** feeling or showing irritability; ill-tempered; peevish: *Francis was cross because he did not get his way.* **2.** resulting from or exhibiting irritability: *a cross word, a cross look.* **3.** lying or passing across or crosswise: *cross ventilation.* **4.** crossbred; hybrid. [Old English *cros* horizontal post crossed by a vertical post, from Old Norse *kross,* from Old Irish *cros,* from Latin *crux.* Doublet of CRUX.] —**cross′ly,** *adv.* —**cross′ness,** *n.*

cross- combining form **1.** lying or passing across: *crossbeam, crosspiece.* **2.** running counter; opposing; opposite: *cross-purposes, crosscurrent.* **3.** resembling or forming a cross: *cross-stitch, skull and crossbones.* **4.** involving interchange or reciprocal action: *cross-reference.* [From CROSS.]

cross·bar (krôs′bär′) *n.* **1.** bar fixed across a structure: *crossbar on a bicycle.* **2.** transverse line: *crossbar on the letter H.*

cross·beam (krôs′bēm′) *n.* any large beam that crosses another or extends from wall to wall.

cross·bill (krôs′bil′) *n.* any of a group of finchlike songbirds, genus *Loxia,* of the evergreen forests of North America, Europe, and Asia.

Crossbill

cross·bones (krôs′bōnz′) *n.pl.* see **skull and crossbones.**

cross·bow (krôs′bō′) *n.* weapon widely used in the Middle Ages, consisting of a bow mounted crosswise at the front of a grooved stock along which arrows, stones, or other missiles are released. —**cross·bow·man** (krôs′bō′man), *n.*

cross·breed (krôs′brēd′, -brēd′) **-bred, -breed·ing.** *v.t.* to breed (plants or animals) with those of different varieties or lines, or sometimes of different species, in order to produce hybrids; hybridize. —*v.i.* to undergo such breeding. —*n.* individual or type produced by crossbreeding; hybrid.

Crossbow

cross·coun·try (krôs′kun′trē) *adj., adv.* **1.** across open country or fields instead of following roads: *cross-country skiing, a cross-country running race.* **2.** from one end of a country to the other.

cross·cur·rent (krôs′kur′ənt) *n.* **1.** current, as in a stream, flowing across the main current. **2.** contrasting or contradictory tendency or movement: *a crosscurrent of opinion.*

cross·cut (krôs′kut′) *adj.* **1.** adapted or used for cutting crosswise: *a crosscut blade.* **2.** cut across or transversely. —*v.t., v.i.* **-cut, -cut·ting.** to cut across.

crosscut saw, saw having beveled teeth shaped like knives, used for cutting wood across the grain.

Teeth of crosscut saw

Teeth of ripsaw

crosse (krôs) *n.* lacrosse stick. [See LACROSSE.]

cross-ex·am·ine (krôs′ig zam′in) **-ined, -in·ing.** *v.t.* **1.** to question (a witness who has already testified for the opposing side) to determine the reliability of his testimony or character. **2.** to question (someone) again to check the reliability of previous answers; question closely. —**cross′-ex·am·i·na′tion, cross′-ex·am′in·er,** *n.*

Crosscut saw

cross-eye (krôs′ī′) *n.* strabismus in which one or both eyes turn inward toward the nose.

cross-eyed (krôs′īd′) *adj.* having one or both eyes turned inward toward the nose.

cross·fer·ti·li·za·tion (krôs′furt′əl i zā′shən) *n.* cross-pollination.

cross·fer·ti·lize (krôs′furt′əl īz′) **-lized, -liz·ing.** *v.t.* to cross-pollinate.

cross·fire (krôs′fīr′) *n.* **1.** intersecting lines of fire from two or more

positions: *The photographer was caught in the crossfire between the police and the bank robber.* **2.** rapid or animated exchange: *a crossfire of insults.*

cross-grained (krôs′grānd′) *adj.* **1.** having the grain running transversely or irregularly; having a gnarled grain: *cross-grained wood.* **2.** stubborn; contrary.

cross·hatch (krôs′hach′) *v.t.* to mark or shade with sets of parallel lines that cross each other.

cross·ing (krô′sing) *n.* **1.** act of going across: *an Atlantic crossing.* **2.** place or point of intersection, as of roads. **3.** place where something, as a street, may be crossed. **4.** act of crossbreeding.

cross·ing-o·ver (krô′sing ō′vər) *n.* exchange of segments, or of genes in the segments, between chromosomes during meiosis.

cross·jack (krôs′jak′, krô′jik) *n.* square sail on the lower yard of a mizzenmast.

cross-leg·ged (krôs′leg′id, -legd′) *adj., adv.* with the ankles crossed and the knees crossed: *The children sat cross-legged on the floor.*

cross·let (krôs′lit) *n.* small cross, esp. one used as a heraldic device.

cross·o·ver (krôs′ō′vər) *n.* **1.** a crossing-over. **2.** short secondary railroad track for switching trains from one main track to another.

cross·patch (krôs′pach′) *n. Informal.* cross, ill-tempered person; grouch.

cross·piece (krôs′pēs′) *n.* piece of any material placed or lying across something else.

cross·pol·li·nate (krôs′pol′ə nāt′) **-nat·ed, -nat·ing.** *v.t.* to subject to cross-pollination.

cross·pol·li·na·tion (krôs′pol′ə nā′shən) *n.* fertilization of a flower or plant by pollen from another, esp. as transferred by wind, water, insects, or birds. Distinguished from **self-pollination.**

cross-pur·pose (krôs′pur′pəs) *n.* **1.** opposing or conflicting purpose. **2. at cross-purposes.** unintentionally opposing or hindering each other's efforts.

cross-ques·tion (krôs′kwes′chən) *v.t.* to question closely or repeatedly; cross-examine. —*n.* question asked in cross-examining.

cross-re·fer (krôs′ri fur′) **-ferred, -fer·ring.** *v.t.* to refer from one part to another. —*v.i.* to make a cross-reference.

cross-ref·er·ence (krôs′ref′ər əns) *n.* reference from one part, as in a book or index, to another part for additional information.

cross·road (krôs′rōd′) *n.* **1.** road crossing another or a secondary road leading from one main road to another. **2. crossroads. a.** place where roads intersect. **b.** in rural areas, a small community at such a place. **c.** central meeting place, as of people or cultures. **3. at the crossroads.** the point where an important decision must be made. ▲ construed as singular in defs. 2b and c, as either singular or plural in 2a.

cross·ruff (krôs′ruf′) *n.* in bridge or whist, a play in which each of two partners alternately leads a card that the other will be able to trump. —*v.i.* to engage in such a play.

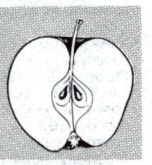

cross section *n.* **1.** plane section produced by cutting an object, esp. at right angles to an axis. **2.** piece cut in this manner. **3.** diagram or representation of such a cut. **4.** sampling considered representative or typical of the whole: *a cross section of public opinion.*

Cross section
of an apple

cross-stitch (krôs′stich′) *n.* **1.** stitch made by crossing one another, forming an X. **2.** needlework made with this stitch. —*v.t., v.i.* to embroider or sew with a cross-stitch.

cross street, street that crosses another, esp. one crossing a main thoroughfare.

cross·town (krôs′toun′) *adj.* going across a town or city: *a crosstown bus, crosstown traffic.* —*adv.* across a town or city: *We traveled crosstown on a slow, old bus.*

cross·trees (krôs′trēz′) *n.pl.* two horizontal bars attached to a masthead on a sailing ship to spread the rigging and support the top.

cross vine, bignonia.

cross·walk (krôs′wôk′) *n.* lane marked off for use by pedestrians in crossing a street.

cross·way (krôs′wā′) *n.* crossroad.

cross·wise (krôs′wīz′) *also,* **cross·ways.** *adv.* **1.** so as to be crossed; across; transversely. **2.** *Archaic.* in the form of a cross.

cross·word puzzle (krôs′wurd′) puzzle in which words or phrases are filled in on a pattern of numbered squares in answer to a list of correspondingly numbered clues. The words usually intersect each other in such a way that they read both across and down.

crotch (kroch) *n.* **1.** region of the human body where the legs fork from the pelvis. **2.** fork or angle formed by two diverging parts, as by the branches of a tree. **3.** forked pole used as a support. [Old French *croche* hook, from *croc;* of Scandinavian origin.]

at; āpe; cär; end; mē; it; īce; hot; ōld; fôrk; wood; fōōl; oil; out; up; ūse; turn; sing; thin; this; zh in treasure; ə in ago, taken, pencil, lemon, circus.

241

crotch·et (kroch′it) *n.* **1.** peculiar, whimsical, or perverse notion. **2.** small hook or hooked instrument. **3.** *British.* quarter note in music. [Old French *crochet* small hook, diminutive of *croc* hook; of Scandinavian origin.]

crotch·et·y (kroch′ə tē) *adj.* full of perverse or eccentric notions; cantankerous. —**crotch′et·i·ness,** *n.*

cro·ton (krōt′ən) *n.* **1.** any tropical herb, shrub, or tree of the genus *Croton,* one species of which was formerly cultivated for its seeds, which yield a purgative oil. **2.** any tropical evergreen tree or shrub, genus *Codiaeum,* cultivated for its bright, attractive foliage. [Modern Latin *Croton,* from Greek *krotōn* tick, castor-oil plant; probably because its seed resembles a tick.]

crouch (krouch) *v.i.* **1.** to stoop or bend low, esp. with the knees bent, as an animal preparing to spring or trying to hide. **2.** to cringe or cower humbly or servilely. —*v.t. Archaic.* to bend (something) low. —*n.* act of crouching; crouching posture. [Old French *crochir* to become bent, from *croc* hook; of Scandinavian origin.]

croup[1] (krōōp) *n.* inflammation of the throat and windpipe, esp. in children, characterized by a high-pitched, barking cough and difficult breathing and caused by infection or allergy. [Imitative.] —**croup′y,** *adj.*

croup[2] (krōōp) *n.* rump of a horse or other animal. [Old French *cro(u)pe;* of Germanic origin.]

crou·pi·er (krōō′pē ər, krōō′pē ā′) *n.* attendant at a gambling table, as in roulette, who rakes in chips or other lost bets and pays winners or, in many cases, has charge of the entire game. [French *croupier* originally, one who rides (behind another) on the rump; hence, assistant, from *cro(u)pe* rump of a horse. See CROUP².]

crou·ton (krōō′ton, krōō ton′) *n.* small cube of toasted or fried bread, often served in soup or used as a garnish. [French *croûton* bit of crust, diminutive of *croûte* crust, from Latin *crusta* crust, shell.]

crow[1] (krō) *crowed* or *(def. 1)* *crew, crowed, crow·ing. v.i.* **1.** to utter the shrill cry of a rooster. **2.** to utter a delighted, happy cry, as a baby does. **3.** to boast in triumph; exult. —*n.* **1.** cry of a rooster. **2.** delighted, happy cry, as that made by a baby. [Old English *crāwan* to utter the cry of a rooster.]

crow[2] (krō) *n.* **1.** any of various omnivorous birds, genus *Corvus,* having glossy black plumage, a heavy, black bill, and a harsh, croaking cry or caw. Length: 17-21 inches. **2.** any of various similar birds, as the raven, magpie, or jay. **3.** crowbar. **4. as the crow flies,** in a straight line. **5. to eat crow.** *Informal.* to be forced to humble oneself, as by admitting a mistake. [Old English *crāwe* bird of the genus *Corvus.*]

Crow² *(def. 1)*

Crow (krō) *pl.,* **Crows** or **Crow.** *n.* **1.** member of a Siouan tribe of North American Indians formerly living along the Missouri River in the Great Plains. **2.** language of the Crow, a member of the Siouan language family. [Translation of Crow *Absaroke* crow², bird people.]

crow·bar (krō′bär′) *n.* bar of iron or steel with a wedge-shaped end that is sometimes slightly bent and forked, used as a lever or pry.

crowd (kroud) *n.* **1.** large number of people gathered together; throng: *We tried to make our way through the crowd.* **2.** *Informal.* particular group of people; set; clique: *the college crowd, my cousin and her crowd.* **3.** attendance; audience: *The comedian's act drew a large crowd.* **4.** people in general; the masses: *far from the madding crowd's ignoble strife* (Gray, 1750). **5.** large number of things collected or grouped together: *I saw a crowd, a host of golden daffodils* (Wordsworth, 1804). —*v.t.* **1.a.** to push or shove: *Please don't crowd me.* **b.** to force (with *off* or *out*): *We crowded him off the platform. He was crowded out of the running when other candidates appeared.* **2.a.** to fill to excess, as by pressing or thronging: *He crowded the shelves with books. Swimmers crowded the beaches.* **b.** to press or force (into a close space); cram: *He crowded everything into the trunk and then could not close it.* **3. to crowd (on) sail.** to raise as many sails as possible in order to achieve maximum speed. —*v.i.* **1.** to gather or congregate closely or in large numbers: *We crowded around the table to get our food.* **2.** to press forward; advance by pushing: *to crowd into a bus.* [Old English *crūdan* to press.] **Syn.** *n.* **1. Crowd, throng, mob** mean a large number of people gathered closely together in one place. **Crowd** is the most general term and may describe any large group of people: *The singer's concert drew a large crowd.* **Throng** may be used interchangeably with **crowd** but suggests more movement on the part of the group: *A throng of fans pressed toward the singer after his performance.* **Mob** suggests larger numbers, usually undisciplined and unruly, and still greater movement: *The angry mob outside the courthouse surged forward to demand the prisoner's release.*

crowd·ed (krou′did) *adj.* **1.** filled with a crowd; packed: *crowded sidewalks.* **2.** gathered, pressed, or clustered uncomfortably close

together: *the crowded conditions of the city's ghettos.* —**Syn. 2.** see **close.**

crow·foot (krō′foot′) *pl., (def. 1)* **-foots** or *(defs. 2, 3)* **-feet.** *n.* **1.** any of various flowering plants, esp. one of the genus *Ranunculus,* as the buttercup and peony, whose leaves are deeply divided into three lobes, thus resembling a crow's foot. **2.** device consisting of a number of small cords passed through a long block and used for various purposes, as to suspend an awning. —*adj.* of or designating a family, Ranunculaceae, of herbs and woody plants of the temperate and arctic regions of the Northern Hemisphere, with distinct and unconnected flower parts, including the buttercup, anemone, and peony.

crown (kroun) *n.* **1.** covering for the head, often of jewels and precious metal, worn as a symbol of sovereignty. **2.** wreath, band, or other circular ornament for the head: *She wore a crown of flowers.* **3.** something resembling a crown in shape, as the corona of a flower. **4.** power or authority of a monarch. **5.** *also,* **the Crown.** sovereign ruler; monarch. **6.a.** highest part of something; top: *the crown of a hill.* **b.** the head. **c.** upper part of a hat or other head covering. **7.** exalting attribute; chief ornament: *They were the pride, the joy, the crown of his old age* (Southey, 1829). **8.** highest or most perfect state or form of anything; culmination. **9.** distinction for achievement or victory; honor; reward. **10.a.** portion of a tooth visible above the gum. **b.** artificial substitute for this portion, usually made of gold, porcelain, or plastic. **11.** crest of an animal, esp. of a bird. **12.** uppermost part of a tree or shrub, formed of the branches and foliage. **13.** any of various coins, often stamped with a crown or crowned head, as the krona of Sweden. **14.** former British silver coin, worth five shillings. —*v.t.* **1.** to make a monarch of; invest with royal power and dignity; enthrone: *They crowned the new king shortly after his father's death.* **2.** to surmount; top: *She crowned the dessert with whipped cream.* **3.** to add the finishing touch to; complete; consummate: *Fame crowned his career.* **4.** to recognize officially as: *He was crowned heavyweight champion.* **5.** to endow with honor or dignity. **6.** to make a king of in checkers. **7.** to put an artificial crown on (a tooth). **8.** *Informal.* to hit on the head: *She crowned him with the frying pan.* [Old French *corone* crown (as of a monarch), from Latin *corōna* wreath, crown, from Greek *korōnē* something bent. Doublet of CORONA.]

crown colony, colony under the authority of the British Crown and largely administered by the British government.

crown glass **1.** hard glass of low refraction, used in optical instruments. **2.** window glass blown and whirled into flat, circular sheets with a lump left in the center by the blower's rod.

crown prince, male heir apparent to a throne, esp. the eldest son of a ruling monarch.

crown princess **1.** wife of a crown prince. **2.** female heir apparent to a throne.

crow's-foot (krōz′foot′) *pl.,* **-feet.** *n.* **1.** crow's-feet. wrinkles near the outer corners of the eyes. **2.** three-pointed embroidered design, sometimes used to finish the ends of seams or the corners of pockets.

crow's-nest (krōz′nest′) *n.* **1.** small enclosed platform or other structure near the top of a ship's mast, used for maintaining a lookout. **2.** any similar structure ashore.

Crow's-foot *(def. 2)*

cro·zier (krō′zhər) crosier.

cru·ces (krōō′sēz) a plural of **crux.**

cru·cial (krōō′shəl) *adj.* **1.** extremely important; critical; decisive: *a crucial decision, a crucial battle.* **2.** trying; severe. [French *crucial* cross-shaped, decisive, from Latin *crux* cross; referring to the choosing of a road at a crossroad.] —**cru′cial·ly,** *adv.*

cru·ci·ate (krōō′shē it, -āt′) *adj.* **1.** cross-shaped. **2.** *Botany.* having leaves or petals arranged in the form of a cross. [Modern Latin *cruciatus* cross-shaped, from Latin *crux* cross.]

cru·ci·ble (krōō′sə bəl) *n.* **1.** hard, heat-resistant vessel for melting such substances as chemicals, metals, and ores. **2.** severe test or trial. [Medieval Latin *crucibulum* melting pot, night lamp (possibly placed before a crucifix), from Latin *crux* cross.]

crucible steel, high-grade steel prepared in crucibles that distribute carbon content uniformly, used for tools and cutlery.

cru·ci·fix (krōō′sə fiks′) *n.* **1.** cross with the crucified figure of Christ upon it. **2.** any cross considered as a Christian symbol. [Old French *crucefis,* going back to Latin *cruci fīxus* fixed to a cross.]

cru·ci·fix·ion (krōō′sə fik′shən) *n.* **1.** act of crucifying; being crucified. **2. Crucifixion. a.** the execution of Christ on the Cross. **b.** picture, statue, or other representation of this.

cru·ci·form (krōō′sə fôrm′) *adj.* in the form of a cross; cross-shaped. [Latin *cruc-,* stem of *crux* cross + -FORM.]

cru·ci·fy (krōō′sə fī′) **-fied, -fy·ing.** *v.t.* **1.** to put to death by nailing or otherwise affixing to a cross. **2.** to treat cruelly; persecute; torment. **3.** to destroy the power or influence of; subdue; mortify: *to crucify the flesh.* [Old French *crucifier* to nail to a cross, going back to Latin *cruci fīgere* to fix to a cross.] —**cru′ci·fi′er,** *n.*

crud (krud) *n. Slang.* **1.** deposit or accumulation of filth or grease. **2.** nonsense; rubbish. [Earlier form of CURD.]

crude (krōōd) **crud·er, crud·est.** *adj.* **1.** lacking skill, finish, or completeness; rough; unpolished: *a crude drawing, a crude theory.* **2.** lacking tact, taste, or refinement; uncultured; rude: *crude behavior.* **3.** in a natural or raw state; unrefined: *crude oil, crude rubber.* **4.** coarse; vulgar: *crude jokes.* **5.** *Archaic.* immature; unripe: *I come to pluck your berries harsh and crude* (Milton, 1637). [Latin *crūdus* raw.] —**crude′ly,** *adv.* —**crude′ness,** *n.*

cru·di·ty (krōō′də tē) *pl.,* **-ties.** *n.* **1.** quality or state of being crude. **2.** that which is crude.

cru·el (krōō′əl) **cru·el·er, cru·el·est;** *also, British.* **cru·el·ler, cru·el·lest.** *adj.* **1.** willing or inclined to inflict suffering; indifferent to or enjoying the pain or distress of others. **2.** causing grief, pain, or suffering; exhibiting cruelty: *a cruel winter, cruel punishment.* [Old French *cruel* severe, harsh, from Latin *crūdēlis.*] —**cru′el·ly,** *adv.* —**cru′el·ness,** *n.*

cru·el·ty (krōō′əl tē) *pl.,* **-ties.** *n.* **1.** quality or state of being cruel. **2.** an action or occurrence that is cruel.

cru·et (krōō′it) *n.* small glass bottle for holding vinegar, oil, or other dressings. [Anglo-Norman *cruet,* diminutive of Old French *cruie* earthen pot; of Germanic origin.]

Cruet

cruise (krōōz) **cruised, cruis·ing.** *v.i.* **1.** to sail about unhurriedly, often without a specific destination, as for pleasure or reconnaisance purposes. **2.** to travel or move about in a similar way: *The police car cruised through the area. The taxi cruised along the street looking for a fare.* **3.** to move at the speed of maximum efficiency, as an aircraft or automobile. —*v.t.* to cruise over or around in: *The pleasure boat cruised the Mediterranean. We cruised the park looking for our lost dog.* —*n.* act of cruising, esp. a sea voyage. [Dutch *kruisen* to cross, to sail to and fro, from *kruis* cross, from Latin *crux.*]

cruis·er (krōō′zər) *n.* **1.** warship less heavily armed than a battleship, having a long cruising radius and designed for speed and maneuverability. **2.** power-driven boat, as a motorboat or cabin cruiser. **3.** police squad car. **4.** one who or that which cruises.

cruising radius, maximum distance that an aircraft or ship can travel before its fuel is exhausted.

cruising speed, speed at which an aircraft, powered boat, or vehicle operates at sustained maximum efficiency.

crul·ler (krul′ər) *also,* **krul·ler.** *n.* small cake made of sweetened dough cut into strips which are twisted together and fried in deep fat. [Dutch *krulle* literally, curled cake, from *krullen* to curl.]

crumb (krum) *n.* **1.** tiny fragment, as of bread, cake, or similar food. **2.** small bit of something; scrap: *crumbs of information.* **3.** soft inner part of bread. **4.** *Slang.* worthless or contemptible person. —*v.t.* **1.** to break into crumbs. **2.** to prepare for cooking by covering or dressing with crumbs. **3.** to clear the crumbs from: *to crumb a table.* [Old English *cruma* fragment.]

crum·ble (krum′bəl) **-bled, -bling.** *v.t.* to break into small fragments: *She crumbled the bread and fed it to the pigeons.* —*v.i.* **1.** to fall into small fragments: *The yellowed pages crumbled at a touch.* **2.** to fall apart or be destroyed; disintegrate: *Our hopes for winning the game crumbled when our best player got hit on the arm by a wild pitch.* [Modification (influenced by CRUMB) of earlier *crimble,* going back to Old English *cruma* fragment.]

crum·bly (krum′blē) **-bli·er, -bli·est.** *adj.* liable to crumble; easily crumbled; friable. —**crum′bli·ness,** *n.*

crumb·y (krum′ē) **crumb·i·er, crumb·i·est.** *adj.* **1.** full of crumbs. **2.** soft, like the inner part of bread. **3.** *Slang.* crummy.

crum·my (krum′ē) **crum·mi·er, crum·mi·est.** *adj. Slang.* inferior; miserable; shabby. [Possibly obsolete *crum* crooked (from Old English *crumb*) + -Y¹.]

crum·pet (krum′pit) *n.* soft, unsweetened batter cake that is first baked on a griddle, then usually toasted and buttered. [Probably from Middle English *crompid (cake)* literally, curled up (cake), going back to Old English *crump* crooked.]

crum·ple (krum′pəl) **-pled, -pling.** *v.t.* to press or crush (something) into irregular folds or creases: *to crumple paper.* —*v.i.* **1.** to become wrinkled or shriveled: *The fender crumpled when it hit the wall.* **2.** to give way; collapse: *The wounded soldier crumpled to the ground.* —*n.* irregular fold or crease. [Obsolete *crump* to curl up (going back to Old English *crump* crooked) + -LE.]

crunch (krunch) *v.t.* **1.** to chew or bite with a crushing or crackling sound; chew noisily: *to crunch carrots.* **2.** to crush or grind noisily: *The car wheels crunched the gravel.* —*v.i.* **1.** to chew noisily: *He crunched on some celery.* **2.** to produce or emit a crunching or crackling sound: *The dry leaves crunched under our feet.* **3.** to move or proceed with such

a sound: *The ship crunched through the ice.* —*n.* **1.** sound of crunching. **2.** act of crunching. [Imitative.]

crup·per (krup′ər, kroop′-) *n.* **1.** leather strap attached to the back of a saddle and passing over the horse's back and around its tail to prevent the saddle from sliding forward. See **harness** for illustration. **2.** rump of a horse; croup. [Old French *cropière* saddle strap, from *crope* rump. See CROUP².]

cru·ral (kroor′əl) *adj.* of or relating to a leg or leglike structure. [Latin *crūrālis,* from *crūs* leg.]

cru·sade (krōō sād′) *n.* **1.** *also,* **Crusade.** any of the military expeditions undertaken by European Christians between 1096 and 1270 to recover the Holy Land from the Muslims. **2.** any war or military expedition undertaken under papal sanction, esp. during the Middle Ages. **3.** any vigorous campaign for the advancement of a cause, esp. for reform or improvement: *a crusade against crime.* —*v.i.* **-sad·ed, -sad·ing.** to engage in a crusade. [Blend of French *croisade* and Spanish *cruzada,* both meaning "expedition to the Holy Land of Christians wearing the cross" and going back to Latin *crux* cross.] —**cru·sad′er,** *n.*

cruse (krōōz, krōōs) *n. Archaic.* earthenware jug, pot, or bottle. [Middle Dutch *cruyse* pot.]

crush (krush) *v.t.* **1.** to press or squeeze with such force as to damage, deform, or destroy. **2.** to break into fragments or small particles, as by grinding or pounding: *to crush ice.* **3.** to put down; subdue completely; quell: *to crush an uprising.* **4.** to depress or burden grievously; overwhelm: *crushed by the bad news.* **5.** to embrace or hug forcibly: *Aunt Martha crushed her dear nephew to her breast.* **6.** to crowd or press upon. —*v.i.* to become crushed. —*n.* **1.** act of crushing; being crushed. **2.** thick or closely pressed crowd: *I was caught in the crush at the parade.* **3.** *Informal.* **a.** infatuation. **b.** object of an infatuation. [Old French *cruis(s)ir* to break, crack; of Germanic origin.]

crust (krust) *n.* **1.a.** outer, often hard or crisp, part of bread. **b.** piece of this. **c.** any dry, hard piece of bread. **2.** outer coating or layer of certain foods: *pie crust. The fried chicken has a thick crust on it.* **3.** any hard or brittle outer coating; surface layer: *The lake was covered with a thin crust of ice.* **4.** hard outer layer of the earth. **5.** *Slang.* insolence; audacity. —*v.t., v.i.* **1.** to cover or become covered with a crust. **2.** to form into a crust. [Old French *crouste* crust of bread, from Latin *crusta* crust of bread, rind, shell.]

crus·ta·cean (krus tā′shən) *n.* any of a diverse, widely distributed group of chiefly aquatic arthropods, class Crustacea, including lobsters, crabs, shrimp, crawfish, barnacles, and wood lice. Crustaceans breathe through gills, have two pairs of antennae, and in the most familiar species have shells that are hard and limy. —*adj.* of or relating to crustaceans. [Modern Latin *Crustacea,* going back to Latin *crusta* rind, shell + -AN.]

crus·ta·ceous (krus tā′shəs) *adj.* **1.** of or like a crust or shell. **2.** having a crust or shell. **3.** crustacean.

crust·y (krus′tē) **crust·i·er, crust·i·est.** *adj.* **1.** having or resembling a crust. **2.** ill-tempered and harsh in manner or speech. —**crust′i·ly,** *adv.* —**crust′i·ness,** *n.*

crutch (kruch) *n.* **1.** staff used by the lame as a support in walking, esp. one having a grip for the hand and either a crosspiece that fits under the armpit or a curved piece that fits around the forearm. **2.** anything resembling a crutch in shape or function, as a forked leg rest on a sidesaddle. **3.** anything that gives support. [Old English *crycc* staff.]

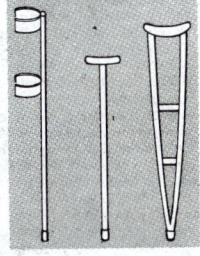

Crutches

crux (kruks) *pl.,* **crux·es** or **cru·ces.** *n.* **1.** pivotal, fundamental, or decisive point: *the crux of the matter, the crux of an argument.* **2.** **Crux.** the Southern Cross. **3.** *Archaic.* difficult or perplexing problem. [Latin *crux* cross, torture, trouble. Doublet of CROSS.]

cru·zei·ro (krōō zār′ō) *n.* monetary unit of Brazil equal to 100 centavos.

cry (krī) **cried, cry·ing.** *v.i.* **1.** to shed tears, esp. as an expression of emotion; weep: *The children cried when they had to leave their friends.* **2.** to call loudly; shout: *The victims cried for help. The stricken man cried out in pain.* **3.** (of an animal) to make its characteristic call. **4. to cry (out) for.** to be in urgent need of; demand: *The situation cries out for attention.* **5. to cry off.** to withdraw from an agreement or undertaking. —*v.t.* **1.** to utter loudly; exclaim: *She cried herself sick. The child cried himself to sleep.* **2.** to affect (oneself) in a specified way by weeping: *She cried herself sick. The child cried himself to sleep.* **3.** to announce or advertise publicly: *to cry one's wares.* **4. to cry down.** to deprecate; disparage. **5. to cry one's eyes** (or **heart**) **out.** to weep inconsolably or profusely. **6. to cry up.** to praise highly; extol. **7. to cry wolf.** to give a false alarm. —*n. pl.,* **cries.** **1.** loud call or shout,

at; āpe; cär; end; mē; it; īce; hot; ōld; fôrk; wood; fōōl; oil; out; up; ūse; turn; sing; thin; <u>th</u>is; zh in treasure; ə in ago, taken, pencil, lemon, circus.

243

esp. one that expresses emotion: *a cry of joy, the bloodcurdling cries of charging rebels.* **2.** fit of weeping: *She felt much better after a good cry.* **3.** entreaty; appeal. **4.** public proclamation or advertisement: *a street vendor's cry.* **5.** public outcry; clamor; demand: *a cry for justice.* **6.** rallying call; slogan; watchword. **7.** (of an animal) characteristic call. **8.** (of hounds) a pack. **9. a far cry. a.** a long way: *It's a far cry from New York to San Francisco.* **b.** something very different: *The published book is a far cry from the early manuscript.* **10. in full cry.** in full pursuit, as a pack of hounds. [Old French *crier* to cry out, shout, from Latin *quirītāre* to cry out, shriek; literally, to call for the assistance of the *Quirītēs,* or Roman citizens.]

cry·ba·by (krī′bā′bē) *pl.* **-bies.** *n.* person, esp. a child, who cries or complains often.

cry·ing (krī′ing) *adj.* **1.** that cries. **2.** demanding immediate attention or remedy: *a crying shame, a crying need.*

cryo- *combining form* cold; freezing; frost: *cryogen.* [Greek *kryos* frost.]

cry·o·gen (krī′ə jən) *n.* mixture that causes freezing; refrigerant. [CRYO- + -GEN.]

cry·o·gen·ics (krī′ə jen′iks) *n.,pl.* branch of physics dealing with the structure and properties of materials at very low temperatures. **A** construed as singular. [CRYO- + -GEN + -ICS.] —**cry′o·gen′ic,** *adj.*

cry·o·lite (krī′ə līt′) *n.* natural or synthetic fluoride of sodium and aluminum, used chiefly in making aluminum. Formula: Na₃AlF₆. [CRYO- + Greek *lithos* stone.]

cry·o·sur·ger·y (krī′ə sur′jər ē) *n.* surgery using the application of extremely low temperatures to destroy diseased or damaged tissue. [CRYO- + SURGERY.]

cry·o·ther·a·py (krī′ə ther′ə pē) *n.* use of extremely low temperatures in medical treatment. [CRYO- + THERAPY.]

crypt (kript) *n.* underground chamber or vault used chiefly as a burial place, esp. one beneath the main floor of a church. [Latin *crypta* vault, cave, from Greek *kryptē,* from *kryptos* hidden. Doublet of GROTTO.]

cryp·tic (krip′tik) *adj.* **1.** having an ambiguous or hidden meaning; enigmatic: *a cryptic remark.* **2.** *Zoology.* serving to conceal; protective: *cryptic coloring.* Also, **cryp′ti·cal.** [Late Latin *crypticus* concealed, from Greek *kryptikos* obscuring, from *kryptos* hidden.] —**cryp′ti·cal·ly,** *adv.*

crypto- *combining form* hidden; secret: *cryptogram.* [Greek *kryptos.*]

cryp·to·gram (krip′tə gram′) *n.* message written in cipher or code. [CRYPTO- + -GRAM¹.] —**cryp′to·gram′mic,** *adj.*

cryp·to·graph (krip′tə graf′) *n.* **1.** cryptogram. **2.** system of cipher writing; cipher. [CRYPTO- + -GRAPH.]

cryp·tog·ra·phy (krip tog′rə fē) *n.* science of writing and deciphering cryptograms. [CRYPTO- + -GRAPHY.] —**cryp·tog′ra·pher, cryp·tog′ra·phist,** *n.* —**cryp·to·graph·ic** (krip′tə graf′ik), *adj.*

crys·tal (krist′əl) *n.* **1.** rock crystal. **2.** a solid bounded by plane surfaces, whose atoms, molecules, or ions are arranged in an orderly and repeated pattern: *crystals of salt.* **3.a.** glass having a high degree of transparency and brilliance. **b.** drinking glasses, bowls, vases, or other objects made of this glass. **4.** transparent covering over the face of a watch. **5.** piece of quartz or similar substance that produces certain electric impulses when subjected to pressure, as from radio waves, used esp. in some kinds of radios or microphones. —*adj.* **1.** composed of crystal: *a crystal ashtray, a crystal goblet.* **2.** resembling crystal; clear; transparent: *crystal waters.* [Old French *cristal* rock crystal, from Latin *crystallum* ice, rock crystal (because it resembles ice), from Greek *krystallos.*]

crystal ball, ball of transparent glass, crystal, or similar material considered to reveal future or distant events when gazed into.

crystal detector, device for changing the alternating current in a radio or television receiver into direct current, consisting of a semiconducting crystal in contact with a conductor or with another crystal.

crystal gazing, act or practice of gazing into a crystal ball, supposedly to discover future events.

crys·tal·line (krist′əl in, -īn′) *adj.* **1.** consisting of crystal or crystals. **2.** having the structure of a crystal. **3.** resembling crystal; clear; pure: *a crystalline lake.*

crystalline lens, lens of the eye in vertebrates and the cephalopods.

crys·tal·lize (krist′əl īz′) **-lized, -liz·ing.** *v.t.* **1.** to cause to form crystals or become crystalline: *The chemist crystallized salt as part of his experiment.* **2.** to give a definite or fixed form to. **3.** to coat or cover with sugar. —*v.i.* **1.** to form into crystals; become crystalline. **2.** to assume a definite or fixed form: *Her suspicions crystallized into certainty.* —**crys′tal·li·za′tion,** *n.*

crys·tal·log·ra·phy (krist′əl og′rə fē) *n.* science of the form, structure, and physical and chemical properties of crystals. [Greek *krystallos* ice, rock crystal + -GRAPHY.] —**crys·tal·lo·graph·ic** (krist′əl ō graf′ik), **crys′tal·lo·graph′i·cal,** *adj.*

crys·tal·loid (krist′əl oid′) *n.* substance, usually capable of crystallization, which, when dissolved in liquid, will diffuse readily through a

membrane. —*adj. also,* **crys′tal·loi·dal.** resembling a crystal or a crystalloid. [Greek *krystalloeidēs* like ice, like crystal, from *krystallos* ice, rock crystal.]

crystal set, radio receiver with a crystal detector rather than vacuum tubes or transistors.

Cs, cesium.

CS **1.** Civil Service. **2.** Christian Science.

CSC, Civil Service Commission.

CST, Central Standard Time.

ct., cent.

Ct., Connecticut.

cten·o·phore (ten′ə fôr′, tē′nə-) *n.* comb jelly. [Modern Latin *Ctenophora,* from Greek *kten-,* stem of *kteis* comb + *-phoros* bearing.]

cts., cents.

Cu., copper. [Late Latin *cuprum.* See COPPER.]

cu., cubic.

cub (kub) *n.* **1.** young animal of certain species, as bears, foxes, wolves, lions, tigers, or the like. **2.** awkward, coarse, or inexperienced youth. **3.** beginner or apprentice. **4.** Cub Scout. [Of uncertain origin.]

Cu·ba (kū′bə) *n.* island country in the Caribbean, the largest and westernmost island of the West Indies. Capital, Havana. Area, 44,218 sq. mi. Pop. (1969 est.), 8,250,000. —**Cu′ban,** *adj., n.*

cub·by·hole (kub′ē hōl′) *n.* small, enclosed space. Also, **cub′by.** [Obsolete English *cub* stall¹, shed (from Middle Dutch *cubbe*) + -Y² + HOLE.]

cube (kūb) *n.* **1.** solid figure with six equal, square faces. **2.** something resembling this figure in shape: *a cube of sugar, an ice cube.* **3.** the product of a number or quantity and its square; third power of a number. The cube of 2 is 8, that is, $2^3 = 2 \times 2 \times 2 = 8$. —*v.t.,* **cubed, cub·ing.** **1.** to cut or form into cubes or cubelike shapes: *to cube potatoes.* **2.** to raise (a number or quantity) to the third power by multiplying it by its square. [Latin *cubus* solid square, die², cubic number, from Greek *kybos.*]

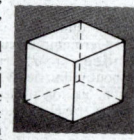

Cube

cu·beb (kū′beb) *n.* **1.** cigarette made from the crushed berries of a tropical plant, *Piper cubeba,* of the pepper family. It was formerly thought that smoking it relieved certain respiratory ailments. **2.** dried, unripe berry from which these cigarettes were made. **3.** climbing, woody, evergreen plant bearing these berries, cultivated in Java and Sumatra. [Middle French *cubèbe* this berry, going back to Arabic *kabābah.*]

cube root, number or quantity which, when multiplied by its square, produces a given number or quantity. The cube root of 8 is 2.

cu·bic (kū′bik) *adj.* **1.** of or having three dimensions: *cubic foot, cubic measure.* **2.** relating to or involving the cube of a number; of the third power: *a cubic equation.* **3.** cubical.

cu·bi·cal (kū′bi kəl) *adj.* shaped like a cube. —**cu′bi·cal·ly,** *adv.*

cu·bi·cle (kū′bi kəl) *n.* small room, compartment, or partitioned area. [Latin *cubiculum* bedroom, from *cubāre* to recline, sleep.]

cubic measure, unit or system of units for measurement of volume.

cub·ism (kū′biz′əm) *n.* movement in art, esp. painting, begun in the early twentieth century, characterized by abstract representations of objects by the use of geometric forms and overlapping planes. —**cu′bist,** *adj., n.* —**cu·bis′tic,** *adj.*

cu·bit (kū′bit) *n.* ancient unit of measure based on the length of the forearm from the elbow to the fingertips. Its value varied from one people to another but usually ranged between 18 and 22 inches. [Latin *cubitum* elbow, cubit.]

cu·boid (kū′boid) *adj.* shaped like a cube. Also, **cu·boi′dal.**

cub reporter, young and inexperienced newspaper reporter.

Cub Scout, member of a subdivision of the Boy Scouts for boys from eight to ten years of age.

Cu·chu·lain (koo kul′in, -KHool′-) *n.* Irish legendary hero of almost supernatural courage and strength who single-handedly defended Ulster against invaders.

cuck·old (kuk′əld) *n.* husband of an unfaithful wife. —*v.t.* to make a cuckold of. [Old French *cucuault* a cuckold, from *cucu* cuckoo; because the female cuckoo frequently changes her mate. See CUCKOO.] —**cuck′old·ry,** *n.*

cuck·oo (koo′koo, kook′oo) *pl.* **-oos.** *n.* **1.** any bird of the family Cuculidae, found in tropical and temperate regions throughout the world, esp. the European cuckoo, *Cuculus canorus,* which, like various other species of the family, lays its eggs in the nests of other birds. **2.** call of the cuckoo or an imitation of it. —*adj. Informal.* crazy; silly. [Old French *cucu* this bird; imitative of the bird's call.]

Cuckoo

cuckoo clock, clock with a toy cuckoo that pops out on the hour,

at; āpe; cär; end; mē; it; īce; hot; ōld; fôrk; wood; fōol; oil; out; up; ūse; turn; sing; thin; this; zh in treasure; ə in ago, taken, pencil, lemon, circus.

or at shorter intervals, and announces the time by a sound similar to a cuckoo's call.

cu. cm., cubic centimeter; cubic centimeters.

cu·cul·late (kū′kə lāt′, kū kul′it) *adj.* shaped like a hood or cowl. [Late Latin *cucullātus* hooded, from Latin *cucullus* cap, hood.]

cu·cum·ber (kū′kum′bər) *n.* **1.** fleshy, green-skinned fruit of a climbing plant, *Cucumis sativus,* of the gourd family, usually eaten in salads or pickled. **2.** the plant itself. **3. cool as a cucumber.** entirely self-possessed; calm. [Old French *coucombre* the plant, going back to Latin *cucumis.*]

cud (kud) *n.* partially digested, barely chewed food that cattle and other ruminants regurgitate from the first stomach back into the mouth for a thorough second chewing. [Old English *cudu.*]

cud·dle (kud′əl) **-dled, -dling.** *v.i.* to lie close and snug; nestle; snuggle. —*v.t.* to hold (someone or something) closely in one's arms, esp. to make warm and snug; hug and caress fondly. —*n.* warm or fond embrace. [Of uncertain origin.] —**cud′dly,** *adj.*

cud·dy (kud′ē) *pl.* **-dies.** *n.* **1.** small cabin on a boat or ship. **2.** small room, closet, or cupboard. [Of uncertain origin.]

cudg·el (kuj′əl) *n.* **1.** short, thick club. **2. to take up the cudgels (for).** to enter into a contest or controversy (in defense of someone). —*v.t.,* **-eled, -el·ing;** *also, British,* **-elled, -el·ling. 1.** to beat with or as with a cudgel. **2. to cudgel one's brains.** to think hard. [Old English *cycgel* a club.]

cue¹ (kū) *n.* **1.** signal, before or during a stage performance, for an actor or other participant to begin some action: *The slamming of a door was the actor's cue to run on stage.* **2.** any similar signal to begin: *The candidate's appearance in the hall was the band's cue to play.* **3.** guiding suggestion; hint. **4.** *Archaic.* prescribed or necessary course of action. **5.** *Archaic.* frame of mind; mood. —*v.t.,* **cued, cu·ing.** to give a cue to. [Earlier *q,* abbreviation of Latin *quandō* when; originally, a guide to actors in written copies of plays to direct them when to come in.]

cue² (kū) *n.* **1.** long, tapering stick used in billiards and pool. It is supposed to hit only the cue ball, not the other balls. **2.** queue *(def. 2).* [Old French *coe, cue* tail, stalk¹, going back to Latin *cōda,* form of *cauda* tail.]

cue ball, white ball intended to be hit by the cue and in turn to strike and move one or more of the other balls.

cuff¹ (kuf) *n.* **1.** band, fold, or similar piece at the bottom of a sleeve, usually at the wrist. **2.** turned-up fold on the bottom of a trouser leg. **3.** sheathlike part or fold on a glove which covers the wrist or lower arm. **4.** detachable piece of material designed to be worn over the wrist end of a sleeve for decoration or protection. **5.** handcuff. **6. off the cuff.** *Informal.* with little or no preparation; spontaneously. **7. on the cuff.** *Informal.* on credit. [Middle English *cuffe* glove; of uncertain origin.]

cuff² (kuf) *v.t.* to strike with or as with the side or back of the hand: *His angry friend cuffed him on the head.* —*n.* blow, esp. with the side or back of the hand. [Possibly from Middle English *cuffe* glove (suggesting "a striking with a glove"). See CUFF¹.]

cuff link, one of a pair of linked buttons or ornamental buttons with a device for fastening the two sides of a French cuff of a shirt.

cu. ft., cubic foot; cubic feet.

cui bo·no (kwē′ bō′nō, kī) *Latin.* **1.** for whose benefit. **2.** to what use or good purpose.

cu. in., cubic inch; cubic inches.

cui·rass (kwi ras′) *n.* **1.** piece of armor consisting of a breastplate and a back plate. **2.** the breastplate alone. [Middle French *cuirasse,* from *cuir* leather, from Latin *corium;* with reference to the earlier use of leather for breastplates.]

cui·ras·sier (kwēr′ə sēr′) *n.* mounted soldier wearing a cuirass.

cui·sine (kwi zēn′) *n.* **1.** manner or style of cooking or preparing food: *the cuisine of Spain.* **2.** food prepared, as at a restaurant: *The cuisine here is excellent.* [French *cuisine,* from Late Latin *coquīna* kitchen, cookery, from Latin *coquere* to cook.]

cuisse (kwis) *also,* **cuish** (kwish). *n.* part of a suit of plate armor used to protect the thigh. See **armor** for illustration. [Old French (plural) *cuisseaux* armor for the thighs, going back to Latin *coxa* hip.]

cul-de-sac (kul′də sak′, kool′-) *pl.* **culs-de-sac** or **cul-de-sacs.** *n.* **1.** street or passage closed at one end; blind alley; dead end. **2.** situation in which further progress or advance is impossible; impasse. **3.** pouch or cavity in the body that is open only at one end. [French *cul-de-sac* blind alley; literally, bottom of a sack; *cul* bottom, from Latin *cūlus* backside; *sac* bag, from Latin *saccus.* See SACK¹.]

cu·lex (kū′leks) *pl.* **-li·ces** (-lə sēz). *n.* any mosquito of the genus *Culex,* esp. *C. pipiens,* the most common mosquito of North America and Europe. [Latin *culex* gnat.]

Cuirass

cu·li·nar·y (kū′lə ner′ē, kul′ə-) *adj.* of, relating to, or used in cooking or the kitchen. [Latin *culīnārius* relating to a kitchen, from *culīna* kitchen.]

cull (kul) *v.t.* **1.** to pick out from a group; select. **2.** to pick, as flowers; gather. **3.** to examine for quality and make a selection from; pick over: *to cull a basket of blueberries.* —*n.* something selected, esp. to be put aside as inferior. [Old French *coillir* to collect, from Latin *colligere.*]

culm¹ (kulm) *n.* coal dust; refuse of coal; slack. [Of uncertain origin.]

culm² (kulm) *n.* jointed, usually hollow, stem of certain grasses. See **wheat** for illustration. [Latin *culmus* stalk¹.]

cul·mi·nate (kul′mə nāt′) **-nat·ed, -nat·ing.** *v.i.* to reach the highest or most decisive point; come to a climax or final result (with *in*): *The border clashes culminated in the outbreak of war.* —*v.t.* to bring to a close or to the highest point; complete; climax: *The chairman culminated his speech with a call to arms.* [Late Latin *culminātus,* past participle of *culmināre* to crown, exalt, from Latin *culmen* top, summit.]

cul·mi·na·tion (kul′mə nā′shən) *n.* point at which something culminates; highest point; climax.

cu·lotte (kōō′lot, kū′-, kōō lot′, kū-) *also,* **cu·lottes.** *n.* women's wide trousers that may be short or long, designed to look like a skirt. [French *culottes,* from *cul* bottom, backside, from Latin *cūlus* backside.]

cul·pa·ble (kul′pə bəl) *adj.* deserving blame or censure. [Old French *culpaole,* from Latin *culpābilis,* from *culpāre* to blame.] —**cul′pa·bil′i·ty, cul′pa·ble·ness,** *n.* —**cul′pa·bly,** *adv.*

cul·prit (kul′prit) *n.* one guilty of some offense or crime: *The police caught the culprit as he was leaving town.* [Anglo-Norman *cul. pri(s)t,* short for *culpable—prist* guilty—ready: *culpable* (see CULPABLE) + *prist* ready, going back to Latin *praestō* ready, at hand. In the law courts of medieval England, when the accused pleaded "not guilty," the prosecutor replied "guilty—ready" for "He is guilty; I am ready (to prove the accusation)."]

cult (kult) *n.* **1.** particular form or system of religious worship. **2.** enthusiastic devotion of a group to a particular person, thing, or idea. **3.** object of such devotion. **4.** followers of a cult; devoted adherents. [Latin *cultus* cultivation, reverence.] —**Syn. 1.** see **sect.**

cul·ti·va·ble (kul′tə və bəl) *adj.* capable of being cultivated. Also, **cul·ti·vat·a·ble** (kul′tə vā′tə bəl).

cul·ti·vate (kul′tə vāt′) **-vat·ed, -vat·ing.** *v.t.* **1.** to prepare and use (land) for raising crops; till. **2.** to promote or improve the growth of (a plant or crop) by labor or attention: *to cultivate roses, to cultivate corn.* **3.** to loosen the soil around growing plants in order to uproot the weeds, aerate the soil, and reduce water loss. **4.** to promote the growth or advancement of; foster; develop: *to cultivate good habits, to cultivate a taste for opera.* **5.** to improve, as by study, training, or exercise; refine: *to cultivate one's mind.* **6.** to seek familiarity with; court the acquaintance or friendship of: *He cultivates politicians.* [Medieval Latin *cultivatus,* past participle of *cultivare* to till², going back to Latin *cultus,* past participle of *colere.*]

cul·ti·vat·ed (kul′tə vā′tid) *adj.* **1.** (of soil) prepared for growing crops. **2.** produced or improved by cultivation. Distinguished from **wild. 3.** improved by education or training; cultured; refined.

cul·ti·va·tion (kul′tə vā′shən) *n.* **1.** act of cultivating soil or plants. **2.** improvement or development of something, as by study or training. **3.** culture; refinement.

cul·ti·va·tor (kul′tə vā′tər) *n.* **1.** one who cultivates. **2.** farm or garden implement for uprooting weeds and loosening the ground around growing plants.

cul·tur·al (kul′chər əl) *adj.* of, relating to, or used to develop culture: *cultural activities.* —**cul′tur·al·ly,** *adv.*

cultural lag, failure of one aspect of a culture to develop or progress as rapidly as another. Also, **culture lag.**

Cultivators

cul·ture (kul′chər) *n.* **1.** sum total of the beliefs, accomplishments, and behavior patterns of a group of people, acquired by members of the group through social learning and transmitted from one generation to another. **2.** intellectual and artistic content of this. **3.** knowledge of intellectual and artistic accomplishments and of what is considered to be fine in taste and manners. **4.** improvement or refinement of the mind or body, as by education and training: *physical culture.* **5.** cultivation of the soil. **6.a.** development of microorganisms or living cells in a prepared medium favorable to their growth. **b.** product of such development. **7.** care and raising of plants or animals, esp. with an interest in improving the species. —*v.t.,* **-tured, -tur·ing. 1.** to grow (microorganisms or living cells) in a prepared medium. **2.** to inoculate with a

prepared culture: *to culture milk.* [Latin *cultūra* cultivation, care, agriculture.]

cul·tured (kul′chərd) *adj.* **1.** having or exhibiting culture; educated; refined: *a cultured man, cultured speech.* **2.** produced or raised by cultivation or under artificial conditions: *a cultured virus.*

culture medium, substance or preparation in which microorganisms or living cells may be grown for research or testing.

cul·tus (kul′təs) *-tus·es* or *-ti* (-tī). *n.* religious cult. [Latin *cultus.* See CULT.]

cul·ver·in (kul′vər in) *n.* **1.** long, heavy cannon of the sixteenth and seventeenth centuries. **2.** crude musket used in medieval times. [Old French *coulevrine,* from *couleuvre* snake, going back to Latin *colubra;* with reference to the snakelike shape.]

cul·vert (kul′vərt) *n.* any structure that provides for the free flow of water under such passages as roads, sidewalks, and railroads. [Of uncertain origin.]

Culvert

Cu·mae (kū′mē) *n.* ancient city in southwestern Italy. It was the earliest Greek settlement in the western Mediterranean.

cum·ber (kum′bər) *v.t.* **1.** to hinder or obstruct; hamper. **2.** to trouble; burden. [Possibly from Old French *combrer* to hinder, from Late Latin *cumbrus* barrier; of uncertain origin.]

Cum·ber·land Gap (kum′bər lənd) natural pass through the Cumberland Mountains near the point where Tennessee, Virginia, and Kentucky meet.

Cumberland Mountains, rugged plateau in the Appalachian Mountains that extends from southwestern West Virginia to northwestern Alabama. Also, **Cumberland Plateau.**

cum·ber·some (kum′bər səm) *adj.* not easily managed or carried; unwieldy. —**cum′ber·some·ly,** *adv.* —**cum′ber·some·ness,** *n.*

cum·brous (kum′brəs) *adj.* cumbersome. —**cum′brous·ly,** *adv.* —**cum′brous·ness,** *n.*

cum·in (kum′in) *also,* **cum·min.** *n.* **1.** aromatic, hot-tasting, seedlike fruit of an herb, *Cuminum cyminum,* of the parsley family, used in curry powder and in flavoring such foods as cheese, meat, and pickles. **2.** the small, delicate herb itself, widely cultivated in southern Europe and India. [Old English *cymen* this herb, from Latin *cumīnum,* from Greek *kymīnon;* of Semitic origin.]

cum lau·de (koom lou′dē, kum lô′də) with honors or praise. Distinguished from **magna cum laude** and **summa cum laude.** ▲ used to signify graduation with honors from a college or university. [Modern Latin *cum laude.*]

cum·mer·bund (kum′ər bund′) *n.* broad sash worn around the waist, esp. with a tuxedo. [Hindi *kamar-band* sash, loin band, going back to Persian *kamar* waist, loins + *band* band.]

Cummerbund

cum·quat (kum′kwot) kumquat.

cu·mu·late (*v.,* kū′myə lāt′; *adj.,* kū′myə lit, -lāt′) *-lat·ed, -lat·ing. v.t., v.i.* to accumulate. —*adj.* accumulated. [Latin *cumulātus,* past participle of *cumulāre* to heap.]

cu·mu·la·tion (kū′myə lā′shən) *n.* **1.** act of accumulating. **2.** that which is accumulated; heap; mass.

cu·mu·la·tive (kū′myə lə tiv, -lā′tiv) *adj.* **1.** increasing in size, strength, or value, as by accumulation or successive additions: *the cumulative effect of smoking.* **2.** arising or gained from accumulation: *cumulative knowledge.* **3.** (of unpaid interest or dividends) accumulating and due to be paid in the future. —**cu′mu·la·tive·ly,** *adv.* —**cu′mu·la·tive·ness,** *n.*

cu·mu·lo·cir·rus (kū′myə lō sir′əs) *n.* small, filmy cumulus cloud. [CUMULUS + CIRRUS.]

cu·mu·lo·nim·bus (kū′myə lō nim′bəs) cumulus cloud billowing upward in the shape of a mountain or tower, often producing thunderstorms. [CUMULUS + NIMBUS.]

cu·mu·lous (kū′myə ləs) *adj.* (of clouds) of or resembling a cumulus.

cu·mu·lus (kū′myə ləs) *pl.* **-li** (-lī′). *n.* **1.** dense cloud made up of rounded mounds or heaps billowing upward from a flat base. **2.** *Archaic.* heap; pile; accumulation. [Latin *cumulus* heap.]

cu·ne·ate (kū′nē it, āt′) *adj.* tapering to a point at one end; wedge-shaped, as a leaf. [Latin *cuneātus,* from *cuneus* wedge.]

cu·ne·i·form (kū nē′ə fôrm′) *n.* system of writing characterized by wedge-shaped characters, as used in ancient times by the Sumerians, Babylonians, Assyrians, and Persians. —*adj.* wedge-shaped. [Latin *cuneus* wedge + -FORM.]

Cuneiform

cun·ner (kun′ər) *n.* saltwater fish, *Tautogolabrus adspersus,* commonly found off the North Atlantic coast of the United States. [Of uncertain origin.]

cun·ning (kun′ing) *adj.* **1.** artfully shrewd or crafty; sly: *a cunning opponent.* **2.** cute or appealing; charming: *a cunning toy.* **3.** *Archaic.* skillful; expert. —*n.* **1.** skill in deception; craftiness; slyness: *His plan showed a good deal of cunning.* **2.** skill in performance or workmanship; expertness. [Middle English *cunning* knowing, present participle of *cunnen* to know, from Old English *cunnan* to know, be able.] —**cun′ning·ly,** *adv.* —**cun′ning·ness,** *n.* —Syn. *adj.* **1.** see sly.

cup (kup) *n.* **1.** small, open vessel, often with a handle, used chiefly for drinking. **2.** amount contained in a cup; contents of a cup: *I'd like a cup of soup.* **3.** unit of capacity equal to eight fluid ounces or half a pint. **4.** part of a chalice vessel that contains the liquid. Distinguished from **stem** and **base.** **5.** ornamental cup-shaped vessel given as a prize, esp. in sports. **6.** something resembling a cup in shape, as the calyx of a flower. **7.** one's lot or fate; share: *bitter cup of humiliation.* **8.** *also,* **cups.** intoxicating drink, or the habit of drinking: *The jolly prince . . . loving his cups and ease* (Thackeray, 1861). **9.a.** chalice used in Communion. **b.** consecrated wine used in Communion. **10.a.** metal container in a hole on a golf course. **b.** the hole itself. **11.** *Medicine.* small, bowl-shaped glass used in cupping. **12. in one's cups.** drunk. —*v.t.,* **cupped, cup·ping. 1.** to shape like a cup: *to cup one's hands.* **2.** to place in or as in a cup: *He cupped his chin in his hand.* **3.** *Medicine.* to subject to cupping. [Old English *cuppe* drinking vessel, from Late Latin *cuppa,* form of Latin *cūpa* vat, cask.]

cup·bear·er (kup′bâr′ər) *n.* attendant, as at a feast, who fills and serves the cups.

cup·board (kub′ərd) *n.* **1.** closet or cabinet with shelves, esp. for dishes or food. **2.** any small closet or cabinet.

cup·cake (kup′kāk′) *n.* small cake baked in a cup-shaped container.

cup·ful (kup′fool′) *pl.,* **-fuls.** *n.* amount that a cup holds.

Cu·pid (kū′pid) *n.* **1.** Roman god of love and son of Venus, usually represented as a winged boy with bow and arrows. His Greek counterpart is Eros. **2.** *also,* **cupid.** any representation of a naked winged boy, esp. with bow and arrows, considered as a symbol of love. [Latin *Cupīdō* the god of love, personification of *cupīdō* desire, from *cupere* to desire.]

cu·pid·i·ty (kū pid′ə tē) *n.* eager desire for possession, esp. of wealth; avarice; greed. [Latin *cupiditās* desire.]

cup of tea *Informal.* something one enjoys or excels in; something suited to one's taste.

cu·po·la (kū′pə lə) *n.* **1.** rounded or dome-like structure rising above a roof. **2.** rounded roof or ceiling; dome. [Italian *cupola* dome, from Late Latin *cūpula* little cask, diminutive of Latin *cūpa* vat, cask.]

cup·ping (kup′ing) *n.* method of drawing blood to the surface of the skin by applying a heated glass cup that creates a partial vacuum as it cools. It is not commonly used in modern medicine.

Cupola

cu·pre·ous (kōō′prē əs, kū′-) *adj.* of, containing, or resembling copper. [Late Latin *cupreus* of copper, from *cuprum* copper. See COPPER.]

cu·pric (kōō′prik, kū′-) *adj.* of, relating to, or containing copper, esp. copper with a positive valence of 2.

cu·prite (kōō′prīt, kū′-) *n.* red, lustrous, translucent mineral compound, which is an important copper ore. Formula: Cu_2O [Late Latin *cuprum* copper + -ITE[1]. See COPPER.]

cu·prous (kōō′prəs, kū′-) *adj.* of, relating to, or containing copper, esp. copper with a positive valence of 1.

cur (kur) *n.* **1.** worthless or bad-tempered dog; mongrel. **2.** despicable person. [Possibly from Old Norse *kurr* grumbling; because of the growling of such a dog.]

cur. 1. currency. **2.** current.

cur·a·ble (kyoor′ə bəl) *adj.* capable of being cured. —**cur·a·bil′i·ty,** **cur′a·ble·ness,** *n.* —**cur′a·bly,** *adv.*

cu·ra·çao (kyoor′ə sō′, koor′ə sou′) *also,* **cu·ra·çoa.** *n.* sweet liqueur flavored with dried peel of bitter oranges. [From CURACAO; because originally made with oranges from Curaçao.]

Cu·ra·çao (kyoor′ə sō′, koor′ə sou′) *n.* island off the coast of Venezuela. Area, 173 sq. mi. Pop. (1967), 141,393.

cu·ra·cy (kyoor′ə sē) *pl.,* **-cies.** *n.* position, duties, or term of office of a curate.

cu·ra·re (kyoo rär′ē) *n.* any of various poisons obtained as a dark-brown resinous extract from certain South American plants, used by natives as an arrow poison. When specially prepared and purified, it is used in medicine to relax muscles during surgery and to treat certain muscular disorders. [Spanish *curare;* of Carib origin.]

cu·ras·sow (kyoor′ə sō′, kyoor ras′ō) *n.* any of several turkeylike birds, family Cracidae, native to mountainous regions of South and Central America, having a crest of stiff, curled feathers and a long tail. Length: 20–40 inches. [Form of *Curaçao*, Caribbean island where the bird was first found.]

cu·rate (kyoor′it) *n.* clergyman who assists the pastor, rector, or vicar of a parish. [Medieval Latin *curatus* one having a spiritual charge, priest, going back to Latin *cūra* care.]

Curassow

cur·a·tive (kyoor′ə tiv) *adj.* **1.** having the tendency or power to cure or remedy: *curative treatment, curative measures.* **2.** of, relating to, or used in the cure of disease: *curative medicine.* —*n.* that which cures; remedy.

cu·ra·tor (kyoor rā′tər, kyoor′ə tər) *n.* person, as in a museum, art gallery, or zoo, in charge of all or part of the materials collected or exhibited. [Latin *cūrātor* guardian, overseer.] —**cu·ra·to·ri·al** (kyoor′ə tôr′ē əl), *adj.* —**cu·ra′tor·ship′,** *n.*

curb (kurb) *n.* **1.** *also, British.* **kerb.** border of concrete, stone, or other material along the edge of a street or sidewalk; outer edge of a sidewalk: *You parked the car too far from the curb.* **2.** something which restrains or controls; check: *The budget committee recommended a curb on national spending.* **3.** chain or strap fastened to a horse's bit and passing under its lower jaw, used to check the horse when the reins are pulled. Also, **curb strap. 4.** enclosing, confining, or reinforcing framework or border, as that around the top of a well. —*v.t.* **1.** to restrain or control with or as with a curb strap; check: *to curb a horse, to curb one's appetite.* **2.** to provide with a curb. **3.** to walk (a dog) along the edge of a street rather than on the sidewalk for the elimination of its waste matter. [Old French *courber* to bend, from Latin *curvāre.*]

curb bit, horse's bit having a curb strap attached, designed so that a slight pull on the reins will exert gentle pressure on the horse's tongue or jaw, causing the horse to stop quickly.

curb·ing (kur′bing) *n.* material forming a curb or used for making one.

curb market, over-the-counter market. Also, **curb exchange.** [CURB + MARKET; because it was originally conducted on the sidewalk or street.]

curb roof, roof consisting of two slopes on each side, the lower two steeper than the upper.

curb·stone (kurb′stōn′) *also, British,* **kerb·stone.** *n.* stone or row of stones along the edge of a street or sidewalk.

cur·cu·li·o (kur kyōō′lē ō′) *pl.* **-li·os.** *n.* any of various weevils of Eurasia and North America, that cause damage to fruit and nuts. Also, **snout beetle.** [Latin *curculiō* weevil.]

curd (kurd) *n.* **1.** *also,* **curds.** coagulated portion of milk, produced by natural or artificial souring, from which cheese is made. Distinguished from **whey. 2.** any substance resembling this. —*v.t., v.i.* to form into or become curd. [Of uncertain origin.]

cur·dle (kurd′əl) **-dled, -dling.** *v.t.* to change into curd; coagulate; thicken. —*v.i.* **1.** to become curd; coagulate; thicken. **2.** to seem to thicken or congeal, as from horror or fear: *an icy sickness curdling o'er my heart* (Byron, 1818). **3. to make (one's) blood curdle.** to fill (someone) with horror or fear; terrify. [CURD + -LE.]

cure (kyoor) *n.* **1.** restoration to a healthy or sound condition; recovery. **2.** something that restores health; remedy. **3.** particular method or course of remedial or medicinal treatment. **4.** something that corrects an undesirable condition or situation. —*v.t.,* **cured, cur·ing. 1.a.** to restore to a healthy or sound condition; make well. **b.** to correct an undesirable situation: *to cure the nation's ills.* **2.** to get rid of or rid (someone) of; remedy: *to cure a sore throat. That certainly cured me of biting my nails.* **3.** to prepare for preservation, as by drying, smoking, or similar process: *to cure fish, to cure hay.* **4.** to subject (a material such as tobacco, leather, or rubber) to chemical or physical processes in order to prepare for use or produce desired qualities. —*v.i.* **1.** to effect a cure. **2.** to be or become preserved or processed by curing: *The meat was hung up in the smokehouse to cure.* [Old French *curer* to take care of, heal, from Latin *cūrāre.*] —**cur′er,** *n.*
Syn. *v.t.* **1. Cure, heal, remedy** mean to correct or make well an unhealthy or undesirable condition. **Cure** is more frequently used in reference to a disease and suggests complete restoration to normal health: *Antibiotics help to cure many diseases that were formerly fatal.* **Heal** is interchangeable with *cure* without loss of meaning but is more often used in the sense of restoring to wholeness an affected or injured part: *This ointment heals burns, wounds, and cuts.* **Remedy** implies a specific corrective treatment that relieves, counteracts, or alleviates an abnormal condition that causes harm and damage: *These reading exercises are designed to remedy speech defects.*

cu·ré (kyoo rā′, kyoor′ā) *n.* parish priest, esp. in France. [French *curé,* from Medieval Latin *curatus.* See CURATE.]

cure-all (kyoor′ôl′) *n.* something that supposedly will cure all diseases or evils; panacea.

cur·few (kur′fyōō) *n.* **1.** order or rule requiring persons to observe certain regulations, as to remain indoors, during specified hours, esp. at night. **2.a.** hour at which such an order or rule becomes effective. **b.** period during which it is in effect. **3.a.** sounding of a bell or other signal at evening time. **b.** bell or other signal so used. [Anglo-Norman *coeverfu* signal for putting out or covering fires at night (a medieval practice); literally, cover fire, from Old French *covrir* to cover (from Latin *cooperīre*) + *feu* fire (going back to Latin *focus* hearth).]

cu·ri·a (kyoor′ē ə) *pl.* **cu·ri·ae** (kyoor′ē ē′). *n.* **1.** one of the thirty divisions into which the three ancient Roman tribes were divided. **2.** building where such a division met, as for worship or public deliberation. **3.** *also,* **Curia.** Curia Romana. **4. Curia.** building where the senate of ancient Rome met. **5.** medieval council, assembly, or court of justice. [Latin *cūria* division of the Roman tribes, Roman senate house.]

Cu·ri·a Ro·ma·na (kyoor′ē ə rō mä′nə) body of officials who assist the pope in the government of the Roman Catholic Church.

cu·rie (kyoor′ē, kyoo rē′) *n.* unit of measurement of radioactivity, equal to 3.70 x 10¹⁰ disintegrations per second. [From Marie CURIE.]

Cu·rie (kyoor′ē, kyoo rē′, koo-) **1. Ma·rie Sklo·dow·ska** (sklô-dôf′skä). 1867–1934, Polish-French chemist and physicist who with her husband discovered radium in 1898. **2. Pierre** (pyer) 1859–1906, her husband; French physicist and chemist.

cu·ri·o (kyoor′ē ō′) *pl.* **cu·ri·os.** *n.* object valued as a curiosity or for its quaintness: *She collects old china figurines and other curios.* [Short for CURIOSITY.]

cu·ri·os·i·ty (kyoor′ē os′ə tē) *pl.* **-ties.** *n.* **1.** desire for knowledge of something, esp. of something new, strange, or unknown. **2.** object that arouses interest by its rarity or strangeness. [Latin *cūriōsitās* desire of knowledge.]

cu·ri·ous (kyoor′ē əs) *adj.* **1.** eager to know or learn. **2.** arousing attention because of rarity or strangeness; odd; unusual: *a curious Greek coin.* **3.** *Archaic.* painstaking; careful. [Latin *cūriōsus* careful, inquisitive, from *cūra* care.] —**cu′ri·ous·ly,** *adv.* —**cu′ri·ous·ness,** *n.*

cu·ri·um (kyoor′ē əm) *n.* man-made radioactive element first produced by bombardment of plutonium 239 with helium ions. Symbol: **Cm** See element for table. [Modern Latin *curium,* from Pierre and Marie CURIE.]

curl (kurl) *v.t.* **1.** to twist or form into ringlets or coils, as the hair. **2.** to bend or form into a curved or spiral shape: *She curled her lips in disdain.* —*v.i.* **1.** to take the form of ringlets or coils, as of hair. **2.** to assume a curved or spiral shape. **3.** to play the game of curling. **4. to curl up.** to sit or lie down in a comfortable position, as with the back curved and the legs drawn up. —*n.* **1.** coiled or curved lock of hair; ringlet. **2.** something having a curved or spiral shape. **3.** act of curling; being curled. [Possibly from Middle Dutch *krul* curly.]

curl·er (kur′lər) *n.* one who or that which curls, esp. a device on which hair is wound to make it curl.

cur·lew (kur′lōō) *n.* any of various migratory wading birds, family Scolopacidae, native to arctic and temperate regions, having long legs, a long, slender, downcurved bill, and, usually, brown plumage. [Old French *courlieu;* imitative of the bird's call.]

Curlew

curl·i·cue (kur′li kyōō′) *also,* **curl·y·cue.** *n.* fancy curve, twist, or flourish, as in handwriting. [CURLY + CUE².]

curl·ing (kur′ling) *n.* game played on the ice in which curling stones are slid toward a circular target, the object being to come as close as possible to the target.

curling iron, metal rod or other instrument, used when heated for curling the hair.

curling stone, large, rounded block of granite or other heavy material, having a handle on one side, used in the game of curling.

Curling stone

curl·pa·per (kurl′pā′pər) *n.* strip of paper designed to hold a lock of hair that is curled.

curl·y (kur′lē) **curl·i·er, curl·i·est.** *adj.* **1.** tending to curl. **2.** having curls. —**curl′i·ness,** *n.*

cur·mud·geon (kər muj′ən) *n.* surly, bad-tempered, or stingy person, esp. an old man. [Of uncertain origin.]

cur·rant (kur′ənt) *n.* **1.a.** edible, tart berry of any of several shrubs, genus *Ribes,* used esp. for making jelly, syrup, and wine. **b.** shrub on which this berry grows. **2.** small, seedless raisin used esp. in certain baked goods, as cakes, pies, and buns. [Anglo-Norman *(raisin de)*

at; āpe; cär; end; mē; it; īce; hot; ōld; fôrk; wood; fōol; oil; out; up; ūse; turn; sing; thin; this; zh in treasure; ə in ago, taken, pencil, lemon, circus.

247

Corauntz (raisin of) Corinth, going back to Greek *Korinthos* Corinth, from which such raisins were first exported.]

cur·ren·cy (kur'ən sē) pl., **-cies.** n. 1. current medium of exchange; money in actual use. 2. general use, acceptance, or circulation; popularity; prevalence: *The story gained wide currency.*

cur·rent (kur'ənt) adj. 1. belonging to the present time; in progress: *current fashions, the current year.* 2. generally used or accepted; prevalent: *current usage.* 3. passing from person to person; widely circulated. —n. 1. continuous movement, as of water; a flowing; flow: *a river with a rapid current.* 2. portion of a body of water or of air flowing continuously in a definite direction: *an ocean current.* 3. noticeable course, movement, or tendency; trend: *the current of modern political thought.* 4.a. flow of electricity in an electric circuit or through any conducting body or medium. b. rate of such flow, measured in amperes. [Old French *corant,* present participle of *courre,* to run, from Latin *currere.*] —**cur'rent·ly,** adv. —**cur'rent·ness,** n.
Syn. adj. 1. **Current, present** mean used or happening at a certain time, usually now. **Current** implies that the existence or occurrence is only at that time: *the current crop of young writers, current events.* **Present** suggests that a thing or condition existed in the past in either the same or different form and may change in the future: *The present practice is to hold auditions on Monday mornings.* See also **modern.**

current density, amount of electric current passing through a given area in a conductor.

cur·ri·cle (kur'i kəl) n. open, two-wheeled carriage, similar to but heavier than a chaise, made to be drawn by two horses. [Latin *curriculum* course, racecourse, chariot.]

cur·ric·u·lar (kə rik'yə lər) adj. of or relating to a curriculum.

cur·ric·u·lum (kə rik'yə ləm) pl., **-lums** or **-la** (-lə). n. 1. all the courses of study offered at a school, college, or university. 2. group or sequence of courses leading to a particular degree, certificate, or license. [Latin *curriculum* course, racecourse, chariot; with reference to a course of study.]

cur·rish (kur'ish) adj. like a cur; snarling; bad-tempered. —**cur'rish·ly,** adv. —**cur'rish·ness,** n.

cur·ry¹ (kur'ē) **-ried, -ry·ing.** v.t. 1. to rub down and clean (a horse or other animal) with a brush or currycomb. 2. to treat (hides or leather), esp. with grease, oil, or wax, to give a desired degree of flexibility. 3. **to curry favor,** to seek to win favor or ingratiate oneself, as by flattery. [Old French *correier* to prepare, arrange, going back to Latin *cum* with + an unrecorded Germanic word.] —**cur'ri·er,** n.

cur·ry² (kur'ē) pl., **-ries.** n. 1. condiment prepared from turmeric and various dried, ground spices. Also, **curry powder.** 2. dish, as a stew, seasoned with either of these. —v.t., **-ried, -ry·ing.** to flavor or prepare with curry. [Tamil *kari* sauce.]

cur·ry·comb (kur'ē kōm') n. brush with rows of teeth rather than bristles, usually of metal or rubber, for currying a horse or similar animal. —v.t. to rub down or groom with a currycomb.

curse (kurs) n. 1. invocation of evil or harm upon someone or something, as through the intercession of divine or supernatural power. 2. evil or harm so invoked. 3. word or words used in swearing; profane oath. 4. that which brings or causes evil or harm. 5. something cursed or accursed. —v.t., **cursed** or **curst, curs·ing.** 1. to call down evil or harm upon; damn: *The patriarch cursed them for their idolatry.* 2. to use profane language against; swear at. 3. to cause evil, harm, or suffering to; torment; afflict: *He was cursed with poor health. Fate seemed to have cursed him and his brother.* —v.i. to utter curses; swear; blaspheme. [Old French *curs* invocation of harm.]

curs·ed (kur'sid, kurst) also, **curst** (kurst). v. past tense and past participle of **curse.** —adj. 1. deserving a curse; detestable; abominable. 2. under a curse; damned. —**curs'ed·ly,** adv. —**curs'ed·ness,** n.

cur·sive (kur'siv) adj. (of writing or type) having the letters joined together with flowing strokes. —n. 1. cursive letter or character. 2. type resembling cursive handwriting. [Medieval Latin *cursivus* running, from Latin *cursus,* past participle of *currere* to run.] —**cur'sive·ly,** adv.

cur·so·ri·al (kur sôr'ē əl) adj. 1. adapted or fitted for running. 2. having limbs adapted for running.

cur·so·ry (kur'sər ē) adj. not thorough; rapid and superficial; hasty. [Late Latin *cursōrius* hasty, from Latin *cursor* runner.] —**cur'so·ri·ly,** adv. —**cur'so·ri·ness,** n.

curst (kurst) v. a past tense and past participle of **curse.** —adj. cursed.

curt (kurt) adj. rudely brief or abrupt: *a curt nod, a curt greeting.* [Latin *curtus* cut short.] —**curt'ly,** adv. —**curt'ness,** n. —**Syn.** see abrupt.

cur·tail (kər tāl') v.t. to cut short or cut down; shorten in duration or extent; reduce. [Modification (influenced by TAIL) of obsolete *curtal* horse with a docked tail, from Middle French *courtault,* from *court* short, from Latin *curtus* cut short.] —**cur·tail'ment,** n.

cur·tain (kur'tin) n. 1. piece or pieces of cloth or other material hung, as at a window, as a decoration or screen. 2. *Theater.* a. the screen used to conceal the major part of the stage from the view of the audience. b. beginning or end of a performance, act, or scene, usually indicated by opening or closing the curtain. 3. anything that screens or covers like a curtain: *a curtain of fog.* 4. that part of a wall which connects two bastions, towers, or similar structures. 5. **curtains.** *Slang.* death; disaster. —v.t. to provide, shut off, or cover with or as with a curtain. [Old French *curtine* a cloth hanging, as for a bed, from Late Latin *cortina* small enclosure, a hanging around a small enclosure, from Latin *cōrs* enclosure.]

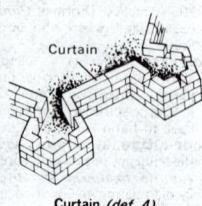
Curtain

Curtain *(def. 4)*

curtain call, reappearance of a performer or performers on the stage to acknowledge the applause of the audience, usually at the end of a performance.

curtain raiser 1. short entertainment given before the main performance, as a short play before a full-length one. 2. any introductory event.

curtain wall, exterior enclosing wall, as of a skyscraper, often consisting largely of glass, which does not serve to support a roof.

cur·te·sy (kur'tə sē) pl., **-sies.** n. *Archaic.* right of a husband to hold for life the real property left by his dead wife, provided they have had children capable of inheriting. [Form of COURTESY.]

Cur·tiss, Glenn Ham·mond (kur'tis; glen ham'ənd) 1878–1930, U.S. inventor and pioneer in aviation.

curt·sy (kurt'sē) pl., **-sies.** also, **curt·sey.** n. gesture of respect or greeting by women and girls, made by bending the knees and lowering the body slightly. —v.i., **-sied, -sy·ing.** to make a curtsy. [Form of COURTESY.]

cu·rule chair (kyoor'ool) official seat reserved for the highest magistrates of ancient Rome, originally resembling a folding stool with curved legs. [Latin *curūlis* relating to a chariot or to the Roman official seat (which originally was placed on a chariot), from *currus* chariot.]

cur·va·ceous (kur vā'shəs) adj. (of a woman) having a full figure; shapely.

Curule chair

cur·va·ture (kur'və chər) n. 1. quality of being curved; instance of curving. 2. something curved. 3. amount of curving, esp. the rate of deviation of an arc from a plane or a straight line. 4. abnormal curving, as of a bodily structure or part, esp. the spine.

curve (kurv) n. 1. continuously bent line having no straight parts or angles, as the arc of a circle. 2. a curving or something curved: *a curve in the road.* 3. baseball or softball pitched so that it veers from a straight path as it passes the batter. 4. *Mathematics.* set of points whose coordinates are determined by an equation. 5. *Statistics.* any line that is plotted from coordinates and represents the changing value of a given variable: *population curve, production curve.* —v.i., **curved, curv·ing.** 1. to have or assume the form of a curve. 2. to move in the course of a curve. —v.t. to cause to curve. [Latin *curvus* bent, crooked.]

cur·vet (kur vet', kur'vit; v., kər vet', kur'vit) n. leap made by a horse in which first the forelegs and then the hind legs are raised so that all four legs are briefly off the ground at the same time. —v.i., **-vet·ted** or **-vet·ed, -vet·ting** or **-vet·ing.** 1. to make a curvet. 2. to leap about; prance; frisk. —v.t. to cause to curvet. [Italian *corvetta* leap, diminutive of *corvo* curve, going back to Latin *curvus* bent, crooked.]

cur·vi·lin·e·ar (kur'vi lin'ē ər) adj. consisting of or enclosed by a curved line or lines. Also, **cur'vi·lin'e·al.**

Cus·co (kōōs'kō) Cuzco.

Cush (kush) n. 1. in the Bible, the eldest son of Ham. 2. land inhabited by the Biblical descendants of Ham, usually identified with what is now Ethiopia.

cush·ion (koosh'ən) n. 1. bag or casing filled with soft or resilient material, as padding, foam rubber, or air, used for resting on or against. 2. something resembling a cushion in shape or function, esp. any device used to absorb shock, as padding or a layer of air. 3. anything which lessens the severity of or protects against harm, loss, or need; buffer: *The old man had saved over the years as a cushion against adversity.* 4. resilient padding around the inside rim of a billiard table, for the balls to rebound against. —v.t. 1. to absorb the shock or effect of: *to cushion a blow.* 2. to place or seat on or as on a cushion; support: *She cushioned the baby's head in her lap.* 3. to furnish with a cushion or cushions. [Old French *coissin, coussin* cushion (for sitting on), going back to Latin *coxa* hip (which a cushion supports).]

Cush·it·ic (koosh it'ik) also, **Kush·it·ic.** n. group of Hamitic lan-

at; āpe; cär; end; mē; it; īce; hot; ōld; fôrk; wood; fōōl; oil; out; up; ūse; turn; sing; thin; this; zh in treasure; ə in ago, taken, pencil, lemon, circus.

guages, including Somali, spoken chiefly in Ethiopia and eastern Africa.

cush·y (koosh′ē) **cush·i·er, cush·i·est.** *adj. Slang.* comfortable; easy: *He's got a nice, cushy job.* [Modification of Hindi *khush* pleasant, from Persian *khūsh.*]

cusk (kusk) *pl.,* **cusks** *or* **cusk.** *n.* **1.** saltwater food fish, *Brosme brosme,* related to the cod and found in the northern Atlantic. **2.** burbot. [Possibly modification of earlier *tusk* the saltwater food fish; of Scandinavian origin.]

cusp (kusp) *n.* **1.** point or pointed end; apex; peak. **2.** either point of a crescent moon. **3.** point or protuberance on the grinding surface or crown of a tooth. [Latin *cuspis* point.]

Cusps

cus·pid (kus′pid) *n.* canine tooth. [Latin *cuspid-,* stem of *cuspis* point.]

cus·pi·dal (kus′pid əl) *adj.* **1.** of or relating to a cusp. **2.** ending in a point.

cus·pi·date (kus′pə dāt′) *adj.* having a cusp or cusps; ending in a point.

cus·pi·dor (kus′pə dôr′) *n.* spittoon. [Portuguese *cuspidouro* place for spitting, from *cuspir* to spit, going back to Latin *cōnspuere* to spit on.]

cuss (kus) *Informal. v.t., v.i.* to curse; swear or swear at. —*n.* **1.** odd or perverse person or animal. **2.** curse. [Form of CURSE.]

cuss·ed (kus′id) *adj. Informal.* **1.** cursed. **2.** stubborn; perverse; mean. —**cuss′ed·ness,** *n.*

cus·tard (kus′tərd) *n.* sweet dessert made from eggs, sugar, milk, and flavoring, either baked or boiled. [Middle English *crustade* pie made with crust, from Old French *croustade,* going back to Latin *crusta* rind, shell, crust.]

custard apple **1.** fleshy, edible fruit of any of a large group of shrubs and small trees, genus *Annona,* esp. of *A. reticulata,* grown in tropical and subtropical regions of the Americas. **2.** shrub or tree bearing this fruit. **3.** any of several other tropical American trees or shrubs cultivated for their fruits.

Cus·ter, George Arm·strong (kus′tər; ärm′strông′) 1839–76, U.S. general killed in one of the wars with the Indians.

cus·to·di·al (kəs tō′dē əl) *adj.* of or relating to custody or custodians.

cus·to·di·an (kəs tō′dē ən) *n.* **1.** one who has care or custody of a person or thing; guardian; keeper. **2.** one responsible for the maintenance and care of a building; janitor. —**cus·to′di·an·ship′,** *n.*

cus·to·dy (kus′tə dē) *pl.,* **-dies.** *n.* **1.** restraint; care; guardianship: *She was in her grandmother's custody.* **2.** state of being kept by or in the charge of officers of the law; confinement; imprisonment: *He was taken into custody immediately after the robbery.* [Latin *custōdia* watching, guard.]

cus·tom (kus′təm) *n.* **1.** established social habit or practice of a group, transmitted from one generation to another; convention: *the custom of trimming Christmas trees. We studied the customs of the Aztecs.* **2.** usual manner of doing or acting; habitual practice; habit: *He arrived early to dust the shop, as was his custom.* **3.** habitual patronage of a business establishment. **4. customs. a.** taxes or duties levied by a government on goods imported from foreign countries. **b.** governmental agency responsible for inspecting imported goods and for assessing and collecting duties on them. **5.** *Law.* established usage or practice of a group which, by long continuance, has acquired the force of law. **6.** tax, rent, tribute, or service regularly given to a feudal lord by his tenants. —*adj.* **1.** dealing or specializing in made-to-order goods. **2.** custom-made. [Old French *custume* usage, going back to Latin *cōnsuētūdō* usage, habit. Doublet of COSTUME.] —**Syn.** *n.* **1.** see **habit.**

cus·tom·ar·y (kus′tə mer′ē) *adj.* according to or based on custom; usual; habitual. —**cus′tom·ar′i·ly,** *adv.* —**cus′tom·ar′i·ness,** *n.*

cus·tom-built (kus′təm bilt′) *adj.* built to individual specifications.

cus·tom·er (kus′tə mər) *n.* **1.** one who is shopping or who buys, esp. one who deals regularly at a given establishment. **2.** *Informal.* anyone with whom a person has to deal: *a tough customer.*

cus·tom·house (kus′təm hous′) *pl.,* **-hous·es.** *also,* **cus·toms·house.** *n.* office building where customs are collected and where ships or their cargoes are cleared.

cus·tom-made (kus′təm mād′) *adj.* made to individual order.

cut (kut) *v.t.,* **cut·ting.** *v.t.* **1.** to separate or divide into parts with a sharp-edged instrument; sever; slice (often with *up*): *to cut the meat into cubes. We cut the rope and pushed off from the dock. Cut up the carrots and put them in the pot.* **2.** to penetrate, slit, or wound with a sharp edge; make an incision in; pierce (often with *open*): *I cut my arm on the jagged glass. She cut her foot open.* **3.** to remove or detach with or as with a sharp-edged instrument; separate or sever from the main body (often with *out* or *off*): *to cut the branches from the tree. He threatened to cut off the prisoner's head. The doctor cut out his tonsils. They cut three steers from the herd.* **4.** to make shorter by removing a portion with a sharp-edged instrument; trim; clip: *to cut one's nails, to cut one's*

hair, to cut a hedge. **5.** to hew or fell (often with *down*): *to cut timber, to cut down a tree.* **6.** to make, form, or shape with or as with a sharp-edged instrument (often with *out*): *to cut gems, to cut out a pattern for a dress. We cut a hole in the ice.* **7.** to make smaller or less; reduce; decrease (often with *down* or *back*): *to cut prices, to cut expenses down. They were forced to cut back production.* **8.** to omit or eliminate; remove (often with *off* or *out*): *I'll cut you out of my will. His part was cut from the play. Smoking may cut ten years off your life.* **9.** to interrupt or put an end to; discontinue or stop (often with *out* or *off*): *to cut out the nonsense. He cut the motor and removed the key. Let's cut out the nonsense. I cut him short in the middle of his explanation.* **10.** to shorten, abridge, or edit by removing parts (often with *down*): *This article is too long and has to be cut.* **11.** to cross or intersect: *One line cuts another at right angles.* **12.** to break down, dissolve, or emulsify: *a detergent that cuts grease.* **13.** to reduce the concentration or strength of; weaken; dilute: *to cut whiskey with water.* **14.** to cause emotional pain or distress to; hurt the feelings of: *Her sarcasm cut me to the quick.* **15.** to hit or strike sharply, as with a whip. **16.** to perform; present: *to cup a caper, to cut a fine figure.* **17.** to break (a deck of cards) at random into two or more parts and put them back together in a different order, as before dealing. **18.** to grow (a tooth or teeth) through the gum: *The baby is cutting his first tooth.* **19.** to make a recording of: *He cut that album last year.* **20.a.** in motion pictures, to suspend or terminate the filming of (a scene). **b.** to edit (film) by removing or rearranging sequences. **21.** *Informal.* to be absent from, esp. without official permission: *to cut a class.* **22.** *Informal.* to pretend not to recognize or be acquainted with; snub: *She cut him in the street without a word.* **23. to cut (someone) in.** *Slang.* to include (someone) in the division or distribution of (profits or loot): *The gang cut him in on the take.* —*v.i.* **1.** to act or function as a sharp edge; make an incision: *This saw cuts well. The blade didn't cut deep enough. The glass had cut into his foot.* **2.** to use a sharp-edged instrument: *The barber cut with a deft hand.* **3.** to admit of being cut: *Silk cuts easily.* **4.** to go, proceed, or move, esp. quickly, abruptly, or by the shortest or most direct route: *He cut through the playground on the way. The tug boat cut across the harbor. We cut down the alley.* **5.** to cross or pass obliquely or diagonally: *The road cuts through the swamp.* **6.** to change direction sharply or suddenly; veer; swerve: *He cut to the right to avoid hitting the dog.* **7.** to penetrate like a sharp-edged instrument: *The bitter wind cut through his jacket. The tight belt cut into her flesh. This soap cuts through grease.* **8.** to divide a deck of cards, as before dealing: *They cut for high card.* **9.** to shift, esp. abruptly or suddenly, from one shot or scene to another, as in television or motion pictures: *The cameras cut to the front of the house.* **10.** *Informal.* to absent oneself from a class, lecture, or similar session or meeting: *I'll cut and come with you.*

to cut back. a. to prune (a plant) by removing the ends of branches or shoots. **b.** in football, to reverse or change suddenly the direction of a run toward the opposing goal line.

to cut down. a. to remodel or reduce in size or amount: *to cut down on smoking.* **b.** to strike or kill with or as with a sword.

to cut in. a. to break or move into suddenly or out of turn: *He cut in at the head of the line.* **b.** to break or join in abruptly, as on a conversation; interrupt: *The sponsor cut in with a commercial.* **c.** to interrupt a dancing couple to take the place of one partner.

to cut loose. to act or speak without restraint or inhibition: *She cut loose and told him just what she thought of him.*

to cut off. a. to shut out; isolate; separate: *He was cut off from all his friends when he studied abroad.* **b.** to stop the passage or movement of; intercept: *The posse cut him off at the pass. The supplies were cut off.* **c.** to disinherit: *The rebellious granddaughter was cut off without a dime.*

to cut out. a. to plan or prepare; arrange: *He had plenty of work cut out for him.* **b.** to oust and take the place of; supplant, as a rival. **c.** *Informal.* to leave, esp. suddenly or hastily: *He cut out as soon as the bell rang.*

to cut up. a. *Informal.* to affect deeply; distress; sadden. **b.** *Informal.* to behave in a mischievous, boisterous, or unruly manner.

—*n.* **1.** slice, blow, or stroke with or as with a sharp-edged instrument: *the clean cut of a saber. She gave her horse a cut with her whip.* **2.** opening or wound made by such a movement: *He bandaged the cut on his face.* **3.** piece or part, esp. of meat, cut or cut off: *a cut of tobacco, a fine cut of beef.* **4.** reduction; decrease: *They took a cut in salary.* **5.** manner or shape in which a thing is cut; style; fashion: *the cut of a dress, cut of her jib.* **6.** omission or removal of a part: *The editor made several cuts in the manuscript.* **7.** something, as a remark or action, that hurts the feelings. **8.** a cutting of a deck of cards. **9.** passage or channel made by cutting, digging, or blasting. **10.** stroke or swing at the ball, as in baseball. **11.** *Informal.* absence, esp. an unexcused one, from a class, lecture, or similar session or meeting: *You're allowed four cuts per semester.* **12.** *Informal.* percentage, commission, or share, as of profits or loot: *The salesman got a 7 percent cut on all sales.* **13.** *Printing.*

engraved block or plate from which a picture is printed, or the picture so printed. **14. a cut above.** a degree better than; superior to: *His honesty showed he was a cut above the rest of the boys.* —*adj.* **1.** that has been cut: *a cut finger, freshly cut flowers.* **2.** formed, shaped, or finished by or as by cutting: *cut diamonds, a face with finely cut features.* **3. cut and dried** (or **dry**). **a.** fixed or settled, as though arranged, determined, or dealt with beforehand. **b.** lacking freshness or spontaneity; dull; uninteresting; routine. **4. cut out.** suited or fit by nature: *He's not cut out to be a soldier. She's not cut out for that kind of work.* [Middle English *cutten, kitten* to make an incision into, sever, trim, reap, divide; of uncertain origin.]

cu·ta·ne·ous (kū tā′nē əs) *adj.* of or relating to the skin. [Modern Latin *cutaneus*, from Latin *cutis* skin.]

cut·a·way (kut′ə wā′) *n.* man's formal coat for daytime wear, cut so as to slope back from the waistline to the tails. —*adj.* having or showing parts or sections removed, as in a drawing: *The cutaway drawing showed the inner parts of the camera.*

Cutaway

cut·back (kut′bak′) *n.* reduction or curtailment, esp. a sharp one: *a cutback in production, a cutback in government spending.*

cute (kūt) **cut·er, cut·est.** *adj. Informal.* **1.** charmingly pretty or attractive; adorable; appealing: *a cute baby, a cute dress. She and her boyfriend made a cute couple.* **2.** clever; shrewd: *a cute trick.* **3.** flippant or impudent; obnoxious. [Short for ACUTE.] —**cute′ly,** *adv.* —**cute′ness,** *n.*

cut glass, glass shaped or decorated by cutting and polishing with an abrasive wheel.

cu·ti·cle (kū′ti kəl) *n.* **1.** tough skin surrounding the base and sides of a fingernail or toenail. **2.** outer skin; epidermis. **3.** *Botany.* waxy layer covering the outer surface of epidermal cells on the leaves and stems of plants. It retards moisture loss and gives leaves their shiny appearance. [Latin *cuticula*, diminutive of *cutis* skin.]

cu·tie (kū′tē) *also,* **cu·tey.** *n. Informal.* someone or something that is very cute. [CUTE + -IE.]

cu·tin (kū′tin) *n.* waxy substance present in the epidermis of plant cells that forms the cuticle. [Latin *cut(is)* skin + -IN[1].]

cu·tis (kū′tis) *n.* dermis. [Latin *cutis* skin.]

Cutlass

cut·lass (kut′ləs) *also,* **cut·las.** *n.* short sword with a flat, wide, slightly curved blade adapted more for slashing than for thrusting. [French *coutelas*, going back to Latin *cultellus* little knife, diminutive of *culter* knife.]

cutlass fish, any of various saltwater fish, family Trichiuridae, usually found in tropical seas, having large sharp teeth and a dorsal fin that runs the length of its body and gradually tapers to form a thin tail. [CUTLASS + FISH; with reference to its shape.]

cut·ler (kut′lər) *n. Archaic.* one who makes, sharpens, repairs, or deals in cutlery. [Old French *cotelier* maker of knives, from *coutel* knife, from Latin *cultellus* little knife. See CUTLASS.]

Cutlass fish

cut·ler·y (kut′lər ē) *n.* **1.** cutting instruments collectively, esp. those used in eating or serving food. **2.** business or trade of a cutler.

cut·let (kut′lit) *n.* **1.** thin slice of meat cut from the leg or ribs that is broiled or fried: *veal cutlet.* **2.** croquette of meat, fish, or other food having a shape similar to such a slice of meat: *a chicken cutlet, a vegetable cutlet.* [French *côtelette* literally, small rib, diminutive of *côte* rib, from Latin *costa* rib, side.]

cut·off (kut′ôf′) *n.* **1.** a stopping or cutting off, esp. of the flow of steam or other fluid into the cylinder of an engine. **2.** point at which this is done. **3.** mechanism or device for cutting off the flow of something, as steam or other fluid. **4.** shorter road or route cutting across or through something; short cut. **5.** new and shorter channel formed when a stream cuts across a bend in its course.

cut·out (kut′out′) *n.* **1.** something, as a figure, cut out or designed to be cut out: *paper cutouts of fairy-tale figures.* **2.** device for letting exhaust gases from an internal-combustion engine pass directly into the air rather than through the muffler.

cut·o·ver (kut′ō′vər) *adj.* (of land) having most or all of the trees cut down; cleared of trees or usable timber.

cut·purse (kut′purs′) *n.* pickpocket. [CUT + PURSE; referring to the theft of purses in earlier times by cutting them from belts or girdles.]

cut-rate (kut′rāt′) *adj.* sold or selling at reduced or cheap prices: *cut-rate drugs, a cut-rate drugstore.*

cut·ter (kut′ər) *n.* **1.** one who cuts, esp. one whose job entails cutting: *glass cutter, dress cutter, a cutter of diamonds.* **2.** that which cuts; device or machine for cutting. **3.** single-masted sailboat, usually carrying a mainsail, forestay sail, and a jib, similar to a sloop but having its mast set nearer the center of the boat. **4.** any ship used by the Coast Guard. **5.** small, light sleigh, usually made to be drawn by one horse.

cut·throat (kut′thrōt′) *n.* one who cuts throats; murderer or murderous thug. —*adj.* **1.** ruthless; merciless: *cutthroat competition.* **2.** *Archaic.* cruel; murderous.

cut·ting (kut′ing) *adj.* **1.** adapted to cut; sharp; edged: *a cutting edge.* **2.** that hurts the feelings; sarcastic: *a cutting reply.* **3.** piercingly chilling; penetrating: *a cutting wind.* —*n.* **1.** act of one who or that which cuts. **2.** something made or obtained by cutting. **3.** shoot or other part cut from a plant and used to grow a new plant. **4.** *British.* newspaper or magazine clipping. —**cut′ting·ly,** *adv.*

cut·tle (kut′əl) *n.* **1.** cuttlefish. **2.** cuttlebone. [Old English *cudele* cuttlefish.]

cut·tle·bone (kut′əl bōn′) *n.* hard internal shell or plate of cuttlefish, used for making polishing powder and often placed in cages to provide birds with minerals and with something on which to peck and sharpen their beaks.

cut·tle·fish (kut′əl fish′) *pl.,* **-fish** or **-fish·es.** *n.* any of a group of saltwater mollusks, genus *Sepia*, found in warm, shallow waters of the Atlantic and Indian oceans, having arms that bear suckers and a limy shell covered by a muscular mantle. When in danger, it may release an inky fluid. [CUTTLE + FISH.]

Cuttlefish

cut·up (kut′up′) *n. Informal.* one who clowns, plays tricks, or behaves in a mischievous or boisterous manner.

cut·wa·ter (kut′wô′tər, -wot′ər) *n.* **1.** forward edge of a ship's prow. **2.** angular edge of a bridge pier, designed to resist the effects of moving water or ice.

cut·worm (kut′wurm′) *n.* **1.** larva or caterpillar of any of several moths, family Noctuidae, that feed at night on the leaves and stems of most cultivated crops and garden plants. **2.** any of several caterpillars, as the army worm.

Cu·vi·er, Georges (kū′vē ā′, kōōv yā′) 1769–1832, French naturalist who founded the science of comparative anatomy.

Cuy·a·hog·a Falls (kī′ə hô′gə, -hō′-, kə hō′gə) city in northeastern Ohio, principally a residential suburb of Akron. Pop. (1970), 49,678.

Cuz·co (kōōs′kō) *also,* **Cus·co.** *n.* city in southern Peru, in the Andes. It was the capital of the Inca empire. Pop. (1969 est.), 105,400.

cwt., hundredweight.

-cy *suffix* (used to form nouns) **1.** quality, state, condition, or fact of being: *bankruptcy, accuracy, secrecy.* **2.** office, position, or rank of: *captaincy, curacy.* [Latin *-cia, -tia,* and Greek *-keiā, -kiā, -teiā, -tiā,* often through French *-cie, -tie.*]

cy·an·a·mide (sī an′ə mid, sī′ə nam′id) *also,* **cy·an·a·mid.** *n.* **1.** calcium cyanamide, used in making ammonia. **2.** highly reactive compound, available as colorless crystals or in water solution, prepared from calcium cyanamide. Formula: $NCNH_2$.

cy·a·nate (sī′ə nāt′) *n.* any salt containing the radical OCN. [CYAN(O-) + -ATE[2].]

cy·an·ic (sī an′ik) *adj.* **1.** of, relating to, or containing cyanogen. **2.** blue. [CYAN(O) + -IC.]

cyanic acid, an unstable, colorless, poisonous liquid. Formula: HOCN

cy·a·nide (sī′ə nīd′, -nid) *also,* **cy·a·nid** (sī′ə nid). *n.* any of several very poisonous compounds containing the cyanogen radical, CN, combined with a metal or another radical, esp. **potassium cyanide,** KCN, and **sodium cyanide,** NaCN. They are used esp. as pesticides and in the extraction of metal from ore.

cyano- *combining form* **1.** characterized by bluish coloring; blue: *cyanosis.* **2.** *Chemistry.* of or containing the cyanogen radical, CN. [Greek *kyanos* dark-blue color.]

cy·an·o·gen (sī an′ə jən) *n.* **1.** compound of carbon and nitrogen in the form of a colorless, poisonous gas with a sharp, penetrating odor, used in synthesizing organic compounds. Formula: NCCN **2.** univalent radical, CN, contained in all cyanide compounds. [CYANO- + -GEN literally, producing blue; with reference to the dark-blue pigment, Prussian blue, in which it was first found.]

cy·a·no·sis (sī′ə nō′sis) *n.* blueness of the skin or mucous membranes, caused by lack of oxygen in the blood. [Modern Latin *cyanosis*, from Greek *kyanōsis* dark-blue color.]

Cyb·e·le (sib′ə lē) *n.* fertility goddess of ancient Asia Minor, whose worship later spread to Greece and Rome.

cy·ber·nate (sī′bər nāt′) **-nat·ed, -nat·ing.** *v.t.* to automate. [CYBERN(ETICS) + -ATE¹.] —**cy′ber·na′tion**, *n.*

cy·ber·net·ics (sī′bər net′iks) *n.,pl.* science dealing with the similarities between communication and control processes, such as feedback, in the brain and in electronic machines, esp. computers. ▲ construed as singular. [Greek *kybernētēs* pilot (from *kybernān* to steer) + -ICS.] —**cy′ber·net′ic**, *adj.*

cy·cad (sī′kad) *n.* any of a group of primitive evergreen plants, family Cycadaceae, found in tropical and subtropical climates. The plants resemble palms and have seed-bearing cones. [Modern Latin *Cycas*, from Greek *kykas*, incorrect recording of *koīkas*, accusative plural of *koix* palm².]

Cyc·la·des (sik′lə dēz) *n.,pl.* group of Greek islands in the Aegean Sea off the southeastern coast of Greece. Land area, 1023 sq. mi. Pop. (1961), 99,959.

cyc·la·men (sī′klə mən, sik′lə-) *n.* **1.** showy flower of any of a group of plants, genus *Cyclamen*, of the primrose family, having pink, purple, rose, or white petals. **2.** widely cultivated plant bearing this flower, having heart-shaped leaves that are often patterned with silver. [Modern Latin *cyclamen*, from Greek *kyklamīnos*, from *kyklos* circle; because of its bulbous roots.]

cy·cle (sī′kəl) *n.* **1.** complete course or series of events or phenomena that recur regularly in a definite sequence. **2.** period of time during which such a course or series occurs and completes itself. **3.** unicycle, bicycle, tricycle, or motorcycle. **4.** group of stories, poems, or plays about a central figure, event, or theme: *The Arthurian cycle deals with the adventures of King Arthur and his knights.* **5.** *Physics.* complete round or series of changes in a quantity which varies periodically, as alternating current. **6.** *Archaic.* long period of time; age. —*v.i.,* **-cled, -cling. 1.** to ride a cycle, esp. a bicycle: *We cycled through the park.* **2.** *Archaic.* to pass through cycles. [Late Latin *cyclus* circle, recurring period, from Greek *kyklos* circle, wheel.]

cy·clic (sī′klik, sik′lik) *adj.* **1.** moving or occurring in cycles. **2.** of or relating to a cycle. **3.** of, relating to, or characterized by an arrangement of atoms in a ring or closed chain. Also, **cy′cli·cal.** —**cy′cli·cal·ly**, *adv.*

cy·clist (sī′klist) *n.* one who rides a cycle. Also, **cy′cler.**

cy·cloid (sī′kloid) *adj.* resembling a circle; having a circular shape. —*n.* curve traced by a point on the circumference of a circle when the circle is rolled along a straight line in its plane. —**cy·cloi′dal,** *adj.*

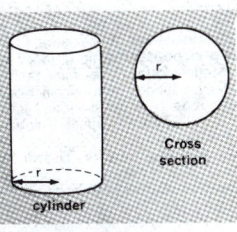
Cycloid

cy·clom·e·ter (sī klom′ə tər) *n.* **1.** instrument for recording the revolutions of a wheel, often used to measure the distance traveled by a wheeled vehicle. **2.** instrument for measuring circular arcs. [Greek *kyklos* circle, wheel + -METER.]

cy·clone (sī′klōn) *n.* **1.** atmospheric disturbance in which winds rotate around a moving center of low atmospheric pressure. Cyclone winds circle clockwise in the Northern Hemisphere, counterclockwise in the Southern. Distinguished from **anticyclone. 2.** any violent windstorm, as a hurricane or a tornado. [Modification of Greek *kyklōma* wheel, coil of a snake, from *kyklos* circle, wheel.] —**cy·clon·ic** (sī klon′ik), *also,* **cy·clon′i·cal,** *adj.* —**cy·clon′i·cal·ly,** *adv.*

Cy·clo·pe·an (sī′klə pē′ən) *adj.* **1.** of, relating to, or characteristic of the Cyclopes. **2.** cyclopean, huge or massive; gigantic.

cy·clo·pe·di·a (sī′klə pē′dē ə) *also,* **cy·clo·pae·di·a.** *n.* encyclopedia. [Short for ENCYCLOPEDIA.]

cy·clo·pe·dic (sī′klə pē′dik) *also,* **cy·clo·pae·dic.** *adj.* encyclopedic.

Cy·clops (sī′klops) *pl.,* **Cy·clo·pes** (sī klō′pēz). *n. Greek Mythology.* one of a group of one-eyed giants having the eye located in the middle of the forehead. [Latin *Cyclops,* from Greek *Kyklōps* literally, round-eyed, from *kyklos* circle + *ōps* eye.]

cy·clo·ram·a (sī′klə ram′ə, -rä′mə) *n.* **1.** large picture or series of pictures represented on the wall of a circular room so as to appear in natural perspective to a spectator standing in the center. **2.** large, often curved, piece of scenery used to surround the back of a stage. [Greek *kyklos* circle + *horama* view.] —**cy′clo·ram′ic,** *adj.*

cy·clo·stome (sī′klə stōm′, sik′lə-) *n.* any of various primitive, eel-like freshwater or saltwater vertebrates that have no jaws and have a large, round, sucking mouth, as the lamprey. [Greek *kyklos* circle, wheel + STOMA mouth.] —**cy·clos′to·mate′, cy′clo·stom′a·tous,** *adj.*

cy·clo·thy·mi·a (sī′klə thī′mē ə, sik′lə-) *n.* emotional disorder in which periods of liveliness and excitement alternate with periods of depression. [Modern Latin *cyclothymia*, going back to Greek *kyklos* circle, wheel + *thȳmos* spirit, soul, mind.] —**cy′clo·thy′mic,** *adj.*

cy·clo·tron (sī′klə tron′) *n.* device that accelerates elementary particles and ions in a flat, spiral orbit of increasing radius by means of an alternating electric field. [Greek *kyklos* circle + -*tron* means, device; referring to the spiral motion produced.]

cyg·net (sig′nit) *n.* young swan. [Diminutive of French *cygne* swan, going back to Latin *cygnus,* from Greek *kyknos.*]

Cyg·nus (sig′nəs) *n.* constellation in the northern sky, conventionally depicted as a swan. See CYGNET. [Latin *cygnus* swan.]

cyl., cylinder.

cyl·in·der (sil′ən dər) *n.* **1.** solid bounded by two equal, parallel circles and a curved surface that is generated by a straight line moving parallel to itself with its ends always on the circumferences of the circles. **2.** something resembling a cylinder in shape. **3.** part of a revolver that contains chambers for cartridges and which, by revolving, moves each cartridge into position to be fired. **4.** piston chamber of an engine or pump. See *piston* for illustration. [Latin *cylindrus* the solid, from Greek *kylindros* literally, roller, from *kylindein* to roll.]

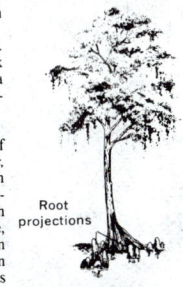
Cross section
cylinder
Cylinder

cy·lin·dri·cal (sə lin′dri kəl) *adj.* **1.** having the form of a cylinder; shaped like a cylinder. **2.** of or relating to a cylinder. Also, **cy·lin′dric.** —**cy·lin′dri·cal·ly,** *adv.*

cym·bal (sim′bəl) *n.* musical percussion instrument consisting of a circular, slightly concave metal plate that produces a ringing sound when clashed against another cymbal or struck, as with a drumstick. [Old English *cymbal* and Middle French *cymbale,* both from Latin *cymbalum,* from Greek *kymbalon,* from *kymbē* hollow of a vessel, cup.]

cyme (sīm) *n.* broad, flat-topped flower cluster in which the central flowers open first. See *inflorescence* for illustration. [Latin *cȳma* young sprout of a cabbage, from Greek *kȳma* something swollen, wave, young sprout of a plant.]

cy·mose (sī′mōs, sī mōs′) *adj.* relating to, bearing, or resembling a cyme.

Cym·ric (kim′rik, sim′-) *adj.* of or relating to the Welsh people or their language. —*n.* the Welsh language.

Cym·ry (kim′rē) *n.,pl.* the Welsh people.

cyn·ic (sin′ik) *n.* **1.** one who disbelieves in or doubts the sincerity, goodness, or selflessness of human motives and actions. **2.** Cynic. member of a group of Greek philosophers of the fourth century B.C. who held that virtue was the goal of life and that it could be achieved by living a natural and simple life, disdaining possessions and social conventions. —*adj.* **1.** Cynic. of or relating to the Cynics or their doctrines. **2.** *Archaic.* cynical. [Latin *cynicus* a Cynic philosopher, from Greek *kynikos* literally, doglike, from *kyōn* dog; because of the currish behavior attributed to the Cynic philosophers.]

cyn·i·cal (sin′i kəl) *adj.* having or showing disbelief in or doubt about the sincerity, goodness, or selflessness of human motives and actions: *a cynical young man, a cynical attitude, a cynical smile.* —**cyn′i·cal·ly,** *adv.*

cyn·i·cism (sin′ə siz′əm) *n.* **1.** cynical disposition, character, or quality. **2.** expression of such a disposition, character, or quality; cynical remark, act, or opinion. **3.** Cynicism. doctrines or practices of the Cynics.

cy·no·sure (sī′nə shoor′, sin′ə-) *n.* person or thing that attracts attention; center or object of attraction, interest, or admiration. [Latin *Cynosūra* constellation of the Little Bear (which served as a guide to navigators), from Greek *kynosoura* literally, dog's tail.]

Cyn·thi·a (sin′thē ə) *n.* **1.** Artemis; Diana. **2.** the moon. [Latin *Cynthia,* from Greek *Kynthiā* literally, (goddess) of *Kynthos,* a mountain of Delos, where Apollo and Artemis were born.]

cy·pher (sī′fər) cipher.

cy·press (sī′prəs) *n.* **1.** any of a group of evergreen trees or shrubs, genus *Cupressus,* found in southern Europe, Asia, and North America, having closely overlapping, scale-like leaves and woody cones. **2.** North American deciduous, cone-bearing tree, genus *Taxodium,* found esp. in southern swampy lands and noted for its swollen trunk base and conical root projections when growing in water. **3.** the wood of any of these trees. [Old French *cypres* the European cypress or its wood, from Latin *cupressus,* from Greek *kyparissos.*]

Root projections

Cypress (*def. 2*)

Cyp·ri·an (sip′rē ən) *n.* Cypriot.

cyp·ri·noid (sip′rə noid′) *n.* any of a group of freshwater fish, family Cyprinidae, including carps, barbels, goldfish, chubs, breams, and most

at; āpe; cär; end; mē; it; īce; hot; ōld; fôrk; wood; fōol; oil; out; up; ūse; turn; sing; thin; this; zh in treasure; ə in ago, taken, pencil, lemon, circus.

251

freshwater minnows. —*adj.* resembling or belonging to any of the fish of this group. Also, **cyp·ri·nid** (sip′rə nid). [Latin *cyprīnus* carp (from Greek *kyprînos*) + -OID.]

Cyp·ri·ot (sip′rē ət) *also,* **Cyp·ri·ote.** *n.* **1.** member or close descendant of the people of Cyprus. **2.** ancient or modern Greek dialect of Cyprus. —*adj.* of or relating to Cyprus, its people, or their language.

cyp·ri·pe·di·um (sip′rə pē′dē əm) *pl.,* **-di·a** (-dē ə). *n.* lady's slipper. [Modern Latin *cypripedium*, probably from Greek *Kypris* Aphrodite + *pedīlon* slipper; with reference to the shape of the flower.]

Cy·prus (sī′prəs) *n.* island country in the eastern Mediterranean, south of Turkey. Capital, Nicosia. Area, 3572 sq. mi. Pop. (1970 est.), 634,000.

Cy·re·ne (sī rē′nē) *n.* ancient Greek city in North Africa in what is now eastern Libya.

Cy·ril·lic alphabet (si ril′ik) alphabet based on the Greek alphabet, dating from the ninth century A.D., used for Russian, Bulgarian, Serbian, and certain other languages. [From *St. Cyril*, ninth-century Greek Christian missionary to the Slavs, said to be its inventor.]

Cy·rus (sī′rəs) *n.* **1. the Great.** died 529 B.C., king of Persia from c.558 to 529 B.C. and founder of the Persian empire. **2. the Younger.** died 401 B.C., Persian prince.

cyst (sist) *n.* **1.** abnormal sac in the body encased by a distinct membrane and usually containing liquid or semisolid substances. **2.a.** protective outer membrane formed around an organism, such as a protozoan, during reproduction or in response to unfavorable environmental conditions. **b.** such a membrane and the organism so enclosed. **3.** any of various saclike structures in plants or animals. [Modern Latin *cystis*, from Greek *kystis* bladder, pouch.]

cyst·ic (sis′tik) *adj.* **1.** of, relating to, or resembling a cyst. **2.** having or containing a cyst or cysts. **3.** of or relating to the gall bladder or to the urinary bladder.

cystic fibrosis, inherited disease, usually appearing in infancy, affecting the ducts of certain glands and characterized by inadequate functioning of the pancreas and chronic infection of the respiratory system.

cys·ti·tis (si stī′tis) *n.* inflammation of the urinary bladder.

cys·to·scope (sis′tə skōp′) *n.* instrument used to examine the urinary bladder. —**cys·to·scop·ic** (sis′tə skop′ik) *adj.*

Cyth·e·re·a (sith′ə rē′ə) *n.* Aphrodite; Venus. [Latin *Cytherea* Venus, from Greek *Kythereia* Aphrodite; literally, (goddess) of *Kythēra*, Greek island in the Aegean Sea where the goddess was worshiped.] —**Cyth′e·re′an,** *adj.*

cyto- *combining form* cell: *cytoplasm.* [Greek *kytos* hollow vessel.]

cy·to·gen·e·sis (sī′tō jen′ə sis) *n.* origin and development of cells. [CYTO- + GENESIS.]

cy·to·ge·ne·tics (sī′tō ji net′iks) *n.,pl.* branch of genetics that deals with the study of those parts of cells that contribute to heredity, as chromosomes and genes. ▲ construed as singular. [CYTO- + GE-NETICS.] —**cy′to·ge·net′ic;** *also,* **cy′to·ge·net′i·cal,** *adj.* —**cy′to·ge·net′i·cal·ly,** *adv.* —**cy·to·ge·net·i·cist** (sī′tō jə net′ə sist), *n.*

cy·tol·o·gy (sī tol′ə jē) *n.* branch of biology that deals with the study of cells, including such aspects as their formation, structure, and function. [CYTO- + -LOGY.] —**cy·to·log·ic** (sī′tə loj′ik); *also,* **cy′to·log′i·cal,** *adj.* —**cy·to·log′i·cal·ly,** *adv.* —**cy·tol′o·gist,** *n.*

cy·to·plasm (sī′tə plaz′əm) *n.* all the protoplasm of a cell outside the nucleus. See **cell** for illustration. [CYTO- + -PLASM.] —**cy′to·plas′mic,** *adj.*

cy·to·sine (sī′tō sēn′, -zēn) *n.* pyrimidine base that is an essential constituent of DNA and RNA. Formula: $C_4H_5N_3O$

C.Z., Canal Zone.

czar (zär) *also,* **tsar, tzar.** *n.* **1.** any of the emperors of Russia before the Revolution of 1917. **2.** one having great or absolute power or authority, as a dictator or magnate. [Russian *tsar* Russian emperor, going back to Latin *Caesar.* See CAESAR.]

czar·das (chär′däsh) *n.* **1.** Hungarian dance consisting of a slow, melancholy introduction followed by a rapid and spirited section. **2.** music for such a dance. [Magyar *csárdás*, from *csárda* tavern.]

czar·e·vitch (zär′ə vich′) *also,* **tsar·e·vitch, tzar·e·vitch.** *n.* **1.** eldest son of a Russian czar. **2.** originally, any son of a Russian czar. [Russian *tsarevich*, from *tsar*. See CZAR.]

cza·rev·na (zä rev′nə) *also,* **tsa·rev·na, tza·rev·na.** *n.* **1.** wife of a czarevitch. **2.** originally, any daughter of a Russian czar. [Russian *tsarevna*, from *tsar*. See CZAR.]

cza·ri·na (zä rē′nə) *also,* **tsa·ri·na, tza·ri·na.** *n.* wife of a Russian czar; empress of Russia. [German *Zarin*, feminine of *Zar* czar, from Russian *tsar*. See CZAR.]

czar·ism (zär′iz′əm) *also,* **tsar·ism, tzar·ism.** *n.* autocratic or absolute government or rule, esp. the government of Russia under the czars. [CZAR + -ISM.]

czar·ist (zär′ist) *also,* **tsar·ist, tzar·ist.** *adj.* of, relating to, or characteristic of a czar or czarism. —*n.* follower or supporter of a czar or of czarism. [CZAR + -IST.]

Czech (chek) *n.* **1.a.** member of the most westerly branch of the Slavs, including the Bohemians and Moravians. **b.** Czechoslovak. **2.** language belonging to the western division of the Slavic languages, spoken chiefly in Czechoslovakia; Bohemian. —*adj.* of or relating to Czechoslovakia, its people, or their language.

Czech·o·slo·vak (chek′ə slō′vak, -väk) *n.* member or close descendant of the people of Czechoslovakia. —*adj.* of or relating to Czechoslovakia, its people, or their language. Also, **Czech·o·slo·va·ki·an** (chek′ə slə vä′kē ən, -vak′ē ən).

Czech·o·slo·va·ki·a (chek′ə slə vä′kē ə, -vak′ē ə) *n.* landlocked country in central Europe. Capital, Prague. Area, 49,370 sq. mi. Pop. (1970 est.), 14,450,000.

Cze·sto·cho·wa (cheN′stə kō′və) *n.* city in south-central Poland. Pop. (1965 est.), 175,000.

at; āpe; cär; end; mē; it; īce; hot; ōld; fôrk; wood; fōōl; oil; out; up; ūse; turn; sing; thin; this; zh in treasure; ə in ago, taken, pencil, lemon, circus.

d, D (dē) *pl.,* **d's, D's.** *n.* **1.** fourth letter of the English alphabet. **2.** shape of this letter or something having such a shape. **3.** fourth item in a series or group. **4.** *Music.* **a.** second note or tone of the diatonic scale of C major. See **do**² for illustration. **b.** scale or key that has this note or tone as its tonic.

D 1. Roman numeral for 500. **2.** deuterium. **3.** didymium. **4.** *Physics.* density.

d. 1. died. **2.** pence: *3d.* **3.** dead. **4.** dime. **5.** dollar. **6.** day; days. **7.** date. **8.** diameter. **9.** degree. **10.** delete. **11.** daughter. **12.** drachma.

D. 1. Democrat. **2.** December. **3.** Dutch. **4.** department. **5.** doctor. **6.** duchess. **7.** duke.

D.A., district attorney.

dab¹ (dab) **dabbed, dab·bing.** *v.t.* **1.** to pat with something soft or moist: *A nurse dabbed the wound with cotton.* **2.** to apply with a light, quick touch: *The artist dabbed green paint on the canvas.* —*v.i.* to pat or stroke, as with something soft or moist: *The girl dabbed at the stain on her dress.* —*n.* **1.** small, moist mass of something: *a dab of clay.* **2.** little bit. **3.** light, quick pat: *She gave her nose a dab with a powder puff.* [Possibly imitative.] —**dab'ber,** *n.*

dab² (dab) *n.* any of various flounders, order Pleuronectiformes. [Possibly from DAB¹.]

dab·ble (dab'əl) **-bled, -bling.** *v.i.* **1.** to do something superficially or occasionally (with *in* or *at*): *to dabble at painting.* **2.** to splash or play gently, as in water: *to dabble in water.* **3.** to splash or dip (something) gently, as in water. [Probably DAB¹ + -LE.] —**dab'bler,** *n.*

Dac·ca (dak'ə) *n.* capital and largest city of Bangladesh. Pop. (1970 est.), 600,000.

dace (dās) *pl.,* **dac·es** or **dace.** *n.* any of various minnows found in small streams of North America and Europe, esp. the **blacknose dace,** *Rhinichthys atratulus,* the most abundant of American minnows, and the **European dace,** *Leuciscus leuciscus.* [Old French *dars,* from Late Latin *dardus* javelin; of Germanic origin; referring to its swift movement.]

da·cha (dä'chə) *n.* Russian country house. [Russian *dacha* literally, a giving.]

Dach·au (dä'ĸʜou) *n.* city in southern Germany, near Munich, site of a Nazi concentration camp.

dachs·hund (däks'hoont', -hoond', dash'ənd) *n.* dog of a breed of German origin, having a long body, very short legs, a long, tapered head, drooping ears, and a red, tan, or black-and-tan coat. Height: 9 inches at the shoulder. [German *Dachshund,* from *Dachs* badger + *Hund* dog; because it was once used for hunting badgers.]

Dachshund

Da·cia (dā'shə) *n.* ancient Roman province in southern Europe, in what is now Romania. —**Da'cian,** *adj.*

Da·cron (dāk'ron, dak'-) *n. Trademark.* **1.** synthetic textile fiber that is long-wearing, wrinkle-resistant, stretch-resistant, and quick-drying, used for many items, esp. clothing. **2.** yarn or fabric that is made of this fiber.

dac·tyl (dakt'əl) *n.* **1.a.** in modern English verse, a metrical foot consisting of one accented syllable followed by two unaccented syllables. The line *Think' of her mourn'fully, gent'ly and hu'manly* contains four dactyls. **b.** in classical verse, a metrical foot consisting of one long syllable followed by two short syllables. **2.** line of verse made up of such feet. **3.** finger or toe; digit. [Latin *dactylus* the classical meter, from Greek *daktylos* finger, toe, the classical meter; because its three metrical feet suggest the three joints of a finger.] —**dac·tyl·ic** (dak til'ik), *adj.*

dactylo- *also,* **dactyl-.** *combining form* finger or toe; digit: *dactylography.* [Greek *daktylos.*]

dac·tyl·o·gram (dak til'ə gram') *n.* fingerprint. [DACTYLO- + -GRAM¹.]

dac·ty·log·ra·phy (dakt'əl og'rə fē) *n.* scientific study of fingerprints, used as a technique of crime detection. [DACTYLO- + -GRAPHY.]

dad (dad) *n. Informal.* father. [Said to be from baby talk.]

Da·da (dä'dä, -də) *also,* **da·da.** *n.* movement in art and literature during the early twentieth century characterized by the use of ridicule, nonsense, and deliberate irrationality to reflect what was considered to be the meaninglessness of the modern world and all of human culture, esp. the arts. Also, **Da'da·ism.** [French *dada* hobby, hobbyhorse (used arbitrarily as a name for their movement by the Dadaists), from baby talk.] —**Da'da·ist,** *n.* —**Da·da·ist'ic,** *adj.*

dad·dy (dad'ē) *pl.,* **-dies.** *n. Informal.* father.

dad·dy-long·legs (dad'ē lông'legz') *pl.,* **-legs.** *n.* any of a group of harmless arachnids, order Phalangida, which are related to the spider and have long, slender legs but do not spin webs. Also, **har'vest·man.**

Daddy-longlegs

da·do (dā'dō) *pl.,* **-does** or **-dos.** *n.* **1.** portion of a pedestal between the base and the cornice. **2.** lower part of an interior wall if decorated differently from the rest of the wall, as with paneling or ornamentation. [Italian *dado* cube, pedestal, from Latin *datum* thing given, noun use of neuter of *datus,* past participle of *dare* to give.]

Daed·a·lus (ded'əl əs) *n. Greek Legend.* a skillful craftsman and inventor who designed the labyrinth in Crete and was later imprisoned in it with his son Icarus. Daedalus then invented artificial wings, with which they escaped.

dae·mon (dē'mən) *n.* demon (*defs.* 5, 6).

daf·fo·dil (daf'ə dil') *n.* **1.** trumpet-shaped flower of any of several plants, genus *Narcissus,* of the amaryllis family, commonly having yellow petals which surround the base of a central tube of any of various colors. **2.** plant bearing this flower, cultivated throughout the world, having tall, stiff, bladelike leaves and growing from a bulb. **3.** brilliant yellow color. [Probably from Dutch *(de) affodil* (the) asphodel, from Old French *affrodile, asphodile* asphodel, through Latin, from Greek *asphodelos.*]

daff·y (daf'ē) **daff·i·er, daff·i·est.** *adj. Informal.* **1.** silly; foolish. **2.** crazy; insane. [Obsolete English *daff* fool (of uncertain origin) + -Y¹.]

daft (daft) *British. adj.* **1.** crazy; insane. **2.** silly; foolish. [Middle English *daffte* gentle, foolish, from Old English *gedæfte* mild, gentle.] —**daft'ly,** *adv.* —**daft'ness,** *n.*

da Ga·ma, Vas·co (də gä'mə, gam'ə; väs'kō) c.1469–1524, Portuguese navigator.

dag·ger (dag'ər) *n.* **1.** small, swordlike weapon having a pointed blade, used for thrusting and stabbing. **2.** mark (†) used in printing to denote a reference to a footnote or other supplementary note. **3. to look daggers at.** to look at with hatred or anger. [Possibly from obsolete *dag* to stab; of uncertain origin.]

Daffodil

Da·gon (dā'gon) *n.* chief god of the Philistines and the Phoenicians, represented as half man and half fish.

da·guerre·o·type (də ger'ə tīp', -ger'ē ə tīp') *n.* **1.** early photographic process in which light-sensitized, silvered copper plates were exposed and then developed with mercury vapor. **2.** picture produced by this process. [French *daguerréotype,* from Louis *Daguerre,* 1789–1851, French inventor of the process.]

at; āpe; cär; end; mē; īce; hot; ōld; fôrk; wood; fōōl; oil; out; up; ūse; turn; sing; thin; this; zh in treasure; ə in ago, taken, pencil, lemon, circus.

253

dahl·ia (dal′yə, däl′-) *n.* **1.** flower head of any of a group of leafy plants, genus *Dahlia*, of the composite family, growing in various bright colors. **2.** leafy plant bearing this flower head, cultivated throughout the world from seeds or from cuttings of the tuberous roots. [Modern Latin *Dahlia*, from Anders *Dahl*, eighteenth-century Swedish botanist.]

Da·ho·mey (də hō′mē) *n.* country in western Africa, formerly part of French West Africa, now called Benin. Capital, Porto-Novo. Area, 44,713 sq. mi. Pop. (1975 est.), 3,100,000. —**Da·ho′man,** *adj., n.*

Dail Eir·eann (dôl âr′ən, doil) lower house of the National Parliament of the Republic of Ireland. [Irish *Dáil Éireann* literally, assembly of Ireland.]

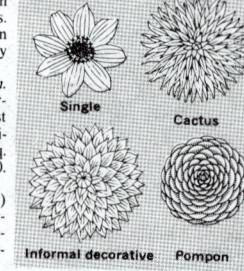

Single

Cactus

Informal decorative   Pompon

Dahlias

dai·ly (dā′lē) *adj.* relating to or happening every day or every weekday: *a daily routine, daily pay.* —*n. pl.*, **-lies.** newspaper appearing every day or every weekday. —*adv.* day after day; every day: *His column is published daily.* [Old English *dæglīc* relating to every day, from *dæg* day.]

daily double, system of betting on horse races in which a better, in order to win, must select the winner in each of two specified races on the same day.

dai·mio (dī′myō) *pl.*, **-mio** or **-mios.** *n.* chief territorial baron or feudal noble of Japan who was a vassal of the emperor. [Japanese *daimyō*, from *dai* great + *mio* name.]

dain·ty (dān′tē) *adj.* **-ti·er, -ti·est.** *adj.* **1.** delicately beautiful or graceful: *a dainty porcelain vase.* **2.** having delicate tastes or fastidious habits; refined: *Few little boys are dainty eaters.* **3.** pleasing to the palate; delicious. —*n. pl.*, **-ties.** delicious bit of food; delicacy. [Old French *daintie* pleasure, tidbit, from Latin *dignitās* worth. Doublet of DIGNITY.] —**dain′ti·ly,** *adv.* —**dain′ti·ness,** *n.*

dai·qui·ri (dī′kər ē, dak′ər ē) *n.* cocktail made of rum, lime or lemon juice, and sugar. [From *Daiquiri* Cuban town from which the rum for this cocktail originally came.]

Dai·ren (dī′ren′) *n.* city in southern Manchuria, in China. Pop. (1957), 950,000.

dair·y (dâr′ē) *pl.*, **dair·ies.** *n.* **1.** business establishment concerned with the manufacture and distribution of milk and milk products. **2.** room or building where milk and milk products are processed and stored. **3.** business of producing milk and milk products; dairying. **4.** store that sells milk and milk products. **5.** dairy farm. [Middle English *deierie* place where milk and milk products are processed and stored, from *deie* dairymaid, from Old English *dæge* (female) maker of bread.]

dairy cattle, cows bred and raised esp. for milk production.

dairy farm, farm principally concerned with the raising of dairy cattle and the production of milk.

dair·y·ing (dâr′ē ing) *n.* business of a dairy.

dair·y·maid (dâr′ē mād′) *n.* girl or woman who works in a dairy; milkmaid.

dair·y·man (dâr′ē mən) *pl.*, **-men.** *n.* man who owns or is employed by a dairy or dairy farm.

da·is (dā′is, dās) *n.* slightly raised platform, as for a throne, speaker's desk, or seats for guests of honor. [Old French *deis* high table, from Late Latin *discus* table, from Latin *discus* quoit, dish, from Greek *diskos* round plate, quoit. Doublet of DESK, DISCUS, DISH, DISK.]

dai·sy (dā′zē) *pl.*, **-sies.** *n.* **1.** flower head of any of various plants of the composite family, having petal-like rays surrounding a yellow disk. The **oxeye daisy,** *Chrysanthemum leucanthemum*, bears white flowers and is particularly common in the eastern United States. **2.** plant bearing such flowers. [Old English *dægesēage* literally, day's eye; named partly for its round yellow center resembling the sun, partly for its closing at night and opening in the day.]

Da·kar (dä kär′) *n.* capital and largest city of Senegal. Pop. (1969 est.), 581,000.

Da·ko·ta (də kō′tə) *n.* **1.** former territory of the United States, consisting of what is now North Dakota and South Dakota. **2. the Dakotas.** North Dakota and South Dakota. **3.** member of a Siouan tribe of North American Indians formerly living on the Great Plains. Also, **Sioux. 4.** language of the Dakotas, a member of the Siouan family of languages. [Dakota *dakota* literally, allies.]

Da·lai La·ma (dä lī′ lä′mə) spiritual and political leader of Tibetan Buddhists. Also, **Grand Lama.**

dale (dāl) *n.* valley. [Old English *dæl*.]

Da·li, Sal·va·dor (dä′lē; säl′və dôr′) 1904—, Spanish painter.

Dal·las (dal′əs) *n.* city in northeastern Texas. Pop. (1970), 844,401.

dalles (dalz) *n.,pl.* rapids of a river flowing through a deep rock gorge. [French *dalles*, plural of *dalle* gutter, from Old Norse *dæla.*]

dal·li·ance (dal′ē əns) *n.* **1.** wasting of time; loitering. **2.** flirtation or playfulness.

dal·ly (dal′ē) **-lied, -ly·ing.** *v.i.* **1.** to waste time; linger; delay: *If you dally any longer, we will be late.* **2.** to toy or play; trifle: *to dally with temptation.* —*v.t.* to waste (time) (with away): *He dallied away the entire morning.* [Old French *dalier* to converse, chat; possibly of Germanic origin.]

Dal·ma·tia (dal mā′shə) *n.* region in western Yugoslavia, on the coast of the Adriatic Sea.

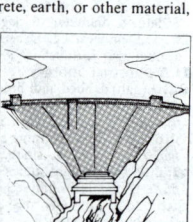

Dalmatian

Dal·ma·tian (dal mā′shən) *n.* **1.** large dog of a breed believed to have been developed in Dalmatia, having a short-haired white coat speckled with small black or brown spots. Height: 21 inches at the shoulder. Also, **coach dog. 2.** native or inhabitant of Dalmatia. —*adj.* of or relating to Dalmatia.

Dal·ton, John (dôlt′ən) 1766–1844, English chemist and physicist.

Da·ly City (dā′lē) *n.* city in west-central California, a suburb of San Francisco. Pop. (1970), 66,922.

dam¹ (dam) *n.* **1.** structure made of concrete, earth, or other material, erected across a stream to hold back water. **2.** any similar barrier. **3.** body of water held back by a dam. —*v.t.*, **dammed, dam·ming. 1.** to hold back by a dam; furnish with a dam. **2.** to restrain or confine, as if with a dam (with *up*): *The boy dammed up his anger.* [Of Germanic origin.]

dam² (dam) *n.* **1.** female parent of a four-footed animal. **2.** *Archaic.* mother. [Form of DAME.]

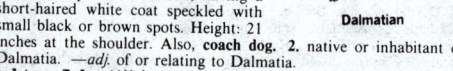

dam·age (dam′ij) *n.* **1.** harm or injury causing loss, as in value or usefulness: *The earthquake caused great damage.* **2. damages.** *Law.* money claimed or allowed as compensation for injury or loss. **3.** *also,* **damages.** *Informal.* cost or price. —*v.t.*, **-aged, -ag·ing.** to cause damage to: *to damage a car, to damage a person's reputation.* —*v.i.* to suffer damage: *This cloth damages easily.* [Old French *damage* harm, from *dam* loss, from Latin *damnum*.] —**dam′age·a·ble,** *adj.* —**Syn.** *v.t.* see **hurt.**

dam·a·scene (dam′ə sēn′, dam′ə sēn′) **-scened, -scen·ing.** *v.t.* **1.** to ornament (metal) with wavy patterns. **2.** to ornament (metal) with designs etched into the surface and inlaid with gold or silver. —*n.* work produced by damascening. —*adj.* of or relating to damask or to the art of damascening. [Latin *Damascēnus* of Damascus (once famous for such work), from Greek *Damaskēnos.* See DAMASCUS STEEL.]

Da·mas·cus (də mas′kəs) *n.* capital and largest city of Syria, one of the oldest continuously inhabited cities in the world. Pop. (1968 est.), 789,840.

Damascus steel, tough steel whose surface is decorated with a wavy pattern resembling watermarks, originally made at Damascus. It was used for sword blades during the Middle Ages. Also, **damask steel.**

dam·ask (dam′əsk) *n.* **1.** reversible fabric made of various fibers woven with elaborate patterns or designs, used for such items as tablecloths and napkins. **2.a.** Damascus steel. **b.** the patterns on Damascus steel. **3.** deep pink or rose color. —*adj.* **1.** made of or resembling damask. **2.** deep pink or rose-colored. **3.** of or from Damascus. —*v.t.* **1.** to damascene. **2.** to ornament or weave with the elaborate pattern or design of damask fabric. [Italian *damasco* fabric of Damascus (where such cloth was first made), going back to Hebrew *d'meseq* fabric of Damascus, and also to Hebrew *Dammeseq* Damascus.]

damask rose, variety of rose, *Rosa damascena*, having fragrant pink or red flowers, cultivated in Europe as a source of perfume.

dame (dām) *n.* **1.** *British.* **a.** woman upon whom an honorary rank equivalent to that of a knight have been conferred. **b.** wife or widow of a knight or baronet. **2.** formerly, a woman of rank, position, or authority; lady. **3.** elderly woman. **4.** *Slang.* any woman or girl. [Old French *dame* lady, from Latin *domina* lady, mistress. Doublet of DUENNA.]

damn (dam) *v.t.* **1.** to declare (something) to be bad, worthless, or a failure: *The critics damned the play.* **2.** to curse or swear at: *In his anger, he damned us all.* **3.** to be the ruin of; cause to fail: *His actions damned him.* **4.** to condemn to eternal punishment in hell. —*v.i.* **1.** to swear; curse. **2. to damn with faint praise.** to praise so grudgingly as to imply

at; āpe; cär; end; mē; it; īce; hot; ōld; fôrk; wood; fōol; oil; out; up; ūse; turn; sing; thin; this; zh in treasure; ə in ago, taken, pencil, lemon, circus.

condemnation. —*n.* **1.** utterance of damn as an expression of anger or annoyance. **2.** negligible amount; slightest bit: *That's not worth a damn.* **3. to give a damn.** *Informal.* to care; be concerned. ▲ used chiefly in negative phrases: *He doesn't give a damn about the election.* —*adj., adv.* damned. —*interj.* expression of anger or disappointment. [Old French *damner* to harm, condemn, from Latin *damnāre* to condemn.]

dam·na·ble (dam′nə bəl) *adj.* deserving condemnation; outrageous; detestable. —**dam′na·bly,** *adv.*

dam·na·tion (dam nā′shən) *n.* **1.** act of damning; being damned. **2.** condemnation to eternal punishment in hell. —*interj.* damn.

dam·na·to·ry (dam′nə tôr′ē) *adj.* conveying, imposing, or causing condemnation; damning.

damnd·est (dam′dist) *also,* **damned·est.** *Informal. adj.* **1.** most abominable; outrageous: *That story contained some of the damndest lies.* **2.** most exceptional or extraordinary: *We had the damndest experience yesterday.* —*n.* utmost; best: *I will try my damndest to be there.*

damned (damd) *adj.* **1.** condemned as bad, worthless, or a failure. **2.** *Informal.* outrageous: *a damned nuisance.* **3.** condemned to eternal punishment in hell. —*adv. Informal.* very; utterly: *That's a damned clever idea.*

damn·ing (dam′ing, -ning) *adj.* that damns or condemns; condemnatory: *damning testimony.*

Dam·o·cles (dam′ə klēz′) *n.* courtier of Dionysius, king of Syracuse, who extolled the happiness of kings. Dionysius showed him the dangers of wealth and power by inviting him to a magnificent banquet which Damocles enjoyed until he saw a sword suspended above his head by a single hair.

dam·oi·selle (dam′ə zel′) *also,* **dam·o·sel, dam·o·zel.** *n. Archaic.* damsel.

Da·mon and Pythias (dā′mən) *n. Roman Legend.* two Greek youths celebrated for their devoted friendship. Damon pledged his life for his friend Pythias, who had been condemned to death.

damp (damp) *adj.* slightly wet; moist: *a damp cloth, a damp cellar, damp weather.* —*n.* **1.** moisture; humidity. **2.** that which checks or discourages. **3.** harmful gas found esp. in mines, such as firedamp. —*v.t.* **1.** to dampen. **2.** to reduce in intensity; check; dull: *to damp a fire, to damp a sound, to damp one's spirits.* [Middle Dutch or Middle Low German *damp* vapor.] —**damp′ly,** *adv.* —**damp′ness,** *n.*

damp·en (dam′pən) *v.t.* **1.** to make damp; moisten. **2.** to diminish the force or intensity of; check; depress: *Discourteous treatment often dampens a person's spirits.* —*v.i.* to become damp.

damp·er (dam′pər) *n.* **1.** one who or that which depresses or checks: *to put a damper on one's hopes.* **2.** movable plate in a flue, for regulating the draft, as in a fireplace, stove, or furnace. **3.** device for deadening vibration, esp. of piano strings.

damp·ing-off (dam′ping ôf′) *n.* disease of young plants, esp. seedlings and cuttings, caused by any of several parasitic fungi which attack roots or stems, causing them to decay and die.

dam·sel (dam′zəl) *n.* young unmarried woman; maiden. [Old French *dameisele,* going back to Latin *domina* lady, mistress.]

damsel fly, any of a group of brightly colored insects, suborder Zygoptera, closely related to the dragonfly, but distinguished by a more slender body and the folded position of its wings when at rest.

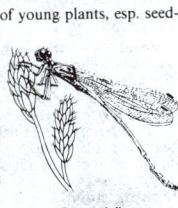

Damsel fly

dam·son (dam′zən) *n.* **1.** small, round, dark-purple fruit of a plum tree, *Prunus insititia,* having a tart flavor and used mainly in preserves. **2.** tree bearing this fruit, originally cultivated in Asia Minor. [Latin *(prūnum) Damascēnum* (plum) of Damascus.]

Dan (dan) *n.* **1.** in the Old Testament, one of the sons of Jacob. **2.** tribe of Israel descended from him, which settled in northern Palestine. **3.** village in northeastern Israel, in ancient times the northernmost city of Palestine. **4. from Dan to Beersheba.** from one limit or extreme to the other.

Dan. 1. Daniel. **2.** Danish.

Da·na, Richard Henry (dā′nə) 1815–82, U.S. author.

Dan·a·e (dan′ā ē′) *also,* **Dan·a·ë.** *n. Greek Legend.* the mother of Perseus by Zeus, who appeared to her in the form of a shower of gold.

Dan·a·i·des (də nā′ə dēz′) *also,* **Dan·a·ï·des.** *n. Greek Legend.* the fifty daughters of Danaus, who, except for one, killed their husbands on their wedding night at their father's command. Their punishment was to draw water with broken vessels forever in Hades.

Da Nang (dä′ näng′) *also,* **Da·nang.** port city in northern South Vietnam, on the South China Sea. Pop. (1961 est.), 110,800.

Dan·a·us (dan′ā əs) *also,* **Dan·a·üs.** *n. Greek Legend.* a king of Argos and father of the Danaides.

dance (dans) *danced, danc·ing. v.i.* **1.** to move the body or feet rhyth-

micially and in a prescribed or improvised pattern, usually in time to music. **2.** to move about in a lively or excited way; leap about: *The man danced with joy.* **3.** to bob up and down: *The sunlight danced on the water's surface.* —*v.t.* **1.** to perform or take part in (a dance): *to dance the polka.* **2.** to cause to dance: *He danced her around the room.* **3.** to bring about a particular condition by dancing. *She danced her cares away.* **4. to dance attendance on.** to wait on constantly and obsequiously. —*n.* **1.** definite series of rhythmical steps or movements, usually done to music: *The waltz is a well-known dance.* **2.** act or instance of dancing. **3.** *also,* **the dance.** art of dancing. **4.** social gathering for dancing: *There will be a dance Friday night at the country club.* **5.** one round of dancing: *He was her partner for the last dance.* **6.** piece of music written for dancing: *Strauss composed many dances.* —*adj.* of or for dancing: *a dance band.* [Old French *danser* to move rhythmically with steps; possibly of Germanic origin.]

dance of death, allegory popular in medieval art, in which a skeleton representing Death leads people in a dance to the grave. Also, **danse macabre.**

danc·er (dan′sər) *n.* one who dances, esp. one whose profession is dancing.

dan·de·li·on (dand′əl ī′ən) *n.* **1.** yellow flower of any of a group of plants, genus *Taraxacum,* of the composite family, esp. *T. officinale,* the common dandelion. **2.** plant bearing this flower, having a cluster of leaves around the base of a hollow stalk and found growing wild in temperate regions throughout the world. [French *dent de lion* literally, tooth of the lion (from the shape of its toothlike leaves), going back to Latin *dēns* tooth + *dē* from, of + *leō* lion.]

dan·der (dan′dər) *n. Informal.* **1.** temper; anger. **2. to get one's dander up.** to make or become angry. [Of uncertain origin.]

Dan·die Din·mont terrier (dan′dē din′mont) long-bodied terrier of a breed originally developed in Scotland for hunting small game, having hind legs longer than the front legs, a curly top-knot, and a shaggy coat. Height: 8–11 inches at the shoulder. [From *Dandie Dinmont* a character who owned two such terriers in Sir Walter Scott's novel *Guy Mannering* (1815).]

Dandie Dinmont terrier

dan·dle (dan′dəl) -dled, -dling. *v.t.* **1.** to move (someone or something) up and down on one's knees or in one's arms: *to dandle a child.* **2.** to fondle; pamper; pet. [Of uncertain origin.] —**dan′dler,** *n.*

dan·druff (dan′drəf) *n.* small, white or grayish scales of dead skin shed from the scalp. [Possibly from dialectal English *dander* scales on the skin + Middle English *roufe* scab (of Scandinavian origin).]

dan·dy (dan′dē) *pl.* **-dies.** *n.* **1.** man who is excessively concerned about the neatness and elegance of his dress and appearance; fop. **2.** *Informal.* very fine example of its class: *That dress is a dandy.* —*adj.* **-di·er, -di·est. 1.** characteristic of or resembling a dandy; foppish. **2.** *Informal.* very good; excellent. [Possibly from a nickname for *Andrew,* or a shortened form of earlier *jack-a-dandy* fop.]

Dane (dān) *n.* member or close descendant of the people of Denmark.

Dane·law (dān′lô′) *also,* **Dane·lagh.** *n.* **1.** region in east and northeast England ruled by the Danes during the ninth and tenth centuries. **2.** body of laws enforced by the Danes in this region. [Old English *Dena lagu* Danes' law; of Scandinavian origin.]

dan·ger (dān′jər) *n.* **1.** exposure or liability to harm, injury, evil, or loss; risk; peril: *the danger in skating on thin ice.* **2.** instance or cause of harm, risk, or peril: *Narrow, winding roads are a danger to drivers.* [Old French *dangier* power (hence, power to harm), jurisdiction, going back to Latin *dominium* power, sovereignty.]

Syn. 1. Danger, hazard, peril, risk mean a threat of damage or harm. **Danger,** the general term, gives no indication of how immediate the threat is or whether it is inevitable: *There is danger in climbing a high mountain.* **Hazard** suggests chance and implies a greater or lesser probability of harm in the very nature of a situation: *He became accustomed to the hazards of driving in heavy traffic.* **Peril** suggests a high probability of harm and implies an impending threat: *The present generation lives in great peril of nuclear war.* **Risk** suggests both the probability of harm and a voluntary acceptance of the chances: *There is risk involved in stock market speculation.*

dan·ger·ous (dān′jər əs) *adj.* **1.** full of danger; risky; hazardous: *Mining is a dangerous occupation.* **2.** likely to cause harm: *A tiger is a dangerous animal.* —**dan′ger·ous·ly,** *adv.* —**dan′ger·ous·ness,** *n.*

dan·gle (dang′gəl) -gled, -gling. *v.i.* **1.** to hang or swing loosely. **2.** to follow a person longingly or closely, as for a favor; be a hanger-on (often with *after*): *to dangle after a well-known man.* —*v.t.* **1.** to make (something) swing loosely. [Possibly from Danish *dangle* to bob[1].] —**dan′gler,** *n.*

dangling participle, participle that does not clearly relate to the

word it is supposed to modify. In the sentence *After working all morning, the lunch was brought out to us,* *working* is a dangling participle because it does not modify the word *lunch.*

Dan·iel (dan′yəl) *n.* **1.** in the Bible, a Hebrew prophet who was held captive in Babylon and whose faith in God saved him from death in a lions' den. **2.** book of the Old Testament containing the story of Daniel and his prophecies.

Dan·ish (dā′nish) *adj.* of or relating to Denmark, the Danes, or their language. —*n.* **1.** North Germanic language spoken by the people of Denmark, a member of the Indo-European family of languages. **2.** *Informal.* Danish pastry.

Danish pastry, sweet, rich pastry made with raised dough.

dank (dangk) *adj.* disagreeably damp; moist and cold. [Probably of Scandinavian origin.] —**dank′ly,** *adv.* —**dank′ness,** *n.*

d'An·nun·zi·o, Ga·bri·e·le (dä noōn′tsē ō′; gä′brē el′ä) 1863–1938, Italian novelist, poet, and dramatist.

dan·seuse (dän sœz′) *pl.,* **-seuses** (-sœz′) *n.* female ballet dancer. [French *danseuse* female dancer, going back to Old French *danser* to dance. See DANCE.]

Dan·te (dän′tē, dän′tā) *n.* 1265–1321, Italian poet.

Dan·te A·li·ghie·ri (dän′tä ä′lē gyär′ē) Dante.

Dan·ton, Georges (dan′tən; zhôrzh) 1759–94, leader in the French Revolution.

Dan·ube (dan′ūb) *n.* second longest river in Europe, flowing eastward from the southern part of West Germany to the Black Sea. —**Dan·u′·bi·an,** *adj.*

Dan·zig (dan′sig) *n.* Gdansk.

Daph·ne (daf′nē) *n.* *Greek Mythology.* nymph who escaped from her pursuer, Apollo, by being changed into a laurel tree.

daph·ni·a (daf′nē ə) *n.* any of a group of tiny crustaceans, genus *Daphnia,* that inhabit freshwater ponds and puddles throughout the world. [Modern Latin *Daphnia,* possibly from DAPHNE.]

dap·per (dap′ər) *adj.* **1.** smart in dress or appearance; neat; trim. **2.** small and active. [Dutch *dapper* brave, quick.] —**dap′per·ly,** *adv.* —**dap′per·ness,** *n.*

dap·ple (dap′əl) *adj.* spotted; variegated: *a dapple horse.* Also, **dap-pled.** —*n.* **1.** spot or dot, as on an animal's skin or coat. **2.** animal having a spotted coat. —*v.t., v.i.,* **-pled, -pling.** to mark or become marked with spots. [Of uncertain origin.]

dap·ple-gray (dap′əl grā′) *adj.* gray, variegated with spots of a darker shade.

DAR, Daughters of the American Revolution, a society of women descended from Americans who fought on or gave aid to the Colonial side in the American Revolution.

Darby and Joan (där′bē; jōn′) any happily married elderly couple. [From a couple so named and described in an eighteenth-century English ballad.]

Dar·da·nelles (därd′ən elz′) *n.* narrow strait between European Turkey and Asiatic Turkey, connecting the Aegean Sea with the Sea of Marmara. In ancient times it was known as the Hellespont.

dare (dâr) **dared** or *(archaic)* **durst, dar·ing.** *v.t.* **1.** to challenge (someone) to do something, esp. as proof of courage or ability: *Bill dared him to climb the wall.* **2.** to be bold enough to attempt or undertake; have courage for: *to dare the ascent of a mountain.* **3.** to meet boldly and defiantly: *He dared the elements by climbing the treacherous mountain.* —*v.i.* **1.** to have boldness or courage to do or try something; venture: *No one dared to skate on the thin ice.* **2. I dare say.** I suppose or believe; I have no doubt. —*n.* challenge: *to give someone a dare.* [Old English *dearr* (I) venture, from *durran* to venture.] —**dar′er,** *n.*

Dare, Virginia (dâr) born 1587, first child born of English parents in North America.

dare·dev·il (dâr′dev′əl) *n.* recklessly daring person. —*adj.* reckless; rash. —**dare′dev′il·ry, dare′dev′il·try,** *n.*

Dar es Sa·laam (där′es sə läm′) capital and largest city of Tanzania. Pop. (1967), 272,821.

Dar·i·en (dâr′ē en′) *n.* **1. Isthmus of.** former name of the Isthmus of Panama. **2. Gulf of.** gulf of the Caribbean Sea, between Panama and Colombia.

dar·ing (dâr′ing) *n.* adventurous courage; boldness. —*adj.* courageous and adventurous; fearless. —**dar′ing·ly,** *adv.*

Da·ri·us I (də rī′əs) c.549–c.485 B.C., king of Persia from 521 to c.485. Also, **Darius the Great.**

Dar·jee·ling (där jē′ling) *n.* very fine variety of black tea from the mountainous regions of northern India. [From *Darjeeling,* district in India where this tea is grown.]

dark (därk) *adj.* **1.** partially or wholly devoid of light: *a dark night; a dark room.* **2.** reflecting or radiating little light: *a dark color.* **3.** of a deep shade; nearly black: *a dark blue.* **4.** not light-complexioned or fair; swarthy: *a dark girl.* **5.** gloomy; cheerless; dismal: *Don't always look on the dark side of things.* **6.** having a morose appearance or disposition; sullen: *a face dark with anger, a dark mood.* **7.** hidden from

view or knowledge; mysterious: *a deep, dark secret.* **8.** spiritually or mentally blind; unenlightened; ignorant: *a dark era of history.* **9.** difficult to comprehend or explain; obscure in meaning: *a dark subject, a dark passage in a book.* **10.** evil; wicked; heinous: *a dark purpose, dark deeds.* —*n.* **1.** partial or total absence of light: *The child was afraid of the dark.* **2.** night; nightfall: *They crept away after dark.* **3.** dark color or shade: *There are many lights and darks in that painting.* **4. in the dark.** **a.** in concealment, obscurity, or secrecy: *The senator kept his political intentions in the dark.* **b.** in a state of ignorance; uninformed: *We were in the dark about his plans.* [Old English *deorc* devoid of light, gloomy, wicked.] —**dark′ly,** *adv.* —**dark′ness,** *n.*

Syn. *adj.* **1. Dark, dim, gloomy** describe lack of illumination. **Dark** suggests the absence of light, but it may mean that there is insufficient light: *Even at midday that is a dark apartment.* **Dim** implies lack of clarity because of insufficient light: *The dim shapes of the trees loomed beyond the headlights.* **Gloomy** suggests interference with illumination: *By afternoon the storm clouds had made the day gloomy.*

Dark Ages *also,* **dark ages. 1.** period in European history from about A.D. 476 to about A.D. 1000, between the fall of the western Roman Empire and the rise of medieval civilization. **2.** formerly, the Middle Ages as a whole, from about A.D. 476 to about A.D. 1450.

Dark Continent, Africa.

dark·en (där′kən) *v.t., v.i.* to make or become dark or darker. —**dark′en·er,** *n.*

dark horse 1. unexpected winner, esp. in a horse race, about whom little is known and whose chances of success had been considered slight. **2.a.** one who is mentioned as a possible nominee for political office but who is considered unlikely to receive the nomination. **b.** one who unexpectedly receives a nomination for political office.

dark·ish (där′kish) *adj.* somewhat dark.

dark lantern, lantern whose light can be concealed by a dark slide or cover.

dark·ling (därk′ling) *Archaic. adv.* in the dark. —*adj.* **1.** dark; dim; obscure. **2.** taking place in the dark.

dark·room (därk′rōōm′, -rōom′) *n.* room in which photographs are developed, arranged so that all actinic light is excluded.

dark·some (därk′səm) *adj.* *Archaic.* **1.** dark; darkish. **2.** gloomy; cheerless.

dar·ling (där′ling) *n.* **1.** one who is very dear or much loved. **2.** favorite: *That actress was once the darling of movie audiences.* —*adj.* **1.** dearly loved; cherished. **2.** *Informal.* charmingly attractive; cute: *What a darling dress!* [Old English *dēorling* one dearly loved, from *dēore* dear.]

darn[1] (därn) *v.t., v.i.* to mend, as a tear or hole in clothing, by sewing interlacing stitches across the gap. —*n.* **1.** place mended by darning. **2.** act of darning. [Of uncertain origin.]

darn[2] (därn) *Informal.* damn. ▲ used as a euphemism. [Milder form of DAMN.]

dar·nel (där′nəl) *n.* annual rye grass, *Lolium temulentum,* often found in grain fields. It is a weed pest and its seeds may become poisonous. [Of uncertain origin.]

darn·er (där′nər) *n.* **1.** one who darns. **2.** darning needle. **3.** hard, round device of wood or other material placed under a hole to be darned. Also, **darning ball.**

darn·ing (där′ning) *n.* **1.a.** act of mending with interlaced stitches; **b.** the result of such a process. **2.** articles that have been darned or are to be darned.

darning needle 1. long needle with a large eye, used for darning. **2.** dragonfly.

Dar·row, Clarence S. (dar′ō) 1857–1938, U.S. lawyer.

dart (därt) *n.* **1.a.** slender, oblong projectile with a short metal point in front and feathers

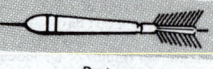

Dart

or featherlike projections in the rear, used in playing certain games. **b. darts,** game in which such projectiles are thrown at a target. **2.** slender, pointed weapon to be thrown or shot, such as that used in blowguns by some Indian tribes of North and South America. **3.** sudden, swift movement. **4.** tapered tuck sewn in a garment to give it a better fit. **5.** stinger of an insect. —*v.i.* to spring or start suddenly and swiftly: *The rabbit darted from the bushes.* —*v.t.* **1.** to throw or emit suddenly and rapidly: *The lizard darted its tongue at the insect.* **2.** to send suddenly: *to dart a glance at a person.* [Old French *dart,* accusative of *darz* javelin, from Late Latin *dardus* of Germanic origin.]

dart·er (där′tər) *n.* **1.** one who or that which moves suddenly and swiftly. **2.** any of several small freshwater fish, family Percidae, closely related to the perch, that swims in quick, darting movements and is found in North America east of the Rockies. Length: to 8 inches. **3.** snakebird.

Dar·win, Charles (där′win) 1809–82, English naturalist and pioneer in the study of evolution.

at; āpe; cär; end; mē; it; īce; hot; ōld; fôrk; wood; fōōl; oil; out; up; ūse; turn; sing; thin; this; zh in treasure; ə in ago, taken, pencil, lemon, circus.

Dar·win·i·an (där win′ē ən) *adj.* of or relating to Charles Darwin or his theory of evolution. —*n.* advocate of Darwinism.

Dar·win·ism (där′wi niz′əm) *n.* theory of evolution propounded by Charles Darwin, which states that all species of plants and animals developed by inheriting slight variations from earlier forms, and that those organisms having traits best suited to their environment survive through the process of natural selection. —**Dar′win·ist,** *adj.,n.*

dash (dash) *v.i.* **1.** to move with speed and violence; rush: *The dog dashed after the rabbit.* **2.** to strike or hit with violence; smash: *Waves dashed against the ship.* **3. to dash off.** to hurry away; leave quickly. —*v.t.* **1.** to strike violently against: *The waves dashed the shore.* **2.** to shatter or break with force or violence; smash: *The storm dashed the ship against the rocks.* **3.** to throw, knock, or thrust violently and suddenly: *He dashed the chair against the door.* **4.** to splash; spatter: *The boys dashed each other with water.* **5.** to ruin or frustrate: *to dash one's hopes.* **6.** to daunt; depress. **7.** to put to shame; abash. **8.** to mix with a small quantity of something else: *to dash wine with water.* **9. to dash off.** to make, write, or complete quickly or hastily: *He dashed off a letter to his client.* —*n.* **1.** sudden rush or movement: *The prisoner made a dash for freedom.* **2.** small quantity added or mixed in: *a dash of pepper.* **3.** short race that is run or swum at top speed: *the 50-yard dash.* **4.** hasty stroke, as of a pen. **5.a.** splashing of water or other liquid on or against something. **b.** sound of splashing. **6.** spirited energy and style: *The man has dash and verve.* **7.** short horizontal line (—) used in writing or printing, as for showing a pause or break in a sentence or indicating an omission. **8.** *Telegraphy.* long signal used in conjunction with a shorter one to represent numbers or letters, as in Morse code. Distinguished from **dot. 9.** dashboard. [Probably imitative.]

dash·board (dash′bôrd′) *n.* **1.** panel equipped with instruments and gauges, located in front of the driver in an automobile or similar vehicle. **2.** screen placed on the front of an open vehicle, as a buggy or buckboard, to prevent mud or water from being splashed into it.

dash·er (dash′ər) *n.* **1.** one who or that which dashes. **2.** plunger of a churn. See **churn** for illustration.

dash·ing (dash′ing) *adj.* **1.** courageous and spirited. **2.** showy; stylish. —**dash′ing·ly,** *adv.*

das·tard (das′tərd) *n.* mean, base coward; sneak. —*adj.* dastardly. [Of uncertain origin.]

das·tard·ly (das′tərd lē) *adj.* mean and despicably cowardly; sneaking. —**das′tard·li·ness,** *n.*

dat., dative.

da·ta (dā′tə, dat′ə, dä′tə) *n.,pl.* information from which inferences or conclusions can be drawn; facts and figures. ▲ It is now considered acceptable to use either a plural or singular verb with *data: The data indicate that our theory is wrong. The data for the project was collected.* [Plural of DATUM.]

data processing, rapid organization and analysis of large amounts of information by machines, as digital computers.

date[1] (dāt) *n.* **1.** day of the month: *Today's date is May 15.* **2.** specific point or period of time when something occurs: *The date of his death is uncertain. The date of her birth is July 15, 1944.* **3.** inscription, as on a coin or statue, stating when something was written or made: *The cornerstone bears the date 1954.* **4.** *Informal.* appointment or social engagement for a specified time or place: *The friends made a date for next Tuesday.* **5.** *Informal.* person of the opposite sex with whom such an appointment or engagement is made: *John picked up his date at her house.* **6.** period of time or age to which something belongs: *The chariot is of Roman date.* **7.** time during which something lasts; duration. **8. out of date.** no longer in vogue or use; old-fashioned: *Bustles are out of date.* **9. to date.** up to and including the present time: *I have received only three replies to date.* **10. up to date. a.** conforming to the latest style or thought; modern: *The minister was up to date in his thinking.* **b.** to the present time: *The accountant brought all his records up to date.* —*v.t.* **1.** to furnish or mark with a date: *The secretary dated the letter.* **2.** to determine or fix the time of; assign a date to: *Archaeologists dated the fossil after much study.* **3.** *Informal.* to go on a date with (a member of the opposite sex): *Tom dated Alice yesterday.* **4.** to show the age of: *The wrinkles on her face dated her.* —*v.i.* **1.** to belong to, or have origin in, a particular time or era (often with *from*): *This custom dates from the seventeenth century.* **2.** to have appointments or engagements with members of the opposite sex: *Maggie dates frequently.* [Old French *date* (in time), going back to Latin *data,* feminine of *datus* given, past participle of *dare* to give; from the expression used to date a letter in ancient Rome: *(epistola) data Romae* (letter) given at Rome (as on a specified date).] —**Syn.** *n.* **4.** see **appointment.**

date[2] (dāt) *n.* **1.** oval-shaped edible fruit of the date palm, having thick, sweet flesh. **2.** date palm. [Old French *date* this fruit, through Latin, from Greek *daktylos* this fruit, finger; from the supposed resemblance of its shape to a finger.]

dat·ed (dā′tid) *adj.* **1.** marked with a date. **2.** old-fashioned: *dated slang. That book now seems dated.*

date·less (dāt′lis) *adj.* **1.** without a date; bearing no date: *The letter was dateless.* **2.** old but retaining permanent interest or worth. **3.** so old as to be undatable; immemorial. **4.** having no limit or end.

date·line (dāt′līn′) *n.* line in a piece of printed material, as an article or newspaper, which supplies its place and date of origin.

date line, International Date Line.

date palm, tall, tropical tree, *Phoenix dactylifera,* of the palm family, having a straight, shaggy trunk topped with divided leaves and bearing thick clusters of fruit.

da·tive (dā′tiv) *n.* **1.** grammatical case in Latin, Russian, and several other Indo-European languages which indicates the indirect object of a verb. In English this case is usually denoted by the use of *to* or *for* preceding the object or by word order: *Please hand that book to me. Please hand me that book.* **2.** word in this case. —*adj.* of, designating, or belonging to the dative. [Latin *dativus* of giving, as in the grammatical term *casus dativus* literally, case of giving.]

da·tum (dā′təm, dat′əm, dä′təm) *pl.,* **da·ta.** *n.* **1.** known or assumed fact from which a conclusion can be inferred. **2.** something used as a basis for measurements or calculations. [Latin *datum* something given, from neuter of *datus,* past participle of *dare* to give.]

dau., daughter.

daub (dôb) *v.t.* **1.** to coat, cover, or smear with a soft adhesive substance, as plaster, grease, or clay: *to daub a wall with plaster.* **2.** to spread a soft adhesive substance on or over: *to daub paint on a canvas.* **3.** to paint (something) coarsely or inartistically. —*v.i.* to paint something coarsely or inartistically. —*n.* **1.** smear or smudge; spot: *The boys had daubs of dirt on their legs.* **2.** substance used for daubing, as plaster or clay. **3.** crudely painted picture. **4.** act or instance of daubing. [Old French *dauber* to whitewash, plaster, from Latin *dealbāre,* going back to *dē* down + *albus* white.] —**daub′er,** *n.*

Dau·det, Alphonse (dō dā′; al fons′) 1840–97, French author.

daugh·ter (dô′tər) *n.* **1.** female offspring, considered in relationship to one or both of her parents. **2.** female descendant: *Ruth was a daughter of Abraham.* **3.** female considered in relation to something that functions in a way similar to a parent: *a daughter of the revolution.* **4.** anything considered as female in relation to its source or origin: *The romance languages are daughters of Latin.* [Old English *dohtor* female offspring or descendant.]

daugh·ter-in-law (dô′tər in lô′) *pl.,* **daugh·ters-in-law.** *n.* wife of one's son.

daugh·ter·ly (dô′tər lē) *adj.* of, relating to, or proper for a daughter.

Dau·mier, Ho·no·ré (dōm yā′; ō nō rā′) 1808–79, French painter.

daunt (dônt) *v.t.* **1.** to overcome with fear; intimidate. **2.** to discourage; dishearten: *The spirit of their chief was not daunted by misfortune* (Gibbon, 1781). [Old French *danter* to tame, subdue, from Latin *domitāre.*]

daunt·less (dônt′lis) *adj.* fearless; courageous; daring. —**daunt′less·ly,** *adv.*

dau·phin (dô′fin) *n.* oldest son of a king of France, used as a title from 1349 to 1830. [Old French *daulphin, dauphin* literally, dolphin; originally referring to the three *dolphins* in the coat of arms of a noble French family that, in 1349, gave the province *Dauphiné* to the king of France on condition that the oldest son of the king of France would thereafter have the title *dauphin.* See DOLPHIN.]

dau·phin·ess (dô′fi nis) *n.* wife of a dauphin. Also, **dau·phine** (dō′fēn).

dav·en·port (dav′ən pôrt′) *n.* **1.** large upholstered sofa, esp. one that is convertible into a bed. **2.** writing desk or table, often with drawers. [Supposedly named after the first maker of the desk.]

Dav·en·port (dav′ən pôrt′) **1. John.** 1597–1670, Puritan clergyman, a founder of the colony of New Haven. **2.** city in eastern Iowa. Pop. (1970), 98,469.

Da·vid (defs. *1, 2* dā′vid; def. *3* dä vēd′) *n.* **1.** c.1040–c.970 B.C., the second king of Judah and Israel, from c.1010 to c.970 B.C. He was the successor to Saul and the father of Solomon. **2. Saint.** died A.D. c.601, patron saint of Wales. **3. Jacques Lou·is** (zhäk lōō′ē). 1748–1825, French painter. [Hebrew *Dāwid* literally, beloved.]

da Vin·ci, Le·o·nar·do (də vin′chē; lē′ə när′dō) Leonardo da Vinci.

Da·vis, Jefferson (dā′vis) 1808–89, U.S. political leader, president of the Confederate States of America, from 1861 to 1865.

dav·it (dav′it, dā′vit) *n.* **1.** one of a pair of movable or curved arms that can project over the stern or side of a boat or ship, used esp. to carry a small boat or to raise it from or lower it into the water. **2.** similar device used for raising or lowering the anchor of a ship. [Earlier *david;* an example of the use of a name for a tool, as in BILLY, JACK.]

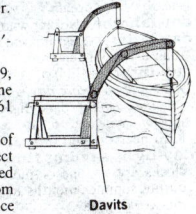

Davits

at; āpe; cär; end; mē; it; īce; hot; ōld; fôrk; wood; fōōl; oil; out; up; ūse; turn; sing; thin; this; zh in treasure; ə in ago, taken, pencil, lemon, circus.

Da·vy, Sir Humphry (dā′vē) 1778–1829, English chemist.

Da·vy Jones (dā′vē jōnz′) spirit of the sea; the sailor's devil.

Davy Jones's locker, bottom of the ocean, esp. as the grave of those who drown at sea.

daw (dô) *n.* jackdaw. [Probably from an unrecorded Old English word.]

daw·dle (dôd′əl) **-dled, -dling.** *v.t., v.i.* to waste (time); idle; linger (often with *away*): *to dawdle the afternoon away. The child dawdled over his breakfast.* [Of uncertain origin.] —**daw′dler,** *n.*

dawn (dôn) *n.* **1.** first appearance of light in the morning; daybreak. **2.** beginning or first appearance: *the dawn of a new era, the dawn of civilization.* —*v.i.* **1.** to begin to grow light in the morning; to become day. **2.** to begin to be clear, understood, or perceived (with *on* or *upon*): *It suddenly dawned on him that he was being deceived.* **3.** to begin to appear, develop, or open: *The space age dawned in the twentieth century.* [From earlier *dawning* daybreak; probably of Scandinavian origin.]

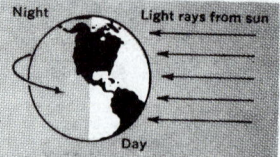

Night   Light rays from sun

Day

Day and night

day (dā) *n.* **1.** period of light between the rising and setting of the sun: *June 21 is the longest day of the year.* **2.** light of day; daylight. **3.a.** length of time required for the earth to complete one rotation on its axis, approximately 24 hours. Also, **solar day. b.** interval of time required for the earth to complete one rotation measured against the vernal equinox, having as its duration, 23 hours, 56 minutes, and 4.09 seconds. Also, **sidereal day. c.** length of time required by a heavenly body to complete one rotation on its axis. **4.a.** part of a day passed in a particular way or place: *a day in court.* **b.** hours of a day devoted to work: *He worked a seven-hour day.* **5.** day regarded as a point or unit of time when something happens or which fixes a date: *He came on the third day and left on the fifth.* **6.** *also,* **Day.** specific period of 24 hours set aside for a particular purpose or observance: *election day, her wedding day.* **7.** period of existence, power, action, success, or influence: *Knighthood has had its day.* **8.** *also,* **days.** particular time or period; era: *in those days, in King Arthur's day.* **9.** *usually,* **days.** span of existence; lifetime: *He spent his days eking out a living.* **10.** chance; opportunity: *Your day will come soon.* **11.** contest or struggle: *The runner carried the day by winning three races.*

day after day, every day.

day by day, each day; daily.

day in, day out, every day.

from day to day, lacking foresight or provision for the future; from one day to the next: *They lived from day to day.*

the other day, in the recent past; not long ago.

to call it a day. *Informal.* to stop engaging in an activity. [Old English *dæg* period between the rising and setting of the sun, length of time required for the earth to complete one rotation on its axis.]

Day·ak (dī′ak, -ək) Dyak.

day·bed (dā′bed′) *also,* **day bed.** *n.* sofa that can be converted into a bed.

day·book (dā′book′) *n.* **1.** in bookkeeping, book in which business transactions are recorded chronologically. **2.** diary or journal.

day·break (dā′brāk′) *n.* time each morning when daylight first appears; dawn.

day care center, day nursery.

day coach, railroad passenger car equipped only with seating facilities, as distinguished from sleeping, dining, or other specialized cars.

day·dream (dā′drēm′) *n.* visionary fancy experienced while awake, esp. one of happy, pleasant thoughts, hopes, or ambitions. —*v.i.* to indulge in or have daydreams: *Chuck daydreamed during his history class.* —**day′dream′er,** *n.*

day laborer, worker who is paid by the day, esp. an unskilled worker.

day letter, telegram sent during the day which is cheaper but slower than a regular telegram.

day·light (dā′līt′) *n.* **1.** light of day. **2.** daytime. **3.** dawn: *The milkman was up before daylight.* **4.** public view: *He brought the matter out into the daylight.* **5.** daylights. *Informal.* wits; sense: *to beat the daylights out of someone.* **6.** to see daylight. *Informal.* **a.** to understand. **b.** to near the end or conclusion of a difficult task.

day·light-sav·ing time (dā′līt′sā′ving) system of time in which clocks are set one or more hours ahead of standard time, used esp. during summer months to provide more daylight hours at the end of the working day.

day lily **1.** yellow, orange, or red flower of any of a group of plants, genus *Hemerocallis,* of the lily family. The flowers live for only one day. **2.** the long-leaved plant that bears these flowers.

day·long (dā′lông′) *adj.* lasting all day. —*adv.* through the whole day.

day nursery, nursery for the care of small children during the day, esp. those of mothers who work. Also, **day care center.**

Day of Atonement, Yom Kippur.

Day of Judgment, Judgment Day.

day school **1.** school that holds classes only during the day. **2.** private school whose students live at home. Distinguished from **boarding school.**

days of grace, extension of time given for payment of a note or bill of exchange after its due date.

day·star (dā′stär′) *n.* **1.** morning star. **2.** *Archaic.* sun.

day·time (dā′tīm′) *n.* period of time between the rising and setting of the sun.

Day·ton (dāt′ən) *n.* city in southwestern Ohio. Pop. (1970), 243,601.

Day·to·na Beach (dā tō′nə) city in northeastern Florida. Pop. (1970), 45,327.

daze (dāz) **dazed, daz·ing.** *v.t.* to stun or stupefy, as by a blow; bewilder; confuse: *The boxer dazed his opponent.* —*n.* dazed state or condition: *The accident left him in a daze.* [Of Scandinavian origin.]

daz·zle (daz′əl) **-zled, -zling.** *v.t.* **1.** to dim or overpower the vision of with an excess of light: *The bright morning sun dazzled him.* **2.** to overpower, confound, or impress, as by brilliance, splendor, or ostentation: *The quarterback's outstanding play dazzled his opponents.* —*v.i.* **1.** to be overpowered or blinded by light. **2.** to excite admiration by brilliance or showiness. —*n.* act of dazzling; being dazzled. [DAZE + -LE.] —**daz′zler,** *n.* —**daz′zling·ly,** *adv.*

dbl., double.

DC, direct current.

D.C., District of Columbia.

D.C.L., Doctor of Civil Law.

D.D., Doctor of Divinity.

D-day (dē′dā′) *n.* **1.** day on which the Allied forces invaded France during World War II; June 6, 1944. **2.** day on which an operation commences or is to commence.

D.D.S., Doctor of Dental Surgery.

DDT, white or cream-colored powdery compound with a faint odor, poisonous to humans and animals upon contact, formerly widely used as an insecticide. [Abbreviation of *d(ichloro) d(iphenyl)t(richloroethane).*]

de- *prefix* **1.** removed from; away; off: *deport, delay, dethrone.* **2.** down: *demote, degrade.* **3.** to do the opposite of, reverse, or undo: *demoralize, decompose.* **4.** thoroughly; completely: *deplore, declaim.* [Either Latin *dē* from, away, down, or Latin *dis* apart, away, un-, exceedingly.]

dea·con (dē′kən) *n.* **1.** in some Christian churches, a cleric or layman who assists the priest or minister in the services or who helps administer the business affairs of the church. **2.** *Roman Catholic Church.* **a.** cleric who helps conduct worship for a year before becoming a priest. **b.** priest who assists the celebrant at a solemn high mass. [Old English *deacon* servant or minister of the Christian church, from Latin *diāconus,* from Greek *diākonos* originally, servant.]

dea·con·ess (dē′kə nis) *n.* woman who is a church assistant, esp. one who does medical or social work.

dea·con·ry (dē′kən rē) *pl.* **-ries.** *n.* **1.** position or office of a deacon. **2.** deacons collectively.

dead (ded) *adj.* **1.** no longer living; having died; lifeless. **2.** resembling death; still: *a dead faint, a dead sleep.* **3.** not endowed with life; inanimate: *dead matter.* **4.** lacking sensation; numb. **5.** unresponsive; insensitive: *He was dead to all sense of shame.* **6.** destitute of spiritual life or energy. **7.** lacking significance, usefulness, or interest: *a dead issue, the dead past.* **8.** lacking power, force, or effectiveness: *dead laws.* **9.** lacking social or intellectual activity or interest; dull; quiet: *a dead town.* **10.** lacking resilience or elasticity: *a dead tennis ball.* **11.** (of colors) lacking luster or brightness. **12.** without fire; extinguished: *a dead fire, a dead cigar.* **13.** commercially inactive, useless, or unprofitable: *dead capital.* **14.** not operating or functioning: *The telephone is dead.* **15.** no longer active or in existence: *a dead volcano.* **16.** no longer in use: *a dead language.* **17.** barren; infertile; unproductive: *dead soil.* **18.** *Electricity.* not connected to a source for charge or current: *a dead battery.* **19.** complete; absolute: *dead certainty, a dead silence.* **20.** sure; certain; unerring: *a dead shot.* **21.** exact; direct: *He hit the target at dead center.* **22.** characterized by a complete and sudden cessation of action or motion; abrupt: *a dead stop.* **23.** *Informal.* very tired; exhausted. **24.** *Informal.* fated; doomed. **25.** *Sports.* out of play; not in the game. **26.** (of sounds) without resonance; muffled. **27.** *Printing.* already used or rejected, as type. —*adv.* **1.** completely; absolutely; entirely: *dead tired, dead sure.* **2.** directly; straight: *dead ahead.* —*n.* **1. the dead.** dead persons collectively. **2.** time of greatest intensity, as of coldness, darkness, or quiet: *the dead of night, the dead of winter.* [Old English *dēad* no longer living, lifeless.] —**dead′ness,** *n.*

at; āpe; cär; end; mē; it; īce; hot; ōld; fôrk; wood; foōl; oil; out; up; ūse; turn; sing; thin; this; zh in treasure; ə in ago, taken, pencil, lemon, circus.

Syn. *adj.* **1. Dead, inanimate, lifeless** mean not alive. **Dead** implies that what was once alive is now no longer so: *Sweep the dead leaves from the walk.* **Inanimate** refers to something that has never been alive: *Rocks are inanimate objects.* **Lifeless** emphasizes lack of vital spirit and may be used of things that never were alive as well as those that have died: *His window looked out on a wall of lifeless brick.*

dead·beat (ded′bēt′) *n. Slang.* **1.** one who avoids paying his bills. **2.** idle person; loafer.

dead center, in mechanics, the position of a crank at which it is in a direct line with the connecting rod.

dead·en (ded′ən) *v.t.* **1.** to lessen the activity, force, or intensity of; weaken: *to deaden sound.* **2.** to lessen the sensitivity of; numb; dull: *The dentist deadened the nerve with novocaine.* **3.** to deprive of luster or brilliancy.

dead·end (ded′end′) *adj.* that is a dead end: *a dead-end street, a dead-end job.*

dead end 1. street, alley, or passage closed at one end. **2.** situation or point from which no progress can be made.

dead·eye (ded′ī′) *n.* **1.** round, laterally flattened wooden block, encircled by a rope or iron band and pierced with three holes, used esp. to extend the shrouds and stays of a ship. **2.** *Informal.* expert marksman.

dead·fall (ded′fôl′) *n.* **1.** trap constructed so that a weight falls upon and kills or holds down an animal. **2.** tangled mass of fallen trees and underbrush.

dead·head (ded′hed′) *n. Informal.* **1.** dull, spiritless person. **2.** nonpaying spectator or passenger, esp. a passenger who rides on a public conveyance free of charge.

dead heat, race in which two or more competitors reach the finish line at the same time; tie.

dead letter 1. letter that lies unclaimed or cannot be delivered, esp. because of a wrong address. **2.** something that has lost its former importance, as a law or ordinance that is no longer enforced or valid but has not been formally repealed.

dead-letter office (ded′let′er) department of the post office which receives and handles dead letters.

dead·line (ded′līn′) *n.* predetermined time by which something must be completed; time limit: *The deadline for the first edition of the paper was 5:00 A.M.*

dead·lock (ded′lok′) *n.* standstill resulting from the exertion of force by opposing factions: *A compromise broke the deadlock between labor and management.* —*v.t., v.i.* to bring or come to a deadlock.

dead·ly (ded′lē) *-li·er, -li·est. adj.* **1.** causing or tending to cause death; fatal: *a deadly blow.* **2.** aiming to kill or destroy; to the death; mortal: *deadly enemies.* **3.** extremely effective or dangerous: *deadly aim.* **4.** resembling death: *a deadly pallor.* **5.** very great; extreme; excessive. —*adv.* **1.** in a manner resembling death: *deadly pale.* **2.** *Informal.* very; extremely: *deadly serious.* —**dead′li·ness,** *n.*
Syn. *adj.* **Deadly, mortal, fatal, lethal** mean causing death. **Deadly** implies the likelihood of death resulting: *Arsenic is a deadly poison.* **Mortal** implies that death has either already taken place or is inevitable: *The king suffered a mortal wound in battle.* **Fatal** suggests almost the same, but implies an interval of time before death occurs: *Cancer can be a fatal disease.* **Lethal** implies inevitable death, coming from the nature of the thing involved or the purpose for which the thing is used: *A machine gun is a lethal weapon.*

deadly nightshade, belladonna.

deadly sins, seven deadly sins.

dead·man's float (ded′manz′) floating position in swimming, face down with the arms stretched out in front.

dead·pan (ded′pan′) *Informal. adj., adv.* with a blank or expressionless face. —*v.i.* **-panned, -pan·ning.** to act or speak in an emotionless and expressionless manner.

dead pan *Informal.* **1.** expressionless face; poker face. **2.** one who has or assumes such a face.

dead point, dead center.

dead reckoning, calculation of the present position of a boat, ship, or aircraft without astronomical observations, by using the records of its speed and last known position and the compass readings of the course steered.

Dead Sea, salt lake between Israel and Jordan.

Dead Sea Scrolls, ancient manuscripts, dating from 100 B.C. to A.D. 100, found in caves near the western shore of the Dead Sea, containing portions of almost all the books of the Old Testament and a manual of discipline for the members of a Jewish monastic order, believed by many scholars to have been the Essenes.

dead weight 1. heavy, oppressive weight, as of an inert body. **2.** oppressive burden: *the dead weight of debt.* **3.** weight of a ship, truck, or other means of transportation when not loaded.

dead·wood (ded′wo͝od′) *n.* **1.** dead portion of a woody plant. **2.** anything useless or valueless.

deaf (def) *adj.* **1.** wholly or partly unable to hear. **2.** unwilling to

hear or listen; heedless: *He was deaf to their pleas.* [Old English *dēaf*] —**deaf′ly,** *adv.* —**deaf′ness,** *n.*

deaf·en (def′ən) *v.t.* **1.** to make deaf. **2.** to stun or overwhelm with noise.

deaf-mute (def′mūt′) *n.* person who cannot hear or speak.

deal[1] (dēl) *dealt, deal·ing. v.i.* **1.** to be engaged or concerned; have to do (with *with* or *in*): *This book deals with dogs. Science deals in facts.* **2.** to act or conduct oneself (often with *with*): *to deal fairly with a person. The police dealt roughly with the rioters.* **3.** to take action with regard to; consider (with *with*): *I will deal with the problem now.* **4.** to do business; trade (with *in* or *with*): *to deal in antiques. She deals with the local butcher.* **5.** to distribute cards to the players of a card game: *It's your turn to deal.* —*v.t.* **1.** to distribute (cards) among the players of a card game: *He dealt seven cards.* **2.** to give to a person as a share; distribute (often with *out*): *She dealt out cookies to the children.* **3.** to administer; render: *to deal a blow.* —*n.* **1.** *Informal.* **a.** business transaction: *to close the deal for a merger.* **b.** bargain: *to get a good deal on a used car.* **2.** *Informal.* private or secret arrangement, esp. in commerce or politics, entered into for mutual advantage. **3.** *Informal.* treatment, arrangement, or plan: *a fair deal, a dirty deal.* **4.** *Card games.* **a.** act of distributing cards to the various players. **b.** cards so distributed; hand. **c.** player's right or turn to distribute the cards: *It's your deal.* **d.** single round of playing cards; hand. **5.** *Archaic.* indefinite quantity, degree, or extent: *He dealt seven cards.* **6. a great** (or **good**) **deal. a.** large amount or quantity: *You've spent a good deal of time on that.* **b.** to a great extent or degree; very much: *She travels a great deal.* [Old English *dǣlan* to divide.] —**Syn.** *v.t.* **2.** see **distribute.**

deal[2] (dēl) *n.* **1.** plank of pine or fir wood of any of several standard sizes. **2.** pine or fir wood used for these planks. —*adj.* made of deal. [Middle Low German or Middle Dutch *dele* plank, floor.]

deal·er (dē′lər) *n.* **1.** one who is engaged in buying and selling: *an antique dealer.* **2.** person who distributes the cards in a card game.

deal·er·ship (dē′lər ship′) *n.* **1.** authorization to sell a particular commodity in a certain area. **2.** individual distributor or agency having such authorization.

deal·ing (dē′ling) *n.* **1.** act of distributing. **2. dealings.** relations, transactions, or communications with others, esp. in business.

dealt (delt) past tense and past participle of **deal**[1].

dean (dēn) *n.* **1.** administrator of a college or university who is in charge of the discipline, activities, studies, and guidance of the students: *the academic dean, the dean of women.* **2.** head of a faculty or division of a school, college, or university: *dean of the graduate school.* **3.** chief official of a cathedral or collegiate church. **4.** senior member in length of service, as of an association or group: *the dean of American literary critics.* [Old French *deien* sergeant, mayor's deputy, from Late Latin *decānus* one in charge of ten persons, from Latin *decem* ten.] —**Syn. 2.** see **principal.**

dean·er·y (dē′nər ē) *pl.* **-er·ies.** *n.* **1.** office, position, or jurisdiction of a dean. **2.** place of residence of a dean.

dear (dēr) *adj.* **1.** held in tender affection; beloved: *a dear friend.* **2.** highly esteemed. ▲ used as a salutation in letters: *Dear Sir.* **3.** high-priced; costly; expensive. **4.** heartfelt; earnest: *our dearest congratulations.* —*n.* beloved person; darling. —*adv.* **1.** affectionately; fondly: *She held him very dear.* **2.** at a high price. —*interj.* exclamation of emotion, as surprise, astonishment, or distress. [Old English *dēore* beloved, costly.] —**dear′ly,** *adv.* —**dear′ness,** *n.*

Dear·born (dēr′bərn, -bôrn) *n.* city in southeastern Michigan, near Detroit. Pop. (1970), 104,199.

dearth (durth) *n.* **1.** scant supply; scarcity; lack. **2.** *Archaic.* scarcity of food; famine. [Middle English *derthe,* from *dere* costly, dear, from Old English *dēore.*] —**Syn. 1.** see **scarcity.**

dear·y (dēr′ē) *pl.* **dear·ies.** *also,* **dear·ie.** *n. Informal.* dear one; darling.

death (deth) *n.* **1.** permanent cessation of all vital functions in a plant or animal; end of life; dying. **2.** state or condition of being dead. **3.** ending or destruction of anything; extinction: *the death of feudalism, the death of silent movies.* **4.** *usually,* **Death.** figure thought of as representing death, usually symbolized by a skeleton carrying a scythe. **5.** cause of dying: *This cold will be the death of me.* **6.** manner of dying: *a martyr's death.* **7.** wholesale slaughter; bloodshed: *The empire fell amidst death and destruction.* **8. at death's door,** close to death; dying. **9. to put to death,** to execute. **10. to death,** to the extreme: *You scared me to death.* [Old English *dēath.*]

death·bed (deth′bed′) *n.* **1.** bed on which a person dies. **2.** last hours of life.

death·blow (deth′blō′) *n.* **1.** blow that causes death. **2.** that which causes the end or destruction of something.

death cup, any of several poisonous mush-

Death cup

at; āpe; cär; end; mē; it; īce; hot; ōld; fôrk; wood; fōōl; oil; out; up; ūse; turn; sing; thin; this; zh in treasure; ə in ago, taken, pencil, lemon, circus.

259

rooms, genus *Amanita,* characterized by a cuplike swelling at the base of the stem. Also, **destroying angel.**

death duty *British.* inheritance tax.

death·ful (deth′fəl) *adj.* **1.** deadly; fatal: *deathful conditions.* **2.** resembling death; deathly: *a deathful hue.*

death house, building or part of a prison where prisoners condemned to death await execution. Also, **death row.**

death·less (deth′lis) *adj.* never dying; immortal; eternal. **—death·less·ness,** *n.*

death·like (deth′līk′) *adj.* characteristic of or resembling death.

death·ly (deth′lē) *adj.* **1.** characteristic of or resembling death: *a deathly pallor.* **2.** causing death; deadly: *a deathly blow.* —*adv.* **1.** in a deathlike manner. **2.** extremely; very: *deathly ill.*

death mask, cast, usually made of plaster, of the face of a dead person.

death rate, proportion of the number of deaths to the total population of a given area, usually stated in terms of the number of deaths per thousand per year.

death's-head (deths′hed′) *n.* human skull, or a figure representing it, used to symbolize death.

death's-head moth, large Old World moth, *Acherontia atropos,* having markings on its thorax which resemble a human skull.

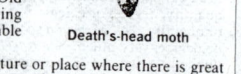

Death's-head moth

death·trap (deth′trap′) *n.* **1.** structure or place where there is great risk of death, as from fire. **2.** any extremely dangerous situation.

Death Valley, deep desert basin in southeastern California. It is the hottest and driest place in the United States and contains the lowest point in the Western Hemisphere.

death·watch (deth′wŏch′) *n.* **1.** vigil kept beside a dying or dead person. **2.** guard set over a condemned prisoner prior to his execution. **3.** any of several destructive beetles, family Anobiidae, that burrow into wood. It makes a ticking sound that was once believed to be an omen of death.

de·ba·cle (di bä′kəl, -bak′əl) *n.* **1.** sudden and complete downfall or collapse; rout; ruin. **2.** breaking up of ice in a river. **3.** sudden, violent rush of water. [French *débâcle* collapse, from *débâcler* to unbar, free, going back to Latin *dis-* un-² + *baculum* stick.]

de·bar (di bär′) *v.t.* **-barred, -bar·ring.** **1.** to shut out; exclude; bar. **2.** to prohibit; prevent. [French *débarrer* to unbar, from *de-* un-² (from Latin *dis-*) + *barrer* to bar, from Old French *barre* rod. See BAR.] **—de·bar′ment,** *n.*

de·bark (di bärk′) *v.t.* to bring to land or unload from a ship or airplane. —*v.i.* to land; disembark. [French *débarquer* to land, from *dé-* away (from Latin *dis-*) + *barque* ship. See BARK³.] **—de·bar·ka·tion** (dē′bär kā′shən), *n.*

de·base (di bās′) **-based, -bas·ing.** *v.t.* to lower in quality, value, or character; adulterate: *to debase coinage, to debase oneself by lying.* [DE- + BASE².] **—de·base′ment, de·bas′er,** *n.*

de·bat·a·ble (di bā′tə bəl) *adj.* open to discussion or dispute; capable of being debated; questionable; moot.

de·bate (di bāt′) *n.* **1.** discussion or argument; dispute: *There was much debate concerning his statement.* **2.** formal discussion of the arguments for and against a question or issue, esp. a public contest in which two people or teams argue opposite sides of a given topic. —*v.t.* **-bat·ed, -bat·ing.** **1.** to argue about or discuss, as at a public meeting. **2.** to deliberate upon; consider. **3.** to discuss or dispute in a formal debate. —*v.i.* **1.** to discuss or argue a matter by giving opposing viewpoints. **2.** to deliberate; consider. **3.** to participate in a formal debate. [Old French *debatre* to argue, fight, going back to Latin *dē-* down + *battuere* to beat.] **—Syn.** *v.t.* **1.** see *discuss.*

de·bauch (di bôch′) *v.t.* to lead away from morality; pervert; deprave. —*v.i.* to indulge in debauchery; dissipate. —*n.* **1.** debauchery. **2.** act or instance of debauching. [Old French *desbaucher* to lead away from; literally, to roughhew (timber for a beam), from *des-* (from Latin *dis-* away from) + *bauch* beam (of Germanic origin).] **—de·bauch′er,** *n.* **de·bauch′ment,** *n.*

deb·au·chee (deb′ô chē′, -shē′) *n.* one who indulges in debauchery; lewd or depraved person.

de·bauch·er·y (di bô′chər ē) *pl.,* **-er·ies.** *n.* excessive indulgence in sensual pleasures.

de·ben·ture (di ben′chər) *n.* bond backed only by the assets and credit of the issuer. [Latin *dēbentur* there are owing, from *dēbēre* to owe; probably at one time the first word of documents concerning debt.]

de·bil·i·tate (di bil′ə tāt′) **-tat·ed, -tat·ing.** *v.t.* to impair the strength of; weaken: *Disease debilitated him.* [Latin *dēbilitātus,* past participle of *dēbilitāre* to weaken.] **—de·bil′i·ta′tion,** *n.*

de·bil·i·ty (di bil′ə tē) *pl.,* **-ties.** *n.* lack of strength or vigor; feebleness. [Old French *debilite,* from Latin *dēbilitās.*]

deb·it (deb′it) *n.* **1.** entry of a debt in an account. **2.** item entered in an account as a debt. **3. debits,** sum total of such entries. **4.** left-hand side or column of an account where such entries are recorded. —*v.t.* **1.** to enter (a debt) in an account. **2.** to charge with a debt: *to debit an account with $300.00.* [Latin *dēbitum* debt, what is owing, from *dēbēre* to owe. Doublet of DEBT.]

deb·o·nair (deb′ə nār′) *also,* **de·bo·naire.** *adj.* **1.** urbane; courteous. **2.** light-hearted; gay; cheerful. [Old French *debonaire* genial, from *de bon aire* of good stock or disposition, going back to Latin *dē* of + *bonus* good + *ārea* open space.] **—deb′o·nair′ly,** *adv.* **—deb′o·nair′ness,** *n.*

Deb·o·rah (deb′ər ə) *n.* in the Old Testament, a Jewish prophetess and judge who rallied the Israelites against the Canaanites.

de·bouch (di boosh′, -bouch′) *v.i.* **1.** to march out from a narrow or confined area into the open, as a body of soldiers. **2.** to come forth or emerge from; issue. —*v.t.* to cause to come forth or emerge. —*n.* opening, esp. in military fortifications, for the passage of troops. [French *déboucher* to emerge; literally, to come out of the mouth, going back to Latin *dis-* away + *bucca* mouth.]

de·bouch·ment (di boosh′mənt, -bouch′-) *n.* **1.** act or process of debouching. **2.** mouth or outlet, as of a river.

de·brief (dē′brēf′) *v.t.* to question or instruct a person, as a pilot or astronaut, at the end of a mission or term of service. **—de′brief′ing,** *n.*

de·bris (də brē′, dā′brē) *also,* **dé·bris.** *n.* **1.** scattered remains, as of something broken or destroyed; rubbish. **2.** accumulation of rock fragments: *The landslide left massive debris.* [French *débris* rubbish, from Old French *debrisier* to shatter, from *de-* down (from Latin *dē*) + *brisier* to break (of Celtic origin).]

De Bro·glie, Louis Victor (də brô′yə) 1892—, French physicist.

Debs, Eugene Victor (debz) 1855–1926, U.S. socialist and labor leader.

debt (det) *n.* **1.** something that is owed to another: *a debt of $1000.* **2.** liability or obligation to pay or render something to another. **3.** state or condition of owing or being obligated: *to be in debt, to get out of debt.* **4.** sin; trespass. [Old French *dete* what is owing, from Latin *dēbitum,* from *dēbēre* to owe. Doublet of DEBIT.]

debt of honor, debt that is not legally enforceable, depending for its payment on the honor of the debtor, as in gambling.

debt·or (det′ər) *n.* one who owes something to another.

de·bunk (di bungk′) *v.t. Informal.* to expose or ridicule as false, pretentious, or exaggerated: *to debunk the claims made in an advertisement.* [DE- + BUNK².]

De·bus·sy, Claude (deb′yoo sē′, dāb′-; klôd) 1862–1918, French composer.

de·but (dā bū′, di-, dā′bū) *also,* **dé·but.** *n.* **1.** first public appearance, as of a performer on stage. **2.** formal introduction of a young lady into society. **3.** beginning, as of a career or course of action. [French *début* a first play (in a game), first appearance, from *débuter* to play first, make one's début, from *dé-* from (from Latin *dis-* apart) + *but* aim (of Germanic origin).]

deb·u·tante (deb′yoo tänt′, -yə-) *also,* **dé·bu·tante.** *n.* young lady who is making her formal entrance into society.

dec. **1.** deceased. **2.** decimeter. **3.** declaration. **4.** decrease.

Dec., December.

deca- *also,* **dec-.** *combining form for: decagon.* [Greek *deka.*]

dec·ade (dek′ād) *n.* **1.** period of ten years. **2.** group, series, or set of ten. [French *décade,* from Late Latin *decas,* from Greek *dekas* group of ten, from *deka* ten.]

dec·a·dence (dek′ə dəns) *n.* **1.** process of decay; deterioration: *the gradual decadence of an empire.* **2.** period or condition of decline, as in morals, art, or literature. [French *décadence* decay, from Medieval Latin *decadentia,* going back to Latin *dē* away + *cadere* to fall (in the sense of falling away from what is good).]

dec·a·dent (dek′ə dənt) *adj.* **1.** characterized by or undergoing deterioration. **2.** of or relating to the decadents. —*n.* **1.** one who is decadent. **2.** any of a group of French and English writers of the late nineteenth century whose work reflected a morbid outlook on life and an extreme concern with purity of style and form. **—dec′a·dent·ly,** *adv.*

dec·a·gon (dek′ə gon′) *n.* plane figure having ten sides and ten angles. [Modern Latin *decagonum,* from Greek *dekagônon,* from *deka* ten + *gônia* corner, angle.]

Regular decagon

Concave decagon

Decagons

dec·a·gram (dek′ə gram′) *also,* **dec·a·gramme, dek·a·gram.** *n.* metric unit of weight, equal to 10 grams. [French *décagramme,* going back to Greek *deka* ten + *gramma* small weight.]

dec·a·he·dron (dek′ə hē′drən) *pl.,* **-drons** or **-dra**

at; āpe; cär; end; mē; it; īce; hot; ōld; fôrk; wood; fōōl; oil; out; up; ūse; turn; sing; thin; this; zh in treasure; ə in ago, taken, pencil, lemon, circus.

(-drə). *n.* solid figure bounded by ten plane surfaces. [DECA- + Greek *hedra* base[1], seat.]

de·cal (dē′kal, di kal′) *n.* design or picure prepared for transfer by the process of decalcomania.

de·cal·co·ma·ni·a (di kal′kə mā′nē ə) *n.* **1.** art or process of transferring designs or pictures from specially treated paper to glass, wood, or other surfaces. **2.** decal. [French *décalcomanie,* from *décalquer* to transfer a tracing (going back to Latin *dē* from, off + *calcāre* to trample) + *manie* craze (from Latin *mania* madness).]

dec·a·li·ter (dek′ə lē′tər), *also,* **dec·a·li·tre, dek·a·li·ter.** *n.* metric measure of volume, equal to 10 liters. See **weights and measures** for table. [French *décalitre,* from Greek *deka* ten + *lītrā* pound[1].]

Dec·a·logue (dek′ə lôg′, -log′) *also,* **Dec·a·log.** *n.* in the Bible, the Ten Commandments. [Late Latin *decalogus,* from Greek *dekalogos,* from *deka* ten + *logos* speech, word.]

dec·a·me·ter (dek′ə mē′tər) *also,* **dec·a·me·tre, dek·a·me·tre.** *n.* metric measure of length, equal to 10 meters. See **weights and measures** for table. [French *décamètre,* from Greek *deka* ten + *metron* measure.]

de·camp (di kamp′) *v.i.* **1.** to leave an encampment; break camp. **2.** to depart quickly or secretly; run away. [French *décamper* to make off; literally, to leave the field, going back to Latin *dis-* away + *campus* field.] —**de·camp′ment,** *n.*

dec·a·nal (dek′ən əl, di kān′əl) *adj.* of or relating to a dean or deanery [Late Latin *decānus* dean + -AL[1]. See DEAN.]

de·cant (di kant′) *v.t.* **1.** to pour off (a liquid) gently without disturbing the sediment: *to decant wine.* **2.** to pour from one container to another. [Medieval Latin *decanthare* to pour out, from *de* down + *canthus* edge of a jug, going back to Greek *kanthos* corner of the eye.]

de·cant·er (di kan′tər) *n.* decorative bottle with a stopper.

de·cap·i·tate (di kap′ə tāt′) **-tat·ed, -tat·ing.** *v.t.* to cut off the head of; behead. [Late Latin *dēcapitātus,* past participle of *dēcapitāre,* from Latin *dē* off + *caput* head.] —**de·cap′i·ta′tion,** *n.*

dec·a·pod (dek′ə pod′) *n.* **1.** any crustacean, order Decapoda, having ten legs or arms, as a lobster or crab. **2.** any mollusk, order Decapoda, having ten arms or tentacles, as a squid or cuttlefish. —*adj.* having ten legs or arms. [Modern Latin *Decapoda,* from Greek *deka* ten + *pod-,* stem of *pous* foot.]

dec·a·syl·la·ble (dek′ə sil′ə bəl) *n.* line of verse having ten syllables. —**dec′a·syl·lab′ic,** *adj.*

de·cath·lon (di kath′lon) *n.* athletic contest consisting of ten different track and field events. The contestant scoring the highest total points for all events is the winner. [DECA- + Greek *athlon* contest.]

De·ca·tur (də kā′tər) *n.* **1.** Stephen. 1779–1820, U.S. naval officer. **2.** city in central Illinois. Pop. (1970), 90,397.

de·cay (di kā′) *v.i.* **1.** destructive decomposition, as of organic tissue; rot: *bacterial decay, tooth decay.* **2.** gradual deterioration, as in strength or quality: *a decay in health, the decay of an empire.* **3.** product of decay. **4.** spontaneous transformation of an atomic nucleus of a radioactive element into another isotope of the same element or into a nucleus of a different element. —*v.i.* **1.** to rot; decompose. **2.** to undergo a gradual loss, as in quality or strength. **3.** *Physics.* to undergo decay. —*v.t.* to cause to decay. [Dialectal Old French *decair* to fall off, decline, going back to Latin *dē* away + *cadere* to fall.]

Syn. *v.t.* **1.** Decay, decompose, disintegrate, putrefy mean to break down from a sound to an unsound state. **Decay** suggests a gradual change for the worse: *His teeth have begun to decay.* **Decompose** stresses a separation into elemental parts, a change from a complex to a simpler state: *The bones are the last part of the body to decompose after death.* **Disintegrate** suggests a breaking up so that the object loses its unity: *The pavement disintegrated under the force of the drill.* **Putrefy** emphasizes the disagreeable effect on the senses of something that is decomposing: *In gangrene, the flesh putrefies and sloughs off.*

Dec·can (dek′ən) *n.* **1.** plateau region occupying most of the peninsula of India. Also, **Deccan Plateau. 2.** peninsula that constitutes the southern part of India.

de·cease (di sēs′) *n.* death. —*v.i.* **-ceased, -ceas·ing.** to die. [Old French *deces* death, from Latin *dēcessus* departure, death.]

de·ceased (di sēst′) *adj.* dead. —*n.* **the deceased.** dead person or persons.

de·ce·dent (di sēd′ənt) *n. Law.* deceased person. [Latin *dēcēdēns,* present participle of *dēcēdere* to depart, die.]

de·ceit (di sēt′) *n.* **1.** act or practice of concealing or misrepresenting the truth; lying. **2.** device intended to deceive; artifice; trick. **3.** quality of being deceitful; deception. [Old French *deceite* act of deceiving, deception, from *decevoir* to deceive. See DECEIVE.]

Syn. 1. Deceit, deception, guile mean deliberate misrepresentation of facts or truth. **Deceit** implies habitual repetition of intentional distortion of the truth: *He came to believe that deceit was the only road to business success.* **Deception** is used of a deed that distorts the fact, but it is not necessarily habitual nor is it necessarily dishonest: *A magician must be skilled in the use of deception.* **Guile** implies subtle treachery and wily

dishonesty: *His promotions were obtained by guile rather than by merit.*

de·ceit·ful (di sēt′fəl) *adj.* **1.** given to deceiving; lying: *a deceitful person.* **2.** tending to deceive; false: *a deceitful act.* —**de·ceit′ful·ly,** *adv.* —**de·ceit′ful·ness,** *n.*

de·ceive (di sēv′) **-ceived, -ceiv·ing.** *v.t.* to make (someone) believe that which is false; mislead; delude. —*v.i.* to use deceit. [Old French *deceivr,* from Latin *dēcipere.*] —**de·ceiv′er,** *n.* —**de·ceiv′ing·ly,** *adv.*

de·cel·er·ate (dē sel′ə rāt′) **-at·ed, -at·ing.** *v.t., v.i.* to decrease the speed (of); slow down. [DE- + (AC)CELERATE.] —**de·cel′er·a′tion,** **de·cel′er·a′tor,** *n.*

De·cem·ber (di sem′bər) *n.* the twelfth and last month of the year, containing thirty-one days. [Latin *December* name of the tenth month in the early Roman calender (in which March was the first month), from *decem* ten.]

de·cem·vir (di sem′vər) *pl.,* **-virs** or **-vi·ri** (-və rī′). *n.* **1.** in ancient Rome, member of either of two councils of ten men, one elected in 451 B.C., the other in 450 B.C., whose duties were to codify and publish the laws. **2.** member of any council of ten men. [Latin *decemvir* one of ten men, going back to *decem* ten + *vir* man.]

de·cem·vi·rate (di sem′vər it, -və rāt′) *n.* **1.** authoritative body of ten men. **2.** government by decemvirs.

de·cen·cy (dē′sən sē) *pl.,* **-cies.** *n.* **1.** conformity to standards of propriety or good taste, as in speech, behavior, or dress: *He had the decency to admit his error.* **2.** decencies. **a.** socially accepted or proper acts or observances. **b.** requirements for a respectable or comfortable manner of living.

de·cen·ni·al (di sen′ē əl) *adj.* **1.** of or continuing for ten years. **2.** occurring every ten years. —*n.* a tenth anniversary or its celebration. [Latin *decennium* period of ten years + -AL[1].]

de·cen·ni·um (di sen′ē əm) *pl.,* **-cen·ni·ums** or **-cen·ni·a** (-sen′ē ə). *n.* period of ten years; decade. [Latin *decennium,* going back to Latin *decem* ten + *annus* year.]

de·cent (dē′sənt) *adj.* **1.** conforming to or satisfying approved standards of society, as in moral character or social conduct; respectable: *a decent family.* **2.** in accordance with standards of good taste; proper: *It is not decent to pry into other people's business.* **3.** not obscene; modest; chaste: *decent language.* **4.** kind; generous: *It was very decent of you to help me.* **5.** fairly good; passable; satisfactory: *a decent salary.* He did a decent job. **6.** *Informal.* adequately clothed; dressed: *Before entering, they knocked and asked, "Are you decent?"* [Latin *decēns,* present participle of *decēre* to be fitting.] —**de′cent·ly,** *adv.* —**de′cent·ness,** *n.*

de·cen·tral·ize (dē sen′trə līz′) **-ized, -iz·ing.** *v.t.* to redistribute most of the centralized power, authority, or production, as of a government or industry, by transfer to smaller units: *to decentralize a school system.* —*v.i.* to be or become decentralized. **3.** not obscene; modest; —**de·cen′tral·i·za′tion,** *n.*

de·cep·tion (di sep′shən) *n.* **1.** act of deceiving; being deceived. **2.** that which deceives or is intended to deceive; trick. [Late Latin *dēceptiō* a deceiving, from Latin *dēcipere* to deceive.] —**Syn. 1.** see **deceit.**

de·cep·tive (di sep′tiv) *adj.* characterized by or having the power or tendency to deceive. —**de·cep′tive·ly,** *adv.* —**de·cep′tive·ness,** *n.* —**Syn.** see **misleading.**

deci- *combining form* one tenth of: *deciliter, decimeter.* [Latin *decimus* tenth, from *decem* ten.]

dec·i·bel (des′ə bel′, -bəl) *n.* unit for measuring the intensity of sound. [DECI- + BEL.]

de·cide (di sīd′) **-cid·ed, -cid·ing.** *v.i.* **1.** to make up one's mind; resolve: *We decided to take the bus.* **2.** to make a judgment; come to a conclusion: *The judge decided in favor of the plaintiff.* —*v.t.* **1.** to determine or settle, as a dispute or question: *I will decide who goes first.* **2.** to determine the result (of): *The last touchdown decided the game.* **3.** to cause (someone) to come to a decision: *What decided you?* [Latin *dēcīdere* to cut off, determine.]

Syn. *v.t.* Decide, determine, resolve, settle[1] mean to reach a decision. **Decide** suggests consideration of a matter for a time, with further doubt or vacillation ended by making one's judgment: *They decided to buy the smaller car.* **Determine** implies a firm decision, not only unshakable but clear in its essential details: *The engineers determined the route the road must follow over the mountains.* **Resolve** suggests making up one's mind on a course of action, either positive or negative: *She resolved to stay within the budget.* **Settle** stresses the end of vacillation either by reaching a decision or by having one imposed: *The judge told them to settle the claim between themselves.*

de·cid·ed (di sī′did) *adj.* **1.** definite; unquestioned: *a decided advantage, a decided improvement in her grades.* **2.** determined; resolute; unwavering: *to speak in a decided tone of voice.* —**de·cid′ed·ly,** *adv.* —**de·cid′ed·ness,** *n.*

de·cid·u·ous (di sij′ōō əs) *adj.* **1.** (of trees, shrubs, and other plants) shedding leaves annually. Distinguished from **evergreen. 2.** falling off

ăt; āpe; cär; end; mē; it; īce; hot; ōld; fôrk; wood; fōōl; oil; out; up; ūse; turn; sing; thin; this; zh in treasure; ə in ago, taken, pencil, lemon, circus.

261

or shed at a particular season or stage of growth: *deciduous petals, deciduous antlers.* **3.** not permanent or enduring; transitory. [Latin *dēciduus* falling down.]

dec·i·gram (des′ə gram′) *also,* **dec·i·gramme.** *n.* metric unit of weight, equal to one tenth of a gram. [French *décigramme,* from Latin *decimus* tenth + Greek *gramma* small weight.]

dec·i·li·ter (des′ə lē′tər) *also,* **dec·i·li·tre.** *n.* metric measure of volume, equal to one tenth of a liter. [French *décilitre,* from Latin *decimus* tenth + Greek *lítrā* pound¹.]

de·cil·lion (di sil′yən) *n.* **1.** in the United States and France, the cardinal number that is represented by 1 followed by 33 zeros. **2.** in Great Britain and Germany, the cardinal number that is represented by 1 followed by 60 zeros. [Latin *decem* ten + (M)ILLION.] —**de·cil′lionth,** *adj., n.*

dec·i·mal (des′ə məl) *adj.* relating to or based on the number 10; proceeding by tens. —*n.* decimal fraction. [Latin *decimus* tenth (from *decem* ten) + -AL¹.]

decimal fraction, fraction whose denominator is equal to ten or a power of ten. The fractions ⁵/₁₀ and ⁷⁵/₁₀₀ expressed as decimal fractions are .5 and .75.

decimal point, period placed before a decimal fraction, which indicates, by the number of figures following it, the size of the denominator.

decimal system, system of computation having the number 10 as its base.

dec·i·mate (des′ə māt′) **-mat·ed, -mat·ing.** *v.t.* **1.** to destroy or kill a large number or proportion of: *The final battle decimated the enemy's ranks.* **2.** to select by lot and execute one out of every ten of. **3.** to destroy a tenth part of. [Latin *decimātus,* past participle of *decimāre* to take by lot every tenth man for punishment. In ancient Rome an army revolt was punished by taking every tenth soldier and executing him.] —**dec′i·ma′tion, dec′i·ma′tor,** *n.*

dec·i·me·ter (des′ə mē′tər) *also,* **dec·i·me·tre.** *n.* metric measure of length, equal to one tenth of a meter. [French *décimètre,* from Latin *decimus* tenth + Greek *metron* measure.]

de·ci·pher (di sī′fər) *v.t.* **1.** to make out the meaning of (something illegible, obscure, or difficult to understand): *to decipher messy handwriting, to decipher a riddle.* **2.** to interpret or translate (something written in code) by using a key; decode: *to decipher a message.* [DE- + CIPHER.] —**de·ci′pher·a·ble,** *adj.* —**de·ci′pher·er, de·ci′pher·ment,** *n.*

de·ci·sion (di sizh′ən) *n.* **1.** act of making up one's mind: *He hesitated because of the difficulty of the decision.* **2.** act of deciding something, as a controversy or question, by reaching a conclusion or making a judgment: *The decision will be left to the court.* **3.** judgment or conclusion reached or given as a result of deciding: *The umpire's decision was final. What is your decision?* **4.** quality of being decided; firmness; determination: *a man of decision.* **5.** in boxing, a victory determined by points instead of by a knockout or a technical knockout. [Latin *dēcīsiō* a cutting down, settlement.] —**Syn. 3.** see **verdict.**

de·ci·sive (di sī′siv) *adj.* **1.** settling controversy or uncertainty; conclusive: *a decisive victory.* **2.** characterized by decision; resolute: *a decisive man.* —**de·ci′sive·ly,** *adv.* —**de·ci′sive·ness,** *n.*

deck (dek) *n.* **1. a.** platform or other horizontal surface serving as the floor in a boat or ship. **b.** space between any two such surfaces, or an uncovered area, as on an upper deck, constituting one of the levels of a ship. **2.** any similar horizontal surface. **3.** complete set of playing cards, usually fifty-two. **4. on deck.** *Informal.* **a.** on hand and ready for action. **b.** ready and waiting for one's turn: *The next batter was on deck.* **5. to clear the deck** (or **decks**). to remove obstacles or impediments in preparation for action, as combat. **6. to hit the deck.** *Slang.* **a.** to fall into a prone position. **b.** to get out of bed. **c.** to get ready for action. —*v.t.* **1.** to dress or adorn; ornament: *to deck the halls with holly.* **2.** to provide with a deck. **3.** *Slang.* to knock down. [Middle Dutch *dec* roof, covering.]

-decker combining form having one or more decks, layers, floors, or levels: *a double-decker bus, a triple-decker sandwich.*

deck hand, sailor who performs general tasks either above or below deck.

deck·house (dek′hous′) *n.* cabin or room built on the upper deck of a ship.

deck·le (dek′əl) *n.* **1.** in papermaking, a wooden frame which forms paper size by confining the pulp within specified limits. **2.** deckle edge. [German *Deckel,* diminutive of *Decke* cover.]

deck·le-edged (dek′əl ejd′) *adj.* having a deckle edge.

deckle edge, rough, raw edge of paper, esp. that made with a deckle.

de·claim (di klām′) *v.i.* **1.** to speak or recite publicly; give an oration. **2.** to speak in a loud, rhetorical manner. **3.** to make an impassioned verbal attack; inveigh: *to declaim against political corruption.* —*v.t.* to utter or recite loudly and rhetorically. [Latin *dēclāmāre* to cry aloud, deliver a speech.] —**de·claim′er,** *n.*

dec·la·ma·tion (dek′lə mā′shən) *n.* **1.** act of declaiming. **2.** art of

speaking or reciting publicly; public speaking. **3.** formal, prepared public speech or recitation. **4.** loud, emotional talk; harangue.

de·clam·a·to·ry (di klam′ə tôr′ē) *adj.* **1.** of or relating to declamation. **2.** loud and rhetorical.

dec·la·ra·tion (dek′lə rā′shən) *n.* **1.** act of declaring. **2.** that which is declared; announcement. **3.** formal statement, or a document containing such a statement: *a declaration of war.* **4.** statement of goods liable to taxation, or a document containing such a statement. **5.** in bridge, a contract.

Declaration of Independence, document declaring the thirteen American colonies independent of Great Britain, written chiefly by Thomas Jefferson and adopted on July 4, 1776, by the Continental Congress.

de·clar·a·tive (di klar′ə tiv) *adj.* making a statement or affirmation: *a declarative sentence.* Also, **de·clar·a·to·ry** (di klar′ə tôr′ē).

de·clare (di klār′) **-clared, -clar·ing.** *v.t.* **1.** to make known publicly or formally; announce; proclaim: *the legislature declared a new state holiday.* **2.** to state emphatically; assert. **3.** to make a full statement or account of, as goods for taxation. **4.** to disclose or prove. **5.** in bridge, to make (the final bid); announce (the contract). —*v.i.* to announce, as an opinion or choice: *The newspaper declared for the Republican candidate.* [Latin *dēclārāre* to make clear, going back to *dē* thoroughly + *clārus* clear.] —**de·clar′er,** *n.*

Syn. *v.t.* **2. Declare, proclaim, announce** signify to make known publicly. **Declare** is to make known explicitly, often something of great importance or significance: *Congress has the power to declare war.* **Proclaim** is to make known officially to a widespread audience something of great importance or significance: *The president proclaimed a state of emergency.* **Announce** is to make known something of general or special interest, often something previously unknown: *The magazine announced the winners of its photography contest.*

de·clas·si·fy (dē klas′ə fī′) **-fied, -fy·ing.** *v.t.* to remove from a secret or restricted classification, as government documents.

de·clen·sion (di klen′shən) *n.* **1.** inflection of nouns, pronouns, and adjectives with regard to case, gender, and number. **2.** class of words whose inflections are the same. **3.** downward slope or bend; descent. **4.** sinking into a lower or inferior condition; deterioration. [Old French *declinaison* grammatical declension, decline, from Latin *dēclīnātiō* turning aside, inflection.]

de·clin·a·ble (di klī′nə bəl) *adj.* capable of being declined grammatically.

dec·li·na·tion (dek′lə nā′shən) *n.* **1.** leaning, bending, or sloping downward; inclination. **2.** angular difference between the direction in which a magnetic compass points and the direction of the true North Pole. Also, **magnetic declination.** **3.** angular distance, as of a star or planet, from the celestial equator in a system of coordinates used to state the position of celestial objects. It is similar to geographic latitude. **4.** polite refusal.

North celestial pole

Star

Declination

Earth

Celestial equator

South celestial pole

Declination

de·cline (di klīn′) **-clined, -clin·ing.** *v.t.* **1.** to refuse politely: *to decline an invitation.* **2.** to give the inflected forms of (a noun, pronoun, or adjective). **3.** to cause to bend or slope downward; incline. —*v.i.* **1.** to refuse politely. **2.** to fall into an inferior or impaired condition; weaken: *His health was declining. The nation declined as a world power.* **3.** to fall or become less: *Prices on the stock market declined.* **4.** to bend or slope downward or aside. **5.** to draw to a close or end; wane: *The day declined.* **6.** to stoop, as to an unworthy object; condescend. —*n.* **1.** decrease, as in influence, strength, value, or amount: *the decline of the nobility, a decline in population. The decline in the nation's influence abroad was evident.* **2.** a falling; sinking. **3.** downward bend or slope. **4.** period during which something is drawing to a close or weakening: *He was approaching the decline of his life.* [Old French *decliner* to bend down, incline, reject grammatically, from Latin *dēclīnāre.*] —**Syn.** *v.t.* **1.** see **refuse¹.**

de·cliv·i·ty (di kliv′ə tē) *pl.* **-ties.** *n.* downward slope. Opposed to **acclivity.** [Latin *dēclīvitās* sloping place.]

de·coct (di kokt′) *v.t.* to extract the essence or flavor of by boiling, usually in water. [Latin *dēcoctus,* past participle of *dēcoquere* to boil down.]

de·coc·tion (di kok′shən) *n.* **1.** act or process of boiling something, usually in water, to extract the soluble properties. **2.** extract obtained by such a process.

de·code (dē kōd′) **-cod·ed, -cod·ing.** *v.t.* to convert from code into ordinary language by using a key: *to decode a secret message.* —**de·cod′er,** *n.*

at; āpe; cär; end; mē; it; īce; hot; ōld; fôrk; wood; fo͞ol; oil; out; up; ūse; turn; sing; thin; this; zh in treasure; ə in ago, taken, pencil, lemon, circus.

dé·colle·tage (dā′kol täzh′, -kol ə-) *n.* low-cut neckline, as of a dress or blouse.

dé·colle·té (dā′kol tā′, -kol ə-) *adj.* **1.** having a low-cut neckline. **2.** having the neck and shoulders exposed; wearing a low-necked garment. [French *décolleté*, past participle of *décolleter* to uncover the neck and shoulders, going back to Latin *dē* away + *collum* neck.]

de·col·or·ize (dē kul′ə rīz′) *v.t.* to deprive of color; bleach. —**de·col′or·i·za′tion,** **de·col′or·iz′er,** *n.*

de·com·pose (dē′dəm pōz′) -posed, -pos·ing. *v.t., v.i.* **1.** to putrefy; rot. **2.** to separate into constituent parts or elements. —**de·com·po·si·tion** (dē′kom pə zish′ən), *n.* —**Syn. 1.** see decay.

de·com·press (dē′kəm pres′) *v.t.* to cause to undergo decompression.

de·com·pres·sion (dē′kəm presh′ən) *n.* reduction or removal of pressure, esp. of high atmospheric pressure on the human body.

decompression chamber, chamber of special construction in which pressure on the body is gradually reduced, esp. one used to treat bends by slowly bringing a person back to normal atmospheric pressure.

de·con·tam·i·nate (dē′kən tam′ə nāt′) -nat·ed, -nat·ing. *v.t.* **1.** to rid of contamination. **2.** to make (a contaminated area or object) safe by removing harmful materials, as poison gas, bacteria, or radioactive wastes. —**de·con·tam′i·na′tion,** *n.*

de·con·trol (dē′kən trōl′) -trolled, -trol·ling. *v.t.* to remove controls from, esp. government controls: *to decontrol housing.* —*n.* removal of controls.

de·cor (dā kôr′) *also,* **dé·cor.** *n.* **1.** decorative scheme and style, as of a room. **2.** scenery, as in a theatrical or television presentation. [French *décor,* from *décorer* to adorn, from Latin *decorāre.*]

dec·o·rate (dek′ə rāt′) -rat·ed, -rat·ing. *v.t.* **1.** to furnish with ornaments; adorn; embellish: *We decorated the Christmas tree.* **2.** to plan and execute the scheme, style, and design of (a room or rooms), as by selecting and arranging furnishings, choosing fabrics, paint, or wallpaper, or adding ornamentation. **3.** to confer honor upon, as with a medal: *to decorate a soldier for valor.* [Latin *decorātus,* past participle of *decorāre* to adorn.]

Syn. 1. Decorate, adorn, beautify mean to make something more appealing to the senses by adding to it. **Decorate** suggests additions that add aesthetic interest: *Adding brightly colored accessories decorates a room with dark upholstered furniture.* **Adorn** implies beauty in the thing added: *That necklace would adorn the neck of even the most beautiful woman.* **Beautify** suggests simply that something adds beauty to or underscores the beauty of what it is joined to: *An attempt was made to beautify the streets by planting trees at the curb.*

dec·o·ra·tion (dek′ə rā′shən) *n.* **1.** act or process of decorating. **2.** something to decorate; ornament; adornment. **3.** mark of honor, as a medal or ribbon.

Decoration Day, Memorial Day.

dec·o·ra·tive (dek′ər ə tiv, -ə rā′tiv) *adj.* relating, tending, or serving to decorate; ornamental. —**dec′o·ra·tive·ly,** *adv.* —**dec′o·ra·tive·ness,** *n.*

dec·o·ra·tor (dek′ə rā′tər) *n.* one who decorates, esp. an interior decorator.

dec·o·rous (dek′ər əs, di kôr′əs) *adj.* characterized by decorum; proper; suitable. [Latin *decōrus.*] —**dec′o·rous·ness,** *n.*

de·co·rum (di kôr′əm) *n.* **1.** conformity to the approved standards of good taste; propriety, as in behavior or speech. **2.** *also,* **decorums.** proprieties. [Latin *decōrum* that which is seemly.]

de·cou·page (dā′kōō päzh′) *also,* **dé·cou·page.** *n.* **1.** art or technique of decorating objects or surfaces, usually with paper cutouts. **2.** work produced by this technique. [French *découpage* a cutting out, from *découper* to cut out; literally, to divide by a blow, going back to Latin *dē* away + *colaphus* blow¹ (from Greek *kolaphos*).]

de·coy (*v.,* di koi′; *n.,* dē′koi′, di koi′) *n.* **1.** artificial bird used to lure birds into a trap or within gunshot range. **2.** one who or that which lures, as into danger or deception: *She was used as a decoy to trap the murderer.* **3.** trick; deception: *The phone call was a decoy.* —*v.t.* **1.** to lure (wildfowl or other animals) into a trap or within gunshot range. **2.** to lure by or as by a decoy. —*v.i.* to become lured by or as by a decoy. [Dutch *de kooi* literally, the cage, from *de* the + *kooi* (from Latin *cavea*).]

de·crease (*v.,* di krēs′; *n.,* dē′krēs, di krēs′) -creased, -creas·ing. *v.i.* **1.** to become less; diminish; abate: *The number of traffic accidents decreased last year.* —*v.t.* to cause to become less; reduce: *to decrease speed, to decrease crime.* —*n.* **1.** act or process of decreasing; lessening. **2.** amount by which something decreases or is decreased. [Anglo-Norman *decreiss-,* a stem of *decreistre* to grow less, going back to Latin *dēcrēscere.*] —**de·creas′ing·ly,** *adv.*

Syn. v.i. Decrease, diminish, dwindle, abate mean to become less. **Decrease** suggests a gradual shrinking or decline: *The percentage of those voting continued to decrease.* **Diminish** implies a tangible or visible reduction in size, as by removal of a part: *The supply of food was greatly diminished.* **Dwindle** suggests a perceptible reduction in size or magnitude, with an implied vanishing point: *The crowd of supporters dwindled when they realized their candidate had lost.* **Abate** suggests a moderation of something burdensome or beyond normal, esp. violence: *The outbreaks of rioting have begun to abate.*

de·cree (di krē′) *n.* **1.** *Law.* decision or order issued by a court: *a divorce decree.* **2.** official decision or order; edict. —*v.t.* **-creed, -cree·ing.** to order, decide, or appoint by decree. —*v.i.* to issue a decree. [Old French *decree, decret* decision, ordinance, from Latin *dēcrētum,* from *dēcernere* to decide.] —**Syn. 2.** see verdict.

dec·re·ment (dek′rə mənt) *n.* **1.** act or process of decreasing. **2.** amount lost by decrease. **3.** *Mathematics.* amount by which the value of a variable decreases. [Latin *dēcrēmentum* decrease.]

de·crep·it (di krep′it) *adj.* broken down or enfeebled by old age or overuse. [Latin *dēcrepitus* literally, making no noise (in the sense of "moving about quietly like an old person"), from *dē* away + *crepitus,* past participle of *crepare* to make noise.] —**de·crep′it·ly,** *adv.*

de·crep·i·tude (di krep′ə tōōd′, -tūd′) *n.* decrepit state or condition; feebleness, as from old age.

decresc., decrescendo.

de·cre·scen·do (dē′krə shen′dō, dā-) *pl.* **-dos.** *Music. n.* **1.** gradual decrease in loudness or force; diminuendo. **2.** passage in which this occurs. —*adj., adv.* with a gradual decrease in loudness or force. [Italian *decrescendo* decreasing, from *decrescere* to decrease, from Latin *dēcrēscere.*]

de·cre·tal (di krēt′əl) *n.* **1.** papal decree or letter determining some question of ecclesiastical law, esp. a papal response to an appeal. **2. Decretals.** collection of such decrees or letters, forming part of the canon laws. —*adj.* of, relating to, or containing a decree. [Medieval Latin *decretale* decree, from Late Latin *dēcrētālis* relating to a decree, from Latin *dēcrētum* decree.]

de·cri·al (di krī′əl) *n.* act of decrying; condemnation.

de·crim·i·na·lize (dē krim′ə nə līz′) -lized, -liz·ing. *v.t.* to make legal or lawful: *to decriminalize the use or possession of marijuana.* —**de·crim′i·na·li·za′tion,** *n.*

de·cry (di krī′) -cried, -cry·ing. *v.t.* **1.** to denounce or disparage openly; condemn publicly: *The defendant's lawyer decried capital punishment.* **2.** to depreciate officially: *The government decried the foreign coins.* [Old French *descrier* to cry down, disparage, going back to Latin *dis-* un-² + *quirītāre* to cry out.] —**Syn. 1.** see disparage.

de·cum·bent (di kum′bənt) *adj.* **1.** (of stems or branches) lying or trailing on the ground with the end tending to climb. **2.** lying down. [Latin *dēcumbēns,* present participle of *dēcumbere* to lie down.]

de·cur·rent (di kur′ənt) *adj.* extending down and growing along the stem, as the base of certain leaves. [Latin *dēcurrēns,* present participle of *dēcurrere* to run down.]

dec·us·sate (*v.,* dek′ə sāt′, di kus′āt; *adj.,* dek′ə sāt′, di kus′it) -sat·ed, -sat·ing. *v.t., v.i.* to cross or cut in the form of an X. —*adj.* **1.** having the form of an X. **2.** (of leaves or branches) arranged in pairs, each of which is at right angles to the pair above and below it. [Latin *decussātus,* past participle of *decussāre* to divide crosswise (in the form of an X), from *decussis* the number ten (for which the symbol was X).]

ded·i·cate (ded′ə kāt′) -cat·ed, -cat·ing. *v.t.* **1.** to set apart for or devote to a deity or a sacred purpose; consecrate: *They dedicated the temple to Athena.* **2.** to set apart for or devote to a special purpose or use: *Part of the building was dedicated to chemical research.* **3.** to give or devote (oneself) entirely or earnestly to some person or purpose: *He dedicated himself to the cause of science.* **4.** to inscribe (a book or other artistic composition) to a friend or patron as a testimony, as of affection, respect, or gratitude. **5.** to open or unveil formally to the public. [Latin *dēdicātus,* past participle of *dēdicāre* to proclaim, consecrate.]

ded·i·ca·tion (ded′ə kā′shən) *n.* **1.** act of dedicating; being dedicated. **2.** inscription in a book or other artistic work, dedicating it to a friend, patron, or cause.

ded·i·ca·tive (ded′ə kā′tiv) *adj.* dedicatory.

ded·i·ca·to·ry (ded′ə kə tôr′ē) *adj.* of the nature of, constituting, or serving as a dedication.

de·duce (di dōōs′, -dūs′) -duced, -duc·ing. *v.t.* **1.** to derive or draw as a conclusion from something known or assumed; infer. **2.** to trace, as the course, descent, or derivation of. [Medieval Latin *deducere* to infer logically, from Latin *dēdūcere* to lead down.] —**de·duc′i·ble,** *adj.* —**Syn. 1.** see conclude.

de·duct (di dukt′) *v.t.* to take away or subtract from a total. [Latin *dēductus,* past participle of *dēdūcere* to lead down, lead away, subtract.] —**de·duct′i·ble,** *adj.*

de·duc·tion (di duk′shən) *n.* **1.** act of deducting; subtraction. **2.** that which is deducted. **3.** reasoning from one or more principles or premises to a conclusion which necessarily or logically follows; reasoning from the general to the particular. Distinguished from **induction.** **4.** that which is deduced; inference; conclusion: *a brilliant deduction.*

---

at; āpe; cär; end; mē; it; īce; hot; ōld; fôrk; wood; fōōl; oil; out; up; ūse; turn; sing; thin; this; zh in treasure; ə in ago, taken, pencil, lemon, circus.

263

de·duc·tive (di duk′tiv) *adj.* of, employing, or based on deduction. —**de·duc′tive·ly,** *adv.*

deed (dēd) *n.* **1.** something done; act. **2.** worthy or notable act; feat; exploit. **3.** sealed document signifying or proving the transfer of real estate. **4.** action or performance, esp. in contrast to words. **5. in deed.** in fact or reality. —*v.t.* to convey or transfer (real estate) by deed. [Old English *dǣd* act, action.] —**Syn.** *n.* **1.** see **act.**

deem (dēm) *v.t., v.i.* to think; believe; judge: *He deemed it wise to accept the new position.* [Old English *dēman.*]

deep (dēp) *adj.* **1.** extending far downward from the surface or top: *a deep well, deep water, a deep hole, a deep cut, a deep box.* **2.** great in degree; intense; extreme: *deep love, deep differences, deep distress, a deep sleep.* **3.** extending far inward or backward from the front or outer edge: *a deep shelf, a deep room. The dress had a deep border of lace at the neck.* **4.** difficult to understand or penetrate; abstruse: *Philosophy is too deep for me.* **5.** completely occupied; absorbed; engrossed: *deep in thought.* **6.** coming from or extending to a depth: *a deep sigh, a deep plunge.* **7.** penetrating; profound: *a deep thinker. He was a man of deep insight.* **8.** to a large extent: *deep in debt.* **9.** going beyond that which is obvious or understood: *The statement had deep significance.* **10.** dark and rich in color: *a deep brown.* **11.** low in pitch: *a deep voice, the deep tones of an organ.* **12.** having a specified dimension downward, inward, or backward: *a pool 12 feet deep, a shelf 24 inches deep, a line of men four deep.* **13.** closely guarded: *a deep, dark secret.* **14.** tall and dense: *deep grass.* **15.** sly; cunning: *a deep scheme.* **16. to go off the deep end.** to act irrationally. —*adv.* **1.** in, at, to, or with a great depth; deeply: *We went deep into the jungle. She reached deep into the bowl.* **2.** far on (in time); late: *The meeting continued deep into the night.* —*n.* **1.** part of greatest intensity: *the deep of winter, the deep of night.* **2. the deep.** the sea. [Old English *dēop* extending far downward or inward, profound.] —**deep′ly,** *adv.* —**deep′ness,** *n.*

deep-dish pie (dēp′dish′) pie, usually containing fruit, baked in a deep dish and having only a top crust.

deep·en (dē′pən) *v.t., v.i.* to make or become deep or deeper.

deep fat, fat used in deep-frying.

deep-fry (dēp′frī′) **-fried, -fry·ing.** *v.t.* to fry in a deep pan of fat or oil.

deep-laid (dēp′lād′) *adj.* made with great cunning, care, or secrecy: *a deep-laid plot.*

deep-root·ed (dēp′rōō′tid, -root′id) *adj.* **1.** firmly fixed or established; deep-seated: *a deep-rooted hatred.* **2.** having roots that extend far below the surface.

deep-sea (dēp′sē′) *adj.* of, in, or relating to the deeper parts of the ocean: *deep-sea fishing.*

deep-seat·ed (dēp′sē′tid) *adj.* firmly fixed or established; deeply implanted: *a deep-seated fear.*

deep-set (dēp′set′) *adj.* placed deeply: *deep-set eyes.*

deep South, region of the United States generally including Alabama, Georgia, Mississippi, and Louisiana.

deer (dēr) *pl.* **deer.** *n.* any of numerous cloven-hoofed, cud-chewing mammals, family Cervidae, typically having deciduous paired antlers in the male, as the white-tailed deer, the moose, the elk, and the reindeer. Height: 13 inches to 6 feet at the shoulder. [Old English *dēor.*]

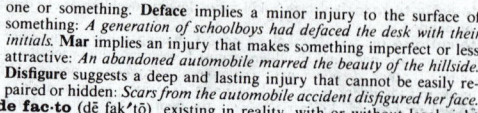

Deer

deer·hound (dēr′hound′) *n.* large, shaggy-haired dog of a breed originally developed in Scotland, formerly used for hunting deer. Height: 31 inches at the shoulder. Also, **Scottish deerhound.**

deer mouse, any of various nocturnal mice, genus *Peromyscus*, of North and Central America, having buff or brown fur with white markings on the underside and legs. Length: 7½ inches.

deer·skin (dēr′skin′) *n.* **1.** hide of a deer. **2.** leather made from this hide.

Deerhound

def. 1. defendant. **2.** defense. **3.** definition. **4.** definite. **5.** defined. **6.** defective. **7.** deferred.

de·face (di fās′) **-faced, -fac·ing.** *v.t.* to spoil or destroy the surface or appearance of: *to deface a monument with chalk marks.* [Old French *desfacier* to disfigure, going back to Latin *dis-* away, apart + *faciēs* face.] —**de·face′ment, de·fac′er,** *n.*

Syn. Deface, mar, disfigure mean to damage the appearance of some-

one or something. **Deface** implies a minor injury to the surface of something: *A generation of schoolboys had defaced the desk with their initials.* **Mar** implies an injury that makes something imperfect or less attractive: *An abandoned automobile marred the beauty of the hillside.* **Disfigure** suggests a deep and lasting injury that cannot be easily repaired or hidden: *Scars from the automobile accident disfigured her face.*

de fac·to (dē fak′tō) existing in reality, with or without legal right or sanction; actual: *de facto segregation, the de facto ruler.* ▲ distinguished from **de jure.** [Latin *dē factō* literally, from the fact.]

de·fal·cate (di fal′kāt, -fôl′-) **-cat·ed, -cat·ing.** *v.i.* to misappropriate money entrusted to one's care; embezzle. [Medieval Latin *defalcatus,* past participle of *defalcare* to take away, to cut off with a sickle, going back to Latin *dē* away + *falx* sickle.] —**de·fal′ca·tor,** *n.*

de·fal·ca·tion (dē′fal kā′shən, -fôl-) *n.* **1.** misappropriation of money entrusted to one's care; embezzlement. **2.** amount misappropriated.

def·a·ma·tion (def′ə mā′shən, dē′fə-) *n.* act or instance of defaming or being defamed; slander or libel.

de·fam·a·to·ry (di fam′ə tôr′ē) *adj.* injurious to the reputation; slanderous or libelous.

de·fame (di fām′) **-famed, -fam·ing.** *v.t.* to attack or ruin the good name or reputation of; slander or libel. [Old French *diffamer, defamer,* from Latin *diffamāre,* from *dis-* apart, away + *fama* rumor, reputation.] —**de·fam′er,** *n.*

de·fault (di fôlt′) *n.* **1.** failure to do something required. **2.** failure to meet a financial obligation. **3.** failure to take part in or complete a scheduled game or contest. **4.** failure to take a required step in a legal action, esp. to appear in court. **5. in default.** in a condition of having failed or neglected to do something required. **6. in default of.** in the absence of; through lack of. —*v.i.* **1.** to fail or neglect to do something required. **2.** to fail to meet a financial obligation. **3.a.** to fail to take part in or complete a scheduled game or contest. **b.** to lose a game or contest by default. **4.a.** to fail to take a required step in a legal action at the specified time, esp. to fail to appear in court. **b.** to lose an action by default. [Old French *defaute* lack, fault, going back to Latin *dē* from, away + Late Latin *fallita* deficiency (from Latin *fallere* to fail).] —**de·fault′er,** *n.*

de·feat (di fēt′) *v.t.* **1.** to overcome in a contest or conflict of any kind; win a victory over; beat: *to defeat an opponent in tennis, to defeat the enemy in battle.* **2.** to prevent the success of; thwart; frustrate: *to defeat a purpose, to defeat a person's hopes.* —*n.* **1.** act of overcoming or fact of being overcome in a contest or conflict. **2.** frustration; thwarting. [Old French *de(s)fait,* past participle of *desfaire* to undo, going back to Latin *dis-* un-² + *facere* to do.]

Syn. *v.t.* **1. Defeat, conquer, overcome, vanquish** mean to gain victory over. **Defeat** implies a clear decision, but not necessarily a final one: *Defeated in his attempt to pass the other runner, Jones waited for him to tire.* **Conquer** suggests gaining control after a series of efforts: *Alexander the Great conquered Persia.* **Overcome** implies surmounting an obstacle, opponent, or difficulty by force or strategy: *The senator overcame his opponent in the primary.* **Vanquish** suggests a definitive victory over an adversary, esp. in a single conflict: *The troops vanquished the guard at the city's gates and soon controlled the capital.*

de·feat·ism (di fē′tiz′əm) *n.* state of mind or behavior characteristic of a defeatist.

de·feat·ist (di fē′tist) *n.* one who expects defeat or prematurely accepts it as inevitable. —*adj.* of or characteristic of a defeatist.

def·e·cate (def′ə kāt′) **-cat·ed, -cat·ing.** *v.i.* to excrete waste from the bowels. [Latin *defaecatus,* past participle of *defaecāre* to cleanse from dregs.] —**def′e·ca′tion,** *n.*

de·fect (*n.* dē′fekt, di fekt′; *v.* di fekt′) *n.* **1.** imperfection, flaw, or weakness; fault; blemish: *a defect in a glass bowl.* **2.** lack of something essential to completeness; deficiency: *a speech defect.* —*v.i.* to desert a group, country, or cause, esp. for another of opposing policies or principles. [Latin *defectus* a want, failure.] —**de·fec′tor,** *n.* —**Syn.** **1.** see **blemish.**

de·fec·tion (di fek′shən) *n.* desertion from a group, country, or cause, esp. for another of opposing policies or principles.

de·fec·tive (di fek′tiv) *adj.* **1.** having a defect or defects; imperfect; incomplete: *a house with defective wiring.* **2.** *Grammar.* lacking one or more of the usual forms of conjugation or other inflection. *Ought* and *must* are defective verbs. **3.** having subnormal mental ability. —*n.* one who is subnormal mentally or physically. —**de·fec′tive·ly,** *adv.* —**de·fec′tive·ness,** *n.* —**Syn.** *adj.* **1.** see **faulty.**

de·fend (di fend′) *v.t.* **1.** to guard against attack, injury, or danger; protect: *the troops defended the city.* **2.** to support, justify, or maintain by word or action: *to defend one's rights.* **3.** *Law.* **a.** to plead the case or cause of (an accused person). **b.** to contest (a charge or suit). —*v.i.* to make a defense. [Old French *defendre* to protect, from Latin *defendere.*] —**de·fend′er,** *n.*

Syn. *v.t.* **1. Defend, guard, protect, shield** mean to shelter something

at; āpe; cär; end; mē; it; īce; hot; ōld; fôrk; wood; fōōl; oil; out; up; ūse; turn; sing; thin; this; zh in treasure; ə in ago, taken, pencil, lemon, circus.

from attack or injury. **Defend** implies an active resistance against someone or something: *We shall defend our island, whatever the cost may be* (Churchill, 1940). **Guard** suggests maintaining a careful watch for possible danger: *Two soldiers guarded the entrance to the fort.* **Protect** implies a covering, screen, or bulwark to deter attack or injury by anything harmful: *A football player wears a helmet to protect his head.* **Shield** suggests a screen or covering interposed against actual attack: *He shielded his eyes against the bright sunlight.*

de·fend·ant (di fen′dənt) *n.* person against whom a civil or criminal action is brought in a court of law.

de·fense (di fens′) *also, British,* **de·fence.** *n.* **1.** act of guarding against attack, injury, or danger; protection: *to be engaged in the defense of a city.* **2.** one who or that which protects; means of protection: *The dike was the town's only defense against flooding.* **3.** support or justification by word or deed: *The governor spoke in defense of his new proposal.* **4.** argument, speech, or writing that so supports or justifies: *The historian's defense of his thesis lacked clarity.* **5.a.** act or method of defending oneself, one's side, or one's goal, as in a sport or game. **b.** defending team, players, or side. **6.a.** arguments presented by a defendant or his lawyer. **b.** defendant and his lawyer or lawyers collectively. [Old French *defense* act of protecting, means of protecting, from Latin *dēfensa* a defending.]

de·fense·less (di fens′lis) *adj.* having no defense; helpless; unprotected. —**de·fense′less·ly,** *adv.* —**de·fense′less·ness,** *n.*

defense mechanism 1. attitude or behavior unconsciously adopted by a person to limit his awareness of painful or unpleasant feelings, such as guilt or anxiety. Rationalization and repression are defense mechanisms. **2.** self-protective reaction of an organism to stimuli, as the production of antitoxins.

de·fen·si·ble (di fen′sə bəl) *adj.* **1.** capable of being defended in argument; justifiable: *a defensible action.* **2.** capable of being defended against attack, injury, or danger: *a defensible coastline.* —**de·fen′si·bil′i·ty, de·fen′si·ble·ness,** *n.* —**de·fen′si·bly,** *adv.*

de·fen·sive (di fen′siv) *adj.* **1.** serving to defend; protective: *defensive armor.* **2.** formed or carried on for the purpose of resisting attack or aggression: *defensive warfare.* **3.** having or using defenses: *a defensive attitude, a defensive person.* —*n.* **1.** position or attitude of defense. **2. on the defensive.** assuming a protective attitude. —**de·fen′sive·ly,** *adv.* —**de·fen′sive·ness,** *n.*

de·fer¹ (di fur′) *-ferred, -fer·ring. v.t.* **1.** to put off to a future time; postpone: *to defer judgment on a matter.* **2.** to postpone the induction of (a person) into the armed forces. —*v.i.* to put off action; delay. [Old French *differer,* from Latin *differre* to delay, carry in different directions. Doublet of DIFFER.] —**de·fer′ra·ble,** *adj.* —**Syn.** *v.t.* **1.** see **delay.**

de·fer² (di fur′) *-ferred, -fer·ring. v.i.* to submit in judgment or opinion; yield respectfully: *He deferred to his friend's wishes.* [French *déférer,* from Latin *dēferre* to carry down, offer.]

Syn. Defer, yield, submit mean to give way to someone else in recognition of greater force or eminence. **Defer** suggests respect for another's authority or knowledge: *Philip . . . had the good sense to defer to the long experience and the wisdom of his father* (Prescott, 1855). **Yield** implies a bending to force, either physical, emotional, or intellectual: *The danger at last forced the king to yield to the Scotch demands* (Green, 1874). **Submit** suggests losing or avoiding a struggle against superior force: *After a siege of six weeks the embattled garrison finally submitted to the invaders.*

def·er·ence (def′ər əns) *n.* **1.** courteous respect or regard: *to have deference for one's elders.* **2. in deference to.** respectful acknowledgment of the authority of; out of respect for: *Flags were flown at half-mast in deference to the slain leader.* —**Syn. 1.** see **honor.**

def·er·ent (def′ər ənt) *adj.* deferential.

def·er·en·tial (def′ə ren′shəl) *adj.* characterized by or showing deference; respectful. —**def′er·en′tial·ly,** *adv.*

de·fer·ment (di fur′mənt) *n.* a putting off or delay; postponement: *a deferment from military service.* Also, **de·fer′ral.**

de·ferred (di furd′) *adj.* **1.** put off for a time; postponed. **2.** with payments or benefits until a certain date: *deferred stock.* **3.** classified as temporarily exempt from military draft.

de·fi·ance (di fī′əns) *n.* **1.** bold or open resistance to authority, an adversary, or an opposing force; contempt of opposition or authority. **2.** challenge to meet in a fight or contest. **3. to bid defiance to.** to defy. **4. in defiance of.** with disregard for; in spite of.

de·fi·ant (di fī′ənt) *adj.* characterized by or showing defiance; openly or boldly resisting. [French *défiant,* present participle of *défier* to defy. See DEFY.] —**de·fi′ant·ly,** *adv.*

de·fi·cien·cy (di fish′ən sē) *pl., -cies. n.* **1.** state of being deficient; lack of something essential: *a mental deficiency, a vitamin deficiency.* **2.** amount of shortage or lack; deficit.

deficiency disease, disease, as scurvy or rickets, caused by a lack of some essential element in the diet.

de·fi·cient (di fish′ənt) *adj.* **1.** not adequate in quantity or supply; insufficient: *a diet deficient in vitamins.* **2.** lacking something essential; incomplete; imperfect: *mentally deficient.* [Latin *dēficiēns,* present participle of *dēficere* to be wanting.] —**de·fi′cient·ly,** *adv.*

def·i·cit (def′ə sit) *n.* **1.** amount by which something, esp. a sum of money, falls short of what is due, required, or expected; shortage. **2.** loss in business operations. **3.** any shortage: *a deficit in the gold supply.* [French *déficit* deficiency, shortage in keeping accounts, from Latin *dēficit* it is wanting, from *dēficere* to be wanting.]

deficit spending, government fiscal policy of spending beyond tax receipts by borrowing funds from public banks and expanding the public debt. Also, **deficit financing.**

de·fi·er (di fī′ər) *n.* one who defies.

de·file¹ (di fīl′) *-filed, -fil·ing. v.t.* **1.** to spoil the purity of; profane; taint: *to defile a temple.* **2.** to make filthy, dirty, or impure; pollute: *to defile a stream with garbage.* [Modification of obsolete *defoul,* partly from Old French *defouler* to trample on, violate (going back to Latin *dē* down + *fullō* fuller; with reference to treading cloth to full it), and partly going back to Old English *fȳlan* to make foul.] —**de·file′ment, de·fil′er,** *n.* —**Syn. 2.** see **pollute.**

de·file² (di fīl′, dē′fīl′) *-filed, -fil·ing. v.i.* to march in a line or by files. —*n.* narrow passage in a mountain region, esp. one that permits travel only in a narrow line. [French *défiler* to march in files; earlier, to unravel, going back to Latin *dis-* apart + *filum* thread.]

de·fine (di fīn′) *-fined, -fin·ing. v.t.* **1.** to state the meaning or meanings of (a word or phrase): *Can you define the word "cafeteria"?* **2.** to describe the essential nature or characteristics of; explain: *to define the concepts used in an argument.* **3.** to fix or set forth precisely or authoritatively: *The Constitution defines the powers of the president.* **4.** to determine the limits or extent of: *rivers that define a country's borders.* **5.** to make clear or distinct in outline or form: *The contrast in color helped to define the forms in the painting.* —*v.i.* to formulate a definition. [Old French *definer* to determine, describe, from Latin *dēfīnīre* to limit, determine, going back to *dē* down + *fīnis* end, boundary.] —**de·fin′a·ble,** *adj.* —**de·fin′er,** *n.*

def·i·nite (def′ə nit) *adj.* **1.** clearly defined; precise; exact: *He has definite ideas on that subject.* **2.** positive; certain; sure: *It is definite that Mr. Smythe will be the new principal.* **3.** having precise limits. **4.** *Botany.* determinate. [Latin *dēfīnītus,* past participle of *dēfīnīre* to limit, determine. See DEFINE.] —**def′i·nite·ly,** *adv.* —**def′i·nite·ness,** *n.* —**Syn.** see **explicit.**

definite article, the article *the,* which limits or specifies the noun it modifies. Distinguished from **indefinite article.**

def·i·ni·tion (def′ə nish′ən) *n.* **1.** statement of the meaning of a word or phrase. **2.** statement of the essential nature or characteristics of a thing. **3.** action of stating the meaning of a word or phrase, or the essential nature or characteristics of a thing. **4.** action of making or being made clear in outline or form. **5.** power of a lens to produce clear, sharp images. **6.** sharpness of outline; distinctness; clearness. **7.** accuracy with which the sound or image of a source is reproduced on a receiver.

de·fin·i·tive (di fin′ə tiv) *adj.* **1.** most nearly accurate and complete: *the definitive edition of the works of Yeats.* **2.** conclusive; final; decisive: *a definitive answer.* **3.** serving to limit or define. —**de·fin′i·tive·ly,** *adv.* —**de·fin′i·tive·ness,** *n.*

de·flate (di flāt′) *-flat·ed, -flat·ing. v.t.* **1.** to reduce in size by releasing air or gas from: *to deflate a tire.* **2.** to reduce in importance, esp. something blown up or exaggerated: *to deflate a person's ego.* **3.** to reduce, esp. in amount, size, or level: *to deflate prices.* —*v.i.* to collapse or contract, as through loss of air or gas: *The tire deflated.* [DE- + (IN)FLATE.] —**de·fla′tor,** *n.*

de·fla·tion (di flā′shən) *n.* **1.** reduction of something that is blown up, as by air or exaggeration. **2.** decline in general price level resulting from a reduction in money supply or spending.

de·fla·tion·ar·y (di flā′shə ner′ē) *adj.* relating to, causing, or characterized by deflation.

de·flect (di flekt′) *v.t., v.i.* to turn or cause to turn aside; bend or deviate from a straight course. [Latin *dēflectere* to bend aside.] —**de·flec′tive,** *adj.* —**de·flec′tor,** *n.*

de·flec·tion (di flek′shən) *also, British,* **de·flex·ion.** *n.* **1.** act of deflecting; being deflected; turning away; deviation. **2.** amount of such turning or deviation. **3.** amount an indicator on a measuring instrument moves or deviates from the zero reading on its scale.

def·lor·a·tion (def′lə rā′shən, dē′flə-) *n.* act of deflowering; being deflowered.

de·flow·er (dē flou′ər) *v.t.* **1.** to take away the virginity of (a woman). **2.** to spoil the beauty or purity of; ravish; violate. **3.** to strip of flowers.

De·foe, Daniel (də fō′) *also,* **De Foe.** c.1660–1731, English author.

de·fo·li·ant (dē fō′lē ənt) *n.* chemical agent for defoliating plants, chiefly used in farming to remove unwanted leaves and in warfare to destroy crops or plant life.

---

at; āpe; cär; end; mē; it; īce; hot; ōld; fôrk; wood; fōol; oil; out; up; ūse; turn; sing; thin; this; zh in treasure; ə in ago, taken, pencil, lemon, circus.

de·fo·li·ate (dē fō′lē āt′) -at·ed, -at·ing. *v.t.* **1.** to strip of leaves. **2.** to destroy (a forest, jungle, or other area of vegetation): *Chemical warfare defoliated a wide area.* —*v.i.* to lose leaves. [Late Latin *dēfoliātus,* past participle of *dēfoliāre* to strip off leaves, from Latin *dē* from + *folium* leaf.] —**de·fo′li·a′tion,** *n.*

de·for·est (dē fôr′ist, -for′-) *v.t.* to clear or strip of forests or trees. —**de·for′est·a′tion,** *n.*

De For·est, Lee (də fôr′əst, -for′-) 1873–1961, U.S. inventor.

de·form (di fôrm′) *v.t.* **1.** to spoil the form of; make misshapen. **2.** to make ugly; mar the beauty of; disfigure. [Latin *dēfôrmāre* to disfigure.]

de·for·ma·tion (dē′fôr mā′shən, def′ər-) *n.* **1.** act of deforming; being deformed. **2.** result or instance of being deformed; deformity.

de·formed (di fôrmd′) *adj.* **1.** misshapen, esp. in body or limbs; distorted. **2.** ugly; offensive.

de·form·i·ty (di fôr′mə tē) *pl.,* **-ties.** *n.* **1.** improperly formed or distorted part of the body. **2.** condition of being deformed. **3.** moral disfigurement or defect.

de·fraud (di frôd′) *v.t.* to deprive by fraud of something rightfully due; cheat; swindle: *to defraud a person of his property.* [Latin *dēfraudāre.*] —**de·fraud·a·tion** (dē′frô dā′shən). **de·fraud′er,** *n.* —Syn. see cheat.

de·fray (di frā′) *v.t.* to pay (costs or expenses): *The college raised its tuition to help defray additional administrative expenses.* [French *défrayer,* from *de-* (see DE-) + *frai* cost (of Germanic origin).] —**de·fray′a·ble,** *adj.* —**de·fray′al, de·fray′ment,** *n.*

de·frock (dē frok′) *v.t.* to unfrock.

de·frost (di frôst′) *v.t., v.i.* **1.** to make or become free of frost or ice: *to defrost a refrigerator.* **2.** to thaw.

de·frost·er (di frôs′tər) *n.* device that removes or prevents the formation of ice or frost, as in a refrigerator or on an automobile windshield.

deft (deft) *adj.* skillful and nimble; dexterous; adroit: *deft fingers, deft handling of a difficult situation.* [Old English *gedæfte* gentle.] —**deft′ly,** *adv.* —**deft′ness,** *n.* —Syn. see dexterous.

de·funct (di fungkt′) *adj.* no longer existing or active; dead; extinct: *that company is defunct.* [Latin *dēfūnctus,* past participle of *dēfungī* to finish, die.]

de·fy (di fī′) -fied, -fy·ing. *v.t.* **1.** to resist openly or boldly; face (opposition or authority) with contempt: *to defy the law.* **2.** to resist completely or successfully; withstand: *That problem defies solution.* **3.** to challenge; dare: *He defied his opponents to equal his record.* [Middle French *defier* to challenge; earlier, to renounce faith, going back to Latin *dis-* apart + *fīdus* faithful.]

deg., degree; degrees.

De·gas, Ed·gar (dā gä′; ed gär′) 1834–1917, French painter.

de Gaulle, Charles (də gōl′, -gôl′; shärl) 1890–1970, French general and political leader, president of France from 1959 to 1969.

de·gauss (dē gous′) *v.t.* to neutralize the magnetic field of (an object, as a television receiver or steel ship) by the use of special coils designed for this purpose. The coils produce a magnetic field equal but opposite to that of the object. [From Karl F. *Gauss,* 1777–1855, German scientist.]

de·gen·er·a·cy (di jen′ər ə sē) *n.* **1.** state of being degenerate, esp. in moral character. **2.** process of degenerating; deterioration.

de·gen·er·ate (*v.,* di jen′ə rāt′; *adj.,* n., di jen′ər it) -at·ed, -at·ing. *v.i.* **1.** to become worse or inferior in condition, character, or quality; deteriorate. **2.** to become a less complex organism; regress to a lower, less developed type. —*adj.* having become worse or inferior in condition, character, or quality; deteriorated; degraded. —*n.* **1.** one who is morally degraded. **2.** one who has deteriorated or regressed, as from a higher physical or cultural standard. [Latin *dēgenerātus,* past participle of *dēgenerāre* to deteriorate, going back to *dē-* down, from + *genus* race, kind.] —**de·gen′er·ate·ly,** *adv.* —**de·gen′er·ate·ness,** *n.*

de·gen·er·a·tion (di jen′ə rā′shən) *n.* **1.** process of degenerating. **2.** state of being degenerate. **3.** progressive deterioration of tissue caused by disease or injury and leading to structural or functional impairment of an organ or other body part.

de·gen·er·a·tive (di jen′ə rā′tiv, -ər ə tiv) *adj.* **1.** relating to, characterized by, or causing degeneration: *a degenerative disease.* **2.** tending to degenerate.

de·glu·ti·tion (dē′glōō tish′ən, deg′lōō-) *n.* act, power, or process of swallowing. [French *déglutition* swallowing, from Latin *dēglūtīre* to swallow down.]

deg·ra·da·tion (deg′rə dā′shən) *n.* **1.** act of degrading; being degraded. **2.** state of being lowered in character, quality, or estimation.

de·grade (di grād′) -grad·ed, -grad·ing. *v.t.* **1.** to lower in character or quality, esp. moral character; debase; corrupt: *Lying degrades a man.* **2.** to bring into contempt or low esteem; dishonor. **3.** to reduce in rank or position. **4.** to wear down by erosion. [Old French *degrader* to deprive of rank, going back to Latin *dē* down + *gradus* grade, rank, step.]

de·grad·ed (di grā′did) *adj.* lowered in character or quality; corrupt; debased.

de·grad·ing (di grā′ding) *adj.* tending to degrade; debasing; humiliating.

de·gree (di grē′) *n.* **1.** one of a series of stages or steps in a process or course: *The child learned to walk by degrees.* **2.** intensity, amount, or extent: *a high degree of intelligence, a burn of the first degree.* **3.** relative social or official rank or position: *a man of low degree.* **4.** relative condition, manner, or respect: *A small contribution and a large one may be equally charitable, each in its own degree.* **5.** unit of temperature measurement, varying according to the scale used. ▲ The symbol for degrees (°) is often used with figures: *70° Fahrenheit.* **6.** rank or title given by an academic institution for completion of a course of study or as an honorary distinction: *a master's degree in history.* **7.** step in a line of genealogical descent. **8.** *Mathematics.* unit of measurement for angles or arcs, equal to ¹⁄₃₆₀ of the circumference of a circle. **9.** *Geography.* unit of angular distance on the earth's surface measured from a specified meridian and the equator. **10.** *Law.* relative seriousness of a particular crime: *murder in the first degree.* **11.** *Algebra.* **a.** rank of a monomial term as determined by the sum of the exponents of the variables. The terms x^4 and xy^3 are both of the fourth degree. **b.** rank of a polynomial as determined by the sum of the exponents of the term of the highest degree. The equation $xy^4 = yz$ is of the fifth degree. **12.** *Grammar.* one of the three forms of comparison of adjectives or adverbs. For the adjective *good, good* is the positive degree, *better* is the comparative degree, and *best* is the superlative degree. **13.** *Music.* **a.** note or tone of a scale. **b.** interval between consecutive notes or tones of a scale. **c.** line or space on a staff. **14. to a degree. a.** to a great extent or amount; exceedingly: *He was proud to a degree.* **b.** somewhat. [Old French *degre* step, stair, rank, going back to Latin *dē* down + *gradus* step, grade, rank.]

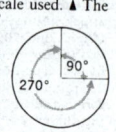

Degree
(def. 8)

de·gree-day (di grē′dā′) unit representing one degree of difference in the average temperature for a given day from a standard, usually 65° Fahrenheit, used for estimating fuel requirements.

De Groot, Huig (də кнrōt′; hoikh) see **Grotius, Hugo.**

de·hisce (di his′) -hisced, -hisc·ing. *v.i.* to burst open, as the capsule or seed pod of a plant. [Latin *dēhīscere* to gape.]

de·his·cence (di his′əns) *n.* bursting open, as of certain ripe fruits or anthers when the seeds or pollen grains are discharged.

de·his·cent (di his′ənt) *adj.* characterized by dehiscence; bursting open.

de·horn (dē hôrn′) *v.t.* to remove the horns from.

de·hu·man·ize (dē hū′mə nīz′, dē ū′-) -ized, -iz·ing. *v.t.* to deprive of human qualities; make inhuman or mechanical: *Confinement in a concentration camp can dehumanize a person.* —**de·hu′man·i·za′tion,** *n.*

de·hu·mid·i·fi·er (dē′hū mid′ə fī′ər, dē′ū-) *n.* device for removing moisture from the air.

de·hu·mid·i·fy (dē′hū mid′ə fī′, dē′ū-) -fied, -fy·ing. *v.t.* to remove moisture from (air or other gases). —**de·hu·mid′i·fi·ca′tion,** *n.*

de·hy·drate (dē hī′drāt) -drat·ed, -drat·ing. *v.t.* **1.** to remove water or its chemical equivalents from (a chemical compound). **2.** to remove water from; dry: *to dehydrate foods.* —*v.i.* to lose water; become dry. —**de′hy·dra′tion,** *n.*

de·ice (dē īs′) -iced, -ic·ing. *v.t.* to remove ice from or prevent ice from forming on.

de·ic·er (dē ī′sər) *n.* device or substance that prevents or removes formations of ice, as on an airplane wing.

de·i·fi·ca·tion (dē′ə fi kā′shən) *n.* **1.** act of deifying; being deified. **2.** state of being deified; that which has been deified.

de·i·fy (dē′ə fī′) -fied, -fy·ing. *v.t.* **1.** to make a god of. **2.** to worship as a god; regard as an object of worship: *to deify an emperor.* **3.** to glorify or idealize: *to deify wealth.* [Old French *deifier* to make a god of, from Late Latin *deificāre,* going back to Latin *deus* a god + *facere* to make.] —**de′i·fi′er,** *n.*

deign (dān) *v.i.* to think worthy of oneself; condescend: *He would not deign to consider such an offer.* —*v.t.* to condescend to grant or give: *He deigned no reply.* [Old French *deignier* to think worthy, from Latin *dignāri.*]

de·ism (dē′iz′əm) *n.* **1.** belief that the universe and its natural laws were created by God, but that the natural laws govern its operation, not the will of God. **2.** belief in God as the source of existence, stressing dependence upon reason rather than revelation and rejecting the rituals of organized religion. [Latin *deus* a god + -ISM.] —**de′ist,** *n.* —**de·is′tic;** also, **de·is′ti·cal,** *adj.* —**de·is′ti·cal·ly,** *adv.*

de·i·ty (dē′ə tē) *pl.,* **-ties.** *n.* **1.** god or goddess; divine being. **2.** state or attributes of being a god; divine nature; divinity. **3. the Deity.** God. [Old French *deite* divinity, divine nature, from Late Latin *deitās,* from Latin *deus* a god.]

at; āpe; cär; end; mē; it; īce; hot; ōld; fôrk; wood; fōōl; oil; out; up; ūse; turn; sing; thin; this; zh in treasure; ə in ago, taken, pencil, lemon, circus.

dé·jà vu (dā′zhä voo′) illusion of having already experienced something that is actually being experienced for the first time. [French *déjà vu* literally, already seen.]

de·ject (di jekt′) *v.t.* to make low in spirits; dishearten; depress. [Latin *dējectus,* past participle of *dēicere* to throw down.]

de·ject·ed (di jek′tid) *adj.* low in spirits; disheartened; depressed. —**de·ject′ed·ly,** *adv.* —**de·ject′ed·ness,** *n.*

de·jec·tion (di jek′shən) *n.* lowness of spirits; depression; sadness. —**Syn.** see **depression.**

de ju·re (dē joor′ē) by right; according to law: *the de jure ruler.* Distinguished from **de facto.** [Latin *dē jūre* by right.]

deka-, variant of **deca-.**

dek·a·gram (dek′ə gram′) decagram.

De Kalb, Baron Jo·hann (də kalb′; yō′hän) 1721–80, German general in the American army during the American Revolution.

dek·a·li·ter (dek′ə lē′tər) decaliter.

dek·a·me·ter (dek′ə mē′tər) decameter.

de Koo·ning, Wil·lem (də kōō′ning; vil′əm, wil′-) 1904—, U.S. painter.

del. 1. delegate. 2. delete.

Del., Delaware.

De·la·croix, Eu·gène (də lä krwä′; œ zhen′) 1798–1863, French painter.

De la Mare, Walter (də lə mâr′) 1873–1956, English writer.

Del·a·ware (del′ə wâr′) *n.* 1. state in the eastern United States. Capital, Dover. Area, 2057 sq. mi. Pop. (1970), 548,104. Abbreviation, **Del.** 2. river in the eastern United States, flowing from southeastern New York State between Pennsylvania and New Jersey into Delaware Bay.

Delaware Bay, inlet of the Atlantic Ocean between Delaware and New Jersey.

de·lay (di lā′) *v.t.* 1. to put off to a future time; postpone: *The umpires delayed the start of the game because of the rain.* 2. to make late; hinder the progress of; detain: *Heavy traffic delayed us.* —*v.i.* to put off or slow down action; linger; procrastinate: *You'll lose your chance if you delay.* —*n.* 1. act of delaying; state of being delayed: *The delay was caused by a derailment.* 2. amount of time something is delayed: *a brief delay.* [Old French *delaier* to postpone, from *de-* (see DE-) + *laier* to leave (of uncertain origin).] —**de·lay′er,** *n.*

Syn. *v.t.* 1. **Delay, defer,** **postpone** mean to put off something for the time being. **Delay** suggests keeping something from happening at a normal or expected time: *The chairman delayed the start of the ceremonies until the guest of honor arrived.* **Defer** implies that the action will be resumed at an indefinite later time: *The meeting was deferred until after New Year's Day.* **Postpone** connotes a definite time at which to renew an action: *Bad bweather forced the general to postpone the invasion until June 6.*

de·le (dē′lē) **-led, -le·ing.** *v.t.* to cross out or take out; delete. ▲ usually used in the imperative as a direction in printing and represented by the symbol ℘. [Latin *dēlē,* imperative singular of *dēlēre* to destroy, wipe out.]

de·lec·ta·ble (di lek′tə bəl) *adj.* highly pleasing or delightful, esp. to the taste; delicious. [Latin *dēlectābilis* delightful.] —**de·lec′ta·ble·ness,** **de·lec′ta·bly,** *adv.*

de·lec·ta·tion (dē′lek tā′shən) *n.* delight; pleasure; enjoyment.

del·e·ga·cy (del′ə gə sē) *pl.,* **-cies.** 1. act of delegating; being delegated. 2. position or authority of a delegate. 3. body or committee of delegates.

del·e·gate (*n.,* del′ə gāt′, -git; *v.,* del′ə gāt′) *n.* 1. one given authority to represent or act for another or others; representative; deputy. 2. formerly, a representative of a territory in the U.S. House of Representatives. A delegate could speak, but not vote. 3. member of the lower house of the state legislature in Maryland, Virginia, and West Virginia. —*v.t.,* **-gat·ed, -gat·ing.** 1. to commit or entrust (power, authority, or responsibility) to another or others. 2. to appoint or send as a delegate: *The club, delegated Bill to attend the national convention.* [Latin *dēlēgātus,* past participle of *dēlēgāre* to send, assign.] —**Syn.** 1. see **agent.**

del·e·ga·tion (del′ə gā′shən) *n.* 1. group of persons authorized to represent others: *A delegation of war veterans marched in the parade.* 2. act of delegating; being delegated.

de Les·seps, Ferdinand Marie (də les′əps) 1805–94, French diplomat and engineer.

de·lete (di lēt′) **-let·ed, -let·ing.** *v.t.* to cross out or take out (anything written or printed); omit; cancel. [Latin *dēlētus,* past participle of *dēlēre* to destroy, wipe out.] —**Syn.** see **erase.**

del·e·te·ri·ous (del′i tēr′ē əs) *adj.* causing harm; injurious; hurtful: *a deleterious drug.* [Medieval Latin *dēleterius* noxious, from Greek *dēlētērios.*] —**del′e·te′ri·ous·ly,** *adv.* —**del′e·te′ri·ous·ness,** *n.*

de·le·tion (di lē′shən) *n.* 1. act of deleting; being deleted. 2. that which has been deleted.

---

delft (delft) *n.* glazed earthenware usually decorated with a blue and white glaze in patterns inspired by Chinese porcelains, originally made in Delft, the Netherlands. Also, **delft′ware′.**

Del·hi (del′ē, -hī) *n.* city in northern India, near New Delhi. Pop. (1969 est.), 2,874,454. Also, **Old Delhi.**

de·lib·er·ate (*adj.,* di lib′ər it; *v.,* di lib′ə rāt′) *adj.* 1. carefully thought out or planned; intentional; studied: *He made a deliberate attempt to ignore their biting comments.* 2. careful and slow in deciding; not hasty or rash: *a man deliberate in his dealings with others.* 3. unhurried in action or movement; slow: *the deliberate steps of an ailing man.* —*v.i.,* **-at·ed, -at·ing.** 1. to consider or reflect carefully. 2. to confer in order to consider and decide something: *The council deliberated behind closed doors.* —*v.t.* to think over or debate carefully; weigh: *The Senate has been deliberating the question for three days.* [Latin *dēlīberātus,* past participle of *dēlīberāre* to weigh well, reflect, consult, going back to *dē* thoroughly + *lībra* a pair of scales.] —**de·lib′er·ate·ly,** *adv.* —**de·lib′er·ate·ness,** *n.*

Delft plate

Syn. *adj.* 1. **Deliberate, intentional, voluntary** indicate something done by choice rather than by accident or because of an external force. **Deliberate** implies that the action is carefully considered beforehand, and that its consequences are clearly understood: *The group decided to commit several acts of deliberate violence.* **Intentional** suggests a premeditated attempt to achieve a definite purpose: *Her omission of his name from the guest list was intentional.* **Voluntary** stresses an exercise of the will and the absence of outside pressures: *His resignation from the company was purely voluntary.*

de·lib·er·a·tion (di lib′ə rā′shən) *n.* 1. careful consideration with the aim of reaching a decision. 2. discussion and consideration by a group of the reasons for and against something. 3. slowness and care in decision or action: *He spoke with deliberation.*

de·lib·er·a·tive (di lib′ər ā′tiv) *adj.* 1. relating to deliberation; having the function of deliberating: *Congress is a deliberative assembly.* 2. characterized by deliberation or careful consideration. —**de·lib′er·a′tive·ly,** *adv.* —**de·lib′er·a′tive·ness,** *n.*

del·i·ca·cy (del′i kə sē) *pl.,* **-cies.** 1. exquisite fineness of structure, texture, quality, or form; daintiness; frailty: *the delicacy of a fabric.* 2. rare or choice food: *caviar and other delicacies.* 3. susceptibility to disease or injury; physical weakness. 4. need of tact, skill, or care in treatment: *a problem of great delicacy.* 5. tact; consideration. 6. fineness of perception, taste, or skill; sensitivity: *the delicacy of an epicure's palate.* 7. sensitivity in measurement or response; accuracy: *the delicacy of a galvanometer.* 8. sensitivity to what is becoming, proper, or modest.

del·i·cate (del′i kit) *adj.* 1. exquisitely fine or dainty in structure, quality, texture, or form: *a delicate piece of lace, a delicate pattern of shadows and light.* 2. pleasing to the senses in a soft, mild, or subtle way: *a delicate perfume, a delicate color, a delicate flavor.* 3. easily damaged; fragile: *a delicate flower, a delicate wine glass.* 4. extremely susceptible to disease or injury: *a delicate child.* 5. requiring tact in handling; ticklish: *a delicate topic of conversation.* 6. requiring great skill and precision in execution: *a delicate brain operation.* 7. finely sensitive in measurement or response; minutely accurate: *A barometer is a delicate instrument.* 8. scarcely perceptible; subtle: *a delicate shade of meaning.* 9. finely skilled or sensitive: *a delicate touch, a delicate palate.* 10. sensitive to or in accord with what is becoming, proper, or modest. 11. tactful; considerate. [Latin *dēlicātus* dainty, charming, luxurious.] —**del′i·cate·ly,** *adv.* —**del′i·cate·ness,** *n.*

del·i·ca·tes·sen (del′i kə tes′ən) *n.* 1. store that specializes in prepared foods, as cooked meats. 2. such foods collectively, usually served cold. [German *Delikatessen,* plural of *Delikatesse* choice food, through French, going back to Latin *dēlicātus* dainty, charming, luxurious.]

de·li·cious (di lish′əs) *adj.* highly pleasing or delightful, esp. to the taste or smell: *delicious fruit, a delicious meal.* —*n.* **Delicious.** sweet red or yellow apple. [Old French *delicieus* fine, delicate, from Late Latin *dēlīciōsus* pleasant, from Latin *dēlicia* delight, pleasure.] —**de·li′cious·ly,** *adv.* —**de·li′cious·ness,** *n.*

de·light (di līt′) *n.* 1. high degree of pleasure; joy. 2. something that gives great pleasure: *Her dancing was a delight to watch.* —*v.t.* to give great pleasure or joy to; please highly: *The play delighted the children.* —*v.i.* to have or take great pleasure: *The gourmet delighted in eating French food.* [Old French *delitier* to rejoice, please, from Latin *dēlectāre* to charm.] —**Syn.** *v.t.* see **please.**

de·light·ed (di lī′tid) *adj.* highly pleased; gratified: *I'd be delighted to go with you.* —**de·light′ed·ly,** *adv.* —**de·light′ed·ness,** *n.* —**Syn.** see **glad′.**

de·light·ful (di līt′fəl) *adj.* highly pleasing; giving delight. —**de·light′ful·ly,** *adv.* —**de·light′ful·ness,** *n.*

---

at; āpe; cär; end; mē; it; īce; hot; ōld; fôrk; wood; fōōl; oil; out; up; ūse; turn; sing; thin; this; zh in treasure; ə in ago, taken, pencil, lemon, circus.

267

de·light·some (di līt′səm) *adj. Archaic.* delightful.

De·li·lah (di lī′lə) *n.* **1.** in the Old Testament, the mistress of Samson, who betrayed him to the Philistines by cutting off his hair, thereby depriving him of his strength. **2.** any treacherous, seductive woman.

de·lim·it (di lim′it) *v.t.* to mark or fix the limits of; bound; demarcate. Also, **de·lim′i·ta′tion,** *n.*

de·lin·e·ate (di lin′ē āt′) **-at·ed, -at·ing.** *v.t.* **1.** to draw or indicate the outline of; sketch out: *The map clearly delineated boundaries.* **2.** to represent by a drawing or sketch. **3.** to depict in words; describe; portray: *to delineate a character in a novel.* [Latin *dēlīneātus,* past participle of *dēlīneāre* to sketch out, going back to *de-* down + *līnea* line.] —**de·lin′e·a′tive,** *adj.* —**de·lin′e·a′tor,** *n.* —**Syn. 2.** see portray.

de·lin·e·a·tion (di lin′ē ā′shən) *n.* **1.** act or process of delineating; being delineated. **2.a.** pictorial representation. **b.** description in words.

de·lin·quen·cy (di ling′kwən sē) *pl.,* **-cies. 1.** failure or neglect of duty or obligation. **2.** fault; offense; misdeed. **3.** juvenile delinquency.

de·lin·quent (di ling′kwənt) *adj.* **1.** failing in or neglectful of a duty or obligation; guilty of a violation against the law. **2.** due and unpaid, as taxes or accounts. —*n.* one who is delinquent, esp. a juvenile delinquent. [Latin *dēlinquēns,* present participle of *dēlinquere* to fail, offend.] —**de·lin′quent·ly,** *adv.*

del·i·quesce (del′ə kwes′) **-quesced, -quesc·ing.** *v.i.* **1.** to melt or become liquid by absorbing moisture from the air. **2.** to melt away. **3.** *Botany.* **a.** to become soft or liquid upon maturing, as certain fungi. **b.** to branch out into many small subdivisions. [Latin *dēliquēscere* to melt.] —**del′i·ques′cence,** *n.*

del·i·ques·cent (del′ə kwes′ənt) *adj.* **1.** able to melt and form a solution by absorbing moisture directly from the air. Some salts are deliquescent. **2.** *Botany.* branching out into many small subdivisions, as the elm or oak.

de·lir·i·ous (di lēr′ē əs) *adj.* **1.** affected with delirium. **2.** characteristic of or caused by delirium: *delirious fantasies.* **3.** wildly excited: *delirious with joy.* —**de·lir′i·ous·ly,** *adv.* —**de·lir′i·ous·ness,** *n.*

de·lir·i·um (di lēr′ē əm) *pl.,* **-lir·i·ums** or **-lir·i·a** (-lēr′ē ə). *n.* **1.** temporary mental disturbance that may occur during high fevers, intoxication, and metabolic and nutritional disorders. Delirium is characterized by confusion, restlessness, disorientation, excitement, and illusions or hallucinations. **2.** wild excitement or emotion. [Latin *dēlīrium* madness; literally, a going out of the furrow (in plowing), going back to *de-* from + *līra* furrow.]

delirium tre·mens (trē′mənz) violent form of delirium, usually caused by excessive and prolonged drinking of alcoholic liquor, characterized by restlessness, muscular tremors, and terrifying hallucinations. Also, **d.t.'s.** [Modern Latin *delirium tremens* literally, trembling delirium.]

De·li·us, Frederick (dē′lē əs) 1862–1934, English composer.

de·liv·er (di liv′ər) *v.t.* **1.** to carry or take to a particular place or person: *to deliver mail, to deliver groceries.* **2.** to give forth in words or sound; utter; pronounce: *to deliver a speech.* **3.** to send forth; discharge. **4.a.** to strike: *to deliver a blow.* **b.** to throw; pitch: *The pitcher delivered a curve ball.* **5.** to surrender or hand over; transfer: *to deliver a town into the hands of the enemy.* **6.a.** to assist in the birth of; assist in giving birth: *to deliver a baby, to deliver a woman of triplets.* **b.** to give birth to. **7.** to give forth; afford; yield. **8.** to set free; liberate; rescue; save: *The Lord delivered the Israelites from bondage.* **9.** *Informal.* to bring or supply (something needed or promised): *to deliver votes in an election.* **10. to be delivered of,** to give birth to. **11. to deliver oneself of,** to express in words; utter. —*v.i.* **1.** to give birth. **2.** to make deliveries: *Does that supermarket deliver?* [Old French *delivrer* to set free, from Late Latin *dēlīberāre,* going back to Latin *de-* from + *līber* free.] —**de·liv′er·a·ble,** *adj.* —**de·liv′er·er,** *n.*

de·liv·er·ance (di liv′ər əns) *n.* **1.** act of setting free; fact of being set free; liberation; rescue. **2.** judgment or opinion expressed formally or publicly.

de·liv·er·y (di liv′ər ē) *pl.,* **-er·ies.** *n.* **1.a.** act of carrying or taking something to a particular place or person: *The laundry makes deliveries on Tuesdays.* **b.** that which is carried or brought: *Two items were missing from the delivery.* **2.** act or manner of speaking, singing, or giving forth in sound: *Her delivery was too weak for such a rousing song.* **3.** act or manner of sending forth, discharging, or striking: *a pitcher with an awkward delivery.* **4.** act of giving birth. **5.** a giving up; handing over; surrender. **6.** a setting free or saving; release or rescue.

dell (del) *n.* small, usually wooded, secluded glen or valley. [Old English *dell* deep hollow, valley.]

De·los (dē′los, del′ōs) *n.* small Greek island in the Cyclades, regarded by the ancient Greeks as the birthplace of Apollo and Artemis.

de·louse (dē lous′, -louz′) **-loused, -lous·ing.** *v.t.* to remove lice from.

Del·phi (del′fī) *n.* ancient city in central Greece, site of the Delphic oracle.

Del·phic (del′fik) *adj.* **1.** relating to Delphi, the oracle of Apollo at

Delphi, or Apollo himself. **2.** obscure in meaning; ambiguous. Also, **Del·phi·an** (del′fē ən).

Delphic oracle, oracle or prophetess of Apollo at Delphi, famed for giving ambiguous advice or prophecies.

del·phin·i·um (del fin′ē əm) *n.* any of a large group of plants, genus *Delphinium,* of the crowfoot family, bearing dense spikes of showy flowers, usually blue or purple. Also, **lark′spur′.** [Modern Latin *Delphinium,* from Greek *delphīnion,* from *delphīs* dolphin; from the dolphinlike shape of its flowers.]

del Sar·to, Andrea (del sär′tō) Andrea del Sarto.

del·ta (del′tə) *n.* **1.** fourth letter of the Greek alphabet (Δ, δ), corresponding to English *D, d.* **2.** anything shaped like a triangle. **3.** usually triangular area of land formed by deposits of silt, sand, and pebbles at the mouth of a river.

River

Delta

del·ta-wing (del′tə wing′) *adj.* (of an airplane) having wings that resemble the triangular shape of the Greek letter delta.

del·toid (del′toid) *n.* broad, triangular muscle covering the shoulder joint and serving to flex and extend the arm and to raise it away from the side of the body. —*adj.* **1.** shaped like a delta; triangular. **2.** relating to the deltoid muscle. [Greek *deltoeidēs* delta-shaped, from *delta* the Greek letter; of Semitic origin. See DELTA.]

de·lude (di lōōd′) **-lud·ed, -lud·ing.** *v.t.* to mislead the mind or judgment; deceive: *The dishonest politician attempted to delude the voters.* [Latin *dēlūdere.*] —**de·lud′er,** *n.* —**de·lud′ing·ly,** *adv.*

del·uge (del′ūj) *n.* **1.** overflowing of water; great flood or downpour; inundation. **2.** anything that overwhelms or rushes like a flood: *a deluge of tourists during the holiday season.* **3. the Deluge,** in the Old Testament, the great flood in the time of Noah. —*v.t.,* **-uged, -ug·ing. 1.** to flood with water; inundate. **2.** to overwhelm by any great rush: *The network was deluged with irate letters from its viewers.* [Old French *deluge* flood, from Latin *dīluvium.*]

de·lu·sion (di lōō′zhən) *n.* **1.** false impression or belief: *delusions of grandeur, the delusion that wealth leads to happiness.* **2.** false belief held despite evidence to the contrary, characteristic of certain types of mental illness. **3.** act of deluding; being deluded. **4.** state of being deluded. [Latin *dēlūsiō* a deceiving.] —**Syn. 2.** see **illusion.**

de·lu·sive (di lōō′siv) *adj.* **1.** apt or tending to delude; misleading; deceptive. **2.** like a delusion; false; unreal. Also, **de·lu·so·ry** (di lōō′sər ē). —**de·lu′sive·ly,** *adv.* —**de·lu′sive·ness,** *n.*

de·luxe (di luks′, -lōōks′) *adj.* exceptionally fine in quality or elegance: *deluxe accomodatiions.* [French *de luxe* literally, of luxury, from Late Latin *dē* of + Latin *luxus* luxury.]

delve (delv) **delved, delv·ing.** *v.i.* **1.** to make careful investigation or examination; search for information: *The board of inquiry delved into the question of possible fraud.* **2.** *Archaic.* to dig. [Old English *delfan* to dig.]

Dem., Democrat; Democratic.

de·mag·net·ize (dē mag′nə tīz′) **-ized, -iz·ing.** *v.t.* to deprive of magnetic properties. —**de·mag′net·i·za′tion,** *de·mag′net·iz′er,* *n.*

dem·a·gog·ic (dem′ə goj′ik, -gog′-) *adj.* of, relating to, or characteristic of a demagogue. Also, **dem′a·gog′i·cal.** —**dem′a·gog′i·cal·ly,** *adv.*

dem·a·gogue (dem′ə gog′) *also,* **dem·a·gog.** *n.* public leader or agitator who appeals to the passions and prejudices of the people in order to obtain power or to further his own interests. [Greek *dēmagōgos* popular leader, from *dēmos* people + *agōgos* leader.]

dem·a·gogu·er·y (dem′ə gog′ər ē) *n.* actions, practices, or principles of a demagogue. Also, **dem·a·gog·y** (dem′ə goj′ē, -gog′ē).

de·mand (di mand′) *v.t.* **1.** to ask for with insistence or urgency: *The customer loudly demanded a refund.* **2.** to ask for with authority; claim as a right: *The judge demanded silence in the courtroom.* **3.** to ask to know; request to be told: *to demand the truth.* **4.** to call for; require as necessary or useful; need: *work which demands careful attention.* —*v.i.* to make a demand. —*n.* **1.** act of demanding. **2.** authoritative or insistent request: *to meet the demands of a blackmailer.* **3.** claim, need, or requirement: *the demands of one's job.* **4.** expressed or existing desire; call: *a demand for excellent teaching.* **5.** *Economics.* **a.** desire for a commodity or service combined with the ability to purchase it. **b.** quantity of a commodity which buyers are willing to purchase at a certain price at a given time. **6.** *Archaic.* inquiry; question. **7. in demand.** sought after; wanted: *That author is in great demand as a lecturer.* **8. on demand,** on presentation; on being requested: *a note payable on demand.* [Old French *demander* to ask, ask for, from Late Latin *dēmandāre* to ask, from Latin *dēmandāre* to entrust.] —**de·mand′a·ble,** *adj.* —**de·mand′er,** *n.*

Syn. *v.t.* **1. Demand, claim, require** imply making a request for something necessary or desired. **Demand** suggests an arbitrary manner, as

at; āpe; cär; end; mē; it; īce; hot; ōld; fôrk; wood; fōōl; out; up; ūse; turn; sing; thin; this; zh in treasure; ə in ago, taken, pencil, lemon, circus.

if from authority: *He demanded an explanation of her behavior.* **Claim** implies the belief that one has a right to what is asked for: *He claimed the money that was lying on the floor.* **Require** implies that what is asked for is needed: *John's history professor requires a great deal of outside reading.*

demand deposit, bank deposit that can be withdrawn by the depositor without advance notice. Checking accounts are demand deposits.

de·mand·ing (di man′ding) *adj.* requiring much care or attention; making demands: *demanding work, a demanding child.* —**de·mand′·ing·ly,** *adv.*

de·mar·cate (di mär′kāt, dē′mär kāt′) -**cat·ed,** -**cat·ing.** *v.t.* **1.** to mark or fix the limits or boundaries of; delimit. **2.** to separate or distinguish. [From DEMARCATION.]

de·mar·ca·tion (dē′mär kā′shən) *n.* **1.** marking or fixing of limits or boundaries. **2.** limits or boundaries so fixed. **3.** separation; differentiation. [Spanish *demarcación* a marking off of bounds, going back to *de-* completely (from Latin *dē* down) + *marcar* to mark (of Germanic origin).]

deme (dēm) *n.* administrative subdivisions of ancient Attica. [Greek *dēmos* district, people.]

de·mean¹ (di mēn′) *v.t.* to lower the dignity or status of; degrade; debase: *The scientist demeaned himself by taking credit for another man's work.* [DE- + MEAN²; modeled on DEBASE.]

de·mean² (di mēn′) *v.t.* to behave, conduct, or comport (oneself): *He demeaned himself well at the reception.* [Old French *demener* to conduct, going back to Latin *dē* down + *mināre* to drive (cattle).]

de·mean·or (di mē′nər) *also, British,* **de·mean·our** *n.* way one behaves and bears oneself; manner; deportment; conduct. [Middle English *demenure,* from *demenen* to conduct, from Old French *demener.* See DEMEAN².]

de·ment·ed (di men′tid) *adj.* insane; mad; crazed. [Past participle of archaic *dement* to drive mad, from Late Latin *dēmentāre,* going back to Latin *dē* from + *mēns* mind.]

de·men·tia (di men′shə) *n.* deterioration or loss of mental faculties, resulting from either organic or emotional causes. [Latin *dēmentia* madness, going back to *dē* from + *mēns* mind.]

dementia prae·cox (prē′koks) schizophrenia. ▲ no longer used in psychiatry. [Modern Latin *dementia praecox* literally, premature insanity.]

de·mer·it (dē mer′it) *n.* **1.** mark against a person for unsatisfactory work or behavior. **2.** quality or act that deserves blame; fault. [Old French *demerite* misdeed, blame, going back to Latin *dē* down + *merēre* to deserve.]

de·mesne (di mān′, -mēn′) *n.* **1.** *Law.* the possession of land as one's own. **2.** manor house and the adjoining untenanted land belonging to a feudal lord. **3.** land of an estate. **4.** domain; realm. **5.** region; district; territory. [Old French *demeine* domain, belonging to a lord, from Latin *dominicus* relating to a master, from *dominus* master.]

De·me·ter (di mē′tər) *n.* Greek goddess of agriculture and the fertility and fruits of the earth. Her Roman counterpart is Ceres.

demi- *prefix* less than usual; not complete; half: *demigod.* [French *demi* half, from Medieval Latin *dimedius,* from Latin *dīmidius.*]

dem·i·god (dem′ē god′) *n.* **1.a.** inferior or lesser god. **b.** offspring of a god and a mortal. **2.** person who is regarded as having godlike qualities. —**dem′i·god′dess,** *n.*

dem·i·john (dem′ē jon′) *n.* narrow-necked bottle of glass or earthenware, usually enclosed in wicker and holding from one to ten gallons. [Modification of French *dame-jeanne* literally, Lady Jane (humorous name for a bottle). See DAME.]

de·mil·i·ta·rize (dē mil′ə tə rīz′) -**ized,** -**iz·ing.** *v.t.* **1.** to remove or prohibit military installations, troops, or action in (an area or zone); declare neutral: *The two warring nations agreed to demilitarize a four-mile strip of land between their countries.* **2.** to remove military character from. **3.** to place under civilian rather than military control. —**de·mil′i·ta·ri·za′tion,** *n.*

demilitarized zone, specified area in which all military installations or forces are prohibited by agreement of two or more nations.

dem·i·mon·daine (dem′ē mon dān′) *n.* woman of the demimonde.

dem·i·monde (dem′ē mond′) *n.* class of women of doubtful reputation and social standing. [French *demi-monde* literally, half-world, from *demi-* (see DEMI-) + *monde* world (from Latin *mundus* world).]

de·mise (di mīz′) *n.* **1.** death: *We lamented her early demise.* **2.** cessation; end: *the demise of the feudal system.* **3.** transfer of an estate for life or for a limited number of years; lease. **4.** transfer of sovereignty upon the death, abdication, or removal of a sovereign. —*v.t.,* -**mised,** -**mis·ing.** **1.** to transfer (an estate) for life or for a limited number of years; lease. **2.** to transfer (sovereignty) upon the death, abdication, or

removal of a sovereign. —*v.i.* to pass by bequest, inheritance, or succession. [Old French *demise,* feminine past participle of *demettre* to dismiss, send away, from Latin *dīmittere.*]

dem·i·sem·i·qua·ver (dem′ē sem′ē kwä′vər) *n.* thirty-second note in music.

dem·i·tasse (dem′ē tas′, -täs′) *n.* **1.** small cup of black, usually strong, coffee. **2.** small cup in which such black coffee is served. [French *demi-tasse,* from *demi-* (see DEMI-) + *tasse* cup (from Arabic *tass* basin, from Persian *tast* cup).]

de·mo·bi·lize (dē mō′bə līz′) -**lized,** -**liz·ing.** *v.t., v.i.* **1.** to disband or dismiss (troops or an army); remove from military service: *He was demobilized in 1945.* **2.** to change from a state of readiness for war; put on a peacetime basis: *The country demobilized its industries after the war.* —**de·mo′bi·li·za′tion,** *n.*

de·moc·ra·cy (di mok′rə sē) *pl.,* -**cies.** *n.* **1.** government by the people, who rule either directly, as through town meetings and referendums, or indirectly, through freely elected representatives. **2.** nation, state, or other political entity having such a government. **3.** political and social equality in spirit and practice. [Middle French *democratie* popular government, through Medieval Latin, from Greek *dēmokratiā,* from *dēmos* people + *-kratiā* rule.]

dem·o·crat (dem′ə krat′) *n.* **1.** one who believes in or advocates democracy as a principle of government. **2.** one who believes in and practices political and social equality. **3.** Democrat. member of the Democratic Party.

dem·o·crat·ic (dem′ə krat′ik) *adj.* **1.** of, relating to, or advocating democracy as a principle or form of government. **2.** relating to, characterized by, or exhibiting political and social equality. **3.** of or meant for all the people **4.** Democratic. of, relating to, or characteristic of the Democratic Party. —**dem′o·crat′i·cal·ly,** *adv.*

Democratic Party, one of the two major political parties in the United States, evolving from the parties of Thomas Jefferson and Andrew Jackson. It adopted its present name about 1828.

Dem·o·crat·ic-Re·pub·li·can Party (dem′ə krat′ik ri pub′li kən) U.S. political party opposed to the Federalist Party, founded in 1792 under the leadership of Thomas Jefferson. It was succeeded by the Democratic Party.

de·moc·ra·tize (di mok′rə tīz′) -**tized,** -**tiz·ing.** *v.t., v.i.* to make or become democratic. —**de·moc′ra·ti·za′tion,** *n.*

De·moc·ri·tus (di mok′rə təs) c.460–370 B.C., Greek philosopher.

de·mod·u·late (dē moj′ə lāt′, -mod′yə-) *v.t.* to separate (information) from a radio carrier wave; detect. —**de·mod′u·la′tion, de·mod′u·la′tor,** *n.*

De·mo·gor·gon (dē′mə gôr′gən) *n.* demon or devil, often associated with the mysterious and evil spirit of creation in ancient and medieval mythology.

de·mog·ra·phy (di mog′rə fē) *n.* statistical study of human populations, including their size, structure, distribution, and composition. [Greek *dēmos* people + -GRAPHY.] —**de·mog′ra·pher,** *n.* —**de·mo·graph·ic** (dē′mə graf′ik), *adj.* —**de·mo·graph′i·cal·ly,** *adv.*

dem·oi·selle (dem′wä zel′, dem′ə-) *n.* **1.** young lady; damsel. **2.** crane, *Anthropoides virgo,* of Asia, Europe, and northern Africa, having long white plumes behind the eyes. **3.** damselfly. [French *demoiselle* young lady, going back to Latin *domina* lady.]

Demoiselle

de·mol·ish (di mol′ish) *v.t.* **1.** to tear down or apart; destroy the structure of: *to demolish an old apartment building.* **2.** to destroy or ruin completely: *New evidence demolished their argument.* [Old French *demoliss-,* a stem of *demolir,* from Latin *dēmōlīrī* to tear down.] —**de·mol′ish·er, de·mol′ish·ment,** *n.*

Syn. 2. Demolish, raze, wreck mean to destroy something, usually by pulling down or by smashing. Demolish implies complete ruin and a heaping up of small, unusable pieces: *The crew demolished the building in half a day.* Raze suggests a leveling to the ground: *Whole blocks of slum dwellings were razed in the development program.* Wreck implies that the destruction is violent and unintentional: *The force of the blast wrecked several small houses.*

dem·o·li·tion (dem′ə lish′ən, dē′mə-) *n.* **1.** act of demolishing; state of being demolished; destruction. **2.** demolitions. explosives, esp. for military use. —**dem·o·li′tion·ist,** *n.*

demolition bomb, bomb with a high explosive force, used esp. to destroy large structures.

de·mon (dē′mən) *n.* **1.** evil spirit; devil. **2.** extremely wicked or cruel person. **3.** something regarded as a personification of evil or as an evil

influence. **4.** one who shows great skill or energy in some activity: *a demon on ice skates, a demon for work.* **5.** *also,* **dae·mon.** attendant or guiding spirit; genius. **6.** *also,* **dae·mon.** *Greek Mythology.* a supernatural being lower in rank than a god. [Late Latin *daemōn* evil spirit, from Latin *daemōn* spirit, from Greek *daimōn* divinity, fate.]

de·mon·e·tize (dē mon′ə tīz′, -mun′-) -**tized, -tiz·ing.** *v.t.* **1.** to deprive (currency) of its standard value as money. **2.** to withdraw from use as money. —**de·mon′e·ti·za′tion,** *n.*

de·mo·ni·ac (di mō′nē ak′) *adj.* **1.** of, like, or characteristic of a demon or evil spirit; devilish. **2.** caused by or as by a demon or evil spirit; wild; frantic. **3.** acting as if possessed by a demon or evil spirit. Also, **de·mo·ni·a·cal** (dē′mə nī′ə kəl). —*n.* one supposedly possessed by a demon. —**de′mo·ni′a·cal·ly,** *adv.*

de·mon·ic (di mon′ik) *adj.* **1.** of, relating to, or characteristic of a demon. **2.** inspired, as by a demon or guiding spirit.

de·mon·ism (dē′mə niz′əm) *n.* **1.** belief in demons. **2.** demonolatry. **3.** demonology.

de·mon·ol·a·try (dē′mə nol′ə trē) *n.* worship of demons.

de·mon·ol·o·gy (dē′mə nol′ə jē) *n.* **1.** study of demons or of beliefs about them. **2.** treatise or doctrine about demons.

de·mon·stra·ble (di mon′strə bəl, dem′ən-) *adj.* capable of being proved or made evident. —**de·mon′stra·bil′i·ty,** *n.* —**de·mon′stra·bly,** *adv.*

dem·on·strate (dem′ən strāt′) -**strat·ed, -strat·ing.** *v.t.* **1.** to reveal or make evident; prove by reasoning: *Recent events demonstrate the need for a change in policy.* **2.** to describe, explain, or exhibit by actual performance or by use of experiments or examples: *to demonstrate a chemical law in the laboratory.* **3.** to make a show of; express openly; manifest: *to demonstrate one's feelings, to demonstrate one's strength.* **4.** to show the uses or merits of (a product): *to demonstrate a washing machine in a department store.* —*v.i.* to make or take part in a public demonstration: *to demonstrate in favor of cleaner air.* [Latin *dēmonstrātus,* past participle of *dēmonstrāre* to show.]

dem·on·stra·tion (dem′ən strā′shən) *n.* **1.** act or process of proving or making evident. **2.** that which serves as proof or evidence. **3.** exhibition and explanation by actual performance or by the use of experiments or examples: *a demonstration of the law of gravity.* **4.** open expression; show: *a demonstration of grief.* **5.** gathering, meeting, or parade to show public feeling toward a particular issue or person: *a demonstration against a proposed highway.* **6.** display of the uses or merits of a product. **7.** process of proving that, from certain premises, certain conclusions must follow.

de·mon·stra·tive (di mon′strə tiv) *adj.* **1.** given to or characterized by open display of feelings, esp. affectionate ones. **2.** serving to indicate or show clearly; explanatory; illustrative. **3.** having the power of proving; conclusive. **4.** *Grammar.* indicating and distinguishing the particular person or thing referred to. *This* and *that* are demonstrative pronouns. —*n.* demonstrative pronoun or adjective. —**de·mon′stra·tive·ly,** *adv.* —**de·mon′stra·tive·ness,** *n.*

dem·on·stra·tor (dem′ən strā′tər) *n.* **1.** one who demonstrates, esp. a person who takes part in a demonstration of public feeling. **2.** thing used for demonstration, as a sample product used in demonstrations to customers.

de·mor·al·ize (di môr′ə līz′, -mor′-) -**ized, -iz·ing.** *v.t.* **1.** to lower or destroy the morale of; deprive of courage, confidence, or hope; dishearten: *A series of defeats demoralized the army.* **2.** to corrupt the morals of. **3.** to throw into disorder. —**de·mor′al·i·za′tion,** *n.*

De·mos·the·nes (də mos′thə nēz′) c.384–322 B.C., Greek orator and statesman.

de·mote (di mōt′) -**mot·ed, -mot·ing.** *v.t.* to reduce to a lower grade or rank: *to demote a soldier from corporal to private.* [DE- + (PRO)MOTE.] —**de·mo′tion** (di mō′shən), *n.*

de·mot·ic (di mot′ik) *adj.* **1.** of or relating to the common people; popular. **2.** of or relating to the simplified form of hieratic writing of ancient Egypt. [Greek *dēmotikos* relating to the people, popular, going back to *dēmos* people.]

de·mount (dē mount′) *v.t.* to remove from a mounting or setting, as a motor or gun. —**de·mount′a·ble,** *adj.*

de·mul·cent (di mul′sənt) *adj.* soothing. —*n.* soothing substance, esp. a medicinal mucilage or oil used to relieve irritation caused by inflammation or abrasion. [Latin *dēmulcēns,* present participle of *dēmulcēre* to soothe.]

de·mur (di mur′) -**murred, -mur·ring.** *v.i.* **1.** to raise objection or exception; object: *to demur at using force. He demurred at first, but then agreed to go.* **2.** to enter a legal demurrer. —*n.* *also,* **de·mur′ral. 1.** objection raised or exception taken. **2.** act of demurring. [Old French *demourer* to tarry, from Latin *dēmorārī.*]

de·mure (di myoor′) -**mur·er, -mur·est.** *adj.* **1.** quiet and modest; shy; reserved. **2.** affectedly modest; coy. [DE- + obsolete *mure* calm, from Old French *mēur* grave, mellow, from Latin *mātūrus* ripe.] —**de·mure′ly,** *adv.* —**de·mure′ness,** *n.*

de·mur·rage (di mur′ij) *n.* **1.** detention of a ship, railroad car, or other commercial conveyance due to the failure of the shipper to load or unload his cargo by a specified time. **2.** payment owed or made to the carrier by the shipper for such a delay.

de·mur·rer (di mur′ər) *n.* **1.** legal request that a case be dismissed on the ground that even if the facts as stated by the opposite party are true, they are insufficient to warrant an action. **2.** objection or exception; demur. **3.** one who demurs.

den (den) *n.* **1.** lair or secluded place inhabited by a wild animal: *a bear's den.* **2.** retreat or secluded place used esp. as a hideout or secret headquarters: *a den of thieves.* **3.** private room, usually small and cozy, for relaxation or study. **4.** small, squalid room or dwelling. [Old English *denn* lair of a wild beast.]

Den., Denmark.

de·nar·i·us (di när′ē əs) *pl.,* **-nar·i·i** (-när′ē ī′). *n.* **1.** silver coin of ancient Rome. **2.** gold coin of ancient Rome, worth 25 silver denarii. [Latin *dēnārius,* from *dēnārius* containing ten, from *dēnī* ten each; originally referring to a coin worth ten asses (see AS²). Doublet of DENIER², DINAR.]

de·na·tion·al·ize (dē nash′ən əl īz′) -**ized, -iz·ing.** *v.t.* **1.** to remove from national control or ownership, as an industry. **2.** to deprive of nationality; divest of national character or rights. —**de·na′tion·al·i·za′tion,** *n.*

de·nat·u·ral·ize (dē nach′ər ə līz′) -**ized, -iz·ing.** *v.t.* **1.** to deprive of original or true nature; make unnatural. **2.** to deprive of the status and rights of naturalization or citizenship. —**de·nat′u·ral·i·za′tion,** *n.*

de·na·ture (dē nā′chər) -**tured, -tur·ing.** *v.t.* **1.** to make a substance, as alcohol, unfit for drinking or eating without destroying its other useful properties. **2.** to change the nature of. **3.** to alter (a protein) so that its original properties are removed or greatly changed. —**de·na′tur·a′tion,** *n.*

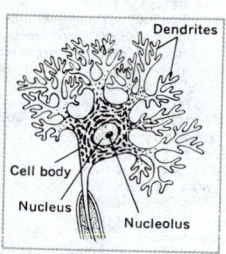

Dendrites

Cell body

Nucleus

Nucleolus

Dendrite

denatured alcohol, ethyl alcohol made unfit for drinking by the addition of small amounts of foreign materials.

den·drite (den′drīt) *n.* **1.** branching treelike marking found on certain stones or minerals. **2.** stone or mineral having such markings. **3.** crystallized treelike form, as of gold. **4.** small branched fiber that extends from a neuron and conducts nerve impulses to the cell body. [Greek *dendrītēs* relating to a tree, from *dendron* tree.] —**den·drit·ic** (den-drit′ik), *adj.*

Den·eb (den′eb) *n.* bluish-white giant star, one of the brightest in the sky and the brightest in the constellation Cygnus.

den·gue (deng′gā, -gē) *n.* acute, infectious tropical or subtropical disease, usually occurring in epidemics, caused by a virus transmitted by a mosquito, and characterized by headache, fever, skin rash, and severe pain in the joints and muscles. [Spanish *dengue* this disease, from Swahili *dinga* cramplike attack.]

de·ni·al (di nī′əl) *n.* **1.** act of declaring something to be untrue; contradiction: *a defendant's denial of the charges against him.* **2.** act of refusing something asked for or desired: *a denial of a request for funds.* **3.** refusal to acknowledge a connection with or responsibility for; disavowal: *his denial of his family.* **4.** refusal to accept or believe in something, as a doctrine: *a denial of his former belief in socialism.* **5.** self-denial.

de·ni·er¹ (di nī′ər) *n.* one who denies. [DENY + -ER¹.]

den·ier² (*def. 1* den′yər, də nēr′; *def. 2* də nēr′) *n.* **1.** unit of weight for expressing the fineness of silk, rayon, or nylon yarn, based on the standard of a yarn weighing one gram for each 9000 meters. **2.** former coin of France and Western Europe, originally of silver and later of copper, varying in value. [Old French *denier* penny, from Latin *dēnārius* the Roman coin, containing ten, from *dēnī* ten each. Doublet of DENARIUS, DINAR.]

den·i·grate (den′ə grāt′) -**grat·ed, -grat·ing.** *v.t.* to cast aspersions on; blacken the reputation of; slander; defame. [Latin *dēnigrātus,* past participle of *dēnigrāre* to blacken, defame.] —**den′i·gra′tion, den′i·gra′tor,** *n.*

den·im (den′im) *n.* **1.** heavy, twilled cotton fabric woven with a colored warp and white filling, used for such items as work clothes and sportswear. **2.** denims, overalls or trousers made of this fabric. [Short for French (*serge*) *de Nîm(es)* serge of Nîmes, a French city where the fabric was first made.]

Den·is, Saint (den′is) died A.D. c.258, patron saint of France.

de·ni·tri·fy (dē nī′trə fī′) -**fied, -fy·ing.** *v.t.* **1.** to remove nitrogen or its compounds from. **2.** to reduce (nitrates) to nitrites, ammonia,

at; āpe; cär; end; mē; it; īce; hot; ōld; fôrk; wood; fōōl; out; up; ūse; turn; sing; thin; *this*; zh in treasure; ə in ago, taken, pencil, lemon, circus.

or nitrogen, as in soil by the action of certain microorganisms. —**de·ni′tri·fi·ca′tion,** *n.*

den·i·zen (den′ə zən) *n.* **1.** inhabitant; dweller; occupant. **2.** *British.* foreigner admitted to residence and certain rights in a country. **3.** anything that has become adapted to a new place or condition, as a plant or animal naturalized in an area to which it is not originally native. [Anglo-Norman *deinzein* literally, one living within, from *deinz* within, going back to Latin *dē* from + *intus* within.]

Den·mark (den′märk) *n.* country in northern Europe, between the North and Baltic seas. Capital, Copenhagen. Area, 16,619 sq. mi. Pop. (1969 est.), 4,910,000.

de·nom·i·nate (di nom′ə nāt′) *-nat·ed, -nat·ing.* *v.t.* to give a name to; name; designate. [Latin *dēnōminātus,* past participle of *dēnōmināre* to name.]

de·nom·i·nate number (di nom′ə nit, -nāt′) number that specifies a concrete quantity by limiting a unit of measurement. In the expression *5 pounds, 5* is a denominate number.

de·nom·i·na·tion (di nom′ə nā′shən) *n.* **1.** religious group or sect: *a man of Lutheran denomination.* **2.** class of one kind of unit in a system of numbers, measures, or values: *The cashier gave the customer change in bills of the same denomination.* **3.** name for a thing or class of things; designation. **4.** act of denominating. —**Syn. 1.** see **sect.**

de·nom·i·na·tion·al (di nom′ə nā′shən əl) *adj.* relating to or controlled by a religious denomination or sect; sectarian: *a denominational school.* —**de·nom′i·na′tion·al·ly,** *adv.*

de·nom·i·na·tion·al·ism (di nom′ə nā′shən əl iz′əm) *n.* strict adherence to a denomination or its principles; sectarianism.

de·nom·i·na·tive (di nom′ə nā′tiv, -nə tiv) *adj.* **1.** giving or constituting a qualifying name; naming. **2.** derived from a noun or adjective. *To elbow* is a denominative verb formed from the noun *elbow.* —*n.* word derived from a noun or adjective.

de·nom·i·na·tor (di nom′ə nā′tər) *n.* **1.** number below or to the right of the line in a fraction, indicating the number of equal parts into which the whole is divided; divisor. In the fraction $1/2$, 2 is the denominator. **2.** characteristic that is held in common; standard.

de·no·ta·tion (dē′nō tā′shən) *n.* **1.** specific or literal meaning of a word or phrase, as distinct from what it suggests. Distinguished from **connotation.** **2.** act of denoting; being denoted. **3.** that which denotes; name; sign; indication.

de·no·ta·tive (dē′nō tā′tiv) *adj.* denoting or capable of denoting. —**de′no·ta′tive·ly,** *adv.*

de·note (di nōt′) *-not·ed, -not·ing.* *v.t.* **1.** to be an indication or sign of: *A frown often denotes displeasure.* **2.** to be a name or designation of; mean: *The word "dentist" denotes a doctor whose work is the care of teeth.* **3.** to be a mark or symbol for: *The sign ° denotes degrees.* [Latin *dēnotāre* to indicate.]

de·noue·ment (dā′nōō mäN′) *also,* **dé·noue·ment.** *n.* **1.** final outcome, solution, or unraveling of a plot in a play, story, or other literary work. **2.** point in the plot where this occurs. **3.** any final outcome or solution. [French *dénouement* an unraveling (esp. of a plot), from *denouer* to unravel, going back to Latin *dis-* apart + *nōdus* knot.]

de·nounce (di nouns′) *-nounced, -nounc·ing.* *v.t.* **1.** to attack or condemn publicly; censure openly: *to denounce the injustices of war.* **2.** to inform against; accuse: *He denounced the offenders to the authorities.* **3.** to give formal notice of the termination of (a treaty, armistice, or other agreement). [Old French *denoncier* to announce, declare, from Latin *dēnūntiāre.*] —**de·nounce′ment, de·nounc′er,** *n.* —**Syn.** *v.t.* **2.** see **accuse.**

de no·vo (dē nō′vō) from the beginning; anew. [Latin *dē novō.*]

dense (dens) **dens·er, dens·est.** *adj.* **1.** having its constituent parts closely packed together; thick; compact: *a dense forest, a dense crowd.* **2.** stupid; thick-headed; dull. **3.** difficult to penetrate; intense; profound; extreme. **4.** *Photography.* (of a developed negative) relatively opaque; having good contrast between light and dark areas. [Latin *dēnsus* thick.] —**dense′ly,** *adv.* —**dense′ness,** *n.* —**Syn. 1.** see **close.**

den·si·ty (den′sə tē) *pl.,* **-ties.** *n.* **1.** quality or condition of being closely packed together; thickness; compactness. **2.** *Physics.* ratio of the mass of a substance to its volume: *Iron has a greater density than wood.* **3.** quantity per unit of area, volume, length, or time, as the average number of people or dwellings in a given area. **4.** stupidity. **5.** *Electricity.* **a.** amount of electricity per unit area at a given point on a surface. **b.** current density. **6.** *Photography.* degree of opaqueness of a developed negative.

dent (dent) *n.* **1.** hollow or depression in a surface made by a blow or pressure: *a dent in an automobile fender.* **2.** effective headway; progress: *He worked all night, but barely made a dent in the work.* —*v.t.* to make a hollow or depression in. —*v.i.* to become dented. [Form of DINT.]

dent. **1.** dental. **2.** dentist. **3.** dentistry.

den·tal (den′təl) *adj.* **1.** of, for, or relating to the teeth. **2.** of or relating to dentistry. **3.** *Phonetics.* of, designating, or characterized by dentals. —*n. Phonetics.* consonant sound formed by putting the tip of the tongue

against the back of the upper front teeth. [Modern Latin *dentalis,* from Latin *dēns* tooth.]

dental caries, caries.

dental floss, strong waxed thread used to clean between the teeth.

den·tal·ize (den′əl īz′) *-ized, -iz·ing.* *v.t.* to pronounce as a dental sound. —**den′tal·i·za′tion,** *n.*

den·tate (den′tāt) *adj.* **1.** *Botany.* (of leaves) having toothlike projections along the edge. **2.** having teeth or toothlike projections; toothed; notched. [Latin *dentātus* toothed, from *dēns* tooth.] —**den·ta′tion,** *n.*

den·ti·frice (den′tə fris) *n.* paste, powder, or liquid used for cleaning the teeth. [French *dentifrice,* from Latin *dentifricium* powder for cleaning teeth, from *dēns* tooth + *fricāre* to rub.]

den·tin (den′tin) *also,* **den·tine** (den′tēn, den tēn′). *n.* hard, calcified material forming the major part of a tooth, covered by the enamel in the crown and the cementum in the root. [From Latin *dēns* tooth.]

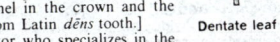

Dentate leaf

den·tist (den′tist) *n.* doctor who specializes in the health and care of the teeth and gums. [French *dentiste,* from *dent* tooth, from Latin *dēns* tooth.]

den·tist·ry (den′tis trē) *n.* **1.** branch of medical science dealing with the health and care of the teeth. **2.** work done by a dentist.

den·ti·tion (den tish′ən) *n.* **1.** process of teething. **2.** kind, number, and arrangement of the teeth characteristic of any animal. [Latin *dentītiō* teething, going back to *dēns* tooth.]

den·ture (den′chər) *n.* **1.** set of artificial teeth. **2.** set of teeth. [French *denture* set of teeth, from *dent* tooth, from Latin *dēns.*]

de·nude (di nōōd′, -nūd′) *-nud·ed, -nud·ing.* *v.t.* **1.** to strip or divest of all covering; make bare: *to denude the land of trees.* **2.** *Geology.* to expose or uncover (rock) by the erosion of overlying matter. [Latin *dēnūdāre* to lay bare, uncover, going back to *dē* down + *nūdus* bare.] —**de·nu·da·tion** (dē′nōō dā′shən, -nū-, den′yoo-), *n.*

de·nun·ci·a·tion (di nun′sē ā′shən) *n.* **1.** public expression of censure; open condemnation. **2.** act of informing the public authorities that a crime has been committed. **3.** formal declaration that an agreement, as a treaty or armistice, is to be terminated. **4.** *Archaic.* declaration of intended evil; threat. [Latin *dēnūntiātiō* declaration.] —**de·nun′ci·a·to′ry,** *adj.*

Den·ver (den′vər) *n.* capital and largest city of Colorado, in the north-central part of the state. Pop. (1970), 514,678.

de·ny (di nī′) *-nied, -ny·ing.* *v.t.* **1.** to declare (something) to be untrue; contradict: *The defendant denied the allegations.* **2.** to refuse to believe or accept as being valid or true; reject: *to deny the constitutionality of a law.* **3.** to refuse to give or grant: *to deny a request, to deny a passport.* **4.** to refuse to acknowledge; disavow: *To save his life, Galileo denied his theories.* **5. to deny oneself.** to practice self-denial; abstain from. [Old French *denoier* to oppose, reject, forbid, from Latin *dēnegāre* to reject, refuse.]

Syn. 1. Deny, contradict, gainsay mean to state that something is not true. **Deny** suggests clear rejection of something as untrue: *He denied that he had stolen the watch.* **Contradict** implies not only the untruth of something but that the opposite is true: *He contradicted the testimony of the previous witness.* **Gainsay,** essentially a literary word, suggests argument or proof to the contrary: *The evidence is clear and can hardly be gainsaid.*

de·o·dar (dē′ə där′) *n.* **1.** pyramid-shaped evergreen tree, *Cedrus deodara,* of the pine family, found mostly in the Himalayas and California, bearing needlelike bluish-green leaves and oval reddish-brown cones. **2.** fragrant, durable wood of this tree. [Hindi *dewdār* this tree; literally, divine tree, going back to Sanskrit *dēvas* divine + *dāru* wood.]

de·o·dor·ant (dē ō′dər ənt) *n.* substance that prevents or counteracts unpleasant odors, esp. a preparation used on the body to disguise or destroy perspiration odor. —*adj.* capable of preventing or counteracting unpleasant odors: *a deodorant soap, a deodorant spray.* [DE- + ODOR + -ANT.]

de·o·dor·ize (dē ō′də rīz′) *-ized, -iz·ing.* *v.t.* to counteract or destroy the unpleasant odor of. —**de·o′dor·i·za′tion, de·o′dor·iz′er,** *n.*

De·o vo·len·te (dē′ō vō len′tē) *Latin.* God willing.

de·ox·i·dize (dē ok′sə dīz′) *-dized, -diz·ing.* *v.t.* **1.** to remove oxygen from. **2.** to reduce from the state of an oxide. —**de·ox′i·di·za′tion, de·ox′i·diz′er,** *n.*

de·ox·y·ri·bo·nu·cle·ic acid (dē ok′si rī′bō nōō klē′ik, -nū-) see DNA.

dep. **1.** depart. **2.** departure. **3.** department. **4.** deponent. **5.** deposit. **6.** depot. **7.** deputy.

Dep., dependency.

de·part (di pärt′) *v.i.* **1.** to go away; leave: *The ship departs at noon.* **2.** to deviate; diverge: *to depart from tradition, to depart from one's customary way of dressing.* **3.** to die: *Lord, now lettest thou thy servant depart in peace* (Luke 2:29). —*v.t.* to go away from; leave. ▲ now used

at; āpe; cär; end; mē; it; īce; hot; ōld; fôrk; wood; fōōl; oil; out; up; ūse; turn; sing; thin; <u>th</u>is; zh in treasure; ə in ago, taken, pencil, lemon, circus.

chiefly in the phrase *to depart this life.* [Old French *departir* to divide (as in phrase *se departir de* to divide oneself from, leave), going back to Latin *dis-* apart + *partīre* to divide.] —**Syn.** *v.i.* 2. see **diverge.**

de·part·ed (di pär′tid) *adj.* 1. dead. 2. past; gone: *departed glory.* —*n.* **the departed.** person or persons who have died.

de·part·ment (di pärt′mənt) *n.* 1. separate part or division of an organization or government, established for a specific purpose: *the police department, the sales department of a company, the shoe department of a store.* 2. division of an educational institution devoted to a particular area of learning: *the physics department.* 3. *usually,* **Department.** major division of the executive branch of the U.S. government: *the Department of Agriculture.* 4. administrative district of France. 5. *Informal.* particular area of interest or proficiency: *Woodworking is not my department.* [French *département* administrative division, line¹, province, from *departir* to divide. See DEPART.] —**de·part·men·tal** (di pärt′ment′əl, dē′pärt-), *adj.*

de·part·men·tal·ize (di pärt′ment′əl īz′, dē′pärt-) **-ized, -iz·ing.** *v.t., v.i.* to divide into departments. —**de·part·men′tal·i·za′tion,** *n.*

department store, large retail store selling a variety of merchandise arranged in separate departments.

de·par·ture (di pär′chər) *n.* 1. act of departing or leaving. 2. deviation, as from a standard or course of action; divergence: *a departure from custom.* 3. setting out, as on a course of action: *This bill marks a new departure in civil-rights legislation.* 4. *Archaic.* death.

de·pend (di pend′) *v.i.* 1. to place confidence in; rely (with *on* or *upon*): *You can depend on Jim to get the job done.* 2. to rely for what is necessary or desirable (with *on* or *upon*): *The student depends on his relatives for support. Britain depends on other countries for oil.* 3. to be influenced or determined (by something); to be contingent (with *on* or *upon*): *Price depends on costs and demand. Whether I accept the job depends on how much the salary is.* 4. to hang down: *Icicles depended from the eaves.* 5. **it depends.** it is contingent on unspecified circumstances. [Old French *dependre* to hang from, rely, from Latin *dēpendēre* to hang from, be dependent on.]

de·pen·da·ble (di pen′də bəl) *adj.* capable of being depended on; reliable. —**de·pen′da·bil′i·ty,** *n.* —**de·pen′da·bly,** *adv.*

de·pen·dence (di pen′dəns) *also,* **de·pen·dance.** *n.* 1. state of relying on another for what is necessary or desirable. 2. state of being influenced or determined by something else; being contingent. 3. subjection or subordination to someone or something. 4. trust; reliance.

de·pen·den·cy (di pen′dən sē) *pl.,* **-cies.** *also,* **de·pen·dan·cy.** *n.* 1. country or territory that is not fully self-governing and does not form an integral part of the governing country. 2. dependence. 3. something subordinate or dependent; subordinate part.

de·pen·dent (di pen′dənt) *also,* **de·pen·dant.** *adj.* 1. relying on another for what is necessary or desirable. 2. subordinate: *dependent territory.* 3. influenced or determined by something; contingent. 4. hanging down; pendent. —*n.* one who depends on another for support or aid. —**de·pen′dent·ly,** *adv.*

dependent clause, clause that functions as a noun, adjective, or adverb within a sentence and cannot stand alone. In the sentence *After the girls had played tennis for an hour, they decided to go for a swim,* the clause *After the girls had played tennis for an hour* is a dependent clause. Distinguished from **independent clause.** Also, **subordinate clause.**

dependent variable *Mathematics.* variable whose values depend on the values of other variables. Distinguished from **independent variable.**

de·pict (di pikt′) *v.t.* 1. to represent by or as by drawing or painting; picture; portray. 2. to portray in words; describe: *to depict a character in a novel.* [Latin *dēpictus,* past participle of *dēpingere.*] —**Syn.** 1. see **portray.**

de·pic·tion (di pik′shən) *n.* 1. result of depicting, as a picture or descriptive account. 2. act of depicting.

dep·i·late (dep′ə lāt′) **-lat·ed, -lat·ing.** *v.t.* to remove hair from. [Latin *dēpilātus,* past participle of *dēpilāre* to remove hair, going back to *dē* from + *pilus* hair.] —**dep′i·la′tion,** *n.*

de·pil·a·to·ry (di pil′ə tôr′ē) *pl.,* **-ries.** *n.* agent for removing hair, esp. a cosmetic preparation used to remove unwanted hair from the body. —*adj.* capable of removing hair.

de·plane (dē plān′) **-planed, -plan·ing.** *v.i.* to get out of an airplane after landing.

de·plete (di plēt′) **-plet·ed, -plet·ing.** *v.t.* 1. to reduce considerably, as in amount or substance: *War depleted the country's resources.* 2. to use up; exhaust: *The campers' food supplies were depleted after three days.* [Latin *dēplētus,* past participle of *dēplēre* to empty out, exhaust.] —**de·ple′tion,** *n.*

Syn. 2. **Deplete, drain, exhaust** mean to draw off all or part of a substance. **Deplete** suggests a harmful reduction of quantity: *Water pollution has depleted the wildlife of the bay.* **Drain** connotes a gradual drawing off with emptiness the probable end: *Heavy expenses had*

drained his bank account. **Exhaust** implies an emptying or a using up, but with the contents transformed into some other substance or performing some service as they are consumed: *At the end of the climb his strength was exhausted.*

de·plor·a·ble (di plôr′ə bəl) *adj.* 1. to be disapproved of: *deplorable behavior.* 2. to be regretted: *the deplorable decline of his singing ability.* 3. wretched; miserable: *deplorable living conditions.* —**de·plor′a·bly,** *adv.*

de·plore (di plôr′) **-plored, -plor·ing.** *v.t.* 1. to disapprove of strongly: *The minister deplored the use of violence to bring about social change.* 2. to be very sorry about; regret deeply; lament: *to deplore the untimely death of a friend.* [Latin *dēplōrāre* to lament, weep bitterly.]

de·ploy (di ploi′) *v.t.* 1. to place in a desired position according to a plan; position strategically: *to deploy missiles, to deploy pieces in the game of chess.* 2. to widen the front of (a military unit or troops) in battle formation. —*v.i.* to be or become deployed. [French *déployer* to unfold, from Latin *displicāre* to unfold, scatter.] —**de·ploy′ment,** *n.*

de·po·lar·ize (dē pō′lə rīz′) **-ized, -iz·ing.** *v.t.* to destroy the polarity or polarization of. —**de·po′lar·i·za′tion, de·po′lar·iz′er,** *n.*

de·pone (di pōn′) **-poned, -pon·ing.** *v.i., v.t. Archaic.* to state under oath; testify; depose. [Medieval Latin *deponere* to testify, from Latin *dēponere* to put aside.]

de·po·nent (di pō′nənt) *adj.* in Greek and Latin grammar, denoting a verb that is passive in form and active in meaning. —*n.* 1. deponent verb. 2. *Law.* one who gives written testimony under oath. [Medieval Latin *deponens,* present participle of *deponere* to testify, from Latin *dēponere* to put aside; in grammar having the sense of "putting aside the active voice."]

de·pop·u·late (dē pop′yə lāt′) **-lat·ed, -lat·ing.** *v.t.* to reduce the population of, as by death or expulsion: *Heavy bombing depopulated the country.* —**de·pop′u·la′tion, de·pop′u·la′tor,** *n.*

de·port (di pôrt′) *v.t.* 1. to expel (an undesirable alien) from a country: *to deport a foreign spy.* 2. to behave or conduct (oneself): *Mary always deports herself like a lady.* [Old French *deporter* to banish, behave, from Latin *dēportāre* to carry off.] —**Syn.** 1. see **banish.**

de·por·ta·tion (dē′pôr tā′shən) *n.* expulsion of an undesirable alien from a country.

de·por·tee (dē′pôr tē′) *n.* person who has been deported or sentenced to deportation.

de·port·ment (di pôrt′mənt) *n.* behavior; conduct; bearing: *the deportment of a gentleman.*

de·pos·al (di pō′zəl) *n.* act of deposing from office; being deposed.

de·pose (di pōz′) **-posed, -pos·ing.** *v.t.* 1. to remove from a throne or other high office: *The rebels deposed the king.* 2. *Law.* to state in a deposition. —*v.t. Law.* to make a deposition; testify. [Old French *deposer* to put down, testify, going back to Latin *dē* from, away + Late Latin *pausāre* to place, from Latin *pausāre* to halt, rest, from *pausa.* See PAUSE.]

de·pos·it (di poz′it) *v.t.* 1. to put (money or valuables) in a bank or other place for safekeeping: *to deposit five dollars in a savings account.* 2. to set or lay down; place: *He deposited his packages on the table.* 3. to leave as a layer; precipitate: *The river deposited silt at its mouth.* 4. to give as partial payment or security. —*n.* 1. something put in a place for safekeeping, esp. money in a bank. 2. something given as partial payment or security: *a deposit of $150 on a new car.* 3. something that has settled: *a deposit of dust on the window sill.* 4. natural layer or accumulation, as of a mineral: *large deposits of iron ore.* 5. depository (*def. 1*). 6. act of depositing. 7. **on deposit.** placed in a bank or other place for safekeeping. [Latin *dēpositus,* past participle of *dēpōnere* to put down, put aside, entrust.]

de·pos·i·tar·y (di poz′i ter′ē) *pl.,* **-tar·ies.** *n.* 1. one who or that which is entrusted with something for safekeeping. 2. depository (*def. 1*).

dep·o·si·tion (dep′ə zish′ən, dē′pə-) *n.* 1. removal from a throne or other high office. 2. sworn, written statement given by a witness out of court, intended to be used as testimony in court. 3. act or process of laying down, esp. by a natural process. 4. thing deposited; deposit.

de·pos·i·tor (di poz′ə tər) *n.* one who makes a deposit, esp. a person who deposits money in a bank.

de·pos·i·to·ry (di poz′ə tôr′ē) *pl.,* **-ries.** *n.* 1. place where something is deposited for safekeeping. 2. depositary (*def. 1*).

de·pot (*def. 1* dē′pō; *defs. 2, 3* dep′ō) *n.* 1. railroad station or bus terminal. 2.a. place where military materiel is stored or processed before distribution. b. place where military personnel are assembled, trained, and classified. 3. storehouse; warehouse. [French *dépôt* a deposit, warehouse, from Latin *dēpositum* a deposit, something put down.]

de·prave (di prāv′) **-praved, -prav·ing.** *v.t.* to make morally bad; corrupt; pervert. [Latin *dēpravāre,* from *dē* down + *pravus* wicked.]

de·praved (di prāvd′) *adj.* morally bad; corrupt; perverted: *a depraved man.* —**Syn.** see **corrupt.**

de·prav·i·ty (di prav′ə tē) pl., **-ties.** n. **1.** state of being depraved; corruption. **2.** depraved act or practice.

dep·re·cate (dep′rə kāt′) **-cat·ed, -cat·ing.** v.t. to express disapproval of; disparage; belittle. [Latin *dēprecātus*, past participle of *dēprecārī* to avert by prayer, pray for.] —**dep′re·ca′tion, dep′re·ca′tor,** n. —**dep·re·ca·to·ry** (dep′rə kə tôr′ē), adj.

de·pre·ci·ate (di prē′shē āt′) **-at·ed, -at·ing.** v.t. **1.** to lower the price or market value of. **2.** to belittle; deprecate. —v.i. to fall in value or price. [Latin *dēpretiātus*, past participle of *dēpretiāre* to lower the price of, from *dē* down + *pretium* price.] —**Syn.** v.t. **2.** see **disparage**.

de·pre·ci·a·tion (di prē′shē ā′shən) n. **1.** decrease in value, as a result of deterioration, age, or obsolescence: *the depreciation of a car over the years.* **2.** *Accounting.* allowance made for such a decrease. **3.** decline in the purchasing power or exchange value of money. **4.** deprecation; disparagement.

de·pre·ci·a·to·ry (di prē′shē ə tôr′ē) adj. tending to disparage.

dep·re·da·tion (dep′rə dā′shən) n. act of laying waste; plundering; ravaging. [French *déprédation*, Late Latin *dēpraedātiō*, going back to Latin *dē* down + *praeda* booty.]

de·press (di pres′) v.t. **1.** to lower in spirits; make gloomy; sadden: *The death of his dog depressed the boy.* **2.** to lessen in force, vigor, or activity; weaken: *The sedative depressed the patient's pulse rate.* **3.** to lower in price or value. **4.** to press or push down: *to depress the accelerator in an automobile.* [Latin *dēpressus*, past participle of *dēprimere* to press down.] —**de·press′ing·ly,** adv.

de·pres·sant (di pres′ənt) adj. tending to reduce nervous, muscular, or other vital life activities. —n. **1.** drug or other substance that reduces the activity of various body functions. Anesthetics, sedatives, and narcotics are depressants. **2.** anything that depresses.

de·pressed (di prest′) adj. **1.** low in spirits; dejected; sad. **2.** decreased in activity, force, value, or price. **3.** undergoing economic depression; having a high rate of unemployment and a low standard of living: *a depressed area.* **4.** pressed down: *a depressed key on a typewriter.* **5.** flattened down; broader than high.

de·pres·sion (di presh′ən) n. **1.** sunken place or surface; hollow: *The potter made a depression in the clay.* **2.** emotional state characterized by pessimism; dejection. **3.a.** period marked by a severe reduction in business activity, a rise in unemployment, and falling wages and prices. **b.** **the Depression.** business depression lasting from 1929 to 1939. Also, **the Great Depression. 4.** decrease in activity, force, or price. **5.** act of pressing down. **6.** area of low atmospheric pressure. —**Syn. 2.** *Depression, dejection* describe states of unhappiness. *Depression* suggests discouragement and lack of energy: *Not even a trip to the seashore could bring her out of her depression.* *Dejection* implies a temporary mood: *His dejection after the exam came from realizing that he knew the answers to the questions he had missed.*

de·pres·sive (di pres′iv) adj. **1.** relating to or characterized by mental depression. **2.** tending to cause depression.

de·pres·sor (di pres′ər) n. **1.** one who or that which depresses. **2.** medical instrument used to press down a part of the body: *a tongue depressor.* **3.a.** muscle that draws down a part of the body. **b.** nerve that acts to lower the heart rate and blood pressure when stimulated.

dep·ri·va·tion (dep′rə vā′shən) n. **1.** act of depriving or being deprived. **2.** loss; privation.

de·prive (di prīv′) **-prived, -priv·ing.** v.t. **1.** to take away from; dispossess; divest: *The proposed highway will deprive the children of their playground.* **2.** to keep from having or enjoying; withhold from: *to deprive a citizen of his right to vote.* [Old French *depriver* to take from, going back to Latin *dē* down + *privāre* to rob, bereave.]

de·pro·gram (dē prō′gram, -grəm) **-grammed, gramming** or **-gramed, -graming.** v.t. to try to change the firm beliefs of (a person), esp. by coercive methods.

dept., department.

depth (depth) n. **1.** distance or extension downward, inward, or from front to back: *the depth of an elevator shaft, the depth of an incision, the depth of a theater stage.* **2.** quality of being deep; deepness. **3.** intensity or strength: *depth of color, the depth of her indignation.* **4.** profundity or complexity of thought or feeling: *the depth of an analysis, a man of depth.* **5.** *also,* **depths. a.** most extreme or intense stage or state: *the depths of despair.* **b.** deepest, innermost, or most remote part: *the depths of the jungle.* **6. depths.** deplorably low moral or intellectual state. **7.** lowness of pitch. [Middle English *depthe* deepness, going back to Old English *dēop* deep.]

depth charge, explosive charge designed to go off under water at a predetermined depth, used esp. against submarines. Also, **depth bomb.**

dep·u·ta·tion (dep′yə tā′shən) n. **1.** one authorized to represent or act for another; delegation. **2.** act of deputing; being deputed.

de·pute (di pūt′) **-put·ed, -put·ing.** v.t. **1.** to appoint as one's substitute, delegate, or agent. **2.** to transfer, as work or authority, to another. [Old French *deputer* to assign, from Late Latin *dēputāre* to allot, from Latin *dēputāre* to consider.]

dep·u·tize (dep′yə tīz′) **-tized, -tiz·ing.** v.t. to appoint as deputy. —v.i. to act as deputy.

dep·u·ty (dep′yə tē) pl., **-ties.** n. **1.** person appointed or authorized to represent or act for another or others. **2.** assistant with power to take charge in his superior's absence: *a sheriff's deputy.* **3.** member of the lower house of certain legislatures, as in France and Italy. —adj. acting as deputy. [French *député* delegate, from *deputer* to depute. See DE-PUTE.] —**Syn. 1.** see **agent**.

De Quin·cey, Thomas (də kwin′sē) 1785–1859, English essayist.

der. 1. derivation. **2.** derivative. **3.** derived.

de·rail (dē rāl′) v.t. to cause to run off the rails: *to derail a train.* —v.i. to run off the rails. —**de·rail′ment,** n.

de·range (di rānj′) **-ranged, -rang·ing.** v.t. **1.** to disorder (someone's) mental functioning; make insane. **2.** to disturb the normal functioning of, as a machine. **3.** to disturb the order or arrangement of; disarrange. [French *déranger* to disarray, going back to Old French *des-* (from Latin *dis-* apart) + *ranger* to rank (of Germanic origin).]

de·ranged (dē rānged′) adj. **1.** mentally disordered; insane. **2.** disordered.

de·range·ment (di rānj′mənt) n. **1.** disorder of the mind; insanity. **2.** disturbance of order or normal functioning; disorder.

der·by (dur′bē; British där′bē) pl., **-bies.** n. hard, round man's hat with a narrow curled brim. Also, **bowl′er.**

Der·by (dur′bē; British där′bē) pl., **-bies.** n. **1.a.** Epsom Derby. **b.** Kentucky Derby. **2.** any similar horse race. **3. derby.** any large race or contest, esp. one open to all who wish to compete. [From the twelfth earl of *Derby*, who instituted the Epsom Derby in 1780.]

Der·by (dur′bē; British där′bē) n. **1.** county in central England. Also, **Der·by·shire** (dur′bē shēr′; British där′bē shēr′). **2.** city in this county. Pop. (1968 est.), 221,300.

der·e·lict (der′ə likt′) n. **1.** degraded social outcast; vagrant; tramp. **2.** property abandoned by the owner or guardian, esp. a ship abandoned at sea. —adj. **1.** neglectful of one's duty; negligent; delinquent: *The sentry was derelict in failing to notice the approach of the enemy.* **2.** abandoned by the owner or guardian: *a derelict ship, a derelict child.* [Latin *dērelictus,* past participle of *dērelinquere* to abandon.]

der·e·lic·tion (der′ə lik′shən) n. **1.** neglect of one's duty; delinquency: *The guard's dereliction allowed the prisoners to escape.* **2.** act of abandoning; being abandoned; desertion.

de·ride (di rīd′) **-rid·ed, -rid·ing.** v.t. to treat with contempt or scorn; mock; ridicule. [Latin *dērīdēre.*] —**de·rid′er,** n. —**de·rid′ing·ly,** adv. —**Syn.** see **mock**.

de ri·gueur (də ri gûr′, də rē gœr′) French. required by etiquette, fashion, or custom; in good form; proper.

de·ri·sion (di rizh′ən) n. contempt; mockery; ridicule. [Late Latin *dērīsiō* mockery, from Latin *dērīdēre* to mock.]

de·ri·sive (di rī′siv) adj. expressing or characterized by derision; mocking; ridiculing: *derisive laughter.* Also **de·ri·so·ry** (də rī′sər ē, -zər ē). —**de·ri′sive·ly,** adv. —**de·ri′sive·ness,** n.

deriv. 1. derivation. **2.** derivative. **3.** derived.

der·i·va·tion (der′ə vā′shən) n. **1.** act of deriving; being derived. **2.** source or origin from which something is derived: *a legend of Irish derivation.* **3.** development; descent: *to trace the derivation of a custom.* **4.** something derived; derivative. **5.a.** process of tracing the origin and development of a word. **b.** statement of this; etymology. **6.** formation of a new word from an existing word, root, or stem, esp. by the addition of a prefix or suffix. The word *happiness* is a derivation from the adjective *happy* and the suffix *-ness.*

de·riv·a·tive (di riv′ə tiv) adj. obtained or characterized by derivation; not original: *a derivative theory, derivative words.* —n. **1.** something derived. **2.** chemical substance obtained or regarded as being obtained from another specific substance by modification or by partial substitution of components. **3.** word formed from another by derivation: *"Sorrowful" is a derivative of "sorrow."* **4.** *Mathematics.* the limit of the ratio of change in a function to the corresponding change in a variable in it, as the latter change approaches zero. —**de·riv′a·tive·ly,** adv.

de·rive (di rīv′) **-rived, -riv·ing.** v.t. **1.** to get or obtain, as from a source or origin (with *from*): *to derive pleasure from reading, a style of painting derived from primitive art.* **2.** to obtain by some process of reasoning; infer: *to derive a principle from various arguments.* **3.** to trace the origin of (something, as a word) from or to its source. **4.** to obtain (a chemical compound or substance) from another, as by substituting different elements or radicals. —v.i. to proceed from a source; originate: *The word "democracy" derives from Greek.* [Late Latin *dērīvāre* to flow, from Latin *dērīvāre* to draw off (a liquid), divert, from *dē* away + *rīvus* stream.] —**de·riv′a·ble,** adj. —**de·riv′er,** n.

der·ma (dur′mə) n. **1.** dermis. **2.** skin; integument. [Modern Latin *derma,* from Greek *derma* skin.]

der·mal (dur′məl) adj. of or relating to the skin.

der·ma·ti·tis (dur′mə tī′tis) n. inflammation of the skin.

der·ma·tol·o·gist (dur′mə tol′ə jist) *n.* physician specializing in dermatology.

der·ma·tol·o·gy (dur′mə tol′ə jē) *n.* branch of medical science dealing with the skin and its diseases.

der·mis (dur′mis) *n.* layer of skin beneath the epidermis, containing blood vessels, nerves, and other structures; corium. See **skin** for illustration. [Modern Latin *dermis*, from **EPIDERMIS**.]

der·o·gate (der′ə gāt′) **-gat·ed, -gat·ing.** *v.t.* to lessen the importance or merit of; belittle: *The writer derogated the works of his fellow authors.* —*v.i.* to take away; detract. [Latin *dērogātus*, past participle of *dērogāre.*] —**der′o·ga′tion,** *n.*

de·rog·a·to·ry (di rog′ə tôr′ē) *adj.* tending to lessen in importance or estimation; disparaging; belittling: *derogatory comments.* Also, **de·rog′a·tive.** —**de·rog′a·to′ri·ly,** *adv.*

der·rick (der′ik) *n.* **1.** machine for lifting and moving heavy objects, usually stationary and consisting of a vertical support to which a slanted boom with hoisting tackle is attached. **2.** framework over an oil well or other drill hole that supports the drilling machinery. [From *Derrick,* surname of a seventeenth-century hangman at Tyburn Prison in London; because its shape suggests a gallows.]

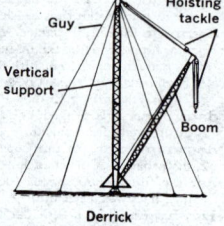

Derrick

der·ri·ère (der′ē âr′) *also,* **der·ri·ere.** *n.* buttocks; rump; rear. [French *derrière,* going back to Latin *dē retrō* from the back.]

der·ring-do (der′ing dōō′) *n.* courageous behavior or feats; daring. [Middle English *dorryng don* daring to do. See **DARE, DO.**]

der·rin·ger (der′in jər) *n.* short-barreled pistol of large caliber. [From Henry *Deringer,* a nineteenth-century American gunsmith, who invented it.]

der·vish (dur′vish) *n.* member of any of various Muslim religious orders known for certain violent forms of worship, as howling and whirling. [Turkish *dervīsh* literally, beggar, from Persian *dārvīsh* poor, a monk.]

de·sal·i·nate (dē sal′ə nāt′) **-nat·ed, -nat·ing.** *v.t.* to remove salt from: *to desalinate sea water.* —**de·sa′li·ni·za′tion,** *n.*

de·salt (dē sôlt′) *v.t.* to desalinate.

des·cant (*n.* des′kant; *v.* des kant′, dis-) *n. Music.* additional ornamental melody that is sung or played above another melody, usually by several soprano voices or instruments. —*v.i.* **1.** to comment at length; discourse; enlarge (with *on* or *upon*). **2.** *Music.* to sing or play a descant. [Dialectal Old French *descant* ornamental accompaniment in music, counterpoint, going back to Latin *dis-* apart + *cantus* song.]

Des·cartes, Re·né (dā kärt′; rə nā′) 1596–1650, French philosopher and mathematician.

de·scend (di send′) *v.i.* **1.** to move or pass from a higher place to a lower one; come or go downward: *We rode up, but descended on foot.* **2.** to slope or extend downward: *a mountain path that descends to a lake.* **3.** to come down by inheritance: *an estate that descends through the eldest son.* **4.** to come down from an earlier source or ancestor; be derived, as by birth or transmission: *His family descends from the first French colonists.* **5.** to come in force or in overwhelming numbers; attack or visit suddenly (with *on* or *upon*): *The hounds descended on their prey. A troop of friends descended on us over the weekend.* **6.** to pass from greater to less, or from higher to lower, in any scale or series. **7.** to pass from the general to the specific. **8.** to lower oneself; stoop. —*v.t.* to come or go downward on or along: *to descend a mountain trail.* [Old French *descendre* to go down, from Latin *dēscendere.*]

de·scen·dant (di sen′dənt) *n.* one who is descended from a particular ancestor or group of ancestors; offspring: *a descendant of William the Conqueror.* —*adj. also,* **de·scen·dent.** **1.** coming or going downward. **2.** descending from an original source or ancestor.

de·scent (di sent′) *n.* **1.** movement or passage from a higher level to a lower one: *the descent of an elevator.* **2.** downward slope or inclination: *a hill with a steep descent.* **3.** derivation, as by ancestry or transmission; birth: *Our family is of Russian descent.* **4.** way or passage leading downward; means of descending. **5.** fall to a lower state or condition; decline. **6.** sudden attack or visit. **7.** hereditary succession to an estate or title. [Old French *descente* sudden fall, succession, from *descendre* See **DESCEND.**]

de·scribe (di skrīb′) **-scribed, -scrib·ing.** *v.t.* **1.** to represent or give a picture of in words; tell or write about: *The boy's essay described his activities during the previous summer. Can you describe the man you saw at the window?* **2.** to draw or trace the outline of: *to describe a circle with a compass.* [Latin *dēscrībere* to write down, copy.] —**de·scrib′a·ble,** *adj.* —**de·scrib′er,** *n.*

de·scrip·tion (di skrip′shən) *n.* **1.** act of setting forth or portraying in words; verbal or written representation. **2.** statement or account that describes. **3.** kind; sort; variety: *dogs of every description.* **4.** act of tracing in outline.

de·scrip·tive (di skrip′tiv) *adj.* having the quality or function of describing; characterized by description: *a descriptive adjective.* —**de·scrip′tive·ly,** *adv.* —**de·scrip′tive·ness,** *n.*

de·scry (di skrī′) **-scried, -scry·ing.** *v.t.* **1.** to catch sight of; make out from afar or through obscurity; espy: *to descry land in the distance.* **2.** to discover by observation; detect: *to descry a flaw in an opponent's argument.* [Old French *descrier* to proclaim, decry. See **DECRY.**]

des·e·crate (des′ə krāt′) **-crat·ed, -crat·ing.** *v.t.* to destroy the sanctity of; treat with irreverence; profane: *to desecrate a tomb.* [**DE-** (**CON**)**SECRATE.**] —**des′e·crat′er;** *also,* **des′e·cra′tor,** *n.* —**des′e·cra′tion,** *n.*

de·seg·re·gate (dē seg′rə gāt′) **-gat·ed, -gat·ing.** *v.t., v.i.* to eliminate racial segregation (in). —**de·seg′re·ga′tion,** *n.*

de·sen·si·tize (dē sen′sə tīz′) **-tized, -tiz·ing.** *v.t.* **1.** to make less sensitive. **2.** to make an exposed photographic film or plate less sensitive to light in order to allow development in light that is brighter than usual. **3.** to reduce or eliminate the sensitivity of (a person, organ, or tissue) to an allergen or other external stimulus. —**de·sen′si·ti·za′tion, de·sen′si·tiz′er,** *n.*

des·ert[1] (dez′ərt) *n.* **1.a.** hot, dry, sandy region with little or no vegetation or animal life: *Many kinds of cactus grow on the desert.* **b.** any expanse of land with little or no vegetation or animal life: *the polar deserts of Antarctica.* **2.** unproductive area, period, or activity; wasteland: *a cultural desert.* —*adj.* **1.** relating to, inhabiting, or occurring in a desert: *desert plants.* **2.** uninhabited; desolate: *a desert island.* [Old French *desert* wilderness, from Late Latin *dēsertum* waste, from Latin *dēserere* to abandon.]

de·sert[2] (di zurt′) *v.t.* **1.** to depart from; abandon; forsake: *to desert one's wife and children.* **2.** to abandon (military service) with the intention of remaining away permanently. **3.** to fail (one) when needed or expected: *His faith deserted him in his hour of need.* —*v.i.* **1.** to abandon one's duty, post, or cause. **2.** to abandon military service with the intention of remaining away permanently. [French *déserter* to forsake, abandon, going back to Latin *dēsertus,* past participle of *dēserere.*] —**de·sert′er,** *n.*

Syn. *v.t.* **1. Desert, abandon, forsake** mean to leave someone or something. **Desert** suggests leaving in violation of obligation, debt, or responsibility: *The hunter deserted his injured comrades.* **Abandon** implies leaving behind as no longer useful or wanted: *The settlers abandoned the town when the mines became exhausted.* **Forsake** suggests renouncing a person or thing with which there had been close attachment: *The senator forsook his political party and joined the opposition.*

de·sert[3] (di zurt′) *n. also,* **deserts.** that which is deserved; deserved reward or punishment: *to get one's just deserts.* [Old French *deserte* merit, from *deservir* to merit. See **DESERVE.**]

de·ser·tion (di zur′shən) *n.* **1.** act of deserting. **2.** abandonment of one's spouse without consent or legal justification. **3.** state of being deserted.

de·serve (di zurv′) **-served, -serv·ing.** *v.t.* to have a right to; be worthy of; merit: *His first play deserved the criticism it received.* —*v.i.* to be worthy; merit. [Old French *deservir* to merit, from Late Latin *dēservīre,* from Latin *dēservīre* to serve well.] —**de·serv′er,** *n.* —**Syn.** *v.t.* see **merit.**

de·serv·ed·ly (di zur′vid lē) *adv.* according to merit; justly; rightfully: *He was deservedly praised for his efforts.*

de·serv·ing (di zur′ving) *adj.* **1.** worthy; meritorious: *This plan is deserving of your attention.* **2.** worthy of help, esp. financial aid: *The scholarship will be given to a deserving student.* —**de·serv′ing·ly,** *adv.*

des·ha·bille (dez′ə bēl′) dishabille.

des·ic·cate (des′i kāt′) **-cat·ed, -cat·ing.** *v.t.* **1.** to dry up completely. **2.** to preserve (food) by drying. —*v.i.* to become dry. [Latin *dēsiccātus,* past participle of *dēsiccāre* to dry up, going back to *dē* thoroughly + *siccus* dry.] —**des′ic·ca′tion,** *n.*

do·sid·er·a·tum (di sid′ə ra′təm, -rä′təm) *pl.,* **-ta** (-tə). *n.* thing desired or required. [Latin *dēsīderātum* (something) longed for, from *dēsīderāre* to long for.]

de·sign (di zīn′) *n.* **1.** preliminary plan, sketch, or outline made to serve as a guide or pattern: *an architect's design for a new house.* **2.** arrangement or combination of parts, details, or colors so as to achieve a particular effect; pattern of an artistic work: *a blue and green design in a carpet.* **3.** art of making designs: *a school of design.* **4.** example of artistic work: *His design was exhibited in the annual show.* **5.** plan, scheme, or project to be carried out. **6.** *also,* **designs.** secret or sinister plot or scheme (usually with *upon, on,* or *against*): *The greedy men had designs on her fortune.* **7.** prearranged purpose for something; aim; intention: *The design of the plot was to oust the dictator.* **8. by design.** on purpose; intentionally; deliberately. —*v.t.* **1.** to make a

at; āpe; cär; end; mē; it; īce; hot; ōld; fôrk; wood; fōol; oil; out; up; ūse; turn; sing; thin; this; zh in treasure; ə in ago, taken, pencil, lemon, circus.

preliminary plan, sketch, or outline of; make a pattern for: *to design an advertisement, to design an automobile.* **2.** to plan and fashion with artistic skill; arrange parts, details, or colors of: *to design a dress, to design a formal garden.* **3.** to form in the mind; plan out; conceive; contrive: *The president designed a new foreign policy.* **4.** to have as an aim or purpose; intend: *The experiment is designed to test the new drug.* —*v.i.* **1.** to make plans, sketches, or outlines, esp. of an original, artistic nature. **2.** to originate and execute a plan or scheme. [French *désigner* to indicate, denote, from Latin *dēsignāre* to mark out, denote.]

des·ig·nate (*v.,* dez′ig nāt′; *adj.,* dez′ig nit, -nāt′) **-nat·ed, -nat·ing.** *v.t.* **1.** to point out or indicate by means of a distinctive mark, sign, or name; specify; signify: *The limits of your property are designated on the map.* **2.** to call by a particular term or title; name; entitle. **3.** to select for a particular purpose or duty; appoint to an office: *He was designated to lead the expedition. Smith was designated chairman of the school board.* —*adj.* selected but not yet serving; appointed. ▲ The adjective **designate** usually follows the noun it modifies and is often joined to it by a hyphen: *The incumbent chairman as well as the chairman-designate were present.* [Latin *dēsignātus,* past participle of *dēsignāre* to mark out, denote.] —**des′ig·na′tor,** *n.*

des·ig·na·tion (dez′ig nā′shən) *n.* **1.** act of pointing out or indicating something: *the designation of a time and place to meet.* **2.** distinguishing name, title, or mark. **3.** selection for a particular purpose or office; appointment: *The president is responsible for the designation of ambassadors.*

de·sign·ed·ly (di zī′nid lē) *adv.* by design; intentionally.

de·sign·er (di zī′nər) *n.* one who designs, esp. a person who creates designs or patterns for manufacture or construction: *a dress designer, a package designer, a book designer.*

de·sign·ing (di zī′ning) *adj.* **1.** having ulterior motives; scheming: *crafty and designing men.* **2.** displaying planning or forethought. —*n.* practice or art of making designs or patterns.

de·sir·a·ble (di zīr′ə bəl) *adj.* **1.** worth having or pursuing; desirable goals. **2.** possessing qualities worthy of desire; pleasing; beautiful; excellent: *a desirable woman.* —**de·sir′a·bil′i·ty, de·sir′a·ble·ness,** *n.* —**de·sir′a·bly,** *adv.*

de·sire (di zīr′) **-sired, -sir·ing.** *v.t.* **1.** to have a strong wish for; long for; crave: *Both nations desired peace, but neither would accept compromise.* **2.** to express a wish for; request: *He desired information about vacationing in the mountains.* —*v.i.* to have or feel desire. —*n.* **1.** state or condition of longing; wish: *a desire for wealth.* **2.** expressed wish; request. **3.** thing desired: *He finally attained his desire.* **4.** sexual longing; passion; lust. [Old French *desirer* to long for, from Latin *dēsīderāre.*] —**Syn.** *n.* **1.** see **wish.**

de·sir·ous (di zīr′əs) *adj.* having desire; desiring: *desirous of fame.* —**de·sir′ous·ly,** *adv.*

de·sist (di zist′, -sist′) *v.i.* to cease some action; stop (usually with *from*): *to desist from useless labor.* [Old French *desister,* from Latin *dēsistere* to stand aside, cease.] —**Syn.** see **stop.**

desk (desk) *n.* **1.** article of furniture having a flat or sloping surface and usually drawers or compartments, used esp. for reading or writing. **2.** reading stand with a sloping top, used esp. to hold a book that is read in a church service. **3.** booth or counter at which certain duties or services are performed, as the place in a hotel where guests register. **4.** division or department of an organization or office: *the city desk of a newspaper.* **5.** stand used to support sheet music. [Medieval Latin *desca* the article of furniture, table, from Italian *desco,* from Late Latin *discus* table, from Latin *discus* quoit, dish, from Greek *diskos* round plate, quoit. Doublet of DAIS, DISCUS, DISH, DISK.]

Des Moines (də moin′) capital and largest city of Iowa, in the south-central part of the state. Pop. (1970), 200,587.

des·o·late (*adj.,* des′ə lit; *v.,* des′ə lāt′) *adj.* **1.** destitute of inhabitants; deserted: *desolate ruins, a desolate beach.* **2.** left alone; without companionship; lonely: *a desolate old man.* **3.** laid waste; devastated: *The forest was left desolate by the fire.* **4.** destitute of joy or comfort; miserable; wretched; forlorn: *the desolate poor.* **5.** dreary; cheerless: *a desolate month far from home.* —*v.t.* **-lat·ed, -lat·ing. 1.** to lay waste; devastate: *The land was desolated by floods.* **2.** to deprive of inhabitants: *Plague desolated the town.* **3.** to make miserable, wretched, or forlorn: *He was desolated by the bad news.* [Latin *dēsōlātus,* past participle of *dēsōlāre* to abandon, going back to *dē* thoroughly + *sōlus* alone.] —**des′o·late·ly,** *adv.* —**des′o·late·ness,** *n.*

des·o·la·tion (des′ə lā′shən) *n.* **1.** act of making desolate; devastation: *the desolation of life and land by war.* **2.** ruined or deserted condition: *He found the old house in complete desolation.* **3.** desolate place or region. **4.** loneliness; sadness: *His desolation was complete in the months following her death.*

De So·to, Her·nan·do (də sō′tō; er nän′dō) c.1500–42, Spanish explorer in America who discovered the Mississippi River.

de·spair (di spâr′) *n.* **1.** complete loss of hope or expectation: *He was filled with despair by his failures.* **2.** someone or something that causes

---

loss of hope: *The child was the despair of his mother.* —*v.i.* to lose or give up hope; be without hope (usually with *of*): *She despaired of ever seeing her son again.* [Old French *desperer* to lose hope, from Latin *dēspērāre,* going back to *dē* away + *spēs* hope.]

Syn. *n.* **1. Despair, desperation** mean loss of hope. **Despair** suggests the feeling that all further efforts are futile and that defeat is inevitable: *The besieged garrison was overcome by despair when the reinforcements did not arrive.* **Desperation** suggests a loss of hope so intense that it goads one into a reckless and last-ditch action regardless of consequences or danger: *In desperation the cornered man lunged at his enemy.*

de·spair·ing (di spâr′ing) *adj.* feeling or showing despair; hopeless: *a despairing lover, a despairing cry.* —**de·spair′ing·ly,** *adv.* —**de·spair′ing·ness,** *n.*

des·patch (dis pach′) dispatch.

des·per·a·do (des′pə rä′dō, -rā′dō) *pl.* **-does** or **-dos.** *n.* bold, desperate, or reckless criminal. [Probably modification (influenced by Spanish ending *-ado*) of obsolete *desperate* wretch. See DESPERATE.]

des·per·ate (des′pər it, -prit) *adj.* **1.** reckless through hopelessness; ready to run any risk; rash; violent: *a desperate criminal.* **2.** done without regard to what happens afterward; irresponsibly or violently reckless: *desperate acts.* **3.** having little or no hope of improvement or recovery; extremely bad; hopeless: *desperate circumstances, a desperate illness.* **4.** deep; extreme: *desperate poverty.* [Latin *dēspērātus,* past participle *dēspērāre* to lose hope. See DESPAIR.] —**des′per·ate·ly,** *adv.* —**des′per·ate·ness,** *n.*

des·per·a·tion (des′pə rā′shən) *n.* recklessness arising from loss of hope: *In desperation they resorted to violence.* —**Syn.** see **despair.**

des·pi·ca·ble (des′pi kə bəl, di spik′ə-) *adj.* to be scorned; contemptible; vile: *despicable cruelty.* [Late Latin *dēspicābilis* contemptible, from Latin *dēspicārī* to despise.] —**des′pi·ca·ble·ness,** *n.* —**des′pi·ca·bly,** *adv.*

de·spise (di spīz′) **-spised, -spis·ing.** *v.t.* to look down on; regard as contemptible; scorn. [Old French *despis-,* a stem of *despire* to scorn, insult, from Latin *dēspicere,* from *dē* down + *spicere* to look.] —**de·spis′er,** *n.*

de·spite (di spīt′) *prep.* in spite of; notwithstanding: *He went to work despite his sickness.* —*n.* **1.** act of contemptuous disregard; insult; injury. **2.** *Archaic.* malice; spite. **3.** *Archaic.* contempt; scorn. **4. in despite of,** in spite of. [Old French *despit* spite, anger, from Latin *dēspectus* a looking down, contempt.]

de·spite·ful (di spīt′fəl) *adj.* *Archaic.* malicious; spiteful.

Des Plaines (des plānz′) city in northeastern Illinois. Pop. (1970), 57,239.

de·spoil (di spoil′) *v.t.* to deprive of possessions by force; rob; pillage; plunder: *The marauders despoiled the countryside.* [Old French *despoillier* to strip, make bare, from Latin *dēspoliāre* to plunder.] —**de·spoil′er, de·spoil′ment,** *n.*

de·spo·li·a·tion (di spō′lē ā′shən) *n.* act of despoiling; being despoiled.

de·spond (di spond′) *v.i.* to lose heart or hope; be depressed. —*n. Archaic.* despondency. [Latin *dēspondēre* to give up, lose.]

de·spon·den·cy (di spon′dən sē) *pl.* **-cies.** *n.* loss of hope; depression of spirit; dejection. Also, **de·spon′dence.**

de·spon·dent (di spon′dənt) *adj.* discouraged; depressed; dejected: *She was despondent when her brother became ill.* —**de·spon′dent·ly,** *adv.*

des·pot (des′pət, -pot) *n.* **1.** one who governs with unlimited authority; absolute ruler; autocrat. **2.** tyrant; oppressor. [Old French *despot* chief lord, from Greek *despotēs* master, tyrant.]

des·pot·ic (des pot′ik, dis-) *adj.* of or like a despot or despotism; tyrannical; arbitrary. —**des·pot′i·cal·ly,** *adv.*

des·pot·ism (des′pə tiz′əm) *n.* **1.** rule of a despot; exercise of absolute authority; autocracy. **2.** tyrannical rule; oppression. **3.** government or state ruled by a despot.

des·sert (di zurt′) *n.* course served at the end of a meal, usually a sweet food, as cake, pie, or ice cream. [French *dessert,* from *desservir* to clear a table, going back to Latin *dis-* away + *servīre* to serve.]

des·sert·spoon (di zurt′spōōn′) *n.* spoon intermediate in size between a teaspoon and a tablespoon.

des·ti·na·tion (des′tə nā′shən) *n.* **1.** place to which a person is going or a thing is directed; intended end of a journey: *His destination is Paris.* **2.** end or purpose for which something is set apart. **3.** act of appointing or setting apart for a particular purpose or use.

des·tine (des′tin) **-tined, -tin·ing.** *v.t.* **1.** to intend or set apart for a particular purpose or use: *That land is destined for the new hospital.* **2.** to appoint or fix beforehand; preordain; predetermine: *The proposal was destined to be defeated. He is destined for greatness.* **3.** to direct to a certain destination: *This ship is destined for America.* [Old French *destiner* to fix, determine, from Latin *dēstināre* to make firm, establish.]

des·ti·ny (des′tə nē) *pl.* **-nies.** *n.* **1.** what is fated to happen to someone or something; lot; fortune: *He believed it was his destiny to lead his*

people to freedom. **2.** what is fated to happen; foreordained course of events: *A consistent man believes in destiny, a capricious man in chance* (Disraeli, 1826). **3.** power or agency that foreordains the course of events; fate: *Destiny willed it so.* **—Syn. 1.** see **fate.**

des·ti·tute (des′tə tōot′, -tūt′) *adj.* **1.** lacking the necessities of life; in absolute want: *The villagers were left destitute by the flood.* **2.** entirely lacking; wanting; devoid (with *of*): *a plain destitute of trees, a story destitute of wit.* [Latin *dēstitūtus,* past participle of *dēstituere* to set down, abandon.] **—Syn. 1.** see **poor.**

des·ti·tu·tion (des′tə tōo′shən, -tū′-) *n.* **1.** lack of the necessities of life; absolute want; dire poverty. **2.** deficiency; deprivation; lack.

de·stroy (di stroi′) *v.t.* **1.** to break into pieces; demolish; ruin; wreck: *to destroy a house, to destroy a city by bombing. Locusts destroyed the crops.* **2.** to put an end to; do away with: *to destroy an opportunity, to destroy a person's hopes.* **3.** to kill: *The horse with the broken leg had to be destroyed.* **4.** to counteract the effect of; detract from; make useless: *to destroy an argument, to destroy a person's influence.* [Old French *destruire* to ruin, cause to decline, going back to Latin *dēstruere* to pull down.]

de·stroy·er (di stroi′ər) *n.* **1.** one who or that which destroys. **2.** small, fast, highly maneuverable warship, armed with guns, depth charges, torpedoes, and sometimes guided missiles, used esp. as an antiaircraft vessel and to escort convoys and attack submarines.

destroyer escort, warship similar to a destroyer but smaller and slower, used chiefly to escort convoys.

destroying angel, death cup.

de·struct (di strukt′) *n.* intentional destruction of a rocket or other missile that fails to function properly after it has been launched. *—adj.* designed to destroy such a rocket or missile: *a destruct mechanism. —v.i.* to be destroyed automatically. *—v.t.* to destroy. [From DESTRUCTION.] **—de·struc′tor,** *n.*

de·struc·ti·ble (di struk′tə bəl) *adj.* capable of being destroyed. **—de·struc′ti·bil′i·ty,** *n.*

de·struc·tion (di struk′shən) *n.* **1.** act of destroying: *the destruction of a city by bombing.* **2.** fact or condition of being destroyed; ruin: *The tornado left destruction in its wake.* **3.** cause or means of destroying. [Latin *dēstructiō* a pulling down.]
Syn. 1. Destruction, ruin, devastation mean very great damage that reduces a thing to a formless or useless state. **Destruction** implies a pulling down, wrecking, or annihilation so thorough that restoration is impossible: *The Roman senate ordered the destruction of Carthage.* **Ruin** implies a falling apart or tumbling down through natural decay, neglect, or dilapidation but falls short of suggesting complete destruction: *Long exposure to the elements caused the ruin of the monument.* **Devastation** implies a ravaging or laying waste that results in the utter desolation of a widespread territory: *The devastation caused by the cyclone left thousands homeless.*

de·struc·tive (di struk′tiv) *adj.* **1.** tending to destroy: *a destructive rodent, a destructive habit, a tax destructive of business expansion.* **2.** causing destruction: *destructive policies, destructive wars.* **3.** tending to overthrow, tear down, or discredit: *destructive criticism.*

destructive distillation, chemical process consisting of the decomposition of an organic substance, as wood or coal, by heating it in a closed vessel, and the simultaneous collection of the volatile matter produced. Charcoal can be produced from wood by means of destructive distillation.

des·ue·tude (des′wə tōod′, -tūd′) *n.* disuse; obsolescence: *an ancient custom that has fallen into desuetude.* [Latin *dēsuētūdō.*]

des·ul·to·ry (des′əl tôr′ē) *adj.* **1.** shifting from one thing to another; not methodical; irregular; disconnected: *desultory movements, a desultory conversation.* **2.** occurring suddenly or by chance; random: *a desultory thought.* [Latin *dēsultōrius* relating to a leaper, fickle, from *dēsultor* leaper; originally referring to a performer in the circus of ancient Rome who leaped from horse to horse.] **—des′ul·to′ri·ly,** *adv.* **—des′ul·to′ri·ness,** *n.*

de·tach (di tach′) *v.t.* **1.** to unfasten and separate; disconnect: *to detach three cars from a train, to detach the price tag from a gift.* **2.** to send away on a special mission: *A patrol boat was detached to search the harbor.* [French *détacher* to untie, from *dé-* (going back to Latin *dis-* apart) + *(at)tacher* to fasten. See ATTACH.] **—de·tach′a·bil′i·ty,** *n.* **—de·tach′a·ble,** *adj.* **—de·tach′a·bly,** *adv.*

de·tached (di tacht′) *adj.* **1.** not connected; unattached: *a detached house, a detached retina.* **2.** not interested or involved emotionally; unconcerned: *a detached observer, a detached view of British politics.*

de·tach·ment (di tach′mənt) *n.* **1.** act of detaching; being detached; separation. **2.** group of military or naval units, esp. personnel, assigned to special duty: *A detachment of ten men remained behind to guard the prisoners.* **3.** act of assigning or state of being assigned to special duty. **4.** a standing apart; aloofness: *Her detachment from their mutual problems was resented by others in the group.* **5.** lack of prejudice or bias; impartiality: *He was unable to examine the issue with detachment.*

de·tail (di tāl′, dē′tāl) *n.* **1.** small or secondary part of a whole; item; particular: *the details of a contract. Modern scholars know few details of the life of Shakespeare.* **2.** treatment of matters item by item; attention to particulars: *to go into detail. A pedantic person has great fondness for detail.* **3.** description or report of particulars; minute account. **4.** small or secondary part of a work of art or architecture, as a painting, statue, or building, esp. when represented or considered separately. **5.** *Military.* **a.** small group of men assigned to a particular service or duty: *A detail of soldiers patrolled the troubled area.* **b.** act of selecting such a group. **c.** particular duty assigned to such a group. **6. in detail,** part by part; minutely: *He described the day's events in detail. —v.t.* **1.** to relate or describe minutely; give particulars of: *He detailed the experiments leading up to his discovery.* **2.** to assign to or send on special duty: *Troops were detailed to guard the frontiers.* [Old French *detail* piece cut off, from *detailler* to cut in pieces, going back to Latin *dē* thoroughly + *tālea* twig, cutting.]

de·tailed (di tāld′, dē′tāld) *adj.* **1.** having many details: *a detailed description of the accident.* **2.** showing careful attention to detail: *The detective made a detailed examination of the room.*

de·tain (di tān′) *v.t.* **1.** to keep from proceeding; hold back; delay: *He was detained by a flat tire on his way home.* **2.** to keep in custody; confine: *to detain a person accused of a crime.* [Old French *detenir* to hold back, from Latin *dētinēre* to hold off, delay.] **—de·tain′er,** *n.* **—de·tain′ment,** *n.*

de·tect (di tekt′) *v.t.* **1.** to find out the conduct or character of; expose; uncover: *to detect someone stealing, to detect a thief.* **2.** to discover the presence, existence, or fact of: *to detect smoke. Do I detect a French accent in your speech?* **3.** *Radio.* **a.** to demodulate. **b.** to rectify. [Latin *dētectus,* past participle of *dētegere* to uncover.] **—de·tect′a·ble;** *also,* **de·tect′i·ble,** *adj.*

de·tec·tion (di tek′shən) *n.* **1.** a finding out or being found out; exposure or discovery: *the detection of a crime, the detection of a thief.* **2.** *Radio.* **a.** demodulation. **b.** rectification.

de·tec·tive (di tek′tiv) *n.* person, usually a policeman, who makes investigations to obtain evidence and information, esp. for the solution of crime and the arrest of criminals. *—adj.* **1.** relating to detectives and their work: *a detective story.* **2.** used for the purpose of detection: *detective methods.*

de·tec·tor (di tek′tər) *n.* **1.** one who or that which detects. **2.** *Radio.* **a.** demodulator. **b.** rectifier.

dé·tente (dā tänt′, -tänt′) *also,* **de·tente.** *n.* a relaxing or slackening of tension or strained relations, esp. a relaxation of political tension between two countries. [French *détente* a loosening, easing, from *détendre* to relax, slacken, going back to Latin *dis-* apart + *tendere* to stretch.]

de·ten·tion (di ten′shən) *n.* **1.** act of detaining or keeping from proceeding. **2.** state of being detained; delay. **3.** a keeping in custody; confinement, esp. as a temporary measure preceding trial. [Late Latin *dētentiō* a keeping back, from Latin *dētinēre* to hold off, delay.]

de·ter (di tur′) **-terred, -ter·ring.** *v.t.* to discourage or restrain from acting or proceeding, esp. by arousing fear or doubt: *The huge waves deterred him from going swimming.* [Latin *dēterrēre* to frighten from.] **—de·ter′ment,** *n.*

de·ter·gent (di tur′jənt) *n.* any cleansing agent, esp. one made synthetically and resembling soap in its cleansing action but not in its chemical composition. *—adj.* cleansing; purging. [Latin *dētergēns,* present participle of *dētergēre* to wipe off.]

de·te·ri·o·rate (di tēr′ē ə rāt′) **-rat·ed, -rat·ing.** *v.i.* to become worse; lessen in quality, character, or value; depreciate: *to deteriorate with age. —v.t.* to make worse; impair. [Late Latin *dēteriōrātus,* past participle of *dēteriōrāre* to make worse, from Latin *dēterior* worse.] **—de·te′ri·o·ra′tion,** *n.*

de·ter·mi·na·ble (di tur′mi nə bəl) *adj.* **1.** capable of being determined. **2.** *Law.* liable to be terminated. **—de·ter′mi·na·bly,** *adv.*

de·ter·mi·nant (di tur′mi nənt) *n.* **1.** something that determined. **2.** *Mathematics.* square array of numbers with a numerical value determined by a prescribed set of rules. Determinants are used esp. in solving algebraic problems in which variables having the same value occur simultaneously in two or more equations. *—adj.* determining. **—Syn.** *n.* **1.** see **cause.**

de·ter·mi·nate (di tur′mi nit) *adj.* **1.** having defined limits; fixed; definite: *a determinate quantity.* **2.** conclusive; settled; decided: *a determinate rule.* **3.** determined; resolute. **4.** *Botany.* (of an inflorescence) having stems all of which end in flower buds, with the central flowers opening first, as in the cyme. **—de·ter′mi·nate·ly,** *adv.* **—de·ter′mi·nate·ness,** *n.*

de·ter·mi·na·tion (di tur′mi nā′shən) *n.* **1.** act of reaching a decision; deciding. **2.** ascertainment after consideration, observation, investigation, or calculation; a finding out: *the determination that an ore bears uranium.* **3.** decision or conclusion: *the judge's determination in the case.* **4.** settlement on a course of action; fixing of purpose: *the presi-*

at; āpe; cär; end; mē; it, īce; hot; ōld; fôrk; wood; fōōl; oil; out; up; ūse; turn; sing; thin; this; zh in treasure; ə in ago, taken, pencil, lemon, circus.

dent's determination not to seek reelection. **5.** fixed purpose; resoluteness: *a man of great determination in the face of obstacles.*

de·ter·mi·na·tive (di tur'mi nā'tiv, -nə tiv) *adj.* serving or tending to determine. —*n.* something that serves or tends to determine.

de·ter·mine (di tur'min) *-mined, -min·ing. v.t.* **1.** to settle or decide a dispute, debate, or question: *The jury determined the sentence.* **2.** to ascertain after consideration, observation, investigation, or calculation; find out: *to determine the species of an animal, to determine the best method of solving a problem.* **3.** to decide upon: *The dramatist determined the title of his new play.* **4.** to be the cause or deciding factor of; bring about as a result; regulate: *The chairmanship of a committee in Congress is determined by seniority.* **5.** to give an aim, purpose, or direction to; direct; impel: *An impoverished boyhood determined him to become financially successful.* **6.** to fix or settle definitely or beforehand; decide the form or character of: *Genes determine one's stature and hair color.* **7.** to fix or define the geometrical position of. **8.** to fix the bounds of; limit. **9.** *Law.* to put an end to; conclude; terminate: *to determine an estate.* —*v.i.* **1.** to come to a decision; resolve. **2.** *Law.* to come to an end; cease to exist: *Under his will, his estate determined with the death of the last stated heir.* [Old French *determiner* to conclude, from Latin *dēterminare* to limit, fix, going back to *dē* thoroughly + *terminus* boundary, end.] —**Syn.** *v.t.* **1.** see **decide. 6.** see **fix.**

de·ter·mined (di tur'mind) *adj.* having or showing determination or fixed purpose; resolute. —**de·ter'mined·ly,** *adv.* —**de·ter'mined·ness,** *n.*

de·ter·min·er (di tur'mi nər) *n.* **1.** one who or that which determines. **2.** word belonging to a class of noun modifiers that includes articles, demonstratives, possessive adjectives, and other words. Determiners always precede the noun they modify, occupying either the first position in a noun phrase or the second position after another determiner. *Our* in the phrase *our house* and *the* in the phrase *the blue car* are determiners.

de·ter·min·ism (di tur'mi niz'əm) *n.* **1.** doctrine that all human actions and historical events are determined by antecedent causes and conditions. **2.** doctrine that all events conform in a regular, orderly fashion to unchangeable laws of the universe. —**de·ter'min·ist,** *n.* —**de·ter·min·is'tic,** *adj.*

de·ter·rence (di tur'əns, -ter'-) *n.* act of deterring.

de·ter·rent (di tur'ənt, -ter'-) *adj.* deterring; discouraging; restraining. —*n.* one who or that which deters: *The article argues that capital punishment is a deterrent to crime.* —**de·ter'rent·ly,** *adv.*

de·test (di test') *v.t.* to dislike intensely; hate; loathe; abominate. [Old French *detester,* from Latin *dētestārī* to curse while calling a god to witness, hate, going back to *dē* thoroughly + *testis* witness.] —**de·test'er,** *n.* —**Syn.** see **hate.**

de·test·a·ble (di tes'tə bəl) *adj.* deserving to be detested; hateful; abominable. —**de·test'a·ble·ness,** *n.* —**de·test'a·bly,** *adv.*

de·tes·ta·tion (dē'tes tā'shən) *n.* **1.** intense hatred or dislike. **2.** person or thing that is detested.

de·throne (dē thrōn') *-throned, -thron·ing. v.t.* **1.** to remove from a throne; depose. **2.** to remove from any high position. —**de·throne'·ment, de·thron'er,** *n.*

de Tocqueville, Alexis. see **Tocqueville, Alexis de.**

det·o·nate (det'ən āt') *-nat·ed, -nat·ing. v.t., v.i.* to explode or cause to explode suddenly and with a loud noise: *to detonate dynamite. The dynamite detonated.* [Latin *dētonātus,* past participle of *dētonāre* to thunder down.] —**det'o·na'tion,** *n.*

det·o·na·tor (det'ən ā'tər) *n.* **1.** device used to detonate an explosive. **2.** an explosive.

de·tour (dē'toor, di toor') *n.* **1.** road used temporarily when the main road cannot be traveled. **2.** deviation from a direct course; indirect way. —*v.i., v.t.* to make or cause to make a detour. [French *détour* circuit, from *détourner* to turn away, going back to Latin *dis-* apart + *tornāre* to turn. See TURN.]

de·tract (di trakt') *v.i.* to take something away; diminish; lessen, esp. in value or reputation (with *from*): *That scratch detracts from the beauty of the table.* —*v.t.* to take (something) away; divert. [Latin *dētractus,* past participle of *dētrahere* to take away, disparage.] —**de·trac'tor,** *n.*

de·trac·tion (di trak'shən) *n.* **1.** act of disparaging or belittling the reputation or worth of a person. **2.** a taking away; detracting.

de·trac·tive (di trak'tiv) *adj.* tending to detract; disparaging; belittling. —**de·trac'tive·ly,** *adv.*

de·train (dē trān') *v.i., v.t.* to get off or take off a railroad train.

det·ri·ment (de'trə mənt) *n.* **1.** damage, injury, or harm: *He is able to pursue several hobbies without detriment to his work.* **2.** something that causes damage, injury, or harm: *His lack of political experience is a great detriment to his candidacy.* [Latin *dētrīmentum* damage; literally, a rubbing away.]

det·ri·men·tal (de'trə men'təl) *adj.* causing damage; injurious; harmful: *Poor eating habits are detrimental to health.* —**det'ri·men'tal·ly,** *adv.*

de·tri·tus (di trī'təs) *n.* **1.** fragments of rock, as gravel or sand, torn away from a larger mass by such forces as erosion or glacial ice. **2.** any accumulation of disintegrated material or debris. [Latin *dētrītus* a rubbing away.]

De·troit (di troit') *n.* **1.** city in Michigan, in the southeastern part of the state. Pop. (1970), 1,511,482. **2.** river between southeastern Michigan and southern Ontario, Canada.

de trop (də trō') *French.* **1.** too much; too many. **2.** in the way; unwelcome.

Deu·ca·li·on and Pyrrha (dōō kā'lē ən) *Greek Mythology.* husband and wife who were the only mortals to survive a great flood sent by Zeus and became the ancestors of the renewed human race.

deuce[1] (dōōs, dūs) *n.* **1.** playing card having two symbols of the suit it represents on its center. **2.a.** face of a die having two spots. **b.** throw of dice that totals two. **3.** *Tennis.* a tie score of forty points or more each in a game, or five games or more each in a set. **4.** *Informal.* two, esp. in games and sports. [Old French *deus* two, from Latin *duōs,* accusative of *duo* two.]

deuce[2] (dōōs, dūs) *interj. Informal.* bad luck; the devil. ▲ used as a mild oath or exclamation: *What the deuce was that?* [Probably from DEUCE[1]; referring to the lowest or losing throw at dice.]

deu·ced (dōō'sid, dūs', dōōst, dūst) *adj. Informal.* devilish; excessive; confounded. —*adv.* devilishly; excessively. —**deu'ced·ly,** *adv.*

de·us ex ma·chi·na (dē'əs eks mak'i nə, dā'əs) **1.** in classical drama, a god appearing on stage unexpectedly to resolve difficulties in the plot. **2.** any person or thing intervening to resolve difficulties in a plot, story, or situation, esp. when the intervention is improbable, contrived, or artificial. [Latin *deus ex māchinā* literally, a god from a machine; because a god was brought on stage in classical drama by a mechanical contrivance.]

Deut., Deuteronomy.

deu·te·ri·um (dōō tēr'ē əm, dū-) *n.* stable isotope of hydrogen having one neutron and one proton in the nucleus and about twice the atomic weight of ordinary hydrogen. Symbols: **D** or **H**[2] Also, **heavy hydrogen.** [Modern Latin *deuterium,* from Greek *deuteros* second.]

deu·ter·on (dōō'tə ron', dū'-) *n.* nucleus of a deuterium atom.

Deu·ter·on·o·my (dōō'tə ron'ə me, dū'-) *n.* fifth book of the Old Testament. The Mosaic laws, first set forth in Exodus, are restated here. [Late Latin *Deuteronomium,* from Greek *Deuteronomion* literally, second or repeated law, from *deuteros* second + *nomos* law.]

deut·sche mark (doi'chə) *also,* **Deutsche mark.** monetary unit of West Germany, equal to 100 pfennigs.

Deutsch·land (doich'länt') see **Germany.**

De Va·le·ra, Ea·mon (dev'ə lãr'ə, -lēr'ə; ã'mən) 1882–1975, Irish political leader, born in the United States.

de·val·u·ate (dē val'ū āt') *-at·ed, -at·ing. v.t.* **1.** to lessen the value of. **2.** to lower the legal value of (a currency). —**de·val'u·a'tion,** *n.*

de·val·ue (dē val'ū) *-val·ued, -val·u·ing. v.t.* to devaluate.

dev·as·tate (dev'əs tāt') *-tat·ed, -tat·ing. v.t.* **1.** to lay waste; make desolate; ravage; destroy. **2.** to overwhelm; overpower. [Latin *dēvastātus,* past participle of *dēvastāre* to lay waste.] —**dev'as·tat'ing·ly,** *adv.* —**dev'as·ta'tor,** *n.*

dev·as·ta·tion (dev'əs tā'shən) *n.* act of devastating or state of being devastated; destruction; desolation. —**Syn.** see **destruction.**

de Ve·ga, Lope. see **Vega, Lope de.**

de·vel·op (di vel'əp) *v.t.* **1.** to bring into existence or activity: *He developed an interest in sports at an early age.* **2.** to change (something or someone) gradually through successive stages or periods: *The demand for speed and comfort has developed the automobile greatly over the past 40 years.* **3.** to bring to a more advanced state; cause to grow; expand: *Only by hard work can he develop his skills as a painter.* **4.** to bring into activity; put to use: *to develop natural resources.* **5.** to construct houses or other buildings on (land). **6.** to work out in detail; enlarge upon; clarify: *The rest of the book merely developed the ideas of the first chapter.* **7.** to make known; reveal; disclose, esp. gradually. **8.** *Photography.* to treat (an exposed film or printing paper) with a chemical developer to make the latent image visible. —*v.i.* **1.** to come into existence or activity: *A series of volcanic eruptions developed along the fault.* **2.** to change gradually through successive stages or periods; evolve: *The small river port developed into one of our great cities.* **3.** to grow into a more advanced state; mature; expand: *He developed into a strong leader.* **4.** to become known; be revealed: *Several new facts developed after the case had already been decided.* [French *développer* to unfold, probably going back to Latin *dis-* apart + blend of Medieval Latin *faluppa* wisp of straw, and Latin *volvere* to roll.] —**de·vel'op·a·ble,** *adj.*

de·vel·op·er (di vel'ə pər) *n.* **1.** someone or something that develops. **2.** *Photography.* chemical solution that makes the latent image visible on a film, plate, or print.

de·vel·op·ment (di vel'əp mənt) *n.* **1.** act or process of developing: *Economic development is essential to the advancement of depressed na-*

tions. **2.** state or condition of having been developed: *muscular development.* **3.** step or stage of advancement: *full development.* **4.** event or happening: *political developments.* **5.** group of houses or other buildings, often of similar design, usually constructed by one builder.

de·vel·op·men·tal (di vel′əp men′təl) *adj.* characterized by development; evolutionary. —**de·vel′op·men′tal·ly,** *adv.*

de·vi·ant (dē′vē ənt) *n.* one who deviates, esp. a person whose behavior deviates from what is considered normal by a group or society. —*adj.* deviating from a standard or norm, esp. from accepted norms of social behavior: *deviant conduct, deviant tendencies.*

de·vi·ate (*v.,* dē′vē āt′; *n., adj.,* dē′vē it) **-at·ed, -at·ing.** *v.i.* to turn aside (from a course of action, standard, line of thought, or the like); diverge: *Although a Democrat, he often deviates from the party line.* —*v.t.* to cause to turn aside. —*n.* one who deviates; deviant. —*adj.* that deviates; deviant. [Late Latin *dēviātus,* past participle of *dēviāre* to go aside, from Latin *dē* away + *via* way.] —**de′vi·a′tor,** *n.* —Syn. *v.i.* see **diverge.**

de·vi·a·tion (dē′vē ā′shən) *n.* **1.** act of deviating; divergence: *A creature of habit, he abhorred any deviation from routine.* **2.** amount of divergence.

de·vice (di vīs′) *n.* **1.** something contrived for a particular purpose; invention; mechanism. **2.** plan or scheme; trick: *By a subtle device, he gained access to the vault.* **3.** ornamental figure or design. **4.** picture, design, or other emblem, usually symbolic and often accompanied by a motto, used as a heraldic bearing. **5.** motto; emblem. **6. to leave (someone) to his own devices.** to permit (someone) to do as he wishes, esp. in a situation where some degree of control might be expected. [Old French *devis, devise* invention, plan, emblem, division, from *deviser* to divide. See **DIVISE.**]

dev·il (dev′əl) *n.* **1.** *also,* **Devil.** supernatural figure thought to be the supreme ruler of hell, the great spirit and principle of evil, the opponent of God, and the tempter and spiritual enemy of man, often represented as a creature having horns, a tail, and cloven feet; Lucifer; Satan. ▲ used with *the.* **2.** any subordinate evil spirit; demon. **3.** wicked, cruel, or ill-natured person. **4.** person of great cleverness, energy, impudence, or recklessness. **5.** wretched or pitiful person: *The poor devil hasn't had a decent meal in weeks.* **6.** something evil or undesirable. **7.** something difficult or trying: *He was in a devil of a spot.* **8.** apprentice or errand boy in a printing house. Also, **printer's devil. 9.** any of various machines for tearing or cleaning.

between the devil and the deep (blue sea). between two equally unpleasant or dangerous alternatives; in a tight spot.

like the devil. with violence, cunning, or other quality attributed to the devil; to an extreme; excessively: *The wind blew like the devil for two hours.*

the devil take the hindmost. let the slowest, last, or least able one take care of himself.

the devil to pay. serious trouble or difficulty ahead; trouble to be overcome.

to give the devil his due. to acknowledge someone's ability or success even though he is of bad character or is disliked.

to go to the devil. to go to ruin; degenerate morally.

to raise the devil. *Slang.* **a.** to cause a disturbance or commotion. **b.** to have a gay, noisy time.

—*v.t.,* **-iled, -il·ing;** *also, British,* **-illed, -il·ling. 1.** to tease; torment; bedevil. **2.** to prepare (food) by chopping fine and seasoning, esp. with exceptionally hot condiments, as mustard or pepper: *to devil eggs.* **3.** to tear to pieces in or with a devil *(def. 9).* —*interj.* **the devil.** used to lend emphasis or express disgust, anger, surprise, or vexation: *What the devil is this?* [Old English *dēofol* the devil, demon, wicked person, from Late Latin *diabolus* the devil, demon, from Greek *diabolos* the devil, slanderer, from *diaballein* to slander.]

dev·il·fish (dev′əl fish′) *pl.,* **-fish** or **-fish·es.** *n.* **1.** manta *(def. 1).* Also, **devil ray. 2.** any of several large cephalopods, esp. the octopus.

dev·il·ish (dev′ə lish, dev′lish) *adj.* **1.** relating to the devil or a devil; malicious; cruel. **2.** mischievous. **3.** *Informal.* extreme; excessive. —*adv. Informal.* extremely. —**dev′il·ish·ly,** *adv.* —**dev′il·ish·ness,** *n.*

dev·il-may-care (dev′əl mā kār′) *adj.* carefree.

dev·il·ment (dev′əl mənt) *n.* devilish activity; mischief.

dev·il·ry (dev′əl rē) *pl.,* **-ries.** *n.* deviltry.

devil's advocate. 1. one who supports an obviously inferior cause, esp. for the sake of argument. **2.** in the Roman Catholic Church, an official appointed to present the argument against a proposed beatification or canonization.

devil's darning needle, dragonfly.

devil's food cake, rich, dark chocolate cake.

Devil's Island, island off the coast of French Guiana, formerly a French penal colony.

dev·il·try (dev′əl trē′) *pl.,* **-tries.** *n.* **1.** diabolical action; wickedness. **2.** mischievous behavior.

de·vi·ous (dē′vē əs) *adj.* **1.** departing from the direct way; winding;

roundabout; wandering: *a devious route.* **2.** not straightforward, frank, or direct: *a devious explanation.* [Latin *dēvius* out of the way, from *dē* from + *via* way.] —**de′vi·ous·ly,** *adv.* —**de′vi·ous·ness,** *n.*

de·vise (di vīz′) **-vised, -vis·ing.** *v.t.* **1.** to think out; invent; plan; contrive: *to devise a secret code.* **2.** *Law.* to give or transmit (real property) by will. —*n.* **1.** the willing of real property. **2.** will or clause in a will disposing of real property. **3.** real property given by will. [Old French *deviser* to divide, regulate, design, talk, going back to Latin *dividere* to divide.] —**de·vis′a·ble,** *adj.* —**de·vis′er,** *n.* —Syn. *v.t.* **1. Devise, contrive, invent** mean to find a way to do, make, or solve something. **Devise** stresses mental effort and experimentation that bring into being something new or different: *That scholar has devised a new method of teaching foreign languages.* **Contrive** emphasizes ingenuity and cleverness in planning or designing: *The prisoners contrived a means of escape.* **Invent** emphasizes fabricating something new through the exercise of imagination, study, or labor: *This machine was invented by an American scientist.*

de·vis·ee (di vī′zē, dev′ə zē′) *n. Law.* one to whom real property is given by will.

de·vi·sor (di vī′zər) *n. Law.* one who gives real property by will.

de·vi·tal·ize (dē vīt′əl īz′) **-ized, -iz·ing.** *v.t.* **1.** to deprive of vitality; weaken; exhaust. **2.** to make lifeless. —**de·vi′tal·i·za′tion,** *n.*

de·void (di void′) *adj.* not possessing; lacking (with *of*): *devoid of reason. The project was disorganized and devoid of leadership.* [Originally past participle of obsolete *devoid* to empty out, from Old French *desvoidier,* going back to Latin *dis-* apart + *vacāre* to be empty.]

dev·o·lu·tion (dev′ə loo′shən) *n.* **1.** a passing down through successive stages. **2.** transfer or passing from one person to another, as of a right, title, or property. **3.** regression of an organism to a lower or less complex form; retrograde evolution; degeneration. [Medieval Latin *devolutio* passing of property to an heir, from Latin *dēvolvere* to roll down.] —**dev′o·lu′tion·ar′y,** *adj.*

de·volve (di volv′) **-volved, -volv·ing.** *v.t.* to transfer or delegate (work or responsibility) to another. —*v.i.* to pass on to anyone; be transferred (with *on, upon,* or *to*): *The kingdom devolved upon the heir apparent. Upon his retirement, the business devolved to his son.* [Latin *dēvolvere* to roll down.]

Dev·on (dev′ən) *n.* **1.** county in southwestern England. Pop. (1961), 823,751. Also, **Dev·on·shire** (dev′ən shēr′). **2.** small, hardy breed of cattle originally raised in Devon.

De·vo·ni·an (də vō′nē ən) *n.* period of the Paleozoic era coming between the Mississippian and the Silurian periods, characterized by an abundance of primitive fish and the appearance of amphibians. See **geology** for table. —*adj.* **1.** of, relating to, or characteristic of this period. **2.** of or relating to Devon, England.

de·vote (di vōt′) **-vot·ed, -vot·ing.** *v.t.* **1.** to give or apply, as oneself or one's time, effort, or attention, to some person or purpose: *She devoted all her energies to her family. He devoted himself to study.* **2.** to set apart solemnly; dedicate: *A large part of his time was devoted to worship.* **3.** to set apart for a particular use or purpose; dedicate. [Latin *dēvōtus,* past participle of *dēvovēre* to vow, give up.]

de·vot·ed (di vō′tid) *adj.* **1.** ardent; loyal; faithful: *a devoted friend, a devoted musician.* **2.** dedicated to some purpose: *hours devoted to study.* —**de·vot′ed·ly,** *adv.* —**de·vot′ed·ness,** *n.*

dev·o·tee (dev′ə tē′) *n.* **1.** one devoted to anything; enthusiast: *a devotee of boating.* **2.** one ardently devoted to religion; zealot. —Syn. **1.** see **enthusiast.**

de·vo·tion (di vō′shən) *n.* **1.** strong attachment or affection; loyalty; faithfulness: *His devotion to the party is unquestionable. Their mutual devotion gave them great strength.* **2.** act of devoting; being devoted: *We appreciated his devotion of time and money to the project.* **3.** religious piety; devoutness. **4. devotions.** religious worship; prayers.

de·vo·tion·al (di vō′shən əl) *adj.* relating to religious devotion; used in worship. —**de·vo′tion·al·ly,** *adv.*

de·vour (di vour′) *v.t.* **1.** to eat up greedily or ravenously: *The lion devoured its prey. The boy devoured his dinner.* **2.** to consume, waste, or destroy: *Time and war have devoured many ancient monuments.* **3.** to take in greedily or eagerly with the senses or the mind: *to devour a book.* **4.** to absorb or engross completely: *to be devoured by grief.* **5.** to swallow up; engulf. [Old French *devorer* to tear to pieces, to feed on prey, from Latin *dēvorāre* to gulp down, consume.] —**de·vour′er,** *n.* —**de·vour′ing·ly,** *adv.*

de·vout (di vout′) *adj.* **1.** devoted to worship and prayer; religious; pious: *a devout order of monks.* **2.** expressing devotion or piety: *devout prayer.* **3.** earnest; sincere: *You have my devout wishes for your safety.* [Old French *devot* devoted, from Latin *dēvōtus,* past participle of *dēvovēre* to vow, give up.] —**de·vout′ly,** *adv.* —**de·vout′ness,** *n.* —Syn. **1.** See **pious.**

De Vries, Hu·go (də vrēs′; *Dutch* hoo′gō) 1848–1935, Dutch botanist.

dew (doo, dū) *n.* **1.** moisture from the air that condenses in small drops upon cool surfaces during the night. **2.** any light moisture in small

at; āpe; cär; end; mē; it; īce; hot; ōld; fôrk; wood; fōōl; oil; out; up; ūse; turn; sing; thin; <u>th</u>is; zh in treasure; ə in ago, taken, pencil, lemon, circus.

drops, as tears or perspiration. **3.** anything fresh, pure, or refreshing like dew: *the dew of youth.* —*v.t.* to moisten with or as with dew; bedew. [Old English *dēaw* moisture from the air that condenses upon cool surfaces.]

dew·ber·ry (dōō′ber′ē, dū′-) *pl.,* **-ries.** *n.* **1.** sweet, black edible berry of any of several trailing or climbing shrubs, genus *Rubus,* of the rose family, similar to the blackberry. **2.** shrub bearing this berry.

dew·claw (dōō′klô′, dū′-) *n.* **1.** small, vestigial inner toe on the foot of certain dogs. **2.** false hoof above the true hoof in deer, cattle, hogs, and other animals.

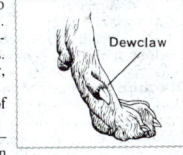

Dewclaw

Dewclaw on a dog's leg

dew·drop (dōō′drop′, dū′-) *n.* drop of dew.

Dew·ey (dōō′ē, dū′ē) **1.** George. 1837–1917, U.S. admiral in the Spanish-American War. **2.** John. 1859–1952, U.S. philosopher and educator.

Dewey decimal system, system used in libraries for classifying books and other publications according to subject matter. It uses the numbers 000 to 999 to designate major categories and decimal numbers to indicate special subdivisions of these fields. [From Melvil *Dewey,* 1851–1931, U.S. librarian, who devised it.]

dew·fall (dōō′fôl′) *n.* **1.** formation of dew. **2.** time of evening when dew begins to form.

dew·lap (dōō′lap′, dū′-) *n.* **1.** loose fold of skin under the throat of cattle and other animals. **2.** any similar part, as the wattle of a turkey or other fowl, or a pendulous fold of flesh on the human throat.

DEW line (dōō, dū) chain of radar stations across North America above the Arctic Circle, maintained to provide advance warning of the approach of hostile aircraft or missiles. [Abbreviation of *D(istant) E(arly) W(arning)*.]

Dewlap

dew point, temperature at which dew forms or vapor condenses into liquid.

dew·y (dōō′ē, dū′ē) **dew·i·er, dew·i·est.** *adj.* **1.** moist with dew: *dewy grass.* **2.** of dew: *dewy mists.* **3.** resembling or suggestive of dew; gentle; ephemeral; refreshing: *dewy slumber.* —**dew′i·ly,** *adv.* —**dew′i·ness,** *n.*

dex·ter (deks′tər) *adj.* **1.** of or on the right-hand side. **2.** *Heraldry.* situated on the bearer's right, and thus to the left of a viewer. Distinguished from *sinister.* [Latin *dexter* on the right side, skillful.]

dex·ter·i·ty (deks ter′ə tē) *n.* **1.** skill in using the hands or body. **2.** mental skill.

dex·ter·ous (deks′trəs, -tər əs) *also,* **dex·trous.** *adj.* having or showing physical or mental skill. —**dex′ter·ous·ly,** *adv.* —**dex′ter·ous·ness,** *n.*

Syn. Dexterous, deft, adroit mean skillful in the use of one's physical and mental powers. **Dexterous** emphasizes expertness and facility in the movement or manipulation of one's hands, limbs, or body: *Magicians and acrobats are dexterous.* **Deft** emphasizes lightness, sureness, and grace in handling or execution perfected through the training of natural powers: *Only a deft pianist can play the works of Beethoven.* **Adroit** emphasizes resourcefulness and artfulness enabling one to cope effectively and readily with difficult situations: *The diplomat handled the problem in an adroit manner.*

dex·tral (deks′trəl) *adj.* **1.** on the right side. **2.** right-handed. —**dex·tral·i·ty** (deks tral′ə tē), *n.* —**dex′tral·ly,** *adv.*

dex·trin (deks′trin) *also,* **dextrine** (deks′trēn, -trin). *n.* gummy substance obtained from the partial chemical breakdown of starch, used esp. as an adhesive. [French *dextrine,* from Latin *dexter* on the right side; because it turns the plane of polarization to the right.]

dex·trose (deks′trōs) *n.* colorless, crystalline sugar found in many plants and in blood. Formula: $C_6H_{12}O_6$ Also, **corn sugar, grape sugar.**

dey (dā) *pl.,* **deys.** *n.* **1.** any of various Turkish governors of Algiers from 1710 until the French conquest in 1830. **2.** any of various former rulers of Tunis or Tripoli. [French *dey,* from Turkish *dāī* maternal uncle (title formerly given to elderly people).]

D.F., Defender of the Faith.

dg., decigram; decigrams.

dhole (dōl) *pl.,* **dholes** *or* **dhole.** *n.* wild dog, *Cuon alpinus,* native to India and other parts of Asia, that usually hunts in packs, preying on deer, pigs, goats, and other large animals. Length: 3½ feet, including tail. [Of uncertain origin.]

Dhole

dhow (dou) *n.* sailing ship, usually single-masted and lateen-rigged, used in Arabia and northern and eastern Africa. [Of uncertain origin.]

di-¹ *prefix* **1.** twice; double; twofold: *dicotyledon.* **2.** *Chemistry.* containing two identical atoms, groups, or radicals. [Greek *di-,* from *dis* twice.]

di-², form of **dis-¹** before *b, d, l, m, n, r, s, v,* and sometimes before *g* and *j,* as in *direct, divert.*

di-³, form of **dia-** before vowels, as in *diorama.*

Dhow

dia- *prefix* **1.** through; between; across: *diagonal, diacritical, dialogue.* **2.** apart; away. [Greek *dia* through, apart.]

di·a·be·tes (dī′ə bē′tis, -tēz) *n.* disorder of metabolism characterized by deficiency of insulin and a resulting excess of sugar in the blood. Also, **diabetes mel·li·tus** (mə-lī′təs). [Late Latin *diabētēs,* from Greek *diabētēs,* from *diabainein* to pass through; with reference to the excessive urination characteristic of the disease.]

di·a·bet·ic (dī′ə bet′ik) *adj.* of, relating to, or having diabetes. —*n.* person having diabetes.

di·a·ble·rie (dē ä′blər ē) *n.* **1.** dealings with the devil; sorcery; witchcraft. **2.** deviltry; mischief. **3.** demonology. [French *diablerie* witchcraft, mischief, from *diable* devil, from Late Latin *diabolus* devil. See DEVIL.]

di·a·bol·ic (dī′ə bol′ik) *adj.* **1.** befitting the devil; very cruel or wicked; fiendish. **2.** relating to the devil or devils. Also, **di′a·bol′i·cal.** [Late Latin *diabolicus* devilish, from Greek *diabolikos,* from *diabolos* devil. See DEVIL.] —**di′a·bol′i·cal·ly,** *adv.* —**di′a·bol′i·cal·ness,** *n.*

di·ab·o·lism (dī ab′ə liz′əm) *n.* **1.** dealings with the devil; sorcery; witchcraft. **2.** devilish action or behavior; deviltry. **3.** belief in or worship of the devil or devils. **4.** character or nature of a devil.

di·ac·o·nal (dī ak′ə nəl) *adj.* of or relating to a deacon. [Late Latin *diāconālis,* from Latin *diāconus* deacon. See DEACON.]

di·ac·o·nate (dī ak′ə nit, -nāt′) *n.* **1.** rank or office of a deacon. **2.** body of deacons.

di·a·crit·ic (dī′ə krit′ik) *n.* diacritical mark. —*adj.* diacritical. [Greek *diakritikos* able to distinguish, separative, from *diakrinein* to distinguish.]

di·a·crit·i·cal (dī′ə krit′i kəl) *adj.* **1.a.** serving to distinguish; distinctive. **b.** serving to distinguish sounds and values of letters. **2.** capable of distinguishing. —**di′a·crit′i·cal·ly,** *adv.*

diacritical mark, mark or sign (as ¨ , ˆ , ˜ , ´ , or `) placed over, under, or across a letter to indicate pronunciation or as part of the spelling.

di·a·dem (dī′ə dem′) *n.* **1.** crown. **2.** cloth headband, often set with jewels and precious metals, formerly worn as a crown by Oriental rulers. **3.** royal power, authority, or dignity. [Latin *diadēma* royal headdress, from Greek *diadēma* band, fillet, royal headdress, from *dia* around; literally, apart + *dein* to bind.]

di·aer·e·sis (dī er′ə sis) *pl.,* **-ses** (-sēz′). *n.* dieresis.

di·ag·nose (dī′əg nōs′, -nōz′)-**nosed, -nos·ing.** *v.t.* to make a diagnosis of. —*v.i.* to make a diagnosis.

di·ag·no·sis (dī′əg nō′sis) *pl.,* **-ses** (-sēz). *n.* **1.a.** act or process of determining the nature of a disease or other harmful condition by careful examination and study of symptoms: *a thorough diagnosis of her ailment.* **b.** conclusion reached by such examination: *His diagnosis was that she had measles.* **2.a.** investigation and study of facts to determine the essential characteristics of something: *He made a complete diagnosis of the housing problem.* **b.** conclusion reached by such investigation: *His diagnosis was that additional dwellings were urgently needed.* **4.** *Biology.* short technical description for scientific classification. [Modern Latin *diagnosis,* from Greek *diagnōsis* a distinguishing.]

di·ag·nos·tic (dī′əg nos′tik) *adj.* relating to or helpful in diagnosis.

di·ag·nos·ti·cian (dī′əg nos tish′ən) *n.* one who makes diagnoses, esp. a specialist in medical diagnoses.

di·ag·o·nal (dī ag′ən əl) *adj.* **1.** *Geometry.* **a.** connecting, as a straight line, two nonadjacent angles of a figure. **b.** connecting, as a plane, two nonadjacent edges of a solid figure. **2.** having an oblique direction; slanting. **3.** having oblique lines, markings, or parts: *diagonal hatching, diagonal cloth.* —*n.* **1.** diagonal straight line or plane. **2.** anything extending diagonally. **3.** fabric woven, with diagonal lines. [Latin *diagōnālis* from one angle to another nonadjacent angle of a figure, from Greek *diagonios,* from *dia* through, across + *gōnia* angle¹, corner.] —**di·ag′o·nal·ly,** *adv.*

Line   Plane

Diagonals

di·a·gram (dī′ə gram′) *n.* **1.** geometrical figure serving to illustrate

a proposition. **2.** set of lines, figure, plan, or sketch giving the outline or general scheme of an object or area or showing the course or results of an action or process: *a diagram of the grasshopper's anatomy, a diagram of the disposition of troops before a battle.* —*v.t.,* **-gramed, -gram·ing;** *also, British.* **-grammed, -gram·ming.** to represent by a diagram; make a diagram of: *to diagram a sentence.* [Latin *diagramma* scale, gamut, from Greek *diagramma* figure marked out by lines, scale', list.] —**Syn.** *v.t.* see **map.**

di·a·gram·mat·ic (dī'ə grə mat'ik) *adj.* **1.** in the form of a diagram. **2.** in outline; sketchy. Also, **di·a·gram·mat'i·cal.** —**di·a·gram·mat'i·cal·ly,** *adv.*

dial (dī'əl, dīl) *n.* **1.** graduated surface on which the amount or degree of something is indicated by a moving pointer or index, as the face of a clock, compass, meter, or gauge. **2.** movable disk or other device on a radio or television for tuning in to a station or channel. **3.** rotating disk on a telephone, for selecting the numbers and letters of the telephone being called. **4.** sundial. —*v.t.* **-aled, -al·ing;** *also, British.* **-alled, -al·ling.** **1.** to tune in (a radio or television station or program). **2.** to call by means of a telephone dial: *to dial a wrong number.* **3.** to indicate by means of a dial. —*v.i.* to operate or use a dial, as in telephoning. [Medieval Latin *dialis* relating to a day, daily, from Latin *diēs* day.]

dial. **1.** dialect. **2.** dialectal.

di·a·lect (dī'ə lekt') *n.* **1.** form of language spoken in a specific area which differs enough from the standard language in its grammar, pronunciation, vocabulary, and idioms to be a distinct entity, but not enough to be a distinct language: *the Scottish dialect of English, the Sicilian dialect of Italian.* **2.** one of a group of languages belonging to a specific family: *French, Italian, Spanish, Portuguese, and Romanian are Romance dialects.* **3.** language distinctly used by a specific group, as a profession or social class; jargon. **4.** manner of expressing oneself; idiom. [Latin *dialectus* way of speaking, from Greek *dialektos* speech, language of a region.] —**Syn. 1.** see **idiom.**

di·a·lec·tal (dī'ə lekt'əl) *adj.* relating to or characteristic of dialect or a dialect. —**di·a·lec'tal·ly,** *adv.*

di·a·lec·tic (dī'ə lek'tik) *n.* **1.** *also,* **dialectics.** method of logical argumentation involving a series of questions and answers to test the truth of a theory or opinion. **2.** logical argumentation. **3.** method of logic used by Georg Hegel and later by Karl Marx, based on a progression of thought through the interplay, or clash, of one idea (thesis) with its opposite (antithesis), which leads to the resolution of these ideas in a conclusion (synthesis). —*adj.* **1.** relating to or practicing logical discussion. **2.** dialectal. [Latin *dialectica (ars)* logic, from Greek *dialektikē (technē)* (art) of discussion by question and answer.]

di·a·lec·ti·cal (dī'ə lek'ti kəl) *adj.* dialectic.

dialectical materialism, philosophy formulated by Karl Marx and Friedrich Engels from Georg Hegel's dialectic, which views historical change as the result of conflict between economic groups.

di·a·lec·ti·cian (dī'ə lek'tish'ən) *n.* **1.** one who is skilled in dialectic; logician. **2.** one who studies dialects.

di·a·lec·tol·o·gy (dī'ə lek tol'ə jē) *n.* study of dialects. —**di'a·lec·tol'o·gist,** *n.*

di·a·logue (dī'ə lôg', -log') *also,* **di·a·log.** *n.* **1.** conversation between two or more persons. **2.** literary work in the form of a conversation between two or more persons. **3.** conversation in a literary work or dramatic presentation: *a play with witty dialogue.* **4.** exchange of ideas; discussion. —*v.t.,* **-logued, -logu·ing.** to express in the form of a dialogue. [Old French *dialoge* conversation between two people, from Latin *dialogus* conversation, from Greek *dialogos.*]

dial tone, steady humming sound in a dial telephone, indicating to the user that a call may be dialed.

di·al·y·sis (dī al'ə sis) *pl.,* **-ses** (-sēz') *n.* method of separating colloidal particles from the liquid of a crystalloid solution by using a semipermeable membrane through which the liquid, but not the particles, will diffuse. [Latin *dialysis* separation, from dialyze.]

di·a·lyt·ic (dī'ə lit'ik) *adj.* relating to or characterized by dialysis.

di·a·lyze (dī'ə līz') **-lyzed, -lyz·ing.** *v.t.* to subject to dialysis.

diam., diameter.

di·a·mag·net·ism (dī'ə mag'nə tiz'əm) *n.* **1.** form of magnetism produced by the movement of electrons around the nucleus of an atom. **2.a.** property of some substances that causes them to be repelled by both poles of a magnet. **b.** position at right angles to a magnet's lines of force taken by such substances. **c.** force causing this phenomenon. **3.** science dealing with such substances and phenomena. —**di·a·mag·net·ic** (dī'ə mag net'ik), *adj.* —**di'a·mag·net'i·cal·ly,** *adv.*

di·am·e·ter (dī am'ə tər) *n.* **1.** straight line passing through the center of a circle or sphere and bounded by the circumference or surface. **2.** length of such a line; width or thickness of something: *the diameter of a pipe. Redwoods average ten*

to twenty-one feet in diameter. [Old French *diametre* diameter of a circle, from Greek *diametros,* from Greek *diametros* a diagonal, diameter of a circle, from *dia* through + *metron* measure.]

di·a·met·ri·cal (dī'ə met'ri kəl) *adj.* **1.** of or along a diameter: *He took a diametrical measurement of the tree.* **2.** directly opposite; completely contrary: *The two candidates have diametrical views on that issue.* Also, **di'a·met'ric.**

di·a·met·ri·cal·ly (dī'ə met'rik lē) *adv.* **1.** as or along a diameter; straight through: *The sphere was cut diametrically.* **2.** directly; completely: *While they were diametrically opposed on most issues, occasionally they could agree.*

dia·mond (dī'mənd, dī'ə-) *n.* **1.** transparent to opaque, usually colorless, mineral consisting of pure carbon in a crystalline form, the hardest natural substance known. It is used in transparent, cut form as a precious gem; imperfect forms are used for industrial purposes, as grinding and cutting. **2.** piece cut from this mineral, esp. when cut and polished for use as a gem. **3.** drill or other tool having a diamond tip. **4.** *Geometry.* plane figure with four equal sides, forming two acute and two obtuse angles; rhombus; lozenge. **5.a.** playing card with red diamond-like designs on it. **b. diamonds.** suit of such cards. **6.** *Baseball.* **a.** the infield. **b.** the entire field. **7. diamond in the rough. a.** diamond in its natural state. **b.** person who has good qualities but lacks polish. —*adj.* **1.** resembling, made of, or set with a diamond or diamonds. **2.** of or designating the sixtieth or seventy-fifth anniversary of an event. [Old French *diamant* the gem, lodestone, from Medieval Latin *diamas* the gem, adamant, modification of Latin *adamas,* from Greek *adamās.* See ADAMANT.]

Diamondback

dia·mond·back (dī'mənd bak', dī'ə-) *n.* **1.** large, poisonous rattlesnake, *Crotalus adamanteus,* having diamond-shaped markings on its back, found in the southeastern United States. Length: to 8 feet. **2.** edible, freshwater turtle, *Malaclemys terrapin,* with diamond-shaped markings on its shell, found in Atlantic coastal waters from Massachusetts to northern Mexico. Length: 6-8 inches. Also (*def.* 2), **diamondback terrapin.**

Di·an·a (dī an'ə) *n.* Roman goddess of the moon, the woods, and the hunt, also worshipped as the protectress of women. Her Greek counterpart is Artemis.

di·a·pa·son (dī'ə pā'zən, -sən) *n.* **1.** either of two principal stops in a pipe organ which extend through the entire range of the organ. **Open diapason** gives full, majestic tones; **stopped diapason** gives powerful, flutelike tones. **2.** entire range of a voice or instrument. **3.** fixed standard of musical pitch. **4.** tuning fork. **5.** full, deep outpouring of harmonious sound. [Latin *diapāsōn* octave, from Greek *dia pāsōn (chordōn symphōnia)* (concord) through all (notes of the scale), octave.]

dia·per (dī'pər, dī'ə-) *n.* **1.** baby's undergarment consisting of a soft, absorbent, thickly folded cloth or other material, drawn up between the legs and fastened at the waist. **2.** pattern made up of small, constantly repeated, and usually geometric, figures. **3.** white cotton or linen cloth woven with such a pattern. —*v.t.* **1.** to put a clean diaper on (a baby). **2.** to decorate with an overall, repeated pattern. [Old French *dia(s)pre* fine cloth, from Medieval Latin *diasprus* made of diaper cloth, from Middle Greek *diaspros* pure white.]

di·aph·a·nous (dī af'ə nəs) *adj.* translucent; transparent. [Greek *diaphanēs* transparent.] —**di·aph'a·nous·ly,** *adv.* —**di·aph'a·nous·ness,** *n.*

di·a·pho·re·sis (dī'ə fə rē'sis) *n.* profuse perspiration, especially when artificially induced. [Late Latin *diaphorēsis* a sweat, from Greek *diaphorēsis* perspiration.]

di·a·phragm (dī'ə fram') *n.* **1.** membrane of muscle and connective tissue between the chest cavity and the abdominal cavity, used in inhaling and exhaling. **2.** any member or partition that serves to separate. **3.** disk used in the conversion of sound to electrical impulses or the reverse, as in a telephone or microphone. **4.** adjustable mechanism for controlling the amount of light admitted through the lens of a camera, microscope, or similar optical

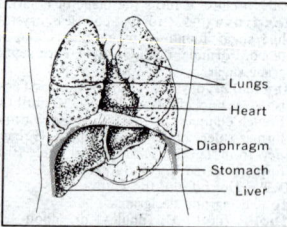

— Lungs
— Heart
— Diaphragm
— Stomach
— Liver

Diaphragm

Center

Diameter

Diameter

at; āpe; cär; end; mē; it; īce; hot; ōld; fôrk; wood; fōōl; oil; out; up; ūse; turn; sing; thin; this; zh in treasure; ə in ago, taken, pencil, lemon, circus.

equipment. [Late Latin *diaphragma* midriff, from Greek *diaphragma* partition, midriff.]

di·a·phrag·mat·ic (dī′ə frag mat′ik) *adj.* relating to or like a diaphragm.

di·a·rist (dī′ər ist) *n.* one who keeps a diary.

di·ar·rhe·a (dī′ə rē′ə) *also*, **di·ar·rhoe·a**, *n.* frequent and loose bowel movements caused by irritation or inflammation of the mucous membrane lining of the intestine. [Late Latin *diarrhoea*, from Greek *diarrhoia* literally, a flowing through.]

di·a·ry (dī′ər ē) *pl.*, **-ries.** *n.* **1.** daily record of events, esp. of the writer's personal experiences and observations. **2.** book for keeping such a record. [Latin *diārium* daily allowance, daily record, from *diēs* day.]

Di·as, Bar·tho·lo·me·u (dē′əs; bär′too loo mā′oo) c.1450–1500, Portuguese navigator who was the first to sail around the southern tip of Africa.

Di·as·po·ra (dī as′pər ə) *n.* **1.** dispersion of the Jews among communities outside Palestine after their captivity in Babylon and after the capture of Jerusalem by the Romans in A.D. 70. **2.** all the Jews thus dispersed. **3.** *also*, **diaspora**, scattering of any group of people; dispersion. [Greek *diasporā* a scattering.]

di·a·stase (dī′ə stās′) *n.* enzyme in green plants that changes starch into sugar. [French *diastase* enzyme, from Greek *diastasis* separation.]

di·as·to·le (dī as′tə lē′) *n.* period of normal dilation or relaxation of the heart, alternating rhythmically with the period of contraction, or systole. [Greek *diastolē* dilation.] **—di·a·stol·ic** (dī′ə stol′ik), *adj.*

di·a·ther·my (dī′ə thur′mē) *n.* method of treating muscular disorders and injuries by heating body tissues with high-frequency electric currents. [DIA- + Greek *thermē* heat.] **—di′a·ther′mic**, *adj.*

di·a·tom (dī′ə tom′) *n.* any of a large group of microscopic, one-celled, aquatic algae that have bivalve walls composed mostly of silica. [Modern Latin *Diatoma*, from Greek *diatomos* cut in half.]

di·a·to·ma·ceous (dī′ə tə mā′shəs) *adj.* relating to, consisting of, or containing diatoms or their fossil remains: *a diatomaceous earth.*

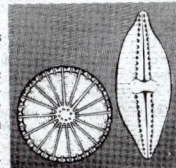

Diatoms

di·a·tom·ic (dī′ə tom′ik) *adj.* having two atoms in each molecule.

di·a·ton·ic (dī′ə ton′ik) *adj. Music.* of or relating to a standard eight-toned major or minor scale having no chromatic alteration. [Late Latin *diatonicus*, from Greek *diatonikos*, going back to *dia* through + *tonos* tone.] **—di′a·ton′i·cal·ly**, *adv.*

di·a·tribe (dī′ə trīb′) *n.* bitter and violent criticism; invective. [Latin *diatriba* learned discussion, from Greek *diatribē* discussion; literally, a wearing away, as of time.]

Di·az, Bartholomew (dē′əs) *see* Dias, Bartolomeu.

di·ba·sic (dī bā′sik) *adj.* **1.** (of an acid) containing two hydrogen atoms replaceable by two atoms or radicals of a base forming salts. **2.** containing two univalent atoms or radicals.

dib·ble (dib′əl) *n.* pointed hand tool used to make holes in the ground for planting seeds or young plants. [Of uncertain origin.]

dice (dīs) *n.,pl.* **1.** small cubes of wood, plastic, or other material, marked on each side with a different number of spots, the number varying from one to six, used in games of chance, usually in a pair. **2.** gambling game played with dice. **3. no dice.** *Slang.* **a.** no luck or success. **b. no.** ▲ used in answering a request. **—v.t., diced, dic·ing.** **1.** to cut into small cubes: *to dice carrots.* **2.** to decorate with a pattern of squares; checker. **3.** to lose by gambling with dice. **—v.i.** to play at dice. **—dic′er,** *n.*

di·chlo·ride (dī klôr′īd, -id) *n.* chloride containing two atoms of chlorine; bichloride.

di·chot·o·mous (dī kot′ə məs) *adj.* **1.** divided or dividing into two parts or branches. **2.** relating to or involving dichotomy.

di·chot·o·my (dī kot′ə mē) *pl.*, **-mies.** *n.* **1.** division into two parts. **2.** *Logic.* division of a class into two contradictory subclasses. **3.** branching by repeated divisions into two parts; bifurcation. [Greek *dichotomiā* a cutting in two.]

di·chro·mate (dī krō′māt) *n.* chromate containing two atoms of chromium; bichromate.

di·chro·mat·ic (dī′krō mat′ik) *adj.* **1.** having or showing two colors. **2.** *Zoology.* exhibiting two color phases independent of those correlated with age, sex, or season, as certain species of insects, birds, and fish. **—di·chro·ma·tism** (dī krō′mə tiz′əm), *n.*

dick·cis·sel (dik sis′əl) *n.* small finch, *Spiza americana*, found in the central United States, the male of which has a light-brown body and a yellow breast with a black patch below the throat. Length: 6–7 inches. [Imitative of its cry.]

dick·ens (dik′ənz) *interj.* the devil; deuce. ▲ used as a mild oath or exclamation: *Where the dickens is my coat?*

Dick·ens, Charles (dik′inz) 1812–70, English novelist.

Dick·en·si·an (di ken′zē ən) *adj.* of, relating to, or suggestive of Charles Dickens or his writings.

dick·er (dik′ər) *v.i.* to trade by petty bargaining; haggle: *to dicker over the price of a head of lettuce.* **—n. 1.** petty bargaining. **2.** petty bargain. [Possibly from earlier *dicker* set of ten pelts, going back to Latin *decūria* a set of ten, from *decem* ten; from the haggling of fur traders over hides or pelts.]

dick·ey (dik′ē) *pl.*, **-eys.** *n.* **1.** article of clothing, usually having a collar, filling in the neckline of a shirt or dress. **2.** false shirt front designed to be worn under a jacket. **3.** child's bib or pinafore. **4.** shirt collar. **5.** any small bird. Also, **dickey bird. 6.** donkey. [From *Dick*, nickname for *Richard*.]

Dick·in·son, Emily (dik′in sən) 1830–86, U.S. poet.

Dick test (dik) test to determine whether a person is susceptible or immune to scarlet fever, made by injecting scarlet fever toxin into the skin. [Named after George and Gladys *Dick*, U.S. physicians who devised it in 1923.]

dick·y (dik′ē) *pl.*, **dick·ies.** *n.* dickey.

di·cli·nous (dī klī′nəs) *adj.* **1.** (of plants) having the stamens and pistils on separate flowers. **2.** (of flowers) unisexual. [DI-¹ + Greek *klinē* bed + -OUS.]

di·cot·y·le·don (dī kot′əl ēd′ən) *n.* plant that has two cotyledons in the embryo. Dicotyledons constitute one of the two classes of flowering plants. Also, **di·cot** (dī′kot). See **cotyledon** for illustration. **—di·cot′y·le′don·ous**, *adj.*

dict. 1. dictionary. **2.** dictator.

dic·ta (dik′tə) a plural of **dictum**.

Dic·ta·phone (dik′tə fōn′) *Trademark. n.* instrument to record and reproduce speech, esp. used for the recording or dictating of business correspondence or the like. [Latin *dictāre* to dictate + Greek *phōnē* sound, voice.]

dic·tate (*v.,* dik′tāt, dik tāt′; *n.,* dik′tāt) **-tat·ed, -tat·ing.** *v.t.* **1.** to say or read aloud (something) to be recorded: *He dictated the letter to his secretary.* **2.** to prescribe with authority, as commands, terms, rules: *The victorious nation dictated the conditions of peace. Conscience dictates truthfulness.* **—v.i. 1.** to say or read aloud something to be recorded: *The teacher dictated in French to the class.* **2.** to give orders; exercise authority. **—n.** authoritative principle, rule, or command: *dictates of reason. Everyone is subject to the dictates of law.* [Latin *dictātus*, past participle of *dictāre* to say often, dictate (for writing).]

dic·ta·tion (dik tā′shən) *n.* **1.** act of dictating something to be recorded: *We listened carefully to the teacher's dictation.* **2.** that which is dictated or recorded: *Part of the French exam was a dictation.* **3.** authoritative prescription or command: *He received the dictation of the court without resentment.*

dic·ta·tor (dik′tā′tər, dik tā′-) *n.* **1.** ruler who exercises absolute authority, esp. one considered an oppressor or tyrant. **2.** one who prescribes or suggests authoritatively: *a dictator of fashion.* **3.** in ancient Rome, absolute ruler appointed to serve temporarily in time of emergency. **4.** one who dictates something to be recorded.

dic·ta·to·ri·al (dik′tə tôr′ē əl) *adj.* **1.** relating to or characteristic of a dictator: *dictatorial powers.* **2.** overbearing; dogmatic; dictatorial individual. **—dic′ta·to′ri·al·ly**, *adv.*

dic·ta·tor·ship (dik′tā′tər ship′) *n.* **1.** office or tenure of a dictator. **2.** state or government ruled by a dictator. **3.** form of government in which absolute authority is held by a dictator. **4.** any prescriptive authority: *literary dictatorship.* **—Syn. 1.** see **totalitarianism.**

dic·tion (dik′shən) *n.* **1.** manner of expression in speaking or writing, esp. in the choice and arrangment of words: *The diction of poetry is often different from the language of common speech.* **2.** degree of distinctness in uttering speech sounds; enunciation: *A singer must have clear diction.* [Latin *dictiō* a saying, speech.]

dic·tion·ar·y (dik′shə ner′ē) *pl.*, **-ar·ies.** *n.* **1.** book containing words of a language arranged in an alphabetical listing, together with definitions, pronunciations, etymologies, and other information about their uses, forms, and functions. **2.** book containing words of one language listed alphabetically, with their equivalent meanings in another language: *an Italian-English dictionary.* **3.** book containing and defining words used in a special area of interest or knowledge, usually listed alphabetically: *a sports dictionary, a dictionary of cooking terms.* [Medieval Latin *dictionarium* literally, book of sayings or words, from Latin *dictiō* a saying.]

dic·tum (dik′təm) *pl.*, **-tums** or **-ta** (-tə). *n.* **1.** formal authoritative statement or opinion: *Their conclusions amounted to a dictum which they insisted everyone must heed.* **2.** maxim; saying: *His favorite dictum was "A penny saved is a penny earned."* [Latin *dictum* saying, something said, from *dicere* to say.]

did (did) past tense of **do¹.**

di·dac·tic (dī dak′tik) *adj.* **1.** intended to instruct; informative: *a didactic treatise.* **2.** morally instructive; aphoristic: *Parables are didactic*

at; āpe; cär; end; mē; it; īce; hot; ōld; fôrk; wood; fōōl; oil; out; up; ūse; turn; sing; thin; this; zh in treasure; ə in ago, taken, pencil, lemon, circus.

281

tales. **3.** overly inclined to instruct or moralize; pedantic: *His lectures were didactic rather than truly informative.* Also, **di·dac'ti·cal.** [Greek *didaktikos* skilled in teaching, from *didaskein* to teach.] **—di·dac'ti·cal·ly,** *adv.* **—di·dac·ti·cism** (dī dak'tə siz'əm), *n.*

di·dac·tics (dī dak'tiks) *n.* science or art of teaching.

did·dle (did'əl) **-dled, -dling.** *v.t. Informal.* to cheat; swindle. **—v.i.** to waste time (usually with *away*): *He diddled away the day.* [Possibly from Jeremy *Diddler,* a character who swindles in James Kenney's play *Raising the Wind* (1803).]

Di·de·rot, De·nis (dē'də rō'; də nē') 1713–84, French writer, philosopher, and encyclopedist.

did·n't (did'ənt) did not.

di·do (dī'dō) *pl.,* **-dos** or **-does.** *n. Informal.* prank; antic. [Of uncertain origin.]

Di·do (dī'dō) *n. Roman Legend.* founder and queen of Carthage. In the *Aeneid,* she falls in love with Aeneas and kills herself when he leaves Carthage.

didst (didst) *Archaic.* second person singular, past tense of **do¹:** *Thou didst.*

di·dym·i·um (dī dim'ē əm) *n.* mixture of two rare-earth elements, neodymium and praseodymium, formerly thought to be an element.

die¹ (dī) **died, dy·ing.** *v.i.* **1.** to cease to live; suffer death; become dead: *Many civilians died in World War II.* **2.** to pass out of existence; come to an end: *The pony express died with the coming of the telegraph.* **3.** to lose force, strength, or active qualities; cease to flourish: *The wind suddenly died as the sailboat neared shore.* **4.** to stop functioning: *The engine died.* **5.** to pass or fade away gradually: *The smile died on his lips. The music died in the distance.* **6.** to suffer unbearable unpleasantness or physical stress: *He was dying of boredom in the isolated cabin.* **7.** *Informal.* to want very much; desire strongly: *He is dying for a hamburger. I am dying to see him again.* **8. to die away.** to fade away gradually: *The sound of his voice died away.* **9. to die down.** to come to an end or subside gradually: *The fire was left to die down by itself.* **10. to die hard.** to struggle against extinction or resist yielding to the very end: *Racial hatred dies hard.* **11. to die off.** to die successively until all are gone. **12. to die out. a.** to end gradually: *Neighborhood shops are dying out because of the big department stores.* **b.** to cease or end completely. [Old Norse *deyja* to cease to live.]

die² (dī) *pl.,* **(def. 1) dice** or **(def. 2) dies.** *n.* **1.** small cube, usually one of a pair, marked with a different number of spots on each side, used in games of chance. **2.** any of various machines or devices used to impress, finish, trim, or give a particular shape to a relatively unformed object or a molten substance. **3. the die is cast.** the decisive step is taken; the course of action is irrevocably decided. [Old French *de* one of a pair of dice, from Latin *datum* something given (as by chance), from *dare* to give.]

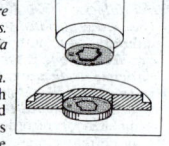
Die²
Die for stamping one side of a coin

die·hard (dī'härd') *also,* **die·hard.** *adj.* resisting vigorously or obstinately to the very end: *a die-hard political conservative.* **—n.** one who refuses to change or modify his views.

di·e·lec·tric (dī'i lek'trik) *n.* substance that does not conduct electricity. **—adj.** nonconducting.

Dien·bien·phu (dyen'byen'fōō') *n.* town in northwestern North Vietnam. Its capture from the French by the Vietminh in 1954 marked the end of French military power in Indochina.

di·er·e·sis (dī er'ə sis) *pl.,* **-ses** (-sēz') *n.* two dots (¨) placed over a vowel to show that it is pronounced in a separate syllable. [Late Latin *diaeresis* dividing of one syllable into two, from Greek *diairesis* division, separation.]

die·sel (dē'zəl, -səl) *n.* **1.** diesel engine. **2.** vehicle powered by a diesel engine. **—adj.** of or for a diesel engine: *diesel fuel.*

diesel engine, internal-combustion engine in which fuel oil, injected into the cylinder, is ignited by the heat produced by the compression of air in the cylinder, rather than by a spark furnished by a spark plug. Also, **diesel motor.** [From Rudolf *Diesel,* 1858–1913, its German inventor.]

die·sink·er (dī'sing'kər) *n.* person who engraves dies for shaping or stamping.

Di·es I·rae (dē'ās ēr'ā) medieval Latin hymn which describes the Day of Judgment, usually sung at masses for the dead. [Latin *diēs īrae* day of wrath, the first two words of this hymn.]

di·et¹ (dī'ət) *n.* **1.** food and drink usually eaten by a person or animal; customary daily fare: *a vegetable diet. A lion's diet consists of meat.* **2.** regulated course of food and drink prescribed for reasons of health or weight control: *He lost twenty pounds the first month of his diet.* **3.** food considered as a nutrient or for its effects on the body. **4.** anything provided or consumed habitually: *a diet of criticism, a steady diet of books.* **—v.i.** to eat according to prescribed rules: *She dieted for several*

weeks to lose weight. [Old French *diete* daily fare, from Latin *diaeta* mode of living, from Greek *diaita.*] **—di'et·er,** *n.*

di·et² (dī'ət) *n.* **1.** formal assembly: *A diet of church officials met to consider changes in the liturgy.* **2.** legislative council or assembly, as the national legislature of Japan or the assembly of the estates of the Holy Roman Empire. [Medieval Latin *dieta* public assembly, appointed day, day's work, from Latin *diēs* day.]

di·e·tar·y (dī'ə ter'ē) *adj.* relating to diet: *Certain dietary rules must be observed for good health.* **—n. pl., -tar·ies.** regulated allowance of food.

di·e·tet·ic (dī'ə tet'ik) *adj.* **1.** relating to diet or to regulation of the use of food. **2.** prepared for use in special diets: *Dietetic sweets are made without sugar.* **—di'e·tet'i·cal·ly,** *adv.*

di·e·tet·ics (dī'ə tet'iks) *n.* branch of the science of nutrition dealing with the nutritional needs of both healthy and sick persons, meal planning, and the preparation and serving of food.

di·e·ti·tian (dī'ə tish'ən) *also,* **di·e·ti·cian.** *n.* person trained in dietetics, usually employed by an institution or other organization.

dif-, form of **dis-**¹ before *f,* as in *diffuse.*

diff. 1. difference. **2.** different.

dif·fer (dif'ər) *v.i.* **1.** to be dissimilar or distinct in nature, form, or qualities; be not the same; be unlike: *The brothers differ in their interests. Wisdom differs from cunning.* **2.** to disagree; dissent: *He differs with the other members of his party on that issue.* **3.** to argue; quarrel: *He and his wife differed constantly.* [Old French *differer* to be different, delay, from Latin *differre* to carry in different directions, be different, delay. Doublet of DEFER¹.]

dif·fer·ence (dif'ər əns, dif'rəns) *n.* **1.** state or quality of being unlike or different; dissimilarity: *Was there a difference between your answers and his?* **2.** instance of such dissimilarity: *We noticed a difference in her attitude.* **3.** distinguishing characteristic: *The only difference between the two cars is the price.* **4.** amount by which one quantity is greater or less than another; remainder left after subtracting one quantity from another: *The difference between six and five is one.* **5.a.** disagreement in opinion: *They managed to settle their differences.* **b.** instance of disagreement; dispute: *A difference arose between the neighbors over the height of the fence.* **6. to make a difference. a.** to distinguish; discriminate: *The law makes a difference between offensive and criminal behavior.* **b.** to affect or change a situation; matter: *Your support will certainly make a difference in our cause.* **7. to split the difference. a.** to divide equally what is left over. **b.** to compromise by reaching a middle course.

dif·fer·ent (dif'ər ənt, dif'rənt) *adj.* **1.** characterized by dissimilarity; not alike: *very different approaches to teaching.* **2.** separate; distinct: *We went to different schools.* **3.** not ordinary; unusual: *This new book is quite different.* **—dif'fer·ent·ly,** *adv.* **—dif'fer·ent·ness,** *n.*
Syn. 1. Different, diverse, divergent, disparate mean not alike. **Different** emphasizes a total or partial dissimilarity in one or more characteristics or details: *Paula wears a different outfit every day.* **Diverse** suggests a marked distinction and conspicuous contrast: *People of Europe speak diverse languages.* **Divergent** implies a branching off in different directions so that an ultimate agreement or reconciliation is impossible: *I was confused by the divergent accounts of the two witnesses.* **Disparate** suggests being so unlike in kind and nature as to be incongruous and incompatible: *Dr. Jekyll and Mr. Hyde were disparate personalities.*

dif·fer·en·ti·a (dif'ə ren'shē ə) *pl.,* **-ti·ae** (shē ē'). *n.* distinguishing quality or characteristic, esp. one that distinguishes one species from all others of the same genus. [Latin *differentia* difference.]

dif·fer·en·tial (dif'ə ren'shəl) *adj.* **1.** relating to or exhibiting a difference or differences: *A differential diagnosis distinguishes between two similar diseases.* **2.** constituting or making a difference; distinguishing: *Each case presents differential features which make it unique.* **3.** depending on a difference or distinction: *differential customs duties.* **4.** *Mathematics.* of or relating to differentials. **5.** *Mechanics.* relating to the difference of two or more motions, pressures, temperatures, or other measurable physical qualities. **—n. 1.** differential amount, factor, wage, or rate. **2.** *Mathematics.* infinitesimal difference between consecutive values of a continuously varying quantity. **3.** system of gears that enables the opposite driving wheels of a motor vehicle to rotate at different speeds when the vehicle rounds a curve. Also *(def. 3).* **differential gear.** **—dif'fer·en'tial·ly,** *adv.*

differential calculus, see calculus.

dif·fer·en·ti·ate (dif'ə ren'shē āt') **-at·ed, -at·ing.** *v.t.* **1.** to constitute the difference in; serve to distinguish between: *Coloring differentiates the sexes in many birds.* **2.** to perceive or express the differences in; distinguish between: *He differentiated his own motives from those of his friends.* **—v.i. 1.** to become different or specialized: *Some reptilian scales apparently differentiated and became feathers.* **2.** to perceive or express a difference: *He never learned to differentiate between good and evil.* **—dif'fer·en'ti·a'tion,** *n.*

dif·fi·cult (dif'ə kult', -kəlt) *adj.* **1.** hard to do or perform; demand-

ing considerable effort; not easy: *Crossing the river was a difficult task.* **2.** hard to understand or solve; perplexing: *That is a difficult problem. He is a difficult poet.* **3.** hard to deal with, please, persuade, or satisfy: *a difficult child. She was the most difficult customer the salesman had to deal with that day.* [From DIFFICULTY.] —**Syn. 1.** see **hard.**

dif·fi·cul·ty (dif′ə kul′tē, -kəl tē) *pl.*, **-ties.** *n.* **1.** fact or condition of being difficult: *a task of great difficulty, the difficulty of learning to drive a car.* **2.** something that is difficult to do or understand: *We encountered many difficulties during the climb.* **3.** considerable effort; struggle: *I speak French with difficulty. I had no difficulty in getting the boat through the rapids.* **4.** embarrassing state of affairs, esp. financial trouble; dilemma: *He was careless with his money and ended up in great difficulties.* **5.** disagreement; estrangement; quarrel: *There was always some difficulty between them.* [Latin *difficultās* trouble, poverty, going back to *dis* apart + *facilis* easy.]

dif·fi·dence (dif′ə dəns) *n.* lack of confidence in oneself; shyness.

dif·fi·dent (dif′ə dənt) *adj.* lacking confidence in oneself; shy. [Latin *diffīdēns*, present participle of *diffīdere* to distrust.] —**dif′fi·dent·ly,** *adv.*

dif·fract (di frakt′) *v.t.* **1.** to break in pieces; break up. **2.** to cause to undergo diffraction. [Latin *diffractus*, past participle of *diffringere* to break in pieces.]

dif·frac·tion (di frak′shən) *n.* **1.** bending of the path of a ray of light as it passes through a narrow slit or is deflected around the edge of a solid or opaque object. The diffracted light wave spreads out to form a pattern of light and dark regions or the colored bands of the spectrum. **2.** similar phenomenon in other waves, as sound, electricity, or X-rays.

diffraction grating, any of several devices made by cutting very fine parallel slits or grooves in glass, metal, or plastic plates, used to produce a spectrum from rays of light by means of diffraction.

dif·fuse (*adj.*, di fūs′; *v.*, di fūz′) *adj.* **1.** widely spread out; not concentrated; dispersed: *diffuse light.* **2.** using many words; wordy; verbose: *a diffuse writer.* —*v.t.*, **-fused, -fus·ing. 1.** to spread widely; scatter in all directions; disperse: *The colors of the sunset were diffused across the sky. He so diffused his talents that he never became a real success in anything.* **2.** to cause (gases or liquids) to intermingle by diffusion. —*v.i.* **1.** to spread out; be or become scattered or dispersed. **2.** to intermingle by diffusion: *Every gas diffuses at a certain rate.* [Latin *diffūsus*, past participle of *diffundere* to pour forth.] —**dif·fuse′ly,** *adv.* —**dif·fuse′ness,** *n.*

dif·fus·i·ble (di fū′zə bəl) *adj.* capable of being diffused.

dif·fu·sion (di fū′zhən) *n.* **1.** a diffusing or being diffused; a spreading or scattering widely; dispersion: *the diffusion of knowledge. There was a rapid diffusion of the news.* **2.** wordiness in speech or writing; verbosity. **3.** gradual mixing together of the molecules of gases or of liquids due to the movement of the molecules without the application of external force. **4.** scattering of light when it passes through a material like frosted glass or fog or is reflected from a rough surface. —**dif·fu′sion·al,** *adj.*

dif·fu·sive (di fū′siv) *adj.* **1.** tending to diffuse. **2.** characterized by diffusion.

dig (dig) **dug** or (archaic) **digged, dig·ging.** *v.t.* **1.** to break up or turn over and remove (earth), as with a shovel, the hands, claws, or snout. **2.** to make or form by or as by digging; hollow out; excavate: *to dig a hole, to dig a tunnel.* **3.** to obtain or extract by digging: *to dig potatoes.* **4.** to discover or obtain by close search or investigation (often with *up* or *out*): *to dig up old records. It took him weeks to dig out the truth from the conflicting evidence.* **5.** to poke; prod: *He dug the horse with his spurs.* **6.** to thrust or plunge: *He dug his heels into the ground.* **7.** *Slang.* **a.** to understand. **b.** to like, appreciate, or be in rapport with. —*v.i.* **1.** to break up, remove, or turn over the earth, as with a shovel, hands, claws, or snout: *The dog was digging in the yard for bones.* **2.** to make a way by or as by digging; make an excavation: *He dug through the dirt under the wall.* **3. to dig in. a.** *Military.* to dig trenches or holes for defensive purposes. **b.** *Informal.* to gain a firm footing; entrench (oneself). **c.** *Informal.* to begin to work hard or intensively. **d.** *Informal.* to begin to eat. **4. to dig into.** *Informal.* **a.** to begin to work hard at. **b.** to begin to eat (something) with enthusiasm. —*n.* **1.** act of digging. **2.** *Informal.* a thrust or poke: *a dig in the ribs.* **3.** *Informal.* sarcastic remark; cutting statement; gibe: *He made a dig about her strange outfit.* **4.** archaeological site or excavation. [French *diguer* to make a dike, hollow out the ground, from *digue* dike, from Middle Dutch *dijc*.]

di·gest (*v.*, dī jest′, di-; *n.*, dī′jest) *v.t.* **1.** to break down (food materials) by the process of digestion. **2.** to grasp and assimilate mentally: *He read rapidly but did not digest anything.* **3.** to condense and arrange systematically; summarize. **4.** to bear with patience; endure; tolerate. **5.** *Chemistry.* to soften or decompose (a substance) with the aid of heat and moisture; dissolve. —*v.i.* **1.** to undergo digestion: *Protein digests slowly.* **2.** to digest food. —*n.* systematically arranged collection or summary, esp. of literary, historical, legal, or scientific material;

compilation: *a digest of court decisions.* [Latin *dīgestus*, past participle of *dīgerere* to carry apart, dissolve.] —**di·gest′er,** *n.*

di·gest·i·ble (di jes′tə bəl, dī-) *adj.* capable of being digested; easily digested. —**di·gest′i·bil′i·ty,** *n.*

di·ges·tion (di jes′chən, dī-) *n.* **1.** process by which food materials are broken down into simple compounds chemically so as to be assimilated by the body. **2.** ability to digest: *The patient's digestion is good.* **3.** mental assimilation; understanding.

di·ges·tive (di jes′tiv, dī-) *adj.* **1.** relating to or serving digestion: *the digestive system.* **2.** aiding digestion: *a digestive medicine.* —*n.* medicine or substance that aids digestion. —**di·ges′tive·ly,** *adv.*

dig·ger (dig′ər) *n.* **1.** one who digs. **2.** tool or machine for digging. **3. Digger.** one of a tribe of North American Indians who dug roots for food.

digger wasp, any of a group of solitary wasps, family Sphecidae, that dig their nests in the ground.

dig·gings (dig′ingz) *n.,pl.* **1.** place where digging is done, as a mine. **2.** materials dug out. **3.** *Informal.* living quarters.

dight (dīt) **dight** or **dight·ed, dight·ing.** *v.t., v.i. Archaic.* **1.** to dress; adorn. **2.** to prepare; equip. [Old English *dihtan* to compose, arrange, from Latin *dictāre* to dictate.]

dig·it (dij′it) *n.* **1.** finger or toe. **2.** any of the ten Arabic numerals from 0 through 9. Sometimes 0 is excluded. **3.** former unit of measure, equal to the breadth of a finger, or about ¾ inch. [Latin *digitus* finger, toe; with reference to counting with the fingers (and toes).]

dig·i·tal (dij′it əl) *adj.* **1.** relating to or resembling a digit or digits. **2.** having digits. —*n.* key on a keyboard instrument played with the finger. —**dig′i·tal·ly,** *adv.*

digital computer, computer that operates with numbers, particularly the digits 0 and 1, or with alphabetical symbols of language, used esp. to solve problems that require exact answers. Distinguished from **analog computer.**

dig·i·tal·is (dij′i tal′is, -tā′lis) *n.* **1.** drug used for stimulating the heart, prepared from the dried leaves of the common foxglove. **2.** foxglove. [Modern Latin *digitalis*, from Latin *digitālis* relating to the finger, from *digitus* finger; from the fingerlike shape of the flower's corollas.]

dig·i·tate (dij′i tāt′) *adj.* **1.** having fingers or toes. **2.** *Botany.* palmate. [Latin *digitātus* having fingers or toes, from *digitus* finger, toe.]

dig·i·ti·grade (dij′i tə grād′) *adj.* walking on the toes, as cats and dogs. Distinguished from **plantigrade.** [French *digitigrade*, from Latin *digitus* finger, toe + *gradī* to walk.]

dig·ni·fied (dig′nə fīd′) *adj.* marked by dignity of manner or style; noble; stately.

dig·ni·fy (dig′nə fī′) **-fied, -fy·ing.** *v.t.* **1.** to give dignity to; honor; ennoble: *The proceedings were dignified by the presence of the governor.* **2.** give a high-sounding name to; confer unmerited distinction upon: *They dignified the violence by calling it a patriotic demonstration.* [Old French *dignifier* to make worthy, from Late Latin *dignificāre*, from Latin *dignus* worthy + *facere* to make.]

dig·ni·tar·y (dig′nə ter′ē) *pl.*, **-tar·ies.** *n.* one who has a high position or office, as in government or the church: *Several foreign dignitaries were entertained by the president.*

dig·ni·ty (dig′nə tē) *pl.*, **-ties.** *n.* **1.** nobility of character or manner; stateliness; serenity: *Even in great adversity, he retained his dignity.* **2.** state or quality of being worthy, honorable, esteemed, or excellent: *The real dignity of a man lies in what he is, not in what he has.* **3.** degree of excellence; relative importance or position; rank. **4.** high office, rank, or title. [Old French *dignete* high rank, high office, from Latin *dignitās* worth. Doublet of DAINTY.]

di·graph (dī′graf′) *n.* two letters used to represent one sound, as *oa* in *boat* or *sh* in *ship.* [DI-¹ + Greek *graphē* writing.]

di·gress (di gres′, dī-) *v.i.* to deviate or depart from the main subject in speaking or writing. [Latin *digressus*, past participle of *dīgredī* to go apart, deviate.] —**Syn.** see **diverge.**

di·gres·sion (di gresh′ən, dī-) *n.* **1.** act of digressing. **2.** something that digresses.

di·gres·sive (di gres′iv, dī-) *adj.* tending to digress; marked by digression: *digressive essays.* —**di·gres′sive·ly,** *adv.* —**di·gres′sive·ness,** *n.*

di·he·dral (dī hē′drəl) *adj.* having two plane surfaces; formed by the intersection of two planes: *a dihedral angle.* —*n.* dihedral angle. [DI-¹ + Greek *hedrā* base, seat.]

Di·jon (dē zhôN′) *n.* city in east-central France. Pop. (1968), 145,357.

dike (dīk) *also,* **dyke.** *n.* **1.** embankment or dam intended to prevent flooding, esp. by the ocean. **2.** ditch or watercourse. **3.** bank of earth

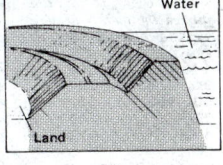

Dike

thrown up in digging a ditch. **4.** low dividing wall of earth or stone. **5.** a raised causeway **6.** barrier; obstacle. **7,** *Geology.* mass of igneous rock, often long and narrow, which was intruded while molten into a fissure in older rock. —*v.t.* **diked, dik·ing. 1.** to provide, protect, or surround with a dike or dikes. **2.** to drain with a dike. [Old English *dīc* ditch.]

di·lan·tin (dī lan′tin) *n.* drug used to reduce the number of seizures in epilepsy. Also, **dilantin sodium.** Trademark: Dilantin. [Short for *di(pheny)l(hyd)ant(o)in.*]

di·lap·i·dat·ed (di lap′ə dā′tid) *adj.* fallen into ruin or decay; broken down; neglected: *The houses were dilapidated beyond repair.* [From earlier *dilapidate* to fall into decay, from Latin *dīlapidātus,* past participle of *dīlapidāre* to throw away; literally, to scatter like stones, going back to *dis* apart + *lapis* stone.]

di·lap·i·da·tion (di lap′ə dā′shən) *n.* **1.** condition of ruin or decay: *They found several of the slum houses in complete dilapidation.* **2.** process of falling into decay or ruin: *the dilapidation of ancient Greek temples.*

dil·a·ta·tion (dil′ə tā′shən, dī′lə-) *n.* dilation.

di·late (dī lāt′, di-) **-lat·ed, -lat·ing.** *v.t.* to make larger or wider; cause to expand: *to dilate the chest in exercise.* —*v.i.* **1.** to become larger or wider; expand: *The ballon dilated with air.* **2.** to speak or write at length; enlarge (with *on* or *upon*): *He dilated upon his achievements for over an hour.* [Old French *dilater* to enlarge, widen from Latin *dīlātāre.*] —**di·lat′a·ble,** *adj.* —**Syn.** *v.i.* **1.** see **expand.**

di·la·tion (dī lā′shən, di-) *n.* **1.** act of dilating; being dilated. **2.** dilated part.

di·la·tor (dī lā′tər, di-) *n.* **1.** one who or that which dilates. **2.** muscle that dilates or expands a part of the body, as the muscle that widens the iris of the eye. **3.** instrument for dilating wounds or canals or openings of the body.

dil·a·to·ry (dil′ə tôr′ē) *adj.* **1.** tending to delay; tardy; slow: *He is often dilatory in paying his bills.* **2.** tending to cause delay, gain time, or defer action: *a dilatory policy, dilatory tactics.* [Late Latin *dīlātōrius* delaying, from Latin *dīlātor* delayer.] —**dil′a·to′ri·ly,** *adv.* —**dil′a·to′ri·ness,** *n.*

di·lem·ma (di lem′ə) *n.* **1.** situation requiring a choice between equally undesirable alternatives; difficult choice: *The dilemma he faced was whether to reveal that his friend stole the money or to let an innocent man take the blame.* **2.** any difficult or perplexing problem or predicament. **3.** argument presenting an adversary with two or more equally unfavorable alternatives. [Late Latin *dilemma* double proposition, from Greek *dilēmma,* from *di-* (see DI-¹) + *lēmma* assumption.]

dil·et·tante (dil′ə tänt′, -tant′, -tän′tē, -tan′tē) *pl.* **-tantes** or **-tan·ti** (-tän′tē, -tan′-). *n.* **1.** one who pursues an art or science superficially or merely for amusement; dabbler. **2.** lover of the fine arts. *adj.* relating to or characteristic of a dilettante. [Italian *dilettante* lover of the arts, dabbler, from *dilettare* to delight, from Latin *dēlectāre.*]

dil·et·tant·ism (dil′ə tänt′iz′əm, -tan′-) *n.* quality or actions characteristic of a dilettante.

dil·i·gence¹ (dil′ə jəns) *n.* persistent attention to one's work or duty; constant effort; industry. [Old French *diligence* application, speed, from Latin *dīligentia* carefulness.]

dil·i·gence² (dil′ə jəns) *n.* public stagecoach formerly used in Europe, esp. in France. [Short for French *carrosse de diligence* literally, coach of speed. See DILIGENCE¹.]

dil·i·gent (dil′ə jənt) *adj.* **1.** attentive and persistent in whatever is undertaken; industrious: *a diligent student.* **2.** pursued with painstaking care and effort: *a diligent search.* [Old French *diligent* attentive, eager, from Latin *dīligēns* careful, attentive.] —**dil′i·gent·ly,** *adv.*

dill (dil) *n.* **1.** dried seedlike fruit and fresh or dried leaves of an annual Old World herb, *Anethum graveolens,* of the parsley family, chiefly used as a spice to flavor pickles and other foods. **2.** the plant itself, cultivated throughout the world, bearing light-green, threadlike leaves and large clusters of small yellow flowers. [Old English *dile* the plant.]

dill pickle, pickled cucumber flavored with dill.

dil·ly-dal·ly (dil′ē dal′ē) **-lied, -ly·ing.** *v.i.* **1.** to waste time; loiter; trifle. **2.** to vacillate.

di·lute (di lōōt′, dī-) **-lut·ed, -lut·ing.** *v.t.* **1.** to thin or weaken by the addition of a liquid: *She diluted the concentrated fruit juice with water.* **2.** to weaken or reduce the strength, force, or purity of by adding another element: *Admitting six new teams to the professional league diluted the quality of play.* —*v.i.* to become diluted. —*adj.* diluted; weak: *a dilute acid.* [Latin *dīlūtus,* past participle of *dīluere* to wash away, dissolve.]

di·lu·tion (di lōō′shən, dī-) *n.* **1.** act of diluting; being diluted. **2.** something diluted.

di·lu·vi·al (di lōō′vē əl, dī-) *adj.* **1.** relating to a flood or deluge. **2.** *Geology.* deposited by a glacier, flooding river, or the like, as rock debris. [Late Latin *dīluviālis* relating to a flood, from Latin *dīluvium* flood.]

dim (dim) **dim·mer, dim·mest.** *adj.* **1.** obscure from lack of light; shadowy; dark: *a dim corner of a basement.* **2.** lacking brilliance or luster; dull: *dim colors.* **3.** not clear to the senses; indistinct; faint; obscure: *a dim sound, the dim outline of a figure in the distance.* **4.** not clear to the mind; vague; confused: *a dim recollection of the accident.* **5.** not clearly understood; confused: *The issue is dim in my mind.* **6.** not seeing or hearing clearly: *Her eyes were dim with tears.* **7.** not understanding clearly: *She is rather dim about the importance of keeping records.* **8.** discouraging; unfavorable; pessimistic: *to take a dim view of something. The prospects of the strike being ended soon are dim.* —*v.t.,* **dimmed, dim·ming.** to make dim: *He dimmed the car's headlights.* —*v.i.* to grow or become dim: *His memory of the event dimmed as the years passed.* [Old English *dimm* dark.] —**dim′ly,** *adv.* —**dim′ness,** *n.* —**Syn.** *adj.* **1.** see **dark. 3.** see **faint.**

dim. 1. diminuendo. **2.** diminutive.

dime (dīm) *n.* coin of the United States equal to ten cents or one-tenth of a dollar. [Old French *dime* tenth part, from Latin *decima (pars)* tenth (part), from *decem* ten.]

dime novel, sensational or melodramatic novel having no literary merit, originally costing ten cents.

di·men·sion (di men′shən) *n.* **1.** any measurable extent, as length, breadth, thickness, or height: *The room's dimensions are twelve feet by ten feet.* **2.** size; extent; magnitude: *The dimensions of this problem have not yet been fully realized by the public.* [French *dimension* a measuring, from Latin *dīmēnsiō.*] —**di·men′sion·al,** *adj.* —**di·men′sion·al·ly,** *adv.*

dime store, five-and-ten.

dimin. 1. diminuendo. **2.** diminutive.

di·min·ish (di min′ish) *v.t.* **1.** to make smaller or less, as size, amount, or degree: *Unforeseen events diminished his savings. Several unpopular decisions diminished the governor's popularity.* **2.** to reduce in power, authority, rank, or importance; degrade: *His constant attempts to diminish his colleagues' achievements eventually caused his dismissal.* —*v.i.* to become smaller or less; decrease: *The campers' food supply gradually diminished as the days wore on.* [Blend of obsolete *diminue* to lessen, reduce (going back to Latin *dēminuere*), and archaic *minish* to lessen, reduce (going back to Latin *minūtus* small).] —**Syn.** *v.i.* see **decrease.**

di·min·u·en·do (di min′ū en′dō) *pl.* **-dos.** *Music. adj. adv.* with gradually decreasing loudness or force; decrescendo. —*n.* **1.** gradual decrease in loudness or force; decrescendo. **2.** passage played diminuendo. [Italian *diminuendo* diminishing, present participle of *diminuire* to lessen, reduce, from Latin *dēminuere.*]

dim·i·nu·tion (dim′ə nōō′shən, -nū′-) *n.* act of diminishing; being diminished; reduction; decrease. [Old French *diminution* a lessening, from Latin *dēminūtiō* decrease.]

di·min·u·tive (di min′yə tiv) *adj.* **1.** small in size; little; tiny. **2.** *Grammar.* expressing smallness, familiarity, or affection: *a diminutive suffix.* —*n.* **1.** small kind or variety of something. **2.** word formed from another either by change in structure or by addition of a suffix, expressing smallness, familiarity, or affection. *Piglet* is a diminutive of *pig.* The nickname *Joe* is a diminutive of *Joseph.* [Old French *diminutif* expressing smallness, from Late Latin *dīminūtīvus, dēminūtīvus,* from Latin *dēminuere* to lessen.]

dim·i·ty (dim′ə tē) *pl.* **-ties.** *n.* sheer, crisp cotton fabric, usually woven with cords at intervals in a striped or checkered arrangement, used for such items as blouses, dresses, or curtains. [Italian *dimito* a coarse cotton cloth, from Medieval Latin *dimitum* cloth woven with two threads, from Greek *dimitos* of double thread.]

dim·mer (dim′ər) *n.* **1.** device which dims an electric light, esp. a stage light or automobile headlight. **2.** one who or that which dims.

dim·out (dim′out′) *n.* dimming or concealment of night lighting, esp. in a city to make it less visible from the air in case of an aerial attack.

dim·ple (dim′pəl) *n.* **1.** small indentation in the surface of the human body, esp. as formed in the cheek or chin in the act of smiling. **2.** similar indentation on any surface: *The falling rain made dimples on the water.* —*v.t.,* **-pled, -pling.** to mark with dimples: *A smile dimpled her cheeks.* —*v.i.* to form dimples: *Her face dimpled as she recognized him.* [Probably from an unrecorded Old English word.]

din (din) *n.* loud, continuous noise or clamor; rattle or clatter that goes on for some time: *the din of machines in a factory, the din of a New Year's Eve party.* —*v.t.,* **dinned, din·ning. 1.** to assail or harass with a din: *The jet planes dinned the surrounding area day and night.* **2.** to utter or press noisily or with persistent repetition: *He is incessantly dinning his complaints into my ear.* —*v.i.* to make a din. [Old English *dyne* noise.]

di·nar (di när′) *n.* **1.** monetary unit of various countries, as Yugoslavia, Iraq, Iran, Algeria, and Tunisia. **2.** ancient gold coin used in Arab countries. [Arabic *dīnār* name of a gold coin, from Late Greek *dēnarion* denarius, from Latin *dēnārius* denarius, containing ten. Doublet of DENARIUS, DENIER².]

Di·nar·ic Alps (di nar′ik) mountain range in southern Europe, mostly in Yugoslavia, part of the eastern Alps.

dine (dīn) dined, din·ing. *v.i.* **1.** to eat dinner. **2. to dine out.** to eat dinner away from home. —*v.t.* **1.** to provide with dinner; give a dinner for: *to dine a prominent politician.* **2.** to eat (with *on* or *upon*): *to dine on roast beef.* [Old French *disner* to have dinner, going back to Latin *dis-* away + *jējūnium* fast[2]; in the sense of "away from fasting" or "breaking a fast."]

din·er (dī′nər) *n.* **1.** one who dines. **2.** dining car. **3.** restaurant housed in a building designed to resemble such a car, usually having an informal atmosphere and offering a relatively inexpensive menu.

di·nette (dī net′) *n.* alcove or small room used for dining. [DINE + -ETTE.]

ding (ding) *n.* sound made by a bell, or any sound resembling it. —*v.i.*, *v.t.* to make or cause to make a ringing sound. [Imitative.]

ding·bat (ding′bat′) *n. Informal.* **1.** any small object, as a stone, used for throwing. **2.** dingus. [Of uncertain origin.]

ding-dong (ding′dông′, -dong′) *n.* **1.** sound of repeated strokes made by a bell. **2.** any similar sound. —*adj. Informal.* closely contested: *a ding-dong battle.* [Imitative.]

din·gey (ding′gē) *pl.*, **-geys.** *n.* dinghy.

din·ghy (ding′gē) *pl.*, **-ghies.** *also,* **din·gey, din·gy.** *n.* any of various small open boats, propelled either by oars or by an outboard motor or fitted with a small mast for sailing. They are often used as tenders for larger boats. [Hindi *ḍiṅgī* small boat.]

din·gle (ding′gəl) *n.* small, deep, wooded valley; dell. [Of uncertain origin.]

din·go (ding′gō) *pl.*, **-goes.** *n.* wolflike wild dog, *Canis dingo,* of Australia, having pointed, erect ears, reddish-brown fur, and a long, bushy tail. Height: 2 feet at the shoulder. [Native Australian name.]

Dingo

ding·us (ding′əs) *n. Informal.* gadget or other thing whose name is unknown or forgotten; thingamabob. [Dutch *dinges.*]

din·gy[1] (din′jē) **-gi·er, -gi·est.** *adj.* **1.** not bright and fresh; discolored; dull: *The sheets looked dingy even after she washed them.* **2.** shabby; dreary; squalid: *He lived in a dingy one-room apartment.* [Of uncertain origin.] —**din′gi·ly,** *adv.* —**din′gi·ness,** *n.*

din·gy[2] (ding′gē) *pl.*, **-gies.** *n.* dinghy.

dining car, railroad car in which meals are served to passengers.

dining room, room in which meals are served as eaten, as in a home or hotel.

dink·ey (ding′kē) *pl.*, **-eys.** *also,* **din·ky.** *n.* small locomotive used for shunting cars or hauling freight in a railroad yard.

dink·y[1] (ding′kē) **dink·i·er, dink·i·est.** *adj. Informal.* small; insignificant.

dink·y[2] (ding′kē) *pl.* **-kies.** *n.* dinkey.

din·ner (din′ər) *n.* **1.** principal meal of the day. **2.** formal meal in honor of some person or occasion; banquet. [French *dîner,* noun use of infinitive *dîner* to dine, going back to Latin *dis-* (see DIS-[1]) + *jējūnium* fast[2].]

dinner jacket, tuxedo.

din·ner·ware (din′ər wâr′) *n.* dishes, glasses, and tableware used for table service.

di·no·saur (dī′nə sôr′) *n.* member of a large group of extinct four-limbed reptiles, orders Saurischia or Ornithischia, of the Mesozoic era. Remarkable for their enormous size and relatively small brain capacity, some species grew to eighty-seven feet in length and weighed up to fifty tons. [Modern Latin *Dinosauria,* from Greek *deinos* terrible + *sauros* lizard.]

di·no·sau·ri·an (dī′nə sôr′ē ən) *adj.* of, relating to, or like a dinosaur. —*n.* dinosaur.

dint (dint) *n.* **1.** exertion; force; power. ▲ now used chiefly in the phrase *by dint of: by dint of argument, by dint of effort.* **2.** dent. —*v.t.* **1.** to make a dent in. **2.** to impress or drive in with force. [Old English *dynt* blow[1].]

di·oc·e·san (dī os′ə sən) *adj.* of or relating to a diocese. —*n.* bishop of a diocese.

di·o·cese (dī′ə sis, -sēz′, -sēs′) *n.* ecclesiastical district under a bishop's authority. [Old French *diocise,* from Latin *dioecēsis* district, diocese, from Greek *dioikēsis* administration, diocese.]

Di·o·cle·tian (dī′ə klē′shən) 245–313, Roman emperor from 284 to 305.

di·ode (dī′ōd) *n.* vacuum tube or semiconductor with two terminals, used chiefly as a rectifier. [DI-[1] + -ODE.]

di·oe·cious (dī ē′shəs) *adj.* having male and female flowers borne on separate or different plants, as the holly tree. [Modern Latin *Dioecia* (from Greek *di-* double + *oikos* house) + -OUS.]

Di·og·e·nes (dī oj′ə nēz′) c.412–323 B.C., Greek philosopher, one of the leaders of the Cynic school of philosophy.

Di·o·me·des (dī′ə mē′dēz) *n. Greek Legend.* king of Argos and one of the bravest of the Greek heroes in the Trojan War.

Di·o·ny·si·a (dī′ə nish′ē ə, -nis′ē ə) *n.,pl.* ancient Greek festivals in honor of the god Dionysus, esp. those held in Athens. The origin of Greek drama is attributed to certain dramatic and ritualistic features of these festivals and to contests among poets and dramatists staged at them.

Di·o·nys·i·ac (dī′ə nis′ē ak′) *adj.* of or relating to Dionysus or the Dionysia.

Di·o·ny·sian (dī′ə nish′ən, -nis′ē ən) *adj.* **1.** Dionysiac. **2.** wildly uninhibited; frenzied; orgiastic.

Di·o·ny·sus (dī′ə nī′səs) *also,* **Di·o·ny·sos.** *n. Greek Mythology.* the son of Zeus and Semele, a mortal. As the god of fertility and wine, Dionysus was often worshiped with orgiastic rites. His Roman counterpart was Bacchus.

di·o·ra·ma (dī′ə ram′ə, -rä′mə) *n.* **1.** partly translucent picture, viewed through a small opening, in which various realistic effects are produced by means of lighting and other devices. **2.** exhibit consisting of sculptured figures, stuffed animals, or other models, placed in a naturalistic setting against a curved, painted background, creating an illusion of depth and realism. [DI-[1] + Greek *horāma* sight.]

di·o·rite (dī′ə rīt′) *n.* dark green or brown granular igneous rock consisting chiefly of feldspar and hornblende. [French *diorite,* from Greek *diorizein* to distinguish.]

Di·os·cu·ri (dī′əs kyoor′ī) *n.,pl. Classical Mythology.* Castor and Pollux. [Greek *Dioskouroi* literally, sons of Zeus, from *Dios,* genitive of *Zeus* Zeus + *kouroi,* plural of *kouros* boy, son.]

di·ox·ide (dī ok′sīd, -sid) *also,* **di·ox·id** (dī ok′sid). *n.* oxide containing two atoms of oxygen per molecule.

dip (dip) dipped *or* dipt, dip·ping. *v.t.* **1.** to put or let down into something, esp. a liquid, for a moment: *to dip a pen into an inkwell. He dipped his hand into the bowl to pick the winning lottery ticket.* **2.** to obtain or lift up and out by or as by scooping: *to dip water from a boat.* **3.** to lower and raise again quickly: *to dip a flag in a salute.* **4.** to immerse (sheep or other animals) in a disinfectant solution. **5.** to dye by immersing in a liquid. **6.** to make (a candle) by repeatedly plunging a wick into melted tallow or wax. **7.** to galvanize, plate, or coat by immersion in a prepared solution. —*v.i.* **1.** to plunge into and then emerge from water or other liquid, esp. quickly: *The oars dipped quietly.* **2.** to sink or go down: *The sun dipped below the horizon. Prices dipped at the end of the week.* **3.** to incline or slope downward: *The land dips as it meets the sea.* **4.** to reach into, esp. to take something out: *She dipped into her purse.* **5.** to study, engage in, or occupy oneself with briefly or superficially (with *into*): *He dipped into the classics.* **6.** (of an airplane) to drop suddenly just before climbing. —*n.* **1.** act of dipping, esp. a brief immersion in water: *a dip in the ocean.* **2.** liquid preparation into which something is dipped, as for dyeing or disinfecting. **3.** sudden drop or decline. **4.** downward inclination or slope: *a dip in the road.* **5.** amount or degree of such an inclination. **6.** creamy mixture of foods intended to be scooped up on crackers or the like, often served as an hors d'oeuvre. **7.** quantity of something taken out or up by dipping. **8.** hollow or depression in the land. **9.** sudden rapid drop of an airplane, followed by a climb. **10.** candle made by the repeated plunging of a wick into melted tallow or wax. **11.** *Geology.* angle at which a stratum or similar formation is inclined from a horizontal plane. **12.** *Slang.* pickpocket. [Old English *dyppan* to immerse.]

Syn. *v.t.* **Dip, immerse, plunge, submerge** mean to insert into a liquid. **Dip** suggests momentarily entering the liquid, either partially or completely: *He dipped the bread into the gravy.* **Immerse** implies being completely covered for a time by the liquid: *The meat must be thoroughly immersed in the sauce.* **Plunge** indicates a sudden, forceful, complete immersion: *The boy jumped out of bed and plunged his face into a basin of cold water.* **Submerge** emphasizes being completely covered for a considerable time: *The huge waves submerged the beach house.*

diph·the·ri·a (dif thēr′ē ə, dip-) *n.* contagious disease caused by a bacterium and characterized by fever, the formation of false membranes which may block the throat, and the production of a toxin which may affect the heart muscle. [Modern Latin *diphtheria,* from French *diphthérie,* from Greek *diphtherā* leather; from the formation of a leathery false membrane characterizing the disease.] —**diph·the′ri·al, diph·the′ri·an,** *adj.*

diph·the·rit·ic (dif′thə rit′ik, dip′-) *adj.* **1.** of, relating to, or resembling diphtheria or its symptoms. **2.** affected with or suffering from diphtheria. Also, **diph·ther·ic** (dif thër′ik, dip-).

diph·thong (dif′thông′, -thong′, dip′-) *n.* **1.** vowel sound produced by the combining, during pronunciation, of two vowel sounds within one syllable. The *ou* in *mouse* and the *ai* in *main* are diphthongs. **2.** digraph. **3.** ligature (def. 4). [French *diphthongue* two vowel sounds pronounced as one syllable, from Late Latin *diphthongus,* from Greek

diphthongos having two sounds, from *dis* double + *phthongos* sound.]
—**diph·thon·gal** (dif thông′gəl, -thong′-, dip-) *adj.*

diph·thong·ize (dif′thŏng īz′, -thong-, dip′-) **-ized, -iz·ing.** *v.t.* to make a diphthong of; pronounce as a diphthong. —*v.i.* to become a diphthong. —**diph′thong·i·za′tion,** *n.*

dipl-, form of **diplo-** before vowels.

diplo- *combining form* double: *diploid.* [Greek *diplous* twofold, double.]

dip·loid (dip′loid) *adj.* **1.** double; twofold. **2.** *Biology.* having twice the normal number of chromosomes. —*n.* cell having twice the haploid number of chromosomes. [DIPLO- + -OID.]

di·plo·ma (di plō′mə) *pl.,* **-mas** or **-ma·ta** (-mə tə). *n.* **1.** certificate granted by a school, college, or other institution to a graduating student, indicating successful completion of a program or curriculum. **2.** any certificate conferring some privilege or honor. **3.** official or state document; charter. [Latin *diplōma* document granting a privilege, from Greek *diplōma* literally, something folded double (probably because it was originally folded double and sealed), from *diplous* double.]

di·plo·ma·cy (di plō′mə sē) *pl.,* **-cies.** *n.* **1.** art or practice of managing international relations between nations and conducting negotiations between governments. **2.** skill in dealing with other people; tact: *He exhibited remarkable diplomacy by not pointing out her mistakes.* [French *diplomatie* diplomatic service, from *diplomate* member of the diplomatic service, going back to Greek *diplōma.* See DIPLOMA.]

dip·lo·mat (dip′lə mat′) *n.* **1.** one who is employed or skilled in international diplomacy, esp. an official who is assigned to a foreign country, or to an international organization or conference, as a representative of his government. **2.** any individual who is skillful in dealing with others; tactful person.

dip·lo·mat·ic (dip′lə mat′ik) *adj.* **1.** of, relating to, or connected with international diplomacy. **2.** possessing or exhibiting skill or tact in dealing with other people. Also, **dip′lo·mat′i·cal.** —**dip′lo·mat′i·cal·ly,** *adv.*

diplomatic corps, all of the foreign diplomats stationed in the capital of a country.

diplomatic immunity, immunity of members of a diplomatic corps from taxes, duties, and legal proceedings in a foreign country.

di·plo·ma·tist (di plō′mə tist) *n.* diplomat.

dip needle, instrument used to find the direction of the earth's magnetic force with respect to the horizon.

di·pole (di′pōl′) *n.* any object or system having two magnetic poles or two electrical charges which are opposite in sign but equal in magnitude. [DI-¹ + POLE².] —**di′po′lar,** *adj.*

dip·per (dip′ər) *n.* **1.** one who or that which dips. **2.** long-handled cup or vessel for scooping up liquids; ladle. **3. Dipper.** the Big Dipper or the Little Dipper. **4.** water ouzel. **5.** digging implement attached by a rigid handle to the boom of certain excavating machines.

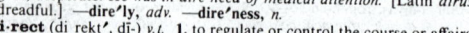

Dipper

dip·so·ma·ni·a (dip′sə mā′nē ə) *n.* abnormal compulsion to drink alcoholic liquor, esp. in excessive amounts. [Modern Latin *dipsomania,* from Greek *dipsos* thirst + *maniā* madness.]

dip·so·ma·ni·ac (dip′sə mā′nē ak′) *n.* one who is affected with dipsomania. —**dip·so·ma·ni·a·cal** (dip′sō mə nī′ə kəl) *adj.*

dip·stick (dip′stik′) *n.* graduated metal rod used for measuring the level of a liquid in a container, esp. of oil in the crankcase of an automobile.

dipt (dipt) a past tense and a past participle of **dip.**

dip·ter·ous (dip′tər əs) *adj.* **1.** of or belonging to an order, Diptera, of insects that have only one pair of wings, including the gnat, mosquito, and housefly. **2.** *Botany.* having only one pair of wing-like parts. Also, **dip′ter·an.** [Greek *dipteros* having two wings.]

dip·tych (dip′tik) *n.* **1.** double painting or carving consisting of two panels hinged together, esp. one depicting a religious subject and used as an altarpiece. **2.** ancient writing tablet consisting of two hinged pieces of wood or ivory whose inner surfaces are waxed for writing on with a stylus. [Late Latin *diptycha* writing tablet with two leaves, from Greek *diptycha* pair of writing tablets, from *diptychos* folded, doubled.]

Diptych

dire (dīr) **dir·er, dir·est.** *adj.* **1.** causing great fear or suffering; dreadful; horrible; disastrous: *a dire calamity, dire prophecies.* **2.** extremely ur-

gent; desperate: *He was in dire need of medical attention.* [Latin *dīrus* dreadful.] —**dire′ly,** *adv.* —**dire′ness,** *n.*

di·rect (di rekt′, dī-) *v.t.* **1.** to regulate or control the course or affairs of; manage: *to direct traffic, to direct the affairs of state.* **2.** to give authoritative instructions to; order; command: *The general directed the troops to attack.* **3.** to tell or show (someone) the way: *Can you direct me to the nearest phone booth?* **4.** to cause to move in a particular direction; turn; aim: *to direct one's gaze, to direct one's energies.* **5.** to intend (words) to be heard or attributed to by someone; address: *Direct your remarks to the entire class.* **6.** to lead, guide, or supervise the production or performance of: *to direct a film. He directed many Shakespearean plays in London.* **7.** to write the destination on: *to direct a letter.* —*v.i.* **1.** to give guidance or commands. **2.** to be a director, as of an orchestra, film, or play. —*adj.* **1.** proceeding in a straight line or by the shortest course; undeviating; straight: *a direct route.* **2.** without obstruction or intervening influence or agencies; immediate: *direct contact.* **3.** straightforward; plain; honest: *a direct manner.* **4.** in an unbroken line of descent: *a direct heir, a direct ancestor.* **5.** exact; absolute; complete: *the direct antithesis.* **6.** in the exact words of the speaker or author: *a direct quotation.* **7.** of or by the action of the people or electorate without intervention of representatives: *direct election of senators.* **8.** *Astronomy.* moving from west to east among the stars. Distinguished from **retrograde.** —*adv.* directly. [Latin *dīrectus,* past participle of *dīrigere* to straighten, guide.] —**di·rect′ness,** *n.* —**Syn.** *v.t.* **1.** see **manage. 2.** see **command.**

direct current, electric current in which the flow of electrons is in one direction only. Distinguished from **alternating current.**

direct discourse, form of discourse in which a person's words are quoted exactly, as *She said, "I don't like cats."* Distinguished from **indirect discourse.**

di·rec·tion (di rek′shən, dī-) *n.* **1.** act of directing. **2.** guidance or control; management: *The recruits are under the direction of a sergeant.* **3.** line or course along which something moves, faces, or lies: *The direction of the airplane changed from north to northeast. He was walking in the direction of the park.* **4.** *also,* **directions.** instruction about how to proceed or act: *He gave us directions to town. The directions on the package were to put the vegetables in cold water.* **5.** tendency or line of development: *efforts in the direction of reform.* **6.** order; command. **7.** supervision and organization of the elements and presentation of a play, film, or other performance. **8.** *Music.* word, phrase, or sign indicating how a particular note, chord, or passage is to be played. **9.** address, as on a letter or package. [Latin *dīrectiō* a making straight; directing.]

Syn. 5. Direction, course, trend, tendency mean a movement that evolves or goes in a certain way. **Direction** stresses the line followed: *His poetry appears to have taken a new direction.* **Course** suggests a line having a definite beginning and end and which may or may not be straight: *He wanted to interfere and simply permitted events to take their course.* **Trend** suggests a general movement that may be marked by detours: *Recent elections show a trend toward conservatism.* **Tendency** implies an underlying reason for one line or bearing to have preference: *The tendency of the middle class is to be politically conservative.*

di·rec·tion·al (di rek′shən əl, dī-) *adj.* **1.** of or relating to direction in space. **2.** *Electronics.* **a.** designed to determine the direction from which signals come. **b.** able to send or receive signals from one direction only. **3.** indicating direction: *directional signals in an automobile.*

direction finder, radio receiving device which determines the direction of incoming radio signals, usually by means of a rotating antenna in the form of a loop or rectangle.

di·rec·tive (di rek′tiv, dī-) *n.* order, regulation, or instruction, esp. one issued by a higher authority, such as a military command. —*adj.* serving to direct, guide, or prescribe.

di·rect·ly (di rekt′lē, dī-) *adv.* **1.** in a direct line or manner; straight: *The car came directly toward us.* **2.** without the intervention of a medium or agent: *He was directly responsible for the confusion.* **3.** without delay; at once: *He returned directly.* **4.** exactly; precisely: *His political views are directly opposed to mine.*

direct object, word or words designating the person or thing that receives the action expressed by a transitive verb. In *we saw him,* the direct object is *him.* Distinguished from **indirect object.**

di·rec·tor (di rek′tər, dī-) *n.* **1.** one who or that which directs: *a camp director, a funeral director.* **2.** one who supervises and guides the performers and technicians in the production of a film, play, television program, or other show or performance. **3.** one of a group of board members of a company or institution chosen to control or govern its overall affairs. —**di·rec′tor·ship, di·rec′tress,** *n.*

di·rec·tor·ate (di rek′tər it, dī-) *n.* **1.** office or position of director. **2.** body of directors.

di·rec·to·ri·al (di rek′tôr′ē əl, dī′rek-) *adj.* **1.** of or relating to a director or directorate. **2.** that directs; directive.

di·rec·to·ry (di rek′tər ē, dī-) *pl.,* **-ries.** *n.* **1.** alphabetical or classified

at; āpe; cär; end; mē; it; īce; hot; ōld; fôrk; wood; fōol; oil; out; up; ūse; turn; sing; thin; this; zh in treasure; ə in ago, taken, pencil, lemon, circus.

list, as of the names, addresses, or occupations of a specific group of people: *a telephone directory.* **2.** board or tablet listing the locations of the occupants, offices, or departments in a building or store. **3.** book or collection of rules, esp. one containing directions for religious worship. **4.** body of directors; directorate. **5. Directory.** executive branch of the Revolutionary government in France from 1795 to 1799, consisting of five men selected by the French legislature. —*adj.* serving to direct or guide.

direct primary, election in which those registered as members of a political party vote directly for the candidates of their party, rather than for delegates to a nominating convention.

direct proportion, mathematical relationship of two variables when one equals the other multiplied by a constant. Distinguished from **inverse proportion.**

di·rec·trix (di rek′triks, dī-) *pl.,* **di·rec·trix·es** or **di·rec·tri·ces** (di-rek′trə sēz′, dī-, dī′rek trī′sēz). *n.* Geometry. fixed line which guides the motion of another line as it generates a surface or guides the motion of a point as it generates a curve. The circle forming the base of a cone is a directrix.

direct tax, tax levied directly on the persons who must pay it, as an income or inheritance tax. Distinguished from **indirect tax.**

dire·ful (dīr′fəl) *adj.* dire; dreadful; terrible. —**dire′ful·ly,** *adv.* —**dire′ful·ness,** *n.*

dirge (durj) *n.* song, hymn, or tune of grief or mourning, esp. one performed at a funeral or memorial ceremony; lament. [Latin *dīrige* direct (imperative of *dīrigere* to direct), the first word of an antiphon in the Roman Catholic office for the dead.]

dir·ham (di ram′) *n.* standard monetary unit of Morocco equal to one hundred moroccan francs. [Arabic *dirham,* from Greek *drachmē.* See DRACHMA.]

dir·i·gi·ble (dir′ə jə bəl, də-rij′ə-) *n.* motor-driven, rigid airship that can be steered. —*adj.* that can be directed, controlled, or steered. [Latin *dīrigere* to straighten, guide + -IBLE.]

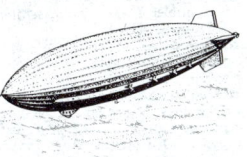

Dirigible

dirk (durk) *n.* dagger. —*v.t.* to stab with a dirk. [Of uncertain origin.]

dirn·dl (durnd′əl) *n.* **1.** woman's dress with a fitted bodice and a full skirt gathered at the waist. **2.** skirt of this style. Also *(def. 2),* **dirndl skirt.** [Short for German *Dirndlkleid* peasant costume for girls, from *Dirndl* young girl, diminutive of *Dirne* girl + *Kleid* dress.]

dirt (durt) *n.* **1.** any filthy, foul, or soiling substance, as mud, dust, or excrement: *Wash that dirt off your hands.* **2.** earth or soil, esp. when loose: *He filled all the flowerpots with dirt.* **3.** something despised, mean, or worthless: *They treated him like dirt.* **4.** corruption; immorality. **5.** obscene writing, pictures, or speech; pornography. **6.** *Informal.* gossip, esp. of a malicious nature. **7. to do (someone) dirt.** *Slang.* to harm or foil maliciously. [Old Norse *drit* excrement.]

dirt-cheap (durt′chēp′) *adj.* very inexpensive. —*adv.* at a very low price.

dirt farmer *Informal.* farmer who works his own land, as distinguished from one who hires others to work his land.

dirt·y (dur′tē) **dirt·i·er, dirt·i·est.** *adj.* **1.** soiled with or as with dirt; not clean; filthy: *a dirty towel.* **2.** imparting dirt; soiling: *Digging the hole was a hard and dirty job.* **3.** low or sordid; despicable: *a dirty trick. War is a dirty business.* **4.** obscene; indecent; smutty: *a dirty joke.* **5.** unfair; unsportsmanlike: *a dirty fighter.* **6.** *Informal.* resentful; insulting; spiteful: *He gave me a dirty look. I'm sick of her dirty cracks about my work.* **7.** (of colors) not clear or bright; impure. **8.** (of nuclear devices) producing a large amount of radioactive fallout. **9.** (of weather) unsettled; stormy. —*v.t., v.i.* **dirt·ied, dirt·y·ing.** to make or become dirty; soil. —**dirt′i·ly,** *adv.* —**dirt′i·ness,** *n.*

dirty work *Informal.* **1.** tiresome, unpleasant, or unrewarding job or part of a job: *We got the credit, and we did the dirty work.* **2.** dishonest or unethical actions; foul play.

Dis (dis) *n.* Roman Mythology. **1.** ruler of the underworld, identified with the Greek god Hades or Pluto. **2.** land of the dead; the underworld.

dis-[1] *prefix* **1.** opposite of; absence of; not: *disobedience, dishonesty.* **2.** undoing of; reverse of: *disconnect, disaffirm.* **3.** apart; away: *dismiss, disperse.* **4.** deprivation of; expulsion from: *dispossession, disbarment.* **5.** completely; thoroughly: *disannul.* [Latin *dis* apart, away, un-[2], exceedingly.]

dis-[2], form of **di-**[1] before *s,* as in *dissyllable.*

dis·a·bil·i·ty (dis′ə bil′ə tē) *pl.* **-ties.** *n.* **1.** loss or lack of ability; disabled condition; incapacity: *disability arising from injury.* **2.** that which disables; handicap: *His lack of training was a serious disability.* **3.** lack of legal capability to do something; legal incapacity.

Syn. 1. Disability, inability, incapacity indicate lack of power to do something. **Disability** implies loss of power, either complete or under given circumstances, or suggests what causes the loss of power: *His speech disability disqualified him as an announcer.* **Inability** stresses absence of power, whatever the cause: *His inability to sense the mood of an audience made him an inept orator.* **Incapacity** suggests absence of power to function, esp. under certain circumstances: *He demonstrated an incapacity to control his speech whenever he became nervous.*

dis·a·ble (dis ā′bəl) **-bled, -bling.** *v.t.* **1.** to deprive of ability or power; cripple; incapacitate. **2.** to make legally incapable. —**dis·a′ble·ment,** *n.*

dis·a·bled (dis ā′bəld) *adj.* having a disability; crippled.

dis·a·buse (dis′ə būz′) **-bused, -bus·ing.** *v.t.* to free from false or mistaken ideas (often with *of*): *to disabuse people of their superstitions.*

dis·ac·cord (dis′ə kôrd′) *v.i.* to be out of accord or harmony; clash; disagree. —*n.* lack of accord or harmony; disagreement.

dis·ad·van·tage (dis′əd van′tij) *n.* **1.** that which interferes with or prevents success; drawback; handicap: *the disadvantages of a poor education.* **2.** loss; injury; detriment: *It was to our disadvantage to stay.* **3. at a disadvantage,** in an unfavorable or inferior situation or state: *Competing with older children put him at a disadvantage.* —*v.t.* **-taged, -tag·ing.** to subject to a disadvantage. [Old French *desavantage* unfavorable condition, from *des-* (from Latin *dis-* apart) + *avantage* advance. See ADVANTAGE.]

dis·ad·van·taged (dis′əd van′tijd) *adj.* lacking what is regarded as essential for a decent standard of living; underprivileged.

dis·ad·van·ta·geous (dis ad′vən tā′jəs) *adj.* attended with or causing disadvantage; unfavorable; detrimental. —**dis·ad′van·ta′geous·ly,** *adv.* —**dis·ad′van·ta′geous·ness,** *n.*

dis·af·fect (dis′ə fekt′) *v.t.* to alienate the affection or loyalty of; estrange. —**dis′af·fec′tion,** *n.*

dis·af·fil·i·ate (dis′ə fil′ē āt′) **-at·ed, -at·ing.** *v.t., v.i.* to sever affiliation (with). —**dis′af·fil′i·a′tion,** *n.*

dis·af·firm (dis′ə furm′) *v.t.* **1.** to deny; contradict. **2.** *Law.* **a.** to refuse to abide by (a settlement or agreement); repudiate. **b.** to reverse or set aside, as a decision; annul. —**dis·af·fir·ma·tion** (dis′af ər mā′shən), *n.*

dis·a·gree (dis′ə grē′) **-greed, -gree·ing.** *v.i.* **1.** to differ in opinion; dissent: *I disagree with your first statement.* **2.** to quarrel; dispute; argue: *We disagreed violently, and she ran out crying.* **3.** to fail to agree or harmonize; differ; conflict: *Newspaper accounts of the robbery disagreed. Your answer disagrees with mine.* **4.** to cause physical discomfort or ill effects; be upsetting or unsuitable (with *with*): *Hot weather disagrees with her.*

dis·a·gree·a·ble (dis′ə grē′ə bəl) *adj.* **1.** not to one's taste or liking; unpleasant; offensive: *a disagreeable odor, a disagreeable task.* **2.** bad-tempered; quarrelsome. —**dis·a·gree′a·bil′i·ty, dis·a·gree′a·ble·ness,** *n.* —**dis·a·gree′a·bly,** *adv.*

dis·a·gree·ment (dis′ə grē′mənt) *n.* **1.** failure to agree; difference; discrepancy: *the disagreement apparent between his testimony and yours.* **2.** difference of opinion: *their disagreement about the political situation.* **3.** quarrel; dispute; argument: *He had a loud disagreement with his boss.* **Syn. 2. Disagreement, discord, dissension** mean lack of common ground between two or more parties. **Disagreement** usually refers to difference of opinion: *There was no disagreement as to what course to take in the developing crisis.* **Discord** implies a noisy or vigorous dispute resulting from lack of concord: *One aim of propaganda is to sow discord among the enemy.* **Dissension** suggests a break or disruption resulting from such a dispute: *Dissension among the troops was severe but never quite reached the point of mutiny.*

dis·al·low (dis′ə lou′) *v.t.* **1.** to deny the truth or validity of: *to disallow a claim.* **2.** to refuse to allow; prohibit. —**dis′al·low′ance,** *n.*

dis·an·nul (dis′ə nul′) *v.t.* to abolish completely; annul. —**dis′an·nul′ment,** *n.*

dis·ap·pear (dis′ə pēr′) *v.i.* **1.** to pass from sight; vanish: *The sun disappeared below the horizon.* **2.** to cease to exist or be known: *That species disappeared in the Ice Age.* **Syn. 1. Disappear, fade, vanish** mean to become lost to sight. **Disappear** is the general word: *The sun disappeared behind a cloud.* **Fade** suggests a gradual disappearance, either complete or partial: *The train faded into the distance.* **Vanish** implies a complete passing from sight, usually suddenly, often with the suggestion of something mysterious: *He glanced away for a moment, and when he looked back, the little man had vanished.*

dis·ap·pear·ance (dis′ə pēr′əns) *n.* act or fact of disappearing.

dis·ap·point (dis′ə point′) *v.t.* **1.** to fail to fulfill the hope, desire, or expectation of (someone): *His poor showing disappointed us.* **2.** to prevent the realization or fulfillment of (something); thwart; frustrate: *to disappoint a person's hopes.* [Old French *desapointier* to frustrate, from *des-* (from Latin *dis-* apart) + *apoint(i)er* to arrange. See APPOINT.]

dis·ap·point·ment (dis′ə point′mənt) *n.* **1.** act or fact of disap-

pointing. **2.** state or feeling of being disappointed: *She couldn't hide her disappointment.* **3.** one who or that which disappoints: *He was a disappointment to his family.*

dis·ap·pro·ba·tion (dis ap′rə bā′shən) *n.* disapproval; censure.

dis·ap·prov·al (dis′ə proo̅o̅′vəl) *n.* **1.** act of disapproving. **2.** unfavorable opinion or feeling; dislike; censure.

dis·ap·prove (dis′ə proo̅o̅v′) **-proved, -prov·ing.** *v.t.* **1.** to have or express an unfavorable opinion of; regard with disfavor; censure; condemn: *We disapprove his rash conduct.* **2.** to refuse to approve or sanction; reject: *to disapprove a request.* —*v.i.* to have or express an unfavorable opinion (often with *of*): *We disapproved of their unethical actions.* —**dis′ap·prov′ing·ly,** *adv.*

dis·arm (dis ärm′) *v.t.* **1.** to deprive of a weapon or weapons: *The sheriff disarmed the prisoners.* **2.** to overcome the hostility or suspicion of; win over: *His charming manner disarmed us.* **3.** to deprive of the means to attack, defend, or injure; make harmless. **4.** to make harmless by removing a fuse or other detonating mechanism: *to disarm a bomb, to disarm a mine.* —*v.i.* **1.** to lay down arms. **2.** to reduce, limit, or eliminate military weapons, equipment, or forces.

dis·ar·ma·ment (dis är′mə mənt) *n.* act of disarming, esp. the reduction, limitation, or elimination of military weapons, equipment, or forces.

dis·arm·ing (dis är′ming) *adj.* tending to overcome hostility or suspicion; winning: *a disarming smile.* —**dis·arm′ing·ly,** *adv.*

dis·ar·range (dis′ə rānj′) **-ranged, -rang·ing.** *v.t.* to disturb the arrangement of; create disorder in: *She searched through the closet, disarranging everything.* —**dis′ar·range′ment,** *n.*

dis·ar·ray (dis′ə rā′) *n.* **1.** lack of orderly arrangement; disorder; confusion. **2.** disorder or incompleteness of clothing. —*v.t.* **1.** to throw into disorder or confusion. **2.** *Archaic.* to undress. —**Syn.** *n.* **1.** see **confusion.**

dis·as·sem·ble (dis′ə sem′bəl) **-bled, -bling.** *v.t.* to take apart: *to disassemble an engine.*

dis·as·so·ci·ate (dis′ə sō′shē āt′, -sē-) **-at·ed, -at·ing.** *v.t.* to cut off association, connection, or identification with; separate from: *I disassociated myself from their company. The candidate disassociated himself from the party's former position.* —**dis′as·so′ci·a′tion,** *n.*

dis·as·ter (di zas′tər) *n.* any event causing much suffering, distress, or loss; sudden or great misfortune; calamity. [French *désastre,* going back to Latin *dis-* (see DIS-¹) + *astrum* star, from Greek *astron;* with reference to the belief that when the stars are against one, great misfortune occurs.]

Syn. Disaster, calamity, catastrophe mean an extremely unfortunate occurrence. **Disaster** suggests destruction that brings widespread ruin, either from a natural phenomenon or from an accident, carelessness, or failure: *The hurricane's violent winds and torrential rains brought disaster to the coastal town.* **Calamity** refers more to the effect of widespread misfortune on people than it does to the physical effects: *The calamity of the dust storms drove many Oklahoma farmers from their land in the 1930s.* **Catastrophe** suggests a final and irreparable misfortune: *The officers strove to keep the retreat from becoming a catastrophe.*

dis·as·trous (di zas′trəs) *adj.* causing or accompanied by disaster; calamitous: *a disastrous flood, a disastrous mistake.* —**dis·as′trous·ly,** *adv.*

dis·a·vow (dis′ə vou′) *v.t.* to deny knowledge of or responsibility for; refuse to acknowledge; repudiate: *to disavow a statement, to disavow a belief.*

dis·a·vow·al (dis′ə vou′əl) *n.* act of disavowing; repudiation.

dis·band (dis band′) *v.t.* to break up the organization of; dissolve: *to disband a regiment.* —*v.i.* to cease to function as an organized body; disperse: *The club disbanded after three meetings.* —**dis·band′ment,** *n.*

dis·bar (dis bär′) **-barred, -bar·ring.** *v.t.* to expel (a lawyer) officially from the legal profession; deprive of the right to practice law. —**dis·bar′ment,** *n.*

dis·be·lief (dis′bi lēf′) *n.* lack of belief; refusal to believe. —**Syn.** see **unbelief.**

dis·be·lieve (dis′bi lēv′) **-lieved, -liev·ing.** *v.t., v.i.* to fail to believe in (someone or something). —**dis′be·liev′er,** *n.*

dis·bur·den (dis burd′ən) *v.t.* **1.** to rid of a burden or load: *to disburden a ship, to disburden an animal.* **2.** to relieve of something burdensome or oppressive: *to disburden one's conscience.* —*v.i.* to get rid of a burden or load.

dis·burse (dis burs′) **-bursed, -burs·ing.** *v.t.* to pay out (funds); expend. [Old French *desbourser* to take money from a purse, pay, going back to Latin *dis-* apart + Late Latin *bursa* purse. See PURSE.] —**dis·burs′er,** *n.* —**Syn.** see **spend.**

dis·burse·ment (dis burs′mənt) *n.* **1.** act of disbursing. **2.** money disbursed; expenditure.

disc (disk) *n.* **1.** phonograph record. **2.** disk. [Form of DISK.]

disc. 1. discount. **2.** discovered.

dis·cant (dis′kant, dis kant′) descant.

dis·card (*v.,* dis kärd′; *n.,* dis′kärd′) *v.t.* **1.** to cast aside, reject, or give up as useless, worthless, or unwanted: *to discard an outdated theory.* **2.a.** to throw away or put aside (an unwanted card or cards). **b.** to play (a card other than trump or the suit led). —*v.i.* to discard a card or cards. —*n.* **1.** act of discarding; being discarded. **2.** one who or that which is discarded. **3.** card or cards discarded. [DIS-¹ + CARD¹.]

dis·cern (di surn′, -zurn′) *v.t.* **1.** to recognize as different and distinct; separate or discriminate mentally; distinguish: *to discern good from evil.* **2.** to detect or recognize, as by intellect or sensation; perceive: *I could barely discern him in the fog. He discerned her plan immediately.* —*v.i.* to distinguish or discriminate: *to discern between truth and falsehood.* [Old French *discerner,* from Latin *discernere* to separate, distinguish.] —**dis·cern′er,** *n.*

Syn. *v.t.* **2. Discern, perceive, recognize, distinguish** mean to see something clearly. **Discern** implies seeing something and differentiating it from confusing impressions: *He could discern the shadowy figure of a man standing among the trees.* **Perceive** suggests the use of sight to determine what a thing really is: *As the vehicle drew nearer, he perceived it to be a police car.* **Recognize** implies identifying, from its characteristics, something known or belonging to a class of known things: *None of the onlookers recognized the movie star in her wig and dark glasses.* **Distinguish** suggests separating the impressions received from one or several things from all other such impressions: *It is possible to distinguish the male of the species from the female by means of the male's bright coloring.* See also **see.**

dis·cern·i·ble (di sur′nə bəl, -zur′-) *adj.* capable of being discerned; perceptible: *There is no discernible difference between the two chairs.* —**dis·cern′i·bly,** *adv.*

dis·cern·ing (di sur′ning, -zur′-) *adj.* having or showing discernment; discriminating; perceptive: *a discerning judge of character, discerning taste in art.* —**dis·cern′ing·ly,** *adv.*

dis·cern·ment (di surn′mənt, -zurn′-) *n.* **1.** act of discerning. **2.** keenness of perception, judgment, or understanding; insight.

dis·charge (*v.,* dis chärj′; *n.,* dis′chärj′, dis chärj′) **-charged, -charg·ing.** *v.t.* **1.** to release from service, office, or employment; dismiss: *to discharge a worker, to discharge a servant, to discharge a soldier from the army.* **2.** to release from care or custody; set at liberty: *to discharge a prisoner, to discharge a patient.* **3.** to let go or clear out; remove: *The boat discharged its passengers at the pier.* **4.** to remove the contents of; unload: *to discharge a ship.* **5.** to fulfill the requirements of; carry out; execute: *to discharge an errand, to discharge a duty.* **6.** to fire; shoot: *to discharge a bow, to discharge a gun.* **7.** to send forth; emit: *The river discharged its water into the bay. The motor discharged fumes.* **8.** to give vent to or express: *to discharge pent-up emotion.* **9.** to relieve of responsibility, duty, or obligation: *to discharge a jury.* **10.** to pay off; settle: *to discharge a debt.* **11.** to rid of an electric charge; withdraw electricity from: *to discharge a battery.* **12.** *Law.* to annul or set aside (a court order). **13.** to remove (color or dye) from textiles, as by chemical bleaching. —*v.i.* **1.** to emit or send forth contents: *The wound discharges constantly. The smaller pipes discharged into the main one.* **2.** to go off, as a firearm; fire. **3.** to get rid of or deliver a charge or load. **4.** to lose an electrical charge. —*n.* **1.** dismissal from service, office, or employment. **2.** release from care or custody: *the discharge of a prisoner.* **3.** something that dismisses or releases, as a certificate discharging one from military service. **4.** act of firing off, as a weapon or missile. **5.** a carrying out; performance; execution: *to be faithful in the discharge of one's duties.* **6.** a flowing or letting out; emission; ejection: *the discharge of pus from a wound.* **7.** rate or amount of outflow. **8.** that which is discharged or emitted: *a watery discharge from sore eyes.* **9.** a relieving from responsibility, duty, or obligation. **10.** a paying off or settling: *the discharge of a debt.* **11.** act of removing a charge or burden; unloading: *the discharge of cargo.* **12.** transference of electricity between two charged bodies. **13.** *Law.* dismissal or annulment, as of a court order. [Old French *descharger* to unload, from *des-* (from Latin *dis-* apart) + *charger* to load. See CHARGE.] —**dis·charge′a·ble,** *adj.* —**dis·charg′er,** *n.*

dis·ci·ple (di sī′pəl) *n.* **1.** follower or adherent of a particular teacher or doctrine: *Plato was a disciple of Socrates.* **2.** any of the early followers of Jesus, esp. one of the Apostles. **Disciple.** member of the Disciples of Christ. [Old English *discipul,* from Latin *discipulus* pupil.] —**dis·ci′ple·ship′,** *n.*

Disciples of Christ. Protestant denomination organized in 1809, that rejects all creeds, holds that the Bible is the only basis for Christian faith and practice, and administers baptism by immersion.

dis·ci·plin·a·ble (dis′ə plin′ə bəl) *adj.* **1.** capable of being taught by discipline and training. **2.** subject to or deserving discipline.

dis·ci·pli·nar·i·an (dis′ə pli när′ē ən) *n.* one who enforces or advocates strict discipline. —*adj.* disciplinary.

dis·ci·pli·nar·y (dis′ə pli ner′ē) *adj.* of, relating to, or used in discipline: *disciplinary measures.*

at; āpe; cär; end; mē; it; īce; hot; ōld; fôrk; wood; fōo̅l; oil; out; up; ūse; turn; sing; thin; this; zh in treasure; ə in ago, taken, pencil, lemon, circus.

dis·ci·pline (dis′ə plin) *n.* **1.** training that molds, corrects, or perfects something, as the mental faculties or moral character: *Your writing would benefit from the discipline of hard work.* **2.** orderly, obedient, or restrained conduct; self-control; self-restraint: *You showed real discipline in being so tactful.* **3.** acceptance of or submission to authority and control; order: *discipline among troops, to maintain discipline in the classroom.* **4.** punishment given to train or correct; chastisement: *She felt the child's behavior demanded severe discipline.* **5.** branch of instruction or knowledge; field of study: *Mathematics and physics are related disciplines.* **6.** set or system of rules for conduct: *The members observed a most exact discipline.* —*v.t.* **1.** to train to be obedient; keep in order or under control: *to discipline troops.* **2.** to develop or train, as by instruction or exercise: *to discipline one's mind.* **3.** to punish; chastise. [Latin *disciplina* instruction, knowledge.] —**dis′ci·plin′er,** *n.*

disc jockey *also,* **disk jockey.** announcer or master of ceremonies on a radio program of recorded music.

dis·claim (dis klām′) *v.t.* **1.** to renounce any claim to, responsibility for, or connection with; disavow; deny: *He disclaims all pretensions to artistic skill. She disclaimed knowledge of the letter's contents.* **2.** to renounce a legal right or claim to: *He disclaimed a share in his uncle's estate.* **3.** to reject or deny the claim or authority of. —*v.i.* to renounce or repudiate a legal right or claim.

dis·claim·er (dis klā′mər) *n.* **1.** a disclaiming act, notice, or instrument. **2.** one who disclaims.

dis·close (dis klōz′) *-closed, -clos·ing.* *v.t.* **1.** to make known; reveal: *to disclose a secret, to disclose one's intentions.* **2.** to expose to view; lay bare; uncover: *The excavation disclosed the ruins of an ancient city.* —**dis·clos′er,** *n.* —**Syn. 1.** see **reveal.**

dis·clo·sure (dis klō′zhər) *n.* **1.** act of disclosing. **2.** that which is disclosed.

dis·cog·ra·phy (dis kog′rə fē) *pl.* **-phies.** *n.* list of phonograph records, esp. a comprehensive listing of the recordings of a particular performer or in a particular category. [DISC + -GRAPHY.]

dis·coid (dis′koid) *adj.* **1.** having the form of a disk. **2.** (of some composite flowers) having only disk flowers, with no rays. Also, **dis·coi′dal.** —*n.* disk or disklike object.

dis·col·or (dis kul′ər) *also, British,* **dis·col·our.** *v.t.* to change or spoil the color of; fade; stain. —*v.i.* to become discolored.

dis·col·or·a·tion (dis kul′ə rā′shən) *also, British,* **dis·col·our·a·tion.** *n.* **1.** act of discoloring; being discolored. **2.** discolored spot or mark; stain. Also, **dis·col′or·ment.**

dis·com·bob·u·late (dis′kəm bob′yə lāt′) *-lat·ed, -lat·ing.* *v.t. Informal.* to confuse; upset.

dis·com·fit (dis kum′fit) *v.t.* **1.** to throw into confusion; disconcert; abash: *I was quite discomfited by her question.* **2.** to defeat the plans or expectations of; frustrate; thwart. **3.** *Archaic.* to defeat or overthrow in battle; rout. [Old French *desconfit,* past participle of *desconfire* to defeat, going back to Latin *dis-* apart + *conficere* to bring about, preserve.]

dis·com·fi·ture (dis kum′fi chər) *n.* act of discomfiting; being discomfited.

dis·com·fort (dis kum′fərt) *n.* **1.** lack of comfort; uneasiness, hardship, pain: *the discomfort of sleeping on rocky ground.* **2.** that which causes discomfort; inconvenience; hardship. —*v.t.* to make uncomfortable or uneasy.

dis·com·mode (dis′kə mōd′) *-mod·ed, -mod·ing.* *v.t.* to cause inconvenience to; disturb; trouble.

dis·com·pose (dis′kəm pōz′) *-posed, -pos·ing.* *v.t.* **1.** to disturb the composure of; make uneasy: *The speaker was not discomposed by the jeers of the crowd.* **2.** to disturb the order of; disarrange.

dis·com·po·sure (dis′kəm pō′zhər) *n.* state of being discomposed; agitation; disturbance.

dis·con·cert (dis′kən surt′) *v.t.* **1.** to disturb the self-possession or composure of; embarrass; confuse: *Forgetting his lines greatly disconcerted the actor.* **2.** to throw into disorder or confusion; frustrate, as a plan. —**dis′con·cert′ed·ly, dis′con·cert′ing·ly,** *adv.* —**dis′con·cert′ed·ness,** *n.*

dis·con·nect (dis′kə nekt′) *v.t.* to sever or break the connection of or between: *to disconnect a locomotive from a train. The repairman disconnected the television set before fixing it.* —**dis′con·nec′tion,** *n.*

dis·con·nect·ed (dis′kə nek′tid) *adj.* **1.** lacking order, connection, or logic; incoherent; disjointed: *a disconnected speech, disconnected thoughts.* **2.** not connected; separate; detached. —**dis′con·nect′ed·ly,** *adv.* —**dis′con·nect′ed·ness,** *n.*

dis·con·so·late (dis kon′sə lit) *adj.* **1.** without cheer, hope, or comfort; dejected; inconsolable: *He was disconsolate after his father's death.* **2.** causing or characterized by dejection or gloom; cheerless. [Medieval Latin *disconsolatus* comfortless, from Latin *dis-* apart + *consōlātus,* past participle of *consōlārī* to comfort.] —**dis·con′so·late·ly,** *adv.* —**dis·con′so·late·ness, dis·con·so·la′tion** (dis kon′sə lā′shən), *n.*

dis·con·tent (dis′kən tent′) *n.* lack of contentment; dissatisfaction;

restlessness: *There was much discontent among the players after the team lost its first six games.* Also, **dis′con·tent′ment.** —*v.t.* to make discontented.

dis·con·tent·ed (dis′kən ten′tid) *adj.* uneasy in mind; not contented; dissatisfied; restless. —**dis′con·tent′ed·ly,** *adv.* —**dis′con·tent′ed·ness,** *n.*

dis·con·tin·u·ance (dis′kən tin′yōō əns) *n.* **1.** discontinuation. **2.** interruption or termination of a law suit by court order at the request of the plaintiff.

dis·con·tin·u·a·tion (dis′kən tin′yōō ā′shən) *n.* act of discontinuing; being discontinued.

dis·con·tin·ue (dis′kən tin′ū) *-tin·ued, -tin·u·ing.* *v.t.* **1.** to break off or cease from; put an end or halt to; stop: *We discontinued the project because of a lack of funds.* **2.** to cease to take, give, use, or receive: *He discontinued his subscription to the magazine.* **3.** to bring about discontinuance of (a law suit). —*v.i.* to come to an end; cease: *Publication of the paper discontinued.* —**dis′con·tin′u·er,** *n.*

dis·con·ti·nu·i·ty (dis′kon tə nōō′ə tē, -nū′-) *pl.,* **-ties.** *n.* **1.** lack of continuity. **2.** gap or break.

dis·con·tin·u·ous (dis′kən tin′ū əs) *adj.* not continuous; interrupted; intermittent. —**dis′con·tin′u·ous·ly,** *adv.* —**dis′con·tin′u·ous·ness,** *n.*

dis·cord (dis′kôrd) *n.* **1.** lack of agreement, concord, or harmony; disagreement; dissension; conflict: *discord between nations, discord among the various factions of a political party.* **2.** mingling or clashing of harsh or unpleasing sounds; din. **3.** *Music.* lack of harmony in notes sounded simultaneously; dissonance. Opposed to **concord.** [Old French *descorde* a quarrel, from *descorder* to quarrel, from Latin *discordāre* to differ.] —**Syn. 1.** see **disagreement.**

dis·cor·dance (dis kôrd′əns) *n.* **1.** state or fact of being discordant; disagreement. **2.** discord of sounds; harsh or dissonant noise. Also, **dis·cor′dan·cy.**

dis·cord·ant (dis kôrd′ənt) *adj.* **1.** not in agreement, concord, or harmony; disagreeing; dissenting; conflicting: *discordant opinions.* **2.** harsh, clashing, or disagreeable in sound; dissonant; inharmonious: *the discordant noises of the train station.* —**dis·cord′ant·ly,** *adv.*

dis·co·thèque (dis′kə tek′, -kō-) *n.* establishment for dancing to recorded or sometimes live music, often having food and beverages available. [French *discothèque* record library, nightclub featuring music by records, from Greek *diskos* round plate, quoit + *thēkē* container.]

dis·count (*n.,* dis′kount′; *v.,* dis′kount′, dis kount′) *n.* **1.** deduction of a specified amount or percentage, as from a price or other amount charged or owed: *to sell a radio at a 25% discount from the retail price.* **2.** interest deducted beforehand in purchasing, selling, or lending money on a note, bill, or other negotiable paper. **3.** discount rate. **4.** act of discounting. **5. at a discount.** at less than the regularly charged price. —*v.t.* **1.** to reduce the cost or value of; offer for sale at a reduced price: *That store discounts all its merchandise.* **2.** to deduct (a specified amount or percentage) from the total amount otherwise charged or owed: *to discount 15% from the price of a car.* **3.** to take little or no account of; minimize; disregard. **4.** to make allowance for exaggeration or bias in: *Discount his stories of his daring exploits.* **5.** to lessen the effect or importance of by taking into account in advance. **6.** to purchase, sell, or lend money on (negotiable paper) after deducting a certain amount from its face value. —*v.i.* **1.** to lend money, deducting the interest in advance. **2.** to sell merchandise at a discount. [Old French *desconter, descompter* to relate, reckon off, going back to Latin *dis-* apart + *computāre* to count.] —**dis′count·a·ble,** *adj.* —**dis′count·er,** *n.*

dis·coun·te·nance (dis kount′ən əns) *-nanced, -nanc·ing.* *v.t.* **1.** to look upon with disfavor or disapproval; discourage; frown on: *to discountenance a proposal.* **2.** to abash; disconcert.

discount house, establishment where merchandise is sold at a price lower than the usual or advertised retail price. Also, **discount store.**

discount rate, rate of interest charged in advance for discounting notes, bills, and other negotiable paper.

dis·cour·age (dis kur′ij) *-aged, -ag·ing.* *v.t.* **1.** to lessen the courage, hope, or confidence of; dishearten: *The hardships she faced discouraged her.* **2.** to dissuade or deter (with *from*): *Bad weather discouraged us from going on the picnic.* **3.** to try to prevent by expressing disapproval of; frown upon: *The principal discouraged unexcused absences.* **4.** to prevent, obstruct, or hinder, as by opposition or difficulty: *Strict laws were passed in an attempt to discourage crime. The scarcity of rainfall discouraged agriculture.* [Old French *descourager* to dishearten, going back to Latin *dis-* apart + *cor* heart.]

dis·cour·age·ment (dis kur′ij mənt) *n.* **1.** act of discouraging; being or feeling discouraged. **2.** that which discourages: *The unfavorable reviews of his first novel were a great discouragement to him.*

dis·course (*n.,* dis′kôrs; *v.,* dis kôrs′) *n.* **1.** communication of thought by speech; conversation; talk. **2.** formal, extended, spoken or written treatment of a given subject, as a treatise, lecture, or sermon. —*v.i.,* **-coursed, -cours·ing. 1.** to speak or write formally and at length

on a subject (with *on* or *upon*). **2.** to converse; talk; confer. [Late Latin *discursus* conversation, from Latin *discursus* a running to and fro.] **—dis·cours'er,** *n.* **—Syn.** *n.* 1. see **talk.**

dis·cour·te·ous (dis kûr'tē əs) *adj.* not courteous; rude; impolite. **—dis·cour'te·ous·ly,** *adv.* **—dis·cour'te·ous·ness,** *n.*

dis·cour·te·sy (dis kûr'tə sē) *pl.,* **-sies.** *n.* **1.** lack of courtesy; rudeness; impoliteness. **2.** discourteous act.

dis·cov·er (dis kuv'ər) *v.t.* **1.a.** to come upon or gain sight or knowledge of (something previously unseen or unknown) for the first time: *Wilhelm Roentgen discovered X rays.* **b.** to learn of the existence of; come to know of: *He discovered his mistake too late. I discovered Shakespeare at an early age.* **2.** Archaic. to make known; reveal. [Old French *descovrir* to uncover, disclose, from Late Latin *discooperīre,* from Latin *dis-* apart + *cooperīre* to cover.] **—dis·cov'er·a·ble,** *adj.* **—dis·cov'er·er,** *n.*

dis·cov·er·y (dis kuv'ə rē) *pl.,* **-er·ies.** *n.* **1.** act of discovering: *Columbus' discovery of America took place by accident.* **2.** something discovered: *Pasteur employed his discoveries to solve many medical problems.*

dis·cred·it (dis kred'it) *v.t.* **1.** to cause to be doubted or disbelieved; destroy belief, confidence, or trust in: *New information discredited the old report.* **2.** to damage the credit or reputation of; bring into disrepute; disgrace: *The unsportsmanlike play of the football team discredited the entire school.* **3.** to refuse to believe or give credit to; disbelieve: *I discredit all those rumors.* **—**n. **1.** lack or loss of credit, reputation, or esteem: *He brought discredit on the whole family.* **2.** lack or loss of belief, confidence, or trust; doubt: *The results of later experiments brought the original theory into discredit.* **3.** that which discredits: *His corrupt activities were a discredit to the Senate.*

dis·cred·it·a·ble (dis kred'i tə bəl) *adj.* bringing discredit; injurious to reputation: *a discreditable attempt to deceive others.* **—dis·cred'it·a·bly,** *adv.*

dis·creet (dis krēt') *adj.* having or showing discernment and careful judgment in speech and action; prudent; circumspect: *He was discreet enough not to reveal what his friend had told him.* [Old French *discret,* from Medieval Latin *discretus* capable of distinguishing, from Latin *discrētus,* past participle of *discernere* to separate, distinguish.] **—dis·creet'ly,** *adv.* **—dis·creet'ness,** *n.*

dis·crep·an·cy (dis krep'ən sē) *pl.,* **-cies.** *n.* **1.** lack of agreement or consistency; difference; contradiction; variance: *There was little discrepancy in the testimony of the two witnesses.* **2.** instance of this. Also, **dis·crep'ance.**

dis·crep·ant (dis krep'ənt) *adj.* lacking agreement or consistency; at variance; conflicting: *discrepant reports of an accident by the two motorists involved.* [Latin *discrepāns,* present participle of *discrepāre* to sound discordantly, be different.] **—dis·crep'ant·ly,** *adv.*

dis·crete (dis krēt') *adj.* **1.** detached from others; separate; distinct: *a whole formed of discrete units. The word "heart" has several discrete meanings.* **2.** consisting of distinct or individual parts. [Latin *discrētus,* past participle of *discernere* to separate, distinguish.] **—dis·crete'ly,** *adv.* **—dis·crete'ness,** *n.*

dis·cre·tion (dis kresh'ən) *n.* **1.** quality of being discreet; good judgment; caution; prudence. **2.** freedom or power to act according to one's own judgment; independent choice or determination: *We left the matter to his discretion.* **3.** at one's discretion. according to one's own judgment.

dis·cre·tion·ar·y (dis kresh'ə ner'ē) *adj.* left to or determined by one's own discretion; limited only by judgment: *The ambassador was invested with discretionary powers.*

dis·crim·i·nate (*v.,* dis krim'ə nāt'; *adj.,* dis krim'ə nit) **-nat·ed, -nat·ing.** *v.i.* **1.** to show prejudice or partiality: *to discriminate against a minority group, to discriminate in favor of one's friends.* **2.** to note or observe a difference; make a distinction; distinguish: *to discriminate between good and bad poetry.* **—**v.t. **1.** to perceive or note the difference in or between; distinguish: *to learn to discriminate good from evil.* **2.** to make or constitute a difference in or between; differentiate: *abilities which discriminate one person from another.* **—**adj. making or perceiving careful or exact distinctions. [Latin *discrīminātus,* past participle of *discrīmināre* to separate.] **—dis·crim'i·nate·ly,** *adv.* **—dis·crim'i·na'tor,** *n.*

dis·crim·i·nat·ing (dis krim'ə nā'ting) *adj.* **1.** perceiving and making distinctions with accuracy; discerning: *a discriminating judge of character.* **2.** attentive to small details; particular; fastidious: *to be discriminating in one's choice of clothes.* **3.** making or constituting a difference; differentiating. **4.** differential, as a tariff. **—dis·crim'i·nat'ing·ly,** *adv.*

dis·crim·i·na·tion (dis krim'ə nā'shən) *n.* **1.** act of discriminating. **2.** prejudice or partiality in attitudes or actions: *The applicants were judged without discrimination as to race, color, or creed.* **3.** power or ability to perceive distinctions or differences; discernment: *She showed taste and discrimination in furnishing her home.*

dis·crim·i·na·tive (dis krim'ə nā'tiv) *adj.* discriminating. **—dis·crim'i·na'tive·ly,** *adv.*

dis·crim·i·na·to·ry (dis krim'ə nə tôr'ē) *adj.* **1.** characterized or marked by prejudice, esp. racial prejudice: *discriminatory practices in hiring personnel.* **2.** discriminating. **—dis·crim'i·na·to'ri·ly,** *adv.*

dis·cur·sive (dis kur'siv) *adj.* wandering from one subject to another; rambling; digressive: *a discursive lecture.* **—dis·cur'sive·ly,** *adv.* **—dis·cur'sive·ness,** *n.*

dis·cus (dis'kəs) *n.* **1.** heavy circular plate, now usually of wood with a smooth metal rim around its edges, hurled for distance in athletic contests. **2.** act or contest of hurling this plate. [Latin *discus* quoit, dish, from Greek *diskos* round plate, quoit. Doublet of DAIS, DESK, DISH, DISK.]

Discus

dis·cuss (dis kus') *v.t.* to exchange or present ideas or opinions about; consider or examine in conversation or writing; talk or write about: *The council discussed plans for a new city hall. The next chapter discusses the Renaissance.* [Late Latin *discussus,* past participle of *discutere* to discuss, investigate, from Latin *discutere* to shatter, disperse.]

Syn. Discuss, argue, debate, dispute mean to engage in conversation with others about the merits of a subject of mutual interest. **Discuss** suggests an examination of everyone's information and ideas on the subject: *The board met to discuss the spring sales campaign.* **Argue** supposes divergent opinions and a taking of sides so that two or more opposing views are presented: *They argued the proposal that women be permitted to become members of the club.* **Debate** usually refers to open, formal argument on some well-defined and previously agreed upon subject: *The legislature debated the school bills for several weeks.* **Dispute** implies emotional involvement and with vehement espousal of the side one has chosen: *Several citizens rose to dispute the speaker's claim that his views reflected those of the entire community.*

dis·cus·sion (dis kush'ən) *n.* act or instance of discussing: *the legislature's discussion of the proposed highway. There will be a discussion after the lecture.*

dis·dain (dis dān') *n.* feeling of contempt and aversion for something or someone regarded as unworthy or beneath one; scorn: *He treats his classmates with disdain.* **—**v.t. **1.** to consider unworthy or beneath oneself; look down on; scorn: *Despite his misfortunes he disdained all help or pity.* [Old French *desdeignier* to scorn, going back to Latin *dis-* un-² + *dignāri* to think worthy.]

dis·dain·ful (dis dān'fəl) *adj.* feeling or showing disdain; scornful. **—dis·dain'ful·ly,** *adv.* **—dis·dain'ful·ness,** *n.*

dis·ease (di zēz') *n.* **1.** disturbance in the function or structure of an organ or group of organs in an organism, resulting from a specific cause or causes, as infection, characterized by particular symptoms, and producing particular effects: *Arthritis is a chronic disease. Many antibiotic drugs are used to combat disease.* **2.** any disordered or harmful condition: *poverty, prejudice, and other diseases of society.* [Old French *desaise* sickness, discomfort, from *des-* (from Latin *dis-* apart) + *aise.* See EASE.] **—dis·eased',** *adj.*

dis·em·bark (dis'im bärk') *v.t.,* *v.i.* to put or get off a ship or airplane: *to disembark passengers at a port. We disembarked at New York.* **—dis·em·bar·ka·tion** (dis em'bär kā'shən), *n.*

dis·em·bar·rass (dis'im bar'əs) *v.t.* to relieve or free from something that embarrasses, entangles, or encumbers.

dis·em·bod·y (dis'im bod'ē) **-bod·ied, -bod·y·ing.** *v.t.* to separate or free, as a spirit, from the body or from physical existence. **—dis·em·bod'i·ment,** *n.*

dis·em·bow·el (dis'im bou'əl) **-eled, -el·ing;** *also,* British. **-elled, -el·ling.** *v.t* to take out the bowels or entrails of; eviscerate. **—dis·em·bow'el·ment,** *n.*

dis·en·chant (dis'in chant') *v.t.* to free from enchantment or strip of pleasant illusion; disillusion: *She had pictured the author as young and handsome, but she was disenchanted when she met him.* **—dis·en·chant'er,** dis'en·chant'ment, *n.*

dis·en·cum·ber (dis'in kum'bər) *v.t.* to relieve or free from an encumbrance.

dis·en·fran·chise (dis'in fran'chīz) **-chised, -chis·ing.** *v.t.* **1.** to deprive of the rights and privileges of citizenship, esp. of the right to vote. **2.** to deprive of a franchise, privilege, or right. Also, **dis·fran'chise.** **—dis'en·fran'chise·ment,** *n.*

dis·en·gage (dis'in gāj') **-gaged, -gag·ing.** *v.t.* **1.** to release or loosen from something that holds, connects, or entangles; detach; free: *She disengaged her hand from his.* **2.** to free, as from engagement, promise, or obligation. **—**v.i. to release, detach, or free oneself. **—dis'en·gage'ment,** *n.*

dis·en·tail (dis'in tāl') *v.t.* Law. to free (an estate) from entail. **—dis'en·tail'ment,** *n.*

at; āpe; cär; end; mē; it; īce; hot; ōld; fôrk; wood; fōōl; oil; out; up; ūse; turn; sing; thin; **th**is; zh in treasure; ə in ago, taken, pencil, lemon, circus.

dis·en·tan·gle (dis'in tang'gəl) **-tan·gled, -tan·gling.** *v.t.* to free from entanglement; extricate; untangle. —*v.i.* to become disentangled. —**dis'en·tan'gle·ment,** *n.*

dis·en·throne (dis'in thrōn') **-throned, -thron·ing.** *v.t.* to dethrone; depose. —**dis'en·throne'ment,** *n.*

dis·en·twine (dis'in twīn') **-twined, -twin·ing.** *v.t., v.i.* to untwine; disentangle.

dis·es·tab·lish (dis'is tab'lish) *v.t.* **1.** to deprive of fixed or established character or status. **2.** to withdraw exclusive state recognition or support from (a church). —**dis'es·tab'lish·ment,** *n.*

dis·es·teem (dis'is tēm') *v.t.* to have a low opinion of or little regard for; hold in low esteem. —*n.* lack of esteem; disfavor: *He is held in disesteem by most of his colleagues.*

dis·fa·vor (dis fā'vər) *n.* **1.** displeasure or lack of favor; dislike; disapproval: *a subject who incurrred the king's disfavor. She looked on their behavior with disfavor.* **2.** state of being regarded unfavorably: *a political candidate in disfavor with his party. That theory fell into disfavor in the nineteenth century.* **3.** unkind or detrimental act; disservice. —*v.t.* to regard or treat unfavorably.

dis·fig·ure (dis fig'yər) **-ured, -ur·ing.** *v.t.* to spoil or destroy the beauty or appearance of; deform; mar. —**dis·fig'ur·er,** *n.* —**Syn.** see deface.

dis·fig·ure·ment (dis fig'yər mənt) *n.* **1.** act of disfiguring; being disfigured. **2.** that which disfigures; deformity; blemish. Also, **dis·fig·u·ra·tion** (dis fig'yə rā'shən).

dis·fran·chise (dis fran'chīz) **-chised, -chis·ing.** *v.t.* to disenfranchise. —**dis·fran'chise·ment,** *n.*

dis·gorge (dis gôrj') **-gorged, -gorg·ing.** *v.t.* **1.** to throw up (something swallowed); vomit. **2.** to eject or pour (something) forth, esp. with force; discharge: *The volcano disgorged lava and smoke. The bus disgorged its passengers at the station.* **3.** to give up unwillingly. **4.** to empty (oneself) of something. [Old French *desgorger* to vomit, going back to Latin *dis-* apart + Late Latin *gurges* throat, from Latin *gurges* whirlpool, abyss.]

dis·grace (dis grās') *n.* **1.** loss of honor, respect, or favor; shame; ignominy: *the disgrace which his behavior brought upon the family.* **2.** state or condition of being dishonored or out of favor: *to live in disgrace. The senator resigned in disgrace.* **3.** one who or that which brings about shame, dishonor, or reproach: *His practices were a disgrace to his profession. These slum conditions are a disgrace to the city.* —*v.t.,* **-graced, -grac·ing. 1.** to bring shame, dishonor, or reproach to or upon: *to disgrace the family name.* **2.** to dismiss from favor or grace; treat with disfavor: *The king disgraced the disloyal courtier.* [French *disgrâce* misfortune, disfavor, going back to Latin *dis-* apart + *grātia* favor.]

dis·grace·ful (dis grās'fəl) *adj.* characterized by, deserving, or causing disgrace; shameful; disreputable: *disgraceful behavior.* —**dis·grace'ful·ly,** *adv.* —**dis·grace'ful·ness,** *n.*

dis·grun·tle (dis grunt'əl) **-tled, -tling.** *v.t.* to put in a bad humor; make dissatisfied, displeased, or cross. [Dis-¹ + earlier *gruntle* to grumble, from GRUNT.]

dis·guise (dis gīz') **-guised, -guis·ing.** *v.t.* **1.** to alter the appearance or dress of so as to make recognition difficult or impossible; conceal the identity of: *The children disguised themselves as ghosts on Halloween.* **2.** to conceal or obscure the existence or true state or character of: *to disguise the truth, to disguise the taste of a medicine. She disguised her sadness with a happy smile.* —*n.* **1.** something that disguises: *A mustache was part of his disguise. Her serene manner was only a disguise.* **2.** act of disguising. **3.** state of being disguised: *a blessing in disguise.* [Old French *desguisier* to dress so as to be unrecognizable, from *des-* (from Latin *dis-* apart) + *guise* manner, fashion. See GUISE.] —**dis·guis'er,** *n.* —**Syn.** see mask.

dis·gust (dis gust') *n.* strong distaste or aversion aroused by something offensive; repugnance; loathing. —*v.t.* to arouse aversion, repugnance, or loathing in; sicken. [Middle French *desgouster* to loathe, going back to Latin *dis-* apart + *gustāre* to taste.]

dis·gust·ed (dis gus'tid) *adj.* filled with disgust. —**dis·gust'ed·ly,** *adv.*

dis·gust·ing (dis gus'ting) *adj.* causing disgust; repugnant; offensive. —**dis·gust'ing·ly,** *adv.*

dish (dish) *n.* **1.a.** container, usually shallow and slightly concave, made of porcelain, earthenware, or other material, used chiefly for holding or serving food. **b. dishes.** table utensils collectively, esp. those of porcelain, earthenware, or similar material: *Clear the table and wash the dishes.* **2.** serving of food on or in a dish; dishful: *a dish of ice cream.* **3.** food prepared in a particular way: *a new recipe for a tasty chicken dish. Spaghetti is my favorite dish.* **4.** hollow or depression like that of a dish. **5.** something resembling a dish in shape or function. **6.** radio, radar, or television antenna with a bowl-shaped reflector. **7.** *Slang.* attractive girl or woman. —*v.t.* **1.** to put or serve in a dish (usually with *up* or *out*): *to dish up dinner. Dish out the meat.* **2.** to shape

like a dish; make concave. **3.** *British. Slang.* to defeat, ruin, or cheat. **4.** *Slang.* to dispense or deal out; give (with *out*): *to dish out foreign aid to underdeveloped nations.* **5. to dish it out.** *Slang.* to abuse someone physically or verbally; administer punishment. [Old English *disc* plate, from Latin *discus* quoit, dish, from Greek *diskos* round plate, quoit. Doublet of DAIS, DESK, DISCUS, DISK.]

dis·ha·bille (dis'ə bēl') *also,* **des·ha·bille.** *n.* **1.** state of being carelessly or only partially dressed. **2.** garment worn in this state. [French *déshabillé* undress, from *déshabiller* to undress, from *dés-* (from Latin *dis-* un-²) + *habiller* to dress. See HABILIMENT.]

dis·har·mo·ny (dis här'mə nē) *pl.,* **-nies.** lack of harmony or agreement; discord: *disharmony between rival factions of a political party.* —**dis'har·mo'ni·ous,** *adj.* —**dis'har·mo'ni·ous·ly,** *adv.*

dish·cloth (dish'klôth') *n.* cloth for washing dishes. Also, **dish'rag'.**

dis·heart·en (dis härt'ən) *v.t.* to cause to lose hope or courage; discourage; depress: *The bad news disheartened him.*

di·shev·el (di shev'əl) **-eled** or **-elled, -el·ing** or **-el·ling.** *v.t.* to disarrange or put into disorder, as hair or clothing.

di·shev·eled (di shev'əld) *also,* **di·shev·elled.** *adj.* **1.** rumpled or tousled; mussed: *disheveled hair.* **2.** untidy; unkempt: *his disheveled appearance.* [Old French *deschevele,* past participle of *descheveler* to disarrange the hair, going back to Latin *dis-* apart + *capillus* hair.]

dish·ful (dish'fool') *n.* amount that a dish holds.

dis·hon·est (dis on'ist) *adj.* **1.** not honest; given to lying, stealing, or other untruthful or fraudulent acts: *a dishonest politician. She was dishonest in giving her opinion.* **2.** characterized by or showing a lack of honesty: *a cowardly, dishonest act.* —**dis·hon'est·ly,** *adv.*

dis·hon·es·ty (dis on'is tē) *pl.,* **-ties.** *n.* **1.** lack of honesty or integrity. **2.** dishonest act or statement.

dis·hon·or (dis on'ər) *also, British,* **dis·hon·our.** *n.* **1.** lack or loss of honor or reputation; shame; disgrace: *to prefer death to dishonor.* **2.** that which causes or is the source of shame or disgrace. **3.** refusal or failure to accept or pay, as a check or note. —*v.t.* **1.** to deprive of honor; bring shame or discredit to; disgrace. **2.** to refuse or fail to accept or pay, as a check or note, when due. [Old French *deshonor* shame, going back to Latin *dis-* apart + *honor* reputation. See HONOR.]

dis·hon·or·a·ble (dis on'ər ə bəl) *adj.* **1.** characterized by or causing dishonor; shameful; disgraceful: *dishonorable conduct.* **2.** lacking honor; without honor: *a dishonorable man, a dishonorable discharge from the army.* —**dis·hon'or·a·ble·ness,** *n.* —**dis·hon'or·a·bly,** *adv.*

dish·pan (dish'pan') *n.* pan in which to wash dishes.

dish·rag (dish'rag') *n.* dishcloth.

dish·tow·el (dish'tou'əl) *n.* towel for drying dishes.

dish·wash·er (dish'wô'shər, -wosh'ər) *n.* **1.** machine for washing dishes and cooking utensils. **2.** person who washes dishes and cooking utensils; a worker employed to do so.

dish·wa·ter (dish'wô'tər, -wot'ər) *n.* water in which dishes and cooking utensils are or have been washed.

dis·il·lu·sion (dis'i loo'zhən) *v.t.* to free from or deprive of illusion; disenchant: *Admirers of the mayor were disillusioned by the scandals in his administration.* —*n.* disillusionment.

dis·il·lu·sion·ment (dis'i loo'zhən mənt) *n.* **1.** act of disillusioning. **2.** fact or state of being disillusioned.

dis·in·cli·na·tion (dis in'klə nā'shən) *n.* slight distaste or aversion; unwillingness: *a disinclination to do hard work.*

dis·in·cline (dis'in klīn') **-clined, -clin·ing.** *v.t., v.i.* to make or be unwilling or averse.

dis·in·fect (dis'in fekt') *v.t.* to destroy disease-causing microorganisms in: *to disinfect a hospital room.* —**dis'in·fec'tion,** *n.* —**dis'in·fec'tor,** *n.*

dis·in·fect·ant (dis'in fek'tənt) *n.* substance used to destroy disease-causing microorganisms. —*adj.* serving to disinfect: *a disinfectant soap.*

dis·in·gen·u·ous (dis'in jen'ū əs) *adj.* lacking frankness, candor, or sincerity; not straightforward; artful. —**dis'in·gen'u·ous·ly,** *adv.* —**dis'in·gen'u·ous·ness,** *n.*

dis·in·her·it (dis'in her'it) *v.t.* to deprive (an heir) of an inheritance or the right to inherit. —**dis'in·her'it·ance,** *n.*

dis·in·te·grate (dis in'tə grāt') **-grat·ed, -grat·ing.** *v.i.* **1.** to break up into particles, fragments, or parts: *This type of rock disintegrates under pressure.* **2.** to deteriorate by or as if by breaking into constituent parts: *The empire disintegrated under his rule.* **3.** *Physics.* to decay. —*v.t.* to cause to disintegrate. —**dis·in'te·gra'tor,** *n.* —**Syn.** *v.i.* see decay.

dis·in·te·gra·tion (dis in'tə grā'shən) *n.* **1.** act or process of disintegrating; being disintegrated. **2.** *Physics.* decay.

dis·in·ter (dis'in tur') **-terred, -ter·ring.** *v.t.* **1.** to remove from a grave or tomb; dig up: *to disinter a body to perform an autopsy.* **2.** to bring to light; unearth; reveal: *to disinter previously unknown facts about an author's early life.* —**dis'in·ter'ment,** *n.*

dis·in·ter·est (dis in'trist, -in'tər ist) *n.* **1.** lack of interest; indiffer-

ence. **2.** freedom from self-interest or bias; impartiality. —*v.t.* to rid of interest or interested motives.

dis·in·ter·est·ed (dis in′tris tid, -in′tər is-, -in′tə res′-) *adj.* **1.** free from self-interest; not influenced by personal motives; impartial; unbiased: *disinterested advice, a disinterested decision.* **2.** uninterested; indifferent. —**dis·in′ter·est·ed·ly,** *adv.* —**dis·in′ter·est·ed·ness,** *n.*

dis·join (dis join′) *v.t.* to prevent or undo the joining of; separate. —*v.i.* to become separated, disunited, or detached.

dis·joint (dis joint′) *v.t.* **1.** to take apart or separate at the joints; dismember: *to disjoint a turkey.* **2.** to put out of joint; dislocate. **3.** to disturb or destroy the order, connection, or coherence of: *Racial or religious strife disjoints the whole framework of society.* —*v.i.* to come apart at the joints; become out of joint. **4.** *Mathematics.* (of sets) having no elements in common. [Old French *desjoint*, past participle of *desjoindre* to disunite, from Latin *disjungere* to separate.]

dis·joint·ed (dis joint′tid) *adj.* **1.** lacking order, coherence, or unity: *a rambling and disjointed letter.* **2.** taken apart or separated at or as if at the joints: *a disjointed fowl.* **3.** out of joint; dislocated: *a disjointed shoulder.* —**dis·joint′ed·ly,** *adv.* —**dis·joint′ed·ness,** *n.*

dis·junc·tion (dis jungk′shən) *n.* **1.** act of disjoining; being disjoined; separation. **2.** *Logic.* **a.** a disjunctive proposition. **b.** relation existing between the terms of such a proposition.

dis·junc·tive (dis jungk′tiv) *adj.* **1.** causing or tending to separate or divide. **2.** *Grammar.* indicating alternation, opposition, or contrast. In the phrase *poorer but wiser for his experience* the word *but* is a disjunctive conjunction. **3.** *Logic.* involving a choice between alternatives. *It is day or it is night* is a disjunctive proposition. —*n.* **1.** *Grammar.* disjunctive conjunction. **2.** *Logic.* disjunctive proposition.

disk (disk) *also,* **disc, disc.** *n.* **1.** flat, circular platelike object. **2.** something resembling a disk in shape, as one of the circular, usually sharp-edged plates mounted on the shaft of a disk harrow. **3.** *Astronomy.* circular, apparently flat shape of a heavenly body when viewed from earth: *the disk of Venus.*

Disk of a sunflower

4. *Botany.* center of the flower of certain composite plants, composed of small disk flowers. **5.** *Anatomy.* any flat, circular organ or structure, as a platelike growth of cartilage between adjacent vertaebrae. **6.** *Archaic.* discus. [Latin *discus* quoit, disk, from Greek *diskos* round plate, quoit. Doublet of DAIS, DESK, DISCUS, DISH.]

disk flower *Botany.* any one of the small tubular flowers which make up the flower head of certain composite plants, as the thistle.

disk harrow, harrow consisting of a series of sharp disks that are set on a rotating shaft, used in cultivating ground.

disk jockey, disc jockey.

dis·like (dis līk′) *n.* **1.** feeling of disapproval, distaste, or aversion: *He has a strong dislike for cold weather.* —*v.t.,* **-liked, -lik·ing.** to consider disagreeable; regard with aversion or disapproval: *She dislikes doing housework.*

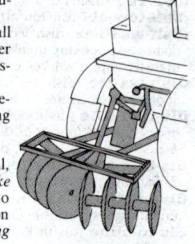

Disk harrow

Syn. *n.* **Dislike, distaste, aversion** mean a negative attitude toward someone or something. **Dislike** simply suggests a recognized feeling that someone or something arouses displeasure: *He disliked the custom of greeting everyone with a smile.* **Distaste** implies active opposition to something: *His distaste for modern music caused him to cancel his subscription to the concerts.* **Aversion** suggests a physical reaction causing one to turn away from something unpleasant: *A cat has a natural aversion to water.*

dis·lo·cate (dis′lō kāt′) **-cat·ed, -cat·ing.** *v.t.* **1.** to upset the order of; throw into confusion; disrupt: *Their national economy was dislocated by war.* **2.** to put out of proper place or order; displace. **3.a.** to put (a bone) out of joint. **b.** to cause (any part of the body) to be in an abnormal position. —**dis·lo·ca′tion,** *n.*

dis·lodge (dis loj′) **-lodged, -lodg·ing.** *v.t.* **1.** to move or force out of a place or position (with *from*): *The avalanche dislodged large rocks from the cliff. The hounds managed to dislodge the bear from its den.* —**dis·lodg′ment;** *also,* **dis·lodge′ment.**

dis·loy·al (dis loi′əl) *adj.* not loyal; unfaithful: *a disloyal friend, to be disloyal to one's country.* —**dis·loy′al·ly,** *adv.*

dis·loy·al·ty (dis loi′əl tē) *pl.* **-ties.** *n.* **1.** lack of loyalty; unfaithfulness; falseness. **2.** disloyal act.

dis·mal (diz′məl) *adj.* **1.** marked by or causing gloom or depression; dreary; miserable; cheerless: *a grimy, dismal industrial town.* **2.** disas-

trously bad; dreadful; terrible: *The project was a dismal failure.* [Anglo-Norman *dis mal* evil days, from Latin *diēs malī,* originally referring to certain days considered unlucky by the Romans.] —**dis′mal·ly,** *adv.* —**dis′mal·ness,** *n.*

Dismal Swamp, coastal swamp extending for over twenty miles in southeastern Virginia and northeastern North Carolina.

dis·man·tle (dis mant′əl) **-tled, -tling.** *v.t.* **1.** to pull down or take apart; disassemble: *to dismantle a machine.* **2.** to strip of covering, furniture, or equipment: *to dismantle a ship.* [Middle French *desmanteller* to remove a cloak, raze, going back to Latin *dis-* apart + *matellum* napkin, cloak.] —**dis·man′tle·ment,** *n.*

dis·mast (dis mast′) *v.t.* to take or break off the masts of (a ship).

dis·may (dis mā′) *v.t.* **1.** to fill with fear or apprehension; make afraid; daunt: *The soldier was dismayed at the sight of the enemy forces.* **2.** to trouble or discourage greatly; depress; dishearten: *The speaker was dismayed by the audience's lack of interest.* —*n.* feeling of alarm or uneasiness; frightened amazement: *the citizens' dismay at learning of the defeat of their army.* [Middle English *dismayen* to dishearten, from an unrecorded Old French form which was partly of Latin and partly of Germanic origin.]

dis·mem·ber (dis mem′bər) *v.t.* **1.** to cut or tear off the limbs or members of; tear limb from limb. **2.** to divide into parts or sections, as a country; partition. —**dis·mem′ber·ment,** *n.*

dis·miss (dis mis′) *v.t.* **1.** to send away or give permission to leave: *to dismiss a patient from the hospital. The child was dismissed from the room.* **2.** to discharge, as from a position or job; fire: *to dismiss an employee for stealing.* **3.** to put aside from attention or serious consideration; reject: *She dismissed the idea because it was impractical. He dismissed the story as a mere rumor.* **4.** to deal with or have done with, esp. quickly: *Before we dismiss this matter, we'll hear one more report.* **5.** to send (an action or suit) out of court without further hearing: *The judge dismissed the case because of lack of evidence.* [Modification (influenced by *dis-*[1]) of Latin *dīmissus,* past participle of *dīmittere* to send away.]

dis·miss·al (dis mis′əl) *n.* **1.** act of dismissing; a being dismissed. **2.** written or spoken order dismissing someone, as from a job.

dis·mis·sion (dis mish′ən) *n.* *Archaic.* dismissal.

dis·mount (dis mount′) *v.i.* to get off or down, as from a horse; alight: *She dismounted gracefully.* —*v.t.* **1.** to remove (something) from its setting, support, or mounting. **2.** to knock off or bring down, as from a horse; unseat. **3.** to take apart; disassemble; dismantle.

Dis·ney, Walt(er) (Elias) (diz′nē) 1901–66, U.S. motion-picture producer.

dis·o·be·di·ence (dis ə bē′dē əns) *n.* refusal or failure to obey.

dis·o·be·di·ent (dis ə bē′dē ənt) *adj.* refusing or failing to obey; disobedient. —**dis′o·be′di·ent·ly,** *adv.*

dis·o·bey (dis′ə bā′) *v.t., v.i.* to refuse or fail to obey: *He disobeyed the lieutenant's orders. That fresh child always disobeys.*

dis·o·blige (dis′ə blīj′) **-bliged, -blig·ing.** *v.t.* **1.** to act contrary to the wishes or convenience of; fail to accommodate. **2.** to give offense to; slight; affront.

dis·or·der (dis ôr′dər) *n.* **1.** lack of order or regular arrangement; confusion: *The room was in disorder after the party.* **2.** breach of peace or public order, as a riot; disturbance: *The police tried to quiet the disorders in the streets.* **3.** disturbance of physical or mental health or functions; sickness; ailment: *a disorder of the digestive system.* —*v.t.* **1.** to disturb the order or regular arrangement of; throw into confusion; disarrange: *Noisy demonstrations disordered the political convention.* **2.** to disturb or upset the physical or mental health or functions of. —**Syn.** *v.* **1.** see **confusion.**

dis·or·dered (dis ôr′dərd) *adj.* **1.** in disorder; confused; disarranged. **2.** disturbed in physical or mental health or functions.

dis·or·der·ly (dis ôr′dər lē) *adj.* **1.** lacking order or regular arrangement; messy; untidy: *The papers lay in a disorderly pile.* **2.** causing a disturbance; uncontrolled; unruly: *a disorderly crowd.* **3.** violating public peace, order, or decency; guilty of disorderly conduct. —*adv.* in a disorderly manner. —**dis·or′der·li·ness,** *n.*

disorderly conduct, any behavior that is considered a petty violation of public peace, order, or decency.

dis·or·gan·ize (dis ôr′gə nīz′) **-ized, -iz·ing.** *v.t.* to upset or destroy the organization, systematic arrangement, or order of; throw into confusion and disorder: *Heavy shelling by the enemy disorganized the army's retreat.* —**dis·or′gan·i·za′tion,** *n.*

dis·or·gan·ized (dis ôr′gə nīzd′) *adj.* lacking organization, systematic arrangement, or order: *a disorganized project, a novel with a badly disorganized plot.*

dis·or·i·ent (dis ôr′i ent′) *v.t.* **1.** to disturb one's sense of direction or position; cause to lose one's bearings; mix up; confuse. —**dis·o′ri·en·ta′tion,** *n.*

dis·own (dis ōn′) *v.t.* to refuse to recognize as one's own, as by not acknowledging responsibility for or connection with; repudiate; reject;

at; āpe; cär; end; mē; it; īce; hot; ōld; fôrk; wood; fōōl; oil; out; up; ūse; turn; sing; thin; this; zh in treasure; ə in ago, taken, pencil, lemon, circus.

deny: *to disown an heir. The senator disowned several controversial statements that had been attributed to him.*

dis·par·age (dis par′ij) **-aged, -ag·ing.** *v.t.* **1.** to speak critically or slightingly of; belittle: *The candidate disparaged his opponent's record in office.* **2.** to bring discredit upon; lower in esteem or reputation. [Old French *desparagier* originally, to cause to marry beneath one, from *des-* (from Latin *dis-* apart) + *parage* equality of rank (going back to Latin *pār* equal).] —**Syn. 1. Disparage, decry, depreciate, belittle** mean to express the opinion that something is of little worth. **Disparage** suggests an indirect approach, a damning with faint praise: *She never failed to disparage his accomplishments by pointing to his brother's eminence.* **Decry** implies open expression of one's opinion that something is of small value: *He decried the suggestions of the planning commission as impractical.* **Depreciate** suggests attributing lesser worth to something than the expected value: *In his memoirs he depreciates the assistance rendered by the American troops.* **Belittle** implies an effort to bring someone or something to insignificance: *Those who had belittled Russian engineering were astonished when the first Sputnik was launched.*

dis·par·age·ment (dis par′ij mənt) *n.* **1.** act of disparaging. **2.** that which belittles or discredits.

dis·par·ag·ing (dis par′ij ing) *adj.* slighting; belittling: *disparaging remarks.* —**dis·par′ag·ing·ly,** *adv.*

dis·pa·rate (dis par′it, dis′pər-) *adj.* essentially or distinctly different; unlike; dissimilar: *disparate points of view.* [Latin *disparātus,* past participle of *disparāre* to separate.] —**dis·par′ate·ly,** *adv.* —**dis·par′ate·ness,** *n.* —**Syn.** see **different.**

dis·par·i·ty (dis par′ə tē) *pl.,* -**ties.** *n.* lack of agreement or similarity; inequality or difference: *a disparity in their ages, a disparity between his words and his actions.*

dis·part (dis pärt′) *v.t., v.i.* *Archaic.* to divide into parts; separate.

dis·pas·sion (dis pash′ən) *n.* freedom from passion, emotion, or bias; calm objectivity; impartiality: *He viewed the controversy with dispassion.*

dis·pas·sion·ate (dis pash′ə nit) *adj.* free from passion, emotion, or bias; impartial: *an honest, dispassionate judge.* —**dis·pas′sion·ate·ly,** *adv.* —**dis·pas′sion·ate·ness,** *n.*

dis·patch (dis pach′) *also,* **des·patch.** *v.t.* **1.** to send off quickly to a specific destination or for a specific purpose: *to dispatch an official messenger, to dispatch a telegram.* **2.** to finish or dispose of quickly or promptly: *to dispatch a business deal.* **3.** to put to death; kill. —*n.* **1.** act of dispatching. **2.** quickness; promptness; speed: *The urgency of the situation called for great dispatch.* **3.** written message sent off quickly or promptly, esp. an official government or military communication. **4.** news story or report, as by a special reporter or from a news service: *a dispatch from the scene of the battle.* **5.** agency or service for quick and prompt conveying of goods or messages. [Spanish *despachar* to speed, send, from Old French *despeechier* to set free, going back to Latin *dis-* un-[2] + *pedica* shackle.] —**Syn.** *v.t.* **2.** see **send.**

dis·patch·er (dis pach′ər) *also,* **des·patch·er.** *n.* **1.** one who dispatches. **2.** one who schedules and directs the arrivals and departures of trains, buses, taxicabs, and other means of transportation.

dis·pel (dis pel′) **-pelled, -pel·ling.** *v.t.* to drive away or cause to disappear or by as by scattering; disperse: *His reassuring words dispelled our doubts.* [Latin *dispellere.*]

dis·pen·sa·ble (dis pen′sə bəl) *adj.* **1.** that can be dispensed with or done without; unessential; unimportant: *to eliminate dispensable items from a budget.* **2.** capable of being dispensed or administered: *dispensable funds.* **3.** subject to dispensation; pardonable, as an offense or sin. —**dis·pen′sa·bil′i·ty, dis·pen′sa·ble·ness,** *n.*

dis·pen·sa·ry (dis pen′sər ē) *pl.,* -**ries.** *n.* **1.** room in which medicines and medical supplies are dispensed: *a hospital dispensary.* **2.** place where medicines and medical treatment are given without charge or for a small fee.

dis·pen·sa·tion (dis′pən sā′shən) *n.* **1.** act of dispensing; giving out; distribution: *The dispensation of supplies in the disaster area was delayed.* **2.** that which is dispensed or distributed: *His widow received a dispensation from the government.* **3.** specific system of administration; management: *the Roman Empire under the dispensation of Augustus.* **4.** official exemption or release, as from an obligation or law, esp. exemption by ecclesiastical authority from a church law: *a papal dispensation.* **b.** official document authorizing or containing such an exemption. **5.** *Theology.* **a.** divine arrangement, provision, or ordering of events, as by providence or nature. **b.** religious system believed to be divinely instituted: *Mosaic dispensation.* —**dis′pen·sa′tion·al,** *adj.*

dis·pen·sa·to·ry (dis pen′sə tôr′ē) *pl.,* -**ries.** *n.* **1.** book describing the composition, preparation, and use of medicines. **2.** *Archaic.* dispensary.

dis·pense (dis pens′) **-pensed, -pens·ing.** *v.t.* **1.** to give or deal out in portions; distribute: *to dispense political favors, to dispense clothing to the needy. This machine dispenses gum.* **2.** to prepare and give out (medicine), esp. by prescription. **3.** to carry out or apply; administer:

to dispense justice. **4.** to exempt or release, as from an obligation or law, esp. a church law. **5. to dispense with.** ′ **a.** to get along without; forgo: *He dispensed with the financial support of his parents.* **b.** to do away with, as a requirement; make unnecessary: *Our handshake dispensed with the need for a contract.* [Old French *dispenser* to distribute, from Latin *dispēnsāre* to weigh out, distribute, regulate.] —**Syn. 1.** see **distribute.**

dis·pens·er (dis pen′sər) *n.* **1.** one who or that which dispenses: *a dispenser of justice. Providence is the dispenser of our fortunes.* **2.** container or mechanical device which dispenses something in convenient units or portions: *a razor-blade dispenser, a soap dispenser.*

dis·peo·ple (dis pē′pəl) **-pled, -pling.** *v.t.* to depopulate.

dis·per·sal (dis pur′səl) *n.* act of dispersing; being dispersed; dispersion: *the dispersal of a mob.*

dis·perse (dis purs′) **-persed, -pers·ing.** *v.t.* **1.** to break up and send off in different directions; scatter: *The police dispersed the crowd.* **2.** to drive away or cause to vanish; dispel: *The winds dispersed the mist.* **3.** to spread about or abroad; diffuse; disseminate: *The lips of the wise disperse knowledge* (Proverbs 15:7). **4.** *Physics.* to separate (radiation) into its component parts according to frequency or wavelength. A beam of white light can be dispersed by being passed through a prism. —*v.i.* to break up and go in different directions; scatter; dissipate: *The congregation dispersed when the service ended.* [Latin *dispersus,* past participle of *dispergere* to scatter.] —**Syn.** *v.t.* **1.** see **scatter.**

dis·per·sion (dis pur′zhən, -shən) *n.* **1.** act of dispersing; being dispersed. **2.** *Physics.* separation of radiation into its component parts according to frequency or wavelength.

dis·per·sive (dis pur′siv) *adj.* dispersing or tending to disperse.

dis·pir·it (dis pir′it) *v.t.* to depress or lower the spirits of; discourage: *The failure of his experiments greatly dispirited the scientist.*

dis·pir·it·ed (dis pir′ə tid) *adj.* depressed; dejected; discouraged. —**dis·pir′it·ed·ly,** *adv.* —**dis·pir′it·ed·ness,** *n.*

dis·place (dis plās′) **-placed, -plac·ing.** *v.t.* **1.** to take the place of; replace; supplant: *Television has displaced motion pictures as America's most popular form of entertainment.* **2.** to move or shift from the usual or proper place or position. **3.** to remove from a position or office: *to displace an officer of the government.* **4.** *Physics.* to shift (a certain weight or volume of fluid) from its original place and occupy its space.

displaced person, homeless person driven or taken from his own country or region, usually as a result of war.

dis·place·ment (dis plās′mənt) *n.* **1.** act of displacing; being displaced. **2.** distance which something has moved from its original place or position. **3.** *Physics.* weight of the volume of fluid displaced by a body floating or immersed in it. The weight of the fluid displaced by a floating body equals the weight of the body itself. **4.** *Geology.* occurrence of a break or movement in a rock, as at a joint or fault. **5.** *Psychology.* unconscious transference of an emotion or attitude to something other than the object that originally aroused it.

dis·play (dis plā′) *v.t.* **1.** to expose to view; cause to be seen; exhibit; show: *to display a poster.* **2.** to manifest or make obvious, often unintentionally; reveal: *to display fear, to display one's ignorance.* **3.** to make a prominent or ostentatious show of; show off; flaunt: *The woman proudly displayed her furs.* **4.** to spread out so as to be viewed; unfold; unfurl: *to display a sail, to display a banner.* —*n.* **1.** act of displaying; exhibition; manifestation: *a display of anger, a display of courage.* **2.** that which is displayed or exhibited: *The display was tastefully arranged.* **3.** ostentatious show: *a vulgar display of wealth.* [Old French *despleier* to unfold, show, from Medieval Latin *displicāre* to unfold, from Latin *displicāre* to scatter.] —**Syn.** *n.* **2.** see **show.**

dis·please (dis plēz′) **-pleased, -pleas·ing.** *v.t.* to fail to please; cause annoyance to; offend; vex: *His conduct displeased his family.* —*v.i.* to cause displeasure or annoyance.

dis·pleas·ure (dis plezh′ər) *n.* **1.** state or feeling of being displeased; annoyance; disapproval. **2.** *Archaic.* discomfort; uneasiness; pain. **3.** *Archaic.* offense; injury.

dis·port (dis pôrt′) *v.t.* to amuse or divert (oneself). —*v.i.* to play; frolic. —*n.* *Archaic.* amusement; diversion; play. [Old French (*se*)*desporter* to amuse (oneself); literally, to carry (oneself) away, going back to Latin *dis-* apart + *portāre* to carry.]

dis·pos·a·ble (dis pō′zə bəl) *adj.* **1.** capable of being disposed of, esp. designed to be discarded after being used: *disposable diapers.* **2.** free to be used; available: *disposable income, disposable property.*

dis·pos·al (dis pō′zal) *n.* **1.** act of getting rid of something; throwing away: *the disposal of refuse.* **2.** act of dealing with or settling (something): *the disposal of certain business matters.* **3.** a transferring of something to another, as by gift or sale: *the disposal of money in a will, the disposal of merchandise.* **4.** a particular ordering or position; arrangement: *the disposal of the troops into three columns.* **5. at one's disposal.** available for use as one pleases: *The car will be at your disposal this week.*

dis·pose (dis pōz′) **-posed, -pos·ing.** *v.t.* **1.** to give a tendency or

at; āpe; cär; end; mē; it; īce; hot; ōld; fôrk; wood; fōōl; oil; out; up; ūse; turn; sing; thin; this; zh in treasure; ə in ago, taken, pencil, lemon, circus.

293

inclination to; make receptive or willing: *His prejudice disposed him to rule in their favor.* **2.** to make susceptible or subject: *A weak constitution disposed him to frequent illness.* **3.** to place in a particular order or position; arrange: *The farmer disposed the plants in rows.* **4.** Archaic. to control or direct; regulate: *to dispose the affairs of the empire.* —*v.i.* **1.** to determine or control the course of events; ordain: *Man proposes, God disposes* (Thomas à Kempis, 1450). **2. to dispose of.** **a.** to get rid of; throw away: *to dispose of garbage.* **b.** to deal or finish up with; settle: *He quickly disposed of the matter.* **c.** to part with, as by gift or sale; transfer to another: *The widow disposed of her husband's property.* **d.** to consume (food or drink). [Old French *disposer* to arrange, modification (influenced by Old French *poser* to place) of Latin *disponere* to arrange.] —**dis·pos′er,** *n.*

dis·posed (dis pōzd′) *adj.* having a specified tendency or inclination: *He's not disposed to work hard.*

dis·po·si·tion (dis′pə zish′ən) *n.* **1.** one's prevailing way of thinking or feeling; temperament; nature: *an irritable disposition, a pleasant disposition.* **2.a.** habitual tendency, inclination, or willingness: *a disposition to accept the ideas of others.* **b.** organic tendency or inclination: *the disposition of sugar to dissolve in water.* **3.** a placing in or being placed in a particular order; arrangement: *the disposition of trees in an orchard.* **4.** regulation, management, or final settlement, as of legal affairs. **5.** a transferring of something to another, as by gift or sale: *the disposition of property after a death.* **6.** power to deal with or settle.
Syn. 1. Disposition, temperament, temper, character mean the dominant impression given by the traits or qualities of a person or group. **Disposition** implies a permanent tendency to react to things in a certain way: *A fellow of cheerful disposition, he was a pleasure to work with.* **Temperament** is the mixture of physical and mental qualities that define a person: *He is a man of such temperament as to prefer a sedentary life.* **Temper** suggests characteristic traits which are acquired and a certain state of mind, permanent or temporary: *She is a woman of even temper. He has been in a vile temper all morning.* **Character** implies the total of qualities, esp. moral ones, seen by others: *The outburst was entirely out of character for so calm a man.*

dis·pos·sess (dis′pə zes′) *v.t.* **1.** to put out of occupancy or possession, esp. of real property, by legal action: *The landlord dispossessed the tenants for not paying rent.* **2.** to deprive of the possession (of something): *an exile dispossessed of his rights.* —**dis′pos·ses′sion, dis′pos·ses′sor,** *n.*

dis·praise (dis prāz′) -**praised, -prais·ing.** *v.t.* to express disapproval of; censure. —*n.* act or instance of dispraising; censure.

dis·prize (dis prīz′) -**prized, -priz·ing.** *v.t.* Archaic. to hold in low esteem.

dis·proof (dis prōōf′) *n.* **1.** act of disproving; refutation. **2.** that which disproves, as evidence.

dis·pro·por·tion (dis′prə pôr′shən) *n.* **1.** lack of proportion or symmetry; disparity. **2.** instance of this. —*v.t.* to make disproportionate. —**dis′pro·por′tion·al·ly,** *adv.*

dis·pro·por·tion·al (dis′prə pôr′shən əl) *adj.* disproportionate. —**dis′pro·por′tion·al·ly,** *adv.*

dis·pro·por·tion·ate (dis′prə pôr′shə nit) *adj.* out of proportion, as in size, amount, or degree; lacking proportion. —**dis′pro·por′tion·ate·ly,** *adv.* —**dis′pro·por′tion·ate·ness,** *n.*

dis·prove (dis prōōv′) -**proved, -prov·ing.** *v.t.* to prove to be false, incorrect, or invalid; refute: *The official deed disproved the miner's claim.* —**dis·prov′a·ble, adj.** —**dis·prov′al,** *n.*

dis·put·a·ble (dis pū′tə bəl, dis′pyə-) *adj.* that can be disputed or called into question; arguable; debatable. —**dis·put′a·bil′i·ty,** *n.* —**dis·put′a·bly,** *adv.*

dis·pu·tant (dis pū′tənt) *n.* one who takes part in a dispute. —*adj.* engaged in dispute; disputing.

dis·pu·ta·tion (dis′pyoo tā′shən) *n.* **1.** act of disputing. **2.** formal debate in which parties attack and defend a question or thesis, as a philosophical or theological theory.

dis·pu·ta·tious (dis′pyoo tā′shəs) *also,* **dis·put′a·tive.** *adj.* given to disputing; contentious; argumentative. —**dis′pu·ta′tious·ly,** *adv.* —**dis′pu·ta′tious·ness,** *n.*

dis·pute (dis pūt′) -**put·ed, -put·ing.** *v.t.* **1.** to debate or quarrel about; discuss; argue: *The issue was disputed at the council meeting.* **2.** to deny or question, as the validity, accuracy, or existence of; express doubt or opposition to: *to dispute someone's authority, to dispute a claim. I won't dispute you on that point.* **3.** to compete for the possession of; strive or contend for. **4.** to oppose; resist. —*v.i.* to engage in argument, discussion, or debate: *The politicians disputed with each other on various issues.* —*n.* **1.** difference of opinion; argument or debate. **2.** quarrel. [Old French *desputer* to discuss, debate, quarrel, from Latin *disputāre* to examine, discuss.] —**dis·put′er,** *n.* —**Syn.** *v.t.* see **discuss** *v.t.* **1.** see **argument.**

dis·qual·i·fi·ca·tion (dis kwol′ə fi kā′shən) *n.* **1.** act of disqualifying; being disqualified. **2.** that which disqualifies.

dis·qual·i·fy (dis kwol′ə fī′) -**fied, -fy·ing.** *v.t.* **1.** to make unfit or

unqualified; incapacitate; disable: *Ill health disqualified him from military service.* **2.** to make or declare ineligible or unsuitable: *Her age disqualifies her for voting.* **3.** to bar from competition or deprive of a victory or award because of an infraction of rules: *The officials disqualified him from the race for knocking down another runner.*

dis·qui·et (dis kwī′it) *v.t.* to make uneasy, anxious, or restless; disturb; alarm: *The bad news disquieted him.* —*n.* lack of tranquility; uneasiness; anxiety; unrest.

dis·qui·et·ing (dis kwī′i ting) *adj.* causing disquiet; disturbing. —**dis·qui′et·ing·ly,** *adv.*

dis·qui·e·tude (dis kwī′i tōōd′, -tūd′) *n.* state of uneasiness or unrest; anxiety.

dis·qui·si·tion (dis kwə zish′ən) *n.* formal treatise or discourse; dissertation. [Latin *disquīsītiō* a search into, inquiry.]

Dis·rae·li, Benjamin (diz rā′lē) 1804–81, Earl of Beaconsfield, English statesman.

dis·re·gard (dis′ri gärd′) *v.t.* to pay no attention to; treat without due regard or respect; ignore: *We disregarded the gossip and rumors. He disregarded my feelings in this matter.* —*n.* lack of attention or due regard; neglect: *his disregard for the regulations.* —**Syn.** *v.t.* see **ignore.**

dis·rel·ish (dis rel′ish) *v.t.* to have a distaste for; dislike. —*n.* distaste; dislike.

dis·re·mem·ber (dis′ri mem′bər) *v.t., v.i.* Informal. to forget.

dis·re·pair (dis′ri pâr′) *n.* state of being in need of repairs: *The old house had fallen into disrepair.*

dis·rep·u·ta·ble (dis rep′yə tə bəl) *adj.* **1.** not in good repute; not reputable, respectable, or decent. **2.** not respectable in appearance; shabby: *a disreputable old jacket.* —**dis·rep′u·ta·ble·ness,** *n.* —**dis·rep′u·ta·bly,** *adv.*

dis·re·pute (dis′ri pūt′) *n.* lack or loss of reputation; ill repute; discredit; disfavor: *The old theory had fallen into disrepute.*

dis·re·spect (dis′ri spekt′) *n.* lack of respect, reverence, or courtesy: *to show disrespect for one's parents.*

dis·re·spect·ful (dis′ri spekt′fəl) *adj.* having or showing disrespect. —**dis′re·spect′ful·ly,** *adv.* —**dis′re·spect′ful·ness,** *n.*

dis·robe (dis rōb′) -**robed, -rob·ing.** *v.t., v.i.* to undress: *The tailor disrobed the mannequin. The girl disrobed quickly.*

dis·rupt (dis rupt′) *v.t.* **1.a.** to throw into disorder; upset: *His behavior disrupted the class.* **b.** to interrupt or impede the normal continuation of; cause to break down: *The tornado disrupted telephone communication.* **2.** to break or burst apart; split; rupture. [Latin *disruptus,* past participle of *disrumpere* to break into pieces.] —**dis·rupt′er,** *n.*

dis·rup·tion (dis rup′shən) *n.* **1.** act of disrupting; being disrupted. **2.** break; interruption.

dis·rup·tive (dis rup′tiv) *adj.* causing or tending to cause disruption: *a disruptive influence, disruptive interruptions.* —**dis·rup′tive·ly,** *adv.* —**dis·rup′tive·ness,** *n.*

dis·sat·is·fac·tion (dis′sat is fak′shən) *n.* **1.** condition or feeling of being dissatisfied; discontent. **2.** that which dissatisfies.

dis·sat·is·fac·to·ry (dis′sat is fak′tər ē) *adj.* not satisfying; causing discontent; unsatisfactory.

dis·sat·is·fied (dis sat′is fīd′) *adj.* **1.** not satisfied; displeased: *The dissatisfied stockholders criticized the company's management.* **2.** showing discontent or displeasure: *a dissatisfied look.*

dis·sat·is·fy (dis sat′is fī′) -**fied, -fy·ing.** *v.t.* to fail to satisfy; cause discontent to; disappoint; displease.

dis·sect (di sekt′, dī-) *v.t.* **1.** to cut apart or divide into parts, as for the purpose of study or scientific examination: *to dissect a frog.* **2.** to examine carefully and critically; analyze in great detail: *The teacher dissected the poem and explained it to the class.* [Latin *dissectus,* past participle of *dissecāre* to cut asunder.]

dis·sect·ed (di sek′tid, dī-) *adj.* **1.** cut apart or divided into parts. **2.** (of certain leaves) divided into many fine segments or lobes.

dis·sec·tion (di sek′shən, dī-) *n.* **1.** act of dissecting. **2.** that which has been dissected, as an animal being studied. **3.** detailed analysis or criticism.

dis·sec·tor (di sek′tər, dī-) *n.* **1.** one who dissects. **2.** instrument used in dissecting.

dis·sem·ble (di sem′bəl) -**bled, -bling.** *v.t.* **1.** to disguise or conceal the real nature of, as feelings or intentions: *He dissembled his excitement by acting bored.* **2.** to put on a false appearance of; pretend; feign: *The corrupt man dissembled virtue.* —*v.i.* to disguise or conceal, as one's true character, feelings, or intentions, by false pretense; act hypocritically. [Modification (influenced by *resemble*) of obsolete *dissimule,* from Old French *dissimuler* to hide one's thoughts, deny, from Latin *dissimulāre* to disguise.] —**dis·sem′bler,** *n.*

dis·sem·i·nate (di sem′ə nāt′) -**nat·ed, -nat·ing.** *v.t.* to scatter widely; spread abroad; diffuse: *to disseminate information.* [Latin *dissēminātus,* past participle of *dissēmināre* to scatter seed.] —**dis·sem′i·na′tion, dis·sem′i·na′tor,** *n.* —**Syn.** see **spread.**

dis·sen·sion (di sen′shən) *n.* difference of opinion or disagreement,

at; āpe; cär; end; mē; it; īce; hot; ōld; fôrk; wood; fōōl; oil; out; up; ūse; turn; sing; thin; this; zh in treasure; ə in ago, taken, pencil, lemon, circus.

often heated or angry; discord: *dissension in the ranks of an army.* —Syn. see **disagreement.**

dis·sent (di sent′) *v.i.* **1.** to differ in opinion or feeling; withhold approval; disagree (often with *from*): *Many people dissented from the policy of the government. Of the ten board members, only one dissented.* **2.** to refuse to conform to the rules, doctrines, or beliefs of an established church. —*n.* **1.** difference of opinion or feeling; disagreement. **2.** refusal to conform to rules, doctrines, or beliefs of an established church. [Latin *dissentīre* to disagree.]

dis·sent·er (di sen′tər) *n.* **1.** one who dissents. **2.** *also,* **Dissenter.** one who refuses to conform to the rules, doctrines, or beliefs of an established church, esp. the Church of England.

dis·sen·tient (di sen′shənt) *adj.* dissenting. —*n.* dissenter. —**dis·sen′tience,** *n.*

dis·sent·ing (di sen′ting) *adj.* expressing dissent: *a dissenting opinion.* —**dis·sent′ing·ly,** *adv.*

dis·sen·tious (di sen′shəs) *adj.* characterized by or inclined to dissension; quarrelsome.

dis·ser·ta·tion (dis′ər tā′shən) *n.* extended formal treatise or discourse upon a given subject, esp. one written for a doctoral degree; thesis. [Latin *dissertātiō* discourse.]

dis·ser·vice (di sur′vis) *n.* ill turn; harm; injury: *He unintentionally did them a disservice.*

dis·sev·er (di sev′ər) *v.t.* **1.** to sever; separate. **2.** to divide into parts. —*v.i.* to separate or part.

dis·si·dence (dis′ə dəns) *n.* dissent; disagreement.

dis·si·dent (dis′ə dənt) *adj.* dissenting; disagreeing: *dissident views on an issue.* —*n.* one who disagrees; dissenter. [Latin *dissidēns,* present participle of *dissidēre* to sit apart, disagree.]

dis·sim·i·lar (dis′ə lər) *adj.* not similar or alike; different. —**dis·sim′i·lar·ly,** *adv.*

dis·sim·i·lar·i·ty (dis′ə lar′ə tē) *pl.,* **-ties.** *n.* **1.** lack of similarity; difference. **2.** instance of this; point of difference.

dis·si·mil·i·tude (dis′si mil′ə tōōd′, -tūd′) *n.* dissimilarity; difference.

dis·sim·u·late (di sim′yə lāt′) **-lat·ed, -lat·ing.** *v.t., v.i.* to disguise or conceal (one's feelings or intentions) by pretense; dissemble. [Latin *dissimulātus,* past participle of *dissimulāre* to disguise, hide.] —**dis·sim′u·la′tion, dis·sim′u·la′tor,** *n.*

dis·si·pate (dis′ə pāt′) **-pat·ed, -pat·ing.** *v.t.* **1.** to disperse or drive away; scatter; dispel: *illusions dissipated by reasoning.* **2.** to expend wastefully or foolishly; fritter away; squander: *In three years he dissipated the family fortune.* —*v.i.* **1.** to become dispersed or scattered; be dispelled: *By noon the mist had dissipated.* **2.** to indulge in dissolute or extravagant pleasures. [Latin *dissipātus,* past participle of *dissipāre* to scatter, squander.]

dis·si·pat·ed (dis′ə pā′tid) *adj.* given to or characterized by indulgence in dissolute or extravagant pleasures; intemperate. **2.** scattered; wasted; squandered.

dis·si·pa·tion (dis′ə pā′shən) *n.* **1.** act of dissipating; being dissipated. **2.** excessive indulgence in dissolute or extravagant pleasures; intemperance.

dis·so·ci·ate (di sō′sē āt′, -shē-) **-at·ed, -at·ing.** *v.t.* **1.** to break the association or connection between; regard as separate or distinct: *He dissociated the two concepts in his mind.* **2.** to disassociate. **3.** to subject to dissociation. —*v.i.* to undergo dissociation. [Latin *dissociātus,* past participle of *dissociāre* to disunite.] —**dis·so′ci·a′tive,** *adj.*

dis·so·ci·a·tion (di sō′sē ā′shən, -shē-) *n.* **1.** act of dissociating; being dissociated. **2.** *Chemistry.* **a.** decomposition of a substance into its constituent substances by some change in physical conditions, as heating, usually accompanied by a reverse change that produces small amounts of the original substance. **b.** decomposition of the molecules of an electrolyte into ions, usually accompanied by some recombination of ions into molecules. **3.** *Psychology.* separation or process of separation of an idea or feeling from the main body of consciousness.

dis·sol·u·ble (di sol′yə bəl) *adj.* capable of being dissolved. —**dis·sol′u·bil′i·ty, dis·sol′u·ble·ness,** *n.*

dis·so·lute (dis′ə lōōt′) *adj.* showing or characterized by lack of moral restraints; wanton; debauched: *a dissolute young man, a dissolute life.* [Latin *dissolūtus* loose, past participle of *dissolvere* to loosen.] —**dis′so·lute′ly,** *adv.* —**dis′so·lute′ness,** *n.*

dis·so·lu·tion (dis′ə lōō′shən) *n.* **1.** act of dissolving; being dissolved. **2.** separation into parts; disintegration. **3.** a breaking up; termination. **4.** separation of soul and body; death.

dis·solve (di zolv′) **-solved, -solv·ing.** *v.t.* **1.** to cause to pass into solution: *He dissolved the sugar in water.* **2.** to separate into parts; disintegrate. **3.** to put an end to; terminate: *to dissolve a partnership.* **4.** to cause to break up, disperse, or disappear. **5.** *Law.* to destroy the binding power, authority, or force of; set aside; annul, as a marriage or injunction. —*v.i.* **1.** to pass into solution: *Salt dissolves in water.* **2.** to dwindle or disappear gradually; fade away: *His prospects for win-*

ning the elections were dissolving rapidly. **3.** to come to an end; terminate. **4.** to break up; disperse. **5.** to be overcome or emotionally moved: *to dissolve in tears.* **6.** to lessen the brightness of a motion-picture or television image gradually until the screen goes black or until a succeeding image appears. —*n.* in motion pictures or television, an act or instance of dissolving. [Latin *dissolvere* to loosen, separate, disunite.] —**dis·solv′a·ble,** *adj.* —**dis·solv′er,** *n.*

dis·so·nance (dis′ə nəns) *n.* **1.** harsh, unpleasant, or inharmonious sound or combination of sounds. **2.** lack of harmony or agreement; incongruity; disagreement. **3.** *Music.* inharmonious blending of tones that seem to be incomplete and require resolution. Distinguished from **consonance.** Also, **dis′so·nan·cy.**

dis·so·nant (dis′ə nənt) *adj.* **1.** harsh or unpleasant in sound; inharmonious. **2.** lacking harmony or agreement; at variance; incongruous: *dissonant views on a subject.* **3.** *Music.* marked by or containing a dissonance. [Latin *dissonāns,* present participle of *dissonāre* to disagree in sound, differ.]

dis·suade (di swād′) **-suad·ed, -suad·ing.** *v.t.* to deter (someone), as from an action or intention, by persuasion or advice: *He dissuaded her from leaving the club.* [Latin *dissuādēre* to advise against.]

dis·sua·sion (di swā′zhən) *n.* act, fact, or process of dissuading.

dis·sua·sive (di swā′siv) *adj.* tending or intended to dissuade. —**dis·sua′sive·ly,** *adv.* —**dis·sua′sive·ness,** *n.*

dis·syl·la·ble (di sil′ə bəl, dis′sil′-, dī′sil′-) *also,* **di·syl·la·ble** (dī′sil′ə bəl, di·sil′-). *n.* word consisting of two syllables, as *pony* or *amen.* [DI-¹ + SYLLABLE.] —**dis′syl·lab′ic,** *adj.*

dist. 1. distance. **2.** district.

dis·taff (dis′taf) *n.* **1.** stick used for spinning, usually cleft at one end, on which wool, flax, cotton, or other fibers are held and from which they are drawn off and twisted into thread by hand onto a spindle. **2.** woman's work, concerns, or domain. **3.** women in general; the female sex. —*adj.* of, relating to, or characteristic of a woman; female. [Old English *dīstæf* stick for spinning.]

Distaff

Spindle

Distaff

distaff side, maternal branch or female side of a family. Distinguished from **spear side.**

dis·tain (di stān′) *v.t. Archaic.* **1.** to discolor; stain; dye. **2.** to dishonor; disgrace; sully. [Old French *desteindre* to remove the color from, going back to Latin *dis-* apart + *tingere* to dye.]

dis·tal (dis′təl) *adj.* located away from the place or point of attachment or origin, as a limb or bone. Distinguished from **proximal.** [DIST(ANT) + -AL¹.]

dis·tance (dis′təns) *n.* **1.** extent of space, esp. between any two points or objects: *to walk a distance of three miles. They followed us down the road for a distance.* *Astronomers can measure the distance of the moon from the earth. The distance from my house to school is two blocks.* **2.** far off point or place; remote region or position: *to view something at a distance. We saw a car in the distance.* **3.** quality, state, or fact of being distant; remoteness: *'Tis distance lends enchantment to the view* (Campbell, 1799). **4.** extent of separation in time. **5.** lack of friendliness or familiarity; coolness of manner; aloofness; reserve. —*v.t.,* **-tanced, -tanc·ing. 1.** to leave far behind, as in a race; outdistance. **2.** to place or hold at a distance.

dis·tant (dis′tənt) *adj.* **1.** far away or apart in space: *a distant land, a distant planet. The highway is eight miles distant from our house.* **2.** far away or off in time: *distant centuries, the distant past.* **3.** to, at, or from a distance: *a distant rumble of thunder.* **4.** far apart or remote, as in relationship, connection, or degree: *a distant cousin, a distant resemblance, a distant hope.* **5.** not friendly or familiar; cool in manner; aloof; reserved: *She's been very distant toward me since our argument.* [Latin *distāns,* present participle of *distāre* to stand apart.] —**dis′tant·ly,** *adv.*

dis·taste (dis′tāst′) *n.* lack of taste, liking, or affinity (for something); dislike; disinclination: *a distaste for spinach, to have a distaste for hard work.* —Syn. see **dislike.**

dis·taste·ful (dis tāst′fəl) *adj.* causing dislike; unpleasant; disagreeable; offensive. —**dis·taste′ful·ly,** *adv.* —**dis·taste′ful·ness,** *n.*

dis·tem·per¹ (dis tem′pər) *n.* **1.** highly contagious virus disease of dogs and certain other mammals, characterized by fever, watery discharges from the nose and eyes, lack of appetite, and loss of strength. **2.** any of various other animal diseases with similar symptoms. **3.** *Archaic.* mental or physical disorder or sickness; ailment. **4.** *Archaic.* disturbance or disorder, esp. of a political or civil nature. —*v.t. Archaic.* **1.** to upset or unbalance the functions of; throw out of order; disorder. **2.** to disturb; confuse; ruffle. [Late Latin *distemperāre* to put out of

at; āpe; cär; end; mē; it; īce; hot; ōld; fôrk; wood; fōōl; oil; out; up; ūse; turn; sing; thin; this; zh in treasure; ə in ago, taken, pencil, lemon, circus.

295

order, mix badly, from Latin *dis-* apart + *temperāre* to mix in proper proportion, regulate.]

dis·tem·per² (dis tem′pər) *n.* **1.** painting medium prepared by mixing pigments with a glutinous medium, as egg yolks or glue, used primarily for scene painting or mural decoration. **2.** art or method of painting with this medium. **3.** painting done in this medium. —*v.t.* to paint in or with distemper. [Old French *destemper* to soak, mix, going back to Latin *dis-* completely + *temperāre* to mix in proper proportion.]

dis·tem·per·a·ture (dis tem′pər ə chər) *n.* *Archaic.* disordered condition, esp. of the mind or body.

dis·tend (dis tend′) *v.t.* to enlarge by or as by pressure from within; stretch out; swell; expand: *Water pressure had distended the weak spot in the hose.* —*v.i.* to become distended; swell: *His stomach distended during the course of his illness.* [Latin *distendere* to stretch out, swell out.] —**Syn.** *v.i.* see **expand.**

dis·ten·si·ble (dis ten′sə bəl) *adj.* capable of being distended. —**dis·ten′si·bil′i·ty,** *n.*

dis·ten·tion (dis ten′shən) *also,* **dis·ten·sion.** *n.* act of distending; being distended.

dis·tich (dis′tik) *n.* two lines of verse, often rhymed, usually expressing a complete thought; couplet. [Latin *distichon,* from Greek *distichon.*]

dis·till (dis til′) -tilled, -till·ing, *also, British.* **dis·til.** *v.t.* **1.** to heat (a liquid or other substance) until evaporation takes place and then condense the vapor given off, as for purification or concentration: *to distill water.* **2.** to extract, produce, or purify by distilling: *to distill whiskey, to distill alcohol from grain.* **3.** to obtain, as if by distilling; extract the essence of: *to distill wisdom from experience, to distill a moral from a story.* **4.** to give forth or let fall in drops. —*v.i.* **1.** to undergo distillation. **2.** to fall or exude in drops; trickle. [Latin *distillāre* to drip, going back to *dē* down + *stilla* a drop; because during distillation cooled vapors fall as drops into a container.]

dis·til·late (dist′l it, -āt′, di stil′it) *n.* **1.** product obtained by distillation; liquid condensed from vapor during distillation. **2.** any concentration, essence, or abstraction.

dis·til·la·tion (dist′əl ā′shən) *n.* **1.** act or process of separating the more volatile parts of a liquid or other substance from those less volatile by heating until evaporation takes place and then condensing the vapor thus produced. **2.** distillate (def. 1). **3.** act of distilling; being distilled. **4.** essential or concentrated quality of something; extract; essence.

Distillation

dis·tilled (dis tild′) *adj.* obtained, produced, or purified by distilling.

dis·till·er (dis til′ər) *n.* **1.** one who or that which distills. **2.** person or corporation that makes distilled liquors, as rye, bourbon, or vodka.

dis·till·er·y (dis til′ər ē) *pl.,* -er·ies. *n.* place where distilling is performed, esp. an industrial plant where distilled liquors are made.

dis·tinct (dis tingkt′) *adj.* **1.** not identical; separate: *The twins had distinct personalities.* **2.** different in quality or kind: *The Spanish temperament is distinct from that of the Portuguese.* **3.** clearly perceptible; clear; plain: *The sound of the drums was distinct even from a distance.* **4.** unquestionable; definite: *a distinct improvement.* [Latin *distinctus,* past participle of *distinguere* to distinguish.] —**dis·tinct′ness,** *n.*

dis·tinc·tion (dis tingk′shən) *n.* **1.** act of making or noting a difference: *to make a distinction between fiction and nonfiction.* **2.** condition or quality of being distinct; difference: *The distinction between the two arguments is not clear.* **3.** distinguishing mark or characteristic: *Toby has the distinction of being the tallest boy in the class.* **4.** quality that merits special recognition; excellence: *acts of distinction, to write with distinction.* **5.** mark or symbol of special recognition or honor.

dis·tinc·tive (dis tingk′tiv) *adj.* serving to distinguish or having a distinguishing quality; characteristic: *the distinctive scent of roses.* —**dis·tinc′tive·ly,** *adv.* —**dis·tinc′tive·ness,** *n.*

dis·tinct·ly (dis tingkt′lē) *adv.* **1.** in a distinct manner; clearly; plainly. **2.** unquestionably; definitely.

dis·tin·gué (dēs′tang gā′, dis tang′gā) *adj.* having a distinguished appearance or manner. [French *distingué,* past participle of *distinguer* to separate, honor, from Latin *distinguere* to distinguish.]

dis·tin·guish (dis ting′gwish) *v.t.* **1.** to recognize or indicate as different; differentiate: *to distinguish gold from brass.* **2.** to be a distinctive characteristic or quality of; characterize: *Brilliant red plumage distinguishes the male cardinal from the female.* **3.** to perceive clearly; discern: *We could see three men approaching but could not distinguish their*

faces. **4.** to separate into categories; classify. **5.** to make prominent or worthy of special recognition: *Martin Luther King distinguished himself as a nonviolent civil rights leader.* ▲ usually used in the reflexive in def. 5. —*v.i.* to recognize or indicate a difference; differentiate (usually with *between* or *among*): *to distinguish between a genuine signature and a forgery.* [Latin *distinguere* to separate.] —**dis·tin′guish·a·ble,** *adj.* —**dis·tin′guish·a·bly,** *adv.* —**Syn.** *v.t.* **3.** see **discern.**

dis·tin·guished (dis ting′gwisht) *adj.* **1.** marked or characterized by excellence; celebrated; eminent: *a distinguished statesman.* **2.** having an air of distinction; dignified. —**Syn. 1.** see **illustrious.**

dis·tort (dis tôrt′) *v.t.* **1.** to twist or bend out of shape; change the natural or usual form of: *The curved mirror distorted Bobby's image.* **2.** to misrepresent, as statements, facts, or meaning: *The editor distorted the author's meaning when he rewrote the sentence.* [Latin *distortus,* past participle of *distorquēre* to twist.]

dis·tor·tion (dis tôr′shən) *n.* **1.** act of distorting. **2.** state of being distorted. **3.** anything that is distorted.

dis·tract (dis trakt′) *v.t.* **1.** to cause (the mind or attention) to be turned away; divert: *Noise distracted the writer from his work.* **2.** to turn (the mind) in different or conflicting directions at once; unsettle; confuse: *A barrage of questions from customers distracted the new salesgirl.* **3.** to disturb or agitate the mind of: *Worry about her soldier son distracted the mother.* [Latin *distractus,* past participle of *distrahere* to pull apart, perplex.] —**dis·tract′ed·ly, dis·tract′ing·ly,** *adv.*

dis·trac·tion (dis trak′shən) *n.* **1.** act of turning away, as the mind or attention. **2.** that which draws away the mind or attention. **3.** that which diverts and relieves the mind; amusement. **4.** emotional agitation or disturbance.

dis·trait (dis trā′) *adj.* absent-minded; inattentive. [French *distrait,* past participle of *distraire* to distract, from Latin *distrahere* to pull apart, perplex.]

dis·traught (dis trôt′) *adj.* **1.** mentally confused or bewildered; distracted: *Indecision made him distraught.* **2.** crazed. [Modification of obsolete *distract* distracted, from Latin *distractus,* past participle of *distrahere* to pull apart, perplex.]

dis·tress (dis tres′) *n.* **1.** suffering of body or mind; anxiety; grief. **2.** dangerous condition marked by extreme or desperate need: *The besieged people were rescued from their distress.* —*v.t.* to cause pain, anxiety, grief, or suffering to; afflict: *The bad news from home distressed him.* [Old French *destrece* misfortune, anguish, going back to Latin *districtus,* past participle of *distringere* to draw asunder.] —**dis·tress′ing·ly,** *adv.*

Syn. *n.* **1. Distress, affliction, misery, suffering** indicate trouble affecting one physically or emotionally. **Distress** suggests physical or mental stress, causing considerable discomfort and continuing for some time but capable of being relieved: *A long automobile trip causes her great distress.* **Affliction** means suffering of body or of mind of some duration, usually with the implication that it is imposed as punishment or trial: *In commemoration of their hard sojourn in Egypt, the Jews call the unleavened Passover bread the bread of affliction.* **Misery** refers to circumstances of extreme hardship and often chronic distress: *The cyclone brought misery to thousands of people.* **Suffering** suggests constant, continuing pain or hardship: *UNESCO works to relieve the suffering of children throughout the world.* —*v.t.* see **trouble.**

dis·tress·ful (dis tres′fəl) *adj.* **1.** causing or bringing distress; painful. **2.** feeling or expressing distress. —**dis·tress′ful·ly,** *adv.*

dis·trib·ute (dis trib′ūt) -ut·ed, -ut·ing. *v.t.* **1.** to separate and give out in shares; deal out: *to distribute clothing to the flood victims, to distribute pamphlets.* **2.** to scatter or spread out, as over an area or surface: *to distribute seed over plowed land.* **3.** to divide and arrange according to a classification or function. [Latin *distribūtus,* past participle of *distribuere* to divide.]

Syn. 1. Distribute, dispense, deal¹ mean to divide and give out in shares. **Distribute** suggests separating some amount, equally or unequally, according to plan, and then giving out these portions: *The foreman distributed the work every morning.* **Dispense** stresses those who receive what is given out by plan: *Medical supplies were dispensed only to those who obviously needed them.* **Deal** suggests piecemeal delivery of rather limited portions: *Ammunition was dealt out to those squads actually on the firing line.*

dis·tri·bu·tion (dis′trə bū′shən) *n.* **1.** act of distributing; being distributed. **2.** manner in which something is distributed: *an even distribution of color on the canvas.* **3.** that which is distributed. **4.** *Economics.* allocation of goods and income of a society among the members of the society. **5.** system or process of distributing produce or commodities to distributors or consumers.

dis·trib·u·tive (dis′trib′yə tiv) *adj.* **1.** of or relating to distribution. **2.** *Grammar.* referring to each member of a group considered individually. *Each* and *every* are distributive adjectives. —*n.* distributive word or expression. —**dis·trib′u·tive·ly,** *adv.*

distributive law *Mathematics.* law which states that the product of a

compound expression and a factor, as $x\ (y\ +\ z)$. remains the same whether one takes the sum of the individual products $xy\ +\ xz$. or first takes the sum of y and z. and then multiplies by x: $3\ (4\ +\ 5) = 3\ \times\ 4\ +\ 3\ \times\ 5 = 3\ \times\ 9$.

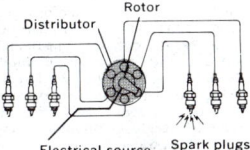

Distributor · Rotor · Electrical source · Spark plugs

Distributor

dis·trib·u·tor (dis trib′yə tər) *n.* **1.** one who or that which distributes. **2.** person or company that sells produce or commodities, usually of a particular type, to retailers or consumers. **3.** device that distributes electric current to the spark plugs of a gasoline engine so that they fire in proper sequence.

dis·trict (dis′trikt) *n.* **1.** territorial division, as of a country, state, or city, marked off for a special purpose: *a school district, an election district.* **2.** region or locality having a particular characteristic: *the poorer districts of the city.* —*v.t.* to divide or organize into districts. [Late Latin *districtus* territory in which a lord may exercise power, from Latin *distringere* to draw asunder.]

district attorney, lawyer who serves as a prosecutor for a federal or state judicial district.

District of Columbia, federal district in the eastern United States between Maryland and Virginia, coextensive with the city of Washington, the capital of the United States. It is conventionally known as Washington, D.C. Area, 69 sq. mi. Pop. (1970), 756,510. Abbreviation, D.C.

dis·trust (dis trust′) *v.t.* to have no trust or confidence in; be suspicious of; doubt. —*n.* lack of trust or confidence; suspicion; doubt.

dis·trust·ful (dis trust′fəl) *adj.* having or showing distrust; suspicious; doubtful: *distrustful of slogans, a distrustful nature.* —**dis·trust′ful·ly,** *adv.* —**dis·trust′ful·ness,** *n.*

dis·turb (dis turb′) *v.t.* **1.** to agitate the mind of; make uneasy or anxious: *The bad news disturbed him.* **2.** to interrupt; break in upon; bother: *Don't disturb me while I am working.* **3.** to destroy or interfere with the peace or tranquility of: *riots disturbing the country.* **4.** to upset the order or arrangement of, as by moving out of position: *The child disturbed the flower arrangement.* **5.** to inconvenience. [Latin *disturbāre* to drive asunder, throw into confusion.] —**dis·turb′er,** *n.*

Syn. 1. Disturb, agitate, perturb, upset mean to put into an unsettled or disordered state of mind. **Disturb** suggests hindrance of normal functioning and resulting difficulties: *The dream so disturbed him that he could not sleep.* **Agitate** implies a stirring up to the point where physical action betrays inner turmoil: *His rudeness continued to agitate her and her hand trembled as she lifted her notebook.* **Perturb** suggests deeply felt alarm: *Thoroughly perturbed by the threat, he nevertheless contrived to look calm.* **Upset** implies a physical reaction accompanying emotional distress so that one's actions seem out of the ordinary: *The news upset her so much that she wept uncontrollably.*

dis·turb·ance (dis tur′bəns) *n.* **1.** act of disturbing; being disturbed. **2.** that which disturbs. **3.** commotion or tumult, esp. a public disorder: *He went to see what the disturbance was about.* **4.** mental agitation or uneasiness; anxiety.

di·sul·fide (dī sul′fīd) *n.* compound in which two atoms of sulfur are combined with another atom or radical.

dis·un·ion (dis ūn′yən) *n.* **1.** a breaking apart; severance; separation. **2.** lack of agreement or unity; dissension; discord.

dis·u·nite (dis′ū nīt′) *v.t.* **1.** to break the union of; sever; separate. **2.** to cause dissension between; alienate. —*v.i.* to come apart; become separate.

dis·u·ni·ty (dis ū′nə tē) *n.* lack of unity; disunion; dissension.

dis·use (*n.*, dis ūs′; *v.*, dis ūz′) *n.* condition or state of not being used or practiced: *a custom fallen into disuse.* —*v.t.* **-used, -us·ing.** to use no longer.

ditch (dich) *n.* **1.** long, narrow hole dug in the ground, usually used for drainage, irrigation, or protection; trench. —*v.t.* **1.** to land (a disabled aircraft) on water and abandon it. **2.a.** to throw into a ditch. **b.** to derail (a train). **3.** to dig a ditch in or around. **4.** *Slang.* to get rid of; get away from: *She ditched him. He ditched the police.* —*v.i.* to land a disabled aircraft on water and abandon it: *We had to ditch.* [Old English *dīc* dike.]

dith·er (dith′ər) *n.* state of nervous excitement, agitation, or confusion: *The news threw her into a dither.* —*v.i.* to be in a dither. [Form of dialectal English *didder* to shake; probably imitative.]

dith·y·ramb (dith′i ram′, -ramb′) *n.* **1.** in ancient Greece, wild, boisterous choric hymn or chant sung in honor of Dionysus. **2.** boisterous, enthusiastic, or emotional writing or speech. [Latin *dīthyrambus* the ancient Greek hymn, from Greek *dīthyrambos.*]

dith·y·ram·bic (dith′ə ram′bik) *adj.* **1.** of or like a dithyramb. **2.** wildly emotional or enthusiastic.

dit·to (dit′ō) *pl.* **-tos.** *n.* **1.** the same (as appeared or was mentioned before or above), often symbolized by ditto marks. **2.** ditto mark. **3.** copy; duplicate. —*v.t.* **-toed, -to·ing.** to duplicate or repeat: *to ditto a copy of the agreement.* —*adv.* as before; likewise. —*interj.* the same; agreed. [Dialectal Italian *ditto* (thing) said, past participle of *dire* to say, from Latin *dīcere.*]

ditto mark, one of a pair of small marks (″) placed under something written or printed to indicate that it is to be repeated.

dit·ty (dit′ē) *pl.* **-ties.** *n.* short, light song. [Old French *ditie* kind of poem, from Latin *dictātum* (thing) dictated, from *dictāre* to say often, dictate.]

ditty bag, small bag used by sailors to hold small items, as needles, thread, and buttons. [Possibly from obsolete *dutty* coarse calico, probably from Hindi *dhōtī* loincloth.]

ditty box, small box used like a ditty bag.

di·u·ret·ic (dī′yə ret′ik) *adj.* causing an increase in the secretion of urine excreted by the kidneys. —*n.* diuretic medicine. [Late Latin *diurēticus* that promotes urine, from Greek *diourētikos,* going back to *dia* through + *ouron* urine.]

di·ur·nal (dī urn′əl) *adj.* **1.** occurring or performed every day; daily: *the diurnal rotation of the earth.* **2.** of or occurring during the daytime: *diurnal noises.* **3.** more active during the day than at night: *a diurnal animal.* **4.** (of a flower) opening during the day and closing at night. **5.** lasting only one day. [Latin *diurnālis* daily, going back to *diēs* day. Doublet of JOURNAL.]

di·ur·nal·ly (dī urn′əl ē) *adv.* every day; daily.

div. **1.** divided. **2.** dividend. **3.** division; divisor. **4.** divorced.

di·va (dē′və) *pl.* **-vas.** *n.* famous female opera singer; prima donna. [Italian *diva,* from Latin *dīva* goddess; because of the exalted position of opera singers in Italy.]

di·va·gate (dī′və gāt′) **-gat·ed, -gat·ing.** *v.i.* **1.** to wander about; stray. **2.** to digress, as in speech. [Latin *dīvagātus,* past participle of *dīvagārī* to wander about.] —**di′va·ga′tion,** *n.*

di·va·lent (dī vā′lənt) *adj.* bivalent.

di·van (di van′, -vän′, dī′van) *n.* **1.** long, low upholstered couch or sofa, usually having no back or arms. **2.a.** formerly, court or council of state in Turkey and some other Middle Eastern countries. **b.** room where such a court or council convened. **3.** smoking room. [Turkish *dīvān* council of state (that met in a chamber with a long couch along the walls), from Persian *dīvān* council of state, royal court.]

dive (dīv) **dived** or **dove, dived, div·ing.** *v.i.* **1.a.** to plunge headfirst, as into water. **b.** to go down underwater: *The men dived for pearls.* **2.** (of an airplane) to descend rapidly at a steep angle. **3.** to dash, leap, or drop suddenly and quickly, esp. headfirst downward: *to dive into a doorway, to dive for a gun, to dive under the covers.* **4.** to enter into or become deeply involved in something: *Walter dove into the thick of the activities.* —*v.t.* to send (an airplane) into a dive. —*n.* **1.a.** headfirst plunge, as into water. **b.** downward movement underwater: *The submarine made a dive for the bottom.* **2.** (of an airplane) steep, rapid descent. **3.** any rapid or headlong dash, leap, or drop. **4.** *Informal.* cheap, disreputable place, as for drinking or gambling. [Old English *dȳfan* to immerse, dip.]

dive bomber, fighter plane equipped to carry one or more bombs that are usually released at the low point of a steep dive.

div·er (dī′vər) *n.* **1.** one who dives into water, esp. one who takes part in diving competitions. **2.** one whose job involves going underwater, as for pearls, exploration, or salvage work. **3.** any of various diving birds, as the loon.

di·verge (di vurj′, dī-) **-verged, -verg·ing.** *v.i.* **1.** to move or extend in different directions from a common point or from each other; draw apart; branch out: *The rays of light diverged.* **2.** to differ, as in character, form, or opinion: *The dialects seem to diverge completely.* **3.** to turn aside or deviate, as from a course, line of thought, or norm: *to diverge from the truth.* —*v.t.* to cause to diverge. [Modern Latin *dīvergere* to go in different directions, from Latin *dis-* apart + *vergere* to bend.]

Syn. *v.i.* **1.** Diverge, depart, deviate, digress mean to turn from a course. **Diverge** suggests a branching of the original course so that a decision must be made between alternatives that separate widely: *After graduation, their careers diverged.* **Depart** implies an alternative that leads away from the beaten track: *The new show departs from the normal pattern of the musical comedy.* **Deviate** suggests a turning away from the expected or the normal: *If he deviates from the method he was taught, his chances of succeeding are slight.* **Digress** implies a side issue or detour that is examined before returning to the route or subject, specifically in speech or writing: *He digressed several times from his prepared remarks.*

di·ver·gence (di vur′jəns, dī-) *n.* **1.** act of diverging; being diverged. **2.** difference, as of opinion. **3.** a turning aside or deviation, as from a norm.

di·ver·gen·cy (di vur′jən sē, dī-) *pl.* **-cies.** *n.* divergence.

di·ver·gent (di vur′jənt, dī-) *adj.* **1.** moving or extending in different

directions; diverging. **2.** differing, as in opinion. **3.** deviating, as from a norm. —**di·ver′gent·ly,** *adv.* —*Syn.* **2.** see **different.**

diverging lens *n.* lens that is thinner in the middle than at the edges. These lenses form virtual images rather than real images.

di·vers (dī′vərz) *adj.* various; several. [Old French *divers* differing, various, from Latin *dīversus.*]

di·verse (di vurs′, dī-) *adj.* **1.** markedly different; unlike. **2.** varied; diversified: the *diverse nature of pleasure.* [Form of DI-VERS.] —**di·verse′ly,** *adv.* —**di·verse′-ness,** *n.* —*Syn.* **1.** see **different.**

Diverging lenses

di·ver·si·fi·ca·tion (di vur′sə fi kā′-shən, dī-) *n.* act of diversifying; being diversified.

di·ver·si·fy (di vur′sə fī′, dī-) -**fied,** -**fy·ing.** *v.t.* **1.** to make diverse; give variety to; vary. **2.** to make or distribute (investments) among various types of securities. —*v.i.* to invest or deal in various lines or products. [Medieval Latin *diversificare* to make unlike, from Latin *diversus* different + *facere* to make.]

di·ver·sion (di vur′zhən, dī-) *n.* **1.** act of diverting; being diverted: *The diversion of a stream.* **2.** distraction of attention: *to create a diversion.* **3.** something that distracts the attention; amusement; entertainment; pastime: *His favorite diversion was music.* **4.** an attack or action intended to draw the enemy away from the main point of operation. —*Syn.* **3.** see **amusement.**

di·ver·sion·ar·y (di vur′zhə ner′ē, dī-) *adj.* of or relating to a diversion, esp. serving to distract the enemy: *diversionary tactics.*

di·ver·si·ty (di vur′sə tē, dī-) *pl.* -**ties. 1.** condition, quality, or instance of being diverse. **2.** variety; multiformity: *diversity of opinion.* —*Syn.* **2.** see **variety.**

di·vert (di vurt′, dī-) *v.t.* **1.** to turn aside; change the direction or course of; deflect: *to divert traffic, to divert funds.* **2.** to distract the attention of. **3.** to amuse; entertain. [Middle French *divertir* to alter, avert, amuse, from Latin *divertere* to separate, turn in different ways.]

di·ver·tic·u·lum (dī′vər tik′yə ləm) *pl.* -**la** (-lə). *n.* pouch or sac opening out from a hollow organ, as the intestine. [Latin *dīverticulum* bypass, bypath.]

di·ver·ti·men·to (di vur′tə men′tō) *pl.* -**ti** (-tē) or -**tos.** *n.* instrumental musical composition, usually of a light character, consisting of several short movements. [Italian *divertimento* amusement, going back to French *divertir* to amuse. See DIVERT.]

di·ver·tisse·ment (di vur′tis mənt; *French* dē ver tēs män′) *n.* **1.** diversion; entertainment. **2.** short ballet or other entertainment, usually performed during the course of a longer work, as an opera or full length ballet. **3.** *Music.* divertimento. [French *divertissement,* from *divertir* to amuse. See DIVERT.]

di·vest (di vest′, dī-) *v.t.* **1.** to deprive or dispossess (someone), as of rights, authority, or possessions. **2.** to rid or free (oneself): *He divested himself of all responsibility.* **3.** to strip, as of clothing. [Medieval Latin *divestire* to undress, going back to Latin *dis-* apart + *vestīre* to clothe.]

di·vide (di vīd′) -**vid·ed,** -**vid·ing.** *v.t.* **1.** to separate into parts or pieces, as by cutting; split up: *to divide an orange.* **2.** to separate into parts or pieces and distribute; share: *to divide profits among shareholders.* **3.** to make or cause to be separate or apart by or as by a boundary or partition: *The fence divides their land from ours.* **4.** to separate or arrange into groups or categories; classify: *The children were divided according to reading level.* **5.** to separate into opposing sides or opinions; cause dissension in or between; disunite. **6.** *Mathematics.* **a.** to perform the operation of a division on. **b.** to be an exact divisor of. —*v.i.* **1.** to become separated into parts; branch. **2.** to become disunited; disagree. **3.** to perform mathematical division. **4.** to vote by separating into two groups, as by standing up or forming two lines. —*n.* ridge or other land elevation separating two regions drained by different river systems; watershed. [Latin *dīvidere* to separate.]

di·vid·ed (di vī′did) *adj.* **1.** separated into parts or pieces: *minutely divided particles.* **2.** disunited, as by conflicting interests or opinions; disagreeing. **3.** shared; distributed: *a divided allegiance.* **4.** *Botany.* separated to the base or the midrib or deeply indented so as to form distinct segments, as certain leaves.

div·i·dend (div′ə dend′, -dənd) *n.* **1.** number or quantity that is to be divided by another. In dividing 15 by 3, the dividend is 15. **2.** net earnings of a corporation for any given period of time, paid to the stockholders and representing their share of the profits of the business. **3.** portion of such earnings given to each stockholder, usually in the form of money, according to the amount and kind of stock owned. [Latin *dīvidendum* thing to be divided, from *dīvidere* to separate.]

di·vid·er (di vī′dər) *n.* **1.** one who or that which divides. **2.** dividers, instrument for measuring and marking distances; compass.

div·i·na·tion (div′ə nā′shən) *n.* **1.** art or practice of foretelling the future or discovering that which is hidden or unknown, as by occult means. **2.** act of divining. **3.** that which is divined; a prophecy or guess.

di·vine (di vīn′) *adj.* **1.** of or relating to God or a god: *divine will.* **2.** given by or coming from God or a god: *divine forgiveness.* **3.** addressed or devoted to God or a god; sacred; religious: *divine worship.* **4.** mirroring the nature or characteristics of God or a god; heavenly: *divine beauty.* **5.** having superhuman qualities; supremely excellent or gifted: *the divine Homer.* **6.** *Informal.* **a.** extremely pleasurable or delightful. **b.** very attractive; lovely. —*v.t.* -**vined,** -**vin·ing. 1.** to foretell or foresee (the future) or discover (something hidden or unknown), as by occult means. **2.** to conjecture or perceive by insight or intuition; guess. **3.** to discover, as water, by using a divining rod. —*v.i.* **1.** to practice divination; prophesy. **2.** to conjecture; guess. —*n.* **1.** clergyman. ▲ often used pejoratively. **2.** theologian. [Latin *dīvīnus* relating to a deity, prophet, from *dīvus* godlike, god.] —**di·vine′ly,** *adv.* —**di·vine′ness,** *n.* **di·vin′er,** *n.*

divine right of kings, doctrine that monarchs derive their authority from God and are accountable only to Him.

diving bell, large, hollow watertight container open at the bottom and filled with compressed air, used for work under water.

diving board, flexible board fastened at one end and extending over water, upon which a diver jumps to gain momentum in executing a dive.

diving suit, suit with a helmet used for working under water. It is usually waterproof and is supplied with air through tubes from the surface or from portable tanks worn by the diver.

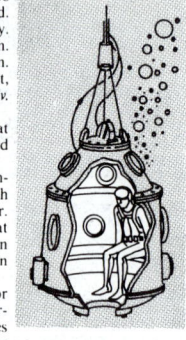

Diving bell

divining rod, forked branch or stick supposedly able to indicate underground water or minerals by bending downward when held at the ends.

di·vin·i·ty (di vin′ə tē) *pl.* -**ties.** *n.* **1.** state or quality of being God or a god: *the divinity of Christ.* **2.** godlike nature, esp. supreme excellence: *To lift the woman's fall'n divinity . . .* (Tennyson, 1847). **3.** divine being; deity; god. **4.** theology. **5.** soft, creamy candy made of sugar, egg whites, corn syrup, flavoring, and usually nuts. **6.** the **Divinity,** God.

di·vis·i·ble (di viz′ə bəl) *adj.* **1.** capable of being divided. **2.** capable of being divided without a remainder. —**di·vis′i·bil′i·ty,** *n.*

di·vi·sion (di vizh′ən) *n.* **1.** act or process of dividing; being divided. **2.** one of the parts into which something is divided, as for a specific purpose; section: *a division of a book, the marketing division of a company.* **3.** that which divides, as a boundary or partition. **4.** lack of agreement; dissension; discord. **5.** operation that determines how many times one number is contained in another number. **6.** in modern armies, basic organizational unit composed of infantry, artillery, and armor, with supporting elements, forming part of a corps and constituting the smallest unit capable of independent sustained combat. **7.** *Botany.* second largest unit of classification for plants, kingdom being the largest. [Latin *dīvīsiō* separation.] —**di·vi′sion·al,** *adj.*

division of labor, specialization of tasks in the process of making a product whereby the total operation is divided into a series of steps, each step being performed by a different worker or workers.

di·vi·sive (di vī′siv) *adj.* causing or tending to cause dissension or discord. —**di·vi′sive·ly,** *adv.* —**di·vi′sive·ness,** *n.*

di·vi·sor (di vī′zər) *n.* **1.** number or quantity by which another is to be divided. **2.** number that divides another without leaving a remainder.

di·vorce (di vôrs′) *n.* **1.** legal dissolution of a marriage. **2.** any complete separation: *a divorce of word and deed.* —*v.t.* -**vorced,** -**vorc·ing. 1.** to free oneself from (one's spouse) by divorce: *He divorced his wife.* **2.** to legally dissolve the marriage of: *The judge divorced the couple.* **3.** to separate; sever; disunite: *He divorced himself from the controversy.* [Old French *divorce* dissolution of marriage, from Latin *dīvortium* separation, dissolution of marriage.] Also, **di·vorce′ment.**

di·vor·cé (di vôr′sā′) *n.* divorced man.

di·vor·cée (di vôr′sē′, -sā′) *n.* divorced woman.

div·ot (div′ət) *n.* piece of turf torn up by a golf club in making a stroke.

di·vulge (di vulj′) -**vulged,** -**vulg·ing.** *v.t.* to make known, as a secret; disclose. [Latin *dīvulgāre* to make common, going back to *dis-* apart + *vulgus* the common people.] —**di·vul′gence, di·vulg′er,** *n.* —*Syn.* see **reveal.**

Dix·ie (dik′sē) *n.* the South, esp. the part of the South that was in the Confederacy. Also, **Dixie Land.** [Possibly from the Mason-*Dixon* line dividing the North from the South prior to the Civil War; possibly from French *dix* ten, printed on ten-dollar bills put out by a Louisiana bank before the Civil War.]

at; āpe; cär; end; mē; it; īce; hot; ōld; fôrk; wood; fōōl; oil; out; up; ūse; turn; sing; thin; this; zh in treasure; ə in ago, taken, pencil, lemon, circus.

Dix·ie·crat (dik′sē krat′) *n.* conservative Democrat from a Southern state who opposes the national policies of the Democratic Party, esp. one who left the party in 1948.

Dix·ie·land (dik′sē land′) style of jazz originating in New Orleans, characterized by a fast, lively, two-beat rhythm and improvised solo performances.

di·zen (dī′zən, diz′ən) *v.t. Archaic.* to dress in finery; deck out; bedizen. [Middle Low German *dise* bunch of flax on a distaff.]

diz·zy (diz′ē) **-zi·er, -zi·est.** *adj.* **1.** having the sensation of whirling, with a tendency to fall; giddy: *The children ran in a circle until they were dizzy.* **2.** thrown into a confused state or bewildered: *She's dizzy from all the excitement.* **3.** causing or tending to cause giddiness or confusion: *a dizzy pace. a dizzy height.* **4.** *Informal.* foolish; silly; inane: *a dizzy blonde.* —*v.t.* to make giddy or confused: *The ride on the roller coaster dizzied us.* [Old English *dysig* foolish.] —**diz′zi·ly,** *adv.* —**diz′zi·ness,** *n.*

Dja·kar·ta (jə kär′tə) *also.* **Ja·kar·ta.** *n.* capital, largest city, and chief commercial and industrial center of Indonesia, a seaport on the northwestern coast of Java. It was formerly known as Batavia. Pop. (1961), 2,906,533.

dl., deciliter; deciliters.

D. Lit., D. Litt., Doctor of Literature. Also, **D. Litt.**

dm., decimeter; decimeters.

DMZ, demilitarized zone.

DNA, nucleic acid found in the chromosomes of all living cells, consisting of a ladder-shaped strand made up of alternating units of sugar and phosphate connected by a nitrogen base. It transmits all hereditary information from parent to child, and determines the exact structure of all the protein produced by the cells. [Abbreviation of *d*(eoxyribo) *n*(ucleic) *a*cid.]

Dne·pro·pe·trovsk (dnye′prŏ pe trŏfsk′) *n.* city in the south-western Soviet Union, in the Ukraine. Pop. (1970 est.), 863,000.

Dnie·per (nē′pər, dnye′per) *n.* river flowing through the European part of the Soviet Union into the Black Sea.

Dnies·ter (nēs′tər, dnyes′ter) *n.* river flowing through the European part of the Soviet Union into the Black Sea.

do¹ (dōō) **did** or *(archaic)* **didst, done,** or *(archaic)* **done;** Present: *sing.,* first person, **do;** second, **do** or *(archaic)* **do·est** or **dost;** third, **does** or *(archaic)* **do·eth** or **doth;** *pl.,* **do.** *v.t.* **1.** to perform or carry out, as an action: *He always does his duty. They did everything they could to make him comfortable. We watched him do a jig.* **2.** to produce, as by creative effort; make: *to do a sketch. I'm doing my report on Shakespeare.* **3.** to bring to an end; complete; finish: *She interrupted him before his speech was done. He arrived after dinner was done.* **4.** to deal with or take care of; attend to. ▲ used as a substitute for a specific verb of action: *to do (wash or set) one's hair, to do (launder) the wash, to do (cook) the meat to a turn, to do (decorate) a room in blue.* **5.** to work out; solve: *I can't do this problem. He's doing the crossword puzzle now.* **6.** to bring about or impart to: *It will not do you any good to lie. His honest stand does him credit. It'll do you good to get away.* **7.** to put forth; exert: *I'll do my utmost to help you. Do your best.* **8.** to give or grant; render: *to do a favor, to show someone a good time, to do justice to.* **9.** to work at, esp. as a vocation: *What are you planning to do when you graduate? What does he do for a living?* **10.** to satisfy the needs of; serve; suffice: *The money will do us for a while.* **11.** to present or enact, as a play or reading: *We did only comedies this season.* **12.** to cover (a distance); traverse: *He did 200 miles a day.* **13.** to travel at a speed of: *She does seventy-five on the highway.* **14.** *Informal.* to serve (time), as during a term in prison: *He did ten years for armed robbery.* **15.** *Informal.* to cheat; swindle: *He did him out of $1,000.* **16.** *Informal.* to visit or tour, esp. as a sightseer: *We did Spain in two weeks.* —*v.i.* **1.** to behave or conduct oneself: *Do as you are told. When in Rome, do as the Romans do. Do unto others as you'd have them do unto you.* **2.** to be active or exert oneself; work; strive: *to do or die.* **3.** to fare or manage; get along: *The patient is doing well. We can do without your comments. He's doing well in school.* **4.** to serve the purpose; be satisfactory; suffice: *This hotel won't do. This will do just fine. That jacket won't do for skiing.* **5.** to be fitting or proper: *It won't do for us to be late.* **6.** *Informal.* to happen; occur: *What's doing this weekend?* **7.** **to do away with. a.** to kill; murder: *to do away with an enemy.* **b.** to put an end to; eliminate; abolish: *The law did away with slavery.* **8.** **to do in.** *Informal.* **a.** to kill; murder: *He was done in by gangsters.* **b.** to tire or wear out; exhaust: *He felt done in after the long trip. All that walking really did me in.* **9.** **to do by.** to act toward; treat: *The company does well by its employees.* **10.** **to do for. a.** to take care of, esp. to cook and keep house for: *She does for Mrs. Jones.* **b.** *Informal.* to defeat, ruin, or destroy: *Now we're done for.* —*auxiliary verb* **1.** used without specific meaning: **a.** to ask a question: *Do you need a new coat?* **b.** to form negative expressions: *I do not want any. He did not find it.* **c.** to form inverted constructions after some adverbs, such as *rarely* or *little: little does he realize.* **2.** used to give emphasis: *Do be quiet! I do enjoy his company.*

3. used as a substitute for a verb already used, to avoid repetition: *He speaks as well as you do. Did you go? I did.* **4. to make do.** to get along or manage: *We can make do without the extra money.* [Old English *dōn* to make, cause, perform, carry out, act.]

do² (dō) *n. Music.* first and last of the series of syllables used to name the eight tones of the diatonic scale. In the **fixed-do** method, do is always the note or tone C, while in **movable-do,** it is the keynote of any given diatonic scale. [Italian *dō,* possibly a modification of *ut,* formerly first note in singing. See GAMUT.]

Do²
Notes of the scale

do., ditto.

D.O.A., dead on arrival.

do·a·ble (dōō′ə bəl) *adj.* capable of being done.

doat (dōt) dote.

dob·bin (dob′in) *n.* horse, esp. a gentle, plodding one; workhorse. [Form of *Robin,* a familiar form of the masculine name *Robert.*]

Do·ber·man pin·scher (dō′bər mən pin′shər) dog of a breed originally developed in Germany, having a long head, slender legs, and usually a sleek, black or brown coat with rust-colored markings, often used as a guard dog. Height: 27 inches at the shoulder.

dob·son fly (dob′sən) North American insect, whose larva, the hellgrammite, is used as bait by anglers. [Of uncertain origin.]

do·cent (dō′sənt) *n.* **1.** lecturer or guide at a museum, esp. an art museum. **2.** lecturer or teacher, esp. one who is not on the regular faculty, as in some American universities. [Latin *docēns,* present participle of *docēre* to teach.]

doc·ile (dos′əl) *adj.* easily managed, trained, or taught; tractable: *a docile pet, a docile child.* [Latin *docilis* teachable, from *docēre* to teach.] —**do·cil·i·ty** (do sil′ə tē), *n.*

Doberman pinscher

dock¹ (dok) *n.* **1.** structure built along the shore or out from the shore, typically secured by piles and serving as a landing place where boats and ships can be tied up and passengers and cargo loaded and discharged; wharf; pier. **2.** area of water between two adjoining piers where boats and ships can be moored; slip. **3.** dry dock. —*v.t.* **1.** to bring (a boat or ship) to a dock. **2.** to bring together or couple two or more orbiting objects, as spacecraft, in space. —*v.i.* **1.** to moor at or come into a dock. **2.** (of orbiting objects) to come together or couple in space. [Middle Dutch *docke* pier.]

dock² (dok) *n.* **1.** solid, fleshy part of an animal's tail. **2.** stump of a tail left after clipping or cropping. —*v.t.* **1.** to cut the end off or shorten, as the tail of a horse or dog; clip; crop; bob. **2.** to deduct a part from; reduce: *to dock one's wages or paycheck.* **3.** to deduct from the wages of: *The company docked him a day's pay for being absent.* [Possibly from Old English *-docca,* as in *fingerdocca* finger muscle.]

dock³ (dok) *n.* place in a criminal court where the defendant stands or sits during trial. [Flemish *dok* cage.]

dock⁴ (dok) *n.* any of various plants, genus *Rumex* related to buckwheat, typically having large, wavy-edged leaves. [Old English *docce.*]

dock·age¹ (dok′ij) *n.* **1.** charge made for using a dock. **2.** facilities for docking a boat or ship. **3.** the docking of boats or ships. [DOCK¹ + -AGE.]

dock·age² (dok′ij) *n.* act of deducting, as from wages. [DOCK² + -AGE.]

dock·et (dok′it) *n.* **1.** list or calendar of cases to be tried by a court of law. **2.** list of legal judgments given in a specific court. **3.** record or summary of the proceedings in a law court. **4.** book containing such a record or summary. **5.** any list or calendar of matters to be acted upon; agenda. **6.** label or tag attached, as to a package or document, listing its contents. —*v.t.* **1.** to enter in a docket. **2.** to put a label or tag on, as a package or document. [Of uncertain origin.]

dock·yard (dok′yärd′) *n.* place containing docks, workshops, and warehouses where boats and ships can be built, equipped, and repaired.

doc·tor (dok′tər) *n.* **1.** one who is licensed to practice any of various branches of medicine, as pediatrics, neurosurgery, or psychiatry; physician or surgeon. **2.** one who is licensed to practice any of several related sciences, as dentistry, osteopathy, or veterinary medicine. **3.** one who holds the highest graduate degree conferred by a university, as in law, philosophy, or divinity. **4.** witch doctor; medicine man. **5.** *Archaic.* an eminently learned person. —*v.t.* **1.** to treat medicinally; apply remedies to. **2.** to tamper with; falsify: *to doctor evidence.* **3.** *Informal.* to modify or improve by special treatment (often with *up*): *to doctor up a food dish with spices.* —*v.i.* to practice medicine. [Latin *doctor* teacher.]

doc·tor·al (dok′tər əl) *adj.* of, relating to, or studying for a doctorate: *a doctoral thesis, a doctoral candidate.*

doc·tor·ate (dok′tər it) *n.* **1.** highest graduate degree given by educational institutions, usually representing several years of advanced study and research. **2.** such a degree awarded as an honor.

doctor's degree, doctorate.

doc·tri·naire (dok′tri när′) *adj.* theoretical; impractical; visionary. —*n.* one who theorizes without a sufficient regard to practical considerations; impractical theorist; visionary.

doc·tri·nal (dok′trin əl) *adj.* of, relating to, or based on doctrine: *a doctrinal controversy.*

doc·trine (dok′trin) *n.* **1.** particular principle or position or body of principles that is taught or advocated, as of a religion or government; tenet or tenets; dogma: *the doctrines of Catholicism.* **2.** that which is taught; teachings: *political doctrine.* [Old French *doctrine* teachings, from Latin *doctrina* learning, teaching.]
Syn. 1. Doctrine, dogma, tenet mean a principle held as a basic authoritative premise. **Doctrine** suggests acceptance on proof, at least on proof held sufficient by those adhering to the doctrine: *With its entry into World War II, the United States rejected the doctrine of isolationism.* **Dogma** implies acceptance on authority, no proof being considered necessary: *The tentative speculation of another age often hardens into dogma in a new one.* **Tenet** suggests a single rule or practical application of a body of doctrine: *One tenet of isolationism is the unwillingness to trade with other nations.*

doc·u·ment (*n.,* dok′yə mənt; *v.,* dok′yə ment′) *n.* something written or printed that furnishes evidence, support, proof, or information about a particular object or subject, as a deed, record, or map. —*v.t.* **1.** to support or prove with facts, evidence, or examples. **2.** to provide with documents. [Old French *document,* lesson, written evidence, from Latin *documentum* lesson, proof, example.]

doc·u·men·ta·ry (dok′yə men′tər ē, -men′trē) *adj.* **1.** relating to, supported by, or consisting of documents: *documentary proof.* **2.** presenting factual material. —*n., pl.* **-ries.** documentary motion picture, television program, or radio program.

doc·u·men·ta·tion (dok′yə mən tā′shən, -men-) *n.* **1.** preparation, furnishing, or citation of documents or documentary evidence: *She completed the documentation for her book.* **2.** documentary evidence or proof: *The case was thrown out of court because he had no documentation for his accusation.*

dod·der[1] (dod′ər) *v.i.* **1.** to move feebly and unsteadily; totter: *an old man doddering down the street.* **2.** to tremble or shake, as from age. [Form of obsolete *dadder* to tremble; of uncertain origin.]

dod·der[2] (dod′ər) *n.* any of various leafless, twining, parasitic weeds, genus *Cuscuta,* related to the morning glory, that have no chlorophyll and are equipped with hundreds of tiny suckers for absorbing nourishment from the host plant. [Possibly of Germanic origin.]

do·dec·a·gon (dō dek′ə gon′) *n.* plane figure having twelve sides and twelve angles. [Greek *dōdekagōnon,* from *dōdeka* twelve + *gōnia* angle.]

do·dec·a·he·dron (dō dek′ə hē′drən, dō′dek ə-) *pl.* **-drons** or **-dra** (-drə). *n.* solid figure having twelve faces. [Greek *dōdekaedros* having twelve faces, from *dōdeka* twelve + *hedra* seat, face.]

Dodecahedron

dodge (doj) **dodged, dodg·ing.** *v.t.* **1.** to avoid, as a blow, by moving aside quickly or suddenly. **2.** to evade, as an issue, by strategy, deception, or cunning. —*v.i.* **1.** to move quickly or suddenly: *The escaped prisoner dodged in and out among the crowd.* **2.** to use evasive techniques: *She usually dodges when asked her opinion.* —*n.* **1.** act of dodging. **2.** trick used to cheat or deceive. **3.** clever scheme or device. [Of uncertain origin.]

dodg·er (doj′ər) *n.* **1.** one who dodges, esp. one who uses evasion or trickery: *a tax dodger.* **2.** small handbill. **3.** type of bread or cake made of cornmeal that is baked or fried, popular in the southern United States.

Dodg·son, Charles L. (doj′sən) see **Car·roll, Lewis.**

do·do (dō′dō) *pl.* **-dos** or **-does.** *n.* any of various extinct, flightless birds, genera *Raphus* and *Pezohaps,* found on the Mascarene Islands of the Indian Ocean until the end of the eighteenth century, having a large head, heavy hooked bill, and a short tail of curly feathers. Weight: 40–50 pounds. [Portuguese *doudo* fool; because of its foolish appearance, with a large body and tiny wings.]

Dodo

doe (dō) *n.* adult female animal, as of the deer, antelope, or rabbit. [Old English *dā* female deer.]

do·er (doo′ər) *n.* one who does (something), esp. a person of action and vigor: *He's a doer, not a talker.*

does (duz) present indicative, third person singular, of **do**[1].

doe·skin (dō′skin′) *n.* **1.** skin of a female deer. **2.** leather made from it. **3.** any of several slightly napped fabrics made of wool, cotton, or rayon, used for coats, suits, and sportswear.

does·n't (duz′ənt) does not.

do·est (doo′ist) *Archaic.* present indicative, second person singular, of **do.**

do·eth (doo′ith) *Archaic.* present indicative, third person singular, of **do.**

doff (dof, dôf) *v.t.* **1.** to take off or remove, as clothing, esp. to lift (the hat) in salutation. **2.** to rid oneself of; discard: *She has doffed her old mannerisms.* [Contraction of *do off* to put off.]

dog (dôg) *n.* **1.** domesticated mammal, *Canis familiaris,* of which there are more than 200 distinct breeds that vary greatly in appearance. **2.** any of various other animals of the dog family, Canidae, as the wolf, fox, coyote, and jackal. **3.** male of any of these animals. **4.** any of various animals resembling or suggestive of a dog. **5.** worthless, contemptible fellow. **6.** any of various mechanical devices to catch, hold, or grip. **7.** andiron. **8.** *Informal.* person: *He's a sly dog. She's a lucky dog.* **9.** dogs. *Slang.* feet. **10. to go to the dogs,** to ruin; deteriorate. **11. to put on the dog.** *Informal.* to make an ostentatious display; be pretentious. —*v.t.,* **dogged, dog·ging. 1.** to follow closely or pursue persistently; hound. **2.** to fasten or hold with any of various mechanical devices. [Old English *docga* a domesticated canine.]

dog·bane (dôg′bān′) *n.* any of various plants, genus *Apocynum,* having clusters of small, white or pink bell-shaped flowers.

dog·ber·ry (dôg′ber′ē) *pl.* **-ries.** *n.* **1.** berrylike fruit of any of several plants, esp. the mountain ash. **2.** tree or shrub bearing this fruit.

dog biscuit 1. type of hard biscuit for dogs made of several ingredients, as ground bones and scraps of meat. **2.** hard biscuit used as army rations.

dog·cart (dôg′kärt′) *n.* **1.** light, open, one-horse carriage, usually two-wheeled, having two transverse seats set back to back and, originally, a space for dogs beneath the rear seat. **2.** small cart drawn by one or more dogs.

Dogcart

dog·catch·er (dôg′kach′ər) *n.* person employed or elected to pick up and impound stray, homeless, or unlicensed dogs.

dog days, hot, sultry days of July and August. [Translation of Latin *diēs canīculārēs;* because the Romans believed that Sirius, called the dog star, which rose with the sun in July and August, increased the excessive heat of the season.]

doge (dōj) *n.* chief magistrate in either of the former republics of Genoa and Venice. [Dialectal Italian *doge,* from Latin *dux* leader. Doublet of DUCE, DUKE.]

dog-ear (dôg′ēr′) *also,* **dog's-ear.** *n.* turned-down corner of a page, as of a book. —*v.t.* to turn down the corner of (a page). —**dog′-eared′,** *adj.*

dog-eat-dog (dôg′ēt′dôg′) *adj.* marked by or characterized by ruthless, unlimited competition: *a dog-eat-dog world.*

dog·face (dôg′fās′) *n. Slang.* soldier in the U.S. Army, esp. an infantryman.

dog·fight (dôg′fīt′) *n.* **1.** fight between or as between dogs; rough, violent dispute, contest, or brawl. **2.** combat between fighter planes.

dog·fish (dôg′fish′) *pl.,* **-fish** or **-fish·es.** *n.* any of a group of relatively small sharks, found in warm and temperate seas, having long, slender, grayish-green bodies, pointed snouts, and large asymmetrically forked tails.

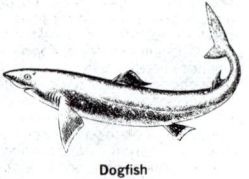
Dogfish

dog·ged (dô′gid) *adj.* stubborn; persevering; unyielding: *dogged courage.* [DOG + -ED[2].] —**dog′ged·ly,** *adv.* —**dog′ged·ness,** *n.*

dog·ger (dô′gər) *n.* two-masted ship having a broad beam, used principally by fishermen in the North Sea. [Middle Dutch *dogger* fishing boat.]

Dog·ger Bank (dô′gər) one of the world's chief fishing grounds, in the North Sea, off the northwestern coast of Europe.

dog·ger·el (dô′gər əl) *n.* poor or trivial poetry having no artistic merit in content or form. —*adj.* resembling or composed of such poetry. [Probably from DOG.]

dog·gy (dô′gē) *pl.* **-gies.** *also,* **dog·gie.** *n.* dog, esp. a little or pet dog. —*adj.* **-gi·er, -gi·est.** of or like a dog.

at; āpe; cär; end; mē; it; īce; hot; ōld; fôrk; wood; fōōl; oil; out; up; ūse; turn; sing; thin; this; zh in treasure; ə in ago, taken, pencil, lemon, circus.

dog·house (dôg′hous′) *n.* **1.** small house or shelter for a dog. **2. in the doghouse.** *Informal.* in disfavor.

do·gie (dō′gē) *also,* **do·gy.** *n.* in the western United States, stray or motherless calf on the range. [Said to be from *dough guts,* applied to an orphaned calf whose belly swells when fed on grass.]

dog in the manger, one who selfishly prevents others from using what he himself cannot or will not use.

dog·ma (dôg′mə) *pl.* **-mas** or **-ma·ta** (-mə tə). *n.* **1.** a doctrine or system of doctrines formally propounded by a church or religious body and held to be authoritative. **2.** principle, belief, or tenet, usually formally stated and viewed as authoritative: *a political dogma.* **3.** system of such principles, beliefs, or tenets: *communist dogma.* [Latin *dogma,* from Greek *dogma* opinion.] —**Syn. 2.** see **doctrine.**

dog·mat·ic (dôg mat′ik) *adj.* **1.** asserting or stating beliefs or opinions in a positive, authoritative, and often arrogant manner: *dogmatic writing, a dogmatic lecturer.* **2.** of or relating to dogma; doctrinal. Also, **dog·mat′i·cal.** —**dog·mat′i·cal·ly,** *adv.*

dog·ma·tism (dôg′mə tiz′əm) *n.* positive, authoritative, often arrogant assertion of opinions or beliefs.

dog·ma·tist (dôg′mə tist) *n.* one who expresses dogmas or who is dogmatic.

dog·ma·tize (dôg′mə tīz′) **-tized, -tiz·ing.** *v.i.* to speak or write dogmatically. —*v.t.* to assert or state as a dogma.

do-good·er (dōō′good′ər) *n.* *Informal.* idealistic or eager reformer or philanthropist. ▲ often used derisively.

dog paddle, rudimentary stroke in swimming with the body in an almost upright position, the hands paddling at the surface, and the legs performing rough kicks. —*v.t.* to perform a dog paddle.

dog rose, shrub rose, *Rosa canina,* having single white or pink flowers.

dog's-ear (dôgz′ēr′) *n.* dog-ear.

dog sled *also,* **dog sledge.** sled that is drawn by one or more dogs.

dog's life, wretched or difficult life.

dog tag 1. small, metal disk or plate attached to the collar of a dog indicating ownership. **2.** *Informal.* oblong tag worn on a chain usually around the neck, by a member of the armed forces for identification purposes.

dog-tired (dôg′tīrd′) *adj.* extremely tired.

dog·tooth violet (dôg′tōōth′) *also,* **dog's-tooth violet. 1.** drooping purple or reddish flower of a plant, *Erythronium denscanis,* of the lily family. Also, **ad′der's-tongue′. 2.** plant bearing this flower, having two mottled leaves and a bulbous stem. **3.** any of several related plants, as the common North American species *Erythronium americanum,* bearing yellow flowers.

dog·trot (dôg′trot′) *n.* gentle, easy trot.

dog·watch (dôg′wŏch′, -woch′) *n.* either of the two short watches on a ship, one from 4 to 6 P.M. and the other from 6 to 8 P.M.

dog·wood (dôg′wood′) *n.* **1.** any of a group of hardy ornamental trees or shrubs, genus *Cornus,* bearing berrylike fruit and greenish-yellow flowers sur-

Dogwood flowers and fruit

rounded by pink or white petal-like leaves. **2.** the hard, heavy wood of this tree.

do·gy (dō′gē) *pl.,* **-gies.** *n.* dogie.

Do·ha (dō′hə) *n.* capital of the sheikdom of Qatar. Pop. (1963 est.), 45,000.

doi·ly (doi′lē) *pl.,* **-lies.** *n.* small, ornamental piece of material, as of linen, lace, or paper, used as a decoration or to protect a surface upon which an object is placed. [Said to be from an eighteenth-century English cloth merchant named *Doily.*]

do·ings (dōō′ingz) *n.* **1.** activities, proceedings, or events: *social doings.* **2.** behavior; conduct.

doit (doit) *n.* **1.** formerly, a small Dutch copper coin. **2.** trifling amount of quantity; bit. [Dutch *duit* this coin.]

do-it-your·self (dōō′it yər self′) *adj.* *Informal.* designed for construction or use by a person without professional training or assistance: *a do-it-yourself bookcase kit.*

dol·ce (dōl′chä) *Music. adj.* sweet; soft. —*adv.* sweetly; softly. [Italian *dolce* sweet, from Latin *dulcis.*]

dol·ce far nien·te (dōl′chä fär nyen′tā) *Italian.* pleasant idleness.

dol·drums (dōl′drəmz, dol′-) *n.* **1.** dull, listless, or depressed mood; low spirits. **2.** certain regions of the ocean along the equator, characterized by calms, very light or constantly shifting winds, and heavy precipitation. **3.** state of inactivity or stagnation, as in business; slump. [Of uncertain origin.]

dole¹ (dōl) *n.* **1.** that which is distributed in charity, as money, food, or clothing. **2.** anything distributed sparingly; small portion. **3.** act of

giving out or distributing of something, esp. of charitable gifts. **4.** relief paid by a government to the unemployed. **5.** *Archaic.* one's destiny or lot. **6. to go (or be) on the dole.** to receive relief payments from the government. —*v.t.* **doled, dol·ing. 1.** to distribute in charity. **2.** to give or distribute in small quantities (often with *out*). [Old English *dāl* portion.]

dole² (dōl) *n.* *Archaic.* sorrow; grief; mental distress. [Old French *doel,* going back to Latin *dolēre* to grieve.]

dole·ful (dōl′fəl) *adj.* full of or expressing grief or sorrow; sad: *a doleful cry, a doleful look.* —**dole′ful·ly,** *adv.* —**dole′ful·ness,** *n.*

dole·some (dōl′səm) *adj.* *Archaic.* doleful.

doll (dol) *n.* **1.** child's toy made to resemble the human figure, esp. that of a baby. **2.** pretty but shallow girl or woman. **3.** pretty or delightful child. **4.** *Slang.* pleasant or attractive person. —*v.t., v.i.* *Informal.* to dress or adorn smartly or ostentatiously (with *up*). [From *Doll,* pet name for *Dorothy* woman's name.]

dol·lar (dol′ər) *n.* **1.** standard monetary unit of the United States equivalent to one hundred cents. **2.** monetary unit of certain other countries, as Canada, New Zealand, Australia, and various British dependencies. **3.** piece of paper currency or silver or gold coin equivalent to one dollar. [Low German *daler* German silver coin, from German *T(h)aler,* abbreviation of *Joachimst(h)aler,* a coin so called because it was first coined in *Joachimsthal,* a Bohemian city, in the early sixteenth century.]

dollar diplomacy, U.S. policy of using the power of the government to promote the interests of U.S. businessmen abroad, esp. the U.S. policy in Latin America and China during the early decades of the twentieth century.

dol·lop (dol′əp) *n.* lump, blob, or portion, as of paint or ice-cream.

dol·ly (dol′ē) *pl.,* **doll·ies.** *n.* **1.** doll. ▲ used as a child's term. **2.** any of several frames with wheels for moving heavy loads. **3.** wheeled platform on which a camera may be moved about a motion-picture or television set. **4.** small locomotive running on narrow-gauge tracks, used as in railroad yards, quarries, and construction sites. —*v.t.* **doll·ied, doll·y·ing.** to move with a dolly. —*v.i.* to move a camera on a motion-picture or television dolly.

dol·man (dol′mən, dōl′-) *pl.,* **-mans.** *n.* **1.** formerly, woman's coat with dolman sleeves or capelike flaps instead of sleeves. **2.** jacket worn like a cape with the sleeves hanging loose. **3.** long outer robe worn by the Turks, having narrow sleeves. [French *dolman* jacket, through German and Magyar, from Turkish *dōlāmān* long robe.]

dolman sleeve, sleeve that has a very wide armhole but is tapered to fit snugly around the wrist.

dol·men (dol′mən, dōl′-) *n.* prehistoric structure, usually regarded as a tomb, consisting of a large, unhewn stone slab resting on two or more unhewn stones placed upright. Also, **crom′-lech.** [French *dolmen,* probably from Cornish *tolmēn* hole of stone.]

Dolmen

do·lo·mite (dō′lə mīt′, dol′ə-) *n.* **1.** mineral of calcium magnesium carbonate, whose crystals usually exhibit a pink or white color, but are sometimes gray, green, brown, or black. Formula: $CaMg(CO_3)_2$. **2.** rock consisting primarily of this mineral. [From the eighteenth-century French geologist Déodat de *Dolomieu.*]

do·lor (dō′lər) *n.* sorrow; grief; anguish. [Old French *dolour,* from Latin *dolor.*]

do·lor·ous (dō′lər əs, dol′ər-) *adj.* expressing or causing pain or sorrow: *a dolorous cry.* —**do′lor·ous·ly,** *adv.* —**do′lor·ous·ness,** *n.*

dol·phin (dol′fin, dôl′-) *n.* **1.** any of various mammals, family Delphinidae, related to the whale, found in all seas and in some freshwater rivers, having a curved dorsal fin, scaleless black, brown, or gray skin, two flippers that are modified front legs, and usually a beaklike snout. Length: 8–30 feet. **2.** edible, saltwater gamefish, *Coryphaena hippurus,* found in warm waters, having long dorsal fins and a powerful, deeply-forked tail. It is remarkable for its changes of color when taken from the water. Also *(def. 2),* **do·ra′do.** [Old French *daulphin* this mammal, going back to Latin *delphīnus,* from Greek *delphīs.*]

Dolphin

dolphin kick, kick in swimming in which both legs are moved up and down together in an undulating motion.

dolphin striker, martingale *(def. 2b).*

dolt (dōlt) *n.* dull, stupid person; blockhead. [Middle English *dult* blunt, from *dul* dull. See DULL.] **—dolt′ish,** *adj.* **—dolt′ish·ly,** *adv.* **—dolt′ish·ness,** *n.*

-dom *suffix* (used to form nouns) **1.** office, rank, or domain of: *earldom. kingdom.* **2.** state or condition of being: *freedom. wisdom.* **3.** totality of all those who are, as of a specified rank, condition, or state: *officialdom.* [Old English *-dōm* office, state, condition.]

dom. 1. domestic. **2.** dominion.

do·main (dō mān′) *n.* **1.** territory over which dominion is exercised by a sovereign or government; realm. **2.** field or sphere, as of knowledge, action, or influence: *the domain of science.* **3.** land owned by one person or family; estate. **4.** *Mathematics.* set of values which the independent variable in a relation or function may have. [French *domaine* estate, sphere, going back to Latin *dominicus* relating to a master, from *dominus* master.]

dome (dōm) *n.* **1.** hemispherical roof erected over a circular or many-sided base. **2.** something resembling this in shape: *the dome of a mountain.* **3.** stately, impressive structure or mansion. **4.** *Slang.* the head. **—v.t. domed, dom·ing. 1.** to cover with or as with a dome. **2.** to shape or form like a dome. **—v.i.** to rise or swell into a shape resembling a dome. [French *dôme* vault, cupola, from Italian *duomo* cupola (a characteristic part of Italian cathedrals), cathedral, house (of God), from Latin *domus* house.]

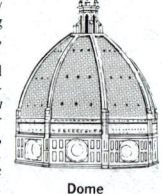

Dome

Domes·day Book (dōmz′dā′, dōmz′-) document recording a detailed survey of landholdings in England in the eleventh century, ordered by William the Conqueror. [Middle English form of DOOMSDAY; because it was considered the final word on the data contained.]

do·mes·tic (də mes′tik) *adj.* **1.** of or relating to the home, household, or family: *domestic life, domestic problems.* **2.** devoted to or fond of things involving the home and family: *a domestic sort of person.* **3.** living with or near man and cared for by him; domesticated; tame: *Cows and dogs are domestic animals.* **4.** of or made in one's own country or the country under consideration: *domestic trade policies. While in France he always drank domestic wine.* **—n.** household servant. [Latin *domesticus* relating to a household, from *domus* house.] **—do·mes′ti·cal·ly,** *adv.*

do·mes·ti·cate (də mes′tə kāt′) **-cat·ed, -cat·ing.** *v.t.* **1.a.** to develop (a strain of plants or animals) for a specific product or purpose useful to human beings and usually depending on human care. **b.** to adapt an animal to live with man; tame: *to domesticate a cheetah.* **2.** to make fond of or accustom to home, household affairs, and family life: *to domesticate a bachelor.* **—do·mes′ti·ca′tion,** *n.*

do·mes·tic·i·ty (dō′mes tis′ə tē) *pl.* **-ties.** *n.* **1.** home and family life. **2.** devotion to the home and family. **2. domesticities.** household affairs.

domestic science, home economics.

dom·i·cile (dom′ə sīl′, -sil, dō′mə-) *also,* **dom·i·cil** (dom′ə sil). *n.* **1.** place of settled or established residence; home, house, or dwelling. **2.** official or legal residence. **—v.t., -ciled, -cil·ing.** to establish in a domicile. [Old French *domicile* house, from Latin *domicilium* dwelling.]

dom·i·cil·i·ar·y (dom′ə sil′ē er′ē, dō′mə-) *adj.* of or relating to a domicile.

dom·i·cil·i·ate (dom′ə sil′ē āt′) **-at·ed, -at·ing.** *v.t.* to domicile. **—v.i.** to dwell; reside.

dom·i·nance (dom′ə nəns) *n.* fact or state of being dominant. Also, **dom′i·nan·cy.**

dom·i·nant (dom′ə nənt) *adj.* **1.** exercising chief authority, influence, or control; commanding or prevailing, as over all others: *the dominant political party of the country. The dominant influence in her life was her father.* **2.** most prominent or conspicuous: *the dominant color in a room.* **3.** relating to or designating one of a pair of hereditary characteristics that appears in an organism by masking or prevailing over the other when both are present in a genetic make-up. Opposed to **recessive. 4.** *Music.* of, based upon, or relating to the dominant. **—n. 1.** *Genetics.* dominant hereditary characteristic. **2.** *Music.* fifth tone of a diatonic scale. D is the dominant in the key of G. [Old French *dominant* ruling, predominating, from Latin *domināns,* present participle of *dominārī* to be master, rule.] **—dom′i·nant·ly,** *adv.*

Syn. *adj.* **1. Dominant, predominant, preponderant, paramount** mean occupying the highest position. **Dominant** suggests having the most power or force and thus ruling or controlling: *His was the dominant voice at the convention.* **Predominant** implies most influence, at least for the time spoken of: *During the second act, interest in the heroine becomes predominant.* **Preponderant** suggests having the most weight, as from numbers or wealth, but not firmly controlling: *The preponderant voice*

in the faculty for some time has been that of the engineering school. **Paramount** indicates supremacy because of rank, position, status, or the like: *Finding a place to live had become his paramount interest.*

dom·i·nate (dom′ə nāt′) **-nat·ed, -nat·ing.** *v.t.* **1.** to exercise control or rule over, as by will or strength; govern: *The Greeks once dominated a large portion of that area. His personality dominated the other members of the committee.* **2.** to occupy a commanding or towering position over; loom over: *The skyscraper dominates the skyline.* **3.** to have an outstanding or preeminent place or position in; affect most prominently or conspicuously: *Fear dominates their lives.* **—v.i. 1.** to have or exercise control or preeminence. **2.** to occupy a commanding or towering position. [Latin *dominātus,* past participle of *dominārī* to be master, rule.] **—dom′i·na′tor,** *n.*

dom·i·na·tion (dom′ə nā′shən) *n.* **1.** act of dominating; being dominated. **2.** exercise of control or influence; rule; sway: *to be under someone's domination.* **3. dominations,** dominions *(def. 5).*

dom·i·neer (dom′ə nēr′) *v.t., v.i.* **1.** to rule arrogantly or despotically; be overbearing; tyrannize; bully. **2.** to occupy a commanding or towering position. [Dutch *domineren* to rule, from French *dominer,* from Latin *dominārī* to be master, rule.]

dom·i·neer·ing (dom′ə nēr′ing) *adj.* bossy; overbearing; tyrannical. **—dom′i·neer′ing·ly,** *adv.*

Dom·i·nic, Saint (dom′ə nik) 1170–1221, Spanish priest and founder of the Roman Catholic order of Dominicans.

Dom·i·ni·ca (dom′ə nē′kə, də min′i kə) *n.* British island in the eastern West Indies, one of the Windward Islands. Area, 290 sq. mi. Pop. (1965 est.), 66,000.

Do·min·i·can (də min′i kən) *adj.* **1.** of or relating to Saint Dominic or the religious order founded by him. **2.** of, characteristic of, or relating to the Dominican Republic. **—n. 1.** member of the Roman Catholic mendicant order of friars and nuns founded by Saint Dominic in 1215. **2.a.** citizen of the Dominican Republic. **b.** close descendant of the people of the Dominican Republic.

Dominican Republic, nation occupying the eastern part of the island of Hispaniola, in the central West Indies. Capital, Santo Domingo. Area, 18,816 sq. mi. Pop. (1970), 4,011,589.

dom·i·nie (dom′ə nē, dō′mə-) *n.* **1.** *Scottish, British.* schoolmaster. **2.** minister of the Dutch Reformed Church. **3.** *Informal.* any minister. [Latin *dominē,* vocative of *dominus* master; formerly a reverent greeting to clergymen.]

do·min·ion (də min′yən) *n.* **1.** sovereign or supreme authority; power or right to rule. **2.** territory or country under the authority of a particular ruler or government. **3.** control, influence, or sway: *the dominion of prejudice.* **4.** *also,* **Dominion,** formerly, any of several self-governing states belonging to the British Empire, as Canada and Australia. **5. dominions,** the fourth of the nine orders of angels. [Old French *dominion* power, rule, going back to Latin *dominium* right of ownership, domain.] **—Syn. 1.** see **power.**

Dominion Day, in Canada, a legal holiday commemorating the federation of Canada into a dominion in 1867. July 1.

dom·i·no[1] (dom′ə nō′) *pl.* **-noes** or **-nos.** *n.* **1.** small mask covering the upper part of the face, esp. the eyes. **2.** loose cloak with a hood, usually worn with such a mask as a disguise at a masquerade. **3.** one who wears a domino. [French *domino* priest's black hooded cloak, going back to Latin *dominus* master.]

dom·i·no[2] (dom′ə nō′) *pl.* **-noes.** *n.* **1.** a small black tile divided into halves, each half being either blank or having from one to six white dots, used in dominoes. **2. dominoes.** any of several games usually played with twenty-eight of these tiles. [From DOMINO[1]; because of the black backs of the pieces used in the game.]

Do·mi·tian (də mish′ən) A.D. 51–96, Roman emperor from A.D. 81 to 96, son of Emperor Vespasian.

Dom·ré·my (dōn rā mē′) village in northeastern France, the birthplace of Joan of Arc. Also, **Dom·ré·my·la·Pu·celle** (dōn rā mē′-la poo sel′).

don[1] (don) *n.* **1. Don.** Sir. ▲ Spanish form of respectful address for a man, usually before the first name only: *Don Pedro.* **2.** Spanish nobleman or gentleman. **3.** *Informal.* head, fellow, or tutor of a college at Oxford or Cambridge University. **4.** *Archaic.* distinguished or important person. [Spanish *don* mister, Spanish title, from Latin *dominus* master.]

don[2] (don) **donned, don·ning.** *v.t.* to put on, as clothing. [Contraction of *do on.*]

Don (don) *n.* river flowing through the central Soviet Union into the Sea of Azov.

Do·ña (dōn′yə) *n.* **1.** Lady; Madam. ▲ Spanish form of respectful address for a married woman, usually before the first name only: *Doña Maria.* **2. doña.** Spanish noblewoman or lady. [Spanish *doña,* from Latin *domina* mistress, lady.]

do·nate (dō′nāt, dō nāt′) **-nat·ed, -nat·ing.** *v.t.* to give, esp. to a fund or charitable cause; contribute. [From DONATION.]

Syn. Donate, contribute, bestow mean to give a gift. **Donate** suggests

a worthy cause: *Everyone was asked to donate a day's pay to the combined city charities.* **Contribute** implies adding something to a general effort: *She contributed a couple of dollars toward buying the Christmas decorations for the office.* **Bestow** suggests assistance, esp. charity, on the part of the giver and appreciation on the part of the receiver: *The committee decided to bestow the scholarship on the younger man.*

Don·a·tel·lo (don′ə tel′ō) n. c.1386–1466, Florentine sculptor.

do·na·tion (dō nā′shən) n. **1.** act of giving; contributing: *a yearly donation of clothing.* **2.** gift; contribution: *a sizable donation to the needy.* [French *donation* present, from Latin *dōnātiō* a presenting.]

done (dun) v. past participle of **do.** —adj. **1.** completed; finished; through. **2.** cooked sufficiently. **3.** socially acceptable: *Picking one's teeth at the dinner table isn't done.*

do·nee (dō nē′) n. recipient of a gift or donation.

Do·nets Basin (do nets′) most important coal-mining and industrial area in the Soviet Union, in the European part of the country.

dong (dông, dong) n. deep sound of or as of a bell. —v.i. to make such a sound.

Don·i·zet·ti, Gae·ta·no (don′i zet′ē; gī-tä′nō) 1797–1848, Italian composer of operas.

don·jon (dun′jən, don′-) n. strongly fortified inner tower of a castle; keep. [Archaic form of DUNGEON.]

Don Juan (don wän′, hwän′) **1.** legendary Spanish nobleman, famous as a seducer of women and as a reckless adventurer. **2.** any man who is a rake or seducer.

don·key (dong′kē, dung′-) pl. **-keys.** n. **1.** domestic animal, *Equus asinus asinus,* resembling a small horse but having longer ears and a shorter mane and often used as a beast of burden; domestic ass. Height: 4½ feet at the shoulder. **2.** stupid or obstinate person. [Diminutive of DUN²; influenced in form by MONKEY.]

Donkey

donkey engine, small auxiliary engine, used as for pumping or hoisting.

don·na (don′ə, dô′nə) n. **1.** Italian noblewoman or lady. **2.** **Donna.** lady; madam. ▲ Italian form of respectful address for a married woman, usually before the first name only. [Italian *donna,* from Latin *domina* mistress, lady.]

Donne, John (dun) c.1573–1631, English poet and clergyman.

don·ny·brook (don′ē brook′) n. rough, noisy brawl; free-for-all. [From *Donnybrook* Fair, held regularly until 1855 at Donnybrook, Ireland, and notorious for disorderly conduct.]

do·nor (dō′nər) n. **1.** one who donates. **2.** person or animal used as a source of biological material, as blood or organs. [Anglo-Norman *donour* giver, Latin *dōnātor.*]

Don Qui·xo·te (don′ kē hō′tē, -tā, don kwik′sət) **1.** tragicomic novel by Cervantes that satirized chivalric romances. **2.** its hero, a chivalrous, idealistic, impractical old man who believes he is a knight and attempts to fight evil and injustice.

don't (dōnt) do not: *Don't go.* ▲ When used in place of *doesn't,* it is generally considered substandard English.

do·nut (dō′nut′, -nət) doughnut.

doo·dad (dōō′dad′) n. *Informal.* **1.** small, fancy, ornament; bauble. **2.** doohickey.

doo·dle (dōō′dl) -dled, -dling. v.t., v.i. to draw or scribble idly or aimlessly, as while talking. —n. design or drawing produced by doodling. [Possibly from dialectal English *doodle* to waste time; of uncertain origin.]

doo·dle·bug¹ (dōō′dl bug′) n. larva of the ant lion. [Possibly dialectal English *doodle* to waste time (of uncertain origin) + BUG.]

doo·dle·bug² (dōō′dl bug′) n. *Informal.* **1.** divining rod or similar device to locate underground deposits. **2.** buzz bomb. [Possibly from DOODLEBUG¹.]

doo·hick·ey (dōō′hik′ē) pl. **-eys.** n. *Informal.* any gadget or small object. ▲ used as a substitute when the name of the gadget or object is forgotten or unknown.

doom (dōōm) n. **1.** that which cannot be escaped, esp. something adverse; fate; destiny. **2.** death, ruin, or destruction. **3.** sentence or judgment, esp. an adverse judicial sentence. **4.** Last Judgment. —v.t. **1.** to pronounce judgment or sentence against; condemn. **2.** to destine, esp. to an adverse or terrible fate: *plans doomed to fall through.* **2.** *Archaic.* to decree or ordain, as a sentence. [Old English *dōm* judgment, sentence, power.]

Dooms·day (dōōmz′dā′) *also,* **dooms·day.** n. **1.** Judgment Day. **2.** any day of final judgment. [Old English *dōmes dæg* Judgment Day.]

Doomsday Book, Domesday Book.

door (dôr) n. **1.** movable structure, usually hinged, sliding, or rotating,

that serves to open or close an entrance or opening, as into a building, vehicle, or cupboard. **2.** doorway: *She's standing in the door.* **3.** room or building to which a door belongs: *Her room is four doors away.* **4.** any means of entrance or exit; access: *no door of escape.* [Old English *dor* gate.]

door·bell (dôr′bel′) n. bell or buzzer activated by a button or other device at or near a door as a signal that someone is at the door and wishes to be admitted.

door·jamb (dôr′jam′) n. vertical piece forming the side of a doorway.

door·keep·er (dôr′kē′pər) n. one who guards an entrance.

door·knob (dôr′nob′) n. handle on a door, used to open it.

door·man (dôr′man, -mən) pl. **-men.** n. attendant at the door of a building, as a hotel, department store, or apartment house, who assists people entering and leaving, as by opening the door and hailing taxicabs.

door·mat (dôr′mat′) n. **1.** mat placed before a doorway, used for wiping the shoes of those entering. **2.** one who allows himself to be taken advantage of.

door·nail (dôr′nāl′) n. **1.** nail having a large head, used to strengthen or ornament doors. **2.** **dead as a doornail.** dead beyond question.

door·plate (dôr′plāt′) n. plate, usually of metal, placed on or near a door, typically bearing the occupant's name and street number.

door·post (dôr′pōst′) n. doorjamb.

door·sill (dôr′sil′) n. sill of a door.

door·step (dôr′step′) n. step or steps leading from an outside door to the ground.

door·way (dôr′wā′) n. **1.** opening in a wall that is closed by a door. **2.** means of access: *the doorway to the Orient.*

door·yard (dôr′yärd′) n. yard around a house, esp. near the door.

dope (dōp) n. **1.** *Informal.* stupid, dull-witted person. **2.** *Informal.* any narcotic, as heroin. **3.** *Slang.* secret or inside information. **4.** clear mixture used to fasten a covering to an object, as tissue to a model airplane, and to strengthen and waterproof it. —v.t. **doped, dop·ing. 1.** *Slang.* to give dope to; drug (often with *up*): *He was all doped up. The jockey doped the horse.* **2.** to treat with or apply dope to. **3. to dope out.** *Slang.* to figure out or plan. [Dutch *doop* sauce, from *doopen* to dip, mix.]

do·pey (dō′pē) **-pi·er, -pi·est.** adj. *Informal.* **1.** mentally slow; stupid. **2.** dulled or sluggish from or as from a narcotic, in a stupor or daze.

Dop·pler effect (dop′lər) *Physics.* apparent or observed change in the frequency of a wave, light, or other wave as the distance between the wave source and the observer changes. The frequency becomes lower as the distance between the source and the observer increases.

dor (dôr) n. European dung beetle or tumblebug, *Geotrupes stercorarius.* Also, **dor·bee·tle** (dôr′bēt′əl). [Old English *dora* bumblebee.]

do·ra·do (dō rä′dō) pl. **-dos.** n. dolphin (def. 2).

Dor·cas (dôr′kəs) n. in the New Testament, woman who made clothes for the poor.

Do·ri·an (dôr′ē ən) adj. of or relating to Doris, its inhabitants, or its culture. —n. member of one of the four major Greek tribes of antiquity. The Dorians settled in the Peloponnesus, Crete, the Italian peninsula, and Sicily.

Dor·ic (dôr′ik, dor′-) adj. **1.** of or relating to the oldest, simplest, and most refined of the three orders of classical Greek architecture, characterized by columns having no base and unadorned capitals consisting of annulets, echinus, and abacus. **2.** Dorian. —n. one of the three principal dialects of ancient Greece.

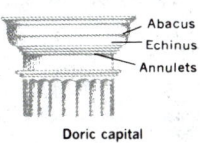

Abacus
Echinus
Annulets

Doric capital

Do·ris (dôr′is) n. small region in the central part of ancient Greece.

Dor·king (dôr′king) n. any of a breed of domestic fowl having a large, heavy body and five toes on each foot. [From *Dorking,* an English market town.]

dorm (dôrm) n. *Informal.* dormitory. [Short for DORMITORY.]

dor·man·cy (dôr′mən sē) n. state of being dormant.

dor·mant (dôr′mənt) adj. **1.** characterized by a state of temporary inactivity; not operating: *a dormant volcano, dormant talents.* **2.** sleeping. **3.** (of animals and plants) characterized by a partial suspension of animation or vegetation: *Some plants and animals are dormant during the winter.* [Old French *dormant,* present participle of *dormir* to sleep, from Latin *dormīre.*] —**Syn. 1.** see **latent.**

dor·mer (dôr′mər) n. **1.** vertical window projecting from a sloping roof. Also, **dormer window.** **2.** roofed projection containing such a window. [Old French *dormeor* room for sleeping, from Latin *dormītōrium.* Doublet of DORMITORY.]

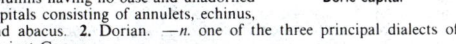

Dormer

dor·mi·to·ry (dôr′mə tôr′ē) pl. **-ries.** n. **1.** building having many

bedrooms and providing sleeping and living accommodations, as for students at a college. **2.** room containing a number of beds, as in a school. [Latin *dormītōrium* room for sleeping. Doublet of DORMER.]

dor·mouse (dôr′mous′) *pl.*, **-mice.** *n.* any of various squirrel-like rodents, suborder Myomorpha, native to Europe, Africa, and Asia, typically having brown or gray fur, and hibernating for up to six months of the year. Length: to 2 feet. [Possibly from dialectal English *dorm* to sleep (from Old French *dormir*, from Latin *dormīre*) + MOUSE.]

dor·sal (dôr′səl) *adj.* of, on, or near the back: *a dorsal fin.* [Late Latin *dorsālis*, from Latin *dorsum* back.] —**dor′sal·ly**, *adv.*

Dort·mund (dôrt′moont′) *n.* city in northwestern West Germany. Pop. (1968), 646,401.

Dormouse

do·ry[1] (dôr′ē) *pl.*, **-ries.** *n.* deep, flat-bottomed rowboat having high sides that slope upward and outward, often used by fishermen. [Of uncertain origin.]

do·ry[2] (dôr′ē) *pl.*, **-ries.** *n.* **1.** the John Dory. **2.** walleye *(def. 4).* [French *dorée* the John Dory; literally, gilded, going back to Latin *dēaurātus* gilded; because of its color.]

dos·age (dō′sij) *n.* **1.** amount of a medicine or other medical treatment in a single dose. **2.** the giving of such a dose.

dose (dōs) *n.* **1.** amount of a medicine or other medical treatment prescribed to be given or taken at one time. **2.** amount, esp. of something painful or unpleasant: *The bully was given a dose of his own medicine.* —*v.t.*, **dosed, dos·ing.** to give, as medicine, to: *to dose a person with antibiotics.* [French *dose* quantity, dose of medicine, through Medieval Latin, from Greek *dosis* a giving.]

do·sim·e·ter (dō sim′ə tər) *n.* device to be carried or worn on the body, used to register the amount of radiation to which a person has been exposed.

dos·si·er (dô′sē ā′, -sē ər) *n.* collection of detailed documents or papers relating to some subject or person. [French *dossier* a bundle, package of papers labeled on the back, from *dos* back, from Latin *dorsum* back.]

dost (dust) *Archaic.* present indicative, second person singular, of **do.** ▲ used with thou.

Dos·to·yev·sky, Feo·dor (dos′tə yef′skē, dos′toi-; fyô′dôr) 1821–81, Russian novelist and short-story writer.

dot[1] (dot) *n.* **1.** small, usually round, mark; speck or very small spot: *He made a dot on the paper with his pencil. The ship was a dot on the horizon.* **2.** shorter of the two sounds used in telegraphic codes, as in Morse code. Distinguished from **dash. 3.** *Music.* **a.** point placed after a note or rest which increases its time by one-half. **b.** point placed over or under a note indicating staccato. **4. on the dot.** at exactly the specified time. —*v.t.*, **dot·ted, dot·ting. 1.** to mark with a dot or dots. **2.** to be scattered over or about: *Houses dotted the landscape.* [Old English *dott* head of a boil.]

dot[2] (dot) *n.* dowry *(def. 1).* [French *dot*, from Latin *dōs*.]

dot·age (dō′tij) *n.* **1.** state of being feeble-minded, esp. because of old age; senility. **2.** foolish or excessive affection. [From DOTE.]

dot·ard (dō′tərd) *n.* one whose mind is feeble, esp. from old age. [From DOTE.]

dote (dōt) **dot·ed, dot·ing.** *also,* **doat.** *v.i.* **1.** to lavish extreme or excessive affection: *The grandparents doted on the child.* **2.** to be feeble-minded, esp. because of old age. [Middle English *doten* to be silly, possibly from Middle Low German *doten.*] —**dot′er**, *n.*

doth (duth) *Archaic.* present indicative, third person singular, of **do.**

dot·ing (dō′ting) *adj.* **1.** foolishly or excessively fond or indulgent: *doting parents.* **2.** feeble-minded; senile. —**dot′ing·ly**, *adv.*

dotted swiss, light, often sheer, cotton fabric, having a pattern of small, raised dots.

dot·ter·el (dot′ər əl) *n.* migratory plover, *Endromias morinellus*, native to northern Eurasia, having a short bill and black, white, and russet plumage. Length: 10 inches. [From DOTE; possibly because of its supposed foolishness.]

dot·ty (dot′ē) **-ti·er, -ti·est.** *adj. Informal.* crazy; eccentric.

Dou·ay Bible (doo′ā) English translation from the Latin of the authorized Roman Catholic Vulgate Bible of St. Jerome. Also, **Douay Version.** [From *Douai*, France, where this translation of the Old Testament was published in 1609–10.]

dou·ble (dub′əl) *adj.* **1.** twice as great or as many (as the usual), as in size, amount, or degree; multiplied by two: *a double blanket, double strength, double capacity.* **2.** having or forming two identical or similar parts; paired; coupled; or repeated: *a double dresser, a double line in front of the theater.* **3.** having a twofold relation, character, or application; combining two in one; dual or ambiguous: *a double role, a double meaning.* **4.** characterized by duplicity; deceitful; false: *to lead a double life.* **5.** *Botany.* having more than one set of petals or sepals. —*adv.*

in pairs or twos; doubly; twofold: *to see double, to ride a motorcycle double.* —*n.* **1.** that which is twice as much (as the usual), as in size, amount, or value: *Ten is the double of five.* **2.** one who or that which closely resembles or looks exactly like another; duplicate: *He's the double of his father.* **3.** actor, singer, or other performer who can substitute for another, as in a motion picture, esp. in performing dangerous physical feats. **4.** *Baseball.* hit that enables a player to reach second base safely without benefit of an error on the part of an opponent. **5.** *Bridge.* **a.** call indicating that the player feels a previous bidder cannot fulfill his bid, that doubles or increases the point value of the bid. **b.** strength in a hand sufficient to justify making such a call. **c.** conventional call used as a signal to inform one's partner of the strength of one's hand and, frequently, as a request to the partner to bid his best suit. **6. doubles.** game, as tennis, having two players on each side. **7. on the double. a.** quickly. **b.** in double time. —*v.t.*, **-bled, -bling. 1.** to make twice as great, as in size, amount, or degree; multiply by two: *to double a sum, to double one's weight.* **2.** to fold or bend, as to make two layers or thicknesses: *to double a bandage, to double a sheet of paper over.* **3.** to be or contain twice the quantity or number of: *The enemy's force doubles ours.* **4.** to turn, esp. sharply and suddenly, and trace the same or similar course (often with *back*): *to double in one's tracks, to double back across a field.* **5.** to clench (the fist) (often with *up*). **6.** (of a ship) to sail or go around, as a projecting piece of land: *to double Cape Horn.* **7.** *Baseball.* to advance (a base runner) by making a two-base hit. **8.** *Music.* to duplicate a note in a higher or lower octave. **9.** *Bridge.* to challenge (an opponent's bid) by calling a double. —*v.i.* **1.** to become twice as great; be multiplied by two: *Costs have doubled during this year.* **2.** to serve two purposes or perform in two capacities: *He doubled as coach and captain of the team. This sofa doubles as a bed.* **3.** to bend or fold: *He doubled up with pain. She doubled over with laughter.* **4.** to serve as a double; be a substitute: *to double for the star in a play.* **5.** *Baseball.* to make a two-base hit. **6.** *Informal.* to go out on a double date: *We doubled with them last week.* **7. to double up.** *Informal.* to share accommodations with another. [Old French *dou(b)le* twofold, from Latin *duplus.* Doublet of DUPLE.]

double bar *Music.* double vertical line on the staff marking the end of a section, movement, or piece. See **bar** for illustration.

dou·ble-bar·reled (dub′əl bar′əld) *adj.* **1.** having two barrels, as a firearm. **2.** that can be taken in two ways; ambiguous: *a double-barreled remark.* **3.** having two purposes.

double bass (bās) musical instrument, largest and deepest-toned of the violin family, usually having four strings, and played in an upright position; bass viol; contrabass.

double bassoon, large bassoon, largest and deepest-toned member of the oboe family, pitched an octave lower than the ordinary bassoon.

double bed, bed large enough for two adults, having a standard width of fifty-four inches.

double boiler, cooking utensil consisting of a pair of nested pots, the upper one containing the food that is cooked gently by the heat generated from the boiling water in the lower pot.

dou·ble-breast·ed (dub′əl bres′tid) *adj.* (of garments, as coats or jackets) overlapping enough to make two thicknesses across the breast and having two rows of buttons, of which only one row is usually used to button the garment.

dou·ble-check (dub′əl chek′) *v.i., v.t.* to check again, esp. for accuracy; countercheck.

double check, act or instance of double-checking; countercheck.

double chin, fat fold of flesh under the chin.

dou·ble-cross (dub′əl krôs′) *v.t. Informal.* to deceive or betray (someone) by failing to act as one has promised; be treacherous to. —**dou′ble-cross′er**, *n.*

double cross *Informal.* act of betrayal; treachery.

double dagger, reference mark (‡) used in printing to denote a note or cross reference.

dou·ble-date (dub′əl dāt′) **-dat·ed, -dat·ing.** *v.i. Informal.* to go on a double date.

double date *Informal.* social engagement involving two couples.

dou·ble-deal·er (dub′əl dē′lər) *n.* one who acts with duplicity.

dou·ble-deal·ing (dub′əl dē′ling) *n.* deceitful behavior; duplicity. —*adj.* given to or characterized by duplicity.

double eagle, gold coin of the United States, worth twenty dollars, withdrawn from circulation in 1934.

dou·ble-edged (dub′əl ejd′) *adj.* **1.** having two cutting edges: *a double-edged sword.* **2.** acting or applicable both for and against: *a double-edged argument.*

dou·ble en·ten·dre (doo′bəl än tän′drə, än tänd′) *n.* word or expression having two meanings, one of which is usually indecent or indelicate. [Obsolete French *double entendre*, going back to Latin *duplus* twofold + *intendere* to apply oneself to.]

double entry, self-balancing method of bookkeeping in which each transaction is recorded as both a debit and a credit.

at; āpe; cär; end; mē; it; īce; hot; ōld; fôrk; wood; foōl; oil; out; up; ūse; turn; sing; thin; this; zh in treasure; ə in ago, taken, pencil, lemon, circus.

double exposure 1. act of making two exposures on the same film or plate, as for a composite photograph. 2. print made from a film or plate so exposed.

double-faced (dub'əl fāst') *adj.* 1. having two faces or aspects. 2. (of a fabric) having the nap finished or patterned on both sides. 3. two-faced; hypocritical.

double feature, program showing two full-length motion pictures.

dou·ble-head·ed nail (dub'əl hed'id) nail with two heads so that it can be easily removed, used esp. in making temporary structures.

dou·ble-head·er (dub'əl hed'ər) *n.* 1.a. two baseball games played on the same day, in close succession, by the same teams. b. two basketball games played on the same day, in close succession, by two different sets of teams. 2. train pulled by two locomotives.

double jeopardy, condition of being retried for the same offense for which one has already been tried and judged.

dou·ble-joint·ed (dub'əl join'tid) *adj.* having extremely flexible joints that permit movement of the body into unusual angles or positions.

dou·ble-park (dub'əl pärk') *v.t., v.i.* to park (a motor vehicle) next to one that is already legally parked parallel to the curb.

double play, baseball play in which two base runners are put out.

double pneumonia, pneumonia affecting both lungs.

dou·ble-quick (dub'əl kwik') *adj.* very quick; hurried; rapid: *He appeared in double-quick time.* —*n.* double time *(def. 1).* —*v.t., v.i.* to march or cause to march in double time.

dou·ble-reed (dub'əl rēd') *Music. adj.* of or designating any of a group of wind instruments, as the oboe and and bassoon, having a reed with two tongues which vibrate together and produce sounds when wind is forced between them. —*n.* double-reed instrument. All double-reeds are members of the oboe family.

double sharp *Music.* 1. symbol (×, ⊗) which, when placed before a note, indicates that the pitch must be raised two half tones. 2. note or tone so raised.

double standard, code of moral behavior in many societies whereby men are permitted greater freedom than women, esp. sexual freedom.

double star 1. two stars which appear to be one unless viewed through a telescope. 2. binary star.

dou·blet (dub'lit) *n.* 1. close-fitting waist-length jacket, with or without sleeves, worn esp. by men in Western Europe from about 1400 to 1650. 2. pair of similar or equal things; couple. 3. either of such a pair. 4. one of two or more words in a language, derived from the same original word but differing in form and, usually, in meaning, as *cloak* and *clock.* 5. *also,* doublets. pair of dice so thrown that the two upper surfaces are identical. [Old French *doublet* something folded, diminutive of *do(u)ble.* See DOUBLE.]

double take, delayed reaction, as to a joke or surprising situation, characterized by initial blankness or acceptance and followed by a sudden understanding or recognition.

double talk 1. deliberately deceptive or ambiguous talk. 2. nonsensical speech made to appear or sound intelligible by mixing actual words with meaningless syllables.

dou·ble-think (dub'əl thingk') *n.* thinking that ignores the conflict between opposite versions of a factual matter given at the same time, accepting both as true. —*v.i.* **-thought, -think·ing.** to think in this way.

dou·ble-time (dub'əl tīm') **-timed, -tim·ing.** *v.i.* to move in double time. —*v.t.* to cause to move in double time.

double time 1. *Military.* rapid marching rate of 180 three-foot steps per minute. 2. rate of pay that is twice one's normal pay rate.

dou·ble-tree (dub'əl trē') *n.* crossbar, as on a carriage, plow, or wagon, to each end of which singletrees are attached when two draft animals are harnessed abreast.

dou·bloon (dub loon') *n.* former gold coin of Spain and Spanish America. [Spanish *doblón,* from *doble* double, from Latin *duplus* twofold; because originally worth double the pistole.]

dou·bly (dub'lē) *adv.* in a twofold manner or degree; twice as.

doubt (dout) *v.t.* to be unconvinced or uncertain about; hesitate to believe or accept; distrust; question: *to doubt the truth of a story. Do you doubt my word?* —*v.i.* to be wavering or undecided in opinion or belief; be unconvinced, uncertain, or distrustful: *He who doubts will establish truths for himself.* —*n.* 1. feeling of disbelief, uncertainty, or distrust: *to remove all doubt about a subject. He had doubts about her sincerity.* 2. state or condition of being uncertain or undecided; condition or state of affairs giving rise to uncertainty: *The outcome of the elections was in doubt.* 3. **no doubt.** a. without question; certainly. b. most likely; probably. 4. **without doubt.** without question; certainly. [Old French *doter* to fear, hesitate, from Late Latin *dubitāre* to fear, from Latin *dubitāre* to doubt.] —**doubt'er,** *n.*

doubt·ful (dout'fəl) *adj.* 1. having, showing, or experiencing doubt: *She had a doubtful look on her face. I'm doubtful about his prospects for success.* 2. subject to or causing doubt; not clear or sure; undecided; uncertain: *The outcome of the war was doubtful. It's doubtful whether*

we'll go. 3. indistinct or obscure, as in character, meaning, or appearance; vague; ambiguous. 4. of questionable, suspect, or equivocal character: *a doubtful reputation.* —**doubt'ful·ly,** *adv.* —**doubt'ful·ness,** *n.*

Syn. 2. **Doubtful, dubious** mean hesitant or unsure about the truth, soundness, value, or the like of something or someone. **Doubtful** implies a distinctly negative judgment: *That Bacon wrote the plays attributed to Shakespeare is doubtful.* **Dubious,** though negative, suggests hesitation or suspicion rather than a contrary judgment: *He was dubious about the results and suggested repeating the experiments.*

doubting Thomas, one who is habitually doubtful and refuses to believe anything without proof; skeptic.

doubt·less (dout'lis) *adv.* 1. unquestionably; certainly. 2. probably. Also, **doubt'less·ly.** —*adj.* free from doubt or uncertainty.

douche (dōōsh) *n.* 1. jet of water or other liquid directed into or onto a body part, organ, or cavity for cleansing or medicinal purposes. 2. application of such a jet. 3. device, as a spray or syringe, for administering such an application. —*v.t.* **douched, douch·ing.** to apply a douche to. —*v.i.* to use a douche; take a douche. [French *douche* shower (bath), from Italian *doccia* canal, pipe, shower (bath), going back to Latin *ductiō* a leading, pipe.]

dough (dō) *n.* 1. soft, thick mass worked or kneaded from a mixture of flour or meal, liquid, and other ingredients for use in baking. 2. any soft, thick, pasty mass. 3. *Slang.* money. [Old English *dāg, dāh* flour paste for baking.]

dough·boy (dō'boi') *n. Informal.* soldier in the United States army, esp. during World War I. [Possibly because the brass buttons on Civil War infantry uniforms resembled the dumplings of those times known as *doughboys.*]

dough·nut (dō'nut', -nət) *also,* **do·nut.** *n.* small, usually ring-shaped, cake made of dough, usually leavened and sweetened, cooked by frying in deep fat.

dough·ty (dou'tē) **-ti·er, -ti·est.** *adj.* steadfast and courageous; valiant: *our doughty hero.* [Old English *dohtig.*] —**dough'ti·ly,** *adv.* —**dough'ti·ness,** *n.*

dough·y (dō'ē) **dough·i·er, dough·i·est.** *adj.* of or like dough in consistency or appearance; pasty.

Doug·las, Stephen A. (dug'ləs) 1813–61, U.S. statesman who was Abraham Lincoln's opponent in the presidential election of 1860.

Douglas fir 1. evergreen timber tree, *Pseudotsuga menziesii,* of the pine family, found in western North America, having reddish-brown ridged bark and bearing oval cones. It may grow to a height of 200 feet and is surpassed in size only by the sequoia of California. Also, **Douglas spruce.** 2. hard, strong wood of this tree, used chiefly in building construction.

Doug·lass, Frederick (dug'ləs) 1817–95, Afro-American anti-slavery orator and journalist.

dour (door, dour) *adj.* 1. sullenly gloomy; grim; forbidding. 2. unyielding; obstinate. [Latin *dūrus* hard.] —**dour'ly,** *adv.* —**dour'ness,** *n.*

douse (dous) **doused, dous·ing.** *v.t.* 1. to plunge into water or other liquid: *He doused the torch in a bucket.* 2. to throw water or other liquid over; drench: *They doused me with the hose.* 3. *Informal.* to put out; extinguish: *Douse the lights.* 4. to lower (a sail) quickly and suddenly. [Of uncertain origin.]

dove[1] (duv) *n.* 1.a. any small or medium-sized bird of the pigeon family, Columbidae, including the mourning dove and turtledove. b. completely white bird of this family, often regarded as a symbol of peace or good fortune. 2. innocent, gentle, or loving person. 3. **Dove.** the Holy Ghost. 4. person who advocates peaceful solutions to international conflicts. Opposed to hawk. [Possibly from Old Norse *dūfa* pigeon.]

dove[2] (dōv) a past tense of **dive.**

dove·cote (duv'kōt') *also,* **dove·cot** (duv'kot'). *n.* small house or boxlike shelter for doves or pigeons, usually having compartments and placed on a pole or other structure.

dove·kie (duv'kē) *also,* **dove·key,.** *n.* small auk, *Plautus alle,* native to the Arctic and north Atlantic regions.

Do·ver (dō'vər) *n.* 1. port town in southeastern England, noted for its white cliffs. Pop. (1961), 35,554. 2. **Strait of.** strait separating southeastern England from northern France, and connecting the English Channel with the North Sea. 3. capital of Delaware, in the east-central part of the state. Pop. (1970), 17,488.

dove·tail (duv'tāl') *n.* 1. wedge-shaped tenon designed to interlock with a mortise of similar shape to form a joint. 2. joint formed by the interlocking of such tenons and mortises. —*v.t.* 1. to fit together or join by means of dovetails. 2. to fit together precisely, compactly, or harmoniously.

Dovetails

dow·a·ger (dou'ə jər) *n.* 1. widow who holds property or a title derived from her deceased husband. ▲ often used as an additional title to differentiate her from the wife of her husband's

heir: *a dowager queen, a dowager empress.* **2.** dignified, elderly lady, esp. one of imposing appearance or social position. [Old French *douagere* widow who has received a dower, from *douage* a dower, from *douer* to endow, from Latin *dōtāre*, from *dōs* dowry.]

dow·dy (dou′dē) **-di·er, -di·est.** *adj.* lacking style or smartness in dress or appearance; not neat or fashionable; frumpish: *a dowdy woman, a dowdy dress.* —*n. pl.* **-dies. 1.** dowdy woman. **2.** pandowdy. [Of uncertain origin.] —**dow′di·ly,** *adv.* —**dow′di·ness,** *n.*

dow·el (dou′əl) *n.* peg or pin fitting into corresponding holes of two adjacent pieces to hold them together. —*v.t.* **-eled, -el·ing;** *also, British,* **-elled, -el·ling.** to fasten or furnish with dowels. [Middle Low German *dövel* peg, plug.]

dow·er (dou′ər) *n.* **1.** part of a deceased man's real property that is given by law to his widow. **2.** dowry *(def. 1).* **3.** natural gift, talent, or endowment. —*v.t.* to provide with a dower. [Old French *doaire* widow's inheritance, from Medieval Latin *dotarium,* from Latin *dōtāre* to endow, from *dōs* dowry.]

down[1] (doun) *adv.* **1.** from a higher to a lower place, level, or position; in a descending direction; toward the ground: *He stepped down from the ladder. We looked down upon the valley.* **2.** in, on, or to a lower place, level, or position: *She pulled the blinds down.* **3.** to or on the ground, floor, or bottom: *to knock someone down. She stumbled and fell down. They beat the door down.* **4.** to, toward, or in a direction, position, or area considered geographically lower or distant, as to the south on a map: *We drove down from New York to Richmond. They went down to the park after dinner. He's down at the seashore this week.* **5.** below the horizon or surface: *The sun's gone down. The ship went down with forty men.* **6.** to a lower or reduced amount, degree, rate, or pitch: *to slow down, to cut one's expenses down, to mark down the price of milk. Turn down the television set. The temperature went down to zero.* **7.** from a higher to a lower rank or station; in, into, or toward a lower status or condition: *He's gone down in my estimation since the scandal.* **8.** to or in a calmer, less active or intense state: *The crowd quieted down. Things finally settled down.* **9.** to lesser strength or consistency or smaller size: *to water down whiskey, to thin down a liquid, to cut down a dress.* **10.** in or into a prostrate or weakened physical condition; ill: *She came down with a cold.* **11.** in or into a low or depressed mental or emotional condition; dejected: *I feel down about her leaving.* **12.** with seriousness; earnestly: *to get down to work, to get down to business.* **13.** fully; thoroughly: *to be loaded down with work. She was loaded down with packages. He seems weighted down with cares.* **14.** from an earlier time or individual: *down to the present, a tradition followed down through the ages. The dress was handed down to her sister.* **15.** at the time of purchase; in cash: *Pay thirty dollars down and the rest in installments.* **16.** in writing; on paper: *Write down this address. I took down their names.* **17.** all the way through and including: *The board raised everyone's salary from the president down to the secretaries.* **18.** to the point of submission, defeat, or inactivity; in or into subjection or control: *to put down a rebellion, to shout down the opposition.* **19.** so as to overtake or locate the source of; to the origin or actual position: *The hounds hunted down the fox. The reporter tracked down the story.* **20. down with.** do away with; overthrow: *Down with tyranny!* —*adj.* **1.** going or directed downward; descending: *a down staircase.* **2.** in a lower place, level, or position: *The curtain is down.* **3.** completed; done; over: *Four pages down, three to go. Eight assignments down, two to go.* **4.** sick; ill; ailing: *He's down with bronchitis.* **5.** depressed; dejected. **6.** trailing an opponent by a specified number, as of points. **7.** (of a football) no longer in play. **8. down and out. a.** completely bereft, as of money or friends; miserable. **b.** *Boxing.* knocked out. **9. down on.** *Informal.* angry at, annoyed with, or hostile to. —*prep.* **1.** in a descending direction along, through, or into: *to walk down a lane, to glance down a page, three miles down the road.* **2.** during the course of: *down the years, down the ages.* —*v.t.* **1.** to cause to fall; bring, throw, knock, or put down: *He downed his opponent with three blows. The guns downed four bombers.* **2.** *Informal.* to swallow, esp. quickly; gulp: *He downed his milk and ran out.* **3.** *Informal.* to defeat, as in a game. —*n.* **1.** downward movement; descent: *the ups and downs of the business cycle.* **2.** unfavorable change or reversal, as of fortune: *to have one's ups and downs.* **3.** *Football.* any of four successive plays during which a team must advance the ball at least ten yards in order to keep possession of it. [Old English *dūne* from a higher to a lower place, short for *of-dūne* literally, from the hill.]

down[2] (doun) *n.* **1.** fine, soft feathers, as on young birds or under the exterior plumage of certain adult birds: *a pillow stuffed with down.* **2.** any fine, soft hair or fuzz. [Old Norse *dūnn* soft plumage.]

down[3] (doun) *n.* **1.** *also,* **downs.** open, rolling, grassy tract of upland, esp. in southern and southeastern England. **2.** hill, esp. one of sand; dune. [Old English *dūn* hill.]

down·beat (doun′bēt′) *n. Music.* **1.** downward gesture made by a conductor to indicate the first accented beat in a measure. **2.** first beat or the first accented beat in a measure. —*adj.* quiet or gloomy.

down·cast (doun′kast′) *adj.* **1.** low or dejected in spirit; sad; depressed. **2.** directed downward: *She sat there quietly with downcast eyes.* —*n.* act of casting down; overthrow; ruin.

Down East *also,* **down East.** New England, esp. Maine.

Dow·ney (dou′nē) *n.* city in southern California. Pop. (1970), 88,445.

down·fall (doun′fôl′) *n.* **1.** descent to a lower position or standing; fall, as from power or prosperity; ruin: *the downfall of the government. His downfall was caused by his greed.* **2.** person or thing causing this: *Excessive pride was his downfall.* **3.** fall, as of rain or snow, esp. when sudden or heavy. **4.** deadfall *(def. 1).*

down·fall·en (doun′fô′lən) *adj.* fallen; ruined.

down·grade (doun′grād′) *n.* **1.** downward or descending slope, as of a hill or road. **2. on the downgrade.** declining, as in strength or status; becoming worse; deteriorating. —*v.t.* **-grad·ed, -grad·ing. 1.** to lower in rank, position, or salary; demote. **2.** to minimize the importance or worth of; belittle. —*adj., adv.* downhill.

down·heart·ed (doun′här′tid) *adj.* depressed or discouraged in spirit; sad; dejected. —**down′heart′ed·ly,** *adv.* —**down′heart′ed·ness,** *n.*

down·hill (doun′hil′) *adv.* **1.** in a descending or downward direction; toward the bottom of a hill: *The car rolled downhill.* **2.** into or toward a lower or worse level or condition: *Her health has been going downhill for months.* —*adj.* sloping or descending downward on or as on a hill: *a downhill battle.*

Down·ing Street (dou′ning) **1.** street in Westminster London, site of several official residences and offices of the British government. The home and residence of the prime minister is at 10 Downing Street. **2.** the British government or cabinet.

down payment, initial amount paid on a purchase, as in installment buying.

down·pour (doun′pôr′) *n.* heavy, drenching fall of rain.

down·range (doun′rānj′) *adj., adv.* away from a launching site, along the course toward the point designated as the target: *a missile moving downrange.*

down·right (doun′rīt′) *adj.* **1.** thorough; absolute; utter: *downright nonsense. You're a downright liar.* **2.** frankly direct; straightforward; forthright. —*adv.* thoroughly; utterly: *That's downright stupid!*

Downs (dounz) *n.,pl.* two ranges of hills in southern England, south of London.

down·stage (doun′stāj′) *adv.* at or toward the front of the stage. —*adj.* of or relating to the front of the stage. —*n.* front half of the stage.

down·stairs (doun′stārz′) *adv.* **1.** down the stairs; toward the foot of a staircase. **2.** on or to a lower floor or level. —*adj.* situated on a lower or main floor: *a downstairs room.* —*n.* lower or main floor or floors: *They rent the whole downstairs.*

down·stream (doun′strēm′) *adv., adj.* with or in the direction of the current or flow of a stream.

down·swing (doun′swing′) *n.* **1.** downward swing, as of a golf club. **2.** downward trend, esp. in business.

down-to-earth (doun′tōō urth′, -tə-) *adj.* realistic and unpretentious; practical; unaffected.

down·town (doun′toun′) *adv.* to, toward, or in the business center or geographically lower part of a town or city: *Let's go downtown this afternoon. They moved downtown.* —*adj.* of, relating to, or in the business center or geographically lower part of a town or city: *a downtown office, downtown traffic, a downtown branch of a bank.* —*n.* central business district of a town or city.

down·trod·den (doun′trod′ən) *adj.* **1.** abused or subjugated, as by those in power; oppressed: *a downtrodden nation, the downtrodden serfs of the feudal period.* **2.** trampled under foot: *downtrodden grass.* Also, **down′trod′.**

down·turn (doun′turn′) *n.* decline, esp. in business activity.

down under *Informal.* Australia or New Zealand.

down·ward (doun′wərd) *adv. also,* **down·wards. 1.** from a higher to a lower place, level, or condition. **2.** from an earlier time or individual. —*adj.* moving from a higher to a lower place, level, or condition.

down·wind (doun′wind′) *adj.* located or moving in the same direction as that in which the wind is blowing.

down·y (dou′nē) **down·i·er, down·i·est.** *adj.* **1.** of or covered with down. **2.** like down; soft; fluffy. —**down′i·ness,** *n.*

dow·ry (dour′ē) *pl.,* **-ries.** *n.* **1.** money or property that a woman brings to her husband at the time of her marriage. **2.** natural talent or endowment. [Form of DOWER.]

dowse (douz) **dowsed, dows·ing.** *v.i.* to search for underground water or minerals with a divining rod. —**dows′er,** *n.*

dox·ol·o·gy (dok sol′ə jē) *pl.,* **-gies.** *n.* in the Christian Church, hymn or formula praising God. [Medieval Latin *doxologia* hymn of praise, from Greek *doxologia* praise, going back to *doxa* glory + *logos* speaking.]

Doyle, Sir Arthur Co·nan (doil; kō′nən, kō′-) 1859–1930, English writer.

---

doz., dozen; dozens.

doze (dōz) **dozed, doz·ing.** *v.i.* **1.** to sleep lightly, fitfully, or for a short while; be half asleep; nap: *She's dozing on the couch. He's dozing over his newspaper.* **2.** to fall into a light, brief sleep unintentionally (often with *off*): *I dozed off while reading.* —*v.t.* to spend or pass (time) in dozing: *He dozed the afternoon away.* —*n.* light, fitful, or brief sleep. [Probably of Scandinavian origin.] —**doz'er,** *n.*

doz·en (duz'ən) *pl.,* **-ens** *or* **-en.** *n.* group of twelve. [Old French *dozaine,* from *do(u)ze* twelve, from Latin *duodecim.*]

doz·enth (duz'ənth) *adj.* twelfth.

DP, displaced person.

dpt. 1. department. **2.** deponent.

Dr. 1. Doctor. **2.** Drive.

dr. 1. dram; drams. **2.** debtor. **3.** drawer.

drab[1] (drab) *n.* **1.** dull, yellowish-brown or gray color. **2.** thick, strong woolen or cotton cloth of this color, often woven with a twill. —*adj.* **drab·ber, drab·best. 1.** lacking brightness; dull; monotonous; cheerless: *a drab existence.* **2.** of the color drab. [Form of obsolete *drap* cloth, from French *drap* cloth; with reference to the color of undyed cloth. See DRAPE.] —**drab'ly,** *adv.* —**drab'ness,** *n.*

drab[2] (drab) *n.* **1.** slovenly, untidy woman. **2.** prostitute. [Of uncertain origin.]

drachm (dram) *n.* **1.** dram. **2.** drachma.

drach·ma (drak'mə) *pl.,* **-mas** *or* **-mae** (-mē). *n.* **1.** basic monetary unit of Greece. **2.** silver coin of ancient Greece. **3.** unit of weight of ancient Greece. **4.** any of several modern weights, esp. a drachm. [Latin *drachma* coin or weight of ancient Greece, from Greek *drachmē* literally, handful. Doublet of DRAM.]

Dra·co (drā'kō) Athenian lawgiver of the late seventh century B.C., whose code of laws is noted for its harshness.

Dra·co·ni·an (drā kō'nē ən, drə-) *adj.* **1.** of or relating to Draco or his code of laws. **2.** *also,* **draconian.** rigorous; severe; harsh.

draft (draft, dräft) *also,* **draught.** *n.* **1.** current of air in an enclosed space or area: *She felt a draft on her shoulders. The size of the chimney will affect the draft in the furnace.* **2.** device for regulating the flow of air, as in a stove. **3.** preliminary or rough version of something written: *a draft of a proposed law. He's now revising the first draft of his essay.* **4.** sketch, plan, or design of something to be made, as a building. **5.a.** act or process of selecting an individual or individuals for some special purpose: *The senator accepted his party's draft and immediately announced his candidacy.* **b.** act or process of selecting persons, by an act of law, for compulsory military service. **6.** group so selected. **7.** written order directing the payment of a specified amount of money, as from one person or bank to another. **8.** act of drawing or pulling something, as a loaded wagon: *a team of oxen for draft.* **9.a.** act of drinking. **b.** amount taken in one drink. **10.a.** act of inhaling, as smoke or air. **b.** quantity inhaled at one breath. **11.** quantity or dose of liquid for drinking. **12.a.** act of drawing in a fishnet. **b.** amount of fish taken in a net at one time. **13.** *Nautical.* depth of water required for a ship to float. **14. on draft,** ready to be drawn from a tap: *ale on draft.* —*v.t.* **1.** to make a preliminary plan, sketch, or version of. **2.** to select for some special purpose, esp. for compulsory military service. —*adj.* **1.** used for pulling loads: *a draft animal.* **2.** drawn or ready to be drawn from a tap; not bottled: *draft beer.* [Possibly from Old Norse *drāttr* act of pulling.]

draft board, official board of civilians that selects qualified men for compulsory service in the U.S. armed forces.

draft dodger, one who avoids or attempts to avoid compulsory military service.

draft·ee (draf tē', dräf-) *n.* one who is drafted for military service.

drafts·man (drafts'mən, dräfts'-) *also,* **draughts·man.** *pl.,* **-men.** *n.* one who draws or designs plans for machinery, buildings, and other structures and facilities. —**drafts'man·ship,** *n.*

draft·y (draf'tē, dräf'-) **draft·i·er, draft·i·est.** *also,* **draught·y.** *adj.* exposed to or admitting drafts of air: *a drafty hallway.* —**draft'i·ly,** *adv.* —**draft'i·ness,** *n.*

drag (drag) **dragged, drag·ging.** *v.t.* **1.a.** to pull or draw heavily, slowly, or with great effort; haul: *She dragged the heavy suitcase along.* **b.** to cause to move with difficulty or as if by force: *She went shopping for a new dress and dragged me along with her.* **2.** to search the bottom of, as with a net or hook; dredge: *to drag a pond for a sunken rowboat.* **3.** to continue tediously or for a painfully long period of time; protract (often with *out*): *to drag out a lonely existence, to drag out a story.* **4.** to introduce or bring in, as something irrelevant or unnecessary (often with *in* or *up*): *He dragged up that corny old story again. Why drag him into the argument?* **5. to drag one's feet.** *Informal.* to act with deliberate slowness; fail to act promptly. —*v.i.* **1.** to be drawn or hauled along; trail to or as to the ground: *Her skirt dragged behind her.* **2.** to move heavily, slowly, or with great effort: *His feet dragged as he walked along despondently.* **3.** to progress or pass slowly, tediously, or laboriously: *The days dragged on, one by one. The movie drags in the middle.*

4. to search, as with a net, hook, or dredge: *to drag for treasure.* **5.** to fall behind; lag. —*n.* **1.** person or thing that hinders or slows down: *His lack of business sense proved to be a drag on his career.* **2.** something that retards movement, as a brake on a wheel. **3.** resistance that acts in a direction opposite to the motion of a body, as an airplane, moving through a fluid, as air, causing it to slow down. **4.** something that is used in searching the bottom of a body of water, as a net, hook, or dredge. **5.** slow, heavy, or difficult movement. **6.** something that is pulled or hauled along a surface. **7.** strong sledlike device, usually homemade, consisting of a wooden platform that is dragged along the ground to move rocks or other heavy loads. **8.** heavy harrow, usually homemade and consisting of planks fastened together. **9.** large coach having seats inside and on top, usually designed to be drawn by four horses. **10.** *Informal.* puff, as on a cigarette. **11.** *Slang.* one who or that which is dull, boring, or vapid. [Old English *dragan* to draw, pull, or Old Norse *draga* to draw.] —**Syn.** *v.t.* **1.a.** see **pull.**

drag·gle (drag'əl) **-gled, -gling.** *v.t.* to make wet or dirty, as by dragging through mud. —*v.i.* **1.** to become wet or dirty, as by being dragged through mud. **2.** to straggle.

drag·net (drag'net') *n.* **1.** net, usually bag-shaped, to be towed over the bottom of a body of water for catching fish or the like. **2.** system or operation for locating, gathering in, or catching something or someone, as a wanted criminal.

drag·o·man (drag'ə mən) *pl.,* **-mans** *or* **-men.** *n.* in the Near East, an interpreter or guide for travelers. [Obsolete French *dragoman.* through Italian, Middle Greek, Arabic, and Aramaic, going back to Akkadian *targumānu* interpreter.]

drag·on (drag'ən) *n.* **1.** mythical monster with a scaly reptilelike body and claws, often represented as having wings and breathing fire and smoke. **2.** fierce person. **3.** strict, watchful female chaperon. **4.** flying dragon. [Old French *dragon* this mythical monster, from Latin *dracō* serpent, reptile monster, from Greek *drakōn.*]

drag·on·fly (drag'ən flī') *pl.,* **-flies.** *n.* any of a large group of slender-bodied insects, suborder Anisoptera, found near fresh water and feeding on mosquitoes and other insects. They have broad heads, compound eyes, and two pairs of membranous, veined wings, which may grow to a spread of 7½ inches. Also, **darning needle, devil's darning needle.**

Dragonfly

drag·on·nade (drag'ə nād') *n.* **1.** persecution directed by Louis XIV in the seventeenth century against French Protestants, in which soldiers were billeted in Protestant homes. **2.** any persecution in which soldiers are used. [French *dragonnade* brutal religious persecution, from *dragon.* See DRAGOON.]

dra·goon (drə gōōn') *n.* **1.** any heavily armed cavalryman. **2.** formerly, a mounted infantryman armed with a musket. —*v.t.* **1.** to coerce or persecute by the use of dragoons or other troops. **2.** to force or pressure (*into* doing something): *They dragooned him into voting for the bill.* [French *dragon* cavalry soldier; earlier, soldier armed with a firearm called a *dragon* because it emitted fire. See DRAGON.]

drag race *Slang.* race on a short, straight course between automobiles beginning from a dead stop, the winner being the car which accelerates the fastest.

drag strip *Slang.* short, straight course used in a drag race.

drain (drān) *v.t.* **1.** to draw water or other liquid from; empty or dry by drawing off liquid: *to drain a marsh, to drain a bathtub.* **2.** to draw off (a liquid) gradually or completely: *to drain water from a pool.* **3.a.** to use up slowly; exhaust gradually: *The nation's resources were drained by the war. The long hike drained my strength.* **b.** to exhaust physically or emotionally: *The experience drained him of all feeling.* **4.** to drink all the liquid from; empty by drinking: *He drained his glass.* —*v.i.* **1.** to become dry or empty by the flowing off or away of liquid: *The dishes drained. The sink is draining.* **2.** to flow off or away gradually: *The water drained out of the hole in the boat.* **3.** to release or discharge waters: *The river drains into the sea. The pipe drains into the sewer.* —*n.* **1.** channel, pipe, or similar device for drawing off water or other liquid: *The bathtub drain is clogged.* **2.** slow or continuous outflow, withdrawal, or expenditure tending toward exhaustion: *The project was a drain on the institute's funds.* **3.** material or device, as gauze or rubber tubing, used to remove fluid in a body cavity or wound. **4. down the drain.** lost, wasted, or worthless. [Old English *drēahnian* to strain.] —**drain'er,** *n.* —**Syn.** *v.t.* **3.** see **deplete.**

drain·age (drā'nij) *n.* **1.** act or process of draining. **2.** system of natural or artificial drains. **3.** that which is drained off. **4.** area or region drained.

drainage basin, area drained by a river and all its tributaries.

drain·pipe (drān'pīp') *n.* pipe for draining water or other liquid, esp. from a gutter on a roof.

drake (drāk) *n.* male duck. [Of uncertain origin.]

Drake, Sir Francis (drāk) c.1540–96, English admiral and explorer, commander of the first English voyage around the world.

dram (dram) **1.** apothecaries' weight equal to sixty grains, or one-eighth of an ounce. **2.** avoirdupois weight equal to 27.343 grams. **3.** fluid dram. See **weights and measures** for table. **4.** small drink, esp. of alcoholic liquor. **5.** small amount of anything. [Middle French *drame* one eighth of an ounce, handful, going back to Latin *drachma* coin or weight of ancient Greece, from Greek *drachmē* literally, handful. Doublet of DRACHMA.]

dra·ma (drä′mə, dram′ə) *n.* **1.a.** literary composition telling a story and written to be performed. **b.** such a composition dealing with a serious subject in a serious manner. **2.** branch of literature composed of such compositions: *a student of drama, the classical drama.* **3.** art or profession of writing, acting, or producing plays. **4.** situation or series of events having dramatic qualities: *The history of space exploration is an exciting drama.* **5.** dramatic state, quality, or effect: *The witness' unexpected disclosure was filled with drama.* [Late Latin *drāma* play, from Greek *drāma* deed, play.]

dram·a·mine (dram′ə mēn′) *n.* antihistamine used to treat allergies and to prevent motion sickness. Trademark: Dramamine.

dra·mat·ic (drə mat′ik) *adj.* **1.** of or relating to drama; dealing with or employing the forms of drama. **2.** characteristic of or appropriate to drama; exciting; vivid; striking: *a dramatic appeal for clemency for the condemned man, the dramatic events leading to his victory.* —**dra·mat′i·cal·ly,** *adv.*

dramatic monologue, lyric poem in which a single character reveals his personality by addressing a silent listener.

dra·mat·ics (drə mat′iks) *n.* **1.** art or activity of producing or performing plays: *He's taken charge of dramatics.* **2.** exaggerated or theatrical behavior. ▲ construed as singular in def. 1; as plural in def. 2.

dram·a·tis per·so·nae (dram′ə tis pər sō′nē, drä′mə-) **1.** characters in a play. **2.** list of these characters, often with the names of the actors who portray them. [Latin *drāmatis persōnae.*]

dram·a·tist (dram′ə tist, drä′mə-) *n.* one who writes dramas.

dram·a·ti·za·tion (dram′ə ti zā′shən, drä′mə-) *n.* **1.** act of dramatizing. **2.** that which is dramatized; dramatized version or representation.

dram·a·tize (dram′ə tīz′, drä′mə-) -tized, -tiz·ing. *v.t.* **1.** to put into the form of a play; adapt for dramatic performance: *to dramatize a novel.* **2.** to represent in an exaggerated or theatrical way; make seem exciting or spectacular: *Stop dramatizing your problems.*

dram·a·turge (dram′ə turj′, drä′mə-) *n.* dramatist. Also, **dram′a·tur′gist.**

dram·a·tur·gy (dram′ə tur′jē, drä′mə-) *n.* art of writing, producing, or acting in plays. [Greek *drāmatourgiā* composition of plays.] —**dram′a·tur′gic;** also, **dram′a·tur′gi·cal,** *adj.*

dram·shop (dram′shop′) *n. Archaic.* saloon; bar.

drank (drangk) past tense of **drink.**

drape (drāp) draped, drap·ing. *v.t.* **1.** to cover or adorn gracefully with or as with cloth: *to drape a window, to drape a statue.* **2.** to place or arrange, as cloth or clothing, in loose, graceful folds. **3.** to arrange, spread, or let fall casually or carelessly: *He draped himself across the sofa. Don't drape your feet over the chair.* —*v.i.* to hang or fall in folds: *Silk drapes nicely.* —*n.* **1.** *usually,* **drapes.** cloth hung in folds, esp. when used as a window curtain; drapery: *He pulled the drapes back.* **2.** way in which cloth hangs. [French *draper* to cover with cloth, from *drap* cloth, from Late Latin *drappus;* probably of Celtic origin.]

drap·er (drā′pər) *n.* dealer in cloth or dry goods.

drap·er·y (drā′pər ē) *pl.,* -per·ies. *n.* **1.** cloth hung or arranged in loose, graceful folds, esp. when used as a window curtain: *the drapery over the statue. They have blue draperies in their living room.* **2.** the draping or arranging of cloth.

dras·tic (dras′tik) *adj.* having a forceful or severe effect; rigorous; extreme: *The imposition of a curfew was a drastic step.* [Greek *drastikos* active, effective.] —**dras′ti·cal·ly,** *adv.*

drat (drat) *Informal. interj.* darn. —*v.t.* drat·ted, drat·ting. to damn; confound; curse. [Euphemism for *God rot.*]

drat·ted (drat′id) *adj. Informal.* damned; confounded.

drave (drāv) archaic past tense of **drive.**

draught (draft, dräft) *n.* draft.

draughts (drafts, dräfts) *n. British.* the game of checkers. ▲ construed as singular.

draughts·man (drafts′mən, dräfts′-) *pl.,* -men. *n.* draftsman. —**draughts′man·ship′,** *n.*

draught·y (draf′tē, dräf′-) draught·i·er, draught·i·est. *adj.* drafty.

Dra·vid·i·an (drə vid′ē ən) *n.* **1.** family of languages spoken mainly in central and southern India and northern Ceylon. **2.** member of a group of Dravidian-speaking peoples living primarily in this area. —*adj.* of or relating to these languages or these peoples.

draw (drô) drew, drawn, draw·ing. *v.t.* **1.a.** to cause to move in a particular direction or to a particular position by or as by pulling: *He drew her aside and told her the news. She drew her gloves on. I drew the covers over my head.* **b.** to cause to follow behind something that is exerting force; drag; haul: *Three white stallions drew the chariot.* **2.** to remove or bring out, as by pulling from a receptacle; take out: *to draw a sword from a scabbard. He drew the cork from the bottle.* **3.** to produce a likeness of or depict with lines or words; delineate; sketch: *to draw a cartoon. He drew a grim picture of conditons in the slums.* **4.** to cause (a liquid) to flow forth: *to draw blood, to draw water for a bath.* **5.** to stretch, extend, or pull tight: *He drew the bowstring and fired. They drew the skin across the top of the drum and fastened it down.* **6.** to deduce or devise, as by reasoning; formulate: *to draw one's own conclusions. He drew a careful distinction between the two.* **7.** to cause to come; bring; attract: *The concert drew a large audience. A flame draws moths. She drew my attention to that fact.* **8.** to bring forth or result in; elicit; evoke: *to draw enemy fire. His actions drew criticism from his superiors.* **9.** to close; shut: *to draw the drapes.* **10.** to take or get (from a source); receive; derive: *to draw a good salary. I drew inspiration from his writings.* **11.** to write out or draft in proper form (often with *up*): *to draw up a contract. There were two people present when the will was drawn.* **12.** to obtain or select by or as by lot: *to draw the winning card. I drew the toughest assignment of all.* **13.** to take in, as by inhaling or sucking: *He's drawn his last breath. The dust is drawn into the vacuum cleaner.* **14.** to take out (funds); withdraw. **15.** to bring in; accumulate; produce: *The bonds are drawing interest.* **16.** to cause to pucker or shrink; wrinkle; contract: *His forehead was drawn into a frown. Hot water draws wool.* **17.** to disembowel: *to draw a turkey.* **18.** to flatten or shape (metal), as by hammering. **19.** to extract the essence or strength of, as by steeping or infusion: *to draw tea.* **20.** *Card Games.* **a.** to take (a card or cards): *He drew a king and then a deuce.* **b.** to cause (a card or cards) to be played: *to draw an opponent's trump.* **21.** *Medicine.* to cause to soften, drain, or discharge, as by applying a poultice: *to draw an abscess.* **22.** (of a ship) to require (a certain depth of water) in order to float. **23. to draw oneself up.** to straighten up, as in anger or indignation. **24. to draw out. a.** to extend; lengthen; prolong: *to draw out a story until it becomes boring.* **b.** to coax or persuade to talk freely: *to draw out a shy person at a party.* **25. to draw up. a.** to bring to a halt. **b.** to arrange: *He drew up the troops in battle order.* —*v.i.* **1.** to create a likeness or picture with lines; sketch. **2.** to take out a weapon for action: *He drew, aimed, and fired.* **3.** to apply or have recourse to; take (with *on, upon,* or *from*): *to draw on one's savings account. The novelist drew upon his own experiences for the plot. We drew from our reserve of supplies.* **4.** to approach; come; move: *We drew near the town. He drew back suddenly. Night drew near.* **5.** to draw lots: *to draw for a prize. We drew for partners.* **6.** to have an attracting force or influence: *That actor's films usually draw well.* **7.** to exert a pulling or sucking force: *He sat there thoughtfully, drawing on his pipe.* **8.** to wrinkle or pucker; become contracted: *Her eyebrows drew together in a frown.* **9.** to cause or allow a current of air to pass: *The chimney is not drawing well.* **10.** to tie, as in a game. **11.** in hunting, to track game by following its scent. **12. to draw away.** to move ahead. **13. to draw up.** to come to a halt; stop: *The car drew up at the toll bridge.* —*n.* **1.** act of drawing: *He got two hearts on the first draw.* **2.** act of pulling out a gun: *The sheriff was quick on the draw.* **3.** that which is drawn, as a ticket in a lottery. **4.** game or contest in which there is no winner; tie. **5.** something that draws or attracts; attracting force or influence: *He's a big draw at the box office.* **6.** gully or ravine into or through which water drains. **7.** movable part or section of a drawbridge. [Old English *dragan* to drag, pull, go.] —**Syn.** *v.t.* **1.a.** see **pull.**

draw·back (drô′bak′) *n.* **1.** unpleasant or objectionable feature or characteristic; shortcoming; disadvantage: *Living in a large house has its drawbacks as well as its advantages.* **2.** refund of taxes or duties, esp. of duties paid on imported goods or raw materials that are subsequently exported.

draw·bridge (drô′brij′) *n.* bridge that can be wholly or partly raised, lowered, or drawn aside so as to permit or prevent passage.

Drawbridge

draw·ee (drô ē′) *n.* one against whom an order to pay money is written and from whom payment is collected.

drawer (*def. 1* drôr; *def. 2* drô′ər) *n.* **1.** boxlike receptacle that, when fitted into a piece of furniture, as a bureau, is drawn out to be opened and pushed in to be closed. **2.** one who draws, esp. a person who writes an order to pay money.

drawers (drôrz) *n.,pl.* underpants.

draw·ing (drô′ing) *n.* **1.** act of one who or that which draws: *the*

at; āpe; cär; end; mē; it; īce; hot; ōld; fôrk; wood; fōōl; oil; out; up; ūse; turn; sing; thin; this; zh in treasure; ə in ago, taken, pencil, lemon, circus.

drawing of a load, the drawing of blood. **2.** pictorial representation or visual pattern, as a sketch or design, usually made by the use of pencil, pen, crayon, or similar material: *a colorful drawing.* **3.** art or technique of making such a representation or pattern: *Your drawing has improved.* **4.** selection of the winning chance or chances in a lottery or raffle: *The drawing will be held next Saturday.*

drawing board, board on which paper or other material is placed or mounted for making drawings.

drawing card, something or someone, as a popular entertainer, that attracts much attention or a large audience.

drawing room **1.** room for receiving or entertaining guests, as a parlor or formal reception room. **2.** company assembled in such a room. **3.** private compartment in a sleeping car on a train. **4.** formal reception, esp. one held by royalty. [Short for *withdrawing room,* the room into which the ladies *withdrew* after dinner in earlier times.]

draw·knife (drô′nīf′) *pl.,* **-knives.** *n.* tool consisting of a blade with a handle at each end, used for shaving or scraping a surface. Also, **drawing knife, draw′shave′.**

Drawknife

drawl (drôl) *v.t., v.i.* to speak or pronounce slowly, esp. with a drawing out of the vowel sounds. —*n.* act or manner of speech of one who drawls. [Possibly from Dutch *dralen* to linger.] —**drawl′er,** *n.* —**drawl′ing·ly,** *adv.*

drawn (drôn) past participle of **draw.**

drawn butter, melted butter, often thickened and seasoned, used as a sauce for food.

drawn work, ornamental openwork made by drawing out threads from a fabric so as to form a pattern, the remaining threads often being formed into other patterns by needlework.

draw·shave (drô′shāv′) *n.* drawknife.

draw·string (drô′string′) *n.* string, cord, or tape run through a hem, casing, or eyelets, as at the mouth of a bag, which, when pulled, draws together or closes an opening.

dray (drā) *n.* low, strong cart with detachable sides, used for carrying heavy loads. —*v.t.* to carry or transport by dray. [Old English *dræge* dragnet, from *dragan* to pull, drag.]

dray·age (drā′ij) *n.* **1.** act of carrying or transporting by dray. **2.** charge made for this.

dray·man (drā′mən) *pl.,* **-men.** *n.* one whose work is driving a dray.

dread (dred) *v.t.* **1.** to anticipate with fear or anxiety; fear greatly: *He dreads flying.* **2.** to look forward to with misgiving or distaste. **3.** *Archaic.* to be in awe of; venerate. —*n.* **1.** fearful anticipation, as of impending evil or danger; great fear. **2.** person or thing dreaded. **3.** *Archaic.* fearful reverence; awe. —*adj.* causing fear, terror, or awe: *a dread disease.* [Middle English *dreden* to fear greatly, short for Old English *ādrædan* to fear.] —**Syn.** *n.* **1.** see **fear.**

dread·ful (dred′fəl) *adj.* **1.** inspiring fear or awe; dire; terrible: *a dreadful omen.* **2.** *Informal.* very bad; awful: *a dreadful headache, a dreadful movie.* —**dread′ful·ly,** *adv.* —**dread′ful·ness,** *n.*

dread·nought (dred′nôt′) *also,* **dread·naught.** *n.* battleship with heavy armor and high-powered guns. [From *Dreadnought,* a British battleship launched in 1906, the first of the modern type of battleship.]

dream (drēm) *n.* **1.** series of thoughts, images, and sensations seen or experienced during sleep. **2.** fanciful thought entertained while awake, esp. a wild or vain fancy; daydream: *I never thought it would happen—not in my wildest dreams.* **3.** mental state in which dreams occur. **4.** object seen in a dream. **5.** fervent hope or desire; cherished goal: *her dream of becoming a movie star.* **6.** something having great beauty or charm. —*v.i.,* **dreamed** or **dreamt, dream·ing.** **1.** to have a dream or dreams. **2.** to indulge in daydreams or fantasies: *She dreams too much in class. He dreams of going to Europe.* **3.** to think of as at all possible; have any conception of (usually with *of*): *He wouldn't dream of going. There are more things in heaven and earth, Horatio, than are dreamt of in your philosophy* (Shakespeare, *Hamlet*). —*v.t.* **1.** to see or imagine in a dream. **2.** to believe possible; suppose; imagine: *We never dreamed the movie would be so long.* **3.** to spend (time) in reverie or dreaming (often with *away*): *to dream away the hours.* **4. to dream up.** *Informal.* to create or devise in one's imagination; concoct: *to dream up an excuse for being late.* —*adj. Informal.* desirable; ideal: *That's my dream house.* [Old English *drēam* joy, noise, music; Modern English meaning influenced by Old Norse *draumr* vision.]

dream·boat (drēm′bōt′) *n. Slang.* person or thing that is extremely attractive or desirable.

dream·er (drē′mər) *n.* **1.** one who dreams. **2.** one who seems to live in a world of dreams or fantasy; impractical or idle speculator.

dream·land (drēm′land′) *n.* **1.** place where a person is said to be while sleeping; realm of dreams. **2.** delightful or ideal place existing only in the imagination.

dreamt (dremt) a past tense and past participle of **dream.**

dream world, world of illusion and fantasy.

dream·y (drē′mē) **dream·i·er, dream·i·est.** *adj.* **1.** dreamlike; vague; indistinct: *a dreamy recollection.* **2.** given to dreaming or daydreaming: *a dreamy frame of mind.* **3.** soothing; pleasing; soft: *dreamy music.* **4.** of or relating to dreams; full of dreams. **5.** *Informal.* wonderful; ideal. —**dream′i·ly,** *adv.* —**dream′i·ness,** *n.*

drear (drēr) *adj. Archaic.* dreary.

drear·y (drēr′ē) **drear·i·er, drear·i·est.** *adj.* **1.** causing sadness or gloom; dismal; depressing: *a dreary room, the dreary prospects of a lonely life.* **2.** dull or uninteresting; monotonous: *It was the dreariest day of the week.* **3.** sad; melancholy. [Old English *drēorig* sad.] —**drear′i·ly,** *adv.* —**drear′i·ness,** *n.*

Dredge¹

dredge¹ (drej) *n.* **1.** excavating apparatus for removing materials such as mud or sand from the bottom of a body of water. **2.** apparatus equipped with a net for gathering shellfish and other objects from the floor of a harbor, bay, or other body of water. —*v.t.,* **dredged, dredg·ing.** **1.** to clear out, deepen, or enlarge with a dredge: *to dredge a harbor.* **2.** to gather or remove with or as if with a dredge (often with *up*): *to dredge mud. He dredged up various facts for the exposé.* —*v.i.* to use a dredge: *to dredge for oysters.* [Possibly going back to Old English *dragan* to pull, drag.]

dredge² (drej) *v.t.* **dredged, dredg·ing.** to sprinkle or coat with a powdered substance, esp. sugar or flour. [From obsolete *dredge* sweetmeat, from Old French *dragee,* through Latin, from Greek *tragēmata* spices, desserts, sweetmeats.]

dredg·er¹ (drej′ər) *n.* **1.** one who or that which dredges. **2.** boat used in dredging. [DREDGE¹ + -ER¹.]

dredg·er² (drej′ər) *n.* container with a perforated lid, used for sprinkling powdered substances on food. [DREDGE² + -ER¹.]

dregs (dregz) *n.,pl.* **1.** sediment of liquids, esp. of beverages: *dregs of coffee, dregs of wine.* **2.** most worthless or undesirable part: *the dregs of society.* **3.** *also,* **dreg,** last remaining part; residue. [Probably from Old Norse *dreggjar* lees.]

Drei·ser, Theodore (drī′sər, -zər) 1871–1945, U.S. novelist.

drench (drench) *v.t.* **1.** to wet (someone or something) thoroughly; saturate; soak: *The sudden rainfall drenched the sightseers.* **2.** to force (an animal) to swallow a medicine. —*n.* **1.** act of drenching. **2.** something that drenches. **3.** dose of liquid medicine given orally, as with a syringe, to an animal. [Old English *drencan* to give to drink, drown.]

Dres·den (drez′dən) *n.* **1.** city in southern East Germany. Pop. (1968 est.), 499,848. **2.** fine porcelain decorated with elaborate, brightly colored designs, made near Dresden.

dress (dres) **dressed** or **drest, dress·ing.** *v.t.* **1.** to put clothes on; clothe: *The little girl dressed her dolls.* **2.** to supply with clothing: *The wardrobe mistress dressed the entire cast.* **3.** to decorate; adorn; trim: *to dress shop windows.* **4.** to clean or prepare for use or sale: *to dress a chicken, to dress leather.* **5.** to treat (a wound or sore) medicinally: *to dress a burn.* **6.** to comb and arrange (hair). **7.** to groom or curry (an animal): *to dress a horse.* **8.** to cultivate, prune, or fertilize. **9.** to get into proper alignment; adjust to a straight line: *to dress ranks.* **10. to dress down.** *Informal.* to scold or reprimand severely. **11. to dress ship.** to pay honor or respect by hoisting the flags of a ship, often by having a continuous line of flags flying from the bow, between mastheads, and to the stern. —*v.i.* **1.** to put on clothes: *He dressed quickly in the morning.* **2.** to select and wear clothes: *She dresses well.* **3.** to put on or wear formal clothes: *She dressed for the ball.* **4.** to come into proper alignment or form in a straight line, as troops. **5. to dress up.** to put on formal wear or clothing more elaborate than that usually worn. —*n.* **1.** garment for a woman or girl, cut to appear as one piece and usually extending from the neck to just above or below the knees. **2.** clothing; apparel; attire: *Oriental dress, soldiers in battle dress.* **3.** style or choice of clothing; manner of wearing clothes: *conservative in his dress.* **4.** external adornment, covering, or appearance: *trees in autumn dress.* —*adj.* **1.** of or for a dress: *dress material, a dress pattern.* **2.** worn or suitable for a formal or ceremonial occasion: *a dress suit, a dress uniform.* **3.** requiring formal dress: *a dress occasion.* [Old French *dresser* to arrange, set up, going back to Latin *dīrectus* straight, just, past participle of *dīrigere* to straighten, guide.]

dress·er¹ (dres′ər) *n.* **1.** one who dresses something: *a dresser of wounds, a dresser of leather.* **2.** one who assists another in dressing, as for the stage. **3.** one who dresses in a particular way: *a fancy dresser, a good dresser.* **4.** any of several tools or machines used for dressing or preparing materials, as leather or stone. [DRESS + -ER¹.]

dress·er² (dres′ər) *n.* chest of drawers, often with a mirror; bureau.

---

2. sideboard or set of shelves for holding dishes and kitchen utensils. [Old French *dresseur* sideboard, set of shelves, from *dresser* to arrange, set up. See DRESS.]

dress·ing (dres′ing) *n.* **1.** act of one who or that which dresses. **2.** sauce, esp. for salads. **3.** medication or bandage applied to a wound or sore. **4.** mixture of bread or cracker crumbs and other ingredients, usually seasoned, used to stuff poultry, fish, or roasts; stuffing. **5.** manure or other fertilizing material. **6.** that which is applied or added to something in dressing it, as a substance used to stiffen fabrics during manufacture.

dress·ing-down (dres′ing doun′) *n. Informal.* severe scolding or reprimand.

dressing gown, robe, esp. a long, loose one, usually worn before or while dressing or for lounging.

dressing room, room for dressing, as backstage in a theater.

dressing station, station set up near a combat area for giving medical attention to the wounded.

dressing table, table, often with drawers, having a mirror to be used while grooming and dressing oneself. Also, **van′i·ty.**

dress·mak·er (dres′mā′kər) *n.* one whose work is making and altering dresses or other articles of clothing for women. —*adj.* **1.** (of women's clothing) of fine workmanship, as if custom-made or handmade by a dressmaker or tailor. **2.** (of women's clothing) having soft, feminine lines; not severely tailored. —**dress′mak′ing,** *n.*

dress parade, military or naval parade in dress uniform.

dress rehearsal **1.** full rehearsal in costume of a theatrical presentation or similar performance, esp. the final rehearsal in costume. **2.** detailed rehearsal of any planned activity: *a dress rehearsal for a general strike.*

dress suit, man's formal suit for evening wear.

dress·y (dres′ē) **dress·i·er, dress·i·est.** *adj.* **1.** suitable for formal occasions; elegant; elaborate: *a dressy blouse. That outfit is much too dressy to wear to work.* **2.** given to wearing elegant or showy clothes: *She's too dressy for our crowd.* **3.** stylish; fashionable: *a dressy affair.* —**dress′i·ness,** *n.*

drest (drest) a past tense and past participle of **dress.**

drew (droo) past tense of **draw.**

Drey·fus, Alfred (drā′fəs, drī′-) 1859–1935, French army officer of Jewish descent, convicted of treason and imprisoned in 1895, acquitted in 1906.

drib·ble (drib′əl) **-bled, -bling.** *v.i.* **1.** to fall or flow in drops or small quantities; trickle: *Water dribbled from the cracks in the roof.* **2.** to let saliva run from the mouth; drivel; drool. **3.** to come little by little or in small amounts (often with *in*): *Contributions dribbled in slowly.* **4.** to move a ball by dribbling. —*v.t.* **1.** to let flow or fall in drops or small quantities: *The faucet is dribbling cold water.* **2.a.** *Basketball.* to propel (the ball) by successive bounces with the hand. **b.** *Soccer.* to propel (the ball) by successive kicks. —*n.* **1.** small quantity of a liquid falling in drops or flowing in a scanty stream. **2.** small or insignificant quantity; fitful flow: *a dribble of funds.* **3.** act of dribbling a ball. **4.** *Scottish.* drizzling rain. [*Drib* (obsolete form of DRIP) + -LE.] —**drib′bler,** *n.* —**Syn.** *v.i.* **1.** see **drip.**

drib·let (drib′lit) *also,* **drib·blet.** *n.* small amount or part; bit.

dried (drīd) past tense and past participle of **dry.**

dri·er (drī′ər) comparative of **dry.** —*n.* **1.** one who or that which dries. **2.** dryer (*defs. 1, 2*).

dri·est (drī′ist) superlative of **dry.**

drift (drift) *v.i.* **1.** to be moved, driven, or borne along by or as by currents of water or air: *Columns of smoke drifted toward the north. We watched the leaves drift downstream. We've drifted apart over the years.* **2.** to be carried along by the force of circumstances; move aimlessly and without any particular goal or purpose: *to drift from town to town. They drifted through life.* **3.** to accumulate in heaps by the force of wind or water: *The snow drifted against the garage.* —*v.t.* to cause to drift: *The wind drifted the snow.* —*n.* **1.** act or instance of being driven along by or as by currents of water or air. **2.** rate or direction of movement or drifting, esp. of a current of water. **3.** something driven along or heaped up by air or water currents, as a snowdrift. **4.** general course of movement; tendency; trend: *the increasing drift toward urbanization.* **5.** purport; intent; meaning: *the drift of a statement.* **6.** wide current of water, usually slow-moving, as in an ocean. **7.** material, as sand, gravel, or rocks, which has been moved from one place and deposited in another by a glacier or the melted water from a glacier. **8.** deviation of a ship, aircraft, or missile from its course, due esp. to water or air currents. **9.** passage excavated horizontally or nearly horizontally in a mine, esp. one driven along the course of a vein or rock layer. [Partly from Old Norse *drift* snowdrift; partly from Middle Dutch *drift* herd, current.]

drift·age (drif′tij) *n.* **1.** act of drifting. **2.** amount of deviation caused by drifting. **3.** that which has drifted; something driven along or deposited by water or air currents.

drift·er (drif′tər) *n.* **1.** one who or that which drifts, esp. one who moves aimlessly from one job or place to another. **2.** boat with nets, as for fishing or mine sweeping, that drift with the current or tide.

drift·wood (drift′wood′) *n.* wood drifting on or washed ashore by water.

Drill[1]
Electric hand drill

drill[1] (dril) *n.* **1.a.** tool with cutting edges or a pointed end used for boring holes in hard substances, operated by means of a rotary or hammering action. **b.** machine operating such a tool. **2.** training or practice in military exercises, as marching or assembling a weapon. **3.** any strict, methodical training or instruction by repeated exercises and practice: *Our class got lots of drill in algebra.* **4.** exercise used in such training: *rifle drill, a spelling drill.* **5.** sea snail, *Urosalpinx cinerea,* that bores through the shells of oysters and eats their flesh. Also (*def. 5*), **oyster drill.** —*v.t.* **1.** to pierce or bore a hole in (something) with or as with a drill: *The dentist drilled my tooth.* **2.** to make (a hole) by boring: *He drilled three holes in the wall for the brackets. They drilled two wells within one week.* **3.** to train or put through military exercises: *to drill soldiers in marching, to drill recruits.* **4.** to train or instruct by repeated exercises and practice: *The teacher drilled the class in math all morning.* **5.** *Informal.* to impart or implant by constant repetition or strict training (with *into*). —*v.i.* **1.** to bore or make a hole with or as with a drill: *to drill for oil.* **2.** to go through or perform drills: *The platoon drills regularly every day.* [Middle Dutch *drillen* to bore, turn around, brandish.] —**Syn.** *n.* **3.** see **practice.**

drill[2] (dril) *n.* **1.** machine for planting that makes a hole or furrow, drops the seed and sometimes fertilizer or other soil preparation, and then covers it with soil. **2.** small furrow in which seeds are planted. **3.** row of planted seeds. —*v.t.* **1.** to sow (seed) in rows. **2.** to sow or plant, as a field, in drills. —*v.i.* to sow or plant in rows. [Possibly from obsolete *drill* small stream; of uncertain origin.]

drill[3] (dril) *n.* closely woven, durable twilled cotton or linen fabric, used for such items as uniforms and work clothes. Also, **drill′ing.** [Short for *drilling,* modification of German *Drillich* canvas, ticking, going back to Latin *trilix* having three threads, triply woven.]

drill[4] (dril) *n.* West African baboon, *Mandrillus leucophaeus,* related to and resembling, but smaller than, the mandrill. [Probably of West African origin.]

drill·er (dril′ər) *n.* one who or that which drills.

drill·ing[1] (dril′ing) *n.* act of one who or that which drills.

drill·ing[2] (dril′ing) *n.* drill[3].

drill·mas·ter (dril′mas′tər) *n.* **1.** one who conducts military drills, esp. marching drills. **2.** instructor who maintains strict discipline or who teaches by drilling.

drill press, machine tool consisting of one or more drills mounted on a column and having an adjustable horizontal table on which the material to be drilled is placed.

dri·ly (drī′lē) dryly.

drink (dringk) **drank** or (*archaic*) **drunk, drunk** or (*archaic*) **drunk·en** or (*archaic*) **drank, drink·ing.** *v.t.* **1.** to take into the mouth and swallow (liquid): *He drinks milk with his meals.* **2.** to take in or soak up (liquid or moisture); absorb: *The sponge drank up the water. The flowers drank in the rain.* **3.** to swallow the contents of: *I quickly drank my cup of coffee.* **4.** to receive or absorb through the senses or the mind, esp. with eagerness and pleasure (often with *in*): *He drank in the beauty of the woodland scene.* **5.a.** to give or join in (a toast): *The guests drank a toast to his good fortune.* **b.** to honor or wish for with a toast: *I drink your good health.* **6.** to bring to a specified state by drinking: *to drink a glass dry.* —*v.i.* **1.** to take liquid into the mouth and swallow it. **2.** to drink alcoholic liquor, esp. habitually or to excess. **3.** to make or join in a toast (with *to*): *We drink to your continued success.* —*n.* **1.** liquid for drinking; beverage: *meat and drink.* **2.a.** portion of liquid swallowed. **b.** portion of alcoholic liquor. **3.** alcoholic liquor. **4.** habitual or excessive use of alcoholic liquor: *He took to drink.* **5. the drink.** *Slang.* body of water, esp. the ocean. [Old English *drincan* to imbibe.] —**drink′er,** *n.*

drink·a·ble (dring′kə bəl) *adj.* suitable or safe for drinking. —*n. also,* **drinkables.** something to drink; beverage.

drip (drip) **dripped** or **dript, drip·ping.** *v.i.* **1.** to fall in drops: *The rain came through the roof and dripped from the ceiling.* **2.** to have moisture or liquid falling off in drops: *The umbrella dripped all over the floor.* **3.** to be saturated or overflow: *This toast is dripping with butter. His letters drip with self-pity.* —*v.t.* to let (something) fall in drops: *I accidentally dripped paint from the brush.* —*n.* **1.** a falling of liquid in drops. **2.** liquid falling in drops. **3.** sound made by a liquid falling in drops. **4.** projecting molding, as on a cornice, for shedding rainwater. **5.** *Slang.* unattractive, insipid, or disagreeable person. [Old English *dryppan* to let fall in drops.]

at; āpe; cär; end; mē; it; īce; hot; ōld; fôrk; wood; fool; oil; out; up; ūse; turn; sing; thin; this; zh in treasure; ə in ago, taken, pencil, lemon, circus.

Syn. *v.i.* **1. Drip, dribble, trickle, ooze¹** indicate the passage of liquid in small amounts. **Drip** stresses the idea of drops: *Water dripped from the paddle as the canoe glided through the water.* **Dribble** emphasizes a rapid succession of drops, amounting to a small stream: *Water from the spilled glass dribbled from the table top to the rug.* **Trickle** implies a flow of drops that usually cannot be differentiated: *A thin stream of water trickled over the rocks.* **Ooze** suggests liquid coming through narrow openings and condensing into a gentle flow or pool: *Blood oozed from the abrasion on his forehead.*

drip-dry (*adj.*, drip′drī′; *v.*, drip′drī′, -drī′) *adj.* of or designating a fabric or garment that dries quickly when hung dripping wet and requires little or no ironing. —*v.i.* **-dried, -dry·ing.** to dry with few or no wrinkles when hung dripping wet: *a fabric that drip-dries quickly.*

drip grind, fine grind of coffee used in a dripolator.

drip·o·la·tor (drip′ə lā′tər) *n.* coffeepot in which boiling water seeps from a top compartment through the coffee and then into a compartment below.

drip·ping (drip′ing) **1.** act of something that drips. **2. drippings.** melted fat and juices that drip from meat, fowl, or fish while cooking. —*adj.* so as to drip: *dripping wet.*

dripping pan, pan placed under food while it is being cooked to catch and hold the drippings. Also, **drip pan.**

drive (drīv) **drove** or *(archaic)* **drave, driv·en, driv·ing.** *v.t.* **1.** to propel or cause to move by or as by the application of physical force: *The waves drove the ship onto the rocks. The cowboys drove the cattle to market. They drove their attackers off.* **2.** to impel, goad, or force into some act or condition: *The noise is enough to drive one mad. Oppression drove them into open rebellion.* **3.** to put in motion and direct the movement of; steer: *to drive a car. He drove a team of black horses.* **4.** to convey in a car or other vehicle: *He drove them to the party.* **5.** to cause to penetrate by force: *to drive a nail into wood.* **6.** to urge insistently to work or exertion, esp. excessively; overwork: *He's been driving himself lately and needs a vacation badly.* **7.** to carry on or bring about energetically and forcefully; execute vigorously: *He drives a hard bargain.* **8.a.** by force; to go rapidly, as by hitting or throwing with force: *He drove the ball over the fence.* **b.** *Golf.* to strike (the ball) forcefully, esp. from a tee. **9.** to set or keep in motion or operation; supply the motive or power for: *Steam drives the engine.* **10.** to form or produce by penetration: *to drive a tunnel.* **11.** *Hunting.* **a.** to chase (game) into a trap, or into the open toward a hunter. **b.** to cover (an area) in this manner. —*v.i.* **1.** to operate and steer a car or other vehicle: *He drives too fast.* **2.** to go or be conveyed in a vehicle: *They drove through the park.* **3.** to go or be moved along swiftly before an impelling force; be impelled: *The ship drove before the gale.* **4.** to rush, dash, or move forcefully or violently: *The winds drove against the house.* **5.** *Golf.* to strike the ball forcefully, esp. from a tee. **6. to drive at.** to attempt or intend to convey; suggest: *What was his speech driving at?* **7. to let drive.** to aim or release (a blow or missile). —*n.* **1.** trip in a car or other vehicle: *They took a drive in the country.* **2.** driveway or a public road on which to drive: *The winding drive to the house was covered with gravel.* **3.** act of driving, esp. a gathering together and urging or impelling forward, as of logs or animals: *a cattle drive.* **4.** that which is so driven, as a collection of logs floating down a river. **5.** organized group effort for some specific purpose; campaign: *a clothing drive, the club's annual membership drive.* **6.** forceful or dynamic energy or initiative; aggressiveness; vigor: *His drive and enthusiasm helped make the project a success.* **7.** impelling or motivating concern, interest, or longing: *her drive to succeed.* **8.** vigorous or aggressive onward course or movement: *the football team's drive toward the goal line.* **9.** strong, motivating urge or stimulus that incites an animal or person to action: *the hunger drive, the sex drive.* **10.** offensive, large-scale military attack, usually consisting of a series of engagements sustained over a period of time. **11.a.** act or instance of driving a ball, puck, or other object; forceful blow or stroke: *The batter hit a long drive to left field.* **b.** manner in which a ball, puck, or other object is driven, or its flight when driven, as in golf. **12.** part that transmits power to a machine or machine part. **13.** manner in which power is applied to the wheels in a motor vehicle: *rear-wheel drive.* [Old English *drīfan* to force to move on, pursue, rush with violence.]

drive-in (drīv′in′) *n.* **1.** outdoor motion-picture theater where customers remain in their parked cars while viewing a movie projected on a large screen. **2.** any place of business, as a bank or restaurant, designed to serve customers while they remain in their cars. —*adj.* designed to give service to customers while they remain in their cars: *a drive-in restaurant, a drive-in bank.*

driv·el (driv′əl) **-eled, -el·ing;** *also, British,* **-elled, -el·ling.** *v.i.* **1.** to let saliva run from the mouth; dribble; slobber. **2.** to talk in a childish or foolish way; talk nonsense. **3.** to flow like saliva running from the mouth. —*v.t.* to utter childishly or foolishly: *to drivel absurdities.* —*n.* **1.** childish, foolish, or ridiculous talk; nonsense. **2.** saliva flowing from the mouth. [Old English *dreflian* to slobber.] —**driv′el·er;** *also,* **driv′el·ler,** *n.*

driv·en (driv′ən) past participle of **drive.**

driv·er (drī′vər) *n.* **1.** one who or that which drives, esp. one who drives a vehicle. **2.** golf club with a wooden head used to drive balls long distances from the tee; number one wood. **3.** any machine part that transmits motion or power.

driver ant, army ant.

driver's seat, position of control, influence, or leadership.

drive shaft, shaft that transmits power from a source to wheels or to other parts to be driven.

drive·way (drīv′wā′) *n.* private road providing access to a house, garage, or other building.

driv·ing (drī′ving) *adj.* **1.** moving with force, intensity, or violence: *a driving rain.* **2.** active and energetic; vigorous: *a man with a driving personality.* **3.** transmitting power or activating motion.

driving iron, golf club with a metal head having very little loft; number one iron.

driving wheel, wheel that transmits power or motion to some part of a machine.

driz·zle (driz′əl) **-zled, -zling.** *v.i.* to rain steadily in fine, mistlike drops. —*v.t.* to shed or let fall in fine drops. —*n.* fine, misty rain. [Modification of Middle English *dresen* to fall, from Old English *drēosan.*] —**driz′zly,** *adj.*

drogue (drōg) *n.* **1.** funnel-shaped device at the end of the fuel line of a tanker plane, used to aid the coupling of the fuel line to the plane being refueled. **2.** parachute used to slow down a falling body. Also, **drogue parachute. 3.** sea anchor. [Possibly a modification of DRAG.]

droll (drōl) *adj.* amusingly odd or quaint: *a droll fellow, droll antics.* —*n.* Archaic. prankster or buffoon; clown. [French *drôle* funny, odd, from Middle French *drolle* merry fellow, possibly from Middle Dutch *drol* funny little chap.] —**droll′ly,** *adv.* —**droll′ness,** *n.*

droll·er·y (drō′lər ē) *pl.* **-er·ies.** *n.* **1.** quality of being droll; quaint humor. **2.** something droll, as a whimsical drawing or story. **3.** behavior or antics of a droll person; jesting: *his talent for drollery.*

Dromedary

drom·e·dar·y (drom′ə der′ē, drum′-) *pl.* **-dar·ies.** *n.* single-humped camel, *Camelus dromedarius,* native to Arabia and North Africa, valued for riding because of its relatively fast pace. Height: 6 feet at the shoulder. [Late Latin *dromedārius,* from Latin *dromas,* from Greek *dromas* running; because of its speed.]

drone¹ (drōn) *n.* **1.** male bee, esp. a honeybee, that develops from an unfertilized egg and does no work, his only function being to mate once with the queen bee, after which he dies. **2.** one who lives on the labor of others; idler; loafer. **3.** unmanned, self-propelled aircraft or ship controlled by radio signals, as certain reconnaissance planes. [Old English *drān* male bee.]

drone² (drōn) **droned, dron·ing.** *v.i.* **1.** to make a continuous, low, humming sound: *The planes droned overhead.* **2.** to talk in a dull, monotonous tone: *The speaker droned on.* —*v.t.* to say (something) in a dull, monotonous tone. —*n.* **1.** dull, continuous buzzing or humming sound: *the drone of the mosquitoes.* **2.** bass pipe of a bagpipe that makes a continuous unvarying tone. [Possibly from DRONE¹; possibly imitative.]

drool (drōōl) *v.i.* **1.** to let saliva run from the mouth; drivel: *The baby drooled all over his bib.* **2.** to water at the mouth, as in anticipation of food: *He drooled at the thought of a steak dinner.* **3.** *Informal.* to show great delight or pleasure; express great enthusiasm: *He drooled over the painting.* —*v.t.* to let run from the mouth. [From DRIVEL.]

droop (drōōp) *v.i.* **1.** to hang or sink down or incline downwards, as from weakness or exhaustion. **2.** to become weak; lose energy or vigor; flag: *His spirits drooped.* **3.** to become dejected or depressed; lose spirit or courage. —*v.t.* to let hang or sink down; incline downwards: *to droop one's head.* —*n.* act or fact of drooping; drooping position or state: *The droop of his shoulders showed his exhaustion.* [Old Norse *drúpa* to hang the head, sink.] —**droop′ing·ly,** *adv.*

Syn. *v.i.* **1. Droop, wilt¹, sag** indicate decline through loss of strength. **Droop** suggests loss of vigor or strength and thus a bowing or hanging down: *His eyes closed and his head drooped, but he forced himself to read on.* **Wilt** implies loss of freshness and thus a becoming limp: *As the summer day wore on, the freshly laundered dresses wilted.* **Sag** emphasizes loss of firmness and thus a sinking: *His knees sagged as another hard punch struck his body.*

droop·y (drōō′pē) **droop·i·er, droop·i·est.** *adj.* **1.** that droops or tends to droop. **2.** gloomy; melancholy; forlorn. —**droop′i·ly,** *adv.* —**droop′i·ness,** *n.*

drop (drop) dropped or dropt, drop·ping. v.i. **1.** to fall in drops, as a liquid: *Sweat dropped from his brow.* **2.** to fall or descend, esp. rapidly or suddenly: *The knife dropped from his hand. The ground drops sharply near the shore.* **3.** to fall down or sink, as from exhaustion or injury: *He dropped to his knees after the race.* **4.** to fall or decline in degree or amount; become less; diminish; decrease (often with *off*): *Her voice dropped to a whisper. Business dropped off during the summer.* **5.** to fall or move to a position that is lower, inferior, or further back: *He dropped behind the other runners.* **6.** to cease to appear or be seen; disappear; vanish: *He dropped from public notice after the scandal.* **7.** to cease to be of concern; come to an end; lapse: *Let the matter drop.* **8.** to pay a casual or unexpected call; come or stop casually (with *in*, *over*, or *by*): *They dropped in on us as they were passing through town.* **9.** to fall or pass into a particular state, condition, or activity: *to drop off to sleep. We soon dropped back into the old life of sight-seeing and shopping* (Edwards, 1877). **10.** *Archaic.* to move along gently with a current of water or air. **11. to drop off.** to fall asleep. **12. to drop out.** to stop being a member or participant; withdraw; quit: *He dropped out of school. The club disbanded when five members dropped out.* —v.t. **1.** to let fall by or as by releasing hold of: *She dropped her keys on the floor. They dropped the supplies from the plane.* **2.** to cause to descend from one level to another; cause to sink, move, or hang down; lower: *to drop a hem. Conscious that she was being stared at, she dropped her eyes.* **3.** to let fall in drops or small amounts. **4.** to stop pursuing, treating, or dealing with; cease to concern oneself with; abandon: *to drop a course in school. Let's drop that subject and discuss something else.* **5.** to write and send (a letter or note) in an offhand manner: *Drop me a line.* **6.** to utter or refer to in or as in a casual or incidental way: *to drop a hint. He's always trying to impress us by dropping well-known names.* **7.** to let out or leave; deposit (often with *off*): *He stopped the car to drop her at the corner. I'll drop the book off at your house.* **8.** (of animals) to give birth to: *to drop a foal.* **9.** to cause to fall, as by tackling, striking, or shooting; bring down: *He dropped the lion with one shot.* **10.** to leave out; omit: *to drop a stitch in knitting, to drop a letter in pronouncing a word.* **11.** to break off an association or connection with; dismiss; discharge (often with *from*): *The firm dropped ten employees. They were dropped from the club.* **12.** to poach (an egg). **13.** *Slang.* to lose: *He dropped $100 at the racetrack. The team dropped three games in a row.* —n. **1.** small quantity of liquid, shaped like a tiny sphere or pear: *a drop of water, a drop of blood, a drop of oil.* **2.** very small amount of liquid: *Water, water everywhere, nor any drop to drink* (Coleridge, 1798). **3.** very small amount: *She didn't have a drop of pride left.* **4.** something resembling a drop of liquid in shape or size, as an earring, pendant, or piece of candy. **5.** act or instance of dropping; descent; fall: *We watched the drop of the parachutists from the plane.* **6.** sudden decline or decrease: *a drop in prices, a drop in temperature.* **7.** drops. liquid medicine to be administered in drops: *The doctor put drops in my eyes to dilate the pupils.* **8.** distance between a higher and a lower level; distance or depth to which anything drops: *a fifteen-foot drop from the second floor to the street.* **9.** something designed or arranged to fall or slide from above, or to be lowered, as a trap door. **10.** slit or other aperture, as in a mail box, into which something is inserted or dropped. **11.** curtain which can be raised and lowered, used as a backdrop for a presentation or part of a presentation. Also, **drop curtain.** **12. drop in the bucket.** a proportionately small quantity; tiny portion, as of what is needed. **13. at the drop of a hat.** without any hesitation or inducement; immediately. **14. to get (or have) the drop on.** *Informal.* **a.** to aim and be ready to shoot a gun at (a person) before he can draw his gun. **b.** to get (or have) at a disadvantage. [Old English *dropa* globule of liquid.]

drop cookie, cookie made by dropping batter onto a cookie sheet for baking.

drop-forge (drop′fôrj′) -forged, -forg·ing. v.t. to forge (hot metal) into shape with a device employing the force of a dropped weight, as a drop hammer.

drop hammer, device for pounding metal into shape, having a heavy weight which is raised by machinery and then dropped on the metal to be shaped. Also, **drop press.**

drop-kick (drop′kik′) v.t., v.i. to give a drop kick (to).

drop kick kick given to a football just as it reaches the ground after being dropped by the kicker.

drop leaf, hinged section, as of a table, that can be folded down when not in use. —drop′-leaf′, adj.

drop·let (drop′lit) n. tiny drop.

drop-out (drop′out′) also, **drop-out.** n. **1.** student who withdraws from school, esp. high school, before graduating. **2.** one who drops out or withdraws: *dropouts from society.*

drop·per (drop′ər) n. **1.** one who or that which drops. **2.** glass tube with a rubber bulb at one end and a small opening at the other end, used for measuring, transferring, or dispensing liquids in drops.

drop·ping (drop′ing) n. **1.** act of one who or that which drops.

2. droppings. dung of animals. **3.** *also,* **droppings.** that which drops or falls in drops.

drop press, drop hammer.

drop·si·cal (drop′si kəl) adj. of, relating to, or suffering from dropsy.

drop·sy (drop′sē) n. abnormal accumulation of diluted lymph in body tissues or cavities. Also **e·de′ma.** [Middle English *dropesie*, short for *idropesie*, from Old French *idropisie*, from Latin *hydrōpisis*, from Greek *hydrōps*, from *hydōr* water.]

drosh·ky (drosh′kē) pl., -kies. also, **dros·ky** (dros′kē). n. **1.** any of various light, open, four-wheeled carriages, often consisting of a long narrow bench on which passengers sit astride, originating and mostly used in Russia. **2.** any similar carriage. [Russian *drozhki*, diminutive of *drogi* wagon.]

dro·soph·i·la (drō sof′ə lə) pl., -lae (-lē′). n. fruit fly *(def. 1).* [Modern Latin *drosophila*, from Greek *drosos* dew + *philos* loving.]

dross (drôs, dros) n. **1.** waste or impure matter that rises to the surface of molten metals. **2.** any worthless matter; refuse; waste. [Old English *drōs* dregs, dirt.]

drought (drout) *also,* **drouth** (drouth). n. **1.** long period of dry weather; prolonged lack of normal or sufficient rainfall. **2.** prolonged scarcity or shortage; dearth: *a period in history marked by a cultural drought.* **3.** *Archaic.* thirst. [Old English *drūgath* dryness.] —drought′y; *also,* drouth′y, adj.

drove¹ (drōv) past tense of **drive.**

drove² (drōv) n. **1.** group of animals moving or driven along together: *a drove of cattle, a drove of sheep.* **2.** group of human beings moving or acting together; crowd: *On a hot, muggy day people head for the beaches in droves.* **3.** large group, esp. of like things: *Crows flew in droves over the field.* —v.t., v.i. droved, drov·ing. to drive (cattle or other animals). [Old English *drāf* herd, from *drīfan* to drive.]

dro·ver (drō′vər) n. **1.** one who takes a drove of cattle, sheep, or other animals to market. **2.** sheep or cattle dealer.

drown (droun) v.i. to die by suffocation in water or other liquid. —v.t. **1.** to kill by suffocation in water or other liquid. **2.** to cover with or as with a flood; inundate; drench: *The dam broke and its waters drowned the entire valley. He drowned his pancakes in syrup.* **3.** to lessen or smother the sound of by greater loudness; muffle (often with *out*): *The waves drowned out his words.* **4.** to get rid of or obliterate as by immersion; submerge: *to drown one's sorrow in drink.* [Possibly going back to Old English *druncnian* to become drunk, sink.]

drowse (drouz) drowsed, drows·ing. v.i. **1.** to be half asleep; doze: *He was drowsing during the lecture.* **2.** to be or grow inactive, dull, or sluggish: *Let not your prudence . . . drowse* (Tennyson, 1874). —v.t. to pass (time) drowsily or in drowsing (often with *away*): *to drowse away the morning.* —n. act of drowsing; being half asleep. [Possibly going back to Old English *drūsian* to sink, be sluggish.] —Syn. v.i. **1.** see sleep.

drow·sy (drou′zē) -si·er, -si·est. adj. **1.** sleepy or inclined to sleep; half asleep: *I felt drowsy after that large dinner.* **2.** characterized by sleepiness or lethargy: *drowsy villages. My heart aches, and a drowsy numbness pains my sense* (Keats, 1820). **3.** inducing lethargy or sleepiness; lulling: *drowsy summer days.* —drow′si·ly, adv. —drow′si·ness, n.

drub (drub) drubbed, drub·bing. v.t. **1.** to beat severely, as with a stick; cudgel; thrash. **2.** to defeat decisively; rout. [Possibly from Arabic *darb* a beating with a stick.] —drub′ber, n.

drub·bing (drub′ing) n. **1.** severe beating; thrashing. **2.** decisive or humiliating defeat, as in an athletic contest.

drudge (druj) n. **1.** one who works hard at wearying, tedious, or menial tasks. —v.i. drudged, drudg·ing. to work hard at wearying, tedious, or menial way. [Of uncertain origin.]

drudg·er·y (druj′ər ē) pl., -er·ies. n. wearying, tedious, or menial labor: *Her whole life was spent in drudgery.*

drug (drug) n. **1.** any chemical agent that affects living cells, esp. one used to treat disease in man and animals. **2.** substance to which a person may become addicted; narcotic. **3.** commodity for which there is little or no demand or of which there is an overabundance: *a drug on the market.* —v.t. drugged, drug·ging. **1.** to administer drugs to, esp. narcotic drugs: *to drug a patient before an operation. He was drugged and then robbed.* **2.** to add a drug or drugs to (food or drink), esp. narcotic or poisonous drugs: *to drug wine.* **3.** to affect or overcome, as if with a drug: *She was drugged by the music. He was drugged with sleep.* [Old French *drogue* medical ingredient, possibly from Dutch *droog* dry (with reference to dry ingredients).]

drug addict, one who is addicted to narcotics.

drug·gist (drug′ist) n. one licensed to fill prescriptions; pharmacist. **2.** one who owns or operates a drugstore.

drug·store (drug′stôr′) n. store where prescriptions are compounded and where medicines, drugs, medical supplies, and miscellaneous merchandise are sold; pharmacy.

---

at; āpe; cär; end; mē; it; īce; hot; ōld; fôrk; wood; fo͞od; oil; out; up; ūse; turn; sing; thin; this; zh in treasure; ə in ago, taken, pencil, lemon, circus.

dru·id (drōō′id) *also*, **Dru·id.** *n.* member of a priestly order among the ancient Celts of Gaul and the British Isles, which was suppressed by the Romans about A.D. 100 but continued unofficially until the fifth century. Druids functioned as religious leaders, teachers, judges, and poets. [Latin *Druidēs* priests of ancient Gaul; of Celtic origin.] —**dru′id·ess**, **dru′id·ism**, *n.* —**dru·id′ic**; *also*, **dru·id′i·cal**, *adj.*

drum (drum) *n.* **1.** percussion instrument usually consisting of a hollow cylinder or frame with a membrane stretched tightly over one or both ends, played by beating on the membrane, as with sticks or the hands. **2.** sound produced when a drum is beaten. **3.** any similar sound: *the drum of fingers on a table.* **4.** something resembling a drum in shape. **5.** cylindrical metal container, as for oil. **6.** metal cylinder around which something, as cable, is wound. **7.** eardrum. **8.** drumfish. —*v.i.* **drummed, drum·ming. 1.** to beat or play a drum. **2.** to beat or tap rhythmically or repeatedly: *He drummed on the desk with his fingers.* **3.** to sound like a drum; pound; resound: *The noise drummed in my ears.* **4.** (of the partridge and other birds) to make a hollow, thumping sound by beating the wings. **5.** to drum into. to drive or force into by persistent or constant repetition. **6. to drum out (of).** to expel or dismiss (from) in disgrace. **7. to drum up.** to obtain or create by vigorous effort: *to drum up business. He couldn't drum up enough support for the proposed legislation.* —*v.t.* to perform or play on or as on a drum. [Middle Dutch *tromme* the percussion instrument.]

drum·beat (drum′bēt′) *n.* sound of a stroke on a drum.

drum·fish (drum′fish′) *pl.* **-fish** or **-fishes.** *n.* any of various saltwater and freshwater fish, family Sciaenidae, that make a drumming sound.

drum·head (drum′hed′) *n.* skin or membrane stretched over the end or ends of a drum.

drumhead court-martial, court-martial held during military operations to try offenses without delay. [From the former use of a *drumhead* as a table for the judges during such courts-martial.]

drum·lin (drum′lin) *n.* oval mound formed from glacial deposits. [Irish Gaelic *druim* back, ridge + -LIN(G).]

drum major, one who leads or directs a marching band or drum and bugle corps.

drum majorette, girl who twirls a baton while marching with a band or drum and bugle corps, as in a parade. Also, **ma′jor·ette′.**

drum·mer (drum′ər) *n.* **1.** one who or that which drums. **2.** *Informal.* traveling salesman.

drum·stick (drum′stik′) *n.* **1.** stick for beating a drum. **2.** lower part of the leg of a fowl, esp. when cooked.

drunk (drungk) past participle and archaic past tense of **drink.** —*adj.* **1.** without normal control of one's faculties because of excessive drinking of alcoholic liquor; intoxicated; inebriated. **2.** powerfully affected; overwhelmed: *drunk with success, drunk with joy.* —*n. Informal.* **1.** one who is drunk. **2.** one who habitually drinks alcoholic liquor to excess. **3.** drinking spree; binge.

drunk·ard (drung′kərd) *n.* one who habitually drinks alcoholic liquor to excess; one who is often drunk.

drunk·en (drung′kən) archaic past participle of drink. —*adj.* **1.** drunk; intoxicated. **2.** habitually drunk. **3.** caused by or characteristic of the state of being drunk: *a drunken rage, a drunken stupor.* —**drunk′en·ly,** *adv.* —**drunk′en·ness,** *n.*

drunk·o·me·ter (drung kom′ə tər) *n.* device which chemically analyzes the breath to determine the alcoholic content of the blood.

dru·pa·ceous (drōō pā′shəs) *adj.* **1.** of or like a drupe. **2.** producing drupes.

drupe (drōōp) *n.* fleshy fruit containing a hard pit or stone that encloses the seed. Cherries, peaches, and avocados are drupes. [Latin *drup(p)a* overripe olive, from Greek *druppā,* from *drupepēs* ripened on the tree.]

drupe·let (drōōp′lit) *n.* one of the small drupes which form an aggregate fruit such as the raspberry or blackberry.

Dru·ry Lane (drur′ē) street in London, England, noted for its theaters.

Druse (drōōz) *also*, **Druze.** *n.* member of a sect found chiefly in Syria and Lebanon which, although considered a branch of Islam, combines elements of Christianity, Judaism, and other religions. [Arabic *durūz,* plural of *darazī* a Druse, from *Ismail al-Darazī* Ismail the tailor, who founded the sect in the eleventh century.]

dry (drī) **dri·er** or **dry·er, dri·est** or **dry·est.** *adj.* **1.** not wet or damp; free from moisture: *dry clothes, dry kindling.* **2.** exhausted of its supply of water or other liquid; empty of liquid contents: *The well has been dry for a month. My pen ran dry.* **3.** not under or in water: *They stepped from the boat onto dry land.* **4.** having or characterized by little or no rainfall: *the dry season. It was the driest summer in years.* **5.** characterized by the absence or deficiency of normal moisture: *My skin becomes dry in the winter.* **6.** parched or withered through loss or absence of moisture. **7.** free from tears; not accompanied by tears: *dry eyes, a dry sob.* **8.** thirsty: *He was dry after his long walk.* **9.** without butter or other spreads: *dry toast.* **10.** not giving milk: *a dry cow.* **11.** marked by the

absence of liquid discharge, as phlegm: *a dry cough.* **12.** characterized by ironic matter-of-factness; shrewd and witty: *dry humor, a dry remark.* **13.** not interesting; dull; boring: *a dry subject.* **14.** unadorned; plain; bare: *a dry style of writing, dry facts.* **15.** lacking warmth, cordiality, or emotion; indifferent; cold. **16.** consisting of substances which are not liquid; solid: *dry cereal, dry provisions.* **17.** free from sweetness: *a dry wine.* **18.** *Informal.* opposing or prohibiting the manufacture, sale, or use of alcoholic beverages: *a dry state, a dry law.* —*v.t.,* **dried, dry·ing. 1.** to make dry; remove moisture from (often with *off*): *She dried the dishes. He dried off the table.* **2.** to deprive wholly of moisture or stop the flow of; evaporate completely (with *up*): *The sun dried up the puddles.* —*v.i.* **1.** to become dry; lose moisture (often with *off* or *out*): *The clothes dried in the sun. This ink dries quickly.* **2.** to lose all moisture or cease to flow; disappear entirely, as by evaporation (with *up*): *The spring dried up last summer.* **3. to dry up. a.** to become exhausted, barren, or unproductive: *After his third novel, his imagination seemed to dry up.* **b.** *Slang.* to stop talking. ▲ usually used as a command. —*n. pl.,* **drys.** *Informal.* prohibitionist. [Old English *drȳge* free from moisture, arid.]

Syn. *adj.* **1. Dry, arid** mean lacking moisture. **Dry** may suggest less moisture than normal or a thorough absence of moisture: *His mouth was dry with fright. He scuffed in the dry dust.* **Arid** implies a complete absence of moisture: *The arid desert that lay before them showed no sign of plant or animal life.*

dry·ad (drī′əd, -ad) *also,* **Dry·ad.** *pl.* **-ads,** or **-a·des** (-ə dēz′). *n. Greek Mythology.* nymph living in or guarding woods and trees; wood nymph. [Latin *dryas,* from Greek *dryas,* from *drȳs* tree.]

dry battery, battery consisting of dry cells.

dry cell, voltaic cell in which the electrolyte is in a form that does not spill, as a paste or jelly.

dry-clean (drī′klēn′) *v.t.* to subject to dry cleaning.

dry cleaner 1. person or business that does dry cleaning. **2.** substance used in dry cleaning.

dry cleaning. act or process of cleaning garments or other articles of cloth with chemical solvents or other substances.

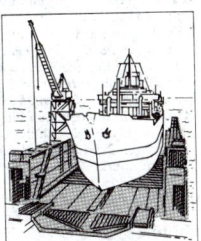

Ship in dry dock

Dry·den, John (drīd′ən) 1631–1700, English poet, dramatist, and critic.

dry-dock (drī′dok′) *v.t.* to put in a dry dock. —*v.i.* to go into a dry dock.

dry dock, any of various watertight structures in which a ship can be docked to allow for such work as repairs, inspection, or cleaning.

dry·er (drī′ər) *n.* **1.** device or appliance for drying: *a hair dryer, a clothes dryer.* **2.** substance added to paints, varnishes, and other materials to make them dry more quickly. **3.** drier (def.1).

dry-farm (drī′färm′) *v.t., v.i.* to practice dry farming (on land).

dry farmer, one who dry-farms.

dry farming, the growing of crops on unirrigated land in semiarid areas by using methods that conserve soil moisture, as contour farming.

dry fly, artificial fly used in fishing that floats on the surface of the water.

dry goods, fabrics and related items, as thread, ribbon, or lace, as distinguished from other merchandise, as hardware or groceries.

dry ice, solid carbon dioxide, made by compressing and cooling the gas, which freezes at −110 degrees Fahrenheit. It is a widely used refrigerant because it changes from a solid back to a gas without becoming liquid. Trademark: **Dry Ice.**

dry·ly (drī′lē) *also,* **dri·ly** *adv.* in a dry manner.

dry measure, system of units for measuring the volume of dry commodities, as grain, vegetables, or fruit. See **weights and measures** for table.

dry·ness (drī′nis) *n.* quality or state of being dry.

dry-nurse (drī′nurs′) **-nursed, -nurs·ing.** *v.t.* to be a dry nurse to.

dry nurse 1. nurse who takes care of a baby without suckling it. Distinguished from **wet nurse. 2.** *Informal.* one who looks after or instructs another, esp. one who instructs a new or inexperienced superior.

dry point 1. technique or process of etching with a sharp needle on copperplate without the use of acid. **2.** needle so used. **3.** print made from a plate that has been etched by this process.

dry rot 1. decay of seasoned timber resulting in its crumbling to a dry powder, caused by any of various fungi. **2.** any of various fungous diseases that attack fruits, vegetables, and other living plants, causing the infected part of the plant to become hard and dry. **3.** fungus causing dry rot. **4.** any concealed or unsuspected inner decay: *a society that succumbed to dry rot.*

dry run 1. *Military.* firing practice, bombing run, or other exercise carried out without the use of live ammunition. **2.** any practice session or trial run; rehearsal.

dry-shod (drī'shod') *adj., adv.* having or keeping one's shoes or feet dry; without getting the feet wet.

dry wash, laundry that has been washed and dried, but not ironed.

d.s. 1. daylight saving. **2.** *Commerce.* days after sight.

D.S. *Music.* repeat a passage or section from the sign ·s· or :S:. ▲ used as a direction to the performer. Also, **d.S., d.s.** [Abbreviation of Italian *dal segno* from the sign.]

D.S., Doctor of Science. Also, **D.Sc.**

DSC, Distinguished Service Cross.

DSM, Distinguished Service Medal.

DSO, Distinguished Service Order.

DST, Daylight Saving Time.

d.t.'s *Informal.* delirium tremens.

du·al (dōō'əl, dū'-) *adj.* **1.** composed or consisting of two; twofold; double: *dual controls, dual ownership.* **2.** designating or relating to two. **3.** in some languages, as Sanskrit and ancient Greek, of or signifying two persons or things. [Latin *duālis* containing two, from *duo* two.]

du·al·ism (dōō'ə liz'əm, dū'-) *n.* **1.** state of being dual; duality. **2.** theory that all the phenomena of the universe can be explained in terms of two distinct essential factors, as body and soul or good and evil. Distinguished from **monism** and **pluralism.** —**du'al·ist,** *n.*

du·al·is·tic (dōō'ə lis'tik, dū'-) *adj.* **1.** of or relating to dualism. **2.** characterized by duality; dual. —**du'al·is'ti·cal·ly,** *adv.*

du·al·i·ty (dōō al'ə tē, dū-) *pl.* **-ties.** *n.* state or quality of being dual.

du·al-pur·pose (dōō'əl-pûr'pəs, dū'-) *adj.* having two functions or uses.

dub¹ (dub) *dubbed, dub·bing. v.t.* **1.** to confer knighthood upon by tapping on the shoulder with a sword; make, or designate as, a knight. **2.a.** to give a title or nickname to; name. **b.** to speak of or refer to as: *He was dubbed a fool. They dubbed him a traitor.* **3.** to make smooth, as by cutting, rubbing, or beating: *to dub wood, to dub leather.* [Old English *dubbian* to designate as a knight.]

dub² (dub) *n. Informal.* clumsy person. [Of uncertain origin.]

dub³ (dub) *dubbed, dub·bing. v.t.* **1.** to provide (a film or other recording) with a new sound track, as one whose dialogue is in another language. **2.** to insert or substitute (music, dialogue, or other sounds) in the sound track of a film or other recording (often with *in*). [Short for DOUBLE.]

Du Bar·ry, Madame (dōō bar'ē, dū-) 1743–93, French countess and mistress of Louis XV of France.

du·bi·e·ty (dōō bī'ə tē, dū-) *pl.* **-ties.** *n.* **1.** state or quality of being dubious. **2.** something doubtful or uncertain; matter of doubt.

du·bi·ous (dōō'bē əs, dū'-) *adj.* **1.** feeling doubt or wavering in opinion; hesitant; skeptical: *I'm dubious about your chances of success.* **2.** of questionable character; suspect: *a dubious reputation.* **3.** causing doubt; ambiguous; equivocal: *a dubious reply.* **4.** of uncertain or unpredictable outcome: *in dubious battle.* [Latin *dubiōsus* doubtful, from *dubium* doubt.] —**du'bi·ous·ly,** *adv.* —**du'bi·ous·ness,** *n.* —**Syn. 1.** see doubtful.

du·bi·ta·ble (dōō'bi tə bəl, dū'-) *adj.* open to doubt; questionable; doubtful. [Latin *dubitābilis,* from *dubitāre* to be uncertain.]

Dub·lin (dub'lin) *n.* capital and largest city of Ireland, in the eastern part of the country. Pop. (1966), 568,772.

Du Bois, W(illiam) E(dward) B(urghardt) (dōō bois') 1868–1963, American educator and civil rights leader.

Du·buque (də bük') *n.* city in eastern Iowa. Pop. (1970), 62,309.

du·cal (dōō'kəl, dū'-) *adj.* of or relating to a duke or duchy. [French *ducal,* from *duc* duke, from Latin *dux* leader.]

duc·at (duk'ət) *n.* **1.** any of several gold or silver coins formerly used in certain European countries. **2.** *Slang.* ticket, as for a sports event. [Italian *ducato* the coin, duchy, from Late Latin *ducātus* duchy, from Latin *dux* leader; with reference to the inscription with the word *ducatus* on ducats issued in Venice in the thirteenth century.]

du·ce (dōō'chā) *n. Italian.* **1.** leader. **2.** il Duce. title assumed by Benito Mussolini as head of the Italian fascist state. [Italian *duce,* from Latin *dux* leader. Doublet of DOGE, DUKE.]

duch·ess (duch'is) *n.* **1.** wife or widow of a duke. **2.** woman holding in her own right a rank equal to a duke's, esp. the female sovereign of a duchy. [Old French *duchesse* wife of a duke, feminine of *duc* duke, from Latin *dux* leader.]

duch·y (duch'ē) *pl.* **duch·ies.** *n.* territory under the rule of a duke or duchess; dukedom.

duck¹ (duk) *n.* **1.** any of various wild or domestic waterfowl, family Anatidae, having

Duck¹

relatively short legs and neck, webbed feet, and usually a broad, flat bill. **2.** female duck, as distinguished from a male or drake. **3.** flesh of a duck used as food. **4.** *British. Informal.* darling; pet. **5.** *Slang.* person; fellow: *He's a queer duck.* [Old English *dūce* waterfowl.]

duck² (duk) *v.t.* **1.** to plunge or thrust under water quickly or suddenly: *We ducked our counselor in the lake.* **2.** to lower or bend (something) suddenly and quickly: *I ducked my head to avoid being hit.* **3.** to avoid or evade: *to duck a blow, to duck a question.* —*v.i.* **1.** to lower the head or body suddenly; crouch, as to avoid being hit: *We all ducked when we heard the shots.* **2.** to move quickly; dart: *to duck in and out of a store. He ducked around the corner when he saw them coming.* —*n.* act of ducking. [From an unrecorded Old English word.]

duck³ (duk) *n.* **1.** any of various very durable cotton fabrics, similar to but lighter in weight than canvas, used for many different items, including small sails, tents, military uniforms, and other articles of clothing. **2. ducks.** trousers made of this. [Dutch *doek* linen cloth, canvas.]

duck⁴ (duk) *n.* amphibious military truck used esp. during World War II. [Modification of its code name, *DUKW*.]

duck-bill (duk'bil') *n.* platypus. Also, **duck-billed platypus.**

ducking stool, device for punishment formerly used in England and colonial America, consisting of a chair in which offenders were tied to be plunged into water, usually attached to a long plank and arranged as a seesaw.

Ducking stool

duck·ling (duk'ling) *n.* young duck.

duck·pin (duk'pin') *n.* **1. duckpins.** bowling game played with pins smaller than those used in tenpins, and a smaller ball. ▲ construed as singular. **2.** pin used in this game.

ducks and drakes 1. game of skimming flat stones or other objects across the surface of water so as to make them skip several times. **2. to make ducks and drakes of** or **play (at) ducks and drakes with.** to handle recklessly; squander.

duck soup *Slang.* something easy to do or accomplish.

duck·weed (duk'wēd') *n.* any of various very small green plants, genus *Lemna,* having no true stems and leaves, that float on still water, often forming a coating on the surface. They are the smallest and simplest of the flowering plants.

duck·y¹ (duk'ē) **duck·i·er, duck·i·est.** *also,* **duck·ie.** *adj. Slang.* fine; delightful; excellent. [DUCK¹ + -Y¹.]

duck·y² (duk'ē) *pl.* **-ies.** *n. British Slang.* dear; darling; pet. [DUCK¹ + -Y².]

duct (dukt) *n.* **1.** tube, pipe, or channel which conveys or conducts something, as a liquid or gas. **2.** tube or channel for carrying a body fluid, esp. a fluid secreted by a gland. **3.** pipe or channel for carrying electric wires, cables, or power. [Latin *ductus* a leading, conducting.] —**duct'less,** *adj.*

duc·tile (dukt'əl) *adj.* **1.** that can be hammered out thin or drawn out into wire without breaking; malleable: *ductile metals.* **2.** easily molded or shaped; pliable; plastic: *Modeling clay is ductile.* **3.** easily controlled or influenced; compliant; tractable: *a ductile person.* [Latin *ductilis* easy to lead, from *dūcere* to lead.] —**duc·til·i·ty** (duk til'ə tē), *n.* —**Syn. 1.** see pliable.

ductless gland, endocrine gland.

dud (dud) *n.* **1.** bomb or shell that fails to explode. **2. duds.** *Informal.* clothing. **3.** *Slang.* person or thing that is a failure. [Of uncertain origin.]

dude (dōōd, dūd) *n.* **1.** man excessively concerned with his clothes, appearance, and manners. **2.** *Informal.* city-bred person, esp. an easterner visiting the western United States. **3.** *Slang.* fellow; guy. [Of uncertain origin.]

dude ranch, ranch operated as a resort for tourists, offering horseback riding, swimming, and other activities.

Du·de·vant, Baroness (dōōd ə vän') see **Sand, George.**

dudg·eon (duj'ən) *n.* feeling of anger, resentment, or offense. ▲ now used chiefly in the phrase *in high dudgeon: to leave in high dudgeon.* [Of uncertain origin.]

due (dōō, dū) *adj.* **1.** owed or owing as a debt; owed and expected to be paid; payable: *The rent will be due on the first of the month. The final payment is due.* **2.** owed or owing as a natural or moral right; that should be given or rendered: *the honor due him.* **3.** appropriate; fitting; proper: *prayers offered in due form.* **4.** adequate; sufficient: *due cause for alarm.* **5.** required or expected to arrive, be present, or be ready: *I am due at the theater in fifteen minutes. The train is due at 5:30.* **6. due to. a.** caused by: *The delay was due to heavy traffic.* **b.** because of: *The project was abandoned due to lack of support.* —*n.* **1.** that which is due. **2. dues.** fee or charge, esp. one paid to a group or organization

at; āpe; cär; end; mē; it; īce; hot; ōld; fôrk; wood; fōōl; oil; out; up; ūse; turn; sing; thin; this; zh in treasure; ə in ago, taken, pencil, lemon, circus.

for the rights of membership. —*adv.* straight; directly; exactly: *We sailed due north.* [Old French *deu*, past participle of *devoir* to owe, from Latin *dēbēre.*]

du·el (dōō′əl, dū′-) *n.* **1.** prearranged formal combat between two people to settle an argument or decide a point of honor, fought in the presence of witnesses or seconds, usually with swords or firearms. **2.** any contest, struggle, or encounter between two contending parties: *a verbal duel, a duel of wits.* —*v.t., v.i.,* **-eled, -eling;** *also, British,* **-elled, -el·ling,** to fight in a duel. [Medieval Latin *duellum* combat between two people, from Latin *duellum,* form of *bellum* war.] —**du′el·er, du′el·ist;** *also, British,* **du′el·ler, du′el·list,** *n.*

du·en·na (dōō en′ə, dū-) *n.* **1.** in Spanish- and Portuguese-speaking countries, a mature woman who serves as the chaperon or escort of a young unmarried girl. **2.** governess; chaperon. [Spanish *dueña* chaperon, mistress, from Latin *domina* mistress, lady.]

due process of law, regular administration of the law carried out according to established legal principles and in such a way that the rights of the individual are protected. Also, **due process.**

du·et (dōō et′, dū-) *n.* musical composition for two performers. [Italian *duetto,* diminutive of *due* two, from Latin *duo* two.]

duff (duf) *n.* stiff flour pudding boiled or steamed in a cloth bag. [Form of DOUGH.]

duf·fel (duf′əl) *also,* **duf·fle.** *n.* **1.** coarse woolen cloth with a thick nap. **2.** equipment or supplies, esp. for camping. [Dutch *duffel* this cloth, from *Duffel,* town near Antwerp, Belgium, where it was first made.]

duffel bag *also,* **duffle bag.** large bag, usually of canvas, used for carrying clothes, equipment, or other belongings.

duff·er (duf′ər) *n. Informal.* clumsy, plodding, or incompetent person, esp. an unskilled golfer.

dug¹ (dug) past tense and past participle of **dig.**

dug² (dug) *n.* nipple; teat; udder. [Of uncertain origin.]

du·gong (dōō′gong′) *n.* plant-eating aquatic mammal, *Dugong dugon,* native to warm, shallow seas from eastern Africa to northern Australia, having a blunt snout, a short, flat tail, a pair of front flippers, a torpedolike body, and a thick gray and white hide. Length: 7–9 feet. Also, **sea cow.** [Malay *dūyōng.*]

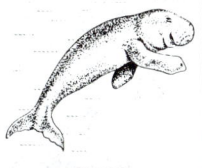
Dugong

dug·out (dug′out′) *n.* **1.** rough shelter or dwelling formed by digging a hole in the ground or in a hillside or other slope, often covered or reinforced with sod or other material. **2.** long, three-sided, roofed structure in which baseball players sit when not at bat or in the field. **3.** canoe or boat made by hollowing out a large log.

Duis·burg (dōōs′bûrg′) *n.* city in northwestern West Germany. Pop. (1968 est.), 465,071.

duke (dōōk, dūk) *n.* **1.** British nobleman of the highest rank. **2.** nobleman of certain other European countries having a similar rank. **3.** prince who rules an independent duchy. **4.** dukes. *Slang.* hands; fists. [Old French *duc* ruler of a duchy, lord, from Latin *dux* leader. Doublet of DOGE, DUCE.]

duke·dom (dōōk′dəm, dūk′-) *n.* **1.** duchy. **2.** office, title, or rank of a duke.

dul·cet (dul′sit) *adj.* soothing or agreeable, esp. to the ear; sweet; pleasant: *her dulcet tones.* [Modification (influenced in spelling by Latin *dulcis* sweet) of Old French *doucet* sweet, diminutive of *doux,* from Latin *dulcis.*]

dul·ci·mer (dul′sə mər) *n.* musical instrument shaped like a trapezoid and having metal strings, played by striking the strings with two leather-covered hammers. [Old French *doulcemer,* form of *doulcemele,* probably going back to Latin *dulcis* sweet + Greek *melos* song; because of its sweet sound.]

Dulcimer

Dul·cin·e·a (dul sin′ē ə, dul′sə nē′ə) *n.* coarse peasant girl whom Don Quixote imagines to be a beautiful lady and with whom he falls in love.

dull (dul) *adj.* **1.** not sharp or pointed; blunt: *a dull ax, a dull blade. The pencil has a dull point.* **2.** not interesting; tedious; boring: *a dull speech, a dull subject.* **3.** lacking in intelligence or mental quickness; slow to learn or understand: *a dull student.* **4.** not keenly felt; not intense: *a dull ache.* **5.** lacking in perception, sensitivity, or responsiveness. **6.** not bright, clear, or vivid: *a dull red, a dull glow, a dull finish on the floor.* **7.** not distinct or ringing in sound; muffled: *a dull thud, the dull roar of the waves.* **8.** not active or brisk; sluggish: *Trading is dull on the stock exchange today.* **9.** not lively or cheerful; depressed;

listless: *moody and dull melancholy* (Shakespeare, *Comedy of Errors*). **10.** (of weather) cloudy or gloomy; overcast. —*v.t.* to make dull: *to dull a blade, to dull the appetite.* —*v.i.* to become dull. [Possibly from an unrecorded Old English word.] —**dull′ness;** *also,* **dul′ness,** *n.* —**dul′ly,** *adv.*

Syn. *adj.* **1. Dull, blunt** mean lacking sharpness. **Dull** implies lack of normal sharpness as a result of overuse or disuse: *Good wood carving cannot be done with dull chisels.* **Blunt** may refer to an edge or point that has lost its sharpness by misuse or to one not meant to be sharp at all: *Use a pen with a blunt point for that kind of lettering.*

dull·ard (dul′ərd) *n.* stupid or slow-witted person; dolt.

dulse (duls) *n.* any of various coarse, edible red seaweeds found on the northern coasts of North America, Asia, and Europe. [Irish Gaelic *duileasg.*]

Du·luth (də lōōth′) *n.* city in northeastern Minnesota. Pop. (1970), 100,578.

du·ly (dōō′lē, dū′-) *adv.* **1.** in a fitting or proper manner; suitably; rightfully: *They were duly sworn in.* **2.** to the extent or degree that is due; adequately; sufficiently: *These proposals should be duly considered.* **3.** when due; at the proper time; punctually: *rent duly paid.*

Du·ma (dōō′mə) *n.* Russian elective legislative assembly which constituted the lower house of parliament, established in 1905 by Czar Nicholas II and dissolved during the revolution of 1917. [Russian *duma* thought, council; of Germanic origin.]

Du·mas (dōō mä′, dū-) **1. A·le·xan·dre** (ä lek sän′drə) 1802–70, French novelist and playwright. **2. Alexandre.** 1824–95, his son; French playwright.

Du Mau·ri·er, George (dōō môr′ē ā′, dū-) 1834–96, English novelist and illustrator.

dumb (dum) *adj.* **1.** lacking the power of speech; mute: *dumb animals, a person who is deaf and dumb.* **2.** temporarily speechless: *dumb with horror. I was struck dumb when I heard the news.* **3.** refraining from speech; silent; taciturn: *He remained dumb, refusing to answer.* **4.** not characterized or accompanied by speech or sound: *Pleasant answered with a short dumb nod* (Dickens, 1865). **5.** *Informal.* stupid; dull-witted; stupid. [Old English *dumb* lacking the power of speech.] —**dumb′ly,** *adv.* —**dumb′ness,** *n.*

Dum·bar·ton Oaks (dum′bär′tən) estate in Washington, D.C., where conferences were held in 1944 to formulate plans for the organization of the United Nations.

dumb·bell (dum′bel′) *n.* **1.** bar with heavy, usually metal, discs or balls at either end, used for exercising. **2.** *Slang.* stupid person.

dumb show **1.** gestures without speech; pantomime. **2.** part of a play presented in pantomime, performed esp. in early English drama.

dumb·wait·er (dum′wā′tər) *n.* **1.** small elevator used to convey dishes, food, rubbish, or other articles from one floor to another. **2.** movable serving table or stand.

dum·dum (dum′dum′) *n.* bullet with a soft nose made so that it will expand on impact, causing a large wound. Also, **dumdum bullet.** [From *Dum Dum,* town near Calcutta, India, where it was formerly manufactured.]

dum·found (dum′found′, dum′found′) *also,* **dumb·found.** *v.t.* to strike dumb, as with amazement; astonish; confound. [DUMB + (CON)FOUND.]

dum·my (dum′ē) *pl.,* **-mies.** *n.* **1.** figure of the human body used to represent or serve as a real person: *department store dummies, a ventriloquist's dummy. The coach had the players tackle dummies during practice.* **2.** imitation object made to resemble the real thing, as a false drawer. **3.** one unable to speak; mute. ▲ now considered offensive. **4.** one seeming to act independently or for his own interests but really serving another. **5.** *Bridge.* **a.** the declarer's partner, whose cards are exposed on the table and played by the declarer. **b.** cards so exposed. **6.** sample, as of a book or magazine, usually consisting of blank pages, arranged to show the size and appearance of a final version. **7.** *Informal.* stupid person; dolt. —*adj.* **1.** imitation; counterfeit; sham: *a dummy rifle, a dummy airplane.* **2.** seeming to act independently but really serving another: *a dummy organization, a dummy stockholder.* **3.** *Bridge.* played with a dummy. [DUMB + -Y¹.]

dump (dump) *v.t.* **1.** to throw down or let fall in a heap or mass; fling down or drop heavily or suddenly: *They dumped the gravel in the driveway. She dumped her books on the bed.* **2.** to unload or empty the contents of (a container), as by overturning: *I dumped out my briefcase on the table.* **3.** *Informal.* to get rid of or throw away by or as by dumping; dispose of: *He went to dump the garbage. Congress dumped the proposal.* **4.** to put (goods) on the market in large quantities and at a low price, esp. on a foreign market at a price lower than that in the home country. —*v.i.* **1.** place where rubbish or refuse is deposited. **2.** pile or heap of rubbish or other discarded materials. **3.** place for temporary storage of military supplies: *an ammunition dump.* **4.** *Slang.* messy, shabby, or unattractive place. [Possibly imitative; possibly of Scandinavian origin.]

dump·cart (dump′kärt′) *n.* cart so constructed that its body can be tilted or its bottom opened to discharge its load.

dump·ling (dump′ling) *n.* **1.** ball of dough that is boiled or steamed. **2.** dessert made by enclosing fruit in a piece of dough and baking or steaming it. [Of uncertain origin.]

dumps (dumps) *n.* gloomy or depressed state of mind; low spirits. ▲ used chiefly in the phrase *down in the dumps.* [Probably from Dutch *domp* haze.]

dump truck, truck so constructed that its rear portion can be tilted to discharge its load through an open tailgate.

dump·y (dum′pē) **dump·i·er, dump·i·est.** *adj.* short and stout; squat. —**dump′i·ly,** *adv.* —**dump′i·ness,** *n.*

dun¹ (dun) **dunned, dun·ning.** *v.t.* **1.** to make repeated and persistent demands upon, esp. for the payment of a debt. **2.** to annoy or harass continually. —*n.* **1.** repeated and insistent demand, esp. for payment of a debt. **2.** one who duns. [Of uncertain origin.]

dun² (dun) *n.* dull grayish-brown color. [Old English *dunn* dark.]

Du·nant, Jean Hen·ri (dōō nän′; zhäN äN rē′) 1829–1910, Swiss philanthropist and founder of the Red Cross.

Dun·bar, Paul Laurence (dun′bär′) 1872–1906, U.S. poet.

Dun·can, Is·a·dor·a (dung′kən; iz′ə dôr′ə) 1878–1927, U.S. dancer.

Dun·can I (dung′kən) d.1040, king of Scotland from c.1034 to 1040. According to tradition, he was murdered by Macbeth.

dunce (duns) *n.* one slow at learning; dull-witted or ignorant person. [From phrase *a Duns man,* applied contemptuously to followers of John Duns Scotus.]

dunce cap also, **dunce's cap.** cone-shaped hat formerly placed on the head of a slow or lazy student in school as a punishment.

Dun·dee (dun dē′) *n.* city in eastern Scotland. Pop. (1968 est.), 184,-381.

dun·der·head (dun′dər hed′) *n.* dull-witted, foolish, or stupid person; blockhead. [Possibly from Dutch *donder* thunder + HEAD; referring to the result of being struck by a thunderbolt.]

dune (dōōn, dūn) *n.* mound, hill, or ridge of sand that is heaped up by the wind. [French *dune,* from Middle Dutch *dunen;* of Celtic origin.]

dung (dung) *n.* **1.** animal excrement; manure. **2.** something vile or foul. —*v.t.* to cover or fertilize with or as with dung. [Old English *dung* excrement.]

dun·ga·ree (dung′gə rē′) *n.* **1.** denim fabric used for such items as work clothes, sportswear, and sails. **2. dungarees.** trousers or work clothes made of this fabric. [Hindi *dūngrī* coarse cotton cloth.]

dung beetle, any of a large group of beetles, family Scarabaeidae, that feed chiefly on the dung of other animals.

dun·geon (dun′jən) *n.* **1.** dark, close cell or prison, esp. one underground: *the dungeon of a castle.* **2.** donjon. [Old French *donjon* donjon, going back to Late Latin *dominiō* tower, dominion, from Latin *dominus* master, lord.]

dung·hill (dung′hil′) *n.* heap of dung.

dunk (dungk) *v.t.* **1.** to dip (something to eat) into a liquid: *to dunk doughnuts into coffee. He dunked the roll in his soup.* **2.** to push or submerge (someone) underwater briefly; duck. [German *tunken* to dip.] —**dunk′er,** *n.*

Dun·kirk (dun′kurk′) also, **Dun·kerque.** *n.* seaport in northern France, scene of the evacuation of Allied troops in 1940. Pop. (1968), 27,504.

dun·lin (dun′lin) *pl.,* **-lins** or **-lin.** *n.* reddish-brown and white sandpiper, *Erolia alpina,* widely distributed throughout the northern hemisphere, which has a black stripe on the abdomen during the breeding season. [DUN² + -LIN(G).]

dun·nage (dun′ij) *n.* **1.** any loose material packed around a cargo to protect it from damage during shipping. **2.** personal belongings; baggage. [Of uncertain origin.]

Dun·sa·ny, Lord Edward (dun sā′nē) 1878–1957, Anglo-Irish dramatist and writer.

Duns Sco·tus, John (dunz skō′təs) c.1266–1308, Scottish theologian and scholastic philosopher.

du·o (dōō′ō, dū′ō) *pl.,* **du·os** or **du·i** (dōō′ē, dū′ē). *n.* **1.** musical ensemble of two performers. **2.** duet. **3.** two persons who perform together or are commonly associated with one another; pair; couple. [Italian *duo* duet, two, from Latin *duo* two.]

du·o·dec·i·mal (dōō′ə des′ə məl, dū′-) *adj.* relating to or based on twelfths or the number twelve; proceeding by twelves: *duodecimal multiplication.* —*n.* number in a duodecimal system. [Latin *duodecimus* twelfth (from *duodecim* twelve) + -AL¹.]

duodecimal system, system of numbers using a base of twelve, rather than ten, as in the decimal system.

du·o·dec·i·mo (dōō′ə des′ə mō′, dū′-) *pl.,* **-mos.** *n.* **1.** page size of approximately 5 by 7½ inches. **2.** book or page of this size. —*adj.* being this size; consisting of pages of this size. Also, **twelve′mo.** [Latin

duodecimō, ablative of *duodecimus* twelfth, from *duodecim* twelve.]

du·o·de·nal (dōō′ə dēn′əl, dū′-, dōō od′ən əl, dū-) *adj.* of or relating to the duodenum.

du·o·de·num (dōō′ə dē′nəm, dū′-, dōō od′ən əm, dū-) *pl.,* **-na** (-nə). *n.* first section of the small intestine, extending from the final portion of the stomach to the jejunum. [Medieval Latin *(intestinum) duodenum (digitorum)* (intestine) of twelve (fingers), from Latin *duodēnī* twelve each, from *duodecim* twelve; because it is approximately the length of twelve finger widths.]

dup., duplicate.

dupe (dōōp, dūp) *n.* **1.** one who is being deluded or tricked, or who unwittingly serves the ends of another: *He was a dupe of the racketeers.* **2.** one easily deceived or deluded. —*v.t.,* **duped, dup·ing.** to make a dupe of; deceive; delude. [French *dupe* deceived person; earlier, hoopoe (of uncertain origin); supposedly referring to the bird's stupidity.] —**dup′er,** *n.*

dup·er·y (dōō′pər ē, dū′-) *pl.,* **-er·ies.** *n.* **1.** act or practice of duping. **2.** state of one who is duped.

du·ple (dōō′pəl, dū′-) *adj.* **1.** double; twofold. **2.** *Music.* having two, or a multiple of two, beats to the measure: *duple time, duple meter.* [Latin *duplus* twofold. Doublet of DOUBLE.]

du·plex (dōō′pleks, dū′-) *adj.* having two parts; double; twofold. —*n.* duplex house or apartment. [Latin *duplex* twofold.]

duplex apartment, apartment having rooms on two floors.

duplex house, house having two separate single-family units.

du·pli·cate (*adj., n.,* dōō′pli kit, dū′-; *v.,* dōō′pli kāt′, dū′-) *adj.* **1.** being an exact copy of an original; exactly like or corresponding exactly to something else: *a duplicate list, a duplicate tax form.* **2.** having or consisting of two corresponding or identical parts; double; twofold. **3.** designating a card game in which all players play the same series of hands, the winners being the partners with the best comparative score: *duplicate bridge.* —*n.* **1.** copy exactly like an original; exact copy: *Keep a duplicate of the letter.* **2.** something corresponding in every respect to something else; counterpart; double: *Your jacket's a duplicate of mine.* **3.** duplicate game of cards, esp. bridge. **4. in duplicate,** in two identical copies: *Type this letter in duplicate.* —*v.t.,* **-cat·ed, -cat·ing. 1.** to copy exactly; reproduce: *to duplicate a letter.* **2.** to do again; repeat: *to duplicate an action.* [Latin *duplicātus,* past participle of *duplicāre* to double.]

Syn. *n.* **1. Duplicate, copy, facsimile, replica** mean something that has close resemblance to or identity with something else. **Duplicate** implies that the object is so like the original that it may serve in its place: *He opened the door with a duplicate key.* **Copy** suggests that the thing is a close imitation of the original but is not identical with it: *He made a copy of the famous painting.* **Facsimile** implies something made to resemble the original in appearance: *The book is a facsimile of the original privately printed edition.* **Replica** is a model imitating the original in spirit, although perhaps differing in some details: *The air show featured a replica of a World War I fighter plane.*

du·pli·ca·tion (dōō′pli kā′shən, dū′-) *n.* **1.** act of duplicating; being duplicated. **2.** copy or counterpart; duplicate.

du·pli·ca·tor (dōō′pli kā′tər, dū′-) *n.* machine for making duplicates, esp. of pages of written or typed material.

du·plic·i·ty (dōō plis′ə tē, dū-) *pl.,* **-ties.** *n.* hypocritical deceit or treachery; dissimulation; double-dealing. [Late Latin *duplicitās* a being double, from Latin *duplex* twofold.]

du·ra·bil·i·ty (door′ə bil′ə tē, dyoor′-) *pl.,* **-ties.** *n.* quality of being durable; ability to resist wear, decay, or change.

du·ra·ble (door′ə bəl, dyoor′-) *adj.* **1.** able to resist wear or decay: *a durable floor, durable shoes.* **2.** able to resist change or stress; stable; enduring: *a durable friendship.* [Old French *durable* lasting, from Latin *dūrābilis,* from *dūrāre* to last.] —**du′ra·ble·ness,** *n.* —**du′ra·bly,** *adv.*

du·ral·u·min (doo ral′yə min, dyoor′-) *n.* strong, light alloy of aluminum which contains copper, maganese, and magnesium. Trademark: Duralumin. [German *Dural* (from *Düren,* German city where it was first made) + ALUMIN(UM).]

du·ra ma·ter (door′ə mā′tər, dyoor′-) tough, fibrous membrane that is the outermost of the three coverings of the brain and spinal cord. Also, **du′ra.** [Medieval Latin *dura mater (cerebri)* hard mother (of the brain).]

du·ra·men (doo rā′mən, dyoo-) heartwood.

du·rance (door′əns, dyoor′-) *n.* forced confinement or imprisonment. ▲ used chiefly in the phrase *in durance vile.* [Old French *durance* duration, from *durer* to last, from Latin *dūrāre.*]

du·ra·tion (doo rā′shən, dyoo-) *n.* length of time during which anything continues or exists; continuance in time: *for the duration of the war, a peace of short duration.* [Medieval Latin *duratio* hardness, perseverance, from Latin *dūrāre* to last, harden.]

Dur·ban (dur′bən) *n.* port city in eastern South Africa. Pop. (1967 est.), 662,894.

dur·bar (dur′bär′) *n.* **1.** court of a native Indian ruler. **2.** formerly,

at; āpe; cär; end; mē; it; īce; hot; ōld; fôrk; wood; fōōl; oil; out; up; ūse; turn; sing; thin; this; zh in treasure; ə in ago, taken, pencil, lemon, circus.

public audience or reception held in India by a native prince or by a British governor or viceroy. **3.** hall or place where such a reception was held. [Hindi *darbār* court, from Persian *darbār*, from *dar* door + *bār* admission.]

Dü·rer, Al·brecht (door'ər, dyoor'-; äl'brɛкнt) 1471–1528, German artist and engraver.

du·ress (doo res', dyoo-, door'is, dyoor'-) *n.* **1.** constraint or coercion used to force someone to do something: *The prisoner signed the confession under duress.* **2.** unlawful confinement or imprisonment. [Old French *duresce* hardness, cruelty, from Latin *dūritia* hardness, severity.]

Dur·ham (dur'əm) *n.* city in north-central North Carolina. Pop. (1970), 95,438.

du·ri·an (door'ē ən) *n.* **1.** oval-shaped, edible fruit of a tree, *Durio zibethinus,* having a soft cream-colored pulp, a thorny rind, and an odor resembling that of Limburger cheese. **2.** tropical tree bearing this fruit, native to the Malay region of Asia. [Malay *dūriān* the fruit, from *dūrī* thorn; referring to the fruit's thorny rind.]

dur·ing (door'ing, dyoor'-) *prep.* **1.** throughout the time or duration of: *I lived in the country during the summer.* **2.** at some point in the course of: *He arrived during the second act.* [Originally present participle of obsolete *dure* to last, from Old French *durer,* from Latin *dūrāre.*]

Durk·heim, É·mile (durk'hīm; ā mēl') 1858–1917, French sociologist.

Du·roc (door'ok, dyoor'-) *n.* hog of a breed originally developed in New York and New Jersey, having a red coat and drooping ears, valued for its meat. Also, **Duroc-Jersey** (door'ok jur'zē, dyoor'-).

dur·ra (door'ə) *n.* sorghum of a variety widely cultivated for its edible grain. [Arabic *dhūrah* millet.]

durst (durst) archaic past tense of **dare.**

du·rum (door'əm, dyoor'-) *n.* any plant belonging to a class of wheat, *Triticum durum,* having hard, amber-colored kernels from which a high-quality flour used primarily in making macaroni, spaghetti, and similar products is produced. Also, **durum wheat.** [Modern Latin *durum,* from Latin *dūrus* hard.]

dusk (dusk) *n.* **1.** time of day just before nightfall; twilight. **2.** shade; darkness; gloom. —*adj.* shadowy; gloomy; dark. [Old English *dox* dark.]

dusk·y (dus'kē) *adj.* **dusk·i·er, dusk·i·est.** **1.** dark in color. **2.** lacking light; shadowy; dim. —**dusk'i·ly,** *adv.* —**dusk'i·ness,** *n.*

Düs·sel·dorf (doos'əl dôrf') *n.* city in northwestern West Germany. Pop. (1968 est.), 686,083.

dust (dust) *n.* **1.** fine, dry particles of earth or other matter, tiny enough to be easily suspended in or carried by air currents. **2.** ground, esp. as the burial place of the dead; earth. **3.** that to which anything, as a dead body, is reduced by decay or disintegration. **4.** low, humble, or poor condition. **5. to bite the dust.** to be killed, esp. in battle. —*v.t.* **1.** to free of dust, as by brushing or wiping: *to dust the table.* **2.** to cover or sprinkle with or as with dust: *to dust a pan with flour, to dust crops with insecticide.* **3.** to strew or sprinkle in the form of dust: *to dust fertilizer on plants.* —*v.i.* **1.** to remove dust, esp. from furniture: *She dusted every day.* **2.** (of a bird) to bathe in dust. [Old English *dūst* powder, particles of earth.]

dust·bin (dust'bin') *n.* *British.* container for refuse or garbage; ashcan.

dust bowl also, **Dust Bowl.** area of dry, dusty land having irregular rainfall and subject to frequent dust storms, esp. one that developed in the Great Plains of the United States in the 1930s.

dust devil, small whirlwind that picks up dust and debris and carries it high into the air.

dust·er (dus'tər) *n.* **1.** one who or that which dusts. **2.** cloth, brush, or other device for removing dust from objects. **3.** loose-fitting, knee-length housecoat. **4.** long, lightweight coat worn, as formerly in open automobiles, to protect clothing from dust.

dust jacket, removable paper cover for a book.

dust·man (dust'mən) *n.* *British.* man whose work is collecting or removing refuse or garbage.

dust·pan (dust'pan') *n.* broad, short-handled shovellike pan for collecting dust swept from a floor.

dust·proof (dust'prōof') *adj.* keeping out dust; protecting from dust.

dust storm, strong wind that carries clouds of dust and silt across dry plains or desert regions.

dust·y (dus'tē) *adj.* **dust·i·er, dust·i·est.** **1.** full of or covered with dust: *a dusty attic.* **2.** like dust; powdery: *a dusty snow.* **3.** of the color of dust; grayish: *dusty pink.* —**dust'i·ly,** *adv.* —**dust'i·ness,** *n.*

Dutch (duch) *adj.* **1.** of or relating to the Netherlands, its people, or their language. **2.** *Informal.* German. —*adv.* **to go Dutch.** *Informal.* to have each person pay his own expenses, as on a date. —*n.* **1. the Dutch. a.** the people of the Netherlands. **b.** *Informal.* the people of Germany. **2.** Germanic language of the Netherlands. **3. in Dutch.**

Informal. in trouble or disfavor: *He's in Dutch with his boss.* [Middle Dutch *dutsch* Dutch (of the Netherlands), German.]

Dutch courage *Informal.* courage inspired or maintained by or as by intoxication.

Dutch door, door divided horizontally so that the upper part can remain open while the bottom part is closed, or vice versa.

Dutch elm disease, disease of elm trees caused by a fungus and transmitted by certain insects, which causes leaves and branches to wilt, finally killing the tree. Also, **elm blight.**

Dutch Guiana, see **Surinam.**

Dutch·man (duch'mən) *pl.* **-men.** *n.* **1.** member or recent descendant of the people of the Netherlands. **2.** *Informal.* German.

Dutch·man's-breech·es (duch'mənz brich'iz) *pl.* **-breech·es.** *n.* **1.** drooping flower of a wild plant, *Dicentra cucullaria,* having white and yellow petals which form a sac resembling pantaloons. **2.** plant bearing this flower, native to woodlands of eastern North America, having stalks and fernlike leaves which grow directly from underground tubers.

Dutch oven 1. heavy metal or ceramic kettle with a tight-fitting cover, used chiefly for preparing meats and stews and sometimes for baking. **2.** metal box having one side which opens, placed before a fire for cooking by reflected heat. **3.** brick oven in which the walls are preheated for cooking.

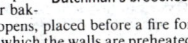

Dutchman's-breeches

Dutch treat *Informal.* meal, entertainment, or outing at which each person pays his own expenses.

Dutch uncle *Informal.* one who criticizes or scolds another bluntly and severely, esp. in an authoritative or patronizing way.

du·te·ous (dōō'tē əs, dū'-) *adj.* dutiful; obedient. —**du'te·ous·ly,** *adv.* —**du'te·ous·ness,** *n.*

du·ti·a·ble (dōō'tē ə bəl, dū'-) *adj.* subject to the payment of customs duty or taxes: *a shipment of dutiable imports.*

du·ti·ful (dōō'ti fəl, dū'-) *adj.* **1.** performing one's duty or duties; having a sense of duty; obedient; respectful: *a dutiful child, a dutiful and loyal subject of the king.* **2.** showing or resulting from a sense of duty: *He displayed a dutiful interest in her complaints.* —**du'ti·ful·ly,** *adv.* —**du'ti·ful·ness,** *n.*

du·ty (dōō'tē, dū'-) *pl.* **-ties.** *n.* **1.** that which one is morally or legally bound to do; obligation: *duty to one's country. It is a father's duty to care for his children properly.* **2.** commitment to or sense of such obligation: *He was motivated by duty alone, and not by any hope of reward.* **3.** act or action required by or involved in one's occupation or position: *One of the duties of a secretary is typing letters.* **4.** obligatory or assigned task or service, esp. military service: *overseas duty.* **5.** tax levied on imported or exported goods; tariff. **6.** obedient or respectful conduct due to a superior or elder. [Anglo-Norman *duete* what is due or owing, from *du,* form of Old French *deu,* past participle of *devoir* to owe. See DUE.]

Syn. 1. Duty, obligation indicate something that ought to be done. **Duty** implies a general moral responsibility and suggests the existence of a code by which immediate action may be required: *Lord Nelson's signal to the ships at Trafalgar was "England expects that every man will do his duty."* **Obligation** suggests a definite action at a definite time to fulfill a requirement: *He was under obligation to submit the report before leaving office.* **3.** see **job.**

du·ty-free (dōō'tē frē', dū'-) *adj., adv.* free of or exempt from customs duties: *duty-free cargo. The goods were shipped duty-free.*

du·um·vir (dōō um'vər, dū-) *pl.* **-virs** or **-vi·ri** (-və rī'). *n.* either of two magistrates in ancient Rome who jointly held the same office. [Latin *duumvir,* going back to *duo* two + *vir* man.]

du·um·vir·ate (dōō um'vər it, dū-) *n.* **1.** any office held jointly by two men, as in ancient Rome. **2.** coalition or partnership of two men, as in a governmental position.

du·vet·yn (dōō'və tēn') *n.* soft, slightly napped fabric made of cotton, wool, or synthetic fibers, used esp. for women's suits and hats.

D.V., (Abbreviation of Latin *Deō volente.*)

Dvo·řák, An·ton (dvôr'zhäk; än'tōn) 1841–1904, Czech musical composer.

dwarf (dwôrf) *n.* **1.** fully grown person, animal, or plant of less than normal size for its species or kind. **2.** in folklore, a little man, often depicted as ugly and misshapen, having unusual powers or skills. **3.** dwarf star. —*v.t.* **1.** to cause to seem small, as by contrast or comparison: *Most professional basketball players dwarf other men. The brilliance of his poetry dwarfed the accomplishments of his contemporaries.* **2.** to prevent from growing to the normal size; hinder the natural development of; stunt. —*adj.* of unusually small stature or size; diminutive. [Old English *dweorg* a being smaller than the normal size.] —**dwarf'ism,** *n.*

dwarf·ish (dwôr′fish) *adj.* like a dwarf; unusually small; diminutive; puny. —**dwarf′ish·ly,** *adv.* —**dwarf′ish·ness,** *n.*

dwarf star, any of a number of faint, relatively small, but usually extremely dense, stars.

dwell (dwel) **dwelt** or **dwelled, dwell·ing.** *v.i.* **1.** to live as a permanent resident; make one's home; reside: *to dwell in the suburbs, to dwell in a cottage by the sea.* **2.** to exist or be present: *a memory that dwells in our hearts.* **3.** to linger over or emphasize in thought, speech, or writing (with *on* or *upon*): *The speaker dwelt at length upon his final point. Don't dwell too much on painful memories.* **4.** to exist or continue in a condition or state: *to dwell in happiness.* [Partly from Old Norse *dvelja* to delay, tarry; partly from Old English *dwellan* to delay, remain.] —**dwell′er,** *n.*

dwell·ing (dwel′ing) *n.* place of residence; house; abode. —**Syn.** see home.

dwin·dle (dwind′əl) **-dled, -dling.** *v.i.* to become gradually smaller or less; shrink; diminish: *The regiment dwindled to a handful of troops. Hopes for their safety dwindled.* —*v.t.* to make gradually smaller or less. [Diminutive of archaic *dwine* to waste away, from Old English *dwīnan.*] —**Syn.** *v.i.* see decrease.

dwt., pennyweight.

DX *Radio.* distance; distant.

Dy, dysprosium.

Dy·ak (dī′ak) *also,* **Day·ak** *n.* member of any of several peoples native to the island of Borneo.

dyb·buk (dib′ək) *pl.,* **dyb·buks** or **dyb·buk·im** (di book′im) *also,* **dib·buk.** *n.* in Jewish folklore, demon or soul of a dead person that enters the body of a living person and takes control. [Hebrew *dibbúq* a joining.]

dye (dī) *n.* **1.** pigment used to impart a particular color to cloth, hair, food, or other materials. It is either obtained from natural substances in plants, animals, and minerals, or produced artificially from coal-tar substances. **2.** color or hue, esp. as produced by dyeing. **3. of the deepest** (or **blackest**) **dye.** of the most pronounced or the worst sort: *a criminal of the deepest dye.* —*v.t.* **dyed, dye·ing.** to impart a particular color to, esp. by soaking in a liquid dye. —*v.i.* to take on color in dyeing. [Old English *déag* color, hue.] —**dye′er,** *n.*

dyed-in-the-wool (dīd′in thə wool′) *adj.* **1.** dyed before being woven into fabric. **2.** thoroughgoing; absolute; complete: *a dyed-in-the-wool scoundrel, a dyed-in-the-wool liberal.*

dye·ing (dī′ing) *n.* act, process, or trade of coloring cloth, hair, or other materials with dye.

dye·stuff (dī′stuf′) *n.* substance used as a dye or as a source of dye.

dye·wood (dī′wood′) *n.* any wood, as logwood, that yields a dyestuff.

dy·ing (dī′ing) *v.* present participle of **die**[1]. —*adj.* **1.** approaching death; about to die: *the last wish of a dying man.* **2.** of death or dying: *to one's dying day, dying words.* **3.** drawing to a close; fading: *a dying flame, a dying institution.* —*n.* death.

dyke (dīk) dike.

dy·nam·ic (dī nam′ik) *adj.* **1.** characterized by energy and vigor; forceful: *a dynamic personality, a dynamic performance.* **2.** characterized by change or activity: *a dynamic economy.* **3.** of or relating to energy or force in motion. Distinguished from **static. 4.** of or relating to dynamics. Also, **dy·nam′i·cal.** [Greek *dynamikos* powerful, from *dynamis* power.] —**dy·nam′i·cal·ly,** *adv.*

dy·nam·ics (dī nam′iks) *n.* **1.** branch of mechanics dealing with bodies in motion. It is often divided into kinetics and kinematics. **2.** motivating or governing forces operating in any field or activity, or the laws by which they act: *the dynamics of human behavior.* **3.** *Music.*

gradations of loudness or softness. ▲ construed as singular in defs. 1, 3; as plural in def. 2.

dy·na·mism (dī′nə miz′əm) *n.* **1.** energy and vigor; forcefulness. **2.** any philosophical system, doctrine, or theory that explains the phenomena of the universe in terms of the action of some pervasive force or energy.

dy·na·mite (dī′nə mīt′) *n.* **1.** explosive consisting of a porous, absorbent material saturated with nitroglycerin, usually packed in cylindrical sticks. **2.** *Slang.* person or thing having an exciting, powerful, or spectacular effect. —*v.t.* **-mit·ed, -mit·ing.** to blow up or destroy with dynamite. [Greek *dynamis* power + -ITE¹.] —**dy′na·mit′er,** *n.*

dy·na·mo (dī′nə mō′) *pl.,* **-mos.** *n.* **1.** electric generator or motor, esp. one which produces a direct current. **2.** *Informal.* energetic, vigorous, forceful person. [Short for *dynamoelectric machine.* See DYNAMOELECTRIC, MACHINE.]

dy·na·mo·e·lec·tric (dī′nə mō′ i lek′trik) *adj.* relating to the conversion of mechanical energy into electric energy, or vice versa. Also, **dy′na·mo·e·lec′tri·cal.** [Greek *dynamis* power + ELECTRIC.]

dy·na·mom·e·ter (dī′nə mom′ə tər) *n.* device for measuring force or power. [Greek *dynamis* power + -METER.]

dy·na·mo·tor (dī′nə mō′tər) *n.* machine that combines motor and generator action and is used to change the voltage of an electric current.

dy·nast (dī′nast, -nəst) *n.* ruler, esp. a hereditary ruler. [Latin *dynastēs,* from Greek *dynastēs.*]

dy·nas·ty (dī′nəs tē) *pl.,* **-ties.** *n.* **1.** succession of rulers of the same family or line of descent. **2.** rule of such a succession. **3.** any family or group that retains prominence or power for a considerable period of time: *a political dynasty.* [Late Latin *dynastīa* rule, kingship, from Greek *dynasteiā* power, domination.] —**dy·nas·tic** (dī nas′tik) *also,* **dy·nas′ti·cal,** *adj.* —**dy·nas′ti·cal·ly,** *adv.*

dyne (dīn) *n.* basic unit of force in the centimeter-gram-second system of units. It is equal to the amount of force that must be applied to one gram to produce an acceleration of one centimeter per second per second. [French *dyne,* from Greek *dynamis* power.]

dys- *combining form* bad; defective; difficult: *dysfunction, dyspepsia.* [Greek *dys-* hard, bad, ill.]

dys·en·ter·y (dis′ən ter′ē) *n.* any of several intestinal disorders characterized by severe diarrhea, often with mucus and bloody discharges, pain, and cramps, caused by any of various organisms, as bacteria, parasites, or viruses. [Latin *dysenteria,* from Greek *dysenteriā,* from *dys-* bad + *entera* intestines.] —**dys′en·ter′ic;** *also.* **dys′en·ter′i·cal,** *adj.*

dys·func·tion (dis fungk′shən) *n.* abnormal or impaired functioning, as of an organ.

dys·gen·ic (dis jen′ik) *adj.* relating to or having a detrimental effect upon hereditary traits.

dys·lex·i·a (dis lek′sē ə) *n.* inability to read effectively, often affecting children, caused by an unknown factor or factors. [Modern Latin *dyslexia,* from Greek *dys-* bad + *lexis* speech.] —**dys·lex′ic,** *adj.*

dys·pep·si·a (dis pep′shə, -sē ə) *n.* indigestion. [Latin *dyspepsia,* from Greek *dyspepsia.*]

dys·pep·tic (dis pep′tik) *adj.* **1.** of, relating to, or suffering from dyspepsia. **2.** gloomy; despondent; irritable. Also, **dys·pep′ti·cal.** —*n.* one who suffers from dyspepsia. —**dys·pep′ti·cal·ly,** *adv.*

dys·pro·si·um (dis prō′sē əm, -shē-) *n.* rare-earth element that is more magnetic than any other substance known. Symbol: **Dy** See **element** for table. [Modern Latin *dysprosium,* from Greek *dysprositos* hard to get at; because it was originally isolated only with great difficulty.]

dz., dozen; dozens.

at; āpe; cär; end; mē; it; īce; hot; ōld; wood; fōōl; oil; out; up; ūse; turn; sing; thin; this; zh in treasure; ə in ago, taken, pencil, lemon, circus.

E

e, E (ē) *pl.* **e's, E's.** *n.* **1.** fifth letter of the English alphabet.
2. fifth item in a series or group. **3.** *Music.* **a.** third note or tone of the
diatonic scale of C major. See **do²** for illustration. **b.** scale or key that
has this note or tone as its tonic.
e- *prefix* form of **ex-¹** before consonants except *c, f, p, q, s, t,* as in *evade*
and *emit.*
E 1. east. **2.** *Physics.* energy. **3.** English. **4.** excellent.
E. 1. east. **2.** English.
ea., each.
each (ēch) *adj.* being one of two or more individuals considered separately or singly: *Each player on the team wore a uniform.* —*pron.*
1. every individual, as of a group or number: *Each did what he had to
do.* **2. each other.** each of two or more in reciprocal action or relation:
*The cousins love each other dearly. The dogs barked ferociously at each
other.* ▲ *Each other* and *one another* are commonly used interchangeably, but in formal writing *each other* is often used for reference to two,
one another for reference to more than two: *Those two professors dislike
each other. At last we all understand one another.* —*adv.* for each;
apiece: *These cookies are a nickel each.* [Old English *ǣlc* every.]
Syn. adj. Each, every indicate all of the individual parts of a group,
one by one. **Each** stresses the individuality of the unit within the group:
Each man will clean his own rifle. **Every** implies that any unit is a
member of the group and represents all the others: *Rifles must be
cleaned every day.*
ea·ger (ē'gər) *adj.* **1.** filled with keen desire and enthusiasm; impatiently anxious: *She was eager to start her vacation.* **2.** characterized by
or showing keen desire or enthusiasm: *an eager look.* [Anglo-Norman
egre keen, harsh, from Latin *ācer* sharp, ardent.] —**ea'ger·ly,** *adv.*
—**ea'ger·ness,** *n.*
Syn. 1. Eager, anxious, keen¹ mean filled with great desire. **Eager**
suggests an earnest impatience: *They were eager to begin their vacation.*
Anxious implies uneasiness and some-
what negative feeling about events to
come: *They were anxious to reach the city
before sundown.* **Keen** emphasizes sharp
enthusiasm and intense desire: *He developed a keen interest in sailing.*
eager beaver *Informal.* one who is
overly zealous, diligent, or ambitious.
ea·gle (ē'gəl) *n.* **1.** any of various hawklike birds of prey, family Accipitridae,
having keen eyesight, a sharply hooked
bill, strong talons, and typically brown,
gray, or black plumage with white markings. Wingspan: 6 or more feet. **2.a.** any
of various representations of an eagle,
often used as a symbol or emblem. **b.** standard, seal, or other object
bearing such a representation, as the national seal of the United States.
3. golf score of two strokes less than par for any hole. **4.** formerly, gold
coin of the United States, worth ten dollars. [Anglo-Norman *egle* the
bird, from Latin *aquila.*]
ea·gle-eyed (ē'gəl īd') *adj.* able to perceive or discern clearly; keenly
observant; sharp-sighted.
ea·glet (ē'glit) *n.* young eagle.
ea·gre (ē'gər, ā'gər) *n.* tidal bore.
-ean, form of **-an,** as in *European, crustacean.*
ear¹ (ēr) *n.* **1.** in vertebrates, the organ of hearing. In man and other
mammals the ear typically consists of three parts: the external ear, the
middle ear, and the inner ear. **2.** in man and other mammals, the outer,
visible part of this organ: *The dog pricked up his ears at the noise.*
3. sense of hearing: *music pleasing to the ear.* **4.** keen or sensitive ability
to appreciate, understand, or perceive differences in or refinements of
(something heard): *an ear for poetry. That girl has no ear for music.*

Eagle

5.a. favorable attention: *to have the king's ear.* **b.** attention: *Give every
man thine ear, but few thy voice* (Shakespeare, *Hamlet*). **6.** something
resembling the outer, visible part
of the ear in shape or position, as
the handle of a pitcher.
to be all ears. to be eagerly attentive.
to bend (someone's) ear. *Informal.* to talk to someone for a
long time and become boring
or annoying.
to be up to one's (or the) ears.
to be deeply or thoroughly involved or immersed: *He was up
to his ears in work.*
to fall on deaf ears. to receive
no attention; be disregarded or
unheeded: *His complaints fell
on deaf ears.*
**to go in one ear and out the
other.** to leave no impression;
be heard but not remembered or heeded: *His advice went in one ear
and out the other.*
to keep (or have) an ear to the ground. to pay attention to or keep
well-informed about, esp. current trends or happenings.
to lend an (or one's) ear. to pay attention; listen.
to play by ear. to play (a musical instrument or piece) without the
aid of written music: *Tom plays the piano by ear.*
to play it by ear. *Informal.* to act without prior planning, according
to the way a situation develops.
to turn a deaf ear. to refuse to pay attention.
[Old English *ēare* the organ of hearing.]
ear² (ēr) *n.* spike of cereal plants, esp. of corn, that contains the grains
or seeds. —*v.i.* to form ears. [Old English *ēar* spike of corn.]
ear·ache (ēr'āk') *n.* pain in the middle or inner ear.
ear·drop (ēr'drop') *n.* earring with a pendant.
ear·drum (ēr'drum') *n.* thin membrane that separates the external
ear from the middle ear and vibrates when sound waves strike it; tympanic membrane. See **ear¹** for illustration.
ear·flap (ēr'flap') *n.* on a cap or hat, a part or parts that can be turned
down to cover the ears, esp. to keep them warm.
ear·ful (ēr'fool') *n. Informal.* **1.** surprising or especially interesting
news or gossip. **2.** enough or too much of something heard. **3.** a
scolding.
earl (url) *n.* British nobleman ranking below a marquis and above a
viscount. The wife or widow of an earl is a countess. [Old English *eorl*
warrior, nobleman.]
ear·lap (ēr'lap') *n.* earflap.
earl·dom (url'dəm) *n.* **1.** rank, title, or territory of an earl.
2. earls collectively.
ear lobe. lower fleshy part of the visible external ear.
ear·ly (ur'lē) **-li·er, -li·est.** *adj.* **1.** relating to or occurring in the
beginning of a period of time or of a course or series: *the early part of
the century. The early reports were less accurate than the later ones.*
2. coming, occurring, or doing something before the customary or
expected time: *an early marriage, an early riser.* **3.** belonging to a period
far back in time: *the early church.* **4.** occurring in the near future: *We
would like to hold the meeting at an early date.* —*adv.* **1.** in or near
the beginning of a period of time or of a course or series: *He met her
early in his teens. It's still too early to know who will win.* **2.** before the
customary or expected time: *He arrived at work early.* **3.** far back in
time; in remote times. [Old English *ǣrlīce* near the start of a time
period, from *ǣr* before + *-līce* -ly¹.] —**ear'li·ness,** *n.*

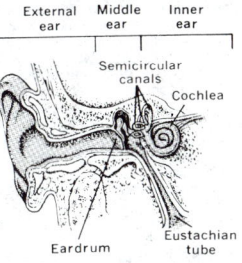

External ear · Middle ear · Inner ear
Semicircular canals
Cochlea
Eardrum
Eustachian tube
Human ear

---

early bird *Informal.* one who does something before others do, esp. one who rises or arrives early.

ear·mark (ēr′märk′) *n.* **1.** mark of identification, usually a cut, made on the ear of an animal to indicate ownership. **2.** any distinguishing or identifying mark or feature; characteristic; sign: *It has all the earmarks of a great novel.* —*v.t.* **1.** to make an earmark on. **2.** to set aside, as for a specific purpose; reserve: *The state earmarked too little money for conservation.*

ear·muffs (ēr′mufs′) *n.,pl.* pair of ear coverings, usually connected by an adjustable metal band, to be worn for protection against the cold.

earn (urn) *v.t.* **1.** to receive or gain in return for work done or services rendered: *to earn a salary.* **2.** to acquire or get as a result of effort or merit; deserve: *The clerk really earned that promotion.* **3.** to produce as income; yield: *The bonds earn five percent interest.* [Old English *earnian* to deserve, labor for.] —**earn′er,** *n.* —**Syn.** **2.** see **merit.**

ear·nest¹ (ur′nist) *adj.* **1.** sincere, intense, or serious in purpose or feeling: *an earnest person, an earnest student.* **2.** showing or characterized by sincere feeling or conviction: *an earnest apology, an earnest plea.* **3.** of a serious or important nature: *an earnest matter.* **4. in earnest.** with sincere or serious intent. [Old English *eornoste* serious.] —**ear′nest·ly,** *adv.* —**ear′nest·ness,** *n.*

ear·nest² (ur′nist) *n.* something giving assurance or indication of something to come, as a deposit of money or a token or pledge. [Modification of earlier *erles* earnest money, through Old French, Latin, and Greek, from Hebrew *'ērābōn* pledge.]

earnest money, partial payment of money as a token or pledge to bind a contract or secure a sale.

earn·ings (ur′ningz) *n.,pl.* money earned, esp. as wages or profits.

ear·phone (ēr′fōn′) *n.* listening device held at or worn over the ear, as a radio or telephone receiver.

ear·plug (ēr′plug′) *n.* rubber or plastic plug inserted into the ear to keep out water or noise.

ear·ring (ēr′ring′) *n.* ornament attached to or suspended from the ear lobe.

ear·shot (ēr′shot′) *n.* distance within which a sound, esp. the human voice, can be heard.

ear·split·ting (ēr′split′ing) *adj.* painfully loud; deafening: *an ear-splitting crash.*

earth (urth) *n.* **1.** also, **Earth.** planet on which man lives, the fifth largest planet of the solar system and third in order of distance from the sun. **2.** solid portion of this planet; land; the ground. **3.** soil; dirt. **4.** the inhabitants of this planet collectively, esp. the human inhabitants. **5.a.** abode of mortal man, often in contrast to heaven and hell. **b.** worldly pursuits and interests in contrast to spiritual concerns; human affairs: *Weary of earth and laden with my sin* (Stone, 1866). **c.** *Archaic.* mortal body of man. **6.** hole or lair of a fox or other burrowing animal. **7.** ground *(def. 8).* **8.** any of several metallic oxides which are difficult to reduce, esp. iron oxide. **9. down to earth.** simple and straightforward. **10. to come back** (or **down**) **to earth,** to stop dreaming; return to reality. [Old English *eorthe* ground, world.]

earth·born (urth′bôrn′) *also,* **earth-born.** *adj.* **1.** mortal; human: *earthborn cares.* **2.** of earthly origin; not divine.

earth·bound (urth′bound′) *also,* **earth-bound.** *adj.* **1.** headed for or going toward the earth: *The rocket ship was earthbound.* **2.** bound by earthly or materialistic ties or interests: *earthbound attitudes.*

earth·en (ur′thən) *adj.* **1.** made of earth: *an earthen floor, earthen ramparts.* **2.** made of baked clay: *an earthen jug.*

earth·en·ware (ur′thən wâr′) *n.* pottery made of a coarse and slightly porous grade of clay baked at a low temperature.

earth·light (urth′līt′) *n.* earthshine.

earth·ling (urth′ling) *n.* inhabitant of the earth; human being.

earth·ly (urth′lē) *-li·er, -li·est. adj.* **1.** of or relating to the earth, esp. as opposed to heaven; worldly; secular: *earthly possessions.* **2.** possible; imaginable: *of no earthly use.* —**earth′li·ness,** *n.*

earth·quake (urth′kwāk′) *n.* a shaking or movement of a part of the earth's surface, caused by the sudden shifting of rock along an existing fracture or fault or by volcanic or other disturbances.

earth science **1.** any or all of the sciences, as geology, geography, oceanography, and geophysics, dealing with the origin and physical features of the earth. **2.** course of study which surveys the basic facts of geology, meteorology, and astronomy, emphasizing the history of the earth's features rather than merely describing them.

earth·shak·ing (urth′shā′king) *adj.* influencing or challenging basic beliefs or attitudes; of fundamental or profound significance: *an earth-shaking discovery.*

earth·shine (urth′shīn′) *n.* faint illumination of the dark portion of the moon by sunlight reflected from the earth's surface.

earth·ward (urth′wərd) *adj.* moving toward the earth. —*adv.* also, **earthwards.** toward the earth: *The plane plunged earthward.*

earth·work (urth′wurk′) *n.* **1.** fortification made of earth. **2.** excavation and piling up of earth in engineering operations.

earth·worm (urth′wurm′) *n.* any of several cylindrical, segmented worms, order Terricolae, found throughout the world, which live in the soil. Also, **an′gle·worm**.

earth·y (ur′thē) **earth·i·er, earth·i·est.** *adj.* **1.** containing, resembling, or characteristic of earth or soil: *an earthy smell, an earthy color.* **2.** natural and hearty; uninhibited; lusty. **3.** unrefined; coarse; gross. —**earth′i·ness,** *n.*

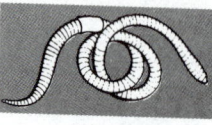

Earthworm

ear trumpet, trumpet-shaped instrument for collecting and concentrating sound waves when held to the ear, formerly used by the partially deaf.

ear·wax (ēr′waks′) *n.* waxy, yellowish substance produced by small glands that line the canal of the external ear. It serves to trap foreign bodies and protect the skin of the external canal from infection. Also, **ce·ru′men.**

ear·wig (ēr′wig′) *n.* any of a group of beetlelike insects, family Forficulidae, having a hard, slender body, threadlike antennae, and a pair of horny pincers at the end of the abdomen. [Old English *ēarwicga,* from *ēare* ear + *wicga* insect; from an earlier belief that it crawled into the ears of sleeping people.]

ease (ēz) *n.* **1.** freedom from pain, discomfort, toil, or worry; comfort: *a life of ease.* **2.** freedom from great effort or difficulty; facility: *to swim with ease.* **3.** freedom from stiffness, formality, or constraint; naturalness; poise: *the ease of his manner.* **4. at ease.** *Military.* in a relaxed standing position with the feet apart and the hands behind the back. ▲ often used as a command to assume such a position. —*v.t.,* **eased, eas·ing.** **1.** to free from pain, discomfort, or worry; make comfortable; relieve (often with *of*): *The good news eased the boy's mind. The nurse eased him of his suffering.* **2.** to make less; lighten; alleviate: *Tranquilizers often ease nervous tension.* **3.** to lessen the pressure, tension, or strain of (something); loosen: *to ease a tight waistband, to ease a rope.* **4.** to move or place (something) slowly and carefully: *to ease a bolt into place.* **5.** to facilitate: *to ease credit.* —*v.i.* **1.** to lessen in severity, tension, speed, or pressure (often with *up* or *off*). **2.** to move slowly and carefully. **3. to ease up on,** to reduce or relax the pressure on: *The driver eased up on the accelerator.* [Old French *aise* comfort, opportunity, from Latin *adjacēns,* present participle of *adjacēre* to lie near.]

Syn. *n.* **1. Ease, comfort** refer to a state in which there is an absence of stress or exertion. **Ease** suggests that there is no work or obligation pressing and that there is a place and sufficient time in which to relax: *Work is alone noble. . . . A life of ease is not for any man, nor for any god* (Carlyle, 1843). **Comfort** implies contentment and enjoyment of good things, as well as an absence of stress or pressure: *He lived a life of comfort among his children in his old age.*

ease·ful (ēz′fəl) *adj.* characterized by or giving ease; peaceful; restful. —**ease′ful·ly,** *adv.* —**ease′ful·ness,** *n.*

ea·sel (ē′zəl) *n.* upright frame or tripod used chiefly to support an artist's canvas or a blackboard. [Dutch *ezel* literally, little ass, from Latin *asinus* ass; because, like a beast of burden, it supports something.]

ease·ment (ēz′mənt) *n.* right or privilege of a landowner or tenant to use the land owned by another.

eas·i·ly (ēz′ə lē) *adv.* **1.** without difficulty, discomfort, or great effort; with ease. **2.** without a doubt; beyond question; certainly. **3.** very likely.

eas·i·ness (ēz′ē nis) *n.* quality or state of being easy.

east (ēst) *n.* **1.** general direction of the sunrise in relation to an observer on earth. **2.** one of the four cardinal points of the compass, lying directly opposite west and 90 degrees right of north. **3.** *also,* **East.** any region situated toward this direction in relation to a specified point of reference. **4. the East. a.** Asia and the islands close to it; the Orient. **b.** Communist nations, esp. the Soviet Union and its satellites in eastern Europe. **5.a.** region in the United States east of the Allegheny Mountains, esp. the area north of Maryland. **b.** the Northeast. **6. down East.** *Informal.* **a.** Maine, esp. the east coast of Maine. **b.** in or toward Maine. —*adj.* **1.** toward or in the east. **2.** coming from the east: *an east wind.* —*adv.* toward the east. [Old English *ēast* in the direction of the sunrise.]

East Berlin, Soviet sector of divided Berlin and capital of East Germany, in northeastern Germany. Pop. (1968 est.), 1,082,229.

east·bound (ēst′bound′) *adj.* going east.

East·er (ēs′tər) *n.* **1.** Christian feast commemorating Christ's resurrection, celebrated on the Sunday after the first full moon following the vernal equinox. **2.** Sunday on which this feast is celebrated. Also (*def. 2*), **Easter Sunday.** [Old English *ēastre* this feast, from *Ēastre* the Teutonic goddess of the dawn whose rites were also celebrated in the spring.]

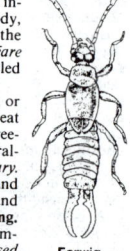

Earwig

at; āpe; cär; end; mē; it; īce; hot; ōld; fôrk; wood; fōol; oil; out; up; ūse; turn; sing; thin; this; zh in treasure; ə in ago, taken, pencil, lemon, circus.

Easter egg, decorated egg or imitation of one, used as an Easter ornament or gift.

Easter Island, Chilean island in the eastern South Pacific, noted for enormous ancient stone statues found there.

east·er·ly (ēs′tər lē) *adj., adv.* **1.** toward the east. **2.** from the east.

east·ern (ēs′tərn) *adj.* **1.** to, toward, or in the east: *an eastern exposure.* **2.** *also,* **Eastern.** of, relating to, or characteristic of the east or East: *an eastern accent.* **3. Eastern.** Oriental: *Eastern philosophy.* **4.** coming from the east.

Eastern Church 1. the Orthodox or Uniate Church. **2.** any of various independent Christian churches, as the Coptic Church, deriving from the church of the Byzantine Empire.

east·ern·er (ēs′tər nər) *n.* **1.** one who was born or lives in the east. **2.** *usually,* **Easterner.** one who was born or lives in the eastern part of the United States.

Eastern Hemisphere, half of the earth east of the Greenwich meridian, including Europe, Asia, Africa, and Australia.

east·ern·most (ēs′tərn mōst′) *adj.* farthest east.

Eastern Orthodox Church, Orthodox Church.

Eastern Roman Empire, Byzantine Empire.

Eastern Standard Time, the local civil time of the seventy-fifth meridian west of Greenwich, England, used in the eastern United States. It is five hours earlier than Greenwich time.

East·er·tide (ēs′tər tīd′) *n.* ecclesiastical season extending from Easter to Trinity Sunday.

East Germany, Communist country in north-central Europe, consisting of the Soviet zone of divided Germany. Capital, East Berlin. Area, 41,815 sq. mi. Pop. (1968 est.), 16,000,000. Its official name is the **German Democratic Republic.**

East Indies 1. Netherlands East Indies, sometimes including India and peninsular Southeast Asia. **2.** Malay Archipelago. Also, **East India.**

East Lansing, city in south-central Michigan, a residential suburb of adjoining Lansing. Pop. (1970), 47,540.

East Orange, city in northeastern New Jersey. Pop. (1970), 75,471.

East Pakistan, See Bangladesh.

East Providence, city in eastern Rhode Island. Pop. (1970), 48,151.

East Prussia, historic region in north-central Europe on the Baltic Sea, formerly a German province. After World War II, it was divided between Poland and the Soviet Union.

East River, navigable strait in New York City connecting New York Bay with Long Island Sound and separating Manhattan and the Bronx from Brooklyn and Queens.

East St. Louis, city in southwestern Illinois. Pop. (1970), 69,996.

east·ward (ēst′wərd) *adv. also,* **east·wards.** toward the east: *to travel eastward.* —*adj.* toward or in the east. —*n.* eastward direction, point, or part.

eas·y (ē′zē) **eas·i·er, eas·i·est.** *adj.* **1.** requiring little effort; presenting few difficulties; not difficult: *an easy task, an easy test.* **2.** free from discomfort, trouble, or anxiety: *an easy mind.* **3.** not oppressive, demanding, or harsh; lenient: *easy terms of payment, an easy teacher.* **4.** providing or characterized by comfort or rest; comfortable: *an easy ride.* **5.** free from stiffness, formality, or awkwardness; relaxed: *an easy style of speaking.* **6.** readily influenced, persuaded, or overcome; yielding; credulous: *He was an easy victim.* **7.** not readily agitated; even-tempered; easygoing: *an easy disposition.* **8.** not hurried or forced; gentle: *an easy trot, an easy pace.* **9.** not binding or tight: *an easy fit.* **10.** well-off; affluent: *in easy circumstances.* **11.** *Economics.* **a.** (of money) in abundance and available for loans, esp. at lower interest rates. **b.** (of a market) characterized by decreased demand and often lower prices. Opposed to **tight. c.** (of a commodity) in abundance and available, esp. at lower prices. **12. to be on easy street.** *Informal.* to be well-to-do; be in comfortable circumstances. —*adv.* **1.** *Informal.* easily. **2. to go easy** (on or **with**). *Informal.* **a.** to use moderately; be sparing. **b.** to treat leniently or gently. **3. to take it easy.** *Informal.* **a.** to refrain from exertion; relax: *The girls took it easy after their long hike.* **b.** to stay calm. [Old French *aisie,* past participle of *aisier* to put at ease, from *aise* comfort. See EASE.]

Syn. *adj.* **1. Easy, effortless, simple** indicate absence of difficulty. **Easy** suggests a task that requires no great physical or mental exertion to accomplish: *He pointed out an easy way to pass the exam.* **Effortless** implies an apparent lack of difficulty that often masks great skill: *They watched the hawks in their effortless hovering.* **Simple** connotes absence of complexity and therefore ease of understanding, doing, or the like: *Tom makes the hardest job seem simple.*

easy chair, comfortable chair, esp. a padded armchair.

eas·y·go·ing (ē′zē gō′ing) *adj.* **1.** inclined to be calm and unhurried; good-natured; relaxed. **2.** having an easy gait or step.

easy mark, *Informal.* one who is easily fooled or taken advantage of.

eat (ēt) **ate, eat·en, eat·ing.** *v.t.* **1.** to take in through the mouth and swallow, esp. to chew and swallow, as solid food. **2.** to wear away gradually; waste; corrode: *Rust has eaten away the surface.* **3.** to destroy

or consume by or as by eating (often with *away* or *up*): *a fortune quickly eaten up by gambling.* **4.** to make, as by gnawing or corroding: *The acid ate holes in the material. The termites ate their way through the log.* **5. to eat one's words.** to retract what one has said or bitterly regret some statement. **6. to eat up.** *Slang.* **a.** to take pleasure or delight in; show enthusiasm for. **b.** to believe without question; accept eagerly. —*v.i.* **1.** to take or consume food; have a meal: *We eat at six o'clock. The starving dog ate ravenously.* **2.** to wear away gradually or destroy, as by gnawing or corroding (with *through* or *into*). **3.** to chew or bore (with *through* or *into*). —*n. pl.,* **eats.** *Slang.* food. [Old English *etan* to consume food, devour, destroy.] —**eat′er,** *n.*

eat·a·ble (ē′tə bəl) *adj.* fit to be eaten; edible. —*n. also,* **eatables.** something fit to eat; food.

eat·ing (ē′ting) *n.* **1.** *Informal.* food with reference to the flavor or quality it displays when eaten: *This chicken is good eating.* **2.** act of one who or that which eats. —*adj.* good or fit to be eaten, esp. raw: *eating apples.*

Eau Claire (ō′ klār′) city in western Wisconsin. Pop. (1970), 44,619.

eau de Co·logne (ō′ də kə-lōn′) cologne. [French *eau de Cologne* literally, water of Cologne.]

eau de vie (ō′ də vē′) *French.* brandy.

eaves (ēvz) *n.,pl.* lower edge of a sloping roof projecting beyond the sides of a building. [Old English *efes.*]

eaves·drop (ēvz′drop′) **-dropped, -drop·ping.** *v.i.* to listen secretly to a private conversation. [Earlier *eavesdrip,* from Old English *yfesdrype* water that drips from the eaves; referring to standing under the eaves from which rainwater dripped in order to overhear a conversation in a house.] —**eaves′drop′per,** *n.*

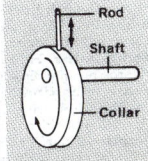

Eaves

ebb (eb) *n.* **1.** the receding of the tide from shore; flowing out of the tide. **2.** point or condition of decline or decay: *The actor's fame was at a low ebb.* **3.** gradual lessening or weakening; decline; decay: *the ebb of strength during an illness.* —*v.i.* **1.** to flow out or recede, as the tide. **2.** to become less or weaker; decline; fail: *Hope for the lost child began to ebb.* [Old English *ebba* the receding of the tide.]

ebb tide 1. falling or receding tide. Opposed to **flood tide. 2.** time or point of this.

eb·on (eb′ən) *n., adj. Archaic.* ebony.

eb·on·ite (eb′ə nīt′) *n.* hard, black vulcanized rubber used for plumbing, electrical equipment, and bowling balls. [EBON(Y) + -ITE¹.]

eb·on·y (eb′ə nē) *pl.,* **-on·ies.** *n.* **1.** hard, heavy, deep-black heartwood of any of several trees, genus *Diospyros,* used esp. for piano keys, knife handles, cabinets, and carvings. **2.** tree yielding this wood, native to Africa, Ceylon, and the East Indies. —*adj.* **1.** made of ebony. **2.** like ebony, esp. in color; black. [Earlier *eban,* from Old French *ebany, ebaine* the tree, from Latin *ebenos,* from Greek *ebenos;* of Egyptian origin.]

e·bul·lient (i bul′yənt) *adj.* **1.** overflowing or bubbling over with excitement or enthusiasm; exuberant: *The winner was ebullient.* **2.** boiling or bubbling up: *lava in an ebullient state.* [Latin *ēbulliēns,* present participle of *ēbullīre* to bubble or boil over.] —**e·bul′lience, e·bul′lien·cy,** *n.* —**e·bul′lient·ly,** *adv.*

eb·ul·li·tion (eb′ə lish′ən) *n.* **1.** act or state of boiling or bubbling up. **2.** sudden outburst or overflowing, as of emotions.

ec-, form of **ex-²** before consonants, as in *eclipse.*

é·car·té (ā′kär tā′) *n.* card game for two people, played with a deck of thirty-two cards, consisting of sevens up through aces. [French *écarté,* past participle of *écarter* to discard, going back to Latin *ex* out of, away + *charta* paper; from the discarding of cards in the game. See CARD¹.]

Ec·bat·a·na (ek bat′ən ə) *n.* capital of ancient Media.

ec·ce ho·mo (ech′ā hō′mō) *Latin.* **1.** "Behold the man," spoken in the Vulgate (John 19:5) by Pilate as he presented Christ crowned with thorns. **2. Ecce Homo.** representation of Christ crowned with thorns.

ec·cen·tric (ik sen′trik, ek-) *adj.* **1.** deviating from established or conventional practices or patterns; peculiar; odd: *eccentric behavior, an eccentric family.* **2.** *Mathematics.* not having the same center: *eccentric circles.* **3.** not situated in the center, as an axis; having its axis set off center, as a wheel; off center. —*n.* **1.** one who deviates from the

Rod
Shaft
Collar

Eccentric (def. 2)

at; āpe; cär; end; mē; it; īce; hot; ōld; fôrk; wood; fōōl; oil; out; up; ūse; turn; sing; thin; this; zh in treasure; ə in ago, taken, pencil, lemon, circus.

321

established or conventional pattern. **2.** disk set off center on a revolving shaft in order to change circular motion into reciprocating motion. [Late Latin *eccentricus* out of the center, from Greek *ekkentros.*] **—ec·cen'tri·cal·ly,** *adv.*

ec·cen·tric·i·ty (ek'sen tris'ə tē) *pl.,* **-ties.** *n.* **1.** deviation from established or conventional practices or patterns; whimsical oddity. **2.** act or characteristic that is unusual or odd; peculiarity. **3.** state or quality of being eccentric: *the eccentricity of an axis.* **4.** amount or degree by which something is eccentric.

eccl., ecclesiastic; ecclesiastical. Also, **eccles.**

Eccl., Ecclesiastes. Also, **Eccles.**

Ec·cle·si·as·tes (i klē'zē as'tēz) *n.* in the Old Testament, book dealing with the worthlessness and vanity of human life, traditionally ascribed to King Solomon. [Greek *ekklēsiastēs* preacher, one who addresses an assembly, from *ekklēsiā* assembly, church.]

ec·cle·si·as·tic (i klē'zē as'tik) *n.* clergyman or other person officially in the service of the church. **—***adj.* ecclesiastical. [Late Latin *ecclesiasticus* relating to the church, from Greek *ekklēsiastikos*, going back to *ekklēsiā* assembly, church.]

ec·cle·si·as·ti·cal (i klē'zē as'ti kəl) *adj.* of or relating to the church or the clergy. **—ec·cle'si·as'ti·cal·ly,** *adv.*

Ec·cle·si·as·ti·cus (i klē'zē as'ti kəs) *n.* book of the Old Testament which is part of the Protestant Apocrypha and is included in the canon of the Douay Bible. It is a collection of prayers and proverbs.

ECG, electrocardiogram.

ech·e·lon (esh'ə lon') *n.* **1.** formation of military, naval, or air units in a stepwise arrangement, with each successive unit behind and to one side of the preceding one. **2.a.** subdivision of a military headquarters: *a rear echelon.* **b.** part of a command to which a principal combat mission is assigned: *a support echelon.* **3.a.** particular level of command, authority, or responsibility: *the lower echelons of the bureaucracy.* **b.** group occupying such a level: *The higher echelon is in conference today.* **—***v.t., v.i.* to move in or form into a steplike arrangement. [French *échelon* rung of a ladder, from *échelle* ladder, from Latin *scāla.*]

e·chid·na (i kid'nə) *pl.,* **-nas** or **-nae** (-nē). *n.* any of various egg-laying, anteating mammals, genera *Tachyglossus* and *Zaglossus,* native to Australia, Tasmania, and New Guinea, having thick, grayish-brown fur, yellow and black spines, a horny, toothless snout, and a long tongue. Length: 15–30 inches. Also, **spiny anteater.** [Latin *echidna* viper, from Greek *echidna.*]

Echidna

e·chi·no·derm (i kī'nə durm', ek'i nə-) *n.* any of a large, widespread group of saltwater sea animals, as the starfish and sea urchin, phylum Echinodermata, having a limy, internal shell, spiny skin, and a radially symmetrical shape. [Modern Latin *Echinodermata,* from Greek *echinos* hedgehog, sea urchin + *derma* skin.]

e·chi·nus (i kī'nəs) *pl.,* **-ni** (-nī). *n.* **1.** sea urchin. **2.** convex molding below the abacus of a Doric capital, or a corresponding member in other capitals. [Latin *echinus* sea urchin, hedgehog, from Greek *echinos.*]

ech·o (ek'ō) *pl.,* **ech·oes.** *n.* **1.a.** repetition of a sound produced by the reflection of sound waves from an obstructing surface. **b.** sound so produced. **2.** any repetition or close imitation, as of the ideas or opinions of another. **3.** one who closely imitates another, as in speech, opinions, or dress. **4.** *Electronics.* radio wave or radar pulse reflected back to a transmitter or receiver. **5. Echo.** *Greek Mythology.* a nymph who pined away with love for Narcissus until only her voice remained. **—***v.t.* **1.** to resound with or send back the sound of: *The cavern walls echoed his cries.* **2.** to repeat or closely imitate, as the ideas or opinions of another; repeat in imitation: *disciples echoing the thoughts of their leader.* **3.** to repeat or closely imitate the words, ideas, or actions of (another): *The young child echoed her older brother.* **—***v.i.* **1.** to resound with or send back an echo; reverberate: *The corridor echoed with footsteps.* **2.** to be repeated by or as if by an echo: *His laughter echoed through the house. Her words echoed in his ears.* [Latin *ēchō* repercussion of sound, from Greek *ēchō* sound, noise.] **—ech'o·er,** *n.*

e·cho·ic (i kō'ik) *adj.* **1.** resembling an echo. **2.** formed in imitation of sounds; onomatopoeic.

ech·o·la·li·a (ek'ō lā'lē ə) *n.* meaningless repetition of one person's words by another. [ECHO + Greek *laliā* chatter.]

ech·o·lo·ca·tion (ek'ō lō kā'shən) *n.* determination of the location of objects by sending out sound waves and measuring the time and direction of their return. Bats and some fish use echolocation.

é·clair (ā klâr') *n.* oblong pastry shell filled with whipped cream or custard and usually topped with chocolate icing. [French *éclair* literally, lightning, from *éclairer* to illuminate, going back to Latin *ex* out + *clārus* clear.]

é·clat (ā klä') *n.* **1.** dazzling or striking effect; conspicuous success;

brilliance: *The guitarist performed with great éclat.* **2.** great applause or praise; acclaim: *The new symphony was received with éclat.* **3.a.** fame; renown. **b.** *Archaic.* notoriety. [French *éclat* burst, brightness, from *éclater* to burst out, shine; of Germanic origin.]

ec·lec·tic (ek lek'tik) *adj.* **1.** selecting what seems best from various doctrines, systems, or sources: *an eclectic painter.* **2.** composed of elements selected from various sources: *an eclectic musical program.* **—***n.* one who uses an eclectic method or approach, as in science, art, or philosophy. [Greek *eklektikos* selecting, going back to *eklegein* to select.] **—ec·lec'ti·cal·ly,** *adv.*

ec·lec·ti·cism (ek lek'tə siz'əm) *n.* **1.** use or advocacy of an eclectic method. **2.** eclectic method or system, as of philosophy.

e·clipse (i klips') *n.* **1.** apparent partial or total darkening of one celestial body by its passage through the shadow of another. In a **solar eclipse** the moon passes between the sun and the earth, totally or partially blocking the sun's rays and darkening certain areas of the earth. In a **lunar eclipse** the earth moves between the sun and the moon,

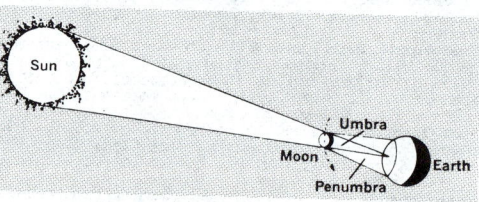

Solar eclipse

blocking the sun's rays and totally or partially darkening the moon. **2.** any overshadowing or dimming, as of reputation or importance. **—***v.t.,* **e·clipsed, e·clips·ing. 1.** to cause an eclipse of; darken. **2.** to overshadow or dim, esp. by comparison; outshine; surpass. [Old French *eclipse* astronomical eclipse, from Latin *eclīpsis,* from Greek *ekleipsis* a leaving out, astronomical eclipse.]

e·clip·tic (i klip'tik) *n.* path that the sun appears to follow annually around the celestial sphere. **—***adj.* also, **e·clip'ti·cal.** of or relating to eclipses or to the ecliptic. **—e·clip'ti·cal·ly,** *adv.*

ec·logue (ek'lôg', -log') *n.* short pastoral poem, esp. in the form of dialogue between shepherds. [Latin *ecloga* short poem, from Greek *eklogē* selection.]

ecol. 1. ecological. **2.** ecology.

é·cole (ā kôl') *n. French.* school.

e·col·o·gy (ē kol'ə jē) *n.* **1.a.** relationship of living organisms to their environment and to each other: *the ecology of a region.* **b.** branch of biology that deals with this. Also, **bi'o·nom'ics.** **2.** *Sociology.* study of the relationship of groups of people to their environment and to each other. [German *Ökologie* biological ecology, from Greek *oikos* house + *-logiā* -logy.] **—e·co·log·ic** (ek'ə loj'ik, ē'kə-); also, **ec·o·log'i·cal, e·co·log'i·cal,** *adv.* **—e·col'o·gist,** *n.*

econ. 1. economic. **2.** economics. **3.** economy.

ec·o·nom·ic (ek'ə nom'ik, ē'kə-) *adj.* **1.** of or relating to the production, distribution, and consumption of wealth, goods, and services, as of a nation: *economic policy, economic development.* **2.** of or relating to the science of economics: *economic theory.* **3.** of or relating to money matters or concerns; financial: *We gave up the house because of economic considerations.* **4.** economical.

ec·o·nom·i·cal (ek'ə nom'i kəl, ē'kə-) *adj.* **1.** prudent in the use of resources; avoiding extravagance; frugal; thrifty: *an economical person, economical habits.* **2.** operating cheaply or at a saving; inexpensive: *an economical car.* **3.** free from waste, superfluousness, or excess. **4.** *Archaic.* **—Syn. 1.** see **thrifty.**

ec·o·nom·i·cal·ly (ek'ə nom'ik lē, ē'kə-) *adv.* **1.** in a frugal manner; without waste. **2.** from an economic viewpoint.

ec·o·nom·ics (ek'ə nom'iks, ē'kə-) *n.* **1.** science that deals with the production, distribution, and consumption of wealth, goods, and services, with the means of supplying the material needs of mankind, and with such related problems as capital, labor, and taxation. **2.** economic aspects or factors: *the economics of bridge construction.* ▲ construed as singular in def. 1, as plural in def. 2.

e·con·o·mist (i kon'ə mist) *n.* **1.** one trained or skilled in economics; expert in economics. **2.** *Archaic.* one who is frugal.

e·con·o·mize (i kon'ə mīz') **-mized, -miz·ing.** *v.i.* to avoid waste or needless expenditure; reduce expenses: *If we don't start economizing soon, we will have no money at all. We can economize on groceries this week.* **—***v.t.* to use sparingly or to the best advantage: *to economize fuel, to economize one's time and effort.* **—e·con'o·miz'er,** *n.*

e·con·o·my (i kon'ə mē) *pl.,* **-mies.** *n.* **1.** sum total of the production,

at; āpe; cär; end; mē; it; īce; hot; ōld; fôrk; wood; fōōl; oil; out; up; ūse; turn; sing; thin; this; zh in treasure; ə in ago, taken, pencil, lemon, circus.

distribution, and consumption of wealth, goods, and services, as of a nation: *That nation's economy is growing rapidly.* **2.** particular system of managing the production, distribution, and consumption of wealth, goods, and services; structure or organization of economic life: *an agrarian economy, an economy based on the gold standard.* **3.a.** careful or frugal management of money or other material resources; avoidance of extravagance; thrift: *During a recession it is wise to practice economy.* **b.** instance or means of economizing: *economies used in running a household.* **4.** efficient, sparing, or judicious use; use (of something) to the best advantage: *an economy of effort, an author who draws his characters with an economy of detail.* **5.** orderly arrangement or regulation of parts or functions: *the economy of nature.* [Latin *oeconomia* management of a household, from Greek *oikonomiā*, going back to *oikos* house + *nemein* to manage.]

ec·ru (ek′rōō, ā′krōō) *also*, **é·cru**, *n.* pale yellowish-brown color; light tan. [French *écru* raw, unbleached, going back to Latin *ex* out of, utterly + *crūdus* raw.]

ec·sta·sy (ek′stə sē) *pl.* **-sies.** *n.* **1.** state of overwhelming joy or delight; rapture: *We were in ecstasy at the thought of going home.* **2.** state of being completely absorbed by an emotion: *an ecstasy of fear.* **3.** trance, esp. one thought to accompany mystic, prophetic, or poetic inspiration. [Old French *extasie* rapture, trance, from Late Latin *ecstasis* trance, from Greek *ekstasis* trance; literally, standing outside oneself.]

ec·stat·ic (ek stat′ik) *adj.* **1.** overwhelmed with joy or delight; enraptured. **2.** like, resulting from, or characterized by ecstasy. —*n.* **1.** one who is subject to ecstasies or trances. **2.** ecstatics. rapturous emotions; ecstasies. —**ec·stat′i·cal·ly,** *adv.*

ecto- *combining form* outside; external; outer: *ectoderm, ectoplasm.* [Greek *ektos* outside.]

ec·to·derm (ek′tə durm′) *n.* outermost of the three cell layers of the gastrula, from which develop the outer layer of skin, the nervous system, and the sense organs. [ECTO- + Greek *derma* skin.] —**ec′to·der′mal, ec′to·der′mic,** *adj.*

ec·to·morph (ek′tə môrf′) *n.* person having a thin, bony body. Distinguished from **endomorph** and **mesomorph.** [ECTO + Greek *morphē* form, shape.] —**ec′to·mor′phic,** *adj.*

ec·to·plasm (ek′tə plaz′əm) *n.* **1.** outer layer of the cytoplasm of a cell. **2.** supposed materialization of a spirit called forth by a medium. [ECTO- + -PLASM.]

Ec·ua·dor (ek′wə dôr′) *n.* country on the northwestern coast of South America. Capital, Quito. Area, 109,483 sq. mi. Pop. (1969 est.), 5,890,000. —**Ec′ua·do′ri·an,** *adj., n.*

ec·u·men·i·cal (ek′yə men′i kəl) *also*, **oec·u·men·i·cal.** *adj.* **1.** world-wide in scope; universal. **2.** of, representing, or relating to all Christian churches: *an ecumenical council.* **3.** promoting world-wide Christian unity: *an ecumenical movement.* [Late Latin *oecūmenicus* universal, from Greek *oikoumenikos,* going back to *oikos* house.]

ec·u·me·nism (ek′yə mə niz′əm) *n.* movement to reunite all Christian churches.

ec·ze·ma (ek′si mə, eg zē′mə) *n.* skin disorder characterized by redness, itching, scaly patches, and, sometimes, tiny blisters that break and release a watery fluid. [Greek *ekzema,* from *ekzein* to boil over.]

-ed[1] *suffix* used to form the past tense of regular verbs: *I walked to work last week.* [Old English *-de, -ede, -ode, -ade.*]

-ed[2] *suffix* **1.** used to form the past participle of regular verbs: *I have walked to work every day this month.* **2.** used to form adjectives from nouns: **a.** characterized by or equipped with; having: *a blue-eyed baby, a fringed curtain.* **b.** having the characteristics of; like: *a bigoted neighbor, dogged pursuit.* **3.** used to form adjectives from adjectives ending in *-ate,* with the same general meaning: *bipinnated, dentated.* [Old English *-ed, -od, -ad.*]

ed. *pl.,* **eds. 1.** edition. **2.** editor. **3.** edited.

e·da·cious (i dā′shəs) *adj.* given to eating or consuming; devouring; voracious. [Latin *edāc-,* stem of *edāx* voracious + -OUS.] —**e·dac′i·ty** (i das′ə tē) *n.*

E·dam cheese (ē′dəm, ē′dam) mild, solid, yellow cheese, usually round and flattened and enclosed in red paraffin. [From *Edam,* Dutch village where it was originally produced.]

Ed.B., Bachelor of Education.

Ed.D., Doctor of Education.

Ed·da (ed′ə) *pl.,* **Ed·das.** *n.* either of two thirteenth-century collections of Icelandic literature. The **Poetic,** or **Elder, Edda** contains anonymous poems dealing primarily with Scandinavian mythology and heroic legends; the **Prose,** or **Younger, Edda** contains Scandinavian myths and heroic lore as well as commentaries on the techniques of ancient Icelandic court poetry. [Old Norse *edda,* possibly from *ōthr* spirit, poetry.] —**Ed·da·ic** (e dā′ik), **Ed′dic,** *adj.*

ed·dy (ed′ē) *pl.,* **-dies.** *n.* **1.** current, as of air or water, moving against the main current, with a circular or whirling motion; small whirlwind or whirlpool. **2.** course or movement, esp. one departing from a

main current or trend: *eddies of political thought.* —*v.i.,* **-died, -dy·ing.** to move in an eddy; move with a circular motion; whirl: *Smoke eddied from the chimney.* [Possibly from Old Norse *itha* whirlpool.]

Ed·dy, Mary Baker (ed′ē) 1821–1910, founder of the Christian Science Church.

e·del·weiss (ād′əl vīs′) *n.* **1.** starlike flower head of a plant, *Leontopodium alpinum,* of the composite family, having tiny yellow flowers surrounded by white, petal-like leaves. **2.** plant bearing this flower head, found on high mountains in Europe and Asia. [German *Edelweiss,* from *edel* noble + *weiss* white.]

e·de·ma (i dē′mə) *pl.,* **-ma·ta** (-mə tə). *n.* dropsy. [Modern Latin *oedema,* from Greek *oidēma* swelling.]

E·den (ēd′ən) *n.* **1.** Garden of Eden. **2.** any delightful region or place; paradise. **3.** state of perfect or supreme happiness. [Hebrew *'ēden* Garden of Eden; literally, delight.]

Edelweiss

e·den·tate (ē den′tāt) *n.* any of a group of mammals, order Edentata, having few or no teeth, including armadillos, sloths, and anteaters. —*adj.* **1.** of, relating to, or belonging to this order. **2.** toothless. [Latin *ēdentātus* toothless, going back to *ex* out of + *dēns* tooth.]

edge (ej) *n.* **1.** line or place at which an object or area begins or ends; extreme or outermost border: *the edge of a table, the water's edge.* **2.** thin, sharp, cutting side of the blade of a cutting instrument, weapon, or tool. **3.** line where surfaces of a solid meet. **4.** sharpness or intensity; keenness: *Eating the cracker took the edge off his appetite.* **5.** Informal. favorable position; margin of superiority; advantage: *to have a slight edge on one's opponent.* **6.** on edge. tense, nervous, or impatient. —*v.t.,* **edged, edg·ing. 1.** to furnish with a border; form a border on: *to edge a fabric with fringe. Tulips edged the garden.* **2.** to advance or move slowly or gradually: *He edged the large crate across the floor.* **3.** to increase the cutting quality of; sharpen, as a blade. —*v.i.* to advance or move slowly, gradually, or sidewise. [Old English *ecg* cutting side of a blade, sword.]

Syn. *n.* **1.** Edge, border, rim indicate an outer limit or end of something. Edge suggests sharpness or abruptness, as where two planes intersect, or distinctness, as where a physical body ends: *The edge of the leaf is serrated.* Border is the line separating one surface from another or the area immediately surrounding that line: *A border of flowers was planted along the fence.* Rim suggests a curved edge: *Nothing upsets him more than finding lipstick on the rim of a clean glass.*

edge·wise (ej′wīz′) *also*, **edge·ways** (ej′wāz′) *adv.* **1.** with the edge forward. **2.** on, by, with, or toward the edge.

edg·ing (ej′ing) *n.* something that forms or is attached along a border, as a fringe; trimming.

edg·y (ej′ē) *adj.* **1.** on edge; uneasy; irritable. **2.** sharp. —**edg′i·ly,** *adv.* —**edg′i·ness,** *n.*

ed·i·ble (ed′ə bəl) *adj.* that can be eaten; fit to eat; not poisonous. —*n. also,* **edibles.** something fit to eat; food. [Late Latin *edibilis* eatable, from Latin *edere* to eat.] —**ed′i·bil′i·ty, ed′i·ble·ness,** *n.*

e·dict (ē′dikt) *n.* **1.** official decree from a sovereign or other authority, publicly proclaimed and having the force of law. **2.** any authoritative command or prohibition. [Latin *ēdictum* proclamation.]

ed·i·fi·ca·tion (ed′ə fi kā′shən) *n.* act of edifying; being edified; intellectual or moral enlightenment or improvement: *to read the classics for one's own edification.*

ed·i·fice (ed′ə fis) *n.* building or other structure, esp. one that is large and impressive: *There is the edifice where the Supreme Court holds court.* [Old French *edifice* building, from Latin *aedificium.*]

ed·i·fy (ed′ə fī′) **-fied, -fy·ing.** *v.t.* to enlighten and improve, esp. morally or spiritually; instruct. [Old French *edifier* to build, from Latin *aedificāre.*] —**ed′i·fi′er,** *n.*

e·dile (ē′dīl) aedile.

Ed·in·burgh (ed′ən bur′ō; *British* ed′ən brə) *n.* capital of Scotland, in the east-central part of the country. Pop. (1968), 470,404.

Ed·i·son, Thomas Al·va (ed′i sən; al′və) 1847–1931, U.S. inventor.

ed·it (ed′it) *v.t.* **1.** to correct, revise, and prepare for publication. **2.** to collect, arrange, and annotate (literary material) for publication. **3.** to review, cut, and arrange for or as for public presentation: *to edit a film, to edit a tape.* **4.** to direct the preparation and editorial policies of, as a newspaper or periodical. [From EDITOR.]

edit. 1. edition. **2.** editor. **3.** edited.

e·di·tion (i dish′ən) *n.* **1.** particular form in which a book or other literary work is published: *a two-volume edition, a pocket edition.* **2.a.** total number of copies of a publication printed from the same plates or type: *the latest edition of a book. Color illustrations were added in the new edition of the book.* **b.** copy belonging to such a printing: *We*

have the Sunday edition of the newspaper delivered. [Latin *ēditiō* a bringing forth, publishing.]

ed·i·tor (ed'ə tər) *n.* one who edits. [Latin *ēditor* one who brings forth or produces.]

ed·i·to·ri·al (ed'ə tôr'ē əl) *n.* article or statement, as in a newspaper or on television, expressing the official opinion or viewpoint of the editor or owner on a particular topic. —*adj.* of, relating to, or characteristic of an editor, editing, or an editorial: *an editorial staff, editorial duties, an editorial comment.*

ed·i·to·ri·al·ize (ed'ə tôr'ē ə līz') **-ized, -iz·ing.** *v.i.* **1.** to express opinions in or as in an editorial. **2.** to insert or introduce editorial comments into a factual report.

ed·i·to·ri·al·ly (ed'ə tôr'ē ə lē) *adv.* in or as in an editorial; in the capacity of an editor: *to comment editorially on a subject.*

ed·i·tor·ship (ed'ə tər ship') *n.* position, functions, or authority of an editor.

Ed·mon·ton (ed'mən tən) *n.* provincial capital and largest city of Alberta, Canada, in the south-central part of the province. Pop. (1968), 376,925.

E·dom (ē'dəm) *n.* in the Old Testament, a region south of Palestine given to Esau.

E·dom·ite (ē'də mīt') *n.* descendant of Esau; inhabitant of Edom.

EDT, Eastern Daylight Time.

ed·u·ca·ble (ej'ə kə bəl) *adj.* capable of being educated. Also, **ed·u·cat·a·ble** (ej'ə kā'tə bəl).

ed·u·cate (ej'ə kāt') **-cat·ed, -cat·ing.** *v.t.* **1.** to develop knowledge, skills, ability, or character in, esp. by formal schooling or instruction; give knowledge or skill to; teach. **2.** to provide with training (for some particular purpose): *He was educated for the priesthood.* **3.** to develop and improve by teaching and training; cultivate, as a taste or aptitude: *to educate one's mind.* **4.** to provide schooling for; send to school: *The cost of educating children in the United States has risen enormously.* [Latin *ēducātus,* past participle of *ēducāre* to bring up, rear.] —**Syn. 1.** see **teach.**

ed·u·cat·ed (ej'ə kā'tid) *adj.* **1.** having an education, esp. one above the average. **2.** showing evidence of having been taught, trained, or instructed; cultivated: *educated speech.* **3.** based on some information or experience: *an educated guess.*

ed·u·ca·tion (ej'ə kā'shən) *n.* **1.** act or process of educating; systematic instruction. **2.** knowledge, skill, or ability developed or obtained by such a process; learning. **3.a.** course of scholastic instruction or formal schooling in an institution of learning: *a college education, a liberal arts education.* **b.** program of instruction of a specified kind: *driver education.* **4.** field of study dealing with the problems, methods, and theories of teaching and learning. [Latin *ēducātiō* a bringing up, rearing.]

Syn. 1. Education, schooling, instruction, training indicate the obtaining or giving of knowledge or proficiency. **Education** suggests both the process and the result of developing the mind's capacity and scope: *Human history becomes more and more a race between education and catastrophe* (Wells, 1919). **Schooling** implies formal direction in a school or classroom, with knowledge at least of fundamentals being imparted: *Six weeks' was all the schooling I got* (Thackeray, 1844). **Instruction** suggests the agency of an informal person who imparts knowledge systematically: *Abraham . . . gave him hospitable entertainment and wise instruction* (Taylor, 1657). **Training** suggests discipline as a teaching method, with a limited goal either in achievement or in time: *It would be absurd to assign the genius of Mozart to training* (Rogers, 1879).

ed·u·ca·tion·al (ej'ə kā'shən əl) *adj.* **1.** of or relating to education. **2.** giving or providing information or knowledge; instructive. —**ed'·u·ca'tion·al·ly,** *adv.*

ed·u·ca·tive (ej'ə kā'tiv) *adj.* **1.** that educates or tends to educate; educational. **2.** of or relating to education.

ed·u·ca·tor (ej'ə kā'tər) *n.* **1.** one whose profession it is to educate others; one trained in teaching. **2.** specialist or authority in the field of education.

e·duce (i dōōs', i dūs') *v.t.* **1.** to bring out; draw forth; elicit. **2.** to infer from data; deduce. [Latin *ēdūcere* to bring out.] —**e·duc'i·ble,** *adj.*

Ed·ward I (ed'wərd) 1239–1307, king of England from 1272 to 1307.

Edward II, 1284–1327, king of England from 1307 to 1327.

Edward III, 1312–77, king of England from 1327 to 1377.

Edward IV, 1442–83, king of England from 1461 to 1470 and 1471 to 1483.

Edward V, 1470–83, king of England in 1483, who was murdered in the Tower of London.

Edward VI, 1537–53, king of England from 1547 to 1553, son of Henry VIII and Jane Seymour.

Edward VII, 1841–1910, king of England from 1901 to 1910, son of Queen Victoria.

Edward VIII, 1894–1972, king of England in 1936, who abdicated and received the title duke of Windsor.

Ed·ward·i·an (ed wär'dē ən, -wôr'-) *adj.* of, relating to, or characteristic of the reign of Edward VII of England, under whom styles were excessively ornate and manners and attitudes overly genteel and pompous.

Edward the Black Prince, 1330–76, Prince of Wales and son of Edward III of England.

Edward the Confessor, c.1004–66, king of England from 1042 to 1066.

-ee *suffix* (used to form nouns from verbs) **1.** one who is affected by or is the recipient of a specified action or process: *appointee, payee.* **2.** one who performs a specified action or is in a specified condition: *escapee, standee.* [Anglo-Norman and Old French past participial ending *-e,* from Latin *-ātus.* See **-EE**.]

E.E., Electrical Engineer.

EEG, electroencephalogram.

eel (ēl) *pl.,* **eels** or **eel.** *n.* **1.** any of various scaleless, snakelike fish, order Anguilliformes, widely distributed in both salt and

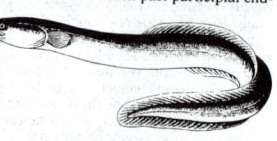

Eel *(def. 1)*

fresh water, having narrow fins that form a continuous line with the body. Length: to 10 feet. **2.** any of various similar fish, such as the electric eel and lamprey. [Old English *ǣl* the fish of the order Anguilliformes.]

eel·grass (ēl'gras') *n.* either of two grasses that grow in shallow waters throughout the world, *Vallisneria americana,* found in fresh water and having short stems and grasslike leaves, and *Zostera marina,* found in salt water and having branching stems and long, ribbonlike leaves.

eel·pout (ēl'pout') *n.* any of various eel-like saltwater fish, family Zoarcidae, related to the blenny. [Old English *ǣlepūte.*]

e'en (ēn) *adv. Archaic.* even.

e'er (ār) *adv. Archaic.* ever.

-eer *suffix* **1.** (used to form nouns) **a.** one who makes or produces (that which is indicated by the stem): *pamphleteer, sonneteer, profiteer.* **b.** one who is concerned or has to do with (that which is indicated by the stem): *auctioneer, engineer.* **2.** (used to form verbs) to be concerned or have to do with: *to electioneer.* [French *-ier,* from Latin *-ārius.* See **-ARY**.]

ee·rie (ēr'ē) **-ri·er, -ri·est.** *also* **ee·ry.** *adj.* **1.** strange and frightening, so as to arouse superstitious fear; weird; uncanny. **2.** nervously uneasy; fearful. [Old English *earg* timid.] —**ee'ri·ly,** *adv.* —**ee'ri·ness,** *n.*

ef-, form of ex-¹ before *f,* as in *efficient.*

ef·face (i fās') **-faced, -fac·ing.** *v.t.* **1.** to make indistinct or destroy by or as by rubbing out; obliterate; erase: *hieroglyphics effaced by wind and sand.* **2.** to make (oneself) inconspicuous. [French *effacer* to erase, going back to Latin *ex* out of, away + *faciēs* form, face.] —**ef·face'·a·ble,** *adj.* —**ef·face'ment, ef·fac'er,** *n.* —**Syn. 1.** see **erase.**

ef·fect (i fekt') *n.* **1.** something brought about by a cause or agent; result; consequence; outcome. **2.a.** power or ability to bring about a result; efficacy: *to deliver a blow with great effect.* **b.** influence or impact (often with *on* or *upon*): *the sobering effect of bad news.* **3.** state or fact of being operative or in force; operation: *to put a plan into effect. The new rule is in effect as of today.* **4.** overall or distinctive impression produced upon the human senses: *This painter achieves dramatic effects by his use of color.* **5.** something, as a technique, used to produce a distinctive impression or achieve a certain result: *Tom is in charge of lighting effects for the production.* **6.** general or basic meaning; intent (with *to*): *The governor's speech was to the effect that the state would preserve its wildlife.* **7.** effects. property; possessions; goods: *personal effects, household effects.* **8.** in effect. **a.** in actual fact; in reality. **b.** for all practical purposes; in essence; virtually. **9.** to take effect. to begin to operate or produce results. —*v.t.* to bring about; produce as a result; cause; accomplish: *to effect an escape.* [Latin *effectus* accomplishment, performance.]

Syn. *n.* **1. Effect, result, consequence** indicate something that can be traced to a cause. **Effect** suggests only those specific things or events that can be shown to be caused directly and esp. immediately: *The effects of the medicine were beneficial to the patient.* **Result** suggests the final end of a cause's action: *All the damage is the result of the hurricane.* **Consequence** suggests anything that results from a cause, either immediately or through a series of effects: *If you break the law, you must take the consequences.* **4.** see **accomplish.**

ef·fec·tive (i fek'tiv) *adj.* **1.** producing or capable of producing an intended or desired result: *an effective method, an effective argument.* **2.** in effect or force; operative; active. **3.** producing a striking impression; impressive: *an effective speaker.* **4.** fit for action or duty:

at; āpe; cär; end; mē; it; īce; hot; ōld; fôrk; wood; fōōl; oil; out; up; ūse; turn; sing; thin; this; zh in treasure; ə in ago, taken, pencil, lemon, circus.

Effective forces numbered 10,000. —**ef·fec'tive·ly,** *adv.* —**ef·fec'- tive·ness,** *n.*

ef·fec·tu·al (i fek'chŏŏ əl) *adj.* **1.** effective (*def. 1*). **2.** legally valid or binding, as an agreement or document. —**ef·fec·tu·al·i·ty** (i fek'- chŏŏ al'ə tē), **ef·fec'tu·al·ness,** *n.*

ef·fec·tu·al·ly (i fek'chŏŏ ə lē) *adv.* in an effectual manner; with complete effect; thoroughly.

ef·fec·tu·ate (i fek'chŏŏ āt') -at·ed, -at·ing. *v.t.* to bring about or cause; accomplish; effect. [Medieval Latin *effectuatus,* past participle of *effectuare* to bring to pass, from Latin *effectus* accomplishment.]

ef·fem·i·na·cy (i fem'ə nə sē) *n.* state or quality of being effeminate.

ef·fem·i·nate (i fem'ə nit) *adj.* having more feminine qualities or traits than are suitable to or usual in a male; womanish; unmanly. [Latin *effēminātus* past participle of *effēmināre* to make womanish.] —**ef·fem'i·nate·ly,** *adv.* —**ef·fem'i·nate·ness,** *n.*

ef·fen·di (i fen'dē) *pl.,* **-dis.** *n.* **1.** sir; master. ▲ Turkish title of respect. **2.** in Muslim countries, a man of property, education, or authority. [Turkish *efendi* master, sir, going back to Greek *authentēs* master.]

ef·fer·ent (ef'ər ənt) *adj.* carrying away from a central organ or point. Efferent nerves carry impulses from the central nervous system to the muscles and organs. Opposed to **afferent.** [Latin *efferēns,* present participle of *efferre* to carry out.]

ef·fer·vesce (ef'ər ves') -vesced, -vesc·ing. *v.i.* **1.a.** to give off bubbles of gas, as carbonated beverages do; bubble. **b.** (of a gas) to form or issue forth in bubbles. **2.** to show liveliness or exhilaration; be exuberant. [Latin *effervēscere* to boil over.]

ef·fer·ves·cence (ef'ər ves'əns) *n.* **1.** act or process of bubbling up. **2.** liveliness; exuberance. Also, **ef'fer·ves'cen·cy.**

ef·fer·ves·cent (ef'ər ves'ənt) *adj.* **1.** giving off bubbles of gas; bubbling. **2.** lively; exuberant.

ef·fete (i fēt', i fĕt') *adj.* having lost strength or vigor; worn-out; exhausted: *an effete and decadent civilization.* [Latin *effētus* exhausted (by bearing young), worn-out.] —**ef·fete'ness,** *n.*

ef·fi·ca·cious (ef'i kā'shəs) *adj.* producing or capable of producing the desired or intended effect. —**ef'fi·ca'cious·ly,** *adv.*

ef·fi·ca·cy (ef'i kə sē) *pl.,* **-cies.** *n.* power to produce the desired or intended effect; effectiveness. [Latin *efficācia* efficiency.]

ef·fi·cien·cy (i fish'ən sē) *pl.,* **-cies.** *n.* **1.** quality of being efficient. **2.** ratio of the useful work or energy output of an organism or machine to the energy supplied to it.

efficiency apartment, small, usually one-room apartment having kitchen facilities and a bathroom.

efficiency expert, one who devises more efficient and productive methods of utilizing the material and human resources of a business or industrial plant. Also, **efficiency engineer.**

ef·fi·cient (i fish'ənt) *adj.* **1.** producing or capable of producing a desired effect with a minimum of effort or waste: *an efficient worker.* **2.** actually producing an effect; causative: *an efficient cause.* [Latin *efficiēns,* present participle of *efficere* to produce.] —**ef·fi'cient·ly,** *adv.*

ef·fi·gy (ef'i jē) *pl.,* **-gies.** *n.* **1.** representation or likeness of a person, esp. a sculptured image: *a bronze effigy of the late king.* **2.** crude representation of a disliked or hated person: *a straw effigy.* **3. to burn** (or **hang**) **in effigy.** to burn or hang publicly a crude representation of someone as an expression of public contempt. [Latin *effigiēs* image.]

ef·flo·resce (ef'lə res') -resced, -resc·ing. *v.i.* **1.** to blossom forth; bloom; flower. **2.** *Chemistry.* **a.** to change either wholly or partially from crystals to a powder by loss of water of crystallization when exposed to air. **b.** to become covered with a crust of particles resulting from evaporation or chemical change. [Latin *efflorēscere* to blossom.]

ef·flo·res·cence (ef'lə res'əns) *n.* **1.** act, state, or period of flowering. **2.** result of growth and development; culmination. **3.** *Chemistry.* **a.** act or process of efflorescing. **b.** powder or deposit formed by this process. **4.** any eruption or rash on the skin.

ef·flo·res·cent (ef'lə res'ənt) *adj.* **1.** blossoming forth; blooming; flowering. **2.** *Chemistry.* **a.** changing from a crystalline to a powdery form. **b.** covered with a powdery crust.

ef·flu·ence (ef'lŏŏ əns) *n.* **1.** a flowing out or forth. **2.** that which flows out or forth; emanation.

ef·flu·ent (ef'lŏŏ ənt) *adj.* flowing out or forth. —*n.* **1.** that which flows out or forth. **2.** stream flowing out of a larger stream, lake, or reservoir. [Latin *effluēns,* present participle of *effluere* to flow out.]

ef·flu·vi·um (i flŏŏ'vē əm) *pl.,* **-vi·a** (-vē ə) or **-vi·ums.** *n.* vapor or odor, esp. one that is noxious. [Latin *effluvium* a flowing out.]

ef·flux (ef'luks) *n.* **1.** a flowing out. **2.** that which flows out. [Latin *efflūxus,* past participle of *effluere* to flow out.]

ef·fort (ef'ərt) *n.* **1.** expenditure of physical or mental energy; exertion: *Control of the mob took great effort.* **2.** attempt, esp. a strong or serious attempt: *She made an effort to get to school on time.* **3.** product or result of exertion; achievement: *a new literary effort.* [French *effort* endeavor, from Old French *esforcier* to force, make greater, going back to Latin *ex* out of, utterly + *fortis* strong.]

Syn. 1. Effort, exertion, endeavor mean an active attempt, physical or mental, to accomplish something. **Effort** implies expenditure of time and energy to attain some end, often by a single try, however extended: *He made an effort to call her, but her line was busy.* **Exertion** suggests a straining to do something: *Bill saved himself from being swept over the falls only by tremendous exertion.* **Endeavor** suggests continued exertion: *The life of Angelico was almost entirely spent in the endeavor to imagine the beings belonging to another world* (Ruskin, 1856).

ef·fort·less (ef'ərt lis) *adj.* displaying or requiring little or no effort; easy: *an effortless task, effortless grace.* —**ef'fort·less·ly,** *adv.* —**ef'fort- less·ness,** *n.* —**Syn.** see **easy.**

ef·fron·ter·y (i frun'tər ē) *n.* shameless boldness or impudence; insolence. [French *effronterie,* going back to Late Latin *effrōns* shameless, barefaced, from Latin *ex* out of, away + *frōns* forehead.]

ef·ful·gence (i ful'jəns) *n.* great brightness or splendor; radiance. [Latin *effulgēns,* present participle of *effulgēre* to shine forth.]

ef·ful·gent (i ful'jənt) *adj.* shining brightly; radiant. [Latin *effulgēns,* present participle of *effulgēre* to shine forth.]

ef·fuse (i fūz') -fused, -fus·ing. *v.t.* **1.** to pour out or forth. —*v.i.* to emanate; exude. **2.** (of a gas) to flow through a porous material or very small opening. [Latin *effūsus,* past participle of *effundere* to pour forth.]

ef·fu·sion (i fū'zhən) *n.* **1.** act of effusing. **2.** that which is effused. **3.** unrestrained outpouring or expression, as of feelings or ideas. **4.** *Medicine.* **a.** escape of fluid from its natural vessel into body cavities or tissues. **b.** fluid that so escapes.

ef·fu·sive (i fū'siv) *adj.* showing or expressing excessive feeling; overly demonstrative; gushing: *an effusive person, her effusive thanks.* —**ef·fu'sive·ly,** *adv.* —**ef·fu'sive·ness,** *n.*

eft (eft) *n.* newt in its immature, land stage. [Old English *efeta.*]

eft·soon (eft sŏŏn') also, **eft·soons.** *adv.* Archaic. **1.** soon afterward; forthwith. **2.** again. **3.** repeatedly; often. [Old English *eftsōna* again.]

e.g., for example. [Abbreviation of Latin *exemplī grātiā.*]

e·gad (i gad') *interj.* by God. ▲ used as a mild oath.

e·gal·i·tar·i·an (i gal'ə tār'ē ən) also, **e·qual·i·tar·i·an.** *adj.* of, relating to, or asserting belief in the equality of all men, esp. with respect to political, economic, and legal rights. —*n.* one who advocates or adheres to egalitarian beliefs. [French *égalitaire* based on equality (from *égalité* equality, from Latin *aequālitās*) + -IAN.] —**e·gal'i·tar'i·an·ism,** *n.*

e·gest (i jest') *v.t.* to discharge or excrete, as from the body. [Latin *ēgestus,* past participle of *ēgerere* to carry out.] —**e·ges'tion,** *n.* —**e·ges'tive,** *adj.*

egg¹ (eg) *n.* **1.** reproductive body produced in the female sex organs of most animals, usually rounded or oval and consisting of an ovum, nutrient substances, as yolk or oil, and a protective membranous covering or shell. **2.a.** hard-shelled egg produced by a bird, esp. by a hen or other domestic fowl, used as food: *He went to the store to get a dozen eggs.* **b.** contents of this: *Beat four eggs and then add milk.* **3.** reproductive cell produced in the female sex organs of most animals; ovum. Also, **egg cell. 4.** something resembling or shaped like a hen's egg. **5.** Slang. person; fellow: *He's a good egg.* **6. to lay an egg.** Slang. to fail completely, esp. before an audience. **7. to put** (or **have**) **all one's eggs in one basket.** to risk everything on a single chance or in a single enterprise. —*v.t.* to cover (food) with beaten egg before cooking. [Old Norse *egg* bird's egg.]

egg² (eg) *v.t.* to incite or urge, as with taunts or dares; goad (often with *on*): *She egged him on to play the trick.* [Old Norse *eggja.*] —**Syn.** see **urge.**

egg·beat·er (eg'bē'tər) *n.* **1.** kitchen utensil, usually having rotary blades, for beating eggs, whipping cream, and mixing cooking ingredients. **2.** Slang. helicopter.

egg·head (eg'hed') *n.* Informal. an intellectual; highbrow.

egg·nog (eg'nog') *n.* drink made of raw eggs beaten up with milk or cream, sugar, and spices, and often containing an alcoholic beverage, as rum. [EGG¹ + earlier *nog* strong ale (of uncertain origin).]

egg·plant (eg'plant') *n.* **1.** oval-shaped fruit of a plant, *Solanum melongena,* variety *esculentum,* usually blackish-purple, cooked and eaten as a vegetable. **2.** this plant.

egg·shell (eg'shel') *n.* **1.** hard, brittle covering of a bird's egg. **2.** pale yellow or ivory color. —*adj.* **1.** of the color eggshell. **2.** thin and fragile. **3.** having little or no gloss; slightly glossy: *an eggshell enamel.*

e·gis (ē'jis) aegis.

eg·lan·tine (eg'lən tīn', -tēn') *n.* sweetbrier. [French *églantine,* from Old French *aiglent,* going back to Latin *acus* needle.]

Eggplant

e·go (ē′gō, eg′ō) *pl.* **e·gos.** *n.* **1.** the self as a thinking, feeling, acting being, conscious of being distinct from its own thoughts and from the selves of others. **2.a.** confidence in oneself; self-image; self-esteem. **b.** *Informal.* conceit; self-centeredness; egotism. **3.** *Psychoanalysis.* the conscious part of the psyche which is shaped by contact with the external world and which deals with reality by mediating between the impulses of the id and the demands of the superego. [Latin *ego* I.]

e·go·cen·tric (ē′gō sen′trik, eg′ō-) *adj.* **1.** viewing everything in relation to oneself; excessively concerned with one's own activities and needs; self-centered. —*n.* egocentric person. —**e·go·cen·tric·i·ty** (ē′gō-sen tris′ə tē, eg′ō-), *n.*

e·go·ism (ē′gō iz′əm, eg′ō-) *n.* **1.** arrogant conceit; egotism. **2.** excessive concern with one's own welfare and interests; selfishness. —**Syn. 1.** see **egotism.**

e·go·ist (ē′gō ist, eg′ō-) *n.* **1.** arrogantly conceited person; egotist. **2.** selfish or self-centered person. —**e·go·is′tic;** *also,* **e·go·is′ti·cal,** *adj.* —**e·go·is′ti·cal·ly,** *adv.*

e·go·ma·ni·a (ē′gō mā′nē ə, eg′ō-) *n.* excessive or abnormal egotism. —**e·go·ma′ni·ac,** *n.*

e·go·tism (ē′gə tiz′əm, eg′ə-) *n.* **1.** inflated sense of self-importance. **2.** excessive reference to or dwelling upon oneself, as in speech or writing; boastfulness. **3.** selfishness.

Syn. 1. **Egotism, egoism, conceit** indicate satisfaction with oneself. **Egotism** suggests vanity and frequent speech and behavior indicating the belief that one is of paramount importance and interest to others: *In his egotism he turns every conversation into a discussion of himself.* **Egoism** implies a thoroughgoing selfishness but without any suggestion of blatant expression: *Little Elsa kept all her toys to herself with the natural egoism of a child.* **Conceit** suggests belief in one's superiority with some degree of arrogance: *The singer was puffed up with conceit.*

e·go·tist (ē′gə tist, eg′ə-) *n.* **1.** one characterized by egotism; conceited, boastful person. **2.** selfish or self-centered person; egoist.

e·go·tis·ti·cal (ē′gə tis′ti kəl, eg′ə-) *adj.* **1.** relating to or characterized by egotism. **2.** inclined to think too highly of oneself; conceited. Also, **e·go·tis′tic.** —**e·go·tis′ti·cal·ly,** *adv.*

e·gre·gious (i grē′jəs) *adj.* **1.** conspicuously bad; glaring; outrageous; flagrant: *an egregious error.* **2.** *Archaic.* distinguished; remarkable. [Latin *ēgregius* excellent; literally, chosen from the herd, from *ex* out of + *grex* herd.] —**e·gre′gious·ly,** *adv.* —**e·gre′gious·ness,** *n.*

e·gress (ē′gres) *n.* **1.** act of going out, as from a building; emergence. **2.** place or means of going out; way out; exit. **3.** right to go out. [Latin *ēgressus* a going out.]

e·gret (ē′grit, eg′rit) *n.* **1.** any of various herons, order Ciconiiformes, that bears tufts of long, lacy feathers on the back, crown, and breast during the breeding season. **2.** lacy feather of the egret. [French *aigrette*, from Provençal *aigreta* heron, from *aigron*; of Germanic origin.]

Egret

E·gypt (ē′jipt) *n.* country in northeastern Africa, now officially known as the United Arab Republic. Ancient Egypt was the center of one of the world's earliest and greatest civilizations.

E·gyp·tian (i jip′shən) *n.* **1.** native or inhabitant of Egypt. **2.** Hamitic language of the ancient Egyptians, from which Coptic descends. —*adj.* of or relating to Egypt, its people, or their culture.

Egyptian cotton, fine, silky cotton with long fibers, grown chiefly in Egypt.

E·gyp·tol·o·gy (ē′jip tol′ə jē) *n.* study of ancient Egypt. —**E′gyp·tol′o·gist,** *n.*

eh (ā) *interj.* exclamation expressing surprise, doubt, or failure to hear what was said.

ei·der (ī′dər) *n.* **1.** any of various sea ducks of the arctic and subarctic regions of the Pacific and North Atlantic oceans. The female of the common eider, *Somateria mollissima*, is the source of eiderdown. Also, **eider duck.** **2.** eiderdown. [Icelandic *æthr* the eider duck.]

ei·der·down (ī′dər doun′) *n.* **1.** small, soft feathers, or down, from the breast of the female common eider, used to stuff pillows and quilts. **2.** quilt filled with eiderdown.

ei·det·ic (ī det′ik) *adj.* of or relating to the faculty of recalling visual images in much detail and with great accuracy. [Greek *eidētikos* relating to images, from *eidos* form.] —**ei·det′i·cal·ly,** *adv.*

Eif·fel Tower (ī′fəl) iron and steel tower in Paris, France.

eight (āt) *n.* **1.** the cardinal number that is one more than seven. **2.** symbol representing this number, as 8 or VIII. **3.** something having this many units or members, as a playing card. —*adj.* numbering one more than seven. [Old English *eahta*.]

eight ball **1.** black pool ball bearing the number eight encircled with white. **2.** pool game in which the eight ball must be pocketed last in order to win the game. **3. behind the eight ball.** *Slang.* in an unfavorable or disadvantageous position.

eight·een (ā tēn′) *n.* **1.** the cardinal number that is eight more than ten. **2.** symbol representing this number, as 18 or XVIII. **3.** something having this many units or members. —*adj.* numbering eight more than ten. [Old English *eahtatȳne.*]

eight·eenth (ā tēnth′) *adj.* **1.** (the ordinal of eighteen) next after the seventeenth. **2.** being one of eighteen equal parts. —*n.* one of eighteen equal parts; 1/18.

eight·fold (āt′fōld′) *adj.* **1.** eight times as great or numerous. **2.** having or consisting of eight parts. —*adv.* so as to be eight times greater or more numerous.

eighth (ātth) *adj.* **1.** (the ordinal of eight) next after the seventh. **2.** being one of eight equal parts. —*n.* **1.** one of eight equal parts; 1/8. **2.** *Music.* octave (*defs.* 1a, b, c).

eighth note *Music.* note having one-eighth the time value of a whole note; quaver. See **note** for illustration.

eight·i·eth (ā′tē ith) *adj.* **1.** (the ordinal of eighty) next after the seventy-ninth. **2.** being one of eighty equal parts. —*n.* one of eighty equal parts; 1/80.

eight·y (ā′tē) *pl.,* **eight·ies.** *n.* **1.** the cardinal number that is eight times ten. **2.** symbol representing this number, as 80 or LXXX. **3. the eighties.** number series from eighty to eighty-nine. ▲ used esp. when referring to the eighth decade of a century or of a person's life. —*adj.* being one more than seventy-nine. [Old English *eahtatig.*]

Ein·stein, Albert (īn′stīn) 1879–1955, German-American physicist who developed the theory of relativity.

ein·stein·i·um (īn stī′nē əm) *n.* man-made, radioactive element, first discovered in the fallout of a hydrogen bomb explosion. Symbol: **Es** See **element** for table. [From Albert *Einstein.*]

Einstein's equation, mass-energy equation.

Eir·e (ār′ə, īr′ə) *n.* see **Ireland, Republic of.**

Ei·sen·how·er, Dwight D. (ī′zən hou′ər; dwīt) 1890–1969, U.S. general and thirty-fourth president of the United States, from 1953 to 1961.

ei·ther (ē′thər, ī′thər) *adj.* **1.** one or the other (of two): *Use either arm.* **2.** one and the other (of two); each: *He could write with either hand.* —*pron.* one or the other (of two): *Either will do as well.* ▲ In formal writing, *either,* like *neither,* takes a singular verb: *Either of the dogs is a good watchdog.* In informal speech and writing, a plural verb is often used: *Are either of you taking lessons?* When there are two subjects, one singular and one plural, the verb agrees with the subject closest to it: *Either Tim or his brothers have to shovel the snow. Either the shirts or the sweater is a good buy.* —*conj.* one or the other of two or more choices. ▲ used with *or* to indicate the first of two or more possibilities: *Either go or don't go. You may come either tonight, tomorrow, or next week.* —*adv.* any more so; also. ▲ used for emphasis after a negative: *She can't do it, and I can't either. That's mine; no, it isn't either.* [Old English *ǣgther* each of two.]

e·jac·u·late (i jak′yə lāt′) **-lat·ed, -lat·ing.** *v.t.* **1.** to eject or discharge suddenly, as seminal fluid. **2.** to utter suddenly and briefly; exclaim. —*v.i.* to eject or discharge a fluid. [Latin *ējaculātus,* past participle of *ējaculārī* to throw out.]

e·jac·u·la·tion (i jak′yə lā′shən) *n.* **1.** act of ejaculating. **2.** sudden ejection or discharge, as of seminal fluid; emission. **3.** sudden, brief emotional utterance; exclamation.

e·jac·u·la·to·ry (i jak′yə lə tôr′ē) *adj.* **1.** of the nature of or resembling an exclamatory utterance. **2.** of or adapted for sudden ejection: *an ejaculatory duct.*

e·ject (i jekt′) *v.t.* **1.** to throw out or discharge; emit: *The furnace ejected smoke.* **2.a.** to expel or drive out, esp. by force; cause to leave. **b.** to evict. [Latin *ējectus,* past participle of *ējicere* to throw out.]

e·jec·tion (i jek′shən) *n.* **1.** act of ejecting; being ejected. **2.** that which is ejected, as lava.

e·ject·ment (i jekt′mənt) *n.* **1.** dispossession; eviction. **2.** *Law.* action to regain possession of real property.

e·jec·tor (i jek′tər) *n.* one who or that which ejects.

eke¹ (ēk) **eked, ek·ing.** *v.t.* **1. to eke out.** **a.** to barely manage to make (a living). **b.** to add to in order to make barely sufficient; supply what is lacking to: *to eke out a meal by adding rice to leftovers.* **c.** to make (something) last longer, as by practicing economy; prolong: *to eke out a limited water supply by rationing.* **2.** *Archaic.* to increase; lengthen. [Old English *ēcan, īecan* to increase.]

eke² (ēk) *adv., conj. Archaic.* also; moreover. [Old English *ēac.*]

el (el) *n.* variant of **ell²**.

e·lab·o·rate (*adj.,* i lab′ər it; *v.,* i lab′ə rāt′) *adj.* **1.** worked out with great care or thoroughness; developed in intricate detail; complex: *an elaborate mathematical theory.* **2.** highly detailed; ornate. —*v.i.,* **-rat·ed, -rat·ing.** to give fuller treatment or additional detail; embellish

at; āpe; cär; end; mē; it; īce; hot; ōld; fôrk; wood; fōōl; oil; out; up; ūse; turn; sing; thin; this; zh in treasure; ə in ago, taken, pencil, lemon, circus.

(often with *on* or *upon*): *to elaborate upon a theme.* —*v.t.* **1.** to work out carefully or thoroughly; develop in detail. **2.** *Archaic.* to make; fashion. [Latin *ēlabōrātus,* past participle of *ēlabōrāre* to labor greatly, work out.] —**e·lab′o·rate·ly,** *adv.* —**e·lab′o·rate·ness, e·lab′o·ra′tor,** *n.* —**e·lab′o·ra′tive,** *adj.*

e·lab·o·ra·tion (i lab′ə rā′shən) *n.* **1.** act of elaborating; being elaborated. **2.** that which is elaborated.

E·laine (i lān′) *n. Arthurian Legend.* **1.** beautiful maiden who died of unrequited love for Sir Lancelot. **2.** mother of Sir Galahad.

E·lam (ē′ləm) *n.* ancient kingdom at the head of the Persian Gulf, just east of Babylonia, in what is now western Iran.

E·lam·ite (ē′lə mīt′) *n.* member of the people of ancient Elam.

é·lan (ā län′) *n.* enthusiasm; dash; vivacity. [French *élan,* from *élancer* to throw, going back to Latin *ex* out of + *lancea* lance.]

e·land (ē′lənd) *n.* largest living antelope, genus *Taurotragus,* native to southern Africa and having humped shoulders and long, twisted horns. [Afrikaans *eland,* from Dutch *eland* elk, from obsolete German *elend,* from Lithuanian *elnis.*]

Eland

e·lapse (i laps′) **e·lapsed, e·laps·ing.** *v.i.* (of time) to slip by; pass away. [Latin *ēlapsus,* past participle of *ēlābī* to glide away.]

e·las·mo·branch (i laz′mə brank′) *n.* any of numerous cartilaginous fish, class Chondrichthyes, including the sharks, rays, and skates. [Modern Latin *Elasmobranchii* (plural), from Greek *elasmos* metal plate + *branchia* gills; because of the platelike structure of its gills.]

e·las·tic (i las′tik) *adj.* **1.a.** capable of returning to its original size or shape after being distorted: *elastic stockings.* **b.** (of a gas) capable of indefinite expansion. **2.** capable of adapting to fit the circumstances; flexible; accommodating: *an elastic set of rules.* **3.** capable of recovering easily, as from emotional or physical distress; resilient; buoyant: *an elastic temperament.* **4.** marked by springiness; bouncy: *an elastic step.* —*n.* **1.** fabric made stretchable by rubber threads or strands running through it. **2.** rubber band. [Modern Latin *elasticus,* from Greek *elastikos* propulsive, from *elaunein* to drive.] —**e·las′ti·cal·ly,** *adv.*

e·las·tic·i·ty (i las′tə tē, ē′las-) *n.* state or quality of being elastic.

e·las·ti·cized (i las′tə sīzd′) *adj.* made stretchable by interweaving with elastic threads or strands: *an elasticized waistband.*

e·late (i lāt′) **e·lat·ed, e·lat·ing.** *v.t.* to put in high spirits; make joyful; excite. [Latin *ēlātus* elevated.]

e·lat·ed (i lā′tid) *adj.* in high spirits; filled with joy; jubilant. —**e·lat′ed·ly,** *adv.* —**e·lat′ed·ness,** *n.*

e·la·tion (i lā′shən) *n.* feeling of exultant joy; jubilation.

E layer, Heaviside layer.

El·ba (el′bə) *n.* Italian island between Italy and Corsica. Area, 85 sq. mi. Pop. (1961), 28,463.

El·be (el′bə, elb) *n.* river flowing from Czechoslovakia through Germany into the North Sea.

el·bow (el′bō) *n.* **1.** joint between the forearm and the upper arm, esp. the projecting outer part of this joint when the arm is bent. **2.** something having a bend like the elbow, as a curved pipe fitting. **3.** to rub **elbows with.** to associate with (celebrities or prominent people). **4. up to one's** (or **the**) **elbows.** excessively busy; deeply immersed. —*v.t.* **1.** to push with or as with the elbows; thrust aside or shove; jostle. **2.** to make or force (one's way) by or as by pushing with the elbows: *to elbow through a crowd.* —*v.i.* to proceed or advance by or as by pushing with the elbows: *elbow through a crowd.* [Old English *el(n)boga* joint between the forearm and the upper arm.]

elbow grease, *Informal.* energetic physical effort.

el·bow·room (el′bō rōōm′, -room′) *n.* ample room, as to move or work in.

El·brus, Mount (el′brōōs) highest peak of Europe and of the Caucasus Mountains, in the southwestern Soviet Union.

El Ca·jon (el′ kə hōn′) city in southwestern California. Pop. (1970), 52,273.

eld (eld) *n. Archaic.* **1.** old age. **2.** old times; antiquity. [Old English *eldo* old age, from *eald* old.]

eld·er[1] (el′dər) *adj.* **1.** of earlier birth or formation; older. **2.a.** prior or superior, as in rank, position, or validity: *an elder partner in the firm.* **b.** distinguished for superior judgment and longer experience: *an elder statesman.* **3.** earlier; former. —*n.* **1.** one who is older; senior. **2.** one of the older, influential members, as of a family or community.

3. officer in any of various Christian churches, esp. a member of the higher priesthood in the Mormon Church or a presbyter. **4.** aged person. **5.** forefather; predecessor. [Old English *eldra* older, comparative of *eald* old.]

eld·er[2] (el′dər) *n.* any of a group of shrubs and small trees, genus *Sambucus,* that bears edible red or purple-black berries. Also, **el′der·ber′ry.** [Old English *ellærn.*]

el·der·ber·ry (el′dər ber′ē) *pl.,* **-ries.** *n.* **1.** berry of the elder, used esp. for making wines, jellies, and pies. **2.** elder[2].

Flowers

Fruits   Leaf

Elder[2]

eld·er·ly (el′dər lē) *adj.* **1.** approaching old age; past middle age: *an elderly gentleman.* **2.** of, relating to, or characteristic of one approaching old age. —**Syn.** 1. see **aged.**

el·der·ship (el′dər ship′) *n.* **1.** position or responsibilities of an elder in a church. **2.** group or court of elders; presbytery.

elder statesman, retired statesman who unofficially advises government leaders.

eld·est (el′dist) *adj.* oldest; first-born. [Old English *eldesta,* superlative of *eald* old.]

El Do·ra·do (el′ də rä′dō) *pl.,* **-dos.** *also,* **El·do·ra·do. 1.** legendary South American city of great wealth sought by sixteenth-century explorers. **2.** any place of fabulous wealth. [Spanish *El Dorado* literally, the gilded: *el* the (from Latin *ille* that) + *dorado,* past participle of *dorar* to gild (going back to Latin *dē* from + *aurum* gold).]

elec. 1. electric. **2.** electricity. **3.** electrical.

e·lect (i lekt′) *v.t.* **1.** to choose (someone) by vote, as for an office or membership. **2.** to choose; select: *Jack elected biology as his major.* **3.** to select for salvation. ▲ used in the passive voice with God as the implied subject. —*adj.* **1.** elected but not yet formally installed in office. ▲ used in combination after a noun: *senator-elect.* **2.** chosen; select: *elect circles of society.* **3.** selected by God for salvation. —*n.* **the elect. a.** people who are favored or preferred, esp. those belonging to a privileged group. **b.** people selected by God for salvation. [Latin *ēlectus,* past participle of *ēligere* to choose.]

e·lec·tion (i lek′shən) *n.* **1.** act of electing; being elected. **2.** a choosing by vote of a person or persons, as for an office or position. **3.** public vote upon any question officially submitted. **4.** selection by God for salvation.

e·lec·tion·eer (i lek′shə nēr′) *v.i.* to work or campaign for the election of a candidate or political party.

e·lec·tive (i lek′tiv) *adj.* **1.** of or relating to election. **2.** chosen or filled by vote: *an elective office.* **3.** having the power or right to choose by vote: *an elective body.* **4.** open to choice; not required; optional: *an elective course.* —*n.* optional subject in a high school or college curriculum.

e·lec·tor (i lek′tər) *n.* **1.** one who is qualified to vote in an election. **2.** member of the U.S. electoral college. **3.** any of several German princes entitled to elect the emperor of the Holy Roman Empire.

e·lec·tor·al (i lek′tər əl) *adj.* of, relating to, or composed of an election or electors: *an electoral system, the electoral vote.*

electoral college, body of representatives, chosen by popular vote, which formally elects the president and vice-president of the United States. Each state has the same number of electors as it has members in Congress.

e·lec·tor·ate (i lek′tər it) *n.* **1.** all persons qualified to vote in an election. **2.a.** territory of an elector of the Holy Roman Empire. **b.** rank or office of an elector of the Holy Roman Empire.

E·lec·tra (i lek′trə) *n. Greek Legend.* the daughter of Agamemnon and Clytemnestra who urged and helped her brother, Orestes, to kill their mother in revenge for the murder of their father.

e·lec·tric (i lek′trik) *adj.* **1.** of or relating to electricity. **2.** charged with or operated by electricity: *an electric iron.* **3.** resulting from or produced by electricity: *an electric shock.* **4.** producing or conveying electricity: *an electric generator, electric cables.* **5.** exciting; thrilling; electrifying. [Modern Latin *electricus,* from Latin *ēlectrum* amber, from Greek *ēlektron;* because of amber's property of attracting other substances when rubbed.]

e·lec·tri·cal (i lek′tri kəl) *adj.* **1.** electric (defs. 1–4). **2.** dealing with electric phenomena: *electrical engineering.* —**e·lec′tri·cal·ly,** *adv.*

electrical storm, thunderstorm.

electrical transcription 1. phonograph record or magnetic tape recording used to record programs for later broadcast. **2.** a broadcast from such a phonograph record or magnetic tape recording.

electric chair 1. chair used for executing criminals by electrocution. **2.** execution by this means.

electric charge 1. fundamental property of matter. An electron carries a negative electric charge; a proton carries a positive electric charge. **2.** quantity of electricity in or on such a body. Electric charge is measured in coulombs.

electric eel, long, eel-like fish, *Electrophorus electricus,* native to rivers of the Amazon Basin in South America, capable of giving off strong electric shocks that ward off enemies and stun prey.

electric eye, photoelectric cell upon which a beam of light is directed and which, when the beam is interrupted, causes a device to open a door, ring a bell, or perform a similar operation.

e·lec·tri·cian (i lek′trish′ən, ē′lek-) *n.* one who designs, installs, repairs, or maintains electric wiring or equipment.

e·lec·tric·i·ty (i lek′tris′ə tē, ē′lek-) *n.* **1.** energy carried by electrons, protons, and other subatomic particles and capable of producing light, heat, and other effects. **2.** branch of physics that deals with such energy, usually studied in conjunction with magnetism. **3.** electric current.

electric ray, any of a group of rays, family Torpedinidae, with organs on each side of the head that give off electric discharges.

e·lec·tri·fi·ca·tion (i lek′trə fi kā′shən) *n.* act of electrifying; being electrified.

e·lec·tri·fy (i lek′trə fī′) **-fied, -fy·ing.** *v.t.* **1.** to charge with electricity: *to electrify a fence.* **2.** to equip for the use of electricity. **3.** to excite; thrill; startle. —**e·lec′tri·fi·ca′tion,** *n.*

electro- *combining form,* of, relating to, or by means of electricity: *electromagnet, electrocute.* [Greek *ēlektron* amber. See ELECTRIC.]

e·lec·tro·car·di·o·gram (i lek′trō kär′dē ə gram′) *n.* tracing made on a graph by an electrocardiograph.

e·lec·tro·car·di·o·graph (i lek′trō kär′dē ə graf′) *n.* instrument that receives and records electrical impulses that originate in the muscle of the heart as it contracts and relaxes, used esp. to detect and diagnose heart disorders. —**e·lec′tro·car′di·o·graph′ic,** *adj.*

e·lec·tro·chem·i·cal (i lek′trō kem′i kəl) *adj.* of or relating to electrochemistry.

e·lec·tro·chem·is·try (i lek′trō kem′is trē) *n.* branch of chemistry that deals with the relationship between electricity and chemical changes or reactions.

e·lec·tro·cute (i lek′trə kūt′) **-cut·ed, -cut·ing.** *v.t.* **1.** to execute (a criminal) in the electric chair. **2.** to kill by electricity. [ELECTRO- + (EXE)CUTE.] —**e·lec′tro·cu′tion,** *n.*

e·lec·trode (i lek′trōd) *n.* electrical conductor, part of an electric circuit, through which electrons enter or leave a conducting medium, as air, other gases, or chemical solutions. [ELECTRO- + -ODE.]

e·lec·tro·dy·nam·ic (i lek′trō dī nam′ik) *adj.* of or relating to electricity in motion.

e·lec·tro·dy·nam·ics (i lek′trō dī nam′iks) *n.,pl.* branch of physics that deals with electric currents and forces produced by or related to electric currents. ▲ construed as singular.

e·lec·tro·en·ceph·a·lo·gram (i lek′trō en sef′ə lə gram′) *n.* tracing made on a graph by an electroencephalograph.

e·lec·tro·en·ceph·a·lo·graph (i lek′trō en sef′ə lə graf′) *n.* instrument that detects and records electrical activity in the brain. —**e·lec′tro·en·ceph′a·lo·graph′ic,** *adj.*

e·lec·trol·y·sis (i lek′trol′ə·sis, ē′lek-) *n.* **1.** chemical decomposition of a liquefied or dissolved substance into its components by passage of an electric current through the substance. Electrolysis is usually performed in an electrolytic cell. **2.** permanent removal of unwanted body hair by destroying the root cells with an electrified needle. [ELECTRO- + Greek *lysis* a loosing.]

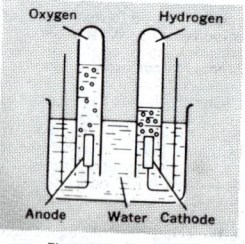

Oxygen   Hydrogen

Anode   Water   Cathode

Electrolysis of water

e·lec·tro·lyte (i lek′trə līt′) *n.*
1. any nonmetallic substance that will conduct an electric current, esp. a liquid solution. **2.** chemical compound, usually an acid, base, or salt, that when liquefied or in solution will dissociate into ions and conduct an electric current. [ELECTRO- + Greek *lytos* that may be loosed or dissolved.]

e·lec·tro·lyt·ic (i lek′trə lit′ik) *adj.* **1.** of, relating to, or produced by electrolysis. **2.** of or relating to an electrolyte.

e·lec·tro·lyt·i·cal·ly (i lek′trə lit′ik lē) *adv.* by means of electrolysis.

electrolytic cell, apparatus consisting of an anode and a cathode

that are immersed in an electrolyte and connected to a source of current, as a battery.

e·lec·tro·lyze (i lek′trə līz′) **-lyzed, -lyz·ing.** *v.t.* to decompose by electrolysis. —**e·lec·tro·ly·za·tion** (i lek′trə li zā′shən), **e·lec′tro·lyz′er,** *n.*

e·lec·tro·mag·net (i lek′trō mag′nit) *n.* iron core with insulated wire wound around it that becomes a magnet when electric current is supplied to it.

e·lec·tro·mag·net·ic (i lek′trō mag net′ik) *adj.* **1.** of or produced by an electromagnet. **2.** of or relating to electromagnetism.

electromagnetic radiation, energy that produces varying electric and magnetic fields as it travels through space from its source to a receiver. X rays, light waves, and radio waves are types of electromagnetic radiation.

electromagnetic wave, wave that consists of varying electric and magnetic fields and that can travel through empty space. Radio waves, light rays, and X rays are electromagnetic waves.

e·lec·tro·mag·net·ism (i lek′trō mag′nə tiz′əm) *n.* **1.** magnetism produced by a current of electricity. **2.** branch of physics that studies the relation between magnetism and electricity.

e·lec·tro·met·al·lur·gy (i lek′trō met′əl ur′jē) *n.* use of electricity in various processes of producing and refining metals.

e·lec·trom·e·ter (i lek′trom′ə tər, ē′lek-) *n.* instrument for measuring electric-potential difference or radiation that ionizes atoms or molecules. [ELECTRO- + -METER.]

e·lec·tro·mo·tive (i lek′trə mō′tiv) *adj.* **1.** producing a flow of electricity. **2.** of or relating to electromotive force.

electromotive force 1. force that causes electric current to flow in a circuit. **2.** amount of energy derived from an electric source.

e·lec·tro·mo·tor (i lek′trə mō′tər) *n.* electric motor.

e·lec·tron (i lek′tron) *n.* subatomic particle that carries the smallest negative electric charge. See **subatomic particle** for table. [Greek *ēlektron* amber. See ELECTRIC.]

e·lec·tro·neg·a·tive (i lek′trō neg′ə tiv) *adj.* **1.** having a negative electric charge. **2.** tending to move to the positive pole, or anode, in electrolysis. **3.** nonmetallic.

electron gun, device consisting of a series of electrodes at one end of a cathode-ray tube, such as a television picture tube, that emits and focuses a beam of electrons.

e·lec·tron·ic (i lek′tron′ik, ē′lek-) *adj.* **1.** of or relating to electrons or electronics. **2.** produced or operating by the action of electrons, as in a radio or radar. —**e·lec′tron′i·cal·ly,** *adv.*

e·lec·tron·ics (i lek′tron′iks, ē′lek-) *n.,pl.* scientific study and practical application of the motion of electrons and other charged particles in a vacuum and in gases, including such motion through empty spaces in the crystalline structure of semiconducting materials. ▲ construed as singular.

electron microscope, device that produces magnified images by means of a beam of electrons rather than a beam of light. It has much higher power than an ordinary microscope.

electron tube, sealed container in which electrons move through a vacuum or gas, used to produce, amplify, or regulate electrical signals.

electron volt, amount of energy gained by an electron when it is accelerated through a potential difference of one volt.

e·lec·troph·o·rus (i lek′trof′ər əs, ē′lek-) *pl.,* **-troph·o·ri** (-trof′ə rī′). *n.* device for generating charges of static electricity by means of induction. [ELECTRO- + Greek *-phoros* bearing.]

e·lec·tro·plate (i lek′trə plāt′) **-plat·ed, -plat·ing.** *v.t.* to apply a metal coating to the surface of (an object) by means of electrolysis. —*n.* any article, esp. silverware, coated in this way. —**e·lec′tro·plat′er,** *n.*

e·lec·tro·pos·i·tive (i lek′trō poz′ə tiv) *adj.* **1.** charged with positive electricity. **2.** tending to move to the negative pole, or cathode, in electrolysis. **3.** basic; metallic.

e·lec·tro·scope (i lek′trə skōp′) *n.* instrument used to detect and measure electric charges.

e·lec·tro·shock (i lek′trə shok′) *n.* shock therapy in which an electric current is passed through the brain.

e·lec·tro·stat·ic (i lek′trə stat′ik) *adj.* of or relating to electricity at rest or static electric charges.

e·lec·tro·stat·ics (i lek′trə stat′iks) *n.,pl.* branch of physics that studies static electricity. ▲ construed as singular.

e·lec·tro·ther·a·py (i lek′trō ther′ə pē) *n.* use of electricity in treating various mental or physical disorders.

e·lec·tro·type (i lek′trə tīp′) *n.* **1.** duplicate of a printing plate made by the electroplating process. **2.** print made from such a plate. —*v.t., v.i.* **-typed, -typ·ing.** to make such a plate or plates (of). —**e·lec′tro·typ′er,** *n.*

e·lec·tro·va·lent bond (i lek′trō vā′lənt) chemical bond formed between ions of opposite electric charge.

e·lec·trum (i lek′trəm) *n.* natural pale-yellow alloy of gold and silver,

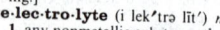

used in ancient times. [Latin *ēlectrum* amber, from Greek *ēlektron*.]

e·lec·tu·ar·y (i lek′chōō er′ē) *pl.*, **-ar·ies.** *n.* medicinal paste made by mixing powdered drugs with syrup or honey and water. [Late Latin *ēlectuārium*, probably modification of Greek *ekleikton*, from *ekleichein* to lick up.]

el·ee·mos·y·nar·y (el′ə mos′ə ner′ē, el′ē ə-) *adj.* **1.** of or relating to charity or alms; charitable. **2.** provided or given as an act of charity; free: *an eleemosynary supply of clothing.* **3.** relying on or supported by charity: *eleemosynary travelers.* [Late Latin *eleēmosynārius* almoner, from Latin *eleēmosyna* alms, from Greek *eleēmosynē* pity.]

el·e·gance (el′ə gəns) *n.* **1.** state or quality of being elegant. **2.** something elegant.

el·e·gan·cy (el′ə gən sē) *pl.*, **-cies.** *n.* elegance.

el·e·gant (el′ə gənt) *adj.* **1.** characterized by tasteful richness, as in dress or furnishings; luxurious. **2.** characterized by grace and refinement, as in manners, taste, or style; polished. **3.** characterized by simplicity and precision. **4.** *Informal.* excellent; fine. [Latin *ēlegāns* tasteful, nice.] —**el′e·gant·ly,** *adv.* —**Syn. 2.** see **graceful.**

el·e·gi·ac (el′ə jī′ak, i lē′jē ak′) *adj.* **1.** of, relating to, or suitable for an elegy. **2.** expressing sorrow or lamentation; mournful; plaintive. **3.** written in elegiacs. —*n.,pl.* **elegiacs.** in classical verse, two lines of dactylic hexameter, the second line of which has only one long or accented syllable in the third and sixth feet.

el·e·gize (el′ə jīz′) **-gized, -giz·ing.** *v.t.* to lament or commemorate in or as in an elegy. —*v.i.* to write an elegy.

el·e·gy (el′ə jē) *pl.*, **-gies.** *n.* **1.** mournful or melancholy poem or musical composition, esp. a lament for the dead. **2.** poem written in elegiacs. [Latin *elegīa* poetic lament, elegiac poem, from Greek *elegeiā*.] —**el′e·gist,** *n.*

elem. 1. element; elements. **2.** elementary.

el·e·ment (el′ə mənt) *n.* **1.** substance that cannot be changed into a less complex substance or substances by ordinary chemical means, such as iron, carbon, oxygen, and hydrogen; substance consisting entirely of atoms having the same atomic number. ▲ See table of elements below. Periodic table of elements appears on the following page. **2.** component or feature of a whole; fundamental part. **3.** natural, suitable, or comfortable environment: *The theater is his real element.* **4.** any of the four substances, earth, water, air, and fire, formerly regarded as composing all physical matter. **5.** any member of a given mathematical set. **6. elements.** bread and wine used in Holy Communion. **7.** *also,* **elements.** part of a military force: *Air elements preceded the ground forces.* **8. the elements.** atmospheric forces, as rain, wind, or snow. [Latin *elementum* first principle, rudiment.]

el·e·men·tal (el′ə ment′əl) *adj.* **1.** of or relating to all or any of the four elements, earth, water, air, and fire. **2.** of or like the forces of nature; primal and powerful. **3.** being an indispensable or integral part; essential. **4.** simple; rudimentary: *the elemental reasoning of a young child.* **5.** of or relating to chemical elements rather than compounds.

el·e·men·ta·ry (el′ə men′tər ē, -trē) *adj.* **1.** relating to or dealing with the fundamentals or first principles of something; basic. **2.** simple and rudimentary. **3.** composed of only one element; not compounded. **Syn. 1. Elementary, fundamental, introductory, rudimentary** indicate the early stages of something or some process. **Elementary** suggests what must necessarily come before anything else: *How can you expect to succeed without even the most elementary knowledge of the field?* **Fundamental** suggests the basic structure, usually a logical or an abstract one, on which something is built: *The first weeks of football practice are spent on fundamental skills like blocking.* **Introductory** implies a preliminary to something more advanced: *The introductory readings in French literature have a simple vocabulary.* **Rudimentary**

ELEMENTS

ELEMENT[1]	SYMBOL	ATOMIC NUMBER	ATOMIC WEIGHT[2]	ELEMENT[1]	SYMBOL	ATOMIC NUMBER	ATOMIC WEIGHT[2]	ELEMENT[1]	SYMBOL	ATOMIC NUMBER	ATOMIC WEIGHT[2]
Actinium	Ac	89	227[3]	Germanium	Ge	32	72.59	Praseodymium	Pr	59	140.907
Aluminum	Al	13	26.982	Gold	Au	79	196.967	Promethium	Pm	61	147[6]
Americium	Am	95	243[3]	Hafnium	Hf	72	178.49	Protactinium	Pa	91	231[3]
Antimony	Sb	51	121.75	Helium	He	2	4.0026	Radium	Ra	88	226[3]
Argon	Ar	18	39.948	Holmium	Ho	67	164.93	Radon	Rn	86	222[3]
Arsenic	As	33	74.922	Hydrogen	H	1	1.00797	Rhenium	Re	75	186.2
Astatine	At	85	210[3]	Indium	In	49	114.82	Rhodium	Rh	45	102.905
Barium	Ba	56	137.34	Iodine	I	53	126.904	Rubidium	Rb	37	85.47
Berkelium	Bk	97	247[3]	Iridium	Ir	77	192.2	Ruthenium	Ru	44	101.07
Beryllium	Be	4	9.012	Iron	Fe	26	55.847[5]	Samarium	Sm	62	150.35
Bismuth	Bi	83	208.98				±0.003	Scandium	Sc	21	44.956
Boron	B	5	10.811[4]	Krypton	Kr	36	83.80	Selenium	Se	34	78.96
			±0.003	Lanthanum	La	57	138.91	Silicon	Si	14	28.086[4]
Bromine	Br	35	79.909[5]	Lawrencium	Lr	103	257[3]				±0.001
			±0.002	Lead	Pb	82	207.19	Silver	Ag	47	107.87[5]
Cadmium	Cd	48	112.4	Lithium	Li	3	6.939				±0.003
Calcium	Ca	20	40.08	Lutetium	Lu	71	174.97	Sodium	Na	11	22.99
Californium	Cf	98	251[3]	Magnesium	Mg	12	24.312	Strontium	Sr	38	87.62
Carbon	C	6	12.011	Manganese	Mn	25	54.938	Sulfur	S	16	32.064
Cerium	Ce	58	140.12	Mendelevium	Md	101	258[3]				±0.003
Cesium	Cs	55	132.905	Mercury	Hg	80	200.59	Tantalum	Ta	73	180.948
Chlorine	Cl	17	35.453[5]	Molybdenum	Mo	42	95.94	Technetium	Tc	43	99[3]
			±0.001	Neodymium	Nd	60	144.24	Tellurium	Te	52	127.6
Chromium	Cr	24	51.996[5]	Neon	Ne	10	20.183	Terbium	Tb	65	158.924
			±0.001	Neptunium	Np	93	237[3]	Thallium	Tl	81	204.37
Cobalt	Co	27	58.933	Nickel	Ni	28	58.71	Thorium	Th	90	232.038
Copper	Cu	29	63.54	Niobium	Nb	41	92.906	Thulium	Tm	69	168.934
Curium	Cm	96	247[3]	Nitrogen	N	7	14.0067	Tin	Sn	50	118.69
Dysprosium	Dy	66	162.50	Nobelium	No	102	254[6]	Titanium	Ti	22	47.9
Einsteinium	Es	99	254[3]	Osmium	Os	76	190.2	Tungsten	W	74	183.85
Erbium	Er	68	167.26	Oxygen	O	8	15.9994	Uranium	U	92	238.03
Europium	Eu	63	151.96	Palladium	Pd	46	106.4	Vanadium	V	23	50.942
Fermium	Fm	100	253[3]	Phosphorus	P	15	30.974	Xenon	Xe	54	131.3
Fluorine	F	9	18.998	Platinum	Pt	78	195.09	Ytterbium	Yb	70	173.04
Francium	Fr	87	223[3]	Plutonium	Pu	94	242[3]	Yttrium	Y	39	88.905
Gadolinium	Gd	64	157.25	Polonium	Po	84	210[6]	Zinc	Zn	30	65.37
Gallium	Ga	31	69.72	Potassium	K	19	39.102	Zirconium	Zr	40	91.22

[1] Elements of atomic numbers 104 and 105 have been tentatively named rutherfordium (104) and hahnium (105) but these names were not official as of January, 1971.

[2] Atomic weights are based upon carbon-12.

[3] Mass number of isotope with longest half-life.

[4] Atomic weight varies.

[5] Figure inexact because of experimental error.

[6] Mass number of best-known isotope.

at; āpe; cär; end; mē; it; īce; hot; ōld; fôrk; wood; fōol; oil; out; up; ūse; turn; sing; thin; this; zh in treasure; ə in ago, taken, pencil, lemon, circus.

PERIODIC TABLE OF THE ELEMENTS

KEY

Atomic number → 56 Ba ← Symbol for element
*Atomic weight 137.34

IA																		0
1 H 1.00797	IIA											IIIA	IVA	VA	VIA	VIIA		2 He 4.0026
3 Li 6.939	4 Be 9.0122				TRANSITION ELEMENTS							5 B 10.811	6 C 12.01115	7 N 14.0067	8 O 15.9994	9 F 18.9984	10 Ne 20.183
11 Na 22.9898	12 Mg 24.312	IIIB	IVB	VB	VIB	VIIB		VIII		IB	IIB	13 Al 26.9815	14 Si 28.086	15 P 30.9738	16 S 32.064	17 Cl 35.453	18 Ar 39.948
19 K 39.102	20 Ca 40.08	21 Sc 44.956	22 Ti 47.90	23 V 50.942	24 Cr 51.996	25 Mn 54.938	26 Fe 55.847	27 Co 58.9332	28 Ni 58.71	29 Cu 63.54	30 Zn 65.37	31 Ga 69.72	32 Ge 72.59	33 As 74.9216	34 Se 78.96	35 Br 79.909	36 Kr 83.8
37 Rb 85.47	38 Sr 87.62	39 Y 88.905	40 Zr 91.22	41 Nb 92.906	42 Mo 95.94	43 Tc (99)	44 Ru 101.07	45 Rh 102.905	46 Pd 106.4	47 Ag 107.87	48 Cd 112.4	49 In 114.82	50 Sn 118.69	51 Sb 121.75	52 Te 127.6	53 I 126.9044	54 Xe 131.3
55 Cs 132.905	56 Ba 137.34	57-71 La	72 Hf 178.49	73 Ta 180.948	74 W 183.85	75 Re 186.2	76 Os 190.2	77 Ir 192.2	78 Pt 195.09	79 Au 196.967	80 Hg 200.59	81 Tl 204.37	82 Pb 207.19	83 Bi 208.98	84 Po (210)	85 At (210)	86 Rn (222)
87 Fr (223)	88 Ra (226)	89-103 Ac	104 **	105 ***													

**proposed names: kurchatovium, rutherfordium
***proposed name: hahnium

LANTHANIDE SERIES	57 La 138.91	58 Ce 140.12	59 Pr 140.907	60 Nd 144.24	61 Pm (145)	62 Sm 150.35	63 Eu 151.96	64 Gd 157.25	65 Tb 158.924	66 Dy 162.5	67 Ho 164.93	68 Er 167.26	69 Tm 168.934	70 Yb 173.04	71 Lu 174.97
ACTINIDE SERIES	89 Ac (227)	90 Th 232.038	91 Pa (231)	92 U 238.03	93 Np (237)	94 Pu (242)	95 Am (243)	96 Cm (247)	97 Bk (247)	98 Cf (251)	99 Es (254)	100 Fm (253)	101 Md (258)	102 No (254)	103 Lr (257)

*For radioactive elements, the mass number of the longest-lived isotope is given in parentheses.

suggests lack of development, with the implication that something more advanced will evolve: *The rudimentary skills of skiing are best learned on the lower slopes.*

el·e·men·ta·ry particle, sub-atomic particle.

el·e·men·ta·ry school, school including the first six or eight grades and sometimes having a kindergarten. Also, **grade school, grammar school.**

African elephant   Indian elephant

el·e·phant (el′ə fənt) *pl.* **-phants** or **-phant.** *n.* any of various thick-skinned mammals, family Elephantidae, native to the tropical regions of Africa and Asia, having a massive head and body, a long, muscular trunk, a pair of ivory tusks, and large, fanlike ears. [Old French *olifant, elefant* elephant, ivory, from Latin *elephantus,* from Greek *elephās,* possibly from Phoenician *āleph* ox.]

elephant bird, any of several extinct, flightless birds that were native to Madagascar. One species grew to a height of almost nine feet.

el·e·phan·ti·a·sis (el′ə fan tī′ə sis) *n.* permanent enlargement and thickening of the skin in parts of the body, esp. the lower extremities, usually caused by parasitic worms that block the flow of lymph. [Latin *elephantiāsis,* going back to Greek *elephās* elephant; because the diseased skin resembles that of an elephant. See ELEPHANT.]

el·e·phan·tine (el′ə fan′tīn, -tīn) *adj.* **1.** like an elephant in size, strength, or movement; huge. **2.** of or relating to an elephant.

el·e·phant's-ear (el′ə fənts ēr′) *n.* any of various plants with large heart-shaped leaves, as the taro, begonia, or caladium.

El·eu·sin·i·an mysteries (el′yoo sin′ē ən) one of the most important religious rites of ancient Greece, honoring Demeter and Persephone and celebrating the annual regeneration of crops.

el·e·vate (el′ə vāt′) **-vat·ed, -vat·ing.** *v.t.* **1.** to raise; lift up. **2.** to raise or improve the moral, intellectual, or cultural level of: *His inspiring speech elevated the audience.* **3.** to raise (a person) in rank or station: *The clerk was elevated to a managerial position.* **4.** to raise the spirits of; cheer up; elate. **5.** to raise the pitch or volume of (the voice). [Latin *elevātus,* past participle of *elevāre* to raise, lift up.] —**Syn. 1.** see **lift.**

el·e·vat·ed (el′ə vā′tid) *adj.* **1.** raised; lifted up; high. **2.** characterized by dignity and refinement; noble. **3.** in high spirits; joyful; elated.

elevated railroad, railroad operating above the ground on an elevated structure, allowing traffic to pass freely underneath.

el·e·va·tion (el′ə vā′shən) *n.* **1.** act of elevating; being elevated. **2.** that which is elevated, as an elevated place. **3.** height above any given

point, esp. above the earth's surface or above sea level; altitude: *The jet reached an elevation of 30,000 feet.* **4.** loftiness; dignity; nobility. **5.** scale drawing in a vertical plane of the front, rear, or side view of a building, machine, or other structure. —**Syn. 3.** see **height.**

el·e·va·tor (el′ə vā′tər) *n.* **1.** movable platform or cage and its hoisting machinery, used for carrying people and things from one level to another, esp. between floors in a building. **2.** anything that raises or lifts up. **3.** building for handling and storing grain or other crops. **4.** airfoil on a horizontal stabilizer of an airplane. See **airplane** for illustration.

e·lev·en (i lev′ən) *n.* **1.** the cardinal number that is one more than ten. **2.** symbol representing this number, as 11 or XI. **3.** something having this many units or members, as a football team. —*adj.* numbering one more than ten. [Old English *endleofan* literally, one left (after ten).]

e·lev·enth (i lev′ənth) *adj.* **1.** (the ordinal of eleven) next after the tenth. **2.** being one of eleven equal parts. —*n.* one of eleven equal parts; $\frac{1}{11}$.

eleventh hour, the last possible moment; just before it is too late.

elf (elf) *pl.* **elves** (elvz). *n.* **1.** small, often mischievous fairy or sprite having magical powers. **2.** small or mischievous person. [Old English *ælf* from Germanic.]

elf·in (el′fin) *adj.* of, characteristic of, or resembling an elf; impish; mischievous: *elfin laughter.* —*n.* elf.

elf·ish (el′fish) also, **elv·ish.** *adj.* elfin. —**elf′ish·ly,** *adv.* —**elf′ish·ness,** *n.*

elf·lock (elf′lok′) *n.* lock of hair tangled as if by elves.

El·gin (el′jin) *n.* city in northeastern Illinois. Pop. (1970), 55,691.

El Gre·co (el grek′ō) c.1541–1614, Spanish painter born in Crete. He was born Domenikos Theotokopoulos.

E·li (ē′lī) *n.* in the Old Testament, the judge and high priest of Israel who trained Samuel to become the leader of Israel.

E·li·a (ē′lē ə) *n.* see **Lamb, Charles.**

E·li·as (i lī′əs) *n.* Elijah.

e·lic·it (i lis′it) *v.t.* to draw forth or bring out; evoke; educe. [Latin *ēlicitus,* past participle of *ēlicere* to draw out.] —**e·lic′i·ta′tion,** *n.*

e·lide (i līd′) **e·lid·ed, e·lid·ing.** *v.t.* **1.** to omit or slur over (a vowel or syllable) in pronunciation. **2.** to suppress; omit. [Latin *ēlīdere* to strike out.]

el·i·gi·bil·i·ty (el′i jə bil′ə tē) *n.* quality or state of being eligible.

el·i·gi·ble (el′i jə bəl) *adj.* **1.** qualified or fit to be chosen. **2.** desirable or suitable, esp. for marriage. **3.** qualified for or allowed to perform some function: *Only citizens are eligible to vote.* —*n.* an eligible person. [French *éligible,* modeled, from Late Latin *ēligibilis* to be preferred, from Latin *ēligere* to choose.] —**el′i·gi·bly,** *adv.*

E·li·jah (i lī′jə) *n.* in the Old Testament, great Hebrew prophet of

at; āpe; cär; end; mē; it; īce; hot; ōld; fôrk; wood; fool; oil; out; up; ūse; turn; sing; thin; this; zh in treasure; ə in ago, taken, pencil, lemon, circus.

the ninth century B.C. who did not die but was carried bodily into heaven in a fiery chariot.

e·lim·i·nate (i lim′ə nāt′) -nat·ed, -nat·ing. *v.t.* **1.** to get rid of; dispose of. **2.** to leave out of consideration; disregard. **3.** to expel (waste materials) from the body; excrete. **4.** to cause (an opponent or team) to be removed from competition by defeating. **5.** *Mathematics.* to remove (an unknown quantity) by combining two or more of the equations in which it occurs. [Latin *ēlīminātus,* past participle of *ēlīmināre* to expel, from *ex* out + *līmen* threshold.] —**Syn. 1.** see **exclude.**

e·lim·i·na·tion (i lim′ə nā′shən) *n.* act or process of eliminating; being eliminated.

El·i·ot (el′ē ət, el′yət) **1. George.** 1819–80, English novelist, born Mary Ann Evans. **2. T(homas) S(tearns).** 1888–1965, English poet, essayist, and critic, born in the United States.

E·lis·a·beth·ville (i liz′ə bəth vil′) see **Lubumbashi.**

E·li·sha (i lī′shə) *n.* in the Old Testament, Hebrew prophet of the ninth century B.C. and successor of Elijah.

e·li·sion (i lizh′ən) *n.* **1.** act or instance of eliding. **2.** suppression or omission of a vowel or a syllable in pronouncing.

e·lite (ā lēt′, i lēt′) *also,* **é·lite.** *n.* **1.** best or most distinguished members, as of a society or social group. **2.** size of type for typewriters providing six lines to the vertical inch and twelve characters to the linear inch. [French *élite* select few, from *élire* to choose, going back to Latin *ēligere.*]

e·lix·ir (i lik′sər) *n.* **1.** in medieval alchemy, substance that was believed able to change base metals, as iron and lead, into gold or to prolong life indefinitely. Also, **philosopher's stone. 2.** sweetened alcoholic solution containing medicine. **3.** cure-all; panacea. **4.** pure essence or essential principle. [Medieval Latin *elixir* the philosopher's stone, from Arabic *al-iksīr,* probably from *al* the + Greek *xērion* dry powder for wounds.]

E·liz·a·beth (i liz′ə bəth) *n.* city in northeastern New Jersey. Pop. (1970), 112,654.

Elizabeth I, 1533–1603, queen of England from 1558 to 1603; daughter of Henry VIII and Anne Boleyn.

Elizabeth II, 1926—, queen of Great Britain and head of the British Commonwealth of Nations since 1952.

E·liz·a·be·than (i liz′ə bē′thən, -beth′ən) *adj.* of, relating to, or characteristic of Queen Elizabeth I of England or her era. —*n.* English person who lived during this time, esp. a writer.

Elizabethan sonnet, Shakespearean sonnet.

elk (elk) *pl.* **elk** *or* **elks.** *n.* **1.** large deer, *Cervus canadensis,* of the mountain regions of western North America, having a predominantly fawn-colored coat. The male has antlers measuring more than 5 feet across. Height: 5 feet at the shoulder. Also, **wap′i·ti. 2.** any of several varieties of large deer native to northern Europe and Asia, of the same species as but larger than the North American moose. [Old English *eolh* a large deer of northern Europe.]

Elk

ell¹ (el) *n.* **1.** the letter L. **2.a.** anything shaped like an L. **b.** extension or wing built at right angles to the main part of a building. [Phonetic representation of letter *l.*]

ell² (el) *n.* formerly, a measure of length, chiefly used in measuring cloth, ranging in length from 27 inches in Holland to 45 inches in England. [Old English *eln* length of the forearm, cubit.]

Elles·mere (elz′mēr) *n.* large Canadian island in the Arctic Ocean northwest of Greenland, the northernmost island of North America. Area, 82,119 sq. mi. Pop. (1961), 141.

el·lipse (i lips′) *n.* closed curve consisting of a set of points in a plane whose respective distances from two fixed points add up to a fixed sum; conic section formed by the intersection of a cone by a plane not parallel to or intersecting the base. [Latin *ellipsis,* from Greek *elleipsis* a falling short, defect, ellipse; because its plane forms with the base of the cone an angle falling short of, or less than, the angle formed by the intersecting plane making a parabola.]

Ellipse
$$AX + AY = BX + BY = CX + CY$$

el·lip·sis (i lip′sis) *pl.,* **-ses** (-sēz). *n.* **1.** omission of a word or words strictly required by grammatical rules to complete the construction of a sentence, but not necessary for comprehending its meaning. *He arrived sooner than expected* instead of *He arrived sooner than he had been expected to arrive* is ellipsis. **2.** mark (. . ., ***, or —) indicating an

omission in writing or printing. [Latin *ellipsis* defect, ellipse. See EL-LIPSE.]

el·lip·soid (i lip′soid) *n.* **1.** solid whose plane sections are all ellipses or circles. **2.** surface of such a solid. —*adj.* relating to or resembling an ellipsoid. Also, **el·lip′soid′al,** *adj.*

el·lip·ti·cal (i lip′ti kəl) *adj.* **1.** of, relating to, or shaped like an ellipse. **2.** of, relating to, or characterized by ellipsis; with a word or words omitted. Also, **el·lip′tic.** —**el·lip′ti·cal·ly,** *adv.*

El·lis, (Henry) Have·lock (el′is; hav′lok) 1859–1939, English psychologist and writer.

Ellis Island, small island in upper New York Bay, the chief U.S. immigrant reception center from 1892 to 1943.

elm (elm) *n.* **1.** any of a group of various tall, hardy trees, genus *Ulmus,* native to the Northern Hemisphere, often grown for ornament or shade. One of the best-known species is the **American elm,** *U. americana,* having a light-gray bark and oval leaves with saw-toothed edges. **2.** the moderately hard, heavy wood of this tree. [Old English *elm* this tree.]

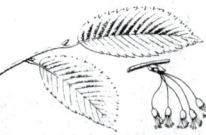

Elm leaves and flowers

Elm·hurst (elm′hurst′) *n.* city in northeastern Illinois. Pop. (1970), 50,547.

el·o·cu·tion (el′ə kū′shən) *n.* **1.** art of public speaking or recitation, including delivery, pronunciation, tone, and gesture. **2.** manner of speaking or reading in public. [Latin *ēlocūtiō* a speaking out, expression.] —**el′o·cu′tion·ar·y,** *adj.* —**el′o·cu′tion·ist,** *n.*

E·lo·him (e lō′him, el′ō hēm′) *n.* in the Old Testament, God. ▲ one of several terms used instead of Yahweh, which the Hebrews believed to be God's true name and too sacred to be spoken.

e·lon·gate (i lông′gāt) -gat·ed, -gat·ing. *v.t., v.i.* to increase in length; lengthen; stretch. —*adj.* **1.** lengthened; stretched. **2.** slender or tapering: *an elongate leaf, an elongate snout.* [Late Latin *ēlongātus,* past participle of *ēlongāre* to prolong, from Latin *ex* out + *longus* long.]

e·lon·ga·tion (i lông′gā′shən, ē′lông-) *n.* **1.** act of elongating; being elongated. **2.** that which is elongated; extension; continuation.

e·lope (i lōp′) **e·loped, e·lop·ing.** *v.i.* **1.** to run away secretly with one's lover, esp. to get married. **2.** to run away; abscond. [Anglo-Norman *aloper,* possibly going back to Latin *ex* away + Middle Dutch *lōpen* to run.] —**e·lope′ment,** **e·lop′er,** *n.*

el·o·quence (el′ə kwəns) *n.* **1.** expressive, effective, and stirring language, as in public speaking: *The speech was full of eloquence and fire.* **2.** art of using such language. **3.** power or quality of being expressive, effective, and stirring: *The eloquence of his plea aroused our sympathy.*

el·o·quent (el′ə kwənt) *adj.* possessing or characterized by eloquence: *an eloquent orator, an eloquent plea.* [Old French *eloquent,* from Latin *ēloquēns,* present participle of *ēloquī* to speak out.] —**el′o·quent·ly,** *adv.*

El Pas·o (el pas′ō) city in westernmost Texas, on the Rio Grande. Pop. (1970), 322,261.

El Sal·va·dor (el sal′və dôr′) country in western Central America. Capital, San Salvador. Area, 8,260 sq. mi. Pop. (1969 est.), 3,390,000. Also, **Sal′va·dor′.**

else (els) *adj.* **1.** other; different: *She reminds me of someone else.* **2.** additional; more; further: *If anyone else comes, we won't have enough chairs.* —*adv.* **1.** in another time, place, or manner; instead: *Where else can we meet?* **2.** under other circumstances; if not; otherwise: *Dress warmly, or else you'll catch cold.* [Old English *elles* otherwise.]

else·where (els′hwâr′, -wâr′) *adv.* in, at, or to another place; somewhere or anywhere else: *This plant is not found elsewhere.*

e·lu·ci·date (i lōō′sə dāt′) -dat·ed, -dat·ing. *v.t.* to make clear; explain: *The senator elucidated his position on foreign policy.* [Late Latin *ēlūcidātus,* past participle of *ēlūcidāre* to enlighten, from Latin *ex* utterly + *lūcidus* bright.] —**e·lu′ci·da′tion,** *n.* —**Syn.** see **interpret.**

e·lude (i lōōd′) **e·lud·ed, e·lud·ing.** *v.t.* **1.** to avoid or escape, as by dexterity or trickery; evade: *The bandit eluded the police.* **2.** to escape discovery, identification, or comprehension by: *The answer to the riddle has eluded us.* [Latin *ēlūdere* to deceive, from *ex* out, away + *lūdere* to play.]

e·lu·sion (i lōō′zhən) *n.* act of eluding; evasion. [Medieval Latin *elusio,* from Latin *ēlūdere* to deceive. See ELUDE.]

e·lu·sive (i lōō′siv) *adj.* **1.** difficult to explain, define, or grasp: *an elusive idea.* **2.** difficult to catch or apprehend: *an elusive criminal.* Also, **e·lu·so·ry** (i lōō′sər ē). —**e·lu′sive·ly,** *adv.* —**e·lu′sive·ness,** *n.*

el·ver (el′vər) *n.* young eel. [Form of earlier *eelfare* brood of young eels, journey of young eels up a river, going back to Old English *ǣl* eel + *fær* journey.]

elves (elvz) plural of **elf.**

elv·ish (el′vish) *adj.* elfin; elfish.

at; āpe; cär; end; mē; it; īce; hot; ōld; fôrk; wood; fōōl; oil; out; up; ūse; turn; sing; thin; this; zh in treasure; ə in ago, taken, pencil, lemon, circus.

E·ly (ē′lē) n. town in eastern England, site of a famous ancient cathedral. Pop. (1968 est.), 10,100.

E·lyr·i·a (i lēr′ē ə) n. city in northern Ohio. Pop. (1970), 53,427.

E·ly·sian (i lizh′ən) adj. **1.** of, relating to, or like Elysium. **2.** blissful; happy.

E·ly·sium (i lizh′əm, i liz′ē əm) n. **1.** Greek Mythology. a happy land where heroes and virtuous people live after death. Also, **Elysian Fields.** **2.** any place or condition of ideal or perfect happiness; paradise; heaven. [Latin *Elysium* the Elysian Fields, from Greek *Élysion (pedion)* Elysian (field).]

el·y·tron (el′ə tron′) pl., **-tra** (-trə). also, **el·y·trum** (el′ə trəm) n. one of the pair of hardened fore wings forming a protective covering over the hind wings in beetles and certain other insects. [Modern Latin *elytron*, from Greek *elytron* sheath.]

em (em) pl., **ems.** Printing. unit of measurement corresponding to the amount of line space occupied by a character that is as wide as the type size is high. A one-em dash in a ten-point font is ten points wide. [Originally referring to the amount of space occupied by the letter M in the various type fonts.]

'em (əm) pron. Informal. them.

em-¹, form of **en-¹** before b, p, and sometimes m, as in embroider, embark.

em-², form of **en-²** before b, m, p, ph, as in embargo, emphasis.

e·ma·ci·ate (i mā′shē āt′) **-at·ed, -at·ing.** v.t. to cause to become abnormally thin; cause to lose much weight or flesh: *emaciated by a long illness.* [Latin *emaciātus,* past participle of *emaciāre* to make thin, going back to *ex* utterly + *maciēs* thinness.] —**e·ma′ci·a′tion,** n.

em·a·nate (em′ə nāt′) **-nat·ed, -nat·ing.** v.i. to come forth or originate from a source; issue: *Light emanates from the sun.* —v.t. to send forth; emit. [Latin *ēmānātus,* past participle of *ēmānāre* to flow out.]

em·a·na·tion (em′ə nā′shən) n. **1.** act of emanating. **2.** that which emanates. **3.** gaseous product of a disintegrating radioactive substance, as thoron or radon.

e·man·ci·pate (i man′sə pāt′) **-pat·ed, -pat·ing.** v.t. to free from bondage, control, or restraint; liberate: *to emancipate a slave, to emancipate oneself from the limitations of conformity.* [Latin *ēmancipātus,* past participle of *ēmancipāre* to set free, going back to *ex* away + *manus* hand + *capere* to take. In ancient Roman custom, a father would take his son by the hand and then let him go, symbolizing the son's release from paternal control.] —**e·man′ci·pa′tion, e·man′ci·pa′tor,** n.

Emancipation Proclamation, proclamation by President Abraham Lincoln on January 1, 1863, that freed all slaves in territory still at war with the Union.

e·mas·cu·late (v., i mas′kyə lāt′; adj., i mas′kyə lit, -lāt′) **-lat·ed, -lat·ing.** v.t. **1.** to deprive of virility or procreative power; castrate. **2.** to deprive of strength, force, or vigor; weaken: *an earthy novel emasculated by censorship.* [Latin *ēmasculātus,* past participle of *ēmasculāre* to castrate, from *ex* out of, away + *musculus* male.] —**e·mas′cu·la′tion, e·mas′cu·la′tor,** n.

em·balm (em bäm′) v.t. **1.** to treat (a dead body) with certain antiseptics and preservatives to temporarily keep it from decaying. **2.** to preserve in fond memory. **3.** Archaic. to perfume. [Old French *embaumer* to annoint with balm or balsam, going back to Latin *in* in, among + *balsamum* balsam. See BALM, BALSAM.] —**em·balm′er,** n.

em·bank (em bangk′) v.t. to protect, enclose, or confine with an embankment, dike, or similar structure.

em·bank·ment (em bangk′mənt) n. **1.** bank of earth, stones, or other materials, used esp. to support a roadbed or to hold back water. **2.** act of embanking.

em·bar·go (em bär′gō) pl., **-goes.** n. **1.** order by a government restraining or prohibiting merchant ships from entering or leaving its ports. **2.** restriction imposed upon commerce by law, esp. upon the import,

Embankment

export, or sale of certain goods: *an embargo on the sale of arms to warring countries, an embargo on goods from Red China.* **3.** restriction; prohibition. —v.t., **-goed, -go·ing.** to put an embargo upon. [Spanish *embargo* arrest, seizure, going back to Latin *in* in + Late Latin *barra.* See BAR.]

em·bark (em bärk′) v.i. **1.** to go aboard a vessel for a trip: *The passengers embarked at San Francisco.* **2.** to set out, as on a venture or course of action: *to embark upon a dangerous undertaking.* —v.t. **1.** to put or take on board a vessel. **2.** to involve (a person) in, or invest (money) in, a commercial venture. [Old French *embarquer* to put on a boat, going back to Late Latin *barca* small boat.]

em·bar·ka·tion (em′bär kā′shən) also, **em·bar·ca·tion,** n. act of embarking.

em·bar·rass (em bar′əs) v.t. **1.** to cause to feel self-conscious, uncomfortable, or ashamed: *Her foolish mistake embarrassed her.* **2.** to burden with debt or financial difficulties. **3.** to encumber; impede. **4.** to make difficult or intricate; complicate. [French *embarrasser* to entangle, obstruct, trouble, through Spanish and Italian, going back to Latin *in* in + Late Latin *barra.* See BAR.]

em·bar·rass·ing (em bar′ə sing) adj. that embarrasses. —**bar′rass·ing·ly,** adv.

em·bar·rass·ment (em bar′əs mənt) n. **1.** act of embarrassing; being embarrassed. **2.** that which embarrasses.

em·bas·sa·dor (em bas′ə dər) n. Archaic. ambassador.

em·bas·sage (em′bə sij) n. Archaic. embassy.

em·bas·sy (em′bə sē) pl., **-sies.** n. **1.** official residence or headquarters of an ambassador in a foreign country. **2.** an ambassador and his staff: *The embassy gave a reception for the visiting dignitaries.* **3.** position or functions of an ambassador. **4.** group of officials charged with a diplomatic assignment to a foreign country: *The king received an embassy from the Vatican.* [Old French *ambassee* mission, delegation, going back to Medieval Latin *ambactia* mission; of Celtic origin.]

em·bat·tle¹ (em bat′əl) **-tled, -tling.** v.t. **1.** to prepare or equip for battle; arrange in battle order. **2.** to prepare for any conflict or struggle; be ready to fight. [Old French *embataillier* to prepare for battle, from *em-* in (from Latin *in*) + *bataille.* See BATTLE.]

em·bat·tle² (em bat′əl) **-tled, -tling.** v.t. to furnish with battlements. [EM-¹ + Old French *bataillier* to furnish with battlements, from *batailles* battlements, plural of *bataille.* See BATTLE.]

em·bay (em bā′) v.t. **1.** to put or force (a vessel) into a bay, as for shelter. **2.** to surround or enclose, as in a bay: *He found himself embayed in a labyrinth* (Bancroft, 1876).

em·bed (em bed′) **-bed·ded, -bed·ding.** also, **im·bed.** v.t. **1.** to set or enclose in a surrounding mass: *The pole was embedded in cement. The arrow was embedded in the tree.* **2.** to instill; implant: *for reasons deeply embedded in the nation's history* (Manchester, 1968). *The idea was embedded in her mind.*

em·bel·lish (em bel′ish) v.t. **1.** to beautify with ornamentation; decorate; adorn: *The jewel case was embellished with pearls and rubies.* **2.** to make (a narrative) more interesting by adding details, usually of a fictitious nature; embroider. [Old French *embelliss-,* a stem of *embellir* to beautify, going back to Latin *in* in + *bellus* handsome.] —**em·bel′lish·ment,** n.

em·ber (em′bər) n. **1.** fragment of wood or coal, smoldering in the ashes of a fire. **2.** embers, smoldering remains of a fire. [Old English *æmerge.*]

Ember days, three days of fasting and prayer observed quarterly by the Anglican Church, certain other Western churches, and, formerly, by the Roman Catholic Church. They occur on the Wednesday, Friday, and Saturday after the first Sunday in Lent, after Pentecost Sunday, after September 14, and after December 13. [Old English *ymbrendagas,* from *ymbryne* period, circuit; literally, a running around (with reference to seasonal fasting) + *dæg* day.]

em·bez·zle (em bez′əl) **-zled, -zling.** v.t. to appropriate by fraud (something entrusted to one's care), esp. money or stocks and bonds: *The bank official embezzled funds.* [Anglo-Norman *enbeseiller* to do away with, destroy, from Old French *en-* in (from Latin *in*) + *besiler* to destroy (of uncertain origin).] —**em·bez′zle·ment, em·bez′zler,** n.

em·bit·ter (em bit′ər) v.t. to make bitter or more bitter: *The failure of his business embittered him.*

em·bla·zon (em blā′zən) v.t. **1.** to inscribe or decorate, esp. with a heraldic device: *a shield emblazoned with a coat of arms.* **2.** to adorn or illuminate with bright colors: *The orbs which emblazoned the canopy of heaven* (Blakey, 1831). **3.** to extol; celebrate: *His deeds were emblazoned by the poets.* —**em·bla′zon·ment,** n.

em·bla·zon·ry (em blā′zən rē) pl., **-ries.** n. **1.** act or art of emblazoning with heraldic devices. **2.** heraldic devices collectively. **3.** brightly colored decoration or display.

em·blem (em′bləm) n. **1.** object, or representation of it, which embodies or personifies something abstract; symbol: *The crown is an emblem of monarchy.* **2.** object or symbolic figure used to identify or represent something: *The soldier wore the emblem of his regiment.* [Latin *emblēma* raised ornament, from Greek *emblēma* embossed ornament.]

em·blem·at·ic (em′blə mat′ik) adj. of, relating to, or serving as an emblem; symbolic: *A gold medal is emblematic of first place in the Olympic games.* Also, **em′blem·at′i·cal.**

em·bod·i·ment (em bod′ē mənt) n. **1.** act of embodying; being embodied. **2.** one who or that which embodies something: *Satan is the embodiment of evil.*

em·bod·y (em bod′ē) **-bod·ied, -bod·y·ing.** v.t. **1.** to give concrete form to: *The old soldier embodied her idea of patriotism.* **2.** to collect

at; āpe; cär; end; mē; it; īce; hot; ōld; fôrk; wood; fō̄ol; oil; out; up; ūse; turn; sing; thin; this; zh in treasure; ə in ago, taken, pencil, lemon, circus.

into, or make part of, an organized whole; incorporate: *The experiments of ten scientists were embodied in the report.* —**Syn. 2. Embody, incorporate, include, embrace** indicate a taking in of something else. **Embody** suggests a thing that already exists or is being assembled and is augmented by the addition: *Not all of President Wilson's Fourteen Points were embodied in the Versailles Treaty.* **Incorporate** implies absorption and assimilation so that the result is uniform or integral: *All their suggestions were incorporated in the final draft of the memorandum.* **Include** suggests only that the thing taken in is contained in the end result: *He detests a salad that includes garlic.* **Embrace** implies that the thing taken in is encompassed: *Primitive art embraces many forms, many peoples, and many ages.*

em·bold·en (em bōld′ən) *v.t.* to make bold or bolder; hearten; encourage.

em·bo·lism (em′bə liz′əm) *n.* obstruction of a blood vessel by a mass of material carried in the blood, as a blood clot or a fat globule. [Late Latin *embolismus* insertion, from Late Greek *embolismos* intercalation, from Greek *emballein* to throw in.]

em·bo·lus (em′bə ləs) *pl.,* **-li** (-lī′). *n.* foreign matter, as a blood clot or fat globule, carried in the blood, causing an obstruction of a blood vessel. [Latin *embolus* piston of a pump, from Greek *embolos* stopper.]

em·bos·om (em booz′əm, -bōō′zəm) *v.t.* **1.** to take to one's heart or bosom; embrace; cherish. **2.** to surround protectively; shelter: *a house embosomed in the woods.*

em·boss (em bôs′, -bos′) *v.t.* **1.** to decorate or cover (a surface) with ornamentation in relief: *Her stationery was embossed with her initials.* **2.** to raise (ornamentation) in relief: *a fleur-de-lis embossed on silver.* [Old French *embosser* to swell in protuberances, from *en-* in (from Latin *in*) + *bosse, boce* protuberance. See BOSS².] —**em·boss′er, em·boss′-ment,** *n.*

em·bou·chure (äm bōō shoor′) *n.* **1.** mouth of a river. **2.** an opening out of a river valley into a plain. **3.a.** mouthpiece of a wind instrument. **b.** position and adjustment of the lips and tongue in playing a wind instrument. [French *embouchure* mouth, mouthpiece, opening, going back to Latin *in* in + *bucca* cheek, mouth.]

em·bow·er (em bou′ər) *v.t.* to cover or shelter in or as in a bower.

em·brace (em brās′) **-braced, -brac·ing.** *v.t.* **1.** to clasp or hold in the arms, esp. as a sign of love or affection; hug. **2.** to take up or adopt: *to embrace the Christian religion. He embraced medicine as his career.* **3.** to avail oneself of: *He eagerly embraced the opportunity for advancement.* **4.** to include; contain: *Botany embraces the study of all plant life.* **5.** to encircle; surround; enclose. —*v.i.* to hug one another: *The young lovers embraced.* —*n.* act of clasping or holding in the arms; hug. [Old French *embracer* to hug, seize, going back to Latin *in* in + *brachium* arm (from Greek *brachion* arm).] —**em·brace′a·ble,** *adj.* —**em·brace′ment,** *n.* —**Syn.** *v.t.* **4.** see **embody.**

em·bra·sure (em brā′zhər) *n.* **1.** opening in a wall or parapet through which a gun may be fired. The sides usually spread outward to permit the gun to be swung through a wider angle of fire. See **battlement** for illustration. **2.** opening in a wall, as for a window, having the sides slanted so that the inside outline is larger than the outside. [French *embrasure* opening of a window, recess, from *embraser* to widen; of uncertain origin.]

em·bro·cate (em′brō kāt′) **-cat·ed, -cat·ing.** *v.t.* to moisten and rub (a part of the body) with liniment or lotion. [Medieval Latin *embrocatus,* past participle of *embrocare* to moisten, from Late Latin *embrocha* lotion, from Greek *embrochē*.]

em·bro·ca·tion (em′brō kā′shən) *n.* **1.** act of embrocating. **2.** liniment or lotion used in embrocating.

em·broi·der (em broi′dər) *v.t.* **1.** to decorate (fabric or other material) with a design in needlework. **2.** to make (a design) on fabric or other material in needlework. **3.** to make (a narrative) more interesting by exaggerating or by adding fictitious details; embellish. —*v.i.* to do embroidery. [EM-¹ + archaic *broider* to ornament with needlework (from French *broder;* of Germanic origin).] —**em·broi′der·er,** *n.*

em·broi·der·y (em broi′dər ē, -drē) *pl.,* **-der·ies.** *n.* **1.** art of decorating fabric or other material with raised designs done in needlework. **2.** embroidered design or work.

em·broil (em broil′) *v.t.* **1.** to involve in conflict or strife: *He tried to embroil me in his quarrel.* **2.** to throw into confusion or disorder. [French *embrouiller* to confuse, from *en-* in (from Latin *in*) + *brouiller* to confuse (of uncertain origin).] —**em·broil′ment,** *n.*

em·bry·o (em′brē ō′) *pl.,* **-bry·os.** *n.* **1.** organism in any of the various stages of its development

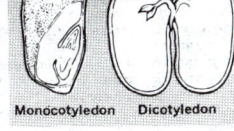

Monocotyledon   Dicotyledon

Embryos of seeds

after fertilization and before hatching or birth. The human embryo is called a fetus after the first six to eight weeks of development. **2.** undeveloped plant within a seed. **3.** beginning or rudimentary stage or form of something. —*adj.* embryonic. [Modern Latin *embryo* fetus, from Greek *embryon.*]

em·bry·ol·o·gist (em′brē ol′ə jist) *n.* specialist in embryology.

em·bry·ol·o·gy (em′brē ol′ə jē) *n.* branch of biology dealing with the formation and development of embryos. —**em·bry·o·log·ic** (em′brē ə loj′ik); *also,* **em′bry·o·log′i·cal,** *adj.*

em·bry·on·ic (em′brē on′ik) *adj.* of, relating to, or of the nature of an embryo.

em·cee (em′sē′) *Informal.* —*n.* master of ceremonies. —*v.t., v.i.* to act as master of ceremonies (of). [Short for *m(aster of) c(eremonies).*]

e·meer (ə mēr′) emir.

e·mend (i mend′) *v.t.* to remove errors from or make changes in the text of (a written work), as a book or document. [Latin *ēmendāre* to correct, from *ex* out, without + *menda* fault.] —**e·mend′a·ble,** *adj.*

e·men·date (ē′mən dāt′, em′ən-) **-dat·ed, -dat·ing.** *v.t.* to emend.

e·men·da·tion (ē′mən dā′shən, em′ən-) *n.* **1.** act of emending. **2.** alteration or correction in the text of a written work.

em·er·ald (em′ər əld, em′rəld) *n.* **1.** bright-green variety of the mineral beryl, prized as a gem. **2.** bright-green color. [Old French *esmeraude* the gem, from Latin *smaragdus,* from Greek *smaragdos;* probably of Semitic origin.]

Emerald Isle, Ireland.

e·merge (i murj′) **e·merged, e·merg·ing.** *v.i.* **1.** to come forth from or as from something that envelops: *The whale emerged from the ocean depths. Ten people emerged from the elevator.* **2.** to come into being or notice: *New evidence emerged from the investigation.* **3.** to rise or come out, as from a difficult or inferior state or condition: *He emerged from the accident unharmed.* [Latin *ēmergere* to rise up, come forth, from *ex* out of + *mergere* to dip.]

e·mer·gence (i mur′jəns) *n.* act or process of emerging.

e·mer·gen·cy (i mur′jən sē) *pl.,* **-cies.** *n.* situation or occurrence demanding immediate action: *In case of emergency, call the police.* —*adj.* for use in an emergency: *an emergency brake, an emergency exit, an emergency room.* —**Syn.** *n.* **Emergency, crisis** both mean a time of urgent need, esp. a time when the course of future events is decided. **Emergency** suggests something unanticipated that suddenly occurs: *It is by presence of mind in untried emergencies that the native metal of a man is tried* (Lowell, 1864). **Crisis** implies that what follows will be decisive for better or worse: *Great crises often call forth gifted leaders* (Bailey, 1956).

e·mer·gent (i mur′jənt) *adj.* emerging.

e·mer·i·tus (i mer′i təs) *adj.* retired from active service, usually because of age, but retaining rank and title: *professor emeritus.* —*n. pl.,* **-ti** (-tī′, -tē). one who is emeritus. [Latin *ēmeritus,* past participle of *ēmerērī* to earn by service.]

e·mer·sion (i mur′zhən, -shən) *n.* act or process of emerging. [From Latin *ēmersus,* past participle of *ēmergere.* See EMERGE.]

Em·er·son, Ralph Wal·do (em′ər sən) 1803–82, U.S. essayist, poet, and philosopher.

em·er·y (em′ər ē, em′rē) *n.* hard black or brown mixture of granular corundum and, usually, magnetite or hematite, used chiefly as an abrasive. [French *émeri,* from Italian *smeriglio,* going back to Greek *smyris* emery powder.]

emery board, small, flat piece of cardboard coated with powdered emery, used esp. in filing the fingernails.

e·met·ic (i met′ik) *n.* medicine that induces vomiting. —*adj.* inducing vomiting: *an emetic drug.* [Latin *emeticus* causing vomiting, from Greek *emetikos* inclined to vomit, from *emetos* vomiting.]

e.m.f., electromotive force. *Also,* **E.M.F.**

em·i·grant (em′i grənt) *n.* one who emigrates. —*adj.* moving from one place or country to settle in another.

em·i·grate (em′ə grāt′) **-grat·ed, -grat·ing.** *v.i.* to move from one place or country to settle in another: *Albert Einstein emigrated from Germany to the United States.* [Latin *ēmigrātus,* past participle of *ēmigrāre* to move away from.]

em·i·gra·tion (em′ə grā′shən) *n.* **1.** act or process of emigrating: *The population of Ireland has decreased because of emigration.* **2.** emigrants collectively.

em·i·gré (em′i grā′) *pl.,* **-grés** (-grāz′). *also,* **é·mi·gré** (French ā mē grā′). *n.* emigrant, esp. one who has fled from a revolution. [French *émigré,* from *émigrer* to emigrate, from Latin *ēmigrāre* to move away from.]

em·i·nence (em′ə nəns) *n.* **1.** superiority, as in rank, power, or achievement; prominence: *The scientist attained a position of eminence in his field.* **2.** elevation of the earth's surface, as a hill. **3. Eminence.** title or form of address for a cardinal of the Roman Catholic Church. ▲ usually preceded by *Your* or *His.*

em·i·nent (em′ə nənt) *adj.* **1.** superior, as in rank, power, or achieve-

---

at; āpe; cär; end; mē; it; īce; hot; ōld; fôrk; wood; fōōl; out; up; ūse; turn; sing; thin; this; zh in treasure; ə in ago, taken, pencil, lemon, circus.

ment; distinguished; prominent: *an eminent writer.* **2.** conspicuous; noteworthy: *an eminent achievement, eminent bravery.* **3.** high; lofty. [Latin *ēminēns*, present participle of *ēminēre* to stand out.] —**em′i‑nent‑ly,** *adv.* —**Syn. 1.** see **illustrious.**

eminent domain, power or right of the government to take privately owned land for public use or for the public welfare, compensation usually being given to the owner.

e‑mir (ə mēr′) *also,* **e‑meer.** *n.* **1.** chief, prince, or military leader in certain Arab or Muslim countries. **2.** descendant of Muhammad. **3.** formerly, any of certain high Turkish officials. [Arabic *amīr* commander.]

em‑is‑sar‑y (em′ə ser′ē) *pl.,* **‑sar‑ies.** *n.* agent, as of a government, on an official or secret mission. [Latin *ēmissārius* scout, spy.] —**Syn.** see **messenger.**

e‑mis‑sion (i mish′ən) *n.* **1.** act or process of emitting. **2.** that which is emitted. [Latin *ēmissiō* a sending out.]

e‑mis‑sive (i mis′iv) *adj.* emitting.

e‑mit (i mit′) **e‑mit‑ted, e‑mit‑ting.** *v.t.* **1.** to send forth or out; give off; discharge: *Fireflies emit light but not heat. Boiling water emits steam.* **2.** to utter: *He did not emit a sound.* **3.** to put into circulation, as paper money. [Latin *ēmittere* to send out.]

Em‑man‑u‑el (i man′ū əl) Immanuel.

em‑met (em′it) *n. Archaic.* ant. [Old English *ǣmete.*]

Em‑met, Robert (em′it) 1778–1803, Irish patriot.

Em‑my (em′ē) *pl.,* **‑mys** or **‑mies.** *n.* one of the gold‑plated statuettes presented annually for outstanding achievement in television acting, programming, and production.

e‑mol‑lient (i mol′yənt) *adj.* making soft or supple; soothing, esp. to the skin. —*n.* medicine or preparation that softens and soothes: *Lanolin is an emollient for the skin.* [Latin *ēmolliēns,* present participle of *ēmollīre* to soften.]

e‑mol‑u‑ment (i mol′yə mənt) *n.* profit or compensation arising from an occupation, service, or position; wages. [Latin *ēmolumentum,* going back to *ex* out + *molere* to grind.]

e‑mote (i mōt′) **e‑mot‑ed, e‑mot‑ing.** *v.i. Informal.* to show or express emotion, esp. in an exaggerated manner, in or as in acting. [From EMOTION.]

e‑mo‑tion (i mō′shən) *n.* **1.** mental state in which a feeling, often intense, as love, hate, or sorrow, is experienced, often accompanied by a physical change or manifestation, as blushing, laughing, or crying. **2.** any of various feelings thus experienced, as love, hate, happiness, or sorrow. [French *émotion,* from *émouvoir* to move, stir up, going back to Latin *ēmovēre* to move out, stir up.] —**Syn. 2.** see **feeling.**

e‑mo‑tion‑al (i mō′shən əl) *adj.* **1.** of, relating to, or characterized by emotion: *an emotional quarrel, an emotional outburst.* **2.** subject to or easily affected by emotion: *an emotional person, an emotional temperament.* **3.** appealing to or arousing emotion: *The lawyer made an emotional plea to the jury.* —**e‑mo′tion‑al‑ly,** *adv.*

e‑mo‑tion‑al‑ism (i mō′shən əl iz′əm) *n.* **1.** tendency to show or be affected by emotion too easily. **2.** appeal to the emotions: *The speech was full of emotionalism.* **3.** display of emotion.

e‑mo‑tive (i mō′tiv) *adj.* **1.** expressing, causing, or appealing to emotion. **2.** of or relating to emotion. —**e‑mo′tive‑ly,** *adv.*

em‑pan‑el (em pan′əl) impanel.

em‑pa‑thize (em′pə thīz′) **‑thized, ‑thiz‑ing.** *v.i.* to experience empathy: *The novelist was able to empathize with the farm workers.*

em‑pa‑thy (em′pə thē) *n.* a sharing through imagination of another's feelings or state of mind without actually going through the same experiences. [Greek *empatheia* passion, going back to *en* in + *pathos* feeling.]

Em‑ped‑o‑cles (em ped′ə klēz′) c.490–c.430 B.C., Greek philosopher.

em‑per‑or (em′pər ər) *n.* male ruler of an empire. [Old French *empereor,* from Latin *imperātor* emperor, ruler, general, commander.]

em‑pha‑sis (em′fə sis) *pl.,* **‑ses** (‑sēz′). *n.* **1.** special importance or significance attached to something: *Too little emphasis was placed on the safety regulations.* **2.** that which is given special importance or significance: *Faith was the emphasis of the sermon.* **3.** vocal accent given to a particular syllable, word, or phrase. [Latin *emphasis* rhetorical stress, from Greek *emphasis* appearance, significance.]

Syn. 1. Emphasis, stress, accent indicate importance given to something by special treatment or force. **Emphasis** implies pushing something forward, marking it specially, or in some other way indicating its presence: *The brilliant colors in the queen's costume give her figure emphasis in the painting.* **Stress** suggests applying weight to something: *Like all weak men he laid an exaggerated stress on not changing one's mind* (Maugham, 1915). **Accent** implies adding contrast of some kind to call attention to something: *The blue in her dress adds an accent that lights up her eyes.*

em‑pha‑size (em′fə sīz′) **‑sized, ‑siz‑ing.** *v.t.* to give emphasis to; stress: *His speech emphasized the use for conservation of wildlife.*

em‑phat‑ic (em fat′ik) *adj.* **1.** spoken or done with emphasis; strongly expressive: *an emphatic denial.* **2.** forceful; insistent: *He remained emphatic on that point.* **3.** striking; significant; decisive: *The jury's verdict was an emphatic vindication of the defendant.* [Greek *emphatikos* expressive, from *emphainein* to exhibit, indicate.] —**em‑phat′i‑cal‑ly,** *adv.*

em‑phy‑se‑ma (em′fə sē′mə) *n.* chronic disease that impairs breathing, characterized by enlargement of the air sacs in the lungs. [Modern Latin *emphysema,* from Greek *emphȳsēma* inflation.]

em‑pire (em′pīr) *n.* **1.** union of countries or territories ruled or controlled by the government of one country. **2.** country or union of countries or territories ruled by an emperor or empress. **3.** absolute power, authority, or control; dominion. **4.** large territory or enterprise under the domination of an individual or group of individuals: *a real‑estate empire.* [Old French *empire* state ruled by an emperor, dominion, from Latin *imperium* dominion, command.]

Em‑pire (*def. 1* em′pīr; *defs. 2, 3* om pēr′) *adj.* **1.** of or relating to the first French Empire (1804–15) under Napoleon Bonaparte. **2.** of or designating a style of furniture of this period, characterized by heavy, massive rectangular forms, classical and Egyptian motifs, and ornamentation with gilded bronze. **3.a.** of or designating a style of women's fashion of this period, characterized by a high waistline, a décolleté bodice, short, puffed sleeves, and a long, loosely fitted straight skirt. **b.** *also,* **empire.** (of a dress) having a high waistline.

em‑pir‑ic (em pir′ik) *n.* **1.** one who relies entirely on observation and practical experience as a source of knowledge. **2.** *Archaic.* charlatan; quack. —*adj.* empirical. [Latin *empīricus* doctor who relies on experience only, from Greek *empeirikos* experienced, going back to *en* in + *peira* experiment.]

em‑pir‑i‑cal (em pir′i kəl) *adj.* **1.** based on or derived from experience, experiment, or observation: *empirical proof.* **2.** relying on practical experience, without regard for, or benefit of, scientific principles or practice, esp. in medicine. —**em‑pir′i‑cal‑ly,** *adv.*

em‑pir‑i‑cism (em pir′ə siz′əm) *n.* **1.** empirical method or practice. **2.** philosophical theory that all knowledge is derived from experience as perceived through the senses. —**em‑pir′i‑cist,** *n.*

em‑place (im plās′) **‑placed, ‑plac‑ing.** *v.t.* to put or place in position.

em‑place‑ment (em plās′mənt) *n.* **1.** prepared position for heavy guns. **2.** setting or putting into position; placement.

em‑ploy (em ploi′) *v.t.* **1.** to engage the services of (someone) for wages, salary, or other compensation; hire: *The store employed extra workers at Christmas.* **2.** to make use of, esp. as a means or instrument: *to employ radar for tracking airplanes.* **3.** to occupy, as time, energy, or attention: *His hobby employs much of his time.* —*n.* state of being employed; service: *The agent was in the employ of a foreign country.* [Old French *employer* to use, from Late Latin *implicāre,* from Latin *implicāre* to infold, involve. Doublet of IMPLICATE, IMPLY.] —**em‑ploy′a‑ble,** *adj.*

Syn. *v.t.* **1. Employ, hire** mean to use the services of a person, esp. for compensation. **Employ** emphasizes the work the person does and suggests regularity of labor, hours, and pay: *The company employed only people with some college education as salesmen.* **Hire** stresses the compensation, with some suggestion that the worker is either in a temporary position or on a probationary period: *He hired another girl to take care of the heavy load of typing.* **2.** see **use.**

em‑ploy‑ee (em ploi′ē, em′ploi ē′) *also,* **em‑ploy‑e.** *n.* one who is employed by a person or business for wages, salary, or other compensation. [French *employé,* noun use of past participle of *employer* to use, give employment to. See EMPLOY.]

em‑ploy‑er (em ploi′ər) *n.* person or business that employs one or more persons for wages, salary, or other compensation.

em‑ploy‑ment (em ploi′mənt) *n.* **1.** act of employing; being employed. **2.** work in which one engages or is employed; job; occupation.

em‑po‑ri‑um (em pôr′ē əm) *pl.,* **‑po‑ri‑ums** or **‑po‑ri‑a** (‑pôr′ē ə) *n.* **1.** large store selling a wide variety of merchandise. **2.** principal center of commerce or trade. [Latin *emporium* trading place, from Greek *emporion,* from *emporos* merchant.]

em‑pow‑er (em pou′ər) *also,* **im‑pow‑er.** *v.t.* **1.** to give power or authority to; authorize: *The ambassador was empowered to sign the treaty.* **2.** to enable; permit: *Technological advancement has empowered man to explore space.*

em‑press (em′pris) *n.* **1.** wife or widow of an emperor. **2.** female ruler of an empire.

em‑prise (em prīz′) *also,* **em‑prize.** *n. Archaic.* **1.** undertaking or enterprise, esp. of an adventurous or daring nature. **2.** knightly daring or prowess; adventurousness. [Old French *emprise,* originally feminine past participle of *emprendre* to undertake, going back to Latin *in* in + *prehendere* to take.]

emp‑ty (emp′tē) **‑ti‑er, ‑ti‑est.** *adj.* **1.** having nothing in it; containing nothing, esp. without the usual or appropriate contents: *an empty glass, an empty classroom.* **2.** lacking force, effect, substance, or value; mean‑

at; āpe; cär; end; mē; it; īce; hot; ōld; fôrk; wood; fōͅol; oil; out; up; ūse; turn; sing; thin; this; zh in treasure; ə in ago, taken, pencil, lemon, circus.

ingless; hollow: *an empty promise, empty dreams.* **3.** *Informal.* hungry. **4. empty of.** devoid or destitute of; lacking: *The streets were empty of traffic at night.* —*v.t.,* **-tied, -ty·ing. 1.** to make empty; remove the contents of: *to empty a wastebasket.* **2.** to transfer the contents of (a container): *She emptied the glass into the sink.* **3.** to take out, pour off, or otherwise remove (the contents of something): *to empty the water out of the tub.* —*v.i.* **1.** to become empty: *The theater emptied when the movie ended.* **2.** to pour or flow out; discharge: *That river empties into the sea. The crowd emptied into the street.* —*n. pl.,* **-ties.** *Informal.* something empty, as a container or bottle. [Old English *ǣmtig* containing nothing, vacant, idle.] —**emp'ti·ly,** *adv.* —**emp'ti·ness,** *n.*
Syn. *adj.* **1. Empty, vacant, bare[1], void** mean lacking in content or lacking the usual and expected content. **Empty** suggests nothing or no one occupying a space, though this use is often relative: *The seats of the auditorium were empty.* **Vacant** implies that the absence of the usual thing or person is temporary: *The position of sales manager is vacant.* **Bare** suggests little or no furnishing: *The walls of the prison cell were bare.* **Void** suggests complete emptiness, esp. with no markings or divisions: *A thousand miles of desert, void of human habitation, lay before him.*
emp·ty-hand·ed (emp'tē han' did) *adj.* **1.** having nothing in the hands; bringing or carrying nothing away. **2.** having gained or acquired nothing.
emp·ty-head·ed (emp'tē hed'id) *adj.* foolish; brainless; stupid.
empty set *Mathematics.* set that has no members. The set of even numbers between 8 and 10 is an empty set.
em·pyr·e·al (em pir'ē əl, em'pī rē'əl) *adj.* of or relating to the empyrean; celestial.
em·py·re·an (em pir'ē ən, em'pī rē'ən) *n.* **1.** in ancient and medieval astronomy, the highest heaven, believed to be the region of pure fire or light. **2.** visible heavens; firmament; sky. —*adj.* empyreal. [Late Latin *empyreus* fiery (from Greek *empyrios,* from *en* in + *pyr* fire) + -AN.]

Emu

e·mu (ē'mū) *n.* flightless bird, *Dromiceius novaehollandiae,* native to Australia, resembling, but smaller than, an ostrich. It can run at speeds up to forty miles per hour. Height: 5–6 feet. [Portuguese *ema* crane, ostrich; possibly from a native word from the Moluccas.]
em·u·late (em'yə lāt') *-lat·ed, -lat·ing. v.t.* **1.** to try to equal or surpass: *The younger players emulated the team's star player.* **2.** to rival or vie with successfully: *Many of the Greek states emulated Tyre in commerce and opulence* (Yeats, 1872). [Latin *aemulātus,* past participle of *aemulārī* to try to equal.] —**em'u·la'tive,** *adj.* —**em'u·la'tor,** *n.*
em·u·la·tion (em'yə lā'shən) *n.* effort or ambition to equal or surpass.
Syn. Emulation, rivalry, competition indicate a desire and striving to equal or surpass someone. **Emulation** stresses the effort to match the accomplishments of another: *The propensity for emulation is probably the strongest and most alert and persistent of the economic motives* (Veblen, 1899). **Rivalry** emphasizes hostile contention: *Jealousies, rivalries, and envy intervene to separate others from our side* (Scott, 1816). **Competition** suggests striving, perhaps amicably, for a prize or tangible reward: *Thou shalt not covet, but tradition approves all forms of competition* (Clough, 1862).
em·u·lous (em'yə ləs) *adj.* **1.** eager to equal or surpass; competitive. **2.** of, of the nature of, or arising from emulation: *an emulous act.* [Latin *aemulus* striving to equal.] —**em'u·lous·ly,** *adv.* —**em'u·lous·ness,** *n.*
e·mul·si·fy (i mul'sə fī') *-fied, -fy·ing. v.t.* to make into an emulsion. —**e·mul'si·fi·ca'tion, e·mul'si·fi'er,** *n.*
e·mul·sion (i mul'shən) *n.* **1.** mixture consisting of very small droplets of one liquid suspended, rather than dissolved, in another liquid. **2.** *Pharmacy.* a milky mixture consisting of very small droplets of one liquid, as fat or oil, suspended in another liquid by means of a substance that keeps them from separating. **3.** light-sensitive coating on photographic film, plates, or paper, consisting of a suspension of silver bromide in gelatin. [Modern Latin *emulsio,* from Latin *ēmulgēre* to milk out, drain.] —**e·mul'sive,** *adj.*
en (en) *n.* *Printing.* unit of measure equal to half the width of an em.
en-[1] *prefix* **1.** (used to form verbs from nouns) **a.** to put in, into, or on: *enthrone, enchain.* **b.** to cover or surround with: *encircle, enshroud.* **2.** (used to form verbs from adjectives and nouns) to cause to be or resemble; make: *enfeeble, enslave.* **3.** used as an intensifier to form verbs from other verbs: *enliven, enwrap.* ▲ the addition of *en-* often does not

alter the meaning of the verb to which it is prefixed. [Old French *en-* in, into, on, from Latin *in.*]
en-[2] *prefix* in; into; on: *energy, enthusiasm.* [Greek *en* in.]
-en[1] *suffix* **1.** (used to form verbs from adjectives) to cause to be or become: *sharpen, madden, harden.* **2.** (used to form verbs from nouns) to cause or come to have: *heighten, strengthen, lengthen.* [Old English *-nian.*]
-en[2] *suffix* (used to form adjectives from nouns) made of or resembling: *silken, wooden, golden.* [Old English *-en* made of.]
-en[3] *suffix* used in the past participles of many strong verbs: *risen, written, sworn.* [Old English *-en.*]
-en[4] *suffix* used in the plural of a few nouns: *children, brethren, oxen.* [Old English *-an.*]
en·a·ble (i nā'bəl) *-bled, -bling. v.t.* to give adequate power, means, ability, or opportunity to; make able: *Tutoring enabled him to pass the test. The bylaws enable the chairman to veto certain proposals.*
en·act (i nakt') *v.t.* **1.** to make into a law, as a bill. **2.** to act out or as on stage; perform.
en·act·ment (i nakt'mənt) *n.* **1.** act of enacting; being enacted. **2.** that which is enacted, as a law.
e·nam·el (i nam'əl) *n.* **1.** glasslike substance, usually opaque, fused to metal, pottery, and other surfaces, used for ornamentation or protection. Enamel is usually made from quartz, feldspar, clay, soda, and borax. **2.** paint, varnish, or other substance that dries to form a hard, glossy coating or surface. **3.** any hard, glossy coating or surface. **4.** hard, glossy substance composed chiefly of calcium and phosphorus, covering the crown of a tooth. **5.** piece made of or coated with enamel. —*v.t.,* **-eled, -el·ing;** *also, British,* **-elled, -el·ling. 1.** to cover or inlay with enamel. **2.** to form a hard, glossy surface on. [Anglo-Norman *enameler* to decorate with enamel, adorn, from *en* on (from Latin *in*) + *amail* the glasslike substance (of Germanic origin).] —**e·nam'el·er;** *also, British,* **e·nam'el·ler,** *n.*
e·nam·el·ware (i nam'əl wār') *n.* metal kitchenware or dinnerware coated with enamel.
en·am·or (in am'ər) *also, British,* **en·am·our.** *v.t.* to inflame with love; charm; captivate. ▲ usually in the passive, with *of: He was enamored of the actress.* [Old French *enamourer,* going back to Latin *in* in + *amor* love.]
en bloc (en blok', än) as a whole; all together. [French *en bloc,* from *en* in (from Latin *in*) + *bloc* lump. See BLOCK.]
en·camp (en kamp') *v.i.* to make or settle in a camp: *They encamped in the valley.* —*v.t.* to place in a camp: *The soldiers were encamped near the river.*
en·camp·ment (en kamp'mənt) *n.* **1.** location or quarters occupied in encamping; camp. **2.** people occupying such a place. **3.** act of encamping; being encamped.
en·case (en kās') *-cased, -cas·ing. also,* **in·case.** *v.t.* to enclose in or as in a case. —**en·case'ment,** *n.*
en·caus·tic (en kôs'tik) *n.* method of painting or decorating in which dry pigments are mixed with melted beeswax and applied to a surface, usually with heated instruments so that the colored wax melts into the surface. —*adj.* of, relating to, or produced by a process of burning into a surface. [Latin *encausticus* done in the encaustic manner, from Greek *enkaustikos* of burning in, from *enkaiein* to burn in.]
-ence *suffix* (used to form nouns from adjectives ending in *-ent*) action, quality, state, or condition of being: *violence, existence, independence, absence.* [Latin *-entia,* often through French *-ence.*]
en·ceinte (en sānt'; *French* än sant') *adj.* pregnant. [French *enceinte,* possibly going back to Latin *inciēns.*]
en·ce·phal·ic (en'sə fal'ik) *adj.* **1.** of or relating to the brain. **2.** situated within the cranial cavity.
en·ceph·a·li·tis (en sef'ə lī'tis) *n.* inflammation of the brain. [Modern Latin *encephalitis,* from Greek *enkephalos* brain + -ITIS.]
en·ceph·a·lon (en sef'ə lon') *n.* brain. [Modern Latin *encephalon,* from Greek *enkephalos,* from *en* in + *kephalē* head.]
en·chain (en chān') *v.t.* to bind with or as with chains; fetter.
en·chant (en chant') *v.t.* **1.** to cast a spell on; bewitch: *Circe enchanted Odysseus' companions.* **2.** to charm or delight greatly: *We were enchanted by the little child.* [Old French *enchanter,* from Latin *incantāre* to chant a magic formula, bewitch, from *in* against + *cantāre* to chant, sing; with reference to the Roman belief in the magical effectiveness of chanted or sung words.] —**en·chant'er,** *n.*
en·chant·ing (en chan'ting) *adj.* very charming or delightful. —**en·chant'ing·ly,** *adv.*
en·chant·ment (en chant'mənt) *n.* **1.** act of enchanting; being enchanted. **2.** that which enchants.
en·chant·ress (en chan'tris) *n.* **1.** witch; sorceress. **2.** alluring, charming, or fascinating woman.
en·chase (en chās') *-chased, -chas·ing. v.t.* **1.** to encase or mount in a setting: *to enchase a jewel.* **2.** to ornament (a surface), as with en-

at; āpe; cär; end; mē; it; īce; hot; ōld; fôrk; wood; fōol; oil; out; up; ūse; turn; sing; thin; this; zh in treasure; ə in ago, taken, pencil, lemon, circus.

335

graved, embossed, or inlaid work. **3.** to engrave or carve (a design) on a surface: *a family crest enchased on silver.* [French *enchâsser* to enshrine, set (jewels), going back to Latin *in* in + *capsa* box, chest.]

en·chi·la·da (en'chi lä'də) *n.* Mexican dish made of a tortilla with a filling, usually of meat or cheese, served with a spicy tomato or chili sauce. [Spanish *enchilada*, from *enchilar* to season with chili, from *en-* in (from Latin *in*) + *chile.* See CHILI.]

en·cir·cle (en sur'kəl) -**cled**, -**cling.** *v.t.* **1.** to form a circle around; surround: *The soldiers encircled the enemy camp.* **2.** to move in a circle around; make a circuit of: *Many artificial satellites encircle the earth today.* —**en·cir'cle·ment**, *n.*

en·clave (en'klāv, än'-) *n.* **1.** country or part of a country completely or partially surrounded by the territory of another country. San Marino and Lesotho are enclaves. **2.** district within a larger geographic unit inhabited by a distinct minority group: *a Chinese enclave in an American city, an enclave of scholars in Oxford.* [French *enclave* piece of enclosed land, from *enclaver* to enclose, going back to Latin *in* in + *clāvis* key.]

en·clit·ic (en klit'ik) *adj.* of or relating to a word that, having no stress of its own, is pronounced as part of the word preceding it. —*n.* enclitic word. [Late Latin *encliticus*, from Greek *enklitikos*, from *enklinein* to lean on.]

en·close (en klōz') -**closed**, -**clos·ing.** *also*, **in·close.** *v.t.* **1.** to close in on all sides with or as with a wall or fence; surround: *a field enclosed by trees.* **2.** to include with a letter or parcel: *The store enclosed an itemized bill with her purchases.* **3.** to contain: *The letter enclosed a check.* [Old French *enclos*, past participle of *enclore* to shut in, going back to Latin *inclūdere.*]

en·clo·sure (en klō'zhər) *also*, **in·clo·sure.** *n.* **1.** act of enclosing; being enclosed. **2.** that which is enclosed. **3.** that which encloses, as a fence or wall.

en·code (en kōd') -**cod·ed**, -**cod·ing.** *v.t.* to convert (a message) into code. —**en·cod'er**, *n.*

en·co·mi·ast (en kō'mē ast') *n.* one who speaks or writes an encomium; eulogist. [Greek *enkōmiastēs*, going back to *enkōmion* eulogy.]

en·co·mi·um (en kō'mē əm) *pl.*, -**mi·ums** or -**mi·a** (-mē ə). *n.* formal expression of praise; eulogy. [Latin *encōmium*, from Greek *enkōmion*, going back to *en* in + *kōmos* revelry.] —**Syn.** see **eulogy.**

en·com·pass (en kum'pəs, -kom'-) *v.t.* **1.** to form a circle around; encircle; surround: *The castle was encompassed by a wide moat.* **2.** to contain or include: *The biography encompasses every aspect of his career.* —**en·com'pass·ment**, *n.*

en·core (äng'kôr, än'-) *interj.* once more; again. —*n.* **1.** call by the audience for the repetition of part of a performance, as of a dance or song, or for the performance of an additional piece. **2.** that which is performed in response to such a call: *The pianist played three encores.* —*v.t.*, -**cored**, -**cor·ing.** to call for an encore of or from. [French *encore* still, again, from Latin *(in) hanc hōram* (to) this hour.]

en·coun·ter (en koun'tər) *v.t.* **1.** to meet unexpectedly or casually; come upon. **2.** to meet in conflict; confront in battle: *We encountered the foe and routed him.* **3.** to be faced with, as opposition or difficulties; experience: *They encountered little resistance to the plan.* —*n.* **1.** unexpected or casual meeting. **2.** meeting of enemies in conflict; skirmish; engagement. [Old French *encontrer* to meet, going back to Latin *in* in + *contrā* against.] —**Syn.** see **meet**[1].

en·cour·age (en kur'ij) -**aged**, -**ag·ing.** *v.t.* **1.** to inspire with courage, hope, or confidence; hearten: *The good news encouraged her.* **2.** to give support to; foster; promote: *Public apathy encourages corruption in government.* [Old French *encoragier* to hearten, from *en-* in (from Latin *in*) + *corage* feelings.] —**Syn.** see **COURAGE.**

en·cour·age·ment (en kur'ij mənt) *n.* **1.** act of encouraging; being encouraged. **2.** that which encourages.

en·cour·ag·ing (en kur'i jing) *adj.* giving, or tending to give, courage, hope, or confidence: *encouraging news, an encouraging smile.* —**en·cour'ag·ing·ly**, *adv.*

en·croach (en krōch') *v.i.* **1.** to intrude gradually on the property or rights of another; trespass (with *on* or *upon*): *He felt that his neighbors encroached on his privacy.* **2.** to go beyond usual or natural limits; make gradual inroads (with *on* or *upon*): *Every spring the river encroached farther on the land.* [Old French *encrochier* to seize upon, from *en-* in (from Latin *in*) + *croc* hook (of Scandinavian origin).] —**Syn.** **1.** see **intrude.**

en·croach·ment (en krōch'mənt) *n.* **1.** act of encroaching. **2.** that which is gained by encroaching.

en·crust (en krust') *also*, **in·crust.** *v.t.* **1.** to cover with or as with a crust or hard coating: *His shoes were encrusted with mud.* **2.** to ornament lavishly, as with jewels or precious metal: *a scabbard encrusted with diamonds and gold.* [Latin *incrustāre* to cover with a crust.]

en·crus·ta·tion (en'krus tā'shən) *also*, **in·crus·ta·tion.** *n.* **1.** act of encrusting; being encrusted. **2.** that which forms a crust or hard coating: *an encrustation of gold, pearls, and jewels.*

en·cum·ber (en kum'bər) *v.t.* **1.** to hinder the motion or action of, as with a burden: *She was encumbered by the bulky package.* **2.** to weigh down or burden, as with debts, duties, or obligations: *He was encumbered with financial responsibilities.* **3.** to obstruct, as with obstacles or unnecessary additions; block: *Discarded furniture encumbered the hallway.* [Old French *encombrer* to block up, obstruct, going back to Latin *in* in + Late Latin *cumbrus* barrier (of uncertain origin).]

en·cum·brance (en kum'brəns) *n.* **1.** that which encumbers; hindrance; burden. **2.** claim attached to real or personal property, as a lien or mortage.

Syn. 1. Encumbrance, burden[1], **impediment** mean something that interferes with the effort to progress. **Encumbrance** suggests a weight that must be carried along, thus limiting the distance or height one may achieve: *The great mass of volunteers . . . were looked upon as a mere encumbrance* (Mariotti, 1851). **Burden** implies a weight or bulk that presses down: *I have found it impossible to carry the heavy burden of responsibility* (Edward VIII, 1936). **Impediment** suggests something that hinders, blocks, or entangles, thus requiring halts during which progress is stopped: *The commissioner . . . wrote in 1868 that the Great Plains was an impediment to western settlement* (Fite, 1966).

-ency *suffix* (used to form nouns from adjectives ending in *-ent*) act, fact, quality, or state of being: *dependency, fluency, emergency.* [Latin *-entia.*]

ency., encyclopedia. Also, **encyc., encycl.**

en·cyc·li·cal (en sik'li kəl) *n.* formal letter written by the pope, addressed to the bishops, and usually pertaining to doctrinal, moral, or disciplinary matters. —*adj.* (of a letter) intended for general circulation; to be read by many or all. [Late Latin *encyclicus*, going back to Greek *en* in + *kyklos* circle.]

en·cy·clo·pe·di·a (en sī'klə pē'dē ə) *also*, **en·cy·clo·pae·di·a.** *n.* comprehensive reference work in one or more volumes, presenting information on all branches of knowledge or on a specific field, usually in articles arranged alphabetically. [Medieval Latin *encyclopaedia* course of general education, going back to Greek *enkyklios paideia* general education, from *enkyklios* circular, general + *paideia* instruction.]

en·cy·clo·pe·dic (en sī'klə pē'dik) *also*, **en·cy·clo·pae·dic.** *adj.* of, like, or relating to an encyclopedia; extensive; comprehensive: *His knowledge of history is encyclopedic.*

en·cy·clo·pe·dist (en sī'klə pē'dist) *also*, **en·cy·clo·pae·dist.** *n.* compiler of or writer for an encyclopedia.

en·cyst (en sist') *v.t.*, *v.i.* to enclose or become enclosed in a cyst or sac. —**en·cyst'ment**, *n.*

end (end) *n.* **1.** point of termination or beginning of something that has greater length than width: *the end of a street, the end of a rope, the end of a line.* **2.** extreme or outermost part of anything that is extended into or occupies space; boundary; limit: *the end of town, the ends of the earth.* **3.** point at which the continuity or duration of something is terminated; conclusion: *the end of the year, the end of a controversy.* **4.** final part: *The end of the book was better than the beginning.* **5.** intended result of an action; purpose; goal: *The end does not always justify the means.* **6.** reason for which something exists: *The end of society is the common . . . good of the people* (Wollaston, 1722). **7.a.** termination of existence; death; destruction: *He came to a sudden and violent end.* **b.** cause or manner of this: *Hard work will be the end of him.* **8.** outcome; consequence. **9.** *also*, **ends.** remnant; fragment. **10.** *Football.* **a.** one of two players whose position is at either the left or right end of the line. **b.** position played by this player. **11. at loose ends.** in an unsettled, undecided, or confused condition: *They were at loose ends as to what to do.* **12. to make (both) ends meet.** to live within one's income: *The married couple had difficulty making ends meet even though they both worked.* **13. on end. a.** in an upright position. **b.** in succession; continuously: *He studied for days on end.* **14. no end.** *Informal.* vast amount; very much: *We had no end of fun at the party.* —*v.t.* **1.** to bring to an end; conclude; finish: *to end a meeting, to end a war.* **2.** to be or form the end of. —*v.i.* **1.** to come to an end: *The play ended at ten o'clock.* **2.** to attain or reach a final state, condition, or objective (often with *up*): *He will end up as president someday.* **3.** *Archaic.* to die. [Old English *ende* extremity, conclusion, final limit.]

Syn. *v.t.* **End, conclude, finish, terminate, close** mean to bring something to a stop. **End** suggests completion, the reaching of a limit: *He looked for a good selection with which to end his recital.* **Conclude** implies a rounding out, in an expected way, formally: *Cato the Elder used to conclude every speech, no matter what the subject, with "Carthage must be destroyed."* **Finish** suggests doing whatever must be done before stopping: *When we finished washing the car, we went for a ride in the country.* **Terminate** implies reaching or being at a predetermined or predicted place or time: *The successful landing on an aircraft carrier terminated the series of test flights.* **Close** suggests shutting or putting a final limit to something open: *He moved to close the nominations.* —*n.* see **objective.**

at; āpe; cär; end; mē; it; īce; hot; ōld; fôrk; wood; fōōl; oil; out; up; ūse; turn; sing; thin; this; zh in treasure; ə in ago, taken, pencil, lemon, circus.

en·dan·ger (en dān′jər) *v.t.* to expose to danger; imperil: *The ship was endangered by the storm.* —Syn. see **imperil.**

en·dear (en dēr′) *v.t.* to make dear or beloved: *The puppy quickly endeared itself to the children.* —**en·dear′ing·ly,** *adv.*

en·dear·ment (en dēr′mənt) *n.* **1.** act of endearing; being endeared. **2.** action or utterance expressive of love or affection: *The lovers whispered endearments to each other.*

en·deav·or (en dev′ər) *also,* **British, en·deav·our.** *v.i.* to make an effort to do or accomplish something; strive; try: *The senator endeavored to gain support for his bill.* —*n.* serious or strenuous attempt to accomplish or achieve something; effort. [Middle English *endeveren* literally, to exert oneself in duty, from EN-¹ + *dever* duty (from Middle French *devoir* duty, from *devoir* to owe, from Latin *dēbēre*).] —Syn. *v.i.* see **try.** *n.* see **effort.**

en·dem·ic (en dem′ik) *adj.* prevalent in or restricted or peculiar to a particular people or locality: *endemic diseases, endemic plants.* —*n.* endemic disease. [Greek *endēmos* native (from *en* in + *dēmos* people) + -IC.]

end·ing (en′ding) *n.* **1.** final part; conclusion: *The story has a sad ending.* **2.** one or more letters or syllables added to a word or word stem, esp. to indicate an inflection.

en·dive (en′dīv, än′dēv) *n.* **1.** creamy white or curly green leaves of a plant, *Cichorium endivia,* of the composite family, usually eaten raw in salads. **2.** the lettucelike plant that bears these leaves, related to chicory. Also, **es′ca·role′.** [Old French *endive* chicory, through Medieval Latin and Middle Greek, going back to Latin *intibus* chicory, endive; possibly of Semitic origin.]

end·less (end′lis) *adj.* **1.** having no limit or end; infinite; boundless: *endless space.* **2.** going on forever; eternal: *Death is a short night followed by an endless day* (Steele, 1711). **3.** perpetually recurring; constant; incessant: *endless repetition, endless interruptions.* **4.** having the ends joined so as to form a circle or loop; continuous: *an endless chain.* —**end′less·ly,** *adv.* —**end′less·ness,** *n.* —Syn. **2.** see **eternal.**

end man, man at either end of a row of performers in a minstrel show, who carries on a comic dialogue with the interlocutor.

end·most (end′mōst′) *adj.* at or nearest to the end; farthest.

endo- combining form within; inside; inner: *endoderm, endogamy.* [Greek *endon.*]

en·do·blast (en′də blast′) *n.* endoderm.

en·do·car·di·tis (en′dō kär dī′tis) *n.* inflammation of the endocardium.

en·do·car·di·um (en′dō kär′dē əm) *n.* thin membrane lining the cavities of the heart. [Modern Latin *endocardium,* from ENDO- + Greek *kardiā* heart.] —**en′do·car′di·al,** *adj.*

en·do·carp (en′də kärp′) *n.* inner layer of a fruit or ripened ovary of certain plants, forming a covering for the cavity containing the seed, as the shell of a cherry or peach stone. [ENDO- + Greek *karpos* fruit.]

en·do·crine (en′də krin, -krīn′, -krēn′) *adj.* **1.** producing internal secretions that pass directly into the blood stream or lymph. **2.** of or relating to an endocrine gland or its secretion. —*n.* **1.** endocrine gland. **2.** secretion of an endocrine gland; hormone. [ENDO- + Greek *krīnein* to separate.]

endocrine gland, any of various ductless glands, as the thyroid and pituitary, that secrete hormones directly into the blood stream or lymph.

en·do·cri·nol·o·gy (en′də kri nol′ə jē, -krī-) *n.* branch of medicine dealing with the endocrine glands and their secretions. —**en′do·cri·nol′o·gist,** *n.*

en·do·derm (en′də durm′) *n.* innermost of the three primary germ layers of animal embryos, that later develops into the lining of most of the digestive and respiratory systems and into certain internal organs, as the liver and pancreas. Also, **en′do·blast′.** [ENDO- + Greek *derma* skin.] —**en′do·der′mal, en′do·der′mic,** *adj.*

en·dog·a·my (en dog′ə mē) *n.* marriage within one's own class, group, or tribe in accordance with custom or law. Distinguished from **exogamy.** [ENDO- + -GAMY.] —**en·do·gam·ic** (en′dō gam′ik), **en·dog′a·mous,** *adj.*

en·dog·e·nous (en doj′ə nəs) *adj.* growing from within; originating internally. Distinguished from **exogenous.** [ENDO- + -GEN + -OUS.]

en·do·lymph (en′də limf′) *n.* fluid contained in the inner ear.

en·do·morph (en′də môrf′) *n.* person having a round, fleshy body. Distinguished from **ectomorph** and **mesomorph.** [ENDO- + *morphē* form, shape.] —**en′do·mor′phic,** *adj.*

en·do·plasm (en′də plaz′əm) *n.* granular inner portion of the cytoplasm of a cell, containing the nucleus, esp. in an amoeba. [ENDO- + -PLASM.]

en·dorse (en dôrs′) *v.t.* **-dorsed, -dors·ing.** *also,* **in·dorse.** *v.t.* to write one's signature on, with or without qualifying comments, on the back of

(a check, draft, note, or similar document) as evidence of its legal transfer or validity. **2.** to give support or approval to; sanction: *The councilmen endorsed the mayor's statement.* [Modification of Middle English *endossen* to write on the back of, from Old French *endosser* literally, to put on the back of, going back to Latin *in* in, on + *dorsum* back.] —**en·dors′er,** *n.* —Syn. **2.** see **approve.**

en·dor·see (en dôr′sē′, en′dôr-) *also,* **in·dor·see.** *n.* one to whom a check, draft, note, or similar document is legally transferred by endorsement.

en·dorse·ment (en dôrs′mənt) *also,* **in·dorse·ment.** *n.* **1.** act of endorsing. **2.** writing, as a signature or comments, placed on the back of a check, draft, note, or similar document as evidence of its legal transfer or validity. **3.** approval; support; sanction: *The chef gave his endorsement to the new frozen food.* **4.** amendment or addition to a contract, record, or legislative bill, esp. an alteration in the coverage provided by an insurance policy; rider.

en·do·skel·e·ton (en′dō skel′ə tən) *n.* internal skeleton which provides support for the body of certain animals, as all vertebrates. Distinguished from **exoskeleton.** —**en′do·skel′e·tal,** *adj.*

en·do·sperm (en′də spurm′) *n.* tissue containing food material, surrounding and providing nourishment for the embryo in a seed plant.

en·do·ther·mic (en′də thur′mik) *adj.* relating to a chemical reaction or other process that is accompanied by the absorption of heat. Distinguished from **exothermic.** Also, **en′do·ther′mal.** [ENDO- + THERMIC.]

en·dow (en dou′) *v.t.* **1.** to give money or property to as a source of permanent income: *The new church was endowed by several parishioners.* **2.** to provide or equip with an ability, talent, or quality (usually with *with*): *a dancer endowed with natural grace.* [Anglo-Norman *endouer* to provide with a dower, from *en-* in (from Latin *in*) + *douer* to give a dowry (from Latin *dōtāre*).]

en·dow·ment (en dou′mənt) *n.* **1.** money or property given to provide a permanent income, as for a church or college. **2.** natural talent, ability, or quality. **3.** act of endowing.

end product 1. final result of a process; outcome. **2.** stable isotope, having no trace of radiation, that is the last member of a radioactive series.

end table, small table placed at the end of a sofa or beside a chair.

en·due (en dōō′, -dū′) *v.t.* **-dued, -du·ing.** *also,* **in·due.** *v.t.* to provide or equip with an ability, talent, or quality; endow: *His writing is endued with clarity and simplicity.* [Old French *enduire* to lead on, put on, introduce, from Latin *indūcere* to lead into; influenced in spelling and meaning by ENDOW and by Latin *induere* to put on.]

en·dur·a·ble (en door′ə bəl, -dyoor′-) *adj.* that can be endured; bearable. —**en·dur′a·bly,** *adv.*

en·dur·ance (en door′əns, -dyoor′-) *n.* **1.** act, fact, or power of bearing up under hardships or difficulties, as pain, stress, or fatigue: *A long-distance runner must have endurance.* **2.** fact, quality, or power of lasting; continued existence: *the endurance of a custom, the endurance of a machine.*

Syn. **1. Endurance, stamina**¹ both mean the ability to withstand physical or mental strain. **Endurance** suggests toughness, the capacity to resist fatigue: *Had we lived, I should have had a tale to tell of the hardihood, endurance, and courage of my companions which would have stirred the heart of every Englishman* (Robert Scott, 1912). **Stamina** implies remaining upright instead of sagging, the ability to keep going despite hardship: *The difficulty of finding food created in these mustangs a stamina which may even have exceeded that of their Arabian ancestors* (Bradley Smith, 1969).

en·dure (en door′, -dyoor′) *v.t.* **-dured, -dur·ing.** *v.t.* **1.** to undergo, as pain, fatigue, stress, or other hardship, without impairment or yielding; stand; bear: *She endured the strenuous hike through the forest without complaint.* **2.** to put up with; tolerate: *She can't endure his rudeness.* —*v.i.* **1.** to continue to be; last. **2.** to suffer without yielding; hold out. [Old French *endurer* to make hard or strong, from Latin *indūrāre* to harden.] —Syn. *v.t.* **1.** see **bear**¹. *v.i.* **1.** see **continue.**

en·dur·ing (en door′ing, -dyoor′-) *adj.* lasting; permanent. —**en·dur′ing·ly,** *adv.*

end·ways (end′wāz′) *also,* **end·wise.** *adv.* **1.** with the end forward or upward. **2.** on end; upright. **3.** lengthwise. **4.** end to end.

En·dym·i·on (en dim′ē ən) *n. Greek Legend.* handsome shepherd loved by Selene, the moon goddess.

end zone, area at either end of a football field between the goal line and the line marking the final boundary of the field.

-ene *suffix* designating certain hydrocarbons, esp. those of the alkene, or olefin, series: *ethylene.*

ENE, east-northeast.

en·e·ma (en′ə mə) *n.* **1.** injection of liquid into the rectum for purgative or diagnostic purposes. **2.** the liquid thus injected or for such an injection. [Greek *enema* injection.]

en·e·my (en′ə mē) *pl.,* **-mies.** *n.* **1.** one who bears hatred for, or wishes

or tries to cause harm to, another. **2.a.** hostile nation or military force. **b.** one belonging to such a nation or force. **3.** something dangerous or injurious: *Disease is an enemy of mankind.* —*adj.* of or relating to a hostile nation or military force. [Old French *enemi* foe, one who bears hatred for another, from Latin *inimīcus* unfriendly, from *in-* not + *amīcus* friend.]

Syn. *n.* **1. Enemy, foe** mean a hostile antagonist. **Enemy** implies deep hatred and a desire to injure, whether an active attempt at harm is being made or not: *Love your enemies, because they tell you your faults* (Franklin, 1756). **Foe** is more rhetorical and suggests a state of active hostilities: *An open foe may prove a curse, but a pretended friend is worse* (Gray, 1727).

en·er·get·ic (en′ər jet′ik) *adj.* having, exerting, or showing energy; vigorous; forceful. —**en′er·get′i·cal·ly,** *adv.*

en·er·gize (en′ər jīz′) **-gized, -giz·ing.** *v.t.* to give energy, force, or strength to. —*v.i.* to exert energy; be active. —**en′er·giz′er,** *n.*

en·er·gy (en′ər jē) *n.*, *pl.* **-gies.** *n.* **1.** capacity for, or tendency toward, forceful action: *The child had more energy than his parents.* **2.** *also,* **energies.** power forcefully or actively exerted: *It took a lot of energy to move the furniture. He put all his energies into helping her.* **3.** vigor or force of expression or action: *a speech marked by honesty and energy, a man of energy.* **4.** *Physics.* capacity for doing work. Energy takes various forms, such as radiant energy, electrical energy, chemical energy, and mechanical energy. [Late Latin *energīa* efficiency, from Greek *energeia* action, efficiency.]

en·er·vate (en′ər vāt′) **-vat·ed, -vat·ing.** *v.t.* to lessen the strength or vitality of; weaken; debilitate: *He was enervated by recurring attacks of malaria.* [Latin *ēnervātus,* past participle of *ēnervāre* to weaken, from *ex* away, out of + *nervus* nerve, sinew.] —**en′er·va′tion, en′er·va′tor,** *n.*

en·fant ter·ri·ble (äN fäN te rē′blə) *pl.,* **en·fants ter·ri·bles** (äN fäN te rē′blə). *French.* person, esp. a young one, whose indiscreet or irresponsible remarks or conduct cause embarrassment to others. [French *enfant terrible* incorrigible child, going back to Latin *infāns* child, baby + *terribilis* frightful, dreadful.]

en·fee·ble (en fē′bəl) **-bled, -bling.** *v.t.* to make feeble; weaken. —**en·fee′ble·ment,** *n.*

en·fi·lade (en′fə lād′) *n.* **1.** gunfire directed from either flank along the length of a line of troops, an enemy position, or other objective. **2.** position vulnerable to such fire. —*v.t.,* **-lad·ed, -lad·ing.** to fire or be in a position to fire along the length of, as a line of troops or an enemy position. [French *enfilade* suite of rooms, string of phrases, raking gunfire, from *enfiler* to thread, going back to Latin *in* in + *fīlum* thread.]

en·fold (en fōld′) *also,* **in·fold.** *v.t.* **1.** to wrap in folds; envelop. **2.** to embrace; clasp.

en·force (en fôrs′) **-forced, -forc·ing.** *v.t.* **1.** to ensure the observance of (a law or rule). **2.** to compel by physical or moral force: *They enforced payment by threats of legal action.* **3.** to give force to; strengthen: *He enforced his case with new evidence.* [Old French *enforcier* to strengthen, going back to Latin *in* in + *fortis* strong.] —**en·force′a·ble,** *adj.* —**en·forc′er,** *n.*

en·force·ment (en fôrs′mənt) *n.* act or process of enforcing.

en·fran·chise (en fran′chīz) **-chised, -chis·ing.** *v.t.* **1.** to grant a franchise to, esp. the right to vote. **2.** to set free, as from slavery; liberate. —**en·fran′chise·ment,** *n.*

eng. **1.** engine; engineer; engineering. **2.** engraved; engraver; engraving.

Eng. **1.** England. **2.** English.

en·gage (en gāj′) **-gaged, -gag·ing.** *v.t.* **1.** to hire or employ (a person) or secure (services, aid, or the like): *to engage two new employees, to engage the professional skills of a surgeon.* **2.** to secure the use of, as lodgings; reserve: *to engage a hotel room.* **3.** to attract and hold (one's attention, interest, or the like); employs; involve: *Her plight engaged his concern.* **4.** to keep busy; occupy: *Housework engages much of her time.* **5.** to bind or pledge (oneself): *We engage ourselves to fulfill certain obligations.* **6.** to pledge to marry; affiance; betroth: *Harry and Gertrude were engaged in January and married in June.* **7.** to meet in combat with; encounter and fight: *The Union soldiers engaged the Confederate soldiers at Gettysburg.* **8.** *Mechanics.* to interlock with; mesh. —*v.i.* **1.** to occupy or involve oneself; take part (with *in*): *Everyone engaged in the search. He engaged in a serious study of the problem.* **2.** to pledge oneself; promise; guarantee: *He engaged to accept the financial responsibility for the project.* **3.** to enter into combat: *The troops engaged with the enemy.* **4.** *Mechanics.* to interlock; mesh: *The gears engaged.* [Old French *engager* to pawn[1], pledge, from *en-* in (from Latin *in*) + *gage* pledge (of Germanic origin).]

en·gage·ment (en gāj′mənt) *n.* **1.** act of engaging; being engaged. **2.** something that engages or binds, as a pledge, agreement, or obligation. **3.** betrothal. **4.** meeting or a promise to meet with someone at a certain time; appointment: *I have an engagement for dinner this eve-*

ning. **5.** employment or period of employment: *The singer signed a contract for a two-week engagement.* **6.** meeting of hostile forces; battle; conflict. —**Syn. 4.** see **appointment.**

en·gag·ing (en gā′jing) *adj.* pleasingly attractive; winning; charming: *Joan has an engaging smile.* —**en·gag′ing·ly,** *adv.* —**en·gag′ing·ness,** *n.*

En·gels, Fried·rich (eng′əlz; frē′driKH) 1820–95, German socialist writer.

en·gen·der (en jen′dər) *v.t.* to develop or bring into being; cause; produce: *The talks engendered several proposals. His attitude engendered much ill will.* —*v.i.* to come into being. [Old French *engendrer,* from Latin *ingenerāre* to produce.]

en·gine (en′jin) *n.* **1.** machine that converts energy into mechanical work. **2.** railroad locomotive. **3.** mechanical contrivance; instrument; device: *engines of war.* **4.** fire engine. **5.** *Archaic.* agency, instrument, or means: *logical analysis, the characteristic engine of* (Blackie, 1871). [Old French *engin* skill, invention, from Latin *ingenium.*]

en·gi·neer (en′ji nēr′) *n.* **1.** person skilled in or practicing any branch of engineering: *an electrical engineer, an aeronautical engineer.* **2.** one who drives or manages an engine, esp. a locomotive. **3.** member of the branch of military force that performs engineering work. **4.** skillful or shrewd manager or leader: *The general was the chief engineer of the victory.* —*v.t.* **1.** to plan, construct, or superintend as an engineer: *to engineer the building of a bridge.* **2.** to manage or lead skillfully or shrewdly: *to engineer the defeat of an opponent. The politician engineered a successful campaign.*

en·gi·neer·ing (en′ji nēr′ing) *n.* science or profession that puts matter and energy to use for man by the practical application of scientific knowledge.

engine house, building for house fire engines.

en·gine·ry (en′jin rē) *n.* engines collectively.

Eng·land (ing′glənd) *n.* largest political division of the United Kingdom, in the southern part of the island of Great Britain. Capital, London. Area, 50,873 sq. mi. Pop. (1961), 43,874,661. [Old English *Engla land* literally, land of the Angles.]

Eng·land·er (ing′glən dər) *n.* member or recent descendant of the people of England.

Eng·lish (ing′glish) *adj.* **1.** of or relating to England or its people. **2.** of, relating to, or expressed in the English language. —*n.* **1. the English,** the people of England collectively. **2.** language of the Germanic branch of the Indo-European family spoken predominantly in the United Kingdom, the United States, Canada, Australia, and New Zealand, and in varying degrees in other parts of the world. The English language is divided into three major periods: **Old English,** A.D. 500–1050, **Middle English,** 1050–1450, and **Modern English,** 1450 to the present. **3.** the English language as spoken in a particular place, at a particular time, or by a particular person or group: *Canadian English, Elizabethan English. The immigrant spoke broken English.* **4.** English translation or equivalent: *"Francis" is the English for the French name "François."* **5.** the English language or its literature as a course of study. **6.** *also,* **english.** spinning motion given to a ball by striking it off-center or by throwing or bowling it with a twist of the wrist. —*v.t.* **1.** to translate into English. **2.** to adopt (a foreign word) into English; anglicize. [Old English *Englisc* relating to the Angles, from *Engle* the Angles.]

English Channel, channel between England and France, connecting the North Sea with the Atlantic Ocean.

English daisy, daisy, *Bellis perennis,* bearing white or pink flowers and growing wild in western Europe.

English horn

English horn, double-reed woodwind instrument of the oboe family, having a pitch one fifth lower than the oboe.

Eng·lish·man (ing′glish mən) *pl.,* **-men.** *n.* member or close descendant of the people of England. —**Eng′lish·wom′an,** *n.*

English muffin, round, flat, unsweetened muffin, usually eaten toasted.

English setter, setter of a breed first developed in England, having a wavy coat that is usually white with dark markings.

English sonnet, Shakespearean sonnet.

English sparrow, house sparrow.

English walnut **1.** oily, sweet,

English setter

at; āpe; cär; end; mē; it; īce; hot; ōld; fôrk; wood; fōol; oil; out; up; ūse; turn; sing; thin; this; zh in treasure; ə in ago, taken, pencil, lemon, circus.

edible nut of a tree, *Juglans regia*, of the walnut family, enclosed in a hard, tan, ridged shell. **2.** the tree that produces this nut.

en·gorge (en gôrj′) **-gorged, -gorg·ing.** *v.t.* **1.** to fill or congest with blood, as a blood vessel or organ. **2.** to swallow greedily; devour. **—en·gorge′ment,** *n.*

engr. 1. engineer; engineering. **2.** engraved; engraver; engraving.

en·graft (en graft′) *also,* **in·graft.** *v.t.* **1.** to graft (a shoot from one tree or plant) into or onto another. **2.** to add permanently into or onto; set firmly; implant.

en·grave (en grāv′) **-graved, -grav·ing.** *v.t.* **1.** to cut or carve letters, figures, or the like into or onto: *Epitaphs are engraved on many tombstones.* **2.** to cut or carve (letters, figures, or the like) into or onto an object or surface: *The boy engraved his initials on the tree.* **3.** to cut or carve (letters, figures, or the like) into a metal plate, stone, wood, or other material for printing. **4.** to print (something) from a metal plate or other material that has been engraved: *to engrave an invitation.* **5.** to impress deeply; fix indelibly: *His dying words were engraved in her mind.* [EN-¹ + GRAVE³.] **—en·grav′er,** *n.*

en·grav·ing (en grā′ving) *n.* **1.** act, art, or process of creating a design, inscription, or picture by cutting lines into a metal plate, stone, wood, or other material. Engravings may be done directly on a finished product, as on jewelry or on the base of a statue, or on a plate from which prints are made, as on some stationery. **2.** design, inscription, or picture engraved on a surface. **3.** engraved printing plate. **4.** printed impression made from such a plate.

en·gross (en grōs′) *v.t.* **1.** to engage or occupy all the attention of; absorb: *The scientist was engrossed in his work. The audience was completely engrossed by the actor's performance.* **2.** to write or copy out in large letters or in a formal manner, as a document. **3.** to buy up large quantities or all of (something, as a commodity) in order to control prices. [Partly from French *en gros* in the lump, wholesale; partly from Anglo-Norman *engrosser* to write in large letters; both going back to Latin *in* in + Late Latin *grossus* thick.] **—en·gross′ment,** *n.*

en·gross·ing (en grō′sing) *adj.* occupying one's full attention; absorbing. **—Syn.** see **interesting.**

en·gulf (en gulf′) *also,* **in·gulf.** *v.t.* to swallow up, as in a gulf or abyss; overwhelm completely: *The avalanche engulfed the small cabin. Civil war engulfed the country.*

en·hance (en hans′) **-hanced, -hanc·ing.** *v.t.* to make greater or heighten, as in beauty, quality, or value; augment; intensify: *The reviews of the poet's most recent book enhanced his reputation.* [Anglo-Norman *enhauncer* to promote, modification of Old French *enhaucier* to raise, going back to Latin *in-* in, on + *altus* high.] **—en·hance′ment,** *n.*

en·har·mon·ic (en′här mon′ik) *adj. Music.* of or relating to notes, as A sharp and B flat, that have different notations but nearly or exactly the same tone when played on instruments using the tempered scale.

e·nig·ma (i nig′mə) *n.* **1.** cryptic or ambiguous statement; riddle. **2.** baffling or perplexing person or thing; mystery: *The ultimate origin of the universe remains an enigma. He was a total enigma to all but his closest friends.* [Latin *aenigma* riddle, from Greek *ainigma*.]

en·ig·mat·ic (en′ig mat′ik, ē′nig-) *adj.* of or like an enigma; mysterious; puzzling. Also, **en′ig·mat′i·cal.** **—Syn.** see **vague.**

En·i·we·tok (en′ə wē′tok, ə nē′wə tŏk′) *n.* large atoll in the Marshall Islands, used as a U.S. testing ground for nuclear weapons.

en·join (en join′) *v.t.* **1.** *Law.* to order (a person or group) to do or to refrain from doing some act, as by an injunction: *The union was enjoined from striking for a period of thirty days.* **2.** to order or direct (a course of action, condition, or the like) on or upon; impose: *Absolute secrecy was enjoined on them.* [Old French *enjoindre* to direct, from Latin *injungere* to join, to charge.]

en·joy (en joi′) *v.t.* **1.** to experience joy or pleasure in: *to enjoy a party.* **2.** to have the use or benefit of: *to enjoy good health.* **3.** to enjoy oneself, to have a good time. [Old French *enjoier* to give joy to, from *en* in (from Latin *in*) + *joie* joy (going back to Latin *gaudium*).]

en·joy·a·ble (en joi′ə bəl) *adj.* giving or capable of giving enjoyment. **—en·joy′a·ble·ness,** *n.* **—en·joy′a·bly,** *adv.*

en·joy·ment (en joi′mənt) *n.* **1.** act or state of enjoying. **2.** that which gives joy, pleasure, or satisfaction: *His work is enjoyment for him.* **3.** joy; pleasure; satisfaction.

en·kin·dle (en kind′əl) *v.t.* **1.** to set on fire; kindle. **2.** to stir up; arouse; excite.

en·lace (en lās′) **-laced, -lac·ing.** *v.t.* **1.** to bind with or as with laces; encircle; enfold. **2.** to intertwine; entangle. [Old French *enlacer* to entangle, going back to Latin *in* in + *laqueāre* to ensnare.]

en·large (en lärj′) **-larged, -larg·ing.** *v.t.* **1.** to increase the size or amount of; make larger: *to enlarge a house. The successful investment enlarged his personal fortune.* **2.** to make a photographic print larger than the original negative. **—v.i. 1.** to become larger. **2. to enlarge on.** to express something at greater length or in more detail. [Old French *enlarg(i)er* to increase, make larger, going back to Latin *in-* in + *largus* abundant.] **—Syn.** *v.t.* see **increase.**

en·large·ment (en lärj′mənt) *n.* **1.** act of enlarging; being enlarged. **2.** thing added so as to enlarge; addition. **3.** enlarged form of something else, esp. a photographic print larger than its original negative.

en·larg·er (en lär′jər) *n.* apparatus for making photographic prints larger than the original negatives.

en·light·en (en līt′ən) *v.t.* to give or reveal knowledge or wisdom to; deliver from prejudice, ignorance, or superstition. **—en·light′en·er,** *n.*

en·light·en·ment (en līt′ən mənt) *n.* **1.** act of enlightening; being enlightened. **2. the Enlightenment.** European philosophical movement of the eighteenth century, characterized by rationalism, skepticism about traditional doctrines, and the empirical method in science.

en·list (en list′) *v.i.* **1.** to join a branch of the armed forces voluntarily. **2.** to join in some cause or enterprise; give support or aid (with *in*). **—v.t. 1.** to engage (someone) for military service; induct. **2.** to persuade to join in some cause or enterprise; secure the support or services of: *Many students were enlisted in the charity drive.*

enlisted man, man in the armed forces who is not a commissioned officer, warrant officer, or cadet.

en·list·ment (en list′mənt) *n.* **1.** act of enlisting; being enlisted. **2.** period of time for which a person enlists.

en·liv·en (en lī′vən) *v.t.* to make lively, active, sprightly, or cheerful; animate: *His witty comments enlivened the discussion.*

en masse (än mas′, en) in a group; all together; as a whole: *The club's officers resigned en masse.* [French *en masse*, going back to Latin *in* in + *massa* lump, mass). See MASS.]

en·mesh (en mesh′) *v.t.* to catch or entangle in or as in a net: *Debts, responsibilities, and expenses will enmesh you* (Shelley, 1822).

en·mi·ty (en′mə tē) *pl.,* **-ties.** *n.* feeling or relation between enemies; ill will; hostility; animosity. [Old French *enemistie*, going back to Latin *inimīcus* unfriendly. See ENEMY.] **—Syn.** see **hostility.**

en·no·ble (i nō′bəl) **-bled, -bling.** *v.t.* **1.** to elevate in nature, quality, or reputation. **2.** to confer a title of nobility on. **—en·no′ble·ment, en·no′bler,** *n.*

en·nui (än wē′) *n.* feeling of listlessness and discontent resulting from inactivity or lack of interest; boredom. [French *ennui*, going back to Latin *in odiō* literally, in hatred.]

E·noch (ē′nək) *n.* **1.** in the Old Testament, the eldest son of Cain. **2.** in the Old Testament, the father of Methuselah.

e·nor·mi·ty (i nôr′mə tē) *pl.,* **-ties.** *n.* **1.** extreme wickedness; outrageousness; heinousness: *the enormity of a crime.* **2.** something wicked or outrageous; heinous crime; atrocity.

e·nor·mous (i nôr′məs) *adj.* **1.** much greater than the usual size, amount, degree, or the like. **2.** *Archaic.* extremely wicked; atrocious; monstrous. [Latin *ēnormis* huge, irregular, from *ex* out of + *norma* carpenter's square, rule.] **—e·nor′mous·ly,** *adv.* **—e·nor′mous·ness,** *n.* **—Syn. 1.** see **huge.**

E·nos (ē′nəs) *n.* in the Old Testament, a son of Seth.

e·nough (i nuf′) *adj.* as much or as many as needed or desired: *enough room, enough money, enough players for a baseball game.* **—n.** quantity or amount that satisfies a need or desire: *There is enough here to feed the whole family.* **—adv. 1.** in a quantity or degree that satisfies a need or desire: *I think the steak is cooked enough. Are you well enough to travel?* **2.** quite; very: *The path up the mountain is steep enough.* **3.** tolerably; fairly: *The children behaved well enough.* **—interj.** that's enough; stop. [Old English *genōg* sufficient, abundant.]

Syn. *adj.* Enough, sufficient, adequate indicate that requirements are met. **Enough** implies that whatever is needed or wanted is present, but not to excess: *He had enough intelligence to see that what he did was wrong.* **Sufficient** suggests that the need or requirement has been filled approximately, neither much over or much under: *We have had sufficient rainfall for a good crop.* **Adequate** implies that a reasonable rather than a rigid requirement has been met comfortably rather than exactly: *He knew no words adequate to convey his thanks.*

e·now (i nou′) *Archaic.* enough.

en·pas·sant (än pä sän′) *French.* **1.** by the way; in passing; incidentally. **2.** in chess, a method of capturing a pawn that, in making its first move of two squares, passes over a square controlled by an opposing pawn. The opposing pawn has the right to capture it by advancing immediately to the square that was passed.

en·quire (in kwīr′) inquire.

en·quir·y (in kwīr′ē, in′kwər ē) inquiry.

en·rage (en rāj′) **-raged, -rag·ing.** *v.t.* to put into a rage; arouse great anger in. [Old French *enrager* to rave, rage, going back to Latin *in* in + *rabiēs* madness, rage.]

en·rapt (en rapt′) *adj.* charmed; enraptured.

en·rap·ture (en rap′chər) **-tured, -tur·ing.** *v.t.* to bring into a state of rapture; delight intensely: *The children were enraptured by the spectacle of the circus.*

en·rich (en rich′) *v.t.* **1.** to make rich or richer: *Revenue from taxes enriched the national treasury.* **2.** to improve, as by adding desirable elements or ingredients: *This tobacco will enrich the blend.* **3.** to increase

the nutritive value of (a food) by the addition of vitamins and minerals in processing. **4.** to make (soil) more fertile. [Old French *enrichir* to make wealthy, adorn, from *en* in (from Latin *in*) + *riche* rich, powerful (of Germanic origin).]

en·rich·ment (en rich′mənt) *n.* **1.** act of enriching; being enriched. **2.** that which enriches.

en·roll (en rōl′) **-rolled, -roll·ing.** *also,* **en·rol.** *v.t.* **1.** to put or record (a name) in a list; register. —*v.i.* **1.** to have or put one's name on a list. **2.** to become a member; join: *to enroll in a history course.* [Old French *enroller* to register, from *en* in (from Latin *in*) + *rolle* roll (from Medieval Latin *rotulus* roll of paper, going back to Latin *rota* wheel).]

en·roll·ment (en rōl′mənt) *also,* **en·rol·ment.** *n.* **1.** act of enrolling; being enrolled. **2.** number of persons enrolled.

en route (än rōōt′, en) on the way: *They will stop en route.* [French *en route,* from *en* (see EN-¹) + *route* road, way. See ROUTE.]

Ens., Ensign.

en·sam·ple (en sam′pəl) *n. Archaic.* example.

en·san·guine (en sang′gwin) **-guined, -guin·ing.** *v.t.* to stain with or as with blood.

en·sconce (en skons′) **-sconced, -sconc·ing.** *v.t.* **1.** to settle or lodge comfortably and securely: *Father is ensconced in the chair by the fireplace.* **2.** to hide or shelter: *He must discover where this Stewart hath ensconced himself* (Scott, 1828). [EN-¹ + earlier *sconce* fortification, from Dutch *schans* bulwark.]

en·sem·ble (än säm′bəl) *n.* **1.** all the parts of something considered as a whole; total effect: *The furniture made a charming ensemble.* **2.** harmonious set of clothes designed as a whole: *Her ensemble consisted of a dress, shoes, a hat, and a coat.* **3.** small group of musicians performing together. **4.** united performance of an entire group of singers, musicians, or the like. [French *ensemble* together, going back to Latin *in* in + *simul* at the same time.]

en·shrine (en shrīn′) **-shrined, -shrin·ing.** *v.t.* **1.** to enclose in or as in a shrine. **2.** to hold sacred; cherish: *His words were enshrined in her memory.* —**en·shrine′ment,** *n.*

en·shroud (en shroud′) *v.t.* to shroud; conceal: *The house was enshrouded in darkness.*

en·sign (*defs. 1,3,4* en′sīn, -sən; *def. 2* en′sən) *n.* **1.** flag or banner, esp. a national or a naval standard. **2.** in the U. S. Navy or Coast Guard, lowest-ranking commissioned officer, ranking below a lieutenant junior grade. **3.** formerly, a British army officer who acted as a standard-bearer. **4.** badge or emblem of rank, office, or authority. [Old French *enseigne* sign, standard, from Latin *insignia,* plural of *insigne* mark, badge, standard. Doublet of INSIGNIA.]

en·sign·ship (en′sən ship′) *n.* rank, office, or commission of an ensign.

en·si·lage (en′sə lij) *n.* **1.** process of preserving green moist fodder for cattle by packing it into an airtight silo or pit. **2.** green fodder preserved in this way. Also, *(def. 2),* **si′lage.** [French *ensilage* putting grain in a silo, from *ensiler* to preserve grain in a silo, from Spanish *ensilar* to preserve grain in a pit, from *en* (from Latin *in*) + *silo* pit. See SILO.]

en·sile (en sīl′) *v.t.* to store (green fodder) in an airtight silo or pit to preserve it.

en·slave (en slāv′) **-slaved, -slav·ing.** *v.t.* to make a slave of; reduce to or as if to slavery. —**en·slave′ment,** *n.*

en·snare (en snâr′) **-snared, -snar·ing.** *also,* **in·snare.** *v.t.* to catch or entangle in or as in a snare; entrap.

en·sue (en sōō′) **-sued, -su·ing.** *v.i.* **1.** to come or happen afterward; arise subsequently; follow: *The first chapters were better than those that ensued.* **2.** to occur as a consequence; result: *The two groups met, and a brief scuffle ensued.* [Old French *ensu-,* a stem of *ensuivre* to follow, going back to Latin *insequi.*] —**Syn. 1.** see **follow.**

en·sure (en shōōr′) **-sured, -sur·ing.** *v.t.* **1.** to make sure or certain; guarantee: *to ensure the success of a venture.* **2.** to make safe or secure; protect: *Vaccinations ensure one against diseases.* [Anglo-Norman *enseurer,* modification of Old French *as(s)eurer* to make sure, assure. See ASSURE.]

-ent *suffix* **1.** (used to form adjectives) being or acting in a specified state or manner: *independent, persistent.* **2.** (used to form nouns) one who or that which performs a specified action: *president, superintendent.* [French *-ent,* from Latin *-ēns* (stem *-ent-*) present participial ending.]

en·tab·la·ture (en tab′lə chər) *n.* horizontal member used in the classi-

cal orders of architecture, supported on columns and composed of the architrave, frieze, and cornice. [Middle French *entablature,* going back to Latin *in* on + *tabula* board, tablet.]

en·tail (en tāl′) *v.t.* **1.** to impose or require as a consequence; involve: *The plan entailed the use of expensive equipment.* **2.** to limit the inheritance of (property) to a specified line of heirs so that it cannot be inherited by anyone else. —*n.* **1.** act of entailing; being entailed. **2.** property that is entailed, as an estate. **3.** rule of descent specified for an estate: *The entail indicated that the estate was to go to male heirs only.* [EN-¹ + Old French *taille* cutting, tax (from *taillier* to cut, limit, tax, from Late Latin *tāliāre* to cut, from Latin *tālea* rod, cutting).] —**en·tail′ment,** *n.*

en·tan·gle (en tang′gəl) **-gled, -gling.** *v.t.* **1.** to catch in or as in a tangle or net; ensnare: *The swimmer was entangled in seaweed.* **2.** to involve, as in difficulties: *An innocent bystander became entangled in the argument.* **3.** to cause to become knotted or tangled; snarl: *to entangle yarn.* **4.** to confuse or complicate: *His reasoning was hopelessly entangled.*

en·tan·gle·ment (en tang′gəl mənt) *n.* **1.** act of entangling; being entangled. **2.** that which entangles.

en·tente (än tänt′; *French* än tänt′) *n.* **1.** broad understanding or agreement between two or more countries, esp. on common diplomatic policies. An entente is less specific and binding than a formal alliance. **2.** countries having such an understanding or agreement. [French *entente* understanding, from *entendre* to hear, understand, from Latin *intendere* to stretch out, apply oneself to.]

entente cor·diale (kôr dyäl′) **1.** friendly, informal collaboration or agreement, esp. between countries. **2. Entente Cordiale.** friendly diplomatic relationship, short of a formal alliance, established before World War I between Great Britain and France against Germany.

en·ter (en′tər) *v.t.* **1.a.** to go or come into: *to enter a room. A sudden thought entered his mind.* **b.** to pass through a surface; penetrate; pierce: *The bullet entered his arm.* **2.** to become a member or participant in; join: *to enter the university, to enter a campaign, to enter a contest.* **3.a.** to cause to be admitted or accepted; enroll (someone or something): *He entered his dog in the competition.* **b.** to set down in writing; make a record of; register: *to enter one's name in a book.* **4.** to take the initial steps in; begin; start: *The organism entered a new phase in its development.* **5.** to place in proper form before a court of law or on record: *to enter a plea of not guilty.* **6.** to register or make a report of (a ship or its cargo) at customs. —*v.i.* **1.a.** to go or come in: *The actor entered when he heard his cue.* **b.** to pierce; penetrate: *The bullet entered above the shoulder.* **2. to enter into. a.** to begin to take part in or engage in: *She entered into politics as a hobby.* **b.** to take an active part in and contribute to: *He entered into the discussion enthusiastically.* **c.** to form a part of; be a constituent element in: *Many factors entered into his decision not to go.* **d.** to consider; discuss; treat: *They entered into the particulars of the subject.* **3. to enter on** (or **upon**). to set out on; begin; start. [Old French *entrer* to go into, begin, from Latin *intrāre* to go into.]

en·ter·ic (en ter′ik) *adj.* intestinal. [Greek *enterikos,* from *entera* intestines.]

en·ter·i·tis (en′tə rī′tis) *n.* inflammation of the lining of the intestines, characterized by diarrhea and sometimes cramps, nausea, and vomiting. [Greek *entera* intestines + -ITIS.]

en·ter·on (en′tə ron′) *n.* alimentary canal; intestine. [Modern Latin *enteron,* from Greek *enteron* an intestine.]

en·ter·prise (en′tər prīz′) *n.* **1.** project or undertaking, esp. one of a difficult, dangerous, or important nature. **2.** readiness to take part in such undertakings; energy; initiative. **3.** business undertaking, organization, or firm. [Old French *entreprise* undertaking, from *entreprendre* to undertake, going back to Latin *inter* among + *prehendere* to take, seize.] —**Syn. 1.** see **project.**

en·ter·pris·ing (en′tər prī′zing) *adj.* showing energy and initiative; venturesome.

en·ter·tain (en′tər tān′) *v.t.* **1.** to hold the attention of so as to divert, interest, or amuse: *The clown entertained the children.* **2.** to have or receive as a guest; give hospitality to: *Every summer they entertain the neighbors at an outdoor party.* **3.** to take into consideration, as an idea or proposal. **4.** to bear in mind; maintain: *He entertained some startling opinions.* —*v.i.* to have or receive guests: *a family that entertains often.* [French *entretenir* to maintain, amuse, provide for, going back to Latin *inter* among + *tenēre* to hold.]

en·ter·tain·er (en′tər tā′nər) *n.* one who entertains, esp. a professional in one of the performing arts.

en·ter·tain·ing (en′tər tā′ning) *adj.* engaging; diverting; amusing. —**en′ter·tain′ing·ly,** *adv.*

en·ter·tain·ment (en′tər tān′mənt) *n.* **1.** act of entertaining; diversion; amusement. **2.** that which entertains, esp. a performance. **3.** the performing arts as a whole: *the world of entertainment.* **4.** reception and treatment of guests; hospitality. —**Syn. 1.** see **amusement.**

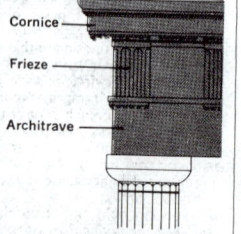

Cornice

Frieze

Architrave

Entablature

at; āpe; cär; end; mē; it; īce; hot; ōld; fôrk; wood; fōōl; oil; out; up; ūse; turn; sing; thin; <u>th</u>is; zh in treasure; ə in ago, taken, pencil, lemon, circus.

en·thrall (en thrôl′) -thralled, -thrall·ing. *also,* **en·thral, in·thrall, in·thral.** *v.t.* **1.** to hold spellbound; captivate; charm: *Everyone was enthralled by her beauty.* **2.** to make a slave of; enslave. —**en·thrall′ment,** *n.*

en·throne (en thrōn′) -throned, -thron·ing. *also,* **in·throne.** *v.t.* **1.** to invest ceremonially with authority, rank, or office, as a sovereign or bishop: *to enthrone a king.* **2.** to put highest of all; exalt; revere. **3.** to place on or as on a throne: *The old man was enthroned at the head of the table.* —**en·throne′ment,** *n.*

en·thuse (en thōōz′) -thused, -thus·ing. *Informal. v.i.* to show enthusiasm. —*v.t.* to make enthusiastic. [From ENTHUSIASM.]

en·thu·si·asm (en thōō′zē az′əm) *n.* eager or fervent interest; ardor; zeal: *He showed great enthusiasm for the plan.* [Greek *enthousiasmos* divine inspiration, going back to *entheos* inspired by a god, possessed, from *en* in + *theos* god.]

en·thu·si·ast (en thōō′zē ast′) *n.* one who is filled with enthusiasm; ardent supporter or follower.
Syn. Enthusiast, zealot, fanatic, fan², devotee indicate intense feeling for or determined occupation with some cause or subject. **Enthusiast** suggests someone whose deep interest in some pursuit often overcomes his connection to ordinary, practical affairs: *It is unfortunate, considering that enthusiasm moves the world, that so few enthusiasts can be trusted to speak the truth* (Balfour, 1918). **Zealot** implies action for a cause and intense devotion to it: *Pennsylvania, too, organized an Antimasonic party, and Thaddeus Stevens was its zealot and its prophet* (Tyler, 1944). **Fanatic** suggests an undeviating determination to follow a course, sometimes to the point of irrationality: *Fanatics have their dreams, wherewith they weave a paradise for a sect* (Keats, 1819). **Fan** is a popular shortening of **fanatic** and is used of one who becomes an avid follower of some form of entertainment, esp. a passive one like motion pictures or a spectator sport: *Ordinarily, a book by a coach is written for other coaches, or for players, and sometimes for the fan* (Glickman, 1952). **Devotee** implies one who faithfully pursues a course, often with religious intensity: *The almighty dollar . . . seems to have no genuine devotees in these peculiar villages* (Irving, 1840).

en·thu·si·as·tic (en thōō′zē as′tik) *adj.* full of enthusiasm; ardent; zealous. —**en·thu′si·as′ti·cal·ly,** *adv.*

en·tice (en tīs′) -ticed, -tic·ing. *v.t.* to attract or lure by offering pleasure or reward; tempt: *They enticed him into joining the conspiracy.* [Old French *enticier* to excite, going back to *in* on + *tītiō* firebrand.] —**en·tic′er,** *n.*

en·tice·ment (en tīs′mənt) *n.* **1.** act of enticing; being enticed. **2.** that which entices.

en·tire (en tīr′) *adj.* **1.** having or including all the parts or elements; total; complete; whole: *The entire faculty was present. He donated the entire sum to charity.* **2.** not broken or impaired; in one piece; intact. **3.** (of leaves) having smooth edges and not divided. [Old French *entier* upright, genuine, from Latin *integer* whole. Doublet of INTEGER.] —**Syn.** **1.** see complete.

en·tire·ly (en tīr′lē) *adv.* **1.** without exception or reservation; wholly; completely. **2.** solely; exclusively.

en·tire·ty (en tīr′tē) *pl.* -ties. *n.* **1.** state of being whole or complete; totality: *The opera was too long to be performed in its entirety.* **2.** that which is entire; whole: *He spent the entirety of his life pursuing success.*

en·ti·tle (en tīt′əl) -tled, -tling. *also,* **in·ti·tle.** *v.t.* **1.** to give the title of; call; designate: *John Bunyan wrote a book entitled "Pilgrim's Progress."* **2.** to give a claim or right to; qualify; authorize: *His high score entitled him to a prize. What entitles you to criticize him?* [Old French *entiteler* to mention, relate, from Late Latin *intitulāre* to give a name to, from Latin *in* in + *titulus* title, label.]

en·ti·ty (en′tə tē) *pl.* -ties. *n.* **1.** something with real and distinct existence, whether objectively or in the mind; an actual thing. **2.** being; existence. [Medieval Latin *entitas* existence, real substance, from Late Latin *ēns* a thing, from Latin *esse* to be.]

en·tomb (en tōōm′) *also,* **in·tomb.** *v.t.* **1.** to place in a tomb; bury. **2.** to serve as a tomb for. —**en·tomb′ment,** *n.*

en·to·mo·log·i·cal (en′tə mə loj′i kəl) *adj.* of or relating to entomology. Also, **en·to·mo·log′ic.**

en·to·mol·o·gy (en′tə mol′ə jē) *n.* branch of zoology dealing with insects. [Greek *entomon* insect + -LOGY.] —**en′to·mol′o·gist,** *n.*

en·tou·rage (än′tōō räzh′) *n.* group of attendants, followers, or companions, esp. one accompanying a person of rank or importance; retinue. [French *entourage* circle of attendants, from *entourer* to surround, from *en-* in (from Latin *in*) + *tour* turn, circuit. See TOUR.]

en·tr'acte (än trakt′) *n.* **1.** interval between two parts of a theatrical performance. **2.** entertainment provided during this interval. [French *entracte* interval between the acts, from *entre* between (from Latin *inter*) + *acte* action, act. See ACT.]

en·trails (en′trālz, -trəlz) *n.,pl.* **1.a.** inner organs of a man or animal; guts; viscera. **b.** intestines; bowels. **2.** *Informal.* inner parts or mech-

anism of anything; innards. [Old French *entrailles* intestines, going back to Latin *interānea,* from *inter* within.]

en·train (en trān′) *v.i., v.t.* to go or put aboard a train.

en·trance¹ (en′trəns) *n.* **1.** act of entering: *Everyone rose at the judge's entrance. The campaign marked his entrance into politics.* **2.** place or means for entering: *an entrance to a building.* **3.** right or power of entering; admittance: *Students were given free entrance to the basketball game.* [Old French *entrance* a going in, passage for entering, beginning, from *entrer* to go into, begin. See ENTER.]

en·trance² (en trans′) -tranced, -tranc·ing. *v.t., v.i.* **1.** to put into a trance. **2.** to fill with joy, delight, or wonder; charm; enchant. [EN-¹ + TRANCE.] —**en·trance′ment,** *n.* —**en·tranc′ing·ly,** *adv.*

en·trance·way (en′trəns wā′) *n.* small chamber or hall through which a larger room or structure can be entered.

en·trant (en′trənt) *n.* **1.** one who enters a contest; contestant; competitor. **2.** one who enters, esp. a new member of a profession or association. [French *entrant,* present participle of *entrer* to go into. See ENTER.]

en·trap (en trap′) -trapped, -trap·ping. *v.t.* **1.** to catch in or as in a trap. **2.** to involve in difficulty or danger by trickery or deception; entangle; ensnare. [Old French *entraper* to pester, catch, from *en-* in (from Latin *in*) + *trape* trap (of Germanic origin).]

en·treat (en trēt′) *also,* **in·treat.** *v.t.* to ask earnestly; beseech; implore. —*v.i.* to appeal; plead. [Old French *entraiter* to treat, of treat, going back to Latin *in* in + *tractāre* to handle.] —**Syn.** *v.t.* see beg.

en·treat·y (en trē′tē) *pl.* -treat·ies. *n.* earnest request; supplication; plea.

en·tree (än′trā) *also,* **en·trée.** *n.* **1.a.** main dish or course at a meal. **b.** food served between courses at a meal, esp. between the fish and meat courses. **2.** freedom, right, or privilege to enter; access; admission. [French *entrée* entrance, first course, from *entrer* to go into. See ENTER.]

en·trench (en trench′) *also,* **in·trench.** *v.t.* **1.** to place in a trench; surround or fortify with trenches. **2.** to establish firmly or securely: *The practice became entrenched in tradition and law.* —*v.i.* to encroach or trespass (with *on* or *upon*): *His work entrenched on his free time.*

en·trench·ment (en trench′mənt) *also,* **in·trench·ment.** *n.* **1.** act of entrenching. **2.** fortification consisting of a trench or trenches, usually with a bank of earth along the side facing the enemy.

en·tre nous (än′trə nōō′) *French.* between ourselves; confidentially.

en·tre·pre·neur (än′trə prə nur′, -noor′) *n.* one who organizes, controls, and assumes the risks of a business or other financial enterprise. [French *entrepreneur* contractor, from *entreprendre* to undertake, going back to Latin *inter* among + *prehendere* to take.]

en·tre·sol (en′tər sol′, en′trə-, än′trə-) *n.* mezzanine. [French *entresol,* going back to Latin *inter* between + *solum* floor, ground.]

en·trust (en trust′) *also,* **in·trust.** *v.t.* **1.** to put something in the trust of; invest or charge with a trust or responsibility: *The chairman was entrusted with the task of settling the dispute.* **2.** to commit the care or safety of; assign responsibility for: *The chemist entrusted the completion of the work to his assistant.*

en·try (en′trē) *pl.* -tries. *n.* **1.** act, right, or an instance of entering. **2.** place for entering; entrance. **3.** written item included in a book, diary, list, or other record: *daily entries in a ship's log. The inventory contained an entry for every object in the warehouse.* **4.a.** word, term, phrase, affix, symbol, abbreviation, or the like, defined or identified in a dictionary, usually set off by boldface type. **b.** such an item together with its definitions or other accompanying information. **5.** that which is entered in a contest or race: *All entries must be twenty-five words or less.* **6.** act of submitting imported goods for inspection at customs for the purpose of estimating the duty to be paid on them. **7.** act of claiming possession of real property by entering or setting foot on it. [Old French *entree* act of entering, place for entering, admittance to a place, beginning, from *entrer* to go into, begin. See ENTER.]

en·twine (en twīn′) -twined, -twin·ing. *v.t., v.i.* to twine together; twist or twine around.

en·twist (en twist′) *v.i., v.t.* to twist together or around.

e·nu·mer·ate (i nōō′mə rāt′, i nū′-) -at·ed, -at·ing. *v.t.* **1.** to name one by one; list: *He enumerated his reasons for resigning.* **2.** to ascertain the number of; count. [Latin *ēnumerātus,* past participle of *ēnumerāre* to reckon up, from *ex* out, utterly + *numerus* number.] —**e·nu′mer·a′tive,** *adj.* —**e·nu′mer·a′tor,** *n.*

e·nu·mer·a·tion (i nōō′mə rā′shən, i nū′-) *n.* **1.** act of enumerating. **2.** catalogue; list.

e·nun·ci·ate (i nun′sē āt′) -at·ed, -at·ing. *v.t.* **1.** to utter (words or speech sounds), esp. in a particular manner; articulate: *It is often difficult to understand someone who does not enunciate his words clearly.* **2.** to state definitely, as a theory or principle. **3.** to announce; proclaim. —*v.i.* to utter words or speech sounds, esp. in a particular manner. [Latin *ēnūntiātus,* past participle of *ēnūntiāre* to declare, disclose, going back to *ex* out, utterly + *nūntius* messenger.] —**e·nun′ci·a′tor,** *n.*

e·nun·ci·a·tion (i nun′sē ā′shən) *n.* **1.** way of pronouncing; pronunciation. **2.** statement; declaration. —**Syn. 1.** see **pronunciation.**

en·vel·op (en vel′əp) *v.t.* to wrap up or cover completely; form a covering about and conceal: *Clouds enveloped the mountain peak.* [Old French *enveloper* to enfold, probably going back to Latin *in in* + a blend of Medieval Latin *faluppa* wisp of straw, and Latin *volvere* to roll.]

en·ve·lope (en′və lōp′, än′-) *n.* **1.** flat, usually paper, wrapper or container, used esp. for mailing letters. **2.** that which envelops; covering; wrapper. **3.a.** outer covering of a balloon or airship, usually made of fabric. **b.** bag containing the gas in a balloon or airship. [French *enveloppe* covering, envelope of a letter, from *envelopper* to wrap up, cover. See ENVELOP.]

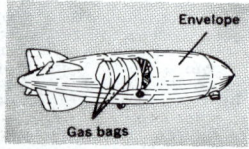

Envelope (def. 3a)

en·vel·op·ment (en vel′əp mənt) *n.* **1.** act of enveloping; being enveloped. **2.** that which envelops; wrapping; covering.

en·ven·om (en ven′əm) *v.t., v.i.* **1.** to fill with venom; make poisonous. **2.** to fill with hate or vindictiveness; embitter: *His thoughts were envenomed by the betrayal.* [Old French *envenimer* to poison, contaminate, going back to Latin *in in* + *venēnum* poison.]

en·vi·a·ble (en′vē ə bəl) *adj.* worthy of envy; desirable. —**en′vi·a·ble·ness,** *n.* —**en′vi·a·bly,** *adv.*

en·vi·ous (en′vē əs) *adj.* characterized by envy; feeling or showing envy. [Old French *envieus* covetous, greedy, exciting envy, from Latin *invidiōsus* full of envy.] —**en′vi·ous·ly,** *adv.* —**en′vi·ous·ness,** *n.*
Syn. Envious, jealous mean to feel resentment at another's good fortune or superiority. **Envious** suggests the gnawing feeling of discontent over the prosperity or success of another and a desire to have that prosperity: *Martha was envious of her sister's popularity.* **Jealous** emphasizes intolerance of a rival because he possesses something which one feels should have come to oneself: *Paul was jealous of Henry's fame as an actor.*

en·vi·ron (en vī′rən, -vī′ərn) *v.t.* to encircle; envelop; surround: *Clear air and grassy plains environ the city.* [Old French *environner* to surround, from *environ* around, from *en-* (from Latin *in*) + *virer* to turn round, veer. See VEER.]

en·vi·ron·ment (en vī′rən mənt, -vī′ərn-) *n.* **1.** all of the surrounding, external factors that actually or potentially affect the development and functioning of a living thing. **2.** surroundings.

en·vi·ron·men·tal (en vī′rən mEnt′əl, -vī′ərn-) *adj.* of or relating to environment. —**en·vi′ron·men′tal·ly,** *adv.*

en·vi·ron·men·tal·ist (en vī′rən mEnt′əl ist, -vī′ərn-) *n.* one who is concerned about the quality of the environment, esp. about the effects of pollution on the earth's atmosphere.

en·vi·rons (en vī′rənz, -vī′ərnz, en′vər ənz) *n.,pl.* surrounding districts, as of a town or city; outskirts.

en·vis·age (en viz′ij) *-aged, -ag·ing. v.t.* to form a mental picture of; visualize, esp. some expected event. [French *envisager* to face, consider, from *en-* in (from Latin *in*) + *visage* face. See VISAGE.]

en·vi·sion (en vizh′ən) *v.t.* to form a conception of; imagine.

en·voy[1] (en′voi, än′-) *n.* **1.a.** diplomat ranking next below an ambassador; minister plenipotentiary. **b.** *Informal.* any diplomat. **2.** anyone sent as messenger or representative of another. [French *envoyé* person sent, from *envoyer* to send, going back to Latin *in viam* on the way.]

en·voy[2] (en′voi, än′-) *n. also,* **en·voi.** concluding stanza of a verse or prose work, usually written as a dedication or summary. Also, **l'en′voy, l'en′voi.** [Old French *envoi* a sending, conclusion, from *envoyer* to send. See ENVOY[1].]

en·vy (en′vē) *pl.* **-vies.** *n.* **1.** one's feeling of discontent or resentment over possession by another of something one wishes to possess. **2.** object of this resentment: *His new car made him the envy of every boy in the neighborhood.* —*v.t.,* **-vied, -vy·ing.** **1.** to feel envy toward (someone); regard with envy. **2.** to feel envy because of: *I envy his good marks.* [Old French *envie* jealousy, grudge, from Latin *invidia* jealousy, from *invidēre* to look maliciously at.] —**en′vi·er,** *n.*

en·womb (en wōōm′) *v.t.* to enclose in, or as in, a womb.

en·wrap (en rap′) **-wrapped, -wrap·ping.** *also,* **in·wrap.** *v.t.* to enfold; envelop (with *in* or *with*).

en·wreathe (en rēth′) **-wreathed, -wreath·ing.** *also,* **in·wreathe.** *v.t.* to encircle or envelop with, or as with, a wreath; wreathe.

en·zo·ot·ic (en′zō ot′ik) *adj.* of or relating to any disease affecting animals in a certain geographical area. —*n.* enzootic disease.

en·zyme (en′zīm) *n.* any one of the chemical substances produced in the living cells of all plants and animals that act as catalysts in the regulation of biological processes. [German *Enzym,* from Middle Greek *enzýmos* leavened, from Greek *en* in + *zýmē* leaven.]

E·o·cene (ē′ə sēn′) *n.* second geological epoch of the Tertiary period of the Cenozoic era, when such animals as the horse, the elephant, and the camel first appeared. —*adj.* of or relating to this epoch. [Greek *ēōs* dawn + *kainos* new.]

e·o·hip·pus (e′ō hip′əs) *n.* early ancestor of the horse, genus *Hyracotherium,* found as a fossil in Eocene deposits in North America and Europe. Height: 10–12 inches. [Modern Latin *Eohippus,* from Greek *ēōs* dawn + *hippos* horse.]

E·o·li·an (ē ō′lē ən) **1.** Aeolian[2]. **2.** eolian. aeolian[1].

E·ol·ic (ē ol′ik) Aeolian[2].

e·o·lith (ē′ə lith′) *n.* any crude stone implement, either naturally shaped or chipped, believed to have been used as a tool by early man. [Greek *ēōs* dawn + *lithos* stone.]

e·o·lith·ic (ē′ə lith′ik) *adj.* of or relating to one of the earliest periods of human culture, at the dawn of the Stone Age, characterized by the use of eoliths.

e·on (ē′ən, ē′on) *also,* **ae·on.** *n.* **1.** very long, indefinite period of time; thousands of years. **2.** largest division of geological time, including at least two eras. [Latin *aeōn* age, from Greek *aiōn.*]

E·os (ē′əs) *n.* Greek goddess of the dawn. Her Roman counterpart is Aurora. [Latin *Ēōs,* from Greek *Ēōs,* from *ēōs* dawn.]

e·o·sin (ē′ə sin) *n.* **1.** reddish coloring matter, obtained from coal tar, used as a dye or stain. **2.** any of several related dyes obtained from coal tar. [Greek *ēōs* dawn + -IN[1]; from the rosy color of the dye.]

ep-, form of **epi-** before vowels and *h,* as in *eponym, ephemeral.*

E·pam·i·non·das (i pam′ə non′dəs) *n.* c.418–362 B.C., Theban general and statesman.

ep·au·let (ep′ə let′ -lət, ep′ə let′) *also,* **ep·au·lette.** *n.* ornamental device designed to be worn on the shoulder of a uniform, as by a military officer, sometimes indicating rank. [French *épaulette,* diminutive of *épaule* shoulder, going back to Late Latin *spatula,* from Latin *spatula* blade. See SPATULA.]

Epaulets

e·pee (ā pā′) *also,* **é·pée.** *n.* **1.** long thin fencing sword with no cutting edge, less flexible than a foil. **2.** bout, series of bouts, or sport of fencing with the epee. [French *épée* this sword, from Latin *spatha* broadsword. See SPATULA.]

Eph., Ephesians.

e·phah (ē′fə) *n.* ancient Hebrew dry measure, a little more than a bushel. [Hebrew *ēphāh* a measure; probably of Egyptian origin.]

e·phed·rine (i fed′rin, ef′ə drēn′, -drin) *n.* crystalline, alkaloid drug used esp. to treat low blood pressure and to relieve hay fever and asthma. Formula: $C_{10}H_{15}NO$ [Modern Latin *Ephedra* (genus name) (from Latin *ephedra* horsetail plant, from Greek *ephedrā*) + -INE[2]; because the drug was first derived from plants of the genus *Ephedra.*]

e·phem·er·a (i fem′ər ə) *pl.,* **-er·as** or **-er·ae** (-ər ē). *n.* **1.** anything or anyone that is ephemeral. **2.** ephemerid.

e·phem·er·al (i fem′ər əl) *adj.* **1.** lasting for a very short time; short-lived; fleeting. **2.** *Biology.* lasting for only a day. [Greek *ephēmeros* lasting for a day (from *epi* for + *hēmerā* day) + -AL[1].]

e·phem·er·id (i fem′ər id) *n.* May fly.

e·phem·er·is (i fem′ər is) *pl.,* **eph·e·mer·i·des** (ef′ə mer′i dēz′). *n.* table or collection of tables showing the predicted positions of celestial bodies, esp. the sun, moon, or planets, during a specified period of time. [Latin *ephēmeris* diary, from Greek *ephēmeris* diary, calendar, from *ephēmeros* lasting for a day.]

E·phe·sian (i fē′zhən) *adj.* of Ephesus or its people. —*n.* **1.** native or inhabitant of Ephesus. **2. Ephesians.** book of the New Testament, written as an epistle by the Apostle Paul to the Christians in Ephesus.

Eph·e·sus (ef′i səs) *n.* ancient city on the west coast of Asia Minor.

eph·od (ef′od, ē′fod) *n.* among the ancient Hebrews, apronlike vestment worn by priests in performing sacred duties and by judges. [Hebrew *ēphōd.*]

eph·or (ef′ôr, -ər) *pl.,* **-ors** or **-o·ri** (-ə rī′). *n.* one of the five chief magistrates elected annually in ancient Sparta to advise the kings. [Latin *ephorus,* from Greek *ephoros,* from *ephorān* to oversee.]

E·phra·im (ē′frē əm, ē′frəm) *n.* **1.** in the Old Testament, the younger son of Joseph. **2.** tribe of Israel descended from him. **3.** the kingdom of Israel.

epi- *prefix* on; upon; near; among: *epidermis, epigram.* [Greek *epi* upon, at, after, to, besides.]

ep·ic (ep′ik) *n.* **1.** long narrative poem, written in an elevated style, celebrating the adventures and achievements of one or more heroic figures of legend, history, or religion. The *Odyssey,* the *Aeneid,* and *Beowulf* are epics. **2.** any written work or play having similar characteristics. **3.** story or series of events worthy of being told in this manner: *the epic of man's exploration of space.* —*adj. also,* **ep′i·cal.** **1.** of or relating to an epic. **2.** like an epic in subject or scope: *an epic novel.* **3.** suitable for an epic in nature, subject, or scope; heroic: *the epic events*

of westward expansion in the United States. **4.** very long or of unusually large size or wide scope: *an epic voyage around the moon.* [Latin *epicus* epic poem, from Greek *epikos,* from *epos* word, song, story.] —**ep′i·cal·ly,** *adv.*

ep·i·ca·lyx (ep′i kā′liks, -kal′iks) *pl.,* **-ca·lyx·es** or **-ca·ly·ces** (-kā′li sēz′, -kal′i-). *n.* involucre resembling a calyx.

ep·i·carp (ep′ə kärp′) *n.* the outer layer of the ripened ovary of a plant, as the skin of a peach or the rind of an orange. See **pericarp** for illustration. [Epi- + Greek *karpos* fruit.]

ep·i·cen·ter (ep′i sen′tər) *n.* point on the earth's surface directly above the underground point where an earthquake begins.

ep·i·cot·yl (ep′ə kot′əl) *n.* part of the stem of a plant embryo or seedling above the cotyledons.

Ep·ic·te·tus (ep′ik tē′təs) *n.* A.D. c.60–140, Greek Stoic philosopher.

ep·i·cure (ep′i kyoor′) *n.* person who cultivates a refined taste for and enjoys good food and drink. [From Epicurus.]

Syn. Epicure, gourmet, gourmand denote a person of refined and discriminating taste in food and drink. **Epicure** is a connoisseur of fine food and drink who delights in the pleasures of the table: *The big hotel was an epicure's paradise.* **Gourmet** is an expert in fine food who has the ability to distinguish delicate differences in flavor, taste, or aroma: *Helen's cooking is so good that it will satisfy even the most demanding gourmet.* **Gourmand** has a less fastidious and sensitive palate but has a hearty appetite and a voluptuous enjoyment of good food: *Paul was a gourmand who spent most of his time in restaurants.*

ep·i·cu·re·an (ep′i kyoo rē′ən, -kyoor′ē ən) *adj.* **1.** given to luxurious tastes or habits, esp. in eating and drinking; of or like an epicure. **2.** fit for an epicure. **3.** Epicurean. of, relating to, or characteristic of Epicurus or his philosophy. —*n.* **1.** epicure. **2.** Epicurean. follower of or believer in Epicurus or his philosophy.

Ep·i·cu·re·an·ism (ep′i kyoo rē′ə niz′əm, -kyoor′ē ə-) *n.* **1.** philosophy founded by Epicurus, which holds that pleasure, sought by the wise man in the lasting virtues of honesty, justice, and friendship, is the highest good of man. **2.** *also,* **epicureanism.** belief in or practice of this philosophy.

Ep·i·cu·rus (ep′i kyoor′əs) *n.* c.342–270 B.C., Greek philosopher.

ep·i·cy·cle (ep′ə sī′kəl) *n.* **1.** *Geometry.* small circle, the center of which moves around the circumference of a larger circle. **2.** *Astronomy.* (in the Ptolemaic system) circle of a planet's orbit, the center of which describes a larger circle as the planet supposedly rotates about the earth.

ep·i·cy·cloid (ep′ə sī′kloid) *n.* *Geometry.* curve generated by a point on a circle rolling on the outside circumference of another circle.

ep·i·dem·ic (ep′ə dem′ik) *n.* **1.** rapid spread or sudden, widespread appearance of a disease in a locality or large area. **2.** disease thus prevalent: *The epidemic was diagnosed as a virulent form of influenza.* **3.** rapid spread or sudden, widespread appearance of something, as an idea, fad, or fashion: *There was an epidemic of young folk singers that year.* —*adj. also,* **ep·i·dem′i·cal.** spreading among and simultaneously affecting many people; widespread. [French *épidémique* widespread, from *épidémie* prevalence of a disease, from Medieval Latin, going back to Greek *epidēmios* among the people.]

ep·i·de·mi·ol·o·gy (ep′ə dē′mē ol′ə jē) *n.* branch of medicine that deals with epidemic diseases. —**ep·i·de·mi·o·log·i·cal** (ep′ə dē′mē ə loj′i kəl), *adj.* —**ep·i·de′mi·o·log′i·cal·ly,** *adv.* —**ep·i·de·mi·ol′o·gist,** *n.*

ep·i·der·mal (ep′ə dur′məl) *adj.* of or relating to the epidermis.

ep·i·der·mis (ep′ə dur′mis) *n.* **1.** protective outer layer of the skin of vertebrates, lacking blood vessels and nerves. See **skin** for illustration. **2.** protective outer layer of various invertebrates. **3.** skinlike outer layer of cells of seed plants and ferns. [Late Latin *epidermis* the surface skin, from Greek *epidermis.*]

e·pig·e·nous (i pij′ə nəs) *adj.* *Botany.* growing on the surface, esp. the upper surface, as fungi on a leaf.

ep·i·glot·tis (ep′ə glot′is) *n.* thin triangular flap of cartilage that covers the entrance to the windpipe during swallowing, preventing foreign matter from entering the lungs. [Greek *epiglōttis,* from *epi* near + *glōtta* tongue.]

ep·i·gram (ep′ə gram′) *n.* **1.** concise, pointed statement expressing a thought in a witty manner, for example: *There is only one thing in the world worse than being talked about, and that is not being talked about* (Wilde, 1871). **2.** short, pithy poem leading to a witty or satirical turn at the end. [Latin *epigramma* short poem, inscription, from Greek *epigramma.*]

ep·i·gram·mat·ic (ep′i grə mat′ik) *adj.* **1.** of, relating to, or using

Epiglottis open

Epiglottis closed

Esophagus

Trachea

Epiglottis

epigrams. **2.** like or suitable to an epigram; witty, pointed, and concise. —**ep′i·gram·mat′i·cal·ly,** *adv.*

ep·i·gram·ma·tist (ep′ə gram′ə tist) *n.* person who composes epigrams.

ep·i·gram·ma·tize (ep′ə gram′ə tīz′) *-tized, -tiz·ing. v.i.* to compose an epigram or epigrams; speak or write epigrammatically. —*v.t.* **1.** to express in the form of an epigram. **2.** to make the subject of an epigram.

ep·i·graph (ep′ə graf′) *n.* **1.** *Archeology.* inscription, as on a building, tomb, or monument. **2.** quotation prefacing a book or a chapter. [From Greek *epigraphē* inscription.]

e·pig·ra·phy (i pig′rə fē) *n.* **1.** inscriptions collectively. **2.** study dealing with the deciphering and interpretation of inscriptions, esp. ancient ones. —**e·pig′ra·pher, e·pig′ra·phist,** *n.*

e·pig·y·nous (i pij′ə nəs) *adj.* *Botany.* with stamens, petals, and sepals appearing to originate at or near the top of the ovary. [Epi- + *gynē* woman + -ous.]

ep·i·lep·sy (ep′ə lep′sē) *n.* disorder of the brain characterized by recurring seizures which may take the form of convulsions or unconsciousness. [Late Latin *epilēpsia,* from Greek *epilēpsiā,* from *epilambanein* to seize.]

ep·i·lep·tic (ep′ə lep′tik) *adj.* of, relating to, or having epilepsy. —*n.* one who has epilepsy.

ep·i·logue (ep′ə lôg′, -log′) *also,* **ep·i·log.** *n.* **1.** passage or section added to the end of a written work as an explanation, summary, or conclusion. **2.** speech or short poem addressed to the audience by one of the actors at the end of a play. [Old French *epilogue* peroration of a speech, from Latin *epilogus,* from Greek *epilogos* peroration, concluding part of a play.]

ep·i·neph·rine (ep′ə nef′rēn, -rin) *also,* **ep·i·neph·rin** (ep′ə nef′rin). *n.* adrenalin.

e·piph·a·ny (i pif′ə nē) *n.* **1.** manifestation or appearance, esp. of a divine or supernatural being. **2.** Epiphany. Christian holy day commemorating the manifestation of Christ on earth. January 6. In the Western Church it commemorates the visit of the Three Wise Men to the infant Jesus. In the Eastern Church it usually commemorates the baptism of Jesus. **3.** sudden understanding or of insight into the essential meaning or nature of something. [Old French *epiphanie* the Epiphany, from Late Latin *epiphania,* from Greek *epiphania* manifestation.]

ep·i·phyte (ep′ə fīt′) *n.* any of various plants, usually having aerial roots, that grow on other plants for support, but are not parasites. Spanish moss and certain orchids are epiphytes. Also, **air plant.** [Epi- + Greek *phyton* plant.] —**ep′i·phyt′ic,** *adj.*

E·pi·rus (i pī′rəs) *n.* region in western Greece, on the Ionian Sea, in ancient times a separate country.

Epis. **1.** Episcopal. **2.** Episcopalian. **3.** Epistle.

e·pis·co·pa·cy (i pis′kə pə sē) *pl.,* **-cies.** *n.* **1.** government of a church by bishops. **2.** bishops collectively. **3.** position, rank, or term of office of a bishop; episcopate.

e·pis·co·pal (i pis′kə pəl) *adj.* **1.** of or relating to bishops. **2.** governed by bishops. **3.** Episcopal. of or relating to the Church of England or the Protestant Episcopal Church. [Late Latin *episcopālis* relating to a bishop, from *episcopus* bishop, overseer, from Greek *episkopos.*]

E·pis·co·pa·lian (i pis′kə pāl′yən, -pā′lē ən) *n.* member of an Episcopal church, as the Protestant Episcopal Church. —*adj.* Episcopal.

e·pis·co·pate (i pis′kə pit, -pāt′) *n.* **1.** position, rank, or term of office of a bishop. **2.** district under authority of a bishop; diocese. **3.** bishops collectively.

ep·i·sode (ep′ə sōd′) *n.* **1.** incident or event that stands out in any series of events: *an amusing episode during their travels.* **2.** incidental narrative or digression separate from the main plot or subject of a literary work. **3.** installment of a dramatic or literary work that is presented in serial form: *an episode of a soap opera.* **4.** digressive, secondary passage or section in a musical composition or movement. [Greek *epeisodion* addition, from *epeisodios* coming in besides, going back to *epi* besides + *eis* into + *hodos* way.] —**Syn.** 1. see **event.**

ep·i·sod·ic (ep′ə sod′ik) *adj.* of the nature of an episode; incidental. Also, **ep′i·sod′i·cal.**

e·pis·te·mol·o·gy (i pis′tə mol′ə jē) *n.* branch of philosophy that analyzes the origin, nature, methods, and validity of human knowledge. [Greek *epistēmē* knowledge + -logy.] —**e·pis′te·mol′o·gist,** *n.*

e·pis·tle (i pis′əl) *n.* **1.** Epistle. **a.** any one of the letters written by an Apostle and contained in the New Testament. **b.** selection from one of these, read as part of a Christian liturgical service. **2.** letter. ▲ often used humorously to describe a long letter in an elevated style. [Old French *epistle* letter, from Latin *epistola* letter, message.]

e·pis·to·lar·y (i pis′tə ler′ē) *adj.* **1.** consisting of letters; carried on by letters; contained in letters: *an epistolary novel.* **2.** of or relating to letters: *an epistolary style.*

---

at; āpe; cär; end; mē; it; īce; hot; ōld; fôrk; wood; fōol; oil; out; up; ūse; turn; sing; thin; this; zh in treasure; ə in ago, taken, pencil, lemon, circus.

ep·i·style (ep′ə stīl′) *n.* architrave. [Latin *epistȳlium,* from Greek *epistȳlion.*]

ep·i·taph (ep′ə taf′) *n.* **1.** brief statement inscribed on a tombstone or other monument in memory of a dead person. **2.** brief eulogy, written as if it were to be inscribed on a tombstone. **3. to write one's own epitaph,** to say or do something that is likely to bring some endeavor to an end: *The politician wrote his own epitaph.* [Latin *epitaphium* funeral oration, from Greek *epitaphion,* from *epi* on + *taphos* tomb.]

ep·i·tha·la·mi·on (ep′ə thə lā′mē ən) *pl.* **-mi·a** (-mē ə). epithalamium.

ep·i·tha·la·mi·um (ep′ə thə lā′mē əm) *pl.* **-mi·ums** or **-mi·a** (-mē ə) *n.* poem or song in honor of a newly married person or couple. [Latin *epithalamium,* from Greek *epithalamion,* from *epi* at + *thalamos* bridal chamber.]

ep·i·the·li·al (ep′ə thē′lē əl) *adj.* of or relating to the epithelium.

ep·i·the·li·oid (ep′ə thē′lē oid′) *adj.* resembling epithelium.

ep·i·the·li·um (ep′ə thē′lē əm) *pl.* **-li·ums** or **-li·a** (-lē ə). *n.* sheet of body tissue, consisting of one or more layers of cells, that covers the entire surface of the body and lines the body cavities and tubes. [Modern Latin *epithelium,* from Greek *epi* on + *thēlē* nipple.]

Squamous Cuboidal Columnar

Epithelium cells

ep·i·thet (ep′ə thet′) *n.* descriptive word or phrase used with or in place of a name: *Homer's epithet for his hero is "great-hearted Odysseus."* [Latin *epitheton,* from Greek *epithēton* something added.]

e·pit·o·me (i pit′ə mē) *n.* **1.** anyone or anything that exemplifies the whole: *That house is the epitome of extravagant taste.* **2.** condensed account or summary, esp. of a literary work; abridgment. [Latin *tomē* abridgment, from Greek *epitomē.*]

e·pit·o·mize (i pit′ə mīz′) **-mized, -miz·ing.** *v.t.* **1.** to be the epitome of: *That painting epitomizes the use of colors to convey mood.* **2.** to make an epitome of.

ep·i·zo·ot·ic (ep′ə zō ot′ik) *adj.* (of diseases) temporarily prevalent in an animal population. —*n.* epizootic disease.

e plu·ri·bus u·num (ē′ ploor′ə bəs ū′nəm) *Latin.* out of many, one. ▲ motto on the official seal of the United States.

ep·och (ep′ək; *British,* ē′pok) *n.* **1.** period of time distinguished by some particular characteristic, development, or course of events. **2.** division of geological time smaller than a period. [Late Latin *epocha* measure of time, fixed point in time from which years are numbered, from Greek *epochē* pause, fixed point in time.] —**Syn. 1.** see **era.**

ep·och·al (ep′ək kal) *adj.* of, relating to, or marking an epoch.

ep·och-mak·ing (ep′ək mā′king) *adj.* introducing something new and important; beginning an epoch.

ep·ode (ep′ōd) *n.* **1.** lyric poem in which a shorter verse follows a longer one. **2.** that part of a lyric ode that comes after the strophe and antistrophe. [Latin *epōdos,* from Greek *epōídos* this part of an ode.]

ep·o·nym (ep′ə nim) *n.* person, either real or legendary, from whom the name of something like a country, a people, or a place derives, or supposedly derives, its name: *Amerigo Vespucci is the eponym of America.* [Greek *epōnymos* given as a name, from *epi* on + *onyma* (dialectal form) name, word.]

ep·on·y·mous (ep on′ə məs) *adj.* giving one's name to something like a country, a people, or a place.

e·pox·y (e pok′sē) *n. Chemistry.* compound formed by polymerization, characterized by powerful adhesion and durability, used esp. in glues and coatings. Also, **epoxy resin.** [EP- + OXY(GEN).]

ep·si·lon (ep′sə lon′, -lən) *n.* fifth letter of the Greek alphabet (E, ε). [Greek *e psīlon* literally, simple *e.*]

Ep·som (ep′səm) *n.* town in southeastern England, near London, noted for horse racing. It is the site of Epsom Downs.

Epsom Derby, annual horse race held at Epson Downs, for three-year-old horses.

Epsom Downs, racetrack where the Epsom Derby is held.

Epsom salts also, **Epsom salt.** hydrated magnesium sulfate, a bitter, crystalline compound used esp. as a laxative and in baths for sore muscles or minor infections. Formula: $MgSO_4 \cdot 7H_2O$ [From *Epsom,* England, where the salt was first obtained from the water of a mineral spring.]

eq. 1. equal. **2.** equivalent. **3.** equation. **4.** equator.

e·qua·bil·i·ty (ek′wə bil′ə tē, ēk′-) *n.* equable condition or quality.

eq·ua·ble (ek′wə bəl, ēk′-) *adj.* **1.** not easily disturbed; tranquil: *an equable state of mind.* **2.** unvarying; steady: *an equable temperature.* **3.** free from inequalities; equal and uniform: *to establish a more equable*

system of taxation. [Latin *aequābilis* uniform, from *aequāre* to make equal.] —**eq′ua·ble·ness,** *n.* —**eq′ua·bly,** *adv.* —**Syn. 2.** see **even'.**

e·qual (ēk′wəl) *adj.* **1.** the same in some measure, as in amount, number, rank, magnitude, or the like: *One tablespoon of the soap in liquid form is equal to one half cup of the same soap in powdered form.* **2.** having the same rights, privileges, and responsibilities: *Men are all equal in the sight of God.* **3.** balanced; even: *That chance to win are equal.* **4.** *Set theory.* having exactly the same elements. **5. equal to,** adequately fit or qualified to; having the strength or ability necessary to: *The young teacher was not equal to the task of controlling and teaching a large class.* —*n.* one who or that which is equal. —*v.t.* **e·qualed, e·qual·ing;** also, *British,* **e·qualled, e·qual·ling. 1.** to be equal to: *Two plus two equals four.* **2.** to make or do something equal to: *No one has equaled his service to the community.* [Latin *aequālis* even, like, from *aequus* just, even.]

Syn. *adj.* **1. Equal, equivalent, identical** denote lack of difference. **Equal** suggests complete correspondence in major characteristics as size, value, number, or area: *The profits were divided into ten equal shares.* **Equivalent** suggests dissimilar things that are freely interchangeable because they are equal in value, quality, or importance: *The vitamin pill is the equivalent of three eggs and a glass of milk.* **Identical** denotes absolute agreement in all details or resembling or matching exactly and in every way: *Mary and Beth are identical twins, but they dress differently.*

e·qual·i·tar·i·an (i kwol′ə tãr′ē ən) *adj.* egalitarian.

e·qual·i·ty (i kwol′ə tē) *n.* equal state or quality of being equal.

e·qual·ize (ēk′wə līz′) **-ized, -iz·ing.** *v.t.* **1.** to make uniform: *to equalize water pressure along the length of a dam.* **2.** to make equal: *Giving runners handicaps according to their demonstrated abilities equalizes the chances of everyone in a race.* —**e′qual·i·za′tion, e′qua·li′zer,** *n.*

e·qual·ly (ēk′wə lē) *adv.* **1.** in an equal manner: *Divide the estate equally among them.* **2.** to an equal degree: *equally talented.*

e·qua·nim·i·ty (ēk′wə nim′ə tē, ek′-) *n.* evenness of mind or temper; calmness. [Latin *aequanimitās* evenness of mind, going back to *aequus* even + *animus* mind.]

e·quate (i kwāt′) **e·quat·ed, e·quat·ing.** *v.t.* **1.** to regard, treat, or represent as equal or comparable: *He equates good manners with real concern for others.* **2.** to regard or represent as usually, or always, related: *to equate wealth and happiness.* **3.** to state the equality of; put in the form of an equation. **4.** to reduce to an average; make correction or allowance in so as to reach a common standard of comparison. [Latin *aequātus,* past participle of *aequāre* to make equal.]

e·qua·tion (i kwā′zhən, -shən) *n.* **1.** *Mathematics.* statement of equality between two quantities or expressions, esp. one using the sign (=). **2.** *Chemistry.* representation of a chemical reaction. Symbols for the original substances appear to the left and those for the resulting substances, to the right of the symbol (=) or (→). $FeS + 2HCl = FeCl_2 + H_2S$ is an equation indicating that ferrous sulfide and hydrochloric acid react to produce ferrous chloride and hydrogen sulfide. **3.** act of equating. **4.** state of being equated.

e·qua·tor (i kwā′tər) *n.* **1.** imaginary line encircling the earth halfway between the North and South poles and from which degrees of latitude are measured. **2.** similar line on any celestial body. **3.** celestial equator. [Medieval Latin *aequator* equalizer, short for *aequator diei et noctis* equalizer of day and night (day and night being of equal length when the sun is over the equator), from Latin *aequāre* to make equal.]

e·qua·to·ri·al (ēk′wə tôr′ē əl, ek′-) *adj.* **1.** of, at, near, or relating to the equator. **2.** like that found at or near the equator.

E·qua·to·ri·al Guinea (ēk′wə tôr′ē əl, ek′-) country in west-central Africa, on the Gulf of Guinea, formerly a Spanish colony. Capital, Santa Isabel. Area, 10,831 sq. mi. Pop. (1969 est.), 286,000.

eq·uer·ry (ek′wər ē) *pl.* **-ries.** *n.* **1.** formerly, officer of a royal or noble household charged with the care of the horses. **2.** personal attendant on any of the members of the British royal family. [French *écurie* stable, from Old French *escuerie* office of a squire, stable, from *escuier* squire, shield-bearer, going back to Latin *scūtum* shield; influenced in form by Latin *equus* horse.]

e·ques·tri·an (i kwes′trē ən) *adj.* **1.** of or relating to horsemen, horsemanship, or horseback riding. **2.a.** mounted on horseback. **b.** (esp. of a statue or portrait) representing a person on horseback: *An equestrian statue of the general stands in the central plaza.* —*n.* rider, esp. a performer on horseback in a circus or other show. [Latin *equester* relating to a horseman (from *eques* horseman, knight, from *equus* horse) + -AN.]

e·ques·tri·enne (i kwes′trē en′) *n.* female equestrian.

equi- *combining form* **1.** equal: *equilibrium, equivalence.* **2.** equally: *equiangular, equidistant.* [Latin *aequus* even, just, like, equal.]

e·qui·an·gu·lar (ēk′wē ang′gyə lər) *adj. Geometry.* having all angles equal: *Regular polygons are equiangular.*

e·qui·dis·tant (ēk′wə dis′tənt) *adj.* equally distant. —**e′qui·dis′tant·ly,** *adv.*

at; āpe; cär; end; mē; it; īce; hot; ōld; fôrk; wood; fōōl; oil; out; up; ūse; turn; sing; thin; this; zh in treasure; ə in ago, taken, pencil, lemon, circus.

e·qui·lat·er·al (ēk'wə lat'ər əl) adj. having all sides equal. —n. geometrical figure having all sides equal. [Late Latin *aequilaterālis* having all sides equal, from Latin *aequus* even, equal + *later-,* stem of *latus* side.]

e·quil·i·brant (i kwil'ə brənt) n. *Physics.* force equal but opposite in direction to a given force and able to balance that force, creating a state of equilibrium.

e·quil·i·brate (i kwil'ə brāt', ēk'wə lī'brāt) -brat·ed, -brat·ing. v.t. 1. to bring into or keep in a state of equilibrium; counterbalance. 2. to be in equilibrium with. —v.i. to be in a state of equilibrium; balance. [Late Latin *aequilibrātus,* past participle of *aequilibrāre* to balance, going back to Latin *aequus* even, equal + *libra* balance.] —e'qui·li·bra'tion, n.

Equilateral triangle

e·qui·lib·ri·um (ēk'wə lib'rē əm) n. 1. state or condition in which forces acting on or within a body or system exactly balance each other: *A cone resting on its base will remain in equilibrium unless additional force is applied to it.* 2. state of balance between powers or factors of any kind: *equilibrium in the international political community.* 3. mental and emotional balance: *He maintains his equilibrium no matter what problems present themselves.* 4. *Physics.* (of a radioactive element) condition in which the rate of radioactive decay is equal to the rate of formation of new atoms. [Latin *aequilibrium* level position, from *aequus* even, equal, + *libra* balance.]

e·quine (ēk'wīn) adj. of, relating to, or like a horse. —n. a horse. [Latin *equīnus* relating to horses, from *equus* horse.]

e·qui·noc·tial (ēk'wə nok'shəl) adj. 1. of or relating to an equinox. 2. occurring at or near the time of an equinox: *an equinoctial storm.* 3. equatorial. —n. storm occurring at or near the time of an equinox.

equinoctial line, celestial equator. Also, **equinoctial circle.**

e·qui·nox (ēk'wə noks') n. 1. time at which day and night are equal all over the earth. Twice a year the sun crosses the celestial equator, northward about March 21, **vernal equinox,** and southward about September 23, **autumnal equinox,** those dates marking the beginning of spring and autumn. 2. either of the two points where the sun crosses the celestial equator. Also *(def. 2),* **equinoctial point.** [Medieval Latin *equinoxium,* modification of Latin *aequinoctium* time of equal days and nights, from *aequus* even, equal + *nox* night.]

e·quip (i kwip') v.t. **e·quipped, e·quip·ping.** to provide or prepare with whatever is necessary for an event or undertaking; provide: *Every boat must be properly equipped to pass Coast Guard inspection.* [French *équiper* to fit out, from Old Norse *skipa* to man a ship, arrange, from *skip* ship.] —**Syn.** see **furnish.**

eq·ui·page (ek'wə pij) n. 1. equipment; gear. 2. carriage, esp. when fully outfitted, with horses, driver, and attendants.

e·quip·ment (i kwip'mənt) n. 1. anything that is used in or provided for equipping someone or something; furnishings; supplies; gear. 2. act of equipping; being equipped. —**Syn.** 1. see **gear.**

e·qui·poise (ek'wə poiz', ek'-) n. 1. state of balance or equilibrium. 2. counterpoise.

e·qui·po·ten·tial (ēk'wə pə ten'shəl) adj. having the same power or potential.

eq·ui·se·tum (ek'wə sē'təm) pl., **-tums** or **-ta** (-tə) n. any of a group of flowerless plants, genus *Equisetum,* including the horsetail, having hollow, jointed stems with conelike, spore-producing structures at the top. [Modern Latin *Equisetum,* from Latin *equisaetum* horsetail plant, from *equus* horse + *saeta* bristle.]

eq·ui·ta·ble (ek'wə tə bəl) adj. 1. characterized by equity; fair; just: *an equitable settlement.* 2. *Law.* relating to, valid in, or existing in equity, as distinguished from common law or civil law. —**eq'ui·ta·ble·ness,** n. —**eq'ui·ta·bly,** adv. —**Syn.** 1. see **fair.**

eq·ui·ta·tion (ek'wə tā'shən) n. horsemanship. [Latin *equitātiō* riding, going back to horse.]

eq·ui·tes (ek'wə tēz') n.,pl. (in ancient Rome) members of the privileged class, originally the cavalry and later the merchants and civil servants. [Latin *equites,* plural of *eques* horseman, knight, from *equus* horse.]

eq·ui·ty (ek'wə tē) pl., **-ties.** n. 1. quality of being impartial, fair, and just. 2. something that is fair and just. 3. *Law.* **a.** justice by ethical judgement and fairness rather than established principles of law. **b.** set of principles dealing with matters for which there are no adequate or fair remedies under the common law or the civil law. Equity was originally separate from the law, but it has come to be considered a branch of the law. **c.** claim or right recognized by a court of equity. 4. money value of a property in excess of any liability or mortgage. [Old French *equite* rectitude, integrity, from Latin *aequitās* equality, fairness, from *aequus* even, equal.]

e·quiv·a·lence (i kwiv'ə ləns) n. state or property of being equivalent.

e·quiv·a·lent (i kwiv'ə lənt) adj. 1. equal, as in value, measure, force, effect, or meaning; corresponding: *a fine equivalent to a week's*

salary. 2. virtually the same; parallel, as in function or effect: *That state's department of commerce is equivalent to our bureau of economic development.* 3. *Geometry.* equal in area or volume, but not alike in shape. 4. *Algebra.* having the same truth set: *equivalent equations.* —n. that which is equivalent. [Late Latin *aequivalēns,* present participle of *aequivalēre* to have equal power, from Latin *aequus* even, just, equal + *valēre* to be worth.] —**Syn.** adj. 1. see **equal.**

e·quiv·o·cal (i kwiv'ə kəl) adj. 1. capable of being interpreted in more than one way; having two or more meanings; ambiguous: *He is notorious for giving equivocal answers to even the most direct questions.* 2. undecided; ambivalent: *an equivocal attitude.* 3. uncertain; doubtful: *The evidence he accumulated was of equivocal value.* 4. questionable; suspicious: *equivocal behavior.* [Late Latin *aequivocus* ambiguous, of equal voice (from Latin *aequus* even, equal + *vocāre* to call) + -AL.]

e·quiv·o·cate (i kwiv'ə kāt') **-cat·ed, -cat·ing.** v.i. to express oneself in terms having more than one possible meaning, esp. to use ambiguous language in order to mislead or avoid committing oneself: *He had equivocated on the issue for many years.* [Late Latin *aequivocātus,* past participle of *aequivocare* to call by the same name, from *aequivocus* ambiguous. See EQUIVOCAL.] —**e·quiv'o·ca'tor,** n.

e·quiv·o·ca·tion (i kwiv'ə kā'shən) n. 1. act of equivocating. 2. equivocal statement.

Er, erbium.

-er¹ *suffix* 1. (used to form nouns from verbs) one who or that which carries out the action of the verb: *driver, grater.* 2. (used to form nouns) **a.** one who is a native or inhabitant of: *northerner, New Yorker.* **b.** one who makes or is professionally concerned with: *clothier, biographer.* **c.** one who or that which is or is characterized by: *three-decker, foreigner.* [Old English *-ere* suffix denoting an agent or agency, going back to Latin *-ārius.*]

-er² *suffix* (used to form nouns) one who or that which is connected with: *officer.* [Old French *-er, -ier,* from Latin *-ārius, -ārium.*]

-er³ *suffix* 1. used to form the comparative degree of adjectives: *colder.* 2. used to form the comparative degree of adverbs: *sooner.* [Old English *-ra* (masculine), *-re* (feminine, neuter), *-or.*]

-er⁴ *suffix* (used to form verbs) repeatedly: *linger, pucker.* [Old English *-rian.*]

e·ra (ēr'ə, er'ə) n. 1. period of time characterized by certain events, conditions, ideas, persons, or things: *Robert Browning and Alfred Tennyson were two famous poets of the Victorian era.* 2. extended period of time beginning with a particular event: *the Christian era.* 3. event or date from which the beginning of a new period of time is reckoned: *the era of space flight.* 4. one of the principal divisions of geological time, including several epochs. [Late Latin *aera* number, epoch (from which time is calculated), from Latin *aera* counters (for calculating), plural of *aes* brass.]

Syn. 1. Era, epoch, period, age denote a division of time. **Era** denotes a span of time characterized by historical change and a new order of things: *The Elizabethan era was a time of expansion and achievement.* **Epoch** properly marks the beginning of an era and is distinguished by formative and crucial events that set it off from the past: *the epoch of space exploration.* **Period** designates any interval or length of time: *Recorded history covers a period of five thousand years.* **Age** denotes an extended period of time marked esp. by a great person or movement: *Don Quixote lived in the age of chivalry.*

e·rad·i·ca·ble (i rad'i kə bəl) adj. that can be eradicated.

e·rad·i·cate (i rad'ə kāt') **-cat·ed, -cat·ing.** v.t. to remove or destroy completely; eliminate; uproot; abolish: *to eradicate weeds, to eradicate a disease.* [Latin *ērādicātus,* past participle of *ērādicāre* to root out, from *ex* out + *rādix* root.] —**e·rad'i·ca'tor,** n.

Syn. Eradicate, uproot, exterminate mean to get rid of something. **Eradicate** means to destroy and eliminate something that had established itself in a region: *Smallpox has been eradicated from the United States.* **Uproot** means to tear up violently by the roots: *The civil war uprooted thousands of families.* **Exterminate** means to wipe out living things by killing them: *Farmers exterminate boll weevils with chemicals.*

e·rad·i·ca·tion (i rad'ə kā'shən) n. act of eradicating; being eradicated.

e·rase (i rās') **e·rased, e·ras·ing.** v.t. 1. to rub, scrape, or scratch out; wipe off: *He erased the notes he had written in the margins.* 2. to remove marks, writing, or recorded information from: *to erase the tapes. Please erase the blackboard.* 3. to remove or destroy completely as if by rubbing or blotting out: *Time had dulled but not erased his memories of the war.* 4. *Slang.* to kill. —v.i. 1. to yield to the act of erasing: *Make light pencil lines so that they will erase easily.* 2. to remove marks, writing, or recorded information: *The tape recorder erases if it is operated in reverse.* [Latin *ērāsus,* past participle of *ērādere* to scrape off, scratch out; with reference to the ancient Roman practice of scratching out words written on a wax tablet by scraping off the wax.] —**e·ras'a·ble,** adj.

Syn. v.t. 1. Erase, delete, efface mean to remove something written or

recorded. **Erase** means to rub or scrape out something written so that the impressions disappear: *The teacher erased the letters on the blackboard.* **Delete** means to exclude or mark for omission: *The editor deleted several passages from the manuscript.* **Efface** means to erase effectively all visible signs or outlines through wear and tear or abrasive action: *Constant use had effaced the legend on the coin.*

e·ras·er (i rā′sər) *n.* device for erasing, esp. a rubber device for removing marks made with a pencil or ink.

E·ras·mus (i raz′məs) *n.* c.1466–1536, Dutch author and humanist.

e·ra·sure (i rā′shər, -zhər) *n.* **1.** act of erasing; being erased. **2.** something that has been erased, as a word, letter, or mark. **3.** place or mark left where something has been erased.

Er·a·to (er′ə tō′) *n.* Greek Muse of lyric poetry, esp. love poetry.

er·bi·um (ur′bē əm) *n.* metallic element of the rare-earth group. Symbol: **Er** See **element** for table. [Modern Latin *erbium,* from the Swedish town *(Ytt)erb(y),* where it was first found.]

ere (ār) *Archaic. prep.* before (in time). —*conj.* **1.** before. **2.** sooner than; rather than. [Old English *ǣr* soon, before.]

Er·e·bus (er′ə bəs) *n.* *Greek Mythology.* **1.** gloomy region of the underworld through which the dead passed on their way to Hades. **2.** personification of darkness.

E·rech·the·um (i rek′thē əm) *n.* beautiful, white marble temple on the Acropolis of Athens, noted as an outstanding example of Ionic architecture.

e·rect (i rekt′) *adj.* in a vertical or upright position or posture; raised: *The dog was trained to stand with ears and tail erect.* —*v.t.* **1.a.** to build; construct: *An apartment house is being erected on that lot.* **b.** to raise or put in a vertical or upright position: *It takes only a few moments to erect a tent.* **2.** to create or set up: *to erect social barriers between people.* **3.** to put together; assemble. **4.** *Geometry.* to construct on a given line: *Erect a perpendicular at this point.* **5.** *Optics.* to restore (an inverted image) to an upright position. **6.** *Archaic.* to establish; found: *to erect a kingdom, to erect a new university.* [Latin *ērēctus,* past participle of *ērigere* to set up.] —**e·rect′ly,** *adv.* —**e·rect′ness,** *n.*

e·rec·tile (i rek′til, -tīl) *adj.* **1.** capable of being raised to an erect position or posture: *erectile feathers on a bird.* **2.** *Physiology.* (of tissue) capable of becoming distended and rigid. —**e·rec·til·i·ty** (i rek′til′ə tē), *n.*

e·rec·tion (i rek′shən) *n.* **1.** act of erecting; state of being erected. **2.** something that is erected, as a building or other structure.

e·rec·tor (i rek′tər) *n.* one who or that which erects.

ere·long (âr lông′) *adv. Archaic.* before long; soon.

er·e·mite (er′ə mīt′) *n. Archaic.* hermit, esp. a religious recluse. [Late Latin *erēmīta,* from Greek *erēmītēs* literally, dweller in a desert, from *erēmiā* desert. Doublet of HERMIT.]

ere·while (âr wīl′, -hwīl′) *adv. Archaic.* some time ago.

Er·furt (âr′foort) *n.* city in southwestern East Germany. Pop. (1968 est.), 193,745.

erg (urg) *n.* unit of work or energy in the centimeter-gram-second system of units. One erg is the work done by a force of one dyne acting through a distance of one centimeter. [Greek *ergon* work.]

er·go (ur′gō) *adv., conj.* Latin. therefore.

er·got (ur′gət, -got) *n.* **1.** disease of rye and other cereal grains caused by a poisonous fungus, *Claviceps purpurea,* in which the grains are replaced by a hard, blackish growth. **2.** this fungus growth itself, used to prepare several drugs useful in medicine. [French *ergot* cock's spur; of uncertain origin; because of the resemblance of the fungus to a cock's spur.]

er·got·ism (ur′gə tiz′əm) *n. Medicine.* ergot poisoning, caused by the eating of infected grain or by misuse of drugs prepared from ergot.

Er·ic·son, Leif (er′ik sən; lēf) *also,* **E·ric·sson.** Norse explorer said to have discovered North America about 1000; son of Eric the Red.

Er·ics·son, John (er′ik sən) 1803–89, Swedish inventor and engineer who built the first ironclad warship, the *Monitor.*

Er·ic the Red (er′ik) born c.950, Norse explorer who in c.982 discovered Greenland.

E·rid·a·nus (i rid′ən əs) *n.* constellation in the southern sky containing the bright star Achernar.

E·rie (ēr′ē) *n.* **1.** Lake. southernmost of the Great Lakes, on the U.S.–Canadian border. **2.** city in Northwestern Pennsylvania, on Lake Erie. Pop. (1970), 129,231.

Erie Canal, waterway across New York, connecting the Hudson River with Lake Erie. The canal is now part of the New York State Barge Canal.

Er·in (er′in, ēr′-) *n. Archaic.* Ireland. [Old Irish *Ērinn,* dative of *Ēriu* Ireland.]

E·rin·y·es (i rin′ē ēz′) *sing.,* **E·rin·ys** (i rin′is, i rī′nis) *n.,pl. Greek Mythology.* the Furies.

E·ris (ēr′is, er′-) *n.* Greek goddess of strife and discord.

Er·i·van (er′ə vän′) Yerevan.

erl·king (url′king′) *n. German and Scandinavian Folklore.* evil spirit who roams the forests, bringing harm to people, esp. to children. [German *Erlkönig.*]

Ermine

er·mine (ur′min) *pl.,* **-mines** *or* **-mine.** *n.* **1.** carnivorous weasel, *Mustela erminea,* of northern regions of North America, Europe, and Asia, having a long, slender body, short legs, a thick, muscular neck, black-tipped tail, and brown coat, which usually changes to white in winter. Length: 7–15 inches including tail. **2.** white, winter fur of this animal used esp. for women's coats, trimming, and the ornamentation of royal or judges' formal robes in some European countries. The black fur of the tail is sometimes inserted at regular intervals on the white for decorative effect. **3.** *Archaic.* rank, office, or functions of a judge. [Old French *ermine,* probably from Medieval Latin *Armenius (mus)* Armenian (mouse), going back to Greek *Armeniā* Armenia.]

erne (urn) *also,* **ern.** *n. Archaic.* sea eagle. [Old English *earn* eagle.]

e·rode (i rōd′) **e·rod·ed, e·rod·ing.** *v.t.* **1.** to wear or wash away gradually, as by rubbing or friction: *The heavy rains had eroded the topsoil on the hills.* **2.** to eat into or eat away; corrode: *Salt water had collected in the bottom of the boat and eroded the metal parts.* **3.** to form (a channel or the like) by a gradual eating or wearing away: *The glacier had eroded a valley in the side of the mountain.* —*v.i.* to become eroded. [Latin *ērōdere* to gnaw away.]

E·ros (ēr′os, er′-) *n.* Greek god of love, son of Aphrodite. His Roman counterpart is Cupid. [Latin *Erōs,* from Greek *Erōs,* from *erōs* love.]

e·ro·sion (i rō′zhən) *n.* gradual wearing or washing away of the soil and rock of the earth's surface by glaciers, running water, waves, or wind: *Soil conservation is intended to curb erosion.* [French *érosion,* from Latin *ērōsiō* a gnawing away.]

e·ro·sive (i rō′siv) *adj.* eroding; causing erosion.

e·rot·ic (i rot′ik) *adj.* **1.** of, relating to, or concerned with sexual love. **2.** arousing or designed to arouse sexual desire. **3.** strongly influenced by sexual love. [Greek *erōtikos* relating to love, from *erōs* love.] —**e·rot′i·cal·ly,** *adv.*

e·rot·i·cism (i rot′ə siz′əm) *n.* **1.** erotic tendency or character. **2.** preoccupation with sex.

ERP, European Recovery Program.

err (ur, er) *v.i.* **1.** to do something wrong; make a mistake; be in error: *He erred in making his decision before he confirmed the facts.* **2.** to do something that is morally wrong; sin. [Old French *errer* to make a mistake, wander, from Latin *errāre* to wander.]

er·rand (er′ənd) *n.* **1.** short trip to do something, usually for someone else: *She had been kept busy all morning, running errands for her mother.* **2.** what one is sent to do; the purpose or object of a trip. [Old English *ǣrende* message, mission.]

er·rant (er′ənt) *adj.* **1.** traveling or roaming in search of adventure; wandering; roving: *the errant knights of the Middle Ages.* **2.** straying from the proper place or correct behavior; erring: *an errant child, errant conduct.* **3.** having no fixed course; erratic: *an errant breeze.* [Partly from Old French *errant,* present participle of *errer* to travel, going back to Latin *iter* journey; partly from Old French *errant,* present participle of *errer* to make a mistake. See ERR.]

er·rant·ry (er′ən trē) *pl.,* **-ries.** *n.* conduct or way of life of a knight-errant.

er·ra·ta (ə rā′tə, ə rä′-) plural of **erratum.**

er·rat·ic (ə rat′ik) *adj.* **1.** having no fixed course; acting or moving irregularly or unpredictably. **2.** deviating from the conventional or usual standard; inconsistent; eccentric. **3.** *Geology.* (of a boulder or rock) at a distance from its original site; moved from its place of origin, esp. by glacial action. [Latin *errāticus* wandering, from *errāre* to wander.] —**er·rat′i·cal·ly,** *adv.*

er·ra·tum (ə rā′təm, ə rä′-) *pl.,* **-ta.** *n.* error in writing or printing. [Latin *errātum* error, from *errāre* to wander.]

er·ro·ne·ous (ə rō′nē əs) *adj.* marked by or containing error; mistaken; incorrect: *an erroneous conclusion.* [Latin *errōneus* wandering.] —**er·ro′ne·ous·ly,** *adv.* —**er·ro′ne·ous·ness,** *n.* —**Syn.** see **wrong.**

er·ror (er′ər) *n.* **1.** something incorrectly done, believed, or stated; something that deviates from what is accurate, proper, or true; mistake: *The total arrived at was obviously an error.* **2.** condition of being mistaken or incorrect (usually preceded by *in*): *They are in error if they think that I am not coming.* **3.** *Baseball.* fielding misplay that allows a base runner to reach a base safely or a batter to remain at bat when, if the play had been made properly, the runner or batter would have been put out. **4.** quantity by which the observed or estimated amount and the correct amount differ: *How large was the error in his calcula-*

tions? **5.** wrongdoing; sin; transgression. [Old French *errour* distress, mistake, from Latin *error* mistake, wandering.] —**Syn. 1.** see **mistake.**

er·satz (er′zäts, -sats) *adj.* serving as a substitute; artificial; false: *ersatz coffee.* —*n.* substitute. [German *Ersatz* replacement.]

Erse (urs) *n.* **1.** Scottish Gaelic. **2.** Irish Gaelic. —*adj.* of or relating to either of these languages or the Celtic people of Scotland and Ireland. [Scottish form of IRISH.]

erst (urst) *adv. Archaic.* formerly; long ago. [Old English *ærst* soonest, first, superlative of *ær* soon, before.]

erst·while (urst′hwīl′, -wīl′) *adv. Archaic.* formerly. —*adj. Archaic.* formerly.

e·ruct (i rukt′) *v.i., v.t.* to belch. [Latin *ēructāre* to belch forth.]

e·ruc·tate (i ruk′tāt) -**tat·ed, -tat·ing.** *v.i., v.t.* to eruct. —**e·ruc′ta′-tion,** *n.*

er·u·dite (er′yoo dīt′, er′oo-) *adj.* scholarly; learned. [Latin *ērudītus* learned, skilled, going back to *ex* out of, from, away + *rudis* rough.] —**er′u·dite′ly,** *adv.* —**er′u·dite′ness,** *n.*

er·u·di·tion (er′yoo dish′ən, er′oo-) *n.* extensive knowledge acquired esp. from reading in the humanities; scholarship; learning.

e·rupt (i rupt′) *v.i.* **1.** to eject something, as lava, suddenly and violently: *The geyser erupts every few hours.* **2.** to burst or break forth: *Enough lava had erupted from the volcano to bury the entire village.* **3.** to break out suddenly and violently: *A fight between the opposing teams erupted during the game.* **4.** to break out, as in a rash: *Many youngsters erupt with acne.* **5.** (of teeth) to break through the gums. —*v.t.* **1.** to throw forth; eject (something, as steam or lava). **2.** to cause to throw forth or eject. [Latin *ēruptus,* past participle of *ērumpere* to break or burst forth.]

e·rup·tion (i rup′shən) *n.* **1.** act of erupting; being erupted. **2.** a violent bursting forth, as of lava from a volcano. **3.a.** a breaking out in a rash. **b.** superficial inflammation of the skin; rash. **4.** a sudden bursting forth; outbreak: *an eruption of laughter.*

e·rup·tive (i rup′tiv) *adj.* **1.** bursting forth; tending to erupt. **2.** causing or accompanied by a rash, as certain diseases. **3.** of or pertaining to volcanic eruptions; formed by a volcano.

-ery *suffix* (used to form nouns) **1.** place of business or place where something is made, stored, or sold: *bakery, brewery.* **2.** place for: *nunnery.* **3.** art, practice, or profession of: *thievery, cookery, archery.* **4.** state of: *slavery.* **5.** characteristics, practices, or principles of: *knavery, popery, trickery.* **6.** collection or group of: *greenery, crockery.* [Old French *-erie,* from *-er, -ier* (see -ER²) + *-ie* (see -Y¹).]

er·y·sip·e·las (er′ə sip′ə ləs, ēr′ə-) *n.* acute infectious skin disease characterized by deep-red inflammation of the skin, caused by a streptococcus. [Greek *erysipelas* erysipelas; literally, red skin.]

e·ryth·ro·cyte (i rith′rə sīt′) *n.* red blood cell.

e·ryth·ro·my·cin (i rith′rə mī′sin) *n.* antibiotic drug used to treat certain penicillin-resistant bacterial infections. [Greek *erythros* red + *mykēs* fungus + -IN¹.]

Er·zu·rum (er′zə room′) *n.* city in northeastern Turkey. Pop. (1965), 105,317.

Es, einsteinium.

E·sau (ē′sô) *n.* in the Old Testament, son of Isaac and Rebecca who sold his birthright to his younger twin brother, Jacob, for a dish of pottage.

es·ca·drille (es′kə dril′) *n.* small unit or squadron of airplanes or warships. [French *escadrille* small squadron, flotilla, from Spanish *escuadrilla,* diminutive of *escuadra* squadron, squad, going back to Latin *ex* out + *quadra* square; because the men in a squadron at one time were formed in a square.]

es·ca·lade (es′kə lād′) *n.* act of scaling the walls of a fortified place, esp. by ladders. [French *escalade* scaling (a wall), from Italian *scalata* scaling, going back to Latin *scālae* (plural) ladder, staircase.]

es·ca·late (es′kə lāt′) -**lat·ed, -lat·ing.** *v.t., v.i.* to increase or enlarge by stages, as in size, scope, intensity, or cost: *to escalate a conflict.* [From ESCALATOR.] —**es′ca·la′tion,** *n.*

es·ca·la·tor (es′kə lā′tər) *n.* moving stairway consisting of a series of steps attached to a continuous chain which transports passengers from one floor or level to another. [Probably blend of ESCAL(ADE) and (ELEV)ATOR.]

escalator clause, provision in the financial terms of a labor contract allowing for increases or decreases, as in wages, under specified conditions, usually in proportion to the cost of living.

es·cal·lop (es kol′əp, -kal′-) *n.* scallop.

es·ca·pade (es′kə pād′) *n.* action or behavior that flouts convention or breaks rules; wild, reckless adventure. [French *escapade* prank; originally, escape, from Italian *scappata* escape, going back to Late Latin *ex cappa* out of one's cape. See ESCAPE.]

es·cape (es kāp′) -**caped, -cap·ing.** *v.i.* **1.** to get away or free, as from restraint or confinement; gain or regain liberty: *The bird escaped from the cage.* **2.** to evade or avoid capture, punishment, or any present or imminent danger: *He escaped from the accident with his life. They chased the bank robber, but he escaped in the crowd.* **3.** to issue forth

from a container or enclosure, esp. gradually: *Gas escaped from the pipe.* —*v.t.* **1.** to get away or free from; elude: *He escaped the mob by ducking out the back door.* **2.** to avoid (something threatening, harmful, or unpleasant): *He narrowly escaped death. He escaped capture.* **3.** to fail to be noticed or recollected by; slip by or away from: *How did you let such a significant fact escape you?* **4.** to be uttered inadvertently or involuntarily by: *No words of kindness escaped her lips.* —*n.* **1.** act of escaping: *His escape was by way of the sea.* **2.** fact or state of having escaped: *His escape brought additional punishment when he was recaptured.* **3.** means of escaping: *His escape from the burning house was a rope ladder.* **4.** way of temporarily avoiding reality: *literature of escape.* **5.** gradual or sudden outflow or leakage, as of gas or water. [Dialectal Old French *escaper* to get away, keep clear of, going back to Late Latin *ex cappa* out of one's cape; with reference to escaping by slipping out of one's cape when seized.]

escape artist, one adept at escaping from handcuffs, ropes, locked rooms, and other forms of confinement, esp. one who does this for the entertainment of others.

escape clause, clause permitting one or both parties to a contract to abstain from performing some or all of the contract's requirements under specified circumstances.

escape mechanism, means of avoiding unpleasant facts or the responsibilities of real life, as by daydreaming.

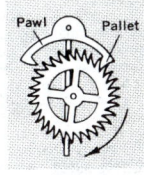

Escapement

es·cape·ment (es kāp′mənt) *n.* **1.** device in a timepiece consisting of a toothed wheel and a pawl. The back-and-forth movement of the pawl allows one tooth of the wheel to escape at each swing, thus controlling the regular movement of a system of gears which moves the hands. **2.** mechanism that regulates the movement of a typewriter carriage during use.

escape velocity, minimum speed a body must attain to pass out of a gravitational field: *Escape velocity from earth is about seven miles per second.*

es·cap·ism (es kā′piz′əm) *n.* tendency to avoid routine and the responsibilities of the real world by constantly engaging the mind in vicarious activities, esp. of the imagination, such as fantasy or passive entertainment. —**es·cap′ist,** *adj., n.*

es·car·got (es′kär gō′) *n.* snail, esp. an edible one. [French.]

es·ca·role (es′kə rōl′) *n.* kind of endive, used esp. in salads. [French *escarole* endive, going back to Late Latin *escariola,* from Latin *esca* food.]

es·carp (es kärp′) *n.* escarpment; scarp.

es·carp·ment (es kärp′mənt) *n.* **1.** steep slope or cliff formed by erosion or faulting. **2.** fortification consisting of a man-made steep slope. [French *escarpment,* from *escarp* scarp, from Italian *scarpa.* See SCARP.]

-esce *suffix* (used to form verbs) begin to be; become: *fluoresce.* [Latin *-ēscere.*]

-escence *suffix* (used to form nouns) state of becoming: *fluorescence.* [Latin *-ēscentia,* from *-ēscēns,* often through French *-escence.* See -ESCENT.]

-escent *suffix* (used to form adjectives) beginning to be; becoming: *fluorescent.* [Latin *-ēscent-,* stem of *-ēscēns,* present participial ending of verbs in *-ēscere* to begin to, often through French *-escent.*]

es·cha·tol·o·gy (es′kə tol′ə jē) *n.* branch of theology dealing with doctrines concerning the last things, as death, judgment, and the final destiny of the soul. [Greek *eschatos* last, extreme + -LOGY.]

es·cheat (es chēt′) *n.* **1.** reversion of property to the state or, in feudal law, to the lord of a manor, when there are no persons legally qualified to inherit it. **2.** property which has so reverted. —*v.i.* to revert by escheat. —*v.t.* to cause (property) to revert by escheat. [Old French *eschete* what falls to one, inheritance, from *escheoir* to fall to one's share, fall out, from Latin *ex* out + *cadere* to fall.] —**es·cheat′a·ble,** *adj.*

es·chew (es choo′) *v.t.* to abstain from; stand aloof from; shun: *to eschew wickedness.* [Old French *eschiver* to shun; of Germanic origin.]

Es·co·ri·al (es kôr′ē əl) *also,* **Es·cu·ri·al.** *n.* huge granite structure built in the sixteenth century near Madrid, including a monastery, palace, church, and royal crypt.

es·cort (*n.,* es′kort; *v.,* es kort′) *n.* **1.** person or persons who accompany another as a courtesy or honor or to protect, esp. a man who accompanies a woman to a public function. **2.** one or more ships or airplanes accompanying another: *a fighter escort, a destroyer escort.* **3.** act of accompanying as a courtesy or honor or to protect. —*v.t.* to act as an escort; accompany as a courtesy or honor or to protect. [French *escorte* guide, from Italian *scorta,* from *scorgere* to guide, going back to Latin *ex* out + *corrigere* to set right.] —**Syn.** *v.t.* see **accompany.**

es·cri·toire (es′krə twär′) *n.* writing desk. [Early French *escritoire,* from Late Latin *scriptorium* place for writing, from Latin *scribere* to write.]

es·crow (es′krō, es krō′) *n.* *Law.* **1.** document, as a deed or bond, or money or other property deposited with a third party to be returned only upon fulfillment of certain conditions. **2. in escrow,** held by a third party pending the fulfillment of certain conditions. [Old French *escroe* scroll, shred; of Germanic origin.]

es·cu·do (es kōō′dō) *pl.,* **-dos.** *n.* **1.a.** monetary unit of Portugal, equal to 100 centavos. **b.** Portuguese coin having this value. **2.a.** monetary unit of Chile equal to 100 centesimos. **b.** Chilean coin having this value. **3.** formerly, any of several gold or silver coins of Spain, Portugal, or their colonies. [Spanish and Portuguese *escudo* coin, shield, from Latin *scūtum* shield.]

es·cu·lent (es′kyə lənt) *adj.* suitable for food; edible. —*n.* something fit for food, esp. an edible plant: *Mallow and chicory are wild esculents.* [Latin *ēsculentus* eatable, good to eat, from *ēsca* food.]

Es·cu·ri·al (es kyoor′ē əl) Escorial.

es·cutch·eon (es kuch′ən) *also,* **scutch·eon.** *n.* **1.** shield or shield-shaped surface carrying armorial bearings. It is the central figure in the coat of arms and is often shown separately, as on stationery, jewelry, or other personal or family possessions. **2. blot on the escutcheon.** stain on one's reputation; something dishonorable or disgraceful. [Dialectal Old French *escuchon* shield, coat of arms, going back to Latin *scūtum* shield.]

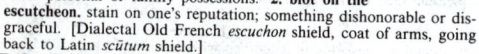

Escutcheon

Esd., Esdras.

Es·dras (ez′drəs) *n.* **1.** in the Douay Bible, the prophet Ezra. **2.** either of two canonical books in the Douay Bible, I Esdras corresponding to the book of Ezra, and II Esdras, considered a continuation of the history in I Esdras, corresponding to the book of Nehemiah in other versions. **3.** either of two apocryphal books of the Protestant (I Esdras and II Esdras) or Catholic (III Esdras and IV Esdras) Old Testament.

-ese *suffix* **1.** (used to form nouns) **a.** native inhabitant, or close descendant of: *Burmese.* **b.** language of: *Japanese.* **c.** style or diction characteristic of a particular area, person, or group: *journalese.* **2.** (used to form adjectives) of, relating to, or originating in: *Chinese.* [Old French *-eis,* from Latin *-ēnsis* belonging to, originating in.]

ESE, east southeast.

Es·ki·mo (es′kə mō′) *pl.,* **-mos** or **-mo.** *n.* **1.** one of a Mongoloid race of once-nomadic hunters living in Alaska, northern Canada, Greenland, and northeastern Siberia. **2.** language spoken by these people. —**Es′ki·mo′an,** *adj.*

Eskimo dog, dog of a sturdy breed native to Greenland and northern Canada, having a thick, shaggy coat, broad chest, and curved bushy tail, and used by the Eskimos to draw heavy sleds. The name is often also applied to the Alaskan malamute, Siberian husky, and Samoyed.

e·soph·a·gus (i sof′ə gəs, ē sof′-) *pl.,* **-gi** (-jī′). *also,* **oe·soph·a·gus.** *n.* muscular passageway or canal through which food passes from the pharynx to the stomach; gullet. [Modern Latin *oesophagus,* from Greek *oisophagos* literally, carrier of food.]

es·o·ter·ic (es′ə ter′ik) *adj.* **1.** understood by or intended for the initiated only; of or for a chosen few, as secret rites or doctrines. **2.** difficult to understand; abstruse; recondite. **3.** private; concealed; confidential: *esoteric aims, esoteric pleasures.* [Greek *esōterikos* inner, going back to *esō* within.] —**es′o·ter′i·cal·ly,** *adv.*

esp., especially.

ESP, extrasensory perception.

es·pal·ier (is pal′yər) *n.* **1.** method of training trees and shrubs to grow in a flattened horizontal position against either a framework or a wall. **2.** tree or shrub trained to grow this way. **3.** framework or other surface upon which plants are thus trained. —*v.t.* (of a tree of shrub) to train on or provide with a framework or surface on which to grow in a flattened horizontal position. [French *espalier* framework or wall on which plants are trained, row of plants so trained, from Italian *spalliera,* from *spalla* shoulder (suggesting a support), from Late Latin *spatula,* from Latin *spatula* blade. See SPATULA.]

Es·pa·ña (es pä′nyä) *n.* Spanish. Spain.

es·par·to (es pär′tō) *n.* any of several species of tough grass, esp. *Stipa tenacissima* and *Lygeum spartum,* native to the Mediterranean region, used to make paper, cord, and baskets. Also, **esparto grass.** [Spanish *esparto,* from Latin *spartum,* from Greek *sparton* rope, esparto.]

es·pe·cial (es pesh′əl) *adj.* special; particular; extraordinary. [Old French *especial* special, from Latin *speciālis* particular, special, from *speciēs* a particular kind, sight, appearance.]

es·pe·cial·ly (es pesh′ə lē, -pesh′lē) *adv.* particularly; principally; exceptionally: *The sea is rough here, especially in the winter.*

Syn. Especially, particularly, principally, mainly, specifically denote above all or most importantly. **Especially** means to a special extent or

degree or standing apart uniquely: *He is especially famous for his abstract paintings.* **Particularly** emphasizes the individual characteristics that differentiate something from all others of its class: *This dictionary is particularly useful for students.* **Principally** means primarily or chiefly and singles out for attention the special status or circumstances of the thing described: *The company deals principally in paper products.* **Mainly** means for the most part and often describes what is outstanding or conspicuous in a numerical sense: *The audience consisted mainly of women.* **Specifically** designates that which has a specific and definite application, manner, or purpose: *He asked specifically for French wine.*

Es·pe·ran·to (es′pə rän′tō, -ran′-) *n.* artificial language with simplified grammar and vocabulary based on the major European languages. [From Dr. *Esperanto,* the pen name of its originator, Dr. L. L. Zamenhof, 1859–1917, the name meaning, in Esperanto, one who is hoping.]

es·pi·al (is pī′əl) *n.* **1.** act of watching or spying. **2.** act of catching sight of; notice.

es·pi·o·nage (es′pē ə näzh′, -nij) *n.* practice of spying, esp. the use of spies by one government to discover the military or political secrets of other countries or by one firm to discover the business or manufacturing secrets of another. [French *espionnage* spying, from *espion* spy, from Old French *espier* to spy; of Germanic origin.]

es·pla·nade (es′plə näd′, -nād′) *n.* **1.** open, level space used for public walking or as a roadway; promenade. **2.** open space between a fortress and a town or a shore, designed to expose an attacking enemy to defensive fire. [French *esplanade,* from *esplaner* to level, from Latin *explānāre* to flatten, explain.]

es·pous·al (is pou′zəl) *n.* **1.** act of espousing; adoption; advocacy: *espousal of a doctrine.* **2.** *also,* **espousals.** ceremony of betrothal or marriage.

es·pouse (is pouz′) **-poused, -pous·ing.** *v.t.* **1.** to marry; wed. **2.** to promise or give in marriage. **3.** to take up or adopt, as a cause; advocate; embrace: *to espouse living outdoors.* [Old French *espouser* to marry, from Latin *spōnsāre* to betroth, marry.]

es·pres·so (es pres′ō) *n.* strong coffee, usually made by forcing steam upward through finely ground dark-roasted coffee beans. [Italian *(caffè) espresso* literally, pressed out (coffee), from *esprimere* to press out, express, from Latin *exprimere.* See EXPRESS.]

es·prit (es prē′) *n.* lively wit; esprit; vivacity. [French *esprit* soul, mind, from Latin *spīritus* breath, soul, mind. Doublet of SPIRIT, SPRITE.]

es·prit de corps (es prē′ də kôr′) feeling of mutual regard existing in a group and its members that all are working together toward some common goal. [French *esprit de corps* literally, spirit of a body (of people). See ESPRIT, CORPS.]

es·py (es pī′) **-pied, -py·ing.** *v.t.* to catch sight of; discern; see. [Old French *espier* to watch, spy upon; of Germanic origin.]

Esq., Esquire.

-esque *suffix* (used to form adjectives) **1.** in the style of; like the style of: *Romanesque.* **2.** like: *picturesque.* [French *-esque,* from Italian *-esco;* of Germanic origin.]

es·quire (es kwīr′, es′kwīr) *n.* **1.** formerly, young aspirant to knighthood who attended a medieval knight; squire. **2.** man belonging to the English gentry, ranking immediately below a knight. **3.** *Archaic.* English landholder; country gentleman; squire. **4. Esquire.** Mr. or Dr. ▲ used as a title of respect or courtesy following a man's surname and usually abbreviated: *Thomas Williams, Esq.* [Old French *escuier* squire, shield-bearer, from Late Latin *scūtārius* shield-bearer, from Latin *scūtum* shield.]

ess (es) *n.* **1.** the letter S. **2.** something shaped like an S.

-ess *suffix* used to form feminine nouns: *lioness.* [Old French *-esse,* from Late Latin *-issa,* from Greek *-issa.*]

es·say (*n.,* es′ā, *def.2 also* e sā′; *v.,* e sā′) *n.* **1.** literary composition, usually shorter and less detailed than a thesis, often informal and personal in tone, and expressing the author's opinions, theories, and analysis of a particular subject. **2.** effort or attempt to do something; endeavor. —*v.t.* to try; attempt. [Old French *essai* trial, going back to Late Latin *exagium* a weighing, from Latin *exigere* to weigh, examine.] —**es·say′er,** *n.*

Syn. *n.* **1. Essay, article, paper, composition** designate a piece of prose writing. **Essay** denotes a brief literary exposition distinguished by organization of facts or ideas and a systematic presentation of the author's personal views on a subject: *The professor wrote an essay on Homer.* **Article** denotes a piece of writing that forms an independent part of a magazine, book, or newspaper: *The encyclopedia contains an excellent article on space flight.* **Paper** is a monograph or treatise on a learned subject intended for publication in a scholarly journal or to be read before a professional society: *Dr. Jones read a paper on Armenian art before the Antiquarian society.* **Composition** is a literary exercise or theme on a definite subject written as part of a course in high school: *Paul received an A for his composition on modern drama.*

es·say·ist (es′ā ist) *n.* writer of essays.

Es·sen (es′ən) *n.* city in northwestern West Germany. Pop. (1968 est.), 702,252.

es·sence (es′ons) *n.* **1.** that which gives a thing its nature; necessary and fundamental part; distinctive feature. **2.a.** substance containing the basic ingredients or characteristic properties of a thing in concentrated form; extract. **b.** such a concentrate or extract, as vanilla flavoring, in a solution of alcohol. **3.** perfume. [French *essence* being, nature, perfume, from Latin *essentia* being or essence of a thing, from *esse* to be.] —Syn. **1.** see **heart.**

Es·sene (es′ēn, e sēn′) *n.* member of an ancient Jewish monastic order. —**Es·se′ni·an,** *adj.*

es·sen·tial (i sen′shəl) *adj.* **1.** necessary for the existence or continuance of something; indispensable: *Industrial growth is essential to the health of a nation's economy.* **2.** basic; fundamental; intrinsic. **3.** of, like, or consisting of an essence or extract. —*n.* necessary or fundamental element or quality; indispensable part: *He outlined the essentials of his plan.* [Late Latin *essentiālis* relating to being, from Latin *essentia* being. See ESSENCE.] —Syn. *adj.* **1.** see **necessary.**

es·sen·tial·ly (i sen′shə lē) *adv.* in essence; fundamentally.

essential oil, any of various volatile oils that give a plant its characteristic flavor or fragrance. They are extracted from plant tissues and used to make perfumes and flavorings.

-est[1] *suffix* **1.** used to form the superlative degree of adjectives: *coldest.* **2.** used to form the superlative degree of adverbs: *soonest.* [Old English *-est, -ost.*]

-est[2] *suffix* used to form the archaic second person singular of verbs: *doest.* [Old English *-est, -ast.*]

est. 1. established. **2.** estate. **3.** estimated. **4.** estuary.

EST, Eastern Standard Time.

es·tab·lish (es tab′lish) *v.t.* **1.** to set up permanently; found: *to establish a colony, to establish a university.* **2.** to settle (oneself) securely or permanently; set up in business: *The lawyer established himself in his new offices.* **3.** to introduce and secure permanent acceptance for; gain recognition of: *to establish a hypothesis, to establish one's reputation.* **4.** to put beyond dispute; show convincingly; prove: *to establish a motive, to establish a claim.* **5.** to make (a church), by law or decree, the official religion of a nation, financially supported by the government. [Old French *establiss-*, a stem of *establir* to found, install, decide, from Latin *stabilīre* to make firm.]

established church, church recognized as the official religion of a nation and financially supported by the government.

es·tab·lish·ment (es tab′lish mənt) *n.* **1.** act of establishing; being established. **2.** something established, as a household, business, or institution: *Stores and restaurants are private establishments; the police and the courts are public establishments.* **3.** act, by law or decree, of making a religion the official religion of a nation. **4. the Establishment. a.** group of people or institutions that, directly or indirectly, have dominant influence in a nation or society. **b.** British. the Church of England.

es·tate (es tāt′) *n.* **1.** large piece of land, esp. with a large house, owned by one person; landed property: *His country estate includes a large forest.* **2.** property or possessions, esp. everything owned by a person at his death or on becoming bankrupt. **3.** condition or circumstances of a person or thing; status; rank: *When I am grown to man's estate, I shall be very proud and great* (Stevenson, 1885). **4.** one of the groups or classes into which the people of a nation are divided with regard to political rights and powers. **5. the three estates.** (in late medieval and early modern Europe) clergy, nobility, and common people. **6. the fourth estate.** journalists collectively; the press. [Old French *estat* possession, state, from Latin *status* position, condition.]

Es·tates-Gen·er·al (es tāts′jen′ər əl) *n.* States-General *(def. 1).*

es·teem (es tēm′) *v.t.* **1.** to consider good or important; regard favorably; value highly: *to esteem someone's opinion, to esteem skill.* **2.** to judge to be; consider; regard: *He esteemed himself lucky to escape with a suspended sentence.* *—n.* **1.** favorable opinion; high regard; respect: *His acts of charity won him much esteem.* **2.** opinion; judgment; consideration: *In their esteem, the bill was worthless.* [Old French *estimer* to determine the value of, from Latin *aestimāre* to value.]

es·ter (es′tər) *n.* organic compound formed by the reaction of an alcohol with an acid, occurring naturally as animal or vegetable fat, oil, and wax. [German *Ester,* abbreviation of *Essigäther* acetic ether, going back to Latin *acētum* vinegar + *aethēr.* See ETHER.]

Es·ther (es′tər) *n.* **1.** in the Old Testament, Jewish queen of the king of Persia. She saved her people from a slaughter plotted by the Persian minister Haman. **2.** book of the Old Testament that tells her story.

es·thete (es′thēt) aesthete.

es·thet·ic (es thet′ik) *adj.* aesthetic. —**es·thet′i·cal·ly,** *adv.*

es·thet·ics (es thet′iks) aesthetics.

Es·tho·ni·a (es tō′nē ə, es thō′-) *n.* Estonia. —**Es·tho′ni·an,** *adj., n.*

es·ti·ma·ble (es′tə mə bəl) *adj.* **1.** worthy of favorable opinion; deserving high regard or respect. **2.** capable of being estimated or valued; calculable. —**es′ti·ma·bly,** *adv.*

es·ti·mate (*n.,* es′tə mit, -māt′; *v.,* es′tə māt′) *n.* **1.** judgment or opinion of the value, quality, extent, or other property of something; rough calculation; approximation: *an estimate of the height of a mountain, an estimate of the age of an antique.* **2.** statement made by one assigned to or seeking to be assigned to do a job as to the probable or approximate cost, duration, and the like of the work: *A company which wants a contract with the government must submit a detailed estimate.* *—v.t.,* **-mat·ed, -mat·ing. 1.** to make a rough judgment or calculation of (the value, quality, extent, or other property of something); form an approximation of. **2.** to make a judgment or form an opinion about. [Latin *aestimātus,* past participle of *aestimāre* to value.] —**es′ti·ma′-tor,** *n.*

Syn. *v.t.* **1. Estimate, evaluate, rate**[1] mean to determine the value or worth of something. **Estimate** means to judge subjectively and in a tentative way: *He estimated the crowd at ten thousand.* **Evaluate** means to pass an exact judgment of value: *The book evaluates President Kennedy's administration.* **Rate** means to assign comparative value or determine the rank of something in relation to others of the same kind: *The critic rated Dickens far above Hardy as a novelist.*

es·ti·ma·tion (es′tə mā′shən) *n.* **1.** judgment; opinion: *The project was a feasible one in their estimation.* **2.** rough calculation; approximation; estimate: *His estimation of their time of arrival was not far wrong.* **3.** favorable opinion; esteem; regard: *His talent was held in the highest estimation.*

es·ti·val (es′tə vəl, es tī′-) *also,* **aes·ti·val.** *adj.* of or relating to summer. [Latin *aestīvālis* relating to summer, going back to *aestās* summer.]

es·ti·vate (es′tə vāt′) **-vat·ed, -vat·ing.** *also,* **aes·ti·vate.** *v.i.* **1.** to spend the summer. **2.** to spend the summer in a dormant, torpid state, as some snakes, fish, and other animals. Distinguished from **hibernate.** [Latin *aestivātus,* past participle of *aestivāre* to spend the summer.]

Es·to·ni·a (es tō′nē ə) *n.* republic of the Soviet Union, in the northwestern part of the country, on the Baltic Sea. Official name: Estonian Soviet Socialist Republic. Capital, Tallinn. Area, 17,400 sq. mi. Pop. (1969 est.), 1,316,000.

Es·to·ni·an (es tō′nē ən) *adj.* of or relating to Estonia or its people. *—n.* **1.** native or inhabitant of Estonia. **2.** language of the Finno-Ugric subfamily of the Ural-Altaic family, spoken predominantly in Estonia.

es·top (es top′) **-topped, -top·ping.** *v.t.* **1.** Law. to bar or impede by estoppel. **2.** Archaic. to stop up; obstruct. [Old French *estoper* to stop, going back to Latin *stuppa* tow[2]; with reference to stopping up something with tow; hence, impeding. See STOP.]

es·top·pel (es top′əl) *n.* Law. prevention of a party from asserting or denying a fact or claim that is inconsistent with his previous statements or acts.

es·trange (es trānj′) **-tranged, -trang·ing.** *v.t.* **1.** to turn (someone) from kindness or affection to indifference or hostility; alienate the friendliness of. **2.** to keep apart or stay away; dissociate: *He estranged himself from the group.* [Old French *estrangier* to alienate, from Late Latin *extrāneāre* to treat as a stranger, from *extrāneus* strange, foreign.] —**es·trange′ment,** *n.*

es·tray (es trā′) *n.* something that has strayed, esp. a stray domestic animal whose owner is unknown.

es·tro·gen (es′trə jən) *n.* any of a group of hormones, secreted primarily by the ovaries or female sex glands, that cause the body to produce the secondary female sex characteristics and function with progesterone to control menstruation, to prepare the uterus for pregnancy, and to help the body maintain pregnancy. [Latin *oestrus* frenzy (from Greek *oistros*) + -GEN.]

es·tu·ar·y (es′chōo er′ē) *pl.,* **-ar·ies.** *n.* **1.** mouth or lower course of a river where the current meets the sea and is affected by the tides. **2.** arm or inlet of the sea. [Latin *aestuārium* marsh, inlet, from *aestus* heat, tide.]

-et *suffix* used to form the diminutive of nouns: *islet.* ▲ This meaning has lost its force in most words. [Old French *-et;* of uncertain origin.]

e·ta (ā′tə, ē′tə) *n.* seventh letter of the Greek alphabet (H, η).

et al. 1. and others. [Latin *et aliī.*] **2.** and elsewhere. [Latin *et alibī.*]

eta meson, subatomic particle of the meson group. See **subatomic particle** for table.

etc., et cetera.

et cet·er·a (et set′ər ə, set′rə), and so forth; and the rest; and others. [Latin *et cētera* (neuter plural) and the rest.]

et·cet·er·as (et set′ər əz, -set′rəz) *n.,pl.* miscellaneous other things; odds and ends.

etch (ech) *v.t.* **1.** to engrave by means of a corrosive, esp. to engrave a printing plate with acid. **2.** to sketch or delineate by this method. *—v.i.* to make plates or designs by this method. [Dutch *etsen,* from German *ätzen* to eat into, corrode, etch.] —**etch′er,** *n.*

etch·ing (ech′ing) *n.* **1.** art or process of engraving in which lines are scratched with a needle on a wax-coated plate, usually of metal, and acid or another corrosive is used to bite the design into the exposed

at; āpe; cär; end; mē; it; īce; hot; ōld; fôrk; wood; fōōl; oil; out; up; ūse; turn; sing; thin; this; zh in treasure; ə in ago, taken, pencil, lemon, circus.

349

surface. **2.** etched figure, design, or plate. **3.** impression or print from an etched plate.

e·ter·nal (i turn′əl) *adj.* **1.** existing throughout all time; infinite in duration; lasting forever. **2.** forever the same; never changing; immutable: *eternal laws of nature.* **3.** seeming to last or continue forever; perpetual; incessant: *the eternal noise of construction.* —*n.* **the Eternal.** God. [Late Latin *aeternālis* everlasting, from Latin *aeternus.*] —**e·ter′nal·ly,** *adv.*

Syn. *adj.* **1. Eternal, everlasting, endless** denote having infinite duration. **Eternal** suggests the absence of a beginning and end and is applied chiefly to God or any other principle that is independent of time: *The eternal God is your dwelling place* (Deut. 33:27). **Everlasting** means enduring endlessly and is usually applied to earthly things that last, or seem to last, forever: *The soldiers swore everlasting loyalty to their king.* **Endless** suggests infinite duration in space as well as in time: *Some philosophers conceive life as an endless cycle of births and deaths.*

Eternal City, Rome.

eternal flame, fire that is kept burning continually for symbolic or memorial purposes.

e·ter·ni·ty (i tur′nə tē) *pl.*, **-ties.** *n.* **1.** time without beginning or end; all time; infinite time. **2.** quality or state without time or beyond time; timelessness. **3.** all future time, esp. the infinite time or condition after death. **4.** seemingly endless length of time; extremely long or indefinite duration: *He waited an eternity for her.* [Old French *eternite* time without beginning or end, from Latin *aeternitās* duration, immortality.]

e·ter·nize (i tur′nīz) **-nized, -niz·ing.** *v.t.* **1.** to prolong the existence or duration of infinitely or indefinitely. **2.** to perpetuate the fame or memory of; immortalize.

-eth *suffix* used to form the archaic third person singular of verbs: *doeth.* [Old English *-eth, -th.*]

eth·ane (eth′ān) *n.* colorless, odorless, flammable gas present in natural gas and also obtained from petroleum refining and coal distillation. Formula: C_2H_6 [ETHER + -ANE.]

eth·a·nol (eth′ə nôl′) *n.* alcohol *(def. 1).*

e·ther (ē′thər) *n.* **1.a.** colorless, volatile, flammable liquid with a strong, sweetish odor, used esp. as an anesthetic and as a solvent. Formula: $(C_2H_5)_2O$ **b.** any of a group of organic compounds in whose molecules two carbon atoms are separated by an oxygen atom. **2.** *also,* **ae·ther. a.** upper regions of the atmosphere or the space beyond; heavens. **b.** *Physics.* hypothetical medium once assumed to fill all space and to transmit light and other forms of radiation. [Latin *aethēr* upper air, from Greek *aithēr.*]

e·the·re·al (i thēr′ē əl) *also,* **ae·the·re·al.** *adj.* **1.** very light and delicate; exquisite; spiritual: *Her ethereal nature seemed to shrink from coarse reality* (Disraeli, 1847). **2.** of or relating to heaven or the heavens; celestial: *Joan of Arc heard the ethereal voices of angels.* **3.** of or relating to the upper regions of the atmosphere, or the space beyond: *The ethereal aurora lit the vast snows.* **4.** of or relating to the ether formerly supposed to fill space. —**e·the′re·al·ly,** *adv.*

e·the·re·al·ize (i thēr′ē ə līz′) **-ized, -iz·ing.** *v.t.* to make ethereal. —**e·the′re·al·i·za′tion,** *n.*

e·ther·i·fy (i ther′ə fī′, ē′thər-) **-fied, -fy·ing.** *v.t.* to convert into an ether.

e·ther·ize (ē′thə rīz′) **-ized, -iz·ing.** *v.t.* **1.** to subject to the influence of ether; anesthetize with ether. **2.** to etherify.

eth·ic (eth′ik) *adj., n.* ethical; moral system.

eth·i·cal (eth′i kəl) *adj.* **1.** of or relating to standards of morality; pertaining to a science or system of ethics. **2.** in accordance with accepted standards of conduct, esp. the standards or code of a profession: *It is not ethical for a lawyer to reveal information a client has told him in confidence.* [Latin *ēthicus* moral (from Greek *ēthikos,* from *ēthos* custom, character) + -AL.] —**eth′i·cal·ly,** *adv.* —**Syn.** see **moral.**

Ethical Culture, movement founded in New York in 1876, whose members stress the inviolability of human personality and the relation of man to man as the essential human problem.

eth·ics (eth′iks) *n.* **1.** branch of philosophy that deals with the pursuit of the good, the meaning and justification of moral codes, and the criteria for evaluating right and wrong. **2.** standards of conduct or code of behavior, as of a profession: *ethics of the legal profession.* ▲ construed as singular in def. 1; construed as plural in def. 2.

E·thi·op (ē′thē op′) *adj., n. Archaic.* Ethiopian.

E·thi·o·pi·a (ē′thē ō′pē ə) *n.* **1.** country in eastern Africa. Capital, Addis Ababa. Area, 457,268 sq. mi. Pop. (1969 est.), 24,769,000. Also, **Ab′ys·sin′i·a. 2.** ancient country in northeastern Africa, south of Egypt.

E·thi·o·pi·an (ē′thē ō′pē ən) *adj.* **1.** of or relating to Ethiopia or its inhabitants. **2.** *Archaic.* Negro. —*n.* **1.** native or inhabitant of Ethiopia.

E·thi·op·ic (ē′thē op′ik, -ō′pik) *n.* ancient Semitic language of Ethiopia, still used in the Christian church of that country. Also, **Ge·ez′.** —*adj.* of, in, or having to do with this language or church.

eth·moid (eth′moid) *adj.* relating to a bone situated in the upper nasal cavity or in the walls and septum of the nose, containing many perforations for the filaments of the olfactory nerve. —*n.* the ethmoid bone. [Greek *ēthmoeidēs* like a sieve, perforated, from *ēthmos* sieve + *eidos* form.]

eth·nic (eth′nik) *adj.* **1.** of or relating to a group of people having distinctive characteristics in common, as language, culture, history, race, or national origin. **2.** of or relating to a people not Christian or Jewish; heathen; pagan. Also, **eth′ni·cal.** [Latin *ethnicus* pagan, from Greek *ethnikos* national, foreign, from *ethnos* race, nation.]

ethno- *combining form* race, nation, or people: *ethnology.* [Greek *ethnos.*]

eth·nog·ra·phy (eth nog′rə fē) *n.* branch of anthropology dealing with description of individual cultures.

eth·no·log·i·cal (eth′nə loj′i kəl) *adj.* of or relating to ethnology. Also, **eth′no·log′ic.** —**eth′no·log′i·cal·ly,** *adv.*

eth·nol·o·gy (eth nol′ə jē) *n.* branch of anthropology dealing with cultures, esp. of living peoples, and specifically with the comparative study of human culture as a whole. [ETHNO- + -LOGY.] —**eth·nol′o·gist,** *n.*

e·thol·o·gy (eth ol′ə jē, ē thol′-) *n.* science which deals with the individual and group behavior of animals in their natural environment. [Greek *ēthologiā* the depiction of character, from *ēthos* custom, character + -logiā. See -LOGY.]

eth·yl (eth′əl) *n.* **1.** univalent organic radical present in many compounds, as ether and ethyl alcohol. Formula: C_2H_5 **2.** Trademark. **Ethyl.** a poisonous lead compound added to gasoline to reduce knocking. Formula: $Pb(C_2H_5)_4$ **b.** gasoline or other motor fuel containing this. [ETH(ER) + -YL.]

ethyl alcohol, alcohol *(def. 1).*

eth·yl·ene (eth′ə lēn′) *n.* colorless, flammable gas of the alkene, or olefin, series, used esp. in making organic compounds, as polyethylene, and for coloring and ripening certain fruits. Formula: C_2H_4 [ETHYL + -ENE.]

ethylene glycol, clear, colorless alcohol, used as an antifreeze. Formula: $HOCH_2CH_2OH$ Also, **gly′col.**

e·ti·o·late (ē′tē ō lāt′) **-lat·ed, -lat·ing.** *v.t.* **1.** to cause (a green plant) to bleach by excluding sunlight. [French *étioler* to make pale (probably from *éteule* stalk¹, going back to Latin *stipula*) + -ATE¹.] —**e′ti·o·la′tion,** *n.*

e·ti·ol·o·gy (ē′tē ol′ə jē) *n.* **1.** analysis of the origins and causes of something. **2.** scientific or philosophical discipline that deals with origins or causes. **3.** study or theory of the causes of disease. [Late Latin *aetiologia* a bringing of proofs, from Greek *aitiologiā* giving the cause of something.] —**e·ti·o·log·i·cal** (ē′tē ō loj′i kəl), *adj.* —**e′ti·ol′o·gist,** *n.*

et·i·quette (et′i kit, -ket′) *n.* **1.** forms of proper or polite behavior in society; good manners; decorum. **2.** rules governing proper or formal conduct in a specific area, as a profession or official ceremony: *Protocol is the etiquette of diplomacy.* [French *étiquette* label, ticket, ceremonial, from Old French *estiquier* to attach, from Dutch *stikken* to stitch; with reference to an earlier custom of "attaching" a "ticket" with the rules of the day in army posts or courts.]

Et·na, Mount (et′nə) high active volcano in northeastern Sicily. Also, **Aetna, Mount.**

E·ton College (ēt′ən) England's largest and most famous preparatory school for boys, located at Eton, a town near London.

E·to·ni·an (ē tō′nē ən) *adj.* of or relating to Eton College, England. —*n.* one educated at Eton College, England.

Eton jacket, short, black jacket, or the type worn by students at Eton College, England, having broad lapels and reaching only to the waist.

E·tru·ri·a (i troor′ē ə) *n.* ancient country in west-central Italy.

E·tru·ri·an (i troor′ē ən) *adj., n.* Etruscan.

E·trus·can (i trus′kən) *adj.* of or relating to Etruria or its people. —*n.* **1.** native or inhabitant of Etruria. **2.** extinct language of ancient Etruria.

et seq., and the following; and what follows. [Latin *et sequēns* and *et sequentia*.]

-ette *suffix* **1.** used to form the diminutive of nouns: *kitchenette.* **2.** used to form feminine nouns: *suffragette.* **3.** (used to form nouns) substitute for or imitation of: *leatherette.* [French *-ette,* feminine of *-et.* See -ET.]

é·tude (ā′tōōd, ā′tüd, ā tōōd′, ā tüd′) *n.* musical composition for a solo instrument designed to develop the performer's technical ability. [French *étude* study, from Latin *studium* zeal, application.]

et·y·mo·log·i·cal (et′ə mə loj′i kəl) *adj.* of or relating to etymology. —**et′y·mo·log′i·cal·ly,** *adv.*

et·y·mol·o·gist (et′ə mol′ə jist) *n.* specialist in etymology.

et·y·mol·o·gy (et′ə mol′ə jē) *pl.*, **-gies.** *n.* **1.** history of a word, tracing it from its origin to its present form, including the changes in

at; āpe; cär; end; mē; it; īce; hot; ōld; fôrk; wood; fōōl; oil; out; up; ūse; turn; sing; thin; this; zh in treasure; ə in ago, taken, pencil, lemon, circus.

spelling and meaning that have taken place. **2.** study of the history of words. [French *étymologie* science of explaining the origin and derivation of words, from Latin *etymologia* analysis of the origins of words, from Greek *etymologiā,* from *etymon* true sense of a word according to its origin + *-logiā.* See -LOGY.]

Eu, europium.

eu- *prefix* good or well: *euphemism.* [Greek *eū* well, *eus* good.]

Eu·boe·a (ū bē′ə) *also,* **Ev·voi·a.** *n.* largest Greek island in the Aegean Sea, just off the eastern coast of the Greek peninsula. Area, 1457 sq. mi. Pop. (1961), 166,097. —**Eu·boe′an,** *n., adj.*

eu·ca·lyp·tus (ū′kə lip′təs) *pl.,* **-tus·es** *or* **-ti** (-tī). *n.* any evergreen tree or shrub, genus *Eucalyptus,* found in Australia and widely cultivated in warm climates for its hard, durable wood, resins, and oils, and as an ornamental. [Modern Latin *Eucalyptus* literally, well-covered, from Greek *eū* well + *kalyptos* covered; with reference to the covering of its buds.]

Eu·cha·rist (ū′kə rist) *n.* Holy Communion. [Latin *eucharistia* thanksgiving, the Lord's Supper, from Greek *eucharistiā,* going back to *eū* well + *charis* grace, favor.] —**Eu′cha·ris′tic,** *adj.*

eu·chre (ū′kər) *n.* card game for two to seven players, using a deck of fifty-two cards or a variable number of the highest cards in the deck depending on the number of players. —*v.t.* **eu·chred, eu·chring. 1.** to prevent (the maker of trumps) from winning three tricks. **2.** *Informal.* to defeat (someone), as by trickery; outwit. [Of uncertain origin.]

Eu·clid (ū′klid) *n.* **1.** c.323–285 B.C., Greek mathematician. **2.** city in northeastern Ohio, an industrial suburb of adjoining Cleveland. Pop. (1970), 71,552.

Eu·clid·e·an (ū klid′ē ən) *also,* **Eu·clid·i·an.** *adj.* of or relating to Euclid or a system of geometry based on his axioms.

Eu·gene (ū jēn′) *n.* city in western Oregon. Pop. (1970), 76,346.

eu·gen·ic (ū jen′ik) *adj.* **1.** relating to the improvement of the human race according to the principles of eugenics. **2.** of or concerning eugenics. [Greek *eugenēs* well-born (from *eū* well + *genos* race, kind) + -IC.] —**eu·gen′i·cal·ly,** *adv.*

eu·gen·i·cist (ū jen′i sist) *n.* specialist in or advocate of eugenics. Also, **eu·gen′ist.**

eu·gen·ics (ū jen′iks) *n.* science that deals with the improvement of hereditary factors of the human race by a careful selection of parents. ▲ construed as singular.

Eu·gé·nie (œ zhā nē′) *n.* 1826–1920, wife of Napoleon III and empress of France.

eu·lo·gist (ū′lə jist) *n.* one who eulogizes.

eu·lo·gis·tic (ū′lə jis′tik) *adj.* of or relating to eulogy; praising. Also, **eu′lo·gis′ti·cal.** —**eu′lo·gis′ti·cal·ly,** *adv.*

eu·lo·gi·um (ū lō′jē əm) *pl.,* **-gi·ums** *or* **-gi·a** (-jē ə). *n.* eulogy.

eu·lo·gize (ū′lə jīz′) *-gized, -giz·ing.* *v.t.* to praise highly in speech or writing; deliver a eulogy about. —**eu′lo·giz′er,** *n.*

eu·lo·gy (ū′lə jē) *pl.,* **-gies.** *n.* strong praise or commendation, esp. when delivered formally in speech or writing, as in honor of the dead. [Greek *eulogiā* praise, from *eū* well + *legein* to speak.]
Syn. Eulogy, encomium, panegyric, tribute denote praise expressed in speech or writing. **Eulogy** designates a studied speech or oration lauding the virtues and achievements of a recently deceased person: *The bishop delivered the eulogy as the body of the general lay in state.* **Encomium** denotes warm or high praise extolling an unusual achievement or quality: *The astronaut received many encomiums from the press.* **Panegyric** denotes elaborate, high-flown, and rhetorical acclaim: *Cicero's panegyric upon Cato is a model of Latin prose.* **Tribute** denotes spoken or written praise on formal occasions: *On Memorial Day, speakers pay tribute to our armed forces.*

Eu·men·i·des (ū men′i dēz′) *n.,pl.* **1.** *Greek Mythology.* the Furies. **2.** Greek play by Aeschylus. ▲ construed as plural in def. 1, as singular in def. 2. [Latin *Eumenides,* going back to Greek *eumenēs* favorable, kindly, from *eū* well + *menos* temper, mind, intent; a euphemistic epithet to propitiate the Furies.]

eu·nuch (ū′nək) *n.* **1.** castrated man. **2.** castrated man in the service of an Oriental ruler as a court official or supervisor of a harem. [Latin *eunūchus* castrated person, from Greek *eunouchos,* from *eunē* bed + *echein* to hold, keep; with reference to the employment of eunuchs in the Orient to guard the bedchambers of women.]

eu·pep·sia (ū pep′shə, -pep′sē ə) *n.* good digestion. [Modern Latin *eupepsia,* from Greek *eupepsiā* good digestion, going back to *eū* well + *peptein* to digest.]

eu·pep·tic (ū pep′tik) *adj.* **1.** having good digestion. **2.** promoting good digestion.

eu·phe·mism (ū′fə miz′əm) *n.* **1.** substitution of a mild or indirect word or phrase for a blunter or harsher one. **2.** word or phrase thus used. In the sentence *He put the dog to sleep, put to sleep* is a euphemism for *kill.* [Greek *euphēmismos* use of auspicious words, going back to *eū* well + *phēmē* saying, speech.] —**eu′phe·mist,** *n.*

eu·phe·mis·tic (ū′fə mis′tik) *adj.* of or using euphemisms; serving as a euphemism. —**eu′phe·mis′ti·cal·ly,** *adv.*

eu·phon·ic (ū fon′ik) *adj.* **1.** of or relating to euphony. **2.** pleasant-sounding; euphonious. Also, **eu·phon′i·cal.** —**eu·phon′i·cal·ly,** *adv.*

eu·pho·ni·ous (ū fō′nē əs) *adj.* pleasant and agreeable in sound; pleasant to hear. —**eu·pho′ni·ous·ly,** *adv.* —**eu·pho′ni·ous·ness,** *n.*

eu·pho·ni·um (ū fō′nē əm) *n.* brass musical instrument, used esp. in military and marching bands, having four valves and producing tones resembling, but higher and mellower than, a tuba's. [Modern Latin *euphonium,* from Greek *euphōnos* sweet-voiced.]

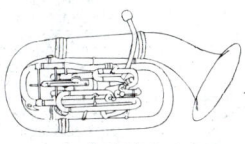
Euphonium

eu·pho·ny (ū′fə nē) *n.* **1.** quality of having a pleasant sound; pleasing effect of sounds free from harshness. **2.** *Phonetics.* tendency for sounds to change to make pronunciation easier. [French *euphonie* an agreeable sound, from Greek *euphōniā* sweetness of voice.]

eu·phor·bi·a (ū fôr′bē ə) *n.* any plant of the genus *Euphorbia,* that includes the spurges. [Latin *euphorbea;* said to be named after *Euphorbus,* an ancient Greek physician.]

eu·pho·ri·a (ū fôr′ē ə) *n.* **1.** feeling of well-being and happiness. **2.** *Psychology.* exaggerated sense of well-being and happiness. [Modern Latin *euphoria,* from Greek *euphoriā* well-being, going back to *eū* well + *pherein* to bear.] —**eu·pho′ric,** *adj.*

Eu·phra·tes (ū frā′tēz) *n.* river in southwestern Asia, flowing from east-central Turkey through Syria and Iraq into the Persian Gulf. It joins the Tigris River in southeastern Iraq.

Eu·phros·y·ne (ū fros′ə nē) *n.* *Greek Mythology.* one of the three Graces.

eu·phu·ism (ū′fū iz′əm) *n.* **1.** elaborate and affected literary style fashionable in England at the end of the sixteenth and beginning of the seventeenth centuries, characterized by antitheses, similes, mythological and historical allusions, consonance, and alliteration. **2.** any similar, affected style of writing; artificial or exaggerated elegance of language; bombast. [From the affected style of two romances by the English writer John Lyly, c.1554–1606, in which *Euphues* was the principal character; from Greek *euphuēs* excellent.] —**eu′phu·is′tic,** *adj.* —**eu′phu·is′ti·cal·ly,** *adv.*

Eur. **1.** Europe. **2.** European.

Eur·a·sia (yoo rā′zhə, -shə) *n.* Europe and Asia, considered as a single continent.

Eur·a·sian (yoo rā′zhən, -shən) *adj.* **1.** of or relating to Eurasia. **2.** of mixed European and Asian descent. —*n.* one who is of mixed European and Asian descent.

Eur·at·om (yoo rat′əm) *n.* organization consisting of France, West Germany, Italy, Belgium, the Netherlands, and Luxembourg, that directs research into the peaceful uses of atomic energy. [Abbreviation of *Eur(opean) Atom(ic) Energy Community.*]

eu·re·ka (yoo rē′kə) *interj.* used as an exclamation of triumph upon discovering something or solving a problem. [Greek *heurēka* I have found (it); the supposed exclamation made by Archimedes upon discovering the test for the purity of gold.]

Eu·rip·i·des (yoo rip′ə dēz′) *n.* c.485–406 B.C., Greek dramatist.

Eur·o·dol·lars (yoor′ō dol′ərz) *n.,pl.* U.S. dollars deposited in foreign banks, mainly in Europe, and lent to other banks or commercial borrowers, serving as a medium of international finance and world trade.

Eu·ro·pa (yoo rō′pə) *n.* *Greek Mythology.* Phoenician princess abducted by Zeus in the form of a white bull. [Latin *Europa,* from Greek *Europē;* probably of Semitic origin and originally having the sense of "land of the setting sun."]

Eu·rope (yoor′əp) *n.* continent between Asia and the Atlantic. Area, 4,063,000 sq. mi. Pop. (1967 est.), 633,214,000. [From EUROPA, who supposedly was the first person to set foot on the continent.]

Eu·ro·pe·an (yoor′ə pē′ən) *adj.* of or relating to Europe or its population. —*n.* **1.** native or inhabitant of Europe. **2.** person of European ancestry.

European Free Trade Association, organization for economic cooperation, in competition with the Common Market, consisting of Great Britain, Norway, Sweden, Denmark, Austria, Switzerland, and Portugal.

Eu·ro·pe·an·ize (yoor′ə pē′ə nīz′) *-ized, -iz·ing.* *v.t.* to make European, as in appearance or culture.

European plan, system of hotel operation in which the charge for rooms is separate from the charge for meals. Distinguished from **American plan.**

European Recovery Program, Marshall Plan.

eu·ro·pi·um (yoo rō′pē əm) *n.* metallic element of the rare-earth

at; āpe; cär; end; mē; it; īce; hot; ōld; fôrk; wood; fōol; oil; out; up; ūse; turn; sing; thin; this; zh in treasure; ə in ago, taken, pencil, lemon, circus.

group used esp. in nuclear reactors and in color television tubes. Symbol: **Eu** See **element** for table. [Modern Latin, from EUROPE.]

Eu·ryd·i·ce (yoo rid′ə sē) *n.* *Greek Mythology.* wife of Orpheus, killed by the bite of a snake. Hades agreed to release her from the underworld, but Orpheus, who had promised not to look at her until they were back in the upper world, looked back and thus lost her.

Eu·sta·chi·an tube (ū stā′kē ən, -shən) canal or passage extending from the pharynx to the middle ear. It equalizes the air pressure on the inside of the eardrum with the atmospheric pressure on the outside. See **ear** for illustration. [From the sixteenth-century Italian anatomist Bartolommeo *Eustachio,* who described it.]

Eu·ter·pe (ū tur′pē) *n.* Greek Muse of music and lyric poetry. [Latin *Euterpe,* from Greek *Euterpē,* from *eu* well + *terpein* to please.]

eu·tha·na·sia (ū′thə nā′zhə) *n.* **1.** painless killing of a person suffering from an agonizing and incurable disease, esp. during the terminal stage. Also, **mercy killing.** **2.** tranquil, painless death. [Greek *euthanasiā* easy death, from *eu* well + *thanatos* death.]

eu·then·ics (ū then′iks) *n.* study of the control of environmental conditions, like housing or sanitation, with the aim of improving the human race. ▲ construed as singular. [Greek *euthenein* to thrive + -ICS.]

Eux·ine Sea (ūk′sin) see **Black Sea.**

EVA, extravehicular activity.

e·vac·u·ate (i vak′ū āt′) **-at·ed, -at·ing.** *v.t.* **1.a.** to leave or vacate; to clear people from: *The troops evacuated their position. Police evacuated the theater.* **b.** to remove all the air from; create a vacuum in: *to evacuate a container.* **c.** to discharge waste matter from: *to evacuate the bladder.* **2.a.** to cause to leave or vacate: *Firemen evacuated the tenants.* **b.** to remove entirely: *to evacuate air from a container.* **c.** to expel or discharge; void: *to evacuate urine from the bladder.* [Latin *ēvacuātus,* past participle of *ēvacuāre* to empty out, from *ex* out + *vacuus* empty.] —**e·vac′u·a′tor,** *n.*

e·vac·u·a·tion (i vak′ū ā′shən) *n.* **1.** act of evacuating; process of being evacuated: *evacuation of troops, evacuation of a container.* **2.a.** expulsion of waste matter from the body, esp. from the bladder or bowels. **b.** waste matter so discharged; feces.

e·vac·u·ee (i vak′ū ē′, i vak′ū ē′) *n.* someone removed from an area of danger or disaster: *The evacuees from the flood area were housed in the school.*

e·vade (i vād′) **e·vad·ed, e·vad·ing.** *v.t.* **1.** to avoid, as by artifice or cunning; elude: *He evaded his pursuers.* **2.** to escape or avoid the responsibility of: *to evade the draft, to evade taxes.* **3.** to avoid answering: *to evade a question.* **4.** to remain hidden from; baffle: *The key to the code evaded all his efforts.* —*v.i.* to avoid honesty or directness; to be evasive: *Please answer the question; do not evade.* [Latin *ēvādere* to escape.] —**e·vad′er,** *n.* —**Syn.** *v.t.* **1.** see **avoid.**

e·val·u·ate (i val′ū āt′) **-at·ed, -at·ing.** *v.t.* **1.** to establish the value or the amount of; appraise: *to evaluate a stamp collection.* **2.** to determine the meaning or importance of; assess: *The diplomat was asked to evaluate the talks. The scientists were still evaluating their data.* **3.** to compute the numerical value of. [From EVALUATION.] —**Syn.** **2.** see **estimate.**

e·val·u·a·tion (i val′ū ā′shən) *n.* **1.** act or process of evaluating. **2.** result of evaluating; appraisal; judgment. [French *évaluation* estimate, from *évaluer* to estimate, going back to Latin *ex* out + *valēre* to be worth.]

ev·a·nesce (ev′ə nes′) **-nesced, -nesc·ing.** *v.i.* to fade away gradually, like smoke or vapor; dissipate; vanish. [Latin *ēvānēscere* to vanish.]

ev·a·nes·cence (ev′ə nes′əns) *n.* **1.** gradual dissipation; fading away: *the evanescence of dew in the summer sun.* **2.** tendency to fade away or become indistinct; quality of being insubstantial.

ev·a·nes·cent (ev′ə nes′ənt) *adj.* tending to fade away or pass away; impermanent; insubstantial.

e·van·gel (i van′jəl) *n.* **1.** the good news of the redemption of the world through Christ. **2.** good tidings. **3.** evangelist. **4. Evangel. a.** any one of the four Gospels. **b.** any of the four Evangelists. [Old French *evangile* gospel, from Church Latin *evangelium,* from Greek *euangelion* good news, gospel, going back to *eu* well + *angellein* to announce.]

e·van·gel·i·cal (ē′van jel′i kəl, ev′ən-) *adj.* **1.** of, in, or according to the four Gospels or the New Testament. **2.** of or relating to the Protestant churches, as the Methodist and Baptist, that conform to the doctrine that faith in Christ's atonement is the way to salvation and that the Bible, esp. the New Testament, is the sole religious authority. **3.** evangelistic. Also, **e·van·gel′ic.** —**e·van·gel′i·cal·ly,** *adv.*

e·van·gel·i·cal·ism (ē′van jel′i kə liz′əm, ev′ən-) *n.* **1.** doctrines or principles of an evangelical church. **2.** advocacy or support of such doctrines.

e·van·gel·ism (i van′jə liz′əm) *n.* **1.** zealous preaching or promulgation of the Gospel, as by itinerant preachers; work of evangelists. **2.** evangelicalism.

e·van·gel·ist (i van′jə list) *n.* **1.** preacher of the Gospel, esp. a zealous or itinerant one. **2. Evangelist.** one of the four authors of the Gospels; Matthew, Mark, Luke, or John.

e·van·gel·is·tic (i van′jə lis′tik) *adj.* **1.** of or relating to the Evangelists. **2.** of or relating to evangelists or evangelism.

e·van·gel·ize (i van′jə līz′) **-ized, -iz·ing.** *v.t.* **1.** to preach the Gospel to. **2.** to convert to Christianity. —*v.i.* to do the work of an evangelist. —**e·van′gel·i·za′tion,** *n.*

Ev·ans, Mary Ann (ev′ənz) see **Eliot, George.**

Ev·ans·ton (ev′ən stən) *n.* city in northeastern Illinois, principally a residential suburb of adjoining Chicago. Pop. (1970), 79,808.

Ev·ans·ville (ev′ənz vil′) *n.* city in southwestern Indiana. Pop. (1970), 138,764.

e·vap·o·rate (i vap′ə rāt′) **-rat·ed, -rat·ing.** *v.i.* **1.** to be changed from a liquid or solid into a gas; become gaseous. **2.** to give off moisture: *Let the mixture simmer until it has evaporated to half its volume.* **3.** to fade away or disappear; be dissipated: *His anger evaporated as the misunderstanding was explained.* —*v.t.* **1.** to cause (a liquid or solid) to change into a gaseous state; convert into a vapor: *The sun soon evaporated the morning dew.* **2.** to drive off or remove moisture from, as by heating: *If sea water is evaporated, a residue of salt will remain.* [Latin *ēvapōrātus,* past participle of *ēvapōrāre* to disperse in vapor, from *ex* out + *vapor* exhalation, steam.]

evaporated milk, unsweetened canned milk, which is thickened by evaporating some of the water from whole milk.

e·vap·o·ra·tion (i vap′ə rā′shən) *n.* **1.** change from a liquid or solid state into vapor; vaporization. **2.** extraction or removal of moisture or liquid: *Powdered milk is produced by complete evaporation of whole milk.*

e·vap·o·ra·tor (i vap′ə rā′tər) *n.* apparatus for evaporating.

e·va·sion (i vā′zhən) *n.* **1.** act of evading something, as a duty or a question; avoidance, as by cleverness or deceit: *He was charged with tax evasion. He responded to criticism of his theory with vague evasions.* **2.** means of evading something: *Changing the subject in response to a question is an evasion.* [Late Latin *ēvāsiō* is a going out, escape, from Latin *ēvādere* to escape.]

e·va·sive (i vā′siv, -ziv) *adj.* that evades or tends to evade; characterized by evasion; elusive: *evasive answers, an evasive person.*

eve (ēv) *n.* **1.** evening or day preceding a holiday or other important day. **2.** period just before: *the eve of the election, the eve of the invasion.* **3.** evening. [Form of EVEN².]

Eve (ēv) *n.* in the Bible, the first woman, Adam's wife.

e·ven¹ (ē′vən) *adj.* **1.** without slope or hills; completely flat; level: *an even piece of ground, even country.* **2.** having no roughness, indentations, or other irregularities; smooth: *an even surface, an even hemline.* **3.** at the same level; of uniform height: *The tip of the ski was even with his eyes.* **4.** in or extending along the same plane; parallel: *They moved the desk to make it even with the others.* **5.** of uniform quality throughout; equally distributed: *an even coat of paint.* **6.** free from variations or sudden changes; regular; constant: *an even rhythm, even spacing.* **7.** not easily aroused; calm; tranquil: *an even disposition.* **8.** fully revenged: *"Now I'm even with you." he said, grinning.* **9.** equitable; fair: *an even bargain, an even hand in meting out justice.* **10.** being approximately equal or the same: *His chances for death or survival are even.* **11.** identical or equal, as in quantity, measure, or size: *an even score.* **12.** without fractional parts; exact: *an even hundred yards. He ran the mile in four minutes even.* **13.** having nothing owed to one or owing nothing; balanced. **14.** exactly divisible by two. Opposed to **odd.** **15.** denoted by or having such numbers: *the even pages of a book.* —*adv.* **1.** at the very same moment; while; just: *It is happening even now.* **2.** in the very same way; exactly; precisely; quite: *It occurred even as I'd thought it would.* **3.** as a matter of fact; really; actually; indeed: *She was happy, even joyous.* **4.** though it may seem improbable or unlikely: *Even to his enemies he was kind.* **5.** all the way; fully: *The sick man was in good spirits even to his death.* **6.** in comparison; still; yet: *The advice is even more applicable to you.* **7.** with no variation; smoothly: *If you keep it adjusted, the motor will run even.* **8. to break even.** *Informal.* to have one's gains equal one's losses. **9. to get even. a.** to obtain revenge upon; retaliate: *I'll get even for that remark.* **b.** to settle one's accounts. **10. even if.** for all that; although. —*v.t.* to make smooth, level, or equal: *to even a road surface, to even an account.* —*v.i.* to become smooth, level, or equal (often with *out*). [Old English *efen* level, equal.] —**e′ven·er, e′ven·ness,** *n.* —**e′ven·ly,** *adv.*

Syn. *adj.* **6. Even, equable, uniform** denote unvarying sameness. **Even** suggests steadiness, consistency in character, and a constant level of activity: *She spoke with an even voice.* **Equable** designates natural constancy and freedom from marked variations or inequalities: *The workmen were paid equable wages.* **Uniform** suggests sameness of parts or units and an unvarying conformity to a fixed standard: *The Bahama Islands have a uniform climate.*

e·ven² (ē′vən) *n.* evening. [Old English *æfen.*]

at; āpe; cär; end; mē; it; īce; hot; ōld; fôrk; wood; fōōl; oil; out; up; ūse; turn; sing; thin; this; zh in treasure; ə in ago, taken, pencil, lemon, circus.

e·ven·hand·ed (ē′vən han′did) *adj.* unbiased; fair; just.
eve·ning (ēv′ning) *n.* **1.** late afternoon and early nighttime; period from twilight to bedtime. **2.** last part or closing period, as of a life. —*adj.* of, relating to, or occurring in the evening: *evening classes, the evening meal.* [Old English *ǣfnung* close of the day.]
evening dress, formal clothing, designed to be worn in the evening. Also, **evening clothes.**
evening gown, woman's evening dress, usually floor-length.
evening primrose, any of various plants, genus *Oenothera,* widely distributed in North America and Europe, esp. *O. biennis,* the common evening primrose, having narrow, lance-shaped leaves and spikes of yellow flowers that open at night and are closed during the day.
evening star, first planet, most often Venus or rarely Mercury, to appear after sunset in the western sky.

Evening primrose

e·ven·song (ē′vən sông′) *n.* **1.** (in the Anglican Church) prayer service said or sung at evening. **2.** (in the Roman Catholic Church) vespers. **3.** *Archaic.* evening. [Old English *ǣfensang* vespers, from *ǣfen* evening + *sang* song.]
e·vent (i vent′) *n.* **1.** anything that happens, esp. an incident or occurrence of some importance: *The signing of the Declaration of Independence was an important historical event.* **2.** result, conclusion; outcome of anything: *There is no merit . . . in learning wisdom after the event* (Jowett, 1875). **3.** any of the contests in a program or series of sports: *the main event, the third event in the track meet.* **4. at all events,** in any event; under any circumstances. **5. in any event,** in any case; at any rate; whatever happens. **6. in the event of.** if (something specified) should occur; in case of. [Latin *ēventus* occurrence, result.]
Syn. 1. Event, episode, incident refer to something that happens. Event applies to a relatively noteworthy occurrence that grows out of earlier happenings: *The program describes the historic events of 1970.* Episode refers to a distinctive or discrete event having sharp identity and unity within a larger sequence: *The novel deals with the romantic episodes of her early life.* Incident is an episode of lesser duration that stands apart from or is subordinate to a chain of related events: *The sailor related two incidents of his voyage to the South Seas.*
e·ven-tem·pered (ē′vən tem′pərd) *adj.* not easily disturbed, excited, or angered; calm.
e·vent·ful (i vent′fəl) *adj.* **1.** marked by important or striking occurrences: *The changes which fourteen eventful years had produced* (Macaulay, 1848). **2.** having important issues or results; momentous: *an eventful meeting between heads of state.*
e·ven·tide (ē′vən tīd′) *n.* evening.
e·ven·tu·al (i ven′chŏo əl) *adj.* **1.** resulting from preceding events; final; ultimate: *The eventual decision came after weeks of deliberation.* **2.** in prospect at some indefinite time in the future; bound to occur: *The eventual death of the dictator will bring chaos.*
e·ven·tu·al·i·ty (i ven′chŏo al′ə tē) *pl.* **-ties.** *n.* possible event, occurrence, or condition; contingency; possibility: *One can plan for, but not act upon, eventualities.*
e·ven·tu·al·ly (i ven′chŏo ə lē) *adv.* in the end; ultimately; finally.
e·ven·tu·ate (i ven′chŏo āt′) *-at·ed, -at·ing.* *v.i.* **1.** to turn out finally; culminate; result (often with *in*): *The incidents eventuated in war.* **2.** to come about; result as a consequence: *They feared that an economic crisis would eventuate when the currency was devalued.*
ev·er (ev′ər) *adv.* **1.** at any time: *Did you ever go to Ireland?* **2.** at all times; always: *He was ever at our beck and call.* **3.** throughout all the time; *They lived happily ever after.* **4.** in any possible way: *She ran as fast as ever she could.* **5. ever so.** *Informal.* very; exceedingly; extremely. **6. ever and anon.** now and then; occasionally. Also, **ever and anon. 7. for ever.** forever; eternally. **8. for ever and a day.** forever; eternally; always. **9. for ever and ever.** forever; eternally. ▲ In informal speech *ever* is used to intensify a question or exclamation: *What ever do you mean? Was it ever hot at the beach today!* [Old English *ǣfre* always.]
Ev·er·est, Mount (ev′ər ist) highest mountain in the world, located in the Himalayas on the border between Nepal and Tibet.
Ev·er·ett (ev′ər it, ev′rit) *n.* **1.** city in eastern Massachusetts. Pop. (1970), 42,485. **2.** city in western Washington. Pop. (1970), 53,622.
ev·er·glade (ev′ər glād′) *n.* **1.** large tract of low marshland partly covered with tall grass. **2. Everglades.** extensive region of marshlands and swamps in southern Florida.
ev·er·green (ev′ər grēn′) *adj.* (of plants, trees, and shrubs) having green foliage throughout the year. Distinguished from **deciduous.** —*n.* **1.a.** plant, shrub, or tree that retains its foliage for more than one

growing season, replacing its leaves gradually, thus having green foliage throughout the year. **2.** evergreens. evergreen twigs or branches used for decoration, as at Christmas.
ev·er·last·ing (ev′ər las′ting) *adj.* **1.** existing, continuing, or lasting forever; having infinite duration: *The mighty God, the everlasting Father* (Isaiah 9:6). **2.** existing, continuing, or lasting indefinitely; perpetual: *And I will give unto thee . . . an everlasting possession* (Genesis 7:8). **3.** endlessly recurring without an end; interminable; tiresome: *tedious, everlasting stories of his adventures.* —*n.* **1.** all time; past and future; eternity: *from everlasting to everlasting thou art God* (Psalms: 90). **2. the Everlasting.** God. —*Syn. adj.* **2.** see **eternal.**
ev·er·more (ev′ər môr′) *adv.* **1.** for and at all times; forever; eternally. **2. for evermore.** forever.
e·ver·si·ble (i vur′sə bəl) *adj.* capable of being everted.
e·ver·sion (i vur′zhən, -shən) *n.* act of everting; state of being everted. [Old French *eversion* an upsetting, overthrow, from Latin *ēversiō* a turning out, overthrowing.]
e·vert (i vurt′) *v.t.* to turn outward or inside out. [Latin *ēvertere* to turn out.]
e·ver·tor (i vur′tər) *n.* muscle that rotates an organ or part outward.
eve·ry (ev′rē) *adj.* **1.** each without excepting any (of the units of an aggregate); all (of a collective or aggregate number) taken one by one: *Every student in the class was in the room.* **2.** all possible; the utmost: *I have every respect for him as a writer.* **3.** at a regular interval of: *The pills should be taken every four hours.*
every bit. in every respect; entirely; quite: *She's every bit as good a cook as her mother.*
every now and then (or **again**). from time to time; occasionally.
every once in a while. from time to time; occasionally.
every other. each alternate; each second: *They took turns driving every other week.*
every so often. from time to time; occasionally.
every which way. *Informal.* in all directions; in total disorder. [Old English *ǣfre* always + *ǣlc* each.] —*Syn.* **1.** see **each.**
eve·ry·bod·y (ev′rē bod′ē, -bud′ē) *pron.* every person.
eve·ry·day (ev′rē dā′) *adj.* **1.** of or relating to every day; daily: *the everyday business of one's life.* **2.** suitable for ordinary days: *She changed from her everyday clothes to her Sunday best.* **3.** commonplace; ordinary; usual: *an everyday occurrence.*
eve·ry·one (ev′rē wun′, -wən) *pron.* every person; everybody: *Everyone agreed that it was a good move.*
eve·ry·thing (ev′rē thing′) *pron.* **1.** every thing; all things; all. **2.** what is important, highly valued, or very much wanted: *For you to go too means everything to him.*
eve·ry·where (ev′rē hwâr′, -wâr′) *adv.* in every place; in all places: *They traveled everywhere in England.*
e·vict (i vikt′) *v.t.* **1.** to expel (a tenant) from land or a building, esp. by legal process; dispossess: *The tenant was evicted for nonpayment of rent.* [Latin *ēvictus,* past participle of *ēvincere* to overcome, conquer.] —**e·vic′tion,** *n.*
ev·i·dence (ev′ə dəns) *n.* **1.** that which serves to prove or disprove a belief or conclusion; proof: *He produced much experimental data as evidence for his theory.* **2.** that which is legally presented to a court, as a document or the testimony of a witness, for the purpose of proving or disproving an issue in question. **3.** that which makes something evident; indication; sign: *Her silence was evidence of her grief.* **4. in evidence.** plainly perceived; noticeably present: *The effects of the war were very much in evidence.* —*v.t.,* **-denced, -denc·ing.** to give proof of; show clearly; demonstrate: *Lines of people waiting to buy tickets evidenced the play's success.* [Old French *evidence* clearness, from Latin *ēvidentia.*]
Syn. n. 1. Evidence, testimony, proof mean grounds cited to uphold or deny a statement. Evidence implies an intention to prove or disprove something to a person or group held to be capable of determining truth: *The student presented evidence that his thesis was based on original research.* Testimony stresses a declaration as to the truth or falsity of something, esp. under oath: *The witnesses' testimony tended to uphold the defendant's alibi.* Proof implies evidence so conclusive as to eliminate doubt: *The photograph was proof enough that the two men knew each other.*
ev·i·dent (ev′ə dənt) *adj.* easily seen or understood; clear; apparent: *It was evident that he had their approval.* [Latin *ēvidēns.*]
ev·i·den·tial (ev′ə den′shəl) *adj.* **1.** based on or relying on evidence. **2.** of, having the nature of, or furnishing evidence.
ev·i·dent·ly (ev′ə dənt lē, -dent′-) *adv.* clearly; apparently; obviously.
e·vil (ē′vəl) *adj.* **1.** morally bad; wicked; sinful: *evil thoughts.* **2.** causing trouble or injury; harmful; pernicious: *an evil custom, evil laws.* **3.** characterized by or threatening misfortune or suffering; disastrous; unlucky: *an evil omen, evil times.* **4.** resulting from bad character or conduct: *an evil reputation.* —*n.* **1.** that which is morally bad; sin;

at; āpe; cär; end; mē; it; īce; hot; ōld; fôrk; wood; fŏŏl; oil; out; up; ūse; turn; sing; thin; this; zh in treasure; ə in ago, taken, pencil, lemon, circus.

353

wickedness. **2.** that which causes misfortune, suffering, or injury: *a necessary evil. Evil befell him.* [Old English *yfel* bad.] —**e′vil·ly,** *adv.* —**e′vil·ness,** *n.* —**Syn.** *adj.* **1.** see **bad¹.**

e·vil·do·er (ē′vəl dōō′ər) *n.* one who does evil. —**e′vil·do′ing,** *n.*

evil eye, eye or glance superstitiously believed to have the power to inflict harm or misfortune.

e·vil-mind·ed (ē′vəl mīn′did) *adj.* having evil thoughts; malicious; malignant.

Evil One, Satan.

e·vince (i vins′) **e·vinced, e·vinc·ing.** *v.t.* **1.** to make clear or evident; reveal clearly: *The evidence evinced the guilt of the defendant.* **2.** to exhibit (a quality, feeling, or condition): *He evinced a total lack of consideration for his friends.* [Latin *ēvincere* to overcome, conquer.] —**e·vin′ci·ble,** *adj.*

e·vis·cer·ate (i vis′ə rāt′) **-at·ed, -at·ing.** *v.t.* **1.** to remove the viscera, esp. the intestines, from; disembowel. **2.** to deprive of an essential part: *The bill was eviscerated before being passed by the legislature.* [Latin *ēviscerātus,* past participle of *ēviscerāre* to disembowel, from *ex* out + *viscera* internal organs.] —**e·vis′cer·a′tion,** *n.*

ev·o·ca·tion (ē′vō kā′shən, ev′ə-) *n.* act of evoking.

e·voc·a·tive (i vok′ə tiv) *adj.* tending to evoke. —**e·voc′a·tive·ly,** *adv.*

e·voke (i vōk′) **e·voked, e·vok·ing.** *v.t.* to call forth or bring out; elicit: *His question evoked an angry response. The song evoked memories.* [Latin *ēvocāre.*]

ev·o·lu·tion (ev′ə lōō′shən) *n.* **1.** gradual process of development or growth through a series of stages: *the evolution of music, the evolution of socialism.* **2.** result of this process. **3.** *Biology.* **a.** theory that all living plants and animals arose from one simple form of life and gradually developed into widely different and more complicated forms through natural processes of change over millions of generations. **b.** continuous adaptation of organisms to their environment by genetic transmission. **4.** movement, esp. one of a series: *the evolutions of a dancer, the evolutions of a machine.* **5.** releasing or giving off, as of gas, heat, or sound; emission. **6.** *Mathematics.* process of extracting the root of a number. Opposed to **involution** in def. 6. [Latin *ēvolūtiō* unrolling of a scroll, opening of a book.]

ev·o·lu·tion·ar·y (ev′ə lōō′shə ner′ē) *adj.* **1.** of, relating to, or resulting from gradual development or growth. **2.** of, relating to, or in accordance with the biological theory of evolution.

ev·o·lu·tion·ist (ev′ə lōō′shə nist) *n.* believer in or adherent of evolution, esp. biological evolution. —**ev′o·lu′tion·ism,** *n.*

e·volve (i volv′) **e·volved, e·volv·ing.** *v.t.* **1.** to develop gradually; work out: *to evolve a theory.* **2.** *Biology.* to develop by a process of change to a more highly organized condition. **3.** to release or give off, as a gas; emit. —*v.i.* **1.** to undergo gradual development or growth. **2.** *Biology.* to be developed by a process of change to a more highly organized condition; undergo evolution. [Latin *ēvolvere* to unroll.] —**e·volve′ment,** *n.*

Ev·voi·a (ev′ē ä) Euboea.

ewe (ū) *n.* female sheep. [Old English *ēowu.*]

ew·er (ū′ər) *n.* wide-mouthed pitcher, used esp. for holding or pouring water. [Anglo-Norman *ewer,* form of Old French *aiguier,* going back to Latin *aquārius* relating to water, from *aqua* water.]

ex (eks) *prep.* **1.** *Commerce.* free of charges until removed from (a specified place or thing): *ex warehouse, ex dock.* **2.** *Finance.* exclusive of; without: *an ex dividend stock.* [Latin *ex* out of, without.]

ex-¹ *prefix* **1.** out of or from: *excursion, exit, export.* **2.** thoroughly; completely: *exhilarate, exasperate.* **3.** former; previous. ▲ followed by a hyphen and used to form a compound: *an ex-minister, an ex-president.* [Latin *ex* out, out of, away, from, utterly, without.]

ex-² also, **ec-.** *prefix* from; forth; out: *exorcise, exodus.* [Greek *ex* out of.]

ex-³ form of **exo-** before vowels, as in *exegesis.*

Ex., **1.** example. **2.** examined. **3.** exchange. **4.** execute.

Ex., Excellency.

ex·ac·er·bate (ig zas′ər bāt′, ek sas′-) **-bat·ed, -bat·ing.** *v.t.* **1.** to make more intense or severe; aggravate, as pain, disease, or anger. **2.** to irritate, provoke, or exasperate (a person). [Latin *exacerbātus,* past participle of *exacerbāre* to irritate, aggravate, from *ex* utterly + *acerbus* harsh, bitter.] —**ex·ac′er·ba′tion,** *n.*

ex·act (ig zakt′) *adj.* **1.** strictly accurate; precise; correct: *exact time, exact measurements.* **2.** being that which is needed or required: *I gave him a check for the exact amount.* **3.** duplicating in every detail; corresponding perfectly: *an exact likeness.* **4.** characterized by accuracy: *an exact thinker.* —*v.t.* **1.** to demand and get by or as by force or authority: *to exact payment, to exact obedience.* **2.** to call for; require: *The problem*

exacted hours of concentration. [Latin *exāctus,* past participle of *exigere* to drive out, demand, measure.] —**ex·act′ness,** *n.* —**Syn.** *adj.* **1.** see **correct.**

ex·act·ing (ig zak′ting) *adj.* **1.** rigorously demanding; strict; severe: *an exacting master.* **2.** requiring great skill, accuracy, care, or attention: *an exacting task.*

ex·ac·tion (ig zak′shən) *n.* **1.** act of exacting. **2.** that which is exacted, as taxes, duties, or tribute.

ex·act·i·tude (ig zak′tə tōōd′, -tūd′) *n.* quality of being exact; accuracy; precision.

ex·act·ly (ig zakt′lē) *adv.* **1.** in an exact manner; accurately; precisely: *He followed my instructions exactly.* **2.** just; quite: *It happened exactly as you described it.*

exact science, a science, such as mathematics or physics, that theoretically allows exact analysis and prediction.

ex·ag·ger·ate (ig zaj′ə rāt′) **-at·ed, -at·ing.** *v.t.* **1.** to represent (something) as greater than it is; overstate; overemphasize: *to exaggerate the seriousness of a problem, to exaggerate a person's faults.* **2.** to increase or enlarge abnormally. —*v.i.* to represent a thing as greater than it is; overstate: *Fishermen often exaggerate when describing a fish.* [Latin *exaggerātus,* past participle of *exaggerāre* to heap up, magnify, going back to *ex* out + *agger* heap.] —**ex·ag′ger·a′tor,** *n.*

ex·ag·ger·a·tion (ig zaj′ə rā′shən) *n.* **1.** act of exaggerating; being exaggerated. **2.** instance of exaggerating; overstatement.

ex·alt (ig zôlt′) *v.t.* **1.** to praise; glorify; extol: *He exalted honesty above all other virtues.* **2.** to elevate, as in rank, character, or esteem: *Angels . . . whom the supreme King exalted to such power* (Milton, 1667). [Latin *exaltāre* to raise, from *ex* out + *altus* high.]

ex·al·ta·tion (eg′zôl tā′shən, ek′sôl-) *n.* **1.** act of exalting; being exalted. **2.** feeling of great exhilaration; rapture; elation.

ex·am (ig zam′) *n.* *Informal.* examination.

ex·am·i·na·tion (ig zam′ə nā′shən) *n.* **1.** act or process of examining; being examined. **2.** test, esp. of knowledge, skill, or qualifications: *an examination in chemistry.* **3.** medical checking and testing of the body or a part of it, as by a dentist or physician. **4.** interrogation of a witness in a court of law for the purpose of eliciting any knowledge which the witness may have of the matter before the court.

ex·am·ine (ig zam′in) **-ined, -in·ing.** *v.t.* **1.** to look at closely and carefully; investigate; inspect; scrutinize: *She examined the merchandise before buying it.* **2.** to test, esp. in order to ascertain the knowledge, skill, or qualifications of: *to examine applicants for a job.* **3.** to subject (a person or organ) to medical checking and testing. **4.** *Law.* to subject (a witness) to an examination. [Old French *examiner* to question, test, from Latin *exāmināre* to weigh, test, from *exāmen* a weighing.] —**ex·am′in·er,** *n.* —**Syn. 1.** see **scrutinize.**

ex·am·i·nee (ig zam′ə nē′) *n.* one who is being examined or is a candidate for an examination.

ex·am·ple (ig zam′pəl) *n.* **1.** particular thing that belongs to and is representative of a whole; sample; illustration: *The instructor gave us several examples of the artist's work. That was but one example of his kindness.* **2.** one who or that which is worthy of imitation; model: *His politeness is a good example for others to follow.* **3.** problem or exercise used to illustrate a rule, method, or process, as in arithmetic. **4.** instance or object, as of punishment, intended to serve as a warning or deterrent to others: *The judge made an example of the criminal by giving him a harsh sentence.* **5.** to set an example. to act so as to inspire imitation; serve as a model for others. **6. for example.** by way of illustration. **7.** without example. without equal or precedent. [Old French *essample, example* illustration, pattern, from Latin *exemplum* sample, pattern.]

Syn. 1. Example, specimen, sample indicate something showing the qualities of a larger body or mass from which it is taken. **Example** suggests that the thing is typical: *This painting is a good example of the artist's realistic period.* **Specimen** implies that the thing chosen is easily separated but quite representative: *That is a good specimen of his handwriting.* **Sample** suggests that the thing chosen is a small part but has all the qualities of the larger unit: *As part of their advertising campaign, they distributed samples of the new detergent.* **2.** see **model.**

ex·as·per·ate (ig zas′pə rāt′) **-at·ed, -at·ing.** *v.t.* to irritate greatly; provoke to anger; infuriate: *Constant interruption of his work exasperated him.* [Latin *exasperātus,* past participle of *exasperāre* to make rough, provoke, going back to *ex* utterly + *asper* rough.] —**ex·as′per·at′ing·ly,** *adv.*

ex·as·per·a·tion (ig zas′pə rā′shən) *n.* act of exasperating; being exasperated.

Exc., Excellency.

Ex·cal·i·bur (eks kal′ə bər) *n.* sword of King Arthur. [Old French *Escalibor,* from Medieval Latin *Caliburnus,* possibly from Irish *Caladbolg* literally, hard belly, name of a sword famous in Irish folklore.]

ex ca·the·dra (eks′ kə thē′drə, kath′ə drə) from the seat of authority; with authority: *an ex cathedra judgment.* [Latin *ex cathedrā* literally, from the chair.]

Ewer

at; āpe; cär; end; mē; it; īce; hot; ōld; fôrk; wood; fōol; oil; out; up; ūse; turn; sing; thin; this; zh in treasure; ə in ago, taken, pencil, lemon, circus.

ex·ca·vate (ĕks′kə vāt′) -vat·ed, -vat·ing. *v.t.* **1.** to remove by digging: *to excavate earth.* **2.** to uncover by digging; unearth: *to excavate an ancient burial site.* **3.** to make by hollowing out; dig: *to excavate a tunnel.* **4.** to make a hole in; hollow out: *They excavated the mountainside for a tunnel.* [Latin *excavātus,* past participle of *excavāre* to hollow out, from *ex* out + *cavus* hollow.]

ex·ca·va·tion (ĕks′kə vā′shən) *n.* **1.** act or process of excavating. **2.** hole made by excavating: *A new building will go up at the site of that excavation.* **3.** that which is uncovered by excavating, as ruins.

ex·ca·va·tor (ĕks′kə vā′tər) *n.* one who or that which excavates, esp. a machine used for digging, as a steam shovel.

ex·ceed (ik sēd′) *v.t.* **1.** to go beyond the limit of: *He has exceeded his authority.* **2.a.** to go beyond in quantity, degree, or rate: *to exceed the speed limit. The contributions exceeded $10,-000.* **b.** to be greater than or superior to; surpass; excel: *His knowledge of history exceeds mine.* [Old French *exceder,* from Latin *excēdere* to go beyond, surpass.] —**Syn. 2.** see **excel.**

Excavator

ex·ceed·ing (ik sē′ding) *Archaic. adj.* unusuⁱ y great; surpassing. —*adv.* exceedingly.

ex·ceed·ing·ly (ik sē′ding lē) *adv.* unusually; extremely.

ex·cel (ik sel′) -celled, -cel·ling. *v.t.* to be better or greater than, as in ability or quality; surpass; outdo. —*v.i.* to be superior to others; surpass others: *He excels in music and art.* [Latin *excellere.*]

Syn. *v.t.* **Excel, exceed, surpass, outdo** mean to do better or more than someone or something else. **Excel** suggests greater accomplishment: *He excels all other composers of his period.* **Exceed** implies having greater extent, volume, number, or the like: *Unfortunately, the rate of his expenditures exceeds his income.* **Surpass** suggests a criterion of some kind: *The response to our financial appeal surpassed anything we expected.* **Outdo** sometimes implies emulation, though usually it stresses only going beyond what is expected: *His latest book outdoes anything he has written previously.*

ex·cel·lence (ĕk′sə ləns) *n.* **1.** fact or condition of excelling; superiority, as in quality, ability, or worth. **2.** something in which a person or thing excels.

ex·cel·len·cy (ĕk′sə lən sē) *pl.,* **-cies.** *n.* **1.** excellence. **2. Excellency.** title of honor used in referring to or addressing certain dignitaries, as governors or ambassadors. ▲ often preceded by *His* or *Your.*

ex·cel·lent (ĕk′sə lənt) *adj.* remarkably good; superior; exceptional. [Latin *excellēns,* present participle of *excellere* to surpass.] —**ex′cel·lent·ly,** *adv.*

ex·cel·si·or (ik sel′sē ər) *n.* fine shavings, as of wood or paper, used as a packing material or for stuffing.

ex·cept (ik sept′) *prep.* **1.** with the exception of; excluding; but: *All the boys went home except Jack.* **2. except for.** were it not for; but for. —*conj.* **1.** only; but: *I would go with you, except that I have to work that day.* **2.** *Archaic.* unless. —*v.t.* to leave out; omit; exclude: *Certain people were excepted from the curfew.* —*v.i.* to take exception; object (often with *to*): *to except to a statement.* [Latin *exceptus,* past participle of *excipere* to take out.]

ex·cept·ing (ik sep′ting) *prep.* except. —*conj. Archaic.* unless.

ex·cep·tion (ik sep′shən) *n.* **1.** act of excepting; being excepted. **2.** one who or that which differs or is excluded, as from a general class or rule. **3.** objection; complaint. **4.** formal objection to the ruling of a court during the course of a trial. **5. to take exception. a.** to object; protest. **b.** to take offense; feel resentful.

ex·cep·tion·a·ble (ik sep′shə nə bəl) *adj.* liable to objection. —**ex·cep′tion·a·bly,** *adv.*

ex·cep·tion·al (ik sep′shən əl) *adj.* out of the ordinary; unusual; extraordinary: *exceptional talent, an exceptional student.* —**ex·cep′tion·al·ly,** *adv.* —**Syn.** see **extraordinary.**

ex·cerpt (*n.,* ĕk′sûrpt; *v.,* ik sûrpt′) *n.* passage or scene selected from a larger work, as a book; extract: *excerpts from a film. He read excerpts from his poetry.* —*v.t.* to take out a passage or scene from; extract; quote: *to excerpt a novel.* [Latin *excerptum* extract, from *excerpere* to select.]

ex·cess (ĕk′ses, ik ses′) *n.* **1.** amount greater than needed or desired; more than enough; superfluity: *an excess of water, an excess of money.* **2.** amount or degree by which one thing exceeds another: *an excess of income over spending.* **3.** action or behavior that goes beyond what is usual, proper, just, or necessary. **4.** immoderate indulgence, as in food or drink; intemperance. **5. in excess of.** to a greater amount or degree than: *His bank balance was in excess of five hundred dollars.* **6.** **excess.** too much: *to drink to excess.* —*adj.* being more than what is usual or required; extra: *excess baggage. excess fat, excess detail.* [Old French *exces* superfluity, from Latin *excessus* departure, deviation.]

ex·ces·sive (ik ses′iv) *adj.* beyond what is necessary, usual, just, or proper; immoderate: *excessive noise, excessive force.* —**ex·ces′sive·ly,** *adv.* —**ex·ces′sive·ness,** *n.*

Syn. Excessive, immoderate, inordinate, intemperate, exorbitant mean going beyond what is normal or proper. **Excessive** suggests an amount or quantity too great for what is required: *The summer rains were excessive and flooded the fields.* **Immoderate** implies going beyond bounds, esp. in emotional matters: *His speech was received by the opposition with immoderate laughter.* **Inordinate** suggests lack of judgment or regulation: *They asked an inordinate price for the house.* **Intemperate** implies lack of control: *His talk turned out to be an intemperate attack on bankers.* **Exorbitant** suggests a rather sharp or extreme divergence from the normal: *The new job made exorbitant demands on his time.*

ex·cess-prof·its tax (ĕk′ses prof′its) tax on business profits above a certain average defined as normal for a specified period of years, usually applied in time of war or high defense spending.

ex·change (iks chānj′) -changed, -chang·ing. *v.t.* **1.** to give and receive reciprocally; interchange: *to exchange gifts, to exchange marriage vows. The United States and Great Britain exchange ambassadors.* **2.** to part with in return for something regarded as equivalent; trade: *to exchange dollars for francs.* **3.** to give up for something in return: *to exchange a life of ease for one of hard labor.* **4.** to return (a purchase) for something else: *She exchanged the blouse for a smaller one.* —*v.i.* **1.** to make an exchange. **2.** to be received as an equivalent: *For many years the British pound exchanged for about five U.S. dollars.* —*n.* **1.** act of giving or receiving reciprocally; mutual transfer: *an exchange of prisoners of war.* **2.** act of giving one thing in return for something regarded as an equivalent: *the exchange of a purchase.* **3.** substitution of one thing or state for another. **4.** that which is given or received in return for something else: *a poor exchange.* **5.** place where things, as commodities or securities, are bought, sold, or traded: *a jewelry exchange.* **6.** central office, station, or system where groups of telephone lines are connected, providing communication in a town or part of a large city. **7.a.** system of settling financial accounts by using negotiable instruments, as bills of exchange or drafts, instead of money. **b.** bill of exchange. **8.** conversion or transferral of money of one country into its equivalent in money of another country, allowing for differences in value between the two. **9.** rate or price of one currency in terms of another; rate of exchange. **10. exchanges.** negotiable instruments, as checks or drafts, presented for collection through a clearing house. [Old French *eschangier* to give and receive reciprocally, barter, going back to Late Latin *ex* out + *cambiāre* to barter, change (probably of Celtic origin).]

ex·change·a·ble (iks chān′jə bəl) *adj.* that can be exchanged. —**ex·change′a·bil′i·ty,** *n.*

ex·cheq·uer (ĕks′chek′ər, iks chek′ər) *n.* **1.** royal or national treasury. **2.** any treasury, as of an organization. **3. Exchequer. a.** department of the British government that manages the national finances, including the collection and spending of the public revenue. **b.** contents of the Exchequer. [Old French *eschequier* chessboard, counting table (so called because the English king's accounts were once reckoned with counters on a checkered cloth resembling a chessboard), from *eschec* a check (at chess). See CHECK.]

ex·cise¹ (ĕk′sīz, -sīs) *n.* indirect tax levied on the manufacture, sale, or consumption of certain commodities within a country, as liquor, tobacco, or gasoline. Also, **excise tax.** [Middle Dutch *excijs,* from Old French *acceis* tax, going back to Latin *ad* to + *cēnsus* register of citizens, tax, property.]

ex·cise² (ik sīz′) -cised, -cis·ing. *v.t.* to remove by or as by cutting: *to excise a tumor, to excise a paragraph from an essay.* [Latin *excīsus,* past participle of *excīdere* to cut out.] —**ex·ci·sion** (ek sizh′ən), *n.*

ex·cise·man (ĕk′sīz mən) *pl.,* **-men.** official of the British government who collects excises and enforces the laws relating to them.

ex·cit·a·ble (ik sī′tə bəl) *adj.* **1.** capable of being excited; easily excited. **2.** (of an organ or organism) capable of reacting to a stimulus. —**ex·cit′a·bil′i·ty, ex·cit′a·ble·ness,** *n.* —**ex·cit′a·bly,** *adv.*

ex·ci·ta·tion (ĕk′sī tā′shən) *n.* **1.** act of exciting; being excited. **2.** production of a magnetic field by electricity, as in an electric generator. **3.** effect of a stimulus on an organ or organism.

ex·cite (ik sīt′) -cit·ed, -cit·ing. *v.t.* **1.** to stir up the mind or emotions of: *The idea of a picnic excited the children. His inflammatory speech excited the mob.* **2.** to call forth; evoke: *to excite fear, to excite a person's curiosity.* **3.a.** to stir to action; put in motion. **b.** to increase the activity of (an organ or organism); stimulate. **4.** to raise (an atom, molecule, or other particle) to an energy level higher than normal. **5.** to produce

at; āpe; cär; end; mē; it; īce; hot; ōld; fôrk; wood; fōōl; oil; out; up; ūse; turn; sing; thin; this; zh in treasure; ə in ago, taken, pencil, lemon, circus.

a magnetic field, as in an electric generator. [Latin *excitāre* to callout, rouse, stir up.]

ex·cit·ed (ik sī′tid) *adj.* **1.** stirred up; aroused; agitated. **2.** (of an atom, molecule, or other particle) at a higher energy level than normal. —**ex·cit′ed·ly**, *adv.*

ex·cite·ment (ek sīt′mənt) *n.* **1.** act of exciting; being excited. **2.** that which excites.

ex·cit·er (ik sī′tər) *n.* **1.** one who or that which excites. **2.** electric generator or battery that supplies current to produce a magnetic field in an electric motor or generator.

ex·cit·ing (ik sī′ting) *adj.* causing excitement; stirring; thrilling. —**ex·cit′ing·ly**, *adv.*

ex·claim (iks klām′) *v.t., v.i.* to speak or cry out suddenly or vehemently, as in anger or surprise. [Latin *exclāmāre*.]

ex·cla·ma·tion (eks′klə mā′shən) *n.* **1.** act of exclaiming. **2.** that which is exclaimed.

exclamation point, punctuation mark (!) used after a word, phrase, or sentence to indicate an exclamation, as of surprise or anger. Also, **exclamation mark.**

ex·clam·a·to·ry (iks klam′ə tôr′ē) *adj.* using, containing, or expressing exclamation.

ex·clude (iks klōōd′) -**clud·ed**, -**clud·ing.** *v.t.* **1.** to prevent from entering; shut or keep out: *All those under twenty years of age were excluded from the club.* **2.** to fail to consider or include; leave out; omit: *He excluded certain passages from the original book in the new edition.* **3.** to put out; expel; eject. [Latin *exclūdere* to shut out.] **Syn. 2. Exclude, eliminate, omit** mean to shut out or keep from joining or becoming part of. **Exclude** implies refusal to permit entry: *Only a very tight gasket is guaranteed to exclude water.* **Eliminate** suggests that what is refused is already in, or a part of, and must be removed: *Even the most thorough proofreading will not eliminate all the errors.* **Omit** implies leaving out or removing part, esp. by oversight: *The typist omitted the last line of the letter.*

ex·clu·sion (iks klōō′zhən) *n.* act of excluding; being excluded. [Latin *exclūsiō* a shutting out.]

ex·clu·sive (iks klōō′siv) *adj.* **1.** belonging to a single individual or group; not divided or shared: *exclusive rights, exclusive ownership.* **2.** open to or admitting only a certain select group, esp. as with regard to social standing or wealth: *an exclusive club.* **3.** given to or appearing in only one source: *an exclusive news item. The actress granted the reporter an exclusive interview.* **4.** high-priced: *an exclusive restaurant, an exclusive dress shop.* **5.** each excluding the other; incompatible: *mutually exclusive concepts.* **6.** complete; entire: *The matter will be given our exclusive attention.* **7.** leaving out; excluding (with *of*): *The price is fifty dollars, exclusive of the sales tax.* —**ex·clu′sive·ly**, *adv.* —**ex·clu′sive·ness**, *n.*

ex·com·mu·ni·cate (*v.*, eks′kə mū′nə kāt′; *n.*, eks′kə mū′nə kit) -**cat·ed**, -**cat·ing.** *v.t.* to expel from membership in a church by ecclesiastical authority; deny (a person) the right to participate in the services of or receive the benefits of a church. —*n.* one who has been excommunicated. [Church Latin *excommūnicātus*, past participle of *excommūnicāre* to expel from membership in a church, going back to Latin *ex* out of + *commūnis* general.]

ex·com·mu·ni·ca·tion (eks′kə mū′nə kā′shən) *n.* **1.** act of excommunicating; being excommunicated. **2.** ecclesiastical pronouncement by which one is excommunicated.

ex·co·ri·ate (eks kôr′ē āt′) -**at·ed**, -**at·ing.** *v.t.* **1.** to strip off or abrade the skin of. **2.** to reprove scathingly; censure; berate: *He excoriated them for their apathy.* [Latin *excoriātus*, past participle of *excoriāre* to strip of its skin, from *ex* from + *corium* skin.] —**ex·co′ri·a′tion**, *n.*

ex·cre·ment (eks′krə mənt) *n.* waste matter discharged from the body, esp. from the bowels; feces. [Latin *excrēmentum* refuse.] —**ex·cre·men′tal**, *adj.*

ex·cres·cence (iks kres′əns) *n.* **1.** any abnormal or disfiguring outgrowth or addition, as a wart or mole. **2.** normal outgrowth, as hair or fingernails.

ex·cres·cent (eks kres′ənt) *adj.* constituting an abnormal or superfluous outgrowth or addition. [Latin *excrēscēns*, past participle of *excrēscere* to grow out.]

ex·cre·ta (eks krē′tə) *n.,pl.* waste matter discharged from the body, as sweat or urine. [Latin *excrēta* literally, things sifted out, neuter plural of *excrētus*. See EXCRETE.]

ex·crete (eks krēt′) -**cret·ed**, -**cret·ing.** *v.t.* to discharge (waste matter) from the body; separate (waste products) from the blood or tissues: *The kidneys excrete the waste products of metabolism.* [Latin *excrētus*, past participle of *excernere* to sift out.]

ex·cre·tion (eks krē′shən) *n.* **1.** act of excreting. **2.** matter excreted, as sweat or urine.

ex·cre·to·ry (eks′krə tôr′ē) *adj.* of, relating to, or for excretion: *an excretory duct.* Also, **ex·cre·tive** (eks krē′tiv).

ex·cru·ci·ate (iks krōō′shē āt′) -**at·ed**, -**at·ing.** *v.t.* **1.** to cause severe

pain to; torture. **2.** to subject to mental distress; torment. [Latin *excruciātus*, past participle of *excruciāre* to torture, going back to *ex* utterly + *crux* cross.] —**ex·cru′ci·a′tion**, *n.*

ex·cru·ci·at·ing (iks krōō′shē ā′ting) *adj.* causing or inflicting extreme pain or suffering; agonizing; torturous. —**ex·cru′ci·at′ing·ly**, *adv.*

ex·cul·pate (eks′kul pāt′, eks kul′pāt) -**pat·ed**, -**pat·ing.** *v.t.* to declare free from blame or a charge of guilt; exonerate. [Ex-¹ + Latin *culpātus*, past participle of *culpāre* to blame.] —**ex′cul·pa′tion**, *n.*

ex·cur·sion (iks kur′zhən, -shən) *n.* **1.** short trip made esp. for pleasure or a special purpose: *an excursion to the museum, an excursion into the country.* **2.** short trip on a train, ship, or other public conveyance, offered at reduced rates, often including other specified services and a return trip: *We took the weekend excursion to the seashore.* **3.** group of people taking such a trip. [Latin *excursiō* a running out.]

ex·cur·sion·ist (iks kur′zhə nist, -shə-) *n.* one who goes on an excursion.

ex·cur·sive (iks kur′siv) *adj.* tending to wander off a subject; rambling; digressive. —**ex·cur′sive·ly**, *adv.* —**ex·cur′sive·ness**, *n.*

ex·cus·a·ble (iks kū′zə bəl) *adj.* capable of being forgiven; pardonable: *an excusable error.* —**ex·cus′a·bly**, *adv.*

ex·cuse (*v.*, iks kūz′; *n.*, iks kūs′) -**cused**, -**cus·ing.** *v.t.* **1.** to grant pardon or forgiveness to: *Please excuse me for inconveniencing you.* **2.** to release or exempt, as from duty, obligation, or attendance: *The jury was excused. He was excused from football practice for the rest of the week.* **3.** to accept as understandable or regard with indulgence; disregard; overlook: *Knowing how upset she was, we excused her rudeness.* **4.** to serve as a reason or explanation for; justify: *Ignorance does not excuse disobedience of the law.* **5.** to attempt to free from blame: *He excused himself by pleading ignorance.* **6. to excuse oneself. a.** to make an apology for oneself. **b.** to ask to be released, as from attendance, obligation, or duty. —*n.* **1.** reason given in explanation; justification: *a written excuse. Oversleeping is no excuse for being late.* **2.** act of excusing. **3.** *Informal.* example; specimen (with *for*): *That's a poor excuse for a sailboat.* [Old French *excuser* to cancel, exclude, seek to free from, from Latin *excūsāre* to free from blame, from *ex* from + *causa* lawsuit, cause.] —**ex·cus′er**, *n.* **Syn. 1, 2. Excuse, pardon, forgive, condone** indicate an overlooking of someone's offense or failing to impose punishment. **Excuse** suggests a minor offense, such as a social error, perhaps considered too slight for punishment: *He asked her to excuse his brusqueness, as he was late for an appointment.* **Pardon** implies a freeing from punishment, or removal of the penalty, for a relatively serious fault: *He could neither understand nor pardon the boy's deliberate lie.* **Forgive** is less formal than **pardon** and suggests a personal willingness to forgo even resentment: *She is far too indulgent when she forgives all her son's faults.* **Condone** implies extreme tolerance of or lack of opposition to an infraction or violation: *By not punishing the culprit, the proctor seemed to condone breaking the curfew.*

exec. **1.** executive. **2.** executor.

ex·e·cra·ble (ek′sə krə bəl) *adj.* **1.** abominable; detestable: *Lynching is an execrable custom.* **2.** of inferior quality; very bad. —**ex′e·cra·ble·ness**, *n.* —**ex′e·cra·bly**, *adv.*

ex·e·crate (ek′sə krāt′) -**crat·ed**, -**crat·ing.** *v.t.* **1.** to condemn scathingly; curse. **2.** to abhor; detest; abominate. —*v.i.* to utter curses; swear. [Latin *ex(s)ecrātus*, past participle of *ex(s)ecrārī* to curse.]

ex·e·cra·tion (ek′sə krā′shən) *n.* **1.** act of cursing or condemning. **2.** expression of abomination; curse. **3.** utter hatred; abhorrence; loathing. **4.** one who or that which is execrated.

ex·e·cute (ek′sə kūt′) -**cut·ed**, -**cut·ing.** *v.t.* **1.** to carry out; fulfill: *to execute a command, to execute a plan.* **2.** to put into effect, as a law; administer; enforce. **3.** to put to death in accordance with a legal sentence. **4.** to produce, esp. in accordance with a plan or design: *to execute a sculpture.* **5.** to perform or play, as a piece of music: *The pianist executed the sonata perfectly.* **6.** to carry out or make valid, as a will, deed, or contract, by doing whatever is legally required. [Old French *executer* to carry out, kill, from *executeur* one who carries out, from Late Latin *ex(s)ecūtor*, from Latin *ex(s)equī* to follow up, pursue.] —**Syn. 1.** see **perform.**

ex·e·cu·tion (ek′sə kū′shən) *n.* **1.** a carrying out or putting into effect: *the execution of a plan.* **2.** the carrying out of a legally imposed death sentence. **3.** performance or production, as of a work of art or piece of music. **4.** method or technique used in producing or performing something, as a work of art or piece of music. **5.** a carrying out or making valid by doing whatever is legally required. **6.** court document directing a judgment to be put into effect.

ex·e·cu·tion·er (ek′sə kū′shə nər) *n.* one who carries out a legally imposed death sentence.

ex·ec·u·tive (ig zek′yə tiv) *adj.* **1.** of, relating to, or suitable for the management of affairs, as in business or industry: *executive talents, an*

at; āpe; cär; end; mē; it; īce; hot; ōld; fôrk; wood; fōol; oil; out; up; ūse; turn; sing; thin; this; zh in treasure; ə in ago, taken, pencil, lemon, circus.

executive position. **2.** concerned with the administration and enforcement of laws or the affairs of government: *The police are part of the executive branch of government.* —*n.* **1.** one who directs or manages affairs, as of a corporation: *A meeting of the company's senior executives was called.* **2.a.** branch of government responsible for administering and enforcing the laws and for managing the affairs of a nation. **b.** person or persons constituting this branch of government.

Executive Mansion 1. White House (*def. 1).* **2.** official residence of the governor of a state.

executive officer, officer who is second in command of a military or naval unit.

executive session, meeting of a legislative body or its leaders, esp. one that is closed to the public.

ex·ec·u·tor (ig zek′yə tər; *def. 2 also* ek′sə kū′tər) *n.* **1.** person named in a will to carry out its provisions. **2.** one who carries out or puts into effect. [Old French *executeur* one who carries out. See EXECUTE.]

ex·ec·u·trix (ig zek′yə triks′) *pl.,* **ex·ec·u·trix·es** or **ex·ec·u·tri·ces** (ig zek′yə tri′sēz). *n.* female executor (*def. 1).*

ex·e·ge·sis (ek′sə jē′sis) *pl.,* **-ses** (-sēz). *n.* critical analysis or interpretation of a word, sentence, or passage, esp. of the Bible. [Greek *exēgēsis* interpretation.]

ex·e·get·ic (ek′sə jet′ik) *adj.* of or relating to exegesis; expository; explanatory. Also, **ex′e·get′i·cal.**

ex·em·plar (ig zem′plər, -plär) *n.* **1.** one who or that which is worthy of imitation; model; archetype. **2.** typical example or instance. [Old French *exemplaire* sample, pattern, going back to Latin *exemplum.*]

ex·em·pla·ry (ig zem′plər ē, eg′zəm pler′ē) *adj.* **1.** serving as a model; worthy of imitation; commendable: *exemplary conduct.* **2.** serving as a warning: *exemplary punishment.* **3.** serving as a typical example or instance; illustrative. [Late Latin *exemplāris* that serves as a pattern, from Latin *exemplum* sample, pattern.]

ex·em·pli·fi·ca·tion (ig zem′plə fi kā′shən) *n.* **1.** act of exemplifying. **2.** that which exemplifies; illustration; example.

ex·em·pli·fy (ig zem′plə fī′) **-fied, -fy·ing.** *v.t.* to serve as an example of; show by example. [Medieval Latin *exemplificare* to copy out, from Latin *exemplum* pattern, sample + *facere* to make.]

ex·em·pli gra·ti·a (eg zem′plī grä′shē ə) *Latin.* for (the sake of) example; for instance.

ex·empt (ig zempt′) *v.t.* to free from something to which others are subject, as a duty or requirement; excuse: *He was exempted from the test.* —*adj.* freed, as from a duty or obligation; excused: *Church property is exempt from real estate taxes.* [Latin *exēmptus,* past participle of *eximere* to take out, free.]

ex·emp·tion (ig zemp′shən) *n.* **1.** act of exempting; being exempted. **2.a.** deduction from taxable income allowed for oneself and one's dependents. **b.** oneself or one's dependents, used as a basis for such a deduction.

Syn. 1. Exemption, immunity mean freedom from some obligation, esp. a legal one. **Exemption** suggests avoidance of a duty required of others whose status is similar to that of the one exempted: *The new law imposes stricter limits on exemptions from the draft.* **Immunity** implies the existence of a protected or privileged class or category recognized as free, sometimes for natural reasons, from some obligation, burden, or restriction applicable to others: *The law establishes a tax immunity for certain industries.*

ex·er·cise (ek′sər sīz′) *n.* **1.** physical activity performed, esp. the training or improvement of the body: *Walking is good exercise.* **2.** specific activity designed or performed for practice, improvement, or development: *a piano exercise, exercises in mathematics.* **3.** active use or performance: *the exercise of patience, the exercise of power.* **4.** *also,* **exercises.** ceremony, program, or proceedings: *The graduation exercises consisted of speeches and the presentation of awards.* —*v.t.,* **-cised, -cis·ing. 1.** to put through exercises: *to exercise the body, to exercise a horse.* **2.** to make active use of; employ: *to exercise one's strength, to exercise one's constitutional rights.* **3.** to perform or fulfill, as functions or duties: *to exercise the duties of governor.* **4.** to bring to bear; exert: *to exercise influence.* **5.a.** to occupy the attention of. **b.** to make uneasy; worry; trouble. —*v.i.* to perform exercises: *He exercises in the gymnasium three times a week.* [Old French *exercice* training, practice, from Latin *exercitium* physical exercise.] —**ex′er·cis′a·ble,** *adj.* —**Syn.** *n.* **1.** see **practice.**

ex·er·cis·er (ek′sər sī′zər) *n.* **1.** one who exercises. **2.** apparatus used for exercising the body.

ex·ert (ig zurt′) *v.t.* **1.** to employ actively or put forth: *to exert power, to exert one's influence.* **2. to exert oneself.** to put forth great effort; try hard. [Latin *ex(s)ertus,* past participle of *ex(s)erere* to stretch or thrust out.]

ex·er·tion (ig zur′shən) *n.* **1.** vigorous use of energy; strenuous effort: *Climbing a mountain involves great physical exertion.* **2.** act or process

of putting forth or into action: *The problem demanded the exertion of considerable thought.* —**Syn. 1.** see **effort.**

ex·e·unt (ek′sē ənt) *Latin.* they go out. ▲ used as a stage direction to indicate that the two or more actors specified are to leave the stage.

ex·fo·li·ate (eks fō′lē āt′) **-at·ed, -at·ing.** *v.t., v.i.* **1.** to remove or shed in layers, flakes, or scales, as skin or bark. **2.** *Geology.* to wear away or come off in scales or sheets, as weathered rock. —**ex·fo′li·a′tion,** *n.* —**ex·fo′li·a′tive,** *adj.*

ex·ha·la·tion (eks′hə lā′shən) *n.* **1.** act or process of exhaling. **2.** that which is exhaled, as air or an odor.

ex·hale (eks hāl′, eks′āl) **-haled, -hal·ing.** *v.t.* **1.** to expel (air) from the lungs. **2.** to give off or release vapor or an odor: *He exhaled smoke in my face.* **3.** to give off; emit. **4.** to draw off in the form of vapor; evaporate. —*v.i.* **1.** to expel air from the lungs: *We inhale and exhale in breathing.* **2.** to be given off or rise as vapor. [Latin *exhālāre* to breathe out.]

ex·haust (ig zôst′) *v.t.* **1.** to make extremely weak or tired; deprive of strength or energy: *Shopping all day exhausted us.* **2.** to use up completely; consume entirely: *to exhaust one's resources, to exhaust one's patience.* **3.** to empty completely by removing the contents of; drain: *to exhaust a reservoir.* **4.** to study, develop, or treat thoroughly: *to exhaust a subject.* **5.** to draw out, as air or other gases, from or as from a container. **6.** to withdraw air or other gases from a scientific apparatus to produce a partial vacuum within the apparatus. —*v.i.* **1.** to escape or be emitted, as gases or steam. —*n.* **1.** escape or discharge, as of used steam or gases from an engine cylinder. **2.** waste products, as steam or gases, that escape or are discharged. **3.** means or passage, as a pipe, by which such waste products escape or are discharged. **4.** air or other gases withdrawn from a room by a fan. [Latin *exhaustus,* past participle of *exhaurīre* to draw out.] —**ex·haust′ed·ly,** *adv.* —**ex·haust′i·bil′i·ty,** *n.* —**ex·haust′i·ble,** *adj.* —**Syn.** *v.t.* **1.** see **fatigue. 3.** see **deplete.**

ex·haus·tion (ig zôs′chən) *n.* **1.** act or process of exhausting; being exhausted. **2.** lack of strength or energy; extreme fatigue.

ex·haus·tive (ig zôs′tiv) *adj.* overlooking or omitting nothing; thorough; comprehensive: *an exhaustive survey, an exhaustive study.* —**ex·haus′tive·ly,** *adv.* —**ex·haus′tive·ness,** *n.*

ex·haust·less (ig zôst′lis) *adj.* incapable of being exhausted; inexhaustible. —**ex·haust′less·ly,** *adv.* —**ex·haust′less·ness,** *n.*

ex·hib·it (ig zib′it) *v.t.* **1.** to put on a public display of; show publicly: *to exhibit paintings.* **2.** to make evident; reveal: *to exhibit a talent, to exhibit bravery, to exhibit emotion.* **3.** to submit (something) to a court or judicial officer as evidence. **4.** to put something on public display; give an exhibition: *Two new artists are exhibiting at the gallery.* —*n.* **1.** public display or show: *We went to see the exhibit of his sculptures.* **2.** object or collection of objects displayed publicly, as at an exhibition. **3.** document or object submitted to a court or judicial officer that is accepted and identified as evidence. [Latin *exhibitus,* past participle of *exhibēre* to hold forth, display.]

ex·hi·bi·tion (ek′sə bish′ən) *n.* **1.** act of exhibiting: *an exhibition of bravery.* **2.** public display or show: *a skiing exhibition, an automobile exhibition.* —**Syn. 2.** see **show.**

ex·hi·bi·tion·ism (ek′sə bish′ə niz′əm) *n.* **1.** act or practice of attracting attention to oneself by behaving in an intentionally conspicuous manner. **2.** compulsive tendency to publicly expose the sex organs for sexual pleasure or excitement. —**ex′hi·bi′tion·ist,** *n.* —**ex′hi·bi′·tion·is′tic,** *adj.*

ex·hib·i·tor (ig zib′i tər) *also,* **ex·hib·it·er.** *n.* one who or that which exhibits or presents an exhibition.

ex·hil·a·rate (ig zil′ə rāt′) **-rat·ed, -rat·ing** *v.t.* to make cheerful, lively, or excited; enliven; invigorate. [Latin *exhilarātus,* past participle of *exhilarāre* to gladden, going back to *ex* utterly + Greek *hilaros* gay.] —**ex·hil′a·rat′ing·ly,** *adv.* —**ex·hil′a·ra′tive,** *adj.*

ex·hil·a·ra·tion (ig zil′ə rā′shən) *n.* **1.** exhilarated feeling or condition. **2.** act of exhilarating.

ex·hort (ig zôrt′) *v.t.* to try to persuade by appeal, argument, or warning; urge strongly: *He exhorted the crew to mutiny.* —*v.i.* to give advice or warning. [Latin *exhortārī* to encourage, stimulate.] —**ex·hort′er,** *n.*

ex·hor·ta·tion (eg′zôr tā′shən ek′sôr-) *n.* **1.** act of exhorting. **2.** that which exhorts or is intended to exhort, as a sermon or appeal.

ex·hor·ta·tive (ig zôr′tə tiv) *adj.* serving or intended to exhort. Also, **ex·hor′ta·to′ry.**

ex·hu·ma·tion (eks′hū mā′shən) *n.* act of exhuming: *the exhumation of a corpse.*

ex·hume (eks hūm′, ig zōōm′, -zūm′) **-humed, -hum·ing.** *v.t.* **1.** to remove (something buried, esp. a corpse) from the earth; dig up. **2.** to bring to light; disclose; reveal: *to exhume hidden facts, to exhume an ancient theory.* [Medieval Latin *exhumare* to unearth, from Latin *ex* out of + *humus* ground.]

ex·i·gen·cy (ek′sə jən sē) *pl.,* **-cies.** *n.* **1.** situation or occurrence

at; āpe; cär; end; mē; it; īce; hot; ōld; fôrk; wood; fōōl; oil; out; up; ūse; turn; sing; thin; this; zh in treasure; ə in ago, taken, pencil, lemon, circus.

357

requiring prompt action, assistance, or attention; emergency. **2.** *also,* **exigencies.** pressing demand or necessity; urgency. Also, **ex′i·gence.**

ex·i·gent (ek′sə jənt) *adj.* **1.** requiring prompt action, assistance, or attention; urgent; pressing. **2.** unusually or unreasonably demanding; exacting. [Latin *exigēns,* present participle of *exigere* to drive out, demand.] —**ex′i·gent·ly,** *adv.*

ex·ig·u·ous (ig zig′ū əs, ik sig′-) *adj.* scanty; diminutive; meager. [Latin *exiguus.*] —**ex·i·gu·i·ty** (ek′sə gū′ə tē), **ex·ig′u·ous·ness,** *n.* —**ex·ig′u·ous·ly,** *adv.*

ex·ile (eg′zīl, ek′sīl) **-iled, -il·ing.** *v.t.* to expel (a person) from his country or home by law or decree: *He was exiled for political reasons.* —*n.* **1.** expulsion or voluntary absence from one's country or home; state of being exiled: *Exile was the fate of many citizens after the revolution. James Joyce lived in exile for many years.* **2.** one who is expelled from or voluntarily leaves his country or home; expatriate. **3. the Exile.** captivity of the Jews in Babylon during the sixth century B.C. [Old French *exil* banishment, from Latin *ex(s)ilium.*] —**Syn.** see **banish.**

ex·ist (ig zist′) *v.i.* **1.** to have reality; be real: *He does not believe ghosts exist.* **2.** to continue to have being or life: *The prisoners could not exist on bread and water. Democracy could no longer exist under those conditions.* **3.** to be present or found; occur: *Outside of zoos, koalas exist only in Australia.* [Latin *ex(s)istere* to come forth, be.] —**Syn. 1.** see **live¹.**

ex·ist·ence (ig zis′təns) *n.* **1.** state or fact of existing. **2.** condition or mode of existing; living; life: *a struggle for existence, a meager existence.* **3.** all that exists.

ex·ist·ent (eg zis′tənt) *adj.* **1.** now existing; present; extant: *the existent economic situation.* **2.** having existence; living: *The dodo is no longer existent.*

ex·is·ten·tial (eg′zis ten′shəl, ek′sis-) *adj.* **1.** of or relating to existentialism. **2.** of or involving the question of one's life or one's choices and their value and meaning. **3.** of or relating to existence: *Primitive man grappled daily with the existential problems of finding food and shelter.*

ex·is·ten·tial·ism (eg′zis ten′shə liz′əm, ek′sis-) *n.* philosophical view that stresses concreteness and individuality in existing things and human experience. Religious proponents stress the individual's personal discovery of God, while the nonreligious emphasize the individual's self-determination through personal decisions and actions in an otherwise meaningless universe. —**ex′is ten′tial·ist,** *adj., n.*

ex·it (eg′zit, ek′sit) *n.* **1.** way out; egress: *We left by the rear exit.* **2.** act of leaving; departure. **3.** departure of a performer from the stage. —*v.i.* **1.** to leave; go out; depart: *They exited from the back door.* **2.** *Latin.* he or she goes out. ▲ used as a stage direction to indicate that the actor specified is to leave the stage. [Partly from Latin *exitus* a going out; partly from Latin *exit* (he) goes out.]

ex li·bris (eks lī′bris, lē′-) **1.** from the library (of). ▲ appearing followed by the owner's name as an inscription in or on a book. **2.** bookplate. [Latin *ex librīs* from the books (of).]

exo- *combining form* outside; external: *exoskeleton.* [Greek *exō,* from *ex* out of.]

ex·o·bi·ol·o·gy (ek′sō bī ol′ə jē) *n.* branch of biology which deals with the effects of extraterrestrial environments on living organisms and with the search for extraterrestrial life. —**ex′o·bi·ol′o·gist,** *n.*

Exod., Exodus.

ex·o·dus (ek′sə dəs) *n.* **1.** departure, esp. of a mass of people: *an exodus from the cities to the suburbs.* **2. the Exodus.** departure of the Israelites from Egypt under the leadership of Moses. **3. Exodus.** second book of the Old Testament, containing an account of this departure. [Latin *exodus* second book of the Old Testament, from Greek *exodos* a going out.]

ex of·fi·ci·o (eks′ ə fish′ē ō′) by virtue of or because of one's office or position: *A ship's captain may ex officio perform marriages on the high seas.* [Latin *ex* out of + *officiō,* ablative of *officium* office, duty.]

ex·og·a·my (ek sog′ə mē) *n.* marriage outside one's own tribe, class, or group in accordance with custom or law. Opposed to **endogamy.** [EXO- + -GAMY.] —**ex·og′a·mous,** *adj.*

ex·og·e·nous (ek soj′ə nəs) *adj.* having an external origin; due to external causes. Distinguished from **endogenous.** [Modern Latin *exogenus* growing on the outside (from EXO- + -GEN) + -OUS.]

ex·on·er·ate (eg zon′ə rāt′) **-at·ed, -at·ing.** *v.t.* to free from blame or guilt; prove or declare innocent; exculpate: *He was fully exonerated by the new evidence.* [Latin *exonerātus,* past participle of *exonerāre* to free from a burden, from *ex* from + *onus* burden.] —**ex·on′er·a′tion,** *n.* —**Syn.** see **absolve.**

ex·or·bi·tance (ig zôr′bə təns) *n.* unreasonable excessiveness, as of prices or demands. Also, **ex·or′bi·tan·cy.**

ex·or·bi·tant (ig zôr′bə tənt) *adj.* exceeding what is proper, reasonable, or usual; excessive: *exorbitant prices, exorbitant demands.* [Late Latin *exorbitāns,* present participle of *exorbitāre* to go out of the track, from Latin *ex* out of + *orbita* track.] —**ex·or′bi·tant·ly,** *adv.* —**Syn.** see **excessive.**

ex·or·cise (ek′sôr sīz′) **-cised, -cis·ing.** *also,* **ex·or·cize.** *v.t.* **1.** to drive

out (an evil spirit), as by prayers or incantations. **2.** to free (a person or place) from an evil spirit. [Late Latin *exorcizāre,* from Greek *exorkizein* to bind by oath, conjure.] —**ex′or·cis′er,** *n.*

ex·or·cism (ek′sôr siz′əm) *n.* **1.** act or fact of exorcising. **2.** ritual used in exorcising. —**ex′or·cist,** *n.*

ex·or·cize (ek′sôr sīz′) **-cized, -ciz·ing.** to exorcise.

ex·or·di·um (ig zôr′dē əm, ik sôr′-) *pl., **-di·ums** or **-di·a** (-dē ə) *n.* beginning or introductory part, as of a speech or dissertation. [Latin *exōrdium.*] —**ex·or′di·al,** *adj.*

ex·o·skel·e·ton (ek′sō skel′ə tən) *n.* protective external skeleton, as that of crustaceans, insects, turtles, or lobsters. Opposed to **endoskeleton.** [EXO- + SKELETON.]

ex·o·sphere (ek′sō sfēr′) *n.* outermost layer of the earth's atmosphere, that begins at an altitude of about 400 miles and gradually merges with interplanetary space. [EXO- + SPHERE.] —**ex·o·spher·ic** (ek′sō sfer′ik), *adj.*

ex·o·ter·ic (ek′sə ter′ik) *adj.* **1.** capable of being understood by or suitable for the general public; not esoteric. **2.** not intended for or restricted to a select group, as of disciples. **3.** popular; well-known. [Greek *exōterikos* external, going back to *exō* outside.]

ex·o·ther·mic (ek′sō thur′mik) *adj.* relating to a chemical reaction or other process that is accompanied by the liberation of heat. Opposed to **endothermic.** Also, **ex′o·ther′mal.**

ex·ot·ic (ig zot′ik) *adj.* **1.** of foreign origin or character; not native: *exotic flowers, exotic birds.* **2.** strangely beautiful or fascinating; strikingly unusual. [Latin *exōticus* foreign, from Greek *exōtikos,* from *exō* outside.] —**ex·ot′i·cal·ly,** *adv.*

exp. 1. expenses. **2.** export. **3.** exported. **4.** express.

ex·pand (iks pand′) *v.t.* **1.** to make larger, as in size, extent, or scope; enlarge: *to expand one's chest. Heat expands metal.* **2.** to stretch or spread (something) out; unfold: *The bird expanded its wings.* **3.** to develop or express (something) in fuller form or greater detail: *to expand an idea.* **4.** to develop a number, algebraic expression, or function to its completed or fullest form according to given rules. $(a + b)^2$ expanded is $a^3 + 3a^2b + 3ab^2 + b^3$. —*v.i.* **1.** to increase, as in size, extent, or volume: *Metal expands when heated. The baseball league expanded by adding four new teams.* **2.** to stretch or spread out; unfold. **3. to expand on** (or **upon**). to discuss in greater detail: *The professor expanded on the topic.* [Latin *expandere* to spread out. Doublet of SPAWN.] —**ex·pand′a·ble,** *adj.*

Syn. *v.i.* **1.** Expand, swell, distend, dilate mean to increase in dimension. Expand suggests a spread in every direction, as by growing, blossoming, or opening out: *The great law of culture is: Let each . . . expand if possible, to his full growth* (Carlyle, 1827). Swell implies growth beyond a level or beyond normal, usual, or established bounds, as by pressure from within: *You can't make money like that and not swell out* (H. G. Wells, 1905). Distend suggests pressure from within stretching something abnormally and perhaps violently or painfully: *I could see his veins swell and his nostrils distend with indignation* (Irving, 1835). Dilate simply indicates a stretching to become wider, with no suggestion of pressure: *The pupils dilate to admit more light.*

ex·panse (iks pans′) *n.* wide, unbroken stretch or area, as of land or water: *a vast expanse of desert.* [Latin *expānsum,* noun use of neuter past participle of *expandere* to spread out.]

ex·pan·si·ble (iks pan′sə bəl) *adj.* capable of being expanded. —**ex·pan′si·bil′i·ty,** *n.*

ex·pan·sile (iks pan′səl) *adj.* of, relating to, capable of, or causing expansion.

ex·pan·sion (eks pan′shən) *n.* **1.** act of expanding; being expanded. **2.** amount or degree of enlargement or increase: *The bird's wing expansion is six feet.* **3.** expanded part or form. **4.** number, algebraic expression, or function in its expanded form. The expansion of $(x + y)^2$ is $x^2 + 2xy + y^2$; the expansion of 125 is $(1 × 10 × 10) + (2 × 10) + (5 × 1)$. [Late Latin *expānsiō* a spreading out, from Latin *expandere* to spread out.]

ex·pan·sion·ism (iks pan′shə niz′əm) *n.* policy of expanding a nation's territory, esp. at the expense of other nations. —**ex·pan′sion·ist,** *n.* —**ex·pan′sion·is′tic,** *adj.*

ex·pan·sive (iks pan′siv) *adj.* **1.** capable of expanding or tending to expand. **2.** extending widely; broad; extensive. **3.** generous and outgoing; demonstrative; open. **4.** *Psychiatry.* characterized by inappropriate or exaggerated euphoria and delusions of power or importance. —**ex·pan′sive·ly,** *adv.* —**ex·pan′sive·ness,** *n.*

ex parte (eks pär′tē) on, from, or in the interest of one side only. [Latin *ex* from + *parte,* ablative of *pars* part, side.]

ex·pa·ti·ate (eks pā′shē āt′) **-at·ed, -at·ing.** *v.i.* to write or speak at length or in detail; elaborate (with *on* or *upon*): *He expatiated for hours on his adventures.* [Latin *ex(s)patiātus,* past participle of *ex(s)patiārī* to go out of the way, digress.] —**ex·pa′ti·a′tion, ex·pa′ti·a′tor,** *n.*

ex·pa·tri·ate (*v.,* eks pā′trē āt′; *adj., n.,* eks pā′trē it, -āt′) **-at·ed, -at·ing.** *v.t.* **1.** to expel (a person) from his native country. **2.** to volun-

at; āpe; cär; end; mē; it; īce; hot; ōld; fôrk; wood; fool; oil; out; up; ūse; turn; sing; thin; this; zh in treasure; ə in ago, taken, pencil, lemon, circus.

tarily withdraw (oneself) from one's native country: *Many American writers expatriated themselves to Europe after World War I.* —*n.* one who is expatriated; exile. —*adj.* expatriated. [Medieval Latin *expatriātus,* past participle of *expatriāre* to banish, from Latin *ex* out of + *patria* native land.] —**ex·pa′tri·a′tion,** *n.*

ex·pect (iks pekt′) *v.t.* **1.** to look forward to the occurrence or coming of; regard as certain or probable; anticipate: *They had expected a larger group at the meeting.* **2.** to look for as just, proper, necessary, or due; require: *to expect an explanation, to expect a reward.* **3.** *Informal.* to presume; suppose: *I rather expect he doesn't intend to come.* —*v.i.* **to be expecting.** *Informal.* to be pregnant. [Latin *ex(s)pectāre* to look for, hope.]
Syn. *v.t.* **1. Expect, anticipate, await** mean to look forward to something that will happen. **Expect** indicates certainty about the coming event: *I've been expecting that letter for a week.* **Anticipate** implies some foreknowledge of the effects, whether good or bad, of what is coming: *They anticipated extensive damage from the approaching storm.* **Await** stresses the waiting for, and often the preparing for, the event: *With some uneasiness, they awaited the birth of their first baby.*

ex·pect·an·cy (iks pek′tən sē) *pl.,* **-cies.** *n.* **1.** an expecting; expectation. **2.** that which is expected, esp. on the basis of statistical probability. **3.** life expectancy.
ex·pect·ant (iks pek′tənt) *adj.* **1.** having or exhibiting expectation: *an expectant look, an expectant heir, an expectant attitude.* **2.** waiting in expectation. **3.** awaiting the birth of a child: *an expectant mother.* —**ex·pect′ant·ly,** *adv.*
ex·pec·ta·tion (eks′pek tā′shən) *n.* **1.** act of expecting. **2.** state or condition of expecting; mental attitude of one who expects. **3.** *also,* **expectations.** ground for expecting; prospect or hope, as of future good or success. **4.** that which is expected. **5.** degree of probability that something will occur. **6.** state of being expected: *a sum of money in expectation.*
ex·pec·to·rant (iks pek′tər ənt) *adj.* aiding or promoting the discharge of phlegm or mucus from the respiratory tract. —*n.* medicine that promotes and facilitates expectoration.
ex·pec·to·rate (iks pek′tə rāt′) **-rat·ed, -rat·ing.** *v.i.* **1.** to discharge phlegm, mucus, or other congestive matter from the respiratory tract by coughing up and spitting. **2.** to spit. —*v.t.* to discharge from the respiratory tract by coughing up and spitting. [Latin *expectorātus,* past participle of *expectorāre* to drive from the breast, from *ex* out of + *pectus* breast.] —**ex·pec′to·ra′tion,** *n.*
ex·pe·di·en·cy (iks pē′dē ən sē) *pl.,* **-cies.** *n.* **1.** state or quality of being expedient. **2.** concern for that which is conducive to immediate results or personal advantage rather than for what is right or just. **3.** that which is expedient. Also, **ex·pe′di·ence.**
ex·pe·di·ent (iks pē′dē ənt) *adj.* **1.** conducive to or promoting immediate results or personal advantage; based on self-interest rather than consideration for what is right or just. **2.** suitable or desirable for a given situation or purpose; appropriate. —*n.* means employed to bring about a desired result; means to an end. [Latin *expediēns,* present participle of *expedīre* to free the feet, extricate, make ready, from *ex* out + *pēs* foot.] —**ex·pe′di·ent·ly,** *adv.*
ex·pe·dite (eks′pə dīt′) **-dit·ed, -dit·ing.** *v.t.* **1.** to hasten the process or progress of; speed up; facilitate: *to expedite the shipment of a carton of fruit.* **2.** to do quickly and efficiently: *to expedite a task.* [Latin *expedītus,* past participle of *expedīre.* See EXPEDIENT.] —**Syn. 1. see quicken.**
ex·pe·dit·er (eks′pə dī′tər) *also,* **ex·pe·di·tor.** *n.* one who expedites, esp. one who is responsible for expediting the flow of materials so that a production schedule will be maintained.
ex·pe·di·tion (eks′pə dish′ən) *n.* **1.** journey, excursion, or voyage made for a specific purpose, as exploration: *an expedition to the North Pole.* **2.** body of persons or things, as ships or equipment, involved in such a journey. **3.** efficient promptness; dispatch: *to perform one's work with expedition.*
ex·pe·di·tion·ar·y (eks′pə dish′ə ner′ē) *adj.* of, relating to, or composing an expedition.
ex·pe·di·tious (eks′pə dish′əs) *adj.* quick and efficient: *Use the most expeditious means possible to finish this job.* —**ex′pe·di′tious·ly,** *adv.* —**ex′pe·di′tious·ness,** *n.*
ex·pel (iks pel′) **-pelled, -pel·ling.** *v.t.* **1.** to drive out or discharge by force; force out: *to expel water from a hose.* **2.** to oust or compel to leave: *to expel a student from school.* [Latin *expellere* to drive out.]
ex·pend (iks pend′) *v.t.* **1.** to pay out; spend. **2.** to use up; consume: *to expend one's energy.* [Latin *expendere* to weigh out, pay. Doublet of SPEND.] —**Syn. 1.** see **spend.**
ex·pend·a·ble (iks pen′də bəl) *adj.* **1.** capable of being expended. **2.** that may be sacrificed without negative effect, often in order to gain a larger advantage. **3.** *Military.* consumed in use and not subject to inventory, as ammunition. —*n.* someone or something considered expendable. —**ex·pend′a·bil′i·ty,** *n.*

ex·pend·i·ture (iks pen′di chər) *n.* **1.** act of expending. **2.** that which is expended, as money, time, or effort.
ex·pense (iks pens′) *n.* **1.** spending or consumption of money; expenditure: *The project involved great expense.* **2.** object or cause of spending money: *The rent on his apartment was his biggest monthly expense.* **3.** money spent in order to buy or do something; cost: *We cannot afford the expense of a new car.* **4.** loss, injury, or sacrifice: *The war was won at great expense to both countries.* **5. expenses. a.** costs or charges incurred in the undertaking of some action or activity: *traveling expenses.* **b.** money paid in reimbursement of these costs. **5. at the expense of. a.** by the loss, injury, or sacrifice of: *He devoted his time to football at the expense of his studies.* **b.** so as to be paid for by: *He took a trip at the expense of the company.* [Late Latin *expēnsa* outlay, money to defray costs, from Latin *expendere* to weigh out, pay; with reference to a former practice of determining the amount of payment required by weighing in a scale.]
expense account 1. arrangement between a company and an employee whereby the company pays for all charges incurred in the performance of the employee's duties, as travel, hotel, and food costs. **2.** record of such expenses.
ex·pen·sive (iks pen′siv) *adj.* involving great expense; costly. —**ex·pen′sive·ly,** *adv.* —**ex·pen′sive·ness,** *n.* —**Syn.** see **valuable.**
ex·pe·ri·ence (iks pēr′ē əns) *n.* **1.** particular event or events encountered, perceived, or participated in, often over a period of time: *a frightening experience. He told us of his war experiences.* **2.** such an event or events in general; accumulation of such events. **3.** actual participation in, contact with, or perceiving of such an event or events: *the experience of being hungry. Experience is the best teacher.* **4.** knowledge, skill, or understanding acquired through this, often over a period of time: *The job requires three years' experience as an accountant. She doesn't have any experience in dealing with children.* —*v.t.,* **-enced, -enc·ing.** to have happen to one; encounter and feel; undergo: *to experience love. He experienced prejudice for the first time.* [Old French *experience* testing, acquired knowledge, from Latin *experientia* proof, trial.]
Syn. *v.t.* **Experience, feel, undergo** indicate taking part, passively or actively, in an event or occurrence. **Experience** suggests only that the event, of whatever kind or quality, occurs with one participating: *He experienced a chill.* **Feel** implies being mentally or emotionally stirred or otherwise affected by what happens: *He felt some misgivings about going.* **Undergo** suggests that what happens is to some extent distressing or distasteful, or at least not pleasant, yet must be endured: *He underwent a thorough physical examination.*
ex·pe·ri·enced (iks pēr′ē ənst) *adj.* made skillful, knowledgeable, or wise through experience: *an experienced politician, an experienced carpenter.*
ex·pe·ri·en·tial (iks pēr′ē en′shəl) *adj.* relating to or derived from experience; empirical. *experiential knowledge.*
ex·per·i·ment (*v.,* iks per′ə ment′; *n.,* iks per′ə mənt) *n.* **1.** action or procedure designed to discover, test, or illustrate something, as a hypothesis or principle; text: *Franklin's experiments showed that lightning is an electrical discharge.* **2.** conducting of such procedures; experimentation: *to demonstrate the validity of a theory by experiment.* —*v.i.* to make an experiment or experiments: *Gregor Mendel developed his theories of heredity by experimenting with garden peas. A good cook experiments with different ingredients.* [Latin *experimentum* proof, test.] —**ex·per′i·ment′er,** *n.*
ex·per·i·men·tal (iks per′ə ment′əl) *adj.* **1.** relating to, derived from, or based on experiments: *experimental evidence.* **2.** used for experimentation: *an experimental drug.* **3.** of the nature of an experiment: *experimental.* **4.** derived from or based on experience; empirical. —**ex·per′i·men′tal·ly,** *adv.*
ex·per·i·men·ta·tion (iks per′ə mən tā′shən) *n.* act or process of experimenting.
ex·pert (eks′purt; *adj. also* iks purt′) *n.* one having special skill or knowledge in something; specialist; authority: *an expert in mathematics, an expert on foreign affairs.* —*adj.* **1.** highly skilled or knowledgeable: *an expert skier, an expert marksman.* **2.** characteristic of or from an expert; authoritative: *expert advice.* [Old French *expert* able, knowing, clever, from Latin *expertus,* past participle of *experīrī* to try, test, prove.] —**ex·pert′ly,** *adv.* —**ex·pert′ness,** *n.*
Syn. *adj.* **1. Expert, adept, skilled, proficient** indicate great competence or superior ability arising from training. **Expert** suggests thorough schooling, deep knowledge, and wide practice: *Thanks to his expert driving, we reached the airport on time, despite the heavy traffic.* **Adept** implies a knowledge and ability not everyone can achieve: *The old woodsman was still very adept at whittling little figures of animals.* **Skilled** suggests knowledge and ability made apparent in practice: *She is a skilled harpsichordist.* **Proficient** suggests ease and excellence: *She has become proficient in karate.*
ex·per·tise (ek′spər tēz′) *n.* expert knowledge or skill. [Middle French *expertise,* from *expert* skillful. See EXPERT.]

ex·pi·a·ble (eks′pē ə bəl) *adj.* capable of being expiated.

ex·pi·ate (eks′pē āt′) **-at·ed, -at·ing.** *v.t.* to make amends for; atone for: *to expiate one's sins.* [Latin *expiātus,* past participle of *expiāre* to atone for, going back to *ex* utterly + *pius* devout.]

ex·pi·a·tion (eks′pē ā′shən) *n.* **1.** act of expiating. **2.** that which expiates; means of atonement.

ex·pi·a·to·ry (eks′pē ə tôr′ē) *adj.* serving to or intended to expiate.

ex·pi·ra·tion (eks′pə rā′shən) *n.* **1.** closing or ending; termination; close: *the expiration of a contract.* **2.** act of breathing out air; exhalation. of air from the lungs.

ex·pir·a·to·ry (iks pīr′ə tôr′ē) *adj.* relating to or used in the expiration of air from the lungs.

ex·pire (iks pīr′) **-pired, -pir·ing.** *v.i.* **1.** to come to an end; terminate: *The lease expires on May 1. My subscription expires with the March issue.* **2.** to expel air from the lungs; exhale. **3.** to die. **4.** to die out: *The sparks expired in the ashes.* —*v.t.* to expel (air) from the lungs. [Latin *ex(s)pīrāre* to breathe out, die.]

ex·pi·ry (iks pīr′ē, eks′pər ē) *n. pl.* **-ries.** *n.* expiration; termination.

ex·plain (iks plān′) *v.t.* **1.** to make clear or understandable: *The pilot explained why the landing was delayed. The doctor explained to us the nature of Mother's illness.* **2.** to reveal the meaning of; interpret: *to explain a prophecy.* **3.** to give the reason or reasons for; account for: *to explain one's behavior.* **4. to explain away.** to give reasons so as to justify or minimize the importance of: *to explain away a friend's faults.* —*v.i.* to give an explanation. [Latin *explānāre* to flatten, make plain.] —**ex·plain′a·ble,** *adj.* —**Syn.** *v.t.* **2.** see **interpret.**

ex·pla·na·tion (eks′plə nā′shən) *n.* **1.** act or process of explaining: *a teacher's explanation of a problem.* **2.** that which clarifies or accounts for something: *Is there any explanation for his strange behavior?* **3.** interpretation given in explaining something; meaning.

ex·plan·a·to·ry (iks plan′ə tôr′ē) *adj.* serving or tending to explain: *explanatory notes.*

ex·ple·tive (eks′plə tiv) *n.* **1.** word, syllable, or phrase added to fill out a sentence or to complete the rhythmical pattern in a line of verse but contributing nothing to the content. In the sentence *There are six birds on the roof,* the word *there* is an expletive. **2.** exclamation or oath. —*adj.* also, **ex·ple·to·ry** (eks′plə tôr′ē). added to fill out a sentence or to complete the rhythm in a line of verse. [Late Latin *explētīvus* serving to fill out, from Latin *explēre* to fill out.]

ex·plic·a·ble (eks plik′ə bəl, eks′plə kə-) *adj.* capable of being explained. [Latin *explicābilis,* from *explicāre* to explain.]

ex·pli·cate (eks′plə kāt′) **-cat·ed, -cat·ing.** *v.t.* **1.** to explain clearly and in detail. **2.** to develop, as a principle or proposition. [Latin *explicātus,* past participle of *explicāre* to unfold, explain.]

ex·pli·ca·tion (eks′plə kā′shən) *n.* **1.** act or process of explicating. **2.** explanation, as of a passage in a text; interpretation. **3.** detailed account or description.

ex·pli·ca·tive (eks plik′ə tiv, eks′plə kā′tiv) *adj.* serving to explicate; explanatory. Also, **ex·pli·ca·to·ry** (eks plik′ə tôr′ē, eks′plə kə-).

ex·plic·it (eks plis′it) *adj.* clear and definite; leaving nothing unexplained: *explicit orders. He gave explicit instructions not to be disturbed.* [Latin *explicitus,* form of *explicātus,* past participle of *explicāre* to unfold, explain.] —**ex·plic′it·ly,** *adv.* —**ex·plic′it·ness,** *n.*

Syn. Explicit, definite, express, specific indicate something that is sharply precise. **Explicit** suggests that nothing is left to inference, that all pertinent details are clearly and unambiguously explained: *The playwright has given explicit directions about how to play the scene.* **Definite** implies that anything needing clarification is thoroughly explained, but that the explanation is limited precisely to that matter: *He left definite instructions that Jones was not to be admitted under any circumstances.* **Express** suggests a firmness and explicitness that leave no possibility of mistaking the meaning: *His express answer eliminated the jury's last doubts.* **Specific** implies selection of detail so exact as to leave no ambiguity: *They were told to limit the experiment to the specific problem of the influence of diet.*

ex·plode (iks plōd′) **-plod·ed, -plod·ing.** *v.i.* **1.** to burst suddenly and violently with a loud noise; blow up: *The bottle exploded in the fire.* **2.** to expand suddenly and violently because of chemical reactions or nuclear fission or fusion, giving off light, heat, and noise: *The nitroglycerin exploded on impact.* **3.** to break forth violently or noisily: *to explode with rage.* **4.** to increase rapidly: *The country's population has exploded in the last few years.* —*v.t.* **1.** to cause (something) to burst suddenly and violently with a loud noise. **2.** to cause to expand suddenly and violently by chemical reaction or nuclear fission or fusion, giving off light, heat, and noise. **3.** to bring into disrepute; refute: *to explode a theory.* [Latin *explōdere* to drive off the stage by clapping, from *ex* away + *plaudere* to clap the hands.]

ex·ploit (*n.,* eks′ploit, iks ploit′; *v.,* iks ploit′) *n.* notable, heroic deed; feat: *military exploits.* —*v.t.* **1.** to use unjustly or unfairly for selfish profit or advantage: *to exploit the poor, to exploit laborers.* **2.** to make practical use of; use or develop profitably: *to exploit natural resources.* [Old French *esploit* achievement, deed, from Latin *explicitum* some-

thing unfolded or settled, from *explicāre* to unfold, explain.] —**ex·ploit′a·ble,** *adj.* —**ex·ploit′er,** *n.*

ex·ploi·ta·tion (eks′ploi tā′shən) *n.* act of exploiting, esp. for selfish profit or advantage.

ex·plo·ra·tion (eks′plə rā′shən) *n.* act or instance of exploring, esp. for the purpose of discovering previously unknown regions or investigating unfamiliar ones.

ex·plor·a·to·ry (iks plôr′ə tôr′ē) *adj.* of, relating to, or for exploration: *an exploratory voyage, exploratory surgery.* Also, **ex·plor′a·tive.**

ex·plore (iks plôr′) **-plored, -plor·ing.** *v.t.* **1.** to travel over or in (previously unfamiliar or unknown regions) in order to discover or investigate: *to explore the surface of the moon.* **2.** to examine or look through or into closely; scrutinize: *The historian explored the causes of the revolution.* **3.** to examine closely (an organ, wound, or diseased part) in order to make a diagnosis, as by probing or experimental surgery. —*v.i.* to make an exploration. [Latin *explōrāre* to search out; originally, to cry out (in the sense of drawing forth game at a hunt by cries).]

ex·plor·er (iks plôr′ər) *n.* one who or that which explores.

ex·plo·sion (iks plō′zhən) *n.* **1.** act of bursting or expanding suddenly and violently: *an atomic explosion.* **2.** loud noise caused by exploding: *The explosion was deafening.* **3.** sudden, violent outburst of emotion: *an explosion of rage.* **4.** large, rapid increase: *a population explosion.* [Latin *explōsiō* a driving off by clapping.]

ex·plo·sive (iks plō′siv) *adj.* **1.** of, relating to, or of the nature of an explosion: *an explosive laugh.* **2.** tending or liable to explode or cause an explosion: *explosive chemicals, an explosive situation.* **3.** Phonetics. plosive. —*n.* **1.** substance that can explode. **2.** Phonetics. plosive. —**ex·plo′sive·ly,** *adv.* —**ex·plo′sive·ness,** *n.*

ex·po·nent (iks pō′nənt, eks′pō′-) *n.* **1.** one who explains or interprets something: *Thomas Huxley was an exponent of the theory of evolution.* **2.** one who or that which represents or advocates something, as an idea, principle, or cause: *Martin Luther King was an exponent of nonviolence.* **3.** numeral or symbol placed at the upper right side of another numeral or symbol to indicate the power to which the latter is to be raised or how many times it is to be taken as a factor. In 4^3 the exponent is 3, indicating $4 \times 4 \times 4$; in A^2 the exponent is 2, indicating $A \times A$; in 5^x the exponent is *x,* indicating 5 multiplied by itself *x* times. [Latin *expōnēns,* present participle of *expōnere* to set forth, explain.]

ex·po·nen·tial (eks′pō nen′shəl) *adj.* of or relating to mathematical exponents, esp. those involving unknown or variable quantities as exponents.

ex·port (*v.,* iks pôrt′, eks′pôrt′; *n.,* eks′pôrt′) *v.t.* to carry or send (commodities) to other countries for sale or trade: *Columbia exports coffee to the United States.* —*n.* **1.** that which is exported: *The leading export of Australia is wool.* **2.** act of exporting: *They prohibited the export of certain raw materials during the war.* [Latin *exportāre* to carry out or away.] —**ex·port′er,** *n.*

ex·por·ta·tion (eks′pôr tā′shən) *n.* **1.** act of exporting. **2.** that which is exported.

ex·pose (iks pōz′) **-posed, -pos·ing.** *v.t.* **1.** to place in contact with or leave open to the action or influence of (with *to*): *The metal was exposed to corrosives and extreme temperatures. The child has never been exposed to the measles.* **2.** to bare to (something), as danger, ridicule, or criticism: *He exposed himself to the taunts of the crowd.* **3.** to make known; disclose: *to expose a conspiracy, to expose a crime.* **4.** to reveal the actions, character, or identity of; unmask: *to expose a spy.* **5.** to show openly or publicly; display: *New fashions are exposing more and more of the body.* **6.** to abandon in an open and unprotected place so as to cause death: *Oedipus was exposed by his parents.* **7.** to submit (a photographic film or plate) to the action of light. [Old French *exposer* to lay out, place in view, make known, modification (influenced by French *poser* to place, put) of Latin *expōnere* to set forth, exhibit, explain.] —**ex·pos′er,** *n.*

ex·po·sé (eks′pō zā′) *n.* **1.** public disclosure of something secret or discreditable, as a scandal or crime. **2.** book or article making such a disclosure. [French *exposé* statement, account, from *exposer* to set forth, explain, show. See EXPOSE.]

ex·posed (iks pōzd′) *adj.* **1.** open to view; unconcealed: *exposed beams.* **2.** without protection; unsheltered.

ex·po·si·tion (eks′pə zish′ən) *n.* **1.** extensive or elaborate public show or display, as of industrial products; collection of exhibitions. **2.** act or process of setting forth or explaining facts or ideas. **3.** detailed statement or explanation of facts or ideas, esp. in writing. **4.** initial section in certain musical forms, esp. the sonata and fugue, in which the theme or themes of the movement or composition are introduced. [Latin *expositiō* a setting forth, a showing.]

ex·pos·i·tor (iks poz′ə tər) *n.* one who expounds something. [Late Latin *expositor,* from *exposuī* to set out, explain.]

ex·pos·i·to·ry (iks poz′ə tôr′ē) *adj.* of, relating to, of the nature of, or containing exposition; explanatory: *a course in expository writing.*

ex post fac·to (eks′ pōst′ fak′tō) made or done after something but having retroactive effect: *An ex post facto law applies to actions that took place prior to the enactment of the law.* [Late Latin *ex post facto* from what is done afterwards, from Latin *ex* from + *post* after + *factum,* neuter past participle of *facere* to do.]

ex·pos·tu·late (iks pos′chə lāt′) -lat·ed, -lat·ing. *v.i.* to reason earnestly with a person against something to which one is opposed; remonstrate (with *with*): *The senator expostulated with his colleagues concerning the advisability of passing the bill.* [Latin *expostulātus,* past participle of *expostulāre* to demand urgently.] —**ex·pos′tu·la′tor,** *n.* —**ex·pos·tu·la·to·ry** (iks pos′chə lə tôr′ē), **ex·pos′tu·la′tive,** *adj.*

ex·pos·tu·la·tion (iks pos′chə lā′shən) *n.* act of expostulating; earnest protest.

ex·po·sure (iks pō′zhər) *n.* **1.** act of exposing; being exposed: *the exposure of widespread corruption in the police department. Public exposure of the entire body is frowned on in most societies.* **2.** lack of protection from the elements resulting in harm to the body, esp. serious harm: *One of the stranded climbers died of exposure; the others all suffered greatly.* **3.** position in relation to sunlight, wind, or points of the compass: *a room with a southern exposure.* **4.a.** act of subjecting a photographic film or plate to actinic light. **b.** length of time light falls on a photographic film or plate, at a certain lens opening, controlled by the lens aperture and shutter speed of the camera. **c.** section of film for one photograph. [EXPOSE + -URE.]

exposure meter, light meter.

ex·pound (iks pound′) *v.t.* **1.** to set forth in detail: *to expound a theory.* **2.** to clarify the meaning of; explain; interpret. —*v.i.* to make a statement; explain a point of view (usually with *on*). [Old French *esponre* to explain, from Latin *expōnere* to set forth, explain.] —**ex·pound′er,** *n.* —**Syn.** *v.t.* **2.** see **interpret.**

ex·press (iks pres′) *v.t.* **1.** to put into words; verbalize: *She found it very difficult to express her opinions.* **2.** to give an outward indication of; manifest: *He expressed his love for life in everything he did.* **3.** to make known or convey; communicate: *The artist's work expresses his feeling of alienation.* **4.** to represent, as by a figure, symbol, or formula; indicate: *The sign* ÷ *expresses division.* **5.** to send (something) by any means of rapid transportation or delivery: *to express a package.* **6.** to press out; squeeze out: *to express the juice from grapes.* **7.** to **express oneself. a.** to put one's thoughts or opinions into words: *He expressed himself eloquently.* **b.** to communicate one's thoughts or feelings through artistic or creative activity, as music or painting. —*adj.* **1.** particular or sole; special: *He came here for the express purpose of seeing her.* **2.** clear and unmistakable; unambiguous: *to give express orders.* **3.** of or relating to a system of rapid transportation or delivery: *an express company.* **4.** quick, direct, and making few or no intermediate stops: *an express train, an express bus.* **5.** designed for rapid and direct traveling: *an express highway.* —*adv.* by a system of rapid transportation or delivery: *to send a package express.* —*n.* **1.** system for the rapid and direct transportation or delivery of goods or money. **2.** company engaged in such transportation or delivery. **3.** goods transported by such a system. **4.** means of conveyance, as a train, bus, or elevator, which is quick and direct and makes few or no intermediate stops. [Latin *expressus,* past participle of *exprimere* to press out, represent, describe.] —**ex·press′i·ble,** *adj.* —**Syn.** *adj.* **2.** see **explicit.**

ex·press·age (iks pres′ij) *n.* **1.** transportation of goods by express. **2.** charge for such transportation.

ex·pres·sion (iks presh′ən) *n.* **1.** act of expressing or communicating something in words, as thoughts, opinions, or ideas. **2.** outward indication of or means of conveying: *Crying is an expression of grief. All of his novels were an expression of his rebellion against society.* **3.** particular look, action, or vocal intonation indicating something, as a thought or feeling: *His face wore an expression of disapproval.* **4.** quality or manner of communicating feeling or meaning: *His voice lacked expression.* **5.** particular word or phrase: *"Look before you leap" is a familiar expression.* **6.** symbol or combination of symbols used to indicate a mathematical quantity or operation. **7.** act of pressing out.

ex·pres·sion·ism (iks presh′ə niz′əm) *n.* movement in the arts originating in Europe about the time of World War I, characterized by the artist's concern with the expression of his personal ideas and feelings about his subject, rather than with the realistic representation of it.

ex·pres·sion·less (iks presh′ən lis) *adj.* revealing little or no feeling: *an expressionless face.*

ex·pres·sive (iks pres′iv) *adj.* **1.** serving to indicate; expressing (with *of*): *He spoke in a manner expressive of his anger.* **2.** full of or conveying much feeling or meaning: *an expressive tone, an expressive look.* **3.** of, relating to, or concerned with expression. —**ex·pres′sive·ly,** *adv.* —**ex·pres′sive·ness,** *n.*

Syn. 2. Expressive, significant, meaningful indicate something bearing or alluding to a meaning. **Expressive** suggests clear representation of what is meant to be described: *The successful pantomimist is trained to make expressive gestures.* **Significant** implies having real and consequen-

tial meaning, sometimes explicit but often hidden or cryptic: *A psychiatrist might find his lapse of memory significant.* **Meaningful** suggests simply that something has meaning, with no implications as to its importance or significance: *He made several meaningful pauses during his speech.*

ex·press·ly (iks pres′lē) *adv.* **1.** particularly or solely; specially. **2.** in clear and unmistakable terms; plainly: *We were expressly warned against feeding the bears.*

ex·press·man (iks pres′mən) *pl.,* **-men.** *n.* one who is employed by an express company, esp. one who picks up or delivers parcels and other articles.

ex·press·way (iks pres′wā′) *n.* wide, usually divided highway with limited points of access or exit, designed for rapid and direct traveling.

ex·pro·pri·ate (iks prō′prē āt′) -at·ed, -at·ing. *v.t.* **1.** to take (private property) from a person or business, esp. for public use by right of eminent domain. **2.** to deprive (a person) of ownership or possession. [Medieval Latin *expropriatus,* past participle of *expropriare* to deprive of property, from Latin *ex* out of + *proprium* property.] —**ex·pro′pri·a′tion, ex·pro′pri·a′tor,** *n.*

ex·pul·sion (iks pul′shən) *n.* act of expelling; being expelled. [Latin *expulsiō* a driving out.]

ex·pul·sive (iks pul′siv) *adj.* serving or tending to expel.

ex·punge (iks punj′) **-punged, -pung·ing.** *v.t.* **1.** to delete or erase (something written): *to expunge passages from a manuscript.* **2.** to wipe out or destroy; obliterate. [Latin *expungere* to erase.] —**ex·pung′er,** *n.*

ex·pur·gate (eks′pər gāt′) **-gat·ed, -gat·ing.** *v.t.* to remove obscene or otherwise objectionable passages or words from: *to expurgate a book.* [Latin *expurgātus,* past participle of *expurgāre* to purge out, cleanse.] —**ex′pur·ga′tion, ex′pur·ga′tor,** *n.*

ex·qui·site (eks′kwi zit, iks kwiz′it) *adj.* **1.** marked by rare and delicate beauty, charm, or perfection: *an exquisite face.* **2.** marked by excellence, as in design, execution, or craftsmanship: *a vase of exquisite workmanship.* **3.** intensely sharp; keen; acute: *exquisite pain, exquisite delight.* **4.** extremely refined or elegant: *exquisite taste.* **5.** keenly sensitive or discriminating: *an exquisite palate.* [Latin *exquīsītus* choice, past participle of *exquīrere* to search out.] —**ex′qui·site·ly,** *adv.* —**ex′qui·site·ness,** *n.*

ex·tant (eks′tənt, iks tant′) *adj.* not lost, destroyed, or extinct; still existing: *The only extant copy of the book is in a private collection.* [Latin *ex(s)tāns,* present participle of *ex(s)tāre* to exist, stand out.]

ex·tem·po·ral (iks tem′pər əl) *adj. Archaic.* extemporaneous.

ex·tem·po·ra·ne·ous (iks tem′pə rā′nē əs) *adj.* **1.** spoken, performed, or composed with little or no preparation; impromptu: *The winner of the award made a few extemporaneous remarks.* **2.** prepared or thought out in advance but not read or memorized: *an extemporaneous political address.* **3.** skilled at or given to speaking with little or no preparation: *The master of ceremonies was a good extemporaneous speaker.* **4.** made for the occasion; improvised. [Late Latin *extemporāneus* unexpected, from Latin *ex tempore* at the moment. See EXTEMPORE.] —**ex·tem′po·ra′ne·ous·ly,** *adv.* —**ex·tem′po·ra′ne·ous·ness,** *n.*

ex·tem·po·rar·y (iks tem′pə rer′ē) *adj.* extemporaneous. —**ex·tem′po·rar′i·ly,** *adv.*

ex·tem·po·re (iks tem′pər ē) *adv.* with little or no preparation; offhand; extemporaneously: *He spoke extempore.* —*adj.* extemporaneous; impromptu. [Latin *ex tempore* at the moment; literally, from the time.]

ex·tem·po·rize (iks tem′pə rīz′) **-rized, -riz·ing.** *v.t., v.i.* to speak, make, perform, or compose (something) extempore; improvise. —**ex·tem′po·ri·za′tion,** *n.*

ex·tend (iks tend′) *v.t.* **1.** to lengthen in a specified direction or for a given distance: *The builders extended the road for three more miles.* **2.** to open or spread out to full length: *The bird extended its wings.* **3.** to straighten or stretch out (a part of the body) to its fullest length: *The dancer extended her leg.* **4.** to increase the duration of; prolong or continue: *We extended our visit.* **5.** to offer or give: *We extended our sympathy to the family. The store extended credit privileges to us.* **6.** to hold out; put forth: *He extended his hand in friendship.* **7.** to enlarge or widen, as in size or area; expand: *The ancient Romans extended their empire into Asia.* **8.** to broaden, as in scope, range, or meaning; make more comprehensive: *We extended the definition so as to include that usage.* —*v.i.* **1.** to continue or be continued for a specified distance or point in time; stretch out: *The driveway extends from the house to the highway. The meeting extended late into the night.* **2.** to cover an area; reach: *The country's trade extended from Europe to China.* [Latin *extendere* to stretch out.] —**ex·tend′i·ble,** *adj.*

ex·tend·ed (iks ten′did) *adj.* **1.** prolonged or continued: *an extended vacation, an extended conversation.* **2.** enlarged or broadened, as in area, scope, or range; extensive: *an extended empire.* **3.** opened or stretched out.

ex·ten·si·ble (iks ten′sə bəl) *adj.* capable of being extended. —**ex·ten′si·bil′i·ty,** *n.*

ex·ten·sile (iks ten′səl) *adj.* **1.** capable of being stuck out or protruded: *an extensile tongue.* **2.** extensible.

ex·ten·sion (iks ten′shən) *n.* **1.** act of extending; being extended. **2.** that by which something is enlarged or prolonged; that which extends something: *I was given a three-month extension for filing my tax return. He added a two-room extension to the house.* **3.** act of straightening or stretching out a part of the body, esp. a limb. Opposed to **flexion**. **4.** additional telephone connected to the same line as the principal one. [Late Latin *extēnsiō* a stretching out, from Latin *extendere* to stretch out.]

ex·ten·sive (iks ten′siv) *adj.* **1.** covering or extending over a large area; great in extent; vast: *an extensive estate.* **2.** broad, as in scope, effect, or range; comprehensive or far-reaching: *extensive influence, extensive research.* **3.** large in amount, degree, or number: *He has extensive real estate holdings in foreign countries.* —**ex·ten′sive·ly,** *adv.* —**ex·ten′sive·ness,** *n.*

ex·ten·sor (iks ten′sər, -sôr) *n.* any muscle that straightens or stretches out a part of the body, esp. a limb. Opposed to **flexor.** [Late Latin *extēnsor* one who stretches, from Latin *extendere* to stretch out.]

ex·tent (iks tent′) *n.* **1.** space, amount, degree, or limit to which something extends or is extended: *the extent of a survey, the extent of his duties. She agrees with us to a certain extent.* **2.** extended area or space: *A large extent of the country was uninhabited.* [Anglo-Norman *extente, estente* area in space, noun use of feminine past participle of Old French *estendre* to stretch out, from Latin *extendere.*]

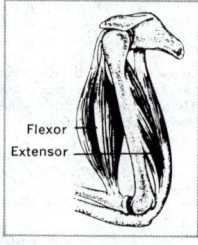

Flexor

Extensor

Extensor in the arm

ex·ten·u·ate (iks ten′ū āt′) **-at·ed, -at·ing.** *v.t.* to lessen the seriousness of (something), as a fault or offense, by serving as or giving an excuse for it: *The boy's youth does not extenuate his crime.* [Latin *extenuātus,* past participle of *extenuāre* to make thin, lessen, from *ex* out + *tenuis* thin.] —**ex·ten′u·a′tion,** *n.*

ex·ten·u·at·ing (iks ten′ū ā′ting) *adj.* tending to extenuate something, esp. a crime: *extenuating circumstances.*

ex·te·ri·or (eks tēr′ē ər) *n.* **1.** external surface or part; outside: *the exterior of a building.* **2.** outward appearance or demeanor: *It is difficult to judge a person by his exterior.* —*adj.* **1.** of, relating to, or situated on the outside; outer; external: *an exterior surface, exterior paint.* **2.** coming or acting from without: *exterior help, exterior causes.* [Latin *exterior* outer, outward, comparative of *exterus* outward, external.]

Syn. *adj.* **1. Exterior, outside, external, outer** indicate being situated beyond or on the surface or limit of something. **Exterior** suggests being on a surface or boundary: *The paint is specifically intended for exterior wood.* **Outside** implies being at or beyond the boundaries or limits: *The outside walls and the roof require insulation.* **External** suggests separation from what is contained inside the limits: *Pressure from within, rather than external force, caused the ultimate collapse of the Roman empire.* **Outer** implies comparative distance from a center or from inner parts: *The prisoner managed to escape from his cell, but was captured before he reached the outer walls.*

ex·ter·mi·nate (iks tur′mə nāt′) **-nat·ed, -nat·ing.** *v.t.* to destroy (living things); wipe out; annihilate: *to exterminate household pests.* [Late Latin *exterminātus,* past participle of *extermināre* to destroy, from Latin *extermināre* to banish; literally, to drive beyond the boundaries, from *ex* out of + *terminus* boundary.] —**Syn.** see **abolish, eradicate.**

ex·ter·mi·na·tion (iks tur′mə nā′shən) *n.* total destruction; annihilation.

ex·ter·mi·na·tor (iks tur′mə nā′tər) *n.* one who or that which exterminates, esp. a person whose business is exterminating cockroaches, termites, rats, and other vermin.

ex·ter·nal (iks turn′əl) *adj.* **1.** of, relating to, or situated on the outside; outer: *an external covering.* **2.** originating or acting from without: *an external force, external causes.* **3.** relating to outward appearance; superficial. **4.** of or relating to foreign countries; not confined within a single country: *external affairs.* **5.** on or to be used on the outside of the body: *Rubbing alcohol is for external use only.* **6.** existing outside the mind or independently of perception; objective. —*n. also,* **externals.** outward form, appearance, feature, or circumstance; superficiality: *a person who puts too much weight on externals in judging others.* [Latin *externus* outward + -AL¹.] —**ex·ter′nal·ly,** *adv.* —**Syn.** *adj.* **2.** see **exterior.**

external ear, the outer, visible part of the ear and the passage leading to the eardrum.

ex·ter·nal·i·ty (eks′tər nal′ə tē) *pl.,* **-ties.** *n.* **1.** quality or state of being external. **2.** external thing or aspect.

ex·ter·nal·ize (iks turn′əl īz′) **-ized, -iz·ing.** *v.t.* **1.** to give external existence to; make external. **2.** to attribute to external causes or factors: *to externalize one's problems.* —**ex·ter′nal·i·za′tion,** *n.*

ex·ter·o·cep·tor (eks′tər ə sep′tər) *n.* organ in or near the skin or mucous membrane responding to stimuli from outside the body, as pressure or temperature. [Latin *exterus* on the outside, outward + (RE)CEPTOR.]

ex·ter·ri·to·ri·al (eks′tər ə tôr′ē əl) extraterritorial. —**ex′ter·ri·to′ri·al·i·ty,** *n.* —**ex′ter·ri·to′ri·al·ly,** *adv.*

ex·tinct (iks tingkt′) *adj.* **1.** no longer in existence: *an extinct species. The passenger pigeon is extinct.* **2.** inactive; extinguished: *an extinct volcano.* [Latin *ex(s)tinctus,* past participle of *ex(s)tinguere* to quench, kill.]

ex·tinc·tion (iks tingk′shən) *n.* **1.** state or condition of being or becoming extinct: *Efforts have been made to prevent the extinction of the buffalo.* **2.** act of extinguishing; being extinguished.

ex·tin·guish (iks ting′gwish) *v.t.* **1.** to put out; quench: *to extinguish a fire.* **2.** to put an end to; destroy: *to extinguish hope.* **3.** to obscure, as by some superior quality; eclipse: *His discovery extinguished the achievements of his colleague.* [Latin *ex(s)tinguere* to quench, kill + -*ish* (as in PERISH).] —**ex·tin′guish·a·ble,** *adj.*

ex·tin·guish·er (iks ting′gwi shər) *n.* **1.** one who or that which extinguishes. **2.** fire extinguisher.

ex·tir·pate (eks′tər pāt′, iks tur′pāt) **-pat·ed, -pat·ing.** *v.t.* **1.** to remove or destroy completely; eradicate: *The church strove to extirpate heresy.* **2.** to tear up by the roots; uproot. [Latin *ex(s)tirpātus,* past participle of *ex(s)tirpāre* to pluck out by the stem, from *ex* out + *stirps* stem.] —**ex′tir·pa′tion,** *n.*

ex·tol (eks tōl′, -tol′) **-tolled, -tol·ling.** *also,* **ex·toll.** *v.t.* to praise highly; laud: *She extolled his virtues.* [Latin *extollere* to raise up.]

ex·tort (iks tôrt′) *v.t.* to obtain (something) by threats, force, abuse of authority, or other type of oppression: *to extort money, to extort a confession.* [Latin *extortus,* past participle of *extorquēre* to twist out.] —**ex·tort′er,** *n.*

ex·tor·tion (iks tôr′shən) *n.* **1.** obtaining of money or another valuable thing by threats, force, abuse of authority, or other type of oppression, esp. as done by a public official. **2.** that which has been extorted.

ex·tor·tion·ate (iks tôr′shə nit) *adj.* **1.** grossly excessive; exorbitant: *an extortionate price.* **2.** characterized by extortion. —**ex·tor′tion·ate·ly,** *adv.*

ex·tor·tion·ist (iks tôr′shə nist) *n.* one who is guilty of or practices extortion. Also, **ex·tor′tion·er.**

ex·tra (eks′trə) *adj.* more than what is usual, expected, or needed: *extra work, extra books, extra pay.* —*n.* **1.** something in addition to what is usual, expected, or needed. **2.** additional charge or expense: *The dinner cost eight dollars without the extras.* **3.** special edition of a newspaper, issued at a time other than that of a regular edition, to carry the account of an extraordinary news event. **4.** one employed to play a minor, usually nonspeaking, part, esp. in a crowd scene, in a motion picture or other production. —*adv.* unusually; extraordinarily: *an extra large size, extra dry wine.* [Probably short for EXTRAORDINARY.]

Syn. *adj.* **Extra, additional** mean beyond a normal or required amount. **Extra** suggests greater number, quantity, or the like: *He packed an extra shirt in case he had to stay another day.* **Additional** implies something more that is attached or included: *He returned every summer for additional training.*

extra- *prefix* outside; beyond; besides: *extraordinary, extracurricular.* [Latin *extrā.*]

ex·tract (*v.,* iks trakt′; *n.,* eks′trakt) *v.t.* **1.** to draw or pull out by effort or force: *to extract a tooth.* **2.** to obtain (a substance) by a chemical or mechanical process, as by pressing, cooking, or distilling: *to extract salt from sea water, to extract wine from grapes.* **3.** to obtain by force, threats, or similar oppression; extort: *to extract information.* **4.** to derive (something, as pleasure or happiness) from a particular source: *He extracted some satisfaction from the incident.* **5.** to take out or select, as a passage from a book. **6.** to deduce, as a principle or doctrine; infer. **7.** to find (the root of a number). —*n.* **1.** that which is extracted, esp. a passage from a book. **2.** concentrated preparation containing the essence of a substance: *vanilla extract.* [Latin *extractus,* past participle of *extrahere* to draw out.] —**ex·tract′a·ble;** *also* **ex·tract′i·ble,** *adj.*

ex·trac·tion (iks trak′shən) *n.* **1.** act of extracting; being extracted. **2.** descent; lineage: *He is of Swedish extraction.* **3.** that which is extracted.

ex·trac·tive (iks trak′tiv) *adj.* **1.** tending or serving to extract. **2.** capable of being extracted. **3.** relating to, of the nature of, or produced by extraction. —*n.* that which is extracted.

ex·trac·tor (iks trak′tər) *n.* **1.** one who or that which extracts, as a device for extracting teeth. **2.** part of a firearm that withdraws the spent cartridge from the chamber.

at; āpe; cär; end; mē; it; īce; hot; ōld; fôrk; wood; fōōl; oil; out; up; ūse; turn; sing; thin; this; zh in treasure; ə in ago, taken, pencil, lemon, circus.

ex·tra·cur·ric·u·lar (eks′trə kə rik′yə lər) *adj.* not part of the regular academic program or course of study: *Working on the school paper is an extracurricular activity.*

ex·tra·dit·a·ble (eks′trə dī′tə bəl) *adj.* subject to or warranting extradition: *an extraditable crime.*

ex·tra·dite (eks′trə dīt′) -dit·ed, -dit·ing. *v.t.* **1.** to surrender or turn over (an accused individual or fugitive) to the legal jurisdiction of another nation or state. **2.** to obtain the extradition of. [From EXTRADITION.]

ex·tra·di·tion (eks′trə dish′ən) *n.* surrender of an accused individual or fugitive by one state or nation to the legal jurisdiction of another. [French *extradition,* from Latin *ex* out + *trāditiō* a delivering up, surrender.]

ex·tra·dos (eks′trə dos′, -dōs′, eks trā′dos) *n.* exterior curve or surface of an arch or vault. [French *extrados,* from Latin *extrā* outside + French *dos* back (from Latin *dorsum*).]

ex·tra·mu·ral (eks′trə myoor′əl) *adj.* involving participants from more than one school or organization. [EXTRA- + Latin *mūrālis* relating to a wall, from *mūrus* wall.]

ex·tra·ne·ous (eks trā′nē əs) *adj.* **1.** not pertinent; irrelevant: *That statement is extraneous to this discussion.* **2.** of external origin; not belonging; foreign: *extraneous matter.* [Latin *extrāneus* external, foreign. Doublet of STRANGE.]

ex·traor·di·nar·y (iks trôr′də ner′ē, eks′trə ôr′də-) *adj.* **1.** beyond or above the usual or ordinary; very unusual or remarkable; exceptional; *extraordinary strength, extraordinary intelligence.* **2.** additional to the regular staff, as of officials; specially appointed or employed: *an envoy extraordinary.* [Latin *extraōrdinārius* out of the usual order, from *extrā ōrdinem* outside the (usual) order.] —**ex·traor′di·nar′i·ly,** *adv.*

Syn. 1. Extraordinary, exceptional, unusual, remarkable indicate something so uncommon as to be noteworthy. **Extraordinary** implies a degree of wonder, as at a natural prodigy: *His extraordinary height singled him out even among basketball players.* **Exceptional** suggests something falling outside the normal rule or measure: *He has discovered two small paintings of exceptional worth.* **Unusual** implies rarity and singularity: *He has an unusual accent.* **Remarkable** suggests something so uncommon as to require notice: *Hailstones of remarkable size fell in Nebraska yesterday.*

ex·trap·o·late (iks trap′ə lāt′, eks′trə pə-) -lat·ed, -lat·ing. *v.t.* **1.** *Mathematics.* to estimate (the value of a quantity or function that lies outside the range of known values) on the basis of values already determined. **2.** to estimate or infer (future events or developments) on the basis of current conditions and trends; predict or project without strict statistical indications. —*v.i.* to perform extrapolation. [EXTRA- + (INTER)POLATE.] —**ex·trap′o·la′tion,** *n.*

ex·tra·sen·so·ry (eks′trə sen′sər ē) *adj.* beyond the range of normal sense perception.

extrasensory perception, ability to perceive external objects, thoughts, or events without the aid of the senses.

ex·tra·ter·res·tri·al (eks′trə tə res′trē əl) *adj.* originating in or inhabiting regions outside the earth and its atmosphere.

ex·tra·ter·ri·to·ri·al (esk′trə ter′ə tôr′ē əl) *adj.* **1.** outside the jurisdiction of the laws of the country in which it is situated: *extraterritorial property, extraterritorial rights.* **2.** outside the territory of a country: *extraterritorial waters.*

ex·tra·ter·ri·to·ri·al·i·ty (eks′trə ter′ə tôr′ē al′ə tē) *n.* **1.** immunity from the jurisdiction of local law, as accorded foreign diplomats and their residences. **2.** jurisdiction of a country's laws outside its own territory, as over its citizens living in other countries.

ex·trav·a·gance (iks trav′ə gəns) *n.* **1.** lavish or immoderate spending of money. **2.** extreme or unreasonable excess, as in speech or behavior. **3.** instance of excess or wastefulness: *With his present income, the purchase of a car would be an extravagance.*

ex·trav·a·gant (iks trav′ə gənt) *adj.* **1.** lavish or immoderate in the spending of money. **2.** characterized by immoderation or a disregard for limits in the spending of money: *an extravagant purchase, extravagant tastes, extravagant living.* **3.** beyond reasonable limits; unrestrained: *extravagant demands.* **4.** unreasonably high; exorbitant: *extravagant prices.* [Medieval Latin *extravagans,* present participle of *extravagari* to wander outside (bounds), from Latin *extrā* beyond + *vagārī* to wander.] —**ex·trav′a·gant·ly,** *adv.*

Syn. 2. Extravagant, wasteful, prodigal indicate excessive spending or consumption. **Extravagant** suggests economic waste and thoughtless dissipation of what one has: *His extravagant habits soon exhausted all the money he had inherited.* **Wasteful** implies inefficient use of money or resources, so that more than necessary is expended: *The process is too wasteful to be useful industrially.* **Prodigal** suggests reckless waste originating in having no need for thought of economy: *America has been prodigal with her natural resources.*

ex·trav·a·gan·za (eks trav′ə gan′zə) *n.* lavish, elaborate show or theatrical production; spectacle. [Italian *(e)stravaganza* oddness, eccentricity, going back to Medieval Latin *extravagans.* See EXTRAVAGANT.]

ex·tra·ve·hic·u·lar activity (eks′trə və hik′yə lər) any of various maneuvers or experiments performed or occurring outside a vehicle in outer space.

ex·tra·ver·sion (eks′trə vur′zhen, -shən) extroversion.

ex·tra·vert (eks′trə vurt′) extrovert.

ex·treme (iks trēm′) -trem·er, -trem·est. *adj.* **1.** of the highest or greatest degree; exceedingly great or severe: *extreme pain, extreme pleasure, extreme danger.* **2.** going beyond what is usual or considered as moderate or reasonable: *extreme fashions, extreme views, extreme measures.* **3.** at the outermost limit; farthest: *He sat on my extreme right.* —*n.* **1.** greatest or highest degree: *Starvation is the extreme of hunger.* **2.** something extreme, as an action, condition, or measure. **3.** outermost limit; farthest point: *Red is at one extreme of the visible spectrum.* **4.** extremes. complete opposites: *Joy and grief are extremes.* **5. to go to extremes.** to use extreme measures; do something excessive or drastic. **6.** *Mathematics.* first or fourth term of a proportion. In the proportion *a:b-c:d, a* and *d* are the extremes. Opposed to **mean.** [Old French *extreme* outermost, ultimate, from Latin *extrēmus* outermost, superlative of *exterus* outward.] —**ex·treme′ness,** *n.*

ex·treme·ly (iks trēm′lē) *adv.* very; exceedingly: *extremely tired, an extremely difficult problem.*

extremely high frequency, radio frequency between 30,000 and 300,000 megacycles.

extreme unction, see anointing of the sick.

ex·trem·ism (iks trē′miz′əm) *n.* tendency to be extreme, esp. in politics: *Extremism in the defense of liberty is no vice* (Goldwater, 1964).

ex·trem·ist (iks trē′mist) *n.* one who advocates extreme measures or holds extreme views, esp. in politics. —*adj.* of or relating to extremism or extremists.

ex·trem·i·ty (iks trem′ə tē) *pl.,* -ties. *n.* **1.** farthest or outermost part or point; very end. **2.** limb of the body. **3. extremities.** hands and feet. **4.** greatest or highest degree: *the extremity of pain.* **5.** *usually,* **extremities.** extreme measure or action. **6.** extreme condition, as of need or danger: *Florence was reduced to the last extremity* (Gibbon, 1781).

ex·tri·ca·ble (eks′tri kə bəl) *adj.* capable of being extricated.

ex·tri·cate (eks′trə kāt′) -cat·ed, -cat·ing. *v.t.* to set free or remove, as from entanglement or difficulty: *He extricated himself from debt.* [Latin *extrīcātus,* past participle of *extrīcāre* to disentangle, from *ex* out of + *trīcae* trifles, perplexities.] —**ex′tri·ca′tion,** *n.*

ex·trin·sic (eks trin′sik) *adj.* **1.** not inherent in, or essential to, the nature of a thing; extraneous: *That statement is extrinsic to the discussion.* **2.** coming or acting from without; external. [Late Latin *extrīnsecus* outer, from Latin *extrīnsecus* from without.] —**ex·trin′si·cal·ly,** *adv.*

ex·tro·ver·sion (eks′trə vur′zhen, -shən) *n.* preoccupation with things outside oneself rather than with one's own inner experiences. Opposed to **introversion.** [*Extro-,* form of EXTRA- + Late Latin *versiō* a turning (from Latin *vertere* to turn).]

ex·tro·vert (eks′trə vurt′) *also,* ex·tra·vert. *n.* **1.** one whose attention is largely directed outside himself. **2.** active, outgoing person. Opposed to **introvert.** [*Extro-,* form of EXTRA- + Latin *vertere* to turn.] —**ex′tro·vert′ed,** *adj.*

ex·trude (iks trōōd′) -trud·ed, -trud·ing. *v.t.* **1.** to force or push out, as by squeezing. **2.** to shape (plastic or metal) by forcing through a die or mold. —*v.i.* to protrude. [Latin *extrūdere* to thrust out.]

ex·tru·sion (iks trōō′zhen) *n.* act or process of extruding. [From EXTRUDE, on the model of *intrusion* and *intrude.*]

ex·tru·sive (iks trōō′siv) *adj.* **1.** tending to extrude. **2.** having been forced out through the earth's surface: *Solidified lava is extrusive rock.*

ex·u·ber·ance (ig zōō′bər əns) *n.* state or quality of being exuberant. Also, ex·u′ber·an·cy.

ex·u·ber·ant (ig zōō′bər ənt) *adj.* **1.** overflowing with high spirits, enthusiasm, or vigor; elated: *an exuberant personality. He was exuberant when he heard the news.* **2.** lavish; effusive: *exuberant praise.* **3.** prolific; fertile: *an exuberant imagination, exuberant growth.* [Latin *exūberāns,* present participle of *exūberāre* to grow luxuriantly, be abundant, going back to *ex* utterly + *ūber* fertile.] —**ex·u′ber·ant·ly,** *adv.*

ex·u·da·tion (eks′yoo dā′shən, ek′sə dā′-, eg′zə-) *n.* **1.** act of exuding. **2.** that which is exuded, as sweat.

ex·ude (ig zōōd′, ik sōōd′) -ud·ed, -ud·ing. *v.t.* **1.** to discharge (a substance) gradually, as through pores; ooze forth. **2.** to give forth: *to exude warmth, to exude charm.* —*v.i.* to come out gradually; ooze out: *Sap exuded from the pine tree.* [Latin *ex(s)ūdāre* to sweat out.]

ex·ult (ig zult′) *v.i.* to rejoice greatly; be joyful: *to exult in triumph.* [Latin *ex(s)ultāre,* from *ex* out + *salīre* to leap.] —**ex·ult′ing·ly,** *adv.*

ex·ult·ant (ig zult′ənt) *adj.* triumphantly joyful; jubilant; elated. —**ex·ult′ant·ly,** *adv.*

ex·ul·ta·tion (eg′zul tā′shən, ek′sul-) *n.* triumphant joy; jubilation; elation.

ex·urb (eks′urb, egz-′) *n.* residential area between the suburbs of a city and the country. [EX-¹ + (SUB)URB.] —**ex·ur′ban,** *adj.*

ex·ur·ban·ite (ek sur′bə nīt′, eg zur′-) *n.* one who lives in an exurb.

ex·ur·bi·a (ek sur′bē ə, eg zur-′) *n.* exurbs collectively.

-ey *suffix* form of **-y¹,** as in *gooey.*

ey·as (ī′əs) *n.* 1. young hawk taken from the nest to be trained for falconry. 2. nestling. [Earlier *nyas,* from Old French *niais* nestling, going back to Latin *nīdus* nest. The phrase *a nyas* came to be divided incorrectly as *an eyas.* For a similar development, see ADDER.]

eye (ī) *n.* **1.a.** an organ of vision. **b.** organ of sight in vertebrate animals, typically one of a pair of spherical, hollow bodies set within a socket in the skull. 2. iris of this organ, esp. with respect to its color: *She has blue eyes.* 3. area surrounding this organ, including the eyelids: *a swollen eye.* 4. this organ with respect to its capacity for seeing: *His eyes are not as good as they used to be.* 5. look; glance; gaze: *He cast an eye at the money.* 6. attentive or close watch: *Please keep an eye on the road. The police are keeping an eye on him.* 7. ability to discriminate, perceive, or judge with the eye: *to have an eye for beauty.* 8. *also,* **eyes.** point of view; opinion; judgment: *In the eyes of his fellow citizens, he was an honest man.* 9. something resembling the eye in shape, position, or function, as the bud of a potato or the hole at the end of a needle through which the thread passes. 10. small, cloudless center of a hurricane, having very light winds and low pressure. 11. center or focus, as of light, power, or influence: *Athens, the eye of Greece, mother of arts* (Milton, 1671).

an eye for an eye. punishment or retribution similar or equivalent to the injury or damage suffered.

in the public eye. often noticed by the public; widely known: *He was in the public eye all his life.*

to catch (someone's) eye. to attract (someone's) attention.

to give (someone) the eye. *Slang.* to look at (someone) with desire, invitation, or admiration.

to make eyes at. to look at flirtatiously or amorously.

to see eye to eye. to agree completely.

to set (or lay) eyes on. to catch sight of; see.

to shut one's eyes to. to refuse to see or think about; ignore.

with an eye to. with a view to; with the purpose of.

—*v.t.,* **eyed, ey·ing** or **eye·ing.** to look at; watch carefully: *He eyed her every movement.* [Old English *ēage* organ of sight, eye of a needle.]

eye·ball (ī′bôl′) *n.* ball-shaped portion of the eye, enclosed by the eyelids and the eye socket.

eye·brow (ī′brou′) *n.* 1. bony ridge projecting over the eye. 2. fringe of hair growing on this.

eye·cup (ī′kup′) *n.* small cup with a rim shaped to fit closely over the eye, used in washing the eyes or applying medicine to them.

eye·drop·per (ī′drop′ər) *n.* dropper for administering eye medicine.

eye·ful (ī′fool′) *n.* 1. *Informal.* full or satisfying look. 2. *Slang.* girl or woman who is very attractive to the eye.

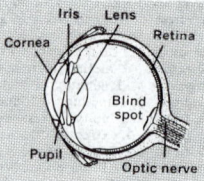

Iris Lens
Cornea Retina
Blind spot
Pupil
Optic nerve

Human eye

eye·glass (ī′glas′) *n.* 1. glass lens, as a monocle, used to aid or correct poor vision. 2. **eyeglasses.** pair of glass lenses mounted in frames, used to aid or correct poor vision. 3. eyepiece. 4. eyecup.

eye·lash (ī′lash′) *n.* 1. one of the stiff hairs growing on the edge of the eyelid. 2. *also,* **eyelashes.** fringe of these hairs that helps to keep foreign matter out of the eyes.

eye·less (ī′lis) *n.* without eyes; blind.

eye·let (ī′lit) *n.* 1. small hole in a material, as leather or cloth, for the passage of a cord or lace: *Shoelaces are passed through eyelets.* 2. metal or plastic ring lining such a hole to reinforce it. 3. small hole edged with stitches, used to make a pattern or edging in embroidery. 4. any of various fabrics, esp. cotton, decorated with this pattern. [Old French *oeillet* little eye, small hole, diminutive of *oeil* eye, from Latin *oculus;* Modern English spelling influenced by EYE.]

eye·lid (ī′lid′) *n.* movable, protective fold of skin capable of closing over the eyeball.

eye opener *Informal.* 1. something surprising or enlightening, as a piece of news or an experience. 2. drink of alcoholic liquor taken after awakening.

eye·piece (ī′pēs′) *n.* lens or combination of lenses nearest to the eye of the user in an optical instrument, esp. a telescope or microscope.

eye shadow, tinted cosmetic cream, powder, or liquid applied to the eyelids.

eye·shot (ī′shot′) *n.* range of vision.

eye·sight (ī′sīt′) *n.* 1. power or faculty of seeing; sight: *A hawk has keen eyesight.* 2. range of vision; view.

eye socket, bony cavity in which the eyeball is located; orbit.

eye·sore (ī′sôr′) *n.* something ugly or unpleasant to look at: *That old shack is an eyesore.*

eye·spot (ī′spot′) *n.* sensory structure present in many lower animals, as protozoa, flatworms, and certain echinoderms. It is believed to be used for distinguishing between light and dark.

eye·stalk (ī′stôk′) *n.* jointed, movable stalk upon which the eye is borne in certain crustaceans, as lobsters, crayfish, and shrimp.

Eyestalks

Head of a crayfish

eye·strain (ī′strān′) *n.* tired or irritated condition of the eyes caused by defects in vision that are uncorrected, use under poor conditions, or excessive use, as extended watching of motion pictures.

eye·tooth (ī′tōōth′) *n., pl.* **-teeth.** either one of the two canine teeth in the upper jaw between the incisors and the bicuspids.

eye·wash (ī′wosh′, ī′wôsh′) *n.* 1. liquid solution used to clean or bathe the eyes. 2. *Slang.* nonsense; hogwash.

eye·wit·ness (ī′wit′nis) *n.* one who has actually seen something happen and therefore can testify concerning it.

ey·rie (âr′ē, ēr′ē) *pl.,* **-ries.** *also* **ey·ry,** *n.* aerie.

Ezek., Ezekiel.

E·ze·ki·el (i zē′kē əl) *also,* **E·ze·chi·el.** 1. Hebrew prophet of the sixth century B.C. 2. book of the Old Testament containing his writings and prophecies.

Ez·ra (ez′rə) *n.* 1. Hebrew scribe and prophet of the fifth century B.C., who led a revival of Judaism among the Jews returning to Jerusalem from the Exile. 2. book of the Old Testament partially credited to him, relating this period of Jewish history. Also, **Es′dras.**

at; āpe; cär; end; mē; it; īce; hot; ōld; fôrk; wood; fōōl; oil; out; up; ūse; turn; sing; thin; this; zh in treasure; ə in ago, taken, pencil, lemon, circus.

f, F (ef) *pl.*, **f's, F's.** *n.* **1.** sixth letter of the English alphabet. **2.** *Music.* **a.** fourth note or tone of the diatonic scale of C major. See **do²** for illustration. **b.** scale or key having this note or tone as its tonic.

F, fluorine.

f. 1. female. **2.** feminine. **3.** forte. **4.** franc. **5.** farthing.

F. 1. Fahrenheit. **2.** French. **3.** Friday. **4.** February.

fa (fä) *n. Music.* fourth of the series of syllables used to name the eight tones of the diatonic scale. See **do²** for illustration. [See GAMUT.]

Fa·bi·an (fā′bē ən) *adj.* **1.** characterized by prolonged harassment of an opponent, while avoiding direct conflict: *Fabian tactics.* **2.** of or relating to the Fabian Society. —*n.* member of the Fabian Society. [Latin *Fabiānus* relating to *Fabius Maximus*, Roman general who helped to win the Second Punic War by avoiding a direct conflict with Hannibal.]

Fabian Society, English socialist organization founded in 1884, advocating the gradual introduction of socialism through legislation rather than revolutionary means.

fa·ble (fā′bəl) *n.* **1.** short story meant to teach a moral, esp. one using animals or inanimate objects as characters. **2.** legend; myth. **3.** falsehood; fabrication. —*v.t.* **-bled, -bling.** to tell or write about as if true: *The house is fabled to have been inhabited by ghosts.* [Old French *fable* story, tale, from Latin *fābula.*]

fa·bled (fā′bəld) *adj.* **1.** described or told about in fables; mythical; legendary. **2.** not real; fictitious; invented.

fab·li·au (fab′lē ō′) *pl.* **-aux** (-ōz′). *n.* short, metrical tale relating an incident of ordinary human life, usually in a comic or bawdy way, popular in France and England in the twelfth and thirteenth centuries. [French *fabliau*, going back to Old French *fable*. See FABLE.]

fab·ric (fab′rik) *n.* **1.** woven, knitted, or otherwise fabricated material, usually made from natural or synthetic fibers; cloth. **2.** system of connected or related parts; framework; structure: *Inflation is weakening the fabric of our economy.* [French *fabrique* factory, a making, from Latin *fabrica* workshop. Doublet of FORGE¹.]

fab·ri·cate (fab′rə kāt′) **-cat·ed, -cat·ing.** *v.t.* **1.** to make up; invent: *She fabricated a story to explain her lateness.* **2.** to manufacture, construct, or process, esp. by assembling or creating standardized parts. [Latin *fabricātus*, past participle of *fabricārī* to build, from *fabrica* workshop.]

fab·ri·ca·tion (fab′rə kā′shən) *n.* **1.** process of manufacturing or constructing. **2.** something fabricated, esp. a false statement.

fab·u·list (fab′yə list) *n.* **1.** inventor or writer of fables. **2.** liar.

fab·u·lous (fab′yə ləs) *adj.* **1.** incredible; amazing: *She spent fabulous sums of money on her wardrobe.* **2.** *Informal.* exceptionally good; wonderful: *We had a fabulous time at the party.* **3.** of or like a fable; imaginary; legendary: *She read about a winged dragon and other fabulous monsters.* [Latin *fābulōsus*, from *fābula* story, tale.] —**fab′u·lous·ly,** *adv.* —**fab′u·lous·ness,** *n.*

fa·çade (fə säd′) *n.* **1.** front of a building. **2.** false front or outward appearance; illusion; pretense: *a façade of prosperity.* [French *façade* front of a building, from Italian *facciata*, going back to Latin *faciēs* face.]

face (fās) *n.* **1.** front of the head. **2.** look or expression; countenance: *to put on a happy face.* **3.** distorted or peculiar expression; grimace: *to make faces in the mirror.* **4.** boldness; impudence; effrontery: *She had the face to insult him in public.* **5.** dignity; self-respect; prestige: *to lose face, to save face.* **6.** front, principal, or outward surface of something: *the face of a cliff, on the face of the earth.* **7.** surface or side of something that is marked, finished, or otherwise prepared for use: *the face of a clock.* **8.** outward appearance: *to put a new face on an old issue.* **9.** *Geometry.* one of the surfaces or sides of a solid: *a cube has six faces.* **10.** topographical appearance of land. **11.** *Economics.* face value. **12.** *Printing.* **a.** surface of a piece of type, which carries the letter or character to be printed. **b.** style or design of this surface.

face to face. facing each other: *The two men stood face to face.*

face to face with. in the presence of; near; confronting.

in the face of. a. when confronted with or near: *He ran in the face of danger.* **b.** notwithstanding; despite.

on the face of it. from its outward appearance; seemingly.

to fly in the face of. to act in defiance of or in direct opposition to.

to (one's) face. directly and boldly in one's presence: *Would you ever say that to his face?*

to show one's face. to make an appearance.

—*v.t.*, **faced, fac·ing. 1.** to have or turn the face toward; front on: *to stand facing the camera. The house faces the park.* **2.** to cause to turn in a particular direction: *Face the plant toward the light.* **3.** to meet openly; confront: *to face a new situation. What problems are facing you?* **4.** to confront boldly; meet with courage: *to face the consequences.* **5.** to realize and admit; accept: *to face the facts.* **6.** to cover or line a surface with. **7.** to smooth or dress the surface of: *to face stone.* **8.** to turn (the face of a playing card) upward. —*v.i.* **1.** to be turned or placed with the face in a particular direction: *The house faced west.* **2.** to turn in a particular direction: *He faced left.* **3.** *Hockey.* to start or resume play with a face-off (with *off*). **4. to face up to. a.** to confront boldly; resist courageously. **b.** to admit and accept. [Old French *face* visage, going back to Latin *faciēs* form, visage.] —**fac′er,** *n.* —**Syn.** *v.t.* **4.** see meet¹.

face card, jack, queen, or king, and sometimes, an ace in a deck of cards.

face lifting 1. cosmetic plastic surgery to tighten sagging or wrinkled skin of the face. **2.** any procedure that renovates or modernizes: *The old city hall was getting a face lifting.*

face-off (fās′ôf′) *n.* act of starting or resuming play in hockey when the referee drops the puck between the sticks of two opposing players.

face-plate (fās′plāt′) *n.* disk which holds work for rotation in a lathe or other machine.

face powder, cosmetic powder applied to the face to dull the shine, conceal blemishes, or otherwise improve its appearance.

fac·et (fas′it) *n.* **1.** any of the small, polished plane surfaces of a cut gem. **2.** any of various sides or aspects: *the many facets of a problem, the many facets of a person's personality.* **3.** fillet between the flutings of a column. **4.** any of the segments of the external surface of the compound eye of an insect or crustacean. —*v.t.*, **-et·ed, -et·ing;** *also, British,* **-et·ted, -et·ting.** to cut facets on. [French *facette* little face, small surface, diminutive of *face* face, visage. See FACE.]

Gem with nine facets showing

fa·ce·tious (fə sē′shəs) *adj.* characterized by flippant humor; not appropriately serious; frivolously amusing: *a facetious young man, a facetious comment.* [French *facétieux*, from *facétie* jest, from Latin *facētia.*] —**fa·ce′tious·ly,** *adv.* —**fa·ce′tious·ness,** *n.*

face value 1. value appearing on currency, stamps, and financial instruments. **2.** apparent value: *to accept promises at face value.*

fa·cial (fā′shəl) *adj.* of, for, or relating to the face. —*n.* massage or other treatment to beautify the face. —**fa′cial·ly,** *adv.*

fac·ile (fas′əl) *adj.* **1.** acting or working with skill and ease; fluent; dexterous: *a facile pen, a facile mind.* **2.** requiring little effort; easily accomplished or done: *a facile task, a facile victory.* **3.** having a mild disposition; easygoing; mild-tempered. **4.** *Archaic.* easily moved or persuaded; yielding. [Latin *facilis* easy, from *facere* to do.] —**fac′ile·ly,** *adv.* —**fac′ile·ness,** *n.*

fa·cil·i·tate (fə sil′ə tāt′) **-tat·ed, -tat·ing.** *v.t.* to make easier; assist in the success, completion, or operation of: *Zip codes are used to facilitate mail service.*

fa·cil·i·ty (fə sil′ə tē) *pl.* **-ties.** *n.* **1.** ease of doing or accomplishing; freedom from difficulty or impediment. **2.** skill or ability; aptitude;

at; āpe; cär; end; mē; it; īce; hot; ōld; fôrk; wood; fōōl; oil; out; up; ūse; turn; sing; thin; this; zh in treasure; ə in ago, taken, pencil, lemon, circus.

dexterity; fluency: *language facility.* **3.** something, as a building or piece of equipment, that provides a convenience or serves a particular purpose: *a cabin with cooking facilities, the inadequate hospital facilities in this city.* **4.** *Archaic.* tendency to be easily moved or persuaded.

fac·ing (fā′sing) *n.* **1.a.** fitted piece of fabric, sewn inside or outside along an edge of a garment to reinforce or trim it. **b.** fabric used for this. **2.** covering in front for ornamentation, protection, or other purposes: *a house with marble facing.* **3. facings.** cuffs, collar, and trimmings of certain military coats.

fac·sim·i·le (fak sim′ə lē) *n.* **1.** exact copy or reproduction. **2.** high-speed transmission of pictures and printed material by telegraph or radio, as in wirephoto systems. **3. in facsimile.** as an exact copy: *This inscription is produced in facsimile.* [Latin *fac simile* make like, from *fac* make, imperative of *facere* to make + *simile,* neuter of *similis* like.] —**Syn. 1.** see **duplicate.**

fact (fakt) *n.* **1.** something known to be true or real; that which has actually occurred: *Restrict your story to the facts.* **2.** something said to be true or real; that which has supposedly occurred: *The writer's facts are far from trustworthy.* **3.** quality or state of being actual; actuality; reality; truth: *to distinguish fact from fiction.* **4.** thing done, esp. a criminal or evil act: *His remorse came after the fact.* **5. as a matter of fact.** actually; really. **6. in fact.** actually; really. **7. in point of fact.** actually; really. [Latin *factum* deed, act, from *facere* to do. Doublet of FEAT.]

fac·tion (fak′shən) *n.* **1.** group of people within a larger group, esp. a dissenting one acting to promote its own ends. **2.** strife or dissension within an organization. [French *faction* factious party, from Latin *factiō* a doing, party. Doublet of FASHION.]

fac·tion·al (fak′shən əl) *adj.* of or characteristic of a faction; partisan.

fac·tious (fak′shəs) *adj.* **1.** inclined to produce faction; causing dissension: *a factious and seditious spirit.* **2.** of, relating to, or characterized by faction: *factious disputes.* [Latin *factiōsus* seditious, from *factiō* a doing, party.]

fac·ti·tious (fak tish′əs) *adj.* not natural, real, or spontaneous; not conforming to actual conditions; artificial. [Latin *factīcius,* from *facere* to do, make.] —**fac·ti′tious·ly,** *adv.* —**fac·ti′tious·ness,** *n.*

fac·tor (fak′tər) *n.* **1.** one of several elements that bring about a result or contribute to the formation of a thing or circumstance. **2.** any of the numbers or algebraic expressions which, when multiplied together, form a product. The factors of 14xy are 2, 7, x, and y. **3.** financial agent or business organization that purchases the accounts receivable of a company, assuming the full risk and responsibility for their collection. **4.** gene. **5.** one who transacts business for another; commission merchant. —*v.t.* to break up (a mathematical product) into its factors. [Latin *factor* doer, maker, from *facere* to do, make.]

fac·tor·age (fak′tər ij) *n.* **1.** commission charged by a factor or agent. **2.** business of such an agent; buying and selling on commission.

fac·to·ri·al (fak tôr′ē əl) *n.* product of an integer and all lower positive integers. The factorial of 3, written as 3!, is $3 \times 2 \times 1 = 6$.

fac·tor·ize (fak′tə rīz′) **-ized, -iz·ing.** *v.t.* to factor.

fac·to·ry (fak′tər ē) *pl.* **-ries.** *n.* building or group of buildings for the manufacture of goods. [Partly from Medieval Latin *factoria* agency; partly from Late Latin *factōrium* oil mill; literally, place where things are made, both from Latin *factor* doer, maker. See FACTOR.]

fac·to·tum (fak tō′təm) *n.* person employed to do all kinds of work. [Medieval Latin *factotum,* from Latin *fac* do (imperative of *facere* to do) + *tōtum* the whole.]

fac·tu·al (fak′chōō əl) *adj.* **1.** of or relating to facts. **2.** consisting of or based on facts: *a factual account.* —**fac′tu·al·ly,** *adv.*

fac·u·la (fak′yə lə) *pl.* **-lae** (-lē′). *n.* luminous eruption of hot gases near the sunspots on the surface of the sun. [Latin *facula* small torch, diminutive of *fax* torch.]

fac·ul·ty (fak′əl tē) *pl.* **-ties.** *n.* **1.** one of the natural powers of the mind or body: *the faculty of speech, in full possession of one's faculties.* **2.** special skill or aptitude; gift; talent: *a faculty for putting people at their ease.* **3.** teachers and administrators of an educational institution, esp. the teaching staff. **4.** department of learning in an educational institution. [Old French *faculte* ability, from Latin *facultās* ability, power.]

fad (fad) *n.* popular practice, interest, or fashion followed enthusiastically for a short time. [Of uncertain origin.] —**fad′dist,** *n.*

fad·dish (fad′ish) *adj.* **1.** of or characteristic of a fad. **2.** given to following fads. —**fad′dish·ly,** *adv.* —**fad′dish·ness,** *n.*

fade (fād) **fad·ed, fad·ing.** *v.i.* **1.** to lose color, brightness, or distinctness: *fabrics that won't fade in the wash.* **2.** to lose freshness, vigor, or strength; wither: *The roses faded after three days.* **3.** to disappear gradually; die down: *The sound of the footsteps faded away.* **4.** *Motion Pictures, Radio, and Television.* **a.** to fade in. to become gradually clearer or louder. **b.** to fade out. to become gradually less clear or less loud. —*v.t.* **1.** to cause to fade: *Sunlight faded my curtains.* **2.** *Informal.* to cover the bet of (the roller) in dice. [Old French *fader* to make faint

or insipid, from *fade* tasteless, weak, going back to a blend of Latin *vapidus* tasteless, insipid + *fatuus* foolish.] —**Syn.** *v.i.* **3.** see **disappear.**

fade-in (fād′in′) *n.* in motion pictures, radio, and television, gradual appearance of an image or sound.

fade-out (fād′out′) *n.* in motion pictures, radio, and television, gradual disappearance of an image or sound.

fae·cal (fē′kəl) fecal.

fae·ces (fē′sēz) feces.

fa·er·ie (fā′ər ē, fār′ē) *pl.* **-ies.** *also,* **fa·er·y.** *Archaic.* *n.* **1.** fairyland. **2.** fairy. —*adj.* fairy.

Faer·oe Islands (fār′ō) group of islands in the north Atlantic, between the Shetland Islands and Iceland. Area, 540 sq. mi. Pop. (1968 est.), 38,000.

Faf·nir (fäf′nər, fäv′nir) *n.* *Norse Legend.* the giant who, in the form of a dragon, guarded a treasure. He was killed by Sigurd.

fag¹ (fag) **fagged, fag·ging.** *v.t.* to tire by hard work; exhaust (often with *out*): *After the race, I was completely fagged out.* —*v.i.* **1.** to work hard; toil. **2.** *British. Informal.* to act as a fag, as in certain English public schools. —*n.* **1.** *British. Informal.* boy who does menial work for an older boy, as in certain English public schools. **2.** hard, menial work; drudgery. [Of uncertain origin.]

fag² (fag) *n.* *Slang.* cigarette. [From FAG END.]

fag end 1. frayed or unfinished end, as of a piece of cloth or rope. **2.** last and worst part of anything; remnant.

fag·ot (fag′ət) *also,* **fag·got.** *n.* **1.** bundle of sticks, twigs, or branches, used esp. for fuel. **2.** bundle of iron or steel pieces to be welded, esp. into bars. —*v.t.* **1.** to make into a fagot; bind together. **2.** to ornament with fagoting. [Old French *fagot* bundle of sticks, probably going back to Greek *phakelos* bundle.]

fag·ot·ing (fag′ə ting) *also,* **fag·got·ing.** *n.* **1.** ornamental effect in textiles made by drawing a number of parallel threads out of the fabric and tying the cross threads together in the middle. **2.** decorative, open-work stitch used to connect two edges.

Fahr., Fahrenheit.

Fahr·en·heit (far′ən hīt′) *adj.* of, according to, or designating the temperature scale on which the freezing point of water is at 32 degrees and the boiling point is at 212 degrees under standard atmospheric pressure. See **thermometer** for illustration. [From Gabriel Daniel *Fahrenheit,* 1686–1736, German physicist who devised this scale.]

fai·ence (fī äns′, fā-) *also,* **faï·ence.** *n.* variety of earthenware, usually highly decorated and having an opaque glaze. [French *faïence,* from *Faenza,* Italian town where it supposedly was first made.]

fail (fāl) *v.i.* **1.** to be unsuccessful in achieving something attempted, desired, or expected: *The plan failed when it was actually tested.* **2.** to be deficient or negligent, as in one's duties or obligations. **3.** to be unsuccessful in passing an examination or subject. **4.** to become weaker, as in health or strength: *The old man's eyesight failed.* **5.** to cease functioning; die out: *The radio tubes failed.* **6.** to be insufficient; fall short; run out: *The water supply failed.* **7.** to become insolvent; go bankrupt. —*v.t.* **1.** to neglect or not do: *He failed to make his point.* **2.** to prove to be of no use or assistance to; disappoint: *His friends failed him in his hour of need.* **3.** to abandon; desert: *His courage failed him.* **4.a.** to receive a grade of failure in (an examination or subject). **b.** to give a grade of failure to (a student). —*n.* **without fail.** definitely; certainly. [Old French *faillir* to be wanting, going back to Latin *fallere* to deceive, disappoint.]

fail·ing (fā′ling) *n.* **1.** shortcoming; fault: *His chief failing is lack of interest.* **2.** failure. —*prep.* in the absence of; without: *Failing a reply, we will cancel your subscription.* —**Syn. 1.** see **fault.**

faille (fīl, fāl) *n.* ribbed fabric, usually made with silk or rayon yarn, used for such items as women's handbags and suits. [French *faille;* of uncertain origin.]

fail-safe (fāl′sāf′) *adj.* **1.** of, relating to, or designating a system which prevents the dropping of bombs or the firing of missiles without confirmation from a specified authority. **2.** of, relating to, or designating a secondary system or part of a system that takes over operation or prevents accident in case of failure of the primary system, as in electronic or mechanical devices.

fail·ure (fāl′yər) *n.* **1.** being unable to achieve something attempted, desired, or expected. **2.** one who or that which is unsuccessful. **3.** omission or neglect of (something required): *failure to comply with the law.* **4.a.** failing to pass an examination or subject. **b.** grade or mark indicating this. **5.** a weakening, as of health or strength. **6.** a ceasing to function; dying out: *a power failure.* **7.** a falling short; insufficiency: *a crop failure.* **8.** insolvency; bankruptcy.

fain (fān) *Archaic. adv.* with pleasure; gladly. —*adj.* **1.** glad; inclined. **2.** willing, but not eager. **3.** eager; desirous. [Old English *fægen* glad.]

faint (fānt) *adj.* **1.** hardly perceptible; dim; indistinct: *faint colors, a faint cry.* **2.** without enthusiasm or strength; feeble; half-hearted: *faint praise, a faint attempt.* **3.** weak and dizzy; likely to faint: *faint with hunger.* **4.** without courage; cowardly. ▲ used only in the phrase *a faint*

at; āpe; cär; end; mē; it; īce; hot; ōld; fôrk; wood; fŏŏl; oil; out; up; ūse; turn; sing; thin; this; zh in treasure; ə in ago, taken, pencil, lemon, circus.

heart. —*n.* brief loss of consciousness because of a temporary decrease in the amount of blood that flows to the brain. —*v.i.* **1.** to go off into a faint; swoon. **2.** *Archaic.* to lose courage; weaken. [Old French *feint* weak, cowardly, past participle of *feindre* to simulate, dissemble. See FEIGN.] —**faint′er, faint′ness,** *n.* —**faint′ly,** *adv.*
Syn. *adj.* **1. Faint, dim, indistinct** indicate lack of clarity or definiteness. **Faint** implies absence of strength: *The candle shed a faint light in the room.* **Dim** suggests darkness or lack of enough vividness to make a sharp impression: *As night fell, the room became dim.* **Indistinct** implies that distinguishing characteristics, such as outline, are so blurred that they cannot be separated from everything surrounding: *The mountain was an indistinct mass against the dark sky.*
faint-heart·ed (fānt′här′tid) *adj.* lacking courage; timid. —**faint′-heart′ed·ly,** *adv.* —**faint′-heart′ed·ness,** *n.*
fair¹ (fār) *adj.* **1.** free from bias or prejudice; impartial; just: *a fair decision.* **2.** according to accepted rules or standards; legitimate: *a fair play in a game.* **3.** moderately good or acceptable; average: *He has a fair chance of winning.* **4.** light in coloring; blond: *a fair complexion.* **5.** not cloudy; clear; bright; sunny: *fair weather for the weekend.* **6.** pleasing in appearance; attractive; beautiful. **7.** legitimately open to attack or pursuit: *Deer are fair game in the hunting season.* **8. fair and square.** *Informal.* honest; just. —*adv.* **1.** in a fair manner; according to rule. **2.** directly; straight; squarely. **3. fair and square.** *Informal.* honestly; justly. **4. to bid fair.** to seem likely or favorable. —*n. Archaic.* woman, esp. a beloved or beautiful one. [Old English *fæger* beautiful, pleasing.] —**fair′ness,** *n.* —**Syn.** *adj.* **1.** see **just¹.**
fair² (fār) *n.* **1.** exhibition, as of livestock and agricultural products, or cultural and industrial displays of different nations, often with shows, competitions, and other entertainment. **2.** exhibition and sale of articles for some charitable cause; bazaar: *a church fair.* **3.** periodic gathering of people to exhibit and sell goods: *a book fair.* [Old French *feire* market, from Late Latin *fēria*, from Latin *fēriae* holidays; from the ancient custom of holding fairs on religious holidays.]
fair ball, a batted baseball that is not a foul.
Fair·banks (fār′bangks′) *n.* city in east-central Alaska. Pop. (1970), 14,771.
fair catch, catch of a punted football made by a player who signals that he will not advance the ball and who therefore cannot be tackled.
fair-com·plex·ioned (fār′kəm plek′shənd) *adj.* having light skin.
fair copy, neat and exact copy of a document after final correction.
Fair Deal, domestic policy of President Harry S Truman after his election in 1948.
fair·ground (fār′ground′) *n.* outdoor place where fairs are held.
fair-haired (fār′hārd′) *adj.* **1.** having light-colored hair. **2.** favorite: *He was his mother's fair-haired boy.*
fair·ing (fār′ing) *n.* auxiliary part fitted to an airplane or other machine to produce a smooth outline that reduces drag.
fair·ish (fār′ish) *adj.* moderately good, well, or large.
fair·lead (fār′lēd′) *n.* any of various devices used aboard a boat or ship to guide lines and prevent them from chafing, esp. a strip of wood or metal with holes in it used to guide the running rigging of a sailing craft. Also, **fair′lead′er.**
fair·ly (fār′lē) *adv.* **1.** justly; impartially; honestly: *We were not treated fairly.* **2.** somewhat; moderately: *a fairly large fortune.* **3.** actually; completely: *The audience fairly roared its approval.*
fair-mind·ed (fār′mīn′did) *adj.* not prejudiced or biased; impartial; just. —**fair′-mind′ed·ness,** *n.*
fair sex, women.
fair-spo·ken (fār′spō′kən) *adj.* speaking or spoken smoothly and courteously; civil.
fair trade, trade under an agreement that forbids a retailer to sell certain products for less than a minimum price specified by the manufacturer or distributor.
fair·way (fār′wā′) *n.* **1.** area on a golf course between the tee and putting green. **2.** navigable channel or course through a river, harbor, or bay.
fair-weath·er (fār′weth′ər) *adj.* **1.** not reliable or helpful in time of distress or need: *a fair-weather friend.* **2.** suitable only in good weather.
fair·y (fār′ē) *n. pl.* **fair·ies.** *n.* tiny imaginary being supposed to possess magic powers. —*adj.* **1.** of or relating to fairies. **2.** resembling a fairy. [Old French *faerie* enchantment, from *fae* the imaginary being, from Late Latin *fāta* the imaginary being, goddess of fate, from Latin *fāta* (plural) the Fates.]
fair·y·land (fār′ē land′) *n.* **1.** imaginary land of the fairies. **2.** any enchanting, beautiful place.
fairy ring, ring of mushrooms growing in the ground, supposedly formed by fairies dancing at night.
fairy tale 1. story, usually for children, about imaginary beings or magical events. **2.** incredible or highly imaginative story, esp. one designed to delude.
fait ac·com·pli (fā tä kôN plē′) something done that no longer can

be changed or reversed. [French *fait accompli* literally, accomplished fact, going back to Latin *factum* deed + *ad* to + *complēre* to fulfill.]
faith (fāth) *n.* **1.** belief not based on proof: *to accept a statement on faith.* **2.** confidence, reliance, or trust: *to have faith in one's doctor.* **3.** belief in God or the doctrines of a religion. **4.** system of religious belief: *the Protestant faith.* **5.** anything believed strongly. **6.** loyalty; fidelity. **7. bad faith.** dishonesty; insincerity. **8. in faith.** truly; indeed. **9. in good faith.** with good intentions; honestly. **10. to break faith.** **a.** to be disloyal to one's principles or beliefs. **b.** to break a promise. **11. to keep faith. a.** to adhere to one's principles or beliefs. **b.** to keep a promise. [Old French *feit* trust, belief, from Latin *fidēs.*] —**Syn. 1.** see **belief.**
faith·ful (fāth′fəl) *adj.* **1.** steadfast in loyalty and devotion; trustworthy: *a faithful companion.* **2.** steadfast in keeping one's word or doing one's duty: *a faithful worker.* **3.** accurate; true; exact: *a faithful translation.* —*n.* **the faithful. a.** the followers or adherents of a religion. **b.** the loyal adherents of any cause or group. —**faith′ful·ly,** *adv.* —**faith′ful·ness,** *n.*
Syn. *adj.* **1. Faithful, loyal, steadfast** mean firmly devoted as to a cause or person. **Faithful** suggests obedience to what honor demands, as to a duty to which one is bound by oath: *He was faithful to his promise.* **Loyal** implies continued devotion to a person or cause under any circumstances: *He remained loyal to me in spite of the scandalous gossip.* **Steadfast** implies unwavering steadiness in holding to a cause: *Elizabeth . . . proved herself the steadfast friend and protector of the Protestant exiles* (Smiles, 1867).
faith healing, method of trying to cure disease by prayer and religious faith.
faith·less (fāth′lis) *adj.* **1.** not trustworthy or loyal: *a faithless husband.* **2.** without faith or belief, esp. religious belief. —**faith′less·ly,** *adv.* —**faith′less·ness,** *n.*
fake¹ (fāk) *n.* one who or that which is not genuine; fraud; sham: *It's not a genuine antique, it's a fake.* —*v.t.,* **faked, fak·ing. 1.** to pretend; feign: *to fake illness.* **2.** to make (something) seem genuine; counterfeit: *The records were faked to show an improvement in sales that didn't exist.* **3.** to improvise: *I don't know the dance step, but I can fake it.* —*v.i.* to practice faking. —*adj.* not genuine; false; sham; counterfeit: *a fake fireplace.* [Of uncertain origin.] —**fak′er, fak′er·y,** *n.*
fake² (fāk) *n.* one of the turns or loops of a coiled rope or cable. —*v.t.,* **faked, fak·ing.** to coil (a rope or cable). [Of uncertain origin.]
fa·kir (fə kēr′, fā′kər) *n.* **1.** member of a Muslim sect who takes vows of poverty and lives by begging. **2.** Hindu ascetic. [Arabic *faqīr* poor.]
Fa·lange (fā′lanj, fə lanj′; *Spanish* fä län′hä) *n.* fascist party in Spain, founded in 1933, the official party of the government under Francisco Franco. [Spanish *Falange,* from *falange* phalanx, from Latin *phalanx* (stem *phalang-*). See PHALANX.] —**Fa·lan·gist** (fə lan′-jist), *n.*
fal·cate (fal′kāt) *adj.* shaped like a sickle; curved; hooked. [Latin *falcātus,* from *falx* sickle.]
fal·chion (fôl′chən, -shən) *n.* **1.** sword of the Middle Ages with a

Falchion

broad, curved blade. **2.** *Archaic.* any sword. [Old French *fauchon* curved short sword, going back to Latin *falx* sickle.]
fal·con (fal′kən, fôl′-, fô′kən) *n.* **1.** any of various hawklike birds of prey, family Falconidae, having short, hooked bills, pointed wings, and gray or brown plumage, usually with buff or white markings, esp. those of the genus *Falco,* as the peregrine falcon. Length: 6–25 inches. **2.** female of any of various hawks trained for falconry. [Old French *faucon,* from Late Latin *falcō,* from Latin *falx* sickle; because of its hooked claws.]
fal·con·er (fôl′kə nər, fal′-, fô′kə-) *n.* **1.** one who hunts with falcons. **2.** breeder or trainer of falcons.
fal·con·ry (fôl′kən rē, fal′-, fô′kən-) *n.* **1.** sport of hunting with falcons; hawking. **2.** art of training falcons to hunt game.
fal·de·ral (fal′də ral′) *also,* **fal·de·rol** (fal′də rol′), *n.* folderol.
fall (fôl) fell, fall·en, fall·ing. *v.i.* **1.** to come down from a higher place by the force of gravity; drop: *The radio fell off the shelf. Snow fell during the night. The curtain fell after the first act.* **2.** to come down suddenly or involuntarily from an erect position: *to fall on one's knees before a king. She swooned and fell.* **3.** to become lower or less, as in quantity, quality, intensity, or degree: *His voice fell to a whisper. Production fell sharply. His popularity is falling.* **4.** to strike; land: *The spear fell wide of its victim.* **5.** to take place; happen; occur: *Easter falls late this year.* **6.** to come as if by descending: *Night fell upon the town. Silence fell as he entered the room.* **7.** to pass into a specified mental or physical condition; become: *to fall ill, to fall in love.* **8.** to be defeated, captured, or conquered: *The city fell after the long siege.* **9.** to be overthrown;

lose power, as a government: *The dictatorship fell during the revolution.* **10.** to decline in estimation, rank, or dignity: *He fell into disgrace.* **11.** to be wounded or killed, as in battle. **12.** to come down in pieces or ruins; collapse: *Several buildings fell during the earthquake.* **13.** to yield to temptation; sin: *Adam fell when he ate the apple.* **14.** to be classified or divided (with *into*): *His argument falls into three parts.* **15.** to show sadness or disappointment: *Her face fell.* **16.** to hang down: *The dress fell in gentle folds. The ringlets fell around her shoulders.* **17.** to come by chance or lot: *It fell to him to tell his brother the bad news.* **18.** to slope or extend downward: *Their property falls gently toward the brook.* **19.** to pass by inheritance or right: *The estate falls to the eldest son.* **20.** to come at a specified place; be positioned: *The accent falls on the last syllable. The perpendicular falls on the midpoint of the line.* **21.** to be cast down: *Her eyes fell.* **22.** to be uttered: *The words fell from his lips.*

  to fall away. a. to withdraw friendship, support, or allegiance; desert. **b.** to become thin or emaciated. **c.** to decline gradually; fade; perish. **d.** *Nautical.* to be blown, or drift, clear of.
  to fall back. to retreat; recede.
  to fall back on. a. to have recourse to; rely on. **b.** to retreat to.
  to fall behind. to fail to keep up: *to fall behind in one's work, to fall behind in the car payments.*
  to fall down on. *Informal.* to fail in: *to fall down on the job.*
  to fall flat. to fail to produce the intended or desired effect: *His performance fell flat.*
  to fall for. *Informal.* **a.** to fall in love with. **b.** to be deceived or tricked by.
  to fall foul (or afoul) of. a. to come into conflict with; clash. **b.** *Nautical.* to collide or become entangled with.
  to fall in. a. to take a proper place in a military formation. **b.** to sink inwardly; cave in.
  to fall in with. a. to meet and join company with: *He fell in with the thieves.* **b.** to agree or comply with; be agreeable or favorable to: *The measure falls in with popular demand.*
  to fall off. a. to become less; diminish; drop: *The demand for the product fell off.* **b.** *Nautical.* to veer to leeward.
  to fall on (or upon). a. to attack vigorously; assault. **b.** to come upon; discover; find.
  to fall out. a. to have a quarrel; argue. **b.** to leave a proper place in a military formation. **c.** to happen; occur.
  to fall short. a. to fail to meet a certain standard, goal, or requirement (with *of*): *a basketball shot that fell short of the basket. Contributions fell short of the expected amount.* **b.** to be or prove deficient; give out.
  to fall through. to come to nothing; fail: *Their plans fell through.*
  to fall to. a. to set about; begin: *He fell to work.* **b.** to begin to attack. **c.** to start eating. **d.** to move or come into place; shut.
  to fall under. a. to be classified as; be included in: *a case that falls under the jurisdiction of a lower court.* **b.** to be or come under the operation or influence of; be subjected to: *to fall under a spell.*
  —*v.t.* to fell or cut down (a tree or trees). —*n.* **1.** act of coming down from a higher place by the force of gravity: *the fall of a meteor.* **2.** amount that comes down: *a six-inch fall of rain.* **3.** distance through which anything falls: *It's a short fall from the window to the ground.* **4.** sudden or involuntary drop from an erect position: *to take a fall on the ice.* **5.** defeat; capture; destruction: *the fall of Troy.* **6.** loss of power or influence; overthrow: *the fall of the Roman Empire.* **7.** decline in estimation, rank, or dignity: *a fall from favor.* **8.** act of yielding to temptation; moral ruin; sin. **9.** reduction or decrease, as in value, quality, or quantity: *a fall in prices.* **10.** a hanging down: *the fall of her hair about her shoulders.* **11.** downward slope or direction. **12.** *also,* **Fall.** autumn. **13. falls.** waterfall; cascade. ▲ usually construed as singular. **14.** woman's hairpiece, usually styled with the natural hair to add length or fullness. **15.** *Wrestling.* **a.** act of throwing and holding one's opponent on his back with both shoulders touching the mat for a specified number of seconds. **b.** match or division of a match. **16.** *Nautical.* apparatus used for hoisting, esp. that part, as a rope, which is actually pulled on to raise the object. **17. the Fall (of Man).** disobedience to God by Adam and Eve in eating the forbidden fruit, resulting in their loss of innocence and acquiring of original sin. **18. to ride for a fall.** to endanger one's position; put oneself in jeopardy. —*adj.* of, relating to, or suitable for the autumn: *fall clothing.* [Old English *feallan* to drop.]

fal·la·cious (fə lā′shəs) *adj.* **1.** based on or containing a fallacy; logically unsound: *a fallacious conclusion.* **2.** deceptive; misleading; delusive: *a fallacious peace, fallacious hopes.* —**fal·la′cious·ly,** *adv.* —**fal·la′cious·ness,** *n.*

fal·la·cy (fal′ə sē) *pl.* **-cies.** *n.* **1.** false or mistaken belief; misconception: *the ancient fallacy that the planets revolve around the earth.* **2.** false or illogical reasoning; unsound argument. **3.** deceptiveness; unsoundness: *the fallacy of his argument.* [Latin *fallācia* deceit.]

fal·lal (fal′lal′) *n.* piece of finery; trifling ornament.

fall·en (fô′lən) *v.* past participle of **fall.** —*adj.* **1.** having come down

from a higher place; dropped: *fallen snow.* **2.** degraded or disgraced: *a fallen woman, a fallen idol.* **3.** captured, overthrown, or defeated: *a fallen village.* **4.** having died, esp. in battle. **5.** on the ground; prostrate.

fall guy *Slang.* one who is made a victim or is left to take the blame for another's crime or mistake; scapegoat.

fal·li·ble (fal′ə bəl) *adj.* **1.** capable of being deceived or mistaken; liable to err. **2.** liable to be erroneous; inaccurate. [Medieval Latin *fallibilis* deceitful, prone to slip, from Latin *fallere* to deceive.] —**fal′li·bil′i·ty,** *n.* —**fal′li·bly,** *adv.*

fall·ing-out (fô′ling out′) *pl.,* **fall·ings-out** or **fall·ing-outs.** *n.* quarrel or estrangement: *The boys were pals again soon after their falling-out.*

falling sickness *Archaic.* epilepsy.

falling star, meteor.

fall line 1. boundary between two plateaus or other land masses, often marked by waterfalls and rapids. **2. Fall Line.** boundary east of the Appalachian Mountains between the Atlantic coastal plains and the Piedmont region.

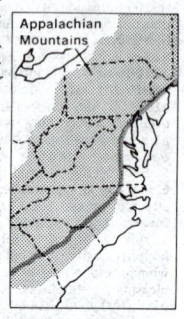

Appalachian Mountains

Fall Line

Fal·lo·pi·an tube (fə lō′pē ən) *also,* **fal·lo·pi·an tube.** either of the pair of slender tubes in female mammals through which eggs pass from the ovaries to the uterus; oviduct. [From Gabriello *Fallopio,* 1523–62, the Italian anatomist who first described these tubes.]

fall·out (fôl′out′) *n.* radioactive dust particles which result from nuclear explosions and fall to the earth from the atmosphere.

fallout shelter, place, usually underground, designed or selected as a shelter from fallout after nuclear explosion.

fal·low¹ (fal′ō) *adj.* (of land) tilled or untilled and left unseeded for one or more growing seasons. —*n.* **1.** fallow land. **2.** tilling of land and leaving it unseeded for one or more growing seasons in order to improve it agriculturally. —*v.t.* to make (land) fallow in order to improve it agriculturally. [Old English *fealh* arable land.]

fal·low² (fal′ō) *n.* pale yellowish-brown color. [Old English *fealu.*]

fallow deer, small European deer, *Dama dama,* usually having a yellowish coat with white spots. Height: 3 feet at the shoulder.

Fallow deer

Fall River, city in southeastern Massachusetts. Pop. (1970), 96,898.

false (fôls) **fals·er, fals·est.** *adj.* **1.** not true; incorrect; erroneous: *a false conclusion, a false accusation.* **2.** not genuine or natural; artificial: *false eyelashes, false modesty.* **3.** misleading; deceptive: *a false impression.* **4.** disloyal; unfaithful: *a false friend.* **5.** untruthful: *a false witness.* **6.** substituting for a similar structure for decoration, protection, or temporary support: *a false pocket, a false front on an old building.* **7.** *Music.* inaccurate or not true in pitch: *a false note.* —*adv.* **to play (someone) false,** to deceive or cheat (someone). [Latin *falsus* deceptive, spurious, past participle of *fallere* to deceive.] —**false′ly,** *adv.* —**false′ness,** *n.*

  Syn. *adj.* **1.** see **wrong.** **2. False, counterfeit** mean resembling and seeming to be something else that is real or genuine. **False** implies intentional or unintentional deception: *Her teeth are false, but they look very natural.* **Counterfeit** suggests a copying with the intent to deceive or defraud: *The bank clerk spotted the counterfeit money.*

false alarm 1. fire alarm erroneously or deliberately sounded when no real fire or danger exists. **2.** any warning or indication of danger when no real danger exists.

false arrest, illegal arrest of a person.

false bottom 1. horizontal partition, as in a suitcase or drawer, which looks like the bottom but which conceals a lower, secret compartment. **2.** base of a glass, bottle, or other container that is raised or narrowed to make the capacity of the container look greater than it really is.

false face, mask.

false-heart·ed (fôls′här′tid) *adj.* pretending faithfulness and loyalty; deceitful: *a false-hearted friend.*

false·hood (fôls′hood′) *n.* **1.** false statement; lie: *to tell falsehoods about one's past.* **2.** quality of being false; absence of truth: *to distinguish between falsehood and truthfulness.* **3.** that which is false, as a theory or idea. —**Syn. 1.** see **lie¹.**

  at; āpe; cär; end; mē; it; īce; hot; ōld; fôrk; wood; fōōl; oil; out; up; ūse; turn; sing; thin; this; zh in treasure; ə in ago, taken, pencil, lemon, circus.

false imprisonment, unlawful imprisonment or detention of a person.

false pretenses, intentional misrepresentation of fact in order to defraud, esp. of money or property.

false ribs, ribs not attached to the breastbone, as the five lower pairs of ribs in man.

false start 1. poor or inadequate beginning: *to solve a problem after a false start.* **2.** incorrect beginning in a race.

false step 1. stumble. **2.** unwise action; blunder.

false teeth, complete or partial set of artificial teeth used in place of real teeth that have been extracted or are missing.

fal·set·to (fôl set'ō) *pl.,* **-tos.** *n.* **1.** unnaturally or artificially high-pitched voice used by a male singer, esp. a tenor. **2.** singer with such a voice. —*adj.* of or having the quality of a falsetto: *falsetto notes.* —*adv.* in falsetto. [Italian *falsetto* falsetto voice, diminutive of *falso* untrue, counterfeit, from Latin *falsus,* past participle of *fallere* to deceive.]

fal·si·fy (fôl'sə fī') **-fied, -fy·ing.** *v.t.* **1.** to change with the intent to deceive; make false: *to falsify the date of one's birth, to falsify an accident report.* **2.** to give a false account of; misrepresent: *This book falsifies the events of the Civil War.* **3.** to prove to be false; disprove: *No man can falsify any material fact here stated* (Jefferson, 1830). —*v.i.* to tell falsehoods; lie. [Late Latin *falsificāre* to make false, from Latin *falsus* (see FALSE) + *facere* to make.] —**fal'si·fi·ca'tion, fal'si·fi'er,** *n.*

fal·si·ty (fôl'sə tē) *pl.,* **-ties.** *n.* **1.** quality or condition of being false; untruthfulness. **2.** that which is false; falsehood.

Fal·staff, Sir John (fôl'staf) fat, brazen, swaggering old knight, given to drinking, jesting, and good-natured lying, in Shakespeare's *Henry IV* and *The Merry Wives of Windsor.*

Fal·staff·i·an (fôl staf'ē ən) *adj.* of or characteristic of Falstaff or his band of ragged soldiers and comrades.

fal·ter (fôl'tər) *v.i.* **1.** to act with hesitation or uncertainty; waver: *The child faltered for a moment before joining the group. Our hopes will not falter in adversity.* **2.** to speak with hesitation; stammer: *He faltered every time he mentioned the accident.* **3.** to move unsteadily; stumble; totter. —*v.t.* to utter haltingly or brokenly. [Of uncertain origin.] —**fal'ter·er,** *n.* —**fal'ter·ing·ly,** *adv.* —Syn. *v.i.* **1.** see hesitate.

fame (fām) *n.* widespread reputation, esp. for great achievement: *to seek fame and fortune.* —*v.t.* **famed, fam·ing.** *Archaic.* to make famous. [Old French *fame* reputation, rumor, from Latin *fāma.*]

famed (fāmd) *adj.* well-known; famous.

fa·mil·i·al (fə mil'yəl) *adj.* of, relating to, or characteristic of a family.

fa·mil·iar (fə mil'yər) *adj.* **1.** commonly seen, heard, or experienced; well-known: *a familiar tune. Smog is a familiar occurrence in that city.* **2.** well-acquainted; conversant (with *with*): *He is familiar with the book.* **3.** close; intimate: *to be on familiar terms with one's neighbors.* **4.** informal; friendly; unconstrained: *an easy and familiar manner.* **5.** unduly intimate; presumptuous; forward. **6.** (of animals) domesticated. —*n.* **1.** close familiar friend or associate. **2.** *Folklore.* spirit or demon supposed to attend a person. **3.** domestic servant in the household of a Roman Catholic bishop or the pope. [Latin *familiāris* relating to a household, from *familia* household.] —**fa·mil'iar·ly,** *adv.* Syn. *adj.* **1.** see common. **3. Familiar, intimate¹, close** indicate a close personal relationship. **Familiar** suggests the open, informal give-and-take of members of the same family: *She gave a last-minute party for her familiar friends.* **Intimate** implies deep understanding based on close and often extended companionship: *Be courteous to all, but intimate with few, and let those few be well tried before you give them your confidence* (Washington, 1783). **Close** suggests a relationship so near that the intrusion of others is difficult if at all possible: *Only his closest friends attended the graduation ceremony.*

fa·mil·i·ar·i·ty (fə mil'ē ar'ə tē) *pl.,* **-ties.** *n.* **1.** close acquaintance with something: *familiarity with a subject.* **2.** absence of formality; friendliness or intimacy: *to be on terms of familiarity.* **3.** undue intimacy; forwardness. **4.** action or conduct suitable only for one of intimate acquaintance: *to resent the familiarities of a stranger.*

fa·mil·iar·ize (fə mil'yə rīz') **-ized, -iz·ing.** *v.t.* **1.** to make (oneself or someone else) accustomed or well-acquainted (with *with*): *Familiarize yourself with the new equipment before you attempt to use it.* **2.** to make (something) well known: *Movies have familiarized the customs of the old West.* —**fa·mil'iar·i·za'tion,** *n.* —Syn. **1.** see accustom.

fam·i·ly (fam'ə lē, fam'lē) *pl.,* **-lies.** *n.* **1.** parents and their children. **2.** children of the same parents. **3.** one's spouse and children: *I'm taking my family to the beach.* **4.** group of people connected by blood or marriage; relatives. **5.** group of people descended from a common ancestor; house, line, or clan. **6.** group of people who form one household. **7.** group of things related by common or similar characteristics: *a family of musical instruments.* **8.** *Biology.* group of related animals or plants forming a category ranking below an order and above a genus. Zebras, asses, and horses belong to the horse family. **9.** *Linguis-*

tics. group of related languages descended from a common parent language. The English language belongs to the Indo-European family. —*adj.* **1.** of or relating to, or suitable for, a family. **2. in the family way.** pregnant. [Latin *familia* household, from *famulus* servant.]

family circle 1. members of a family considered as an intimate group. **2.** section in the upper balcony of a theater or opera house containing inexpensive seats.

family man 1. man with a family. **2.** man who is devoted to his family.

family name, hereditary last name common to the members of a certain family; surname.

family tree 1. genealogical chart or diagram showing the ancestry, relationships, and descent of all the members of a family. **2.** ancestors and descendants in a given family collectively.

fam·ine (fam'in) *n.* **1.** extreme and widespread scarcity of food. **2.** extreme scarcity of anything; dearth: *a rice famine.* **3.** *Archaic.* starvation. [French *famine,* going back to Latin *famēs* hunger.]

fam·ish (fam'ish) *v.i., v.t.* **1.** to be or make intensely hungry; starve. [Modification of Middle English *famen,* shortened from Old French *afamer,* going back to Latin *ad* to + *famēs* hunger.]

fam·ished (fam'isht) *adj.* intensely hungry; starving: *We were famished after the long ride home.*

fa·mous (fā'məs) *adj.* having fame or celebrity; well-known; renowned: *a famous author.* [Old French *fameus* renowned for good or ill, from Latin *fāmōsus* renowned, from *fāma* rumor, reputation.] Syn. **Famous, renowned, celebrated** mean widely known and of good reputation. **Famous** suggests extensive good repute within a given group or at a given time: *She was famous for the glamorous roles she played in films of the forties.* **Renowned** implies still wider and longer lasting recognition: *Peace hath her victories no less renowned than War* (Milton, 1652). **Celebrated** suggests public attention and acclaim: *The building being demolished was once celebrated for its innovative architecture.*

fa·mous·ly (fā'məs lē) *adv.* **1.** remarkably well; splendidly: *We got along famously.* **2.** with renown.

fan¹ (fan) *n.* **1.** device for producing a current of air, as a hand-held, collapsible object of various materials, as paper, ivory, or feathers, which, when opened, is shaped like a sector of a circle. **2.** anything resembling an open fan, as the tail of a peacock. **3.** mechanical device consisting of several blades attached to a central hub and rotated by a motor, used for producing a current of air to cool, heat, or ventilate. **4.** winnowing machine. —*v.t.,* **fanned, fan·ning. 1.** to move (air) with or as with a fan: *The bird's wings fanned the air and rustled the leaves.* **2.** to direct a current of air upon or toward, with or as with a fan: *to fan the flame.* **3.** to blow gently or refreshingly upon, as if driven by a fan: *The cool breeze fanned his hot face.* **4.** to sweep or drive away with or as with a fan: *to fan smoke from one's face.* **5.** to stir up; excite; stimulate: *to fan the dissension between the two parties.* **6.** to spread out (something) like a fan. **7.** to winnow. **8.** *Baseball.* to cause (a batter) to strike out. —*v.i.* **1.** to spread out like a fan. **2. to fan out.** *Baseball.* to strike out. [Old English *fann* winnowing implement, from Latin *vannus.*]

fan² (fan) *n. Informal.* enthusiastic devotee or admirer, as of a sport or performer. [Short for FANATIC.] —Syn. see **enthusiast.**

fa·nat·ic (fə nat'ik) *n.* one whose devotion to a cause or belief is marked by excessive, often irrational enthusiasm or zeal: *a religious fanatic, to be a fanatic about punctuality.* —*adj.* fanatical. [Latin *fānāticus* inspired by a divinity, frenzied, from *fānum* temple.] —Syn. *n.* see **enthusiast.**

fa·nat·i·cal (fə nat'i kəl) *adj.* irrationally enthusiastic; excessively zealous. —**fa·nat'i·cal·ly,** *adv.*

fa·nat·i·cism (fə nat'ə siz'əm) *n.* excessive or irrational enthusiasm or zeal.

fan·cied (fan'sēd) *adj.* imagined; imaginary: *her real and fancied accomplishments.*

fan·ci·er (fan'sē ər) *n.* one who has a special liking for or interest in something: *a bird fancier.*

fan·ci·ful (fan'si fəl) *adj.* **1.** produced or suggested by fancy; imaginary; unreal: *She told the children a fanciful story.* **2.** showing fancy in design or construction; quaint in appearance: *a fanciful costume.* **3.** influenced by fancy; imaginative; whimsical: *a fanciful mind.* —**fan'ci·ful·ly,** *adv.* —**fan'ci·ful·ness,** *n.*

fan·cy (fan'sē) *pl.,* **-cies.** *n.* **1.** imagination, esp. of a capricious or whimsical nature: *The unicorn is a product of men's fancy.* **2.** that which is imagined by the fancy; mental image: *a pleasing fancy.* **3.** idea or opinion based on few or no facts; notion; supposition: *a mere fancy.* **4.** capricious preference or inclination; fondness; liking: *to have a fancy for liche nuts. She took a fancy to the boy.* —*adj.,* **-ci·er, -ci·est. 1.** made or designed to please the fancy; highly decorated; ornamental; elaborate: *fancy embroidery on a shirt.* **2.** of highest quality; superior; choice: *fancy fruits and vegetables.* **3.** *Informal.* extravagant (in cost or price): *to charge fancy prices.* **4.** dealing in fancy goods; geared to

extravagant or elegant taste: *a fancy restaurant.* **5.** displaying or requiring great skill or grace; intricate: *fancy footwork.* **6.** (of animals) bred for excellence of specific qualities. —*v.t.* **-cied, -cy·ing. 1.** to picture mentally; imagine: *He fancies himself a great general. Fancy that!* **2.** to have a fondness for; like. **3.** to believe without proof or certainty; suppose; presume. [Contraction of FANTASY.] —**Syn.** *n.* **1.** see **imagination.**

fancy dress, masquerade costume.

fan·cy-free (fan′sē frē′) *adj.* **1.** free to marry or fall in love. **2.** carefree.

fan·cy·work (fan′sē wurk′) *n.* ornamental needlework, as embroidery or tatting.

fan·dan·go (fan dang′gō) *pl.*, **-gos.** *n.* **1.** lively dance of Spanish origin performed in three-quarter time, usually with castanets. **2.** music for such a dance. [Spanish *fandango;* of uncertain origin.]

fane (fān) *n. Archaic.* temple; church. [Latin *fānum* temple.]

fan·fare (fan′fãr′) *n.* **1.** flourish, call, or short tune sounded by bugles, trumpets, or other brass instruments, used esp. for military and ceremonial occasions. **2.** ostentatious noise, excitement, fuss, or activity, as in celebration or promotion of something. [French *fanfare* flourish of trumpets; probably imitative.]

Fangs

fang (fang) *n.* **1.** long, pointed tooth, as of a carnivore, with which a beast slashes or holds its prey. **2.** one of the two sharp, slender, hollow or grooved teeth with which a poisonous snake injects venom. **3.** any pointed, tapered projection. [Old English *fang* a seizing, from Old Norse *fang* capture.]

fan·jet (fan′jet′) *n.* type of aircraft equipped with turbofan engines.

fan·light (fan′līt′) *n.* semicircular window over a door or larger window, with sash bars radiating like an open fan.

fan mail, letters of admiration received by a performer, author, or other celebrity.

fan·tail (fan′tāl′) *n.* **1.** tail, end, or other part resembling an open fan. **2.** domestic pigeon having a fan-shaped tail.

Fanlight

fan-tan (fan′tan′) *n.* **1.** card game in which from two to eight players, using a deck of fifty-two cards, discard cards in a certain sequence. The winner is the first player to play all of his cards. **2.** Chinese gambling game in which the players bet on the number of beans or counters that will remain after an uncounted pile of them, under a bowl, has been counted off by fours. [Chinese (Mandarin) *fan t'an* the Chinese game; literally, repeated division.]

fan·ta·si·a (fan tā′zhə, -zhē ə, fan′tə-zē′ə) *n.* **1.** fanciful musical composition not conforming to strict style or form. **2.** medley of familiar tunes or themes embellished with interludes and flourishes. [Italian *fantasia* imagination, fantasia, from Latin *phantasia* fancy, idea, from Greek *phantasiā* imagination, perception, appearance. Doublet of FANTASY.]

Fantail *(def. 2)*

fan·ta·size (fan′tə sīz′) **-sized, -siz·ing.** *v.i.* to escape from reality by creating fanciful mental images; daydream.

fan·tas·tic (fan tas′tik) *adj.* **1.** strikingly unusual or strange in appearance, as though conceived by unrestrained fancy or imagination; bizarre; grotesque: *Driftwood sometimes takes fantastic shapes.* **2.** existing in the mind only; imaginary; irrational: *the fantastic fears of children.* **3.** *Informal.* particularly good; splendid: *a fantastic view of the city from the mountain top.* **4.** extraordinary; remarkable; amazing: *to consume a fantastic amount of food.* Also, **fan·tas′ti·cal.** [Medieval Latin *fantasticus* disordered, strange, imaginary, from Late Latin *phantasticus* imaginary, from Greek *phantastikos* able to produce the appearance of something, from *phantazein* to make visible.] —**fan·tas′ti·cal·ly,** *adv.* —**Syn. 1.** see **grotesque.**

fan·ta·sy (fan′tə sē, -zē) *pl.* **-sies.** *also,* **phan·ta·sy.** *n.* **1.** unrestrained imagination or fancy. **2.** unreal or grotesque mental image: *fantasies brought on by drugs.* **3.** fanciful or imaginative creation or invention, such as science fiction. **4.** *Psychology.* daydream or train of fanciful mental images, usually in the form of a wish fulfillment, through which a person escapes from reality. **5.** caprice; whim. **6.** fantasia. [Old French *fantasie* imagination, fancy, from Latin *phantasia* fancy, idea, from Greek *phantasiā* imagination, perception, appearance. Doublet of FANTASIA.] —**Syn. 1.** see **imagination.**

far (fär) **far·ther** or **fur·ther, far·thest** or **fur·thest.** *adv.* **1.** at or to a great distance in space: *to travel far from home.* **2.** at or to an advanced

or remote point in time, degree, or extent: *to continue far into the night. That painting is far from finished.* **3.** to or at a specific distance, point in time, or degree: *Billy's practical jokes always go too far.* **4.** to a great degree; very much: *far better, far wiser.*

as far as. to the distance, degree, or extent that: *Read as far as you can in ten minutes.*

by far. to a great degree; very much: *That is by far the best choice.*

far and away. without a doubt; very much: *Tom is far and away the best actor for the part.*

far and wide (or near). to, from, or in all areas, including distant ones; everywhere: *The fans came from far and wide to greet their idol.*

far be it from me. I do not have the desire or courage: *Far be it from me to criticize such an expert.*

how far. to what distance, extent, or degree.

in so far (or insofar) as. to the degree or extent that.

so far. a. up to now. **b.** up to a certain point or extent: *You can go just so far in being candid.*

so far as. to the degree or extent that.

so far so good. up to now everything has been satisfactory.

to go far. a. to achieve success; accomplish much: *With his musical talent he should go far.* **b.** to last a long time; cover a considerable extent: *The cookies didn't go far among those hungry boys.* **c.** to have a positive effect on; help: *The testimony went far in clarifying the sequence of events.*

—*adj.* **1.** distant or remote in time or space: *the far future, the far north.* **2.** more distant; farther: *the far side of the moon.* **3.** extending over a long distance and time: *a far journey.* [Old English *feor(r)* at a distance, remote, beyond.]

far·ad (far′əd, -ad) *n.* unit of capacitance. An object that stores one coulomb of charge when raised to a potential of one volt has a capacitance of one farad. [From Michael *Faraday.*]

far·a·day (far′ə dē′, -dā′) *n.* in electrolysis, quantity of electricity necessary to deposit or dissolve one gram equivalent of a substance. It is equivalent to 96,500 coulombs. [From Michael *Faraday.*]

Far·a·day, Michael (far′ə dē′, -dā′) 1791–1867, English physicist and chemist.

far·a·dize (far′ə dīz′) **-dized, -diz·ing.** *v.t.* to stimulate or treat (a nerve or muscle) by means of induced electricity. —**far′a·di·za′tion, far′a·diz′er,** *n.*

far·a·way (fär′ə wā′) *adj.* **1.** at a great distance; remote: *faraway places.* **2.** dreamy; pensive: *a faraway look in her eyes.*

farce (färs) *n.* **1.a.** humorous play in which the situation and characters are greatly exaggerated. **b.** broad humor used in such a play. **2.** hollow pretense; mockery; absurdity: *The meeting turned out to be a farce.* —*v.t.,* **farced, farc·ing.** to fill out (a speech, play, or composition) with wit or humor. [French *farce* stuffing, humorous play, going back to Latin *farcīre* to stuff; originally used to denote comic interludes "stuffed" between the acts of medieval religious plays.]

far·ceur (fär sûr′) *n.* **1.** one who writes or acts in a farce. **2.** joker; wag. [French *farceur* writer or actor of farce, from *farce* stuffing, humorous play. See FARCE.]

far·ci·cal (fär′si kəl) *adj.* of, relating to, or characteristic of a farce; absurd; ludicrous. —**far·ci·cal·i·ty** (fär′si kal′ə tē), **far′ci·cal·ness,** *n.* —**far′ci·cal·ly,** *adv.*

far cry, great distance; long way: *a far cry from the truth.*

far·cy (fär′sē) *n.* disease of horses that affects the lymph glands. It is a form of glanders. [French *farcin,* from Late Latin *farcīminum,* from Latin *farcīre* to stuff; because the diseased animal was "stuffed" with pustules.]

far·del (färd′əl) *n. Archaic.* bundle; burden. [Old French *fardel,* going back to Arabic *farda* package, load for a camel.]

fare (fãr) *n.* **1.** cost of a ride on a bus, airplane, or other conveyance. **2.** passenger carried on such a conveyance. **3.** food and drink. —*v.i.,* **fared, far·ing. 1.** to be in a specified state, esp. with regard to good or bad fortune; get along: *He fared well at his last job.* **2.** to turn out; result; happen: *It fared well with us.* **3.** to eat and drink; dine. **4.** *Archaic.* to go; travel. [Old English *faran* to go, travel, get along, happen.] —**far′er,** *n.*

Far East, countries of eastern Asia, as Japan and China.

fare·well (fãr′wel′) *interj.* good-by and good luck. ▲ used as a parting salutation. —*n.* **1.** parting word; good-by: *They said their farewells and left.* **2.** act of parting; departure; leave-taking: *See how the morning . . . takes her farewell of the glorious sun!* (Shakespeare, *Henry VI*). —*adj.* of or relating to a farewell; last: *a farewell luncheon, a farewell speech.*

far-fetched (fär′fecht′) *adj.* not natural or reasonable; forced; strained: *a far-fetched comparison.*

far-flung (fär′flung′) *adj.* extending over a great distance; widespread.

Far·go (fär′gō) *n.* largest city in North Dakota, in the eastern part of the state. Pop. (1970), 53,365.

at; āpe; cär; end; mē; it; īce; hot; ōld; fôrk; wood; fŏŏl; oil; out; up; ūse; turn; sing; thin; this; zh in treasure; ə in ago, taken, pencil, lemon, circus.

fa·ri·na (fə rē′nə) *n.* **1.** flour or meal made from cereal grains, nuts, or starchy roots, used as a breakfast cereal or in puddings. **2.** starch. [Latin *farīna* meal², ground corn.]

far·i·na·ceous (far′ə nā′shəs) *adj.* **1.** of, relating to, or containing flour or meal. **2.** containing starch; starchy.

far·i·nose (far′ə nōs′) *adj.* yielding farina: *farinose plants.*

far·kle·ber·ry (fär′kəl ber′ē) *pl.,* **-ries.** *n.* spreading shrub or small tree, *Vaccinium arboreum,* found in the southern United States, bearing small, smooth, inedible black berries. [Of uncertain origin.]

farm (färm) *n.* **1.** area of land used to raise crops, livestock, or poultry. **2.** tract of water used for the cultivation of fish or other forms of marine life: *an oyster farm.* **3.** farm team. —*v.t.* **1.** to cultivate (land). **2.** to let out the labor or services of (a person) for hire. **3.** to contract for the maintenance and care of (a person or institution) for a fixed amount. **4.** *Archaic.* to collect proceeds or profits of (a tax or business) and keep what is collected after paying a fixed sum. **5.** *Archaic.* to let or lease (land or the authority to collect taxes) to another in return for a fixed amount or percentage (usually with *out*): *to farm out land.* **6. to farm out. a.** to assign (a baseball player) to a minor-league team. **b.** to arrange to have done by someone not directly associated with a main organization; subcontract. —*v.i.* to be engaged in agricultural farming. [Old French *ferme* rural property, lease, from Medieval Latin *firma* fixed payment, from Latin *firmāre* to strengthen, fix; a farm was originally a tax or rent based on property and later came to mean the property itself.]

farm·er (fär′mər) *n.* **1.** one who engages in agricultural farming. **2.** one who undertakes to perform certain duties or services at a fixed price, such as caring for children or paupers: *a farmer of infants* (Dickens, 1838). **3.** *Archaic.* one who contracts to collect taxes and keep what is collected after paying a fixed sum for the privilege.

Farm·er-La·bor Party (fär′mər lā′bər) U.S. political party, organized in 1918 to represent small farmers and city workers, that merged with the Democratic Party in 1944.

farm·hand (färm′hand′) *n.* one who works on a farm, esp. a hired laborer.

farm·house (färm′hous′) *n.* house on a farm, esp. one in which the owner or manager lives.

farm·ing (fär′ming) *n.* **1.** cultivation of crops, livestock, or poultry; agriculture. **2.** *Archaic.* practice of leasing the authority to collect taxes.

farm·stead (färm′sted′) *n.* farm and its buildings.

farm team, minor-league baseball team owned by or associated with a major-league club to train its recruits. Also, **farm, farm club.**

farm·yard (färm′yärd′) *n.* yard enclosed by or surrounding farm buildings.

far·o (fār′ō) *n.* card game using a deck of fifty-two cards, in which any number of players bet against the house as to the order in which cards will be drawn from the dealing box. [Modification of PHARAOH; because the Egyptian *Pharaoh* was once depicted on one of the cards.]

far-off (fär′ôf′) *adj.* distant; remote.

far-out (fär′out′) *adj. Slang.* unconventional; avant-garde; extreme: *a far-out taste in music.*

far·ra·go (fə räg′ō, -rä′gō) *pl.,* **-goes.** *n.* confused mixture; hodgepodge; medley. [Latin *farrāgō* medley, mixed fodder.]

far-reach·ing (fär′rē′ching) *adj.* having wide influence, effect, or range.

far·ri·er (far′ē ər) *n. British.* blacksmith who shoes horses. [Old French *ferrier,* from Latin *ferrārius,* from *ferrum* iron.]

far·ri·er·y (far′ē ər ē) *pl.,* **-er·ies.** *n. British.* work or establishment of a farrier.

far·row (far′ō) *n.* litter of pigs. —*v.i., v.t.* to give birth to (pigs). [Old English *fearh* young pig.]

far·see·ing (fär′sē′ing) *adj.* **1.** able to see distant objects. **2.** having foresight; planning ahead wisely.

far·sight·ed (fär′sī′tid) *adj.* **1.** able to see distant objects more clearly than those nearby; hyperopic. Distinguished from **nearsighted.** **2.** having foresight; planning ahead; prudent: *a farsighted leader, a farsighted plan.* —**far′sight′ed·ly,** *adv.* —**far′sight′ed·ness,** *n.*

far·ther (fär′thər) comparative of **far.** —*adv.* **1.** at or to a more distant or remote point in space: *The raft drifted farther and farther from the dock.* **2.** to a greater degree or extent; more completely: *to go a step farther in carrying out a plan.* —*adj.* **1.** more distant or remote. **2.** further. (def. 1). [Middle English *ferther,* form of FURTHER and used as a comparative of FAR.]

far·ther·most (fär′thər mōst′) *adj.* most distant or remote; farthest.

far·thest (fär′thist) superlative of **far.** —*adv.* **1.** at or to the most distant or remote point in space: *Jane sat farthest from the hostess.* **2.** to the greatest degree or extent; most completely: *He went farthest in defense of their actions.* —*adj.* most distant or remote: *the farthest hill.* [Form of FURTHEST and used as a superlative of FAR.]

far·thing (fär′thing) *n.* **1.** British monetary unit and coin equal to one-fourth of a British penny, no longer legal tender. **2.** anything of

little or no value; trifle. [Old English *fēorthung* the coin; literally, a little fourth, from *fēortha* fourth.]

far·thin·gale (fär′thing gāl′) *n.* framework for expanding a woman's skirt, worn in the sixteenth and seventeenth centuries. [Modification of Middle French *verdugalle,* from Spanish *verdugado* (referring to the rods of which it was made), from *verdugo* rod, shoot of a tree, going back to Latin *viridis* green.]

fas·ces (fas′ēz) *sing.,* **fas·cis** (fas′is). *n.,pl.* bundle of rods bound with a red cord and carried before a magistrate in ancient Rome as a symbol of authority. [Latin *fascēs,* plural of *fascis* bundle.]

fas·ci·a (fash′ē ə)*pl.,* **fas·ci·ae** (fash′ē ē′). *n.* **1.** band, sash, or fillet. **2.** subcutaneous sheet of fibrous tissue which holds muscles and various organs of the body in place. [Latin *fascia* band, fillet.]

fas·ci·cle (fas′i kəl) *n.* **1.** small bundle. **2.** division of a book published in installments. **3.** close cluster, as of flowers, leaves, or fruits. [Latin *fasciculus* small bundle, bunch, diminutive of *fascis* bundle.] —**fas·cic·u·lar** (fə sik′yə-lər, fa-), **fas·cic·u·late** (fə sik′yə lit, fa-), *adj.* —**fas·cic′u·late·ly,** *adv.*

Fasces

fas·ci·nate (fas′ə nāt′) **-nat·ed, -nat·ing.** *v.t.* **1.** to attract and hold the close interest of by some compelling quality or charm; captivate: *The magician's tricks fascinated the children in the audience.* **2.** to transfix, as by inspiring terror or awe: *A serpent fascinates its prey.* [Latin *fascinātus,* past participle of *fascināre* to enchant.] —**fas′ci·na′tor,** *n.*

fas·ci·nat·ing (fas′ə nā′ting) *adj.* intensely interesting; captivating; irresistible: *a fascinating plot.* —**fas′ci·nat′ing·ly,** *adv.*

fas·ci·na·tion (fas′ə nā′shən) *n.* **1.** act of fascinating; being fascinated. **2.** strong attraction; charm; enchantment: *The room's fascination was in its decor.*

fas·cine (fa sēn′, fə-) *n.* bundle of sticks bound at short intervals, used for fortification, as in filling ditches and lining trenches. [French *fascine,* going back to Latin *fascis* bundle.]

fas·cism (fash′iz′əm) *n.* **1. Fascism.** nationalist movement that controlled Italy from 1922 to 1943 under the dictatorship of Benito Mussolini. Originally based on opposition to Communism and socialism, Fascism established rigid economic controls and attempted to organize most phases of Italian life. **2.** any similar movement, such as German Naziism or the Falange in Spain, which advocates a nationalist dictatorship, private ownership of property but state control of the economy, and suppression of opposing political movements, particularly socialism and Communism. **3.** *also,* **Fascism.** doctrines or methods of such movements. [Italian *Fascismo* Italian fascism, from *fascio* bundle, political group, from Latin *fascis* bundle; with reference to the *fasces* of ancient Rome. See FASCES.]

fas·cist (fash′ist) *n.* **1. Fascist.** member of the ruling political party in Italy under the dictatorship of Benito Mussolini. **2.** member of any similar political party. **3.** one who advocates or supports fascism. —*adj. also,* **Fascist.** of, relating to, or supporting fascism or fascists.

Fa·sci·sti (fä shē′stē) *n.,pl.* members of the Fascist movement in Italy.

fash·ion (fash′ən) *n.* **1.** style considered as a standard of taste: *the glass of fashion, and the mold of form* (Shakespeare, *Hamlet*). **2.** clothing; apparel: *spring fashions.* **3.** prevailing custom or style, as in dress, home furnishings, speech, or behavior; current practice: *the latest fashion in men's clothing.* **4.** manner; way: *to act in a carefree fashion.* **5.** *Archaic.* fashionable people collectively. **6. after** (or **in) a fashion.** to some extent but not too well or completely: *to solve a problem after a fashion.* —*v.t.* **1.** to give form to; shape; mold: *to fashion a boot out of leather. His character was fashioned like his father's.* **2.** *Archaic.* to adapt; accommodate; fit. [Old French *façon* appearance, form, from Latin *factiō* a doing, party. Doublet of FACTION.]

Syn. *n.* **3. Fashion, vogue, style** mean the contemporary way of doing things, esp. in dress. **Fashion** emphasizes popularity, wide prevalence, or general acceptance at any particular time and suggests the importance of novelty and being up-to-date as a standard of or guide to dress: *Your severe clothes are out of fashion; you should be wearing bright prints, long ruffled skirts, lots of accessories, and stagy makeup.* **Vogue** emphasizes the latest original designs worn by those who set fashion and thus suggests the importance of chic, sophistication, and daring as an element of fashion: *Some of the best-dressed women are already wearing sheer, revealing fabrics that will be the vogue this summer.* **Style** suggests that fashion is more than the sum of its parts, a product and expression either of a period or a personality, conferring distinction and reflecting taste: *That dress is so classic, it will always be in style.*

fash·ion·a·ble (fash′ə nə bəl) *adj.* **1.** conforming to current styles or practices; in fashion; stylish: *a fashionable hairdo.* **2.** of, relating to, or frequented by people of fashion: *a fashionable resort.* —**fash′ion·a·ble·ness,** *n.* —**fash′ion·a·bly,** *adv.*

fashion plate 1. one who dresses in the latest style. 2. illustration showing new or current fashions in dress.

fast[1] (fast) *adj.* 1. acting or moving with speed; quick; rapid: *a fast train, a fast thinker.* 2. accomplished in relatively little time; performed rapidly: *a fast game, to make a fast retreat.* 3. (of a clock or watch) ahead of the true time. 4. suitable for or promoting rapid movement: *a fast race track.* 5. characterized by the reckless pursuit of pleasure; dissipated: *fast living.* 6. firmly attached; secure; tight: *a fast knot, a fast grip on a child's arm.* 7. loyal; steadfast; faithful: *fast friends.* 8. (of colors) not easily faded. 9. resistant ▲ used in combination, as in: *acid-fast.* 10. *Photography.* allowing for a short exposure time: *fast film.* —*adv.* 1. in a firm manner; securely; tightly: *to hold fast, to stick fast.* 2. soundly; deeply: *to be fast asleep.* 3. with speed; quickly; rapidly: *to move fast.* 4. in a wild, dissipated manner; recklessly: *to live fast.* 5. *Archaic.* close; near: *fast by.* 6. **to play fast and loose.** to act recklessly and insincerely; be irresponsible. [Old English *fæst* firm, fixed.] —**Syn.** *adj.* 1. see **quick.**

fast[2] (fast) *v.i.* 1. to eat little or no food or only certain kinds of food, esp. as a religious observance. —*n.* 1. act of fasting. 2. day or period of fasting. [Old English *fæstan* to abstain from food.]

fast day, day on which fasting is observed, esp. as a religious observance.

fas·ten (fas'ən) *v.t.* 1. to attach firmly to something else; join: *to fasten a corsage to a dress.* 2. to make fast; close tightly; secure: *to fasten a seatbelt.* 3. to direct steadily or fix (one's eyes or mind). —*v.i.* 1. to become attached or firmly joined: *This snap won't fasten.* 2. to take a firm hold; concentrate (with *on*): *to fasten on a plan* [Old English *fæstnian* to make firm, secure.] —**fas'ten·er,** *n.*

fas·ten·ing (fas'ə ning) *n.* 1. that which fastens, as a hook, bolt, or button. 2. act of making fast.

fast-food (fast'fōōd') *adj.* serving foods that can be cooked quickly, such as hamburgers, frankfurters, and fried chicken: *a fast-food restaurant.*

fas·tid·i·ous (fas tid'ē əs) *adj.* exacting or particular, esp. in matters of taste; difficult to please or satisfy: *a woman who is fastidious about her clothes.* [Latin *fastīdiōsus* full of disgust, disdainful, from *fastīdium* loathing.] —**fas·tid'i·ous·ly,** *adv.* —**fas·tid'i·ous·ness,** *n.*

fast·ness (fast'nis) *n.* 1. quality or state of being securely fixed. 2. swiftness; rapidity. 3. secure place: *an impenetrable fastness.*

fat (fat) *n.* 1. any of a group of oily or greasy substances, white or yellow in color, found esp. in deposits in certain tissues of animals and some plants, for which they serve as reserve sources of energy. Fats constitute one of the three major food compounds, together with carbohydrates and proteins. 2. animal tissue consisting mainly of such a substance; adipose tissue. 3. fat or oil used in cooking: *bacon fat, to fry in deep fat.* 4. obesity; corpulence. 5. best or richest part of anything; luxury. 6. *Chemistry.* any of a class of organic compounds, such as olein, formed by the reaction of fatty acids and glycerol. 7. **The fat is in the fire.** a. something has been started that cannot be stopped. b. something has been done to make matters worse. 8. **to chew the fat.** to talk or chat, usually at leisure. —*adj.* **fat·ter, fat·test.** 1. having excess flesh or fat; obese; plump: *a fat man, a fat turkey.* 2. containing much fat, oil, or grease; fatty: *fat cheese, fat gravy.* 3. containing much; full; abundant: *a fat wallet, a fat letter.* 4. profitable; lucrative: *That fat job pays well.* 5. gross; stupid. —*v.t., v.i.* **fat·ted, fat·ting.** to fatten. [Old English *fætt* plump, obese, fatty.] —**fat'ly,** *adv.* —**fat'ness,** *n.* —**Syn.** *adj.* 1. **Fat, stout, portly** indicate a body of more than usual bulk or thickness. **Fat** implies fullness, whether slight or great, not coming from muscular development, and is often derogatory: *Who ever hears of fat men heading a riot, or herding together in turbulent mobs* (Irving, 1809). **Stout** suggests a squared effect coming from more than usual girth: *The gentleman was middle-aged and stout.* **Portly** implies, in addition, impressive dignity and stately bearing: *The judge was portly.*

fa·tal (fāt'əl) *adj.* 1. causing death; lethal: *a fatal heart attack.* 2. causing destruction or harm; disastrous: *a fatal mistake.* 3. extremely important or decisive; fateful: *the fatal hour.* 4. influencing or controlling man's fate. [Latin *fātālis* destined, deadly, from *fātum* oracle, destiny.] —**Syn.** 1. see **deadly.**

fa·tal·ism (fāt'əl iz'əm) *n.* 1. doctrine that all events and conditions are predetermined by fate and cannot be altered by man. 2. acceptance of all events and conditions as inevitable; submission to fate. —**fa'tal·ist,** *n.* —**fa'tal·is'tic,** *adj.* —**fa'tal·is'ti·cal·ly,** *adv.*

fa·tal·i·ty (fā tal'ə tē, fə-) *n., pl.* **-ties.** 1. death resulting from a disaster; fatal accident: *highway fatalities.* 2. capability of causing death; deadly effect: *the fatality of some diseases.* 3. quality or condition of being predetermined or influenced by fate. 4. predetermined liability to disaster or danger. 5. fate or destiny.

fa·tal·ly (fāt'əl ē) *adv.* 1. so as to cause death or disaster; mortally: *to be fatally ill.* 2. as determined by fate; inevitably.

fa·ta mor·ga·na (fä'tə môr gä'nə) mirage, esp. the one seen in the Strait of Messina between Italy and Sicily. [Italian *fata Morgana* Mor-

gan le Fay, going back to Late Latin *fāta* fairy (see FAIRY) + Greek *margarítēs* pearl; because her magic power was once believed to cause mirages.]

fat·back (fat'bak') *n.* fatty strip from the back of a hog, usually salted and dried.

fat cat *Slang.* 1. one who is wealthy, esp. one expected to make substantial contributions to a political party or campaign. 2. one who receives special privileges.

fate (fāt) *n.* 1. power that is believed to predetermine events and over which man has no control. 2. that which is believed to be caused by fate; inescapable lot or fortune: *It was his fate to die young.* 3. final state; outcome: *the fate of an appeal to a higher court.* 4. doom; death; disaster. —*v.t.* **fat·ed, fat·ing.** to predetermine. ▲ now used only in the passive: *The team was fated to win.* [Latin *fātum* oracle, destiny; literally, what is spoken, from *fārī* to speak.] —**Syn.** *n.* 1. **Fate, destiny, lot** indicate what is ordained or predetermined in one's life. **Fate** implies a supernatural power guiding one to an inevitable end: *When fate summons, monarchs must obey* (Dryden, 1682). **Destiny** stresses the concept of predetermination: *A consistent man believes in destiny, a capricious man in chance* (Disraeli, 1826). **Lot** suggests the portion or share that man draws by chance for his life: *She believes it is her lot in life to be an old drudge.*

fat·ed (fā'tid) *adj.* 1. predetermined by fate; destined. 2. destined to disaster; doomed.

fate·ful (fāt'fəl) *adj.* 1. of great consequence; decisive; momentous: *a fateful battle.* 2. prophetic; portentous: *a fateful prediction.* 3. controlled or influenced by fate. 4. causing death or disaster; deadly. —**fate'ful·ly,** *adv.* —**fate'ful·ness,** *n.*

Fates (fāts) *n.,pl. Classical Mythology.* Clotho, Lachesis, and Atropos, the three goddesses who controlled human life and destiny. Also, **fatal sisters.**

fat·head (fat'hed') *n. Informal.* stupid person; fool; blockhead. —**fat'head'ed,** *adj.*

fa·ther (fä'thər) *n.* 1. male parent. 2. man who acts or is regarded as a male parent; guardian or provider. 3. man who originates, invents, or founds something: *Gutenberg was the father of printing.* 4. *also,* **Father.** ecclesiastical title of respect used with or without a name to address a priest or another clergyman. 5. **Father. a. God. b.** the first person of the Trinity. 6. male ancestor; forefather. 7. one of the leaders or elders, as of a city or assembly. ▲ usually used in the plural: *the city fathers.* 8. senator in ancient Rome. 9. **Fathers of the Church.** leaders of the early Christian Church whose writings on Church doctrines and teachings are considered authoritative. Also (def. 9), **Church Fathers.** —*v.t.* 1. to be the father of. 2. to act as a father toward: *to father an orphan.* 3. to originate, invent, or establish. 4. to acknowledge or represent oneself as the father or author of. [Old English *fæder* male parent, forefather, God.]

father confessor 1. priest who hears confession. 2. someone in whom one confides.

fa·ther·hood (fä'thər hood') *n.* state of being a father.

fa·ther-in-law (fä'thər in lô') *pl.,* **fa·thers-in-law.** *n.* father of one's husband or wife.

fa·ther·land (fä'thər land') *n.* country in which a person or his ancestors were born.

fa·ther·less (fä'thər lis) *adj.* 1. having no living father. 2. lacking a father's support or recognition.

fa·ther·ly (fä'thər lē) *adj.* 1. of, relating to, or characteristic of a father: *fatherly advice.* 2. like a father in behavior or attitude: *a fatherly uncle.* —*adv.* in a fatherly manner. —**fa'ther·li·ness,** *n.*

Father's Day, day set aside in honor of fathers, observed annually on the third Sunday in June.

fath·om (fath'əm) *pl.,* **fath·oms** or **fath·om.** *n.* unit of measure equal to six feet, used esp. in nautical measurements, as the depth of water. See **weights and measures** for table. —*v.t.* 1. to determine the depth of (water); sound. 2. to understand fully: *He could not fathom the seer's remark.* [Old English *fæthm* length of the outstretched arms, grasp.] —**fath'om·a·ble,** *adj.*

fath·om·less (fath'əm lis) *adj.* 1. of immeasurable depth. 2. unable to be fully understood; incomprehensible.

fa·tid·ic (fā tid'ik, fə-) *adj.* of or relating to prophecy; prophetic. Also, **fa·tid'i·cal.** [Latin *fātidicus.*]

fa·tigue (fə tēg') *n.* 1. loss of strength resulting from physical or mental exertion; weariness; exhaustion. 2. cause of such weariness; toil; exertion: *the fatigues of an election campaign.* 3. weakening of a material, esp. metal, caused by continued use or excessive strain. 4. condition of decreased response or functioning which occurs when a muscle has been repeatedly contracted without rest. 5. manual or general labor performed by military personnel, as cleaning the grounds or doing other maintenance work. Also, **fatigue duty.** 6. **fatigues.** heavy-duty, two-piece uniform worn by military personnel when in the field or performing work details. Also, **fatigue clothes.** —*v.t.* 1. to cause weariness in;

tire out. **2.** to weaken, as metal, by continued use or excessive strain. [French *fatigue* weariness, from Old French *fatiguer* to weary, from Latin *fatigāre*.]
Syn. *v.t.* **1. Fatigue, tire¹, exhaust** indicate decrease or loss of energy or power. **Fatigue** implies almost complete depletion of strength as a result of normal activity: *She's so easily fatigued since her illness.* **Tire** suggests gradual disappearance of strength, alertness, or the like: *Watching TV for three hours tired his eyes.* **Exhaust** implies thorough draining of energy as a result of extraordinary effort: *The explorers were exhausted by their long trek through the desert.*
fat·ling (fat′ling) *n.* young animal fattened for slaughter.
fat·ten (fat′ən) *v.t.* **1.** to make fat or plump; fill out. **2.** to enrich or make more substantial. —*v.i.* to grow or become fat. —**fat′ten·er,** *n.*
fat·ty (fat′ē) *-ti·er, -ti·est. adj.* **1.** made or containing fat, esp. in large amounts. **2.** resembling fat; greasy. —**fat′ti·ness,** *n.*
fatty acid, any of several hydrocarbon compounds consisting of a long chain of carbon atoms with an acid group, —COOH, at one end.
fa·tu·i·ty (fə tōō′ə tē, -tū′-) *pl.* **-ties.** *n.* **1.** smug stupidity or foolishness. **2.** that which is fatuous, as an action or statement. [Latin *fatuitās* foolishness.]
fat·u·ous (fach′ōō əs) *adj.* smugly stupid or foolish; inane. [Latin *fatuus* foolish.] —**fat′u·ous·ly,** *adv.* —**fat′u·ous·ness,** *n.*
fau·bourg (fō′boor, -boorg) *n.* **1.** suburb. **2.** district within a city. [French *faubourg* suburb, modification (influenced by French *faux* false, because a suburb was not regarded as a true city) of Old French *forsbourc* literally, what is outside the town, going back to Latin *foris* outside + Late Latin *burgus* fortress; of Germanic origin.]
fau·ces (fô′sēz) *n.,pl.* cavity at the back of the mouth, opening into the pharynx. [Latin *faucēs.*]
fau·cet (fô′sit) *n.* device that regulates the flow of liquid from a pipe or container by means of a valve. [French *fausset* spigot, possibly from *fausser* to damage, falsify, going back to Latin *falsus* false, deceptive.]
faugh (fô) *interj.* expression of disgust. [Imitative.]
Faulk·ner, William (fôk′nər) 1897–1962, U.S. novelist and short-story writer.
fault (fôlt) *n.* **1.** something that impairs character, appearance, or structure; flaw: *The roof collapsed because of a fault in the beams. Jack's temper is not his only fault.* **2.** responsibility for a mistake or wrongdoing: *That error in subtraction is my fault.* **3.** mistake; error: *The faults in the manuscript have been corrected.* **4.** *Geology.* break in a rock mass.

Fault (def. 4)

The mass on one side of the break is displaced with respect to the mass on the other side. **5.a.** failure to serve the ball into the prescribed area of the court in tennis, squash, and similar games. **b.** ball served in this manner. **6.** *Hunting.* loss of the scent by the dogs. **7. at fault. a.** open to or deserving blame; wrong: *The boys are not at fault in this case.* **b.** at a loss; puzzled. **c.** (of hunting dogs) off or unable to find the scent. **8. to a fault.** excessively; extremely: *to be generous to a fault.* **9. to find fault (with).** to look for and point out a fault; complain; criticize: *You are always finding fault. John's aunt seems to find fault with everything.* —*v.t.* **1.** to find fault with; blame. **2.** *Geology.* to cause or produce a fault in. —*v.i.* **1.** *Geology.* to develop a fault. **2.** *Archaic.* to commit an error; blunder. [Old French *faute* default, lack, gap, going back to Latin *fallere* to deceive.]
Syn. *n.* **1. Fault, failing, weakness** indicate a flaw or shortcoming, as in character. **Fault** suggests a lack of what is needed for perfection, not necessarily blameworthy or even significantly serious: *It is well that there is no one without a fault, for he would not have a friend in the world* (Hazlitt, 1823). **Failing** implies a falling short with no suggestion of blame or wrong: *One trait more remains to be noticed in the character of this remarkable man; that is, his bigotry, the failing of the age* (Prescott, 1843). **Weakness** suggests a shortcoming of limited scope, a minor defect: *Credulity is the man's weakness, but the child's strength* (Lamb, 1833).
fault·find·er (fôlt′fīn′dər) *n.* one who looks for and points out faults; one who criticizes excessively.
fault·find·ing (fôlt′fīn′ding) *n.* act of criticizing or pointing out faults. —*adj.* disposed to pointing out faults; critical.
fault·less (fôlt′lis) *adj.* without a fault; perfect. —**fault′less·ly,** *adv.* —**fault′less·ness,** *n.*
fault·y (fôl′tē) *fault·i·er, fault·i·est. adj.* having faults or defects. —**fault′i·ly,** *adv.* —**fault′i·ness,** *n.*
Syn. Faulty, defective, imperfect indicate something falling short of perfection. **Faulty** suggests that the flaw is apparent when the person or thing is active, in operation, or in motion: *The accident was caused by faulty brakes.* **Defective** implies the absence of something essential to proper action or the like: *He wore thick lenses to improve defective vision.* **Imperfect** suggests a lack that prevents complete efficiency

or ideal development: *The cylinder will continue to leak oil if the imperfect piston ring is not replaced.*
faun (fôn) *n. Roman Mythology.* a minor rural deity having the body of a man and the ears, horns, legs, and tail of a goat. It is identified with the Greek satyr. [Latin *Faunus.*]
fau·na (fô′nə) *pl.* **-nas** or **-nae** (-nē). *n.* animals characteristic of a particular region, time, or environment: *the fauna of the African plains.* Distinguished from **flora.** [Modern Latin *fauna,* from Late Latin *Fauna* rural goddess in Roman mythology.] —**fau′nal,** *adj.*
Faust (foust) *n. German Legend.* magician and philosopher who sold his soul to the devil in return for knowledge and power.
fauv·ism (fō′viz′əm) *n.* French art movement in the early 1900s that emphasized bold, violent colors and freely distorted forms. [French *fauvisme,* from *(les) fauves* (the) wild animals (from a critic's reference to the painters' bold style); of Germanic origin.] —**fauv′ist,** *n.*
faux pas (fō′pä′) *pl.,* **faux pas** (fō′päz′, -päz′). embarrassing mistake; blunder, esp. a social one. [French *faux pas* literally, false step, going back to Latin *falsus* deceptive + *passus* step.]
fa·vor (fā′vər) *also, British.* **fa·vour.** *n.* **1.** act of kindness or good will: *to ask a favor of a friend.* **2.** friendly regard; approval; liking: *The tutor looked on his pupil with favor.* **3.** excessive consideration or kindness; partiality: *Some colleges show favor toward the children of their alumni.* **4.** state or condition of being liked, highly regarded, or approved: *a politician in favor with the people.* **5.** something given, as a souvenir at a party, as a token of affection; gift. **6.** state of being ahead of one's opponent in a contest: *The score is 12 to 6, our favor.* ▲ usually used with a possessive to indicate the side that is ahead. **7.** *Archaic.* letter, esp. a business letter. **8. in favor of. a.** in support of; advocating: *The students were in favor of reform.* **b.** to the advantage of: *The jury decided in favor of the defendant.* **c.** payable to, as a check. **9. in (one's) favor.** to (one's) advantage or interest: *A high-school diploma is in your favor when applying for a job.* **10. to find favor.** to be regarded with approval; become accepted: *a plan that found favor with the mayor.* —*v.t.* **1.** to show favor to; oblige: *Favor us with a reply.* **2.** to approve of; like: *to favor long hair.* **3.** to show special consideration for; be partial to: *to favor one son over another, a state legislature that favors rural areas.* **4.** to endorse; support: *The facts favored Tom's theory rather than Jim's.* **5.** to prove advantageous to; facilitate; assist: *Crowded conditions favor the spread of disease.* **6.** to treat with gentleness; spare: *to favor a sprained ankle.* **7.** to resemble in facial features; look like: *Harold favors his father's side of the family.* [Old French *favor* kindness, partiality, support, from Latin *favor* good will, partiality.]
fa·vor·a·ble (fā′vər ə bəl) *also, British.* **fa·vour·a·ble.** *adj.* **1.** approving; complimentary: *That movie received a favorable review.* **2.** in one's favor; advantageous: *favorable conditions for sailing, a favorable impression.* **3.** granting something desired or requested; affirmative: *a favorable reply.* **4.** promising; optimistic: *a favorable diagnosis.* —**fa′vor·a·ble·ness,** *n.* —**fa′vor·a·bly,** *adv.*
Syn. 4. Favorable, auspicious, promising mean likely to come out well. **Favorable** indicates that everyone and everything involved seem to cooperate toward a happy result: *All the polls point to a favorable response from the voters.* **Auspicious** suggests particular signs pointing to a good outcome: *His quick checkmating of Jones was an auspicious beginning in the chess tournament.* **Promising** implies that something has happened that points to good or better things to come: *For a man new to politics, he has begun a career that is most promising.*
fa·vored (fā′vərd) *also, British.* **fa·voured.** *adj.* **1.** regarded or treated with favor or partiality: *a favored child.* **2.** endowed with special advantages or superior qualities: *a favored group of musicians.* **3.** having a certain kind of appearance or features. ▲ used in combination, as in *ill-favored, well-favored.*
fa·vor·ite (fā′vər it) *also, British.* **fa·vour·ite.** *adj.* regarded with special liking or favor; preferred: *a favorite baseball team.* —*n.* **1.** one who or that which is preferred or liked best: *Mystery stories are my favorites.* **2.** one who is treated with partiality by a superior. **3.** in a contest, the competitor considered most likely to win. [Obsolete French *favorit* favored, from Italian *favorito,* past participle of *favorire* to favor, going back to Latin *favor* good will.]
favorite son, political leader nominated as a presidential candidate by the delegates of his state at a national nominating convention.
fa·vor·it·ism (fā′vər i tiz′əm) *also, British.* **fa·vour·it·ism.** *n.* **1.** show of special favor toward one or more persons to the neglect of others; partiality. **2.** state promoting the interests of one.
Fawkes, Guy (fôks) 1570–1606, English conspirator.
fawn¹ (fôn) *n.* **1.** deer less than one year old. **2.** light yellowish-brown

Fawn

color. [Old French *faon* young deer, going back to Latin *fētus* offspring.]

fawn² (fôn) *v.i.* **1.** to seek notice or favor by acting in a servile manner; be obsequious: *People fawned on the politician.* **2.** (of dogs) to show affection, as by wagging the tail. [Middle English *faunen* to show fondness as a dog does, to show fondness servilely, from Old English *fagnian* to rejoice.] —**fawn′er,** *n.* —**fawn′ing·ly,** *adv.*

fay¹ (fā) *n.* fairy.

fay² (fā) *n. Archaic.* faith.

Fay·ette·ville (fā′it vil′) *n.* city in south-central North Carolina. Pop. (1970), 53,510.

faze (fāz) *fazed, faz·ing. v.t. Informal.* to disrupt the composure of; disconcert: *Nothing fazes him.* [Form of obsolete *feeze* to drive away, worry, from Old French *fēsian* to drive away.]

FBI, Federal Bureau of Investigation.

FCC, Federal Communications Commission.

F clef, bass clef in music. See **clef** for illustration.

Fe, iron. [Latin *ferrum.*]

fe·al·ty (fē′əl tē) *pl.* **-ties.** *n.* **1.** loyalty and duty owed by a vassal or feudal tenant to his lord. **2.** *Archaic.* faithfulness; loyalty. [Old French *fealte* fidelity, from Latin *fidēlitās* faithfulness. Doublet of FIDELITY.]

fear (fēr) *n.* **1.** apprehensive and agitated feeling caused by the awareness or expectation of danger, pain, or evil; dread: *to tremble with fear at the sight of a gunman. Flash floods sent fear through the village.* **2.** state of feeling this emotion: *to live in fear.* **3.** feeling of concern or anxiety; solicitude: *the fear that a sick dog will not recover.* **4.** cause for fear or alarm; danger: *There was no fear of his failing the exam.* **5.** awe or reverence, esp. toward God. **6. for fear of.** in order to avoid or prevent: *We left early for fear of missing the last train home.* **7. for fear that** (or lest). in case: *She hid her jewelry for fear that it would be stolen while she was away.* —*v.t.* **1.** to regard with fear; be afraid of; dread: *Many children fear the dark.* **2.** to feel concerned or anxious about: *I fear that we will be late for the show.* **3.** to feel awe or reverence for: *to fear God.* —*v.i.* **1.** to feel fear; be afraid. **2.** to be concerned or anxious; have misgivings: *to fear for one's safety.* [Old English *fǣr* danger, panic.]

Syn. *n.* **1. Fear, fright, dread** indicate the emotional confusion that seizes a person when facing danger. **Fear** suggests a state of extreme apprehension, usually where courage has fled: *His fear of high places kept him away from the windows.* **Fright** suggests sudden and immediate fear: *His fright as he lost his footing was almost comical to behold.* **Dread** implies the feeling that something dangerous or disagreeable, often undefined, will occur: *The dread of being assaulted kept him from leaving his room after dark.*

fear·ful (fēr′fəl) *adj.* **1.** feeling fear; afraid; apprehensive: *a child fearful of a barking dog.* **2.** causing fear; dreadful; frightening: *Those were fearful years.* **3.** showing fear; produced by fear: *a fearful look.* **4.** *Informal.* very bad; appalling; offensive: *fearful manners.* —**fear′ful·ly,** *adv.* —**fear′ful·ness,** *n.*

fear·less (fēr′lis) *adj.* without fear; intrepid; brave. —**fear′less·ly,** *adv.* —**fear′less·ness,** *n.*

Syn. Fearless, intrepid mean showing no fear when faced with danger. **Fearless** explicitly stresses freedom from fear: *a fearless bullfighter.* **Intrepid** connotes fortitude in the face of hardship or the unknown: *an intrepid explorer of the Arctic.*

fear·some (fēr′səm) *adj.* **1.** causing or instilling fear; frightening. **2.** feeling fear; frightened; apprehensive. —**fear′some·ly,** *adv.* —**fear′some·ness,** *n.*

fea·sance (fē′zəns) *n. Law.* performance, as of a duty or condition.

fea·si·ble (fē′zə bəl) *adj.* **1.** capable of being done or carried out; practicable: *a feasible design for a bridge, a feasible system of defense.* **2.** capable of being used successfully; suitable: *a feasible site for a dam.* **3.** likely; probable: *a hasty but feasible explanation.* [Old French *faisible* capable of being done, from *fais-,* a stem of *faire* to do, make, from Latin *facere.*] —**fea′si·bil′i·ty, fea′si·ble·ness,** *n.* —**fea′si·bly,** *adv.* —**Syn.** **1.** see **characteristic.**

feast (fēst) *n.* **1.** elaborate and lavish meal, esp. one prepared for many guests on a special occasion. **2.** periodic celebration or time of celebration commemorating a religious occasion, other event, or person. **3.** something that provides great pleasure; treat: *Snow-capped mountains and alpine flowers are a feast for anyone's eyes.* —*v.t.* **1.** to provide great pleasure for. **2.** to provide a feast for; entertain lavishly. —*v.i.* **1.** to have or partake of a feast; eat lavishly. [Old French *feste* festival, going back to Latin *fēsta* festivals.]

Syn. *n.* **1. Feast, banquet** indicate a ceremonious and often elaborate meal for a number, usually a large number, of persons. **Feast** suggests observance of a celebration with unlimited food and drink: *Belshazzar the king made a great feast to a thousand of his lords* (Daniel 5:1). **Banquet** stresses the formality of the occasion: *A banquet was given by the city to honor the hero.*

feat (fēt) *n.* noteworthy act or deed, esp. one displaying exceptional skill or strength: *Climbing that mountain was quite a feat.* [Old French *fait* deed, exploit, from Latin *factum,* thing done, deed, from *facere* to do. Doublet of FACT.]

feath·er (feth′ər) *n.* **1.** one of the outgrowths from a bird's skin, consisting of a horny, tubular shaft with soft, flexible barbs on either side. **2.** something resembling a feather in appearance or lightness, as a fringe of hair on the leg of a dog or a feather-shaped flaw in a precious stone. **3.** pieces of feather or featherlike parts attached to the base of an arrow to guide its flight. **4.** kind; class; species: *literary quacks of every feather* (Carlyle, 1857). **5.** act of feathering an oar or propeller. **6.** *Archaic.* attire; dress: *I saw him in full clerical feather* (Thackeray, 1855). **7. feather in one's cap.** accomplishment to be proud of; praiseworthy act. **8. in fine (good, or high) feather.** in good condition or form, esp. in health or spirits: *Jim was in fine feather and kept us laughing for hours.* —*v.t.* **1.** to cover, line, or adorn with feathers. **2.** to supply with a feather or feathers: *to feather an arrow.* **3.** to turn (the blade of an oar) parallel to the water's surface after a stroke, keeping it in that position until the beginning of the next stroke. **4.** to bring (an airplane propeller blade) parallel to the line of flight in order to decrease wind resistance. **5. to feather one's nest.** to enrich oneself, esp. by taking advantage of a position of trust. —*v.i.* **1.** to grow feathers. **2.** to move, grow, or expand like feathers: *The ivy feathered over the edge of the wall.* [Old English *fether* plume.]

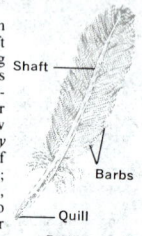

Shaft

Barbs

Quill

Feather

feather bed, soft, warm quilt or mattress filled with feathers.

feath·er·bed·ding (feth′ər bed′ing) *n.* the padding of a work force with more personnel than are necessary to do the work, esp. as practiced by labor unions to preserve jobs.

feath·er·brain (feth′ər brān′) *n.* flighty, weak-minded person. —**feath′er·brained′,** *adj.*

feath·er·edge (feth′ər ej′) *n.* very thin, often fragile edge, as of a tapered board. —**feath′er·edged′,** *adj.*

feath·er·stitch (feth′ər stich′) *n.* embroidery stitch that resembles small branches or feathers on a stem. —*v.i., v.t.* to embroider with this stitch.

Featherstitch

feath·er·weight (feth′ər wāt′) *n.* **1.a.** boxer competing in the second from the lowest weight class (118–126 lbs.). **b.** wrestler or weight lifter in a similar class. **2.** one who or that which is small or very light. **3.** one who or that which is insignificant. —*adj.* **1.** relating to featherweights. **2.** trivial; insignificant.

feath·er·y (feth′ər ē) *adj.* **1.** covered with or having feathers. **2.** resembling feather; light in weight; flimsy.

feat·ly (fēt′lē) *adv. Archaic.* properly; skillfully; neatly.

fea·ture (fē′chər) *n.* **1.** distinctive or prominent part or characteristic of something. **2.** part of the face, as the eyes, mouth, or chin. **3.** full-length motion picture, esp. one shown as a main attraction. **4.** anything presented as a main or special attraction, as an item specially priced for sale or a particular act in a variety show. **5.** story, article, or column of special interest, often appearing in a prominent place in a newspaper or magazine. —*v.t.,* **-tured, -tur·ing. 1.** to give a prominent place to: *The concert features a guitarist and singer.* **2.** to resemble in features; look like. **3.** *Slang.* to form a notion of; imagine: *I can't feature going there.* —*v.i.* to play an important part: *Local school issues featured prominently in the campaign.* [Old French *feture* fashion, form, from Latin *factūra* formation, a making.] —**Syn.** *n.* **1.** see **characteristic.**

fea·tured (fē′chərd) *adj.* **1.** presented as a special attraction: *a featured guest on a panel.* **2.** having a specified kind of facial features. ▲ used in combination, as in *a fine-featured woman.*

fea·ture·less (fē′chər lis) *adj.* having no distinctive or prominent features; uninteresting.

Feb., February.

feb·ri·fuge (feb′rə fūj′) *adj.* reducing or removing fever, as a medicine. —*n.* febrifuge medicine or agent. [French *fébrifuge,* from Latin *febris* fever + *fugāre* to drive away.]

fe·brile (fē′bril, feb′ril) *adj.* **1.** of, relating to, or causing fever. **2.** affected with fever; feverish. [Medieval Latin *febrilis* relating to fever, from Latin *febris* fever.]

Feb·ru·ar·y (feb′rōō er′ē, feb′rū-) *pl.* **-ar·ies.** *n.* second month of the year, containing twenty-eight days in regular years and twenty-nine days in leap years. [Latin *Februārius* month of purification; because *februa,* the Roman festival of purification, was observed on February 15.]

at; āpe; cär; end; mē; it; īce; hot; ōld; fôrk; wood; fōōl; oil; out; up; ūse; turn; sing; thin; this; zh in treasure; ə in ago, taken, pencil, lemon, circus.

fe·cal (fē′kəl) *also,* **fae·cal.** *adj.* of or relating to feces.
fe·ces (fē′sēz) *also,* **fae·ces.** *n.,pl.* waste matter discharged from the bowels; excrement. [Latin *faecēs,* plural of *faex* dregs.]
feck·less (fek′lis) *adj.* **1.** ineffective; weak; feeble. **2.** irresponsible; careless. [Scottish *feckless* ineffective, feeble, from *feck* (short for EFFECT) + -LESS.]
fe·cund (fē′kənd, fek′ənd) *adj.* fertile; fruitful; productive: *fecund earth, a fecund era in art.* [Latin *fēcundus.*] —**Syn.** see **fertile.**
fe·cun·date (fek′ən dāt′, fē′kən-) -**dat·ed, -dat·ing.** *v.t.* **1.** to fertilize; impregnate. **2.** to make fertile, fruitful, or productive.
fe·cun·di·ty (fi kun′də tē) *n.* quality or power of being fecund; fertility; fruitfulness; productiveness.
fed (fed) *v.* past tense and past participle of **feed.** —*adj.* **fed up.** *Informal.* disgusted, annoyed, or bored.
fed·er·al (fed′ər əl) *adj.* **1.** of, relating to, or formed by an agreement between states or other groups establishing a central governing body to control matters of common concern, with each of the individual states or groups maintaining control over its own internal affairs. **2.** *also,* **Federal.** of, relating to, or designating a central government formed in this way, esp. the central government of the United States as distinguished from the governments of the individual states. **3.** *Federal.* of, relating to, or supporting the Union during the American Civil War. **4.** *Federal.* of or relating to the Federalist Party. —*n.* **Federal.** one who supported the Union during the American Civil War, esp. a Union soldier. [Latin *foeder-,* stem of *foedus* league, treaty + -AL¹.]
Federal Bureau of Investigation, agency of the U.S. Department of Justice which investigates violations of federal law and subversive activities against the United States.
Federal Communications Commission, agency of the U.S. government that regulates wire, cable, and radio communications media.
fed·er·al·ism (fed′ər ə liz′əm) *n.* **1.a.** federal principle or system of government. **b.** advocacy of such a system of government. **2.** **Federalism.** principles of the Federalist Party.
fed·er·al·ist (fed′ər ə list) *n.* **1.** one who advocates a federal system of government. **2.** **Federalist.** member or supporter of the Federalist Party.
Federalist Party, political party in the United States, from 1788 to 1816, supporting the Constitution and advocating a strong central government. Its principal leader was Alexander Hamilton. Also, **Federal Party.**
fed·er·al·ize (fed′ər ə līz′) -**ized, -iz·ing.** *v.t.* **1.** to unite in a federal union. **2.** to place under the control of a federal government.
Federal Republic of Germany, West Germany.
Federal Reserve Bank, any of the twelve district banks belonging to the Federal Reserve System.
Federal Reserve Board, board that directs the Federal Reserve System, composed of seven members appointed by the president of the United States and confirmed by the Senate.
Federal Reserve System, central banking system of the United States, controlled by the federal government through the Federal Reserve Board and operated through a system of twelve Federal Reserve Banks which are privately owned by commercial banks and which regulate the member banks in their respective districts. It was established in 1913 by the Federal Reserve Act to stabilize the economy by regulating the flow of currency and credit in accordance with business practices.
fed·er·ate (*v.,* fed′ə rāt′; *adj.* fed′ər it) -**at·ed, -at·ing.** *v.t., v.i.* to unite in a federal union. —*adj.* united in a federation or alliance. [Latin *foederātus,* past participle of *foederāre* to establish by treaty, from *foedus* treaty.]
fed·er·a·tion (fed′ə rā′shən) *n.* **1.** act of federating; formation of a federal union by agreement between states, nations, or other groups. **2.** union so formed, esp. as a form of government: *a federation of Western nations to promote peace, a federation of labor unions.*
fed·er·a·tive (fed′ə rā′tiv) *adj.* of or relating to a federation or the formation of a federation.
fe·do·ra (fi dôr′ə) *n.* soft felt hat with a curved brim and a lengthwise crease in the crown. [Supposedly from *Fédora,* a play by Victorien Sardou, 1831–1908, French dramatist.]
fee (fē) *n.* **1.** charge or payment for a service or privilege: *an initiation fee, a registration fee.* **2.** *Archaic.* gratuity; tip: *a waiter's fee.* **3.** estate in land held from a feudal lord; fief. **4.** fee simple. [Anglo-Norman *fee* fief; of Germanic origin.]
fee·ble (fē′bəl) -**bler, -blest.** *adj.* **1.** lacking physical strength; weak; infirm: *a feeble old woman, a feeble body.* **2.** lacking force, durability, or effectiveness; inadequate: *a feeble cry, a feeble objection.* **3.** lacking intelligence or moral judgment: *a feeble mind.* [Anglo-Norman *feble* lacking strength, from Latin *flēbilis* lamentable, from *flēre* to weep.]
—**fee′ble·ness,** *n.* —**fee′bly,** *adv.*

fee·ble-mind·ed (fē′bəl mīn′did) *adj.* **1.** lacking normal intelligence; mentally deficient. **2.** not sensible; foolish; absurd: *a feebleminded plan.* **3.** *Archaic.* indecisive; irresolute. —**fee′ble-mind′ed·ly,** *adv.* —**fee′ble-mind′ed·ness,** *n.*
feed (fēd) **fed, feed·ing.** *v.t.* **1.** to give food or nourishment to; provide with food: *to feed an infant three times a day, to feed a weary traveler.* **2.** to provide as food or nourishment: *to feed grain to cattle.* **3.** to yield or serve as food or nourishment for: *Three acres of wheat will feed many people.* **4.** to provide with something that is used for the growth, maintenance, or operation of: *to feed a fire, to feed a computer. Melting snow from the mountains feeds the rivers each spring.* **5.** to supply (material to be used or consumed): *to feed data into a computer, to feed water into an engine.* **6.** to give satisfaction to; gratify: *to feed one's ego, to feed a woman's vanity.* **7.** *Sports.* **a.** to deliver (the ball or puck) to a teammate who is in a more favorable position. **b.** to deliver the ball or puck to (such a teammate). **8.** to provide (an actor) with cues or lines. —*v.i.* **1.** (of animals) to eat. **2.** **to feed on** (or **upon**). **a.** to consume, as food or nourishment; prey: *Vultures feed on dead animals.* **b.** to receive support or satisfaction from: *to feed on hope.* —*n.* **1.a.** food for animals; fodder. **b.** amount of such food given at one time. **2.a.** act or process of supplying material, as to a machine: *to slow up the feed of paper to the printing press.* **b.** material so supplied or used. **c.** mechanical part that supplies such material. **3.** *Informal.* meals; food. [Old English *fēdan* to feed, to nourish.]
feed·back (fēd′bak′) *n.* **1.** *Electronics.* the return of a portion of the output of a machine, system, or process to the input, esp. in order to correct, control, or modify the output. **2.** process by which a continuing action is controlled or corrected. When a person reaches to catch a ball, the feedback of information to his brain about the relative position of his hand and the ball enables the brain to guide his hand correctly.
feed·bag (fēd′bag′) *n.* bag that holds feed for a horse, fastened in place below the animal's mouth by straps wrapped around the head or muzzle. Also, **nose′bag′.**
feed·er (fē′dər) *n.* **1.** one who or that which supplies food or feeds material to a machine. **2.** anything that carries something or leads into a main line, such as a tributary, branch railroad, or side road leading into a highway. **3.** conductor that supplies electrical energy to some point in an electrical distribution system.
feel (fēl) **felt, feel·ing.** *v.t.* **1.** to perceive or examine by touching or handling; touch: *to feel the difference in the fabrics.* **2.** to be aware of through the sense of touch or a similar physical sensation: *to feel the cold, to feel the rain on one's face.* **3.** to be conscious of or affected by (an emotion): *to feel hope for the future.* **4.** to be aware of through an emotional or intellectual perception: *Not a word was spoken, but she could feel the hostility in the room.* **5.** to be moved or emotionally affected by: *He felt the loss deeply.* **6.** to hold as an opinion; believe: *Many people felt that the law was discriminatory.* **7.** to experience the impact of; suffer under: *to feel the full force of an attack.* **8.** to find (one's way) by or as by touching; grope: *The blind boy felt his way up the stairs. She had to feel her way for a while in her new job.* **9. to feel out.** to try to discover the attitudes of (someone) or the nature of (a situation) in a cautious and indirect way: *Let's feel out our parents and see if they'll let us go.* —*v.i.* **1.** to be aware of being in a specified condition or state of mind: *to feel uncertain, to feel fine.* **2.** to produce the sensation or feeling of being; seem: *The water feels warm. Today feels like spring.* **3.** to search or explore by touch; grope: *The doctor felt for broken bones.* **4.** to have sympathy or compassion (with *for*): *to feel for a crippled child.* **5.** to have or be capable of the sense of touch. **6. to feel like.** *Informal.* to have an inclination for; desire: *Maybe Tom feels like helping out.* **7. to feel (like) oneself.** to seem to be in one's usual good health or mood: *I don't feel like myself today—I'm so grouchy.* **8. to feel up to.** to feel capable of or ready for: *The swimmer does not feel up to racing today.* —*n.* **1.** quality of an object as perceived by touch: *the cold feel of snow.* **2.** perception of this quality by the sense of touch. **3.** sense of touch. **4.** general sensation or feeling: *to like the feel of a beach at sunset.* **5.** innate ability, appreciation, or understanding: *to have a feel for music.* [Old English *fēlan* to touch, perceive.] —**Syn.** *v.t.* **4.** see **experience.**
feel·er (fē′lər) *n.* **1.** organ of touch in an animal's body, esp. the antenna of an insect or crustacean. **2.** act, remark, or plan used to feel out a person or group: *After years of battle, a peace feeler was sent to the warring nations.*
feel·ing (fē′ling) *n.* **1.** capacity to perceive by touch; sense of touch: *He rubbed his numb foot to restore the feeling.* **2.** physical sensation perceived through or as through the sense of touch: *a feeling of dampness, a feeling of hunger.* **3.** emotion, as joy, fear, or anger: *a feeling of security.* **4.** awareness or consciousness; impression: *a feeling of security.* **5.** **feelings.** sensitivities; susceptibilities: *The criticism hurt his feelings.* **6.** capacity for emotion, esp. sympathy or compassion: *a man of deep feeling, to have great feeling for the afflicted.* **7.** opinion; sentiment: *It is my feeling that the bill should be passed.* **8.** foreboding; premonition: *I have a feeling that*

something is wrong. **9.** character or quality as perceived by the emotions or intellect; impression made on a person: *The big empty room had a cold feeling.* **10.** emotional quality or impression conveyed by a work of art or an artistic performance. **11.** appreciation and sensitivity: *a feeling for abstract art.* —*adj.* **1.** affected by emotion; sensitive. **2.** expressing emotion. —**feel′ing·ly,** *adv.*

Syn. 3. Feeling, emotion, passion mean mental reaction to a stimulus that does not physically affect the body. **Feeling** is the general term: *Since she often has to deal with people who have angry complaints, she has learned to disguise her real feelings.* **Emotion** suggests a strong and stirring feeling: *The director was so moved by the workers' tribute to her, she could hardly express the emotion she felt.* **Passion** implies a deep emotion so strong that it overmasters all other considerations: *In a passion of anger he struck the policeman.*

fee simple, estate in land, in which the owner has unconditional rights of disposition.

feet (fēt) plural of **foot.** —*n.* **1. on one's feet. a.** in a standing position: *A dentist is on his feet all day.* **b.** in a stable or secure position: *The new job put him back on his feet.* **c.** in a restored state of health: *to be back on one's feet after a long illness.* **2. to stand on one's own (two) feet,** to be independent.

fee tail, estate in land, in which inheritance is limited to a particular class of heirs.

feign (fān) *v.t.* **1.** to put on a false appearance of; pretend; simulate: *to feign sickness, to feign joy.* **2.** to invent, as a story or excuse, and assert as true; fabricate. —*v.i.* to make believe; pretend. [Old French *feign-,* a stem of *feindre* to simulate, dissemble, from Latin *fingere* to form, make.] —**Syn.** *v.t.* **1.** see **pretend.**

feint (fānt) *n.* **1.** deceptive blow or movement, esp. one used in boxing, fencing, or warfare to divert attention from the real point of attack. **2.** false appearance or show; pretense: *to make a feint of listening to someone.* —*v.i.* to make a deceptive blow or movement. [French *feinte* pretense, dissimulation, from *feindre* to simulate. See FEIGN.]

feld·spar (feld′spär′) *also,* **fel·spar.** *n.* any of a group of aluminum silicate minerals containing sodium, potassium, and calcium, used commercially in the manufacture of glass. [Modification of German *Feldspat* literally, field spar; influenced in form by SPAR¹.] —**feld·spath·ic** (feld spath′ik), *adj.*

fe·lic·i·tate (fi lis′ə tāt′) -**tat·ed, -tat·ing.** *v.t.* to wish happiness to; congratulate. [Late Latin *fēlīcitātus,* past participle of *fēlīcitāre* to make happy, from Latin *fēlīcitās* happiness.] —**Syn.** see **congratulate.**

fe·lic·i·ta·tion (fi lis′ə tā′shən) *n.* expression of pleasure over another's happiness or good fortune; congratulation. ▲ usually used in the plural.

fe·lic·i·tous (fi lis′ə təs) *adj.* **1.** well-chosen; appropriate; apt: *a felicitous reply.* **2.** being adept at appropriate and effective expression: *The congressman was an extremely felicitous speaker.* **3.** marked by happiness or good feeling: *a felicitous occasion.* —**fe·lic′i·tous·ly,** *adv.* —**fe·lic′i·tous·ness,** *n.*

fe·lic·i·ty (fi lis′ə tē) *pl.,* **-ties.** *n.* **1.** great happiness; bliss. **2.** particular instance of such happiness. **3.** source of happiness; blessing. **4.** adeptness at appropriate or graceful expression: *to write with felicity.* **5.** instance of such adeptness; appropriate expression. [Old French *felicite* happiness, from Latin *fēlīcitās.*] —**Syn. 1.** see **happiness.**

fe·line (fē′līn) *adj.* **1.** of or relating to cats or the cat family. **2.** resembling a cat, as in stealthiness or grace: *feline movements.* —*n.* animal belonging to the cat family, such as a lion, tiger, or leopard. [Latin *fēlīnus* relating to a cat, from *fēlēs* cat.]

fell¹ (fel) past tense of **fall.**

fell² (fel) *v.t.* **1.** to strike and knock down; cause to fall: *to fell an opponent, to fell a deer.* **2.** to cut down (a tree or trees). **3.** in sewing, to finish (a seam) by joining the edges, turning them under, and stitching them to the fabric. —*n.* **1.** timber cut down in one season. **2.** felled seam. [Old English *fellan* to cause to fall, cut down.] —**fell′er,** *n.*

fell³ (fel) *adj.* **1.** cruel; savage; dreadful. **2.** *Archaic.* intensely painful or destructive; deadly: *a fell poison.* [Old French *fel* cruel, fierce, from Medieval Latin *fello* villain; of uncertain origin.]

fell⁴ (fel) *n.* skin or hide of an animal; pelt. [Old English *fel(l).*]

fell⁵ (fel) *n. British.* tract of high wasteland; moor; down. [Old Norse *fjall* mountain, hill.]

fel·lah (fel′ə) *pl.,* **fel·la·hin** or **fel·la·heen** (fel′ə hēn′). *n.* peasant or laborer in Arabic-speaking countries. [Arabic *fellāh.*]

fel·loe (fel′ō) felly.

fel·low (fel′ō) *n.* **1.** man or boy: *What a clever fellow he is.* **2.** person in general; individual; anyone: *He won't give a fellow a chance.* **3.** companion; comrade; associate. **4.** *Informal.* beau; suitor; boyfriend. **5.** member of a learned society. **6.** graduate student who holds a fellowship at a university or college. **7.** one of a pair, as of shoes or gloves; mate; match. **8.** one who is equal to another in rank, character, or ability; peer: *That mathematician has no fellow in his field.* **9.** *Archaic.*

worthless or disreputable person. —*adj.* belonging to the same class or group; joined by a common interest, activity, or condition: *fellow workers, fellow Americans.* [Old English *fēolaga* partner, from Old Norse *fēlagi,* from *fē* cattle, money + *lag* a laying down.]

fellow feeling, sympathy; understanding.

fel·low·ship (fel′ō ship′) *n.* **1.** companionship; camaraderie; friendliness: *the warm fellowship between an older and younger brother.* **2.** sharing of beliefs, experiences, or other matters of common interest; mutual participation. **3.** group of people joined by common interests, beliefs, or goals; brotherhood; society. **4.** position or sum of money granted to a graduate student in a university or college to enable him to continue his studies: *a teaching fellowship, a fellowship in Asian studies.*

fellow traveler, nonmember who supports or sympathizes with the program of a group or political party, esp. the Communist Party.

fel·ly (fel′ē) *pl.,* **-lies.** *also,* **fel·loe.** *n.* rim or section of the rim of a wheel, into which the outer ends of the spokes are inserted. [Old English *felg.*]

fel·on¹ (fel′ən) *n.* one who has committed a felony. —*adj. Archaic.* wicked; cruel; malicious. [Old French *felon* villain, from Medieval Latin *fello;* of uncertain origin.]

fel·on² (fel′ən) *n.* deep and painful infection in a finger or toe, usually near the nail; whitlow. [Of uncertain origin.]

fe·lo·ni·ous (fə lō′nē əs) *adj.* **1.** of, relating to, or having the nature of a felony: *a felonious assault.* **2.** *Archaic.* malicious; villainous: *a felonious deed.* —**fe·lo′ni·ous·ly,** *adv.* —**fe·lo′ni·ous·ness,** *n.*

fel·o·ny (fel′ə nē) *pl.,* **-nies.** *n.* any of several crimes, as murder, rape, or burglary, designated by statute to be graver than a misdemeanor, commonly punishable in the United States by a minimum penalty of imprisonment in a penitentiary for at least a year and a maximum penalty of death.

fel·site (fel′sīt) *n.* light-colored, very fine-grained volcanic rock composed chiefly of quartz and feldspar. [FEL(SPAR) + -ITE¹.]

fel·spar (fel′spär) feldspar.

felt¹ (felt) past tense and past participle of **feel.**

felt² (felt) *n.* **1.** nonwoven fabric, usually composed of wool, hair, or fur, made by subjecting layers of fibers to heat, moisture, and pressure, which causes them to shrink and become firmly interlocked. It is used for such items as hats and table pads. **2.** any fabric resembling this. —*adj.* of or relating to felt. —*v.t.* **1.** to make into felt. **2.** to cover with felt. [Old English *felt* felt cloth.]

felt·ing (fel′ting) *n.* **1.** felted cloth; felt. **2.** process by which felt is made.

fe·luc·ca (fə luk′ə) *n.* long, narrow ship with oars or lateen sails, or both, used esp. along the Mediterranean coast. [Italian *feluca,* from Arabic *fulk* ship.]

fem., female; feminine.

fe·male (fē′māl) *adj.* **1.** of or relating to the sex that bears young or produces eggs. **2.** feminine *(def. 1).* **3.** of or relating to a plant that bears pistillate flowers. **4.** (of an object or device) having a hollowed part into which a corresponding part fits, as an electric socket. —*n.* female person, animal, or plant. [Old French *femelle* being of the female sex, from Latin *fēmella* young woman, diminutive of *fēmina* woman; Modern English spelling influenced by MALE.]

Syn. *n.* **Female, woman, lady** mean an adult human being not of the male sex. **Female** stresses the difference according to sex and is generally applicable to any age group from babyhood through old age, esp. in statistical or scientific usage: *Check the box marked male or female on the application.* **Woman** emphasizes the adult female human being as an individual: *She belonged to a group of women that did work for the church.* **Lady** suggests a woman of refinement, breeding, dignity: *Today I pronounced a word which should never come out of a lady's lips* (Fleming, c.1811).

fem·i·nine (fem′ə nin) *adj.* **1.** of, characteristic of, or relating to a woman: *feminine taste, feminine interests.* **2.** having characteristics regarded as womanly, as gentleness and delicateness. **3.** (of a man) effeminate; womanish. **4.** of or relating to the female sex. **5.** *Grammar.* of the gender that includes words applying to females or to things regarded as female. —*n. Grammar.* **1.** feminine gender. **2.** word or other element belonging to the feminine gender. [Latin *fēminīnus* of the feminine gender, from *fēmina* woman.]

feminine rhyme, rhyme of two words which terminate in an unaccented syllable or syllables, as *after* and *laughter* or *nourishing* and *flourishing.*

fem·i·nin·i·ty (fem′ə nin′ə tē) *n.* **1.** quality or state of being femi-

Felucca

at; āpe; cär; end; mē; it; īce; hot; ōld; fôrk; wood; fōōl; oil; out; up; ūse; turn; sing; thin; this; zh in treasure; ə in ago, taken, pencil, lemon, circus.

nine: *The modern woman is sometimes accused of lacking femininity.*
2. effeminacy; womanishness. **3.** *Archaic.* women collectively.

fem·i·nism (fem′ə niz′əm) *n.* **1.** doctrine advocating the same social, economic, and political rights for women as those granted to men. **2.** movement to secure such rights for women. —**fem′i·nis′tic,** *adj.*

fem·i·nist (fem′ə nist) *n.* one who believes in or supports feminism.

femme fa·tale (fem′ fə tal′ -täl′) *pl.,* **femmes fa·tales** (fem′ fə talz′, -tälz′). **1.** seductively attractive woman. [French *femme fatale,* going back to Latin *fēmina* woman + *fātālis* deadly. See FATAL.]

fem·o·ral (fem′ər əl) *adj.* of or relating to the femur or thigh. [Latin *femor-,* stem of *femur* thigh + -AL¹.]

fe·mur (fē′mər) *pl.,* **fe·murs** or **fem·o·ra** (fem′ər ə). *n.* long bone of the upper leg, extending from the pelvis to the knee; thighbone. See **tibia** for illustration. [Latin *femur* thigh.]

fen¹ (fen) *pl.,* **fen.** *n.* *British.* marshy lowland; swamp; bog. [Old English *fenn* marsh, mud.]

fen² (fun) *n.* in mainland China, monetary unit equal to one hundredth of a yuan. [Chinese (mandarin) *fen.*]

fence (fens) *n.* **1.** structure, often made of wire mesh or wood, used to bound, enclose, or protect an area; barrier: *a fence around a construction site.* **2.a.** one who receives and sells stolen goods. **b.** place where such goods are received and sold. **3. on the fence.** undecided about something; not committed to any side. **4. to mend one's fences.** to make amends in order to restore one's position or friendly relations. —*v.t.,* **fenced, fenc·ing. 1.** to surround with a fence or other enclosure (often with *in*): *to fence a garden, to fence in cattle.* **2.** to separate with a fence or other structure (often with *off*): *to fence the small dogs from the large ones, to fence off an area of the park.* **3.** *Archaic.* to defend; ward off. —*v.i.* **1.** to engage in the sport of fencing. **2.** to avoid answering directly; parry with words. **3.** to deal in stolen goods. [Short for DE-FENCE.]

fenc·er (fen′sər) *n.* **1.** one who engages in fencing with a foil, épée, or similar weapon. **2.** one who makes or repairs fences.

fenc·ing (fen′sing) *n.* **1.** art, act, or practice of using a foil, épée, or similar weapon in attack and defense. **2.** parrying of words or arguments, esp. to avoid answering directly. **3.** material used in making fences. **4.** fences collectively.

Fencing

fend (fend) *v.t.* **1.** to offer resistance; parry. **2. to fend for oneself.** to provide or shift for oneself: *The children can fend for themselves while you're gone.* —*v.t.* to ward off or keep away; repel (often with *off*): *to fend off an angry mob.* [Short for DEFEND.]

fend·er (fen′dər) *n.* **1.** one of the metal guards projecting over the wheels of an automobile, bicycle, or other vehicle to protect against splashed water or mud; mudguard. **2.** metal frame or screen placed in front of a fireplace to protect against escaping coals or sparks. **3.** metal frame projecting from the front of a locomotive or streetcar, used to push obstacles from the tracks; cowcatcher. **4.** any of various cushioning devices, as cork-filled pads or braids of rope, used on the side of a ship to prevent damage from chafing or impact when docking or lying alongside another vessel. [FEND + -ER¹.]

fen·es·tra·tion (fen′is trā′shən) *n.* arrangement of windows in a building. [Latin *fenestrātus,* past participle of *fenestrāre* to furnish with windows (going back to *fenestra* window) + -ION.]

Fe·ni·an (fē′nē ən, fēn′yən) *n.* **1.** member of an Irish secret society organized in New York in 1858 to promote Irish independence from Great Britain. **2.** *Irish Legend.* member of an ancient band of warriors, the subject of a cycle of tales. —*adj.* of or relating to the Fenians. [Blend of Old Irish *Féne,* the ancient inhabitants of Ireland, and Old Irish *Fiann,* a group of Irish heroes in the period of Finn, a legendary king of Ireland.]

fen·nec (fen′ik) *n.* fawn-colored fox, *Fennecus zerda,* of desert regions of northern Africa, having very long, broad ears. Length: 24 inches including tail. [Arabic *fanak.*]

fen·nel (fen′əl) *n.* **1.** aromatic seeds of a plant, *Foeniculum vulgare,* of the parsley family, which taste like licorice and are used as a flavoring in certain foods and liqueurs. **2.** the plant itself, widely cultivated for its seeds, bearing bright-green feathery leaves and clusters of yellow flowers. [Old English *finul, fenol* the plant, going back to Latin *fēniculum,* diminutive of *fēnum* hay.]

fen·ny (fen′ē) *adj.* **1.** having the characteristics of a fen; swampy. **2.** of or found in a fen.

feoff (fēf) *fief.*

fe·ral (fēr′əl) *adj.* **1.** not domesticated; wild; untamed. **2.** relating to

or characteristic of a wild beast; brutal; savage. [Latin *fera* wild beast + -AL¹.]

fer·de·lance (fer′dəl ans′, -äns′) *n.* extremely poisonous tropical American snake, *Bothrops atrox,* related to the rattlesnake. [French *fer de lance* literally, spearhead (with reference to its shape), iron of a spear, going back to Latin *ferrum* iron + *dē* from + *lancea* spear.]

Fer·di·nand I [Latin *ferminōn* and′) died 1065, emperor of Spain from 1056 to 1065; king of Castile and León from 1037 to 1065.

Ferdinand V, 1452–1516, Spanish king of Aragon who in 1469 married Queen Isabella I of Castile. They united all Spain under the rule of one monarchy and sponsored Columbus' voyages.

fer·ment (*v.,* fer ment′; *n.,* fur′ment) *v.i.* **1.** to undergo chemical fermentation. **2.** to be excited or agitated; seethe: *A plan fermented in his mind.* —*v.t.* **1.** to cause chemical fermentation in. **2.** to cause excitement in; agitate; stir up; foment: *Youth ferments your blood* (Pope, 1704). *Poverty helped to ferment the revolution.* —*n.* **1.** substance or agent causing chemical fermentation, as the enzymes secreted by yeast or certain bacteria. **2.** state of excitement, agitation, or unrest: *intellectual ferment.* [Latin *fermentum* leaven, from *fervēre* to boil; with reference to the bubbles formed in moistened dough causing it to rise, resembling the bubbles in boiling liquids.]

fer·men·ta·tion (fur′men tā′shən) *n.* **1.** chemical reaction or series of chemical reactions in carbohydrates that is caused by enzymes, resulting in the formation of bubbles of gas. Fermentation causes milk to turn sour and the juice of grapes to turn into wine. **2.** process of undergoing this reaction. **3.** excitement; agitation; unrest.

Fer·mi, En·ri·co (fur′mē; en rē′kō) 1901–54, Italian-American physicist who directed the building of the first nuclear reactor.

fer·mi·um (fur′mē əm) *n.* man-made radioactive element produced by bombarding a lighter element, such as plutonium, with neutrons. Symbol: **Fm** See **element** for table. [Modern Latin *fermium,* from Enrico *Fermi.*]

fern (furn) *n.* **1.** any of a large group of plants that constitute a major division, Filicophyta, of the plant kingdom. Ferns lack flowers, usually bear large feathery leaves, and generally reproduce in alternating sporophyte and gametophyte generations. **2.** large, feathery leaves of certain of these plants, widely used in flower arrangements. [Old English *fern.*]

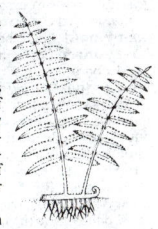

Fern

fern·er·y (fur′nər ē) *pl.,* **-er·ies.** *n.* **1.** place in which ferns are grown, as a case or stand. **2.** collection of growing ferns.

fern·y (fur′nē) *adj.* **1.** of or like ferns: *ferny frost on the windowpane.* **2.** abounding or overgrown with ferns: *the forest's ferny floor* (De la Mare, 1912).

fe·ro·cious (fə rō′shəs) *adj.* **1.** savage; cruel; fierce: *ferocious beasts.* **2.** *Informal.* very intense: *a ferocious headache.* [Latin *ferōc-,* stem of *ferōx* wild, fierce + -OUS.] —**fe·ro′cious·ly,** *adv.* —**fe·ro′cious·ness,** *n.* —**Syn. 1.** see **fierce.**

fe·roc·i·ty (fə ros′ə tē) *pl.,* **-ties.** *n.* state or quality of being ferocious; fierceness. [Latin *ferōcitās.*]

-ferous *suffix* containing; producing; bearing: *coniferous, carboniferous.* [Latin *-fer* bearing, producing (from *ferre* to bear) + -OUS.]

Fer·ra·ra (fə rär′ə) *n.* city in northeastern Italy. Pop. (1968 est.), 156,931.

fer·ret (fer′it) *n.* any of various weasel-like mammals, genus *Mustela,* of Europe, Asia, and North America, usually having yellowish-white fur and pink eyes, esp. a domesticated variety, *M. putorius furo,* used by hunters to flush game from burrows. Length: to 2 feet including tail. —*v.t.*

Ferret

1. to hunt (game) with a ferret; drive out of hiding, as in hunting with a ferret: *to ferret rabbits.* **2.** to search out; bring to light (with *out*): *to ferret out the facts.* —*v.i.* **1.** to hunt with ferrets: *to ferret for rabbits.* **2.** to search: *He ferreted through old bookshops to find rare books.* [Old French *furet* the animal, going back to Latin *fūr* thief.]

fer·ric (fer′ik) *adj.* of or containing iron, esp. in the higher oxidation state. [Late *ferrum* iron + -IC.]

ferric oxide, dark-red compound of iron in its higher oxidation state and oxygen, used esp. in pigments and in recording tapes. Formula: Fe_2O_3

Fer·ris wheel (fer′is) large, upright, revolving wheel with seats hung at regular intervals within its rim, used as an amusement ride. [From G. W. G. *Ferris,* 1859–96, American engineer who invented it.]

ferro- *combining form* relating to, containing, or derived from iron: *ferrochromium.* [Latin *ferrum* iron.]

at; āpe; cär; end; mē; it; īce; hot; ōld; fôrk; wood; fō͞od; oil; out; up; ūse; turn; sing; thin; this; zh in treasure; ə in ago, taken, pencil, lemon, circus.

fer·ro·chro·mi·um (fer′ō krō′mē əm) *n.* alloy of iron and chromium used in making hard steel.

fer·ro·con·crete (fer′ō kon′krēt, -kon krēt′) *n.* reinforced concrete.

fer·ro·mag·net·ic (fer′ō mag net′ik) *adj.* of or relating to a substance, as iron or steel, that is able to become highly magnetic.

fer·ro·man·ga·nese (fer′ō mang′gə nēs′, -nēz′) *n.* alloy of iron, manganese, and varying amounts of carbon, used in making hard steel.

fer·rous (fer′əs) *adj.* of or containing iron, esp. in the lower oxidation state. [Latin *ferrum* iron + -OUS.]

fer·ru·gi·nous (fə rōō′jə nəs) *adj.* **1.** like or containing iron. **2.** rust-colored; reddish-brown. [Latin *ferrūginus* rusty, from *ferrūgō* rust, from *ferrum* iron.]

fer·rule (fer′əl, fer′ōōl) *also,* **fer·ule.** *n.* metal ring or cap put around the end of a shaft, as of a cane, tool handle, stem of a pipe, or umbrella, to give added strength or protect against splitting. [Modification (influenced by Latin *ferrum* iron) of earlier *verrel,* from Old French *virole,* from Latin *viriola* little bracelet, diminutive of *viriae* bracelets.]

fer·ry (fer′ē) *pl.,* **-ries.** *n.* **1.** boat or other craft used to convey people, vehicles, and goods over a designated route, esp. across a river or other narrow body of water. **2.** place of embarkation at either end of such a route: *They waited at the ferry for the boat to return.* **3.a.** service of conveying people, vehicles, and goods across a river or other body of water by boat: *The ferry has been terminated.* **b.** legal right to operate and collect toll for such service. **4.** system for delivery of airplanes by flying them to their destination. —*v.t.,* **-ried, -ry·ing. 1.** to convey across a narrow body of water by a boat or other craft: *They ferried the storm victims to the mainland.* **2.** to cross (a body of water) in a ferryboat: *to ferry the Mississippi.* **3.** to deliver (an airplane) by the ferry system. —*v.i.* to cross a body of water in a ferryboat. [Old English *ferian* to carry, convey.]

fer·ry·boat (fer′ē bōt′) *n.* boat used as a ferry.

fer·ry·man (fer′ē mən) *pl.,* **-men.** *n.* one who owns, operates, or works on a ferry.

fer·tile (furt′əl) *adj.* **1.** producing or capable of producing crops or vegetation abundantly: *fertile soil.* **2.** capable of reproducing; able to produce young, eggs, seeds, pollen, or the like. **3.** capable of developing into a new individual: *a fertile egg.* **4.** producing offspring abundantly; prolific. **5.** causing or aiding productiveness: *fertile rain.* **6.** mentally productive; inventive: *a fertile imagination.* [Latin *fertilis* fruitful, from *ferre* to bear′.] —**fer′tile·ly,** *adv.*

Syn. 1.,2. Fertile, fruitful, fecund indicate the ability to bear offspring or produce growth in profusion. **Fertile** suggests inherent conditions that promote life and growth: *From ancient times, the valley of the Nile has been made fertile by the river's floods.* **Fruitful** implies something that promotes growth or actually bears young itself: *The valleys to the north are more fruitful.* **Fecund** suggests prolific yield: *He spent years developing fecund citrus plants.*

Fertile Crescent, crescent-shaped region of fertile land extending from the eastern coast of the Mediterranean to the northern coast of the Persian Gulf, site of several early civilizations.

fer·til·i·ty (fər til′ə tē) *n.* state or quality of being fertile; fecundity; productiveness.

fer·ti·li·za·tion (furt′əl ī zā′shən) *n.* **1.** a fertilizing or being fertilized. **2.** *Biology.* the uniting of a sperm cell with an egg cell to form a cell that will develop into a new individual.

fer·ti·lize (furt′əl īz′) **-lized, -liz·ing.** *v.t.* **1.** to make fertile; render productive: *Rain fertilizes the soil.* **2.** to spread fertilizer, such as manure or nitrates, on (land). **3.** *Biology.* to make (an egg cell) capable of reproducing a new individual by fertilization. —**fer′ti·liz′a·ble,** *adj.*

fer·ti·liz·er (furt′əl ī′zər) *n.* **1.** any of a wide variety of substances added to the soil to promote the growth and yield of plants by ensuring that the proper kinds and amounts of nutritional elements, as nitrogen, potassium, and phosphorus are present. **2.** one who or that which fertilizes.

fer·ule[1] (fer′əl, -ōol) *n.* **1.** flat stick, as a ruler, used to punish school children by striking them, esp. on the hand. **2.** punishment; discipline. —*v.t.,* **-uled, -ul·ing.** to punish with a ferule. [Late Latin *ferula* rod.]

fer·ule[2] (fer′əl, -ōol) *n.* ferrule.

fer·ven·cy (fur′vən sē) *n.* great warmth or intensity of feeling; ardency, devotion, or zeal.

fer·vent (fur′vənt) *adj.* **1.** having or showing great warmth or intensity of feeling; ardent: *fervent prayers, fervent support of a political movement.* **2.** hot; burning; glowing: *fervent rays.* [Latin *fervēns,* present participle of *fervēre* to boil, glow.] —**fer′vent·ly,** *adv.* —**Syn. 1.** see **impassioned.**

fer·vid (fur′vid) *adj.* **1.** extremely fervent; intense; impassioned: *Fervid devotion to a cause sometimes leads to rash acts.* **2.** very hot; burning: *fervid heat.* [Latin *fervidus* burning, vehement.] —**fer′vid·ly,** *adv.* —**fer′vid·ness,** *n.*

fer·vor (fur′vər) *also,* **British, fer·vour.** *n.* **1.** great warmth or intensity of feeling; ardor: *moral fervor, patriotic fervor.* **2.** heat; warmth.

[Old French *fervor* ardor, from Latin *fervor* raging heat.] —**Syn. 1.** see **passion.**

Fes (fes) Fez.

fes·cue (fes′kū) *n.* **1.** any of a large group of grasses, genus *Festuca,* having long narrow leaves and often growing in dense tufts, found in temperate and cooler regions throughout the world. Most species are used for pasture, although some are cultivated as lawn grasses. **2.** small stick or straw formerly used to point out the letters in teaching children to read. [Old French *festu* straw, stalk[1], going back to Latin *festūca.*]

fess (fes) *also,* **fesse.** *n.* wide horizontal band forming the middle third of a heraldic shield. [Old French *fesse,* *faisse* band[2], strip[2], from Latin *fascia* band[2].]

fes·tal (fes′təl) *adj.* relating to or befitting a feast or holiday; joyous; convivial; festive. [Latin *festum* feast, holiday + -AL[1].]

fes·ter (fes′tər) *v.i.* **1.** to form pus. **2.** to become more virulent; rankle, as a feeling of resentment or irritation: *Rebellion festered in the provinces.* **3.** to putrefy; rot. —*v.t.* **1.** to cause pus to form in. —*n.* small sore that forms pus. [Old French *festre* ulcer, from Latin *fistula* tube, ulcer.]

Fess

fes·ti·val (fes′tə vəl) *n.* **1.** particular feast, holiday, or celebration, marked by special observances and recurring periodically, esp. annually: *a harvest festival, the festival of Pentecost.* **2.** any occasion for celebration: *a victory festival, a festival commemorating the fiftieth anniversary of the city's founding.* **3.** period or program of activities and cultural events such as performances and exhibitions: *a Shakespeare festival, a jazz festival.* **4.** merrymaking; conviviality: *a time of festival and mirth.* —*adj.* relating to or befitting a festival; festive: *festival crowds, a festival mood.* [Old French *festival* relating to a festival or holiday, going back to Latin *festum* feast, holiday.]

Festival of Lights, Hanukkah.

fes·tive (fes′tiv) *adj.* relating to or suitable for a festival; festal; gay: *It was a festive New Year's celebration.*

fes·tiv·i·ty (fes tiv′ə tē) *pl.,* **-ties.** *n.* **1.** rejoicing and gaiety, typical of a celebration or other joyous occasion. **2. festivities.** festive activities; merrymaking: *Costume balls and street processions are part of the Mardi Gras festivities in New Orleans.* **3.** festival.

fes·toon (fes tōōn′) *n.* **1.** ornamental string or chain of flowers, leaves, ribbons, or other decorative elements suspended in a curve between two points. **2.** carved, molded, or painted ornament resembling this. —*v.t.* **1.** to decorate with festoons: *The walls were festooned with crepe paper and flowers.* **2.** to arrange in festoons. **3.** to connect by festoons. [French *feston* garland, from Italian *festone* garland, festal ornament, going back to Latin *festum* feast, holiday, with reference to the use of garlands in celebrating holidays.]

fe·tal (fēt′əl) *also,* **foe·tal.** *adj.* of, relating to, or having the character of a fetus.

fetch (fech) *v.t.* **1.** to go after and bring back; come and take back; get: *to fetch a chair from another room.* **2.** to cause to come; succeed in bringing; draw forth; elicit: *to fetch tears, to fetch an answer.* **3.** to be sold for; bring, as a price: *The car should fetch at least $2000.* **4.a.** to draw or take in (a breath). **b.** to give forth with or as with effort, as a groan or sigh; heave. **5.** to deduce; infer. **6.** *Informal.* to attract; allure; interest. **7.** *Informal.* to give (a blow); strike: *He fetched him a blow on the head.* **8.** *Informal.* to come to; arrive at. —*v.i.* **1.** to go after or get something and bring it back. **2.** *Hunting.* (of dogs) to retrieve game. **3.** *Nautical.* (of ships) **a.** to move to a point or place. **b.** to swing around; veer: *The boat fetched into the wind.* **4. to fetch and carry.** to perform menial tasks or services. **5. to fetch up.** *Informal.* to come to or arrive at a particular point and stop: *The travelers fetched up at the inn.* —*n.* act of fetching. **2.** trick; dodge; artifice. [Old English *feccan* to bring, go and get.] —**Syn.** *v.t.* **1.** see **bring.**

fetch·ing (fech′ing) *adj.* *Informal.* attractive; alluring. —**fetch′ing·ly,** *adv.*

fete (fāt) *also,* **fête.** *n.* **1.** festival. **2.** elaborate function or entertainment, often held outdoors. —*v.t.* **fet·ed, fet·ing.** to entertain at or honor with a fete: *He was feted by all the local dignitaries.* [French *fête* holiday, festival, from Old French *feste* festival. See FEAST.]

fet·id (fet′id, fē′tid) *also,* **foet·id.** *adj.* having an offensive smell; stinking: *a fetid swamp.* [Latin *fetidus* stinking.] —**fet′id·ly,** *adv.* —**fet′id·ness,** *n.*

fet·ish (fet′ish, fē′tish) *also,* **fet·ich.** *n.* **1.** object believed to have magical or supernatural powers. **2.** anything to which excessive devotion, concern, or reverence is given: *He made a fetish of frugality.* **3.** *Psychology.* **a.** something that is an object of fetishism. **b.** fetishism. [French *fétiche* object having magic power, from Portuguese *feitiço* amulet used as a charm, sorcery, from Latin *facticius* artificial, made by art.]

fet·ish·ism (fet′i shiz′əm, fē′ti-) *also,* **fet·ich·ism.** *n.* **1.** belief in or devotion to fetishes. **2.** blind devotion to or excessive concern with

at; āpe; cär; end; mē; it; īce; hot; ōld; fôrk; wood; fōōl; oil; out; up; ūse; turn; sing; thin; this; zh in treasure; ə in ago, taken, pencil, lemon, circu-

something. **3.** *Psychology.* abnormal feeling of sexual excitement aroused by an inanimate object or by a part of the body not normally considered erotic, as the foot. —**fet′ish·ist;** *also,* **fet′ich·ist,** *n.*

fet·lock (fet′lok′) *n.* **1.** tuft of hair on the back part of the leg of a horse or similar animal, just above the hoof. **2.** part of the leg where this tuft grows. [Probably of Germanic origin.]

fe·tor (fē′tər) *n.* strong, offensive smell; stench. [Latin *fētor.*]

fet·ter (fet′ər) *n.* **1.** chain or shackle for the feet to restrain movement. **2. fetters.** anything that confines or restrains: *Artists have always rebelled against the fetters of convention.* —*v.t.* **1.** to bind with fetters; shackle: *The prisoners were fettered for the night.* **2.** to confine; restrain: *An educated person should not be fettered by prejudice.* [Old English *feter* chain for the feet.]

fet·tle (fet′əl) *n.* condition or state of the body and mind: *He is in fine fettle.* [Middle English *fetlen* to gird up, from Old English *fetel* belt, girdle.]

fe·tus (fē′təs) *pl.,* **-tus·es.** *also,* **foe·tus.** *n.* animal embryo in its later stages of development, esp. a developed human embryo. [Latin *fētus* offspring.]

feud[1] (fūd) *n.* **1.** bitter mutual hostility between families, tribes, or clans, usually lasting for generations and marked by violent clashes. **2.** lasting strife or hostility between individuals or groups: *a feud between two scholars.* **3.** quarrel; contention: *to have a feud with the government about taxes.* —*v.i.* to carry on a feud: *The actress is feuding with her co-star.* [Old French *fe(i)de* lasting hostility, from Old High German *fehida* quarrel, hatred.]

feud[2] *n.* fief. [Medieval Latin *feudum;* of Germanic origin.]

feu·dal (fūd′əl) *adj.* **1.** relating to or characteristic of feudalism: *feudal law.* **2.** of or relating to a fief: *feudal rights.* [Medieval Latin *feudalis* relating to a fief, from *feudum* fief. See FEUD[2].] —**feu′dal·ly,** *adv.*

feu·dal·ism (fūd′əl iz′əm) *n.* **1.** system of political and social organization prevalent in western Europe during the Middle Ages, based upon the relation between a lord who provided land and protection and a vassal who in return pledged military and certain other services to the lord. **2.** any of various similar political systems. —**feu′dal·is′tic,** *adj.*

feu·dal·i·ty (fū dal′ə tē) *pl.,* **-ties.** *n.* **1.** state or quality of being feudal. **2.** feudalism. **3.** feudal holding; fief.

feudal system, feudalism.

feu·da·to·ry (fū′də tôr′ē) *adj.* **1.** under feudal allegiance to a lord: *a feudatory noble.* **2.** (of land) held by feudal tenure. —*n. pl.,* **-ries. 1.** one holding land by feudal tenure; vassal. **2.** fief.

feud·ist[1] (fū′dist) *n.* one who engages in a feud. [FEUD[1] + -IST.]

feud·ist[2] *n.* writer or authority on feudal law. [FEUD[2] + -IST.]

fe·ver (fē′vər) *n.* **1.** a body temperature higher than normal. **2.** any of various diseases marked by higher than normal body temperature. **3.a.** state of intense emotion, as of excitement, anxiety, or restlessness: *a fever of anticipation.* **b.** strong but temporary enthusiasm. —*v.t.* to affect with or as with fever. [Old English *fēfor* abnormally high body temperature, from Latin *febris.*]

fe·ver·few (fē′vər fū′) *n.* bushy plant, *Chrysanthemum parthenium,* of the composite family, native to Europe and eastern North America, having daisylike flower heads and deeply lobed leaves with a strong acrid odor. [Old English *feferfuge,* from Latin *febrifugia* a plant that was said to alleviate fever, from *febris* fever + *fugāre* to drive away.]

fe·ver·ish (fē′vər ish) *adj.* **1.** having fever, esp. a slight degree of fever: *a feverish patient.* **2.** indicating or characteristic of fever: *feverish symptoms.* **3.** tending to cause fever. **4.** excited, agitated, or restless, as if from fever: *feverish joy. There was feverish activity in the barracks as the men prepared for the general's visit.* Also, **fe′ver·ous.** —**fe′ver·ish·ly,** *adv.* —**fe′ver·ish·ness,** *n.*

fe·ver·root (fē′vər rōot′, -root′) *n.* any of several coarse plants, genus *Triosteum,* of the honeysuckle family, found in northern temperate regions, having white, yellow, or purple flowers.

fever sore, cold sore. Also, **fever blister.**

few (fū) *adj.* not many: *Few people attended.* —*n.* **1.** not many persons or things; a small number: *Many are called, but few are chosen* (Matthew, 22:14). *He sold only a few of the papers.* **2. the few.** the minority: *The new tax law benefits the few at the expense of the many.* **3. quite a few.** *Informal.* a considerable number; a good many. [Old English *fēawe, fēa* not many.] —**few′ness,** *n.*

fey (fā) *adj.* **1.** seemingly under a spell; enchanted; possessed. **2.** having an unwordly attitude or manner; visionary. [Old English *fǣge* doomed to die.]

fez (fez) *pl.,* **fez·zes.** *n.* brimless felt cap, usually red, having a conical shape and a flat crown and ornamented with a tassel, worn esp. by men in the Middle East. [French *fez,* from Turkish *fez,* from *Fez,* where it was chiefly manufactured.]

Fez (fez) *also,* **Fes.** *n.* city in north-central Morocco. Population (1969), 280,000.

ff, fortissimo.

ff. 1. and the following (pages, lines, sections, or the like). **2.** folios.

FHA, Federal Housing Administration.

fi·an·cé (fē′än sā′, fē än′sä) *n.* man to whom a woman is engaged to be married. [French *fiancé,* originally past participle of *fiancer* to betroth, going back to Latin *fīdus* trusty, faithful.]

fi·an·cée (fē′än sā′, fē än′sā) *n.* woman to whom a man is engaged to be married. [French *fiancée,* feminine of *fiancé.*]

fi·as·co (fē as′kō) *pl.,* **-cos** *or* **-coes.** *n.* complete or humiliating failure. [Italian *fiasco* bottle, utter failure, from *(far) fiasco* (to make) a bottle, fail (sense development not explained), possibly from Late Latin *flascō* wine bottle; of Germanic origin.]

fi·at (fī′ət, -at) *n.* **1.** authoritative order or decree. **2.** authorization; sanction. [Latin *fiat* let it be done, from *fierī* to be done, become.]

fiat money, paper currency made legal tender by the decree of a government, but not based on or convertible into gold or silver.

fib (fib) *n.* a lie about something unimportant; trivial lie. —*v.i.,* **fibbed, fib·bing.** to tell a fib. [Possibly from obsolete *fible-fable* nonsense; repetition with vowel change of FABLE.] —**fib′ber,** *n.* —**Syn.** *n.* see **lie**[1].

fi·ber (fī′bər) *also, British,* **fi·bre.** *n.* **1.** any fine threadlike part of a substance; filament: *asbestos fiber, cotton fiber, nerve fiber.* **2.a.** substance composed of threadlike parts or filaments: *hemp fiber.* **b.** the filaments collectively. **3.** composition or structure of a filamentous substance; texture: *cloth of coarse fiber.* **4.** essential character, nature, or strength: *moral fiber, the fiber of an argument.* [French *fibre* thread, filament, from Latin *fibra.*]

fi·ber·board (fī′bər bôrd′) *n.* stiff sheet material made from processed cellulose fiber, particularly wood fiber, used for panels, partitions, or the like.

fi·ber·glass (fī′bər glas′) *also,* **fi·ber·glas.** *n.* durable nonflammable material of fine threads of glass, used for insulation, textiles, boat bodies, and many other purposes. Trademark: Fiberglas.

fi·bril (fī′bril) *n.* **1.** small or slender fiber. **2.** root hair. [Modern Latin *fibrilla,* diminutive of Latin *fibra* thread, filament.]

fi·bril·la·tion (fī′bri lā′shən) *n.* malfunction of the heart in which rapid erratic contractions of the individual muscle fibers replace the normal heartbeat.

fi·brin (fī′brin) *n.* fibrous, insoluble protein formed during the clotting of blood. [Latin *fibra* thread, filament + -IN[1].]

fi·brin·o·gen (fī brin′ə jen′) *n.* soluble protein in the blood plasma from which fibrin is formed. [FIBRIN + -GEN.]

fi·brin·ous (fī′bri nəs) *adj.* relating to or having the properties of fibrin.

fi·broid (fī′broid) *adj.* made up of or resembling fibers or fibrous tissue. —*n.* benign tumor made up of fibrous tissue.

fi·bro·sis (fī brō′sis) *n.* abnormal increase in the amount of fibrous tissue in an organ, part, or tissue. [Latin *fibra* thread, filament + -OSIS.]

fi·brous (fī′brəs) *adj.* made up of, having, or resembling fibers.

fi·bro·vas·cu·lar (fī′brō vas′kyə lər) *adj.* composed of fibers and ducts that convey a fluid, as sap: *the fibrovascular tissue of wood.*

fib·u·la (fib′yə lə) *pl.,* **-lae** (-lē) *or* **-las.** *n.* **1.** outer and more slender of the two bones of the human lower leg, extending from the knee to the ankle. **2.** similar bone in the hind leg of an animal. **3.** ornamental brooch or pin worn in ancient Greece and Rome. [Latin *fībula* clasp, buckle, brooch.] —**fib′u·lar,** *adj.*

-fic *suffix* (used to form adjectives) making; causing: *scientific, terrific.* [Latin *-ficus,* from *facere* to do, make.]

-fication *suffix* (used to form nouns) a making or causing: *falsification, purification.* [French *-fication,* from Latin *-ficātiō,* going back to *facere* to make, do.]

Fich·te, Jo·hann Gott·lieb (fiкн′tə; yō′hän got′lēp) 1762–1814, German philosopher.

fich·u (fish′ōō) *n.* triangular scarf or kerchief of lightweight material, as lace, formerly worn by women about the neck to cover the shoulders. [French *fichu,* from *ficher* to fix, fasten, going back to Latin *fīgere.*]

fick·le (fik′əl) *adj.* inconstant; changeable; capricious: *a fickle girl, fickle winds.* [Old English *ficol* deceitful, false.] —**fick′le·ness,** *n.*

Syn. Fickle, inconstant, capricious indicate changeability or instability, esp. emotionally or in matters of

Fez

Fichu

at; āpe; cär; end; mē; it; īce; hot; ōld; fôrk; wood; fōōl; oil; out; up; ūse; turn; sing; thin; this; zh in treasure; ə in ago, taken, pencil, lemon, circus.

379

trust. **Fickle** suggests a flaw of character, an ingrown inability to remain steady or true: *He proved to be fickle and invited someone else to the dance.* **Inconstant** implies a natural and perhaps basic tendency to change often: *Television audiences are inconstant in their tastes, changing their favorite programs from season to season.* **Capricious** suggests unpredictable change, esp. as dictated by whim: *She became bored quickly, but was capricious about what she wanted next.*

fic·tion (fĭk′shən) *n.* **1.** narrative literature, esp. prose works such as novels and short stories, dealing with partly or completely imaginary characters and events. **2.** something feigned, invented, or imagined, as a story, explanation, or statement: *to distinguish fact from fiction.* **3.** act of feigning or imagining; false conclusion: *It was a fiction of his mind that others were plotting against him.* **4.** *Law.* something assumed as fact that in reality may not be fact, as for argument's sake. [Latin *fictiō* a feigning, forming.]

fic·tion·al (fĭk′shən əl) *adj.* relating to or having the nature of fiction. —**fic′tion·al·ly,** *adv.*

fic·tion·al·ize (fĭk′shən əl īz′)-**ized, -iz·ing.** *v.t.* to make into fiction; give a fictional account of. —**fic′tion·al·i·za′tion,** *n.*

fic·ti·tious (fĭk tĭsh′əs) *adj.* **1.** not corresponding to fact; invented; imaginary: *fictitious claims.* **2.** assumed for deception; not genuine; false: *a fictitious excuse.* **3.** fictional: *Sherlock Holmes is a fictitious character.* [Latin *fictīcius* feigned, artificial.] —**fic·ti′tious·ly,** *adv.* —**fic·ti′tious·ness,** *n.*

fid (fĭd) *n.* **1.** square bar of wood or metal for supporting a topmast. **2.** conical pin of hard wood used to open the strands of rope in splicing. [Of uncertain origin.]

-fid *suffix* (used to form adjectives) split; cleft; lobed: *bifid.* [Latin *-fidus* divided, split, from *findere* to cleave, split.]

fid·dle (fĭd′əl) *n.* **1.** violin or other instrument of the violin family. ▲ now chiefly a familiar or jocular term. **2. fit as a fiddle,** in excellent health or physical condition. **3. to play second fiddle,** to take a minor or subordinate position. —*v.i.* **-dled, -dling. 1.** *Informal.* to play a fiddle. **2.** to make aimless or nervous movements, as with the fingers or hands; fidget: *She fiddled nervously with her pencil.* **3.** to act idly or frivolously; trifle: *He fiddled over his work and did not finish anything.* —*v.t.* **1.** *Informal.* to play (a tune) on a fiddle. **2.** to waste in an idle or frivolous way (often with *away*): *to fiddle away one's time.* [Old English *fithele* the instrument, probably from Medieval Latin *vitula,* possibly from Latin *vitulārī* to be joyful.]

fid·dle-de-dee (fĭd′əl dē dē′) *n., interj. Informal.* nonsense.

fid·dle-fad·dle (fĭd′əl fad′əl) *n., interj. Informal.* nonsense.

fid·dler (fĭd′lər) *n.* **1.** one who fiddles. **2.** fiddler crab.

fiddler crab, any of a widespread group of burrowing crabs, genus *Uca,* the male of which has one claw much larger than the other. [Possibly because it seems to hold the claw as a fiddle is held while being played.]

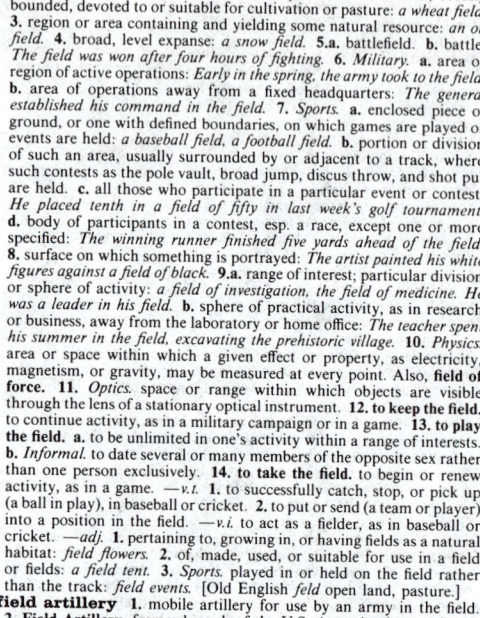
Fiddler crab

fid·dle·stick (fĭd′əl stik′) *n.* **1.** violin bow. **2.** something insignificant or absurd.

fid·dle·sticks (fĭd′əl stiks′) *interj. Informal.* nonsense.

fi·del·i·ty (fĭ del′ə tē, fī-) *pl.,* **-ties.** *n.* **1.** observance of or faithfulness to duties, obligations, or vows. **2.** steadfast loyalty. **3.** adherence to factual truth: *The novel was written with strict fidelity to historical facts.* **4.** accuracy of reproduction: *The translation was made with complete fidelity to the original.* **5.** degree of accuracy with which electronic devices, such as radios or recorders, reproduce original sound. [Latin *fidēlitās* faithfulness. Doublet of FEALTY.] —**Syn.** *see* **loyalty.**

fidg·et (fĭj′ĭt) *v.i.* to make restless movements; be nervous or uneasy: *The audience fidgeted in their seats.* —*v.t.* to cause to fidget; make restless or uneasy. —*n.* **1.** one who fidgets: *He is a terrible fidget.* **2. the fidgets,** state of being restless or of making nervous movements: *I had the fidgets all morning waiting for my interview.* [From dialectal English *fidge* to move restlessly; probably from Scandinavian origin.]

fidg·et·y (fĭj′ə tē) *adj.* restless; uneasy.

fi·du·ci·ar·y (fĭ dōō′shē er′ē, -dū′-) *adj.* **1.** of, relating to, or designating a trust, trustee, or trusteeship: *a fiduciary guardian, a fiduciary relationship.* **2.** held in trust: *a fiduciary estate.* **3.** depending upon public confidence for value or currency, as fiat money. —*n. pl.,* **-ar·ies.** trustee. [Latin *fīdūciārius* relating to a thing held in trust, from *fīducia* trust.]

fie (fī) *interj.* used to express shock or disapproval. ▲ now usually used humorously as a mild or pretended reproach. [Old French *fi,* possibly from Latin *fī* an expression of disgust at a bad smell.]

fief (fēf) *n.* **1.** land held by a vassal; estate held in feudal tenure. **2.** office and rights of a vassal holding land in feudal tenure. Also, **fee, feoff.** [Old French *fief* estate held in feudal tenure; of Germanic origin.]

field (fēld) *n.* **1.** piece of land, usually covered with vegetation and

having few or no trees or structures. **2.** piece of cleared land, usually bounded, devoted to or suitable for cultivation or pasture: *a wheat field.* **3.** region or area containing and yielding some natural resource: *an oil field.* **4.** broad, level expanse: *a snow field.* **5.a.** battlefield. **b.** battle: *The field was won after four hours of fighting.* **6.** *Military.* **a.** area or region of active operations: *Early in the spring, the army took to the field.* **b.** area of operations away from a fixed headquarters: *The general established his command in the field.* **7.** *Sports.* **a.** enclosed piece of ground, or one with defined boundaries, on which games are played or events are held: *a baseball field, a football field.* **b.** portion or division of such an area, usually surrounded by or adjacent to a track, where such contests as the pole vault, broad jump, discus throw, and shot put are held. **c.** all those who participate in a particular event or contest: *He placed tenth in a field of fifty in last week's golf tournament.* **d.** body of participants in a contest, esp. a race, except one or more specified: *The winning runner finished five yards ahead of the field.* **8.** surface on which something is portrayed: *The artist painted his white figures against a field of black.* **9.a.** range of interest; particular division or sphere of activity: *a field of investigation, the field of medicine. He was a leader in his field.* **b.** sphere of practical activity, as in research or business, away from the laboratory or home office: *The teacher spent his summer in the field, excavating the prehistoric village.* **10.** *Physics.* area or space within which a given effect or property, as electricity, magnetism, or gravity, may be measured at every point. Also, **field of force. 11.** *Optics.* space or range within which objects are visible through the lens of a stationary optical instrument. **12. to keep the field.** to continue activity, as in a military campaign or in a game. **13. to play the field. a.** to be unlimited in one's activity within a range of interests. **b.** *Informal.* to date several or many members of the opposite sex rather than one person exclusively. **14. to take the field.** to begin or renew activity, as in a game. —*v.t.* **1.** to successfully catch, stop, or pick up (a ball in play), in baseball or cricket. **2.** to put or send (a team or player) into a position in the field. —*v.i.* to act as a fielder, as in baseball or cricket. —*adj.* **1.** pertaining to, growing in, or having fields as a natural habitat: *field flowers.* **2.** of, made, used, or suitable for use in a field or fields: *a field tent.* **3.** *Sports.* played in or held on the field rather than the track: *field events.* [Old English *feld* open land, pasture.]

field artillery 1. mobile artillery for use by an army in the field. **2. Field Artillery.** former branch of the U.S. Army in charge of such weapons.

field corn, any of several varieties of corn used primarily for feeding livestock and for grinding into grain.

field day 1. day set aside for athletic contests, games, and races. **2.** day or time of unusual opportunity, as for fun: *The children had a field day when their parents went away for the weekend.*

field·er (fēl′dər) *n.* **1.** *Baseball.* any of the players in the field attempting to put out the side at bat, esp. an outfielder. **2.** any player with such defensive duties in softball, cricket, or similar ball games.

fielder's choice *Baseball.* play in which a fielder chooses to try to put out a base runner rather than the batter. If the batter reaches first base safely as a result of this, he is not credited with a hit.

field·fare (fēld′fâr′) *n.* thrush, *Turdus pilaris,* native to Europe and Asia, having a gray head, nape, and tail, brown back, black and rust breast, and white belly. Length: 10 inches. [Old English *feldefare* literally, field-traveler, from *feld* open land + *faran* to travel.]

field glasses, compact, portable binoculars, used esp. outdoors. Also, **field glass.**

field goal 1. *Football.* play in which the ball is place-kicked or drop-kicked from scrimmage over the crossbar and between the posts of the opponent's goal. It scores three points. **2.** *Basketball.* goal made while the ball is in play. It scores two points.

field gun, mobile artillery piece for field use. Also, **field′piece′.**

field hockey, game played on a grassy field by two teams of eleven players each, in which wooden sticks with curved ends are used to hit a ball along the ground, the object being to drive the ball into the opponent's goal.

field hospital, temporary hospital for emergency treatment close to a combat area.

field house 1. building used for indoor athletic events, as track and field or basketball. **2.** building near an athletic field, having dressing rooms, showers, and the like for the athletes, and facilities for storing sports equipment.

Field·ing, Henry (fēl′dĭng) 1707–54, English novelist.

field jacket, jacket designed to be worn by soldiers in the field.

field magnet, magnet used to produce and maintain a magnetic field, esp. in an electric motor or generator.

field marshal, officer of highest rank in the armies of some nations, such as Great Britain.

field mouse, any of various mice living in fields and meadows.

field officer, colonel, lieutenant colonel, or major; officer ranking below a general officer and above a company officer.

at; āpe; cär; end; mē; it; īce; hot; ōld; fôrk; wood; fōōl; oil; out; up; ūse; turn; sing; thin; this; zh in treasure; ə in ago, taken, pencil, lemon, circus.

field of fire, area which a weapon or a group of weapons can cover effectively with fire from a given position.
field of force, field *(def. 10)*.
field-piece (fēld′pēs′) *n.* field gun.
field-stone (fēld′stōn′) *n.* undressed stone, esp. when used as constructional material.
field trial 1. competition in which sporting dogs are judged on the basis of their performance in the field, under natural hunting conditions. **2.** actual use of a new machine, product, or the like, to test its performance, acceptance, or weaknesses. Also *(def. 2),* **field test.**
field trip, trip away from the classroom for direct observation and study, as to a museum or to examine plants or animals in their natural environment.
field winding, winding of a field magnet.
field-work (fēld′wurk′) *n.* temporary work or fortification erected by troops operating in the field.
field work, observation, investigation, and study done in the field, as by botanists, geologists, sociologists, or other scientists.
fiend (fēnd) *n.* **1.a.** evil spirit; devil; demon. **b. the Fiend.** the Devil; Satan. **2.** extremely wicked or cruel person. **3.** *Informal.* **a.** one who is much involved with or highly skilled in a particular field, interest, or activity: *a bridge fiend.* **b.** one who is addicted to a practice or habit, esp. an injurious one: *a dope fiend.* [Old English *fēond* enemy, devil.]
fiend·ish (fēn′dish) *adj.* extremely wicked or cruel; diabolic. —**fiend′ish·ly,** *adv.* —**fiend′ish·ness,** *n.*
fierce (fērs) **fierc·er, fierc·est.** *adj.* **1.** cruel or violent in nature or behavior; savage; ferocious: *a fierce bear.* **2.** violent in force or activity; raging: *a fierce storm, fierce fighting.* **3.** vehement; intense; ardent: *a fierce contest.* **4.** *Slang.* very bad; disagreeable: *a fierce headache.* [Old French *f(i)ers* wild, savage, from Latin *ferus.*] —**fierce′ly,** *adv.* —**fierce′ness,** *n.*
Syn. 1. Fierce, savage, ferocious indicate wild fury. **Fierce** implies wild, active attack with absence of restraint or any suggestion of care: *There was a short, fierce struggle.* **Savage** suggests lack of any moderating limitations on behavior, such as those civilization is supposed to impose: *His savage lashing of the horse led to immediate disqualification by the judges.* **Ferocious** implies the utmost in cruelty, savagery, and violence: *The ferocious animals, starved for days, charged into the arena.*
fier·y (fīr′ē, fī′ər ē) **fier·i·er, fier·i·est.** *adj.* **1.** containing or composed of fire; aflame; flaming: *a fiery furnace.* **2.** hot as fire; burning: *the fiery sun.* **3.** suggestive of fire; flashing; glowing: *fiery red, a fiery sunset, fiery eyes.* **4.a.** like fire in character or quality; ardent; impetuous; passionate: *a fiery speech.* **b.** excitable; fierce; irritable: *a fiery temper.* **5.** causing a burning sensation: *fiery whiskey.* **6.** easily set on fire; flammable. **7.** inflamed, as a sore. —**fier′i·ly,** *adv.* —**fier′i·ness,** *n.*
fi·es·ta (fē es′tə) *n.* **1.** religious festival, esp. saint's day as celebrated in Spain or Latin America. **2.** any festive celebration; holiday. [Spanish *fiesta* feast, festival, going back to Latin *fēsta* festivals.]
fife (fīf) *n.* shrill-toned musical instrument of the flute family, often used with drums in marching bands. —*v.t., v.i.* **fifed, fif·ing.** to play on a fife. [German *Pfeife* this instrument, pipe, going back to Latin *pīpāre* to chirp.] —**fif′er,** *n.*
fif·teen (fif′tēn′) *n.* **1.** the cardinal number that is five more than ten. **2.** symbol representing this number, as 15 or XV. **3.** something having this many units or members. [Old English *fīftyne.*]

Fife

fif·teenth (fif′tēnth′) *adj.* **1.** (the ordinal of fifteen) next after the fourteenth. **2.** being one of fifteen equal parts. —*n.* **1.** that which is next after the fourteenth. **2.** one of fifteen equal parts; 1/15.
fifth (fifth) *adj.* **1.** (the ordinal of five) next after the fourth. **2.** being one of five equal parts. —*n.* **1.** that which is next after the fourth. **2.** one of five equal parts; 1/5. **3.** one-fifth of a gallon, used as a measure of liquor. **4.** *Music.* **a.** tone, esp. the dominant, five diatonic degrees from a given tone. **b.** interval of five degrees between two tones of the diatonic scale. **c.** harmonic combination of two tones separated by this interval. —*adv.* in the fifth place.
Fifth Avenue, street in Manhattan, New York City, known for its shops, museums, and wealthy residential areas.
fifth column, group of persons within a country who sympathize with and secretly aid its enemies. [From a statement by Emilio Mola, 1887–1937, Spanish nationalist general, during the Spanish Civil War; he said that he was marching on Madrid with four columns and had a *fifth column* of sympathizers and agents within the city.]
fifth columnist, member of a fifth column.
fifth·ly (fifth′lē) *adv.* in the fifth place.

fifth wheel 1. horizontal ring placed over the front axle of a carriage or other vehicle to support the body during turns. **2.** spare wheel of a four-wheeled vehicle. **3.** *Informal.* unnecessary or superfluous person or thing.
fif·ti·eth (fif′tē ith) *adj.* **1.** (the ordinal of fifty) next after the forty-ninth. **2.** being one of fifty equal parts. —*n.* **1.** that which is next after forty-ninth. **2.** one of fifty equal parts; 1/50.
fif·ty (fif′tē) *pl.* **-ties.** *n.* **1.** the cardinal number that is five times ten. **2.** symbol representing this number, as 50 or L. **3.** something having this many units or members. **4. the fifties.** number series from fifty to fifty-nine. ▲ used esp. in reference to the fifth decade of a century or of a person's life. —*adj.* numbering five times ten. [Old English *fīftig.*]
fif·ty-fif·ty (fif′tē fif′tē) *adj. Informal.* **1.** sharing equally; equal: *a fifty-fifty division of the profits.* **2.** as likely to turn out one way as another; even: *The mission has a fifty-fifty chance of success.* —*adv.* equally: *to share fifty-fifty.*
fifty pence, coin of the United Kingdom equal to fifty pennies or half a pound.
fig¹ (fig) *n.* **1.** small, sweet edible fruit of a tree, *Ficus carica,* of the mulberry family, consisting of a fleshy sac containing many tiny seedlike structures. **2.** shrub or small tree bearing this fruit, grown mainly in the Mediterranean region and California. **3.** the merest trifle; least bit: *I don't care a fig for it.* [Old French *figue* the fruit, through Provençal, going back to Latin *fīcus* the fruit, the tree.]

Leaves
Fruit
Cross section

Fig¹

fig² (fig) *n. Informal.* **1.** dress; array: *in full fig.* **2.** condition; form: *in good fig.* [Of uncertain origin.]
fig. 1. figure; figures. **2.** figurative; figuratively.
fig·eat·er (fig′ē′tər) *n.* large, destructive green and red beetle, *Cotinis nitida,* that feeds on ripe fruit. Also, **June bug.**
fight (fīt) *n.* **1.** physical struggle between two opposing individuals or groups; battle; conflict: *There was a fight between the two gangs.* **2.** contest between two boxers; boxing match. **3.** dispute; quarrel: *They had a fight over the issue.* **4.** any struggle, esp. one to gain some objective or goal: *a fight for control of the government.* **5.** power or inclination to contest; pugnacity: *He had no fight left in him.* —*v.t.* **fought, fight·ing. 1.** to engage (someone) in physical struggle or combat: *The British fought the Americans in 1776.* **2.** to oppose in a boxing match: *The champion fought three opponents last year.* **3.** to struggle against or contend with in any manner: *He fought his desire to run from the scene. The ship fought the storm.* **4.** to carry on or wage (a battle, contest, or struggle): *The battle was fought on an open plain. The lawyer fought the case well.* **5.** to gain or make (one's way) by struggle: *He fought his way through the crowd.* **6.** to cause to fight; manage the fighting of. **6. to fight it out.** to fight until a decisive result is attained. **7. to fight off. a.** to repel by fighting: *The garrison fought off the attackers.* **b.** to struggle to get rid of or avoid: *to fight off a cold. The motorist fought off the effects of fatigue.* —*v.i.* **1.** to take part in a physical struggle or combat; try to subdue or overcome an opponent: *The two armies fought for eight hours.* **2.** to contend or struggle, as to gain an end; strive energetically: *They fought for equal rights.* **3. to fight shy of.** to avoid or evade confrontation with: *to fight shy of an issue.* [Old English *feohtan* to contend, struggle.]
Syn. n. 1. Fight, struggle, combat, conflict indicate a contest, esp. a close and bitter one. **Fight** suggests open contention between two parties, esp. two individuals: *He had a fight with his brother and was lucky to get away with just a bloody nose.* **Struggle** implies vigorous effort, esp. in the face of an onslaught or of unfavorable odds: *The victim put up a heroic struggle against his assailant.* **Combat** suggests an individual struggle that occurs within the context of an armed battle: *The two soldiers met in hand-to-hand combat.* **Conflict** suggests a wider clash, esp. one that is a result of opposing ideas or ideologies: *The two nations have not, as yet, engaged in open conflict.*
fight·er (fī′tər) *n.* **1.** one who fights. **2.** professional boxer. **3.** fast, manueverable airplane designed for use against enemy airplanes or ground forces, usually with a crew of one or two men.
fighter bomber, airplane that can perform the functions of both a fighter and a bomber.
fighting chance *Informal.* possibility of success contingent on a long, hard struggle.
fig·ment (fig′mənt) *n.* something imagined or made up; fiction: *The boy's story of seeing a dragon was a figment of his imagination.* [Latin *figmentum* a fiction, something made.]
fig·ur·a·tion (fig′yə rā′shən) *n.* **1.** act of shaping figures or marking

at; āpe; cär; end; mē; it; īce; hot; ōld; fôrk; wood; fōōl; oil; out; up; ūse; turn; sing; thin; this; zh in treasure; ə in ago, taken, pencil, lemon, circus.

with figures. **2.** figure; configuration; shape. **3.** figurative representation.

fig·ur·a·tive (fig′yər ə tiv) *adj.* **1.** characteristic of a figure of speech; not literal; metaphorical: *To throw caution to the wind* is a figurative expression. **2.** containing or using figures of speech; flowery: *figurative poetry.* **3.** representing symbolically; emblematic: *a figurative ceremony.* **4.** pictorial or plastic in representation: *figurative sculpture.* —**fig′·ur·a·tive·ly,** *adv.* —**fig′ur·a·tive·ness,** *n.*

fig·ure (fig′yər) *n.* **1.** symbol representing a number as 0, 1, 2, 3, 4, 5. **2. figures.** use of such symbols in calculating; arithmetic: *She is good at figures.* **3.** amount or value as expressed in figures; price; sum: *The figure asked for the house was too high.* **4.** visible external form or appearance of anything; shape; outline: *He saw the figure of a man silhouetted in the window.* **5.** human body or form, or its appearance, esp. as matching an ideal: *a slender figure, a fine figure of a man.* **6.** impression or conspicuous appearance: *He cut a comical figure.* **7.** person, esp. one of importance or distinction; character: *a well-known figure, a figure famous in local history.* **8.** someone or something that represents or symbolizes another person, thing, or a principle: *a figure of evil, a figure of strength.* **9.** representation or likeness, esp. of the human form: *The figure of an angel appears on the coin.* **10.** pictorial diagram; illustration; drawing. **11.** design; pattern: *The cloth had bold figures woven into it.* **12.** *Geometry.* bounded surface or space; series of lines, solids, or surfaces having a definite shape: *The circle is a plane figure; the sphere is a solid figure.* **13.** set or series of movements, as in dancing or skating. **14.** figure of speech. **15.** *Music.* series of notes or chords forming a short, distinct phrase or theme; subject; motif. —*v.t.,* **-ured, -ur·ing. 1.** to represent or depict in any way, as in a picture or diagram: *The sculptor figured the girl in clay.* **2.** to ornament or cover with a design or pattern: *The paper was figured with a holiday design.* **3.** *Informal.* **a.** to think; believe: *She figured she would be next.* **b.** to reach a conclusion about; decide: *They figured he was the best man available.* **4.** to have a mental picture of; imagine. **5. to figure out. a.** to solve by using figures; compute: *to figure out the answer to an arithmetic problem.* **b.** to arrive at the explanation or solution of; understand: *He figured out who the murderer was before the end of the book.* **6.** *Music.* to mark (the bass) with figures to indicate accompanying chords or intended harmony. —*v.i.* **1.** to be conspicuous or prominent; take part: *He figured in the conspiracy.* **2. to figure on.** *Informal.* **a.** to depend on; rely on: *They figured on him to complete his part of the job.* **b.** to include in plans; take into consideration: *We didn't figure on the presence of outsiders.* **c.** to plan on: *They figured on going if the weather was nice.* [Old French *figure* form, shape, face, from Latin *figūra* thing made, form.] —**fig′ur·er,** *n.* —**Syn.** *n.* **4.** see **shape.**

fig·ured (fig′yərd) *adj.* **1.** decorated with figures or designs: *figured wallpaper.* **2.** represented by figures; pictured: *a figured motif.* **3.** *Music.* (of the bass part) having the accompanying chords indicated by figures.

figure eight, traced line resembling the numeral 8, as formed in flying, skating, or embroidery.

fig·ure·head (fig′yər hed′) *n.* **1.** person having nominal authority but no real power or responsibility: *The emperor of Japan is a figurehead.* **2.** carved, ornamental figure on the bow of a ship.

figure of speech, form of expression in which words are intentionally used out of their literal sense or in fanciful or incongruous combinations, so as to produce a vivid, fresh, or poetic effect. Simile, metaphor, hyperbole, and synecdoche are figures of speech.

fig·ur·ine (fig′yə rēn′) *n.* small carved or molded figure; statuette. [French *figurine,* from Italian *figurina,* diminutive of *figura* shape, form, image, from Latin *figūra* thing made, form.]

fig·wort (fig′wurt′) *n.* **1.** any of a large group of strong-smelling, weedy plants, genus *Scrophularia,* found growing in damp places throughout the Northern Hemisphere, bearing oval, toothed leaves and loose clusters of small, tubular, greenish-yellow or purple flowers. **2.** any plant of the same family, as the snapdragon or foxglove.

Fi·ji (fē′jē) *n.* island country in the southwestern Pacific, just west of the International Date Line. Land area, 7036 sq. mi. Pop. (1973 est.), 550,000.

Fi·ji·an (fē′jē ən, fi jē′ən) *adj.* relating to the Fiji Islands, their people, or the language spoken there. —*n.* language of the Melanesian group of the Malayo-Polynesian family, spoken predominantly in the Fiji Islands.

Fiji Islands, Fiji.

fil·a·ment (fil′ə mənt) *n.* **1.** very fine thread or

Figured bass

(musical notation: 5 6 6 / 3 3 4)

Written

Played

Filament

threadlike structure; fiber: *a filament of a spider's web, filaments of lint.* **2.** wire that gives off light when an electric current passes through it. **3.** wire in a vacuum tube that emits electrons when heated by the passage of an electric current and that often acts as a cathode. **4.** stalklike part of a stamen that supports the anther in some flowers. [Modern Latin *filamentum,* going back to Latin *filum* thread.] —**fil′a·men′tous,** *adj.*

fi·lar·i·a (fi lār′ē ə) *pl.,* **-lar·i·ae** (-lār′ē ē′). *n.* any of various threadlike roundworms, phylum Nematoda, that live as parasites in the blood and tissues of man and other vertebrate animals. Filariae are usually transmitted by mosquitoes and other arthropods. [Modern Latin *Filaria,* from Latin *filum* thread.] —**fi·lar′i·al,** *adj.*

fil·a·ri·a·sis (fil′ə rī′ə sis) *n.* any of various tropical diseases, as elephantiasis, caused by the presence of filariae in the body, esp. the lymph vessels.

fil·bert (fil′bərt) *n.* **1.** thick-shelled, edible nut of either of two European shrubs, *Corylus maxima* or *C. avellana.* Also, **ha′zel·nut′. 2.** shrub producing this nut, widely cultivated in southern Europe and the northwestern United States. [From dialectal French *noix de filbert* literally, nut of (St.) Philibert; because this nut becomes ripe around St. Philibert's day (August 22).]

filch (filch) *v.t.* to steal (things of small value); pilfer. [Of uncertain origin.] —**filch′er,** *n.* —**Syn.** see **steal.**

file¹ (fīl) *n.* **1.** any device, as a folder or cabinet, in which papers, cards, records, or documents are arranged in order for easy reference. **2.** collection of items thus arranged. **3.a.** line of persons, animals, or things placed one behind another. **b.** line or row of soldiers standing one behind another. Distinguished from **rank. 4.** any row of squares on a chessboard running from one player toward the other, each named for the piece at its head: *king's bishop's file.* Distinguished from **rank.** See **chessboard** for illustration. **5. on file.** arranged in order and kept for reference; in a file. —*v.t.* **filed, fil·ing. 1.** to keep (papers or similar items) arranged in order. **2.** to place in a file: *She filed the letters under the names of the correspondents.* **3.** to file submit legally or officially; enter on a record: *to file a report, to file one's income tax return.* **4.** to send in (a news story) to a newspaper office. —*v.i.* **1.** to march or move in a file: *The soldiers filed out of the barracks.* **2.** to make application: *He filed for a hunting permit. She filed for divorce.* **3.** to register as a candidate for a political office. [Partly from Old French *file* row, from Late Latin *fila* string of things; partly from Old French *fil* thread; both from Latin *filum* thread.] —**fil′er,** *n.*

file² (fīl) *n.* steel tool having one or more closely ridged surfaces used to smooth, form, or wear away hard substances. —*v.t.* **filed, fil·ing.** to cut, smooth, or grind down with a file. [Old English *fēol, fīl* the tool.] —**fil′er,** *n.*

file clerk, office worker employed to keep files and records in order.

file·fish (fīl′fish′) *pl.,* **-fish** or **-fish·es.** *n.* any of several tropical salt-water fish, family Balistidae, having scales set closely together in fine ridges and one or more sharp dorsal spines.

fi·let (fi lā′, fil′ā) *n.* **1.** net or lace with a square mesh. **2.** fillet *(def. 3).* [French *filet* fish net, from Old French *filé* what has been spun, yarn, from Old Provençal *filat* literally, made of threads, from *fil* thread, from Latin *filum.*]

fi·let mi·gnon (fi lā′ min yon′) small, thick steak from the tip of the tenderloin, noted for its tenderness.

fil·i·al (fil′ē əl) *adj.* **1.** relating to or befitting a son or daughter: *filial obedience.* **2.** *Genetics.* relating to or designating a generation following the parental generation. [Late Latin *fīliālis* befitting a son, from Latin *fīlius* son.] —**fil′i·al·ly,** *adv.*

fil·i·bus·ter (fil′ə bus′tər) *n.* **1.a.** method of delaying or stopping action on a legislative issue by the use of lengthy speeches, prolonged debate, or other obstructive tactics. **b.** member of a legislature, esp. in the U.S. Senate, who obstructs the passage of a bill by such measures. Also, **fil′i·bus′ter·er. 2.** pirate; freebooter; buccaneer. **3.** adventurer who engages in unlawful warfare against a foreign country, esp. a U.S. adventurer involved in an armed expedition into a Latin American country during the nineteenth century. —*v.i.* **1.** to obstruct legislative action by use of filibuster, as by prolonged speeches. **2.** to engage in unlawful warfare against a foreign country. —*v.t.* **1.** to obstruct the passage of (a bill) by filibuster. [Spanish *filibustero* buccaneer, from French

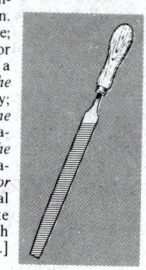

File²

Filefish

filibustier buccaneer, robber, from Dutch *vrijbuiter,* going back to *vrij* free + *buit* booty. Doublet of FREEBOOTER.]

fil·i·gree (fil′ə grē′) *n.* **1.** delicate, lacelike ornamental work of intertwined gold or silver wire. **2.** anything ornate, delicate, or fanciful: *The sun shining through the leaves made a green and gold filigree.* —*adj.* resembling, made of, or ornamented with filigree: *filigree earrings.* —*v.t.,* **-greed, -gree·ing.** to adorn with or work in filigree. [Modification of earlier *filigrane* filigree work, from French *filigrane,* from Italian *filigrana,* going back to Latin *fīlum* thread + *grānum* seed; because metal threads are used.]

fil·ings (fī′lingz) *n.,pl.* particles removed by a file.

Fil·i·pi·no (fil′ə pē′nō) *pl.,* **-nos.** *n.* native or inhabitant of the Philippine Islands. —*adj.* Philippine.

fill (fil) *v.t.* **1.** to supply with as much as can be held or contained; make full, as a container or space: *to fill a bucket with water.* **2.** to occupy the whole capacity or extent of: *Flowers filled the garden. The crowd filled the auditorium.* **3.** to spread over or throughout; pervade; permeate: *Smoke filled the room. Angry shouts filled the air.* **4.** to sate with or as with food; feed: *She filled her stomach.* **5.** to fulfill; satisfy; meet: *His contribution fills the need for additional funds.* **6.** to supply or make up whatever is required or asked for: *to fill an order, to fill a prescription.* **7.a.** to stop up or close by putting something in; plug: *to fill a hole in a wall.* **b.** to put a filling in (a tooth). **8.** to hold or occupy, as a position or office; discharge the duties of: *to fill the office of treasurer.* **9.** to place or appoint a person for: *to fill a vacancy.* **10.** *Nautical.* **a.** to distend (a sail) by pressure of the wind. **b.** to trim (a yard) so that the wind will distend the sail. **11.** to build up, as low ground or an embankment, by adding stone and earth. **12. to fill the bill.** to fulfill or supply the requirements of satisfactorily. **13. to fill in. a.** to fill entirely with something: *The men filled in the hole with dirt.* **b.** to complete by inserting something: *to fill in a questionnaire.* **c.** to insert to make something complete: *Fill in your name on the application form.* **14. to fill someone in on.** to supply a person with additional information about: *They filled him in on the rest of the plan.* **15. to fill out.** to complete by inserting something: *to fill out an application.* **16. to fill up.** to make completely full: *to fill up the gas tank of a car.* —*v.i.* **1.** to become full: *The room filled with smoke.* **2. to fill in.** to act as a substitute: *He filled in for the chairman during the meeting.* **3. to fill out.** to become larger, fuller, or more rounded: *The thin child gradually filled out as he grew older.* **4. to fill up.** to become completely full. —*n.* **1.** quantity sufficient to fill; enough to satiate a desire or need; full supply: *Eat your fill.* **2.** something used to fill: *Stone and gravel were used as fill for the hole.* **3. to have one's fill.** to have enough or too much. [Old English *fyllan* to make full.]

fill·er (fil′ər) *n.* **1.** one who or that which fills. **2.a.** material used to fill a gap, to even the grain of wood, to stiffen fabric, or to increase the bulk of something. **b.** item, esp. a brief paragraph, used to fill space in a newspaper or magazine. **c.** sheaf of paper for a looseleaf notebook.

fil·lér (fē′lār, fil′ār) *pl.,* **-lér.** *n.* monetary unit of Hungary, equal to one hundredth of a forint. [Magyar *fillér.*]

fil·let (fil′it; *n. def. 3, v. def. 2,* fi lā′) *n.* **1.** narrow band or ribbon for binding or adorning the hair. **2.** narrow band or strip of any material. **3.** *also,* **fi·let.** lean, boneless piece or slice of fish or meat. —*v.t.* **1.** to bind or adorn with a fillet. **2.** to cut (fish or meat) into fillets. [Old French *filet* little thread, diminutive of *fil* thread, from Latin *fīlum.*]

fill-in (fil′in′) *n.* **1.** person or thing filling a gap or vacancy. **2.** *Informal.* summary of relevant facts to increase someone's understanding, as of a situation.

fill·ing (fil′ing) *n.* **1.** that which is used to fill something: *pie filling.* **2.** substance, as amalgam or cement, put into a cavity in a tooth. **3.** threads running from side to side across the warp threads in a woven fabric; woof. **4.** act of filling.

filling station, gas station.

fil·lip (fil′ip) *n.* **1.a.** snap of a finger that has been pressed down by the thumb and suddenly released. **b.** smart tap given by such a means. **2.** something that serves to arouse, excite, or enliven; stimulus: *That news was a fillip to my spirits.* —*v.t.* **1.** to tap or strike with a fillip. **2.** to project or drive by or as by a fillip. **3.** to rouse; stimulate. —*v.i.* to make a fillip. [Probably imitative.]

Fill·more, Mil·lard (fil′môr; mil′ərd) 1800–74, thirteenth president of the United States, from 1850 to 1853.

fil·ly (fil′ē) *pl.,* **-lies.** *n.* female colt. [Old Norse *fylja.*]

film (film) *n.* **1.** thin layer, sheet, covering, or membrane: *The windows were covered by a film of dirt.* **2.** thin, flexible roll or strip used in making photographs, usually of cellulose acetate coated with a light-sensitive emulsion. **3.a.** such a roll or strip containing pictures to be projected on a screen: *The film was rewound for the next showing.* **b.** motion picture: *We saw a good film.* **4. films. a.** motion pictures collectively: *She was a star in films twenty years ago.* **b.** the motion picture industry. **5.** thin veil or haze that blurs: *a film of tears.* —*v.t.* **1.** to cover or obscure by a thin layer or haze. **2.a.** to photograph with a motion picture camera: *He filmed the football game.* **b.** to make a motion picture of: *to film a popular novel.* —*v.i.* **1.** to become covered or obscured by a thin layer or haze. **2.a.** to be suitable for filming: *Some plays do not film well.* **b.** to make a motion picture. [Old English *filmen* membrane.]

film·ic (fil′mik) *adj.* of or relating to motion pictures.

film·strip (film′strip′) *n.* length of film containing still pictures for projection on a screen, often used as a teaching aid.

film·y (fil′mē) **film·i·er, film·i·est.** *adj.* **1.** composed of or resembling a thin layer; gauzy: *filmy material.* **2.** covered with or as with a thin layer; hazy: *a filmy vision.* —**film′i·ness,** *n.*

fil·ter (fil′tər) *n.* **1.** device for straining solids or impurities from a liquid or gas. **2.** porous material used in such a device, as sand, charcoal, or paper. **3.** device that allows certain electrical frequencies to pass and restricts others. —*v.t.* **1.** to pass (liquid or gas) through a filter; strain: *The water was filtered through charcoal.* **2.** to act as a filter for. **3.** to separate or remove, as impurities, solid particles, or other matter, by or as by a filter: *The solid particles were filtered from the solution.* —*v.i.* to pass through or as through a filter: *Sunlight filtered through the leaves.* [Medieval Latin *filtrum* strainer made of felt; of Germanic origin.]

fil·ter·a·ble (fil′tər ə bəl) *also,* **fil·tra·ble** (fil′trə bəl). *adj.* **1.** capable of being filtered. **2.** capable of passing through a filter that stops bacteria: *a filterable virus.* —**fil′ter·a·bil′i·ty,** *adv.*

filter bed, pond or tank having a false bottom covered with sand or gravel, serving to filter water or sewage.

filter paper *n.* porous paper used to strain suspended solids from liquids.

filth (filth) *n.* **1.** something that is foul or putrid; offensive dirt or refuse: *Industrial filth pollutes the air and water.* **2.** foul condition. **3.** moral defilement or corruption; obscenity. **4.** obscene language. [Old English *fȳlth* putrid matter, rottenness.]

filth·y (fil′thē) **filth·i·er, filth·i·est.** *adj.* **1.** of the nature of or containing filth; dirty; foul: *filthy streets.* **2.** morally foul; obscene. **3.** highly unpleasant or objectionable; contemptible: *That was a filthy accusation.* —**filth′i·ly,** *adv.* —**filth′i·ness,** *n.*

fil·trate (fil′trāt) *n.* liquid that has been separated by filtration. —*v.t.,* **-trat·ed, -trat·ing.** to filter.

fil·tra·tion (fil trā′shən) *n.* act of filtering; being filtered.

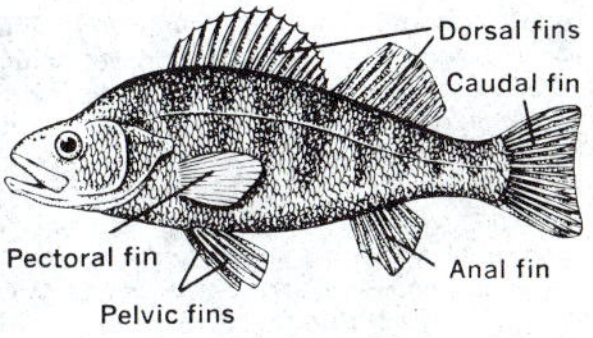

Fin[1]

fin[1] (fin) *n.* **1.** one of the movable structures extending from the body of a fish, supported by bone or cartilage, and enabling the fish to swim, guide, and balance itself in the water. **2.** similar structure of other aquatic animals, as whales and some porpoises. **3.** something resembling a fin in shape or function. **4.** vertical surface attached longitudinally to an aircraft or rocket to provide stability. **5.** fin-shaped appendage of a submarine or boat. —*v.t.,* **finned, fin·ning.** to cut the fins from (a fish). —*v.i.* to move the fins violently, as a whale when dying. [Old English *finn* the movable structure of a fish.]

fin[2] (fin) *n.* *Slang.* five-dollar bill. [Yiddish *finf* five, going back to Old High German *finf.*]

fi·na·gle (fi nā′gəl) **-gled, -gling.** *v.t.* *Informal.* **1.** to get or manage (something) by trickery or deceit; wangle: *He finagled a free ticket to the game.* **2.** to cheat or trick (someone): *He finagled them out of their money.* —*v.i.* to use trickery or deceit; cheat. [Of uncertain origin.] —**fi·na′gler,** *n.*

fi·nal (fīn′əl) *adj.* **1.** relating to or coming at the end; last; ultimate: *the final chapter, the final revision of a manuscript.* **2.** precluding further action, controversy, or change; deciding; conclusive: *a final decision, the final word on a subject.* **3.** relating to or constituting an end or purpose: *a final cause.* —*n.* **1.** something that is last or terminal. **2.** *also,* **finals. a.** the last examination of a school or college course: *He is studying for the history final.* **b.** the last and decisive game, match, or trial in a series of athletic contests: *Our team reached the finals of the basketball tournament.* [Late Latin *fīnālis* relating to the end, concluding, from Latin *fīnis* end.] —**Syn.** *adj.* **1.** see **last[1].**

fi·na·le (fi nä′lē) *n.* **1.** last part or conclusion of any performance or course of action. **2.** concluding part of a piece of music or of a performance, as a play or opera. [Italian *finale* end, close, from Late Latin *fīnālis* concluding. See FINAL.]

fi·nal·ist (fīn′əl ist) *n.* one who takes part in the final match or event of a series of games or contests.

fi·nal·i·ty (fī nal′ə tē, fi-) *pl.,* **-ties.** *n.* **1.** state or quality of being final,

settled, or complete; conclusiveness; decisiveness: *She stated her position with finality.* **2.** something final, as a final act or utterance.

fi·nal·ize (fīn′əl īz′) **-ized, -iz·ing.** *v.t.* to put into final or finished form; bring to completion: *We must finalize our plans.*

fi·nal·ly (fīn′əl ē) *adv.* **1.** at the end; in conclusion; ultimately: *We finally reached our destination.* **2.** completely; irrevocably; decisively: *We must deal with this problem finally and effectively.*

fi·nance (fi nans′, fī-, fī′nans) *n.* **1.** theory and management of monetary affairs of individuals, businesses, or governments, including such matters as credit, banking, and investment. **2. finances.** monetary affairs or resources of a government, organization, or individual; budgetary balance; funds; revenue; income. —*v.t.,* **-nanced, -nanc·ing. 1.** to provide money for: *His parents financed his college education.* **2.** to manage the finances of: *The organization was skillfully financed.* [Old French *finance* end, payment, wealth, from *finer* to end, pay, settle, going back to Latin *finire* to end.]

fi·nan·cial (fi nan′shəl, fī-) *adj.* relating to finance or financiers: *financial skills, a financial crisis.* —**fi·nan′cial·ly,** *adv.*

fin·an·cier (fin′ən sēr′, fī′nan′-) *n.* **1.** one skilled in financial matters. **2.** one engaged in financial operations on a large scale. [French *financier,* from *finance* ready money, money resources. See FINANCE.]

fin·back (fin′bak′) *n.* whale, *Balaenoptera physalus,* having a wedge-shaped head, long, slender body, and a large dorsal fin; rorqual. Length: to 85 feet. Also, **fin whale, finback whale.**

finch (finch) *n.* any of a large group of songbirds, family Fringillidae, that typically have a cone-shaped bill and stout body and feed on seeds, as the sparrow, bunting, canary, and cardinal. Length: 4–11 inches. [Old English *finc.*]

Finch

find (fīnd) found, find·ing. *v.t.* **1.** to come upon accidentally; meet with by chance; happen on: *I found a wallet on the sidewalk.* **2.** to ascertain by calculation; get at or obtain (the solution to a problem): *to find the sum of several numbers.* **3.** to discover or obtain by or as by search or effort: *to find a place to live, to find a cure for a disease, to find the right man for a job.* **4.** to discover, learn, or become aware of through experience, investigation, or observation: *I found I couldn't study past midnight. They found that the fire had been set deliberately.* **5.** to recover (something lost): *She found the missing necklace under the couch.* **6.** to gain or recover the use of: *He finally found his voice and replied to her shocking accusation.* **7.** to gain knowledge of through sensation; feel; perceive: *He found that he was sinking in the mud.* **8.** to get or obtain by arrangement or management: *I haven't found time to read that book.* **9.** to arrive at; reach: *Water finds its level.* **10.** to determine and declare: *The jury found the defendant guilty.* **11.** to feel or think to be; consider; regard: *to find the climate too humid. He found the play very amusing.* **12.** to provide; supply; furnish: *to find a room for a guest.* **13. to find oneself. a.** to discover one's abilities or talents and the best manner or way to employ them: *After changing jobs many times, he finally found himself.* **b.** to perceive oneself to be (in some specified place or mental or physical condition): *He found himself in a dilemma.* **14. to find out. a.** to learn; discover: *He found out that prices were much higher in the city.* **b.** to detect or discover the identity or true character of (a person or thing): *The investigator found him out before he could commit the crime.* —*v.i.* to arrive at a decision after judicial inquiry: *The jury found for the plaintiff.* —*n.* **1.** act or instance of finding: *The archaeologist's summer dig resulted in a startling find.* **2.** something that is found, esp. something of value: *She made a find at the antique auction.* [Old English *findan* to come upon, attain.]

find·er (fīn′dər) *n.* **1.** one who or that which finds. **2.** small extra lens or other device built in or attached to a camera for sighting the object or area to be photographed. Also, **view′find′er. 3.** small telescope attached to a larger one to help sight the objects to be viewed by the more powerful telescope.

fin de siè·cle (faN də sye′klə) *French.* end of the century, esp. as used of the last years of the nineteenth century, thought of as being a period of artistic and social sophistication, innovation, and decadence.

find·ing (fīn′ding) *n.* **1.** act of one who finds; discovery. **2.** something that is found: *research findings.* **3.** *also,* **findings.** result or conclusions of a judicial or other inquiry: *A finding of murder in the first degree was announced by the court.* **4. findings.** tools and incidental materials used by a workman.

fine¹ (fīn) **fin·er, fin·est.** *adj.* **1.** of superior grade or quality; very good; excellent: *a fine speech, fine linen.* **2.** very satisfactory; enjoyable: *We had a fine time.* **3.** highly accomplished; of superior ability; skilled: *a fine musician.* **4.** characterized by or displaying elegance or refinement; polished: *fine manners.* **5.** delicate, as in structure, texture, or workmanship: *fine facial features, fine embroidery.* **6.** capable of delicate discrimination; highly perceptive: *a fine eye for color.* **7.** subtle; refined:

a fine point in an argument. **8.a.** extremely thin; slender: *a fine thread.* **b.** extremely small: *the fine print in a contract.* **9.** consisting or composed of minute particles; not coarse: *fine sand.* **10.** sharp; keen: *the fine edge of a razor.* **11.** overly decorated; showy; ornate: *fine feathers.* **12.** handsome; good-looking: *a fine young man.* **13.** free from clouds or rain; clear; bright: *fine weather.* **14.** free from impurities or foreign matter; clear; pure: *fine gold.* **15.** containing a stated proportion of pure metal, as gold or silver. Commercial silver is usually 999 fine, containing 999 parts of silver in 1000 parts of the metal. —*adv.* **1.** finely. **2.** *Informal.* very well: *He's doing fine in school.* [Old French *fin* perfect, exact, going back to Latin *finis* end, limit.]

fine² (fīn) *n.* **1.** sum of money exacted as penalty for an offense: *There is a fine of fifty dollars for littering.* **2. in fine.** in conclusion; finally. —*v.t.,* **fined, fin·ing.** to subject to or punish by a fine: *to fine a motorist for speeding.* [Old French *fin* end, settlement, from Medieval Latin *finis* final payment, from Latin *finis* end, limit.]

fi·ne³ (fē′nā) *n. Music.* the end. ▲ a direction marking the end of a repeated section or movement. [Italian *fine* end, limit, from Latin *finis.*]

fine arts, those arts having a purely aesthetic function as their basic purpose, including painting, drawing, and sculpture, and sometimes architecture, literature, music, drama, and the dance.

fine-drawn (fīn′drôn′) *adj.* drawn out to extreme fineness or subtlety.

fine-grained (fīn′grānd′) *adj.* having a fine, close grain.

fine·ly (fīn′lē) *adv.* in a fine manner.

fine·ness (fīn′nis) *n.* **1.** state or quality of being fine. **2.** proportion of pure gold or silver in an alloy, usually stated in parts per thousand.

fin·er·y (fī′nər ē) *pl.,* **-er·ies.** *n.* fine or showy dress or ornaments; elaborate adornment. [FINE¹ + -ERY.]

fine-spun (fīn′spun′) *adj.* **1.** spun or drawn out to extreme fineness or delicacy. **2.** excessively subtle or refined.

fi·nesse (fi nes′) *n.* **1.** refinement or subtlety of execution, skill, or discernment: *The pianist displayed great finesse and virtuosity.* **2.** smooth or artful handling of a delicate situation; craft; cunning; stratagem: *Bismarck was a master of finesse in politics.* **3.** *Bridge.* attempt to take a trick by playing the lower of two cards not in sequence, in the hope that the intervening card is in the hand of an opponent who has already played. —*v.i.,* **-nessed, -ness·ing. 1.** to use finesse. **2.** *Bridge.* to make a finesse. —*v.t.* **1.** to bring about or change by finesse. **2.** *Bridge.* to make a finesse with (a card). [Old French *finesse* delicacy, fineness, from *fin.* See FINE¹.]

fin·ger (fing′gər) *n.* **1.** one of the five separate parts of the end of the hand, esp. the four excluding the thumb; digit. **2.** part of a glove which is made to receive or cover one of these. **3.** anything resembling a finger in shape or use: *The fingers of the sun's rays shone above the horizon.* **4.a.** unit of measure equal to the breadth of a finger, approximately ¾ inch. **b.** length of a finger, approximately 4½ inches. **5. to burn one's fingers.** to bring suffering or loss upon oneself by meddling or interfering. **6. to have a finger in the pie.** to take part in something; have a share in doing something. **7. to put one's finger on.** to indicate or point out precisely or correctly. **8. to put the finger on.** *Slang.* **a.** to inform on, as to the police; betray. **b.** to indicate or point out, as a victim to be killed. **9. to twist around one's little finger.** to be able to handle or control completely or with ease; make subservient. —*v.t.* **1.** to touch, feel, or handle with the fingers; toy with: *She fingered the silk gently.* **2.** *Music.* **a.** to play (a musical instrument) with the fingers. **b.** to mark (musical notes or a piece of music) with figures indicating a specific fingering to be used. **3.** to point out or identify (as the victim of an impending crime): *The driver fingered the bank messenger.* —*v.i.* **1.** to touch, feel, or handle something with the fingers. **2.** *Music.* **a.** to use the fingers in a certain way in playing a musical instrument. **b.** (of musical instruments) to be arranged for playing with the fingers. [Old English *finger* one of the end parts of the hand.]

finger board, strip of wood on the neck of a violin, guitar, or similar instrument, against which strings are pressed by the fingers.

finger bowl, small bowl containing water for rinsing the fingers during or after a meal.

fin·ger·ing (fing′gər ing) *n.* **1.** act of touching or handling with the fingers. **2.a.** action, method, or technique of using the fingers in playing a musical instrument. **b.** numerals or other notations on a piece of music indicating which fingers are to be used in playing its notes.

Finger Lakes, group of eleven long, narrow, glacial lakes in west-central New York.

fin·ger·ling (fing′gər ling) *n.* **1.** young or small fish, esp. a salmon or trout no longer than a finger. **2.** something very small.

fin·ger·nail (fing′gər nāl′) *n.* horny substance that develops from the skin and forms a hard plate on the upper surface of the end of a finger.

finger painting 1. technique of painting by spreading paint on dampened paper with the fingers or palms. **2.** painting made in this way.

at; āpe; cär; end; mē; it; īce; hot; ōld; fôrk; wood; fōōl; oil; out; up; ūse; turn; sing; thin; th̄is; zh in treasure; ə in ago, taken, pencil, lemon, circus.

finger post, sign or guidepost in the shape of a hand with a pointing finger, indicating direction.

fin·ger·print (fing′gər print′) *n.* impression of the markings on the inner surface of the tip of a finger or thumb, esp. such an impression made with ink and used for purposes of identification. —*v.t.* to take finger-prints of.

fin·ger·tip (fing′gər tip′) *n.* **1.** last joint of a finger, esp. its very end. **2. to have at one's fingertips.** to have immediate access to or knowledge of.

fin·i·al (fin′ē əl) *n.* **1.** terminal ornament at the apex of a spire, gable, or other architectural member. **2.** apex or terminal ornament. [Form of FINAL.]

fin·i·cal (fin′i kəl) *adj.* finicky. [FINE¹ + -ICAL.] —**fin′i·cal·ly,** *adv.*

fin·ick·ing (fin′i king) *adj.* finicky.

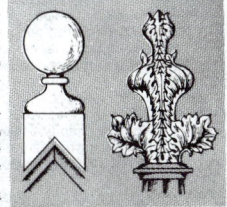

Finials

fin·ick·y (fin′i kē) *adj.* excessively fastidious, exacting, or precise; fussy: *She is a finicky eater.* —**fin′ick·i·ness,** *n.*

fi·nis (fin′is, fī′nis) *n.* end; conclusion. [Latin *fīnis.*]

fin·ish (fin′ish) *v.t.* **1.** to bring to an end; come to the end of; end: *to finish speaking, to finish a meal.* **2.** to bring to completion; complete: *to finish a task, to finish a dress.* **3.** to use up or consume completely (often with *up*): *to finish one ream of paper. He finished up the can of soda.* **4.** to complete and perfect in detail; put final and perfecting touches on (often with *up*): *to finish a statue.* **5.** to perfect (someone), as in social graces or education: *She was finished at the best school in the East.* **6.** to treat and give a certain surface, quality, or effect to, as cloth or wood: *He used clear varnish to finish the cabinet.* **7.** *Informal.* to defeat, destroy, or kill: *The scandal finished his political career.* **8. to finish off. a.** to bring to completion; end: *She finished off the thread with a knot.* **b.** to cause the defeat, death, or destruction of: *He finished off his opponent with a right to the jaw.* —*v.i.* **1.** to reach or come to an end: *She finished before the allotted time was up.* **2. to finish with. a.** to bring to completion; end: *I finished with the first draft this morning.* **b.** to sever relations with; cease to have anything to do with. —*n.* **1.** last stage of any action; conclusion; end: *the finish of a race, a fight to the finish. The game had a thrilling finish.* **2.** something that ends, perfects, or completes: *Some walls have a plaster finish.* **3.** condition or quality of being finished; perfection; completion. **4.** polish or perfection, as in education or social manners. **5.** manner in which a surface is finally treated; effect produced by the finishing process: *a rough finish.* [Old French *finiss-*, a stem of *finir* to end, from Latin *fīnīre.*] —**fin′ish·er,** *n.* —**Syn.** *1. see* **end.**

fin·ished (fin′isht) *adj.* **1.** ended; concluded: *The project is finished.* **2.** completed in all details: *a finished product.* **3.** perfected; polished: *The ballet is a finished work.* **4.** highly skilled or accomplished: *a finished dancer.*

finishing school, private school, emphasizing social and cultural attainments, that prepares women for entrance into society.

fi·nite (fī′nīt) *adj.* **1.a.** having a beginning and an end; having limits or bounds: *an essay describing the universe as infinite and our galaxy as finite.* **b.** subject to human or natural limitations or conditions: *finite beings.* **2.** *Mathematics.* **a.** that can be equaled or completed by counting. **b.** neither infinite nor infinitesimal. **c.** of or relating to a set containing a limited number of elements. **3.** *Grammar.* (of a verb or verb phrase) limited by person, number, tense, and mood; capable of serving as a predicate. In the sentence *He attends college, attends* is a finite verb. —*n.* that which is finite. [Latin *fīnītus,* past participle of *fīnīre* to end.] —**fi′nite·ly,** *adv.* —**fi′nite·ness,** *n.*

fin·i·tude (fin′ə tōōd′, -tūd′, fī′nə-) *n.* quality or condition of being finite.

fink (fingk) *n. Slang.* **1.a.** strikebreaker. **b.** labor spy. **2.** informer. **3.** obnoxious or contemptible person.

Fin·land (fin′lənd) *n.* **1.** nation in northeastern Europe, on the Baltic Sea. Capital, Helsinki. Area, 130,119 sq. mi. Pop. (1970 est.), 4,695,000. **2. Gulf of.** arm of the Baltic Sea between Finland and Estonia.

Finn (fin) *n.* **1.** native or inhabitant of Finland. **2.** one whose native language is Finnish or a Finnic language.

fin·nan had·die (fin′ən had′ē) smoked haddock. Also, **finnan haddock.** [Modification of earlier *Findhorn haddock,* from *Findhorn,* fishing town in Scotland.] + HADDOCK.]

Finn·ic (fin′ik) *adj.* **1.** of or relating to Finland or the Finns. **2.** of, relating to, or designating a branch of the Finno-Ugric subfamily of the Ural-Altaic family of languages, including esp. Finnish, Lapp, and Estonian. —*n.* Finnic branch of Finno-Ugric.

Finn·ish (fin′ish) *adj.* **1.** of or relating to Finland, the Finns, or their language. —*n.* language spoken predominantly in Finland, a member of the Finno-Ugric subfamily of the Ural-Altaic family of languages.

Fin·no-U·gric (fin′ō ōōg′rik, -ūg′-) *n.* subfamily of the Ural-Altaic family of languages, including Finnish, Estonian, and Hungarian.

fin·ny (fin′ē) *adj.* **1.** having fins. **2.** resembling a fin. **3.** relating to or abounding in fish: *the finny deep.*

fiord (fyôrd) *also,* **fjord.** *n.* deep, narrow inlet of the sea between high, steep banks or cliffs, esp. one along the coast of Norway. [Norwegian *fiord,* from Old Norse *fjörthr.*]

fir (fur) *n.* **1.** any of a group of pyramid-shaped evergreen trees, genus *Abies,* of the pine family, widely distributed in temperate and cooler climates, bearing cones that grow erect on the branches. **2.** any of certain other trees of the pine family. [Old English *furh.*]

Fir twig with cone

fire (fīr) *n.* **1.** flame, heat, and light given off in combustion. **2.a.** mass of burning material, as wood, coal, or other fuel: *He added another log to the fire.* **b.** some material arranged to be burned: *He lit the fire with one match.* **3.** destructive burning: *a forest fire. The fire which started in the kitchen spread throughout the house.* **4.** any combustible preparation. **5.** something resembling or suggestive of fire because of its glow, luminosity, heat, or brilliance: *the fire of the sunset, the fire of a diamond.* **6.** intense emotional feeling or spirit; fervor; passion: *the fire of love, words of fire.* **7.** liveliness of imagination; capacity for ardor or zeal; animation: *the fire of youth.* **8.** fever or inflammation of the body or a part of the body: *the fire of disease.* **9.** severe trial; overwhelming trouble: *the fire of affliction.* **10.** discharge of firearms; shooting: *The faint crackle of carbine fire wafted across the hills* (R. M. Utley, 1960). **11.** rapid or intense series of verbal outbursts: *a fire of questions.*

between two fires. physical or verbal attack from both sides.

on fire. a. burning; ignited. **b.** inflamed or overwhelmed with intense emotional feeling; eager; zealous; passionate.

to catch fire. to become ignited; begin to burn.

to go through fire and water. to experience or endure great danger, hardships, or trials.

to hang fire. a. to fail or be slow to discharge: *The artillery hung fire, and the enemy got through the line.* **b.** to be slow in acting; hesitate. **c.** to be delayed: *The deal hung fire for several weeks.*

to lay a fire. to arrange material so that it may be burned.

to open fire. a. to begin to shoot: *They opened fire on the enemy.* **b.** to begin; commence.

to play with fire. to do or meddle with something dangerous or risky.

to set fire to. to cause to burn; ignite.

to set on fire. a. to cause to burn; ignite. **b.** to arouse an intense emotional feeling or spirit in; inflame; excite.

to set the world on fire. to achieve great success or fame; become renowned.

to strike fire. a. to produce a spark, as by friction. **b.** to evoke a response.

to take fire. a. to become ignited; begin to burn. **b.** to become aroused, excited, or zealous.

under fire. a. exposed to the enemy's shooting or attack. **b.** exposed to verbal assault; subjected to criticism or censure.

—*v.t.,* **fired, fir·ing. 1.** to supply with fuel; tend the fire of: *He fired the engine.* **2.** to expose to the action of fire; process by the use of heat; bake: *to fire pottery.* **3.** to cause to shine or glow as if on fire: *The setting sun fires the western sky.* **4.** to cause to explode, esp. by application of fire: *to fire gunpowder.* **5.** to discharge, as a gun or bullet: *to fire a shotgun.* **6.** to arouse the feelings or passions of; inflame; excite: *to fire one's anger.* **7.** to animate; inspire: *to fire a boy's imagination.* **8.** *Informal.* to direct or hurl forcibly or suddenly: *He fired the puck toward the goal. The lawyer fired questions at the witness.* **9.** *Informal.* to dismiss from a position; discharge: *The firm fired seven employees.* —*v.i.* **1.** to discharge artillery or firearms; shoot: *The enemy fired on the town.* **2.** to go off, as a gun. **3.** to become inflamed, angered, or excited: *She fired at his accusations.* **4.** to show a certain result or reaction after being fired in a kiln: *The glaze fired poorly and cracked.* **5.** to throw or discharge a missile. **6. to fire away.** *Informal.* to begin or start, esp. with energy or rapidity. **7. to fire up.** **a.** to start a fire, as in an engine, furnace, or boiler. **b.** to become irritated, angry, or excited. [Old English *fȳr* flame, burning material.] —**fir′er,** *n.*

fire alarm 1. signal calling attention to a fire. **2.** apparatus for giving such a signal.

fire·arm (fīr′ärm′) *n.* weapon from which shot is discharged by means of gases created by the rapid burning of an explosive charge, esp. such a weapon normally carried and fired by one man, as a rifle, pistol, or shotgun.

fire·ball (fīr′bôl′) *n.* **1.** something resembling a ball of fire, as the sun

at; āpe; cär; end; mē; it; īce; hot; ōld; fôrk; wood; fōōl; oil; out; up; ūse; turn; sing; thin; this; zh in treasure; ə in ago, taken, pencil, lemon, circus.

385

or a globular burst of lightning. **2.** brilliant meteor; shooting star. **3.** luminous sphere of hot gases that forms after the detonation of a nuclear weapon. **4.** *Informal.* dynamic, energetic person or thing: *He is a real fireball.*

fire·boat (fīr′bōt′) *n.* boat equipped with apparatus for fighting fires.

fire·bomb (fīr′bom′) *n.* bomb or missile designed to cause a fire. —*v.t.* to attack with a firebomb or firebombs. —**fire′bomb′er,** *n.*

fire·box (fīr′boks′) *n.* chamber in which fuel is burned, as in a furnace, boiler, or locomotive.

fire·brand (fīr′brand′) *n.* **1.** piece of burning wood. **2.** one who stirs up unrest or dissension; agitator.

fire·break (fīr′brāk′) *n.* strip of land plowed or cleared to check the spread of fire.

fire·brick (fīr′brik′) *n.* brick that can stand great heat, used to line furnaces and fireplaces.

fire·bug (fīr′bug′) *n.* *Informal.* one who purposely sets destructive fires; incendiary; pyromaniac.

fire clay, clay that can resist high temperatures, used for making such things as crucibles or firebricks.

fire company, company of men established to put out fires.

fire·crack·er (fīr′krak′ər) *n.* paper cylinder containing an explosive and an attached fuse, discharged as a noisemaker.

fire·damp (fīr′damp′) *n.* gas formed in coal mines, composed primarily of methane, dangerously explosive when mixed with certain proportions of air.

fire department 1. municipal department organized and equipped to prevent and put out fires. **2.** men of this department.

fire·dog (fīr′dôg′) *n.* andiron.

fire drill, practice drill, esp. in school or aboard ship, involving the procedures to be followed in case of fire.

fire·eat·er (fīr′ē′tər) *n.* **1.** performer who pretends to eat fire. **2.** hot-headed person always ready to fight or quarrel.

fire engine, truck designed to carry equipment with which to fight fire, esp. one that has a pumping apparatus to spray water or chemicals on the fire.

fire escape 1. metal stairway attached to the outside of a building for use as a means of escape in case of fire. **2.** any device for similar use, as a ladder.

fire extinguisher, apparatus containing chemicals for extinguishing fires.

fire·fight·er (fīr′fī′tər) *n.* fireman *(def. 1).*

fire·fly (fīr′flī′) *pl.* **-flies.** *n.* any of a number of soft-bodied beetles, family Lampyridae, widely distributed throughout the world, that have specialized abdominal organs that give off flashes of phosphorescent light as a mating signal. Also, **lightning bug.**

Firefly

fire·house (fīr′hous′) *n.* building housing a fire company and its equipment. Also, **fire station.**

fire hydrant, hydrant.

fire insurance, insurance covering property damage or loss by fire.

fire·less (fīr′lis) *adj.* without fire.

fireless cooker, insulated container that retains heat long enough to allow food to cook or be kept warm without further heating of the container.

fire·light (fīr′līt′) *n.* light from a fire, esp. an open fire.

fire·lock (fīr′lok′) *n.* *Archaic.* any of various types of gunlocks, as the flintlock, in which sparks were produced to ignite the priming.

fire·man (fīr′mən) *pl.* **-men.** *n.* **1.** man employed to extinguish and prevent fires; member of a fire department; firefighter. **2.** man who tends the fire in a furnace or steam engine, esp. on a locomotive; stoker. **3.** enlisted man in the navy who tends engineering machinery.

Fi·ren·ze (fē ren′zā) *n.* Italian. Florence.

fire·place (fīr′plās′) *n.* open structure or recess in which a fire is built, esp. such a recess opening into a room at the base of a chimney.

fire·plug (fīr′plug′) *n.* hydrant for supplying water in case of fire.

fire pot 1. that part of a stove or furnace in which the fire is made. **2.** crucible.

fire·pow·er (fīr′pou′ər) *n.* *Military.* **1.** amount of fire that may be delivered by any particular weapon, unit, or weapon system. **2.** ability to deliver such fire.

fire·proof (fīr′prōōf′) *adj.* resistant to fire; comparatively incombustible. —*v.t.* to make resistant to fire.

fire sale, special sale of goods damaged by fire.

fire screen, metal screen placed in front of a fireplace to prevent sparks from entering the room.

fire ship, ship loaded with combustibles and explosives and directed so that it will explode when it reaches an enemy position, as a ship or bridge.

fire·side (fīr′sīd′) *n.* **1.** space around a fireplace; hearth. **2.** home or home life. —*adj.* of, in, or near the hearth or home.

fire station, firehouse.

fire tower, watchtower, usually overlooking a forest, where a lookout is posted to watch for and report fires.

fire·trap (fīr′trap′) *n.* building that is highly flammable or lacks adequate means of escape in case of fire.

fire wall 1. wall of fire-resistant material to prevent the spread of fire from one room or compartment to another. **2.** fireproof plate behind the engine of an automobile or aircraft.

fire·ward·en (fīr′wôrd′ən) *n.* official charged with the prevention and extinguishing of fires, esp. forest fires.

fire·wa·ter (fīr′wô′tər, -wot′ər) *n.* *Informal.* hard liquor, esp. whiskey. [Possibly translation of an Algonquian expression such as *scoutiouabou* firewater.]

fire·weed (fīr′wēd′) *n.* weedy plant, *Epilobium angustifolium,* of the evening primrose family, found throughout Eurasia and North America, bearing narrow, lance-shaped leaves and striking clusters of purple-pink, red, or white flowers. It often appears in areas cleared by fires.

fire·wood (fīr′wood′) *n.* wood for fuel.

fire·works (fīr′wurks′) *n.,pl.* **1.** combustible or explosive devices ignited to produce a brilliant display of light or loud noises. **2.** a show or display in which such devices are exploded. **3.** *Informal.* any loud or dramatic controversy or clash: *political fireworks.*

fir·ing (fīr′ing) *n.* **1.** act or process of subjecting to fire or intense heat, as in baking and glazing pottery. **2.** discharge of firearms. **3.** fuel, as firewood or coal.

firing line 1. line from which shooting is done, as in battle or on a firing range. **2.** foremost position in any action or activity.

firing pin, that part of a firearm that strikes the primer to explode the charge.

firing squad 1. detachment assigned to execute a person condemned to death by shooting. **2.** detachment of troops assigned to fire a volley of shots as a tribute at a military funeral.

fir·kin (fur′kin) *n.* **1.** measure of capacity equal to one-fourth of a barrel. **2.** wooden cask or tub used for holding food, as butter or fish.

firm¹ (furm) *adj.* **1.** relatively solid or compact in structure or texture; unyielding to pressure: *firm footing.* **2.** securely fixed; not easily moved; stable: *a firm foundation.* **3.** unalterably fixed or settled; immutable: *a firm belief, firm convictions.* **4.** steadfast and unwavering; resolute: *a firm friendship, firm believers.* **5.** having or indicating determination or firmness; steady: *a firm hand.* **6.** not fluctuating widely; steady, as prices. —*adv.* firmly: *The stock market held firm. The men stood firm in their demands.* —*v.t., v.i.* to make or become firm (often with *up*). [Old French *ferme* strong, from Latin *firmus* steadfast, strong.] —**firm′ly,** *adv.* —**firm′ness,** *n.*

Syn. *adj.* **1.** Firm, hard, solid indicate something that will not be permanently distorted by force. **Firm** implies an elastic compactness that yields only slightly to pressure and soon recovers its original shape: *They sought firm ground away from the bog.* **Hard** suggests an unyielding rigidity: *The plastic has a very hard surface, but it is brittle.* **Solid** implies stability that resists being changed because of its mass, density, and strength: *Their furniture was of oak, solid and ornate, made to last a lifetime.*

firm² (furm) *n.* **1.** company or partnership of two or more persons for carrying on a business; business establishment. **2.** name or title under which a company carries on business. [Spanish *firma* signature, from *firmar* to confirm, sign, from Late Latin *firmāre* to confirm by signature, from Latin *firmāre* to strengthen.]

fir·ma·ment (fur′mə mənt) *n.* expanse of the heavens; sky. [Latin *firmāmentum* support, extent of the sky.]

fir·man (fur′mən, fər män′) *n.* edict or decree issued by an oriental sovereign. [Persian *fermān* order.]

first (furst) *adj.* **1.** (the ordinal of one) preceding all others in an order or series. **2.** preceding all others in time; earliest: *George Washington was the first President of the United States.* **3.** foremost in importance, estimation, dignity, or excellence; superior; highest; best: *First in war, first in peace, and first in the hearts of his countrymen* (Lee, 1799). **4.** *Music.* (of a performer or instrument) playing or singing the instrumental or vocal part of highest pitch or principal melodic importance: *first violin. He sings first tenor.* **5.** denoting or being the lowest forward gear of a mechanical transmission, as in an automobile. —*adv.* **1.** before all other persons or things, as in order, rank, or importance: *He was chosen first.* **2.** before any other action, time, or event: *First, apologize to him.* **3.** for the first time: *I first heard of it yesterday.* **4.** in preference to something else; rather; sooner: *He would starve first.* —*n.* **1.** one who or that which is first, as in rank, importance, order, time, or place: *The program was the first of its type.* **2.** first day of a month: *Bills are received on the first.* **3.** beginning: *From the first, he was part of the project.* **4.** winning place, as in a race or contest: *First went to the American team.* **5.** lowest forward gear, as of an automobile. **6. firsts.** commercial articles of the highest quality or finest grade. **7. at first,** in the beginning; at the start. **8. first and last,** altogether

at; āpe; cär; end; mē; it; īce; hot; ōld; fôrk; wood; fōōl; oil; out; up; ūse; turn; sing; thin; this; zh in treasure; ə in ago, taken, pencil, lemon, circus.

all. **9. from the first.** from or at the beginning. [Old English *fyrst* earliest, foremost.]

first aid, emergency treatment given to an ill or injured person before full medical care can be obtained. —**first′-aid′,** *adj.*

first base 1. *Baseball.* **a.** base that a batter must try to reach first after hitting the ball. See **baseball** for illustration. **b.** position of a player stationed in the area near this base. **2. to get to first base.** *Slang.* to make initial progress toward some goal.

first-born (furst′bôrn′) *adj.* first brought forth; born first; eldest. —*n.* the first-born child.

first cause 1. cause not stemming from any other. **2. First Cause.** *Theology.* God.

first-class (furst′klas′) *adj.* **1.** of the highest rank or best quality: *She gave a first-class performance.* **2.** designating a class of mail consisting primarily of letters, parcels, and other written or sealed matter meeting certain governmental limits, as size or weight, and carrying the highest regular postage rate. **3.** designating the best-equipped or most luxurious accommodations on a ship, airplane, or other conveyance. —*adv.* by first-class mail or conveyance: *We sent the package first-class.*

first class 1. first-class travel accommodations. **2.** first-class mail.

First Day, Sunday. ▲ used by the Society of Friends.

first fruits 1. earliest produce of the season. **2.** first profits, products, or results of anything.

first-hand (furst′hand′) *adj.* direct from the original source or producer: *first-hand knowledge of an event.* —*adv.* from the original source: *to learn of something first-hand.*

first lady 1. wife of the president of the United States or of a state governor. **2.** leading or outstanding woman in a particular field or profession: *the first lady of the theater.*

first lieutenant, officer in the U.S. Army, Air Force, and Marine Corps ranking above a second lieutenant and below a captain.

first-ling (furst′ling) *n.* **1.** first of its class or kind. **2.** first product or result. **3.** first offspring of an animal.

first-ly (furst′lē) *adv.* in the first place; first.

first night, opening night, as of a play or opera.

first-night-er (furst′nī′tər) *n.* one who regularly attends opening performances, as of plays or operas.

first person, verb, pronoun, or inflected form that indicates the speaker, as the pronoun *I,* or a group in which the speaker is included, as *we.*

first quarter, half moon that follows a new moon.

first-rate (furst′rāt′) *adj.* **1.** of the highest class, quality, or importance: *a first-rate military power.* **2.** *Informal.* excellent; very good: *a first-rate tennis player.* —*adv. Informal.* excellently.

first sergeant, senior noncommissioned officer of a company or similar unit.

first string, players that comprise the regular or starting lineup of an athletic team, as distinguished from substitutes. —**first′-string′,** *adj.*

first water 1. highest degree of quality in a diamond or other gem. **2.** highest degree, grade, or quality: *a scoundrel of the first water.*

firth (furth) *n.* long, narrow arm of the sea; lower part of an estuary. [Old Norse *fjörthr.*]

fisc (fisk) *n. Archaic.* royal or state treasury; exchequer. [Latin *fiscus* purse, treasury; originally, a basket used to hold money.]

fis-cal (fis′kəl) *adj.* **1.** relating to the treasury, finances, or revenues of a government: *fiscal policy.* **2.** relating to money matters; financial. —*n.* public prosecutor in some countries. [Late Latin *fiscālis* relating to the treasury, from Latin *fiscus* treasury. See FISC.] —**fis′cal-ly,** *adv.*

fiscal year, any twelve-month period used as a basis for settling financial accounts in a business or government. The fiscal year of the U.S. government begins July 1.

fish (fish) *n. pl.* **fish** or **fish-es.** *n.* **1.** cold-blooded, aquatic vertebrate having gills for respiration, fins for mobility, and, usually, a scaly external covering for protection. Fish, which outnumber all other backboned animals, comprise three classes of the subphylum Vertebrata. **2.** any of various other animals that inhabit the water, as a porpoise, starfish, or cuttlefish. **3.** flesh of fish used as food. **4.** *Informal.* person thought to have the characteristics of a fish, as lack of emotion or intelligence: *a cold fish, a poor fish.* **5.** flat strip, as of iron or wood, fastened alongside another either to strengthen it or to join two separate parts. **6. like a fish out of water.** ill at ease, as if out of one's customary or familiar environment. **7. other fish to fry.** other more important things to attend to. —*v.t.* **1.** to catch or try to catch fish in: *to fish a stream.* **2.** to catch or try to catch (fish): *to fish eels.* **3.** to search for, as by groping; find, and bring to the surface; get as by fishing (often with *up* or *out*): *She fished the keys out of her purse.* **4. to fish out.** to deplete of fish; exhaust the supply of fish in. —*v.i.* **1.** to catch or try to catch fish: *They fished all day.* **2.** to get or try to get by cunning or artifice: *She fished for an invitation to the party.* **3. to fish in troubled waters.** to take advantage of a disturbance or troubled situation to achieve one's ends. [Old English *fisc* animal that lives in water.]

fish and chips, fish fillets and potatoes, cut into short, broad strips and deep fried.

fish-bowl (fish′bōl′) *n.* **1.** glass bowl serving as an aquarium for small fish. **2.** area of activity completely exposed to public view or scrutiny.

fish cake, fried patty or ball made of chopped fish, usually cod, and mashed potato. Also, **fish ball.**

fish-er (fish′ər) *n.* **1.** fisherman. **2.** any animal that catches fish for food. **3.** carnivorous North American mammal, *Martes pennanti,* of the marten family, having a long body, short legs, and a pointed face. Length: 40 inches including tail. **4.** dark-brown fur of this animal.

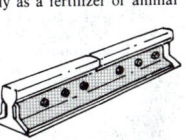

Fisher (def. 3)

fish-er-man (fish′ər mən) *pl.,* **-men.** *n.* **1.** one who fishes as an occupation or for sport. **2.** boat used in commercial fishing.

fish-er-y (fish′ər ē) *pl.,* **-er-ies.** *n.* **1.** occupation or industry of catching fish or taking other products from seas, lakes, or rivers. **2.** place for catching fish or other sea products; fishing ground. **3.** fish hatchery.

fish glue, glue derived from bones and waste parts of fish, used in paints and sizes.

fish hatchery, establishment for the hatching and growing of fish under controlled conditions.

fish hawk, osprey.

fish-hook (fish′hook′) *n.* hook, usually barbed, for catching fish.

fish-ing (fish′ing) *n.* **1.** occupation or sport of catching fish. **2.** place to catch fish.

fishing rod, long pole, usually made of wood, metal, or fiberglass, with a line, hook, and usually a reel attached to it, used to catch fish.

fishing tackle, equipment used by a fisherman, as rods, lines, hooks, and nets.

fish ladder, arrangement of successive ascending pools of water by which fish can pass around a dam or waterfall in swimming upstream.

fish line, line, usually with a hook attached, used for fishing.

fish meal, ground, dried fish, used chiefly as a fertilizer or animal feed.

fish-mon-ger (fish′mung′gər) *n.* one who deals in fish.

fish-net (fish′net′) *n.* **1.** net for catching fish. **2.** meshed fabric resembling the netting used for catching fish.

fish-plate (fish′plāt′) *n.* plate for fastening two rails or beams end to end, as on a railroad track.

Fishplate

fish pole, fishing rod.

fish-pond (fish′pond′) *n.* pond containing fish, esp. a pond stocked with edible fish for sport or food.

fish stick, fish fillet in the shape of a long, flattened bar that is breaded and fried.

fish story *Informal.* exaggerated or improbable story. [From the belief that fishermen habitually exaggerate in describing the size of fish.]

fish-tail (fish′tāl′) *adj.* resembling a fish's tail in shape or action. —*v.i.* to move in the manner of a fish's tail: *The car's rear end fishtailed as it sped around the sharp curve.*

fish-wife (fish′wīf′) *pl.,* **-wives.** *n.* **1.** woman who sells fish. **2.** coarse, abusive woman.

fish-y (fish′ē) **fish-i-er, fish-i-est.** *adj.* **1.** resembling a fish, as in odor or taste. **2.** consisting of fish. **3.** abounding in fish. **4.** *Informal.* improbable; unlikely: *a fishy story.* **5.** *Informal.* of questionable character; suspicious: *He was involved in some kind of fishy business.* **6.** vacant of expression; dull: *a fishy stare.* —**fish′i-ly,** *adv.* —**fish′i-ness,** *n.*

Fiske, John (fisk) 1842–1901, U.S. philosopher and educator.

fis-sile (fis′əl) *adj.* **1.** capable of being split or divided. **2.** fissionable. **3.** tending to split. [Latin *fissilis* that may be split, from *findere* to split.]

fis-sion (fish′ən) *n.* **1.** act of splitting or breaking apart. **2.** *Physics.* splitting of a heavy atomic nucleus into two lighter ones, occurring when the nucleus is bombarded by and absorbs a neutron. When fission is initiated in a nuclear reactor, the energy released during the fission process can be utilized as an efficient power source. **3.** *Biology.* method of reproduction in which the parent cell divides to form two or more new individuals. Many single-celled plants and animals reproduce by means of fission. —*v.i., v.t.* to undergo or cause to undergo fission. [Latin *fissiō* a cleaving.]

fis-sion-a-ble (fish′ən ə bəl) *adj.* (of an element or isotope) capable of undergoing nuclear fission. Uranium, plutonium, and thorium are fissionable materials.

fission bomb, atomic bomb.

fis-sure (fish′ər) *n.* **1.** long, narrow opening; cleft or crack: *a fissure in a rock.* **2.** a splitting apart or being split; cleavage. —*v.t., v.i.* **-sured,**

at; āpe; cär; end; mē; it; īce; hot; ōld; fôrk; wood; fōōl; oil; out; up; ūse; turn; sing; thin; this; zh in treasure; ə in ago, taken, pencil, lemon, circus.

387

-sur·ing. to split apart; cleave. —*v.i.* to become split; crack. [Latin *fissūra* a cleft.]

fist (fist) *n.* **1.** hand clenched with fingers doubled into the palm. **2.** *Informal.* grasp; grip; clutch. **b.** hand. **c.** handwriting. **3.** *Printing.* index mark. —*v.t.* to strike with the fist. [Old English *fӯst* clenched hand.]

fist·ful (fist′fŏol′) *n.* handful.

fist·ic (fis′tik) *adj. Informal.* of or relating to boxing or fist fighting; pugilistic.

fist·i·cuffs (fis′ti kufs′) *n.,pl.* **1.** a fight with the fists, esp. bare fists. **2.** the art of boxing.

fis·tu·la (fis′cha la) *pl.,* **-las** or **-lae** (-lē) *n.* tubelike passage that connects body cavities or organs that are normally not connected, either congenital or resulting from the improper healing of a wound or abscess. [Latin *fistula* tube, ulcer.]

fis·tu·lous (fis′cha las) *adj.* **1.** of, relating to, or resembling a fistula. **2.** hollow and cylindrical, like a pipe or reed; tubelike. **3.** having or consisting of tubelike parts.

fit¹ (fit) **fit·ter, fit·test.** *adj.* **1.** adapted to or qualified for an end, object, or purpose; appropriate; suited: *This dress style is fit for a long, slender figure.* **2.** becoming; meet; right; proper: *a fit occasion to honor him.* **3.** possessing the necessary qualifications; competent: *He is fit to lead the expedition.* **4.** ready; prepared: *The fruit will be fit to eat in three days.* **5.** in good physical or mental condition; healthy: *He is fit enough to run twice that distance.* —*v.t.,* **fit·ted, fit·ting. 1.** to be suitable or proper for; be adapted to; befit: *Let the punishment fit the crime. The time when screech-owls cry . . . best fits the work we have in hand* (Shakespeare, *Macbeth*). **2.** to be of the proper or correct size or shape for: *The coat fits her well.* **3.** to make fit or suitable; alter; adjust: *to fit a speech to the occasion.* **4.** to make ready; prepare; qualify: *The course fits you for the position.* **5.** to supply with what is necessary or suitable; equip (often with *out* or *up*): *The society fitted out the members of the expedition with all needed supplies.* **6.** to adjust, join, or insert precisely: *to fit the pieces of a jigsaw puzzle together.* **7.** to make or arrange to conform or correspond to something else: *We will fit our plans to yours.* —*v.i.* **1.** to be suitable, proper, or becoming. **2.** to be of the proper size or shape: *Does the coat fit?* **3.** to be in harmony or accord; be adapted (with *in* or *into*). —*n.* **1.** manner in which something fits: *a loose fit.* **2.** thing that fits or is fitted: *The dress is a perfect fit.* [Of uncertain origin.] —**fit′ly,** *adv.* —**fit′ness,** *n.*

Syn. *adj.* **2. Fit, suitable, appropriate** indicate that something is proper or right for a purpose. **Fit** suggests that something has the correct attributes, such as being in good physical condition or having the qualities needed for the purpose: *It was a dinner fit for royalty and included many delicacies and exotic foods.* **Suitable** implies meeting, however roughly, whatever requirements are necessary: *She refused to go to the party until she had a suitable dress.* **Appropriate** suggests being exactly right for a specific purpose: *He selected an appropriate birthday card for his mother.*

fit² (fit) *n.* **1.a.** acute, sudden attack of illness, esp. a chronic one: *a fit of the gout.* **b.** sudden attack or seizure, esp. when resulting in unconsciousness: *a fainting fit.* **2.** sudden, quickly passing outburst of emotion or feeling: *a fit of anger, a fit of laughter.* **3.** impulsive and irregular effort or activity: *In a fit of meticulousness, she cleaned the whole house.* **4. by** (or **in**) **fits and starts,** in a spasmodic or irregular manner. **5. to have** (or **throw**) **a fit.** *Informal.* to show extreme anger; become upset. [Old English *fitt* conflict.]

fitch (fich) *n.* the buff-gray, black-tipped fur of the European polecat, used to make coats and jackets. [Middle Dutch *vitsche* polecat.]

fit·ful (fit′fal) *adj.* characterized by irregular or intermittent behavior; spasmodic. [FIT² + -FUL.] —**fit′ful·ly,** *adv.* —**fit′ful·ness,** *n.*

fit·ter (fit′ar) *n.* **1.** one who fits. **2.** one who fits or alters garments. **3.** one who adjusts or assembles parts or machinery. **4.** one who supplies, installs, and fixes fittings and fixtures of any kind. **5.** one who furnishes all necessary equipment and supplies for an undertaking, esp. an expedition.

fit·ting (fit′ing) *adj.* suitable; proper; appropriate: *fitting praise, a fitting conclusion.* —*n.* **1.** act of one who fits. **2.** trying on of an article of clothing so that it can be marked for adjustments. **3.** accessory part or attachment used to adjust something: *a pipe fitting.* **4. fittings.** furnishings, fixtures, or decorations, as for a house or automobile. —**fit′ting·ly,** *adv.* —**fit′ting·ness,** *n.* —**Syn.** *adj.* see **proper.**

Fitz·Ger·ald, Edward (fits jer′ald) 1809–83, English poet and translator.

Fitz·ger·ald, F(rancis) Scott (Key) (fits jer′ald) 1896–1940, U.S. novelist and short-story writer.

Fiu·me (fū′mā) *n.* Rijeka.

five (fīv) *n.* **1.** the cardinal number that is one more than four. **2.** symbol representing this number, as 5 or V. **3.** something having this many units or members, as a men's basketball team or a playing card. —*adj.* numbering one more than four. [Old English *fīf.*]

five-and-ten (fīv′an ten′) *n.* store offering a wide variety of inexpensive merchandise. Also, **dime store, five-and-dime, five-and-ten-cent store.** [Because such stores originally sold many articles costing five or ten cents.]

five·fold (fīv′fōld′) *adj.* **1.** five times as great or numerous. **2.** having or consisting of five parts. —*adv.* so as to be five times greater or more numerous.

Five Nations, Iroquois.

five pence, coin of the United Kindgom equal to five pennies or ¹/₂₀ of a pound.

fives (fīvz) *n.* English game similar to handball.

five-year plan (fīv′yĕr′) **1.** any of several programs for the national economic development of the Soviet Union, intended to be completed within a five-year period. **2.** any similar plan in another country.

fix (fiks) **fixed** or **fixt, fix·ing.** *v.t.* **1.** to make firm, stable, or secure; fasten tightly: *to fix a stake in the ground.* **2.** to establish firmly in the mind. **3.** to place permanently; set; station: *The chair was fixed next to the desk.* **4.** to settle or arrange definitely; set: *to fix a price.* **5.** to determine or specify with certainty; establish as fact: *to fix Plato's birthplace.* **6.** to direct or hold, as the eyes or attention, steadily: *He fixed his gaze on her.* **7.** to attract and hold fast, as with the eyes; arrest: *to fix the attention of an audience.* **8.** to make rigid or motionless: *to be fixed with admiration.* **9.** to place, assign, or impose upon: *to fix blame, to fix a responsibility.* **10.** to mend; repair: *to fix a broken chair.* **11.** to treat so as to make permanent or lasting: *to fix colors in a fabric.* **12.** to cause (insoluble gaseous nitrogen) to combine with other substances into a soluble compound. **13.** *Photography.* to treat (a photograph) with a chemical solution so that it will not fade. **14.** *Informal.* to put in order; get ready; arrange (often with *up*): *She fixed up the room for her guest.* **15.** *Informal.* to prearrange or influence the result of (a contest) to one's advantage, as by a bribe: *to fix a race, to fix a basketball game.* **16.** to prepare (food or a meal): *to fix dinner.* **17.** *Informal.* to get revenge upon; get even with; punish: *I'll fix him yet!* **18.** to spay; castrate: *to fix a cat.* **19. to fix up.** *Informal.* **a.** to mend; repair: *He fixed up the broken chair.* **b.** to provide what is needed for; accommodate: *We fixed him up for the evening at our house.* —*v.i.* **1.** to become firm, stable, secure, or permanent: *The stain fixes if you wash it in cold water.* **2.** *Informal.* to get ready; prepare: *She is fixing to leave.* **3. to fix on** (or **upon).** to decide on; choose; select: *He fixed on her as his secretary.* —*n.* **1.** *Informal.* position from which it is difficult to escape; difficulty; predicament: *She got herself into a fix by accepting two dates for the same dance.* **2.** *Informal.* prearrangement of the result or outcome of a contest, as an athletic event, by illegal means. **3.** *Slang.* dosage of a narcotic. **4.** position of a ship or aircraft, as determined by observations or from radio signals. [Latin *fīxus,* past participle of *fīgere* to fasten.] —**fix′a·ble,** *adj.* —**fix′er,** *n.*

Syn. *v.t.* **4. Fix, set, determine** indicate making something firm and definite. **Fix** suggests deciding on a position for something from which it is not to be moved and placing it there as if it were anchored: *The judge fixed the date for the trial as June 14.* **Set** implies making arrangements for something to occur, as by stating its limitations or by putting it in a definite position: *They set the last week in July as the deadline for going to press.* **Determine** suggests that all relevant factors are taken into account before making a definite arrangement: *The committee determined who would handle the shopping for the party.* **10.** see **mend.**

fix·a·tion (fik sā′shan) *n.* **1.** a fixing; fixing. **2.** treatment to make permanent a dye or color, as in film. **3.** conversion of atmospheric nitrogen into useful nitrogen compounds such as soil nitrates and ammonia. **4.** obsessive preoccupation or attachment.

fix·a·tive (fik′sa tiv) *n.* something that serves to fix or make permanent, esp. a substance sprayed on a charcoal or crayon drawing to preserve it. —*adj.* serving to fix or make permanent.

fixed (fikst) *adj.* **1.** made firm in position; securely placed or fastened; not movable: *fixed seats.* **2.** stationary or unchanging in relative position. **3.** steadily intent or directed; rigid; set: *fixed teeth, a fixed stare.* **4.** not fluctuating; settled; unalterable: *a fixed rate of interest.* **5.** definite; resolute: *a fixed purpose.* **6.** *Chemistry.* **a.** not volatile. **b.** incorporated into a stable compound. **7.** *Informal.* prearranged privately or dishonestly as to outcome or decision: *a fixed race.* **8.** *Informal.* provided with something, as money: *He is well fixed.* —**fix·ed·ly** (fik′sid lē) *adv.* —**fix′ed·ness,** *n.*

fixed star, star that, because of its great distance from the earth, appears to remain in the same position in relation to other stars.

fix·ings (fik′singz) *n.,pl. Informal.* accessories; trimmings; garnishes: *a turkey dinner with all the fixings.*

fix·i·ty (fik′sa tē) *pl.,* **-ties.** *n.* **1.** state or quality of being fixed; stability; permanence. **2.** something that is fixed into position.

fixt (fikst) a past tense and past participle of **fix.**

fix·ture (fiks′char) *n.* **1.** anything fixed or securely fastened into position, esp. a permanently attached part or accessory of a house: *bathroom fixtures.* **2.** person or thing permanently established or regarded as fixed

at; āpe; cär; end; mē; it; īce; hot; ōld; fôrk; wood; fōol; oil; out; up; ūse; turn; sing; thin; this; zh in treasure; a in ago, taken, pencil, lemon, circus.

in a particular place or job. [Modification (influenced by *mixture*) of obsolete *fixure* fixed condition, from Late Latin *fixūra* a fastening, from Latin *figere* to fasten.]

fizz (fiz) *v.i.* to make a hissing or sputtering sound. —*n.* **1.** hissing sound. **2.** effervescent beverage, as champagne or soda water. **3.** mixed drink made with liquor, soda water, and flavorings: *a gin fizz.* [Imitative.]

fiz·zle (fiz'əl) -zled, -zling, *v.i.* **1.** to make a hissing or sputtering sound: *The wet wood fizzled in the fireplace.* **2.** *Informal.* to fail or end feebly, esp. after a good start (often with *out*): *All our plans fizzled out.* —*n.* **1.** hissing or sputtering sound. **2.** *Informal.* abortive effort; failure. [FIZZ + -LE.]

fizz·y (fiz'ē) fizz·i·er, fizz·i·est. *adj.* fizzing; effervescent.

fjord (fyôrd) fiord.

Fl, fluorine.

fl. 1. floor. **2.** florin. **3.** flourished. **4.** fluid.

Fla., Florida.

flab·ber·gast (flab'ər gast') *v.t.* *Informal.* to astonish; confound. [Possibly blend of FLABBY and AGHAST.]

flab·by (flab'ē) -bi·er, -bi·est. *adj.* **1.** lacking firmness; soft; flaccid: *flabby skin.* **2.** lacking substance or force; weak: *flabby logic.* [Form of earlier *flappy,* from FLAP + -Y¹.] —**flab'bi·ly,** *adv.* —**flab'bi·ness,** *n.*

flac·cid (flak'sid) *adj.* lacking firmness or elasticity; limp; weak: *flaccid muscles.* [Latin *flaccidus* flabby.] —**flac·cid'i·ty,** *n.*

fla·con (flak'ən, flä kôṅ') *n.* small stoppered bottle or flask. [French *flacon* bottle, phial, from Old French *flascon* bottle. See FLAGON.]

flag¹ (flag) *n.* **1.** piece of cloth or bunting of various sizes, colors, and symbolic emblems or devices, used to represent something, as a country or organization, or as a signaling device. **2.** something suggesting a flag, as the bushy tail of a dog or the tail of a deer. **3.** flags. **a.** feathers on the second joint of a bird's wing. **b.** long feathers on the lower parts of certain bird's legs. —*v.t.,* **flagged, flag·ging. 1.** to put a flag or flags over or on; decorate or adorn with flags. **2.** to stop or signal with or as with a flag: *to flag a taxicab.* **3.** to communicate (information) by signaling with a flag or flags: *to flag a message.* **4.** to decoy (game) by waving a flag or similar object to attract attention. **5. to flag down.** to signal something to stop by using a flag or by a waving motion: *to flag down a train.* [Possibly from FLAG³.]

flag² (flag) *n.* **1.** any of various irises having sword-shaped leaves and blue, yellow, purple, or white flowers. **2.** flower of any these plants. **3.** sweet flag. [Of uncertain origin.]

flag³ (flag) flagged, flag·ging. *v.i.* **1.** to run low in interest or activity; grow weak or tired; lose vigor: *His interest flagged.* **2.** to hang down; become limp; droop: *When the wind died down, the sails flagged.* [Of uncertain origin.]

flag⁴ (flag) *n.* flagstone. —*v.t.,* flagged, flag·ging. to pave with flagstones. [Old Norse *flaga* slab of stone.]

Flag Day, June 14, the anniversary of the adoption in 1777 of the Stars and Stripes as the official flag of the United States.

flag·el·lant (flaj'ə lənt, flə jel'ənt) *n.* one who whips, esp. one who whips himself or has himself whipped for religious reasons or for sexual excitement. —*adj.* flagellating. [Latin *flagellāns,* present participle of *flagellāre.* See FLAGELLATE.]

flag·el·late (flaj'ə lāt') *adj.* **1.** having a flagellum or flagella. **2.** shaped like a flagellum. Also, **flag'el·lat·ed.** —*v.t.,* -lat·ed, -lat·ing. to whip; scourge. [Latin *flagellātus,* past participle of *flagellāre* to scourge, going back to *flagrum* whip.] —**flag'el·la'tion,** *n.*

fla·gel·lum (flə jel'əm) *pl.,* -la (-lə) or -lums. *n.* **1.** long, whiplike projection that serves as an organ of locomotion in certain cells, bacteria, and protozoa. **2.** whip. [Latin *flagellum* whip, diminutive of *flagrum.*]

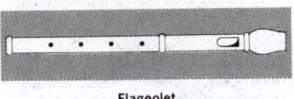

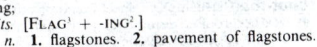

Flagellum of a protozoan

flag·eo·let (flaj'ə let') *n.* wind instrument of the flute family, similar to the recorder, and having six finger holes, four on the top and two on the underside. [French *flageolet* pipe, flute, diminutive of Old French *flageol* flute, through Provençal, going back to Latin *flāre* to blow.]

Flageolet

flag·ging¹ (flag'ing) *adj.* weakening; tiring; drooping: *flagging spirits.* [FLAG³ + -ING².]

flag·ging² (flag'ing) *n.* **1.** flagstones. **2.** pavement of flagstones. **3.** act of paving with flagstones. [FLAG⁴ + -ING¹.]

fla·gi·tious (flə jish'əs) *adj.* **1.** guilty of atrocious acts or extreme wickedness: *a flagitious ruler.* **2.** extremely wicked or atrocious; hei-

nous: *the flagitious crimes he had committed.* [Latin *flāgitiōsus* shameful, from *flāgitium* shameful act.] —**fla·gi'tious·ly,** *adv.* —**fla·gi'tious·ness,** *n.*

flag·man (flag'mən) *pl.,* -men. *n.* **1.** one who carries a flag. **2.** person who signals with a flag or lantern, esp. at a railroad crossing.

flag officer, naval officer above the rank of captain, entitled to display a flag indicating his rank.

flag of truce, white flag used to signal a desire for a conference with the enemy or for a cessation of hostilities.

flag·on (flag'ən) *n.* **1.** large vessel for liquids, having a handle, a spout, and usually a cover. **2.** large bottle used to hold alcoholic beverages, as wine or ale. **3.** contents of a flagon. [Old French *flascon* bottle, from Late Latin *flascō;* possibly of Germanic origin.]

flag·pole (flag'pōl') *n.* pole on which a flag is raised and displayed.

flag rank, naval rank above captain, including commodore, rear admiral, vice-admiral, and admiral.

fla·grant (flā'grənt) *adj.* glaring; notorious; scandalous: *flagrant violations of the law. Such a flagrant display of cowardice was unforgivable.* [Latin *flagrāns,* present participle of *flagrāre* to burn.] —**fla'gran·cy,** *n.* —**fla'grant·ly,** *adv.*

Syn. Flagrant, glaring, gross indicate something openly and scandalously bad. **Flagrant** implies a conspicuous and thus unavoidably obvious misdeed: *His flagrant disobedience could not be tolerated.* **Glaring** suggests the impossibility of hiding an obtrusive wrong: *The witness left several glaring inconsistencies in his testimony.* **Gross** implies something so monstrous or beyond normal bounds that it cannot be overlooked or condoned: *His gross refusal to respect the wishes of the bereaved parents was inexcusable.*

flag·ship (flag'ship') *n.* ship carrying the commanding officer of a fleet.

flag·staff (flag'staf') *n.* flagpole.

flag station, railroad station at which trains stop only on signal. Also, **flag stop.**

flag·stone (flag'stōn') *n.* large, flat stone, used for paving.

flail (flāl) *n.* instrument for threshing grain by hand, consisting of a wooden staff at the end of which a stouter, shorter pole is hung so as to swing freely. —*v.t.* **1.** to strike with or as with a flail; thresh. **2.** to wave or swing, esp. violently or swiftly: *The frightened woman flailed her arms wildly at the hornets swarming about her* —*v.i.* **1.** to toss or thrash about. [Old French *flaiel* scourge, from Latin *flagellum* whip. See FLAGELLUM.]

flair (flâr) *n.* **1.** perceptiveness; discernment. **2.** natural talent or aptitude: *an author's flair for the dramatic. He has a flair for acting.* [French *flair* sense of smell, discernment, from *flairer* to smell, going back to Latin *fragrāre* to smell sweet.]

flak (flak) *n.* **1.** antiaircraft fire. **2.** fragments from exploding shells fired at enemy aircraft. **3.** *Slang.* criticism or abuse: *The senator had not expected his proposal to meet with so much flak.* [Abbreviation of German *Fl(ieger)a(bwehr)k(anone)* antiaircraft gun; literally, gun warding off aviators.]

flake (flāk) *n.* **1.** small, thin particle of light substance: *soap flakes.* **2.** thin, scalelike piece or layer split or peeled from the surface of something; chip: *paint flakes.* —*v.t.,* flaked, flak·ing. **1.** to chip or peel off in flakes: *He flaked the arrowhead carefully.* **2.** to form into flakes. **3.** to spot or cover with or as with flakes: *His hair was flaked with white.* —*v.i.* **1.** to peel off in flakes: *The plaster cracked and flaked.* **2.** to become spotted with or as with flakes. [Probably of Scandinavian origin.]

flak·y (flā'kē) flak·i·er, flak·i·est. *adj.* **1.** resembling or consisting of flakes: *a flaky mineral.* **2.** separating easily into flakes: *a flaky pie crust.* —**flak'i·ly,** *adv.* —**flak'i·ness,** *n.*

flam·beau (flam'bō) *pl.,* -beaux (-bōz) or -beaus. *n.* **1.** flaming torch. **2.** large, decorated candlestick. [French *flambeau* torch, from Old French *flamble* flame, going back to Latin *flamma.*]

flam·boy·ant (flam boi'ənt) *adj.* **1.** extravagantly ornate; overly decorated; showy; florid: *a flamboyant writing style, flamboyant fashions.* **2.** brilliant; resplendent: *a flamboyant sunset.* **3.** designating a style of architecture, as French Gothic of the fifteenth and sixteenth centuries, characterized by florid decoration and wavy, flamelike tracery in windows and openwork. [French *flamboyant,* present participle of *flamboyer* to flame, blaze, going back to Latin *flamma* blaze, flame.] —**flam·boy'ance, flam·boy'an·cy,** *n.* —**flam·boy'ant·ly,** *adv.* —**Syn. 1.** see ornate.

flame (flām) *n.* **1.** one of the tongues of light emitted from a fire: *The flames shot in every direction.* **2.** ignited gas or vapor that gives off light and heat: *Lower the flame under the frying pan.* **3.** condition or state of visible combustion; blaze: *The house was in flames.* **4.** something resembling or suggesting a flame: *The sun was a flame on the horizon.* **5.** bright or glowing light; flamelike color or appearance; brilliance: *the flame of a jewel;* possibly of Germanic origin.] **6.** strong emotional feeling; passion; ardor: *the flame of love.* **7.** *Slang.* sweetheart: *He was my first flame.* —*v.i.,* **flamed,**

at; āpe; cär; end; mē; it; īce; hot; ōld; fôrk; wood; fŏŏl; oil; out; up; ūse; turn; sing; thin; this; zh in treasure; ə in ago, taken, pencil, lemon, circus.

389

flam·ing. 1. to burn with flames; burst into flame; blaze: *The fire flamed intensely.* **2.** to light up or glow as if with flames; grow hot or red: *His face flamed with embarrassment.* **3.** to emit or display a flamelike color or appearance; shine like flame; glow brilliantly: *The autumn woods flamed with color.* **4.** to become aroused or excited; break out with violence or passion: *She flamed with rage at the very thought of such injustice.* **5. to flame up** (or **out**). to burst out suddenly with or as with violence or emotion. —*v.t.* to subject to the action of fire or flame. [Old French *flam(m)e* blaze, tongue of light emitted from a fire, from Latin *flamma*.] —**flam′er,** *n.*

fla·men (flā′men) *pl.* **fla·mens** or **flam·i·nes** (flam′ə nēz′). *n.* priest in ancient Rome devoted to the service of one particular deity. [Latin *flāmen.*]

fla·men·co (flə meng′kō) *n.* type of vigorous dance associated with the Andalusian gypsies of Spain, characterized by slow twisting arm and hand movements, stamping of the feet, clapping of the hands, and the use of castanets.

flame·out (flām′out′) *n.* sudden cessation of functioning in a jet engine.

flame thrower, weapon or instrument that projects a stream of burning fuel.

flam·ing (flā′ming) *adj.* **1.** in flames; blazing; fiery. **2.** flamelike; brilliant: *flaming orange.* **3.** ardent; passionate; vehement: *a flaming speech.* —**flam′ing·ly,** *adv.*

fla·min·go (flə ming′gō) *pl.* **-gos** or **-goes.** *n.* any of various wading birds, genus *Phoenicopterus,* of tropical and subtropical regions, having long, thin legs and neck, a down-curved beak, webbed feet, and plumage that ranges from pinkish-white to deep crimson. Height: to 5 feet. [Portuguese *flamingo,* through Spanish and Provençal, going back to Latin *flamma* blaze, flame; because of its color.]

Flamingo

Fla·min·i·an Way (flə min′ē ən) one of the principal ancient Roman roads in central Italy, leading north from Rome to the Adriatic.

flam·ma·ble (flam′ə bəl) *adj.* capable of being set on fire easily; combustible. —*n.* something flammable. —**flam′ma·bil′i·ty,** *n.*

Flan·ders (flan′dərz) *n.* historic region of northwestern Europe, in western Belgium, northern France, and southwestern Netherlands.

flange (flanj) *n.* projecting rim or collar on an object, designed to keep it in place, as on railroad wheels, to attach it to another object, as on pipes, or for various other purposes. —*v.t.,* **flanged, flang·ing.** to provide with a flange. [Probably form of obsolete *flanch* projection, from Old French *flanche,* form of *flanc* side, flank. See FLANK.]

flank (flangk) *n.* **1.** part between the ribs and the hip on either side of an animal or human being. **2.** cut of meat, esp. beef, from this part of an animal. **3.** outer side of the human thigh. **4.** *Military.* the side of a unit, formation, position, or fortification. **5.** side or lateral part of something: *the flanks of a building.* —*v.t.* **1.** to be located at the side of: *Two statues flanked the entrance of the municipal library.* **2.a.** to defend or guard the flank of. **b.** to attack the flank of. **c.** to move around the flank of. —*v.i.* to be located at the side of something; be in a flanking position (with *on* or *upon*). [Old French *flanc* side; of Germanic origin.]

flank·er (flang′kər) *n.* **1.** one who or that which flanks. **2.** member of a body of soldiers protecting the flank of an army. **3.** projecting extension at either side of a fortification. **4.** offensive back in football who lines up in a flanking position.

flan·nel (flan′əl) *n.* **1.** soft cotton fabric, napped on one or both sides, used for such items as nightgowns, infants' wear, and shirts. Also, **cotton flannel, flan′nel·ette′. 2.** soft woolen fabric having a slightly napped surface. Also, **wool flannel. 3. flannels.** *a.* clothes made of flannel. *b.* warm woolen underwear. [Earlier *flannen,* from Welsh *gwlanen* woolen article, from *gwlân* wool.]

flan·nel·ette (flan′əl et′) *also,* **flan·nel·et.** *n.* flannel (*def. 1*).

flap (flap) *flapped,* **flap·ping.** *v.t.* **1.** to move up and down, esp. with a muffled, slapping sound: *The birds flapped their wings. He flapped his arms wildly.* **2.** to cause to move in a swaying or rippling manner, esp. with noise: *The wind flapped the shutters.* **3.** to strike with something broad and flat; slap. **4.** to toss, throw down, or swing shut suddenly or noisily: *He flapped the newspaper on the floor.* —*v.i.* **1.** to move the wings or arms up and down, esp. with a muffled, slapping sound: *The bird flapped across the sky.* **2.** to sway or wave loosely, esp. with noise: *The curtains flapped in the breeze.* —*n.* **1.a.** flapping motion. **b.** the muffled, slapping sound produced by flapping. **2.** part of an envelope

folded down in closing or sealing it. **3.** blow given with something broad and flat; slap. **4.** piece of material attached at one edge only so that it may move as though hinged, esp. one covering the opening of a pocket. **5.** hinged section, usually on the trailing edge of an airplane wing, that is used to increase lift during a take-off or a landing. See **airplane** for illustration. [Probably imitative.]

flap·jack (flap′jak′) *n.* pancake.

flap·per (flap′ər) *n.* **1.** one who or that which flaps. **2.** young bird not yet able to fly. **3.** *Informal.* young woman, esp. in the 1920s, who is unconventional in dress and behavior.

flare (flâr) *flared,* **flar·ing.** *v.i.* **1.** to burn with a very bright light, esp. for only a short time: *The torch flared in the darkness.* **2.** to burst into a sudden blaze (often with *up*): *The campfire flared up in the sudden wind.* **3.** to break out in sudden or violent emotion or activity (often with *up* or *out*): *She flared up at his remark. Rebellion flared up in the outlying provinces.* **4.** to open or spread outward: *Her skirt flared from the waist.* —*v.t.* **1.** to cause to flare. **2.** to signal with flares. —*n.* **1.** bright or glaring light, usually lasting only a short time. **2.a.** fire or blaze of light used for signaling or illumination. **b.** device producing such a light. **3.** sudden outburst, as of emotion or activity: *a flare of resentment.* **4.a.** a widening or spreading outward. **b.** the thing or part that spreads out: *the flare of a skirt.* [Possibly blend of FLAME + GLARE.]

flare-up (flâr′up′) *n.* **1.** sudden outburst of flame or light. **2.** *Informal.* sudden outburst: *a flare-up of violence at a political rally.*

flar·ing (flâr′ing) *adj.* **1.** blazing brightly or unsteadily. **2.** showy; gaudy. **3.** widening or spreading gradually outward.

flash (flash) *n.* **1.** sudden, brief burst, as of light or flame: *a flash of lightning.* **2.** very brief period of time; instant; moment: *He was there in a flash.* **3.** sudden outburst or brief display, as of thought or understanding: *a flash of merriment, a flash of inspiration.* **4.** brief bulletin or report of very recent or urgent news. **5.** ostentatious or vulgar display; showiness. **6.** flashlight. **7. flash in the pan.** someone or something initially promising or successful but ultimately a failure. —*v.i.* **1.** to burst forth in sudden, brief light or fire: *Lightning flashed in the sky.* **2.** to reflect or burst forth with light in sudden brilliance; shine; gleam: *The swords flashed in the sun. Her eyes flashed with anger.* **3.** to burst suddenly into view or perception: *An idea flashed into his mind.* **4.** to come or move suddenly or quickly: *The car flashed by.* —*v.t.* **1.** to cause to flash: *He flashed the light in her eyes.* **2.** to emit or send forth in a sudden flash or flashes: *The flagship flashed a signal to the fleet.* **3.** to communicate by flashes, as by telegraph or radio: *The news was flashed all over the country.* **4.** *Informal.* to make an ostentatious display of; show off: *He flashed a roll of fifty-dollar bills.* **5.** to show suddenly and briefly: *The detective flashed his badge.* **6.** to cover with a protective material, as sheet metal; provide with or use flashing. **7.** to cover or coat (glass) with a thin layer or film of differently colored glass. —*adj.* **1.** happening or done very quickly: *flash freezing.* **2.** flashy; showy; ostentatious. [Probably imitative.] —**flash′er,** *n.*

Syn. *v.i.* **2.** Flash, shine, glitter, sparkle indicate a bright light, esp. a momentary or intermittent light. **Flash** suggests a quick, intense beam of short duration: *The mirror flashed in the sunlight.* **Shine** implies brightness that is reflected or comes from within and may be of some duration: *The lights of the harbor shine across the bay.* **Glitter** suggests a sequence of brilliant, cold sparks: *Glass from the shattered headlight glittered in the sun.* **Sparkle** implies many bright flashes of light: *The grass sparkled with dew as the sun rose.*

flash·back (flash′bak′) *n.* **1.** break in the normal time sequence of a motion picture, radio script, novel, or play, during which a scene or episode describing earlier events is inserted. **2.** scene or episode thus inserted.

flash bulb, incandescent light bulb filled with metal foil that gives off a single bright flash when ignited, used for taking photographs.

flash burn, burn caused by exposure to intense thermal radiation, esp. from an atomic explosion.

flash·card (flash′kärd′) *n.* any of a set of cards bearing information, as words or numbers, on either or both sides, used in classroom drills or in private study, as of a foreign language.

flash·cube (flash′kūb′) *n.* cubical camera accessory containing four flash bulbs that can be ignited in sequence by tripping the shutter mechanism of the camera.

flash flood, sudden, violent flood caused by heavy rainfall.

flash gun, battery-powered camera attachment or accessory that holds and ignites a flash bulb.

flash·ing (flash′ing) *n.* sheet metal or other protective material used as weatherproof covering over joints and angles, as of a roof where it meets the edges of walls or chimneys.

flash lamp, electric lamp that produces a brief, very bright light, used in taking photographs.

flash·light (flash′līt′) *n.* **1.** portable electric lamp powered by batter-

at; āpe; cär; end; mē; it; īce; hot; ōld; fôrk; wood; fōōl; oil; out; up; ūse; turn; sing; thin; this; zh in treasure; ə in ago, taken, pencil, lemon, circus.

ies. **2.** bright, flashing light used for signaling, as from a lighthouse. **3.** burst of artificial light used for taking photographs.

flash point, lowest temperature at which the vapor of a combustible substance will ignite.

flash·y (flash′ē) **flash·i·er, flash·i·est.** *adj.* **1.** momentarily brilliant; sparkling; flashing. **2.** showy; gaudy: *a flashy car.* —**flash′i·ly,** *adv.* —**flash′i·ness,** *n.*

flask (flask) *n.* **1.** any of various bottle-shaped containers, usually made of glass or metal, esp. a small, broad, flattened container, as for liquor, made to be carried in the pocket. **2.** rounded glass container with a long neck used in laboratory work, esp. for heating liquids. **3.** box or frame for holding a sand mold in a foundry. [Partly from Middle French *flasque* container for gunpowder; partly from Italian *fiasco* bottle; from Late Latin *flasca, flascō* (wine) bottle; possibly of Germanic origin.]

flat¹ (flat) **flat·ter, flat·test.** *adj.* **1.** extended horizontally with little or no slope or inclination: *A flat roof has poor drainage.* **2.** without projection; relatively smooth or even; level: *The plasterer made the surface flat.* **3.** lying or stretched at full length; spread out: *He was flat on his back.* **4.** placed or having an entire length or surface in contact with something: *Stand with your back flat against the wall.* **5.** having little depth or thickness; shallow: *a flat sheet of metal.* **6.** having relatively little curvature or projection: *a flat face.* **7.** plain; positive; absolute; downright: *a flat denial, a flat refusal.* **8.** fixed; unchangeable; uniform: *a flat rate.* **9.** lacking in interest, vigor, or animation; lifeless; dull; monotonous: *a flat performance.* **10.** having little or no flavor or sparkle; stale; tasteless; insipid: *flat food.* **11.** not clear or sharp in sound; lacking resonance: *a flat voice.* **12.a.** having little or no feeling of depth; without relief or projection. **b.** not shiny or glossy: *flat paint.* **c.** uniform in color or shading: *a flat tint.* **d.** without emphasizing contour or shadows: *flat lighting.* **13.** containing little or no air; deflated: *flat tire.* **14.** exact; precise. **15.** *Informal.* lacking or short of money. **16.** *Music.* **a.** below the true, regular, or intended pitch. **b.** one half step or half note lower than natural pitch. **c.** having a flat in the signature. —*n.* **1.** flat part or surface: *the flat of a sword, the flat of the hand.* **2.** piece or expanse of level ground. **3.** tract of low-lying marshy land; swamp. **4.** *also,* **flats.** level, partially submerged ground near a river; shoal. **5.** something that is flat. **6.** shallow box or container in which seedlings are grown. **7.** flatcar. **8.** piece of theatrical scenery, consisting of a frame, usually of wood, with a fabric, as canvas, stretched over it. **9.** flats. women's shoes having low heels. **10.** *Informal.* tire from which air is escaping or has escaped. **11.** *Music.* **a.** tone or note lowered one half step or half note below its natural pitch. **b.** character (♭) that indicates such a tone or note. —*adv.* **1.** in a flat manner; flatly: *to lie flat on the ground. The ladder was placed flat against the wall.* **2.** exactly; precisely: *He ran a mile in four minutes flat.* **3.** *Music.* below the true pitch: *She sang flat.* **4. to fall flat.** to fail completely; prove uninteresting or ineffective: *His joke fell flat.* —*v.t.,* **flat·ted, flat·ting. 1.** to make flat. **2.** *Music.* to sing or play flat. —*v.i.* to become flat. [Old Norse *flatr* level.] —**flat′ly,** *adv.* —**flat′ness,** *n.* —**Syn.** *adj.* **2. see level.**

flat² (flat) *n.* apartment or suite of rooms on one floor of a building. [Modification (influenced by FLAT¹) of Scottish *flet* interior of a house, from Old English *flet* floor, dwelling.]

flat·boat (flat′bōt′) *n.* large boat with a flat bottom and square ends, used for transport on rivers or canals.

flat·car (flat′kär′) *n.* railroad car consisting of a platform without sides or roof, used for transporting freight.

flat·fish (flat′fish′) *pl.,* **-fish** *or* **-fish·es.** any of any group of food fishes, order Pleuronectiformes, that have flattened bodies. In the adult both eyes are on the pigmented side of the body, which is always turned toward the surface of the water. Halibut, flounder, and sole are flatfishes. See **flounder** for illustration.

flat·foot (*def. 1,* flat′foot′; *def. 2,* flat′foot′) *pl.,* **-feet.** *n.* **1.a.** condition in which the arch of the foot is abnormally low and most or all of the sole touches the ground. **b.** foot with an abnormally low arch. **2.** *Slang.* policeman, esp. one who walks a beat.

flat·foot·ed (flat′foot′id) *adj.* **1.** having flat feet. **2.** *Informal.* direct; uncompromising; resolute: *a flat-footed refusal.* **3.** *Informal.* off one's guard; not ready; unprepared: *to be caught flat-footed.* —**flat′-foot′ed·ness,** *n.*

Flat·head (flat′hed′) *n.* **1.** member of any of several North American Indian tribes that practiced or were said to practice artificial flattening of the skulls of their babies, including the Chinook, Choctaw, Catawba, and Natchez. **2.** Salish (*def. 1*).

flat·i·ron (flat′ī′ərn) *n.* heavy iron for pressing clothes, esp. one which must be heated in an oven or fireplace before it can be used.

flat·ten (flat′ən) *v.t.* **1.** to make flat or flatter. **2.** to make prostrate; knock down: *The boxer flattened his opponent.* —*v.i.* **1.** to become flat or flatter. **2.** to fall or lie prostrate. **3. to flatten out.** to spread out and indicate, as in flying. —**flat′ten·er,** *n.*

flat·ter (flat′ər) *v.t.* **1.** to praise excessively or insincerely. **2.** to try to please or gain the favor of by praising excessively. **3.** to gratify the vanity of: *She was flattered by the invitation.* **4.** to represent or portray favorably, too favorably, or as more attractive than is actually the case: *The painting flatters him.* **5. to flatter oneself.** to have a vain hope, conviction, or feeling; delude oneself (with *that*): *She flattered herself that he was coming because of her.* —*v.i.* to flatter someone or something; use flattery. [Old French *flater* to soothe, caress; of Germanic origin.] —**flat′ter·er,** *n.* —**flat′ter·ing·ly,** *adv.*

flat·ter·y (flat′ər ē) *pl.,* **-ter·ies.** *n.* **1.** act of flattering; excessive or insincere praise. **2.** flattering remark or speech.

flat·tish (flat′ish) *adj.* somewhat flat.

flat·top (flat′top′) *n.* *Informal.* aircraft carrier.

flat·u·lent (flach′ə lənt) *adj.* **1.** having gas or air in the stomach or intestines. **2.** producing gas in the stomach or intestines. **3.** empty; boastful; vain; pretentious: *flatulent speech.* [French *flatulent* windy, going back to Latin *flātus* blowing.] —**flat′u·lence,** *n.* —**flat′u·lent·ly,** *adv.*

flat·ware (flat′wār′) *n.* **1.** table utensils, as knives, forks, and spoons. **2.** dishes that are more or less flat, as plates, platters, or saucers.

flat·wise (flat′wīz′) *also,* **flat·ways** (flat′wāz′). *adj.* in a flat position; with the flat side in contact; not edgewise.

flat·worm (flat′wurm′) *n.* any of a large group of soft, flat-bodied worms, phylum Platyhelminthes, that exhibit bilateral symmetry, including the planaria, the parasitic fluke, and the tapeworm.

Flau·bert, Gus·tave (flō bâr′; gōōs tàv′) 1821–80, French novelist.

flaunt (flônt, flänt) *v.t.* **1.** to obtrude oneself impudently or ostentatiously on the public view; make a gaudy display. **2.** to wave or flutter freely or conspicuously: *banners flaunting.* —*v.i.* **1.** to show or display ostentatiously or impudently: *People were offended by the way he flaunted his wealth.* —*n.* act of flaunting. [Of uncertain origin.] —**flaunt′ing·ly,** *adv.*

flau·tist (flō′tist) flutist.

fla·vor (flā′vər) *also, British.* **fla·vour.** *n.* **1.** particular or characteristic taste: *Adding pepper to the stew will give it a spicy flavor.* **2.** substance having such a taste: *You can choose from ten different flavors at that ice cream parlor.* **3.** characteristic, distinctive, or predominant quality; aura: *stories having a quaint flavor.* **4.** flavoring. **5.** *Archaic.* odor; aroma: *the flavor of the rose.* —*v.t.* to give flavor to: *to flavor apple pie with cinnamon.* [Old French *flaur* odor, going back to Latin *flāre* to blow.] —**Syn. 1. see taste.**

fla·vor·ful (flā′vər fəl) *adj.* full of flavor; tasty. Also, **fla·vor·some, fla′vor·y.**

fla·vor·ing (flā′vər ing) *n.* something, as an extract, added to food or drink to give or heighten flavor: *Connie added lemon flavoring to the cookies.*

flaw¹ (flô) *n.* **1.** something that detracts from or mars completeness, soundness, or perfection: *a tragic flaw in his character. There's a flaw in your plan.* **2.** broken, faulty, or weak spot; crack; fissure: *It was a large diamond, but it had a flaw.* —*v.t., v.i.* to make or become defective. [Possibly from Old Norse *flaga* slab of stone.] —**Syn.** *n.* **1. see blemish.**

flaw² (flô) *n.* sudden gust of wind, often accompanied by rain or snow; squall. [Possibly from Middle Dutch *vlāghe* stroke¹, storm.]

flaw·less (flô′lis) *adj.* having no flaw; perfect: *a flawless emerald. a flawless complexion. He gave a flawless performance.* —**flaw′less·ly,** *adv.* —**flaw′less·ness,** *n.* —**Syn. see perfect.**

flax (flaks) *n.* **1.** fiber that is obtained from the stem of a plant, *Linum usitatissimum,* and processed to be spun into the thread used to make linen and such products as rope and rugs. **2.** the plant itself, cultivated throughout the world, having small, lance-shaped leaves and clusters of blue, white, or pink flowers. **3.** any of certain plants resembling flax. [Old English *fleax* the plant.]

flax·en (flak′sən) *adj.* **1.** relating to, resembling, or made of flax: *flaxen thread.* **2.** having a pale-yellow color like that of flax fiber or straw: *flaxen hair.*

flax·seed (flaks′sēd′, flak′-) *n.* seed of flax, valued chiefly as a source of linseed oil; linseed.

flay (flā) *v.t.* **1.** to strip off the skin or outer covering of, as by lashing. **2.** to criticize or scold severely or harshly. [Old English *flēan* to skin.] —**flay′er,** *n.*

flea (flē) *n.* **1.** any of a large group of wingless, parasitic insects, order Siphonaptera, that feed on the blood of warm-blooded animals. They have strong legs for leaping and sharp mouth parts for piercing the skin and sucking blood, and may transmit certain diseases, as bubonic plague. Length: to 1/8 of an inch. **2.** water flea. **3.** any of several beetles that leap like fleas. Also, **flea**

Flea

beetle. **4. a flea in one's ear.** an irritating hint or sharp, stinging rebuke or rebuff. [Old English *flēa* the wingless, parasitic insect.]

flea·bane (flē'bān') *n.* any of a large group of plants, genus *Erigeron*, of the composite family, that were believed to repel or destroy fleas.

flea-bit·ten (flē'bit'ən) *adj.* **1.** bitten by or infested with fleas: a *flea-bitten dog.* **2.** having a gray or white coat, marked with reddish-brown spots or streaks. **3.** *Informal.* in poor condition; run-down; decrepit.

flea market, outdoor market that sells cheap or used goods.

fleck (flek) *n.* **1.** small patch or streak; spot, as of light or color: *flecks of sunlight on the water, black marble with flecks of white in it.* **2.** small particle; flake; speck: *flecks of dust.* —*v.t.* to mark with flecks; spot; speckle. [Probably from Old Norse *flekkr* spot.]

flec·tion (flek'shən) *n.* **1.** act of bending; being bent. **2.** bent part; bend. **3.** *Anatomy.* flexion. [Form of FLEXION.]

fled (fled) past tense and past participle of **flee.**

fledge (flej) **fledged, fledg·ing.** *v.t.* **1.** to furnish (an arrow) with feathers. **2.** to rear (a young bird) until it is able to fly. —*v.i.* (of a young bird) to grow the feathers needed for flight; acquire full plumage (often with *out*). [Old English *-flycge* (found in *unflycge* without feathers, unfledged).]

fledg·ling (flej'ling) *also,* **fledge·ling,** *n.* **1.** young bird just fledged. **2.** young or inexperienced person.

flee (flē) **fled, flee·ing.** *v.i.* **1.** to run away, as from danger or pursuers; take flight: *The robbers fled down the alley. The squirrel fled when he saw us.* **2.** to move or pass away swiftly: *cars fleeing by. Color fled from her cheeks. His troubles fled.* —*v.t.* to run away or try to escape from: *citizens forced to flee the besieged city.* [Old English *flēon* to run away from, avoid.] —**fle'er,** *n.*

fleece (flēs) *n.* **1.** coat of wool covering a sheep or similar animal. **2.** quantity of wool sheared from a sheep or similar animal at any one time. **3.** something resembling fleece: *fleeces of descending snow.* **4.** fabric with a thick nap or pile resembling the wool of sheep, used for such purposes as lining coats or gloves. —*v.t.,* **fleeced, fleec·ing. 1.** to shear the fleece from. **2.** to deprive of money or property by deception; cheat; swindle. [Old English *flēos* coat of wool of a sheep or similar animal.] —**fleec'er,** *n.*

fleec·y (flē'sē) **fleec·i·er, fleec·i·est.** *adj.* **1.** made of or covered with fleece. **2.** resembling fleece: *fleecy clouds in a clear blue sky.* —**fleec'i·ness,** *n.*

fleer (flēr) *v.i.* to laugh or grin sneeringly. —*v.t.* to mock; deride. —*n.* sneering look or laugh. [Probably of Scandinavian origin.]

fleet¹ (flēt) *n.* **1.** group of warships organized under one command. **2.** group, as of boats or vehicles, organized into or regarded as a unit or operated by a single company: *a fleet of taxis, a fleet of barges, the fleet of a steamship company.* [Old English *flēot* ship, from *flēotan* to float.]

fleet² (flēt) *adj.* swift; fast: *fleet of foot.* —*v.i.* to move or pass swiftly. [Old English *flēotan* to float, swim.] —**fleet'ly,** *adv.* —**fleet'ness,** *n.*

fleet admiral, officer in the U.S. Navy of the highest rank.

fleet·ing (flē'ting) *adj.* lasting a short time; passing quickly; transitory; brief: *a fleeting glimpse, a fleeting moment.* —**fleet'ing·ly,** *adv.* —**fleet'ing·ness,** *n.*

Flem·ing (flem'ing) *n.* **1.** Belgian whose native language is Flemish. **2.** one of the people of historic Flanders.

Flem·ing, Sir Alexander (flem'ing) 1881–1955, Scottish bacteriologist and codiscoverer of penicillin.

Flem·ish (flem'ish) *adj.* of or relating to Flanders, its people, or their language. —*n.* **1. the Flemish.** the people historically inhabiting Flanders and those who have descended from them. **2.** Germanic language of the Indo-European family resembling Dutch and spoken chiefly in northern Belgium and northwestern France.

flesh (flesh) *n.* **1.** part of the body of a human being or animal that covers the bones, consisting mainly of muscle and fat, esp. the muscular tissue of this part. **2.** surface of the human body; skin. **3.** parts of an animal used as food; meat, esp. as distinguished from fish or fowl. **4.** soft, pulpy portion of fruits or vegetables, as distinguished from the core, seeds, or skin. **5.** body of man, as opposed to the soul or spirit: *The spirit is willing, but the flesh is weak.* **6.** sensual or physical nature of man, as distinguished from the moral or spiritual nature: *to satisfy the desires of the flesh.* **7.** human beings collectively; humanity; mankind. **8.** light pinkish or yellowish tan color. **9. one's (own) flesh and blood.** one's offspring, immediate family, or other blood relatives. **10. to be (only) flesh and blood.** to have human feelings, limitations, or weaknesses; be human. **11. in the flesh.** physically present before one's eyes; in person: *He's taller in the flesh than he seems in pictures.* —*v.t.* to remove the adhering flesh from (a skin or hide). —*v.i.* to put on flesh; become fleshy (with *out*): *She has fleshed out since we last saw her.* [Old English *flǣsc* part of the body covering the bones, meat.]

flesh-col·ored (flesh'kul'ərd) *adj.* having a light pinkish or yellowish tan color.

flesh fly, any of several flies, family Sarcophagidae, whose larvae infest the wounds, wastes, or decaying flesh of animals.

flesh·ly (flesh'lē) **-li·er, -li·est.** *adj.* **1.** sensual; carnal. **2.** of or relating to the flesh or body; bodily; physical. —**flesh'li·ness,** *n.*

flesh·pot (flesh'pot') *n.* **1.** place offering unrestrained or luxurious pleasure or entertainment: *the fleshpots of the Orient.* **2.** fleshpots. material or sensual luxuries; physical comforts.

flesh wound, superficial wound that does not extend beyond the flesh or affect a bone or vital organ.

flesh·y (flesh'ē) **flesh·i·er, flesh·i·est.** *adj.* **1.** having much flesh; plump; fat. **2.** of or like flesh. **3.** firm and pulpy: *a fleshy fruit, fleshy leaves.* —**flesh'i·ness,** *n.*

fletch (flech) *v.t.* to attach feathers to (an arrow).

Fletch·er, John (flech'ər) 1579–1625, English playwright who collaborated with Francis Beaumont.

Fleurs-de-lis

fleur-de-lis (flur'də lē', -lēs', floor'-) *pl.,* **fleurs-de-lis** (flur'də lēz', floor'-) *n.* **1.** heraldic design or device, representing a lily or iris. **2.** distinctive armorial bearing of the former royal family of France. **3.** iris (*defs.* 2, 3). [French *fleur de lis* lily flower; *fleur* flower (from Latin *flōs*) + *de* of (from Latin *dē* from) + *lis* lily (from Latin *līlium*).]

flew (flōō) past tense of **fly².**

flex (fleks) *v.t.* **1.** to bend: *to flex one's arm, to flex a bow.* **2.** to tighten or contract: *to flex one's muscles.* —*v.i.* to tighten or contract a muscle or muscles. [Latin *flexus,* past participle of *flectere* to bend.]

flex·i·ble (flek'sə bəl) *adj.* **1.** able to bend without breaking; not stiff or rigid; easily bent. **2.** able to adjust easily to change; adaptable: *a flexible schedule, flexible rules.* [Latin *flexibilis* pliant, from *flexus,* past participle of *flectere* to bend.] —**flex'i·bil'i·ty, flex'i·ble·ness,** *n.* —**flex'i·bly,** *adv.*

Syn. 1. Flexible, pliant, supple, limber¹ mean giving or bending easily without breaking. **Flexible** implies little or no resistance to the bending force and no tendency to retain original form: *The wire is flexible.* **Pliant** suggests easy bending to the force that is applied: *Leather that has been soaked and kneaded becomes pliant.* **Supple** implies that any form or conformation is easily attained: *He cut a supple willow branch to make a hoop frame.* **Limber** adds to this a suggestion of resistance to being bent and a tendency to be more awkward when handled: *It takes some work to make a new rope limber enough to work with.*

flex·ion (flek'shən) *n.* **1.** *Anatomy.* act of bending, esp. a limb or other part of the body. Opposed to **extension. 2.** flection. [Latin *flexiō* bending.]

flex·or (flek'sər) *n.* any muscle that bends a part of the body, esp. a limb. Opposed to **extensor.** [Modern Latin *flexor,* from Latin *flexus.* See FLEX.]

flex·ure (flek'shər) *n.* **1.** act of bending; being bent. **2.** bent part; bend; curve. [Latin *flexūra* a bending.]

flib·ber·ti·gib·bet (flib'ər tē jib'ət) *n.* frivolous or flighty person, esp. a woman. [Of uncertain origin.]

flick¹ (flik) *n.* **1.** light, quick, snapping movement or stroke: *with a flick of the wrist. He gave his horse a flick with his whip.* **2.** sound made by such a movement or stroke. —*v.t.* **1.** to remove (something) with a light, quick, snapping movement or stroke, as of the hand: *to flick the crumbs from one's lap, to flick ashes from a cigarette.* **2.** to cause to move or snap with a light, quick movement: *to flick a towel at someone.* **3.** to strike with a light, quick stroke, as with a whip: *to flick a horse's rump.* [Probably imitative.]

flick² (flik) *also,* **flicks.** *n.* *Slang.* motion picture; movie. [From FLICKER¹.]

flick·er¹ (flik'ər) *v.i.* **1.** to shine or burn with an unsteady or wavering light: *The match flickered in the draft.* **2.** to move back and forth with a quick, fluttering movement; quiver; tremble: *Shadows flickered on the wall.* —*n.* **1.** unsteady or wavering light. **2.** slight indication or stirring; brief appearance: *a flicker of hope, a flicker of fear.* **3.** quick fluttering or quivering movement: *the flicker of an eyelid.* [Old English *flicorian* to flutter, hover.]

flick·er² (flik'ər) *n.* any of various woodpeckers, genus *Colaptes,* native to areas from Alaska to southern Chile, having a slightly curved, slender bill and brightly marked plumage. Length: 12 inches. [FLICK¹ + -ER¹.]

Flicker²

flied (flīd) a past tense and past participle of **fly².**

at; āpe; cär; end; mē; it; īce; hot; ōld; fôrk; wood; fōōl; oil; out; up; ūse; turn; sing; thin; this; zh in treasure; ə in ago, taken, pencil, lemon, circus.

fli·er (flī′ər) *also,* **fly·er.** *n.* **1.** one who or that which flies, esp. an aviator. **2.** one who or that which moves swiftly, as an express train. **3.** *Informal.* risky financial investment or speculation, as on the stock market. **4.** small handbill or leaflet, as one used in advertising.

flight¹ (flīt) *n.* **1.** act, manner, or power of flying: *the graceful flight of the butterfly. Flight is natural to birds.* **2.** distance or course traveled by a flying object, as an airplane or bird. **3.** group flying or passing through the air together: *a flight of swallows, a flight of arrows.* **4.** trip made by or in an aircraft. **5.** aircraft making a scheduled trip. **6.** basic tactical unit of an air force, consisting of from two to five aircraft. **7.** swift movement or passage: *the flight of time.* **8.** a departure from or soaring above or beyond the ordinary: *a flight of fancy.* **9.** continuous series of stairs or steps between adjacent floors or landings. [Old English *flyht* act of flying.]

flight² (flīt) *n.* **1.** act of fleeing. **2. to put to flight.** to cause to flee; rout. **3. to take (to) flight.** to retreat or flee. [Probably from an unrecorded Old English word.]

flight attendant, one employed to provide passenger service on an airplane.

flight deck, upper deck of an aircraft carrier, on which aircraft take off and land.

flight feather, one of the strong, stiff feathers that form the major portion of the wing and tail of a bird and are essential to flight.

flight·less (flīt′lis) *adj.* (of birds) incapable of flying, as an ostrich.

flight·y (flī′tē) **flight·i·er, flight·i·est.** *adj.* guided by whim or impulse rather than by reason or mature judgment; irresponsible; capricious. —**flight′i·ly,** *adv.* —**flight′i·ness,** *n.*

flim·flam (flim′flam′) *Informal. n.* **1.** trickery or deception. **2.** foolish talk; rubbish; nonsense. —*v.t.* **-flammed, -flam·ming.** to trick or deceive; swindle; cheat. [Probably of Scandinavian origin.]

flim·sy (flim′zē) **-si·er, -si·est.** *adj.* **1.** lacking strength, solidity, or substance; thin; frail: *The blouse was made of a flimsy material. The platform is too flimsy to support our weight.* **2.** lacking validity or effectiveness; not convincing or adequate; weak: *a flimsy excuse.* —*n. pl.,* **-sies.** thin paper used to make multiple copies, as in newspaper work. [Of uncertain origin.] —**flim′si·ly,** *adv.* —**flim′si·ness,** *n.*

flinch (flinch) *v.i.* to draw back or away, as from something painful, dangerous, or unpleasant; shrink; wince: *She always flinches at loud noises. He flinches from facing the future.* —*n.* act of flinching. [Old French *flenchir* to bend, turn aside; probably of Germanic origin.]

fling (fling) **flung, fling·ing.** *v.t.* **1.** to throw, esp. with force or violence: *He flung up his hands in disgust. She flung her coat over her shoulders. The horse flung his rider to the ground.* **2.** to send or put suddenly or violently, as if by throwing; thrust: *to fling someone into prison.* **3.** to enter into vigorously or completely: *She flung herself into the campaign.* —*v.i.* to move suddenly or violently; rush headlong. —*n.* **1.** act of flinging. **2.** period of freely indulging oneself, as in pleasures or adventure: *to have a fling before settling down.* **3.** lively or spirited dance, esp. the Highland fling. **4. to have (or take) a fling at.** to have a try at; make an attempt at. [Probably of Scandinavian origin.] —**Syn.** *v.t.* **1.** toss.

flint (flint) *n.* **1.** hard, fine-grained variety of quartz, usually dull gray in color, that produces sparks when struck against steel. **2.** piece of this, esp. as used for kindling a fire or spark. **3.** piece of flint used to produce sparks in cigarette lighters. [Old English *flint* rock.]

Flint (flint) *n.* city in southeastern Michigan. Pop. (1970), 193,317.

flint glass, glass containing lead, used esp. in making lenses.

flint·lock (flint′lok′) *n.* **1.** gunlock in which a flint was struck against steel to produce sparks and ignite the gunpowder in the pan. **2.** firearm with such a gunlock.

flint·y (flin′tē) **flint·i·er, flint·i·est.** *adj.* **1.** consisting of, containing, or resembling flint. **2.** hard; unyielding; cruel: *a flinty heart, a flinty look.* —**flint′i·ly,** *adv.* —**flint′i·ness,** *n.*

flip¹ (flip) **flipped, flip·ping.** *v.t.* **1.** to toss with a quick, jerking movement so as to cause to turn over in the air: *to flip a coin.* **2.a.** to turn over, esp. with a quick, jerking movement: *to flip the pages of a book. He flipped the cards over as he dealt them.* **b.** to move with a quick, jerking movement: *to flip one's lid* or **wig** or **top**). *Slang.* **3.** to react angrily, violently, or excitedly; lose self-control. —*v.i.* **1.** to move or turn with a jerk: *The fish flipped onto its back.* **2.** to turn, glance at, or proceed quickly; leaf (with *through*): *He casually flipped through the pages.* **3.** *Slang.* to react violently or excitedly (often with *over* or *out*). —*n.* quick turning or jerking movement. —*adj.* **flip·per, flip·pest.** *Informal.* impertinent; saucy; flippant: *a flip remark. Don't be flip with me.* [Probably imitative.]

flip² (flip) *n.* sweetened drink containing an alcoholic beverage, spices, eggs, and sometimes milk. [Probably from FLIP¹; because the drink is prepared by flipping the ingredients.]

flip·pant (flip′ənt) *adj.* lacking proper respect or seriousness: *a flippant remark, a flippant attitude.* [FLIP¹ + -ANT.] —**flip′pan·cy,** *n.* —**flip′pant·ly,** *adv.*

flip·per (flip′ər) *n.* **1.** broad, flat limb, as of a seal, dolphin, penguin, or turtle, adapted for swimming. **2.** one of a pair of broad, paddle-shaped shoes, usually of rubber, worn as an aid in swimming or skin diving. Also, (*def. 2*), **fin.**

flirt (flurt) *v.i.* **1.** to act romantically or affectionately in an enticing, coy, or playful manner; be coquettish: *She flirted with every boy at the party.* **2.** to approach or handle carelessly, casually, or lightly; trifle or toy with: *to flirt with danger, to flirt with an idea. The candidate flirted with the liberal wing of the party.* —*v.t. Archaic.* to move or toss with a quick, jerking movement. —*n.* one who flirts or is coquettish. [Of uncertain origin.]

flir·ta·tion (flur tā′shən) *n.* **1.** act or instance of flirting. **2.** brief or casual romance.

flir·ta·tious (flur tā′shəs) *adj.* **1.** inclined to flirt or be coquettish: *a flirtatious girl.* **2.** characteristic of a flirt: *flirtatious behavior.* —**flir·ta′tious·ly,** *adv.* —**flir·ta′tious·ness,** *n.*

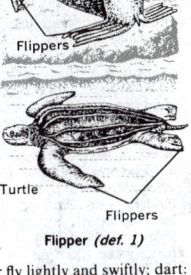

Sea lion

Flippers

Turtle

Flippers

Flipper (def. 1)

flit (flit) **flit·ted, flit·ting.** *v.i.* **1.** to move or fly lightly and swiftly; dart: *Butterflies flitted among the flowers.* **2.** to pass lightly and swiftly: *The days flit by. Thoughts flitted through her mind.* [Possibly from Old Norse *flytja* to carry.]

flitch (flich) *n.* side of a hog salted and cured. [Old English *flicce.*]

flit·ter (flit′ər) flutter. [FLIT + -ER¹.]

fliv·ver (fliv′ər) *n. Slang.* old, cheap, or dilapidated automobile. [Of uncertain origin.]

float (flōt) *v.i.* **1.** to rest on or at the surface of or be suspended in a liquid: *This bar of soap won't float. He was floating on his back. Bits of cork floated in the glass of wine.* **2.** to move or be carried along gently on or at the surface of liquid: *The toy sailboat floated across the lake. Our raft floated downstream. We watched the logs floating towards the mill.* **3.** to remain suspended or be carried along in the air or some other gas: *The clouds floated across the sky. Leaves floated down from the trees.* **4.** to hover or move as if suspended or carried along in this manner: *the rumors were floating all about town. Strains of music floated across the lawn.* **5.** to move effortlessly or gracefully, as if buoyed up: *She floated down the stairs.* **6.** to move about aimlessly or in a random or unsettled way; drift: *He floated from job to job.* —*v.t.* **1.** to cause to float: *to float a raft, to float lumber down a river.* **2.** to offer for sale, as stocks or bonds; put on the market: *to float an issue of stock.* **3.** to obtain or negotiate: *to float a loan.* **4.** to flood or irrigate. —*n.* **1.** object that floats or helps something else to float in a liquid, as a raft anchored near a shore for use by swimmers. **2.** tableau or exhibit carried on a vehicle or wheeled platform in parades or pageants. **3.** drink consisting of ice cream floating in a beverage, as soda. **4.** piece of cork or other material, used to support the end of a fishing line and indicate by its bobbing movement the presence of a fish. **5.** air-filled sac that serves to keep certain animals afloat, as in the Portuguese man-of-war. **6.** hollow metal ball or other device that floats on the surface of a body of liquid and is attached to a valve that regulates the level, supply, or outflow of the liquid, as in a carburetor, cistern, or boiler. [Old English *flotian* to rest on the surface of a liquid.]

float·er (flō′tər) *n.* **1.** one who or that which floats. **2.** one who votes illegally, esp. for pay, in several voting districts.

float·ing (flō′ting) *adj.* **1.** that floats. **2.** not appropriated to any fixed, permanent investment; available for use: *floating capital.* **3.** *Medicine.* displaced, esp. downward, from the usual position: *a floating kidney.*

floating debt, debt due within a short period of time but having no specified date for repayment and bearing no fixed interest rate.

floating island, dessert made of boiled custard with meringue, whipped cream, or other topping floating on the surface.

floating ribs, ribs attached to the backbone but not to the breastbone. In man the bottom two pairs of ribs are floating ribs.

floc·cu·lent (flok′yə lənt) *adj.* resembling, having, or covered with tufts of wool or any soft, fluffy substance. [Latin *floccus* tuft of wool + -*ulentus* full of.] —**floc′cu·lence,** *n.*

flock¹ (flok) *n.* **1.** group of animals of one kind gathered or herded together: *a flock of goats, a flock of geese, a shepherd and his flock.* **2.** large number or group: *a flock of reporters. I've a flock of things to do.* **3.** members of a church; congregation, esp. in relation to its pastor. —*v.i.* to move or gather in crowds: *People flocked to the beaches.* [Old English *flocc* band.]

flock² (flok) *n.* **1.** finely powdered wool or other fiber applied to a surface, as wallpaper, as a decorative or protective coating. **2.** waste

at; āpe; cär; end; mē; it; īce; hot; ōld; fôrk; wood; fo͞ol; oil; out; up; ūse; turn; sing; thin; this; zh in treasure; ə in ago, taken, pencil, lemon, circus.

wool, cotton, or other fabric, cut up and used to stuff such items as mattresses and cushions. **3.** tuft, as of wool or hair. —*v.t.* to cover or fill with flock. [Old French *floc* tuft of wool, from Latin *floccus*.]

floe (flō) *n.* **1.** field or sheet of floating ice. **2.** detached floating portion of such a field or sheet. Also, **ice floe.** [Norwegian *flo* layer, from Old Norse *flō*.]

flog (flog, flôg) **flogged, flog·ging.** *v.t.* to beat or whip severely, esp. as punishment. [Possibly modification of Latin *flagellāre* to whip.] —**flog'ger,** *n.*

flood (flud) *n.* **1.** great flow, rise, or overflowing of water, esp. over ordinarily dry land; deluge. **2.** great outpouring or abundance; overwhelming quantity: *a flood of tears, a flood of words.* **3.** flood tide. **4.** *also,* the Flood. in the Old Testament, the great deluge that occurred in the time of Noah. **5.** *Informal.* floodlight. —*v.t.* **1.** to cover or cause to be covered with a flood; inundate: *The valley was flooded when the dam broke. The pipes burst and our basement was flooded.* **2.** to fill or overwhelm, as with a flood: *The stage was flooded with light. The box office was flooded with requests for tickets.* **3.** to supply excessively: *to flood an engine with gasoline.* —*v.i.* **1.** to rise in a flood; overflow. **2.** to become filled with or submerged under a flood: *Our cellar floods after a heavy rain.* **3.** to flow, pour out, or stream in or as in a flood. [Old English *flōd* flood tide, deluge, body of flowing water.]

flood control, attempt to prevent or reduce the occurrence of floods, as by the use of dams, artificial channels, or soil conservation.

flood·gate (flud'gāt') *n.* **1.** gate in a waterway designed to control the flow of water. **2.** something that controls or restrains a flow or outburst.

flood·light (flud'līt') *n.* **1.** lamp that provides a broad beam of bright light. **2.** broad beam of light projected by such a lamp. —*v.t.,* **-light·ed,** or **-lit, light·ing.** to illuminate with a floodlight.

flood plain, plain formed by sedimentary deposits, adjacent to and subject to flooding by a river.

flood tide, rising or incoming tide. Opposed to **ebb tide.**

floor (flôr) *n.* **1.** lower enclosing surface of a room, building, or similar structure. **2.** any surface resembling a floor in position or function; bottom surface: *the ocean floor, the forest floor, the floor of a cave.* **3.** platform or level structure or area used for a specific purpose: *a threshing floor.* **4.** level or story of a building. **5.** part of a room or building, as in a legislative house or stock exchange, where members sit, speak, and conduct business: *The bill was debated at length on the floor of the Senate.* **6.** members of an assembly; audience: *questions from the floor.* **7.** in parliamentary procedure, right or privilege to speak to the assembly: *The chairman gave him the floor.* **8.** lower limit or minimum, as of an amount charged or paid: *a group demanding that the government fix a wage floor.* —*v.t.* **1.** to cover or furnish with a floor: *to floor a house, to floor a porch.* **2.** to knock unconscious or knock down, as to the floor: *The boxer floored his opponent.* **3.** to depress (the accelerator of a motor vehicle) all the way to the floor. **4.** *Informal.* to bewilder or surprise completely; flabbergast; dumbfound: *I was floored by the news.* [Old English *flōr* bottom of a room or house.] **Syn.** *n.* **4.** **Floor, story²** mean one of the levels of rooms of a building. **Floor** suggests the height of such a level between one ceiling and the next and the specific location of a room or set of rooms in relation to others above or below it: *My apartment is on the third floor.* **Story** implies the series of floors one above the other all taken together as a unit of comparison: *The house is two stories high.*

floor·ing (flôr'ing) *n.* **1.** material for making floors. **2.** floor; floors collectively.

floor lamp, tall lamp that stands on the floor.

floor leader, member of a legislative assembly who is chosen to assist the majority or minority leader in managing his party's forces and legislative strategy for a certain period of time or during deliberations on a specific bill.

floor-length (flôr'length') *adj.* reaching to the floor.

floor plan, scale drawing or plan of the sections or spaces of a room, floor, or building, drawn as if seen from above.

floor show, entertainment consisting of singing, dancing, or comic acts, as presented on the dance floor of a nightclub.

floor·walk·er (flôr'wô'kər) *n.* person employed in a department store or other large store to supervise sales and services.

floo·zy (flōō'zē) *pl.,* **-zies.** *n.* *Slang.* disreputable, cheaply dressed girl or woman. [Of uncertain origin.]

flop (flop) **flopped, flop·ping.** *v.i.* **1.** to drop or fall loosely, clumsily, or heavily: *to flop into a chair, to flop into bed.* **2.** to move, swing, or flap about loosely or clumsily: *The spaniel's ears flopped about its face.* **3.** *Informal.* to be completely unsuccessful; fail totally: *The play flopped.* —*n.* **1.** act of flopping: *He took a flop on the ice.* **2.** sound of flopping; thud: *She fell down with a flop.* **3.** *Informal.* total failure. [Form of FLAP.] —**flop'per,** *n.*

flop·house (flop'hous') *n.* cheap, shabby rooming house or hotel, esp. one having many beds to a room.

flop·py (flop'ē) **-pi·er, -pi·est.** *adj.* *Informal.* that flops or tends to flop: *a large straw hat with a floppy brim.* —**flop'pi·ly,** *adv.* —**flop'pi·ness,** *n.*

flo·ra (flôr'ə) *pl.,* **flo·ras** or **flo·rae** (flôr'ē). *n.* plants or plant life characteristic of a particular region or period. Distinguished from **fauna.** [Latin *Flōra.* See FLORA.]

Flo·ra (flôr'ə) *n.* Roman goddess of flowers. [Latin *Flōra,* from *flōr-,* stem of *flōs* flower.]

flo·ral (flôr'əl) *adj.* of, relating to, or like flowers: *a floral arrangement, a perfume with a floral fragrance.*

floral envelope *Botany.* perianth.

Flor·ence (flôr'əns) *n.* city in central Italy. It was one of the world's greatest centers of Renaissance art. Also, *Italian,* **Firenze.**

Flor·en·tine (flôr'ən tēn', flôr'-) *adj.* **1.** of or relating to Florence, its people, or their culture. **2.** *also,* **florentine.** relating to or having a dull, brushed finish engraved with finely traced lines: *florentine gold.* —*n.* native or inhabitant of Florence.

flo·res·cence (flō res'əns, flə-) *n.* act, state, or period of blooming or blossoming. [Modern Latin *florescentia,* from Latin *flōrēscere* to begin to blossom.] —**flo·res'cent,** *adj.*

flo·ret (flôr'it) *n.* **1.** small flower. **2.** *Botany.* one of the small flowers that make up the flower head of a composite plant, as the dandelion, or of a plant of certain other kinds, as the clover. [Old French *florete,* diminutive of *flor* flower, from Latin *flōs.*]

flo·ri·cul·ture (flôr'ə kul'chər) *n.* cultivation of flowers or ornamental flowering plants. [Latin *flōr-,* stem of *flōs* flower + CULTURE.] —**flo'ri·cul'tur·al,** *adj.* —**flo'ri·cul'tur·ist,** *n.*

flor·id (flôr'id, flor'-) *adj.* **1.** flushed with redness; ruddy: *a florid complexion.* **2.** excessively or elaborately ornate; flowery: *The author has a very florid style of writing.* [Latin *flōridus* full of flowers, from *flōs* flower.] —**flor'id·ly,** *adv.* —**flo·rid'i·ty, flor'id·ness,** *n.* —**Syn. 2.** see **ornate.**

Flor·i·da (flôr'ə də, flor'-) *n.* state on the southeastern peninsula of the United States. Capital, Tallahassee. Area, 58,560 sq. mi. Pop. (1970), 6,789,443. Abbreviation, **Fla.**

Florida Keys, chain of small islands off the southern coast of Florida.

flor·in (flôr'in, flor'-) *n.* **1.** coin of the United Kingdom equal to two shillings. **2.** guilder. **3.** formerly, gold coin issued at Florence in 1252. **4.** formerly, any of various other gold or silver coins issued in different European countries since 1252. [Old French *florin* coin of Florence, from Italian *fiorino,* from *fiore* flower, from Latin *flōs*; because the Florentine coin was decorated with the emblem of Florence, the lily.]

Flor·is·sant (flôr'ə sənt) *n.* city in eastern Missouri, principally a residential suburb of St. Louis. Pop. (1970), 65,908.

flo·rist (flôr'ist, flor'-) *n.* one who sells flowers and ornamental plants. [Latin *flōr-,* stem of *flōs* flower + -IST.]

floss (flôs, flos) *n.* **1.** short silk fibers or waste. **2.** soft, loosely twisted silk thread made from such fibers, used for embroidery. **3.** soft, silky fibers or fluff found in cotton, corn, milkweed, and other plants. **4.** dental floss. [French *floche* flossy, shaggy, possibly going back to Latin *flūxus* weak, frail.]

floss·y (flô'sē, flos'ē) **floss·i·er, floss·i·est.** *adj.* of or like floss.

flo·ta·tion (flō tā'shən) *n.* **1.** act or state of floating. **2.** method of separating a mineral in an ore from waste materials or from other minerals by using a chemical solution that the ore particles water resistant and causes them to float. [FLOAT + -ATION.]

flotation collar, large inflatable tube of rubber or other material placed around a spacecraft or other vehicle to keep it afloat, as when landing on a body of water.

flo·til·la (flō til'ə) *n.* **1.** fleet of small vessels; small fleet. **2.** in the U.S. Navy, group of small ships, as destroyers, usually consisting of two or more squadrons. [Spanish *flotilla* small fleet¹, diminutive of *flota* fleet¹, from Old French *flote,* from Old Norse *floti* fleet¹, raft.]

flot·sam (flot'səm) *n.* **1.** wreckage found floating on the sea of a ship or of cargo cast or swept overboard from a wrecked or imperiled ship. Distinguished from **jetsam. 2.** flotsam and jetsam (*defs.* 2,3). [Anglo-Norman *floteson* floating wreckage, from Old French *floter* to float; of Germanic origin.]

flotsam and jetsam 1. wreckage of a ship or its cargo floating on the water or washed ashore. **2.** worthless or miscellaneous things; trifles; odds and ends. **3.** unemployed drifters or vagrants; transients.

flounce¹ (flouns) **flounced, flounc·ing.** *v.i.* **1.** to go with abrupt, agitated, or impatient movements of the body, as in anger or petulance: *She answered them indignantly and flounced back to her seat.* **2.** to move in a showy, flamboyant manner, as if to attract attention: *She flounced about the room in her new evening gown.* —*n.* act or instance of flouncing; abrupt or impatient movement: *She sat down with a flounce.* [Probably of Scandinavian origin.]

flounce² (flouns) *n.* wide strip of cloth, gathered along one edge and attached as a trimming, as on a dress or a sofa. —*v.t.,* **flounced, flounc-**

at; āpe; cär; end; mē; it; īce; hot; ōld; fôrk; wood; fōōl; oil; out; up; ūse; turn; sing; thin; this; zh in treasure; ə in ago, taken, pencil, lemon, circus.

ing. to trim or furnish with a flounce or flounces. [Earlier *frounce* wrinkle, fold, from Old French *fronce,* from *froncer* to wrinkle, fold; of Germanic origin.]

floun·der¹ (floun′dər) *v.i.*
1. to move with stumbling or plunging motions; struggle awkwardly or clumsily: *The boat floundered in the surf. We floundered about in the swamp for hours.* **2.** to proceed in a stumbling, awkward, or confused manner: *to flounder through a speech.* —*n.* act or movement of floundering. [Possibly blend of FOUNDER¹ and BLUNDER.]

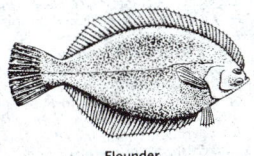

Flounder

floun·der² (floun′dər) *pl.,* **-ders** or **-der.** *n.* flatfish of either of two families, Bothidae and Pleuronectidae, valued as both a food and a game fish. [Old French *flondre;* of Scandinavian origin.]

flour (flour, flou′ər) *n.* **1.** soft, powdery substance obtained by grinding and sifting grain, esp. wheat, used chiefly as a basic ingredient in baked goods and other foods. **2.** any soft powdery substance. —*v.t.* to cover or sprinkle with flour. [Form of FLOWER in the sense of "finest part" (of the grain).]

flour·ish (flûr′ish) *v.i.* **1.** to grow or develop vigorously or prosperously; thrive: *Crops flourish in rich soil. His business is flourishing.* **2.** to reach or be at the peak of development or achievement: *a civilization that flourished thousands of years ago.* —*v.t.* **1.** to wave about with bold or sweeping gestures; brandish: *to flourish a sword, to flourish a baton.* **2.** to display ostentatiously; flaunt. —*n.* **1.** a brandishing: *He bowed to her with a flourish of his hat.* **2.** ostentatious or dramatic display or gesture: *She entered the room with a flourish.* **3.** decorative stroke or embellishment in writing. **4.** elaborate, ornamental passage or series of notes, as a trill or fanfare, added to a musical work. [Old French *floriss-,* a stem of *florir* to flower, bloom, going back to Latin *flōrēre* to flower, bloom.] —**Syn.** *v.i.* **1.** see prosper.

flour·y (flour′ē) *adj.* **1.** of, relating to, or resembling flour. **2.** covered with or as with flour.

flout (flout) *v.t.* to treat with disdain or contempt; scoff at; defy: *to flout the authorities, to flout tradition.* —*n. Archaic.* disdainful or contemptuous remark or act. [Middle English *flouten* to play the flute, from Old French *flauter,* from *flaute, fleute.* See FLUTE.] —**flout′er,** *n.*

flow (flō) *v.i.* **1.** (of a fluid) to move or pass along steadily and smoothly: *The river flows northward. The electricity flowed through the wire.* **2.** to move along steadily, smoothly, or readily, as in a stream: *Money continued to flow in. Conversation flowed freely.* **3.** to issue or proceed, as from a source: *Orders for supplies flowed from the manager's office.* **4.** to appear to move with harmonious, continuous motion; have smooth continuity: *The lines in the painting flowed together.* **5.** to be full or plentiful; overflow: *Her heart was flowing with happiness.* **6.** to hang, fall, or ripple loosely: *Her skirts flowed from her waist.* **7.** to come in or advance; rise, as the tide: *the waters ebb and flow.* **8.** to menstruate. —*n.* **1.** act or manner of flowing: *to stop the flow of blood, to move in a steady flow.* **2.** menstruation. **3.** any continuous, uninterrupted movement; outpouring; stream: *the flow of traffic.* **4.** that which flows. **5.** amount that flows in a given time. **6.** the incoming or rising of the tide. [Old English *flōwan* to move in a stream.]

flow chart, schematic diagram showing a sequence of operations, as for a computer program or industrial process. Also, **flow sheet.**

flow·er (flou′ər) *n.* **1.** the part of a flowering plant composed of the reproductive organs and their surrounding, usually brightly colored petals; blossom; bloom. **2.** plant cultivated for the beauty of its blossoms. **3.** state or time of blossoming: *an orchard in flower.* **4.** finest or choicest part or example: *the flower of the country's youth, the flower of chivalry.* **5.** finest or most flourishing period: *in the flower of manhood, when knighthood was in flower.* **6.** decorative feature or embellishment, esp. a figure of speech. **7. flowers.** *Chemistry.* substance in the form of a fine powder, produced by condensation or sublimation. ▲ construed as singular. —*v.i.* **1.** to produce flowers; bloom: *Cherry trees flower in the early spring.* **2.** to be at or reach fullest development or growth: *His writing ability flowered early.* —*v.t.* to decorate or cover with flowers or a floral design. [Old French *flo(u)r* blossom, finest part, from Latin *flōr-,* stem of *flōs* blossom.]

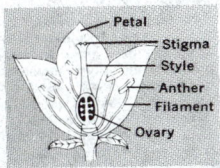

Parts of a flower

Petal
Stigma
Style
Anther
Filament
Ovary

flow·ered (flou′ərd) *adj.* **1.** having or covered with flowers: *a flowered slope.* **2.** having or decorated with a floral design: *a flowered blouse.*

flow·er·et (flou′ər it) *n.* small flower; floret.

flower girl, young girl who carries flowers and precedes the bride at a wedding.

flower head *Botany.* inflorescence consisting of a dense cluster of tiny flowers.

flowering plant, any of a large group of plants including trees and shrubs whose seeds are borne enclosed in an ovary. They constitute the largest division of the plant kingdom, including more than half of all known species. Also, **an′gi·o·sperm′.**

flow·er·pot (flou′ər pot′) *n.* pot, usually clay, in which to grow plants.

flow·er·y (flou′ər ē) **-er·i·er, -er·i·est.** *adj.* **1.** covered with or resembling flowers. **2.** using or containing elaborate, elegant, or highly embellished language; florid. **3.** having or decorated with a floral design. —**flow′er·i·ly,** *adv.* —**flow′er·i·ness,** *n.*

flown (flōn) past participle of *fly².*

fl. oz., fluid ounce.

flu (flōō) *n.* influenza.

flub (flub) **flubbed, flub·bing.** *Informal. v.t.* to bungle: *He flubbed his lines in the second act.* —*n.* bungling error; blunder. [Of uncertain origin.]

fluc·tu·ate (fluk′chōō āt′) **-at·ed, -at·ing.** *v.i.* **1.** to change, vary, or move up and down continually or irregularly; be wavering, unsteady, or unstable: *fluctuating prices. The stock market fluctuates daily.* **2.** *Archaic.* to move in or as in waves. [Latin *flūctuātus,* past participle of *flūctuāre* to wave, from *flūctus* wave.] —**fluc′tu·a′tion,** *n.*

flue (flōō) *n.* **1.** passage, as in a chimney, for conveying smoke, hot air, or waste gas. **2.** flue pipe. **3.** air passage in such a pipe. [Of uncertain origin.]

flu·ent (flōō′ənt) *adj.* **1.** spoken or written smoothly and effortlessly: *fluent poetry.* **2.** capable of speaking or writing smoothly and effortlessly: *a fluent speaker. He is fluent in Spanish.* **3.** characterized by smoothness and grace: *fluent motion.* [Latin *fluēns,* present participle of *fluere* to flow.] —**flu′en·cy,** *n.* —**flu′ent·ly,** *adv.*

flue pipe, organ pipe whose tone is produced by a current of air striking the mouth, or opening, of the pipe.

fluff (fluf) *n.* **1.** soft, light, downy material: *The kitten looked like a ball of fluff.* **2.** soft, downy mass: *a fluff of golden hair about her face* (Garrett, 1885). **3.** *Informal.* error or blunder, esp. one made by a performer in the delivery of his lines. —*v.t.* **1.** to shake, pat, or puff out into a soft, downy mass; make fluffy: *to fluff up a pillow. The bird fluffed its feathers. She fluffed her hair out with her fingers.* **2.** *Informal.* to make an error or blunder in. [Probably modification of obsolete *flue* downy material, from Flemish *vluwe,* from French *velu* shaggy, going back to Latin *villus* shaggy hair.]

fluff·y (fluf′ē) **fluff·i·er, fluff·i·est.** *adj.* consisting of, covered with, or resembling fluff: *a fluffy sweater. Beat the egg whites until fluffy.* —**fluff′i·ly,** *adv.* —**fluff′i·ness,** *n.*

flu·id (flōō′id) *n.* **1.** substance, as a liquid or gas, that is capable of flowing, has no definite shape, and adapts itself to the shape of any container that confines it. **2.** any liquid: *Stay in bed and drink plenty of fluids.* —*adj.* **1.** capable of flowing; not solid; liquid or gaseous. **2.** of, relating to, or consisting of fluids. **3.** changing readily; not fixed, firm, or stable: *the fluid political situation.* [Latin *fluidus* flowing, liquid.] —**flu·id′i·ty,** *n.* —**flu′id·ly,** *adv.*

fluid dram, liquid measure of capacity equal to ⅛ of a fluid ounce. See **weights and measures** for table.

flu·id·ic (flōō id′ik) *adj.* relating to or like a fluid.

flu·id·ics (flōō id′iks) *n.* science concerned with the study and application of the properties of flowing gases and liquids, esp. as they can be used to replace mechanical and electronic devices in performing various functions, as amplification. ▲ construed as singular.

fluid mechanics, branch of physics that deals with fluids in motion and at rest, including aerodynamics, hydrodynamics, and hydrostatics.

fluid ounce, liquid measure of capacity equal to ¹⁄₁₆ of a pint. See **weights and measures** for table.

fluke¹ (flōōk) *n.* **1.** either of the two flat, triangular pieces on an anchor that catch in the bottom. **2.** barb or barbed head, as of an arrow, harpoon, or spear. **3.** either of the lobes, or horizontal fins, of a whale's tail. [Possibly from FLUKE³; because of the similarity of shape.]

fluke² (flōōk) *n.* unexpected or accidental stroke or turn, esp. of good luck; chance happening. [Of uncertain origin.]

fluke³ (flōōk) *n.* **1.** any of various flatfish, esp. some flounder. **2.** any of a group of parasitic flatworms, class Trematoda, that infest many kinds of animals, including snails, fish, birds, and mammals. Also, **trem′a·tode.** [Old English *flōc* flatfish.]

fluk·y (flōō′kē) **fluk·i·er, fluk·i·est.** *adj.* **1.** unexpected or accidental, as a stroke of good luck. **2.** uncertain; changeable: *a fluky breeze.* —**fluk′i·ness,** *n.*

flume (flōōm) *n.* **1.** deep, narrow passage or ravine through which a stream runs. **2.** artificial chute or trough, esp. an inclined one, that

at; āpe; cär; end; mē; it; īce; hot; ōld; fôrk; wood; fōōl; oil; out; up; ūse; turn; sing; thin; this; zh in treasure; ə in ago, taken, pencil, lemon, circus.

395

carries water, as for conveying logs or furnishing water power. [Old French *flum* river, from Latin *flūmen*.]

flum·mer·y (flum′ər ē) *pl.*, **-mer·ies.** *n.* **1.** any of various sweet, puddinglike dishes. **2.** empty flattery; utter nonsense. [Welsh *llymru* jellied and boiled sour oatmeal.]

flum·mox (flum′əks) *v.t. Informal.* to throw into confusion; bewilder; perplex. [Imitative.]

flung (flung) past tense and past participle of **fling.**

flunk (flungk) *Informal. v.t.* **1.** to fail to pass; fail: *to flunk an exam, to flunk a course. He flunked his physical and was medically disqualified.* **2.** to give a failing grade or mark to: *His teacher flunked him.* —*v.i.* **1.** to fail, as in an examination: *He flunked because he didn't study. She flunked in math.* **2.** **to flunk out.** to be dismissed, as from a school, because of failure: *He flunked out last semester.* —*n.* failure, as in an examination or course. [Possibly blend of FLINCH and FUNK.]

flunk·ey (flung′kē) *pl.*, **-eys.** *n.* flunky.

flunk·y (flung′kē) *pl.*, **flunk·ies.** *n.* **1.** one who fawningly serves and tries to please another; servile follower or hanger-on. **2.** footman or other male servant, esp. one who wears livery and performs menial tasks; lackey. [Possibly modification of earlier *flanker* person stationed at another's *flank* or side. See FLANK.]

flu·or (floor, flŏŏ′ər, -ôr) *n.* fluorite. [Latin *fluor* a flowing; referring to its use as a flux in smelting.]

flu·o·resce (floo res′, flô-, flŏŏ′ə res′) **-resced, -resc·ing.** *v.i.* to produce or show fluorescence.

flu·o·res·cence (floo res′əns, flô-, flŏŏ′ə res′-) *n.* **1.** emission of light from a substance that is absorbing radiant energy, such as X rays or ultraviolet rays, and instantaneously emitting it as visible light. Fluorescence continues only as long as the substance is exposed to the source of energy. Distinguished from **phosophorescence. 2.** light so emitted. [FLUOR(SPAR) + -ESCENCE; because this phenomenon was first observed in the mineral *fluorspar*, in 1852.]

flu·o·res·cent (floo res′ənt, flô-, flŏŏ′ə res′-) *adj.* producing, resulting from, or showing fluorescence.

fluorescent lamp, electric lamp that produces ultraviolet light and converts it into visible light.

flu·o·ri·date (floor′ə dāt′, flôr′-) **-dat·ed, -dat·ing.** *v.t.* to add a fluoride to (drinking water), esp. to reduce tooth decay. —**flu′o·ri·da′·tion,** *n.*

flu·o·ride (floor′īd, flôr′-, flŏŏ′ə rīd′) *n.* compound consisting of fluorine and another element or radical. [FLUOR + IDE. See FLUORINE.]

flu·o·ri·nate (floor′ə nāt′, flôr′-) **-nat·ed, -nat·ing.** *v.t.* to treat or combine with fluorine. —**flu′o·ri·na′tion,** *n.*

flu·o·rine (floor′ēn, flôr′-, flŏŏ′ə rēn′) *n.* the most reactive nonmetallic element in the form of a greenish-yellow gas that is poisonous and very corrosive. Symbol: **F** See **element** for table. [FLUOR + -INE²; because this element was first discovered in the mineral *fluor*.]

flu·o·rite (floor′īt, flôr′-, flŏŏ′ə rīt′) *n.* transparent to translucent mineral occurring in various colors, composed chiefly of calcium fluoride, used esp. as a flux to help melt iron ore in steel production. Also, **fluor′spar′.** [FLUOR + -ITE¹.]

flu·o·ro·car·bon (floor′ō kär′bən, flôr′-, flŏŏ′ər ō-) *n.* any of a group of organic compounds containing both carbon and fluorine, having great chemical stability and resistance to heat, widely used as refrigerants, lubricants, and insulators.

flu·o·ro·scope (floor′ə skōp′, flôr′-) *n.* instrument used to examine internal structures or parts, as of the body. It consists of an X-ray machine and a fluorescent screen which registers patterns of light and shadow cast by the different amounts of X rays allowed to pass through the internal structures or parts. —*v.t.*, **-scoped, -scop·ing.** to examine with a fluoroscope. [FLUOR(ESCENCE) + -SCOPE.] —**fluor·o·scop·ic** (floor′ə skop′ik, flôr′-), *adj.* —**flu′o·ro·scop′i·cal·ly,** *adv.*

fluor·os·co·py (floo ros′kə pē, flô-, flŏŏ′ə ros′-) *n.* examination conducted by means of a fluoroscope.

flu·or·spar (flŏŏ′ər spär′) *n.* fluorite. [FLUOR + SPAR³.]

flur·ry (flur′ē) *pl.*, **-ries.** *n.* **1.** sudden or nervous movement, commotion, or agitation; stir: *a flurry of activity, a flurry of excitement.* **2.** light, scattered snowfall, accompanied by gusts of wind. **3.** *Archaic.* brief, sudden gust: *a flurry of wind.* [Obsolete *flurr* to scatter, whir of imitative origin) + -Y¹.]

flush¹ (flush) *v.i.* **1.** to glow or become suffused with a reddish color: *His face flushed with embarrassment.* **2.** to become red in the face, as from emotion; blush: *He flushed when he saw her.* **3.** to flow or rush suddenly or copiously: *Water flushed through the pipes.* **4.** to become cleaned or emptied through a sudden, rapid rush or flow, as of water. —*v.t.* **1.** to cause to redden: *The child was flushed with fever.* **2.** to clean, empty, or wash with a sudden, rapid rush or flow, as of water: *to flush out a drain.* **3.** to stir up or fill, as with pride, elation, or excitement: *He was flushed with success.* —*n.* **1.** reddish color or glow. **2.** rush or surge of elation, excitement, or other emotion. **3.** glowing vigor or

freshness: *the first flush of spring.* **4.** rapid, sudden rush or flow, as of water. **5.** brief, sudden feeling of being hot. [Possibly from FLUSH¹.]

flush² (flush) *adj.* **1.** having immediate contact; directly abutting or adjacent; touching: *The table was flush against the wall.* **2.** even or level, as with a surface; forming one plane; being in exact alignment: *The building is flush with the street.* **3.** well or abundantly supplied, esp. with money: *He's feeling particularly flush since it's payday.* **4.** abundant or plentiful, as money. **5.** prosperous: *flush times.* —*adv.* **1.** in immediate or direct contact: *He set the bureau flush against the wall.* **2.** in an even or level manner, so as to form one plane or be in exact alignment: *They placed the second picture flush with the first.* **3.** directly; squarely: *to hit someone flush on the chin.* [Probably from FLUSH¹.]

flush³ (flush) *v.t.* to drive from cover or from a hiding place, esp. to startle from cover, as birds: *to flush a quail. The police flushed out the fugitive.* —*v.i.* to start up or flee from cover. [Possibly imitative.]

flush⁴ (flush) *n.* in card games, hand or set of cards all of one suit. A **royal flush** consists of the five highest cards of a particular suit; a **straight flush** consists of any five consecutive cards of a particular suit. [French *flux* literally, a flowing, from Latin *flūxus.*]

flus·ter (flus′tər) *v.t.* to cause to be embarrassed or at a loss; agitate and confuse. —*n.* state of agitated confusion. [Probably of Scandinavian origin.]

Flute

flute (floot) *n.* **1.** reedless musical instrument of the woodwind family, consisting of a hollow cylinder with fingerholes or keys along its length, played through a mouth hole near one end, and producing a high-pitched tone. **2.a.** shallow, rounded groove on the shaft of a column. **b.** any similar groove, esp. a decorative one, as on silverware or in a ruffle or piecrust. —*v.i.*, **flut·ed, flut·ing. 1.** to play on a flute. **2.** to produce a sound like that of a flute. —*v.t.* **1.** to utter with a sound like that of a flute. **2.** to make flutes in. [Old French *flaute, fleute* this musical instrument; possibly of imitative origin.]

flut·ing (floo′ting) *n.* **1.** ornamentation or decoration with flutes or grooves. **2.** groove or a series of grooves; flutes or grooves collectively. **3.** act of making such flutes or grooves.

flut·ist (floo′tist) *also*, **flau·tist.** *n.* one who plays the flute.

flut·ter (flut′ər) *v.i.* **1.** to wave or flap quickly and irregularly: *The flag fluttered in the breeze.* **2.** to fly, hover, or flap the wings lightly, gracefully, and with quick, irregular movements: *Butterflies fluttered among the flowers.* **3.** to fall or move with light, irregular motion: *Her eyelashes fluttered and she opened her eyes. Some leaves fluttered to the ground.* **4.** to move about lightly, quickly, or in a nervous, excited manner: *She fluttered about the room.* **5.** to beat quickly and irregularly, as the heart. —*v.t.* to cause to flutter: *She fluttered her eyelashes at him.* —*n.* **1.** a fluttering; quick, irregular movement: *the flutter of her pulse.* **2.** state of nervous confusion or excitement: *to be in a flutter.* **3.** *Medicine.* rhythmical but abnormally rapid contraction of the heart. [Old English *flotorian* to float about, flap the wings.] —**flut′ter·er,** *n.*

flutter kick, kick in swimming in which the legs are moved alternately up and down with the feet pointed out to the back.

flu·vi·al (floo′vē əl) *adj.* relating to, found in, or produced by a river: *fluvial deposits.* [Latin *fluviālis*, from *fluvius* river.]

flux (fluks) *n.* **1.** constant change or movement. **2.** a flowing or flow. **3.** flowing in of the tide. **4.** *Metallurgy.* a substance, as lime, that promotes the fusion of metals or minerals, used chiefly in metal refining. **b.** substance, as rosin, used in soldering to promote the flowing of the solder. **5.** *Physics.* **a.** rate of flow of fluids, particles, or energy, such as light or other radiant energy, through a given area. **b.** magnetic flux. **6.** *Medicine.* abnormal, excessive discharge of liquid matter from the body. —*v.t.* to treat, as metal, with a flux. [Latin *flūxus* a flowing.]

flux·ion (fluk′shən) *n.* act of flowing; flow or flux.

fly¹ (flī) *pl.*, **flies.** *n.* **1.** any of a large group of insects, order Diptera, including houseflies, mosquitoes, and gnats, that have sucking mouth parts and one pair of transparent wings. **2.** any of various other flying insects. **3.** fishhook decorated, as with feathers or other material, so as to resemble an insect. **4.** **fly in the ointment.** something that detracts from or spoils the value, usefulness, or enjoyment of something else. [Old English *flȳge, flēoge* winged insect.]

fly² (flī) *(v.i. defs. 1–7, v.t.)* **flew, flown, fly·ing** *or (v.i. def. 8)* **flied, fly·ing.** *v.i.* **1.** to move through the air by using wings, as a bird does. **2.** to operate, move, or travel in an aircraft or spacecraft: *The pilot flew to Chicago. They flew to Los Angeles last night.* **3.** to pass, move, or be propelled through the air by wind or other force: *Bullets flew in all directions. The spray flew into our faces.* **4.** to wave or flutter in the air: *A flag flew from the ship's mast.* **5.** to move or pass swiftly; speed: *She flew up the stairs when she heard the child crying. The summer flew by.*

at; āpe; cär; end; mē; it; īce; hot; ōld; fôrk; wood; fŏŏl; oil; out; up; ūse; turn; sing; thin; this; zh in treasure; ə in ago, taken, pencil, lemon, circus.

6. to change rapidly and suddenly from one state, condition, or position to another; pass abruptly into a particular state: *to fly into a rage. The door flew open. The clay pigeon flew apart when the pellets struck it.* **7.** to run away; flee. **8.** *Baseball.* to hit a fly ball: *The batter flied to left field.* **9.** **to fly at** (or **into**). to attack or lash out at suddenly and violently. **10. to fly in the face** (or **teeth**) **of.** to defy openly or brazenly: *to fly in the face of the law.* **11. to let fly.** to discharge or hurl with force or violence: *to let fly a stone, to let fly an oath.* **12. to fly out.** *Baseball.* to be put out by hitting a fly ball that is caught by an opposing player before it touches the ground. —*v. t.* **1.** to cause to move through or float in the air: *to fly a kite. The ship flew the flag of its country.* **2.** to operate (an aircraft or spacecraft): *He flew a bomber during the war.* **3.** to traverse or pass over, as in an aircraft: *They flew the Atlantic Ocean in five hours.* **4.** to take part in or perform (something) in an aircraft or spacecraft: *The pilot had flown fifteen missions.* **5.** to carry or transport by air: *They flew supplies to the city.* **6.** to flee from; avoid; shun. —*n. pl.* **flies.** **1.** opening in the front of a pair of trousers, usually having a zipper, buttons, or other fastening, concealed by a flap of material. **2.** flap at the entrance of a tent. **3.** piece of canvas pitched in front of or over a tent to provide extra protection. **4.** flyleaf. **5.** *Baseball.* fly ball. **6.** flywheel. **7.** light carriage used for public transportation, as a hackney or hansom. **8.** **flies.** *Theater.* space above and behind the proscenium of a stage. **9. on the fly.** while still in flight; before touching the ground: *to catch a ball on the fly.* [Old English *flēogan* to move with wings through the air, flee.] —**fly·a·bil·i·ty,** *n.* —**fly·a·ble,** *adj.*
Syn. *v. i.* **1.** Fly, soar, sail mean to move through the air on or as on wings. **Fly** suggests rapid movement, whether by motion of wings, by motor or jet propulsion, or by any other means: *The peregrine falcon flies a hundred miles per hour.* **Soar** implies flight high above the ground, esp. the upward flight or the effortless movement on air currents characteristic of hawks or gliders: *The naturalists spent weeks watching seabirds soar from the cliffs to dive for prey in the waters below.* **Sail** suggests the easy, floating motion of a bird with wings spread using the winds like a sailing ship: *Kites of many shapes and colors sailed through the air above the sandy beach.*
fly agaric, very poisonous mushroom, *Amanita Muscaria.*
fly·a·way (flī′ə wā′) *adj.* tending to muss or become disarranged; loosely streaming: *flyaway hair.*
fly ball *Baseball.* ball hit high into the air. Also, **fly.**
fly-blown (flī′blōn′) *adj.* **1.** covered or tainted with the eggs or larvae of flies. **2.** tainted; impure; corrupt.
fly-by-night (flī′bī nīt′) *adj.* not established or operating on a sound or permanent basis; not to be trusted, esp. in financial matters: *a fly-by-night scheme, a fly-by-night business.* —*n.* one who or that which is fly-by-night, esp. someone who cheats his creditors by departing secretly.
fly casting, act or method of casting a fishing line using artificial flies and a longer, more flexible rod than that used when fishing with bait. Also, **fly fishing.**

Tyrant flycatcher

fly-catch·er (flī′kach′ər) *n.* any insect-eating bird of either of two large families, the **tyrant flycatchers,** family Tyrannidae, of North and South America, and the **Old World flycatchers,** family Muscicapidae, of the Eastern Hemisphere. Length: 3½–16 inches.
fly·er (flī′ər) flier.
flying boat, airplane having a fuselage shaped like the hull of a boat, enabling it to float on water.
flying buttress, masonry support carried on a half arch, springing from a pier or other structure and resting against a wall for the purpose of resisting thrust, used esp. in Gothic architecture.
flying colors, complete and triumphant success: *He passed all his exams with flying colors.* [From the custom of displaying or raising the colors, that is, one's flag, to indicate victory.]
Flying Dutchman 1. legendary Dutch sea captain who, condemned for his pride, was to sail a phantom ship until Judgment Day or until he found a woman whose love would redeem him. **2.** his ghostly ship supposed to appear at sea, esp. off the Cape of Good Hope, and considered a bad omen.
flying fish, any of a group of saltwater fish, family Exocoetidae, that are found in warm waters and have one to two pairs of winglike, pectoral fins that enable them to leap into the air and glide for some distance. They are valued as both food and game fish.
Flying Fortress, heavy four-engine bomber used by the U.S. Air Force during World War II.

flying fox, any of various tropical bats, family Pteropidae, having a foxlike face and, often, gray or black fur with yellow markings on the shoulders. It is the largest of all bats. Wingspan: to 5 feet.
flying gurnard, gurnard.
flying jib, small, triangular sail set out beyond the jib on an extension of the jib boom.
flying machine, airplane or other aircraft that is heavier than air.
flying saucer, any of various unidentified flying objects allegedly having a saucerlike or disklike shape and presumed to be from outer space. Also, **flying disk.**
flying squirrel, any of various squirrel-like rodents, family Sciuridae, of the forests of Europe, Asia, and North America, having winglike membranes between the front and hind legs which enable it to make long, gliding leaps through the air. Length: to 3 feet.

Flying squirrel

flying start 1. start of a race in which the contestants begin moving before reaching the starting line. **2.** any swift, promising, or vigorous start or beginning: *The tremendous reception the candidate received launched his campaign with a flying start.*
fly·leaf (flī′lēf′) *pl.* **-leaves.** *n.* blank sheet of paper at the beginning or end of a book or other bound printed matter.
fly·o·ver (flī′ō′vər) *n.* low-altitude flight over a specific area by one or more aircraft, often as part of a display or exhibition.
fly·pa·per (flī′pā′pər) *n.* paper covered with a sticky or poisonous substance, placed so as to catch or kill flies.
fly speck 1. tiny spot of excrement left by a fly. **2.** any very small or hardly noticeable spot.
fly swatter, device for swatting or killing flies or other insects, usually a square sheet of wire mesh attached to a long handle.
fly-trap (flī′trap′) *n.* **1.** any of various plants that trap insects, as the Venus's-flytrap or the pitcher plant. **2.** any device for catching flies.
fly·way (flī′wā′) *n.* particular air route along which migratory birds regularly travel.
fly·weight (flī′wāt′) *n.* athlete competing in the lowest weight class in boxing and wrestling.
fly·wheel (flī′hwēl′, -wēl′) *n.* heavy wheel driven by an engine shaft, serving to regulate and make more uniform the speed of an engine.
Fm, fermium.
fm. 1. fathom. **2.** from.
FM 1. method of radio broadcasting by which a signal is transmitted over radio carrier waves by altering the frequency of the waves. **2.** broadcasting system using this method. **3.** of, relating to, or using an FM broadcasting system: *an FM radio, an FM station.* Distinguished from **AM.** [Abbreviation of *frequency modulation.*]
f number, number that expresses the size to which the lens opening in a camera is adjusted and indicates the amount of light admitted by the lens at that setting. The lower the f number the wider the lens opening.
foal (fōl) *n.* young offspring of a horse, donkey, zebra, or other member of the horse family, esp. one under one year of age. —*v. i., v. t.* to give birth to (a foal). [Old English *fola.*]
foam (fōm) *n.* **1.** frothy mass of bubbles, as that formed on the surface of a liquid by violent agitation or by fermentation: *the foam formed by breaking waves, the foam left in a glass of beer.* **2.** similar frothy mass, as of saliva or sweat: *After the race, the horse's flanks were covered with foam.* **3.** thick, frothy mass that results when a liquid under pressure is released from its container, as shaving cream, or a substance used in fire fighting to smother flames. —*v. i.* **1.** to form or produce foam: *The water foamed and bubbled when the soap flakes were added.* **2.** to flow or gush in a foam: *The soda foamed over the top of the glass.* **3. to foam at the mouth.** *Informal.* to be extremely or uncontrollably angry; be enraged or furious. [Old English *fām* froth, spume.]
foam rubber, synthetic spongy rubber chiefly used in mattresses and upholstery and for insulation.
foam·y (fō′mē) **foam·i·er, foam·i·est.** *adj.* covered with, consisting of, or resembling foam. —**foam′i·ly,** *adv.* —**foam′i·ness,** *n.*
fob[1] (fob) *n.* **1.** short chain or ribbon attached to a watch and often worn hanging from a watch pocket. **2.** ornament worn at the end of such a chain or ribbon. **3.** watch pocket, as in the front of a vest or just below the waistband in trousers. [Probably of Germanic origin.]
fob[2] (fob) **fobbed, fob·bing.** *v.t.* **1.** *Archaic.* to trick; cheat. **2. to fob off. a.** to dispose of (something worthless) by trickery or deception; palm off. **b.** to put (someone) off by trickery or deception. [Possibly from German *foppen* to jeer at, fool.]
F.O.B., free on board.
fo·cal (fō′kəl) *adj.* of, at, or relating to a focus. —**fo′cal·ly,** *adv.*

at, āpe; cär; end; mē; it; īce; hot; ōld; fôrk; wood, fōol; oil; out; up; ūse; turn; sing; thin; this; zh in treasure; ə in ago, taken, pencil, lemon, circus.

397

fo·cal·ize (fō′kə līz′) -ized, -iz·ing. v.t., v.i. to focus. —**fo′cal·i·za′tion,** n.

focal length, distance from the center of a lens or mirror to the focus. Also, **focal distance.**

Foch, Fer·di·nand (fosh, fôsh; fer′dē nän′) 1851–1929, French marshal.

fo′c's'le (fōk′səl) forecastle.

fo·cus (fō′kəs) pl., **-cus·es** or **-ci** (-sī). n. **1.a.** point at which converging rays, esp. light rays, meet, after being refracted by a lens or reflected by a mirror. Also, **real focus.** **b.** point from which diverging rays, esp. light rays, appear to originate,

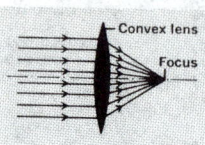

Convex lens

Focus

Focus

after having undergone such refraction or reflection. Also, **virtual focus.** **2.** focal length. **3.** adjustment, as of a lens or the eye, necessary to produce a clear image: *My binoculars aren't in focus.* **4.** condition of being distinct, comprehensible, or clearly defined: *His explanation brought the meaning of the events into focus for us.* **5.** central point or center, as of activity, interest, or importance: *The downtown area was the focus of the disturbance.* **6.** *Geometry.* fixed point or one of two fixed points used in determining an ellipse, parabola, or hyperbola. **7.** *Pathology.* chief center at which a disease develops or is localized or from which it spreads. **8.** center or point of origin of an earthquake. —v.t., **-cused, -cus·ing;** also, British, **-cussed, -cus·sing.** **1.** to bring to a focus or into focus: *to focus a camera. Unless the object is properly focused, the photograph will be blurred.* **2.** to fix; concentrate: *Focus your attention on the speaker.* —v.i. to become focused. [Latin *focus* hearth; because the hearth was once the center of the home.]

fod·der (fod′ər) n. food for livestock, obtained by cutting and drying any of various grasses, as alfalfa or the stalks and leaves of corn. —v.t. to feed with fodder. [Old English *fōdor* food for cattle.]

foe (fō) n. **1.** enemy. **2.** one who opposes or rivals another, as in a game or contest; adversary: *They've been political foes for years.* **3.** one who is opposed in viewpoint to or acts to the detriment of (something): *a foe of religion, a foe to all measures of reform.* [Old English *fāh* hostile, *gefā* adversary.] —**Syn. 1.** see **enemy.**

foehn (fān; German foen) also, **föhn.** n. warm, dry wind that blows down the side of a mountain. [German *Föhn,* going back to Latin *favōnius* the west wind.]

foe·tal (fē′təl) fetal.

foe·tid (fē′tid) fetid.

foe·tus (fē′təs) fetus.

fog (fôg, fog) n. **1.** suspension of very small water droplets in the air, at or close to the earth's surface. **2.** any hazy or smoggy condition of the atmosphere, as one caused by smoke or dust. **3.** state of mental confusion or bewilderment; daze: *I was really in a fog after the exam.* **4.** hazy blur on developed photographic film caused by chemical action or by stray light or other radiation. —v.t., **fogged, fog·ging. 1.** to cover, envelop, or obscure with or as with fog. **2.** to produce a hazy blur on (photographic film). **3.** to confuse; bewilder. —v.i. **1.** to become covered, enveloped, or obscured with or as with fog. **2.** (of photographic film) to become clouded with a hazy blur. [Probably of Scandinavian origin.]

fog bank, dense, low-lying mass of fog, esp. over a body of water.

fog·bound (fôg′bound′, fog′-) adj. shut in, surrounded, or immobilized by fog: *The airplane was fogbound at the airport.*

fog·gy (fôg′gē, fog′ē) **-gi·er, -gi·est.** adj. **1.** full of or obscured by fog: *a foggy day.* **2.** confused or unclear; vague; cloudy: *foggy thinking.* —**fog′gi·ly,** adv. —**fog′gi·ness,** n.

fog·horn (fôg′hôrn′, fog′-) n. horn or similar device for sounding warning signals, as to boats, during a fog.

fo·gy (fō′gē) pl., **-gies.** also, **fo·gey.** n. old-fashioned or very conservative person. [Of uncertain origin.]

föhn (fān; German foen) foehn.

foi·ble (foi′bəl) n. minor weakness or failing of character; flaw; shortcoming. [French *foible,* form of *faible* weak, from Latin *flēbilis* mournful.]

foil¹ (foil) v.t. to interfere with or prevent from being successful; frustrate; thwart. [Old French *fouler* to trample on, hurt, full cloth, going back to Latin *fullō* a fuller.] —**Syn.** see **frustrate.**

foil² (foil) n. **1.** metal hammered or rolled into a very thin, flexible sheet. **2.** person or thing that, by comparison or contrast, serves to set off or enhance the qualities of another: *In the play his shallowness is a perfect foil for the hero's sincerity.* **3.** leaf-shaped space or arc, as in the tracery of Gothic architecture. **4.** thin piece

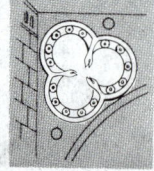

Foil² (def. 3)

of bright metal placed under a gem to add brilliancy or color. [Old French *foil* leaf, from Latin *folium* leaf.]

foil³ (foil) n. long, flexible, four-sided fencing sword that tapers from the hilt to the point, which is blunted or padded to prevent injury. [Of uncertain origin.]

foist (foist) v.t. to pass off or offer wrongfully as genuine or valuable; impose slyly or deceitfully; palm off. [Probably from dialectal Dutch *vuisten* to take in the fist, from *vuist* fist.]

fold¹ (fōld) v.t. **1.** to bring one part of (something) over another, as by bending; bend or double over on itself: *to fold a paper in half. Fold the towels up and put them away.* **2.** to close, collapse, or make more compact by bending or laying parts together (often with *up*): *Fold the chairs and lean them against the wall.* **3.** to bring together and interlock or intertwine: *She folded her hands in her lap. He folded him arms over his chest.* **4.** to bring the (wings) close to the body. **5.** to enfold in or as in the arms; embrace; clasp: *She folded the crying child to her breast.* **6.** to cover or wrap; enclose: *Fold all the dishes in newspaper.* **7.** to coil or wind: *He folded his arm about her waist.* **8.** *Cooking.* to add or blend (an ingredient) into a mixture by repeatedly turning one part over another gently (often with *in*): *Next fold the eggs in.* —v.i. **1.** to become folded; be capable of being folded: *Paper folds more easily than cardboard.* **2.** *Informal.* to end or close due to financial failure (often with *up*): *The business folded. The play folded up within a month.* —n. **1.** part that is folded; layer; pleat: *Her dress hung in graceful folds. He was hidden in the folds of the curtain.* **2.** hollow or space produced by folding: *She cuddled the child in the fold of her arms until he stopped crying.* **3.** mark or crease produced by folding: *Cut the paper along the fold.* **4.** *Geology.* deformation, or bend, in a layer of rock, caused by forces within the earth. [Old English *fealdan* to wrap, double together, bend.] —**fold′a·ble,** adj.

fold² (fōld) n. **1.** pen or other enclosure for livestock, esp. for sheep. **2.** sheep or other animals kept together in such a pen. **3.** flock of sheep. **4.** group, as the congregation of a church, under the guidance of a leader or adhering to common beliefs or values. [Old English *falod* pen².]

-fold suffix **1.** (a specified number of) times as much or as great: *a hundredfold increase.* **2.** having (a specified number of) parts: *a threefold disaster, a twofold problem.* [Old English *-feald.*]

fold·er (fōl′dər) n. **1.** holder or container for loose papers, usually a folded sheet of light cardboard. **2.** sheet of printed material, as a circular, timetable, or map, folded rather than stitched or bound into a number of pagelike sections. **3.** one who or that which folds.

fol·de·rol (fol′də rol′) also, **fal·de·ral** (fal′də ral′). n. **1.** mere nonsense. **2.** trivial ornament; trifle.

folding door, door having two or more hinged sections that open by folding back.

fo·li·a (fō′lē ə) a plural of **folium.**

fo·li·a·ceous (fō′lē ā′shəs) adj. **1.** of, relating to, or resembling the leaf of a plant. **2.** consisting of thin, leaflike plates or layers, as certain rocks. [Latin *foliāceus* leafy, from *folium* leaf.]

fo·li·age (fō′lē ij) n. **1.** growth of leaves on a tree or other plant; leaves collectively. **2.** representation of leaves, flowers, and branches, as in architectural ornamentation. [Modification (influenced by Latin *folium* leaf) of French *feuillage* leafage, from *feuille* leaf, from Latin *folia* leaves, plural of *folium.*]

fo·li·ate (adj., fō′lē it, -lē āt′; v., fō′lē āt′) adj. having leaves; leafy. —v.i., **-at·ed, -at·ing. 1.** to put forth leaves, as a tree. **2.** to split into thin, leaflike plates or layers. —v.t. to decorate with foliage or with leaf-shaped ornaments. [Latin *foliātus* leafy, from *folium* leaf.]

fo·li·a·tion (fō′lē ā′shən) n. **1.** act of putting forth leaves; being in leaf. **2.** arrangement of leaves in a bud. **3.** decoration with foliage or with leaf-shaped ornaments.

fol·ic acid (fō′lik) chrystalline vitamin of the vitamin B complex group, used in treating anemia. [Latin *folium* leaf + -IC + ACID; because found in green leaves.]

fo·li·o (fō′lē ō′) pl., **-li·os.** n. **1.** sheet of paper folded once to form two leaves, or four pages, as of a book or manuscript. **2.** book or manuscript, usually more than 11 inches in height, made up of sheets folded in this way. **3.** page number, as of a book. **4.** leaf, as of a book, numbered only on the front side. —adj. of or having the size or form of a folio. [Latin *foliō,* ablative of *folium* leaf (of a tree, of paper).]

fo·li·um (fō′lē əm) pl., **-li·ums** or **-li·a** (-lē ə). n. thin layer or stratum, as of a rock. [Latin *folium* leaf.]

folk (fōk) pl., **folk** or **folks.** n. **1.** also, **folks.** people: *city folk, old folks.* **2. folks.** *Informal.* one's family or relatives, esp. one's parents: *I'm going home to see my folks tomorrow.* **3.** *Archaic.* nation or race; a people. —adj. of the common people; originating or widespread among the common people: *a folk custom.* [Old English *folc* a people, nation, crowd.]

folk dance 1. dance originating among the common people of a region or country and handed down from generation to generation. **2.** music for such a dance.

at; āpe; cär; end; mē; it; īce; hot; ōld; fôrk; wood; fōōl; out; up; ūse; turn; sing; thin; this; zh in treasure; ə in ago, taken, pencil, lemon, circus.

folk etymology 1. change in the form of a word or phrase due to an incorrectly assumed etymology, for example: **humble pie** for the earlier form "umble pie". **2.** incorrectly assumed etymology, for example: **sirloin** which was once thought to have come into the language when an English King knighted the loin of beef.

folk·lore (fōk′lôr′) *n.* **1.** tales, beliefs, customs, or other traditions of a people, handed down from generation to generation orally or by performance, rather than in writing. **2.** study of such material. —**folk′lor′ic, folk′lor·is′tic,** *adj.* —**folk′lor′ist,** *n.*

folk music 1. traditional music, usually of anonymous origin, of the common people of a region or country, reflecting their customs, characteristics, and occupations. **2.** music written in imitation of the style and character of such music.

folk singer, singer who specializes in the performance of folk songs.

folk song 1. traditional song, usually originating among the common people and handed down orally from generation to generation, often having a simple tune and appearing in various versions. **2.** song written in imitation of the style and character of such song.

folk·sy (fōk′sē) **-si·er, -si·est.** *adj. Informal.* unaffected and neighborly; friendly and unpretentious. —**folk′si·ly,** *adv.* —**folk′si·ness,** *n.*

folk tale, prose narrative, as a tale or legend, that is part of the folklore of a people and is sometimes handed down in writing as well as orally, often appearing in several different versions. Also, **folk story.**

folk·way (fōk′wā′) *n.* customary way of acting common to a people or group.

fol·li·cle (fŏl′i kəl) *n.* **1.** small cavity, sac, or gland in the body. Hair grows from follicles. **2.** a dry fruit that splits open along one seam when it is ripe and releases its seeds, as a milkweed pod. [Latin *folliculus* little bag, diminutive of *follis* bellows, bag.]

fol·low (fŏl′ō) *v.t.* **1.** to go, proceed, or come after; move behind in the same direction: *The dog followed the boy obediently. We followed them in our car.* **2.** to come or occur after in sequence, order, or time; succeed: *Spring follows winter. The riot followed a night of disorder.* **3.** to proceed along or hold to the course of; go along: *to follow a path. Follow the river to the fork.* **4.** to conform to, comply with, or act in accordance with; obey: *I was only following orders. Follow the directions on the package.* **5.** to watch or observe closely or steadily: *to follow a tennis match. He followed her movements from across the room.* **6.** to be actively interested in or attentive about; keep abreast of: *Have you been following this serial on television? We closely followed his career as a novelist.* **7.** to grasp the continuity or logic of; keep up with and understand: *I don't follow your reasoning.* **8.** to use or take as a model; imitate: *Follow his example.* **9.** to employ oneself in; make a living from: *to follow a profession.* **10.** to accept as a guide or leader; support or advocate the opinions or cause of: *He follows Freud.* **11.** to come after or take place as a consequence or result; result from: *Disaster followed the flood.* **12.** to try to overtake, capture, or keep under surveillance; pursue; chase: *The detective followed the suspect for three days.* **13.** *Archaic.* to accompany; attend. **14. to follow out,** to carry out or comply with fully. **15. to follow through,** to proceed with or pursue to an end or conclusion; complete. **16. to follow up. a.** to pursue to a conclusion or check thoroughly: *The reporter followed up on the story.* **b.** to reinforce or increase the effect of by further action: *They followed up one devastating attack with another.* —*v.i.* **1.** to proceed, come, or occur after. **2.** to come as a logical consequence: *Your statement doesn't follow from the original premise.* **3. to follow through.** to continue the motion of a stroke after hitting the ball, as in tennis or golf. [Old English *folgian* to go or come after.]

Syn. *v.i.* **1. Follow, ensue, succeed** mean to come after or later. **Follow** is the general term to indicate that something is subsequent to another in time, place, order, or importance: *We weren't prepared for what followed.* **Ensue** is often applied to the final event or climax of a given order: *After the play, a lively discussion ensued.* **Succeed** is often applied to one person replacing another and emphasizes the sequence rather than the particular event: *The prince usually succeeds to the throne after the king's death.*

fol·low·er (fŏl′ō ər) *n.* **1.** one who follows another, or the opinions or cause of another, as a supporter, disciple, or admirer; adherent. **2.** one who or that which follows. **3.** part of a machine that receives motion from or follows the motion of another part. **4.** *Archaic.* servant; attendant.

fol·low·ing (fŏl′ō ing) *adj.* **1.** coming after or next in sequence, order, or time: *the following morning.* **2.** about to be mentioned, related, or set forth: *He did it for the following reasons.* —*n.* **1.** body of followers: *an actor who has a large following.* **2. the following. a.** those about to be mentioned, related, or set forth: *The following are the alternatives we discussed.* **b.** that which comes after or next in sequence, order, or time.

fol·low-through (fŏl′ō thrōō′) *n.* **1.a.** act or manner of continuing the motion of a stroke after hitting the ball, as in tennis or golf.

b. part of the stroke itself after the ball has been hit. **2.** act of proceeding with to an end or conclusion.

fol·low-up (fŏl′ō up′) *n.* **1.** act of following up. **2.** something, as a letter or procedure, used in following up. —*adj.* of or relating to an act or instance of following up: *a follow-up visit, follow-up care.*

fol·ly (fŏl′ē) *pl.,* **-lies.** *n.* **1.** quality or state of being foolish; lack of good sense or understanding; foolishness. **2.** something foolish; foolish act, idea, or practice. **3.** foolish and costly undertaking, as a ruinous investment or purchase. [Old French *folie* madness, foolishness, from *fol* fool, from Latin *follis* bellows, bag, windbag.]

Fol·som man (fōl′səm) prehistoric man believed to have lived on the North American continent about 10,000 years ago.

Fo·mal·haut (fō′məl hôt′, -mə lō′) *n.* white star, one of the brightest in the sky and the brightest in the constellation Piscis Austrinus. [Arabic *fum'l-haut* literally, mouth of the fish.]

fo·ment (fō ment′) *v.t.* **1.** to promote or incite; instigate: *to foment rebellion, to foment trouble.* **2.** to apply heat and moisture to (a part of the body) to reduce pain or inflammation. [Late Latin *fōmentāre* to restore with poultices, foster, from Latin *fōmentum* poultice.] —**fo·ment′er,** *n.*

fo·men·ta·tion (fō′men tā′shən) *n.* **1.** incitement, as to rebellion or unrest; instigation. **2.a.** application of heat and moisture to a part of the body to reduce pain or inflammation. **b.** hot, moist application so applied.

fond (fŏnd) *adj.* **1.** having strong liking or affection for (with *of*): *fond of chocolates, fond of animals.* **2.** affectionate; tender; loving: *a fond embrace.* **3.** excessively loving or weakly indulgent; doting: *a fond and foolish aunt.* **4.** entertained with great affection; deeply felt; cherished: *my fondest wish, fond dreams of glory.* **5.** *Archaic.* foolish. [Of uncertain origin.] —**fond′ness,** *n.*

fon·dant (fŏn′dənt) *n.* smooth, creamy confection, made of sugar, used as a filling or icing or eaten as candy. [French *fondant* sweetmeat, from *fondre* to melt, from Latin *fundere;* because it melts readily when eaten.]

Fond du Lac (fŏn′ də lak′) city in eastern Wisconsin. Pop. (1970), 35,515.

fon·dle (fŏn′dəl) **-dled, -dling.** *v.t.* to stroke or touch lovingly or tenderly; caress. [Obsolete *fond* to be fond of, caress (from FOND) + -LE.] —**fon′dler,** *n.*

fond·ly (fŏnd′lē) *adv.* **1.** in a fond manner. **2.** with naive or complacent credulity: *She fondly believed she still loved him. We fondly imagined the war would soon end.*

fon·due (fon dōō′) *n.* **1.** dish containing melted cheese, seasonings, wine and often brandy, served as a dip for cubes of bread. **2.** dish made of melted cheese, eggs, butter, milk, and seasonings and usually baked. **3.** dish consisting of hot oil into which chunks of meat, esp. beef, are dipped and cooked quickly, usually served with a variety of sauces. [French *fondue* dish of melted cheese and eggs, from *fondre* to melt, from Latin *fundere.*]

font¹ (font) *n.* **1.** receptacle, often of stone, used to hold the water for baptism. **2.** receptacle for holy water; stoup. **3.** fountain; source: *the font of life, a font of wisdom.* [Old English *font* baptismal font, from Latin *fōns* spring, fountain.]

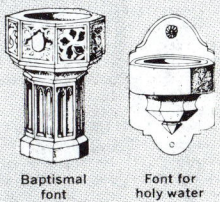

Baptismal font

Font for holy water

Fonts¹

font² (font) *n. Printing.* complete assortment of printing type of one size and style. [French *fonte* a casting (of metals), from *fondre* to melt, cast, from Latin *fundere* to melt, pour.]

Fon·taine·bleau (fŏn′tən blō′) *n.* town in north-central France, near Paris, site of a palace formerly used by French kings.

Foo·chow (fōō′chou′) *n.* port city in southeastern China. Pop. (1957 est.), 616,000.

food (fōōd) *n.* **1.** that which is eaten or otherwise assimilated by an organism to sustain life, provide energy, and promote the growth and repair of tissues; nourishment. **2.** nourishment that is solid rather than liquid or eaten rather than drunk: *food and drink.* **3.** something that sustains or stimulates or serves for consumption or use: *food for thought. What food fed his first hopes?* (Wordsworth, 1801). [Old English *fōda* nourishment.]

food chain *Ecology.* sequence of the organisms of a community, in which each member of the sequence feeds upon the member below it.

food poisoning, gastrointestinal disorder caused by eating foods that are naturally toxic or that have been contaminated with chemicals or by harmful bacteria or their toxins, usually characterized by nausea, vomiting, and severe abdominal cramps.

at; āpe; cär; end; mē; it; īce; hot; ōld; fôrk; wood; fōōl; oil; out; up; ūse; turn; sing; thin; this; zh in treasure; ə in ago, taken, pencil, lemon, circus.

food·stuff (fo͞od′stuf′) *n.* substance suitable for or used as food.

fool (fo͞ol) *n.* **1.** one who lacks judgment or good sense; unwise or silly person. **2.** clown formerly kept by a king or nobleman to provide entertainment for the household; jester. **3.** one who has been tricked, taken advantage of, or made to appear foolish; dupe: *to make a fool of someone. I am Fortune's fool* (Shakespeare, *Romeo and Juliet*). **4. to be nobody's fool.** to be wise or shrewd. —*v.t.* **1.** to make a fool of; deceive; trick: *Her disguise didn't fool anyone. You shouldn't have been fooled by his ridiculous stories.* **2.** to spend wastefully or unwisely; fritter (with *away*): *to fool the whole afternoon away, to fool away one's money.* —*v.i.* **1.** to act like a fool; be silly (often with *around*). **2.** to act or speak in a jesting or playful manner; tease; joke: *Don't be offended; I was only fooling.* **3.** *Informal.* to spend time idly, aimlessly, or foolishly (with *around*): *The team was just fooling around on the court and not really practicing.* **4.** to play or meddle foolishly, aimlessly, or thoughtlessly; toy; tamper (often with *with*): *It's cruel to fool with his emotions. Don't fool with that gun.* —*adj. Informal.* foolish; silly: *a fool notion.* [Old French *fol* madman, foolish person, from Latin *follis* bellows, bag, windbag.]

fool·er·y (fo͞o′lər ē) *pl.*, **-er·ies.** *n.* foolish action or behavior.

fool·har·dy (fo͞ol′här′dē) **-di·er, -di·est.** *adj.* bold or daring in a foolish or unthinking way; rash; reckless: *a foolhardy young man, a foolhardy thing to do.* —**fool′har′di·ly,** *adv.* —**fool′har′di·ness,** *n.*

fool·ish (fo͞o′lish) *adj.* **1.** marked by or showing a lack of understanding or good sense; unwise; silly: *a foolish move. You were foolish to expect anything else.* **2.** ridiculous; absurd: *You look foolish in that dress.* —**fool′ish·ly,** *adv.* —**fool′ish·ness,** *n.*

fool·proof (fo͞ol′pro͞of′) *adj.* devised or made so as to be proof against error, misuse, or failure; unfailing: *a foolproof recipe.*

fools·cap (fo͞olz′kap′) *n.* **1.** writing paper varying in size from about 12 by 15 inches to 13½ by 17 inches. **2.** fool's cap. [Because the writing paper once had a FOOL'S CAP as a watermark.]

fool's cap *also,* **fools cap. 1.** jester's cap or hood, usually having several drooping peaks from which bells are hung. **2.** dunce cap.

fool's errand, profitless or pointless undertaking.

fool's gold, any of various minerals, as pyrite, that look like gold.

fool's paradise, state of deceptive or illusory happiness based on false hopes or beliefs.

foot (fo͝ot) *pl.*, **feet.** *n.* **1.** in certain vertebrates, the terminal part of the leg, on which the body stands. **2.** in invertebrate animals and plants, any structure or organ used by the organism for locomotion or for attaching itself to surfaces or objects. **3.** this part of the human body considered as the organ or source of movement or motion: *They drove, but we came on foot. After paddling to shore, they proceeded by foot.* **4.** step or manner of movement: *swift of foot. He walked with a heavy foot.* **5.** something resembling a foot in shape, position, or function, as the part of a sewing machine that holds the cloth in place. **6.** part that covers or encloses the foot: *the foot of a stocking, the foot of a boot.* **7.** lowest or supporting part: *the foot of a mountain, the foot of a ladder, the foot of a vase.* **8.** part far from or opposite the head: *the foot of a bed. Sit at the foot of the table.* **9.** measure of length equal to twelve inches. See **weights and measures** for table. **10.** basic unit of rhythm in poetry, consisting of a group of stressed and unstressed syllables. The line *The time/ you won / your town / the race* has four feet. **11.** *Archaic.* unmounted soldiers; infantry. **12. to put one's foot down.** to take a firm position; act firmly and decisively. **13. to put one's foot in it** (or in one's mouth). *Informal.* to make an embarrassing slip, mistake, or blunder. **14. to put one's best foot forward. a.** to try to appear at one's best, esp. in order to make a good impression. **b.** to do one's best. **15. to start** (or get) **off on the right foot.** to begin in a good manner. **16. to start** (or get) **off on the wrong foot.** to begin in a poor manner. **17. under foot,** in the way. —*v.t.* **1.** to make or renew the foot of; furnish with a foot: *to foot a sock. The throne was footed with gold.* **2.** *Informal.* to pay, as a bill. **3.** to foot it. to walk, run, or dance. [Old English *fōt* terminal part of the leg, measure of length equal to twelve inches.]

foot·age (fo͝ot′ij) *n.* length or amount, as of lumber of motion-picture film, measured in feet.

foot-and-mouth disease (fo͝ot′ən mouth′) highly contagious virus disease of cattle, pigs, and other cloven-hoofed animals, causing blisters in the mouth and around the hoofs. Infected animals are often quarantined and destroyed because the disease spreads so rapidly. Also, **hoof-and-mouth disease.**

foot·ball (fo͝ot′bôl′) *n.* **1.a.** game played between two teams, officially of eleven players each, on a field one hundred yards long with goals at each end, in which points are made by getting a ball across the opponent's goal line. **b.** elliptical ball used in this game, usually leather-covered and having an inflatable rubber bladder inside. **2.a.** any of several similar games, as rugby or soccer. **b.** ball used in any of these games. **3.** person or thing tossed about or passed back and forth like a football, as from one group to another: *The issue soon became a political football.*

foot·board (fo͝ot′bôrd′) *n.* **1.** piece at the foot of a bedstead. **2.** board or small platform used to support or rest the feet.

foot brake, brake operated by pressure of the foot, as in an automobile.

foot·bridge (fo͝ot′brij′) *n.* bridge for pedestrians only.

foot·can·dle (fo͝ot′kand′əl) *also,* **foot·can·dle.** *n.* unit for measuring illumination, equal to the amount of illumination produced by an international candle at a distance of one foot.

foot·ed (fo͝ot′id) *adj.* **1.** having a foot or feet: *a footed goblet.* **2.** having a specified kind or number of feet. ▲ used in combination, as in *flat-footed, a four-footed animal.*

foot·fall (fo͝ot′fôl′) *n.* footstep or its sound.

foot·gear (fo͝ot′gēr′) *n.* footwear.

foot·hill (fo͝ot′hil′) *n.* low hill at the foot of a mountain or mountain range.

foot·hold (fo͝ot′hōld′) *n.* **1.** place where one may stand or tread securely; hold or support for the feet, as in climbing. **2.** secure position, esp. a firm base for further progress or advancement: *Once it gained a foothold, the disease spread rapidly.*

foot·ing (fo͝ot′ing) *n.* **1.** secure or firm placing of the feet: *to lose one's footing.* **2.** hold or support for the feet: *The icy ledge provided no footing.* **3.** established or secure position or foundation: *to put an enterprise on a sound footing.* **4.** terms of social intercourse or relationship; mutual relation; standing: *We're on a friendly footing.*

foot·less (fo͝ot′lis) *adj.* **1.** lacking a foot or feet. **2.** having no basis; insubstantial. **3.** *Informal.* awkward; inept.

foot·lights (fo͝ot′līts′) *n.,pl.* **1.** lights in one or more rows along the front of a stage, either recessed in the stage floor or resting on it. **2. the footlights.** acting as a profession; the stage.

foot·lock·er (fo͝ot′lok′ər) *n.* small trunk for the belongings of a soldier or camper and often kept at the foot of his bed.

foot·loose (fo͝ot′lo͞os′) *adj.* free to travel about or live as one pleases; free from attachments or responsibilities.

foot·man (fo͝ot′mən) *pl.*, **-men.** *n.* male servant in livery who assists a butler with various duties, as serving, cleaning, and answering the door. He may also attend an automobile or carriage. [FOOT + MAN; because he originally accompanied his master's carriage on *foot.*]

foot·mark (fo͝ot′märk′) *n.* footprint.

foot·note (fo͝ot′nōt′) *n.* **1.** explanatory note, comment, or reference, usually below the text on a page and indicated in the body of the text by a number or symbol referring to it. **2.** subordinate addition to a major statement or event: *an essay viewing all subsequent research as only a footnote to Einstein's work.* —*v.t.*, **-not·ed, -not·ing.** to furnish with or add a footnote or footnotes to.

foot·pace (fo͝ot′pās′) *n. Archaic.* slow or walking pace.

foot·pad (fo͝ot′pad′) *n. Archaic.* highwayman who goes on foot.

foot·path (fo͝ot′path′) *n.* path for pedestrians.

foot·pound (fo͝ot′pound′) *n.* unit of work or energy, equal to the amount of energy required to raise one pound through a vertical distance of one foot.

foot·pound-sec·ond (fo͝ot′pound′sek′ənd) *adj.* of, relating to, or being a system of measurement in which the foot is the unit of length, the pound is the unit of mass, and the second is the unit of time.

foot·print (fo͝ot′print′) *n.* mark or impression made by a foot: *footprints in the sand, dirty footprints all over the kitchen floor.*

foot·rest (fo͝ot′rest′) *n.* something, as a small stool or platform, on which the feet may be rested or propped.

foot soldier, soldier trained or equipped to fight on foot; infantryman.

foot·sore (fo͝ot′sôr′) *adj.* having sore or tired feet, as from much walking.

foot·stalk (fo͝ot′stôk′) *n.* pedicel or peduncle.

foot·step (fo͝ot′step′) *n.* **1.** step or tread of the foot: *the baby's first awkward footsteps. Each footstep brought him closer to home.* **2.** sound made by this: *I heard his footsteps in the hall.* **3.** distance covered in a step: *It's just a footstep away.* **4.** footprint. **5.** step by which to ascend or descend, as on a carriage. **6. to follow in someone's footsteps.** to imitate or succeed someone.

foot·stool (fo͝ot′sto͞ol′) *n.* low stool on which to place the feet when sitting.

foot·way (fo͝ot′wā′) *n.* footpath.

foot·wear (fo͝ot′wâr′) *n.* articles to be worn on the feet, as shoes or slippers.

foot·work (fo͝ot′wurk′) *n.* **1.** use or management of the feet, as in boxing or dancing. **2.** adroit or skillful management; maneuvering.

foot·worn (fo͝ot′wôrn′) *adj.* **1.** worn or trodden down by footsteps: *a footworn trail.* **2.** weary from walking; footsore: *a footworn traveler.*

fop (fop) *n.* man or boy who is overly concerned about or affected in his manner and appearance; dandy. [Possibly from Dutch *foppen* to fool, dupe, from German *foppen* to fool, jeer at.]

fop·per·y (fop′ər ē) *pl.*, **-per·ies.** *n.* **1.** behavior, clothing, or manner of a fop. **2.** something foppish.

at; āpe; cär; end; mē; it; īce; hot; ōld; fôrk; wood; fo͞ol; oil; out; up; ūse; turn; sing; thin; this; zh in treasure; ə in ago, taken, pencil, lemon, circus.

fop·pish (fop′ish) *adj.* like or characteristic of a fop. —**fop′pish·ly,** *adv.* —**fop′pish·ness,** *n.*

for (fôr; *unstressed* fər) *prep.* **1.** to the length, extent, or duration of: *to agree for the moment. She stayed for an hour. They hiked for five miles. You can see for miles from the roof.* **2.** used with or adapted to; suited or appropriate to: *a closet for linens, a dress for the occasion, a movie for adults only, a time and a place for everything.* **3.** as a result of; by reason of; because of: *to jump for joy, a city known for its beauty, a man respected for his honesty. He handled it carefully for fear of breaking it.* **4.** in defense, support, or approval of; in favor or on the side of: *to vote for a measure, to demonstrate for civil rights, to stand up for one's rights. I'm all for it.* **5.** to or in the amount of: *a check for fifty dollars. He's liable for the whole sum.* **6.** at the cost or price of: *He bought the book for five dollars. We sold our car for $400.* **7.** in exchange as the equivalent of or in requital or payment of: *an eye for an eye, to swap pelts for supplies, five points for each correct answer.* **8.** in order to find, keep, or obtain: *to run for one's life, to work for a living, to compete for a prize, to sue for damages. She's looking for a job.* **9.** meant to be received by or belong to; sent or given to: *Any mail for me? There's a package for you. I bought presents for everybody.* **10.** as a substitute of; in place of; instead of: *to use saccharin for sugar. Russell stood in for Bob.* **11.** focused upon or directed toward: *his love for her. She had a caving for chocolate.* **12.** appreciative of or discerning about; sensitive or responsive to: *an eye for color, an ear for music.* **13.** in the interest or behalf of; as representative of: *to act for a client. She spoke for the group. Say hello for me.* **14.** in honor of: *The child was named for her grandmother. A banquet was given for him.* **15.** with respect or regard to; concerning: *pressed for time. So much for that topic. Trust to luck for the rest.* **16.** considering the nature or usual characteristics of, in spite of being: *It's very cool for August. She's strong for a girl. He's tall for his age.* **17.** becoming, permissible, or assigned to; up to: *It's for you to decide. It's not for me to say.* **18.** in spite or regardless of; notwithstanding; despite: *For all I know, he could have left. For all his fancy manners, he's still a boor.* **19.** in order to reach or go toward: *He set out for London. She just left for school.* **20.** with the aim, object, or purpose of; with a view to: *money set aside for his education. I read for pleasure. The house was insulated for warmth.* **21.** in order to be, become, or do: *to run for president, to volunteer for a task. He was hired for the job.* **22.** to serve as; as: *We had eggs for breakfast. I'll have salad for my first course.* **23.** in proportion to: *For every rainy day there were four sunny ones.* **24.** as being: *to know for a fact, to take for granted. Don't take me for a fool. The account was mistaken for history.* **25.** to take care of or accommodate: *There's enough meat left for three people. There's room for you in the back.* **26.** corresponding or equivalent to: *an English word for every French word in the translation.* **27.** necessary in order to gain admission to: *Did you get the tickets for the play?* **28.** at or during (a specified time or occasion): *She made an appointment for one o'clock. I met them for the first time last week.* —*conj.* seeing that; inasmuch as; because: *Let's go, for it is late.* [Old English *for* on account of, instead of, because of.]

for- *prefix* **1.** away; off: *forget.* **2.** extremely; completely: *forlorn.* [Old English *for-.*]

for., foreign.

for·age (fôr′ij, for′-) *n.* **1.** food for livestock, esp. when obtained by grazing, consisting of leaves and stalks, as of grasses and legumes. **2.** search for food or provisions. —*v.i.,* **-aged, -ag·ing. 1.** to hunt or search about for food or provisions: *The birds foraged in the snow. The troops foraged near the village.* **2.** to make a search; rummage: *The little girl foraged in the attic for old clothes to play with.* —*v.t.* **1.** to obtain by hunting or searching about: *to forage some vegetables for the meal.* **2.** to obtain food or provisions from: *to forage the countryside.* **3.** to supply, as horses, with food or provisions. **4.** *Archaic.* to plunder; loot. [Old French *fourage* pillage, from *forre* fodder; of Germanic origin.] —**for′ag·er,** *n.*

fo·ra·men (fə rā′mən) *pl.* **-ram·i·na** (-ram′ə nə). *n.* natural opening in a bone or membrane. [Latin *forāmen* opening.]

foramen mag·num (mag′nəm) large opening in the skull through which the spinal cord passes to become the medulla oblongata.

for·a·min·i·fer (fôr′ə min′ə fər, for′-) *n.* any of a large group of one-celled, chiefly saltwater invertebrates, order Foraminifera, having perforated calcium or silicate shells that, when accumulated, form chalk and limestone deposits. [Latin *forāmen* opening, hole + *ferre* to bear.]

for·as·much as (fôr′əz much′ az) in view of the fact that; because; since.

for·ay (fôr′ā, for′ā) *n.* attack or raid, as for plunder or spoils. —*v.t., v.i.* to raid; plunder. [Middle English *forraien* to raid, from *forrier* forager, from Old French *forrier,* from *forre* to forage, from *forre* fodder. See FORAGE.]

for·bear[1] (fôr bâr′) **-bore, -borne, -bear·ing.** *v.i.* **1.** to abstain or refrain: *to forbear from quarreling.* **2.** to control oneself, as when provoked; be patient. —*v.t.* to abstain or refrain from: *to forbear laughing.* [Old English *forberan.*]

for·bear[2] (fôr′bâr) forebear.

for·bear·ance (fôr bâr′əns) *n.* **1.** act of forbearing: *forbearance from sin.* **2.** self-control; restraint; patience: *She showed great forbearance during his long illness.*

for·bid (fər bid′, fôr-) **-bade** (-bad′, -bād′) or **-bad** (-bad′), **-bid·den** or *(archaic)* **-bid, -bid·ding.** *v.t.* **1.a.** to command (someone) not to do something; refuse to allow: *I forbid you to go out.* **b.** to prohibit (something); ban: *to forbid the wearing of make-up.* **2.** to command to keep away from; bar or exclude from: *I forbid you the car.* **3.** to stand in the way of or make impossible; hinder; prevent: *The snowstorm forbids air travel.* [Old English *forbēodan* to prohibit, restrain.] —**Syn. 1.** Forbid, prohibit mean to order that something not be done. **Forbid** suggests a direct command from an authority who expects to be obeyed: *The airline forbids smoking on take-off and landing.* **Prohibit** implies a legal order, as by statute, or a less arbitrary command: *The law prohibits smoking on the subways.*

for·bid·den (fər bid′ən, fôr-) *adj.* not permitted; prohibited: *Gambling is forbidden.*

Forbidden City, walled area in the center of Peking, China enclosing the palaces and grounds of the former Chinese emperors. It was closed to the public for many centuries.

forbidden fruit 1. in the Old Testament, the fruit of the tree of knowledge, forbidden to Adam and Eve. **2.** something desired but forbidden, as unlawful pleasure.

for·bid·ding (fər bid′ing, fôr-) *adj.* appearing to be threatening, hostile, or dangerous; grim; ominous: *a forbidding manner, forbidding cliffs.* —**for·bid′ding·ly,** *adv.*

for·bore (fôr bôr′) past tense of **forbear**[1].

for·borne (fôr bôrn′) past participle of **forbear**[1].

force (fôrs) *n.* **1.a.** power or energy; strength: *great force of character.* **b.** impetus or intensity of effect: *The leaves broke the force of his fall.* **2.a.** strength, constraint, or power exerted upon an object: *He used force to open the door.* **b.** use of such power; physical coercion: *They dragged him off by force.* **3.** power to convince, influence, or control; efficacious power: *the forces of his logic, the force of circumstances.* **4.** that which exerts such power; agency of movement or change: *the forces of nature. He explained the forces contributing to feudalism's decline.* **5.a.** fighting strength or military organization, esp. of a nation: *our naval forces. The country mobilized its forces for war.* **b.** individuals comprising or belonging to this; body of armed men: *Our forces suffered severe casualties.* **6.** group of people organized or available for some purpose or activity: *the police force. The party rallied its forces.* **7.** *Law.* binding effect; validity: *the force of a contract.* **8.** *Physics.* that which causes bodies to move or change their motion: *gravitational force.* **9. in force. a.** in effect; operative. **b.** in great numbers. —*v.t.,* **forced, forc·ing. 1.** to make (someone) do something, as by threats or physical violence; constrain: *She forced the child to take the pill. He was forced to resign.* **2.** to bring or cause to come into a particular state or condition; drive: *Various conditions forced prices down last summer.* **3.** to get or obtain by or as by force; extort; wrest: *They forced a confession out of him.* **4.** to bring forth or produce by or as by effort: *to force a smile.* **5.** to propel or cause to move, as against resistance: *to force enemy troops back. The nurse forced the food into his mouth.* **6.** to cause to open or give way by using force; break open: *to force a lock.* **7.** to press or impose on by or as by force: *He forced his attentions on her.* **8.** to make or effect by force: *to force a passage through a mountain, to force one's way through a crowd.* **9.** to overpower or capture by force: *They forced the enemy's stronghold.* **10.** to urge or exert to the utmost; strain, as the voice. **11.** to hasten the growth or development of (plants) by artificial means. **12.** *Card Games.* **a.** to compel (an opponent) to trump if he wishes to take a trick. **b.** to cause a player to play (a certain card). **c.** to compel (a player) to play so as to show the strength of his hand. **13.** *Baseball.* **a.** to cause (a base runner) to be put out by making a hit that compels him to move to the next base. **b.** to cause (a base runner on third base) to score a run by walking the batter when the bases are loaded (often with *in*). **c.** to allow (a run) to be scored in this way. [Old French *force* strength, might, going back to Latin *fortis* strong.] —**force′a·ble, -force′er,** *adv.* —**Syn. v.t. 1.** Force, compel, oblige, constrain mean to cause someone to submit or act in a certain way. **Force** implies coercion, as by the threat of bodily harm: *The floods forced them to turn back.* **Compel** suggests that no other course but the one required may be taken, with the threat of impending punishment otherwise: *The bandit compelled the rider to dismount.* **Oblige** implies that what is done is necessary because of some form of social authority or pressure: *Visitors are obliged to remove their hats.* **Constrain** suggests a narrowing of choices by the establishing of restrictions until only the required way is open: *The professor felt constrained to answer the attack on the university's policies.* —*n.* **2.a.** see **violence.**

at; āpe; cär; end; mē; it; īce; hot; ōld; fôrk; wood; fōol; oil; out; up; ūse; turn; sing; thin; this; zh in treasure; ə in ago, taken, pencil, lemon, circus.

401

forced (fôrst) adj. **1.** imposed or compelled by force; compulsory: *forced labor.* **2.** brought forth or produced by or as by effort; affected; strained: *forced gaiety.* **3.** done as the result of or in an emergency: *a forced landing.*

forced march, unusually long march undertaken and performed under pressure.

force field, field *(def. 10).*

force·ful (fôrs′fəl) adj. full of force; powerful; vigorous; effective: *a forceful argument.* —**force′ful·ly,** adv.

force·meat (fôrs′mēt′) n. finely chopped, seasoned meat that is served separately or used for stuffing. [Obsolete *force*, form of obsolete *farce* to stuff (from Old French *farsir*, from Latin *farcīre*) + MEAT.]

for·ceps (fôr′səps, -seps) *pl.,* **-ceps.** n. pincerlike instrument used for holding or manipulating objects, esp. in surgery. [Latin *forceps* pincers, from *formus* hot + *capere* to hold; because it was sometimes used to hold hot things.]

force pump, pump that delivers liquid under pressure by the action of a valveless piston that forces the liquid through a pipe.

for·ci·ble (fôr′sə bəl) adj. **1.** effected by or involving the use of force or violence: *a forcible entry.* **2.** characterized by or having force; powerful; effective. —**for′ci·bly,** adv.

ford (fôrd) n. shallow place where a river, stream, or other body of water may be crossed, as by wading. —v.t. to cross (a body of water) at a shallow place, as by wading. [Old English *ford* the shallow place.] —**ford′a·ble,** adj.

Ford (fôrd) **1. Gerald R.** 1913—, thirty-eighth president of the United States, from 1974 to 1976. **2. Henry.** 1863–1947, U.S. automobile manufacturer and industrialist.

fore[1] (fôr) adj. at or toward the front; forward: *the fore part of a ship.* —n. **1.** Nautical. foremast or bow of a boat or ship. **2. to the fore.** in or into a prominent position: *He came to the fore as their candidate.* —adv. Nautical. at or toward the bow of a boat or ship. [Old English *fore* for, before.]

fore[2] (fôr) interj. in golf, warning cry to persons ahead, made just before the ball is hit. [Probably short for BEFORE.]

fore- prefix **1.** situated at or near the front; in front: *foremast, forelock.* **2.** before in time or order; prior; beforehand: *forenamed, foretell.* [Old English *fore-* before.]

fore-and-aft (fôr′ən aft′) adj. leading or lying in the direction of a ship's length; from bow to stern: *a fore-and-aft sail.*

fore and aft 1. from the bow to the stern of a ship; lengthwise. **2.** in, at, or toward both the bow and the stern of a ship.

fore-and-aft-rigged (fôr′ən-aft′rigd′) adj. fitted with fore-and-aft sails.

fore·arm[1] (fôr′ärm′) n. part of the arm between the elbow and wrist.

fore·arm[2] (fôr ärm′) v.t. to prepare or arm beforehand.

fore·bear (fôr′bār) *also,* **forbear.** n. ancestor; forefather. [FORE- + -ER¹ (-ber¹).]

fore·bode (fôr bōd′) **-bod·ed,** **-bod·ing.** v.t. **1.** to be a warning or indication of; predict; portend: *omens that forebode disaster.* **2.** Archaic. to have a premonition of (an approaching misfortune or evil). —**fore·bod′er,** n.

fore·bod·ing (fôr bō′ding) n. feeling that something evil is going to happen; premonition, inner certainty, or dread of an approaching misfortune: *The news filled me with foreboding.*

fore·brain (fôr′brān′) n. part of the brain which includes the cerebrum, the thalamus, and the hypothalamus.

fore·cast (fôr′kast′) **-cast** or **-cast·ed, -cast·ing.** v.t. **1.** to predict, esp. on the basis of observation or analysis of information and data: *to forecast the weather, to forecast election results.* **2.** to be an advance indication of; foreshadow: *events that forecast an outbreak of war.* —n. prediction, esp. one made on the basis of observation or analysis of information and data. —**fore′cast′er,** n. —**Syn.** v.t. **1.** see **predict.**

fore·cas·tle (fōk′səl, fôr′kas′əl) *also,* **fo′c's'le.** n. **1.** part of a ship's upper deck forward of the foremast. **2.** forward section of a merchant ship, in which the sailor's quarters are located. [FORE- + CASTLE. A ship's forward section was formerly equipped for sea warfare with a battlement resembling that of a *castle.*]

fore·close (fôr klōz′) **-closed, -clos·ing.** v.t. **1.** to subject (a person, mortgage, or lien) to the process of foreclosure. **2.** to exclude; prevent: *to foreclose all discussion.* —v.i. to foreclose a mortgage or lien.

[Old French *forclos,* past participle of *forclore* to exclude, going back to Latin *forīs* outside + *claudere* to shut.]

fore·clo·sure (fôr klō′zhər) n. legal proceeding in which one who has subjected his property to a mortgage or lien is deprived of the right to redeem it for having failed to meet the conditions thereof.

fore·deck (fôr′dek′) n. forward part of a ship's main deck.

fore·doom (fôr dōōm′) v.t. to doom or condemn in advance.

fore·fa·ther (fôr′fä′thər) n. **1.** ancestor. **2.** predecessor from whom national or traditional descent is claimed: *our forefathers who framed the Constitution.*

fore·fend (fôr fend′) forfend.

fore·fin·ger (fôr′fing′gər) n. index finger.

fore·foot (fôr′foot′) *pl.,* **-feet.** n. **1.** one of the front feet of a four-legged animal. **2.** forward part of a ship's keel where it meets the stem.

fore·front (fôr′frunt′) n. place or part in front; most advanced position; vanguard.

fore·gath·er (fôr gath′ər) forgather.

fore·go[1] (fôr gō′) **-went, -gone, -go·ing.** v.t. to forgo.

fore·go[2] (fôr gō′) **-went, -gone, -go·ing.** v.t., v.i. Archaic. to go before; precede. [Old English *foregān.*]

fore·go·ing (fôr′gō′ing) adj. going before; preceding: *the foregoing example, in the foregoing quotation.*

fore·gone (fôr′gôn′) adj. that has gone before or gone by; previous; past: *in a foregone era.*

foregone conclusion, inevitable or forseen outcome or result.

fore·ground (fôr′ground′) n. **1.** part of a picture or scene perceived as nearest to the spectator's eye. Opposed to **background. 2.** most conspicuous or prominent position; forefront.

fore·hand (fôr′hand′) adj. performed or made with the arm extended outward from the body and the palm of the hand toward the front: *a forehand stroke.* Also, **fore·hand·ed.** —n. forehand stroke, as in tennis. Distinguished from **backhand.**

fore·head (fôr′id, -hed′, for′-) n. part of the face above the eyes. [Old English *forhēafod.*]

for·eign (fôr′ən, for′-) adj. **1.** belonging to, derived from, or characteristic of another country; not native: *a foreign accent, foreign currency, on foreign soil.* **2.** outside one's own country: *foreign lands.* **3.** related to, carried on, or dealing with other countries: *foreign trade, foreign policy.* **4.** not typical or characteristic (often with *to): Aggressiveness is foreign to his disposition.* **5.** strange; unfamiliar: *a concept foreign to my way of thinking.* **6.** having little or no relation; not pertinent; irrelevant: *foreign to our purpose.* **7.** not normally occurring in or belonging to the place where found: *a foreign body in the eye, foreign matter in the bloodstream.* [Old French *forain* alien, strange, going back to Latin *forās* outside.] —**for′eign·ness,** n.

foreign affairs, dealings or diplomatic relations of a country with other countries.

for·eign-born (fôr′ən bôrn′, for′-) adj. born in a foreign country.

for·eign·er (fôr′ə nər, for′-) n. one born in another country; citizen or native of another country.

foreign exchange 1. the transaction of financial affairs and settling of accounts or debts by persons, businesses, or governments of one country with those of another. **2.** bills of exchange drawn in one country and made payable in another.

for·eign·ism (fôr′i niz′əm, for′-) n. something peculiar to or characteristic of a foreign people or language, as a word, idiom, or custom.

foreign legion 1. military unit composed chiefly of foreign volunteers serving in a national army. **2.** also, **Foreign Legion.** such a unit in the French army, traditionally assigned to military operations and service outside of France.

foreign minister, in certain countries, the minister of a governmental cabinet who conducts and supervises foreign affairs.

foreign office, in certain countries, department of a government that handles foreign affairs.

fore·judge (fôr juj′) **-judged, -judg·ing.** v.t. to prejudge.

fore·know (fôr nō′) **-knew, -known, -know·ing.** v.t. to know beforehand.

fore·knowl·edge (fôr′nol′ij, fôr nol′ij) n. knowledge of something before it exists or occurs.

fore·la·dy (fôr′lā′dē) *pl.,* **-la·dies.** n. forewoman.

fore·land (fôr′land′) n. promontory or area of high land jutting into the sea.

fore·leg (fôr′leg′) n. **1.** one of the front legs of a four-legged animal. **2.** one of the front legs of any of various insects.

fore·limb (fôr′lim′) n. front limb, as a foreleg, wing, fin, or arm.

fore·lock (fôr′lok′) n. lock or tuft of hair growing just above the forehead.

fore·man (fôr′mən) *pl.,* **-men.** n. **1.** overseer of a body of workers or of a particular operation or section of a plant. **2.** chairman and spokesman of a jury.

fore·mast (fôr′mast′, -məst) n. mast nearest the bow of a ship.

Fore-and-aft-rigged schooner

Force pump

Outlet
Piston
Water
Valve
Valve

at; āpe; cär; end; mē; it; īce; hot; ōld; fôrk; wood; fōōl; oil; out; up; ūse; turn; sing; thin; this; zh in treasure; ə in ago, taken, pencil, lemon, circus.

fore·most (fôr′mōst′) *adj.* first in position, rank, or importance: *the foremost dramatist of his time.* —*adv.* before any other or anything else, as in position or rank; in the first place: *He was first and foremost a scholar.* [Old English *formest,* superlative of *forma* first, in turn a superlative of FORE¹; Modern English spelling influenced by FORE¹ and by association with MOST.]

fore·name (fôr′nām′) *n.* first or given name.

fore·named (fôr′nāmd′) *adj.* previously named or mentioned.

fore·noon (fôr′nōōn′) *n.* period between sunrise and noon; morning. —*adj.* of, relating to, or occurring in the forenoon.

fo·ren·sic (fə ren′sik) *adj.* **1.** relating to, appropriate for, or used in courts of law or public discussion and debate. **2.** relating to argumentation; argumentative; rhetorical. Also, **fo·ren′si·cal.** [Latin *forēnsis* relating to the forum (from *forum* public place, market place) + -IC.] —**fo·ren′si·cal·ly,** *adv.*

forensic medicine, science concerned with the application of the medical sciences to the purposes of the law, as the use of pathology to determine the cause of a death.

fore·or·dain (fôr′ôr dān′) *v.t.* to ordain or appoint beforehand; predestine; preordain. —**fore·or·dain′ment, fore′or·di·na′tion,** *n.*

fore·part (fôr′pärt′) *also,* **fore part.** *n.* first, front, or early part.

fore·paw (fôr′pô′) *n.* paw of a foreleg; front paw.

fore·quar·ter (fôr′kwôr′tər) *n.* **1.** front half of a side of beef or other meat, including the leg, shoulder, and adjacent parts. **2.** **forequarters,** forelegs, shoulders, and adjacent parts of an animal.

fore·reach (for rēch′) *v.i.* to catch up with or move ahead of a ship (with *on* or *upon*).

fore·run (fôr run′) **-ran, -run, -run·ning.** *v.t. Archaic.* **1.** to be a sign or prediction of; foreshadow. **2.** to go before; precede.

fore·run·ner (fôr′run′ər) *n.* **1.** one who or that which precedes another, as in a line of descent or development; predecessor; ancestor: *an essay in which the bicycle was viewed as the forerunner of the motorcycle.* **2.** sign of something to come; omen. **3.** one who or that which announces in advance the approach of something or someone; herald.

fore·said (fôr′sed′) *adj.* aforesaid.

fore·sail (fôr′sāl′, -səl) *n.* **1.** lowest sail, bent to the foreyard, on the foremast of a square-rigged ship. **2.** principal sail on the foremast of a schooner.

fore·see (fôr sē′) **-saw, -seen, -see·ing.** *v.t.* to know or see beforehand: *It was easy to foresee the consequences.* [Old English *forēsēon.*] —**fore·see′a·ble,** *adj.* —**fore·se′er,** *n.*

fore·shad·ow (fôr shad′ō) *v.t.* to show or indicate beforehand; presage: *The surrender of the city foreshadowed the fate of the country at large.*

fore·shank (fôr′shangk′) *n.* in cattle, upper foreleg.

fore·sheet (fôr′shēt′) *n.* **1.** rope attached to one of the clews of a foresail for the purpose of adjusting the angle of the sail. **2.** **foresheets,** forward spaces, not occupied by thwarts, in an open boat.

fore·shore (fôr′shôr′) *n.* that part of the shore between the high-water mark and low-water mark, uncovered at low tide.

fore·short·en (fôr shôrt′ən) *v.t.* in drawing, to shorten or reduce parts of (an object) in order to create an illusion of perspective, depth, and distance.

fore·sight (fôr′sīt′) *n.* **1.** care, provision, or thought for the future; prudence. **2.** act or ability of foreseeing what is likely to happen.

fore·sight·ed (fôr′sī′tid, fôr sī′tid) *adj.* having or marked by foresight. —**fore′sight′ed·ly,** *adv.* —**fore′sight′ed·ness,** *n.*

fore·skin (fôr′skin′) *n.* fold of skin that covers the end of the penis; prepuce. It is removed in circumcision.

for·est (fôr′ist, for′-) *n.* **1.** area of land, usually an extensive area, covered with a dense growth of trees and underbrush: *We were lost in the forest.* **2.** the trees themselves: *to cut down a forest.* —*v.t.* to plant or cover with trees; make into a forest. [Old French *forest* woodland, from Late Latin *forestis* open or unfenced wood, from Latin *forīs* outside.]

fore·stall (fôr stôl′) *v.t.* **1.** to hinder, prevent, or thwart by action taken in advance: *Tax reforms forestalled an economic crisis.* **2.** to buy up or divert, as goods not yet on the market, in order to sell at a higher price. [Middle English *forestallen* to obstruct, going back to Old English *foresteall* interception.] —**fore·stall′er,** *n.*

for·est·a·tion (fôr′is tā′shən, for′-) *n.* the planting or care of forests.

fore·stay (fôr′stā′) *n.* rope or cable that runs from the head of a ship's foremast to the stem and helps support the foremast.

for·est·er (fôr′is tər, for′-) *n.* one who practices or has been trained in forestry.

forest ranger, officer supervising the care of a forest, esp. a public forest.

for·est·ry (fôr′is trē, for′-) *n.* science that deals with the care and management of forests, including their protection, the harvesting and cultivation of trees, and the planting of new timber crops.

fore·taste (*n.,* fôr′tāst′; *v.,* fôr tāst′) *n.* brief experience, taste, or

sample of something to come. —*v.t.* **-tast·ed, -tast·ing.** to have a foretaste of.

fore·tell (fôr tel′) **-told, -tell·ing.** *v.t.* **1.** to tell of beforehand; give a prophecy of. **2.** to show or indicate beforehand; be an omen of; foreshadow.
Syn. 1. Foretell, prophesy mean to tell something of the future. **Foretell** suggests an announcement of coming events or the anticipation of eventualities through foreknowledge without indicating the nature or source of such foreknowledge: *The astrologer foretold the death of the king.* **Prophesy** implies the prediction made by a person possessing occult knowledge, divine guidance, or extraordinary foresight: *Isaiah prophesied the fall of the Assyrian empire.*

fore·thought (fôr′thôt′) *n.* advance planning; consideration for the future.

fore·to·ken (*v.,* fôr tō′kən; *n.,* fôr′tō′kən) *v.t.* to indicate or betoken beforehand; foreshadow. —*n.* sign or indication of something to come; omen. [Old English *foretācn* omen, sign.]

fore·top (fôr′top′, -təp) *n.* platform at the top of the foremast.

fore·top·gal·lant (fôr′top gal′ənt, fôr′tə-) *adj.* of, relating to, or designating the mast, sails, yards, and other parts immediately above the fore-topmast.

fore·top·mast (fôr′top′mast′, -məst) *n.* section of a mast next above the foremast.

fore·top·sail (fôr′top′sāl′, -səl) *n.* sail set on the fore-topmast.

for·ev·er (fô rev′ər, fə-) *adv.* **1.** to the end of time; without ever ending; eternally: *He promised to love her forever.* **2.** incessantly; constantly: *She was forever complaining about her job.*

for·ev·er·more (fô rev′ər môr′, fə-) *adv.* forever.

fore·warn (fôr wôrn′) *v.t.* to warn in advance.

fore·wom·an (fôr′woom′ən) *pl.,* **-wom·en.** *n.* **1.** woman who oversees a body of workers or a particular operation or section of a plant. **2.** woman chairman or spokesman of a jury.

fore·word (fôr′wurd′, -wərd) *n.* preface or introductory statement, as in a book. —**Syn.** see **introduction.**

fore·yard (fôr′yärd′) *n.* lowest yard on the foremast of a square-rigged ship.

for·feit (fôr′fit) *v.t.* to lose or lose the right to as a penalty for some offense, error, or omission: *to forfeit a claim. The team forfeited the game when they failed to show up.* —*n.* **1.** that which is lost as a penalty for some offense, error, or omission. **2.** act of forfeiting. —*adj. Archaic.* forfeited or liable to be forfeited. [Old French *forfait* crime, fine², from *forfaire* to transgress; literally, to act beyond (the law), going back to Latin *forīs* outside + *facere* to do.]

for·fei·ture (fôr′fi chər) *n.* **1.** act of forfeiting. **2.** that which is forfeited.

for·fend (fôr fend′) *also,* **fore·fend.** *v.t. Archaic.* to ward off; prevent; forbid.

for·gat (fər gat′) archaic past tense of **forget.**

for·gath·er (fər gath′ər) *also,* **fore·gath·er.** *v.i.* to meet or gather together; assemble.

for·gave (fər gāv′) past tense of **forgive.**

forge¹ (fôrj) *n.* **1.** furnace or hearth in which metal is heated and softened so that it can be worked into shape, as by hammering. **2.** workshop in which metals are heated in such an apparatus and then worked into shape; smithy. —*v.t.,* **forged, forg·ing. 1.** to heat (metal) in a forge and then work into shape. **2.** to make or work into shape; form; fashion: *to forge an agreement.* **3.** to copy, sign, or alter for purposes of deception or fraud; counterfeit; falsify: *to forge a signature, to forge a passport.* —*v.i.* **1.** to commit forgery. **2.** to work at a forge. [Old French *forge* works where one melts iron, going back to Latin *fabrica* workshop. Doublet of FABRIC.] —**forg′er,** *n.*

forge² (fôrj) **forged, forg·ing.** *v.i.* **1.** to advance or progress with increased speed or efficiency: *We forged ahead on the project.* **2.** to move forward slowly but steadily, as if with difficulty: *The ferry forged through the choppy bay.* [Of uncertain origin.]

for·ger·y (fôr′jər ē) *pl.,* **-ger·ies.** *n.* **1.** crime of copying, falsifying, or altering written or printed matter for the purpose of fraud. **2.** that which is forged; fraudulent imitation: *The Rembrandt he purchased was a forgery.*

for·get (fər get′) **-got** *or (archaic)* **-gat, -got·ten** *or* **-got, -get·ting.** *v.t.* **1.** to be unable to recall: *I have forgotten how to do it.* **2.** to omit or neglect unintentionally; overlook: *She forgot to pay the bill.* **3.** to fail to take through carelessness or thoughtlessness; leave behind inadvertently: *I forgot my keys.* **4.** to put out of mind deliberately; cease to think of: *Try to forget what happened.* **5.** to neglect willfully and intentionally; slight; disregard: *Once he became a success, he soon forgot his old friends.* **6. to forget oneself.** to act improperly or in an unbecoming manner; lose self-control. —*v.i.* to cease or neglect to think (often with *about*): *I forgot about the food cooking on the stove.* [Old English *forgitan* to lose memory of, neglect.] —**for·get′ta·ble,** *adj.* —**for·get′ter,** *n.*

for·get·ful (fər get′fəl) *adj.* **1.** likely to forget; having a poor memory.

at; āpe; cär; end; mē; it; īce; hot; ōld; fôrk; wood; fōōl; oil; out; up; ūse; turn; sing; thin; this; zh in treasure; ə in ago, taken, pencil, lemon, circus.

403

2. inattentive; neglectful; careless: *forgetful of his duty.* **3.** *Archaic.* that causes to forget; causing oblivion. —**for·get′ful·ly,** *adv.* —**for·get′-ful·ness,** *n.*

for·get-me-not (fər get′mē not′) *n.* **1.** trumpet-shaped blue or white flower of any of a group of plants, genus *Myosotis.* **2.** the small plant that bears these flowers, widely cultivated in gardens.

forg·ing (fôr′jing) *n.* **1.** act of one who or that which forges. **2.** forged piece of metal.

for·give (fər giv′) **-gave, -giv·en, -giv·ing.** *v.t.* **1.** to cease to blame or feel resentment against (someone): *I've already forgiven you.* **2.** to cease to feel resentment of or demand a penalty for (something); grant pardon for: *to forgive an insult, to forgive a sin.* **3.** to require no payment of (a debt); cancel; remit. —*v.i.* to grant pardon: *He forgives easily.* [Old English *forgifan* to give, remit.] —**for·giv′a·ble,** *adj.* —**for·giv′er,** *n.* —**Syn.** *v.t.* see **excuse.**

Forget-me-not

for·give·ness (fər giv′nis) *n.* **1.** act of forgiving; being forgiven. **2.** disposition or willingness to forgive.

for·giv·ing (fər giv′ing) *adj.* having or showing forgiveness: *a forgiving nature, a forgiving glance.* —**for·giv′ing·ly,** *adv.* —**for·giv′ing·ness,** *n.*

for·go (fôr gō′) **-went, -gone, -go·ing.** *also,* **fore·go.** *v.t.* to abstain or refrain from; give up; do without: *to forgo the usual formalities.* [Old English *forgān* to pass over, neglect.] —**for·go′er,** *n.*

for·got (fər got′) past tense and a past participle of **forget.**

for·got·ten (fər got′ən) a past participle of **forget.**

fo·rint (fôr′int) *n.* monetary unit of Hungary equal to one hundred fillérs. [Magyar *forint,* from Italian *fiorino* coin of Florence. See FLORIN.]

fork (fôrk) *n.* **1.** any of various-sized utensils having a handle at one end and two or more prongs at the other, used esp. for lifting or handling food. **2.** something resembling a fork in shape, as any of various agricultural tools used for such purposes as digging or lifting. **3.a.** a branching or dividing into branches, as of a road or river. **b.** point at which such a branching occurs. **c.** any one of these branches or divisions. —*v.t.* **1.** to lift, spear, or pitch with or as with a fork: *We forked the hay into the wagon.* **2.** to make or put into the shape of a fork. **3.** *Slang.* to hand over; give up; pay (with *over, out,* or *up*). —*v.i.* to divide into branches: *The road forks further ahead.* [Old English *forca* pronged instrument, from Latin *furca* two-pronged fork, fork-shaped stake.]

forked (fôrkt, fôr′kid) *adj.* shaped like a fork; divided into forks: *a forked road, a forked tongue, forked lightning.*

fork·ful (fôrk′fool′) *pl.,* **fork·fuls** or **forks·ful.** *n.* as much as a fork will hold.

for·lorn (fôr lôrn′) *adj.* **1.** dejected; hopeless; wretched. **2.** abandoned; forsaken; deserted. **3.** *Archaic.* deprived or bereft *of.* [Old English *forloren,* past participle of *forlēosan* to lose.] —**for·lorn′ly,** *adv.* —**for·lorn′ness,** *n.*

forlorn hope 1. undertaking that is almost certain to fail; vain hope. **2.** group of men chosen to perform some perilous or desperate undertaking. [Modification of Dutch *verloren hoop* literally, lost company or troop.]

form (fôrm) *n.* **1.** outline or external contour of something, not including its substance or color; shape. **2.** body or figure: *A large form loomed ahead of us in the darkness.* **3.** external appearance: *the many myths in which Zeus assumed the form of an animal.* **4.** particular state, structure, or character in which something appears or exists: *water in the form of ice. Her resentment took the form of forgetting his name.* **5.** kind; variety: *Democracy is a form of government. A rose is a form of plant life.* **6.** manner or style of arranging and organizing parts, esp. in an orderly or effective way, as in a literary or musical composition: *These papers will be graded on form as well as content. His work introduced a new form into the writing of novels.* **7.** orderly or systematic arrangement or progression; organization: *Your ideas are fuzzy and lack form.* **8.** way of doing something, esp. with regard to established standards of technique: *Dick worked to improve his form in diving.* **9.** fitness of mind or body, as for performance; condition: *He is in top form.* **10.** document having blank spaces for insertion of required information: *an order form. The applicant filled out a form.* **11.** prescribed or set order of words or wording; formula. **12.** something, as a frame or mold, that holds, supports, or gives or determines shape: *a dressmaker's form, to pour concrete into a form.* **13.** behavior or conduct with regard to decorum or the usages of society: *It was bad form to act that rudely.* **14.** customary or established practice or ritual; ceremony; formality: *There are certain forms that must be followed in diplomatic circles. We shook hands as a matter of form.* **15.** grade or class in a secondary school. **16.** *British.* long, backless seat or bench. **17.** *Grammar.* any of

the ways in which a word may appear as a result of inflection or modification in spelling or pronunciation. *Men* is the plural form of *man; was* is a form of the verb *to be; disc* and *disk* are variant forms. **18.** linguistic form. **19.** *Printing.* body of type or other material properly arranged and locked in a frame for printing or electrotyping. —*v.t.* **1.** to give shape or form to; fashion: *to form patties out of meat.* **2.** to make or produce: *He tried to form a sentence without a verb.* **3.** to serve to make up or constitute; be an element of: *Students formed the bulk of the crowd.* **4.** to construct in the mind; conceive; devise: *to form a plan, to form an opinion.* **5.** to combine into; organize; establish: *The workers formed a union. Some of the factions formed a coalition.* **6.** to develop; acquire: *to form a habit.* **7.** to shape or mold, as by discipline or instruction: *His mind was formed by study of the classics.* **8.** to place or arrange in order. **9.** *Grammar.* to construct or produce (a word) by adding, subtracting, or changing elements. —*v.i.* **1.** to take shape: *The water formed into icicles on the window.* **2.** to come into existence; be produced: *Mold formed on the stale bread. Ice won't form on the lake until the temperature is lower.* [Old French *forme* shape, figure, from Latin *forma.*] —**Syn.** *n.* **1.** see **shape.**

-form *suffix* (used to form adjectives). **1.** having the form of: *cruciform.* **2.** having (a specified number of) forms: *multiform, uniform.* [Latin *-formis,* from Latin *forma* shape, figure, pattern.]

for·mal (fôr′məl) *adj.* **1.** characterized by or given to observance, esp. strict observance, of the requirements of form, convention, or etiquette: *You needn't be so formal with me.* **2.** marked by or requiring ceremony or elaborate detail or dress: *a formal wedding, a formal banquet.* **3.** appropriate for or worn at elaborate or state occasions: *formal dress.* **4.** that is a matter of form only; perfunctory; nominal: *The king is the formal head of state.* **5.** of or relating to form or structure, as distinguished from content: *the formal elements of the poem.* **6.** done or made so as to be binding and valid: *a formal contract, a formal agreement.* **7.** received in school; academic: *formal education.* **8.** (of language) relating to or characterized by grammar, syntax, and pronunciation that conforms to traditional standards of correctness and avoids the use of colloquial, informal, or contracted forms. **9.** having a regular, symmetrical, or orderly pattern or arrangement: *formal gardens.* **n.** something formal, as a dance or evening gown. [Latin *formālis* relating to a form, having a set form, from *forma* shape, figure, pattern.] —**for′-mal·ly,** *adv.*

form·al·de·hyde (fôr mal′də hīd′) *n.* colorless, poisonous gas with a sharp, suffocating odor, used esp. in solution as a disinfectant and preservative, and in the manufacture of synthetic resins. Formula: HCHO [FORM(IC ACID) + ALDEHYDE.]

For·ma·lin (fôr′mə lin) *n.* *Trademark.* solution of approximately 37 percent formaldehyde in water.

form·al·ism (fôr′mə liz′əm) *n.* strict observance of or adherence to prescribed or traditional forms, as in art or religion. —**for′mal·ist,** *n.* —**for′mal·is′tic,** *adj.*

for·mal·i·ty (fôr mal′ə tē) *pl.,* **-ties.** *n.* **1.** state or quality of being formal: *the formality of the occasion.* **2.** observance of or attention to the requirements of form, convention, or etiquette: *She treated all of us with great formality.* **3.** established, proper, or customary act, practice, or procedure: *His will was executed with all the due legal formalities.* **4.** something that is a matter of form only; requirement or outward observance of convention or etiquette: *He was already assured of the job and his interview was a mere formality.*

for·mal·ize (fôr′mə līz′) **-ized, -iz·ing.** *v.t.* **1.** to make formal. **2.** to give a definite or official form to: *to formalize an agreement.* —**for′mal·i·za′tion, for′mal·iz′er,** *n.*

for·mat (fôr′mat) *n.* **1.** arrangement or general make-up of a book, magazine, or other publication, including size, shape, and type size. **2.** general organization or style, as of a television program: *the format of a quiz show.* [French *format* format (of a book), from German *Format* size (of a book), form, shape, from Latin *formātus* formed, past participle of *formāre* to form, shape.]

for·ma·tion (fôr mā′shən) *n.* **1.** act or process of forming; being formed: *the formation of good habits.* **2.** that which is formed: *The cloud formation covered the sun.* **3.** manner in which something is formed or arranged; disposition of parts; arrangement: *The troops lined up in parade formation.* **4.** *Geology.* masses of rock or deposits of minerals that have the same characteristics or origin.

form·a·tive (fôr′mə tiv) *adj.* **1.** giving or capable of giving form; helping to develop, shape, or mold: *a formative influence.* **2.** of or relating to growth, formation, or development: *the formative years of childhood.* **3.** *Grammar.* of, relating to, or characteristic of a grammatical element, as an affix, that, when added to words, changes their meanings or functions, or acts as a means of word formation —*n.* formative element, as an affix.

for·mer¹ (fôr′mər) *adj.* **1.** being first (of two) mentioned or understood. Distinguished from **latter.** ▲ often preceded by *the* and used absolutely: *Sally and Helen are the same age, but the former is shorter*

at; āpe; cär; end; mē; it; īce; hot; ōld; fôrk; wood; fōōl; oil; out; up; ūse; turn; sing; thin; this; zh in treasure; ə in ago, taken, pencil, lemon, circus.

than the latter. **2.** belonging to, being of, or occurring in the past; previous; earlier: *our former governor, in former times.* [Middle English *formere,* from *forme* first, from Old English *forma.* See FOREMOST.]

form·er² (fôr′mər) *n.* one who or that which forms. [FORM + -ER¹.]

for·mer·ly (fôr′mər lē) *adv.* in time past; once; previously.

form·fit·ting (fôrm′fit′ing) *adj.* (of clothing) conforming closely to the shape of the body: *a formfitting sweater, formfitting ski pants.*

for·mic (fôr′mik) *adj.* **1.** of or relating to ants. **2.** relating to or derived from formic acid.

For·mi·ca (fôr mī′kə) *n. Trademark.* laminated plastic covering resistant to water, heat, and most chemicals, used esp. for kitchen and bathroom surfaces. [FOR + MICA; because when first introduced, it was used in place of the mineral *mica.*]

formic acid, colorless, pungent liquid that is irritating to the skin, found esp. in ants and spiders and in some plants, and also produced synthetically, used in dyeing. Formula: HCOOH [Latin *formīca* ant + ACID; because it was originally obtained from the fluid that the red ant secretes when it bites, which causes pain.]

for·mi·da·ble (fôr′mi də bəl) *adj.* **1.** exciting fear, dread, or awe, as by reason of strength, size, or power: *a formidable enemy.* **2.** difficult to deal with, perform, or overcome: *a formidable task.* **3.** arousing admiration or wonder; strikingly impressive: *a formidable accomplishment.* [Latin *formīdābilis* terrible, from *formīdāre* to dread.] —for′·mi·da·bil′i·ty, *n.* —for′mi·da·bly, *adv.*

form·less (fôrm′lis) *adj.* lacking a definite or regular shape; shapeless. —**form′less·ly,** *adv.* —**form′less·ness,** *n.*

form letter, one of a number of duplicate copies of a letter written in such a way that it may be sent to various individuals or groups.

For·mo·sa (fô mō′sə) *n.* Taiwan.

for·mu·la (fôr′myə lə) *pl.,* **-las** or **-lae.** *n.* **1.** prescribed or conventional form or method for doing something; fixed rule: *There is no formula for achieving international peace.* **2.** set order or form of words, as used in conventional expressions or ceremonial, legal, or similar proceedings. **3.** representation, using symbols and numbers, of the composition of a chemical compound. An **empirical formula** gives the proportion of the constituents, as in H_2O; a **structural formula** gives, in addition, the approximate arrangement of the atoms in a molecule, as H-O-H. **4.** conventionally used rule or principle stated as an equation in algebraic form. The formula $A = \pi r^2$ states that the area equals the product of pi and the radius squared. **5.** recipe or prescription: *a formula for mixing paints.* **6.** mixture of milk or a milk substitute, water, and a sugar, used to feed infants. **7.** formal statement of religious faith or doctrine. [Latin *formula* small pattern, method, diminutive of *forma* shape, plan, pattern.]

for·mu·lar·y (fôr′myə ler′ē) *pl.,* **-lar·ies.** *n.* **1.** collection or system of formulas. **2.** formula. **3.** book containing a list of pharmaceutical substances and formulas for medicinal preparations. —*adj.* relating to or resembling a formula.

for·mu·late (fôr′myə lāt′) **-lat·ed, -lat·ing.** *v.t.* **1.** to put or state in precise and systematic form: *to formulate one's ideas.* **2.** to devise or develop: *He formulated a plan of attack.* **3.** to reduce to or express in a formula. —**for′mu·la′tion, for′mu·la′tor,** *n.*

for·ni·cate (fôr′nə kāt′) **-cat·ed, -cat·ing.** *v.i.* to commit fornication. [Late Latin *fornicātus,* past participle of *fornicārī* to commit fornication, from Latin *fornix* arch, brothel; with reference to the location of ancient Roman brothels under an arch or in a cave.] —**for′ni·ca·tor,** *n.*

for·ni·ca·tion (fôr′nə kā′shən) *n.* sexual intercourse between two persons of the opposite sex who are unmarried or who are not married to each other.

for·sake (fôr sāk′) **-sook** (-sook′), **-sak·en, -sak·ing.** *v.t.* **1.** to give up or renounce completely, as an idea or belief. **2.** to leave or desert completely: *to forsake one's friends.* [Old English *forsacan* to give up.] —**for·sak′er,** *n.* —**Syn. 2.** see DESERT².

for·sooth (fôr sooth′) *adv. Archaic.* in truth; indeed. [Old English *forsōth.*]

For·ster, E(dward) M(organ) (fôr′stər) 1879-1970, English novelist.

for·swear (fôr swâr′) **-swore, -sworn, -swear·ing.** *v.t.* **1.** to give up or renounce completely or on oath; abjure. **2.** to deny emphatically or on oath: *to forswear smoking.* **3.** to forswear oneself, to perjure oneself. —*v.i.* to swear falsely. [Old English *forswerian* to swear falsely.]

for·sworn (fôr swôrn′) *adj.* perjured.

for·syth·i·a (fôr sith′ē ə) *n.* any of a group of shrubs, genus *Forsythia,* widely cultivated as ornamentals, bearing bell-shaped, yellow flowers that grow in clusters along the stems and usually

Forsythia

appear before the leaves do. [From William *Forsyth,* 1737-1804, an English botanist who introduced it from China.]

fort (fôrt) *n.* **1.** fortified structure or enclosure that can be defended against an enemy; fortification. **2.** permanent military post. **3. to hold the fort.** *Informal.* to keep things in operation; carry on. [Old French *fort* stronghold, from *fort* strong, from Latin *fortis.*]

For·ta·le·za (fôr′tə lā′zə) *n.* city on the northeastern coast of Brazil. Pop. (1968 est.), 846,069.

Fort-de-France (fôr də fräns′) *n.* capital and largest city of Martinique. Pop. (1961), 84,811.

forte¹ (fôrt) *n.* that in which one excels; strong point: *Mathematics is his forte.* [French *fort* strength, from *fort* strong, from Latin *fortis.*]

for·te² (fôr′tā) *Music. adj.* loud and forceful. —*adv.* loudly and forcefully. —*n.* forte note, chord, or passage. [Italian *forte* strong, loud, from Latin *fortis* strong.]

forth (fôrth) *adv.* **1.** forward in time, place, or order; onward: *from this day forth.* He came forth to receive his degree. **2.** out into view or consideration, as from concealment, obscurity, or latency: *The tree put forth leaves. New arguments were brought forth.* **3. and so forth,** and so on; et cetera. [Old English *forth* forward, onward.] —**Syn. 1.** see forward.

Forth, Firth of (fôrth) inlet of the North Sea, in southeastern Scotland.

forth·com·ing (fôrth′kum′ing) *adj.* **1.** about to appear or occur; approaching in time: *the forthcoming election.* **2.** available or ready when required or expected: *Relief will be forthcoming for those left homeless by the flood.*

forth·right (fôrth′rīt′) *adj.* **1.** going straight to the point; straightforward; frank: *forthright criticism.* **2.** proceeding in a straight line or course; direct: *a forthright line of attack.* —*adv.* in a direct or straightforward course or manner. —**forth′right′ly,** *adv.* —**forth′right′ness,** *n.*

forth·with (fôrth′with′, -with′) *adv.* without delay; at once; immediately: *The doctor came forthwith.*

for·ti·eth (fôr′tē ith) *adj.* **1.** (the ordinal of forty) next after the thirty-ninth. **2.** being one of forty equal parts. —*n.* **1.** that which is next after the thirty-ninth. **2.** one of forty equal parts; $\frac{1}{40}$.

for·ti·fi·ca·tion (fôr′tə fi kā′shən) *n.* **1.** act, art, or science of fortifying. **2.** that which fortifies, as a wall or ditch. **3.** fortified military work or place of defense.

for·ti·fy (fôr′tə fī′) **-fied, -fy·ing.** *v.t.* **1.** to provide or protect with defensive works; strengthen against attack: *The Great Wall fortified China against barbarian invasions.* **2.** to strengthen structurally: *They fortified the dam against the flood.* **3.** to give physical strength or endurance to: *Good eating habits help to fortify the body against disease.* **4.** to give support by confirming; corroborate: *Each of the lawyer's arguments was fortified by facts.* **5.** to give mental or moral strength to: *The men's spirits were fortified by their captain's fearlessness.* **6.** to strengthen with alcohol: *to fortify wine.* **7.** to enrich (food), as with vitamins and minerals: *to fortify bread.* —*v.i.* to erect defensive works. [Old French *fortifier* to strengthen, going back to Latin *fortis* strong + *facere* to make.]

for·tis·si·mo (fôr tis′i mō′) *Music. adj.* very loud. —*adv.* very loudly. —*n. pl.,* **-mos** or **-mi** (-mē′). fortissimo note, chord, or passage. [Italian *fortissimo,* superlative of *forte* loud, strong. See FORTE².]

for·ti·tude (fôr′tə tood′, -tūd′) *n.* courage or strength of mind in the face of pain, danger, or adversity. [Latin *fortitūdō.*]

Fort Knox, military reservation in northern Kentucky, site of the U.S. gold bullion depository.

Fort-La·my (fôr lä mē′) *n.* capital of Chad, in the southwestern part of the country. Pop. (1964 est.), 99,000.

Fort Lau·der·dale (lô′dər dāl′) city in southeastern Florida. Pop. (1970), 139,590.

fort·night (fôrt′nīt′) *n.* two weeks. [Old English *fēowertīene niht* fourteen nights.]

fort·night·ly (fôrt′nīt′lē) *adv.* once every two weeks. —*adj.* occurring, issued, or appearing every two weeks. —*n. pl.,* **-lies.** something published every two weeks, as a magazine.

Fortran (fôr′tran′) *n.* computer coding system using modified mathematical notation for solving scientific problems. [Short for *for(mula) tran(slation).*]

for·tress (fôr′tris) *n.* **1.** fortified place; stronghold; fort. **2.** any place or thing providing security: *God is our fortress* (Shakespeare, *Henry VI,* Part I). —*v.t.* to furnish or protect with or as with a fortress. [Old French *forteresse* strong place, going back to Latin *fortis* strong.] —**Syn. 1.** see stronghold.

Fort Smith, city in western Arkansas. Pop. (1970), 62,802.

for·tu·i·tous (fôr too′ə təs, fôr tū′-) *adj.* **1.** happening by chance; accidental; casual: *a fortuitous encounter.* **2.** fortunate; lucky: *fortuitous circumstances.* [Latin *fortuītus* casual, accidental, going back to *fors* chance.] —**for·tu′i·tous·ly,** *adv.* —**for·tu′i·tous·ness,** *n.*

at; āpe; cär; end; mē; it; īce; hot; ōld; fôrk; wood; fōōl; oil; out; up; ūse; turn; sing; thin; this; zh in treasure; ə in ago, taken, pencil, lemon, circus.

405

for·tu·i·ty (fôr tōō′ə tē, fôr tū′-) *pl.*, **-ties.** *n.* **1.** quality of being fortuitous. **2.** accidental occurrence; chance.

for·tu·nate (fôr′chə nit) *adj.* **1.** having good fortune; lucky. **2.** bringing good fortune; favorable: *fortunate circumstances.* [Latin *fortūnātus*, past participle of *fortūnāre* to make prosperous, to prosper, from *fortūna* chance, luck.] —**for′tu·nate·ly,** *adv.*

for·tune (fôr′chən) *n.* **1.** that which happens or is going to happen to a person, whether good or bad: *She told our fortune by looking into a crystal ball.* **2.** luck, esp. when good: *He has fortune on his side. It was his good fortune to meet her where he did.* **3.** *also,* **Fortune,** force, often personified, that controls the future; destiny; fate. **4.** great wealth; riches: *He has accumulated a fortune in diamonds and pearls. She inherited a fortune from her grandmother.* **5.** amount of wealth: *He made a small fortune in mining.* **6.** conditions of prosperity or success. [Old French *fortune* chance, from Latin *fortūna* fate, chance, luck.] —**Syn. 1.** see **chance.**

fortune cookie, thin, folded cookie containing a piece of paper with a prediction or other message.

fortune hunter, one who seeks to gain wealth, esp. through marriage.

for·tune·tell·er (fôr′chən tel′ər) *n.* one who professes to foretell future events in a person's life. —**for′tune·tell′ing,** *n., adj.*

Fort Wayne (wān) city in northeastern Indiana. Pop. (1970), 177,-671.

Fort Worth (wurth) city in northeastern Texas. Pop. (1970), 393,-476.

for·ty (fôr′tē) *pl.*, **-ties.** *n.* **1.** the cardinal number that is four times ten. **2.** symbol representing this number, as 40 or XL. **3.** something having this many units or members. **4. the forties.** number series from forty through forty-nine. ▲ used esp. in reference to the fourth decade of a century or of a person's life. —*adj.* numbering four times ten. [Old English *fēowertig*.]

for·ty-nin·er (fôr′tē nī′nər) *n.* one who went to California seeking gold in the gold rush of 1849.

forty winks *Informal.* short nap.

fo·rum (fôr′əm) *n.* **1.** public square or marketplace of an ancient Roman city, where public assemblies met, and where most legal and political activities took place. **2. the Forum,** the political, commercial, social, and religious center of ancient Rome. **3.** assembly, meeting, or other medium for discussion of issues or questions of public interest. **4.** court; tribunal. [Latin *forum* marketplace, public place.]

for·ward (fôr′wərd) *adv.* **1.** *also,* **forwards.** toward what is ahead or in front; onward: *He took three steps forward and two back. He stepped forward to accept the trophy.* **2.** toward the future: *from this day forward.* **3.** into view or consideration; forth: *to bring forward an opinion.* **4.** at the front; in front: *The ship's boiler room was forward of the steward's cabin.* —*adj.* **1.** situated in, at, near, or toward the front: *the forward column of an army, the forward cabins of a ship.* **2.** moving or directed toward a point in front: *a forward movement.* **3.** toward the future: *a forward look.* **4.** well-advanced or progressive, as in thinking. **5.** impertinent; presumptuous; bold: *She was a very forward young lady.* —*v.t.* **1.** to send onward or ahead, esp. to a new address: *They forwarded his mail to his new address.* **2.** to help along; promote; advance: *to forward one's interests, to forward a cause.* —*n.* player whose position is at or near the front line in certain games, as basketball or hockey. [Old English *foreweard* onward.]

Syn. *adv.* **1. Forward, onward, forth** indicate movement ahead. **Forward** suggests movement past things which then lie behind, as in place, time, or sequence: *In case they walk straight forward, in half an hour they shall meet men* (Berkeley, 1732). **Onward** implies a goal toward which movement is taking place: *Onward to the fortress rode the three* (Tennyson, 1859). **Forth** suggests movement toward the foreground, as from obscurity into full view: *Forth comes the pocket mirror* (Cowper, 1785).

for·ward·er (fôr′wər dər) *n.* one who or that which forwards, esp. a person or company acting as an agent in receiving or delivering goods for reshipment to the proper destination.

for·ward·ly (fôr′wərd lē) *adv.* impertinently; presumptuously; boldly.

for·ward·ness (fôr′wərd nis) *n.* **1.** impertinence; presumptuousness; boldness. **2.** condition of being well-advanced or progressive: *The forwardness of his policies are in keeping with the times.*

forward pass, passing of a football from behind the line of scrimmage toward the opponent's goal.

fos·sa (fos′ə) *pl.*, **fos·sae** (fos′ē). *n.* shallow depression, pit, or cavity, as in a bone. [Latin *fossa* ditch.]

fosse (fos) *also,* **foss.** *n.* ditch or moat, esp. one in a fortification. [Old French *fosse* pit, from Latin *fossa* ditch.]

fos·sil (fos′əl) *n.* **1.** remains or traces of an animal or plant of ancient geological times, preserved in rock in the earth's crust. **2.** *Informal.* one who or that which is outmoded or antiquated. —*adj.* **1.** relating to,

of the nature of, or forming a fossil. **2.** dug from the earth: *Oil is a fossil fuel.* **3.** belonging to the past; outmoded; antiquated. [Latin *fossilis* dug up, from *fossus,* past participle of *fodere* to dig.]

fos·sil·if·er·ous (fos′ə lif′ər əs) *adj.* containing fossils.

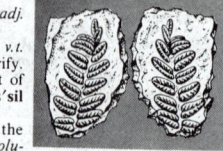
Fossil

fos·sil·ize (fos′ə līz′) -ized, -iz·ing. *v.t.* **1.** to change into a fossil; petrify. **2.** to make antiquated, rigid, or out of date. —*v.i.* **1.** to become a fossil. —**fos′sil·i·za′tion,** *n.*

fos·ter (fôs′tər) *v.t.* **1.** to promote the growth or development of: *The revolution was fostered by sympathetic foreigners.* **2.** to bring up (a child); rear. **3.** to cling to, as a feeling; cherish: *He fostered a feeling of pride over his recent success.* [Old English *fōstrian* to nourish, feed.]

Fos·ter, Stephen Col·lins (fôs′tər; kol′inz) 1826–84, U.S. composer of popular songs.

fos·ter·age (fôs′tər ij) *n.* **1.** rearing of a foster child. **2.** condition of being a foster child. **3.** act of promoting the growth or development of something.

foster brother, boy in relation to the child or children of his foster parents.

foster child, child reared by a foster parent or parents.

foster father, man who rears a child not his own.

foster home, home in which a foster child is reared.

fos·ter·ling (fôs′tər ling) *n.* foster child.

foster mother, woman who rears a child not her own.

foster parent, man or woman who rears a child not his or her own.

foster sister, girl in relation to the child or children of her foster parents.

Fou·cault, Jean (fōō kō′; zhän) 1819–68, French physicist.

foul (foul) *adj.* **1.** extremely offensive to the senses, esp. to the sense of smell: *a foul odor.* **2.** containing dirt or other offensive matter: *foul air, foul water.* **3.** extremely filthy or soiled: *foul clothing.* **4.** obscene, abusive, or profane: *foul language.* **5.** stormy; inclement: *foul weather.* **6.** (of food) rotten or spoiled. **7.** morally offensive; vile; abominable: *a foul deed.* **8.** treacherous; dishonest. **9.** entangled or obstructed; jammed: *a foul anchor.* **10.** (of a ship) having the bottom covered or encumbered with foreign matter, as seaweed or barnacles. **11.** *Sports.* contrary to or violating the rules; unfair. **12.** *Baseball.* outside the foul line: *The ball was foul.* **13.** *Printing.* having many corrections or changes indicated on it: *foul copy.* —*n.* **1.** *Sports.* an infraction of the rules. **2.** foul ball. —*v.t.* **1.** to make dirty; soil or pollute: *They fouled the water by throwing in garbage.* **2.** to entangle or obstruct (something); jam: *The ship fouled the underwater cable.* **3.** to clog or choke (something) with foreign matter: *Dirt fouled the carburetor.* **4.** to dishonor; disgrace: *The scandal fouled her reputation.* **5.** to cover or encumber (a ship's bottom) with foreign matter, as seaweed or barnacles. **6.** *Sports.* to commit a foul against: *The boxer fouled his opponent by hitting him below the belt.* **7.** *Baseball.* to hit (a ball) into foul territory. **8. to foul up.** *Informal.* to mix or mess up completely; throw into disorder or confusion: *He fouled up the project.* —*v.i.* **1.** to be or become dirty. **2.** to become entangled or obstructed; jam: *The rope fouled on the anchor.* **3.** to be or become clogged or choked. **4.** *Sports.* to commit a violation of the rules. **5.** *Baseball.* to hit a foul ball. **6. to foul out. a.** *Baseball.* to be retired by hitting a foul ball that is caught before it touches the ground. **b.** *Basketball.* to be put out of the game for having committed a particular number of fouls. **7. to foul up.** *Informal.* to make a mistake. —*adv.* afoul: *to run foul of the law.* [Old English *fūl* dirty, rotten, stinking, abominable, abusive.] —**foul′ly,** *adv.*

fou·lard (fōō lärd′) *n.* **1.** soft, lightweight fabric made of silk, rayon, cotton, or similar fibers, usually having a small printed motif, esp. for neckties, scarves, and dresses. **2.** scarf or necktie made of this fabric. [French *foulard;* of uncertain origin.]

foul ball *Baseball.* a batted ball that goes outside the foul lines.

foul line 1. *Baseball.* either of the lines that extends from home plate through first or third base to the limits of the playing field. **2.** *Basketball.* free throw line. **3.** *Bowling.* line across the alley that the bowler may not touch or cross when bowling the ball.

foul-mouthed (foul′mouthd′, -mouth′) *adj.* using obscene, abusive, or profane language.

foul·ness (foul′nis) *n.* **1.** state or quality of being foul. **2.** foul matter; filth. **3.** moral impurity; sinfulness.

foul play, unfair or treacherous action, esp. when violent.

foul shot, free throw.

foul tip, pitched baseball that the batter barely deflects off his bat into foul territory.

foul-up (foul′up′) *n.* *Informal.* complete mix-up or mess.

found¹ (found) *v.* past tense and past participle of **find.**

found² (found) *v.t.* **1.** to bring into being; set up or establish: *to found a college, to found a political party.* **2.** to rest for support; base; ground: *a house founded on rock. My argument is founded on fact.* [Old French *fonder* to establish, from Latin *fundāre* to lay the bottom of, establish, from *fundus* bottom, base.]

found³ (found) *v.t.* **1.** to melt and pour (metal) into a mold. **2.** to form or make by pouring molten metal into a mold; cast. [Old French *fondre* to melt, cast (metal), from Latin *fundere* to pour, melt, cast (metal).]

foun·da·tion (foun dā'shən) *n.* **1.** act of founding; being founded; establishment. **2.** that on which anything is based or supported; basis: *the foundations of society.* **3.** supporting portion or base of a wall or building, usually of masonary, constructed partly or wholly below the surface of the ground. **4.** endowed institution or organization, esp. one that grants money for scientific research or scholarly work. **5.** fund for the maintenance of an institution or organization; endowment. **6.** foundation garment. —**Syn. 2.** see **base¹**.

foundation garment, any of various undergarments, as a girdle, corset, or brassiere, designed to give shape and support to the body.

foun·der¹ (foun'dər) *v.i.* **1.** to fill with water and sink, as a boat. **2.** to fall down or give way: *Several buildings foundered in the earthquake.* **3.** to fail completely: *The business foundered because of quarreling among the partners.* **4.** to stumble and become lame or otherwise disabled: *The horse foundered on the rocky path.* —*v.t.* to cause to founder. [Old French *fondrer* to sink, from *fond* bottom, from Latin *fundus.*]

found·er² (foun'dər) *n.* one who founds or establishes: *the founders of a colony.* [FOUND² + -ER¹.]

found·er³ (foun'dər) *n.* one who founds or casts metal. [FOUND³ + -ER¹.]

found·ling (found'ling) *n.* deserted infant of unknown parents. [Middle English *fundling,* from *funden,* past participle of *finden* to find + -LING¹. See FIND.]

found·ry (foun'drē) *pl.,* **-ries.** *n.* **1.** place where metal is melted and cast. **2.** act or process of founding metal. [French *fonderie,* from *fondre* to melt, cast (metal). See FOUND³.]

fount (fount) *n.* **1.** source. **2.** fountain; spring. [From FOUNTAIN.]

foun·tain (foun'tən) *n.* **1.** stream of water made to rise or spout upward artificially, as to provide water for drinking or to serve as an ornament. **2.** structure designed for such a stream to rise and fall into. **3.** spring of water issuing from the earth. **4.** source or origin of anything: *a heart, the fountain of sweet tears* (Wordsworth, 1802). **5.** soda fountain. **6.** reservoir or compartment for holding a supply of ink, oil, or other liquid. [Old French *fontaine* spring, from Late Latin *fontāna,* from Latin *fōns.*]

foun·tain·head (fount'ən hed') *n.* **1.** spring from which a stream flows; source of a stream. **2.** primary source or origin of anything.

Fountain of Youth, legendary spring whose waters were said to have the power to restore youth and health.

fountain pen, pen having a reservoir or replaceable cartridge that automatically feeds a steady supply of ink to the writing point.

four (fôr) *n.* **1.** the cardinal number that is one more than three. **2.** symbol representing this number, as 4 or IV. **3.** something having this many units or members, as a playing card. **4. on all fours. a.** on all four feet: *The cat landed on all fours.* **b.** on hands and knees: *We were on all fours looking for the lost contact lens.* —*adj.* numbering one more than three. [Old English *fēower.*]

four·di·men·sion·al (fôr'di men'shən əl) *adj.* relating to or having four dimensions.

four-eyed fish, any of a group of fish, genus *Anableps,* of tropical America, having horizontally divided eyes able to see above and below the water's surface simultaneously.

four-flush·er (fôr'flush'ər) *n. Slang.* one who bluffs or fakes. [From an expression used in poker, meaning a player who pretends to have a five-card flush when he has only four cards of a suit.]

four·fold (fôr'fōld') *adj.* **1.** four times as great or as numerous. **2.** having or consisting of four parts. —*adv.* so as to be four times greater or more numerous.

four-foot·ed (fôr'foot'id) *adj.* having four feet.

Four Freedoms, human rights set forth as essential to a free society by President Franklin D. Roosevelt in a message to Congress on January 6, 1941. They are freedom of speech, freedom of worship, freedom from want, and freedom from fear.

four-hand·ed (fôr'han'did) *adj.* **1.** for or played by four players: *a four-handed card game.* **2.** intended for two performers, as a piano duet. **3.** having four feet resembling hands in shape or function.

Four-H clubs *also,* **4-H clubs.** educational and recreational organization for youth, sponsored by the U.S. Department of Agriculture, designed to provide training in the fields of agriculture and home economics. [Because it is the purpose of these clubs to improve their members' Heads, Hearts, Hands, and Health.]

four hundred, most exclusive social set: *a banker whose family belongs to the four hundred.* [Probably from the claim in 1889 by society leader Ward McAllister that only four hundred people were accepted in the best social circles of New York City.]

Fou·rier (foor'ē ā', foor yā') **1. Fran·cois** (frän swä'). 1772–1837, French socialist. **2. Jean** (zhäN). 1768–1830, French mathematician and physicist.

four-in-hand (fôr'in hand') *n.* **1.** necktie tied in a slip knot with the ends hanging down vertically. **2.** team of four horses driven by one person. **3.** vehicle drawn by such a team.

four-let·ter word (fôr'let'ər) any of several short words regarded as obscene or objectionable.

four-o'clock (fôr'ə klok') *n.* any of a large group of plants, genus *Mirabilis,* found chiefly in tropical America, having red, white, yellow, or striped trumpet-shaped flowers that open in the late afternoon and close in the morning.

four-post·er (fôr'pōs'tər) *n.* bedstead with four tall corner posts designed to support a canopy or curtains.

four·score (fôr'skôr') *adj., n.* four times twenty; eighty.

four·some (fôr'səm) *n.* group of four persons or things, as four people playing golf together. —*adj.* relating to, consisting of, or designed for a group of four.

four·square (fôr'skwâr') *adj.* **1.** square. **2.** frank; forthright. **3.** unyielding; firm. —*adv.* squarely; firmly: *He stands foursquare for religious freedom.*

four·teen (fôr'tēn') *n.* **1.** the cardinal number that is four more than ten. **2.** symbol representing this number, as 14 or XIV. **3.** something having this many units or members. —*adj.* numbering four more than ten. [Old English *fēowertēne.*]

Fourteen Points, statement of the peace aims of the United States and its allies made by President Woodrow Wilson on January 8, 1918.

four·teenth (fôr'tēnth') *adj.* **1.** (the ordinal of fourteen) next after the thirteenth. **2.** being one of fourteen equal parts. —*n.* **1.** that which is next after the thirteenth. **2.** one of fourteen equal parts; ¹/₁₄.

fourth (fôrth) *adj.* **1.** (the ordinal of four) next after the third. **2.** being one of four equal parts. —*n.* **1.** that which is next after the third. **2.** one of four equal parts; ¼. **3.** *Music.* **a.** tone, esp. the subdominant, four diatonic degrees from a given tone. **b.** interval of four degrees between two tones of the diatonic scale. **c.** harmonic combination of two tones separated by this interval. **4.** fourth forward gear, as of an automobile. **5. the Fourth.** Independence Day. —*adv.* in the fourth place.

fourth-class (fôrth'klas') *adj.* designating mail matter consisting of merchandise and sent for the lowest rate. Also, **parcel post.** —*adv.* by fourth-class mail.

fourth dimension, dimension in addition to the three spatial dimensions of length, width, and depth. In the theory of relativity, time is regarded as the fourth dimension.

fourth estate see **estate.**

fourth·ly (fôrth'lē) *adv.* in the fourth place.

Fourth of July, Independence Day.

four-wheel (fôr'hwēl', -wēl') *adj.* **1.** *also,* **four'-wheeled'.** having four wheels. **2.** acting on or controlled by four wheels: *four-wheel drive.* —**four'-wheel'er,** *n.*

fo·ve·a (fō'vē ə) *pl.,* **-ve·ae** (-vē ē'). *n.* small pit or depression in the surface of a structure or organ, esp. the eye. [Latin *fovea* small pit.] —**fo've·al,** *adj.*

fovea cen·tra·lis (sen trā'lis) small pit in the retina of the eye, where the vision is most acute.

fowl (foul) *pl.,* **fowl** or **fowls.** *n.* **1.** domestic hen or rooster; chicken. **2.** any of various related domestic or wild birds, as the turkey, duck, pheasant, or grouse. **3.** flesh of such a bird used as food. **4.** any bird; birds collectively. —*v.i.* to hunt or catch wild birds. [Old English *fugol* bird.] —**fowl'er,** *n.*

fowl·ing (fou'ling) *n.* hunting of wild birds for sport.

fowling piece, light gun for shooting wild birds.

fox (foks) *n.* **1.** any of various wild, carnivorous mammals of the genus *Vulpes* and related genera, belonging to the dog family, but smaller than a wolf, and having a pointed muzzle, large erect ears, a bushy tail, and a thick coat. Height: 12–16 inches at the shoulder. **2.** fur of a fox. **3.** sly, crafty person. —*v.t. Informal.* to trick or deceive; outwit: *He foxed his pursuers by taking another route.* [Old English *fox* this animal, crafty person.]

Fox

Fox (foks) *n.* **1. Charles James.** 1749–1806, English statesman. **2. George.** 1624–91, English religious leader, founder of the Society of Friends.

fox·glove (foks'gluv') *n.* any plant, genus *Digitalis*, of the figwort family, widely cultivated and bearing white, yellow, or purple thimble-shaped flowers on long spikes. The **common**, or **purple, foxglove**, *D. purpurea*, is grown as a garden flower and for its leaves which yield the drug digitalis. [Old English *foxes glōfa* literally, fox's glove.]

fox·hole (foks'hōl') *n.* hole dug in the ground by soldiers as shelter from enemy fire.

fox·hound (foks'hound') *n.* large, swift hound, usually having a tan, black, and white coat, raised esp. to hunt foxes. Height: to 25 inches at the shoulder.

fox hunting, sport in which the participants, on horseback, follow hounds that trail a fox.

fox·tail (foks'tāl') *n.* **1.** tail of a fox. **2.** any of various weedy grasses bearing soft, brushlike flower spikes that resemble the tails of foxes.

fox terrier, dog of a breed originally used to drive foxes from their burrows, having a long head, short tail, and a smooth- or wire-haired white coat with tan or black and tan markings. Height: 15 inches at the shoulder.

fox-trot (foks'trot') -trot·ted, -trot·ting. *v.i.* to dance the fox trot.

fox trot 1. dance performed in 2/4 or 4/4 time, combining slow steps and short, quick ones. **2.** music for this dance.

fox·y (fok'sē) fox·i·er, fox·i·est *adj.* **1.** foxlike; sly; crafty. **2.** discolored or stained. —**fox'i·ly,** *adv.* —**fox'i·ness,** *n.*

foy·er (foi'ər, foi'ā) *n.* **1.** lobby of a theater, hotel, or other public building. **2.** entrance hall in a house or apartment. [French *foyer* hearth, home, lobby of a theater, going back to Latin *focus* hearth. Formerly, theaters often had hearths in their lobbies.]

Fr, francium.

fr. 1. fragment. **2.** franc. **3.** from.

Fr. 1. Father. **2.** France. **3.** French. **4.** Friar. **5.** Friday.

Fra (frä) *n.* Brother. ▲ used as the title of a monk or friar. [Italian *fra,* short for *frate,* from Latin *frāter.*]

fra·cas (frā'kəs) *n.* noisy disturbance, quarrel, or fight; brawl. [French *fracas,* from *fracasser* to shatter, from Italian *fracassare,* possibly going back to a blend of Latin *frangere* to break and *quassāre* to shake.]

frac·tion (frak'shən) *n.* **1.a.** one or more of the equal portions of a whole quantity. **b.** mathematical expression representing part of some whole quantity or the ratio of two quantities, shown in the form of a numerator over a denominator. —$^0/_b$, $^2/_3$, $1/\sqrt{2}$, and $(x^2 - 2y)/(x^2 - y^2)$ are fractions. **2.** small portion or disconnected part; fragment. **3.** component of a liquid mixture separated by crystallization or distillation. Gasoline and kerosene are fractions of crude oil. **4.** act of breaking the bread in the Eucharist. [Church Latin *frāctiō* a breaking, from Latin *frāctus,* past participle of *frangere* to break.]

frac·tion·al (frak'shən əl) *adj.* **1.** of, relating to, or constituting a fraction or fractions. **2.** small or unimportant; insignificant. **3.** *Chemistry.* separating into fractions: *fractional distillation.*

frac·tious (frak'shəs) *adj.* **1.** unruly; rebellious: *a fractious youth.* **2.** quarrelsome; irritable; cranky: *a fractious temperament.* —**frac'tious·ly,** *adv.* —**frac'tious·ness,** *n.*

frac·ture (frak'chər) -tured, -tur·ing. *v.t., v.i.* to break; split; crack. —*n.* **1.** act of breaking; broken. **2.** break; split; crack. **3.** break or split in a bone. **4.** characteristic appearance or texture of the freshly broken surface of a mineral. [Latin *frāctūra* a breach, cleft.] —**Syn.** *v.t.* see **crack.**

frae (frā) *prep. Scottish.* from.

frag·ile (fraj'əl, -īl) *adj.* easily broken, damaged, or destroyed; delicate. [Latin *fragilis.* Doublet of **FRAIL.**] —**frag'ile·ly,** *adv.* —**fra·gil·i·ty** (frə jil'ə tē), *n.*

Syn. Fragile, frail, brittle mean tending to break easily. **Fragile** suggests that the substance of which a thing is made may result in its breaking if it is not handled with care: *The movers carefully packed the fragile china into cartons.* **Frail** implies that a thing is of weak construction and that it will tend to collapse under strain: *The frail wooden bridge cracked and swayed in the heavy winds.* **Brittle** suggests hardness of such rigidity that the thing may easily break if pressure is applied unwisely: *The bones of an aged person are often quite brittle.*

frag·ment (*n.,* frag'mənt; *v.,* frag'ment) *n.* **1.** part broken off; small detached portion: *fragments of broken pottery.* **2.** incomplete or isolated bit: *fragments of news.* **3.** part of something left incomplete or

unfinished: *Schubert's Unfinished Symphony is a fragment.* —*v.t., v.i.* to break into fragments. [Latin *fragmentum* a piece.]

frag·men·tal (frag men'təl) *adj.* **1.** fragmentary. **2.** *Geology.* composed or consisting of broken pieces of rock or other previously existing solid material: *fragmental rock.*

frag·men·tar·y (frag'mən ter'ē) *adj.* composed of fragments; broken; incomplete: *fragmentary remains, fragmentary knowledge. The dazed victim was able to give only a fragmentary description.* Also, **frag·men·tal** (frag men'təl).

frag·men·ta·tion (frag'mən tā'shən) *n.* **1.** act or process of breaking into fragments. **2.** the scattering of the fragments of a bomb, shell, or grenade. —*adj.* that scatters fragments upon explosion: *a fragmentation grenade.*

fragmentation bomb, aerial bomb that scatters the fragments of its casing over a wide area when it explodes.

Fra·go·nard, Jean Ho·no·ré (frä gō när'; zhän ō nō rä') 1732–1806, French painter.

fra·grance (frā'grəns) *n.* **1.** sweet or pleasing smell. **2.** state or quality of being fragrant.

fra·grant (frā'grənt) *adj.* having a sweet or pleasing smell. [Latin *fragrāns,* present participle of *fragrāre* to smell sweet.] —**fra'grant·ly,** *adv.*

frail (frāl) *adj.* **1.** lacking in strength; weak: *The child was too frail to take part in active sports.* **2.** easily broken, damaged, or destroyed; delicate; fragile. **3.** morally weak; easily tempted. [Old French *fraile* weak, brittle, from Latin *fragilis* easily broken. Doublet of **FRAGILE.**] —**frail'ness,** *n.* —**Syn.** *2.* see **fragile.**

frail·ty (frāl'tē) *pl.* -ties. *n.* **1.** state or quality of being frail; weakness: *the frailty of human trust.* **2.** fault or failing arising from moral weakness: *mankind's frailties.*

frame (frām) *n.* **1.** structure into which something is set, used for support or protection: *a window frame, a picture frame. I broke the frames of my eyeglasses.* **2.** structure composed or constructed of parts fitted and joined together, serving as an underlying support; skeleton; framework. **3.** body, esp. the human body, with reference to its physical structure; build: *She has a thin frame.* **4.** general or established form, arrangement, or system: *the frame of the Constitution.* **5.** one of the individual pictures on a length of motion-picture film. **6.** the total television picture transmitted by one scan of the electronic beam. **7.** figure, such as a box, in which numbers are put to solve equations. In the equation $3 + \square = 5$, if the number 2 is put in the frame, the equation is true. **8.** machine built on, within, or in the shape of a frame: *a spinning frame.* **9.** one of the ten divisions of a game of bowling; one turn at bowling. **10.** *Informal.* an inning in a baseball game. **11.** *Slang.* frame-up. —*v.t.,* **framed, fram·ing. 1.** to enclose or set in or as in a frame: *to frame a painting. He framed his college diploma. The house was framed by a background of trees.* **2.** to form or construct mentally; conceive: *to frame an idea.* **3.** to give expression to or utter: *to frame a reply.* **4.** to shape or adapt, as to a purpose: *That law was framed to protect freedom of speech.* **5.** to draw up; devise: *to frame a plan of action.* **6.** *Slang.* to cause (an innocent person) to appear guilty by using false evidence. [Old English *framian* to be profitable, avail.] —**fram'er,** *n.*

frame house, house constructed on a wooden framework, usually covered with boards or shingles.

frame of mind, mental or emotional state; mood.

frame of reference, set or system, as of facts or ideas, that serves to define or direct one's thinking.

frame-up (frām'up') *n. Slang.* conspiracy or scheme to make an innocent person appear guilty through the use of false evidence.

frame·work (frām'wurk') *n.* **1.** structure usually rigid, serving to support, enclose, or give shape to something: *the framework of a building.* **2.** basic structure or arrangement of the parts of something: *the framework of a novel, the framework of society.*

franc (frangk) *n.* monetary unit and coin of France, Belgium, Switzerland, Luxembourg, and several African countries. [Old French *franc,* short for Medieval Latin *Francorum rex* king of the Franks, inscribed on some fourteenth-century French gold coins. See **FRANK.**]

France (frans; *French* fräns) *n.* **1.** country in western Europe. Capital, Paris. Area, 210,039 sq. mi. Pop. (1970 est.), 50,620,000. **2. A·na·tole** (ä nä tôl') 1844–1924, French author, born Jacques Anatole Thibault.

fran·chise (fran'chīz) *n.* **1.** right to vote; suffrage. **2.** privilege or authorization granted to an individual or group, esp. by a government or corporation: *The store was granted a franchise to sell that brand of cosmetics.* **3.** geographical area for which such a privilege is granted. [Old French *franchise* freedom, from *franc* free. See **FRANK.**]

Fran·cis I (fran'sis) **1.** 1494–1547, king of France from 1515 to 1547. **2.** title of Francis II as emperor of Austria.

Francis II, 1768–1835, last emperor of the Holy Roman Empire, from 1792 to 1806, and as Francis I, first emperor of Austria, from 1804 to 1835.

Foxglove

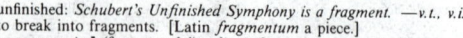
Smooth-haired fox terrier

Fran·cis·can (fran sis′kən) *adj.* **1.** of or relating to St. Francis of Assisi. **2.** belonging to a religious order of the Roman Catholic Church founded by St. Francis in the thirteenth century, now divided into three independent branches. —*n.* member of this order.

Francis Ferdinand, 1863–1914, archduke of Austria whose assassination led to the outbreak of World War I.

Francis Joseph I, 1830–1916, emperor of Austria from 1848 to 1916 and king of Hungary and Bohemia.

Francis of As·si·si, Saint (ə sē′zē) c.1181–1226, Italian friar, founder of the Franciscan order.

fran·ci·um (fran′sē əm) *n.* rare, radioactive, metallic element. Symbol: Fr See element for table. [Modern Latin *francium,* from *France;* named by the French chemist Marguerite Perey.]

Franck, Cé·sar (frangk; sä zär′) 1822–90, French composer, born in Belgium.

Fran·co, Fran·cis·co (frang′kō; fran sis′kō) 1892–1975, Spanish political and military leader.

Franco- combining form French: *Franco-American.*

fran·gi·ble (fran′jə bəl) *adj.* easily broken; fragile. [Old French *frangible,* going back to Latin *frangere* to break.] —**fran′gi·bil′i·ty,** *n.*

frank[1] (frangk) *adj.* **1.** open or unreserved in speech; outspoken; candid: *Frank criticism of the article enabled the author to improve his writing.* **2.** clearly manifest; undisguised; open: *There was frank enmity between the two men.* —*v.t.* **1.** to mark (a letter, package, or other mail), as with a signature, for delivery without charge. **2.** to send (mail) without charge by marking in this way. —*n.* **1.a.** right or privilege to send mail without charge. **b.** mark indicating this right or privilege. **2.** letter, package, or other mail sent without charge. [Old French *franc* free, pure, from Medieval Latin *francus* a Frank, free; of Germanic origin. The Franks were associated with freedom because, as rulers of Gaul, they alone had freedom there.] —**frank′ly,** *adv.* —**frank′-ness,** *n.*

Syn. *adj.* **1.** Frank, candid, blunt, outspoken mean openly truthful. Frank suggests freedom and openness: *They sat down to have a frank discussion about his future.* Candid implies absence of any dissimulation, an honesty that hides nothing pertinent: *It was his candid opinion that a policy change would have to occur.* Blunt suggests a straightforward approach that makes no effort to moderate what is said so as to avoid hurting feelings: *He was blunt with her about her illness.* Outspoken implies saying what comes to mind, with nothing held back: *That senator is the most outspoken critic of our foreign policy.*

frank[2] (frangk) *n. Informal.* frankfurter.

Frank (frangk) *n.* member of a Germanic people living along the Rhine River in the third century A.D. In the late fifth and early sixth centuries, the Franks expanded into Gaul, giving their name to present-day France. [Old English *Franca;* of Germanic origin; said to be from the Franks' national weapon, in Old English *franca* javelin.]

Frank·en·stein (frang′kən stīn′) *n.* **1.** medical student in Mary Wollstonecraft Shelley's novel *Frankenstein,* who creates a monster that eventually destroys him. **2.** monster created by him. **3.** anything that threatens or destroys its creator.

Frank·fort (frangk′fərt) *n.* **1.** capital of Kentucky, in the north-central part of the state. Pop. (1970), 21,356. **2.** Frankfurt.

frank·furt (frangk′fərt) *n.* frankfurter.

Frank·furt (frangk′fərt) *n.* city in central West Germany. Pop. (1968 est.), 660,575. Also, **Frank′fort.**

frank·furt·er (frangk′fər tər) *n.* **1.** reddish variety of smoked and seasoned sausage made of beef or beef and pork and shaped in cylindrical pieces. **2.** such a sausage served hot in a long, soft roll, often with mustard, relish, or sauerkraut. Also, **hot dog.** [German *Frankfurter* of Frankfurt.]

Frank·furt·er, Fe·lix (frangk′fər tər) 1882–1965, U.S. jurist, born in Austria.

frank·in·cense (frang′kin sens′) *n.* fragrant resin obtained from various Asian and African trees, genus *Boswellia,* esp. *B. carteri.* It is used for embalming, as an incense, and in the manufacture of perfumes and face powders. [Old French *franc encens* pure incense, from Medieval Latin *francus* free + Late Latin *incēnsum* incense. See FRANK, INCENSE[1].]

Frank·ish (frang′kish) *adj.* of or relating to the Franks. —*n.* extinct language of the Franks, belonging to the western branch of the Germanic languages.

frank·lin (frangk′lin) *n.* in England in the fourteenth and fifteenth centuries, a landowner of free, but not noble birth, ranking next below the gentry. [Medieval Latin *franccolanus,* going back to *francus* free. See FRANK.]

Frank·lin (frangk′lin) **1.** Benjamin. 1706–90, U.S. scientist, author, statesman, and inventor. **2.** Sir John. 1786–1847, English explorer.

fran·tic (fran′tik) *adj.* marked by extreme or uncontrollable emotion, as of grief, pain, or rage; wildly excited; frenzied. [Old French *frenetique* seized with frenzy, from Latin *phrenēticus* mad, from Greek

phrenētikos, from *phrenītis* delirium, from *phrēn* mind.] —**fran′ti·cal·ly;** also, **fran′tic·ly,** *adv.* —**fran′tic·ness,** *n.*

Franz Jo·sef Land (franz jō′səf, fränts yō′zef) group of islands in the Arctic Ocean belonging to the Soviet Union. Land area, approx. 7000 sq. mi.

frap·pé (*adj.,* *defs. 1, 2* fra pā′; *n., def. 3* frap) *adj.* iced; chilled. —*n.* **1.** sweetened fruit juice mixture partially frozen to a mushy consistency. **2.** liqueur or other beverage poured over shaved ice. **3.** frappe, sweet dish or beverage made with ice cream, as a milkshake. [French *frappé* struck, iced, past participle of *frapper* to strike, ice; probably imitative.]

fra·ter·nal (frə turn′əl) *adj.* **1.** relating to or befitting a brother; brotherly. **2.** of or relating to a fraternal order. **3.** (of twins) developed from two separate fertilized egg cells, and thus having different hereditary characteristics. Distinguished from **identical.** [Medieval Latin *fraternalis* brotherly, from Latin *frāternus,* from *frāter* brother.] —**fra·ter′nal·ly,** *adv.*

fraternal order, association of men organized for their mutual benefit or attainment of a common goal. Also, **fraternal association, fraternal society.**

fra·ter·ni·ty (frə tur′nə tē) *pl.,* **-ties.** *n.* **1.** society of male students, often having chapters in various institutions, organized esp. for social purposes and usually designated by a Greek letter name. **2.** state or quality of being brotherly; brotherhood. **3.** group of people sharing the same interests or profession, or having other common ties: *the medical fraternity.* **4.** fraternal order. [Old French *fraternite* brotherhood, from Latin *frāternitās,* going back to *frāter* brother.]

frat·er·nize (frat′ər nīz′) -nized, -niz·ing. *v.i.* **1.** to associate closely with someone in a friendly or brotherly way. **2.** to associate in a friendly or intimate way with the citizens of an enemy or conquered country. —**frat′er·ni·za′tion,** *n.*

frat·ri·cide[1] (frat′rə sīd′) *n.* act of killing one's brother or sister. [Latin *frātricidium,* from *frāter* brother + *-cīdium.* See -CIDE[1].] —**frat′ri·cid′al,** *adj.*

frat·ri·cide[2] (frat′rə sīd′) *n.* one who kills his brother or sister. [Latin *frātricīda,* from *frāter* brother + *-cīda.* See -CIDE[2].]

Frau (frou) *pl.,* **Fraus** or *(German)* **Frau·en** (frou′ən). *n.* married woman; wife. ▲ German form of polite address for a married woman, equivalent to *Mrs.* [German *Frau.*]

fraud (frôd) *n.* **1.** deceit or trickery, esp. deliberate deception practiced to cheat another of rights or property: *He was found guilty of fraud.* **2.** act or instance of such deceit or trickery. **3.** one who deceives; phony; imposter. **4.** that which is intended to deceive; sham. [Old French *fraude* guile, from Latin *fraus* guile, deceit.]

fraud·u·lent (frô′jə lənt) *adj.* **1.** given to or using fraud; deceitful; dishonest: *a fraudulent businessman.* **2.** proceeding from, achieved by, or characterized by fraud: *a fraudulent deal.* [Latin *fraudulentus* deceitful, from *fraus* deceit.] —**fraud′u·lence, fraud′u·len·cy,** *n.* —**fraud′u·lent·ly,** *adv.*

fraught (frôt) *adj.* filled or accompanied (with *with*): *fraught with grief, a mission fraught with danger.* [Past participle of obsolete *fraught* to load (a ship), from *fraught* cargo, load, from Middle Dutch *vracht.*]

Fräu·lein (froi′līn) *pl.,* **-leins** or *(German)* **-lein.** *n.* unmarried woman; young lady. ▲ German form of polite address for an unmarried woman, equivalent to *Miss.* [German *Fräulein.*]

fray[1] (frā) *n.* **1.** noisy quarrel, fight, or disturbance; brawl. **2.** heated dispute or contest. [Form of AFFRAY.]

fray[2] (frā) *v.t.* **1.** to cause (something, as cloth or rope) to separate into loose threads, esp. along the edges; ravel. **2.** to wear the surface of, as by rubbing. **3.** to strain or irritate, as the nerves. —*v.i.* to become frayed; ravel. [French *frayer* to rub against, from Old French *freier* to rub, from Latin *fricāre.*]

fraz·zle (fraz′əl) -zled, -zling. *v.t., v.i.* **1.** to wear to shreds; fray. **2.** to tire out; exhaust. —*n. Informal.* state of being frazzled. [Possibly blend of FRAY[2] and obsolete *fasel* to ravel.]

freak (frēk) *n.* **1.** abnormally developed person, animal, or plant; monstrosity. **2.** anything odd, unusual, or unexplainable. **3.** sudden whim; caprice. —*adj.* abnormal, odd, unusual, or bizarre: *a freak accident.* [Of uncertain origin.]

freak·ish (frē′kish) *adj.* **1.** relating to or characteristic of a freak; abnormal. **2.** odd, unusual, or unexplainable: *a freakish turn of events.* **3.** whimsical; capricious. —**freak′ish·ly,** *adv.* —**freak′ish·ness,** *n.*

freck·le (frek′əl) *n.* small yellowish or brownish spot on the skin due to accumulation of pigment, often caused by exposure to the sun. —*v.t., v.i.,* **-led, -ling.** to mark or become marked with freckles. [Old Norse *freknur* the small spots on the skin.]

freck·led (frek′əld) *adj.* marked with or full of freckles. Also, **freck′ly.**

Fred·er·ick I (fred′rik, -ər ik) **1.** Frederick Barbarossa. **2.** 1657–1713, king of Prussia from 1701 to 1713.

---

at; āpe; cär; end; mē; it; īce; hot; ōld; fôrk; wood; fōōl; oil; out; up; ūse; turn; sing; thin; this; zh in treasure; ə in ago, taken, pencil, lemon, circus.　　**409**

Frederick II 1. 1194–1250, German king who was emperor of the Holy Roman Empire from 1220 to 1250. 2. Frederick the Great.

Frederick III, 1463–1525, elector of Saxony from 1486 to 1525 and protector of Martin Luther.

Frederick IX, 1899—, king of Denmark since 1947.

Frederick Bar·ba·ros·sa (bar′bə ros′ə) c.1123–90, emperor of the Holy Roman Empire from 1152 to 1190.

Fred·er·icks·burg (fred′riks burg′) *n.* city in northeastern Virginia, site of a Confederate victory in the Civil War in 1862. Pop. (1970), 14,450.

Frederick the Great, 1712–86, king of Prussia from 1740 to 1786.

Frederick William, 1620–88, elector of Brandenburg from 1640 to 1688.

Frederick William I, 1688–1740, king of Prussia from 1713 to 1740.

Frederick William II, 1744–97, king of Prussia from 1786 to 1797.

Frederick William III, 1770–1840, king of Prussia from 1797 to 1840.

free (frē) **fre·er, fre·est.** *adj.* 1. having personal liberty or rights; independent in thought or action; not under another's control. 2.a. having or existing under a government that allows civil, political, or religious liberty: *a free country, a free society.* b. not subject to foreign domination or control; autonomous. 3. not held, imprisoned, or confined, as by a court or legal charges; acquitted: *The prisoner was now free.* 4. released from or unhindered by a specified thing or condition, as obligation, pain, or discomfort (with *from* or *of*): *free from care, free of family ties.* 5. devoid of or without something (with *from* or *of*): *The administration was free from corruption.* 6. allowed or permitted (to do something): *He is free to come and go as he chooses.* 7. given or provided without cost or payment; gratis: *We received a free ticket to the show.* 8. not busy; available: *I'll be free at two o'clock for the conference.* 9. not motivated, controlled, or determined by anything other than one's own limitations or nature: *a free choice.* 10. open and unreserved in expressing one's thoughts, feelings, or opinions; frank; outspoken: *She was very free in discussing her personal problems.* 11. generous; liberal: *a free spender. She is quite free with her money.* 12. unimpeded or unrestrained, as in motion or movement; unhampered: *free access to a place.* 13. not adhering strictly to the original; not literal: *a free translation.* 14. not attached, bound, or fastened; loose: *the free end of a rope.* 15. coming or appearing in profusion; heavy: *a free flow of blood.* 16. easy and graceful; smooth: *a bold, free stroke.* 17. unrestrained by decency or propriety: *She was too free in her behavior.* 18. made, done, or given willingly or voluntarily. 19. clear of obstruction or impediment; open. 20. exempt from or not subject to, as regulations or taxes. 21. *Chemistry.* not part of a compound; uncombined: *free oxygen, free copper.* —*adv.* 1. without cost or payment: *He was admitted free.* 2. in a free manner; easily: *The children ran free across the meadow.* 3. into an unconfined or unrestrained condition; loose: *The horse broke free.* 4. **to set free.** to liberate, as from confinement, restraint, or obligation; release: *The prisoner was set free. He was set free from his debts.* 5. **to make free with.** to use, treat, or act toward (a person or thing) with an undue amount of liberty or familiarity: *He made free with his father's money.* —*v.t.,* **freed, free·ing.** 1. to release, as from burden, constraint, or obligation: *They freed the prisoners. He was freed of his financial obligations. She freed herself of worry.* 2. to clear or disentangle (a person or thing) from some obstruction or hindrance: *They freed the traffic lane by removing the stalled car.* [Old English frēo, frī having liberty.] —**free′ly,** *adv.* —**free′ness,** *n.*

free and easy, unrestrained by formality or conventionality; unceremonious; natural: *a free and easy manner.*

free association, psychiatric procedure in which a patient says whatever comes to mind without restriction or embarrassment. The thoughts and feelings he expresses disclose the content of his unconscious mind.

free·board (frē′bôrd′) *n.* that part of the side of a ship that is out of the water.

free·boot·er (frē′bōō′tər) *n.* one who plunders; pirate. [Dutch *vrijbuiter* robber, going back to *vrij* free + *buit* booty. Doublet of FILIBUSTER.] —**free′boot′ing,** *n.*

free·born (frē′bôrn′) *adj.* 1. not in slavery or servitude; born free. 2. of or relating to those born free.

free city, city having an autonomous government and constituting an independent state, as certain medieval cities.

free coinage, system under which a government is legally required to mint coins for private persons from specified bullion, as gold or silver, with or without a fixed charge.

freed·man (frēd′mən) *pl.,* **-men.** *n.* one legally freed from slavery. —**freed′wom′an,** *n.*

free·dom (frē′dəm) *n.* 1. political independence, as of a people or nation. 2. liberation, as from slavery, confinement, or imprisonment.

3. independence of thought, choice, or action; personal liberty. 4. ability or liberty to move or act without interference, coercion, or restraint: *He has the freedom to do as he pleases.* 5. absence of or release from a specified condition or thing: *freedom from fear.* 6. possession of a particular privilege, right, or immunity: *The government has the freedom to levy taxes.* 7. frankness or familiarity in manner or speech; informality. 8. unrestricted access or use: *We were given the freedom of his library.* 9. ease, as of movement or action; facility. 10. state or condition of being free. [Old English *frēodōm.*]

Syn. 4. *Freedom, liberty* mean the absence of outside rule over one's thoughts, beliefs, or actions. *Freedom* implies that determination of what it is right to do or think is an internal matter, personally or politically, and not to be decided by an outsider: *An artist needs freedom to express himself effectively.* *Liberty* suggests having the power to do those things that freedom permits one to do: *They that can give up essential liberty to obtain a little temporary safety deserve neither liberty nor safety* (Franklin, 1759).

freedom of the seas, principle that all ocean areas, other than territorial waters, are open to any ship without interference.

free energy *Physics.* that portion of the energy of a system which is available to do work.

free enterprise, economic system based on private ownership and operation of the means of production with a minimum of government control. Also, **private enterprise.**

free fall 1. state or condition of falling unrestrained after jumping from an aircraft and before opening the parachute: *The skydiver was in free fall.* 2. period of time that elapses before the opening of the parachute. 3. state or condition of a body, as a space vehicle, when it is subject only to gravitational and inertial forces, and is not guided, under thrust, or slowed down by a parachute or other braking device.

free-fall·ing (frē′fô′ling) *adj.* characterized by free fall: *a free-falling missile.*

free flight, free and unhampered motion of a body along a trajectory, subject only to gravitational and inertial forces.

free-for-all (frē′fər ôl′) *n.* 1. disorderly or noisy fight or quarrel. 2. contest, game, or other activity in which anyone may take part.

free-form (frē′fôrm′) *adj.* characterized by a shape or design not adhering to any regular or rigid pattern: *free-form sculpture, free-form furniture.*

free gold, formerly, gold or gold certificates held by the U.S. Treasury in excess of the amount needed to back gold certificates or meet other Federal Reserve requirements.

free·hand (frē′hand′) *adj.* drawn or sketched by hand without using measurements or instruments, as rulers: *a freehand diagram.* —*adv.* by hand without measurements or instruments: *to draw freehand.*

free hand, unrestricted liberty or action: *Give him a free hand and he will get the job done.*

free·hand·ed (frē′han′did) *adj.* openhanded; generous.

free·hold (frē′hōld′) *n.* 1. piece of land held for life with the right to transfer it to one's heirs. 2. the holding of land in this way. —**free′hold′er,** *n.*

free-lance (frē′lans′) *adj.* relating to or working as a free lance. —*v.i.* **-lanced, -lanc·ing.** to work as a free lance. —**free-lanc′er,** *n.*

free lance 1. writer, artist, or other professional whose services are not sold exclusively to, or committed under contract to, any single buyer. 2. one who works for or supports a variety of causes without being fully or exclusively committed to any organization. 3. mercenary in the Middle Ages, esp. one of rank, who would fight for anyone who paid his price.

free list, list of goods not subject to tariff duties.

free·load (frē′lōd′) *v.i. Informal.* to act as a freeloader.

free·load·er (frē′lō′dər) *n. Informal.* one who makes a practice of living at the expense of others.

free love, doctrine or practice of free choice in sexual relations, without legal marriage or other restraints.

free·man (frē′mən) *pl.,* **-men.** *n.* 1. one who is free from bondage of any kind. 2. one who has full civil and political rights.

Free·ma·son (frē′mā′sən) *n.* member of an international fraternal and service society that grew out of the medieval stonemasons' organizations. Also, **Ma′son.**

Free·ma·son·ry (frē′mā′sən rē) *n.* 1. principles, practices, and doctrines of the Freemasons. 2. Freemasons collectively. Also, **Ma′son·ry.** 3. **freemasonry.** instinctive sympathy and understanding among people with common interests and experiences.

free on board, delivered aboard or into a carrier by the seller without charge to the buyer.

free port 1. port of zone where customs duties are not charged on foreign goods to be shipped elsewhere rather than imported. 2. port open to all traders on equal terms.

free·sia (frē′zhə, -zē ə, -zhē ə) *n.* South African plant, genus *Freesia,* of the iris family, having fragrant funnel-shaped white or yellow flowers

at; āpe; cär; end; mē; it; īce; hot; ōld; fôrk; wood; fōōl; oil; out; up; ūse; turn; sing; thin; this; zh in treasure; ə in ago, taken, pencil, lemon, circus.

and narrow sword-shaped leaves. [Modern Latin *Freesia*, from Friedrich H. T. *Freese*, 1795–1876, a German doctor.]

free silver, free coinage of silver, esp. at a fixed ratio to gold coined at the same time.

free soil, U.S. territory in which slavery was prohibited before the Civil War.

Free-Soil Party (frē'soil') U.S. political party formed in 1848 to oppose the extension of slavery into the western territories and the admission of new slave states to the Union. It also urged the granting of free land in the territories to small homesteaders.

free-spo·ken (frē'spō'kən) *adj.* given to speaking frankly or without reserve; outspoken.

free-stand·ing (frē'stan'ding) *adj.* standing alone or independently on its own foundation apart from any supporting framework: *freestanding sculpture.*

Free State 1. U.S. state in which slavery was prohibited before the Civil War. 2. Irish Free State.

free-stone (frē'stōn') *adj.* having a pit that is easily separated from the pulp: *a freestone peach, a freestone plum.* Distinguished from **clingstone.** —*n.* 1. any fine-grained stone, as limestone or sandstone, that can be cut easily in any direction without splitting. 2. a freestone fruit, as a peach.

free-style (frē'stīl') *adj.* in swimming, using or allowing any stroke the swimmer chooses. —*n.* freestyle race or event: *He won the 200-meter freestyle.* —**free'styl·er,** *n.*

free-think·er (frē'thing'kər) *n.* one who forms his opinions by relying on reason rather than authority or tradition, esp. in matters of religion. —**free'think'ing,** *adj., n.*

free thought, thought or belief, esp. in religious matters, formed by relying on reason, rather than authority or tradition.

free throw *Basketball.* privilege granted to a player to take an unhindered shot from the free throw line because of a foul made by a member of the opposing team. Also, **foul shot.**

free throw line *Basketball.* line fifteen feet from the front of the backboard, behind which a player stands while shooting a free throw. Also, **foul line.**

Free·town (frē'toun') *n.* capital of Sierra Leone, on the western coast of the country. Pop. (1969), 100,600.

free trade 1. international commerce free from governmental restrictions, as import and export duties. 2. practice, policy, or system of such commerce.

free-trad·er (frē'trā'dər) *n.* one who advocates or engages in free trade.

free verse, poetry marked by the lack of a regular metrical pattern or rhyme scheme.

free·way (frē'wā') *n.* multiple-lane highway, usually divided, with limited points of access or exit, designed for rapid and direct traveling.

free·will (frē'wil') *adj.* given or done freely or of one's own accord; voluntary: *a freewill offering.*

free will 1. power of determining one's own actions; free choice; voluntary decision: *He did it of his own free will.* 2. doctrine that man's ability to choose between alternatives is not completely determined by divine will or external circumstances, and that he is therefore responsible for his actions.

free-world (frē'wurld') *adj.* of or relating to the free world.

free world, non-Communist countries collectively.

freeze (frēz) froze, fro·zen, freez·ing. *v.i.* 1. to change from a liquid to a solid form or state. When water freezes, it is called ice. 2. to become covered, obstructed, or clogged with ice: *The water pipes froze. The lake froze last night.* 3. to be or become extremely cold: *He froze while waiting for the bus during the snowstorm.* 4. to become hard or rigid because of cold: *The wet clothes froze on the clothesline. The steaks froze in the freezer.* 5. to adhere or become fixed because of cold: *The windshield wiper froze to the window.* 6. to become motionless or unable to move by an intense, sudden surge of emotion, as fear or shock: *She froze in her tracks when she saw him.* 7. to be at or near the temperature at which water becomes ice: *It is freezing tonight.* 8. to be destroyed or damaged by frost or extreme cold: *The orange crop froze this winter.* 9. to become formal, unfriendly, or aloof (often with *up*): *The child froze up around strangers.* —*v.t.* 1. to cause a liquid to change to a solid state or form; cause to become ice: *The cold weather froze the lake.* 2. to cover, obstruct, or clog (something) with ice. 3. to cause to adhere or become fixed to (something) by the action of cold or frost. 4. to make very cold; chill: *She was frozen to the bones.* 5. to preserve (food) by rapid reduction of its temperature: *to freeze a steak.* 6. to damage or destroy by exposure to extreme cold or frost. 7. to render (a part of the body) insensitive, as to pain, by subjecting to extreme cold; anesthetize. 8. to cause to become or remain motionless or stiff through a sudden surge of emotion, as fear or shock. 9. to fix (a person or thing) at a definite level or amount: *His salary was frozen at $150 per week.* 10. to prevent collection, use, or liquidation (of funds or other assets)

by governmental decree. 11. to prohibit further production, sale, or use of (a raw material): *to freeze gold.* 12. *Sports.* to attempt to retain possession of (a ball or puck) so that the opponent will not have an opportunity to score, as in the closing minutes of play. 13. **to freeze out.** *Informal.* to drive or force out, as by unfriendliness or severe competition: *The man was frozen out of the club by those who disliked him.* —*n.* 1. act of freezing; being frozen. 2. period of weather characterized by extremely cold temperature. 3. *Sports.* attempt to freeze a ball or puck. [Old English *frēosan* to turn to ice.]

freeze-dry (frēz'drī') **-dried, -dry·ing.** *v.t.* to dry (something, as food or serum) while frozen in a high vacuum, esp. for preservation.

freez·er (frē'zər) *n.* 1. refrigerator or compartment that freezes food rapidly and preserves it for long periods of time. 2. apparatus for freezing ice cream.

freezer burn, condition or appearance of frozen food caused by improper packaging or temperature control, or too long a period of storage. Freezer burn produces a loss of color, flavor, and nutritional value.

freezing point, temperature at which a liquid freezes. The freezing point of water at the standard atmospheric pressure of 14.7 lbs./sq. in. is 32 degrees Fahrenheit, or 0 degrees centigrade.

Frei·burg (frī'burg', -boork') *n.* city in southwestern West Germany. Pop. (1968 est.), 161,448.

freight (frāt) *n.* 1. transportation of goods by means of land, air, or water. It is usually less expensive and slower than express. 2. goods transported by such means; cargo. 3. charge for the transportation of goods by such means. 4. freight train. —*v.t.* 1. to load with goods for transportation. 2. to send as or transport by freight. [Middle Dutch *vrecht*, form of *vracht* cargo, load.] —**Syn.** *n.* 2. see **load.**

freight·age (frā'tij) *n.* 1. transportation of goods. 2. charge for the transportation of goods. 3. goods transported; freight; cargo.

freight car, railroad car for carrying freight.

freight·er (frā'tər) *n.* 1. ship used primarily for transporting cargo. 2.a. one who receives and transports freight. b. one who sends freight. 3. one who loads cargo.

freight train, railroad train composed of freight cars.

Fre·mont (frē'mont) *n.* city in western California, near San Francisco. Pop. (1970), 100,600.

Fré·mont, John Charles (frē'mont) 1813–90, U.S. explorer, soldier, and politician.

French (french) *adj.* of, relating to, or characteristic of France, its people, their language, or their culture. —*n.* 1. **the French.** people of France collectively. 2. one of the Romance languages, spoken as the native language of France. It is also spoken in parts of Belgium, Switzerland, and Canada, and in many former French colonies. [Old English *frencisc* relating to France, from *franca.* See **FRANK.**]

French and Indian War, war in North America between the French and their Indian allies and the English from 1754 to 1763, as a result of which France was forced to give up all her Canadian territory to England.

French chalk, fine-grained white talc used for marking lines on cloth or removing grease.

French Community, political association established in 1958, consisting of France, its overseas departments and territories, and several independent countries in Africa that formerly were French colonies.

French cuff, cuff of a sleeve that is folded back and fastened with a cuff link.

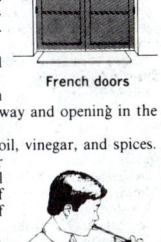

French doors

French doors, pair of doors, usually with glass panes, hinged at opposite sides of a doorway and opening in the middle.

French dressing, salad dressing made of oil, vinegar, and spices.

French Equatorial Africa, former French possession in western and central Africa, comprising the present countries of Chad, Central African Republic, Republic of the Congo, and Gabon.

French fried, fried in deep fat until brown and crisp: *French fried onion rings, French fried potatoes.*

French fry, potato cut into a thin strip and fried in deep fat until brown and crisp.

French Guiana, French overseas territory on the northeastern coast of South America. Area, 35,135 sq. mi. Pop. (1967 est.), 44,392.

French Guinea, Guinea.

French horn, valved brass instrument con-

French horn

at; āpe; cär; end; mē; it; īce; hot; ōld; fôrk; wood; fo͞ol; oil; out; up; ūse; turn; sing; thin; this; zh in treasure; a in ago, taken, pencil, lemon, circus.

sisting of a long, coiled tube ending in a flared bell, and producing a rich, mellow tone.

French Indochina, former French dependency in Southeast Asia, comprising the present countries of North Vietnam, South Vietnam, Laos, and Cambodia.

French leave, informal, secret, or hurried departure. [From the eighteenth-century French custom of leaving a social affair without saying good-by to the host or hostess.]

French·man (french′mən) *pl.*, **-men.** *n.* member or close descendant of the people of France. **—French′wom′an,** *n.*

French pastry, rich pastry, usually elaborately shaped and fancily decorated, often filled with custard, preserved fruit, or whipped cream.

French Polynesia, French possession in the eastern South Pacific, consisting of several island groups. Land area, approx. 1520 sq. mi. Pop. (1970 est.), 108,000.

French Revolution, revolution in France from 1789 to 1799 which overthrew the monarchy and aristocracy and gave rise to the First French Republic. It ended with the election of Napoleon I as First Consul in 1799.

French seam, strong, smooth seam sewed on both sides of a fabric, so that no raw edges are exposed.

French Somaliland, French possession on the eastern coast of Africa. Area, 9000 sq. mi. Pop. (1970 est.), 108,000.

French toast, bread dipped in a mixture of egg and milk and then fried.

French West Africa, former French possession, comprising the present countries of Dahomey, Guinea, Ivory Coast, Mali, Mauritania, Niger, Senegal, and Upper Volta.

French West Indies, French island possessions in the West Indies, comprising Martinique, Guadeloupe, and several smaller islands.

French windows, pair of doorlike windows hinged at opposite sides and opening in the middle.

fre·net·ic (fri net′ik) *also.* **phre·net·ic.** *adj.* frenzied; frantic. Also, **fre·net′i·cal.** [Form of PHRENETIC.] **—fre·net′i·cal·ly,** *adv.*

fre·num (frē′nəm) *pl.*, **-nums** or **-na** (-nə). *n.* band or fold of membrane that supports or restrains an organ or part, as the fold under the tongue. [Latin *frēnum* bridle.]

fren·zied (fren′zēd) *adj.* marked by frenzy; frantic.

fren·zy (fren′zē) *pl.*, **-zies.** *n.* state of intense or delirious emotion, as of excitement or agitation. **—v.t., -zied, -zy·ing.** to drive to frenzy; make frantic. [Old French *frenesie* delirium, from Latin *phrenēsis,* going back to Greek *phrēn* mind.]

fre·quen·cy (frē′kwən sē) *pl.*, **-cies.** *n.* **1.** state or fact of being frequent; repeated occurrence: *the frequency of his visits to the doctor.* **2.** number of times an action or occurrence is repeated within a given period; rate of recurrence. **3.** number of cycles per second of an alternating current, electromagnetic radiation, or sound. **4.** *Mathematics.* ratio of the number of times an event occurs to the total number of possible occurrences. [Latin *frequentia* crowd.]

frequency modulation, see FM.

fre·quent (*adj.* frē′kwənt; *v.* fri kwent′, frē′kwənt) *adj.* **1.** happening often, esp. at short intervals; occurring again and again: *There is frequent rainfall on that island.* **2.** appearing often; regular; habitual: *He is a frequent visitor.* **—v.t.** to go to or be in or at often or habitually: *to frequent the theater.* [Latin *frequēns* repeated, crowded.] **—fre′quent·ly,** *adv.* **—fre·quent′er,** *n.*

fres·co (fres′kō) *pl.*, **-coes** or **-cos.** *n.* **1.** art or method of painting on a surface of plaster, esp. while it is still wet, using pigments mixed with water. **2.** picture or design painted in this manner. **—v.t., -coed, -co·ing.** to paint using this method. [Italian *fresco* cool, fresh; of Germanic origin; because it is painted on plaster that is still fresh.]

fresh (fresh) *adj.* **1.** newly applied, made, arrived, obtained, or received: *a fresh coat of paint, fresh fingerprints, fresh coffee, a fresh wound.* **2.** not known, seen, worn, or used before; new: *a fresh shirt, a fresh approach to an old problem. She put fresh linens on the bed.* **3.** most recent; latest: *They received fresh information on the battlefront.* **4.** additional or different; further; another: *a fresh start. The student began a fresh paragraph.* **5.** not spoiled, stale, musty, or rotten: *fresh bread. The meat remained fresh for a day without refrigeration.* **6.** (of food) not artificially preserved, as by salting or pickling: *fresh vegetables.* **7.** not faded; vivid: *His words remained fresh in my mind. The accident was fresh in her memory.* **8.** looking or appearing healthy or youthful: *a fresh complexion.* **9.** cool and invigorating: *a fresh breeze, fresh air.* **10.** (of water) not salty. **11.** not fatigued; vigorous; energetic: *He felt fresh after his rest.* **12.** (of wind) having considerable force; brisk. **13.** inexperienced; untrained. **14.** *Informal.* showing impudence and disrespect; sassy: *The little girl was very fresh to her parents.* **15.** to be **fresh out of.** *Informal.* to have recently sold or exhausted the supply of. [Partly from Old English *fersc* unsalted; partly from Old French *freis* (feminine, *fresche*) new, cool, brisk; of Germanic origin.] **—fresh′ly,** *adv.* **—fresh′ness,** *n.*

fresh·en (fresh′ən) *v.t.* to make fresh. **—v.i. 1.** to become fresh. **2.** to make oneself fresh, as by washing or changing clothes (often with *up*): *We freshened up before going to the party.*

fresh·et (fresh′it) *n.* **1.** sudden rise or overflow of a stream, caused by heavy rains or melted snow. **2.** stream of fresh water flowing into the sea.

fresh·man (fresh′mən) *pl.*, **-men.** *n.* **1.** student in his first year of high school or college. **2.** one who is in his first year of any enterprise or activity. **3.** beginner; novice.

fresh·wa·ter (fresh′wô′tər, -wot′ər) *adj.* of, relating to, or living in fresh water: *a freshwater fish.*

Fres·no (frez′nō) *n.* city in central California. Pop. (1970), 165,972.

fret¹ (fret) **fret·ted, fret·ting.** *v.i.* **1.** to be irritated or worried: *Don't fret about such a minor incident.* **2.** to become corroded or worn away, as by friction. **3.** to become rough or agitated, as water. **—v.t. 1.** to irritate or worry: *Doubts began to fret his mind.* **2.** to wear away or corrode, as by friction: *The acid fretted the metal.* **3.** to roughen or agitate, as water: *The breeze fretted the surface of the water.* **—n. 1.** agitation or uneasiness of mind; vexation. **2.** act of wearing away or corroding. [Old English *fretan* to eat up, consume.]

fret² (fret) *n.* **1.** ornamental pattern, usually consisting of horizontal and vertical straight lines, symmetrically arranged within a band or border. **2.** any ornamental work consisting of such a pattern, often perforated or in relief. **—v.t., fret·ted, fret·ting.** to decorate with a fret. [Old French *freter* to adorn, from *frete* interlaced work; of uncertain origin.]

fret³ (fret) *n.* one of a series of bars or ridges, as of wood or metal, across the fingerboard of instruments of the guitar family, used for regulating the fingering to produce the desired tones. [Of uncertain origin.]

Frets²

fret·ful (fret′fəl) *adj.* inclined to fret; irritable; peevish. **—fret′ful·ly,** *adv.* **—fret′ful·ness,** *n.*

fret saw, compass saw.

fret·work (fret′wurk′) *n.* **1.** ornamental openwork, usually consisting of frets or interlaced patterns. **2.** any pattern, as of light and shade, resembling such openwork.

Freud, Sig·mund (froid; sig′mənd) 1856–1939, Austrian physician and neurologist, the founder of psychoanalysis.

Freud·i·an (froi′dē ən) *adj.* of, relating to, or in accordance with the theories, methods, or teachings of Freud. **—n.** adherent of the theories, methods, or teachings of Freud. **—Freud′i·an·ism,** *n.*

Frey (frā) *n. Norse Mythology.* the god of sun and rain, fertility, love, and marriage.

Frey·a (frā′ə) *n. Norse Mythology.* the goddess of love and beauty, and sister of Frey.

F.R.G.S., Fellow of the Royal Geographical Society.

Fri., Friday.

fri·a·ble (frī′ə bəl) *adj.* easily crumbled or pulverized; *friable rock.* [Latin *friābilis,* from *friāre* to crumble.] **—fri′a·bil′i·ty, fri′a·ble·ness,** *n.*

fri·ar (frī′ər) *n.* man who is a member of any of various monastic orders of the Roman Catholic Church, esp. the Franciscans, Dominicans, Carmelites, and Augustinians. [Old French *frere* brother, friar, from Latin *frāter* brother.]

fri·ar·y (frī′ər ē) *pl.*, **-ar·ies.** *n.* **1.** building or group of buildings where friars live. **2.** brotherhood of friars.

fric·as·see (frik′ə sē′) *n.* dish consisting of meat, esp. chicken, that is cut up, stewed, and served in a sauce made with its own gravy. **—v.t., -seed, -see·ing.** to make (meat) into a fricassee. [French *fricassée* this dish, from *fricasser* to fry; of uncertain origin.]

fric·a·tive (frik′ə tiv) *adj.* (of a speech sound) articulated by forcing the breath through a narrow opening formed by placing the tongue or lips against the palate or teeth. **—n.** a fricative consonant, as *f, v,* or *th.* [Modern Latin *fricativus,* from Latin *fricātus,* past participle of *fricāre* to rub.]

fric·tion (frik′shən) *n.* **1.** rubbing of one object against another. **2.** *Physics.* force that resists motion between two surfaces that are in contact with one another. **3.** conflict or difference, as of ideas, opinions, or temperaments; disagreement: *There is great friction between the two countries.* [Latin *frictiō* a rubbing.]

fric·tion·al (frik′shən əl) *adj.* of, relating to, or produced by friction. **—fric′tion·al·ly,** *adv.*

friction tape, cloth tape treated with an adhesive and moisture-resistant substance, used esp. in electrical work to protect and insulate electric conductors.

Fri·day (frī′dē, -dā) *n.* sixth day of the week. [Old English *Frīgedæg* Frig's day, from *Frīge,* genitive of *Frīg* Frigg + *dæg* day.]

at; āpe; cär; end; mē; it; īce; hot; ōld; fôrk; wood; fool; oil; out; up; ūse; turn; sing; thin; this; zh in treasure; ə in ago, taken, pencil, lemon, circus.

fried (frīd) past tense and past participle of **fry**¹.

friend (frend) *n.* **1.** one who is known intimately and regarded with affection by another; person one knows well and likes. **2.** associate or acquaintance. **3.** one who belongs to the same nation or group as oneself; ally: *Is he friend or foe?* **4.** patron or supporter: *Her name was on the list of friends of the museum.* **5.** **Friend.** member of the Society of Friends. Also, **Quak′er.** **6. to be friends with.** to be a friend of. **7. to make friends with.** to become a friend of. [Old English *frēond* intimate acquaintance, lover.]

friend at court, influential person who has the ability and the disposition to further the interests of another.

friend·less (frend′lis) *adj.* having no friends. —**friend′less·ness,** *n.*

friend·ly (frend′lē) **-li·er, -li·est.** *adj.* **1.** of, relating to, or characteristic of a friend: *a friendly gesture, a friendly letter.* **2.** acting as or like a friend. **3.** favorably disposed; not hostile: *friendly relations between two nations.* **4.** helpful or favorable: *a friendly breeze.* —*adv.* in a friendly manner. —**friend′li·ness,** *n.*

Friendly Islands, Tonga Islands.

friend·ship (frend′ship′) *n.* **1.** state or fact of being friends. **2.** mutual liking or attachment between friends. **3.** friendly feeling or disposition; friendliness: *He offered us his friendship.*

Fries·land (frēz′lənd) *n.* province of the Netherlands, in the northern part of the country. Area, 1312 sq. mi. Pop. (1968), 516,446.

frieze¹ (frēz) *n.* **1.** horizontal band, often decorated with sculpture or other ornamentation, between the cornice and architrave of a building. See **entablature** for illustration. **2.** any decorative horizontal band, as around the top of a wall or building. [French *frise*, possibly from Medieval Latin *frisium, phrygium* embroidery, going back to Latin *Phrygium (opus)* Phrygian (work); possibly because the decorations on a frieze often recalled elaborate embroidery, for which the Phrygians were noted.]

frieze² (frēz) *n.* heavy woolen fabric with a coarse, rough nap on one side. [French *frise*, from Old French *drap de frise* literally, cloth of Friesland.]

frig·ate (frig′it) *n.* **1.** three-masted, square-rigged sailing warship carrying one row of guns broadside, in use from the seventeenth to nineteenth centuries. **2.** naval ship smaller than a cruiser but larger than a destroyer, used for escort and patrol duties. [French *frégate*, from Italian *fregata*; of uncertain origin.]

Frigate

frigate bird, any of various tropical seabirds, genus *Fregata*, having long, pointed wings, predominantly black plumage, and a thin, hooked bill. The male has an inflatable orange throat pouch that becomes bright-red during the breeding season. The frigate bird feeds chiefly on small fish caught on the surface of the sea or stolen from other birds in flight. Also, **man-o'-war bird.**

Frigg (frig) *n.* *Norse Mythology.* the wife of Odin and queen of the gods and goddesses of the sky. Also, **Frig·ga** (frig′ə).

Frigate bird

fright (frīt) *n.* **1.** sudden, violent alarm or fear. **2.** *Informal.* one who or that which is grotesque, shocking, or ridiculous in appearance: *He looked a fright after three months of camping in the mountains.* [Old English *fyrhto* terror, fear.] —**Syn. 1.** see **fear.**

fright·en (frīt′ən) *v.t.* **1.** to make suddenly alarmed or afraid; scare: *The explosion frightened me.* **2.** to drive or compel by scaring (with *away, out, into,* or *off*): *The dog frightened away the squirrels.* —*v.i.* to become suddenly alarmed or afraid: *She frightens easily.* [From FRIGHT.]

fright·ened (frīt′ənd) *adj.* filled with fright; afraid. —**Syn.** see **afraid.**

fright·en·ing (frīt′ən ing) *adj.* that fills one with sudden alarm or fear: *a frightening experience.* —**fright′en·ing·ly,** *adv.*

fright·ful (frīt′fəl) *adj.* **1.** causing fright; terrifying: *a frightful enemy.* **2.** disgusting, shocking, or revolting: *a frightful spectacle of poverty and disease.* **3.** *Informal.* most distressing or unpleasant: *a frightful headache, to make a frightful racket.* **4.** *Informal.* extreme; great: *a frightful snob.* —**fright′ful·ly,** *adv.* —**fright′ful·ness,** *n.*

frig·id (frij′id) *adj.* **1.** intensely cold. **2.** lacking warmth of feeling or enthusiasm; indifferent: *a frigid reception.* [Latin *frigidus* cold.] —**fri·gid′i·ty, frig′id·ness,** *n.* —**frig′id·ly,** *adv.*

Frigid Zone, either of two extremely cold climatic regions, one lying

---

within the Arctic Circle and the other within the Antarctic Circle.

fri·jol (frē′hōl′, frē hōl′) *pl.*, **fri·joles** (frē′hōlz′, frē hō′lēz, -lās). *also.* **fri·jo·le** (frē hō′lē). *n.* any of various beans used for food, esp. in the southwestern United States, Mexico, and other Central and South American countries. [Spanish *frijol* kidney bean, through Portuguese and Latin, going back to Greek *phasēlos* kind of bean.]

frill (fril) *n.* **1.** ornamental trimming consisting of a strip of material, as lace, gathered and attached along one edge and left free along the other; ruffle. **2.** *also,* **frills.** anything showy or superfluous, as an affectation of dress or manner. **3.** ruff of feathers or hair around the necks of some birds, dogs, or other animals. [Of uncertain origin.] —**frill′y,** *adj.*

fringe (frinj) *n.* **1.** border or trimming consisting of hanging threads, cords, tassels, or the like. **2.** anything resembling or suggestive of such a border or trimming: *A fringe of bushes lined the driveway.* **3.** outer edge; border; margin: *the fringes of a city.* **4.** part considered to be marginal or extreme. —*v.t.,* **fringed, fring·ing.** **1.** to furnish with or as with a fringe. **2.** to serve as a fringe for. —*adj.* along the outer edge; marginal: *a fringe area.* [Old French *frenge* border of hanging threads, going back to Latin *fimbriae* (plural) threads, border.]

Fringe

fringe benefit, benefit received by an employee in addition to wages or salary, as pensions, health insurance, or paid vacations.

frip·per·y (frip′ər ē) *pl.* **-per·ies.** *n.* **1.** cheap, showy clothes or ornaments. **2.** showiness or affectation, as in speech or manner; ostentation. [French *friperie* rubbish, old clothes, going back to Old French *frepe* rag; of uncertain origin.]

Fris·co (fris′kō) *n.* *Informal.* San Francisco.

Fri·sian (frizh′ən, frē′zhən) *adj.* of or relating to Friesland, its people, or their language. —*n.* **1.** native or inhabitant of Friesland. **2.** language belonging to the Germanic branch of the Indo-European family of languages, spoken predominantly in Friesland.

frisk (frisk) *v.i.* to leap, skip, or move about playfully; gambol; frolic. —*v.t.* *Informal.* to search (someone), esp. for concealed weapons, by running the hand quickly over the pockets and clothing. [From obsolete *frisk* lively, from Middle French *frisque*; of Germanic origin.]

frisk·y (fris′kē) **frisk·i·er, frisk·i·est.** *adj.* playful; lively. —**frisk′i·ly,** *adv.* —**frisk′i·ness,** *n.*

frith (frith) firth.

frit·il·lar·y (frit′əl er′ē) *pl.* **-lar·ies.** *n.* **1.** any of a group of hardy plants, genus *Fritillaria*, of the lily family, found throughout northern temperate regions, bearing drooping, bell-shaped flowers often checkered with dark-green or purple markings. **2.** any of a group of butterflies, genus *Argynnis* and related genera, having multicolored spots. [Modern Latin *Fritillaria*, from Latin *fritillus* dice box; because of the markings on the petals.]

frit·ter¹ (frit′ər) *v.t.* to waste or squander little by little (often with *away*): *He frittered away his time doing nothing.* [Possibly modification of obsolete *fitter* to break into fragments; of uncertain origin.] —**frit′-ter·er,** *n.*

frit·ter² (frit′ər) *n.* small cake made of sautéed or fried batter, often containing fruit, vegetables, meat, or fish: *an apple fritter, a corn fritter.* [Old French *friture* a frying, going back to Latin *frīctus,* past participle of *frīgere* to roast, fry.]

fri·vol·i·ty (fri vol′ə tē) *pl.* **-ties.** *n.* **1.** quality or condition of being frivolous. **2.** frivolous act or thing.

friv·o·lous (friv′ə ləs) *adj.* **1.** given to trifling or levity; not serious; silly. **2.** of little value or importance; trivial; petty: *frivolous matters.* [Latin *frivolus*.] —**friv′o·lous·ly,** *adv.* —**friv′o·lous·ness,** *n.*

frizz (friz) *frizzed, friz·zing. also,* **friz.** *v.t., v.i.* to form into small, tight curls. —*n. pl.,* **friz·zes.** **1.** something frizzed, esp. hair. **2.** condition of being frizzed. [French *friser* to curl, possibly from *fris-,* a stem of *frire* to fry, from Latin *frīgere* to fry; with reference to the curled appearance of fried meat.]

friz·zle¹ (friz′əl) **-zled, -zling.** *v.t., v.i.* to form into small, tight curls; frizz. —*n.* something frizzled, esp. hair. [FRIZZ + -LE.]

friz·zle² (friz′əl) **-zled, -zling.** *v.t., v.i.* **1.** to fry with a sizzling noise. **2.** to fry until crisp. [Possibly blend of FRY¹ and SIZZLE.]

friz·zly (friz′lē) **-zli·er, -zli·est.** *adj.* having small, tight curls.

friz·zy (friz′ē) **-zi·er, -zi·est.** *adj.* having small, tight curls. —**friz′-zi·ly,** *adv.* —**friz′zi·ness,** *n.*

fro (frō) *adv.* **1.** to and fro. in different directions; back and forth. **2.** *Archaic.* away from; back. [Old Norse *frá*.]

Fro·bish·er, Sir Martin (frō′bi shər) c.1535–94, English explorer and navigator.

frock (frok) *n.* **1.** woman's or girl's dress. **2.** long, loose robe, esp. one worn by monks and friars. **3.** loose outer garment; smock. —*v.t.*

---

invest with the powers of the ministry or priesthood. [Old French *froc* hood; of Germanic origin.]

frock coat, man's coat reaching to the knees, usually double-breasted and fitted at the waist, popular in the late nineteenth century.

Froe·bel, Frie·drich (frō′bəl; frēd′riKH) 1782–1852, German educator, founder of the kindergarten system.

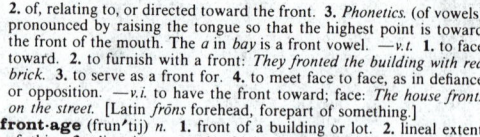
Frock coat

frog¹ (frôg, frog) *n.* **1.** any of a widespread group of web-footed, tail-less amphibians, order Salientia, found mostly near fresh water, and having strong hind legs adapted for leaping. **2.** any of various similar amphibians. **3.** triangular horny pad on the sole of a horse's foot. **4.** device permitting the wheels of a railroad car to pass over a junction at intersecting tracks without difficulty. **5. frog in the (or one's) throat.** slight irritation of the throat causing hoarseness or difficulty in speaking. [Old English *frogga* the amphibian.]

frog² (frôg, frog) *n.* ornamental fastening for clothing, usually made of braid that forms a loop on one side and a button on the other. [Of uncertain origin.]

frog kick, kick in swimming in which the legs are drawn toward the body, knees out and heels together, then pressed out and to the rear.

frog·man (frôg′man′; frôg′-) *pl.,* **-men.** *n.* swimmer specially equipped and trained for underwater reconnaissance and demolition, esp. for military purposes.

Frois·sart, Jean (froi′särt; French frwä-sär′; zhäN) c.1337–1410, French chronicler and poet.

frol·ic (frol′ik) **-icked, -ick·ing.** *v.i.* to move about or play with spirit or gaiety; make merry. —*n.* **1.** gay or spirited activity; romp. **2.** merriment; gaiety. [Dutch *vrolijk* merry, gay, from Middle Dutch *vro* glad.]

frol·ic·some (frol′ik səm) *adj.* gay and spirited; merry.

Frog¹

from (from, frum; *unstressed* frəm) *prep.* **1.** starting at; beginning with: *We flew from New York to Chicago. We waited from six o'clock to ten.* **2.** with a particular person, place, or thing as the source, origin, or instrument: *a letter from John, light from the sun. Our alphabet was derived from the Greek.* **3.** out of: *He took the money from his pocket.* **4.** out of the control, custody, or possession of: *He escaped from jail. The gun was taken from him.* **5.** out of the whole of: *to subtract two from five.* **6.** at a distance to; out of contact with: *She lives about ten miles from my house. The child shied away from me.* **7.** by reason of; because of: *to act from a sense of duty. She shivered from cold.* **8.** as being another or different than: *Can you tell one twin from the other?* **9.** beyond the reach, realm, or possibility of: *He prevented me from getting the job I wanted by giving me a poor reference.* [Old English *from, fram* away, apart, starting at.]

Frog²

frond (frond) *n.* **1.** leaf of a fern or palm. **2.** leaflike part of certain other plants, as a seaweed or lichen. [Latin *frond-,* stem of *frōns* leafy branch, foliage.] —**frond′ed,** *adj.*

front (frunt) *n.* **1.** part which faces, or is regarded as facing, forward; forepart: *the front of the body. I got a stain on the front of my dress.* **2.** first or foremost part: *The introduction is always in the front of the book.* **3.** place or position located directly ahead of or before any person or thing that follows: *He stopped right in front of her.* **4.** part or side that is normally used: *Sign the check on the front.* **5.** side of a building or similar structure containing the main entrance. **6.a.** one's attitude or bearing when confronted with anything, esp. of a dangerous or problematic nature: *He put on a bold front.* **b.** cool assurance; impudence; effrontery. **7.a.** broad movement uniting various groups for the achievement of a common goal, esp. of a political or economic nature: *the labor front.* **b.** area or field of activity or interest: *on the news front.* **8.** land facing or lying along a street, river, or the like; frontage. **9.a.** line or area of contact of two enemy forces: *The strategy was that the enemy divide its forces by fighting on two fronts.* **b.** foremost part of a military position: *The supplies were sent to the front.* **10.** *Informal.* apparently respectable person or thing used to disguise objectives or activities, as of an illegal organization: *The real estate business was a front for the gang's gambling activities.* **11.** *Informal.* outward, usually assumed or feigned appearance, as of wealth or importance. **12.** *Meteorology.* boundary between two air masses of different origin and properties: *a warm front, a cold front.* —*adj.* **1.** situated at, on, or near the front: *the front door of a house, the front page of a newspaper.*

2. of, relating to, or directed toward the front. **3.** *Phonetics.* (of vowels) pronounced by raising the tongue so that the highest point is toward the front of the mouth. The *a* in *bay* is a front vowel. —*v.t.* **1.** to face toward. **2.** to furnish as a front for: *They fronted the building with red brick.* **3.** to serve as a front for. **4.** to meet face to face, as in defiance or opposition. —*v.i.* to have the front toward; face: *The house fronts on the street.* [Latin *frōns* forehead, forepart of something.]

front·age (frun′tij) *n.* **1.** front of a building or lot. **2.** lineal extent of this. **3.** direction toward which the front of something faces. **4.** land abutting on a street, body of water, or the like. **5.** land between the front of a building and another boundary, as a road or body of water.

fron·tal (frunt′əl) *adj.* **1.** of, relating to, or situated at the front. **2.** of or relating to the forehead. —*n. also,* **frontal bone.** bone of the front of the skull, forming the forehead. [Modern Latin *frontalis,* from Latin *frōns* forehead, forepart of something.] —**fron′tal·ly,** *adv.*

fron·tier (frun tēr′) *n.* **1.** settled region of a country lying along the border of unsettled or undeveloped territory. **2.** that part of a country lying along the border of another country; border. **3.** *also,* **frontiers.** any new or unexplored area of a field, as science or philosophy: *the frontiers of medicine.* —*adj.* of, relating to, or situated on the frontier: *a frontier town.* [Old French *frontiere* border of a country, from *front* forehead, front, from Latin *frōns.*] —**Syn.** *n.* **2.** see **boundary.**

fron·tiers·man (frun tērz′mən) *pl.,* **-men.** *n.* one who lives on the frontier.

fron·tis·piece (frun′tis pēs′, fron′-) *n.* illustration facing the title page of a book or division of a book. [French *frontispice* title page, from Late Latin *frontispicium* façade; literally, front view, from Latin *frōns* forehead, forepart + *specere* to look.]

front·let (frunt′lit) *n.* **1.** band or ornament worn on the forehead, esp. a decorative headband of the medieval period. **2.** the forehead of an animal or bird, esp. when distinctively marked.

front office, main office or executive body of a business or other organization.

front-page (frunt′pāj′) *adj.* printed on, or important enough to be printed on, the front page of a newspaper.

front-run·ner (frunt′run′ər) *n.* leading contestant in any competition.

frost (frôst) *n.* **1.** deposit of minute ice crystals formed by the freezing of dew or water vapor on the surface of an exposed object or on the ground. **2.** state or temperature of the atmosphere below the freezing point of water; severe cold. **3.** act of freezing. **4.** coldness of manner, feeling, or action. —*v.t.* **1.** to cover with frost. **2.** to damage or destroy by frost. **3.** to produce a frostlike surface on, as glass. **4.** to cover with frosting. [Old English *forst, frost* extreme cold, frozen vapor.]

Frost, Robert (frôst) 1874–1963, U.S. poet.

frost·bite (frôst′bīt′) *n.* frozen or partially frozen condition of some part of the body as a result of excessive exposure to extreme cold. —*v.t.,* **-bit, -bit·ten.** to affect, injure, or destroy by freezing.

frost·bit·ten (frôst′bit′ən) *adj.* affected or injured by frostbite.

frost·ing (frôs′ting) *n.* **1.** mixture of sugar, a liquid, butter, flavoring, and sometimes egg whites, used to cover baked goods; icing. **2.** dull, frostlike finish, as produced on glass or metal.

frost·y (frôs′tē) *adj.* **frost·i·er, frost·i·est.** **1.** attended with or producing frost: *frosty weather.* **2.** containing or covered with frost: *frosty windows.* **3.** marked by coldness of manner or feeling: *a frosty reception.* **4.** resembling frost; hoary. —**frost′i·ly,** *adv.* —**frost′i·ness,** *n.*

froth (frôth) *n.* **1.** mass of bubbles formed in or on a liquid through agitation or fermentation; foam. **2.** any foamy matter or excretion, as from disease or exertion: *a froth at the mouth of the tired horse.* **3.** something light, trivial, or unsubstantial, as idea or conversation. —*v.i.* to emit or form froth; foam: *The rabid dog frothed at the mouth.* —*v.t.* **1.** to cause to foam. **2.** to cover with froth. [Old Norse *frotha* foam, spray.]

froth·y (frô′thē) **froth·i·er, froth·i·est.** *adj.* **1.** consisting of, covered with, or full of froth; foamy. **2.** unsubstantial or trivial: *a frothy speech.* —**froth′i·ly,** *adv.* —**froth′i·ness,** *n.*

frou-frou (frōō′frōō′) *n.* **1.** a swishing or rustling, as of silk. **2.** *Informal.* affected elegance or excessive ornamentation, as of a man's dress. [French *frou-frou* rustling; imitative.]

fro·ward (frō′wərd, frō′ərd) *adj.* not easily managed; stubborn or disobedient. [FRO + -WARD.] —**fro′ward·ly,** *adv.* —**fro′ward·ness,** *n.*

frown (froun) *n.* **1.** contraction of the brow, as in displeasure or concentration. **2.** any expression of displeasure or disapproval. —*v.i.* **1.** to contract the brow, as in displeasure or concentration. **2.** to look with displeasure or disapproval (with *on* or *upon*): *His parents frowned on his staying out late.* —*v.t.* to express (displeasure or disapproval) by contracting the brow: *to frown defiance.* [Old French *fro(i)-gnier* to look sternly, scowl; of Celtic origin.] —**frown′ing·ly,** *adv.*

Syn. *v.i.* **1.** Frown, scowl, glower mean to assume a facial expression in which the brow is contracted. Frown suggests an expression, perhaps

at; āpe; cär; end; mē; it; īce; hot; ōld; fôrk; wood; fōōl; oil; out; up; ūse; turn; sing; thin; this; zh in treasure; ə in ago, taken, pencil, lemon, circus.

only fleeting, that indicates disapproval, anger, puzzlement, or the like: *A man who . . . when asked to listen, frowned much, though not in an ill temper* (Darwin, 1872). **Scowl** implies a fixed expression of sullen discontent and malevolence: *We met many disbanded soldiers. . . . but beyond scowling at us they did us no harm* (Ramsay, 1882). **Glower** suggests a look of disapproval, anger, or the like directed pointedly at someone: *Mr. Slope saw it, and glowered with jealousy* (Trollope, 1857).

frows·y (frou′zē) **frows·i·er, frows·i·est.** *adj.* frowzy.

frowz·y (frou′zē) **frowz·i·er, frowz·i·est.** *adj.* **1.** having a slovenly appearance; unkempt. **2.** having an unpleasant smell; musty. [Of uncertain origin.] —**frowz′i·ly,** *adv.* —**frowz′i·ness,** *n.*

froze (frōz) past tense of **freeze.**

fro·zen (frō′zən) *v.* past participle of **freeze.** —*adj.* **1.** converted into ice; congealed by cold. **2.** covered, obstructed, or clogged with ice: *a frozen radiator, a frozen lake.* **3.** unable to move: *frozen with fear.* **4.** (of food) preserved by rapid temperature reduction. **5.** damaged or destroyed by frost or extreme cold. **6.** extremely cold; frigid: *a frozen climate.* **7.** maintained at a definite level or amount: *frozen wages.* **8.** cold and unfeeling: *a frozen stare.* —**fro′zen·ly,** *adv.*

FRS, Federal Reserve System.

frt., freight.

fruc·tif·er·ous (fruk tif′ər əs, frook-) *adj.* fruit-bearing.

fruc·ti·fy (fruk′tə fī′, frook′-) -**fied,** -**fy·ing.** *v.t.* to make fruitful or productive; fertilize. —*v.i.* to bear fruit. [Old French *fructifier* to bear fruit, from Late Latin *frūctificāre,* from Latin *frūctus* fruit + *facere* to make.] —**fruc′ti·fi·ca′tion,** *n.*

fruc·tose (fruk′tōs, frook′-) *n.* simple sugar occurring naturally in fruits and honey. Formula: $C_6H_{12}O_6.$ Also, **fruit sugar, lev′u·lose'.** [Latin *frūctus* fruit + -OSE².]

fru·gal (frōo′gəl) *adj.* **1.** avoiding waste; economical; saving: *a frugal woman.* **2.** meager; spare: *a frugal meal.* [Latin *frūgālis* temperate, thrifty; literally, relating to fruit, going back to *frūx* fruit.] —**fru·gal·i·ty** (frōo gal′ə tē), *n.* —**fru′gal·ly,** *adv.* —**Syn. 1.** see **thrifty.**

fruit (frōot) *pl.,* **fruit** or **fruits.** *n.* **1.** any edible plant product. **2.** ripened ovary of a plant. **3.** any useful plant product. **4.** result of an action: *the fruit of hard work.* —*v.i., v.t.* to bear or cause to bear fruit. [Old French *fruit* edible product of a plant, advantageous result, from Latin *frūctus* produce of the earth, result, enjoyment.]

fruit·age (frōo′tij) *n.* **1.** state or process of producing fruit. **2.** fruit collectively. **3.** any result.

fruit cake, rich cake containing preserved or dried fruits, nuts, and spices, and sometimes wine or brandy.

fruit cup, mixture of cut fruits, usually served in a cup or glass as an appetizer or dessert.

fruit·er (frōo′tər) *n.* **1.** ship that carries fruit. **2.** tree or plant that produces fruit. **3.** fruit dealer or grower. Also, **fruit′er·er.**

fruit fly, 1. small fly, *Drosophila melanogaster,* whose larvae feed chiefly on decaying fruit. It is valuable in genetic studies because of the extraordinarily large chromosomes of the larvae and its short life span. Also, **dro·soph′i·la. 2.** any of various other flies, family Trypetidae, whose larvae feed on fruit, leaves, and roots.

fruit·ful (frōot′fəl) *adj.* **1.** producing results; profitable: *a fruitful discussion.* **2.** bearing fruit or offspring in abundance; prolific: *a fruitful tree.* **3.** conducive to productiveness: *fruitful soil.* —**fruit′ful·ly,** *adv.* —**fruit′ful·ness,** *n.* —**Syn. 3.** see **fertile.**

fru·i·tion (frōo ish′ən) *n.* **1.** realization or accomplishment of one's efforts or desires; fulfillment: *After many years he brought his ideas to fruition.* **2.** bearing of fruit. [Old French *fruition* enjoying, from Late Latin *fruitiō* enjoyment, from Latin *fruī* to enjoy.]

fruit·less (frōot′lis) *adj.* **1.** producing no effect or result; useless: *a fruitless effort.* **2.** bearing no fruit or offspring; barren: *a fruitless tree, a fruitless marriage.* —**fruit′less·ly,** *adv.* —**fruit′less·ness,** *n.* —**Syn. 1.** see **vain.**

fruit sugar, fructose.

fruit tree, tree bearing edible fruit.

fruit·y (frōo′tē) **fruit·i·er, fruit·i·est.** *adj.* of, relating to, or suggestive of fruit, as in taste or smell.

frump (frump) *n.* **1.** dowdy, often ill-tempered woman. **2.** one who is staid and old-fashioned.

frump·ish (frum′pish) *adj.* **1.** dowdy or outdated in dress. **2.** staid and old-fashioned in manner. **3.** ill-tempered; cross.

frump·y (frum′pē) **frump·i·er, frump·i·est.** *adj.* frumpish.

frus·trate (frus′trāt) -**trat·ed,** -**trat·ing.** *v.t.* **1.** to keep (someone) from doing or achieving something; disappoint or thwart: *He was frustrated by his poverty.* **2.** to prevent something from being attained or fulfilled; defeat: *to frustrate a plan.* [Latin *frūstrātus,* past participle of *frūstrārī* to disappoint, render vain, from *frūstra* in vain.]

Syn. 2. Frustrate, foil¹, thwart mean to interfere with and defeat another's efforts. **Frustrate** suggests the blocking of attempts to achieve what the other wishes to do: *The team's efforts to score were frustrated by the opposing goalkeeper.* **Foil** implies resistance or hindrance that

eventually discourages effort: *The guards managed to foil the plans of the prisoners to escape.* **Thwart** suggests getting in the way of someone or something that is getting along well toward a goal: *The extravagances of the entertainment committee thwarted the club's drive to cut expenses.*

frus·tra·tion (frus trā′shən) *n.* **1.** act of frustrating; being frustrated. **2.** that which frustrates.

frus·tum (frus′təm) *pl.,* -**tums** or -**ta** (-tə). *n.* **1.** section of a cone or pyramid between the base and a plane parallel to the base and cutting through the solid. **2.** part of any solid between two parallel planes cutting through it. [Latin *frustrum* piece.]

Frustum

fry¹ (frī) **fried, fry·ing.** *v.t., v.i.* to cook in hot fat, usually over direct heat. —*n. pl.,* **fries.** social gathering, usually outdoors, at which food is fried and eaten: *a fish fry.* [Old French *frire* to cook in a frying pan with fat, from Latin *frīgere* to roast, fry.]

fry² (frī) *pl.,* **fry.** *n.* **1.** newly hatched fish. **2.** small adult fish, esp. when living in a large group. **3.** young of certain animals, as the frog. [Probably from Anglo-Norman *frie* spawn, from Old French *freier* to rub, spawn, from Latin *fricāre* to rub.]

fry·er (frī′ər) *n.* **1.** young chicken suitable for frying. **2.** deep pan for frying food. **3.** one who or that which fries.

frying pan, 1. shallow pan with a handle, used for frying food. **2. out of the frying pan into the fire.** from one dangerous or difficult situation to another that is worse.

f stop, any of the settings for the f number of a camera.

ft. 1. feet; foot. **2.** fort. **3.** fortification.

FTC, Federal Trade Commission.

fuch·sia (fū′shə) *n.* **1.** any shrub or small tree, genus *Fuchsia,* of the evening primrose family, native to tropical America, bearing pink, red, or purple clusters of funnel-shaped, usually drooping flowers. **2.** bright purplish-pink color. [Modern Latin *Fuchsia,* from Leonhard Fuchs, 1501–66, a German botanist.]

Fuchsia

fuch·sin (fūk′sin, -sēn) *also,* **fuch·sine.** *n.* synthetic, dark-green, powdery or crystalline mixture containing anilines, used as a red dye.

fud·dle (fud′əl) -**dled,** -**dling.** *v.t.* to stupefy or confuse with or as with liquor; befuddle. —*n.* state of being fuddled. [Of uncertain origin.]

fud·dy-dud·dy (fud′ē dud′ē) *n. Informal.* **1.** one who is old-fashioned. **2.** one who is overly critical or fussy about trifles.

fudge (fuj) *n.* **1.** soft candy made of sugar, milk, butter, flavoring, and sometimes nuts. **2.** nonsense; foolishness. —*interj.* used to express disappointment, annoyance, or disbelief. —*v.t.,* **fudged, fudg·ing. 1.** to evade a direct response to; refuse to commit oneself on, as a subject or issue. **2.** to fake. —*v.i.* **1.** to evade a direct response; refuse to commit oneself on something. **2.** to cheat. [Of uncertain origin.]

Fueh·rer (fyoor′ər, fir′-) Führer.

fu·el (fyoor′əl) *n.* **1.** combustible matter, as coal, wood, or oil, burned as a source of heat and power. **2.** that which sustains or intensifies an emotion, as passion or excitement. —*v.t.,* -**eled,** -**el·ing;** *also, British,* -**elled,** -**el·ling.** to supply with fuel. —*v.i.* to take in fuel. [Old French *fouaille* fagots, anything used for heating, from Late Latin *focālia,* plural of *focāle,* from Latin *focus* hearth.]

fuel cell, device that produces electricity by a direct chemical reaction between a fuel and an oxidizer.

fuel element *Physics.* rod, plate, or other form into which nuclear fuel is fabricated for use in a nuclear reactor.

fuel injection, spraying of liquid fuel directly into the combustion chamber of an internal-combustion engine.

fu·gi·tive (fū′jə tiv) *n.* **1.** one who flees or has fled, as from danger, pursuit, or intolerable circumstances: *a fugitive from tyranny.* —*adj.* **1.** fleeing or having fled, as from danger or pursuit. **2.** not fixed or durable; fleeting: *fugitive thoughts.* **3.** dealing with subjects of passing interest; occasional: *fugitive essays.* [Old French *fugitif* fleeing, from Latin *fugitīvus,* from *fugere* to flee.]

Fugitive Slave Laws, laws passed by the U.S. Congress before the Civil War that made it illegal to aid a runaway slave or prevent his being returned to his master.

fugue (fūg) *n.* polyphonic musical composition, based on one or more short themes or subjects taken up in turn by different voices or instruments and developed according to the rules of counterpoint. [French *fugue* flight, fugue, from Italian *fuga,* from Latin *fuga* flight; possibly because the notes seem to be in flight.]

Füh·rer (fyoor′ər, fir′-) *also,* **Fueh·rer.** *n. German.* **1.** leader. **2. der Führer.** title assumed by Adolf Hitler as head of Nazi Germany.

Fu·ji (fōo′jē) *n.* highest mountain in Japan, in the south-central part of the island of Honshu. Also, **Fu·ji·ya·ma** (fōo′jē yä′mə).

-ful *suffix* **1.** full of or characterized by: *graceful, peaceful.* **2.** tending

or able to: *forgetful, helpful.* **3.** having the qualities of: *manful.* **4.** number or amount that fills or will fill: *spoonful, glassful.* [Old English *-ful,* suffix representing *full* filled, complete.]

ful·crum (fool′krəm, ful′-) *pl.,* **-crums** or **-cra** (-krə). *n.* support or point of support upon which a lever rests, or about which it rotates when in use. [Latin *fulcrum* bedpost, from *fulcīre* to support.]

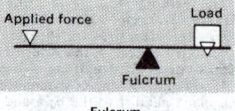

Applied force   Load

Fulcrum

Fulcrum

ful·fill (fool fil′) **-filled, -fill·ing.** *also,* **ful·fil.** *v.t.* **1.** to carry out or bring to completion, as a promise, hope, or prophecy; cause to happen. **2.** to meet (a requirement or condition). **3.** to bring to an end (a period of time or a task); finish. **4.** complete, as in extent, quantity, or number; total: *a full dozen, a full share.* **5. to fulfill oneself.** to realize completely one's potentiality or ambition. [Old English *fullfyllan* to accomplish; literally, to fill full.]

ful·fill·ment (fool fil′mənt) *also,* **ful·fil·ment.** *n.* **1.** act of being fulfilled. **2.** that which fulfills.

full¹ (fool) *adj.* **1.** containing as much or as many as possible; with no empty space: *a full glass of water.* **2.** containing a large number or quantity: *a house full of people.* **3.** having an abundant or ample supply: *The book was full of adventure.* **4.** complete, as in extent, quantity, or number; total: *a full dozen, a full share.* **5.** of or having reached the maximum, as of size, quantity, or amount: *full speed, full strength.* **6.** filled with a sufficient amount of food or drink: *I am full.* **7.** having a rounded outline; well filled out; plump: *full lips, a full face.* **8.** completely absorbed or occupied, as in thought: *He was full of concern for the future.* **9.** filled with emotion: *a full heart.* **10.** having ample resonance and volume: *a full tone, a full voice.* **11.** (of garments) having loose, wide folds or an abundance of cloth: *a full skirt.* **12.** (of sails) completely distended. **13.** (of the tide) high. —*adv.* **1.** straight; directly: *He looked her full in the face.* **2.** to the greatest degree or extent; completely; entirely. **3.** very; exceedingly: *to know full well. Full many a flower is born to blush unseen* (Gray, 1751). —*n.* **1. in full. a.** to or for the entire amount: *He paid the bill in full.* **b.** without abbreviation, condensation, or omission: *They reproduced the document in full.* **2. to the full.** to the utmost extent; completely; entirely: *John's grandfather enjoyed life to the full.* [Old English *full* filled, complete, entire.]

full² (fool) *v.t.* to finish (woolen fabric) by subjecting it to moisture, heat, friction, and pressure, causing it to shrink and giving it a smooth, tight finish. [From FULLER.]

full·back (fool′bak′) *n.* Football. **1.** player on the offensive team who usually lines up farthest behind the front line. **2.** position played by this player.

full-blood·ed (fool′blud′id) *adj.* **1.** of unmixed race, breed, or ancestry. **2.** vigorous; virile; hearty.

full-blown (fool′blōn′) *adj.* **1.** (of flowers) in full bloom: *a full-blown rose.* **2.** fully developed or perfected: *a full-blown beauty.*

full-bod·ied (fool′bod′ēd) *adj.* having a rich flavor and aroma: *a full-bodied wine.*

full dress, formal attire, as worn for ceremonial occasions.

full·er (fool′ər) *n.* one who fulls fabric. [Old English *fullere,* from Latin *fullō.*]

fuller's earth, fine, claylike earth, used as an adsorptive agent, as to remove grease from wool or to decolorize oil.

Ful·ler·ton (fool′ər tən) *n.* city in southern California. Pop. (1970), 85,826.

full-fash·ioned (fool′fash′ənd) *adj.* knitted to conform to the shape of the body, as hosiery.

full-fledged (fool′flejd′) *adj.* **1.** having full rank or status: *a full-fledged citizen.* **2.** completely developed or mature. **3.** (of a bird) having full plumage.

full gainer, gainer *(def. 2a).*

full-grown (fool′grōn′) *adj.* having attained full size or maturity; fully grown.

full house, poker hand made up of three cards of one kind and two of another, as three aces and two fours.

full-length (fool′lengkth′) *adj.* **1.** showing or covering the whole length of an object or figure: *a full-length mirror, a full-length gown.* **2.** being of the original or standard length; unabridged: *a full-length novel.*

full moon. 1. moon when the whole of its face is illuminated, as seen from the earth. **2.** time of month when this occurs.

full·ness (fool′nis) *also,* **ful·ness.** *n.* state or quality of being full.

fullness of time, sufficient length of time; approximate or indicated time.

full-rigged (fool′rigd′) *adj.* (of a ship) having complete rigging for three or more masts and a full set of sails.

full-scale (fool′skāl′) *adj.* **1.** of the same size as the original; of actual size: *a full-scale drawing.* **2.** undertaken to the fullest extent possible or with the fullest use of resources: *a full-scale war.*

full swing, height of activity: *The party was in full swing.*

ful·ly (fool′ē) *adv.* **1.** to the fullest extent or degree; completely; entirely: *to be fully aware of something.* **2.** at least; not less than.

ful·mi·nate (ful′mə nāt′, ful′-) **-nat·ed, -nat·ing.** *v.i.* **1.** to make threats or denunciations; inveigh (often with *against*): *The speaker fulminated against war.* **2.** to explode with sudden violence. —*v.t.* **1.** to threaten or denounce vehemently. **2.** to cause (something) to explode with sudden violence. —*n.* any of several explosive salts used as detonators, as mercury fulminate. [Latin *fulminātus,* past participle of *fulmināre* to thunder, lighten.]

ful·mi·na·tion (ful′mə nā′shən, ful′-) *n.* **1.** act of fulminating. **2.** violent denunciation or censure. **3.** loud, violent explosion.

ful·some (fool′səm) *adj.* offensive to good taste, as excessive or insincere praise. [FULL¹ + -SOME¹; possibly influenced in meaning by Middle English *ful* foul.] —**ful′some·ly,** *adv.* —**ful′some·ness,** *n.*

Ful·ton, Robert (fool′tən) 1765–1815, U.S. inventor who developed the steamboat as a practical means of transportation.

fum·ble (fum′bəl) **-bled, -bling.** *v.i.* **1.** to search or grope clumsily: *He fumbled for his hat.* **2.** to make an awkward attempt: *He fumbled at opening the lock.* **3.** to handle or finger something clumsily or aimlessly: *She fumbled nervously with her necklace.* **4.** in sports, to catch and lose hold of a ball. —*v.t.* **1.** to handle or deal with awkwardly; botch: *She fumbled her chances.* **2.** in sports, to catch and lose hold of (a ball). —*n.* **1.** act of fumbling. **2.** ball that is fumbled. [Dutch *fommelen* to grope.] —**fum′bler,** *n.* —**fum′bling·ly,** *adv.*

fume (fūm) *n.* **1.** *also,* **fumes.** smoke, gas, vapor, or other exhalation, esp. when irritating or offensive. **2.** strongly penetrating odor: *fumes from the city dump.* **3.** state of irritation or rage. —*v.i.,* **fumed, fuming. 1.** to give off fumes. **2.** to rise or pass off in fumes. **3.** to be filled with or show anger or irritation: *The man fumed as he waited in the heavy traffic jam.* —*v.t.* **1.** to expose to fumes. **2.** to give off in fumes. [Old French *fum* smoke, from Latin *fūmus.*]

fumed (fūmd) *adj.* darkened or colored by exposure to ammonia fumes, as oak wood.

fu·mi·gate (fū′mə gāt′) **-gat·ed, -gat·ing.** *v.t.* to expose to fumes, as smoke, esp. for disinfection. [Latin *fūmigātus,* past participle of *fūmigāre,* from *fūmus* smoke + *agere* to do, drive.] —**fu′mi·ga′tion, fu′mi·ga′tor,** *n.*

fun (fun) *n.* **1.** amusement or enjoyment; diversion; recreation. **2.** playfulness or gaiety: *He is full of fun.* **3.** source of amusement: *She is great fun to be with.* **4. for** (or in) **fun,** not seriously; in jest; playfully. **5. like fun,** by no means; not at all. **6. to make fun of** (or **to poke fun at**). to ridicule; mock. —*adj.* providing diversion or amusement; full of fun. [Probably from obsolete *fun* to hoax; of uncertain origin.]

fu·nam·bu·list (fū nam′byə list) *n.* tightrope walker. [Latin *fūnambulus* ropedancer (from *fūnis* rope + *ambulāre* to walk) + -IST.]

func·tion (fungk′shən) *n.* **1.** specific natural or characteristic action or use of anything; purpose: *The function of the kidneys is to excrete wastes from the body.* **2.** special duty or action required of a person, as in an occupation or role: *What is his function on the committee?* **3.** formal social gathering or official ceremony. **4.** *Mathematics.* **a.** quantity whose value is dependent on that of another quantity. **b.** relationship between two sets in which at least one element of the second set is assigned to one element of the first set. —*v.i.* **1.** to operate; work: *The motor functions best when it is kept well lubricated.* **2.** to perform the role of something else; serve: *The cellar functioned as a shelter.* [Latin *functiō* performance.]

func·tion·al (fungk′shən əl) *adj.* **1.** of or relating to a function or functions: *The system has functional problems.* **2.** designed for or adapted to a particular use; having a function: *They design functional buildings.* **3.** capable of functioning: *The system will be functional in five years.* **4.** affecting the function of an organ or part. Distinguished from **organic.** **5.** *Mathematics.* relating to or designating a function. —**func′tion·al·ly,** *adv.*

func·tion·al·ism (fungk′shən əl iz′əm) *n.* doctrine or practice of adapting the form, structure, or material of an object or building to its practical use or function. —**func′tion·al·ist,** *n.*

func·tion·ar·y (fungk′shə ner′ē) *pl.,* **-ar·ies.** *n.* one who serves in a specific function, esp. an official.

function word, word used to express a grammatical relationship in a sentence or phrase, as a conjunction, preposition, or auxiliary verb. In the sentence *I do enjoy swimming, do* is a function word.

fund (fund) *n.* **1.** sum of money or its equivalent accumulated or set aside for a specific purpose: *a fund for a political campaign.* **2.** available supply, as of information or knowledge: *What funds do you have to finance this venture?* —*v.t.* **1.** to provide money or its equivalent for payment of the interest or principal on (a debt). **2.** to provide a fund for: *to fund an organization.*

at; āpe; cär; end; mē; it; īce; hot; ōld; fôrk; wood; fool; oil; out; up; ūse; turn; sing; thin; this; zh in treasure; ə in ago, taken, pencil, lemon, circus.

[Blend of French *fond* bottom, basis, and French *fonds* capital, property, both from Latin *fundus* bottom, piece of land.]

fun·da·men·tal (fun′də ment′əl) *adj.* **1.** relating to or constituting a foundation; basic; essential. **2.** *Music.* of or relating to the lowest tone or root of a chord. —*n.* **1.** anything that forms or serves as the basis of a thing or system, as a principle, rule, or law; essential part. **2.** *Music.* lowest tone or root of a chord. Also, **fundamental note, fundamental tone. 3.** *Physics.* component of a wave that has the lowest frequency. [Late Latin *fundāmentālis* relating to a foundation, from Latin *fundāmentum* foundation.] —**fun′da·men′tal·ly,** *adv.* —**Syn.** *adj.* **1.** see **elementary.**

fun·da·men·tal·ism (fun′də ment′əl iz′əm) *n.* **1.** movement in U.S. Protestantism in the twentieth century, concerned with maintaining a literal interpretation of the Bible. **2.** beliefs associated with this movement. —**fun′da·men′tal·ist,** *n., adj.*

Fun·dy, Bay of (fun′dē) inlet of the Atlantic in eastern Canada, noted for its very high tides.

fu·ner·al (fū′nər əl) *n.* **1.** burial or cremation of the body of a dead person, together with religious services or other accompanying observances. **2.** procession accompanying the body of a dead person to the place of burial or cremation. [Medieval Latin *funeralia* funeral rites, going back to Latin *fūnus* burial, death.]

fu·ner·ar·y (fū′nə rer′ē) *adj.* of, relating to, or intended for a funeral.

fu·ne·re·al (fū nēr′ē əl) *adj.* **1.** of, relating to, or suitable for a funeral. **2.** sad; gloomy; dismal: *a funereal atmosphere.* [Latin *fūnereus,* from *fūnus* burial, death.] —**fu·ne′re·al·ly,** *adv.*

fun·gi (fun′jī) plural of **fungus.**

fungi- also, **fung-.** *combining form* fungus: *fungicide.*

fun·gi·cide (fun′jə sīd′) *n.* any substance used in destroying fungi. [FUNGI- + -CIDE².] —**fun′gi·cid′al,** *adj.*

fun·go (fun′gō) *adj. Baseball.* a high fly hit by a player during fielding practice after he has thrown the ball into the air. [Of uncertain origin.]

fun·goid (fung′goid) *adj.* resembling or characteristic of fungi.

fun·gous (fung′gəs) *adj.* **1.** of, relating to, or caused by a fungus. **2.** springing up or spreading suddenly, but not durable or substantial: *a fungous mushroom.* [Latin *fungōsus* spongy, from *fungus.* See FUNGUS.]

fun·gus (fun′gəs) *pl.,* **fun·gi** or **fun·gus·es.** *n.* **1.** any of a large group of plants that lack chlorophyll, live as parasites or saprophytes, and reproduce sexually or asexually. A fungus usually consists of a network of filaments to which are attached reproductive bodies that in some plants, as the mushroom, are the most conspicuous part. **2.** something that springs up or spreads rapidly, as a mushroom. **3.** diseased, spongy growth on the body. —*adj.* fungous. [Latin *fungus* mushroom, fungous excrescence on the skin, possibly from Greek *sphongos, spongos* sponge.]

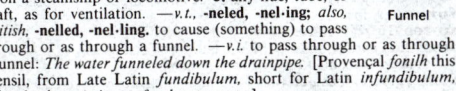

Fungi

fu·nic·u·lar (fū nik′yə lər) *n.* railway system in which two cars attached to both ends of a cable along a steep slope move alternately up and down the slope by counterbalancing and pulling each other. Also, **funicular railway.** —*adj.* of or relating to such a system. [Latin *fūniculus* small rope, diminutive of *fūnis* rope + -AR¹.]

funk (fungk) *Informal. n.* **1.** state of cowardly fear or panic. **2.** one who cowers with fear; coward. **3.** state of depression or moodiness. —*v.t.* **1.** to be afraid of. **2.** to shrink from or try to evade (something) through fear. —*v.i.* to shrink from or try to evade something through fear. [Possibly from Flemish *fonck* fear.]

fun·nel (fun′əl) *n.* **1.** utensil with a tube at one end and a wide, cone-shaped mouth at the other, used to facilitate pouring a substance into a container with a small opening. **2.** cylindrical chimney or smokestack, as on a steamship or locomotive. **3.** any flue, tube, or shaft, as for ventilation. —*v.t.,* **-neled, -nel·ing;** *also, British,* **-nelled, -nel·ling.** to cause (something) to pass through or as through a funnel. —*v.i.* to pass through or as through a funnel: *The water funneled down the drainpipe.* [Provençal *fonilh* this utensil, from Late Latin *fundibulum,* short for Latin *infundibulum,* going back to *in* in + *fundere* to pour.]

Funnel

fun·nies (fun′ēz) *n.* **1.** comic strips. **2.** section of a newspaper containing them.

fun·ny (fun′ē) **-ni·er, -ni·est.** *adj.* **1.** causing laughter or amusement; comical: *a funny joke.* **2.** *Informal.* strange or suspicious; odd. **3.** *Informal.* involving deceit or fraud. [FUN + -Y¹.] —**fun′ni·ly,** *adv.* —**fun′ni·ness,** *n.*

Syn. *adj.* **1. Funny, amusing, comical** indicate something appealing to the sense of humor. **Funny** is the general term: *Everything is funny as* long as it is happening to somebody else (Will Rogers, 1924). **Amusing** stresses the idea of diversion and lack of care evoking a feeling of joy: *There are amusing people who do not interest . . . and interesting people who do not amuse* (Disraeli, 1870). **Comical** suggests that something is so funny that is causes irrepressible laughter: *There was something extremely comical about the short, fat clown waddling about in clothes too big for him.*

funny bone, part of the elbow where the ulnar nerve passes very close to the skin. When it is struck, a sharp, tingling sensation is felt.

fur (fur) *n.* **1.** soft, thick, hairy coat of certain animals. **2.a.** piece of animal skin with such a coat, prepared for use in garments, rugs, and other items. **b.** such skins collectively. **3.** article of apparel, as a coat, made of such skin. **4.** coating of furlike foul matter, as on the tongue in illness. —*v.t.* **furred, fur·ring. 1.** to cover, trim, or line with fur. **2.** to clothe or cover with fur: *She furred herself with ermine.* **3.** to coat with a furlike deposit of foul matter. **4.** to apply furring to (a wall or floor) in order to make a level surface or create air spaces. —*v.i.* to become coated with a furlike deposit of foul matter. [Old French *forrer* to encase, sheathe, from *forre* sheath, case; of Germanic origin.]

fur·be·low (fur′bə lō′) *n.* **1.** frill, ruffle, or similar ornamentation, esp. on women's clothing. **2.** *also,* **furbelows.** any showy or superfluous ornamentation. —*v.t.* to furnish or ornament with furbelows. [Modification of dialectal French *farbella* flounce; of uncertain origin.]

fur·bish (fur′bish) *v.t.* **1.** to make bright by rubbing; polish; burnish: *We furbished the old armor.* **2.** to restore to a fresh or usable condition; renovate (often with *up*). [Old French *forbiss-,* a stem of *forbir* to polish; of Germanic origin.] —**fur′bish·er, fur′bish·ment,** *n.*

fur·cate (fur′kāt) *adj.* forked. —*v.i.,* **-cat·ed, -cat·ing.** to divide into branches; fork. [Late Latin *furcātus* forked, from Latin *furca* fork.]

fur·ca·tion (fər kā′shən) *n.* **1.** division into branches; forking. **2.** forklike branch or part.

fur·fur·al (fur′fə ral′, fur′fyə-) *n.* colorless, organic liquid with an almondlike odor, used esp. in the production of certain plastics and nylon, and as an industrial solvent.

Fu·ries (fyoor′ēz) *n. Classical Mythology.* three hideous female spirits who punished wrongdoers. Also, **E·rin′y·es′, Eu·men′i·des′.**

fu·ri·ous (fyoor′ē əs) *adj.* **1.** extremely angry; enraged: *He was furious that we left without him.* **2.** extremely violent or intense: *a furious wind.* **3.** unrestrained, as in activity, speed, or energy: *They raced down the highway at a furious speed.* [Old French *furieux* given over to rage or madness, from Latin *furiōsus* full of rage, from *furia* rage, madness.] —**fu′ri·ous·ly,** *adv.* —**fu′ri·ous·ness,** *n.*

furl (furl) *v.t.* to roll up and secure, as to a staff or mast: *to furl a flag.* —*v.i.* to become furled. —*n.* **1.** act of furling; being furled. **2.** rolled-up section, as of a flag. [Old French *ferl(i)er* to tie tightly, from *fer(m)* tight (from Latin *firmus* strong) + *lier* to bind (from Latin *ligāre*).]

fur·long (fur′lông) *n.* measure of distance equal to one-eighth of a mile, or 220 yards. See **weights and measures** for table. [Old English *furlang* literally, length of a furrow, from *furh* furrow + *lang* long, tall; because in early times in England the length of a furrow was used as a unit of measure.]

fur·lough (fur′lō) *n.* **1.** official leave of absence from duty, esp. in the armed services. **2.** document authorizing such a leave of absence. —*v.t.* to grant a furlough to. [Dutch *verlof* leave².]

furn. **1.** furnished. **2.** furniture.

fur·nace (fur′nis) *n.* structure or apparatus containing an enclosed chamber for the production of intense heat, as for heating buildings, melting metals, or generating steam power. **2.** any extremely hot place. [Old French *fornais* large oven, from Latin *fornāx* oven.]

fur·nish (fur′nish) *v.t.* **1.** to equip with or as with furniture, fixtures, or appliances: *The newlyweds finally finished furnishing their home.* **2.** to supply; provide: *The soldiers were furnished with rifles. The book furnished us with facts.* [Old French *forniss-,* a stem of *fornir* to supply; of Germanic origin.] —**fur′nish·er,** *n.*

Syn. 2. Furnish, equip, supply¹, provide mean to outfit someone or something with what is needed or usable. **Furnish** suggests fitting out with all that is needed for a particular action: *Several local merchants furnished the boys' baseball team with uniforms.* **Equip** implies materials for functioning well or improving efficiency: *They have equipped the office with the latest business machines.* **Supply** suggests giving what is needed as a regular or routine service: *The union says it can supply enough manpower to meet the factory's needs.* **Provide** implies that materials are ready and available when needed, as in an emergency or some unforeseen demand: *Milk provides all the major nutrients.*

fur·nish·ings (fur′ni shingz) *n.* **1.** furniture, fixtures, or appliances, as for a house or office. **2.** articles of clothing and accessories. **3.** useful or necessary equipment.

fur·ni·ture (fur′ni chər) *n.* **1.** movable articles, as tables, chairs, or beds, used to prepare a room for occupancy or use. **2.** any necessary equipment, as for a ship or factory. [French *fourniture* furnishing, supplying, from *fournir* to supply, provide; of Germanic origin.]

fu·ror (fyoor′ôr) also, **fu·rore**. n. 1. great outburst of enthusiasm or excitement; commotion. 2. frenzy; rage. [Latin *furor* rage, madness.]

furred (furd) adj. 1. having or wearing fur. 2. made, trimmed, or lined with fur. 3. coated with furlike foul matter, as the tongue.

fur·ri·er (fur′ē ər) n. one who deals in or works with furs.

fur·ri·er·y (fur′ē ər ē) pl., **-er·ies.** n. 1. furs collectively. 2. business or work of a furrier.

fur·ring (fur′ing) n. 1. fur trimming or lining. 2. coating of furlike foul matter. 3. thin strips of wood or metal fastened, as to walls or floors, to make a level surface or to provide air spaces.

fur·row (fur′ō) n. 1. long, narrow groove or channel made in the ground by a plow. 2. any long, narrow groove or channel, as a rut or wrinkle. —v.t. 1. to make a furrow or furrows in, as with a plow. 2. to make deep wrinkles in. —v.i. to become furrowed or wrinkled. [Old English *furh* channel made by a plow.]

fur·ry (fur′ē) **-ri·er, -ri·est.** adj. 1. made of or resembling fur. 2. covered with or wearing fur. 3. coated with furlike foul matter, as the tongue. —**fur′ri·ness,** n.

fur·ther (fur′thər) comparative of **far.** —adj. 1. additional; more: *without further delay.* 2. more distant or remote in time, space, or degree; farther: *on the further side.* —adv. 1. at or to a more distant or remote point in time or space: *to move further away.* 2. to a greater degree or extent; more: *to inquire further into a problem.* 3. in addition; moreover. —v.t. to help forward; promote: *to further the cause of peace.* [Old English *furthra* before, and *furthor* to a more advanced point, more (comparative of *forth* forwards, hence).]

fur·ther·more (fur′thər môr′) adv. in addition; moreover; besides.

fur·ther·most (fur′thər mōst′) adj. furthest.

fur·thest (fur′thist) superlative of **far.** —adv. 1. at or to the most distant or remote point in time or space. 2. to the greatest degree or extent; most. —adj. most distant or remote in time, space, or degree. [Superlative of FORTH, formed as a result of taking FURTHER as the comparative of *forth.*]

fur·tive (fur′tiv) adj. 1. done by stealth; secret; surreptitious: *a furtive glance.* 2. shifty; sly: *furtive eyes.* [Latin *furtīvus* stolen, secret, going back to *fūr* thief.] —**fur′tive·ly,** adv. —**fur′tive·ness,** n.

fu·run·cle (fyoor′ung′kəl) n. boil. [Latin *fūrunculus* petty thief, boil, diminutive of *fūr* thief.]

fu·ry (fyoor′ē) pl., **-ries.** n. 1. extreme, uncontrollable anger. 2. fit of such anger. 3. violence; fierceness: *the fury of the storm.* 4. person of fierce or uncontrollable temper. 5. Fury. one of the Furies. 6. like fury. *Informal.* violently or very rapidly. [Old French *furie* madness, rage, from Latin *furia.*]

furze (furz) n. any of a group of spiny shrubs, genus *Ulex,* of the pea family, found in Europe, Asia, and parts of North America, bearing yellow flowers and usually small, scalelike leaves. Also, **gorse, whin.** [Old English *fyrs.*]

fuse¹ (fūz) also, **fuze.** n. 1. safety device, consisting of a strip of metal encased in a container, that is inserted in an electric circuit. The strip will melt and break the circuit if the current becomes excessive. 2. length of cord or tubing filled or saturated with combustible material, used to ignite an explosive charge. [Italian *fuso* spindle, shaft, from Latin *fūsus* spindle.]

fuse² (fūz) **fused, fus·ing.** v.t., v.i. 1. to liquefy by heating; melt. 2. to blend or unite by or as by melting together. [Latin *fūsus,* past participle of *fundere* to pour, melt.]

fu·see (fū zē′) also, **fu·zee.** n. 1. friction match with a large head that will burn in a wind. 2. red or green flare used as a railroad signal. [Old French *fusee* spindleful, going back to Latin *fūsus* spindle.]

fu·se·lage (fū′sə lázh′, -lij, -zə-) n. body of an airplane, accommodating the passengers, cargo, and crew. [French *fuselage,* from *fuselé* spindle-shaped, from *fuseau* spindle, going back to Latin *fūsus.*]

fu·sel oil (fū′zəl) colorless, poisonous oily liquid produced as a byproduct of grain fermentation, used esp. in the manufacture of explosives, pharmaceuticals, and perfumes, and as a solvent for fats, oils, and other substances. [German *Fusel* bad liquor + OIL.]

fu·si·bil·i·ty (fū′zə bil′ə tē) n. 1. quality of being fusible. 2. degree of this quality.

fu·si·ble (fū′zə bəl) adj. capable of being fused or melted.

fu·si·form (fū′zə form′) adj. tapering from the middle toward each end; spindle-shaped. [Latin *fūsus* spindle + -FORM.]

fu·sil (fū′zəl) n. light flintlock musket. [French *fusil* musket; earlier, steel for a tinderbox, going back to Latin *focus* hearth.]

fu·sil·ier (fū′zə lēr′) also, **fu·sil·eer.** n. 1. soldier of any of several regiments of the British army. 2. formerly, a soldier armed with a fusil. [French *fusilier* soldier armed with a musket, from *fusil* musket. See FUSIL.]

fu·sil·lade (fū′sə lād′, -läd′, -zə-) n. 1. simultaneous or continuous discharge of firearms. 2. anything resembling this: *a fusillade of rain, a fusillade of criticism.* —v.t. **-lad·ed, -lad·ing.** to attack or shoot down

by a fusillade. [French *fusillade* discharge of firearms, from *fusiller* to shoot, from *fusil* musket. See FUSIL.]

fu·sion (fū′zhən) n. 1. act or process of fusing; melting together: *the fusion of metals.* 2. state or condition of being fused: *metals in fusion.* 3. union or blending together of different things, as a coalition of political parties. 4. that which is formed by fusing; fused mass. 5. *Physics.* combining of two light nuclei to form a heavier nucleus. It occurs when the light nuclei are heated to extremely high temperatures, releasing huge amounts of energy, as in the explosion of a hydrogen bomb. [Latin *fūsiō* a pouring out, melting.]

fusion bomb, hydrogen bomb.

fuss (fus) n. 1. unnecessary or excessive display, as of excitement, attention, or concern: *She spoiled her children by making a fuss over them. There was a great fuss in the convention hall.* 2. slight quarrel or dispute; spat: *The children had a fuss about who would get the prize.* 3. protest or objection: *There will be a fuss if the train is late again.* —v.i. 1. to make an unnecessary or excessive display, as of excitement, attention, or concern; make a fuss: *She fussed over dinner.* 2. to have a slight quarrel or dispute. [Possibly imitative.] —**fuss′er,** n.

fuss·budg·et (fus′buj′it) n. *Informal.* one who fusses; fussy person.

fuss·y (fus′ē) **fuss·i·er, fuss·i·est.** adj. 1. hard to please; finicky: *She is very fussy about her personal appearance.* 2. requiring much attention to details: *He had a fussy matter to clear up.* 3. elaborately made or trimmed: *a fussy dress.* —**fuss′i·ly,** adv. —**fuss′i·ness,** n.

fus·tian (fus′chən) n. 1. any of various heavy cotton fabrics with a thick nap resembling corduroy or moleskin. 2. coarse, heavy fabric made of cotton and linen, or a similar fabric made of wool, used for clothing in Europe during the Middle Ages. 3. pompous, pretentious writing or speech; bombast. —adj. 1. made of fustian. 2. pompous; bombastic. [Old French *fustaine* coarse cotton cloth, from Medieval Latin *fustaneum,* possibly from Arabic *fūstat* Fostat, a suburb of Cairo, where this type of cloth was first made.]

fus·tic (fus′tik) n. 1. yellow, brown, or green dye made from the wood of a tree, *Chlorophora tinctoria.* 2. the yellowish wood that yields this dye. 3. the tree itself, native to the West Indies and South and Central America. [Spanish *fustoc* this wood, from Arabic *fustuq* pistachio tree, from Greek *pistakē,* from Persian *pistā* pistachio nut.]

fust·y (fus′tē) **fust·i·er, fust·i·est.** adj. 1. having a stale smell; musty; moldy. 2. old-fashioned in appearance or behavior; not up-to-date. [Old French *fuste* odor of a cask, from *fust* tree trunk, cask, from Latin *fūstis* stick, staff.] —**fust′i·ly,** adv. —**fust′i·ness,** n.

fu·tile (fū′til, -tīl) adj. useless or hopeless; ineffective; vain: *They made futile efforts at reaching an agreement.* [Latin *fūtilis* that pours out easily, worthless.] —**fu′tile·ly,** adv. —Syn. see **vain.**

fu·til·i·ty (fū til′ə tē) pl., **-ties.** n. 1. quality of being futile. 2. that which is futile.

fut·tock (fut′ək) n. one of the curved timbers that forms a compound rib in the frame of a wooden ship. [Of uncertain origin.]

fu·ture (fū′chər) adj. 1. that is to be or happen in time to come: *a future occurrence.* 2. relating to or expressing time to come: *a future tense.* —n. 1. time that is to come. 2. that which will be or happen in time to come. 3. opportunity of success or prosperity in time to come: *There is a good future in business.* 4.a. verb tense indicating future action. b. verb in this tense. 5. futures. commodities bought and sold for future receipt or delivery. [Old French *futur* what is to come, from Latin *fūtūrus* about to be, future participle of *esse* to be.]

future life, existence of the soul after death.

future perfect 1. verb tense indicating an action or state of being that is completed before a specified time in the future. 2. verb form in this tense.

fu·tur·ism (fū′chə riz′əm) also, **Fu·tur·ism.** n. movement in art and literature originating in Italy early in the twentieth century and marked by a rejection of traditional forms in order to express the intensity and dynamic energy of the modern, mechanical age. —**fu′tur·ist;** also, **Fu′tur·ist,** n., adj.

fu·tu·ri·ty (fū tur′ə tē, -tyoor′-, choor′-) pl., **-ties.** n. 1. the future. 2. state or quality of being future. 3. future event or prospect.

fuze (fūz) fuse¹.

fu·zee (fū zē′) fusee.

fuzz (fuz) n. fine, loose particles, hair, or fibers: *peach fuzz.* —v.i., v.t. to make or become fuzzy. [From FUZZY.]

fuzz·y (fuz′ē) **fuzz·i·er, fuzz·i·est.** adj. 1. having or covered with fuzz. 2. resembling fuzz. 3. indistinct; blurred: *fuzzy recollections, fuzzy thinking.* [Possibly from Low German *fussig* loose, spongy.] —**fuzz′i·ly,** adv. —**fuzz′i·ness,** n.

-fy suffix 1. to cause to be or become; make: *nullify, pacify.* 2. to become: *solidify.* 3. to make similar to: *countrify.* [French *-fier,* from Latin *-ficāre,* going back to *facere* to do, make.]

fyl·fot (fil′fot′) n. swastika. [Possibly modification of *fill foot;* with reference to *filling* the *foot,* or lower part, of a painted window with a design. See FILL, FOOT.]

at; āpe; cär; end; mē; it; īce; hot; ōld; fôrk; wood; fōol; oil; out; up; ūse; turn; sing; thin; this; zh in treasure; ə in ago, taken, pencil, lemon, circus.

g, G (jē) *pl.*, **g's, G's.** *n.* **1.** seventh letter of the English alphabet. **2.** *Music.* **a.** fifth note or tone of the diatonic scale of C major. See do² for illustration. **b.** scale or key that has this note or tone as its tonic. **3.** unit of measurement of force exerted on bodies undergoing acceleration, equal to the acceleration of gravity, approximately 32.2 feet per second at sea level.

G, German.

g. **1.** gram. **2.** gauge. **3.** guinea.

G. **1.** German. **2.** specific gravity. **3.** Gulf.

Ga, gallium.

Ga., Georgia.

G.A., General Assembly.

gab (gab) *gabbed, gab·bing. Informal. v.i.* to talk idly or excessively; chatter. —*n.* **1.** idle or excessive talk; chatter. **2.** gift of gab. ability to speak fluently or glibly. [Probably imitative.] —**gab′ber,** *n.*

gab·ar·dine (gab′ər dēn′) *n.* **1.** durable, closely woven fabric, having diagonal ribs on its surface, used for such items as sportswear, coats, and suits. **2.** gaberdine (*def. 1*). [Form of GABERDINE.]

Ga·ba·ro·ne (gä′bə rō′nä) *n.* capital of Botswana, in the southeastern part of the country. Pop. (1964), 14,000.

gab·ble (gab′əl) *-bled, -bling. v.i.* to talk rapidly, foolishly, or incoherently; jabber. —*v.t.* to utter rapidly or incoherently. —*n.* rapid, foolish, or incoherent talk. [GAB + -LE.] —**gab′bler,** *n.*

gab·by (gab′ē) *-bi·er, -bi·est. adj. Informal.* very talkative; loquacious.

gab·er·dine (gab′ər dēn′) *n.* **1.** loose cloak or smock, esp. one worn by men in the Middle Ages. **2.** gabardine (*def. 1*). [Spanish *gabardina* coarse frock (probably once worn by pilgrims), probably going back to Middle High German *wallevart* pilgrimage, from Old High German *wallōn* to wander + *vart* journey.]

ga·bi·on (gā′bē ən) *n.* **1.** wicker cylinder filled with earth or stones, formerly used as in military fortifications. **2.** cylinder, usually of metal, filled with earth or stones, used in constructing foundations, as for dams, jetties, and bridges. [French *gabion* the wicker cylinder, from Italian *gabbione* large cage, going back to Latin *cavea* cage, den.]

ga·ble (gā′bəl) *n.* **1.** outside section of wall surface, usually triangular, between the sides of a sloped roof, extending from the level of the eaves to the ridge pole. **2.** end wall of a building, terminating in such a gable. **3.** any architectural feature having the form of a gable, as over a door or window. [Old French *gable* end of a house, from Old Norse *gafl* end of a ridged roof with the triangular piece of wall sheltered by it.]

ga·bled (gā′bəld) *adj.* having or built with a gable or gables.

gable roof, ridged roof that forms a gable either at one or both ends.

Ga·bon (gä bôn′) *n.* country on the west coast of central Africa. Capital, Libreville. Area, 103,347 sq. mi. Pop. (1968 est.), 480,000. —**Gab·o·nese** (gab′ə nēz′, -nēs′, and′gä bə-), *adj., n.*

Ga·bri·el (gā′brē əl) *n.* archangel appointed by God as His divine messenger, venerated by Christians, Jews, and Muslims.

gad¹ (gad) *gad·ded, gad·ding. v.i.* to move about restlessly or aimlessly, as in search of fun or excitement; roam: *The tourists gadded about Paris.* [Possibly from obsolete *gadling* companion, from Old English *gædeling.*] —**gad′der,** *n.*

gad² (gad) *n.* **1.** goad, esp. for driving cattle. **2.** in mining, sharp, pointed tool used to break up ore or rock. —*v.t.* **gad·ded, gad·ding.** to break up (ore or rock) with a gad. [Old Norse *gaddr* goad.]

Gad (gad) *also,* **gad.** *n., interj. Archaic.* God. ▲ used euphemistically as a mild oath.

gad·a·bout (gad′ə bout′) *n. Informal.* one who moves about restlessly or aimlessly, esp. in search of fun or excitement.

gad·fly (gad′flī′) *pl.,* **-flies.** *n.* **1.** any of various large blood-sucking flies, esp. those of the family Tabanidae, as the horsefly, that bites animals, esp. horses and cattle. **2.** one who persistently annoys, irritates, or stirs up others: *a political gadfly.* [GAD² + FLY.]

gad·get (gaj′it) *n. Informal.* small mechanical device or contrivance. [Of uncertain origin.]

gad·o·lin·i·um (gad′əl in′ē əm) *n.* metallic element, one of the rare-earth elements. Symbol: **Gd** See **element** for table. [Modern Latin *gadolinium,* from Johan *Gadolin,* 1760–1852, Finnish chemist.]

Gads·den (gadz′dən) *n.* city in northeastern Alabama. Pop. (1970), 53,928.

Gae·a (jē′ə) *also,* **Gai·a.** *n. Greek Mythology.* the earth goddess who was the mother and wife of Uranus and mother of the Cyclopes and Titans. Also, **Ge.**

Gael (gāl) *n.* **1.** Highlander (*def. 2a*). **2.** one of the Celtic people of Scotland, Ireland, or the Isle of Man. [Scottish Gaelic *Gàidheal.*]

Gael·ic (gā′lik) *adj.* of or relating to the Gaels or their languages. —*n.* languages of the Gaels.

gaff (gaf) *n.* **1.a.** large, sharp hook at the end of a pole, used to help pull large fish out of the water. **b.** pole equipped with such a hook. **2.** sharp metal spur fastened to the leg of a gamecock. **3.** spar for extending the upper edge of a fore-and-aft sail. **4.** to stand the gaff. *Slang.* to bear up well, as under hardship, ridicule, or punishment; be game. —*v.t.* to hook or land (a fish) with a gaff. [French *gaffe* a fishing gaff, from Provençal *gaf* boat hook.]

gaffe (gaf) *n.* social blunder; faux pas. [French *gaffe* a fishing gaff, blunder; retch.]

gaf·fer (gaf′ər) *n.* old man. [Modification of GODFATHER.]

gaff-top·sail (gaf′top′sāl′, -səl) *n.* light sail, usually triangular, set above a gaff, along which the foot of the sail is extended.

gag (gag) *n.* **1.** something stuffed into or put over the mouth to prevent a person from talking or crying out. **2.** any restraint or suppression of freedom of speech. **3.** *Slang.* amusing act or remark; practical joke; joke. —*v.t.* **gagged, gag·ging. 1.a.** to prevent from speaking or crying out by means of a gag: *The kidnapers gagged and bound the child.* **b.** to put a gag into or over (the mouth) to prevent from speaking or crying out. **2.** to restrain or suppress freedom of speech; silence: *The government gagged the revolutionary newspaper.* —*v.i.* to heave with nausea; choke; retch. [Imitative.] —**gag′ger,** *n.* —**Syn.** *v.* **3.** see **joke.**

Ga·ga·rin, Yu·ri (gä gär′in; yōō′rē) 1934–68, Russian cosmonaut, the first man to fly in outer space.

gage¹ (gāj) *n.* **1.** something given as security that an obligation or promise will be fulfilled; pledge. **2.** something, as a glove thrown on the ground by a knight, used as a token of a challenge to fight. **3.** any challenge. —*v.t.,* **gaged, gag·ing.** *Archaic.* to offer as a pledge or security; stake; wager. [Old French *gage* pledge; of Germanic origin.]

gage² (gāj) *n.* gauge. (Form of GAUGE.) —**gag′er,** *n.*

Gage, Thomas (gāj) 1721–87, British general in the American Revolution.

gag·man (gag′man′) *pl.,* **-men.** *n.* one who writes jokes or makes up comic routines for entertainers.

Gai·a (gā′ə) Gaea.

gai·e·ty (gā′ə tē) *pl.,* **-ties.** *also,* **gay·e·ty.** *n.* **1.** quality or state of being gay; cheerfulness. **2.** merrymaking; festivity: *the gaieties of the city during the holiday season.* **3.** brightness or showiness, as of dress; finery. [Old French *gaiete* mirth, from *gai* merry. See GAY.]

gai·ly (gā′lē) *also,* **gay·ly.** *adv.* in a gay manner.

gain (gān) *v.t.* **1.** to obtain, as by effort or striving; get; secure: *to gain the advantage in an argument, to gain time by stalling.* **2.** to get or develop as an increase, addition, advantage, or profit: *to gain momentum, to gain weight, to gain strength.* **3.** (of a timepiece) to run fast by (a specified amount): *My watch gains three minutes each day.* **4.** to obtain in competition or combat; win: *They gained the battle but lost many men.* **5.** to get to; arrive at; reach: *The ship gained the port before the storm struck.* —*v.i.* **1.** to improve, progress, or advance: *to gain in*

---

health, to gain in happiness. **2.** to advance nearer, as to an opponent in a race; come closer (often with *on*): *The black horse is gaining on the brown one.* **3. to gain over.** to win over to one's side, esp. by persuasion. —*n.* **1.** that which is gained, as an increase, addition, advantage, or profit: *a ten-pound gain in weight, a five-point gain on the stock market. Our gain was his loss.* **2. gains.** that which is acquired as profits, earnings, or winnings. **3.** act of gaining; acquisition. [Old French *gaigner* win; of Germanic origin.]
Syn. *v.t.* **1. Gain, acquire, secure, obtain** mean to get something. One **gains** something when one comes to have what is advantageous or valuable: *Mike has gained a reputation as an expert poker player.* **Acquire** stresses long and sustained effort leading to full possession and control of a physical or financial asset: *He has acquired great wealth by trading on the stock market.* **Secure** stresses undoubted possession of something that is difficult to acquire and hard to come by: *Nat has secured a job in an advertising firm.* **Obtain** implies seeking out something very desirable from a specific source and with great effort: *The astronauts obtained rock samples from the moon.*
gain·er (gā′nər) *n.* **1.** one who or that which gains. **2.a.** dive in which the diver faces the water and then does a full backward somersault, entering the water feet first. Also, **full gainer. b.** dive in which the diver does a half backward somersault and enters the water head first. Also *(def. 2b),* **half gainer.**
gain·ful (gān′fəl) *adj.* serving to produce gain; profitable; lucrative. —**gain′ful·ly,** *adv.*
gain·say (gān′sā′) -**said** (-sād′, -sed′), -**say·ing.** *v.t.* **1.** to deny. **2.** to contradict; dispute. **3.** to speak or act against; oppose. [Obsolete *gain-* against (from Old Norse *gegn*) + SAY.] —**gain′say′er,** *n.* —**Syn. 1.** see **deny.**
Gains·bor·ough, Thomas (gānz′bur′ō; *British* gānz′bur′ə) 1727–88, English painter.
gainst (genst; *British* gänst) *also,* '**gainst.** *prep. Archaic.* against.
gait (gāt) *n.* **1.** particular manner of moving on foot: *The young boy walked with a slow and easy gait.* **2.** one of the particular ways in which a horse steps or runs, as a trot or canter. [Old Norse *gata* way, path.]
gait·ed (gā′tid) *adj.* **1.** having a particular gait. ▲ used in combination, as in *slow-gaited horses.* **2.** trained when to use a gait or gaits: *a gaited horse.*
gai·ter (gā′tər) *n.* **1.** covering for the tops of shoes, the ankle, and sometimes the lower leg, similar to a puttee or spats, and made of cloth or leather. **2.** shoe with elastic inserts on the sides. **3.** overshoe with a cloth top. [French *guêtre;* probably of Germanic origin.]
gal., gallon; gallons.
Gal., Galatians.
ga·la (gā′lə, gal′ə) *adj.* of, relating to, or suitable for a festive occasion; festive: *Her birthday was marked with a gala celebration.* —*n.* festive occasion or celebration. [Italian *gala* festivity, finery, from Spanish *gala* court dress, from Arabic *khil'a* robe presented as an honor by an Oriental ruler.]
ga·lac·tic (gə lak′tik) *adj.* of or relating to a galaxy or galaxies, esp. the Milky Way. [Greek *galaktikos* milky, from *gala* milk.]
ga·lac·tose (gə lak′tōs, -tōz) *n.* white sugar obtained from lactose. Formula: $C_6H_{12}O_6$. [Greek *galakt-,* stem of *gala* milk + OSE².]
Gal·a·had (gal′ə had′) **1. Sir.** in Arthurian legend, son of Lancelot and Elaine, the purest and most virtuous knight of the Round Table. According to one account, he was the only knight to find the Holy Grail. **2.** any man of great purity and nobility.
gal·an·tine (gal′ən tēn′) *n.* dish of meat, esp. white meat, as chicken or veal, which is boned, stuffed, and poached, and then chilled and served with its own jelly. [French *galantine,* from Old French *galantine* sauce for fish, going back to Latin *gelātus* frozen, past participle of *gelāre* to freeze.]
Ga·lá·pa·gos Islands (gə lä′pə gōs′) island group in the eastern Pacific, west of and belonging to Ecuador. Land area, 3029 sq. mi. Pop. (1962), 2391.
Gal·a·te·a (gal′ə tē′ə) *n. Greek Legend.* statue of a maiden carved by Pygmalion, who then fell in love with it. Aphrodite brought the statue to life in response to Pygmalion's prayers.
Ga·lati (gä läts′) *also,* **Ga·latz.** *n.* port city in eastern Romania. Pop. (1968 est.), 160,097.
Ga·la·tia (gə lā′shə) *n.* ancient country and later a Roman province, in central Asia Minor. —**Ga·la′tian,** *adj., n.*
Ga·la·tians (gə lā′shənz) *n.* book of the New Testament, an epistle written by the Apostle Paul to the Christians of Galatia.
gal·a·vant (gal′ə vant′) *v.* gallivant.
gal·ax·y (gal′ək sē) *pl.,* -**ax·ies.** *n.* **1.** any of the vast groupings of stars, dust, and gases scattered throughout the universe. **2.** *also,* **Galaxy.** Milky Way. **3.** brilliant or splendid group: *The opening of the show was attended by a galaxy of celebrities.* [Old French *galaxie* the Milky Way, from Latin *galaxiās,* from Greek *galaxiās,* from *gala* milk.]
gale¹ (gāl) *n.* **1.** very strong wind, esp. one having a velocity of from

thirty-two to sixty-three miles per hour. **2.** *Archaic.* gentle breeze. **3.** noisy outburst, as of laughter. [Of uncertain origin.]
gale² (gāl) *n.* sweet gale. [Old English *gagel.*]
Ga·len, Claudius (gā′lən) A.D. 130–c.200, Greek physician and physiologist.
ga·le·na (gə lē′nə) *n.* gray metallic ore, the principal source of lead and an important source of silver. It is found in association with other minerals, esp. zinc. Also, **ga·le·nite** (gə lē′nīt). [Latin *galēna* lead ore.]
Gales·burg (gālz′burg′) *n.* city in northwestern Illinois. Pop. (1970), 36,290.
Ga·li·cia (gə lish′ə) *n.* **1.** historic region in east-central Europe, now divided between Poland and the Ukraine. **2.** region and ancient kingdom in northwestern Spain. —**Ga·li′cian,** *adj., n.*
Gal·i·le·an (gal′ə lē′ən) *adj.* of or relating to Galilee. —*n.* **1.** native or recent descendant of the people of Galilee. **2. the Galilean.** Jesus.
Gal·i·lee (gal′ə lē′) *n.* **1.** small region in northernmost Palestine. **2. Sea of.** small, freshwater lake in northeastern Israel. Also, **Lake Tiberias.**
Gal·i·le·o (gal′ə lē′ō, -lā′ō) *n.* 1564–1642, Italian astronomer, physicist, and mathematician; full name, Galileo Galilei.
gal·i·ot (gal′ē ət) *also,* **gal·li·ot.** *n.* **1.** small, fast galley propelled by oars and sails, formerly used in the Mediterranean. **2.** single-masted Dutch or Flemish merchant ship or fishing boat. [Old French *galiote* small galley, from *galie* large ship. See GALLEY.]
gall¹ (gôl) *n.* **1.** bile *(def. 1).* **2.** something bitter or unpleasant: *the gall of disappointment.* **3.** bitterness of feeling; rancor. **4.** *Informal.* impudence; nerve; effrontery. [Old English *g(e)alla* bile.]
gall² (gôl) *v.t.* **1.** to make sore by rubbing or chafing. **2.** to vex; irritate: *It galled her to hear her friend insulted.* —*v.i.* to become sore or chafed. —*n.* **1.** sore spot on the skin caused by rubbing or chafing. **2.** cause or instance of vexation or irritation. [Old English *gealla* sore spot on skin, probably from Latin *galla* gallnut.]
gall³ (gôl) *n.* abnormal growth or swelling on a plant, usually caused by insects, fungi, or other plant parasites. [Old French *galle,* from Latin *galla* gallnut.]
gal·lant (*adj., defs. 1, 3, 4* gal′ənt; *adj., def. 2, n.,* gə lant′, -länt′, gal′ənt) *adj.* **1.** brave; noble; heroic: *a gallant soldier.* **2.** characterized by politeness and attentiveness to women; courtly. **3.** grand; imposing; stately: *Our royal, good, and gallant ship* (Shakespeare, *The Tempest*). **4.** *Archaic.* gay or showy, as in dress. —*n.* **1.** chivalrous, brave, or noble man. **2.** fashionable or dashing young man. **3.** man who is particularly polite and attentive to women. **4.** suitor; lover. [Old French *galant* brave, gay, present participle of *galer* to make merry, rejoice, from *gale* mirth, pleasure; of Germanic origin.]
gal·lant·ry (gal′ən trē) *pl.,* -**ries.** *n.* **1.** bravery; courage; heroism: *The soldier received a medal for gallantry in combat.* **2.** courtly politeness and attentiveness to women. **3.** courtly action or speech: *to exchange a few gallantries with the lady* (Dickens, 1838).
gall bladder, small, muscular sac that is attached to the liver and in which bile is stored and concentrated.
gal·le·ass (gal′ē as′) *n.* large, three-masted galley propelled by both oars and sails, used chiefly as a war vessel in the Mediterranean in the fifteenth to seventeenth centuries. [Old French *galeace,* from Italian *galeazza* large galley, from Italian *galea* galley, from Medieval Latin *galea.* See GALLEY.]
gal·le·on (gal′ē ən, gal′yən) *n.* large, square-rigged, usually four-masted, sailing ship of the fifteenth to seventeenth centuries, having a square stern and usually three or four decks, used for both commerce and warfare. [Spanish *galeón,* from Medieval Latin *galea.*

Galleon

gal·ler·y (gal′ər ē, gal′rē) *pl.,* -**ler·ies.** *n.* **1.** narrow platform or passage, usually roofed and open on one side, projecting from the interior or exterior wall of a building; balcony. **2.a.** room or building where works of art are exhibited or sold. **b.** collection of works of art for exhibition. **3.** platform or floor projecting from the rear interior wall or side of a building, providing additional seating capacity, esp. the highest of a series of such floors in a theater, usually containing the cheapest seats. **4.a.** that part of the audience occupying the highest gallery of a theater. **b.** that part of the general public regarded as unrefined or uninformed. **5.** group of spectators: *The gallery applauded when the golfer made a difficult putt.* **6.** long, narrow room or passage; hall; corridor. **7.** covered walk or porch, wholly or partially open on one side, the roof of which is supported by pillars; portico. **8.** room or other wholly or partially enclosed area used for a particular activity,

at; āpe; cär; end; mē; it; īce; hot; ōld; fôrk; wood; fōōl; oil; out; up; ūse; turn; sing; thin; <u>th</u>is; zh in treasure; ə in ago, taken, pencil, lemon, circus.

as target shooting or photography. **9.** underground passage, as in a mine or an animal's burrow. **10. to play to the gallery.** *Informal.* to do something or act in a manner aimed at obtaining the praise or approval of the crowd. [Old French *galerie* long room, from Medieval Latin *galeria* long portico; of uncertain origin.]

gal·ley (gal′ē) *pl.,* **-leys.** *n.*
1. long, low ship of ancient and medieval times, propelled chiefly by a row of oars on either side, sometimes by several rows, one above the other. **2.** kitchen of a ship or airplane. **3.** *Printing.*
a. galley proof. **b.** long, shallow tray for holding type that has been set. **4.** large rowboat. [Old French *galie* large ship, from Medieval Latin *galea* large, fast ship, from Middle Greek *galaia;* of uncertain origin.]

Galley

galley proof *Printing.* a proof printed from type set in a galley, used esp. for making corrections in the printed matter before it is made up into pages.

galley slave 1. slave or convict condemned to row in a galley. **2.** drudge.

gall·fly (gôl′flī′) *pl.,* **-flies.** *n.* any of various insects whose eggs, when deposited in plant tissue, cause galls to be formed.

Gal·lic (gal′ik) *adj.* of or relating to Gaul or France or their people. [Latin *Gallicus* relating to the Gauls, from *Gallus* a Gaul.]

gal·lic acid (gal′ik) organic acid distilled from galls on certain plants or produced synthetically, used esp. in making ink and dyes. Formula: C₆H₂(OH)₃COOH

Gal·li·cism (gal′ə siz′əm) *also,* **gal·li·cism.** *n.* idiom or form of expression peculiar to French or anywhere in another language.

gal·li·gas·kins (gal′ə gas′kinz) *n.,pl.* **1.** loose trousers, esp. loose breeches or hose worn in the sixteenth and seventeenth centuries. **2.** leggings. [Earlier *garragascoyne,* from Old French *garguesque,* form of *greguesque* type of hose or breeches associated with Venice, Grecian, from Italian *grechesca,* short for *alla grechesca* in the Grecian manner, from *greco* Greek, from Latin *Graecus;* influenced in form by *galley* and *Gascony* because associated with sailors' hose and Gascony respectively. See GREEK.]

gal·li·na·ceous (gal′ə nā′shəs) *adj.* of or relating to an order, Galliformes, of typically terrestrial birds, as pheasants, grouse, partridges, and all domestic fowl. [Latin *gallīnāceus* relating to poultry, from *gallīna* hen, from *gallus* cock².]

gall·ing (gô′ling) *adj.* extremely annoying; irritating; exasperating: *a galling defeat.*

gal·li·nule (gal′ə nōōl′, -nūl′) *n.* any of several long-toed wading birds of the rail family, of temperate and tropical regions, having a small head, slender body, and typically green, blue, or black plumage, as the **Florida gallinule,** or **moorhen,** *Gallinula chloropus.* Length: 12–14 inches. [Latin *gallīnula* chicken, diminutive of *gallīna* hen, from *gallus* cock¹.]

Gal·lip·o·li (gə lip′ə lē) *n.* peninsula in northwestern Turkey, forming the northern shore of the Dardanelles.

gal·li·pot (gal′ə pot′) *n.* small, glazed, earthenware jar, used esp. by druggists for ointments and other medicines. [GALLEY + POT; possibly because this type of pottery was once transported in galleys.]

gal·li·um (gal′ē əm) *n.* rare, bluish-white, metallic element, found in aluminum ore and zinc ore, having a very low melting point. Symbol: Ga See **element** for table. [Modern Latin *gallium,* from Latin *gallus* cock¹, a translation of part of the name of its discoverer, *Lecoq* de Boisbaudran, 1838–1912, French chemist.]

gal·li·vant (gal′ə vant′) *also,* **gal·a·vant.** *v.i.* to wander about or travel in search of fun or excitement; gad. [Possibly modification of GALLANT.]

gall·nut (gôl′nut′) *n.* nutlike gall, esp. on oaks.

gal·lon (gal′ən) *n.* liquid measure of capacity, in the United States equal to four quarts, 231 cubic inches, or 128 fluid ounces. The British imperial gallon is equal to 277.42 cubic inches or 160 fluid ounces. See **weights and measures** for table. [Old French *galon, jalon,* probably from Medieval Latin *galeta* jug, liquid measure; of uncertain origin.]

gal·loon (gə lōōn′) *n.* narrow band of braid, lace, or other trimming, often made with metallic thread. [French *galon,* from *galonner* to adorn with lace; of uncertain origin.]

gal·lop (gal′əp) *n.* **1.** fastest gait of a horse or other four-footed animal, in which all four feet are off the ground at the same time during each leaping stride. **2.** ride or run at a gallop: *They took one gallop around the field before going back to the barn.* **3.** any rapid pace or action. —*v.i.* **1.** to ride or move at a gallop: *The zebra galloped away from the lion.* **2.** to go or act very fast; hurry; race: *The children galloped home*

from school. —*v.t.* to cause to gallop. [Old French *galoper* to go at a gallop; of Germanic origin.] —**gal′lop·er,** *n.*

gal·lows (gal′ōz) *pl.,* **-lows·es** or **-lows.** *n.* framework, usually consisting of upright beams supporting a crossbar from which criminals are hanged. Also, **gallows tree.** [Old English *gealga.*]

gallows bird *Informal.* one who deserves to be hanged.

gall·stone (gôl′stōn′) *n.* small, hard mass that sometimes forms in the gall bladder or its ducts. When a gallstone becomes lodged in a duct, it produces severe pain.

ga·loot (gə lōōt′) *also,* **gal·loot.** *n.* rough or awkward man. [Of uncertain origin.]

gal·op (gal′əp) *n.* **1.** lively dance in two-four time. **2.** music for this dance. [French *galop,* from *galoper* to dance a galop, from very fast; of Germanic origin.]

ga·lore (gə lôr′) *adv.* in abundance: *The table was covered with food and drink galore.* [Irish *go leór* sufficiently; literally, to sufficiency.]

ga·losh (gə losh′) *pl.,* **-losh·es.** *also,* **go·losh.** *n.* rubber overshoe reaching above the ankle, usually worn in wet or snowy weather. [Old French *galoche* wooden shoe (worn over silk shoes by the nobles in medieval France), probably from Late Latin *gallicula* Gallic shoe, from Latin *gallica (solea)* Gallic (sandal).]

gals., gallons.

Gals·wor·thy, John (gôlz′wur′thē) 1867–1933, English novelist and dramatist.

Gal·va·ni, Lu·i·gi (gäl vä′nē; lōō ē′jē) 1737–98, Italian physician and physicist.

gal·van·ic (gal van′ik) *adj.* **1.** of or relating to direct electric current, esp. one produced by chemical action. **2.** relating to or having the characteristics of a reaction to an electric shock; startling; convulsive.

gal·va·nism (gal′və niz′əm) *n.* **1.** direct current electricity produced by chemical action. **2.** in medicine, therapeutic application of such electricity. [French *galvanisme* such electricity, from Luigi *Galvani,* who discovered it.]

gal·va·nize (gal′və nīz′) **-nized, -niz·ing.** *v.t.* **1.** to stimulate by the application of electric current. **2.** to rouse suddenly into action; startle; excite: *The unexpected news galvanized him into life.* **3.** to cover (metal, esp. iron or steel) with a protective coating of zinc. —**gal′va·ni·za′-tion,** *n.*

gal·va·nom·e·ter (gal′və nom′ə tər) *n.* instrument for detecting and measuring electric current and determining the direction of its flow. [GALVANIC + -METER.] —**gal·va·no·met·ric** (gal′və nō met′rik) *adj.* —**gal′va·nom′e·try,** *n.*

Gal·ves·ton (gal′vis tən) *n.* port city in southeastern Texas. Pop. (1970), 61,809.

Gam·bi·a (gam′bē ə) *n.* country on the western coast of Africa, formerly a British colony and protectorate. Capital, Bathurst. Area, 4361 sq. mi. Pop. (1969 est.), 357,000.

gam·bit (gam′bit) *n.* **1.** chess opening in which a pawn or other piece is risked or sacrificed to gain some advantage. **2.** any opening move or maneuver designed to gain an advantage. [French *gambit* chess opening, from Spanish *gambito,* from Italian *gambetto* a tripping up, from *gamba* leg. See GAMBOL.]

gam·ble (gam′bəl) **-bled, -bling.** *v.i.* **1.** to play games of chance for stakes; risk money. **2.** to risk something of value with the hope of making a gain; wager. —*v.t.* **1.** to bet or wager (something of value): *He gambled his savings on the horse race.* **2.** to lose or squander by gambling (usually with *away*): *He gambled away his fortune.* —*n.* risky or uncertain undertaking: *Investing in the stock was a bad gamble. Driving in the snow was a gamble we had to take.* [Probably modification of Middle English *gamenen* to play at games, from Old English *gamenian* to play, sport.] —**gam′bler,** *n.*

gam·boge (gam bōj′, -bōōzh′) *n.* **1.** a gum resin obtained from any of various trees, genus *Carcinia,* used as a yellow pigment for varnishes, and in medicine as a drastic cathartic for cattle. **2.** any of various tropical evergreen trees yielding this resin, found in Asia, and Polynesia. [Modern Latin *gambogium,* from CAMBODIA, where the resin is found.]

gam·bol (gam′bəl) **-boled, -bol·ing;** *also, British,* **-bolled, -bol·ling.** *v.i.* to run, skip, or leap about in play; frolic: *The children loved to gambol in the woods.* —*n.* running, skipping, or leaping about in play; frolic. [Earlier *gambad(e), gambold,* from French *gambade* leap, spring, from Italian *gambata* kick, from *gamba* leg, from Late Latin *gamba* hoof, leg, going back to Greek *kampē* bend, joint.]

gam·brel (gam′brəl) *n.* hock of a horse or similar animal. [Dialectal Old French *gamberel* crooked stick, from *gambe* leg, from Late Latin *gamba* hoof, leg. See GAMBOL.]

gambrel roof, ridged roof having two slopes on each side, the lower slope being steeper than the upper.

game¹ (gām) *n.* **1.** form of playing; diversion; pastime; amusement: *Hopscotch is a children's game. What we took seriously was only a game to him.* **2.** form of mental or physical competitive play, governed by

specific rules, and testing the skill, endurance, or luck of the participants: *the game of baseball, the game of bridge.* **3.a.** single match between two opposing players or teams: *Our school won the football game.* **b.** one of several divisions in a fixed series or number of contests: *The tennis player won the first game of the set.* **4.** score at any given point in a competition: *In the third inning the game was tied two to two.* **5.** number of points required for winning: *Game was twenty-one.* **6.** equipment used in playing certain games: *The man bought several toys and games for his children.* **7.** particular manner of playing or degree of ability shown in a competition: *His tennis game was average.* **8.** *Informal.* any proceeding, vocation, activity, or undertaking: *the game of diplomacy. The senator had been in the political game for thirty-five years.* **9.** plan, scheme, or trick designed to gain an end: *They spoiled his little game by exposing him as an impostor.* **10.** wild animals, birds, or fish hunted or caught for sport or for food: *He hunted zebra, antelope, and other game in Africa.* **11.** flesh of such animals used for food. **12.** that which is hunted or pursued; quarry; prey: *The hounds got nearer to their game.* **13.** object of ridicule, attack, or pursuit: *His poor performance made him fair game for the critics.* **14. to make game of.** to make fun of; ridicule; tease. **15. to play the game.** *Informal.* to act in accordance with propriety, custom, or expected behavior. —*adj.,* **gam·er, gam·est.** **1.** having a fighting spirit; courageous; plucky: *He was a game fighter.* **2.** *Informal.* having enough spirit or will; ready: *Are you game for a swim in the cold water? He was game for anything.* —*v.i.,* **gamed, gam·ing.** to play games of chance for money or other stakes; gamble. [Old English *gamen* sport, amusement.] —**Syn.** **1.** see **play.**

game² (gām) *adj. Informal.* lame; injured: *a game leg.* [Of uncertain origin.]

game bird, any bird hunted for sport or food, as a pheasant or duck.

game·cock (gām'kok') *n.* rooster bred and trained for fighting.

game fish, fish that puts up a fight when hooked, providing sport for the fisherman.

game fowl **1.** fowl of any of several breeds trained for fighting. **2.** any fowl that is hunted as game.

game·keep·er (gām'kē'pər) *n.* person employed to breed, protect, and care for game in a government preserve or on private lands.

game laws, laws to protect and conserve game by limiting the size and number that may be killed or caught and by restricting the hunting and fishing seasons.

game·ly (gām'lē) *adv.* in a plucky manner.

game·ness (gām'nis) *n.* pluck; courage; endurance.

game·some (gām'səm) *adj.* playful; sportive; frolicsome.

game·ster (gām'stər) *n.* gambler.

gam·ete (gam'ēt, gə mēt') *n. Biology.* either of two mature reproductive cells, the sperm or the ovum, capable of uniting to form a zygote. [Modern Latin *gameta,* from Greek *gametē* wife, and *gametēs* husband.]

game theory, branch of applied mathematics dealing with situations of conflict involving a choice of strategies. It seeks to determine the best strategy for a given play.

ga·me·to·cyte (gə mē'tə sīt') *n. Biology.* cell that produces gametes. [GAMETE + Greek *kytos* hollow vessel.]

ga·me·to·gen·e·sis (gə mē'tə jen'ə sis) *n. Biology.* production of gametes. [GAMETE + GENESIS.] —**gam'e·to·gen'ic,** *adj.*

ga·me·to·phyte (gə mē'tə fīt') *n. Botany.* stage in the life cycle of plants that undergo alternation of generations, during which sex cells, or gametes, are produced. Distinguished from **sporophyte.** [GAMETE + -PHYTE.]

game warden, public official who enforces the game laws in a given district.

gam·in (gam'in) *n.* neglected or homeless child left to roam about the streets; urchin. [French *gamin* boy, urchin; of uncertain origin.]

gam·ing (gā'ming) *n.* act or practice of playing games of chance for money or other stakes; gambling.

gam·ma (gam'ə) *n.* third letter of the Greek alphabet, corresponding to English *G.* g. Symbol: Γ, γ.

gamma glob·u·lin (glob'yə lin) any of a group of proteins in blood plasma. Most gamma globulins are antibodies which protect the body against a recurrence of certain diseases, as measles or polio. It is sometimes given as an injection to immunize a person who has been exposed to a disease.

gamma ray, electromagnetic radiation similar to X rays but of shorter wavelength and greater penetrating power, given off by nuclei of radioactive atoms. It is used for such purposes as detection of internal defects in metal casting and welded structures.

gam·mer (gam'ər) *n.* old woman. [Probably modification of GODMOTHER or GRANDMOTHER.]

gam·mon (gam'ən) *n.* **1.** smoked or cured ham. **2.** lower end of a side of bacon. [Dialectal Old French *gambon* ham, from *gambe* leg. See GAMBREL, GAMBOL.]

gam·o·pet·al·ous (gam'ə pet'əl əs) *adj. Botany.* (of a flower) having the petals wholly or partially united, as the morning glory. Also, **sym·pet'al·ous.** [Greek *gamos* marriage + PETAL + -OUS.]

gam·o·sep·al·ous (gam'ə sep'ə ləs) *adj. Botany.* (of a flower) having the sepals united. [Greek *gamos* marriage + SEPAL + -OUS.]

-gamous *combining form* marrying or uniting sexually: *exogamous, bigamous.* [Greek *gamos* marriage + -OUS.]

gam·ut (gam'ət) *n.* **1.** entire range, scope, or extent of anything: *The actress ran the gamut of emotions in the play.* **2.** entire series of recognized notes or tones in modern music. **3.** major diatonic scale. [From Medieval Latin *gamma,* the note below *a* in Guido d'Arezzo's scale + *ut* (now called DO), another old name for the first note of the scale. The names of the notes of the scale apparently came from syllables in a Latin hymn; *ut* queant laxis resonare fibris, *Mi*ra gestorum *fa*muli tuorum, *Sol*ve polluti *la*bi reatum, *Sancte Iohannes.*]

gam·y (gā'mē) **gam·i·er, gam·i·est.** *adj.* **1.** having the taste or smell of game, esp. game that has been kept uncooked until slightly tainted. **2.** plucky. —**gam'i·ly,** *adv.* —**gam'i·ness,** *n.*

-gamy *combining form* marriage or sexual union: *monogamy, polygamy.* [Greek *-gamia,* from *gamos* marriage.]

gan·der (gan'dər) *n.* **1.** adult male goose. **2.** *Slang.* **to take a gander (at).** to look (at): *Take a gander at his new car!* [Old English *gandra* male goose.]

Gan·dhi (gän'dē, gan'-) **1. In·di·ra** (in dēr'ə). 1917—, prime minister of India since 1966. **2. Mo·han·das K.** (mō'han däs'). 1869–1948, Indian political, social, and religious leader; called Mahatma Gandhi.

gang¹ (gang) *n.* **1.** group of people organized or associated together for illegal or disreputable purposes: *The bank was held up by a gang of robbers.* **2.** group of laborers working together under one foreman; crew. **3.** *Informal.* group of people associated together for social reasons: *Our gang went to the party after the football game.* **4.** set of tools or machines designed to work together. —*v.t.* **1.** to arrange in or as in a gang: *The foreman ganged the men together.* **2.** to attack as a group. —*v.i. Informal.* **1.** to form or act as a gang. **2. to gang up on.** *Slang.* to attack or oppose together: *They ganged up on their little brother.* [Old Norse *gangr* a going.]

gang² (gang) *v.i. Scottish.* to go or walk. [Old English *gangan.*]

Gan·ges (gan'jēz) *n.* river in northern India and East Pakistan flowing from the Himalayas to the Bay of Bengal. It is considered sacred by the Hindus.

gan·gling (gang'gling) *adj.* awkwardly tall and spindling; lank. Also, **gan'gly.** [Probably from GANG².]

gan·gli·on (gang'glē ən) *pl.,* **-gli·a** (-glē ə) *or* **-gli·ons.** *n.* **1.** group of nerve cell bodies outside the brain or spinal cord. **2.** center of force, activity, or energy: *That scene is the chief ganglion of the tale* (Stevenson, 1882). [Greek *ganglion* tumor on a tendon.]

gang·plank (gang'plangk') *n.* movable bridge between a ship and a wharf used for boarding or leaving the ship.

gang plow, set of plows or plowshares which are designed to operate together.

gan·grene (gang'grēn', gang grēn') *n.* death and decay of body tissue caused when the blood supply is cut off or as a result of certain bacterial infections. —*v.t.,* **-grened, -gren·ing.** to cause gangrene in. —*v.i.* to become affected with gangrene. [Latin *gangraena* cancerous ulcer, from Greek *gangraina.*] —**gan·gre·nous** (gang'grə nəs), *adj.*

gang·ster (gang'stər) *n. Informal.* member of a gang of criminals.

gang·way (*n.,* gang'wā'; *interj.,* gang'wā') *n.* **1.** passageway. **2.** *Nautical.* **a.** passageway on either side of the upper deck of a ship. **b.** opening in the side of a ship for boarding passengers or loading freight. **c.** gangplank. —*interj.* get out of the way; make room.

gan·net (gan'it) *n.* any of various web-footed sea birds, genus *Morus,* of coastal islands and waters of most temperate regions, having a long, pointed bill and predominantly white plumage and capable of prolonged flight. Length: to 40 inches. [Old English *ganot.*]

gan·oid (gan'oid) *adj.* of or relating to a large group, Ganoidei, of primitive, bony fishes, including sturgeon, bowfin, and gar, many of which have hard scales of bone overlaid with an enamel-like substance. —*n.* ganoid fish. [French *ganoïde* ganoid fish, from Greek *ganos* brightness.]

gant·let¹ (gônt'lit, gant'-) *also,* **gaunt·let.** *n.* **1.** former military punishment in which the offender had to run between two rows of men who struck him with clubs, whips, or other weapons as he passed. **2.** series or siege of difficulties or troubles. **3. to run the gantlet. a.** to undergo the punishment of the gantlet. **b.** to be besieged by difficulties, opposition, or criticism. [Modification (influenced by GAUNTLET²) of earlier *gantlope,* from Swedish *gatlopp* the military punishment; literally, a running down a lane, from *gata* lane + *lopp* running.]

gant·let² (gônt'lit, gant'-) *variant of* GAUNTLET.

gan·try (gan'trē) *pl.,* **-tries.** *n.* **1.** framework consisting of a horizontal bridge fixed to upright supports which may be stationary or mounted on wheels. Gantries are used to support traveling cranes, winches, and railroad signals. **2.** gantry scaffold. [Possibly modification of Old

at; āpe; cär; end; mē; it; īce; hot; ōld; fôrk; wood; fōōl; oil; out; up; ūse; turn; sing; thin; this; zh in treasure; ə in ago, taken, pencil, lemon, circus.

French *gantier, chantier* wooden frame for barrels, from Latin *cantherius* rafter, trellis, ass, possibly from Greek *kanthēlios* pack ass.]

gantry crane, crane mounted on a gantry.

gantry scaffold, scaffold mounted on tracks for mobility and used to assemble and service a space rocket on its launching pad.

Gan·y·mede (gan′ə mēd′) *n. Greek Mythology.* a beautiful youth who was the favorite of Zeus and cupbearer to the Olympian gods.

gaol (jāl) *n. British.* jail. —**gaol′er,** *n.*

gap (gap) *n.* **1.** break, crack, or opening, as in a wall. **2.** deep ravine or pass through a mountain ridge. **3.** unfilled part or space; break in continuity; hiatus: *There were gaps of a week or more in her diary.* **4.** wide difference or divergence, as of opinion, character, or ideas: *There is a large gap between their political philosophies.* —*v.i.* gapped, gap·ping. to form a gap or opening. —*v.t.* to make a gap or opening in. [Old Norse *gap* chasm.]

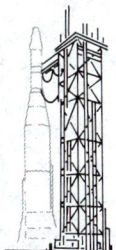

Gantry scaffold

gape (gāp, gap) **gaped, gap·ing.** *v.i.* **1.** to stare with or as with the mouth open, as in wonder or surprise (often with *at*): *The children gaped at the beautiful Christmas tree.* **2.** to open the mouth wide, as when yawning. **3.** to open or be opened wide, as a gap or hole. —*n.* **1.** act or instance of gaping. **2. the gapes. a.** fit of yawning. **b.** disease of birds and poultry, caused by a parasitic worm, the gapeworm, that infests the trachea, producing gasping and choking. [Old Norse *gapa* to open the mouth.] —**gap′er,** *n.*

gape·worm (gāp′wurm, gap′-) *n.* nematode worm, *Syngamus trachea,* that causes the gapes in birds.

gar (gär) *pl.,* **gars** or **gar.** *n.* any of a group of predatory fish, order Semionotiformes, usually found in shallow, weedy waters of eastern North

Gar

and Central America, having elongated jaws and a long, narrow body covered with bony scales. Length: to 12 feet. Also, **gar′fish′, gar pike.** [Old English *gār* spear; probably because of its shape.]

G.A.R., Grand Army of the Republic.

ga·rage (gə räzh′, -räj′; *British* gar′ij) *n.* private or commercial building where automobiles are kept, repaired, or serviced. —*v.t.,* **-raged, -rag·ing.** to put or keep in a garage. [French *garage* place for storage, storing away, from Middle French *garer* to take care, protect; of Germanic origin.]

Gar·and rifle (gar′ənd) .30 caliber, gas-operated, automatic or semiautomatic rifle used by the U.S. ground troops in World War II. [From John C. *Garand,* twentieth-century American inventor, who was its designer.]

garb (gärb) *n.* **1.** clothing or attire, esp. a particular or distinctive form of dress: *military garb.* **2.** outward appearance, form, or covering: *the principal's customary garb of strictness.* —*v.t.* to clothe; dress: *The old woman was garbed in a flowing gown of black and white lace.* [Middle French *garbe* grace, good fashion, from Italian *garbo* grace; of Germanic origin.]

gar·bage (gär′bij) *n.* **1.** waste material, esp. animal or vegetable matter that has been thrown away, as food scraps from a kitchen. **2.** anything worthless or offensive: *The book she's reading is garbage.* [Of uncertain origin.]

garbage disposal, machine that is attached to a sink and disposes of garbage by grinding it up to be carried away with the waste water.

gar·ble (gär′bəl) **-bled, -bling.** *v.t.* **1.** to make unfair selections from (facts or a text) in order to give a false impression or distort: *The witness garbled his account of the accident.* **2.** to confuse or mix up unintentionally: *to garble a telephone message.* —*n.* act or instance of garbling: *The message was such a garble that no one could understand it.* [Italian *garbellare* to sift, from Arabic *gharbala,* going back to Latin *crībrum* sieve.] —**gar′bler,** *n.*

Gar·ci·a Lor·ca, Fer·nan·do (gär sē′ə lôr′kə; fer nän′dō) 1899–1936, Spanish poet and dramatist.

gar·çon (gär sôN′) *pl.,* **-cons** (-sôN′). *n. French.* **1.** young man; boy. **2.** waiter. **3.** male servant.

gar·den (gärd′ən) *n.* **1.** plot of ground where flowers, vegetables, herbs, or other small plants are cultivated. **2.** fertile, well-cultivated area or region. **3.** *also,* **gardens.** park or other piece of ground used by the public for recreation or amusement. —*adj.* **1.** of a garden. **2.** common; ordinary: *a boring, garden variety novel.* —*v.i.* to cultivate or work in a garden. —*v.t.* to cultivate as a garden: *He gardened the lot behind his house.* [Dialectal Old French *gardin* plot of ground with plants; of Germanic origin.]

garden apartment. 1. ground-floor apartment rented with an adjoining garden. **2.** apartment building, usually having landscaped grounds and only two or three stories of units.

Garden City, city in southeastern Michigan, principally a residential suburb of Detroit. Pop. (1970), 41,864.

gar·den·er (gärd′nər) *n.* one who cultivates or tends a garden professionally or as a hobby.

Garden Grove, city in southern California, near Los Angeles. Pop. (1970), 122,524.

gar·de·nia (gär dēn′yə, -dē′nē ə) *n.* **1.** fragrant yellow or white flower of any of a group of evergreen shrubs and small trees, genus *Gardenia,* having waxy, dish-shaped petals, as the cape jasmine, *G. jasminoides,* often grown commercially for corsages. **2.** shrub or tree bearing this flower, having shiny oval leaves, widely cultivated in many parts of the world. [Modern Latin *Gardenia,* from Alexander *Garden,* 1730–91, American botanist.]

Gardenia (cape jasmine)

Garden of Eden, in the Bible, the original home of Adam and Eve.

Gar·eth (gar′ith) *n.* in Arthurian legend, a knight of the Round Table, brother of Sir Gawain, and nephew of King Arthur.

Gar·field, James A. (gär′fēld′) 1831–81, twentieth president of the United States from March 4 to September 19, 1881.

gar·fish (gär′fish′) *pl.,* **-fish** or **-fish·es.** *n.* gar.

Gar·gan·tu·an (gär gan′chōō ən) *adj.* enormous; gigantic; huge. [*Gargantua* giant in Rabelais' satire *Gargantua and Pantagruel* + -AN.]

gar·get (gär′gət) *n.* inflammation of the udder in cows, ewes, and other domestic mammals. [Old French *gargate* throat, gullet; of imitative origin.]

gar·gle (gär′gəl) **-gled, -gling.** *v.i.* to wash or rinse the mouth or upper portion of the throat with a liquid kept in motion by an exhalation of the breath. —*v.t.* **1.** to use (a liquid) for gargling: *to gargle salt water.* **2.** to wash or rinse (the throat or mouth) by gargling. —*n.* liquid used for gargling. [French *gargouiller* to gurgle, from Old French *gargouille* throat; of imitative origin.]

gar·goyle (gär′goil) *n.* **1.** waterspout, usually in the form of a grotesque human or animal figure, projecting from the gutter of a building to throw off rainwater. **2.** decorative projection on a building resembling this. [Old French *gargouille* throat, waterspout; of imitative origin.]

Gar·i·bal·di, Giu·sep·pe (gar′ə bôl′dē; jōō zep′ē) 1807–82, Italian patriot and general.

gar·ish (gâr′ish) *adj.* excessively bright or ornate; flashy; gaudy. [Of uncertain origin.]

gar·land (gär′lənd) *n.* **1.** wreath of flowers, leaves, vines, or similar materials usually worn about the head for decoration, esp. as a token of honor. **2.** collection of short literary pieces, esp. poems; anthology. **3.** *Nautical.* ring of rope lashed to a spar for use in hoisting it aboard or wound around the head of a mast to prevent the shrouds from chafing. —*v.t.* to decorate with or form into a garland or garlands. [Old French *garlande* the wreath; of uncertain origin.]

Gargoyle

Gar·land (gär′lənd) *n.* city in northeastern Texas, principally an industrial suburb of Dallas. Pop. (1970), 81,437.

gar·lic (gär′lik) *n.* **1.** strong tasting bulb of a plant, *Allium sativum,* of the lily family, used as a spice. The bulb is composed of separate sections called cloves. **2.** plant itself, widely cultivated in most parts of the world, having long, flat, ridged leaves and bearing clusters of small pink or purple flowers. [Old English *gārlēac* the plant, from *gār* spear + *lēac* leek; with reference to the shape of its leaves.]

gar·lick·y (gär′li kē) *adj.* containing or tasting or smelling of garlic.

gar·ment (gär′mənt) *n.* **1.** article of clothing. **2.** outer covering or appearance: *to put these forms into the garment of words* (Macdonald, 1866). —*v.t.* to clothe. [Old French *garnement* robe, equipment, from *garnir* to protect, adorn. See GARNISH.]

gar·ner (gär′nər) *v.t.* to gather and store in or as in a granary; accumulate; reap: *The businessman garnered large profits from the venture.* —*n.* **1.** place for storing grain; granary. **2.** store of anything: *a great garner of knowledge.* [Old French *gernier* granary, from Latin *grānārium.*]

gar·net (gär′nit) *n.* **1.** any of a group of hard, vitreous, silicate minerals with a glassy to resinous luster and a transparent to translucent appearance. It occurs in various colors, the deep-red variety being the

at; āpe; cär; end; mē; it; īce; hot; ōld; fôrk; wood; fōōl; oil; out; up; ūse; turn; sing; thin; this; zh in treasure; ə in ago, taken, pencil, lemon, circus.

423

most commonly used as a gem. **2.** deep-red color. [Old French *grenat* the precious stone, going back to Latin *grānātum* pomegranate; stone probably so called because of its similarity in color and shape to the seeds of the pomegranate.]

gar·nish (gär′nish) *v.t.* **1.** to decorate; embellish; trim: *The queen's robes were garnished with gems and fur.* **2.** to decorate (food) with something that adds color or flavor: *The fish was garnished with lemon slices.* **3.** to garnishee. —*n.* **1.** something placed on or around served food to enhance its appearance and flavor: *to serve steak with a garnish of parsley.* **2.** decoration; embellishment; trimming. [Old French *garniss-*, a stem of *garnir* to protect, equip, adorn; of Germanic origin.]

gar·nish·ee (gär′ni shē′) **-nish·eed, -nish·ee·ing.** *v.t.* **1.** to attach (a debtor's money or property in the possession or control of another person) by legal authority. **2.** to warn (a person in control or possession of a defendant's money or property) to hold that money or property pending settlement of the suit. —*n.* one served with a garnishment.

gar·nish·ment (gär′nish mənt) *n.* **1.** decoration; embellishment; trimming. **2.** warning to a person in control or possession of money or property belonging to a defendant to hold that money or property pending settlement of the suit. **3.** warning or summons to a person to appear in court in an action in which he is not a party.

gar·ni·ture (gär′ni chər) *n.* that which garnishes; decoration; embellishment; trimming. [French *garniture*, from *garnir* to provide, adorn; of Germanic origin.]

Ga·ro·fa·lo (gä rō′fä lō′) *n.* whirlpool in the Strait of Messina, believed to be the Charybdis mentioned in Homer's *Odyssey*.

ga·rotte (gə rot′, -rōt′) *n.* garrote. —*v.t.,* **-rot·ted, rot·ting.** to garrote. —**ga·rot′ter,** *n.*

gar·ret (gar′it) *n.* uppermost floor or room of a house directly below the roof; attic. [Old French *garite* watchtower, place of refuge, from *garir* to defend; of Germanic origin.]

Gar·rick, David (gar′ik) 1717–79, English actor, theater manager, and playwright.

gar·ri·son (gar′ə sən) *n.* **1.** military post. **2.** soldiers stationed in a town or post. —*v.t.* **1.** to station soldiers in (a town or post). **2.** to station (soldiers) in a garrison: *The army garrisoned a battalion in the captured town.* [Old French *garison* defense, provision, from *garir* to defend; of Germanic origin.]

Gar·ri·son, William Lloyd (gar′ə sən) 1805–79, U.S. editor and abolitionist.

gar·rote (gə rot′, -rōt′) *also,* **ga·rotte.** *n.* **1.** former Spanish method of execution by strangulation with a cord or an iron collar tightened by a screw. **2.** cord or collar used. **3.** strangling, esp. with the intent of robbing. —*v.t.,* **-rot·ed, -rot·ing.** **1.** to execute with a garrote. **2.** to strangle, esp. with the intent of robbing. [Spanish *garrote* cudgel to twist cord, method of execution by strangling; possibly of Celtic origin.] —**gar·rot′er,** *n.*

gar·ru·li·ty (gə rōō′lə tē) *n.* quality of being garrulous; talkativeness.

gar·ru·lous (gar′ə ləs, gar′yə-) *adj.* given to too much talking, esp. about unimportant matters; talkative; loquacious. [Latin *garrulus,* from *garrīre* to chatter.] —**gar′ru·lous·ly,** *adv.* —**gar′ru·lous·ness,** *n.* —**Syn.** see **talkative.**

gar·ter (gär′tər) *n.* **1.** band or strap, usually elastic, worn to hold up a stocking or sock. **2. Garter. a.** see **Order of the Garter. b.** badge of this order. **c.** membership in this order. —*v.t.* to fasten or support with a garter. [Dialectal Old French *gartier* band to support hose, from *garet* bend of the knee; probably of Celtic origin.]

garter snake, any of a group of harmless, brownish or greenish snakes, genus *Thamnophis,* found in North and Central America, typically having yellow stripes along the body. Length: to 2 feet.

Gar·y (gâr′ē; gar′ē) *n.* city in northwestern Indiana. Pop. (1970), 175,415.

gas (gas) *pl.,* **gas·es.** *n.* **1.** form of matter characterized by the ability of its atoms or molecules to move about readily and independently. It has no definite shape or volume and expands to fill its container. Distinguished from **solid** and **liquid. 2.** any gas or gaseous mixture other than air. **3.** any combustible gas or gaseous mixture used for heating or lighting, as natural gas. **4.** any gas or gaseous mixture used as an anesthetic, as laughing gas. **5.** chemical substance, as mustard gas or tear gas, which is intentionally dispersed in the air to irritate, stupefy, or kill. **6.** *Informal.* gasoline. **7.** *Mining.* combustible mixture of firedamp with air. **8.** presence of gas in the stomach or intestines; flatulence. **9.** *Slang.* anything extraordinary, exciting, or satisfying. **10.** *Slang.* empty or boastful talk: *He gave us a lot of gas about how important he is.* **11. to step on the gas. a.** to press or step down on the accelerator of a vehicle. **b.** to hurry; go faster. —*v.t.,* **gassed, gas·sing. 1.** to irritate, stupefy, or kill with gas, as in chemical warfare. **2.** to supply with gas or gasoline (often with *up*): *Dad gassed the car up before the long drive.* **3.** to treat with gas: *to gas lime with chlorine.* —*v.i.* **1.** to give off gas. **2.** *Slang.* to talk idly or boastfully. [Dutch *gas* this

form of matter (that is not liquid or solid), adaptation of Greek *chaos* empty space, chaos, by J. B. van Helmont, 1577–1644, Belgian chemist.]

gas burner, part of a gas fixture at which the gas is burned, esp. one which distributes the flame.

gas chamber, sealed room in which people are executed by poisonous gas.

Gas·con (gas′kən) *n.* **1.** member or close descendant of the people of Gascony. **2.** dialect of the French language spoken in Gascony. **3. gascon.** boastful person; braggart. —*adj.* of or relating to Gascony, its people, or their language. [French *Gascon,* going back to Latin *Vasco* one of the people inhabiting the Pyrenees in ancient times.]

gas·con·ade (gas′kə nād′) *n.* boastful or blustering talk. —*v.i.* **-ad·ed, -ad·ing.** to boast or bluster. [French *gasconnade* boasting, from *gascon* (see GASCON); because the Gascons were noted for bragging.]

Gas·co·ny (gas′kə nē) *n.* historic region and former province of southwestern France.

gas engine, internal combustion engine, esp. one that uses natural gas or gases derived from petroleum.

gas·e·ous (gas′ē əs, gash′əs) *adj.* of, relating to, of the nature of, or in the form of gas.

gas fitter, person who assembles, installs, and repairs gas pipes and fixtures.

gash (gash) *n.* long, deep cut or wound: *The doctor closed the gash with ten stitches.* —*v.t.* to make a gash in: *The swimmer gashed his foot on a rock.* [Earlier *garsh,* from Old French *garser* to scarify, incise, possibly going back to Late Latin *charaxāre* to scratch, engrave, from Greek *charassein.*]

gas·i·fy (gas′ə fī′) **-fied, -fy·ing.** *v.t., v.i.* to make into or become a gas. —**gas′i·fi·ca′tion,** *n.*

gas jet 1. burner or nozzle of a gas fixture at which the gas is burned. **2.** flame of gas issuing from this.

gas·ket (gas′kit) *n.* **1.** ring, disk, or other piece of packing used to make a joint or closure, as in a pipe or piston, leakproof. **2.** *Nautical.* cord or rope used to secure furled sails to the yard or boom. [French *garcette* little girl, thin rope, diminutive of *garce* wench, feminine of Old French *gars* boy; possibly of Germanic origin.]

gas·light (gas′līt′) *n.* **1.** light produced by the burning of illuminating gas. **2.** gas burner or gas jet.

gas main, large underground pipe which carries gas to smaller subsidiary pipes.

gas mantle, tube, made by impregnating fabric with oxides of cerium and thorium, which glows brightly when placed over a hot gas flame. Also, **man′tle.**

gas mask, mask worn over the mouth, nose, and eyes, designed to filter contaminated air to make it suitable for breathing.

gas·o·line (gas′ə lēn′, gas′ə lēn′) *also,* **gas·o·lene** *n.* highly flammable and volatile fuel consisting of a mixture of hydrocarbons, used chiefly for internal-combustion engines. It is obtained by cracking or distilling petroleum, by polymerization, or by condensing natural gas. [GAS + -*ol* (suffix from Latin *oleum* oil) + -INE².]

gas·om·e·ter (gas om′ə tər) *n.* **1.** apparatus for holding and measuring gas. **2.** tank or reservoir for storing gas. [French *gazomètre,* from *gaz* gas, from Dutch *gas* (see GAS) + *mètre* (see -METER).]

gasp (gasp) *v.i.* to draw in the breath suddenly, sharply, or with difficulty, as in fear, surprise, or exhaustion. —*v.t.* to utter while gasping: *The excited child gasped the news to us.* —*n.* **1.** act or instance of gasping. **2. at the last gasp.** at the point of death; at the end. [Old Norse *geispa* to yawn.]

gas station, establishment that sells gasoline, oil, and other items necessary to keep motor vehicles operating, often having repair facilities as well. Also, **filling station, service station.**

gas·sy (gas′ē) **-si·er, -si·est.** *adj.* **1.** full of or containing gas. **2.** resembling or of the nature of gas.

Gas·to·ni·a (gas tō′nē ə) *n.* city in southern North Carolina. Pop. (1970), 47,142.

gas·tric (gas′trik) *adj.* of, relating to, or near the stomach. [Greek *gastr-,* stem of *gastēr* stomach + -IC.]

gastric juice, digestive fluid secreted by glands in the stomach lining, containing hydrochloric acid and certain enzymes, such as pepsin and rennin.

gas·trin (gas′trin) *n.* hormone that stimulates the flow of gastric juice.

gas·tri·tis (gas trī′tis) *n.* inflammation of the mucous membrane lining the stomach, characterized by nausea and cramplike pain. [Modern Latin *gastritis,* from Greek *gastēr* stomach + -ITIS.]

gas·tro·in·tes·ti·nal (gas′trō in tes′tən əl) *adj.* of or relating to the stomach and the intestines, considered collectively.

gas·tro·nom·ic (gas′trə nom′ik) *adj.* of or relating to gastronomy. Also, **gas′tro·nom′i·cal.**

gas·tron·o·my (gas tron′ə mē) *n.* art or science of good eating. [French *gastronomie,* going back to Greek *gastēr* stomach + *nomos* law.]

at; āpe; cär; end; mē; it; īce; hot; ōld; fôrk; wood; fōōl; oil; out; up; ūse; turn; sing; thin; **th**is; zh in treasure; ə in ago, taken, pencil, lemon, circus.

gas·tro·pod (gas′trə pod′) *n.* any of a widespread group of univalved mollusks, class Gastropoda, including the snail, slug, and whelk, that moves by means of a muscular foot on the ventral surface of its body. Most gastropods have a single-chambered, usually spiral, shell. —*adj.* of or relating to gastropods. [Modern Latin *Gasteropoda* (plural), from Greek *gastēr* stomach + *pod-*, stem of *pous* foot.]

gas·tru·la (gas′trə lə) *n.* stage of embryonic development following the blastula, in which the ectoderm, mesoderm, and endoderm are formed. [Modern Latin *gastrula*, diminutive of Greek *gastēr* stomach.]

gas·tru·late (gas′trə lāt′) *-lat·ed, -lat·ing. v.i.* to form a gastrula. —**gas′tru·la′tion,** *n.*

gas well, well producing natural gas.

gat¹ (gat) *Archaic.* a past tense of **get.**

gat² (gat) *n. Slang.* pistol. [Short for GATLING GUN.]

gate (gāt) *n.* **1.** movable barrier, usually swinging on hinges, used to close off a passage, as in a wall or fence. **2.** opening for entrance or exit in a wall or fence; gateway. **3.** structure built on either side and sometimes across the top of such an opening. **4.** *Archaic.* gateway (def. 2). **5.** device to control the flow of a fluid, esp. water, as through a pipe, dam, or lock. **6.a.** number of people who pay to see a sports event, play, or other contest or performance. **b.** total amount of money received from these people: *The race drew in a gate of $2,000.* **7. to get the gate.** *Slang.* to be dismissed, rejected, or sent away. **8.** *Slang.* **to give (someone) the gate.** to dismiss, reject, or send away: *The coach gave him the gate for missing practice.* [Old English *geat* barrier, door, opening.]

gate crasher, one who gains admittance to a party or other private gathering without being invited or to a performance or game without having a ticket.

gate·house (gāt′hous′) *n.* house or other structure built next to or over a gate, used esp. as the keeper's quarters.

gate·keep·er (gāt′kē′pər) *n.* one in charge of a gate.

gate·post (gāt′pōst′) *n.* either of two posts on each side of a gate, to one of which the gate is hinged.

Gates, Ho·ra·tio (gāts; hə rā′shō) 1728–1806, U.S. General during the American Revolutionary War.

Gates·head (gāts′hed′) *n.* city in northeastern England. Pop. (1968 est.), 100,600.

gate·way (gāt′wā′) *n.* **1.** opening for entrance or exit in a wall or fence which is or may be closed with a gate. **2.** means of entering someplace or achieving something: *the gateway to the West, the gateway to happiness.*

gath·er (gath′ər) *v.t.* **1.** to bring together in one place or group: *The general gathered his army and marched forward.* **2.** to bring together from various places or sources; accumulate: *The bird gathered twigs for its nest. He gathered a large fortune before his death.* **3.** to raise or collect by selecting from among various things; cull: *The teacher gathered the best of our essays for the school magazine.* **4.** to pick and harvest, as fruit or crops: *The farmer gathered the corn in August.* **5.** to gain gradually; increase little by little: *The ball gathered speed as it rolled down the hill.* **6.** to learn or realize by observation or reasoning; deduce; infer: *I gather it was he who called. He gathered from the evidence that she was guilty.* **7.** to prepare or collect (something, as one's energies) for an effort: *He gathered his strength for the fight.* **8.** to take and hold; enfold: *She gathered her child in her arms.* **9.** to wrap or draw closer, as a garment: *She gathered the shawl about her shoulders to keep out the wind.* **10.** to draw (cloth) into pleats, folds, or puckers along a line of stitching; shirr: *The drapes were gathered at the top.* **11.** to wrinkle (one's brow): *He gathered his brow in a frown.* **12. to be gathered to one's fathers.** to die. **13. gather up. a.** to pick up and assemble: *The child gathered up his toys and put them away. The repairman gathered up his tools.* **b.** to draw or bring closer together; to make smaller or more compact: *He gathered up the rope and put it into a box.* —*v.i.* **1.** to come together or assemble: *Students gathered in the auditorium.* **2.** to increase by accumulation; collect: *Sweat gathered on his brow.* **3.** to form pus and come to a head, as a boil or sore. —*n.* pleat, fold, or pucker made by gathering cloth. [Old English *gaderian* to bring together, come together, collect, from *geador* together.]

Syn. *v.t.* **1., 2. Gather, assemble, collect** mean to bring together to form a group. **Gather** is the term with the broadest range of application and suggests the bringing together of widely scattered things with no implication of the manner of their subsequent arrangement: *That author is gathering materials for his next book.* **Assemble** suggests a coming together in a purposive manner and is usually used of people who congregate to form a group united in some common interest: *The headmaster assembled the students in the auditorium.* **Collect** implies not only a gradual gathering but also a discriminating selection in accordance with some principle or purpose and an orderly arrangement of what is so gathered: *Joan collects stamps.*

gath·er·ing (gath′ər ing) *n.* **1.** act of one who or that which gathers. **2.** that which is gathered. **3.** meeting, assembly, or crowd. **4.** series of

gathers in a garment or fabric. **5.** boil; abscess. —**Syn. 3.** see **meeting.**

Gat·ling gun (gat′ling) earliest effective machine gun consisting of from six to ten barrels mounted in a circle on a frame, the whole assembly being rotated by a hand crank. [From Richard J. *Gatling,* 1818–1903, its American inventor.]

gauche (gōsh) *adj.* lacking social grace; awkward; boorish; tactless. [French *gauche* left, awkward, from *gauchir* to turn aside, warp; of Germanic origin.]

gau·che·rie (gō′shə rē′) *n.* **1.** quality of being gauche. **2.** gauche act or statement. [French *gaucherie* awkwardness, from *gauche* left, awkward. See GAUCHE.]

Gatling gun

gau·cho (gou′chō) *pl.* **-chos.** *n.* cowboy of the pampas of South America, esp. of mixed Spanish and Indian descent. [Spanish *gaucho* herdsman, horseman, rustic, possibly from Quechua *wáhcha* poor person.]

gaud (gôd) *n.* cheap, tasteless, or showy ornament or trinket. [Old French *gaudir* to rejoice, going back to Latin *gaudēre.*]

gaud·y (gô′dē) **gaud·i·er, gaud·i·est.** *adj.* tastelessly bright or ornate; showy; garish. —**gaud′i·ly,** *adv.* —**gaud′i·ness,** *n.*

gauge (gāj) *also,* **gage.** *n.* **1.** standard measure or scale of measurements. **2.** instrument or device used for measuring or indicating measurements: *a gasoline gauge.* **3.** means of estimating or judging; standard; criterion: *His performance on the test is a gauge of his ability.* **4.a.** distance between two rails on a railroad. The standard U.S. gauge is 56.5 inches. **b.** distance between opposite wheels on an axle, as on an automobile. **5.** diameter of the bore of a gun, esp. a shotgun. —*v.t.,* **gauged, gaug·ing. 1.** to determine accurately the dimensions, amount, force, or capacity of, esp. with a gauge; measure: *to gauge the depth of a well, to gauge the speed of the wind.* **2.** to estimate; judge; appraise: *He gauged the worth of the gem. It was difficult to gauge what his family's reaction would be.* **3.** to make conform to a standard of measurement. [Dialectal Old French *gauge* gauging rod; possibly of Germanic origin.] —**gauge′a·ble,** *adj.* —**gaug′er,** *n.* —**Syn.** *n.* **3.** see **standard.**

Gau·guin, Paul (gō gan′; pōl) 1848–1903, French painter.

Gaul (gôl) *n.* **1.** ancient region in western Europe, consisting of present-day France, Belgium, northern Italy, and parts of Germany, Switzerland, and the Netherlands. **2.** one of the Celtic people who inhabited this region. **3.** Frenchman. [French *Gaule* the country of the Gauls, from Latin *Gallia,* from *Gallus* native of Gaul, Gallic.]

Gaull·ist (gō′list, gô′-) *n.* in French politics, a supporter or follower of Charles de Gaulle.

gaunt (gônt) *adj.* **1.** extremely thin and hollow-eyed, as from hunger or illness; haggard. **2.** desolate, bare, and gloomy; grim; bleak. [Possibly of Scandinavian origin.]

gaunt·let¹ (gônt′lit) *also,* **gant·let. 1.** heavy glove, usually made of leather covered with armor plate or mail, used in medieval times to protect the hand. **2.a.** glove having a long, flaring cuff extending above the wrist. **b.** cuff of such a glove. **3. to take up the gauntlet.** to accept a challenge. **4. to throw or (fling) down the gauntlet.** to challenge, as to combat. [Old French *gauntelet* armored glove, diminutive of *gant* glove; of Germanic origin.]

(def. 1)   (def. 2)
Gauntlets

gaunt·let² (gônt′lit) gantlet¹.

gauss (gous) *pl.,* **gauss.** centimeter-gram-second unit of magnetic induction.

Gau·ta·ma (gō′tə mə, gou′-) *also,* **Go·ta·ma.** Buddha.

Gau·tier, Thé·o·phile (gō tyā′; tā ō fēl′) 1811–72, French poet, critic, and novelist.

gauze (gôz) *n.* **1.** very thin, light-weight cloth woven from any of various fibers, used for such items as bandages, surgical dressings, and curtains. **2.** thin haze, mist, or fog. [French *gaze* light, transparent, thin cloth; supposedly because it first came from GAZA.]

gauz·y (gô′zē) **gauz·i·er, gauz·i·est.** *adj.* resembling gauze; thin; transparent. —**gauz′i·ness,** *n.*

gave (gāv) past tense of **give.**

gav·el (gav′əl) *n.* small mallet used by the person presiding at a trial, meeting, or other gathering to call for attention or order. [Of uncertain origin.]

Gavel

ga·vi·al (gā′vē əl) *n.* large, freshwater reptile, family Gavialidae,

related to and resembling crocodiles and alligators, found along rivers in India and Pakistan. Length: to 21 feet. [French *gavial,* modification of Hindi *ghariyāl* crocodile.]

ga·votte (gə vot′) *n.* **1.** dance of French origin, resembling the minuet, but much faster and livelier. **2.** music for such a dance. [French *gavotte* the dance, from Provençal *gavato,* from *Gavot* native of the Alps; supposedly originally a dance of this people.]

Ga·wain (gä′win, gô′-, gə-wān′) *n.* in Arthurian legend, knight of the Round Table, brother of Sir Gareth, and nephew of King Arthur.

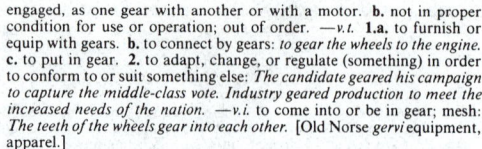
Gavial

gawk (gôk) *v.i. Informal.* to stare stupidly; gape: *They gawked at the unfamiliar sight.* [Possibly modification of obsolete *gaw,* from Old Norse *gā* to heed.]

gawk·y (gô′kē) **gawk·i·er, gawk·i·est.** *adj.* awkward; ungainly. —**gawk′i·ly,** *adv.* —**gawk′i·ness,** *n.*

gay (gā) **gay·er, gay·est.** *adj.* **1.** full of joy and fun; merry; happy. **2.** brightly colored or showy. **3.** given to or full of lightheartedness or pleasure: *They lead a gay life, free from responsibility and worry.* [Old French *gai* merry; possibly of Germanic origin.] —**gay′ness,** *n.*

Gay, John (gā) 1685–1732, English poet and dramatist.

gay·e·ty (gā′i tē) gaiety.

gay·ly (gā′lē) gaily.

gaz. 1. gazette. **2.** gazetteer.

Ga·za (gä′zə, gaz′ə, gā′zə) *n.* historic city in the Gaza Strip. It was once a major Philistine city.

Gaza Strip, territory on the southeastern coast of the Mediterranean Sea, between Egypt and Israel, formerly part of Palestine. Pop. (1967 est.), 450,000.

gaze (gāz) **gazed, gaz·ing.** *v.i.* to look steadily or fixedly, as in admiration or wonder, or with rapt attention. —*n.* steady or fixed look. [Possibly of Scandinavian origin.]

ga·ze·bo (gə zē′bō, -zä′-) *pl.,* **-bos** or **boes.** *n.* summerhouse or similar structure affording a view of the surrounding area.

ga·zelle (gə zel′) *pl.,* **-zelles** or **-zelle.** *n.* any of various graceful antelopes, genus *Gazella,* native to hot, dry regions of northern Africa and southern Asia, having a fawn-colored coat with black and white markings, curving, ridged horns, and large, lustrous eyes. It can run as fast as sixty miles per hour. Height: 2–3 feet at the shoulder. [French *gazelle,* from Arabic *ghazāl.*]

ga·zette (gə zet′) *n.* **1.** newspaper or similar periodical. **2.** official publication, as of a government or institution, esp. any of several journals containing public notices published by the British government. —*v.t.,* **-zet·ted, -zet·ting.** to publish, list, or announce in a gazette. [French *gazette* newspaper, from Italian *gazzetta* originally, coin of little worth (because in sixteenth-century Venice it cost a *gazzetta* (coin) to read a government newspaper), probably diminutive from Latin *gaza* wealth, from Greek *gaza,* from Persian *ganj* treasure.]

gaz·et·teer (gaz′ə tēr′) *n.* dictionary or list of geographical names. [French *gazetier* writer for a gazette, geographical dictionary, from *gazette* newspaper. See GAZETTE.]

G.B., Great Britain.

G clef, treble clef.

Gd, gadolinium.

Gdansk (gə dänsk′) *n.* port city in northern Poland, formerly the free city of Danzig. Pop. (1968), 364,000.

Gdy·nia (gə din′yə) *n.* port city in north-central Poland. Pop. (1968), 179,200.

Ge, germanium.

gear (gēr) *n.* **1.** mechanical assembly of fixed and moving interacting parts for transmitting or changing motion. **2.** device, esp. a wheel, with projections or teeth spaced evenly on its perimeter, designed to mesh with corresponding projections on another such device. **3.** mechanism or part of a mechanism within a machine, performing a specific function: *steering gear.* **4.** any equipment used for a specific purpose: *The fisherman's gear consisted of rods and reels.* **5.** personal belongings; movable property; household effects: *They loaded their gear into the moving van.* **6. in gear. a.** engaged, as one gear with another or with a motor. **b.** in proper working order; ready for use. **7. out of gear. a.** not

Gazelle

engaged, as one gear with another or with a motor. **b.** not in proper condition for use or operation; out of order. —*v.t.* **1.a.** to furnish or equip with gears. **b.** to connect by gears: *to gear the wheels to the engine.* **c.** to put in gear. **2.** to adapt, change, or regulate (something) in order to conform to or suit something else: *The candidate geared his campaign to capture the middle-class vote. Industry geared production to meet the increased needs of the nation.* —*v.i.* to come into or be in gear; mesh: *The teeth of the wheels gear into each other.* [Old Norse *gervi* equipment, apparel.]

Syn. *n.* **4. Gear, equipment, tackle** mean materials used in a specific activity. **Gear** refers to movable professional equipment and paraphernalia as tools, implements, or outfit needed for a particular activity, service, or task: *The plumber stowed all his gear in a canvas bag.* **Equipment** may be applied to a set of materials and external aids designed for use in a particular undertaking and including instruments, supplies, and furnishings: *Twenty porters were needed to carry the equipment of the Himalayan expedition.* **Tackle** may be applied to the usual and necessary equipment and apparatus used in a specific activity or recreation: *Don't forget the fishing tackle on your trip.*

gear·box (gēr′boks′) *n.* transmission, as of an automobile or other vehicle.

gear·ing (gēr′ing) *n.* apparatus for the transmission of motion or power; system of gears.

gear·shift (gēr′shift′) *n.* device for engaging or disengaging any of several sets of gears in a transmission system.

gear train, system of more than one set of gears working in conjunction with one another.

gear·wheel (gēr′hwēl′, -wēl′) *n.* cogwheel.

geck·o (gek′ō) *pl.,* **geck·os** or **geck·oes.** *n.* any of a widespread group of harmless, tropical lizards, family Gekkonidae, having pads on the bottom of the toes covered with minute hooks which enable it to walk on walls and ceilings. [Malay *gēkoq;* from the sound of its cry.]

gee¹ (jē) *interj.* to the right; faster. ▲ used to direct horses, mules, and certain other animals. —*v.t., v.i.,* **geed, gee·ing.** to turn to the right or move faster. [Of uncertain origin.]

gee² (jē) *interj.* used to express enthusiasm or surprise. [Euphemism for JESUS.]

geese (gēs) a plural of **goose.**

Ge·ez (gē ez′, gā-) *n.* Ethiopic.

Ge·hen·na (gə hen′ə) *n.* **1.** in the New Testament, hell. **2.** place of torment and suffering. [Church Latin *gehenna* hell, from Greek *geenna,* from Hebrew *gē'hinnōm* literally, valley of Hinnom (a valley near Jerusalem, where children were sacrificed to the god Moloch).]

Gei·ger counter (gī′gər) electronic device which is used to detect and measure the intensity of ionizing radiation. [From Hans *Geiger,* 1882–1945, German physicist, one of its inventors.]

gei·sha (gā′shə, gē′-) *pl.,* **-shas** or **-sha.** *n.* Japanese girl who has been trained to sing, dance, and provide entertainment in a teahouse. [Japanese *gēisha* artiste, from *gei* art + *sha* person.]

gel (jel) *n.* jellylike, solid substance, formed by a colloidal dispersion of a solid in a liquid. —*v.t., v.i.,* **gelled, gel·ling.** to form into a gel: *Pudding gels when cooled.* [From GELATIN.]

gel·a·tin (jel′ət ən) *also,* **gel·a·tine** (jel′ət ən, ə tēn′) *n.* **1.** colorless, tasteless protein substance obtained from skin, bones, and other animal tissues. It is soluble in hot water and is used in jellies, desserts, and other foods, and in the manufacture of drugs and photographic film. **2.** preparation or product made primarily with or resembling gelatin. [French *gélatine* the protein substance from animal tissues, from Italian *gelatina* jelly, gelatinous substance, from *gelata* jelly, frost, going back to Latin *gelātus,* past participle of *gelāre* to freeze.]

ge·lat·i·nous (jə lat′ən əs) *adj.* **1.** of the nature of or resembling gelatin. **2.** consisting of or containing gelatin.

geld (geld) **geld·ed** or **gelt, geld·ing.** *v.t.* to castrate (a horse or similar animal). [Old Norse *gelda.*]

geld·ing (gel′ding) *n.* gelded animal, esp. a gelded horse.

gel·id (jel′id) *adj.* very cold; icy. [Latin *gelidus* cold, from *gelū* frost.]

gelt (gelt) a past tense and past participle of **geld.**

gem (jem) *n.* **1.** cut and polished precious or, sometimes, semiprecious stone; jewel. **2.** one who or that which is considered perfect, extremely beautiful, or precious: *This novel is a gem.* **3.** muffin. —*v.t.,* **gemmed, gem·ming.** to set or adorn with or as with gems: *Tiny blossoms gemmed the branches of the tree.* [Old French *gemme* jewel, from Latin *gemma* bud, jewel.]

Ge·ma·ra (gə mär′ə, -môr′ə) *n.* commentary on and supplement to the Mishnah, which together form the Talmud. [Aramaic *gemārā* completion.]

gem·i·nate *v.* (jem′ə nāt′; *adj.,* jem′ə nit, -nāt′) **-nat·ed, -nat·ing.** *v.t., v.i.* to make or become double; form into identical pairs. —*adj.* formed or combined in a pair or pairs; coupled. [Latin *geminātus,* past participle of *gemināre* to double, from *geminus* twin, double.] —**gem′i·na′tion,** *n.*

at; āpe; cär; end; mē; it; īce; hot; ōld; fôrk; wood; fōōl; oil; out; up; ūse; turn; sing; thin; this; zh in treasure; ə in ago, taken, pencil, lemon, circus.

Gem·i·ni (jem′ə nī′) *n.,pl.* **1.** constellation in the northern sky containing the bright stars Castor and Pollux, and conventionally depicted as the mythological brothers for whom these stars are named. **2.** third sign of the zodiac. See **zodiac** for illustration. ▲ construed as singular in both definitions. [Latin *geminī* twins, plural of *geminus* twin, double.]

gem·ma (jem′ə) *pl.,* **gem·mae** (jem′ē). *n. Biology.* bud or budlike structure on a plant, that becomes detached and develops into a new individual. [Latin *gemma* bud, jewel.]

gem·mate (jem′āt) **-mat·ed, -mat·ing.** *v.i.* to form or reproduce by gemmae. [Latin *gemmātus,* past participle of *gemmāre* to bud, from *gemma* bud, jewel.] —**gem·ma′tion,** *n.*

gem·mip·a·rous (je mip′ər əs) *adj. Botany.* forming or reproducing by gemmae. [GEMMA + Latin *-parus,* from *parere* to bring forth, produce.]

gem·mule (jem′ūl) *n.* **1.** internal bud composed of several cells inside a heavy coat of organic material, formed by freshwater sponges as a method of reproduction. **2.** gemma. [Latin *gemmula* little bud, diminutive of *gemma* bud.]

gems·bok (gemz′bok′) *pl.,* **-boks** or **-bok.** *n.* swift, South African antelope, *Oryx gazella,* having very long, straight horns, a long, tufted tail, and a sandy-gray coat with striking dark markings on the side and brown and white markings on the face. Height: 46 inches at the shoulder. [Afrikaans *gemsbok* male chamois, from German *Gemsbock,* from *Gemse* chamois (from Late Latin *camox*) + *Bock* male, buck[1]. See CHAMOIS.]

Gemsbok

gem·stone (jem′stōn′) *n.* mineral or petrified material that can be used in jewelry when cut and polished.

gen. 1. gender. **2.** general. **3.** genitive. **4.** genus.

Gen. 1. General. **2.** Genesis.

-gen *suffix* (used to form nouns) **1.** that which produces: *oxygen, estrogen.* **2.** that which is produced: *antigen.* [Greek *-genēs* born, produced, often through French *-gène.*]

gen·darme (zhän′därm) *pl.,* **-darmes** (-därmz). *n.* **1.** armed policeman in France and French-speaking parts of certain other European countries. **2.** *Slang.* any policeman. [French *gendarme,* from *gens d'armes* men at arms, going back to Latin *gēns* nation, people + *dē* from + *arma* weapons.]

gen·der (jen′dər) *n.* **1.** grammatical classification of words, used primarily in Indo-European and Semitic languages, which distinguishes chiefly between masculine and feminine, but which in some languages also includes the classifications neuter, animate, and inanimate. **2.** any one of such classes. **3.** *Informal.* quality or condition of being of the male or female sex; sex. [Old French *gendre* kind, sort, from Latin *genus.*]

gene (jēn) *n.* one of the units located on a chromosome that determine the characteristics an organism inherits from its parent or parents. [Greek *genos* descent, race, and Greek *genea* race, breed.]

ge·ne·al·o·gist (jē′nē ol′ə jist, -al′-, jen′ē-) *n.* one who traces or studies genealogies.

ge·ne·al·o·gy (jē′nē ol′ə jē, -al′-, jen′ē-) *pl.,* **-gies.** *n.* **1.** study of the descent of persons or families from an ancestor or ancestors. **2.** account or chart of such a descent for a particular person or family: *Her genealogy went back to the American Revolution.* **3.** direct descent from an ancestor or progenitor; pedigree; lineage. [Late Latin *geneālogia* account of a descent, from Greek *geneālogiā* tracing a descent, going back to *geneā* race, breed + *-logia* (see -LOGY).] —**ge·ne·a·log·i·cal** (jē′nē ə loj′i kəl, jen′ē-), *adj.* —**ge′ne·a·log′i·cal·ly,** *adv.*

gen·er·a (jen′ər ə) plural of **genus.**

gen·er·al (jen′ər əl) *adj.* **1.** concerned with or affecting all or the whole: *to work for the general good.* **2.** common to or occurring among many or most; widespread; prevalent: *a word in general use, general unrest.* **3.** not limited in scope or application: *a general principle.* **4.** not concerned with details or specifics: *a general idea, to speak in a general way.* **5.** not restricted to one class, type, or group: *general merchandise, a general term for several kinds of heart ailments.* **6.** concerned with or skilled in all branches, as of business or learning; not specialized. **7.** of superior rank; highest; chief. —*n.* **1.a.** in the U.S. Army and Air Force, an officer ranking below general of the army or general of the air force and above lieutenant general. **b.** general officer. **c.** in the U.S. Marine Corps, officer of the highest rank. **2.** head of any of a number of religious orders: *general of the Dominicans.* **3.** *Archaic.* the public; people. **4. in general. a.** for the most part;

commonly. **b.** without regard to specific details. **c.** considering all persons or things mentioned. [Old French *general* universal, Latin *generālis* relating to a species, relating to all, from *genus* kind, sort.]

Syn. *adj.* **1. General, common, universal** mean belonging to, characteristic of, or affecting all or most of a group. **General** stresses extensiveness and broad applicability to all or most of a wide group with possible exceptions: *The article expressed the general opinion about the new administration.* **Common** stresses what belongs typically to or is shared equally among all or most members of a class or group: *Freedom is the common heritage of Americans.* **Universal** is the most emphatic of these terms to describe what is so all-embracing that it applies to all and each one of a group without exception, restriction, or limitation: *Food is a universal need.*

General Assembly 1. highest deliberative assembly of the United Nations, in which every member of the United Nations has one vote. **2.** legislative body of the state of New Jersey.

General Court, legislative body of Massachusetts or New Hampshire.

general delivery 1. department of the post office which handles mail that addressees pick up at a post office window. **2.** mail sent through this department.

gen·er·al·is·si·mo (jen′ər ə lis′ə mō′) *pl.,* **-mos.** *n.* commander in chief of all the military forces of a country, or of several armies in the field. [Italian *generalissimo,* superlative of *generale* a general, from *generale* universal, from Latin *generālis.* See GENERAL.]

gen·er·al·i·ty (jen′ə ral′ə tē) *pl.,* **-ties.** *n.* **1.** undetailed or unspecific statement, phrase, or idea, esp. one that is too broad or vague to be meaningful: *to speak in generalities.* **2.** greater part or number; main body; majority: *The generality of man's problems are usually minor.* **3.** quality or condition of being general.

gen·er·al·i·za·tion (jen′ər ə li zā′shən) *n.* **1.** act or process of generalizing. **2.** that which results from this process, as a general statement.

gen·er·al·ize (jen′ər ə līz′) **-ized, -iz·ing.** *v.i.* **1.** to treat a subject without going into details or specifics; use generalities. **2.** to infer a general rule or principle from particular facts or instances. —*v.t.* **1.** to give a more general form to; state in general terms. **2.** to formulate (a general rule or principle) from particular facts or instances. **3.** to form a general conclusion or principle from.

gen·er·al·ly (jen′ər ə lē) *adv.* **1.** in most cases; usually; as a rule: *We generally walk home.* **2.** for the most part; commonly: *a generally accepted theory.* **3.** without regard to specific details: *Generally speaking, the book was good.*

general officer, in the U.S. Army, Air Force, or Marine Corps, any officer holding a rank above that of a colonel.

general of the air force, in the U.S. Air Force, officer of the highest rank.

general of the army, in the U.S. Army, officer of the highest rank.

general paresis, disease of the brain caused by syphilis and characterized by progressive loss of physical and mental faculties. Also, **pa·re′sis.**

general practitioner, physician who does not limit his practice to a specific branch of medicine.

gen·er·al·pur·pose (jen′ər əl pur′pəs) *adj.* suitable for more than one use: *a general-purpose machine.*

gen·er·al·ship (jen′ər əl ship′) *n.* **1.** military skill of a general. **2.** skill in management of any sort; leadership. **3.** rank, office, or function of a general.

general staff 1. in the U.S. Army and Marine Corps, group of officers in the headquarters of a division, brigade, or similar or larger unit, who assist their commanders in planning, coordinating, and supervising operations. **2.** any group of individuals who act in an advisory capacity.

general store, store that carries a large variety of items but is not divided into departments.

general strike, strike that involves all the workers in an industry or in an entire area or country.

gen·er·ate (jen′ə rāt′) **-at·ed, -at·ing.** *v.t.* **1.** to produce or cause to be; bring into existence: *to generate electricity in an atomic power plant. Publicity was used to generate interest in the new film.* **2.** to produce (offspring); beget. **3.** *Mathematics.* to trace out a line, surface, plane figure, or solid by moving a point, line, or plane: *A line moved around a circle, remaining always parallel to itself, generates a cylinder.* [Latin *generātus,* past participle of *generāre* to produce.]

gen·er·a·tion (jen′ə rā′shən) *n.* **1.** group of individuals born at about the same time: *the younger generation.* **2.** one step or degree in the line of natural descent, as of people, animals, or plants. Grandfather, father, and son comprise three generations. **3.** period of time between the birth of one generation and the next. **4.** act or process of causing to be or bringing into existence; production: *the generation of new jobs in an expanding economy.* **5.** act or process of producing offspring; procreation. **6.** *Mathematics.* formation of a line, surface, or plane figure by

---

at; āpe; cär; end; mē; it; īce; hot; ōld; fôrk; wood; fō͞ol; oil; out; up; ūse; turn; sing; thin; this; zh in treasure; ə in ago, taken, pencil, lemon, circus.

the motion of a point, line, or plane. [Latin *generātiō* a generating.]

gen·er·a·tive (jĕn'ə rā'tiv) *adj.* **1.** of or relating to production of offspring. **2.** having the ability to produce or bring into existence.

gen·er·a·tor (jĕn'ə rā'tər) *n.* **1.** device that converts mechanical energy into electrical energy. **2.** apparatus for the production of gas or steam. **3.** one who generates. [Latin *generātor* producer.]

gen·er·a·trix (jĕn'ə rā'triks) *pl.*, **gen·er·a·tri·ces** (jĕn'ər ə trī'sēz). *n. Mathematics.* point, line, or plane which generates a line, plane figure, or solid. [Latin *generātrix* she that produces.]

ge·ner·ic (jə nĕr'ik) *adj.* **1.** of, relating to, or applied to a whole kind, class, or group; general. **2.** of, relating to, or characteristic of a genus of plants or animals. [Latin *gener-*, stem of *genus* kind, sort + -IC.]

gen·er·os·i·ty (jĕn'ə rŏs'ə tē) *pl.*, **-ties.** *n.* **1.** quality of being unselfish; willingness to give or share freely. **2.** quality of being noble-minded and free from pettiness; magnanimity; graciousness. **3.** generous act.

gen·er·ous (jĕn'ər əs) *adj.* **1.** characterized by or showing a willingness to give or share freely; unselfish: *a generous gift, a generous donor.* **2.** noble-minded and gracious; free from pettiness; magnanimous: *a generous nature.* **3.** plentiful; abundant: *a generous helping.* **4.** fertile: *generous soil.* **5.** (of wine) rich and strong in flavor. [Latin *generōsus* of noble birth, noble, from *genus* sort, kind, race.] —**gen'er·ous·ly,** *adv.*

gen·e·sis (jĕn'ə sis) *pl.*, **-ses** (-sēz'). *n.* coming into being of anything; origin; creation. [Latin *genesis* birth, creation, from Greek *genesis* origin, creation.]

Gen·e·sis (jĕn'ə sis) *n.* first book of the Old Testament, which gives an account of the origin of the world, of man, and of the Hebrew people.

ge·net·ic (jə nĕt'ik) *adj.* **1.** of or relating to genetics. **2.** of, relating to, or produced by a gene or genes. **3.** of or relating to the origin and development of anything. [From GENESIS, on the model of *antithesis, antithetic.*] —**ge·net'i·cal·ly,** *adv.*

genetic code, arrangement of the sections of a DNA molecule that determines the characteristics of an organism.

genetic engineer, one who is an expert in genetic engineering.

genetic engineering, the biological and biochemical manipulation of genes to create a new microorganism, such as a new virus, or to alter the genetic makeup of a microorganism.

ge·net·i·cist (jə nĕt'ə sist) *n.* expert in genetics.

ge·net·ics (jə nĕt'iks) *n.* branch of biology that deals with the principles of heredity and the inherited similarities and differences found in organisms. ▲ construed as singular.

Ge·ne·va (jə nē'və) *n.* **1.** city in southwestern Switzerland. Pop. (1969 est.), 169,500. **2.** Lake. narrow, crescent-shaped lake between southwestern Switzerland and eastern France. Also, **Lake Leman.**

Geneva Convention, international agreement regulating the wartime treatment of sick and wounded soldiers and prisoners of war. It was first adopted in 1864 at Geneva, Switzerland.

Ge·ne·van (jə nē'vən) *adj.* of, relating to, or characteristic of Geneva or its people. —*n.* native or inhabitant of the city of Geneva.

Gen·e·vieve, Saint (jĕn'ə vēv') A.D. c.422–512, patron saint of Paris.

Genghis Khan (gĕng'gis kän', jĕng'-) *also,* **Jen·ghis Khan, Jen·ghiz Khan.** 1162–1227, Mongol conqueror of central Asia.

gen·ial (jēn'yəl, jē'nē əl) *adj.* **1.** pleasant and cheerful; friendly; cordial: *a genial host.* **2.** favorable to life or growth: *a genial climate.* [Latin *geniālis* pleasant, from Latin *genius* guardian spirit, spirit of social enjoyment.] —**gen'ial·ly,** *adv.* —**ge·ni·al·i·ty** (jē'nē al'ə tē), *n.*

ge·nie (jē'nē) *also,* **jin·ni.** *n.* in Arab folklore and literature, spirit having magic powers, capable of assuming human or animal form. [French *génie* (from Latin *genius* guardian spirit), used to translate Arabic *jinnī* spirit.]

ge·ni·i (jē'nē ī') plural of **genius** (*defs.* 6, 7, 9).

gen·i·tal (jĕn'ə təl) *adj.* of or relating to the sex organs or reproduction. [Latin *genitālis.*]

gen·i·ta·li·a (jĕn'ə tā'lē ə, -tāl'yə) *n.,pl.* genitals.

gen·i·tals (jĕn'ə təlz) *n.,pl.* reproductive organs, esp. the external sex organs.

gen·i·ti·val (jĕn'ə tī'vəl) *adj.* of, in, or belonging to the genitive case.

gen·i·tive (jĕn'ə tiv) *n.* **1.** grammatical case in Latin, Greek, and certain other Indo-European languages that indicates possession, source or origin, or the object of certain prepositions, corresponding to the possessive case in English. **2.** word or construction in this case. —*adj.* of, belonging to, or designating this case. [Latin *(casus) genitīvus* genitive (case); literally, relating to origin.]

gen·i·to·u·ri·nar·y (jĕn'ə tō yoor'ə nĕr'ē) *adj.* of or relating to the genital and urinary organs.

gen·ius (jēn'yəs) *pl.*, *genii* (*defs.* 1–5, 8) **ge·ni·us·es** (*defs.* 6, 7, 9) **ge·ni·i,** *n.* **1.** extraordinary mental power, esp. as shown by creative or inventive achievement in science or the arts: *Leonardo da Vinci was a man of genius.* **2.a.** one who has such power: *Beethoven was a genius.* **b.** person having a very high intelligence quotient. **2.** great aptitude or talent for a particular thing: *She has a genius for drawing.* **4.** one who

has such an aptitude: *He is a genius at diplomatic negotiations.* **5.** distinctive character or spirit, as of a nation, age, group, or institution: *the genius of Christianity.* **6.** guardian spirit, as of a person or place. **7.** either of two warring spirits, one good and one evil, assumed to be fighting for control over one's fate. **8.** one who exerts a powerful influence over another: *an evil genius.* **9.** supernatural being; spirit; jinn. [Latin *genius* guardian spirit, talent, inclination.]

Gen·o·a (jĕn'ō ə) *n.* port city in northwestern Italy. Pop. (1968) 843,632. Also, *Italian,* **Ge·no·va** (jĕ'nō vä').

gen·o·cide (jĕn'ō sīd') *n.* deliberate and methodical annihilation of a national or racial group. [Greek *genos* race + -CIDE[1].] —**gen'o·cid'al,** *adj.*

Gen·o·ese (jĕn'ō ēz' -ēs') *pl.*, **-ese.** *n.* member or recent descendant of the people of Genoa. —*adj.* of or relating to Genoa or its people.

gen·o·type (jĕn'ə tīp') *n.* **1.** hereditary constitution or genetic makeup of an organism. Opposed to **phenotype.** **2.** group or class of organisms having the same genetic makeup. [Greek *genos* origin, race, kind + TYPE.]

gen·re (zhän'rə; *French* zhän'rə) *n.* **1.** kind; type; sort. **2.** particular class or style of work in literature or art: *O. Henry was a master of the genre of the short story.* **3.** style of painting depicting scenes and events from everyday life. —*adj.* being or relating to a genre: *a genre painting. The western is a genre film.* [French *genre* kind, style, from Latin *genus* kind, sort.]

gens (jenz) *pl.*, **gen·tes** (jĕn'tēz). *n.* **1.** in ancient Rome, a group of families descended from a common male ancestor and united by a common name and by certain religious, social, and political functions. **2.** group of individuals related through a common ancestor in the male line and sharing the same surname; tribe; clan. [Latin *gēns.*]

gent (jent) *n. Slang.* gentleman.

Gent (KHent) *Flemish.* Ghent.

gen·teel (jen tēl') *adj.* **1.** polite in manner or behavior; well-bred or refined. **2.** of, relating to, or suitable for those who are well-bred or refined. **3.** refined or polite to the point of excessiveness or affectation. [Old French *gentil* nobly born, from Latin *gentīlis* of the same clan, from *gēns* clan. Doublet of GENTILE, GENTLE, JAUNTY.] —**gen·teel'ly,** *adv.* —**gen·teel'ness,** *n.*

gen·tian (jĕn'shən) *n.* any of a large group of plants, genus *Gentiana,* found in temperate and mountainous regions, bearing stalkless leaves and tubular, often blue, flowers. [Latin *gentiāna,* said to be from *Gentius,* an ancient king of Illyria who supposedly discovered its medicinal use.]

gentian violet, dark green powdery or crystalline substance that forms a purple solution used esp. as an antiseptic and as a biological stain.

gen·tile (jĕn'tīl) *also,* **Gen·tile.** *n.* **1.** one who is not a Jew, esp. a Christian as distinguished from a Jew. **2.** among Mormons, one who is not a Mormon. **3.** heathen; pagan. —*adj.* **1.** of, relating to, or designating any people who are not Jewish. **2.** among Mormons, of, relating to, or designating any people who are not Mormon. **3.** heathen; pagan. [Late Latin *gentīlis* heathen, foreign, from Latin *gentīlis* of the same clan, from *gēns* clan. Doublet of GENTEEL, GENTLE, JAUNTY.]

gen·til·i·ty (jen til'ə tē) *pl.*, **-ties.** *n.* **1.** refinement or good manners characteristic of one who is well-bred. **2.** position belonging to the upper classes; social superiority.

gen·tle (jĕn'təl) **-tler, -tlest.** *adj.* **1.** mild and kindly in manner, nature, or tone: *to be gentle when speaking to a young child.* **2.** not severe, rough, or loud; soft; moderate: *the gentle tapping of the rain.* **3.** easily handled; docile; tame: *a gentle horse.* **4.** gradual in rate; not extreme or abrupt: *a gentle slope.* **5.** of good family or birth; wellborn. **6.** characteristic of or like one of good family; respectable; polite; refined. **7.** *Archaic.* chivalrous; noble: *a gentle knight.* [Old French *gentil* nobly born, noble, from Latin *gentīlis* of the same clan, from *gēns* clan. Doublet of GENTEEL, GENTILE, JAUNTY.] —**gen'tle·ness,** *n.* —**gen'tly,** *adv.*

Syn. 2. Gentle, mild, tender[1] indicate a lack of roughness, harshness, violence, or intensity. **Gentle** suggests that emotions or actions are being deliberately controlled: *The doctor bandaged the boy's leg with a gentle touch.* **Mild** implies that the thing is not as rough or harsh as it might have been: *The newspaper editorials contained only mild criticism of the mayor's controversial decision.* **Tender** suggests softness stemming from sympathy or a desire not to disturb or harm: *The mother's tender words soothed the weeping child.*

gen·tle·folk (jĕn'təl fōk') *n.,pl.* people of good family and breeding.

gen·tle·man (jĕn'təl mən) *pl.*, **-men.** *n.* **1.** man who is honorable, courteous, and considerate. **2.** man of good family and high social standing. **3.** any man. ▲ used in the plural as a polite form of address. **4.** man's personal servant; valet. **5.** in English history, a man ranking above a yeoman but below the nobility.

gen·tle·man-farm·er (jĕn'təl mən fär'mər) *n.* man of wealth who owns a farm but usually does not work on it.

gen·tle·man·ly (jent′əl mən lē) *adj.* having the character, behavior, or appearance of a gentleman; courteous; well-bred. —**gen′tle·man·li·ness,** *n.*

gentleman's agreement, unwritten agreement guaranteed only by the honor of the parties involved, and not legally binding. Also, **gentlemen's agreement.**

gentleman's gentleman, man's personal servant; valet.

gen·tle·wom·an (jent′əl woom′ən) *pl.,* **-wom·en.** *n.* **1.** woman of good family and high social standing. **2.** well-mannered, refined woman; lady. **3.** formerly, a woman attending a lady of rank.

gen·try (jen′trē) *n.* **1.** people of good family or high social standing. **2.** class in England ranking below the nobility and above the yeomanry; upper middle class. **3.** people of any particular area, class, or group: *the sporting gentry.* [Earlier *gentrise,* from Old French *genterise* rank, nobility, going back to *gentil* nobly born, noble. See GENTLE.]

gen·u·flect (jen′yoo flekt′) *v.i.* to bend the knee, as in worship or respect. [Late Latin *genuflectere,* from Latin *genū* knee + *flectere* to bend.]

gen·u·flec·tion (jen′yoo flek′shən) *n.* act of bending the knee, as in worship or respect.

gen·u·ine (jen′ū in) *adj.* **1.** actually being what it seems or is claimed to be; real; true: *genuine pearls, a genuine antique.* **2.** actually proceeding from its reputed source or author: *The painting is a genuine Rembrandt.* **3.** free from affectation or hypocrisy; sincere: *a genuine expression of sympathy, a genuine effort to help.* [Latin *genuīnus* native, innate, natural.] —**gen′u·ine·ly,** *adv.* —**gen′u·ine·ness,** *n.*
Syn. 1. Genuine, authentic indicate that something is just what it is supposed to be. **Genuine** suggests that the item may be traced to a source to prove what it really is: *The woman's coat was genuine mink.* **Authentic** implies that facts may be checked for the underlying truth: *This photograph is the only authentic record of how that street looked in 1900.*

ge·nus (jē′nəs) *pl.,* **gen·er·a** or **ge·nus·es.** *n.* **1.** category of plant and animal classification ranking next below the family and next above the species. The scientific designation of an organism or group of related organisms consists of the genus, which is capitalized, followed by the species, which is not capitalized, as *Canis latrans,* the coyote, or *Taraxacum officinale,* the common dandelion. **2.** *Logic.* a class of individuals or things divided into subordinate groups or species. **3.** kind; sort; class. [Latin *genus* kind, sort.]

geo- combining form earth; of the earth: *geology, geography.* [Greek *gē* earth.]

Geo., George.

ge·o·cen·tric (jē′ō sen′trik) *adj.* **1.** as measured or viewed from the earth's center. **2.** based on the idea that the earth is the center of the universe: *a geocentric astronomic system.* Also, **ge′o·cen′tri·cal.** —**ge′o·cen′tri·cal·ly,** *adv.*

ge·o·chem·is·try (jē′ō kem′is trē) *n.* branch of chemistry dealing with the chemical composition of the earth's crust and the chemical changes occurring there. —**ge′o·chem′i·cal,** *adj.* —**ge′o·chem′ist,** *n.*

ge·ode (jē′ōd) *n.* **1.** round stone having a cavity lined with crystals. **2.** the cavity itself. [Latin *geōdēs* a precious stone, from Greek *geōdēs* earthlike, from *gē* earth.]

ge·o·des·ic (jē′ə des′ik, -dē′sik) *n.* shortest line segment that joins two points lying on a surface, esp. a curved surface. Also, **geodesic line.** —*adj.* **1.** of or relating to geodesy. **2.** of or relating to geodesic lines.

geodesic dome, light, strong hemispherical dome, usually made of triangular planes and covered with plastic sheeting.

ge·od·e·sy (jē od′ə sē) *n.* science concerned with determining the shape and dimensions of the earth and with the mapping of large areas of its surface. It employs the methods of surveying and of astronomical and gravitational measurement and observation. [Greek *geōdaisiā* division of the earth, from *gē* earth + *daiesthai* to divide.]

ge·o·det·ic (jē′ə det′ik) *adj.* **1.** of or relating to geodesy. **2.** geodesic. —**ge′o·det′i·cal·ly,** *adv.*

Geof·frey of Mon·mouth (jef′rē; mon′məth) A.D. c.1100–54, English bishop and chronicler.

geog., geography; geographical; geographer.

ge·og·ra·pher (jē og′rə fər) *n.* an expert in or student of geography.

ge·o·graph·i·cal (jē ə graf′i kəl) *adj.* of or relating to geography. Also, **ge′o·graph′ic.** —**ge′o·graph′i·cal·ly,** *adv.*

geographical mile, measure of length equal to 1/60 of a degree of the earth's equator or approximately 6080 feet.

ge·og·ra·phy (jē og′rə fē) *pl.,* **phies.** *n.* **1.** study of the characteristics of particular places on the surface of the earth, and of all the physical and cultural factors affecting these characteristics. Geography includes the study of the earth's natural surface, its climate, the distribution of plant, animal, and human life, and the effects of human activity on an area. **2.** topographical features of a place or region: *the geography of Siberia.* [Latin *geōgraphia* description of the earth's surface, from Greek *geōgraphiā* writing about the earth, from *gē* earth + *graphein* to write.]

geol., geology; geological; geologist.

ge·o·log·i·cal (jē′ə loj′i kəl) *adj.* of or relating to geology. Also, **ge′o·log′ic.** —**ge′o·log′i·cal·ly,** *adv.*

ge·ol·o·gist (jē ol′ə jist) *n.* an expert in or student of geology.

ge·ol·o·gy (jē ol′ə jē) *pl.,* **-gies.** *n.* **1.** science that deals with the earth's structure, composition, and history, including the changes that have taken place on the earth's surface and the processes by which such changes have occurred. ▲ For a record of the earth's geological history, see the table on the following page. **2.** structure and composition of the earth in a given area. [Modern Latin *geologia,* from Greek *gē* earth + *-logiā* (see -LOGY.)]

geom., geometry; geometric; geometrician.

ge·o·mag·net·ic (jē′ō mag net′ik) *adj.* of or relating to the magnetic properties of the earth. —**ge′o·mag′ne·tism,** *n.*

ge·om·e·ter (jē om′ə tər) *n.* geometrician. [Latin *geōmetrēs,* from Greek *geōmetrēs* one who measures land.]

ge·o·met·ric (jē′ə met′rik) *adj.* **1.** of or relating to geometry. **2.** consisting of or decorated by straight lines, angles, circles, triangles, or similar forms. Also, **ge′o·met′ri·cal.** —**ge′o·met′ri·cal·ly,** *adv.*

ge·om·e·tri·cian (jē om′ə trish′ən, jē′ə mə-) *n.* an expert in or student of geometry.

geometric mean *Mathematics.* the *n*th root of the product of *n* numbers. The geometric mean of 3, 6, and 12 is the cube root of 216, or 6.

geometric progression *Mathematics.* series in which each number other than the first is the product of the preceding number and a constant factor. 1½, 3, 6, 12, and 24 is a geometric progression, as is 1/3, 1/9, 1/27. Distinguished from **arithmetic progression.**

ge·om·e·try (jē om′ə trē) *pl.,* **-tries.** *n.* **1.** branch of mathematics that deals with the properties, measurements, and relations of points, lines, angles, plane figures, and solids. **2.** particular system of geometry. **3.** shape or design: *the geometry of a building.* [Old French *geometrie* this branch of mathematics, from Latin *geōmetria,* from Greek *geōmetriā,* from *geō* + *-metriā* measurement.]

ge·o·mor·phol·o·gy (jē′ō môr fol′ə jē) *n.* science that deals with the physical features of the surface of the earth and the geological processes by which they are produced. —**ge′o·mor′pho·log′i·cal,** *adj.*

ge·o·phys·ics (jē′ō fiz′iks) *n.* branch of earth science dealing with the physical nature, motions, atmosphere, and hydrosphere of the earth. It includes seismology, oceanography, meteorology, and geodesy. —**ge′o·phys′i·cal,** *adj.* —**ge′o·phys′i·cist,** *n.*

ge·o·pol·i·tics (jē′ō pol′ə tiks) *n.* **1.** study of the effects of physical geography on politics. **2.** any political doctrine, as in Nazi Germany, asserting the right of aggressive expansion for geographic reasons. —**ge′o·po·lit′i·cal,** *adj.* —**ge′o·pol′i·ti′cian,** *n.*

George (jôrj) **1.** David Lloyd. see Lloyd George. **2.** Henry. 1839–97, U.S. economist and journalist. **3.** Saint. died A.D. c.303, Christian martyr; patron saint of England. **4.** Lake. lake in eastern New York.

George I **1.** 1660–1727, king of England from 1714 to 1727. He was the first king from the house of Hanover. **2.** 1845–1913, king of Greece from 1863 to 1913.

George II **1.** 1683–1760, king of England from 1727 to 1760 and son of George I. **2.** 1890–1947, king of Greece from 1922 to 1923, and from 1935 to 1947.

George III. 1738–1820, king of England from 1760 to 1820 and grandson of George II.

George IV, 1762–1830, king of England from 1820 to 1830 and son of George III.

George V, 1865–1936, king of England from 1910 to 1936 and son of Edward VII.

George VI, 1895–1952, king of England from 1936 to 1952 and son of George V.

George·town (jôrj′toun′) *n.* capital and largest city of Guyana, a port on the northern coast of the country. Pop. (1969), 97,190.

George Town, *also,* **George·town.** see Penang.

Geor·gette (jôr jet′) *n.* sheer lightweight silk fabric having a pebbly, crepe-like surface, used for such items as dresses and blouses. Also, **Georgette crepe.** [From Madame *Georgette* de la Plante, famous nineteenth-century French dressmaker.]

Geor·gia (jôr′jə) *n.* **1.** state in the southeastern United States. Capital, Atlanta. Area, 58,876 sq. mi. Pop. (1970), 4,589,575. Abbrev., **Ga.** **2.** republic of the Soviet Union, in the southwestern part of the country, bordering Turkey and the Black Sea, formerly an independent country. Official name: **Georgian Soviet Socialist Republic.** Area, approx. 26,900 sq. mi. Pop. (1967 est.), 4,611,000.

Geor·gian (jôr′jən) *adj.* **1.** of or relating to the reigns of the first four Georges, kings of England from 1714 to 1830. **2.** of, relating to, or designating the style of architecture, art, or decoration of this period. **3.** of or relating to the state of Georgia or the republic of Georgia. —*n.* **1.** native or inhabitant of the state of Georgia or the republic of Georgia. **2.** person living in England during the Georgian period.

STANDARD GEOLOGICAL TIME SCALE

Years Ago	Time Units			Events and Characteristics*
10 thousand	QUARTER-NARY PERIOD		Recent or Holocene epoch	Warm climate melts glaciers. Civilization spreads and flourishes.
2 million			Pleistocene epoch	The Ice Ages. Glaciers advance and retreat many times in North America and Europe. Early man appears.
	CENOZOIC ERA	TERTIARY PERIOD	Pliocene epoch	Many of the world's mountain ranges are uplifted. *Throughout the Cenozoic the land masses drift toward their Holocene positions. Separation of Australia from Antarctica and of North America from northern Europe is completed. India collides with Asia, forming Himalayas.*
11 million			Miocene epoch	Tremendous volcanic activity. Spread of grasses and grazing animals. Birds important.
25 million			Oliogocene epoch	Monkeys and apes appear. Tropical forests throughout the world.
40 million			Eocene epoch	Early horses, rhinoceroses, and camels appear.
58 million			Paleocene epoch	Beginning of Age of Mammals as first placental mammals appear. Flowering plants are dominant.
70 million	MESOZOIC ERA		Cretaceous period	Intense environmental changes accompany the building of mountains and retreat of seas. Dinosaurs and many other species become extinct. Rocky Mountains form. *South Atlantic Ocean opens as South America completes separation from Africa.*
135 million			Jurassic period	Height of Age of Reptiles, particularly dinosaurs. First known birds and flowering plants. Much of Europe and Asia submerged. *North America drifts away from Africa and Europe. Africa and South America begin to separate.*
190 million			Triassic period	Dinosaurs appear and become dominant. Widespread formation of sandstone as newly formed mountains are eroded; much volcanic activity. *Pangaea begins to split into two great land masses, Laurasia and Gondwana.*
225 million	PALEOZOIC ERA		Permian period	Mammal-like reptiles and coniferlike plants appear. Many species become extinct because of environmental changes after vast upheavals of the earth's crust. *There is a single great land mass called Pangaea (all lands).*
280 million		CARBON-IFEROUS PERIOD	Pennsylvanian subperiod	Land mostly low-lying and covered with lush, coal-forming vegetation in swamps. In the Pennsylvanian, or Upper Carboniferous, reptiles appear, and amphibians and insects are abundant.
305 million			Mississippian subperiod	
345 million			Devonian period	Amphibians, first-known insects and spiders, and forests (tree ferns) appear. Urals and Appalachians begin to form.
395 million			Silurian period	Land plants (club mosses) appear. Limestone deposited in widespread seas. Mountain-building in western Europe and northern Siberia at end of period.
430 million			Ordovician period	Corals, sponges, shellfish, and first vertebrates (fish) appear. Beginning of mountain formation in New England near end of period.
500 million			Cambrian period	Animals develop hard shells and skeletons that remain as fossils. All invertebrate phyla appear. Land areas covered by sea during much of the period.
570 million	**PRECAMBRIAN ERA**			Since Precambrian rocks are strongly metamorphosed and often buried by younger rocks, little is known of the long history of these eras. Imprints of algae have been found on all continents, but otherwise fossilized plant and animal remains are rare.
4.5 billion				THE ORIGIN OF THE EARTH

*Italicized statements describe movements of the continents about the surface of the earth, called continental drift. The dates and the sequence shown for these movements are tentative.

Georgian Bay, large northeastern arm of Lake Huron, in Ontario, Canada.

ge·o·tax·is (jē'ō tak'sis) *n.* involuntary movement of an organism 'in response to the force of gravity. —**ge·o·tac·tic** (jē'ō tak'tic), *adj.* —**ge'o·tac'ti·cal·ly,** *adv.*

ge·o·ther·mal (jē'ō thur'məl) *adj.* of or relating to the heat of the earth's interior. Also, **ge'o·ther'mic.**

ge·ot·ro·pism (jē ot'rə piz'əm) *n.* involuntary movement or growth of an organism in response to the force of gravity. **Positive geotropism** is a tendency to move or grow toward the earth's gravitational pull, as the roots of a plant do. **Negative geotropism** is a tendency to move or grow away from the earth's gravitational pull, as plant stems do. [GEO- + Greek *tropē* turning + -ISM.] —**ge·o·trop·ic** (jē'ə trop'ik), *adj.* —**ge'o·trop'i·cal·ly,** *adv.*

Geranium

ger., gerund.

Ger. 1. German. **2.** Germany.

ge·ra·ni·um (jə rā'nē əm) *n.* **1.** any of a group of plants, genus *Pelargonium,* widely cultivated for their showy clusters of red, pink, or white flowers. **2.** any of various other plants of the geranium family, having lobed leaves and small, usually white or purple flowers. **3.** flower of any of those plants. [Latin *geranium* cranesbill, from Greek *geranion,* from *geranos* crane; because its seed pod is shaped like a crane's bill.]

ger·bil (jûr'bil) *also,* **ger·bille.** *n.* any of various burrowing rodents, genus *Gerbillus,* native to desert regions of southern Africa and Asia, having a slender, tufted tail and a short, soft coat that is usually gray, brown, or reddish. Length: to 9 inches, including the tail. [French *gerbille,* from Modern Latin *gerbillus,* diminutive of *gerboa, jerboa.* See JERBOA.]

ger·fal·con (jûr fal'kən, -fôl'-) gyrfalcon.

ger·i·at·rics (jer'ē at'riks) *n.* branch of medicine that deals with the physiology, diseases, and hygiene of old age and aging. ▲ construed as singular. [Greek *gēras* old age + *iātros* physician + -ICS.] —**ger'·i·at'ric,** *adj.* —**ger·i·a·tri·cian** (jer'i·at'rist, n.

germ (jûrm) *n.* **1.** any microorganism, esp. one that causes disease. **2.** rudimentary stage in the development of an organism. **3.** rudimentary form of anything; initial stage: *the germ of a plan.* [French *germe* rudimentary stage of an organism or a thing, from Latin *germen* offshoot, embryo.]

ger·man (jûr'mən) *adj.* **1.** having the same parents. **2.** having the same grandparents. ▲ placed after the noun it modifies and connected by a hyphen: *brother-german, cousin-german.* [Old French *germain* having the same parents, from Latin *germānus.*]

Ger·man (jûr'mən) *adj.* of or relating to Germany, its people, their language, or their culture. —*n.* **1.** member or recent descendant of the people of Germany. **2.** Germanic language of the Indo-European family of languages, spoken predominantly in Germany, Austria, and parts of Switzerland. It includes the subdivisions High German and Low German. [Latin *Germānus* of the Germans, a German; possibly of Celtic origin.]

German Democratic Republic, East Germany.

ger·man·der (jər man'dər) *n.* any of a group of plants, genus *Teucrium,* of the mint family, bearing bluish, white, or purple flowers. [Old French *germandree,* through Latin, going back to Greek *chamaidrŷs* literally, tree on the ground.]

ger·mane (jər mān') *adj.* directly related; pertinent; relevant: *The speaker's comments were in no way germane to the issue.* [Form of GERMAN.] —**Syn.** see pertinent.

Ger·man·ic (jər man'ik) *adj.* **1.** German. **2.** Teutonic. —*n.* branch of the Indo-European language family that includes English, German, Dutch, and Flemish in its western division, Norwegian, Swedish, Danish, and Icelandic in its northern division, and the extinct Gothic language in its eastern division.

Ger·man·ism (gûr'mə niz'əm) *n.* **1.** word, phrase, or usage originating in Germany or peculiar to the German language. **2.** custom or belief characteristic of or peculiar to Germany and its people. **3.** devotion to or support of Germany and its institutions.

ger·ma·ni·um (jər mā'nē əm) *n.* grayish-white metallic element, widely used in the manufacture of semiconductor devices, such as transistors. Symbol: Ge See **element** for table. [Modern Latin *germanium,* from Latin *Germānia* land of the Germans.]

Ger·man·ize (gûr'mə nīz') -ized, -iz·ing. *v.t.* **1.** to cause to conform to or acquire German traits, institutions, or beliefs: *Three years of living in Berlin had completely Germanized him.* **2.** *Archaic.* to translate into German. —*v.i.* to conform to or acquire German characteristics or institutions. —**Ger'man·i·za'tion,** *n.*

German measles, contagious disease usually producing a pink blotchy rash. It is most common in young people and is esp. serious for women early in pregnancy. Also, **ru·bel'la.**

German shepherd, intelligent, wolflike dog of a breed developed in Germany, having a thick coat of black, brown, or gray fur, often trained for use as a watchdog, guard dog, or Seeing Eye dog. Height: 25 inches at the shoulder. Also, **police dog, Al·sa'tian.**

German shepherd

German silver, nickel silver.

Ger·man·town (jûr'mən toun') *n.* section of Philadelphia, the site of a Revolutionary War battle in which the British were victorious.

Ger·ma·ny (jûr'mə nē) *n.* country in north-central Europe, divided into West Germany and East Germany since 1949. Area, approx. 138,000 sq. mi. Pop. (1966 est.), 76,000,000. Also, *German,* **Deutsch'land'.**

germ cell, male or female reproductive cell; sperm or egg. Distinguished from **somatic cell.**

ger·mi·cide (jûr'mə sīd') *n.* agent that kills germs, esp. those causing disease. [GERM + -CIDE².] —**ger'mi·cid'al,** *adj.*

ger·mi·nal (jûr'mən əl) *adj.* **1.** of, relating to, or characteristic of germs or germ cells. **2.** in a very early stage of development: *a germinal idea.*

ger·mi·nant (jûr'mə nənt) *adj.* that germinates; sprouting.

ger·mi·nate (jûr'mə nāt') -nat·ed, -nat·ing. *v.i.* to start to grow or develop, as from a seed. —*v.t.* to cause to sprout. [Latin *germinātus,* past participle of *germināre* to sprout, bud, from *germen* a sprout, bud.] —**ger'mi·na'tive,** *adj.* —**ger'mi·na'tion, ger'mi·na'tor,** *n.*

germ layer, any of the three principal layers of embryonic cells from which the various tissues and bodily systems develop. These layers are the ectoderm, mesoderm, and endoderm.

germ plasm, substance in germ cells that contains the material of heredity.

germ theory, theory that infectious and contagious diseases are caused and transmitted by the activity of microorganisms.

germ warfare, biological warfare.

Ge·ron·i·mo (jə ron'ə mō') *n.* c.1829–1909, Apache Indian chief.

ger·on·tol·o·gy (jer'ən tol'ə jē) *n.* scientific study of the processes and problems of aging. —**ger·on·to·log·i·cal** (jə ront'əl oj'i kəl), *adj.* —**ger'on·tol'o·gist,** *n.*

ger·ry·man·der (jer'ē man'dər, ger'-) *n.* **1.** arrangement of voting districts in a state or other political unit to give one political party an unfair advantage. **2.** district arranged in this way. —*v.t.* **1.** to subject (a state or other political unit) to a gerrymander. **2.** to manipulate unfairly in order to gain an advantage. [Elbridge *Gerry,* 1744–1814, U.S. political leader + (SALA)MANDER; from the salamanderlike shape of a Massachusetts election district rearranged in 1812 during Gerry's governorship of the state.]

Gersh·win, George (gursh'win) 1898–1937, U.S. composer.

ger·und (jer'ənd) *n.* verb form ending in *-ing* that functions as a noun. In the sentence *Swimming is good exercise,* the word *swimming* is a gerund. [Late Latin *gerundium* verb form that functions as a noun, going back to Latin *gerendum* that which is to be done, gerund of *gerere* to do.] —**ge·run·di·al** (jə run'dē əl), *adj.*

ge·run·dive (jə run'div) *n.* verbal adjective in Latin that is similar to a gerund in form, used primarily to express necessity or obligation. [Late Latin *gerundīvus (modus)* gerund (mood), from *gerundium.* See GERUND.]

Ge·ry·on (jēr'ē ən, ger'-) *n.* Greek Mythology. a three-bodied, winged giant killed by Hercules, who then stole his cattle.

ges·so (jes'ō) *n.* **1.** mixture of plaster of Paris and glue or other materials used as a ground in painting or gilding or in the making of bas-reliefs and plaster casts and molds. **2.** prepared surface or ground for painting made of such a mixture. [Italian *gesso* chalk, plaster, from Latin *gypsum* chalk. See GYPSUM.]

gest (jest) *also,* **geste.** *n.* Archaic. **1.** notable deed or exploit. **2.** tale of achievement or adventure, esp. one in verse; romance. [Old French *geste* deed, exploit, from Latin *gesta* deeds.]

ge·stalt (gə shtält', -shtôlt') *pl.* **-stalts** or **-stalten** (-shtält'ən, -stôlt'-). *also,* **Ge·stalt.** *n.* unified pattern of experience whose properties cannot be derived from the parts of the whole or from their relationships. [German *Gestalt* form, shape, aspect.]

Gestalt psychology, school of psychology based on the belief that experience is a unified pattern and is more than the sum of its smaller, independent events. It emphasizes that an event cannot be analyzed in isolation because of its interaction with other events and their relation to the whole.

Ge·sta·po (gə stä'pō) *n.* secret police force of Nazi Germany. [Abbreviation of German *Ge(heime) Sta(ats)po(lizei)* secret state police.]

ges·tate (jes'tāt) -tat·ed, -tat·ing. *v.i.* to carry developing young in

the uterus: *Dogs gestate for approximately sixty days.* [From GESTA-TION.]

ges·ta·tion (jes tā′shən) *n.* **1.** period from conception to birth during which the unborn young are carried in the uterus; pregnancy. **2.** development or conception in the mind, as of a project, plan, or idea. [Latin *gestātiō* a carrying.] —**ges·ta′tion·al,** *adj.*

ges·tic·u·late (jes tik′yə lāt′) **-lat·ed, -lat·ing.** *v.i.* to make or use emphatic or expressive gestures, as in speaking. —*v.t.* to indicate or express by gestures. [Latin *gesticulātus,* past participle of *gesticulārī* to make gestures.] —**ges·tic′u·la′tor,** *n.*

ges·tic·u·la·tion (jes tik′yə lā′shən) *n.* **1.** emphatic or expressive gesture. **2.** act of gesticulating.

ges·ture (jes′chər) *n.* **1.** movement of the head, body, or limbs, used to express a thought or feeling or to emphasize what is said: *He used hand gestures to indicate distress.* **2.** something said or done for effect or as a symbol: *to shake hands as a gesture of friendship.* —*v.i.* **-tured, -tur·ing.** to make or use gestures: *The policeman gestured for us to proceed.* [Medieval Latin *gestura* bearing, behavior, from Latin *gestus,* past participle of *gerere* to perform.]

Ge·sund·heit (gə zoont′hīt′) *interj.* German. used to wish good health to someone who has just sneezed.

get (get) **got** or *(archaic)* **gat, got** or **got·ten, get·ting.** *v.t.* **1.** to obtain possession of; receive; acquire: *to get a good price for a car.* **2.** to achieve; earn; gain: *The team got three touchdowns.* **3.** to go for and return with; fetch: *Please get me a glass of water.* **4.** to lay hold of; capture: *The police got the escaped prisoner.* **5.** to cause to become; cause to be in a specified condition: *to get a bill passed by Congress. His problems often get him down.* **6.** to cause (something) to move: *to get a stalled car off the road.* **7.** to become ill with; suffer from; catch: *to get the measles.* **8.** to ascertain by calculation or experiment: *If you add three and seven, you get ten.* **9.** to establish communication with; reach: *Please get the doctor on the phone.* **10.** to prevail upon; induce; persuade: *She got her brother to walk the dog.* **11.** to learn through study; master; memorize: *He got the grammar lesson without difficulty.* **12.** to receive as punishment: *The criminal got six years.* **13.** to make ready; prepare: *to get lunch.* **14.** to arrive in time or go aboard: *to get the ten o'clock train.* **15.** to possess; have (with *have* or *has*): *Guess what I've got in my hand. She's got blonde hair.* **16.** (of animals) to beget. **17.** *Informal.* to be obliged (to do something); be a necessity (with *have* or *has*): *You've got to look for a new job.* **18.** *Informal.* to understand; comprehend: *I get the idea.* **19.** *Informal.* to cause a response of annoyance or excitement in: *His arrogance always gets me.* **20.** *Informal.* to puzzle; baffle. **21.** *Slang.* to hit: *The ball got him in the eye.* **22.** *Slang.* to overcome, destroy, or kill. —*v.i.* **1.** to come to or reach a certain place or position: *to get to shore safely, to get to work on time.* **2.** to move, come, or go: *to get into an elevator, to get down from a ladder, to get nowhere in trying to reach a decision.* **3.** to be in or come to be in a specified condition or become: *to get lost, to get ready to leave, to get caught in the rain.* **4.** to gain or acquire wealth: *Getting and spending, we lay waste our powers* (Wordsworth, 1806). **5.** *Informal.* to go away immediately; be off.
to get about. to get around *(defs. a–c).*
to get across. a. to make intelligible or understandable: *to use visual aids to get across a lesson.* **b.** to be intelligible or understandable: *The explanation got across to the group.*
to get along. see **along.**
to get around. a. to move or go from place to place. **b.** to be circulated; become known: *The rumor got around quickly.* **c.** to be active socially: *He gets around a lot for a newcomer.* **d.** to influence, outwit, or obtain a favor from (someone), esp. through flattery: *A little girl can usually get around her father.* **e.** to avoid; evade; circumvent: *to get around taking out the garbage.*
to get around to. to do after a delay.
to get at. a. to arrive at; reach. **b.** to find out; ascertain: *to get at the truth.* **c.** to apply oneself to: *to get at one's work.* **d.** to attempt to clarify; mean: *I don't see what you're getting at.* **e.** *Informal.* to tamper with or influence underhandedly; bribe.
to get away. a. to leave; depart. **b.** to escape. **c.** to start, as in a horse race.
to get away with. *Informal.* to do (something) without being noticed, caught, or punished: *to get away with a crime.*
to get back. a. to return to a former condition or place: *to get back from a trip.* **b.** to recover: *to get back one's strength.*
to get back at. *Slang.* to take revenge on.
to get by. *Informal.* **a.** to pass without notice. **b.** to barely manage; survive.
to get down to. to start to consider or take action on: *to get down to work.*
to get in. a. to enter; go in: *They got in through the hole in the fence.* **b.** to come in; arrive: *The train got in at noon.* **c.** to insert, as in conversation: *to get in a word or two.* **d.** to become friendly, involved, or associated: *He got in with the wrong crowd.*

to get it. *Informal.* to receive a scolding or punishment.
to get off. a. to move down from or out of. **b.** to start; depart: *to get off on time.* **c.** to be released or escape, as from punishment. **d.** to help to reduce the penalty for: *The lawyer got his client off with merely a fine.* **e.** to write and send: *to get off a telegram.* **f.** to take off; remove. **g.** *Informal.* to utter or deliver, esp. a joke. **h.** *Slang.* to have the audacity (to do something): *Where does he get off saying that?*
to get on. a. to move up on or onto: *to get on a horse.* **b.** to get along.
to get out. a. to go away; depart. **b.** to escape, as from danger, difficulty, or obligation. **c.** to take out. **d.** to become known; leak out: *No one could discover how the secret got out.* **e.** to publish; issue: *to get out a daily newspaper.* **f.** to say with difficulty: *He got out a weak hello.*
to get out of. a. to depart from; leave: *to get out of bed.* **b.** to escape from danger, difficulty, obligation, or something undesirable: *to get out of shoveling the snow.* **c.** to help to remove or escape from: *He got his friend out of difficulty.* **d.** to elicit or obtain from: *They finally got the information out of him.* **e.** to go beyond (sight, reach, or earshot).
to get over. a. to recover from: *to get over a cold.* **b.** to overcome; surmount. **c.** *Informal.* to get across.
to get there. to achieve a goal; succeed.
to get through. a. to complete; finish: *to get through dinner quickly.* **b.** to manage to survive: *to get through the day after a sleepless night.*
to get through to. a. to make or become clear or convincing to. **b.** to establish communication with; reach.
to get to. a. to reach; contact. **b.** to succeed in doing something: *They got to take a trip last August.* **c.** *Informal.* to produce a strong emotion in, as anger, joy, or melancholy: *Those old tunes really get to me.*
to get together. a. to come together, esp. informally; meet; assemble. **b.** to bring together; gather; collect: *to get together pictures for an album.* **c.** to come to or reach an agreement, esp. after discussion or negotiation.
to get up. a. to rise from bed or sleep. **b.** to bring oneself to a sitting or standing position. **c.** to mount; climb; ascend. **d.** to bring into existence; arrange; organize: *to get up an excursion to a museum.* **e.** to work up; develop; arouse. **f.** to dress in a certain style, esp. an unusual one. **g.** to produce (a book or similar item) in a certain style. —*n.* **1.** return of a shot thought to be out of reach in tennis, handball, and similar games. **2.** offspring of an animal. [Old Norse *geta* to obtain, beget, learn.]

get·a·way (get′ə wā′) *n.* *Informal.* **1.** act of escaping: *The thief made a fast getaway.* **2.** act of starting a race.

Geth·sem·a·ne (geth sem′ə nē) *n.* **1.** in the New Testament, a garden on the Mount of Olives, east of Jerusalem, the scene of Jesus' agony, betrayal, and arrest. **2. gethsemane.** any scene or occasion of intense suffering.

get-to·geth·er (get′tə geth′ər) *n.* *Informal.* informal meeting, gathering, or party.

Get·tys·burg (get′iz burg′) *n.* town in southern Pennsylvania, the site of a decisive Union victory in 1863 during the Civil War. Pop. (1970), 7275.

get-up (get′up′) *n.* *Informal.* **1.** style of dress, esp. an unusual one; outfit. **2.** style of production or finish, as of a book; arrangement.

get-up-and-go (get′up′ən gō′) *n.* *Informal.* drive; vigor; energy.

gew·gaw (gū′gô, gōō′-) *n.* gaudy, worthless plaything or ornament; showy trifle; bauble. —*adj.* showy but without value; gaudy. [Of uncertain origin.]

gey·ser (gī′zər) *n.* natural hot spring from which steam and hot water burst into the air after being heated below the surface by surrounding masses of hot rock. [Icelandic *Geysir* a noted hot spring in Iceland; literally, gusher, from *geysa* to gush.]

gey·ser·ite (gī′zə rīt′) *n.* variety of opaline silica deposited around the edges of geysers and hot springs.

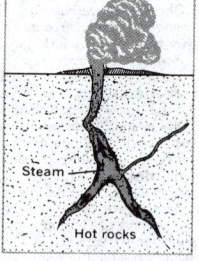
Geyser

G-force (jē′fôrs′) *n.* force exerted on a body by gravity or by reaction to acceleration or deceleration, as when an aircraft or rocket changes speed or direction. [G(RAVITY) + FORCE.]

Gha·na (gä′nə) *n.* country in western Africa, on the Gulf of Guinea, consisting of the former British territories of the Gold Coast and Togoland. Capital, Accra. Area, 92,100 sq. mi. Pop. (1969 est.), 8,600,000.

ghast·ly (gast′lē) **-li·er, -li·est.** *adj.* **1.** horrible; dreadful: *ghastly damage from a flood.* **2.** deathly pale; ghostlike: *a ghastly look.* **3.** *Informal.* extremely bad or unpleasant: *a ghastly mistake.* —*adv.* in a ghastly

at; āpe; cär; end; mē; it; īce; hot; ōld; fôrk; wood; fōōl; oil; out; up; ūse; turn; sing; thin; this; zh in treasure; ə in ago, taken, pencil, lemon, circus.

manner; dreadfully. [Old English *gástlíc* spiritual, ghostly, from *gást* spirit, ghost + *-lic* (see -LY²).] —**ghast′li·ness,** *n.*

Syn. *adj.* **1. Ghastly, gruesome, grisly** mean shockingly dreadful. **Ghastly** may be applied to what inspires horror and intense dread: *The ghastly scars on his face spoke of his harrowing experiences.* **Gruesome** evokes the fear and aversion aroused by something sinister or violent: *His gruesome description of the massacre horrified the audience.* **Grisly** suggests that the sense of horror is so strong that it causes one to shudder: *The scene of the accident provided a grisly sight.*

ghat (gôt) *also,* **ghaut.** *n.* **1.** in India, a passage or stairway leading to a river or river landing. **2.** in India, a mountain pass. [Hindi *ghāt* landing place, from Sanskrit *ghattah.*]

Ghats (gôts) *n.,pl.* two mountain ranges along the eastern and western coasts of southern India.

ghee (gē) *n.* in India, a clarified, semiliquid butter made by boiling and straining the milk of cows and buffaloes. [Hindi *ghī,* from Sanskrit *ghrta.*]

Ghent (gent) *n.* port city in northwestern Belgium. Pop. (1968), 153,-301. Also, **Flemish, Gent.**

gher·kin (gur′kin) *n.* **1.** small, prickly, many-seeded cucumber, *Cucumis anguria,* pickled and eaten usually as a relish. Also, **bur gherkin. 2.** slender cucumber vine bearing this cucumber, found in the United States and the West Indies. **3.** small, immature common cucumber used for pickling. [Dutch *gurken,* plural of *gurk* cucumber, through Low German and Polish, from Middle Greek *agouros,* from Persian *angārah.*]

ghet·to (get′ō) *pl.,* **-tos** or **-toes.** *n.* **1.** section of a European city where Jews were required to live. **2.** section of a city, esp. a slum area, in which members of a minority group live because of social discrimination or economic pressure. [Italian *ghetto* Jewish quarter, possibly from dialectal Italian *ghèto, gèto* foundry, going back to Latin *jactus* a casting; probably so called from *Ghèto,* a Venetian island set aside for Jews in 1516 that contained a foundry.]

Ghib·el·line (gib′ə lin, -lēn′) *n.* member of the aristocratic political faction in medieval Italy that supported the authority of the German emperors in opposition to the pope. The Ghibellines were opposed to the Guelphs.

Ghi·ber·ti, Lo·ren·zo (gē ber′tē; lō ren′tsō) 1378–1455, Florentine sculptor, goldsmith, and painter.

ghost (gôst) *n.* **1.** spirit of a dead person, thought of as making its presence known to the living in a visible form or in some other way; specter. **2.** shadowy outline or semblance of something; slightest bit: *a ghost of a smile, a ghost of a chance.* **3.** image on a television screen that is a fainter duplicate of the desired image, resulting from reflection of the television signals from tall buildings or other surfaces. **4.** haunting memory of something: *to be troubled by the ghost of an early failure.* **5. Ghost.** Holy Ghost. **6.** spelling game for two or more players whose object is to avoid completing a word of four or more letters. **7.** *Informal.* ghost-writer. **8. to give up the ghost,** to die. —*v.t., v.i. Informal.* to ghostwrite. [Old English *gást* spirit, soul.]

Syn. *n.* **1. Ghost, specter, apparition** indicate a manifestation of something not tangibly present, esp. of a dead person. **Ghost** implies the soul or spirit of someone who has died: *The castle is said to be haunted by a ghost.* **Specter** suggests something that terrorizes the one who sees it: *The specter of death appears like a human skeleton.* **Apparition** implies the sudden appearance of a spirit: *The apparition vanished to reappear at once on the staircase.*

ghost dance, religious dance practiced by certain North American Indian tribes in the late nineteenth century, intended to establish communication with the dead and to bring about a return to former conditions.

ghost·ly (gôst′lē) **-li·er, -li·est.** *adj.* **1.** relating to or characteristic of a ghost; spectral: *The scarecrow took on a ghostly shape in the dim light.* **2.** *Archaic.* of or relating to the spirit or soul; spiritual. —**ghost′li·ness,** *n.*

ghost town, town that has been deserted, esp. a mining town in the western U.S. abandoned after the nearby mines closed.

ghostwrite (gôst′rīt′) **-wrote, -writ·ten, -writ·ing.** *v.t., v.i.* to be a ghost-writer or write (something) as a ghost-writer: *His assistant ghostwrites his speeches.*

ghost-writer (gôst′rī′tər) *n.* one who writes a speech, article, book, or other work for someone else to whom the work is attributed.

ghoul (gōōl) *n.* **1.** *Oriental Legend.* a horrible demon believed to rob graves and feed on human corpses. **2.** anyone who robs graves. **3.** one who enjoys revolting acts or horrible things. [Arabic *ghūl* the demon.] —**ghoul′ish,** *adj.* —**ghoul′ish·ly,** *adv.* —**ghoul′ish·ness,** *n.*

GHQ, General Headquarters.

GI (jē′ī′) *pl.,* **GI's, GIs.** *Informal. n.* enlisted man in any of the branches of the U.S. military service, esp. the Army. —*adj.* **1.** of, relating to, or characteristic of GI's: *a GI haircut.* **2.** issued by the U.S. government for use by the armed forces: *GI boots.* **3.** conforming strictly to military regulations. —*v.t.,* **GI'd, GI'ing.** to clean thoroughly, as in preparation for inspection: *to GI a barracks.* [Abbreviation of *G(overnment) I(ssue),* used in the U.S. Army in official supply lists and later applied more widely by soldiers. Before World War II, GI was used officially in the U.S. Army only as an abbreviation for *g(alvanized) i(ron)* trash cans.]

GI 1. gastrointestinal. **2.** government issue.

Gia·co·met·ti, Al·ber·to (jä′kō met′ē; äl ber′tō) 1901–66, Swiss sculptor and painter.

gi·ant (jī′ənt) *n.* **1.** in folklore and legend, a huge and powerful creature having human form. **2.** one who or that which is extraordinary in strength, importance, size, or ability: *Isaac Newton was an intellectual giant. That company is a giant in the field of electronics.* **3.** *Greek Mythology.* one of a race of huge beings who fought against and were defeated by the Olympian gods. —*adj.* of, relating to, or characteristic of a giant; huge: *a giant telescope.* [Old French *geant* huge person, legendary huge creature, going back to Latin *gigās* one of the huge mythical beings, from Greek *gigās.*] —**gi′ant·ess,** *n.*

gi·ant·ism (jī′ən tiz′əm) gigantism.

giant panda, panda *(def. 1).*

giant star, bright, comparatively large star.

giaour (jour, jou′ər) *n.* among Muslims, one who does not believe in Islam, esp. a Christian. [Turkish *giaur* infidel, from Persian *gaur,* form of *gābr* fire worshiper.]

gib¹ (gib) *n.* piece of metal or other material, often wedge-shaped, used to hold parts of a machine in place. —*v.t.,* **gibbed, gib·bing.** to hold in place with a gib. [Of uncertain origin.]

gib² (gib) *n.* male cat, esp. one that has been castrated. [Contraction of the proper name *Gilbert* used for a cat.]

Gib., Gibraltar.

gib·ber (jib′ər, gib′-) *v.t., v.i.* to speak rapidly and unintelligibly; jabber. —*n.* gibberish. [Imitative.]

gib·ber·el·lin (jib′ə rel′in) *n.* growth-regulating hormone that increases the length of the shoots of plants. [Modern Latin *Giberella* (from Latin *gibber* hump on the back) + -IN¹.]

gib·ber·ish (jib′ər ish, gib′-) *n.* **1.** rapid, unintelligible chatter. **2.** meaningless or obscure spoken or written language; nonsense.

gib·bet (jib′it) *n.* **1.** gallows. **2.** upright post with a projecting arm from which the bodies of executed criminals were suspended. —*v.t.,* **-bet·ed, -bet·ing. 1.** to hang (a corpse) on a gibbet. **2.** to put to death by hanging. **3.** to expose to public scorn or ridicule. [Old French *gibet* staff, gallows, diminutive of *gibe* staff, club; possibly of Germanic origin.]

gib·bon (gib′ən) *n.* any of various small tree-dwelling anthropoid apes, genera *Hylobates* and *Symphalangus,* of southeastern Asia and the East Indies, having long, slender limbs and a predominantly black, brown, or pale gray coat. Height: 3 feet. [French *gibbon;* supposedly from a language of India.]

Gib·bon, Edward (gib′ən) 1737–94, English historian and author.

Gibbon

gib·bous (gib′əs) *adj.* **1.** of or relating to that phase in which the moon or a planet appears more than half full but less than full. See **moon** for illustration. **2.** hunchbacked. [Latin *gibbōsus* humpbacked, crooked, from *gibbus* hump.] —**gib′bous·ly,** *adv.* —**gib′bous·ness,** *n.*

gibe (jīb) *also,* **jibe.** *v.i.* **-gibed, -gib·ing.** derisive remark; jeer; taunt. —*v.i.,* **gibed, gib·ing.** to utter gibes; jeer. —*v.t.* to utter gibes at. [Possibly from Old French *giber* to handle roughly; of uncertain origin.] —**gib′er,** *n.*

GI Bill of Rights, federal legislation providing disability compensation, medical care, educational assistance, and other benefits for veterans of the U.S. armed forces. Also, **GI Bill.**

gib·let (jib′lit) *n. usually, giblets.* any of the edible visceral parts of a fowl, such as the heart, liver, or gizzard. [Old French *gibelet* stewed game, possibly going back to *gibier* hunting, game; of Germanic origin.]

Gi·bral·tar (ji brôl′tər) *n.* **1.** British crown colony and seaport on a promontory near the southern tip of Spain, site of a large, heavily fortified naval base. Area, 2¼ sq. mi. Pop. (1965), 24,875. **2. Rock of.** **a.** great rock formation on and near which this colony is situated, known to ancient geographers as one of the Pillars of Hercules. **b.** *Informal.* one who or that which has lasting strength and stability. **3. Strait of.** body of water connecting the Mediterranean Sea with the Atlantic Ocean, separating northern Africa from the southern tip of Spain.

gid·dy (gid′ē) **-di·er, -di·est.** *adj.* **1.** having a reeling or swimming sensation in one's head; dizzy. **2.** causing or tending to cause dizziness. **3.** frivolous; flighty; light-hearted. [Old English *gidig, gydig* foolish, mad.] —**gid′di·ly,** *adv.* —**gid′di·ness,** *n.*

gid·dy·ap (gid'ē ap', gid yap') *interj.* used as a command to make a horse start or go faster. Also, **gid·dap** (gi dap').

Gide, An·dré (zhēd; än drā') 1869–1951, French writer.

Gid·e·on (gid'ē ən) *n.* in the Old Testament, Israelite who saved his people from the Midianites and served as judge of Israel.

Gideons International, service organization of Christian business and professional men that provides Bibles for hotels, hospitals, the armed services, and institutions, founded in 1899.

gift (gift) *n.* 1. something given; present; donation: *a graduation gift.* 2. natural ability or endowment; talent: *a gift for writing.* 3. act, power, or right of giving. 4. **to look a gift horse in the mouth.** to find fault with something given. [Old Norse *gipt* present.]

Syn. 1. **Gift, present**[2] indicate something given. **Gift** suggests something formally bestowed upon a person or institution: *The statue was a gift from one of the museum's wealthiest patrons.* **Present** implies affection or good will as motive for the giving: *Among his birthday presents was a set of electric trains from his father.*

gift·ed (gif'tid) *adj.* having natural ability; talented: *a gifted artist, a special class for gifted children.*

gig[1] (gig) *n.* 1. light, open, two-wheeled carriage drawn by a single horse. 2. long, light ship's boat propelled by oars, sails, or a motor. [Possibly of Scandinavian origin.]

Gig[1] (def. 1)

gig[2] (gig) *n.* 1. fishing spear. 2. device made of hooks fastened back to back, used to catch fish by their bodies. —*v.t., v.i.* **gigged, gig·ging.** to catch or spear (fish) with a gig. [Short for earlier *fishgig* harpoon, form of *fisgig,* from Spanish *fisga,* from *fisgar* to thrust into, fasten, going back to Latin *figere.*]

gi·gan·tic (jī gan'tik) *adj.* of, characteristic of, or suited to a giant; huge; enormous. [Latin *gigant-,* stem of *gigās* giant + -IC. See GIANT.] —**gi·gan'ti·cal·ly,** *adv.*

gi·gan·tism (jī gan'tiz'əm, jī'gan-) *n.* abnormal size or stature of the body, or abnormal growth of certain parts of the body. This condition is usually caused by improper functioning of the pituitary gland. Also, **gi'ant·ism.**

gig·gle (gig'əl) **-gled, -gling.** *v.i.* to laugh in a silly, high-pitched, or nervous way. —*n.* silly, high-pitched, or nervous laughter. [Imitative.] —**gig'gler,** *n.*

gig·gly (gig'lē) **-gli·er, -gli·est.** *adj.* inclined to giggle.

gig·o·lo (jig'ə lō') *pl.* **-los.** *n.* 1. man kept as a lover and supported by a woman. 2. man paid as an escort or dancing partner for a woman. [French *gigolo,* from *gigue* leg; of Germanic origin.]

gig·ot (jig'ət) *n.* 1. leg-of-mutton sleeve. 2. leg of lamb, mutton, or veal for cooking. [French *gigot* leg of mutton, diminutive of Old French *gigue* leg, fiddle (in the Middle Ages shaped like a leg of mutton); of Germanic origin.]

Gi·la monster (hē'lə) large, sluggish, poisonous lizard, *Heloderma suspectum,* native to desert regions of northern Mexico and the southwestern United States. It has a black or brown scaly body with orange or yellow blotches. Length: 2 feet, including the tail. [From the *Gila* River in Arizona, near which this lizard is found.]

Gila monster

Gil·bert, Sir William Schwenck (gil'bərt; shwenk) 1836–1911, English humorist and librettist who collaborated with the composer Sir Arthur Sullivan.

Gilbert and El·lice Islands (el'is) British island group in the west-central Pacific. Land area, approx. 124 sq. mi. Pop. (1968), 53,517.

gild[1] (gild) **gild·ed** or **gilt, gild·ing.** *v.t.* 1. to coat with or as with a thin layer of gold. 2. to adorn, esp. with a golden light or color; brighten attractively. 3. to give a deceptively better appearance to. 4. **to gild the lily.** to add needless decoration or ornamentation to something that is beautiful in its own right. [Old English *gyldan* to cover with a thin layer of gold.] —**gild'er,** *n.*

gild[2] (gild) guild.

gild·er (gil'dər) guilder.

gild·ing (gil'ding) *n.* 1. art or process of covering surfaces with a thin layer of gold or similar material. 2. thin layer of gold or similar material used in this process. 3. deceptively attractive covering or appearance.

Gil·e·ad (gil'ē əd) *n.* mountainous region in ancient Palestine east of the Jordan River, between the Dead Sea and the Sea of Galilee.

Gil·ga·mesh (gil'gə mesh') *n.* in Babylonian and Sumerian legend, a king who is the hero of a long epic poem.

gill[1] (gil) *n.* 1. respiratory organ of fish and most other aquatic animals, consisting of a thin layer of tissue well supplied with blood, capable of absorbing oxygen from water and releasing carbon dioxide from the blood. 2. one of the thin, bladelike structures radially arranged on the underside of the cap of a mushroom. 3. **gills.** *Informal.* the flesh around a person's chin or under the jaws. 4. **green around the gills.** *Informal.* sickly or nervous in appearance. 5. also, **gills.** the wattles of a fowl. [Of Scandinavian origin.]

Gills

Gill[1] (def. 1)

gill[2] (jil) *n.* liquid measure equal to one fourth of a pint. [Old French *gille* wine measure, from Late Latin *gillō* water pot; possibly of Semitic origin.]

gil·lie (gil'ē) *pl.* **gil·lies.** also, **gil·ly.** *n.* 1. attendant of a hunter or fisherman in the Scottish Highlands. 2. male servant, esp. of a Highland chief. [Scottish Gaelic *gille* lad, servant.]

gil·ly·flow·er (jil'ē flou'ər) also, **gil·li·flow·er.** *n.* any of various flowers having a spicy, clovelike fragrance, as *Mathiola incana,* the most common variety of stock. [Old French *gilofre, girofle* clove, from Medieval Latin *caryophyllum,* from Greek *karyophyllon;* the Modern English spelling is due to an incorrect association with *flower.*]

gilt (gilt) *v.* a past tense and past participle of **gild**[1]. —*adj.* covered with gold or a golden color; gilded. —*n.* gold or similar material used in gilding.

gilt-edged (gilt'ejd') *adj.* 1. having gilded edges: *a gilt-edged book.* 2. of the highest quality or value.

gim·bals (jim'bəlz, gim'-) *n.,pl.* mounting arrangement that allows a body to move freely or an instrument, as a ship's compass, to remain level regardless of the motion of the object that supports it. Gimbals consist of two rings, one inside another, with the axes perpendicular to one another and pivoted so that each one can rotate freely about its own axis. [Earlier *gimmal,* from Old French *gemel* a twin, from Latin *gemellus.*]

Gimbals

Gyroscope mounted on gimbals

gim·crack (jim'krak') *n.* gaudy, useless object; trifle; bauble. —*adj.* gaudy, but cheap and useless. [Of uncertain origin.]

gim·let (gim'lit) *n.* small pointed screw tool with a cross handle, used for boring holes. [Middle French *guimbelet,* probably from Middle Dutch *wimmelkijn.*]

gim·mick (gim'ik) *n. Slang.* 1. clever feature or idea, esp. one that is used to attract attention. 2. hidden feature, esp. one that is not advantageous; catch. 3. small device or gadget, esp. one that is hidden or is used to deceive. [Of uncertain origin.]

gimp[1] (gimp) *n.* narrow strip of fabric, sometimes stiffened with wire, used for trimming borders of garments, curtains, or furniture. [Dutch *gimp;* of uncertain origin.]

Gimlet

gimp[2] (gimp) *Slang. n.* 1. one who limps. 2. limp; hobble. —*v.i.* to limp; hobble. [Of uncertain origin.] —**gim'py,** *adj.*

gin[1] (jin) *n.* 1. strong aromatic alcoholic liquor, distilled from grains and flavored with juniper berries. 2. similar liquor flavored with other substances, as angelica root or licorice. [Short for earlier *geneva,* from obsolete Dutch *genever* juniper, from Old French *genevre,* going back to Latin *jūniperus.*]

gin[2] (jin) *n.* 1. machine for separating cotton from its seed. 2. trap or snare, as for game. —*v.t.,* **ginned, gin·ning.** 1. to separate (cotton) from its seeds with a gin. 2. to trap or snare (game). [Shortened from Old French *engin* machine, skill, from Latin *ingenium* skill, invention.] —**gin'ner,** *n.*

gin[3] (jin) *n.* gin rummy.

gin[4] (jin) **gan** or **gun, gin·ning.** *v.t., v.i. Archaic.* to begin.

gin·ger (jin'jər) *n.* 1. any of a group of plants, genus *Zingiber,* widely cultivated in tropical and subtropical regions for their edible roots. 2. pungent, aromatic spice ground from these roots, used in cooking and in medicine. 3. the root itself, often candied or preserved in syrup. 4. *Informal.* liveliness; high spirits; pep. 5. dull tawny or reddish-brown color. [Old English *gingifer* ginger, ginger root, through Latin and Greek, going back to Sanskrit *çr̥ngavēram* ginger plant, from *çr̥ngam* horn + *vera* body; because the root is shaped like a horn.]

ginger ale, carbonated soft drink flavored with ginger.

ginger beer, carbonated soft drink made with yeast and flavored with ginger.

gin·ger·bread (jin'jər bred') *n.* 1. dark, sweet cake or cookie flavored with ginger and molasses. 2. gaudy and tasteless ornamentation, as on furniture or buildings. —*adj.* cheap and showy; gaudy.

gin·ger·ly (jin′jər lē) *adv.* with extreme caution; carefully; timidly: *to walk gingerly on thin ice.* —*adj.* extremely cautious or wary. —**gin′ger·li·ness,** *n.*

gin·ger·snap (jin′jər snap′) *n.* thin, crisp cooky flavored with ginger and molasses.

gin·ger·y (jin′jər ē) *adj.* **1.** having the pungent and spicy flavor of ginger; like ginger. **2.** having the dull tawny or reddish-brown color of ginger. **3.** lively, snappy, or outspoken, as a comment.

ging·ham (ging′əm) *n.* strong, medium-weight dyed cotton fabric, usually woven in checks, stripes, or plaids. [French *guingan,* from Malay *ginggang* striped, striped cotton.]

gin·gi·vi·tis (jin′jə vī′təs) *n.* inflammation of the gums. [Latin *gingiva* gum + -ITIS.]

gink·go (ging′kō) *pl.,* **-goes.** *also,* **ging·ko.** *n.* large tree with fan-shaped leaves, *Ginkgo biloba,* native to China. The female form is noted for its foul-smelling yellow, plumlike fruit. Male ginkgoes are popular as ornamental or shade trees. [Japanese *ginkyo,* from *gin* silver + *kyō* apricot.]

gin rummy (jin) variation of the card game rummy in which two players, or sometimes more, form matched sets of cards until one of the players has matched all the cards in his hand or has ten points or less of unmatched cards. [GIN¹ + RUMMY²; *gin* was probably suggested by *rum* since rum is the first syllable of RUMMY² and since both are alcoholic beverages.]

gin·seng (jin′seng) *n.* **1.** either of two low plants, genus *Panax,* cultivated in North America and Asia, having a thick branched root and bearing toothed leaves, each consisting of five leaflets, and small, pale-green, flowers. **2.** root of these plants, used in medicine by the Chinese. [Chinese (Mandarin) *jen shen* man image; referring to the shape of the root, which resembles the Chinese character for man.]

Gior·gio·ne (jôr jō′nē) *n.* c.1478–1510, Italian painter.

Giot·to (jot′ō) *n.* c.1266–1337, Italian painter, born Giotto di Bondone.

Gip·sy (jip′sē) Gypsy.

gipsy moth, gypsy moth.

gi·raffe (jə raf′) *n.* cud-chewing African mammal, genus *Giraffa,* the tallest living animal, having a very long neck, long slender legs, two or four small bony horns, and a coat with brown patches outlined with white. Height: to 19 feet. [French *girafe,* from Arabic *zarāfah.*]

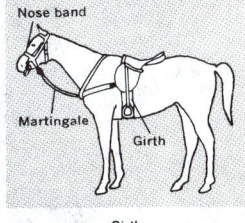
Giraffe

Gi·rau·doux, Jean (zhēr′ō dōō′; zhän) 1882–1944, French playwright and novelist.

gird¹ (gurd) **girt** or **gird·ed, gird·ing.** *v.t.* **1.** to surround or encircle with a belt or girdle. **2.** to fasten or secure with a belt or girdle. **3.** to encircle, as with a belt; enclose; hem in. **4.** to prepare (oneself) for action. **5.** to invest; clothe; equip; endue. [Old English *gyrdan* to surround, encircle.]

gird² (gurd) *v.t., v.i.* to jeer; gibe; scoff (at). —*n. Archaic.* biting remark; gibe. [Of uncertain origin.]

gird·er (gur′dər) *n.* large horizontal beam, usually made of steel, used to support joists and other beams, as for a floor or the framework of a bridge or building. [GIRD¹ + -ER¹.]

gir·dle (gurd′əl) *n.* **1.** flexible undergarment worn esp. by women to support or shape the waist, abdomen, or hips; corset. **2.** belt or band worn around the waist. **3.** anything that encircles in the manner of a belt. **4.** complete ring around the trunk or branch of a tree cut through the bark, preventing the flow of sap and nutrients above that point and causing the tree to die. **5.** bony arch supporting a limb or limbs: *the pelvic girdle.* **6.** outer rim of a cut gem. —*v.t.,* **-dled, -dling. 1.** to encircle with a belt or girdle. **2.** to encircle, as with a belt; surround. **3.** to cut a girdle through the bark of a tree. [Old English *gyrdel* belt, from *gyrdan* to surround, encircle.] —**gir′dler,** *n.*

girl (gurl) *n.* **1.** female child. **2.** young, unmarried woman. **3.** female servant or employee. **4.** *Informal.* sweetheart. **5.** *Informal.* woman of any age, single or married. [Of uncertain origin.]

girl Friday, female employee, esp. in an office, with a wide variety of duties. [Patterned after MAN FRIDAY.]

girl·friend (gurl′frend′) *n. Informal.* female friend, esp. a sweetheart.

girl·hood (gurl′hood′) *n.* **1.** time or state of being a girl. **2.** girls collectively.

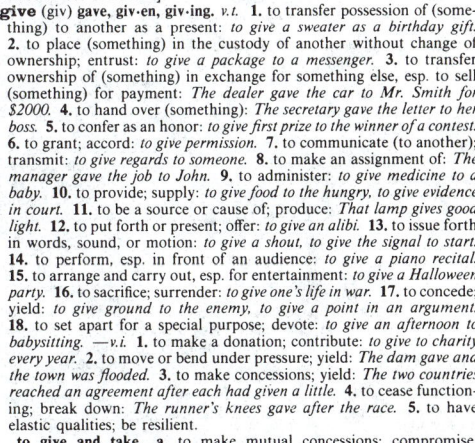
Joists
Girder
Girder

girl·ish (gur′lish) *adj.* **1.** of or relating to girls or girlhood. **2.** suitable for a girl or girls. —**girl′ish·ly,** *adv.* —**girl′ish·ness,** *n.*

girl scout, member of the Girl Scouts.

Girl Scouts, worldwide organization founded to provide young girls with the opportunity to participate in community service and to develop character and physical fitness.

Gi·ron·dist (jə ron′dist) *n.* member of a political party that advocated moderate republican principles during the French Revolution, from 1791 to 1793. —*adj.* of or relating to this party.

girt¹ (gurt) a past tense and past participle of **gird¹.**

girt² (gurt) *v.t., v.i.* **1.** to gird. **2.** to measure in girth. [Form of GIRD¹.]

girth (gurth) *n.* **1.** distance around something; circumference: *the girth of a pillar, the girth of a person's waist.* **2.** strap or band, usually of leather or webbing, that is passed under the belly of a horse or other animal to keep a saddle or pack in place. **3.** band or girdle. —*v.t.* **1.** to surround; encircle; gird. **2.** to fasten or fit with a girth. —*v.i.* to measure in girth. [Old Norse *gjörth* girdle, hoop.]

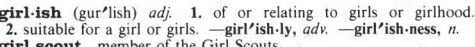
Nose band
Martingale
Girth
Girth

gist (jist) *n.* main idea; central point: *the gist of a speech.* [Old French *gist* it lies, from *gesir* to lie², *gesir en* to depend on, from Latin *jacére* to lie².]

git·tern (git′ərn) *n.* medieval musical instrument similar to a guitar, having wire strings. [Old French *guiterne* cithern, guitar, from Latin *cithara.* See CITHARA.]

give (giv) **gave, giv·en, giv·ing.** *v.t.* **1.** to transfer possession of (something) to another as a present: *to give a sweater as a birthday gift.* **2.** to place (something) in the custody of another without change of ownership; entrust: *to give a package to a messenger.* **3.** to transfer ownership of (something) in exchange for something else, esp. to sell (something) for payment: *The dealer gave the car to Mr. Smith for $2000.* **4.** to hand over (something): *The secretary gave the letter to her boss.* **5.** to confer as an honor: *to give first prize to the winner of a contest.* **6.** to grant; accord: *to give permission.* **7.** to communicate (to another); transmit: *to give regards to someone.* **8.** to make an assignment of: *The manager gave the job to John.* **9.** to administer: *to give medicine to a baby.* **10.** to provide; supply: *to give food to the hungry, to give evidence in court.* **11.** to be a source or cause of; produce: *That lamp gives good light.* **12.** to put forth or present; offer: *to give an alibi.* **13.** to issue forth in words, sound, or motion: *to give a shout, to give the signal to start.* **14.** to perform, esp. in front of an audience: *to give a piano recital.* **15.** to arrange and carry out, esp. for entertainment: *to give a Halloween party.* **16.** to sacrifice; surrender: *to give one's life in war.* **17.** to concede; yield: *to give ground to the enemy, to give a point in an argument.* **18.** to set apart for a special purpose; devote: *to give an afternoon to babysitting.* —*v.i.* **1.** to make a donation; contribute: *to give to charity every year.* **2.** to move or bend under pressure; yield: *The dam gave and the town was flooded.* **3.** to make concessions; yield: *The two countries reached an agreement after each had given a little.* **4.** to cease functioning; break down: *The runner's knees gave after the race.* **5.** to have elastic qualities; be resilient.
to give and take. **a.** to make mutual concessions; compromise. **b.** to exchange on equal terms.
to give away. **a.** to give as a gift; donate. **b.** to present (the bride) to the bridegroom in a marriage ceremony. **c.** to reveal; expose: *The boy gave away his hiding place when he sneezed.*
to give back. to return; restore.
to give forth. to emit; issue: *The dog gave forth a howl.*
to give in. **a.** to end opposition; yield: *The father gave in and·let his son drive the car.* **b.** to deliver or present.
to give it to. *Informal.* to administer punishment; berate; scold: *Ann's mother gave it to her for being late.*
to give off. to put forth; emit: *The flowers gave off a sweet fragrance.*
to give out. **a.** to issue or distribute; pass (something) out: *to give out samples, to give out a summons.* **b.** to make public; announce. **c.** to become exhausted, broken down, or used up: *The swimmer gave out after ten laps. The old car finally gave out.*
to give over. **a.** to relinquish; surrender. **b.** to cease; finish. **c.** to set aside (for a specified purpose); devote: *The guidance counselor gave over afternoons for interviews with students.*
to give rise to. to produce; cause.
to give up. **a.** to relinquish; surrender; yield: *to give up ground to the enemy.* **b.** to stop; cease: *to give up eating between meals.* **c.** to acknowledge that one has failed and stop trying. **d.** to abandon as

hopeless or useless: *to give up the search for a lost dog.* **e.** to devote completely or sacrifice: *to give up one's life.*

to give way. a. to yield under pressure; break down: *The thin ice gave way under the skater.* **b.** to make room for; make way. **c.** to lose one's self-control.
—*n.* **1.** quality of being elastic. **2.** tendency to yield to force or pressure. [Of Scandinavian origin.] —**giv′er,** *n.*

Syn. *v.t.* **1. Give, present², confer** indicate delivering something to someone to be his own. **Give** is the general term: *He gave his friend two tickets to the game.* **Present** suggests formal giving: *They presented him with a watch when he retired.* **Confer** implies patronage or favor or the bestowing of an official honor: *The college conferred an honorary degree on the famous poet.*

give-and-take (giv′ən tāk′) *n.* **1.** mutual yielding or concession; compromise. **2.** good-natured exchange of talk; repartee; banter.

give·a·way (giv′ə wā′) *n.* *Informal.* **1.** unintentional revelation; exposure. **2.** something given away or sold at a very low price, as to promote sales. **3.** radio or television program on which prizes are given away to contestants.

giv·en (giv′ən) *adj.* **1.** presented; bestowed. **2.** inclined; disposed; prone: *given to allergic reactions. He is given to spreading gossip.* **3.** stated; specified: *to do something on a given day.* **4.** granted or assigned as a basis of calculating or reasoning: *Given a = b and b = c, then a = c.* **5.** executed, dated, and delivered, as an official document.

given name, name given to a person at birth or baptism; first name. Distinguished from **surname.**

Gi·za (gē′zə) *also,* **Gi·zeh.** *n.* city in northern Egypt, on the Nile near Cairo, site of the Sphinx and the Pyramids. Pop. (1966 est.), 571,249.

giz·zard (giz′ərd) *n.* **1.** second and muscular part of the stomach of a bird, in which partially digested food from the first part of the stomach is finely ground. **2.** first stomach of an insect. **3.** *Slang.* the human stomach. [Old French *giser* second stomach of a bird, going back to Latin *gigeria* (plural) cooked entrails of poultry.]

Gk., Greek.

gla·brous (glā′brəs) *adj.* (of leaves) free of hair, down, or fuzz. [Latin *glaber* without hair, smooth + -OUS.]

gla·cé (gla sā′) *adj.* **1.** covered with icing or sugar; glazed. **2.** frozen; iced. **3.** having a smooth, shiny surface; glossy: *glacé silk.* [French *glacé* iced, glazed, past participle of *glacer* to ice, glaze, from Latin *glaciāre* to turn into ice.]

gla·cial (glā′shəl) *adj.* **1.** of, relating to, or produced by ice or glaciers. **2.** of or relating to a period of time when glaciers covered large areas of the earth, esp. the Pleistocene. **3.** extremely cold; icy: *glacial rivers.* **4.** coldly indifferent; unfriendly: *a glacial manner.* **5.** *Chemistry.* tending to assume a crystalline structure: *glacial acetic acid.* [Latin *glaciālis* icy, from *glaciēs* ice.] —**gla′cial·ly,** *adv.*

glacial epoch, ice age.

gla·ci·ate (glā′shē āt′, -sē-) *-at·ed, -at·ing.* *v.t.* **1.** to cover with ice. **2.** to subject to or change by glacial action. [Latin *glaciātus,* past participle of *glaciāre* to turn into ice.] —**gla′ci·a′tion,** *n.*

gla·cier (glā′shər) *n.* large mass of ice moving slowly over some land surface or down a valley, formed over long periods from the accumulation of snow in areas where the amount of snow that falls exceeds the amount that melts. [French *glacier,* from *glace* ice, going back to Latin *glaciēs.*]

gla·ci·ol·o·gy (glā′shē ol′ə jē, -sē-) *n.* branch of geology concerned with the study of glaciers. —**gla·ci·o·log·i·cal** (glā′sē ə loj′i kəl), *adj.* —**gla′ci·ol′o·gist,** *n.*

gla·cis (glā′sis, glas′is) *pl.,* **-cis** *or* **-cis·es.** *n.* **1.** gently sloping surface; incline. **2.** sloping surface in front of a fortification, exposing attackers to defensive fire. [French *glacis,* from Old French *glacier* to slip, slide, from Latin *glaciāre* to turn into ice.]

glad¹ (glad) **glad·der, glad·dest.** *adj.* **1.** feeling or expressing joy, pleasure, or satisfaction, esp. about a particular condition or event; happy. **2.** causing joy or pleasure; pleasing: *glad tidings.* **3.** very willing: *Tom will be glad to go with you.* [Old English *glæd* bright, cheerful.] —**glad′ly,** *adv.* —**glad′ness,** *n.*

Syn. 1. Glad, happy, delighted, joyful mean expressing feelings of pleasure. **Glad** is generally used to convey a degree of pleasure ranging from pleased satisfaction to a feeling of elation: *The sailors were glad to see land on the horizon.* **Happy** suggests enjoyment brought about by the fulfillment of one's desires: *The child was happy pounding away at his new drum.* **Delighted** implies a quick and lively emotional reaction that is keenly felt and vividly expressed: *Ben uttered a delighted hurrah when he opened the package.* **Joyful** evokes the sense of jubilation and rejoicing arising from a particularly happy cause or occasion: *Everyone joined in the joyful singing of the Christmas carols.*

glad² (glad) *n.* *Informal.* gladiolus.

glad·den (glad′ən) *v.t.* to make glad.

glade (glād) *n.* open space in a wood or forest. [Of uncertain origin.]

glad·i·a·tor (glad′ē ā′tər) *n.* **1.** slave, captive, or paid professional who engaged in public combat in the arenas of ancient Rome. **2.** one who engages in physical or verbal combat. [Latin *gladiātor* swordsman, from *gladius* sword; probably of Celtic origin.] —**glad·i·a·to·ri·al** (glad′ē ə tôr′ē əl), *adj.*

glad·i·o·la (glad′ē ō′lə) *n.* gladiolus.

glad·i·o·lus (glad′ē ō′ləs) *pl.,* **-li** (-lī) *or* **-lus·es.** *n.* **1.** funnel-shaped, showy flower of any of a large group of plants, genus *Gladiolus,* having no stalk and growing in long clusters along one side of the stem. **2.** leafy plant bearing this flower, having stiff, sword-shaped leaves and a stem that grows directly from a corm. It is native to the Mediterranean region and Africa. [Latin *gladiolus* little sword, diminutive of *gladius* sword; referring to the plant's sword-shaped leaves. See GLADIATOR.]

glad·some (glad′səm) *adj.* **1.** causing joy or pleasure. **2.** glad. —**glad′some·ly,** *adv.* —**glad′some·ness,** *n.*

Glad·stone, William Ew·art (glad′stōn′, -stən; ū′ərt) 1809–98, British statesman, prime minister four times between 1868 and 1894.

Gladstone bag, lightweight, hinged suitcase that opens flat into two compartments. Also, **Glad′stone′.** [From William Ewart *Gladstone.*]

glam·or·ize (glam′ə rīz′) *-ized, -iz·ing.* *v.t.* to make glamorous. —**glam′or·i·za′tion, glam′or·iz′er,** *n.*

glam·or·ous (glam′ər əs) *also,* **glam·our·ous.** *adj.* full of glamour; alluring. —**glam′or·ous·ly,** *adv.* —**glam′or·ous·ness,** *n.*

glam·our (glam′ər) *also,* **glam·or.** *n.* **1.** elusive or alluring beauty or charm attached to a person or object. **2.** *Archaic.* a magic spell; magic. [Modification of GRAMMAR; because of the earlier association of learning with magic.]

glance (glans) *n.* **1.** brief or hurried look; glimpse. **2.** flash or gleam of light; glint. **3.** swift, oblique impact and deflection. —*v.i.,* **glanced, glanc·ing. 1.** to take a brief or hurried look: *The girls glanced in the store windows as they rode by.* **2.** to be deflected and move off at an oblique angle: *The bullet glanced off the rock.* **3.** to make an incidental or passing allusion, as in speaking or writing. **4.** to gleam or flash with light; glint: *The sequins on the singer's dress glanced under the spotlights.* —*v.t.* to cause (something) to strike a surface so that it is deflected at an oblique angle. [Modification of obsolete *glace* to glide, slip, from Old French *glacier* to slip, slide, from Latin *glaciāre* to turn into ice.]

gland (gland) *n.* **1.** any cell, tissue, or organ that produces and discharges one or more substances that are utilized by or discharged from the body. Important glands include the thyroid and pituitary glands and the pancreas. **2.** secreting structure in certain plants, as a hair or small prominence, usually located on the surfaces of stems, leaves, or flowers. [French *glande* organ of secretion, going back to Latin *glandula* gland of the throat, diminutive of *glāns* acorn.]

glan·ders (glan′dərz) *n.* highly contagious, usually fatal, bacterial disease of horses, mules, and related animals that can affect the respiratory system and skin. It is communicable to man and certain other animals. [Old French *glandres,* plural of *glandre* glandular swelling, from Latin *glandula.* See GLAND.]

glan·du·lar (glan′jə lər) *adj.* **1.** of, relating to, or affecting a gland: *a glandular disease.* **2.** consisting of or containing a gland or glands: *a glandular mass of tissue.* Also, **glan′du·lous.**

glandular fever, infectious mononucleosis.

glare (glâr) *n.* **1.** strong, usually unpleasant light, as from sunlight reflected on a shiny surface. **2.** piercing, hostile stare. **3.** offensively showy appearance; gaudiness. —*v.i.,* **glared, glar·ing. 1.** to shine with a strong, harsh brilliancy. **2.** to stare piercingly and with hostility. **3.** to be offensively showy or conspicuous. —*v.t.* to express with a glare: *to glare defiance at a person.* [Middle Low German *glaren* to gleam.]

glar·ing (glâr′ing) *adj.* **1.** emitting or reflecting a harsh light; unpleasantly bright. **2.** extremely conspicuous; flagrant: *a glaring mistake.* **3.** staring piercingly and with hostility. —**glar′ing·ly,** *adv.* —**Syn. 2.** see **flagrant.**

glar·y (glâr′ē) *adj.* **glar·i·er, glar·i·est.** *adj.* dazzling; glaring.

Glas·gow (glas′gō, -kō) largest city and chief port of Scotland, in the southern part of the country. Pop. (1968), 956,195.

glass (glas) *n.* **1.** hard, brittle, usually transparent material made by melting a mixture of sand, soda, and lime. The characteristic that distinguishes glass from other materials is that it cools from the liquid state to a hardened state without developing a crystalline structure, thus retaining the amorphous molecular structure characteristic of liquids. **2.** any substance, artificial or natural, that has similar properties or composition: *glass of phosphorus, glass of lead.* **3.** open container, esp. of glass, usually without a handle, used chiefly for drinking. **4.a.** glassful: *I'd like half a glass of water.* **b.** drink: *She gave him a glass of wine.* **5.** something partially or entirely made of glass, as a window or a mirror. **6.** glassware. **7. glasses. a.** eyeglasses. **b.** binoculars. —*adj.*

at; āpe; cär; end; mē; it; īce; hot; ōld; fôrk; wood; fōōl; oil; out; up; ūse; turn; sing; thin; this; zh in treasure; ə in ago, taken, pencil, lemon, circus.

Gladiolus

1. made of glass: *a glass bottle.* **2.** fitted with or covered with glass: *a glass door.* —*v.t.* **1.** to enclose or protect with glass (with *in*): *They glassed in the open porch.* **2.** *Archaic.* to reflect, as a mirror. [Old English *glæs* the hard, brittle substance.]

glass blower, one who engages in glass blowing.

glass blowing, art or process of shaping a mass of molten glass into various shapes or objects by blowing a controlled stream of air through a tube into the mass.

glass·ful (glas′fool′) *pl.* **-fuls.** *n.* quantity that can be contained in a drinking glass.

glass·house (glas′hous′) *n.* *British.* greenhouse.

glass·ine (gla sēn′) *n.* thin, glazed, transluscent paper, used esp. for book jackets, envelopes, and envelope windows.

glass snake, any of several legless, snakelike lizards, genus *Ophisaurus,* found in the United States, Europe, and Asia. When it is struck, its fragile tail readily breaks into several wiggling pieces which can distract an enemy while the lizard escapes. Length: 1–3½ feet.

glass·ware (glas′wār′) *n.* objects of glass fashioned by hand or produced by machine, esp. drinking glasses.

glass wool, fibers of spun glass having a woollike appearance, used esp. for insulation and filtration.

glass·wort (glas′wurt′) *n.* any of a small group of low-growing wild plants, genus *Salicornia,* of the goosefoot family, that grows in saltwater marshes or on lake shores and bears fleshy, jointed stems and small scalelike leaves. Also, **sam′phire.** [Because formerly used in manufacturing glass.]

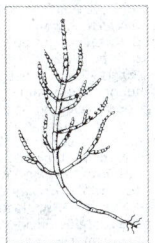
Glasswort

glass·y (glas′ē) **glass·i·er, glass·i·est.** *adj.* **1.** resembling or having properties of glass; smooth and shiny: *the glassy surface of a lake on a windless day.* **2.** having a fixed, expressionless, or lifeless look: *a glassy stare.* **3.** having a fixed, unintelligent, or expressionless look: *glassy eyes.* —**glass′i·ly,** *adv.* —**glass′i·ness,** *n.*

glass·y-eyed (glas′ē īd′) *adj.* having a fixed, lifeless expression in one's eyes.

Glas·we·gian (glas wē′jən, -jē ən) *adj.* of or relating to Glasgow. —*n.* native or inhabitant of Glasgow.

Glau·ber's salt (glou′bərz) hydrated sodium sulfate, used as a mild laxative and in the dyeing industry. [From Johann R. *Glauber,* 1604–68, a German chemist who first made it.]

glau·co·ma (glô kō′mə, glou-) *n.* serious eye disease characterized by increased pressure in, and gradual hardening of, the eyeball. It may lead to damage of the retina and gradual loss of sight. [Latin *glaucōma* cataract of the eye, from Greek *glaukōma,* from *glaukos* gray.]

glau·cous (glô′kəs) *adj.* **1.** having a bluish-green color. **2.** (of plants or plant parts) covered with a whitish powder, as plums or grapes. [Latin *glaucus* bluish-green, grayish, gleaming, from Greek *glaukos.*]

glaze (glāz) **glazed, glaz·ing.** *v.t.* **1.** to overlay or cover with a smooth, glossy coating: *She glazed the doughnuts with sugar. The pottery was glazed to make it shiny.* **2.** to furnish or fit with glass. **3.** to cover (a painting) with a transparent coating to modify the tone. —*v.i.* to become glassy or glazed: *His eyes glazed with pain.* —*n.* **1.** smooth, glossy covering or coating. **2.** any substance used to produce such a coating. [Middle English *glasen* to fit with glass, make a glassy coating, from *glas* glass, from Old English *glæs.*] —**glaz′er,** *n.*

gla·zier (glā′zhər) *n.* one who installs glass panes, as in windows.

glaz·ing (glā′zing) *n.* **1.** act or business of a glazier. **2.** glass used for this. **3.** glaze. **4.** process or art of applying a glaze.

gleam (glēm) *n.* **1.** flash or beam of bright light. **2.** reflected brightness, as from a polished surface: *the gleam of a new car.* **3.** subdued or transient light; glow: *the distant gleam of the candle, the gleam of the polished floor.* **4.** faint or fleeting manifestation: *a gleam of humor, a gleam of understanding.* —*v.i.* **1.** to shine with subdued or transient light: *The polished floor gleamed.* **2.** to be manifested faintly or fleetingly: *A light gleamed in the fog. Hope gleamed for an instant.* [Old English *glæm* brightness, splendor.] —**Syn.** *n.* **1.** see **glimmer.**

glean (glēn) *v.t., v.i.* **1.** to collect slowly and assiduously. **2.** to gather (grain or other remains of a crop) left on a field after reaping. [Old French *glener* to gather grain left after reaping, from Late Latin *glennāre;* of Celtic origin.] —**glean′a·ble,** *adj.* —**glean′er,** *n.*

glean·ings (glē′ningz) *n.,pl.* things acquired by gleaning.

glebe (glēb) *n.* *British.* portion of land assigned to a clergyman and considered as part of his income during his tenure of office. [Latin *glēba* soil¹, clod.]

glee (glē) *n.* **1.** joy; delight; merriment. **2.** unaccompanied song for three or more male voices, popular in the eighteenth century. [Old English *glēo* joy, mirth, music.]

glee club, group organized for singing choral music.

glee·ful (glē′fəl) *adj.* full of glee; merry; joyous. —**glee′ful·ly,** *adv.* —**glee′ful·ness,** *n.*

glee·man (glē′mən) *pl.,* **-men.** *n.* a medieval minstrel.

glee·some (glē′səm) *adj.* *Archaic.* gleeful.

glen (glen) *n.* small, narrow, usually secluded valley. [Scottish Gaelic *gleann.*]

Glen·dale (glen′dāl′) *n.* city in southwestern California, adjoining Los Angeles. Pop. (1970), 132,752.

glen·gar·ry (glen gar′ē) *pl.,* **-ries.** *n.* Scottish cap made of wool, having straight sides and a crease lengthwise across the crown, often with short ribbons at the back. [From *Glengarry,* a valley in Scotland.]

Glenn, John (glen) 1921—, U.S. astronaut, the first American to orbit the earth.

glib (glib) **glib·ber, glib·best.** *adj.* **1.** superficial; insincere: *a glib compliment.* **2.** fluent and polished: *He was a glib speaker.* **3.** easy; informal; offhand: *a glib manner.* [Probably modification of Dutch *glibberig* slippery.] —**glib′ly,** *adv.* —**glib′ness,** *n.*

glide (glīd) **glid·ed, glid·ing.** *v.i.* **1.** to move smoothly, continuously, and effortlessly: *The figure skater glided over the ice.* **2.** to pass gradually and imperceptibly, as time. **3.** *Aeronautics.* to maintain flight or descend slowly without the use of a motor or engine. —*n.* **1.** act of moving smoothly and effortlessly. **2.** *Aeronautics.* act of gliding. **3.** *Music.* slur. **4.** *Phonetics.* **a.** transitional sound produced when the voice shifts from the articulation of one sound to that of another sound. **b.** semivowel. [Old English *glīdan* to slide, slip.] —**Syn.** *v.i.* **1.** see **slide.**

Glengarry

glid·er (glī′dər) *n.* **1.** aircraft constructed of lightweight materials and designed to fly without the aid of an engine, relying on rising air currents to remain aloft. **2.** one who or that which glides. **3.** piece of furniture resembling a couch, usually used outdoors, suspended from a frame that permits a backward and forward movement.

glim (glim) *n.* *Slang.* **1.** an eye. **2.** candle, lamp, or other source of light. [Possibly short for GLIMMER or GLIMPSE.]

Glider

glim·mer (glim′ər) *n.* **1.** dim, wavering light. **2.** faint notion; inkling: *a glimmer of hope.* —*v.i.* **1.** to shine with a dim, wavering light; flicker. **2.** to appear faintly. [Probably of Scandinavian origin.]

Syn. *n.* **1. Glimmer, shimmer, glint, gleam** indicate an unsteady, usually weak, light. **Glimmer** implies rapidly varying strength so that the beam of light seems to shake: *Far across the moor could be seen the glimmer of a farmhouse window.* **Shimmer** suggests soft glimmering light: *The shimmer of moonlight on a mountain lake is thought to be very romantic.* **Glint** implies sharp, bright flashes: *On the battlements they saw the glint of armor.* **Gleam** suggests quick brightness seen against the dark or through something more or less transparent: *He saw the gleam of the trout deep in the stream.*

glim·mer·ing (glim′ər ing) *n.* glimmer.

glimpse (glimps) *n.* **1.** brief view; passing glance: *He caught a glimpse of the driver's face as the car sped by.* **2.** transient appearance; trace: *His statement contained a glimpse of the truth.* —*v.t.,* **glimpsed, glimps·ing.** to catch a brief view of; see momentarily. —*v.i.* to look quickly; glance (with *at*). [Probably of Germanic origin.]

glint (glint) *n.* **1.** bright quick flash; gleam. **2.** sparkle or luster, as of metal. —*v.i.* **1.** to shine; gleam. **2.** to move quickly; dart: *Rays of light glinted off the lake's surface.* [Possibly from dialectal Swedish *glinta* to slip, gleam.] —**Syn.** *n.* **1.** see **glimmer.**

glis·sade (gli säd′, -säd′) *n.* **1.** act of gliding over snow or ice, as in skiing. **2.** gliding or sliding dance step, esp. in ballet. [French *glissade* a sliding, from *glisser* to slide, a blend of Old French *glier* to glide (of Germanic origin) and Old French *glacier* to slide. See GLACIS.]

glis·san·do (gli sän′dō) *pl.,* **-di** (-dē). *n. Music.* **1.** gliding effect performed in various ways, as by rapidly running one finger over the white keys of a piano or sliding one finger along the string of a stringed instrument. **2.** glissando passage. —*adj.* of or performed with a gliding effect. [Possibly modification (using Italian present participle ending *-ando*) of French *glissade* a sliding. See GLISSADE.]

glis·ten (glis′ən) *v.i.* to shine or sparkle with or as with reflected light: *Tears glistened on her cheeks.* —*n.* gleam; sparkle. [Old English *glisnian* to glitter.]

glit·ter (glit′ər) *v.i.* **1.** to shine with scattered light; sparkle: *The jewels glittered.* **2.** to be superficially attractive or showy. —*n.* **1.** brilliance;

at; āpe; cär; end; mē; it; īce; hot; ōld; fôrk; wood; fōol; oil; out; up; ūse; turn; sing; thin; <u>th</u>is; zh in treasure; ə in ago, taken, pencil, lemon, circus.

437

showiness; splendor: *the glitter of New York City's theater district.*
2. small bits of sparkling material, used for ornamentation. [Old Norse *glitra* to sparkle.] —**glit′ter·y,** *adv.* —**Syn.** *v.i.* **1.** see **flash.**
gloam·ing (glō′ming) *n.* twilight; dusk. [Old English *glōmung.*]
gloat (glōt) *v.i.* to ponder with smugness or satisfaction: *He gloated over his rival's misfortune.* [Old Norse *glotta* to smile scornfully.] —**gloat′er,** *n.* —**gloat′ing·ly,** *adv.*
glob (glob) *n.* **1.** small drop. **2.** large, rounded mass or lump: *a glob of paint.* [Possibly blend of GLOBE and BLOB.]
glob·al (glō′bəl) *adj.* **1.** of or relating to the entire world; worldwide: *global warfare.* **2.** shaped like a globe; spherical. —**glob′al·ly,** *adv.*
glo·bate (glō′bāt) *adj.* shaped like a globe; globular.
globe (glōb) *n.* **1.** the earth; world. **2.** sphere on which a map of the earth or of the heavens appears. **3.** solid spherical body; sphere. **4.** anything spherical or spherelike, as a glass covering for a light bulb. [Latin *globus* ball.] —**Syn.** *n.* **3.** see **ball¹.**
globe·fish (glōb′fish′) *pl.,* **-fish** or **-fish·es.** *n.* any of various spiny-finned fish, family Tetraodontidae, of tropical seas, that can inflate their bodies into a globular form with air or water. Also, **puff′er.**
globe·flow·er (glōb′flou′ər) *n.* any of several plants, genus *Trollius,* of the crowfoot family, bearing globe-shaped, usually yellow flowers.
globe·trot·ter (glōb′trot′ər) *n.* one who travels extensively, esp. as a sightseer. —**globe′trot′ting,** *n., adj.*
glo·bose (glō′bōs, glō bōs′) *adj.* having the form of a globe; globular. [Latin *globōsus* round as a ball, from *globus* ball.]
glob·u·lar (glob′yə lər) *adj.* **1.** having the shape of a globe; spherical. **2.** composed of globules.
glob·ule (glob′ūl) *n.* small ball or drop: *a globule of oil.* [Latin *globulus* little ball, diminutive of *globus* ball.]
glob·u·lin (glob′yə lin) *n.* any of a group of proteins found in many kinds of plant and animal cells, insoluble in water but readily soluble in dilute salt solutions. Globulins occur in seeds, milk, egg yolks, muscle cells, and blood plasma. [GLOBULE + -IN¹.]

glock·en·spiel (glok′ən spēl′, -shpēl′) *n.* musical percussion instrument consisting of a series of metal bars mounted in a frame, played by striking with two small hammers. [German *Glockenspiel* chimes, from *Glocke* bell + *Spiel* play.]
glom·er·ate (glom′ər it, -ə rāt′) *adj.* having the form of a compact rounded mass; clustered. [Latin *glomerātus,* past participle of *glomerāre* to form into a ball or heap, from *glomus* ball.]
glom·er·ule (glom′ə rōol′) *n.* dense flower cluster, esp. a cyme. [Modern Latin *glomerulus,* from Latin *glomer-,* stem of *glomus* ball.]

Glockenspiel

gloom (glōōm) *n.* **1.** depressing or sullen atmosphere. **2.** dejection; sadness: *Gloom was reflected in his voice.* **3.** complete or partial darkness; dimness: *The car's headlights pierced the gloom.* —*v.i.* **1.** to be or look sullen, depressed, or displeased. **2.** to be or become dark or dismal. [Middle English *gloumen* to look sullen; of uncertain origin.]
gloom·y (glōō′mē) **gloom·i·er, gloom·i·est.** *adj.* **1.** depressing; dismal; dreary: *There was a gloomy atmosphere in the losing candidate's head-quarters.* **2.** melancholy; depressed; dejected: *He looked gloomy.* **3.** dark; dim. —**gloom′i·ly,** *adv.* —**gloom′i·ness,** *n.* —**Syn.** **3.** see **dark.**
Glo·ri·a (glôr′ē ə) *n.* **1.a.** any of several hymns of praise to God, beginning with the Latin word *Gloria,* as the Gloria in Excelsis Deo or the Gloria Patri. **b.** second part of the ordinary of the Mass, the Gloria in Excelsis Deo, sung or said between the Kyrie eleison and the Credo. **c.** musical setting for any of these. **2. gloria. a.** halo or nimbus, esp. in art. **b.** closely woven, lightweight fabric made of nylon, rayon, acetate, and various other materials, used chiefly for umbrellas. [Latin *glōria* honor, praise, fame.]
Glo·ri·a in Ex·cel·sis De·o (glôr′ē ə in ek sel′sis dā′ō) hymn of praise beginning with the words *Glory to God in the highest.*
Glo·ri·a Pa·tri (glôr′ē ə pä′trē) hymn of praise beginning with the words *Glory be to the Father.*
glo·ri·fi·ca·tion (glôr′ə fi kā′shən) *n.* **1.** act of glorifying. **2.** state of being glorified. **3.** transformation of something into a more magnificent form.
glo·ri·fy (glôr′ə fī′) **-fied, -fy·ing.** *v.t.* **1.** to exalt with praise; honor: *The Romans glorified Caesar.* **2.** to make glorious; procure glory for: *His success glorified his profession.* **3.** to cause to appear or seem more glorious or splendid than it actually is: *The author glorified the life of the peasants.* [Old French *glorifier* to honor greatly, from Church Latin *glōrificāre* to make glorious, from Latin *glōria* praise, fame + *facere* to make.] —**glo′ri·fi′er,** *n.*
glo·ri·ous (glôr′ē əs) *adj.* **1.** magnificent; splendid: *a glorious day, a*

glorious sunset. **2.** possessing or deserving glory; famous; renowned: *a glorious career.* **3.** conferring glory: *a glorious deed.* **4.** *Informal.* extremely enjoyable or delightful: *We had a glorious time.* [Old French *glorios* blessed, famous, splendid, from Latin *glōriōsus* famous, full of glory, from *glōria.* See GLORY.] —**glo′ri·ous·ly,** *adv.* —**glo′ri·ous·ness,** *n.*
glo·ry (glôr′ē) *pl.,* **-ries.** *n.* **1.** exalted praise, honor, or distinction; fame; renown: *They did the deed for glory alone. His assistant actually made the discovery, but he received all the glory.* **2.** one who or that which brings such praise, honor, distinction, or renown; source of pride: *The glory of the tropical region was its climate. He was a glory to his profession.* **3.** resplendent beauty; magnificence: *The sun shone in all its glory.* **4.** state or condition of ultimate magnificence or prosperity: *That country was in its glory during the years just before the war.* **5.** highest degree of self-satisfaction or pleasure: *He was in his glory in front of the television cameras.* **6.** praise and honor offered in adoration: *Give glory to God.* **7.** external splendor and bliss of heaven: *The angels accepted him into glory.* **8.** halo or nimbus. —*v.i.,* **-ried, -ry·ing. 1.** to rejoice proudly; exult (with *in*): *They gloried in the war's end.* **2.** to be extremely delighted; revel: *He gloried in his newly-gained authority.* [Old French *glorie, gloire* great renown, from Latin *glōria* honor, praise, fame.]
gloss¹ (glôs, glos) *n.* **1.** superficial shine, as of satin or a polished surface; luster. **2.** deceptive appearance; semblance: *After his gloss of politeness wore off, she found she did not like him.* —*v.t.* **1.** to put a superficial shine or luster on. **2.** to minimize or attempt to hide (often with *over*): *to gloss over the faults of a friend. He glossed over his selfishness with a display of generosity.* [Possibly of Scandinavian origin.] —**Syn.** *n.* **1.** see **luster.**
gloss² (glôs, glos) *n.* **1.** explanation or interpretation, as of a text; commentary. **2.** glossary. **3.** notation or translation placed in between the lines or in the margin of a text, esp. of an ancient or medieval manuscript. —*v.t.* **1.** to comment on, as a word or text; explain; interpret. **2.** to give a false or superficial explanation of (often with *over* or *away*): *He glossed away the problem with a glib panacea.* [Latin *glōssa* word needing explanation, from Greek *glōssa* tongue, language.] —**gloss′er,** *n.*
glos·sa·ry (glôs′ər ē, glos′ər ē) *pl.,* **-ries.** *n.* alphabetized list of glosses, esp. of specialized, foreign, or obscure words. [Latin *glōssārium,* from *glōssa* word needing explanation. See GLOSS².] —**glos·sar′i·al,** *adj.*
glos·so·la·li·a (glô′sə lā′lē ə, glos′ə-) *n.* **1.** incomprehensible speech associated with religious ecstasy; speaking in tongues. **2.** imaginary, unintelligible language associated with the insane. [Modern Latin *glossolalia,* going back to Greek *glōssa* language + *lalein* to talk.]
gloss·y (glô′sē, glos′ē) **gloss·i·er, gloss·i·est.** *adj.* **1.** having a shiny surface; lustrous. **2.** having a false air or appearance of sophistication: *They were not taken in by the glossy advertisement promoting the product.* —*n. pl.,* **gloss·ies.** photograph printed on smooth, glossy paper. —**gloss′i·ly,** *adv.* —**gloss′i·ness,** *n.*
glot·tal (glot′əl) *adj.* **1.** of or relating to the glottis. **2.** *Phonetics.* articulated in the glottis, as *h* in English.
glottal stop, speech sound produced by closing the glottis and then suddenly releasing the breath with a slight gulping sound.
glot·tis (glot′is) *n.* narrow opening in the larynx between the vocal cords. [Greek *glōttis* mouth of the windpipe, from *glōtta* tongue.]
glove (gluv) *n.* **1.** covering for the hand made of fabric or leather, usually with separate sections that conform in shape to each finger. **2.a.** any of several coverings for the hand used in various sports, as baseball, hockey, or golf. **b.** boxing glove. **3. to fit like a glove.** to fit or suit perfectly. **4. to handle with kid gloves.** to treat extremely gently and tactfully. —*v.t.,* **gloved, glov·ing. 1.** to cover or provide with gloves. **2.** to catch (a ball) with a glove. [Old English *glōf* covering for the hand.]
glove compartment, small storage space in the dashboard of an automobile.
glow (glō) *n.* **1.** shine from or as from a heated substance; incandescence. **2.** richness and warmth, as of color: *the golden glow of her hair, the glow of the autumn moon, the glow of health.* **3.** enthusiastic or ardent feeling or appearance: *a glow of pleasure.* —*v.i.* **1.** to shine from or as if from intense heat: *The candle glowed. The face of the clock glowed in the dark.* **2.** to be bright and warm, as in color: *The sunset glowed with color. Her cheeks glowed as she described her vacation.* **3.** to be or look enthusiastic or ardent: *Her eyes glowed with pleasure.* [Old English *glōwan* to shine, to shine with heat.]
glow·er (glou′ər) *v.i.* to look at angrily or threateningly; scowl: *The motorist glowered at the driver who had cut in front of him.* —*n.* angry or threatening stare. [Possibly of Scandinavian origin.] —**glow′er·ing·ly,** *adv.* —**Syn.** *v.i.* see **frown.**
glow·ing (glō′ing) *adj.* **1.** incandescent: *glowing coals.* **2.** ardent; enthusiastic: *glowing praise. She described her trip in glowing terms.*

at; āpe; cär; end; mē; it; īce; hot; ōld; fôrk; wood; fōōl; oil; out; up; ūse; turn; sing; thin; this; zh in treasure; ə in ago, taken, pencil, lemon, circus.

3. having the facial coloring caused by excitement or health; radiant. **4.** rich and warm; vivid: *a glowing red.* —**glow′ing·ly,** *adv.*

glow·worm (glō′wurm′) *n.* any of various insects or larvae that give off light, as the larva of the firefly.

glox·in·i·a (glok sin′ē ə) *n.* low-growing tropical plant, *Sinningia speciosa,* native to the rain forests of Brazil, often cultivated for its large, velvety leaves and showy, tubular or bell-shaped flowers. [Modern Latin *Gloxinia,* from Benjamin P. *Gloxin,* an eighteenth-century German botanist.]

glu·ca·gon (glōō′kə gən) *n.* hormone secreted by the pancreas that raises the level of sugar in the bloodstream.

glu·ci·num (glōō sī′nəm) *n.* former name of beryllium. Also, **glu·cin·i·um** (glōō sin′ē əm). [Modern Latin *glucinum,* going back to Greek *glykys* sweet; because some of its salts have a sweet taste.]

glu·cose (glōō′kōs) *n.* **1.** simple sugar occurring in plants and in the blood of man and animals that is an important source of energy for the body. Formula: $C_6H_{12}O_6$ **2.** thick, yellowish syrup made from starch, used in foods, in intravenous feedings, in the curing of tobacco, and in the tanning industry. [Greek *glykys* sweet + -OSE².]

glue (glōō) *n.* **1.** adhesive consisting of impure gelatin derived from various animal proteins, widely used in the manufacture of furniture, paints, and plywood. **2.** any sticky substance used as an adhesive. —*v.t.,* **glued, glu·ing.** to stick together or fasten with or as with glue. [Old French *glu,* from Late Latin *glūs,* from Latin *glūten.*]

glue·y (glōō′ē) **glu·i·er, glu·i·est.** *adj.* **1.** resembling glue; viscous. **2.** full of or smeared with glue: *a gluey surface.*

glum (glum) **glum·mer, glum·mest.** *adj.* gloomy; morose. [From Middle English *glomen, gloumen* to look sullen. See GLOOM.] —**glum′ly,** *adv.* —**glum′ness,** *n.*

glut (glut) **glut·ted, glut·ting.** *v.t.* **1.** to gratify completely; satiate: *A feast glutted his hunger.* **2.** to supply (a market) with goods to excess; oversupply. —*n.* **1.** excess of something, esp. a commodity. **2.** great quantity. [Old French *gloutir* to gulp down, from Latin *gluttīre.*]

glu·te·al (glōō′tē əl, glōō tē′əl) *adj.* of or relating to the buttocks.

glu·ten (glōō′tən) *n.* tough, sticky protein substance obtained from grains, esp. wheat and rye, used to make bread dough rise. [Latin *glūten* glue.] —**glu′te·nous,** *adj.*

glu·ti·nous (glōō′tən əs) *adj.* like glue; sticky. —**glu′ti·nous·ly,** *adv.*

glut·ton¹ (glut′ən) *n.* **1.** one who eats to excess or takes pleasure in eating excessively. **2.** one who has an excessive fondness or capacity for something: *a glutton for work, a glutton for punishment.* [Old French *gluton* greedy eater, from Latin *gluttō.*]

glut·ton² (glut′ən) *n.* wolverine. [Translation of German *Vielfrass* wolverine, glutton¹ (from *viel* much + *fressen* to devour).]

glut·ton·ous (glut′ən əs) *adj.* given to excessive eating; greedy; voracious. —**glut′ton·ous·ly,** *adv.* —**glut′ton·ous·ness,** *n.*

glut·ton·y (glut′ən ē) *pl.,* **-ton·ies.** *n.* excess in eating; greediness.

glyc·er·in (glis′ər in) *also,* **glyc·er·ine** (glis′ər in, -ə rēn′). *n.* colorless, syrupy, sweet liquid obtained from fats or produced synthetically, used esp. in making nitroglycerin, medicines, soaps, and certain plastics. Formula: $C_3H_5(OH)_3$ [French *glycérine,* from Greek *glykeros* sweet.]

glyc·er·ol (glis′ə rôl′) *n.* glycerin.

gly·co·gen (glī′kə jən) *n.* one of the forms in which sugar is stored in the body of animals and, when needed, converted into simple sugar glucose. [Greek *glykys* sweet + -GEN.]

gly·col (glī′kôl) *n.* ethylene glycol.

glyph (glif) *n.* **1.** figure carved in relief, representing a word or idea; hieroglyph. **2.** *Architecture.* vertical channel or groove, as in a Doric frieze. [Greek *glyphē* carving, from *glyphein* to hollow out, carve.]

gm., gram; grams.

G-man (jē′man′) *pl.,* **-men.** *n. Informal.* agent of the Federal Bureau of Investigation. [Short for G(*overnment*) *man.*]

Gmc., Germanic.

gnarl (närl) *n.* twisted, knotty protuberance, as on a tree. —*v.t.* to twist or make knotted and rugged like an old tree. [From GNARLED.] —**gnarl′y,** *adj.*

gnarled (närld) *adj.* **1.** having many rough, twisted knots, as a tree trunk or branches. **2.** (of the hands) rough and slightly deformed, with prominent knuckles. [Probably modification of earlier *knurled* knotted, from KNURL.]

gnash (nash) *v.t.* **1.** to strike, grate, or grind (the teeth) together, as in anger or pain. **2.** to bite by violently grinding the teeth. [Probably of Scandinavian origin.]

gnat (nat) *n.* **1.** any of various mosquitolike insects, order Diptera, having sharp, piercing mouth parts. Some suck blood; others feed on plants. **2.** *British.* mosquito. **3. to strain at a gnat,** to object to some unimportant thing. [Old English *gnætt* small fly with two wings.]

gnaw (nô) **gnawed, gnawed** *or* **gnawn, gnaw·ing.** *v.t.* **1.** to bite (something) repeatedly with the teeth: *The dog gnawed the bone.* **2.** to make

by gnawing: *The rat gnawed a hole through the box.* **3.** to cause constant discomfort, pain, or trouble to. —*v.i.* **1.** to bite repeatedly. **2.** to torment or trouble (with *on, at,* or *into*): *His guilt gnawed at his conscience.* [Old English *gnagan* to bite repeatedly.]

gnaw·ing (nô′ing) *n.* dull, constant sensation of pain or discomfort, as from hunger.

gneiss (nīs) *n.* metamorphic rock composed of layers of light-colored feldspar and quartz alternating with darker layers of other minerals. [German *Gneis,* possibly from Middle High German *gneiste* spark; because it sparkles.]

gnome¹ (nōm) *n.* in folklore, dwarf who inhabits a mountain grotto or a mine in the earth. [French *gnome,* from Modern Latin *gnomus,* said to be from Greek *gnōmē* intelligence (supposedly because gnomes had knowledge of the riches of the earth).]

gnome² (nōm, nō′mē) *n.* short, pithy saying; maxim; aphorism. [Greek *gnōmē* maxim, intelligence.]

gno·mic (nō′mik, nom′ik) *adj.* **1.** containing or consisting of gnomes; aphoristic. **2.** of or designating a writer of maxims. [Greek *gnōmikos* relating to maxims, didactic, from *gnōmē* maxim.]

gno·mon (nō′mon) *n.* triangular piece on a sundial, the projecting end of which shows the time of day by casting a shadow on the face of the dial. [Latin *gnōmōn,* from Greek *gnōmōn* one that knows, interpreter, gnomon.]

Gnos·tic (nos′tik) *n.* one who believes in Gnosticism. —*adj.* of or relating to Gnosticism or Gnostics. [Greek *gnōstikos* relating to knowing, going back to *gignōskein* to know; because the Gnostics claimed to have a superior knowledge of spiritual matters.]

Gnos·ti·cism (nos′tə siz′əm) *n.* ancient religious movement whose members believed that most men are completely material and therefore doomed, but that God sent Christ to the few who possess a divine spark and thus can be saved.

GNP, gross national product.

gnu (nōō, nū) *pl.,* **gnus** *or* **gnu.** *n.* any of several swift African antelope, genera *Connochaetes* and *Gorgon,* having an oxlike head, short horns that curve sharply upward, and horselike legs, body, and tail. Also, **wil′de·beest′.** Height: to 4½ feet at the shoulder. [Modification of Kaffir *nqu.*]

Gnu

go¹ (gō) **went, gone, go·ing.** *v.i.* **1.** to move or pass along; travel: *to go by train. The car is going too fast.* **2.** to move away; depart; leave: *I have to go now. He comes and goes as he pleases.* **3.a.** to advance or move toward someone or something or in a particular direction: *to go right, to go downstairs. He went to his aunt's house for dinner. We must go to the authorities to report the accident.* **b.** to move or proceed with a specific goal or purpose: *He went to dress for dinner.* **4.** to be in or maintain action or movement; operate: *The machines are kept going day and night.* **5.** to be given or awarded: *The estate went to his children when he died.* **6.** to be, appear, continue, or be habitually in a particular state or condition: *to go unrewarded, to go in rags, to go naked.* **7.** to pass into a particular state or condition; become: *to go insane. Will the state go Republican after all these years?* **8.** to enter into a state or condition of: *to go into hiding, to go into mourning.* **9.** to be contributed or put: *Months of research went into his term paper.* **10.** to be appropriated, spent, or applied: *Most of the money went for food.* **11.** to proceed or be guided: *We have to go by the rules.* **12.** to extend, reach, or lead: *Our land goes as far as the eye can see. The stairs go to the basement. The road goes east from here. The ribbon won't go around the package.* **13.** to pass away; cease: *The pain has gone.* **14.** to be given up or discarded: *The two old chairs must go.* **15.** to cease to exist; be abolished: *The old laws must go.* **16.** to be compatible or suitable; harmonize: *Red wine goes with meat. The shoes go with the bag.* **17.** to pass; elapse: *When you are busy, time goes quickly. The day went slowly.* **18.** to put or subject oneself: *She'd go to any expense for him. He went to a lot of trouble for us.* **19.** to have recourse; resort; appeal: *We may have to go to court to settle the matter.* **20.** to be consumed: *The food went quickly because we were hungry.* **21.** to pass from person to person; circulate: *The flu went through the family. News of the plane crash went around like wildfire.* **22.** to be sold: *The sofa went for $50 at the auction.* **23.** to result in a specified manner; turn out: *The election went against him. Things went well.* **24.** to be known: *She went by the name of Smith.* **25.** to fail, break down, or give way: *The old man's eyesight started to go. The bridge went under the pressure.* **26.** to hold up or out; endure; last: *The boxer couldn't go two more rounds.* **27.** to be expressed or phrased; have a particular form or arrangement: *How does the poem go? I'll sing the song the way it should go.* **28.** to contribute to a result or consequence; help: *His conduct just goes to show*

that he's a rude person. **29.** to have a usual or proper place; belong: *These sheets go in the linen closet.* **30.** to be able to be accommodated or contained; fit: *Will the books go in that box? All the information will go on two pages.* **31.** to be capable of being divided: *Four goes into eight two times.* **32.** to continue or carry one's actions to or beyond a certain point: *How far will you go before you get hurt?* **33.** to emit or make a certain sound. **34.** to be compared with or ranked among others of its kind: *This is a luxury hotel, as hotels go.* **35.** to be about or intending to do something: *It is going to rain. We are going to leave.* **36.** to attack (with *at* or *for*): *The dog went for the thief.* **37.** to work or function properly or as intended. **38.** to be acceptable, satisfactory, or authoritative: *Whatever he says goes. Anything goes in this school.* **39.** to die.
to go. 1. left; remaining: *We have six days to go before the holidays.* **2.** *Informal.* to be prepared and packaged to be taken out of an eating establishment: *One hamburger to go.*
to go about. a. to be occupied with or busy at: *to go about one's business.* **b.** to set about; begin: *How does one go about getting the information?* **c.** *Nautical.* to change from one tack to another; change direction.
to go after. to go in pursuit of; chase.
to go against. to be contrary to or antagonize; oppose: *It goes against my principles.*
to go along. to agree; cooperate (often with *with*): *So far we go along with you. We'll go along if you complete your end of the bargain.*
to go (along) with. to accompany.
to go around. to be sufficient to provide or give a portion to all: *Will there be enough to go around?*
to go at. to undertake or work at: *He went at the job with vigor.*
to go back on. *Informal.* **a.** to fail to keep or fulfill; break: *He went back on his word.* **b.** to be unfaithful or disloyal to; betray: *He went back on his friends.*
to go beyond. to exceed; surpass.
to go by. to pass unnoticed or be disregarded: *We'll let the error go by this time.*
to go down. a. to be recorded or remembered: *He'll go down in history.* **b.** to suffer defeat; lose.
to go for. *Informal.* **a.** to try to secure or obtain: *He went for the money instead of the car.* **b.** to favor or support: *The state went for the Democrats.* **c.** to be strongly attracted by or interested in: *He goes for anything concerning money.*
to go for broke. to put forth or risk everything in order to gain or achieve something.
to go hard with. to cause or result in hardship, trouble, or suffering for.
to go in (or out) for. *Informal.* to like or engage in.
to go into. a. to examine or discuss: *We can't go into all the causes of the war at this time.* **b.** to enter or take up, as a profession or study: *She went into medicine.*
to go in with. to join: *He went in with his friend on the deal.*
to go off. a. to explode or be discharged: *The gun went off accidentally.* **b.** to ring: *My alarm went off at 6 A.M.* **c.** *Informal.* to take place; happen; occur: *Everything went off as expected.* **d.** to be sent: *The proofs went off to the printer.*
to go on. a. to continue: *The work must go on. The party went on until midnight.* **b.** to take place; happen; occur: *What's going on? You won't believe what went on last night.* **c.** to approach; near: *It's going on two years since we last saw her.* **d.** to proceed: *He went on to name the conspirators.* **e.** *Informal.* to chatter; rant: *She went on about the injustices to females.* **f.** to admit of being put on: *These shoes won't go on.*
to go out. a. to be extinguished: *The fire went out.* **b.** to become obsolete or out-of-date: *Those shoes went out about ten years ago.* **c.** to attend social functions or date. **d.** to be moved, esp. by love or sympathy toward: *My heart went out to him.* **e.** to strike: *The workers went out for better pay.* **f.** to be a candidate; try: *She went out for the cheerleading squad.* **g.** to play the first nine holes of an 18-hole golf course. **h.** to get rid of the last card in one's hand in one round or for the entire game.
to go over. a. to examine carefully: *The accountant went over the books.* **b.** to read, rehearse, or review: *He went over his notes before the exam. The actor went over his lines many times. She went over her story three times.* **c.** to do again: *She had to go over the floor with a mop.* **d.** to be successful: *The party went over.*
to go steady. to date someone exclusively and for an extended period of time.
to go through. a. to perform thoroughly or in detail: *We went through the scene three times during rehearsal.* **b.** to undergo; experience: *She went through one hardship after another.* **c.** to search or examine thoroughly: *The thief went through all the drawers.* **d.** to spend or wear out completely: *She goes through money quickly. A child can go through three pairs of shoes in a month.* **e.** to be accepted or

approved: *Her application went through, and she was hired.* **f.** to read, rehearse, or review.
to go through with. to carry out to the finish; complete: *Are you prepared to go through with it?*
to go together. to date someone exclusively and for an extended period of time.
to go to one's head. to cause (someone) to become overly excited or self-confident: *The compliment went to her head.*
to go to pieces. to become extremely upset.
to go under. a. to be overwhelmed or defeated. **b.** to sink: *The ship went under with 1000 passengers.* **c.** to fail: *His business went under because of competition from the large corporations.* **d.** to yield to the influence of a drug; become unconscious.
to go up. a. to move toward or approach: *She went up to him and slapped his face.* **b.** to be raised or constructed: *Barricades went up along the street.*
to go with. *Informal.* to date (someone) exclusively and for an extended period of time.
to go without saying. to be taken for granted; be obvious.
to let go. a. to release or set free: *He let the bird go. He let her hand go.* **b.** to allow to pass by without taking action or notice: *I'll let it go for the time being.* **c.** to fail to maintain in or as in proper working order or good condition: *He let the business go.*
to let oneself go. a. to allow (oneself) to be uninhibited. **b.** to fail to maintain oneself properly or attractively.
—*v.t.* **1.** to proceed along, with, or according to; follow: *Are you going my way?* **2.** *Informal.* to bet or bid: *to go a dollar on the first race.* **3.** to share or participate in the manner of or to the extent of: *to go halves, to go partners.* **4.** to furnish (bail) (with *for*): *He went bail for his friend.* **5.** *Informal.* to put up with; tolerate: *I can't go any more of her complaining.* **6.** to be able to pay or afford. **7.** to go it alone. to do something without assistance or support. **8. to go (someone) one better.** *Informal.* to outdo or excel (someone) in some manner or degree; surpass. —*n. pl.*, **goes. 1.** act of going: *the come and go of the tide.* **2.** *Informal.* spirit; energy; vigor: *She was full of go.* **3.** *Informal.* try; attempt: *to have a go at something.* **4.** *Informal.* success: *He was determined to make a go of the business.* **5.** *Archaic.* fashion; rage. **6. no go.** *Informal.* not to be done; useless; hopeless: *The launching was no go until everything was checked out thoroughly.* **7. on the go.** *Informal.* constantly active or in motion: *He was on the go from 8:00 A.M. to 11:00 P.M.* [Old English *gān* to move along, proceed, be in a particular condition.]
Syn. *v.i.* **1. Go, leave¹** indicate moving from a place. **Go** implies little more than the reverse of "come": *She told him to go.* **Leave** suggests a less casual going and often requires an explanation, such as an indication of means or place of departure: *I may have to leave in a hurry. Our plane leaves from Kennedy Airport.*
go² (gō) *n.* Japanese game for two players played with stonelike black and white counters on a board divided into squares. [Japanese *go.*]
go·a (gō′ə) *n.* black-tailed gazelle, *Procapra picticaudata,* of Tibet, the male of which has horns that curve backward. Height: 25 inches at the shoulder. [Tibetan *dgoba.*]
Go·a (gō′ə) *n.* former Portuguese possession, now part of India, on the western coast of India.
goad (gōd) *n.* **1.** sharp-pointed stick used for driving cattle or oxen. **2.** anything that drives or urges; stimulus. —*v.t.* to urge or prod with or as with a goad. [Old English *gād* pointed stick used for driving cattle.] —**Syn.** *v.t.* see **urge.**
go·a·head (gō′ə hed′) *n.* *Informal.* permission, signal, or order to proceed: *The captain gave the go-ahead to his soldiers.*
goal (gōl) *n.* **1.** object to which effort is directed; aim. **2.** area or object into, or through which, players try to get a ball or puck in order to score. **3.** act of getting a ball or puck into, or through, such an area or object. **4.** point or points made by such an act. **5.** position of goalkeeper: *John played goal for the hockey team.* [Middle English *gōl* boundary, limit; of uncertain origin.] —**Syn. 1.** see **objective.**
goal·ie (gō′lē) *n.* goalkeeper.
goal·keep·er (gōl′kē′pər) *n.* player who defends the goal in certain games, as ice hockey, field hockey, lacrosse, and soccer. Also, **goal′ie, goal′tend′er.**
goal line, either of two lines marking the goals in a game.
goal post, either of two structures consisting of a pair of posts supporting a crossbar, situated on either the end line or the goal line, as in football.
goal·tend·er (gōl′ten′dər) *n.* goalkeeper.
goat (gōt) *pl.,* **goats** or **goat.** *n.* **1.** any of various wild or domesticated cloven-hoofed, cud-chewing mammals, family

Goat

Bovidae, esp. genus *Capra,* having hollow horns and frequently a beard-like tuft of hair under the chin. Height: 30–35 inches at the shoulder. **2.** lecherous man. **3.** *Informal.* **a.** one who is made to take the blame or punishment for others; scapegoat. **b.** one who is the butt of a joke. **4. to get one's goat.** *Informal.* to cause to become angry, annoyed, or irritated. [Old English *gāt* the female of this animal.]

goat·ee (gō tē′) *n.* small pointed beard on a man's chin. [From GOAT; because it resembles a goat's beard.]

goat·herd (gōt′hurd′) *n.* one who tends goats.

goat·skin (gōt′skin′) *n.* **1.** skin of a goat. **2.** leather made from it. **3.** container made from this skin, used esp. for wine.

goat·suck·er (gōt′suk′ər) *n.* nightjar.

gob¹ (gob) *n. Informal.* **1.** mass or lump. **2. gobs.** large quantity; a lot: *gobs of money.* [Old French *gobe* lump, mouthful, from *gober* to swallow; possibly of Celtic origin.]

gob² (gob) *n. Informal.* sailor in the U.S. Navy. [Of uncertain origin.]

gob·bet (gob′it) *n. Archaic.* piece or fragment, esp. of raw flesh or meat. [Old French *gobet* piece, bit, diminutive of *gobe* lump. See GOB¹.]

gob·ble¹ (gob əl) **-bled, -bling.** *v.t.* **1.** to eat (food) hastily and greedily. **2.** *Informal.* to seize eagerly or greedily (often with *up*). —*v.i.* to eat hastily and greedily. [GOB¹ + -LE.]

gob·ble² (gob′əl) **-bled, -bling.** *v.i.* to make the throaty sound characteristic of a male turkey. —*n.* such a sound. [Imitative.]

gob·ble·dy·gook (gob′əl dē gook′) *n. Informal.* speech or writing that is wordy, involved, and not easily understood. [Possibly based on GOBBLE².]

gob·bler (gob′lər) *n.* male turkey.

Gob·e·lin (gob′ə lin; *French* gō blaN′) *n.* fine, handwoven tapestry, esp. of the late seventeenth and eighteenth centuries, valued for the richness of the colors and the workmanship and artistry with which it was executed. [From *Gobelin,* family of French dyers who founded a factory for making tapestries in Paris in the fifteenth century.]

go·be·tween (gō′bi twēn′) *n.* one who acts as an intermediary.

Go·bi (gō′bē) *n.* large desert in east-central Asia. Area, approx. 500,000 sq. mi.

gob·let (gob′lit) *n.* **1.** drinking vessel, usually of glass, with a base and stem. **2.** *Archaic.* bowl-shaped drinking vessel without handles. [Old French *gobelet* cup, diminutive of *gobel* large drinking bowl; possibly of Celtic origin.]

gob·lin (gob′lin) *n.* ugly, mischievous sprite or elf, esp. one that is evil and malicious. [Old French *gobelin,* from Medieval Latin *gobelinus,* possibly going back to Greek *kobálos* evil spirit.]

go·by (gō′bē) *pl.* **-bies** or **-by.** *n.* any of any group of colorful saltwater fish, family Gobiidae, found in temperate and tropical coastal waters and usually having pelvic fins that join to form a ventral sucker by which it attaches itself to the bottom. One species, *Mistichthys luzonensis,* is the smallest living vertebrate. Length: ½–4 inches. [Latin *gobius* gudgeon, from Greek *kōbios.*]

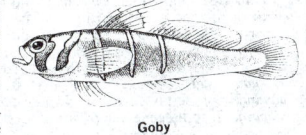
Goby

go·by (gō′bī′) *n. Informal.* passing by without notice: *to give someone the go-by.*

go·cart (gō′kärt′) *n.* **1.** small wagon for young children to ride in or pull. **2.** small, light framework mounted on rollers, used to support a baby learning to walk. **3.** light carriage. **4.** handcart. **5.** go-kart.

God (god) *n.* **1.** eternal, almighty being who is the creator, sustainer, and ruler of the universe; Supreme Being. **2. god. a.** any of various beings, as in Greek and Roman mythology and certain primitive religions, regarded as immortal, as personifying or controlling a specific aspect or element of nature, or as having special powers over the lives and affairs of man. **b.** male god. **c.** image of a god that is an object of worship; idol. **d.** one who or that which is made an object of worship, devotion, or admiration: *The powerful king was a god to his subjects.* [Old English *god.*]

god·child (god′chīld′) *n. pl.* **-chil·dren.** *n.* one for whom a person is sponsor, as at baptism.

God·dard, Robert Hutch·ings (god′ərd; huch′ingz) 1882–1945, U.S. pioneer rocket scientist.

god·daugh·ter (god′dô′tər) *n.* female godchild.

god·dess (god′is) *n.* **1.** female god. **2.** extraordinarily beautiful woman.

god·fa·ther (god′fä′thər) *n.* man who sponsors a child, as at baptism. —*v.t.* to act as a godfather to.

god·for·sak·en (god′fər sā′kən) *adj.* wretched; miserable.

God·head (god′hed′) *n.* **1.** the Deity; God. **2.** *also,* **godhead.** divine nature; divinity.

god·hood (god′hood′) *n.* state or quality of being divine; divinity.

Go·di·va (gə dī′və) *n.* wife of an English nobleman of the eleventh century. According to legend, she rode naked through the streets of Coventry so that her husband would remove an unpopular tax.

god·less (god′lis) *adj.* **1.** not believing in a god or God. **2.** wicked. —**god′less·ness,** *n.*

god·like (god′līk′) *adj.* befitting or like a god or God.

god·ly (god′lē) **-li·er, -li·est.** *adj.* **1.** devoutly observant of the laws of God; pious. **2.** *Archaic.* godlike. —**god′li·ness,** *n.*

god·moth·er (god′muth′ər) *n.* woman who sponsors a child, as at baptism. —*v.t.* to act as a godmother to.

god·par·ent (god′pâr′ənt) *n.* godfather or godmother.

God's acre, cemetery, esp. in a churchyard.

god·send (god′send′) *n.* something that is needed or desired and arrives or occurs unexpectedly, as if sent by God: *The inheritance was a godsend to the poor girl.*

god·son (god′sun′) *n.* male godchild.

God·speed (god′spēd′) *n.* success; good luck.

god·wit (god′wit) *n.* any of various wading birds, genus *Limosa,* which breed in the Arctic tundra and usually winter south of the equator. They have a slender body, long slender legs, and a long, narrow, slightly upturned bill. Length: 14–20 inches. [Of uncertain origin.]

Godwit

Goe·thals, George W. (gō′thəlz) 1858–1928, U.S. army engineer in charge of constructing the Panama Canal.

Goe·the, Jo·hann Wolf·gang von (gur′tə; *German* gœ′tə; yō′hän völf′gäng′) 1749–1832, German poet, playwright, novelist, and scientist.

Gog and Magog (gog) in the New Testament, the two nations who, led by Satan, will war with the kingdom of God at Armageddon.

go·get·ter (gō′get′ər, -get′-) *n. Informal.* energetic, aggressive, and enterprising person.

gog·gle (gog′əl) *n.* **goggles.** large, close-fitting spectacles used to protect the eyes, as from sparks, dust, or wind. Skiers, motorcyclists, and welders often wear goggles. —*v.i.* **-gled, -gling. 1.** to roll one's eyes or stare with bulging eyes. **2.** (of eyes) to roll or bulge: *The frog's hideous eyes goggling out of his head* (Thackeray, 1855). —*v.t.* to roll (one's eyes). —*adj.* (of eyes) rolling, bulging, or staring. [Of uncertain origin.]

gog·gle-eyed (gog′əl īd′) *adj.* having rolling, bulging, or staring eyes.

Gogh, Vincent van, see van Gogh, Vincent.

Go·gol, Ni·ko·lai (gō′gol; ni kə lī′) 1809–52, Russian author.

Goi·del·ic (goi del′ik) *n.* branch of the Celtic group of the Indo-European family of languages, which includes Irish Gaelic, Scottish Gaelic, and Manx. [Old Irish *Gōidel* a Gael + -IC.]

go·ing (gō′ing) *n.* **1.** act of moving away or departing: *Her going was unexpected.* **2.** condition of a surface or the environment, as for walking, driving, or flying: *The going was muddy because of heavy rain. The going was bumpy during our flight.* **3.** *Informal.* condition or circumstance which affects or impedes action or progress: *It was tough going during exams.* —*adj.* **1.** in action or movement; operating; functioning: *The machine is going.* **2.** doing or conducting business successfully: *The store is now a going concern.* **3.** current; prevalent: *the going price for a used car.* **4.** *Informal.* in existence: *the funniest joke going.*

go·ing-o·ver (gō′ing ō′vər) *n. Informal.* **1.** careful, intensive search, check, or examination: *The police gave the room a going-over.* **2.** severe beating.

goings on, actions, behavior, or incidents, esp. when disapproved of: *The police investigated the strange goings on at the old house.*

goi·ter (goi′tər) *also,* **goi·tre.** *n.* enlargement of the thyroid gland causing a swelling in the neck. It is often caused by improper functioning of the thyroid or a deficiency of iodine in the diet. Also, **stru′ma.** [French *goître,* from Old French *goitron* throat, going back to Latin *guttur.*]

go-kart (gō′kärt′) *also,* **go-cart.** *n.* small vehicle consisting of a bare frame on wheels and a low-powered gasoline engine, used esp. for racing.

Gol·con·da (gol kon′də) *n.* **1.** ancient city in southern India, famous in the sixteenth century for its wealth and diamond mines. **2.** *also,* **golconda.** mine or other source of wealth.

gold (gōld) *n.* **1.** heavy, soft, lustrous metallic element, used esp. as

a standard for currency, in jewelry, and in electronic devices. Symbol: **Au** See **element** for table. **2.** coin made of this metal. **3.** wealth; riches. **4.** bright-yellow color. **5.** anything resembling gold, as in value, beauty, or luster: *a heart of gold.* —*adj.* **1.** relating to, containing, or made of gold: *a gold bracelet, a gold tooth.* **2.** bright yellow: *She bought gold shoes to match her dress.* **3.** resembling gold. [Old English *gold* this metal, coin made of this metal, wealth.]

gold·beat·ing (gōld′bē′ting) *n.* act or process of beating gold into very thin sheets to make gold leaf. —**gold′beat′er,** *n.*

gold-brick (gōld′brik′) *Slang. v.i.* to shirk work or duty, esp. by pretending to be ill. —*n.* person, esp. in the armed forces, who shirks work or duty. Also, **gold′brick′er.**

gold certificate, certificate issued by the U.S. government, formerly circulated as money, stating that a certain amount of gold has been deposited in the Treasury for redemption on demand. Only Federal Reserve Banks now hold gold certificates.

Gold Coast, former British possession in western Africa, now part of Ghana.

gold digger *Slang.* woman who uses feminine charm to get money and gifts from men.

gold dust, gold in very small particles or as a fine powder.

gold·en (gōld′ən) *adj.* **1.** made of or containing gold. **2.** having the color or luster of gold: *the golden sun.* **3.** excellent or very valuable: *a golden opportunity.* **4.** very happy and prosperous; flourishing: *the golden days of youth.* **5.** of or marking the fiftieth year or event in a series: *Our parents recently celebrated their golden wedding anniversary.*

Golden Age **1.** *Classical Mythology.* theoretical first or early period in man's history, supposed to be a time of peace, innocence, plenty, longevity, and absence of laws. **2. golden age.** period, as in a country's history, during which the highest level of prosperity, achievement, or progress is reached.

golden calf **1.** in the Old Testament, golden statue of a calf which the Israelites persuaded Aaron to make for them to worship. **2.** wealth or material possessions regarded as being of supreme value.

golden eagle, eagle, *Aquila chrysaëtos,* widely distributed throughout the Northern Hemisphere and having dark-brown feathers with golden tints on the head and back of the neck. Length: 33 inches.

gold·en·eye (gōld′ən ī′) *pl.,* **-eyes** or **-eye.** *n.* diving duck, genus *Bucephala,* found in woods and forests in most parts of the Northern Hemisphere and having bright-yellow eyes. The male is black and white and the female is brown and white. Length: 17–23 inches.

Golden Fleece *Greek Legend.* a sheepskin from a golden ram, kept in a grove guarded by a dragon. It was stolen by Jason and the Argonauts.

golden glow, tall plant, *Rudbeckia laciniata,* of the composite family, found in North America and bearing showy double flower heads consisting of yellowish or greenish disk flowers surrounded by yellow, petal-like rays.

golden mean, course that avoids extremes and pursues moderation.

gold·en·rod (gōld′ən rod′) *n.* any of a large group of plants, genus *Solidago,* of the composite family, found in north temperate regions of the world and widely distributed as a weed in eastern North America. They bear many small yellow flower heads in spikes on tall, branching stalks.

golden rule, rule of conduct, set forth by Jesus in the Sermon on the Mount, that one should treat others as one wishes to be treated.

gold-filled (gōld′fild′) *adj.* made of or containing a base metal covered with a layer of gold.

gold-finch (gōld′finch′) *n.* **1.** European songbird, *Carduelis carduelis,* having yellow markings on its wings. **2.** any of several American finches, genus *Spinus,* esp. the **American** or **common goldfinch,** *Spinus tristis,* the male of which has bright-yellow and black summer plumage. [Old English *goldfinc* the European songbird.]

Goldfinch

gold-fish (gōld′fish′) *pl.,* **-fish** or **-fish·es.** *n.* freshwater fish, *Carassius auratus,* native to southeastern Asia, and ranging in color from gold to black. Many domestic varieties are raised in home aquariums and outdoor ponds.

gold·i·locks (gōl′dē loks′) *n.* hardy plant, *Linosyris vulgaris,* of the composite family, found growing wild in rocky places and along gravelly riverbanks in Europe and bearing small, pale-yellow flower heads.

gold leaf, gold beaten into extremely thin sheets, used in gilding.

gold mine **1.** mine from which ore yielding gold is obtained. **2.** any source of great wealth or profit: *His business turned out to be a gold mine.*

gold rush, sudden rush of people to an area where gold has been discovered, as to California in 1849 and to the Klondike in 1897.

gold·smith (gōld′smith′) *n.* one who fashions or deals in objects made from gold, as jewelry. [Old English *goldsmith.*]

Gold·smith, Oliver (gōld′smith′) 1730–74, English poet, novelist, and playwright.

gold standard, monetary system that defines the basic currency unit of a country in terms of a specified amount of gold.

go·lem (gō′lem, -ləm) *n.* *Jewish Legend.* an artificial being made in the shape of a man and given life by incantation. [Yiddish *goylem,* from Hebrew *gōlem* formless mass.]

golf (golf, gôlf) *n.* game played on a golf course with a small, hard ball and a set of golf clubs, the object being to sink the ball in a succession of holes with as few strokes as possible. —*v.i.* to play this game. [Of uncertain origin.] —**golf′er,** *n.*

golf club **1.** any of various clubs with long thin shafts and wooden or iron heads, used to hit the ball in golf. **2.** private club that maintains such facilities as a golf course and clubhouse.

golf course, area of land laid out in nine or eighteen holes, each having obstacles or traps, and consisting of a tee, fairway, and a green. Also, **golf links.**

Gol·go·tha (gol′gə thə) *n.* **1.** Calvary. **2. golgotha. a.** any place of suffering or sacrifice. **b.** place of burial. [Greek *golgothā* Calvary, transliteration of Aramaic *gogolthā* skull, from Hebrew *gulgōleth* skull, name of the skull-shaped hill near Jerusalem where Christ was crucified.]

Go·li·ath (gə lī′əth) *n.* in the Old Testament, the Philistine giant whom David killed with a stone shot from a sling.

gol·li·wog (gol′ē wog′) *also,* **gol·li·wogg.** *n.* **1.** grotesque black doll. **2.** grotesque person. [From *Golliwogg,* name of a doll in a series of children's books, possibly patterned after POLLIWOG.]

go·losh (gə losh′) *n.* galosh.

Go·mor·rah (gə môr′ə, -mor′ə) see **Sodom.**

Gom·pers, Samuel (gom′pərz) 1850–1924, U.S. labor leader and first president of the American Federation of Labor.

go·nad (gō′nad, gon′ad) *n.* sex organ in which reproductive cells develop and in which sex hormones are produced in vertebrates. The ovaries are the female gonads, and the testes are the male gonads. [Modern Latin *gonad-,* stem of *gonas,* from Greek *gonē* seed, genitals.]

Gon·court (gôn koōr′) **1.** **Ed·mond de** (ed môn′də) 1822–96, French author. **2. Jules de** (zhool-də). 1830–70, French author and brother of Edmond.

gon·do·la (gon′də lə) *n.* **1.** long, narrow, flat-bottomed boat with high peaks at the ends, propelled at the stern by one man with an oar or pole, and used on the canals of Venice. **2. gondola car. 3.** small cabin suspended from an overhead cable which is supported by vertical pylons. **4.** car suspended from a dirigible or balloon. [Italian *gondola* Venetian boat, diminutive of *gonda,* possibly going back to Greek *kondy* drinking vessel; with reference to a gondola's shape.]

Gondola with gondolier

gondola car, railroad freight car with low sides and no top, used for hauling bulk commodities.

gon·do·lier (gon′də lēr′) *n.* man who rows or poles a gondola.

gone (gôn, gon) *v.* past participle of **go.** —*adj.* **1.** moved away; left; departed. **2.** used up or spent: *The supplies are all gone.* **3.** dead. **4.** beyond hope or recovery; lost; ruined: *But don't talk so, as if it were a gone case* (Stowe, 1852). **5.** characterized by weakness or faintness: *He had a sad, gone look on his face.* **6. to be far gone.** to be much advanced or deeply involved: *The epidemic was too far gone to be stopped.* **7. to be gone on.** *Informal.* to be infatuated or in love with (someone or something).

gon·er (gô′nər, gon′ər) *n.* *Informal.* one who or that which is dying, ruined, lost, or beyond help or recovery.

gon·fa·lon (gon′fə lən) *n.* banner or flag hung vertically from a crossbar, rather than a pole, often composed of, or ending in, several streamers, esp. such a banner or flag used by various medieval Italian republics. [Italian *gonfalone;* of Germanic origin.]

gong (gông, gong) *n.* **1.** Oriental musical instrument consisting of a metal disk, usually with an upturned rim, that makes a loud, resonant tone when struck. **2.** saucer-shaped bell sounded by a mechanical hammer. [Malay *gōng* the musical instrument.]

gon·o·coc·cus (gon′ə kok′əs) *pl.,* **-coc·ci** (-kok′sī). *n.* bacterium that causes gonorrhea. —**gon′o·coc′cal, gon·no·coc·cic** (gon′ə kok′sik), *adj.*

gon·or·rhe·a (gon′ə rē′ə) *also,* **gon·or·rhoe·a.** *n.* contagious venereal disease that causes inflammation of the genital and urinary organs. It can usually be cured with penicillin, but if left untreated, leads to serious complications. [Late Latin *gonorrhoea,* from Greek *gonorrhoia,* from *gonos* seed + *rhoiā* flow; because mistakenly thought to be a discharge of semen.]

goo (gōō) *n.* *Informal.* any sticky substance, as glue. [Possibly modification of GLUE.]

at; āpe; cär; end; mē; it; īce; hot; ōld; fôrk; wood; fōōl; oil; out; up; ūse; turn; sing; thin; this; zh in treasure; ə in ago, taken, pencil, lemon, circus.

goo·ber (gōō′bər) *n. Informal.* peanut. Also, **goober pea.** [Bantu *nguba.*]

good (good) **bet·ter, best.** *adj.* **1.** above average or commendable: *good food, a good movie. She has many good qualities.* **2.** characterized by or possessing moral excellence; virtuous: *He was a good man.* **3.** agreeable; pleasant: *good news. She was in a good frame of mind. The perfume smells good.* **4.** kind or benevolent: *He was always good to me. The queen was good to her subjects.* **5.** competent or skillful: *She was a good dancer. He was good at figures.* **6.** honorable: *He was a member in good standing. John has a good reputation among his colleagues.* **7.** safe or correct; reliable: *good advice, a good risk. He is a good judge of character.* **8.** satisfactory for or suitable to a specific purpose: *It's a good day for sailing. Old clothes are good for making dust rags.* **9.** genuine or valid: *He had a good excuse for his tardiness. That was a good criticism of the book.* **10.** satisfyingly full or adequate: *I had a good night's sleep.* **11.** beneficial; advantageous: *Milk is good for children. The promotion was good for his career.* **12.** representative; typical: *That is a good example of Greek architecture.* **13.** having the necessary or desired requirements; qualified: *He was a good man for the job.* **14.** sound; unimpaired: *good eyesight. The car was in good condition. The old man was in good health.* **15.** fairly great, as in amount or extent; more than a little; considerable: *a good deal of trouble. Cleaning the house took a good part of the day. We saw a good number of people at the party.* **16.** well-behaved; obedient: *She was always good as a child.* **17.** best or most formal: *She used her good china and crystal for the dinner party.* **18.** thorough: *She did a good job of confusing us. Her parents gave her a good scolding.* **19.** favorable; approving: *She had a good opinion of him.* **20.** entire; complete: *The town is a good day's trip from here. He played for a good hour.* **21.** pleasing to the eye; attractive: *a good figure.* **22.** loyal or devout: *a good Democrat, a good Catholic.* **23.** fresh; unspoiled: *Is the meat still good?* **24.** right; proper: *He speaks good English. It was good that they should be respected and obeyed* (Macaulay, 1849). **25. as good as.** virtually; almost; practically: *He was as good as dead.* **26. no good.** worthless or useless: *This old radio is no good.* **27. good for. a.** able to survive, endure, or remain valid or functioning for (a specified period): *The car is good for another 2000 miles. The check is good for 90 days.* **b.** able or willing to pay, repay, or give (something): *Is he good for the money? His father is always good for at least ten dollars.* **c.** worth: *The coupon is good for five dollars of merchandise.* —*n.* **1.** benefit; advantage: *He worked for the good of all. It's for your own good.* **2.** that which is morally or ethically excellent, honorable, or correct: *There is much good in him.* **3.** good people: *Only the good will receive eternal happiness.* **4. to come to no good.** to end in disgrace or moral corruption. **5. for good (and all).** for the last time; finally; permanently. **6. to the good.** as a profit or advantage: *We have fifty dollars to the good.* —*adv.* **1.** *Informal.* well. **2. to be in good with.** to have the approval, confidence, or friendship of: *He is in good with the teacher.* **3. to get in good with.** to obtain the approval, confidence, or friendship of. **4. good and.** *Informal.* completely; entirely: *He was good and angry.* **5. to make good. a.** to fulfill: *He made good his promise.* **b.** to make up for; repay or replace: *He made good part of the debt.* **c.** to be successful: *After years of acting in minor roles, he finally made good.* **d.** to succeed in doing: *The army made good its retreat.* **e.** to prove; substantiate. [Old English *gōd* satisfactory, excellent, kind, pleasant, thorough, full.]

Good Book, Bible.

good·by (good′bī′) also, **good·bye.** *interj.* farewell. —*n. pl.,* **-bys.** farewell: *After the necessary good-bys he went on his trip.* [Contraction of *God be with you* (or *ye*).]

good·bye (good′bī′) good-by.

good cheer 1. feeling of joy or optimism; high spirits: *to be of good cheer.* **2.** good food or drink: *Have some good cheer.* **3.** feasting and merrymaking; revelry.

good day, salutation of greeting or farewell used in the daytime.

good evening, salutation of greeting or farewell used in the evening.

good-for-noth·ing (good′fər nuth′ing, -nuth′-) *adj.* useless or worthless. —*n.* one who is idle, worthless, or useless.

Good Friday, Friday of Holy Week, commemorating the crucifixion of Jesus.

good-heart·ed (good′här′tid) *adj.* kind or generous. —**good′-heart′ed·ly,** *adv.* —**good′-heart′ed·ness,** *n.*

Good Hope, Cape of 1. cape at the southernmost tip of Africa, on the Atlantic. **2.** province in the southern part of the Republic of South Africa. Area, 278,465 sq. mi. Pop. (1960), 5,355,368. Also (*def. 2*), **Cape Colony, Cape Province.**

good-hu·mored (good′hū′mərd, -ū′mərd) *adj.* having or showing a cheerful, pleasant, or amiable mood or feeling. —**good′-hu′mored·ly,** *adv.* —**good′-hu′mored·ness,** *n.*

good·ish (good′ish) *adj.* fairly good or large.

good-look·ing (good′look′ing) *adj.* pleasing or attractive in appearance.

good·ly (good′lē) **-li·er, -li·est.** *adj.* **1.** considerable, as in amount or degree: *Their trip cost them a goodly sum of money.* **2.** *Archaic.* **a.** of good quality: *The land which sent forth such goodly stores* (Freeman, 1871). **b.** having a pleasing or attractive appearance. [Old English *gōdlīc* good-looking.] —**good′li·ness,** *n.*

good·man (good′man) *pl.,* **-men.** *n. Archaic.* **1.** master or male head, esp. of a household. **2.** man below the rank of gentleman; mister.

good morning, salutation of greeting or farewell in the morning.

good-na·tured (good′nā′chərd) *adj.* having or showing a pleasant or kindly disposition; agreeable. —**good′-na′tured·ly,** *adv.* —**good′-na′tured·ness,** *n.*

Good Neighbor Policy, U.S. policy toward Latin America, urging political and economic cooperation and a system of mutual defense, established by President Franklin D. Roosevelt in 1933.

good·ness (good′nis) *n.* **1.** state or quality of being good. **2.** moral excellence; virtue. **3.** kindness, benevolence, or generosity: *He did it out of the goodness of his heart.* **4.** best or most valuable part of something. **5.** God. ▲ used as a euphemism: *Goodness knows.* [Old English *gōdnes* virtue, kindness.]

Syn. 2. Goodness, virtue indicate fine moral nature. **Goodness** suggests those innate character traits considered most noble in man, such as kindness or sympathy: *She has more goodness in her little finger than he has in his whole body* (Swift, 1738). **Virtue** implies acquisition and practice of those qualities that cause a man to do what is morally right: *Virtue is the roughest way, but proves at night a bed of down* (Wotton, 1651).

goods (goodz) *n.,pl.* **1.** merchandise; wares: *sporting goods.* **2.** movable personal property; belongings: *They lost all their worldly goods.* **3.** fabric; material; cloth. **4. to deliver the goods.** *Slang.* to do or produce what is expected, promised, or required. **5. to get the goods on.** *Slang.* to get evidence or proof of guilt or wrongdoing. **6. to have the goods on.** *Slang.* to have evidence or proof of guilt or wrongdoing. [Plural of GOOD.]

Good Samaritan 1. in the New Testament, traveler who aided a fellow traveler who had been beaten and robbed. **2.** one who is compassionate and helpful toward others.

Good Shepherd, Jesus Christ.

good-sized (good′sīzd′) *adj.* fairly big or large.

good speed, Godspeed.

good-tem·pered (good′tem′pərd) *adj.* not easily angered or irritated.

good·wife (good′wīf′) *pl.,* **-wives.** *n. Archaic.* **1.** mistress of a household. **2.** woman below the rank of lady. [GOOD + WIFE]

good will also, **good·will. 1.** kindness or benevolence: *a feeling of good will toward others.* **2.** cheerful consent; willingness: *He accepted the task with good will.* **3.** intangible asset of a business, resulting from the good relations it has established with the public.

good·y¹ (good′ē) *pl.,* **good·ies.** *Informal. n.* **1.** also, **goodies.** something very tasty and sweet, as candy or cookies. **2. goodies.** choice or special things: *He had some goodies in his record collection.* —*interj.* great or wonderful. [GOOD + -Y².]

good·y² (good′ē) *pl.,* **good·ies.** *n. Archaic.* married woman of humble station. ▲ used as a title or term of address. [Short for GOODWIFE.]

Good·year, Charles (good′yēr′) 1800–60, U.S. inventor and discoverer of the process of vulcanizing rubber.

good·y-good·y (good′ē good′ē) *adj.* sentimentally good; affectedly pious. —*n. pl.,* **-good·ies.** goody-goody person.

goo·ey (gōō′ē) **goo·i·er, goo·i·est.** *adj. Informal.* sticky. [GOO + -EY.]

goof (gōōf) *Informal. n.* **1.** stupid or clumsy mistake; blunder. **2.** stupid, silly, or blundering person. —*v.i.* **1.** to make a stupid or clumsy mistake; blunder. **2. to goof off** (or **around**). to avoid work or duty or do nothing. —*v.t.* to make a mess of; botch (often with *up*): *He really goofed up that assignment.* [Possibly form of obsolete *goff* fool, from French *goffe* awkward, stupid, from Italian *goffo;* of uncertain origin.]

goof-off (gōōf′ôf′) *n. Slang.* one who habitually avoids work or duty or does nothing.

goof·y (gōō′fē) **goof·i·er, goof·i·est.** *adj. Slang.* stupid, silly, or ridiculous. —**goof′i·ness,** *n.*

goo·gol (gōō′gol, -gəl) *n.* numeral 1 followed by 100 zeros, written as 10^{100}. [Coined by the American mathematician Edward Kasner, 1878–1955.]

goo·gol·plex (gōō′gol pleks′, -gəl-) *n.* numeral one followed by a googol of zeros, written as $10^{10^{100}}$. [GOOGOL + (DU)PLEX.]

goon (gōōn) *n. Slang.* **1.** hoodlum or thug, esp. one hired as a strikebreaker or to intimidate workers. **2.** stupid, rough, or clumsy person. [Partly from dialectal English *gooney* booby (of uncertain origin); partly from Alice the *Goon,* subhuman character in the American comic strip *Thimble Theatre* by E. C. Segar, 1894–1938.]

goo·ney (gōō′nē) *n.* albatross. Also, **gooney bird.**

goose (gōōs) *pl.* (*defs.* 1–4) **geese** or (*def.* 5) **goos·es.** *n.* **1.** any of various wild or domesticated web-footed water birds, family Anatidae, found throughout most of the world, resembling, but larger than, a duck and usually having a longer neck. Wild geese are usually a combination of gray, brown, black, and white, while domesticated geese are often gray or white. **2.** female goose. Distinguished from **gander.** **3.** flesh of a goose used as food. **4.** foolish, silly person. **5.** tailor's smoothing iron with a handle shaped like a goose's neck. **6. to cook one's goose.** *Informal.* to ruin one's chances. [Old English *gōs* this bird.]

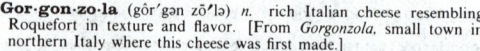

Goose

goose·ber·ry (gōōs′ber′ē, gōōz′-) *pl.,* **-ries.** *n.* **1.** tart edible berry of any of a group of thorny shrubs, genus *Ribes,* widely cultivated in many parts of Europe and North America. **2.** thorny shrub bearing this berry. [Possibly GOOSE + BERRY.]

goose egg *Slang.* **1.** nothing; zero. **2.** score of zero.

goose flesh, temporary, rough condition of the skin caused by the contraction of tiny muscles near the surface, usually resulting from cold or fear. Also, **goose bumps, goose pimples.**

goose·foot (gōōs′fŏōt′) *pl.,* **-foots.** *n.* any of a group of weedy plants, genus *Chenopodium,* found throughout the world, bearing coarse, often broad leaves, clusters of small greenish flowers, and usually having a strong, unpleasant odor. Also, **pig′weed′.**

goose·neck (gōōs′nek′) *n.* something long and curved like a goose's neck, as an s-shaped pipe or a flexible support for a desk lamp.

goose·step (gōōs′step′) **-stepped, -step·ping.** *v.i.* to march in a goose step.

goose step, marching step in which the legs are held straight and kicked high with the knees unbent.

G.O.P., Grand Old Party.

go·pher (gō′fər) *n.* **1.** any of various burrowing rodents, family Geomyidae, found throughout North and Central America, having large cheek pouches. Length: 5–17 inches. Also, **pocket gopher. 2.** ground squirrel. [Possibly from French *gaufre* honeycomb; of Germanic origin; because it honeycombs the earth as it burrows.]

Gopher

Gor·di·an knot (gôr′dē ən) *n.* **1.** *Greek Legend.* intricate knot that could be untied only by the person who should rule Asia. Alexander the Great, instead of trying to untie it, cut through it with his sword. **2. to cut the Gordian knot.** to find and use quick, drastic, or bold means to solve or eliminate a problem or difficulty. [From *Gordius,* legendary king of Phrygia, who first tied the knot.]

Gordon setter, setter of a breed that originated in Scotland, having a black-and-tan coat. [From the fourth duke of *Gordon,* who first popularized the breed in the nineteenth century.]

gore¹ (gôr) *n.* blood that has been shed, esp. when thick or clotted. [Old English *gor* filth.]

gore² (gôr) **gored, gor·ing.** *v.t.* (of an animal) to pierce with a horn or tusk: *The bull gored the matador.* [Possibly from Old English *gār* spear (suggesting piercing with a sharp weapon).]

gore³ (gôr) *n.* triangular or tapered piece of fabric, used esp. in making umbrellas or certain skirts or sails to provide fullness. —*v.t.,* **gored, gor·ing.** to make or furnish with a gore or gores: *The seamstress gored the skirt.* [Old English *gāra* triangular piece of land.]

Gor·gas, William Craw·ford (gôr′gəs; krô′fərd) 1854–1920, U.S. Army physician.

gorge (gôrj) *n.* **1.** deep, narrow opening or passage between steep and rocky sides of walls or mountains. **2.** mass which stops up or clogs a passage: *an ice gorge.* **3.** *Archaic.* throat; gullet. **4. to make one's gorge rise.** to provoke anger or disgust. —*v.t.,* **gorged, gorg·ing. 1.** to stuff with food: *He gorged himself at dinner.* **2.** to swallow or devour greedily: *He gorged his food.* —*v.i.* to stuff oneself with food. [Old French *gorge* throat, probably going back to Latin *gurges* abyss.] —**gorg′er,** *n.*

gor·geous (gôr′jəs) *adj.* **1.** richly or brilliantly colored; resplendent. **2.** *Informal.* beautiful, attractive, or delightful: *a gorgeous woman.* [Old French *gorgias* fine, elegant; of uncertain origin.] —**gor′geous·ly,** *adv.* —**gor′geous·ness** *n.*

gor·get (gôr′jit) *n.* **1.** piece of armor used to protect the throat. **2.** covering for the neck worn by women during the Middle Ages to fill in the neckline of a dress. [Old French *gorgete* little throat, diminutive of *gorge* throat. See GORGE.]

Gor·gon (gôr′gən) *n.* **1.** *Greek Legend.* any one of three sisters who had snakes for hair and whose appearance was so horrible that anyone who looked at them was turned to stone. **2. gorgon.** very ugly or hideous woman. [Latin *Gorgō,* from Greek *Gorgō,* from *gorgos* fearful.]

Gor·gon·zo·la (gôr′gən zō′lə) *n.* rich Italian cheese resembling Roquefort in texture and flavor. [From *Gorgonzola,* small town in northern Italy where this cheese was first made.]

go·ril·la (gə ril′ə) *n.* **1.** herbivorous ape, *Gorilla gorilla,* of equatorial Africa, having a massive body, short legs, long arms, and a gray or black coat. It is the largest and most powerful anthropoid ape. Height: to 6 feet. **2.** *Informal.* muscular, ugly, or brutal man. **3.** *Slang.* hoodlum; thug. [Greek *gorilla* wild, hairy person; supposedly of African origin, according to an account of the travels in West Africa of the Carthaginian Hanno (about the fifth century B.C.).]

Gorilla

Gor·ki (gôr′kē) *also,* **Gor·ky. 1. Max·im** (mäk sēm′). 1868–1936, Russian novelist, short story writer, and playwright. **2.** city in the European Soviet Union, on the Volga River, formerly known as Nizhni Novgorod. Pop. (1970 est.), 1,170,000.

gor·mand (gôr′mənd) gourmand.

gor·mand·ize (gôr′mən dīz′) **-ized, -iz·ing.** *v.i.* to eat like a glutton; gorge. [From obsolete *gormandize* gluttony, from Old French *gourmandise,* from *gourmand* glutton; of uncertain origin.] —**gor′mand·iz′er,** *n.*

gorse (gôrs) *n.* furze. [Old English *gorst.*]

gor·y (gôr′ē) **gor·i·er, gor·i·est.** *adj.* **1.** covered with gore; bloody. **2.** characterized by bloodshed or carnage: *a gory clash of two armies.* **3.** resembling gore; disgusting; horrible: *He spared us the gory details.* —**gor′i·ly,** *adv.* —**gor′i·ness,** *n.*

gosh (gosh) *interj.* used to express pleasure or surprise. [Euphemism for GOD.]

gos·hawk (gos′hôk′) *n.* powerful, short-winged hawk, *Accipiter gentilis,* of northern North America and Eurasia, formerly used in falconry. Length: to 26 inches. [Old English *gōshafoc,* from *gōs* goose + *hafoc* hawk.]

Go·shen (gō′shən) *n.* **1.** in the Old Testament, fertile region in northern Egypt inhabited by the Israelites before the Exodus. **2.** any land of plenty.

gos·ling (goz′ling) *n.* young goose.

gos·pel (gos′pəl) *n.* **1.** teachings of Jesus and the Apostles. **2. Gospel. a.** any one of the first four books of the New Testament, attributed to Matthew, Mark, Luke, and John. **b.** excerpt from one of these books read as part of a religious service. **3.** something accepted or regarded as absolutely true. **4.** doctrine or precept regarded as being of major importance and serving as a guide for action: *The insurgents preached the gospel of revolution.* —*adj.* of, relating to, or according to the gospel: *a gospel singer.* [Old English *gōdspel* teachings of Jesus and the Apostles, from *gōd* good + *spel* tidings.]

gos·sa·mer (gos′ə mər) *n.* **1.** fine filmy cobweb, seen esp. in autumn floating in the air or suspended from bushes or grass. **2.** any light or filmy substance. **3.** light, delicate, gauzelike fabric. —*adj.* of or like gossamer; light, filmy, or delicate. [Middle English *gossomer* fine film of cobwebs; literally, goose summer; probably because it is most common in early November, the time of St. Martin's summer, which was also the season for eating geese in England. See GOOSE, SUMMER.]

gos·sip (gos′ip) *n.* **1.** idle talk or rumors, often malicious, esp. about the personal affairs of other people. **2.** one who is given to repeating gossip. **3.** *Archaic.* **a.** friend, esp. a woman. **b.** godparent. —*v.i.,* **-sip·ing.** to repeat gossip. —*v.t.* to repeat as gossip: *The old women gossiped the story all over town.* [Old English *godsibb* godparent, from *god* God + *sibb* relative; from the association of a godparent with a friend, who in turn was associated with a person of idle talk.] —**gos′sip·er,** *n.*

gos·sip·y (gos′ə pē) *adj.* **1.** inclined to or fond of gossip. **2.** full of gossip.

gos·soon (go sōōn′) *n.* **1.** lad; boy. **2.** boy servant. [Earlier *garsoon,* from Old French *garçon* menial; possibly of Germanic origin.]

got (got) past tense and a past participle of **get.**

Go·ta·ma (gō′tə mə) Gautama.

Gö·te·borg (yœ′tə bôr′yə) *n.* port city located in southwestern Sweden. Pop. (1968 est.), 444,131. Also, **Goth·en·burg** (goth′ən burg′, got′-).

Goth (goth) *n.* member of a powerful Germanic people that invaded the Roman Empire in the third, fourth, and fifth centuries A.D., including the Visigoths, who captured Rome itself, and the Ostrogoths. [Late Latin *Gothī* (plural); of Gothic origin.]

Goth·am (*def. 1* goth′əm, gō′thəm; *def. 2* got′əm, gō′thəm) *n.* **1.** New York City. **2.** village in England, noted in legend for the foolishness of its inhabitants.

Goth·ic (goth′ik) *adj.* **1.** of or relating to a style of architecture developed in Europe between the twelfth and sixteenth centuries, characterized esp. by pointed arches, rib vaulting, and flying buttresses.

2. of or relating to the Goths, their language, or culture. **3.** *also,* **gothic.**
a. of, relating to, or characteristic of a literary genre emphasizing elements of the grotesque, horrible, violent, and mysterious. **b.** of, relating to, or characteristic of the Middle Ages; medieval. **c.** uncivilized; barbarous. —*n.* **1.a.** typeface characterized by straight unornamental lines. **b.** black letter. **2.** extinct German language of the Indo-European family, formerly spoken by various Germanic peoples such as the Visigoths. [Late Latin *Gothicus* relating to the Goths, from *Gothī* Goths. See GOTH.]

Gothic cathedral

got·ten (got′ən) a past participle of **get.**
Göt·ting·en (gœt′ing ən) *n.* city in eastern West Germany, noted for its university. Pop. (1968 est.), 112,560.
gouache (gwäsh, gōō äsh′) *n.*
1. method of painting with watercolors in which the pigments are mixed with zinc white and gum to produce an opaque effect similar to that of oils. **2.** painting done by this method. **3.** pigment used in this method. [French *gouache,* from Italian *guazzo* puddle, going back to Latin *aqua* water.]
Gou·da cheese (gou′də, gōō′-) Dutch cheese resembling Edam cheese in texture and flavor. [From *Gouda,* Dutch city where it originated.]
gouge (gouj) *n.* **1.** tool similar to a chisel but having a concave blade, used for cutting rounded grooves or holes in wood.

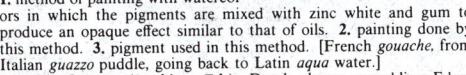

Gouge

2. groove or hole made by or as by a gouge. **3.** *Informal.* poke. **4.** *Slang.* act of cheating or defrauding. —*v.t.,* **gouged, goug·ing.**
1. to cut or scoop out with or as with a gouge. **2.** to dig, tear, or poke (with *out*): *to gouge out an eye.* **3.** *Slang.* to cheat or defraud. [French *gouge* chisel, from Late Latin *gubia;* possibly of Celtic origin.]
gou·lash (gōō′läsh) *n.* stew made of beef or veal and vegetables, usually seasoned with paprika. [Magyar *gulyás (hús)* herdsman's (meat).]
Gou·nod, Charles Fran·çois (gōō-nō′; shärl frän swä′) 1818–93, French composer.
gourd (gôrd, gōōrd) *n.* **1.** hard-shelled fruit of any of a group of trailing or climbing vines of the gourd family, usually brightly colored, esp. the calabash gourd. **2.** vine bearing this fruit, growing in most tropical and temperate regions of the world. **3.** dried shell of a gourd, used esp. as a drinking vessel or dipper. **4.** any of various other plants of the gourd family, as the watermelon, cucumber, squash, and pumpkin. [Old French *gourde,* going back to Latin *cucurbita.*]

Gourds

gourde (gōōrd) *n.* monetary unit of Haiti equal to 100 centimes. [French *gourde* silver coin, dollar, feminine of *gourd* dull, heavy (suggesting a heavy coin), from Latin *gurdus* dull.]
gour·mand (gōōr′mənd) *also,* **gor·mand.** *n.* one who is fond of fine food and drink. [French *gourmand* glutton; of uncertain origin.] —**Syn.** see epicure.
gour·met (gōōr mā′) *n.* one who is a connoisseur of fine food and drink. [French *gourmet;* earlier, wine merchant's assistant; of uncertain origin; influenced in meaning by GOURMAND.] —**Syn.** see epicure.
gout (gout) *n.* **1.** metabolic disease, possibly inherited, characterized by swelling of the joints and a high level of uric acid in the blood. It often affects the big toe. **2.** drop or clot, esp. of blood. [Old French *goute,* from Latin *gutta* drop; because it was associated in medieval times with drops of humors or fluids in the body that affected the joints. See HUMOR.]
gout·y (gou′tē) **gout·i·er, gout·i·est.** *adj.* **1.** of, relating to, or of the nature of gout. **2.** resulting from or causing gout. **3.** affected with or subject to gout. **4.** swollen, as with gout. —**gout·i·ly,** *adv.* —**gout′i·ness,** *n.*
gov. **1.** governor. **2.** government. Also, **Gov.**
gov·ern (guv′ərn) *v.t.* **1.** to rule, control, or direct by right of authority. **2.** to direct or influence; guide: *Concern for his own welfare governed his actions.* **3.** to serve as or constitute a rule or law for: *The law there stated clearly governs this case* (Lopes, 1890). **4.** to hold in

check; restrain; curb: *I appeal to you to govern your temper* (Dickens, 1870). **5.** *Grammar.* to require the use of (a particular case, mood, or other form): *Transitive verbs govern the objective case.* —*v.i.* to exercise or have control, authority, or influence; rule. [Old French *governer* to rule, steer (a ship), from Latin *gubernāre,* from Greek *kybernān.*] —**gov′ern·a·ble,** *adj.* —**Syn.** *v.t.* **1.** see rule.
gov·ern·ance (guv′ər nəns) *n.* exercise of control or authority; rule.
gov·ern·ess (guv′ər nis) *n.* woman employed to teach and train children in a private household.
gov·ern·ment (guv′ərn mənt, -ər mənt) *n.* **1.** organization or body through which control or administration, as of a city or state, is exercised: *He works for the federal government.* **2.** system or established form of ruling by which a given political unit is governed: *parliamentary government, democratic government.* **3.** control or authority over the affairs of a state, city, or other political unit; rule. **4.** body of elected officials holding power. **5.** holding in check; regulation. —**gov′ern·men′tal,** *adj.* —**gov′ern·men′tal·ly,** *adv.*
government issue, supplied by the government.
gov·er·nor (guv′ər nər) *n.* **1.** official elected as the chief executive of a state or commonwealth of the United States. **2.** official appointed to govern, as over a province, colony, or territory. **3.** one who manages or directs a social organization or financial institution: *the board of governors of the club, a governor of a bank.* **4.** automatic device for regulating the speed of an engine by controlling the rate at which fuel or steam is admitted to the engine. [Old French *gouverneur* ruler, pilot, from Latin *gubernātor.*]
governor general *pl.,* **governors general** or **governor generals.** governor who has subordinate or deputy governors under him, as in certain British overseas territories.
gov·er·nor·ship (guv′ər nər ship′) *n.* functions, position, or term of office of a governor.
govt. government. Also, **Govt.**
gown (goun) *n.* **1.** woman's dress, esp. a formal dress. **2.** long, loose outer garment worn to signify the wearer's office, profession, or status; robe: *a judge's gown.* **3.** long, loose garment, as a nightgown or dressing gown. **4.** faculty and students of a college or university: *town and gown.* —*v.t.* to dress in a gown. [Old French *goune* long coat, from Late Latin *gunna* fur, fur garment; of uncertain origin.]
Go·ya, Fran·cis·co (gô′yə; fran sis′kō) 1746–1828, Spanish painter and etcher.
G.P., general practitioner.
gph, gallons per hour.
GPU, OGPU.
gr. **1.** grade. **2.** grain; grains. **3.** gram; grams. **4.** grammar. **5.** gross. **6.** group.
Gr. **1.** Greek. **2.** Greece. **3.** Grecian.
Graaf·i·an follicle (grä′fē ən, graf′ē-) one of many small, round sacs in the ovary of a mammal in which ova are developed. [From Regnier de Graaf, 1641–73, Dutch anatomist.]
grab (grab) **grabbed, grab·bing.** *v.t.* **1.** to grasp or snatch suddenly or forcibly: *Tom grabbed the candy bar away from his brother.* **2.** to obtain forcibly, unscrupulously, or illegally: *The conquering nation grabbed the land from the natives.* —*v.i.* to make a grasping or snatching motion (often with *at* or *for*): *The drowning man grabbed desperately for the life preserver.* —*n.* **1.** act of grabbing. **2.** forcible, unscrupulous, or illegal seizure or acquisition, as of land or power. **3.** any of various mechanical devices used to grip or clutch something that is to be lifted. **4. up for grabs.** *Informal.* open or available to any taker or successful competitor: *When she resigned, her job was up for grabs.* [Middle Dutch *grabben* to grasp.] —**grab′ber,** *n.* —**grab′by,** *adj.*
grab bag **1.** receptacle filled with wrapped articles, from which a person draws one without knowing in advance what it is. **2.** miscellaneous collection of things: *The book was a grab bag of jokes, gossip, and serious criticism.*
Grac·chus (grak′əs), **Ga·ius** (gā′əs) 153–121 B.C., and **Ti·be·ri·us** (tī bēr′ē əs) c.163–133 B.C., Roman tribunes who attempted to aid the impoverished plebeians by peaceful reforms, such as the redistribution of land. Also, **the Grac·chi** (grak′ī).
grace (grās) *n.* **1.** harmony or beauty of form, movement, or expression: *The ballerina danced with grace.* **2.** short prayer or blessing before or after a meal. **3.** sense of propriety; consideration: *He had the grace to leave.* **4.** freely given good will, beneficence, or mercy: *The people had rights only by the grace of the king.* **5.** *Theology.* **a.** unmerited and freely bestowed divine assistance, favor, and love, esp. in saving one from eternal damnation. **b.** divine influence which operates in man to inspire virtue. **c.** divine influence or intervention: *By the grace of God the children were rescued by the firemen.* **6.** any attractive or charming quality or feature: *Speaking French and playing the piano are social graces.* **7.** grace period. **8.** *Music.* embellishment or ornament consisting of an additional note or notes not essential to the melody or harmony, esp. a grace note or appoggiatura. **9. Grace.** worship; eminence.

ᴀ used to address or speak of royalty, nobility, or clergy: *Yes, Your Grace.* **10. Graces.** three young and beautiful Greek goddesses, Aglaia, Thalia, and Euphrosyne, who personified loveliness and charm. **11. in the bad graces of.** disliked or disapproved by; in disfavor with. **12. in the good graces of.** liked or approved by; in favor with. **13. with bad grace.** with obvious reluctance; insincerely; unwillingly: *The apology was made with bad grace.* **14. with good grace.** willingly; gladly; sincerely. **15. to fall from grace.** *Informal.* to lose the favor or approval of others. —*v.t.,* **graced, grac·ing. 1.** to add grace or beauty to; adorn: *The lovely park graced the urban scene.* **2.** to favor or honor (something): *You graced the party with your presence.* **3.** *Music.* to add grace notes or other embellishments to. [Old French *grace* favor, thanks, pardon, charm, from Latin *grātia* favor, thanks, charm.]

grace·ful (grās′fəl) *adj.* characterized by harmony or beauty of form, movement, or expression. —**grace′ful·ly,** *adv.* —**grace′ful·ness,** *n.*
Syn. Graceful, elegant, lithe indicate movement or manner showing beauty. **Graceful** suggests lack of awkwardness in rhythmic physical movement: *They sailed off in a graceful waltz.* **Elegant** implies harmony of movement: *She made an elegant curtsy to the queen.* **Lithe** suggests coordinated smooth twisting or bending physical movement: *The lithe movements of the dancer suggest the twining serpent.*

grace·less (grās′lis) *adj.* **1.** lacking beauty or harmony of form, movement, or expression. **2.** lacking a sense of propriety; inconsiderate. —**grace′less·ly,** *adv.* —**grace′less·ness,** *n.*

grace note *Music.* ornamental note having no inherent time value, added to embellish the melody or harmony.

grace period, extension or allowance of time after an official due date: *If the tuition is paid within the five-day grace period, no fine is assessed.*

gra·cious (grā′shəs) *adj.* **1.** having or showing kindness and courtesy: *a gracious host.* **2.** prosperous, leisurely, and comfortable: *gracious living.* **3.** merciful; compassionate. [Old French *gracieux* charming, pleasant, from Latin *grātiōsus* popular, obliging, from *grātia* favor.] —**gra′cious·ly,** *adv.* —**gra′cious·ness,** *n.*

grack·le (grak′əl) *n.* **1.** any of several North American blackbirds, family Icteridae, having a long, wedge-shaped tail and iridescent black plumage. Length: 1–1½ feet. **2.** any of several Asian starlings, family Sturnidae, as the myna. [Latin *grāculus* jackdaw.]

grad (grad) *n. Informal.* graduate: *The old grads came back for their fifth reunion.*

grad. 1. graduate. **2.** graduated.

gra·date (grā′dāt) **-dat·ed, -dat·ing.** *v.t., v.i.*
to pass or cause to pass through a series of imperceptible stages or degrees, as from one color to another. [From GRADATION.]

Grackle *(def. 1)*

gra·da·tion (grā dā′shən) *n.* **1.** gradual progression or change by a series of steps, stages, or degrees, as of size or intensity. **2.** step, stage, or degree in such a series. **3.** act or process of arranging in steps, stages, or degrees. **4.** ablaut. [Latin *gradātiō* series of steps, from *gradus* step.]

grade (grād) *n.* **1.** step or degree in a scale, as of quality, merit, or value: *an inferior grade of ore.* **2.** stage in an orderly process or progression. **3.a.** any one of the divisions, equal to one school year, which together make up the elementary and secondary curriculum. **b.** pupils in any of these divisions: *The play was presented by the third grade.* **4.** number or letter indicating the level, merit, or quality of a student's work or conduct; mark: *He received a failing grade on the term paper. She got a grade of seventy-nine on the test.* **5.a.** slope, as of a road or railroad track. **b.** amount or degree of slope: *There was a grade of thirty feet in the road.* **6.** class or group of people or things that are the same or equal, as in quality, rank, or value. **7.** military rank or rating: *Before being discharged, he reached the grade of sergeant.* **8.** (of food) classification according to certain standards, as of quality or size. **9.** animal that is the result of crossbreeding a pure-blooded animal with one of another breed or of mixed stock. **10. the grades.** elementary school. **11. to make the grade.** *Informal.* to be successful in reaching or attaining a desired goal or objective. **12. at grade.** at the same level or degree of slope. **13. up to grade.** conforming to established standards. —*v.t.,* **grad·ed, grad·ing. 1.** to arrange or classify by grades; sort. **2.** to give or assign a mark to: *to grade term papers.* **3.** to make (ground) more level; reduce the slope of. **4.** to improve (livestock) by crossbreeding a pure-blooded animal with one of another breed or mixed stock (often with *up*). —*v.i.* **1.** to be of a particular grade. **2.** to pass through a series of imperceptible stages or degrees; change gradually: *The colors graded from dark red to bright pink.* [Latin *gradus* step, degree.]

grade crossing, place where a railroad track crosses a road or another railroad track at the same level.

grad·er (grā′dər) *n.* **1.** one who or that which grades. **2.** pupil in a specified grade in school: *a twelfth grader.*

grade school, elementary school.

gra·di·ent (grā′dē ənt) *n.* **1.** amount or degree of slope, as of a road or railroad track; grade. **2.** sloping surface, as of a road or railroad track. **3.** *Physics.* rate at which a variable quantity, as temperature or pressure, changes in a certain direction. —*adj.* **1.** rising or descending gradually by regular degrees of inclination. **2.** (of animals) capable of or adapted for walking. [Latin *gradiēns,* present participle of *gradī* to walk, go.]

grad·u·al (graj′ōō əl) *adj.* **1.** moving, changing, or progressing slowly or by degrees: *The change was so gradual that we hardly noticed it.* **2.** rising or descending with a slight degree of inclination; not steep or abrupt. —*n.* **1.** antiphon sung between the Epistle and the Gospel in the Mass. **2.** book containing the words and music of the parts of the Mass sung by the choir. [Medieval Latin *gradualis* in steps, by degrees, from Latin *gradus* step, degree.] —**grad′u·al·ly,** *adv.* —**grad′u·al·ness,** *n.*

grad·u·al·ism (graj′ōō ə liz′əm) *n.* policy of approaching a goal, esp. a political or social goal, by slow stages. —**grad′u·al·ist,** *n.* —**grad·u·al is′tic,** *adj.*

grad·u·ate (*v.,* graj′ōō āt′; *n., adj.,* graj′ōō it) **-at·ed, -at·ing.** *v.i.* **1.** to receive an academic diploma or degree signifying the completion of a course of study: *He graduated last year.* **2.** to change gradually; pass by degrees: *His mood graduated from mild irritation to anger.* —*v.t.* **1.** to grant an academic diploma or degree to (someone) in recognition of the completion of a course of study: *The university graduated a class of 500.* **2.** to arrange or place in a series of steps, stages, or degrees. **3.** to mark with, or divide into, degrees, units, or similar divisions: *to graduate a thermometer.* —*n.* **1.** one who has been granted an academic diploma or degree upon completion of a course of study. **2.** container, as a cylinder or beaker, marked with units for measuring the amount of liquid. —*adj.* **1.** that is engaged in postgraduate work or studies: *a graduate student.* **2.** of, relating to, or for graduates: *graduate courses.* [Medieval Latin *graduatus,* past participle of *graduari* to take a degree, from Latin *gradus* step, degree.]

graduate school, school, usually part of a university, offering academic degrees beyond the baccalaureate.

grad·u·a·tion (graj′ōō ā′shən) *n.* **1.** act of graduating; being graduated. **2.** ceremony of conferring diplomas or degrees, as at a school or university; commencement. **3.** mark or series of marks, as on a cylinder or beaker, indicating degrees or quantity.

Grae·co-Ro·man (grē′kō rō′mən) Greco-Roman.

graf·fi·to (grə fē′tō) *pl.* **-ti** (-tē). *n.* **1.** ancient drawing or inscription on a wall, rock, or other surface. **2. graffiti.** any inscription or drawing on a wall, sidewalk, or other surface. [Italian *graffito* drawing or writing on a wall, diminutive of *graffio* scratch, going back to Latin *graphium* stylus (used to scratch writing or wax), from Greek *grapheion.*]

graft[1] (graft) *v.t.* **1.** to insert (a scion) from one plant, esp. a tree, into a cut or slit in another or the same plant so that the two pieces will grow together and eventually form one plant. **2.** to propagate (a new plant) by grafting. **3.** to transplant (tissue) from one part of the body to another or from one person to another. **4.** to unite or incorporate as by grafting. —*v.i.* **1.** to insert a scion from one plant into another or the same plant. **2.** to be or become grafted. —*n.* **1.** scion, as a bud or stem part, that has been grafted. **2.** place where a scion has been inserted. **3.** plant propagated by grafting. **4.** tissue surgically transplanted from one part of the body to another or from one person to another. **5.** act or process of grafting. [Earlier *graff,* from Old French *grafe* stylus, young shoot, from Latin *graphium* stylus, from Greek *grapheion,* from *graphein* to write; because a shoot used in grafting resembles a stylus.] —**graft′er,** *n.*

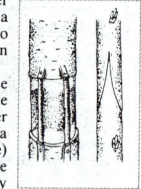

Graft[1]

graft[2] (graft) *n.* **1.** act of gaining profit or advantages by dishonest or unethical means, esp. through one's political influence or position. **2.** that which is acquired by such means. —*v.i.* to practice graft. —*v.t.* to obtain by graft. [Of uncertain origin.] —**graft′er,** *n.*

gra·ham (grā′əm) *adj.* made from or consisting of unsifted whole-wheat flour: *graham crackers.* [From Sylvester *Graham,* 1794–1851, American dietary reformer.]

Grail (grāl) *n.* Holy Grail. [Old French *graal,* from Medieval Latin *gradalis* dish; of uncertain origin.]

grain (grān) *n.* **1.a.** edible seed or seedlike fruit of various cereal grasses, as rye, wheat, or corn. **b.** such seeds collectively: *They threshed the grain.* **c.** plants that produce such seeds. **2.** tiny, hard particle: *a grain of sand.* **3.a.** arrangement or direction of fibers or layers of different composition, density, or color, as in wood or stone. **b.** markings or patterns resulting from this. **4.** smallest unit of weight in the avoirdupois, apothecaries', and troy measurement systems, equal to 64.8 milligrams. **5.** texture of a substance, as compared with others of its

at; āpe; cär; end; mē; it; īce; hot; ōld; fôrk; wood; fōōl; oil; out; up; ūse; turn; sing; thin; this; zh in treasure; ə in ago, taken, pencil, lemon, circus.

type: *The salt used on city streets to melt snow is of coarser grain than table salt.* **6.** smallest possible quantity; tiny bit: *There is a grain of truth in his statement.* **7.** character or temperament: *Inefficiency goes against the American grain.* **8.** markings or texture formed on the outer side of a piece of leather by the cavities that remain after the hair has been removed. **9.** threads or fibers that run parallel with the selvage in a piece of fabric. —*v.t.* **1.** to produce an imitation grain upon, as by painting or stamping: *to grain plastic to look like leather.* **2.** to make (something) form into grains. **3.** to remove the hair from (leather) so as to bring out the grain. [Old French *grain* seedlike fruit of cereals, small quantity, ground piece of a substance, from Latin *grānum* seed.] —**grain′er,** *n.*

grain alcohol, alcohol (*def. 1*).

grain elevator, building for the storage of grain.

grain·y (grā′nē) **grain·i·er, grain·i·est.** *adj.* **1.** of or resembling grains; granular. **2.** having a grain, as wood. —**grain′i·ness,** *n.*

gram (gram) *also, British,* **gramme.** *n.* unit of mass in the metric system, equal to $\frac{1}{28}$ of an ounce or $\frac{1}{1000}$ of a kilogram. See **weights and measures** for table. [French *gramme,* from Greek *gramma* a small weight.]

-gram[1] combining form something written or drawn: *telegram, diagram.* [Greek *gramma* something written, letter of the alphabet.]

-gram[2] combining form of a gram; grams: *centigram, kilogram.* [From GRAM.]

gram. **1.** grammar. **2.** grammarian. **3.** grammatical.

gram atom, quantity of a chemical element having a weight in grams numerically equal to the atomic weight of the element. One gram atom of aluminum, which has an atomic weight of 27, weighs 27 grams. Also, **gram-atomic weight.**

gram equivalent, quantity of a substance, expressed in grams, needed to supply or react with one mole of hydrogen ions. Also, **gram-equivalent weight.**

gra·mer·cy (grə mur′sē) *interj. Archaic.* many thanks. [Old French *grand merci.* See GRAND, MERCY.]

gram·mar (gram′ər) *n.* **1.a.** structures and forms of a language, and the rules governing the use of these structures and forms, considered as a whole. **b.** systematic study of these structures and forms. **2.** book dealing with such forms and structures: *a French grammar.* **3.** speech or writing judged according to its conformity to established usage: *The language student's pronunciation and grammar were very good.* **4.** fundamental principles or rules of an art, science, or field of knowledge: *He learned the grammar of his profession.* [Old French *gramaire* science of the rules of language, book of such rules, from Latin *grammatica* science of the rules of language, philology, from Greek *grammatikē.*]

gram·mar·i·an (grə mâr′ē ən) *n.* student or expert in grammar.

grammar school **1.** elementary school. **2.** secondary school, esp. in England, in which college preparatory subjects, such as Latin and Greek, are emphasized.

gram·mat·i·cal (grə mat′i kəl) *adj.* **1.** of or relating to grammar. **2.** conforming to the established rules of grammar: *That sentence was not grammatical.* —**gram·mat′i·cal·ly,** *adv.* —**gram·mat′i·cal·ness,** *n.*

gramme (gram) *gram.*

gram molecule, mole. Also, **gram-molecular weight.**

gram·o·phone (gram′ə fōn′) *n.* phonograph. Trademark: Gramophone. [Inversion of PHONOGRAM.]

Gram·pi·ans (gram′pē ənz) *n.,pl.* mountain range in central Scotland separating the Highlands from the Lowlands. Also, **Grampian Hills.**

gram·pus (gram′pəs) *pl.,* **-pus·es.** *n.* **1.** dolphin, *Gramphidelphis griseus,* found in all seas except those in polar regions. **2.** killer whale. [Modification (influenced by GRAND) of Middle English *graspeys,* from Old French *graspeis, craspois* whale, seal[1]; literally, fat fish, going back to Latin *crassus piscis* fat fish.]

Gra·na·da (grə nä′də) *n.* historic city in southern Spain, site of the Alhambra and formerly the capital of a Moorish kingdom. Pop. (1968), 158,375.

gra·na·ry (grā′nər ē, gran′ər ē) *pl.,* **-ries.** *n.* storehouse for threshed grain. [Latin *grānārium,* from *grānum* grain, seed.]

Gran Cha·co (grän′ chä′kō) vast lowland region in south-central South America. Area, approx. 250,000 sq. mi.

grand (grand) *adj.* **1.** imposing or impressive, as in magnitude, scope, or magnificence: *a grand palace.* **2.** noble or dignified, as in character or manner. **3.** most important; main; principal: *The party was held in the grand ballroom.* **4.** complete; comprehensive: *The grand total was 2164.* **5.** highest or very high in rank or office. **6.** lofty and dignified in subject, treatment, or expression: *the grand style of the classical epic poem.* **7.** admired or respected because of age, position, or experience: *The ex-president became the grand old man of the Republican Party.* **8.** *Informal.* very good or excellent: *We had a grand time at the party.* —*n.* **1.** grand piano. **2.** *Slang.* a thousand dollars: *The thieves stole ten*

grand from the bank. [French *grand* great, tall, lofty, from Latin *grandis.*] —**grand′ly,** *adv.* —**grand′ness,** *n.*
Syn. *adj.* **1. Grand, stately, majestic** mean impressive. **Grand** is impressive because of magnitude and splendor in size and general effect: *London has many grand cathedrals.* **Stately** is impressive because of poised dignity, grace of proportion, and regal bearing: *The queen walked at a stately pace across the hall.* **Majestic** is impressive because of commanding appearance and lofty and august style or character: *In the distance we saw the majestic Rocky Mountains.*

gran·dam (gran′dəm, -dam′) *also,* **gran·dame** (gran′dām′, -dəm). *n. Archaic.* **1.** grandmother. **2.** old woman. [Anglo-Norman *graund dame* grandmother, going back to Latin *grandis* great + *domina* lady, mistress.]

Grand Army of the Republic, organization of Union veterans of the Civil War, founded in 1866.

grand-aunt (grand′ant′, -änt′) *n.* aunt of one's father or mother; great-aunt.

Grand Bank *also,* **Grand Banks.** shoal off the eastern coast of Newfoundland, in the North Atlantic. It is a major fishing area.

Grand Canal **1.** canal in eastern China, one of the longest and oldest in the world. **2.** large canal in Venice, Italy, the city's main thoroughfare.

Grand Canyon, large canyon on the upper course of the Colorado River, in northwestern Arizona, regarded as one of the most spectacular natural wonders of the world.

grand·child (grand′chīld′) *pl.,* **-chil·dren.** *n.* child of one's son or daughter.

Grand Cou·lee (kōō′lē) large dam on the Columbia River, in east-central Washington.

grand·daugh·ter (gran′dô′tər) *n.* daughter of one's son or daughter.

grand duchess **1.** wife or widow of a grand duke. **2.** in certain European countries, woman holding in her own right the sovereignty of a grand duchy. **3.** in czarist Russia, a princess of the royal family.

grand duchy, territory under the rule of a grand duke or grand duchess.

grand duke **1.** in certain European countries, sovereign of a grand duchy, ranking next below a king. **2.** in czarist Russia, a prince of the royal family.

gran·dee (gran dē′) *n.* **1.** Spanish or Portuguese nobleman of the highest rank. **2.** any person of high rank or great importance. [Spanish *grande* nobleman of the highest rank, from *grande* great, from Latin *grandis.*]

gran·deur (gran′jər, -joor) *n.* state or quality of being majestic or imposing; magnificence; splendor. [French *grandeur,* from *grand* great, from Latin *grandis.*]

grand·fa·ther (grand′fä′thər, gran′-) *n.* **1.** father of one's father or mother. **2.** forefather; ancestor.

grandfather clock *also,* **grandfather's clock.** clock having a pendulum and enclosed in a tall, usually wooden, cabinet that stands on the floor.

grand·fa·ther·ly (grand′fä′thər lē, gran′-) *adj.* **1.** of a grandfather. **2.** like or characteristic of a grandfather; kindly; benevolent: *He gave her a grandfatherly pat on the head.*

gran·dil·o·quence (gran dil′ə kwəns) *n.* quality of being grandiloquent.

gran·dil·o·quent (gran dil′ə kwənt) *adj.* using or characterized by a lofty, pompous, or pretentious style in speech or writing. [Latin *grandiloquus* speaking loftily (from *grandis* great + *loquī* to speak) + -ENT.] —**gran·dil′o·quent·ly,** *adv.*

gran·di·ose (gran′dē ōs′) *adj.* **1.** imposing or impressive; magnificent. **2.** pompous or pretentious: *He wrote in a grandiose style.* [French *grandiose* majestic, imposing, from Italian *grandioso,* from *grande,* great, from Latin *grandis.*] —**gran′di·ose·ly,** *adv.* —**gran·di·os·i·ty** (gran′dē os′ə tē), *n.*

grand jury, jury summoned to hear accusations in criminal cases and bring indictments if there is enough evidence for a trial.

Grand Lama, Dalai Lama.

grand larceny, larceny in which the goods stolen equal or exceed a specified statutory value. Distinguished from **petit larceny.**

grand·ma (grand′mä′, gram′-, gram′ə) *n. Informal.* grandmother. Also, **grand·ma·ma, grand·mam·ma** (grand′mə mä′-, -mä′mä)

grand mal (gran′ mal′) most severe form of epilepsy, characterized by sudden loss of consciousness and convulsions. [French *grand mal* literally, great sickness, going back to Latin *grandis* great + *malus* bad.]

grand·moth·er (grand′muth′ər, gran′-) *n.* **1.** mother of one's father or mother. **2.** female ancestor.

grand·moth·er·ly (grand′muth′ər lē, gran′-) *adj.* **1.** of a grandmother. **2.** like or characteristic of a grandmother; kindly; benevolent.

grand·neph·ew (grand′nef′ū, gran′-) *n.* son of one's nephew or niece.

---

at; āpe; cär; end; mē; it; īce; hot; ōld; fôrk; wood; fōōl; oil; out; up; ūse; turn; sing; thin; this; zh in treasure; ə in ago, taken; pencil, lemon, circus.　　447

grand·niece (grand′nēs′, gran′-) *n.* daughter of one's nephew or niece.

Grand Old Party, Republican Party of the United States.

grand opera, opera in which the entire text is sung.

grand·pa (grand′pä′, gran′-, gram′pə) *n. Informal.* grandfather. Also, **grand·pa·pa** (grand′pə pä′, -pä′pə).

grand·par·ent (grand′pâr′ənt) *n.* grandfather or grandmother.

grand piano, piano having horizontally arranged strings in a harp-shaped case. Distinguished from **upright piano.**

Grand Prairie, city in northeastern Texas, near Dallas. Pop. (1970), 50,904.

Grand Rapids, city in western Michigan. Pop. (1970), 197,649.

grand·sire (grand′sīr′) *n. Archaic.* **1.** grandfather. **2.** ancestor; forefather. **3.** old man.

grand slam 1. *Bridge.* winning of all thirteen tricks in a round of play. **2.** *Baseball.* home run with the bases loaded. **3.** *Golf.* winning of all of a specified number of tournaments.

grand·son (grand′sun′, gran′-) *n.* son of one's son or daughter.

grand·stand (grand′stand′) *n.* **1.** seating area accommodating spectators, as at an outdoor sports event or parade. **2.** spectators seated in such an area: *The entire grandstand cheered when our team won.* —*v.i. Informal.* to perform an action or conduct oneself in an unnecessarily showy or flamboyant manner in order to impress those watching.

grandstand play, action, esp. in sports, performed in an unnecessarily showy or flamboyant manner in order to impress those watching.

grand tour, formerly, extended tour of the principal cities and places of interest in continental Europe, considered to be part of the education of young men and women of wealthy families.

grand·un·cle (grand′ung′kəl) *n.* uncle of one's father or mother; great-uncle.

grange (grānj) *n.* **1.** *British.* farm and the buildings on it. **2. Grange. a.** fraternal organization, founded in 1867, to promote the interests and welfare of farm families and rural communities in the United States. **b.** lodge or local branch of this organization. [Old French *grange* barn, farm, going back to Latin *grānum* seed, grain.]

grang·er (grān′jər) *n.* **1.** farmer. **2. Granger.** member of a Grange.

gran·ite (gran′it) *n.* hard, durable igneous rock composed of feldspar and quartz with specks of darker minerals, often used for buildings and monuments. [Italian *granito* literally, speckled, grained, going back to *grano* grain, from Latin *grānum;* because it has a grained appearance.] —gra·nit·ic (grə nit′ik), *adj.*

gran·ite·ware (gran′it wâr′) *n.* **1.** ironware covered with gray, stonelike enamel. **2.** type of fine, hard pottery.

gran·ny (gran′ē) *pl.,* **-nies.** *also,* **gran·nie.** *n. Informal.* **1.** grandmother. **2.** old woman. **3.** fussy, meddling person.

granny knot, knot like a square knot but with the ends crossing in the wrong way, causing it to jam easily.

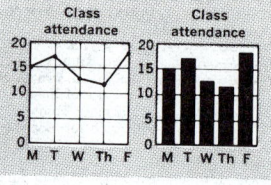

Granny knot

grant (grant) *v.t.* **1.** to give (what is asked for); confer: *We granted him permission to go.* **2.** to admit to be true, as for the sake of argument; concede: *I'll grant that that fact is correct, but the rest of your argument is wrong.* **3.** to bestow or confer, as property, a right, or a privilege, esp. by a formal act: *The king of England granted a charter to the colonists.* **4.** to transfer (real property), esp. by deed. —*n.* **1.** act of granting. **2.** that which is granted, as a right or privilege. **3.** transferal of real property, esp. by deed. **4.** one of certain tracts of land in New Hampshire, Vermont, or Maine, originally granted by the state to an individual, group of individuals, or an institution. **5. to take for granted. a.** to assume to be true. **b.** to accept, possess, or regard without due thought, consideration, or acknowledgment: *She took her friends for granted.* [Old French *granter,* form of *creanter* to guarantee, promise, going back to Latin *crēdere* to trust, believe.] —**grant′a·ble,** *adj.* —**grant′er,** *n.*

Syn. *v.t.* **2. Grant, concede** mean to acknowledge or accept as true, esp. in an argument. **Grant** suggests an effort to clear away nonessential hindrances to an understanding: *I grant that your argument is valid.* **Concede** implies a grudging willingness not to contest some point, either because it is not essential or because one's argument relative to the point is weak: *He finally conceded the point.*

Grant, Ulysses S(impson) (grant) 1822–85, U.S. general and eighteenth president of the United States from 1869 to 1877.

grant·ee (gran′tē) *n.* one to whom a grant is made.

grant·or (gran′tər, gran tôr′) *n.* one who makes a grant.

gran·u·lar (gran′yə lər) *adj.* **1.** consisting of, containing, or resembling grains or granules. **2.** having a granulated surface. —**gran·u·lar·i·ty** (gran′yə lar′ə tē), *n.* —**gran′u·lar·ly,** *adv.*

gran·u·late (gran′yə lāt′) **-lat·ed, -lat·ing.** *v.t.* **1.** to form into grains or granules. **2.** to roughen the surface of; raise in granules. —*v.i.* to

become roughened on the surface; develop granulations. —**gran′u·la′tive,** *adj.* —**gran′u·la′tor,** *n.*

gran·u·la·tion (gran′yə lā′shən) *n.* **1.** act or process of granulating; being granulated. **2.a.** roughened surface, as of a wound or ulcer that is healing. **b.** granule on such a surface.

gran·ule (gran′ūl) *n.* minute particle; grain. [Late Latin *grānulum,* diminutive of *grānum* grain, seed.]

gran·u·lose (gran′yə lōs′) *n.* that part of a starch granule which is soluble.

grape (grāp) *n.* **1.** smooth, thin-skinned edible fruit of any of a group of climbing woody vines, genus *Vitis,* growing in large clusters, and usually green or purple in color. Grapes are used to make wine and eaten dried or raw as a fruit. **2.** vine bearing this fruit, grown in warm temperate regions throughout the world, and having large clusters of small greenish flowers; grapevine. [Old French *grape* bunch of grapes; originally, hook (with reference to plucking clusters of grapes by a hook); of Germanic origin.]

grape·fruit (grāp′frōōt′) *n.* **1.** large, round, edible citrus fruit of an evergreen tree, *Citrus paradisi,* having a thick skin that ranges in color from pale yellow to reddish brown and tart, pink or white, juicy pulp. Also, **pom′e·lo′.** **2.** tree that bears this fruit, cultivated in warm regions of the world, esp. in the United States. [Because this *fruit* grows in clusters like *grapes.*]

grape hyacinth 1. spikelike cluster of small blue or white bell-shaped flowers of any of a group of plants, genus *Muscari,* of the lily family. **2.** plant bearing this flower cluster, widely cultivated, and having long narrow leaves.

grape·shot (grāp′shot′) *n.* cluster of small iron balls formerly used as a charge for cannon.

grape sugar, dextrose.

grape·vine (grāp′vīn′) *n.* **1.** vine bearing grapes. **2.** *Informal.* secret or informal means of spreading information, esp. from person to person.

graph (graf) *n.* **1.** diagram representing the changes of and the relationship between two or more elements by means of various forms of notation, as a series of dots, bars, or lines. **2.** *Mathematics.* locus of a function or equation plotted on coordinate axes. —*v.t.* to express or represent by a graph: *to graph the weekly profits of a business.* [Short for *graphic formula.* See GRAPHIC, FORMULA.]

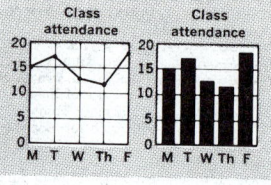

Class attendance — Line graph

Class attendance — Bar graph

-graph *combining form* **1.** machine or other apparatus that writes or records: *telegraph, seismograph.* **2.** that which is written or recorded: *autograph.* [Greek *-graphos* written, writing, writer (from *graphein* to write), often through French *-graphe* and Latin *-graphus.*]

graph·ic (graf′ik) *adj.* **1.** vividly descriptive; lifelike: *The book gave a graphic description of the fight.* **2.** of, relating to, or represented by a graph: *a graphic representation of rising business profits.* **3.** of or relating to the graphic arts. **4.** of, relating to, or expressed by writing: *Letters are graphic symbols.* Also, **graph′i·cal.** [Latin *graphicus* relating to painting or drawing, from Greek *graphikos,* from *graphein* to write, draw.] —**graph′i·cal·ly,** *adv.*

Syn. 1. Graphic, vivid, picturesque indicate sharpness, as in description, that recalls reality clearly to the mind. **Graphic** suggests an impression as definite as a picture: *The audience thrilled to his graphic description of the ascent.* **Vivid** implies intense clarity that seems to impress itself on the senses as if it were actually being experienced: *Crane is responsible for the most vivid war novel in American literature.* **Picturesque** suggests selection of detail, as by a painter or a writer, to emphasize certain aspects of a scene: *He gave a picturesque description of the little village.*

graphic arts 1. those forms of representation in which impressions are made from blocks, plates, and the like, as in etching or lithography. **2.** all forms of visual artistic representation on a flat surface, as drawing, painting, and photography.

graph·ite (graf′īt) *n.* soft, black crystalline form of carbon, commonly used as a lubricant when mixed with oil and as lead for pencils when mixed with clay. Also, **plum·ba′go.** [German *Graphit,* from Greek *graphein* to write; because used for pencils.]

graph paper, paper ruled in small squares on which to draw graphs, diagrams, or charts.

-graphy *combining form* **1.** process or form of writing, describing, or recording: *photography, biography.* **2.** descriptive science: *oceanography.* [Greek *-graphia* description of (from *graphein* to write), often through French *-graphie* and Latin *-graphia.*]

grap·nel (grap′nəl) *n.* **1.** grappling iron. **2.** small anchor with three to six flukes at the end of the shank. [Diminutive of Old French *grapin* hook, from *grape;* of Germanic origin.]

grap·ple (grap′əl) **-pled, -pling.** *v.t.* to seize or hold with or as with a grappling iron. —*v.i.* **1.** to contend or attempt to deal (usually with *with*). **2.a.** to struggle in hand-to-hand combat; wrestle: *He grappled with his assailant.* **b.** to seize another or each other in a close grip, as in wrestling. **3.** to use a grappling iron. —*n.* **1.** act or instance of grappling. **2.** grappling iron. [Middle French *grappil* grappling iron, from Old French *grape* hook. See GRAPNEL.] —**grap′pler,** *n.*

Grapnel

grappling iron, any of various devices having one or more hooks or clamps, used esp. for grasping or holding something.

grasp (grasp) *v.t.* **1.** to take hold of firmly with or as with the hand: *to grasp a baseball bat.* **2.** to understand; comprehend: *It's a hard concept to grasp.* **3.** to take possession of eagerly or greedily. —*v.i.* **1.** to make the motion of grasping. **2. to grasp at. a.** to catch at; try to seize: *to grasp at a life preserver.* **b.** to accept eagerly: *He grasped at the opportunity.* —*n.* **1.** act or instance of grasping. **2.** power or ability to obtain: *Happiness was within his grasp.* **3.** comprehension; understanding: *He had a grasp of algebra.* **4.** firm control; possession: *They freed the country from the grasp of the enemy.* [Possibly from an unrecorded Old English word.] —**Syn.** *v.t.* **1.** see **take.**

grasp·ing (gras′ping) *adj.* **1.** greedy; avaricious. **2.** that grasps. —**grasp′ing·ly,** *adv.* —**grasp′ing·ness,** *n.* —**Syn. 1.** see **greedy.**

grass (gras) *n.* **1.** any of a large group of plants, family Gramineae, having fibrous roots, jointed, usually hollow, stems, narrow leaves, and often bearing spikelets of small flowers. Wheat, rye, oats, corn, sugarcane, rice, and bamboo are grasses. **2.** any of a number of such plants covering lawns, pastures, or fields, as **Kentucky blue grass,** *Poa pratensis,* or **creeping bent grass,** *Agrostis palustris,* which are grown for lawns and golf courses. **3.** land on which grass grows, as a lawn or pasture. **4.** *Slang.* marijuana. **5. to let the grass grow under one's feet,** to waste time or miss chances or opportunities. —*v.t.* to cover with grass or turf. [Old English *græs* herbage.]

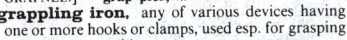

grass·hop·per (gras′hop′ər) *n.* any of a widespread group of chirping, winged insects, order Orthoptera, having long, powerful hind legs used for jumping.

Grasshopper

grass·land (gras′land′) *n.* **1.** land on which grass grows, used for pasturage. **2.** land or territory where grass is the predominant type of vegetation.

grass-roots (gras′rōōts′) *adj.* of, relating to, or coming from the common people, esp. in rural areas: *He had grass-roots support.*

grass roots, common people, esp. from rural areas, considered as the originators of political feelings or cultural forms.

grass snake, any of various harmless grayish-green snakes, commonly seen in the grass or garden.

grass widow, woman who is divorced, separated, or living apart from her husband.

grass widower, man who is divorced, separated, or living apart from his wife.

grass·y (gras′ē) *adj.* **1.** covered with or abounding in grass. **2.** consisting of or containing grass. **3.** resembling grass, esp. in color. —**grass′i·ness,** *n.*

grate¹ (grāt) *n.* **1.** framework of parallel or crossed bars set in or over an opening, as in a window, door, or drain; grating. **2.** framework or basket of iron bars to hold burning fuel, as in a fireplace or furnace. **3.** fireplace. **4.** screen used in mining to sift and grade crushed ore. —*v.t.* **grat·ed, grat·ing.** to fit or furnish with a grate or grating. [Medieval Latin *grata* grating¹, lattice, going back to Latin *crātis* hurdle, wickerwork.]

grate² (grāt) **grat·ed, grat·ing.** *v.t.* **1.** to reduce to small particles or shreds by rubbing against a rough or sharply indented surface: *to grate cheese.* **2.** to rub together so as to produce a harsh, scraping sound; grind: *to grate one's teeth.* —*v.i.* **1.** to have an annoying or irritating effect: *Her selfish attitude grates on my nerves.* **2.** to produce a harsh, scraping sound by rubbing: *The cell door grated on its rusty hinges.* [Old French *grater* to scratch, scrape; of Germanic origin.]

grate·ful (grāt′fəl) *adj.* **1.** thankful and appreciative for kindness or benefits received. **2.** pleasing; welcome; agreeable: *a grateful shower of rain.* [Obsolete *grate* agreeable (from Latin *grātus* pleasing) + -FUL.] —**grate′ful·ly,** *adv.* —**grate′ful·ness,** *n.* **Syn. 1.** Grateful, thankful, appreciative indicate the feeling or expression of gratitude. **Grateful** suggests gratitude for having received some

kindness or other favor from another person: *I shall always be grateful for his advice.* **Thankful** implies awareness of one's good fortune or acknowledgment of divine rather than human help: *I am always thankful for my good health.* **Appreciative** suggests thanks arising from recognition of the real importance or significance of what one has received: *She made a short, appreciative speech of acceptance.*

grat·er (grāt′ər) *n.* **1.** kitchen utensil having a rough surface of sharp, raised edges above each of a number of indentations, used to grate vegetables, cheese, spices, and other foods. **2.** one who or that which grates.

grat·i·fi·ca·tion (grat′ə fi kā′shən) *n.* **1.** act of gratifying; being gratified. **2.** source or cause of pleasure or satisfaction.

grat·i·fy (grat′ə fī′) **-fied, -fy·ing.** *v.t.* **1.** to give pleasure or satisfaction to; please: *The news that they were well gratified us.* **2.** to satisfy, indulge, or humor, as a feeling, need, or desire: *She gratified her grandchild's every whim.* [Latin *grātificāri* to please, do a favor to, going back to *grātus* pleasing + *facere* to make, do.] —**grat′i·fi′er,** *n.* —**Syn. 1.** see **please.**

grat·i·fy·ing (grat′ə fī′ing) *adj.* that gratifies; pleasing or satisfying. —**grat′i·fy′ing·ly,** *adv.*

grat·ing¹ (grā′ting) *n.* framework of parallel or crossed bars set in or over an opening, as a window or sewer, serving as a cover, guard, or screen. [GRATE¹ + -ING¹.]

grat·ing² (grā′ting) *adj.* **1.** producing or characterized by a harsh or irritating sound: *a grating, rusty hinge, a grating cough.* **2.** annoying; irritating. [GRATE² + -ING².]

grat·is (grat′is, grā′tis) *adv.* without charge, cost, or payment; free: *No one will give anything for that which can be obtained gratis* (Mill, 1848). —*adj.* given or provided without charge, cost, or payment. [Latin *grātīs,* going back to *grātia* favor.]

grat·i·tude (grat′ə tōōd′, -tūd′) *n.* quality or condition of being grateful, as for a kindness or favor. [Late Latin *grātitūdō,* from Latin *grātus* pleasing, thankful.]

gra·tu·i·tous (grə tōō′ə təs, -tū′-) *adj.* **1.** given or provided without obligation of payment or return; free. **2.** without good reason or cause; unjustifiable; unwarranted: *A gratuitous and unfounded supposition* (Lingard, 1844). [Latin *grātuītus* done without pay, free.] —**gra·tu′i·tous·ly,** *adv.* —**gra·tu′i·tous·ness,** *n.*

gra·tu·i·ty (grə tōō′ə tē, -tū′-) *pl.,* **-ties.** *n.* gift, esp. of money, given in return for services rendered; tip: *He gave a gratuity to the waiter.* [Medieval Latin *gratuitas* free gift, from Latin *grātuītus* done without pay.]

grat·u·lant (grach′ə lənt) *adj.* congratulatory. [Latin *grātulāns,* present participle of *grātulārī* to express joy.]

grat·u·late (grach′ə lāt′) **-lat·ed, -lat·ing.** *v.t. Archaic.* **1.** to greet with joy; hail. **2.** to congratulate. [Latin *grātulātus,* past participle of *grātulārī* to express joy.] —**grat′u·la′tion,** *n.* —**grat′u·la·to′ry,** *adj.*

gra·va·men (grə vā′mən) *pl.,* **-vam·i·na** (-vam′i nə). *n. Law.* **1.** grievance. **2.** significant part or gist of an accusation or complaint. [Medieval Latin *gravamen* grievance, going back to Latin *gravis* heavy.]

grave¹ (grāv) *n.* **1.** burial place, esp. an excavation in the earth, for the interment of a body. **2.** place or occasion of loss. **3.** *also,* **the grave.** death: *The paths of glory lead but to the grave* (Gray, 1750). **4. to have one foot in the grave.** to be near death, as from old age or illness. **5. to turn (over) in one's grave.** to be supposedly distressed or displeased after one's death by the actions of the living. [Old English *græf* place of burial.]

grave² (grāv; *adj. def. 4, n. also,* gräv) **grav·er, grav·est.** *adj.* **1.** of great importance; weighty: *grave decisions.* **2.** of a threatening nature; dangerous; critical: *a grave illness.* **3.** earnest and dignified; sober: *a grave, humorless man.* **4.** of or relating to a diacritical mark (`) placed over a vowel to indicate correct pronunciation, as in French *père,* to distinguish between two words identically spelled, as in French *à* and *à,* to indicate that a final syllable is pronounced, as in English *learnèd,* or to indicate that a final syllable is stressed, as in Italian *città.* **5.** (of colors) somber. —*n.* grave accent. [Latin *gravis* heavy, important.] —**grave′ly,** *adv.* —**grave′ness,** *n.* **Syn. adj. 3.** Grave, solemn, somber indicate a mood or temperament characterized by the absence of levity or superficiality. **Grave** implies a dignified demeanor suggesting concentration on weighty and important matters: *The president addressed the Congress with a grave voice.* **Solemn** stresses the rather ceremonious dignity with which affairs of importance are handled: *There was a solemn hush in the cathedral as the mourners filed past the casket.* **Somber** stresses a melancholy seriousness: *The judge pronounced the sentence in somber tones.*

grave³ (grāv) **graved, graved** or **grav·en, grav·ing.** *v.t.* **1.** to form or shape by carving; sculpt. **2.** to engrave on a hard substance; incise. **3.** to impress deeply; fix firmly, as in the memory. [Old English *grafan* to dig, engrave.]

grave⁴ (grāv) **graved, grav·ing.** *v.t.* to clean (a ship's bottom), esp. by removing accumulated material and coating with pitch. [Probably from

Old French *grave* sandbank, shore of sand; of Celtic origin; because boats were drawn up on the shore to be graved.]

grav·el (grav′əl) *n.* mixture of pebbles and small rock fragments, often mixed with sand, used esp. for roads and walks. —*v.t.* **-eled, -el·ing**; *also, British,* **-elled, -el·ling.** **1.** to cover or lay with gravel. **2.** to puzzle; perplex; confound. **3.** *Informal.* to irritate; annoy. [Old French *gravele* small stones or pebbles mixed with sand, diminutive of *grave* sandbank, coarse sand; of Celtic origin.]

grav·el·ly (grav′ə lē) *adj.* **1.** consisting of, containing, or like gravel. **2.** (of voices) harsh; grating.

grav·en (grā′vən) a past participle of **grave**[3].

graven image, idol.

grav·er (grā′vər) *n.* **1.** burin. **2.** engraver, sculptor, or stonecarver.

grave·stone (grāv′stōn′) *n.* stone marking a grave.

grave·yard (grāv′yärd′) *n.* cemetery.

graveyard shift *Informal.* work shift usually beginning at midnight.

grav·i·tate (grav′ə tāt′) **-tat·ed, -tat·ing.** *v.i.* **1.** to move or tend to move as a result of the force of gravity. **2.** to move or be attracted as the result of a natural tendency or strong influence (with *to* or *toward*): *The new students in the class gravitated toward each other.* **3.** to sink or fall. [Modern Latin *gravitatus,* past participle of *gravitare,* from Latin *gravitās* weight.]

grav·i·ta·tion (grav′ə tā′shən) *n.* **1.** force of mutual attraction that exists between any two bodies in the universe. It is directly proportional to the product of the masses of the two bodies and inversely proportional to the square of the distance between them. **2.** act or process of gravitating. **3.** movement toward or attraction to someone or something as the result of a natural tendency or strong influence. —**grav′i·ta′tion·al,** *adj.* —**grav′i·ta′tion·al·ly,** *adv.*

grav·i·ton (grav′ə ton′) *n.* hypothetical elementary particle, having no mass or electric charge, representing a quantum of gravitational energy. [From GRAVITY.]

grav·i·ty (grav′ə tē) *pl.,* **-ties.** *n.* **1.** gravitational force that the earth exerts on bodies at or near its surface. The pull of gravity on a body is called the weight of the body. **2.** gravitation. **3.** weight; heaviness: *the center of gravity.* **4.** serious or critical nature: *He was not aware of the gravity of the problem.* **5.** dignity of manner or character; solemnity; seriousness. **6.** lowness of pitch, as of musical tones. [Latin *gravitās* weight, dignity, importance.]

gra·vure (grə vyoor′, grā′vyər) *n.* photogravure. [French *gravure* engraving, print, from *graver* to engrave, imprint; of Germanic origin.]

gra·vy (grā′vē) *pl.,* **-vies.** *n.* **1.** juice that exudes from meat during and after cooking. **2.** thickened sauce made by blending this juice with other ingredients, as flour and seasonings. **3.** *Slang.* money or profit acquired or obtained easily. [Middle English *grave* spiced sauce, as for meats, possibly a misreading of Old French *grane* literally, grained (since gravies may be seasoned with grains of spices), from Latin *grānātus* having many grains, from *grānum* grain, seed.]

gravy boat, boat-shaped dish, usually having a pouring spout on one end and a handle on the other, used for serving gravy or sauce.

gravy train *Informal.* **1.** job, position, or situation from which a person receives money or other gain with little or no work. **2.** *to ride the gravy train,* to receive money or other gain with little or no work.

gray (grā) *also,* **grey,** *adj.* **1.** of or having a color that is a blend of black and white. **2.** dark, gloomy, or dismal: *a gray day.* **3.** gray-headed. **4.** (of a knitted or woven fabric) not yet dyed, bleached, or otherwise processed. —*n.* achromatic color produced by blending black and white. —*v.t., v.i.* to make or become gray. [Old English *græg* color produced by blending black and white.] —**gray′ly,** *adv.* —**gray′-ness,** *n.*

Gray, Thomas (grā) 1716–71, English poet.

gray·beard (grā′bērd′) *n.* old man.

Gray Friar, Franciscan friar.

gray·head·ed (grā′hed′id) *adj.* **1.** having gray hair. **2.** old.

gray·hound (grā′hound′) greyhound.

gray·ish (grā′ish) *adj.* somewhat gray.

gray·lag (grā′lag′) *n.* wild, gray goose, *Anser anser,* found in Europe, considered to be the ancestor of the domestic goose. Length: 30–35 inches. [GRAY + LAG; because it migrates later than other migratory geese.]

gray·ling (grā′ling) *n.* **1.** any of several troutlike, silver-blue or purple fish, genus *Thymallus,* found in cold, running streams, having a large dorsal fin, and valued as both a food and a game fish. Length: 12–16 inches. **2.** any of several grayish or brownish butterflies, family Nymphalidae, esp. *Eumenis semele,* common in Europe.

gray market, purchasing and selling of scarce goods at exorbitant prices. It is not illegal, but is considered unethical because it takes unfair advantage of market demand.

gray matter, **1.** grayish tissue in the brain and spinal cord containing numerous cell bodies and the dendrites of nerve cells. **2.** *Informal.* intelligence; brains: *She's sweet but a little short on gray matter.*

gray squirrel, squirrel, genus *Sciurus,* found in both urban and rural areas of the United States, having gray fur. There are two species, **the eastern gray squirrel,** *S. carolinensis,* and **the western gray squirrel,** *S. griseus.* Length: 15–28 inches.

graze[1] (grāz) **grazed, graz·ing.** *v.i.* to feed on growing grass and other herbage: *Cattle and sheep grazed in the meadow.* —*v.t.* **1.** to put (livestock) to feed on growing grass and other herbage: *They grazed the herd in the north pasture.* **2.** to feed on (growing grass and other herbage). **3.** to tend (livestock) while they graze. [Old English *grasian* to feed on herbage.]

graze[2] (grāz) **grazed, graz·ing.** *v.t.* **1.** to scrape the skin from slightly in passing: *The bullet grazed the young lady's temple* (Scott, 1814). **2.** to touch or rub against lightly in passing. —*v.i.* **1.** to move so as to touch, rub, or scrape something lightly in passing. —*n.* **1.** act or instance of grazing. **2.** scratch, scrape, or superficial wound caused by grazing. [Possibly from GRAZE[1]; possibly originally referring to bullets grazing or touching grass and rebounding.]

gra·zier (grā′zhər) *n. British.* one who grazes cattle, esp. for market.

graz·ing (grā′zing) *n.* pasture land; pasturage.

Gr. Br., Great Britain. Also, **Gr. Brit.**

grease (*n.,* grēs; *v.,* grēs, grēz) *n.* **1.** soft animal fat, esp. when it has been melted or rendered: *bear grease, bacon grease.* **2.** viscous, semisolid substance, used esp. as a lubricant. **3.** shorn wool that has not been cleaned. —*v.t.* **greased, greas·ing.** **1.** to smear or lubricate with grease. **2.** to cause to operate more easily, freely, or smoothly; facilitate: *to grease the wheels of progress.* **3. to grease (someone's) palm** (or **hand**). to bribe or tip. [Old French *graisse* animal fat, going back to Latin *crassus* thick, fat.] —**greas′er,** *n.*

grease cup, lubricating device, as in certain machines, consisting of a cup that feeds grease to the bearing or other part to which it is attached.

grease monkey *Informal.* mechanic, esp. one who works on automobiles or airplanes.

grease paint, thick make-up having a heavy oil or wax base, used esp. by actors and actresses.

grease·wood (grēs′wood′) *n.* **1.** spiny, evergreen shrub, *Sarcobatus vermiculatus* of the goosefoot family, abundant in dry, alkaline regions of the western plains of North America, having a hard, yellow wood, used esp. as fuel. **2.** any of several related plants, as the creosote bush. [GREASE + WOOD; possibly because the wood contains some oil and burns easily.]

greas·y (grē′sē, -zē) **greas·i·er, greas·i·est.** *adj.* **1.** smeared or soiled with grease. **2.** containing excessive grease or fat. **3.** resembling grease, as in consistency or appearance; slippery. **4.** *Informal.* disagreeably unctuous: *The salesman had a greasy manner.* —**greas′i·ly,** *adv.* —**greas′i·ness,** *n.*

great (grāt) *adj.* **1.** extraordinary in ability or achievement; eminent: *a great writer, a great baseball player.* **2.** of more than ordinary importance, distinction, or effect: *a great occasion, a great honor, a great achievement.* **3.** very large: *a great expanse of land, a great variety of colors.* **4.a.** of unusual extent; extreme: *great poverty.* **b.** to a degree far beyond normal: *a great believer in the power of faith.* **5.** of long duration: *a great while.* **6.** exhibiting nobility or loftiness, as of character or purpose: *Great souls suffer in silence* (Schiller, 1787). **7.** largest or most important among others of its kind: *the great hall of the castle.* **8.** belonging to the generation before the relative specified: *great-great-grandfather.* **9.** *Informal.* very good; exceptional: *We had a great vacation.* —*adv. Informal.* very well: *You're doing great.* —*n.* one who or that which is extraordinary or outstanding. [Old English *grēat* large, thick, massive.] —**great′ness,** *n.*

Syn. *adj.* **3.** Great, large, big indicate extent, size, or dimensions above average. Great is the most formal word and suggests something imposing or impressive: *The great redwoods towered above us as we stood in the clearing.* Large is somewhat formal and implies that the thing is being judged in terms of its physical measurements: *The advertisement states that the apartment has large rooms.* Big has an informal connotation and suggests bulk, mass, or volume: *He is too big to fit into that suit.*

great ape, any anthropoid ape, as a gorilla or chimpanzee.

great-aunt (grāt′ant′, -änt′) *n.* sister of one's grandmother or grandfather; grandaunt.

Great Barrier Reef, largest barrier reef in the world, along the northeastern coast of Australia.

Great Basin, vast region in the western United States, consisting mostly of arid or semiarid land characterized by numerous small basins separated by short mountain ranges. It lies between the Sierra Nevada mountain range on the west and the Rocky Mountains on the east and includes most of Nevada. Area, approx. 200,000 sq. mi.

Great Bear Lake, lake in the western part of the Northwest Territories, in Canada.

Great Britain **1.** United Kingdom. **2.** island off the western coast

at; āpe; cär; end; mē; it; īce; hot; ōld; fôrk; wood; fōōl; oil; out; up; ūse; turn; sing; thin; this; zh in treasure; ə in ago, taken, pencil, lemon, circus.

of Europe comprising England, Scotland, and Wales, largest of the British Isles. Area, 94,214 sq. mi. Also, **Brit′ain.**

great circle, any circle on a sphere formed by a plane intersecting the surface of the sphere and passing through the center of the sphere.

great·coat (grāt′kōt′) *n.* heavy overcoat.

Great Dane, dog of a breed noted for its size and strength, having a square muzzle and a smooth, short-haired coat. Height: 32 inches at the shoulder.

Great Divide 1. Continental Divide. **2.** borderline between life and death: *to cross the Great Divide.*

great·er (grā′tər) *adj.* designating a city and its suburbs: *the greater metropolitan area.*

Greater Antilles, island group of the West Indies, including Cuba, Jamaica, Hispaniola, and Puerto Rico.

Great Dane

Greater London, administrative unit of England comprising the City of London and the thirty-two London boroughs. Area, 616 sq. mi. Pop. (1968), 7,763,800.

Great Falls, largest city of Montana, in the west-central part of the state. Pop. (1970), 60,091.

great-grand·child (grāt′gran′chīld′) *pl.* **-chil·dren.** *n.* child of one's grandchild.

great-grand·daugh·ter (grāt′gran′dô′tər) *n.* daughter of one's grandchild.

great-grand·fa·ther (grāt′gran′fä′thər, -gran′-) *n.* father of one's grandmother or grandfather.

great-grand·moth·er (grāt′gran′muth′ər, -gran′-) *n.* mother of one's grandmother or grandfather.

great-grand·par·ent (grāt′gran′pâr′ənt, -par′-, -gran′-) *n.* mother or father of one's grandmother or grandfather.

great-grand·son (grāt′gran′sun′, -gran′-) *n.* son of one's grandchild.

great-heart·ed (grāt′här′tid) *adj.* **1.** having a generous and forgiving nature; magnanimous. **2.** brave.

great horned owl, dark-brown horned owl, *Bubo virginianus,* found throughout North and South America. Height: 2 feet.

Great Lakes, group of five large freshwater lakes along the border between the United States and Canada, including Lakes Superior, Michigan, Huron, Erie, and Ontario.

great·ly (grāt′lē) *adv.* **1.** in or to a great degree; very much: *I would greatly appreciate your help.* **2.** in a great manner; nobly; magnanimously.

Great Mogul, title of the ruler of the Mogul empire.

great-neph·ew (grāt′nef′ū) *n.* son of one's nephew or niece; grandnephew.

great-niece (grāt′nēs′) *n.* daughter of one's nephew or niece; grandniece.

Great Plains, vast plateau region in western North America, extending from Alberta, Canada, to Texas, consisting mostly of flat or rolling, generally treeless, plains.

Great Pyramid, tomb of Cheops at Giza, the largest structure erected in ancient times, and the greatest of the Pyramids.

Great Russian, member of the Russian-speaking people living in the central and northeastern part of the Soviet Union.

Great Salt Lake, lake in northwestern Utah, the largest salt lake in North America and one of the saltiest bodies of water in the world.

great seal, principal seal of a government, placed on documents as proof of their official approval.

Great Slave Lake, lake in the southwestern part of the Northwest Territories, in Canada.

Great Smoky Mountains, mountain range in the southeastern United States, between Tennessee and North Carolina, part of the Appalachian Mountains. Also, **Smoky Mountains, Great Smokies.**

Great Spirit, chief god in the religion of certain North American Indian tribes.

great-un·cle (grāt′ung′kəl) *n.* brother of one's grandmother or grandfather; granduncle.

Great Wall of China, defensive wall extending about 1500 miles along the boundary between north and northwest China and Mongolia. It was originally built in the third century B.C. as a defense against Huns and other invaders from Mongolia. Also, **Great Wall, Chinese Wall.**

Great War, World War I.

Great White Way, brightly lighted theater district on Broadway near Times Square in New York City.

greave (grēv) *n.* armor for the leg below the knee. See **armor** for illustration. [Old French *greve* shin, armor for the leg; of uncertain origin.]

grebe (grēb) *n.* any of various water birds, family Podicipedidae, having soft, lustrous plumage that in winter is typically gray or black above and white below, legs set far back on the body, and lobed toes rather than webbed feet. Length: 9–24 inches. [French *grèbe;* of uncertain origin.]

Grebe

Gre·cian (grē′shən) *adj.* Greek. —*n.* a Greek.

Gre·co-Ro·man (grē′kō rō′mən, grek′ō-) *also,* **Grae·co-Ro·man.** *adj.* of or characteristic of ancient Greece and Rome: *Greco-Roman art.*

Greece (grēs) *n.* country at the southern end of the Balkan Peninsula. Ancient Greece was a great intellectual and artistic center and a major influence on Western culture. Capital, Athens. Area, 50,944 sq. mi. Pop. (1969 est.), 8,835,000.

greed (grēd) *n.* excessive, usually selfish, desire to have or acquire something, esp. wealth. [From GREEDY.]

greed·y (grē′dē) **greed·i·er, greed·i·est.** *adj.* **1.** excessively eager to have or acquire something; wanting more than one's share. **2.** wanting to eat or drink too much or too quickly; gluttonous. [Old English *grǣdig.*] —**greed′i·ly,** *adv.* —**greed′i·ness,** *n.*

Syn. 1. Greedy, grasping, avaricious, covetous indicate a keen desire to possess something, esp. wealth. **Greedy** suggests a lack of moderation and a continuing desire to acquire something far beyond one's needs or rightful share: *Greedy for power, the general conceived a plan to overthrow the government.* **Grasping** suggests aggressive and selfish accumulation by unscrupulous means: *She displayed a grasping ambition that won her few friends.* **Avaricious** implies an obsessive drive to acquire money or wealth, and often suggests stinginess: *The avaricious manager paid the boxer only a tiny portion of the profits of the bout.* **Covetous** implies an inordinate desire to have more, esp. of something owned by someone else: *He was covetous of his neighbor's land in the valley.*

Greek (grēk) *adj.* of or relating to Greece, its people, their language, or culture. —*n.* **1.** member or close descendant of the people of Greece. **2.** Indo-European language spoken predominantly in Greece and surrounding areas in varying forms since prehistoric times. **3.** *Informal.* language or subject matter that cannot be understood: *It's all Greek to me.* [Old English *Grēcas* (plural) natives of Greece, from Latin *Graecī,* plural of *Graecus* native of Greece, Grecian, from Greek *Graikos* native of Greece.]

Greek cross, cross having four arms of equal length.

Greek fire, incendiary material that burned on contact with water, used as a weapon in ancient and medieval warfare. It was first used by the Byzantine Greeks.

Greek cross

Greek Orthodox Church 1. Orthodox Church. **2.** established church of Greece, a self-governing member of the Orthodox Church.

Gree·ley, Horace (grē′lē) 1811–72, U.S. journalist, author, and politician.

green (grēn) *n.* **1.** color between yellow and blue in the spectrum. **2.** something that imparts this color, as a dye or paint. **3.** grassy, usually level, open plot of land used for a particular purpose: *village green.* **4.** *Golf.* area around a cup, having very thick, closely cut grass. Also, **putting green. 5. greens. a.** green leaves or stems of certain plants, as turnips, lettuce, spinach, or dandelions, used for food: *She washed the salad greens and mixed them with the dressing.* **b.** freshly cut leaves or branches used for decoration: *The mantelpiece was decorated with greens for the holiday.* **6. the Green.** national color of the Irish Republic. —*adj.* **1.** having the color green. **2.** covered with growing plants, grass, or green foliage; verdant: *green pastures.* **3.** not fully grown or mature; not ripe: *green tomatoes.* **4.** consisting of edible green leaves or other plant parts: *a tossed green salad.* **5.a.** having little or no training or experience; immature, as in judgment: *a green recruit.* **b.** easily fooled; gullible; naive. **6.** having a pale, sickly color, as from nausea or fear: *Their faces were green when they came off the roller coaster.* **7.** not dried, cured, or otherwise ready for use: *green lumber.* **8.** full of vitality; lively: *a fresh, green memory.* **9.** characterized by unusually mild weather: *a green winter.* **10. to be green with envy.** to be sick with jealousy; be extremely envious. —*v.i.* to become green: *The land greened with the coming of spring.* —*v.t.* to make green: *The sunshine greened the vines on the slope.* [Old English *grēne* of the color green, verdant.] —**green′ness,** *n.*

green·back (grēn′bak′) *n.* **1.** paper currency not backed by gold or silver, first issued by the U.S. government in 1862 to finance the Union effort in the Civil War and slowly retired until 1879, when those still in circulation were made convertible into gold. **2.** any piece of U.S. paper currency. [GREEN + BACK¹; because the back is usually printed in green ink.]

at; āpe; cär; end; mē; it; īce; hot; ōld; fôrk; wood; fōōl; oil; out; up; ūse; turn; sing; thin; this; zh in treasure; ə in ago, taken, pencil, lemon, circus.

451

Greenback Party. U.S. political party organized by farm leaders in 1874 and active through the 1880s. It favored the continued issuing of greenbacks not redeemable for gold or silver as the only U.S. paper currency. —**Green'back'er,** n.

Green Bay, port city in east-central Wisconsin. Pop. (1970), 87,809.

green bean, string bean.

green·belt (grēn'belt') n. strip of land that adjoins or surrounds a community and is left undeveloped or is used for recreational areas, parks, or similar public facilities.

green·bri·er (grēn'brī'ər) n. any of a large group of vines or shrubs, genus *Smilax,* of the lily family, bearing clusters of white, yellow, or green flowers and usually having prickly stems.

green corn, young tender ears of corn, used esp. for roasting.

Greene (grēn) **1. Nathanael.** 1742–86, U.S. general in the American Revolution. **2. Gra·ham** (grā'əm) 1904—, English author.

green·er·y (grē'nər ē) pl. **-er·ies.** n. green plants or foliage; verdure.

green-eyed (grēn'īd') adj. **1.** having green eyes. **2.** jealous.

green·finch (grēn'finch') n. any of several finches, genus *Chloris,* esp. *C. chloris,* of Europe and western Asia, the male of which is olive-green with yellow and black markings.

green·gage (grēn'gāj') n. sweet plum, *Prunus domestica,* having a greenish-yellow skin and flesh. [From the English botanist Sir William *Gage,* who brought it to England from France about 1725.]

green·gro·cer (grēn'grō'sər) n. *British.* person who sells fresh vegetables and fruit. —**green'gro'cer·y,** n.

green·horn (grēn'hôrn') n. *Informal.* **1.** inexperienced person; novice. **2.** person easily fooled or imposed upon. [GREEN + HORN; in allusion to the green or young horns of oxen not fully grown.]

green·house (grēn'hous') n. building or similar structure having the roof and sides of glass or transparent plastic that traps the heat of the sun and in which plants can be cultivated throughout the year.

green·ing (grē'ning) n. any of several apples having a greenish-yellow skin when ripe and a tart flavor, used esp. for cooking.

green·ish (grē'nish) adj. somewhat green.

Green·land (grēn'lənd, -land') n. Danish island northeast of the mainland of North America, lying mostly within the Arctic Circle. It is the largest island in the world. Area, 840,000 sq. mi. Pop. (1967 est.), 43,792.

green light 1. green traffic signal indicating permission to proceed. **2.** *Informal.* authorization or permission to proceed with a particular project or activity: *Mother gave us the green light to go on the camping trip.*

green manure 1. crop, as clover or alfalfa, that is plowed under while still green to enrich the soil. **2.** manure that has not yet decayed.

Green Mountains, mountain range extending along the entire length of central Vermont, part of the Appalachian Mountains.

green onion, scallion (def. 1).

green pepper, unripe sweet pepper.

green plant, any plant containing chlorophyll.

green·room (grēn'rōōm', -room') n. lounge in a theater for the use of the performers.

Greens·bor·o (grēnz'bur'ō) n. city in north-central North Carolina. Pop. (1970), 144,076.

green soap, soft soap made chiefly from potassium hydroxide and vegetable oils, used esp. in treating skin disorders.

green-stick fracture (grēn'stik') partial fracture in which only one side of a bone is broken.

green·sward (grēn'swôrd') n. green grass; grassy ground.

green tea, tea made from leaves that have been steamed to prevent fermentation.

green thumb, special talent for making plants grow.

green turtle, large sea turtle, *Chelonia mydas,* found in warm waters throughout the world, having a green shell, and used for food, esp. in soup.

Green·ville (grēn'vil') n. **1.** city in northwestern South Carolina. Pop. (1970), 61,208. **2.** port city in western Mississippi, on the Mississippi River. Pop. (1970), 39,648.

Green·wich (def. *1* grin'ij, -ich, grēn'-; def. *2* grēn'ich, grin'-, grēn'wich') n. **1.** borough of Greater London, England, former site of an astronomical observatory. The prime meridian passes through Greenwich. Pop. (1968 est.), 229,700. **2.** city in southwestern Connecticut, on Long Island Sound. Pop. (1970), 59,755.

Green·wich Time (grin'ij, -ich, grēn'-) the time at the prime meridian in Greenwich, England, used as the standard time by which the time zones of the world are established.

Green·wich Village (grēn'ich) section of lower Manhattan, New York City, noted as an artists' and writers' quarter and for its bohemian atmosphere. Also, **the Village.**

green·wood (grēn'wood') n. forest when green, as in the summer.

greet (grēt) v.t. **1.** to speak to or welcome in a friendly or polite way, as upon meeting: *She greeted her guests at the door.* **2.** to meet or receive in a specified way: *The pianist was greeted with applause.* **3.** to present itself to: *The morning sun greeted us as we came out on deck.* [Old English *grētan* to approach, address.] —**greet'er,** n.

greet·ing (grē'ting) n. **1.** act or words of a person who greets another or others. **2.** greetings. friendly wishes or message, esp. from someone absent: *He sent greetings on my birthday.* —*interj.* **greetings.** hello.

greeting card, card¹ (def. 5).

gre·gar·i·ous (gri gâr'ē əs) adj. **1.** enjoying and seeking the company of others; sociable; outgoing. **2.** living in flocks, herds, or similar groups, as sheep. [Latin *gregārius* relating to a flock¹, from *grex* flock¹.] —**gre·gar'i·ous·ly,** adv. —**gre·gar'i·ous·ness,** n.

Gre·go·ri·an (gri gôr'ē ən) adj. of, relating to, or introduced by one of several popes named Gregory, esp. Pope Gregory I or Pope Gregory XIII.

Gregorian calendar, calendar currently in use in the Western Hemisphere and other countries. Introduced as a reform of the Julian calendar by Pope Gregory XIII in 1582, it provides for an ordinary year of 365 days and a leap year of 366 days.

Gregorian chant, plainsong used in the liturgy of the Roman Catholic and certain other churches. [From Pope *Gregory* I, who collected and edited the great body of church songs.]

Greg·o·ry I, Saint (greg'ər ē) A.D. c.540–604, pope from 590 to 604. Also, **Gregory the Great.**

Gregory VII, Saint, 1020–85, pope from 1073 to 1085.

Gregory XIII, 1502–85, pope from 1572 to 1585. He introduced the Gregorian calendar.

Gregory of Tours, Saint, A.D. c.538–594, Frankish bishop and historian.

grem·lin (grem'lin) n. small, mischievous spirit blamed for sudden or unaccountable mishaps. [Of uncertain origin.]

Gre·na·da (gri nā'də) n. island country in the West Indies, one of the Windward Islands. Land area, 133 sq. mi. Pop. (1975 est.), 100,000.

gre·nade (gri nād') n. small explosive missile that can be thrown by hand or launched from a rifle with a grenade launcher. [French *grenade* small bomb, pomegranate, going back to Latin *grānātus* having many grains, from *grānum* grain, seed; because a grenade resembles a pomegranate both in shape and in its "grains" of gunpowder.]

grenade launcher, device attached to the muzzle or barrel of a rifle, used to fire grenades.

gren·a·dier (gren'ə dēr') n. **1.** member of the first regiment of infantry in the British Army attached to the royal household. Also, **Grenadier Guard. 2.** formerly, a soldier who threw hand grenades. [French *grenadier,* soldier who throws grenades, pomegranate tree, from *grenade* small bomb, pomegranate. See GRENADE.]

gren·a·dine (gren'ə dēn', gren'ə dēn') n. **1.** syrup made from fruit, esp. pomegranates, used as a flavoring. **2.** thin, openwork fabric, woven from any of various fibers, used esp. for women's dresses. [French *grenadine* rough-grained silk, syrup made from the juice of the pomegranate, from *grenade* pomegranate. See GRENADE.]

Gre·no·ble (gri nō'bəl) n. city in southeastern France. Pop. (1968), 161,616.

Gren·ville (gren'vil') **1. George.** 1712–70, English statesman. **2. Sir Richard.** c.1542–91, English naval commander.

Gret·na Green (gret'nə) village in southern Scotland that became notorious in the eighteenth century as a place where runaway couples from England could be married.

grew (grōō) past tense of **grow.**

grew·some (grōō'səm) gruesome.

grey (grā) gray.

Grey (grā) **1. Charles, 2nd Earl.** 1764–1845, English statesman and prime minister from 1830 to 1834. **2. Sir Edward.** 1862–1933, 1st Viscount of Fallodon, English statesman. **3. Lady Jane.** 1537–54, great-granddaughter of Henry VII of England and queen of England for nine days in 1553. She was executed as a usurper to the crown. **4. Zane** (zān). 1875–1939, U.S. author.

grey·hound (grā'hound') n. **1.** one of a breed of slender swift dogs, having a smooth blue-gray, black, white, brown, or red short-haired coat, raised esp. for racing or hunting. Height: 26 inches at the shoulder. **2.** swift ocean liner. [Old English *grīghund* the dog.]

Greyhound

grid (grid) n. **1.** arrangement of parallel or intersecting bars or wires with openings between them; grating: *The heat came through grids in the floor.* **2.** something resembling or arranged in a manner similar to this: *The scenery was hung from a grid over the stage. The city was*

crisscrossed by a grid of railroad tracks. **3.** pattern of intersecting parallel lines used to form a system of coordinates, as on a map or chart. **4.** metal plate that forms an electrode in a storage battery. **5.** electrode in a vacuum tube, used to control the flow of electrons. **6.** interconnected system of electric generating stations and electric transmission and distribution devices that serves a large area. —*adj.* of or relating to football or a football field: *a full grid schedule for Saturday.* [Short for GRIDIRON.]

grid·dle (grid′əl) *n.* heavy, flat metal pan or surface, used for cooking. —*v.t.* **-dled, -dling.** to cook on a griddle. [Anglo-Norman *gridil* grate¹, going back to Latin *crāticula* small gridiron.]

grid·dle·cake (grid′əl kāk′) *n.* pancake.

grid·i·ron (grid′ī′ərn) *n.* **1.** football field. **2.** grill (def. 1). [Middle English *gredire* griddle, form of *gredil*, from Anglo-Norman *gridil* grate¹; Modern English spelling influenced by association with IRON. See GRIDDLE.]

grid leak, resistor placed in a vacuum tube to allow excess electrons on the grid to leak off.

grief (grēf) *n.* **1.** intense emotional suffering caused by trouble, remorse, or loss; mental anguish; deep sorrow. **2.** cause of such suffering or sorrow: *The loss of her dog was the greatest grief the child had known.* **3. to come to grief,** to meet with disaster; fail. [Old French *grief* sorrow, from *grever.* See GRIEVE.]

grief-strick·en (grēf′strik′ən) *adj.* overcome by grief; deeply anguished.

Grieg, Ed·vard (grēg; ed′värd) 1843–1907, Norwegian composer.

griev·ance (grē′vəns) *n.* **1.a.** real or imagined wrong that causes anger, resentment, or distress: *He composed a list of grievances to give to his boss.* **b.** complaint arising from such a wrong: *They met to discuss the grievances of their employees.* **2.** resentment or anger caused by such a wrong: *She harbored many grievances against her employers for many years.*

grieve (grēv) *grieved, griev·ing. v.i.* to feel grief; mourn. —*v.t.* to cause to feel grief; deeply sadden; distress. [Old French *grever* to burden, from Latin *gravāre.*]

griev·ous (grē′vəs) *adj.* **1.** causing grief or anguish: *a grievous loss, a grievous injury.* **2.** of a very serious nature; grave; outrageous: *a grievous crime, a grievous complaint.* **3.** expressing grief; sorrowful; mournful: *a grievous wail of pain.* —**griev′ous·ly,** *adv.* —**griev′ous·ness,** *n.*

grif·fin (grif′ən) *also,* **grif·fon, gryph·on.** *n.* mythical creature usually depicted with the head and wings of an eagle and the body and legs of a lion. [Old French *griffon,* going back to Latin *grȳphus,* form of *grȳps,* from Greek *grȳps,* possibly from *grȳpos* curved; because of its hooked beak.]

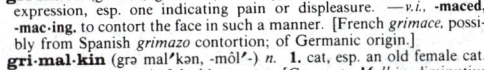

Griffin

Grif·fith, D(avid) W(ark) (grif′ith; wôrk) 1875–1948, U.S. motion-picture director and producer.

grill (gril) *n.* **1.a.** cooking utensil consisting of a framework of parallel metal bars or wires on which food is placed to be cooked over an open fire. **b.** heavy, flat metal cooking surface. **2.** food, esp. a dish of meat, that has been cooked on such a utensil or surface. **3.** grillroom. —*v.t.* **1.** to broil on or as on a grill: *to grill a cheese sandwich, to grill hamburgers.* **2.** to question or cross-examine closely and relentlessly: *The police grilled the suspect.* [French *gril* gridiron, going back to Latin *crāticula* small gridiron.]

grille (gril) *n.* grating, often of ornamental metalwork, used to cover or enclose a space or as a screen or gate. [French *grille* grill, grating¹, going back to Latin *crāticula* small gridiron.]

grill·room (gril′rōōm′, -room′) *n.* restaurant or dining room, as in a hotel, that features grilled foods.

grill·work (gril′wûrk′) *n.* a grille or a pattern of grilles: *the grillwork of an automobile.*

Grille

grilse (grils) *pl.,* **grilse.** *n.* young salmon on its first return from the sea to fresh water. [Of uncertain origin.]

grim (grim) *grim·mer, grim·mest. adj.* **1.** having a stern, forbidding, or formidable quality or appearance: *She wore a cold, grim smile. The room was dingy and grim.* **2.** that will not yield easily; resolute; uncompromising: *grim determination.* **3.** fierce; merciless: *horns locked in grim battle.* **4.** having a ghastly, repellent, or sinister nature; horrifying: *a grim pastime.* [Old English *grim* fierce, cruel.] —**grim′ly,** *adv.* —**grim′ness,** *n.*

gri·mace (grim′is, gri mās′) *n.* wry or otherwise contorted facial expression, esp. one indicating pain or displeasure. —*v.i.* **-maced, -mac·ing.** to contort the face in such a manner. [French *grimace,* possibly from Spanish *grimazo* contortion; of Germanic origin.]

gri·mal·kin (grə mal′kən, -môl′-) *n.* **1.** cat, esp. an old female cat. **2.** bad-tempered, spiteful old woman. [GRAY + *Malkin,* diminutive of *Maud,* feminine proper name.]

grime (grīm) *n.* dirt, esp. sooty dirt, covering or rubbed into a surface: *The windows were black with grime.* —*v.t.,* **grimed, grim·ing.** to cover with grime; soil: *The walls were grimed from the smoke and grease in the air.* [Flemish *grijm* soot, from Middle Dutch *grīme.*]

Grimm (grim) **1.** Ja·kob (yä′kop). 1785–1863, German philologist and folklorist. **2.** Wil·helm (vil′helm). 1786–1859, his brother and collaborator.

grim·y (grī′mē) *grim·i·er, grim·i·est. adj.* full of or covered with grime; filthy: *a grimy napkin, a grimy face.* —**grim′i·ness,** *n.*

grin (grin) *grinned, grin·ning. v.i.* **1.** to smile broadly. **2.** to draw back the lips and show the teeth, as in scorn or anger: *He grinned maliciously.* —*v.t.* to express by smiling broadly: *She grinned her acceptance of the plan.* —*n.* facial expression made by grinning, esp. a broad smile. [Old English *grennian* to show the teeth, as in pain or anger.] —**grin′ner,** *n.* —**Syn.** *n.* see **smile.**

grind (grīnd) *ground, grind·ing. v.t.* **1.** to crush or chop into small particles or powder; mill; pulverize: *to grind corn into meal.* **2.** to wear down, smooth, or sharpen by abrasion: *to grind a lens.* **3.** to produce by crushing: *to grind pepper from peppercorns.* **4.** to rub together, press down, or move in a harsh or noisy manner: *to grind one's teeth.* **5.** to operate by turning a crank: *to grind a coffee mill.* **6.** to oppress harshly: *The laborers were mercilessly ground down by their cruel overseers.* **7.** to impart or implant by constant effort or repetition (with *into*): *Showing respect for my elders is something that has been ground into me from early childhood.* **8.** to produce mechanically without imagination or special effort (with *out*): *to grind out dime novels.* —*v.i.* **1.** to perform the operation of crushing, sharpening, or smoothing. **2.** to become ground. **3.** to rub together, press down, or move in a harsh or noisy manner. —*n.* **1.** size of the particles of a material that has been crushed: *different grinds of coffee, a coarse grind of pepper.* **2.** act of grinding. **3.** hard, tedious work or study: *the grind of working a 12-hour day.* **4.** harsh, gnashing sound, as that caused by two surfaces rubbing against one another: *the annoying grind of the machinery.* **5.** *Informal.* one who is thought to spend too much time and effort at his studies or work. [Old English *grindan* to reduce to small particles, make a grating noise.]

grind·er (grīn′dər) *n.* **1.** one who or that which grinds. **2.** one of the back teeth; molar.

grind·stone (grīnd′stōn′) *n.* **1.** stone disk that can be revolved on an axle to sharpen or smooth something, as a knife blade. **2. to keep** (or **have** or **put**) **one's nose to the grindstone.** to work steadily or very diligently at one's job.

grin·go (gring′gō) *pl.,* **-gos.** *n.* in Latin America, a foreigner, esp. an American or Englishman. ▲ used disparagingly. [Spanish *gringo* gibberish, foreigner, probably modification of *griego* Greek, from Latin *Graecus* native of Greece. See GREEK.]

grip (grip) *n.* **1.** firm hold; tight grasp: *I tried to get a good grip on the dog's collar.* **2.** ability to hold firmly; strength of such a hold: *His grip weakened as he tired.* **3.a.** manner of holding or taking hold of something, esp. a piece of sports equipment. **b.** special manner of shaking or clasping hands, esp. one used by members of a secret or fraternal organization. **4.** firm control; mastery; power: *to get a grip on oneself. The people were in the grip of the dictator.* **5.** mental grasp; knowledge of: *He is just beginning to get a grip on the subject.* **6.** that part of an object, esp. certain pieces of sports equipment, by which it is supposed to be held: *The golf clubs had black leather grips.* **7.** mechanical device or part that holds something firmly. **8.** satchel, usually a small one. **9. to come to grips with.** to face and deal with in a firm, decisive manner. —*v.t.* **gripped, grip·ping. 1.** to take hold of firmly and tightly with or as with the hand: *He gripped the rifle between his knees.* **2.** to attract and keep the interest of. —*v.i.* to take hold firmly. [Partly from Old English *gripe* grasp; partly from Old English *gripa* handful.] —**grip′per,** *n.*

gripe (grīp) *griped, grip·ing. Informal. v.i.* to complain; grumble. —*v.t.* to irritate; annoy. —*n.* complaint. [Old English *grīpan* to seize.]

grippe (grip) *n.* influenza. [French *grippe,* from *gripper* to seize; of Germanic origin.]

Gris, Juan (grēs; hwän) 1887–1927, Spanish painter.

gris·ly (griz′lē) **-li·er, -li·est.** *adj.* causing one to feel horror, revulsion, or fear; gruesome: *the grisly sight of the battleground.* [Old English *grislīc* horrible.] —**gris′li·ness,** *n.* —**Syn.** see **ghastly.**

grist (grist) *n.* **1.** *Archaic.* grain to be ground. **2. grist for one's mill.** anything that can be used to one's profit. [Old English *grīst* act of grinding.]

at; āpe; cär; end; mē; it; īce; hot; ōld; fôrk; wood; fōōl; oil; out; up; ūse; turn; sing; thin; this; zh in treasure; ə in ago, taken, pencil, lemon, circus.

453

gris·tle (gris′əl) *n.* cartilage or cartilaginous tissue, esp. in meat. [Old English *gristle.*]

gris·tly (gris′lē) **-tli·er, -tli·est,** *adj.* consisting of, containing, or resembling gristle.

grist mill, mill for grinding grain.

grit (grit) *n.* **1.** very small, hard granules, as of sand or stone. **2.** strength of mind and spirit: *It took grit to stick out the storm in that boat.* **3.** coarse-grained sandstone. —*v.t.* **grit·ted, grit·ting.** to grind or tightly clamp together (the teeth), as in determination or anger: *He gritted his teeth as he entered the dentist's office.* —*v.i.* to make a grinding or gnashing sound. [Old English *grēot* dust, sand, gravel.]

grits (grits) *n.,pl.* **1.** coarsely ground hominy, used as a cereal and in bread and puddings. Also, **hominy grits. 2.** coarsely ground, hulled grain. [Old English *gryttan,* plural of *grytt* bran, chaff[1].]

grit·ty (grit′ē) **-ti·er, -ti·est.** *adj.* **1.** of, containing, or resembling grit: *a gritty substance.* **2.** covered or soiled with or as with grit: *gritty hands.* **3.** having or showing strength of mind and spirit; courageous. —**grit′ti·ness,** *n.*

griz·zled (griz′əld) *adj.* **1.** gray or mixed with gray: *a grizzled beard.* **2.** gray-haired. [From earlier *grizzle* gray, from Old French *grisel,* diminutive of *gris;* of Germanic origin.]

griz·zly (griz′lē) *pl.,* **-zlies.** *n.* grizzly bear. —*adj.* **-zli·er, -zli·est.** grayish; grizzled.

grizzly bear, long-clawed bear, *Ursus horribilis,* of western North America, having a massive head and body and usually brown or gray fur. Height: to 8 feet when standing erect.

Grizzly bear

groan (grōn) *n.* deep mournful sound, as one uttered in grief, pain, or mock disapproval. —*v.i.* **1.** to utter such a sound: *He groaned when he tried to move his broken arm.* **2.** to make a sound resembling this: *The roof creaked and groaned under the weight of the snow.* **3.** to be overburdened, oppressed, or strained: *The shelves groan with books. The nation groans under the tyrant's rule.* —*v.t.* to express or utter with a groan: *The fans groaned their disappointment when their team lost.* [Old English *grānian* to lament, murmur.] —**groan′er,** *n.*

groat (grōt) *n.* English silver coin with fourpence, issued from the thirteenth through the seventeenth centuries. [Middle Dutch *groot* thick (coin).]

groats (grōts) *n.,pl.* hulled grain, esp. oats or wheat, usually coarsely ground. [Old English *grotan* (plural).]

gro·cer (grō′sər) *n.* one who owns or manages a grocery. [Old French *grossier* wholesale dealer, from Medieval Latin *grossarius,* from Late Latin *grossus* great, large; because he sold in great quantities or by the gross.]

gro·cer·y (grō′sər ē) *pl.,* **-cer·ies.** *n.* **1.** store that sells food and household supplies. **2. groceries.** goods, esp. food, carried by such a store.

grog (grog) *n.* **1.** drink made by diluting a strong alcoholic liquor, as rum, with water. **2.** any alcoholic beverage. [From "Old *Grog,*" nickname of English Admiral Edward Vernon, because he wore a grogram cloak. He instituted the dilution of rum with water in the British Navy in 1740.]

grog·gy (grog′ē) **-gi·er, -gi·est.** *adj.* not fully alert or awake; in a dazed or unsteady condition: *He's groggy until he has his coffee in the morning.* [GROG + -Y[1].] —**grog′gi·ly,** *adv.* —**grog′gi·ness,** *n.*

grog·ram (grog′rəm) *n.* coarse, loosely woven fabric made of silk, mohair, wool, or combinations of these, formerly used for such items as cloaks and coats. [French *gros grain* coarse grain; because of its coarse texture. See GROSS, GRAIN.]

grog·shop (grog′shop′) *n.* *British.* saloon.

groin (groin) *n.* **1.** fold or hollow on either side of the front of the body where the thigh joins the trunk. **2.** *Architecture.* curved edge formed by the intersection of two vaults. —*v.t.* *Architecture.* to furnish or build with groins. [Possibly from Old English *grynde* abyss; probably originally, depression.]

grom·met (grom′it) *n.* **1.** ring, as of metal or plastic, that reinforces a hole in material, as leather or cloth. **2.** *Nautical.* ring of rope or metal used for various purposes, as to hold oars in place or to fasten the edges of sails to spars. [Obsolete French *gromette* curb of a bridle, from *gourmer* to curb; of uncertain origin.]

grom·well (grom′wəl) *n.* any of several plants, genus *Lithospermum,* found in Europe and the northeastern United States, bearing clusters of small, funnel-shaped flowers and having smooth white seeds resembling stones. [Old French *gromil,* possibly from *gres* sandstone (of Germanic origin) + *mil* (see MILLET).]

Gro·my·ko, An·drei An·dre·ie·vich (grō mē′kō; än drä′ än-drä′yə vich) 1909—, Soviet diplomat and statesman.

Gro·ning·en (grō′ning ən) *n.* city in the northeastern Netherlands. Pop. (1968 est.), 156,299.

groom (grōōm, groom) *n.* **1.** bridegroom. **2.** one who washes, curries, and otherwise takes care of animals, esp. horses. **3.** one of several officers of the English royal household. **4.** *Archaic.* manservant. —*v.t.* **1.** to wash, curry, and otherwise take care of (an animal, esp. a horse). **2.** to make neat, tidy, and attractive in appearance: *She groomed herself carefully before the interview. He groomed his lawn and garden meticulously.* **3.** to train or prepare (someone) for some purpose, as political office. [Of uncertain origin.]

grooms·man (grōōmz′mən, groomz′-) *pl.,* **-men.** *n.* male attendant of the bridegroom at a wedding, esp. the best man.

groove (grōōv) *n.* **1.** long, narrow channel or depression cut in a surface, as in a phonograph record or tree. **2.** narrow, limited manner of doing things; routine; rut: *He fell back into the old groove again.* **3.** situation or activity for which one is best suited by ability or interest: *Acting has always been his groove.* **4. in the groove.** *Slang.* functioning or performing smoothly and expertly; in good form: *The musicians were in the groove after a short time.* —*v.t.,* **grooved, groov·ing.** to make a groove or grooves in: *He grooved the board to fit the other tightly.* [Middle Dutch *groeve* channel, furrow.]

groov·y (grōō′vē) **groov·i·er, groov·i·est.** *adj.* *Slang.* having what is considered to be a very pleasing or commendable quality; great: *a groovy person, groovy music.*

grope (grōp) **groped, grop·ing.** *v.i.* **1.** to feel about with or as with the hands: *He groped for the door handle in the dark hall.* **2.** to search blindly and uncertainly; try desperately to think of: *He groped for a solution to his problem.* —*v.t.* to find (one's way) by groping: *He groped his way in the dark.* [Old English *grāpian* to seize, touch.] —**grop′ing·ly,** *adv.*

Gro·pi·us, Walter (grō′pē əs) 1883–1969, German architect.

gros·beak (grōs′bēk′) *n.* any of various birds of the finch or weaverbird families, having a stout, cone-shaped bill, as the **rose-breasted grosbeak,** *Pheuticus ludovicianus,* and the **evening grosbeak,** *Hesperiphona vespertina.* [French *grosbec,* from *gros* great, thick + *bec* beak. See GROSS, BEAK.]

Grosbeak

gro·schen (grō′shən) *pl.,* **-schen.** *n.* **1.** in Austria, 1/100 of a schilling. **2.** former silver coin of Germany. [German *Groschen,* going back to Late Latin *grossus* thick, great.]

gros·grain (grō′grān′) *n.* closely woven, ribbed fabric, often of silk or rayon, used chiefly for ribbons. [French *gros grain* coarse grain. See GROGRAM.]

gross (grōs) *adj.* **1.** with nothing deducted; total; entire: *On gross earnings of $1000, his net income was only $650.* **2.** extremely obvious or reprehensible; glaring; flagrant: *a gross mistake, a gross injustice.* **3.** not refined; coarse; vulgar: *gross behavior, a gross joke.* **4.** excessively or repulsively fat. **5.** *Archaic.* thick; heavy; dense. —*n.* **1.** total amount, as of income, before deductions: *The gross for the year was $50,000.* **2.a.** unit of quantitative measure equivalent to twelve dozen. **b.** group or quantity of twelve dozen items. —*v.t.* to earn a total of before deductions: *The company grossed $1 million.* [Old French *gros* great, thick, coarse, from Late Latin *grossus.*] —**gross′ly,** *adv.* —**gross′ness,** *n.* —**Syn.** *adj.* **2.** see **flagrant. 3.** see **coarse.**

gross national product, total value of all the goods and services produced by a country during a certain period of time, before any deductions or allowances are made.

grosz (grōsh) *pl.,* **gro·szy** (grō′shē). *n.* in Poland, 1/100 of a zloty.

Grosz, George (grōs) 1893–1959, German-American painter and graphic artist.

gro·tesque (grō tesk′) *adj.* **1.** distorted, deformed, or otherwise unnatural or ugly, as in shape or appearance: *All the human figures in the painting were grotesque.* **2.** amusingly or fantastically absurd; ludicrous; incongruous: *a grotesque situation. She wore her hat at a grotesque angle.* **3.** of or relating to art characterized by a fantastic combination of human and animal forms with foliage, scrolls, and other ornamental patterns. —*n.* ornamentation having characteristics of the grotesque style of art. [French *grotesque* strange painting, from Italian *(pittura) grottesca* strange (painting), from *grotta* cave; because of the strange nature of paintings found in certain old grottoes in Italy. See GROTTO.] —**gro·tesque′ly,** *adv.* —**gro·tesque′ness,** *n.*

Syn. *adj.* **1. Grotesque, bizarre, fantastic** indicate something that seems unnaturally or unusually distorted in shape, form, appearance, or character. **Grotesque** suggests an absurd or ludicrous combination of incongruous elements: *The audience comes to recognize the tragedy behind the grotesque figure of the dwarf.* **Bizarre** implies that which is eccentric or strange because of a clash of opposing qualities that seemingly should

at; āpe; cär; end; mē; it; īce; hot; ōld; fôrk; wood; fōōl; oil; out; up; ūse; turn; sing; thin; this; zh in treasure; ə in ago, taken, pencil, lemon, circus.

not exist side by side: *The building is a bizarre combination of classical Greek, Gothic, and Georgian architectural elements.* **Fantastic** suggests an exaggerated or imaginative invention, conception, or design: *Marco Polo's descriptions of his travels seemed fantastic to his countrymen.*

gro·tes·quer·ie (grō tes′kər ē) *also,* **gro·tes·quer·y.** *n.* **1.** something that is grotesque. **2.** grotesque character or style.

Gro·ti·us, Hugo (grō′shē əs) 1583–1645, Dutch jurist, statesman, and writer who is regarded as the father of international law; born Huig de Groot.

grot·to (grot′ō) *pl.,* **-toes** *or* **-tos.** *n.* **1.** cave. **2.** excavation or structure made to resemble a cave, as one designed as a shrine or retreat. [Italian *grotta* cave, going back to Latin *crypta,* from Greek *kryptē* vault. Doublet of CRYPT.]

grouch (grouch) *n.* **1.** one who is very irritable, sulky, or ill-tempered. **2.** complaint. **3.** sulky or grumbling mood. —*v.i.* to grumble or sulk. [Form of obsolete *grutch* to complain, from Old French *grouch(i)er* to murmur; of Germanic origin.]

grouch·y (grou′chē) **grouch·i·er, grouch·i·est.** *adj.* in a bad mood, either habitually or momentarily; irritable; sulky. —**grouch′i·ly,** *adv.* —**grouch′i·ness,** *n.*

ground[1] (ground) *n.* **1.a.** solid surface of the earth: *The ground was covered with snow. After months at sea, the ground felt good beneath his feet.* **b.** material, as soil, sand, or clay, at or near the earth's surface: *Dig deep into ground. The ground is too sterile to support plant life.* **2. grounds.** land surrounding or attached to a house, institution, or other building: *The college grounds were beautifully planted.* **3.** *also,* **grounds.** area or piece of land, esp. one designated for a particular use: *parade ground, picnic grounds.* **4.** *also,* **grounds.** that on which something is established or rests; basis; foundation: *grounds for suspicion. Their friendship is on shaky ground.* **5.** subject area or material, as for discussion, study, or work: *The writer found himself on unfamiliar ground. The teacher covered a great deal of ground in one hour.* **6.** that which serves as the underlying surface or background: *The wallpaper is printed with a red floral design on a green ground.* **7. grounds.** particles that settle at the bottom of a liquid or are left over in the container that held it; dregs: *Throw out the coffee grounds.* **8.a.** connection between an electric circuit or device, as a television and the earth, established through a conductor. **b.** electric conductor itself.

  from the ground up. from the beginning or most elementary to the end or most complex; completely; thoroughly.

  on one's own (or **home**) **ground. a.** in a familiar place or situation. **b.** dealing with a subject that one is well versed in.

  to break ground. to begin some undertaking, esp. the construction of a building: *They broke ground for the new school last spring.*

  to cut the ground from under (one's) **feet.** to render someone's defense or argument invalid.

  to gain ground. a. to make progress: *They gained ground in their effort to end the strike.* **b.** to become more popular or widespread: *Their candidate had gained ground since the primary election.*

  to give ground. to withdraw from or as from attack; retreat; yield.

  to hold (or **stand**) **one's ground.** to maintain one's position; not retreat, yield, or withdraw.

  to lose ground. a. to move farther away from one's goal; go backwards: *to lose ground in the negotiations.* **b.** to decline in popularity; become less widespread: *The television program was rapidly losing ground in the ratings.*

  to run into the ground. a. to overdo or overwork (something) to the point where it is useless; wear out: *to run a discussion into the ground, to run a car into the ground.* **b.** to disprove or criticize severely: *to run someone's argument into the ground.*

  to shift one's ground. to change one's position or opinion.

  —*adj.* **1.** of, on, at, or near the surface of the earth. —*v.t.* **1.** to place or set on the ground; bring to or cause to touch the ground: *The boxer grounded his opponent.* **2.** to provide a firm foundation or basis for; establish, as on some fact or circumstance; base: *His argument is grounded on fact. Their fears were grounded in superstition.* **3.** to instruct in the basic principles or elements of a subject: *He grounded himself thoroughly in mathematics.* **4.** *Aviation.* to forbid (a person or aircraft) to fly; confine to the ground: *The plane was grounded for three hours because of bad weather. The pilot was grounded for misconduct.* **5.** to connect an electric circuit or other device, as a radio, with the earth by means of a wire or other conductor. **6.** to cause (a boat or ship) to run aground: *The captain grounded his ship on the shoal.* **7.** to furnish with or place on an underlying surface or background. —*v.i.* **1.** to fall to or strike the ground: *The kite grounded because the wind stopped.* **2.** (of a boat or ship) to run aground. **3.** *Baseball.* **a.** to hit a ground ball: *He grounded to the shortstop.* **b.** to ground out. **to ground out.** to hit a ground ball that puts one out at first base. [Old English *grund* bottom, foundation, earth, land.]

ground[2] (ground) past tense and past participle of **grind.**

ground alert, state of readiness in which airplanes and their crews stand by awaiting orders to take off.

ground ball *Baseball.* batted ball that strikes the ground in the infield and then rolls or moves along in low bounces.

ground cover, low-growing plants, such as ivy, that provide dense cover for an area of ground, esp. one that is difficult to plant, as a slope.

ground crew, personnel responsible for the servicing and maintenance of aircraft.

ground-ef·fect machine (ground′i fekt′) hovercraft.

ground·er (groun′dər) *n.* ground ball.

ground floor 1. floor in a building that is level or nearly level with the ground. **2. to be** (or **get**) **in on the ground floor.** to be involved in some activity, as a business deal or project, from or soon after its beginning.

ground glass, glass which has had its surface roughened so that it will diffuse light and not be transparent.

ground hemlock, low-growing yew, *Taxus canadensis,* found in North America, sometimes grown as a hedge because it can be easily trimmed into various shapes.

ground·hog (ground′hôg′, -hog′) *n.* woodchuck.

Groundhog Day, day when the groundhog, according to popular belief, emerges from hibernation. If he sees his shadow, he returns underground for another six weeks of winter. February 2.

ground ivy, creeping ivy, *Nepeta hederacea,* of the mint family, found in North America, Europe, and Asia, bearing round or kidney-shaped leaves and light-blue, tube-shaped flowers.

ground·less (ground′lis) *adj.* having no real cause or reason: *a groundless fear.* —**ground′less·ly,** *adv.* —**ground′less·ness,** *n.* —Syn. see **unfounded.**

ground·ling (ground′ling) *n.* **1.** animal or plant that lives or grows close to the ground. **2.** fish that lives at the bottom of the water. **3.** spectator who stood in the pit of the theater in Elizabethan times. **4.** person of unrefined or uncritical taste, esp. with regard to literature and the theater.

ground loop, sharp, uncontrollable turn made by an airplane while taxiing, taking off, or landing.

ground-mass (ground′mas′) *n.* material in which the crystals of porphyry are embedded.

ground·nut (ground′nut′) *n.* **1.** any of several plants of the pea family having edible tubers, roots, or underground seed pods, esp. the peanut. **2.** edible tuber, root, or seed of such a plant.

ground pine 1. any of several club mosses, esp. *Lycopodium obscurum.* **2.** creeping European herb, *Ajuga chamaepitys,* having a pine-like odor.

ground plan 1. plan of any floor of a building. **2.** first or fundamental plan of any kind.

ground rule, basic principle or statement of procedure that governs a particular situation or activity.

ground·sel (ground′səl) *n.* any of a large group of plants, including trees and shrubs, genus *Senecio,* of the composite family, many of which bear showy, yellow flower heads, esp. *S. vulgaris,* a common weed in North America. [Old English *grundeswelge,* earlier *gundaeswelg(i)ae,* probably from *gund* pus + *swelgan* to swallow; probably because it was used to reduce abscesses.]

ground·sill (ground′sil′) *n.* lowest horizontal timber used as a foundation in a wooden framework, as of a building.

ground speed, speed of an aircraft relative to the ground. Distinguished from **air speed.**

ground squirrel 1. any of various rodents of North America, Eurasia, and Africa that live in burrows in the ground, usually having gray or light-brown fur, often with striped or spotted markings. Length: 8–21 inches, including tail. Also, **go′pher.** **2.** chipmunk or prairie dog.

ground state, most stable state of an atom or other particle when its energy level is lowest.

ground swell 1. broad, deep waves or rolling sea, caused by an often distant storm or seismic disturbance. **2.** rising wave or surge, as of emotion: *There was a ground swell of public opinion.*

Ground water

ground water, water that has flowed or seeped beneath the surface of the earth and saturated the soil and other porous material below. It is the source of water for wells and underground springs.

ground wave, radio wave that travels along the surface of the earth, rather than being reflected by the air or clouds.

ground·work (ground′wurk′) *n.* preliminary work or material on which something is built or based; foundation: *He completed the groundwork for his thesis a year ago.*

---

at; āpe; cär; end; mē; it; īce; hot; ōld; fôrk; wood; fo͞ol; oil; out; up; ūse; turn; sing; thin; this; zh in treasure; ə in ago, taken, pencil, lemon, circus.

ground zero, point on the surface of land or water that is at or directly above or below the center of the explosion of a nuclear bomb.

group (grōōp) *n.* **1.** number of persons, figures, or things that form or are regarded as forming a unit: *a group of houses, a group of saints in a painting.* **2.** number of persons or things classed together because of similarities: *a peer group, an ethnic group.* **3.** administrative and tactical military unit consisting of two or more battalions or squadrons. **4.** number of chemical elements having similar properties and arranged in a vertical column on the periodic table. **5.** configuration of atoms attached to different molecules, giving similar properties to a family of compounds. The amino group symbol is NH_2. —*v.t.* to arrange or place in a group: *The chaperon grouped the younger children together.* —*v.i.* to form or belong to a group: *The skiers grouped around the fire.* [French *groupe* assemblage, unit, cluster, from Italian *groppo* assemblage; earlier, knot; of Germanic origin.] —**Syn.** *n.* **1.** see **company.**

group·er (grōō′pər) *pl.*, **-ers** or **-er.** *n.* any of a number of spiny-rayed saltwater fish, family Serranidae, including many food fish found in warm waters. They have huge

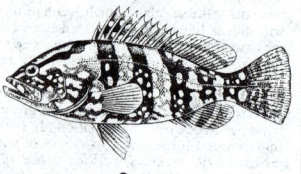

Grouper

mouths and sharp teeth, and some may weigh as much as 1000 pounds. [Portuguese *garoupa*; probably of native South American origin.]

group·ing (grōō′ping) *n.* **1.** act of placing in a group: *The grouping of slow readers was a help to the teacher.* **2.** set of things arranged in a group: *There was an attractive grouping of prints on one wall.*

group therapy, form of psychotherapy in which a group of patients, usually under the supervision of a therapist, attempt to understand and deal with their emotional problems, esp. through discussion.

grouse¹ (grous) *pl.*, **grouse** or **grous·es.** *n.* any of a group of fowl-like game birds, family Tetraonidae, including the ruffed grouse, prairie chicken, capercaillie, and sage grouse, having brown, black, or gray feathers, often with white markings, and feathered legs. Length: 1–3 feet. [Of uncertain origin.]

grouse² (grous) groused, grous·ing. *Informal.* *v.i.* to grumble; complain. —*n.* complaint. [Of uncertain origin.] —**grous′er,** *n.*

grout (grout) *n.* **1.** thin mortar used to fill cracks and crevices, as between stones or bricks. **2.** finishing coat of plaster for walls and ceilings. —*v.t.* to fill up or finish with grout. [Old English *grūt* coarse meal.]

grove (grōv) *n.* **1.** small forested area or group of trees without underbrush. **2.** group of fruit trees, esp. citrus trees: *an orange grove.* [Old English *grǣf* group of trees.]

grov·el (gruv′əl, grov′-) **-eled, -el·ing;** *also, British,* **-elled, -el·ling.** *v.i.* **1.** to act in a demeaning or servile manner, as through fear; abase oneself: *The servant groveled in hopes of securing his master's favor.* **2.** to lie or crawl face downward, as in fear or humility: *The subjects groveled before their king.* [From obsolete *groveling* prone, from obsolete *gruf* on the face, from Old Norse *ā grūfu.*] —**grov′el·er;** *also, British,* **grov′el·ler,** *n.*

grow (grō) grew, grown, grow·ing. *v.i.* **1.** to increase or become larger by a natural process of development: *She grew two inches this year.* **2.** to expand or increase, as in size, amount, or degree: *His savings account began to grow rapidly. The father's hope grew. His taste for fine food grew.* **3.** to be produced and develop; thrive; flourish: *Orchids grow wild in the jungles of South America.* **4.** to come into existence; arise. **5.** to come to be by degrees: *The days seem to grow longer. John grew old.* **6.** to become fixed to or united by or as by a natural growth process: *The graft grew to the skin. The two trees intertwined and grew together.* **7. to grow on,** to become increasingly acceptable, attractive, or pleasurable to: *The character's strange mannerisms grew on me.* **8. to grow out of. a.** to outgrow. **b.** to develop or arise from: *Arguments often grow out of misunderstandings.* **9. to grow up. a.** to advance to or reach maturity or full growth: *He wanted to be a fireman when he grew up.* **b.** to come into existence; develop: *A dispute had grown up between them.* —*v.t.* **1.** to cause to grow; raise; cultivate: *The farmer grows tomatoes.* **2.** to allow to grow: *He grew a mustache.* **3.** to cover with a growth: *The lawn was grown with weeds.* [Old English *grōwan* to increase, spring up, sprout.]

grow·er (grō′ər) *n.* **1.** one who grows something, as wheat or potatoes. **2.** plant that grows in a certain way: *a rapid grower.*

growing pains **1.** emotional problems encountered by adolescents during the process of maturing. **2.** difficulties arising in the early development of something new, as a project or a new business. **3.** pains in the limbs during childhood and youth, thought to be caused by growing.

growl (groul) *v.i.* **1.** to make a deep, harsh, guttural sound, in anger or as a threat: *The bear growled at us.* **2.** to speak or make an angry sound or sounds like this: *He growled at being disturbed.* —*v.t.* to express by growling: *He growled a reply.* —*n.* **1.** deep, harsh, rumbling sound made by an angry animal. **2.** any sound or utterance resembling this. [Probably imitative.] —**growl′er,** *n.*

grown (grōn) *v.* past participle of **grow.** —*adj.* having attained one's full growth or maturity; adult: *a grown woman.*

grown-up (adj. grōn′up′; n. grōn′up′) adj. **1.** adult: *She seems more grown-up this year.* **2.** characteristic of or suitable for adults: *grown-up clothes.* —*n.* adult: *The grown-ups watched as the children played.*

growth (grōth) *n.* **1.** process of growing toward full size or maturity; development: *the growth of a child, the growth of a plant.* **2.** increase, as in size, importance, or power: *the growth of industry, a rapid growth in popularity, the growth of human knowledge.* **3.** that which grows or has grown: *They cleared a month's growth of weeds from the garden.* **4.** mass of new tissue that results from an abnormal increase in cells and serves no useful function for the body; tumor; neoplasm.

grub (grub) *n.* **1.** soft, wormlike larva of an insect, esp. of a beetle. **2.** *Informal.* food. **3.** *Informal.* unkempt, sloppy person. —*v.i.* grubbed, grub·bing. **1.** to dig in the ground; root: *Trained pigs are used to grub for truffles.* **2.** to work very hard, esp. doing menial or dreary work; drudge: *to grub for a meager existence.* —*v.t.* **1.** to dig up by the roots; uproot: *to grub out the mushrooms in the lawn.* **2.** to clear (ground) of plants, roots, and stumps. **3.** *Slang.* to borrow without intending to return or repay: *He is notorious for grubbing cigarettes.* [Possibly from an unrecorded Old English word.] —**grub′ber,** *n.*

grub·by (grub′ē) **-bi·er, -bi·est.** *adj.* **1.** dirty; grimy; filthy: *Please wash your grubby hands. He looked grubby after playing outside all day.* **2.** infested with grubs. —**grub′bi·ness,** *n.*

grub·stake (grub′stāk′) *n.* **1.** money or supplies advanced to a prospector in return for a share of his profits. **2.** money or assistance advanced for any project. —*v.t.,* **-staked, -stak·ing.** to supply with a grubstake.

Grub Street, needy, inferior writers; literary hacks collectively. [From *Grub Street* (now Milton Street), London, where a number of poor and inferior writers once lived.]

grudge (gruj) *n.* strong feeling of ill will, anger, or resentment: *She's held a grudge against me for years.* —*v.t.,* **grudged, grudg·ing.** to begrudge. [Old French *groucier, grouch(i)er* to grumble, murmur; of Germanic origin.] —**grudg′ing·ly,** *adv.*

gru·el (grōō′əl) *n.* thin porridge made by boiling meal, esp. oatmeal, in water or milk. [Old French *gruel,* diminutive of *gru* oatmeal; of Germanic origin.]

gru·el·ing (grōō′ə ling, grōō′ling) *also,* **gru·el·ling.** *adj.* very difficult or punishing; exhausting: *a grueling experience.*

grue·some (grōō′səm) *also,* **grew·some.** *adj.* inspiring horror, revulsion, or fear; frightful; repulsive. [Dialectal English *grue* to feel horror (probably of Scandinavian origin) + -SOME¹.] —**grue′some·ness,** *n.* —**Syn.** see **ghastly.**

gruff (gruf) *adj.* **1.** (of the voice) deep and rough. **2.** abrupt or stern in manner; brusque. [Dutch *grof* coarse, heavy, blunt.] —**gruff′ly,** *adv.* —**gruff′ness,** *n.*

grum·ble (grum′bəl) **-bled, -bling.** *v.i.* **1.** to mutter in discontent; complain in a grouchy or sullen manner. **2.** to rumble. —*v.t.* to express by grumbling. —*n.* **1.** mutter of discontent or complaint. **2.** rumble. [French *grommeler* to complain, from Old French *gromer* to growl, mutter, from Middle Dutch *grommen* to growl.] —**grum′bler,** *n.*

grump (grump) *n.* **1.** ill-tempered, complaining person. **2.** *usually,* **grumps.** fit of bad humor. —*v.i.* to sulk or complain. [Possibly imitative.]

grump·y (grum′pē) **grump·i·er, grump·i·est.** *adj.* in an irritable or gloomy mood; surly; ill-tempered: *Lack of sleep made me grumpy.* [From obsolete *grump* sulkiness (probably imitative) + -Y¹.] —**grump′i·ly,** *adv.* —**grump′i·ness,** *n.*

Grun·dy, Mrs. (grun′dē) one who has narrow-minded and prudish views regarding personal conduct, manners, and morals. [From *Mrs. Grundy,* a character referred to in the play *Speed the Plough* (1798) by Thomas Morton, in which the question "What will Mrs. Grundy say?" is constantly asked.] —**Grun′dy·ism,** *n.*

grun·ion (grun′yən) *n.* saltwater food fish, *Leuresthes tenuis,* found in the coastal waters of southern and Lower California, noted for spawning on the beach at high tide before it is carried back out to sea by the waves. Length: 5–7 inches. [Probably from Spanish *gruñón* grunter, from *gruñir* to grunt, from Latin *grunnīre.*]

grunt (grunt) *v.i.* **1.** short, deep, hoarse sound, as that made by a hog. **2.** any of a group of tropical saltwater fish, family Pomadasyidae, that make a similar sound by rubbing their teeth together. —*v.i.* **1.** to make the short, deep, hoarse sound of a hog. **2.** to make a similar sound, as in effort or discontent. —*v.t.* to utter or express with a grunt: *He grunted a surly reply.* [Old English *grunnettan* to utter a sound like that of a hog.] —**grunt′er,** *n.*

Gru·yère (grōō yâr′, gri-) *n.* variety of firm, light-yellow cheese that is made from whole milk and resembles Swiss cheese in flavor. [From *Gruyère*, Swiss district where this cheese was first made.]

gryph·on (grif′ən) griffin.

G-suit (jē′sōōt′) *n.* suit designed to counteract the effects of rapid acceleration or deceleration or of the force of gravity, worn by a pilot or astronaut.

gt., great.

Gt. Br., Great Britain. Also, **Gt. Brit.**

Gua·da·la·ja·ra (gwäd′əl ə här′ə) *n.* city in southwestern Mexico. Pop. (1969), 1,352,109.

Gua·dal·ca·nal (gwäd′əl kə nal′) *n.* mountainous island in the southwestern Pacific, one of the Solomon Islands. It was the scene of prolonged and bitter fighting between American and Japanese forces in World War II. Area, 2500 sq. mi. Pop. (1966 est.), 24,000.

Gua·de·loupe (gwäd′əl ōōp′) *n.* two French islands in the West Indies, part of the Leeward Islands. Area, 583 sq. mi. Pop. (1967) 312,-724.

Guam (gwäm) *n.* island in the western Pacific, east of the Philippines. It is administered by the United States. Area, 212 sq. mi. Pop. (1970 est.), 86,926.

gua·na·co (gwä nä′kō) *pl.* **-cos.** *n.* wild, hoofed mammal, *Lama guanicoe*, of the Andes Mountains, thought to be the ancestor of the domesticated llama and alpaca. Height: 3½ feet at the shoulder. [Spanish *guanaco*, from Quechua *huanacu* wild sheep.]

Guanaco

gua·nine (gwä′nēn) *n.* purine base that is an essential constituent of DNA and RNA. Formula: $C_5H_5N_5O$

gua·no (gwä′nō) *pl.,* **-nos.** *n.* **1.** waste matter of sea birds, widely used as fertilizer, found in large deposits on islands off the coast of Peru. **2.** any similar fertilizer. [Spanish *guano* manure of sea birds, from Quechua *huanu* dung.]

Guan·tá·na·mo Bay (gwän tä′nə mō′) inlet of the Caribbean in southeastern Cuba, site of a U.S. naval base.

gua·ra·ni (gwär′ə nē′) *pl.,* **-ni** or **-nis.** *n.* monetary unit of Paraguay, equal to one-hundred centimos. [Spanish *guaraní*, from the *Guarani* people.]

Gua·ra·ni (gwär′ə nē′) *pl.,* **-nis** or **-nies.** *n.* **1.** member of any of several South American Indian tribes formerly living in what is now Paraguay and parts of Bolivia and Brazil. **2.** one of the descendants of these Indians and the early Spanish settlers, now constituting more than half the population of Paraguay. **3.** their language, belonging to the Tupi-Guarani language family.

guar·an·tee (gar′ən tē′) *n.* **1.** assurance given by a seller to a buyer that his product is or will be as it is represented or will be repaired or replaced if it proves defective within a certain period of time; warranty. **2.** anything that assures a certain outcome or condition: *Beauty is no guarantee of popularity.* **3.** one who receives a guaranty. **4.** guarantor. —*v.t.,* **-teed, -tee·ing. 1.a.** to give assurance of the quality of; give a guarantee for: *The manufacturer guaranteed the toaster for one year.* **b.** to agree to be responsible for the debts or obligations of another; make a guaranty. **2.** to make sure or certain: *By shopping early she hoped to guarantee that there would be a good selection.* **3.** to state or otherwise affirm (something); promise: *I guarantee we will leave tomorrow.* **4.** to give security to; ensure: *The policy would guarantee them against fire and theft.* [Modification of GUARANTY.]

guar·an·tor (gar′ən tôr′, -tər) *n.* one who makes or gives a guarantee.

guar·an·ty (gar′ən tē′) *pl.,* **-ties.** *n.* **1.** agreement or promise to be responsible for the debts or obligations of another person in case of his default. **2.** something given or retained as security. **3.** guarantee; warranty. **4.** guarantor. —*v.t.,* **-tied, -ty·ing.** to guarantee. [Anglo-Norman *guarantie* warranty, from Old French *garantir* to warrant, from *garant* warrant, protection; of Germanic origin.]

guard (gärd) *v.t.* **1.** to watch over or tend carefully so as to keep safe from harm; defend; protect: *The dog guarded the house. The shepherd guarded his flock.* **2.** to maintain close supervision or surveillance over, as to prevent escape or trouble: *Ten men guarded the prisoners at night.* **3.** to prevent or regulate entrance or exit through: *Two soldiers guarded the gate of the fort.* **4.** to keep in check; control: *to guard one's feelings.* **5.** in goal games, to attempt to prevent (an opponent) from scoring. **6.** to provide a cover or other protective device for. —*v.i.* to take precautions (with *against*): *to guard against illness. He guarded against repeating the mistake.* —*n.* **1.** person or group that guards: *a prison guard, a museum guard, a guard made up of ten soldiers.* **2.** any cover,

attachment, or other device that protects against loss, injury, or damage: *She put a guard on her ring because it was too large.* **3.** careful or restraining watch or supervision: *A sentry kept guard at the door.* **4.** that which guards or protects; defense; safeguard: *Reason is a guard against rash actions.* **5.** Football. **a.** one of two players positioned at the right and the left of the center. **b.** position played by such a player. **6.** Basketball. **a.** one of two primarily defensive players positioned toward the rear of the court. **b.** position played by such a player. **7.** posture of defense or readiness, as in boxing or fencing. **8. guards.** any of several units of soldiers in the British army attached to the royal household. **9. on** (one's) **guard.** prepared or watchful, as for danger, difficulties, or attack; vigilant; alert. **10. off** (one's) **guard.** unprepared, as for danger, difficulties, or attack; not alert: *They were caught off guard by the enemy.* **11. to stand guard. a.** to serve as a sentry. **b.** to keep a protective watch: *The mother bear stood guard over her injured cub.* [Old French *garder* to keep, watch over, protect; of Germanic origin.] —**guard′er,** *n.* —**Syn.** *v.t.* **1.** see **defend.**

guard cell Botany. one of a pair of bean-shaped cells, scattered throughout the epidermis of a leaf, whose responses to heat and light control the amount of transpiration and respiration that take place through the stoma.

guard·ed (gär′did) *adj.* **1.** cautious; prudent: *a guarded reply.* **2.** closely watched, defended, or restrained. —**guard′ed·ly,** *adv.* —**Syn. 1.** see **cautious.**

guard hair, long, coarse outer hair serving to protect the soft inner fur in certain animals.

guard·house (gärd′hous′) *n.* **1.** building used as a temporary jail for military personnel who have been convicted of minor offenses or are awaiting court-martial. **2.** building used to house military personnel on guard duty.

guard·i·an (gär′dē ən) *n.* **1.** one who guards or watches over; protector: *The clergy were the guardians of morality* (Froude, 1856). **2.** one who is legally entrusted with the care of the person, property, or rights of a minor or other individual who is considered incapable of managing his own affairs. —*adj.* protecting: *a guardian angel.* [Anglo-Norman *gardein* warden, keeper, from Old French *garder.* See GUARD.] —**guard′i·an·ship′,** *n.*

guard·rail (gärd′rāl′) *n.* railing for support or protection, as on a staircase or a highway.

guard·room (gärd′rōōm′, -room′) *n.* room used to accommodate military personnel on guard duty.

guards·man (gärdz′mən) *pl.,* **-men.** *n.* **1.** man who serves as a guard. **2.** soldier in the National Guard. **3.** soldier in a guards regiment of the British army.

Guar·ner·i (gwä när′ē) *n.* family of Italian violin makers of the seventeenth and eighteenth centuries.

Guar·ner·i·us (gwär när′ē əs) *pl.,* **-us·es.** *n.* violin made by a member of the Guarneri family.

Gua·te·ma·la (gwä′tə mä′lə) *n.* **1.** northernmost country of Central America. Capital, Guatemala City. Area, 42,042 sq. mi. Pop. (1965 est.), 4,438,000. **2.** Guatemala City. —**Gua′te·ma′lan,** *adj., n.*

Guatemala City, capital and principal city of Guatemala, in the southern part of the country. It is the largest city in Central America. Pop. (1967 est.), 577,100.

gua·va (gwä′və) *n.* **1.** round or pear-shaped berrylike fruit of any of a group of trees or shrubs, genus *Psidium*, of the myrtle family, having a sweet, firm flesh that may be white, yellow, or deep pink, used for making jellies and other sweets. **2.** tree or shrub bearing this fruit, grown in tropical America, having large oval leaves and white flowers. The most widely cultivated species is the **common guava,** *P. guajava*, having a scaly bark and hairy twigs. [Spanish *guayaba* the fruit; of South American Indian origin.]

Guay·a·quil (gwī′ə kēl′) *n.* largest city and chief port of Ecuador, in the western part of the country. Pop. (1969), 738,591.

gua·yu·le (gwä yōō′lē) *n.* low-growing shrub, *Parthenium argentatum*, of the composite family, found in desert areas, chiefly in Mexico and Texas, bearing narrow, silvery leaves and small, white, daisylike flower heads, and having tissues that yield granules of natural rubber. [Spanish *guayule*, from Nahuatl *cuauhuli* literally, tree gum, from *cuahuitl* tree + *uli* gum.]

gu·ber·na·to·ri·al (gōō′bər nə tôr′ē əl, gū′-) *adj.* of or relating to a governor or the office of governor. [Latin *gubernator* ruler, pilot + -IAL.]

gudg·eon (guj′ən) *n.* **1.** freshwater fish of Europe, easily caught and often used for bait. **2.** any of various similar fish, as the minnow. [Old French *goujon* this freshwater fish, from Latin *gōbius*, form of *gōbius* (see GOBY).]

Gud·run (good′rōōn) *n.* wife of the Norse hero Sigurd.

Guelph (gwelf) *also,* **Guelf.** *n.* member of a medieval Italian party that supported the pope's opposition to German emperors controlling Italy. The Guelphs were opposed by the Ghibellines.

---

at; āpe; cär; end; mē; it; īce; hot; ōld; fôrk; wood; fōōl; oil; out; up; ūse; turn; sing; thin; this; zh in treasure; ə in ago, taken, pencil, lemon, circus.

guer·don (gurd′ən) *Archaic.* *n.* reward; recompense. —*v.t.* to reward. [Old French *guerdon* a reward, modification (influenced by Latin *dōnum* gift) of Old High German *widarlōn*.]

Guern·sey (gurn′zē) *pl.,* **-seys.** *n.* **1.** British island in the English Channel. Area, approx. 25 sq. mi. Pop. (1967), 45,884. **2.** any of a breed of dairy cattle originally developed in the Channel Islands, typically having a reddish or fawn coat with white markings. Weight: to 1700 pounds. **3.** **guernsey,** close-fitting knitted woolen shirt worn by sailors.

guer·ril·la (gə ril′ə) *also,* **gue·ril·la.** *n.* one who fights as a member of an armed band, usually of local origin, that does not form a part of a regular military unit. —*adj.* of, relating to, or by guerrillas: *guerrilla warfare.* [Spanish *guerrilla* skirmish, diminutive of *guerra* war, from Old High German *werra* discord.]

guess (ges) *v.t.* **1.** to form an opinion or estimate of (something) from incomplete or uncertain knowledge or evidence: *Without a clock he could only guess what time it was.* **2.** to judge (something) correctly by doing this: *He guessed the answer to the teacher's question.* **3.** to think; believe; suppose: *I guess we'll leave now.* —*v.i.* **1.** to form an opinion or estimate from incomplete or uncertain knowledge or evidence (often with *at*): *He guessed at the height of the building.* **2.** to judge something correctly by guessing. —*n.* opinion, estimate, or conclusion formed by guessing. [Probably of Scandinavian origin.] —**guess′er,** *n.*

Syn. *v.t.* **1.** **Guess, conjecture, surmise** indicate an assumption made on less than conclusive evidence. **Guess** suggests a decision made haphazardly or on the basis of slight evidence: *The children tried to guess where the candy was hidden.* **Conjecture** implies a plausible choice made from substantial but incomplete evidence: *They conjectured that the president would arrive at noon.* **Surmise** suggests reaching a conclusion by intuition: *I surmise that he has lost interest, though he has not said so.*

guess·work (ges′wurk′) *n.* process or result of guessing: *We got there by guesswork. The theory is mere guesswork.*

guest (gest) *n.* **1.** one who is received and entertained by another, as for a party, meal, or visit. **2.** one who pays for accommodations, food, or other services, as at a hotel, boarding house, or restaurant. **3.** organism that shares the food supply or dwelling of another. —*v.i.* to be a guest. [Old Norse *gestr* visitor, stranger.]

guest room, room used esp. for the accommodation of overnight guests.

guff (guf) *n.* *Slang.* empty talk; nonsense. [Probably imitative.]

guf·faw (gu fô′, gə-) *n.* loud, boisterous burst of laughter. —*v.i.* to laugh loudly and boisterously. [Imitative.]

Gui·a·na (gē ä′nə, -an′ə) *n.* region in northeastern South America on the Atlantic, including Guyana, French Guiana, Surinam, and parts of Venezuela and Brazil.

Gui·a·nas, The (gē ä′nəs, -an′əs) three small territories in northeastern South America occupying part of Guiana: British Guiana (now Guyana), Dutch Guiana (now Surinam), and French Guiana.

guid·ance (gīd′əns) *n.* **1.** act or process of guiding; leadership; direction: *She wrote a term paper under the teacher's guidance.* **2.** that which guides. **3.** service of a school providing counseling and evaluation of pupils to help them and their parents with future educational and vocational plans.

guide (gīd) *n.* **1.** one who guides, esp. one who is employed to lead or conduct tours, hunting expeditions, or the like. **2.** one who or that which directs another in his conduct or course of action: *They were dangerous guides, the feelings* (Tennyson, 1859). **3.** guidebook. **4.** book explaining or outlining the basic elements of some subject: *a guide to medieval literature.* **5.** part of a machine, serving to steady or direct motion. *A power saw has a guide to keep wood in position as it is being sawed.* **6.** member of a military formation who sets the pace and direction of a march. **7.** guidepost. —*v.t.,* **guid·ed, guid·ing. 1.** to show the way to; lead; conduct: *We guided the lost tourist across town.* **2.** to direct the course or motion of: *The teacher guided the girl's fingers on the piano keys.* **3.** to lead or direct, as the actions, affairs, or motives of; regulate: *He always let his conscience guide him.* —*v.i.* to act as a guide. [Old French *guider* to lead, modification of earlier *gvier;* of Germanic origin.] —**guid′er,** *n.* —**Syn.** *v.* **4.** see **manual.** *v.t.* **1.** see **lead**[1].

guide·book (gīd′book′) *n.* book of directions and information for travelers and tourists.

guided missile, missile that is guided during its flight by external means, as transmitted electronic impulses, or by internal means, as a heat-seeking device.

guide·post (gīd′pōst′) *n.* post at a roadside or intersection to which are attached directions for travelers.

Gui·do d'A·rez·zo (gwē′dō dä rät′sō) c.990–c.1050, Italian musical theorist.

gui·don (gīd′ən) *n.* **1.** flag, streamer, or pennant of a military unit. **2.** soldier who carries the guidon. [French *guidon* banner, from Italian *guidone,* from *guida* guide, from *guidare* to lead; of Germanic origin.]

guild (gild) *also,* **gild.** *n.* **1.** in the Middle Ages, a group of merchants or artisans in one trade or craft, organized to uphold standards and to protect the interests of members. **2.** any association of persons with similar interests or aims. [Old English *gildi* payment, fraternity.]

guil·der (gil′dər) *also,* **gil·der.** *n.* **1.** basic monetary unit in the Netherlands. **2.** any of several gold or silver coins formerly used in the Netherlands, Germany, and Austria. Also, **gul′den.** [Modification of Dutch *gulden.* See **GULDEN.**]

guild·hall (gild′hôl′) *n.* hall in which a guild meets.

guilds·man (gildz′mən) *pl.,* **-men.** *n.* member of a guild.

guile (gīl) *n.* cunning; deceit; slyness: *He used guile to escape punishment for his crime.* [Old French *guile;* of Germanic origin.] —**Syn.** deceit.

guile·ful (gīl′fəl) *adj.* full of guile; deceitful; cunning. —**guile′ful·ly,** *adv.* —**guile′ful·ness,** *n.*

guile·less (gīl′lis) *adj.* without guile; candid. —**guile′less·ly,** *adv.* —**guile′less·ness,** *n.*

guil·le·mot (gil′ə mot′) *n.* any of several web-footed birds, genera *Uria* and *Cepphus,* of the auk family, inhabiting the northern regions of the Atlantic and Pacific oceans, having a narrow, pointed bill and black or black-and-white plumage. [French *guillemot* diminutive of *Guillaume* William.]

guil·lo·tine (*n.* gil′ə tēn′, gē′ə-; *v.* gil′ə tēn′, gē′ə-) *n.* machine consisting of a heavily weighted knife that falls between two grooved posts, used for beheading people. It was adopted as the legal means of execution in France during the French Revolution. —*v.t.,* **-tined, -tin·ing.** to behead by the guillotine. [French *guillotine* this machine, from Joseph I. *Guillotin,* 1738–1814, French physician said to have invented it.]

guilt (gilt) *n.* **1.** state or fact of having done wrong, esp. of having committed a crime: *The police worked day and night to prove the man's guilt.* **2.** feeling of remorse for real or imagined wrongdoing. **3.** *Archaic.* guilty conduct. [Old English *gylt* crime, offense.]

guilt·less (gilt′lis) *adj.* **1.** free from guilt; innocent. **2.** having no knowledge or experience of something.

guilt·y (gil′tē) **guilt·i·er, guilt·i·est.** *adj.* **1.** having committed an offense; deserving of blame or punishment: *Who is guilty of taking the last piece of cake?* **2.** convicted of a crime: *The jury found him guilty of arson.* **3.** experiencing or showing guilt or a sense of guilt: *After he stole the fruit, the little boy suffered from a guilty conscience. The boy who broke the window had a guilty look on his face.* **4.** involving, relating to, or characterized by guilt. [Old English *gyltig* criminal.] —**guilt′i·ly,** *adv.* —**guilt′i·ness,** *n.*

guimpe (gimp, gamp) *n.* short blouse designed to be worn under certain dresses, as jumpers. [French *guimpe* wimple, veil; of Germanic origin.]

guin·ea (gin′ē) *n.* **1.** former English gold coin last minted in 1813 and fixed in value in 1717 at twenty-one shillings. **2.** in England, sum of money equal to twenty-one shillings. **3.** guinea fowl.

Guin·ea (gin′ē) *n.* **1.** country in western Africa, on the Atlantic, formerly the colony of French Guinea. Capital, Conakry. Area, 94,925 sq. mi. Pop. (1969 est.), 3,890,000. **2.** **Gulf of.** great bay of the Atlantic, on the west coast of Africa. **3.** historic region of western Africa, on the Atlantic coast of the continent. Also, **Guinea Coast.**

guinea fowl, any of various pheasant-like fowl, family Numididae, native to Africa, having dark-gray feathers speckled with white, widely domesticated and raised for its flesh, esp. the common species, *Numida meleagris.* Length: 17–30 inches.

guinea hen 1. female guinea fowl. **2.** guinea fowl.

guinea pig 1. rabbitlike rodent, genus *Cavia,* having a large head, small rounded ears, a stout body, and a long or short coat that may be solid or variegated, used for biological and medical research and kept as a pet. Length: 6–10 inches. **2.** any person or thing used in experimentation.

Guin·e·vere (gwin′ə vēr′) *n.* wife of King Arthur and mistress of Lancelot.

guise (gīz) *n.* **1.** external appearance or aspect; semblance: *Blessings in the guise of disasters* (Macaulay, 1849). **2.** assumed or false appearance; pretense: *They exploited us under the guise of friendship.* **3.** *Archaic.* style or manner of dress; garb. [Old French *guise* way, manner; of Germanic origin.]

Guillotine

Guinea fowl

Guinea pig

at; āpe; cär; end; mē; it; īce; hot; ōld; fôrk; wood; fōōl; oil; out; up; ūse; turn; sing; thin; this; zh in treasure; ə in ago, taken, pencil, lemon, circus.

gui·tar (gi tär′) *n.* musical instrument having a somewhat violinlike body, a long, fretted neck, and strings, usually six, that are plucked or strummed with the fingers or a plectrum. [French *guitare,* from Spanish *guitarra,* from Arabic *qîtāra* stringed instrument like a guitar, from Greek *kitharā* type of lyre. Doublet of CITHARA, ZITHER.]

Gui·zot, Fran·çois (gē zō′; frän-swä′) 1787–1874, French statesman.

Gu·ja·ra·ti (gooj′ə rä′tē) *n.* Indo-Iranian language of the Indo-European family, spoken in India.

gulch (gulch) *n.* deep, narrow ravine with steep sides, esp. one cut by a stream or torrent. [Possibly from dialectal English *gulch* to swallow; or imitative origin.]

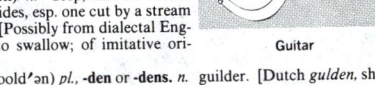

Guitar

gul·den (gool′dən) *pl.* **-den** or **-dens.** *n.* guilder. [Dutch *gulden,* short for *gulden florijn* golden florin.]

gules (gūlz) *n. Heraldry.* the color red. In representations without color, it is indicated by parallel vertical lines. [Old French *gueules* red; originally, scarfs of red fur for the neck, plural of *gueule* throat, from Latin *gula.*]

gulf (gulf) *n.* **1.** body of water forming an indentation in the shoreline of an ocean or sea, usually larger and deeper than a bay. **2.** deep hollow in the earth; chasm. **3.** any wide separation or interval; gap: *It is imperative to eliminate the great gulf between the rich and the poor.* **4.** that which engulfs or swallows up, esp. a whirlpool. [Old French *golfe* bay[1], whirlpool, from Italian *golfo,* going back to Greek *kolpos* bosom, hollow, bay[1].]

Gulf States, five Southern states bordering the Gulf of Mexico: Florida, Alabama, Mississippi, Louisiana, and Texas.

Gulf Stream, warm ocean current flowing northeast across the North Atlantic Ocean from the Gulf of Mexico along the eastern coast of North America to the northern coast of Europe.

gulf·weed (gulf′wēd′) *n.* any of a group of tropical marine seaweeds, genus *Sargassum,* found floating in large masses in the Gulf Stream and the Sargasso Sea, consisting of branches of leaflike blades having small berrylike sacs filled with air that keep it afloat.

gull¹ (gul) *n.* any of several graceful, long-winged birds, family Laridae, found on most seacoasts and near other large bodies of water, having webbed feet, a thick, slightly hooked beak, and usually clear white plumage with black wing tips. Length: 8–30 inches. Also, **sea gull.** [Probably from Cornish *guilan* or Welsh *gwylan.*]

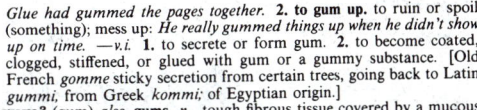

Gull¹

gull² (gul) *Archaic. v.t.* to deceive; cheat; dupe: *Mr. Brown was gulled into a bad business deal.* —*n.* one who is easily deceived or cheated; dupe. [Possibly from obsolete *gull* to swallow, from *gull* throat, from Old French *gole,* from Latin *gula.*]

Gul·lah (gul′ə) *n.* **1.** member or recent descendant of a group of Negroes living along the coast of South Carolina and Georgia and on the Sea Islands. **2.** dialect of these people, consisting of mixed African and English elements.

gul·let (gul′it) *n.* **1.** tube or passage through which food passes from the mouth to the stomach; esophagus. **2.** throat. [Old French *goulet* neck of a bottle or vase, water passage, diminutive of *gole* throat, from Latin *gula.*]

gul·li·ble (gul′ə bəl) *adj.* easily deceived, cheated, or duped; credulous. [GULL² + -IBLE.] —**gul′li·bil′i·ty,** *n.* —**gul′li·bly,** *adv.*

gul·ly (gul′ē) *pl.,* **-lies.** *n.* ditch or channel cut in the earth by running water; small ravine. —*v.t.,* **-lied, -ly·ing.** to make a gully in. [Modification of GULLET.]

gulp (gulp) *v.t.* **1.** to swallow hastily, greedily, or in large amounts (often with *down*): *He gulped his sandwich down and ran out.* **2.** to choke back or stifle as if by swallowing (often with *down*): *He gulped down his anger and smiled.* —*v.i.* to draw in or swallow air, as in surprise or fear. —*n.* **1.** act of gulping. **2.** amount swallowed at one time; mouthful: *a gulp of milk.* [Middle Dutch *gulpen* to guzzle; imitative.]

gum¹ (gum) *n.* **1.** thick sticky juice, secreted by various plants and trees, that dissolves or softens in cold water and hardens when exposed to air or heat. **2.** any natural plant or tree secretion, as resin. **3.** preparation made from such substances, used in manufacturing textiles, adhesives, dyes, and paints. **4.** chewing gum. **5.** mucilage, glue, or similar adhesive: *There is no gum on the back of this stamp.* **6.** gum tree. —*v.t.,* **gummed, gum·ming. 1.** to coat, clog, stiffen, or glue with gum or a gummy substance: *The machine gummed the back of the stamps.*

Glue had gummed the pages together. **2. to gum up.** to ruin or spoil (something); mess up: *He really gummed things up when he didn't show up on time.* —*v.i.* **1.** to secrete or form gum. **2.** to become coated, clogged, stiffened, or glued with gum or a gummy substance. [Old French *gomme* sticky secretion from certain trees, going back to Latin *gummi,* from Greek *kommi;* of Egyptian origin.]

gum² (gum) *also,* **gums.** *n.* tough fibrous tissue covered by a mucous membrane surrounding the necks of the teeth. [Old English *gōma* palate.]

gum ammoniac, ammoniac.

gum arabic, gum obtained from any of several trees, genus *Acacia,* esp. *A. senegal,* used chiefly in the manufacture of candies, adhesives, inks, textiles, and medicines. Also, **acacia.**

gum·bo (gum′bō) *pl.,* **-bos.** *n.* **1.** okra. **2.** highly seasoned soup thickened with okra pods and usually containing other vegetables and meat or fish. **3.** silty soil found in parts of the southern and western United States that becomes very sticky when wet. [Of Bantu origin.]

gum·boil (gum′boil′) *n.* small abscess on the gum.

gum·drop (gum′drop′) *n.* small, jellylike piece of candy made of gum arabic or gelatin, sweetened, variously flavored and colored, and usually coated with sugar.

gum·my (gum′ē) **-mi·er, -mi·est.** *adj.* **1.** of, containing, or resembling gum; sticky. **2.** covered or clogged with gum or a similar substance. **3.** secreting gum or a similar substance. —**gum′mi·ness,** *n.*

gump·tion (gump′shən) *n. Informal.* courage and energy; initiative; resourcefulness: *It took a lot of gumption to do a job that hard.* [Of unknown origin.]

gum resin, mixture of certain gum and resin, usually obtained by cutting the outer covering of certain plants.

gum·shoe (gum′shoo′) *Slang. n.* **1.** detective. —*v.i.,* **-shoed, -shoe·ing.** to go around quietly and stealthily; sneak.

gum tree, any of various gum-producing trees, as the sapodilla, tupelo, sour gum, sweet gum, and several trees of the genus *Eucalyptus.*

gun (gun) *n.* **1.** any of various weapons, as a pistol, rifle, or cannon, consisting of a metal tube through which a projectile is shot in a flat trajectory by the force of an explosive. **2.** similar device that discharges a projectile: *a dart gun.* **3.** any device resembling a gun in form or use: *They painted the wall with a spray gun.* **4.** firing of a gun as a signal or salute: *The gun started the race.* **5.** one skilled in the use of guns: *a hired gun, the fastest gun in the West.* **6. to give it** (or **her**) **the gun.** to cause to start or speed up, esp. a motor vehicle. **7. to go great guns.** to work or proceed with great skill, speed, and efficiency. **8. to spike (someone's) guns.** to ruin or foil someone's plans; defeat. **9. to stick to one's guns.** to be firm despite opposition; refuse to retreat or yield. —*v.t.,* **gunned, gun·ning. 1.** *Informal.* to shoot (a person or animal) with a gun (often with *down*). **2.** *Slang.* to open the throttle of so as to increase the speed: *The driver gunned the engine.* —*v.i.* **1.** to shoot or hunt with a gun. **2. to gun for. a.** *Informal.* to look for in order to harm or kill. **b.** *Slang.* to try to obtain; seek: *He was gunning for a promotion.* [Short for Old Norse *Gunnhildr,* feminine proper name (from *gunnr* war + *hildr* battle); applied to a type of weapon.]

gun·boat (gun′bōt′) *n.* small, armed ship used for patrolling rivers and coastal waters.

gun·cot·ton (gun′kot′ən) *n.* highly explosive form of nitrocellulose made by treating cotton with a mixture of concentrated nitric and sulfuric acids.

gun·fire (gun′fīr′) *n.* shooting of a gun or guns.

gung ho (gung′hō′) *Informal.* very enthusiastic; eager: *They were gung ho about the party.* [Probably from Chinese (Mandarin) *kung ho* work together.]

gun·lock (gun′lok′) *n.* part of the mechanism in certain guns by which the charge is exploded.

gun·man (gun′mən) *pl.,* **-men.** *n.* man armed with a gun, esp. a criminal.

gun metal 1. any of various metallic alloys with a grayish color used for making such items as chains, buckles, and other trinkets. **2.** kind of bronze formerly used for making guns. **3.** dark-gray color with a bluish tinge. —**gun′-met′al,** *adj.*

Gun·nar (goon′är, -ər) *n. Norse Legend.* brother of Gudrun and husband of Brynhild.

gun·nel¹ (gun′əl) *n.* gunwale. [Form of GUNWALE.]

gun·nel² (gun′əl) *n.* slender fish, *Pholis gunnellus,* of the blenny family, found in the North Atlantic. Length: to 12 inches. [Of uncertain origin.]

gun·ner (gun′ər) *n.* **1.** serviceman who operates or helps to operate a firearm. **2.** naval warrant officer in charge of ordnance. **3.** one who hunts with a gun.

gun·ner·y (gun′ər ē) *n.* **1.** use and firing of guns. **2.** guns collectively.

gun·ny (gun′ē) *pl.,* **-nies.** *n.* strong, coarse fabric of jute or hemp, used esp. for making sacks or bags. [Hindi *gōnī* sack, from Sanskrit *gōnī.*]

gun·ny·sack (gun′ē sak′) *n.* sack or bag made of gunny. Also, **gunny bag.**

gun·point (gun′point′) *n.* **1.** end of a gun barrel. **2. at gunpoint.** under threat of being shot.

gun·pow·der (gun′pou′dər) *n.* explosive consisting of charcoal, sulfur, and potassium nitrate, used esp. in bullets, artillery shells, fireworks, and blasting.

gun room 1. room where guns are kept or displayed. **2.** junior officers' quarters on a British warship.

gun·run·ning (gun′run′ing) *n.* smuggling of firearms and ammunition into a country. —**gun′run′ner,** *n.*

gun·shot (gun′shot′) *n.* **1.** shot fired from a gun. **2.** range of a gun. **3.** firing of a gun.

gun-shy (gun′shī′) *adj.* easily frightened by the firing of a gun.

gun·smith (gun′smith′) *n.* one who makes or repairs firearms.

gun·stock (gun′stok′) *n.* wooden support or handle to which the barrel of a gun is attached.

Gun·ther (goon′tər) *n.* in the *Nibelungenlied,* king of Burgundy and husband of Brunhild.

Gunwales

gun·wale (gun′əl) *also,* **gun·nel.** *n.* upper edge of the side of a ship or boat. [GUN + WALE because it once supported a ship's guns.]

gup·py (gup′ē) *pl.,* **-pies.** *n.* small, slender fish, *Lebistes reticulatus,* native to the fresh waters of Trinidad and northern South America, the male of which is brightly colored. It is widely raised in home aquariums. Length: to 2 inches. [From R. J. L. *Guppy,* British clergyman in Trinidad, who gave specimens to the British Museum.]

Guppy

gur·gle (gur′gəl) **-gled, -gling.** *v.i.* **1.** to flow irregularly with a bubbling sound: *The stream gurgled around the rocks.* **2.** to make a bubbling sound: *The baby cooed and gurgled with delight.* —*v.t.* to utter with a gurgling sound: *She gurgled her thanks.* —*n.* act or sound of gurgling. [Probably imitative.]

Gur·kha (gur′kə, goor′-) *n.* member of a Hindu people living in Nepal, famous as soldiers.

gur·nard (gur′nərd) *pl.,* **-nards** or **-nard.** *n.* any of various tropical, saltwater fish, family Dactylopteridae, having enlarged pectoral fins that enable them to glide for short distances in the air. Also, **flying gurnard.** [Old French *gornard* literally, grunter, from *gronir* to grunt, going back to Latin *grunnīre;* because it grunts when removed from water.]

Gurnard

gu·ru (goo′roo, goo roo′) *n.* **1.** holy man and religious and spiritual teacher, esp. in the Hindu religion. **2.** *Informal.* respected leader or teacher. [Hindi *gurū* teacher, priest, from Sanskrit *guruh* weighty, venerable.]

gush (gush) *v.i.* **1.** to flow or rush out suddenly and abundantly: *Water gushed from the broken pipe.* **2.** to emit a sudden, abundant flow of something (with *with*): *The cut gushed with blood.* **3.** *Informal.* to be overly or insincerely enthusiastic or emotional in speech or writing. —*v.t.* to emit in a sudden and abundant flow. —*n.* **1.** sudden rush or outflow: *a gush of water.* **2.** that which gushes forth. **3.** *Informal.* display of extravagant and insincere emotion or enthusiasm. [Probably imitative.]

gush·er (gush′ər) *n.* **1.** oil well from which oil flows abundantly without being pumped. **2.** one who gushes.

gush·y (gush′ē) **gush·i·er, gush·i·est.** *adj.* overly emotional or enthusiastic; effusive. —**gush′i·ness,** *n.*

gus·set (gus′it) *n.* **1.** triangular piece of material inserted into a garment or other article to reinforce or expand some part. **2.** triangular metal brace or bracket used to reinforce a corner or angle of a structure. [Old French *gousset* piece of armor or cloth inserted under the armhole, diminutive of *gousse* husk of a bean; of uncertain origin; because it supposedly resembled a bean husk.]

gust (gust) *n.* **1.** sudden, strong rush of wind or air. **2.** any sudden burst or outflow, as of rain, fire, or sound. **3.** outburst of emotion, as anger or enthusiasm. [Old Norse *gustr* blast.]

gus·ta·to·ry (gus′tə tôr′ē) *adj.* of or relating to the sense of taste or the act of tasting. [Latin *gustātus,* past participle of *gustāre* to taste + -ORY.]

Gus·ta·vus I (gus tā′vəs, -tä′-) 1496–1560, king of Sweden from 1523 to 1560.

Gustavus II, 1594–1632, king of Sweden from 1611 to 1632.

Gustavus IV, 1778–1837, king of Sweden from 1792 to 1809.

Gustavus V, 1858–1950, king of Sweden from 1907 to 1950.

Gustavus VI, 1882–1973, king of Sweden from 1950–1973.

gus·to (gus′tō) *n.* great enthusiasm and enjoyment: *He ate with gusto.* [Italian *gusto* taste, liking, from Latin *gustus* taste.]

gust·y (gus′tē) **gust·i·er, gust·i·est.** *adj.* characterized by or coming in gusts; windy; blustery: *the gusty weather of late October.* —**gust′i·ly,** *adv.* —**gust′i·ness,** *n.*

gut (gut) *n.* **1.** digestive tract or any part of it, esp. the stomach or intestine. **2. guts. a.** *Slang.* courage; pluck; spirit; fortitude: *She had the guts to admit she was wrong. It took guts to play when he was injured.* **b.** entrails; bowels. **3.** catgut. **4.** narrow passage or channel, as a strait or gorge. —*v.t.* **gut·ted, gut·ting. 1.** to remove the entrails of; disembowel; eviscerate. **2.** to destroy the inside of: *Fire gutted the house.* [Old English *guttas* (plural) bowels, entrails.]

Gu·ten·berg, Jo·hann (goot′ən bûrg′; yō′hän) c.1400–c.1468, German printer, probably the first European to print from movable type.

gut·sy (gut′sē) **-si·er, -si·est.** *adj. Slang.* courageous, bold, or vital.

gut·ta-per·cha (gut′ə pur′chə) *n.* pliable, pale-gray material obtained from the latex of several evergreen trees found in Malaya and the East Indies, esp. *Palaquium gutta.* It is used esp. in electrical insulation, in dentistry, and as waterproofing. [Malay *getah* gum, balsam + *percha* tree from which it comes.]

Gutter

gut·ter (gut′ər) *n.* **1.** narrow channel, ditch, or low area along the side of a street or road to carry off surface water. **2.** trough fixed under or along the eaves of a roof to carry off rain water. **3.** any channel or groove, as at the side of a bowling alley. **4.** place or way of life characterized by poverty, filth, squalor, and immorality: *the slang of the gutter.* —*v.t.* to form gutters in or furnish with gutters. —*v.i.* **1.** to flow in streams. **2.** (of a candle) to melt rapidly so that the wax or tallow runs down the sides in channels. [Old French *goutiere* channel, from *goute* drop, from Latin *gutta.*]

gut·ter·snipe (gut′ər snīp′) *n. Informal.* poor, neglected child who spends much time in the streets.

gut·tur·al (gut′ər əl) *adj.* **1.** of or relating to the throat. **2.** having a harsh, rasping quality, as a sound produced in the throat: *a fierce, guttural growl.* **3.** *Phonetics.* pronounced with the back of the tongue raised toward the soft palate. —*n.* guttural sound. [Modern Latin *gutturalis,* from *guttur* throat.] —**gut′tur·al·ly,** *adv.*

gut·ty (gut′ē) **-ti·er, -ti·est.** *adj. Slang.* gutsy.

guy¹ (gī) *n.* rope, chain, wire, or rod used to steady or secure something. —*v.t.,* **guyed, guy·ing.** to steady or secure with a guy. [Old French *guie* guide, from *guier* to guide; of Germanic origin.]

guy² (gī) *Informal. n.* man; fellow. —*v.t.,* **guyed, guy·ing.** to make fun of; tease. [From *Guy* Fawkes, leader of a conspiracy to blow up the British Parliament in 1605.]

Guy·an·a (gī an′ə) *n.* country on the northeastern coast of South America, formerly the colony of British Guiana. Capital, Georgetown. Area, 83,000 sq. mi. Pop. (1969 est.), 742,000.

guz·zle (guz′əl) **-zled, -zling.** *v.t., v.i.* to drink greedily or excessively. [Of uncertain origin.] —**guz′zler,** *n.*

gym (jim) *n.* **1.** gymnasium. **2.** course in physical education in a school or college.

gym·kha·na (jim kä′nə) *n.* **1.** sports car event over a planned course in which driving skill, rather than speed, is tested. **2.** meet consisting of various sports contests. [Modification (influenced by GYMNASIUM) of Hindi *gend-khāna* ball house, racket court: *khāna* house, from Persian *khāna.*]

gym·na·si·um (jim nā′zē əm) *pl.,* **-si·ums** or **-si·a** (-zē ə) *n.* **1.** room or building provided with equipment for physical exercise or training and for indoor sports. **2. Gymnasium.** secondary school in various European countries, emphasizing classical studies, esp. Greek and Latin. [Latin *gymnasium* athletic school, school, from Greek *gymnasion,* going back to *gymnos* naked; because ancient Greek athletes exercised naked.]

gym·nast (jim′nast) *n.* one skilled in gymnastics. [Greek *gymnastēs* trainer of athletes.]

gym·nas·tic (jim nas′tik) *adj.* of or relating to gymnastics. —**gym·nas′ti·cal·ly,** *adv.*

at; āpe; cär; end; mē; it; īce; hot; ōld; fôrk; wood; foõl; out; up; ūse; turn; sing; thin; this; zh in treasure; ə in ago, taken, pencil, lemon, circus.

gym·nas·tics (jim nas′tiks) *n.,pl.* **1.** physical exercises, with or without apparatus, designed to develop strength, agility, coordination, and balance. **2.** art, practice, or sport of such exercises. ▲ construed as singular in def. 2.

gym·no·sperm (jim′nə spurm′) *n.* any of a large group of plants whose seeds are not enclosed in ovaries and are generally borne in cones. Gymnosperms are usually characterized by thin needlelike leaves, as in pines, yews, spruces, and junipers. [Modern Latin *Gymnospermae,* from Greek *gymnospermos,* from *gymnos* naked + *sperma* seed.] —**gym′no·sper′mous,** *adj.*

gy·ne·col·o·gist (gī′nə kol′ə jist, jin′ə-) *n.* doctor who specializes in gynecology.

gy·ne·col·o·gy (gī′nə kol′ə jē, jin′ə-) *n.* branch of medicine dealing with the functions and diseases of women. [Greek *gynaik-,* stem of *gynē* woman + -LOGY.]

gy·noe·ci·um (jə nē′sē əm, gī-) *pl.,* **-ci·a** (-sē ə). *n.* pistil or pistils of a flower considered as a unit. [Modern Latin *gynoecium,* modification (influenced by Greek *oikion* house) of *gynaeceum,* going back to Greek *gynaikeion* women's apartment, from *gynē* woman.]

gyp (jip) **gypped, gyp·ping.** *Slang. v.t., v.i.* to cheat, swindle, or defraud. —*n.* **1.** fraud; swindle. **2.** cheat; swindler. [Probably short for GYPSY.]

gyp·soph·i·la (jip sof′ə lə) *n.* any of a group of plants, genus *Gypsophila,* found in northern temperate regions of the world, bearing clusters of small white or pink flowers on branching stalks with few leaves. Baby's breath is one of the most familiar species. [Modern Latin *Gypsophila,* going back to Greek *gypsos* chalk, gypsum + *philos* loving, dear.]

gyp·sum (jip′səm) *n.* natural hydrated calcium sulfate, a common mineral used esp. in the production of plaster of Paris, and as a fertilizer. Alabaster is a type of gypsum. Formula: CaSO₄·2H₂O [Latin *gypsum* chalk, plaster, from Greek *gypsos* chalk; of Semitic origin.]

Gyp·sy (jip′sē) *pl.,* **-sies.** *also,* **Gip·sy,** *n.* **1.** *also, gypsy.* member of a migratory Caucasian people having dark skin and black hair, who left northwestern India over 1000 years ago and appeared in Europe around the fourteenth century. Now scattered throughout the world, they are noted as musicians, fortune tellers, horse traders, and tinkers. **2.** Rom-

any *(def. 2).* **3.** *gypsy.* one who resembles or leads the life of a Gypsy. [Modification of *Egyptian;* from the mistaken belief that Gypsies came from Egypt.]

gypsy moth, insect pest, *Porthetria dispar,* native to Europe and Japan, now found in the northeastern United States, whose larvae attack the leaves of trees. The female is unable to fly.

gy·rate (jī′rāt, jī rāt′) **-rat·ed, -rat·ing.** *v.i.* to move in a circle or spiral, esp. around an axis or fixed point; whirl; rotate: *The dancing couples gyrated around the room.* [Latin *gȳrātus,* past participle of *gȳrāre* to turn around, from *gȳrus* circle, from Greek *gȳros.*] —**gy·ra′tor,** *n.*

gy·ra·tion (jī rā′shən) *n.* act of gyrating; circular or spiral motion.

gy·ra·to·ry (jī′rə tôr′ē) *adj.* moving in a circle or spiral; revolving; whirling.

gyr·fal·con (jur′fal′kən, -fôl′-) *also,* **ger·fal·con.** *n.* falcon, *Falco rusticolus,* living mainly in the Arctic. It is the largest of the falcons. Length: 2 feet. [Old French *gerfaucon;* of Germanic origin.]

gy·ro (jī′rō) *pl.,* **-ros.** *n.* **1.** gyrocompass. **2.** gyroscope.

gyro- *combining form* **1.** gyrating; rotating: *gyroscope.* **2.** gyroscope: *gyrocompass.* [Greek *gȳros* circle.]

gy·ro·com·pass (jī′rō kum′pəs, -kom′-) *n.* compass using a rapidly spinning gyroscope to indicate the north. It indicates true north rather than magnetic north. [GYRO- + COMPASS.]

gy·ro·scope (jī′rə skōp′) *n.* wheel mounted so that the axis on which it spins can point in any direction. When the wheel is spinning, the axis sets itself in a fixed direction and resists changes from that direction. Gyroscopes are used as stabilizers, compasses, and automatic pilots. [GYRO- + -SCOPE.] —**gy·ro·scop·ic** (jī′rə skop′ik), *adj.*

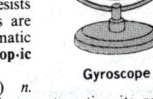

Gyroscope

gy·ro·sta·bi·liz·er (jī′rō stā′bə lī′zər) *n.* gyroscopic device for stabilizing a ship by counteracting its rolling motion.

gyve (jīv) *n.* fetter or shackle, esp. for the leg. —*v.t.,* **gyved, gyv·ing.** to bind with or as with fetters; shackle: *I will gyve thee in thine own courtship* (Shakespeare, *Othello*). [Of uncertain origin.]

at; āpe; cär; end; mē; it; īce; hot; ōld; fôrk; wood; fōōl; oil; out; up; ūse; turn; sing; thin; this; zh in treasure; ə in ago, taken, pencil, lemon, circus.

h, H (āch) *pl.,* **h's, H's.** **1.** eighth letter of the English alphabet. **2.** shape of this letter or something having such a shape.

H **1.** anything in the shape of an H. **2.** henry. **3.** hydrogen. **4.** *Physics.* intensity of a magnetic field.

H. **1.** hour; hours. **2.** harbor. **3.** height. **4.** high. **5.** hard. **6.** hardness. **7.** *Baseball.* hit; hits. **8.** hundred. **9.** husband. **10.** *Music.* horn.

ha (hä) *interj.* **1.** *also,* **hah.** used to express a sudden feeling, as of surprise, joy, triumph, or scorn. **2.** used repetitively to express laughter.

Haar·lem (här′ləm) *n.* city in the western Netherlands, near the North Sea. Pop. (1968), 173,463.

Hab., Habakkuk.

Ha·bak·kuk (hə bak′ək, hab′ə kuk′) *n.* **1.** Hebrew prophet of the seventh century B.C. **2.** book of the Old Testament containing his prophecies. Also, in Douay Bible, **Ha·bac′uc.**

ha·be·as cor·pus (hā′bē əs kôr′pəs) writ or order commanding that a person imprisoned or detained be brought before a court or judge to determine if he is being imprisoned or detained lawfully. [Latin *habeās corpus* literally, you may have the body.]

hab·er·dash·er (hab′ər dash′ər) *n.* **1.** one who sells men's furnishings, as neckties, shirts, and gloves. **2.** *British.* one who sells notions, as buttons, thread, and ribbons. [Possibly from Anglo-Norman *hapertas* fabric, cloth; of uncertain origin.]

hab·er·dash·er·y (hab′ər dash′ər ē) *pl.,* **-er·ies.** *n.* **1.** merchandise sold by a haberdasher. **2.** haberdasher's shop.

hab·er·geon (hab′ər jən) *n.* **1.** *also,* **hau·ber·geon.** sleeveless jacket or short coat of mail or scale armor. **2.** hauberk. [Old French *haubergeon,* diminutive of *hauberc.* See HAUBERK.]

ha·bil·i·ment (hə bil′ə mənt) *n.* **1.** garb or attire of a particular occupation or occasion. **2.** clothing. ▲ usually used in the plural in both definitions. [French *habillement* clothing, from Old French *(h)abiller* to dress; originally, to get ready, prepare a log of wood, from *a* to (from Latin *ad*) + *bille* tree trunk, large branch (of Celtic origin).]

hab·it (hab′it) *n.* **1.** action that has become nearly automatic through deliberate or unconscious repetition: *Jaywalking is a bad habit.* **2.** tendency to act in a customary way: *The driver turned left by force of habit.* **3.** addiction. **4.** type of dress characteristic of a particular profession, rank, religious order, or activity: *a nun's habit.* **5.** customary pattern of behavior: *of lax habits.* **6.** characteristic form or manner of growth of an animal or plant: *Ivy has a climbing habit.* —*v.t.* to dress or clothe. [Old French *habit* practice, dress, from Latin *habitus* condition, dress.]

Syn. *n.* **1.** Habit, custom, practice mean a usual way of doing something which has become established over a long period of time. Habit applies to a person's action that happens so often that it is done naturally and without thinking: *He has a habit of humming while he works.* Custom usually applies to long-established behavior by a group or nation: *It is an English custom to drink tea in the afternoon.* Practice may be used of either a person or a group and applies to an action which has been made a habit deliberately and by choice: *It is his practice to arrive at work half an hour before the other employees.*

hab·it·a·ble (hab′ə tə bəl) *adj.* suitable for living in; inhabitable. —**hab′it·a·bil′i·ty, hab′it·a·ble·ness,** *n.* —**hab′it·a·bly,** *adv.*

hab·i·tant (hab′ə tənt; *def. 2 also French* à bē tän′) *n.* **1.** inhabitant. **2.** *also,* **ha·bi·tan,** farmer of French descent who has settled in Canada or Louisiana. [French *habitant* inhabitant, from *habiter* to dwell, from Latin *habitāre.*]

hab·i·tat (hab′ə tat′) *n.* **1.** area or region in which an animal or plant naturally lives or grows, as salt water or the desert. **2.** place where a person or thing is most frequently found. **3.** dwelling place; habitation. [Latin *habitat* it dwells.]

hab·i·ta·tion (hab′ə tā′shən) *n.* **1.** dwelling place; living quarters. **2.** act of inhabiting; occupancy: *to be fit for human habitation.* **3.** settlement: *the habitations of pioneers.* [Latin *habitātiō.*]

ha·bit·u·al (hə bich′ōō əl) *adj.* **1.** done by habit; resulting from habit: *habitual optimism.* **2.** being something or acting in a certain way by habit: *a habitual latecomer.* **3.** commonly occurring or used; usual: *India's habitual monsoon season.* —**ha·bit′u·al·ly,** *adv.* —**ha·bit′u·al·ness,** *n.* —**Syn. 1.** see **chronic.**

ha·bit·u·ate (hə bich′ōō āt′) -**at·ed, -at·ing.** *v.t.* to familiarize through habit; accustom: *The action was more frank and fearless than any I was habituated to indulge in* (Charlotte Brontë, 1847). [Late Latin *habituātus,* past participle of *habituāre* to bring into a condition, from Latin *habitus* condition.] —**Syn.** see **accustom.**

hab·i·tude (hab′ə tōōd′, -tūd′) *n.* **1.** disposition to act in a customary way. **2.** habitual action; custom. [French *habitude* custom, from Latin *habitūdō* condition.]

ha·bit·u·é (hə bich′ōō ā′) *n.* one who frequents (a specified place): *a habitué of auctions.* [French *habitué,* from *habituer* to accustom, from Late Latin *habituāre.* See HABITUATE.]

Habs·burg (haps′bûrg′; *German* häps′boork′) Hapsburg.

ha·ci·en·da (hä′sē en′də, ä′sē-) *n.* **1.** landed estate, country house, ranch, or plantation. **2.** in southwestern United States and Spanish America, low, sprawling ranch house with wide porches. [Spanish *hacienda* landed estate, domestic work, from Latin *facienda* things to be done, from *facere* to do.]

hack¹ (hak) *v.t.* **1.** to cut or chop irregularly with heavy blows, as with a hatchet or cleaver. **2.** to clear or break up (land), as with a hoe. **3.** to cut (a story or other piece of writing) ruthlessly and ineptly; mangle. —*v.i.* **1.** to deal cutting blows; chop. **2.** to emit short, harsh, repeated coughs. **3. to hack around.** *Slang.* to be idle; waste time; fool around. —*n.* **1.** rough gash, cut, or notch made by or as by a heavy blow. **2.** sharp tool or implement used for hacking, as a pick, hatchet, or cleaver. **3.** short, harsh, repeated cough. [Old English *-haccian* to cut.] —**hack′er,** *n.*

hack² (hak) *n.* **1.** one who renounces a talent, training, independence, or integrity and hires himself out solely for money or other reward; hireling. **2.** one hired to write banal or pedestrian material; literary drudge. **3.** carriage for hire; hackney. **4.** old, worn-out horse. **5.** *Informal.* **a.** taxicab. **b.** taxicab driver. **6.** *British.* **a.** horse kept for hire or for general work. **b.** horse for riding. —*v.i.* **1.** *Informal.* to drive a taxicab. **2.** *British.* to ride on horseback on a road at an ordinary pace. —*adj.* **1.** relating to someone hired as a hack or his work: *a hack writer, a hack job.* **2.** trite; hackneyed. [Short for HACKNEY.]

hack·a·more (hak′ə môr′) *n.* kind of halter consisting of a coil of rope or rawhide that can be tightened around the nose of a horse, used to break horses. [Spanish *jáquima,* going back to Arabic *shakīma′* bridle bit, curb.]

hack·ber·ry (hak′ber′ē) *pl.,* **-ries.** *n.* **1.** any of a large group of shrubs and trees, genus *Celtis,* of the elm family, found throughout the Northern Hemisphere, having gray bark and tiny flowers. **2.** cherrylike fruit of this tree. [Form of *hagberry;* of Scandinavian origin.]

Hack·en·sack (hak′ən sak′) *n.* city in northeastern New Jersey. Pop. (1970), 35,911.

hack·ie (hak′ē) *n.* *Slang.* taxicab driver.

hack·le (hak′əl) *n.* **1.a.** any of the long, slender feathers on the neck of certain birds, esp. the domestic rooster. **b.** neck plumage, as of the domestic rooster. **2.** artificial fishing fly made with hackles, often without wings. Also, **hackle fly.** **3. hackles.** erectile hairs along the neck and back of an animal, esp. a dog. **4.** board set with metal teeth, used to comb and clean flax, hemp, or jute. Also, **hatch′el. 5. to get one's hackles up.** to be ready for an argument or fight. —*v.t.* **-led, -ling. 1.** to equip (a fishing fly) with hackles. **2.** to comb (flax, hemp, or jute) with a hackle. Also (*def. 2*), **hatch′el.** [Possibly from an unrecorded Old English word.] —**hack′ler,** *n.*

hack·le² (hak′əl) **-led, -ling.** *v.t.* to cut or chop roughly; hack. [HACK¹ + -LE.]

at; āpe; cär; end; mē; it; īce; hot; ōld; fôrk; wood; fōōl; oil; out; up; ūse; turn; sing; thin; this; zh in treasure; ə in ago, taken, pencil, lemon, circus.

hack·man (hak′mən) *pl.,* **-men.** *n.* **1.** driver of a hack. **2.** *Slang.* taxicab driver.

hack·ma·tack (hak′mə tak′) *n.* tamarack. [Of Algonquian origin.]

hack·ney (hak′nē) *pl.,* **-neys.** *n.* **1.** horse used for ordinary riding or driving. **2.** carriage for hire. **3.** *Archaic.* one who is hired to do menial work; drudge. —*adj.* **1.** let out, employed, or done for hire. **2.** hackneyed. —*v.t.* to make trite or banal by overuse. [Possibly from *Hackney,* an English town (now a borough of London) once famous for its horses.]

hack·neyed (hak′nēd) *adj.* used too frequently; trite; banal.

hack·saw (hak′sô′) *n.* saw having a narrow, fine-toothed blade held firm in a frame, used esp. for cutting metal.

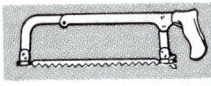
Hacksaw

had (had; *unstressed* həd, əd) past tense and past participle of **have.** ▲ often used to express necessity or preference: *You had better study tonight if you want to pass tomorrow's examination.*

had·dock (had′ək) *pl.,* **-dock** or **-docks.** *n.* commercially valuable food fish, *Melanogrammus aeglefinus,* of the cod family, widely distributed in North Atlantic coastal waters, having five fins, a barbel, and a black line running along each side of the body from the gills to the tail. Weight: usually from 2–4 pounds.

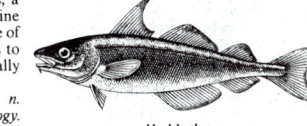
Haddock

Ha·des (hā′dēz) *n.* **1.** *Greek Mythology.* **a.** place to which the dead go; underworld. **b.** god who ruled the underworld; Pluto. **2. hades.** hell. [Greek *Haidēs* the lower world.]

hadj (haj) *also,* **hajj.** *n.* pilgrimage to Mecca which each Muslim is required to make at least once during his life. [Arabic *hajj* pilgrimage.]

hadj·i (haj′ē) *also,* **haj·ji.** *n.* Muslim who has made the required pilgrimage to Mecca. ▲ used as a title of respect. [Arabic *hājjī* pilgrim, from *hajj.* See HADJ.]

had·n't (had′ənt) had not.

Ha·dri·an (hā′drē ən) *n.* 76–138, Roman emperor from 117 to 138; born Publius Aelius Hadrianus.

hadst (hadst) *Archaic.* second person singular past tense of **have.**

ha·fiz (hä′fiz) *n.* Muslim who has memorized the Koran. ▲ used as a title of respect. [Arabic *hāfiz.*]

haf·ni·um (haf′nē əm) *n.* gray metallic element resembling zirconium in physical and chemical properties. Symbol: **Hf** See **element** for table. [Modern Latin *hafnium,* from Latin *Hafnia* Copenhagen.]

haft (haft) *n.* handle of a knife, sword, or other tool or weapon; hilt. —*v.t.* to furnish with or set in a haft. [Old English *hæft* a handle.]

hag (hag) *n.* **1.** ugly, repulsive, often vicious old woman. **2.** witch. **3.** hagfish. [Short for Old English *hægtesse* witch.] —**hag′gish,** *adj.* —**hag′gish·ly,** *adv.* —**hag′gish·ness,** *n.*

Hag., Haggai.

Ha·gar (hā′gär, -gər) *n.* in the Old Testament, the concubine of Abraham and mother of Ishmael, driven with her son into the desert because of the jealousy of Sarah, Abraham's wife.

Ha·gen (hä′gən) *n.* in the *Nibelungenlied,* the king's henchman who murders the hero Siegfried and steals the Nibelungs' treasure.

Ha·gers·town (hā′gərz toun′) *n.* city in northwestern Maryland. Pop. (1970), 35,862.

hag·fish (hag′fish′) *pl.,* **-fish** or **-fish·es.** *n.* any of a group of eel-like saltwater fish, family Myxinidae, having a round, sucking mouth surrounded by tentacles and a tongue with comblike teeth. Some attach themselves by mouth to other fish, bore into their bodies, and feed on their organs. Length: usually under 2½ feet. Also, **hag.**

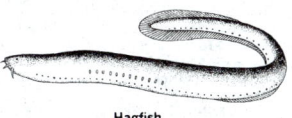
Hagfish

Hag·ga·dah (hə gä′də) *pl.,* **-doth** (-dōs, -dôt). *n.* Also, **Hag·ga·da.** *n.* **1.** book of services for the celebration of the Jewish festival of Passover, including prayers, the story of the Exodus, legends, and songs. **2.** nonlegal part of rabbinical literature, including explanations, legends, and parables. Distinguished from **Halakah** in both definitions. [Hebrew *haggādāh* narrative.] —**hag·gad′ic** (hə gad′ik, -gä′dik), *adj.* —**hag·ga′dist,** *n.*

Hag·ga·i (hag′ē ī′, hag′ī) *n.* **1.** Hebrew prophet of the sixth century B.C. **2.** book of the Old Testament containing his prophecies. Also, in Douay Bible, **Ag′ge·us.**

hag·gard (hag′ərd) *adj.* having a worn look, as from fatigue, anxiety, hunger, or other suffering; gaunt. [Old French *hagard* wild, wild hawk; of Germanic origin.] —**hag′gard·ly,** *adv.* —**hag′gard·ness,** *n.*

hag·gis (hag′is) *n.* Scottish dish consisting of the heart, lungs, and liver of a sheep or calf, combined with suet, onions, oatmeal, and seasonings and boiled in the stomach of the animal. [Possibly from dialectal English *hag* to chop, hew; of Scandinavian origin.]

hag·gle (hag′əl) *v.i.* to bargain in a petty way, esp. about price or terms of an agreement; dicker. —*v.t.* to cut roughly; mangle; hack. —*n.* act or instance of bargaining in a petty way. [From dialectal English *hag* to chop, hew (of Scandinavian origin) + -LE.] —**hag′gler,** *n.*

hag·i·ol·o·gy (hag′ē ol′ə jē, hā′jē-) *pl.,* **-gies.** *n.* **1.** literature dealing with the lives and legends of saints. **2.** work or collection on this subject. **3.** list of the saints. [Greek *hagios* holy + -LOGY.]

hag·rid·den (hag′rid′ən) *adj.* tormented as if by a witch; harassed.

Hague, The (hāg) city in the western Netherlands, seat of the national government. Pop., metropolitan area (1969), 738,078.

hah (hä) ha.

ha-ha (hä′hä′) *interj.* used to express amusement or scorn.

Hai·fa (hī′fə) *n.* port city in northwestern Israel, on the Mediterranean Sea. Pop. (1968), 212,300.

hai·ku (hī′kōō) *pl.,* **-ku.** *n.* **1.** Japanese verse form in three lines containing seventeen syllables, five in the first line, seven in the second, and five in the third. **2.** poem written in this form, usually on a subject from nature. [Japanese *haiku.*]

hail¹ (hāl) *v.t.* **1.** to greet enthusiastically with shouts of approval; acclaim: *Millions of people hailed the astronauts.* **2.** to attract the attention of through motions or calls: *Let's hail a taxi.* **3.** to acknowledge with greeting; salute: *They hailed him as their commander.* —*v.i.* **1.** to call out in order to greet or to attract attention, as to a passing ship. **2. to hail from.** to have come from (a particular place, such as a birthplace or point of departure). —*n.* **1.** greeting or shout of acclaim. **2.** call intended to attract attention. **3.** act of hailing. **4. within hail.** close enough to hear a call or greeting; within earshot. —*interj.* greetings. ▲ used as an expression of acclaim, greeting, or salutation. [Earlier *be hail,* from obsolete *hail* healthy, from Old Norse *heill.*] —**hail′er,** *n.*

hail² (hāl) *n.* **1.** small, usually round pieces of layered ice that fall in a shower, esp. during thunderstorms. **2.** heavy shower of anything: *a hail of stones and dirt.* —*v.i.* to pour down hail (often with *it*): *It hailed for an hour.* —*v.t.* to pour down or shower something heavily (often with *on* or *upon*). [Old English *hægl, hagol* this kind of falling ice.]

Hai·le Se·las·sie (hī′lē sə las′ē) 1892–1975, emperor of Ethiopia from 1930 to 1936 and from 1941 to 1975.

hail·fel·low (*adj.,* hāl′fel′ō; *n.,* hāl′fel′ō) *adj.* cordial or friendly, esp. in a superficial manner. —*n.* also, **hail fellow.** congenial companion; comrade. Also, **hail fellow well met.** [From earlier greeting *hail, fellow.*]

Hail Mary, Ave Maria.

hail·stone (hāl′stōn′) *n.* pellet of hail.

hail·storm (hāl′stôrm′) *n.* storm in which hail falls.

Hai·phong (hī′fong′) *n.* port city in northeastern North Vietnam. Pop. (1960), 182,496.

hair (hâr) *n.* **1.** fine, threadlike outgrowth of the skin of mammals. **2.** such growths collectively, as on the head of humans or the bodies of animals. **3.** fine, threadlike outgrowth of the outer layer of plants. **4.** extremely small amount or distance; least degree: *to miss a train by a hair.* **hair of the dog (that bit one).** *Informal.* drink of an alcoholic beverage believed to relieve a hangover.

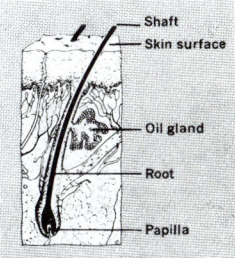
Root of a hair

not to turn a hair. to give no indication of disturbance or embarrassment; remain calm.

to a hair. with utmost exactness; precisely.

to get in one's hair. *Informal.* to annoy (someone); pester.

to let one's hair down. to relax completely; be informal.

to make one's hair stand on end. to frighten or terrify (someone).

to split hairs. to make petty or overly subtle distinctions.

to tear one's hair (out). to be most utterly exasperated.

—*adj.* **1.** of or containing hair: *a hair mattress.* **2.** for the hair: *a hair dryer.* [Old English *hær* fine, threadlike outgrowth of the skin of mammals.]

hair·breadth (hâr′bredth′, -bretth′) hair's-breadth.

at; āpe; cär; end; mē; it; īce; hot; ōld; fôrk; wood; fōōl; oil; out; up; ūse; turn; sing; thin; this; zh in treasure; ə in ago, taken, pencil, lemon, circus.

463

hair·brush (hâr'brush') *n.* brush used for grooming the hair.

hair·cloth (hâr'klôth') *n.* stiff, coarse cloth made of horsehair or camel's hair, used chiefly as an interlining or stiffening material.

hair·cut (hâr'kut') *n.* act of cutting the hair or style in which it is cut.

hair·do (hâr'dōō') *pl.* **-dos.** *n.* style in which the hair, esp. of a woman, is arranged; coiffure.

hair·dress·er (hâr'drĕs'ər) *n.* one whose job is to style, cut, and arrange hair, esp. women's hair.

hair·line (hâr'līn') *n.* **1.** outline of hair on the head, esp. around the forehead. **2.** very thin or fine line, as in printing.

hair net, net worn on the head to keep the hair in place.

hair·piece (hâr'pēs') *n.* quantity of artificial or natural hair made into a removable wig, toupee, switch, or fall and worn to cover baldness or as part of a hair style.

hair·pin (hâr'pĭn') *n.* small, two-pronged U-shaped pin usually made of wire, shell, or plastic, used by a woman to keep her hair or a hairpiece in place. —*adj.* shaped like a hairpin: *a hairpin curve in the road.*

hair·rais·ing (hâr'rā'zĭng) *adj. Informal.* causing great fear; terrifying.

hair's·breadth (hârz'brĕdth', -brĕtth') *also,* **hairs·breadth** *or* **hair·breadth.** *n.* extremely small space or distance: *to lose by a hair's-breadth.* —*adj.* very narrow or close.

hair shirt, rough shirt made of horsehair, worn next to the skin as penance or self-punishment.

hair·split·ting (hâr'splĭt'ĭng) *n.* act of making distinctions that are too subtle; pettiness. —*adj.* characterized by overly subtle distinctions or pettiness. —**hair'split'ter,** *n.*

hair·spring (hâr'sprĭng') *n.* fine coiled spring in a watch or clock that regulates the movement of the balance wheel.

hair·trig·ger (hâr'trĭg'ər) *adj.* reacting at once to the slightest stimulus: *a hair-trigger temper.*

hair trigger, trigger that can discharge a firearm with very slight pressure.

hair·y (hâr'ē) **hair·i·er, hair·i·est.** *adj.* **1.** covered with hair; having much hair; hirsute. **2.** of or resembling hair: *a hairy sweater.* —**hair'i·ness,** *n.*

Hai·ti (hā'tē) *n.* **1.** country in the Caribbean, on the western part of the island of Hispaniola. Capital, Port-au-Prince. Area, 10,714 sq. mi. Pop. (1969 est.), 4,768,000. **2.** Hispaniola.

Hai·ti·an (hā'shən, -tē ən) *n.* **1.** member or close descendant of the people of Haiti. dialect of French spoken in Haiti. Also, (*def. 2*), **Haitian Creole.** —*adj.* of or relating to Haiti, the Haitians, their dialect, or their culture.

hajj (haj) *hadj.*

haj·ji (haj'ē) *hadji.*

hake (hāk) *pl.* **hake** *or* **hakes.** *n.* any of several valuable food fish, family Gadidae, related to the cod, found in cold and temperate seas. Weight:

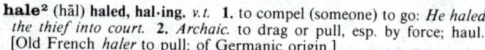

Hake

up to 8 pounds. [Possibly from Old Norse *haki* hook; because of the shape of its lower jaw.]

ha·kim¹ (hä kēm') *also,* **ha·keem.** *n.* in Muslim countries, a learned man, esp. a physician. [Arabic *hakim.*]

ha·kim² (hä kēm') *n.* in Muslim countries, a ruler, judge, or governor. [Arabic *hakim.*]

Hak·luyt, Richard (hak'lit) c.1552–1616, English geographer and historian.

Ha·ko·da·te (hä'kō dä'tā) *n.* port city on the southern coast of Hokkaido, Japan. Pop. (1968), 249,000.

Ha·la·kah (hä lä'кнä) *also,* **Ha·la·chah.** *n.* in Judaism, civil and ritual law of rabbinical literature. Distinguished from **Haggadah.** [Hebrew *halākhāh* rule, tradition.]

hal·berd (hal'bərd) *also,* **hal·bert** (hal'bərt). *n.* poleax with a long spear and hook-shaped blade, used as a weapon, esp. in fifteenth- and sixteenth-century Europe. [French *hallebarde,* from Middle High German *helmbarde* literally, ax with a long handle, from *helm* handle + *barde* ax.]

hal·berd·ier (hal'bər dēr') *n.* soldier or guard armed with a halberd.

hal·cy·on (hal'sē ən) *adj.* undisturbed; peaceful; happy: *to yearn for the halcyon days of that springtime long ago.* —*n.* kingfisher, the bird with the legendary power of calming the sea at the winter solstice to protect its floating nest during the period of incubation. [Latin *halcyōn* kingfisher, from Greek *(h)alkyōn.*]

Halberd

hale¹ (hāl) **hal·er, hal·est.** *adj.* in good physical condition; healthy; robust. Also, **hale and hearty.** [Old English *hāl.*]

hale² (hāl) **haled, hal·ing.** *v.t.* **1.** to compel (someone) to go: *He haled the thief into court.* **2.** *Archaic.* to drag or pull, esp. by force; haul. [Old French *haler* to pull; of Germanic origin.]

Hale (hāl) **1. Edward Everett.** 1822–1909, U.S. author and Unitarian clergyman. **2. Nathan.** 1755–76, U.S. patriot hanged as a spy by the British.

half (haf) *pl.* **halves.** *n.* **1.** either of two equal parts into which anything is or may be divided: *A pint is half of a quart. She will be away for a year and a half.* **2.** either of two approximately equal parts: *to be awake half the night, to eat half a cantaloupe.* **3.** *Sports.* **a.** either of two time periods into which certain games are divided. **b.** intermission period between two halves of a sporting event, as in football or basketball. **c.** one of the two divisions of an inning in baseball. **d.** halfback. **4.** *Informal.* half dollar. **5. by half,** by a great deal; considerably. **6. in half.** into two equal or approximately equal parts. **7. one's better half.** *Informal.* one's husband or wife; spouse. —*adj.* **1.** being one of two equal parts; forming a half. **2.** being or amounting to approximately one half. **3.** lacking in some part; incomplete; partial: *half answers.* ▲ often used in combination with a noun to form compound words, as *half-breed* or *half moon.* —*adv.* **1.** to exactly or approximately half of the full amount, degree, or capacity: *The theater was half empty.* **2.** to a great extent; nearly: *The house was half hidden by the trees.* **3.** not completely; partially; *to leave an apple half eaten.* ▲ often used in combination with an adjective to form compound words, as *half-baked.* **4. not half bad.** rather good. [Old English *h(e)alf* side, either of two equal parts.]

half-and-half (haf'ən haf') *n.* **1.** mixture that is half one thing and half another, esp. a liquid composed of half milk and half cream. **2.** *British.* mixture of two malt beverages, esp. one composed of half bitter ale and half mild ale. —*adj.* that is half one thing and half another. —*adv.* in two equal parts.

half·back (haf'bak') *n.* **1.** either of two football players whose positions are behind the line of scrimmage and who are used as ball carriers, esp. in plays around the ends. **2.** position played by either of these players.

half-baked (haf'bākt') *adj.* **1.** not completely cooked; underdone. **2.** *Informal.* badly planned; incomplete; inadequate: *a half-baked plan.* **3.** *Informal.* lacking experience or common sense; stupid: *half-baked technicians.*

half-blood (haf'blud') *n.* **1.** one who is related to another through one parent only. **2.** half-breed.

half blood, relationship between persons who have only one parent in common.

half-blood·ed (haf'blud'id) *adj.* **1.** born of parents of different races. **2.** being related to another through one parent only.

half boot, boot reaching about halfway between the ankle and the knee.

half-breed (haf'brēd') *n.* one whose parents are of different races, esp. an offspring of a Caucasian and an American Indian. —*adj.* half-blooded; hybrid.

half brother, brother related through one parent only.

half-caste (haf'kast') *n.* **1.** anyone of mixed race; half-breed. **2.** offspring of one European and one Asian parent; Eurasian.

half cock, position in which the hammer of a gun is raised halfway, causing the trigger to be locked.

half-cocked (haf'kokt') *adj.* **1.** (of a gun) having the hammer at the position of half cock. **2.** lacking adequate forethought or planning; rash: *a half-cocked scheme for getting rich.* **3. to go off half-cocked** (or **at half cock**). **a.** (of a gun) to fire prematurely. **b.** *Informal.* to act or speak too hastily or without adequate forethought.

half crown, former British coin equal to two-and-one-half shillings.

half dollar, coin of the United States equal to fifty cents.

half eagle, former gold coin of the United States equal to five dollars.

half gainer, gainer (*def. 2b*).

half-heart·ed (haf'här'tid) *adj.* lacking interest or enthusiasm; indifferent; perfunctory. —**half'heart'ed·ly,** *adv.* —**half'heart'ed·ness,** *n.*

Syn. Half-hearted, lukewarm, indifferent indicate lack of complete involvement or interest. **Half-hearted** suggests that passion or enthusiasm is absent: *The boys made a half-hearted effort to climb the hill.* **Lukewarm** implies a coolness that is really neither for nor against: *The lawyer's lukewarm summation weighed heavily against his client.* **Indifferent** implies neutrality, a lack of concern for any specific course of action or solution: *The boy was indifferent to his sister's dating problems.*

half hitch, knot made by passing the end of a rope around the rope, then through the loop thus formed, and finally drawing the end tight.

Half hitch

half-hour (haf'our') *n.* **1.** half of an hour; thirty minutes.

2. point thirty minutes past a given hour: *The bus runs on the half-hour.* —*adj.* of, lasting for, or occurring at the half-hour. —**half′-hour′ly,** *adv., adj.*

half-life (haf′līf′) *n.* time required by any given quantity of a radioactive isotope to decay to half that quantity.

half-line (haf′līn′) *n.* part of a straight line extending in one direction from a point on the line.

half-mast (haf′mast′) *n.* position about halfway down from the top of a mast, staff, or pole, used esp. as a sign of mourning or as a distress signal. Also, **half′-staff′.**

half moon 1. moon when only half of its disk appears illuminated. See *moon* for illustration. **2.** anything in the shape of a half moon.

half nelson, wrestling hold made from behind by hooking one arm under the opponent's corresponding arm and pressing the hand across the back of his neck.

half note, musical note having one-half the time value of a whole note. Also, **min′im.** See *note* for illustration.

half-pen-ny (hā′pə nē, hāp′nē) *pl.,* **half-pence** (hā′pəns) or **half-pen-nies.** *n.* coin of Great Britain equal to half a penny. —*adj.* **1.** having the value of a halfpenny. **2.** having very little value; insignificant.

half-plane (haf′plān′) *n.* part of a plane extending in one direction from a line in the plane.

half sister, sister related through one parent only.

half-slip (haf′slip′) *n.* slip that extends from the waist down.

half-sole (haf′sōl′) **-soled, -sol-ing.** *v.t.* to repair (a shoe or boot) by putting on a new half sole.

half sole, that part of the sole of a shoe or boot extending from the arch to the toe.

half sovereign, former gold coin of Great Britain equal to ten shillings.

half-space (haf′spās′) *n.* part of space extending in one direction from a plane.

half-staff (haf′staf′) *n.* half-mast.

half step 1. *Music.* difference in pitch between any two adjacent keys on a keyboard instrument. Also, **half tone, sem′i-tone′. 2.** military marching step fifteen inches in length.

half-tim-bered (haf′tim′bərd) *adj.* (of a building) constructed of a framework of timbers, having the spaces filled with masonry or plaster.

half-tone (haf′tōn′) *n.* **1.** picture consisting of dots that vary in size in proportion to the gradations of tones of the subject, with the small dots representing the light tones and the large dots representing the dark tones. **2.** photoengraving process by which such a picture is made, used esp. for reproducing photographs and other pictures with tones, as in books. **3.** any intermediate tone between a high light and a deep shadow in art or photography.

half tone, half step *(def. 1).*

half-track (haf′trak′) *also,* **half·track.** *n.* armored, military vehicle having wheels in front and caterpillar tracks in the rear.

half-way (haf′wā′) *adv.* **1.** at or to the midway point; half the distance: *to climb halfway up a mountain.* **2. to meet halfway,** to agree to make concessions to; compromise with: *The union met management halfway on the request for raises.* —*adj.* **1.** midway between two points. **2.** partial; inadequate: *halfway measures.*

half-wit (haf′wit′) *n.* **1.** mentally retarded or feeble-minded person. **2.** foolish, idiotic, or stupid person. —**half′-wit′-ted,** *adj.*

hal-i-but (hal′ə bət, hol′-) *pl.,* **-but** or **-buts.** *n.* **1.** either of two large flatfishes, genus *Hippoglossus,* found in northern waters of the Atlantic and Pacific oceans and highly valued as a source of food and vitamin oil. Weight: Atlan-

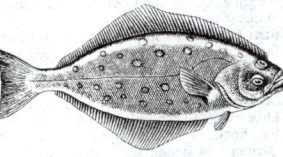

Atlantic halibut

tic halibut—up to 700 pounds. Pacific halibut—female, up to 500 pounds; male, up to 50 pounds. **2.** any of several related flatfishes. [Middle English *hāly* HOLY + *butte* flatfish; because it was eaten on holy days.]

Hal-i-car-nas-sus (hal′ə kär nas′əs) *n.* ancient city in southwestern Asia Minor, site of the famous mausoleum that was one of the seven wonders of the ancient world.

hal-ide (hal′īd, -id, hā′līd, -lid) *n.* binary compound of a halogen with an element or radical, as sodium chloride. [Greek *hals* salt + -IDE.]

hal-i-dom (hal′ə dəm) *also,* **hal-i-dome** (hal′ə dōm′). *n. Archaic.* **1.** holy place; sanctuary. **2.** anything regarded as holy; sacred relic. [Old English *hāligdōm,* from *hālig* holy + *-dōm* state, condition.]

Hal-i-fax (hal′ə faks′) *n.* port city in southeastern Canada and the capital of Nova Scotia. Pop. (1966), 86,792.

hal-ite (hal′īt, hā′līt) *n.* rock salt. [Greek *hals* salt + -ITE².]

hal-i-to-sis (hal′ə tō′sis) *n.* condition in which the breath has an unpleasant or offensive odor. [Latin *hālitus* breath + -OSIS.]

hall (hôl) *n.* **1.** passageway through a building; corridor. **2.** passageway or room at the entrance to a building; vestibule or lobby. **3.** room or building in which public meetings, entertainment, or lectures are held: *a concert hall.* **4.a.** room or building in a school, college, or university set aside for a particular purpose: *a residence hall, the dining hall.* **b.** occupants of such a room or building. **5.** building housing public offices. **6.** *British.* manor house on the estate of a nobleman. [Old English *heall* large roofed place.]

Hall, Charles Martin (hôl) 1863–1914, U.S. chemist.

Hal-le (hä′lə) *n.* city in west-central East Germany. Pop. (1968), 263,928.

hal-le-lu-jah (hal′ə lōō′yə) *also,* **hal-le-lu-iah, al-le-lu-ia.** *interj.* praise ye the Lord! ▲ used in songs of praise or thanksgiving. —*n.* hymn or other musical composition based on the word *hallelujah.* [Hebrew *hallelūyāh.*]

Hal-ley, Ed-mund (hal′ē; ed′mənd) 1656–1742, English astronomer, noted for his research on comets.

Halley's comet, a comet that can be seen from the earth approximately every seventy-six years. It was last seen in 1910. [From Edmund HALLEY, who discovered this comet's cycle.]

hal-liard (hal′yərd) halyard.

hall-mark (hôl′märk′) *n.* **1.** official symbol stamped on gold and silver items to guarantee their high quality or purity. **2.** any mark that indicates high quality or purity. **3.** distinguishing quality or characteristic: *Suspense is a hallmark of a good mystery.* —*v.t.* to stamp with a hallmark. [From the *mark* indicating quality or purity that was stamped on gold or silver articles in the Goldsmiths' *Hall* in London, the center of the guild of goldsmiths in charge of certification.]

hall of fame 1. room or building containing tablets, busts, or other commemorative items honoring eminent people: *the baseball hall of fame.* **2. Hall of Fame.** such a building in New York City commemorating famous Americans.

hal-loo (hə lōō′) *also,* **hal-loa** (hə lō′). *interj.* used to attract attention or to urge on hounds in fox hunting. —*n. pl.,* **-loos,** call or cry of *halloo.* —*v.i., v.t.,* **-looed, -loo-ing. 1.** to call in order to attract the attention of (someone). **2.** to urge on (hounds) with cries of *halloo.* **3.** to shout. [Possibly from Old French *halloer* to follow with shouts; imitative.]

hal-low (hal′ō) *v.t.* **1.** to make or select as holy; sanctify; consecrate. **2.** to regard or honor as sacred or holy; venerate. [Old English *hālgian.*]

hal-lowed (hal′ōd, -ō id) *adj.* **1.** made holy; sanctified; consecrated. **2.** regarded as sacred or holy; venerated. —**hal′lowed-ness,** *n.*

Hal-low-een (hal′ō wēn′, -ō ēn′, hol′-) *also,* **Hal-low-e′en.** *n.* the eve of All Saints' Day, now celebrated by children in costumes and masks who collect treats and threaten to play tricks. October 31. [Short for *all hallow even* eve of All Saints, from ALL + *hallow* (from Old English *hālga* holy person) + EVEN².]

Hal-low-mas (hal′ō məs, -mas′) *n.* All Saints' Day.

hal-lu-ci-nate (hə lōō′sə nāt′) **-nat-ed, -nat-ing.** *v.i.* to have hallucinations.

hal-lu-ci-na-tion (hə lōō′sə nā′shən) *n.* **1.** false sensory perception in which a person experiences as real something that is not there. **2.** that which is falsely perceived: *The voices he heard were actually hallucinations.* [Latin *hallūcinātiō* wandering of the mind, possibly going back to Greek *halýein* to be distraught, wander.]

hal-lu-cin-o-gen (hə lōō′si nə jen′, hal′yə sin′ə-) *n.* any of several drugs that cause hallucinations, such as mescaline or LSD. [HALLUCIN(ATION) + -GEN.] —**hal-lu′cin-o-gen′ic,** *adj.*

hall-way (hôl′wā′) *n.* **1.** passageway through a building; corridor; hall. **2.** entrance hall; foyer.

ha-lo (hā′lō) *pl.,* **-los** or **-loes.** *n.* **1.** in artistic representation, a ring or disk of light surrounding the head of a deity, saint, or other sacred figure; nimbus. **2.** circle of light that appears to surround the sun, moon, or other celestial body, caused by the reflection and refraction of light by ice crystals in the earth's upper atmosphere. **3.** aura of glory or splendor surrounding a person or thing held in high esteem or reverence. —*v.t.* to surround or invest with a halo. [Latin *halōs* circle of light appearing to surround the sun or moon, from Greek *halōs* threshing floor (around which the oxen moved in a circular path), disk of the sun or moon.]

hal-o-gen (hal′ə jən) *n.* any of the very active nonmetallic elements fluorine, chlorine, bromine, iodine, or astatine that combine readily with metals to form salts. [Greek *hals* salt + -GEN.]

Hals, Frans (häls; fräns) c.1580–1666, Dutch portrait painter.

halt¹ (hôlt) *n.* **1.** temporary cessation of movement; stop. **2. to call a halt,** to bring to a stop. —*v.t., v.i.* to stop or cause to stop. —*interj.* stop. ▲ used esp. as a military command. [German *Halt.*]

halt² (hôlt) *v.i.* **1.** to proceed imperfectly or faultily as in speech, logic, or meter in verse; falter. **2.** to be indecisive; hesitate; vacillate.

at; āpe; cär; end; mē; it; īce; hot; ōld; fôrk; wood; fōōl; oil; out; up; ūse; turn; sing; thin; this; zh in treasure; ə in ago, taken, pencil, lemon, circus.

3. *Archaic.* to be lame; limp. —*adj. Archaic.* unable to walk without limping; lame. —*n. Archaic.* lameness; limp. [Old English *h(e)alt* lame.] —**halt′ing,** *adj.* —**halt′ing·ly,** *adv.*

hal·ter (hôl′tər) *n.* **1.** rope or strap usually designed to fit around the nose and over or behind the ears, used for leading or tying an animal. **2.** abbreviated bodice, worn by women and girls, usually fastening behind the neck and across the lower back, leaving the arms and back bare. **3.** rope used for hanging someone; noose. **4.** death by hanging. —*v.t.* **1.** to put a halter on or secure with a halter: *to halter a horse.* **2.** to hang (someone). [Old English *hælfter* rope with a noose for leading a horse.]

hal·vah (häl vä′, häl′vä) *n.* sweet, flaky candy consisting esp. of ground sesame seeds and honey. [Yiddish *halva,* going back to Arabic *halwā* candy.]

halve (hav) **halved, halv·ing.** *v.t.* **1.** to divide into two equal parts. **2.** to share equally. **3.** to reduce to half. **4.** to play (a hole) in golf in the same number of strokes as one's opponent. [Middle English *halven,* from HALF.]

halves (havz) plural of **half. 1. by halves. a.** incompletely; imperfectly. **b.** half-heartedly. **2. to go halves.** to share equally; divide in half.

hal·yard (hal′yərd) *also,* **hal·liard.** *n. Nautical.* rope or tackle used for hoisting or lowering something, such as a sail, yard, or flag. [Modification (influenced by YARD²) of Middle English *halier,* from *halen* to HALE², pull.]

ham (ham) *n.* **1.** meat from the hind leg or shoulder of a hog, usually cured and smoked. **2.** hind leg of an animal, esp. a hog. **3. hams.** back part of the thighs and the buttocks. **4.** back or bend of the knee. **5.** *Informal.* actor who overacts or who exaggerates his performance. **6.** *Informal.* amateur radio operator. —*v.i., v.t.,* **hammed, ham·ming.** *Informal.* (of an actor) to act in an exaggerated way; overact (usually with *up*). [Old English *hamm* bend of the knee.]

Ham (ham) *n.* in the Old Testament, second son of Noah, considered to be the ancestor of the African races.

Ham·a·dan (ham′ə dan′) *n.* city in northwestern Iran. Pop. (1963 est.), 114,600.

ham·a·dry·ad (ham′ə drī′əd, -ad) *n.* wood nymph in Greek and Roman mythology who inhabited or took the shape of a tree. [Latin *Hamādryades* (plural), from Greek *Hamādryades,* from *hama* together with + *drŷs* tree; because the life of each nymph was connected with that of her tree.]

Ha·man (hā′mən) *n.* in the Old Testament, the prime minister of Persia who was executed when his plot to massacre the Jews was discovered by Esther, the queen.

Ham·burg (ham′bûrg′; *German* häm′boork′) *n.* port city in northern West Germany, on the Elbe River. Pop. (1968), 1,826,411.

ham·burg·er (ham′bûr′gər, -bər-) *n.* **1.** ground beef. **2.** such meat shaped into a round, flat patty, and cooked. **3.** sandwich consisting of such a patty in a round bun. Also, **burg′er, ham′burg′.** [Short for *Hamburger steak,* from *Hamburg* German city.]

hame (hām) *n.* either of two curved wood or metal pieces, located on either side of a draft animal's collar, to which the traces and other straps are fastened. [Middle Dutch *hame* yoke for the neck.]

Ha·mil·car Bar·ca (hə mil′kär bär′kə, häm′əl kär′) 270–c.228 B.C., Carthaginian general and father of Hannibal.

Ham·il·ton (ham′əl tən) *n.* **1. Alexander.** 1757–1804, U.S. statesman and first secretary of the treasury. **2. Edith.** 1867–1963, U.S. classical scholar, educator, and author. **3.** port city in southern Ontario, Canada, at the western end of Lake Ontario. Pop. (1966), 298,121. **4.** city in southwestern Ohio. Pop. (1960), 72,354. **5.** capital and chief city of Bermuda. Pop. (1960), 2763.

Ham·ite (ham′īt) *n.* **1.** descendant of Ham. **2.** one of a group of people in northern and eastern Africa, most of whom speak a Hamitic language, such as the Berbers.

Ham·it·ic (ha mit′ik, hə-) *n.* group of languages belonging to the Semito-Hamitic language family. These languages, including Berber, Somali, ancient Egyptian, and Coptic, are spoken predominantly in northern and eastern Africa. —*adj.* of or relating to Ham, the Hamites, or their languages.

ham·let (ham′lit) *n.* cluster of houses in the country; small rural village. [Old French *hamelet,* diminutive of *hamel* village, diminutive of *ham;* of Germanic origin.]

Ham·let (ham′lit) *n.* central character in William Shakespeare's play *Hamlet.*

Ham·mar·skjöld, Dag (hä′mər shôld′, -shəld, ham′ər-; *däg*) 1905–61, Swedish statesman and secretary general of the United Nations from 1953 to 1961.

ham·mer (ham′ər) *n.* **1.** tool with a solid head, usually of metal, set crosswise on a handle, usually used for driving nails and beating or shaping metal. **2.** anything resembling such a tool in shape or function, as the lever that strikes a bell in a clock. **3.** part of a gun that strikes the firing pin, causing the gun to go off; cock. **4.** any of the padded

mallets in a piano which, when activated by the depression of a key, strike the strings. **5.** *Anatomy.* largest and outermost of the three small bones in the middle ear, shaped like a hammer. Also, **mal′le·us. 6.** metal sphere of various weights attached to a wire, used for throwing in track and field contests. **7.** small mallet used by an auctioneer to indicate that an item has been sold. **8. to come** (or **go**) **under the hammer.** to be for sale or sold at auction. **9. hammer and tongs,** with great energy and force; vigorously; violently. —*v.t.* **1.** to strike repeatedly with, or as with, a hammer; drive; pound: *to hammer nails into a wall.* **2.** to pound into shape or form with a hammer: *to hammer a bowl out of metal.* **3.** to fasten with a hammer, as by nailing: *to hammer a picture hook.* **4.** to force by constant repetition, as of words, ideas, or actions: *They could not hammer any common sense into him.* —*v.i.* **1.** to strike blows repeatedly with, or as with, a hammer; pound: *The carpenter hammered all day.* **2. to hammer away** (**at**). **a.** to work industriously or persistently on: *He hammered away at the chemistry problem for an hour.* **b.** to repeat for emphasis or to make something understood: *The mayor hammered away at the need for federal aid.* **3. to hammer out. a.** to pound into shape or form with a hammer: *to hammer out a tray.* **b.** to flatten or remove with, or as with, a hammer: *to hammer out a dent.* **c.** to work out with great care and effort, esp. in collaboration with another person: *It took many meetings to hammer out a settlement.* **d.** to bring about by pounding: *He hammered out a tune on his xylophone.* [Old English *hamor* tool with a head and a handle.] —**ham′mer·er,** *n.*

hammer and sickle, communist emblem, consisting of a crossed sickle and hammer and symbolizing the alliance of workers and peasants.

ham·mer·head (ham′-ər hed′) *n.* **1.** shark whose head extends on each side in a broad, flat lobe, resembling a double-headed hammer. **2.** head of a hammer.

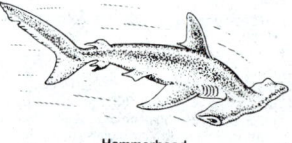

Hammerhead

hammer lock, wrestling hold in which an opponent's arm is twisted and held in a right-angle position behind his back.

ham·mock (ham′ək) *n.* swinging bed made from a long piece of canvas, leather, or netting hung between two vertical supports, such as trees or poles. [Spanish *hamaca;* of Carib origin.]

Ham·mond (ham′ənd) *n.* city in northwestern Indiana. Pop. (1970), 107,790.

Ham·mu·ra·bi (hä′moo rä′bē) *n.* Babylonian king of the eighteenth century B.C., noted for his code of laws.

ham·per¹ (ham′pər) *v.t.* to obstruct the action or progress of; impede: *Stalled cars hampered snow-removal efforts.* [Of uncertain origin.]

ham·per² (ham′pər) *n.* large basket or other receptacle, usually with a cover: *a hamper for soiled clothes.* [Earlier *hanaper,* from Old French *hanapier* basket for cups, from *hanap* cup; of Germanic origin.]

Hamp·ton (hamp′tən) *n.* city in southeastern Virginia. Pop. (1970), 120,779.

Hampton Roads, a channel of the Chesapeake Bay in southeastern Virginia, site of the battle in 1862 between the *Monitor* and the *Merrimac.*

ham·ster (ham′stər) *n.* any of various burrowing, mouselike rodents, family Cricetidae, found in Europe, Asia, and Africa, having a stout body, stumpy tail, and large cheek pouches. Length: 6 inches. [German *Hamster.*]

ham·string (ham′string′) *n.* **1.** tendon at the back of the human knee. **2.** great tendon at the back of the hock of a quadruped. —*v.t.,* **-strung** (-strung′), **-string·ing. 1.** to cripple or disable (a person or animal) by cutting the hamstring. **2.** to destroy the efficiency of; make ineffective.

Han (hän) *n.* **1.** Chinese dynasty, 206 B.C. to A.D. 220, during which some contact was made with the West and Buddhism was introduced. **2.** river in east-central China, flowing southeast from the Yangtze.

Han·cock, John (han′kok′) 1737–93, U.S. patriot and statesman, first signer of the Declaration of Independence.

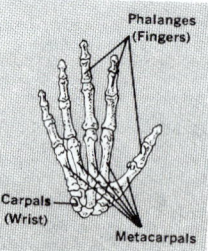

Phalanges (Fingers)

Carpals (Wrist)

Metacarpals

Bones of the hand

hand (hand) *n.* **1.** end of the forelimb in man, consisting of the wrist, five fingers including an opposable thumb, and the metacarpus, the area

at; āpe; cär; end; mē; it; īce; hot; ōld; fôrk; wood; fōōl; oil; out; up; ūse; turn; sing; thin; this; zh in treasure; ə in ago, taken, pencil, lemon, circus.

between the wrist and the fingers. It is used esp. for holding and grasping. **2.** end of a limb in animals which corresponds in function to the human hand, such as that of an ape. **3.** anything resembling a hand in shape or function, as the pointers on a clock or the pointer on a sign to indicate direction. **4.** *also,* **hands. a.** personal possession: *The letter fell into the wrong hands.* **b.** custody; care: *She is in good hands.* **c.** control; power: *to take the law into one's own hands.* **5.** direction in relation to the position of the hand; side: *She was at his left hand.* **6.** workman employed in manual labor; laborer: *the hands on a farm.* **7.** one who produces a particular kind of work: *The book was translated by several hands.* **8.** member of a group or crew: *All hands on deck.* **9.** workmanship; skill; performance: *the hand of a master.* **10.** manner of doing something: *a deft hand.* **11.** participation or influence in something; share; role: *Each of them had a hand in the matter.* **12.** person in reference to his skill at doing something: *She was an old hand at diving.* **13.** aid; assistance: *He gave me a hand in moving the piano.* **14.** round of applause; clapping: *to give the performer a hand.* **15.a.** single round of a card game. **b.** cards held by a player during a round. **c.** any of the players. **16.** person or thing through which something passes; source. ▲ used with an ordinal number: *to get information at first hand.* **17.** handwriting style; penmanship: *an illegible hand.* **18.** person's signature. **19.** promise or pledge, as of marriage or to seal an agreement. **20.** unit of measure equal to four inches, or the approximate breadth of the hand, used in expressing the height of a horse.

at hand. a. accessible or ready for use. **b.** near in time; close.
at the hand (or **hands**) **of.** by the action of: *to suffer at the hands of the enemy.*
by hand. with the hands, as opposed to mechanical means: *to wash clothes by hand.*
from hand to hand. from one person to another.
from hand to mouth. using everything for one's immediate needs without considering the future: *to live from hand to mouth.*
hand and foot. a. with both hands and feet restricted: *bound hand and foot.* **b.** totally; diligently: *to wait on someone hand and foot.*
hand in (or **and**) **glove.** in close association and cooperation; intimately: *to work hand in glove.*
hand in hand. a. holding each other's hand. **b.** in close cooperation; together.
hand over fist. rapidly and in great quantity: *to make money hand over fist.*
hands down. with great ease; effortlessly: *to win hands down.*
hands off. do not interfere or touch; keep away. ▲ used as a command.
hands up. hold your hands over your head. ▲ used as a command, esp. by someone pointing a gun.
in hand. a. in one's possession. **b.** under one's control: *The police had the mob well in hand.* **c.** in the process of being carried out: *to concentrate on the matter in hand.*
off one's hands. out of one's control or responsibility.
on hand. a. readily available for use: *to have cash on hand.* **b.** present: *There was a large crowd on hand to greet the president.*
on one's hands. in one's possession or control, esp. as a burden: *He had time on his hands.*
on the one hand. from one side or viewpoint.
on the other hand. from another side or viewpoint, esp. the opposite one.
out of hand. a. out of one's control: *The dog got out of hand.* **b.** without delay or hesitation; immediately: *to act out of hand.* **c.** ended; finished.
the upper hand. superior position; advantage.
to change hands. to pass from one owner to another.
to eat out of one's hand. to be completely devoted to or controlled by someone: *The king had his subjects eating out of his hand.*
to force one's hand. to compel someone to act before he had intended to act.
to hand. a. within reach; accessible. **b.** in or into one's possession: *to bring land to hand.*
to have one's hands full. to be occupied with as much as or more than one can do: *She had her hands full with five children.*
to join hands. a. to become business partners or associates. **b.** to get married.
to keep one's hand in. to maintain one's interest or skill in; to remain proficient in.
to lay one's hands on. a. to get possession of; seize. **b.** to injure or harm; attack. **c.** to touch in blessing or consecration, as in the rites of confirmation.
to tie one's hands. to thwart one's efforts; prevent one from acting.
to try one's hand at. to make an attempt at doing (something).
to turn (or **put**) **one's hand to.** to begin to work at; undertake: *He turned his hand to painting.*
to wash one's hands of. to refuse to associate with or be responsible for any longer.

with a heavy hand. a. lacking sensitivity; clumsily. **b.** in an oppressive manner; overbearingly.
with a high hand. in an autocratic way; arrogantly.
—*v.t.* **1.** to give or pass with the hand; transmit: *He handed the book to the librarian.* **2.** to lead or assist with the hand: *He handed the lady into a taxicab.* **3. to hand down. a.** to pass along in succession, as to one's heirs: *The wedding dress was handed down from mother to daughter.* **b.** to announce (a decision) to the court. **4. to hand in.** to give, as to someone in authority; deliver: *He handed in his resignation.* **5. to hand on.** to pass along in succession; hand along. **6. to hand out.** to give out to people; distribute. **7. to hand over.** to yield or give up to another. —*adj.* **1.** of, relating to, or for the hand or hands: *one's hand size, hand lotion.* **2.** performed or operated by hand: *a hand tool.* **3.** suited to be held in or worn on the hand: *a hand mirror.* [Old English *hand* end of the arm from wrist to fingers, possession, custody, authority, direction.]

hand·bag (hand′bag′) *n.* **1.** bag or case, as of leather, used by women for carrying small articles, such as cosmetics and a wallet; pocketbook. **2.** small traveling suitcase.
hand·ball (hand′bôl′) *n.* **1.** game in which the players, normally two or four, alternately hit a small rubber ball against a wall with the hand, which is usually gloved. **2.** small rubber ball used in this game.
hand·bar·row (hand′bar′ō) *n.* flat, rectangular frame having handles at each end for lifting and carrying loads.
hand·bill (hand′bil′) *n.* written or printed announcement or advertisement, intended to be distributed by hand.
hand·book (hand′bŏŏk′) *n.* **1.** concise book of information or instructions on a particular subject; manual: *photography handbook.* **2.** travel guidebook. —*Syn.* **1.** see manual.
hand brake, brake operated by pressure of the hand, as on a bicycle.
hand·breadth (hand′bredth′, -bretth′) *n.* unit of linear measurement, based on the width of the hand, varying from 2½ to 4 inches.
hand·cart (hand′kärt′) *n.* small cart pushed or drawn by hand; pushcart.
hand·cuff (hand′kuf′) *n.* either of a pair of metal rings joined by a short chain, designed to be locked around the wrist of a person to be restrained, such as a prisoner. ▲ usually used in the plural. —*v.t.* to restrain by enclosing the wrists in handcuffs; manacle.

Handcuffs

hand·ed (han′did) *adj.* **1.** of, characterized by, performed with, or designed to be used by (a specified) hand: *a left-handed pitch, left-handed scissors.* **2.** of, characterized by, or performed with (a specified number of) hands or people: *a four-handed piano duet, a game of three-handed bridge.* ▲ used in combination with other adjectives and hyphenated in both definitions.
Han·del, George Frederick (hand′əl) 1685–1759, British composer, born in Germany.
hand·ful (hand′fŏŏl′) *pl.,* **-fuls.** *n.* **1.** amount that the hand can hold at one time. **2.** small number or quantity. **3.** *Informal.* someone or something that is as much as one can handle: *That unruly child is a real handful.*
hand grenade, small explosive missile designed to be thrown by hand, detonated by a fuse.
hand·gun (hand′gun′) *n.* firearm that can be held and fired with one hand; pistol; revolver.
hand·hold (hand′hōld′) *n.* something that can be grasped with the hand, as for support.
hand·i·cap (hand′dē kap′) *n.* **1.** race or contest in which opponents of unequal ability are given certain advantages or disadvantages in an attempt to equalize the competition. **2.** advantage or disadvantage given in such a contest. **3.** anything that places a person at a disadvantage and hampers his achievement, esp. a physical disability. —*v.t.,* **-capped, -cap·ping. 1.** to place at a disadvantage; hamper: *His poor eyesight handicaps him in his work.* **2.** (in a contest) to give one or more handicaps to: *to handicap the opponent.* **3.** to try to predict the winners of (races or other contests): *to handicap the races.* [From *hand in cap;* possibly alluding to a way of drawing lots.] —**hand′i·cap′per,** *n.*
hand·i·craft (han′dē kraft′) *n.* **1.** trade, occupation, or art in which great skill with the hands is required, as in working with mosaics or leather. **2.** skill in working with the hands; manual expertise. **3.** object made or work done by a skilled hand. [Modification (influenced by HANDIWORK) of obsolete *handcraft* manual skill, from Old English *handcræft.*] —**hand′i·crafts′man,** *n.*
hand·i·work (han′dē wurk′) *n.* **1.** work done by hand. **2.** product of one's work or action. [Old English *handgeweorc.*]
hand·ker·chief (hang′kar chif, -chēf′) *n.* **1.** soft piece of cloth, usually square, used esp. to wipe the nose or brow or worn as an accessory. **2.** larger piece of cloth worn around the head or neck; kerchief. [HAND + KERCHIEF.]

---

at; āpe; cär; end; mē; it; īce; hot; ōld; fôrk; wood; fōōl; oil; out; up; ūse; turn; sing; thin; this; zh in treasure; ə in ago, taken, pencil, lemon, circus.

han·dle (hand′əl) *n.* **1.** that part of an object which is intended to be grasped by the hand: *to carry a suitcase by the handle.* **2.** that which provides an opportunity for achieving an end: *He took care to give her no handle against him* (Langhorne, 1770). **3.** *Slang.* individual's name. **4. to fly off the handle.** to become very angry suddenly. —*v.t.,* **-dled, -dling. 1.** to touch or hold with the hand or hands: *Please do not handle the glassware.* **2.** to work at with the hands: *to handle clay skillfully.* **3.** to represent, manage, control, or train: *to handle a group of children, to handle a fighter. Which lawyer will handle your case?* **4.** to act on or toward; deal or cope with: *to handle a problem, to handle a customer politely.* **5.** to have business dealings in; specialize or trade in: *That company handles exports.* —*v.i.* to act or respond to being handled: *This drill handles nicely.* [Old English *handlian* to touch with the hands, deal with, from HAND.]
Syn. *v.t.* **Handle, manipulate** mean to manage or use with skill. **Handle** means to manage or use with the hands, or as if with hands, in an easy and competent manner: *The mother taught the child to handle a knife and fork.* **Manipulate** means to manage or control effectively and implies technical skill in handling something: *The man manipulated the puppets by wires and strings.*

handlebar mustache, thick mustache extending in a prominent curve to either side.

han·dle·bars (hand′əl bärz′) *also,* **han·dle·bar.** *n.* usually curved steering bar connected with the front wheel of a bicycle, motorcycle, or similar vehicle, having right and left ends extending toward the rider, often with a grip for the rider to hold.

han·dler (hand′lər) *n.* **1.** one who or that which handles anything. **2.** one who helps to train a boxer or is his second during a boxing match. **3.** one who trains or shows a dog or other animal.

hand·made (hand′mād′) *adj.* made by hand rather than by machine.

hand·maid (hand′mād′) *n.* female servant or personal attendant. Also, **hand′maid′en.**

hand-me-down (hand′mē doun′) *n.* piece of clothing previously worn by one person, given to another for additional wear.

hand organ, portable musical instrument combining features of a pipe organ and a music box, played by means of a hand crank.

hand·out (hand′out′) *n.* **1.** food, clothing, or money given out to a beggar. **2.** prepared news story or statement released to the press for free publication. **3.** anything handed out without charge.

hand·pick (hand′pik′) *v.t.* **1.** to collect or pick by hand. **2.** to choose carefully, as for quality: *to hand-pick fabric for a dress.* **3.** to select personally or for a particular reason, esp. for self-serving reasons: *to hand-pick a commissioner.*

hand·rail (hand′rāl′) *n.* railing designed to be grasped by the hand, used esp. as a guard on stairs or at the edge of a balcony.

hand·saw (hand′sô′) *n.* saw operated by hand.

hand·sel (hand′səl) *also,* **han·sel.** *n.* **1.** gift given as a token of good luck at the beginning of something new, as a new year. **2.** first experience of anything, considered as a sample of what is to come. **3.** first installment, given as a promise of further payment. —*v.t.,* **-seled** or **-selled, -sel·ing** or **-sel·ling. 1.** to give a handsel to. **2.** to inaugurate with ceremony. **3.** to do or experience for the first time. [Old Norse *handsal* concluding a bargain by shaking hands, promise; literally, hand sale.]

hand·set (hand′set′) *n.* telephone handle containing both the receiver and the transmitter.

hand·shake (hand′shāk′) *n.* act of clasping and shaking each other's right hand as a sign of greeting, friendliness, or agreement.

hand·some (han′səm) **-som·er, -som·est.** *adj.* **1.** having a pleasing, often dignified appearance; good-looking: *a handsome man, a handsome desk.* **2.** considerable in size or quantity; relatively large: *a handsome contribution to medical research.* **3.** characterized by generosity; gracious. [Middle English *handsom* easy to handle, from HAND + -SOME¹.] —**hand′some·ly,** *adv.* —**hand′some·ness,** *n.* —**Syn. 1.** see **beautiful.**

hand·spike (hand′spīk′) *n.* bar used as a lever.

hand·spring (hand′spring′) *n.* kind of somersault in which one rotates the body in a full circle either forward or backward, starting from a standing position, springing onto one or both hands, and returning to a standing position.

hand·stand (hand′stand′) *n.* act of balancing the body in an upright position, with the feet in the air and the palms of the hands flat on the floor or ground.

hand-to-hand (hand′tə hand′) *adj.* in direct contact; at close quarters: *hand-to-hand combat.*

hand-to-mouth (hand′tə mouth′) *adj.* concerned only with one's immediate needs: *a hand-to-mouth existence.*

hand·work (hand′wurk′) *n.* work done by hand; handiwork.

hand·writ·ing (hand′rī′ting) *n.* **1.** writing done by hand, as distinguished from typewriting or printing. **2.** style of writing; penmanship: *The boy's handwriting was hard to read.*

hand·writ·ten (hand′rit′ən) *adj.* written by hand: *handwritten invitations.*

hand·y (han′dē) **hand·i·er, hand·i·est.** *adj.* **1.** at hand; nearby; accessible: *That's a handy place for the telephone.* **2.** able to use the hands skillfully; dexterous: *to be handy at woodworking.* **3.** convenient to handle; easily manipulated: *a handy carrying case.* —**hand′i·ly,** *adv.* —**hand′i·ness,** *n.*

Han·dy, W(illiam) C(hristopher) (han′dē) 1873–1958, U.S. Negro blues musician and composer.

hand·y·man (han′dē man′) *pl.,* **-men.** *n.* one who is skilled in or works at various small jobs.

hang (hang) **hung** or *(v.t. def. 3, v.i. def. 3)* **hanged, hang·ing.** *v.t.* **1.** to fasten or attach (an object) from above only, without any support from below; suspend: *to hang wet towels on a clothesline.* **2.** to attach (an object), as with a hinge, to allow for free movement at the point of attachment: *to hang a garden gate.* **3.** To suspend (a person) by the neck, as from a gallows, until he is dead: *to hang a man for treason.* **4.** to turn in a downward direction; droop: *to hang one's head in grief.* **5.** to furnish, cover, or decorate with anything that is suspended or attached: *to hang a room with tapestries.* **6.** to attach (wallpaper) to a wall. **7.** to attach or suspend (pictures) for display. **8.** (of a juror) to prevent (a jury) from reaching a verdict, as by withholding one's vote; deadlock. **9.** to fasten or attach in a well-balanced position: *to hang a scythe to a handle.* **10. hang it.** *Slang.* I give up; damn it. ▲ used to express anger, annoyance, or frustration. —*v.i.* **1.** to be attached to or suspended from something above without any support from below; dangle: *A mobile hung from a hook in the ceiling. Monkeys hang by their tails.* **2.** to be fastened in a way that allows for free movement at the point of attachment: *A door hangs on its hinges.* **3.** to die by hanging: *The murderer hanged for his crime.* **4.** to cling, esp. for support; hold fast: *The fisherman hung onto the capsized boat.* **5.** to be contingent or dependent: *The defendant's fate hung on the jury's decision.* **6.** to be in a suspenseful or undecided state; vacillate; waver: *The sick man hung between life and death for two days.* **7.** to bend forward or downward; droop: *The tree hangs over the house.* **8.** to be suspended, usually without motion, above something; hover: *Polluted air hangs over the city.* **9.** to be imminent; threaten: *The prospect of war hung over the country.* **10.** to be completely attentive; listen intently (often with *on* or *upon*): *The audience hung on the poet's words.* **11.** to fit the figure with ease: *That dress hangs nicely.* **12.** to be on display, esp. in a gallery or museum: *Rembrandt's paintings hang in many museums.*
to be hung up. *Slang.* **a.** to be hampered or detained by; be temporarily handicapped by: *to be hung up on a problem.* **b.** to be fond of or smitten with.
to hang around (or **about**). *Informal.* **a.** to linger or loiter: *Let's hang around a while.* **b.** to spend much time: *He hangs around with older boys.*
to hang back. to be reluctant to proceed; hesitate.
to hang fire. a. (of a gun) to be slow to fire. **b.** to pause in an activity before completing it; delay; hesitate.
to hang on. a. to persist; persevere: *to hang on until graduation.* **b.** *Informal.* to keep a telephone line open while one party is elsewhere: *I'll look for Jack if you'll hang on.*
to hang one on. *Slang.* **a.** to hit or strike with the fist. **b.** to get very drunk.
to hang out. a. to lean out of: *The dog hung out the car window.* **b.** *Slang.* to spend much time; hang around: *The group usually hangs out at Bob's house.*
to hang together. a. to keep together; be united: *Those opposed to the proposal hung together.* **b.** to be related in a logical way; be coherent: *Your ideas do not hang together.*
to hang up. a. to suspend from or as from a hanger or peg. **b.** to end a telephone conversation by replacing the receiver in its cradle. **c.** to hamper the progress of; detain.
—*n.* **1.** way in which something hangs or falls: *the hang of a dress.* **2.** particular way of doing something; knack: *to get the hang of riding a bicycle.* **3.** general meaning; gist: *to get the hang of a conversation.* **4. to give a hang.** to be concerned or interested; care: *Jack's date didn't give a hang about football.* [Partly from Old English *hōn* (past tense *heng*) to suspend; partly from Old English *hangian* to be suspended; partly from Old Norse *hanga* to suspend.]

han·gar (hang′ər, -gar) *n.* **1.** building for sheltering and servicing aircraft. **2.** shed. [French *hangar* shed; of uncertain origin.]

hang·bird (hang′burd′) *n.* any of various birds that build a hanging nest, esp. the Baltimore oriole.

Hang·chow (hang′chou′) *n.* port city in eastern China. Pop. (1957 est.), 784,000.

hang·dog (hang′dôg′) *adj.* sneaking or degraded in manner or appearance.

hang·er (hang′ər) *n.* **1.** frame or device on which something is hung, esp. one that fits under the shoulders of a garment such as a coat.

at; āpe; cär; end; mē; it; īce; hot; ōld; fôrk; wood; fōol; oil; out; up; ūse; turn; sing; thin; <u>th</u>is; zh in treasure; ə in ago, taken, pencil, lemon, circus.

2. loop or ring for hanging something, as at the back of the neck of a coat. **3.** one who hangs things: *wallpaper hanger.*

hang·er-on (hang′ər ôn′, -on′) *pl.,* **hang·ers-on.** *n.* one who clings to or hangs around a person, group, or place, esp. for personal gain; parasite.

hang·ing (hang′ing) *n.* **1.** execution in which a person is hanged, as from a gallows. **2.** something, often of fabric, which hangs as from a wall or window. —*adj.* **1.** attached to something above without any support from below; dangling. **2.** leaning over; overhanging. **3.** placed on a steep slope. **4.** deserving punishment by hanging: *a hanging offense.*

hang·man (hang′mən) *pl.,* **-men.** *n.* one who hangs condemned persons; executioner.

hang·nail (hang′nāl′) *n.* piece of skin partially torn away and hanging loose at the side or base of a fingernail. [Modification (influenced by HANG) of earlier *agnail,* from Old English *angnægl,* from *ang-* (only in compounds) painful + *nægl* nail.]

hang·out (hang′out′) *n. Informal.* place to which a person or group goes much of the time.

hang·o·ver (hang′ō′vər) *n.* **1.** unpleasant aftereffect, as nausea or a headache, from drinking too much alcoholic liquor. **2.** something remaining from a past time or condition, such as a family custom.

hang·up (hang′up′) *n. Informal.* **1.** psychological problem that temporarily handicaps a person; mental block. **2.** anything that hampers progress; snag.

hank (hangk) *n.* **1.** loop or coil, as of hair. **2.** skein, esp. one of yarn containing a specific number of yards varying according to the material. A hank of cotton or silk yarn contains 840 yards; a hank of worsted yarn, 560 yards. [Of Scandinavian origin.]

han·ker (hang′kər) *v.i.* to yearn or crave; desire strongly (with *after, for,* or an infinitive). [Probably from Flemish *hankeren* to long for.]

han·ker·ing (hang′kər ing) *n.* strong desire; yearning; craving.

Han·kow (han′kou′) *n.* former city in east-central China, now part of Wuhan.

han·ky-pan·ky (hang′kē pang′kē) *n. Slang.* deceitful or underhanded activity; trickery. [Rhyming modification of HOCUS-POCUS; possibly influenced by *hand* or *hankerchief* with reference to their use in jugglery.]

Han·na, Mark (han′ə) 1837–1904, U.S. politician; full name, Marcus Alonzo Hanna.

Han·ni·bal (han′ə bəl) *n.* c.247–c.183 B.C., Carthaginian general who led Carthage against Rome in the Second Punic War.

Ha·noi (ha noi′, hä-) *n.* capital, port, and largest city of North Vietnam, in the northeastern part of the country. Pop. (1960), 414,620.

Han·o·ver (han′ō′vər) *n.* **1.** *also,* **Han·no·ver.** historic region and former province of Prussia, in the northern part of present-day West Germany. **2.** *also,* **Han·no·ver.** city in northern West Germany. Pop. (1968), 524,516. **3.** royal family that reigned in Great Britain from 1714 to 1901, beginning with George I and ending with Queen Victoria. **4.** member of this family.

Han·o·ve·ri·an (han′ō vēr′ē ən) *adj.* **1.** of, relating to, or characteristic of Hanover. **2.** of or relating to the English royal family of Hanover. —*n.* **1.** native or inhabitant of Hanover. **2.** member or supporter of the English royal family of Hanover.

hanse (hans) *n.* **1.** medieval guild or association of merchants. **2.** payment made to this guild, such as membership fee or a toll levied on nonmembers. **3. Hanse.** Hanseatic League. [Old French *hanse* guild of merchants, from Middle Low German *hanse,* from Old High German *hansa* troop of soldiers.]

Han·se·at·ic (han′sē at′ik) *adj.* of or relating to the Hanseatic League or the cities that formed it.

Hanseatic League. association of cities in northern Germany established in 1241 for the purpose of mutual defense and the promotion of free trade among its members.

han·sel (han′səl) handsel.

Han·sen's disease (han′sənz) leprosy. [From A.G.H. *Hansen* (1841–1912), Norwegian physician who discovered the bacterium causing the disease.]

han·som (han′səm) *n.* low, two-wheeled, covered carriage for two passengers, drawn by one horse, with the driver's seat elevated behind the cab. Also, **hansom cab.** [From Joseph A. *Hansom,* a nineteenth-century English architect who designed such cabs.]

Hansom

Ha·nuk·kah (hä′nə kə; *Hebrew* KHä nōō kä′) *also,* **Cha·nu·kah.** *n.* Jewish holiday, celebrated for eight days, commemorating the rededication of the Temple of Jerusalem after the victory of the Maccabees over the king of ancient Syria. [Hebrew *hanukkāh* dedication.]

Han·yang (hän′yäng′) *n.* former city in east-central China, now part of Wuhan.

hap (hap) *Archaic. n.* **1.** chance; luck; lot. **2.** occurrence; happening. —*v.i.* **happed, hap·ping.** to occur by chance; happen. [Old Norse *happ* chance, good luck.]

hap·haz·ard (hap′haz′ərd) *adj.* characterized by a lack of order, direction, or planning; random; aimless. —**hap′haz′ard·ly,** *adv.* —**Syn.** see random.

hap·less (hap′lis) *adj.* unlucky; unfortunate.

hap·loid (hap′loid) *adj.* having a single set of unpaired chromosomes characteristic of germ cells, as distinguished from the full number of chromosomes present in other living cells. [Greek *haploeidēs* single, from *haplous* single, simple + *-oeidēs* -OID.]

hap·ly (hap′lē) *adv. Archaic.* by chance; perhaps.

hap·pen (hap′ən) *v.i.* **1.** to take place; occur: *The accident happened last week.* **2.** to be or occur by chance; take place without planning or apparent reason: *His birthday just happens to be the same day as mine.* **3.** to have the occasion or luck; chance: *I happened to be there at the right time.* **4.** to come or go by chance (with *along* or *by*). **5. to happen on** (or **upon**). to meet or find accidentally. **6. to happen to. a.** to be done to; befall: *Something terrible must have happened to the family.* **b.** to be the fate of; become of: *What ever happened to old-fashioned gallantry?* [Middle English *happenen* to befall, from *happen,* from *hap* chance. See HAP.]

Syn. 1. **Happen, occur** denote to take place. **Happen** is the common word and means to come to pass with or without cause: *Those terrible traffic jams usually happen around Christmas.* **Occur** is slightly more formal and may be more specific in terms of place or event: *The accident occurred at the intersection.*

hap·pen·ing (hap′ə ning) *n.* **1.** that which happens; event; occurrence. **2.** meeting, event, or performance characterized by spontaneous group activity. —**Syn.** 1. see occurrence.

hap·pi·ly (hap′ə lē) *adv.* **1.** with pleasure, joy, or contentment. **2.** luckily; fortunately. **3.** aptly; appropriately.

hap·pi·ness (hap′ē nis) *n.* **1.** quality or state of being joyous, glad, or contented. **2.** good fortune; luck. **3.** aptness.

Syn. 1. **Happiness, joy, felicity** indicate a state of enjoyment. **Happiness** suggests a general inner feeling of satisfaction: *It is a rare person who finds happiness in solitude.* **Joy** implies a heightened, more active feeling of pleasure, usually derived from a specific source: *The child brought them great joy.* **Felicity** is a more formal term also suggesting an active appreciation of pleasure: *The felicity he found in married life more than compensated for the independence enjoyed in bachelorhood.*

hap·py (hap′ē) **-pi·er, -pi·est.** *adj.* **1.** having, showing, or providing pleasure, joy, or contentment: *a happy home, a happy occasion.* **2.** lucky; fortunate: *a happy discovery.* **3.** particularly well-suited; apt; felicitous: *a happy choice of words.* [HAP + -Y.] —**Syn.** 1. see glad.

hap·py-go-luck·y (hap′ē gō luk′ē) *adj.* free from worry; carefree.

Haps·burg (haps′burg′; *German* häps′bŏork′) *also,* **Habs·burg.** *n.* ruling family of Europe from 1273 to 1918, which governed Austria from 1282 to 1918, the Holy Roman Empire from 1438 to 1806, Spain from 1516 to 1700, and Hungary from 1526 to 1918.

har·a·kir·i (har′ə kēr′ē) *also,* **har·a·kar·i** (har′ə kar′ē), **har·i·kar·i.** *n.* **1.** suicide by cutting open the abdomen with a knife, a ritual suicide in Japan committed to redeem honor or express grief. **2.** any form of suicide for honorable purposes. [Japanese *hara-kiri* suicide by disembowelment, from *hara* belly + *kiri* to cut.]

ha·rangue (hə rang′) *n.* long noisy speech, often pompous or didactic, delivered in a vehement manner; tirade. —*v.t.* **-rangued, -rangu·ing.** to address with a harangue. —*v.i.* to deliver a harangue. [Middle French *harangue* oration, from Medieval Latin *harenga* meeting, speech made at a meeting; of Germanic origin.]

har·ass (har′əs, hə ras′) *v.t.* **1.** to bother or annoy repeatedly; torment. **2.** to trouble (an enemy) by repeated raids or attacks. [French *harasser,* from Old French *harer* to set a dog on, from *hare* a cry used to do this; of Germanic origin.] —**har′ass·ment,** *n.* —**Syn.** 1. see pester.

Har·bin (här′bin) *n.* city in northeastern China. Pop. (1965 est.), 1,552,000.

har·bin·ger (här′bin jər) *n.* one who or that which goes before to announce or indicate the arrival of someone or something; herald: *a harbinger of impending evil.* —*v.t.* to act as a harbinger of; foretell. [Old French *herbergere* provider of lodging, from *herbergier* to provide lodging for, from *herberge* lodging; of Germanic origin; supposedly so called because this person went ahead of an army or important individual to secure lodging.]

har·bor (här′bər) *also, British,* **har·bour.** *n.* **1.** protected place on a coastline of a sea, lake, or river and used as a shelter for ships and boats. **2.** any place of shelter. —*v.t.* **1.** to give shelter or protection to; conceal: *to harbor a criminal.* **2.** to keep or foster in the mind: *to harbor a grudge.* —*v.i.* to take shelter in a harbor. [Old English *hereboru* lodgings, quarters, from *here* army + *beorg* protection.]

Syn. *n.* **1. Harbor, port**[1] indicate a place where a ship may dock safely. **Harbor** suggests any such place, natural or artificial: *The harbor is full of ships arriving and departing.* **Port** emphasizes the loading and unloading of cargo and passengers and is extended to all the facilities connected with these activities: *The West Coast ports are expected to be tied up by the strike.*

har·bor·age (här′bər ij) *also, British,* **har·bour·age.** *n.* **1.** shelter for ships and boats. **2.** any shelter; lodging.

harbor master, officer in charge of enforcing the regulations of a harbor.

hard (härd) *adj.* **1.** not readily penetrated, indented, or crushed; resistant to pressure; firm to the touch: *the hard surface of a tiled floor.* **2.** requiring or involving considerable physical or mental effort to do or make: *a hard task, a hard decision.* **3.** not easy to understand, master, or explain: *a hard problem.* **4.** requiring much effort in dealing with: *He was hard to get along with.* **5.** causing or involving something unpleasant, as sorrow, pain, or discomfort; severe; oppressive: *a hard ·life. He had a hard time of it.* **6.** lacking feeling; stern; strict: *a hard heart, a hard taskmaster.* **7.** showing or carried on with great energy, vigor, or industriousness: *a hard day's work.* **8.** exacting or rigorous in terms: *a hard bargain.* **9.** having or done with great force or strength: *a hard blow.* **10.** not easily negated or explained away; undeniable; actual: *cold, hard facts.* **11.** unpleasantly severe or harsh to the physical or aesthetic senses: *a hard color. She had a hard face.* **12.** firmly formed; tight: *a hard knot.* **13.** containing much alcohol: *hard liquor.* **14.** (of water) containing calcium and magnesium salts that interfere with the sudsing and cleansing action of soap. **15.** (of currency) readily convertible into gold or other currencies; worth full face value in purchasing power. **16.** high and firm; stable: *hard prices, a hard market.* **17.** *Phonetics.* **a.** (of *c* and *g*) pronounced with the sound of *k* in *cat* and *g* in *good.* **b.** (of consonants) pronounced without vibration of the vocal cords; voiceless. **18. hard and fast.** unalterable; obligatory; strict: *a hard and fast rule.* **19. hard of hearing.** partially deaf. **20. hard up.** *Informal.* **a.** without any money; broke. **b.** in need of (something): *He was hard up for a job.* **21. to be hard on.** to treat roughly or harshly; be cruel, oppressive, or painful to: *The sergeant was hard on the new recruits. Children are hard on shoes.* —*adv.* **1.** with effort or energy; strenuously; persistently: *to work hard.* **2.** with force or strength: *It rained hard.* **3.** with difficulty: *to breathe hard.* **4.** so as to be or become solid or firm: *frozen hard.* **5.** with a deep emotional reaction, as of grief or bitterness: *She took the tragic news hard.* **6.** firmly; tightly; securely: *The child held hard to her mother's hand.* **7.** with resistance or reluctance: *to die hard.* **8.** in close proximity; near: *The dogs were hard upon the fox.* **9.** *Nautical.* to the extreme limit; to the fullest extent: *hard alee, hard aport.* **10. to be hard put to.** to have much difficulty or trouble: *He was hard put to find an excuse for his lateness.* [Old English *heard* solid, unfeeling, severe.] —**hard′ness,** *n.*

Syn. *adj.* **1.** see **firm**[1]. **2. Hard, difficult, arduous, laborious** indicate a need for effort in accomplishing something. **Hard,** the general term, simply implies that physical or mental effort must be made: *The piano was hard to move.* **Difficult** stresses that skill rather than force is required: *That is one of the most difficult arias in all opera.* **Arduous** implies that great effort and persistence is required: *They applied themselves to the arduous task of cleaning up the flood damage.* **Laborious** also suggests the need for extended effort, but has the additional implication that careful attention must be given to detail: *He was involved with the laborious problem of preserving the scrolls.*

hard·bit·ten (härd′bit′ən) *adj.* unyielding; tough.

hard·boiled (härd′boild′) *adj.* **1.** (of eggs) boiled until yolk and white are hard. **2.** *Informal.* tough; insensitive; callous.

hard cash *Informal.* **1.** ready cash. **2.** coin as distinguished from paper money.

hard cider, apple cider that has fermented.

hard coal, anthracite.

hard·core (härd′kôr′) *adj.* **1.** most dedicated or extreme; inveterate: *a hard-core conservative.* **2.** unchanging; lasting: *hard-core unemployment.*

hard·en (härd′ən) *v.i.* **1.** to become rigid and firm to the touch. **2.** to become capable of great mental or physical endurance. **3.** to become insensitive or cruel. **4.** to become rigid, unyielding, or strengthened. **5.** (of prices) to become stable or to rise. —*v.t.* **1.** to make rigid and firm to the touch. **2.** to make unfeeling or callous. **3.** to make tough or hardy; inure. **4.** to strengthen or make rigid or unyielding.

hard goods, items that can be used for a long time, as furniture or appliances.

hard·hack (härd′hak′) *n.* hardy shrub, *Spiraea tomentosa,* of the rose family, found in eastern North America, bearing narrow clusters of small pink, purple, or white flowers. Also, **stee′ple·bush′.**

hard·head·ed (härd′hed′id) *adj.* **1.** practical; shrewd. **2.** stubborn; obstinate.

hard·heart·ed (härd′här′tid) *adj.* pitiless; cruel; unfeeling.

har·di·hood (här′dē hood′) *n.* boldness; daring; audacity.

har·di·ness (här′dē nis) *n.* **1.** physical endurance; strength. **2.** boldness; daring.

Har·ding, Warren Ga·ma·liel (här′ding; gə mãl′yəl) 1865–1923, twenty-ninth president of the United States, from 1921 to 1923.

hard labor, compulsory labor imposed on imprisoned criminals as part of the punishment for some crimes.

hard landing, landing of a spacecraft on the moon or another body in outer space at so high a speed that the vehicle or its payload is damaged.

hard·ly (härd′lē) *adv.* **1.** only just; barely: *We could hardly see in the dim light.* **2.** not quite; not: *He's hardly the type to do such a thing.* **3.** probably not; not likely: *He'll hardly do it now that we're gone.* **4.** with difficulty or effort: *a hardly fought battle.*

Syn. 1. Hardly, barely, scarcely refer to the narrow margin by which something is done. **Hardly** suggests scantiness or inadequacy: *The music was so soft they could hardly hear it.* **Barely** implies that there is an absence of appreciable margin: *We barely made the last train.* **Scarcely** suggests an even narrower, almost imperceptible margin: *They had scarcely begun when they were told to stop.*

hard palate, bony structure in the front of the roof of the mouth which separates the mouth from the nasal cavity.

hard·pan (härd′pan′) *n.* **1.** layer of hard, impenetrable earth underneath soft soil. **2.** hard, unbroken ground. **3.** firm foundation of anything.

hard sauce, uncooked, creamy mixture of butter, sugar, and flavoring, used as a topping for dishes, as plum pudding.

hard sell, aggressive and usually highly pressured or insistent method of selling or advertising.

hard·shell (härd′shel′) *adj.* **1.** (of certain shellfish) having a hard shell. **2.** rigid; uncompromising.

hard·ship (härd′ship′) *n.* cause or condition of difficulty, pain, or suffering, as poverty or illness.

hard·tack (härd′tak′) *n.* unleavened bread, shaped into a hard, dry biscuit, traditionally eaten by sailors. Also, **pilot biscuit, sea biscuit, ship biscuit.**

hard·top (härd′top′) *n.* automobile having the general design of a convertible, but with a non-folding rigid top.

hard·ware (härd′wâr′) *n.* **1.** metal articles or parts, as tools, nails and screws, fittings, or cutlery. **2.** physical equipment of a computer, as distinguished from theory, programs, or data. **3.** weapons, esp. heavy equipment.

hard·wood (härd′wood′) *n.* **1.** any of a large group of trees having broad leaves that are shed every year, as the oak, beech, or maple. **2.** wood of such a tree, usually denser, heavier, and harder than softwood, used to make such items as furniture, flooring, and athletic equipment. **3.** any hard, compact, heavy wood.

har·dy (här′dē) *·di·er, ·di·est. adj.* **1.** able to endure hardship or harsh physical conditions; strong; robust. **2.** (of plants) able to endure the cold of winter without protection. **3.** bold; daring; audacious. [Old French *hardi* bold, stout; originally past participle of *hardir* to make bold; of Germanic origin.]

Har·dy, Thomas (här′dē) 1840–1928, English novelist and poet.

hare (hâr) *pl.* **hares** *or* **hare.** *n.* any of various rodentlike mammals, family Leporidae, related to and usually larger than the rabbit, having very long ears, hind legs and feet, a short tail, white, brown, or gray fur, and a divided upper lip. Length: to 25 inches. [Old English *hara.*]

Hare

hare·bell (hâr′bel′) *n.* plant having a slender stem with bright blue, bell-shaped flowers, *Campanula rotundifolia,* of the bellflower family, found in Europe, Asia, and North America; bluebell.

hare·brained (hâr′brānd′) *adj.* foolish; flighty; reckless.

hare·lip (hâr′lip′) *n.* birth defect consisting of a vertical split in the lip which often impairs speech. —**hare′lipped′,** *adj.*

har·em (hâr′əm) *n.* **1.** part of a Muslim house where the women live. **2.** women of a Muslim household. [Arabic *haram, harīm* forbidden, women's quarters; because men are forbidden to enter.]

Har·greaves, James (här′grēvz) c.1720–78, English weaver who invented the spinning jenny.

har·i·cot (har′ə kō′) *n.* unripe pod or ripe seeds of any of several beans, as the kidney bean or haricot bean. [French *haricot* kidney bean, from Nahuatl *ayacotl* bean.]

har·i·kar·i (har′ē kar′ē) hara-kiri.

hark (härk) *v.i.* **1.** to listen. ▲ used chiefly in the imperative. **2. to hark back.** to return to some previous point of reference; go back; revert. [Middle English *herkien,* probably from an unrecorded Old English word.]

at; āpe; cär; end; mē; it; īce; hot; ōld; fôrk; wood; fōol; oil; out; up; ūse; turn; sing; thin; this; zh in treasure; ə in ago, taken, pencil, lemon, circus.

hark·en (här′kən) *also.* **heark·en.** *v.i.* to pay close attention; listen carefully. [Old English *heorcnian.*]

Har·lem (här′ləm) *n.* district of New York City, in Manhattan, including one of the largest Negro communities in the United States.

har·le·quin (här′lə kwin, -kin) *n.* **1. Harlequin.** stock character in sixteenth-century Italian commedia dell'arte, later adapted to English pantomime, traditionally appearing in a skin-tight costume in a brightly colored, diamond pattern carrying a small wooden sword. **2.** buffoon. —*adj.* having brightly colored diamonds; parti-colored. [Obsolete French *harlequin,* from earlier *Herlequin* legendary leader of a demon host, possibly going back to Old English *Herla cyning* King Herla (who was probably originally identical with Woden); modern meaning from Italian *arlecchino* buffoon, from obsolete French *harlequin,* which an Italian troupe of actors in France used for the name of the buffoon in their plays.]

harlequin bug, small, colorful bug, *Murgantia histrionica,* having bright red, orange, and yellow markings, found in North and Central America, destructive to cabbage, turnips, and related plants. Also, **cal′ico·back′.**

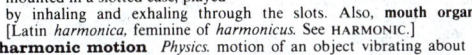
Harlequin bug

Har·lin·gen (här′lin jin) *n.* city in southernmost Texas. Pop. (1970), 33,503.

har·lot (här′lət) *n.* prostitute. [Old French *harlot* rascal, vagabond; of uncertain origin.]

har·lot·ry (här′lə trē) *n.* prostitution.

harm (härm) *n.* **1.** injury; damage; hurt: *bodily harm.* **2.** moral injury; evil; wrong: *I meant no harm.* —*v.t.* to do damage to; hurt. [Old English *hearm* injury, evil.] —**Syn.** *v.t.* see **hurt.**

harm·ful (härm′fəl) *adj.* causing or able to cause harm; injurious; damaging. —**harm′ful·ly,** *adv.* —**harm′ful·ness,** *n.*

harm·less (härm′lis) *adj.* not capable of causing harm; not injurious or damaging. —**harm′less·ly,** *adv.* —**harm′less·ness,** *n.*

har·mon·ic (här mon′ik) *adj.* **1.** of or relating to musical harmony. **2.** of or relating to a higher tone or tones produced along with the main tone or tones when a musical note is played. [Latin *harmonicus* relating to harmony, from Greek *harmonikos* skilled in music, harmonious, from *harmoniā* joining, concord. See HARMONY.]

har·mon·i·ca (här mon′i kə) *n.* musical wind instrument consisting of a series of metallic reeds mounted in a slotted case, played by inhaling and exhaling through the slots. Also, **mouth organ.** [Latin *harmonica,* feminine of *harmonicus.* See HARMONIC.]

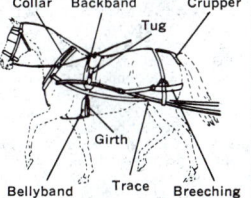
Harmonica

harmonic motion *Physics.* motion of an object vibrating about a fixed point, as a pendulum does.

har·mon·ics (här mon′iks) *n.,pl.* **1.** science of musical sounds. ▲ construed as singular. **2.** secondary sounds or overtones produced along with the main tone when a musical note is played.

har·mo·ni·ous (här mō′nē əs) *adj.* **1.** characterized by agreement in feelings, thoughts, or actions; in accord: *a harmonious gathering.* **2.** having elements that combine agreeably or pleasingly: *a harmonious mixture of light and color.* **3.** agreeable or pleasing to the ear; sweetsounding. —**har·mo′ni·ous·ly,** *adv.*

har·mo·ni·um (här mō′nē əm) *n.* reed organ; melodeon. [French *harmonium,* from Latin *harmonia.* See HARMONY.]

har·mo·nize (här′mə nīz′) **-nized, -niz·ing.** *v.i.* **1.** to arrange, sing, or play in harmony. **2.** to be in agreement. —*v.t.* **1.** to bring into agreement; make harmonious. **2.** to add notes, usually of lower pitch, to (a melody) so as to form chords; add harmony to.

har·mo·ny (här′mə nē) *pl.,* **-nies.** *n.* **1.a.** combination of simultaneously sounded musical notes so as to form chords. **b.** chordal structure of a musical work, as distinguished from its melody and rhythm. **c.** science or study of the structure, relations, and combination of chords. **2.** any sweet or pleasant sound. **3.** agreement of feeling, thoughts, or actions; good relations: *to live in harmony.* **4.** agreement or pleasing arrangement among the various elements of a whole. **5.** collation of parallel passages from different authors or sources, esp. the four Gospels, showing their points of agreement and disagreement. [Latin *harmonia* agreement of sounds, concord, from Greek *harmoniā,* from *harmos* joint.]

har·ness (här′nis) *n.* **1.** gear of

Collar Backband Crupper
Tug
Girth
Bellyband Trace Breeching
Harness

a draft animal, which includes a combination of straps and bands by which the animal is attached to the load it is pulling, and the bridle by which the animal is controlled and guided. **2.** gear of a riding or pack animal, as the bridle or halter and saddle. **3.** *Archaic.* armor for a knight, soldier, or horse. **4. in harness,** in or at one's routine work. —*v.t.* **1.** to put a harness on. **2.** to control and make use of: *to harness water power to generate electricity.* **3.** *Archaic.* to put armor on. [Old French *harneis* armor, equipment; possibly of Scandinavian origin.]

harness racing, sport in which horses pull twowheeled sulkies in trotting or pacing races.

harp (härp) *n.* musical instrument consisting of a series of strings of varying length set in an upright, triangular frame with a curved top, played by plucking the strings with the fingers. —*v.i.* **1.** to play on a harp. **2. to harp on.** to refer to continually and annoyingly. [Old English *hearpe* this musical instrument.]

Harp

Har·pers Ferry (här′pərz) town in northeastern West Virginia, site of John Brown's raid on a government arsenal in 1859.

harp·ist (här′pist) *n.* one who plays the harp.

har·poon (här poon′) *n.* barbed spearlike missile with a rope attached, used to spear whales and other sea animals. —*v.t.* to strike, catch, or kill with a harpoon. [Probably from Dutch *harpoen* a harpoon, from Old French *harpon* clamp, clasp, from *harper* to seize; probably of Scandinavian origin.] —**har·poon′er,** *n.*

harp·si·chord (härp′sə kôrd′) *n.* stringed musical instrument, with a keyboard, esp. widely used from 1550 to 1750. It resembles a grand piano, but has the wire strings plucked by leather or quill points, and produces a guitarlike tone. [Obsolete French *harpechorde,* from *harpe* harp (of Germanic origin) + *chorde* string (from Latin *chorda* string of a musical instrument). See CHORD².]

Harpoon

Har·py (här′pē) *pl.,* **-pies.** *n.* **1.** *Greek Mythology.* foul-smelling, ugly monster having an old woman's head and the body, wings, and claws of a bird. **2. harpy.** one who is always angry and who preys upon other people. [Latin *harpyia,* from Greek *harpyiai* (plural) Harpies of mythology; literally, snatchers.]

har·que·bus (här′kwə bəs) *n. also,* **ar·que·bus.** *n.* early portable firearm, a predecessor of the musket. [French *arquebuse,* from Middle Dutch *hakebusse* literally, hook gun, from *hake* hook + *busse* gun (going back to Latin *buxus;* see BOX¹); referring to the hook that was cast on the gun.]

har·ri·dan (har′id ən) *n.* mean, shrewish woman. [Supposedly modification of French *haridelle* worn-out horse; of uncertain origin.]

har·ri·er¹ (har′ē ər) *n.* **1.** hunting dog of a breed developed in England, resembling the English foxhound, originally raised for hunting hares. Height: 20 inches at the shoulder. **2.** runner in a cross-country race. [HARE + -IER.]

har·ri·er² (har′ē ər) *n.* **1.** one who or that which harries. **2.** any of various hawks, genus *Circus,* whose plumage is gray or brown above and white below, that preys on rodents, frogs, and other small animals. Wingspan: 4 feet. [HARRY + -ER¹.]

Har·ris, Joel Chan·dler (har′is; chand′lər) 1848–1908, U.S. writer.

Har·ris·burg (har′is bûrg′) *n.* capital of Pennsylvania, in the southeastern part of the state. Pop. (1970), 68,061.

Har·ri·son (har′i sən) *n.* **1. Benjamin.** 1833–1901, twenty-third president of the United States, from 1889 to 1893. **2. William Henry.** 1773–1841, ninth president of the United States, from March 4 to April 4, 1841; grandfather of Benjamin Harrison.

har·row (har′ō) *n.* heavy frame with upright disks or teeth, drawn by a tractor to break up and level plowed land. —*v.t.* **1.** to draw a harrow over (land). **2.** to make uneasy or disturbed; distress. [Of uncertain origin.] —**har′row·er,** *n.*

Har·row (har′ō) *n.* one of England's oldest and best-known boys' preparatory schools, founded in 1571. It is located in Harrow-on-the-Hill, a borough of London.

har·ry (har′ē) **-ried, -ry·ing.** *v.t.* **1.** to trouble constantly; torment; vex. **2.** to rob or pillage, as in a raid or attack. [Old English *hergian* to make raids, lay waste, from *here* army.]

harsh (härsh) *adj.* **1.** rough or unpleasant to any of the physical senses: *a harsh sound.* **2.** cruel; severe: *harsh treatment, a harsh winter.*

at; āpe; cär; end; mē; it; īce; hot; ōld; fôrk; wood; fōōl; oil; out; up; ūse; turn; sing; thin; <u>th</u>is; zh in treasure; ə in ago, taken, pencil, lemon, circus.

471

[Probably of Scandinavian origin.] —**harsh′ly,** *adv.* —**harsh-ness,** *n.*

hart (härt) *pl.,* **harts** or **hart.** *n.* stag, esp. a male red deer, usually after its fifth year. Distinguished from **hind²**. [Old English *heorot.*]

Harte, (Francis) Bret (härt; bret) 1839–1902, U.S. short-story writer.

har·te·beest (här′tə bēst′, härt′bēst′) *pl.,* **-beests** or **-beest.** *n.* reddish-brown African antelope, genus *Alcelaphus,* having a long, narrow head and ringed, U-shaped horns that bend backward at the tips. Height: 4 feet at the shoulder. [Obsolete Afrikaans *hartebeest,* from Dutch *hert* hart + *beest* beast (from Old French *beste* BEAST.)]

Hart·ford (härt′fərd) *n.* capital and largest city in Connecticut, in the central part of the state. Pop. (1970), 158,017.

harts·horn (härts′hôrn′) *n.* smelling salts. [So called because formerly obtained chiefly from a hart's horns.]

har·um-scar·um (hâr′əm skâr′əm) *adj.* reckless; rash. —*adv.* in a reckless or rash manner. [Possibly from obsolete *hare* to frighten (of uncertain origin) + SCARE.]

ha·rus·pex (hə rus′peks′, har′əs) *pl.,* **ha·rus·pi·ces** (hə rus′pə sēz′). *n.* member of a group of priests in ancient Etruria or Rome who divined the will of the gods by observing the entrails of sacrificed animals, patterns of lightning, and the flight of birds. [Latin *haruspex* literally, inspector of entrails.]

Har·vard (här′vərd) *n.* private accredited university in Cambridge, Massachusetts, the oldest college in the United States.

har·vest (här′vist) *n.* **1.** act of gathering a crop when it is ripe. **2.** crop that is gathered; season's yield of a crop: *a large harvest.* **3.** time of year when ripened crops are gathered. **4.** product or result of any action, effort, or labor: *Their cruelty brought a harvest of sorrow.* —*v.t.* **1.** to gather, as a crop: *to harvest corn.* **2.** to gather the crop from: *to harvest the wheat fields.* **3.** to reap or get as a result or product of: *to harvest the fruits of one's labors.* —*v.i.* **1.** to gather a crop. [Old English *hærfest* autumn, the season for gathering crops.]

har·vest·er (här′vis tər) *n.* **1.** any of various machines for harvesting field crops, esp. a reaper. **2.** one who harvests.

harvest home **1.** last harvest of the year; the close of harvesting. **2.** old English festival celebrating the close of harvesting. **3.** song sung at this festival.

har·vest·man (här′vist mən) *pl.,* **-men.** *n.* **1.** daddy-longlegs. **2.** man who harvests.

harvest moon, full moon occurring nearest the autumnal equinox.

Har·vey, William (här′vē) 1578–1657, English physiologist who discovered the circulation of the blood.

Harz Mountains (härts) low mountain range in north-central Germany.

has (haz) third person singular present indicative of **have.**

has-been (haz′bin′) *n. Informal.* one who or that which is no longer popular, powerful, or effective.

Has·dru·bal (haz′drŏŏ′bəl) *n.* **1.** died 221 B.C., Carthaginian general, brother-in-law of Hannibal. **2.** died 207 B.C., Carthaginian general, brother of Hannibal.

hash (hash) *n.* **1.** mixture of cooked meat and potatoes and often onions or other vegetables, esp. one that is chopped fine and either browned, fried, or baked. **2.** mess; jumble; muddle. **3. to make a hash of.** *Informal.* to make a mess of; bungle. **4. to settle one's hash.** *Informal.* to treat (someone) harshly; subdue. —*v.t.* **1.** to chop into small pieces. **2.** to consider or discuss carefully; review (often with *over*): *to hash over a decision.* [Old French *hacher* to hack, from *hache* ax; of Germanic origin.]

hash·ish (hash′ēsh, -ish) *also,* **hash·eesh** (hash′ēsh). *n.* dried flowering top parts of a hemp plant, *Cannabis sativa.* It is smoked or chewed as a narcotic. [Arabic *hashīsh.*]

hash mark **1.** *Slang.* service stripe. **2.** either of two short lines which intersect with and divide each five-yard line on a football field into three equal parts.

Has·i·dism (has′i diz′əm) *n.* mystical religious movement among Jews which stresses virtue, religious joy, and the possibility of communion with God through emotional prayer. [Hebrew *hāsīdh* pious + -ISM.] —**Ha·sid′ic,** *adj.*

has·n't (haz′ənt) has not.

hasp (hasp) *n.* any of several clasps or fastenings, esp. a hinged metal clasp which fits over a staple and is fastened by a pin or padlock, used to keep a door, window, or box closed. [Old English *hæpse.*]

Hasp

has·sle (has′əl) *Informal. n.* **1.** heated argument; squabble. **2.** bother; irritation; struggle. —*v.i.* **-sled, -sling.** to squabble; fight. —*v.t.* to bother or irritate. [Possibly blend of HAGGLE and TUSSLE.]

has·sock (has′ək) *n.* **1.** low, cushioned stool used for resting the feet, sitting, or kneeling on. **2.** tuft of coarse grass. [Old English *hassuc* coarse grass. The stool was formerly made of coarse grass.]

hast (hast) *Archaic.* second person singular present indicative of **have.** ▲ used with *thou.*

has·tate (has′tāt) *adj.* (of leaves) shaped like the head of a spear. [Latin *hastātus* armed with a spear, from *hasta* spear.]

haste (hāst) *n.* **1.** swiftness of motion or action; hurry; speed: *She departed in great haste in order to make the train.* **2.** rash or careless hurry: *Haste makes waste.* **3. to make haste.** to move quickly; hurry. —*v.t., v.i.,* **hast·ed, hast·ing.** *Archaic.* to hasten. [Old French *haste* speed; of Germanic origin.] —**Syn. 1.** see **hurry.**

has·ten (hā′sən) *v.t.* to cause to move or act quickly; speed up: *That mistake will hasten his downfall.* —*v.i.* to move or act quickly; hurry: *He hastened to her side.*

Has·tings (hās′tingz) *n.* city in southeastern England on the English Channel, site of William the Conqueror's decisive victory over the Saxons in 1066.

hast·y (hās′tē) **hast·i·er, hast·i·est.** *adj.* **1.** swift in motion or action; hurried; quick: *a hasty meal.* **2.** characterized by careless hurry; rash: *to be hasty in drawing conclusions.* **3.** showing anger or easily made angry; impatient: *hasty words, a hasty temper.* —**hast′i·ly,** *adv.* —**hast′i·ness,** *n.*

hasty pudding **1.** mush made of flour or oatmeal boiled with water or milk. **2.** mush made of corn meal.

hat (hat) *n.* **1.** any of various coverings for the head, usually having a brim and crown. **2. to pass the hat.** to take up a collection; ask for contributions. **3. to take off one's hat to.** to praise or congratulate. **4. to talk through (one's) hat.** to speak ignorantly; talk nonsense. **5. to toss one's hat into the ring.** to enter into a competition, esp. as a candidate for office. **6. under one's hat.** in confidence; private. —*v.t.* **hat·ted, hat·ting.** to furnish or cover with a hat. [Old English *hæt.*]

hat·band (hat′band′) *n.* cloth band around the crown of a hat, just above the brim.

hat·box (hat′boks′) *n.* round box or piece of luggage for a hat.

hatch¹ (hach) *v.t.* **1.** to cause young to be brought forth from (the egg): *to hatch eggs in an incubator.* **2.** to bring forth (young) from the egg: *The hen hatched the chickens yesterday.* **3.** to devise or bring forth, as a plan or plot; scheme. —*v.i.* **1.** to come forth from the egg: *The chicks hatched by pecking through their shells.* **2.** (of eggs) to produce young: *All the eggs hatched today.* —*n.* **1.** act of hatching. **2.** brood of young hatched. [Probably from an unrecorded Old English word.] —**hatch′er,** *n.*

hatch² (hach) *n.* **1.a.** opening in a ship's deck for access to lower decks or to the ship's hold. **b.** similar opening in the floor or roof of a building. Also, **hatch′way′.** **2.** cover or trap door for such openings. **3.** lower half of a door or gate with two movable parts. **4. down the hatch.** drink up; eat up. [Old English *hæc* half-door, gate.]

hatch³ (hach) *v.t.* to mark with fine parallel or crossed lines, as for shading in drawing and engraving. —*n.* one of these lines. [Old French *hacher* to hack. See HASH.]

hatch·el (hach′əl) *n.* hackle¹ (def. 4). —*v.t.* hackle¹ (def. 2). [Form of HACKLE¹.]

hatch·er·y (hach′ər ē) *pl.,* **-er·ies.** *n.* place where eggs are hatched, esp. those of fish or poultry.

hatch·et (hach′it) *n.* **1.** small, short-handled ax designed to be used with one hand. **2.** tomahawk. **3. to bury the hatchet.** to stop fighting; make peace. [Old French *hachette,* diminutive of *hache* ax; of Germanic origin.]

hatch·ing (hach′ing) *n.* **1.** use of fine, parallel, or crossed lines chiefly for shading effects in drawing or engraving. **2.** pattern of lines so created. [HATCH³ + -ING¹.]

hatch·ment (hach′mənt) *n.* square tablet set diagonally bearing the coat of arms of a deceased person. [Earlier *achement, atcheament,* form of ACHIEVEMENT.]

hatch·way (hach′wā′) *n.* hatch² (def. 1).

hate (hāt) **hat·ed, hat·ing.** *v.t.* **1.** to have an intense dislike for: *to hate cruelty.* **2.** to think of as unpleasant or distasteful; be unwilling: *She hates to sew.* —*v.i.* to feel intense dislike. —*n.* **1.** intense dislike or animosity; hatred. **2.** one who or that which is hated. [Old English *hatian* to detest.] —**hat′er,** *n.*

Syn. 1. Hate, detest, abhor, loathe indicate strong dislike. **Hate** implies deep emotion and is used often to indicate personal animosity: *The two rivals hated each other from the start.* **Detest** suggests an even stronger, but less personal dislike and is often accompanied by a feeling of disdain: *She detests men who smoke cigars.* **Abhor** implies a strong dislike of something to the point of repugnance or revulsion: *I abhor*

physical violence. **Loathe** suggests total revulsion: *That girl loathes snakes.*

hate·ful (hāt′fəl) *adj.* **1.** deserving or arousing hatred; detestable: *a hateful crime.* **2.** feeling or showing hate; full of hate. —**hate′ful·ly,** *adv.* —**hate′ful·ness,** *n.*
Syn. 1. Hateful, odious, obnoxious, offensive refer to something arousing great dislike or aversion. **Hateful** implies a feeling of active hostility: *Her conduct toward that salesgirl is hateful.* **Odious** emphasizes the distasteful or disgusting quality of that which arouses such dislike: *The book describes the odious atrocities of war.* **Obnoxious** refers to that which offends one to the point of actual discomfort and is often used of social behavior: *The hecklers in the crowd became so obnoxious that they were asked to leave.* **Offensive** suggests the arousing of active displeasure and, although not as strong as *obnoxious,* is also used widely of social behavior: *His language is more offensive than his manners.*
hath (hath) *Archaic.* third person singular present indicative of **have.**
hat·pin (hat′pin′) *n.* long, sometimes decorative, pin for fastening a woman's hat to her hair.
hat·rack (hat′rak′) *n.* rack or pole with hooks used to hold hats.
ha·tred (hā′trid) *n.* intense dislike or animosity. [Middle English *hatereden,* going back to Old English *hete* intense dislike + *rǣden* condition.]
hat·ter (hat′ər) *n.* one who makes or sells hats.
Hat·ter·as, Cape (hat′ər əs) cape on an island off the eastern coast of North Carolina, site of many shipwrecks.
hau·ber·geon (hô′bər jən) *n.* habergeon (*def. 1*).
hau·berk (hô′burk′) *n.* long coat of chain mail or scale armor worn in feudal Europe. [Old French *hauberc;* of Germanic origin.]
haugh·ty (hô′tē) **-ti·er, -ti·est.** *adj.* having or showing excessive pride in oneself and great disdain for others. [From obsolete *haught* (from Old French *haut* high, from Latin *altus*) + -Y¹.] —**haugh′ti·ly,** *adv.* —**haugh′ti·ness.** *n.* —**Syn.** see **proud.**
haul (hôl) *v.t.* **1.** to pull or draw with force; drag; tug: *We hauled the cart up the hill.* **2.** to transport, as in a truck or car: *Railroads haul freight cross-country.* **3.** *Nautical.* to change the course of (a vessel), esp. to sail closer to the wind. **4. to haul up.** to force to appear, as before a court or judge. —*v.i.* **1.** to pull; tug. **2.** (of the wind) to change direction; shift: *The wind hauled to the south.* **3.** *Nautical.* to change course, esp. to sail closer to the wind. **4. to haul off. a.** to draw back the arm to deliver a blow. **b.** *Nautical.* to change course or move away from an object. —*n.* **1.** forceful pull or tug. **2.** that which is obtained or taken, as by catching or winning: *a big haul of money.* **3.** distance over which a load is hauled: *a long haul.* **4.** that which is hauled; quantity transported. [Form of HALE².] —**haul′er,** *n.*
haul·age (hô′lij) *n.* **1.** act or process of hauling. **2.** force used in hauling. **3.** fee charged for hauling.
haunch (hônch) *n.* **1.** part of the body including the hip, buttock, and upper thigh in man and four-footed animals. **2.** leg and loin of an animal, as a deer or sheep, used for food. [Old French *hanche* hip; of Germanic origin.]
haunt (hônt) *v.t.* **1.** (of ghosts or spirits) to visit or inhabit. **2.** to appear to, or come to the mind of, persistently: *The face of his dead wife haunts him.* **3.** to visit often; frequent: *to haunt the movies.* —*n.* **1.** place often visited; hangout: *That restaurant was his favorite haunt.* **2.** *Informal.* ghost. [Old French *hanter* to frequent; of Germanic origin.]
haunt·ed (hôn′tid) *adj.* visited or inhabited by ghosts: *a haunted house.*
haunt·ing (hôn′ting) *adj.* appearing or coming to the mind persistently; hard to forget: *a haunting melody.* —**haunt′ing·ly,** *adv.*
Haupt·mann, Ger·hart (houpt′män′; ger′härt′) 1862–1946, German playwright, novelist, and poet.
haut·boy (hō′boi′, ō′boi′) *n.* oboe. [French *hautbois,* from *haut* high (from Latin *altus*) + *bois* wood (from Late Latin *boscus*). See BUSH.]
haute (ōt) *adj.* elevated or developed to a high degree of refinement; fashionable or influential: *haute couture, haute cuisine.* [French *haute,* feminine of *haut* high, from Latin *altus.*]
hau·teur (hō tur′) *n.* haughtiness; arrogance. [French *hauteur,* from *haut* high, from Latin *altus.*]
Ha·van·a (hə van′ə) *n.* **1.** capital and chief port of Cuba, on the northwestern coast of the island. Pop. (1966), 990,000. **2.** cigar made from Cuban tobacco.
have (hav; *unstressed* həv, əv) **had, hav·ing. Present:** *sing.,* first person, **have;** second, **have** or (*archaic*) **hast;** third, **has** or (*archaic*) **hath;** *pl.,* **have.** *v.t.* **1.** to hold in one's hand or bear on one's person: *The girl has a scarf around her neck.* **2.** to own or be in possession of: *The man has four dollars in his wallet.* **3.** to be related to or connected with by a bond similar to that of possession: *The king has many enemies.* **4.** to contain or be characterized by: *The year has twelve months.* **5.** to harbor, esp. in the mind: *Do you have any doubts? I don't know what he has against us.* **6.** to exhibit or exercise: *One must have patience when dealing with children.* **7.** to cause to or cause to be: *Please have*

the matter taken care of. **8.** to engage in; carry on: *to have a discussion. The boys had a fight.* **9.** to experience; undergo: *We had a good time. She had a frightening dream.* **10.** to be affected with; suffer from: *Jane had the mumps when she was ten years old.* **11.** to be obliged to do or deal with: *I have a lot of errands this afternoon.* **12.** to make arrangements for and carry out: *The senator had a dinner party for the ambassador.* **13.** to give birth to. **14.** to be obligated, compelled, or necessitated: *I have to go to the grocery store.* ▲ used with an infinitive. **15.** to eat or drink: *We always have eggs for breakfast.* **16.** to invite or entertain as a guest: *We had Mary over for dinner last week.* **17.** to receive, take, or obtain: *The play had bad reviews. Used cars can be had for as little as $500.* **18.** to permit or tolerate: *I won't have you talk to me like that.* **19.** to maintain or assert: *Rumor has it that they eloped.* **20.** to possess knowledge of or understand: *He has a little Greek, but no Latin.* **21.** *Informal.* to cheat or deceive: *You've been had.* **22.** *Informal.* to hold at a disadvantage: *The boxer has his opponent now.* **23.** an auxiliary verb used with past participles to form the perfect tenses, expressing completed action: *We have done the work. We had done the work. We shall have done the work.* **24. to have it in for.** *Informal.* to have or hold a grudge against. **25. to have it out.** to settle (a matter) by fighting or discussion. **26. to have had it. a.** to have experienced or put up with all that one is able. **b.** to have come to the end, as of a career; be finished. —*v.i.* **to have to do with. a.** to have as a relation to or connection with: *What does this have to do with you?* **b.** to associate with as a friend, companion, or partner. —*n. usually,* **the haves.** person or country that has much property, wealth,. or resources: *the haves and the have-nots.* [Old English *habban* to hold, possess.]
have·lock (hav′lok′) *n.* white cloth covering for a military cap, having a flap that hangs over the back of the neck. [From Sir Henry *Havelock,* nineteenth-century British general in India.]
ha·ven (hā′vən) *n.* **1.** harbor; port. **2.** place of safety or shelter; refuge. —*v.t.* to shelter in or as in a haven. [Old English *hæfen* harbor, from Old Norse *höfn.*]
have-not (hav′not′) *n.* person or country having little or no property, wealth, or resources.
have·n't (hav′ənt) have not.
Ha·ver·hill (hā′vər il, -vrəl) *n.* city in northeastern Massachusetts. Pop. (1970), 46,120.
hav·er·sack (hav′ər sak′) *n.* bag, usually suspended at one's side by a strap, used to carry food and other provisions. [French *havresac,* from German *Habersack* oat sack.]
hav·oc (hav′ək) *n.* **1.** general destruction; devastation; ruin. **2. to play havoc with.** to devastate. **3. to cry havoc.** to give the signal for pillage and destruction. [Anglo-Norman *havok,* form of Old French *havot* plunder; possibly of Germanic origin.]
Ha·vre (hä′vrə, -vər) *n.* Le Havre.
haw¹ (hô) *n.* **1.** fruit of any hawthorn. **2.** hawthorn. [Old English *haga* hedge, hawthorn.]
haw² (hô) *v.i.* to hesitate in speaking; grope for words. ▲ usually used in the phrase *to hem and haw.* —*n.* stammering sound made by a speaker when hesitating between words. [Imitative.]
haw³ (hô) *interj.* to the left. ▲ used to direct horses, mules, and certain other animals. —*v.t., v.i.* to turn to the left. [Of uncertain origin.]
Ha·wai·i (hə wī′ē, -wä′ē) *n.* **1.** state of the United States, comprising the Hawaiian Islands. It is the only island state and the only state not on the North American continent. Capital, Honolulu. Land area, 6424 sq. mi. Pop. (1970), 748,575. **2.** largest of the Hawaiian Islands. Area, 4021 sq. mi. Pop. (1970), 61,586.
Ha·wai·ian (hə wī′ən, -wä′yən) *adj.* of or relating to Hawaii, its people, or their language. —*n.* **1.** member or close descendant of the people of Hawaii. **2.** language belonging to the Polynesian branch of the Malayo-Polynesian family of languages, spoken predominantly in Hawaii.
Hawaiian Islands, island chain in the North Pacific constituting the state of Hawaii, formerly known as the Sandwich Islands.

Hawk

hawk¹ (hôk) *n.* **1.** any of various birds of prey, genera *Accipiter* and *Buteo,* having a sharp, hooked beak, strong talons, and short, rounded wings. Length: to 2 feet. **2.** any of various other birds of prey, as the eagle, buzzard, and kite. **3.** one who preys on others; swindler. **4.** person, esp. one in public office, who advocates or supports the use of aggressive military force. —*v.i.* to hunt game with trained hawks; engage in falconry. [Old English *hafoc* bird of prey used in falconry.] —**hawk′ish,** *adj.*
hawk² (hôk) *v.t.* to offer (goods) for sale by calling out in public: *He hawked his wares in the marketplace.* [From HAWKER².]

hawk³ (hôk) *v.i.* to clear the throat noisily by coughing. —*v.t.* to bring up (phlegm) by coughing. —*n.* noisy effort to clear the throat. [Imitative.]

hawk·er¹ (hô′kər) *n.* falconer. [Old English *hafocere*.]

hawk·er² (hô′kər) *n.* one who hawks goods. [Low German *höker*.]

hawk-eyed (hôk′īd′) *adj.* having keen vision.

hawk·ing (hô′king) *n.* falconry.

hawk moth, any of a group of large, stout-bodied moths, family Sphingidae, noted for their strong, rapid flight.

hawks·bill (hôks′bil′) *also,* **hawk's-bill.** *n.* saltwater turtle, *Eretmochelys imbricata,* found in warm waters, whose brown-and-yellow, shieldlike shell is the major commercial source of tortoise shell. Length: 2–3 feet. Weight: to 160 pounds. Also, **hawksbill turtle.**

hawk·weed (hôk′wēd′) *n.* any of a large group of plants, genus *Hieracium,* of the composite family, found growing as a weed in Europe and North and South America, bearing yellow or orange daisylike flower heads and usually having hairy leaves and stems.

hawse (hôz) *n.* **1.** that part of a ship's bow where the hawseholes are located. **2.** hawsehole. **3.** the space from the hawsehole in the bow of a moored ship to the point where the anchor cable enters the water. **4.** arrangement of the two anchor cables of a ship that is moored with both a port anchor and a starboard one. [Old Norse *hāls* neck, ship's bow.]

hawse·hole (hôz′hōl′) *n.* hole on either side of the bow of a ship through which the anchor cable or hawser is passed.

Hawsehole

Hawser

Hawse

haw·ser (hô′zər) *n.* heavy rope or cable used esp. for mooring or towing ships. [Anglo-Norman *hauceor,* from Old French *haucier, halcier* to hoist, going back to Latin *altus* high.]

haw·thorn (hô′thôrn′) *n.* any of a large group of thorny shrubs or trees, genus *Crataegus,* of the rose family, found esp. in eastern North America and bearing small red, yellow, or black fruits which are sometimes used to make jelly. [Old English *hagathorn,* from *haga* hedge + *thorn* thorn.]

Haw·thorne (hô′thôrn′) **1. Nathaniel.** 1804–64, U.S. novelist and short-story writer. **2.** city in southern California, a residential suburb of Los Angeles. Pop. (1960), 33,035.

hay (hā) *n.* **1.** any of various plants, as grass, alfalfa, or clover, cut and dried for use as feed for livestock. **2. that** (or it) **ain't hay.** *Slang.* that's a lot of money: *He makes $50,000 a year and that ain't hay.* **3. to hit the hay.** *Slang.* to go to bed. **4. to make hay while the sun shines.** to profit from, or take full advantage of, an opportunity. —*v.i.* to mow, dry, and store hay. —*v.t.* to feed with hay. [Old English *hēg* grass cut and dried for fodder.]

hay·cock (hā′kok′) *n.* small, cone-shaped pile of hay.

Hay·dn, Franz Joseph (hīd′ən; fränts) 1732–1809, Austrian composer.

Hayes, Rutherford B. (hāz) 1822–93, nineteenth president of the United States, from 1877 to 1881.

hay fever, allergy caused by breathing pollen in the air, characterized by inflammation of the air passages, itching of the eyes, and sneezing.

hay·fork (hā′fôrk′) *n.* **1.** pitchfork. **2.** mechanical device for moving or loading hay.

hay·loft (hā′lôft′) *n.* loft in a stable or barn for storing hay.

hay·mak·er (hā′mā′kər) *n. Slang.* powerful punch that results in, or is intended to result in, the person hit being knocked unconscious.

hay·mow (hā′mou′) *n.* **1.** hayloft. **2.** pile of hay stored in a barn.

hay·rack (hā′rak′) *n.* **1.** rack or frame for holding hay on which livestock may feed. **2.** framework mounted on a wagon to increase its capacity for holding hay or other bulky material. **3.** wagon equipped with such a framework.

hay·rick (hā′rik′) *n.* haystack.

hay·seed (hā′sēd′) *n.* **1.** seed of any of various grasses. **2.** clinging bits of straw, chaff, and seed that fall from hay during processing. **3.** *Slang.* person from the country; country bumpkin; hick.

hay·stack (hā′stak′) *n.* pile of hay, usually cone-shaped, stored outdoors.

Hay·ward (hā′wərd) *n.* city in western California, an industrial suburb of Oakland. Pop. (1970), 93,058.

hay·wire (hā′wīr′) *n.* wire used for baling hay. —*adj. Informal.* **1.** out of order; broken down. **2.** crazy.

haz·ard (haz′ərd) *n.* **1.** exposure to danger, harm, or loss; risk; peril. **2.** potential source of danger or harm: *Icy roads are a hazard to motorists.* **3.** fortuitous event; accident: *On what hazards turns our fate* (Lytton, 1843). **4.** any obstruction, as sand, water, or a bunker, on a golf course. **5.** dice game from which craps developed. —*v.t.* **1.** to venture: *I'll hazard a guess.* **2.** to expose to danger, harm, or loss; risk. [Old French *hasard* game played with dice, risk, accident, from Spanish

azar unfortunate throw at dice, accident, possibly from Arabic *yasara* he played at dice.] —**Syn.** *n.* **1.** see **danger.**

haz·ard·ous (haz′ər dəs) *adj.* **1.** involving danger; risky: *a hazardous trek through the jungle.* **2.** involving or dependent upon chance. —**haz′ard·ous·ly,** *adv.* —**haz′ard·ous·ness,** *n.*

haze¹ (hāz) *n.* **1.** fine suspension of mist, smoke, dust, or other particles in the air: *An early morning haze limited visibility on the highway.* **2.** vagueness of mind or mental confusion. (See HAZY.)

haze² (hāz) *hazed, haz·ing. v.t.* to harass, humiliate, and play pranks on, often with some physical abuse, esp. as part of initiation in certain colleges and universities. [Old French *haser* to vex, annoy; of uncertain origin.] —**haz′er,** *n.*

ha·zel (hā′zəl) *n.* **1.** any of a group of shrubs or trees, genus *Corylus,* grown in the United States and Europe, having oval, tooth-edged leaves and clusters of small flowers. **2.** hazelnut. **3.** reddish-brown or yellowish-brown color, like that of the hazelnut. —*adj.* **1.** of or relating to the hazel. **2.** reddish or yellowish brown in color. [Old English *hæsel* hazel tree.]

ha·zel·nut (hā′zəl nut′) *n.* light brown, round or oval, edible nut of a hazel. Also, **fil′bert.**

Hazelnut

Ha·zle·ton (hā′zəl tən) *n.* city in eastern Pennsylvania. Pop. (1970), 30,426.

Haz·litt, William (haz′lit) 1778–1830, English critic and essayist.

ha·zy (hā′zē) -**zi·er, -zi·est.** *adj.* **1.** characterized or obscured by haze: *a hazy day, a hazy view.* **2.** lacking intellectual clarity; vague: *His knowledge of the subject was hazy.* [Of uncertain origin.] —**ha′zi·ly,** *adv.* —**ha′zi·ness,** *n.*

H-bomb (āch′bom′) *n.* hydrogen bomb.

H.C., House of Commons.

h.c.f., highest common factor.

hd. 1. head. **2.** hand.

hdqrs., headquarters.

he (hē; *unstressed* ē) *sing.,* nominative, **he;** possessive, **his;** objective, **him;** *pl.,* nominative, **they;** possessive, **their, theirs;** objective, **them.** *pron.* **1.** male person or animal, or an object personified as male, that has been previously mentioned. **2.** a person; anyone: *He makes no friend who never made a foe* (Elaine, 1859). —*n. pl.,* **hes.** male person or animal. [Old English *hē,* masculine pronoun of the third person singular.]

He, helium.

H.E. 1. His Eminence. **2.** His Excellency.

head (hed) *pl.,* **heads** or *(def. 14)* **head.** *n.* **1.** anterior or upper part of the body of a vertebrate animal, containing the brain, organs of sight, hearing, taste, and smell, and part of the organs of speech. **2.** corresponding part of any animal or organism. **3.** top or uppermost part of anything: *Jane paused at the head of the stairs.* **4.** foremost part or end of anything; front: *the head of a line.* **5.** part associated with, or regarded as forming, the top or uppermost end: *Our father always sat at the head of the table.* **6.** part resembling a head in position or shape: *the head of a pin, the head of a hammer.* **7.** one to whom others are subordinate; chief; leader: *The old man was the head of the tribe.* **8.** the head regarded as the center of intelligence, memory, or imagination: *John has a good head on his shoulders.* **9.** mental ability; aptitude: *Jack has a good head for figures.* **10.** dominant rank or position; command: *The lawyer was placed at the head of the crime commission.* **11.** most honorable or prominent position or place: *Mary graduated at the head of her class.* **12.** self-control; poise: *John always lost his head when discussing politics.* **13.** conclusion, culmination, or crisis: *Jane's threat to run away brought matters to a head.* **14.** single person or animal, esp. when considered as one of a number: *The cowboys rounded up fifty head of cattle after the stampede.* **15. heads.** obverse of a coin. Opposed to **tails. 16.** the head considered as a unit in measuring: *John is a head taller than his brother.* **17.** representation of the head, as on a frieze. **18.** foam or froth on the surface of certain liquids, esp. beer. **19.** compact cluster of leaves, as of cabbage or lettuce, growing from a main stem. **20.** source, as of a river or stream. **21.** tip or point, as of a boil or abscess, where pus has accumulated and is at the point of breaking through the skin. **22.** pressure, as of a fluid: *a head of steam.* **23.** *Botany.* flower head. **24.** projecting, usually high, point of a coast; headland. **25.** tightly stretched membrane covering the end or ends of a percussion instrument, as a drum or tambourine. **26.** heading. **27.** headway. **28.** *Nautical.* **a.** forward part of a ship; bow. **b.** upper corner or top of a sail. **c.** toilet.

head and shoulders above. greatly superior to.

head over heels. a. in a somersault: *He tumbled head over heels down the stairs.* **b.** completely; thoroughly: *He was head over heels in love with her.*

one's head off. *Informal.* too much; excessively: *He talked his head off.*

at; āpe; cär; end; mē; it; īce; hot; ōld; fôrk; wood; foōl; oil; out; up; ūse; turn; sing; thin; this; zh in treasure; ə in ago, taken, pencil, lemon, circus.

on (or **upon**) **one's head.** as one's responsibility.

out of (or **off**) **one's head.** *Informal.* crazy; insane.

over one's head. a. beyond one's power or ability to comprehend. **b.** beyond one's power to handle or manage.

to go over (**someone's**) **head.** to bypass (someone) and go to a higher authority: *She went over her supervisor's head.*

to go to one's head. a. to make one dizzy or intoxicated. **b.** to make one conceited.

to keep one's head above water. a. to stay afloat. **b.** to manage to avoid disaster, loss, or failure.

to make head or tail of. to understand: *He wasn't able to make head or tail of the book.*

to put heads together. to consult together; confer.

to take it into one's head. to conceive the idea, notion, or intention.

to turn one's head. to make one overly confident or conceited. —*adj.* **1.** chief; principal; commanding. **2.** situated at the top or front. **3.** coming from in front. —*v.t.* **1.** to be or go at the top or front of: *The professors headed the procession. Your name heads the list.* **2.** to be the chief or leader of; be in charge of; direct: *to head a project.* **3.** to turn or direct the course of: *The captain headed the ship northward.* **4.** to go around the head of, as a stream. **5.** to cut off the head of: *to head fish.* **6.** to fit or furnish with a head. **7.** *Soccer.* to hit (the ball) with the head. **8. to head off.** to get in front of and turn back or aside; intercept. —*v.i.* **1.** to move in a certain direction or toward a specified point: *Don and Sherry headed for the mountains for their vacation.* **2.** (of streams) to originate; rise. **3.** to come to or form a head. [Old English *hēafod* part of the body containing the brain and sense organs, highest point, chief, source.]

head·ache (hed′āk′) *n.* **1.** pain in the head. **2.** *Informal.* source or cause of annoyance, trouble, or worry.

head·band (hed′band′) *n.* narrow band, usually of cloth, worn around the head to hold the hair in place or as an ornament.

head·board (hed′bôrd′) *n.* board that forms the head of a bedstead.

head·cheese (hed′chēz′) *n.* food made from the boiled meat of the head and feet of a hog or calf, finely chopped, seasoned, and chilled to form a jellylike mass.

head·dress (hed′dres′) *n.* **1.** covering or decoration for the head. **2.** style in which the hair is arranged; coiffure.

head·ed (hed′id) *adj.* **1.** having a head or heading. **2.** grown or formed into a head, as cabbage. **3.** having a specified kind of head or number of heads. **⚊** used in combination: *clear-headed, a three-headed monster.*

head·er (hed′ər) *n.* **1.a.** one who or that which removes heads, esp. a machine which removes the heads from grain. **b.** one who or that which puts on or makes heads, as for rivets or nails. **2.** brick or stone laid with its end toward the face of a wall. **3.** in a floor or roof, a beam framed between two joists and supporting the ends of the tailpieces. **4. to take a header.** to fall or plunge head-first.

head·first (hed′fûrst′) *adv.* **1.** with the head going in front. Also, **head′fore′most′.** **2.** without due consideration; impetuously.

head gate 1. upstream gate of a canal or river lock. **2.** floodgate of a race, sluice, or other channel for the control of water.

head·gear (hed′gēr′) *n.* covering for the head, esp. one worn for protection: *Football players wear special headgear.*

head·hunt·ing (hed′hun′ting) *n.* custom of cutting off the head of an enemy and preserving it as a trophy. —**head′·hunt′er,** *n.*

head·ing (hed′ing) *n.* **1.a.** that part of a written work which describes or sets apart a section of the text. **b.** division or section of a subject of discourse; topic. **2.** part serving as or forming the top or front. **3.** direction or course, as of a ship or aircraft, as indicated on the compass.

head·land (hed′lənd) *n.* point of land, usually high, projecting out into the water; cape; promontory.

head·less (hed′lis) *adj.* **1.** having no head; beheaded. **2.** having no leader or chief. **3.** foolish; stupid; brainless.

head·light (hed′līt′) *n.* bright light mounted at the front of an automobile, motorcycle, or other vehicle.

head·line (hed′līn′) *n.* one or more lines of type at the top of an article, as in a newspaper, summarizing or highlighting the contents and printed in larger type than the body of the article. —*v.t.*, **-lined, -lining. 1.** to provide with a headline, as a newspaper article. **2.** to be the main attraction of a theatrical presentation: *A tap dance act headlined the vaudeville show.*

head·lin·er (hed′lī′nər) *n.* one who or that which is the main attraction of a theatrical presentation.

head·lock (hed′lok′) *n.* wrestling hold in which the arm or arms encircle the opponent's head.

head·long (hed′lông′) *adv.* **1.** headfirst (*def. 1*). **2.** without deliberation; recklessly; impetuously. **3.** with unrestrained speed or force. —*adj.* **1.** made or moving with the head foremost: *He took a headlong dive into the cold lake.* **2.** rash; impetuous. [Modification of Middle English *hedling* headfirst, precipitate, from *hed* HEAD + -LING².]

head·man (hed′man′, -mən) *pl.*, **-men.** *n.* chief; leader.

head·mas·ter (hed′mas′tər) *n.* principal or head of a school, esp. a private elementary or secondary school. —**head′mas′ter·ship′, head′mis′tress,** *n.* —Syn. see **principal.**

head·most (hed′mōst′) *adj.* most advanced; foremost.

head·on (hed′ôn′, -on′) *adj., adv.* with the head or front end foremost: *a head-on collision, to collide head-on.*

head·phone (hed′fōn′) *n.* electronic receiver held against or worn over the ear.

head·piece (hed′pēs′) *n.* **1.** covering for the head, as a hat, cap, or helmet. **2.** pair of headphones. **3.** *Printing.* decorative design, usually at the beginning of a book or chapter or at the top of a page.

head pin, front pin of the triangle of pins in bowling.

head·quar·ters (hed′kwôr′tərz) *n.* **1.** center of operations from which a commanding officer, chief, or other leader, as of an army or police force, issues orders. **2.** center of operations, as of a business; main office. **3.** entire staff of a center of operations. **⚊** construed as singular or plural in all definitions.

head register, head tone.

head·rest (hed′rest′) *n.* support for the head.

head·sail (hed′sāl′, -sǝl) *n.* any sail set forward of the foremast, as a jib.

head·set (hed′set′) *n.* pair of headphones.

head·ship (hed′ship′) *n.* position or office of a person in charge.

heads·man (hedz′mən) *pl.*, **-men.** *n.* one who beheads condemned criminals; public executioner.

Headset

head·stall (hed′stôl′) *n.* part of a bridle or halter that fits around the head of an animal.

head·stand (hed′stand′) *n.* balancing of the body on the head in an upside-down vertical position, usually assisted by the hands.

head start 1. advantage of starting a race ahead of others. **2.** similar advantage in any competition.

head·stock (hed′stok′) *n.* part of a machine that supports a revolving or working part or parts, as the part supporting the spindle of a lathe.

head·stone (hed′stōn′) *n.* **1.** stone, usually with an inscription, set at the head of a grave; tombstone. **2.** principal stone in a structure, as a cornerstone or keystone.

head·strong (hed′strông′) *adj.* **1.** determined to have one's own way or do as one pleases; willful. **2.** characterized by or proceeding from obstinate willfulness.

Syn. 1. Headstrong, willful suggest being unyielding or ungovernable by temperament or nature. **Headstrong** stresses unreasonable insistence on having one's own way, even to the point of foolhardiness: *Because of his headstrong action, he was suspended for thirty days.* **Willful** emphasizes stubborn adherence to one's own ideas and wishes without regard to reason or advice: *His willful disobedience could not be tamed by his parents.*

head tone, tone produced in the higher registers of a vocal range, bringing the cavities of the head and nose into sympathetic vibration. Also, **head register, head voice.**

head·wait·er (hed′wā′tər) *n.* man who supervises the waiters in a restaurant and sometimes is responsible for taking reservations and seating guests.

head·wa·ters (hed′wô′tərz, -wot′ərz) *n.,pl.* small streams at the source of a river that unite to form the main channel.

head·way (hed′wā′) *n.* **1.** forward motion or progress: *The ship made little headway in the storm.* **2.** clear space overhead, as under a bridge. **3.** interval of time or distance between two trains, ships, or other vehicles traveling over the same route.

head wind, wind blowing from the direction in which something, as a ship, is moving.

head·work (hed′wûrk′) *n.* mental labor or effort; thought.

head·y (hed′ē) **head·i·er, head·i·est.** *adj.* **1.** tending to make one dizzy or giddy; intoxicating: *the heady aroma of poppies.* **2.** headstrong; willful. —**head′i·ly,** *adv.* —**head′i·ness,** *n.*

heal (hēl) *v.i.* **1.** to close, as a wound, or knit, as a broken bone: *The wound healed without leaving a scar.* **2.** to become whole or sound; get well: *Her arm healed quickly.* —*v.t.* **1.** to restore to health or sound-

Section of a roof captions:

Tail beams

Rafter

Headers

Rafter

Trimmers

Opening

Header (def. 3)
Section of a roof

ness; cure: *The doctor healed the sick child.* **2.** to effect the cure or remedy of, as a wound. **3.** to remedy, repair, or remove: *The breach in our ranks might be healed tomorrow* (Trevelyan, 1887). **4.** to free from an evil or distressing state or condition; purify; cleanse: *Heal me with your pardon* (Tennyson, 1847). [Old English *hælan* to make whole, cure repair.] —**heal′er,** *n.* —**Syn.** *v.t.* **1.,2.** see **cure.**

health (helth) *n.* **1.** soundness of body and mind; freedom from defect or disease. **2.** condition of body and mind: *The doctor said the boy was in very good health.* **3.** toast drunk in a person's honor expressing a wish for his well-being: *We drank a health to him before his ship sailed.* [Old English *hælth* soundness of body or mind.]

health food, any of certain foods to which some people ascribe special nutritional or therapeutic properties.

health·ful (helth′fəl) *adj.* **1.** promoting health; wholesome. **2.** healthy *(def. 1).* —**health′ful·ly,** *adv.* —**health′ful·ness,** *n.*

health·y (hel′thē) **health·i·er, health·i·est.** *adj.* **1.** having good health; well: *a healthy young woman.* **2.** characteristic of or showing good health or sound condition: *a healthy appearance, a healthy outlook on life.* **3.** conducive to health; healthful. **4.** *Informal.* considerable or great in amount, size, or intensity: *She kept a healthy distance from the tiger.* —**health′i·ly,** *adv.* —**health′i·ness,** *n.*

heap (hēp) *n.* **1.** collection of things randomly piled together; mass: *a heap of clothes on the floor.* **2.** also, **heaps.** *Informal.* a large number or quantity; lot: *We saw heaps of people that we knew.* —*v.t.* **1.** to make into a heap; pile. **2.** to fill (something) full or more than full: *She heaped the dish with mashed potatoes.* **3.** to cast or bestow in large measure: *to heap insults on his memory* (Bright, 1861). [Old English *hēap* pile of things, crowd.]

heap·ing (hē′ping) *adj.* filled above the normal capacity: *The recipe called for a heaping teaspoon of salt.*

hear (hēr) **heard** (hurd), **hear·ing.** *v.t.* **1.** to be able to perceive (sound) by means of the ear. **2.** to pay attention to; listen: *We heard both sides of the argument before we made a decision.* **3.** to be informed of: *We heard the news on the radio.* **4.** to give a formal, official, or legal hearing to: *The judge heard the testimony of all the witnesses.* **5.** to listen with compliance; accede to; grant: *His prayers were heard.* **6.** to attend and listen to as part of an audience. **7. to hear out.** to listen to until the end: *Hear me out before you decide.* —*v.i.* **1.** to perceive or be able to perceive sound by means of the ear. **2.** to receive information; be told; learn (with *of, about,* or *from*): *What have you heard about the situation? Have you ever heard of him?* **3. to hear of.** to allow, consider, or agree to: *I will not hear of your leaving.* ▲ usually with the negative. **4. to hear tell.** *Informal.* to learn: *I hear tell you're getting married.* —*interj.* **hear, hear.** well done or well spoken. [Old English *hēran* to perceive sound, listen.] —**hear′er,** *n.*

Syn. *v.i.* **1. Hear, listen** mean to perceive sound by the ear. **Hear** suggests the physical act of perceiving sound: *Deaf men cannot hear.* **Listen** implies giving heed or paying attention to what is heard: *The audience listened very carefully to the president's speech.*

hear·ing (hēr′ing) *n.* **1.** faculty or sense by which sound is perceived; ability to hear: *She has acute hearing.* **2.** act or process of perceiving sound: *Hearing your voice brought back happy memories.* **3.** opportunity to be heard; audience: *We were granted a hearing to air our grievances.* **4.** investigation or trial before a judge or any person or group invested with judicial power. **5.** distance within which sound may be heard; earshot: *The child was told to play within hearing of the house.*

hearing aid, small electronic device that amplifies sound, worn to compensate for poor hearing.

hark·en (här′kən) harken.

hear·say (hēr′sā′) *n.* information received by word of mouth rather than by personal knowledge; gossip; rumor.

hearsay evidence, evidence given by a witness proceeding from what another person has told him rather than personal knowledge. It is admissible as testimony in very rare instances.

hearse (hurs) *n.* vehicle for conveying a dead person from one place to another before or after a funeral service. [Old French *herce* harrow, frame holding candles, as at a funeral, going back to Latin *hirpex* harrow, from Samnite *hirpus* wolf; with reference to the resemblance of the teeth of a wolf to the teeth of a harrow.]

Hearst, William Randolph (hurst) 1863–1951, U.S. editor and newspaper publisher.

heart (härt) *n.* **1.** hollow, muscular organ that pumps the blood through the body by means of rhythmic contractions and dilations. **2.** region of the body containing the heart; bosom. **3.** one's innermost feelings or thoughts: *He knew in his heart that they would never meet again.* **4.** the heart considered as the center of the emotions, esp. of love and affection: *He spoke from his heart.* **5.** love and affection: *The little girl won our hearts.* **6.** disposition; nature: *She has a kind heart.* **7.** capacity for kindness or compassion for others: *He has no heart.* **8.** mental state; mood: *a heavy heart.* **9.** firmness of will; spirit; courage: *to lose heart.* **10.** energy; enthusiasm; ardor: *She put all her heart into*

her work. **11.** person, esp. one who is admired or loved: *a dear heart.* **12.** center or innermost part of anything: *in the heart of the city, hearts of lettuce.* **13.** main, vital, or most essential part: *Let's get to the heart of the matter.* **14.** anything shaped like the heart: *She wore a diamond heart around her neck. They cut out paper hearts.* **15.** playing card bearing one or more red, heart-shaped figures. **16. hearts. a.** suit of such playing cards. **b.** card game played with a fifty-two card deck in which the players either try to get none or all of the cards of this suit.

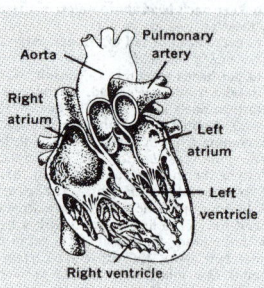

Human heart

after one's own heart. conforming perfectly to one's own ideas, tastes, or desires.

by heart. from memory or by rote: *She knew the poem by heart.*

from (the bottom of) one's heart. with deepest feeling; sincerely.

heart and soul. with all of one's affections and energies; completely; wholly: *She loved him heart and soul.*

in one's heart of hearts. in the deepest and most intimate part of one's feelings or nature: *In his heart of hearts, he knew she was right.*

to break one's heart. to cause one to feel great sorrow, disappointment, or grief: *The old man broke my heart with his sad story.*

to eat one's heart out. a. to feel great sorrow, grief, or remorse. **b.** to pine away: *She ate her heart out while he was gone.*

to have a change of heart. to change one's feelings, attitude, or opinion.

to have one's heart in one's mouth. to be terrified or very excited.

to have one's heart in the right place. to have good intentions; mean well.

to have the heart. to be hard-hearted or cruel enough.

to lose one's heart to. to fall in love with.

to set one's heart on. to desire strongly; long for.

to take to heart. a. to consider seriously or carefully: *She took the advice to heart.* **b.** to be deeply affected or worried by.

to wear one's heart on one's sleeve. to behave in a manner that plainly exposes one's feelings.

with all one's heart. a. with great sincerity or earnestness. **b.** very willingly; gladly.

[Old English *heorte.*]

Syn. 13. Heart, core, essence denote the central or vital part of a thing. **Heart** means the part, function, or principle in which the force or life of something is thought to reside: *The dynamo is the heart of that power plant.* **Core** implies the center around which something is formed as well as the inmost and most intimate part: *Infantry forms the core of the army.* **Essence** suggests the intrinsic and indispensable properties which make a thing what it is: *Simplicity is the essence of good taste.*

heart·ache (härt′āk′) *n.* emotional anguish; sorrow; grief.

heart·beat (härt′bēt′) *n.* one pulsation of the heart, consisting of one complete contraction and dilation.

heart·break (härt′brāk′) *n.* overwhelming sorrow or grief. —**heart′break′er,** *n.* —**heart′break′ing·ly,** *adv.*

heart·bro·ken (härt′brō′kən) *adj.* overwhelmed with sorrow or grief. —**heart′bro′ken·ly,** *adv.*

heart·burn (härt′burn′) *n.* **1.** burning sensation under the breastbone, produced by stomach acid rising into the esophagus. **2.** something that angers or saddens.

heart·ed (här′tid) *adj.* having or marked by a (specified kind of) disposition. ▲ used in combination, as in *light-hearted, good-hearted.*

heart·en (härt′ən) *v.t.* to give heart to; encourage; cheer: *The story of his success heartened us.*

heart·felt (härt′felt′) *adj.* deeply and earnestly felt; sincere; genuine: *He gave us his heartfelt congratulations.*

hearth (härth) *n.* **1.** floor of a fireplace, often extending out into the room. **2.** family circle; home; fireside. **3.** the lowest part of a blast furnace. [Old English *heorth.*]

hearth·stone (härth′stōn′) *n.* **1.** stone forming a hearth. **2.** family circle; home; fireside.

heart·i·ly (härt′əl ē) *adv.* **1.** with genuine sincerity or cordiality; earnestly. **2.** with enthusiasm or zeal; eagerly; vigorously: *to laugh heartily.* **3.** with a good appetite: *After the day's labors they ate heartily.* **4.** completely; thoroughly; exceedingly.

at; āpe; cär; end; mē; it; īce; hot; ōld; fôrk; wood; fōōl; oil; out; up; ūse; turn; sing; thin; this; zh in treasure; ə in ago, taken, pencil, lemon, circus.

heart·land (härt′land′) *n.* geographic area whose control is considered vital to a nation for strategic and economic reasons.

heart·less (härt′lis) *adj.* **1.** without kindness or compassion; unfeeling; cruel. **2.** without courage or enthusiasm; spiritless. —**heart′·less·ly,** *adv.* —**heart′less·ness,** *n.*

heart murmur, abnormal sound, as a rumbling or blowing, produced in the heart in addition to the normal rhythmic beating.

heart-rend·ing (härt′ren′ding) *adj.* causing much sorrow or anguish.

hearts·ease (härts′ēz′) *also,* **heart's-ease.** *n.* **1.** peace of mind. **2.** a pansy of the variety *hortensis,* cultivated as a garden flower. **3.** lady's-thumb.

heart·sick (härt′sik′) *adj.* deeply depressed or unhappy; despondent.

heart·sore (härt′sôr′) *adj.* heartsick.

heart-strick·en (härt′strik′ən) *adj.* deeply affected by grief, fear, or dismay. Also, **heart′struck′.**

heart·strings (härt′stringz′) *n.,pl.* strongest feelings or affections: *The sad story touched their heartstrings.*

heart-to-heart (härt′tə härt′) *adj.* frank; sincere; candid: *a heart-to-heart talk.*

heart·wood (härt′wood′) *n.* central portion of the wood of a tree, composed of nonliving cells and usually harder and darker than the surrounding sapwood. Also, **du·ra′·men.**

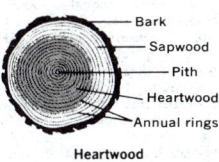

— Bark
— Sapwood
— Pith
— Heartwood
— Annual rings

Heartwood

heart·y (här′tē) **heart·i·er, heart·i·est.** *adj.* **1.** full of affection, warmth, or kindness; cordial; friendly: *a hearty welcome.* **2.** enthusiastic; vigorous; unrestrained: *a hearty laugh.* **3.** of sound health; strong and well. **4.** satisfying to the appetite; full; nourishing. **5.** requiring or using abundant nourishment: *a hearty appetite.* —*n. pl.,* **heart·ies.** bold, good fellow or comrade, esp. a sailor. [HEART + -Y².] —**heart′·i·ness,** *n.*

heat (hēt) *n.* **1.** state or quality of being hot. **2.** degree of hotness; temperature. **3.** great warmth; high temperature: *The heat in the room is stifling.* **4.** sensation or perception of hotness or warmth: *He felt the heat of the fire on his face.* **5.** warmth provided, as for a house, by any of various heating mechanisms: *We turned on the heat as soon as we got home.* **6.** hot weather or climate: *It's very difficult to work in this heat.* **7.** most intense or violent stage; point of greatest vehemence or activity: *in the heat of the battle.* **8.** intensity of feeling, esp. of anger or excitement. **9.** indication of high temperature, as by the color of a body or object. **10.** *Physics.* form of energy represented by the random motion of molecules, atoms, or smaller particles of a body. It is transferred from body to body by contact or by electromagnetic radiation. **11.** period during which female animals are able to conceive. **12.a.** single trial or effort in a contest, as a race, used to determine the contestants who will compete in the final. **b.** single division of a harness race. **13.a.** single heating operation, as of iron, in a furnace. **b.** material so heated. **14.** *Informal.* great pressure: *The heat was on to get the road paved before winter.* —*v.t., v.i.* **1.** to make or become hot or warm. **2.** to make or become excited. [Old English *hætu* great warmth, warmth of feeling.]

heat barrier, thermal barrier.

heat·er (hē′tər) *n.* **1.** apparatus that produces or gives heat or warmth. **2.** *Slang.* pistol.

heath (hēth) *n.* **1.a.** open wasteland overgrown with heather or low bushes; moor. **b.** shrub or shrubs growing upon such land. **2.** any of a large group of shrubs, genus *Erica,* found in southern Africa and Mediterranean regions as well as Europe, bearing needlelike leaves and tiny white, pink, or red tubular flowers. —*adj.* designating a family, Ericaceae, of widely distributed shrubs and small trees, including ornamentals, such as the rhododendron, azalea, and heather, and plants cultivated for their fruit, such as the cranberry and blueberry. [Old English *hæth* open wasteland, plants growing on it.]

hea·then (hē′thən) *pl.,* **-thens** *or* **-then.** *n.* **1.** one who does not believe in the God of the Bible; one who is not a Christian, Jew, or Muslim. **2.** any irreligious, uncivilized, or uncultured person. —*adj.* **1.** of or relating to heathens; pagan. **2.** irreligious, uncivilized, or uncultured. —**hea′then·ism, hea′then·ry,** *n.* —**Syn.** *n.* **1.** see **pagan.** [Old English *hæthen* pagan; originally, dweller on a heath, from *hæth* open wasteland; referring to the first converts to Christianity, who were city dwellers, while the inhabitants of remote rural areas were then pagan.] —**hea′then·ish,** *adj.*

hea·then·dom (hē′thən dəm) *n.* **1.** heathen practices or beliefs; paganism. **2.** heathen countries or people.

hea·then·ish (hē′thə nish) *adj.* **1.** of or relating to heathens. **2.** like or characteristic of heathens; barbarous.

heath·er (heth′ər) *n.* **1.** small pink bell-shaped flower of a shrub, *Calluna vulgaris,* of the heath family, growing in dense clusters. **2.** low,

evergreen shrub bearing this flower, having small, scalelike leaves. It grows wild and is particularly abundant in Scotland. [Of uncertain origin.]

heath·er·y (heth′ər ē) *adj.* **1.** of or resembling heather. **2.** covered with heather.

heat lightning, flashes of lightning occurring too far away for the thunder to be heard, seen near the horizon, esp. on summer evenings.

heat shield, covering on a spacecraft designed to protect it against the intense heat caused by friction during reentry.

heat·stroke (hēt′strōk′) *n.* serious condition caused by exposure to high temperatures, characterized by high fever, rapid pulse, and weakness or unconsciousness.

heat wave, period of extremely hot weather.

heave (hēv) **heaved** *or* (*nautical*) **hove, heav·ing.** *v.t.* **1.** to lift or raise with force or effort: *All afternoon we heaved bales of hay up onto the truck.* **2.** to throw, esp. with great effort: *He heaved a rock through the window.* **3.** to utter or emit, as a groan or sigh, with much effort or pain. **4.** to cause to rise or swell: *He heaved his chest.* **5.** *Nautical.* **a.** to raise or haul up, as an anchor. **b.** to pull, raise, or haul with or as with a rope or cable. **6. to heave to,** to bring (a ship) to a standstill; make (a ship) lie to. —*v.i.* **1.** to rise and fall continuously in a rhythmic manner: *The ship heaves with the waves.* **2.** to rise and swell; bulge: *His chest heaves with every breath.* **3.** to retch; vomit. **4.** *Nautical.* **a.** to pull, haul, or push with force or effort, as on a capstan or rope. **b.** (of a ship) to move or proceed in some direction. **5. to heave in** (or **into**) **sight,** to come into view over the horizon, as a ship when approaching or being approached. —*n.* **1.** act or effort of heaving. **2. heaves.** chronic, respiratory disease of horses. ▲ construed as singular. —*interj.* **heave ho.** pull or push hard together. [Old English *hebban* to lift.]

Heather

heav·en (hev′ən) *n.* **1.** in Christian theology, the abode of God, the angels, and those who are saved. **2. Heaven.** the Supreme Being. **3.** *also,* **heavens.** space above and around the earth; firmament; sky. **4.** happy, pleasing, or beautiful place. **5.** state of bliss or supreme happiness. **6. to move heaven and earth.** to do all that one can possibly do. [Old English *heofon.*]

heav·en·ly (hev′ən lē) *adj.* **1.** of, belonging to, or in heaven; divine; holy. **2.** of, relating to, or in the sky: *The sun and moon are heavenly bodies.* **3.** fit for or characteristic of heaven. —**heav′en·li·ness,** *n.*

heav·en·ward (hev′ən wərd) *adv.* toward heaven. Also, **heav′en·wards.** —*adj.* directed toward heaven.

heav·i·er-than-air (hev′ē ər thən âr′) *adj.* having a weight that is greater than that of air, as an airplane.

heavier-than-air craft, aircraft that is maintained in flight by the aerodynamic forces acting on its support surfaces.

heav·i·ly (hev′ə lē) *adv.* **1.** with great weight or burden: *The moving van was heavily loaded with furniture.* **2.** densely; thickly: *a heavily populated area.* **3.** slowly, clumsily, or laboriously: *to walk heavily.* **4.** to a great or excessive degree; severely: *The poor peasants were heavily taxed.* **5.** in an oppressive manner: *His sins weighed heavily on his mind.*

heav·i·ness (hev′ē nis) *n.* state or quality of being heavy.

Heav·i·side layer (hev′ē sīd′) highly ionized second layer of the ionosphere existing at fifty-five to seventy-five miles. Certain radio waves can be transmitted by repeated bouncing between the earth and this layer. [From Oliver *Heaviside* (1850–1925), English physicist.]

heav·y (hev′ē) **heav·i·er, heav·i·est.** *adj.* **1.** hard to lift or move; of great weight: *The furniture was very heavy.* **2.** having relatively much weight in proportion to size; of great specific gravity: *a heavy metal.* **3.** having more than the usual weight: *heavy paper, heavy wool.* **4.** of an unusually large amount, size, volume, or quantity: *a heavy rainfall, heavy traffic.* **5.** of great force, intensity, momentum, or impact: *a heavy blow.* **6.** acting, operating, or indulging on a large scale or to an excessive degree: *a heavy investor, a heavy drinker.* **7.** hard to bear or endure; oppressive; severe: *The judge imposed a heavy sentence against the defendant.* **8.** difficult to do, accomplish, or deal with; trying; laborious: *heavy going.* **9.** causing sorrow; sad; grievous: *heavy news.* **10.** expressing or feeling grief; sorrowful; despondent: *a heavy heart.* **11.** of great importance; grave; serious: *a heavy responsibility.* **12.** profound or intense: *a heavy silence.* **13.** weighted down; laden; burdened: *trees heavy with fruit.* **14.** broad, thick, or coarse: *She drew a heavy line through the sentence.* **15.** strong or lingering: *a heavy odor.* **16.** considerable or pronounced: *a heavy accent. The teacher put a heavy stress on that part of the work.* **17.** acting or moving slowly, clumsily, or with difficulty: *a heavy gait.* **18.** lacking animation; ponderous; tedious; dull: *a heavy style of writing.* **19.** overcast; gloomy. **20.** loud and deep; resounding. **21.** not having leavened or risen properly, as bread. **22.** (of food) not easily digestible. **23.** hindering passage or progress: *heavy underbrush.* **24.** in a theatrical presentation, designating a role that is tragic, serious, or villainous. **25.** pregnant: *heavy with child.*

26. (of an isotope) having a greater atomic weight than other isotopes of the same element. **27.** *Military.* **a.** of large size; massive: *heavy guns.* **b.** heavily armed or equipped: *heavy cavalry.* **28.** *Slang.* profound; important. *—n. pl.,* **heav·ies. 1.** tragic, serious, or villainous role in a theatrical presentation. **2.** actor portraying such a role. *—adv.* **1.** heavily. **2. to hang heavy.** to pass slowly and tediously, as time. [Old English *hefig* of great weight, important, oppressive, grievous.] **Syn.** *adj.* **1,2. Heavy, weighty, ponderous** mean of greater than normal weight. **Heavy** means great weight in proportion to its size and suggests a burden that is difficult to carry, lift, or cope with: *Trucks frequently carry heavy loads.* **Weighty** denotes real rather than relative or apparent weight: *The bridge was supported by ten weighty girders.* **Ponderous** suggests massiveness, bulk, and unwieldiness: *The elephant is a ponderous animal.*

heav·y-du·ty (hev′ē dōō′tē, -dū′-) *adj.* **1.** designed, made, or constructed for sturdiness and durability: *The work clothes were made of heavy-duty material.* **2.** having a high import or export tax rate.

heav·y-hand·ed (hev′ē han′did) *adj.* **1.** clumsy; awkward. **2.** oppressive; harsh; cruel: *heavy-handed tyranny.* **—heav′y-hand′ed·ly,** *adv.* **—heav′y-hand′ed·ness,** *n.*

heav·y-heart·ed (hev′ē här′tid) *adj.* sad; melancholy; depressed. **—heav′y-heart′ed·ness,** *n.*

heavy hydrogen, deuterium.

heavy water, water whose molecules contain atoms of hydrogen or oxygen whose mass is greater than the ordinary, esp. deuterium oxide (D₂O), which is composed of heavy hydrogen and ordinary oxygen. It is used as a moderator in nuclear reactors.

heav·y·weight (hev′ē wāt′) *n.* **1.** person or animal of much more than average weight. **2.** athlete who competes in the highest weight class in boxing, wrestling, or weight lifting. **3.** *Informal.* influential, important, or intelligent person.

Heb., Hebrew; Hebrews.

heb·dom·a·dal (heb dom′əd əl) *adj.* weekly. Also, **heb·dom′a·dar′y.** [Late Latin *hebdomadālis,* from Latin *hebdomas* seven, a week, from Greek *hebdomas.*] **—heb·dom′a·dal·ly,** *adv.*

He·be (hē′bē) *n.* Greek goddess of youth, cupbearer to the gods until replaced by Ganymede. [Latin *Hēbē,* from Greek *Hēbē,* from *hēbē* youth.]

He·bra·ic (hi brā′ik) *adj.* of, relating to, or characteristic of the Hebrews, their language, or culture. [Late Latin *Hebrāicus,* from Greek *Hebraikos,* from *Hebraios* Jew, Jewish. See HEBREW.] **—He·bra′i·cal·ly,** *adv.*

He·bra·ism (hē′brā iz′əm, -brē-) *n.* **1.** Hebrew idiom. **2.** Hebrew character, thought, or practice.

He·bra·ist (hē′brā ist, -brē-) *n.* **1.** expert in, or student of, the Hebrew language, literature, and culture. **2.** adherent of Hebrew thought, traditions, ethics, or religion.

He·bra·is·tic (hē′brā is′tik, -brē-) *adj.* of, relating to, or characteristic of Hebraism or Hebraists.

He·brew (hē′brōō) *n.* **1.** member of one of the Jewish tribes of ancient times. **2.** language originally spoken by the ancient Jews, belonging to the Semitic group of the Semito-Hamitic family of languages. It is an official language of Israel and the religious language of Judaism. *—adj.* Hebraic. [Old French *hebreu,* from Late Latin *Hebraeus* Jew, Jewish, from Greek *Hebraios,* from Aramaic *'ebrāyā* Jew, ancient Hebrew language, from Hebrew *'ibrī* literally, one from across (the river).]

Hebrew calendar, calendar which begins with the assumed date of the Creation, 3761 B.C., and varies in the number of days per year from 353 to 385. It is used for dating Jewish religious observances and is the official calendar of Israel.

He·brews (hē′brōōz) *n.* book of the New Testament, the Epistle to the Hebrews, attributed to Saint Paul.

Heb·ri·des (heb′rə dēz′) *n.* Scottish island group off the northwestern coast of Scotland. Land area, 2812 sq. mi. Pop. (1965 est.), 46,000.

He·bron (hē′brən) *n.* town in Israeli-occupied western Jordan. It is one of the world's oldest settlements. Pop. (1967 est.), 43,000.

Hec·a·te (hek′ə tē, hek′it) *n.* Greek goddess who had power over the moon, the earth, and the realm of the dead, and was also associated with sorcery.

hec·a·tomb (hek′ə tōm′, -tōōm′) *n.* **1.** any great slaughter or sacrifice. **2.** in ancient Greece and Rome, a public sacrifice of a hundred oxen or other animals at one time. [Latin *hecatombē,* from Greek *hekatombē,* from *hekaton* hundred + *bous* ox.]

heck·le (hek′əl) **-led, -ling.** *v.t.* to harass and annoy (a speaker) with questions, taunts, and gibes. [Form of HACKLE¹; referring to the teasing of flax with a comb.] **—heck′ler,** *n.* **—Syn.** see bait.

hect-, form of hecto- before vowels, as in *hectare.*

hec·tare (hek′târ) *n.* metric measure of area equal to 10,000 square meters, or 2.471 acres. [French *hectare* literally, 100 ares, from Greek *hekaton* hundred + French *are.* See ARE².]

hec·tic (hek′tik) *adj.* **1.** characterized by great excitement, agitation,

haste, and activity: *a hectic day.* **2.** relating to or having hectic fever. [Late Latin *hectica (febris)* continuous (fever), from Greek *hektikos (pyretos)* continuous or consumptive (fever), from *hexis* condition of (the body).] **—hec′ti·cal·ly,** *adv.*

hectic fever, daily rise in bodily temperature accompanying tuberculosis, usually occurring in the afternoon or evening.

hecto- combining form hundred: *hectometer.* [French *hecto-,* from Greek *hekaton.*]

hec·to·gram (hek′tə gram′) *also, British,* **hec·to·gramme.** *n.* metric measure of weight equal to 100 grams, or 3.527 ounces avoirdupois.

hec·to·graph (hek′tə graf′) *n.* duplicating machine in which the ink impression from an original copy is transferred onto a gelatin-coated surface from which other copies may be made. *—v.t.* to make copies of with a hectograph. **—hec′to·graph′ic,** *adj.* **—hec′to·graph′i·cal·ly,** *adv.*

hec·to·li·ter (hek′tə lē′tər) *also, British,* **hec·to·li·tre.** *n.* metric measure of capacity equal to 100 liters, 2.8378 bushels, or 26.4 U.S. gallons.

hec·to·me·ter (hek′tə mē′tər) *also, British,* **hec·to·me·tre.** *n.* metric measure of length equal to 100 meters, one-tenth of a kilometer, or 328.08 feet.

hec·tor (hek′tər) *v.t., v.i.* to bluster, brag, or bully. *—n.* brawling, swaggering fellow; bully. [From HECTOR.]

Hec·tor (hek′tər) *n. Greek Legend.* eldest son of King Priam of Troy, killed by Achilles. [Latin *Hector,* from Greek *Hektōr,* from *hektōr* holding fast.]

Hec·u·ba (hek′yə bə) *n. Greek Legend.* wife of King Priam of Troy and mother of Hector.

he'd (hēd; *unstressed* ēd) **1.** he had. **2.** he would.

hedge (hej) *n.* **1.** row of shrubs or small trees planted close together, forming a fence or barrier. **2.** any barrier or boundary. **3.** act or means of protecting oneself against loss or risk. *—v.t.,* **hedged, hedg·ing. 1.** to surround, enclose, or separate with a hedge. **2.** to protect oneself from losing money on (a bet or investment) by making another bet or investment that would compensate for any possible loss on the first. **3.** to surround as with a barrier so as to hinder or obstruct free movement. *—v.i.* **1.** to avoid giving a direct answer or committing oneself. **2.** to protect oneself from losing money on a bet or investment by making another bet or investment that would compensate for any possible loss on the first. [Old English *hecg* row of bushes planted as a boundary.] **—hedg′er,** *n.*

hedge·hog (hej′hôg′, ′-hog′) *n.* **1.** any of various insect-eating mammals, family Erinaceidae, having a pointed snout and a thick mass of

Hedgehog

sharp, hard spines. When frightened or attacked, it rolls up into a tight ball with only its spines exposed. Length: 1 foot. **2.** porcupine. **3.** *Military.* obstacle strung with barbed wire.

hedge·hop (hej′hop′) **-hopped, -hop·ping.** *v.i.* to fly close to the ground, rising over obstacles as they occur. **—hedge′-hop′per,** *n.*

hedge·row (hej′rō′) *n.* row of shrubs or small trees planted close together, forming a fence or barrier; hedge.

hedge sparrow, sparrowlike European warbler, *Prunella modularis,* that frequents gardens and other cultivated land.

He·djaz (hē jaz′, he jäz′) Hejaz.

he·don·ism (hēd′ən iz′əm) *n.* **1.** theory that pleasure is the highest good. **2.** pursuit of pleasure as a way of life. [Greek *hēdonē* pleasure + -ISM.]

he·don·ist (hēd′ən ist) *n.* one who advocates or practices hedonism. **—he′don·is′tic,** *adj.* **—he′don·is′ti·cal·ly,** *adv.*

hee·bie-jee·bies (hē′bē jē′bēz) *n.,pl. Informal.* fit of nervousness; jitters. [Coined by the American comic-strip cartoonist Billy De Beck, 1890–1942.]

heed (hēd) *v.t.* to pay careful attention to; mind. *—v.i.* to pay careful attention; notice. *—n.* careful attention; notice: *Let us take heed, and be on our guard against deceptions* (Jowett, 1875). [Old English *hēdan* to take notice.] **—heed′er,** *n.*

heed·ful (hēd′fəl) *adj.* giving or taking heed; attentive; mindful. **—heed′ful·ly,** *adv.* **—heed′ful·ness,** *n.*

heed·less (hēd′lis) *adj.* not attentive; unmindful. **—heed′less·ly,** *adv.* **—heed′less·ness,** *n.*

hee·haw (hē′hô′) *n.* **1.** braying sound made by a donkey. **2.** loud, rude laugh. *—v.i.* **1.** to bray. **2.** to laugh in a loud, rude manner. [Imitative.]

heel¹ (hēl) *n.* **1.** rounded, projecting rear part of the human foot, below the ankle. **2.** corresponding part of the hind leg of an animal. **3.** fleshy, rounded part of the palm of the hand, near the wrist. **4.** that part of a stocking, shoe, or other piece of footwear that covers

the heel. **5.** thick, built-up part of a shoe or boot that is under or raises the heel: *Certain shoe styles have lower heels.* **6.** anything resembling the human heel in shape, function, or position. **7.** *Informal.* dishonest, contemptible man, esp. with regard to his treatment of women. **8. down at the heel** (or **heels**). poor or shabby. **9. to kick up one's heels.** to enjoy oneself; have fun. **10. on** (or **upon**) **the heels of.** close behind or immediately after. **11. to take to one's heels.** to run away; flee. —*v.t.* **1.** to furnish with a heel or heels: *to heel a shoe.* **2.** to follow on the heels of. —*v.i.* to follow closely. [Old English *hēla* rear part of the human foot.]

heel² (hēl) *v.t., v.i.* to lean or cause to lean to one side. —*n.* act of heeling; list. [Modification of obsolete *heeld, hield* to lean, from Old English *hieldan.*]

heel·er (hē′lər) *n.* **1.** one who heels shoes. **2.** ward heeler.

heel·tap (hēl′tap′) *n.* **1.** lift of a shoe. **2.** small amount of liquor left in a glass after drinking.

heft (heft) *Informal. v.t.* **1.** to test the weight of by lifting. **2.** to lift up; heave. —*n.* **1.** weight; heaviness. **2.** greater part; bulk. [From HEAVE.]

heft·y (hef′tē) **heft·i·er, heft·i·est.** *adj. Informal.* **1.** big and strong; muscular. **2.** heavy; weighty. [HEFT + -Y¹.]

He·gel, Ge·org Wil·helm Frie·drich (hā′gəl; gā′ôrk vil′helm frē′driкн) 1770–1831, German philosopher.

he·gem·o·ny (hi jem′ə nē, hej′ə mō′nē) *pl., -nies. n.* leadership or domination, esp. of one state over other independent states, as in a political union or geographic area. [Greek *hēgemoniā.*]

He·gi·ra (hi jīr′ə, hej′ər ə) *also,* **He·ji·ra.** *n.* **1.** flight of the Prophet Muhammad from Mecca to Medina in A.D. 622, marking the establishment of Islam. **2. hegira.** sudden departure or flight; exodus. [Arabic *hijrah.*]

Hei·deg·ger, Martin (hī′deg′ər, -də gər) 1889—, German existentialist philosopher.

Hei·del·berg (hīd′əl burg′) *n.* city in west-central West Germany, site of a noted university. Pop. (1968), 122,031.

heif·er (hef′ər) *n.* young cow that has not borne a calf. [Old English *hēahfore.*]

Hei·fetz, Ja·scha (hī′fits; yä′shə) 1901—, American violinist.

heigh (hī, hā) *interj. Archaic.* used to attract attention, give encouragement, or express surprise or pleasure.

heigh-ho (hī′hō′, hā′-) *interj. Archaic.* used to express surprise, happiness, sadness, or weariness.

height (hīt) *n.* **1.** distance or measurement from bottom to top: *The height of the statue is eleven feet.* **2.** state or condition of being relatively tall or high: *Height is an advantage in playing basketball.* **3.** distance above a given level, as the sea or horizon. **4.** *also,* **heights.** high point or place: *The climbers scaled the heights.* **5.** greatest degree; culmination: *the height of fashion.* **6.** highest point or part of something; summit. [Old English *hēahthu.*]

Syn. 1. Height, altitude, elevation refer to distance extending upward. **Height** indicates the vertical extent or measure of space between the base and the top: *Sequoia trees rise to a height of several hundred feet.* **Altitude** applies to the vertical elevation of an object above a given level, esp. above the surface of the earth: *The plane was flying at an altitude of 10,000 feet.* **Elevation** applies to the vertical height above sea level on the surface of the earth: *The town is situated at an elevation of 200 feet.*

height·en (hīt′ən) *v.t.* **1.** to make high or higher; increase the height of. **2.** to increase (something), as in amount, degree, or intensity. —*v.i.* **1.** to become high or higher. **2.** to increase, as in amount or degree. —**height′en·er,** *n.*

heil (hīl) *interj. German.* hail.

Hei·ne, Hein·rich (hī′nə; hīn′riкн) 1797–1856, German poet and essayist.

hei·nous (hā′nəs) *adj.* extremely wicked; atrocious; odious: *Hitler was guilty of committing heinous crimes.* [Old French *haïneus,* from *haïne* hate, from *haïr* to hate; of Germanic origin.] —**hei′nous·ly,** *adv.* —**hei′nous·ness,** *n.*

heir (âr) *n.* **1.** one who inherits or is entitled to inherit property after the death of its former owner. **2.** one who succeeds to or is entitled to succeed to a hereditary title, rank, or office. **3.** one who inherits something or benefits from something established in the past: *an heir to western civilization.* [Old French *(h)eir,* from Latin *hēres.*]

heir apparent *pl.,* **heirs apparent.** one who will become heir to a throne, title, or inheritance if he outlives the ancestor.

heir·ess (âr′is) *n.* female heir, esp. one who has inherited or will inherit great wealth.

heir·loom (âr′loom′) *n.* personal possession handed down, as in a family, from generation to generation. [HEIR + LOOM¹.]

heir presumptive *pl.,* **heirs presumptive.** one who will become heir to a throne, title, or inheritance if an heir more closely related to the ancestor is not born.

heir·ship (âr′ship′) *n.* **1.** state or condition of being an heir. **2.** right of inheritance.

He·jaz (hē jaz′, he jäz′) *also,* **Hed·jaz.** *n.* former independent kingdom in the northwestern part of the Arabian peninsula, on the Red Sea, now part of Saudi Arabia.

He·ji·ra (hē jīr′ə, hej′ər ə) Hegira.

Hel (hel) *n. Teutonic Mythology.* **1.** daughter of Loki and goddess of the underworld. **2.** region of the underworld that she ruled, where those who died of sickness or old age, and not in battle, were sent.

held (held) past tense and past participle of **hold¹.**

Hel·en (hel′ən) *n.* Helen of Troy.

Hel·e·na (hel′ə nə) *n.* capital of Montana, in the west-central part of the state. Pop. (1970), 22,730.

Helen of Troy *Greek Legend.* the very beautiful queen of King Menelaus. When she was carried off by Paris, the Greeks, in revenge, waged war against Troy.

Hel·go·land (hel′gō land′) *n.* small West German island in the North Sea, off the northwestern coast of Germany, near which the British, in 1914, defeated the Germans in a naval battle. Also, **Hel′go·land′.**

hel·i·cal (hel′i kəl) *adj.* of, relating to, or having the form of a helix. —**hel′i·cal·ly,** *adv.*

hel·i·ces (hel′ə sēz′) a plural of **helix.**

hel·i·con (hel′ə kon′, -kən) *n.* very large tuba, carried over the shoulder, used esp. in marching bands.

Hel·i·con (hel′ə kon′, -kən) *n.* mountain range in central Greece. In Greek mythology it was the sacred home of the Muses.

hel·i·cop·ter (hel′ə kop′tər, hē′lə-) *n.* aircraft supported in the air by one or more motor-driven rotors which rotate horizontally above the craft. [French *hélicoptère,* from Greek *heliko-,* stem of *helix* spiral + *pteron* wing.]

Helicopter

Hel·i·go·land (hel′ə gō land′) *n.* Helgoland.

helio- *combining form* of or relating to the sun: *heliocentric.* [Greek *hēlios.* sun.]

he·li·o·cen·tric (hē′lē ō sen′trik) *adj.* **1.** of or relating to the modern or Copernican astronomic system in which the earth and other planets move about the sun. **2.** having or regarding the sun as the center. Opposed to **geocentric** in both definitions. [HELIO- + CENTRIC.]

he·li·o·graph (hē′lē ə graf′) *n.* instrument for signaling by means of mirrors that reflect light from the sun. The signal may be interrupted by a shutter to form a code, such as a telegraphic code. —*v.t., v.i.* to communicate or signal by means of a heliograph.

He·li·os (hē′lē os′) *n.* Greek god of the sun and father of Phaëthon. His Roman counterpart is Sol. [Greek *Hēlios,* from *hēlios* sun.]

he·li·o·stat (hē′lē ə stat′) *n.* instrument consisting of a mirror that turns automatically at about half the speed of the rotation of the earth and reflects sunlight in a fixed direction, as through the fixed tube of a solar telescope.

he·li·o·ther·a·py (hē′lē ō ther′ə pē) *n.* treatment of disease by means of sunlight.

he·li·o·trope (hē′lē ə trōp′, hēl′yə-) *n.* **1.** any of a group of plants and shrubs, genus *Heliotropium,* growing wild in warm regions of the world, bearing clusters of fragrant, tube-shaped white or purple flowers. **2.** reddish purple. **3.** bloodstone. [Latin *hēliotropium,* from Greek *hēliotropion,* from *hēlios* sun + *tropos* turning; referring to the turning of the plant toward the sun.]

he·li·ot·ro·pism (hē′lē ot′rə piz′əm) *n.* involuntary response of plants and certain other organisms that causes them to move or turn toward the sunlight. **Positive heliotropism** is a turning toward the sunlight. **Negative heliotropism** is a turning away from the light. [HELIO- + Greek *tropos* turning + -ISM.]

hel·i·port (hel′ə pôrt′, hel′ə-) *n.* place, as on the top of a building, for helicopters to take off and land.

he·li·um (hē′lē əm) *n.* inert, nonmetallic, extremely light gaseous element with no color or odor, used esp. to inflate lighter-than-air craft and to dilute oxygen and other gases. Symbol: He. **See element** for table. [Modern Latin *helium,* from Greek *hēlios* sun; referring to the initial discovery of helium in the spectrum of the sun.]

he·lix (hē′liks) *pl.,* **hel·i·ces** or **he·lix·es.** *n.* **1.** anything spiral in shape. **2.** three-dimensional curve lying along the surface of a cylinder or cone at a fixed angle. **3.** curved fold of skin and cartilage forming the rim of the outer ear. **4.** small, ornamental volute, as on a Corinthian or Ionic capital. [Latin *helix* spiral, from Greek *helix* spiral, anything twisted.]

hell (hel) *n.* **1.** in Christian theology, the abode of Satan and the fallen angels, where the wicked will be punished after death. **2.** in various

at; āpe; cär; end; mē; it; īce; hot; ōld; fôrk; wood; fool; oil; out; up; ūse; turn; sing; thin; this; zh in treasure; ə in ago, taken, pencil, lemon, circus.

479

religions, the abode of the dead; hades. **3.** any place or condition of great evil, torment, or misery: *The prisons were hells on earth* (Macaulay, 1849). [Old English *hell.*]

he'll (hēl) **1.** he will. **2.** he shall.

Hel·las (hel′əs) *n.* Greece.

hell·bend·er (hel′ben′dər) *n.* large aquatic salamander, *Cryptobranchus alleganiensis,* found in the south-central and eastern United States. Length: to 2 feet.

hell·bent (hel′bent′) *adj. Informal.* stubbornly or recklessly determined to do or achieve something (with *on* or *for*).

hell·cat (hel′kat′) *n.* **1.** evil, bad-tempered, or wrathful woman. **2.** witch.

Hel·le (hel′ē) *n. Greek Legend.* young girl who, while fleeing on the ram with the Golden Fleece, fell into the Hellespont and drowned.

hel·le·bore (hel′ə bôr′) *n.* **1.** any of a group of thick-rooted plants, genus *Helleborus,* often cultivated for their large attractive flowers that grow at the ends of long stalks. **2.** any of various plants of the genus *Veratrum,* esp. *Veratrum viride,* a tall poisonous plant. [Latin *(h)elleborus* the plant *(def. 1),* from Greek *helleboros.*]

Hel·lene (hel′ēn) *n.* a Greek. [Greek *Hellēn* mythical ancestor of the Greeks.]

Hel·len·ic (he len′ik, hə-) *adj.* of or relating to Greece, esp. ancient Greece, its language, history, or culture before the time of Alexander the Great. —*n.* subfamily of the Indo-European language family, to which Greek and its dialects, both ancient and modern, belong.

Hel·le·nism (hel′ə niz′əm) *n.* **1.** culture of the ancient Greeks. **2.** in ancient times, the adoption or imitation of Greek culture: *the Hellenism of the Romans.* **3.** word or idiom peculiar to the Greek language.

Hel·le·nist (hel′ə nist) *n.* **1.** one who in ancient times adopted or imitated the culture of the Greeks. **2.** expert in the study of the ancient Greek language, literature, or culture.

Hel·le·nis·tic (hel′ə nis′tik) *adj.* **1.** of or relating to the period in Greek or Near Eastern history after the death of Alexander the Great in 323 B.C. until the first century B.C. **2.** of, relating to, or having the characteristics of a style in the arts developed during the Hellenistic age. **3.** of or relating to Hellenists.

Hel·le·nize (hel′ə nīz′) **-nized, -niz·ing.** *v.t., v.i.* to make or become Greek, in customs, form, or character.

Hel·les·pont (hel′is pont′) *n.* Dardanelles. [Latin *Hellespontus,* from Greek *Hellēspontos* literally, Sea of Helle. See HELLE.]

hell·fire (hel′fīr′) *n.* fire of, or punishment in, hell: *a sermon full of threats of hellfire and damnation.*

hell·gram·mite (hel′grə mīt′) *n.* larva of a dobson fly. [Of uncertain origin.]

hel·lion (hel′yən) *n.* very devilish, rowdy, or troublesome person.

hell·ish (hel′ish) *adj.* of, like, relating to, or fit for hell; diabolical. —**hell′ish·ly,** *adv.* —**hell′ish·ness,** *n.*

hel·lo (he lō′, hə-) *also,* **hul·lo.** *interj.* used to express greeting, attract attention, or indicate surprise. —*n. pl.,* **-los.** utterance of this interjection. —*v.i. v.t.,* **-loed, -lo·ing.** to say, call, or shout this, as to someone.

helm¹ (helm) *n.* **1.** tiller, wheel, or entire steering apparatus of a ship. **2.** position of control or authority; head. [Old English *helma* tiller.]

helm² (helm) *n. Archaic.* helmet. —*v.t.* to cover or furnish with a helmet. [Old English *helm* helmet.]

hel·met (hel′mit) *n.* any of various protective coverings for the head, as those worn by soldiers or participants in various sports. [Old French *helmet,* diminutive of *helme;* of Germanic origin.]

Helm·holtz, Her·mann von (helm′hōlts′; her′män) 1821–94, German physiologist and physicist.

hel·minth (hel′minth) *n.* parasitic worm, esp. one that invades the intestines. [Greek *helminth-,* stem of *helmins.*]

helms·man (helmz′mən) *pl.,* **-men.** *n.* one at the helm of a ship; steersman.

Hé·lo·ise (el′ō ēz′) c.1101–64, wife of Abélard, whose correspondence with him has become famous as a classic expression of romantic love.

hel·ot (hel′ət) *n.* **1.** *also,* **Helot.** one of a class of serfs in ancient Sparta. **2.** any serf. [Latin *Hēlōtes,* from Greek *Heilōtes,* plural of *Heilōs;* possibly from *Helos,* a town in Laconia whose inhabitants were enslaved by the Spartans.]

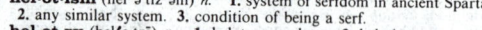

Helm¹

Soldier's helmet

Football helmet

hel·ot·ism (hel′ə tiz′əm) *n.* **1.** system of serfdom in ancient Sparta. **2.** any similar system. **3.** condition of being a serf.

hel·ot·ry (hel′ə trē) *n.* **1.** helots as a class. **2.** helotism.

help (help) *helped* or *(archaic)* **holp,** *helped* or *(archaic)* **hol·pen,** **help·ing.** *v.t.* **1.** to provide with support, as in the performance of a task; be of service to: *He helped his brother paint the room.* ▲ also used elliptically with a preposition or adverb: *He helped the old woman up the stairs.* **2.** to enable (someone or something) to accomplish a goal or achieve a desired effect: *The coach's advice helped the team to win.* **3.** to provide with sustenance or relief, as in time of need or distress; succor: *The Red Cross helped the flood victims.* **4.** to promote or contribute to; further: *The medication helped his recovery.* **5.** to be useful or profitable to; be of advantage to: *It might help you if you read the book.* **6.** to improve or remedy: *Nothing really helped his sinus condition.* **7.** to prevent; stop: *I can't help his rudeness.* **8.** to refrain from; avoid: *I couldn't help smiling when I heard the story.* **9.** to wait on or serve (often with *to*): *The clerk helped us. The hostess helped him to the dessert.* **10. cannot help but.** *Informal.* cannot but. **11. so help me (God).** oath of affirmation. **12. to help oneself to.** to take or appropriate: *The thief helped himself to all the jewels.* —*v.i.* to provide support, as in the performance of a task; be of service. —*n.* **1.** act of providing support, service, or sustenance. **2.** source of support, service, or sustenance. **3.** person or group of persons hired to work for another or others. **4.** means of improving, remedying, or preventing. [Old English *helpan* to aid, succor, benefit.]

Syn. *v.t.* **1. Help, aid, assist** mean to support in a useful way. **Help** is the most common word and means to give support in response to a known or expressed need or for a definite purpose: *Everyone helped to make the school fair a success.* **Aid** means to give relief in times of distress or difficulty: *It is the duty of rich nations to aid the poor.* **Assist** means to serve another person in the performance of his task in a secondary capacity: *The secretary assists the officer by taking care of his correspondence.*

help·er (hel′pər) *n.* one who or that which provides support, as in the performance of a task.

help·ful (help′fəl) *adj.* giving or providing support or service; useful. —**help′ful·ly,** *adv.* —**help′ful·ness,** *n.*

help·ing (hel′ping) *n.* individual portion of food.

help·less (help′lis) *adj.* **1.** unable to take care of oneself; dependent: *He was made quite helpless by the accident.* **2.** without power or strength: *We were helpless in that situation.* **3.** without a source of relief, support, or sustenance: *He left his family destitute and helpless.* **4.** expressing confusion or bewilderment: *With a helpless look, he shrugged and walked away.* —**help′less·ly,** *adv.* —**help′less·ness,** *n.*

help·mate (help′māt′) *n.* companion and helper, esp. a spouse. Also, **help·meet** (help′mēt′).

Hel·sin·ki (hel′sing′kē, hel sing′-) *n.* capital, largest city, and chief port of Finland, on the southern coast of the country. Pop. (1967), 523,051.

hel·ter-skel·ter (hel′tər skel′tər) *adv.* in a hurried, confused, and disorderly manner: *She threw her books and papers helter-shelter on the table.* —*adj.* hurried, confused, and disorderly: *He was a helter-skelter sort of person.* —*n.* hurried, confused, and disorderly activity. [Possibly rhyming expression based on obsolete *skelt* to hasten; of uncertain origin.]

helve (helv) *n.* handle, as of an ax, hatchet, or hammer. [Old English *hielfe.*]

Hel·ve·tia (hel vē′shə) *n. Archaic.* Switzerland. [Modern Latin *Helvetia,* from Latin *Helvētiī* an ancient people inhabiting what is now Switzerland.] —**Hel·ve′tian,** *adj., n.*

Hel·vé·tius, Claude A·dri·en (hel vē′shəs, *French.* el vā syoos′; klôd a drē än′) 1715–71, French philosopher.

hem¹ (hem) *n.* **1.a.** that part of a garment or piece of cloth made by turning the unfinished edge back and fastening it down, usually by sewing: *She ripped the hem of her coat.* **b.** edge formed by this: *The hem is uneven.* **2.** hemline *(def. 1).* —*v.t.,* **hemmed, hem·ming. 1.** to turn back the unfinished edge of (a garment or piece of cloth) and fasten it down, usually by sewing. **2.** to surround; enclose: *The valley was hemmed in by steep cliffs.* [Old English *hem(m)* border of a piece of cloth.]

hem² (hem) *n. interj.* sound resembling the clearing of the throat, made to attract attention or to express hesitation, doubt, or embarrassment. —*v.i.,* **hemmed, hem·ming. 1.** to make this sound. **2.** to hesitate in speaking. **3. to hem and haw.** to hesitate in speaking, esp. in order to avoid making a definite statement. [Imitative.]

he-man (hē′man′) *pl.,* **-men.** *n. Informal.* strong, virile man.

hem·a·tite (hem′ə tīt′, hē′mə-) *n.* hard, translucent mineral consisting mainly of ferric oxide and ranging in color from reddish brown to black. It is the principal ore of iron. [Latin *haematītēs* bloodstone, from Greek *haimatītēs* bloodlike, from *haima* blood.]

hemi- *prefix* half: *hemisphere.* [Greek *hēmi-.*]

at; āpe; cär; end; mē; it; īce; hot; ōld; fôrk; wood; fōōl; oil; out; up; ūse; turn; sing; thin; this; zh in treasure; ə in ago, taken, pencil, lemon, circus.

hem·i·mor·phite (hem′i môr′fīt) n. lustrous, transparent to translucent mineral consisting of zinc silicate. It is an important ore of zinc. Formula: $Zn_4Si_2O_7(OH)_2H_2O$ [HEMI- + Greek *morphē* form, shape + -ITE[1].]

Hem·ing·way, Ernest (hem′ing wā′) 1899–1961, U.S. novelist and short-story writer.

he·mip·ter·ous (hi mip′tər əs) adj. of or belonging to an order, Hemiptera, of true bugs that have beaklike mouth parts. [Modern Latin *Hemiptera* (from HEMI- + Greek *pteron* wing) + -OUS.]

hem·i·sphere (hem′is fēr′) n. 1. one-half of the earth, as divided by the equator or the Greenwich meridian. The equator divides the earth into the Northern and Southern hemispheres; the Greenwich meridian divides it into the Eastern and Western hemispheres. 2. one-half of a sphere formed by a plane passing through the center of the sphere. 3. either of the lateral halves of the cerebrum. [Latin *hēmisphaerium* a half globe, from Greek *hēmisphairion*, from *hēmi-* half + *sphaira* ball, sphere.] —**hem·i·spher·ic** (hem′is fēr′ik) also, **hem′i·spher′i·cal,** adj.

hem·i·stich (hem′i stik′) n. 1. half of a line of verse, esp. as divided by a caesura. 2. line of verse that is incomplete or has less than the usual length. [Latin *hēmistichium* a half verse, from Greek *hēmistichion*, from *hēmi-* half + *stichos* row, verse.]

hem·line (hem′līn′) n. 1. length of a skirt or dress from the waist down: *Hemlines are down this year.* 2. hem (def. 1b).

hem·lock (hem′lok′) n. 1.a. any of a group of tall evergreen trees, genus *Tsuga*, of the pine family, found in North America and Asia, having a pyramidal shape, reddish bark, and flat, blunt needles. One of the best-known species in the United States is the eastern hemlock, *T. canadensis*, whose bark yields tannin. b. soft, coarse-grained wood of this tree. 2.a. poisonous plant, *Conium maculatum*, of the parsley family, found in Europe, Asia, and the Americas, having speckled, hollow stems with many branches and finely divided leaves, and bearing clusters of white flowers. b. poison prepared from this plant. [Old English *hemlic* the poisonous plant.]

he·mo·glo·bin (hē′mə glō′bin, hem′ə-) n. iron-bearing protein matter in the red blood cells carrying oxygen from the lungs to the tissues and carbon dioxide from the tissues to the lungs. [Earlier *haematoglobulin*, from Greek *haimat-*, stem of *haima* blood + Latin *globulus*, diminutive of *globus* ball + -IN.]

he·mo·phil·i·a (hē′mə fil′ē ə, -fēl′yə, hem′ə-) n. hereditary disease that prevents the blood from clotting normally, so that a small injury may result in profuse internal or external bleeding. [Modern Latin *haemophilia*, from Greek *haima* blood + *philiā* fondness for, tendency to.]

he·mo·phil·i·ac (hē′mə fil′ē ak′, -fē′lē ak′, hem′ə-) n. one who is afflicted with hemophilia.

hem·or·rhage (hem′ər ij, hem′rij) n. discharge of blood, esp. one that is severe. —v.i., **-rhaged, -rhag·ing.** to discharge blood. [Latin *haemorrhagia* severe bleeding, from Greek *haimorrhagiā*, from *haima* blood + *rhēgnÿnai* to burst.]

hem·or·rhoids (hem′ə roidz′) n.,pl. enlarged veins on or within the lower part of the rectum. Also, **piles.** [Latin *haemorrhoidae*, from Greek *haimorrhoides*, plural of *haimorrhois* liable to discharge blood, from *haima* blood + *rhein* to flow.] —**hem′or·rhoid′al,** adj.

hemp (hemp) n. 1. strong, durable fiber obtained from the stem of a tall plant, *Cannabis sativa*, used chiefly to make rope and twine. 2. plant from which this fiber is obtained, cultivated in Asia, Europe, and the United States, having a hollow, thin stem and large leaves. 3. any of various drugs obtained from this plant, as marijuana and hashish. [Old English *henep* this plant.]

hemp·en (hem′pən) adj. made of or like hemp.

hem·stitch (hem′stich′) v.t. to stitch across an area of cloth from which cross threads have been removed, gathering several of the remaining threads at a time into small bundles. —n. 1. ornamental needlework that has been hemstitched, often used to decorate borders and hems. Also, **hem′stitch′ing.** 2. single stitch made by hemstitching.

Hemstitch

hen (hen) n. 1. mature female of the domestic fowl. 2. female of other birds, esp. of gallinaceous birds. 3. female of the lobster and various fish. [Old English *henn* female domestic fowl.]

hen·bane (hen′bān′) n. any of a small group of poisonous, bad-smelling plants, genus *Hyoscyamus*, of the nightshade family, found in Mediterranean regions and in eastern North America, bearing hairy leaves and clusters of funnel-shaped yellow flowers marked with purple veins. [HEN + BANE; because of its poisonous effect on fowls.]

hence (hens) adv. 1. as a consequence or result of this fact or circumstance; therefore: *It is winter now, hence the days will be shorter.* 2.a. from this time: *We plan to meet three weeks hence.* b. *Archaic.* from this time onward; henceforth. 3. *Archaic.* a. away from this place; from here: *not more than three miles hence.* b. from this source or origin: *All other faces borrowed hence their light and grace* (Suckling, 1641). c. from this world; from this life: *Before I go hence, and be no more seen* (Psalm 34). [Middle English *hennes* away, from this place or time, going back to Old English *heonan*.]

hence·forth (hens′fôrth′, -fôrth′) adv. from this time on; from now on: *Henceforth he shall be supreme ruler of the kingdom.* Also, **hence′·for′ward.**

hench·man (hench′mən) pl., **-men.** n. 1. willing partner in crime or misdeed: *The duke was the evil king's henchman.* 2. trusted follower. [Middle English *hensman* groom, squire, from Old English *hengest* horse + MAN.]

hen·e·quen (hen′ə kin) also, **hen·e·quin.** n. sisal. [Spanish *henequén;* probably of Taino origin.]

Hen·gist and Hor·sa (heng′gist, hen′jist; hôr′sə) two brothers who are said to have led the Jutes into England in the fifth century A.D.

hen·house (hen′hous′) n. house, coop, or shelter for poultry. Also, **hen′coop′.**

Hen·ley, William Er·nest (hen′le) 1849–1903, English poet, critic, and editor.

hen·na (hen′ə) n. 1. orange dye obtained from the dried leaves of a shrub, *Lawsonia inermis*, used for centuries in Asia and Africa to color various items as hair, fingernails, and fabrics, and used today chiefly in commercial hair rinses. 2. tall, slender shrub from whose leaves this dye is obtained. 3. reddish brown or copper color. —v.t., **-naed, -na·ing.** to color or tint with henna. [Arabic *hinnā′* the shrub.]

hen·ner·y (hen′ər ē) pl., **-ner·ies.** n. place where poultry is kept or raised.

hen party, party or gathering for women only.

hen·peck (hen′pek′) v.t. to domineer over (one's husband) by persistent nagging.

hen·ry (hen′rē) pl., **-ries** or **-rys.** n. *Physics.* unit of electromagnetic inductance in an electric circuit. One henry is the amount of inductance that produces an electromotive force of one volt when the current changes at the rate of one ampere per second. [From Joseph *Henry*, 1797–1878, U.S. physicist.]

Hen·ry (hen′rē) 1. O. 1862–1910, U.S. short-story writer; born William Sidney Porter. 2. Patrick. 1736–99, leading patriot of the American Revolution, statesman, and orator.

Henry I, 1068–1135, king of England from 1100 to 1135.

Henry II 1. 1133–89, king of England from 1154 to 1189; first of the Plantagenet line. 2. 1519–59, king of France from 1547 to 1559.

Henry III, 1207–72, king of England from 1216 to 1272.

Henry IV 1. 1367–1413, king of England from 1399 to 1413; founder of the Lancastrian line. 2. 1553–1610, king of France from 1589 to 1610; first of the Bourbon line. Also, **Henry of Navarre.**

Henry V, 1387–1422, king of England from 1413 to 1422.

Henry VI, 1421–71, king of England from 1422 to 1461 and from 1470 to 1471; last of the Lancastrian line.

Henry VII, 1457–1509, king of England from 1485 to 1509; the first Tudor king.

Henry VIII, 1491–1547, king of England from 1509 to 1547; founder of the Church of England.

Henry of Navarre, Henry IV of France.

hep (hep) adj. *Slang.* hip[3].

he·pat·ic (hi pat′ik) adj. 1. of, relating to, or resembling the liver. 2. acting on or affecting the liver. 3. liver-colored. [Latin *hēpaticus*, from Greek *hēpatikos*, from *hēpar* liver.]

he·pat·i·ca (hi pat′i kə) n. any of a group of low-growing plants, genus *Hepatica*, of the crowfoot family, found in northern temperate regions of the world, bearing three-lobed leaves and small purple, pink, or white flowers. [Medieval Latin *hepatica*, from feminine of Latin *hēpaticus* relating to the liver; because the shape of the leaf resembles that of the liver. See HEPATIC.]

hep·a·ti·tis (hep′ə tī′tis) n. inflammation of the liver, usually caused by a virus, resulting in fever, weakness, and often jaundice. [Modern Latin *hepatitis*, from Greek *hēpar* liver + -ITIS.]

hep·cat (hep′kat′) n. *Slang.* jazz musician or enthusiast, esp. of the 1930s or 1940s.

He·phaes·tus (hi fes′təs) n. ugly and lame Greek god of fire, who was a skilled blacksmith and workman for the other gods. His Roman counterpart is Vulcan.

Hep·ple·white (hep′əl hwīt′, wīt′) adj. of or belonging to a style of furniture noted for subtle and gracefully proportioned curves, extensive use of satinwood, and much painted decoration: *a Hepplewhite chair.* —n. piece of furniture in this style. [From George *Hepplewhite*, eighteenth-century English cabinetmaker, who designed this style of furniture.]

hept-, form of hepta- before vowels, as in *heptarchy.*

hepta- *combining form* seven: *heptagon.* [Greek *hepta*.]

at; āpe; cär; end; mē; it; īce; hot; ōld; fôrk; wood; fōōl; oil; out; up; ūse; turn; sing; thin; this; zh in treasure; ə in ago, taken, pencil, lemon, circus.

hep·ta·gon (hep′tə gon′) *n.* polygon with seven sides and seven angles. [Greek *heptagōnos* having seven angles, from *hepta* seven + *gōniā* angle.] —**hep·tag′o·nal** (hep tag′ən əl), *adj.*

hep·tam·e·ter (hep tam′ə tər) *n.* line of verse consisting of seven metrical feet, for example: *The ships/ that sailed/ the sea/ have reached/ the dis/tant shore.* [HEPTA- + -METER.]

hep·tar·chy (hep′tär′kē) *pl.* **-chies.** *n.* **1.** government by seven rulers. **2.** *also,* **Heptarchy.** group of seven kingdoms or states, each under its own ruler, esp. the seven principal kingdoms of England in the seventh and eighth centuries. [HEPT- + Greek *-archiā* rule.]

Irregular heptagon

her (hur; *unstressed* hər, ər) *pron.* objective case of **she:** *We called her and offered her a ride. —adj.* possessive form of **she:** *her fears, her piano, her accomplishments.* [Old English *hire.*]

her. **1.** heraldry. **2.** heraldic.

He·ra (hēr′ə) *n.* Greek goddess of marriage and the protector of married women, who was the sister and wife of Zeus. Her Roman counterpart is Juno.

Her·a·cles (her′ə klēz′) *also,* **Her·a·kles.** *n.* Hercules.

Her·a·cli·tus (her′ə klī′təs) *n.* c.540–475 B.C., Greek philosopher.

her·ald (her′əld) *v.t.* to proclaim, indicate, or announce; usher in: *Trumpets heralded the hero's arrival. —n.* **1.** formerly, an officer who carried messages between princes or sovereign powers, announced royal or state proclamations, and arranged and supervised various state ceremonies and functions, as tourneys, processions, and funerals. **2.** one who proclaims or announces; messenger. **3.** one who or that which announces or indicates the approach of someone or something; harbinger: *Earthquakes are often the heralds of volcanic eruptions* (Huxley, 1878). **4.** official in charge of heraldry, who grants, records, and regulates the use of coats of arms, traces genealogies, and has the authority to settle certain questions of precedence and protocol. [Old French *herau(l)t* the royal officer; of Germanic origin.]

he·ral·dic (he ral′dik) *adj.* of or relating to heraldry or heralds.

her·ald·ry (her′əl drē) *pl.* **-ries.** *n.* **1.** study and craft of describing and representing coats of arms, granting certain rights to bear certain coats of arms, tracing genealogies, and settling certain questions of precedence. **2.a.** heraldic device or collection of such devices. **b.** coat of arms; armorial bearings. **3.** heraldic ceremony or pomp.

herb (urb, hurb) *n.* **1.a.** any plant whose leaves, stems, seeds, or roots are desired for their flavor or odor or for making medicines. **b.** the leaves, stems, seeds, or roots themselves, often chopped and dried. **2.** any flowering plant that does not form a persistent woody stem but instead dies down at the end of each growing season. [Old French *(h)erbe* grass, green vegetation used to feed animals, from Latin *herba* grass, green crops.]

her·ba·ceous (hur bā′shəs) *adj.* **1.** of, relating to, or of the nature of plants which do not develop a persistent woody stem. **2.** having the texture and color of an ordinary leaf: *flowers with herbaceous petals.* [Latin *herbāceus* grassy, herblike, from *herba.* See HERB.]

herb·age (ur′bij, hur′-) *n.* **1.** soft-stemmed plant life collectively, esp. when suitable for grazing. **2.** green leaves and stems of herbaceous plants.

herb·al (hur′bəl, ur′-) *adj.* of, relating to, or made of herbs. —*n. Archaic.* treatise on herbs or plants.

herb·al·ist (hur′bə list, ur′-) *n.* **1.** dealer in herbs, esp. medicinal herbs. **2.** *Archaic.* expert in the study of herbs or plants.

her·bar·i·um (hur bâr′ē əm) *pl.,* **-bar·i·ums** or **-bar·i·a** (-bâr′ē ə). *n.* **1.** systematically arranged collection of dried plants. **2.** room or building in which such a collection is kept. [Late Latin *herbārium* such a collection, from Latin *herba.* See HERB.]

Her·bart, Jo·hann F. (her′bärt; yō′hän) 1776–1841, German philosopher, psychologist, and educator.

Her·bert (hur′bərt) **1.** George. 1593–1633, English metaphysical poet. **2.** Victor. 1859–1924, Irish-American composer.

her·bi·cide (hur′bə sīd′) *n.* any of a group of organic or inorganic chemical compounds used to kill plants. [HERB + -CIDE².] —**her′bi·ci′dal,** *adj.*

her·bi·vore (hur′bə vôr′) *n.* animal, esp. a mammal, that feeds chiefly on plants, as a cow or a kangaroo. [Modern Latin *Herbivora,* from *herbivorus.* See HERBIVOROUS.]

her·biv·o·rous (hur biv′ər əs) *adj.* feeding chiefly on grass or other plants. [Modern Latin *herbivorus* grass-eating, from Latin *herba* grass + *vorāre* to devour.]

Her·cu·la·ne·um (hur′kyə lā′nē əm) *n.* ancient city in southwestern Italy, buried when Mount Vesuvius erupted in A.D. 79.

her·cu·le·an (hur′kyə lē′ən, hər kū′lē-) *adj.* **1.** requiring great strength or effort: *Moving the boulder was a herculean task.* **2.** *also,* **Herculean.** like Hercules, esp. in strength or courage. **3.** Herculean. of or relating to Hercules: *the twelve Herculean labors.*

Her·cu·les (hur′kyə lēz′) *n.* **1.** *Classical Legend.* the son of Zeus and

a mortal, a hero celebrated for his exceptional strength and bravery. Also, **Her′a·cles, Her′a·kles. 2.** constellation in the northern sky. [Latin *Herculēs* this hero, from Greek *Hēraklēs* literally, glory of Hera, from HERA + *kleos* glory.]

herd¹ (hurd) *n.* **1.** number of animals, esp. large animals, as cattle, sheep, reindeer, or elephants, feeding, traveling, or being kept together. **2.** large number of people; crowd: *a herd of job seekers.* **3.** **the herd.** the masses; the rabble. —*v.t.* **1.** to group (persons or animals) in or as in a herd: *The cowboys herded the cattle and drove them to market.* **2.** to lead or drive in or as in a herd: *The guide herded the tourists into the bus.* —*v.i.* to group or join together in or as in a herd. [Old English *heord* number of animals kept together, flock.]

herd² (hurd) *n.* herdsman. —*v.t.* to take care of; tend: *The old man herds goats in the mountains.* [Old English *hierde* herdsman.]

Her·der, Jo·hann von (her′dər; yō′hän) 1744–1803, German philosopher and literary critic.

herds·man (hurdz′mən) *pl.,* **-men.** *n.* one who owns, tends, or drives a herd. Also, **herd′er.**

here (hēr) *adv.* **1.** at or in this place: *I like it here.* **▲** also used to indicate or emphasize a specific person or thing being referred to: *this person here.* **2.** to or toward this place: *Bring the book here.* **3.** at this point, as in time, action, or thought: *Here the transcript ends. I suggest that we stop here and read the rest tomorrow.* **4.** now to be presented; as follows: *Here are my replies to your questions.* **5.** on or concerning this particular matter or issue: *Here more than anywhere else we must come to an agreement.* **6.** in the present life: *Both here and hence pursue me lasting strife . . .* (Shakespeare, *Hamlet*). **7. here and there. a.** in various places: *The balloons were hung here and there.* **b.** back and forth; to and fro: *He ran here and there looking for her.* **8. neither here nor there.** not pertinent or important. —*n.* **1.** this place: *How can I get to your house from here?* **2.** this life: *the here and now.* —*interj.* **1.** used as an exclamation, as in answering a roll call, calling an animal, or attracting attention. **2. here goes.** here I go. [Old English *hēr* in this place, in this life, at this point, now.]

here·a·bout (hēr′ə bout′) *also,* **here·a·bouts.** *adv.* about or near this place; in this vicinity.

here·af·ter (hēr′af′tər) *adv.* **1.** from now on; after this: *When you see her hereafter, don't speak to her.* **2.** after the present life. —*n.* life after the present life; future life.

here·by (hēr′bī′) *adv.* by virtue of this.

he·red·i·ta·ble (hə red′ə tə bəl) *adj.* heritable. —**he·red′i·ta·bil′-i·ty,** *n.* —**he·red′i·ta·bly,** *adv.*

he·red·i·tar·y (hə red′ə ter′ē) *adj.* **1.** transmitted or transmissible, genetically, from an animal or plant to its offspring. **2.** derived from a custom, belief, or prejudice held by ancestors or predecessors; inherited. **3.** of or relating to inheritance or heredity. **4.** *Law.* **a.** transmitted or transmissible from an ancestor to an heir according to rules of descent. **b.** holding title or possession by inheritance. [Latin *hērēditārius* relating to an inheritance, from *hērēditās* inheritance.]

he·red·i·ty (hə red′ə tē) *pl.,* **-ties.** *n.* **1.** process by which characteristics are transmitted genetically from an animal or plant to its offspring. **2.** total characteristics so transmitted. [Latin *hērēditās* inheritance.]

Here·ford (hur′fərd, her′ə-) *n.* any of a breed of beef cattle having a thick, red coat, white face, and white body markings. Weight: to 2200 pounds. [From *Herefordshire,* English county where the breed was developed.]

here·in (hēr′in′) *adv.* in this place, matter, or circumstance; in this.

here·in·af·ter (hēr′in af′tər) *adv.* afterward in this document, statement, or narrative.

here·in·be·fore (hēr′in bi fôr′) *adv.* in a preceding part of this document, statement, or narrative.

here·in·to (hēr′in′tōō) *adv.* into this place, matter, or circumstance; into this.

here·of (hēr′uv′, -ov′) *adv.* of or concerning this.

here·on (hēr′ôn′, -on′) *adv.* hereupon.

her·e·sy (her′ə sē) *pl.,* **-sies.** *n.* **1.a.** religious belief or doctrine that is at variance with accepted church doctrine. **b.** any belief or doctrine at variance with accepted or established doctrine. **2.** the maintaining of such a belief or doctrine. [Old French *heresie* heretical religious belief or doctrine, going back to Latin *haeresis* sect, heretical religious doctrine, from Greek *hairesis* sect.]

her·e·tic (her′ə tik) *n.* **1.** one who maintains a religious belief or doctrine at variance with accepted church doctrine. **2.** one who maintains any belief or doctrine at variance with accepted or established doctrine. [Old French *heretique* person holding heretical religious views, from Church Latin *haereticus,* from Greek *hairetikos* able to choose.]

he·ret·i·cal (hə ret′i kəl) *adj.* of, relating to, or characterized by heresy: *heretical beliefs, heretical movement.* —**he·ret′i·cal·ly,** *adv.*

here·to (hēr′tōō′) *adv.* to this matter, subject, point, or place.

here·to·fore (hēr′tə fôr′) *adv.* before now; until this time.

---

at; āpe; cär; end; mē; it; īce; hot; ōld; fôrk; wood; fōōl; oil; out; up; ūse; turn; sing; thin; this; zh in treasure; ə in ago, taken, pencil, lemon, circus.

here·un·to (hēr'un tōō') *adv.* to this; hereto.
here·up·on (hēr'ə pŏn', -pon') *adv.* immediately following this.
here·with (hēr with', -with') *adv.* **1.** along or together with this. **2.** by means of this; hereby.
her·it·a·ble (her'ə bəl) *adj.* that can be inherited.
her·it·age (her'ə tij) *n.* **1.** that which is handed down from previous generations or from the past; tradition. **2.** totality of property that has been or may be inherited by someone, including possessions or land. **3.** that which comes from the circumstances of birth; lot: *To earn bread by the sweat of the brow is the common heritage of the sons of Adam* (Maurice, 1872). [Old French *heritage* inheritance, from *heriter* to inherit, from Late Latin *hērēditāre*, from Latin *hērēs* heir.] **Syn. 1.** Heritage, legacy, patrimony denote something that has been handed down from an ancestor or predecessor. **Heritage** has the widest application and refers to anything traditionally passed on from one generation to the succeeding generation or generations: *The Bill of Rights is part of the American heritage.* **Legacy** is used to describe something specifically derived from the past: *The scientific spirit is one of the legacies of the Renaissance.* **Patrimony** refers to the tangible and intangible assets that one inherits: *Natural resources are society's richest patrimony.*
her·maph·ro·dite (hur maf'rə dīt') *n.* **1.** animal that has both male and female reproductive organs. Many species of worms are hermaphrodites. **2.** hermaphrodite brig. —*adj.* hermaphroditic. [Latin *hermaphrodītus* person having the attributes of both sexes, from Greek *hermaphrodītos*, from *Hermaphrodītos* son of *Hermes* and *Aphrodite*, who, according to legend, became united in one body with a nymph.]
hermaphrodite brig, two-masted ship with the foremast square-rigged and the mainmast fore-and-aft-rigged.
her·maph·ro·dit·ic (hur maf'rə dit'ik) *adj.* of, relating to, or characteristic of a hermaphrodite.
Her·mes (hur'mēz) *n.* Greek god of science and invention, who was the swift messenger of the gods, usually pictured with winged sandals and helmet. His Roman counterpart is Mercury.
her·met·ic (hur met'ik) *adj.* **1.** made airtight, as by fusion: *a hermetic seal.* **2.** of or relating to alchemy or other secret lore. **3.** impervious to outward influence; sealed off. Also, **her·met'i·cal.** [Medieval Latin *hermeticus* relating to alchemy, relating to Hermes, from Greek *Hermēs* the god Hermes, who supposedly discovered the secrets of alchemy.]
her·met·i·cal·ly (hur met'ik lē) *adv.* **1.** so as to be airtight: *a hermetically sealed container.* **2.** so as to be impervious to outward influence: *scholars hermetically confined among their books.*
Her·mi·o·ne (hur mī'ə nē) *n.* Greek Legend. the daughter of Menelaus and Helen of Troy.
her·mit (hur'mit) *n.* one who lives a solitary, ascetic life, often from religious motives and in a place far removed from society; recluse. [Old French *(h)ermite*, from Late Latin *(h)erēmīta*, from Greek *erēmītēs* solitary, dweller in a desert, from *erēmiā* desert. Doublet of EREMITE.] —**her·mit'ic,** *adj.*

Snail shell

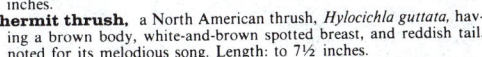

her·mit·age (hur'mi tij) *n.* **1.** habitation of a hermit. **2.** any solitary or secluded dwelling place.
hermit crab, any of a widespread group of soft-bodied, mostly ocean-dwelling crabs that occupy the empty shells of snails, whelks, and similar animals for protection. Length: to 18 inches.

Hermit crab

hermit thrush, a North American thrush, *Hylocichla guttata,* having a brown body, white-and-brown spotted breast, and reddish tail, noted for its melodious song. Length: to 7½ inches.
Her·mon, Mount (hur'mən) mountain on the border between Syria and Lebanon.
her·ni·a (hur'nē ə) *pl.* **-ni·as** or **-ni·ae** (-nē ē'). *n.* condition in which a part of an organ bulges out through the wall of its body cavity; rupture. [Latin *hernia*.] —**her'ni·al,** *adj.*
he·ro (hēr'ō) *pl.* **-roes.** *n.* **1.** man admired and looked up to for his valor, achievements, and noble qualities. **2.** one who performs a particularly courageous act, esp. an act that rescues or protects someone. **3.** principal male character in a story, play, or poem. **4.** in mythology and legend, man, often descended from a god, having great strength and courage and the ability to perform superhuman feats. **5.** sandwich consisting of a small loaf of white bread filled with meat, cheese, onions, etc. [Latin *hērōs* man descended from a god, illustrious man, from Greek *hērōs.*]
He·ro (hēr'ō) *n.* Greek Legend. a priestess of Aphrodite whose lover, Leander, swam the Hellespont every night to visit her. One night he was drowned, and in her sorrow, Hero killed herself.
Her·od (her'əd) *n.* **1.** Herod the Great. **2.** Herod Antipas.
Herod An·ti·pas (an'tə pas') c.20 B.C.–A.D. 39, ruler of Judea from 4 B.C. to A.D. 39, son of Herod the Great.

He·ro·di·as (hə rō'dē əs) *n.* in the New Testament, wife of Herod Antipas, who, together with her daughter, Salome, caused the death of John the Baptist.
He·rod·o·tus (hə rod'ə təs) *n.* c.484–425 B.C., Greek historian, known as the father of history.
Herod the Great, c.73–4 B.C., king of Palestine from 37 to 4 B.C., during whose reign Christ was born. Also, **Her'od.**
he·ro·ic (hi rō'ik) *adj.* **1.** of or appropriate to a hero; individually courageous: *heroic attempts to save the victim's life.* **2.** relating to or describing the deeds of heroes from myth and legend. **3.** on a grand scale; large or impressive. Also, **he·ro'i·cal.** —*n.* **heroics. a.** melodramatic or extravagant language or actions. **b.** heroic verse. —**he·ro'i·cal·ly,** *adv.*
heroic age 1. the era in which the heroes of Greek myth and legend supposedly flourished. **2.** any similar era of great vigor and accomplishments, esp. in the early history of a culture or nation.
heroic couplet, two successive, rhyming lines of verse written in iambic pentameter, for example: *Let such teach others who themselves excel / And censure freely who have written well* (Pope, 1711).
heroic verse, any of several verse forms, adapted to the treatment of heroic or exalted themes. In English, German, and Italian it is iambic pentameter; in French, the Alexandrine; and in Greek and Latin, dactylic hexameter.
her·o·in (her'ō in) *n.* white, crystalline, narcotic drug made from morphine. It is habit-forming and, if taken in overdose, may be fatal. [German *Heroin.*]
her·o·ine (her'ō in) *n.* **1.** woman or girl admired for her valor, achievements, or noble qualities. **2.** woman or girl who performs a difficult or courageous act, esp. an act that saves or protects someone. **3.** principal female character in a story, play, or poem. [Latin *hērōīne* woman descended from a god, illustrious woman, from Greek *hērōīnē,* feminine of *hērōs* person descended from a god, illustrious man.]
her·o·ism (her'ō iz'əm) *n.* **1.** qualities of a hero; courage; fortitude. **2.** courageous conduct that saves or protects someone.
her·on (her'ən) *n.* any of various wading birds, family Ardeidae, of temperate and tropical regions, having a long slender neck, long pointed bill, and long thin legs. Length: 1–6 feet. [Old French *hairon;* of Germanic origin.]
her·on·ry (her'ən rē) *pl.* **-ries.** *n.* place where herons congregate during the breeding season.

Heron

hero worship, immoderate or intense admiration or reverence for a hero or one who is thought of as a hero: *a teenager's hero worship of a movie star.*
her·pes sim·plex (hur'pēz sim'pleks) virus disease of the skin or mucous membrane, characterized by the formation and spreading of blisters. Cold sores are an example of herpes simplex. Also, **her'pes.** [Modern Latin *herpes simplex,* from Latin *herpes* skin eruption that creeps and spreads, from Greek *herpēs* shingles, from *herpein* to creep + Latin *simplex* simple.]
herpes zos·ter (zos'tər) shingles. [Modern Latin *herpes zoster,* from Greek *herpēs* shingles + *zōstēr* belt; because the disease most commonly affects the area around the waist.]
her·pe·tol·o·gy (hur'pə tol'ə jē) *n.* branch of zoology that deals with reptiles and amphibians. [Greek *herpeton* reptile, from *herpein* to creep + -LOGY.]
Herr (her) *pl.* **Her·ren** (her'ən) or **Herrn** (hern). *n.* mister; sir. [German.]
Her·rick, Robert (her'ik) 1591–1674, English lyric poet.

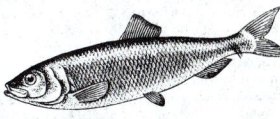

Atlantic herring

her·ring (her'ing) *pl.* **-ring** or **-rings.** *n.* any of a widespread group of bony, saltwater food fish, family Clupeidae, esp. the **Atlantic herring,** *Clupea harengus,* which grows to twelve inches in length. [Old English *hæring.*]
her·ring·bone (her'ing bōn') *n.* pattern of short lines slanting back from either side of a longer line, forming a series of arrowhead shapes resembling the spine of a herring. —*adj.* having or making this pattern.
Her·riot, É·douard (er yō'; ā dwär') 1872–1957, French statesman.
hers (hurz) *pron.* **1.** of, relating to, or be-

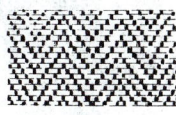

Herringbone

longing to her: *The blue sweater is hers.* **2.** one or ones belonging to her: *His room was neat; hers was messy.* ▲ **Hers** is the absolute form of the possessive pronoun **her**, used when no noun follows.

Her·schel (hur'shəl) **1. Sir William.** 1738–1822, British astronomer; discoverer of the planet Uranus. **2. Sir John.** 1792–1871, his son; British astronomer.

her·self (hur self') *pron.* **1.** emphatic form of **she** or **her**: *She herself was opposed to the idea.* **2.** reflexive form of **her**: *She blamed herself.* **3.** her normal, average, or true self: *She has not been herself lately.*

Hertz·i·an wave (hurt'sē ən) electromagnetic wave, as a radio wave, produced by the acceleration or oscillation of an electric charge. [From Heinrich *Hertz*, 1857–94, German physicist who discovered these waves.]

Herz·l, The·o·dor (her'tsəl; tā'ə dôr') 1860–1904, Hungarian founder of the Zionist movement.

he's (hēz; *unstressed* ēz) **1.** he is. **2.** he has.

He·si·od (hē'sē əd, hes'ē-) *n.* Greek poet of the eighth century B.C.

hes·i·tan·cy (hez'ət ən sē) *pl.,* **-cies.** *n.* quality or condition of being hesitant. Also, **hes'i·tance.**

hes·i·tant (hez'ət ənt) *adj.* **1.** reluctant; unwilling: *The caller was hesitant about giving his name.* **2.a.** full of awkward stops and starts: *The young seaman's speech was hesitant and confused.* **b.** characterized by unsureness; groping; tentative: *Archaeologists find in this period the first hesitant attempts at agriculture.* **3.** slow to act; indecisive: *If the captain is hesitant, the crew will be lost.* —**hes'i·tant·ly,** *adv.*

hes·i·tate (hez'ə tāt') **-tat·ed, -tat·ing.** *v.i.* **1.** to wait or stop a moment; pause briefly: *The salesman hesitated and then rang the doorbell again.* **2.** to be afraid, reluctant, or unwilling (with *to*): *I hesitate to tell you the real truth.* **3.** to delay action because of indecision: *If you hesitate too long, you will miss this opportunity.* **4.** to falter in speech; stammer. [Latin *haesitātus,* past participle of *haesitāre* to stick fast, be undecided, from *haerēre* to stick.] —**hes'i·tat'ing·ly,** *adv.*
Syn. 1. Hesitate, waver, vacillate, falter all mean to show indecision and irresolution. **Hesitate** means to wait or pause briefly because of uncertainty or doubt before making up one's mind: *She hesitated for a moment before saying yes.* **Waver** means to hold back after a decision has been reached and suggests lack of purpose and weakness: *The initial reverses did not make Bruce waver in his determination to win the throne.* **Vacillate** means to hesitate for a prolonged period or shift indecisively between one course of action and another: *The general vacillated for so long that he lost the battle.* **Falter** means to waver in purpose or stumble because of fear, lack of courage, or nervousness: *She faltered at the door, wondering whether she should go out on such a cold day.*

hes·i·ta·tion (hez'ə tā'shən) *n.* **1.** delay due to reluctance or indecision: *The actress accepted the part without hesitation.* **2.** act or instance of stopping; pause: *In this dance there is a hesitation after each step.*

Hes·pe·ri·an (hes pēr'ē ən) *adj.* **1.** of or relating to the west; western. **2.** of or relating to the Hesperides. [Latin *hesperius* western (from Greek *hesperios,* from *hesperos*) + -AN. See HESPERUS.]

Hes·per·i·des (hes per'ə dēz') *n. Greek Mythology.* **1.** the daughters of Atlas who guarded the golden apples given to Hera when she married Zeus. **2.** garden at the western edge of the world where Hera's golden apples were grown and kept. ▲ construed as plural in def. 1 and as singular in def. 2.

Hes·per·us (hes'pər əs) *n.* evening star, esp. Venus. Also, **Hes·per** (hes'pər). [Latin *Hesperus,* from Greek *Hesperos* evening star, relating to the evening, western.]

Hes·se (def. *1* hes'ə; def. 2 hes,'ə) **1. Her·mann** (her'män'). 1877–1962, German-Swiss novelist. **2.** political subdivision of West Germany in the central part of the country. Pop. (1968 est.), 5,333,200.

Hes·sian (hesh'ən) *n.* **1.** native or inhabitant of Hesse. **2.** mercenary from Hesse who fought for the British during the American Revolution. **3.** any mercenary. —*adj.* of or relating to Hesse or its people.

Hessian boots, high, tasseled boots, popular in England during the nineteenth century.

Hessian fly, small, black, two-winged insect, *Phytophaga destructor,* found in nearly all cereal-growing areas of the United States, whose larvae live and feed on wheat and other cultivated grains. [From the *Hessian* mercenaries of the American Revolution, who supposedly brought the insect to America in their straw bedding.]

hest (hest) *n. Archaic.* behest; command. [Old English *hǣs.*]

Hes·ti·a (hes'tē ə) *n.* Greek goddess of the hearth and a daughter of Cronus and Rhea. Her Roman counterpart is Vesta.

he·tae·ra (hi tēr'ə) *pl.,* **-tae·rae** (-tēr'ē). *n.* in ancient Greece, a female companion or prostitute, esp. one who was well educated and associated with men of wealth and rank. [Greek *hetairā,* feminine of *hetairos* companion.]

he·tai·ra (hi tīr'ə) *pl.,* **-tai·rai** (-tī'rī'). *n.* hetaera.

hetero- *combining form* not the same; other: *heterodox.* Opposed to **homo-.** [Greek *heteros* other.]

het·er·o·dox (het'ər ə doks') *adj.* **1.** diverging from accepted beliefs

or doctrines; unorthodox. **2.** holding opinions at variance with accepted beliefs or doctrines. [Greek *heterodoxos* differing in opinion, from *heteros* other + *doxā* opinion.]

het·er·o·dox·y (het'ər ə dok'sē) *pl.,* **-dox·ies.** *n.* **1.** state or quality of being heterodox. **2.** heterodox belief or doctrine.

het·er·o·dyne (het'ər ə dīn') *adj.* of or relating to the process of combining a received carrier wave with a wave originating within the receiver and having a slightly different frequency. Two new frequencies, representing the sum and difference between the original two frequencies, are produced. [HETERO- + DYNE.]

het·er·o·ge·ne·i·ty (het'ər ō jə nē'ə tē) *pl.,* **-ties.** *n.* state or quality of being heterogeneous; dissimilarity.

het·er·o·ge·ne·ous (het'ər ə jē'nē əs, -jēn'yəs) *adj.* **1.** having dissimilar or unrelated parts or elements; not homogeneous: *a heterogeneous nation.* **2.** differing in kind or nature; dissimilar: *A large collection of heterogeneous writings* (Liddon, 1866). [Medieval Latin *heterogeneus,* going back to Greek *heteros* other + *genos* race, kind.] —**het'er·o·ge'ne·ous·ly,** *adv.* —**het'er·o·ge'ne·ous·ness,** *n.*

het·er·o·nym (het'ər ə nim') *n.* word with the same spelling as another, but having a different pronunciation and meaning. *Bow,* the front of a ship, and *bow,* the weapon, are heteronyms. [Greek *heterōnymos* with different designation, from *heteros* other + (dialectal form) *onyma* name, word.]

het·er·o·sex·u·al (het'ər ə sek'shoo əl) *adj.* of, relating to, or characterized by heterosexuality. —*n.* one who manifests or practices heterosexuality.

het·er·o·sex·u·al·i·ty (het'ər ə sek'shoo al'ə tē) *n.* sexual attraction toward members of the opposite sex. Opposed to **homosexuality.**

het·man (het'mən) *pl.,* **-mans.** *n.* Cossack chieftain elected by his community. Also, **at'a·man.** [Polish *hetman* captain, from German *Hauptmann,* from *Haupt* chief + *Mann* man.]

heu·ris·tic (hyoo ris'tik) *adj.* **1.** helping or guiding to discover. **2.** designating an educational approach that encourages a student to learn by making his own investigations and discoveries. [Modern Latin *heuristicus,* from Greek *heuriskein* to discover.]

hew (hū) **hewed, hewed** *or* **hewn, hew·ing.** *v.t.* **1.** to make or shape with cutting blows, as from an ax: *The Indians had hewed steps into the side of the mountain.* **2.** to strike or cut, as with an ax or sword; chop; hack: *The man hewed the block into small pieces. He hewed the dead branches off the tree.* —*v.i.* **1.** to inflict cutting blows. **2.** to conform or adhere (with *to*): *Advancement comes by hewing to proper standards.* [Old English *hēawan* to cut, strike.] —**hew'er,** *n.*

hewn (hūn) a past participle of **hew.**

hex (heks) *v.t.* to put an evil spell on; bewitch. —*n.* **1.** evil spell. **2.** witch. [German *Hexe* witch.]

hexa- also, **hex-.** *combining form* six. [Greek *hex.*]

hex·a·gon (hek'sə gon') *n.* plane figure with six sides and six angles. [Latin *hexagōnum,* from Greek *hexagōnos* having six angles, from *hex* six + *gōniā* angle, corner.]

hex·ag·o·nal (hek sag'ən əl) *adj.* **1.** of, relating to, or having the shape of a hexagon. **2.** (of a solid figure) having a hexagon as a base or cross section.

hex·a·gram (hek'sə gram') *n.* six-pointed star formed of two intersecting equilateral triangles.

hex·a·he·dron (hek'sə hē'drən) *pl.,* **-drons** *or* **-dra** (-drə). *n.* polyhedron with six faces. A regular hexahedron is a cube. [Greek *hexaedron,* going back to *hex* six + *hedrā* seat, base.] —**hex'a·he'dral,** *adj.*

Regular hexagon

Hexagram

hex·am·e·ter (hek sam'ə tər) *n.* line of verse consisting of six metrical feet, esp. the six-foot dactylic verse of classical poetry consisting of five dactyls and a spondee or trochee, for example: *Ghosts' of the/ fear'some O'/ Fla'hertys/ ride' through the/ val'leys of/ Eng'land.* [Latin *hexameter,* from Greek *hexametros* (verse) having six measures, from *hex* six + *metron* measure.]

hex·a·pod (hek'sə pod') *adj.* having six feet. [Greek *hexapod-,* stem of *hexapous,* from *hex* six + *pous* foot.]

hey (hā) *interj.* used to attract attention or to express a sudden feeling as of surprise, pleasure, or annoyance.

hey·day (hā'dā') *n.* period of greatest strength, popularity, or prosperity. [Possibly from Middle English *hey day* literally, high day.]

Hey·wood, Thomas (hā'wood') c.1574–1641, English dramatist.

Hez·e·ki·ah (hez'ə kī'ə) *n.* in the Old Testament, a king of Judah of the eighth century B.C.

hf. 1. half. **2.** high frequency.

Hf, hafnium.

Hg, mercury. [Modern Latin *hydrargyrum,* going back to Greek *hydōr* water + *argyros* silver.]

HG, High German.

H.H. 1. His (or Her) Highness. **2.** His Holiness.

hhd., hogshead.
H-hour (āch′our′) *n.* zero hour.
hi (hī) *interj. Informal.* hello.
H.I., Hawaiian Islands.
Hi·a·le·ah (hī′ə lē′ə) *n.* city in southeastern Florida, a suburb of Miami noted for its race track. Pop. (1970), 102,297.
hi·a·tus (hī ā′təs) *pl.* **-tus·es** or **-tus.** *n.* **1.** break or gap, as in time or the continuity of something: *After a brief hiatus, the argument flared up again.* **2.** slight pause in sound between two successive vowels that are separately pronounced in consecutive syllables or words, as between the *o*'s in *cooperate.* [Latin *hiātus* gap.] —**Syn. 1.** see **interval.**
Hi·a·wath·a (hī′ə woth′ə, hē′-) *n.* **1.** an Indian brave who is the hero of a poem by Longfellow, based on a hero of Chippewa mythology. **2.** Indian chieftain of the sixteenth century, probably Mohawk, credited with founding the Iroquois federation.
hi·ba·chi (hi bä′chē, hē′-) *n.* portable brazier for heating and cooking, consisting of a grill covering a deep container in which charcoal is placed. [Japanese *hibachi,* from *hi* fire + *bachi* bowl.]
hi·ber·nal (hī bûrn′əl) *adj.* of or relating to winter; wintry.
hi·ber·nate (hī′bər nāt′) **-nat·ed, -nat·ing.** *v.i.* **1.** to spend the winter in a dormant or inactive state, as do many mammals, most reptiles and amphibians, a few fish and birds, and certain insects. Distinguished from **estivate. 2.** to be inactive or secluded for any period of time. [Latin *hībernātus,* past participle of *hībernāre* to pass the winter, from *hībernus* wintry.] —**hi′ber·na′tion,** *n.*
Hi·ber·ni·a (hī bûr′nē ə) *n.* Ireland. ▲ used primarily in literature. —**Hi·ber′ni·an,** *n., adj.*
hi·bis·cus (hī bis′kəs, hə-) *pl.* **-cus·es.** *n.* any of a large group of plants, shrubs, or trees, genus *Hibiscus,* found in tropical and temperate regions, bearing large, bell-shaped flowers of various colors. [Latin *hibiscus;* possibly of Celtic origin.]
hic·cup (hik′up, -əp) *also,* **hic·cough** (hik′up, -əp). *n.* **1.** spasm of involuntary inhaling that is stopped suddenly by closure of the vocal cords. **2. hiccups.** condition of being affected by such spasms: *to have the hiccups.* —*v.i.* **-cupped, -cup·ping. 1.** to inhale spasmodically, with a characteristic sound like a catch in the voice. **2.** to make a similar sound. [Imitative.]
hic ja·cet (hik jā′set) **1.** *Latin.* here lies. **2.** epitaph.
hick (hik) *Informal. n.* one who is awkward or unsophisticated, esp. one from a rural area. —*adj.* of or characteristic of a hick or hicks. [From *Hick,* an earlier nickname for Richard.]
Hick·ok, Wild Bill (hik′ok) 1837–76, U.S. frontier marshal; born James Butler Hickok.
hick·o·ry (hik′ər ē, hik′rē) *pl.* **-ries.** *n.* **1.** any of a group of tall trees, genus *Carya,* of the walnut family, found in North America, having gray bark, leaflets with saw-toothed edges, and hard edible nuts. **2.** hard, strong wood of this tree, used esp. for tool handles. **3.** round or oblong edible nut of this tree. Also, **hickory nut.** [Short for *pohickery,* from Algonquian *pawcohiccora* food made of crushed hickory nuts.]
hid (hid) past tense and past participle of **hide¹.**
hi·dal·go (hi dal′gō) *pl.* **-gos.** *n.* Spanish nobleman of the lower rank of the nobility. [Spanish *hidalgo,* earlier *hijo de algo* literally, son with something (i.e., some property), going back to Latin *fīlius* son + *dē* from, of + *aliquid* something.]
hid·den (hid′ən) *v.* a past participle of **hide¹.** —*adj.* not easily seen, found, or known; concealed; secret; obscure.
hide¹ (hīd) **hid, hid·den** or **hid, hid·ing.** *v.* **1.** to put or keep out of sight: *Maria's parents hid the presents for her birthday.* **2.** to keep from the knowledge of others; keep secret: *Sometimes it is difficult to hide your feelings.* **3.** to obstruct the view of; prevent from being seen: *The heavy snowfall hid the tracks that had been made the day before.* —*v.i.* to keep oneself out of sight; conceal oneself: *The rabbit hid in the high grass.* [Old English *hȳdan.*] —**hid′er,** *n.*
Syn. *v.t.* **1. Hide, conceal** mean to keep from being seen or detected. **Hide** is the more common word and implies a keeping or placing of something out of sight: *Squirrels hide nuts for the winter.* **Conceal** is more formal and suggests an intentional covering up of something: *The woman's smile concealed her anger.*
hide² (hīd) *n.* **1.** skin of an animal, esp. one of the larger animals, either raw or tanned. **2.** *Informal.* human skin. **3. neither hide nor hair.** absolutely nothing: *The police could find neither hide nor hair of him.* —*v.t.* **hid·ed, hid·ing.** *Informal.* to give a severe beating to; thrash. [Old English *hȳd* skin.]
hide³ (hīd) *n.* in old English law, a measure of land considered adequate for the support of one family, varying in estimated size from 60 to 120 acres. [Old English *hīgid.*]
hide-and-seek (hīd′ən sēk′) *n.* children's game in which one of the players has to find all of the others, who have hidden themselves. Also, **hide′-and-go-seek′.**
hide·a·way (hīd′ə wā′) *n.* secret or secluded place where one may hide or retreat from the world.

hide·bound (hīd′bound′) *adj.* **1.** stubbornly narrow-minded. **2.** (of an animal) having the skin adhering closely to the bones and muscles, often as a result of undernourishment.
hid·e·ous (hid′ē əs) *adj.* very ugly; repulsive; ghastly; detestable: *a hideous creature, hideous crimes.* [Old French *hideus,* from *hide* terror; of uncertain origin.] —**hid′e·ous·ly,** *adv.* —**hid′e·ous·ness,** *n.*
hide·out (hīd′out′) *n.* place where one can hide, esp. from the police or other authorities.
hid·ing¹ (hī′ding) *n.* **1.** state or place of concealment: *The outlaw went into hiding.* **2.** act of concealing. [From HIDE¹.]
hid·ing² (hī′ding) *n. Informal.* severe beating or thrashing. [From HIDE².]
hie (hī) **hied, hie·ing** or **hy·ing.** *v.i., v.t. Archaic.* to betake oneself quickly; hasten: *Hie thee hence!* [Old English *hīgian.*]
hi·er·arch (hī′ə rärk′) *n.* **1.** one who holds a high position in any hierarchy. **2.** religious leader holding an important office, esp. a high priest. —**hi′er·arch′al,** *adj.*
hi·er·ar·chi·cal (hī′ə rär′ki kəl) *adj.* of or relating to a hierarchy. Also, **hi′er·ar′chic.**
hi·er·ar·chy (hī′ə rär′kē) *pl.* **-chies.** *n.* **1.** organization of persons or things by rank, with each rank subordinate to the one above it: *the governmental hierarchy.* **2.** body of clergy organized in this manner. **3.** church government by such a body of clergy. [Medieval Latin *hierarchia* rule of a priest, from Greek *hierarchiā,* going back to *hieros* sacred + *archein* to rule.]
hi·er·at·ic (hī′ə rat′ik) *adj.* **1.** of, relating to, or used by priests; sacerdotal. **2.** of or relating to an abridged form of hieroglyphics used by ancient Egyptian priests for keeping records. Also, **hi′er·at′i·cal.** [Latin *hierāticus* relating to sacred uses, from Greek *hierātikos* relating to a priest, going back to *hieros* sacred.] —**hi′er·at′i·cal·ly,** *adv.*
hi·er·o·glyph (hī′ər ə glif′, hīr′ə-) *n.* hieroglyphic.
hi·er·o·glyph·ic (hī′ər ə-glif′ik, hīr′ə-) *n.* **1.a.** picture or symbol representing an object,

Hieroglyphics

word, syllable, or sound, used in writing systems by certain ancient peoples, esp. the Egyptians. **b.** any figure or symbol that has an obscure or hidden meaning. **2. hieroglyphics. a.** system of writing that uses hieroglyphics. **b.** any writing that is difficult to read. —*adj.* **1.** of, relating to, or resembling hieroglyphics. **2.** written in hieroglyphics. **3.** difficult to read. Also, **hi′er·o·glyph′i·cal.** [Late Latin *hieroglyphicus* relating to ancient Egyptian writing, from Greek *hieroglyphikos,* from *hieros* sacred + *glyphē* carving.] —**hi′er·o·glyph′i·cal·ly,** *adv.*
hi·er·o·phant (hī′ər ə fant′, hīr′ə-, hī′er-ō-) *n.* **1.** in ancient Greece, a priest who presided at sacred mysteries. **2.** one who interprets esoteric knowledge. [Late Latin *hierophantēs* teacher of religious rites, from Greek *hierophantēs,* from *hieros* sacred + *phainein* to show.]
hi-fi (hī′fī′) *n.* **1.** high fidelity. **2.** equipment for reproduction of sound with high fidelity. —*adj.* of or relating to high fidelity.
hig·gle (hig′əl) **-gled, -gling.** *v.i.* to haggle. [Form of HAGGLE.]
hig·gle·dy-pig·gle·dy (hig′əl dē pig′əl dē) *adv.* in jumbled confusion. —*adj.* jumbled; confused. [Rhyming expression probably based on PIG and suggested by the way pigs huddle together.]
high (hī) *adj.* **1.** extending upward a great or unusual distance; tall: *The walls were strong and high. Her hat had a high crown.* **2.** being or elevated some distance above the ground or some other base: *The bridge is high above the water.* **3.** having a specified elevation: *The building is forty stories high.* **4.** reaching to or performed from a height: *The horse made a high jump over the fence.* **5.** great or above normal, as in force, strength, degree, or value: *The rain stopped, but the high winds continued.* **6.** above or more important than others, as in rank or position: *a high dignitary of the church, the high altar.* **7.** of a noble or lofty nature: *high ideals.* **8.** above the usual or desired amount or price: *Interest rates are high.* **9.** luxurious; extravagant: *living in high style.* **10.** having advanced to or nearing its peak or most complete stage, extent, or degree: *high noon.* **11.** produced or characterized by relatively rapid vibrations; acute in pitch: *a high note.* **12.** of serious consequence; grave: *a high crime against the king.* **13.** exuberant; happy: *in high spirits.* **14.** full of pride; haughty; pretentious: *John had a high and mighty air about him.* **15.** (of meat, esp. wild game) slightly decomposed: *high venison.* **16.** *Informal.* feeling the effect of a liquor or drug; intoxicated. **17.** *Phonetics.* pronounced with the back of the tongue raised toward the roof of the mouth. The *e* in *me* is the high vowel. —*adv.* **1.** at or to a high point, position, or degree: *He climbed high up the mountain. Prices have risen too high.* **2.** in an extravagant manner: *to live high.* **3. high and dry. a.** completely out of water: *The ship was stranded high and dry.* **b.** without aid or assistance; abandoned: *He left his family high and dry.* **4. high and low.** everywhere.

at; āpe; cär; end; mē; it; īce; hot; ōld; fôrk; wood; fŏŏl; oil; out; up; ūse; turn; sing; thin; ṯhis; zh in treasure; ə in ago, taken, pencil, lemon, circus.

—*n.* **1.** high level, place, or position: *The temperature reached a new high.* **2.** arrangement of gears that produces maximum speed. **3.** state of intoxication caused by or as by liquor or drugs. **4. on high. a.** in or at a high place or position; above: *the flag waving on high.* **b.** in heaven. [Old English *hēah* tall, lofty, sublime.]
Syn. *adj.* **1. High, tall, lofty** mean being at or rising to more than average height. **High** is the general word and suggests an upward extension or rising to a conspicuous height: *That is as high a building as I have ever seen.* **Tall** is usually applied to growing things and suggests height in relation to breadth: *The redwoods are very tall trees.* **Lofty** is more poetic and suggests imposing or towering height: *The lofty walls of the castle seemed impregnable.*

high·ball (hī′bôl′) *n.* drink consisting of an alcoholic beverage, as rye or Scotch mixed with water, ginger ale, soda, or other liquid and served with ice in a tall glass.
high·born (hī′bôrn′) *adj.* of noble birth.
high·boy (hī′boi′) *n.* tall chest of drawers supported on legs.
high·bred (hī′bred′) *adj.* **1.** of superior breed or stock. **2.** showing good breeding; well-mannered; refined.
high·brow (hī′brou′) *Informal. n.* one who has or appears to have cultivated tastes or who engages in intellectual pursuits. —*adj.* of, relating to, or suitable for a highbrow.
high·chair (hī′châr′) *n.* chair for feeding an infant or young child, having high legs and a tray extended across the arms.
High Church, group in the Anglican Church that emphasizes church authority, the liturgy, and the sacraments. —**High′-Church′,** *adj.* —**High′-Church′man,** *n.*
high-col·ored (hī′kul′ərd) *adj.* **1.** having a strong or deep color; brilliant; vivid. **2.** florid; red.
high comedy, comedy dealing with polite society and relying on witty dialogue and sophisticated characterization.
higher education, college or university education.
high·er-up (hī′ər up′) *n. Informal.* one occupying a superior position.
high·fa·lu·tin (hī′fə lōōt′ən) *also,* **high·fa·lu·ting** (hī′fə lōō′ting). *adj. Informal.* pompous or pretentious, as in speech or manner. [HIGH + *falutin,* possibly a modification of *fluting,* present participle of FLUTE.]
high fidelity, reproduction of the full range of audible frequencies of a signal so that the original sound is almost exactly duplicated. —**high′-fi·del′i·ty,** *adj.*
high·fli·er (hī′flī′ər) *also,* **high·fly·er.** *n.* **1.** one who or that which flies high. **2.** one who is extravagant or pretentious, as in ideas, ambitions, or tastes.
high-flown (hī′flōn′) *adj.* pretentious or extravagant, as in ambitions, ideas, or language.
high frequency, radio frequency between 3 and 30 megacycles. —**high′-fre′quen·cy,** *adj.*
High German, standard literary and official form of the German language spoken predominantly in Germany, Austria, and parts of Switzerland.
high-grade (hī′grād′) *adj.* of superior quality.
high-hand·ed (hī′han′did) *adj.* arbitrary; overbearing. —**high′-hand′ed·ly,** *adv.* —**high′-hand′ed·ness,** *n.*
high-hat (hī′hat′) **-hat·ted, -hat·ting.** *Informal. v.t.* to treat snobbishly; snub. —*adj.* **1.** stylish; elegant. **2.** snobbish.
high hat, top hat.
high·jack (hī′jak′) *v.t.* to hijack. —**high′jack′er,** *n.*
high jinks (jingks) boisterous, good-natured pranks or fun. [HIGH + *jinks* frolic; of uncertain origin.]
high jump 1. field event in which the contestant jumps, usually from a running start, over a crossbar set between two uprights. **2.** such a jump.
high·land (hī′lənd) *n.* **1.** *also,* **highlands,** hilly or mountainous region of a country. **2.** portion of land, as a hill or plateau, rising above the land in the immediate area. —*adj.* **1.** of, relating to, or characteristic of such a region or portion of land. **2. Highland.** of or relating to the Scottish Highlands.
high·land·er (hī′lən dər) *n.* **1.** native or inhabitant of a highland. **2. Highlander. a.** member of the Gaelic people who inhabit the Highlands of Scotland. **b.** soldier of a regiment recruited from the Scottish Highlands.
Highland fling, lively Scottish folk dance that originated in the Highlands.
Highland Park, city in southeastern Michigan, principally an industrial suburb of Detroit. Pop. (1970), 35,444.
High·lands (hī′ləndz) *n.,pl.* rugged, mountainous region of northern and central Scotland.
high·light (hī′līt′) *n.* **1.** point or area in a painting or picture that is represented as brightly lighted. **2.** the most important, interesting, or memorable part of something: *The lighting of the Christmas tree was the highlight of the evening.* —*v.t.* **-light·ed, -light·ing. 1.** to give

a highlight or highlights to. **2.** to give emphasis or prominence to.
high·ly (hī′lē) *adv.* **1.** in or to a high degree; very much: *a highly motivated student.* **2.** with much approval or praise; very favorably: *The critics think highly of his work.* **3.** at a high price: *The consultant is being highly paid for his advice.*
High Mass, Mass celebrated with the use of choir, music, and incense, in which the celebrant is assisted by a deacon and subdeacon. Distinguished from **Low Mass.**
high-mind·ed (hī′mīn′did) *adj.* **1.** having or characterized by lofty ideals or feelings. **2.** *Archaic.* proud; arrogant. —**high′-mind′ed·ly,** *adv.* —**high′-mind′ed·ness,** *n.*
high·ness (hī′nis) *n.* **1.** state or quality of being high; loftiness. **2. Highness.** used as a form of address in speaking or referring to a member of a royal family, preceded by *His, Her,* or *Your.*
high-pitched (hī′picht′) *adj.* **1.** having a high pitch; shrill. **2.** (of a roof) having a steep slope.
High Point, city in north-central North Carolina. Pop. (1970), 63,204.
high-pres·sure (hī′presh′ər) *adj.* **1.** having, using, or able to withstand pressure higher than normal. **2.** having high barometric pressure. **3.** *Informal.* using aggressive methods of persuasion: *a high-pressure sales approach.* —*v.t.* **-sured, -sur·ing.** to use aggressive methods of persuasion on.
high priest 1. a chief priest. **2.** in the Old Testament, the head of the ancient Jewish priesthood, who presided over the Temple worship. **3.** leader, as of a cult or movement.
high relief, sculpture in which the figures project from the background by half their thickness or more. Also, **alto relievo.**
high rise, building having many stories. —**high′-rise′,** *adj.*
high·road (hī′rōd′) *n.* **1.** main road; highway. **2.** direct and easy course.
high school, school attended after elementary school, usually comprising grades nine through twelve. ▲ often used instead of **senior high school** and distinguished from **junior high school.**
high seas, those portions of seas and oceans that are not within the territorial limits of any country.
high-sound·ing (hī′soun′ding) *adj.* having an imposing or pretentious sound.
high-spir·it·ed (hī′spir′i tid) *adj.* having a proud, courageous, or fiery spirit.
high-strung (hī′strung′) *adj.* extremely tense or nervous; excitable.
hight (hīt) *adj. Archaic.* named; called: *a lady hight Elinore.* [Old English *heht,* past tense of *hātan* to call.]
high-ten·sion (hī′ten′shən) *adj.* having or using a high voltage: *a high-tension wire.*
high-test (hī′test′) *adj.* (of gasoline) very volatile.
high tide 1. the tide at its highest level. **2.** time when this level is reached. **3.** culminating point.
high time 1. later than the proper time but not too late. **2.** *Informal.* rollicking good time.
high-toned (hī′tōnd′) *adj.* **1.** high in tone or pitch. **2.** having or showing an elevated or lofty spirit or character; dignified: *a high-toned speech about responsibility and morality.* **3.** *Informal.* high in quality or social status; fashionable or stylish, often pretentiously so: *a high-toned neighborhood.*
high treason, treason, esp. against a monarch.
high water 1. body of water that has reached its highest level, as during a flood. **2.** high tide.
high-water mark 1. mark indicating the highest level reached by a body of water. **2.** highest point of anything, as of a career.
high·way (hī′wā′) *n.* **1.** public road, esp. one that is extensive and a major route of travel. **2.** any main route or direct course, esp. one to a specific objective: *highway to happiness.* —**Syn. 1.** see **road.**
high·way·man (hī′wā′mən) *pl.,* **-men.** *n.* robber who holds up travelers on a public road.
H.I.H., His (or Her) Imperial Highness.
hi·jack (hī′jak′) *also,* **high·jack.** *v.t.* **1.** to seize or take (a vehicle in transit) by force: *Two men hijacked the airplane.* **2.** to steal (cargo) from a vehicle in transit: *The thieves hijacked a truckload of tires.* [Possibly from the supposed use by robbers of the phrase *"High, Jack"* when ordering a victim to raise his hands.] —**hi′jack′er,** *n.*
hike (hīk) **hiked, hik·ing.** *v.i.* to walk a long distance, esp. for pleasure or exercise. —*v.t.* **1.** to raise, esp. with a sharp movement (with *up*): *He had become thin and was continually hiking up his trousers.* **2.** to increase, as prices; usually sharply: *The ferry hiked the fare to forty cents.* —*n.* **1.** long walk or march. **2.** increase: *a hike in rent.* [Possibly dialectal form of HITCH.] —**hik′er,** *n.*
hi·lar·i·ous (hi lâr′ē əs, hī-) *adj.* **1.** extremely funny; very amusing: *hilarious stories.* **2.** laughing loudly; in a merry mood. —**hi·lar′i·ous·ly,** *adv.* —**hi·lar′i·ous·ness,** *n.*
hi·lar·i·ty (hi lâr′ə tē, hī-) *n.* **1.** great merriment or laughter; boister-

ous gaiety: *The hilarity at the party downstairs kept them up half the night.* **2.** extremely humorous quality or aspect; funniness: *The hilarity of her predicament escaped her.* [French *hilarité* mirth, from Latin *hilaritās*, going back to Greek *hilaros* gay.]

hill (hil) *n.* **1.** portion of the earth's surface that is usually rounded and elevated above the surrounding land but is not as high as a mountain. **2.** small heap or mound, as one made by ants or a mole. **3.** slope, as in a road or on a piece of land: *Stay in gear if you park on a hill.* **4.** small mound or pile of earth in which seed is planted. **5. over the hill.** no longer strong, active, or effective. **6. to go over the hill.** to escape or run away from something, esp. prison. —*v.t.* to form in a small heap or mound. [Old English *hyll* small mountain.]

hill·bil·ly (hil′bil′ē) *pl.,* **-lies.** *n. Informal.* one who lives in or comes from the backwoods or mountain country, esp. from such an area in the southeastern United States.

hill·ock (hil′ək) *n.* small hill or mound.

hill·side (hil′sīd′) *n.* side or slope of a hill.

hill·top (hil′top′) *n.* top of a hill.

hill·y (hil′ē) **hill·i·er, hill·i·est.** *adj.* **1.** having many hills. **2.** like a hill; steep: *a hilly road.* —**hill′i·ness,** *n.*

hilt (hilt) *n.* **1.** handle of a sword, dagger, or similar weapon. **2. to the hilt.** to the furthest degree possible; thoroughly; completely: *The house is mortgaged to the hilt.* [Old English *hilt.*]

hi·lum (hī′ləm) *pl.,* **-la** (-lə). *n.* mark or scar formed on a seed at the point where it was attached to the cone or flower. See **seed** for illustration. Also, **um·bil′i·cus.** [Latin *hīlum* trifle.]

Hil·ver·sum (hil′vər səm) *n.* city in the west-central Netherlands. Pop. (1968), 100,940.

him (him; *unstressed* im) *pron.* objective case of **he:** *We saw him last night at the theater.*

Hilts

H.I.M., His (or Her) Imperial Majesty.

Him·a·la·yas (him′ə lā′əz, hi mäl′yəz) *n.* highest mountain system in the world, extending in an arc across central Asia from the northeastern border of Afghanistan through northern India and Tibet to the northwestern border of Burma. Also, **Himalaya Mountains.** —**Him′·a·la′yan,** *adj.*

Himm·ler, Hein·rich (him′lər; hin′riкн) 1900–45, head of the Gestapo in Nazi Germany.

him·self (him self′) *pron.* **1.** emphatic form of **he** or **him:** *The president himself was unable to solve the problem.* **2.** reflexive form of **him:** *He always talks to himself.* **3.** his usual or normal state or condition: *He hasn't been himself since the accident.* **4.** used in absolute constructions: *Having experienced a similar tragedy himself, he understood their pain.*

hind¹ (hind) *hind·er, hind·most* or *hind·er·most. adj.* situated at the back; rear: *The dog injured one of its hind legs.* [Probably from HINDER².]

hind² (hind) *pl.,* **hinds** or **hind.** *n.* doe, esp. a female red deer in and after its third year. [Old English *hind.*]

hind³ (hind) *n. Archaic.* **1.** farm worker. **2.** peasant. [Old English *hīne* (plural) household servants.]

hind·brain (hind′brān′) *n.* part of the brain that includes the pons, cerebellum, and medulla oblongata.

Hin·de·mith, Paul (hin′də mith′, -mit′) 1895–1963, German-American composer.

Hin·den·burg, Paul von (hin′dən burg′) 1847–1934, German general and field marshal, president of Germany from 1925 to 1934.

hin·der¹ (hin′dər) *v.t.* to make difficult or delay the movement or progress of; hold back: *The storm hindered the search for the missing child. Her stubbornness hinders her in relationships with other people.* [Old English *hindrian.*]

Syn. Hinder, impede, obstruct all mean to slow or stop a movement or action. **Hinder** means to hold back a thing or person in its or his progress and suggests an annoying delay: *Heavy snow hindered construction work.* **Impede** retains the original sense of fettering the feet and means to slow an action or movement by fettering, clogging, or hampering: *The tight bandage impeded the circulation of the blood.* **Obstruct** implies hindering that almost halts the action completely: *Widespread opposition obstructed passage of the bill.*

hin·der² (hin′dər) *adj.* situated at the back or rear. [Old English *hinder* behind.]

hind·er·most (hin′dər mōst′) *adj.* hindmost.

Hin·di (hin′dē) *n.* **1.** Indic language of the Indo-Iranian sub-family of the Indo-European family of languages, spoken predominantly in northern India. **2.** official language of India, derived from Hindustani. [Hindustani *Hindī* relating to India, Indian, from Persian *Hind* India. See HIND².]

hind·most (hind′mōst′) *adj.* farthest back; nearest the rear.

hind·quar·ter (hind′kwôr′tər) *n.* **1.** back half of a side of beef or

other meat, including the leg, loin, and adjacent parts. **2. hindquarters.** hind legs, loins, and adjacent parts of an animal.

hin·drance (hin′drəns) *n.* **1.** one who or that which hinders; obstacle. **2.** act of hindering.

hind·sight (hind′sīt′) *n.* the understanding of an event and its implications after it is over, esp. of what would have been a better course of action.

Hin·du (hin′dōō) *n.* **1.** one who adheres to the teachings, beliefs, or practices of Hinduism. **2.** native or inhabitant of India, esp. northern India. —*adj.* of, relating to, or characteristic of Hindus or Hinduism. [Persian *Hindū* native of India, from *Hind* India, from Sanskrit *Sindhu* Indus River, region of the Indus River.]

Hin·du-Ar·a·bic numerals (hin′dōō ar′ə bik) Arabic numerals.

Hin·du·ism (hin′dōō iz′əm) *n.* predominant religious, philosophical, and social system of India. Its goal is salvation through communion with the Supreme Being, or Brahman, who appears in the form of the three major gods: Brahma, the creator; Vishnu, the sustainer; and Shiva, the destroyer.

Hindu Kush Mountains (koosh′) mountain system of central Asia, largely in northeastern Afghanistan.

Hin·du·stan (hin′dōō stän′, -stan′) *n.* **1.** area of northern India where Hindi is spoken. **2.** the Indian subcontinent.

Hin·du·sta·ni (hin′dōō stä′nē, -stan′ē) *adj.* of, relating to, or characteristic of India, its people, languages, or culture. —*n.* a language including elements of Hindi and Urdu, used as a lingua franca in most of India. [Hindustani *Hindustānī* relating to Hindustan, from Persian *Hindūstān* India; literally, country of the Hindus, from *Hindū* native of India + *stān* country. See HINDU.]

hinge (hinj) *n.* **1.** mechanical device, usually consisting of two metal plates attached to one another by a pin, that forms a movable joint on which something, as a door, can swing, turn, or otherwise move. **2.** joint whose motion is limited to one plane forward or backward, as the elbow or knee joint. **3.** that on which something turns or depends; basic or central principle; critical point. —*v.t.,* **hinged, hing·ing.** to furnish with or attach by a hinge or hinges. —*v.i.* **1.** to hang or turn on a hinge. **2.** to depend or be contingent upon: *The fate of the prisoner hinges upon the jury's decision.* [Middle English *heng* mechanism on which a door is hung, going back to Old English *hangian* to be suspended.]

Hinges

hin·ny (hin′ē) *pl.,* **-nies.** *n.* hybrid offspring of a male horse and a female donkey. Distinguished from **mule¹.** [Latin *hinnus,* from Greek *innós* small mule.]

hint (hint) *n.* subtle sign or indication; slight or covert reference: *There was a hint of spring in the morning air. The girl needed one more hint before she could find the location of the treasure.* —*v.t.* to give a subtle sign or indication of; make a slight reference to: *She hinted to me that she knew about the party.* —*v.i.* to make a subtle reference to or suggestion of (with *at*): *What do you think he's hinting at?* [Possibly a form of obsolete *hent* act of seizing, going back to Old English *hentan* to seize.] —**hint′er,** *n.*

Syn. *v.t.* **Hint, intimate², insinuate** mean to suggest by indirect means. **Hint** implies the use of subtle or veiled suggestions and stresses lack of candor or frankness: *For weeks before Christmas, he hinted that he wanted skis.* **Intimate** usually involves an intelligible but elusive and barely perceptible hint: *The man intimated his displeasure with a grunt.* **Insinuate** suggests something unpleasant indicated in a sly or artful manner: *The political candidate insinuated that one of his opponents was dishonest.*

hin·ter·land (hin′tər land′) *n.* **1.** region or district lying inland from the coast. **2.** region that is remote from urban centers; back country. [German *Hinterland* back country, from *hinter* behind + *Land* land.]

hip¹ (hip) *n.* **1.** projecting part of each side of the human body; where the top of the thighbone joins the side of the pelvis. **2.** corresponding part of the body of animals. **3.** joint between the thighbone and the pelvic bone. **4.** angle formed by the meeting of adjacent sloping sides of a roof. [Old English *hype* the haunch.]

hip² (hip) *n.* ripe fruit of a rosebush. [Old English *hēope.*]

hip³ (hip) *hip·per, hip·pest. adj. Slang.* familiar with or informed about what is happening, esp. about new things. [Of uncertain origin.]

hip·bone (hip′bōn′) *n.* either of two large, irregularly shaped bones consisting of the ilium, ischium, and pubis and forming the two sides of the pelvic cavity.

hipped (hipt) *adj.* **1.** characterized by or having a particular kind of hips. ▲ used in combination, as *narrow-hipped.* **2.** *Architecture.* having a hip or hips, as a roof. [HIP¹ + -ED².]

hip·pie (hip′ē) *n.* any of a number of predominantly young people, esp. of the 1960s, who reject many of the values and practices of

traditional society and who follow their own life style, often characterized by unconventional dress, free expression, and sharing, often involving communal living. [From HIP[1].]

hip·po (hip′ō) *pl.*, **-pos.** *n. Informal.* hippopotamus.

Hip·po (hip′ō) *n.* ancient city of northern Africa, whose ruins are in present-day Algeria, near the Tunisian border.

Hip·poc·ra·tes (hi pok′rə tēz) *n.* c.460–c.370 B.C., Greek physician known as the father of medicine. —**Hip·po·crat·ic** (hip′ə krat′ik), *adj.*

Hippocratic oath, vow, taken by most beginning physicians, that sets forth an ethical code for medical practice and is attributed to Hippocrates.

Hip·po·crene (hip′ə krēn′, hip′ə krē′nē) *n.* spring on Mount Helicon, sacred to the Greek Muses, whose waters were regarded as a source of poetic inspiration. [Latin *Hippocrēnē,* from Greek *Hippokrēnē,* from *hippos* horse + *krēnē* fountain. According to myth, the spring was produced by a stroke of Pegasus' hoof.]

hip·po·drome (hip′ə drōm′) *n.* **1.** in ancient Greece and Rome, an outdoor arena for horse races and chariot races. **2.** arena or similar structure for circuses, horse shows, or other spectacles. [Latin *hippodromos* race course, going back to Greek *hippos* horse + *dromos* course.]

Hip·pol·y·ta (hi pol′ə tə) *also,* **Hip·pol·y·te** (hi pol′ə tē) *n. Greek Mythology.* queen of the Amazons and mother of Hippolytus. Hercules' ninth labor was to bring back her girdle.

Hip·pol·y·tus (hi pol′ə təs) *n.* son of Hippolyta and the Greek hero Theseus. Falsely accused by his stepmother Phaedra of raping her, he was cursed by his father and consequently suffered a violent death.

Hip·pom·e·nes (hi pom′ə nēz′) *n. Greek Mythology.* youth who defeated Atalanta in a race and thereby won her in marriage.

Hippopotamus

hip·po·pot·a·mus (hip′ə pot′ə-məs) *pl.*, **-mus·es** or **-mi** (-mī′). *n.* plant-eating mammal, *Hippopotamus amphibius,* native to parts of central and southern Africa, living in and near rivers and lakes and having a massive, thick-skinned, hairless body, short legs, and the largest mouth of any land animal. Weight: to 4 tons. Length: to 14 feet. [Latin *hippopotamus,* going back to Greek *hippos* horse + *potamos* river.]

hip roof, roof with ends and sides that slope.

hir·cine (hur′sīn, -sin) *adj.* **1.** of, relating to, or resembling a goat, esp. in odor. **2.** lustful. [Latin *hircīnus* relating to a goat, from *hircus* male goat.]

Hip roof

hire (hīr) *hired,* **hir·ing.** *v.t.* **1.** to obtain the use of for a fee. **2.** to grant the use of for a fee (often with *out*). —*v.i.* **to hire out.** to give one's work in return for payment: *He hires out as a house painter in the summer.* —*n.* **1.** payment for the use of an object, services rendered, or labor performed: *A poor worker is usually not worth his hire.* **2.** act of hiring. **3. for hire.** available for use or work in return for payment. [Old English *hȳr* wages, payment for the use of something.] —**Syn.** *v.t.* **1.** see **employ.** **2.** see **lease.**

hire·ling (hīr′ling) *n.* one who hires himself out, esp. to perform an unpleasant or criminal act. —*adj.* mercenary.

Hir·o·hi·to (hēr′ō hē′tō) *n.* 1901—, emperor of Japan since 1926.

Hir·o·shi·ma (hēr′ō shē′mə, hē rō′shē mə) *n.* port city in southwestern Japan, on the island of Honshu. It was the first city to be devastated by an atomic bomb. Pop. (1968), 542,000.

hir·sute (hur′sōot) *adj.* hairy. [Latin *hirsūtus* bristly.] —**hir′sute·ness,** *n.*

his (hiz; *unstressed* iz) *pron.* those or that which belong or relate to him: *We went together with my sisters and his.* —*adj.* of or belonging to him: *his dog.* [Old English *his,* genitive of *hē.* See HE.]

His·pa·ni·a (hi spā′nē ə, -pān′yə) *n. Archaic.* Spain. [Latin *Hispānia.*] —**His·pan·ic** (hi span′ik), *adj.*

His·pan·io·la (his′pən yō′lə) *n.* island in the Greater Antilles, in the Caribbean, divided into the Dominican Republic and Haiti. Area, approx. 30,000 sq. mi.

hiss (his) *v.i.* **1.** to make a sound similar to a prolonged *s: Startled snakes hiss.* **2.** to make such a sound to show disapproval or great dislike: *The angry crowd hissed when the man spoke.* —*v.t.* **1.** to force to silence or drive away by hissing: *The fans hissed the umpire.* **2.** to say or express by hissing: *She hissed an angry reply.* —*n.* sound similar to a prolonged *s.* [Imitative.]

hist (hist) *interj. Archaic.* used to call attention or obtain silence.

hist. **1.** history; historian; historical. **2.** histology.

his·ta·mine (his′tə mēn′, -min) *n.* chemical compound found in certain plant and animal cells which, when released, has such effects on the body as lowering the blood pressure and stimulating the secretion of gastric juice during digestion. It is also released by the body in allergic reactions and causes body tissues to swell. Formula: $C_5H_9N_3$, [Greek *histos* web, tissue + English *amine* (from AM(MONIA) + -INE[2].] —**his′ta·min·ic,** *adj.*

his·tol·o·gy (his tol′ə jē) *n.* **1.** science that deals with the microscopic study of plant and animal tissues. **2.** tissue structure of a plant or animal organism, in whole or in part. [Greek *histos* web, tissue + -LOGY.] —**his·to·log·i·cal** (his′tə loj′i kəl), *adj.* —**his·tol′o·gist,** *n.*

his·to·ri·an (his tôr′ē ən, -tor′-) *n.* **1.** one who writes a history or about history. **2.** one who is an authority on history.

his·tor·ic (his tôr′ik, -tor′-) *adj.* **1.** famous or noteworthy in history: *a historic site.* **2.** historical. **3.** worthy of note or remembrance: *This is a historic moment.*

his·tor·i·cal (his tôr′i kəl, -tor′-) *adj.* **1.** of or relating to history: *historical events, the historical method.* **2.** based on the facts, events, or personages of history rather than on fiction or legend: *historical novel.* [Latin *historicus* relating to history (from Greek *historikos,* from *historiā* history) + -AL[1].] —**his·tor′i·cal·ly,** *adv.*

historical present, present tense used in relating past events.

his·to·ri·og·ra·pher (his tôr′ē og′rə fər) *n.* historian, esp. one who serves officially: *He was appointed as historiographer to the queen.* [Late Latin *historiographus* writer of history, from Greek *historiographos,* from *historiā* history + *graphein* to write.]

his·to·ri·og·ra·phy (his tôr′ē og′rə fē) *n.* **1.** the writing or recording of history. **2.** historical writings collectively, as of a particular school. **3.** the science or study of the writing of history; principles of historical study.

his·to·ry (his′tər ē, his′trē) *pl.*, **-ries.** *n.* **1.** story or record of what has happened in the past, as of a nation, nations, or people, usually including the development of ideas and institutions as well as specific events. **2.** aggregate of past events. **3.** branch of knowledge or study dealing with past events. **4.** noteworthy past: *There is a long history behind that building.* **5.** something that is, or is considered to be, no longer important or of current concern: *That troubled period of his life is history now; we no longer discuss it.* **6.** drama representing historical events. [Latin *historia* narrative of past events, from Greek *historiā* inquiry, information, account, historical narrative. Doublet of STORY[1].]

his·tri·on·ic (his′trē on′ik) *adj.* **1.** insincere or exaggerated in character or manner; overemotional; theatrical: *Her histrionic display of feelings was not convincing.* **2.** of or relating to actors or acting. [Late Latin *histriōnicus* relating to an actor, from Latin *histriō* actor; possibly of Etruscan origin.]

his·tri·on·ics (his′trē on′iks) *n.* **1.** overemotional or theatrical behavior. **2.** dramatic representation; acting; dramatics. ▲ construed as plural in def. 1, as singular in def. 2.

hit (hit) *hit,* **hit·ting.** *v.t.* **1.** to give a physical blow to; strike: *He hit a ball over the fence. The little boy hit him hard enough to blacken his eye.* **2.** to come against forcibly; meet with a physical impact: *The car hit the tree.* **3.** to cause (something) to make forceful contact with: *She hit her head against the shelf.* **4.** to strike, as with a bullet or other projectile, (something aimed at): *He was an expert at darts and could hit the bull's-eye.* **5.** to come to; reach: *She hit the high note perfectly.* **6.** to have a painful, injurious, or otherwise adverse effect on: *The lack of job opportunities hit the town hard that winter.* **7.** to arrive or appear in on, or at: *The news hit the front page this morning.* **8.** to become suddenly discovered or realized by: *The truth hit me at the last moment.* **9.** *Informal.* to attack or otherwise assail: *The guerrillas hit the camp at midnight. The audience hit the speaker with a huge number of questions.* **10.** *Informal.* to start traveling on: *They hit the road at six o'clock every morning.* **11.** *Informal.* to appeal to or agree with; suit: *The proposal for the new building site did not hit him as the best one.* **12.** *Informal.* to ask for (money): *to hit someone for a loan.* **13.** Baseball. to make (a specified base hit): *He hit a home run in the third inning.* —*v.i.* **1.** to give a blow; strike: *The boxer hits hard with his fist.* **2.** to come into forcible contact; collide: *The cars hit with a loud crash.* **3.** to arrive or appear: *The tornado hit without warning.* **4.** to discover or arrive at, esp. by accident (with *on* or *upon*): *We hit upon the solution to the problem.* **5. to hit it off.** *Informal.* to like or get along well with one another: *We really hit it off from the day we met.* —*n.* **1.** blow or strike on something aimed at: *The bomber made a direct hit.* **2.** one who or that which is successful: *The song was a hit. He was a hit with his roommate's sister.* **3.** base hit. **4. hit or miss.** regardless of the result, whether it be success or failure; in a haphazard manner. [Old Norse *hitta* to meet with, light upon.] —**hit′ter,** *n.* —**Syn.** *n.* **1.** see **blow.**

hitch (hich) *v.t.* **1.** to attach, as with a hook, rope, or strap, esp. temporarily; fasten; tie: *He hitched the cars together.* **2.** to harness; yoke (often with *up*): *He hitched the ox to the plow. He hitched up the horses.* **3.** to raise or lift with a jerk; pull abruptly (often with *up*): *He hitched*

the package to his shoulder. *He hitched up his suspenders.* **4.** *Informal.* to marry: *He's getting hitched tomorrow.* ▲ usually construed in the passive. **5.** *Informal.* to obtain by hitchhiking: *He hitched a ride to the station.* —*v.i.* **1.** to become fastened or caught: *The railroad cars were hitched together.* **2.** *Informal.* to hitchhike: *He hitched all the way to Boston.* —*n.* **1.** device used for connecting two things together; fastening; catch: *The hitch between the boat and the dock was slipping.* **2.** that which causes an unforeseen delay; obstacle; catch: *A hitch in the proceedings gave him time to review his notes.* **3.** abrupt movement or pull; jerk: *to give one's trousers a hitch.* **4.** hobble; limp; lameness: *a hitch in one's gait.* **5.** any of various knots used for temporary fastenings. **6.** *Informal.* time spent in military service: *He served a three-year hitch in the navy.* [Of uncertain origin.]

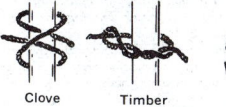

Clove   Timber   Rolling
Types of hitch knots

hitch·hike (hich′hīk′) **-hiked, -hik·ing.** *v.i.* *Informal.* to travel by soliciting free rides from passing motorists. —**hitch′hik′er,** *n.*
hitching post, railing or pole to which animals, esp. horses, may be tied.
hith·er (hith′ər) *adv.* to or toward this place. —*adj.* on or toward this side; nearer. [Old English *hider* to this place.]
hith·er·most (hith′ər mōst′) *adj.* nearest.
hith·er·to (hith′ər tōō′) *adv.* up to this time; until now.
hith·er·ward (hith′ər wərd) *also,* **hith·er·wards.** hither.
Hit·ler, Ad·olf (hit′lər; ad′olf, ä′dolf) 1889–1945, German dictator, born in Austria, chancellor of Nazi Germany from 1933 to 1945.
Hit·ler·ism (hit′lə riz′əm) *n.* policies and practices of Hitler and the Nazis.
Hit·tite (hit′īt) *n.* **1.** member of a people whose civilization dominated Asia Minor and part of Syria between 2000 and 1200 B.C. **2.** extinct language of the Hittites, belonging to the Indo-European family of languages. —*adj.* of or relating to the Hittites or their language. [Hebrew *Hittī* (from Hittite *Hatti* the Hittite people) + -ITE¹.]
hive (hīv) *n.* **1.a.** any nest built by a colony of bees, esp. honeybees. **b.** man-made structure designed for honeybees to build a nest in. **2.** colony of bees inhabiting a hive. **3.** place swarming with busy occupants. **4.** swarming, bustling crowd. —*v.t.* **hived, hiv·ing. 1.** to put (bees) into a hive. **2.** to store up in, or as in, a hive for future use. —*v.i.* **1.** to enter a hive. **2.** to live in, or as in, a hive. [Old English *hȳf* beehive.]

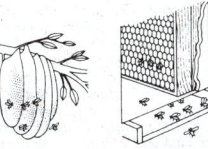

Natural hive   Man-made hive

hives (hīvz) *n.pl.* itching skin rash, characterized by white welts surrounded by red areas, caused by an allergy. ▲ construed as singular or plural. [Of uncertain origin.]
H.J., hic jacet.
hl., hectoliter.
hm., hectometer.
h'm (hm) *interj.* used to express hesitation, doubt, or meditation.
H.M., His (or Her) Majesty.
H.M.S. 1. His (or Her) Majesty's Ship. **2.** His (or Her) Majesty's Service.
ho (hō) *interj.* **1.** used to express pleasure, laughter, surprise, or doubt. **2.** used to attract attention or call attention to: *Land ho!*
Ho, holmium
hoar (hōr) *adj.* hoary. —*n.* hoarfrost. [Old English *hār* gray, gray-haired, old.]
hoard (hōrd) *v.t.* to accumulate and store or hide away —*n.* accumulation of items, stored up and often hidden, esp. for future use. [Old English *hord* accumulated stock, treasure.] —**hoard′er,** *n.*
hoard·ing¹ (hōr′ding) *n.* **1.** act of one who hoards. **2.** *also,* **hoardings.** that which is hoarded. [HOARD + -ING¹.]
hoard·ing² (hōr′ding) *n.* *British.* **1.** temporary board fence around a building under construction or repair. **2.** billboard. [Obsolete *hoard* fence (probably from Old French *hourd* scaffold; of Germanic origin) + -ING¹.]
hoar·frost (hōr′frôst′) *n.* frost, esp. when it forms a white coating on a surface.
hoar·hound (hōr′hound′) *n.* horehound.
hoarse (hōrs) **hoars·er, hoars·est.** *adj.* **1.** sounding deep and harsh or grating: *After his cold, he was left with a hoarse voice.* **2.** having a harsh or grating voice: *He is hoarse after singing for an hour.* [Old English *hās*.] —**hoarse′ly,** *adv.* —**hoarse′ness,** *n.*

hoar·y (hôr′ē) **hoar·i·er, hoar·i·est.** *adj.* **1.** white or gray with or as with age: *the hoary beard of an old man. The leaves were hoary with frost.* **2.** venerable; ancient. —**hoar′i·ness,** *n.*
hoax (hōks) *n.* trick or deception, meant either as a practical joke or as a fraud. —*v.t.* to trick or deceive by a hoax. [Modification of HOCUS.] —**hoax′er,** *n.*
hob¹ (hob) *n.* projection or shelf at the back or side of the interior of a fireplace, used for keeping things warm. [Of uncertain origin.]
hob² (hob) *n.* **1.** hobgoblin; elf. **2. to play** (or **raise**) **hob with.** *Informal.* to cause mischief, trouble, or confusion. [From *Hob*, an earlier nickname for *Robin* or *Robert*.]
Hobbes, Thomas (hobz) 1588–1679, English philosopher.
hob·ble (hob′əl) **-bled, -bling.** *v.i.* to move or walk awkwardly with or as if with a limp: *Howie had to hobble around in his cast for a month.* —*v.t.* **1.** to hold together the front legs or hind legs of (a horse or other animal) by a very short rope, strap, or similar material, esp. to prevent it from moving far. **2.** to impede the action or progress of. **3.** to cause to limp or move unsteadily. —*n.* **1.** rope, strap, or other device used to hobble an animal. **2.** awkward or faltering walk or movement; limp. **3.** *Archaic.* awkward or difficult situation. [Probably of Low German origin.]
hob·ble·de·hoy (hob′əl dē hoi′) *n.* adolescent boy, esp. one who is awkward or gawky. [Of uncertain origin.]
hobble skirt, woman's skirt, popular around the end of World War I, that was very narrow below the knees, making it necessary for the wearer to take small steps when walking.
hob·by (hob′ē) *pl.,* **-bies.** *n.* activity or interest that is undertaken for pleasure or relaxation in one's spare time. [Middle English *hobyn* small horse, form of the name *Robin* or *Robert*; the pursuit of a *hobby* being likened to a child's playing with a toy horse.]
hob·by·horse (hob′ē hôrs′) *n.* **1.** toy horse, usually consisting of a horse's head attached to a pole that a child can straddle and pretend to ride. **2.** rocking horse. [HOBBY + HORSE.]
hob·gob·lin (hob′gob′lin) *n.* **1.a.** mischievous goblin or elf. **b.** frightful apparition. **2.** anything, usually imaginary, that arouses fear or unreasonable concern: *A foolish consistency is the hobgoblin of little minds* (Emerson, 1841). [HOB² + GOBLIN.]
hob·nail (hob′nāl′) *n.* nail with a large head used to protect the soles of heavy boots or shoes. [Archaic *hob* peg + NAIL.]
hob·nob (hob′nob′) **-nobbed, -nob·bing.** *v.i.* to be on close or familiar terms; be friendly (with *with*): *Her family hobnobs with the wealthiest people in the city.* [Earlier *hob* or *nob* give or take, have or have not, hit or miss; with reference to the custom of alternating in treating to drinks, going back to Old English *habban* to have + *nabban* not to have.]
ho·bo (hō′bō) *pl.,* **-bos** or **-boes.** *n.* tramp. [Possibly for *hoe-boy* migrant farm worker.]
Hob·son's choice (hob′sənz) choice of taking that which is offered or nothing at all. [From Thomas *Hobson*, seventeenth-century English owner of a livery stable, who forced customers to rent either the horse nearest the stable door or none.]
Ho Chi Minh (hō′ chē′ min′) 1890?–1969, founder and leader of the Vietminh and president of North Vietnam from 1954 to 1969.
hock¹ (hok) *n.* joint in the hind leg, as of a horse or cow, that is above the fetlock joint and corresponds to the ankle in humans. See **fetlock** for illustration. [Old English *hōh* heel.]
hock² (hok) *n.* white Rhine wine. [Short for obsolete *hockamore*, modification of German *Hochheimer* (wine) of *Hochheim*, German village from which the wine comes.]
hock³ (hok) *Informal.* *v.t.* to pawn. —*n.* **in hock. a.** in the possession of a pawnbroker. **b.** in debt. [Dutch *hok* pen for animals, prison.]
hock·ey (hok′ē) *n.* **1.** game played on ice by two teams, officially of six players each, in which the object is to hit a puck into the opponent's goal. Also, **ice hockey. 2.** field hockey. [Possibly from Old French *hoquet* a stick, diminutive of *hoc* hook; of Germanic origin.]
hockey stick, long stick with a flat curved blade used to hit the puck in ice hockey or the ball in field hockey.
ho·cus (hō′kəs) **-cused, -cus·ing;** *also,* British, **-cussed, -cus·sing.** *v.t.* to play a trick on; hoax. [Short for HOCUS-POCUS.]
ho·cus-po·cus (hō′kəs pō′kəs) *n.* **1.** meaningless words used as a magical-sounding formula in conjuring or performing tricks. **2.** sleight of hand or other magic trick. **3.** any bit of trickery or nonsense; ʟeception. [Coined to imitate Latin.]
hod (hod) *n.* **1.** long-handled tool with an open-ended container consisting of two sides meeting in a V and a third side blocking one end, used for carrying bricks, mortar, and similar materials on the shoulder, esp. to supply workers at a building site. **2.** coal scuttle. [Middle Dutch *hodde* basket.]
hod carrier, worker whose job it is to carry materials such as bricks or mortar in a hod to other workers.
hod·den (hod′ən) *n.* *Scottish.* coarse fabric woven of undyed wool.

It was often made with a combination of black and white fleece and called **hodden gray**. [Of uncertain origin.]

hodge·podge (hoj′poj′) *also,* **hotch·potch.** *n.* jumbled mixture; conglomeration. [Modification of earlier *hotchpot,* from Old French *hochepot,* from *hocher* to shake (of Germanic origin) + *pot* pot (of Germanic origin).]

Hodg·kin's disease (hoj′kinz) disease characterized by progressive enlargement of the lymph glands. [From Thomas *Hodgkin,* 1798–1866, English physician who discovered it.]

hoe (hō) *n.* tool with a wide, thin blade set at an angle to a long handle, used esp. for weeding and loosening soil. —*v.i., v.t.,* **hoed, hoe·ing,** to dig or cultivate with a hoe. [Old French *houe* this tool; of Germanic origin.] —**ho′er,** *n.*

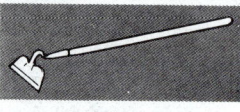

Hoe

hoe·cake (hō′kāk′) *n.* coarse bread made of corn meal, water, and salt, shaped into a flat, thin cake, originally baked on a hoe over a fire.

hoe·down (hō′doun′) *n.* **1.** party or similar social gathering at which square dances are danced. **2.** lively country dance or square dance. [HOE + DOWN¹.]

Hoff·mann, Ernst T. A. (hof′mən; urnst) 1776–1822, German writer, musician, and painter.

hog (hôg, hog) *n.* **1.** domestic pig, esp. one weighing over 120 pounds and raised for its meat. **2.** wild boar. **3.** *Informal.* gluttonous, greedy, or filthy person. **4. to go whole hog.** *Informal.* to do something without reservation or restraint. **5. to live (or eat) high on the hog.** *Informal.* to live or eat very well or in an extravagant manner. **6. to go hog wild.** *Informal.* to go to an extreme or act without restraint. —*v.t.,* **hogged, hog·ging.** *Informal.* to take more than one's share of. [Old English *hogg* a swine.]

ho·gan (hō′gän, -gan) *n.* dwelling of the Navaho Indians usually made of timber and branches covered with earth.

Ho·garth, William (hō′gärth) 1697–1764, English painter and engraver.

hog·back (hôg′bak′, hog′-) *n. Geology.* sharply crested ridge with abruptly sloping sides, often formed by exposure of steeply inclined strata.

hog·gish (hô′gish, hog′ish) *adj.* gluttonous, greedy, or filthy like a hog. —**hog′gish·ly,** *adv.* —**hog′gish·ness,** *n.*

hog·nose snake (hôg′nōz′, hog′-) any of several thick-nosed, harmless North American snakes, family Colubridae, which flatten their bodies and hiss ferociously when disturbed.

hogs·head (hôgz′hed′, hogz′-) *n.* **1.** large cask or barrel, esp. one that can contain from 63 to 140 gallons. **2.** liquid measure, esp. one equal to 63 gallons. See **weights and measures** for table.

hog·wash (hôg′wôsh′, hog′wosh′) *n.* **1.** worthless or nonsensical talk or writing. **2.** refuse fed to hogs; swill.

Hoh·en·stau·fen (hō′ən shtou′fən) *n.* German royal family whose members ruled as kings in Germany or as Holy Roman emperors from 1138 to 1254.

Hoh·en·zol·lern (hō′ən zol′ərn; *German* hō′ən tsôl′ərn) *n.* German royal family founded by Frederick I that included the kings of Prussia from 1701 to 1918 and the emperors of Germany from 1871 to 1918.

hoi·den (hoid′ən) *hoyden.*

hoi pol·loi (hoi′ pə loi′) common people; the masses. ▲ often used mistakenly to mean the elite. [Greek *hoi polloi* the many.]

hoist (hoist) *v.t.* to lift or pull up, esp. by means of some mechanical device: *The sailors hoisted the cargo on board.* —*n.* **1.** apparatus, as a block and tackle or elevator, for hoisting. **2.** act of hoisting. [Earlier *hoise, hysse,* probably from Middle Dutch *hischen, hyssen* to raise up.]

hoi·ty-toi·ty (hoi′tē toi′tē) *adj.* **1.** snobbish; haughty: *The hoity-toity manner of some clubwomen annoys her.* **2.** *Archaic.* giddy; flighty. —*n.* **1.** haughtiness. **2.** *Archaic.* giddy or flighty behavior. [Rhyming expression based on obsolete *hoit* to romp; of uncertain origin.]

ho·key-po·key (hō′kē pō′kē) *n.* mild deception or trickery; funny business. [Modification of HOCUS-POCUS.]

Hok·kai·do (ho ki′dō) *n.* northernmost and second largest island of Japan. Area, 30,132 sq. mi. Pop. (1963), 5,171,800.

ho·kum (hō′kəm) *n.* meaningless or false statement or idea; bunk. [Possibly blend of HOCUS-POCUS and BUNKUM.]

Hol·bein (hōl′bīn) **1. Hans (the Elder)** (häns). c.1460–1524, German painter. **2. Hans (the Younger).** 1497–1543, his son; German painter and engraver.

hold¹ (hōld) *held, held or (archaic)* **hold·en, hold·ing,** *v.t.* **1.** to take and keep in, or as in, the hands or arms; clasp; grip: *The mother held the squirming child on her lap. He held the packages while I unlocked the door.* **2.** to keep up; support; bear: *Will the chair hold my weight?*

3.a. to keep in a specified position; maintain: *The photographer asked her to hold the pose for a few minutes longer.* **b.** to keep in a specified state or condition; have control or influence over: *to hold the audience's attention.* **4.** to keep under control; keep back; check: *The troops held their fire. The little boy held his breath.* **5.** to prevent the movement or escape of; detain: *The deputy held the prisoner at gunpoint. The dam held back the flooding river.* **6.** to set aside or reserve: *to hold theater tickets at the box office, to hold someone's paycheck until his return.* **7.** to be able to contain: *The bus can hold twenty-five people. A sponge holds water.* **8.** to keep or have in, or as in, the mind; harbor: *to hold an opinion, to hold a grudge.* **9.** to keep forcibly against an enemy; defend: *The troops held the territory for one week.* **10.** to have and retain as one's own; possess; occupy: *to hold a high position in government.* **11.** to carry on; engage in: *to hold a conversation, to hold a celebration.* **12.** to convoke; convene: *to hold a meeting.* **13.** to believe or judge to be; think; assert; consider: *They held him responsible. The scientist held that the drug was dangerous.* **14.** *Law.* **a.** to decree: *The jury held him innocent.* **b.** to possess or have title to: *to hold a mortgage.* **15.** *Music.* to sustain (a musical note): *She held high C for fifteen seconds.* —*v.i.* **1.** to remain fast or unbroken; not yield to pressure, strain, or other force: *The anchor held even in the rough seas.* **2.** to keep one's clasp or grip: *The old woman held tightly to the railing as she came down the steps.* **3.** to remain faithful or attached; adhere: *to hold to one's beliefs, to hold to a purpose.* **4.** to remain valid; be in force; apply: *My decision still holds.* **5.** to remain or continue in a state, position, or condition: *The humidity held all day.*

to hold back. a. to keep back; restrain: *John tried to hold the dog back but it got loose.* **b.** to stop or hesitate in one's actions; refrain: *She held back from asking the favor of you.* **c.** to keep in or as in one's possession; retain: *Do not hold back the truth.*

to hold down. a. to keep under subjection or control; repress: *The policemen held down the edgy crowd.* **b.** to have and work at: *His frequent illnesses made it difficult for him to hold down a job.*

to hold forth. a. to talk at great length; lecture; harangue: *The candidate was holding forth on the mistakes of his opponent.* **b.** to offer; propose: *This book holds forth the promise of a paradise on earth.*

to hold in. a. to keep in check; curb; restrain: *He held in the horse with the reins.* **b.** to control or hide (one's feelings or impulses): *She held in the urge to cry.*

to hold off. a. to keep away or at a distance: *The troops held off the enemy. The campers held off the wolves with burning sticks.* **b.** to refrain temporarily from action; delay: *The jury held off giving a decision until hearing more evidence.*

to hold on. *Informal.* **a.** to maintain one's hold or grasp on something: *He held on for dear life.* **b.** to continue; persist: *The custom held on for two generations.* **c.** to stop; wait: *Hold on, don't get so excited!* ▲ used in the imperative.

to hold one's own. to maintain one's condition, advantage, or position; stand one's ground: *He held his own in the contest and finished in first place.*

to hold out. a. to last; endure: *The food supplies held out for a week.* **b.** to maintain or continue resistance: *The men in the besieged fort held out for two weeks.* **c.** to extend; offer; present: *to hold out a promise of new jobs.* **d.** *Informal.* to keep back or delay (something expected or due): *The employer held out the workers' pay as punishment for striking.*

to hold over. a. to keep for future action or consideration; postpone: *The bill was held over for the next session.* **b.** to remain in office or in possession beyond the regular term. **c.** to have or use as an advantage, control, or threat.

to hold up. a. *Informal.* to rob: *The thieves held up the store last night.* **b.** to bring or point attention to: *She held him up as an example to the class.* **c.** to maintain a state or position; last; endure: *She held up under the questioning.* **d.** to stop; delay: *The filibuster held up action on the bill.*

to hold water. to be sound, believable, or consistent; stand up: *Will your argument hold water?*

to hold with. to approve of.

—*n.* **1.a.** act of holding; grasp; grip: *His tight hold on the rope saved him from a bad fall.* **b.** way of gripping with, or as with, the hands: *The wrestler couldn't break loose from his opponent's hold.* **2.** controlling force; strong influence: *The dictator kept a tight hold on his people. Some ideas exert an unshakable hold on man's imagination.* **3.** something that can be grasped, as for support: *The diver found a hold in the coral reef.* **4.** order to put aside or delay (something): *Put a hold on the delivery until the balance is paid.* **5.** prison cell: *The king imprisoned the rebels in the hold of the castle.* **6.** *Music.* sign or symbol indicating a pause. **7.** *Archaic.* fortified place; stronghold. [Old English *h(e)aldan* to detain, keep, support, defend.] —**Syn.** *v.t.* **7.** see **contain.**

hold² (hōld) *n.* space below the deck of a ship, where cargo is stowed. [Middle Dutch *hol* hole, ship's hold.]

hold·back (hōld′bak′) *n.* **1.** that which holds back; check; restraint. **2.** iron or strap on the shaft of a vehicle to which the harness is attached, enabling a horse to stop the vehicle or to back it up.

hold·en (hōl′dən) *Archaic.* a past participle of **hold**[1].

hold·er (hōl′dər) *n.* **1.** one who holds something, esp. an owner or possessor, as of property or a title. **2.** that which holds or aids in holding something: *a napkin holder.* **3.** one who is the legal possessor of a bill, note, or check and is entitled to receive payment on it.

hold·ing (hōl′ding) *n.* **1.** piece of rented land. **2.** *also,* **holdings.** legally held property, esp. stocks or bonds. **3.** *Sports.* act or instance of illegally hindering the movement of an opposing player.

holding company, company that owns the majority of stock of other companies, usually for purpose of control.

hold·up (hōld′up′) *n.* **1.** act of, or attempt at, armed robbery. **2.** stoppage or delay: *There was a holdup of traffic.*

hole (hōl) *n.* **1.** hollow place or cavity in a solid body or surface; pit: *They dug a hole in the ground for the foundation. The apples were riddled with holes made by insects.* **2.** opening in or through something; perforation: *The bullet made a hole in the window.* **3.** any small, dingy, squalid place: *The old man spent his last years in a hole of a room.* **4.** prison cell; dungeon. **5.** flaw; defect; fault: *There were many holes in his alibi.* **6.** pond or deep, calm place in a river, stream, or pond: *a swimming hole, a fishing hole.* **7.** *Informal.* awkward or embarrassing position; predicament: *His lack of manners got him into one hole after another.* **8.a.** *Golf.* small, round cavity into which the ball is hit. **b.** area between a tee and this hole, including the fairway and the putting green. **9. to burn a hole in one's pocket.** (of money) to create a strong desire to spend it. **10. hole in one.** *Golf.* single drive from a tee that goes into the cup. **11. in the hole.** in debt. **12. to make a hole in.** to consume a considerable portion of: *The unexpected bills made a hole in our savings.* —*v.t.,* **holed, hol·ing. 1.** to make a hole or holes in: *The earth was holed along the road for telephone posts.* **2.** to hit or drive, as a ball, into a hole: *He holed the ball on the third stroke.* **3.** to make by or as by digging or boring: *to hole a tunnel through the mountain.* —*v.i.* **1.** to make a hole or holes: *The miners holed through from one shaft to another.* **2. to hole out.** to hit a golf ball into a hole. **3. to hole up. a.** to hibernate, in or as in a hole: *The bear holed up for the winter.* **b.** to seclude or hide oneself: *The couple holed up until the danger passed.* [Old English *hol* hollow place.]

Syn. n. **1.** Hole, cavity, hollow indicate an empty space in a body or surface. Hole is the general term and means an unfilled space in a solid body, usually connecting with the surface: *A gopher lives in a hole in the ground.* Cavity is a more formal way of saying the same thing: *The mining operation left a large cavity in the mountain.* Hollow suggests an unfilled space in the surface of or within a solid body and implies opposition to solid: *There is a hollow in the sequoia's trunk.*

hol·i·day (hōl′ə dā′) *n.* **1.** day when work is suspended by custom or law, as to commemorate a special event. **2.** any day free from work. **3.** *also,* **holidays.** any period when usual occupations are suspended, esp. for leisure or relaxation; vacation: *Christmas holidays, I'm going to take a holiday from trouble and from care.* **4.** holy day. —*adj.* relating or suited to a holiday; gay; festive. [Old English *hāligdæg* holy day.]

ho·li·er-than-thou (hō′lē ər thən thou′) *adj.* showing a feeling of superiority or self-righteousness: *Even his friends disliked his holier-than-thou attitude.*

ho·li·ness (hō′lē nis) *n.* **1.** quality or state of being holy. **2. Holiness.** used as a form of address in speaking or referring to the pope and some patriarchs of the Orthodox Church, preceded by *His* or *Your.* [Old English *hālignes* quality of being holy.]

hol·land (hol′ənd) *n.* linen or cotton fabric, sometimes given a glazed finish, used for such items as window shades and upholstery. [From *Holland,* where it was first made.]

Hol·land (hol′ənd) *n.* **1.** historic region in northwestern Europe, now part of the Netherlands. **2.** the Netherlands.

hol·lan·daise sauce (hol′ən dāz′) rich, creamy sauce made from egg yolks, butter, lemon juice, and seasoning. [French *sauce hollandaise* Dutch sauce; *hollandaise,* feminine of *hollandais* Dutch, from *Hollande* the Netherlands, from Dutch *Holland,* former county of the Netherlands. See SAUCE.]

Hol·land·er (hol′ən dər) *n.* Dutchman.

Hol·lands (hol′əndz) *n.* very dry gin, originally made in Holland, in which the flavoring agent, juniper, is ground up directly with the malt. Also, **Hollands gin.**

hol·ler (hol′ər) *v.t., v.i.* *Informal.* to shout.

hol·lo (hol′ō, hə lō′) halloo.

hol·loa (hol′ō, hə lō′) halloo.

hol·low (hol′ō) *adj.* **1.** having a hole or cavity within; not solid: *an old, hollow tree trunk.* **2.** having a depression or groove in the surface; concave; scooped out. **3.** set deeply within; sunken, as the cheeks or eyes. **4.** deep and muffled in tone, as though reverberating in an empty space. **5.** devoid of worth, sincerity, or substance; false; deceitful: *hollow*

oaths. *They made a hollow truce with the enemy.* **6.** empty: *The divorce left him with a hollow feeling inside.* —*n.* **1.** cavity, depression, or concavity in any surface; empty space; hole. **2.** feeling of emptiness or void. **3.** valley; basin. —*v.t.* to make or form by making hollow (with *out*): *The cook hollowed out the melons.* —*adv.* **to beat all hollow.** to defeat or surpass completely: *Christmas beats all hollow.* [Old English *holh* hole, cave.] —**hol′low·ly,** *adv.* —**hol′low·ness,** *n.* —*Syn. n.* **1.** see hole.

hol·low-eyed (hol′ō īd′) *adj.* having deep-set eyes, often encircled by dark rings due to illness or fatigue.

hol·low·ware (hol′ō wâr′) *n.* dishes, bowls, or serving utensils, usually metalware or earthenware, which have depth.

hol·ly (hol′ē) *pl.,* **-lies.** *n.* **1.** any of a group of trees or woody shrubs, genus *Ilex,* bearing greenish-white flowers, the females of which have bright red, white, or black berries. The best-known species is the evergreen English holly, *I. aquifolium,* bearing glossy spiny-toothed leaves and bright red berries. **2.** shiny leaves and berries of any of several of these trees or shrubs, widely used as Christmas decorations. [Old English *hole(g)n* shrub of the genus *Ilex.*]

hol·ly·hock (hol′ē hok′) *n.* **1.** spikelike stalk of large showy flowers of the plant *Althaea rosea,* growing in various colors. **2.** tall plant bearing these flowers, grown in many parts of the world, having large, wrinkled, heart-shaped leaves and a strong hairy stem. [Middle English *holihoc* marsh mallow, from *holi* holy + *hoc* mallow (from Old English *hoc*). See HOLY.]

Hollyhock

Hol·ly·wood (hol′ē wood′) *n.* **1.a.** section of Los Angeles, noted as the traditional home of U.S. motion-picture and television industries. **b.** U.S. motion-picture industry or its characteristic image. **2.** city in southeastern Florida, on the Atlantic, near Miami. Pop. (1970), 106,873.

Hollywood bed, single bed with or without a headboard, usually supported by four short legs.

holm[1] (hōm) *n.* **1.** low, flat land by a river or stream. **2.** small island in a river or lake. [Old Norse *holmr.*]

holm[2] (hōm) *n.* holm oak. [Short for HOLM OAK.]

Holmes (hōmz) **1.** Oliver Wen·dell (wend′əl). 1809–94, U.S. author and physician. **2.** Oliver Wendell, Jr. 1841–1935, his son, an associate justice of the U.S. Supreme Court from 1902 to 1932. **3.** see Sherlock Holmes.

hol·mi·um (hōl′mē əm) *n.* lustrous metallic element, nearly as heavy as copper, one of the rare-earth elements. Symbol: Ho See **element** for table. [Modern Latin *holmium,* from *Holmia* Stockholm; because it is found near Stockholm.]

holm oak, ornamental evergreen tree, *Quercus ilex,* grown in warm regions of the world, and having broad, leathery leaves. [*Holm* going back to Old English *holegn* holly) + OAK.]

hol·o·caust (hol′ə kôst′, hō′lə-) *n.* **1.** great or complete destruction, esp. due to fire. **2.** sacrifice that is entirely consumed by fire; burnt offering. [Late Latin *holocaustum* whole burnt offering or sacrifice, from Greek *holokauston,* from *holos* whole + *kaustos* burnt.]

Hol·o·cene (hol′ə sēn′, hō′lə-) *adj.* of or relating to the Recent geological epoch. —*n.* Recent geological epoch. [Greek *holos* whole + *kainos* recent.]

ho·lo·gram (hō′lə gram′, hol′ə-) *n.* photographic film or other medium in which the light-wave patterns produced by an object or scene are recorded. When properly illuminated, the hologram produces a realistic three-dimensional image of the object or scene. [Greek *holos* whole + -GRAM[1].]

hol·o·graph (hol′ə graf′, hō′lə-) *adj.* written entirely in the handwriting of the person who signed it: *a holograph document.* —*n.* any document written in this way. [Late Latin *holographus,* going back to Greek *holos* whole + *graphein* to write.]

hol·og·ra·phy (ho log′rə fē) *n.* process involving wave interference, esp. the technique used in producing optical holograms.

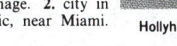

holp (hōlp) *Archaic.* a past tense of **help**.

hol·pen (hōl′pən) *Archaic.* a past participle of **help**.

Hol·stein (hōl′stīn′, -stēn′) *n.* one of a breed of black-and-white dairy cattle. They are the largest of all dairy breeds, the bull weighing at least 2200 pounds.

Hol·stein-Frie·sian (hōl′stīn′ frē′zhən, -stēn′) *n.* Holstein.

hol·ster (hōl′stər) *n.* case, usually of leather, for a pistol, rifle, or similar weapon, attached to a belt at the waist or shoulder or to a horseman's saddle. [Dutch *holster.*] —**hol′stered,** *adj.*

Holster

ho·ly (hō′lē) **-li·er, -li·est.** *adj.* **1.** belonging to, dedicated to, or issuing from God; sacred. **2.** having a sacred quality by religious use or au-

thority; consecrated: *holy bread.* **3.** spiritually pure; free from sin; pious; saintly. **4.** worthy of or inspiring reverence. [Old English *hālig* sacred, pure, saintly.]

Syn. *adj.* **1., 2. Holy, sacred** mean worthy of religious worship and veneration. **Holy** means consecrated to the service of God or possessing sanctity: *Bishops and priests belong to the holy orders.* **Sacred,** opposed to the profane, refers to what is revered as partaking of the nature of God or sanctioned by or serving God: *The Koran is the sacred book of the Muslims.*

Holy Alliance, agreement uniting European monarchs proposed by Alexander I of Russia in 1815, the object of which was to perpetuate existing dynasties and suppress revolutionary movements and similar threats, as that posed by Napoleon.

Holy City, city considered sacred by the followers of a particular religion, as Jerusalem by Jews, Christians, and Muslims.

Holy Communion 1. church service in which bread and wine are consecrated and distributed to members of the congregation in commemoration of the Last Supper. **2.** the bread and wine, or elements, used in this service, esp. when received as a sacrament.

holy day, day set apart for religious observance, as in commemoration of a sacred person or event.

Holy Father, used as a title and form of address of the pope.

Holy Ghost, third person of the Trinity. Also, **Holy Spirit.**

Holy Grail *Medieval Legend.* sacred chalice considered to be either the cup used by Christ at the Last Supper or the vessel that caught the blood of Christ at the Crucifixion.

Holy Land, Palestine.

holy of holies 1. innermost chamber of the Temple in ancient Jerusalem, concealed from public view by a veil. It housed the Ark of the Covenant and could be entered only by the high priest on the Day of Atonement. **2.** any place or thing of special sacredness.

Hol·yoke (hōl'yōk') *n.* city in southwestern Massachusetts, on the Connecticut River. Pop. (1970), 50,112.

holy orders 1. rite or sacrament of ordination. **2.** rank of an ordained Christian minister or priest, esp. in a church with an official hierarchy. **3.** the higher grades of the ministry, as in the Roman Catholic, Anglican, or Orthodox Church. **4. to take holy orders,** to be ordained as a Christian minister or priest.

Holy Roman Empire, empire in western and central Europe that was founded by Charlemagne in 800 and lapsed into anarchy late in the ninth century. It was revived by Otto I of Germany in 962 and lasted until 1806.

Holy Rood 1. cross on which Jesus Christ was crucified. **2. holy rood.** crucifix, esp. one above an ornamented screen at a church altar.

Holy Saturday, Saturday of Holy Week, the day before Easter Sunday.

Holy Scripture, the Bible *(def. 1).*

Holy See, office, authority, or jurisdiction of the pope. Also, **Apostolic See.**

Holy Spirit, Holy Ghost.

ho·ly·stone (hō'lē stōn') *n.* flat piece of soft sandstone used for scouring the wooden decks of ships. —*v.t.,* **-stoned, -ston·ing.** to scrub with a holystone. [HOLY + STONE; supposedly because its users kneel while working.]

Holy Synod, administrative council of a self-governing Orthodox Church.

Holy Thursday 1. Maundy Thursday **2.** in the Anglican Church, Ascension Day.

holy water, water blessed by a priest, used in religious services and devotional acts, as in baptizing or blessing.

Holy Week, week before Easter, beginning with Palm Sunday.

Holy Writ, the Bible *(def. 1).*

hom·age (hom'ij, om'-) *n.* **1.** honor, respect, or reverent regard given or shown: *The university paid homage to the professor by establishing a scholarship in his name.* **2.** formal acknowledgment of allegiance and obligation by a feudal vassal to his lord. **3.** act done or payment made to indicate such acknowledgment. [Old French *homage* duty owed by a vassal to his lord, from *hom* man, vassal, from Latin *homō* man.] —**Syn.** see **honor.**

hom·bre (ōm'brā, -brē) *n.* *Informal.* man; fellow [Spanish *hombre*, from Latin *homō.*]

hom·burg (hom'bûrg') *also,* **Hom·burg.** *n.* felt hat with a brim turned up slightly at the sides and a crown dented lengthwise. [From *Homburg,* Germany, where it was first made.]

home (hōm) *n.* **1.a.** place in which one lives; domicile; residence: *We invited him into our home. I'll be at home if you need me.* **b.** place that can serve as a residence; house: *to get a mortgage on a new home.* **2.** place or environment that is the center of one's familial or domestic attachments: *This life of wandering makes a few days' residence in one place seem like home* (Hawthorne, 1858). **3.** home regarded as representing a familial unit; family; household: *a happy home, a broken home.*

4. country, region, town, or locality where one was born or reared or where one lives: *He lives in Texas now, but his home is Wisconsin. New York's been my home for five years now.* **5.** place or region where something originated, developed, or is commonly or natively found: *Australia is the home of the koala bear.* **6.** place where one feels one belongs or where one finds refuge or satisfaction: *He found a home in that university and taught there for many years.* **7.** institution or establishment for the shelter and care of certain people: *a foundling home, a home for the aged.* **8.** place from which activities are initiated or coordinated; base of operations; headquarters: *The pilot turned the plane around and headed for home.* **9.** goal or place of safety in certain sports and games. **10.** *Baseball.* home plate. **11. at home. a.** at one's ease, as if in one's own home; unconstrained; comfortable: *She always felt at home in her friend's house.* **b.** thoroughly familiar or knowledgeable (in a specified area or subject); proficient: *She was at home in the arts.* **c.** prepared and willing to receive visitors: *Mrs. Jones is at home on Thursdays.* —*adv.* **1.** at, to, or toward home: *to see someone home. He wrote home.* **2.a.** to the place or mark aimed at; so as to penetrate effectively: *The bullet hit home.* **b.** so as to reach or affect intimately and completely; to the very heart: *Her criticism hit home. The examples he used drove his argument home.* —*v.i.* **homed, hom·ing. 1.** to go or return home: *The pigeon homed from a distance of 100 miles.* **2.** to proceed or be directed toward a particular point or target, as by means of radio waves or by heat radiation emanating from the point or target (often with *on*). —*v.t.* to cause, as an aircraft or guided missile, to proceed toward a particular point or target, esp. toward a target emitting heat radiation. [Old English *hām* dwelling, house.]

Syn. *n.* **1.a. Home, house, residence, dwelling** mean the place where a person or persons live. **Home** is the most common word for a place where one lives and often suggests comfort, warmth, or protection: *A man's home is his castle.* **House** refers only to the building itself: *Our house is over fifty years old.* **Residence** is a more dignified and formal word and stresses the fact of physical occupancy: *The prime minister returned to his residence after the meeting.* **Dwelling** is a quainter term, often suggesting a small or lowly structure or shelter where a person, or often an animal, lives: *The poor lived in dwellings of mud and straw.*

home base 1. home plate. **2.** headquarters or base of operations from which activities are coordinated or initiated or around which they are centered. **3.** goal or place of safety in certain sports and games.

home·bod·y (hōm'bod'ē) *pl.,* **-ies.** *n.* one who prefers to stay at home or whose interests center in the home.

home·bred (hōm'bred') *adj.* bred or raised at home; native; domestic.

home brew *also,* **home-brew.** any alcoholic beverage or liquor made at home.

home·com·ing (hōm'kum'ing) *n.* **1.** return to one's home. **2.** annual celebration in many colleges and universities, marked by the return of alumni.

home economics, science, art, and study of managing a household, including such subjects as nutrition, budgeting, and child care.

home fries, boiled potatoes sliced and fried in butter or shortening. Also, **home-fried potatoes.**

home front, civilian sphere or population of a country at war.

home-grown (hōm'grōn') *adj.* grown, produced, or developed locally or at home.

home·land (hōm'land') *n.* one's native or adopted land.

home·less (hōm'lis) *adj.* having no home.

home·ly (hōm'lē) **-li·er, -li·est.** *adj.* **1.** having plain features; not good-looking; unattractive. **2.** of an unsophisticated, familiar, or everyday nature; unpretentious; simple: *homely truths, homely virtues.* —**home'li·ness,** *n.*

home·made (hōm'mād') *adj.* **1.** made at home: *homemade cookies.* **2.** crudely or simply done; not professionally made: *a dress that looks homemade.*

home·mak·er (hōm'mā'kər) *n.* one who manages a household, esp. a housewife.

ho·me·op·a·thy (hō'mē op'ə thē) *n.* method of treating disease with small amounts of drugs which, if given in more concentrated doses to a healthy person, would produce symptoms similar to those of the disease. [Modern Latin *homoeopathia,* from Greek *homoios* like + *-patheia* -PATHY.] —**ho·me·o·path** (hō'mē ə path'), **ho·me·op·a·thist,** *n.* —**ho'me·o·path'ic,** *adj.*

ho·me·o·sta·sis (hō'mē ə stā'sis) *n.* tendency to maintain internal equilibrium of the body, esp. in the composition, temperature, and acidity of the fluid that bathes all the body cells, carrying to them essential material and taking away wastes. This equilibrium is essential for the normal functioning of the body. [Modern Latin *homeostasis,* from Greek *homoios* like + *stasis* a standing still.]

ho·me·o·stat·ic (hō'mē ə stat'ik) *adj.* of or relating to homeostasis.

home plate, flat piece, officially a five-sided, white rubber slab, beside which a baseball player stands to hit the pitched ball and which he must touch after rounding the bases to score a run.

hom·er (hō′mər) *n. Informal.* home run.

Ho·mer (hō′mər) *n.* **1.** great epic poet of ancient Greece and the earliest known poet in European literature, believed to have lived about the eighth century B.C. **2.** **Wins·low** (winz′lō). 1836–1910, U.S. painter, best known for his seascapes.

Ho·mer·ic (hō mer′ik) *adj.* of, relating to, or characteristic of Homer, his poetry, or the period of Greek history about which he wrote.

Homeric laughter, loud, hearty laughter.

home·room (hōm′rōom′, -room′) *n.* class to which students report at the beginning of each school day, at which time attendance is checked and school announcements made before the start of regular classes.

home rule, system under which one political unit within a larger one, as a city within a state, is granted power to manage its own affairs.

home run **1.** hit made by a baseball player that enables him, without benefit of errors on the part of the opponents, to round the bases and score a run. **2.** score made in such a way.

home·sick (hōm′sik′) *adj.* depressed or ill because one is away from one's home or family; a longing for home. —**home′sick′ness,** *n.*

home·spun (hōm′spun′) *adj.* **1.** spun or made at home. **2.** simple and unpretentious in character; unsophisticated. —*n.* **1.** fabric woven of yarn spun at home or by hand. **2.** any of various coarse, strong fabrics woven to resemble this.

home·stead (hōm′sted′) *n.* **1.** any house together with adjacent buildings and the land they are on. **2.** parcel of 160 acres of public land granted to a settler under the Homestead Act of 1862. —*v.t.* to settle on and claim (land), esp. as provided for by the Homestead Act. —*v.i.* to settle and claim a homestead, esp. as provided for by the Homestead Act.

Homestead Act, law passed by the U.S. Congress in 1862 to distribute public land to settlers for farming.

home·stead·er (hōm′sted′ər) *n.* **1.** one who has a homestead. **2.** one granted land under the Homestead Act.

homestead law, law exempting a homestead from attachment or sale for debt.

home stretch **1.** straight part of a track between the last turn and the finish line. **2.** last part of any trip or endeavor.

home·ward (hōm′wərd) *also,* **home·wards.** *adv.* toward home: *to be traveling homeward after a long journey.* —*adj.* directed or going toward home: *the homeward leg of the voyage.*

home·work (hōm′wurk′) *n.* **1.** school lesson to be studied or prepared outside the classroom, usually at home. **2.** any work, esp. preparatory study, that must be done at home or on one's own time, rather than during regular working hours.

home·y (hō′mē) **hom·i·er, hom·i·est.** *adj. Informal.* having homelike qualities; informal and friendly; cozy; comfortable.

hom·i·cid·al (hom′ə sīd′əl) *adj.* **1.** of or relating to homicide. **2.** tending to or leading to homicide; murderous: *a homicidal maniac, a homicidal rage.*

hom·i·cide¹ (hom′ə sīd′) *n.* the killing of one human being by another. [Old French *homicide,* from Latin *homicīdium,* from *homō* man + *-cīdium.* See -CIDE¹.]

hom·i·cide² (hom′ə sīd′) *n.* person who kills another. [Old French *homicide,* from Latin *homicīda,* from *homō* man + *-cīda.* See -CIDE².]

hom·i·let·ic (hom′ə let′ik) *adj.* **1.** of, relating to, or characteristic of a homily or homilies. **2.** of or relating to homiletics. [Greek *homīlētikos* sociable, conversable, going back to *homīlein* to associate with.]

hom·i·let·ics (hom′ə let′iks) *n.pl.* branch of practical theology dealing with the art of writing and preaching sermons. ▲ construed as singular.

hom·i·ly (hom′ə lē) *pl.,* **-lies.** *n.* **1.** sermon, esp. one based on some portion of the Bible. **2.** solemn and usually long discourse, esp. on the subject of morals. [Late Latin *homīlia* sermon, from Greek *homīliā* instruction, sermon.]

homing pigeon, pigeon trained to fly home, often used to carry messages. Also, **carrier pigeon.**

hom·i·nid (hom′ə nid) *n.* any of a family of primates of whom the only surviving species is man.

hom·i·ny (hom′ə nē) *n.* kernels of white corn that have been dried and hulled, and sometimes coarsely ground or crushed, prepared for eating by being mixed with water and boiled. [Possibly of Algonquian origin.]

hominy grits, grits *(def. 1).*

homo- *combining form* same. Opposed to **hetero-.** [Greek *homos.*]

ho·mo·ge·ne·i·ty (hō′mə jə nē′ə tē, hom′ə-) *n.* state or quality of being homogeneous.

ho·mo·ge·ne·ous (hō′mə jē′nē əs, -jēn′yəs, hom′ə-) *adj.* **1.** of the same kind; similar or identical: *two homogeneous parts.* **2.** having similar or identical components or character throughout: *a homogeneous mass.* [Medieval Latin *homogeneus* of the same kind, from Greek *homogenēs,* from *homos* same + *genos* kind, race.] —**ho′mo·ge′ne·ous·ly,** *adv.* —**ho′mo·ge′ne·ous·ness,** *n.*

ho·mog·e·nize (hə moj′ə nīz′) **-nized, -niz·ing.** *v.t.* **1.** to make homogeneous. **2.** to reduce the particles of two or more insoluble substances, as of the fat in milk, to such a small size that they will form a stable emulsion with one another.

hom·o·graph (hom′ə graf′, hō′mə-) *n.* word with the same spelling as another, but of different origin and meaning. *Fair* meaning "beautiful" and *fair* meaning "market place" are homographs. [HOMO + -GRAPH.]

ho·mol·o·gous (hə mol′ə gəs, hō-) *adj.* **1.** corresponding, as in position, proportion, function, or structure. **2.** *Biology.* corresponding in structure and evolutionary origin, but not necessarily serving the same function. The human arm, the wing of a bird, and the foreleg of a horse are homologous. Distinguished from **analogous** in def. 2. [Greek *homologos* agreeing.]

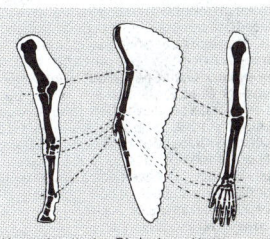

Horse forelimb Bird wing Human arm

Homologous structures

hom·o·logue (hom′ə lôg′) *n.* that which is homologous, as an organ or part.

ho·mol·o·gy (hə mol′ə jē, hō-) *pl.,* **-gies.** *n.* **1.** state or quality of being homologous. **2.** *Biology.* homologous similarity of organs. [Greek *homologiā* agreement.]

hom·o·nym (hom′ə nim′) *n.* word with the same pronunciation as another, but different in meaning. *Boar* and *bore* are homonyms. [Latin *homōnymum* the same word employed to indicate different things, going back to Greek *homōnymos* having the same name.]

hom·o·phone (hom′ə fōn′, hō′mə-) *n.* **1.** letter or group of letters having the same sound as another. The letters *ks* and *x* are homophones. **2.** homonym. [Greek *homos* + Greek *phōnē* sound.]

hom·o·phon·ic (hom′ə fon′ik, hō′mə-) *adj.* **1.** of or having the same sound. **2.** *Music.* having one predominant melodic line with the other parts or voices providing harmony. Opposed to **polyphonic.**

ho·moph·o·nous (hə mof′ə nəs) *adj.* homophonic.

ho·moph·o·ny (hə mof′ə nē) *n.* **1.** state or quality of being homophonic. **2.** homophonic music.

ho·mop·ter·ous (hə mop′tər əs, hō-) *adj.* of or belonging to a diverse group of insects, order Homoptera, including aphids and cicadas, characterized by sucking mouth parts and membranous wings. [Modern Latin *Homoptera,* from HOMO- + Greek *pteron* wing + -OUS.]

Ho·mo sa·pi·ens (hō′mō sā′pē ənz) the human being; modern man; man viewed as the only surviving species of the genus *Homo,* including all existing races. ▲ italicized when used as a Modern Latin taxonomic classification but often used without italics in general contexts, esp. as a facetious or scientific-sounding synonym for *man.* [Latin *homo* man + *sapiens* wise, intelligent.]

ho·mo·sex·u·al (hō′mə sek′shōo əl, -mō-) *adj.* of, relating to, or characterized by homosexuality. —*n.* one who manifests or practices homosexuality.

ho·mo·sex·u·al·i·ty (hō′mə sek′shōo al′ə tē, -mō-) *n.* **1.** sexual attraction toward members of one's own sex. **2.** sexual relations with a member of one's own sex.

ho·mun·cu·lus (hō mung′kyə ləs) *pl.,* **-li** (-lī′). *n.* **1.** little man; manikin. **2.** in occult tradition, a tiny human being that could be developed artificially by an alchemist. [Latin *homunculus,* diminutive of *homō* man.]

Hon. **1.** Honorable. **2.** Honorary.

Hon·do (hon′dō) *n.* Honshu.

Hon·du·ras (hon door′əs, -dyoor′-) *n.* country in northern Central America with coast lines on the Caribbean and the Pacific. Capital, Tegucigalpa. Area, 43,277 sq. mi. Pop. (1969 est.), 2,495,000. —**Hon·du′ran,** *adj., n.*

hone (hōn) *n.* whetstone with a fine grain, used to sharpen the cutting edges of tools, as razors or scissors. —*v.t.* **honed, hon·ing.** to sharpen on or as on a hone. [Old English *hān* a stone.]

hon·est (on′ist) *adj.* **1.** displaying truthfulness, fairness, or trustworthiness, as in character, principles, or actions: *an honest person, an honest effort.* **2.** earned or gotten fairly or legitimately; obtained without deceit: *to make an honest living.* **3.** sincere; frank; open: *to have an honest face, to express honest appreciation.* **4.** of full or stated quality or quantity; genuine; pure: *an honest measure.* **5.** *Archaic.* chaste; virtuous. [Old French *honeste* good, virtuous, from Latin *honestus* honorable.] —**hon′est·ly,** *adv.* —**hon′est·ness,** *n.*

hon·es·ty (on′is tē) *n.* **1.** state or quality of being honest; integrity:

The honesty of his action is not in question. **2.** truthfulness; sincerity; fairness: *He could not, in all honesty, agree to their terms.* **3.** *Archaic.* chastity.
Syn. 1. Honesty, integrity, probity mean uprightness of character and conduct. **Honesty** suggests truthfulness and absence of duplicity, esp. in one's dealings with others: *Honesty is always the best policy* (George Washington, 1796). **Integrity** implies soundness of moral principles and steadfast adherence to a high ethical code: *Knowledge without integrity is dangerous and dreadful* (Samuel Johnson, 1759). **Probity** denotes integrity that has been proved or revealed in one's actions: *Only men of probity should be elected to high offices.*

hon·ey (hun′ē) *pl.,* **hon·eys.** *n.* **1.** thick, sweet liquid, made by bees from the nectar they collect from flowers, used for food and as a sweetening agent. **2.** sweetness. **3.** sweet one; darling; dear. **4.** *Informal.* that which is thought to be exceptionally good or exemplary: *a honey of a boat.* —*adj.* of or like honey; sweet. —*v.t.,* **hon·eyed** or **hon·ied, hon·ey·ing. 1.** to sweeten with or as with honey. **2.** to talk to in a sweet or flattering manner. [Old English *hunig* the sweet liquid made by bees.]

honey bear, kinkajou.

hon·ey·bee (hun′ē bē′) *n.* any bee that makes and stores honey, esp. *Apis mellifera,* the common bee that is widely domesticated.

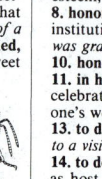

Honeybee

hon·ey·comb (hun′ē kōm′) *n.* **1.** wax structure formed by bees, consisting of six-sided cells arranged back to back, that hangs vertically in the hive, used for storing honey, pollen, eggs, and larvae. **2.** anything resembling this in appearance or structure. —*adj.* resembling a honeycomb: *Termites chew wood in a honeycomb pattern.* —*v.t.* **1.** to make full of holes or cavities like a honeycomb: *The old house was honeycombed with secret passages.* **2.** to penetrate or pervade: *His alibi was honeycombed with inconsistencies.* [Old English *hunig-camb* wax structure formed by bees, from *hunig* honey + *camb* comb.]

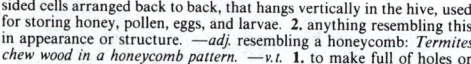

Queen bee

Workers

Honeycomb

hon·ey·dew (hun′ē dōō′, -dū′) *n.* **1.** honeydew melon. **2.** sweet substance secreted on leaves and stems by aphids and certain other plant-sucking insects. It forms a part of the diet of certain kinds of ants. **3.** sweet substance exuded by the leaves of certain plants in hot weather.

honeydew melon, a muskmelon having a smooth creamy-yellow rind and sweet, light-green flesh.

hon·eyed (hun′ēd) *adj.* **1.** sweetened with or full of honey. **2.** sweet as honey, as speech designed to flatter: *His honeyed words fooled no one.*

honey locust, any of a group of tall, thorny trees, genus *Gleditsia,* of the pea family, found in Asia, Africa, and North and South America, bearing long divided leaves, clusters of small greenish flowers, and large flat pods containing sweet pulp.

hon·ey·moon (hun′ē mōōn′) *n.* **1.** vacation taken by a newly married couple, usually right after the wedding and off by themselves. **2.** the very beginning of married life, esp. the first month. **3.** initial, blissful period in any relationship: *The honeymoon is over between Congress and the president.* —*v.i.* to go or be on a honeymoon. [HONEY + MOON]; said to be from an early Scandinavian custom of having a newly married couple drink wine containing honey for the first *moon* (i.e., month) of their marriage.] —**hon′ey·moon′er,** *n.*

hon·ey·suck·le (hun′ē suk′əl) *n.* **1.** any of a group of erect or climbing shrubs, genus *Lonicera,* found throughout the Northern Hemisphere, bearing fragrant, tubular or bell-shaped, white, yellow, or pink flowers. A sweet nectar can usually be obtained from the base of the flower. **2.** any of various similar plants. [Going back to Old English *hunig* honey + *sūcan* to suck; because one can *suck* honey, i.e., sweet nectar, from the flower.]

Hong Kong (hong′kong′, hông′kông′) **1.** British crown colony off the southeastern coast of China. Area, 398 sq. mi. Pop. (1969 est.), 3,990,000. **2.** Victoria.

hon·ied (hun′ēd) *v.* a past tense and past participle of **honey.** —*adj.* honeyed.

honk (hôngk, hongk) *n.* **1.** cry of a goose. **2.** any similar sound, esp. that of the horn of an automobile. —*v.i.* to utter or make such a sound. —*v.t.* to cause (something) to make such a sound: *Stop honking the horn!* [Imitative.] —**honk′er,** *n.*

Ho·no·lu·lu (hon′ə lōō′lōō) *n.* capital, major city, and chief port of Hawaii, on the southern coast of Oahu. Pop. (1970), 324,871.

hon·or (on′ər) *also, British,* **hon·our.** *n.* **1.** strong adherence to or sense

of what is right or moral; integrity: *There is honor even among thieves. A man of honor would not behave in so cowardly a way.* **2.** good name or reputation; position of being respected or esteemed; credit: *The nation's honor was at stake.* **3.a.** source or cause of respect, esteem, or pride: *She was an honor to her profession. It was a great honor to receive the award.* **b.** privilege: *We request the honor of your presence. I have the honor to introduce Mr. Jones.* **4.** glory; renown; fame: *The fewer men, the greater share of honor* (Shakespeare, *Henry V*). **5.** exalted rank or position; dignity; distinction: *The king bestowed the honor of knighthood upon him.* **6. Honor.** used as a form of address in speaking or referring to certain officials, as a judge or mayor, preceded by *His* or *Your.* **7. honors.** something done or conferred as a token of respect, esteem, or distinction: *The hero was buried with full military honors.* **8. honors.** special recognition conferred on a student by an educational institution, for outstanding academic achievement: *The valedictorian was graduated with highest honors.* **9.** chastity or purity in a woman. **10. honors.** the five highest trump cards or the four aces in no-trump. **11. in honor of.** as an expression of respect, esteem, or affection for; in celebration or recognition of. **12. on** (or **upon**) **one's honor.** pledging one's word as to the truth of a statement or the fulfilling of a promise. **13. to do honor to. a.** to treat with great respect or esteem: *to do honor to a visiting dignitary.* **b.** to be a credit to: *to do honor to one's country.* **14. to do the honors.** to perform certain social courtesies, esp. by acting as host or hostess: *Father did the honors and carved the roast.* —*v.t.* **1.** to regard with great respect or esteem: *Honor thy father and thy mother* (Exodus 20:12). **2.** to treat with courtesy or deference: *to honor the flag by saluting it.* **3.** to confer honor or dignity upon; favor; dignify: *The president honored them with his presence.* **4.** to accept as valid for payment or credit: *The bank honored his check. The store would not honor my credit card.* **5.** in square dancing, to curtsy or bow to: *Honor your partner.* [Old French *honor* glory, esteem, chastity, virtue, from Latin *honor* office, dignity, reputation, esteem.]
Syn. *n.* **2. Honor, deference, homage** mean respect or esteem shown to another. **Honor** applies to the feeling as well as the manifestation of respect: *A prophet is not without honor, save in his own country* (Matthew 13:57). **Deference** implies yielding to another's wishes or judgment out of respect for rank, age, dignity, or wisdom: *The flower show was canceled out of deference to the wishes of the queen.* **Homage** suggests high praise or tribute conveyed in a ceremonial manner: *The members of the party paid homage to their leader on his birthday.*

hon·or·a·ble (on′ər ə bəl) *also, British,* **hon·our·a·ble.** *adj.* **1.** characterized by or consistent with principles of morality and integrity; upright: *The young man's intentions were honorable.* **2.** bringing honor or distinction; creditable: *an honorable achievement.* **3.** worthy of honor and respect: *an honorable profession.* **4.** having high rank or eminence; noble; illustrious: *He is descended from an honorable family.* **5.** performed or accompanied with tokens of honor or respect: *The soldier received an honorable discharge at the end of the war.* **6. Honorable.** used as a form of address in speaking of or referring to certain government officials, as members of Congress and cabinet officers or certain members of the nobility. —**hon′or·a·ble·ness;** *also, British,* **hon′our·a·ble·ness,** *n.* —**hon′or·a·bly;** *also, British,* **hon′our·a·bly,** *adv.*

hon·o·rar·i·um (on′ə rār′ē əm) *pl.,* **-rar·i·ums** or **-rar·i·a** (-rār′ē ə). *n.* fee for services rendered, esp. by a professional person: *The visiting lecturer received an honorarium of $300.* [Latin *honōrārium* gift made for admission to a post of honor, fee, going back to *honor* office, dignity, reputation.]

hon·or·ar·y (on′ə rer′ē) *adj.* **1.** designating a title or position conferred as an honor, without the customary requirements, obligations, or salary: *an honorary degree.* **2.** holding such a title or position: *honorary chairman of the fund drive.* **3.** given or made as a token of honor: *Honorary arches were erected to emperors.* **4.** depending on one's honor for fulfillment; not legally binding: *an honorary obligation.* [Latin *honōrārius* relating to honor, from *honor* office, dignity, reputation.]

hon·or·if·ic (on′ə rif′ik) *adj.* conferring honor or respect: *an honorific title.* [Latin *honōrificus* honorable, going back to *honor* office, dignity, reputation + *facere* to make, do.]

honors of war, special concessions given or courtesies shown to a defeated enemy, as permission to retain weapons and flags.

honor system, system in which the individual is trusted to obey rules and carry out responsibilities without direct supervision, used esp. in schools, colleges, and correctional institutions.

hon·our (on′ər) *British.* honor.

Hon·shu (hon′shōō) *n.* largest island of Japan. Area, 88,936 sq. mi. Pop. (1960), 70,353,500.

hooch (hōōch) *n. Slang.* alcoholic beverage, esp. cheap or illegal liquor. [Short for *hoochinoo* a liquor made by the *Hoochinoo,* an Alaskan Indian tribe.]

hood¹ (hood) *n.* **1.** covering for the head and back of the neck, often attached to the neckline of a coat, jacket, or other garment. **2.** anything resembling a hood in form or use, as the loose skin on the neck of a

at; āpe; cär; end; mē; it; īce; hot; ōld; fôrk; wood; fōōl; oil; out; up; ūse; turn; sing; thin; this; zh in treasure; ə in ago, taken, pencil, lemon, circus.

cobra or the collapsible top of a convertible car. **3.** movable metal covering over the engine of an automobile. **4.** ornamental fold of cloth worn over the back of an academic gown. The color and cut of the hood indicate the degree held by the wearer. **5.** covering used in falconry to blind the hawk when it is not pursuing game. —*v.t.* to cover or furnish with or as with a hood. [Old English *hōd* soft covering for the head and neck.]

hood² (hood) *n. Slang.* hoodlum. [Short for HOODLUM.]

Hood, Mount, mountain in the Cascade Range, in northwestern Oregon.

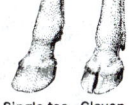

Hood¹ *(def. 4)*

-hood *suffix* **1.** state, quality, or condition of being: *childhood, likelihood.* **2.** entire group, class, or body of: *priesthood, brotherhood.* [Old English *hād* condition, quality.]

hood·ed (hood'id) *adj.* **1.** having, wearing, or covered with a hood. **2.** shaped like a hood.

hood·lum (hōōd'ləm, hood'-) *n. Informal.* **1.** ruffian or rowdy, esp. a teen-age member of a street gang. **2.** gangster; thug. [Of uncertain origin.]

hoo·doo (hōō'dōō) *pl.,* **-doos.** *n.* **1.** voodoo. **2.** *Informal.* one who or that which brings bad luck. **3.** *Informal.* bad luck. —*v.t.,* **-dooed, -doo·ing.** *Informal.* to bring bad luck to. [Form of VOODOO.]

hood·wink (hood'wingk') *v.t.* **1.** to trick or deceive. **2.** *Archaic.* to blindfold. [HOOD + WINK.]

hoof (hoof, hōōf) *pl.,* **hooves** or **hoofs.** *n.* **1.** hard, horny covering on the feet of certain mammals, as horses, cattle, pigs, or deer. **2.** entire foot of such an animal. **3.** human foot. ▲ used humorously. **4. on the hoof.** (of livestock) not butchered; alive. —*v.t., v.i.* **1.** *Informal.* to walk. **2.** *Slang.* to dance. [Old English *hōf* this horny covering.]

Single-toe hoof / Cloven hoof

hoof-and-mouth disease (hoof' ənd mouth', hōōf'-) foot-and-mouth disease.

hoof·beat (hoof'bēt', hōōf'-) *n.* sound made by a hoofed animal when it walks, trots, or runs: *rhythmical hoofbeats fading into the silent night.*

hoofed (hooft, hōōft) *adj.* having hoofs.

hoof·er (hoof'ər, hōō'fər) *n. Slang.* professional dancer, esp. a tap dancer.

hook (hook) *n.* **1.** bent or sharply angled piece of metal, wood, or other firm material, having one or more free ends adapted for catching, suspending, fastening, or holding something: *a meat hook, a coat hook.* **2.** fishhook. **3.** something resembling a hook in shape or use. **4.** sharp bend or angle in the length or course of something, as in a river. **5.** projecting point or spit of land. **6.** *Baseball.* curve. **7.** *Golf.* stroke in which the ball curves in the direction opposite to which the player is facing. **8.** *Boxing.* short, swinging blow made with the arm bent. **9.** *Music.* line on the stem of certain musical notes, indicating the duration of the note. **10. by hook or (by) crook.** by any means, fair or foul; in any way possible: *The dishonest politician was determined to win the election by hook or by crook.* **11. hook, line, and sinker.** completely; entirely: *The gullible girl fell for their story hook, line, and sinker.* **12. off the hook. a.** *Slang.* free from a difficult situation, an obligation, or blame: *His alibi got him off the hook.* **b.** (of a telephone receiver) not on the cradle: *Rob couldn't contact her because her phone was off the hook.* **13. on one's own hook.** *Informal.* by oneself; independently. **14. on the hook.** (of a telephone receiver) on the cradle. —*v.t.* **1.** to attach, fasten, or secure with or as with a hook or hooks: *The sailor hooked the line to the side of the boat. The seamstress hooked the train onto the gown.* **2.** to catch or take hold of with a hook: *The fisherman hooked three trout in the stream.* **3.** to make into the shape of a hook; bend; crook: *The boy hooked his leg over the arm of the chair.* **4.** to catch or win by artifice; entrap: *The young woman was determined to hook a husband.* **5.** to make, as a rug or mat, by pulling yarn or strips of cloth through a piece of fabric by means of a hook. **6.** *Baseball.* to pitch or throw (a ball) so that it curves. **7.** *Golf.* to drive (a ball) so that it curves in the direction opposite to which the player is facing. **8.** *Boxing.* to strike with a hook. **9.** *Informal.* to steal; pilfer: *Someone hooked five dollars from her wallet.* —*v.i.* **1.** to have the form of a hook; curve: *The river hooks at Smithtown.* **2.** to be attached, fastened, or secured with or as with a hook or hooks: *The coat hooks in the front.* **3. to hook up.** to assemble (a mechanical or electrical device) and connect it to a source of power: *The electrician hooked up the doorbell.* **4. to hook up with.** *Informal.* to become connected or joined with; unite: *The French army hooked up with the Americans for the march to Paris.* [Old English *hōc* bent piece of metal, fishhook, type of agricultural implement.]

hook·ah (hook'ə) *also,* **hook·a.** *n.* tobacco pipe of Oriental origin, having a long, flexible tube attached to a vessel of water through which the smoke is drawn and cooled. [Urdu *huqqah,* from Arabic *huqqah* box, water vessel of a hookah.]

hook and eye, clothing fastener consisting of a metallic or plastic hook and a loop or bar to which the hook may be attached.

hooked (hookt) *adj.* **1.** curved or bent like a hook. **2.** having a hook or hooks. **3.** *Slang.* addicted to or obsessed with some practice or thing, esp. narcotics.

hooked rug, rug made by looping yarn or strips of cloth through a piece of fabric, as canvas or burlap.

hook·er (hook'ər) *n.* **1.** small, one-masted fishing boat. **2.** any ship that is old, poorly designed, or hard to maneuver. [Dutch *hoeker* fishing boat, dogger, from *hoek* hook, fishhook.]

hook·up (hook'up') *n.* **1.** arrangement and connection of electric or electronic parts or circuits, esp. a temporary connection, as a network of television stations connected for a particular event: *a nationwide television hookup for the election returns.* **2.** any arrangement or connection of separate or related parts.

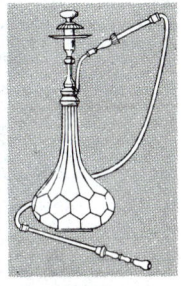

Hookah

hook·worm (hook'wurm') *n.* **1.** any of several small, threadlike parasitic worms, phylum Nematoda, that may infest the intestines of man and other mammals. **2.** hookworm disease. [HOOK + WORM; with reference to the small, hooked, toothlike structures around its mouth with which it attaches itself to the intestinal walls of the host.]

hookworm disease, disease caused by certain hookworms that feed on the host's blood. It is characterized by anemia and tiredness and, in children, by arrested physical and mental development.

hook·y (hook'ē) *n. Informal.* **to play hooky,** to stay out of school without permission or a justifiable excuse; be truant. [Possibly from dialectal English *hook* to make off.]

hoo·li·gan (hōō'lə gən) *n. Slang.* ruffian or hoodlum, esp. a member of a street gang. [Supposedly from *juzgar* to judge, applied to certain rowdies in late-nineteenth-century London.] —**hoo'li·gan·ism,** *n.*

hoop (hōōp, hoop) *n.* **1.** circular band or ring, as of wood or metal, esp. for holding together the staves of a barrel. **2.** child's toy consisting of a large circular band of wood, metal, or plastic which can be rolled along the ground or spun around the body. **3.** circular band of flexible metal, whalebone, or similar support for a hoop skirt. **4.** a croquet wicket. —*v.t.* to bind or fasten with a hoop or hoops. [Old English *hōp* round band, as of wood or metal.]

hoop·la (hōōp'lä, hoop'-) *n. Slang.* boisterous activity or excitement; great noise and fuss. [French *houp-là* interjection used to rouse someone; of uncertain origin.]

hoo·poe (hōō'pōō) *n.* brightly colored bird, *Upupa epops,* of Europe, Asia, and Africa, having a long, slender bill, a fanlike crest, and usually pinkish-brown plumage with black and white markings. Length: 1 foot. [Earlier *hoop,* from French *huppe,* from Latin *upupa;* imitative of the bird's call.]

hoop skirt 1. framework of flexible hoops connected by tapes, formerly worn as a petticoat to make a woman's skirt stand out from her body. **2.** skirt worn with such a framework.

Hoopoe

hoo·ray (hoo rā') hurrah.

hoose·gow (hōōs'gou') *also,* **hoos·gow.** *n. Slang.* jail. [Spanish *juzgado* court of justice, from *juzgar* to judge, from Latin *judicāre.*]

Hoo·sier (hōō'zhər) *n. Informal.* native or resident of Indiana. [Of uncertain origin.]

hoot (hōōt) *n.* **1.** cry of an owl. **2.** cry or shout, esp. one expressing derision or disapproval. **3.** *Informal.* very small or insignificant amount; the least bit: *His advice isn't worth a hoot.* —*v.i.* **1.** to utter the cry of an owl. **2.** to shout or cry out, as in derision or disapproval: *The fans hooted at the outfielder's error.* —*v.t.* **1.** to drive away by hooting: *The speaker's opponents hooted him out of the meeting.* **2.** to assail with cries of derision or disapproval: *They will not listen to him, but laugh at him, and hoot him* (Jowett, 1875). **3.** to express, as derision or disapproval, by hooting: *The crowd hooted their scorn for the congressman's speech.* [Probably imitative of the owl's cry.]

hoot·en·an·ny (hōōt'ən an'ē) *pl.,* **-nies.** *n.* informal gathering or party for singing folk songs. [Of uncertain origin.]

Hoo·ver, Herbert Clark (hōō'vər) 1874–1964, thirty-first president of the United States, from 1929 to 1933.

---

at; āpe; cär; end; mē; it; īce; hot; ōld; fôrk; wood; fōōl; oil; out; up; ūse; turn; sing; thin; this; zh in treasure; ə in ago, taken, pencil, lemon, circus.

Hoover Dam, massive dam on the Colorado River between Nevada and Arizona, formerly known as Boulder Dam.

hooves (hoovz, hōovz) a plural of **hoof.**

hop¹ (hop) hopped, hop·ping. *v.i.* **1.** to make a short leap or series of leaps on one foot: *William hopped up and down to keep warm.* **2.** to move in short leaps on both or all feet at once: *The frog hopped along the shore of the pond.* **3.** to rise or get up quickly: *Russell hopped up and offered the lady his chair.* **4.** *Informal.* to travel, esp. with little or no preparation: *He hopped off to New York for the weekend.* —*v.t.* **1.** to jump over: *to hop a fence.* **2.** *Informal.* to board and ride in (a vehicle), esp. without paying: *The hobo hopped a freight that took him to Houston.* **3. to hop to it.** to move or begin to act quickly. **4. to hop up.** *Informal.* to increase the power of: *The boy hopped up the engine of his car.* —*n.* **1.** act of hopping. **2.** *Informal.* trip, esp. in an airplane: *It's a short hop between Paris and London.* **3.** *Informal.* dance or dancing party. **4.** *Informal.* bounce or rebound: *The ball took a bad hop and the shortstop missed it.* [Old English *hoppian* to leap, dance.]

hop² (hop) *n.* **1. hops.** conelike greenish-yellow fruits of any of a group of plants, genus *Humulus,* of the mulberry family, containing bitter-tasting oils and used in the brewing of beer and other malt beverages. **2.** long-stemmed climbing plant bearing this fruit, having hairy leaves with saw-toothed edges. —*v.t.,* hopped, hop·ping. to flavor or treat with hops. [Middle Dutch *hoppe* this plant.]

hope (hōp) hoped, hop·ing. *v.t.* **1.** to desire with expectation of fulfillment: *Susan hoped her book review would be printed.* **2.** to wish, believe, or trust: *We hope you will enjoy your vacation.* —*v.i.* **1.** to have expectation or desire: *to hope for support from one's friends.* **2.** *Archaic.* to trust; rely. **3. to hope against hope.** to hope for something when there is little or no prospect of fulfillment. —*n.* **1.** desire accompanied by expectation of fulfillment: *Hope springs eternal in the human breast* (Pope, 1732). **2.** that which is hoped for: *The senator staked his career on the hope of winning reelection.* **3.** one on whom or that on which hopes are centered: *The younger generation is the hope of the nation.* **4.** *Archaic.* trust; reliance. [Old English *hopa* expectation, trust.]

hope chest, chest or box in which a young woman keeps linens, clothing, and similar articles in anticipation of marriage.

hope·ful (hōp′fəl) *adj.* **1.** full of or showing hope. **2.** inspiring hope; promising fulfillment: *a hopeful sign.* —*n.* one who is considered likely to succeed or who aspires to success. —**hope′ful·ly,** *adv.* —**hope′-ful·ness,** *n.*

hope·less (hōp′lis) *adj.* **1.** having or feeling no hope: *a mood of hopeless depression.* **2.** inspiring no hope: *a hopeless case.* —**hope′-less·ly,** *adv.* —**hope′less·ness,** *n.*

hop hornbeam, any of a small group of trees, genus *Ostrya,* bearing fruits that resemble hops.

Ho·pi (hō′pē) *pl.,* **-pis** or **-pi.** *n.* **1.** member of a tribe of Pueblo Indians living in northeastern Arizona and New Mexico. **2.** language of the Hopis. [Hopi *hópi* peaceful.]

Hop·kins (hop′kinz) **1.** Gerard Man·ley (man′lē). 1844–89, English poet. **2.** Mark. 1802–87, U.S. educator.

hop·lite (hop′līt′) *n.* heavily armed foot soldier of ancient Greece. [Greek *hoplítēs,* from *hoplon* weapon.]

hop·per (hop′ər) *n.* **1.** one who or that which hops. **2.** container, usually with a wider top than bottom, used to hold something temporarily and to feed it into another container or part.

hop·scotch (hop′skoch′) *n.* children's game played on a course usually consisting of a pattern of numbered squares drawn on the pavement or ground. The players hop into the squares in sequence and try to retrieve a stone or other object that has been tossed into one of the squares. [Hop¹ + the now rare term *scotch* line, incision; of uncertain origin.]

Hor·ace (hôr′is, hor′-) *n.* 65–8 B.C., Roman poet and satirist; born Quintus Horatius Flaccus.

Ho·rae (hôr′ē, hōr′ī) *n.,pl. Greek Mythology.* the Hours.

Ho·ra·tian (hə rā′shən) *adj.* of, relating to, or characteristic of Horace or his poetry.

Ho·ra·ti·us Co·cles (hə rā′shəs kō′klēz) legendary military hero who, by holding off the attacking Etruscans until the bridge across the Tiber could be destroyed, saved Rome.

horde (hôrd) *n.* **1.** large group; swarm; multitude: *A horde of people poured out of the stadium when the game ended.* **2.** nomadic tribe or clan of Mongols. **3.** any nomadic tribe or clan. [French *horde* pack, band, through German and Polish, from Turkish *ordū* camp.]

Ho·reb (hôr′eb) *n.* in the Old Testament, the mountain on which Moses received the Ten Commandments, generally identified with Mount Sinai.

hore·hound (hôr′hound′) *also,* **hoar·hound.** *n.* **1.** bitter, aromatic plant, *Marrubium vulgare,* of the mint family, having whitish, woolly leaves and stems, and bearing clusters of small flowers. **2.** bitter extract obtained from the leaves of this plant. **3.** candy or cough medicine flavored with this extract. [Old English *hārhūne* this plant.]

ho·ri·zon (hə rī′zən) *n.* **1.** line of apparent meeting of the sky and the earth or sea: *Two ships were barely visible on the horizon.* **2.** limit or range of knowledge, perception, interest, or experience: *Meeting new people widened the young man's horizon.* [Old French *horizon* line of apparent meeting of the sky and the earth or sea, from Late Latin *horizōn,* from Greek *horízōn (kuklos)* bounding (circle), going back to *horos* limit.]

hor·i·zon·tal (hôr′ə zont′əl, hor′-) *adj.* **1.** parallel to the horizon; level. Opposed to **vertical.** **2.** contained, measured, or operating in a plane parallel to the horizon: *horizontal distance.* **3.** of, relating to, or near the horizon. —*n.* something horizontal, as a line, plane, direction, or member. —**hor′i·zon′tal·ly,** *adv.*

hor·mone (hôr′mōn) *n.* **1.** any of numerous chemical substances formed in and by the endocrine glands which enter the bloodstream directly and affect the activity of other organs. Hormones regulate body growth, control sexual activity and development, and maintain the body's chemical balance. **2.** similar substance in plants. [Greek *hormōn,* present participle of *hormân* to set in motion, urge on.] —**hor·mo′nal,** *adj.*

horn (hôrn) *n.* **1.** hard, permanent, unbranched projection, usually occurring in pairs, growing on the upper part of the head of various hoofed mammals, including cattle, sheep, antelope, and rhinoceros. **2.** one of the antlers of a deer. **3.** hornlike projection on the head of various other animals, as the tuft of feathers on a horned *owl.* **4.a.** substance of which the horn is composed. **b.** any similar natural or synthetic substance. **5.** vessel or other container formed from or shaped like a horn. **6.a.** *Music.* any of various brass instruments usually consisting of a coiled metal tube that gradually widens into a flaring bell, esp. the French horn. **b.** *Informal.* any brass instrument, esp. a trumpet. **c.** any wind instrument resembling or originally made from the horn of an animal. **7.** device used to sound a warning signal: *The bus driver honked his horn at the children in the street.* **8.** something shaped like a horn, as a cape or peninsula. **9.** either of the pointed extremities of a crescent. **10. to blow one's own horn.** to praise oneself; brag. **11. to draw** (or **pull**) **in one's horns. a.** to restrain oneself: *He drew in his horns just as he was about to explode with anger.* **b.** to withdraw; retract: *His statement was challenged and he drew in his horns.* **12. horns of a dilemma.** two unpleasant alternatives: *to be caught on the horns of a dilemma.* —*v.i.* **to horn in.** *Slang.* to enter without being invited; butt in; intrude: *to horn in on a conversation.* [Old English *horn* hard growth on the head of some animals, container made of a horn, type of wind instrument.]

Horn, Cape (hôrn) cape on an island of Tierra del Fuego, forming the southernmost tip of South America.

horn·beam (hôrn′bēm′) *n.* any of various small trees, genus *Carpinus,* of the birch family, esp. the American hornbeam, *C. caroliniana,* having smooth gray bark and very hard wood.

horn·bill (hôrn′bil′) *n.* any of various songless birds, family Bucerotidae, native to tropical and subtropical forests of Africa, Asia, and the East Indies, usually having a large, colorful bill surmounted by a horny growth. Length: 15–60 inches including the tail.

Hornbill

horn·blende (hôrn′blend′) *n.* translucent mineral of complex composition, ranging from dark green to black, and occurring in both igneous and metamorphic rocks. [German *Hornblende.*]

horn·book (hôrn′book′) *n.* **1.** primer consisting of a page with the alphabet and a prayer or numerals on it, covered with a sheet of transparent horn and fastened in a frame with a handle, formerly used in teaching children to read. **2.** treatise on the rudiments of a subject; primer.

horned (hôrnd) *adj.* having a horn or horns; having a hornlike projection.

horned owl, any of various owls having hornlike ear tufts, esp. the great horned owl.

horned toad, any of a group of insect-eating lizards, genus *Phrynosoma,* common in dry areas of the western United States, having spiny horns on the head and fringed scales along the sides of the body. Length: to 4½ inches. Also, **horn toad.**

Horned toad

Input

Hopper

Output

Hopper

---

at; āpe; cär; end; mē; it; īce; hot; ōld; fôrk; wood; fōōl; oil; out; up; ūse; turn; sing; thin; this; zh in treasure; ə in ago, taken, pencil, lemon, circus.

hor·net (hôr′nit) *n.* **1.** any of various large wasps, family Vespidae, that live in colonies and are often reddish-brown or black with dull markings. The female can inflict a painful sting. Length: ½–1 inch. **2. hornet's nest.** great controversy; much trouble: *to stir up a hornet's nest.* [Old English *hyrnet.*]

horn of plenty, cornucopia.

horn·pipe (hôrn′pīp′) *n.* **1.** lively British folk dance, usually performed solo, formerly popular among sailors. **2.** music for such a dance. **3.** obsolete musical wind instrument having the bell and mouthpiece made of horn.

horn·y (hôr′nē) **horn·i·er, horn·i·est.** *adj.* **1.** made of horn or of something resembling it. **2.** having horns or hornlike growths. **3.** hard like horn; calloused: *horny and rough feet.*

hor·o·loge (hôr′ə lōj′, hor′-) *n.* timepiece, as a clock, watch, sundial, or hourglass. [Old French *hor(o)loge* clock, from Latin *hōrologium* sundial, water clock, from Greek *hōrologion,* going back to *hōrā* season, hour + *-logos* telling.]

ho·rol·o·ger (hə rol′ə jər) *n.* person skilled in horology; clock maker. Also, **ho·rol′o·gist.**

ho·rol·o·gy (hə rol′ə jē) *n.* **1.** science of measuring time. **2.** art of making, regulating, or testing timepieces.

hor·o·scope (hôr′ə skōp′, hor′-) *n.* **1.** prediction about one's personal fate, often with advice, esp. for a particular day. It is based on an interpretation of the positions of the planets at a given time. **2.** appearance of the heavens, specifically with reference to the relative positions of the planets at any particular moment, esp. at the time of a person's birth. **3.** diagram of the twelve signs of the zodiac with relation to the positions of the planets, used in predicting the future. [French *horoscope* nativity, from Latin *hōroscopus,* from Greek *hōroskopos,* from *hōrā* hour + *skopos* watcher.]

hor·ren·dous (hô ren′dəs, ho-) *adj.* horrible; dreadful; frightful. [Latin *horrēndus.*] —**hor·ren′dous·ly,** *adv.*

hor·ri·ble (hôr′ə bəl, hor′-) *adj.* **1.** arousing or tending to arouse horror; terrible; dreadful. **2.** *Informal.* extremely unpleasant, disagreeable, shocking, or ugly: *She has a horrible cold. The weather is horrible today.* [Old French *horrible,* from Latin *horrībilis,* from *horrēre* to bristle, tremble.] —**hor′ri·ble·ness,** *n.* —**hor′ri·bly,** *adv.*

hor·rid (hôr′id, hor′-) *adj.* **1.** causing aversion or horror; dreadful; abominable. **2.** *Informal.* extremely unpleasant; disagreeable or offensive. [Latin *horridus* bristly, frightful.] —**hor′rid·ly,** *adv.* —**hor′rid·ness,** *n.*

hor·rif·ic (hô rif′ik, ho-) *adj.* causing horror; horrifying; horrible.

hor·ri·fy (hôr′ə fī′, hor′-) *-fied, -fy·ing. v.t.* **1.** to cause to feel horror. **2.** *Informal.* to shock greatly and unpleasantly. [Latin *horrificāre* to cause terror.]

hor·ror (hôr′ər, hor′-) *n.* **1.** intense and painful feeling of fear and abhorrence; dread; terror. **2.** great aversion or dislike; loathing: *a horror of snakes.* **3.** quality of causing horror: *the horrors of war.* **4.** one who or that which causes horror. **5.** *Informal.* that which is extremely disagreeable, shocking, or ugly: *That blue dress is a horror.* [Latin *horror* terror.]

hors de com·bat (ôr də kôN bä′) *French.* out of the fight; disabled.

hors d'oeuvre (ôr dœrv′) *pl.,* **hors d'oeuvres.** hot or cold appetizer, as olives, celery, or cheese, served before the main courses of a meal. [French *hors d'oeuvre* literally, outside of work, going back to Latin *forīs* out of doors + *dē* from, of + *opera* work; originally referring to an outbuilding not included in the central architectural plan and later applied to a course separate from the main part of a meal.]

horse (hôrs) *pl.,* **hors·es.** *n.* **1.** four-legged, hoofed mammal, *Equus caballus,* having a long, flowing mane and tail, domesticated since prehistoric times, and used as a beast of burden and a draft animal, and for riding. Height: to 6 feet at the shoulder. **2.** full-grown male horse; stallion or gelding. **3.** any of various animals of the horse family, Equidae, as the zebra or donkey. **4.** gymnastic apparatus consisting of a leather-covered block mounted on four legs, used for vaulting and other exercises. **5.** frame or structure, usually having four legs, used for holding or supporting something. **6.** *Military.* mounted troops; cavalry. **7.** *Slang.* heroin. **8. from the horse's mouth.** from the original or most reliable source: *The information came straight from the horse's mouth.* **9. horse of a different** (or **another**) **color.** something completely different. **10. to be** (or **get**) **on one's high horse.**

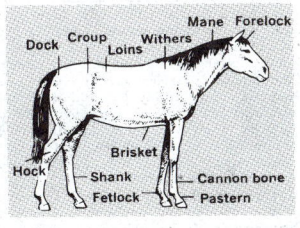

Horse

to assume a haughty or pretentious attitude or manner. **11. to hold one's horses.** to restrain oneself. **12. to horse.** get on your horse; mount. ▲ used esp. as a command to cavalry troops. —*v.t.,* **horsed, hors·ing.** to furnish with a horse or horses: *to horse a cavalry regiment.* —*v.i.* **to horse around.** to engage in horseplay. —*adj.* **1.** of or relating to a horse or horses. **2.** mounted on horses: *horse soldiers.* [Old English *hors* the animal.]

horse·back (hors′bak′) *n.* **1.** back of a horse. **2.** ridge of earth or rock; hogback. —*adv.* sitting or riding on a horse.

horse·car (hôrs′kär′) *n.* **1.** streetcar drawn by horses. **2.** car for transporting horses.

horse chestnut 1. large ornamental tree, *Aesculus hippocastanum,* widely grown in Europe and the United States, bearing pyramid-shaped clusters of white flowers and inedible nuts. **2.** the nut itself, containing two large, shiny, brown seeds.

horse·flesh (hôrs′flesh′) *n.* **1.** horses collectively, esp. for riding, driving, or racing: *The trainer is a good judge of horseflesh.* **2.** flesh of a horse, esp. as used for food.

horse·fly (hôrs′flī′) *pl.,* **-flies.** *n.* **1.** any of a large group of bloodsucking flies, family Tabanidae, having a stout, hairy, usually black or brown body. The female attacks various mammals, including man, and inflicts a painful bite. **2.** any of various other insects, as the botfly, which attack horses and cattle.

Horse Guards, body of cavalry, esp. the cavalry brigade forming the household guard of the British sovereign.

horse·hair (hôrs′hâr′) *n.* **1.** hair of a horse, esp. from the mane or tail. **2.** stiff fabric made with this hair, usually in combination with other fibers, used esp. for upholstery and outer garments. —*adj.* made of, covered, or stuffed with horsehair.

horse·hide (hôrs′hīd′) *n.* **1.** hide of a horse. **2.** leather made from this hide.

horse latitudes, two belts of high atmospheric pressure and predominantly calm, dry weather, extending over the oceans at about 30 degrees north and south of the equator.

horse·laugh (hôrs′laf′) *n.* loud, coarse, or boisterous laugh.

horse·less carriage (hôrs′lis) *Archaic.* automobile.

horse·man (hôrs′mən) *pl.* **-men.** *n.* **1.** man who rides on horseback. **2.** man skilled in riding or handling horses.

horse·man·ship (hôrs′mən ship′) *n.* art of riding or handling horses; equestrian skill.

horse marine 1. member of an imaginary corps of mounted marines. **2.** one who is out of his element; misfit.

horse pistol, large pistol formerly carried by horsemen.

horse·play (hôrs′plā′) *n.* rough, boisterous play or fun.

horse·pow·er (hôrs′pou′ər) *n.* unit for measuring power, or rate of work, as of an engine, equal to 550 foot-pounds per second or 746 watts.

horse·rad·ish (hôrs′rad′ish) *n.* **1.** sharp-tasting white root of a plant, *Armoracia rusticana,* of the mustard family, used as a condiment. **2.** the plant itself, widely cultivated in southeastern Europe and North America.

horse sense *Informal.* plain, practical common sense.

horse·shoe (hôrs′shoo′, hôrsh′-) *n.* **1.** any of several types of U-shaped metal pieces curved to fit the shape of a horse's hoof, attached by means of nails driven into the hard, horny, outer shell of the hoof. **2.** something shaped like a horseshoe. **3. horseshoes.** game for two or more players in which the object is to pitch a U-shaped piece so that it encircles a stake, normally placed 40 feet away from the pitcher, or lands closer to the stake than the opponent's piece. ▲ construed as singular. —*v.t.* **-shoed, -shoe·ing.** to provide with horseshoes.

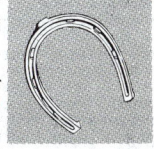

Horseshoe

horseshoe crab, saltwater invertebrate of any of four families, order Xiphosura, having a hard, horseshoe-shaped shell and a stiff, spinelike tail. Length: to 20 inches including the tail. Also, **king crab.**

horse·tail (hôrs′tāl′) *n.* **1.** any of a small group of flowerless plants, genus *Equisetum,* having hollow, jointed stems and scalelike leaves. **2.** tail of a horse, esp. one formerly used in Turkey as a military standard indicating the rank of pasha. Also, **mare's′-tail′.**

horse·whip (hôrs′hwip′, -wip′) *n.* whip used for driving or controlling horses. —*v.t.,* **-whipped, -whip·ping.** to beat with or as with a horsewhip.

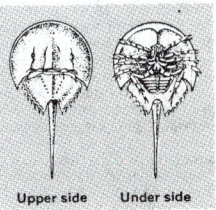

Upper side   Under side

Horseshoe crab

---

horse·wom·an (hôrs′woom′ən) *pl.,* **-wom·en.** *n.* **1.** woman who rides on horseback. **2.** woman skilled in riding or handling horses.

horst (hôrst) *n. Geology.* block of the earth's crust that has been uplifted between two faults. [German *Horst* thicket.]

hors·y (hôr′sē) **hors·i·er, hors·i·est.** *also,* **hors·ey.** *adj.* **1.** relating to, characteristic of, or suggestive of a horse or horses. **2.** interested in or fond of horses or sports involving horses. **3.** *Slang.* large and awkward in appearance or manner. —**hors′i·ly,** *adv.* —**hors′i·ness,** *n.*

hor·ta·tive (hôr′tə tiv) *adj.* hortatory. —**hor′ta·tive·ly,** *adv.*

hor·ta·to·ry (hôr′tə tôr′ē) *adj.* of, relating to, or giving exhortation; serving to urge or encourage. [Late Latin *hortātōrius,* from Latin *hortārī* to encourage.]

hor·ti·cul·ture (hôr′tə kul′chər) *n.* **1.** art or science of growing flowers, fruits, vegetables, and ornamental plants. **2.** cultivation of a garden. [Latin *hortus* garden + *cultūra* cultivating.] —**hor′ti·cul′tur·al,** *adj.* —**hor′ti·cul′tur·ist,** *n.*

Ho·rus (hôr′əs) *n.* a sun god of ancient Egypt, represented as having the head of a falcon.

Hos., Hosea.

ho·san·na (hō zan′ə) *interj.* praise to God. —*n.* **1.** cry of *hosanna.* **2.** any cry or shout of adoration, acclamation, or praise. [Late Latin *hōsanna,* from Greek *hōsanna,* from Hebrew *hōsha′nā* save now, we pray.]

hose (hōz) *pl.,* **hose** or *(def. 1)* **hos·es** or *(defs. 2, 3, archaic)* **hos·en.** *n.* **1.** flexible tube of rubber, canvas, or other material for conveying water or other liquids to a desired point. **2.** stocking or sock. ▲ usually construed as plural. **3.** close-fitting trousers resembling tights, formerly worn by men. —*v.t.,* **hosed, hos·ing.** to spray, wash, or water with a hose. [Old English *hosa* garment for the leg.]

Ho·se·a (hō zē′ə, -zā′ə) *n.* **1.** book of the Old Testament, predicting the doom of Israel. **2.** its author, a Hebrew prophet of the eighth century B.C.

ho·sier (hō′zhər) *n.* person who manufactures or sells hosiery or similar goods.

ho·sier·y (hō′zhər ē) *n.* **1.** stockings and socks. **2.** business of a hosier.

hos·pice (hos′pis) *n.* place of lodging for travelers or pilgrims, esp. one kept by monks. [French *hospice,* from Latin *hospitium* lodging, hospitality, from *hospes* guest, host¹.]

hos·pi·ta·ble (hos′pi tə bəl, hos pit′ə bəl) *adj.* **1.** offering a friendly and generous welcome to guests or strangers. **2.** characterized by or affording welcome and generosity toward guests. **3.** receptive or open in mind or disposition. [Modern Latin *hospitābilis,* going back to Latin *hospitārī* to be a guest.] —**hos′pi·ta·bly,** *adv.*

hos·pi·tal (hos′pit əl) *n.* **1.** institution providing medical, surgical, or psychiatric treatment for the sick or injured. **2.** place providing medical care for animals. **3.** repair shop for specified small items: *a watch hospital, a doll hospital.* [Old French *hospital* place to receive persons in need, from Medieval Latin *hospitale* place to receive guests, going back to *hospes* guest, host¹. Doublet of HOSTEL, HOTEL.]

hos·pi·tal·i·ty (hos′pə tal′ə tē) *pl.,* **-ties.** *n.* act, practice, or quality of being hospitable. [Old French *hospitalite,* from Latin *hospitālitās.*]

hos·pi·tal·i·za·tion (hos′pit əl i zā′shən) *n.* **1.a.** act of hospitalizing; being hospitalized. **b.** period of time during which a person is hospitalized. **2.** form of insurance providing partial or total payment of a patient's hospital expenses.

hos·pi·tal·ize (hos′pit əl īz′) -**ized, -iz·ing.** *v.t.* to admit or put in a hospital as a patient: *The skier was hospitalized with a broken leg.*

host¹ (hōst) *n.* **1.** man who receives or entertains others, usually as guests in his own home. **2.** proprietor of an inn or hotel. **3.** living plant or animal in or upon which a parasite lives and obtains nourishment. —*v.t.* to be or serve as host for. [Old French *hoste* innkeeper, guest, one who entertains a guest, from Latin *hospes* guest, one who entertains a guest.]

host² (hōst) *n.* **1.** large number; multitude: *a host of golden daffodils* (Wordsworth, 1804). **2.** *Archaic.* army. [Old French *host* army, from Medieval Latin *hostis,* from Latin *hostis* enemy, stranger.]
Syn. 1. Host, multitude, legion denote a very large number of persons or things. **Host** suggests a concentration of persons or things in great numbers or in striking array: *On a clear night we can see a host of stars in the sky.* **Multitude** stresses numerousness and suggests a large number considered together: *A large multitude assembled in the park for the festival.* **Legion** suggests an incalculably large number and is often used facetiously: *The big hotel had a legion of waiters.*

host³ (hōst) *also,* **Host.** *n.* wafer of unleavened bread used for Holy Communion in the Roman Catholic Church. [Old French *(h)oiste,* from Late Latin *hostia,* from Latin *hostia* animal sacrificed.]

hos·tage (hos′tij) *n.* person held or given as security that certain promises or conditions will be fulfilled: *King Richard was held as a hostage until the ransom was paid.* [Old French *(h)ostage* surety, pawn, going back to Latin *obses;* probably influenced in form by Latin *hospes* guest, host¹.]

hos·tel (hos′təl) *n.* lodging place, esp. a supervised lodging place for young people. [Old French *hostel* inn, from Medieval Latin *hospitale* place to receive guests, going back to Latin *hospes* guest, host¹. Doublet of HOSPITAL, HOTEL.]

hos·tel·ry (hos′təl rē) *pl.,* **-ries.** *n. Archaic.* inn; hotel.

host·ess (hōs′tis) *n.* **1.** woman who receives or entertains others, usually as guests in her own home. **2.** woman employed, as by a restaurant or nightclub, to greet and assist patrons. **3.** stewardess *(def. 2).* **4.** woman who keeps an inn or hotel.

hos·tile (host′əl, -īl) *adj.* **1.** feeling or exhibiting enmity or antagonism: *The speaker was shouted down by the hostile crowd.* **2.** of or belonging to an enemy: *The battalion encountered hostile forces in the valley.* [Latin *hostīlis* relating to an enemy, from *hostis* enemy.] —**hos′tile·ly,** *adv.*

hos·til·i·ty (hos til′ə tē) *pl.,* **-ties.** *n.* **1.** state of being hostile; antagonism. **2.** hostile act. **3.** **hostilities.** acts of war; warfare; war: *The hostilities ended when the truce was signed.*
Syn. 1. Hostility, enmity, animosity, antagonism apply to the feeling and expression of intense dislike and hatred. **Hostility** suggests open and active opposition: *The hostility of the citizens to the dictator was the main reason for the riot.* **Enmity** indicates a strong, deep-seated feeling of hatred which may be concealed or open: *I will put enmity between thee and the woman* (Genesis 3:15). **Animosity** is the strongest word to express bitter hatred and a desire to hurt one's enemy: *Increasing animosity between the nations inevitably led to the outbreak of war.* **Antagonism** stresses a clash of temperaments and interests: *There was a natural antagonism between the conservationist and the real estate developer.*

hos·tler (hos′lər, os′lər) *also,* **os·tler.** *n.* one who takes care of horses at an inn or stable. [Old French *hostelier* innkeeper, from *hostel* inn. See HOSTEL.]

hot (hot) **hot·ter, hot·test.** *adj.* **1.** having or communicating much heat; having a high temperature: *to make a crease with a hot iron.* **2.** having a relatively high temperature; very warm: *It was surprisingly hot for an autumn day.* **3.** having or showing an abnormally high body temperature: *She is hot with fever.* **4.** having or producing an effect of heat or burning, esp. to the taste buds; pungent; sharp: *Mexican food is usually very hot.* **5.** having or carrying an electrical current or charge, esp. one of high voltage: *a hot wire.* **6.** radioactive, esp. to a high or lethal degree. **7.** showing or characterized by intensity of feeling; angry: *The candidates exchanged hot words over the controversial issue.* **8.** highly controversial: *a hot topic of debate.* **9.** intensely active; violent; raging: *a hot battle.* **10.** in constant use or action: *During the crisis the telephones were kept hot between Moscow and Washington.* **11.** following very closely; close behind: *The police were hot on the heels of the fugitive.* **12.** in certain games, close to the object or answer sought: *She told us we were getting hot when we nearly guessed the secret.* **13.** in hunting, strong or fresh, as a scent or trail. **14.** *Informal.* dangerous; unsafe: *The refugees fled when conditions in their own country became too hot.* **15.** *Informal.* new; fresh: *The book is hot off the press.* **16.** *Music. Informal.* **a.** of or relating to jazz characterized by heavily accented beat, fast tempo, and much improvisation. **b.** playing such music: *a hot piano.* **17.** *Slang.* very eager or enthusiastic; ardent: *She was hot for all the new styles.* **18.** *Slang.* filled with activity; lively; exciting: *They had a hot time at the party.* **19.** *Slang.* unusually lucky: *While the baseball player was hot, his batting average rose thirty points.* **20.** *Slang.* **a.** recently stolen or illegally procured: *The thief tried to sell the hot jewelry.* **b.** wanted by the police. **21.** *Slang.* sexually excited or exciting. **22. hot under the collar.** *Slang.* extremely agitated; very angry. **23. to make it hot for.** *Informal.* to make a situation very difficult or uncomfortable for. —*adv.* in a hot manner. [Old English *hāt* having much heat, excitable, violent.] —**hot′ly,** *adv.* —**hot′ness,** *n.*

hot air *Slang.* empty, boastful, or pretentious talk or writing.

hot·bed (hot′bed′) *n.* **1.** garden frame used for growing plants, in which the soil is heated by decaying manure or by electricity, steam, or hot water pipes. **2.** environment fostering rapid growth or development, esp. of something bad: *The investigation of the department exposed a hotbed of corruption.*

hot-blood·ed (hot′blud′id) *adj.* very excitable; passionate; impulsive; rash.

hot·box (hot′boks′) *n.* journal box on a railroad car or locomotive overheated by friction between the bearings and the shaft or axle.

hot cake **1.** pancake; griddlecake. **2. to go (or sell) like hot cakes.** *Informal.* to be sold quickly and in great quantity.

hotch·potch (hoch′poch′) hodgepodge.

hot cross bun sweet bun sometimes containing small bits of dried fruits, as raisins or citrons, marked with a cross made of icing and traditionally eaten during Lent.

hot dog *Informal.* frankfurter.

ho·tel (hō tel′) *n.* commercial establishment that provides lodging and often food, entertainment, and other services for the public, esp. for

transients. [French *hôtel* large house, inn, from Old French *hostel* inn, from Medieval Latin *hospitale* place to receive guests, going back to Latin *hospes* guest, host¹. Doublet of HOSPITAL, HOSTEL.]

hô·tel de ville (ō tel′də vēl′) *French.* town hall.

hot·foot (hot′foot′) *pl.,* -foots. *Informal. n.* practical joke in which a match is secretly inserted between the sole and upper portion of the victim's shoe and then lit. —*v.i.* to go in great haste; hurry (usually with *it*): *We hotfooted it downtown after school.* —*adv.* in great haste.

hot·head (hot′hed′) *n.* hot-headed person.

hot·head·ed (hot′hed′id) *adj.* **1.** easily angered; quick-tempered. **2.** impetuous; rash. —**hot′-head′ed·ly,** *adv.* —**hot′-head′ed·ness,** *n.*

hot·house (hot′hous′) *n.* greenhouse.

hot pepper, pungent, podlike edible fruit of a pepper plant, esp. *Capsicum frutescens,* variety longum, from which cayenne is made.

hot plate **1.** electrical apparatus usually consisting of one or two burners, used for cooking or heating food. **2.** apparatus that can be heated and is used to keep food warm.

hot pot, dish consisting of lamb or beef and potatoes and other vegetables that have been placed in a tightly covered pot and stewed.

hot·press (hot′pres′) *v.t.* to produce a glossy surface on (paper or fabric) by subjecting it to heat and mechanical pressure. —*n.* machine for hotpressing.

hot rod *Slang.* automobile, esp. an older model, rebuilt or modified for high speeds.

hot seat *Slang.* **1.** electric chair. **2. in the hot seat.** in a difficult or dangerous position or situation.

hot·shot (hot′shot′) *n. Slang.* person who is aggressively and flamboyantly successful at something.

hot spring, natural spring emitting water above 98 degrees Fahrenheit.

Hot Springs, city in west-central Arkansas, near Little Rock, noted as a health resort and tourist center. Pop. (1970), 35,631.

hot·spur (hot′spur′) *n.* impetuous or rash person; hothead.

Hot·ten·tot (hot′ən tot′) *n.* **1.** member of a southern African people, formerly nomadic raisers of sheep and cattle. **2.** language of the Hottentots, belonging to the Khoisan language family. —*adj.* of, relating to, or characteristic of the Hottentots or their language. [Dutch *Hottentot* member of this southern African people, stutterer; said to be an imitative word suggested by the speech of these Africans, which sounded like stuttering to the Dutch.]

hot toddy, toddy *(def. 1).*

hot war, conflict involving actual fighting; open warfare. Distinguished from **cold war.**

hot water *Informal.* state of difficulty; trouble: *a mischievous lad always getting himself into hot water.*

hou·dah (hou′də) howdah.

Hou·di·ni, Har·ry (hoō dē′nē) 1874–1926, U.S. magician and escape artist; born Ehrich Weiss.

hound (hound) *n.* **1.** any of various dogs that are bred and trained to hunt by scent, as the beagle, bloodhound, and foxhound, or by sight, as the deerhound and Irish wolfhound. **2.** any dog. **3.** mean, contemptible person. **4.** *Informal.* one who avidly enjoys something, as a specific pastime or food; devotee; addict: *an autograph hound.* **5. to follow the** (or **ride to**) **hounds.** to participate in a fox hunt. —*v.t.* **1.** to pursue relentlessly or harassingly. **2.** *Informal.* to urge persistently; nag; pester: *Mother hounded me about cleaning my room.* [Old English *hund* dog, detestable person.]

hound's-tooth (houndz′toōth′) *n.* broken-check pattern used chiefly in weaving woolen fabrics. Also, **hound's-tooth check.**

hour (our) *n.* **1.** unit of time equal to ¹⁄₂₄ of a day; sixty minutes. **2.** one of the twelve points on a timepiece indicating such a unit of time: *The bus to the city leaves on the hour.* **3.** definite time of day as indicated by a timepiece: *At what hour should we leave? They met at the appointed hour.* **4.** particular or fixed time for some activity: *The family always gathered at the dinner hour.* **5.** indefinite, usually short period of time: *the hour of death.* **6. hours.** **a.** fixed time devoted to one's work or other regular pursuits: *The doctor had office hours four days a week. Do you work long hours?* **b.** habitual time for retiring and rising: *He keeps late hours and gets very little sleep.* **7.** present time or current situation: *The astronaut was a national hero and the man of the hour.* **8.** measure of distance calculated or stated in terms of the time needed to cover it: *We were an hour away from home.* **9.** measure of longitude equal to ¹⁄₂₄ of a complete circle, or 15 degrees. **10. hours. a.** canonical hours. **b.** prayers or services recited at these times. **11.a.** single period of classroom instruction, usually less than sixty minutes: *The daily schedule is divided into eight hours.* **b.** in colleges and universities, a unit of academic credit, one of which is usually given for each hour of instruction per week. **12. the wee** (or **small**) **hours.** early morning hours: *We didn't get home from the party until the wee hours.* [Old French *(h)ore* ¹⁄₂₄ of a day, time, period, from Latin *hōra* certain space of time, season, hour, from Greek *hōra.*]

hour·glass (our′glas′) *n.* device for measuring time, consisting of a glass vessel with a narrow passage in the middle, through which a quantity of sand or mercury runs from the upper to lower part in exactly one hour.

hour hand, short hand on a clock or watch indicating the hour.

hou·ri (hoor′ē, hour′ē) *pl.,* -ris. *n.* in Islam, one of the eternally young and beautiful girls given as a companion to those who attain paradise. [French *houri,* from Persian *hūrī,* from Arabic *hūrīyah* black-eyed (woman).]

hour·ly (our′lē) *adj.* **1.** done, occurring, or counted every hour: *an hourly check.* **2.** done in the course of or computed on the basis of an hour: *hourly wages.* **3.** frequent; continual. —*adv.* **1.** every hour: *The nurse looked in on the patient hourly.* **2.** frequently; continually.

Hours (ourz) *n.,pl.* Greek goddesses of time and the seasons, the daughters of the earth and the sky. Also, **Ho′rae.**

Hourglass

house (*n.,* hous; *v.,* houz) *pl.,* hous·es (hou′ziz). *n.* **1.** building for human habitation, esp. one in which a family dwells; place of residence: *Come to my house for dinner.* **2.** people, esp. a family, inhabiting a house; household: *The whole house was ill with the mumps. The house was in an uproar.* **3.a.** building in which people live together as a social group or unit: *There were ten fraternity houses on the campus.* **b.** people living in such a building. **c.** *Informal.* club or organization, as a fraternity or sorority: *What house did he pledge?* **4.** anything serving as protection or habitation for an animal: *The snail carries his house on his back.* **5.** building or other structure in which animals or objects are kept: *We visited the monkey house at the zoo.* **6.** structure or area used for a purpose other than human occupation: *We went to hear a folk singer at a coffee house.* **7.** place of worship, as a church or temple. **8.a.** place of entertainment, esp. a theater: *The house was filled for the premiere.* **b.** audience in such a place: *The house gave him a standing ovation.* **9.** *also,* **House. a.** legislative or deliberative body: *Did the bill pass in the House?* **b.** building in which such a body meets. **10.** *also,* **House.** family, esp. of royal or noble blood, including ancestors, descendants, and kindred: *Queen Elizabeth II of England is a member of the House of Windsor.* **11.** business firm or establishment: *a banking and investment house.* **12.** in gambling, one who acts as banker in a game, or the gambling establishment itself: *to bet against the house.* **13. to bring down the house.** *Informal.* to get enthusiastic, prolonged applause. **14. to clean house. a.** to clean a house or put it in order. **b.** to do away with a person, element, or situation which is undesirable. **15. to keep house.** to manage the affairs of a household and perform domestic duties. **16. on the house.** at the expense of the owner; without charge: *Our first drink was on the house.* **17. to put** (or **set**) **one's house in order.** to straighten out one's personal affairs. —*v.t.,* **housed, hous·ing. 1.** to put or receive into a house; provide with a house; shelter; lodge: *They were housed in the old mansion. The colonial structure housed a family of five.* **2.** to store or keep in a house or building: *The art collection was housed in the museum.* **3.** to place in a secure or protected position in, or as in, a house. —*v.i.* to take shelter; reside; dwell: *Graze where you will, you shall not house with me* (Shakespeare, *Romeo and Juliet*). [Old English *hūs* building for human habitation, family, animal habitation.] —**Syn.** *n.* **1.** see **home.**

house·boat (hous′bōt′) *n.* boat or barge with a superstructure that is fitted out as a dwelling.

house·break·ing (hous′brā′king) *n.* act of breaking into and entering a residence with intent to steal or commit some other crime. —**house′break′er,** *n.*

house·bro·ken (hous′brō′kən) *adj.* (of a household pet) trained to excrete outdoors or in a specific place.

house·coat (hous′kōt′) *n.* robe or dresslike garment worn at home.

house·dress (hous′dres′) *n.* dress, usually of a lightweight fabric, to be worn while doing housework.

house·fly (hous′flī′) *pl.,* -flies. *n.* common fly, *Musca domestica,* that lives in and around houses, feeding on food and refuse. It may carry many disease-producing organisms.

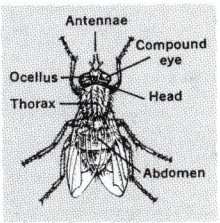

Housefly

house·hold (hous′hōld′) *n.* **1.** all the inhabitants of a house; family and servants. **2.** home and its affairs. —*adj.* **1.** of or relating to a household; domestic: *household chores.* **2.** familiar; common.

Household Cavalry, personal guard of the British sovereign.

house·hold·er (hous'hōl'dər) *n.* **1.** one who owns or occupies a house. **2.** head of a family.

household word, familiar word, name, or phrase: *The astronaut's name became a household word.*

house·keep·er (hous'kē'pər) *n.* **1.** woman who manages the affairs of a household. **2.** woman hired to direct the servants of a household.

house·keep·ing (hous'kē'ping) *n.* maintenance of a household and the managing of its affairs.

house·leek (hous'lēk') *n.* succulent plant, *Sempervivum tectorum,* found in Europe and Asia, bearing thick leaves, usually in rosettes, and hairy, erect, pink flowers.

house·maid (hous'mād') *n.* woman employed to do housework.

housemaid's knee, chronic inflammation in the front of the kneecap, usually caused by kneeling.

house·moth·er (hous'muth'ər) *n.* woman who supervises a group of people, esp. young people, living together, as in a dormitory.

House of Burgesses, popularly elected lower house of the legislature in colonial Virginia.

house of cards, anything unstable or flimsy, that can be easily knocked down.

House of Commons, lower, elective house of either the British or Canadian Parliament. Also, **Com'mons.**

house of correction, place for the confinement and rehabilitation of persons convicted of minor offenses.

House of Delegates, lower branch of the legislature in Maryland, Virginia, and West Virginia.

House of Lords, upper, nonelective house of the British Parliament, composed of the nobility and high-ranking Anglican clergymen.

House of Representatives. **1.** lower elective house of the U.S. Congress and of many state legislatures, in which representation is based on population. **2.** similar legislative body, as in Australia.

house organ, periodical published by a business for its employees or clients.

house party, entertainment of guests, usually for several days, esp. in a home or at a college.

house physician, resident physician, as of a hotel or hospital.

house·plant (hous'plant') *n.* plant grown indoors, esp. one requiring little light.

house sparrow, hardy sparrow, *Passer domesticus,* found in rural and urban areas throughout warm and temperate regions of the world, having dull gray-and-brown plumage with black-and-white markings. Length: 6 inches.

house·top (hous'top') *n.* **1.** roof or top of a house. **2. from the housetops,** loudly and publicly: *The victory was proclaimed from the housetops.*

house·warm·ing (hous'wôr'ming) *n.* party given when new occupants move into a house.

house·wife (hous'wīf'; *def. 2 also* huz'if) *pl.,* **-wives.** *n.* **1.** married woman who manages a home and its affairs. **2.** small case for needles, pins, thread, and similar items.

house·wife·ly (hous'wīf'lē) *adj.* of, relating to, or characteristic of a housewife or her duties.

house·wif·er·y (hous'wīf'fər ē, -wīf'rē) *n.* work or duties of a housewife; housekeeping.

house·work (hous'wurk') *n.* work done in housekeeping, as washing, ironing, cleaning, and cooking.

hous·ing[1] (hou'zing) *n.* **1.** houses collectively: *Housing for the middle class in the city was insufficient.* **2.** act of sheltering or providing houses, as for a group of people. **3.** any shelter or covering. **4.** frame, plate, or casing which supports, secures, or contains a machine or part of a machine. **5.** in carpentry, a slot, groove, or other space made in one structural member for the insertion of another. **6.** part of the mast below the decks of a ship. [HOUSE + -ING[1].]

hous·ing[2] (hou'zing) *n.* ornamental covering for a horse. [Middle English *house* (from Old French *houce;* of Germanic origin) + -ING[1].]

Hous·man, A(lfred) E(dward) (hous'mən) 1859–1936, English poet and scholar.

Hous·ton (hūs'tən) **1.** Samuel. 1793–1863, U.S. frontiersman and statesman, twice president of Texas before it became a state. **2.** city in southeastern Texas. Pop. (1970), 1,232,802.

Hou·yhn·hnm (hōō in'əm, hwin'-) *n.* in Swift's *Gulliver's Travels,* one of a race of horses endowed with the power of reason, who rule over the Yahoos. [Invented by Jonathan Swift to suggest a horse's neighing.]

hove (hōv) *a* past tense and past participle of **heave.**

hov·el (huv'əl, hov'-) *n.* **1.** small, wretched house or shack; hut. **2.** open shed, as for sheltering cattle or tools. [Of uncertain origin.]

hov·er (huv'ər, hov'-) *v.i.* **1.** to remain as if suspended in the air over or around a particular spot. **2.** to linger or remain nearby: *to hover over a sick child. The thought formed in his mind.* **3.** to continue in an indeterminate or irresolute state: *to hover between tears and laughter.*

—*n.* act of hovering. [Middle English *hoveren* to remain in the air, tarry, frequentative of *hoven;* of uncertain origin.

hov·er·craft (huv'ər kraft') *n.* vehicle that can hover or travel over land or water on a thin cushion of high pressure air created beneath the craft by means of fans or rotors. Also, **ground-effect machine.**

how (hou) *adv.* **1.** in what manner or way; by what means: *How do you plan to get there?* **2.** to what degree or extent: *How hot is it outside? How do you like this dress?* **3.** in what state or condition: *How's the weather today? How are you?* **4.** for what reason or purpose; why: *How did you happen to be there?* **5.** with what meaning; to what effect: *How did you mean your last statement?* **6.** by what name: *How is he known?* **7.** *Informal.* what: *How's that?* **8. and how.** *Informal.* that's absolutely true. **▲** used to emphasize one's agreement with a previous statement. **9. how about.** what do you think of; would you like or consider: *How about joining us? How about a drink?* **10. how come.** *Informal.* how does it happen that: *How come he isn't here?* —*n.* manner or method of doing; means: *Have you considered the why and how of this plan?* —*conj.* **1.** the way or manner in which: *He told us how to get there.* **2.** of the way or manner in which: *Be careful how you drive.* **3.** in whatever way or manner: *You can do the job how you like.* [Old English *hū* in what way, to what extent.]

how·be·it (hou bē'it) *adv. Archaic.* however it may be; nevertheless.

how·dah (hou'də) *also,* **hou·dah.** *n.* seat, usually with a railing and canopy, used for riding on the back of an elephant or camel. [Hindustani *haudah,* from Arabic *haudaj.*]

how·dy (hou'dē) *pl.,* **-dies.** *n. Informal.* hello. [Short for *How do you do?*]

Howe (hou) **1.** Elias. 1819–67, U.S. inventor of the sewing machine. **2. Julia Ward** (wôrd) 1819–1910, U.S. writer and social reformer..

how·e'er (hou âr') however.

How·ells, William Dean (hou'əlz) 1837–1920, U.S. author and editor.

how·ev·er (hou ev'ər) *conj.* nevertheless; yet; notwithstanding: *It was a good guess; however, he was wrong.* —*adv.* **1.** in whatever way; by whatever means: *You may use it however and whenever you like.* **2.** to whatever degree or extent: *However far he wandered, he always returned by dusk.* —**Syn. conj.** see **but.**

how·itz·er (hou'it sər) *n.* cannon of medium length used to fire shells at high angles of elevation. [Dutch *houwitser,* from German *Haubitze,* from Czech *houfnice* catapult.]

howl (houl) *v.i.* **1.** to utter the loud, wailing cry as of a dog or wolf. **2.** to utter such a cry, as from pain, rage, grief, scorn, or amusement. —*v.t.* **1.** to utter or express with howling: *to howl one's scorn.* **2.** to force or drive by or as howling: *The audience howled the actor off the stage.* **3. to howl down.** to prevent (a speaker) from being heard by prolonged, usually angry shouting. —*n.* **1.** loud, wailing cry as of a dog or wolf. **2.** any howling sound, esp. a shout or cry of pain, rage, grief, scorn, or amusement. **3.** *Slang.* something extremely funny: *The new comedy is really a howl.* [Probably imitative.] —**Syn. v.i. 1.** see **bark².**

howl·er (hou'lər) *n.* **1.** one who or that which howls. **2.** *Informal.* ridiculous or glaring blunder.

How·rah (hou'rä) *n.* city in northeastern India, near Calcutta. Pop. (1969), 590,385.

how·so·ev·er (hou'sō ev'ər) *adv.* **1.** in whatever way; by whatever means. **2.** to whatever degree or extent.

hoy·den (hoid'ən) *also,* **hoi·den.** *n.* boisterous, ill-mannered, or saucy girl, esp. a tomboy. [Middle Dutch *heiden* heathen, rustic.] —**hoy'den·ish,** *adj.*

Hoyle (hoil) **1.** Edmond. 1672–1769, English lawyer and writer of books on card and board games. **2. according to Hoyle.** according to the rules; fairly or correctly.

HP, horsepower. Also, **hp.**

Hq, headquarters. Also, **HQ.**

hr., hour.

H.R., House of Representatives.

H.R.H., His (or Her) Royal Highness.

H.S., High School.

ht., height.

hub (hub) *n.* **1.** central part of a wheel into which the axle is inserted. **2.** central point of interest, importance, or activity: *An egotist sees himself as the hub of the universe. The seaport was the hub of commerce.* [Form of HOB[1].]

hub·bub (hub'ub) *n.* loud, confused noise, as of many voices or sounds; tumult; uproar. [Probably of Irish origin.]

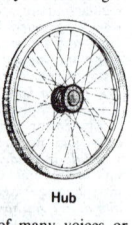

Howdah

Hub

at; āpe; cär; end; mē; it; īce; hot; ōld; fôrk; wood; fōōl; oil; out; up; ūse; turn; sing; thin; this; zh in treasure; ə in ago, taken, pencil, lemon, circus.

hu·bris (hū′bris, hōō′-) *also,* **hy·bris.** *n.* insolence or arrogance resulting from excessive pride or passion. [Greek *hubris* insolence, outrage.]

huck·a·back (huk′ə bak′) *n.* absorbent linen or cotton fabric woven with a rough, uneven surface and used for towels. [Of uncertain origin.]

huck·le·ber·ry (huk′əl ber′ē) *pl.* **-ries.** *n.* **1.** small, shiny blue or black berry of any of a group of shrubs, genus *Gaylussacia,* of the heath family, resembling the blueberry but larger and darker in color, used esp. to make pie fillings and preserves. **2.** low shrub bearing this fruit, growing wild in North and South America and bearing drooping clusters of tiny reddish flowers. [Probably modification of dialectal *hurtleberry,* a form of WHORTLEBERRY.]

huck·ster (huk′stər) *n.* **1.** peddler or hawker of small articles, esp. fruits and vegetables. **2.** mercenary person who does business in a mean and petty way. **3.** *Informal.* person in the advertising business. —*v.t.* to sell or peddle. [Possibly from Middle Dutch *hoekster,* feminine of *hoeker* hawker[1].]

hud·dle (hud′əl) **-dled, -dling.** *v.i.* **1.** to crowd or nestle, as from cold or fear: *The children huddled together like a flock of sheep.* **2.** to draw oneself together; hunch: *The cold wind made the boy huddle inside his coat.* **3.** *Football.* to gather behind the line of scrimmage before a play in order to receive signals. **4.** *Informal.* to meet privately in order to consult or discuss; confer: *The judges huddled before they announced the winner.* —*v.t.* **1.** to drive or crowd together closely. **2.** to draw (oneself) together; hunch (often with *up*). —*n.* **1.** number of persons or things crowded or clustered together; jumble: *In thirty years the huddle of houses grew into a city.* **2.** *Football.* gathering of players behind the line of scrimmage before a play in order to receive signals. **3.** *Informal.* small, private meeting or conference: *The politician's advisers went into a huddle to discuss strategy.* [Of uncertain origin.]

Hud·son (hud′sən) **1.** Henry, died 1611, English navigator and explorer of North America. **2.** W(illiam) H(enry), 1841–1922, English naturalist and writer. **3.** river in eastern New York, flowing southward into New York Bay.

Hudson Bay, large inland sea in northeastern Canada, connected with the Atlantic by Hudson Strait.

Hudson's Bay Company, British joint-stock company chartered in 1670 to carry on the fur trade in what is now Canada.

Hudson seal, muskrat fur that has been dyed and plucked to look like seal.

Hudson Strait, strait connecting Hudson Bay with the Atlantic.

hue¹ (hū) *n.* **1.** the property of a color that determines its position in the spectrum. **2.** color *(def. 2).* [Old English *hīw, hēow* appearance, color.] —**Syn. 1.** see tint.

hue² (hū) *n.* **1. hue and cry.** clamor or public stir, as of alarm or opposition: *The newspaper raised a great hue and cry when the scandal was disclosed.* **2.** *Archaic.* outcry; clamor. [Old French *hu* a cry, from *huer* to shout; imitative.]

huff (huf) *n.* sudden, temporary feeling of anger, irritation, or indignation: *Cindy walked off in a huff when Dan insulted her.* —*v.t.* to make angry; offend. —*v.i.* to puff; blow: *She huffed and puffed and blew out the birthday candles.* [Imitative.]

huff·y (huf′ē) **huff·i·er, huff·i·est.** *adj.* **1.** easily offended; touchy. **2.** offended; sulking. —**huff′i·ly,** *adv.* —**huff′i·ness,** *n.*

hug (hug) **hugged, hug·ging.** *v.t.* **1.a.** to clasp the arms around and hold close, esp. in affection; embrace closely. **b.** to grasp and squeeze tightly with the arms, as a bear does. **2.** to keep close to: *The bicycle rider hugged the curb.* **3.** to cling firmly to; cherish: *The Briton in the blood hugs the homestead still* (Emerson, 1856). —*n.* **1.** strong clasp with the arms, esp. as a sign of affection; embrace. **2.** tight clasp or squeeze with the arms, as in wrestling. [Probably of Scandinavian origin.]

huge (hūj) **hug·er, hug·est.** *adj.* of great size, extent, or degree; extremely large. [Short for Old French *ahuge;* of uncertain origin.] —**huge′ly,** *adv.* —**huge′ness,** *n.*

Syn. Huge, enormous, vast, immense mean extremely large. **Huge** is the common term to indicate extreme largeness and may be preferred when the emphasis is on size, bulk, or capacity: *The room is dominated by a huge fireplace.* **Enormous** stresses dimensions beyond the normal in number or degree: *The truck was carrying an enormous load.* **Vast** may be preferred when extent or range is to be stressed: *The Sahara is a vast desert.* **Immense** refers to that which is beyond measurement or count in magnitude, spread, or scope: *The solar system is part of an immense galaxy called the Milky Way.*

hug·ger-mug·ger (hug′ər mug′ər) *n.* confusion; disorder. —*adj.* confused; disorderly. [Of uncertain origin.]

Hughes, Lang·ston (hūz; lang′stən) 1902–67, U.S. poet.

Hu·go, Vic·tor (hū′gō) 1802–85, French poet, novelist, and dramatist.

Hu·gue·not (hū′gə not′) *n.* French Calvinist, esp. one of the sixteenth or seventeenth century. [French *huguenot,* going back to German (Swiss dialect) *Eidgenoss* confederate.]

huh (hu) *interj.* used to express surprise, contempt, or inquiry.

hu·la (hōō′lə) *n.* traditional Hawaiian dance characterized by highly stylized gestures of the dancers' arms and hands which relate a story. Also, **hu′la-hu′la.** [Of Hawaiian origin.]

hulk (hulk) *n.* **1.** large, clumsy person or thing. **2.a.** body of an old, wrecked, or dismantled ship. **b.** shell of something that has been abandoned, wrecked, or gutted: *Only the hulk of the building remained after the explosion.* **3.** ship used for a prison, storehouse, or similar purpose other than sailing. **4.** *Archaic.* big, unwieldy ship. —*v.i.* to loom or rise bulkily. [Old English *hulc* light ship, possibly from Medieval Latin *holcas* merchantman, from Greek *holkás.*]

hulk·ing (hul′king) *adj.* massive and clumsy; unwieldy.

hull (hul) *n.* **1.a.** outer covering of a seed, as of a nut or grain of rice. **b.** calyx of certain fruits, as strawberries or raspberries. **2.** any outer covering: *Their prejudices were encased within a hull of ignorance.* **3.** frame or body of a ship, exclusive of the masts, sails, yards, and rigging. **4.a.** the part of the body of a seaplane that rests on the water. **b.** frame of a rigid dirigible. —*v.t.* **1.** to remove the hull of. **2.** to strike or pierce the hull of (a ship), as with a shell or torpedo. [Old English *hulu* the outer covering of a seed or fruit.] —**hull′er,** *n.*

Hull (hul) **1.** Cor·dell (kôr′dəl, kôr del′). 1871–1955, U.S. statesman. **2.** port city in northeastern England. Pop. (1968 est.), 294,700. Also *(def. 2).* King′ston·upon-Hull′.

hul·la·ba·loo (hul′ə bə lōō′) *pl.* **-loos.** *n.* great noise, excitement, or confusion; disturbance; uproar.

hul·lo (hə lō′) *Informal.* hello.

hum (hum) **hummed, hum·ming.** *v.i.* **1.** to make a low, continuous murmuring sound: *Bumblebees hummed in the garden. The refrigerator motor hummed.* **2.** to sing with closed lips, not articulating words. **3.** *Informal.* to be in a condition of busy activity: *Things were really humming at the newspaper offices on election night.* —*v.t.* **1.** to sing (something, as a tune) with closed lips, not articulating words. **2.** to bring or put into a specified condition by humming: *to hum an infant to sleep.* —*n.* **1.** low, continuous murmuring sound. **2.** singing with closed lips, not articulating words: *The hum of the chorus contrasted with the soprano's high tones.* **3.** low vocal sound uttered with closed lips, to express some attitude such as hesitation, disagreement, surprise, or approval: *There arose a little hum of approbation from all present* (Trollope, 1877). —*interj.* used to express some attitude such as hesitation, disagreement, surprise, or approval. [Imitative.]

hu·man (hū′mən, ū′mən) *adj.* **1.** of or relating to human beings or humanity: *human evolution, the human condition.* **2.** having or showing the nature, attributes, or good or bad qualities characteristic of human beings: *the milk of human kindness, human frailty. Our pet seems almost human to us.* **3.** having the form of a human being; consisting of human beings: *He is a human adding machine. The police formed a human wall around the building. There are no signs of human life on other planets.* —*n.* human being. [Latin *hūmānus* relating to man, kind, refined.]

human being, erect primate mammal, *Homo sapiens,* distinguished from other animals by extraordinary development of the brain and by the ability to alter the environment to a great degree, esp. through the use of technology, language, and social organization.

Syn. human being, man, person refer to an individual member of the human race. **Human being** is the most general term and emphasizes the distinction from the nonhuman or inhuman: *We are not dealing with statistics but with living human beings. In the story human beings were replaced by robots. No human being would be capable of such cruelty.* **Man** stresses the abstract or universal characteristics of human beings and is often used in anthropological contexts: *the evolution of man. Man is a political animal.* **Person** emphasizes the individuality of a single or specific human being: *She is the most interesting person I've ever known.*

hu·mane (hū mān′, ū mān′) *adj.* **1.** having or showing sympathy and compassion for other human beings or animals; kind; merciful; benevolent. **2.** (of certain branches of learning and literature) tending to refine or civilize: *He received an honorary degree in humane letters.* [Form of HUMAN.] —**hu·mane′ly,** *adv.* —**hu·mane′ness,** *n.*

hu·man·ism (hū′mə niz′əm, ū′mə-) *n.* **1.** any system of thought or action concerned primarily with human interests, needs, values, and ideals, rather than with superhuman beings or concepts of theology. **2.** *also,* **Humanism.** the study of classical Greek and Roman culture, esp. by European scholars in the Renaissance.

hu·man·ist (hū′mə nist, ū′mə-) *n.* **1.** follower or student of any philosophy concerned primarily with human interests, needs, values, and ideals. **2.** student of the humanities, esp. a classical scholar. —**hu′man·is′tic,** *adj.*

hu·man·i·tar·i·an (hū man′ə târ′ē ən, ū man′-) *adj.* concerned with or promoting the general welfare of humanity: *the humanitarian goals of social reformers.* —*n.* one who devotes himself to the welfare of humanity; philanthropist.

hu·man·i·tar·i·an·ism (hū man′ə târ′ē ə niz′əm, ū man′-) *n.* humane or humanitarian principles or action; philanthropy.

hu·man·i·ty (hū man′ə tē, ū man′-) *pl.* **-ties.** *n.* **1.** human beings

at; āpe; cär; end; mē; it; īce; hot; ōld; fôrk; wood; fōōl; oil; out; up; ūse; turn; sing; thin; this; zh in treasure; ə in ago, taken, pencil, lemon, circus.

501

collectively; the human race; mankind: *Each nation contributes something to the fullness of the life of humanity* (Westcott, 1892). **2.** condition or quality of being human; human character or nature: *Without the use of reason and speech, we have no pretensions to humanity* (Monboddo, 1773). **3.** quality of being humane; kindness; benevolence: *Great tenderness of heart, and humanity of disposition* (Burke, 1791). **4. the humanities. a.** branch of learning concerned with human culture, including languages, literature, philosophy, and art. **b.** branch of learning concerned with classical Latin and Greek languages and literature. [Old French *humanite* human nature, kindness, from Latin *hūmānitās*.]

hu·man·ize (hū′mə nīz′, ū′mə-) **-ized, -iz·ing.** *v.t.* **1.** to give or attribute a human character to; make human. **2.** to cause to be kind, merciful, or benevolent; make humane. —**hu′man·i·za′tion,** *n.*

hu·man·kind (hū′mən kīnd′, -kīnd′, ū′mən-) *n.* the human race; humanity; mankind.

hu·man·ly (hū′mən lē, ū′mən-) *adv.* **1.** within human ability or power; by human means: *It isn't humanly possible to run that far.* **2.** in accordance with human nature; in a human manner: *humanly fallible.* **3.** according to human knowledge or experience: *under circumstances never humanly matched* (Butler, 1834).

hum·ble (hum′bəl) **-bler, -blest.** *adj.* **1.** having or showing a low estimate of one's importance or worth; not proud. **2.** low in position, station, or condition; not pretentious: *Be it ever so humble, there's no place like home* (Payne, 1823). **3.** courteous or respectful: *The letter was signed "Your humble servant, Harry Newton."* —*v.t.,* **-bled, -bling. 1.** to make humble in spirit; humiliate. **2.** to make lower in position, station, or condition. [Old French *humble* meek, modest, from Latin *humilis* low, base, from *humus* ground.] —**hum′ble·ness,** *n.* —**hum′bly,** *adv.*

Syn. *adj.* **1. Humble, modest** denote freedom from pride and arrogance. **Humble** suggests innate gentleness and mildness as well as absence of assertiveness and pride: *The man's humble behavior made a favorable impression on the judge.* **Modest** describes a lack of boastfulness and vanity: *Paul was so modest that he took no credit to himself for his good work.*

hum·ble·bee (hum′bəl bē′) *n.* bumblebee. [Middle English *humblybee,* possibly from Middle English *humblen* to buzz (imitative) + BEE.]

humble pie 1. to eat humble pie. to submit to humiliation, esp. to be forced to admit one's mistake and apologize abjectly. **2.** *Archaic.* pie made of the entrails of a deer or other animal. [From the earlier form *umble pie,* from *umbles* entrails, form of *numbles,* from Old French *nombles,* going back to Latin *lumbulus,* diminutive of *lumbus* loin; spelling due to association with *humble* because *umble pie* was usually eaten by the servants while the master ate venison.]

Hum·boldt, Alexander von (hum′bōlt′) 1769–1859, German scientist and explorer of Central and South America.

hum·bug (hum′bug′) *n.* **1.** foolish or empty talk; nonsense. **2.** something intended to deceive or trick; hoax; sham. **3.** one who tries to deceive or trick others; impostor; fraud. —*v.t.,* **-bugged, -bug·ging.** to deceive or trick with false pretense; delude; cheat: *Even we have been humbugged by this pagan rascal* (De Quincey, 1841). [Of uncertain origin.]

hum·ding·er (hum′ding′ər) *n.* *Informal.* unusual, remarkable, or excellent thing or person. [Possibly from HUM + DING; suggesting an object *humming* through the air and *dinging* as it hits its mark.]

hum·drum (hum′drum′) *adj.* lacking variety or excitement; monotonous; tedious; dull: *humdrum routine, a humdrum existence.* —*n.* one who or that which is monotonous, tedious, or dull: *an extended dramatic holiday from the humdrum of the everyday* (Lerner, 1970). [Rhyming compound formed from HUM.]

Hume, David (hūm) 1711–76, Scottish philosopher and historian.

hu·mer·al (hū′mər əl) *adj.* **1.** of, relating to, or near the humerus. **2.** of, relating to, or near the shoulder or shoulders.

hu·mer·us (hū′mər əs) *pl.,* **-mer·i** (-mə rī′). *n.* long bone in the upper arm or forelimb, extending from the shoulder to the elbow. [Latin *(h)umerus* shoulder.]

hu·mid (hū′mid, ū′mid) *adj.* containing or characterized by the presence of much water vapor; moist; damp: *a hot and humid summer day.* [Latin *(h)ūmidus.*] —**hu′mid·ly,** *adv.*

hu·mid·i·fy (hū mid′ə fī′, ū mid′-) **-fied, -fy·ing.** *v.t.* to make more humid or moist, as the air in a room. —**hu·mid′i·fi·ca′tion, hu·mid′i·fi′er,** *n.*

hu·mid·i·ty (hū mid′ə tē, ū mid′-) *n.* **1.** moistness or dampness, esp. of the atmosphere. **2.** *Meteorology.* ratio, ex-

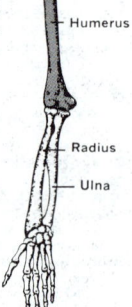

Humerus

— Humerus

— Radius

— Ulna

pressed as a percentage, of the amount of water vapor present in the air to maximum amount the air could hold at the same temperature.

hu·mi·dor (hū′mə dôr′, ū′mə-) *n.* container or storage room for cigars or other tobacco products, containing a device which keeps the air and tobacco moist.

hu·mil·i·ate (hū mil′ē āt′, ū mil′-) **-at·ed, -at·ing.** *v.t.* to lower the pride or dignity of; cause to seem foolish or worthless; mortify. [Late Latin *humiliātus,* past participle of *humiliāre,* from Latin *humilis.* See HUMBLE.] —**hu·mil′i·at′ing·ly,** *adv.*

hu·mil·i·a·tion (hū mil′ē ā′shən, ū mil′-) *n.* **1.** feeling of shame or extreme embarrassment; mortification. **2.** act of humiliating; being humiliated.

hu·mil·i·ty (hū mil′ə tē, ū mil′-) *n.* quality of being humble; lack of pride or arrogance. [Old French *humilite,* from Latin *humilitās* lowness, baseness.]

hum·ming·bird (hum′ing burd′) *n.* any of numerous small, brightly colored birds, family Trochilidae, of North, Central, and South America, having a slender, pointed bill, and narrow wings which beat very rapidly when it flies. It is capable of flying sideways and backwards. Hummingbirds range from 2½ to 8½ inches in length. The **bee hummingbird,** *Calypte helenae,* is the smallest of all living birds. [From the *humming* sound made by its rapidly moving wings.]

Hummingbird

hum·mock (hum′ək) *n.* **1.** low mound of earth or rock; knoll; hillock. **2.** tract of wooded land rising above a plain or swamp. **3.** bump or ridge on an ice field. [Of uncertain origin.] —**hum′mock·y,** *adj.*

hu·mor (hū′mər, ū′mər) *also, British,* **hu·mour.** *n.* **1.** that quality of something that makes it amusing or funny; comicality: *There often is humor in the most difficult situations. David failed to see the humor in my joke.* **2.** ability to perceive, appreciate, or express what is amusing or funny: *a sense of humor, a dour old man who was devoid of humor.* **3.** speech, writing, or action that is amusing or funny: *The movie never rose above the level of slapstick humor.* **4.** temporary state of mind; mood: *The prospect of a vacation put Ruth in a good humor.* **5.** sudden, unpredictable, or capricious inclination; fancy; whim. **6.** *Physiology.* any fluid substance of the body, as blood, bile, lymph, aqueous humor, and vitreous humor. **7.** in ancient and medieval physiology, any of the four body fluids believed to determine, according to their relative proportions in the system, a person's health and temperament. **8. out of humor.** in a bad mood; irritable; cross. —*v.t.* to comply with the moods, wishes, or whims of (someone); indulge: *We humored the old man and listened to his story again.* [Old French *humor* fluid influencing bodily health, temperament, from Latin *(h)ūmor* moisture, fluid. Formerly there were thought to be four humors in the human body: yellow bile or choler (Latin *bīlis* and Greek *cholē*), blood (Latin *sanguis*), phlegm (Greek *phlegma*), and black bile or melancholy (Greek *melas* black + *cholē* bile). If the humors were evenly mixed, the health was good. If any one humor predominated, a person might be *bilious* or *choleric, sanguine, phlegmatic,* or *melancholy.*]

Syn. *v.t.* **Humor, pamper, indulge** mean to yield to someone's wishes or caprices. **Humor** implies a helpful yielding to another's wishes, usually to spare the other unpleasantness: *The customer humored the salesman a while before telling him no.* **Pamper** stresses gratification of another's desires or appetites in such a way as to spoil and soften him: *Some mothers pamper their children with solicitude.* **Indulge** suggests gratification by undue and habitual compliance: *The rich father indulged his son with plenty of pocket money.*

hu·mor·esque (hū′mə resk′) *n.* musical composition written in a light, spirited, or whimsical style; capriccio. [German *Humoreske.*]

hu·mor·ist (hū′mər ist, ū′mər-) *n.* **1.** professional writer or performer of humorous material: *Mark Twain was one of America's greatest humorists.* **2.** person with a good sense of humor.

hu·mor·less (hū′mər lis, ū′mər-) *adj.* without a sense of humor or humorous qualities. —**hu′mor·less·ness,** *n.*

hu·mor·ous (hū′mər əs, ū′mər-) *adj.* characterized by or full of humor; funny; comical: *a humorous writer, a humorous situation.* —**hu′mor·ous·ly,** *adv.* —**hu′mor·ous·ness,** *n.*

hump (hump) *n.* **1.** rounded protuberance, esp. on the back, as that which occurs as a normal feature in camels and bison or as a deformity resulting from curvature of the spine in man. **2.** hillock; knoll; hummock. **3. over the hump.** past the most difficult, critical, or time-consuming part; over halfway. —*v.t.* to bend or arch (something, as the back) so as to form a hump; hunch. [Possibly of Low German origin.]

hump·back (hump′bak′) *n.* **1.** back having a hump. **2.** hunchback (*def. 1*). **3.** black-and-white whale, *Megaptera novaeangliae,* having a humplike dorsal fin and long flippers. Length: 40 feet. —**hump′-backed′,** *adj.*

humph (humpf) *interj.* used to express contempt, dissatisfaction, disbelief, or the like.

hump·y (hum′pē) **hump·i·er, hump·i·est.** *adj.* **1.** having or full of humps. **2.** like a hump.

hu·mus (hū′məs, ū′məs) *n.* organic matter of the soil, consisting of decayed animal or vegetable matter and containing nitrogen and other plant nutrients. [Latin *humus* ground, earth, soil.]

Hun (hun) *n.* **1.** member of a nomadic Asian people who invaded Europe in the fourth and fifth centuries A.D. and helped to destroy the Roman Empire. They were led in the middle of the fourth century by Attila. **2.** barbarous, willfully destructive person. ▲ used esp. as a derogatory epithet for a German during World War I. [Old English (plural) *Hūne* members of this Asian people, from Late Latin *Hūnī;* of Turkic origin.]

hunch (hunch) *v.t.* to draw up, raise, or bend: *The cold air made him hunch his shoulders.* —*v.i.* to assume a bent, stooped, or crouched posture: *Grandpa had to hunch over the paper to read the small print.* —*n.* **1.** *Informal.* intuitive guess or feeling: *I have a hunch it's going to rain.* **2.** rounded protuberance; hump. [Of uncertain origin.]

hunch·back (hunch′bak′) *n.* **1.** one who has a hump on his back resulting from curvature of the spine. **2.** back having such a hump. —**hunch′backed**′, *adj.*

hun·dred (hun′drid) *pl.,* **-dreds** or **-dred.** *n.* **1.** the cardinal number that is ten times ten. **2.** symbol representing this number, as 100 or C. **3a.** formerly, a subdivision of an English county. **b.** similar subdivision in the early United States, still existing in Delaware. —*adj.* numbering ten times ten. [Old English *hundred* ten times ten.]

Hundred Days, period from March 20 to June 28, 1815, during which Napoleon I restored his rule over France. It began with his escape from exile on the island of Elba and ended with his defeat at Waterloo.

hun·dred·fold (hun′drid fōld′) *adj.* **1.** one hundred times as great or as numerous. **2.** having or consisting of one hundred parts. —*adv.* so as to be one hundred times greater or more numerous.

hun·dredth (hun′dridth, -dritth) *adj.* **1.** (the ordinal of hundred) next after the ninety-ninth. **2.** being one of a hundred equal parts. —*n.* **1.** that which is next after the ninety-ninth. **2.** one of a hundred equal parts; 1/100.

hun·dred·weight (hun′drid wāt′) *pl.,* **-weights** or **-weight.** *n.* unit of weight, equal to 100 pounds avoirdupois in the United States or 112 pounds in England. See **weights and measures** for table.

Hundred Years' War, intermittent struggle between England and France from 1337 to 1453, during which England lost all her French possessions except Calais.

hung (hung) a past tense and past participle of **hang.**

Hun·gar·i·an (hung gār′ē ən) *adj.* of, relating to, or characteristic of Hungary, its people, their language, or culture. —*n.* **1.** citizen of Hungary; member or close descendant of the people historically inhabiting Hungary. **2.** language spoken predominantly in Hungary, belonging to the Ural-Altaic family of languages. Also (*def. 2*), **Mag′yar.**

Hun·ga·ry (hung′gər ē) *n.* small, landlocked country in east-central Europe. Capital, Budapest. Area, 35,919 sq. mi. Pop. (1970 est.), 10,331,000.

hun·ger (hung′gər) *n.* **1.** discomfort, pain, or weakness caused by a lack of food: *to die of hunger, a people afflicted with hunger, disease, and ignorance.* **2.** desire or craving for food: *The chocolate temporarily satisfied Ruth's hunger.* **3.** any strong desire or craving: *Excellence is lost sight of in the hunger for sudden performance and praise* (Emerson, 1870). —*v.i.* **1.** to have or feel a need or desire for food: *They shall hunger no more, neither thirst any more* (Revelation 7:16). **2.** to have a strong desire or craving (often with *for* or *after*): *to hunger for attention, to hunger after financial success.* [Old English *hungor* state caused by lack of food, famine.]

hunger strike, self-imposed fast, as by a prisoner or political leader, undertaken to protest something or attain certain demands.

hung jury, jury so divided in opinion that it is unlikely it could ever agree on a verdict and is therefore dismissed by the judge.

hun·gry (hung′grē) **-gri·er, -gri·est.** *adj.* **1.** desiring or needing food. **2.** caused by or characteristic of a lack of or desire for food: *Yond' Cassius has a lean and hungry look* (Shakespeare, *Julius Caesar*). **3.** having a strong desire or craving; eager; longing: *hungry for companionship.* [Old English *hungrig* feeling hunger.] —**hun′gri·ly,** *adv.* —**hun′gri·ness,** *n.*

hunk (hungk) *n. Informal.* large lump or piece; chunk: *The keeper fed the lion a hunk of meat.* [Flemish *hunke.*]

hun·ker (hung′kər) *v.i.* to squat or crouch close to the ground: *to hunker down like a Texas jackrabbit in a snowstorm.* [Possibly of Scandinavian origin.]

hun·ky-do·ry (hung′kē dôr′ē) *adj. Slang.* quite satisfactory; all right; fine. [Of uncertain origin.]

hunt (hunt) *v.t.* **1.** to pursue (game) for the purpose of killing or catching: *to hunt deer, to hunt lions.* **2.** to attempt to obtain or find;

search for: *to hunt strawberries.* **3.** to scour (a region) in pursuit of game: *Indians hunted the prairie for buffalo.* **4.** to search (a place) carefully and thoroughly: *to hunt the woods for a fugitive.* **5.** to pursue or drive with force, violence, or hostility: *The outcasts had been hunted out of society.* **6.** to use or direct (horses or dogs) in pursuing game. —*v.i.* **1.** to pursue game. **2.** to look for; seek (often with *after* or *for*): *to hunt for buried treasure.* **3.** to search thoroughly or carefully: *Susan hunted through her purse for some change.* **4. to hunt down. a.** to pursue until captured or killed. **b.** to search for until found: *to hunt down every piece of evidence.* **5. to hunt up. a.** to search carefully for: *to hunt up all the necessary information.* **b.** to find by searching: *When he returned, he hunted up his old friends.* —*n.* **1.** act or instance of pursuing game: *The men were mounted and ready for the hunt.* **2.** group of persons engaged in or associated for the purpose of hunting game together. **3.** act or instance of seeking something; search: *A hunt was conducted for the missing child.* [Old English *huntian* to pursue game.]

Syn. *v.t.* **1. Hunt, pursue, chase** all mean to go after for the purpose of catching or overtaking. **Hunt** means to follow or search for game or prey for the purpose of killing or capturing: *Sportsmen hunt wild animals in Africa.* **Pursue** means to follow a quarry or enemy for a specific purpose: *The Indians pursued the buffalo herd across the border.* **Chase** means to go after a fleeing object or person in determined pursuit: *The dog chased the thief.*

hunt·er (hun′tər) *n.* **1.** one who pursues game. **2.** one who searches for something. **3.** horse or dog used in hunting.

hunting case, watchcase with a hinged cover to protect the crystal.

hunting horn, horn on which signals are blown during a hunt.

hunting knife, large, sharp knife for killing, skinning, or cutting up game.

Hunting horn

Hunt·ing·ton (hun′ting tən) *n.* port city in western West Virginia, on the Ohio River. Pop. (1970), 74,315.

Huntington Beach, city in southern California, on the Pacific. Pop. (1970), 115,960.

hunt·ress (hun′tris) *n.* female hunter.

hunts·man (hunts′mən) *pl.,* **-men.** *n.* **1.** one who pursues game; hunter. **2.** one who manages a hunt, esp. a fox hunt.

Hunts·ville (hunts′vil′) *n.* city in northern Alabama. Pop. (1970), 137,-802.

hur·dle (hurd′əl) *n.* **1.** obstacle over which a runner must leap in certain track events. **2.** hurdles. pl. either of two track events, **high hurdles** or **low hurdles,** in which the contestants must leap over hurdles while running, the winner being the one who crosses the finish line first. **3.** obstacle, difficulty, or problem: *Getting an education was the biggest hurdle before him.* **4.** movable frame made of sticks or narrow boards, used as a temporary fence or pen. —*v.t.* **-dled, -dling. 1.** to jump over (a hurdle or similar obstacle) in a race. **2.** to overcome or surmount (something, as an obstacle, difficulty, or problem): *to hurdle a fence.* [Old English *hyrdel* movable frame of sticks used as a fence.] —**hur′dler,** *n.*

Hurdle (def. 1)

hur·dy-gur·dy (hur′dē gur′dē) *pl.,* **-dies.** *n.* **1.** any of various mechanized musical instruments, as a barrel organ, played by turning a handle or crank. **2.** obsolete stringed musical instrument shaped somewhat like a guitar, played by turning a hand crank which causes a revolving wheel to make the strings vibrate. [Probably imitative.]

hurl (hurl) *v.t.* **1.** to throw with violence or force; fling. **2.** to utter or emit with vehemence: *The senator's opponent hurled insults and accusations at him.* —*v.i. Baseball.* to pitch: *He began his career hurling for the local team.* —*n.* act of throwing forcibly or violently. [Probably imitative.] —**hurl′er,** *n.* —**Syn.** *v.t.* **1.** see **throw.**

hurl·y-burl·y (hur′lē burl′lē) *pl.,* **-burl·ies.** *n.* disorder; commotion; tumult; turmoil. [Earlier *hurling and burling,* rhyming phrase based on obsolete *hurling* commotion, from HURL.]

Hu·ron (hyoor′ən) *n.* **1. Lake.** second largest of the Great Lakes, on the U.S.-Canadian border. **2.** member of a tribe of North American Indians formerly living east of Lake Huron, now living in Oklahoma. **3.** language of the Huron Indians, a member of the Iroquoian family of languages. [French *huron* boor, disheveled person, from *hure* disheveled head of hair; of uncertain origin; applied by the French in about 1600 to the Huron Indians because of the way they wore their hair.]

hur·rah (hə rä′, hə rô′) *also,* **hoo·ray, hur·ray** (hə rā′). *interj.* used to express joy, triumph, praise, or encouragement. —*n.* shout of joy, triumph, praise, or encouragement. —*v.i.* to shout hurrah; cheer. [Possibly from German *hurra* cry of cheer; imitative.]

hur·ri·cane (hur′ə kān′) *n.* **1.** storm with violent winds of more than seventy-five miles per hour revolving around a calm center and accompanied by heavy rain, high tides, and flooding in coastal regions. **2.** something resembling a hurricane in force or speed; violent outburst or commotion: *a hurricane of emotion.* [Spanish *huracán* violent storm, from Carib *hurakan* name of an evil spirit.]

hurricane deck, light upper deck on a passenger ship, esp. on an American riverboat.

hur·ried (hur′ēd) *adj.* **1.** urged or forced to act, move, or go faster than is easy or natural. **2.** done, performed, or carried on quickly or too quickly: *a hurried glance, a hurried letter full of typographical errors.* —**hur′ried·ly,** *adv.* —**hur′ried·ness,** *n.*

hur·ry (hur′ē) **-ried, -ry·ing.** *v.i.* to move or act with evident or apparent speed; go faster than is easy or natural: *Because we were late we had to hurry. If you don't hurry, you'll miss the train.* —*v.t.* **1.** to cause or urge to act, move, or go with greater speed: *Mother hurried the children along.* **2.** to cause or urge to act, move, or go too quickly; rush: *The judge would not be hurried into making a decision.* **3.** to hasten the preparation, progress, or completion of: *The cook hurried the meal.* —*n. pl.,* **-ries. 1.** act of hurrying: *There is no hurry in the designs of God* (Farrar, 1879). **2.** state or condition of desiring or needing to act, move, or go with greater speed: *He had to leave because he was in a hurry.* [Probably imitative.]

Syn. *n.* **1. Hurry, haste** mean an effort to do something more quickly than usual. **Hurry** suggests undue or excessive quickness accompanied by commotion and agitation: *In the hurry of their preparations, they had forgotten their passports.* **Haste** stresses the urgency of the effort and implies considerable speed: *When he heard footsteps, he left in haste.*

hur·ry-scur·ry (hur′ē skur′ē) *pl.,* **-ries.** *also,* **hur·ry-skur·ry.** *n.* haste, bustle, and confusion. —*adv.* in haste and confusion. —*adj.* hurried and confused. —*v.i.,* **-ried, -ry·ing.** to act in or proceed with haste and confusion. [Rhyming compound based on HURRY.]

hurt (hurt) **hurt, hurt·ing.** *v.t.* **1.** to cause physical pain or injury to. **2.** to do harm to; be detrimental to; damage: *The scandal hurt the mayor's chance for reelection.* **3.** to cause mental pain or suffering to; injure the feelings of: *The insult hurt her deeply.* —*v.i.* **1.** to be painful: *His knee hurts.* **2.** to cause or inflict pain or injury: *The doctor said that the injection wouldn't hurt much.* —*n.* **1.** any physical pain or injury. **2.** mental pain or suffering. **3.** *Archaic.* damage; harm. [Old French *hurter* to strike; of Germanic origin.]

Syn. *v.t.* **1. Hurt, harm, injure, damage** mean to inflict on a person or thing something that causes pain or loss. **Hurt** suggests that pain and suffering are caused without serious impairment: *The dentist's drill hurt him but did not injure him.* **Harm** has a wider application than hurt and implies more serious grief, distress, or suffering: *Thoughtless actions can harm one's reputation.* **Injure** refers to a partial or entire loss of something of value, esp. of a bodily part or function: *The player injured his shoulder during the game.* **Damage** stresses loss to property rather than person: *The collision damaged the car.*

hurt·ful (hurt′fəl) *adj.* causing hurt; painful; injurious. —**hurt′ful·ly,** *adv.* —**hurt′ful·ness,** *n.*

hur·tle (hurt′əl) **-tled, -tling.** *v.i.* **1.** to collide or strike, esp. violently or noisily (with *together* or *against*): *The racing car hurtled against the metal fence.* **2.** to move rapidly, esp. with much force or noise. —*v.t.* to throw or fling violently; hurl. [HURT + -LE.]

hus·band (huz′bənd) *n.* male in a married couple; married man. —*v.t.* to manage carefully and frugally; use, spend, or apply economically: *to husband one's time and energy.* [Old English *hūsbonda* master of a house, from Old Norse *hūsbōndi.*]

hus·band·man (huz′bənd mən) *pl.,* **-men.** *n. Archaic.* farmer.

hus·band·ry (huz′bən drē) *n.* **1.** cultivation of the soil or breeding and raising of livestock; agriculture; farming. **2.** careful or frugal management; thrift; economy.

hush (hush) *n.* silence or stillness, esp. after noise or commotion has ceased: *A hush fell over the audience.* —*v.t.* **1.** to quiet or silence. **2.** to calm; soothe; lull: *He hushed her fears.* **3.** to keep knowledge or discussion of (something) from spreading; impose silence concerning (usually with *up*). —*v.i.* to become quiet or silent. —*interj.* be quiet; be calm. **▲** often said to a baby. [From archaic *husht* (interjection) be quiet; imitative.]

hush money, money paid to keep someone from telling something that he knows.

husk (husk) *n.* **1.** dry outer covering of certain seeds or fruits, as of an ear of corn. **2.** outer shell or covering of something, esp. when useless or worthless. —*v.t.* to remove the husk of: *to husk corn.* [Middle Dutch *huusken* little house, little cover, diminutive of *huus* house, cover.] —**husk′er,** *n.*

husking bee *Informal.* festive social event in which a farmer's neighbors and friends gather to help him husk corn. Also, **husk′ing.**

husk·y¹ (hus′kē) **husk·i·er, husk·i·est.** *adj.* **1.** big and strong: *a husky fellow.* **2.** hoarse and deep in tone, as a voice. —*n. pl.,* **husk·ies.** *Infor-*

mal. big, strong person. [HUSK + -Y¹ (with reference to the toughness or dryness of husks).] —**husk′i·ly,** *adv.* —**husk′i·ness,** *n.*

husk·y² (hus′kē) *pl.,* **husk·ies.** *also,* **Husk·y.** *n.* Siberian husky. [Probably a modification of ESKIMO.]

Huss, John (hus) c.1369–1415, Bohemian religious reformer and national hero.

hus·sar (hə zär′) *n.* member of a light cavalry regiment in any of several European armies. [Magyar *huszar* light cavalry horseman, earlier, pirate, going back to Late Latin *cursārius* pirate, from *cursus* plunder, from Latin *cursus* course. Doublet of CORSAIR.]

Huss·ite (hus′īt) *n.* follower of John Huss or his doctrines. —*adj.* of or relating to the doctrines of John Huss.

hus·sy (huz′ē, hus′ē) *pl.,* **-sies.** *n.* **1.** woman of improper behavior or low character. **2.** impertinent, forward, or mischievous girl; minx. [Modification of Middle English *hūswif* housewife, from *hūs* house + *wif* wife.]

hus·tings (hus′tingz) *n.,pl.* **1.** formerly, a temporary platform from which candidates for the British Parliament were nominated and from which they made speeches. **2.** any place where political speeches are made and campaigning is carried on. **▲** usually construed as singular in both definitions. **3. on the hustings.** on an election campaign. [Old English *hūsting* council, from Old Norse *hūsthing,* from *hūs* house + *thing* assembly.]

hus·tle (hus′əl) **-tled, -tling.** *v.i.* **1.** to move or work quickly or energetically: *She had to hustle to finish the job on time.* **2.** *Slang.* to make money by clever, deceitful, or unscrupulous means. —*v.t.* **1.** to hasten along forcibly; convey hurriedly: *The nurse hustled patients in and out of the office.* **2.** *Informal.* **a.** to obtain (something), esp. by begging: *to hustle a meal.* **b.** to sell (something) illegally or unethically: *to hustle cheap watches.* **c.** to obtain something from (someone) by deceit, trickery, or begging: *They hustled him for five dollars and a free drink.* —*n. Informal.* energy and enthusiasm; drive: *A good shortstop has to have lots of hustle.* [Dutch *hutselen* to shake.]

hus·tler (hus′lər) *n. Informal.* **a.** one who works hard or energetically. **b.** one who earns a living by energetic scheming, begging, or cheating. **2.** *Slang.* prostitute.

hut (hut) *n.* **1.** small, one-story dwelling or shelter, esp. of rough or primitive construction. **2.** large, temporary structure, often made of metal, used by the military to house men and equipment. [French *hutte* cottage, probably from Old High German *hutta.*]

hutch (huch) *n.* **1.** covered pen or box for keeping rabbits or other small animals. **2.** cupboard with open shelves. **3.** chest or bin for storage. [Old French *huche* bin, from Medieval Latin *hutica* chest; of uncertain origin.]

Hutch·in·son (huch′in sən) *n.* city in south-central Kansas. Pop. (1970), 36,885.

Hux·ley (huks′lē) **1. Al·dous** (ôl′dəs). 1894–1963, English author. **2. Julian Sor·rell** (sor′əl). 1877–1975, English biologist. **3. Thomas Henry.** 1825–95, English biologist, grandfather of Aldous and Julian.

Huy·gens, Christian (hī′ganz, hoi′-) *also,* **Huy·ghens.** 1629–95, Dutch physicist, astronomer, and mathematician.

huz·za (hə zä′) *Archaic.* hurrah. [Possibly imitative.]

Hwang Ho (hwäng′ hō′) *also,* **Hwang·ho.** large river in China flowing from the Tibetan highlands into the Yellow Sea. Also, **Yellow River.**

hy·a·cinth (hī′ə sinth′) *n.* **1.** fragrant, funnel-shaped flower of any of a group of plants, genus *Hyacinthus,* of the lily family, growing in spikelike clusters. **2.** plant bearing this flower, native to the Mediterranean region and southern Africa. One of the best known species is *H. orientalis,* widely cultivated as a garden and house plant. **3.** reddish-orange zircon used in jewelry. Also *(def. 3),* **ja′cinth.** [Latin *hyacinthus* iris, larkspur, blue precious stone, from Greek *hyakinthos* bluebell, larkspur, blue precious stone; named after the youth *Hyacinthus* because, according to Greek mythology, the flower sprang from his blood after he was killed by Apollo. Doublet of JACINTH.] —**hy·a·cin·thine** (hī′ə sin′thin), *adj.*

Hyacinth

Hy·a·cin·thus (hī′ə sin′thəs) *n. Greek Mythology.* handsome youth, killed accidentally by a discus thrown by Apollo.

Hy·a·des (hī′ə dēz′) *n.,pl.* **1.** V-shaped group of stars near the Pleiades in the constellation Taurus, believed by ancient astronomers to indicate the approach of rain when they rose with the sun. **2.** *Greek Mythology.* five nymphs who were daughters of the god Atlas and who raised the infant Dionysus. As a reward they were placed among the stars by Zeus.

hy·ae·na (hī ē′nə) hyena.

hy·a·line (hī′ə lin, -līn′) *adj.* resembling glass; glassy; transparent. —*n. Archaic.* glassy or transparent substance or color: *Meadows fluttered with the pearly hyaline of dew* (Blackmore, 1876). [Late Latin *hyalinus* of glass, from Greek *hyalinos,* from *hyalos* glass.]

hy·a·lite (hī'ə līt') *n.* colorless, often transparent, opal that resembles glass. [Greek *hyalos* glass + -ITE[1].]
hy·a·loid (hī'ə loid') *adj.* hyaline.
hy·brid (hī'brid) *n.* **1.** offspring of two animals or plants of different varieties, lines, or breeds that combines differing qualities of the parents. **2.** anything derived from heterogeneous sources or made up of incongruous elements. —*adj.* of, relating to, or of the nature of a hybrid: *a hybrid flower.* [Latin *hybrida* mongrel.]
hy·brid·ism (hī'bri diz'əm) *n.* **1.** condition, quality, or fact of being hybrid. **2.** production of hybrids; crossbreeding.
hy·brid·ize (hī'bri dīz') -ized, -iz·ing. *v.t.* to cause to crossbreed and produce hybrids. —**hy'brid·i·za'tion,** *n.*
hy·bris (hī'bris) hubris.
hyd. **1.** hydraulics. **2.** hydrostatics.
Hyde, Mr. (hīd) see Jekyll and Hyde.
Hyde Park **1.** park in London, England, noted for its speakers' corner where amateur orators make speeches. **2.** village in southeastern New York, on the Hudson, site of the birthplace, home, and burial place of Franklin D. Roosevelt. Pop. (1970), 2805.
Hy·der·a·bad (hī'dər ə bad', -bäd') *n.* **1.** city in south-central India. Pop. (1969), 1,294,800. **2.** city in southeastern West Pakistan. Pop., metropolitan area (1969), 698,000.
hydr-, form of **hydro-** before vowels, as in *hydrate.*
hy·dra (hī'drə) *pl.*, **-dras** or **-drae** (-drē). *n.* **1.** Hydra. *Classical Mythology.* deadly snakelike monster with nine heads and the power to grow two more whenever one was cut off. It was slain by Hercules. **2.** any persistent evil that is difficult to overcome because it tends to reappear: *The hydra of revolt lay stunned and prostrate* (Merivale, 1850). **3.** small freshwater invertebrate, class Hydrozoa, having a tubelike body with a single mouth, or open end, surrounded by thin tentacles that bear clusters of poison-filled stinging cells. If a hydra is cut into pieces, each piece will develop into a complete, new organism. **4.** Hydra. constellation appearing low in the northern sky, conventionally depicted as a serpent. It is the largest of the constellations. [Latin *Hydra* the monster, from Greek *Hydrā,* from *hydōr* water.]

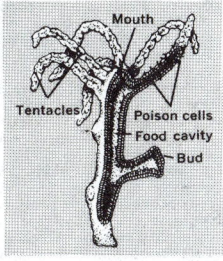

Hydra *(def. 3)*

hy·dran·gea (hī drān'jə) *n.* **1.** large showy flower of any of a group of shrubs or vines, genus *Hydrangea,* growing in clusters of usually white or pink blossoms. **2.** shrub or vine bearing this flower. [Modern Latin *hydrangea,* from Greek *hydōr* water + *angeion* vessel; with reference to the shape of the seed vessel.]
hy·drant (hī'drənt) *n.* street fixture for drawing water directly from a main, consisting of an upright pipe with spouts to which hoses may be attached. Also, **fire hydrant.** [HYDRO- + -ANT.]
hy·drate (hī'drāt) *n.* any crystalline substance formed by the union of a chemical compound with molecules of water in a definite ratio. Copper sulfate is a hydrate. —*v.t.,* **-drat·ed, -drat·ing.** to combine (a chemical compound) with water to form a hydrate; cause to form a hydrate. [HYDRO + -ATE[2].] —**hy·dra'tion,** *n.*
hy·drau·lic (hī drô'lik) *adj.* **1.** operated by water or some other fluid: *a hydraulic jack, hydraulic brakes.* **2.** of or relating to the forces exerted by fluids in motion and at rest or to the science of hydraulics. **3.** hardening under water: *hydraulic cement.* [Latin *hydraulicus* relating to an ancient pipe organ that used water pressure, going back to Greek *hydōr* water + *aulos* pipe.] —**hy·drau'li·cal·ly,** *adv.*
hydraulic ram, pump that uses the energy of moving water to pump part of the water to a higher level.
hy·drau·lics (hī drô'liks) *n.,pl.* branch of fluid mechanics dealing with the study of fluids in motion and at rest and their use to perform work. ▲ usually construed as singular.
hy·dra·zine (hī'drə zēn') *n.* colorless, poisonous liquid having an odor like ammonia, a compound of nitrogen and hydrogen, used esp. as a rocket fuel. Formula: N_2H_4 [HYDR(O)- + French *az(ote)* nitrogen + -INE[2].]
hy·dride (hī'drīd, -drid) *also,* **hy·drid** (hī'drid). *n.* compound of hydrogen with a more electropositive element or radical.
hydro- *combining form* **1.** of or relating to water: *hydrodynamics, hydroplane.* **2.** *Chemistry.* combined with or composed of hydrogen: *hydrocarbon, hydrofluoric acid.* [Greek *hydōr* water.]
hy·dro·car·bon (hī'drə kär'bən) *n.* any of a large group of organic compounds composed solely of the chemical elements hydrogen and carbon. Ethane, C_2H_6, and propane, C_3H_8, are hydrocarbons.

hy·dro·ceph·a·lus (hī'drə sef'ə ləs) *n.* condition characterized by an excessive accumulation of fluid in the cranium, forcing the cranial bones apart, causing enlargement of the head. Also, **hy'dro·ceph'a·ly.**
hy·dro·chlo·ric acid (hī'drə klôr'ik) poisonous, highly corrosive solution of hydrogen chloride, HCl, in water, fumes of which cause severe irritation of the eyes and nose. Also, **muriatic acid.**
hy·dro·cor·ti·sone (hī'drə kôr'tə sōn', -zōn') *n.* hormone produced by the adrenal cortex, used primarily in treating rheumatoid arthritis and various allergic and inflammatory conditions.
hy·dro·cy·an·ic acid (hī'drō sī an'ik) weak, colorless acid that is a deadly poison. It has an almondlike odor and is a solution of a compound of hydrogen, carbon, and nitrogen, HCN, in water, and is used esp. to make plastics and pesticides. Also, **prussic acid.**
hy·dro·dy·nam·ic (hī'drō dī nam'ik) *adj.* of or relating to the forces exerted by fluids in motion or to the science of hydrodynamics. —**hy'dro·dy·nam'i·cal·ly,** *adv.*
hy·dro·dy·nam·ics (hī'drō dī nam'iks) *n.,pl.* branch of fluid mechanics that deals with the forces exerted by fluids in motion. ▲ usually construed as singular.

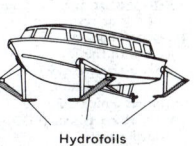

Hydrofoils

hy·dro·e·lec·tric (hī'drō i lek'trik) *adj.* of or relating to electricity generated by water power. —**hy'dro·e·lec'tric'i·ty,** *n.*
hy·dro·fluor·ic acid (hī'drə floor'ik, -flôr'ik) colorless, active, poisonous solution of hydrogen fluoride in water, used esp. to frost and etch glass.
hy·dro·foil (hī'drə foil') *n.* **1.** bladelike or winglike structure under a motor-powered boat that raises the hull out of the water, facilitating high speeds. The hydrofoil is shaped so that pressure on its upper surface decreases when it moves through the water, resulting in an upward lift. **2.** boat fitted with hydrofoils.

Cross section of hydrofoil showing water pressure

hy·dro·gen (hī'drə jən) *n.* nonmetallic element which is a highly flammable gas at normal temperatures. It is colorless, tasteless, and odorless, and is the lightest chemical element. Symbol: **H** See **element** for table. [French *hydrogène,* going back to Greek *hydōr* water + *gennān* to produce; because water is produced when hydrogen is burned.] —**hy·drog·e·nous** (hī droj'ə nəs), *adj.*
hy·dro·gen·ate (hī'drə jə nāt', hī droj'ə-) **-at·ed, -at·ing.** *v.t.* to combine or treat with hydrogen: *Oils are hydrogenated to produce margarine.* —**hy'dro·gen·a'tion,** *n.*
hydrogen bomb, bomb whose enormous destructive power is caused by the fusion of hydrogen atoms to form helium atoms. Its destructive force is similar to but much greater than that of an atomic bomb. Also, **H-bomb.**
hydrogen peroxide, colorless, unstable liquid that is an active oxidizing agent, diluted for use as a bleach and antiseptic. In concentrated form it is highly explosive. Formula: H_2O_2
hy·drog·ra·phy (hi drog'rə fē) *n.* **1.** scientific measurement, charting, and description of the features of oceans, lakes, rivers, and other surface waters, esp. to determine their use for navigation. **2.** those parts of a map representing surface waters. —**hy·dro·graph·ic** (hī'drə graf'ik), *adj.*
hy·droid (hī'droid) *n.* any of various coelenterates having the polyp form as the dominant stage in the life cycle and typically living in delicate branching colonies. They are included in the class Hydrozoa. —*adj.* of or relating to hydroids. [HYDRA + -OID.]
hy·drol·y·sis (hī drol'ə sis) *pl.,* **-ses** (-sēz'). *n.* chemical reaction in which one of the reactants is water. Starch undergoes hydrolysis to form glucose. [HYDRO- + Greek *lysis* a loosing, dissolution.] —**hy'dro·lyt'ic,** *adj.*
hy·dro·lyze (hī'drə līz') **-lyzed, -lyz·ing.** *v.t., v.i.* to undergo or cause to undergo hydrolysis.
hy·drom·e·ter (hī drom'ə tər) *n.* instrument for measuring the specific gravity of liquids.
hy·dro·met·ric (hī'drə met'rik) *adj.* of or relating to hydrometry or a hydrometer. Also, **hy'dro·met'ri·cal.**
hy·drom·e·try (hī drom'ə trē) *n.* determination of specific gravity by means of a hydrometer.
hy·drop·a·thy (hī drop'ə thē) *n.* hydrotherapy. —**hy·dro·path·ic** (hī'drə path'ik), *adj.*
hy·dro·pho·bi·a (hī'drə fō'bē ə) *n.* **1.** rabies. **2.** abnormal fear of water. [Latin *hydrophobia,* from Greek *hydōr* water + *-phobiā* fear of; with reference to the contractions of the mouth and throat caused by this disease, which are intensified by drinking and, eventually, by the mere sight of liquid.] —**hy'dro·pho'bic,** *adj.*

hy·dro·phyte (hī′drə fīt′) *n.* any plant growing in water or very wet soil. Water lilies and seaweeds are hydrophytes.

hy·dro·plane (hī′drə plān′) *n.* **1.** motorboat whose hull is designed to skim over the surface of the water rather than push through it, used esp. in racing. **2.** seaplane.

hy·dro·pon·ics (hī′drə pon′iks) *n.,pl.* science or practice of cultivating plants in a chemical solution rather than in soil. ▲ construed as singular. [HYDRO- + Greek *ponos* work + -ICS.] —**hy′dro·pon′ic,** *adj.*

hy·dro·qui·none (hī′drō kwi nōn′, -kwin′ōn) *n.* white, soluble, crystalline compound, used esp. as a photographic developer. Formula: C₆H₄(OH)₂

hy·dro·sphere (hī′drə sfēr′) *n.* **1.** all the water on the surface of the earth. **2.** all the moisture in the atmosphere surrounding the earth. [HYDRO- + SPHERE.]

hy·dro·stat (hī′drə stat′) *n.* electrical device for detecting the presence of water, as from leakage or overflow. [HYDRO- + Greek *statos* standing.]

hy·dro·stat·ic (hī′drə stat′ik) *adj.* of or relating to the forces exerted by fluids at rest or to the science of hydrostatics.

hy·dro·stat·ics (hī′drə stat′iks) *n.,pl.* branch of fluid mechanics that deals with the forces exerted by fluids at rest. ▲ construed as singular.

hy·dro·ther·a·py (hī′drō ther′ə pē) *n.* scientific treatment of disease by means of water. Also, **hy·drop′a·thy, hy·dro·ther·a·peu·tics** (hī′drō ther′ə pū′tiks).

hy·drot·ro·pism (hī drot′rə piz′əm) *n.* tendency of a plant to grow toward moisture.

hy·drous (hī′drəs) *adj.* (of a chemical compound) containing water, esp. water of crystallization. [HYDRO- + -OUS.]

hy·drox·ide (hī drok′sīd, -sid) *n.* any chemical compound containing one or more hydroxyl radicals.

hy·drox·yl (hī drok′sil) *n.* chemical ion or group consisting of one atom of oxygen and one of hydrogen and having a valence of −1. Formula: OH⁻¹ [HYDR(OGEN) + OX(YGEN) + -YL.]

hy·dro·zo·an (hī′drə zō′ən) *n.* any of various marine and freshwater coelenterates constituting the class Hydrozoa and generally existing in two unlike forms, that of a free-swimming jellyfish or that of an attached polyp which may live in a colony. —*adj.* of or relating to hydrozoans. [Modern Latin *Hydrozoa* class of coelenterates, from HYDRA + Greek *zōion* animal.]

hy·e·na (hī ē′nə) *also,* **hy·ae·na.** *n.* any of various wolflike, carnivorous mammals, family Hyaenidae, of Africa and Asia, having a large head, extremely strong jaws, and front legs longer than the back ones. They feed chiefly on carrion by day, but hunt live prey at night. Height: to 3 feet at the shoulder. [Latin *hyaena,* from Greek *hyaina.*]

Hyena

Hy·ge·ia (hī jē′ə) *n.* Greek goddess of health. [Greek *Hygeiā* or *Hygieia,* from *hygieia* health.]

hy·giene (hī′jēn) *n.* **1.** practices or conditions conducive to good health. **2.** science that deals with maintenance of good health and the prevention of disease. [French *hygiène,* from Greek *hygieinon,* neuter of *hygieinos* healthful.]

hy·gi·en·ic (hī′jē en′ik, hī jē′nik) *adj.* **1.** sanitary. **2.** of or relating to health or hygiene.

hy·gi·en·ist (hī jē′nist, -jen′ist) *n.* one who is trained or expert in the principles of hygiene.

hygro- *combining form* wet; moist; moisture: *hygroscope.* [Greek *hygros* wet.]

hy·grom·e·ter (hī grom′ə tər) *n.* instrument for determining the humidity of the atmosphere.

hy·gro·met·ric (hī′grə met′rik) *adj.* of or relating to hygrometry or a hygrometer.

hy·grom·e·try (hī grom′ə trē) *n.* study of the moisture of the atmosphere.

hy·gro·scope (hī′grə skōp′) *n.* instrument for recording variations in the humidity of the atmosphere.

hy·gro·scop·ic (hī′grə skop′ik) *adj.* readily attracting or absorbing moisture from the atmosphere.

hy·ing (hī′ing) a present participle of **hie.**

Hyk·sos (hik′sos, -sōs) *n.* succession of foreign rulers of Egypt, c.1675–c.1570 B.C.

hy·la (hī′lə) *n.* tree frog. [Modern Latin *Hyla,* from Greek *hylē* wood, forest.]

hy·men (hī′mən) *n.* fold of mucous membrane partially covering the external vaginal opening. Also, **maid′en·head′.** [Greek *hymēn* membrane.]

Hy·men (hī′mən) *n.* Greek god of marriage.

hy·me·ne·al (hī′mə nē′əl) *adj.* of or relating to a wedding or marriage. —*n. Archaic.* wedding song or poem.

hy·me·nop·ter·ous (hī′mə nop′tər əs) *adj.* of, relating to, or belonging to a widespread, varied group of insects, order Hymenoptera, including ants, bees, wasps, and sawflies, characteristically having four membranous wings. [Greek *hymenopteros* membrane-winged, from *hymēn* membrane + *pteron* wing.]

hymn (him) *n.* **1.** song of praise or thanksgiving to God or a god. **2.** any song or ode of praise or joy. —*v.t.* to worship or praise in a hymn. —*v.i.* to sing hymns. [Latin *hymnus* song of praise, from Greek *hymnos.*]

hym·nal (him′nəl) *n.* book or collection of hymns for use in a religious service. Also, **hymn′book′.**

hym·no·dy (him′nə dē) *pl.,* **-dies.** *n.* **1.** hymns collectively, as of a particular period, nation, or church. **2.** the singing or composing of hymns. [Greek *hymnōidiā* singing of hymns.]

hym·nol·o·gy (him nol′ə jē) *n.* **1.** study of hymns. **2.** hymnody *(def. 1).* **3.** the composing of hymns. —**hym·no·log·ic** (him′nə loj′ik); *also,* **hym′no·log′i·cal,** *adj.* —**hym·nol′o·gist,** *n.*

hy·oid (hī′oid) *n.* bone or series of bones at the base of the tongue in vertebrates. In man, it is a single, small, horseshoe-shaped bone. Also, **hyoid bone.** —*adj.* of or relating to the hyoid. [French *hyoïde,* from Greek *hyoeidēs* shaped like the Greek letter *υ* (upsilon), from *υ* upsilon + *eidos* shape.]

hy·o·scine (hī′ə sēn′) *n.* scopolamine.

hyp. **1.** hypothesis. **2.** hypotenuse.

hyper- *prefix* over; above; excessive; excessively: *hypercritical, hypertension.* [Greek *hyper* above, over, beyond.]

hy·per·a·cid·i·ty (hī′pər ə sid′ə tē) *n.* excessive acidity, esp. of gastric juice. —**hy·per·ac·id** (hī′pər as′id), *adj.*

hy·per·bo·la (hī pur′bə lə) *pl.,* **-las.** *n.* open curve with two branches consisting of a set of points in a plane whose distances from two fixed points, or foci, differ by a constant value; conic section formed by the intersection of a plane with the surface of a double cone. [Modern Latin *hyperbola,* from Greek *hyperbolē* literally, a throwing beyond, excess.]

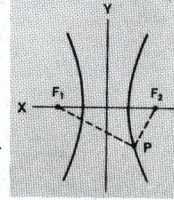

Hyperbola

P = any point on hyperbola; F_1, F_2 = foci; $PF_1 - PF_2$ = a constant.

hy·per·bo·le (hī pur′bə lē) *n.* figure of speech consisting of an extreme exaggeration not meant to be taken literally, for example: *Mother shopped in a million stores today.* [Latin *hyperbole,* from Greek *hyperbolē* a throwing beyond.]

hy·per·bol·ic (hī′pər bol′ik) *adj.* **1.** of, relating to, or using hyperbole; exaggerated or exaggerating. **2.** of, relating to, or having the form of a hyperbola. Also, **hy′per·bol′i·cal.**

hy·per·bo·lize (hī′pur′bə līz′) **-lized, -liz·ing.** *v.t., v.i.* to express with or use hyperbole; exaggerate.

Hy·per·bo·re·an (hī pər bôr′ē ən) *n. Greek Legend.* member of a people who lived happily and virtuously in a land of perpetual spring beyond the north wind. —*adj.* **1.** of or relating to the Hyperboreans. **2.** hyperborean, of or relating to the far north; arctic; frigid. [Late Latin *hyperboreānus* relating to the Hyperboreans, northern, going back to Greek *hyper* beyond + *boreās* north wind.]

hy·per·crit·i·cal (hī′pər krit′i kəl) *adj.* excessively critical. —**hy′per·crit′i·cal·ly,** *adv.*

hy·per·gol·ic (hī′pər gô′lik, -gol′ik) *adj.* of, relating to, or denoting a rocket fuel consisting of a combination of fuel and oxidizer which ignite spontaneously on contact with each other. [HYP(ER-) + Greek *(erg)on* work + Latin *ol(eum)* oil + -IC.]

Hy·pe·ri·on (hī pēr′ē ən) *n. Greek Mythology.* one of the thirteen Titans, son of Uranus and Gaea.

hy·per·me·tro·pi·a (hī′pər mi trō′pē ə) *n.* hyperopia.

hy·per·on (hī′pə ron′) *n.* subatomic particle whose mass is greater than that of a neutron. See **subatomic particle** for table.

hy·per·o·pi·a (hī′pər ō′pē ə) *n.* condition of being able to see distant objects more clearly than those nearby; far-sightedness. Distinguished from **myopia.** Also, **hy′per·me·tro′pi·a.** [Modern Latin *hyperopia,* from Greek *hyper* beyond + *ōps* eye.] —**hy·per·op·ic** (hī′pər op′ik), *adj.*

hy·per·sen·si·tive (hī′pər sen′sə tiv) *adj.* excessively or abnormally sensitive: *hypersensitive skin, to be hypersensitive to criticism.* —**hy′per·sen′si·tive·ness, hy′per·sen′si·tiv′i·ty,** *n.*

hy·per·son·ic (hī′pər son′ik) *adj.* of or relating to the speed of an object moving at Mach 5 or greater, relative to the surrounding medium. [HYPER + SONIC.]

hy·per·ten·sion (hī′pər ten′shən) *n.* **1.** *Medicine.* **a.** high blood pressure. **b.** diseased condition characterized by high blood pressure. **2.** condition of excessive tenseness or edginess.

hy·per·tro·phy (hī pur′trə fē) *pl.,* **-phies.** *n.*. abnormal or excessive growth, esp. of a body part or organ. —*v.i., v.t.,* **-phied, -phy·ing.** to grow or cause to grow abnormally large. [HYPER + Greek *trophē* food.] —**hy·per′tro·phic,** *adj.*

hy·phen (hī′fən) *n.* punctuation mark (-) used to connect two or more elements or words to form a compound word, or to join the syllables of a word which have been separated, as at the end of a line. —*v.t.* to hyphenate. [Late Latin *hyphen* unification of two words, from Greek *hyphen* together, all in one (word), from *hypo* under + *hen,* neuter of *heis* one.]

hy·phen·ate (hī′fə nāt′) **-at·ed, -at·ing.** *v.t.* to separate, connect, or write with a hyphen. —**hy′phen·a′tion,** *n.*

Hyp·nos (hip′nos) *also,* **Hyp·nus.** *n.* Greek Mythology. god of sleep. His Roman counterpart is Somnus.

hyp·no·sis (hip nō′sis) *pl.,* **-ses** (-sēz). *n.* **1.** induced state resembling deep sleep, characterized by extreme suggestibility and loss of will power. **2.** hypnotism (*def. 1*). [Modern Latin *hypnosis,* from Greek *hypnos* sleep + -OSIS.]

hyp·no·ther·a·py (hip′nō ther′ə pē) *n.* treatment of disease, esp. mental illness, by means of hypnotism.

hyp·not·ic (hip not′ik) *adj.* **1.** of or relating to hypnosis or hypnotism: *a hypnotic trance, hypnotic suggestion.* **2.** tending to produce sleep or a trancelike state: *a droning, hypnotic voice. The long stretch of straight highway had a hypnotic effect on the truck driver.* —*n.* **1.** drug or other agent that produces sleep; soporific. **2.** one who is or can be easily hypnotized. [Late Latin *hypnōticus* putting to sleep, from Greek *hypnōtikos,* going back to *hypnos* sleep.] —**hyp·not′i·cal·ly,** *adv.*

hyp·no·tism (hip′nə tiz′əm) *n.* **1.** science, practice, or act of inducing hypnosis. **2.** hypnosis (*def. 1*).

hyp·no·tist (hip′nə tist) *n.* one who induces hypnosis.

hyp·no·tize (hip′nə tīz′) **-tized, -tiz·ing.** *v.t.* **1.** to induce hypnosis in. **2.** to entrance; enthrall; mesmerize. —**hyp′no·tiz′a·ble,** *adj.* —**hyp′no·ti·za′tion, hyp′no·tiz′er,** *n.*

hy·po¹ (hī′pō) *n.* sodium thiosulfate. [Short for HYPOSULFITE.]

hy·po² (hī′pō) *pl.,* **-pos.** *n. Informal.* hypodermic syringe or injection. [Short for HYPODERMIC.]

hypo- *prefix* **1.** under; beneath; below: *hypodermic.* **2.** less than normal; deficient in; lacking: *hypoxia.* [Greek *hypo* under, below.]

hy·po·blast (hī′pō blast′) *n.* endoderm. [HYPO- + Greek *blastos* shoot, bud.]

hy·po·chlo·rous acid (hī′pə klôr′əs) weak, unstable acid that exists only in water solution, formed when chlorine is dissolved in water, used esp. as a disinfectant. Formula: HOCl

hy·po·chon·dri·a (hī′pə kon′drē ə) *n.* neurotic disorder characterized by excessive worry over one's health, imagined diseases and symptoms, and extreme depression. Also, **hy·po·chon·dri·a·sis** (hī′pō kən drī′ə sis). [Late Latin *hypochondria* (plural) abdomen, from Greek *hypochondria,* from *hypo* under + *chondros* cartilage of the breastbone; with reference to the early belief that the abdomen was the seat of depression.]

hy·po·chon·dri·ac (hī′pə kon′drē ak′) *n.* one who is subject to hypochondria. —*adj. also,* **hy·po·chon·dri·a·cal** (hī′pə kən drī′ə kəl). of, relating to, or suffering from hypochondria.

hy·po·cot·yl (hī′pə kot′əl) *n.* part of the stem below the cotyledons in the embryo or seedling stage of a plant. [HYPO- + COTYL(EDON).]

hy·poc·ri·sy (hī pok′rə sē) *pl.,* **-sies.** *n.* act or practice of presenting one's character, feelings, or beliefs as being other than they really are, esp. the feigning of virtue or piety. [Old French *hypocrisie* pretending, from Late Latin *hypocrisis* acting (in a play), pretending, from Greek *hypokrisis*.]

hyp·o·crite (hip′ə krit′) *n.* one who is given to or practices hypocrisy. [Old French *hypocrite* pretender, from Late Latin *hypocrita,* from Greek *hypokritēs* actor, pretender.] —**hyp′o·crit′i·cal,** *adj.* —**hyp′o·crit′i·cal·ly,** *adv.*

hy·po·der·mic (hī′pə dur′mik) *adj.* **1.** lying beneath the skin. **2.** made to be injected under the skin; syringe. —*n.* **1.** instrument used to give injections beneath the skin; syringe. **2.** injection given with a needle or syringe. [HYPO- + Greek *derma* skin + -IC.] —**hy′po·der′mi·cal·ly,** *adv.*

hypodermic syringe, glass barrel with a plunger and hollow needle, inserted in the skin to inject or remove fluids. Also, **hypodermic needle.**

hy·po·gas·tric (hī′pə gas′trik) *adj.* relating to, designating, or situated in the hypogastrium.

hy·po·gas·tri·um (hī′pə gas′trē əm) *pl.,* **-tri·a** (-trē ə). *n.* lower middle region of the abdomen. [Modern Latin *hypogastrium,* from Greek *hypogastrion* the lower belly.]

hy·poph·y·sis (hī pof′ə sis) *pl.,* **-ses** (-sēz′). *n.* pituitary gland. [Greek *hypophysis* attachment underneath; with reference to its position below the brain.]

hy·po·sul·fite (hī′pə sul′fīt) *n.* sodium thiosulfate.

hy·pot·e·nuse (hī pot′ən ōōs′, -ūs′) *also,* **hy·poth·e·nuse** (hī poth′ə nōōs′, -nūs′). *n.* side of a right triangle opposite the right angle. [Latin *hypotēnūsa,* from Greek *hypoteinousa (grammē)* literally, (a) subtending (line), from *hypoteinein* to stretch under.]

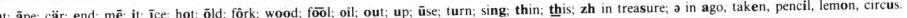

hy·po·thal·a·mus (hī′pə thal′ə məs) *pl.,* **-mi** (-mī′). *n.* small structure lying below the thalamus that controls various internal activities, as the heartbeat, body temperature, sexual drive, and metabolism.

hy·poth·e·cate (hī poth′ə kāt′) **-cat·ed, -cat·ing.** *v.t.* to pledge (property, as a ship or its cargo) as security for a loan or debt without transferring ownership; mortgage. [Medieval Latin *hypothecatus,* past participle of *hypothecare* to pledge, from Late Latin *hypothēca* a pledge, mortgage, from Greek *hypothēkē*.] —**hy·poth′e·ca′tion,** *n.*

hy·poth·e·sis (hī poth′ə sis) *pl.,* **-ses** (-sēz′). *n.* **1.** unproved, tentative explanation or supposition that is based on known facts and can be used as a basis for further experimentation or investigation; theory. **2.** proposition, assumption, or principle put forth as a basis for reasoning or argument. [Greek *hypothesis* a placing under, foundation, supposition.]

hy·poth·e·size (hī poth′ə sīz′) **-sized, -siz·ing.** *v.t.* to suggest or assume as a hypothesis. —*v.i.* to make a hypothesis.

hy·po·thet·i·cal (hī′pə thet′i kəl) *adj.* of the nature of, involving, or based on a hypothesis; theoretical: *a hypothetical example.* Also, **hy′po·thet′ic.** [Greek *hypothetikos* supposed, relating to a hypothesis + -AL¹.] —**hy′po·thet′i·cal·ly,** *adv.*

hy·pox·i·a (hī pok′sē ə) *n.* condition caused by the failure of the body tissue to absorb oxygen, characterized by rapid pulse, labored breathing, and impairment of the senses. [Modern Latin *hypoxia,* from HYPO- + OX(YGEN).]

hy·rax (hī′raks) *pl.,* **-rax·es** or **-ra·ces** (-rə sēz′). *n.* any of various rabbitlike mammals, family Procaviidae, of Africa and the Middle East, having hooflike claws, sharp canine teeth, and a coarse black, brownish-gray, or tan coat. Length: 20 inches. [Greek *hyrax* mouselike shrew.]

hys·sop (his′əp) *n.* **1.** stiff, shrublike plant, *Hyssopus officinalis,* of the mint family, having leaves with a pungent odor that were formerly used for flavoring food and for medicinal purposes. **2.** in the Old Testament, a plant whose twigs were used for sprinkling water in purification ceremonies. [Old English *(h)ysope,* from Latin *hyssōpus* an aromatic plant, from Greek *hyssōpos,* possibly from Hebrew *ēzōb* a plant.]

hys·te·ri·a (his ter′ē ə, -tēr′-) *n.* **1.** excessive, uncontrollable terror, panic, or other strong emotion; frenzy: *an outbreak of mob hysteria. The end of the war was greeted with joyous hysteria.* **2.** neurotic disorder characterized esp. by emotional excitability and disturbances in sensory or motor functions, as loss of sight, for which no organic cause can be found. [Modern Latin *hysteria,* going back to Greek *hysterā* womb; because it was formerly thought that hysteria occurred more frequently in women than in men.]

hys·ter·ic (his ter′ik) *n.* one who is subject to hysteria. —*adj.* hysterical.

hys·ter·i·cal (his ter′i kəl) *adj.* **1.** resembling or caused by hysteria; uncontrollably emotional; frenzied: *hysterical outbursts, hysterical sobbing.* **2.** of, characteristic of, or occurring as a symptom of hysteria: *hysterical blindness.* **3.** suffering from or prone to hysteria. **4.** *Informal.* extremely funny. [Latin *hystericus* subject to uncontrollable feelings (from Greek *hysterikos* relating to the womb, from *hysterā* womb) + -AL¹. See HYSTERIA.] —**hys·ter′i·cal·ly,** *adv.*

hys·ter·ics (his ter′iks) *n.pl.* fit of uncontrollable emotion, esp. of alternate laughing and crying. ▲ often construed as singular.

Cotyledons

Hypocotyl

Roots

Hypocotyl

---

at; āpe; cär; end; mē; it; īce; hot; ōld; fôrk; wood; fōōl; oil; out; up; ūse; turn; sing; thin; this; zh in treasure; ə in ago, taken, pencil, lemon, circus.

i, I (ī) *pl.* **i's, I's.** *n.* **1.** ninth letter of the English alphabet. **2.** shape of this letter or something having such a shape. **3.** Roman numeral for 1.

i., intransitive.

I (ī) *sing.* nominative, **I**; possessive, **my, mine**; objective, **me**; *pl.* nominative, **we**; possessive, **our, ours**; objective, **us.** *pron.* the one who is speaking or writing. —*n.* person; ego. [Old English *ic* the pronoun.]

I, iodine.

I. **1.** Island; Islands. **2.** Isle; Isles.

Ia., Iowa.

I·a·go (ē ä′gō) *n.* villain in Shakespeare's *Othello.*

-ial, form of **-al** after stressed syllables, as in *celestial.*

i·amb (ī′amb) *n.* metrical foot consisting of two syllables, the first unstressed and the second stressed (in English verse) or the first long and the second short (in classical Greek and Latin verse), for example: *That fought/ with us/ upon/ Saint Crisp/in's day.* [Latin *iambus,* from Greek *iambos.*]

i·am·bic (ī am′bik) *adj.* of, relating to, or consisting of iambs. —*n.* **1.** iamb. **2.** *usually.* **iambics.** poetry written in iambs.

-ian, form of **-an,** as in *Australian, simian.*

-iatry *combining form* medical treatment: *psychiatry.* [Modern Latin *-iatria,* from Greek *iātreiā* healing.]

ib., ibidem.

I·ba·dan (ē bä′dän) *n.* largest city of Nigeria, in the southwestern part of the country. Pop. (1969 est.), 727,565.

I·be·ri·a (ī bēr′ē ə) *n.* **1.** large peninsula of southwestern Europe, between the Atlantic and the Mediterranean, occupied by Spain and Portugal. Also, **Iberian Peninsula.** **2.** ancient region in the southern Caucasus, in what is now the eastern part of Soviet Georgia. [Latin *Ibēria,* from Greek *Ibēria.*]

I·be·ri·an (ī bēr′ē ən) *adj.* **1.** of, characteristic of, or relating to Iberia in Europe, its people, or its culture. **2.** of or denoting members of an ancient race that inhabited Iberia in Europe. **3.** of or relating to ancient Iberia in Asia or its inhabitants. —*n.* **1.** inhabitant of ancient Iberia in Europe. **2.** almost completely unknown language formerly spoken in Iberia in Europe. **3.** inhabitant of ancient Iberia in Asia.

i·bex (ī′beks) *pl.* **i·bex·es** or **ib·i·ces** (ib′ə sēz, ī′bə-) or **i·bex.** *n.* mountain-dwelling wild goat, *Capra ibex,* native to Europe, Asia, and northern Africa, having ridged, curving horns which in the male may grow to as much as five feet in length. Height: to 40 inches at the shoulder. [Latin *ibex* chamois.]

ibid., ibidem.

i·bi·dem (i bī′dem) *adv.* in the work previously mentioned or cited. ▲ used mainly in footnotes in the abbreviated form **ibid.** [Latin *ibidem* in the same place.]

-ibility, form of **-ability,** as in *sensibility, flexibility.*

i·bis (ī′bis) *pl.* **i·bis·es** or **i·bis.** *n.* long-legged wading bird of any of several species, family Threskiornithidae, related to the stork and heron, having a long, downward curving bill, esp. the **sacred ibis,** *Threskiornis aethiopica,* which was worshiped by the ancient Egyptians. Height: 3½ feet. [Latin *ibis,* from Greek *ibis;* of Egyptian origin.]

Ibex

Ibis

-ible, form of **-able,** as in *convertible.*

Ib·sen, Hen·rik (ib′sən; hen′rik) 1828–1906, Norwegian dramatist.

-ic *suffix* **1.** (used to form adjectives from nouns) **a.** of or relating to: *psychiatric, Celtic.* **b.** having the qualities of; being or like: *athletic, angelic.* **c.** made of or containing: *alcoholic, granitic.* **d.** characterized by: *cyclic.* **e.** produced or caused by: *seismic.* ▲ Many words ending in *-ic* have more than one of the above meanings. **2.** *Chemistry.* **a.** of a higher oxidation state than a related compound or ion whose name ends in *-ous.* The oxidation state of copper is +2 in *cupric* oxide and +1 in *cuprous* oxide. **b.** designating the most commonly used of a group of related ternary acids. Nitric acid is more commonly used than nitrous acid. [Latin *-icus* or Greek *-ikos,* often through French *-ique.*]

-ical *suffix* **1.** (used to form adjectives from nouns) **a.** of, relating to, characterized by, or caused by: *pontifical, farcical.* **b.** characterized by in a special way: *economical, philosophical.* **2.** (used to form adjectives from nouns ending in *-ic*): of, relating to, or characterized by: *logical, musical.* [Latin *-icālis,* sometimes through French *-ical(e).*]

Ic·a·rus (ik′ər əs) *n.* *Greek Mythology.* youth who escaped from Crete on wings made by his father, Daedalus. As he flew too near the sun, the wax holding the wings melted, and he fell into the sea.

ICBM, intercontinental ballistic missile, ballistic missile with a range of over 3000 miles.

ICC, Interstate Commerce Commission.

ice (īs) *n.* **1.** the solid state of water, normally produced at or below 32 degrees Fahrenheit. **2.** frozen surface, esp. of a body of water, as a lake: *The fisherman cut a hole in the ice.* **3.** something that resembles ice in appearance or consistency. **4.** frozen dessert made of sweetened water and fruit flavoring or fruit juice. **5.** *Slang.* a diamond or diamonds. **6. to cut no ice.** *Informal.* to have little effect or influence: *His excuse cuts no ice with me.* **7. on ice.** *Informal.* **a.** in reserve, as for future consideration: *We'll keep the matter on ice until the next meeting.* **b.** out of communication with others; incommunicado: *The police kept the suspect on ice for several days.* **8. on thin ice,** in a risky or precarious situation. —*v.i.,* **iced, ic·ing,** to become covered with ice (often with *up* or *over*): *The windows have iced up.* —*v.t.* **1.** to cause ice to form on; cover with ice. **2.** to chill or keep cold, esp. with ice: *The hostess iced the champagne.* **3.** to cover or decorate with icing; frost. **4.** to convert into ice. [Old English *īs* frozen water.]

ice age 1. any period of time when glaciers covered much of the surface of the earth. **2. Ice Age.** Pleistocene.

ice bag, waterproof bag for holding ice, used to apply cold to parts of the body, esp. to alleviate pain or lessen swelling.

ice·berg (īs′bûrg′) *n.* large mass of floating ice that has broken off from a glacier or polar icecap. [Probably from Dutch *ijsberg* literally, ice mountain.]

ice·boat (īs′bōt′) *n.* **1.** boatlike, often triangular, frame equipped with runners and sails for sailing on ice. **2.** icebreaker.

ice·bound (īs′bound′) *adj.* **1.** obstructed and made inaccessible by ice: *an icebound coast.* **2.** held fast or impeded by ice: *an icebound ship.*

ice·box (īs′boks′) *n.* **1.** box or chest cooled by blocks of ice, used for storing food and drinks. **2.** *Informal.* refrigerator.

ice·break·er (īs′brā′kər) *n.* ship with a strong prow, used in harbors, rivers, and other waterways to break a navigable channel through ice.

ice·cap (īs′kap′) *n.* dome-shaped glacier covering a land area.

ice cream, frozen dessert made chiefly of milk products, sweeteners, and flavoring.

iced (īst) *adj.* **1.** chilled or kept cold, esp. with ice: *iced tea, iced melon.*

Iceberg

2. covered or coated with ice: *an iced airplane wing.* **3.** covered or decorated with icing: *an iced cupcake.*

ice field, large expanse of floating ice, found esp. in polar regions.

ice floe, floe.

ice hockey, hockey *(def. 1).*

ice·house (īs′hous′) *n.* building for storing ice.

Ice·land (īs′lənd) *n.* island country in the North Atlantic, between Greenland and Norway, formerly a possession of Denmark. Capital, Reykjavik. Area, 39,800 sq. mi. Pop. (1969 est.), 204,000. —**Ice·land·er** (īs′lan′dər, -lən-), *n.*

Ice·lan·dic (īs lan′dik) *adj.* of or relating to Iceland, its people, language, or culture. —*n.* language spoken predominantly in Iceland, belonging to the Germanic branch of the Indo-European language family.

Iceland moss, edible lichen, *Cetraria islandica,* found in the Arctic and in mountainous regions of the Northern Hemisphere, growing in a tangled mass of thin, spiny-edged branches.

ice·man (īs′man′) *pl.,* **-men** (-men′). *n.* one whose job or business is selling or delivering ice.

ice pack 1. ice bag or folded cloth filled with ice and applied to parts of the body, esp. to alleviate pain or lessen swelling. **2.** pack ice.

ice pick, pointed tool used to break or chip ice.

ice sheet, thick layer of ice covering an extensive area of land for a long period of time.

ice-skate (īs′skāt′) **-skat·ed, -skat·ing.** *v.i.* to skate on ice.

ice skate 1. runner, usually of metal, mounted in a frame that has straps and clamps for attaching to the sole of a shoe, used for skating on ice. **2.** bootlike shoe with such a runner permanently attached to it.

ice skating, skating on ice.

ice water 1. water that is chilled with ice or is as cold as ice. **2.** water from melted ice.

ich·neu·mon (ik nōō′mən, -nū′-) *n.* **1.** mongoose native to Africa, *Herpestes ichneumon,* having a gray body and brownish-black feet, considered sacred by the ancient Egyptians. Length: 40 inches including the tail. **2.** ichneumon fly. [Latin *ichneumōn,* from Greek *ichneumōn* literally, tracker. The mongoose was believed to hunt out crocodile's eggs; the ichneumon fly, to hunt spiders.]

ichneumon fly, any of a group of stingless, wasplike insects, family Ichneumonidae, found throughout the world, whose larvae are parasites on many destructive crop pests.

i·chor¹ (ī′kôr, ī′kər) *n.* ethereal fluid supposed by the Greeks to flow in the veins of the gods. [Greek *īchōr.*]

i·chor² (ī′kôr, ī′kər) *n.* thin watery discharge from an ulcer or wound. [Late Latin *ichor* bloody matter, from Greek *īchōr* blood of the gods, watery fluid.]

ich·thy·ol·o·gy (ik′thē ol′ə jē) *n.* branch of zoology that deals with fish. [Greek *ichthŷs* fish + -LOGY.] —**ich·thy·o·log·ic** (ik′thē ə loj′ik), *also,* **ich·thy·o·log·i·cal,** *adj.* —**ich·thy·ol·o·gist,** *n.*

ich·thy·o·saur (ik′thē ə sôr′) *n.* any of an extinct group of fishlike marine reptiles, order Ichthyosauria, of the Mesozoic, having a large head with a thin, elongated snout, and four paddle-like flippers. Length: from 25 to 40 feet. [Modern Latin *Ichthyosaurus,* from Greek *ichthŷs* fish + *sauros* lizard.]

Ichthyosaur

ich·thy·o·sau·rus (ik′thē ə sôr′əs) *pl.,* **-sau·ri** (-sôr′ī) or **-sau·rus·es.** *n.* ichthyosaur.

i·ci·cle (ī′si kəl) *n.* tapered, hanging piece of ice formed by the freezing of dripping water. [Middle English *isikel,* from Old English *īs* ice + *gicel* icicle.]

i·ci·ly (ī sə lē) *adv.* in an icy manner.

i·ci·ness (ī′sē nis) *n.* state or quality of being icy.

ic·ing (ī′sing) *n.* mixture of sugar, butter, flavoring, a liquid, and sometimes egg whites, used to cover or decorate a cake or other baked goods; frosting.

i·con (ī′kon) *also,* **i·kon.** *n.* painted representation of a holy person, as Christ, the Virgin Mary, or a saint. Icons are held in reverence by Christians in the Eastern churches. [Latin *īcōn* image, from Greek *eikōn.*]

i·con·o·clasm (ī kon′ə klaz′əm) *n.* beliefs or behavior of an iconoclast.

i·con·o·clast (ī kon′ə klast′) *n.* **1.** one who attacks traditional or cherished ideas, beliefs, or institutions as being false or harmful. **2.** one who destroys icons and is opposed to their religious use. [Modern Latin *iconoclastes,* going back to Greek *eikōn* image + *-klastēs* breaker.] —**i·con′o·clas′tic,** *adj.*

-ics *suffix* (used to form nouns) **1.** art, science, or field of study: *physics,*

graphics. **2.** procedures, practices, or activities: *gymnastics.* [Plural of -IC, imitating Greek *-ika,* neuter plural of *-ikos,* as in *(ta) ethika* (the) ethics.]

ic·tus (ik′təs) *pl.,* **-tus·es** or **-tus.** *n.* rhythmical or metrical stress. [Latin *ictus* blow, stroke.]

i·cy (ī′sē) **i·ci·er, i·ci·est.** *adj.* **1.** made of, containing, or covered with ice: *icy pavement, icy regions, icy mounds.* **2.** very cold: *icy winds; icy hands.* **3.** without warmth of feeling; coldly indifferent: *an icy stare.*

id (id) *n. Psychoanalysis.* the part of the personality that is inherited and present at birth and is the source of all psychic energy. [Latin *id* it, translation of German *es* it.]

I'd (īd) **1.** I had. **2.** I would. **3.** I should.

-id¹ *suffix* (used to form nouns) **1.** *Mythology.* children of: *nereid.* **2.** *Astronomy.* meteor that seems to originate or radiate from a specified constellation: *Leonid.* [Greek *-id-,* stem of *-is* (feminine) offspring of, often through Latin *-id-,* stem of *-is.*]

-id² *suffix* (used to form nouns) member of a specified family or class: *hominid.* [Modern Latin *-idae* and *-ida,* masculine and neuter plural respectively of *-ides,* from Greek *-idēs,* (masculine) offspring of.]

-id³ *suffix* (used to form adjectives) having a particular quality, state, or conditon: *fluid, morbid, torrid, solid.* [Latin *-idus,* often through French *-ide.*]

id., idem.

ID, identification.

Ida., Idaho.

I·da·ho (ī′də hō′) *n.* state in the western United States. Capital, Boise. Area, 83,557 sq. mi. Pop. (1970), 698,275. Abbreviation, **Ida.** —**I′da·ho′an,** *adj., n.*

Idaho Falls, city in southeastern Idaho. Pop. (1970), 35,318.

-ide *suffix* used in chemistry to indicate a salt whose formula contains only two elements: *sodium chloride, potassium sulfide.* [From (OX)-IDE.]

i·dea (ī dē′ə) *n.* **1.** something formulated by the mind; thought: *You have good ideas, but have difficulty expressing them.* **2.** mental image: *The prisoner's idea of his former life grew dim after a few years.* **3.** abstract form or essence; general concept: *the idea of war, the idea of the good.* **4.** belief; conviction: *The old man had strong ideas about religion.* **5.** vague feeling; inkling: *John had an idea that he met this girl somewhere before.* **6.** plan of action; intention: *Talking with her uncle gave Jane the idea of becoming an artist.* **7.** aim or purpose of something: *The idea of the game is to hit the ball over the net.* [Latin *idea* archetype, model, from Greek *ideā* look, form, model, notion.]

Syn. 1. Idea, thought, conception denote products of conscious mental activity. **Idea** is the most common word and emphasizes a degree of seriousness: *The scientist explained his ideas to the audience.* **Thought** may be expressed or not and suggests an idea formed by reasoning rather than by imagination: *The professor organized his thoughts before delivering his lecture.* **Conception** usually implies that the mental formulation is of something new: *The architect's conception of the buildings included a plaza with a fountain.*

i·de·al (ī dē′əl) *n.* **1.** concept or standard of perfection or excellence: *the ideal of beauty.* **2.** one who or that which is the embodiment of such a concept or standard, esp. one to be admired and imitated: *Florence Nightingale is the ideal of many a young nurse.* **3.** best or most satisfactory situation; eventual aim or goal: *The ideal would be to have a round-the-clock emergency hospital in each district.* —*adj.* **1.** actualizing or embodying standards of perfection or excellence; much better than currently exists: *an ideal society.* **2.** most desirable or suitable: *These boots are ideal for a wet, slushy day.* **3.** existing only as or in a concept; not concrete: *the ideal man.* [Late Latin *ideālis* relating to an archetype or model, from Latin *idea.* See IDEA.] —**Syn.** *adj.* **1.** see **perfect.**

i·de·al·ism (ī dē′ə liz′əm) *n.* **1.** action or belief in accordance with standards of perfection or excellence, rather than in accordance with what currently exists: *the idealism of those who would eliminate hunger and poverty.* **2.** in art and literature, the imaginative treatment of subject matter, usually expressing an ethical or aesthetic standard of perfection rather than the accidental details of nature. Opposed to **realism.** **3.** philosophical theory that reality is essentially mental or spiritual rather than material. **Objective idealism** maintains that reality consists essentially of ideal forms, such as beauty and justice, that exist outside of and independent of anyone's mind. **Subjective idealism** maintains that nothing is real but the perceptions and ideas that exist in one's mind.

i·de·al·ist (ī dē′ə list) *n.* **1.** one who thinks or acts in accordance with ideals. **2.** one who thinks that things are better than they are; dreamer. **3.** one who adheres to or expresses idealism in art, literature, or philosophy. —*adj.* idealistic: *idealist philosophy.*

i·de·al·is·tic (ī dē′ə lis′tik) *adj.* **1.** motivated by standards of perfection or excellence. **2.** tending to ignore practical limitations; unrealistic.

3. tending to think or assume that things are better than they are. 4. of, relating to, or characterized by idealism in art, literature, or philosophy. —i′de·al·is′ti·cal·ly, *adv.*

i·de·al·i·za·tion (ī dē′ə li zā′shən) *n.* 1. act of idealizing; state of being idealized. 2. result of idealizing.

i·de·al·ize (ī dē′ə līz′) -ized, -iz·ing. *v.t.* 1. to portray or represent as ethically or aesthetically perfect, as in art: *portraits that idealize their subjects.* 2. to remember or think of (something) as better than it was or is: *The old man idealized his early days on his father's farm.*

i·de·al·ly (ī dē′ə lē) *adv.* 1. in the best possible manner; perfectly or very well: *Jane's personality suits her ideally to be a doctor.* 2. in accordance with a standard or concept; under the best conditions: *Ideally, each child should receive three shots of the vaccine.*

i·de·a·tion (ī′dē ā′shən) *n.* process of forming ideas.

i·dem (ī′dem, id′em) *pron., adj. Latin.* the same; ditto. ▲ used to refer to something previously mentioned.

i·den·ti·cal (ī den′ti kəl) *adj.* 1. one and the same: *She wore the identical dress on both occasions.* 2. exactly alike: *identical uniforms, identical statements.* 3. (of values or amounts) numerically the same; equal. 4. (of two or more babies born at the same time) developing from a single fertilized egg cell, and thus having the same hereditary material: *identical twins.* Distinguished from *fraternal.* [Medieval Latin *identicus* the same (from Late Latin *identitās* sameness) + -AL¹. See IDENTITY.] —i·den′ti·cal·ly, *adv.* —i·den′ti·cal·ness, *n.* —Syn. 2. see **equal, same.**

i·den·ti·fi·ca·tion (ī den′tə fi kā′shən) *n.* 1. act or process of identifying; state of being identified. 2. something used to give evidence of or to establish one's identity.

i·den·ti·fy (ī den′tə fī′) -fied, -fy·ing. *v.t.* 1.a. to establish that (someone or something) is a particular person or thing: *Mrs. Jones identified the suspect by the scar on his face.* b. to recognize: *How many species of birds can you identify?* 2. to be a means of knowing who or what a person or thing is. 3. to regard or treat as identical; assume to be one and the same: *The Roman goddess Venus is identified with the Greek goddess Aphrodite.* 4. to associate closely (with *with*): *a businessman who identifies money with success.* —*v.i.* to become as one with another or others (with *with*): *She identified with the heroine of the novel.* —i·den′ti·fi′a·ble, *adj.* —i·den′ti·fi′er, *n.*

i·den·ti·ty (ī den′tə tē) *pl.,* -ties. *n.* 1. one's sense of being distinguishable from other persons; individuality: *to suffer a loss of identity.* 2. being a certain person or thing; being who or what one or it is: *The traveler's passport established his identity.* 3. state or condition of being identical: *an identity of interests.* 4. *Mathematics.* statement of equality that is true for all values of a variable. The equation $3x + 2x = 5x$ is true for all values of x and is therefore an identity. [Late Latin *identitās* sameness, from Latin *idem* the same.]

identity element, element in a set which, when added to or multiplied by any other element, yields that element. For addition, 0 is the identity element; for multiplication, 1 is the identity element.

id·e·o·graph (id′ē ə graf′, ī′dē-) *n.* written symbol, such as a character in Chinese, that stands for an object or idea rather than for a word or, as does a letter in English, for a sound. Also, **id·e·o·gram** (id′ē ə-gram′, ī′dē-). [Greek *ideá* form, kind, idea + -GRAPH; literally, idea writing.]

i·de·o·log·i·cal (ī′dē ə loj′i kəl, id′ē-) *adj.* 1. due to or based on ideologies or an ideology: *ideological differences.* 2. of or relating to ideologies or an ideology: *ideological studies.*

i·de·ol·o·gy (ī′dē ol′ə jē, id′ē-) *pl.,* -gies. *n.* 1. total complex of beliefs, attitudes, and concepts that directs and channels the thinking of members of a group, as of a political party or social class. 2. beliefs; ideas: *His ideology is so different from mine that we can't understand each other.* [Greek *ideá* idea, form, kind + -LOGY.]

ides (īdz) *n.,pl.* in the ancient Roman calendar, the fifteenth day of March, May, July, or October, and the thirteenth day of the other months. ▲ construed as singular. [French *ides,* from Latin *īdūs;* possibly of Etruscan origin.]

id·i·o·cy (id′ē ə sē) *pl.,* -cies. *n.* 1. severe mental retardation. 2. excessive silliness or stupidity.

id·i·om (id′ē əm) *n.* 1. any expression peculiar to a language whose meaning cannot be construed from the meanings of the words composing it. *To pull one's leg* is an idiom. 2. language or dialect peculiar to a people or to a specific region: *the classics of the Tuscan idiom* (Gibbon, 1794). 3. distinctive grammatical character of a language. 4. characteristic style or form of expression, esp. in the arts: *He was one of the first artists to appreciate jazz as a distinctly American idiom* (Barbara Rose, 1967). [Late Latin *idīoma* peculiarity in language, from Greek *idīōma,* going back to *idios* one's own.]

Syn. 2. Idiom, dialect denote forms of speech. **Idiom** is a speech form native to or characteristic of a people, class, or linguistic province as a whole, distinguished by peculiarities of usage and modes of expression: *The novels of Mark Twain have enriched the American idiom.* **Dialect**

is a regional form of language with its own distinctive pronunciation, grammar, and vocabulary: *Scottish is a dialect of English.*

id·i·o·mat·ic (id′ē ə mat′ik) *adj.* 1. having the nature of an idiom or idioms: *an idiomatic expression.* 2. characterized by the use of idioms: *idiomatic speech.* 3. peculiar to or characteristic of a particular language. —id′i·o·mat′i·cal·ly, *adv.*

id·i·o·syn·cra·sy (id′ē ə sing′krə sē) *pl.,* -sies. *n.* unusual or distinguishing characteristic of an individual, as a habit or mannerism; peculiarity; eccentricity. [Greek *idiosynkrāsiā* peculiar temperament, from *idios* one's own + *syn* with + *krāsis* mixture.] —id·i·o·syn·crat·ic (id′ē ə sing krat′ik), *adj.* —id′i·o·syn·crat′i·cal·ly, *adv.*

id·i·ot (id′ē ət) *n.* 1. one who is mentally retarded, having a mental age of up to four years. See **mental retardation.** 2. very silly or stupid person; fool. [Latin *idiōta* ignorant person, from Greek *idiōtēs* private person (as opposed to one holding public office), uneducated person.]

id·i·ot·ic (id′ē ot′ik) *adj.* 1. of, relating to, or characteristic of an idiot; very foolish. —id′i·ot′i·cal·ly, *adv.*

i·dle (īd′əl) i·dler, i·dlest. *adj.* 1.a. not engaged in work or activity; unemployed; inactive: *an idle secretary.* b. not in use: *an idle typewriter.* 2. unwilling to work or exert oneself; lazy. 3. having little worth, usefulness, or significance; frivolous: *an idle pastime.* 4. without any basis in fact; groundless: *idle gossip.* 5. leading to no result; ineffective; futile: *idle threats.* —*v.i.* i·dled, i·dling. 1. to spend time doing nothing; be inactive: *He idled around the house all morning.* 2. to move sluggishly or aimlessly: *He idled along the sidewalk.* 3. (of machines) to run slowly, out of gear, or without transmitting power: *The car idled in the driveway.* —*v.t.* 1. to spend (time) doing nothing; waste (often with *away*): *He idled away his entire vacation.* 2. to cause (someone or something) to be inactive: *The strike idled the men for days.* [Old English *idel* empty, useless, inactive.] —i′dle·ness, *n.* —i′dly, *adv.*

i·dler (īd′lər) *n.* 1. one who is lazy or inactive. 2. wheel or gear located between two other wheels or gears that transmits motion from one to the other without altering their direction or speed. Also (*def.* 2). **idle wheel.**

i·dol (īd′əl) *n.* 1. representation of a god, used as an object of worship. 2. in the Old Testament, a false god, esp. of a heathen people. 3. one who is the object of great or excessive admiration or devotion: *The athlete was the idol of many fans.* [Latin *īdōlum* image, form, from Greek *eidōlon.*]

i·dol·a·ter (ī dol′ə tər) *n.* 1. one who worships an idol or idols. 2. one who idolizes another: *The famous singer was surrounded by idolaters.*

i·dol·a·trous (ī dol′ə trəs) *adj.* 1. of, relating to, or characteristic of idolatry. 2. given to worshiping an idol or idols: *an idolatrous people.* 3. given to great or excessive admiration or devotion. —i·dol′a·trous·ly, *adv.*

i·dol·a·try (ī dol′ə trē) *pl.,* -tries. *n.* 1. worship of idols. 2. great or excessive admiration or devotion. [Old French *idolatrie* worship of idols, through Latin, going back to Greek *eidōlolatreiā,* from *eidōlon* image + *latreiā* worship.]

i·dol·ize (īd′əl īz′) -ized, -iz·ing. *v.t.* 1. to look upon with great or excessive admiration or devotion. 2. to worship as an idol. —i′dol·i·za′tion, *n.*

I·dom·e·neus (ī dom′ə nōōs′, -nūs′) *n. Greek Legend.* a king of Crete and leader of the Cretans in the Trojan War.

Id·u·mae·a (id′ū mē′ə) *also,* Id·u·me·a. *n.* Edom.

i·dyll (īd′əl) *also,* i·dyl. *n.* 1. short descriptive pastoral poem or work of prose in which the characters are usually shepherds and the setting is simple, rustic, and peaceful. 2. long descriptive or narrative poem. 3. situation or scene suitable for such a work. [Latin *idyllium* pastoral poem, from Greek *eidyllion* little picture, pastoral poem, diminutive of *eidos* form, picture.]

i·dyl·lic (ī dil′ik) *adj.* 1. of, relating to, or having the nature of an idyll. 2. having natural, simple, or poetic charm: *His home was in an idyllic setting.*

-ie *suffix* (used to form nouns) 1. little or dear: *lassie.* ▲ also used with proper nouns as an expression of affection or intimacy, as in *Susie.* 2. of a certain kind or quality: *sweetie, meanie.* [Form of -Y².]

i.e., that is. [Abbreviation of Latin *id est.*]

-ier *suffix* (used to form nouns) one who is concerned with or has to do with (that which is indicated by the stem): *cashier, financier.* [French -*ier,* from Latin -*ārius.* See -ARY¹.]

if (if) *conj.* 1.a. in case that; supposing that: *If I make a mistake, I'll admit it. If he is sick, will he still come?* b. granting that: *Even if he stays, I can't. If you didn't see him, who did?* 2. on condition that: *I will sing, if you will accompany me.* 3. whether: *I don't know if he will be there.* 4. even though; although: *It was a nice, if humid, day.* 5. if not. perhaps; possibly: *It was a good, if not excellent, play.* 6. used in exclamatory clauses to express wish, surprise, or annoyance: *If we had only known. Well, if it isn't John!* —*n.* condition; supposition. [Old English *gif* supposing that, whether, though.]

at; āpe; cär; end; mē; it; īce; hot; ōld; fôrk; wood; fōōl; oil; out; up; ūse; turn; sing; thin; <u>th</u>is; zh in treasure; ə in ago, taken, pencil, lemon, circus.

If·ni (if′nē) *n.* former Spanish territory in northwestern Africa, on the Atlantic, part of Morocco since 1969. Area, 580 sq. mi. Pop. (1969 est.), 55,000.

ig·loo (ig′lōō) *pl.,* **-loos.** *n.* dome-shaped hut used by Eskimos, usually built of blocks of hardened snow. [Eskimo *igdlu* house.]

Igloo

Ig·na·tius of Loyola, Saint (ig nā′-shəs) 1491–1556, founder of the Jesuits.

ig·ne·ous (ig′nē əs) *adj.* **1.** of, relating to, resembling, or characteristic of fire. **2.** produced by conditions involving great heat or volcanic action, as with rocks formed from molten material within the earth. [Latin *igneus* of fire, fiery, from *ignis* fire.]

ig·nis fat·u·us (ig′nis fach′ōō əs) *pl.,* **ig·nes fat·u·i** (ig′nēz fach′ōō ī′). will-o′-the-wisp. [Modern Latin *ignis fatuus* literally, foolish fire; referring to the unpredictability of its movement.]

ig·nite (ig nīt′) **-nit·ed, -nit·ing.** *v.t.* **1.** to burn or set on fire; kindle. **2.** to cause to glow with heat; make intensely hot. —*v.i.* to begin to burn; catch on fire. [Latin *ignītus,* past participle of *ignīre* to set on fire, from *ignis* fire.] —**ig·nit′a·ble,** *adj.* —**ig·nit′er,** *n.* —Syn. **1.** see **kindle.**

ig·ni·tion (ig nish′ən) *n.* **1.** act of igniting; being ignited. **2.** device or system for igniting the fuel and air mixture within the cylinders of an internal-combustion engine.

ig·no·ble (ig nō′bəl) *adj.* **1.** without honor or worth; mean; base: *an ignoble motive.* **2.** of low birth or position. [Latin *īgnōbilis* unknown, undistinguished, from *in-* not + Old Latin *gnōbilis* famous, of noble birth.] —**ig·no′ble·ness,** *n.* —**ig·no′bly,** *adv.*

ig·no·min·i·ous (ig′nə min′ē əs) *adj.* **1.** marked by or involving dishonor or disgrace; shameful: *ignominious punishment, an ignominious defeat.* **2.** deserving of shame or contempt; despicable. [Latin *īgnōminiōsus* disgraceful, from *īgnōminia.* See IGNOMINY.] —**ig′no·min′i·ous·ly,** *adv.*

ig·no·min·y (ig′nə min′ē) *pl.,* **-min·ies.** *n.* **1.** disgrace; dishonor; infamy. **2.** that which causes or deserves disgrace or dishonor. [Latin *īgnōminia* disgrace, dishonor, from *in-* not + *nōmen* name, reputation.]

ig·no·ra·mus (ig′nə rā′məs, -ram′əs) *pl.,* **-mus·es.** *n.* ignorant person. [From *Ignoramus* (1615), a satirical play by George Ruggle, from Latin *īgnōrāmus* we do not know.]

ig·no·rance (ig′nər əns) *n.* state or quality of being ignorant.

ig·no·rant (ig′nər ənt) *adj.* **1.** lacking in knowledge or education. **2.** uninformed or unaware: *ignorant of the details.* **3.** resulting from or showing lack of knowledge or education: *an ignorant statement.* [Latin *īgnōrāns,* present participle of *īgnōrāre* not to know.] —**ig′no·rant·ly,** *adv.*

ig·nore (ig nôr′) **-nored, -nor·ing.** *v.t.* to refuse to take notice of or recognize; disregard intentionally. [Latin *īgnōrāre* not to know.]
   Syn. **Ignore, disregard, neglect** mean to overlook something or give it inadequate attention. **Ignore** means to refuse deliberately to take notice of something one does not wish to recognize or acknowledge: *The speaker ignored the catcalls and insults of the hecklers.* **Disregard** means to overlook something, esp. in a slighting way, by undervaluing its importance: *The losing team had disregarded its coach's advice.* **Neglect** means to treat with culpable disregard something or someone entitled to care and attention: *The boy was careful never to neglect his dog.*

Ig·o·rot (ig′ə rōt′) *pl.,* **-rots** or **-rot.** *n.* **1.** any of several tribes of the Philippines, living in the mountainous area of north-central Luzon. **2.** their language, a member of the Malayo-Polynesian family of languages. [Spanish *igorrote;* probably of Tagalog origin.]

i·gua·na (i gwä′nə) *n.* **1.** large, greenish-brown, black-banded lizard, *Iguana iguana,* found from Mexico to northern South America, usually living in trees and having a large fold of skin suspended from its throat and a ridge of enlarged scales down the center of the back. Length: to more than 6½ feet. **2.** any of various other lizards, family Iguanidae, as the chuckwalla, *Sauromalus obesus,* of the United States and Mexico. [Spanish *iguana,* from Carib *iwana.*]

Iguana

IGY, International Geophysical Year.

IHS, monogram and symbol representing the name of Jesus. [Late Latin *IHS,* representing Greek ΙΗΣ, short for Greek ΙΗΣΟΥΣ Jesus (in Greek capital letters).]

i·kon (ī′kon) icon.

il-¹, form of **in-¹** before *l,* as in *illegitimate.*

il-², form of **in-²** before *l,* as in *illuminate.*

-ile *also,* **-il.** *suffix* used to form adjectives expressing relation-

ship, similarity, capability, suitability, or liability: *contractile, motile.* [Latin *-ilis, -īlis,* often through French *-il, -ile.*]

il·e·ac (il′ē ak′) *adj.* of or relating to the ileum.

Ile-de-France (ēl də fräns′) *n.* historic region and former province in north-central France, surrounding and including Paris.

il·e·i·tis (il′ē ī′tis) *n.* inflammation of the ileum.

il·e·um (il′ē əm) *pl.,* **il·e·a** (il′ē ə). *n.* last section of the small intestine, extending from the jejunum to the large intestine. [Modern Latin *ileum,* from Latin *īleum* groin, flank.]

i·lex (ī′leks) *n.* holly.

il·i·ac (il′ē ak′) *adj.* of, relating to, or near the ilium.

il·i·um (il′ē əm) *pl.,* **il·i·a** (il′ē ə). *n.* broad upper portion of the hipbone forming the prominence of the hip. [Modern Latin *ilium,* from Latin *īlium* groin, flank.]

Il·i·um (il′ē əm) *n.* Troy (def. 1).

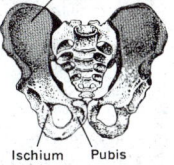
Ilium
Ischium — Pubis
Ilium

ilk (ilk) *n.* kind; sort; class: *he and others of his ilk.* [Old English *ilca* same.]

ill (il) **worse, worst.** *adj.* **1.** not healthy or well; sick. **2.** unsatisfactory; poor: *ill health, ill fortune.* **3.** harsh; hostile; cruel: *ill treatment, ill feeling.* **4.** causing harm, destruction, or inconvenience; adverse: *The war had many ill consequences.* **5. ill at ease.** nervous and uncomfortable: *The shy girl was ill at ease with strangers.* —*adv.* **1.** badly. **2.** imperfectly; poorly: *Such an opinionated statement ill becomes a judge.* **3.** scarcely; hardly: *We can ill afford the time wasted.* —*n.* **1.** affliction; trouble: *the ills of mankind.* **2.** sickness or ailment: *Arthritis is a common ill.* **3.** evil: *Good will be the final goal of ill* (Tennyson, 1850). [Old Norse *illr* bad.]

I'll (īl) **1.** I will. **2.** I shall.

ill. **1.** illustrated. **2.** illustration.

Ill., Illinois.

ill-ad·vised (il′əd vīzd′) *adj.* acting or done without sound advice or sufficient consideration; unwise.

ill-bred (il′bred′) *adj.* badly brought up or trained; unmannerly; rude.

ill-con·sid·ered (il′kən sid′ərd) *adj.* done without proper consideration or forethought; unwise.

ill-de·fined (il′di fīnd′) *adj.* poorly defined or outlined; unclear: *ill-defined areas of responsibility.*

ill-dis·posed (il′dis pōzd′) *adj.* **1.** having a hostile attitude; unfriendly: *The natives are ill-disposed toward us.* **2.** reluctant; disinclined: *The rulers were ill-disposed to receive him.*

il·le·gal (i lē′gəl) *adj.* **1.** not legal; unlawful. **2.** not authorized by official rules, as in sports. —**il·le′gal·ly,** *adv.*

il·le·gal·i·ty (il′ē gal′ə tē) *pl.,* **-ties.** *n.* **1.** state or quality of being illegal; unlawfulness. **2.** illegal act.

il·leg·i·ble (i lej′ə bəl) *adj.* difficult or impossible to read; not legible: *The tiny handwriting on the envelope was illegible.* —**il·leg′i·bil′i·ty, il·leg′i·ble·ness,** *n.* —**il·leg′i·bly,** *adv.*

il·le·git·i·ma·cy (il′i jit′ə mə sē) *pl.,* **-cies.** *n.* state or quality of being illegitimate.

il·le·git·i·mate (il′i jit′ə mit) *adj.* **1.** having no authority; not authorized; not lawful: *an illegitimate ruler.* **2.** born out of wedlock. **3.** contrary to logic or to good usage; improper; incorrect: *an illegitimate conclusion. In this sentence the writer uses an illegitimate construction.* —**il′le·git′i·mate·ly,** *adv.*

ill-fat·ed (il′fā′tid) *adj.* **1.** having a bad fate; doomed from the start: *The ill-fated play closed after the second performance.* **2.** characterized by or causing misfortune; unlucky: *an ill-fated day.*

ill-fa·vored (il′fā′vərd) *adj.* **1.** unpleasant in appearance; ugly. **2.** offensive; disagreeable; objectionable.

ill-found·ed (il′foun′did) *adj.* having a weak or incorrect basis; unsupported: *an ill-founded conviction that he alone was immune to the disease.*

ill-got·ten (il′got′ən) *adj.* acquired by evil or dishonest means: *ill-gotten gains.*

ill-hu·mored (il′hū′mərd, -ū′mərd) *adj.* having or showing a bad temperament or humor; irritable; cross.

il·lib·er·al (i lib′ər əl, i lib′rəl) *adj.* **1.** narrow-minded; bigoted; intolerant. **2.** not generous in giving; stingy. —**il·lib′er·al′i·ty,** *n.*

il·lic·it (i lis′it) *adj.* forbidden by law; not allowed. —**il·lic′it·ly,** *adv.* —**il·lic′it·ness,** *n.*

il·lim·it·a·ble (i lim′i tə bəl) *adj.* incapable of being limited or bounded; limitless. —**il·lim′it·a·bly,** *adv.*

Il·li·nois (il′ə noi′, -noiz′) *n.* **1.** state in the north-central United States. Capital, Springfield. Area, 56,400 sq. mi. Pop. (1970), 11,113,-976. Abbreviation, **Ill. 2.** river flowing from northeastern Illinois into the Mississippi. **3.** member of a confederation of North American Indians of the Algonquian language family, formerly living in northern Illinois, southern Wisconsin, and parts of Iowa and Missouri, now living

in northeast Oklahoma. [French *Illinois;* of Algonquian origin.] —**Il′li·nois′an,** *adj., n.*

il·lit·er·a·cy (i lit′ər ə sē) *pl.,* **-cies.** *n.* 1. inability to read or write. 2. lack of education or culture. 3. error indicative of such an inability or lack.

il·lit·er·ate (i lit′ər it) *adj.* 1. unable to read or write. 2. lacking or indicating a lack of education or culture. —*n.* one who is illiterate. —**il·lit′er·ate·ly,** *adv.* —**il·lit′er·ate·ness,** *n.*

ill-man·nered (il′man′ərd) *adj.* having bad manners; rude.

ill-na·tured (il′nā′chərd) *adj.* having or showing a disagreeable or surly disposition.

ill·ness (il′nis) *n.* 1. condition or period of being ill: *During her illness, Alice stayed indoors.* 2. what one is ill with; disease: *Children are susceptible to various illnesses.*

il·log·i·cal (i loj′i kəl) *adj.* devoid of or contrary to logic. —**il·log·i·cal·i·ty** (i loj′i kal′i tē), **il·log′i·cal·ness,** *n.* —**il·log′i·cal·ly,** *adv.*

ill-starred (il′stärd′) *adj.* ill-fated or unlucky as if under the influence of an evil star.

ill-suit·ed (il′sōō′tid) *adj.* not fit or well adapted; inappropriate: *behavior ill-suited to the occasion.*

ill-tem·pered (il′tem′pərd) *adj.* grouchy; cross.

ill-timed (il′tīmd′) *adj.* coming at the wrong time; badly timed.

ill-treat (il′trēt′) *v.t.* to treat badly or cruelly; maltreat. —**ill′-treat′ment,** *n.*

il·lume (i lōōm′) **-lumed, -lum·ing.** *v.t. Archaic.* to illuminate.

il·lu·mi·nant (i lōō′mi nənt) *n.* something that gives light.

il·lu·mi·nate (i lōō′mi nāt′) **-nat·ed, -nat·ing.** *v.t.* 1. to give light to; light up: *The sun illuminates the sky.* 2. to decorate with lights: *to illuminate a fountain at night.* 3. to throw light upon; elucidate; clarify: *lectures that illuminate history more than any book.* 4. to enlighten or inform: *We were greatly enlightened by the discussion.* 5. to decorate (a scroll, manuscript, or page) with ornamental designs and miniature figures in gold, silver, and brilliant colors, as was done esp. in medieval times. [Latin *illūminātus,* past participle of *illūmināre* to make light, from *in* in + *lūmen* light.]

il·lu·mi·nat·ing (i lōō′mi nā′ting) *adj.* 1. enlightening; instructive. 2. giving light.

il·lu·mi·na·tion (i lōō′mi nā′shən) *n.* 1. act of illuminating; state of being illuminated. 2. amount or supply of light: *poor illumination.* 3. decoration with lights. 4. decoration of a scroll, manuscript, or page of a book with gold or colored designs and figures, as in medieval times. 5. intellectual or spiritual enlightenment.

il·lu·mi·na·tive (i lōō′mi nā′tiv) *adj.* illuminating.

il·lu·mi·na·tor (i lōō′mi nā′tər) *n.* 1. that which illuminates; source of light. 2. any of several devices for projecting, concentrating, or reflecting light. 3. one who illuminates a scroll, manuscript, or page.

il·lu·mine (i lōō′min) **-mined, -min·ing.** *v.t.* to illuminate. [Latin *illūmināre* to illuminate. See ILLUMINATE.]

illus. 1. illustrated. 2. illustrator.

ill-use (*v.,* il′ūz′; *n.,* il′ūs′) **-used, -us·ing.** *v.t.* to treat badly, cruelly, or unfairly; abuse. —*n.* bad, cruel, or unfair treatment.

il·lu·sion (i lōō′zhən) *n.* 1.a. false or misleading idea; misconception. b. general impression that does not correspond to actual fact: *The purchase of a new home gave an illusion of permanence to their relationship.* 2. sensory perception that causes a false or distorted impression; *an optical illusion.* 3. very fine silk net used over wedding gowns and for such items as veils; tulle. [Latin *illūsiō* mocking, deception.]

Illusion (def. 2)
Optical illusion in which the two horizontal lines are equal in length, although they appear unequal

Syn. 1.a. Illusion, delusion mean a false or distorted idea or belief. **Illusion** often suggests an impression or belief fostered by an outside influence or condition which is accepted as real even though it is false or merely apparent: *She had many illusions about herself.* **Delusion** stresses a mistaken belief that is fixed and harmful, usually arising out of a confused state of mind: *The man labored under the delusion that he was constantly being followed.*

il·lu·sion·ist (i lōō′zhə nist) *n.* one who produces illusions for entertainment; magician.

il·lu·sive (i lōō′siv) *adj.* deceptive or unreal; illusory. —**il·lu′sive·ly,** *adv.* —**il·lu′sive·ness,** *n.*

il·lu·so·ry (i lōō′sər ē) *adj.* of the nature of or causing an illusion; deceptive or unreal.

illust. 1. illustration. 2. illustrated.

il·lus·trate (il′əs trāt′, i lus′-) **-trat·ed, -trat·ing.** *v.t.* 1. to make clear or explain, as by the use of examples or comparisons. 2. to provide with pictures, diagrams, or other visual representations that serve to explain or decorate: *An artist was hired to illustrate a book on the birds of the world.* 3. to be or serve as an example, explanation, or instance of: *These*

early stories illustrate the writer's characteristic preoccupation with death. [Latin *illūstrātus,* past participle of *illūstrāre* to light up.]

il·lus·tra·tion (il′əs trā′shən) *n.* 1. something, as an example or comparison, used to clarify or explain. 2. picture, diagram, drawing, or other visual representation used to explain or decorate written or printed matter. 3. act or art of illustrating.

il·lus·tra·tive (i lus′trə tiv, il′əs trā′tiv) *adj.* serving to illustrate. —**il·lus′tra·tive·ly,** *adv.*

il·lus·tra·tor (il′əs trā′tər) *n.* 1. artist who makes or creates illustrations, as for books or magazines. 2. one who or that which illustrates.

il·lus·tri·ous (i lus′trē əs) *adj.* 1. distinguished; renowned; eminent: *an illustrious statesman.* 2. conferring greatness, distinction, or glory: *illustrious acts.* [Latin *illūstris* bright, famous + -OUS.] —**il·lus′tri·ous·ly,** *adv.* —**il·lus′tri·ous·ness,** *n.*

Syn. 1. **Illustrious, distinguished, eminent** mean famous or widely known. **Illustrious** is rich in poetic associations and means glorious and renowned in deeds and heroic in stature: *Hercules was one of the most illustrious heroes of ancient times.* **Distinguished** means marked by distinction and noted for significant achievements and excellence of qualities: *Eisenhower was a distinguished general before he became president.* **Eminent** means particularly outstanding, esp. in relation to one's peers, and indicates a critical evaluation rather than a measure of ephemeral fame or popularity: *Einstein was one of the most eminent scientists of his age.* See also **famous.**

ill will, hostile feeling; enmity.

Il·lyr·i·a (i lēr′ē ə) *n.* ancient country on the east coast of the Adriatic.

I·lo·i·lo (ē′lō ē′lō) *n.* port city in the central Philippines. Pop. (1960), 151,266.

I'm (īm) I am.

im-¹, form of **in-¹** before *b, m, p,* as in *immoral.*

im-², form of **in-²** before *b, m, p,* as in *imbibe.*

im·age (im′ij) *n.* 1. representation or likeness of a person, animal, or thing: *The coin bore an image of the emperor.* 2. picture or idea held in the mind of something that is not actually present to the senses: *I had formed an image of her before we met.* 3. one who or that which closely resembles another; counterpart: *You are the image of your father.* 4. typical example; picture: *He is the image of good health.* 5. description or figure of speech, esp. a metaphor or simile. 6. impression created by a person, group, or organization on the basis of its attitudes, policies, and practices: *The politician wanted to change his public image.* 7. *Optics.* a. representation of an object produced when light rays from the object are focused on a surface, as by a lens or mirror. Also, **real image.** b. representation of an object as seen through a lens or in a mirror, which cannot be focused and viewed on a screen. Also, **virtual image.** 8. change in the emulsion on a photographic plate when such a representation is focused on it. It is invisible until the film is developed. Also, **latent image.** [Old French *image* statue, representation of a divinity, from Latin *imāgō* statue, likeness.]

im·age·ry (im′ij rē) *pl.,* **-ries.** *n.* 1. mental images collectively, as formed by memory or imagination. 2. use of descriptions or figures of speech in writing or speech.

i·mag·i·na·ble (i maj′i nə bəl) *adj.* capable of being imagined. —**i·mag′i·na·bly,** *adv.*

i·mag·i·nar·y (i maj′i ner′ē) *adj.* 1. existing only in the imagination; unreal. 2. of or relating to imaginary numbers.

imaginary number, bi in the complex number $a + bi$, in which i is the square root of negative one, $\sqrt{-1}$, and a and b are real numbers, and b is not equal to zero.

i·mag·i·na·tion (i maj′ə nā′shən) *n.* 1. power or process of forming mental images of what is not actually present to the senses: *I'll have to use my imagination to envisage how the furniture is arranged.* 2. mental ability to create original images or ideas of things never experienced or to reconstruct or combine past experiences to form new images or ideas: *It took a lot of imagination to come up with such an ingenious plan.*

Syn. 1. **Imagination, fancy, fantasy** refer to the faculty or process of forming or projecting mental images. **Imagination** emphasizes the conscious and creative capacity of the mind to form ideal or fictional representations of things not actually present to the senses: *In her imagination, she relived last summer's vacation.* **Fancy** usually involves the conjuring up of whimsical inventions or visions: *Fairies and goblins are creatures of fancy.* **Fantasy** usually suggests that there are no limits to the formation of unreal visions or images: *Henry's fantasies took him to other worlds.*

i·mag·i·na·tive (i maj′ə nə tiv, -nā′tiv) *adj.* 1. having or exhibiting creative ability or a good imagination: *an imaginative child.* 2. produced or characterized by creativity or imagination: *an imaginative story.* —**i·mag′i·na·tive·ly,** *adv.* —**i·mag′i·na·tive·ness,** *n.*

i·mag·ine (i maj′in) **-ined, -in·ing.** *v.t.* 1. to picture (something) in the mind; form a mental image of: *Can you imagine life on the moon?*

at; āpe; cär; end; mē; it; īce; hot; ōld; fôrk; wood; fōōl; oil; out; up; ūse; turn; sing; thin; this; zh in treasure; ə in ago, taken, pencil, lemon, circus.

I imagined him as being older. **2.** to suppose; guess: *I don't imagine they will come if it rains.* —*v.i.* **1.** to picture or conceive in the mind; think: *The book was different from what I had imagined.* **2.** to use the imagination. [Old French *imaginer* to fancy, conceive, from Latin *imāginārī* to fancy.]

im·ag·ism (im′i jiz′əm) *n.* movement in poetry in the early twentieth century that emphasized the use of free verse, colloquial language, a wide range of subjects, and precise, concrete images. —**im′ag·ist,** *n.,* *adj.*

i·ma·go (i mā′gō) *pl.* **i·ma·gos** or **i·mag·i·nes** (i maj′ə nēz′). *n.* **1.** insect in the adult, sexually mature stage following metamorphosis. **2.** *Psychoanalysis.* an idealized concept of a parent or other loved one that is formed in childhood and retained in the unconscious mind in adulthood. [Latin *imāgō* likeness.]

i·mam (i mäm′) *n.* **1.** leader of prayer in a Muslim mosque. **2.** *also,* **Imam.** any of various Muslim leaders having both temporal and religious authority, esp. one claiming descent from Muhammad. [Arabic *imām.*]

im·bal·ance (im bal′əns) *n.* lack of balance.

im·be·cile (im′bə sil) *n.* **1.** one who is mentally retarded, having a mental age of up to eight years. See **mental retardation.** **2.** stupid or foolish person. —*adj.* imbecilic. [French *imbécile* weak, from Latin *imbēcillus* literally, without support, from *in-* not + *bacillus* little staff.]

im·be·cil·ic (im′bə sil′ik) *adj.* stupid or foolish: *imbecilic behavior.*

im·be·cil·i·ty (im′bə sil′ə tē) *pl.* **-ties.** *n.* **1.** moderate mental retardation. **2.** stupidity or foolishness.

im·bed (im bed′) embed.

im·bibe (im bīb′) **-bibed, -bib·ing.** *v.t.* **1.** to take into the mouth and swallow (liquid); drink. **2.** to take in as if by drinking; absorb. **3.** to take in and keep mentally: *Imbibe the precious truths* (Hervey, 1746). —*v.i.* to drink. ▲ often used euphemistically to refer to the drinking of alcoholic beverages. [Latin *imbibere* to drink in.] —**im·bib′er,** *n.*

im·bri·cate (*adj.* im′brə kit, -kāt′; *v.* im′brə kāt′) *adj.* **1.** arranged in a regular, overlapping pattern. **2.** decorated with a regular pattern of overlapping edges. —*v.t.* **-cat·ed, -cat·ing.** to overlap in a regular pattern. [Latin *imbricātus,* past participle of *imbricāre* to cover with tiles, from *imbrex* roof tile.]

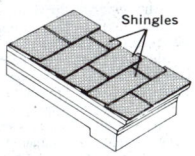
Shingles

Imbricate shingles

im·bri·ca·tion (im′brə kā′shən) *n.* **1.** an overlapping of the edges. **2.** decoration consisting of a regular pattern of overlapping edges.

im·bro·glio (im brōl′yō) *pl.* **-glios.** *n.* **1.a.** complicated dispute or disagreement: *The two neighbors got into an imbroglio over the boundaries of their property.* **b.** confused or complicated state of affairs. **2.** confused heap. [Italian *imbroglio* trouble, intrigue, from *imbrogliare* to confuse; of uncertain origin.]

im·brue (im brōō′) **-brued, -bru·ing.** *v.t.* to stain or soak, esp. with blood. [Old French *embruer* to moisten, possibly going back to Latin *in* in + *bibere* to drink.]

im·bue (im būˊ) **-bued, -bu·ing.** *v.t.* **1.** to pervade, permeate, or inspire, as with emotions, ideals, or opinions: *He was imbued with the spirit of justice.* **2.** to saturate, as with color. [Latin *imbuere* to moisten, stain, accustom.]

im·i·ta·ble (im′ə tə bəl) *adj.* capable of being imitated.

im·i·tate (im′ə tāt′) **-tat·ed, -tat·ing.** *v.t.* **1.** to follow or try to follow the example of: *The child imitated her older sister.* **2.** to reproduce the behavior or mannerisms of: *He imitated the president giving a speech.* **3.** to make a duplicate of: *His handwriting is difficult to imitate.* **4.** to have the appearance of; look like; resemble: *The floors are painted to imitate marble.* [Latin *imitātus,* past participle of *imitārī* to copy.] —**im′i·ta·tor,** *n.*

Syn. 1.,2. **Imitate, copy, mimic, ape** mean to follow or reproduce something very closely. **Imitate** means to emulate a model with fidelity to essentials but varying details: *The young writer tried to imitate Hemingway.* **Copy** means to imitate in every detail in order to resemble the original in every way: *Some American buildings have copied the classical style of ancient Greece.* **Mimic** means to simulate or reproduce another person's voice, mannerisms, or gestures in a clownish manner to achieve the effect of parody: *The actor amused the audience by mimicking some well-known people.* **Ape** means to emulate in a servile manner or with ludicrous results: *Barbara aped her older sister's dress and manners.*

im·i·ta·tion (im′ə tā′shən) *n.* **1.** act of imitating. **2.** result or product of imitating. **3.** reproduction, esp. one that is inferior in quality: *That is not an authentic Wedgwood vase, but merely an imitation.* —*adj.* made to counterfeit something genuine or superior; not genuine: *imitation mink.*

im·i·ta·tive (im′ə tā′tiv) *adj.* **1.** imitating or tending to imitate: *Chil-*

dren are very imitative of their elders. **2.** characterized by imitation: *Portrait painting is an imitative art.* **3.** not genuine: *imitative jewelry.* **4.** onomatopoetic. —**im′i·ta′tive·ly,** *adv.* —**im′i·ta′tive·ness,** *n.*

im·mac·u·late (i mak′yə lit) *adj.* **1.** free from dust, grime, or clutter; extremely clean or neat: *Her house is always immaculate.* **2.** free from spot or stain; unblemished: *an immaculate complexion.* **3.** free from fault; flawless: *He is an immaculate dresser.* **4.** free from sin; undefiled; pure. [Latin *immaculātus* unstained, going back to *in-* not + *macula* spot.] —**im·mac′u·late·ly,** *adv.* —**im·mac′u·late·ness,** *n.*

Immaculate Conception, Roman Catholic dogma that the Virgin Mary was conceived free from original sin.

im·ma·nent (im′ə nənt) *adj.* existing or remaining within; indwelling: *the idea of deity immanent in the universe.* [Late Latin *immanēns,* present participle of *immanēre* to dwell within, from Latin *in* in + *manēre* to remain.] —**im′ma·nence, im′ma·nen·cy,** *n.* —**im′ma·nent·ly,** *adv.*

Im·man·u·el (i man′ū əl) *also,* **Em·man·u·el.** *n.* the Messiah. [Hebrew *'Immānū'ēl* literally, God with us.]

im·ma·te·ri·al (im′ə tēr′ē əl) *adj.* **1.** of little or no significance or value; unimportant: *It is wholly immaterial to me what you decide.* **2.** not consisting of matter; incorporeal. —**im′ma·te′ri·al·ly,** *adv.* —**im′ma·te′ri·al·ness,** *n.*

im·ma·ture (im′ə choor′, -toor′, -tyoor′) *adj.* **1.** not having reached full growth or development; not mature. **2.** foolish, puerile, or infantile: *immature behavior.* —**im′ma·ture′ly,** *adv.* —**im·ma·ture′ness, im′ma·tu′ri·ty,** *n.*

im·meas·ur·a·ble (i mezh′ər ə bəl) *adj.* not capable of being measured; boundless. —**im·meas′ur·a·bly,** *adv.*

im·me·di·a·cy (i mē′dē ə sē) *n.* state or quality of being immediate.

im·me·di·ate (i mē′dē it) *adj.* **1.** occurring or accomplished without delay; instant: *We received an immediate reaction to our proposal. The commander ordered an immediate withdrawal of the troops.* **2.** of, relating to, or involving the present time: *We must take care of our immediate needs.* **3.** close in time or space; near: *the immediate neighborhood. We have no definite plans for the immediate future.* **4.** nearest in line or relationship: *the immediate family. He works closely with his immediate superiors.* **5.** acting or existing without any intervening agency; directly related: *The evidence has no immediate bearing on the case.* [Late Latin *immediātus* next, going back to Latin *in-* not + *medius* middle.] —**im·me′di·ate·ness,** *n.*

im·me·di·ate·ly (i mē′dē it lē) *adv.* **1.** without delay; at once; instantly: *She recognized him immediately.* **2.** without intervening time or space: *We saw him immediately after the accident.* **3.** without intervening agency; directly: *The airplane was immediately overhead.*

im·med·i·ca·ble (i med′i kə bəl) *adj.* incapable of being healed; incurable.

im·me·mo·ri·al (im′ə môr′ē əl) *adj.* extending back beyond memory or record; ancient. —**im′me·mo′ri·al·ly,** *adv.*

im·mense (i mens′) *adj.* of great size, extent, or degree; huge; vast. [Latin *immēnsus* literally, not measured.] —**im·mense′ly,** *adv.* —**im·mense′ness,** *n.* —**Syn.** see **huge.**

im·men·si·ty (i men′sə tē) *pl.* **-ties.** *n.* state or quality of being immense; hugeness; vastness.

im·merge (i murj′) **-merged, -merg·ing.** *v.t.* to immerse. [Latin *immergere* to plunge into.]

im·merse (i murs′) **-mersed, -mers·ing.** *v.t.* **1.** to plunge or dip into water or other liquid so as to cover completely. **2.** to baptize by immersion. **3.** to involve deeply; absorb: *He was immersed in his work.* [Latin *immersus,* past participle of *immergere* to plunge into.] —**Syn.** 1. see **dip.**

im·mer·sion (i mur′zhən, -shən) *n.* **1.** act of immersing; being immersed. **2.** method of baptism in which part or all of the body is submerged in water.

im·mi·grant (im′ə grənt) *n.* one who immigrates. —*adj.* coming into a country or region of which one is not a native in order to make a permanent residence there.

im·mi·grate (im′ə grāt′) **-grat·ed, -grat·ing.** *v.i.* **1.** to come into a country or region of which one is not a native in order to make a permanent residence there. —*v.t.* to bring in as immigrants. [Latin *immigrātus,* past participle of *immigrāre* to go into.]

im·mi·gra·tion (im′ə grā′shən) *n.* act of immigrating.

im·mi·nence (im′ə nəns) *n.* state or quality of being imminent. Also, **im′mi·nen·cy.**

im·mi·nent (im′ə nənt) *adj.* about to happen; impending; threatening. [Latin *imminēns,* present participle of *imminēre* to hang over, threaten.] —**im′mi·nent·ly,** *adv.*

im·mis·ci·ble (i mis′ə bəl) *adj.* not capable of being mixed.

im·mo·bile (i mō′bil, -bēl) *adj.* **1.** incapable of moving or of being moved; fixed. **2.** not moving; motionless. —**im′mo·bil′i·ty,** *n.*

im·mo·bi·lize (i mō′bə līz′) **-lized, -liz·ing.** *v.t.* to make immobile; fix in place. —**im·mo′bi·li·za′tion,** *n.*

at; āpe; cär; end; mē; it; īce; hot; ōld; fôrk; wood; fōōl; oil; out; up; ūse; turn; sing; thin; this; zh in treasure; ə in ago, taken, pencil, lemon, circus.

513

im·mod·er·ate (i mod'ər it) *adj.* exceeding usual or proper limits; not moderate. —**im·mod'er·ate·ly,** *adv.* —**im·mod'er·ate·ness, im·mod·er·a·tion** (i mod'ə rā'shən) , *n.* —**Syn.** see **excessive.**

im·mod·est (i mod'ist) *adj.* **1.** lacking or indicating a lack of shame, esp. about one's body. **2.** tending to take too much praise or credit; boastful. —**im·mod'est·ly,** *adv.* —**im·mod'es·ty,** *n.*

im·mo·late (im'ə lāt') **-lat·ed, -lat·ing.** *v.t.* **1.** to offer in sacrifice, esp. to kill as a sacrificial victim. **2.** to destroy, esp. by burning: *bombing which immolates whole cities.* [Latin *immolātus,* past participle of *immolāre* to sacrifice; literally, to sprinkle meal on a sacrificial victim, from *in* in, on + *mola* meal.] —**im'mo·la'tion, im'mo·la'tor,** *n.*

im·mor·al (i môr'əl, i mor'-) *adj.* violating morality; ethically wrong. —**im·mor'al·ly,** *adv.*

Syn. Immoral, amoral, unmoral mean not moral. **Immoral** means contrary to a moral code and disregarding ethical bounds and constraints: *The villain in that story is an immoral man who uses others to advance his own interests.* **Amoral** means indifferent to or unaffected by moral definition and judgment, thus constituting a passive negation of morality: *The laws of science are by their very nature amoral.* **Unmoral,** a rarer term, suggests a complete lack of morality and of the ability to distinguish between what is morally right and wrong: *Many primitive societies seem to be unmoral.*

im·mor·al·ist (i môr'ə list, i mor'-) *n.* advocate of immorality.

im·mo·ral·i·ty (im'ə ral'ə tē) *pl.,* **-ties.** *n.* **1.** immoral character or quality. **2.** immoral act.

im·mor·tal (i môr'əl) *adj.* **1.** not subject to death; living on after death. **2.** remembered or celebrated through all subsequent time: *Shakespeare's immortal works.* **3.** lasting through all time; existing forever; eternal. —*n.* **1.** immortal being, as a god in Greek mythology. **2.** person remembered or celebrated through all subsequent time. [Latin *immortālis* deathless, everlasting, going back to *in-* not + *mors* death.] —**im·mor'tal·ly,** *adv.*

im·mor·tal·i·ty (im'ôr tal'ə tē) *n.* **1.** supposed power of living on after death; not being subject to death. **2.** fact of being remembered or celebrated through all subsequent time. **3.** existence through all time; fact of being eternal.

im·mor·tal·ize (i môr'əl īz') **-ized, -iz·ing.** *v.t.* to make remembered or celebrated through all ages.

im·mor·telle (im'ôr tel') *n.* an everlasting plant or flower. [French *immortelle,* from Latin *immortālis* deathless. See IMMORTAL.]

im·mov·a·ble (i mōō'və bəl) *adj.* **1.** incapable of moving or being moved; fixed firmly in place; stationary. **2.** not easily altered or shaken; steadfast; unyielding: *Father was immovable in his opinions.* **3.** not easily stirred or affected by emotion: *an immovable audience.* —*n.* **immovables.** property that cannot be moved from place to place, as land; real property. —**im·mov'a·bil'i·ty, im·mov'a·ble·ness,** *n.* —**im·mov'a·bly,** *adv.*

im·mune (i mūn') *adj.* **1.** protected from a disease or infection, as by inoculation. **2.** not susceptible or responsive, as to something disagreeable or harmful: *immune to threats.* **3.** exempt, as from laws. [Latin *immūnis* exempt.]

im·mu·ni·ty (i mū'nə tē) *pl.,* **-ties.** *n.* **1.** resistance to a specific disease or infection because of the presence of antibodies. **2.** freedom or protection from anything disagreeable or harmful: *immunity from attack.* **3.** special exemption, as from laws. [Latin *immūnitās* exemption.] —**Syn. 3.** see **exemption.**

im·mu·nize (im'yə nīz') **-nized, -niz·ing.** *v.t.* to make immune, esp. from disease. —**im'mu·ni·za'tion,** *n.*

im·mu·nol·o·gy (im'yə nol'ə jē) *n.* branch of medical science dealing with immunity from disease.

im·mure (i myoor') **-mured, -mur·ing.** *v.t.* **1.** to enclose within walls in or as in a prison. **2.** to confine the attention of; involve completely; close off: *scientists immured in their work.* [Medieval Latin *immurare* to put within four walls, from Latin *in* in + *mūrus* wall.] —**im·mure'ment,** *n.*

im·mu·ta·ble (i mū'tə bəl) *adj.* not mutable; unchanging. —**im·mu·ta·bil'i·ty, im·mu'ta·ble·ness,** *n.* —**im·mu'ta·bly,** *adv.*

imp (imp) *n.* **1.** young or small demon; mischievous spirit. **2.** mischievous child. [Old English *impa* young shoot, graft, going back to Late Latin *impotus* a graft, from Greek *emphytos* engrafted. In English this word once meant young shoot or offspring of a family and later came to mean mischievous child or young demon.]

imp. 1. imperative. **2.** imperfect. **3.** import; imported. **4.** important. **5.** imprimatur.

im·pact (im'pakt) *n.* **1.a.** impetus or force of one object striking against another: *The car hit the stone wall with great impact.* **b.** action of one object striking against another: *The glass shattered upon impact. At the time of impact, the passenger had his seat belt on.* **2.** forcible impression or influence; strong effect: *the impact of trade on the economy.* [Latin *impactus,* past participle of *impingere* to strike against.]

im·pact·ed (im pak'tid) *adj.* **1.** (of a tooth) pressed between the jawbone and another tooth so that it cannot grow out. **2.** closely packed together or wedged in.

im·pair (im pâr') *v.t.* to lessen the quality, strength, or value of; damage; weaken: *The accident impaired his vision.* [Old French *empeirer,* going back to Latin *in* in + *pējor* worse.]

im·pair·ment (im pâr'mənt) *n.* act of impairing; being impaired.

im·pal·a (im pal'ə, -pä'lə) *n.* slender antelope, *Aepyceros melampus,* native to eastern and southern Africa, having a reddish or golden-brown coat, the male of which has curving black horns. It is noted for its speed and grace and can cover as much as thirty-five feet in one leap. Height: 3 feet at the shoulder. [Of Zulu origin.]

Impala

im·pale (im pāl') **-paled, -pal·ing.** *v.t.* **1.** to fix on a stake or other pointed object by piercing (with *on*). **2.** to torture or put to death in this way. [Medieval Latin *impalare,* going back to Latin *in* in, on + *pālus* stake.] —**im·pale'ment,** *n.*

im·pal·pa·ble (im pal'pə bəl) *adj.* **1.** incapable of being perceived by the sense of touch: *impalpable shadows.* **2.** not readily grasped by the mind; incomprehensible: *impalpable distinctions.* —**im·pal'pa·bil'i·ty,** *n.* —**im·pal'pa·bly,** *adv.*

im·pan·el (im pan'əl) **-eled, -el·ing;** *also,* British, **-elled, -el·ling.** *also,* **em·pan·el.** *v.t.* **1.** to place (someone) on a panel or list, as for jury duty. **2.** to select (a jury) from such a list. —**im·pan'el·ment,** *n.*

im·part (im pärt') *v.t.* **1.** to make known; disclose; tell: *to impart information.* **2.** to bestow; give: *to impart understanding and good will.* [Latin *impartīre* to share with, going back to *in* in + *pars* portion, share.] —**Syn. 1.** see **communicate.**

im·par·tial (im pär'shəl) *adj.* not favoring one more than another; without prejudice; unbiased. —**im·par'tial·ly,** *adv.* —**Syn.** see **just.**

im·par·ti·al·i·ty (im pär'shē al'ə tē) *n.* freedom from bias; fairness.

im·pass·a·ble (im pas'ə bəl) *adj.* that cannot be passed or traveled over, across, or through: *an impassable road.* —**im·pass'a·bil'i·ty, im·pass'a·ble·ness,** *n.* —**im·pass'a·bly,** *adv.*

Syn. Impassable, impenetrable, impervious mean not admitting passage. **Impassable** applies to land or water that is difficult or impossible to cross because of some insurmountable obstacle: *That dirt road is impassable during the rainy season.* **Impenetrable** applies to things that are so thick and dense that nothing can pierce or penetrate them: *Armor plate is impenetrable by ordinary bullets.* **Impervious** refers to materials and substances that are resistant to passage or pervasion by their very nature: *This coating is impervious to water.*

im·passe (im'pas, im pas') *n.* **1.** position or situation from which proceeding or advancing is impossible: *The jury reached an impasse in its deliberations.* **2.** road or passage open only at one end; dead end. [French *impasse,* from *in-* not (from Latin *in-*) + *passer* to go across. See PASS.]

im·pas·si·ble (im pas'ə bəl) *adj.* **1.** incapable of suffering or pain. **2.** not subject to injury or harm; invulnerable. **3.** impassive. [Church Latin *impassibilis* incapable of suffering, going back to Latin *in-* not + *passus,* past participle of *patī* to suffer.]

im·pas·sioned (im pash'ənd) *adj.* filled with passion or strong feeling; fiery; ardent.

Syn. Impassioned, ardent, fervent mean manifesting or characterized by intense feeling. **Impassioned** applies to feelings and expressions of great emotional intensity and sincerity that are capable of stirring equally intense responses: *The president made an impassioned speech for national unity.* **Ardent** suggests vehemence of emotion and depth of commitment and devotion, esp. to a cause or person: *Nathan Hale was an ardent patriot.* **Fervent** usually indicates sustained and heartfelt emotion, sometimes openly and warmly expressed, but not necessarily displayed outwardly: *The soldiers maintained a fervent loyalty to the general who had led them to victory.*

im·pas·sive (im pas'iv) *adj.* not feeling or showing emotion; apathetic; unmoved. —**im·pas'sive·ly,** *adv.* —**im·pas'sive·ness, im'pas·siv'i·ty,** *n.*

im·pa·tience (im pā'shəns) *n.* **1.** inability to tolerate or endure irritation, delay, or opposition; lack of patience. **2.** restless eagerness, as for change or activity.

im·pa·tient (im pā'shənt) *adj.* **1.** unable to tolerate or endure irritation, delay, or opposition. **2.** showing lack of patience: *an impatient expression.* **3.** restlessly eager: *to be impatient for the weekend to come.* **4.** intolerant (with *of*): *Mother was impatient of bad manners.* —**im·pa'tient·ly,** *adv.*

im·peach (im pēch') *v.t.* **1.** to charge (a public official) before a competent tribunal for crime or misconduct in office. **2.** to question,

at; āpe; cär; end; mē; it; īce; hot; ōld; fôrk; wood; fōōl; oil; out; up; ūse; turn; sing; thin; this; zh in treasure; ə in ago, taken, pencil, lemon, circus.

challenge, or cast doubt on: *The defense attorney impeached the credibility of the witness.* [Old French *empe(s)cher* to hinder, from Late Latin *impedicāre* to entangle, from Latin *in* in, on + *pedica* fetter.]

im·peach·a·ble (im pē′chə bəl) *adj.* **1.** liable to be impeached. **2.** making liable to impeachment: *an impeachable offense.* —**im·peach′a·bil′i·ty,** *n.*

im·peach·ment (im pēch′mənt) *n.* **1.** act of impeaching; being impeached. **2.a.** arraignment of a public official before a competent tribunal. **b.** in the United States, the presentation of formal charges against a federal official by the House of Representatives with a trial held before the Senate.

im·pearl (im purl′) *v.t.* **1.** to form into pearl-like drops. **2.** to make pearly. **3.** to adorn with pearls or pearl-like drops.

im·pec·ca·ble (im pek′ə bəl) *adj.* **1.** free from error or defect; faultless; flawless: *impeccable taste, impeccable judgment.* **2.** incapable of sinning or doing wrong; unerring. [Latin *impeccābilis,* from *in-* not + *peccāre* to sin.] —**im·pec′ca·bil′i·ty,** *n.* —**im·pec′ca·bly,** *adv.*

im·pe·cu·ni·ous (im′pi kū′nē əs) *adj.* having no money; poor; penniless. [IN-¹ + Latin *pecūniōsus* rich, from *pecūnia* money, from *pecu* cattle (wealth in early times being computed in terms of the number of cattle owned).] —**im·pe·cu′ni·ous·ly,** *adv.*

im·ped·ance (im pēd′əns) *n.* opposition that an electrical circuit offers to the flow of an alternating current.

im·pede (im pēd′) *-ped·ed, -ped·ing. v.t.* to retard or hinder the progress or action of; obstruct. [Latin *impedīre* literally, to entangle the feet, from *in* in, on + *pēs* foot (originally referring to the fettering of slaves' feet to hinder their movements).] —**Syn.** see **hinder¹.**

im·ped·i·ment (im ped′ə mənt) *n.* **1.** that which impedes; obstruction; obstacle. **2.** physical defect, esp. of speech. [Latin *impedīmentum* hindrance, from *impedīre.* See IMPEDE.] —**Syn. 1.** see **encumbrance, obstacle.**

im·ped·i·men·ta (im ped′e men′tə) *n.,pl.* things that impede, esp. the baggage, equipment, or supplies of an army. [Latin *impedīmenta* baggage, plural of *impedīmentum* hindrance. See IMPEDIMENT.]

im·pel (im pel′) *-pelled, -pel·ling. v.t.* **1.** to drive or urge to some action: *War impelled them to leave the country.* **2.** to propel or cause to move forward: *The boat was impelled by a strong wind.* [Latin *impellere* to drive on or against.]

im·pel·ler (im pel′ər) *n.* **1.** one who or that which impels. **2.** rotor, as of a pump or blower, for transmitting motion.

im·pend (im pend′) *v.i.* **1.** to be about to occur; threaten: *a storm impended.* **2.** to be suspended; hang (with *over*): *The cliffs impend over the road.* [Latin *impendēre.*]

im·pend·ent (im pen′dənt) *adj.* impending.

im·pend·ing (im pen′ding) *adj.* about to occur; threatening: *an impending crisis.*

im·pen·e·tra·ble (im pen′ə trə bəl) *adj.* **1.** that cannot be pierced, entered, or passed through: *an impenetrable forest.* **2.** impervious, as to influences or ideas. **3.** incapable of being comprehended; inscrutable: *an impenetrable mystery.* —**im·pen′e·tra·bil′i·ty,** *n.* —**im·pen′e·tra·bly,** *adv.* —**Syn.** see **impassable.**

im·pen·i·tent (im pen′ə tənt) *adj.* not penitent; obdurate. —**im·pen′i·tence,** *n.* —**im·pen′i·tent·ly,** *adv.*

imper., imperative.

im·per·a·tive (im per′ə tiv) *adj.* **1.** not to be avoided or evaded; absolutely necessary; urgent: *It is imperative that we leave at once.* **2.** of the nature of or expressing a command; commanding; authoritative: *an imperative tone of voice.* **3.** of, relating to, or designating the grammatical mood used to express commands, requests, or exhortations. —*n.* **1.** that which is imperative, as a command or obligation. **2.a.** imperative mood. **b.** verb or verb form in this mood. [Late Latin *imperātīvus* relating to a command, from Latin *imperātum* command.] —**im·per′a·tive·ly,** *adv.* —**im·per′a·tive·ness,** *n.* —**Syn. adj.** see **urgent.**

im·pe·ra·tor (im′pə rā′tər) *n.* **1.a.** Roman emperor. ▲ often used as a title. ▲ a victorious Roman general. ▲ conferred as an honorary title. **2.** any emperor. [Latin *imperātor,* from *imperāre* to command.]

im·per·cep·ti·ble (im′pər sep′tə bəl) *adj.* **1.** too slight, gradual, delicate, or subtle to be easily perceived: *imperceptible changes.* **2.** not perceptible by the mind or senses. —**im′per·cep′ti·bil′i·ty,** *n.* —**im′per·cep′ti·bly,** *adv.*

imperf., imperfect.

im·per·fect (im pur′fikt) *adj.* **1.** not perfect; faulty: *an imperfect diamond.* **2.** not fully developed, formed, or done; incomplete. **3.** of, relating to, or designating the verbal tense that expresses action, usually in the past, that is continuous or not completed. —*n.* the imperfect tense, expressed in English by the use of progressive verb forms, as *was reading.* —**im·per′fect·ly,** *adv.* —**im·per′fect·ness,** *n.* —**Syn. adj. 1.** see **faulty.**

im·per·fec·tion (im′pər fek′shən) *n.* **1.** state or quality of being imperfect. **2.** defect; flaw: *There was an imperfection in the cloth.*

im·per·fo·rate (im pur′fər it, -fə rāt′) *adj.* **1.** having no holes or openings; not perforated. **2.** (of stamps) not separated by rows of perforations.

im·pe·ri·al (im pēr′ē əl) *adj.* **1.** of or relating to an empire or to the rule of an emperor or empress. **2.** of or relating to a country's military, political, or economic power or influence over other countries or tributaries. **3.** of, relating to, or having the rank of emperor or empress. **4.a.** having great dignity; majestic; magnificent. **b.** overbearing; imperious: *a haughty and imperial manner.* **5.** of imposing size or superior quality. **6.** conforming to the official British standard of weights and measures. —*n.* small, pointed beard growing on the chin. [Late Latin *imperiālis* relating to an empire, from *imperium* rule, empire.] —**pe′ri·al·ly,** *adv.*

im·pe·ri·al·ism (im pēr′ē ə liz′əm) *n.* **1.** policy of extending a country's power or influence over other countries by military, political, or economic means. **2.** imperial system of government; rule of an emperor.

im·pe·ri·al·ist (im pēr′ē ə list) *n.* **1.** one who favors or supports imperialism. **2.** one who engages in imperialism. —*adj.* of or relating to imperialism. —**im·pe′ri·al·is′tic,** *adj.* —**im·pe′ri·al·is′ti·cal·ly,** *adv.*

Imperial Valley, low-lying, productive farming region in southeastern California and a small portion of northeastern Baja California, Mexico.

im·per·il (im per′əl) *-iled, -il·ing; also, British, -illed, -il·ling. v.t.* to expose to danger; put in peril.

Syn. Imperil, endanger, jeopardize mean to expose to harm, loss, or injury. **Imperil,** the strongest word, means to expose to a threat or concrete danger and implies that the danger is imminent or certain: *Water pollution imperils all kinds of marine life.* **Endanger** suggests a threat not so immediate or severe and more possible to avoid: *The sudden squall endangered the small boat.* **Jeopardize** implies only a vulnerability or susceptibility to a danger, with the chances of its being avoided generally as great as those of its overtaking one: *Reforms too long delayed or denied have jeopardized peace* (F. Roosevelt, 1944).

im·pe·ri·ous (im pēr′ē əs) *adj.* **1.** dictatorial; domineering; overbearing. **2.** imperative; urgent: *an imperious necessity.* [Latin *imperiōsus* powerful, tyrannical, from *imperium* rule, empire.] —**im·pe′ri·ous·ly,** *adv.* —**im·pe′ri·ous·ness,** *n.*

im·per·ish·a·ble (im per′i shə bəl) *adj.* not subject to destruction or decay; not perishable; enduring. —**im·per′ish·a·bil′i·ty,** *n.* —**im·per′ish·a·bly,** *adv.*

im·pe·ri·um (im pēr′ē əm) *pl.,* **-pe·ri·a** (-pēr′ē ə). *n.* **1.** supreme power or authority. **2.** the right to command, esp. the right to use the force of the state to enforce its laws. [Latin *imperium* rule, empire.]

im·per·ma·nent (im pur′mə nənt) *adj.* subject to change; not permanent; transient. —**im·per′ma·nence,** *n.* —**im·per′ma·nen·cy,** *n.* —**im·per′ma·nent·ly,** *adv.*

im·per·me·a·ble (im pur′mē ə bəl) *adj.* not capable of being permeated; impenetrable.

im·per·mis·si·ble (im′pər mis′ə bəl) *adj.* not permissible. —**im′per·mis′si·bil′i·ty,** *n.* —**im′per·mis′si·bly,** *adv.*

im·per·son·al (im pur′sən əl) *adj.* **1.** not concerned with a particular person or persons; not personal: *an impersonal consideration.* **2.** not existing as a person: *an impersonal deity.* **3.** *Grammar.* **a.** (of a verb) denoting an action by an unspecified subject, used in the third person singular, as *rained* in *It rained for several days.* **b.** (of a pronoun) referring to an indefinite subject. —**im·per·son·al·i·ty** (im pur′sə-nal′ə tē), *n.* —**im·per′son·al·ly,** *adv.*

im·per·son·al·ize (im pur′sən əl īz′) *v.t.* to make impersonal.

im·per·son·ate (im pur′sən nāt′) *-at·ed, -at·ing. v.t.* **1.** to take on or reproduce the appearance, behavior, or mannerisms of: *He was arrested for impersonating a police officer.* **2.** to act the part of (a character) in a play. [IM-² + Latin *persōna* mask + -ATE¹ (suggesting the putting on of a mask, with reference to the use of masks in the ancient Greek or Roman theater).] —**im·per′son·a′tion,** *n.* —**im·per′son·a′tor,** *n.*

im·per·ti·nence (im purt′ən əns) *n.* **1.** offensive boldness or rudeness; insolence. **2.** impertinent act or remark. **3.** lack of pertinence; inappropriateness. —**im·per′ti·nen·cy.**

im·per·ti·nent (im purt′ən ənt) *adj.* **1.** offensively bold or rude; insolent. **2.** not pertinent; inappropriate. —**im·per′ti·nent·ly,** *adv.*

im·per·turb·a·ble (im′pər tur′bə bəl) *adj.* not easily excited or disturbed; calm. —**im′per·turb′a·bil′i·ty,** *n.* —**im′per·turb′a·bly,** *adv.*

im·per·vi·ous (im pur′vē əs) *adj.* **1.** not easily affected, influenced, or disturbed; unreceptive: *impervious to criticism.* **2.** incapable of being passed through or penetrated; impenetrable. —**im·per′vi·ous·ness,** *n.* —**Syn. 2.** see **impassable.**

im·pe·ti·go (im′pə tē′gō, -tī′-) *n.* contagious disease affecting outer layers of the skin, characterized by small blisters that break open and release pus. [Latin *impetīgō,* from *impetere* to attack.]

im·pet·u·os·i·ty (im pech′ōō os′ə tē) *pl.,* **-ties.** *n.* state or quality of being impetuous.

im·pet·u·ous (im pech′ōō əs) *adj.* **1.** rushing headlong into things; impulsive and energetic. **2.** made or done impulsively and suddenly; rash: *an impetuous choice.* **3.** moving with great force or violence; rapid; furious: *impetuous winds.* [Late Latin *impetuōsus* violent, from Latin *impetus* attack.] —**im·pet′u·ous·ness**, *n.*

im·pe·tus (im′pə təs) *n.* **1.a.** momentum of a moving body. **b.** force which puts a body in motion. **2.** strength; push; energy: *The exposure of widespread graft among city officials gave great impetus to demands for reform.* **3.** motive; incentive: *The impetus that produced the age of exploration was the increased need for trade.* [Latin *impetus* attack.]

im·pi·e·ty (im pī′ə tē) *pl.* **-ties.** *n.* **1.** lack of reverence for the gods or a god. **2.** lack of dutifulness or respect toward those deserving of respect. **3.** an impious act.

im·pinge (im pinj′) **-pinged, -ping·ing.** *v.i.* **1.** to come into contact with; come right up to; border: *A full answer to the child's question impinges on the most difficult areas of physics.* **2.** to encroach; infringe: *to impinge upon another's domain.* **3.** to strike or dash; collide (with *on, upon,* or *against*). [Latin *impingere* to strike against.] —**im·pinge′ment**, *n.*

im·pi·ous (im′pē əs) *adj.* **1.** lacking in reverence for a god or a god; irreligious. **2.** undutiful or disrespectful. —**im′pi·ous·ness**, *n.*

imp·ish (im′pish) *adj.* of or like an imp; mischievous: *an impish grin.* —**imp′ish·ly**, *adv.* —**imp′ish·ness**, *n.*

im·plac·a·ble (im plak′ə bəl, -plā′kə-) *adj.* **1.** that cannot be placated or appeased. **2.** unchanging; inexorable; relentless. —**im·plac′a·bil′i·ty**, *n.* —**im·pla′ca·bly**, *adv.*

im·plant (*v.,* im plant′; *n.,* im′plant′) *v.t.* **1.** to fix firmly and deeply; instill: *Nature has implanted fear in all living creatures* (Bacon, 1627). **2.** to set; root; embed: *The old tree stump was firmly implanted in the ground.* **3.** to insert (tissue or a device) in the body by surgery. —*n.* tissue or device surgically inserted in the body.

im·plan·ta·tion (im′plan tā′shən) *n.* **1.** act of implanting; state of being implanted. **2.** something implanted.

im·plau·si·ble (im plô′zə bəl) *adj.* not believable; unlikely: *an implausible explanation.* —**im·plau′si·bil′i·ty**, *n.* —**im·plau′si·bly**, *adv.*

im·ple·ment (*n.,* im′plə mənt; *v.,* im′plə ment′) *n.* **1.** tool; instrument. **2.** one who serves as a tool or agent: *This man was a most useful implement to us everywhere* (Defoe, 1719). —*v.t.* **1.** to put into effect; make actual; carry out: *to implement a decision of the court, to implement a proposal.* **2.** to provide with implements. [Late Latin *implēmentum* a filling up, instrument, from Latin *implēre* to fill, fulfill.]
Syn. n. 1. Implement, tool, instrument refer to devices for performing or facilitating work. **Implement** is a device functionally designed to assist in the performance of a manual or mechanical operation: *That factory makes agricultural implements.* **Tool** is the preferred term when referring to technical implements that are used by artisans, mechanics, and craftsmen in their work: *A carpenter's tools include saws, hammers, and screwdrivers.* **Instrument** is a device that is made with great precision and is used for work requiring a high degree of accuracy, as surgery and science: *The stethoscope is a medical instrument.*

im·pli·cate (im′plə kāt′) **-cat·ed, -cat·ing.** *v.t.* **1.** to claim or show to be also involved, as in a crime or conspiracy: *The suspect implicated his girl friend.* **2.** to connect; involve; include (often with *in*): *Police believe many officials are implicated in the attempt to embezzle funds.* **3.** *Archaic.* to imply. **4.** *Archaic.* to fold or twist together; entangle; intertwine. [Latin *implicātus,* past participle of *implicāre* to infold, imply.] —**Syn. 1. see involve.**

im·pli·ca·tion (im′plə kā′shən) *n.* **1.a.** that which is logically implied; requirement or consequence: *a decision with many implications for the future.* **b.** that which is hinted or suggested, but not directly expressed: *Did you gather the implications of her remark?* **2.** act of implicating or state of being implicated, as in a crime. **3.** act of implying; state of being implied.

im·plic·it (im plis′it) *adj.* **1.** suggested or understood, though not directly expressed: *conclusions that are implicit and must be drawn out by the reader.* **2.** without reservation or doubt; unquestioning; absolute: *implicit faith, implicit confidence.* **3.** contained in the nature of something, though not apparent; latent; potential: *implicit ability.* [Latin *implicitus,* the later past participle of *implicāre* to infold, involve.] —**im·plic′it·ly**, *adv.* —**im·plic′it·ness**, *n.*

im·plied (im plīd′) *adj.* involved, suggested, or required without being directly expressed.

im·pli·ed·ly (im plī′id lē) *adv.* by implication.

im·plode (im plōd′) *v.i.* to explode inward.

im·plore (im plôr′) **-plored, -plor·ing.** *v.t.* **1.** to call upon in supplication; ask earnestly; beseech: *They implored the sheriff to stay and protect them.* **2.** to beg or pray for earnestly: *to implore aid or pardon.* [Latin *implōrāre* to invoke with tears, beseech.] —**im·plor′er**, *n.* —**im·plor′ing·ly**, *adv.* —**Syn. 1. see beg.**

im·plo·sion (im plō′zhən) *n.* explosion inward.

im·ply (im plī′) **-plied, -ply·ing.** *v.t.* **1.** to indicate or suggest without direct statement: *Are you implying that I caused the trouble?* **2.** to involve as a necessary part, condition, or consequence; require the truth of: *"John has left" implies "John has been here."* ▲ see **infer** for usage note. [Middle French *emplier* to infold, involve, from Latin *implicāre.* Doublet of EMPLOY, IMPLICATE.]

im·po·lite (im′pə līt′) *adj.* not having or exhibiting good manners; not courteous; rude. [Latin *impolītus* rough, unpolished.] —**im′po·lite′ly**, *adv.* —**im′po·lite′ness**, *n.*

im·pol·i·tic (im pol′ə tik) *adj.* not conforming to good policy; not politic; inexpedient.

im·pon·der·a·ble (im pon′dər ə bəl) *adj.* not capable of being weighed or evaluated with certainty. —*n.* imponderable thing or factor: *There are too many imponderables for a hasty decision.* —**im·pon′der·a·bil′i·ty, im·pon′der·a·ble·ness**, *n.* —**im·pon′der·a·bly**, *adv.*

im·port (*v.,* im pôrt′; *n.,* im′pôrt′) *v.t.* **1.a.** to bring in (goods) from a foreign country for commercial purposes. **b.** to bring in or introduce from an external or foreign source: *to import ideas.* **2.** to mean: *What do his words import for us?* —*v.i.* to be of importance; matter. —*n.* **1.** that which is imported for commercial purposes. **2.** act of importing goods; importation. **3.** meaning. **4.** consequence; importance: *That is a matter of great import.* [Latin *importāre* to carry in.] —**im·port′a·bil′i·ty, im·port′er**, *n.* ⌐**im·port′a·ble**, *adj.*

im·por·tance (im pôr′təns) *n.* **1.** state or quality of being important. **2.** special authority, social position, or influence.

im·por·tant (im pôr′ənt) *adj.* **1.** having special value, relevance, or meaning: *Your friendship is very important to him.* **2.** having special authority, social position, or influence: *Joel always cultivates the important people and ignores old friends.* **3.** having or giving the impression of a false or exaggerated sense of importance: *He had an important air about him.* [French *important* of consequence, from Medieval Latin *importans,* present participle of *importāre* to be of weight or force, from Latin *importāre* to carry in.] —**im·por′tant·ly**, *adv.*

im·por·ta·tion (im′pôr tā′shən) *n.* **1.** act of importing. **2.** that which is imported.

im·por·tu·nate (im pôr′chə nit) *adj.* annoyingly or stubbornly persistent; insistent: *an importunate salesman, an importunate demand.* —**im·por′tu·nate·ly**, *adv.* —**im·por′tu·nate·ness**, *n.*

im·por·tune (im′pər tōōn′, -tün′, -pôr-, im pôr′chən) **-tuned, -tun·ing.** *v.t.* to trouble with persistent requests or demands. —*adj.* importunate. [Medieval Latin *importunari* to be troublesome, from Latin *importūnus* difficult of access, unsuitable; literally, lacking a harbor, from *in-* not + *portus* harbor.] —**im′por·tune′ly**, *adv.* —**im′por·tun′er**, *n.*

im·por·tu·ni·ty (im′pər tōō′nə tē, -tü′-, -pôr-) *pl.* **-ties.** *n.* **1.** act of importuning. **2.** state of being importunate. **3. importunities.** persistent requests or demands.

im·pose (im pōz′) **-posed, -pos·ing.** *v.t.* **1.** to establish or apply by legal means as an obligation: *to impose taxes, to impose a penalty.* **2.** to inflict or enforce by or as by authority: *to impose one's will on others.* **3.** to thrust (oneself) upon others. **4.** to pass off (something false or worthless) as genuine or valuable. **5.** to arrange (type or plates) for printing so that the printed sheets will be in proper order when folded. —*v.i.* **1.** to thrust oneself upon others; intrude. **2.** to take advantage of (with *on* or *upon*): *He imposed upon my good will.* [French *imposer* to put on, inflict; a modification (influenced by French *poser* to place, put) of Latin *impōnere* to place on, deceive.] —**im·pos′er**, *n.*

im·pos·ing (im pō′zing) *adj.* marked by great size or dignity; exciting awe or admiration; impressive. —**im·pos′ing·ly**, *adv.*

im·po·si·tion (im′pə zish′ən) *n.* **1.** act of imposing. **2.** that which is imposed. **3.** act or process of arranging type or plates for printing so that the printed sheets will be in proper order when they are folded.

im·pos·si·bil·i·ty (im pos′ə bil′ə tē, im′pos-) *pl.* **-ties.** *n.* **1.** state or quality of being impossible. **2.** something impossible.

im·pos·si·ble (im pos′ə bəl) *adj.* **1.a.** not capable of coming into being or occurring; not possible: *It is impossible for a man to live forever.* **b.** not capable of being realized or accomplished; not feasible; impracticable: *That is an impossible scheme.* **2.** not likely to occur; not probable: *Winning the sweepstakes is an impossible dream.* **3.** not capable of being endured; extremely objectionable; intolerable: *He is an impossible person to work with. This is an impossible situation.* **4.** not acceptable as truth; inconceivable: *an impossible story.* —**im·pos′si·bly**, *adv.*

im·post¹ (im′pōst) *n.* duty, esp. on imported goods. [Medieval Latin *impostus,* past participle of *impōnere* to place on.]

im·post² (im′pōst) *n.* uppermost part of

Impost²

at; āpe; cär; end; mē; it; īce; hot; ōld; fôrk; wood; fōōl; out; up; ūse; turn; sing; thin; this; zh in treasure; ə in ago, taken, pencil, lemon, circus.

a pillar, wall, or column, usually serving as a support for an arch. [Italian *imposta* upper part of a column, from *imporre* to place on, from Latin *impōnere*.]

im·pos·tor (im pos′tər) *n.* one who deceives, esp. by assuming the name or character of another. [Late Latin *impostor*, from Latin *impōnere* to place on, deceive.]

im·pos·ture (im pos′chər) *n.* deception, esp. fraudulent impersonation. [Late Latin *impostūra*, from Latin *impōnere* to place on, deceive.]

im·po·tence (im′pət əns) *n.* quality or condition of being impotent. Also, **im′po·ten·cy.**

im·po·tent (im′pət ənt) *adj.* **1.** lacking force or effectiveness; helpless. **2.** physically weak. **3.** (of males) incapable of engaging in sexual intercourse. [Latin *impotēns* powerless.] —**im′po·tent·ly,** *adv.*

im·pound (im pound′) *v.t.* **1.** to shut up in a pound: *to impound a stray dog.* **2.** to seize and put in the custody of a court of law. **3.** to collect (water), as in a reservoir. —**im·pound′er, im·pound′ment,** *n.*

im·pov·er·ish (im pov′ər ish, -pov′rish) *v.t.* **1.** to reduce to poverty. **2.** to deprive, as of strength, richness, or resources: *to impoverish the mind.* [Old French *empoveriss-*, a stem of *empoverir* to make poor, going back to Latin *in* in + *pauper* poor.] —**im·pov′er·ish·ment,** *n.*

im·pow·er (im pou′ər) empower.

im·prac·ti·ca·ble (im prak′ti kə bəl) *adj.* **1.** incapable of being accomplished, carried out, or put into practice: *an economically impracticable plan.* **2.** incapable of being used; unserviceable: *an impracticable mechanism.* —**im·prac′ti·ca·bil′i·ty,** *n.* —**im·prac′ti·ca·bly,** *adv.*

im·prac·ti·cal (im prak′ti kəl) *adj.* not practical. —**im·prac′ti·cal·i·ty** (im prak′ti kal′ə tē), *n.*

im·pre·cate (im′pri kāt′) -cat·ed, -cat·ing. *v.t.* to invoke or call down (evil or harm). [Latin *imprecātus*, past participle of *imprecārī* to call down on.] —**im′pre·ca·tor,** *n.* —**im·pre·ca·to·ry** (im′pri kə tôr′ē), *adj.*

im·pre·ca·tion (im′pri kā′shən) *n.* **1.** act of imprecating. **2.** a curse.

im·pre·cise (im′pri sīs′) *adj.* not precise; inexact; vague. —**im′pre·cise′ly,** *adv.* —**im·pre·ci·sion** (im′pri sizh′ən), *n.*

im·preg·na·ble (im preg′nə bəl) *adj.* **1.** incapable of being taken by force; able to resist attack: *an impregnable fortress.* **2.** incapable of being moved, shaken, or overcome; firm: *impregnable virtue.* [Old French *imprenable* untakable, from Latin *in-*) + *prenable.* See PREGNABLE.] —**im·preg′na·bil′i·ty,** *n.* —**im·preg′na·bly,** *adv.* —**Syn. 1.** see invincible.

im·preg·nate (im preg′nāt) -nat·ed, -nat·ing. *v.t.* **1.** to make pregnant; cause to conceive. **2.** to fertilize, as an ovum. **3.** to cause to be saturated, as with a liquid; permeate. **4.** to imbue or fill, as with ideas or feelings. —*adj.* made pregnant. [Late Latin *impraegnātus*, past participle of *impraegnāre* to make pregnant, from Latin *in* in + *praegnāns* with child.] —**im·preg′na·tor,** *n.*

im·preg·na·tion (im′preg nā′shən) *n.* **1.** act of impregnating; being impregnated. **2.** that with which anything is impregnated.

im·pre·sa·ri·o (im′prə sär′ē ō′) *pl.* **-sa·ri·os.** *n.* one who organizes or manages live entertainment events, esp. ballets, operas, or concerts. [Italian *impresario* manager, from *impresa* undertaking, going back to Latin *in* in, on + *prehendere* to take.]

im·pre·scrip·ti·ble (im′pri skrip′tə bəl) *adj.* that cannot legally be withdrawn or revoked; not subject to invalidation. —**im′pre·scrip′ti·bil′i·ty,** *n.* —**im′pre·scrip′ti·bly,** *adv.*

im·press¹ (*v.,* im pres′; *n.,* im′pres′) **-pressed** or (*archaic*) **-prest, -press·ing.** *v.t.* **1.** to influence or produce a strong effect on the mind or feelings of: *The speaker's sincerity impressed us.* **2.** to strike in a specified manner: *She impressed me as being very rude.* **3.** to fix firmly in the mind or memory: *He had the power to impress his beliefs on others.* **4.** to form or make a mark or design on: *to impress wax.* **5.** to form or make by pressing or stamping: *to impress figures on coins.* **6.** to apply with pressure: *to impress a seal into wax.* —*n.* **1.** act of forming or making a mark or design on something by pressing or stamping. **2.** mark or design made in this way. [Latin *impressus*, past participle of *imprimere* to press into, imprint.] —**im·press′er,** *n.*

im·press² (im pres′) **-pressed** or (*archaic*) **-prest, -press·ing.** *v.t.* **1.** to compel by illegal means to enter the military service, esp. the navy. **2.** to seize (property) for public use. [IN-² + PRESS².]

im·press·i·ble (im pres′ə bəl) *adj.* impressionable. —**im·press′i·bil′i·ty,** *n.*

im·pres·sion (im presh′ən) *n.* **1.** effect or influence produced on the mind, senses, or feelings: *The experience left a lasting impression on me.* **2.** generalized feeling or judgment about someone or something: *My first impression of him proved to be correct.* **3.** notion or belief: *We were under the impression that they were brothers.* **4.** mark or design produced by pressing or stamping: *We made impressions of our hands in the wet concrete.* **5.** impersonation; imitation: *The child gave his impression of a monkey.* **6.** act or process of impressing. **7.a.** process of pressing plates or type onto a surface, esp. paper; printing. **b.** printed

copy. **c.** total number of copies of a book or publication printed at one time. **8.** mold or imprint of a tooth or the teeth and surrounding tissues, made in plaster, wax, or plastic.

im·pres·sion·a·ble (im presh′ə nə bəl, -presh′nə-) *adj.* easily impressed or influenced; very receptive to impressions. —**im·pres′sion·a·bil′i·ty,** *n.*

im·pres·sion·ism (im presh′ə niz′əm) *n.* **1.** method or school of painting developed in the late nineteenth century by French painters, as Monet and Renoir, characterized by a careful study of nature and the direct observation of the effects of light and color on a subject at a given moment. **2.** method and style of musical composition of the late nineteenth and early twentieth centuries, typified by the works of Debussy and Ravel, in which mood, atmosphere, and emotions are subtly evoked by characteristic harmonies and tonal progressions. —**im·pres′sion·ist,** *n., adj.* —**im·pres′sion·is′tic,** *adj.*

im·pres·sive (im pres′iv) *adj.* producing or tending to make a strong impression; exciting attention, emotion, or admiration: *an impressive feat of strength, an impressive display of silver.* —**im·pres′sive·ly,** *adv.* —**im·pres′sive·ness,** *n.*

im·press·ment (im pres′mənt) *n.* **1.** act of impressing men into military service, esp. the navy. **2.** act of seizing property for public use.

im·prest (im prest′) *Archaic.* past tense and past participle of **impress.**

im·pri·ma·tur (im′pri mä′tər, -mā′-) *n.* **1.** official license authorizing or approving the printing and publication of a book or article, esp. such a license granted by prelates of the Roman Catholic Church. **2.** any authorization or sanction; approval. [Modern Latin *imprimatur* let it be printed, from Latin *imprimere* to press into, imprint.]

im·print (*n.,* im′print′; *v.,* im print′) *n.* **1.** mark or depression produced by pressing or stamping: *His head left an imprint on the pillow.* **2.** effect; mark: *Years of poverty left their imprint on his personality.* **3.a.** publisher's name, the place and date of publication, and sometimes a trademark, usually printed on the title page. **b.** printer's name and address on any printed matter. —*v.t.* **1.** to make or produce (a mark or design) by pressing or stamping. **2.** to mark, or produce a mark or design on, by pressing or stamping; print. **3.** to fix firmly in the mind or memory.

im·pris·on (im priz′ən) *v.t.* **1.** to put or keep in prison. **2.** to confine or restrain in any way: *The figures seemed to be imprisoned in the marble.* —**im·pris′on·ment,** *n.*

Syn. 1. Imprison, jail, intern¹, incarcerate mean to confine in or as in a prison. **Imprison** usually suggests a long confinement in penal custody, esp. after sentencing: *The man was imprisoned for grand larceny.* **Jail** implies that the confinement is for a short period, for a minor offense, or while one is awaiting trial: *The judge jailed the young offender for thirty days.* **Intern** has distinct military associations and means to confine to a specified area or within certain limitations: *The crew of the enemy plane was interned until the end of the war.* **Incarcerate,** a more formal term, emphasizes the fact of confinement rather than the duration or conditions: *The state does not incarcerate first offenders.*

im·prob·a·bil·i·ty (im prob′ə bil′ə tē) *pl.* **-ties.** *n.* **1.** quality of being improbable; unlikelihood. **2.** something improbable.

im·prob·a·ble (im prob′ə bəl) *adj.* not probable; unlikely. —**im·prob′a·bly,** *adv.*

im·promp·tu (im promp′tōō, -tū) *adj.* made or done on the spur of the moment; without preparation; offhand: *The president gave an impromptu press conference.* —*n.* anything made or done on the spur of the moment. —*adv.* without preparation. [French *impromptu* unprepared, from Latin *in prōmptū* in readiness.]

im·prop·er (im prop′ər) *adj.* **1.** not in accordance with fact, truth, or established usage; erroneous: *That is an improper usage of the word.* **2.** not in accordance with accepted standards of propriety or good taste; indecorous: *improper behavior.* **3.** not suitable for the purpose or the circumstances; inappropriate. —**im·prop′er·ly,** *adv.*

improper fraction, fraction whose numerator is greater than, or equal to, the denominator, such as ⁸/₅ or ⁶/₆.

improper subset, any subset that is not a proper subset.

im·pro·pri·e·ty (im′prə prī′ə tē) *pl.* **-ties.** *n.* **1.** quality of being improper. **2.** improper act or behavior. **3.** improper usage of a word or of language.

im·prove (im prōōv′) **-proved, -prov·ing.** *v.t.* **1.** to raise to a higher or more desirable quality or condition; increase, as in value or excellence; make better: *to improve one's tennis, to improve one's mind.* **2.** to increase the value of (land or property), as by cultivation or the erection of buildings. —*v.i.* **1.** to become better: *My French improved after a summer in Paris.* **2. to improve on** (or **upon**), to do or make something better or more perfect than: *It is difficult to improve on nature. He improved on the invention.* [Anglo-Norman *emprower* to benefit, turn to profit, from Old French *em-* in (from Latin *in*) + *prou* a benefit, profit (going back to Latin *prōdesse* to be of advantage).] —**im·prov′a·bil′i·ty, im·prov′er,** *n.* —**im·prov′a·ble,** *adj.*

im·prove·ment (im prōōv′mənt) *n.* **1.** act of improving; being improved. **2.** change or addition that improves something, as in quality or value. **3.** one who or that which is better or more perfect than another: *The group's new chairman is an improvement over the past one.*

im·prov·i·dence (im prov′ə dəns) *n.* quality of being improvident; lack of foresight or thrift.

im·prov·i·dent (im prov′ə dənt) *adj.* **1.** lacking foresight; incautious. **2.** neglecting to provide for future needs; thriftless. —**im·prov′i·dent·ly,** *adv.*

im·prov·i·sa·tion (im prov′ə zā′shən, im′prə və-) *n.* **1.** act or art of improvising. **2.** that which is improvised. —**im·prov′i·sa′tion·al,** *adj.*

im·pro·vi·sa·to·ry (im prov′ə zə tôr′ē, im′prə vī′zə-) *adj.* of, relating to, or of the nature of an improviser or improvisation.

im·pro·vise (im′prə vīz′) **-vised, -vis·ing.** *v.t.* **1.** to produce without preparation, esp. to make up and perform extemporaneously: *to improvise a skit.* **2.** to devise or construct from whatever resources are on hand: *to improvise a bookcase out of crates.* —*v.i.* to do or make anything on the spur of the moment. [Italian *improvvisare* to produce without preparation, going back to Latin *imprōvīsus* unforeseen.] —**im′pro·vis′er,** *n.*

im·pru·dence (im prōōd′əns) *n.* **1.** quality of being imprudent. **2.** imprudent action or behavior.

im·pru·dent (im prōōd′ənt) *adj.* lacking prudence or discretion; unwise. [Latin *imprūdēns* not foreseeing.] —**im·pru′dent·ly,** *adv.*

im·pu·dence (im′pyə dəns) *n.* **1.** quality of being impudent; sauciness; insolence. **2.** impudent speech or behavior.

im·pu·dent (im′pyə dənt) *adj.* offensively forward; saucy; insolent. [Latin *impudēns* shameless.] —**im′pu·dent·ly,** *adv.*

im·pugn (im pūn′) *v.t.* **1.** to suggest there is something bad about; question the rightness of: *to impugn a benefactor's motives in making a gift, to impugn the courts and laws.* **2.** *Archaic.* to challenge or attack; fight against; assail: *The outworks of the enemy, from whence they impugn the civil power* (Hobbes, 1651). [Latin *impūgnāre* to fight against.] —**im·pugn′a·ble,** *adj.*

im·pulse (im′puls) *n.* **1.** force that impels one to act without planning or reflection: *A sudden impulse led him to open the window.* **2.** sudden force that causes motion; thrust; push: *The impulse of falling water turns the water wheel.* **3.** motion caused by the sudden application of force. **4.** brief surge or pulsation of power or energy, as of a radio signal. **5.** signal produced and carried by nerve cells to or from the central nervous system. [Latin *impulsus* a pushing against, incitement.]

im·pul·sion (im pul′shən) *n.* **1.** act of impelling. **2.** onward motion resulting from such an act. **3.** impulse: *He felt an impulsion to help them.*

im·pul·sive (im pul′siv) *adj.* **1.** inclined to act on impulse. **2.** resulting from impulse: *Jim later regretted his impulsive decision.* **3.** having the power of producing motion. —**im·pul′sive·ly,** *adv.* —**im·pul′sive·ness,** *n.*

im·pu·ni·ty (im pū′ni tē) *n.* freedom from punishment, penalty, injury, or loss. [Latin *impūnitās* freedom from punishment, going back to *in-* not + *poena* punishment (from Greek *poinē*).]

im·pure (im pyoor′) *adj.* **1.** dirty; unclean: *impure water.* **2.** containing something foreign or extraneous. [Latin *impūrus* unclean.]

im·pu·ri·ty (im pyoor′ə tē) *pl.,* **-ties.** *n.* **1.** quality or state of being impure. **2.** that which makes something impure.

im·pu·ta·tion (im′pyə tā′shən) *n.* **1.** act of imputing. **2.** that which is imputed or charged.

im·pute (im pūt′) **-put·ed, -put·ing.** *v.t.* to charge or attribute (something, esp. something bad): *to impute cowardice to a deserter, to impute his illness to the tropical climate.* [Latin *imputāre* to reckon, charge.] —**im·put′a·ble,** *adj.* —**Syn.** see **attribute.**

in (in) *prep.* **1.** bounded, confined, or enclosed by: *in the closet, in a cage.* **2.** with the location of; among or in the midst of: *a ride in the hill country, a home in San Juan.* **3.** through or into: *You can go in the door on your left.* **4.** during the act of; while; when: *He drowned in attempting to save the child.* **5.** during: *a good place to visit in the winter.* **6.** before the end of: *Repayment is due in sixty days. I'll be there in ten minutes.* **7.** made of: *a statue in bronze, music in triple time.* **8.** by means of; with; using: *to paint in oils.* **9.** covered by; wearing: *a lady in pink, in curlers.* **10.** out of: *One in every four children examined had bad teeth.* **11.** affected by or having: *in sickness and in health.* **12.** within the power, range, or scope of: *in my hearing. He has it in him to be a doctor.* **13.** with the purpose or result of; for: *to strike in self-defense, to say in conclusion.* **14.** engaged at: *in training, in business.* **15.** with the shape of; so as to form: *arranged in rows, to run in circles.* **16.** with respect to; as regards: *Two brothers differ in their outlooks.* **17.** according to: *in my opinion.* **18. in that.** in consequence or view of; because; since. —*adv.* **1.** to or toward a point or place inside: *to come in out of the cold.* **2.** at a specific place, esp. one's home or office: *She stayed in because she was ill.* **3.** into a position of power: *The vote put the Demo-*crats *in.* **4.** into some substance so as to form a part of: *Mix the butter in.* **5.** so as to agree with: *to fall in with our plans.* **6. to be in for.** to be due or destined to do, have, or receive: *to be in for a hard time, to be in for a scolding.* **7. to be in with.** to be on friendly or intimate terms with. **8. to have it in for.** to harbor bad feeling toward; hold a grudge against. —*adj.* **1.a.** having power or control: *the in group.* **b.** pertaining or understandable to a select group: *an in joke.* **2.** leading or going in: *the in door.* **3.** *Informal.* fashionable; popular: *It was an in thing to do.* —*n.* **1.** usually, **ins.** people in office or in power. **2.** means of approach or entry: *to have an in with the boss.* **3. ins and outs. a.** turns and twists, as of a road. **b.** details; intricacies; complexities: *to know the ins and outs of legal procedures.* [Old English *in* within, into, on, among.]

In, indium.

in-¹ *prefix* without; not: *inanimate, inequality.* [Latin *in-* not, sometimes through French *in-* or *en-*.]

in-² *prefix* **1.** in; into: *inquire, invade.* **2.** strongly; fully: *inundate.* [Latin *in* in, into, within, on, toward, against, often through French *in-* or *en-*.]

in-³ *prefix* in; within; into: *insight, indwelling.* [Old English *in* within the limits of something.]

-in¹, form of **-ine²,** as in *lanolin, pectin.*

-in² *combining form* used with verbs to form compound nouns describing a gathering of people for a particular purpose, esp. as a form of protest: *sit-in, teach-in.* [From IN.]

in., inch; inches.

in·a·bil·i·ty (in′ə bil′ə tē) *n.* quality or condition of being unable. —**Syn.** see **disability.**

in ab·sen·tia (in ab sen′shə, -shē ə) *Latin.* during or despite one's absence.

in·ac·ces·si·bil·i·ty (in′ak ses′ə bil′ə tē) *n.* quality or state of being inaccessible.

in·ac·ces·si·ble (in′ak ses′ə bəl) *adj.* not to be reached or approached; not accessible. —**in′ac·ces′si·bly,** *adv.*

in·ac·cu·ra·cy (in ak′yər ə sē) *pl.,* **-cies.** *n.* **1.** quality or conditon of being inaccurate. **2.** error; mistake.

in·ac·cu·rate (in ak′yər it) *adj.* not accurate; incorrect. —**in·ac′cu·rate·ly,** *adv.*

in·ac·tion (in ak′shən) *n.* absence of action; inertness; passivity.

in·ac·tive (in ak′tiv) *adj.* not active; passive; inert. —**in·ac′tive·ly,** *adv.*

in·ac·tiv·i·ty (in′ak tiv′ə tē) *n.* lack of activity.

in·ad·e·qua·cy (in ad′ə kwə sē) *n.* state or quality of being inadequate.

in·ad·e·quate (in ad′ə kwit) *adj.* less than required; not adequate. —**in·ad′e·quate·ly,** *adv.*

in·ad·mis·si·ble (in′ad mis′ə bəl) *adj.* not to be admitted, considered, or allowed; not admissible. —**in′ad·mis′si·bil′i·ty,** *n.* —**in′ad·mis′si·bly,** *adv.*

in·ad·ver·tence (in′əd vurt′əns) *n.* **1.** quality of being inadvertent. **2.** result of being inadvertent.

in·ad·ver·ten·cy (in′əd vurt′ən sē) *pl.,* **-cies.** *n.* inadvertence.

in·ad·ver·tent (in′əd vurt′ənt) *adj.* not sought or intended; unconscious or accidental: *an inadvertent oversight, an inadvertent discovery.* —**in′ad·ver′tent·ly,** *adv.*

in·ad·vis·a·ble (in′əd vī′zə bəl) *adj.* apt to be detrimental; unwise. —**in′ad·vis′a·bil′i·ty,** *n.* —**in′ad·vis′a·bly,** *adv.*

in·al·ien·a·ble (in āl′yə nə bəl, -ā′lē ə-) *adj.* that cannot be given up, taken away, or transferred. —**in·al′ien·a·bil′i·ty,** *n.* —**in·al′ien·a·bly,** *adv.*

in·am·o·ra·ta (in am′ə rä′tə) *pl.,* **-tas.** *n.* woman with whom one is in love. [Italian *innamorata,* from *innamorare* to inspire with love, going back to Latin *in* in + *amor* love.]

in·ane (i nān′) *adj.* **1.** lacking intelligence; empty of meaning; silly and senseless. **2.** empty; void. [Latin *inānis* empty.] —**in·ane′ly,** *adv.*

in·an·i·mate (in an′ə mit) *adj.* **1.** not moving, growing, or feeling; not having the functions of life; not alive: *Rocks are inanimate objects.* **2.** lifeless; dull: *an inanimate expression, inanimate conversation.* —**in·an′i·mate·ly,** *adv.* —**in·an′i·mate·ness,** *n.* —**Syn.** see **dead.**

in·a·ni·tion (in′ə nish′ən) *n.* **1.** emptiness or lack, esp. of intellectual vitality. **2.** exhaustion because of lack of food or water. [Late Latin *inānītiō* emptiness, from *inānīre* to empty.]

in·an·i·ty (i nan′ə tē) *pl.,* **-ties.** *n.* **1.** quality or state of being inane. **2.** something inane, as a remark or act.

in·ap·pli·ca·ble (in ap′li kə bəl, -ə plik′ə bəl) *adj.* not relevant or suitable; not applicable. —**in·ap′pli·ca·bil′i·ty,** *n.*

in·ap·po·site (in ap′ə zit) *adj.* not to the point; inapposite: *inapposite remarks.* —**in·ap′po·site·ly,** *adv.*

in·ap·pre·cia·ble (in′ə prē′shə bəl) *adj.* too small to be given attention; slight; unimportant: *an inappreciable variation in style from one opera to the next.* —**in′ap·pre′cia·bly,** *adv.*

in·ap·pro·pri·ate (in′ə prō′prē it) *adj.* not appropriate; unsuitable.

at; āpe; cär; end; mē; it; īce; hot; ōld; fôrk; wood; fōōl; oil; out; up; ūse; turn; sing; thin; this; zh in treasure; ə in ago, taken, pencil, lemon, circus.

It was inappropriate to laugh at such a solemn moment. —in′ap·pro′-pri·ate·ly, *adv.* —in′ap·pro′pri·ate·ness, *n.*

in·apt (in apt′) *adj.* unsuitable; inappropriate: *an inapt comparison.* —in·apt′ness, *n.*

in·ap·ti·tude (in ap′tə tōōd′, -tūd′) *n.* lack of aptitude or skill.

in·ar·tic·u·late (in′är tik′yə lit) *adj.* **1.** not clearly expressed or pronounced; not having distinct, meaningful units: *The boy's speech was inarticulate because his mouth was full of peanut butter.* **2.** not fluent or ready in expression; not able to express oneself. **3.** not fully expressed; not made definite and clear: *inarticulate pain.* **4.** not capable of speech or expression. **5.** *Biology.* not jointed. [Late Latin *inarticulātus* indistinct, from Latin *in-* not + *articulātus*, past participle of *articulāre.* See ARTICULATE.] —in′ar·tic′u·late·ly, *adv.* —in′ar·tic′u·late·ness, *n.*

in·ar·tis·tic (in′är tis′tik) *adj.* not artistic. —in′ar·tis′ti·cal·ly, *adv.*

in·as·much (in′əz much′) *conj.* **1.** in view of the fact that; since (with *as*). **2.** insofar as (with *as*): *Inasmuch as ye have done it unto one of the least of these my brethren, ye have done it unto me* (Matthew 25:40).

in·at·ten·tion (in′ə ten′shən) *n.* lack of attention: *inattention to details.*

in·at·ten·tive (in′ə ten′tiv) *adj.* not attentive; neglectful. —in′at·ten′tive·ly, *adv.* —in′at·ten′tive·ness, *n.*

in·au·di·ble (in ô′də bəl) *adj.* that cannot be heard. —in·au′di·bly, *adv.*

in·au·gu·ral (in ô′gyər əl, -gər-) *adj.* of, relating to, or for an inauguration: *an inaugural ball.* —n. address by a person being inaugurated, esp. one by a president of the United States. [French *inaugural* relating to inauguration, from *inaugurer* to establish, usher in, from Latin *inaugurāre.* See INAUGURATE.]

in·au·gu·rate (in ô′gyə rāt′, -gə-) -rat·ed, -rat·ing. *v.t.* **1.** to install (an official, as a president or governor) in office with a formal ceremony. **2.** to initiate, esp. with formalities; usher in: *to inaugurate a new policy.* **3.** to begin public use of or access to (something) with a formal opening ceremony: *to inaugurate a bridge.* [Latin *inaugurātus*, past participle of *inaugurāre* to seek guidance from omens (before undertaking an enterprise), consecrate, install.] —in·au′gu·ra′tor, *n.*

in·au·gu·ra·tion (in ô′gyə rā′shən, -gə-) *n.* **1.** formal ceremony installing a person in office. **2.** act or instance of initiating; condition of being initiated. **3.** ceremony formally opening something for public use or access.

in·aus·pi·cious (in′ôs pish′əs) *adj.* not favorable for success; not especially notable or fortunate: *From inauspicious beginnings, the Red Cross grew into a worldwide organization.*

in·be·tween (in′bi twēn′) *adj.* characterized by neither of two opposed or contrasting conditions: *to take an in-between position, neither for nor against the proposal.*

in·board (in′bôrd′) *adj.* inside the hull of a ship: *an inboard engine.* —adv. inside the hull or within the sides of a ship: *to stow cargo inboard, to draw the sails inboard.*

in·born (in′bôrn′) *adj.* deeply ingrained, as if born in a person; natural: *inborn optimism.*

in·bound (in′bound′) *adj.* inward bound.

in·bred (in′bred′) *adj.* **1.a.** resulting from marriages between close relatives over many generations: *an inbred royal line.* **b.** closed in; narrow; self-perpetuating: *an inbred elite.* **2.** inborn; inborn: *your inbred curiosity, and love of experimental learning* (Boyle, 1660).

in·breed (in′brēd′) -bred, -breed·ing. *v.t., v.i.* **1.** to breed with closely related stock. **2.** to make or become closed in, narrow, or self-perpetuating.

in·breed·ing (in′brē′ding) *n.* **1.** breeding among closely related individuals, resulting in certain traits becoming more marked. **2.** practice of remaining closed in, narrow, or self-perpetuating, as in personnel or outlook: *The inbreeding of the general's staff kept out any new ideas.*

inc. 1. incorporated. **2.** including. **3.** included. **4.** inclusive. **5.** increase.

In·ca (ing′kə) *n.* **1.** member of a highly civilized group of Quechua-speaking Indians once dominant in Peru and occupying an area from the southern border of Colombia to central Chile. The Incas had the only true empire in the Americas and were conquered by the Spanish in the sixteenth century. **2.** ruler or member of the nobility of this people. [Spanish *inca* king, prince, noble, from Quechua *inca.*] —In′can, *adj., n.*

in·cal·cu·la·ble (in kal′kyə lə bəl) *adj.* incapable of being exactly determined or calculated, esp. too much or too many to be calculated: *incalculable benefits. David's actions have done incalculable harm to our project.* —in·cal′cu·la·bly, *adv.*

in·can·des·cence (in′kən des′əns) *n.* condition of being or becoming incandescent.

in·can·des·cent (in′kən des′ənt) *adj.* **1.** glowing with heat. **2.** brightly shining; brilliant; sparkling. [Latin *incandēscēns*, present participle of *incandēscere* to become hot, glow.]

incandescent lamp, light bulb in which light is produced by passing an electric current through a thin high-resistance wire or filament, causing it to glow.

in·can·ta·tion (in′kan tā′shən) *n.* **1.** formula of words spoken or chanted in casting a spell or performing or producing other magic. **2.** use of such a formula. [Late Latin *incantātiō* enchantment, from Latin *incantāre.* See ENCHANT.]

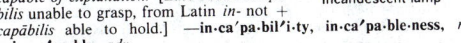

Incandescent lamp

(Bulb, Filament, Lead-in wire, Support rod, Contact, Screw base, Contact)

in·ca·pa·ble (in kā′pə bəl) *adj.* **1.** lacking ability, training, or qualification; not capable; incompetent. **2.** incapable of. **a.** without the capacity or ability for; prevented from: *incapable of walking.* **b.** not open or susceptible to; not allowing or admitting: *incapable of explanation.* [Late Latin *incapābilis* unable to grasp, from Latin *in-* not + *capābilis* able to hold.] —in·ca′pa·bil′i·ty, in·ca′pa·ble·ness, *n.* —in·ca′pa·bly, *adv.*

in·ca·pac·i·tate (in′kə pas′ə tāt′) -tat·ed, -tat·ing. *v.t.* to deprive of power or ability, esp. of power to do physical activity or labor; lay up: *Disease incapacitated many of the soldiers.* —in′ca·pac′i·ta′tion, *n.*

in·ca·pac·i·ty (in′kə pas′ə tē) *pl.*, -ties. *n.* **1.** lack of power or ability. **2.** lack of legal ability to act. —Syn. **1.** see disability.

in·car·cer·ate (in kär′sə rāt′) -at·ed, -at·ing. *v.t.* to imprison. [Medieval Latin *incarcerātus*, past participle of *incarcerāre* to imprison, going back to Latin *in* in + *carcer* prison.] —in·car′cer·a′tion, *n.* —Syn. see imprison.

in·car·na·dine (in kär′nə dīn′, -din, -dēn′) *n.* **1.** crimson color. **2.** pale red, pink color. —v.t., -dined, -din·ing. *Archaic.* to color with incarnadine. [French *incarnadin* flesh-colored, from dialectal Italian *incarnadino,* going back to Latin *in* in + *carō* (stem *carn-*) flesh.]

in·car·nate (*adj.*, in kär′nit, -nāt; *v.*, in kär′nāt) *adj.* **1.** in pure form; personified; itself: *John was a fool, although he thought of himself as sagacity incarnate.* **2.** embodied in flesh, esp. in human form or display: *the incarnate Deity* (J. Wesley, 1738). —v.t., -nat·ed, -nat·ing. **1.** to embody in flesh, esp. in human form. **2.** to embody in pure form; typify. [Late Latin *incarnātus,* past participle of *incarnāre* to make flesh, from Latin *in* in + *carō* flesh.]

in·car·na·tion (in′kär nā′shən) *n.* **1.** assumption of bodily form, esp. human form, by a supernatural being. **2.** one who or that which embodies, personifies, or typifies: *Poor Zloto, the rejected lover, was the incarnation of misery.* **3.** act or process of embodying, personifying, or typifying. **4.** the Incarnation. assumption of human flesh and nature by the Son of God in the historical person of Jesus Christ.

in·case (in kās′) encase.

in·cau·tious (in kô′shəs) *adj.* not cautious; unwary; rash.

in·cen·di·a·rism (in sen′dē ə riz′əm) *n.* practice of an incendiary.

in·cen·di·ar·y (in sen′dē er′ē) *adj.* **1.** causing or designed to cause a fire: *incendiary grenades.* **2.** tending to excite or inflame; inflammatory: *incendiary publications.* **3.** of or relating to arson. —n. pl., -ar·ies. **1.** arsonist. **2.** inflammatory agitator. **3.** bomb, shell, grenade, or other device designed to cause a fire. [Latin *incendiārius* causing a fire, from *incendium* fire.]

in·cense¹ (in′sens′) *n.* **1.** any of several substances, as gums or spices, burned to produce a fragrant aroma. **2.** odor or smoke that is emitted from such a substance. **3.** any pleasant aroma: *the incense of a meadow.* [Late Latin *incēnsum* literally, something burnt, from Latin *incendere* to burn.]

in·cense² (in sens′) -censed, -cens·ing. *v.t.* to make (someone) very angry or indignant: *It incensed the lady to be told to move on.* [Latin *incēnsus,* past participle of *incendere* to burn, anger.]

in·cen·tive (in sen′tiv) *n.* that which urges to action, esp. a promised reward for working harder. [Latin *incentīvus* setting the tune, inciting, from *incinere* to sound.]

Syn. Incentive, inducement, stimulus all mean a motive or motives prompting or impelling a person to act in a certain way. **Incentive** is something that inspires or constitutes an external motive to encourage competitive activity: *The government promised lower taxes as an incentive to attract new business.* **Inducement** is an external motive and impetus in an even narrower sense that serves to entice or lure: *The company offered him a high salary as an inducement to accept the job.* **Stimulus** applies to an impetus that not only quickens the momentum of activity but stimulates and invigorates the mind: *The initial breakthrough on the vaccine was a stimulus for further research.*

in·cep·tion (in sep′shən) *n.* point of beginning or being begun; commencement: *The program was popular from its inception.* [Latin *inceptiō.*]

in·cep·tive (in sep′tiv) *adj. Grammar.* (of verbs or tenses) expressing the beginning of action.

in·cer·ti·tude (in sur′tə tōōd′, -tūd′) *n.* **1.** condition of not being

at; āpe; cär; end; mē; it; īce; hot; ōld; fôrk; wood; fōōl; oil; out; up; ūse; turn; sing; thin; this; zh in treasure; ə in ago, taken, pencil, lemon, circus.

519

sure or certain: *one's incertitude about particular questions.* **2.** instability; insecurity: *the incertitude of one's situation.* [French *incertitude,* going back to Latin *in-* not + Late Latin *certitūdō.* See CERTITUDE.]

in·ces·sant (in ses'ənt) *adj.* continuing without interruption; unceasing: *an incessant flow of commands from headquarters, the incessant buzz of mosquitoes.* [Late Latin *incessāns* unceasing, going back to Latin *in-* not + *cessāre* to stop.] **—in·ces'sant·ly,** *adv.* **—Syn.** see **continual.**

in·cest (in'sest') *n.* marriage or a sexual relationship between two persons who are closely related, as a parent and child or a brother and sister. [Latin *incestum,* from *incestus* unchaste.]

in·ces·tu·ous (in ses'chōō əs) *adj.* **1.** involving incest. **2.** guilty of incest. **—in·ces'tu·ous·ly,** *adv.* **—in·ces'tu·ous·ness,** *n.*

inch (inch) *n.* **1.** linear measure, equal to 1/12 of a foot. **2.** smallest distance, amount, or degree: *The candidate wouldn't retreat an inch from his initial statement.* **3. every inch,** in every respect; totally: *every inch an outfielder.* —*v.i.* to move very slowly, as if an inch at a time: *The captive inched toward the window to get away.* —*v.t.* to move (someone or something) very slowly. [Old English *ynce* 1/12 of a foot, from Latin *uncia* a twelfth part. Doublet of OUNCE¹.]

in·cho·ate (in kō'it) *adj.* **1.** disorderly; chaotic. **2.** *Archaic.* in an initial or early stage; not yet fully developed or formed. [Latin *inchoātus,* past participle of *incho(h)āre* to begin; originally, to harness, from *in* in + *cohum* strap tying the plow beam and the yoke together.]

in·cho·a·tive (in kō'ə tiv) *n.* *Grammar.* inceptive.

In·chon (in'chon') *n.* port city in northwestern South Korea, on the Yellow Sea. Pop. (1966), 525,072.

inch·worm (inch'wurm') *n.* any of a group of caterpillars, family Geometridae, which move by drawing the rear of the body

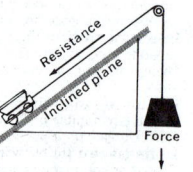

Inchworm

up toward the front, forming a loop, and then stretching the front end forward. Also, **measuring worm, span'worm'.**

in·ci·dence (in'sə dəns) *n.* **1.** rate or frequency of occurrence, esp. in a certain area. **2.** fact of falling on or affecting. **3.** containment of one figure by another figure, as of a point in a line.

in·ci·dent (in'sə dənt) *n.* **1.** occurrence or action, esp. one leading to serious consequences or to a crisis: *The war began with a series of minor incidents in outlying areas.* **2.** distinct event or piece of action, as in a novel, play, or poem; episode. —*adj.* **1.** naturally connected with; belonging to as a part (with *to*): *the great misfortunes and calamities incident to human life* (Steele, 1710). **2.** falling or striking (with *on* or *upon*). [Latin *incidēns,* present participle of *incidere* to happen.] **—Syn.** *n.* **2.** see **event.**

in·ci·den·tal (in'sə dent'əl) *adj.* **1.a.** belonging to as a minor part or a relatively unimportant condition (with *to*): *problems incidental to living in space.* **b.** minor; unimportant: *walking the dog and other incidental tasks.* **2.** not belonging with or pertaining to anything else; thrown in; random: *an incidental remark.* —*n.* that which is incidental.

in·ci·den·tal·ly (in'sə dent'lē, -dent'əl ē) *adv.* **1.** in an incidental manner. **2.** by the way.

in·cin·er·ate (in sin'ə rāt') -**at·ed, -at·ing.** *v.t.* to burn (something) in or as if in an incinerator. [Medieval Latin *incineratus,* past participle of *incinerare* to reduce to ashes, from *in* in + *cinis* ashes.] **—in·cin'er·a'tion,** *n.*

in·cin·er·a·tor (in sin'ə rā'tər) *n.* piece of equipment, as a furnace, used to dispose of garbage or other waste material by burning it to ashes.

in·cip·i·ence (in sip'ē əns) *n.* fact or condition of being incipient.

in·cip·i·ent (in sip'ē ənt) *adj.* in an early stage; just beginning to appear. [Latin *incipiēns,* present participle of *incipere* to begin.]

in·cise (in sīz') -**cised, -cis·ing.** *v.t.* **1.** to cut into. **2.** to make (marks or designs) by cutting; carve; engrave. [French *inciser* to cut into, from Latin *incīsus,* past participle of *incīdere.*]

in·ci·sion (in sizh'ən) *n.* cut or result of carefully cutting into something, esp. flesh, along a thin line; precise cut.

in·ci·sive (in sī'siv) *adj.* penetrating; sharp; acute: *an incisive mind.* [Medieval Latin *incisivus* cutting in, from Latin *incīsus,* past participle of *incīdere* to cut into.] **—in·ci'sive·ly,** *adv.* **—in·ci'sive·ness,** *n.*

in·ci·sor (in sī'zər) *n.* any of the front teeth of the upper or lower jaw having sharp flattened edges used for cutting food. [Modern Latin *incisor* literally, cutter, from Latin *incīsus.* See INCISE.]

Incisors

in·cite (in sīt') -**cit·ed, -cit·ing.** *v.t.* **1.** to move or urge; rouse: *to incite someone to action.* **2.** to cause by urging or arousing; do something to bring about: *to incite a riot.* [Latin *incitāre.*]

in·ci·ta·tion (in'sī tā'shən), **in·cite'er,** *n.*

Syn. 1. Incite, instigate, provoke mean to spur or urge on to action.

Incite tends to refer to agitated activity or a disturbing course of action: *The cries of the hunters incited the birds to fly.* **Instigate** stresses the initial stimulus to a questionable or violent activity: *The plot to overthrow the government was instigated by the military.* **Provoke** implies goading another or others into an angry and vexed reaction: *The book provoked a storm of controversy.*

in·cite·ment (in sīt'mənt) *n.* **1.** act of inciting. **2.** incentive.

in·ci·vil·i·ty (in'sə vil'ə tē) *pl.* **-ties.** *n.* lack of politeness and courtesy. **2.** impolite, discourteous act.

incl. 1. inclosure. **2.** including. **3.** inclusive.

in·clem·ent (in klem'ənt) *adj.* **1.** (of climate or weather) cold or stormy; unfavorable. **2.** harsh; unmerciful. [Latin *inclēmēns* harsh, from *in-* not + *clēmēns* mild, merciful.] **—in·clem'en·cy,** *n.* **—in·clem'ent·ly,** *adv.*

in·cli·na·tion (in'klə nā'shən) *n.* **1.** feeling or disposition that is more favorable to one thing or person than to another; preference; liking: *an inclination to go swimming rather than to stay at home.* **2.** tendency toward or movement in the direction of some quality or condition: *Prices have an inclination to go up.* **3.** act, fact, or state of being or going at an angle or of bending or leaning: *The inclination of the hillside made it hard to stand. The dog showed its interest by an inclination of its ears.* **4.** angle formed between two lines or planes, or between a line and its projection on a plane. [Latin *inclīnātiō* leaning, bending.]

in·cline (*v.,* in klīn'; *n.,* in'klīn', in klīn') -**clined, -clin·ing.** *v.i.* **1.** to be or go at an angle; slope; slant: *The road inclines upward.* **2.** to bend; lean: *The partly deaf man inclined forward to hear the conversation more clearly.* **3.** to have an inclination; be favorable (with *toward* to): *Ed inclines toward becoming a mechanic.* **4.** to tend toward or move in the direction of some quality or condition: *a middle-sized woman, but rather inclining to tall* (Fielding, 1749). —*v.t.* **1.** to cause to bend, lean, slope, or slant: *Incline your head this way.* **2.** to give (someone) an inclination; cause (someone) to be favorable: *Mary's interests inclined her toward sports.* —*n.* plane or surface that goes at an angle: *The wagon rolled down the incline.* [Old French *incliner* to bend, bow¹, from Latin *inclīnāre.*] **—Syn.** *v.i.* **1.** see **slant.**

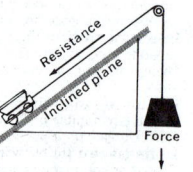

Inclined plane

in·clined (in klīnd') *adj.* **1.** subject to an inclination or tendency: *I am inclined to agree. Prices are inclined to rise.* **2.** sloping or leaning.

inclined plane, any plane surface, as a ramp, set at an angle of less than ninety degrees with a horizontal surface.

in·cli·nom·e·ter (in'klə nom'ə tər) *n.* **1.** instrument for measuring the inclination or slope of anything. **2.** instrument for determining the angle with the horizontal made by an aircraft or ship. [INCLINE + -METER.]

in·close (in klōz') enclose.

in·clo·sure (in klō'zhər) enclosure.

in·clude (in klōōd') -**clud·ed, -clud·ing.** *v.t.* **1.** to have as a part; contain: *The book includes an appendix.* **2.** to cause to be a part; put in: *The director included John in the cast.* **3.** to involve; imply: *Their religion includes opposition to violence.* [Latin *inclūdere* to shut in.] **—in·clud'a·ble;** *also,* **in·clud'i·ble,** *adj.* **—Syn.** see **embody.**

in·clu·sion (in klōō'zhən) *n.* **1.** act of including; state of being included. **2.** that which is included. [Latin *inclūsiō* a shutting up.]

in·clu·sive (in klōō'siv) *adj.* **1.** including the stated limits and everything in between: *five days, Monday to Friday inclusive.* **2.** including (with *of*): *cowboy gear, inclusive of chaps and spurs.* **3.** including everything relevant; comprehensive. **—in·clu'sive·ly,** *adv.* **—in·clu'sive·ness,** *n.*

in·cog·ni·to (in'kög nē'tō, in kog'ni tō') *adj., adv.* having one's identity concealed so as to be unknown; in disguise: *The famous actress attended the party incognito. The hunted man occasionally visited his daughter incognito.* —*n. pl.,* **-tos. 1.** that which makes one incognito; disguise. **2.** one who is incognito. [Italian *incognito* unknown, from Latin *incognitus.*]

in·co·her·ence (in'kō hēr'əns, -her'-) *n.* state or quality of being incoherent. Also, **in'co·her'en·cy.**

in·co·her·ent (in'kō hēr'ənt, -her'-) *adj.* **1.** characterized by confused, disjointed speech or thought; not understandable: *The patient was incoherent when he was brought in.* **2.** lacking cohesiveness, organization, or logical connection; confused; disconnected.

in·com·bus·ti·ble (in'kəm bus'tə bəl) *adj.* that cannot burn. —*n.* incombustible substance. **—in'com·bus'ti·bil'i·ty,** *n.*

in·come (in'kum') *n.* **1.** payment in money or its equivalent, esp. periodic payment, as for services, labor, property, or investments. **2.** amount of such payment, as to a particular person: *a low income.*

income tax, tax levied on personal and corporate incomes, usually graduated, and with certain legally permitted deductions.

in·com·ing (in′kum′ing) *adj.* coming in: *a volunteer to handle all incoming calls.*

in·com·men·su·ra·ble (in′kə men′sər ə bəl, -shər-) *adj.* **1.** having no common basis for comparison; not measurable by the same standards, values, or units. **2.** not in proportion; incommensurate. **3.** having no common divisor. —**in′com·men·su·ra·bil′i·ty,** *n.* —**in′com·men′su·ra·bly,** *adv.*

in·com·men·su·rate (in′kə men′sər it, -shər-) *adj.* **1.** not corresponding or proportionate; not of equal size: *an increase in housing incommensurate with the growth of population.* **2.** having no common basis for comparison; incommensurable. —**in′com·men′su·rate·ly,** *adv.*

in·com·mode (in′kə mōd′) **-mod·ed, -mod·ing.** *v.t.* to inconvenience or make uncomfortable: *The lack of heat and hot water incommoded us.* [Latin *incommodāre.*]

in·com·mo·di·ous (in′kə mō′dē əs) *adj.* inconvenient or uncomfortable, esp. by being too small.

in·com·mu·ni·ca·ble (in′kə mū′ni kə bəl) *adj.* **1.** that cannot be told or conveyed. **2.** that is not likely to be transmitted to others; not catching.

in·com·mu·ni·ca·do (in′kə mū′nə kä′dō) *adj.* without the right or means of communicating with others: *confined to his home incommunicado, with no calls, no mail, and no visitors.* [Spanish *incomunicado,* from *incomunicar* to deprive of communication, going back to Latin *in-* not + *commūnicāre* to impart, share.]

in·com·pa·ra·ble (in kom′pər ə bəl, -kom′prə-) *adj.* **1.** unequaled; matchless: *an incomparable voice.* **2.** that cannot be compared; without a basis for comparison: *two incomparable social systems.* —**in·com′pa·ra·ble·ness,** *n.* —**in·com′pa·ra·bly,** *adv.*

in·com·pat·i·bil·i·ty (in′kəm pat′ə bil′ə tē) *pl.* **-ties.** *n.* **1.** quality or condition of being incompatible. **2.** that which is or makes incompatible.

in·com·pat·i·ble (in′kəm pat′ə bəl) *adj.* not capable of existing or functioning together in harmony; not consistent or congenial: *incompatible roommates. Discrimination is incompatible with democratic principles.* —**in′com·pat′i·bly,** *adv.*

in·com·pe·tence (in kom′pət əns) *n.* state or fact of being incompetent or an incompetent. Also, **in·com′pe·ten·cy.**

in·com·pe·tent (in kom′pət ənt) *adj.* **1.** not having or showing sufficient ability; not capable or adequate: *an incompetent typist, an incompetent repair job.* **2.** not legally qualified. —*n.* **1.** one who lacks sufficient ability. **2.** one who is legally incapable of acting for himself, as because of insanity or feeble-mindedness. —**in·com′pe·tent·ly,** *adv.*

in·com·plete (in′kəm plēt′) *adj.* not complete. [Late Latin *incomplētus,* going back to Latin *in-* not + *complēre* to finish.] —**in′com·plete′ly,** *adv.* —**in′com·plete′ness,** *n.*

in·com·pre·hen·si·ble (in′kom pri hen′sə bəl) *adj.* that cannot be comprehended or understood. —**in′com·pre·hen′si·bil′i·ty,** *n.* —**in′com·pre·hen′si·bly,** *adv.*

in·com·pre·hen·sion (in′kom prə hen′shən) *n.* fact of not comprehending or understanding.

in·con·ceiv·a·ble (in′kən sē′və bəl) *adj.* that cannot be conceived, imagined, or thought of. —**in′con·ceiv·a·bil′i·ty,** *n.* —**in′con·ceiv′a·bly,** *adv.*

in·con·clu·sive (in′kən klōō′siv) *adj.* not leading to a conclusion or result: *The preliminary reports were inconclusive.* —**in′con·clu′sive·ly,** *adv.* —**in′con·clu′sive·ness,** *n.*

in·con·gru·ent (in kong′grōō ənt, in′kən grōō′-) *adj.* not congruent.

in·con·gru·i·ty (in′kən grōō′ə tē) *pl.* **-ties.** *n.* **1.** quality or condition of being incongruous or incongruent. **2.** that which is incongruous.

in·con·gru·ous (in kong′grōō əs) *adj.* **1.** not harmonious; discordant; absurd: *Among the modern chairs and bookshelves, the antique washstand looked very incongruous.* **2.** unfitting; inappropriate: *an incongruous remark.* [Latin *incongruus* inconsistent.]

in·con·se·quence (in kon′sə kwens′, -kwəns) *n.* condition or quality of being inconsequential: *the total inconsequence of his remarks, forceful though they were.*

in·con·se·quent (in kon′sə kwent′, -kwənt) *adj.* **1.** not following from anything; illogical. **2.** not leading to anything; inconsequential. —**in·con′se·quent·ly,** *adv.*

in·con·se·quen·tial (in kon′sə kwen′chəl) *adj.* **1.** not leading to anything important; trivial. **2.** not following from anything; inconsequent.

in·con·sid·er·a·ble (in′kən sid′ər ə bəl) *adj.* small or not worth considering: *inconsiderable amounts of rain.* —**in′con·sid′er·a·bly,** *adv.*

in·con·sid·er·ate (in′kən sid′ər it) *adj.* having or showing insufficient regard for others and their feelings. [Latin *inconsiderātus.*] —**in′con·sid′er·ate·ly,** *adv.* —**in′con·sid′er·ate·ness,** *n.*

in·con·sist·en·cy (in′kən sis′tən sē) *pl.* **-cies.** *n.* **1.** quality or condition of being inconsistent. **2.** that which is or makes inconsistent.

in·con·sist·ent (in′kən sis′tənt) *adj.* **1.** not in agreement; contradictory: *His statements and his actions are inconsistent.* **2.** not keeping to the same thoughts or course of action; lacking constancy or dependability; erratic. —**in′con·sist′ent·ly,** *adv.*

in·con·sol·a·ble (in′kən sō′lə bəl) *adj.* that cannot be consoled; grief-stricken. —**in′con·sol′a·bly,** *adv.*

in·con·so·nant (in kon′sə nənt) *adj.* not in agreement or harmony. —**in′con′so·nant·ly,** *adv.*

in·con·spic·u·ous (in′kən spik′ū əs) *adj.* likely to escape notice; not obvious or easily seen. —**in′con·spic′u·ous·ly,** *adv.* —**in′con·spic′u·ous·ness,** *n.*

in·con·stan·cy (in kon′stan sē) *n.* state or quality of being inconstant.

in·con·stant (in kon′stənt) *adj.* **1.** not faithful or steadfast; fickle. **2.** variable; changeable: *The lamp gave off a flickering and inconstant light.* —**Syn. 1.** see **fickle.**

in·con·test·a·ble (in′kən tes′tə bəl) *adj.* that cannot be disputed or challenged. —**in′con·test′a·bly,** *adv.*

in·con·ti·nence (in kon′tən əns) *n.* condition of being incontinent.

in·con·ti·nent (in kon′tən ənt) *adj.* **1.** lacking self-restraint or moderation, esp. with regard to sexual desires. **2.** not able to control urination or defecation. [Latin *incontinēns* immoderate.]

in·con·tro·vert·i·ble (in kon′trə vur′tə bəl) *adj.* that cannot be argued against or debated; certain: *incontrovertible proof.* —**in′con·tro·vert′i·bly,** *adv.*

in·con·ven·ience (in′kən vēn′yəns) *n.* **1.** quality or state of being inconvenient: *The inconvenience of their out-of-the-way location discouraged business.* **2.** inconvenient situation or thing: *the inconvenience of not having a telephone.* **3.** lack of ease or comfort; difficulty or bother: *The delay caused great inconvenience.* —*v.t.* **-ienced, -ienc·ing.** to cause (someone) to have difficulty or to go out of his or her way: *We hope this delay will not inconvenience you.*

in·con·ven·ient (in′kən vēn′yənt) *adj.* not easy to do, use, or reach; not favorable for one's needs or purposes: *an inconvenient handle on a suitcase, an inconvenient place to meet.* [Latin *inconveniēns* unsuitable.]

in·con·vert·i·ble (in′kən vur′tə bəl) *adj.* that cannot be converted, as from paper money into coins. —**in′con·vert′i·bil′i·ty,** *n.*

in·cor·po·rate (in kôr′pə rāt′) *v.t.* **1.a.** to include (something) as a part; embody: *The bill incorporates many changes.* **b.** to add (something) to (with *in* or *into*): *The general incorporated a warning into his speech.* **2.** to form into a corporation. **3.** to combine or unite into one uniform body. —*v.i.* to become or form a corporation. [Late Latin *incorporātus,* past participle of *incorporāre* to embody, going back to Latin *in* in + *corpus* body.] —**Syn.** *v.t.* **1.** see **embody.**

in·cor·po·rat·ed (in kôr′pə rā′tid) *adj.* **1.** formed into or constituting a corporation. **2.** included, added, or combined.

in·cor·po·ra·tion (in kôr′pə rā′shən) *n.* act of incorporating; state of being incorporated.

in·cor·po·ra·tor (in kôr′pə rā′tər) *n.* **1.** one who incorporates. **2.** one of the organizers of a corporation, named in the incorporating charter.

in·cor·po·re·al (in′kôr pôr′ē əl) *adj.* not consisting of matter; not having body or a body: *an incorporeal ghost.* —**in′cor·po′re·al·ly,** *adv.*

in·cor·rect (in′kə rekt′) *adj.* **1.** not agreeing with fact or truth; not accurate. **2.** not conforming to an acknowledged or approved standard; not proper. —**in′cor·rect′ly,** *adv.* —**in′cor·rect′ness,** *n.*

in·cor·ri·gi·ble (in kôr′ə jə bəl, -kor′-) *adj.* **1.** bad beyond or almost beyond all correction or reform: *an incorrigible child.* **2.** that cannot be corrected or amended: *an incorrigible twitch.* —*n.* one who is incorrigible. —**in·cor′ri·gi·bil′i·ty,** *n.* —**in·cor′ri·gi·bly,** *adv.*

in·cor·rupt·i·ble (in′kə rup′tə bəl) *adj.* **1.** that cannot be induced to act dishonestly; morally strong. **2.** that does not decay or become rotten. —**in′cor·rupt′i·bil′i·ty,** *n.* —**in′cor·rupt′i·bly,** *adv.*

in·crease (in krēs′; *n.* in′krēs′) **-creased, -creas·ing.** *v.t.* to make greater in any respect, as in number, size, intensity, or extent: *to increase enrollment, to increase farm holdings, to increase community involvement.* —*v.i.* **1.** to become greater in any respect. **2.** to grow in numbers; multiply; propagate: *Abou Ben Adhem (may his tribe increase!) awoke one night from a deep dream of peace* (Hunt, 1847). —*n.* **1.** act, process, or instance of increasing. **2.** that by which a given base is increased: *an increase of twelve dozen eggs a day.* **3. on the increase.** increasing. [Anglo-Norman *encress-,* a stem of *encrestre* to grow, augment, from Latin *incrēscere* to grow in or upon.]
Syn. *v.t.* **increase, enlarge, augment** mean to make greater in some respect. **Increase** means to grow or advance progressively through gradual increments, esp. in number, size, intensity, or extent: *The governor increased the state taxes this year.* **Enlarge** means to expand esp. in scope, capacity, or range of application: *By joining the club, Paul*

at; āpe; cär; end; mē; it; īce; hot; ōld; fôrk; wood; fōōl; oil; out; up; ūse; turn; sing; thin; this; zh in treasure; ə in ago, taken, pencil, lemon, circus.

521

enlarged his circle of friends. **Augment** means to increase by addition and grow greater, more numerous, larger, or more intense: *The rains augmented the water in the reservoir.*

in·creas·ing·ly (in krē′sing lē) *adv.* to a greater and greater extent; more and more.

in·cred·i·ble (in kred′ə bəl) *adj.* **1.** that cannot be believed or taken for the truth: *incredible science fiction.* **2.** seemingly impossible; hard to believe: *an incredible leap.* [Latin *incrēdibilis* that cannot be believed.] —**in·cred′i·bil′i·ty,** *n.* —**in·cred′i·bly,** *adv.*

in·cre·du·li·ty (in′krə dōō′lə tē, -dū′-) *n.* unreadiness or unwillingness to believe. —**Syn.** see **unbelief.**

in·cred·u·lous (in krej′ə ləs) *adj.* **1.** not disposed or not willing to believe something; skeptical; unbelieving: *When the discovery was first announced, many scholars were incredulous.* **2.** indicating incredulity: *an incredulous gasp.* [Latin *incrēdulus.*]

in·cre·ment (ing′krə mənt, in′-) *n.* **1.** that which grows or collects on something else or is added on to what is already there: *Flooding left an annual increment of several layers of mud.* **2.** quantity added to the value of a variable, usually a very small quantity. [Latin *incrēmentum* increase.]

in·crim·i·nate (in krim′ə nāt′) **-nat·ed, -nat·ing.** *v.t.* **1.** to charge with a crime or fault: *The contractor incriminated the water commissioner.* **2.** to imply or show the guilt of: *The fact that he ran away seemed to incriminate the boy.* [Late Latin *incrīminātus,* past participle of *incrīmināre* to accuse, from Latin *in* against + *crīmen* charge.] —**in·crim′i·na′tion,** *n.*

in·crim·i·na·to·ry (in krim′ə nə tôr′ē) *adj.* tending to incriminate.

in·crust (in krust′) encrust.

in·crus·ta·tion (in′krus tā′shən) encrustation.

in·cu·bate (ing′kyə bāt′, in′-) **-bat·ed, -bat·ing.** *v.t.* **1.** to keep (eggs) warm for hatching: *The mother hen incubates her eggs by sitting on them.* **2.** to provide and maintain conditions, as of air, moisture, and temperature, suitable for the development of. [Latin *incubātus,* past participle of *incubāre* to lie on.]

in·cu·ba·tion (ing′kyə bā′shən, in′-) *n.* process of incubating; state of being incubated.

incubation period, length of the development stage of a disease from the time of infection until the first appearance of symptoms.

in·cu·ba·tor (ing′kyə bā′tər, in′-) *n.* boxlike apparatus or room with a controlled environment. Incubators are used to keep premature or sick babies until they are stronger or

Incubator

well, to hatch eggs, or to grow various organisms. [Latin *incubātor* one who lies in or on something.]

in·cu·bus (ing′kyə bəs, in′-) *pl.* **-bi** (-bī′) *or* **-bus·es.** *n.* **1.** evil spirit or demon supposed to descend on sleeping people, esp. one who seeks sexual intercourse with sleeping women. **2.** any oppressive burden that is like a nightmare. **3.** nightmare. [Late Latin *incubus* nightmare; literally, that which lies on one, from Latin *incubāre* to lie on.]

in·cu·des (ing kū′dēz) plural of **incus.**

in·cul·cate (in kul′kāt, in′kul kāt′) **-cat·ed, -cat·ing.** *v.t.* to produce or encourage (an attitude or belief) by persistent teaching or indoctrination; implant in the mind: *to inculcate a love of reading in children.* [Latin *inculcātus,* past participle of *inculcāre* to impress on, tread in with the heel, going back to *in* in + *calx* heel.] —**in′cul·ca′tion, in·cul′ca·tor,** *n.*

in·cul·pate (in kul′pāt, in′kul pāt′) **-pat·ed, -pat·ing.** *v.t.* to incriminate. [Late Latin *inculpātus,* past participle of *inculpāre* to blame, going back to Latin *in* on + *culpa* blame.]

in·cum·ben·cy (in kum′bən sē) *pl.,* **-cies.** *n.* **1.** holding of an office and performance of its duties. **2.** term of office of an incumbent. **3.** condition or quality of being incumbent.

in·cum·bent (in kum′bənt) *adj.* **1.** existing or imposed as a duty or obligation; obligatory (with *on* or *upon*): *It was incumbent upon Congress to act.* **2.** holding an office: *an incumbent president.* **3.** lying, leaning, or resting upon something. —*n.* one who holds an office. [Latin *incumbēns,* present participle of *incumbere* to lie or lean on.]

in·cu·nab·u·la (in′kyə nab′yə lə) *sing.,* **-lum** (-ləm). *n.,pl.* **1.** books produced during the early development of printing from movable type, esp. during the fifteenth century. **2.** earliest stages or first traces in the development of anything. [Latin *incūnābula* cradle, infancy, origin.]

in·cur (in kur′) **-curred, -cur·ring.** *v.t.* to bring (something) on oneself by one's own actions: *to incur an expense. The monarch incurred the wrath of the people.* [Latin *incurrere* to run into.]

in·cur·a·ble (in kyoor′ə bəl) *adj.* that cannot be made well, corrected, or remedied. —**in·cur′a·bil′i·ty,** *n.* —**in·cur′a·bly,** *adv.*

in·cu·ri·ous (in kyoor′ē əs) *adj.* **1.** not eager to know or learn; not curious. **2.** not arousing attention; lacking interest: *We may conclude . . . with a not incurious anecdote* (John Brown, 1757). [Latin *incūriōsus* indifferent.] —**in·cu·ri·os·i·ty** (in kyoor′ē os′ə tē), **in·cu′ri·ous·ness,** *n.* —**in·cu′ri·ous·ly,** *adv.*

in·cur·sion (in kur′zhən) *n.* **1.** act or process of spreading, intruding, or running in; inroad: *an incursion of disease.* **2.** sudden attack; raid; invasion. [Latin *incursiō* attack.] —**Syn. 2.** see **invasion.**

in·cur·sive (in kur′siv) *adj.* making incursions.

in·cus (ing′kəs) *pl.,* **in·cu·des.** *n.* one of the three small bones of the middle ear; anvil. [Latin *incūs* anvil.]

ind. **1.** independent. **2.** indicative. **3.** industrial.

Ind. **1.** Indiana. **2.** India. **3.** Indian.

in·debt·ed (in det′id) *adj.* **1.** in the condition of owing gratitude or recognition to; in the debt of (with *to*): *All later playwrights are indebted to Shakespeare.* **2.** owing money; in debt.

in·debt·ed·ness (in det′id nis) *n.* **1.** state of being indebted. **2.** amount owed: *a total indebtedness of $6000.*

in·de·cen·cy (in dē′sən sē) *pl.,* **-cies.** *n.* **1.** quality or condition of being indecent. **2.** that which is indecent.

in·de·cent (in dē′sənt) *adj.* **1.** offensive to someone or to some social standard, esp. a standard of modest dress: *That skimpy outfit is indecent.* **2.** not in accordance with standards of good taste; improper: *an indecent delay in returning a visit.*

in·de·ci·pher·a·ble (in′di sī′fər ə bəl) *adj.* that cannot be deciphered.

in·de·ci·sion (in′di sizh′ən) *n.* inability to decide or to make up one's mind.

in·de·ci·sive (in′di sī′siv) *adj.* **1.** not coming to a decision; characterized by indecision: *an indecisive leader.* **2.** not leading to a decision; inconclusive: *an indecisive contest.* —**in′de·ci′sive·ly,** *adv.* —**in′de·ci′sive·ness,** *n.*

in·de·clin·a·ble (in′di klī′nə bəl) *adj.* having no grammatical inflections; that cannot be declined.

in·dec·o·rous (in dek′ər əs, in′di kôr′əs) *adj.* not in conformity with the approved standards of good taste; improper: *indecorous behavior.* [Latin *indecōrus* unsuitable.] —**in·dec′o·rous·ly,** *adv.* —**in·dec′o·rous·ness,** *n.*

in·de·co·rum (in′di kôr′əm) *n.* lack of decorum; impropriety. [Latin *indecōrum,* neuter of *indecōrus.* See INDECOROUS.]

in·deed (in dēd′) *adv.* really; truly. —*interj.* I don't believe it; you don't say: *A huntsman marry the princess? Indeed!*

indef., indefinite.

in·de·fat·i·ga·ble (in′di fat′ə gə bəl) *adj.* that does not become tired or exhausted. [Latin *indēfatīgābilis,* going back to *in-* not + *dē* extremely + *fatīgāre* to weary.] —**in′de·fat′i·ga·bil′i·ty,** *n.* —**in′de·fat′i·ga·bly,** *adv.*

in·de·fea·si·ble (in′di fē′zə bəl) *adj.* that cannot be set aside, annulled, or forfeited. —**in′de·fea′si·bly,** *adv.*

in·de·fen·si·ble (in′di fen′sə bəl) *adj.* **1.** that cannot be defended against attack: *The fortress, cut off and surrounded, quickly became indefensible.* **2.** that cannot be proved, justified, or excused: *an indefensible use of force.* —**in′de·fen′si·bly,** *adv.*

in·de·fin·a·ble (in′di fī′nə bəl) *adj.* that cannot be defined. —**in′de·fin′a·bly,** *adv.*

in·def·i·nite (in def′ə nit) *adj.* **1.** not clearly defined; not exact: *a lot of vague, indefinite ideas about motherhood.* **2.** having no limits or no precise limits; unmeasured: *a line of indefinite length, time of indefinite duration.* **3.** *Grammar.* not limiting or specifying precisely. [Latin *indēfinītus.*] —**in·def′i·nite·ly,** *adv.* —**in·def′i·nite·ness,** *n.*

indefinite article, the article *a* or *an,* which classifies the noun it modifies as single but unspecified. Distinguished from **definite article.**

in·de·his·cent (in′di his′ənt) *adj. Botany.* not opening at maturity to release its seeds; not dehiscent.

in·del·i·ble (in del′ə bəl) *adj.* **1.** that cannot be removed, washed out, or obliterated: *indelible memories.* **2.** that makes indelible writing or marks: *an indelible laundry-marking pen.* [Latin *indēlēbilis* imperishable.] —**in·del′i·bil′i·ty,** *n.* —**in·del′i·bly,** *adv.*

in·del·i·ca·cy (in del′ə kə sē) *pl.,* **-cies.** *n.* **1.** quality of being indelicate. **2.** that which is indelicate.

in·del·i·cate (in del′ə kit) *adj.* **1.** not tactful or considerate; coarse; crude: *The comment was indelicate at a funeral.* **2.** not in accord with what is becoming, proper, or modest; offensive: *indelicate language.* —**in·del′i·cate·ly,** *adv.* —**in·del′i·cate·ness,** *n.*

in·dem·ni·fi·ca·tion (in dem′nə fi kā′shən) *n.* **1.** act of indemnifying; state of being indemnified. **2.** that which is given to indemnify; indemnity.

in·dem·ni·fy (in dem′nə fī′) **-fied, -fy·ing.** *v.t.* **1.** to compensate (someone) for loss, damage, or expense incurred. **2.** to give security against future damage or loss; insure. [Latin *indemnis* unhurt (from *in-* not + *damnum* harm) + -FY.]

at; āpe; cär; end; mē; it; īce; hot; ōld; fôrk; wood; fōōl; out; up; ūse; turn; sing; thin; this; zh in treasure; ə in ago, taken, pencil, lemon, circus.

in·dem·ni·ty (in dem′nə tē) *pl.*, **-ties.** *n.* **1.** compensation given for loss, damage, or expenses incurred. **2.** agreement or contract to compensate another for damage, loss, or expenses; insurance. [Late Latin *indemnitās* security from loss or harm, from *indemnis*. See INDEMNIFY.]

in·dent[1] (*v.*, in dent′; *n.*, in′dent′, in dent′) *v.t.* **1.** to start (a line of writing, typing, or printing) farther in than the other lines, as at the beginning of a paragraph. **2.** to cut or make toothlike notches on (an edge or border). **3.** *Archaic.* to make identical cuts or tears in (copies of an agreement or contract) that can be matched for identification. —*n.* indentation. [Medieval Latin *indentare* to furnish with teeth, notch, from Latin *in* in + *dēns* tooth.]

in·dent[2] (in dent′) *v.t.* to make a dent or an impression in. [IN-[2] + DENT.]

in·den·ta·tion (in′den tā′shən) *n.* part set or pushed back from the rest; dent or recess: *a series of indentations where the hailstones hit the car roof, an indentation on the coastline that marks the location of a harbor.*

in·den·tion (in den′shən) *n.* practice or result of starting a line of writing, typing, or printing farther in than the other lines: *to begin each new paragraph with an indention.*

in·den·ture (in den′chər) *n.* contract by which a person, as an apprentice, is bound to serve another person for a stated period of time. —*v.t.*, **-tured, -tur·ing.** to bind (a person or persons) by such a contract. [Medieval Latin *indentura* document in duplicate that has been indented or provided with notched matching edges to prevent fraud, from *indentare* to notch. See INDENT[1]. The indentured person kept a copy of the agreement to prove when the period of service was over.]

in·de·pend·ence (in′di pen′dəns) *n.* **1.** state or quality of being independent. **2.** *Archaic.* independency (*def.* 1).

In·de·pend·ence (in′di pen′dəns) *n.* city in western Missouri, near Kansas City. Pop. (1970), 111,662.

Independence Day, holiday observed on July 4, commemorating the adoption of the Declaration of Independence on July 4, 1776. Also, **Fourth of July.**

in·de·pend·en·cy (in′di pen′dən sē) *pl.*, **-cies.** *n.* *Archaic.* **1.** enough money to live on without working; competence. **2.** independence.

in·de·pend·ent (in′di pen′dənt) *adj.* **1.** not influenced, guided, or determined by others: *a program of independent study.* **2.** not subject to external control or rule; politically autonomous: *independent village administrations.* **3.** not depending or contingent on something else (often with *of*): *The seasons change, independent of anyone's wishes.* **4.** not connected with, derived from, or part of anything larger, as a chain or system: *independent evidence, an independent filmmaker.* **5.** not affiliated with or regularly supporting any political party: *the independent voter.* **6.** self-willed; self-reliant: *a very independent young woman.* **7.** not relying on anyone for what is necessary or desirable: *a financially independent person.* —*n.* one who or that which is independent, esp. one who is not affiliated with any political party. —in′de·pend′ent·ly, *adv.*

independent clause, clause within a compound or complex sentence that can stand alone as a complete sentence. In the sentence *After the girls had played tennis for an hour, they decided to go for a swim,* the clause *they decided to go for a swim* is an independent clause. Distinguished from **dependent clause.** Also, **main clause.**

independent variable *Mathematics.* variable to which values are assigned without regard to other variables. Distinguished from **dependent variable.**

in-depth (in′depth′) *adj.* penetrating and comprehensive: *an in-depth study of the crisis in the cities.*

in·de·scrib·a·ble (in′di skrī′bə bəl) *adj.* that cannot be described in words; too unusual, great, or private to be described: *an evening of indescribable beauty.* —in′de·scrib′a·bly, *adv.*

in·de·struc·ti·ble (in′di struk′tə bəl) *adj.* that cannot be destroyed; durable; hardy. —in′de·struc′ti·bil′i·ty, in′de·struc′ti·ble·ness, *n.* —in′de·struc′ti·bly, *adv.*

in·de·ter·mi·na·ble (in′di tur′mi nə bəl) *adj.* that cannot be defined, decided, or fixed with certainty: *a specimen of indeterminable genus, a man of indeterminable age.* —in′de·ter′mi·na·bly, *adv.*

in·de·ter·mi·na·cy (in′di tur′mi nə sē) *n.* state or quality of being indeterminate.

in·de·ter·mi·nate (in′di tur′mi nit) *adj.* without defined limits; indefinite or vague: *phrases of indeterminate meaning, waiting for an indeterminate length of time.* —in′de·ter′mi·nate·ly, *adv.* —in′de·ter′mi·nate·ness, *n.*

in·dex (in′deks) *pl.*, **-dex·es** or **-di·ces.** *n.* **1.a.** alphabetical list that comes at the end of a book, indicating where in the book reference to a person or subject can be found. **b.** any similar list, as on the front page of a newspaper, in the last volume of an encyclopedia, or in regularly issued separate volumes, that refers the user to the place where

something can be found. **2.** that which serves to indicate, guide, or direct, as the pointer on a scale or a compass. **3.** indication; sign: *Good manners are an index of one's upbringing.* **4.** relation of size, function, or capacity of one thing to that of another, expressed in terms of a ratio or formula: *an index of obesity.* **5.** index number: *the consumer price index.* **6. Index.** Index Librorum Prohibitorum. **7.** *Printing.* symbol or character (as ☞) used to direct the reader's attention to a particular note or paragraph. **8.** *Mathematics.* **a.** exponent. **b.** number in a radical expressing the root. In $\sqrt[3]{256}$, the index is 3. —*v.t.* **1.** to make an index of or for: *to index periodicals, to index a book.* **2.** to enter in an index: *to index "Tulip" under the entry "Flower."* [Latin *index* forefinger, indicator, indication.]

index finger, finger next to the thumb; forefinger.

In·dex Li·bro·rum Pro·hib·i·to·rum (in′deks lĭ brôr′əm prō hib′ə tôr′əm) list, now abolished, of books that the Roman Catholic Church forbade its members to read without special permission. [Modern Latin *Index Librorum Prohibitorum* literally, list of forbidden books.]

index number, number which measures relative change, as of stock market prices or the cost of living, sometimes expressed as a percentage of an arbitrary base.

index of refraction, number expressing the ratio of the velocity of light in a vacuum to its velocity in a given substance, used to characterize the substance. Also, **refractive index.**

In·di·a (in′dē ə) *n.* **1.** country in southern Asia. Capital, New Delhi. Area, 1,226,860 sq. mi. Pop. (1969 est.), 536,984,000. **2.** large peninsular region of southern Asia, bounded by the Arabian Sea, Indian Ocean, and Bay of Bengal, and comprising India, Pakistan, and several smaller political units. Until 1947, most of India was under British control.

India ink 1. ink made from a special black pigment, used for both writing and drawing. **2.** pigment used to make this ink, consisting of carbon black and gum often formed into sticks, that came originally from China and Japan but was thought by the British to come from India.

In·di·an (in′dē ən) *n.* **1.** member of any of the tribes of original inhabitants of North and South America. Also, **American Indian. 2.** any one of the languages of these tribes. **3.** native of India. —*adj.* **1.** of or relating to American Indians. **2.** of or relating to India.

In·di·an·a (in′dē an′ə) *n.* state in the north-central United States. Capital, Indianapolis. Area, 36,-291 sq. mi. Pop. (1970), 5,193,-669. Abbreviation, **Ind.** —In′di·an′i·an, *n.*

In·di·an·ap·o·lis (in′dē ə-nap′ə lis) *n.* capital and largest city of Indiana, in the central part of the state. Pop. (1970), 744,624.

Indian clubs

Indian club, bottle-shaped club used in arm exercises.

Indian corn, corn (*defs.* 1,2).

Indian Empire, formerly, the parts of India under British control, including the dependent and semidependent Indian states; British India.

Indian file, single file.

Indian giver, one who wants back or takes back a gift.

Indian meal, corn meal.

Indian Ocean, ocean south of Asia, between Africa and Australia.

Indian paintbrush, any of several plants, genus *Castilleja,* of the figwort family, having brightly colored flowers.

Indian pipe, nongreen, leafless, saprophytic plant, *Monotropa uniflora,* shaped like a smoker's pipe, that bears a single white or pink flower and is found chiefly in dark, damp woodlands of North America and Asia.

Indian pudding, sweet pudding made mainly of corn meal, molasses, and milk.

Indian summer, period of warm, mild weather occurring in autumn, usually after the first frost.

Indian Territory, former region in what is now Oklahoma, where the Cherokee, Creek, Seminole, Chickasaw, and Choctaw Indians of the Southeast were sent in the nineteenth century.

Indian tobacco, a plant of the species *Lobelia inflata,* bearing spikelike clusters of light-blue flowers.

Indian turnip, jack-in-the-pulpit.

Indian pipe

India paper 1. thin, strong, opaque paper, used chiefly for Bibles. **2.** thin, absorbent paper made from vegetable fiber, used in taking proofs from engraved plates. It came originally from China and Japan.

India rubber *also,* **india rubber.** rubber (*def.* 1).

In·dic (in′dik) *adj.* of or relating to India.

indic., indicative.

in·di·cate (in′di kāt′) **-cat·ed, -cat·ing.** *v.t.* **1.** to be a sign of; show:

at; āpe; cär; end; mē; it; īce; hot; ōld; fôrk; wood; fōōl; oil; out; up; ūse; turn; sing; thin; this; zh in treasure; ə in ago, taken, pencil, lemon, circus.

523

A high fever indicates that a person's body is fighting disease. **2.** to direct attention to; point out: *The guide indicated the best trail.* **3.a.** to express briefly or generally; suggest: *The senator indicated that he might resign.* **b.** to state, describe, or make known: *Indicate your preferences on these cards.* **4.** to require or point to (a specific course of treatment): *Paul's condition indicated the need for immediate surgery.* [Latin *indicātus*, past participle of *indicāre* to point out, show.]

in·di·ca·tion (in′di kā′shən) *n.* **1.** act of indicating. **2.** that which indicates; sign: *The study found many indications that the economy was in a recession.* **3.** that which is indicated: *The indication is that we are in for a hard winter.*

in·dic·a·tive (in dik′ə tiv) *adj.* **1.** that points out, shows, or suggests (often with *of*): *a gift indicative of our high regard.* **2.** *Grammar.* of or relating to the verb mood that expresses a relation of objective fact between the subject and the predicate. —*n. Grammar.* indicative mood or a verb in this mood. —**in·dic′a·tive·ly,** *adv.*

in·di·ca·tor (in′di kā′tər) *n.* **1.** one who or that which indicates. **2.** any of various instruments which show the position of, measure, or record something, as an airspeed indicator on an airplane. **3.** pointer on the dial of such an instrument. **4.** substance which indicates chemical conditions or changes, esp. by changing color.

in·di·ces (in′də sēz) a plural of **index**.

in·dict (in dīt′) *v.t.* **1.** to accuse of an offense, as if on legal authority; criticize harshly: *The press indicted the candidate for his lack of concern with the housing problem.* **2.** (of a grand jury) to accuse formally of an act or omission which is punishable by law; return an indictment against. [Modification (influenced by Medieval Latin *indictāre* to accuse) of INDITE.] —**in·dict′er;** *also,* **in·dict′or,** *n.*

in·dict·a·ble (in dī′tə bəl) *adj.* **1.** that one can be indicted for: *an indictable offense.* **2.** that can be indicted.

in·dict·ment (in dīt′mənt) *n.* **1.** legal accusation returned by a grand jury, charging the commission or omission of some act, which is punishable by law. **2.** accusation or criticism.

In·dies (in′dēz) *n.* **1.a.** East Indies. **b.** East Indies together with India and Indochina. **2.** West Indies.

in·dif·fer·ence (in dif′ər əns, -dif′rəns) *n.* **1.** lack of feeling, concern, or care. **2.** insignificance.

in·dif·fer·ent (in dif′ər ənt, -dif′rənt) *adj.* **1.** having or showing a lack of feeling, concern, or care. **2.** not particularly good; routine and average: *an indifferent performance.* **3.** making no important difference one way or the other; not significant: *an indifferent result.* **4.** not interested one way or another; not partial to one more than another. [Latin *indifferēns* making no difference.] —**in·dif′fer·ent·ly,** *adv.* —**Syn. 1.** see **half-hearted.**

in·di·gence (in′di jəns) *n.* poverty.

in·dig·e·nous (in dij′ə nəs) *adj.* originating in a particular place; not brought in from outside; native: *Kangaroos are indigenous to Australia.* [Latin *indigena* native + OUS.] —**in·dig′e·nous·ly,** *adv.* —**Syn.** see **native.**

in·di·gent (in′di jənt) *adj.* not having enough to live on; poor; needy. [Latin *indigēns,* present participle of *indigēre* to need.] —**Syn.** see **poor.**

in·di·gest·i·ble (in′di jes′tə bəl, -dī-) *adj.* that cannot be digested or that is difficult to digest. —**in′di·gest′i·bil′i·ty,** *n.*

in·di·ges·tion (in′di jes′chən, -dī-) *n.* condition characterized by gas, heartburn, belching, and other symptoms that show a disturbance of the normal process of digesting food.

in·dig·nant (in dig′nənt) *adj.* filled with indignation. [Latin *indignāns,* present participle of *indignārī* to be angry at.] —**in·dig′nant·ly,** *adv.*

in·dig·na·tion (in′dig nā′shən) *n.* restrained, dignified anger aroused by meanness, injustice, or ingratitude: *the old man's indignation at being told he had to retire.* [Latin *indignātiō.*] —**Syn.** see **anger.**

in·dig·ni·ty (in dig′nə tē) *pl.,* **-ties.** *n.* act or circumstance that demeans one's worth or character and interferes with one's dignity. [Latin *indignitās.*] —**Syn.** see **insult.**

in·di·go (in′di gō′) *pl.,* **-gos** or **-goes.** *n.* **1.** very dark blue dye obtained from various plants or made synthetically from aniline. **2.** any of the plants from which this dye is obtained, belonging to either of two genera, *Indigofera,* found chiefly in Asia, or *Isatis,* native to Europe. **3.** deep violet-blue color. [Spanish *indigo* the plant and the dye, from Latin *indicum* the dye, from Greek *indikon (pharmakon)* Indian (dye), going back to Persian *Hind* India. See HINDU.]

indigo bunting, North American finch, *Passerina cyanea,* the male of which has deep-blue summer plumage which, in winter, turns brown, the year-round color of the female's plumage. Length: 5½ inches. Also, **indigo bird.**

in·di·rect (in′di rekt′, -dī-) *adj.* **1.** not in a straight line; roundabout: *an indirect course.* **2.** having or depending on something intervening; not immediate: *an indirect influence on his decisions.* **3.** not straightforward and open; devious: *Becky thought of an indirect way of getting what she wanted.* —**in′di·rect′ly,** *adv.* —**in′di·rect′ness,** *n.*

indirect discourse, form of discourse in which a person's words or thoughts are repeated without exact quotation, for example: *She said that she didn't like dresses.* Distinguished from **direct discourse.**

in·di·rec·tion (in′də rek′shən, -dī-) *n.* **1.** roundabout action or procedure. **2.** lack of straightforwardness and openness. **3.** that which lacks straightforwardness and openness. **4.** absence of guidance and control.

indirect lighting, illumination by light reflected from a ceiling, wall, or other surface.

indirect object, word designating the person or thing indirectly affected by an action, with the stated or understood accompaniment of a preposition. In *I gave him a book, him* is the indirect object. Distinguished from **direct object.**

indirect tax, tax, as a customs duty or excise tax, which is passed on to the consumer by raising the price of the goods or service taxed. Distinguished from **direct tax.**

in·dis·cern·i·ble (in′di surn′ə bəl, -zur′-) *adj.* that cannot be detected, perceived, or recognized as distinct: *The spotted fawn was indiscernible among the trees.*

in·dis·creet (in′dis krēt′) *adj.* lacking discernment, prudence, tact, or careful judgment; not discreet. —**in′dis·creet′ly,** *adv.* —**in′dis·creet′ness,** *n.*

in·dis·cre·tion (in′dis kresh′ən) *n.* **1.** quality of being indiscreet. **2.** that which is indiscreet.

in·dis·crim·i·nate (in dis krim′ə nit) *adj.* **1.** not noting differences or making distinctions: *an indiscriminate movie goer.* **2.** random or confused: *indiscriminate arrests.* —**in·dis·crim′i·nate·ly,** *adv.*

in·dis·pen·sa·ble (in′dis pen′sə bəl) *adj.* that cannot be dispensed with; absolutely necessary or essential: *A balanced diet is indispensable for good health.* —**in′dis·pen′sa·bil′i·ty,** *n.* —**in′dis·pen′sa·bly,** *adv.* —**Syn.** see **necessary.**

in·dis·pose (in′dis pōz′) **-posed, -pos·ing.** *v.t.* **1.** to make unwilling or unreceptive. **2.** to make unfit or incapable.

in·dis·posed (in′dis pōzd′) *adj.* **1.** sick. **2.** unwilling; unreceptive.

in·dis·put·a·ble (in′dis pū′tə bəl, in dis′pyə-) *adj.* not subject to dispute; unquestionable. —**in′dis·put′a·bil′i·ty,** *n.* —**in′dis·put′a·bly,** *adv.*

in·dis·sol·u·ble (in′dis sol′yə bəl) *adj.* that cannot be dissolved, destroyed, or abolished. —**in′dis·sol′u·bil′i·ty,** *n.* —**in dis·sol′u·bly,** *adv.*

in·dis·tinct (in′dis tingkt′) *adj.* not distinct. [Latin *indistinctus.*] —**Syn.** see **faint.**

in·dis·tin·guish·a·ble (in′dis ting′gwi shə bəl) *adj.* that cannot be told apart or seen as a distinct thing.

in·dite (in dīt′) **-dit·ed, -dit·ing.** *v.t. Archaic.* to put into writing; compose. [Old French *enditer* to dictate, write down, going back to Latin *in* in + *dictāre* to dictate, write down.]

in·di·um (in′dē əm) *n.* soft, silvery, rare metallic element, used esp. in alloys for jewelry, bearings, and dentures. Symbol: In See **element** for table. [Modern Latin *indium,* from Latin *indicum* blue pigment, indigo; referring to a line of indigo color in the spectrum of indium. See INDIGO.]

in·di·vid·u·al (in′də vij′ōō əl) *adj.* **1.** single; particular; distinct; separate: *each individual dwelling.* **2.** for or by one only: *individual action.* **3.** characteristic of one only: *individual opinions.* —*n.* **1.** single person, esp. as distinct from a group. **2.** single living thing: *No one supposes that all the individuals of the same species are cast in the same actual mold* (Darwin, 1859). [Medieval Latin *individualis* indivisible, from Latin *indīviduus.*] —**in′di·vid′u·al·ly,** *adv.* —**Syn. adj. 1.** see **particular.**

in·di·vid·u·al·ism (in′də vij′ōō ə liz′əm) *n.* **1.** theory and practice that emphasizes the worth, freedom, and well-being of the individual as against the authority of a group, community, or state. **2.** action or thought by each person for his or her own ends without regard for others. **3.** theory that stresses the reality of particular things or the separateness and self-sufficiency of particular things. **4.** individuality.

in·di·vid·u·al·ist (in′də vij′ōō ə list) *n.* **1.** one who practices or advocates individualism. **2.** one who has individuality. —*adj.* individualistic.

in·di·vid·u·al·is·tic (in′də vij′ōō ə lis′tik) *adj.* of, relating to, or characteristic of individualism or individualists.

in·di·vid·u·al·i·ty (in′də vij′ōō al′ə tē) *pl.,* **-ties.** *n.* **1.** quality that distinguishes one person or thing from others; individual character. **2.** condition of being an individual.

in·di·vid·u·al·ize (in′də vij′ōō ə līz′) **-ized, -iz·ing.** *v.t.* **1.** to fit to a particular individual or to different individuals: *to individualize instruction.* **2.** to consider separately; particularize: *to individualize the features of a landscape.* **3.** to make into an individual; bring out the individuality of: *to individualize the characters in a play.*

in·di·vid·u·ate (in′də vij′ōō āt′) **-at·ed, -at·ing.** *v.t.* to make distinct from others; make individual.

---

at; āpe; cär; end; mē; it; īce; hot; ōld; fôrk; wood; fōōl; oil; out; up; ūse; turn; sing; thin; this; zh in treasure; ə in ago, taken, pencil, lemon, circus.

in·di·vid·u·a·tion (in′də vij′ōō ā′shən) *n.* act or process of individuating; state of being individuated.

in·di·vis·i·ble (in′də viz′ə bəl) *adj.* that cannot be divided. —**in′di·vis′i·bil′i·ty,** *n.* —**in′di·vis′i·bly,** *adv.*

In·do·chi·na (in′dō chī′nə) *n.* **1.** peninsula in southeastern Asia between the Bay of Bengal and the South China Sea, consisting of the Malay Peninsula and the nations of North Vietnam, South Vietnam, Burma, Laos, Cambodia, and Thailand. **2.** French Indochina. —**In·do·chi·nese** (in′dō chī′nēz′, -nēs′), *adj., n.*

in·doc·tri·nate (in dok′tri nāt′) -nat·ed, -nat·ing. *v.t.* to teach to or inculcate into (someone) a theory, belief, or principle, esp. one that is partisan or sectarian. [Latin *in* + *doctrīna* learning, teaching + -ATE[1].] —**in·doc′tri·na′tion,** *n.*

In·do-Eu·ro·pe·an (in′dō yoor′ə pē′ən) *adj.* of or relating to the family of languages that includes the majority of those spoken in Europe and the Americas and many of those spoken in Asia. —*n.* this family of languages or the hypothetical prehistoric language from which they are derived.

In·do-I·ra·ni·an (in′dō i rā′nē ən, -ī rä′-) *n.* subfamily of the Indo-European family of languages, including Hindustani, Bengali, Persian, and other languages spoken predominantly in Afghanistan, India, Persia, and certain other Asian countries.

in·do·lence (ind′əl əns) *n.* state or quality of being indolent.

in·do·lent (ind′əl ənt) *adj.* having or showing a dislike or avoidance of work or exertion; lazy; idle. [Late Latin *indolēns* painless, from Latin *in-* not + *dolēns,* present participle of *dolēre* to feel pain.] —**in′do·lent·ly,** *adv.*

in·dom·i·ta·ble (in dom′ə tə bəl) *adj.* that cannot be conquered or dominated; an indomitable will. [Late Latin *indomitābilis,* from Latin *in-* not + *domitāre* to tame.] —**in·dom′i·ta·bly,** *adv.* —**Syn.** see **invincible.**

In·do·ne·sia (in′də nē′zhə, -shə) *n.* country in southeastern Asia composed of islands in the Malay Archipelago, formerly known as the Netherlands East Indies. Capital, Djakarta. Area, 735,268 sq. mi. Pop. (1969 est.), 116,000,000. [Greek *Indos* Indian (going back to Persian *Hind* India) + *nēsos* island. See HINDU.]

In·do·ne·sian (in′də nē′zhən, -shən) *adj.* of or relating to Indonesia or its people. —*n.* native or inhabitant of Indonesia.

Indonesian Borneo, Kalimantan (def. 1).

in·door (in′dôr′) *adj.* **1.** situated or carried on within a house or building: *an indoor swimming pool, an indoor service, an indoor sport.* **2.** meant to be used within a house or building: *indoor carpeting, indoor furniture.*

in·doors (in′dôrz′) *adv.* in or into a house or building: *to play indoors, to move a party indoors when it rains.*

In·dore (in dôr′) *n.* city in central India. Pop. (1961), 394,941.

in·dorse (in dôrs′) endorse.

in·dor·see (in dôr′sē′, in′dôr-) endorsee.

in·dorse·ment (in dôrs′mənt) endorsement.

In·dra (in′drə) *n.* one of the chief gods of the earliest Hindu religion, associated with rain and storms. In the present form of Hinduism, he is of minor rank.

in·du·bi·ta·ble (in dōō′bə tə bəl, -dū′-) *adj.* not to be doubted; certain; unquestionable. —**in·du′bi·ta·bly,** *adv.*

in·duce (in dōōs′, -dūs′) -duced, -duc·ing. *v.t.* **1.** to lead by or as by persuasion or influence; motivate: *We tried to induce them to come with us.* **2.** to bring about; bring on; produce; cause: *The first-aid treatment for some poisons is to induce vomiting.* **3.** to produce (electric current) by induction. [Latin *indūcere* to lead in, persuade.]
Syn. 1. Induce, persuade mean to move or coax another to a course of action. **Induce** suggests influencing a person and overcoming his opposition by providing him with the necessary motivation: *Bert's wife induced him to give up smoking.* **Persuade** usually involves swaying a person's mind and inclining his will by pleading and reasoning: *The saleswoman persuaded the lady to buy the blue dress.*

in·duce·ment (in dōōs′mənt, -dūs′-) *n.* **1.** something attractive that leads someone on: *The sunny day and clear water were irresistible inducements to go swimming.* **2.** act of inducing; state of being induced. —**Syn. 1.** see **incentive.**

in·duct (in dukt′) *v.t.* **1.** to put (someone) through the process of induction into military service. **2.** to bring into a group; admit: *The club inducted four new members.* **3.** to install in an office. [Latin *inductus,* past participle of *indūcere* to lead in.]
Syn. 3. Induct, install, initiate mean to admit as a member or official, esp. in a formal way. **Induct** means to put in office formally by investing with the appropriate insignia of office: *The new governor was inducted into office.* **Install** means to place in possession of an office, rank, or dignity by seating in the official seat: *The new college president was installed before a large crowd.* **Initiate** means to admit as a member of a society, guild, or fraternity with formal ceremony: *The newly elected members were initiated by the president of the club.*

in·duc·tance (in duk′təns) *n.* ability of an electric circuit to produce an electromotive force when the current in the circuit or in a neighboring circuit is changing.

in·duc·tee (in duk′tē) *n.* one who is being inducted, esp. into military service.

in·duc·tion (in duk′shən) *n.* **1.a.** process by which someone is made a member of the military service, including swearing in. **b.** process or ceremony of being brought into a group or installed in an office. **2.** act of inducing: *the induction of a hypnotized state.* **3.** *Electricity.* **a.** act or process of giving an electric charge to an object by bringing it close to a charged object. **b.** act or process of magnetizing an object by placing it in a magnetic field. **c.** act or process of producing an electric current in a conductor by moving the conductor through a magnetic field, or by moving the field itself. **d.** any process by which a body having electric or magnetic properties produces electric or magnetic properties in another body. **4.** method of supporting or of arriving at a general or universal statement by observing a limited number of particular cases. Distinguished from **deduction.** **5.** *Mathematics.* method of proving a law or theorem about numbers by showing that the law or theorem holds for the first number and then showing that if it holds for all the numbers preceding a given number, it also holds for the next following number.

induction coil, electrical device that converts low-voltage direct current into high-voltage pulses.

in·duc·tive (in duk′tiv) *adj.* **1.** of or relating to logical induction: *We attempted to reach a conclusion by the use of inductive reasoning.* **2.** of, relating to, producing, or produced by electrical or magnetic induction. —**in·duc′tive·ly,** *adv.*

in·duc·tor (in duk′tər) *n.* **1.** one who inducts. **2.** device that possesses inductance, used to introduce inductance into a circuit.

in·due (in dōō′, -dū′) endue.

in·dulge (in dulj′) -dulged, -dulg·ing. *v.t.* **1.** to give way to; yield to: *to indulge one's passion for expensive shoes.* **2.** to yield to the whims or wishes of; give in to: *to indulge a child by giving her ice cream.* —*v.i.* to do or use something to an excessive or unhealthy extent, esp. something pleasant (with *in*): *to indulge in card playing, to indulge in a cigar.* [Latin *indulgēre* to be kind to.] —**Syn.** *v.t.* **2.** see **humor.**

in·dul·gence (in dul′jəns) *n.* **1.** act of indulging. **2.** that which is indulged in: *Cigarettes are an indulgence.* **3.** that granted by one who is indulgent; favor. **4.** in the Roman Catholic Church, pardon from punishment for the sin that remains after the guilt has been forgiven.

in·dul·gent (in dul′jənt) *adj.* characterized by indulgence. —**in·dul′gent·ly,** *adv.*

in·du·rate (*v.,* in′də rāt′, -dyə-; *adj.,* in′dər it, -dyər-, in door′-, -dyoor′-) -rat·ed, -rat·ing. *v.t., v.i.* to make or become hard or unfeeling. —*adj.* hard or unfeeling. [Latin *indūrātus,* past participle of *indūrāre* to harden.]

In·dus (in′dəs) *n.* river flowing from Tibet through Kashmir and West Pakistan into the Arabian Sea.

in·dus·tri·al (in dus′trē əl) *adj.* **1.** of or produced by industry: *industrial wastes, industrial output.* **2.** in or connected with industry: *industrial development, industrial wage system.* **3.** having or characterized by highly developed industry: *industrial society.* **4.** made for use in industry: *heavy machinery and other industrial products.* [Partly from French *industrial* relating to industry, from *industrie* work, manufacturing, from Latin *industria* diligence; partly from Latin *industria* + -AL[1].] —**in·dus′tri·al·ly,** *adv.*

in·dus·tri·al·ism (in dus′trē ə liz′əm) *n.* social and economic system based chiefly on large-scale industries, mechanization, and production, rather than on agriculture or commerce.

in·dus·tri·al·ist (in dus′trē ə list) *n.* one who conducts, owns, or engages in an industrial enterprise.

in·dus·tri·al·ize (in dus′trē ə līz′) -ized, -iz·ing. *v.t.* **1.** to create a high proportion of mechanized industry in (a region or country). **2.** to organize as an industry. —**in·dus′tri·al·i·za′tion,** *n.*

Industrial Revolution, economic and social changes occurring first in England and later throughout Europe and the United States in the eighteenth and nineteenth centuries, resulting from innovations in technology and agriculture. The Industrial Revolution brought about a shift from an agrarian to an industrial society.

industrial union, labor union to which all the workers in a given industry, regardless of particular occupation or skill, may belong. Also, **vertical union.**

in·dus·tri·ous (in dus′trē əs) *adj.* hard-working. [Latin *industriōsus* diligent, from *industrius.*] —**in·dus′tri·ous·ly,** *adv.* —**in·dus′tri·ous·ness,** *n.*

in·dus·try (in′dəs trē) *pl.* **-tries.** *n.* **1.** manufacturing concerns as a whole, esp. as constituting a highly mechanized system: *The future of the nation's industry is imperiled by the strike.* **2.** a particular branch of business, trade, or manufacture: *the tourist industry, the aircraft industry.* **3.** leaders or spokesmen of manufacturing concerns; manage-

ment: *Labor is for the new tax proposal, but industry is opposed.* **4.** ability or fact of getting down to hard work or steady effort: *He shows much industry in performing the task.* [Latin *industria* diligence.]

in·dwell·ing (in′dwel′ing) *adj.* that dwells or is located within.

-ine[1] *suffix* used to form adjectives from nouns: of, like, or relating to: *Alpine, feline.* [Latin *-inus, -īnus,* from Greek *-inos,* sometimes through French *-in(e).*]

-ine[2] *suffix* used in chemistry to form nouns: *bromine, fluorine.* [Latin *-īna,* feminine of *-īnus,* sometimes through French *-ine.* See -INE[1].]

in·e·bri·ate (*v.,* i nē′brē āt′; *n.,* i nē′brē it, -āt′) *-at·ed, -at·ing. v.t.* to make inebriated. —*n.* intoxicated person; habitual drunkard. [Latin *inēbriātus,* past participle of *inēbriāre* to make drunk.] —**in·e′bri·a′tion,** *n.*

in·e·bri·at·ed (i nē′brē ā′tid) *adj.* **1.** intoxicated with liquor; drunk. **2.** excited or stupefied, as if with liquor: *inebriated with the exuberance of his own verbosity* (Disraeli, 1878).

in·e·bri·e·ty (in′i brī′ə tē) *n.* condition of being inebriated or of being an inebriate.

in·ed·i·ble (in ed′ə bəl) *adj.* not fit as food; unsuitable for eating: *The burned meat was inedible.*

in·ef·fa·ble (in ef′ə bəl) *adj.* **1.** that cannot be fully captured or described in words. **2.** too sacred to be spoken aloud. [Latin *ineffābilis* unutterable, going back to *in-* not + *ex* out + *fārī* to speak.] —**in·ef′fa·bil′i·ty, in·ef′fa·ble·ness,** *n.* —**in·ef′fa·bly,** *adv.*

in·ef·face·a·ble (in′i fă′sə bəl) *adj.* that cannot be obliterated, erased, or rubbed out. —**in′ef·face′a·bly,** *adv.*

in·ef·fec·tive (in′i fek′tiv) *adj.* not effective. —**in′ef·fec′tive·ly,** *adv.* —**in′ef·fec′tive·ness,** *n.*

in·ef·fec·tu·al (in′i fek′chōō əl) *adj.* that cannot or does not produce a desired result or effect. —**in′ei·fec′tu·al·ly,** *adv.*

in·ef·fi·ca·cious (in ef′ə kā′shəs) *adj.* unable to produce an intended or desired effect; ineffective.

in·ef·fi·ca·cy (in ef′ə kə sē) *n.* inability to produce an intended or desired effect.

in·ef·fi·cien·cy (in′i fish′ən sē) *n.* state, quality, or fact of being inefficient.

in·ef·fi·cient (in′i fish′ənt) *adj.* involving or resulting in too much effort or waste; not efficient: *The business failed because of inefficient management.* —**in′ef·fi′cient·ly,** *adv.*

in·e·las·tic (in′i las′tik) *adj.* not elastic. —**in′e·las·tic′i·ty,** *n.*

in·el·e·gance (in el′ə gəns) *n.* **1.** state or quality of being inelegant. **2.** that which is inelegant.

in·el·e·gan·cy (in el′ə gən sē) *pl.,* **-cies.** *n.* inelegance.

in·el·e·gant (in el′ə gənt) *adj.* not elegant. —**in′el′e·gant·ly,** *adv.*

in·el·i·gi·ble (in el′i jə bəl) *adj.* not qualified or fit to be chosen. —*n.* one who is ineligible. —**in·el′i·gi·bil′i·ty,** —**in·el′i·gi·bly,** *adv.*

in·e·luc·ta·ble (in′i luk′tə bəl) *adj.* that cannot be overcome or escaped from; inevitable: *an ineluctable force.* [Latin *inēluctābilis,* going back to *in-* not + *ēluctārī* to struggle out.] —**in′e·luc′ta·bil′i·ty,** —**in′e·luc′ta·bly,** *adv.*

in·ept (i nept′) *adj.* **1.** incompetent; awkward; clumsy. **2.** poorly done or chosen; not suitable; inappropriate: *an inept comparison.* **3.** foolish; absurd: *an inept policy.* [Latin *ineptus* unsuitable, foolish.] —**in·ept′ly,** *adv.* —**in·ept′ness,** *n.*

in·ept·i·tude (i nep′tə tōōd′, -tūd′) *n.* **1.** quality of being inept. **2.** inept act or remark.

in·e·qual·i·ty (in′i kwol′ə tē) *pl.,* **-ties.** *n.* **1.** fact or condition of not being equal; lack of equality. **2.** mathematical statement that a number or algebraic expression is greater or less than another.

in·eq·ui·ta·ble (in ek′wə tə bəl) *adj.* not fair and just; not equitable. —**in′eq′ui·ta·bly,** *adv.*

in·eq·ui·ty (in ek′wə tē) *pl.,* **-ties.** *n.* **1.** injustice; unfairness. **2.** that which is unfair and unjust.

in·e·rad·i·ca·ble (in′i rad′i kə bəl) *adj.* that cannot be eradicated. —**in′e·rad′i·ca·bly,** *adv.*

in·ert (i nurt′) *adj.* **1.** without power to move or act; not moving: *a lifeless and inert body.* **2.** not reacting or combining readily with other substances; chemically inactive. **3.** inactive; sluggish; slow: *an inert bureaucracy.* [Latin *iners* inactive.]

in·er·tia (i nur′shə) *n.* **1.** tendency not to get started, not to do anything, or to continue too long in the same course. **2.** *Physics.* resistance of a body to any change in its state of rest or motion. [Latin *inertia* inactivity.]

inertial guidance system, system of guidance for a space vehicle using gyroscopic devices, that automatically absorbs and interprets information, as speed and position, and adjusts the vehicle to a planned flight path.

in·es·cap·a·ble (in′is kā′pə bəl) *adj.* that cannot be escaped or avoided; inevitable: *the inescapable conclusion.* —**in′es·cap′a·bly,** *adv.*

in·es·sen·tial (in′i sen′shəl) *adj.* not essential.

in·es·ti·ma·ble (in es′tə mə bəl) *adj.* that cannot be completely assessed or estimated; very great: *of inestimable value.* —**in·es′ti·ma·bly,** *adv.*

in·ev·i·ta·ble (i nev′ə tə bəl) *adj.* that cannot be avoided; obvious or certain: *the inevitable result.* [Latin *inēvītābilis.*] —**in·ev′i·ta·bil′·i·ty,** *n.* —**in·ev′i·ta·bly,** *adv.*

in·ex·act (in′ig zakt′) *adj.* not exact. —**in′ex·act′ness,** *n.* —**in′ex·act′ly,** *adv.*

in·ex·cus·a·ble (in′iks kū′zə bəl) *adj.* that cannot or should not be excused or justified: *Cruelty to animals is completely inexcusable.* —**in′ex·cus′a·bly,** *adv.*

in·ex·haust·i·ble (in′ig zôs′tə bəl) *adj.* **1.** that cannot be depleted or used up easily: *an inexhaustible source of jokes.* **2.** that does not become easily worn out or tired out; tireless: *an inexhaustible swimmer.* —**in′ex·haust′i·bil′i·ty,** *n.* —**in′ex·haust′i·bly,** *adv.*

in·ex·o·ra·ble (i nek′sər ə bəl) *adj.* that does not change or relent, no matter what anyone does or says; unyielding: *inexorable fate.* [Latin *inexōrābilis,* going back to *in-* not + *exōrāre* to gain by entreaty + -ABLE.] —**in·ex′o·ra·bil′i·ty,** —**in·ex′o·ra·bly,** *adv.*

in·ex·pe·di·en·cy (in′iks pē′dē ən sē) *n.* state or quality of being inexpedient. Also, **in′ex·pe′di·ence.**

in·ex·pe·di·ent (in′iks pē′dē ənt) *adj.* not promoting immediate results or advantage; not expedient.

in·ex·pen·sive (in′iks pen′siv) *adj.* involving little expense; not costly. —**in′ex·pen′sive·ly,** *adv.* —**in′ex·pen′sive·ness,** *n.*

in·ex·pe·ri·ence (in′iks pēr′ē əns) *n.* lack of experience: *She was hampered in her new job by inexperience.*

in·ex·pe·ri·enced (in′iks pēr′ē ənst) *adj.* lacking experience.

in·ex·pert (in eks′purt, in′iks purt′) *adj.* not expert.

in·ex·pi·a·ble (in eks′pē ə bəl) *adj.* that cannot be atoned for or made amends for. [Latin *inexpiābilis.*]

in·ex·pli·ca·ble (in eks′pli kə bəl, in eks′pli kə-) *adj.* that cannot be explained. [Latin *inexplicābilis.*] —**in′ex·plic′a·bil′i·ty,** *n.* —**in′·ex·plic′a·bly,** *adv.*

in·ex·plic·it (in′iks plis′it) *adj.* not clear or definite; not explicit.

in·ex·press·i·ble (in′iks pres′ə bəl) *adj.* that cannot be put into words, communicated, or shown outwardly. —**in′ex·press′i·bil′i·ty,** *n.* —**in′ex·press′i·ble·ness,** *n.* —**in′ex·press′i·bly,** *adv.*

in·ex·pres·sive (in′iks pres′iv) *adj.* conveying little feeling or meaning; not expressive.

in ex·ten·so (in′ eks ten′sō) *Latin.* at full length; in full.

in·ex·tin·guish·a·ble (in′iks ting′gwi shə bəl) *adj.* that cannot be put out, destroyed, or obscured: *an inextinguishable flame, an inextinguishable memory.* —**in′ex·tin′guish·a·bly,** *adv.*

in ex·tre·mis (in′eks trē′mis) *Latin.* at the outermost limits, as of endurance, esp. at the point of death.

in·ex·tri·ca·ble (in eks′tri kə bəl, -iks trik′ə bəl) *adj.* **1.** impossible to separate, disentangle, remove, or set free: *an inextricable tangle of threads.* **2.** impossible to solve, straighten out, or escape from: *an inextricable dilemma.* [Latin *inextricābilis* that cannot be disentangled.] —**in·ex′tri·ca·bly,** *adv.*

inf., infinitive.

in·fal·li·ble (in fal′ə bəl) *adj.* **1.** incapable of error: *infallible judgment.* **2.** reliable; unfailing; sure: *an infallible solution.* [Medieval Latin *infallibilis* incapable of error, from Latin *in-* not + Late Latin *fallibilis.* See FALLIBLE.] —**in·fal′li·bil′i·ty,** *n.* —**in·fal′li·bly,** *adv.*

in·fa·mous (in′fə məs) *adj.* **1.** widely known and condemned for wrongdoing. **2.** having or deserving everyone's condemnation; extremely bad: *infamous crimes.* [Medieval Latin *infamosus* ill spoken of, from Latin *infāmis.*]

in·fa·my (in′fə mē) *pl.,* **-mies.** *n.* **1.** state or condition of being widely known and condemned for wrongdoing. **2.** quality of being extremely bad: *the great infamy of these crimes.* **3.** extremely bad act. [Latin *infāmia* bad reputation.]

in·fan·cy (in′fən sē) *pl.,* **-cies.** *n.* **1.** state or period of being an infant. **2.** earliest period of development of anything. **3.** *Law.* state of being under the age of legal responsibility, usually twenty-one, or the period before reaching this age. [Latin *infantia* early childhood; literally, inability to speak.]

in·fant (in′fənt) *n.* **1.** child during the earliest period of his or her life; baby. **2.** *Law.* one who has not reached the age of legal responsibility; minor. —*adj.* **1.** of, relating to, or for an infant. **2.** in the earliest period of development: *an infant industry.* [Latin *infāns* baby; literally, (one) unable to speak.]

in·fan·ta (in fan′tə) *n.* daughter of the monarch of Spain or Portugal. [Spanish and Portuguese *infanta,* feminine of *infante.* See INFANTE.]

in·fan·te (in fan′tā) *n.* son of the monarch of Spain or Portugal other than the first son, not an heir to the throne. [Spanish and Portuguese *infante,* from Latin *infāns.* See INFANT.]

in·fan·ti·cide[1] (in fan′tə sīd′) *n.* killing of an infant. [Late Latin *īnfanticīdium,* from Latin *īnfāns* baby + *-cīdium.* See -CIDE[1].]

at; āpe; cär; end; mē; it; īce; hot; ōld; fôrk; wood; fōōl; oil; out; up; ūse; turn; sing; thin; this; zh in treasure; ə in ago, taken, pencil, lemon, circus.

in·fan·ti·cide² (in fan′tə sīd′) *n.* one who kills an infant. [Late Latin *īnfanticīda*, from Latin *īnfāns* baby + *-cīda.* See *-CIDE².*]

in·fan·tile (in′fən tīl′, -til) *adj.* **1.** too much like an infant or like that of an infant; childish. **2.** of, relating to, or belonging to infancy. [Late Latin *īnfantīlis* relating to an infant, from *īnfāns.* See INFANT.] —**Syn. 1.** see childish.

infantile paralysis, poliomyelitis.

in·fan·ti·lism (in′fən tī liz′əm, -ti-) *n.* condition characterized by overly slow body development and persistence of childish physical, emotional, or intellectual traits in adult life.

in·fan·try (in′fən trē) *pl.* **-tries.** *n.* **1.** soldiers trained and equipped to fight on foot. **2.** branch of an army composed of such soldiers. [French *infanterie,* from Italian *infanteria,* from *infante* child, servant of a knight, foot soldier, from Latin *īnfāns* baby.]

in·fan·try·man (in′fən trē mən) *pl.* **-men.** *n.* male who is in an infantry.

infant school *British.* school for children who are under seven years of age.

in·fat·u·ate (in fach′ōō āt′) **-at·ed, -at·ing.** *v.t.* to affect (someone) with a seemingly great passion or attraction that is really childish or foolish and will pass quickly. [Latin *īnfatuātus,* past participle of *īnfatuāre* to make a fool of, from *in* + *fatuus* foolish.]

in·fat·u·at·ed (in fach′ōō ā′tid) *adj.* affected with a passion or attraction that is childish or foolish and will pass quickly.

in·fat·u·a·tion (in fach′ōō ā′shən) *n.* **1.** act of infatuating; state of being infatuated. **2.** passion or attraction that passes quickly.

in·fect (in fekt′) *v.t.* **1.** to cause disease in by introducing certain microorganisms. **2.** to contaminate with microorganisms that cause disease. **3.** to affect or influence, as with feelings or beliefs. [Latin *īnfectus,* past participle of *īnficere* to put in, stain, taint.]

in·fec·tion (in fek′shən) *n.* **1.** invasion of part of the body by certain microorganisms, as bacteria, viruses, or fungi, whose growth causes disease. **2.** disease or other harmful condition resulting from this. **3.** fact or state of being infected. **4.** communication of a feeling, belief, or state of mind.

in·fec·tious (in fek′shəs) *adj.* **1.** (of a disease) caused or transmitted by infection. **2.** capable of producing infection; containing disease-producing microorganisms. **3.** readily communicated to others; tending to spread: *infectious laughter.* ▲ **Infectious** and **contagious** both refer to diseases that are catching or transmissible. **Infectious** refers to diseases transmitted by germs, as viruses or bacteria, in the air and water. Infectious diseases may or may not also be contagious. Cholera is an infectious disease. **Contagious** designates diseases transmitted by contact or directly from a person afflicted with it. Measles is a contagious disease. —**in·fec′tious·ly,** *adv.* —**in·fec′tious·ness,** *n.*

infectious mononucleosis, contagious but usually not serious blood disease in which there are an excessive number of certain white blood cells in the blood. It is characterized by fever, loss of appetite, and fatigue, and is thought to be caused by a virus. Also, **glandular fever.**

in·fec·tive (in fek′tiv) *adj.* likely to produce infection; infectious.

in·fe·lic·i·tous (in′fə lis′ə təs) *adj.* **1.** unsuitable; inappropriate: *an infelicitous comment.* **2.** unfortunate; unhappy.

in·fe·lic·i·ty (in′fə lis′ə tē) *pl.* **-ties.** *n.* **1.** state or quality of being infelicitous. **2.** that which is inappropriate.

in·fer (in fur′) **-ferred, -fer·ring.** *v.t.* to derive or conclude by reasoning from something known or assumed: *From his grades I inferred he was a good student.* ▲ **Infer** is sometimes used to mean **imply,** but such usage is generally considered improper. It is better not to confuse the two words but to reserve each for a distinct function. To **imply** is to point to a conclusion; to **infer** is to deduce a conclusion *from* something: *Will's stalling implied that he didn't want to go. Holly inferred from Will's stalling that he didn't want to go.* —*v.i.* to draw inferences. [Latin *īnferre* to bring into, deduce.]

in·fer·ence (in′fər əns) *n.* **1.** that which is inferred; conclusion. **2.** act or process of inferring.

in·fer·en·tial (in′fə ren′shəl) *adj.* involving or depending on inference.

in·fe·ri·or (in fēr′ē ər) *adj.* **1.** of poor quality; below average: *The food at that restaurant is inferior.* **2.** low or lower in quality, value, or importance: *She always felt inferior to her older sister.* **3.** low or lower in place or rank; subordinate: *an inferior position.* **4.** (of an organ or part) lower in place or position or directed downward; below in relation to another structure. **5.** (of a plant part) growing below some other part. **6.** between the earth and the sun: *an inferior planet.* —*n.* person who is inferior to others, as in rank or achievement. [Latin *īnferior* lower, comparative of *īnferus* low.] —**in·fe′ri·or′i·ty,** *n.*

inferiority complex *Psychology.* general feeling of personal unworthiness and inadequacy.

in·fer·nal (in furn′əl) *adj.* **1.** of, relating to, or characteristic of hell. **2.** hellish; diabolical. **3.** *Informal.* hateful; outrageous: *an infernal nui-*

sance. [Late Latin *īnfernālis* relating to the underworld, going back to Latin *īnferus* low.] —**in·fer′nal·ly,** *adv.*

in·fer·no (in fur′nō) *pl.* **-nos.** *n.* **1.** hell. **2.** any place resembling hell, esp. one having intense heat: *The furnace room was an inferno.* [Italian *inferno,* from Latin *īnfernus* lying beneath.]

in·fer·tile (in furt′əl) *adj.* not fertile; barren. —**in·fer·til′i·ty,** *n.*

in·fest (in fest′) *v.t.* to overrun or occur in large numbers so as to be harmful or troublesome: *Weeds infested the garden.* [Latin *īnfestāre* to attack, trouble.]

in·fes·ta·tion (in′fes tā′shən) *n.* act of infesting; being infested.

in·fi·del (in′fəd əl, -fə del′) *n.* **1.** one who does not believe in any religion. **2.** among the Muslims, one who does not accept Islam, esp. a Christian. **3.** among Christians, one who does not accept Christianity, esp. a Muslim. —*adj.* **1.** having no religious beliefs. **2.** not accepting a particular faith, esp. Christianity or Islam. **3.** of or relating to unbelievers. [Latin *īnfidēlis* faithless, unbelieving.] —**Syn.** *n.* see pagan.

in·fi·del·i·ty (in′fə del′ə tē) *pl.* **-ties.** *n.* **1.** lack of faith; disloyalty. **2.** marital unfaithfulness; adultery. **3.** lack of belief in a particular religion, esp. Christianity or Islam. **4.** disloyal or adulterous act.

in·field (in′fēld′) *n.* Baseball. **1.** area bounded by the paths connecting the bases. **2.** the first, second, and third basemen and shortstop, collectively.

in·field·er (in′fēl′dər) *n.* Baseball. player who plays a position in the infield.

in·fil·trate (in fil′trāt, in′fil trāt′) **-trat·ed, -trat·ing.** *v.t.* **1.** to move members of a faction or group gradually and secretly into positions of power or responsibility within (an organization or government). **2.** (of troops) to move through (enemy lines) in order to attack from the rear or engage in sabotage or espionage. **3.** to filter into or through; permeate. **4.** to cause (a liquid or gas) to pass through pores or openings. —*v.i.* to pass into or through a substance by filtering.

in·fil·tra·tion (in′fil trā′shən) *n.* **1.** act of infiltrating; being infiltrated. **2.** that which infiltrates.

infin., infinitive.

in·fi·nite (in′fə nit) *adj.* **1.** having no limits or end; boundless. **2.** immeasurably or extremely great; immense; vast. **3.** *Mathematics.* **a.** of or designating a quantity larger than any assigned number. **b.** of or relating to a set containing an unlimited number of elements. —*n.* **1.** that which is infinite. **2.** *Mathematics.* an infinite quantity. **3. the Infinite.** God. [Latin *īnfīnītus* unlimited.] —**in′fi·nite·ly,** *adv.* —**in′fi·nite·ness,** *n.*

in·fin·i·tes·i·mal (in′fi nə tes′ə məl) *adj.* **1.** so small as to be immeasurable or insignificant: *an infinitesimal speck of dust.* **2.** *Mathematics.* of, relating to, or designating a variable that becomes arbitrarily small, approaching zero as a limit. —*n.* *Mathematics.* an infinitesimal quantity. [Modern Latin *infinitesimus* (from Latin *īnfīnītus* unlimited) + *-AL¹.*] —**in′fi·ni·tes′i·mal·ly,** *adv.*

in·fin·i·tive (in fin′ə tiv) *n.* form of a verb expressing existence or action, without indicating person or number. In English, it is often preceded by *to: We want him to go.* [Late Latin *īnfīnītīvus,* from Latin *īnfīnītus* unlimited (because it does not indicate definite persons or numbers).]

in·fin·i·tude (in fin′ə tōōd′, -tūd′) *n.* **1.** quality of being infinite. **2.** infinite quantity, number, or extent.

in·fin·i·ty (in fin′ə tē) *pl.* **-ties.** *n.* **1.** state or quality of being infinite; boundlessness. **2.** something that is infinite, as space or time. **3.** indefinitely or extremely great amount or number. **4.** *Mathematics.* quantity of unbounded magnitude, larger than any assigned number, represented by the symbol ∞. [Latin *īnfīnītās* boundlessness.]

in·firm (in furm′) *adj.* **1.** physically weak, esp. from old age. **2.** lacking firmness of will, purpose, or character; irresolute. [Latin *īnfirmus* feeble, weak.] —**in·firm′ly,** *adv.* —**in·firm′ness,** *n.*

in·fir·ma·ry (in fur′mər ē) *pl.* **-ries.** *n.* place, as in a school or factory, for the care or treatment of the sick or injured. [Medieval Latin *infirmaria* hospital, from Latin *īnfirmus* sick.]

in·fir·mi·ty (in fur′mə tē) *pl.* **-ties.** *n.* **1.** state or quality of being infirm; physical weakness; feebleness. **2.** physical defect or ailment, esp. from old age. **3.** moral weakness or failing.

in·flame (in flām′) **-flamed, -flam·ing.** *v.t.* **1.** to excite to great emotion; stir up. **2.** to make hot, red, swollen, or painful; cause inflammation in. **3.** to increase or intensify, as anger or violence. —*v.i.* to become affected, as a part of the body, with inflammation. [Old French *enflammer* to set on fire, excite, irritate, from Latin *inflammāre* to set on fire.]

in·flam·ma·ble (in flam′ə bəl) *adj.* **1.** capable of being set on fire easily. **2.** easily excited or aroused. —*n.* that which can be set on fire easily. —**in·flam′ma·bil′i·ty,** *n.* —**in·flam′ma·bly,** *adv.*

in·flam·ma·tion (in′flə mā′shən) *n.* **1.** reaction of body tissue to injury, infection, or irritation, characterized by heat, redness, swelling, and pain. **2.** act of inflaming; being inflamed.

in·flam·ma·to·ry (in flam′ə tôr′ē) *adj.* **1.** tending to excite strong

emotion or violent action: *an inflammatory statement.* **2.** of, relating to, or characterized by inflammation.

in·flat·able (in flā′tə bəl) *adj.* that can be distended.

in·flate (in flāt′) *-flat·ed, -flat·ing.* *v.t.* **1.** to cause to swell by filling with air or gas; distend: *to inflate the lungs.* **2.** to enhance or give a boost to: *His sudden fame inflated his ego.* **3.** to increase beyond previous or usual levels, as prices or currency. —*v.i.* to become swollen; puff up. [Latin *īnflātus,* past participle of *īnflāre* to blow into.] —**flat′er;** *also,* **in·fla′tor,** *n.*

in·fla·tion (in flā′shən) *n.* **1.** act of inflating; being inflated. **2.** economic condition characterized by a rise in the average price level, usually caused by an increase in money supply without a corresponding increase in the supply of goods and services.

in·fla·tion·ar·y (in flā′shə ner′ē) *adj.* of, relating to, or causing economic inflation.

in·fla·tion·ist (in flā′shə nist) *n.* one who favors economic inflation.

in·flect (in flekt′) *v.t.* **1.** to change or vary the tone or pitch of (the voice); modulate. **2.** to vary the form of (a word) by inflection. **3.** to turn from a direct line or course; bend: *to inflect rays of light.* [Latin *īnflectere* to change, bend.]

in·flec·tion (in flek′shən) *also, British,* **in·flex·ion.** *n.* **1.** change or variation in the tone or pitch of the voice. **2.a.** process by which the form of a word is changed to express grammatical or syntactical relationships. **b.** word formed by this process. **3.** act of inflecting; being inflected. **4.** bend or angle.
Syn. 1. Inflection, intonation, accent denote quality or variation in speech. **Inflection** denotes a variation in pitch or tone used to convey emotions or distinctions in meaning: *Questions end on a rising inflection.* **Intonation** denotes modulation of pitch and rhythmic quality of speech: *The actor who played Hamlet had a rich and solemn intonation.* **Accent** denotes the manner of oral expression, esp. the patterns of stress and enunciation peculiar to a region, language, or group: *The Rhodes scholar spoke with an Oxford accent.*

in·flec·tion·al (in flek′shən əl) *also, British,* **in·flex·ion·al.** *adj.* of, relating to, or exhibiting grammatical inflection.

in·flex·i·ble (in flek′sə bəl) *adj.* **1.** that cannot be bent; stiff; rigid. **2.** unyielding in mind or purpose; adamant: *He was inflexible once he had made a decision.* **3.** that cannot be changed or altered; immutable: *an inflexible rule.* [Latin *īnflexibilis* that cannot be bent.] —**in·flex′-i·bil′i·ty,** *n.* —**in·flex′i·bly,** *adv.* —**Syn. 1.** see **stiff.**

in·flict (in flikt′) *v.t.* **1.** to cause by or as by striking: *to inflict pain, to inflict a wound.* **2.** to administer or deal: *to inflict a blow.* **3.** to impose (something unwelcome) on someone: *to inflict punishment.* [Latin *īnflīctus,* past participle of *īnflīgere* to dash against, impose upon.]

in·flic·tion (in flik′shən) *n.* **1.** act of inflicting. **2.** that which is inflicted, as pain, punishment, or suffering.

in·flo·res·cence (in′flō res′əns) *n.* **1.a.** mode of arrangement of a cluster of flowers in relation to the stem or stems in the cluster and in relation to each other. **b.** flower cluster. **c.** flowers collectively. **d.** solitary flower. **2.** unfolding of blossoms; flowering. [Modern Latin *inflorescentia,* from Late Latin *īnflōrēscere* to begin to blossom, going back to Latin *in* in + *flōs* flower.] —**in′flo·res′cent,** *adj.*

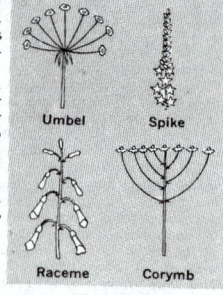

Umbel   Spike

Raceme   Corymb

Inflorescence

in·flow (in′flō′) *n.* **1.** act of flowing in. **2.** that which flows in.

in·flu·ence (in′flōō əns) *n.* **1.a.** power or capacity of persons or things to produce effects on others or to affect the outcome of events, esp. by indirect or invisible means: *The moon exerts an influence on the tides. Do you have any influence with her?* **b.** power to produce effects by virtue of one's wealth, social position, or prestige: *Mr. Jones is a man of influence in this town.* **2.** effect thus produced: *He had a great influence on my career.* **3.** one who or that which possesses or exercises the power to affect others: *His friends were a bad influence on him.* —*v.t.,* **-enced, -enc·ing.** **1.** to change or affect the thought, nature, or behavior of; persuade; sway: *He thought that we could influence her in making up her mind.* **2.** to have or produce an effect on; modify: *He influenced my thinking.* [Medieval Latin *influentia* exertion of power; literally, a flowing in, going back to Latin *in* in + *fluere* to flow; referring to the former belief that forces flowing in from stars and planets influenced human life.] —**Syn.** *n.* **1.a.** see **authority.**

in·flu·en·tial (in′flōō en′shəl) *adj.* having or exerting influence: *He is a very influential man in the government.*

in·flu·en·za (in′flōō en′zə) *n.* highly contagious disease, characterized by fever, headache, coughing, exhaustion, and inflammation of the mucous membranes. Also, **flu.** [Italian *influenza* influence (because the disease was once believed to be caused by the *influence* of the stars), from Medieval Latin *influentia.* See **INFLUENCE.**]

in·flux (in′fluks′) *n.* **1.** continual flow: *the influx of goods into a country. There was a great influx of migrants during the past year.* **2.** act of flowing in, as of a liquid or gas. **3.** place at which a river flows into another body of water; mouth. [Late Latin *īnflūxus* a flowing in, from Latin *influere* to flow in.]

in·fold (in fōld′) enfold.

in·form (in fôrm′) *v.t.* **1.** to communicate information to; make known to; tell: *The police informed him of his rights. Please inform me when the train arrives.* **2.** to inspire with a specific quality or character; animate. —*v.i.* to give or disclose incriminating information (with *on* or *against*): *The leader informed on the gang.* [Latin *īnfōrmāre* to give form to, tell, from *in* in + *fōrma* shape, pattern.]

in·for·mal (in fôr′məl) *adj.* **1.** not bound by or observing fixed customs, rules, or ceremonies: *The meeting of the board of directors was informal.* **2.** characteristic of or suitable for everyday or ordinary use or occasions: *informal clothes, an informal speech.* **3.** lacking or not requiring ceremony or elaborate detail or dress: *an informal atmosphere, an informal wedding. The minister paid an informal visit on us.* **4.** (of language) characteristic of or appropriate for the usual or everyday language used in speech or writing. —**in·for′mal·ly,** *adv.*

in·for·mal·i·ty (in′fôr mal′ə tē) *pl.,* **-ties.** *n.* **1.** state or quality of being informal. **2.** informal act.

in·form·ant (in fôr′mənt) *n.* one who gives or provides information.

in·for·ma·tion (in′fər mā′shən) *n.* **1.** knowledge or facts acquired or derived, as from study, instruction, or observation: *We will write to the company for further information. Where did you get your information?* **2.** act of informing; being informed. **3.** person or service that answers questions and provides facts for the public. **4.** formal accusation filed by a prosecuting officer rather than by a grand jury. —**in′for·ma′tion·al,** *adj.*

information theory, branch of mathematics concerned with the transmission and reception of information, esp. in communications systems.

in·form·a·tive (in fôr′mə tiv) *adj.* giving or providing information; instructive.

in·form·er (in fôr′mər) *n.* **1.** one who informs on others, often for monetary compensation: *He was an informer for the secret police.* **2.** informant.

infra- *prefix* below; beneath: *infrared.* [Latin *īnfrā.*]

in·frac·tion (in frak′shən) *n.* act of breaking or violating something, as a law or rule; infringement: *He committed an infraction of the law by parking overtime.* [Latin *īnfrāctiō* a breaking.]

in·fra·red (in′frə red′) *adj.* relating to, having, or using that portion of the spectrum of electromagnetic radiation whose wavelengths are longer than those of visible light but shorter than those of microwaves. When a body absorbs infrared radiation, the body is heated. [INFRA- + RED.]

in·fre·quen·cy (in frē′kwən sē) *n.* state or quality of being infrequent. Also, **in·fre′quence.**

in·fre·quent (in frē′kwənt) *adj.* not happening or appearing often; not frequent: *infrequent visits from a friend who lives far away.* [Latin *īnfrequēns.*] —**in·fre′quent·ly,** *adv.*

in·fringe (in frinj′) *-fringed, -fring·ing.* *v.i.* to trespass or intrude (with *on* or *upon*): *That law infringes on the rights of the people.* —*v.t.* to break or violate, as a law or agreement. [Latin *īnfringere* to break off, weaken.] —**in·fring′er,** *n.*

in·fringe·ment (in frinj′mənt) *n.* act of infringing.

in·fu·ri·ate (in fyoor′ē āt′) *-at·ed, -at·ing.* *v.t.* to make furious; enrage. [Medieval Latin *infuriatus,* past participle of *infuriare,* from Latin *in* in + *furia* rage.] —**in·fu′ri·at′ing·ly,** *adv.* —**in·fu′ri·a′tion,** *n.*

in·fuse (in fūz′) *-fused, -fus·ing.* *v.t.* **1.** to instill, as principles or qualities (often with *into*): *He infused new life into his weary followers.* **2.** to inspire; imbue (with *with*): *Their mother infused them with a sense of responsibility.* **3.** to steep or soak in a liquid so as to bring out certain qualities. [Latin *īnfūsus,* past participle of *īnfundere* to pour into, moisten.]

in·fu·si·ble (in fū′zə bəl) *adj.* incapable of being fused or melted.

in·fu·sion (in fū′zhən) *n.* **1.** act or process of infusing. **2.** that which is infused in a liquid. **3.** liquid extract obtained by steeping or soaking a substance in a liquid.

in·fu·so·ri·an (in′fū sôr′ē ən) *n.* ciliate. [Modern Latin *Infusoria* a class of protozoans, from Latin *īnfūsus,* past participle of *īnfundere* to pour into; referring to their presence in things soaked in a liquid.]

-ing¹ *suffix* **1.** (used to form nouns from verbs) **a.** act, art, process, or instance of performing the action of the root verb: *her sewing, their meeting, our skating.* **b.** product or result of such action: *to make a*

drawing. The poet gave a reading of his poems. **c.** material used for a specific purpose as indicated by the root verb: *lining, roofing, scaffolding.* **d.** that which performs or does the action of the root verb: *bedding, a covering for the head.* **2.** (used to form nouns from other nouns) of the nature of, belonging to, or involving the noun root: *bookkeeping, fishing, carpeting, ticking.* [Old English *-ing, -ung,* suffix forming nouns of action from verbs.]

-ing² *suffix* **1.** used to form the present participle of verbs: *He is walking. We were talking.* **2.** used to form adjectives from the present participle of verbs: *a charming woman, a leading citizen.* **3.** used to form adjectives from words other than verbs: *swashbuckling.* [Middle English *-ing(e),* form of *-ind, -end,* from Old English *-ende,* suffix forming the present participle.]

in·gen·ious (in jēn′yəs) *adj.* **1.** conceived, made, or executed with cleverness, originality, or imagination: *an ingenious plan, an ingenious contraption.* **2.** characterized by or exhibiting creative ability; imaginative; inventive: *an ingenious designer.* [Latin *ingeniōsus* clever, from *ingenium* natural ability, talent.] —**in·gen′ious·ly,** *adv.* —**in·gen′ious·ness,** *n.* —**Syn.** see **clever.**

in·gé·nue (än′jə nōō′, -nū′; *French* an zhā noo′) *pl.,* -**nues** (-nōōz′, -nūz′; *French* -noo′). *n.* **1.** innocent or unsophisticated girl or young woman. **2.a.** role of such a person in a theatrical presentation. **b.** actress who plays such a role. [French *ingénue,* feminine of *ingénu* artless, from Latin *ingenuus* freeborn, candid.]

in·ge·nu·i·ty (in′jə nōō′ə tē, -nū′-) *pl.,* -**ties.** *n.* **1.** cleverness, originality, or imagination in conceiving, making, or executing something. **2.** cleverness or originality of design, conception, or execution: *The ingenuity of his plan surprised us.* [Latin *ingenuitās* frankness; influenced in meaning by INGENIOUS.]

in·gen·u·ous (in jen′ū əs) *adj.* **1.** straightforward; frank; candid. **2.** innocent and simple; guileless; naive. [Latin *ingenuus* freeborn, candid.] —**in·gen′u·ous·ly,** *adv.* —**in·gen′u·ous·ness,** *n.*

in·gest (in jest′) *v.t.* to take or put into the body, as food or liquid, for digestion. [Latin *ingestus,* past participle of *ingerere* to carry in.]

in·ges·tion (in jes′chən) *n.* act or process of ingesting food or other substances.

In·gle·wood (ing′gəl wood′) *n.* city in southwestern California, an industrial and residential suburb of Los Angeles. Pop. (1970), 89,985.

in·glo·ri·ous (in glôr′ē əs) *adj.* bringing no glory or honor; shameful; disgraceful: *an inglorious past.* —**in·glo′ri·ous·ly,** *adv.* —**in·glo′-ri·ous·ness,** *n.*

in·got (ing′gət) *n.* mass of metal cast into a shape convenient for storage or further processing. [Old English *in* in + *goten* poured, past participle of *gēotan* to pour.]

in·graft (in graft′) engraft.

in·grain (*v.,* in grān′; *adj., n.,* in′grān′) *v.t.* to fix deeply or permanently on the mind or nature: *to ingrain an idea in someone's mind.* —*adj.* **1.** (of yarn or fiber) dyed before weaving or knitting. **2.** made of yarn or fiber dyed before weaving or knitting. —*n.* yarn or fiber dyed before weaving or knitting. [IN-² + obsolete *grain* color, from Old French *graine* seed of plants, cochineal, going back to Latin *grānum* seed; with reference to the resemblance to seeds of the bodies of the insects from which cochineal is made.]

in·grained (in grānd′, in′grānd′) *adj.* **1.** deeply or permanently fixed; firmly established: *ingrained prejudice.* **2.** thorough or habitual: *an ingrained hypocrite.*

in·grate (in′grāt′) *n.* ungrateful person. [Latin *ingrātus* ungrateful.]

in·gra·ti·ate (in grā′shē āt′) *-at·ed, -at·ing. v.t.* to bring (oneself) deliberately into another's favor. [IN-³ + Latin *grātia* favor + -ATE³.]

in·grat·i·tude (in grat′ə tōōd′, -tūd′) *n.* lack of gratitude or appreciation; ungratefulness.

in·gre·di·ent (in grē′dē ənt) *n.* **1.** any one of the component parts of a mixture: *Butter and eggs are two of the ingredients of this sauce.* **2.** component part of anything. [Latin *ingrediēns,* present participle of *ingredī* to enter, begin.]
Syn. 1. Ingredient, constituent, component mean a unit of a compound or composite. **Ingredient** refers to any substance that is, or can be, combined with one or more other substances to form a mixture: *Flour and butter are ingredients of a cake.* **Component** is a functional element that enters into a compound retaining a distinct identity and character of its own: *Transistors and oscillators are components of a radio.* **Constituent** is an essential part, serving to form or make up a whole and helping determine its nature: *Hemoglobin is a constituent of blood.*

In·gres, Jean Au·guste Do·mi·nique (an′grə; zhän ō goost′ dō mē nēk′) 1780–1867, French painter.

in·gress (in′gres) *n.* **1.** act of going in; entrance. **2.** place or means of entrance. **3.** right to go in. [Latin *ingressus* an entrance.]

in·grow·ing (in′grō′ing) *adj.* growing inwards or into something.

in·grown (in′grōn′) *adj.* **1.** grown into the flesh, as a hair or toenail. **2.** innate; inborn: *ingrown prejudice.*

in·gui·nal (ing′gwən əl) *adj.* of, relating to, or located in or near the groin. [Latin *inguinālis,* from *inguen* groin.]

in·gulf (in gulf′) engulf.

in·hab·it (in hab′it) *v.t.* to live in or on: *Many birds inhabit the island.* —*v.i. Archaic.* to live; dwell. [Latin *inhabitāre* to dwell in.] —**hab′it·a·ble,** *adj.*

in·hab·it·ant (in hab′ət ənt) *n.* person or animal that lives permanently in a place; resident. [Latin *inhabitāns,* present participle of *inhabitāre* to dwell in.]

in·hal·ant (in hā′lənt) *n.* medicine to be inhaled. —*adj.* used for inhaling.

in·ha·la·tion (in′hə lā′shən) *n.* act of inhaling.

in·ha·la·tor (in′hə lā′tər) *n.* device used to promote the inhaling of a gas or spray, as an anesthetic or medicinal vapors.

in·hale (in hāl′) *-haled, -hal·ing. v.t.* to draw into the lungs. —*v.i.* to draw something, as air or tobacco smoke, into the lungs. [Latin *inhālāre* to breathe upon.]

in·hal·er (in hā′lər) *n.* **1.** inhalator. **2.** device used to filter the air that is breathed in a particle-laden, noxious, or cold environment. **3.** one who inhales something, esp. tobacco smoke.

in·har·mo·ni·ous (in′här mō′nē əs) *adj.* not in harmony or agreement: *inharmonious sounds.* Also, **in·har·mon·ic** (in′här mon′ik). —**in′har·mo′ni·ous·ly,** *adv.* —**in′har·mo′ni·ous·ness,** *n.*

in·here (in hēr′) *-hered, -her·ing. v.i.* to exist as or form a permanent or essential quality, element, or attribute; be inherent (with *in*): *Knowledge and perception inhere in mind alone* (Bain, 1855). [Latin *inhaerēre* to stick to.] —**in·her·ence** (in hēr′əns, -her′-), **in·her′en·cy,** *n.*

in·her·ent (in hēr′ənt, -her′-) *adj.* existing as or forming a permanent or essential quality, element, or attribute of someone or something. [Latin *inhaerēns,* present participle of *inhaerēre* to stick to.] —**her′ent·ly,** *adv.*
Syn. Inherent, intrinsic, innate refer to that which is or forms the essential character or nature of someone or something. **Inherent** is used more commonly and stresses the inseparability of a quality, element, or attribute from the person or thing itself: *Honesty is inherent in his nature. Such problems are inherent in that kind of situation.* **Intrinsic** usually refers to a quality, element, or attribute that may be evaluated or measured in some way: *Does money have any intrinsic value apart from what it can buy?* **Innate** is usually restricted to more formal or loftier contexts: *There is an innate fallacy in his logic.*

in·her·it (in her′it) *v.t.* **1.** to receive, as property or a title, from a former owner at his death: *I inherited this jewelry from my aunt.* **2.** to receive (a characteristic) through genetic transmission from one's parent or parents. **3.** to receive or come into possession of in any way: *He inherited all of his father's bad habits.* —*v.i.* to come into, or take possession of, an inheritance. [Old French *enheriter* to put in possession of an inheritance, from Late Latin *inhērēditāre* to appoint as heir, going back to Latin *in* in + *hērēs* heir.]

in·her·it·a·ble (in her′i tə bəl) *adj.* **1.** capable of being inherited. **2.** *Archaic.* capable of inheriting; qualified to inherit.

in·her·it·ance (in her′ət əns) *n.* **1.** that which is or may be inherited; legacy: *He received a large inheritance.* **2.** act or fact of inheriting.

inheritance tax, tax imposed on inherited property.

in·her·i·tor (in her′i tər) *n.* one who inherits something; heir.

in·hib·it (in hib′it) *v.t.* **1.** to hold back; check; restrain. **2.** to forbid or prohibit. [Latin *inhibitus,* past participle of *inhibēre.*] —**in·hib′i·tive, in·hib′i·to′ry,** *adj.*

in·hi·bi·tion (in′i bish′ən, in′hi-) *n.* **1.** a restraint or check on some activity or on one's natural impulses: *His inhibitions prevented him from speaking up.* **2.** act of inhibiting; being inhibited.

in·hib·i·tor (in hib′ə tər) *n.* substance that slows down or stops a chemical reaction.

in·hos·pi·ta·ble (in hos′pi tə bəl, in′hos pit′ə bəl) *adj.* **1.** not offering hospitality to guests or visitors; not hospitable; unfriendly. **2.** not providing food, shelter, or other accommodation: *an inhospitable desert.* —**in·hos′pi·ta·bly,** *adv.*

in·hos·pi·tal·i·ty (in hos′pə tal′ə tē) *n.* lack of hospitality.

in·hu·man (in hū′mən, -ū′mən) *adj.* **1.** lacking the feelings or qualities that are considered admirable in, or natural to, a human being; without kindness, pity, or compassion: *The general was inhuman in his treatment of prisoners.* **2.** causing or inflicting extreme or intolerable pain, grief, or suffering; savage: *an inhuman punishment.* **3.** not resembling a human being in form: *inhuman creatures.* [Latin *inhūmānus* savage, cruel.] —**in·hu′man·ly,** *adv.*

in·hu·mane (in′hū mān′, -ū mān′) *adj.* not feeling or showing kindness, pity, or compassion for other human beings or animals; not humane. [Form of INHUMAN.] —**in′hu·mane′ly,** *adv.*

in·hu·man·i·ty (in′hū man′ə tē, -ū man′-) *pl.,* -**ties.** *n.* **1.** quality or condition of being inhuman or inhumane; lack of kindness, pity, or compassion. **2.** instance of this; inhuman act.

in·im·i·cal (in im′i kəl) *adj.* **1.** antagonistic; unfriendly; hostile: *She had an inimical reaction to my suggestion.* **2.** injurious; harmful: *Lack*

at; āpe; cär; end; mē; it; īce; hot; ōld; fôrk; wood; fōōl; oil; out; up; ūse; turn; sing; thin; this; zh in treasure; ə in ago, taken, pencil, lemon, circus.

of sleep is inimical to good health. [Late Latin *inimīcālis* hostile, from Latin *inimīcus* enemy.] —**in·im′i·cal·ly,** *adv.*

in·im·i·ta·ble (in im′ə tə bəl) *adj.* that cannot be imitated; matchless. —**in·im′i·ta·bil′i·ty,** *n.* —**in·im′i·ta·bly,** *adv.*

in·iq·ui·tous (in ik′wə təs) *adj.* characterized by iniquity; unjust or wicked. —**in·iq′ui·tous·ly,** *adv.* —**in·iq′ui·tous·ness,** *n.*

in·iq·ui·ty (in ik′wə tē) *pl.,* **-ties.** *n.* 1. great injustice or wickedness: *the iniquity of slavery.* 2. wicked or unjust act or deed. [Latin *inīquitās* injustice.]

i·ni·tial (i nish′əl) *adj.* of, relating to, or occurring at the beginning; first: *the initial letter of a word, the initial step in a process.* —*n.* 1. first letter of a person's name or of each part of a person's name: *Sara Ann Smith's initials are S.A.S.* 2. first letter of any name or word. —*v.t.,* **-tialed, -tial·ing;** *also, British,* **-tialled, -tial·ling.** to mark or sign with one's initial or initials: *He initialed the report after reading it.* [Latin *initiālis* incipient, from *initium* a beginning.]

i·ni·tial·ly (i nish′ə lē) *adv.* at the beginning.

i·ni·ti·ate (*v.,* i nish′ē āt′; *n., adj.,* i nish′ē it) **-at·ed, -at·ing.** *v.t.* 1. to introduce or begin: *to initiate changes in a law.* 2. to admit (a person) into an organization or group, esp. with formal ceremonies or secret rites. 3. to introduce to or instruct in some subject. —*n.* one who has been initiated into an organization or group. —*adj.* initiated. [Latin *initiātus,* past participle of *initiāre* to begin.] —**i·ni′ti·a′tor,** *n.* —**Syn.** 1. see **induct.**

i·ni·ti·a·tion (i nish′ē ā′shən) *n.* 1. act of initiating; being initiated. 2. ceremonies or special rites by which one is admitted to an organization or group.

i·ni·ti·a·tive (i nish′ə tiv) *n.* 1. first step in an undertaking; active role; lead: *to take the initiative.* 2. power or ability to originate something or take the first step or lead in an undertaking: *He did not have the initiative to start his own business.* 3.a. power or right of the general public to introduce and enact a new law or constitutional amendment. b. procedure by which the general public introduces and enacts legislation.

i·ni·ti·a·to·ry (i nish′ē ə tôr′ē, i nish′ə-) *adj.* 1. introductory; initial. 2. serving to initiate.

in·ject (in jekt′) *v.t.* 1. to force (fluid), as with a syringe, through the skin into a muscle, vein, or the like: *to inject serum into the bloodstream.* 2. to throw in; introduce: *to inject humor into a situation.* [Latin *injectus,* past participle of *inicere* to throw in.] —**in·jec′tor,** *n.*

in·jec·tion (in jek′shən) *n.* 1. act or process of injecting. 2. fluid that is injected. 3. act or process of boosting a spacecraft into a desired trajectory.

in·ju·di·cious (in′jŏo dish′əs) *adj.* showing lack of judgment; not judicious. —**in′ju·di′cious·ly,** *adv.* —**in′ju·di′cious·ness,** *n.*

in·junc·tion (in jungk′shən) *n.* 1. court order requiring the party or parties named to perform, or refrain from performing, some act. 2. command; order; directive: *The crowd ignored the repeated injunctions of the police.* 3. act of enjoining. [Late Latin *injunctiō* command, from Latin *injungere* to join to, enjoin.]

in·jure (in′jər) **-jured, -jur·ing.** *v.t.* 1. to do or cause damage to; harm. 2. to do injustice or wrong to. [From INJURY.] —**Syn.** 1. see **hurt.**

in·ju·ri·ous (in joor′ē əs) *adj.* 1. causing harm or damage. 2. slanderous or abusive. [Latin *injūriōsus* harmful, from *injūria* harm.] —**in·ju′ri·ous·ly,** *adv.* —**in·ju′ri·ous·ness,** *n.*

in·ju·ry (in′jər ē) *pl.,* **-ju·ries.** *n.* 1. damage or harm inflicted on or suffered by a person or thing. 2. injustice or wrong inflicted or suffered. [Latin *injūria.*]

in·jus·tice (in jus′tis) *n.* 1. lack of justice; unfairness. 2. unjust act.

ink (ingk) *n.* 1. any of various colored fluids or pastes used esp. for writing, drawing, or printing. 2. dark pigment ejected by cuttlefish, squids, and other cephalopods when frightened in order to cloud the water and hide them from their enemies. —*v.t.* to mark, cover, or color with ink. [Old French *enque* liquid used for writing, from Late Latin *encaustum* purple ink, from Greek *enkauston,* from *enkaiein* to burn in; referring to the ancient Greek practice of burning in, or making colors of paintings fast, with heat.] —**ink′er,** *n.*

ink·ber·ry (ingk′ber′ē) *pl.,* **-ries.** *n.* 1. evergreen shrub, *Ilex glabra,* of the holly family, native to North America, bearing many branches and small, black fruit. 2. the fruit itself. 3. pokeweed.

ink·horn (ingk′hôrn′) *n.* small container made of horn or similar material, formerly used to hold ink.

ink·ling (ingk′ling) *n.* 1. vague idea or notion: *She had no inkling of what we were talking about.* 2. slight suggestion; hint: *They gave us no inkling as to their plans.* [Of uncertain origin.]

ink·stand (ingk′stand′) *n.* 1. stand or rack for holding containers of ink and pens. 2. inkwell.

ink·well (ingk′wel′) *n.* container for ink, esp. on a desk.

ink·y (ingk′kē) **ink·i·er, ink·i·est.** *adj.* 1. dark or black in color. 2. marked, covered, or stained with ink. —**ink′i·ness,** *n.*

in·laid (in′lād′) *adj.* 1. set flush into a surface as a decoration: *The*

box had inlaid marble on the lid. 2. decorated with a material, as gold or ivory, set flush in the surface: *The table had an inlaid border.*

in·land (in′land′, -lənd) *adj.* 1. of, relating to, or located in the interior of a country or region; away from the coast or border: *an inland city.* 2. carried on or operating within a country or region; domestic: *inland trade.* —*adv.* in or toward the interior of a country or region. —*n.* interior part of a country or region.

in·land·er (in′lan′dər, -lən-) *n.* one who lives inland.

in·law (in′lô′) *n. Informal.* relative by marriage.

in·lay (in lā′) **-laid, -lay·ing.** *v.t.* 1. to set or embed a material, as gold or ivory, into the surface of something so as to form a decorative design flush with that surface. 2. to decorate with a material set flush in the surface: *to inlay a cabinet with ivory.* —*n.* 1. inlaid design or material. 2. filling of gold, porcelain, or the like cemented into a cavity in a tooth.

in·let (in′let′) *n.* 1. narrow channel of water between islands or leading inland from a larger body of water. 2. entrance or opening.

in·mate (in′māt′) *n.* one confined in a prison, asylum, or similar institution. [IN-³ + MATE¹.]

in me·di·as res (in mā′dē äs rās′, in mē′dē äs rēz′) *Latin* into the middle of things. ▲ used esp. of a narrative that begins in the middle of the action rather than at the beginning.

in me·mo·ri·am (in mə môr′ē əm) as a memorial (to); in memory (of). [Latin.]

in·most (in′mōst′) *adj.* innermost. [Old English *innemest,* superlative of *inne* in, within; influenced by MOST.]

inn (in) *n.* 1. small hotel, esp. in the country. 2. restaurant or tavern. [Old English *inn* dwelling.]

in·nate (i nāt′, in′āt) *adj.* 1. possessed at birth; natural; inborn: *innate intelligence.* 2. belonging to or forming the essential character of someone or something. [Latin *innātus,* past participle of *innāscī* to be born in.] —**in·nate′ly,** *adv.* —**in·nate′ness,** *n.* —**Syn.** 2. see **inherent.**

in·ner (in′ər) *adj.* 1. located farther in; interior: *an inner chamber.* 2. of or relating to the mind or soul: *His inner life was rich and fulfilling.* 3. more private or intimate; secret: *one's inner feelings.* 4. not obvious; hidden: *inner meaning.* [Old English *innera,* comparative of *inne* in, within.]

inner ear, area behind the three bones of the middle ear, consisting, in man, of the vestibule, the semicircular canals, and the cochlea.

Inner Mongolia, political subdivision of China, in the northern part of the country. Area, approx. 540,000 sq. mi. Pop. (1957 est.), 9,200,000.

in·ner·most (in′ər mōst′) *adj.* 1. most private or intimate; deepest: *one's innermost feelings.* 2. farthest from the outside; most inward: *the innermost recesses of the mind.*

Inner Temple, one of the four Inns of Court.

inner tube, airtight rubber tube used within a pneumatic tire to maintain a specified air pressure.

in·ning (in′ing) *n.* 1. division of a baseball game in which both teams bat, the visiting team first, until three men on each team are put out. 2. *also,* **innings.** turn or opportunity for action or accomplishment: *Now the other party has its innings.* [IN + -ING¹.]

inn·keep·er (in′kē′pər) *n.* one who owns or manages an inn.

in·no·cence (in′ə səns) *n.* 1. state, quality, or fact of being innocent. 2. *Botany.* bluet.

in·no·cent (in′ə sənt) *adj.* 1.a. not guilty of a specific crime: *The jury found him innocent of murder.* b. free from guilt or wrongdoing: *A defendant is innocent until proved guilty.* 2. free from or unacquainted with moral wrong, sin, or evil; pure. 3. not arising from or involving any evil or malicious intent or motive; harmless: *an innocent prank, an innocent remark.* 4. having or exhibiting the naiveté, ignorance, or unsuspecting nature of one who lacks experience or worldliness. —*n.* 1. person, esp. a child, who is free from or unacquainted with evil or sin. 2. simple, inexperienced, or unworldly person. [Latin *innocēns* harmless, blameless.] —**in′no·cent·ly,** *adv.*

In·no·cent II (in′ə sənt) died 1143, pope from 1130 to 1143.

Innocent III, c.1161–1216, pope from 1198 to 1216, who brought the church to the height of its power in medieval Europe.

Innocent IV, died 1254, pope from 1243 to 1254.

Innocent XI, 1611–89, pope from 1676 to 1689.

in·noc·u·ous (i nok′ū əs) *adj.* harmless; innocent. [Latin *innocuus.*]

in·no·vate (in′ə vāt′) **-vat·ed, -vat·ing.** *v.t.* to introduce (something new): *to innovate a technique.* —*v.i.* to introduce something new; make changes in something. [Latin *innovātus,* past participle of *innovāre* to renew, alter.] —**in′no·va′tive,** *adj.* —**in′no·va′tor,** *n.*

in·no·va·tion (in′ə vā′shən) *n.* 1. something newly introduced; change, as in practice or method: *Anesthesia was a great innovation in medicine.* 2. act of innovating.

Inns·bruck (inz′brook′) *n.* city in western Austria. Pop. (1968 est.), 113,468.

Inns of Court 1. group of four legal societies in Britain that have

the exclusive right to train barristers and to regulate their admission to the British bar. **2.** buildings which house these societies.

in·nu·en·do (in´ū en´dō) *pl.* **-does.** *n.* indirect suggestion, esp. one that is unfavorable; insinuation. [Latin *innuendō* by nodding to, by intimating, ablative gerund or *innuere* to nod to, intimate; referring to the use of a nod to imply something.] **—Syn.** see **insinuation.**

in·nu·mer·a·ble (i nōō´mər ə bəl, i nū´-) *adj.* too numerous to be counted: *There are innumerable stars in the sky.* **—in·nu´mer·a·ble·ness,** *n.* **—in·nu´mer·a·bly,** *adv.*

in·oc·u·late (in ok´yə lāt´) **-lat·ed, -lat·ing.** *v.t.* **1.** to infect (a person or animal) with an organism that causes a disease, in order to produce that disease in a mild form so that immunity will result. **2.** to use (the organism that causes a disease) in the prevention or cure of that disease. **3.** to introduce into (soil) a form of bacteria that will fix nitrogen so it can be used by plants. [Latin *inoculātus,* past participle of *inoculāre* to engraft, implant, from *in* in + *oculus* eye, bud; referring to the similarity between introducing a germ into the body to immunize and grafting a bud onto a plant.] **—in·oc´u·la´tive,** *adj.* **—in·oc´u·la´tor,** *n.*

in·oc·u·la·tion (in ok´yə lā´shən) *n.* **1.** act of inoculating, esp. in order to produce immunity to a disease. **2.** injection given in order to produce immunity to a disease.

in·of·fen·sive (in´ə fen´siv) *adj.* not offensive; unobjectionable; harmless. **—in´of·fen´sive·ly,** *adv.* **—in´of·fen´sive·ness,** *n.*

in·op·er·a·tive (in op´ər ə tiv, -op´ə rā´-) *adj.* not functioning or effective; not operative.

in·op·por·tune (in op´ər tōōn´, -tūn´) *adj.* coming or occurring at a bad time; untimely or inconvenient. **—in·op´por·tune´ly,** *adv.* **—in·op´por·tune´ness,** *n.*

in·or·di·nate (in ôr´də nit) *adj.* excessive; immoderate: *inordinate demands.* [Latin *inōrdinātus* not arranged, going back to *in-* not + *ōrdō* row, arrangement.] **—in·or´di·nate·ly,** *adv.* **—Syn.** see **excessive.**

in·or·gan·ic (in´ôr gan´ik) *adj.* **1.** containing no carbon compounds of high molecular weight; not organic: *an inorganic compound.* **2.** not produced by animals or plants. **3.** not having the organized structure of animals and plants. **—in´or·gan´i·cal·ly,** *adv.*

inorganic chemistry, branch of chemistry concerned with the study of elements and compounds of elements other than carbon, with the exception of certain very simple carbon compounds.

in·pa·tient (in´pā´shənt) *n.* patient who remains in a hospital or similar institution while receiving care and treatment.

in·put (in´pōōt´) *n.* **1.** anything put or taken in. **2.** amount of power or energy that is put into something, as a machine. **3.** information fed into a computer or any other information storage and retrieval system. **4.** information, as electrical or sound signals, fed into a mechanical, electronic, or other device.

in·quest (in´kwest) *n.* **1.a.** judicial or official inquiry made by a jury or other body appointed by law. **b.** jury or body appointed to make such an inquiry. **c.** finding of such a jury or body. **2.** coroner's inquest. [Old French *enqueste* official inquiry, going back to Latin *inquīrere* to search for.]

in·qui·e·tude (in kwī´ə tōōd´, -tūd´) *n.* restlessness or uneasiness.

in·quire (in kwīr´) **-quired, -quir·ing.** *also,* **en·quire.** *v.i.* **1.** to seek knowledge or information by asking a question or questions (often with *after*): *We inquired after his health. She inquired about directions.* **2.** to make an investigation, search, or examination (with *into*): *The police inquired into her background.* —*v.t.* to seek knowledge or information about: *to inquire the way.* [Latin *inquīrere* to search for.] **—in·quir´er,** *n.* **—in·quir´ing·ly,** *adv.*

in·quir·y (in kwīr´ē, in´kwər ē) *pl.* **-quir·ies.** *also,* **en·quir·y.** *n.* **1.** act of inquiring. **2.** investigation, search, or examination. **3.** question; query.

Syn. 2. Inquiry, investigation, probe denote an active attempt to establish truth. **Inquiry** denotes an orderly attempt to uncover facts by questioning rather than by inspection: *The object of scientific inquiry is to discover the laws of nature.* **Investigation** is a systematic and searching attempt to unearth facts through detailed and formal examination: *Government ordered a full investigation of the food industry.* **Probe** is a penetrating investigation or critical inquiry into crime or other unlawful practices: *The press demanded a probe into alleged corruption among public officials.*

in·qui·si·tion (in´kwə zish´ən) *n.* **1.a.** judicial or official inquiry; inquest. **b.** document recording the finding of such an inquiry. **2.** any strict or thorough inquiry or questioning. **3. the Inquisition.** Roman Catholic tribunal established in the thirteenth century for the discovery, examination, and trial of heretics. It was abolished in the early nineteenth century. [Latin *inquīsītiō* a searching for.]

in·quis·i·tive (in kwiz´ə tiv) *adj.* **1.** eager for knowledge; curious. **2.** unduly curious; nosy; prying. **—in·quis´i·tive·ly,** *adv.* **—in·quis´i·tive·ness,** *n.*

in·quis·i·tor (in kwiz´ə tər) *n.* **1.** one who makes or conducts an

inquisition or inquiry. **2. Inquisitor.** official of the Inquisition, esp. the head of the tribunal.

in·quis·i·to·ri·al (in kwiz´ə tôr´ē əl) *adj.* **1.** of, relating to, or like an inquisitor or inquisition. **2.** unduly curious; inquisitive.

in re (in rē´, in rā´) in the matter of; concerning. [Latin.]

I.N.R.I., letters of the Latin words *Iesus Nazarenus, Rex Iudaeorum* (Jesus of Nazareth, King of the Jews) placed on the cross of Christ.

in·road (in´rōd´) *n.* **1.** sudden, hostile attack or raid. **2.** *also,* **inroads.** forcible or destructive encroachment.

in·rush (in´rush´) *n.* sudden rushing or pouring in.

ins. 1. inches. **2.** insurance. **3.** insulated.

in·sane (in sān´) *adj.* **1.** not sane; mentally deranged. **2.** characteristic of or for insane people. **3.** extremely foolish; senseless. [Latin *insānus* not sane.] **—in·sane´ly,** *adv.*

in·san·i·tar·y (in san´ə ter´ē) *adj.* injurious to health; not sanitary. **—in·san´i·ta´tion,** *n.*

in·san·i·ty (in san´ə tē) *pl.* **-ties.** *n.* **1.** state of being insane; mental derangement. **2.** *Law.* weakness or unsoundness of mind sufficient to render a person incapable of distinguishing between right and wrong or of comprehending the nature and consequences of his acts. **3.** extreme folly or senselessness.

in·sa·tia·ble (in sā´shə bəl) *adj.* that cannot be satisfied: *an insatiable thirst.* Also, **in·sa·ti·ate** (in sā´shē it). **—in·sa´tia·bly,** *adv.*

in·scribe (in skrīb´) **-scribed, -scrib·ing.** *v.t.* **1.** to write, carve, engrave, or mark (words or characters) on a surface: *The stonecutter inscribed the date on the tombstone.* **2.** to carve, engrave, or mark words or characters on (a surface): *The jeweler inscribed the locket.* **3.** to write a message or note on (something, as a book) in presenting or giving it to someone. **4.** to draw (a geometric figure) within another figure so that the inner intersects the outer in as many points as possible: *to inscribe a circle within a square.* **5.** to enter (a name) on a list; enroll. [Latin *inscrībere* to write in or on.] **—in·scrib´er,** *n.*

in·scrip·tion (in skrip´shən) *n.* **1.** something inscribed, esp. words or characters written, carved, engraved, or marked on a surface, as of metal or stone: *an inscription on a tombstone.* **2.** message or note written on something, as a book, in presenting or giving it to someone. **3.** act of inscribing. [Latin *inscrīptiō* a writing in or on.]

in·scru·ta·ble (in skrōō´tə bəl) *adj.* that cannot be easily understood; mysterious; enigmatic. [Late Latin *inscrūtābilis* from Latin *in-* not + *scrūtārī* to examine.] **—in·scru´ta·bil´i·ty,** *n.* **—in·scru´ta·bly,** *adv.*

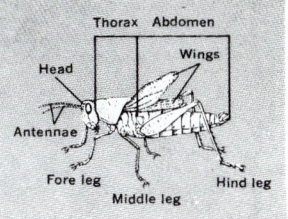

in·sect (in´sekt) *n.* **1.** any of a widely distributed group of invertebrates, class Insecta, characterized by a body divided into three parts with three pairs of legs, and in the adult, usually two pairs of wings. Flies, ants, grasshoppers, and beetles are insects. **2.** any similar crawling animal. [Latin *insectum* literally, (animal) cut into, from *insecāre* to cut into; referring to the segmented body of an insect.]

Parts of an insect

in·sec·ti·cide (in sek´tə sīd´) *n.* chemical for killing insects and related pests. [Latin *insectum* insect + -CIDE².]

in·sec·ti·vore (in sek´tə vôr´) *n.* **1.** any insect-eating animal or plant. **2.** any of certain insect-eating mammals, order Insectivora, as hedgehogs, moles, and shrews. [French *insectivore,* from Modern Latin *insectivorus.* See INSECTIVOROUS.]

in·sec·tiv·o·rous (in´sek tiv´ə rəs) *adj.* **1.** feeding chiefly on insects. **2.** of or relating to mammals belonging to the order Insactivora. [Modern Latin *insectivorus* literally, insect-eating (from Latin *insectum* insect + *vorāre* to devour) + -OUS.]

in·se·cure (in´si kyoor´) *adj.* **1.** liable to give way or fail; unstable or unsafe: *The knot was very insecure.* **2.** not assured; uncertain: *His position with the company was very insecure.* **3.** lacking in self-confidence: *an insecure person.* **—in´se·cure´ly,** *adv.*

in·se·cu·ri·ty (in´si kyoor´ə tē) *pl.* **-ties.** *n.* **1.** state or quality of being insecure. **2.** lack of self-confidence; self-doubt. **3.** *also,* **insecurities.** something insecure.

in·sem·i·nate (in sem´ə nāt´) **-nat·ed, -nat·ing.** *v.t.* to inject or introduce semen into the reproductive tract of (a female); impregnate.

in·sem·i·na·tion (in sem´ə nā´shən) *n.* act of inseminating; being inseminated.

in·sen·sate (in sen´sāt, -sit) *adj.* **1.** without awareness or sensation; inanimate: *The silence and the calm of mute insensate things* (Words-

worth, 1799). **2.** exhibiting a lack of feeling, sensitivity, or perception. **3.** lacking sense or reason; stupid; foolish. —**in·sen′sate·ly,** *adv.*

in·sen·si·bil·i·ty (in sen′sə bil′ə tē) *pl.* **-ties.** *n.* state or quality of being insensible.

in·sen·si·ble (in sen′sə bəl) *adj.* **1.** incapable of feeling, perceiving, or being affected by (with *to*): *insensible to pain, insensible to the suffering of others.* **2.** unaware (with *of*): *We were insensible of the risks involved.* **3.** deprived of sensation; unconscious or numb: *He was insensible for several minutes after being struck on the head.* **4.** too slight, gradual, or subtle to be easily perceived; imperceptible: *insensible transitions.* —**in·sen′si·bly,** *adv.*

in·sen·si·tive (in sen′sə tiv) *adj.* **1.** incapable of feeling, perceiving, or being affected by (with *to*): *insensitive to beauty, insensitive to pain.* **2.** lacking feeling, sensitivity, or perception: *He is a cruel and insensitive person.* —**in·sen′si·tive·ness, in·sen′si·tiv′i·ty,** *n.*

in·sen·ti·ent (in sen′shē ənt, -shənt) *adj.* without feeling, awareness, sensation, or consciousness; inanimate. —**in·sen′ti·ence,** *n.*

in·sep·a·ra·ble (in sep′ər ə bəl, -sep′rə-) *adj.* that cannot be separated. —*n.* **inseparables.** inseparable persons or things. —**in·sep′a·ra·bil′i·ty,** *n.* —**in·sep′a·ra·bly,** *adv.*

in·sert (*v.,* in surt′; *n.,* in′surt) *v.t.* to put, set, or place in: *to insert a bookmark into a book.* —*n.* something inserted or to be inserted, as an extra section or pamphlet inserted in a newspaper, magazine, or other printed matter. [Latin *insertus,* past participle of *inserere* to put in.]

in·ser·tion (in sur′shən) *n.* **1.** act of inserting. **2.** something inserted. **3.** point at which a muscle is attached to the bone that it moves. **4.** act or process of boosting a spacecraft into an orbit around the earth, moon, or other celestial body. **5.** band of lace or other material made so that it can be sewed at each edge between parts of other material.

in·set (*v.,* in set′; *n.,* in′set′) **-set, -set·ting.** *v.t.* to set, put, or place in; insert. —*n.* **1.** something inset or to be inset; insertion. **2.** small map, diagram, or other illustration inserted within the border of a larger one.

in·shore (in′shôr′) *adj.* **1.** near the shore. **2.** moving toward the shore. —*adv.* toward the shore.

in·side (in′sīd′, in′sīd′) *n.* **1.** inner side, surface, or part; interior: *the inside of a car. Pin the money to the inside of your coat.* **2.** inner nature or aspect. **3. insides. a.** internal organs of the body. **b.** internal parts of anything. **4. inside out. a.** reversed so that the inside is outside: *He wore his coat inside out.* **b.** thoroughly; totally: *He knew his work inside out.* —*adj.* **1.** situated on or in the inside. **2.** known to only a few; confidential: *The reporter got the inside story on the murder.* **3.** working or done from within a place or organization: *an inside job. The thieves used an inside man at the factory.* **4.** Baseball. (of a pitch) passing over home plate between the batter and the center of the plate. —*adv.* **1.** on, in, or toward the inside; within. **2.** indoors: *The children played inside all day.* —*prep.* **1.** in or into the inside of; within: *I looked inside the house.* **2. inside of. a.** within; in: *The dress is inside of the box.* **b.** within the space or limits of: *He ran the race inside of an hour.*

in·sid·er (in sī′dər) *n.* **1.** one who is a member, as of a given group, society, or organization. **2.** one who is or can obtain information that is not accessible to everyone.

in·sid·i·ous (in sid′ē əs) *adj.* **1.** slyly treacherous and deceitful: *an insidious manner.* **2.** working or proceeding in a harmful and subtle manner: *an insidious disease.* [Latin *insidiōsus* deceitful, from *insidiae* plot.] —**in·sid′i·ous·ly,** *adv.* —**in·sid′i·ous·ness,** *n.*

in·sight (in′sīt′) *n.* **1.** capacity to see into and understand the inner character or hidden nature of things: *She had great insight into his problems.* **2.** an instance of such understanding.

in·sig·ni·a (in sig′nē ə) *pl.* **-ni·a** or **-ni·as.** *also,* **in·sig·ne** (in sig′nē). *n.* **1.** emblem, badge, medal, or other distinguishing mark, as of office, honor, or position: *The officer wore an insignia on his collar.* **2.** such marks collectively: *military insignia.* **3.** distinguishing mark or sign of anything. [Latin *insignia,* plural of *insigne* mark, badge. Doublet of ENSIGN.]

in·sig·nif·i·cance (in′sig nif′i kəns) *n.* state or quality of being insignificant.

in·sig·nif·i·can·cy (in′sig nif′i kən sē) *pl.* **-cies.** *n.* **1.** insignificance. **2.** insignificant person or thing.

in·sig·nif·i·cant (in′sig nif′ə kənt) *adj.* **1.** being of or having little or no meaning or importance; not significant. **2.** small in size or amount; nominal: *an insignificant sum of money.* **3.** lacking distinction: *an insignificant face.* —**in′sig·nif′i·cant·ly,** *adv.*

in·sin·cere (in′sin sēr′) *adj.* not sincere; hypocritical. —**in′sin·cere′ly,** *adv.*

in·sin·cer·i·ty (in′sin ser′ə tē) *pl.* **-ties.** *n.* **1.** quality of being insincere. **2.** instance of this.

in·sin·u·ate (in sin′ū āt′) **-at·ed, -at·ing.** *v.t.* **1.** to suggest indirectly; intimate: *The prosecutor insinuated that the witness was lying.* **2.** to get in or introduce by subtle or indirect means: *They insinuated themselves into families to betray them* (Sismondi, 1832). [Latin *insinuātus,* past

participle of *insinuāre* to bring in by winding or turning, from *in* in + *sinus* curve, hollow.] —**Syn. 1.** see hint.

in·sin·u·a·tion (in sin′ū ā′shən) *n.* **1.** indirect suggestion; sly hint. **2.** act of insinuating.

Syn. 1. Insinuation, innuendo denote something that is hinted at or implied. **Insinuation** is a sly, artful, or oblique remark, esp. of a derogatory nature: *During election time the air is full of insinuations and rumors.* **Innuendo** is an implication or suggestion still more oblique and veiled and conveyed as much through tone, inflection, and gesture as through remarks: *Jerry's friends showed their disapproval of his actions through innuendo rather than confronting him openly.*

in·sip·id (in sip′id) *adj.* **1.** lacking qualities that arouse interest or excite; dull; colorless: *an insipid person.* **2.** without much taste or flavor; bland. [Late Latin *insipidus* tasteless, from Latin *in-* not + *sapidus* savory¹.] —**in′si·pid′i·ty, in·sip′id·ness,** *n.* —**in·sip′id·ly,** *adv.*

in·sist (in sist′) *v.t.* **1.** to demand (something) firmly and strongly: *The doctor insisted that she get plenty of rest.* **2.** to maintain or assert persistently and positively: *He insisted that he was right.* —*v.i.* **1.** to demand firmly and strongly (with *on* or *upon*): *She insisted on our coming.* **2.** to persist in a course of action (with *on* or *upon*): *If you insist on shouting, I shall leave.* [Latin *insistere* to stand on, persist.]

in·sis·tence (in sis′təns) *n.* **1.** act or instance of insisting. **2.** quality of being insistent. Also, **in·sis′ten·cy.**

in·sis·tent (in sis′tənt) *adj.* **1.** urgent or persistent. **2.** demanding attention or notice: *The insistent ringing of the doorbell woke us.* —**in·sis′tent·ly,** *adv.*

in si·tu (in sī′tōō, -tū) *Latin.* in its original place or position.

in·snare (in snār′) ensnare.

in·so·bri·e·ty (in′sə brī′ə tē) *n.* lack of sobriety.

in·sole (in′sōl′) *n.* **1.** inner sole of a shoe or boot. **2.** layer of material laid on the sole inside a shoe or boot for warmth, waterproofing, or for a better fit.

in·so·lence (in′sə ləns) *n.* **1.** quality of being insolent. **2.** insolent speech or behavior.

in·so·lent (in′sə lənt) *adj.* offensively rude or arrogant. [Latin *insolēns,* from *in-* not + *solēre* to be accustomed.] —**in′so·lent·ly,** *adv.*

in·sol·u·ble (in sol′yə bəl) *adj.* **1.** that cannot be dissolved. **2.** that cannot be solved or explained: *an insoluble crime.* [Latin *insolūbilis* that cannot be loosed, going back to *in-* not + *solvere* to loose.] —**in·sol′u·bil′i·ty,** *n.* —**in·sol′u·bly,** *adv.*

in·solv·a·ble (in sol′və bəl) *adj.* that cannot be solved or explained.

in·sol·ven·cy (in sol′vən sē) *pl.* **-cies.** *n.* state or condition of being unable to pay debts or discharge liabilities; bankruptcy.

in·sol·vent (in sol′vənt) *adj.* **1.** not able to pay debts or discharge liabilities. **2.** of or relating to insolvency or insolvent persons. —*n.* insolvent person.

in·som·ni·a (in som′nē ə) *n.* restless sleep or an inability to fall asleep. [Latin *insomnia* sleeplessness.]

in·so·much (in′sō much′) *adv.* **1.** to such an extent or degree (with *that*). **2.** inasmuch as.

in·sou·ci·ance (in sōō′sē əns) *n.* quality or condition of being insouciant.

in·sou·ci·ant (in sōō′sē ənt) *adj.* free from care or worry; carefree; unconcerned. [French *insouciant,* going back to *in-* not (from Latin *in-*) + *soucier* to care (from Latin *sollicitāre* to move, excite).]

in·spect (in spekt′) *v.t.* **1.** to look at closely and critically, esp. for errors, faults, or flaws. **2.** to examine formally or officially: *to inspect troops.* [Latin *inspectus,* past participle of *inspicere* to look into.] —**Syn.** see scrutinize.

in·spec·tion (in spek′shən) *n.* **1.** act of inspecting, esp. for errors, faults, or flaws. **2.** formal or official examination.

in·spec·tor (in spek′tər) *n.* **1.** person, esp. an appointed official, who inspects. **2.** police officer ranking next below a superintendent. [Latin *inspector* examiner.]

in·spi·ra·tion (in′spə rā′shən) *n.* **1.** stimulation of the mind, feelings, or imagination resulting in creativity or activity. **2.** one who or that which inspires. **3.** something inspired, as an idea or action. **4.** state or quality of being inspired. **5.** divine influence directly exerted upon a mind or soul. **6.** act of breathing in; inhalation.

in·spi·ra·tion·al (in′spə rā′shən əl) *adj.* **1.** giving or tending to give inspiration; inspiring. **2.** resulting from inspiration; inspired. **3.** of or relating to inspiration.

in·spire (in spīr′) **-spired, -spir·ing.** *v.t.* **1.** to have an animating influence on; stimulate; stir: *The minister's words inspired his congregation.* **2.** to be the activating force or creative influence that results in something specified: *His wife inspired his first novel.* **3.** to produce or arouse, as a thought or feeling: *Grandfather inspired love and respect.* **4.** to affect with a specified thought or feeling: *His success inspired him with hope for the future.* **5.** to motivate, guide, or control by divine influence. **6.** to breathe in; inhale. —*v.i.* **1.** to inhale. **2.** to give inspiration. [Latin *inspīrāre* to breathe into.]

in·spir·it (in spir′it) *v.t.* to give life, courage, or spirit to.

in·spis·sate (in spis′āt) -sat·ed, -sat·ing. *v.t.* to thicken, as by evaporation; condense. [Late Latin *inspissātus*, past participle of *inspissāre* to thicken, from Latin *in* in + *spissus* thick.]

inst. 1. institute. 2. institution.

in·sta·bil·i·ty (in′stə bil′ə tē) *n.* lack of stability.

in·stall (in stôl′) *v.t.* 1. to put in position for service or use: *The serviceman installed the air conditioner.* 2. to place (a person) in an office, rank, or position with ceremony: *We installed the new club president today.* 3. to establish in a place or position; settle: *He installed himself at the front desk.* [Medieval Latin *installare* to introduce formally, from Latin *in* in + Late Latin *stallum* seat, stall¹; of Germanic origin.] —**Syn.** 2. see **induct.**

in·stal·la·tion (in′stə lā′shən) *n.* 1. act of installing; being installed. 2. mechanical system or apparatus placed in position for use. 3. military base, including its buildings and subsidiary facilities. 4. military equipment, esp. equipment that is large and permanently placed: *antiaircraft installation.*

in·stall·ment¹ (in stôl′mənt) *also,* **in·stal·ment.** *n.* 1. portion of a sum of money owed, to be paid in specified amounts at regular intervals: *We paid for our car in ten installments.* 2. any of several parts issued, presented, or supplied at regular intervals: *The novel appeared in the magazine in installments.* [IN-² + obsolete *stall* to arrange a payment (from Old French *estaler* to fix, from *estal* position; of Germanic origin) + -MENT.]

in·stall·ment² (in stôl′mənt) *also,* **in·stal·ment.** *n.* installation. [INSTALL + -MENT.]

installment plan, system of paying for goods or services in specified amounts at regular intervals.

in·stance (in′stəns) *n.* 1. example or case: *This is one instance where he is wrong. We cannot be sure in this instance.* 2. **for instance.** by way of illustration; for example. [Medieval Latin *instantia,* from Latin *instantia* being present, urgency.]

in·stant (in′stənt) *n.* 1. very short period of time; moment: *I saw him for just an instant.* 2. particular moment or point in time: *If you don't leave this instant I will scream.* —*adj.* 1. without delay: *We received an instant reply.* 2. pressing; urgent: *an instant need.* 3. (of food products) prepared beforehand and packaged, often in powdered form, and requiring only the addition of a liquid, as water or milk, for quick, final preparation: *instant oatmeal, instant coffee.* 4. *Archaic.* of or relating to the present month: *in my letter of the fifth instant.* [Latin *instāns,* present participle of *instāre* to be present, urge.]

in·stan·ta·ne·ous (in′stən tā′nē əs) *adj.* occurring, accomplished, or coming in an instant or without delay: *The reaction of the audience was instantaneous.* —**in′stan·ta′ne·ous·ly,** *adv.* —**in′stan·ta′ne·ous·ness,** *n.*

in·stant·ly (in′stənt lē) *adv.* without delay; at once.

in·stead (in sted′) *adv.* 1. in place of the person or thing previously mentioned; as a substitute or alternative: *The recipe called for butter, but we used margarine instead.* 2. **instead of.** rather than; in place of: *We went for a walk instead of going straight home.* [Earlier *in stead* in place. See IN, STEAD.]

in·step (in′step′) *n.* 1. arched upper surface of the human foot between the toes and the ankle. 2. part of a shoe, stocking, or other footwear that covers this part of the foot. 3. front part of the hind leg of a horse, from the hock to the pastern joint. [Probably IN + STEP.]

in·sti·gate (in′stə gāt′) -gat·ed, -gat·ing. *v.t.* 1. to cause by inciting: *to instigate a riot.* 2. to urge on; stir up. [Latin *instigātus,* past participle of *instigāre.*] —**in′sti·ga′tor,** *n.* —**Syn.** 1. see **incite.**

in·sti·ga·tion (in′stə gā′shən) *n.* act of instigating.

in·still (in stil′) -stilled, -still·ing. *also,* **in·stil.** *v.t.* 1. to introduce gradually or by degrees: *He instilled a love of beauty into us.* 2. to pour in by drops. [Latin *instillāre* to pour in by drops, from *in* in + *stilla* drop.] —**in′stil·la′tion,** *n.*

in·stinct¹ (in′stingkt) *n.* 1. unlearned, inborn disposition, common to all members of a species, to behave in a fixed way when moved by a particular set of stimuli. 2. natural aptitude or tendency; talent. [Latin *instinctus* impulse, from *instinctus,* past participle of *instinguere* to impel.]

Syn. 1. Instinct, intuition refer to mental faculties outside the level of conscious reasoning. Instinct is an innate, untaught, and unacquired impulse or pattern of behavior, characteristic of a whole natural group or species: *Babies cry by instinct when they are hungry.* Intuition denotes the capacity to pass directly and spontaneously from observation to understanding without the intervention of reason or a logical sequence of ideas: *The old hunter knew by intuition that the quarry would soon be there.*

in·stinct² (in stingkt′) *adj.* charged or imbued (with *with*). [Latin *instinctus* impelled, past participle of *instinguere* to impel.]

in·stinc·tive (in stingk′tiv) *adj.* 1. arising from or done by instinct.

2. of, relating to, or of the nature of instinct. —**in·stinc′tive·ly,** *adv.*

in·sti·tute (in′stə tōōt′, -tūt′) -tut·ed, -tut·ing. *v.t.* 1. to set up or give form to; establish: *to institute an annual observance.* 2. to put into operation; initiate; start: *to institute an investigation.* —*n.* 1.a. organization or society for the promotion of work in a particular field: *a music institute.* b. building or buildings housing such an organization or society. 2. educational institution, often affiliated with a college or university, specializing in the research and teaching of a particular field or subject. 3. something established, as a principle or law. [Latin *institūtus,* past participle of *instituere* to establish.]

in·sti·tu·tion (in′stə tōō′shən, -tū′-) *n.* 1.a. organization, society, or similar establishment devoted to a particular purpose, esp. one of a social, educational, or religious nature. b. building or buildings housing such an establishment. 2. act of instituting; establishment. 3. any activity that is vital to a society as a whole, as its economy, government, religion, or social organization: *Slavery was an institution in the South before the Civil War.* 4. person, practice, or object that has become an established or traditional feature, as of a group or people: *Shooting off fireworks on July 4 is an American institution.*

in·sti·tu·tion·al (in′stə tōō′shən əl, -tū′-) *adj.* 1. of, relating to, or having the nature of an institution. 2. of or relating to an organization pursuing a particular purpose or the building or buildings in which it is housed. 3. (of advertising) intended to promote reputation and good will rather than increase immediate sales.

in·sti·tu·tion·al·ism (in′stə tōō′shən əl iz′əm, -tū′-) *n.* 1. system of institutions or organized societies. 2. belief in established institutions, esp. of religion.

in·sti·tu·tion·al·ize (in′stə tōō′shən əl iz′, -tū′-) *v.t.* 1. to convert into or treat as an institution. 2. to place in an institution, esp. one for the care and treatment of an illness.

in·struct (in strukt′) *v.t.* 1. to furnish with knowledge, information, or skill; teach. 2. to give directions or orders to: *He instructed me to deliver the message.* [Latin *instructus,* past participle of *instruere* to build, provide, teach.] —**Syn.** 1. see **teach.**

in·struc·tion (in struk′shən) *n.* 1. act of teaching. 2. **instructions.** explanations, directions, or orders. 3. knowledge or skill that is taught. —**in·struc′tion·al,** *adj.* —**Syn.** 3. see **education.**

in·struc·tive (in struk′tiv) *adj.* giving or providing information; serving to instruct: *The lecture was instructive and interesting.* —**in·struc′tive·ly,** *adv.* —**in·struc′tive·ness,** *n.*

in·struc·tor (in struk′tər) *n.* 1. one who instructs; teacher. 2. teacher in a college or university who ranks next below an assistant professor. [Medieval Latin *instructor* teacher, from Latin *instructor* preparer.] —**in·struc′tress,** *n.*

in·stru·ment (in′strə mənt) *n.* 1. tool, esp. one designed or used for precise or exacting work: *surgical instruments.* 2. device for producing musical sounds: *a keyboard instrument, a wind instrument.* 3. device for measuring or monitoring the condition or progress of something: *navigational instruments.* 4.a. means by or through which something is done or brought about. b. person used as such. 5. formal or legal document, as a contract, deed, or will. [Latin *instrūmentum* tool, apparatus.] —**Syn.** 1. see **implement.** 4.a. see **mean³.**

in·stru·men·tal (in′strə ment′əl) *adj.* 1. serving as a means; helpful. 2. of, relating to, composed for, or performed on musical instruments: *He composed both vocal and instrumental music.* 3. of, relating to, or done with a tool. —*n.* composition for one or more musical instruments. —**in′stru·men′tal·ly,** *adv.*

in·stru·men·tal·ist (in′strə ment′əl ist) *n.* one who plays a musical instrument.

in·stru·men·tal·i·ty (in′strə men tal′ə tē) *pl.,* -ties. *n.* 1. quality or condition of being instrumental. 2. that which serves, or is used for, some purpose; means.

in·stru·men·ta·tion (in′strə men tā′shən) *n.* 1. arrangement or composition of music for instruments, esp. for an orchestra; orchestration. 2. use of scientific, surgical, or other instruments.

instrument panel, panel on or in which instruments are fixed for monitoring. Also, **instrument board.**

in·sub·or·di·nate (in′sə bôrd′ən it) *adj.* not submitting to authority; disobedient. —*n.* one who is insubordinate. —**in′sub·or′di·nate·ly,** *adv.*

in·sub·or·di·na·tion (in′sə bôrd ən ā′shən) *n.* state, quality, or fact of being insubordinate; disobedience.

in·sub·stan·tial (in′səb stan′shəl) *adj.* 1. not real; imaginary: *insubstantial hopes.* 2. not solid or firm; flimsy.

in·suf·fer·a·ble (in suf′ər ə bəl) *adj.* not to be endured; not tolerable; unbearable: *an insufferable bore.* —**in·suf′fer·a·ble·ness,** *n.* —**in·suf′fer·a·bly,** *adv.*

in·suf·fi·cien·cy (in′sə fish′ən sē) *pl.,* -cies. *n.* deficiency, as in amount or capacity: *an insufficiency of supplies.*

in·suf·fi·cient (in′sə fish′ənt) *adj.* not sufficient; inadequate: *insufficient funds.* —**in′suf·fi′cient·ly,** *adv.*

---

at; āpe; cär; end; mē; it; īce; hot; ōld; fôrk; wood; fōōl; oil; out; up; ūse; turn; sing; thin; this; zh in treasure; ə in ago, taken, pencil, lemon, circus.

in·su·lar (in′sə lər, ins′yə-) *adj.* **1.** of, relating to, or characteristic of an island or its people. **2.** inhabiting or situated on an island. **3.** composing or forming an island. **4.** standing alone; isolated. **5.** narrow-minded; provincial. [Late Latin *insulāris* relating to an island, from Latin *insula* island.]

in·su·lar·i·ty (in′sə lar′ə tē, ins′yə-) *n.* **1.** state or condition of being an island. **2.** narrow-mindedness; provincialism.

in·su·late (in′sə lāt′) -lat·ed, -lat·ing. *v.t.* **1.** to cover or surround with a nonconducting material, as rubber: *to insulate an electric wire.* **2.** to install a layer of material, as rubber, between the exterior and interior walls of (a building, refrigerator, or other structure) to reduce the amount of heat transferred. **3.** to protect or isolate. [Late Latin *insulātus* made into an island, from Latin *insula* island.]

in·su·la·tion (in′sə lā′shən) *n.* **1.** material used in insulating. **2.** act of insulating; being insulated.

in·su·la·tor (in′sə lā′tər) *n.* material or device that prevents the conduction of electric current.

in·su·lin (in′sə lin) *n.* **1.** hormone, secreted by the islets of Langerhans in the pancreas, that regulates the body's use and storage of sugar and other carbohydrates. **2.** preparation containing this hormone, used in treating diabetes. It is obtained from the pancreas .of cattle, sheep, or pigs or is produced artificially. Trademark: Insulin. [Late Latin *insula* island + *in*¹; referring to its discovery in the *islets* of Langerhans.]

in·sult (*v.,* in sult′; *n.,* in′sult′) *v.t.* to speak to or treat with scornful abuse, rudeness, or disrespect. —*n.* rude, scornful, or disrespectful act or remark. [Latin *insultāre* to leap upon, scoff at.]

Syn. Insult, affront, indignity refer to an act or remark that offends or slights. **Insult** is an abusive offense meant to humiliate and mortify: *It is an insult to question a man's honesty.* **Affront** is an overt indication of disrespect calculated to offend, belittle, or scorn, and arousing deep resentment: *Walking out during a speech is an affront to the speaker.* **Indignity** is a gross outrage upon one's dignity and self-respect: *A slave suffers many indignities.* —*v.i.* see **offend.**

in·su·per·a·ble (in sōō′pər ə bəl) *adj.* that cannot be overcome or surmounted: *insuperable obstacles.* —**in·su′per·a·bil′i·ty,** *n.* —**su′per·a·bly,** *adv.*

in·sup·port·a·ble (in′sə pôr′tə bəl) *adj.* unbearable; unendurable.

in·sur·a·ble (in shoor′ə bəl) *adj.* capable of being or fit to be insured.

in·sur·ance (in shoor′əns) *n.* **1.** protection against risk or loss by means of a contract between two parties whereby the insurer guarantees payment of a sum of money to the insured in the event of a specified contingency, as personal disability or loss of life or property, in return for the payment of fixed premiums by the insured. **2.** contract guaranteeing such protection. **3.** amount for which someone or something is insured. **4.** amount paid for insurance; premium. **5.** business of insuring persons or property. **6.** any protection against risk, harm, or loss.

in·sure (in shoor′) -sured, -sur·ing. *v.t.* **1.** to protect (someone or something) against risk or loss by means of insurance; cover with insurance. **2.** to ensure. —*v.i.* to buy or sell insurance. [Form of EN-SURE.]

in·sured (in shoord′) *n.* one who is covered by insurance.

in·sur·er (in shoor′ər) *n.* person or company that insures.

in·sur·gence (in sur′jəns) *n.* act of rebelling against established authority; revolt.

in·sur·gen·cy (in sur′jən sē) *n.* **1.** state or quality of being insurgent. **2.** insurgence.

in·sur·gent (in sur′jənt) *n.* **1.** one who rebels against established authority. **2.** member of a political party who rebels against the policies and decisions of the party. —*adj.* rising in revolt against authority; rebellious. [Latin *insurgēns,* present participle of *insurgere* to rise up.]

in·sur·mount·a·ble (in′sur mount′tə bəl) *adj.* that cannot be overcome. —**in′sur·mount′a·bly,** *adv.*

in·sur·rec·tion (in′sə rek′shən) *n.* act or instance of rebelling against established authority, esp. of a government; revolt. [Latin *insurrēctiō,* from Latin *insurgere* to rise up.] —**in′sur·rec′tion·ar·y,** *adj.* —**in′sur·rec′tion·ist,** *n.* —**Syn.** see insurrection.

in·sus·cep·ti·ble (in′sə sep′tə bəl) *adj.* not susceptible. —**in′sus·cep′ti·bil′i·ty,** *n.*

int. **1.** interest. **2.** international. **3.** intransitive. **4.** interior. **5.** internal.

in·tact (in takt′) *adj.* untouched, whole, or unimpaired. [Latin *intāctus.*]

in·ta·glio (in tal′yō, -täl′-) *pl.* **-glios.** *n.* **1.** design incised or carved deep into the surface of a hard material. **2.** art or process of making such designs. **3.** something, esp. a gem, cut or ornamented with such a design. **4.** incised design used as a mold for producing a design in relief. [Italian *intaglio* engraving, carving, from *intagliare* to cut into, engrave, going back to Latin *in* in + *tālea* stick, cutting.]

Intaglio

in·take (in′tāk′) *n.* **1.** act of taking in. **2.** amount taken in: *The doctors restricted his intake of liquids.* **3.** place in a channel, pipe, or other narrow opening where fluid is taken in.

in·tan·gi·ble (in tan′jə bəl) *adj.* **1.** incapable of being easily defined or evaluated by the mind: *Morale is the intangible factor in warfare.* **2.** incapable of being perceived by the sense of touch: *The soul is intangible.* —*n.* something intangible. —**in·tan′gi·bil′i·ty,** *n.* —**in·tan′gi·bly,** *adv.*

in·te·ger (in′tə jər) *n.* **1.** any of the natural numbers, their additive inverses, or zero. For example, 16, — 16, and 0 are integers. **2.** whole or entire thing or entity. [Latin *integer* whole. Doublet of ENTIRE.]

in·te·gral (in′tə grəl) *adj.* **1.** necessary to the completeness of the whole; essential: *an integral part.* **2.** having no part or element missing; entire. **3.** relating to, produced by, or being an integer. —*n.* **1.** something entire; a whole. **2.** *Mathematics.* quantity that is the limit of a sum. [Late Latin *integrālis* whole, not divided, from Latin *integer* whole.]

integral calculus, see calculus.

in·te·grate (in′tə grāt′) -grat·ed, -grat·ing. *v.t.* **1.** to make accessible or available to all racial groups; desegregate. **2.** to bring (parts) together into a whole. **3.** to make whole by adding or bringing together all necessary parts. **4.** *Mathematics.* to find the integral of. —*v.i.* to become accessible or available to all racial groups. [Latin *integrātus,* past participle of *integrāre* to make whole.] —**in′te·gra′tor,** *n.*

in·te·gra·tion (in′tə grā′shən) *n.* **1.** elimination of racial segregation, as in schools or housing. **2.** act of integrating parts into a whole. **3.** *Mathematics.* process of integrating.

in·te·gra·tion·ist (in′tə grā′shə nist) *n.* one who believes in or favors racial integration.

in·teg·ri·ty (in teg′rə tē) *n.* **1.** moral uprightness; honesty; sincerity. **2.** state, quality, or condition of being complete; wholeness. [Latin *integritās.*] —**Syn.** **1.** see honesty.

in·teg·u·ment (in teg′yə mənt) *n.* natural covering of an animal or plant, as.a husk, skin, shell, or rind. [Latin *integumentum* covering.]

in·tel·lect (int′əl ekt′) *n.* **1.** power of the mind to know, understand, and reason. **2.** intelligence or mental ability, esp. when highly developed. **3.** person of great intelligence. [Latin *intellēctus* understanding.]

in·tel·lec·tu·al (int′əl ek′chōō əl) *adj.* **1.** of or relating to the intellect. **2.** appealing to, involving, or using the intellect: *intellectual pursuits.* **3.** possessing or showing intellect. —*n.* intellectual person. —**in′tel·lec′tu·al·ly,** *adv.*

in·tel·lec·tu·al·ism (int′əl ek′chōō ə liz′əm) *n.* **1.** exercise of the intellect. **2.** devotion to intellectual pursuits. **3.** philosophical doctrine that knowledge is wholly or mainly derived from reason.

in·tel·lec·tu·al·i·ty (int′əl ek′chōō al′ə tē) *pl.* **-ties.** *n.* **1.** quality of being intellectual. **2.** intellectual power or force.

in·tel·lec·tu·al·ize (int′əl ek′chōō ə līz′) -ized, -iz·ing. *v.t.* **1.** to give an intellectual character to; make intellectual. —*v.i.* to think; reason.

in·tel·li·gence (in tel′ə jəns) *n.* **1.** ability to learn from experience, to solve problems rationally, and to modify behavior with changes in environment; faculty of understanding and reasoning. **2.a.** secret information, esp. about an enemy: *Our intelligence shows that the enemy is advancing.* **b.** agency or individuals of a military service engaged in the collection and evaluation of such information. **3.** *also,* **Intelligence.** intelligent or rational being, esp. one that is incorporeal.

intelligence quotient, number used to estimate the rate of mental growth, obtained by dividing a person's mental age by his chronological age, and multiplying by 100.

intelligence test, test used to measure one's mental development in relation to that of others. It may require answering questions or performing manual tasks.

in·tel·li·gent (in tel′ə jənt) *adj.* **1.** having a high degree of intelligence and mental ability; quick to learn. **2.** having or using the faculty of understanding and reasoning; having intelligence: *Man is an intelligent being.* **3.** marked by or indicating intelligence: *The child made a very intelligent comment.* [Latin *intelligēns,* present participle of *intelligere* to understand, from *inter* between + *legere* to choose.] —**in·tel′li·gent·ly,** *adv.*

in·tel·li·gent·si·a (in tel′ə jent′sē ə, -gent′-) *n.,pl.* group of persons having or regarded as having superior intelligence and enlightened opinions; intellectuals collectively. [Russian *intelligentsiya,* going back to Latin *intelligentia* understanding.]

in·tel·li·gi·bil·i·ty (in tel′ə jə bil′ə tē) *n.* state or quality of being comprehensible.

in·tel·li·gi·ble (in tel′ə jə bəl) *adj.* **1.** capable of being understood; comprehensible. **2.** *Philosophy.* that can be known or understood by the intellect alone. [Latin *intelligibilis* comprehensible, from *intelligere* to understand.] —**in·tel′li·gi·bly,** *adv.*

in·tem·per·ance (in tem′pər əns, -prəns) *n.* lack of moderation or restraint, esp. in the use of alcoholic beverages.

at; āpe; cär; end; mē; it; īce; hot; ōld; fôrk; wood; fōōl; oil; out; up; ūse; turn; sing; thin; <u>th</u>is; zh in treasure; ə in ago, taken, pencil, lemon, circus

in·tem·per·ate (in tem′pər it, -prit) *adj.* lacking temperance; excessive. —**in·tem′per·ate·ly,** *adv.* —**in·tem′per·ate·ness,** *n.* —**Syn.** see **excessive.**

in·tend (in tend′) *v.t.* **1.** to have in mind as a purpose; plan: *I intend to write as soon as I arrive.* **2.** to make, design, or mean for a particular purpose, use, person, or body of persons: *The movie is intended for adults only. That remark was intended for you.* **3.** *Archaic.* to direct. —*v.i.* to have a purpose or plan in mind. [Latin *intendere* to stretch out, direct, apply oneself to.]

in·tend·an·cy (in ten′dən sē) *pl.,* **-cies.** *n.* **1.** office, position, or function of an intendant. **2.** intendants collectively. **3.** formerly, a district under the control of an intendant.

in·tend·ant (in ten′dənt) *n.* **1.** formerly, a manager, director, or administrator under the French or Spanish monarchies. **2.** any manager, director, or administrator, as of a public business. [French *intendant,* from Latin *intendēns,* present participle of *intendere.* See INTEND.]

in·tend·ed (in ten′did) *adj.* **1.** meant; intentional. **2.** prospective: *We met his intended wife.* —*n.* prospective husband or wife.

in·tense (in tens′) *adj.* **1.** of a very high degree; very strong: *an intense desire.* **2.** having or showing strong emotion and earnest feeling: *an intense look.* [Latin *intēnsus* stretched out, strained, past participle of *intendere.* See INTEND.] —**in·tense′ly,** *adv.* —**in·tense′ness,** *n.*

in·ten·si·fi·er (in ten′sə fī′ər) *n.* *Grammar.* an intensive.

in·ten·si·fy (in ten′sə fī′) **-fied, -fy·ing.** *v.t.* to make intense or more intense; increase greatly. —*v.i.* to become intense or more intense; grow in intensity. —**in·ten′si·fi·ca′tion,** *n.*

in·ten·si·ty (in ten′sə tē) *pl.,* **-ties.** *n.* **1.** state or quality of being intense. **2.** strength or degree, as of feeling or force: *The pain increased in intensity.* **3.** strength of a form of energy, as heat, light, or sound, per unit of area, volume, or mass.

in·ten·sive (in ten′siv) *adj.* **1.** thorough or concentrated: *intensive research.* **2.** of, relating to, or characterized by intensity. **3.** *Grammar.* indicating force or emphasis. In the sentence *I myself did it, myself* is an intensive pronoun. —*n.* *Grammar.* intensive element, word, or phrase. —**in·ten′sive·ly,** *adv.*

in·tent¹ (in tent′) *n.* **1.** intention; aim. **2.** act or fact of intending. **3.** to (or for) all intents and purposes. in almost every way; practically; virtually. [Old French *entent(e)* purpose, from Late Latin *intentus,* from Latin *intentus* an extending.]

in·tent² (in tent′) *adj.* **1.** having the mind firmly fixed on something: *He was intent on solving our problems.* **2.** firmly directed or fixed: *an intent look.* [Latin *intentus,* past participle of *intendere.* See INTEND.] —**in·tent′ly,** *adv.*

in·ten·tion (in ten′shən) *n.* **1.** that which is intended; purpose; plan: *Her intention was to help you.* **2.** act of intending. **3. intentions.** purposes with respect to marriage. —**Syn.** see **purpose.**

in·ten·tion·al (in ten′shən əl) *adj.* carefully thought out or planned; done on purpose. —**in·ten′tion·al·ly,** *adv.* —**Syn.** see **deliberate.**

in·ter (in tur′) **-terred, -ter·ring.** *v.t.* to put a (dead body) into a grave or tomb; bury. [Old French *enterrer,* going back to Latin *in* in + *terra* earth.]

inter- *prefix* **1.** one with the other; together: *to interact.* **2.** between or among: *intercollegiate, interchange.* [Latin *inter* between, among, during.]

in·ter·act (in′tə rakt′) *v.i.* to act on or influence each other. —**in′ter·ac′tive,** *adj.*

in·ter·ac·tion (in′tə rak′shən) *n.* reciprocal action or influence.

in·ter a·li·a (in′tər ā′lē ə) *Latin.* among other things.

in·ter·bor·ough (in′tər bur′ō) *adj.* between boroughs.

in·ter·breed (in′tər brēd′) **-bred, -breed·ing.** *v.t., v.i.* to crossbreed.

in·ter·ca·lar·y (in tur′kə ler′ē) *adj.* **1.** (of a day or month) added to the calendar to make the calendar year correspond to the solar year. **2.** (of a year) having such a day or month added. **3.** interpolated; inserted. [Latin *intercalārius* relating to insertion, from *intercalāre* to insert.]

in·ter·ca·late (in tur′kə lāt′) **-lat·ed, -lat·ing.** *v.t.* **1.** to add (a day or month) to the calendar. **2.** to interpolate; insert. [Latin *intercalātus,* past participle of *intercalāre* to insert.]

in·ter·ca·la·tion (in tur′kə lā′shən) *n.* **1.** act of intercalating. **2.** that which is intercalated.

in·ter·cede (in′tər sēd′) **-ced·ed, -ced·ing.** *v.i.* **1.** to plead on behalf of another or others. **2.** to act as mediator between opposing parties. [Latin *intercēdere* to go between.]

in·ter·cel·lu·lar (in′tər sel′yə lər) *adj.* situated among or occupying the area between cells.

in·ter·cept (in′tər sept′) *v.t.* **1.** to seize, interrupt, or delay on the way. **2.** to stop the course or progress of; check: *to intercept a missile.* **3.** *Mathematics.* to meet at a point or points. —*n.* in a graph, the distance from the origin to a point at which a straight line or curve intersects a coordinate axis. [Latin *interceptus,* past participle of *intercipere* to interrupt; literally, to catch between.] —**in′ter·cep′tion,** *n.*

in·ter·cep·tor (in′tər sep′tər) *n.* **1.** one who or that which intercepts. **2.** fast-climbing airplane designed to intercept attacking enemy aircraft.

interceptor missile, defensive missile designed to counter enemy forces in the air.

in·ter·ces·sion (in′tər sesh′ən) *n.* **1.** act of interceding. **2.** prayer or plea on behalf of another or others. [Latin *intercessiō* a going between.]

in·ter·ces·sor (in′tər ses′ər) *n.* one who intercedes.

in·ter·ces·so·ry (in′tər ses′ər ē) *adj.* that intercedes on behalf of another or others.

in·ter·change (*v.,* in′tər chānj′; *n.,* in′tər chānj′) **-changed, -chang·ing.** *v.t.* **1.** to put each of (two things) in the place or position of the other. **2.** to give and receive mutually. —*v.i.* to change places one with the other. —*n.* **1.** act or instance of changing places or positions one with the other. **2.** act or instance of giving and receiving mutually. **3.** place where a vehicle may enter or leave a major highway without interfering with the flow of traffic on the highway. [Old French *entrechangier* to change, exchange, going back to Latin *inter* between + Late Latin *cambiāre.* See CHANGE.]

in·ter·change·a·ble (in′tər chān′jə bəl) *adj.* capable of being put or used in place of each other: *The parts are interchangeable.* —**in′ter·change′a·bil′i·ty,** *n.* —**in′ter·change′a·bly,** *adv.*

in·ter·col·le·giate (in′tər kə lē′jit, -jē it) *adj.* carried on or occurring between colleges or universities: *intercollegiate baseball.*

in·ter·com (in′tər kom′) *n.* radio or telephone system which affords internal communication, as between rooms or different areas of a building. [Short for *intercommunication system.*]

in·ter·com·mu·ni·cate (in′tər kə mū′nə kāt′) **-cat·ed, -cat·ing.** *v.i.* to communicate with each other or one another. —**in′ter·com·mu′ni·ca′tion,** *n.*

in·ter·con·nect (in′tər kə nekt′) *v.t., v.i.* to connect or be connected one with the other. —**in′ter·con·nec′tion,** *n.*

in·ter·con·ti·nen·tal (in′tər kon′tə nent′əl) *adj.* **1.** traveling or capable of traveling from one continent to another. **2.** of, relating to, or involving more than one continent.

in·ter·cos·tal (in′tər kos′təl) *adj.* between the ribs: *an intercostal artery.* —*n.* intercostal muscle. [Modern Latin *intercostalis,* from Latin *inter* between + *costa* rib.]

in·ter·course (in′tər kôrs′) *n.* **1.** communication, relations, or dealings between individuals or groups; interchange, as of thoughts, ideas, or feelings: *social intercourse.* **2.** sexual relations. [Old French *entrecours* commerce, from Late Latin *intercursus,* from Latin *intercursus* a running between.]

in·ter·de·nom·i·na·tion·al (in′tər di nom′ə nā′shən əl) *adj.* between, among, or involving different religious denominations.

in·ter·de·part·men·tal (in′tər dē′pärt ment′əl, -di pärt′-) *adj.* between or among departments.

in·ter·de·pen·dence (in′tər di pen′dəns) *n.* dependence on each other or one another; mutual dependence.

in·ter·de·pen·dent (in′tər di pen′dənt) *adj.* dependent on each other or one another; mutually dependent. —**in′ter·de·pend′ent·ly,** *adv.*

in·ter·dict (*v.,* in′tər dikt′; *n.,* in′tər dikt′) *v.t.* **1.** to prohibit; forbid. **2.** to prevent or obstruct by heavy fire, as the advancement of enemy troops. **3.** in the Roman Catholic Church, to exclude from certain rites and sacraments. —*n.* **1.** official or authoritative prohibition. **2.** in the Roman Catholic Church, a punishment in which a person, district, or country is excluded from certain rites and sacraments. [Latin *interdictum* prohibition.]

in·ter·dic·tion (in′tər dik′shən) *n.* **1.** act of interdicting; being interdicted. **2.** an interdict. —**in′ter·dic′to·ry,** *adj.*

in·ter·est (in′trist, -tər ist) *n.* **1.a.** feeling of concern, involvement, or curiosity: *He has no interest in our problems.* **b.** cause or source of such feeling: *His career is his primary interest at the moment. He was eager to know what her interests were.* **c.** power to arouse such feeling: *His theories had little interest for me.* **2.** *also,* **interests.** that which is advantageous, beneficial, or contributes to one's welfare. **3.** money paid for the use or borrowing of money. **4.a.** legal right, claim, or share: *He has a controlling interest in the business.* **b.** something in which one has such a right, claim, or share. **5.** *usually,* **interests.** group having a common concern, esp. in a business or industry: *the mining interests.* **6.** anything given in excess of what is due: *He returned our hospitality with interest.* **7. in the interest (or interests) of.** for the promotion, benefit, or advancement of; in behalf of. —*v.t.* **1.** to stimulate or hold the curiosity or attention of. **2.** to cause (a person) to take an interest in something: *He tried to interest them in politics.* [Noun use of Latin *interest* it is of importance, it concerns.]

in·ter·est·ing (in′tris ting, -tər is-, -tə res′-) *adj.* arousing curiosity or attention. —**in′ter·est·ing·ly,** *adv.*

Syn. Interesting, engrossing, absorbing mean engaging attention or arousing curiosity. **Interesting** is the most widely used but least precise term, running the gamut of meaning from stimulating or entertaining

to exciting and provocative: *The demonstration of fencing techniques was very interesting.* **Engrossing** is usually applied to things and means to hold one's attention in a challenging and fascinating way: *The children found the magician's tricks thoroughly engrossing.* **Absorbing** suggests monopolizing one's attention to the exclusion of all other feelings: *The detective story was so absorbing that Paul did not hear the bell ring.*

in·ter·fere (in'tər fēr') -fered, -fer·ing. *v.i.* **1.** to concern oneself with or intrude in the affairs of others without having been asked; meddle (often *with in*): *She always interferes in matters that don't concern her.* **2.** to interrupt, hinder, or disturb (*with with*): *Constant interruptions interfere with my work.* **3.** *Sports.* to obstruct the action of an opponent by illegal means. **4.** *Physics.* (of waves) to cause interference by acting upon one another. [Old French *(s')entreferir* to strike each other, going back to Latin *inter* between + *ferīre* to strike.]
Syn. 1. Interfere, meddle, tamper mean to concern oneself with what belongs to others. **Interfere** suggests intrusion in an unwanted, unwarranted, or unnecessary fashion as to hamper and frustrate: *Under the Constitution, government cannot interfere in the private lives of citizens.* **Meddle** usually applies to involvement in personal concerns without right or authorization: *The person who constantly meddles in other people's business will have few friends.* **Tamper** indicates altering something, usually in a minor way, either for one's own benefit or to cause harm: *A would-be thief had tampered with the lock.*

in·ter·fer·ence (in'tər fēr'əns) *n.* **1.** act of interfering. **2.a.** disruption of a radio signal by other signals. **b.** radio signals that cause such disruption. **3.** *Football.* **a.** illegal hindering of the intended receiver of a pass. **b.** the blocking of opposing players in order to make way for the ball carrier. **c.** player or players who provide such blocking. **4.** *Physics.* phenomenon produced when two waves arrive at the same point. If the waves are in phase they reinforce one another; if they are out of phase they weaken or neutralize one another.

in·ter·fer·om·e·ter (in'tər fə rom'ə tər) *n.* instrument that uses interference patterns produced by light, sound, or radio waves to measure distances and wavelengths and to analyze spectra. [INTERFER(E) + -METER.]

in·ter·fold (in'tər fōld') *v.t.* to fold together or one within another.

in·ter·fuse (in'tər fūz') -fused, -fus·ing. *v.t.* **1.** to mix together thoroughly; blend. **2.** to spread through; permeate. **3.** to cause to pass into or spread throughout. —*v.i.* to become blended. [Latin *interfūsus,* past participle of *interfundere* to pour between.] —**in'ter·fu'sion,** *n.*

in·ter·im (in'tər im) *n.* time intervening; as between events; meantime. —*adj.* for or occurring during an interim; temporary. [Latin *interim* in the meantime.]

in·te·ri·or (in tēr'ē ər) *n.* **1.** inner side, surface, or part: *The interior of the cave was dark.* **2.** part of a region or country that is away from the coast or border. **3.** representation of the inside of a room or building, as in a painting. —*adj.* **1.** of, relating to, or situated on the inside. **2.** away from the coast or border; inland. [Latin *interior* inner.]

interior decoration, art or business of planning, designing, and furnishing interiors, as of homes or offices, to provide beauty, comfort, and convenience. Also, **interior design.**

interior decorator, one who is engaged in interior decoration.

interj., interjection.

in·ter·ject (in'tər jekt') *v.t.* to throw in between other things; insert abruptly: *to interject a comment.* [Latin *interjectus,* past participle of *intericere* to throw between.]

in·ter·jec·tion (in'tər jek'shən) *n.* **1.** word or phrase belonging to that part of speech that expresses emotion or exclamation and is capable of standing alone. *Oh* and *alas* are interjections. **2.** act of interjecting. **3.** that which is interjected, as a remark or question. —**in'ter·jec'tion·al,** *adj.*

in·ter·lace (in'tər lās') -laced, -lac·ing. *v.t.* **1.** to unite by or as by weaving together; intertwine. **2.** to distribute at intervals; intersperse. —*v.i.* to intertwine.

In·ter·la·ken (in'tər lä'kən) *n.* resort town in central Switzerland. Pop. (1960), 4738.

in·ter·leaf (in'tər lēf') *pl.,* -leaves. *n.* sheet of paper, usually blank, placed between two regular printed leaves of a book, esp. to protect an engraving or color plate.

in·ter·leave (in'tər lēv') -leaved, -leav·ing. *v.t.* to insert an interleaf or interleaves between the regular printed leaves of.

in·ter·line¹ (in'tər līn') -lined, -lin·ing. *v.t.* to sew an interlining in (a garment). [INTER + LINE².]

in·ter·line² (in'tər līn') -lined, -lin·ing. *v.t.* to insert words between the written or printed lines of: *to interline a book.* **2.** to write or print, as comments or corrections, between written or printed lines: *to interline a comment.* [Medieval Latin *interlineare* to write between lines, from Latin *inter* between + *līnea* line.]

in·ter·lin·e·ar (in'tər lin'ē ər) *adj.* **1.** inserted between written or printed lines. **2.** written or printed in different languages or versions in alternate lines.

in·ter·lin·e·a·tion (in'tər lin'ē ā'shən) *n.* **1.** insertion of a word or words between printed or written lines. **2.** word or words so inserted.

in·ter·lin·ing (in'tər lī'ning) *n.* extra lining between the outer fabric and the ordinary lining of a garment.

in·ter·link (in'tər lingk') *v.t.* to link together.

in·ter·lock (in'tər lok') *v.t., v.i.* to lock or fit together closely.

in·ter·loc·u·tor (in'tər lok'yə tər) *n.* **1.** one who takes part in a conversation or dialogue. **2.** man in the middle of a line of performers in a minstrel show who exchanges jokes and puns with the two end men. [Latin *interlocūtus,* past participle of *interloquī* to interrupt in speaking, converse + -OR.]

in·ter·loc·u·to·ry (in'tər lok'yə tôr'ē) *adj.* **1.** of, relating to, or occurring in conversation or dialogue. **2.** interjected into the narrative, conversation, or speech: *interlocutory observations.* **3.** coming between the beginning and end of a law suit or trial, as a temporary or provisional decree.

in·ter·lope (in'tər lōp') -loped, -lop·ing. *v.i.* **1.** to interfere with the affairs of others; intrude. **2.** to encroach upon the rights or violate the domain of others, esp. in trade. [INTER- + LOPE.]

in·ter·lude (in'tər lōōd') *n.* **1.** intervening time, space, or event: *a few brief interludes of sleep* (Livingstone, 1865). **2.** brief passage of music played between parts of a church service, acts of a play, or sections of a long musical composition. [Medieval Latin *interludium* type of comic play given between the acts of a miracle or mystery play, from Latin *inter* between + *lūdus* a play.]

in·ter·lu·nar (in'tər lōō'nər) *adj.* of or relating to the period between the old moon and the new moon when the moon is invisible.

in·ter·mar·riage (in'tər mar'ij) *n.* marriage between persons of different religious faiths, races, or ethnic backgrounds.

in·ter·mar·ry (in'tər mar'ē) -ried, -ry·ing. *v.i.* **1.** to marry outside one's religious, racial, or ethnic group. **2.** to become connected by marriage, as two families, tribes, or races. **3.** to marry within one's own family.

in·ter·me·di·ar·y (in'tər mē'dē er'ē) *pl.,* -ar·ies. *n.* **1.** one who comes between two or more opposing parties in order to bring about an agreement or compromise; mediator: *He served as an intermediary in the negotiations.* **2.** means by which something is brought about; instrument. **3.** intermediate form or stage. —*adj.* **1.** acting as a mediator: *an intermediary agent.* **2.** located or occurring between; intermediate: *intermediary step.* [Latin *intermedius* that which is between + -ARY¹.]

in·ter·me·di·ate¹ (in'tər mē'dē it) *adj.* located or occurring in the middle or between. —*n.* **1.** something intermediate. **2.** intermediary. [Medieval Latin *intermediatus* lying between, from Latin *intermedius* that which is between.]

in·ter·me·di·ate² (in'tər mē'dē āt') -at·ed, -at·ing. *v.i.* to act as an intermediary; mediate. [INTER- + MEDIATE.]

in·ter·ment (in tur'mənt) *n.* act of interring.

in·ter·mez·zo (in'tər met'sō, -med'zō) *pl.,* -mez·zos or -mez·zi (-met'sē, -med'zē). *n.* **1.** short musical or other entertainment performed between the acts of a play or opera. **2.** *Music.* **a.** short, slow movement between the two longer movements of an extended composition, as a symphony. **b.** short, independent instrumental composition. [Italian *intermezzo* interlude, interval, from Latin *intermedius* that which is between.]

in·ter·mi·na·ble (in tur'mi nə bəl) *adj.* prolonged and seemingly endless; long drawn out: *interminable controversy.* [Late Latin *interminābilis* endless, going back to Latin *in-* not + *terminus* end.] —**in·ter'mi·na·bly,** *adv.*

in·ter·min·gle (in'tər ming'gəl) -gled, -gling. *v.t., v.i.* to mingle together.

in·ter·mis·sion (in'tər mish'ən) *n.* **1.** interval between events or periods of activity: *There was a short intermission after the first act of the play.* **2.** act or instance of intermitting. [Latin *intermissiō* interruption.]

in·ter·mit (in'tər mit') -mit·ted, -mit·ting. *v.t., v.i.* to discontinue for a time; suspend; interrupt: *to intermit an action.* [Latin *intermittere* to leave off, pause.]

in·ter·mit·tent (in'tər mit'ənt) *adj.* alternately stopping and starting again; coming at intervals: *intermittent rain.* —**in'ter·mit'tence, in'ter·mit'ten·cy,** *n.* —**in'ter·mit'tent·ly,** *adv.* —**Syn.** see periodic.

in·ter·mix (in'tər miks') *v.t., v.i.* to mix together; intermingle.

in·ter·mix·ture (in'tər miks'chər) *n.* **1.** act of mixing together; being mixed together. **2.** mass of ingredients mixed together. **3.** addition to a mixture: *intermixtures to the population.*

in·tern¹ (in turn') *v.t.* to detain and restrict to a particular place, esp. during a war. [French *interner* to confine, from *interne* inward, from Latin *internus.*] —**Syn.** see imprison.

in·tern² (in'turn') *n.* assistant resident doctor, esp. a recent graduate, serving in a hospital or clinic under the supervision of experienced doctors. —*v.i.* to be an intern. [French *interne* resident medical student

at; āpe; cär; end; mē; it; īce; hot; ōld; fôrk; wood; fōōl; oil; out; up; ūse; turn; sing; thin; this; zh in treasure; ə in ago, taken, pencil, lemon, circus.

in a hospital, going back to Latin *internus* inward.] —**in′tern·ship′**, *n.*

in·ter·nal (in turn′əl) *adj.* **1.** of, relating to, or existing on the inside; interior: *internal organs.* **2.** of or relating to the domestic matters or concerns of a country: *internal security, internal affairs.* **3.** taken internally: *internal medication.* **4.** of, relating to, or dependent upon the nature of a thing; intrinsic: *internal evidence.* **5.** of, relating to, or existing in the mind; subjective: *Sensations and ideas are both internal* (Martineau, 1869). [Latin *internus* inward + -AL¹.] —**in·ter′nal·ly**, *adv.*

in·ter·nal·com·bus·tion engine (in turn′əl kəm bus′chən) engine in which fuel is burned within the engine itself.

internal revenue, governmental income that is derived from taxes other than customs duties.

internal rhyme, rhyme between words within the same line of poetry.

in·ter·na·tion·al (in′tər nash′ən əl) *adj.* **1.** of, relating to, or concerning two or more countries: *international cooperation.* **2.** of or relating to relations between countries. —*n.* **International.** any of several worldwide Socialist or Communist organizations. —**in′ter·na′tion·al·ly**, *adv.*

international candle, unit of measure of light intensity, used internationally until 1948. The present unit is the candela.

International Court of Justice, judicial body of the United Nations created in 1945. Also, **World Court.**

International Date Line *also,* **international date line.** imaginary line running approximately along the 180th meridian, marking the time boundary between one day and the next. Also, **date line.**

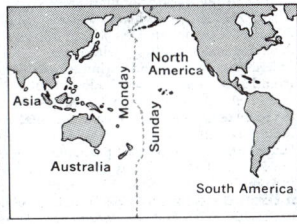

International Date Line

In·ter·na·tio·nale (in′tər nash′ə nal′, -näl′) *n.* revolutionary socialist anthem composed at the time of the Paris Commune of 1871.

International Geophysical Year, period from July 1, 1957, to December 31, 1958, during which scientists from many countries cooperated in the study of the earth. Also, **IGY.**

in·ter·na·tion·al·ism (in′tər nash′ən əl iz′əm) *n.* **1.** doctrine of mutual cooperation among countries and peoples for the benefit of all mankind. **2.** state or quality of being international, as in character, interests, or outlook.

in·ter·na·tion·al·ist (in′tər nash′ən əl ist) *n.* one who advocates or supports internationalism.

in·ter·na·tion·al·ize (in′tər nash′ən əl īz′) **-ized, -iz·ing.** *v.t.* to bring under international control; make international.

international law, body of rules regulating the dealings of countries with one another.

International Phonetic Alphabet, alphabet consisting of letters and symbols that are universally understood, developed to transcribe the sounds of any language.

in·terne (in′turn′) *n.* intern². [Form of INTERN².]

in·ter·ne·cine (in′tər nes′ēn, -nē′sin) *adj.* **1.** mutually destructive. **2.** characterized by much bloodshed. [Latin *internecinus* deadly.]

in·tern·ee (in′tur nē′) *n.* one who is or has been interned.

in·tern·ment (in turn′mənt) *n.* act of interning; being interned.

in·ter·o·cep·tor (in′tər ō sep′tər) *n.* Anatomy. sensory nerve receptor located in and transmitting impulses from the inner organs.

in·ter·pel·late (in′tər pel′āt, in tur′pə lāt′) **-lat·ed, -lat·ing.** *v.t., v.i.* to question formally or publicly an action or policy of the government. [Latin *interpellātus,* past participle of *interpellāre* to interrupt in speaking.] —**in·ter·pel·la·tion** (in′tər pə lā′shən, in tur′-), *n.*

in·ter·pen·e·trate (in′tər pen′ə trāt′) **-trat·ed, -trat·ing.** *v.t.* to penetrate thoroughly; permeate; pervade. —*v.i.* to penetrate each other. —**in′ter·pen′e·tra′tion**, *n.* **in′ter·pen′e·tra′tive**, *adj.*

in·ter·phone (in′tər fōn′) *n.* telephone system that provides communication between rooms or sections of a building or ship; intercom.

in·ter·plan·e·tar·y (in′tər plan′ə ter′ē) *adj.* between the planets.

in·ter·play (in′tər plā′) *n.* reciprocal action or influence; interaction: *an interplay of parts.* —*v.i.* to act on each other; interact.

In·ter·pol (in′tər pōl′) *n.* international police agency that assists the police of member countries in their work. [Short for *inter(national) pol(ice).*]

in·ter·po·late (in tur′pə lāt′) **-lat·ed, -lat·ing.** *v.t.* **1.** to alter or corrupt (a text) by inserting new material: *This ancient poem has been extensively interpolated by medieval scribes.* **2.** to insert (new or false material) into a text: *The actor interpolated several lines of his own into*

the play. **3.** *Mathematics.* to find the value of (a function, as a logarithm) between two known values. —*v.i.* to make an insertion or insertions of new or false material. [Latin *interpolātus,* past participle of *interpolāre.*]

in·ter·po·la·tion (in tur′pə lā′shən) *n.* **1.** act of interpolating; being interpolated. **2.** that which is interpolated; insertion.

in·ter·pose (in′tər pōz′) **-posed, -pos·ing.** *v.t.* **1.** to introduce into a conversation or speech: *to interpose an unnecessary remark.* **2.** to place between; insert: *to interpose an obstacle.* **3.** to put forth or assert in order to intervene: *to interpose authority.* —*v.i.* **1.** to interrupt. **2.** to come between; intervene. [French *interposer* to put between, a modification (influenced by French *poser* to place) of Latin *interpōnere.*] —**in′ter·pos′er**, *n.*

in·ter·po·si·tion (in′tər pə zish′ən) *n.* **1.** act or instance of interposing. **2.** that which is interposed.

in·ter·pret (in tur′prit) *v.t.* **1.** to make clear or understandable; reveal the meaning of; elucidate. **2.** to translate: *The guide interpreted the woman's remarks for us.* **3.** to understand or regard: *The policeman interpreted his offer as a bribe.* **4.** to render or perform so as to bring out the meaning of: *The pianist interpreted the sonata with great feeling.* —*v.i.* **1.** to act as an interpreter; translate: *During our trip abroad he offered to interpret for us.* **2.** to give an interpretation: *Each must interpret for himself* (Hawthorne, 1860). [Latin *interpretārī* to explain.]

Syn. *v.t.* **1. Interpret, explain, expound, elucidate** mean to make clear. **Interpret** usually involves a paraphrasing or translating into familiar and intelligible terms what is not immediately apparent or explicit: *The poet read and then interpreted his poem about nature.* **Explain** suggests unfolding the meaning, sense, or significance to clarify and define what is complex or obscure: *The professor explained how the mechanism works.* **Expound** stresses elaboration and analysis, esp. in a scholarly and methodical fashion, with application of special knowledge and insight: *The preacher expounded some of the difficult passages of the Bible.* **Elucidate** indicates the use of explanation or illustration to make a complex subject clearer: *The secretary of state elucidated the president's foreign policy statement.*

in·ter·pre·ta·tion (in tur′prə tā′shən) *n.* **1.** act of interpreting. **2.** sense that results from interpreting; meaning. **3.** rendition or performance that brings out the meaning of something, as of a musical composition or dramatic role.

in·ter·pre·ta·tive (in tur′prə tā′tiv) *adj.* serving to interpret or interpret; explanatory: *The book contains an interpretative treatment of the subject.* Also, **in·ter·pre·tive** (in tur′prə tiv).

in·ter·pret·er (in tur′prə tər) *n.* **1.** one who gives oral translations from one language to another. **2.** one who renders or performs something so as to bring out the meaning: *He is the leading interpreter of Bach's organ works.*

in·ter·ra·cial (in′tər rā′shəl) *adj.* **1.** between or involving members of different races: *interracial marriage, interracial harmony.* **2.** of or for members of different races: *interracial community facilities.*

in·ter·reg·num (in′tər reg′nəm) *pl.* **-nums** or **-na** (-nə). *n.* **1.** interval between the end of a sovereign's reign and the accession of his successor. **2.** any period without the usual ruling power or authority. **3.** any break in continuity; pause. [Latin *interregnum* time between the end of a sovereign's reign and the accession of his successor, from *inter* between + *regnum* reign.]

in·ter·re·late (in′tər ri lāt′) **-lat·ed, -lat·ing.** *v.t., v.i.* to bring to or come into mutual or close relation. —**in′ter·re·la′tion, in′ter·re·la′tion·ship′**, *n.*

interrog. **1.** interrogation. **2.** interrogative.

in·ter·ro·gate (in ter′ə gāt′) **-gat·ed, -gat·ing.** *v.t.* to examine by questioning formally and methodically: *The policeman interrogated the prisoner for hours.* —*v.i.* to ask questions: *They were granted permission to interrogate.* [Latin *interrogātus,* past participle of *interrogāre* to question.]

in·ter·ro·ga·tion (in ter′ə gā′shən) *n.* **1.** act of interrogating; being interrogated; questioning. **2.** question: *The lawyer's interrogation was couched in the most conciliatory language.*

interrogation point, question mark. Also, **interrogation mark.**

in·ter·rog·a·tive (in′tə rog′ə tiv) *adj.* **1.** of, relating to, or having the form of a question: *an interrogative method.* **2.** Grammar. expressing or introducing a question. *Who* is an interrogative pronoun in the sentence *Who is it?* —*n.* word or construction used in asking a question.

in·ter·rog·a·tor (in ter′ə gā′tər) *n.* one who interrogates; questioner.

in·ter·rog·a·to·ry (in′tə rog′ə tôr′ē) *adj.* interrogative. —*n.* **interrogatories.** Law. formal, usually written, questions or series of questions.

in·ter·rupt (in′tər rupt′) *v.t.* **1.** to break the continuity; break off; cause to stop: *She interrupted her work to answer the phone.* **2.** to break in upon (someone) in the course of an action or speech: *Please do not interrupt me when I am talking.* —*v.i.* to break in upon an action or

at; āpe; cär; end; mē; it; īce; hot; ōld; fôrk; wood; fōōl; oil; out; up; ūse; turn; sing; thin; this; zh in treasure; ə in ago, taken, pencil, lemon, circus.

537

speech: *He always interrupts when someone is speaking.* [Latin *interruptus*, past participle of *interrumpere* to break up, break off.]

in·ter·rupt·er (in′tə rup′tər) *n.* **1.** one who or that which interrupts. **2.** device for interrupting an electrical circuit periodically and automatically.

in·ter·rup·tion (in′tə rup′shən) *n.* **1.** act of interrupting; being interrupted. **2.** that which interrupts. —**Syn. 2.** see **interval.**

in·ter·scho·las·tic (in′tər skə las′tik) *adj.* between or among schools: *interscholastic rivalries.*

in·ter·sect (in′tər sekt′) *v.t.* to divide by passing or lying across: *The river intersected the valley.* —*v.i.* to meet and lie across each other: *The two roads intersect at the bridge.* [Latin *intersectus,* past participle of *intersecāre* to cut apart.]

in·ter·sec·tion (in′tər sek′shən, in′tər sek′-) *n.* **1.** place of intersecting, esp. where two or more roads or streets meet and cross. **2.** act of intersecting; being intersected. **3.** *Mathematics.* **a.** points contained in common by two geometrical figures. **b.** set of all the elements that are found in two or more given sets. —**in′ter·sec′tion·al,** *adj.*

in·ter·space (*n.,* in′tər spās′; *v.,* in′tər spās′) *n.* space between things; interval. —*v.t.,* **-spaced, -spac·ing. 1.** to put a space between. **2.** to occupy or fill the space between.

in·ter·sperse (in′tər spurs′) **-spersed, -spers·ing.** *v.t.* **1.** to scatter at intervals among or between other things: *The author interspersed short stories among the essays in his book.* **2.** to diversify by scattering at intervals among or between (with *with*): *He interspersed his remarks with witticisms.* [Latin *interspersus* strewn, sprinkled upon.] —**in·ter·sper·sion** (in′tər spur′shən), *n.*

in·ter·state (in′tər stāt′) *adj.* between or among two or more states of the United States: *interstate highways.*

Interstate Commerce Commission, an agency of the U.S. government which regulates all ground carriers that cross state lines.

in·ter·stel·lar (in′tər stel′ər) *adj.* between or among the stars.

in·ter·stice (in tur′stis) *pl.,* **-sti·ces** (-stə siz, -sēz′). *n.* narrow space or opening between things or parts; crevice; fissure. [Late Latin *interstitium,* from Latin *inter* between + *stāre* to stand.]

in·ter·sti·tial (in′tər stish′əl) *adj.* **1.** of, relating to, or forming an interstice or interstices: *interstitial spaces.* **2.** situated between the cellular elements of an organ or part: *interstitial tissue.*

in·ter·trib·al (in′tər trī′bəl) *adj.* between tribes.

in·ter·twine (in′tər twīn′) **-twined, -twin·ing.** *v.t., v.i.* to twine together.

in·ter·ur·ban (in′tər ur′bən) *adj.* of or between different cities: *an interurban transit system, interurban commerce.*

in·ter·val (in′tər vəl) *n.* **1.** intervening time or space: *An interval of a year elapsed before we were able to return. We placed the posts at regular intervals of three feet.* **2.** temporary stop or break in the course of something, as of an action or event: *After a brief interval we resumed our conversation.* **3.** difference in pitch between any two notes. [Latin *intervallum* space between ramparts, space between, from *inter* between + *vallum* rampart.]

Syn. 2. Interval, interruption, hiatus mean a breach in continuity. **Interval** usually involves distance between two similar things or conditions in space or time: *I heard from Paul after a long interval.* **Interruption** suggests a break in continuity, uniformity, or series that causes a gap: *The row of houses continued without interruption to the end of the road.* **Hiatus** implies a gap in sequence or continuity wherein some essential links are missing: *There was a hiatus in the subject catalogue of the library.*

in·ter·vene (in′tər vēn′) **-vened, -ven·ing.** *v.i.* **1.** to come between certain events or points in time: *Many years intervened before they met again.* **2.** to come in as a mediator; come between opposing parties; intercede: *The young man intervened in her behalf.* **3.** to come in or between so as to affect, modify, or prevent: *The old man had made many plans, but death intervened.* **4.** to interfere, esp. in the affairs of another country. [Latin *intervenīre* to come between.] —**in′ter·ven′er, in·ter·ven·tion** (in′tər ven′chən), *n.*

in·ter·view (in′tər vū′) *n.* **1.a.** meeting between a writer or reporter and a person from whom information is sought. **b.** broadcast or published report resulting from such a meeting. **2.** meeting for consultation or evaluation. —*v.t.* to have an interview with. [Old French *entrevue* meeting between people for discussion, from *entrevoir* to glimpse, going back to Latin *inter* between + *vidēre* to see.] —**in′ter·view′er,** *n.*

in·ter·weave (in′tər wēv′) **-wove** or **-weaved, -wo·ven** or **-wove** or **-weaved, -weav·ing.** *v.t., v.i.* to weave together.

in·tes·tate (in tes′tāt, -tit) *adj.* without making a will: *He died intestate.* —*n.* one who dies without making a will. [Latin *intestātus,* from *in-* not + *testārī* to make a will.] —**in·tes·ta·cy** (in tes′tə sē), *n.*

in·tes·ti·nal (in tes′tən əl) *adj.* of, relating to, or affecting the intestines. —**in·tes′ti·nal·ly,** *adv.*

intestinal fortitude, courage; steadfastness. [A euphemism for the corresponding meaning of guts. See GUT.]

in·tes·tine (in tes′tin) *n.* usually, **intestines.** that part of the alimentary canal extending from the stomach to the anus. The intestines are divided into the large intestine and the small intestine. —*adj.* domestic: *intestine feuds and disorders.* [Latin *intestīnus* internal, and *intestīnum* gut, both from *intus* within.]

in·thrall (in thrôl′) *also,* **in·thral.** enthrall.

in·throne (in thrōn′) enthrone.

in·ti·ma·cy (in′tə mə sē) *pl.,* **-cies.** *n.* **1.** state of being intimate. **2.** an instance of this. **3.** *also,* **intimacies.** sexual liberties, esp. intercourse.

in·ti·mate¹ (in′tə mit) *adj.* **1.** closely or personally associated; well-acquainted: *a long, intimate friendship.* **2.** of or resulting from great familiarity; close: *He has an intimate knowledge of parliamentary procedure.* **3.** personal or private: *She kept a diary of her most intimate thoughts.* **4.** having sexual relations (with *with*). **5.** intrinsic. —*n.* very close friend or associate. [Modification (influenced by INTIMATE²) of earlier *intime,* from French *intime* inward, close, from Latin *intimus* inmost, superlative of *in* in.] —**in′ti·mate·ly,** *adv.* —**Syn. adj. 1.** see **familiar.**

in·ti·mate² (in′tə māt′) **-mat·ed, -mat·ing.** *v.t.* **1.** to make known indirectly; hint; imply. **2.** *Archaic.* to announce formally; declare. [Late Latin *intimātus,* past participle of *intimāre* to make known, bring into, from Latin *intimus* inmost. See INTIMATE¹.] —**in′ti·mat′er, in′ti·ma′tion,** *n.* —**Syn. 1.** see **hint.**

in·tim·i·date (in tim′ə dāt′) **-dat·ed, -dat·ing.** *v.t.* **1.** to make timid or fearful: *The child was intimidated by the fury of the storm.* **2.** to influence or deter by threats or violence. **3.** to disconcert or overawe: *He intimidated us with his polished, self-assured manner.* [Medieval Latin *intimidatus,* past participle of *intimidare* to frighten, from Latin *in* in + *timidus* fearful.] —**in·tim′i·da′tion,** *n.* —**in·tim′i·da′tor,** *n.*

Syn. 2. Intimidate, cow², bully mean to subdue through coercion. **Intimidate** stresses the winning of submission and obedience by inspiring fear through threats: *The thieves intimidated the shopkeeper with threats that they would kill him.* **Cow** suggests causing inactivity by sapping the courage and paralyzing the will: *The sergeant cowed the recruits with his gruff manner and loud, booming voice.* **Bully** implies a use of force, threats, or arrogant and overbearing treatment: *The teenagers bullied the ten-year-old until he ran home crying.*

in·ti·tle (in tīt′əl) entitle.

in·to (in′tōō, -tə) *prep.* **1.** to the inside of: *He bit into the apple. She came into the kitchen.* **2.** in the direction of; toward: *He rode off into the horizon. She looked into the sky.* **3.** against so as to meet head on: *He bumped into the door. She drove into a pole.* **4.** to the state or form of: *The water turned into ice. The dish broke into many pieces.* **5.** to the midst of a period of time: *It rained into the night.* **6.** separating; dividing: *8 into 16 is 2.* [Old English *intō* to the interior of, within the limits of, from *in* in + *tō* to.]

in·tol·er·a·ble (in tol′ər ə bəl) *adj.* not to be endured; not tolerable; insufferable; unbearable. [Latin *intolerābilis,* from *in-* not + *tolerābilis* bearable.] —**in·tol′er·a·bil′i·ty,** *n.* —**in·tol′er·a·bly,** *adv.*

in·tol·er·ance (in tol′ər əns) *n.* **1.** unwillingness to permit or endure differences of opinion or practice; lack of tolerance. **2.** inability to resist or endure the effects; lack of resistance: *intolerance to penicillin.*

in·tol·er·ant (in tol′ər ənt) *adj.* **1.** unwilling to permit or endure differences of opinion or practice; not tolerant. **2.** unable to resist or endure the effects (usually with *of*): *His system is intolerant of tobacco.* —**in·tol′er·ant·ly,** *adv.*

in·tomb (in tōōm′) entomb.

in·to·nate (in′tō nāt′) **-nat·ed, -nat·ing.** *v.t.* **1.** to utter or pronounce with a particular tone; modulate the voice. **2.** to intone.

in·to·na·tion (in′tō nā′shən, -tə-) *n.* **1.** act of intonating. **2.** manner of intonating; modulation of the voice in speaking; pitch. **3.** *Music.* production of tones that are accurate in pitch. —**Syn. 2.** see **inflection.**

in·tone (in tōn′) **-toned, -ton·ing.** *v.t., v.i.* **1.** to recite in a singing voice or monotone. **2.** to utter with a particular tone. [Medieval Latin *intonare* to utter in a musical tone, from Latin *in* in + *tonus* tone, sound. See TONE.]

in to·to (in tō′tō) *Latin.* as a whole; completely.

in·tox·i·cant (in tok′sə kənt) *n.* any substance that intoxicates, esp. alcoholic liquor. —*adj.* intoxicating.

in·tox·i·cate (in tok′sə kāt′) **-cat·ed, -cat·ing.** *v.t.* **1.** to exhilarate, make unsteady, or put into a stupor by means of alcoholic liquor or

at; āpe; cär; end; mē; it; īce; hot; ōld; fôrk; wood; fōōl; oil; out; up; ūse; turn; sing; thin; this; zh in treasure; ə in ago, taken, pencil, lemon, circus.

a drug. **2.** to excite greatly or enrapture: *The very sounds and smells of the city intoxicated him.* **3.** *Medicine.* to poison. [Medieval Latin *intoxicatus,* past participle of *intoxicare* to poison, from Latin *in* in + *toxicum* poison. See TOXIC.] —in·tox′i·cat·ed·ly, *adv.* —in·tox′i·ca′tion, in·tox′i·ca′tor, *n.* —in·tox′i·ca′tive, *adj.*

intr., intransitive.

intra- *prefix* within; on the inside: *intravenous.* [Latin *intrā.*]

in·trac·ta·ble (in trak′tə bəl) *adj.* **1.** not easily managed; not tractable; stubborn: *an intractable man.* **2.** not easily treated, handled, used, or worked: *an intractable problem, an intractable subject.* —in·trac′ta·bil′i·ty, *n.* —in·trac′ta·bly, *adv.*

in·tra·dos (in′trə dos′, -dōs′, in trā′dos) *n.* interior curve or surface of an arch or vault. [French *intrados,* from Latin *intrā* within + French *dos* back (from Latin *dorsum*).]

in·tra·mu·ral (in′trə myoor′əl) *adj.* consisting of or limited to participants from the same school or organization: *intramural basketball.* [INTRA- + Latin *mūrālis* relating to a wall, from *mūrus* wall.]

in·tran·si·gent (in tran′sə jənt) *adj.* refusing to yield or compromise; uncompromising. —*n.* one who is uncompromising. [French *intransigeant,* from Spanish *intransigente* (name given to a supporter of an extreme leftist party in Spain in 1873–74), going back to Latin *in-* not + *trānsigere* to come to an agreement.] —in·tran′si·gence, in·tran′si·gen·cy, *n.* —in·tran′si·gent·ly, *adv.*

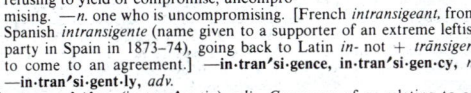

Intrados

in·tran·si·tive (in tran′sə tiv) *adj.* *Grammar.* of or relating to an action that does not require a direct object. The verbs *exist* and *die* are intransitive. —in·tran′si·tive·ly, *adv.*

in·tra·state (in′trə stāt′) *adj.* existing or occurring within a state, esp. of the United States.

in·tra·ve·nous (in′trə vē′nəs) *adj.* existing or taking place within a vein. [INTRA- + VENOUS.] —in′tra·ve′nous·ly, *adv.*

in·treat (in trēt′) entreat.

in·trench (in trench′) entrench.

in·trench·ment (in trench′mənt) entrenchment.

in·trep·id (in trep′id) *adj.* having or showing great bravery and valor; undaunted: *His intrepid spirit enabled him to succeed where others failed.* [Latin *intrepidus,* from *in-* not + *trepidus* alarmed.] —in·tre·pid·i·ty (in′trə pid′ə tē), in·trep′id·ness, *n.* —in·trep′id·ly, *adv.* —Syn. see fearless.

in·tri·ca·cy (in′tri kə sē) *pl.* **-cies.** *n.* **1.** quality or state of being intricate. **2.** something intricate.

in·tri·cate (in′tri kit) *adj.* **1.** perplexingly entangled or involved: *an intricate pattern.* **2.** difficult to analyze or understand: *intricate reasoning.* [Latin *intrīcātus,* past participle of *intrīcāre* to entangle, perplex, from *in* in + *trīcae* trifles, hindrances.] —in′tri·cate·ly, *adv.* —in′tri·cate·ness, *n.* —Syn. **2.** see complex.

in·trigue (*n.,* in′trēg, in trēg′; *v.,* in trēg′) *n.* **1.** use of underhanded and devious means to achieve a goal: *There was much plotting and intrigue in the capitals of Europe before the outbreak of war.* **2.** underhanded and devious scheme or plot: *He exposed the intrigue before harm was done.* **3.** clandestine love affair. —*v.i.,* **-trigued, -trigu·ing.** to carry on an underhanded and devious scheme or plot. —*v.t.* **1.** to excite the curiosity or interest of; fascinate: *The story of the boys' adventures intrigued their friends.* [French *intrigue* plot, liaison, from Italian *intrigo* plot, from *intrigare* to plot, from Latin *intrīcāre.* See INTRICATE.] —in·trigu′er, *n.* —Syn. see plot.

in·trin·sic (in trin′sik, -sik) *adj.* belonging to or basic to something by its very nature. Also, **in·trin′si·cal.** [Old French *intrinseque* inner, from Late Latin *intrinsecus* inward, from Latin *intrinsecus* inwardly.] —in·trin′si·cal·ly, *adv.* —Syn. see inherent.

intro- *prefix* into; inward; within: *introvert.* [Latin *intrō* to the inside, within.]

intro. **1.** introduction. **2.** introductory.

in·tro·duce (in′trə dōōs′, -dūs′) **-duced, -duc·ing.** *v.t.* **1.** to bring into the formal acquaintance of a person or persons: *Our host introduced us to the other guests.* **2.** to bring into use, knowledge, or fashion; institute: *He introduced a new procedure for manufacturing the product.* **3.** to bring into the acquaintance of something: *She introduced him to the ballet.* **4.** to bring forward for consideration; propose: *He introduced a motion to adjourn.* **5.a.** to bring in and settle securely: *The botanist introduced a new species of plant to the region.* **b.** to interject: *He introduced his observations into the discussion.* **6.** to insert. **7.** to start; open; begin: *He introduced his speech with a humorous anecdote.* [Latin *intrōdūcere* to bring in, originate.] —in′tro·duc′er, *n.*

Syn. 1. Introduce, present² mean to cause to be acquainted. **Introduce** means to make two persons, esp. strangers, acquainted face to face or to identify and make known a person to a group: *Mr. Jones introduced his family to the visitors.* **Present** is a more dignified term and means to introduce formally: *The ambassador was presented to the king.*

in·tro·duc·tion (in′trə duk′shən) *n.* **1.** act of introducing; being introduced. **2.** that which serves to introduce, as a preface. **3.** something introduced. **4.** beginning or elementary textbook or treatise. [Latin *intrōductiō* a leading in.]

Syn. 2. Introduction, foreward, preface, prologue mean a preliminary work. An **introduction** prepares the reader for what follows by giving him explanatory or anticipatory information: *Most textbooks have an introduction.* A **foreword** is a brief and simple introduction containing prefatory remarks written in a personal vein usually by someone other than the author: *A famous conductor was asked to write a foreword to a book on music.* A **preface** is an opening discourse that explains the scope, purpose, or method of the book and is intended to prepare the reader for a fuller appreciation of the subject: *George Bernard Shaw's prefaces to his dramas expound his personal philosophy.* A **prologue** is a distinct part of a work, esp. a dramatic or poetic work, that prepares for the later development of the theme by introducing the characters or explaining their background: *Epic dramas have lengthy prologues.*

in·tro·duc·to·ry (in′trə duk′tər ē) *adj.* serving to introduce; prefatory; preliminary. —Syn. see elementary.

in·tro·it (in′trō it, -troit, in trō′it) *n.* **1.** opening portion of the Mass, usually consisting of an antiphon and Gloria Patri. **2.** psalm or anthem sung at the beginning of the Communion service in the Anglican Church. **3.** any hymn, prayer, or response sung or played at the beginning of a religious service. [Latin *introitus* entrance.]

in·tro·spect (in′trə spekt′) *v.i.* to examine one's own thoughts or feelings; practice introspection.

in·tro·spec·tion (in′trə spek′shən) *n.* examination of one's own thoughts or feelings. [Latin *intrōspectus,* past participle of *intrōspicere* to look into + -ION.]

in·tro·spec·tive (in′trə spek′tiv) *adj.* of, characterized by, or given to introspection. —in′tro·spec′tive·ly, *adv.*

in·tro·ver·sion (in′trə vur′zhən, -shən) *n.* preoccupation with one's own inner experiences rather than with things outside oneself. Opposed to **extroversion.** [INTRO- + Late Latin *versiō* a turning (from Latin *vertere* to turn).]

in·tro·vert (in′trə vurt′) *n.* **1.a.** one whose attention is largely directed toward himself. **b.** shy, withdrawn person. Opposed to **extrovert.** **2.** *Biology.* organ or part that is or can be turned inward upon itself. —*v.t.* **1.** to direct (one's attention) toward one's inner experiences. **2.** *Biology.* to turn (an organ or part) inward upon itself. [INTRO- + Latin *vertere* to turn.]

in·trude (in trōōd′) **-trud·ed, -trud·ing.** *v.i.* **1.** to come in as a disturbing or unwelcome addition; enter brusquely or obtrusively: *The inconsiderate young man intruded upon their privacy.* —*v.t.* **1.** to thrust or force in obtrusively. **2.** *Geology.* to penetrate into or between older rock. [Latin *intrūdere* to thrust in.] —in·trud′er, *n.*

Syn. *v.i.* Intrude, trespass, encroach mean to infringe on the rights or property of others. **Intrude** involves thrusting oneself abruptly without right or welcome: *It is considered rude to intrude on a private conversation.* **Trespass** suggests infringement in an unwarranted and offensive manner, esp. in violation of law: *All those who trespass on this land will be prosecuted.* **Encroach** implies gradual and sometimes underhanded inroads on the rights, domain, or property of others: *The settlers constantly encroached on Indian territory.*

in·tru·sion (in trōō′zhən) *n.* **1.** act or instance of intruding; being intruded upon. **2.** that which intrudes: *His presence at the party was a singularly unpleasant intrusion.* **3.** illegal entering into or seizing of another's property. **4.** *Geology.* **a.** penetration of matter, as molten rock, into or between older rock. **b.** body of rock thus formed. [Medieval Latin *intrusio* a thrusting in, from Latin *intrūsus,* past participle of *intrūdere* to thrust in.]

in·tru·sive (in trōō′siv) *adj.* characterized by intrusion; tending to intrude: *intrusive questions, an intrusive appearance.* —in·tru′sive·ly, *adv.* —in·tru′sive·ness, *n.*

in·trust (in trust′) entrust.

in·tu·i·tion (in′tōō ish′ən, -tū-) *n.* **1.** direct or immediate perception of truth. **2.** truth or insight resulting from such perception. **3.** ability to conjecture correctly. [Late Latin *intuitiō* a looking into, from Latin *intuērī* to look upon, consider.] —in′tu·i′tion·al, *adj.* —in′tu·i′tion·al·ly, *adv.* —Syn. **1.** see instinct¹.

in·tu·i·tive (in tōō′ə tiv, -tū′-) *adj.* **1.** of or relating to intuition: *intuitive ability.* **2.** derived from or characterized by intuition: *intuitive knowledge.* **3.** possessing intuition. —in·tu′i·tive·ly, *adv.*

in·un·date (in′ən dāt′, in un′dāt) **-dat·ed, -dat·ing.** *v.t.* **1.** to cover with a flood: *After the heavy rain, the river overflowed its banks and inundated the valley.* **2.** to fill or overwhelm; swamp: *to inundate with*

requests. [Latin *inundātus,* past participle of *inundāre,* from *in* upon + *unda* wave.] —**in′un·da′tion,** *n.*

in·ure (in yoor′) **-ured, -ur·ing.** *v.t.* to make tough or hardy by experience; cause to withstand or endure (with *to*): *The arctic climate inured him to extreme cold.* [IN + obsolete *ure* use, work, from Old French *uevre* work, from Latin *opera.*] —**in·ure′ment,** *n.*

inv. **1.** invented; invention; inventor. **2.** invoice.

in va·cu·o (in vak′ū ō′) *Latin.* in a vacuum.

in·vade (in vād′) **-vad·ed, -vad·ing.** *v.t.* **1.** to enter and attack with an armed force, as for pillage or conquest: *Germany invaded France in 1940.* **2.** to enter and overrun as if to take possession: *Rabbits invaded the garden during the night. Relatives invaded our house last weekend.* **3.** to interfere with; infringe upon; violate: *to invade the privacy of others.* **4.** to penetrate and spread with harmful effects; infect: *Disease germs had invaded his body.* —*v.i.* to make an invasion. [Latin *invādere* to go into, attack.] —**in·vad′er,** *n.*

in·val·id¹ (in′və lid) *n.* one who is disabled by disease or injury. —*adj.* **1.** disabled by disease or injury. **2.** of, for, or for invalids. —*v.t.* **1.** to make an invalid of; disable: *The injury invalided him for life.* **2.** *British.* to discharge or remove from active service because of disease or injury. [French *invalide* infirm, disabled, from Latin *invalidus* infirm.]

in·val·id² (in val′id) *adj.* without force, basis, or authority; not valid: *an invalid contract, invalid reasoning.* [Latin *invalidus* infirm, inadequate.] —**in·val′id·ly,** *adv.*

in·val·i·date (in val′ə dāt′) **-dat·ed, -dat·ing.** *v.t.* to render invalid. —**in·val′i·da′tion,** *n.*

in·va·lid·ism (in′və li diz′əm) *n.* condition of being disabled by disease or injury.

in·va·lid·i·ty (in′və lid′ə tē) *n.* lack of validity.

in·val·u·a·ble (in val′ū ə bəl, -val′yə bəl) *adj.* beyond valuation; incalculable; priceless: *invaluable information.* —**in·val′u·a·bly,** *adv.*

in·var·i·a·ble (in vâr′ē ə bəl) *adj.* unchanging or unchangeable; not variable; uniform: *the invariable and oppressive heat of the African lowlands.* —*n.* that which is unchanging or unchangeable: *the invariables in a function.* —**in·var′i·a·bil′i·ty,** *n.* —**in·var′i·a·bly,** *adv.*

in·va·sion (in vā′zhən) *n.* **1.** entrance of an armed force, as into a country, in order to pillage or conquer; military incursion. **2.** act of invading; being invaded. **3.** intrusion or violation; infringement: *an invasion of one's rights.* [Late Latin *invāsiō* attack, from Latin *invādere.* See INVADE.]

Syn. 1. Invasion, incursion, raid mean entry by force. **Invasion** implies an armed attack on a large scale for conquest or other hostile purposes: *Napoleon's invasion of Russia was a disaster.* **Incursion** is a brief, predatory or harassing inroad or a sudden and unexpected onslaught: *During the war, there were repeated incursions along the border.* **Raid** suggests a swift foray or a military operation on a small but furious scale to gain a specific objective within hostile territory: *The guerrillas made a surprise raid on the naval base.*

in·vec·tive (in vek′tiv) *n.* violent, railing accusation or verbal attack; vehement denunciation; vituperation: *The candidate for mayor directed his invective against the incumbent.* [Late Latin *invectīvus* abusive, from Latin *invehere.* See INVEIGH.]

in·veigh (in vā′) *v.i.* to utter or write a vehement denunciation; make a verbal attack (with *against*). [Latin *invehere* to carry in, attack.]

in·vei·gle (in vā′gəl, -vē′-) **-gled, -gling.** *v.t.* **1.** to lure or induce by deceit, blandishments, or cajolery: *The young man inveigled his friends into lending him large sums of money.* **2.** to acquire by blandishments or cajolery: *The lawyer inveigled a response from the reluctant witness.* [Modification of French *aveugler* to blind, delude, going back to Latin *ab* without + *oculus* eye.] —**in·vei′gle·ment,** **in·vei′gler,** *n.*

in·vent (in vent′) *v.t.* **1.** to conceive and produce by original thought and ingenuity; originate: *to invent a new part for a machine, to invent a new word.* **2.** to make up (something false or fictitious): *to invent rumors.* [Latin *inventus,* past participle of *invenīre* to come upon, find.] —**Syn. 1.** see DEVISE.

in·ven·tion (in ven′chən) *n.* **1.** act or process of inventing. **2.** that which is invented. **3.** fictitious account; false statement. **4.** ability to invent; inventiveness: *a man of much invention.* **5.** *Music.* short, contrapuntal composition written for a keyboard instrument.

in·ven·tive (in ven′tiv) *adj.* **1.** skillful and resourceful; able to invent: *an inventive people.* **2.** of, relating to, or characterized by invention. —**in·ven′tive·ly,** *adv.* —**in·ven′tive·ness,** *n.*

in·ven·tor (in ven′tər) *n.* one who invents, esp. one who conceives and produces something new, as a process or device.

in·ven·to·ry (in′vən tôr′ē) *pl.* **-to·ries.** *n.* **1.** descriptive list of articles in stock at a given time: *The inventory revealed that the store was overstocked.* **2.** any detailed list of articles: *an inventory of books in a library, an inventory of items in an estate.* **3.** articles so listed. **4.** act or process of compiling such a list: *The store was closed for inventory all week.* **5.** list or account resulting from a survey or question-

naire: *a wildlife inventory. an inventory of personality traits.* —*v.t.,* **-to·ried, -to·ry·ing.** to make a detailed list of. [Medieval Latin *inventorium* list, modification of Late Latin *inventārium,* from Latin *inventus,* past participle of *invenīre* to find.] —**in′ven·to′ri·al,** *adj.* —**in′ven·to′ri·al·ly,** *adv.*

in·verse (in vurs′, in′vurs′) *adj.* **1.** reversed in sequence, position, or relation: *an inverse order.* **2.** turned upside down; inverted. —*n.* **1.** that which is the direct opposite; reverse. **2.** *Mathematics.* element in a set which, when added to or multiplied by a given element, yields the identity element for addition or multiplication respectively. The **additive inverse** of 3 is −3; the **multiplicative inverse** of 3 is ⅓. Also, **inverse element.** [Latin *inversus,* past participle of *invertere* to turn about, reverse.] —**in·verse′ly,** *adv.*

in·ver·sion (in vur′zhən, -shən) *n.* **1.** act of inverting; being inverted. **2.** that which is inverted. [Latin *inversiō* transposition, reverse order.]

in·vert (in vurt′) *v.t.* **1.** to turn upside down: *The lens inverted the image.* **2.** to reverse the sequence, position, or relation of. **3.** to subject to or bring about inversion. [Latin *invertere* to turn about or upside down, reverse.] —**in·vert′i·ble,** *adj.*

in·ver·te·brate (in vur′tə brit, -brāt′) *adj.* of or relating to an animal having no backbone; not vertebrate. —*n.* an invertebrate animal.

in·vert·er (in vur′tər) *n.* **1.** one who or that which inverts. **2.** device that converts direct current into alternating current.

in·vest (in vest′) *v.t.* **1.** to use (money) to acquire an interest in existing properties or to create new properties for the purpose of producing profit or income: *to invest one's savings in stocks.* **2.** to expend or devote (something, as time, effort, or money), esp. for personal advantage or merit: *to invest time and effort in a college education. The dowager invested much of her time in charity work.* **3.** to endow or furnish, as with power, authority, or privilege. **4.** to formally install in an office, rank, or position. **5.** to endow, as with qualities or attributes: *His behavior invested him with a certain integrity.* **6.** to cover; envelop: *Fog invested the harbor.* **7.** to surround with armed forces in order to blockade or capture; lay siege to. —*v.i.* to make an investment. [Latin *investīre* to clothe, cover.] —**in·ves′tor,** *n.*

in·ves·ti·gate (in ves′tə gāt′) **-gat·ed, -gat·ing.** *v.t.* to explore systematically in order to uncover facts or gain information; make a thorough examination of. —*v.i.* to make an investigation. [Latin *investīgātus,* past participle of *investīgāre* to trace out, search after, going back to *in* in + *vestīgium* trace, footprint.]

in·ves·ti·ga·tion (in ves′tə gā′shən) *n.* **1.** act or instance of investigating. **2.** careful search for facts or information; thorough examination. —**Syn. 2.** see INQUIRY.

in·ves·ti·ga·tor (in ves′tə gā′tər) *n.* one who investigates, as a detective.

in·ves·ti·ture (in ves′tə chər) *n.* **1.** act or ceremony of formally installing in an office, rank, or position. **2.** that which covers or envelops: *the bright investiture of light.*

in·vest·ment (in vest′mənt) *n.* **1.** act of investing, esp. the use of money to produce profit or income. **2.** amount of money that is invested. **3.** property in which money is invested. **4.** investiture *(def. 1).* **5.** blockade.

in·vet·er·ate (in vet′ər it) *adj.* **1.** confirmed in a habit or practice; habitual: *an inveterate complainer.* **2.** firmly established by tradition or custom; deep-rooted: *inveterate prejudices.* [Latin *inveterātus,* past participle of *inveterāre* to make old, give duration to.] —**in·vet′er·a·cy, in·vet′er·ate·ness,** *n.* —**in·vet′er·ate·ly,** *adv.* —**Syn. 1.** see **chronic.**

in·vid·i·ous (in vid′ē əs) *adj.* **1.** arousing or liable to arouse ill will or hatred; odious: *an invidious task, an invidious word.* **2.** offensively biased: *an invidious comparison.* [Latin *invidiōsus* envious, from *invidia* envy.] —**in·vid′i·ous·ly,** *adv.* —**in·vid′i·ous·ness,** *n.*

in·vig·or·ate (in vig′ə rāt′) **-at·ed, -at·ing.** *v.t.* to fill with strength and energy; give vigor to: *The mountain air invigorated and refreshed him.* [IN-² + VIGOR + -ATE¹.] —**in·vig′or·at′ing·ly,** *adv.* —**in·vig′or·a′tion,** *n.* —**in·vig′or·a′tive,** *adj.*

in·vin·ci·ble (in vin′sə bəl) *adj.* not capable of being vanquished or overcome; unconquerable: *an invincible warrior.* [Late Latin *invincibilis,* from Latin *in-* not + *vincere* to conquer.] —**in·vin′ci·bly,** *adv.* —**in·vin′ci·bil′i·ty, in·vin′ci·ble·ness,** *n.*

Syn. Invincible, indomitable, impregnable mean incapable of being attacked or conquered. **Invincible** suggests that something cannot be subjugated, vanquished, overcome, or displaced: *That football team was once reputed to be invincible.* **Indomitable** stresses determined resistance to all attempts at subjugation and endurance, with fortitude, until all difficulties are overcome: *The general's indomitable spirit saved his country from defeat.* **Impregnable** usually applies to something that is so well protected that it is incapable of being assailed: *A battleship is an impregnable floating fortress.*

in·vi·o·la·ble (in vī′ə lə bəl) *adj.* **1.** that must not be violated; sacrosanct: *an inviolable oath.* **2.** not subject to harm or injury; invulnera-

ble: *an inviolable substance.* —in·vi′o·la·bil′i·ty, *n.* —in·vi′o·la·bly, *adv.*

in·vi·o·late (in vī′ə lit, -lāt′) *adj.* not broken or defiled; not violated: *Our friendship will remain strong and inviolate.*

in·vis·i·ble (in viz′ə bəl) *adj.* 1. not visible. 2. hidden from view. 3. not evident to the mind: *invisible degrees of difference.* —*n.* an invisible being. —in·vis′i·bil′i·ty, *n.* —in·vis′i·bly, *adv.*

in·vi·ta·tion (in′və tā′shən) *n.* 1. act of inviting. 2. spoken or written form with which a person is invited.

in·vite (*v.,* in vīt′; *n.,* in′vīt) -vit·ed, -vit·ing. *v.t.* 1. to make a courteous or formal request for the presence or participation of: *They invited him to their country house for the weekend.* 2. to ask for; solicit: *to invite confidences, to invite assistance.* 3. to tend to bring on; foster: *What you have done can only invite trouble.* 4. to present inducements to; tempt: *The beauty of the place invited them to pause in their hike and rest awhile.* —*n. Informal.* invitation. [Latin *invītāre* to summon, entertain.] —in·vit′er, *n.*

in·vit·ing (in vī′ting) *adj.* tempting; attractive: *The cool, placid lake looked inviting.* —in·vit′ing·ly, *adv.* —in·vit′ing·ness, *n.*

in·vo·ca·tion (in′və kā′shən) *n.* 1. act of invoking, esp. the calling upon in prayer for aid or protection; supplication. 2. prayer used in invoking, esp. one spoken at the beginning of a public ceremony or formal religious service. 3. incantation used to summon a devil or spirit.

in·voice (in′vois′) *n.* itemized account of goods sent to a buyer, indicating the quantities shipped, prices, and other charges. —*v.t.* -voiced, -voic·ing. to make an invoice of. [Earlier *invoyes,* plural of obsolete *invoy* something sent, from Old French *envoy* a sending, going back to Latin *in viam* on the way.]

in·voke (in vōk′) -voked, -vok·ing. *v.t.* 1. to call upon in prayer for aid or protection; make supplication to: *to invoke the Muses.* 2. to call or beg for earnestly; make supplication for: *to invoke God's mercy.* 3. to call forth by charms or incantation; conjure: *to invoke the spirits of the dead.* 4. to call upon as relevant or mandatory: *to invoke one's rights.* 5. to refer to as support, proof, or confirmation; cite. [Latin *invocāre* to call on, implore.] —in·vok′er, *n.*

in·vo·lu·cre (in′və lōō′kər) *n.* circle or circles of bracts surrounding a flower or flower cluster. [Latin *involūcrum* covering, case.]

in·vol·un·tar·y (in vol′ən ter′ē) *adj.* 1. not done willingly or by choice; not voluntary: *an involuntary confession.* 2. occurring without control; unintentional: *an involuntary shudder.* 3. existing or acting without the control of the will: *involuntary muscles.* —in·vol′un·tar′i·ly, *adv.* —in·vol′un·tar′i·ness, *n.* —Syn. 2. see automatic.

Involucre

in·vo·lute (in′və lōōt′) *adj.* 1. involved or intricate: *an involute procedure.* 2. rolled inward toward the upper side from the edge or edges: *involute leaves.* 3. rolled or curled inward around the axis: *an involute shell.* Also, in′vo·lut′ed. [Latin *involūtus,* past participle of *involvere* to roll up, cover.]

in·vo·lu·tion (in′və lōō′shən) *n.* 1. act of involving; being involved. 2. something involved or intricate.

in·volve (in volv′) -volved, -volv·ing. *v.t.* 1. to include as a necessary part, condition, or consequence: *Winning the game involves both skill and perseverance.* 2. to have an effect on; affect: *The decision on tariffs involves more than just the economic well-being of the country.* 3. to draw or bring, as into an unfortunate situation; cause to be associated or concerned: *The young man's heedless remarks involved him in a law suit. The youth was involved in the robbery.* 4. to occupy completely; absorb: *He was involved in reading the book all evening.* 5. to make intricate; complicate: *The lawyer involved his argument with numerous contradictions.* 6. to surround; envelop: *Fog involved the quiet, ghostly city.* [Latin *involvere* to roll up, cover, envelop.] —in·volve′ment, in·volv′er, *n.*

Syn. 3. Involve, implicate both mean to draw a person into a situation from which he cannot extricate himself easily or blamelessly. Involve means to implicate someone in an embarrassing situation or association: *John's extravagant spending habits have frequently involved him in debt.* Implicate means to embroil a person in an incriminating way in a crime or evil: *Four men were implicated in the attempt to hijack a plane.*

in·vul·ner·a·ble (in vul′nər ə bəl) *adj.* 1. not subject to harm or injury; not vulnerable: *an invulnerable person.* 2. not assailable; impregnable; unconquerable: *an invulnerable wall, an invulnerable argument.* —in·vul′ner·a·bil′i·ty, in·vul′ner·a·ble·ness, *n.* —in·vul′ner·a·bly, *adv.*

in·ward (in′wərd) *adv. also,* in·wards. 1. toward the inside, interior, or center: *The door opened inward into the room.* 2. into the mind; into one's own thoughts. —*adj.* 1. directed toward the inside: *an inward motion.* 2. situated within; inner; internal: *an inward vitality.* 3. of or

relating to the mind or thought; mental: *inward vision, inward fears, an inward existence.* [Old English *inneweard* situated within.]

in·ward·ly (in′wərd lē) *adv.* 1. in or on the inside; within: *Inwardly, he was seething with rage.* 2. in the mind or thought; secretly; privately: *He was inwardly assured by her sincerity.* 3. toward the inside.

in·ward·ness (in′wərd nis) *n.* 1. state of being inward. 2. inner nature, quality, or meaning. 3. depth or intensity of feeling or thought. 4. inward preoccupation; spirituality.

in·weave (in wēv′) -wove or -weaved, -wo·ven or -wove or -weaved, -weav·ing. *v.t.* to weave in or weave together.

in·wrap (in rap′) enwrap.

in·wreathe (in rēth′) enwreathe.

in·wrought (in rôt′) *adj.* 1. having something worked in as a decoration: *a brocade inwrought with gold.* 2. being worked into something: *a floral pattern inwrought on silk.*

I·o (ī′ō) *n. Greek Mythology.* young maiden loved by Zeus, who changed her into a white heifer to protect her from Hera.

Io, ionium.

i·o·dide (ī′ə dīd′) *n.* binary compound of iodine with an element or radical.

i·o·dine (ī′ə dīn′, -din, -dēn′) *n.* 1. nonmetallic element consisting of shiny, grayish crystals that vaporize in air, giving off a violet-colored vapor with a pungent, choking odor. Iodine is used esp. in medicine, photography, and analytical chemistry. Symbol: I See **element** for table. 2. antiseptic consisting of iodine dissolved in an alcohol solution of sodium or potassium iodide. [French *iode* this element, from Greek *iōdēs* violet-colored, from *ion* violet + -INE[2].]

i·o·do·form (ī ō′də fôrm′, ī od′ə-) *n.* yellow crystalline iodine compound with a strong medicinal odor, formerly used as a local antiseptic. Formula: CHI₃ [IOD(INE) + (CHLOR)OFORM.]

i·on (ī′ən, ī′on) *n.* atom or group of atoms whose outer electron shell has gained or lost one or more electrons. Positive ions are formed by the loss of electrons. Negative ions are formed by the gain of electrons. [Greek *ion* going, neuter present participle of *ienai* to go.]

-ion *suffix* 1. act of: *notation, completion.* 2. state of: *damnation, suspicion.* 3. result of: *pollution, solution.* [Latin *-iō* (stem *-iōn-*), suffix forming nouns, often through French *-ion.*]

I·o·ni·a (ī ō′nē ə) *n.* ancient region on the western coast of Asia Minor, colonized by the ancient Greeks.

I·o·ni·an (ī ō′nē ən) *adj.* of or relating to Ionia, its people, language, or culture. —*n.* member of one of the four major Greek tribes of antiquity. The Ionians settled in Attica, the Ionian Islands, and Ionia.

Ionian Islands, group of islands in the Ionian Sea off the western coast of Greece. Land area, 1100 sq. mi. Pop. (1961), 212,573.

Ionian Sea, part of the Mediterranean Sea between Greece and Albania on the east and southern Italy and Sicily on the west.

i·on·ic (ī on′ik) *adj.* of or relating to ions.

I·on·ic (ī on′ik) *adj.* 1. of or relating to one of the three orders of classical Greek architecture, characterized by columns having molded bases and capitals composed of spiral volutes or scrolls. 2. of or relating to Ionia, its people, language, or culture. —*n.* one of the three principal dialects of ancient Greece. [Latin *Iōnicus* relating to Ionia, from Greek *Iōnikos,* from *Iōn* legendary Greek hero after whom Ionia is named.]

i·o·ni·um (ī ō′nē əm) *n.* radioactive isotope of thorium. Symbol: Io [From ION; with reference to its ionizing action.]

i·on·i·za·tion (ī′ə ni zā′shən) *n.* process by which ions are formed, in which electrons are gained by or lost from the outer electron shells around atoms.

ionization chamber, instrument used in the study of electrically charged particles.

i·on·ize (ī ə nīz′) -ized, -iz·ing. *v.t., v.i.* to be converted into ions, or produce ions in.

i·on·o·sphere (ī on′ə sfēr′) *n.* highest region of ionized gases in the earth's atmosphere, occurring approximately 40–300 miles above the earth's surface between the stratosphere and exosphere. [ION + SPHERE.]

i·o·ta (ī ō′tə) *n.* 1. ninth letter of the Greek alphabet (Ι, ι), corresponding to the English letter I, i. 2. very small quantity; bit: *He hasn't an iota of proof.* [Greek *iōta* the Greek letter ι, the smallest letter of the Greek alphabet; of Semitic origin. Doublet of JOT.]

IOU (ī′ō′ū′) *n.* informal written acknowledgment of a debt, usually containing only these letters, the amount owed, and the signature of the debtor. [Abbreviation of *I owe you.*]

I·o·wa (ī′ə wə) *n.* state in the north-central United States. Capital, Des Moines. Area, 56,290 sq. mi. Pop. (1970), 2,825,041. Abbreviation: Ia. [From the *Iowa* Indians, supposedly from Dakota *Ayuhwa* sleepy ones.] —I′o·wan, *adj., n.*

Iowa City, city in eastern Iowa. Pop. (1970), 46,850.

IPA, International Phonetic Alphabet.

ip·e·cac (ip′ə kak′) *n.* 1. drug obtained from the roots of a South American plant, *Cephaelis ipecacuanha,* used for medicinal purposes.

Also, **ip·e·cac·u·an·ha** (ip'ə kak'ü an'ə). **2.** the plant itself. [From Portuguese *ipecacuanha,* from Tupi-Guarani *ipe-kaa-guéne* the plant; literally, small plant causing vomit.]

Iph·i·ge·ni·a (if'ə jə nī'ə) *n. Greek Mythology.* a daughter of Agamemnon offered as a sacrifice to Artemis in order to obtain favorable winds for sailing against Troy.

ip·se dix·it (ip'sē dik'sit) assertion made dogmatically or without proof. [Latin *ipse dīxit* he himself said (it).]

ip·so fac·to (ip'sō fak'tō) by that very fact; by the fact itself. [Latin.]

Ips·wich (ips'wich) *n.* city in southeastern England. Pop. (1968 est.), 121,700.

IQ, intelligence quotient.

Ir, iridium.

ir-¹, form of **in-¹** before *r,* as in *irregular.*

ir-², form of **in-²** before *r,* as in *irruption.*

Ir. 1. Ireland. **2.** Irish.

I·ran (i ran', ē rän') *n.* country in southwestern Asia, formerly known as Persia. Capital, Tehran. Area, 636,300 sq. mi. Pop. (1969 est.), 28,237,000.

I·ra·ni·an (i rā'nē ən, ī rā'-) *adj.* of or relating to Iran, its people, their language, or culture. —*n.* **1.** member or close descendant of the people of Iran. **2.** subdivision of the Indo-Iranian branch of the Indo-European language family, which includes Persian and Kurdish.

I·raq (i rak', ē räk') *also,* **I·rak.** *n.* country in southwestern Asia. Capital, Baghdad. Area, 167,925 sq. mi. Pop. (1969), 9,431,000. —**I·ra·qi** (i rä'kē, i rak'ē) *also,* **I·ra'ki,** *adj., n.*

i·ras·ci·ble (i ras'ə bəl) *adj.* **1.** easily irritated or provoked to anger; irritable: *an irascible old man.* **2.** characterized by or arising from anger: *an irascible reply.* [Late Latin *īrāscibilis* irritable, from Latin *īrāscī* to become angry.] —**i·ras'ci·bil'i·ty, i·ras'ci·ble·ness,** *n.* —**i·ras'ci·bly,** *adv.*

i·rate (ī rāt') *adj.* angry; incensed; enraged. [Latin *īrātus,* from *īra* anger.] —**i·rate'ly,** *adv.*

IRBM, intermediate range ballistic missile, a ballistic missile with a range between 300 and 1500 miles.

ire (īr) *n.* anger; wrath. [Old French *ire,* from Latin *īra.*] —**Syn.** see **anger.**

Ire., Ireland.

ire·ful (īr'fəl) *adj.* full of ire; angry; wrathful: *an ireful glance.* —**ire'ful·ly,** *adv.*

Ire·land (īr'lənd) *n.* **1.** one of the British Isles, consisting of the Republic of Ireland and Northern Ireland. Area, 32,596 sq. mi. **2. Republic of.** country in northwestern Europe occupying most of the island of Ireland, formerly known as the Irish Free State, or Eire. Capital, Dublin. Area, 27,137 sq. mi. Pop. (1969 est.), 2,921,000.

ir·i·des·cence (ir'ə des'əns) *n.* quality of being iridescent; play of shimmering and changing colors.

ir·i·des·cent (ir'ə des'ənt) *adj.* displaying shimmering and changing colors, like those reflected by soap bubbles. [Latin *īrid-,* stem of *īris* rainbow + -ESCENT. See IRIS.] —**ir'i·des'cent·ly,** *adv.*

i·rid·i·um (i rid'ē əm) *n.* extremely hard, brittle, silver-white metallic element of the platinum family, used esp. in alloys of platinum and for electrical contacts and chemical apparatus. Symbol: **Ir** See **element** for table. [Modern Latin *iridium,* from Latin *īris* rainbow; referring to the variety of its colors in solutions. See IRIS.]

i·ris (ī'ris) *pl.,* **i·ris·es** or **i·ri·des** (ir'ə dēz', ī'rə-) *n.* **1.** colored, contractile membrane between the cornea and the lens that controls the amount of light entering the eye. **2.** showy flower of any of a large group of plants, genus *Iris,* usually growing directly from an underground bulb and consisting of three erect petals and three drooping petals. **3.** plant bearing this flower, cultivated as a house and garden plant, usually having long, sword-shaped leaves. **4. Iris.** Greek goddess of the rainbow. **5.** rainbow. [Latin *īris* rainbow, from Greek *īris.*]

Iris

I·rish (ī'rish) *adj.* of or relating to Ireland, its people, their language, or culture. —*n.* **1.** the people of Ireland or their close descendants. **2.** Irish Gaelic. **3.** dialect of English spoken by the Irish. ▲ construed as plural in def. 1, as singular in defs. 2 and 3. [Old English *Iras* inhabitants of Ireland.]

Irish Free State, see Ireland *(def. 2).*

Irish Gaelic, Gaelic as spoken in Ireland. Also, **Erse.**

I·rish·man (ī'rish mən) *pl.,* **-men.** *n.* member or close descendant of the people of Ireland. —**I'rish·wom'an,** *fem. n.*

Irish moss, edible reddish or purple seaweed, *Chondrus crispus,* that grows along the rocky Atlantic coasts of North America and northern Europe.

Irish potato, the common white potato.

Irish Sea, arm of the Atlantic Ocean between Ireland and England.

Irish setter, setter of a breed that originated in Ireland, having a coat of silky, reddish hair.

Irish stew, stew made of meat and various vegetables, as carrots, onions, and potatoes.

Irish terrier, short-haired terrier having a reddish, wiry coat. Height: 18 inches at the shoulder.

Irish wolfhound, heavily built, tall hound having a rough, wiry, usually gray coat. Height: to 37 inches at the shoulder.

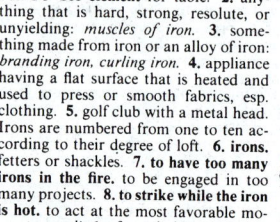

Irish setter

irk (urk) *v.t.* to annoy; vex; bother. [Of uncertain origin.]

irk·some (urk'səm) *adj.* annoying; tiresome: *irksome tasks.* —**irk'some·ly,** *adv.* —**irk'some·ness,** *n.*

Ir·kutsk (ir kootsk') *n.* city in the southern part of the Soviet Union. Pop. (1970 est.), 451,000.

i·ron (ī'ərn) *n.* **1.** gray-white, lustrous metallic element that is very ductile, highly magnetic, and a good conductor of heat and electricity. Symbol: **Fe** See **element** for table. **2.** anything that is hard, strong, resolute, or unyielding: *muscles of iron.* **3.** something made from iron or an alloy of iron: *branding iron, curling iron.* **4.** appliance having a flat surface that is heated and used to press or smooth fabrics, esp. clothing. **5.** golf club with a metal head. Irons are numbered from one to ten according to their degree of loft. **6. irons.** fetters or shackles. **7. to have too many irons in the fire.** to be engaged in too many projects. **8. to strike while the iron is hot.** to act at the most favorable moment. —*adj.* **1.** of or relating to iron. **2.** resolute or unyielding: *an iron will.* **3.** cruel or harsh: *The conquered people had to submit to the tyrant's iron yoke.* **4.** hardy or robust: *an iron constitution.* —*v.t.* to smooth or press with a heated iron: *to iron a shirt.* —*v.i.* to iron fabric, esp. clothes. [Old English *īren, īse(r)n* the metal iron, tool made of iron.]

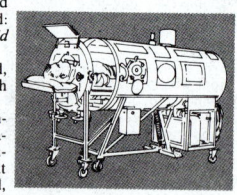

Irish terrier

Iron Age, stage in the development of civilization following the Bronze Age, characterized by the widespread use of iron in tools and weapons.

i·ron·bound (ī'ərn bound') *adj.* **1.** bound with iron. **2.** rigid; inflexible: *an ironbound society.* **3.** rocky; rugged: *an ironbound coast.*

i·ron·clad (ī'ərn klad') *adj.* **1.** covered or protected with iron or steel plates. **2.** difficult to change or break: *an ironclad regulation, an ironclad alibi.* —*n.* nineteenth-century warship covered wholly or partially with iron or steel plates for protection.

iron curtain, imaginary barrier separating the Soviet Union and its Communist satellites from the non-Communist world.

iron hand, very strict, harsh, or inflexible control: *The dictator ruled with an iron hand.* —**i'ron·hand'ed,** *adj.*

iron horse *Informal.* locomotive.

i·ron·ic (ī ron'ik) *adj.* **1.** of, relating to, or characterized by irony: *an ironic situation, an ironic remark.* **2.** given to the use of irony: *an ironic writer.* Also, **i·ron'i·cal.** [Late Latin *īrōnicus,* from Greek *eirōnikos* dissembling, from *eirōneiā* dissimulation.] —**i·ron'i·cal·ly,** *adv.* —**i·ron'i·cal·ness,** *n.*

i·ron·ing (ī'ər ning) *n.* **1.** act or process of pressing or smoothing fabrics or clothing, with a heated iron. **2.** that which is to be ironed: *The ironing piled up while the maid was ill.*

ironing board, padded board, usually on a folding frame, on which fabrics or clothing may be ironed.

iron lung, apparatus used to maintain breathing when normal respiration is impaired. An iron lung consists of a cylindrical tank that encloses the body, except the head, and air pumps that increase and decrease the air pressure in the tank.

Iron lung

i·ron·mon·ger (ī'ərn mung'gər, -mong'-) *n. British.* dealer in ironware or hardware.

iron pyrites, pyrite.

I·ron·sides (ī'ərn sīdz') *n.* **1.** nickname of Oliver Cromwell. **2.** soldiers under Cromwell in the English civil war. ▲ construed as singular in def. 1, as plural in def. 2.

at; āpe; cär; end; mē; it; īce; hot; ōld; fôrk; wood; fōōl; oil; out; up; ūse; turn; sing; thin; <u>th</u>is; zh in treasure; ə in ago, taken, pencil, lemon, circus.

i·ron·stone (ī′ərn stōn′) *n.* **1.** any rock or mineral containing large amounts of iron ore mixed with clay and other impurities. **2.** hard white stoneware.

i·ron·ware (ī′ərn wâr′) *n.* articles that are made of iron, as pots and kettles.

i·ron·weed (ī′ərn wēd′) *n.* any of a large group of plants, genus *Vernonia,* widely distributed in North America, having dark, very hard stems and clusters of usually purple flowers.

i·ron·wood (ī′ərn wood′) *n.* **1.** any of a number of trees having hard, close-grained wood, esp. the hop hornbeam, *Ostrya virginiana.* **2.** hard, durable wood of this tree, used esp. for making tool handles and similar equipment.

i·ron·work (ī′ərn wurk′) *n.* object or structure made of iron: *decorative ironwork.*

i·ron·work·er (ī′ərn wur′kər) *n.* **1.** one engaged in smelting iron or manufacturing iron objects. **2.** one who constructs or repairs structures of metal.

i·ron·works (ī′ərn wurks′) *n.,pl.* establishment where iron is smelted or where iron objects are manufactured. ▲ construed as both singular and plural.

i·ro·ny (ī′rə nē) *pl.,* **-nies.** *n.* **1.a.** form of expression in which the intended meaning is the opposite of that expressed in words: *The speaker's passion for irony gave a sardonic quality to his words.* **b.** instance of this: *She spoke in subtle ironies.* **2.** event or outcome of events opposite to what was, or might naturally have been, expected: *the irony of fate.* **3.** incongruity that results from such an outcome of events: *The fireman whose home had burned down was unable to appreciate the irony of his situation.* **4.** feigned ignorance, esp. when used in an argument or discussion. [Latin *īrōnīa* dissimulation, from Greek *eirōneiā.*]

Ir·o·quoi·an (ir′ə kwoi′ən) *n.* **1.** family of North American Indian languages, including Huron, Iroquois, Cherokee, and others. **2.** member of a tribe speaking one of these languages. —*adj.* of or relating to this family of languages.

Ir·o·quois (ir′ə kwoi′, -kwoiz′) *pl.,* **-quois.** *n.* **1.** member of a confederation of North American Indian tribes speaking Iroquoian languages, formerly living in New York. Originally called the Five Nations (the Seneca, Cayuga, Onondaga, Oneida, and Mohawk), the Iroquois became the Six Nations in 1722 when the Tuscaroras joined the confederation. **2.** member of a tribe belonging to this confederation. **3.** Iroquoian languages spoken by these Indians. —*adj.* of or relating to the Iroquois or their tribes. [French *Iroquois,* from Algonquian *Irinakhoiw* literally, real adders.]

ir·ra·di·ant (i rā′dē ənt) *adj.* emitting rays of light; shining brightly. —ir·ra′di·ance, ir·ra′di·an·cy, *n.*

ir·ra·di·ate (i rā′dē āt′) **-at·ed, -at·ing.** *v.t.* **1.** to shed light upon; brighten; illuminate: *Brilliant flashes of lightning irradiated the night sky.* **2.** to expose (something) to or treat with radiation. **3.** to send out in or as in rays; radiate. —*v.i.* Archaic. to emit rays; shine. [Latin *irradiātus,* past participle of *irradiāre* to cast forth rays.] —ir·ra′di·a′tion, *n.*

ir·ra·tion·al (i rash′ən əl) *adj.* **1.** deprived of or lacking reason; void of understanding; not rational: *The survivors of the crash wandered about in a confused and irrational state.* **2.** contrary to reason; illogical; absurd: *The man's remarks were totally irrational.* **3.** Mathematics. that cannot be expressed as a quotient of integers or as an integer. [Latin *irratiōnālis* without reason, going back to *in-* not + *ratiō* reason.] —ir·ra′tion·al·ly, *adv.* —**Syn.** **2.** see unreasonable.

ir·ra·tion·al·i·ty (i rash′ə nal′ə tē) *pl.,* **-ties.** *n.* **1.** condition or quality of being irrational. **2.** that which is irrational.

irrational number, real number that cannot be expressed as a quotient of integers or as an integer.√2 and π are irrational numbers.

Ir·ra·wad·dy (ir′ə wod′ē) *n.* river in eastern Asia, flowing through Burma into the Bay of Bengal.

ir·re·claim·a·ble (ir′i klā′mə bəl) *adj.* that cannot be reclaimed: *irreclaimable land.* —ir′re·claim′a·bil′i·ty, *n.* —ir′re·claim′a·bly, *adv.*

ir·rec·on·cil·a·ble (i rek′ən sī′lə bəl, i rek′ən sī′-) *adj.* **1.** that cannot be restored to friendly relations; implacable or uncompromising; hostile: *irreconcilable enemies.* **2.** that cannot be brought into harmony; incompatible: *irreconcilable differences.* —*n.* one who refused to be reconciled. —ir′rec′on·cil′a·bly, *adv.*

ir·re·cov·er·a·ble (ir′i kuv′ər ə bəl) *adj.* **1.** that cannot be recovered. **2.** that cannot be remedied or restored; irreparable: *The flood caused irrecoverable damage.* —ir′re·cov′er·a·bly, *adv.*

ir·re·deem·a·ble (ir′i dē′mə bəl) *adj.* **1.** that cannot be bought back or paid off: *an irredeemable mortgage.* **2.** that cannot be converted into coin. **3.** beyond redemption or reform: *an irredeemable criminal.* **4.** that cannot be changed or remedied; hopeless: *an atmosphere of irredeemable gloom.* —ir′re·deem′a·bly, *adv.*

ir·re·den·tist (ir′i den′tist) *n.* **1.** *also,* **Irredentist.** member of an Italian political party, formed in 1878, advocating the incorporation

into Italy of neighboring territories with Italian populations. **2.** one who advocates the incorporation into his country of a territory under foreign rule, claimed because of common linguistic, cultural, or racial characteristics. [Italian *irredentista* Irredentist, from *(Italia) irredenta* unredeemed (Italy), going back to Latin *in-* not + *redemptus,* past participle of *redimere* to buy back.] —ir′re·den′tism, *n.*

ir·re·duc·i·ble (ir′i dōō′sə bəl, -dū′-) *adj.* not reducible. —ir′re·duc′i·bly, *adv.*

ir·ref·ra·ga·ble (i ref′rə gə bəl) *adj.* that cannot be contested or refuted; indisputable: *an irrefragable authority.* [Late Latin *irrefragābilis,* from Latin *in-* not + *refragārī* to oppose.] —ir′ref′ra·ga·bil′i·ty, *n.* —ir′ref′ra·ga·bly, *adv.*

ir·re·fran·gi·ble (ir′i fran′jə bəl) *adj.* **1.** that can or must not be violated or broken; inviolable: *an irrefrangible law.* **2.** Optics. not subject to refraction.

ir·ref·u·ta·ble (i ref′yə tə bəl, ir′i fū′-) *adj.* that cannot be refuted; incontrovertible; indisputable: *irrefutable evidence.* —ir′ref′u·ta·bly, *adv.*

ir·reg·u·lar (i reg′yə lər) *adj.* **1.** not conforming to convention or custom; deviating from the usual rule or practice; unusual: *These procedures are highly irregular.* **2.** not conforming to established law or morality: *He is an irregular and intemperate person.* **3.** not occurring at fixed or uniform intervals: *irregular motions.* **4.** not evenly or uniformly arranged; uneven: *The astronaut walked on the irregular surface of the moon.* **5.** not belonging to the regular army. **6.** Grammar. deviating from the usual or most common pattern of inflection. The verb *to be* is irregular. —*n.* soldier not of the regular army. —ir′reg′u·lar·ly, *adv.* —**Syn.** *adj.* **4.** see rough.

ir·reg·u·lar·i·ty (i reg′yə lar′ə tē) *pl.,* **-ties.** *n.* **1.** quality or state of being irregular. **2.** that which is irregular.

ir·rel·e·vance (i rel′ə vəns) *n.* **1.** quality or fact of being irrelevant. **2.** that which is irrelevant. Also, **ir·rel′e·van·cy.**

ir·rel·e·vant (i rel′ə vənt) *adj.* not bearing upon or connected with the matter at hand; not pertinent; inappropriate. —ir·rel′e·vant·ly, *adv.*

ir·re·li·gion (ir′i lij′ən) *n.* **1.** lack of religion. **2.** hostility to religion.

ir·re·li·gious (ir′i lij′əs) *adj.* **1.** indifferent to or lacking religion; not religious. **2.** showing disrespect or hostility to religious principles; profane. [Latin *irreligiōsus* impious.] —ir′re·li′gious·ly, *adv.*

ir·re·me·di·a·ble (ir′i mē′dē ə bəl) *adj.* not subject to remedy or cure; incurable. —ir′re·me′di·a·bly, *adv.*

ir·re·mis·si·ble (ir′i mis′ə bəl) *adj.* that cannot be pardoned; not remissible; unpardonable: *an irremissible crime.* —ir′re·mis′si·bil′i·ty, *n.* —ir′re·mis′si·bly, *adv.*

ir·re·mov·a·ble (ir′i mōō′və bəl) *adj.* that cannot be removed. —ir′re·mov·a·bil′i·ty, *n.* —ir′re·mov′a·bly, *adv.*

ir·rep·a·ra·ble (i rep′ər ə bəl) *adj.* that cannot be repaired, restored, or made good: *irreparable damage, irreparable loss.* —ir′rep′a·ra·bil′i·ty, *n.* —ir′rep′a·ra·bly, *adv.*

ir·re·place·a·ble (ir′i plā′sə bəl) *adj.* that cannot be replaced: *irreplaceable works of art.*

ir·re·press·i·ble (ir′i pres′ə bəl) *adj.* that cannot be restrained: *irrepressible high spirits.* —ir′re·press′i·bil′i·ty, *n.* —ir′re·press′i·bly, *adv.*

ir·re·proach·a·ble (ir′i prō′chə bəl) *adj.* free from blame or criticism; above reproach; faultless: *irreproachable conduct.* —ir′re·proach′a·bly, *adv.*

ir·re·sist·i·ble (ir′i zis′tə bəl) *adj.* **1.** that cannot be resisted or opposed: *an irresistible power, an irresistible temptation.* **2.** extremely captivating: *an irresistible baby.* —ir′re·sis′ti·bil′i·ty, *n.* —ir′re·sist′i·bly, *adv.*

ir·res·o·lute (i rez′ə lōōt′) *adj.* lacking steadfast determination; vacillating: *a spineless and irresolute man.* —ir·res′o·lute′ly, *adv.* —ir·res′o·lute′ness, ir·res′o·lu′tion, *n.*

ir·re·spec·tive (ir′i spek′tiv) *adv.* without regard to or consideration for; regardless of (with *of*): *We will proceed, irrespective of the consequences.*

ir·re·spon·si·ble (ir′i spon′sə bəl) *adj.* **1.** not trustworthy or dependable; unreliable: *a thoughtless and irresponsible person.* **2.** not carefully considered: *an irresponsible decision.* **3.** not answerable to a higher authority for conduct or action: *an irresponsible government.* **4.** not capable of managing one's affairs: *financially irresponsible.* —ir′re·spon′si·bil′i·ty, *n.* —ir′re·spon′si·bly, *adv.*

ir·re·triev·a·ble (ir′i trē′və bəl) *adj.* that cannot be retrieved. —ir′re·triev′a·bil′i·ty, *n.* —ir′re·triev′a·bly, *adv.*

ir·rev·er·ence (i rev′ər əns) *n.* **1.** fact or quality of being irreverent; lack of reverence. **2.** irreverent act or utterance.

ir·rev·er·ent (i rev′ər ənt) *adj.* not feeling or showing reverence; disrespectful: *an irreverent man, an irreverent attitude.* [Latin *irreverēns.*] —ir·rev′er·ent·ly, *adv.*

ir·re·vers·i·ble (ir′i vur′sə bəl) *adj.* that cannot be reversed, re-

pealed, or undone; irrevocable: *irreversible decisions.* —ir′re·vers′i·bil′i·ty, *n.* —ir′re·vers′i·bly, *adv.*

ir·rev·o·ca·ble (i rev′ə bəl) *adj.* that cannot be revoked or recalled; unalterable. —ir′rev·o·ca·bil′i·ty, *n.* —ir·rev′o·ca·bly, *adv.*

ir·ri·ga·ble (ir′ə gə bəl) *adj.* that can be irrigated.

ir·ri·gate (ir′ə gāt′) -gat·ed, -gat·ing. *v.t.* **1.** to supply (land) with water by means of channels, streams, or pipes: *to irrigate a desert so that crops can be grown.* **2.** to cleanse (a wound or body cavity) with a constant flow of some liquid. [Latin *irrigātus*, past participle of *irrigāre* to moisten.] —ir′ri·ga′tion, ir′ri·ga′tor, *n.*

ir·ri·ta·bil·i·ty (ir′ə tə bil′ə tē) *pl.,* -ties. *n.* **1.** quality or state of being irritable; petulance. **2.** (of a body organ or part) the condition of being excessively or morbidly sensitive, esp. to a slight stimulus. **3.** *Biology.* ability to respond to a stimulus.

ir·ri·ta·ble (ir′ə tə bəl) *adj.* **1.** easily excited to impatience or anger; petulant; irascible. **2.** excessively or morbidly sensitive. **3.** *Biology.* able to respond to a stimulus. [Latin *irrītābilis* easily excited or angered, from *irrītāre* to excite, provoke.] —ir′ri·ta·ble·ness, *n.* —ir′ri·ta·bly, *adv.*

ir·ri·tant (ir′ə tənt) *n.* that which causes irritation. —*adj.* irritating. [Latin *irrītāns,* present participle of *irrītāre* to excite, provoke.]

ir·ri·tate (ir′ə tāt′) -tat·ed, -tat·ing. *v.t.* **1.** to excite to impatience or anger; vex: *The constant bickering of his friends irritated the young man.* **2.** to cause redness, pain, or swelling; inflame: *Cigarette smoke irritates my eyes.* **3.** *Biology.* to stimulate (a body organ or part) to some characteristic action or function. [Latin *irrītātus,* past participle of *irrītāre* to excite, provoke.] —ir′ri·tat′ing·ly, *adv.* —ir′ri·ta′tor, *n.*

ir·ri·ta·tion (ir′ə tā′shən) *n.* **1.** act or process of irritating; being irritated; vexation. **2.** red, painful, or swollen condition.

ir·rupt (i rupt′) *v.i.* **1.** to burst or break in; enter forcibly or violently. **2.** (of animals) to experience a sudden, unchecked increase in population. [Latin *irruptus,* past participle of *irrumpere* to break in.]

ir·rup·tion (i rup′shən) *n.* **1.** act of bursting or breaking in; violent entry; invasion. **2.** sudden, unchecked increase in population. [Latin *irruptiō* a bursting into.]

ir·rup·tive (i rup′tiv) *adj.* **1.** characterized by irruption. **2.** irrupting or tending to irrupt. **3.** *Geology.* intrusive.

Ir·ving (ur′ving) **1. Washington.** 1783–1859, U.S. author. **2.** city in northeastern Texas, near Dallas. Pop. (1970), 97,260.

is (iz) third person singular, present indicative, of **be.** [Old English *is* is.]

is., island.

Is. 1. Isaiah. **2.** Island.

Isa., Isaiah.

I·saac (ī′zək) *n.* in the Old Testament, the son of Abraham and Sarah and the father of Jacob and Esau. [Late Latin *Isaac,* from Greek *Isaak,* from Hebrew *Yitzhāq* literally, he laughs.]

Is·a·bel·la I (iz′ə bel′ə) 1451–1504, Spanish queen of Castile. See **Ferdinand V.**

I·sai·ah (ī zā′ə, ī zī′ə) *n.* **1.** Hebrew prophet of the eighth century B.C. **2.** book of the Old Testament attributed to him. [Hebrew *Yeshaʿyāhū* literally, salvation of Jehovah.]

I·sai·as (ī zā′əs, ī zī′-) *n.* in the Douay Bible, Isaiah.

Is·car·i·ot (is kar′ē ət) *n.* Judas *(def. 1).*

is·chi·um (is′kē əm) *pl.,* -chi·a (-kē ə). *n.* lowest portion of the hipbone. [Latin *ischium* hip joint, from Greek *ischion.*]

-ise, form of **-ize.**

I·seult (i sōōlt′) Isolde.

Is·fa·han (is′fə hän′) *also,* **Is·pa·han.** *n.* city in west-central Iran, the capital of Persia during the seventeenth and eighteenth centuries. Pop. (1966 est.), 424,045.

-ish *suffix* **1.** of, belonging to, or having to do with: *Irish, Polish.* **2.** of the nature or character of; like: *mannish, foolish.* **3.** tending or inclined to: *bookish.* **4.** somewhat: *bluish, youngish.* [Old English *-isc,* suffix forming adjectives.]

Ish·ma·el (ish′mē əl, -mā-) *n.* **1.** in the Old Testament, the son of Abraham and Hagar, driven into the wilderness with his mother, the supposed ancestor of the Arabs. **2.** outcast. [Hebrew *Yishmāʿēl* a son of Abraham in the Bible; literally, God hears.]

Ish·ma·el·ite (ish′mē ə līt′, -mā-) *n.* **1.** descendant of Ishmael. **2.** outcast or wanderer.

Ish·tar (ish′tär) *n.* Babylonian and Assyrian goddess of fertility and love, identified with the Phoenician goddess Astarte.

i·sin·glass (ī′zin glas′, ī′zing-) *n.* **1.** white, odorless, very pure form of gelatin obtained from the air bladders of fish, esp. sturgeon, used to

make glue and clarify liquors. **2.** mica. [Modification (influenced by GLASS) of obsolete Dutch *huizenblas* sturgeon bladder.]

I·sis (ī′sis) *n.* Egyptian goddess of fertility, wife and sister of Osiris. [Latin *Īsis,* from Greek *Īsis;* of Egyptian origin.]

isl., island.

Is·lam (is′lam, iz′-, is läm′) *n.* **1.** religion based on the teachings and writings of Muhammad, asserting that there is only one god, Allah, and that Muhammad is his prophet. **2.** the whole of the Muslim world, including Muslim civilization, and the countries under Muslim rule. [Arabic *islām* submission (to God).] —Is·lam′ic, *adj.*

Is·lam·a·bad (is läm′ä bäd′) *n.* capital of Pakistan, in the northern part of the country. Pop. (1970), 60,000.

Is·lam·ite (is′lə mīt′, iz′-) *n.* Muslim.

is·land (ī′lənd) *n.* **1.** body of land entirely surrounded by water and smaller than a continent. **2.** anything resembling an island: *an island of floating ice, a traffic island. The mountains were islanded in the billowing mist.* [Old English *īgland,* piece of land surrounded by water; Modern English spelling influenced by ISLE.]

is·land·er (ī′lən dər) *n.* native or inhabitant of an island.

isle (īl) *n.* island, esp. a small island. [Old French *isle,* from Latin *īnsula.*]

is·let (ī′lit) *n.* a little island. [Middle French *islette,* diminutive of Old French *isle.* See ISLE.]

islet of Lang·er·hans (läng′ər häns′, -hänz′) any of several small masses of cells lying in the pancreas that function as endocrine glands by secreting insulin into the blood stream. Also, **island of Langerhans.**

ism (iz′əm) *n.* doctrine, theory, or system. [From words ending in -ISM.]

-ism *suffix* **1.** action or practice: *criticism, nepotism.* **2.** condition or state: *giantism, parallelism.* **3.** characteristic conduct or behavior: *patriotism, barbarism, heroism.* **4.** distinguishing feature, aspect, or manner, as of style or language: *colloquialism, Hellenism, classicism.* **5.** doctrine, system, or principle: *socialism, paganism, pragmatism.* [Greek *-ismos, -isma,* often through Latin *-ismus, -isma,* or French *-isme;* suffix used to form nouns.]

is·n't (iz′ənt) is not.

iso- *combining form* equal: *isosceles, isogonic.* [Greek *isos* equal.]

i·so·bar (ī′sə bär′) *n.* **1.** line on a weather map connecting points having the same barometric pressure. **2.** any of two or more atoms that have the same atomic weight but different atomic numbers. [Iso- + Greek *baros* weight.]

i·so·bar·ic (ī′sə bar′ik) *adj.* **1.** of, relating to, or containing isobars. **2.** having or indicating equal barometric pressure.

i·soch·ro·nal (ī sok′rən əl) *adj.* **1.** equal in duration. **2.** characterized by, relating to, or occurring in equal intervals of time. Also, **i·soch′ro·nous.** [Greek *isochronos* equal in time + -AL′.]

i·so·gon·ic (ī′sə gon′ik) *adj.* having equal angles. Also, **i·sog·o·nal** (ī sog′ən əl). [Iso- + Greek *gōniā* angle, corner + -IC.]

i·so·late (ī′sə lāt′, is′ə-) -lat·ed, -lat·ing. *v.t.* **1.** to place or set apart; separate from others; detach: *The writer isolated himself in his study.* **2.** to separate (an infected person) from all contact with others; quarantine. **3.** to obtain (a chemical substance) in pure or uncombined form. [From *isolated,* from Italian *isolato* detached, from *isola* island, from Latin *īnsula.*] —Syn. see SEGREGATE.

i·so·la·tion (ī′sə lā′shən, is′ə-) *n.* **1.** act of isolating. **2.** state of being isolated; solitude: *The patient remained in isolation until she was no longer contagious.*

i·so·la·tion·ism (ī sə lā′shə niz′əm, is ə-) *n.* policy of avoiding political, economic, or military involvements with foreign countries. —i′so·la′tion·ist, *n.*

I·sol·de (i zōl′də, i sōl′-) *n. Medieval Legend.* an Irish princess loved by Tristan. Also, **I·seult′, I·solt** (i sōlt′).

i·so·mer (ī′sə mər) *n.* any of two or more compounds that have the same molecular formula and thus the same chemical composition but that differ in properties due to different arrangements of the atoms in their molecules. [Greek *isomerēs* equally divided, from *isos* equal + *meros* part.] —i·so·mer·ic (ī′sə mer′ik), *adj.*

i·som·er·ism (ī som′ə riz′əm) *n.* change in the chemical properties of a compound due to a change in the arrangement of atoms in a molecule.

i·som·er·ous (ī som′ər əs) *adj.* having an equal number of markings, organs, or other parts.

i·so·met·ric (ī′sə met′rik) *adj.* **1.** of, relating to, or having all measurements equal to one another. **2.** relating to or denoting a system of crystalline forms characterized by three equal axes at right angles to one another. Also, **i′so·met′ri·cal. 3.** of or relating to the contraction of a muscle in which there is increased tension rather than change in length. —*n.pl.* **isometrics.** isometric exercise. ▲ construed as singular. [Greek *isometros* of equal measure, from *isos* equal + *metron* measure + -IC.] —i′so·met′ri·cal·ly, *adv.*

Ilium

Ischium   Pubis

Ischium

isometric exercise, type of exercise accomplished by pitting any of the muscles or parts of the body against an immovable object, as a wall, or against an opposing set of muscles of either equal or greater strength.

i·so·morph (ī sə môrf′) *n.* **1.** organism that is similar in appearance or structure to another, but is of different ancestry. **2.** *Chemistry.* substance isomorphous with another.

i·so·mor·phic (ī′sə môr′fik) *adj.* **1.** similar in appearance or structure, but of different ancestry; morphologically alike. **2.** isomorphous. [Iso- + Greek *morphē* form, shape + -IC.]

i·so·mor·phous (ī′sə môr′fəs) *adj.* (of a substance) able to crystallize in the same or related form as another substance having a dissimilar chemical composition.

i·so·pod (ī′sə pod′) *n.* any of various insectlike crustaceans, order Isopoda, having a flat, segmented body and seven pairs of legs. [Modern Latin *Isopoda* literally, equal-footed, from Greek *isos* equal + *pous* (stem *pod-*) foot.]

i·sos·ce·les (ī sos′ə lēz′) *adj.* having two sides whose lengths are equal: *an isosceles triangle.* [Late Latin *isoscelēs* having equal legs, from Greek *isoskelēs*, from *isos* equal + *skelos* leg.]

i·so·therm (ī′sə thûrm′) *n.* line on a weather map connecting points having the same mean temperature. [Iso- + Greek *thermē* heat.]

i·so·ther·mal (ī′sə thûr′məl) *adj.* **1.** of, relating to, or indicating equal temperatures. **2.** of or relating to an isotherm.

i·so·ton·ic (ī′sə ton′ik) *adj.* **1.** (of solutions) having equal osmotic pressure on both sides of a membrane. **2.** denoting the contraction of a muscle encountering little resistance. [Greek *isotonos* of equal tension or tone (from *isos* equal + *tonos* stretching, tone) + -IC.]

i·so·tope (ī′sə tōp′) *n.* any of two or more kinds of atoms of the same element having the same atomic number but differing mass number. [Iso- + Greek *topos* place.]

i·so·trop·ic (ī′sə trop′ik) *adj. Physics.* having the same physical properties in all directions. Also, **i·sot·ro·pous** (ī sot′rə pəs). [Iso- + Greek *tropos* turn, direction + -IC.]

Is·pa·han (is′pə hän′) *n.* Isfahan.

Is·ra·el (iz′rē əl, -rā-) *n.* **1.** country in southwestern Asia, at the eastern end of the Mediterranean Sea. Capital, Jerusalem. Area, 7993 sq. mi. Pop. (1970 est.), 2,899,000. **2.** in the Old Testament, the patriarch Jacob, who was given this name after he had wrestled with the angel. **3.** the people descended from Jacob; the Hebrew people. **4.a.** ancient kingdom of the Hebrew people, ruled by David and Solomon in the eleventh and tenth centuries B.C. **b.** northern portion of this, established as a separate kingdom by Jeroboam after Solomon's death. [Latin *Isrāēl* another name of Jacob in the Old Testament, from Greek *Isrāēl,* from Hebrew *Yisrā'ēl* literally, he strives with God.]

Is·rae·li (iz rā′lē) *adj.* of or relating to modern Israel, its people, their language, or culture. —*n. pl.,* **-lis.** member or close descendant of the people of modern Israel.

Is·ra·el·ite (iz′rē ə līt′, -rā-) *n.* descendant of the patriarch Jacob; Hebrew. —*adj.* of or relating to the Hebrews.

Is·sei (ēs′sā′) *pl.,* **-sei.** native of Japan who immigrated to the United States. [Japanese *issei* first generation.]

is·su·ance (ish′ōō əns) *n.* act of issuing.

is·sue (ish′ōō) *n.* **1.a.** act of sending or giving out: *an issue of licenses, an issue of supplies.* **b.** act of going, passing, or flowing out: *an issue of blood.* **2.a.** that which is sent or given out, as a certain quantity of magazines, newspapers, stamps, or books, printed and distributed at one time: *the latest issue of the newspaper.* **b.** individual copy of a magazine. **3.** point in question or matter under consideration: *The raising of taxes was the issue under debate.* **4.** offspring. **5.** outcome of an action or course of events; result; consequence. **6.** opening or outlet. **7. at issue. a.** under discussion or consideration; in question. **b.** at variance. **8. to join issue.** to argue on a particular point; debate. **9. to take issue.** to disagree. —*v.t.,* **-sued, -su·ing. 1.a.** to send or give out: *to issue coins, to issue a statement.* **b.** to send forth; discharge; emit. **2.** to publish. —*v.i.* **1.** to go or come out; flow out; pour forth. **2.** to proceed as a result or outcome; be derived. [Old French *issue* result, way, event, from *issir* to go out, from Latin *exīre.*] —**is′su·er,** *n.*

-ist *suffix* **1.** one who does or makes: *tourist, novelist.* **2.** one who practices or has as a profession: *bigamist, scientist, violinist.* **3.** one who adheres to or advocates: *Buddhist, idealist, socialist.* [Greek *-istēs,* through Latin *-ista, -istēs* or French *-iste.*]

Is·tan·bul (is′tan bōōl′, -tän-, is täm′bool) *n.* largest city, major seaport, and commercial and financial center of Turkey, located on both sides of the Bosporus. It was formerly Constantinople and, in ancient times, Byzantium. Pop. (1965), 1,742,978.

isth·mi·an (is′mē ən) *adj.* **1.** of or relating to an isthmus. **2. Isthmian.** of or relating to the isthmuses of Corinth or Panama.

isth·mus (is′məs) *pl.,* **-mus·es.** *n.* narrow strip of land bordered by water and connecting two larger bodies of land. [Latin *isthmus,* from Greek *isthmos* narrow passage.]

is·tle (ist′lē) *n.* fiber obtained from certain tropical American plants, as the henequen, used in making bags, rope, and similar products. [Spanish *ixtle;* of Nahuatl origin.]

it (it) *Sing.,* nominative, **it;** possessive, **its;** objective, **its;** *pl.,* nominative, **they;** possessive, **their, theirs;** objective, **them.** *pron.* **1.** thing or animal previously referred to: *Did you see that automobile? No, I didn't see it.* **2.** subject of an impersonal verb: *It snowed last night.* **3.** anticipatory subject of a verb introducing a phrase or dependent clause: *It is obvious that he likes you.* **4.** indefinite object without definite force: *Go to it! Flaunt it!* [Old English *hit,* neuter pronoun of the third person singular.]

It. **1.** Italy. **2.** Italian.

ital., italic; italics.

Ital. **1.** Italy. **2.** Italian.

I·tal·ian (i tal′yən) *adj.* of or relating to Italy, its people, their language, or culture. —*n.* **1.** member or recent descendant of the people of Italy. **2.** Romance language spoken predominantly in Italy and in parts of Switzerland.

I·tal·ian·ize (i tal′yə nīz′) **-ized, -iz·ing.** *v.t., v.i.* to make or become Italian, esp. in style or character.

Italian sonnet, Petrarchan sonnet.

i·tal·ic (i tal′ik) *adj.* **1.** relating to or designating a style of type whose letters slant to the right. *This sentence is printed in italic type.* **2. Italic.** of or relating to ancient Italy, its people, their languages, or culture. —*n.* **1.** *also,* **italics.** italic type. **2. Italic.** group of languages belonging to the Indo-European language family, including Umbrian, Latin, and the Romance languages. [Latin *Italicus* Italian, from Greek *Italikos,* from *Italia* Italy; with reference to the type invented by the *Italian* printer Aldus Manutius (about 1500).]

i·tal·i·cize (i tal′ə sīz′) **-cized, -ciz·ing.** *v.t.* **1.** to print in italics: *Foreign words are usually italicized.* **2.** to underscore with a single line to indicate italics.

It·a·ly (it′əl ē) *n.* country in southern Europe, on the Mediterranean Sea. Capital, Rome. Area, 116,303 sq. mi. Pop. (1969 est.), 53,170,000.

I·tas·ca, Lake (ī tas′kə) lake in northern Minnesota, a source of the Mississippi River.

itch (ich) *n.* **1.** tickling or stinging sensation in the skin that is relieved by scratching or rubbing. **2.** restless, uneasy desire for something: *He had an itch for authorship* (Eliot, 1863). **3.** scabies. —*v.i.* **1.** to have or cause a tickling or stinging sensation in the skin. **2.** to have a restless, uneasy desire: *He is itching for a fight.* [Old English *giccan* to feel irritation of the skin.]

itch·y (ich′ē) **itch·i·er, itch·i·est.** *adj.* characterized by, having, or causing a tickling or stinging sensation in the skin: *itchy flannels, an itchy feeling.* —**itch′i·ness,** *n.*

-ite[1] *suffix* **1.** native or resident of: *Muscovite, Israelite.* **2.** advocate or adherent of: *pre-Raphaelite, Laborite.* **3.** manufactured product: *dynamite.* **4.** mineral compound of: *calcite.* **5.** fossil: *trilobite.* [Greek *-ītēs,* often through Latin *-īta, -ītēs* or French *-ite;* suffix forming adjectives and nouns.]

-ite[2] *suffix* salt of: *sulfite.* [French *-ite,* modification of -ATE[2].]

i·tem (ī′təm) *n.* **1.** unit or article included in an assemblage, series, or list: *There are many valuable items in his stamp collection.* **2.** bit of information, or a brief newspaper article or paragraph containing such information: *There was an item in Sunday's newspaper about the society's forthcoming convention.* —*adv.* also; likewise. ▲ formerly used before each listing except the first in an inventory. [Latin *item* likewise, also.]

i·tem·ize (ī′tə mīz′) **-ized, -iz·ing.** *v.t.* to set down each item of; list by items: *The accountant itemized the tax deductions.*

it·er·ate (it′ə rāt′) **-at·ed, -at·ing.** *v.t.* to say or do again; repeat. [Latin *interātus,* past participle of *interāre.*] —**it′er·a′tion,** *n.* —**it′er·a·tive,** *adj.*

Ith·a·ca (ith′ə kə) *n.* one of the Ionian islands off the west coast of Greece. It was the home of Ulysses.

i·tin·er·an·cy (ī tin′ər ən sē, i tin′-) *n.* **1.** state or condition of traveling from place to place, esp. for business purposes or in the exercise of duty. **2.** act of so traveling. Also, **i·tin·er·a·cy** (ī tin′ər ə sē, i tin′-).

i·tin·er·ant (ī tin′ər ənt, i tin′-) *adj.* traveling from place to place, esp. for business purposes or in the exercise of duty: *an itinerant judge, an itinerant preacher.* —*n.* one who travels from place to place, esp. for business or duty. [Late Latin *itinerāns,* present participle of *itinerārī* to travel, from Latin *iter* journey.] —**i·tin′er·ant·ly,** *adv.*

i·tin·er·ar·y (ī tin′ər er′ē, i tin′-) *n. pl.,* **-ar·ies.** *n.* **1.** course or plan of travel, or for a journey: *Rome, Amsterdam, and New York were included in her itinerary.* **2.** account or record of travel. **3.** guidebook. —*adj.* of or relating to traveling or a route. [Late Latin *itinerārium* account of a journey, going back to Latin *iter* journey.]

i·tin·er·ate (ī tin′ə rāt′, i tin′-) **-at·ed, -at·ing.** *v.i.* to travel from place to place. [Late Latin *itinerātus,* past participle of *itinerārī.* See ITINERANT.]

---

at; āpe; cär; end; mē; it; īce; hot; ōld; fôrk; wood; fōōl; oil; out; up; ūse; turn; sing; thin; this; zh in treasure; ə in ago, taken, pencil, lemon, circus.

-itis *suffix* inflammation of: *appendicitis*. [Modern Latin *-itis*, from Greek *-itis*, feminine of *-itēs* relating to.]

it'll (it'əl) **1.** it will. **2.** it shall.

its (its) *adj.* of or belonging to it.

it's (its) **1.** it is. **2.** it has.

it·self (it self') *pron.* **1.** emphatic form of **it:** *The book itself is very poorly written.* **2.** reflexive form of **it:** *The cat can wash itself.* **3.** its usual or normal state or condition: *The car is not itself this morning.*

-ity *suffix* state, condition, or quality of being: *suavity, formality, animosity, inferiority*. [French *-ité*, from Latin *-itās*.]

I·van III (ī'vən, i vän') 1440–1505, ruler of Russia from 1462 to 1505. Also, **Ivan the Great.**

Ivan IV, 1530–84, czar of Russia from 1533 to 1584. Also, **Ivan the Terrible.**

I've (īv) I have.

-ive *suffix* **1.** given to: *active, demonstrative, inquisitive.* **2.** of or relating to: *infinitive, native.* [Latin *-īvus*, often through French *-if, -ive.*]

i·vied (ī'vēd) *adj.* covered or overgrown with ivy.

i·vo·ry (ī'vər ē, īv'rē) *pl.,* **-ries.** *n.* **1.** smooth, hard, white substance composing the tusks of elephants, walruses, and certain other mammals. **2.** object or objects made of this substance: *The museum has a fine collection of medieval ivories.* **3.** creamy white color. **4. ivories.** *Slang.* **a.** piano keys. **b.** dice. —*adj.* of or resembling ivory. [Anglo-Norman *ivorie* this substance, from Latin *eboreus* made of ivory, from *ebur* ivory; probably of Egyptian origin.]

Ivory Coast, country in western Africa, on the Gulf of Guinea. Capital, Abidjan. Area, 124,504 sq. mi. Pop. (1969 est.), 4,195,000.

ivory nut, nutlike seed of a South American palm tree, *Phytelephas macrocarpa*, used to make imitation ivory buttons and other objects.

ivory tower, situation, attitude, or condition of withdrawal from practical matters, as into a world of intellectual or artistic pursuits.

i·vy (ī'vē) *pl.,* **i·vies.** *n.* **1.** any of several unrelated creeping vines widely cultivated as decorative coverings for walls and yards, as English ivy, *Hedera helix*, and Boston ivy, *Parthenocissus tricuspidata*. **2.** any of various climbing plants, as poison ivy. [Old English *ifig* climbing evergreen plant.]

Ivy

Ivy League, association of colleges and universities in the northeastern United States, having high scholastic standing and social prestige.

i·wis (ē wis', ī wis') *also,* **y·wis.** *adv.* *Archaic.* certainly; surely. [Old English *gewis* certain.]

I·wo Ji·ma (ē'wō jē'mə) island in the western North Pacific, captured from Japan by the United States in 1945 during World War II and returned in 1968.

IWW, Industrial Workers of the World.

Ix·i·on (ik sī'ən) *n.* *Greek Mythology*. father of the centaurs. Zeus punished Ixion for making advances to Hera by having him bound to a perpetually revolving fiery wheel in Hades.

-ize *suffix* **1.a.** to act upon; make: *civilize, legalize, fertilize.* **b.** to treat like: *idolize.* **2.** to treat or affect with: *oxidize.* **3.** to form into; become: *crystallize.* **4.** to be concerned with or engaged in: *philosophize, characterize.* [Greek *-izein* to act in a certain way, often through Latin *-izāre* or French *-iser*.]

Iz·mir (iz'mēr, iz mēr') *n.* port city in western Turkey, on the Aegean Sea, formerly known as Smyrna. Pop. (1965), 411,626.

at; āpe; cär; end; mē; it; īce; hot; ōld; fôrk; wood; fōōl; oil; out; up; ūse; turn; sing; thin; **th**is; zh in treasure; ə in ago, taken, pencil, lemon, circus.

J

j, J (jā) *pl.*, **j's, J's.** *n.* **1.** tenth letter of the English alphabet. **2.** shape of this letter or something having such a shape.

J, joule.

J. 1. judge. **2.** justice.

Ja., January.

J.A. 1. joint account. **2.** judge advocate.

jab (jab) **jabbed, jab·bing.** *v.t., v.i.* **1.** to poke or thrust sharply, as with something pointed; stab. **2.** to punch or strike with short, quick blows. —*n.* sharp, quick thrust or blow. [Form of archaic *job* to strike; possibly imitative.]

jab·ber (jab′ər) *v.i., v.t.* to talk rapidly, unintelligibly, or nonsensically; chatter. —*n.* rapid, unintelligible, or nonsensical talk; gibberish. [Imitative.] —**jab′ber·er,** *n.*

ja·bot (zha bō′, ja-) *n.* ruffle or similar ornamentation of lace or other material, usually worn down the front of a dress or shirt. [French *jabot* originally, crop of a bird; of uncertain origin.]

ja·cinth (jā′sinth, jas′inth) *n.* hyacinth (*def. 3*). [Old French *jacinte,* from Latin *hyacinthus* larkspur, blue precious stone, from Greek *hyakinthos.* Doublet of HYACINTH.]

jack (jak) *n.* **1.** *also,* **Jack. a.** man or boy; fellow. **b.** one who does manual labor or odd jobs; laborer. ▲ usually used in combination: *lumberjack, steeplejack, jack-of-all-trades.* **c.** sailor; seaman. **2.** any of various mechanical or hydraulic devices, usually portable, used for lifting heavy objects a short distance. **3.** playing card bearing the picture of a young man. Also, **knave. 4.a. jacks.** game played chiefly by children, the object of which is to pick up a number of small, six-pointed metal pieces or similar objects while bouncing and catching a small rubber ball with the same hand. Also, **jack′stones′.** ▲ Jacks and jackstones are construed as singular. **b.** one of the playing pieces used in this game Also, **jack′stone′.** **5.** male donkey; jackass. **6.** small flag flown by a ship, usually to indicate nationality. **7.** electrical device into which a plug may be inserted to make a connection. **8.** *Slang.* money. **9. every man jack,** everyone without exception. —*v.t.* **1.** to lift or move with or as if with a mechanical or hydraulic jack (often with *up*): *to jack up an automobile.* **2.** *Informal.* to increase, as prices (often with *up*): *colleges that jack up fees every year.* [From the masculine proper name *Jack,* from *Jankin,* diminutive of JOHN; possibly influenced by French *Jacques* James.]

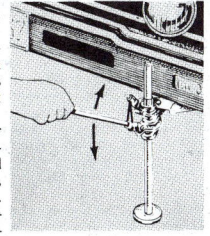

Jack (def. 2)

jack·al (jak′ôl, -ôl) *n.* **1.** any of various foxlike mammals, genus *Thos,* of Africa, Asia, and southeastern Europe, having a pointed face, bushy tail, and usually gray, buff, or reddish-black fur. Jackals often feed on the remains of another animal's prey. Length: 32–38 inches including the tail. **2.** one who does menial or dishonest work for another. [Turkish *chakāl* the animal, from Persian *shaghāl.*]

Jackal

jack·a·napes (jak′ə nāps′) *n.* impertinent, presumptuous, or conceited fellow; upstart. [From earlier *Jack Napes* ape, originally (about 1450) a nickname of the first Duke of Suffolk, whose badge was a ball and chain of the kind fastened on tame *apes.*]

jack·ass (jak′as′) *n.* **1.** male donkey. **2.** stupid or foolish person; blockhead.

jack·boot (jak′boot′) *also,* **jack boot.** *n.* sturdy boot reaching above the knee, originally designed to be worn by cavalrymen.

jack·daw (jak′dô′) *n.* glossy black crow, *Corvus monedula;* of Europe, Asia, and northern Africa, having a gray band around the throat and a gray underside. Length: 13 inches. Also, **daw.**

jack·et (jak′it) *n.* **1.a.** short coat, usually not extending below the hips. **b.** sports jacket; suit jacket. **2.** outer covering or casing, as a removable paper or cardboard cover for a book or phonograph record. —*v.t.* to cover with a jacket; put a jacket on. [Old French *jaquette,* diminutive of *jaque* sleeveless coatlike garment, possibly from *jacques* nickname given to French peasants of the fourteenth century who often wore the *jaque,* from *Jacques* James.]

Jack Frost, figure thought of as representing frost or freezing cold weather.

jack·ham·mer (jak′ham′ər) *n.* machine for drilling rock, pavement, or similar hard materials, operated by compressed air.

jack-in-the-box (jak′in thə boks′) *also,* **jack′-in-a-box′.** *n.* toy consisting of a box containing a grotesque figure, often that of a clown, that springs up when the lid of the box is opened.

jack-in-the-pul·pit (jak′in thə pul′pit) *n.* tall plant, *Arisaema atrorubens,* of eastern North America, bearing one or two long-stalked leaves that grow directly from an underground bulb, and tiny flowers that are enclosed within a spathe.

jack·knife (jak′nīf′) *pl.,* **-knives.** *n.* **1.** large pocketknife. **2.** dive in which the diver bends at the waist and, keeping his legs straight, touches his feet with his hands before straightening out and entering the water hands first. —*v.t., v.i.* **-knifed, knif·ing.** to double up or bend like a jackknife. [Probably *Jack,* nickname of King James I of England (because this knife was popular in England during his reign), + KNIFE.]

jack-of-all-trades (jak′əv ôl′trādz′) *pl.,* **jacks-of-all-trades.** *n.* one who can do many different kinds of work.

jack-o'-lan·tern (jak′ə lan′tərn) *n.* **1.** pumpkin hollowed out and carved so as to resemble a human face, used as a decoration or lantern at Halloween. **2.** will-o'-the wisp (*def. 1*).

jack·pot (jak′pot′) *n.* **1.** top prize or cumulative stakes in any of various games and contests: *a quiz show that offers a $100,000 jackpot. Nick played the slot machine until he won the jackpot.* **2. to hit the jackpot. a.** to win a jackpot. **b.** to have great success or unexpected good fortune.

jack rabbit, any of several North American hares, genus *Lepus,* having very long ears and long, powerful hind legs. Length: to 2 feet.

jack·screw (jak′skroo′) *n.* jack for lifting, operated by means of a screw.

Jack·son (jak′sən) **1. Andrew.** 1767–1845, seventh president of the United States, from 1829 to 1837. **2. Stone·wall** (stōn′wôl′). 1824–63, U.S. Confederate general in the Civil War; born Thomas Jonathan Jackson. **3.** capital and largest city of Mississippi, in the central part of the state. Pop. (1970), 153,968. **4.** city in southern Michigan. Pop. (1970), 45,484.

Jack rabbit

Jack·so·ni·an (jak sō′nē ən) *adj.* of or relating to Andrew Jackson, his principles, or his policies. —*n.* supporter of Andrew Jackson, his principles, or his policies.

Jack·son·ville (jak′sən vil′) *n.* largest city in Florida, a major seaport on the northeastern coast of the state. Pop. (1970), 528,865.

jack·stone (jak′stōn′) *n.* **1.** jackstones. jack (*def. 4a*). **2.** jack (*def. 4b*).

jack·straw (jak′strô′) *n.* **1.** jackstraws. game in which a number of objects, usually thin sticks or light strips of wood or other material, are thrown into a pile and must be picked up one at a time without disturb-

ing the rest of the pile. ▲ construed as singular. **2.** one of the sticks or other objects used in this game.

jack-tar (jak′tär′) *also,* **Jack-tar, Jack Tar.** *n.* sailor; seaman.

Ja-cob (jā′kəb) *n.* in the Old Testament, the son of Isaac and Rebecca and twin brother of Esau. Jacob's twelve sons founded the twelve tribes of Israel. [Late Latin *Jacōbus,* from Greek *Iákōbos,* from Hebrew *Ya'aqōb* literally, he who takes by the heel.]

Jac-o-be-an (jak′ə bē′ən) *adj.* of, relating to, or characteristic of King James I of England or the period of his reign. —*n.* English person who lived during this time, esp. a statesman or writer. [Modern Latin *Jacobaeus,* from Latin *Jacobus* James, Jacob. See JACOB.]

Jac-o-bin (jak′ə bin) *n.* **1.** member of a French revolutionary society organized in 1789 that dominated the government of France during the Reign of Terror, led by Robespierre. **2.** extreme radical, esp. one who advocates violent upheavals to achieve political ends. **3.** Dominican friar. [French *Jacobin,* from Medieval Latin *Jacobinus* relating to Jacob, from Latin *Jacobus.* See JACOB. The reference was to the meetings held by the revolutionary society in a building of the Dominican, or Jacobin, friars.] —**Jac′o-bin′ic;** *also,* **Jac′o-bin′i-cal,** *adj.*

Jac-o-bin-ism (jak′ə bi niz′əm) *n.* **1.** political principles or practices of the Jacobin society. **2.** extreme radicalism, esp. in politics.

Jac-o-bite (jak′ə bīt′) *n.* English or Scottish supporter of James II after his expulsion in 1688, or of his descendants' claims to the throne. [From Latin *Jacobus.* See JACOB, JAMES.]

Jacob's ladder **1.** in the Old Testament, a ladder from earth to heaven that Jacob saw in a dream. **2.** rope ladder used on ships, usually having wooden rungs. **3.** sturdy, leafy plant, *Polemonium caeruleum,* native to Europe and Asia and widely cultivated as a garden plant, having clusters of bell-shaped blue flowers and a ladderlike arrangement of leaves and leaflets.

Jac-que-rie (zhäk rē′) *n.* **1.** revolt of the French peasants against the nobility in 1358. **2.** *also,* **jacquerie.** any peasants' revolt. [French *jacquerie,* from *jacques* scornful nickname given to French peasants by the nobility, from *Jacques* James.]

jade¹ (jād) *n.* **1.** either of two very hard minerals, nephrite or jadeite, that are most commonly deep green to greenish-white and are used for jewelry and carved ornaments. **2.** *also,* **jade green.** color of jade. [French *jade,* from Spanish *(piedra de) ijada* (stone of) colic (because jade was thought to cure colic), going back to Latin *īlia* abdomen.]

jade² (jād) *n.* **1.** old, worn-out, worthless, or ill-tempered horse. **2.** disreputable or worthless woman; hussy. —*v.t., v.i.,* **jad-ed, jad-ing.** to make or become tired or worn-out. [Of uncertain origin.]

jad-ed (jā′did) *adj.* **1.** worn-out; tired. **2.** dulled, as from overindulgence; satiated. —**jad′ed-ly,** *adv.* —**jad′ed-ness,** *n.*

jade-ite (jā′dīt) *n.* mineral that is a variety of jade, usually green or greenish-white, with a glassy or pearly luster. Formula: NaAlSi$_2$O$_6$

jae-ger (jā′gər, jā′-) *also,* **jä-ger.** *n.* any of several brown and white sea birds, genus *Stercorarius,* that resemble gulls. It pursues and harasses weaker birds until they drop their prey, which it then snatches. Length: 18–22 inches. [German *Jäger* hunter.]

Jaf-fa (jaf′ə) *n.* seaport on the Mediterranean coast of Israel, combined with Tel Aviv in 1950 as one city. In ancient times it was known as Joppa.

jag¹ (jag) *n.* sharp, projecting point. —*v.t.,* **jagged, jag-ging. 1.** to cut notches in. **2.** to make uneven or ragged by cutting or tearing. [Of uncertain origin.]

jag² (jag) *n. Informal.* unrestrained outburst or period of overindulgence in some activity; spell; bout: *an eating jag, a laughing jag.* [Of uncertain origin.]

Jag-an-nath (jug′ə nät′, -nôt′) Juggernaut.

jag-ged (jag′id) *adj.* having sharp, projecting points or uneven or irregular edges: *jagged lightning bolts.* —**jag′ged-ly,** *adv.* —**jag′ged-ness,** *n.*

jag-uar (jag′wär, jag′ū är′) *n.* large mammal, *Felis onca,* of the cat family, native to the southwestern United States, Mexico, and Central

Jaguar

and South America, having a coat of short, tawny or golden fur with black spots. Length: to 9 feet including the tail. [Tupi-Guarani *jaguara* carnivorous animal.]

Jah-veh (yä′vā) *also,* **Jah-weh.** *n.* Yahweh.

jai a-lai (hī′ lī′, hī′ə lī′) extremely fast game similar to handball, esp. popular in Spain and Latin America, in which the ball is hooked and caught with a long, curved basket strapped to the wrist. Also, **pe-lo′ta.** [Spanish *jai alai,* from Basque *jai* festival + *alai* merry.]

jail (jāl) *also, British,* **gaol.** *n.* **1.** building for the confinement of persons accused or convicted of breaking the law. **2.** any place of confinement. —*v.t.* to put or keep in jail; imprison. [Old French *jaiole, gaole* prison,

cage, from Medieval Latin *gabiola* cage, going back to Latin *cavea.*] —**Syn.** *v.t.* see **imprison.**

jail-bird (jāl′burd′) *n. Informal.* one who is or has been confined in prison; prisoner or ex-convict.

jail-break (jāl′brāk′) *n.* escape from prison.

jail-er (jā′lər) *also,* **jail-or;** *British,* **gaol-er.** *n.* keeper of a jail.

Jain (jīn) *n.* one who practices Jainism. —*adj.* of or relating to Jainism or the Jains. Also, **Jai-na** (jī′nə). [Hindi *jaina* saint, going back to Sanskrit *jinas* literally, one who overcomes.]

Jain-ism (jī′niz′əm) *n.* ascetic Hindu religion founded in the sixth century B.C. that teaches immortality of the soul and respect for all living things.

Jai-pur (jī′poor) *n.* city in northwestern India. Pop. (1969 est.), 533,-151.

Ja-kar-ta (jə kär′tə) Djakarta.

jake (jāk) *adj. Slang.* fine; all right. [Of uncertain origin.]

jal-ap (jal′əp) *n.* **1.** drug made from the dried roots of a plant, *Exogonium purga,* formerly used as a drastic cathartic. **2.** plant yielding this drug, grown esp. in Mexico and India. [French *jalap,* from Spanish *jalapa* the plant, from *Jalapa,* Mexican town from which the plant was first obtained.]

ja-lop-y (jə lop′ē) *pl.,* **-lop-ies.** *n. Informal.* old or broken-down automobile. [Of uncertain origin.]

jal-ou-sie (jal′ə sē, zhal′oo zē′) *n.* series of horizontal overlapping slats, often made of glass, that can be adjusted to regulate the passage of air and light. [French *jalousie* literally, jealousy, from *jaloux* envious, from Old French *jalous;* because, supposedly, a jealous person can watch through it without being seen. See JEALOUS.]

jam¹ (jam) **jammed, jam-ming.** *v.t.* **1.** to squeeze, force, or press into or through a tight or close space: *Ed jammed all his clothes into one large suitcase.* **2.** to fill or block up completely: *Shoppers jammed the stores at Christmas time.* **3.** to push, place, or thrust violently, esp. to apply (brakes) suddenly with maximum strength. **4.** to cause to become stuck or wedged so as to be unworkable, as a machine or moving part: *Rust and dirt had jammed the gate's old latch.* **5.** to bruise or crush: *The girl jammed her hand when she closed the drawer on it.* **6.** to interfere with (electronic signals) sent out by others, as by operating radio equipment at the same frequency. —*v.i.* **1.** to become stuck fast or wedged: *The key jammed in the lock.* **2.** to become unworkable through the sticking or wedging of some part: *The soldier's rifle jammed.* **3.** to force one's way into a confined space: *Thousands of people jam into the subways during rush hour.* **4.** to take part in a jam session; improvise jazz. —*n.* **1.** mass of people or things so tightly crowded together that movement is difficult or impossible. **2.** act of jamming; being jammed. **3.** *Informal.* difficult or troublesome situation; fix. [Possibly imitative.]

jam² (jam) *n.* food made by boiling fruit with sugar to a thick consistency, used as a spread on bread and other foods. [Probably from JAM¹; referring to fruit pressed tightly together in making jam.]

Jam., Jamaica.

Ja-mai-ca (jə mā′kə) *n.* island country of the Greater Antilles, in the Caribbean, south of Cuba. Capital, Kingston. Area, 4232 sq. mi. Pop. (1970 est.), 1,972,000. —**Ja-mai′can,** *adj., n.*

jamb (jam) *also,* **jambe.** *n.* post or surface forming the side of a doorway, window, or other opening. [French *jambe* leg, side post of a door, from Late Latin *gamba* hoof, leg, going back to Greek *kampē* bend, joint.]

jam-bo-ree (jam′bə rē′) *n.* **1.** noisy or festive gathering or celebration. **2.** large national or international assembly of Boy Scouts. [Of uncertain origin.]

James (jāmz) *n.* **1.** in the New Testament, one of Christ's Apostles, the son of Zebedee and brother of John. Also, **James the Greater. 2.** in the New Testament, one of Christ's Apostles. Also, **James the Less. 3.** an Epistle of the New Testament. **4. Henry.** 1843–1916, U.S. novelist and short-story writer. **5. Jes-se Wood-son** (jes′ē wood′sən). 1847–82, U.S. outlaw. **6. William.** 1842–1910, U.S. psychologist and philosopher; brother of Henry James. [Old French *James* masculine given name, going back to Late Latin *Jacomus,* form of Latin *Jacobus.* See JACOB.]

James I, 1566–1625, king of England from 1603 to 1625, and, as **James VI,** king of Scotland from 1567 to 1625.

James II, 1633–1701, king of England, Scotland, and Ireland from 1685 to 1688. He was deposed by Parliament.

James-town (jāmz′toun′) *n.* **1.** village in southeastern Virginia, the first permanent English settlement in America, founded in 1607. **2.** city in western New York. Pop. (1970), 39,795.

Jam-mu and Kashmir (jum′ōō) Kashmir.

jam-pack (jam′pak′) *v.t. Informal.* to fill or crowd to capacity: *The museum had been jam-packed by tourists all day.*

jam session, informal gathering of jazz musicians to improvise freely on various themes.

at; āpe; cär; end; mē; it; īce; hot; ōld; fôrk; wood; fōōl; oil; out; up; ūse; turn; sing; thin; this; zh in treasure; ə in ago, taken, pencil, lemon, circus.

Jan., January.
jan·gle (jang′gəl) -gled, -gling. v.i. 1. to make a harsh or discordant sound. 2. to quarrel; bicker. —v.t. 1. to cause to make a harsh or discordant sound. 2. to have an upsetting or irritating effect on: *The constant noise jangled his nerves.* —n. 1. harsh or discordant sound. 2. quarrel; bickering. [Old French *jangler* to chatter; of Germanic origin.] —**jan′gler,** n.
Jan·is·sar·y (jan′ə ser′ē) pl., -sar·ies. also, jan·is·sar·y, Jan·i·zar·y, jan·i·zar·y (jan′ə zer′ē). n. soldier in an elite Turkish army corps that served as the sultan's guard and was also a powerful fighting force. The corps was established about 1330 and abolished in 1826. [French *janissaire,* from Italian *giannizzero,* from Turkish *yeñicheri* literally, new troop.]
jan·i·tor (jan′ə tər) n. one employed to clean and service a building or establishment, as an apartment house, school, or office. [Latin *jānitor* doorkeeper, porter, from *jānua* door, from *Jānus* Roman god of gates and doors.] —**jan′i·tress,** n.
Jan·u·ar·y (jan′yōō er′ē) pl., -ar·ies. n. first month of the year, containing thirty-one days. [Latin *Jānuārius* (*mēnsis*) (month) of the god Janus, from *Jānus;* because a feast day of Janus occurred during this month.]
Ja·nus (jā′nəs) n. Roman god of gates and doors who presided over beginnings and endings, conventionally represented as having two faces looking in opposite directions. [Latin *Jānus.*]
Ja·nus-faced (jā′nəs fāst′) adj. two-faced; hypocritical; deceitful.
Jap (jap) n., adj. Slang. Japanese. ▲ usually considered offensive.
Jap. 1. Japan. 2. Japanese.
ja·pan (jə pan′) n. 1. any of various durable, glossy, black lacquers or varnishes, originally from Japan, used for coating objects. 2. work varnished and decorated in the manner developed by the Japanese. —adj. relating to or varnished with japan. —v.t. -panned, -pan·ning. to varnish or lacquer with or as with japan.
Ja·pan (jə pan′) n. 1. island country in the North Pacific, off the eastern coast of Asia. Capital, Tokyo. Land area, 142,727 sq. mi. Pop. (1969 est.), 102,833,000. Also, **Nip·pon′.** 2. **Sea of.** arm of the Pacific separating Japan from the Asian mainland.
Japan Current, warm current in the western North Pacific flowing northeast past southeastern Japan.
Jap·a·nese (jap′ə nēz′, -nēs′) adj. of or relating to Japan, its people, their language, or culture. —n. pl., -nese. 1. member or close descendant of the people of Japan. 2. language of Japan.
Japanese beetle, small destructive beetle, *Popillia japonica,* introduced into the United States from Japan, that has red wings and a greenish oval body, and feeds on various plants.

Japanese beetle

jape (jāp) japed, jap·ing. Archaic. v.i. to joke; jest. —v.t. to make fun of; mock. —n. joke; jest; gibe. [Probably blend of Old French *japer* to yelp (imitative) and Old French *gaber* to mock (from Old Norse *gabba*).] —**jap′er, jap′er·y,** n.
ja·pon·i·ca (jə pon′i kə) n. 1. camellia. 2. Oriental shrub, *Chaenomeles lagenaria,* of the rose family, usually bearing scarlet, pink, or white flowers. Also, **Japanese quince.** [Modern Latin *japonica* literally, Japanese, from *Japonia* Japan. See JAPAN.]
jar[1] (jär) n. 1. wide-mouthed, usually cylindrical container or vessel that is usually made of glass or earthenware. 2. amount contained in a jar; contents of a jar: *The boy ate a whole jar of jam.* [French *jarre* large earthen vessel, from Arabic *jarrah.*]
jar[2] (jär) jarred, jar·ring. v.t. 1. to cause to shake or vibrate; cause to move suddenly by impact or shock: *The explosion jarred the building.* 2. to have a harsh, disturbing, or unpleasant effect on: *The sudden clatter jarred her nerves.* —v.i. 1. to shake, vibrate, or move suddenly from impact or shock. 2. to have an irritating or upsetting effect: *His snide laugh jars on my nerves.* 3. to clash; conflict: *This verse . . . jars with the words which precede and follow* (Arnold, 1873). 4. to make a harsh or discordant sound. —n. 1. shake or sudden movement; shock; jolt. 2. sudden disturbing effect on the mind or senses. 3. harsh or discordant sound or combination of sounds. [Probably imitative.] —**jar′ring·ly,** adv.
jar[3] (jär) n. **on the jar.** ajar; partially open. [Old English *c(i)err* turning.]
jar·di·niere (järd′ən ēr′, zhärd′ən yār′) n. ornamental pot or stand for flowers or plants. [French *jardinière,* feminine of *jardinier* of the garden, from *jardin* garden; of Germanic origin.]
jar·ful (jär′fool) pl., -fuls. n. amount that a jar holds.
jar·gon (jär′gən, -gon) n. 1. confused, unintelligible, or meaningless speech or writing; gibberish. 2. technical or specialized language or phraseology of a particular profession, sect, or other group; cant: *legal*

jargon. 3. mixture of two or more languages or dialects, esp. such a mixture serving as a lingua franca. —v.i. to talk jargon. [Old French *jargon* chatter; probably of imitative origin.] —**Syn.** 2. see **lingo.**
jarl (yärl) n. ancient Scandinavian chieftain or nobleman. [Old Norse *jarl.*]
Jas., James.
jas·mine (jaz′min, jas′-) n. 1. fragrant bell-shaped flower of any of a large group of plants, genus *Jasminum,* of the olive family, growing in yellow, white, or pink. 2. shrub bearing clusters of these flowers, widely cultivated throughout the world. 3. any of several unrelated plants that bear sweet-scented flowers, as the **yellow jessamine,** *Gelsemium sempervirens,* or the **cape jasmine,** *Gardenia jasminoides.* Also, **jes′sa·mine.** [French *jasmin* the shrub, from Arabic *yāsamīn,* from Persian *yāsmīn.*]
Ja·son (jā′sən) n. Greek Legend. hero who led the Argonauts in quest of the Golden Fleece.
jas·per (jas′pər) n. opaque quartz, usually reddish, brown, or yellow. [Old French *jaspre,* from Latin *iaspis* a green precious stone prized by the ancients, from Greek *iaspis;* of Semitic origin.]
ja·to (jā′tō) n. takeoff of an aircraft with the aid of small, auxiliary rocket or jet engines. [J(ET)[1] + A(SSISTED) + T(AKE)O(FF).]
jaun·dice (jôn′dis, jän′-) n. 1. yellow discoloration of the skin, the whites of the eyes, and the mucous membranes, due to an excess of bile pigment in the blood. 2. state of mind or feeling that colors the point of view or distorts the judgment. —v.t. -diced, -dic·ing. to affect so as to distort the judgment; prejudice. [Old French *jaunice* yellowness, from *jaune* yellow, from Latin *galbinus* greenish-yellow.]
jaun·diced (jôn′dist, jän′-) adj. 1. affected with jaundice. 2. affected or distorted by envy, jealousy, bitterness, or similar feeling; prejudiced.
jaunt (jônt, jänt) n. short trip, esp. one taken for pleasure. —v.i. to take such a trip. [Of uncertain origin.]
jaunting car, light, two-wheeled open cart used in Ireland, having lengthwise seats set back to back or face to face.
jaun·ty (jôn′tē, jän′-) -ti·er, -ti·est. adj. 1. lively, carefree, or self-confident in air or manner; sprightly. 2. smart; stylish: *He wore a jaunty cap and jacket.* [French *gentil* nice, pleasing, from Old French *gentil* nobly born, from Latin *gentīlis* of the same clan, from *gēns* race, clan. Doublet of GENTEEL, GENTILE, GENTLE.] —**jaun′ti·ly,** adv. —**jaun′ti·ness,** n.
Jav., Javanese.
Ja·va (jä′və, jav′ə) n. 1. large island of Indonesia, in the Malay Archipelago. Area, approx. 50,000 sq. mi. Pop. (1967 est.), 72,600,000. 2. coffee grown on Java and other nearby islands. 3. also, java. Informal. any coffee.
Java man, extinct primitive man having many apelike features but able to walk erect, whose fossil remains, dating from the early Ice Age, were found in central Java. First classified as *Pithecanthropus erectus,* it is now generally classified as *Homo erectus,* together with Peking man and certain other human fossil remains. Also, **Pith′e·can′thro·pus.**
Jav·a·nese (jav′ə nēz′, -nēs′) adj. of or relating to Java, its people, their language, or culture. —n. pl., -nese. 1. member or close descendant of the people of Java. 2. language belonging to the Malayo-Polynesian family of languages, spoken predominantly in Java.
Java Sea, part of the South Pacific, between Java and Borneo.
jave·lin (jav′lin, jav′ə-) n. 1. light spear, used chiefly as a weapon. 2.a. lightweight, spearlike shaft, about 8½ feet long, made of wood or metal, thrown for distance in athletic contests. b. contest in which it is thrown. Also (def. 2b), **javelin throw.** [Middle French *javeline* long, thin dart; possibly of Celtic origin.]
Ja·velle water (zhə vel′) also, **Ja·vel water.** solution of potassium or sodium hypochlorite in water, used as a bleach and disinfectant. [From French (eau de) *Javel* (water of) Javel, former French town, now part of Paris, where it was first produced.]
jaw (jô) n. 1. either of the two bony structures forming the framework of the mouth and holding the teeth, esp. the lower of these structures. 2. also, **jaws.** part of the face covering these structures; the mouth and its related parts. 3. either of a pair of parts, as of a tool, that can be closed to grasp or hold something: *the jaws of a vise.* 4. **jaws.** any situation or position that suggests the closing or grasping action of a pair of jaws: *the jaws of danger,* to snatch victory *from the jaws of defeat.* 5. one of the sides or walls of a pass, chasm, canyon, or similar opening. 6. Slang. a. impudent or offensive talk. b. talk; chatter. —v.i. Slang. to talk; chatter. [Anglo-Norman *jowe,* Old French *joe* cheek; of uncertain origin.]
jaw·bone (jô′bōn′) n. one of the bones of the jaw, esp. the mandible.
jaw·break·er (jô′brā′kər) n. 1. very hard, usually round candy or chewing gum. 2. Informal. word that is difficult to pronounce.
jay (jā) n. 1. any of various harsh-voiced birds, family Corvidae, related to crows and magpies, often crested and having brightly colored plumage, as the blue jay or the **Canada jay,** *Perisoreus canadensis.* Length: 1 foot. 2. Slang. silly, stupid, gullible, or inexperienced person.

[Middle French *jay* the bird, from Late Latin *gaius;* probably imitative of the bird's sound.]

Jay, John (jā) 1745–1829, U.S. statesman and first chief justice of the United States, from 1789 to 1795.

jay·walk (jā′wôk′) *v.i.* to cross a street without paying attention to traffic regulations or signals. [JAY in the sense of simpleton + WALK.] —**jay′walk′er,** *n.*

jazz (jaz) *n.* **1.** music of a style that was originated by American Negroes, primarily in the southern United States, late in the nineteenth century. It is characterized by improvisation, strong rhythm, syncopation, and unusual tonal effects. **2.** *Slang.* liveliness; animation. **3.** *Slang.* **a.** exaggerated, insincere, or idle talk: *The salesman gave us a lot of jazz about the car.* **b.** information or material of a related or miscellaneous nature: *a book on knights and castles and all that jazz.* —*v.t.* **1.** to play or arrange (music) as jazz. **2. to jazz up.** to make more lively or exciting: *to jazz up a lecture with some funny stories.* [Of uncertain origin.]

jazz·y (jaz′ē) jazz·i·er, jazz·i·est. *adj.* **1.** resembling or characteristic of jazz music. **2.** *Slang.* lively; flashy. —**jazz′i·ly,** *adv.* —**jazz′i·ness,** *n.*

JCS, Joint Chiefs of Staff.

jct., junction.

JD, juvenile delinquent.

jeal·ous (jel′əs) *adj.* **1.** fearful or suspicious of losing to someone else what one wishes to gain or keep, esp. the love or affection of another: *The woman's flirtations made her husband jealous.* **2.** envious or resentful of a person or of that person's attainments or advantages: *The girl was jealous of her friend's good looks.* **3.** arising from feelings of apprehension, suspicion, envy, or resentment: *jealous anger.* **4.** watchful or careful in guarding or keeping something: *jealous of hard-won liberties.* **5.** demanding exclusive worship and faithfulness. [Old French *jalous* fearful or suspicious of rivalry, from Late Latin *zēlōsus* full of fervor, from *zēlus* fervor, jealousy, from Greek *zēlos.*] —**jeal′ous·ly,** *adv.* —**jeal′ous·ness,** *n.* —**Syn. 2.** see **envious.**

jeal·ous·y (jel′ə sē) *pl.,* -ous·ies. *n.* state or quality of being jealous; jealous feeling or attitude.

jean (jēn) *n.* **1.** strong, twilled cotton fabric, used chiefly for sportswear and work clothes. **2. jeans.** trousers or overalls made of this fabric or denim; dungarees. [French *Gênes* Genoa, where this fabric was first produced.]

Jeanne d'Arc (zhän därk′) Joan of Arc.

Jeb·el Mu·sa (jeb′əl mōō′sä) mountain in northern Morocco, known to ancient geographers as one of the Pillars of Hercules.

jeep (jēp) *n.* motor vehicle with four-wheel drive and usually a quarter-ton carrying capacity, used chiefly for transport, esp. by the armed forces. [Supposedly from *G.P.,* abbreviation of general purpose, used by the U.S. Army to designate this vehicle.]

jeer (jēr) *v.i.* to speak or shout in a derisive or mocking manner; scoff. —*v.t.* to treat or address with derision or mockery; taunt. —*n.* derisive or mocking remark; taunt. [Of uncertain origin.] —**jeer′er,** *n.*

Syn. *v.i.* **Jeer, sneer, scoff** mean to show contempt. **Jeer** means to mock or deride in a coarse and loud manner: *The crowd jeered at the losing team.* **Sneer** means to show disdain and contempt by a caustic tone or scornful expression: *Cynics sneer at everything sentimental.* **Scoff** implies to be irreverent in an insulting manner: *Those who came to scoff remained to pray* (Goldsmith, 1724).

Jef·fer·son, Thomas (jef′ər sən) 1743–1826, third president of the United States, from 1801 to 1809.

Jefferson City, capital of Missouri, in the central part of the state. Pop. (1970), 32,407.

Jef·fer·so·ni·an (jef′ər sō′nē ən) *adj.* of, relating to, or characteristic of Thomas Jefferson or his political principles. —*n.* supporter of Thomas Jefferson or his political principles. —**Jef′fer·so′ni·an·ism,** *n.*

Je·hosh·a·phat (ji hosh′ə fat′, -hos′-) *n.* in the Old Testament, a king of Judah in the ninth century B.C.

Je·ho·vah (ji hō′və) *n.* in the Old Testament, God. [Transliteration of Hebrew *JHVH* or *YHWH* (with the addition of vowels), used to refer to God.]

Jehovah's Witnesses, Christian sect, founded in the United States in the late nineteenth century, that believes in the imminent end of the world and is strongly opposed to war and to the authority of the government in matters of conscience.

je·june (ji jōōn′) *adj.* **1.** lacking in nourishment; insubstantial; meager: *a jejune diet.* **2.** lacking interest, significance, or value; dull or empty: *a jejune speech.* **3.** unsophisticated; juvenile: *jejune behavior.* [Latin *jējūnus* fasting, barren, insignificant.] —**je·june′ly,** *adv.* —**je·june′ness, je·ju′ni·ty,** *n.*

je·ju·num (ji jōō′nəm) *pl.,* -na. *n.* middle section of the small intestine, extending from the duodenum to the ileum. [Modern Latin *jējunum,* from Latin *jējūnus* fasting; referring to the belief of the ancient Greek physician Galen that it was empty after death.]

Jek·yll and Hyde (jek′əl, jē′kəl) **1.** two characters in a story by Robert Louis Stevenson, the kindly Dr. Jekyll and the evil Mr. Hyde, who are actually opposing identities of the same person. **2.** one who has or seems to have a personality distinctly split into a good side and an evil side. [From *The Strange Case of Dr. Jekyll and Mr. Hyde* (1886).]

jell (jel) *v.i.* **1.** to become or come to the consistency of jelly. **2.** *Informal.* to assume definite form; become clear: *His political ideas began to jell after he entered college.* —*v.t.* *Informal.* to cause to assume definite form; make clear. —*n.* jelly. [From JELLY.]

jel·lied (jel′ēd) *adj.* **1.** having or brought to the consistency of jelly; congealed. **2.** spread or made with jelly or prepared in jelly.

jel·lo (jel′ō) *n.* gelatin dessert. Trademark: Jell-O.

jel·ly (jel′ē) *pl.,* -lies. *n.* **1.** any food preparation consisting mainly of gelatin or pectin and having a smooth, firm, somewhat elastic consistency and a semitransparent appearance, esp. such a preparation made of boiled fruit juice and sugar. **2.** anything having the consistency of jelly or resembling jelly. —*v.t.,* -lied, -ly·ing. **1.** to make into jelly. **2.** to spread or prepare with jelly. —*v.i.* to become or come to the consistency of jelly. [Old French *gelee* frost, gelatin, going back to Latin *gelāta,* feminine past participle of *gelāre* to freeze, congeal.]

jel·ly·bean (jel′ē bēn′) *also,* **jelly bean.** *n.* small egg-shaped candy having a hard outer coating and a gelatinous center.

jel·ly·fish (jel′ē fish′) *pl.,* -fish or -fish·es. *n.* **1.** any of a group of umbrella-shaped animals, classes Hydrozoa and Scyphozoa, found chiefly in salt water and having a soft, gelatinous body with threadlike tentacles that are studded with stinging cells. **2.** *Informal.* weak, fearful, or indecisive person.

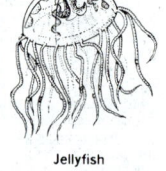

Jellyfish

Jen·ghis Khan (jeng′giz kän′) *also,* **Jen·ghiz Khan.** Genghis Khan.

Jen·ner, Edward (jen′ər) 1749–1823, English physician who discovered vaccination as a means of producing immunity to smallpox.

jen·net (jen′it) *n.* small Spanish horse. [French *genet,* from Spanish *jinete* horseman, from Arabic *Zenāta* a Berber tribe noted for its horsemanship.]

jen·ny (jen′ē) *pl.,* -nies. *n.* **1.** spinning jenny. **2.** female of certain animals, esp. a female wren or female donkey. [From *Jenny,* familiar form of the proper name *Jane.*]

jeop·ard·ize (jep′ər dīz′) -ized, -iz·ing. *v.t.* to expose to loss or injury; endanger; imperil. —**Syn.** see **imperil.**

jeop·ard·y (jep′ər dē) *n.* **1.** danger of loss, injury, or death; peril: *The fireman put his own life in jeopardy to save the child.* **2.** danger of conviction and punishment to which a defendant is exposed when put on trial for a crime. [Old French *jeu parti* game in which the chances are even, even chance; literally, divided game, going back to Latin *jocus* jest, game + *partire* to divide.]

Jeph·thah (jef′thə) *n.* in the Old Testament, a judge of Israel who sacrificed his only daughter to fulfill a rash vow.

Jer., Jeremiah.

jer·bo·a (jər bō′ə) *n.* any of various mouselike, jumping rodents, family Dipodidae, of desert regions of Eurasia and Africa, having very long hind legs, a long tufted tail, and a silky buff-colored coat. Length: 6–18 inches including the tail. [Modern Latin *jerboa,* from Arabic *yarbū* flesh of the loins; referring to the strong muscles in its hind legs.]

Jerboa

jer·e·mi·ad (jer′ə mī′ad) *n.* anguished or doleful complaint or denunciation; lamentation; tale of woe. [French *jérémiade,* from *Jérémie* Jeremiah; referring to *Lamentations,* a book of the Old Testament attributed to Jeremiah.]

Jer·e·mi·ah (jer′ə mī′ə) *also,* in the Douay Bible, **Jer·e·mi·as.** *n.* **1.** Hebrew prophet of the seventh and sixth centuries B.C. who denounced and lamented the evils of his time. **2.** book of prophecies in the Old Testament, attributed to Jeremiah.

Jer·i·cho (jer′ə kō′) *n.* **1.** ancient Palestinian city near the northern tip of the Red Sea. According to the Old Testament, it was miraculously captured by Joshua, whose soldiers toppled the walls of the city by sounding their trumpets. **2.** town in western Jordan on the site of ancient Jericho. Pop. (1961), 10,166.

jerk¹ (jurk) *n.* **1.** sharp, abrupt pull, twist, or similar movement. **2.** sudden, involuntary muscle contraction caused by reflex action. **3.** *Informal.* stupid, dull, or unconventional person. —*v.t.* **1.** to move or throw (something) with a sudden, sharp motion; give a sharp, abrupt pull, twist, or push to. **2.** to utter in an abrupt or sharply broken manner

at; āpe; cär; end; mē; it; īce; hot; ōld; fôrk; wood; fōōl; oil; out; up; ūse; turn; sing; thin; this; zh in treasure; ə in ago, taken, pencil, lemon, circus.

(with *out*). —*v.i.* **1.** to move with a sudden, sharp motion or series of such motions. **2.** to make spasmodic movements. [Probably imitative.]

jerk² (jurk) *v.t.* to cure (meat) by cutting it into strips and drying it, usually in the sun. [Modification of Spanish *charquear*, from *charqui* dried meat, from Quechua *charqui*.]

jer·kin (jur′kin) *n.* short, close-fitting jacket or waistcoat, usually sleeveless and often made of leather, worn chiefly in the sixteenth and seventeenth centuries. [Of uncertain origin.]

jerk·wa·ter (jurk′wô tər) *adj. Informal.* **1.** small and out-of-the-way: *a jerkwater town.* **2.** ridiculously or contemptibly insignificant: *some unknown jerkwater politician.* [An old railroad expression for a remote place where it was necessary to "jerk" or draw water in buckets for trains.]

jerk·y¹ (jur′kē) **jerk·i·er, jerk·i·est.** *adj.* **1.** characterized by abrupt movements; moving with sudden starts and stops: *a jerky subway ride.* **2.** *Informal.* stupid; foolish: *a jerky idea.* [JERK¹ + -Y¹.] —**jerk′i·ly,** *adv.* —**jerk′i·ness,** *n.*

Jerkin

jerk·y² (jur′kē) *n.* meat, esp. beef, that has been jerked. Also, **jerked beef.** [Modification of Spanish *charqui.* See JERK².]

Jer·o·bo·am (jer′ə bō′əm) *n.* **1.** in the Old Testament, founder and first king of the northern kingdom of Israel in the tenth century B.C. After Solomon's death, he led the ten northern tribes in a revolt against Solomon's oppressive successor. **2. jeroboam.** wine bottle having a capacity of about four-fifths of a gallon.

Je·rome, Saint (jə rōm′) A.D. c.342–420, monk and Church Father, author of the Vulgate.

Jer·ry (jer′ē) *pl.,* **-ries.** *also,* **jer·ry.** *n. Slang.* German, esp. a German soldier. [Modification of GERMAN.]

jer·ry-built (jer′ē bilt′) *adj.* built or put together carelessly or hastily or with poor materials: *a jerry-built cottage.* [Possibly a blend of the proper name *Jerry* with JURY².]

jer·sey (jur′zē) *pl.,* **-seys.** *n.* **1.** machine-knitted fabric made of wool, cotton, silk, or man-made fibers, used for clothing. **2.** knitted sweater or shirt made of this or a similar fabric, usually a close-fitting pullover. [From *Jersey,* British island where this fabric was originally made.]

Jer·sey (jur′zē) *pl.,* **-seys.** *n.* **1.** British island in the English Channel, off the coast of France, the largest of the Channel Islands. Area, approx. 45 sq. mi. Pop. (1961), 63,345. **2.** one of a breed of usually fawn-colored dairy cattle originally developed on this island, the female of which produces milk with a very high butterfat content. **3.** *Informal.* New Jersey.

Jersey City, port city in northeastern New Jersey, on the Hudson, opposite New York City. Pop. (1970), 260,545.

Je·ru·sa·lem (jə rōō′sə ləm) *n.* historic city in central Palestine, now capital of Israel. It is a holy city for Jews, Christians, and Muslims. Pop. (1968 est.), 275,000.

Jerusalem artichoke **1.** sunflower of the species *Helianthus tuberosus,* widely cultivated in North America and Europe, having large, rough leaves, yellow flower heads, and a potatolike tuber that is eaten as a vegetable. **2.** the tuber itself. [Modification of Italian *girasole* sunflower (going back to Latin *gȳrāre* to turn + *sōl* sun) + ARTICHOKE.]

jess (jes) *n.* strap, used in falconry, that is fastened around a falcon's leg, to which a leash or bell may be attached. —*v.t.* to fasten a jess or jesses on. [Old French *ges* a throwing, going back to Latin *jactus.*]

jes·sa·mine (jes′ə min) *n.* jasmine.

Jes·se (jes′ē) *n.* in the Old Testament, the father of David.

jest (jest) *n.* **1.** something said or done to provoke laughter; witticism or prank; joke. **2.** frivolous or facetious mood or manner; playfulness; fun: *Many a true word is said in jest.* **3.** mocking remark; jeer. **4.** object of laughter or mockery; laughingstock. —*v.i.* **1.** to speak or act in a playful or facetious manner. **2.** to make humorous or witty remarks. **3.** to utter gibes or taunts; scoff: *He jests at scars, that never felt a wound* (Shakespeare, *Romeo and Juliet*). **4.** to poke fun at; deride. [Old French *geste* exploit, tale, from Latin *gesta* (neuter plural) exploits.] —**Syn.** *n.* **1.** see **joke.**

jest·er (jes′tər) *n.* one who jests, esp. a clown formerly kept in royal courts and noble households to provide entertainment.

Je·su (jē′zōō, jā′-, yā′-) *n. Archaic.* Jesus.

Jes·u·it (jezh′ōō it, jez′-) *n.* member of the Society of Jesus, a Roman Catholic religious order for men that was founded by Ignatius of Loyola in 1534. [Modern Latin *Jesuita,* from JESUS.]

Je·sus (jē′zəs) c.4 B.C.–A.D. c.29, founder of Christianity, considered by Christians to be the Son of God and the Messiah. [Late Latin *Jēsūs* Jesus, Joshua, from Greek *Iēsous,* from Hebrew *Yēshūa'* Joshua, from earlier *Yehōshūa.* See JOSHUA.]

Jesus Christ, Jesus.

jet¹ (jet) *n.* **1.** stream of liquid, gas, or vapor, forcefully or suddenly emitted from a nozzle, spout, or narrow opening. **2.** something issued in or as in such a stream. **3.** nozzle or spout for emitting such a stream: *the gas jets of a stove.* **4.a.** jet plane. **b.** jet engine. —*v.i.* **jet·ted, jet·ting. 1.** to be shot forth in a stream. **2.** to travel by jet plane. —*v.t.* **1.** to shoot (something) forth in a stream. **2.** to transport by jet plane. [Old French *jeter* to throw, going back to Latin *jactāre.*]

jet² (jet) *n.* **1.** dense, deep-black lignite coal capable of taking a high polish, formerly used to make jewelry. **2.** any of several other materials, as black quartz or glass, finished in imitation of this and now used to make jewelry. **3.** deep-black color. —*adj.* **1.** made of or resembling jet. **2.** jet-black. [Old French *jaiet* hard black mineral, from Latin *gagā-tēs,* from Greek *gagātēs* literally, stone of *Gagai,* an ancient town in Asia Minor.]

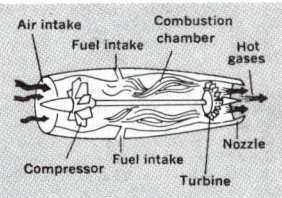

Air intake / Combustion chamber / Fuel intake / Hot gases / Compressor / Fuel intake / Nozzle / Turbine

Gas turbine jet engine

jet-black (jet′blak′) *adj.* black as jet; deep-black.

jet engine **1.** engine that produces propulsive power by burning a mixture of fuel and atmospheric oxygen which is ejected to the rear as hot exhaust gases. **2.** any engine that produces propulsive power by ejecting a stream of fluid.

jet plane, airplane driven by jet propulsion.

jet-pro·pelled (jet′prə peld′) *adj.* driven by jet propulsion.

jet propulsion **1.** propulsion by means of a jet of fluid, as hot gas, whose ejection in one direction causes the ejecting body or vehicle to move in the opposite direction. **2.** propulsion by means of one or more jet engines.

jet·sam (jet′səm) *n.* **1.** cargo or equipment cast overboard in order to lighten a ship in distress. **2.** such discarded cargo or equipment found washed ashore. Distinguished from **flotsam. 3.** discarded, worthless, or miscellaneous things; odds and ends. [Modification of JETTISON.]

jet set, social set composed of people who spend much of their time jetting to various places considered fashionable.

jet stream **1.** high-speed air current, usually found between seven and nine miles above the earth's surface, that moves generally west to east at speeds reaching over 200 miles per hour. **2.** high-speed stream of gas or other fluid ejected from a jet engine.

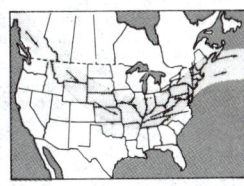

Jet stream

jet·ti·son (jet′ə sən, -zən) *v.t.* **1.** to throw (cargo or equipment) overboard or off, esp. in order to lighten a ship or aircraft in distress. **2.** to cast off or discard (something unwanted, useless, or burdensome). —*n.* **1.** act of jettisoning. **2.** jetsam (*defs. 1, 2*). [Old French *getaison* a throwing, from Latin *jactātiō.*]

jet·ty¹ (jet′ē) *pl.,* **-ties.** *n.* structure of timber, concrete, steel, or a combination of these materials, built out into a body of water in order to influence the current or protect a harbor or coast. **2.** wharf; pier. [Old French *jetee* a throwing, structure "thrown out" to protect a harbor, from *jeter* to throw, going back to Latin *jactāre.*]

jet·ty² (jet′ē) *adj.* resembling or made of jet; black as jet. [From JET².] —**jet′ti·ness,** *n.*

jeu d'es·prit (zhœ' des prē′) *pl.,* **jeux d'es·prit.** *French.* witty remark or piece of writing; witticism.

Jew (jōō) *n.* **1.** member of a geographically dispersed people descended from the group of Semitic tribes who lived in and among ancient Palestine and among whom the beliefs and laws of Judaism were developed and followed; Hebrew. **2.** one whose religion is Judaism. [Old French *giu, juiu,* from Latin *Jūdaeus,* from Greek *Ioudaios,* going back to Hebrew *Yehūdāh* Judah (ancestor of the tribe of Judah in the Bible).]

jew·el (jōō′əl) *n.* **1.** precious stone; gem. **2.** any article of personal adornment, as a ring, bracelet, or brooch, usually made of cut and polished gems in a setting of precious metal. **3.** person or thing of great value or rare excellence. **4.** gem or substitute for a gem used as a bearing, in a watch, because of its durability. —*v.t.,* **-eled, -el·ing;** *also, British.* **-elled, -el·ling.** to set or adorn with or as with jewels. [Old French *jouel, joiel* gem, possibly from Late Latin *jocālia* gems, trinkets, from Latin *jocus* jest, game.]

---

jew·el·er (jōō′ə lər) *also, British,* **jew·el·ler.** *n.* one who makes, repairs, or deals in jewelry.

jew·el·ry (jōō′əl rē) *also, British,* **jew·el·ler·y** *n.* precious stones or other articles, as of gold, silver, or glass, for personal ornamentation; jewels collectively: *costume jewelry.*

jew·el·weed (jōō′əl wēd′) *n.* touch-me-not *(def. 1).*

Jew·ess (jōō′is) *n.* Jewish girl or woman.

jew·fish (jōō′fish′) *pl.* **fish** *or* **-fish·es.** *n.* any of several dark-green or black, rough-scaled sea bass, found in warm waters of the Atlantic and Pacific, valued as food fish.

Jew·ish (jōō′ish) *adj.* of, relating to, belonging to, or characteristic of the Jews or their culture. —*n.* Yiddish.

Jewish calendar, calendar used by the Jews, esp. for dating religious observances. It dates the Creation at 3761 B.C.

Jew·ry (jōō′rē) *pl.,* **-ries.** *n.* **1.** Jews collectively; the Jewish people. **2.** *Archaic.* ghetto. [Old French *juerie,* from *giu.* See JEW.]

jew's-harp (jōō′härp′) *also,* **jews'-harp.** *n.* small musical instrument, held between the teeth when played, that consists of a lyre-shaped metal frame and a flexible metal tongue and that produces a twanging tone when the free end of the tongue is plucked.

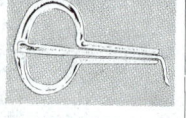

Jew's-harp

Jez·e·bel (jez′ə bel′, -bəl) *n.* **1.** in the Old Testament, the wicked wife of Ahab, king of Israel. **2.** *also,* **jezebel.** shameless or wicked woman.

jg. junior grade.

jib¹ (jib) *n.* **1.** triangular sail set on a stay forward of the mast or foremast, usually smaller than the mainsail. **2. the cut of one's jib.** *Informal.* one's appearance or manner. [Of uncertain origin.]

jib² (jib) **jibbed, jib·bing.** *v.i.* to jibe¹. [Possibly form of JIBE¹.]

jib³ (jib) **jibbed, jib·bing.** *v.i.* to refuse to proceed or advance; balk. —*n.* horse or other animal that jibs. Also, **jib′ber.** [Possibly from JIB².]

jib⁴ (jib) *n.* boom of a crane or derrick. [Possibly short for GIBBET.]

jib boom, spar that extends out from the bowsprit and to which a jib may be attached.

jibe¹ (jīb) **jibed, jib·ing.** *v.i.* **1.** to shift a fore-and-aft sail or its boom from one side of a boat or ship to the other when sailing before the wind. [Modification (influenced by *jib¹*) of obsolete Dutch *gijben,* form of Dutch *gijpen.*]

jibe² (jīb) *n.* gibe. —*v.i., v.t.,* **jibed, jib·ing.** to gibe. [Form of GIBE.] —**jib′er,** *n.*

jibe³ (jīb) **jibed, jib·ing.** *also,* **jive.** *v.i. Informal.* to be in harmony or accord; agree. [Of uncertain origin.]

Jid·da (jid′ə) *n.* port city in western Saudi Arabia, on the Red Sea, near Mecca. Pop. (1965 est.) 194,000.

jif·fy (jif′ē) *pl.* **jif·fies.** *n. Informal.* very short time; moment; instant. Also, **jiff.** [Of uncertain origin.]

jig (jig) *n.* **1.a.** fast, lively dance, usually in triple time. **b.** music for this dance. **2.** device used for guiding a tool, as a drill, or for holding material to be worked on in place during the operation of such a tool. **3.** fishhook, or set of fishhooks, attached to a colorful artificial lure and kept moving in the water to attract fish. **4. the jig is up.** *Informal.* the game is over; all hope or chance of success is gone. —*v.i.,* **jigged, jig·ging. 1.** to dance or play a jig. **2.** to move with a rapid jerking or bobbing motion. **3.** to fish with a jig. **4.** to work with or operate a jig. —*v.t.* **1.** to dance (a jig or other lively dance). **2.** to move (something) with a rapid jerking or bobbing motion. **3.** to cut, form, or produce with the aid of a jig. [Possibly from Old French *giguer* to dance, frolic, from *gigue* fiddle; of Germanic origin.]

jig·ger¹ (jig′ər) *n.* **1.a.** small glass or cup used to measure liquor, holding about an ounce and a half. **b.** amount contained in a jigger. **2.** jig *(def. 3).* **3.** any of various machines or mechanical devices that operate with a jerking motion. **4.a.** light, general-purpose tackle used on a boat or ship. **b.** small sail set in the stern of a yawl or similar boat. **c.** jigger mast. **5.** one who jigs. **6.** *Informal.* any small device, article, or part that one is unable to name more precisely; thingamabob. [JIG + -ER¹.]

jig·ger² (jig′ər) *n.* chigger. [Form of CHIGGER.]

jigger mast 1. aftermost mast of a ship having four or more masts. **2.** mast in the stern of a yawl or similar boat.

jig·gle (jig′əl) **-gled, -gling.** *v.t., v.i.* to move up and down or to and fro with quick, slight, jerking motions. —*n.* jiggling movement. [JIG + -LE.]

jig·saw (jig′sô′) *n.* saw with a narrow blade set vertically in a frame, used to cut curved or irregular lines.

jigsaw puzzle, puzzle consisting of a set of irregularly shaped cardboard or wood pieces that can be fitted together to form a picture.

jilt (jilt) *v.t.* to cast off or desert (a lover or sweetheart). —*n.* woman who jilts a lover or sweetheart. [Contraction of earlier *jillet* flirt, wench, diminutive of *Jill,* female proper name once used as a term for girl or sweetheart.] —**jilt′er,** *n.*

Jim-Crow (jim′krō′) *also,* **jim-crow.** *adj. Informal.* promoting, sanctioning, or effecting segregation of or discrimination against Negroes: *a Jim-Crow law.* —*v.t.* to subject to segregation or discrimination.

Jim Crow *also,* **jim crow.** *Informal.* **1.** segregation of or discrimination against Negroes. Also, **Jim Crow′ism. 2.** Negro. ▲ usually considered offensive in def. 2. [From *Jim Crow,* a name in a nineteenth-century American Negro song.]

jim·my (jim′ē) *pl.,* **-mies.** *n.* short crowbar used esp. by burglars. —*v.t.,* **-mied, -my·ing.** to force or pry open with or as with a jimmy: *to jimmy a window.* [From *Jimmy,* familiar form of JAMES; example of the use of a nickname for a tool.]

jim·son·weed (jim′sən wēd′) *also,* **Jimson weed.** *n.* poisonous, rank-smelling plant, *Datura stramonium,* of the nightshade family, found in the tropics and many parts of North America, having large oval leaves and white or purple trumpet-shaped flowers. Also, **stra·mo′ni·um.** [Modification of *Jamestown weed,* a weed named after *Jamestown,* Virginia.]

jin·gle (jing′gəl) **-gled, -gling.** *v.i.* **1.** to make a light, metallic tinkling or ringing sound: *The coins jingled in his pocket.* **2.** to be full of simple, catchy rhymes or repetitions. —*v.t.* **1.** to cause to make a tinkling or ringing sound: *to jingle keys.* —*n.* **1.** light, metallic tinkling or ringing sound: *the jingle of the cowboy's spurs.* **2.** catchy or repetitious succession of words or sounds, as in poetry, esp. a short, catchy song or piece of verse: *musical jingles used in advertising.* [Imitative.]

jin·gly (jing′glē) *adj.* having, producing, or resembling a jingling sound.

jin·go (jing′gō) *pl.,* **-goes.** *n.* one who is characterized by jingoism. —*adj.* of, relating to, or characteristic of jingoes; characterized by jingoism. [From the phrase *by Jingo,* used in an English chauvinistic song of 1878 opposing Russian expansion; *Jingo* possibly a substitute for *Jesus* to avoid giving offense.] —**jin′go·ist,** *n., adj.* —**jin′go·is′tic,** *adj.*

jin·go·ism (jing′gō iz′əm) *n.* extreme patriotism or chauvinism, marked esp. by the advocacy of an aggressive, warlike foreign policy to promote national interests abroad.

jin·ni (ji nē′, jin′ē) *pl.,* **jinn** (jin). *n.* genie.

jin·rick·sha (jin rik′shô) *also,* **jin·rik·i·sha.** *n.* ricksha. [Japanese *jinrikisha* literally, vehicle drawn by a man's strength, from *jin* man + *riki* strength + *sha* vehicle.]

jinx (jingks) *Informal. n.* **1.** person or that which brings or is believed to bring bad luck. **2.** spell of bad luck; hex: *to put a jinx on someone.* —*v.t.* to bring or try to bring bad luck; hex. [Supposedly from Latin *iynx* wryneck (a bird used in witchcraft), from Greek *iynx.*]

jit·ney (jit′nē) *pl.,* **-neys.** *n. Informal.* car or bus that carries passengers for a small fare, usually over a short regular route. [Of uncertain origin.]

jit·ter (jit′ər) *Informal. v.i.* to be nervous or uneasy; fidget. —*n.* **jitters,** fit of nervousness; extreme anxiety. [Of uncertain origin.] —**jit′ter·y,** *adj.*

jit·ter·bug (jit′ər bug′) *Informal. n.* **1.** lively dance, popular esp. during the 1930s and 1940s, consisting chiefly of improvised movements performed to swing music. **2.** one who does this dance. —*v.i.,* **-bugged, -bug·ging.** to dance the jitterbug.

jiu·jit·su (jōō jit′sōō) *also,* **jiu·jut·su.** *n.* jujutsu.

jive (jīv) *Slang. n.* **1.** jazz, esp. swing music of the late 1930s and 1940s. **2.** jargon of jazz musicians and enthusiasts. **3.** deceptive, glib, or meaningless talk. —*v.t., v.i.,* **jived, jiv·ing.** to deceive by or as by glib talk. [Of uncertain origin.]

jive² (jīv) **jived, jiv·ing.** *v.i. Informal.* to jibe³. [Probably from JIBE³.]

jo (jō) *pl.,* **joes.** *also,* **joe.** *n. Scottish.* sweetheart; dear. [Form of JOY.]

Jo·ab (jō′ab) *n.* in the Old Testament, commander of David's army.

Joan of Arc (jōn′ əv ärk′) 1412–31, French national heroine and military leader during the Hundred Years' War, known as the Maid of Orleans. She was condemned as a witch and heretic and burned at the stake. In 1920 she was canonized. Also, **Jeanne d'Arc.**

job (job) *n.* **1.** position of work; employment: *a part-time job in a publishing company.* **2.** something that has to be done; task, duty, or responsibility: *It's your job to type the memo.* **3.** specific activity or piece of work, esp. when done for a set fee: *The repair job will cost $300.* **4.** specific activity or function performed regularly, esp. a profession or occupation. **5.** quality, product, or result of work. **6.** object or material worked on. **7.** *Informal.* criminal act, esp. a robbery. **8.** *Informal.* difficult or exhausting task: *Waxing the car was quite a job.* **9.** damaging

or thoroughly destructive piece of work. **10. on the job. a.** while working; at work: *He received his most valuable training on the job.* **b.** *Informal.* closely attentive to one's task, duty, or responsibility: *a dependable watchman who was always on the job.* **11. to lie down on the job.** *Informal.* to be lax about one's task, duty, or responsibility. —*v.i.,* **jobbed, job·bing. 1.** to do odd or occasional pieces of work; work by the piece. **2.** to act as a middleman or jobber. —*v.t.* **1.** to buy (goods) in large quantities and sell to dealers in smaller lots. **2.** to sublet (work) among different contractors or workmen. —*adj.* of or for a particular task or piece of work; hired or done by the job. [Originally, a piece of work, possibly from obsolete *job* piece; of uncertain origin.] **Syn.** *n.* **2. Job, task, duty** denote a piece of work or activity that one does or is asked to do. **Job** is the most general term and designates work for which one is responsible, esp. in relation to one's function or role: *It is the stoker's job to feed the furnace.* **Task** is a well-defined piece of work or service directed toward a specific goal: *The statesman set before himself the ambitious task of fighting inflation.* **Duty** is an obligatory labor done in the course of one's occupation or employment, for the performance of which one is answerable to a superior: *The secretary's duties included typing and filing letters.*

Job (jōb) *n.* **1.** in the Old Testament, a righteous man who patiently accepted the trials with which God tested his faith. **2.** book of the Old Testament that tells his story. [Late Latin *Iōb* the Biblical character, from Greek *Iōb,* from Hebrew *Iyyōbh* literally, persecuted.]

job·ber (job′ər) *n.* **1.** one who buys goods, as from a manufacturer, and sells them to retailers; dealer in job lots. **2.** one who does piecework or odd jobs.

job·hold·er (job′hōl′dər) *n.* one who is regularly employed.

job·less (job′lis) *adj.* **1.** without a job; unemployed. **2.** of or relating to people who are unemployed: *an increase in the jobless rate.* —**job′less·ness,** *n.*

job lot 1. miscellaneous collection of goods sold by a manufacturer or wholesaler, usually at reduced prices. **2.** any miscellaneous collection, esp. one composed of items of inferior quality.

Jo·cas·ta (jō kas′tə) *n. Greek Mythology.* queen of Thebes who unknowingly married her own son, Oedipus. When she later discovered his identity, she committed suicide.

jock·ey (jok′ē) *pl.,* **-eys.** *n.* one who rides horses in races, esp. as a profession. —*v.i.* **-eyed, -ey·ing. 1.** to maneuver, esp. to gain an advantage: *to jockey for position.* **2.** to ride a horse in a race. —*v.t.* **1.** to maneuver or manipulate (someone or something): *to jockey a car into a parking space.* **2.** to trick; cheat. **3.** to ride (a horse) in a race. [Diminutive of *Jock,* Scottish nickname for JOHN.]

jock·o (jok′ō) *pl.,* **jock·os.** *n.* any ape or monkey.

jock·strap (jok′strap′) *also,* **jock strap.** *n.* elastic support for the male genitals, worn esp. for athletics. Also, **athletic supporter.**

jo·cose (jō kōs′) *adj.* given to or characterized by joking and jesting; merry; playful. [Latin *jocōsus,* from *jocus* jest, game.] —**jo·cose′ly,** *adv.* —**jo·cose′ness,** *n.*

jo·cos·i·ty (jō kos′ə tē) *pl.,* **-ties.** *n.* **1.** state or quality of being jocose. **2.** jocose act or remark; joke or jest.

joc·u·lar (jok′yə lər) *adj.* **1.** given to or characterized by joking and jesting; merry; playful. **2.** of the nature of or intended as a joke; humorous. [Latin *joculāris,* from *joculus* little jest, diminutive of *jocus* jest, game.] —**joc′u·lar·ly,** *adv.*

joc·u·lar·i·ty (jok′yə lar′ə tē) *pl.,* **-ties.** *n.* **1.** state or quality of being jocular; merriment. **2.** jocular act or remark; joke or jest.

joc·und (jok′ənd, jō′kənd) *adj.* cheerful; merry; carefree. [Old French *jocond* pleasant, going back to Latin *jūcundus.*] —**joc′und·ly,** *adv.*

jo·cun·di·ty (jō kun′də tē) *pl.,* **-ties.** *n.* **1.** state or quality of being jocund; cheerfulness. **2.** jocund act or remark; a pleasantry.

Jodh·pur (jod′poor′) *n.* city in northwestern India. Pop. (1969 est.), 270,404.

jodh·purs (jod′pərz) *n.,pl.* breeches for horseback riding that are loose above the knee and close-fitting from knee to ankle. [From JODHPUR, where they were first widely used.]

joe (jō) *jo.*

Jo·el (jō′əl) *n.* **1.** prophet of the Old Testament. **2.** book of the Old Testament attributed to him.

jo·ey (jō′ē) *pl.,* **-eys.** *n.* young kangaroo. [From a native Australian name.]

jog[1] (jog) **jogged, jog·ging.** *v.i.* **1.** to run or move at a slow, steady, jolting pace or trot: *The runners jogged lazily around the track.* **2.** to proceed in a slow, steady, or monotonous manner (with *on* or *along*): *His life just jogged along.* —*v.t.* **1.** to jolt or cause to move by shaking or jerking: *The rickety wagon jogged us up and down.* **2.** to give a slight push to; nudge. **3.** to stir or stimulate, esp.

Jodhpurs

the memory. —*n.* **1.** shake, push, or nudge. **2.** slow, steady, jolting pace or motion. [Possibly imitative.] —**jog′ger,** *n.*

jog[2] (jog) *n.* irregularity in a line or surface; angle, projection, or recess. [Form of JAG[1].]

jog·gle[1] (jog′əl) **-gled, -gling.** *v.t., v.i.* to shake slightly. —*n.* act or instance of joggling; shake or shaking. [JOG[1] + -LE.]

jog·gle[2] (jog′əl) *n.* **1.** a projection or a corresponding notch on either of two surfaces, fitted together in order to prevent slipping. **2.** joint formed in this way. —*v.t.,* **-gled, -gling.** to join or fasten by means of a joggle or joggles. [Probably from JOG[2].]

jog trot 1. slow, regular trot; jog. **2.** routine or humdrum habit or way of doing something.

Jo·han·nes·burg (jō han′is burg′, yō hä′nis-) *n.* largest city and commercial and industrial center of the Republic of South Africa, in the northeastern part of the country. Pop. (1967 est.), 1,294,800.

john (jon) *n. Informal.* toilet; bathroom. [From JOHN, masculine proper name.]

John (jon) *n.* **1.** one of Christ's Apostles, the brother of James the Greater and reputed author of the fourth Gospel, three Epistles, and Revelation. **2.** one of the four Gospels, the fourth book of the New Testament, attributed to him. **3.** John the Baptist. **4.** c.1167–1216, king of England from 1199 to 1216, who signed the Magna Carta in 1215. [Medieval Latin *Johannes,* masculine proper name, from Latin *Ioannēs,* from Greek *Iōannēs,* from Hebrew *Yōhānān* literally, Jehovah is gracious.]

John XXIII, 1881–1963, pope from 1958 to 1963.

John Bar·ley·corn (bär′lē kôrn′) personification of barley as used in malt liquor, of malt liquor itself, or of intoxicating liquors in general.

John Birch Society, ultraconservative U.S. organization established in 1958, founded primarily to combat alleged communist activities and influence in the United States.

John Bull 1. personification of England or the English. **2.** the typical Englishman.

John Doe 1. unknown or fictitious person. ▲ used esp. in legal documents to designate a fictitious person or a person whose real name is not known. **2.** the average man.

John Dory

John Do·ry (dôr′ē) *pl.,* **John Do·rys.** any of several saltwater fish, family Zeidae, commonly found in coastal waters, having a large, pouting mouth and a thin, yellowish-brown body marked on each side with a black spot ringed in yellow.

John Han·cock (han′kok) *Informal.* person's signature or autograph. [From the large, prominent signature of *John Hancock* on the Declaration of Independence.]

Johnny Ap·ple·seed (ap′əl sēd′) c.1774–1845, U.S. frontiersman, noted for sowing apple seeds throughout the Ohio River valley; born John Chapman.

john·ny·cake (jon′ē kāk′) *n.* flat, crisp bread made of cornmeal, water or milk, flour, and, sometimes, eggs, often baked in a pan or on a griddle. [Of uncertain origin.]

John·ny-come-late·ly (jon′ē kum lāt′lē) *pl.,* **John·ny-come-late·lies** or **John·ies-come-late·ly.** *n. Informal.* one who has recently arrived on the scene.

John·ny-jump-up (jon′ē jump′up′) *n.* wild pansy, *Viola tricolor,* of the violet family. [Referring to its rapid growth.]

John·ny-on-the-spot (jon′ē on thə spot′) *pl.,* **John·nies-on-the-spot** or **John·ny-on-the-spots.** *n. Informal.* one who is on hand and ready to act whenever needed.

John·ny Reb (jon′ē reb′) *Informal.* Confederate soldier.

John·son (jon′sən) **1. Andrew.** 1808–75, seventeenth president of the United States, from 1865 to 1869, impeached and acquitted in 1868. **2. Lyn·don B.** (lin′dən). 1908–73, thirty-sixth president of the United States, from 1963 to 1969. **3. Samuel.** 1709–84, English writer, critic, and lexicographer.

Johns·town (jonz′toun′) *n.* city in southwestern Pennsylvania, site of a great flood in 1889. Pop. (1970), 42,476.

John the Baptist, in the New Testament, the forerunner and baptizer of Jesus, beheaded by Herod Antipas.

joie de vi·vre (zhwä′ də vē′vrə) *French.* keen or zestful enjoyment of life.

join (join) *v.t.* **1.** to bring, put, or fasten together so as to become one or as one: *to join two wires, the coupler that joins the boxcars. John hands and form a circle.* **2.** to come into contact or union with: *This road joins the highway up ahead. This bone joins the other at the shoulder.* **3.** to become a member or part of: *to join the army. Join the fun.* **4.** to come or enter into the company of: *Join us at our table when you're*

at; āpe; cär; end; mē; it; īce; hot; ōld; fôrk; wood; fŏŏl; oil; out; up; ūse; turn; sing; thin; this; zh in treasure; ə in ago, taken, pencil, lemon, circus.

553

done. **5.** to participate with (someone) in some act or activity: *The rest of the family joins me in expressing our gratitude.* **6.** to unite, combine, or bring together in act or purpose: *to join forces.* **7.** to unite or bring together in close association or relationship: *to join a couple in marriage.* **8.** to take a place in, with, or among: *This record now joins the year's top hits.* **9.** *Geometry.* to draw a straight or curved line segment between (points). **10.** *Informal.* to adjoin. **11. to join battle.** to enter into a battle or conflict: *The armies joined battle on the plain.* —*v.i.* **1.** to take part with others; participate (often with *in*): *to join in a conversation.* **2.** to combine or act together in close association; become united or associated (often with *with*): *All segments of the community joined to fight the epidemic.* **3.** to become a member of a group or organization; enlist, as in the armed forces (often with *up*): *He joined up in the last months of the war.* **4.** to come into or be in contact or union: *At what point do the rivers join?* **5.** to meet in battle or conflict: *Our troops joined with enemy forces just outside the city.* —*n.* place or line of joining; seam; joint; junction. [Old French *joindre* to unite, connect, from Latin *jungere.*]

Syn. *v.t.* **1. Join, combine, connect, unite** mean to form or come together as one. **Join** usually stresses the fastening or bringing into contact of separate parts: *The blacksmith joined the pieces of iron with a solder.* **Combine** often involves a blending or mixing for a specified purpose: *The girl combined sugar, butter, and flour to make the dough.* **Connect** suggests a linking or coupling through an intervening medium or element: *A bridge connected the two islands.* **Unite** emphasizes the close joining of a number of distinct things so that they function as an integrated unit: *The twenty-four associations united to form a new organization.*

join·er (joi′nər) *n.* **1.** *Informal.* one who joins many clubs, committees, or other organized activities. **2.** craftsman or carpenter who makes woodwork and furniture, esp. one who constructs articles by joining pieces of wood. **3.** one who or that which joins.

join·er·y (joi′nər ē) *n.* **1.** skill or trade of a joiner. **2.** woodwork, furniture, or other articles made by a joiner.

joint (joint) *n.* **1.** place or structure where two or more bones meet or join, usually freely movable. **2.** any place at which, or structure by which, two or more things or parts are joined or fitted together. **3.** part or section between such places or structures. **4.** one of the portions into which a carcass is cut by a butcher, esp.

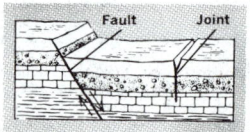

Joint (def. 6)

one containing the bone. **5.** *Botany.* point on a stem from which a leaf or branch grows. **6.** *Geology.* fracture in a rock mass, usually transverse or vertical to the bedding, along which no movement has occurred. **7.** *Slang.* **a.** cheap or disreputable gathering place: *a gambling joint.* **b.** any building, establishment, or place: *Let me out of this joint.* **8.** *Slang.* marijuana cigarette. **9. out of joint. a.** out of place at the joint, as a bone. **b.** in an unfavorable, disordered, or inharmonious state. —*adj.* **1.** belonging to or used by two or more; held or shared in common: *a joint interest in an enterprise.* **2.** performed or produced by two or more in conjunction: *joint efforts, a joint attack.* **3.** sharing or acting with another or others: *joint owners.* **4.** of or involving both houses or branches of a legislature: *a joint session of Congress.* —*v.t.* **1.** to connect by means of a joint or joints. **2.** to divide or cut at the joints, as meat. [Old French *joint* place where two things touch or join, yoke, from *joindre.* See JOIN.]

joint account, bank account in the name of two or more persons, each of whom may deposit or withdraw funds.

Joint Chiefs of Staff, principal military advisory board to the President of the United States, consisting of a chairman, the chiefs of staff of the Army and of the Air Force, the head of the Navy, and, usually, the commandant of the Marine Corps.

join·ted (join′tid) *adj.* **1.** having a joint or joints: *a jointed body.* **2.** having a specified kind of joint. ▲ used in combination in both definitions: *double-jointed.*

joint·ly (joint′lē) *adv.* in conjunction; unitedly; together: *The island is administered jointly by the two countries.*

joint resolution, resolution passed by both houses of Congress and having the force of law if signed by the president.

joint-stock company, business organization whose capital is held in transferable shares of stock by its joint owners, similar to a corporation, but differing in that the shareholders are personally liable for the debts of the business.

join·ture (join′chər) *n.* property settled on a married woman by her husband, to be given to her after his death. [Middle French *jointure* a joining, yoking together, from Latin *junctūra* a joining. Doublet of JUNCTURE.]

joist (joist) *n.* one of a series of parallel beams to which the boards of a floor or the laths of a ceiling are fastened. [Old French *giste* such a beam, bed, going back to Latin *jacēre* to lie.]

joke (jōk) *n.* **1.** anecdote or story, usually having a punch line or funny climax, intended to provoke laughter or amusement: *I've heard that joke before.* **2.** anything said or done to provoke laughter or amusement, as a humorous remark or a prank: *My brother hid the keys as a joke.* **3.** person or thing exciting amusement or ridicule; object

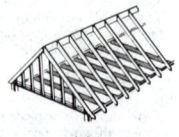

Joists

of laughter or jesting; laughingstock: *Her debut in a starring role was a joke.* **4.** something not to be taken seriously; matter of little or no importance; trifle: *He tried to treat his failure as a joke.* —*v.i.,* joked, jok·ing. **1.** to tell or make jokes; speak or act in a playful, merry way (often with *around*): *Her predicament is nothing to joke about. He's always joking around when he should be working.* **2.** to say something in jest, rather than in earnest: *I'm not joking—I really will tell your mother what you did to your little brother.* [Latin *jocus* jest, game.] —**jok′ing·ly,** *adv.*

Syn. *n.* **1. Joke, jest, gag** denote something said or done to amuse or provoke laughter. **Joke** is a short and funny anecdote or remark, esp. one with an unexpected twist: *The speaker interspersed his speech with a few jokes.* **Jest** is a more literary term and suggests a mocking or bantering remark: *Oscar Wilde's jests ridiculed the foibles of his age.* **Gag** is a humorous anecdote often written into a script and designed to enliven a theatrical routine: *The comedian's gags brought the house down.*

jok·er (jō′kər) *n.* **1.** one who jokes or is given to joking. **2.** either of two extra playing cards provided with a standard deck, often bearing a picture of a jester and used in certain games as a wild card or as trump. **3.** hidden, ambiguous, or seemingly unimportant clause, phrase, or wording in a document, as a piece of legislation, that partially or completely defeats its purpose or changes its original or intended meaning. **4.** *Informal.* **a.** prankster, practical joker, or smart aleck: *Who's the joker who switched the name plates around?* **b.** man or fellow, esp. one who seems unimpressive or worthy of contempt.

Jo·li·et (jō′lē et′) *n.* city in northeastern Illinois. Pop. (1970), 80,378.

Jol·li·et, Louis (jō′lē et′, zhô lē ā′) *also,* **Jo·li·et.** 1645–1700, French-Canadian explorer of the Mississippi River.

jol·li·fi·ca·tion (jol′ə fi kā′shən) *n.* merrymaking; jollity.

jol·li·ty (jol′ə tē) *n., pl.* -ties. **1.** state or quality of being jolly. **2.** *British.* festive occasion or gathering.

jol·ly (jol′ē) -li·er, -li·est. *adj.* **1.** full of fun, good humor, and high spirits: *a jolly old man.* **2.** characterized by or causing mirth, gaiety, or good cheer: *a jolly song, jolly laughter.* **3.** *British. Informal.* **a.** pleasant; agreeable; delightful: *How jolly it will be to see them again!* **b.** great; large; remarkable: *He's gotten himself into a jolly mess.* —*adv. British. Informal.* extremely; very; remarkably: *It was jolly good of you to help.* —*v.t.,* -lied, -ly·ing. *Informal.* to amuse, humor, or flatter so as to put or keep in a good mood (often with *up* or *along*): *We tried to jolly him up.* [Old French *joli(f)* gay, festive, pretty, from Old Norse *jōl* Yule, feast.] —**jol′li·ly,** *adv.* —**jol′li·ness,** *n.*

jolly boat, small, general-purpose boat carried on a ship. [Possibly from Danish *jolle* yawl + BOAT.]

Jolly Rog·er (roj′ər) flag with a skull and crossbones, usually white on a black field, esp. one flown by pirates.

jolt (jōlt) *v.t.* **1.** to cause to move with a rough, jerky motion; jar or shake up with or as with a sudden bump or blow: *The impact of the collision jolted us out of our seats.* **2.** to bring or put abruptly or roughly into a specified state or condition: *to jolt someone back to reality. The interruption jolted her out of her daydream.* —*v.i.* to move in a succession of abrupt, bumpy jerks: *The carriage jolted along the dirt road. The train jolted forward.* —*n.* **1.** rough, jerky motion: *The wagon stopped with a jolt.* **2.** abrupt surprise or emotional shock: *The news gave me quite a jolt.* [Of uncertain origin.]

Jo·nah (jō′nə) *n.* **1.** in the Old Testament, the Hebrew prophet thrown overboard during a storm for disobeying God, swallowed by a large fish, and three days later cast up on land unharmed. **2.** book of the Old Testament containing his story and prophecies. **3.** one whose presence supposedly brings bad luck; jinx.

Jo·nas (jō′nəs) *n.* in the Douay Bible, Jonah.

Jon·a·than (jon′ə thən) *n.* **1.** in the Old Testament, a son of Saul and close friend of David. **2.** apple of a variety having a bright-red color and ripening in the late autumn.

Jones, John Paul (jōnz) 1747–92, Scottish-born U.S. naval hero in the American Revolution; born John Paul.

jon·gleur (jong′glər; *French* zhôn glœr′) *n.* in medieval France and England, a wandering minstrel. [French *jongleur* such a minstrel, juggler, going back to Latin *joculātor* jester.]

jon·quil (jong'kwil, jon'-) *n.* **1.** yellow flower of a plant, *Narcissus jonquilla,* resembling the daffodil, having six petal-like segments surrounding a shallow, cup-shaped structure. **2.** slender plant bearing this flower, having shiny dark-green leaves and grown from bulbs. [French *jonquille* this plant, from Spanish *junquillo,* diminutive of *junco* reed, from Latin *juncus;* because of its reedlike leaves.]

Jon·son, Ben (jon'sən) c.1573–1637, English dramatist and poet.

Jop·pa (jop'ə) *n.* see **Jaffa.**

Jor·dan (jôrd'ən) *n.* **1.** country in southwestern Asia, east of and bordering Israel. It was formerly known as Transjordan. Capital, Amman. Area, 37,-738 sq. mi. Pop. (1969 est.), 2,160,000. **2.** river in southwestern Asia flowing between Israel and Jordan into the Dead Sea. —**Jor·da·ni·an** (jôr dā'-nē ən), *adj., n.*

Jordan almond 1. large almond of a variety from Spain, widely used in confectionery. **2.** almond covered with a hard, colored sugar coating. [Modification of Middle English *jardyne almaunde* literally, garden almond, from Old French *jardin* garden + *almande* almond. See JARDINIERE, ALMOND.]

Jonquil

jo·rum (jôr'əm) *n.* **1.** large drinking bowl. **2.** its contents: *a jorum of punch.* [Supposedly from *Joram,* Old Testament character who brought metal vessels to David.]

jo·seph (jō'zəf, -səf) *n.* long coat or cloak with a cape, worn chiefly by women in the eighteenth century for horseback riding. [Probably from the many-colored coat of the Old Testament JOSEPH.]

Jo·seph (jō'zəf, -səf) *n.* **1.** in the Old Testament, a son of Jacob and Rachel who was sold into slavery by his jealous brothers and who later became a high official in Egypt. **2.** in the New Testament, husband of Mary, the mother of Jesus. [Late Latin *Jōsēph,* a masculine proper name, from Greek *Iōsēph,* from Hebrew *Yōsēph* literally, he adds.]

Jo·se·phine (jō'zə fēn', -sə-) *n.* 1763–1814, first wife of Napoleon Bonaparte and empress of France from 1804 to 1809.

Joseph of Ar·i·ma·the·a (ar'ə mə thē'ə) in the New Testament, a rich disciple who put the body of Jesus in his own tomb.

Jo·se·phus, Fla·vi·us (jō sē'fəs; flā'vē əs) A.D. 37–c.95, Jewish historian and soldier.

josh (josh) *Informal. v.t.* to make good-natured fun of; tease playfully: *He's joshing you.* —*v.i.* to indulge in light-hearted, playful teasing. [Of uncertain origin.] —**josh'er,** *n.*

Josh., Joshua.

Josh·u·a (josh'ōō ə) *n.* **1.** in the Old Testament, the successor of Moses who led the Israelites into Canaan. **2.** book of the Old Testament containing the history of the Israelites from the death of Moses to the settlement in Canaan. [Hebrew *Yehōshūa'* literally, Jehovah is salvation.]

Joshua tree, tall treelike plant, *Yucca brevifolia,* of arid or desert regions of the southwestern United States, having extended, forking branches and bearing clusters of white or greenish-white flowers. [Supposedly from the resemblance of its extended branches to the outstretched arms of *Joshua* as described in the Old Testament.]

Jo·si·ah (jō sī'ə) *n.* in the Old Testament, a seventh-century B.C. king of Judah who instituted a major reform of ancient Judaism.

joss (jos) *n.* image or idol of a Chinese god. [Pidgin English modification of Portuguese *deos* a god, from Latin *deus.*]

joss house, Chinese temple or shrine containing idols.

joss stick, slender stick of dried fragrant paste, burned as incense, as before a joss.

jos·tle (jos'əl) -**tled,** -**tling.** *also,* **jus·tle.** *v.t., v.i.* to bump, push, or shove roughly, as with the elbows in a crowd. —*n.* bump, push, or shove; a jostling. [JOUST + -LE.] —**jos'tler,** *n.*

Jos·u·e (jos'ū ē') *n.* in the Douay Bible, Joshua.

jot (jot) *n.* the least or smallest bit; iota; whit: *Her smug airs didn't impress me a jot.* —*v.t.,* **jot·ted, jot·ting.** to make a brief and hasty note of (often *with down*): *Let me jot down your telephone number.* [Latin *iōta* ita, the Greek letter ι from Greek *iōta* the smallest letter of the Greek alphabet; of Semitic origin. Doublet of IOTA.] —**jot'ter,** *n.*

Jo·tun (yō'tōōn) *also,* **Jo·tunn, Jö·tunn.** *n. Norse Mythology.* one of a race of giants who were enemies of the gods. [Old Norse *jötunn* giant.]

Jo·tun·heim (yō'tōōn hām') *also,* **Jo·tunn·heim, Jö·tunn·heim.** *n.* home of the Jotuns.

joule (jōōl, joul) *n. Physics.* unit of work or energy in the meter-kilogram-second system of units, equal to the work done by a force of one newton acting through a distance of one meter. The joule is equivalent to 10ᐟ ergs. [From James P. *Joule,* 1818–89, English physicist.]

jounce (jouns) *jounced,* **jounc·ing.** *v.t., v.i.* to move or shake up and down roughly; bounce; jolt. —*n.* sudden, rough bump; bounce; jolt.

jour·nal (jurn'əl) *n.* **1.** record or account, esp. one kept daily, of occurrences, experiences, or observations. **2.** official record, usually one kept daily, of proceedings or transactions, as the register of a legislative body. **3.** magazine or periodical, esp. one dealing with matters of current interest in a particular area: *The study appeared in a leading medical journal.* **4.** newspaper, esp. one published daily. **5.** part of a shaft or axle turning within a bearing. **6.** daybook *(def. 1).* [French *journal* newspaper, diary, from Old French *jornal* daily, from Latin *diurnālis,* going back to *diēs* day. Doublet of DIURNAL.]

Syn. 3. Journal, periodical, magazine denote a publication that appears at stated intervals under the same title. **Journal** usually refers to a publication of a group or society that presents news of current interest in a particular area: *That engineering society distributes its journal to all its members.* **Periodical** is any regular publication appearing at intervals of more than a day and less than a year and containing a record of public transactions and occurrences: *That library does not lend current periodicals to members.* **Magazine** is a periodical, often illustrated, that contains a variety of features for the general reader: *Some American magazines are popular throughout the world.*

jour·nal·ese (jurn'əl ēz', -ēs') *n.* slick, superficial style of writing considered to be characteristic of newspapers.

jour·nal·ism (jurn'əl iz'əm) *n.* **1.** the collecting, presenting, or interpreting of facts and opinions about current events and topics of public interest, esp. the writing or publishing of such facts and opinions in newspaper or magazines. **2.** occupation or study of this.

jour·nal·ist (jurn'əl ist) *n.* one whose occupation is journalism, esp. one who edits or writes for a newspaper or magazine.

jour·nal·is·tic (jurn'əl is'tik) *adj.* of, relating to, or characteristic of journalism or journalists. —**jour'nal·is'ti·cal·ly,** *adv.*

jour·ney (jur'nē) *pl.,* -**neys.** *n.* **1.** trip, esp. one over a considerable distance or taking considerable time: *a journey across the United States.* **2.** distance traveled, or that can be traveled, in a specified time: *a four days' journey from here.* —*v.i.,* -**neyed,** -**ney·ing.** to make a trip; travel. —*v.t.* to travel over or through. [Old French *journee* day, a day's travel, a day's work, going back to Latin *diurnus* daily, from *diēs* day.] —**jour'ney·er,** *n.*

Syn. n. 1. Journey, voyage, trip, tour denote travel from one place to another. **Journey** implies that the travel is for a somewhat lengthy period, often over land: *The New Yorkers' journey to California was uneventful.* **Voyage** also implies length of time but is used esp. in reference to travel by ship: *Columbus made four voyages to the new world.* **Trip** implies a relatively short period of travel, esp. for a specified purpose: *The salesman makes two trips to Seattle every week.* **Tour** suggests a circular trip with a planned itinerary, as for sightseeing: *The travel agent suggested a ninety-day tour of Europe.*

jour·ney·man (jur'nē man) *pl.,* -**men.** *n.* **1.** one who has completed his apprenticeship in a trade, craft, or skill, but who is not yet eligible to become a master and works for another. **2.** experienced, qualified, and competent workman. [From obsolete *journey* a day's work (from Old French *journee*) + MAN. See JOURNEY.]

joust (joust) *also,* **just.** *n.* **1.** formal combat, often part of a tournament, between two mounted knights or other individuals armed with lances and other weapons. **2.** jousts. series of such confrontations; tournament. **3.** any combat, confrontation, or struggle resembling a joust. —*v.i.* to engage in a joust. [Old French *jouste,* from *jouster* to meet, joust, tourney, from Late Latin *iuxtāre* to approach, join, from Latin *iuxtā* near.] —**joust'er,** *n.*

Jove (jōv) *n.* **1.** Jupiter *(def. 1).* **2.** *Archaic.* the planet Jupiter. [Latin *Jov-,* stem of oblique cases of *Jupiter.*]

jo·vi·al (jō'vē əl) *adj.* characterized by hearty, good-natured humor and conviviality; merry; jolly. [Late Latin *Joviālis* relating to Jove or Jupiter, from Latin *Jov-.* See JOVE. From the belief that people born under the sign of the planet Jupiter were happy and jolly.] —**jo'vi·al·ly,** *adv.* —**jo'vi·al·ness,** *n.*

jo·vi·al·i·ty (jō'vē al'ə te) *n.* quality or state of being jovial; jollity; merriment.

Jo·vi·an (jō'vē ən) *adj.* of, relating to, or like Jove or the planet Jupiter.

jowl[1] (joul, jōl) *n.* **1.** flabby, sagging flesh hanging from or under the lower jaw. **2.** any similar fleshy part, as the dewlap of cattle or the wattle of fowl. [Old English *ceole* throat.]

jowl[2] (joul, jōl) *n.* **1.** jawbone or jaw, esp. the lower jaw. **2.** cheek. [Old English *ceafl* jaw.]

joy (joi) *n.* **1.** strong feeling of happiness or delight, as that arising from present or expected gratification or good. **2.** that which is the source or cause of such feeling. **3.** expression or manifestation of happiness; outward rejoicing. [Old French *joie,* from Latin *gaudia,* plural of *gaudium.*] —**Syn.** 1. see **happiness.**

joy·ance (joi'əns) *n. Archaic.* enjoyment; delight; gladness.

Joyce, James (jois) 1882–1941, Irish novelist, poet, and short-story writer.

---

at; āpe; cär; end; mē; it; īce; hot; ōld; fôrk; wood; fōōl; oil; out; up; ūse; turn; sing; thin; this; zh in treasure; ə in ago, taken, pencil, lemon, circus.

joy·ful (joi′fəl) *adj.* **1.** full of joy; feeling joy. **2.** showing joy: *a joyful look in his eyes.* **3.** causing joy: *a joyful sight.* —**joy′ful·ly**, *adv.* —**joy′ful·ness**, *n.* —**Syn. 1.** see **glad**[1].

joy·less (joi′lis) *adj.* feeling, expressing, or causing no joy; completely lacking in joy: *a joyless smile, a joyless existence.* —**joy′less·ly**, *adv.* —**joy′less·ness**, *n.*

joy·ous (joi′əs) *adj.* feeling, showing, or causing joy; marked by rejoicing. —**joy′ous·ly**, *adv.* —**joy′ous·ness**, *n.*

joy·ride (joi′rīd′) *Informal. n.* **1.** reckless automobile ride, esp. in a stolen vehicle, taken purely for fun or amusement. **2.** something, as a venture, resembling this; something marked by recklessness, danger, or disregard for consequences. —*v.i.* **-rode, -rid·den, -rid·ing.** to take a joyride. —**joy′rid′er**, *n.*

J.P., justice of the peace.

jr., junior.

Juá·rez (wär′ez; *Spanish* hwä′res) **1. Be·ni·to Pa·blo** (be nē′tō pä′vlō). 1806–72, Mexican statesman, president of Mexico from 1858 to 1865 and from 1867 to 1872. **2.** Ciudad Juárez.

Ju·bal (jōō′bəl) *n.* in the Old Testament, a descendant of Cain and inventor of musical instruments.

ju·bi·lant (jōō′bə lənt) *adj.* joyfully elated or triumphant; exultant: *After the contest the victor was jubilant.* [Latin *jūbilāns,* present participle of *jūbilāre* to shout with joy.] —**ju′bi·lance, ju′bi·lan·cy,** *n.* —**ju′bi·lant·ly,** *adv.*

ju·bi·late (jōō′bə lāt′) **-lat·ed, -lat·ing.** *v.i.* to rejoice; exult. [Latin *jūbilātus,* past participle of *jūbilāre* to shout with joy.]

Ju·bi·la·te (ū′bi lä′tā; jōō′-) *n.* **1.** in the Old Testament, the one-hundredth Psalm, or, in the Douay Bible, the ninety-ninth Psalm. **2.** third Sunday after Easter. [Latin *jūbilāte,* imperative of *jūbilāre* to shout with joy; the first word of the Latin version of the psalm.]

ju·bi·la·tion (jōō′bə lā′shən) *n.* **1.** feeling of elated or triumphant joy. **2.** act of rejoicing; exultation.

ju·bi·lee (jōō′bə lē′, jōō′bə lē′) *n.* **1.a.** special anniversary, esp. a twenty-fifth or fiftieth anniversary. **b.** celebration of such an anniversary. **2.** year, season, or occasion of joyful celebration and rejoicing. **3.** great joy; rejoicing. **4.** among the ancient Hebrews, a year-long celebration held every fifty years, during which time slaves were freed, debts were forgiven, and fields were left uncultivated. **5.** in the Roman Catholic Church, year in which punishment for sin is remitted after repentance and the fulfillment of certain conditions. It occurs every twenty-five years. [Old French *jubile,* from Late Latin *jūbilaeus* year of jubilee among the Hebrews, going back to Greek *iōbēlos,* from Hebrew *yōbēl,* originally, ram's horn; because such a horn was sounded to proclaim the year of jubilee on the Day of Atonement every fiftieth year.]

Ju·dae·a (jōō dē′ə) *n.* Judea. —**Ju·dae′an,** *adj., n.*

Judaeo-, form of **Judeo-**.

Ju·dah (jōō′də) *n.* **1.** in the Old Testament, the fourth son of Jacob and founder of one of the twelve tribes of Israel. **2.** tribe descended from him, the most powerful of the twelve tribes of Israel. **3.** Hebrew kingdom in Palestine, consisting of the tribes of Judah and Benjamin, ruled by the descendants of Solomon until its fall in the sixth century B.C.

Ju·da·ic (jōō dā′ik) *adj.* of or relating to Jews or Judaism. Also, **Ju·da′i·cal.**

Ju·da·ism (jōō′dē iz′əm, -dā-) *n.* **1.** monotheistic religion followed by the Jews, based chiefly on the precepts of the Old Testament and the teachings of the Talmud and marked by the observance of the Mosaic law and adherence to certain principles of ethical conduct. One of the world's major religions, it has three branches: Orthodox, Conservative, and Reform. **2.** observance of the practices and ceremonies of this religion. **3.** cultural, social, and intellectual tradition and heritage associated with this religion.

Ju·da·ize (jōō′dē īz′, -dā-) **-ized, -iz·ing.** *v.t.* to bring into conformity with Judaism. —*v.i.* to conform to Judaism.

Ju·das (jōō′dəs) *n.* **1.** in the New Testament, the Apostle who betrayed Jesus for thirty pieces of silver. Also, **Judas Iscariot. 2.** treacherous betrayer or traitor, esp. one who betrays under the guise of friendship. **3.** *judas* (def. 1).

judas goat also, **Judas goat. 1.** goat used to lead unsuspecting sheep or other animals to their slaughter. **2.** one who betrays unsuspecting persons by leading them to their death or into a trap or ambush.

Judas tree, redbud. [Because *Judas* Iscariot is said to have hanged himself upon such a tree.]

Jude (jōōd) *n.* **1.** one of the twelve Apostles of Jesus. Also, **Jude Thaddeus. 2.** book of the New Testament, often attributed to him.

Ju·de·a (jōō dē′ə) also, **Ju·dae·a.** *n.* southern part of ancient Palestine, esp. when it was under Roman rule. —**Ju·de′an,** *adj., n.*

Judeo- also, **Judaeo-,** combining form Jewish: *Judeo-Christian.* [Latin *Jūdaeus* Jewish, Jew. See JEW.]

Ju·de·o-Chris·tian (jōō dā′ō kris′chən) *adj.* Jewish and Christian: *in the Judeo-Christian tradition.*

Judg., Judges.

judge (juj) **judged, judg·ing.** *v.t.* **1.** to hear and decide by official authority the merits or guilt of; pass sentence in or on: *He judged the case impartially.* **2.** to settle or decide authoritatively, as a contest, competition, or dispute: *Who's judging the first race?* **3.** to form an opinion, estimate, or evaluation of: *Judge him by what he does, not by his appearance. I can't judge the distance in this light.* **4.** to criticize; condemn; censure. **5.** to think; suppose; consider: *I judge him to be loyal.* —*v.i.* **1.** to form an opinion, estimate, or critical evaluation: *Listen to both sides of the story and judge for yourself.* **2.** to act or decide as a judge: *He'll have to judge between four entries.* —*n.* **1.** appointed or elected official who has authority to hear and decide cases in a court of law. **2.** one appointed to decide in any contest, competition, or dispute; arbiter: *The judges awarded first prize to the bay gelding.* **3.** one qualified to form and pronounce an opinion and make critical evaluations (about a particular subject): *I'm no judge when it comes to opera.* **4.** one of the rulers of Israel during the period between the death of Joshua and the reign of Saul. [Old French *juge* official who decides cases in a court of law, from Latin *jūdex* arbiter, juror, from *jūs* law + *dīcere* to say.] —**judg′er,** *n.*

Syn. *n.* **2.** Judge, arbiter, arbitrator refer to a person who hears and decides disputed issues. **Judge** is a person invested with authority to decide what is true in a contest or controversy by weighing the evidence fairly: *The three judges were asked to decide whether the painting was a forgery.* **Arbiter** is a person with wisdom, knowledge, or experience whose verdict on a disputed question is accepted as final: *Editors of fashion magazines are often regarded as arbiters of style.* **Arbitrator** denotes one or more persons constituting a tribunal with the consent of the disputants and with the authority to make a settlement: *The long-standing labor dispute was settled by an arbitrator.*

judge advocate *pl.*, **judge advocates.** staff officer whose duty is to administer military law and advise the commanding officer on legal questions.

judge advocate general *pl.*, **judge advocates general** or **judge advocate generals.** in the U.S. Army, Navy, and Air Force, the head of the legal department of each service.

Judg·es (juj′iz) *n.* book of the Old Testament containing the history of the Israelites from the death of Joshua to the birth of Samuel.

judge·ship (juj′ship′) *n.* position, function, or term of office of a judge.

judg·ment (juj′mənt) also, **judge·ment.** *n.* **1.** faculty of judging; ability to judge, discern, or make decisions wisely: *a man of judgment. She shows good judgment for a girl her age.* **2.** act of judging. **3.** result of judging; opinion or conclusion reached through judging: *In my judgment they've got nothing to worry about. Form your own judgment of what's going on.* **4.** *Law.* **a.** decree, verdict, order, or sentence handed down by a court of law. **b.** obligation arising from such a decree, verdict, or order, as a debt or the duty to fulfill a legal contract. **c.** document embodying such a decree, verdict, or order. **5.** misfortune considered to be sent by God as a punishment for sin. **6.** also, **Judgment.** the Last Judgment. —**judg·men·tal** (juj ment′əl), *adj.* —**Syn. 4.** see **verdict.**

Judgment Day also, **judgment day.** in some religions, the day of God's final judgment of mankind, which is to occur on the day the world ends. Also, **Day of Judgment, Last Judgment, Doomsday.**

ju·di·ca·to·ry (jōō′də kə tôr′ē) *adj.* of or relating to the administration of justice. —*n. pl.*, **-to·ries. 1.** body of persons having judicial authority; court of justice; tribunal. **2.** system of administration of justice. [Late Latin *jūdicātōrius* relating to judging, from Latin *jūdicāre* to judge, decide.]

ju·di·ca·ture (jōō′də kā′chər) *n.* **1.** administration of justice. **2.** right, power, or authority to administer justice; extent of jurisdiction of a judge or court. **3.** court of law. **4.** system of courts of law; judges or courts of law collectively. [Medieval Latin *judicatura* office of a judge, from Latin *jūdicāre* to judge, decide.]

ju·di·cial (jōō dish′əl) *adj.* **1.** of or relating to courts of law, to the administration of justice, or to the application and interpretation of the law: *judicial proceedings, the judicial branch of the government.* **2.** of, relating to, or appropriate to a judge, judges, or the office of a judge: *judicial robes, judicial authority.* **3.** decreed or enforced by a judge or a court: *a judicial decision.* **4.** inclined to make judgments; critical; discriminating; judicious. [Latin *jūdiciālis* relating to law courts, from *jūdicium* judgment, from *jūdex* judge.] —**ju·di′cial·ly,** *adv.*

ju·di·ci·ar·y (jōō dish′ē er′ē) *pl.*, **-ar·ies.** *n.* **1.** branch of government that is invested with judicial power and that interprets and applies the law. **2.** system of courts, as of a country. **3.** judges of these courts collectively. —*adj.* of or relating to judges, courts of law, or judgments made in courts of law.

ju·di·cious (jōō dish′əs) *adj.* **1.** having or exercising good judgment; wise; sensible: *a judicious commander of troops.* **2.** marked by or proceeding from good judgment: *a judicious plan of operations.* [French

at; āpe; cär; end; mē; it; īce; hot; ōld; fôrk; wood; fōol; oil; out; up; ūse; turn; sing; thin; this; zh in treasure; ə in ago, taken, pencil, lemon, circus.

judicieux, going back to Latin *jūdicium* judgment, trial.] —**ju·di′-cious·ly,** *adv.* —**ju·di′cious·ness,** *n.*

Ju·dith (jōō′dĭth) *n.* **1.** in the Old Testament, a Jewish heroine who saved her people by killing an Assyrian general while he slept. **2.** book of the Protestant Apocrypha and of the Douay Bible that relates her story.

ju·do (jōō′dō) *n.* **1.** method of unarmed combat and self-defense related to but less violent than jujitsu and karate. It originated in the Orient and developed from jujitsu. **2.** sport of fighting by this method. [Japanese *jūdō,* from *jū* gentle + *dō* way.]

Ju·dy (jōō′dē) *n.* wife of Punch.

jug (jŭg) *n.* **1.** rounded vessel of earthenware, glass, or other material, with a handle and a narrow neck that usually has a stopper or cap, used chiefly for holding liquids. **2.** pitcher or similar vessel for liquids. **3.a.** jug and its contents: *He passed the jug around, and we all drank from it. There are three jugs of cider stored on the shelf.* **b.** contents of a jug: *She added a jug of milk to the batter.* **4.** *Slang.* jail; prison. —*v.t.,* **jugged, jug·ging. 1.** to put or cook in a jug. **2.** *Slang.* to jail; imprison. [Possibly from *Jug,* an earlier nickname for the proper name *Joan* (used humorously to refer to such a vessel).]

jug·ger·naut (jŭg′ər nôt′) *n.* **1.** any overpowering force or object that advances relentlessly and destroys whatever is in its path. **2.** something, as a custom or belief, to which people blindly devote themselves or are ruthlessly sacrificed. [From JUGGERNAUT.]

Jug·ger·naut (jŭg′ər nôt′) *also,* **Jag·an·nath.** *n.* idol of the Hindu god Krishna, annually drawn in procession on a huge car under whose wheels devotees of the god are said to have thrown themselves to be crushed to death. [Hindi *Jagannāth* lord of the world, from Sanskrit *Jagannātha.*]

jug·gle (jŭg′əl) -**gled, -gling.** *v.t.* **1.** to keep (two or more balls or other objects) in continuous motion from the hands into the air by skillfully tossing and catching in rapid succession: *He can juggle four oranges at once.* **2.** to change or manipulate in order to deceive or defraud: *The embezzler juggled the firm's financial records.* **3.** to attempt to balance or handle; hold, balance, or handle precariously: *He juggled his books and the baseball bats as we walked down the block.* **4.** to deal with or keep in motion at the same time: *This year she's juggling going to school, working part-time, and taking tennis lessons.* —*v.i.* **1.** to perform or entertain as a juggler. **2.** to practice artifice and trickery with the intent of deceiving or defrauding. —*n.* **1.** act of juggling. **2.** trick; deception; fraud. [Old French *jogler* to jest, from Latin *joculārī.*]

jug·gler (jŭg′lər) *n.* **1.** one whose work or occupation is juggling or performing juggling feats: *a circus juggler.* **2.** one who practices deception or fraud. [Old French *jougleor* jester, from Latin *joculātor.*]

jug·gler·y (jŭg′lər ē) *pl.* -**gler·ies.** *n.* **1.** skill or tricks of a juggler; sleight of hand. **2.** trickery; deception; fraud.

Ju·go·slav (ū′gō släv′, -slav′) *n., adj.* Yugoslav. —**Ju′go·sla′vic,** *adj.*

Ju·go·sla·vi·a (ū′gō slä′vē ə) *n.* Yugoslavia. —**Ju′go·sla′vi·an,** *adj., n.*

jug·u·lar (jŭg′yə lər) *adj.* **1.** of or relating to the neck or throat. **2.** of or relating to the jugular vein. —*n.* jugular vein. [Modern Latin *jugularis,* from Latin *jugulum* collarbone, diminutive of *jugum* yoke; because the jugular vein is near the *jugulum,* or collarbone, which *yokes* the shoulder and neck.]

jugular vein, either of the two large blood vessels on either side of the neck that return blood from the head and neck to the heart.

juice (jōōs) *n.* **1.** fluid contained in a plant or in plant tissues, esp. that extracted from a fruit or vegetable for use as a drink. **2.** fluid contained in animal flesh or tissues: *Let the roast cook in its own juices.* **3.** fluid secreted in animal tissue: *gastric juices, intestinal juices.* **4.** *Slang.* electric current; electricity. **5.** *Slang.* vigor; vitality. **6.** *Slang.* gasoline, oil, or other liquid fuel. —*v.t.,* **juiced, juic·ing.** to extract the juice from. [Old French *jus* broth, sauce, from Latin *jūs.*]

juic·er (jōō′sər) *n.* appliance for extracting juice from fruits and vegetables.

juic·y (jōō′sē) **juic·i·er, juic·i·est.** *adj.* **1.** having much juice; succulent: *a juicy orange.* **2.** full of interest; colorful; lively: *some juicy gossip.* —**juic′i·ly,** *adv.* —**juic′i·ness,** *n.*

ju·jit·su (jōō jĭt′sōō) *also,* **jiu·jit·su, ju·jut·su.** *n.* Japanese method of unarmed self-defense or combat, related to judo and karate, that employs skill and anatomical knowledge to use the strength and weight of an opponent to his disadvantage. [Japanese *jūjutsu,* from *jū* gentle + *jutsu* art.]

ju·jube (jōō′jōōb′) *n.* **1.** fruit-flavored, gelatinous candy or lozenge. **2.** edible plumlike fruit of a shrub or small tree, *Zizyphus jujuba,* that is preserved in various ways and made into candy. **3.** shrub or tree bearing this fruit, cultivated in warm regions throughout the world. [Old French *jujube* the plumlike fruit, going back to Latin *zizyphum,* from Greek *zizyphon.*]

juke·box (jōōk′bŏks′) *n.* phonograph, usually coin-operated and en-

cased in a cabinet, that allows for a choice of records to be played, as by pushing one or more of a series of buttons. [From Gullah *juke* disorderly + BOX¹.]

Jul., July.

ju·lep (jōō′ləp) *n.* **1.** mint julep. **2.** sweet drink made of sugar or syrup, flavoring, and water, often taken with medicine. [French *julep,* through Spanish and Arabic, from Persian *gulāb* rose water.]

Jul·ian (jōōl′yən) *adj.* of, relating to, or named for Julius Caesar.

Jul·ian (jōōl′yən) *n.* A.D. c.331–363, Roman emperor from A.D. 361 to A.D. 363 who renounced Christianity and attempted to restore paganism. Also, **Julian the Apostate.**

Julian calendar, calendar established by Julius Caesar, providing for 365 days in a year with every fourth year having 366 days. The number of days in each month and the order of months in the year correspond to the almost universally used present-day Gregorian calendar.

ju·li·enne (jōō′lē en′) *adj.* cut into thin strips: *julienne carrots, julienne potatoes.* —*n.* clear soup containing vegetables cut in such a manner. [French *julienne* the soup, possibly from a chef named *Julien.*]

Ju·liet (jōōl′yət, jōō′lē·ət, -et′) *n.* heroine of Shakespeare's tragedy *Romeo and Juliet.*

Jul·ius Cae·sar (jōōl′yəs sē′zər) see **Caesar, Gaius Julius.**

Ju·ly (joo lī′) *pl.,* **-lies.** *n.* seventh month of the year, containing thirty-one days. [Old French *Jule,* from Latin *Jūlius,* from *Jūlius* Caesar, who was born in this month.]

jum·ble (jŭm′bəl) -**bled, -bling.** *v.t.* **1.** to mix or throw in confusion and disorder: *All the toys were jumbled together in the box.* **2.** to confuse mentally; muddle. —*n.* **1.** confused or disordered mixture, collection, or mass. **2.** state of disorder or confusion. [Probably imitative.]

jum·bo (jŭm′bō) *Informal. adj.* extremely large: *a jumbo ice-cream cone.* —*n. pl.,* **-bos.** person, animal, or thing that is unusually large for its kind. [Probably from *Jumbo,* name of a huge elephant shown by P. T. Barnum.]

jump (jŭmp) *v.i.* **1.** to spring into the air, esp. to spring free from the ground or other surface by a sudden propelling effort, as of the feet and legs: *to jump up to catch a ball. The cat jumped into my lap.* **2.** to move or go suddenly or abruptly, as with a bounding movement: *They jumped to their feet when they heard the alarm go off.* **3.** to start involuntarily, as in surprise or fright: *She always jumps when the phone rings.* **4.** to move with a sudden, spasmodic jerk or twitch: *The electrodes jumped when we switched on the current.* **5.** to increase or rise suddenly: *His temperature jumped sharply.* **6.** to come or pass abruptly, as by omitting necessary intermediate points: *to jump to a hasty conclusion. This book jumps from one topic to another.* **7.** to accept or grab hastily and eagerly (with *at*): *to jump at a chance, to jump at an offer.* **8.** to enter or join with eagerness or vigor (with *in* or *into*): *He jumped into the discussion as soon as the subject came up.* **9.** to attack with abuse; criticize or scold harshly (often with *at* or *on*): *He jumped on me for not agreeing with him.* **10.** *Informal.* to respond, obey, or act without question or delay: *When he gives an order, he expects people to jump.* **11.** *Slang.* to be filled with or show signs of vigorous, pulsating activity; be lively or vibrant: *The place is jumping tonight.* **12.** *Checkers.* to capture an opponent's piece by passing one's own directly over it to a vacant square. **13.** *Bridge.* to make a jump bid. —*v.t.* **1.** to spring over or across: *to jump a fence.* **2.** to cause to jump: *to jump a child on one's knee. He jumped his pony across the brook.* **3.** to pass over or by (something intermediate); skip; bypass: *The typewriter jumped three spaces.* **4.** to move or start before (the proper time or signal); anticipate: *The driver jumped the green light at the corner.* **5.** to leave or depart from (a usual course or track) abruptly: *The locomotive jumped the rail.* **6.** *Informal.* to attack by surprise; pounce upon: *The intruders jumped him as he opened the door.* **7.** *Informal.* to board hastily or by jumping: *to jump a train.* **8.** *Checkers.* to capture (an opponent's piece) by passing one's own piece directly over to a vacant square. **9.** *Bridge.* to make (a jump bid). **10. to jump a claim.** to take possession of something belonging to another, as a mining claim, by fraud or force. **11. to jump bail.** to forfeit one's bail by absconding when free on bail. **12. to jump ship.** to desert from service in a ship's crew. **13. to jump the gun. a.** to start or act prematurely or too hastily. **b.** to leap to a premature conclusion. —*n.* **1.** act of jumping; spring; leap: *The dog cleared the stream with one jump.* **2.** place or thing to be jumped over or across: *There were five jumps in the race. The second jump was a tall hedge.* **3.** distance or space covered by a jump: *a jump of eight feet. His jump set an all-time record.* **4.** sudden start or jerk, as in surprise or fright. **5.** sudden increase or rise: *a jump in prices.* **6.** sudden and abrupt transition, as with omission of something intermediate: *to make a jump from one subject to another.* **7.** any of a number of sports contests in jumping. **8.** leap by parachute from an airplane. **9.** *Checkers.* move made by jumping. **10. to get (or have) the jump on.** *Informal.* to get or have a head start or advantage over. —*adj. Military.* of, relating to,

or used by paratroops: *jump area, jump boots, jump school.* [Probably imitative.]

Syn. *v.i.* **1. Jump, leap, spring** mean to move through space with a single, quick motion. **Jump** means to propel oneself through the air, usually in a swift and sharp curve: *The horse jumped over the ditch.* **Leap** means to jump as with a bound and suggests lightness and vigor: *The monkeys leaped from tree to tree.* **Spring** means to jump with a vaulting motion and emphasizes gracefulness: *The tiger sprang on the unsuspecting lamb.*

jump ball, basketball tossed up by the referee between two opposing players who must jump up and tap the ball to put it into play.

jump bid, bid in bridge that is higher than necessary to reach the next level, usually made to show strength.

jump·er[1] (jum′pər) *n.* **1.** one who or that which jumps. **2.** cable, wire, or other conductor used, usually temporarily, to complete or bypass a circuit. [JUMP + -ER[1].]

jump·er[2] (jum′pər) *n.* **1.** one-piece, sleeveless dress, usually worn over a blouse or sweater. **2.** loose shirt, smock, or jacket worn over other clothes to protect them, as by sailors or workmen. **3.** jumpers, rompers. [From dialectal *jump* jacket, modification of French *jupe* petticoat, skirt, going back to Arabic *jubbah* long woolen garment.]

jumping bean, beanlike seed of any of several plants native to Mexico, genera *Sebastiana* and *Sapium*, containing a small moth larva whose movements cause the seed to jump. Also, **Mexican jumping bean.**

jumping jack, toy figure of a man or animal having jointed limbs that can be made to move by pulling attached strings or a lever.

jump·ing-off place (jum′ping ôf′) **1.** utmost limit or extent, as of anything settled or civilized; remote or isolated place. **2.** starting point for an enterprise.

jump-off (jump′ôf′) *n.* start of an enterprise or activity, as of a planned military attack.

jump shot, basketball shot in which a player jumps into the air and shoots the ball at the basket at the highest point of his jump.

jump-start (jump′stärt′) *v.t.* to start (an automobile engine) by using jumpers connected to the battery of another automobile.

jump·suit (jump′soōt′) *n.* **1.** one-piece garment, combining shirt and trousers, designed to be worn as coveralls by paratroopers. **2.** garment styled like this.

jump·y (jum′pē′) jump·i·er, jump·i·est. *adj.* **1.** easily made to start, as in surprise or fright; nervous; jittery. **2.** moving by jumps or sudden variations. —**jump′i·ness,** *n.*

jun., junior.

Jun., June.

junc., junction.

jun·co (jung′kō) *pl.,* -cos. any of various North American finches, genus *Junco,* usually having gray and white plumage. Length: 5–6½ inches. [Modern Latin *Junco* literally, reed bird, from Spanish *junco* reed, from Latin *juncus.*]

junc·tion (jungk′shən) *n.* **1.** place or station where railroad lines meet or cross. **2.** any place or point where two or more things join or meet. **3.** act of joining; being joined. [Latin *jūnctiō* a joining.]

junc·ture (jungk′chər) *n.* **1.** point in time, esp. one made critical by a concurrence of circumstances: *At this juncture, the outbreak of war seems imminent.* **2.** place at which, or structure by which, two things are joined; joint. **3.** act of joining; being joined. [Latin *jūnctūra* a joining. Doublet of JOINTURE.]

June (joōn) *n.* sixth month of the year, containing thirty days. [Latin *Jūnius,* from *Jūnō,* the queen of the gods in Roman mythology.]

Ju·neau (joō′nō) *n.* capital of Alaska, a port city in the southeastern part of the state. Pop. (1970), 6050.

June·ber·ry (joōn′ber′ē) *pl.,* -ries. *n.* the shadbush or its fruit.

June bug 1. any of several stout, brown beetles, family Scarabaeidae, that emerge as adults in late spring or early summer and are destructive to shrubs and trees. Their larvae feed on the roots of many crops. Also, **June beetle. 2.** figeater.

Jung, Carl Gus·tav (yoong; goos′täf) 1875–1961, Swiss psychiatrist.

Jung·i·an (yoong′ē ən) *adj.* of, relating to, or in accordance with the theories of Jung. —*n.* adherent or advocate of the theories of Jung.

jun·gle (jung′gəl) *n.* **1.a.** dense and tangled mass of tropical vegetation, usually consisting of vines, ferns, low bushes, and young trees. **b.** land overgrown with such a mass, usually inhabited by wild animals. **2.** wild, confused, or tangled growth or mass: *a jungle of skyscrapers, a jungle of red tape.* **3.** scene of ruthless competitor or of a fierce struggle for survival: *the advertising jungle.* **4.** *Slang.* place where hobos camp. [Hindi *jangal* forest, desert, Sanskrit *jāngala* desert.]

June bug

jungle fowl, any of various pheasants, genus *Gallus,* of southern Asia, the East Indies, and some Pacific Islands, the male of which has a long, arched tail, two wattles, and a comb. Jungle fowl are considered to be the ancestors of the domestic chicken.

jungle rot, skin condition or disease usually caused by a fungus and occurring in a tropical, jungle environment.

jun·ior (joōn′yər) *adj.* **1.** younger of two. Distinguished from **senior.** ▲ used after the name of a son whose father has the same name. **2.** of lower position, rank, or standing or of more recent appointment or election: *a junior member of the law firm, the junior senator from New York.* **3.** relating to, enrolled in, or designating the third year of a four-year high school or college program: *the junior class.* **4.** of or for younger people: *the junior department in a store.* **5.** smaller in size than others or than the usual. —*n.* **1.** person who is younger than another: *She's my junior by three years.* **2.** student in the third year of a four-year high school or college. **3.** one who is of lower position, rank, or standing or of more recent appointment. [Latin *jūnior,* comparative of *juvenis* young.]

junior college, school having a two-year course equivalent to the first two years of a four-year college, offering liberal arts courses and special or vocational training, and granting an associate's degree.

junior high school, school usually including grades seven and eight, and sometimes six or nine; any school intermediate between elementary school and senior high school.

ju·ni·per (joō′nə pər) *n.* any of a group of ornamental evergreen shrubs or trees, genus *Juniperus,* of the cypress family, bearing purple berrylike fruits, some of which yield an oil used as a flavoring agent in gin. [Latin *jūniperus.*]

junk[1] (jungk) *n.* **1.** old or discarded material, as metal, wood, or rags, that can be put to some use. **2.** *Informal.* anything regarded as worthless or useless; rubbish; trash. **3.** *Nautical.* **a.** old cable or rope used for making such items as mats, swabs, or gaskets. **b.** hard, salted meat used for food on shipboard. **4.** *Slang.* narcotic drug; narcotic drugs collectively. —*v.t.* *Informal.* to throw away or discard as junk; scrap: *to junk an old car.* [Of uncertain origin.]

junk[2] (jungk) *n.* large flat-bottomed sailing vessel developed in China, having a square prow and lugsails. [Portuguese *junco,* from Javanese *jong* large boat.]

Junk[2]

Jun·ker (yoong′kər) *n.* formerly, a member of the German or Prussian landed aristocracy. [German *Junker,* going back to Old High German *junc* young + *hērro* lord.]

jun·ket (jung′kit) *n.* **1.** trip or excursion, as one made by a government official or businessman, paid for by public or organizational funds and ostensibly for purposes of inspection or other official business. **2.** trip or tour, esp. one undertaken for pleasure. **3.** custardlike food of flavored and sweetened milk curdled by rennet. **4.** feast, banquet, or picnic. —*v.i.* **1.** to go on a junket, esp. at public expense. **2.** to feast, banquet, or picnic. [Probably from Italian *giuncata* originally, a cream cheese taken to market (or served) on reeds, going back to *giunco* reed, from Latin *juncus.*] —**jun′ket·er;** *also,* **jun·ket·eer** (jung′kə tēr′), *n.*

junk·ie (jung′kē) *pl.,* -ies. *also,* **junk·y.** *n.* *Slang.* narcotics addict, esp. one addicted to heroin.

junk·man (jungk′man′) *pl.,* -men. *n.* one who buys or sells scrap material, such a metal, glass, paper, and rags.

junk·yard (jungk′yärd′) *n.* place where junk is collected, stored, or resold.

Ju·no (joō′nō) *pl.,* -nos. *n.* **1.** Roman goddess who was the wife and sister of Jupiter and queen of the gods, protectress chiefly of women and marriage. Her Greek counterpart is Hera. **2.** beautiful, stately woman. [Latin *Juno* this goddess.]

Ju·no·esque (joō′nō esk′) *adj.* having the regal bearing and stately beauty of Juno.

jun·ta (hoon′tə, hŏon′-, jun′-) *n.* **1.** group, often consisting of military officers, that rules a country after a coup d'état or a violent overthrow of an existing, usually elected, government. **2.** legislative or administrative council or committee, esp. in Latin America. [Spanish *junta* a council, assembly, from Latin *juncta,* past participle of *jungere* to connect, unite.]

jun·to (jun′tō) *pl.,* -tos. *n.* small, usually secret group that gathers for some common purpose, esp. for political intrigue. [Spanish *junto,* modification of *junta.* See JUNTA.]

Ju·pi·ter (joō′pə tər) *n.* **1.** Roman god who was the ruler of gods and men, associated esp. with rain and thunder. His Greek counterpart is Zeus. Also, **Jove.** **2.** largest planet of the solar system and fifth in order of distance from the sun. It has twelve known moons. [Latin *Jupiter* this god.]

at; āpe; cär; end; mē; it; īce; hot; ōld; fôrk; wood; foŏl; oil; out; up; ūse; turn; sing; thin; this; zh in treasure; ə in ago, taken, pencil, lemon, circus.

ju·ral (joor′əl) *adj.* **1.** of or relating to law; legal. **2.** of or relating to rights and obligations. [From Latin *jūr-*, stem of *jūs* right, law.]

Ju·ra Mountains (joor′ə) mountain range in eastern France and western Switzerland.

Ju·ras·sic (joo ras′ik) *n.* middle geological period of the Mesozoic era during which time the first known birds and flowering plants appeared. See **geology** for table. —*adj.* of, relating to, or characteristic of this period. [From the *Jura* Mountains, where fossils of the Jurassic period were found.]

ju·rid·i·cal (joo rid′i kəl) *adj.* of or relating to law and to the administration of justice. Also, **ju·rid′ic.** [Latin *jūridicus* (from *jūs* right, law + *dīcere* to say) + -AL¹.] —**ju·rid′i·cal·ly,** *adv.*

ju·ris·dic·tion (joor′is dik′shən) *n.* **1.** limits within which judicial or other authority may be exercised; range or extent of authority. **2.** territory over which authority is exercised. **3.** legal right to exercise authority, esp. the authority to interpret or apply the law. **4.** power of those in authority; authority; control. [Latin *jurisdictiō* administration of justice, from *jūs* right, law + *dictiō* a saying.] —**ju′ris·dic′tion·al,** *adj.* —**Syn. 3.** see **power.**

ju·ris·pru·dence (jur′is prōōd′əns) *n.* **1.** science or philosophy of law. **2.** body or system of laws. **3.** branch or department of law: *medical jurisprudence.* [Late Latin *jūrisprūdentia* the science of law, from Latin *jūs* right, law + *prūdentia* skill.]

ju·rist (joor′ist) *n.* one who is versed or skilled in the law, as a lawyer, judge, or writer on the subject of law. [Medieval Latin *jurista* lawyer, from Latin *jūs* right, law.]

ju·ris·tic (joo ris′tik) *adj.* of or relating to a jurist, to jurisprudence, or to the legal profession. Also, **ju·ris′ti·cal.**

ju·ror (joor′ər) *n.* member of a jury. [Anglo-Norman *jurour* a swearer, from Latin *jūrātor.*]

ju·ry¹ (joor′ē) *pl.* **ju·ries.** *n.* **1.** body of persons selected according to law to hear evidence on a matter submitted to them in a court of law and to render a decision or make a presentment according to the law and the evidence. **2.** committee chosen to select the winners and award the prizes in a contest, exhibition, or other competition. [Old French *juree* oath, legal inquiry, from *jurer* to swear, from Latin *jūrāre.*]

ju·ry² (joor′ē) *adj.* *Nautical.* for temporary use, as in an emergency; makeshift: *a jury mast.* [Of uncertain origin.]

ju·ry·man (joor′ē mən) *pl.* **-men.** *n.* male juror. —**ju′ry·wom′an,** *n.*

just¹ (just) *adj.* **1.** fair, upright, and reasonable in acting or judging; adhering to standards of honesty and morality: *a stern but just ruler, to be just in one's dealings.* **2.** consistent with standards of what is fair, upright, and moral: *a just cause, a legal system providing for just treatment of suspects.* **3.** rightly due or given; deserved; merited: *just deserts.* **4.** having sound, reasonable, or adequate grounds; well-founded: *just indignation.* **5.** legally valid; lawful; legitimate: *a just claim to the throne.* **6.** in accordance with truth or fact; accurate; correct: *a just picture of the incidents that led to the war.* **7.** conforming to standards or requirements; proper: *a just balance.* —*adv.* **1.** precisely: *That's just what we were looking for. It's just as I thought.* **2.** a very little while ago; very recently: *I just saw him. We just finished packing.* **3.** by very little; by a narrow margin: *They stopped just short of the line. He arrived just in the nick of time.* **4.** only; merely: *It's just a cold and nothing to worry about.* **5.** at a short distance; immediately: *It's just south of here.* **6.** *Informal.* simply; utterly; positively: *That movie was just awful.* [Latin *jūstus* upright, fair, from *jūs* right, law.] —**just′ly,** *adv.* —**just′ness,** *n.*

Syn. *adj.* **1. Just, fair¹, impartial** mean free from bias or prejudice in judgment. **Just** denotes that which strictly conforms to what is right, lawful, and true, disentangled from personal considerations: *The king was just even to his enemies.* **Fair** implies equitable treatment of all concerned to the point of conceding all reasonable demands and allowing no undue advantage to anyone: *The American legal system guarantees a fair trial to every citizen.* **Impartial** means scrupulously unbiased and objective and free from favoritism and prejudice: *Umpires must be impartial in their decisions.*

just² (just) *v.* joust. [Form of JOUST.]

jus·tice (jus′tis) *n.* **1.** maintenance of just treatment or of what is just; the administering of merited rewards and punishments or of what is due: *After suffering such unfair treatment, the child felt there was no justice in this world.* **2.** that which is merited or due with regard to standards of what is fair, upright, or moral: *to right wrongs and secure social justice.* **3.** quality of conforming to standards of what is fair, upright, and moral: *No one could deny the justice of their being punished.*

4. maintenance, administration, or procedure of law: *a court of justice.* **5.** conformity to reason, truth, or fact; correctness; rightfulness; validity: *There's much justice in his accusation.* **6.a.** judge of the Supreme Court of the United States. **b.** in certain states, judge of an appellate court. **7. to bring to justice.** to cause to be tried or to be legally punished for wrongdoing. **8. to do justice (to). a.** to treat or deal (with something or someone) fittingly or in a manner showing due appreciation. **b.** to represent or show (something or someone) truly or well. [Old French *justice* equity, righteousness, from Latin *jūstitia.*]

justice of the peace, local public official empowered to try minor cases, hold inquests and hearings, perform civil marriages, and carry out other administrative and judicial duties.

jus·tice·ship (jus′tis ship′) *n.* position, function, or term of office of a justice.

jus·ti·fi·a·ble (jus′tə fī′ə bəl) *adj.* capable of being justified; defensible: *justifiable homicide.* —**jus′ti·fi′a·bil′i·ty, jus′ti·fi′a·ble·ness,** *n.* —**jus′ti·fi′a·bly,** *adv.*

jus·ti·fi·ca·tion (jus′tə fə kā′shən) *n.* **1.** act of justifying; being justified. **2.** fact or circumstance that justifies.

jus·ti·fi·er (jus′tə fī′ər) *n.* one who justifies.

jus·ti·fy (jus′tə fī′) -**fied,** -**fy·ing.** *v.t.* **1.** to show to be just, right, or reasonable; vindicate: *His great success justified our faith in him.* **2.** to provide adequate grounds for; warrant: *Their dangerous negligence justified his firing them on the spot.* **3.** to declare or prove guiltless or blameless; absolve. **4.** *Law.* to show a sufficient reason for (an act or omission) in court. **5.** *Printing.* to adjust (lines of type) to the proper length by spacing. [Old French *justifier* to assert or prove the innocence of, going back to Latin *jūstus* upright, fair + *facere* to make.]

Jus·tin·i·an I (jus′tin′ē ən) A.D. 483–565, emperor of the Byzantine Empire from A.D. 527 to 565. The most comprehensive code of Roman law ever compiled was formulated during his reign.

jus·tle (jus′əl) jostle.

jut (jut) **jut·ted, jut·ting.** *v.i.* to stick out; project; protrude. —*n.* that which juts out; projection or protruding point. [Form of JET¹.]

jute (jōōt) *n.* **1.** strong flexible fiber obtained from either of two plants, genus *Corchorus,* chiefly used to make burlap and twine. **2.** either of the two plants yielding this fiber, grown chiefly in India and Pakistan. [Bengali *jhūto* from Sanskrit *jūta* braid of hair.]

Jute (jōōt) *n.* member of a Germanic tribe, some of whom, along with the Angles and Saxons, invaded and settled in Britain during the fifth century A.D. The Jutes founded the kingdom of Kent.

Jut·land (jut′lənd) *n.* peninsula in northern Europe, comprising the mainland of Denmark and the adjoining part of West Germany. Also, Danish, **Jyl′land.** —**Jut′land·er,** *n.*

Ju·ve·nal (jōō′vən əl) *n.* A.D. c.60–c.140, Roman satirist.

ju·ve·nes·cence (jōō′və nes′əns) *n.* state of growing young or youthful.

ju·ve·nes·cent (jōō′və nes′ənt) *adj.* growing young or youthful. [Latin *juvenēscēns,* present participle of *juvenēscere* to grow young again, from *juvenis* young.]

ju·ve·nile (jōō′vən əl, -və nīl′) *adj.* **1.** designed or appropriate for children or young people: *a juvenile edition, juvenile fashions.* **2.** characteristic of children or young people; childish; immature: *temper tantrums and other juvenile behavior.* **3.** young; youthful. —*n.* **1.** young person; youth. **2.** actor who plays youthful parts. **3.** book for children. [Latin *juvenīlis* youthful, from *juvenis* young.] —**ju′ve·nile·ly,** *adv.* —**ju′ve·nile·ness,** *n.*

juvenile court, court of law having special jurisdiction over children or adolescents under a specified age when they have been apprehended by the police or neglected by parents or legal guardians.

juvenile delinquency, antisocial or illegal behavior by children or adolescents.

juvenile delinquent, child or adolescent of a specified age, usually under eighteen, who is guilty of antisocial or illegal behavior but is too young to be held criminally responsible.

ju·ve·nil·i·a (jōō′və nil′ē ə, -nil′yə) *n.,pl.* works, esp. writings, produced in childhood or youth.

ju·ve·nil·i·ty (jōō′və nil′ə tē) *pl.* -**ties.** *n.* **1.** quality or state of being juvenile. **2.** instance of being juvenile; juvenile act or idea.

jux·ta·pose (juks′tə pōz′) -**posed,** -**pos·ing.** *v.t.* to place (two or more things) s ie by side or close together, esp. for contrast or comparison. [From JUXTAPOSITION.]

jux·ta·po·si·tion (juks′tə pə zish′ən) *n.* act of juxtaposing; being juxtaposed. [Latin *iuxtā* near + POSITION.]

Jyl·land (yil′län′) *n.* Danish. Jutland.

---

at; āpe; cär; end; mē; it; īce; hot; ōld; fôrk; wood; fōol; oil; out; up; ūse; turn; sing; thin; this; zh in treasure; ə in ago, taken, pencil, lemon, circus.

k, K (kā) *pl.,* **k's, K's.** *n.* **1.** eleventh letter of the English alphabet. **2.** shape of this letter or something having such a shape.

K, potassium. [Modern Latin *kalium;* of Arabic origin.

k. **1.** kilogram. **2.** karat. **3.** kopeck. **4.** krone.

K. **1.** king. **2.** knight.

Kaa·ba (kä′bə) *also,* **Caa·ba.** *n.* sacred Muslim shrine at Mecca. It is a small cubical structure containing a black stone said to have been given to Abraham by the archangel Gabriel. [Arabic *ka'bah* square house, from *ka'b* cube.]

kab·a·la (kab′ə lə, kə bä′-) *also,* **kab·ba·la.** cabala.

ka·bob (kə bob′) *n.* shish kebab.

Ka·bu·ki (kə bōō′kē, kä′bōō kē) *n.* form of Japanese drama, originating in the late sixteenth century, characterized by stylized acting, singing, and dancing, elaborate costuming, and the playing of both male and female roles by men. [Japanese *kabuki* literally, art of singing and dancing, from *kabu* singing and dancing + *ki* art.]

Ka·bul (kä′bool) *n.* capital and largest city of Afghanistan, in the east-central part of the country. Pop. (1967 est.), 289,703.

ka·chi·na (kə chē′nə) *n.* any of various supernatural beings worshiped by the Hopi, Zuni, and other Pueblo Indian tribes, esp. one associated with clouds and rain.

Kad·dish (kä′dish) *n.* Jewish prayer in praise of God, recited by mourners or as part of a daily synagogue service. [Aramaic *quaddish* holy.]

Kae·song (kā′sông′) *n.* city in southern North Korea. Pop. (1960), 100,000.

Kaf·fir (kaf′ər) *also,* **Kaf·ir.** *n.* **1.** member of a Negroid people who live in parts of South Africa. **2.** their language, a member of the Bantu family of languages. [Arabic *kāfir* infidel.]

kaf·ir (kaf′ər) *also,* **Kaf·fir.** *n.* edible sorghum, *Sorghum caffrorum,* cultivated for its grain and as a source of forage. Also, **kafir corn.**

Kaf·ka, Franz (käf′kə; *fränts*) 1883–1924, Austrian novelist and short-story writer.

kaf·tan (kaf′tən, kaf tan′) caftan.

kai·ak (kī′ak) kayak.

Kai·feng (kī′feng′) *n.* city in east-central China. Pop. (1953), 299,-100.

Kai·ser (kī′zər) *n.* **1.a.** any of the emperors of Germany from 1871 to 1918. **b.** any of the emperors of Austria from 1804 to 1918. **c.** any of the emperors of the Holy Roman Empire from A.D. 962 to 1806. **2.** kaiser; emperor. [German *Kaiser,* going back to Latin *Caesar,* cognomen of the Roman dictator Gaius Julius *Caesar* that was adopted as a title by certain Roman emperors.]

Ka·la·ha·ri (kä′lə här′ē) *n.* large desert region in the central part of southern Africa. Area, approx. 200,000 sq. mi.

Kal·a·ma·zoo (kal′ə mə zōō′) *n.* city in southwestern Michigan. Pop. (1970), 85,555.

kale (kāl) *also,* **kail.** *n.* **1.** broad, curly, bluish-green leaves of a plant, *Brassica oleracea,* variety *acephala,* of the cabbage family, eaten cooked or raw as a vegetable. **2.** the plant itself, cultivated in many temperate regions of the world. [Form of COLE.]

ka·lei·do·scope (kə lī′də skōp′) *n.* **1.** tube-shaped optical device containing loose bits of colored glass or other small objects which are reflected by a set of mirrors as a series of continually changing symmetrical patterns when the tube is rotated. **2.** anything exhibiting a succession of changing colors, patterns, or phases: *the perpetually shifting kaleidoscope of public opinion.* [Greek *kalos* beautiful + *eidos* form + -SCOPE.] —**ka·lei·do·scop·ic** (kə lī′də skop′ik), *adj.* —**ka·lei′do·scop′i·cal·ly,** *adv.*

kal·ends (kal′əndz) calends.

Ka·le·va·la (kä′lə vä′lä) *n.* national epic poem of Finland, consisting of a compilation of traditional Finnish folk tales.

Ka·li·man·tan (kä′lē män′tän) *n.* part of the Republic of Indonesia comprising approximately three-quarters of Borneo. Area, 208,800 sq. mi. Pop. (1961), 4,067,000. Also, **Indonesian Borneo.**

Ka·li·nin·grad (kə lē′nin grad′) *n.* port city in the westernmost part of the Soviet Union. It was formerly the capital of East Prussia and was known as Königsberg. Pop. (1970), 297,000.

kal·mi·a (kal′mē ə) *n.* any of a small group of broad-leafed, usually evergreen shrubs, genus *Kalmia,* of the heath family, native to North America and bearing clusters of cup-shaped flowers. The mountain laurel is a kalmia. [Modern Latin *Kalmia,* from Peter *Kalm,* 1715–1779, Swedish botanist.]

Kal·muck (kal′muk) *also,* **Kal·muk.** *n.* **1.** member of a group of Mongol tribes, formerly nomadic herdsmen, who settled in the region of the lower Volga River. **2.** their language, a member of the Ural-Altaic family of languages. [Turkish *Kalmuk* part of a nomadic Tartar tribe remaining at home.]

kal·so·mine (kal′sə mīn′, -min) calcimine.

ka·mi·ka·ze (kä′mə kä′zē) *n.* **1.** one of a group of Japanese pilots in World War II whose mission was to dive their planes, which were carrying explosives, onto a ship or other target in a suicidal attempt to destroy it. **2.** airplane flown in such a mission. [Japanese *kamikaze* literally, divine wind, from *kami* god + *kaze* wind.]

Kam·pa·la (käm pä′lə) *n.* capital and largest city of Uganda, in the southern part of the country. Pop. (1959), 46,735.

Kan., Kansas.

Ka·nak·a (kə nak′ə, kan′ə kə) *n.* **1.** a Hawaiian. **2.** any South Sea islander. [Hawaiian *kanaka* man.]

Kan·din·sky, Va·si·ly (kan din′skē; vä sē′lē) 1866–1944, Russian painter.

Kan·dy (kän′dē) *n.* city in south-central Ceylon, site of a famous Buddhist temple. Pop. (1963), 67,800.

kan·ga·roo (kang′gə rōō′) *pl.,* **-roos** or **-roo.** *n.* any of various marsupials, family Macropodidae, of Australia and neighboring islands, having small forelimbs, long hind feet, powerful hind legs adapted for leaping, and a long, muscular tail used for support and balancing and for giving greater force to the leap. For approximately six months after birth, the baby kangaroo is carried in the mother's pouch. Height: 1½–7 feet. [Possibly of native Australian origin.]

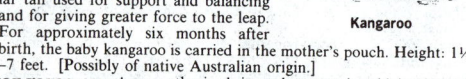

Kangaroo

kangaroo court, unauthorized, irregular court in which trials are hastily arranged, verdicts often decided beforehand, and fair legal procedures ignored.

kangaroo rat, any of various burrowing rodents, genus *Dipodomys,* of the warm, sandy plains of western North America, having small, weak forelegs, strong hind legs which enable it to hop like a kangaroo, and a silky coat of tan or gray fur with white markings. Length: 9–14 inches including the tail.

Kan·pur (kän′poor′) *n.* city in north-central India, on the Ganges, formerly known as Cawnpore. Pop. (1969), 1,163,524.

Kans., Kansas.

Kan·sas (kan′zəs) *n.* state in the west-central United States. Capital, Topeka. Area, 82,264 sq. mi. Pop. (1970), 2,249,071. Abbreviations, **Kans., Kan.** [From the *Kansa* Indians, a Siouan tribe.] —**Kan′san,** *adj., n.*

Kansas City **1.** city in western Missouri. Pop. (1970), 507,087. **2.** city in eastern Kansas adjoining it. Pop. (1970), 168,213.

Kant, Im·ma·nu·el (kant, känt; i mä′nōō el′) 1724–1804, German philosopher.

Kant·ian (kan′tē ən) *adj.* of or relating to Kant or his philosophy. —*n.* follower or adherent of Kant or his philosophy.

at; āpe; cär; end; mē; it; īce; hot; old; fôrk; wood; fōōl; oil; out; up; ūse; turn; sing; thin; this; zh in treasure; ə in ago, taken, pencil, lemon, circus.

ka·o·lin (kā′ə lin) *also,* **ka·o·line.** *n.* fine white clay used chiefly to fill and coat paper and to make pottery and other ceramics. [French *Kaolin,* from Chinese *Kao-ling* name of a mountain (literally, high hill) in China where it was first obtained.]

ka·on (kā′on) *n. Physics.* subatomic particle of the meson group. See **subatomic particle** for table. [*Ka* the letter *k* + (MES)ON.]

ka·pok (kā′pok) *n.* light, fluffy fiber obtained from the seedpods of the silk-cotton tree, used as a stuffing for life preservers, pillows, and mattresses, and as an insulating material. Also, **silk cotton.** [Malay *kāpoq* cotton tree.]

kap·pa (kap′ə) *n.* tenth letter of the Greek alphabet (K, κ), corresponding to English *K, k* and sometimes *C, c*.

kappa meson, kaon.

ka·put (kə poot′, kä-) *adj. Informal.* defeated, destroyed, or ruined. [German *Kaputt,* from French *capot* without tricks (in the game of piquet); literally, hoodwinked, from *capot* hooded cloak, going back to Late Latin *cappa.* See CAPE[1].]

Ka·ra·chi (kə rä′chē) *n.* largest city and former capital of Pakistan, a port in southern West Pakistan, on the Arabian Sea. Pop. (1969), 3,060,000.

kar·a·kul (kar′ə kəl) *n.* **1.** sheep of a breed originally native to central Asia, having a narrow body and a broad tail. The young karakul has a coat of curled, gray or glossy black fur which becomes long, coarse, and gray or brown when the lamb matures. Height: to 3 feet at the shoulder. **2.** caracul. [From *Kara Kul,* lake in Turkestan, where it was first raised.]

kar·at (kar′ət) *also,* **car·at.** *n.* unit of measure used to express the fineness of gold, 24 karats equaling pure gold. Fourteen-karat gold is 14 parts gold and 10 parts alloy.

ka·ra·te (kə rä′tē) *n.* Japanese system of unarmed self-defense in which the hands, elbows, knees, and feet are used to strike an opponent at various vulnerable points of the body. [Japanese *karate* literally, empty hand (in the sense of weaponless).]

Karl-Marx-Stadt (kärl′märks′shtät′) *n.* city in southern East Germany, formerly known as Chemnitz. Pop. (1968 est.), 295,443.

Kar·lo·vy Va·ry (kär′lô vē vär′ē) *n.* town in northwestern Czechoslovakia, a famous health resort. Pop. (1965 est.), 45,200. Also, **Carls′bad;** *German,* **Karls′bad.**

Karls·bad (kärlz′bad′, -bät) *German.* Karlovy Vary.

Karls·ruh·e (kärlz′rōō′ə) *also,* **Carls·ruh·e.** *n.* city in southwestern West Germany. Pop. (1968 est.), 253,995.

kar·ma (kär′mə) *n.* **1.** Hindu and Buddhist doctrine that the morality of a man's actions determines the status of his future incarnations. **2.** fate; destiny. [Sanskrit *karma* action, fate.]

Kar·nak (kär′nak) *n.* village in Egypt, on the Nile, site of a large group of ancient temples. Karnak is located on part of the site of ancient Thebes.

kar·roo (kə rōō′) *pl.,* **-roos.** *also,* **ka·roo.** *n.* **1.** dry tableland of southern Africa. **2. Karroo,** vast plateau region in the southern part of the Republic of South Africa, in Cape of Good Hope province. [Afrikaans *karo,* probably from Hottentot *garo* desert.]

karyo- *combining form* nucleus of a cell: *karyokinesis.* [Greek *karyon* kernel, nut.]

kar·yo·ki·ne·sis (kar′ē ō ki nē′sis, -kī-) *n.* mitosis. [KARYO- + Greek *kinēsis* movement, motion.]

Kash·mir (kash′mēr, kash mēr′) *also,* **Cash·mere.** *n.* area in southern Asia, north of India, disputed by India and Pakistan. Area, approx. 86,024 sq. mi. Pop. (1965 est.), 4,700,000. Also, **Jammu and Kashmir.** —**Kash·mir·i** (kash mēr′ē), *adj., n.*

Kashmir goat, goat native to India, Tibet, and other regions of Asia, raised esp. for its fine, soft undercoat, which is used to make cashmere wool. Also, **Cashmere goat.**

Ka·tan·ga (kə täng′gə, -tang′-) *n.* former province in the southern part of the Belgian Congo and a self-proclaimed independent country from 1960 to 1963, now part of the Democratic Republic of the Congo.

Kat·man·du (kät′män dōō′) *also,* **Kath·man·du.** *n.* capital of Nepal, in the central part of the country. Pop. (1961), 122,500.

Kat·te·gat (kat′ə gat′) *also,* **Cat·te·gat.** *n.* broad arm of the North Sea between Denmark and Sweden.

ka·ty·did (kā′tē did′) *n.* any of a group of large green grasshoppers, family Tettigoniidae, having long threadlike antennae. The male produces a shrill, rasping noise by rubbing its wings together. [Imitative of this sound.]

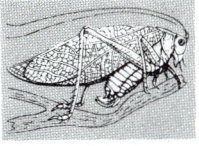
Katydid

Kau·ai (kou′ī) *n.* northernmost island of Hawaii. Area, 551 sq. mi. Pop. (1970), 29,761.

kau·ri (kour′ē) *pl.,* **-ris.** *n.* **1.** tall evergreen tree, *Agathis australis,* found in Australia, New Zealand, and California, having broad flat leaves. Also, **kauri pine. 2.** fine, ever-grained wood of this tree, used in shipbuilding. **3.** resin obtained from this tree, used esp. in making varnish and linoleum. [Of Maori origin.]

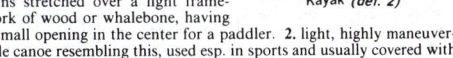

kau·ry (kour′ē) *pl.,* **-ries.** *n.* kauri.

Kay, Sir (kā) rude and boastful knight of the Round Table who was the foster brother and steward of King Arthur.

kay·ak (kī′ak) *also,* **kai·ak.** *n.* **1.** Eskimo canoe made of animal skins stretched over a light framework of wood or whalebone, having a small opening in the center for a paddler. **2.** light, highly maneuverable canoe resembling this, used esp. in sports and usually covered with canvas. [Of Eskimo origin.]

Kayak *(def. 2)*

kay·o (kā′ō′) *n.* knockout in boxing. —*v.t.,* **kay·oed,** **kay·o·ing.** to knock out in boxing.

Ka·zakh·stan (kä′zäk stän′) *n.* republic of the Soviet Union, in the Asian part of the country. Official name: **Kazakh Soviet Socialist Republic.** Area, approx. 1,048,300 sq. mi. Pop. (1965 est.), 11,853,000.

Ka·zan (kä zän′) *n.* city in the European part of the Soviet Union, near the Volga River. Pop. (1970 est.), 869,000.

ka·zoo (kə zōō′) *pl.,* **-zoos.** *n.* toy musical instrument consisting of a tube containing a strip of catgut or a piece of paper that vibrates and produces a harsh buzzing sound when the player hums into the tube. [Probably imitative.]

kc., kilocycle.

K.C., Knights of Columbus.

ke·a (kē′ə) *n.* New Zealand parrot, *Nestor notabilis,* having a sharp, hooked bill and predominantly olive-green plumage. It feeds on fruit and insects in the summer, but in the winter may feed on carrion or attack and kill sheep by tearing their backs to eat the kidney fat. [Of Maori origin.]

Keats, John (kēts) 1795–1821, English poet.

ke·bab (kə bob′) *also,* **ke·bob.** shish kebob.

kedge (kej) **kedged, kedg·ing.** *v.t.* to move (a boat or ship) by pulling on a rope attached to a small anchor that has been dropped at some distance. —*v.i.* (of a boat or ship) to move by kedging. —*n.* small anchor used esp. in kedging. Also, **kedge anchor.** [Of uncertain origin.]

keel (kēl) *n.* **1.** main timber or steel piece extending lengthwise along the center of the bottom of a ship or boat and supporting the entire frame. **2.** part in an aircraft, esp. an airship, corresponding to a ship's keel. **3.** any structure or part resembling a ship's keel. **4.** *Archaic.* ship. **5. on an even keel. a.** in a state of stability; steady; balanced: *His clear-headedness helped keep everyone on an even keel.* —*v.i., v.t.* **1.** to capsize or nearly capsize; turn over: *The boat keeled when the wind came up.* **2. to keel over. a.** to turn bottom up; capsize. **b.** to fall over suddenly; topple; collapse: *to keel over in a faint.* [Old Norse *kjǫlr* lowest timber along the bottom of a ship.]

Keel

keel·boat (kēl′bōt′) *n.* flat-bottomed river boat having a keel but no sails, propelled by being rowed, towed, or poled, formerly used to carry freight in the western United States.

keel·haul (kēl′hôl′) *v.t.* **1.** to drag (a person) under the keel of a ship from one side or end to the other as a form of punishment. **2.** to rebuke or punish severely. [Dutch *kielhalen,* from *kiel* keel + *halen* to haul.]

keel·son (kel′sən, kēl′-) *also,* **kel·son.** *n.* long beam running parallel with and fastened to the main keel of a ship in order to strengthen it. [Of Germanic origin.]

keen[1] (kēn) *adj.* **1.** having a fine cutting edge or point; able to cut or pierce easily; sharp: *a keen sword.* **2.** having or showing great mental sharpness; clever; perceptive: *a keen mind, a keen understanding of a subject.* **3.** highly sensitive or acute, as a sense or sense organ: *keen eyes, a keen sense of smell.* **4.** vividly felt or experienced; intense; strong: *a keen sense of loss. The hounds followed the keen scent.* **5.** of a piercing, penetrating, or cutting nature: *A cold, keen wind blows in from the ocean.* **6.** enthusiastic; eager: *Kate is keen about traveling.* [Old English *cēne* wise, brave.] —**keen′ly,** *adv.* —**keen′ness,** *n.* —**Syn.** See EAGER.

keen[2] (kēn) *Irish. n.* wailing lament for the dead. —*v.i.* to wail loudly for the dead. [Irish *caoinim* I wail.] —**keen′er,** *n.*

keep (kēp) **kept, keep·ing.** *v.t.* **1.** to retain in one's possession, power, or control: *I told Joan she could borrow my sweater but not keep it.* **2.a.** to cause to continue in some specified place, condition, relation, or position: *to keep things in order, to keep the door open, to keep a child*

happy. **b.** to continue to maintain or preserve; continue: *to keep watch over a prisoner, to keep time with the music.* **3.** to store, put, or hold habitually: *Where do you keep your dictionary?* **4.** to have habitually in stock or for for sale: *That market keeps fine meats.* **5.** to have or maintain in one's service or for one's use or enjoyment: *to keep a maid and a gardener, to keep a boat at the lake.* **6.** to maintain by making regular entries in: *to keep account books, to keep a diary.* **7.** to set down regularly so as to have a record: *to keep the score of a basketball game.* **8.** to cause to remain in a place or position; restrain from leaving; detain: *to keep a person in jail, to keep a sick child in quarantine. What could be keeping him this late?* **9.** to hold back; prevent; deter: *Cold weather may keep the plants from budding. She kept herself from laughing.* **10.** to withhold from present use; reserve; save: *to keep some for tomorrow.* **11.** to refrain from divulging: *Can you keep a secret? The newspaper refused to keep the facts from the public.* **12.** to be faithful to; abide by: *to keep one's word, to keep an appointment.* **13.** to observe or celebrate, as with certain rites or ceremonies: *to keep the Sabbath, to keep Christmas.* **14.** to look after the affairs of; manage: *to keep house, to keep a shop.* **15.** to provide the necessities of life for; support: *to keep a large family.* **16.** to protect from harm; guard; defend: *The Lord bless thee, and keep thee* (Numbers 6:24). **17.** to take care of; watch over; tend: *to keep a flock of sheep.* **18.** to stay or remain in, at, or on! *The spectators kept their seats.* **19. to keep back. a.** to retard the progress or growth of: *A slow learner can keep back the whole class.* **b.** to restrain, withhold, or conceal: *to keep back tears, to keep back valuable information.* **20. to keep (something) to oneself.** to refrain from divulging; keep secret; conceal. **21. to keep up. a.** to maintain or continue: *to keep up a correspondence. Keep up the good work.* **b.** to maintain in good order or condition: *The city keeps up the roads and sidewalks.* **c.** to cause to remain awake or out of bed: *Am I keeping you up?* —*v.i.* **1.** to remain or stay in a specified place, condition, relation, or position: *to keep silent, to keep away. Keep off the grass.* **2.** to continue or persevere in some course or action (often with *on*): *to keep moving. He kept on driving despite the snow.* **3.** to restrain oneself; refrain (with *from*): *Ruth couldn't keep from crying at the sad movie.* **4.** to remain in good condition; last without spoiling: *Will this meat keep until tomorrow?* **5.** to be able to last or endure until a later time: *The rest of my news will keep until I see you again.* **6. to keep in with.** *Informal.* to remain in good favor with; continue a friendly relationship with. **7. to keep to. a.** to adhere strictly to; follow closely: *to keep to an agreement.* **b.** to remain in or at: *to keep to one's bed.* **8. to keep to oneself.** to avoid the company of others; remain alone. **9. to keep up. a.** to maintain an equal pace: *Can you keep up, or will we have to walk more slowly?* **b.** to continue: *The noise kept up all night.* **10. to keep up with. a.** to maintain the same speed or rate of progress as: *The slow child could not keep up with the brighter children.* **b.** to remain in contact with: *to keep up with old friends.* **c.** *also,* **to keep up on.** to continue to be informed about: *Have you kept up with the developments in Czechoslovakia? Father keeps up on the latest news.* —*n.* **1.** that which is needed to sustain a person or animal, as food and shelter; means of subsistence: *to earn one's keep.* **2.** care; custody: *The child is in his keep.* **3.** strongest, usually innermost, part of a castle, used as a last defense; donjon. **4. for keeps.** *Informal.* **a.** permanently; forever: *It's yours for keeps.* **b.** with complete seriousness: *The two teams played for keeps.* [Old English *cēpan* to observe, seize.]
Syn. *v.t.* **1. Keep, retain, withhold** mean to continue to have and hold. **Keep** means to hold in one's possession: *The girl kept the abandoned cat she found in the alley.* **Retain** means to hold and preserve against opposition or adverse circumstances: *In spite of his misfortunes Harry has retained a sense of humor.* **Withhold** means to hold back or refrain from granting or relinquishing: *The judge withheld his decision until he had heard all the evidence.*
keep·er (kē′pər) *n.* person who protects, tends, or is responsible for someone or something, as a guard or attendant: *a keeper at a zoo, the keeper of an inn.* ▲ often used in combination: *a shopkeeper, a gamekeeper.*
keep·ing (kē′ping) *n.* **1.** care, custody, or possession: *The jewels were placed in my keeping.* **2. in keeping (with).** consistent; appropriate: *The president's actions are in keeping with his stated goals. Greg's behavior was not in keeping with the solemn occasion.*
keep·sake (kēp′sāk′) *n.* article given or kept to remind one of the giver; memento.
Syn. Keepsake, memento, souvenir apply to something that serves as a reminder. **Keepsake** denotes an article that reminds the keeper of the giver or is retained and cherished as a token of affection, esteem, or regard: *Mary's boy friend gave her a bracelet as a keepsake before he left for college.* **Memento** denotes a small article that serves to renew or keep alive the memory of an event or person: *Every guest received a noisemaker as a memento of the party.* **Souvenir** is an article whose association with an event or place endows it with a special value as a remembrance: *The local shopkeepers sell souvenirs to the tourists.*

keg (keg) *n.* **1.** small barrel, usually holding five to ten gallons. **2.** unit of weight for nails that is equal to 100 pounds. [Old Norse *kaggi* cask.]
Kei·jo (kā′jō′) *n.* Seoul.
Kel·ler, Helen (kel′ər) 1880–1968, U.S. writer and lecturer who was deaf and blind from infancy.
kelp (kelp) *n.* **1.** any of a large group of brown seaweeds, order Laminariales, growing in great masses along the coasts of the Atlantic and Pacific oceans. **2.** ashes of such seaweed, formerly a major source of potassium and iodine, now used mainly as a fertilizer. [Of uncertain origin.]
kel·pie (kel′pē) *pl.,* **-pies.** *also,* **kel·py.** *n.* water spirit in Scottish folklore, usually appearing as a horse, supposed to drown people or warn them of drowning. [Of uncertain origin.]
kel·son (kel′sən) keelson.
Kelt (kelt) Celt.
Kelt·ic (kel′tik) Celtic.
Kelvin scale, temperature scale in which one degree is equal in size to a centigrade degree and zero degrees represents absolute zero (-273.15° centrigrade). [From Lord *Kelvin,* 1824–1907, British scientist.]
Kem·pis, Thomas à (kem′pis) 1380–1471, German churchman and writer.
ken (ken) *n.* range of knowledge, perception, or understanding: *I'm afraid that subject under discussion is beyond my ken.* —*v.t., v.i.,* **kenned** or **kent** (kent), **ken·ning.** *Scottish.* to know; understand. [Partly from Old English *cennan* to make known, declare; partly from Old Norse *kenna* to know.]
Ken·ne·dy, John Fitzgerald (ken′ə dē) 1917–63, thirty-fifth president of the United States, from 1961 to 1963.
ken·nel (ken′əl) *n.* **1.** shelter for a dog or dogs. **2.** *also,* **kennels.** establishment where dogs are bred, trained, or boarded. —*v.t.,* **-neled, -nel·ing;** *also, British,* **-nelled, -nel·ling.** to put or keep in a kennel. [Going back to Latin *canis* dog.]
Ken·nel·ly-Heav·i·side layer (ken′əl ē hev′ē sīd′) Heaviside layer.
ke·no (kē′nō) *n.* gambling game derived from and resembling lotto. [Possibly from French *quine* five winning numbers in a lottery, from Latin *quīnī* five each; because the pieces used in the game are placed in rows of five.]
Ke·no·sha (kə nō′shə) *n.* city in southeastern Wisconsin, on Lake Michigan. Pop. (1960), 67,899.
Kent (kent) *n.* **1.** county in southeastern England. **2.** ancient kingdom in southeastern England.
Kent·ish (ken′tish) *adj.* of or relating to Kent or its people. —*n.* Old English or Middle English dialect spoken in the kingdom of Kent.
Ken·tuck·y (kən tuk′ē) *n.* state in the east-central United States. Capital, Frankfort. Area, 40,395 sq. mi. Pop. (1970), 3,219,311. Abbreviation, **Ky.** [Of Iroquoian origin.] —**Ken·tuck′i·an,** *adj., n.*
Kentucky Derby, race for three-year-old horses, established in 1875 and run annually at Churchill Downs in Louisville, Kentucky.
Ken·ya (ken′yə, kēn′yə) *n.* country in eastern Africa, formerly a British colony and protectorate. Capital, Nairobi. Area, 224,960 sq. mi. Pop. (1969 est.), 10,506,000. —**Ken′yan,** *adj., n.*
kep·i (kep′ē) *pl.,* **kep·is.** *n.* military cap having a flat, circular top inclined toward the front and a visor. [French *képi,* from Swiss German *Käppi,* diminutive of *Kappe* cap, from Late Latin *cappa* hood, cap. See CAP.]

Kepi

Kep·ler, Jo·hann (kep′lər; yō′hän) 1571–1630, German astronomer.
kept (kept) past tense and past participle of **keep.**
ker·a·tin (ker′ə tin) *n.* tough, fibrous protein present in the skin tissue of all vertebrates, forming the chief component of horns, hoofs, hair, nails, feathers, and other outgrowths of the skin. [Greek *kerat-,* stem of *keras* horn + -IN¹.]
kerb (kurb) *n.* *British.* curb *(def. 1).*
ker·chief (kur′chif) *n.* **1.** piece of cloth, usually square, worn over the head or around the neck, esp. by women; scarf. **2.** handkerchief *(def. 1).* [Old French *couvrechief* literally, to cover the head, from *couvrir* to cover + *chef* head (from Latin *caput*). See COVER.]
Ke·ren·sky, A·le·xan·der (ke ren′skē; ä′lek sän′dər) 1881–1970, Russian revolutionary leader.
kerf (kurf) *n.* **1.** cut or notch made by an ax, saw, or other tool. **2.** amount or piece cut off. [Old English *cyrf* act of cutting.]
ker·mis (kur′mis) *also,* **ker·mess, kir·mess.** *n.* **1.** annual fair or festival held in the Low Countries. **2.** any similar fair or entertainment. [Dutch *kermis* church Mass; originally, a religious celebration including a fair, from *kerk* church (going back to Greek *kyriakon*) + *mis* Mass (going back to Late Latin *missa*). See CHURCH, MASS.]

kern (kurn) *also,* **kerne.** *n. Archaic.* medieval Irish or Scottish foot soldier armed with light weapons. [Irish *ceatharn* troop, soldier.]

ker·nel (kurn′əl) *n.* **1.** grain or seed of various plants, as of wheat or corn. **2.** softer, inner part of a seed or fruit. **3.** central, most valuable, or most important part; core; nucleus. [Old English *cyrnel.*]

ker·o·sene (ker′ə sēn′, ker′ə sēn′) *also,* **ker·o·sine.** *n.* colorless, highly volatile liquid distilled from petroleum, widely used as a fuel and cleaning solvent. It consists of a mixture of hydrocarbons. Also, **coal oil.** [Greek *kēros* wax + -ENE; because paraffin is used in distilling it.]

Ker·ry (ker′ē) *pl.,* **-ries.** *n.* one of a breed of small, black dairy cattle, often having white markings, originally developed in Ireland.

Kerry blue terrier, terrier of a breed originally developed in Ireland, having a dark grayish-blue coat of thick, wavy hair. Height: to 19 inches at the shoulder.

ker·sey (kur′zē) *pl.,* **-seys.** *n.* **1.** coarse, ribbed, woolen fabric, woven with a cotton warp, used esp. for work clothes. **2.** heavy, woolen fabric similar to melton, having a lustrous nap, used esp. for overcoats and jackets. [Probably from *Kersey,* village in Suffolk, England, once noted for its trade in woolens.]

kes·trel (kes′trəl) *n.* small falcon, *Falco tinnunculus,* native to Europe and Asia, having predominantly brown plumage, noted for its ability to hover in the air against the wind. Length: about 13½ inches. Also, **wind′hov′er.** [Old French *cresserelle,* going back to Latin *crepitāculum* rattle; because its cry resembles the sound of a rattle.]

ketch (kech) *n.* fore-and-aft-rigged sailing ship with two masts, similar to a yawl, but having the mizzenmast farther forward, ahead of the rudder post. [Possibly from CATCH.]

Ketch

ketch·up (kech′əp) *also,* **catch-up, cat·sup.** *n.* thick, seasoned sauce, usually made of tomatoes, onions, salt, sugar, and spices, and used with many types of food. [Malay *kēchap* fish sauce, probably from dialectal Chinese *ke-tsiap* brine of fish.]

ke·tone (kē′tōn′) *n.* any of a class of organic compounds in which a carbonyl group is attached to each of two carbon atoms that are contained in hydrocarbon radicals. [German *Keton,* short for *Aketon,* from French *acétone* acetone.]

ket·tle (ket′əl) *n.* **1.** any metal container for boiling liquids or for cooking in liquid; pot. **2.** teakettle. **3. kettle of fish.** difficult, disagreeable, or awkward situation: *The simple problem quickly became a fine kettle of fish.* [Old Norse *ketill* caldron, from Latin *catillus* small bowl, diminutive of *catīnus* deep vessel for cooking food.]

ket·tle·drum (ket′əl drum′) *n.* drum consisting of a hollow brass or copper hemisphere with a parchment head that can be tuned to a definite pitch.

key¹ (kē) *pl.,* **keys.** *n.* **1.** instrument that opens or closes a locking mechanism by moving a bolt or tumblers. **2.** device for turning a screw, bolt, nut, or the like, as on a roller skate. **3.** something that serves to disclose, explain, or solve, as a clue in a mystery, a set of answers to problems in a textbook, or the legend of a map.

Kettledrum

4. something that leads to or is a means of attaining something: *the key to success. The miser thought money was the key to happiness.* **5.** something, as a geographical location or position, which provides a means of control, esp. of entry or possession: *The Bosporus is the key to the Black Sea.* **6.** one who or that which is considered the essential or controlling element or force of something: *The quarterback was the key of their team.* **7.** part that works by lever action or by making electrical contact, used in operating an instrument or machine: *a piano key, a telegraph key.* **8.** device, as a pin, bolt, or wedge, put in a hole or space to hold parts together. **9.** *Music.* scale or system of notes in which all the notes bear a definite relationship to, and are based on and named for, a given note which is the keynote: *a symphony in the key of F sharp.* **10.** tone or pitch of the voice: *to speak in a high key.* **11.** characteristic or general tone or level of intensity, as of feeling, action, or expression: *The letter was written in an angry key. The actor's performance was in a subtle, low key.* —*adj.* of great or chief importance; essential, major, or basic: *a key factor in their success, a key battle in the war.* —*v.t.,* **keyed, key·ing. 1.** *Music.* to regulate the pitch or tone of: *to key an instrument to B flat.* **2.** to regulate or adjust (something) so as to suit

a particular activity, state, requirement, or the like: *to key a speech to an occasion.* **3.** to lock or fasten with or as with a key: *to key a door, to key parts together with a wedge.* **4.** to provide (something, as a machine or instrument) with a key or keys. **5.** to finish (an arch) by adding a keystone. **6.** to provide with an explanatory key, legend, table, or the like. **7. to key up.** to make nervous, tense, or excited: *Just thinking about the final exam keys him up.* [Old English *cæg* instrument that locks or unlocks something, explanation.]

key² (kē) *n.* low, coastal island or reef, as those along the southern tip of Florida; cay. [Spanish *cayo,* probably from Old French *cay* retaining wall; of Celtic origin.]

Key, Francis Scott (kē) 1779–1843, U.S. lawyer and author of *The Star-Spangled Banner,* the U.S. national anthem.

key·board (kē′bôrd′) *n.* arrangement or set of keys, as in a piano, harpsichord, typewriter, or key punch.

key fruit, samara.

key·hole (kē′hōl′) *n.* hole through which a key is inserted into a lock.

keyhole saw, compass saw.

Keynes, John May·nard (kānz; mā′nərd) 1883–1946, English economist. **—Keynes′i·an,** *adj., n.*

key·note (kē′nōt′) *n.* **1.** *Music.* note on which a scale or system of tones is based; tonic. **2.** main or dominant idea, principle, theme, or mood: *Economic expansion was the keynote of the nation's foreign policy.* —*v.t.,* **-not·ed, -not·ing.** to give or set the keynote of.

keynote address, speech, as at the convention of a political party, in which important issues and the basic policy to be followed are presented. Also, **keynote speech.**

key punch, machine operated from a keyboard and used to record information in data processing by means of holes punched in cards.

key signature *Music.* sharps or flats placed after the clef at the beginning of each staff, or at any point where there is a change of key, indicating the key of the music which follows.

key·stone (kē′stōn′) *n.* **1.** central, topmost stone of an arch, serving to lock the remaining stones of the arch together. It is usually the last stone to be set in place and is often distinguished in some way, as by projection. **2.** fundamental element or part upon which associated parts depend: *Singapore was the keystone of British power in the Far East.*

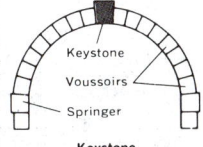
Keystone

Key West 1. island off the coast of southwestern Florida, in the Gulf of Mexico, one of the westernmost Florida Keys. **2.** port city on this island. Pop. (1970), 27,563.

kg., kilogram.

khak·i (kak′ē, kä′kē) *pl.,* **khak·is.** *n.* **1.** dull, yellowish-brown or tan color. **2.** sturdy, twilled cotton fabric of this color. **3. khakis.** garment made of this fabric, esp. a military uniform. [Hindi *khākī* dusty, from Persian *khāk* dust.]

khan¹ (kän, kan) *n.* **1.** any of the medieval emperors of China who also ruled the Tartar, Turkish, and Mongol tribes. **2.** ruler, official, dignitary, or other man of high rank in Iran, Afghanistan, and central Asia. [Turkish *khān* lord, prince.]

khan² (kän, kan) *n.* inn or caravansary in Turkey and neighboring countries. [Arabic *khān,* from Persian *khān.*]

Khar·kov (kär′kof, -kov) *n.* city in the European Soviet Union, in the Ukraine. Pop. (1970), 1,223,000.

Khar·toum (kär tōōm′) *n.* capital of Sudan, in the north-central part of the country, on the Nile. Pop. (1968), 194,000.

khe·dive (kə dēv′) *n.* title of the Turkish viceroys of Egypt from 1867 to 1914. [French *khédive,* going back to Persian *khedīv* prince, sovereign.]

Khmer (kə mer′) *pl.,* **Khmers** or **Khmer.** *n.* **1.** member of a people native to Cambodia, whose civilization reached its peak in the twelfth century. **2.** Cambodian (*def. 2*).

Khmer Republic, official name of Cambodia.

Khoi·san (koi′sän) *n.* family of languages spoken in southwest Africa, comprising Hottentot and Bushman.

Khrush·chev, Ni·ki·ta (kroosh′chef′, -chôf′, krōōsh′-; ni kē′tä) 1894–1971, premier of the Soviet Union from 1958 to 1964.

Khu·fu (kōō′fōō) *n.* Cheops.

Khy·ber Pass (kī′bər) mountain pass between West Pakistan and Afghanistan.

kib·butz (ki boots′, -bōōts′) *pl.,* **-but·zim** (-boot′sēm, -bōōt′-). *n.* collective farm or settlement in modern Israel. [Hebrew *qibbûtz* literally, a gathering.]

kibe (kīb) *n.* chapped or ulcerated chilblain or other sore, esp. one on the heel. [Probably from Welsh *cibi.*]

kib·itz (kib′its) *v.i. Informal.* to act as a kibitzer. [Yiddish *kibitzen,* from German *kiebitzen* to look on.]

at; āpe; cär; end; mē; it; īce; hot; ōld; fôrk; wood; fōōl; oil; out; up; ūse; turn; sing; thin; this; zh in treasure; ə in ago, taken, pencil, lemon, circus.

563

kib·itz·er (kib′it sər) *n. Informal.* **1.** spectator at a card game who gives unwanted advice to the players. **2.** anyone who gives unwanted advice or meddles in the affairs of others. [Yiddish *kibitzer*, going back to German *kiebitzen* to look on.]

kick (kik) *v.t.* **1.** to strike with the foot or feet: *to kick a pebble on the beach.* **2.** to drive, impel, or move by striking with the foot or feet: *to kick a stone into the sewer.* **3.** *Sports.* to score (a goal or point) by kicking the ball over the goal posts or into the goal, as in football or soccer. **4.** (of firearms) to strike in recoiling: *The rifle kicked Tom's shoulder.* —*v.i.* **1.** to strike out with the foot or feet: *The wild bronco kicked and bucked. The swimmer increased his speed by kicking faster.* **2.** *Sports.* to put the ball in play or attempt to score or gain ground by kicking the ball, as in football or soccer. **3.** (of firearms) to recoil when fired. **4.** *Informal.* to object strongly; complain; rebel: *Mike kicked at having so much work to do.*
to kick around. *Informal.* **a.** to treat roughly or inconsiderately. **b.** to wander from place to place: *The sailor has kicked around for years.* **c.** to give consideration or thought to: *to kick around a plan.*
to kick back. *Slang.* to pay back (a portion of money received as a fee, commission, salary, or the like) as a kickback.
to kick in. *Slang.* to contribute as one's share: *Everyone was asked to kick in fifty cents.*
to kick off. a. *Football.* to make a kickoff. **b.** *Informal.* to start; initiate: *The students kicked off the football season with a party.* **c.** *Slang.* to die.
to kick (someone) out. *Informal.* to dismiss, expel, or eject (someone) forcefully or suddenly.
to kick the bucket. *Slang.* to die.
to kick the habit. *Slang.* to free oneself of an addiction, esp. to narcotics.
to kick up. *Informal.* **a.** to cause trouble, pain, or difficulty: *The old man's arthritis kicks up in wet weather.* **b.** to cause or stir up (trouble, confusion, or the like): *The spoiled child kicked up a fuss.*
to kick (someone) upstairs. *Informal.* to promote (someone) to a position which is higher but gives less responsibility or power.
—*n.* **1.** act or power of kicking the foot or feet: *Pete shut the door with a kick. The swimmer has a strong kick.* **2.** sudden recoil, esp. of a gun when fired. **3.** *Sports.* **a.** act or instance of kicking a ball. **b.** ball kicked: *to block a kick.* **c.** distance a ball travels when kicked: *a fifty-yard kick.* **4.** *Slang.* complaint; objection: *What's your kick this time?* **5.** *Slang.* pleasing or exciting sensation; thrill: *Dave gets a kick out of driving a car.* **6.** *Slang.* stimulating or intoxicating power or effect, esp. of alcoholic drink. **7.** *Slang.* temporary but intense period of interest or indulgence: *Claudia was on a knitting kick.* [Of uncertain origin.]
kick·back (kik′bak′) *n.* **1.** illegal or secret payment made by a seller of goods or services to the person who directed a buyer or client to him. **2.** portion of a worker's wages returned to someone, as his supervisor or employer, as the condition under which he gets or keeps his job. **3.** sudden or violent reaction or response.
kick·er (kik′ər) *n.* **1.** one who or that which kicks. **2.** *Slang.* surprising, controversial, or difficult part or point: *It's an easy job, but the kicker is the long hours.*
kick·off (kik′ôf′) *n.* **1.** kick that puts the ball in play in football, as at the beginning of a half. **2.** *Informal.* beginning; commencement: *The dance marked the kickoff of the charity's fund drive.*
kick·shaw (kik′shô′) *n.* **1.** fancy or uncommon dish; delicacy. **2.** trifle; trinket. [Modification of French *quelque chose* trifle, something, going back to Latin *quālis* of what kind + *qui* who + *causa* reason.]
kid (kid) *n.* **1.** young goat. **2.** kidskin. **3.** *Informal.* young person; child; youngster. —*adj. Informal.* (of a brother or sister) younger. —*v.t.*, **kid·ded, kid·ding.** *Informal.* **1.** to make fun of; tease: *They kidded Jim about his freckles.* **2.** to deceive (someone) as a joke; fool: *Sam tried to kid us into believing his story.* —*v.i.* **1.** to engage in good-humored fooling or teasing; joke. [Old Norse *kith* young goat.] —**kid′der,** *n.*
Kidd, William (kid) c.1645–1701, British pirate known as Captain Kidd.
Kid·dush (kid′oosh, ki doosh′) *n.* Jewish prayer recited over wine on the eve of the Sabbath or a festival. [Hebrew *quiddūsh* sanctification.]
kid glove **1.** glove made of kidskin or similar leather. **2.** *kid gloves.* tactful, gentle, or cautious treatment: *Cindy is sensitive and unpredictable and must be handled with kid gloves.*
kid·nap (kid′nap′) *v.t.*, **-naped** or **-napped, -nap·ing** or **-nap·ping.** to seize or detain (a person) against his will, esp. for the purpose of receiving a ransom. [KID child + *nap*, form of NAB.] —**kid′nap·er,** *n.; also,* **kid′nap·per,** *n.*
Syn. Kidnap, abduct mean to carry off a person illegally. **Kidnap** means to seize a person by force or fraud and hold him against his will, esp. as a hostage for ransom: *Terrorists kidnaped the minister and demanded $10,000 from the government for his release.* **Abduct** usually means to

kidnap a girl, esp. for illegal or immoral purposes: *Two masked men abducted the girl from her home.*
kid·ney (kid′nē) *pl.*, **-neys.** **1.** either of a pair of organs lying against the back of the abdominal cavity that filter urea, various salts, and other wastes out of the bloodstream, forming urine which is collected in the bladder. **2.** kidney of certain animals, used as food. **3.** nature; disposition; temperament: *a man of my kidney* (Shakespeare, *The Merry Wives of Windsor*). [Middle English *kidenei,* from *kiden-,* of uncertain meaning and origin + *ei* egg, from Old English *æg* egg.]

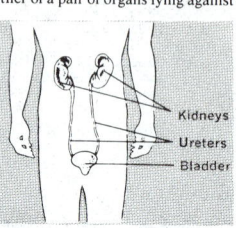
Kidneys
Ureters
Bladder

kidney bean **1.** kidney-shaped seed of any of various varieties of a plant, *Phaseolus vulgaris,* of the pea family, cooked and eaten as a vegetable. **2.** the plant itself, widely cultivated throughout the world.
kid·skin (kid′skin′) *n.* leather made from the skin of young goats, used for such items as gloves and shoes.
Kiel (kēl) *n.* city in northern West Germany. Pop. (1968), 268,905.
Kiel Canal, canal in northern West Germany connecting the Baltic and North seas.
Kier·ke·gaard, Sø·ren Aa·bye (kẽr′kə gärd′; sœ′rən ô′boo) 1813–55, Danish philosopher and theologian.
Ki·ev (kē′ef, -ev) *n.* port city on the Dnieper River, in the southwestern Soviet Union, capital and largest city of the Ukraine. Pop. (1970), 1,632,000.
Ki·ga·li (ki gä′lē) *n.* capital of Rwanda, in the central part of the country. Pop. (1962 est.), 4000.
Ki·ku·yu (ki kōō′ū) *pl.*, **-yus** or **-yu.** *n.* **1.** member of a Bantu tribe of northern Kenya. **2.** their language, a member of the Bantu family of languages.
Ki·lau·e·a (kē′lou ā′ə) *n.* active volcano in Hawaii.
Kil·i·man·ja·ro, Mount (kil′ə mən jär′ō) highest mountain in Africa, in northeastern Tanzania, near the Kenya border.
kill¹ (kil) *v.t.* **1.** to deprive of life; cause the death of: *Car accidents kill thousands of Americans every year. The sergeant killed three enemy soldiers.* **2.** to put an end to; destroy; extinguish: *A drink of water killed the taste of the medicine.* **3.** to destroy or spoil the effect of, as by contrast or incongruity: *The ugly fence kills the beauty of the house.* **4.** to destroy the active qualities of; neutralize: *Too many consecutive plantings killed the soil.* **5.** to delete, cancel, or stop the publication of (something, as a line, paragraph, or article): *The editor killed the story in the late edition.* **6.** to defeat or veto: *to kill a proposed law.* **7.** to hit (a ball in tennis) to an opponent with such force that it is impossible to return it. **8.** to pass (time) aimlessly or unproductively: *Ed killed an hour by wandering through the town.* **9.** *Informal.* to overcome completely, as with amusement or embarrassment: *The joke killed the audience. It kills him to admit he is wrong.* **10.** *Informal.* to affect with severe pain, discomfort, or fatigue: *My back is killing me.* **11.** *Informal.* to stop or turn off: *to kill a motor. Kill the lights.* —*v.i.* **1.** to cause death; be fatal: *An overdose of this drug can kill.* **2.** to commit murder: *to kill without a motive.* —*n.* **1.** act or instance of killing, esp. in hunting: *The hunters moved in for the kill.* **2.** animal or animals killed in hunting: *The tiger dragged its kill into the jungle.* [Possibly from an unrecorded Old English word.]
Syn. *v.t.* **1. Kill, murder, slay, assassinate** mean to deprive of life or bring about death. **Kill** is the general word meaning to cause the death of a person, animal, or plant in any way: *A late frost killed many flowers last spring.* **Murder** means to kill a person in a premeditated and criminal manner: *The bandits murdered the man for his money.* **Slay** means to kill violently and deliberately and is now usually used in a literary context: *The king slew his enemies on the battlefield.* **Assassinate** especially means to murder a prominent person for political motives: *President Kennedy was assassinated in Dallas in 1963.*
kill² (kil) *n.* channel, creek, or stream. [Dutch *kil.*]
Kil·lar·ney (ki lär′nē) *n.* **1.** town in southwestern Ireland. Pop. (1961), 6825. **2.** Lakes of. three famous lakes near this town.
kill·dee (kil′dē′) *pl.*, **-dees** or **-dee.** *n.* killdeer.
kill·deer (kil′dēr′) *pl.*, **-deers** or **-deer.** *n.*

Killdeer

North American wading bird, *Charadrius vociferus,* having a brown back, a white throat, breast, and abdomen, and two black bands across the breast. Length: 9–11 inches. [Imitative of its cry.]

at; āpe; cär; end; mē; it; īce; hot; ōld; fôrk; wood; fōol; oil; out; up; ūse; turn; sing; thin; <u>th</u>is; zh in treasure; ə in ago, taken, pencil, lemon, circus.

kill·er (kil′ər) *n.* **1.** one who or that which kills. **2.** killer whale.

killer whale, any of various black-and-white, carnivorous dolphins, genus *Orcinus,* inhabiting all oceans of the world. The killer whale preys on fish, penguins, seals, sea lions, and even whales. Length: to 30 feet. Also, **gram′pus.**

kill·ing (kil′ing) *n.* **1.** act of one who or that which kills, esp. murder. **2.** *Informal.* sudden great profit or success: *to make a killing in a real-estate deal.* —*adj.* **1.** causing or likely to cause death; deadly; fatal: *a killing blow.* **2.** extremely tiring; exhausting: *a killing amount of work.*

kill·joy (kil′joi′) *n.* one who spoils or lessens the enjoyment of others.

kiln (kil, kiln) *n.* furnace or oven for burning, baking, or drying, as in making bricks, pottery, or charcoal. —*v.t.* to burn, bake, or dry in a kiln. [Old English *cylene* oven, from Latin *culīna* kitchen.]

ki·lo (kē′lō, kil′ō) *pl., n.* **1.** kilogram. **2.** kilometer.

kilo- *prefix* one thousand: *kilocycle, kiloliter.* [French *kilo-,* from Greek *chīlioi.*]

kil·o·cal·o·rie (kil′ə kal′ər ē) *n.* large calorie. See **calorie.**

kil·o·cy·cle (kil′ə sī′kəl) *n.* **1.** unit equal to 1000 cycles. **2.** unit equal to 1000 cycles per second, used in measuring the frequency of electromagnetic waves.

kil·o·gram (kil′ə gram′) *also, British,* **kil·o·gramme.** *n.* unit of mass and weight in the metric system equal to 1000 grams, or 2.2046 pounds avoirdupois. [French *kilogramme,* going back to Greek *chīlioi* thousand + *gramma* small weight.]

kil·o·gram-me·ter (kil′ə gram′mē′tər) *n.* unit of work or energy, equal to about 7.2 foot-pounds. A kilogram-meter is the amount of energy required to raise a mass of one kilogram to a height of one meter.

kil·o·li·ter (kil′ə lē′tər) *also, British,* **kil·o·li·tre.** *n.* unit of capacity in the metric system equal to 1000 liters, or one cubic meter; 264.17 U.S. gallons or 1.308 cubic yards. [French *kilolitre,* going back to Greek *chīlioi* thousand + *litra* pound.]

ki·lom·e·ter (ki lom′ə tər, kil′ə mē′-) *also, British,* **kil·o·me·tre** (kil′ə mē′tər). *n.* unit of length in the metric system equal to 1000 meters, or 3280.8 feet. [French *kilomètre,* going back to Greek *chīlioi* thousand + *metron* measure.] —**kil·o·met·ric** (kil′ə met′rik), *adj.*

kil·o·ton (kil′ə tun′) *n.* **1.** unit of weight equal to 1000 tons. **2.** unit of explosive force equivalent to that produced by the detonation of 1000 tons of TNT.

kil·o·watt (kil′ə wot′) *n.* unit of electrical power equal to 1000 watts.

kil·o·watt-hour (kil′ə wot′our′) *n.* unit of electrical energy equal to the energy consumed by a machine working at a steady rate of one kilowatt for one hour.

kilt (kilt) *n.* pleated skirt usually made of tartan and reaching to the knees, esp. one worn by men in the Scottish Highlands. —*v.t. Scottish.* to tuck up or fasten (the skirts) around the body. [Of Scandinavian origin.]

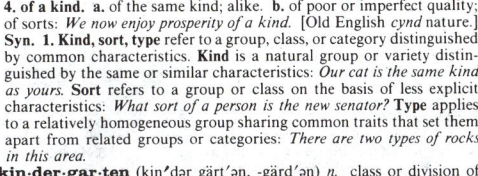
Plaid

Kilt

Kilt

kil·ter (kil′tər) *n. Informal.* good condition; order. ▲ now used chiefly in the phrase *out of kilter: That toaster is out of kilter.* [Of uncertain origin.]

Kim·ber·ley (kim′bər lē) *n.* city in the Republic of South Africa, center of the world's diamond industry. Pop. (1961 est.), 79,000.

ki·mo·no (ki mō′nə, -nō) *pl., n.* **-nos.** *n.* **1.** loose robe or gown tied with a sash, traditionally worn as an outer garment by Japanese men and women. **2.** loose dressing gown similar to this. [Japanese *kimono* clothing.]

kin (kin) *n.* **1.** one's whole family; one's relatives; kindred; kinsfolk. **2.** kinsman; relative: *She is no kin of mine.* **3.** next of kin. person or persons most closely related to one: *The police notified the victim's next of kin.* —*adj.* **1.** related: *She is not kin to me.* **2.** closely similar; akin: *a parliament that is kin to Great Britain's.* [Old English *cynn* kind², family.]

-kin *suffix* little; small: *lambkin.* [Middle Dutch *-kijn, -kin.*]

kind¹ (kīnd) *adj.* **1.** gentle, considerate, and friendly in nature or behavior; good-hearted: *a kind person, to be kind to animals. It was kind of you to help her.* **2.** proceeding from or characterized by good-heartedness: *kind words, a kind act.* [Old English *cynde* natural, native.]

kind² (kīnd) *n.* **1.** class, sort, or grouping; variety; type: *The whale is a kind of mammal. There are many kinds of games to play.* **2. in kind. a.** in goods or produce, rather than in money. **b.** with something comparable: *She insulted him, and he repaid her in kind.* **3. kind of.** *Informal.* somewhat; rather: *I'm getting kind of hungry. It's kind of late.*

Kimono

4. of a kind. a. of the same kind; alike. **b.** of poor or imperfect quality; of sorts: *We now enjoy prosperity of a kind.* [Old English *cynd* nature.]

Syn. 1. Kind, sort, type refer to a group, class, or category distinguished by common characteristics. **Kind** is a natural group or variety distinguished by the same or similar characteristics: *Our cat is the same kind as yours.* **Sort** refers to a group or class on the basis of less explicit characteristics: *What sort of a person is the new senator?* **Type** applies to a relatively homogeneous group sharing common traits that set them apart from related groups or categories: *There are two types of rocks in this area.*

kin·der·gar·ten (kin′dər gärt′ən, -gärd′ən) *n.* class or division of school for children from four to six years old, preceding the first grade of elementary school. [German *Kindergarten* literally, children's garden, from *Kind* child + *Garten* garden.]

kin·der·gart·ner (kin′dər gärt′nər, -gärd′-) *also,* **kin·der·gar·ten·er.** *n.* child who attends kindergarten.

kind-heart·ed (kīnd′här′tid) *adj.* having or showing kindness or sympathy: *a kind-hearted person, kind-hearted actions.* —**kind′-heart′ed·ly,** *adv.* —**kind′-heart′ed·ness,** *n.*

kin·dle (kind′əl) **-dled, -dling.** *v.t.* **1.** to set on fire; light. **2.** to arouse, stir up, or excite (emotions or the like): *to kindle a person's anger, to kindle a revolt.* **3.** to make bright or glowing; light up: *The setting sun kindled the evening sky.* —*v.i.* **1.** to catch fire; begin to burn: *A dry forest is likely to kindle with the smallest spark.* **2.** to become aroused or stirred up, as the emotions. **3.** to become bright or glowing: *His face kindled with excitement.* [Old Norse *kynda* to light a fire + -LE.] —**kin′dler,** *n.*

Syn. *v.t.* **1. Kindle, ignite, light¹** mean to set on fire. **Kindle** indicates that the fire is started gradually, as with wood or straw: *The campers learned how to kindle a fire without matches.* **Ignite** suggests the application of a spark to a highly inflammable substance which then bursts suddenly into flame: *An electric spark ignites the gasoline in an automobile engine.* **Light** implies that a flame is applied to an object which then burns brightly or glows with intense heat: *Peter lighted his cigarette.*

kin·dling (kind′ling) *n.* material for starting a fire, esp. small pieces of dry wood.

kind·ly (kīnd′lē) **-li·er, -li·est.** *adj.* **1.** having or showing kindness; kind; benevolent: *a kindly face, a kindly smile, kindly people.* **2.** having a favorable effect; pleasant; agreeable: *a kindly breeze on a hot day.* —*adv.* **1.** in a kind or gentle manner: *to speak kindly to a child.* **2.** favorably; agreeably: *Fate did not look kindly upon their venture.* **3.** as a favor; please: *Kindly remove your foot from the table.* **4.** enthusiastically; cordially: *We thank you kindly.* **5. to take kindly to.** to like or accept: *He does not take kindly to criticism.* [Old English *cyndelic* natural.] —**kind′li·ness,** *n.*

kind·ness (kīnd′nis) *n.* **1.** quality or state of being kind; good will. **2.** kind act; favor: *We thanked our hostess for her many kindnesses.* —**Syn. 1.** see **benevolence.**

kin·dred (kin′drid) *n.* **1.** one's whole family; one's relatives. —*adj.* **1.** like; allied; similar: *a kindred spirit, kindred pursuits.* **2.** related by history or derivation; having common ancestors: *kindred languages.* [Old English *cynn* family, kind², + *rēden* condition.]

kine (kīn) *n.,pl. Archaic.* cows; cattle. [Old English *cȳna* of cows, genitive plural of *cū* cow¹.]

kin·e·mat·ics (kin′ə mat′iks) *n.* branch of mechanics dealing with the motion of moving bodies, without reference to the mass or force involved in the motion. [Greek *kīnēma* motion + -ICS.] —**kin′e·mat′ic,** *adj.*

kin·e·scope (kin′ə skōp′) *n.* **1.** motion-picture record of a television program. **2.** picture tube. —*v.t.* **-scoped, -scop·ing.** to make a kinescope of. [Greek *kīnētos* moving + -SCOPE.]

kin·es·the·sia (kin′əs thē′zhə) *n.* sensation of movement, weight, resistance, and position in the muscles and joints, perceived through the nerves. [Modern Latin *kinesthesia,* from Greek *kīnein* to move + *aisthēsis* perception.] —**kin·es·thet·ic** (kin′əs thet′ik), *adj.*

ki·net·ic (ki net′ik) *adj.* **1.** of or relating to motion. **2.** produced or caused by motion. [Greek *kīnētikos* of putting in motion, going back to *kīnein* to move.]

kinetic energy, energy possessed by a body because of its motion. Distinguished from **potential energy.**

ki·net·ics (ki net′iks) *n.* branch of mechanics that deals with the effects of forces in causing or changing the motion of bodies.

kin·folk (kin′fōk′) *also,* **kin·folks.** kinsfolk.

king (king) *n.* **1.** male ruler who holds limited or absolute sovereignty over a nation or state for life, usually by hereditary rights. **2. King.** God or Christ. **3.** person or thing supreme or preeminent in a given sphere: *the king of the jungle, an oil king, the king of popular music.* **4.** playing card bearing a picture of a king. **5.** principal piece in the game of chess, ordinarily capable of moving only one square in any

King *(def. 5)*

direction. The object of the game is to checkmate the opponent's king. **6.** piece in the game of checkers that has moved across the board to the opponent's side, and has been crowned, thus entitling it to move both forward and backward. [Old English *cyning* male ruler of a state.]

King, Martin Luther, Jr. (king) 1928–68, U.S. clergyman and civil rights leader.

King Arthur, see Arthur.

king·bird (king′burd′) *n.* any of various flycatchers, genus *Tyrannus,* found throughout North and South America. Length: 8–9 inches.

king·bolt (king′bōlt′) *n.* vertical bolt connecting the body of a wagon or other vehicle with the front axle, or the body of a railroad car with a truck, and serving as a pivot in turning. Also, **king′pin′.**

king crab 1. largest edible crab, *Paralithodes kamtschatica,* having a small triangular body and very long legs. It is found in the northern Pacific Ocean. **2.** horseshoe crab.

king·craft (king′kraft′) *n.* art of ruling as a king; royal statesmanship.

king·dom (king′dəm) *n.* **1.** nation or state ruled by a king or queen. **2.** realm, region, or sphere in which some condition or quality is supreme or prevails: *a cattle kingdom, the kingdom of the intellect.* **3.** one of the three primary divisions of nature: *the animal kingdom, the vegetable kingdom, the mineral kingdom.* **4.** spiritual realm of God. [Old English *cyningdōm* kingship.]

king·fish (king′fish′) *pl.,* **-fish** or **-fish·es.** *n.* any of several saltwater food and game fish, family Sciaenidae, esp. the northern kingfish, *Menticirrhus saxatilis,* found along the Atlantic coast of the United States, having a dark-gray body, and weighing up to three pounds. Length: to 18 inches.

king·fish·er (king′fish′ər) *n.* any of various brightly colored birds, family Alcedinidae, found throughout temperate and tropical regions of the world, having a large, usually crested head and a long, pointed bill. It feeds on fish, insects, reptiles, and sometimes small mammals or birds.

King James Version, English translation of the Bible authorized by King James I and published in 1611, widely used by Protestants. Also, **Authorized Version.**

king·let (king′lit) *n.* **1.** weak or insignificant king. **2.** any of various greenish songbirds, genus *Regulus,* related to and resembling warblers, often having a somewhat concealed orange, yellow, or red crest. Length: 4 inches.

king·ly (king′lē) **-li·er, -li·est.** *adj.* characteristic of, like, or suitable for a king; royal; regal: *a kingly bearing, kingly pride.* —*adv.* in a kingly manner; regally; royally. —**king′li·ness,** *n.* —**Syn.** *adj.* see royal.

king·pin (king′pin′) *n.* **1.** pin that is positioned in the center and in front of the other pins in bowling. **2.** kingbolt. **3.** *Informal.* chief person in a group or sphere: *the kingpin of organized crime.*

king post, vertical post connecting the apex of a triangular truss, as of a roof, with the tie beam.

Kings (kingz) *n.* **1.** in the Protestant Bible, either of two books (I Kings or II Kings) of the Old Testament, containing the history of the Jewish monarchy from the reign of Solomon to the fall of Jerusalem in 586 B.C. **2.** in the Douay Bible, one of four books of the Old Testament, equivalent to I and II Samuel and I and II Kings of the Protestant Bible.

king salmon, large salmon, *Oncorhynchus tschawytscha,* found throughout the northern Pacific Ocean, commercially important as a food fish. Also, **chi·nook′.**

king's English, standard, correct, or accepted English usage or speech, esp. that of Great Britain. Also, **queen's English.**

king·ship (king′ship) *n.* **1.** position, office, or dignity of a king. **2.** government by a king; monarchy.

king-size (king′sīz′) *adj.* larger or longer than is ordinary: *a king-size cigarette, a king-size portion of meat.* Also, **king′-sized′.**

king snake, any of a group of nonpoisonous snakes, genus *Lampropeltis,* of varied marking and coloration, found from southern Canada to northern South America. It feeds on other snakes and on rodents, lizards, frogs, and other small animals.

Kings·ton (king′stən) *n.* capital, largest city, and chief port of Jamaica, on the southeastern coast of the island. Pop. (1960), 123,403.

Kings·ton-up·on-Hull (king′stən ə pon′hul′) *n.* Hull (*def. 2*).

king truss, truss having a king post.

kink (kingk) *n.* **1.** tight curl or sharp twist, as in a hair, wire, or rope. **2.** painful muscle spasm or cramp; crick: *He got a kink in his back after doing physical exercise for the first time in two years.* **3.** *Informal.* imperfection or flaw, as in the plan or operation of something: *The engineer got the kinks out of the design.* **4.** *Informal.* mental quirk, eccentricity, or whim. —*v.i., v.t.* to form or cause to form a kink or kinks. [Dutch *kink* twist in a rope.]

kin·ka·jou (king′kə jōō′) *n.* small, slender, yellowish-brown mammal, *Potos flavus,* related to the raccoon, native to the tropical forests of Mexico and Central and South America, having a long prehensile tail and soft woolly fur. Length: 42 inches including the tail. Also, **honey bear.** [French *kinkajou;* of Algonquian origin.]

Kinkajou

kink·y (king′kē) **kink·i·er, kink·i·est.** *adj.* full of kinks; tightly curled or twisted: *kinky hair.* —**kink′i·ness,** *n.*

kins·folk (kinz′fōk′) *also,* **kin·folk, kin·folks.** *n.,pl.* one's relatives collectively; family.

Kin·sha·sa (kin shä′sə) *n.* capital and largest city of the Democratic Republic of the Congo, a port in the western part of the country, formerly known as Léopoldville. Pop. (1967), 901,520.

kin·ship (kin′ship′) *n.* **1.** family relationship. **2.** any relationship or close connection: *the kinship between botany and zoology.*

kins·man (kinz′mən) *pl.,* **-men.** *n.* male relative.

kins·wom·an (kinz′woom′ən) *pl.,* **-wom·en.** *n.* female relative.

ki·osk (kē′osk, kē osk′) *n.* **1.** small structure with one or more open sides, used esp. as a newsstand, bandstand, telephone booth, or subway entrance. **2.** light, open pavilion or summerhouse, often having its roof supported by columns, common in Turkey and Iran. [French *kiosque,* from Turkish *kiüshk* pavilion, from Persian *kūshk* palace.]

kip (kip) *n.* untanned hide of a small or young animal. [Middle Dutch *kip* bundle of hides.]

Kip·ling, Rud·yard (kip′ling; rud′yərd) 1865–1936, English poet, short-story writer, and novelist.

kip·per (kip′ər) *v.t.* to cure (fish) by splitting, cleaning, and salting, and then drying, smoking, or preserving. —*n.* **1.** fish, esp. herring, salmon, or sea trout, that has been kippered. **2.** male salmon or sea trout during or shortly after the spawning season. [Old English *cypera* kind of salmon, possibly from *coper* copper (with reference to the coloring of the salmon). See COPPER.]

Kir·ghiz (kir gēz′) *pl.,* **-ghiz** or **-ghiz·es.** *n.* **1.** member of a Turkic-speaking Mongolian people, living mainly in west-central Asia. **2.** their language, a member of the Ural-Altaic family of languages.

Kir·ghi·zia (kir gē′zhə) *n.* republic of the Soviet Union, in the Asian part of the country, bordering northwestern China. Official name: **Kirghiz Soviet Socialist Republic.** Area, 76,650 sq. mi. Pop. (1963 est.), 2,379,000. Also, **Kir·ghiz·stan** (kir gē stän′).

kirk (kurk) *n.* **1.** *Scottish.* church. **2. the Kirk,** the established Presbyterian Church of Scotland, as distinguished from the Church of England or the Episcopal Church of Scotland. [Old Norse *kirkja* church, from Old English *cirice.* See CHURCH.]

kir·mess (kur′mis) *n.* kermis.

kir·tle (kurt′əl) *n.* *Archaic.* **1.** woman's skirt, gown, or petticoat. **2.** man's short coat or tunic. [Old English *cyrtel,* going back to Latin *curtus* short.]

Kish·i·nev (kish′ə nef′) *n.* city in the southwestern Soviet Union, capital of Moldavia. Pop. (1970), 357,000.

kis·met (kiz′met′, -mət) *n.* fate; destiny. [Turkish *qismet,* from Arabic *qisma(t).*]

kiss (kis) *v.t., v.i.* **1.** to touch with the lips as a sign of greeting, affection, desire, or respect: *The mother kissed her child. They kissed and said good-by.* **2.** to touch lightly or softly: *When the sweet wind did gently kiss the trees* (Shakespeare, *Merchant of Venice*). —*n.* **1.** a touching with the lips as a sign of greeting, affection, desire, or respect. **2.** light or gentle touch. **3.** any of several small candies, esp. of chocolate, usually individually wrapped in foil or paper. [Old English *cyssan* to touch with the lips.] —**kiss′a·ble,** *adj.*

kiss·er (kis′ər) *n.* **1.** one who kisses. **2.** *Slang.* the face.

kit[1] (kit) *n.* **1.** set of tools, instruments, or equipment for a specific purpose: *a repair kit, a first-aid kit.* **2.** collection of personal effects or articles, esp. for traveling. **3.** bag, case, box, or other container for storing or carrying a kit: *The television repairman kept spare tubes in his kit.* **4.** set of parts or materials to be assembled: *Jack built a model of a rocket from a kit.* **5.** *Informal.* collection of persons or things; lot. ▲ now used chiefly in the phrase *kit and caboodle: He sold the whole kit and caboodle to a junk dealer.* [Middle Dutch *kitte* large wooden bowl, tankard.]

kit[2] (kit) *n.* kitten.

Kit·a·kyu·shu (kē′tä kū′shōō) *n.* city at the northwestern tip of Kyushu, Japan. Pop. (1968), 1,050,000.

kitch·en (kich′ən) *n.* **1.** room or place specially equipped or set apart for the preparation and cooking of food. **2.** facilities, equipment, or staff of a kitchen. **3.** cuisine: *This restaurant has an international kitchen that includes French and Italian dishes.* [Old English *cycene* place for cooking food, going back to Latin *coquīna,* from *coquere* to cook.]

at; āpe; cär; end; mē; it, īce; hot; ōld; fôrk; wood; fōōl; oil; out; up; ūse; turn; sing; thin; this; zh in treasure; ə in ago, taken, pencil, lemon, circus.

Kitch·e·ner (kich′ə nər) n. city in southern Ontario, Canada. Pop. (1966), 93,255.

kitch·en·ette (kich′ə net′) also, **kitch·en·et**. n. small, compactly arranged kitchen, frequently an alcove off or a section of a larger room.

kitchen garden, garden where vegetables and fruit are grown for home use.

kitchen midden, prehistoric mound of kitchen refuse consisting mainly of shells and bones, marking the location of a primitive human habitation. Also, **mid′den.** [Translation of Danish *køkkenmödding*.]

kitchen police *Military*. **1.** duty of assisting the cook by performing kitchen chores. **2.** enlisted men assigned to such duty.

kitch·en·ware (kich′ən wâr′) n. kitchen utensils, such as pots and pans.

kite (kīt) n. **1.** lightweight frame, usually of wood covered with paper or cloth, flown in the air at the end of a long string for sport or recreation. **2.** any of various hawks, family Accipitridae, having a hooked bill, a forked tail, and long, narrow wings. **3.** any of several light, lofty sails spread only in a light wind. —*v.i.* **kit·ed, kit·ing.** *Informal.* to move or fly with or as with the swift, gliding motion of a kite. [Old English *cȳta* a bird of prey.]

kith (kith) n. **1. kith and kin.** one's friends, acquaintances, and relatives collectively. **2.** *Archaic.* one's friends and acquaintances collectively. [Old English *cȳththu* relationship.]

kit·ten (kit′ən) n. young cat. [Blend of dialectal *kitling* (of Scandinavian origin) and Old French *chaton,* diminutive of *chat* cat, from Late Latin *cattus*. See CAT.]

kit·ten·ish (kit′ən ish) adj. playful or cute, esp. in a coquettish manner. —**kit′ten·ish·ly,** adv. —**kit′ten·ish·ness,** n.

kit·ti·wake (kit′ē wāk′) n. sea gull, genus *Rissa*, native to Arctic regions, having white plumage with gray and black markings on the wings and a very short hind toe. Length: 16–18 inches. [Imitative of its cry.]

kit·ty¹ (kit′ē) pl., **-ties.** n. kitten or cat. [KIT² + -Y².]

kit·ty² (kit′ē) pl., **-ties.** n. **1.a.** pool in a card game into which each player contributes, used esp. to pay expenses or buy refreshments. **b.** stakes in a card game, esp. poker; pot. **2.** money pooled by a group of people for some special purpose. [KIT¹ + -Y².]

kit·ty-cor·ner (kit′ē kôr′nər) n. catty-corner.

Kitty Hawk, village in northeastern North Carolina where the first successful airplane flight was made in 1903 by Wilbur and Orville Wright.

Kiu·shu (kū′shōō) Kyushu.

ki·va (kē′və) n. large chamber in a Pueblo Indian dwelling, usually completely or partly underground, used esp. for religious ceremonies and social gatherings. [Of Hopi origin.]

Ki·wa·nis (ki wä′nis) n. international association of men's business and professional clubs, founded in Detroit in 1915, pledged to promote higher standards in business and professional life. —**Ki·wa·ni·an** (ki wä′nē ən), n., adj.

ki·wi (kē′wē) pl., **-wis.** n. any of several flightless birds, genus *Apteryx,* native to the forests of New Zealand, having a rounded body, a very long, slender bill, and brownish-gray, furlike feathers. Length: 19–33 inches. Also, **ap′ter·yx.** [Of Maori origin.]

Kiwi

KKK, Ku Klux Klan.

kl., kiloliter.

Klan (klan) n. Ku Klux Klan.

Klans·man (klanz′mən) pl., **-men.** n. member of the Ku Klux Klan.

Klee, Paul (klā; poul) 1879–1940, Swiss artist.

Kleen·ex (klē′neks) n. *Trademark.* disposable paper tissue which serves as a handkerchief.

Klein bottle (klīn) *Geometry.* one-sided surface theoretically formed by taking the neck of a bottle, passing it through the side of the bottle, and joining it to an opening at the bottom of the bottle.

Klein bottle

klep·to·ma·ni·a (klep′tə mā′nē ə) n. obsessive and uncontrollable impulse or tendency to steal, esp. when one has no economic need for the article involved. [Greek *kleptēs* thief + *maniā* madness.] —**klep′to·ma′ni·ac′,** n.

klieg light (klēg) bright arc lamp used esp. in filming motion pictures. [From the brothers John H. and Anton T. *Kliegl,* German-American developers of this light.]

Klon·dike (klon′dīk) n. noted gold-mining region in the west-central Yukon, Canada. Area, approx. 800 sq. mi.

km., kilometer.

K-me·son (kā′mē′son, -mes′on) n. kaon.

knack (nak) n. special skill, ability, or method for doing something easily or proficiently: *a knack for writing, to have a knack for saying funny things.* [Possibly identical with obsolete *knack* sharp blow; imitative.]

knap·sack (nap′sak′) n. bag, usually of canvas or leather, for carrying clothes, equipment, or other supplies, designed to be strapped over the shoulders and carried on the back. [Dutch *knapzak,* from *knappen* to eat + *zak* bag.]

Knapsack

knap·weed (nap′wēd′) n. coarse plant, *Centaurea nigra,* of the composite family, widely distributed throughout North America and Europe, having a wiry stem and bearing oblong leaves and reddish-purple flowers. [Archaic *knop* bud of a flower, knob (possibly from Old English *cnop* knob) + WEED¹.]

knave (nāv) n. **1.** unprincipled, deceitful, or disloyal man; scoundrel. **2.** in card games, a jack. **3.** *Archaic.* **a.** male servant. **b.** man of humble birth. [Old English *cnafa* boy, servant.]

knav·er·y (nā′vər ē) pl., **-er·ies.** n. behavior characteristic of a knave; deceitfulness; trickery.

knav·ish (nā′vish) adj. of, relating to, or characteristic of a knave; unprincipled; deceitful. —**knav′ish·ly,** adv. —**knav′ish·ness,** n.

knead (nēd) v.t. **1.** to mix or work (a substance, as dough or clay) into a uniform mass, esp. by pressing and squeezing with the hands. **2.** to manipulate by pressing and squeezing with the hands; massage: *The team's trainer kneaded the pitcher's sore arm.* **3.** to make or shape by or as by kneading: *to knead a statue of clay, to knead a person's character.* [Old English *cnedan* to make into a dough.] —**knead′er,** n.

knee (nē) n. **1.a.** joint of the human leg between the thigh and the lower leg. **b.** region around this joint. **2.** any joint similar or corresponding to the human knee, as the carpal joint in the foreleg of hoofed mammals. **3.** part of a garment, esp. trousers, covering the knee. **4. to bring to one's knees,** to force to submit or yield. —*v.t.,* **kneed, knee·ing.** to strike or touch with the knee. [Old English *cnēo* joint between the thigh and lower leg.]

knee breeches, breeches reaching to or just below the knees.

knee·cap (nē′kap′) n. flat, triangular, movable bone at the front of the knee, protecting the joint from injury. Also, **knee′pan′, pa·tel′la.**

knee-deep (nē′dēp′) adj. **1.** so deep as to reach the knees: *The river is only knee-deep at this point.* **2.** sunk to the knees: *knee-deep in mud.* **3.** deeply involved or concerned: *knee-deep in work.*

knee-high (nē′hī′) adj. so high or tall as to reach the knees: *The meadow was covered with knee-high grass.*

kneel (nēl) **knelt** or **kneeled, kneel·ing.** *v.i.* to rest on the bent knee or knees: *to kneel down to scrub the floor, to kneel before an altar.* [Old English *cnēowlian,* from *cnēo* knee.] —**kneel′er,** n.

knee·pad (nē′pad′) n. protective covering for the knee, worn esp. when engaging in certain sports, as football or ice hockey.

knee·pan (nē′pan′) n. kneecap.

knell (nel) n. **1.** tolling of a bell, esp. the sound of a bell rung slowly and solemnly, as after a death. **2.** an omen of death, failure, or impending doom: *Not receiving the requested funds was the death knell for the project.* **3.** any mournful sound: *a knell of sobbing voices.* —*v.i.* **1.** (of a bell) to ring slowly and solemnly, as after a death; toll. **2.** to sound mournfully or ominously. —*v.t.* **1.** to summon or proclaim by or as by a knell. **2.** to sound a bell.] [Old English *cnyllan* to sound a bell.]

knelt (nelt) a past tense and past participle of **kneel.**

knew (nōō, nū) past tense of **know.**

Knick·er·bock·er (nik′ər bok′ər) n. **1.** descendant of the early Dutch settlers of New York. **2.** native or resident of New York. [From Diedrich *Knickerbocker,* pseudonym used by Washington Irving for his *History of New York* (1809).]

knick·ers (nik′ərz) n.pl. loose-fitting trousers extending to and gathered just below the knee. Also, **knick′er·bock′ers.** [From KNICKERBOCKER; because of their resemblance to the breeches worn by the Dutch in the illustrations for Irving's book.]

knick·knack (nik′nak′) also, **nick·nack.** n. small decorative object. [Repetition of obsolete *knack* toy (with vowel change); imitative.]

knife (nīf) pl., **knives.** n. **1.** cutting instrument consisting of one or more sharp-edged blades attached to a handle. **2.** cutting blade of a tool or machine. —*v.t.,* **knifed, knif·ing. 1.** to cut or stab with a knife. **2.** *Informal.* to slander, betray, or harm (someone), esp. in an underhanded way. —*v.i.* to move or cut a way through something with or as with a knife: *The boat knifed through the water.* [Old English *cnīf* a cutting tool with a blade and handle.]

knife-edge (nīf′ej′) n. **1.** sharp, cutting part of the blade of a knife. **2.** anything very sharp or penetrating: *The knife-edge of analysis revealed the solution.* **3.** wedge with a fine edge which acts as a fulcrum for a scale, beam, pendulum, or similar instrument.

knife pleat, one of a set of narrow pleats turned in the same direction. See **pleat** for illustration.

knight (nīt) *n.* **1.a.** in the Middle Ages, a mounted soldier who gave military service to a king or lord in return for the right to hold land. **b.** such a soldier, usually of noble birth, who, after serving an apprenticeship as a page and squire, was raised to honorable military rank by a king or lord and was pledged to chivalrous behavior. **2.** man upon whom an honorary, nonhereditary dignity has been conferred by the sovereign in recognition of personal merit or for services rendered to the crown or a country. In Great Britain a knight ranks next below a baronet and is entitled to use *Sir* before his given name. **3.** man devoted to the service or protection of another, esp. a lady; champion. **4.** piece in the game of chess shaped like a horse's head, which may move one square either horizontally or vertically and then one square diagonally. —*v.t.* to raise to the rank of knight: *The king knighted the soldier for his valor.* [Old English *cniht* boy, servant, vassal.]

knight·er·rant (nīt′er′ənt) *pl.,* **knights·er·rant.** *n.* medieval knight who traveled in search of adventure, esp. to display military skill, bravery, and chivalry.

knight·er·rant·ry (nīt′er′ən trē) *pl.,* **knight·er·rant·ries.** *n.* **1.** conduct, actions, or practices characteristic of a knight-errant. **2.** conduct inspired by noble but impractical ideals; quixotic behavior.

knight·hood (nīt′hood′) *n.* **1.** rank, dignity, or vocation of a knight. **2.** behavior or qualities befitting a knight; chivalry. **3.** knights collectively.

knight·ly (nīt′lē) *adj.* of, relating to, or characteristic of a knight: *knightly deeds, knightly valor.* —**knight′li·ness,** *n.*

Knights of Columbus, international fraternal and service organization of Roman Catholic men founded in 1882.

Knight Templar *pl.,* *(def. 1)* **Knights Templars** or *(def. 2)* **Knights Templar. 1.** Templar *(def. 1).* **2.** member of an order of Freemasons.

knit (nit) **knit·ted** or **knit, knit·ting.** *v.t.* **1.** to make (a fabric or garment) by interlocking loops of yarn or thread, either by hand by the use of knitting needles, or by machine. **2.** to join or fasten closely and securely: *Love knitted the family together.* **3.** to draw (the brows) together in wrinkles; furrow. —*v.i.* **1.a.** to make a fabric or garment by interlocking loops of yarn or thread. **b.** to make a basic stitch in knitting. **2.** to come together securely, as the parts of a broken bone. **3.** (of the brows) to come together in wrinkles. —*n.* fabric or garment made by knitting. [Old English *cnyttan* to tie by knotting.] —**knit′ter,** *n.*

knit·ting (nit′ing) *n.* **1.** action of a person or thing that knits. **2.** knitted fabric or garment.

knitting needle, long, slender rod, either straight or curved, having a blunt point at one or both ends, used in knitting.

knit·wear (nit′wâr′) *n.* clothing made of knitted fabric.

knives (nīvz) plural of **knife.**

knob (nob) *n.* **1.** rounded protuberance or lump. **2.** rounded handle or dial, as for opening a door or drawer or for operating a radio or television. **3.** rounded, usually isolated, hill or mountain. [Middle Low German *knobbe* knot, bud.] —**knobbed,** *adj.*

knob·by (nob′ē) **-bi·er, -bi·est.** *adj.* **1.** covered with knobs or lumps. **2.** shaped like a knob: *knobby knees.*

knock (nok) *v.t.* **1.** to strike with a sharp, hard blow; hit: *The falling branch knocked him on the head.* **2.** to drive or force by hitting: *The batter knocked the ball out of the park.* **3.** to drive or bring (something) violently against something else; cause to collide: *They accidentally knocked heads when they stood up. Dan knocked his knee against the leg of the table.* **4.** to hit or push so as to cause to fall: *to knock a glass over.* **5.** to make or render by striking: *to knock a hole in a wall, to knock a person unconscious.* **6.** to find fault with; disparage: *The critics knocked his latest play.* —*v.i.* **1.** to strike a resounding blow or series of blows, esp. with the fist; rap: *I knocked on the door but nobody answered. Did you hear someone knock?* **2.** to come into collision; bump: *Fear made his knees knock.* **3.** to make a pounding, clanking, or rattling sound, as an engine with faulty combustion.

to knock about (or **around**). *Informal.* **a.** to treat roughly or inconsiderately. **b.** to wander from place to place.

to knock down. a. to take apart or disassemble, as for shipping or storage. **b.** to dispose of (an article) to a bidder at an auction by a knock with the auctioneer's gavel; sell to the highest bidder. **c.** *Informal.* to lower (a purchase price); reduce: *During the sale prices were knocked down twenty percent or more.* **d.** *Slang.* to receive as wages or salary; earn: *to knock down $150 a week.*

to knock it off. *Slang.* to stop it.

to knock off. *Informal.* **a.** to stop or discontinue: *to knock off work for lunch.* **b.** to stop work: *to knock off every day at 5 o'clock.* **c.** to deduct (an amount or sum): *to knock off ten dollars from the retail price.* **d.** to make or accomplish hastily, roughly, or easily: *The author knocked off the book in less than a month.* **e.** to kill.

to knock out. a. to render unconscious: *A blow on the head knocked him out.* **b.** to defeat (an opponent) in boxing by hitting him so that he falls to the canvas and is unable to rise to his feet within the prescribed time. **c.** *Informal.* to tire or exhaust completely: *The long drive really knocked me out.* **d.** *Informal.* to destroy the power or effectiveness of: *The storm knocked out electricity in the town. Bombing raids knocked out the enemy's artillery.* **e.** *Informal.* to make or accomplish hastily, roughly, or easily: *The artist knocked out a sketch in fifteen minutes.*

to knock out of the box. *Baseball.* to get so many hits against (an opposing pitcher) that he is removed from the game.

to knock over (or **off**). *Slang.* to rob or burglarize: *to knock over a bank.*

to knock together. to make or put together hastily or roughly.

—*n.* **1.** act or instance of knocking; sharp, hard blow: *Bill got a knock on the head in the fight.* **2.** sound produced by a blow or series of blows, as that produced by rapping on a door with the fist in order to gain admittance. **3.** pounding, clanking, or rattling sound, esp. one in an automobile engine caused by faulty combustion. **4.** *Informal.* misfortune; setback. **5.** *Slang.* harsh or hostile criticism; adverse remark: *The actor's performance received more knocks than praise.* [Old English *cnocian* to strike with a hard blow.]

knock·a·bout (nok′ə bout′) *n.* small, one-masted sailboat, rigged with a mainsail and a jib. —*adj.* **1.** suitable or appropriate for rough use or wear, as a garment. **2.** rough; noisy; boisterous: *knockabout comedy.*

knock·down (nok′doun′) *adj.* **1.** powerful enough to knock down or overwhelm: *a knockdown blow.* **2.** made so as to be easily taken apart or put together. —*n.* **1.** act or instance of knocking down, esp. in a boxing match. **2.** something that is easily taken apart or put together, esp. a piece of furniture.

knock·er (nok′ər) *n.* **1.** one who or that which knocks. **2.** hinged knob, ring, or other device, usually made of metal, fastened to a door for use in knocking.

knock·knee (nok′nē′) *n.* **1.** abnormal condition of inward curvature of the leg or legs, causing the knees to knock or rub together in walking. **2. knock-knees.** legs having such curvature. —**knock′-kneed,** *adj.*

knock·out (nok′out′) *n.* **1.** defeat of an opponent in boxing by a blow that knocks him down so that he is unable to rise to his feet within the prescribed time: *The knockout occurred in the fourth round.* **2.** blow that causes unconsciousness. **3.** *Informal.* someone or something that is extremely attractive, striking, or impressive: *Joe's date at the party was a real knockout.* —*adj.* causing a knockout: *a knockout punch.*

knoll (nōl) *n.* small, rounded hill or mound; hummock; hillock. [Old English *cnoll.*]

Knos·sos (nos′əs, knos′-) *also,* **Cnossus.** *n.* ancient city on the northern coast of Crete, center of the Minoan civilization.

knot¹ (not) *n.* **1.** fastening formed by intertwining rope, string, or the like, esp. with one free end being passed through a loop and drawn tight. **2.** lump, knob, or tangle formed by the intertwining of thread, cord, or the like: *Ethel combed the knots out of her hair.* **3.** piece of material, as ribbon or lace, folded or tied into a knot and worn as an ornament or accessory. **4.** small group or cluster of persons or things: *A knot of people waited on the platform for the train.* **5.** something intricate, involved, or difficult to solve: *It is too hard a knot for me* (Shakespeare, *Twelfth Night*). **6.** thing that forms or maintains a union; any tie or bond, esp. the bond of marriage. **7.a.** hard, cross-grained lump of wood formed in a tree trunk at the point where a branch grows out from the tree. **b.** cross section of such a lump, appearing as a roundish, cross-grained section in a piece of cut lumber. **8.** enlargement or swelling, as in a muscle or gland; node; lump. **9.a.** one of a series of equal divisions of a log line, marked by pieces of cloth or knotted string, and used to measure a ship's rate of speed. **b.** unit of speed of one nautical mile per hour, approximately equal to 6080 feet per hour, or 1.15 statue miles. **c.** one nautical mile. **10. to tie the knot.** *Informal.* to get married. —*v.t.* **knot·ted, knot·ting. 1.** to tie in a knot; form a knot or knots in: *Carol knotted the string around the package.* **2.** to secure or fasten with or by a knot: *to knot one's hair with a ribbon.* —*v.i.* to become tangled or snarled. [Old English *cnotta* fastening formed by intertwining parts of rope, strings, or the like, something intricate.]

knot² (not) *n.* any of several sandpipers, genus *Calidris,* that breed in Arctic regions, esp. *C. canutus,* having a reddish breast during the breeding season. [Of uncertain origin.]

Knight *(def. 4)*

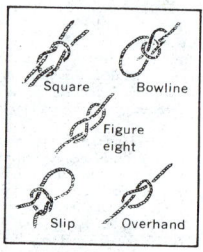

Square   Bowline

Figure
eight

Slip   Overhand

Knots

knot·grass (not′gras′) *n.* low-growing plant, *Polygonum aviculare,* of the buckwheat family, found as a weed throughout the world, having a wiry stem with a knotlike swelling at each joint, and bearing small, bluish-gray leaves and tiny, pink-edged flowers.

knot·hole (not′hōl′) *n.* hole in a board or other piece of cut wood where a knot has fallen out or been removed.

knot·ted (not′id) *adj.* having or covered with knots, knobs, or bumps.

knot·ty (not′ē) **-ti·er, -ti·est.** *adj.* **1.** having, covered with, or full of knots or bumps, as wood: *knotty pine.* **2.** difficult to understand, solve, or explain; puzzling: *a knotty problem.* —**knot′ti·ness,** *n.*

knout (nout) *n.* whip formerly used for flogging criminals, esp. in Russia. —*v.t.* to flog with a knout. [Russian *knut* (knotted) whip, from Old Norse *knūtr* knot.]

know (nō) **knew, known, know·ing.** *v.t.* **1.** to be cognizant, conscious, or aware of: *He knows exactly what he's doing.* **2.** to perceive or comprehend with clearness and certainty; regard or accept as fact or truth: *William refused to compromise because he knew that he was right.* **3.** to have a practical understanding of, experience with, or skill in, esp. through instruction, study, or practice: *to know how to type.* **4.** to have learned by committing to memory; be able to repeat: *The actress knew her part.* **5.** to be acquainted or familiar with, as through experience or through information or report: *Alas! poor Yorick. I knew him, Horatio* (Shakespeare, *Hamlet*). **6.** to be able to identify; recognize: *You won't know him with his beard.* **7.** to be able to distinguish: *to know good music from bad music.* **8.** to meet with, experience, or undergo: *The peasants had known hunger all their lives.* —*v.i.* **1.** to have understanding or knowledge: *The goal of science is not to speculate but to know.* **2.** to be cognizant, conscious, or aware (with *of*): *I know of the town but I've never been there.* —*n.* **in the know.** *Informal.* having special or secret information. [Old English *cnāwan* to recognize, be familiar with, understand.] —**know′a·ble,** *adj.* —**know′er,** *n.*

Syn. *v.t.* **2. Know, understand** mean to achieve a clear idea of something. **Know** emphasizes the certainty of one's grasp and awareness of something: *Do you know the solution to this problem?* **Understand** stresses not only an awareness of the facts but also an insight into their meaning, significance, and implication: *To understand the present, we must study the past.*

know-how (nō′hou′) *n. Informal.* knowledge of how to do something; practical skill.

know·ing (nō′ing) *adj.* **1.** suggesting secret or private knowledge about something: *a knowing smile.* **2.** showing discernment or cunning; clever; shrewd: *a knowing judge of human nature.* **3.** having knowledge; well-informed: *He is very knowing about horses.* **4.** deliberate; intentional. —**know′ing·ly,** *adv.*

knowl·edge (nol′ij) *n.* **1.** familiarity, understanding, awareness, or information acquired through experience, study, or observation: *Her knowledge of zoology was limited.* **2.** fact of knowing: *The knowledge that the car might skid made Bill drive more slowly.* **3.** that which is or can be perceived or learned. **4.** sum or range of that which is or can be perceived or learned. **5.** specific information or facts concerning a given matter: *Have you any knowledge of his whereabouts?* **6.** to (the best of) one's knowledge. so far as one is aware. [Middle English *l nowleche* fact of knowing, acquaintance, going back to Old English *cnāwan* to be familiar with, understand.]

knowl·edge·a·ble (nol′i jə bəl) *adj.* having knowledge; well-informed. —**knowl′edge·a·bil′i·ty, knowl′edge·a·ble·ness,** *n.* —**knowl′edge·a·bly,** *adv.*

known (nōn) past participle of **know.**

know-noth·ing (nō′nuth′ing) *n.* **1.** ignorant person. **2. Know-Nothing.** member of a secretive American political party, prominent from 1853 to 1856, that was opposed to the political influence exercised by immigrants.

Knox, John (noks) c.1505–72, Scottish religious reformer, the founder of Presbyterianism.

Knox·ville (noks′vil′) *n.* city in eastern Tennessee, on the Tennessee River. Pop. (1970), 174,587.

knuck·le (nuk′əl) *n.* **1.** joint of a finger, esp. one connecting a finger to the hand. **2.** cut of meat, esp. of ham or veal, consisting of the knuckle joint and the flesh immediately above and below it. **3. knuckles.** brass knuckles. —*v.i.,* **-led, -ling. 1.** to put the knuckles on the gound when shooting a marble. **2. to knuckle down.** *Informal.* to apply oneself earnestly. **3. to knuckle under.** to give in; submit; yield. —*v.t.* to press, rub, or hit with the knuckles. [Of Germanic origin.]

knurl (nurl) *n.* **1.** knot, knob, lump, or similar protuberance. **2.** one of a series of small ridges on the edge of a metal object, as a coin or thumbscrew. —*v.t.* to make knurls on; mill. [Possibly diminutive of earlier *knur* gnarl (of uncertain origin).]

knurl·y (nur′lē) **knurl·i·er, knurl·i·est.** *adj.* having knurls or knots; gnarled.

KO also, **kay·o.** *Slang. n.* knockout in boxing. —*v.t.,* **KO'd, KO'ing.** to knock out in boxing.

ko·a·la (kō ä′lə) *n.* tree-dwelling marsupial, *Phascolarctos cinereus,* native to Australia, having a chubby, tail-less body covered with gray-ish-blue fur, large, bushy ears, and a black nose. Length: 34 inches. [Of native Australian origin.]

Koala

Ko·be (kō′bē, -bā) *n.* port city in Japan, on the southern coast of Honshu. Pop. (1968), 1,253,-000.

Ko·blenz (kō′blents′) *also,* **Co·blenz.** *n.* city in western West Germany. Pop. (1968), 102,462.

Koch, Robert (kok, kôĸʜ) 1843–1910, German bacteriologist and physician.

Ko·di·ak (kō′dē ak′) *n.* U.S. island off the coast of southwestern Alaska. Area, approx. 3465 sq. mi.

K. of C., Knights of Columbus.

Koh·i·noor (kō′ə noor′) *also,* **Koh·i·nor, Koh·i·nur.** *n.* very large diamond that was found in India, weighing 108.93 carats, now one of the British crown jewels. [Persian *kōh-i nūr* literally, mountain of light.]

kohl (kōl) *n.* cosmetic preparation used by women in certain Middle Eastern and Asian countries to darken the skin around the eyes. [Arabic *kohl* powder of antimony.]

kohl·ra·bi (kōl′rä′bē) *pl.,* **-bies.** *n.* cultivated plant, *Brassica caulorapa,* of the cabbage family, having a white or purple, thick, round stem that resembles a turnip and is eaten as a vegetable. [German *Kohlrabi,* through Italian, from Latin *caulis* cabbage + *rāpa* turnip.]

Ko·ko·mo (kō′kə mō′) *n.* city in north-central Indiana. Pop. (1970), 44,042.

ko·la (kō′lə) *n.* **1.** evergreen tree, *Cola acuminata,* widely cultivated in tropical regions of the world, having leathery oval leaves, and bearing kola nuts and clusters of small bell-shaped yellow flowers. Also, **kola nut tree. 2.** dried extract of kola nuts, used chiefly to flavor soft drinks. [Of West African origin.]

kola nut, also, **cola nut.** bitter brown seed of the kola, borne in thick, fleshy pods.

Pod
Kola nuts

ko·lin·sky (kə lin′skē) *pl.,* **-skies.** *n.* **1.** yellow weasel, *Mustela sibirica,* native to Asia and eastern Europe. Length: 18–21 inches including the tail. **2.** tawny fur of this animal, frequently dyed to resemble sable. [Russian *kolinski* relating to *Kola,* a region in the northwestern Soviet Union where the best grade of this fur is found.]

Köln (kœln) *n.* German. Cologne.

Kol Ni·dre (kōl nid′rä) Jewish prayer of atonement recited in the service on the eve of Yom Kippur.

Kö·nigs·berg (German kœ′niks berk′) *n.* see **Kaliningrad.**

koo·doo (kōō′dōō′) *pl.,* **-doos.** *n.* kudu.

kook·a·bur·ra (kook′ə bur′ə) *n.* Australian kingfisher, *Dacelo novaeguineae,* having a large head, a stout, pointed bill and brown and white plumage. Length: 17 inches. [Of native Australian origin.]

ko·peck (kō′pek) *also,* **ko·pek, co·peck.** *n.* copper or bronze coin of the Soviet Union, equivalent to ¹⁄₁₀₀ of a ruble. [Russian *kopeika,* from *kop'e* spear; because the coin once depicted the czar holding a spear.]

Ko·ran (kō rän′, -ran′, kô-) *n.* the sacred book of the Muslims, containing the religious and moral code of Islam. Muslims believe that it contains the word of Allah, revealed by the archangel Gabriel to the prophet Muhammad. [Arabic *Qur'ān* a reading, recitation.] —**Ko·ran′ic,** *adj.*

Ko·re·a (kə rē′ə, kô-) *n.* country in eastern Asia, divided into North Korea and South Korea in 1948. Area, 85,030 sq. mi. Also, **Cho′sen′.**

Ko·re·an (kə rē′ən, kô-) *adj.* of or relating to Korea, its people, or their language. —*n.* **1.** member or close descendant of the people of Korea. **2.** language of Korea, unrelated to any known language family.

Korean War, war between North Korea, aided by Communist China, and South Korea, aided by the United States and other United Nations members, which lasted from June 1950 until July 1953.

ko·ru·na (kôr′ə nä′) *pl.,* **ko·ru·nas** or **ko·ru·ny** (kôr′ə nē) or **ko·run** (kôr′ōōn). *n.* monetary unit and coin of Czechoslovakia. [Czech *koruna* literally, crown, from Latin *corōna.* See **CROWN.**]

Kos·ci·us·ko, Thad·de·us (kos′ē us′kō, kosh choosh′kō; thad′-ē əs) 1746–1817, Polish patriot who served in the American army during the American Revolution.

ko·sher (kō′shər) *adj.* **1.** conforming to or in accordance with Jewish ceremonial law, esp. those laws affecting food and its preparation: *kosher meat, a kosher restaurant.* **2.** *Slang.* legitimate; proper; legitimate. —*v.t.* to prepare (food) in accordance with Jewish ceremonial law. —*n.* kosher food. [Hebrew *kāshēr* fit, proper.]

---

at; āpe; cär; end; mē; it; īce; hot; ōld; fôrk; wood; fōōl; oil; out; up; ūse; turn; sing; thin; this; zh in treasure; ə in ago, taken, pencil, lemon, circus.

Kos·suth, Louis (kos'ooth) 1802–94, Hungarian patriot and statesman.

Ko·sy·gin, A·lek·sei (kō sē'gin; ä lek sā') 1904—, Soviet political leader, premier of the Soviet Union since 1964.

kou·miss (kōo'mis) *also,* **kou·mis.** *n.* kumiss.

kow·tow (kou'tou', -tou') *also,* **ko·tow** (kō'tou', -tou'). *v.i.* **1.** to kneel and touch the forehead to the ground as an expression of deep respect, submission, or worship. **2.** to act in an obsequious manner; show servile deference: *The young man refused to kowtow to his boss.* —*n.* act of kowtowing. [Chinese (Mandarin) *k'o t'ou,* to touch the forehead on the ground to show respect, from *k'o* to strike + *t'ou* head.] —**kow'tow'er;** *also,* **ko'tow'er,** *n.*

Ko·zhi·kode (kō'zhə kōd') *n.* port city on the southwestern coast of India, formerly known as Calicut. Pop. (1969), 315,786.

KP, kitchen police.

Kr, krypton.

kraal (kräl) *n.* **1.** village of southern African natives, typically surrounded by a fence or stockade. **2.** fenced enclosure in southern Africa for livestock, as cattle or sheep. —*v.t.* to enclose (livestock) in a kraal. [Afrikaans *kraal* village, enclosure, pen, from Portuguese *curral* pen for cattle, from *correr* to run, from Latin *currere*.]

krait (krīt) *n.* any of several very poisonous snakes, genus *Bungarus,* related to the cobra and found in southeastern Asia and adjacent islands. [Hindi *karait*.]

Krak·a·to·a (krak'ə tō'ə) *also,* **Kra·ka·tau** (krak'ə tou'). *n.* uninhabited volcanic island between Java and Sumatra, in Indonesia, noted as the site of a catastrophic volcanic eruption in 1883.

Krak·ów (krä'kou, krak'ou) *n.* city in southern Poland. Pop. (1968), 560,300.

Kras·no·dar (kräs'nō där') *n.* city in the western Soviet Union, in the Russian Republic. Pop. (1970), 465,000.

Kras·no·yarsk (kras'nə yärsk') *n.* city in the Asian Soviet Union, in the Russian Republic. Pop. (1970), 648,000.

K ration, packaged emergency field ration used by U.S. military forces.

Kre·feld (krā'felt') *n.* city in western West Germany, on the Rhine. Pop. (1968), 224,807.

Kreis·ler, Fritz (krīs'lər; frits) 1875–1962, U.S. violinist and composer, born in Austria.

Krem·lin (krem'lin) *n.* **1.** citadel of Moscow, the former royal residence of the czars, now the administrative center of the Soviet Union. **2.** government of the Soviet Union. **3.** *kremlin.* citadel of any Russian city. [French *kremlin,* from Russian *kreml'* citadel; of Tartar origin.]

kreut·zer (kroit'sər) *also,* **kreu·zer.** *n.* former coin of Germany or Austria. [German *Kreuzer,* from *Kreuz* cross, going back to Latin *crux;* because it originally bore the design of a cross.]

Kriem·hild (krēm'hilt') *n. German Legend.* Siegfried's wife who avenges his murder.

krim·mer (krim'ər) *n.* loosely curled, usually gray fur resembling Persian lamb and astrakhan, made from the pelts of young lambs raised in the Crimean peninsula region. [German *Krimmer,* from Russian *Krim* Crimea; of Tartar origin.]

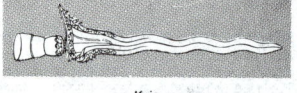

Kris

kris (krēs) *n.* Malay dagger or short sword with a wavy, double-edged blade. [Malay *krīs*.]

Krish·na (krish'nə) *n.* one of the most important Hindu gods, worshiped as an incarnation of Vishnu. [Sanskrit *Kṛṣṇāh* literally, black, dark.]

Kriss Krin·gle (kris' kring'gəl) Santa Claus. [German *Christkindl* little Christ child, from *Christ* Christ + *Kind* child. See CHRIST.]

kro·na (krō'nə) *pl.* **-nor** (-nôr). *n.* monetary unit and coin of Sweden. [Swedish *krona,* going back to Latin *corōna.* See CROWN.]

kró·na (krō'nə) *pl.* **-nur** (-nər). *n.* monetary unit and coin of Iceland. [Icelandic *króna,* going back to Latin *corōna.* See CROWN.]

kro·ne¹ (krō'nə) *pl.* **-ner** (-nər). *n.* monetary unit and coin of Denmark and Norway. [Danish and Norwegian *krone,* going back to Latin *corōna.* See CROWN.]

kro·ne² (krō'nə) *pl.* **-nen** (-nən). *n.* **1.** former gold coin of Germany. **2.** former monetary unit and silver coin of Austria. [German *Krone,* going back to Latin *corōna.* See CROWN.]

Kro·nos (krō'nos) Cronus.

krul·ler (krul'ər) cruller.

kryp·ton (krip'ton) *n.* colorless, inert gaseous element used esp. to fill electric lamps. Symbol: **Kr** See element for table. [Greek *krypton,* neuter of *kryptos* hidden; since it remained undiscovered for so long.]

Kt *Chess.* knight.

Kua·la Lum·pur (kwä'lə loom poor') capital of Malaysia, on the Malay Peninsula. Pop. (1963 est.), 500,000.

Ku·blai Khan (kōo'blī kän', -blə) c.1215–94, ruler of the Mongol empire from 1260 to 1294; grandson of Genghis Khan.

ku·dos (kōo'dŏs, -dos, kū'-) *n.* praise; renown. ▲ construed as singular. [Greek *kydos*.]

ku·du (kōo'dōo) *also,* **koo·doo.** *n.* African antelope, genus *Strepsiceros,* having long, spirally twisted horns. There are two species: the **greater kudu,** *S. strepsiceros,* having a reddish or grayish body marked with vertical white stripes, and the **lesser kudu,** *S. imberbis,* having a dark-gray, heavily striped body. [Of Hottentot origin.]

Greater kudu

Kui·by·shev (kwē'bə shef') *n.* city in the European Soviet Union, on the Volga River, formerly known as Samara. Pop. (1964 est.), 928,000.

Ku Klux Klan (kōo' kluks' klan', kū' kluks' klan') **1.** white-supremacist organization founded in the southern United States after the Civil War to reestablish the political and social dominance that white Southerners lost under Reconstruction. It declined in the 1870s. **2.** society founded in 1915, modeled on the original Ku Klux Klan. It sought to rid the country of the supposedly harmful influence of certain minority groups, as Catholics, Jews, and Negroes. [Possibly a modification of Greek *kyklos* circle + CLAN.]

ku·lak (kōo läk') *n.* wealthy or landed peasant in Russia who resisted the program of collectivization of agriculture of the Soviet government in the 1920s and 1930s. [Russian *kulak* rich peasant; literally, fist.]

ku·miss (kōo'mis) *also,* **kou·miss, kou·mis.** *n.* **1.** alcoholic drink usually made from fermented mare's or camel's milk, drunk esp. by nomads in western and central Asia. **2.** similar drink made from cow's milk. [Russian *kumys* fermented mare's milk; of Tartar origin.]

küm·mel (kim'əl, koom'-) *n.* colorless liqueur usually flavored with caraway seeds, cumin, or anise. [German *Kümmel* caraway seed, this liqueur, going back to Latin *cumīnum* cumin.]

kum·quat (kum'kwot) *also,* **cum·quat.** *n.* **1.** small, oval, orange or yellow fruit of any of a group of evergreen shrubs or trees, genus *Fortunella,* having a sweet rind and sour pulp. **2.** shrub or tree bearing this fruit, grown in many tropical and temperate regions of the world. [Chinese (Cantonese) *kam kwat* golden orange.]

Kun·ming (koon'ming') *n.* city in southwestern China. Pop. (1957 est.), 880,000.

Kuo·min·tang (kwō min tang', -täng') *n.* Chinese nationalist party organized in the early twentieth century by Sun Yat-sen, and later led by Chiang Kai-shek. [Chinese (Mandarin) *kuo* nation + *min* people + *tang* party.]

Kurd (koord, kurd) *n.* member of a Muslim people, formerly nomadic, who live predominantly in Kurdistan.

Kurd·ish (kur'dish, koor'-) *adj.* of or relating to the Kurds or their language. —*n.* language of the Kurds, belonging to the Indo-Iranian branch of the Indo-European language family.

Kur·di·stan (kur'də stan', -stän') *n.* highland region that includes parts of Iran, Iraq, Turkey, and Syria, and is inhabited chiefly by Kurds.

Ku·re (kōo'rā) *n.* city in the southwestern part of Honshu, Japan. Pop. (1968), 237,000.

Ku·rile Islands (kyoor'əl, kyoo rēl') *also,* **Ku·ril Islands.** chain of islands north of Japan, belonging to the Soviet Union.

Kush (kush) Cush.

Kush·it·ic (kush it'ik) Cushitic.

Ku·wait (kə wāt') *n.* **1.** country in the northeastern part of the Arabian peninsula, formerly under British protection. Capital, Kuwait. Area, 8000 sq. mi. Pop. (1968 est.), 555,000. **2.** capital and chief city of this country. Pop. (1965), 99,609. —**Ku·wai·ti** (kə wā'tē), *adj., n.*

kw., kilowatt.

kwash·i·or·kor (kwä'shē ôr'kər) *n.* serious nutritional disease occurring in children, esp. in Africa, caused by a protein deficiency.

kwh, kilowatt-hour. Also, **kw-h, kw-hr, kw.-hr.**

Ky., Kentucky.

ky·mo·graph (kī'mə graf') *n.* instrument used for measuring and recording variations in fluid pressure, as in blood pressure or the pulse. [Greek *kȳma* something swollen, wave + -GRAPH.]

Kyo·to (kyō'tō) *n.* city in the west-central part of Honshu, Japan, former capital of the country. Pop. (1968), 1,410,000.

Ky·ri·e e·le·i·son (kēr'ē ā' i lā'i son') **1.** liturgical prayer containing the words "Kyrie eleison" or "Lord, have mercy," esp. part of the ordinary of the Mass, sung or said before the Gloria. **2.** *also,* **kyrie.** musical setting for this. [Greek *Kyrie eleēson* Lord, have mercy.]

Kyu·shu (kū'shōo) *n.* southernmost island of Japan. Pop. (1965), 12,370,100.

at; āpe; cär; end; mē; it; īce; hot; ōld; fôrk; wood; fōōl; oil; out; up; ūse; turn; sing; thin; this; zh in treasure; ə in ago, taken, pencil, lemon, circus.

l, L (el) *pl.* **l's, L's.** *n.* **1.** twelfth letter of the English alphabet. **2. L.** shape of this letter or something having such a shape.

L, Roman numeral for 50.

l. **1.** liter. **2.** league. **3.** lira; lire. **4.** line. **5.** length. **6.** lake. **7.** law. **8.** latitude. **9.** left.

L., Latin.

la (lä) *n. Music.* sixth of the series of syllables used to name the eight tones of the diatonic scale. See **do²** for illustration. [See GAMUT.]

La, lanthanum.

La., Louisiana.

L.A., Los Angeles.

lab (lab) *n. Informal.* laboratory.

Lab. **1.** Labrador. **2.** Labourite.

la·bel (lā′bəl) *n.* **1.a.** any attachment, as a gummed piece of paper or a small square of cloth, affixed to an article to identify its contents, owner, or manufacturer or to show its destination. **b.** statement on or as on such an attachment. **2.** brand of a product, as of a phonograph record. **3.** short descriptive or characterizing phrase applied to a person, group, thing, or idea: *Tom has been given the label of "playboy" by his friends.* —*v.t.,* **-beled, -bel·ing;** *also, British,* **-belled, -bel·ling.** **1.** to put a label on. **2.** to describe or characterize by means of a label: *to label a product "flammable," to label a person "unteachable."* [Old French *label* ribbon, strip²; of Germanic origin.] —**la′bel·er;** *also, British,* **la′bel·ler,** *n.*

la·bel·lum (lə bel′əm) *pl.,* **-bel·la** (-bel′ə). *n. Botany.* inner petal of an orchid, usually larger and different in shape and markings from the other two. [Latin *labellum* little lip, diminutive of *labrum* lip.]

la·bi·al (lā′bē əl) *adj.* **1.** of, relating to, or characteristic of the lips. **2.** *Phonetics.* articulated primarily by the lips. —*n. Phonetics.* vowel or consonant sound made by the lips. [Medieval Latin *labialis* relating to the lips, from *labium* lip.]

la·bi·ate (lā′bē āt′, -it) *adj.* having lips or parts resembling lips. [Modern Latin *labiatus,* from Latin *labium* lip.]

la·bi·o·den·tal (lā′bē ō dent′əl) *Phonetics. adj.* articulated with the lower lip and upper front teeth. —*n.* sound made by the lower lip and upper front teeth. [Latin *labium* lip + DENTAL.]

la·bi·um (lā′bē əm) *pl.,* **-bi·a** (-bē ə). *n.* lip or liplike part. [Latin *labium* lip.]

la·bor (lā′bər) *also, British,* **la·bour.** *n.* **1.** physical or mental exertion; work; toil. **2.** specific piece of work; task: *Hercules was given twelve labors to perform.* **3.** economic group that performs manual work for wages. **4.** labor unions collectively. **5.** exertion and contractions of childbirth. —*v.i.* **1.** to do work; perform labor: *a hand who labors in the field.* **2.** to move slowly and with difficulty: *The old man labored up the steep hill.* **3.** to suffer from a disadvantage, burden, or trouble (with *under*): *to labor under extremely difficult circumstances.* **4.** to undergo the exertion and contractions of childbirth. —*v.t.* to spend too much time on or work out in too much detail; belabor. [Old French *labour* toil, trouble, from Latin *labor* toil, pain.]

lab·o·ra·to·ry (lab′rə tôr′ē, lab′ər ə-) *pl.,* **-ries.** *n.* **1.** room, building, or workshop designated and equipped for teaching science or for making scientific experiments or tests. **2.** factory that develops and manufactures chemical or pharmaceutical products. **3.** educational program involving practical experience, observation, or experimentation: *a laboratory on crime prevention.* [Medieval Latin *laboratorium* workshop, from Latin *laborāre* to work.]

Labor Day, legal holiday in honor of labor, observed in the United States and Canada on the first Monday in September.

la·bored (lā′bərd) *adj.* done with effort; not easy; forced: *labored breathing, a labored style of writing.*

la·bor·er (lā′bər ər) *n.* worker, esp. one who performs manual work for wages.

la·bo·ri·ous (lə bôr′ē əs) *adj.* **1.** requiring much work, esp. much

tedious work: *Checking all the names was a slow, laborious job.* **2.** industrious. [Latin *labōriōsus,* from *labor* toil.] —**la·bo′ri·ous·ly,** *adv.* —**la·bo′ri·ous·ness,** *n.* —Syn. **1.** see **hard.**

la·bor·ite (lā′bə rīt′) member or supporter of a labor party.

labor party, political party that supports or represents the interests of labor.

labor-sav·ing (lā′bər sā′ving) *adj.* that saves people work, esp. manual work: *The dishwasher is a labor-saving appliance.*

labor union, association of workers organized to advance their mutual interests, esp. in improving wages and working conditions.

la·bour (lā′bər) *British.* labor.

La·bour·ite (lā′bə rīt′) *n.* member or supporter of the Labour Party.

Labour Party, British political party that represents the laboring class and supports welfare legislation and the nationalizing of basic industry, formed by an alliance of trade union and intellectual socialist groups.

Lab·ra·dor (lab′rə dôr′) *n.* **1.** region in eastern Canada, on the Atlantic, part of the province of Newfoundland. **2.** peninsula in eastern Canada, between the Atlantic and Hudson Bay.

Labrador retriever, sturdy hunting dog commonly used to retrieve game birds and waterfowl, having a dense coat of short black, brown, or yellowish hair and a thick tail. Height: 23 inches at the shoulder.

Labrador retriever

la·bur·num (lə bur′nəm) *n.* any of a group of shrubs or small trees, genus *Laburnum,* of the pea family, bearing hanging clusters of yellow flowers and leaves divided into three leaflets. [Latin *laburnum.*]

lab·y·rinth (lab′ə rinth′) *n.* **1.** set of winding, interconnected passages or pathways in which it is easy to get lost or lose one's way; maze. **2.** any intricate, complicated, and confusing arrangement, situation, or subject. **3. Labyrinth.** *Greek Mythology.* underground maze in Crete designed by Daedalus to contain the Minotaur. **4.** inner ear. [Latin *labyrinthos* maze, from Greek *labyrinthos.*]

lab·y·rin·thine (lab′ə rin′thin, -thēn) *adj.* **1.** of or being a labyrinth. **2.** intricate; complicated. Also, **lab·y·rin·thi·an** (lab′ə rin′thē ən).

lac¹ (lak) *n.* reddish-brown resinous substance deposited on trees, esp. in India and Burma, by the female lac insect, used to make shellac and varnish. [Hindi *lākh,* going back to Sanskrit *lākshā.*]

lac² (lak) *also,* **lakh.** *n.* **1.** in India, sum or amount of 100,000, esp. 100,000 rupees. **2.** in India, any great number. [Hindi *lākh* 100,000, from Sanskrit *lākshā* originally, mark.]

lace (lās) *n.* **1.** long, thin piece, as of string or leather, passed or threaded through edges to pull or hold them together. **2.** ornamental, patterned, openwork fabric made by interweaving fine thread. **3.** ornamental braid, usually gold or silver, used for trimming such items as military uniforms and hats. —*v.t.,* **laced, lac·ing.** **1.a.** to pull together or tighten with a lace or laces (often with *up*): *to lace up a corset. Lace your shoes.* **b.** to fasten or tighten (laces) (often with *up*). **2.** to ornament or trim with lace. **3.** to interlace; intertwine: *The man laced his fingers together in contemplation.* **4.** to add a dash of liquor to. **5.** to streak with or as with lines of color: *The brown fabric was laced with white.* **6.** to beat; thrash. —*v.i.* **1.** to fasten by means of a lace or laces: *shoes that lace rather than button.* **2. to lace into.** to attack with or as if with blows. [Old French *las* noose, snare, going back to Latin *laqueus.*] —**lac′er,** *n.*

Lac·e·dae·mon (las′ə dē′mən) *n.* Sparta. —**Lac·e·dae·mo·ni·an** (las′ə di mō′nē ən), *adj., n.*

lac·er·ate (las′ə rāt′) **-at·ed, -at·ing.** *v.t.* **1.** to tear; cut. **2.** to wound;

at; āpe; cär; end; mē; it; īce; hot; ōld; fôrk; wood; fōōl; oil; out; up; ūse; turn; sing; thin; this; zh in treasure; ə in ago, taken, pencil, lemon, circus.

571

hurt: *to lacerate someone's feelings.* [Latin *lacerātus*, past participle of *lacerāre* to tear[1], rend.]

lac·er·a·tion (las′ə rā′shən) *n.* **1.** act of lacerating. **2.** jagged tear; wound.

lace·wing (lās′wing′) *n.* any of a group of brown or green insects, families Chrysopidae and Hemerobiidae, having four long, narrow, transparent wings veined in a lacelike pattern.

lach·es (lach′ēz) *n. Law.* failure to do something that one should do or delay in asserting a right or making a claim. [Old French *laschesse* neglect, from *lasche* loose, relaxed, going back to Latin *laxus* loose, open.]

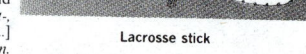
Lacewing

Lach·e·sis (lak′ə sis) *n. Greek Mythology.* one of the three Fates, who assigned to each man his lot or destiny. [Latin *Lachesis*, from Greek *Lachesis*; literally, disposer of lots, from *lanchanein* to obtain by lot.]

lach·ry·mal (lak′rə məl) *also,* **lac·ri·mal.** *adj.* of or relating to tears. [Medieval Latin *lachrymalis* relating to tears, from Latin *lacrima* tear[2].]

lach·ry·ma·to·ry (lak′rə mə tôr′ē) *pl.* **-ries.** *n.* any of various small thin-necked vases found in ancient Roman tombs, formerly supposed to have been used to hold the tears of mourners. —*adj.* of, relating to, or producing tears.

lach·ry·mose (lak′rə mōs′) *adj.* shedding tears or causing the shedding of tears; tearful or sad. [Latin *lacrimōsus* tearful, weeping, from *lacrima* tear[2].] —**lach′ry·mose′ly,** *adv.*

lac·ing (lā′sing) *n.* **1.** lace. **2.** beating; thrashing.

lac insect, scale insect, *Laccifera lacca,* found esp. in India and Burma, the female of which deposits lac on trees.

lack (lak) *v.t.* **1.** to be without or have too little of; be deficient in; need: *a personality that lacks warmth.* **2.** to be missing, short of, or less than (a portion of a total): *John lacks an inch of being six feet tall.* —*v.i.* to be missing or needing (with *in*): *What the rookie baseball player lacks in ability, he more than makes up in dedication.* —*n.* **1.** state of being without or having too little: *The meeting ended because of lack of order.* **2.** that which is needed. [Possibly from Middle Dutch *lac* fault.]

Syn. **1.** Lack, want, denote the fact or state of being without something essential or required. **Lack** denotes the total or partial absence of something that is necessary for completion or fullness: *The drought was caused by a lack of rain.* **Want** denotes a pressing and dire lack of something desirable: *The boy showed a deplorable want of tact and courtesy.* **Need** emphasizes urgent necessity arising out of absence or scarcity: *The sick man is in need of sleep.*

lack·a·dai·si·cal (lak′ə dā′zi kəl) *adj.* lifeless and uninterested; listless. [From earlier *lackadaisy,* lengthened form of LACKADAY.] —**lack′a·dai′si·cal·ly,** *adv.*

lack·a·day (lak′ə dā′) *interj. Archaic.* alas and alack. [Short for ALACKADAY.]

lack·ey (lak′ē) *pl.* **-eys.** *n.* **1.** servile subordinate or follower. **2.** low-ranking male servant, esp. a footman. —*v.i., v.t.,* **-eyed, -ey·ing.** to serve as a lackey. [French *laquais* footman, flunky, possibly through Spanish, Italian, and Greek, going back to Turkish *ulak* courier.]

lack·lus·ter (lak′lus′tər) *also, British,* **lack·lus·tre.** *adj.* that lacks brilliance or any other special qualities; dull: *a lackluster performance.*

la·con·ic (lə kon′ik) *adj.* characterized by the use of few words to express much; terse; concise. [Latin *Lacōnicus* relating to Laconia, a country of ancient Greece where the Spartans lived, from Greek *Lakōnikos,* from *Lakōn* a Spartan; with reference to the concise speech of the Spartans.] —**la·con′i·cal·ly,** *adv.*

lac·o·nism (lak′ə niz′əm) *n.* **1.** laconic style of expression. **2.** laconic phrase or expression.

lac·quer (lak′ər) *n.* **1.** fast-drying varnish usually consisting of a cellulose derivative in a mixture of solvents, plasticizers, and resins. **2.** varnish obtained from the sap of an oriental sumac tree, *Rhus verniciflua,* formerly widely used on furniture. **3.** wooden articles or decorative work covered with such varnish. —*v.t.* to coat with or as with lacquer. [Obsolete French *lacre* sealing wax, from Portuguese *laca* lac[1], from Hindi *lākh.* See LAC[1].] —**lac′quer·er,** *n.*

lacrimal glands, small glands in the upper part of the eye socket that secrete tears.

la·crosse (lə krôs′) *n.* game for two teams of ten players each, played with lacrosse sticks whose netlike pockets are used for catching, carrying, or throwing the ball into the opponent's goal. [French *la crosse* the lacrosse stick, from *la* the + *crosse* lacrosse stick, bishop's staff (of Germanic origin); because the Indians' lacrosse sticks reminded the early French settlers in Canada of a *crosse,* or bishop's staff.]

La Crosse (lə krôs′) port city in western Wisconsin, on the Mississippi. Pop. (1970), 51,153.

lacrosse stick, racket used in lacrosse, consisting of a long handle that curves around a netlike pocket at one end.

lac·tase (lak′tās) *n.* enzyme present in yeast and the intestines of animals, that hydrolyzes lactose into glucose and galactose. [Latin *lact-,* stem of *lac* milk + -ASE.]

Lacrosse stick

lac·tate (lak′tāt) *n.* salt or ester of lactic acid. —*v.i.* **-tat·ed, -tat·ing.** to produce or secrete milk.

lac·ta·tion (lak tā′shən) *n.* formation and secretion of milk by the mammary glands. —**lac·ta′tion·al,** *adj.*

lac·te·al (lak′tē əl) *n.* any of the lymphatic vessels of the small intestine that carry chyle to the blood. —*adj.* **1.** of or like milk; milky. **2.** of or relating to the lacteals. [Latin *lacteus* milky (from *lac* milk) + -AL[1].]

lac·tic (lak′tik) *adj.* of, relating to, or obtained from milk. [Latin *lact-,* stem of *lac* milk + -IC.]

lactic acid, colorless, odorless syrupy compound formed in sour milk, in fermenting molasses, and in muscles, and also produced synthetically. Formula: $CH_3CHOHCOOH$

lac·tif·er·ous (lak tif′ər əs) *adj.* **1.** conveying milk. **2.** yielding or secreting milk or a milky fluid. —**lac·tif′er·ous·ness,** *n.*

lac·to·fla·vin (lak′tō flā′vin, lak′tō flā′-) *n.* riboflavin.

lac·tom·e·ter (lak tom′ə tər) *n.* instrument for determining the specific gravity and thereby the richness of milk. [Latin *lact-,* stem of *lac* milk + -METER.]

lac·tose (lak′tōs) *n.* white crystalline compound present in milk. Also, **milk sugar.** Formula: $C_{12}H_{22}O_{11}$ [Latin *lact-,* stem of *lac* milk + -OSE[2].]

la·cu·na (lə kū′nə) *pl.* **-nas** or **-nae** (-nē). *n.* **1.** space in which something has been left out; gap. **2.** small cavity in bone or tissue. [Latin *lacūna* hole, pond. Doublet of LAGOON.]

la·cus·trine (lə kus′trin) *adj.* **1.** of or relating to lakes. **2.** found or formed in or near lakes.

lac·y (lā′sē) **lac·i·er, lac·i·est.** *adj.* of or resembling lace. —**lac′i·ness,** *n.*

lad (lad) *n.* **1.** young fellow; boy. **2.** *Informal.* fellow; man. [Of uncertain origin.]

lad·der (lad′ər) *n.* **1.** device used in climbing, usually made of two parallel side pieces with a series of cross pieces, or rungs, connecting them. **2.** any means of ascent or arrangement of ascending steps or levels: *the ladder of success.* [Old English *hlæder* frame with steps for ascending or descending.]

lad·die (lad′ē) *n. Scottish.* lad.

lade (lād) **lad·ed, lad·ed** or **lad·en, lad·ing.** *v.t.* **1.** to load, esp. cargo. **2.** to ladle. —*v.i.* **1.** to take on a load, as of cargo. **2.** to ladle liquid. [Old English *hladan* to load, draw (water).]

lad·en (lād′ən) *adj.* **1.** loaded: *a ship laden with riches.* **2.** weighed down; burdened: *laden with cares.*

lad·ing (lā′ding) *n.* **1.** act of loading. **2.** that which is loaded; freight; cargo.

la·dle (lād′əl) *n.* long-handled spoon with a cup-shaped bowl for dipping liquids. —*v.t.* **-dled, -dling.** to dip out with or carry in a ladle. [Old English *hlædel* large spoon, from *hladan* to draw (water).] —**la′dler,** *n.*

La·do·ga, Lake (lä′də gä′) largest freshwater lake in Europe, in the northwestern Soviet Union.

la·dy (lā′dē) *pl.* **-dies.** *n.* **1.** woman, esp. an older woman: *Two ladies sat on the porch.* **2.** mistress of a household. **3.** girl or woman with good manners or feminine qualities. **4.** **Lady.** in Great Britain, a marchioness, countess, viscountess, or baroness; a daughter of a duke, marquis, or earl; the wife of a baronet or knight; or the wife of a man holding the courtesy title of Lord. ▲ used as a title. **5.** woman who exercised authority over a feudal manor. **6.** woman who is the object of a man's love or devotion. **7.** wife. [Old English *hlæfdīge* mistress of a household; literally, loaf-kneader; with reference to the duties of the mistress of a house in early times.] —**Syn. 3.** see **female.**

la·dy·bird (lā′dē burd′) *n.* ladybug.

la·dy·bug (lā′dē bug′) *n.* any of a group of beetles, family Coccinellidae, that has a round, humped body, often bright red or orange with black spots, and feeds on aphids and other insect pests.

Ladybug

Lady Day, Annunciation.

la·dy·fin·ger (lā′dē fĭng′gər) *also,* **lady's finger.** *n.* small sponge cake resembling a finger in size and shape.

la·dy-in-wait·ing (lā′dē in wā′tĭng) *pl.,* **la·dies-in-wait·ing.** *n.* lady appointed to be an attendant of a queen or princess.

la·dy-kill·er (lā′dē kĭl′ər) *n. Informal.* man who is very popular with women, esp. one who is insensitive to their feelings.

la·dy·like (lā′dē līk′) *adj.* like or suitable for a lady.

la·dy·love (lā′dē lŭv′) *n.* woman who is the object of a man's love; sweetheart.

la·dy·ship (lā′dē shĭp′) *n.* rank, status, or position of a lady. ▲ also used as a title.

la·dy's-slip·per (lā′dēz slĭp′ər) *also,* **lady slipper.** *n.* any of a group of hardy orchids, genus *Cypripedium,* that bear flowers having a lower petal with a shoelike pouch. Also, **moccasin flower.**

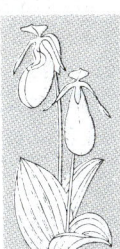

Lady's-slipper

la·dy's-thumb (lā′dēz thŭm′) *n.* weedy plant, *Polygonum persicaria,* of the buckwheat family, found in damp regions in Europe and North America, having small pink flowers borne on spikes. Also, **hearts′ease′.**

La·e·trile (lā′ə trĭl) *n. Trademark.* drug made from the pits of apricots, thought by many to cure cancer.

La·fa·yette (lăf′ē et′, lä′fē-) **1. Marquis de.** 1757–1834, French general and statesman. **2.** city in southern Louisiana. Pop. (1970), 68,908.

La Fon·taine, Jean de (lä fŏn tān′; *French* lä fôN ten′) 1621–95, French poet and fable writer.

lag (lăg) **lagged, lag·ging.** *v.i.* **1.** to fail to keep up or keep pace (often with *behind*): *The little girl lagged behind because she was tired. The turtle lagged behind, but then caught up.* **2.** to slacken; fall off; slump: *a business that lags in summer.* —*n.* act, instance, or amount of lagging. [Probably of Scandinavian origin.] —**lag′ger,** *n.*

la·ger (lä′gər) *n.* light-bodied beer that is prepared by slow fermentation at low temperature and kept for months before being used. [Short for German *Lagerbier* beer brewed for keeping, from *Lager* storehouse + *Bier* beer.]

lag·gard (lăg′ərd) *n.* one who or that which lags. —*adj.* that lags; slow; backward.

la·gniappe (lăn yăp′, lăn′yăp) *also,* **la·gnappe.** *n.* **1.** gift that comes with a purchase. **2.** anything given as an extra; bonus. [French *lagniappe* gift that comes with a purchase, from Spanish *la ñapa* the addition, going back to Latin *illa,* feminine of *ille* that + Quechua *yapa* addition.]

lag·o·morph (lăg′ə môrf′) *n.* any of numerous mammals constituting the order Lagomorpha, having two pairs of upper incisors and comprising the hares, rabbits, and pikas. [Modern Latin *Lagomorpha,* from Greek *lagōs* hare + *morphē* form.] —**lag′o·mor′phic,** **lag′o·mor′phous,** *adj.*

la·goon (lə gōōn′) *n.* **1.** shallow body of water partly or completely enclosed within an atoll. **2.** shallow body of sea water partly cut off from the sea by a narrow strip of land. [Italian *laguna* pool, from Latin *lacūna* hole, pond. Doublet of LACUNA.]

La·gos (lä′gŏs, lā′gos) *n.* capital and chief port of Nigeria, in the southwestern part of the country. Pop. (1969), 841,749.

La·hore (lə hôr′) *n.* capital of West Pakistan, in the eastern part of the province, on the border with India. Pop. (1969), 1,823,000.

la·ic (lā′ĭk) *adj.* of, relating to, or belonging to the laity. [Latin *lāicus* relating to the people. See LAY².]

laid (lād) past tense and past participle of LAY¹.

lain (lān) past participle of LIE².

lair (lâr) *n.* home or resting place, esp. of a wild animal. [Old English *leger* bed.]

laird (lârd) *n. Scottish.* owner of a large estate; lord. [Scottish form of LORD.]

lais·sez-faire (lĕs′ā fâr′, lā′zā-) *adj.* **1.** of or based on laissez faire: *laissez-faire economics.* **2.** that does not interfere; hands-off: *a laissez-faire attitude.*

lais·sez faire (lĕs′ā fâr′, lā′zā-) economic theory developed in the eighteenth century that opposed mercantilism and supported the growth of free enterprise and capitalism. It claims that economic laws guarantee well-being as long as each individual is left alone to pursue his own interest with a minimum of interference or regulation by the government. [French *laissez faire* allow (people) to do (what they please), going back to Latin *laxāre* to loosen, relax + *facere* to do, make.]

la·i·ty (lā′ə tē) *pl.,* **-ties.** *n.* **1.** those who are members of a church but are not ordained for religious work. Distinguished from **clergy.** **2.** those who are not members of a certain profession or who are not trained in a particular speciality: *Lawyers use many terms not familiar to the laity.* [LAY² + -ITY.]

La·ius (lā′əs) *n. Greek Legend.* king of Thebes killed unknowingly by his son Oedipus.

lake¹ (lāk) *n.* **1.** inland body of salt or fresh water. **2.** any large pool of liquid. [Old French *lac* pond, from Latin *lacus* pond, large reservoir for water.]

lake² (lāk) *n.* **1.** any of various pigments and coloring compounds consisting of an organic dye, as cochineal, bonded to an inorganic base. **2.** deep red or purplish-red color. [Form of LAC¹.]

Lake Charles, port city in southwestern Louisiana. Pop. (1970), 77,998.

Lake District, region in northwestern England, noted for its scenic mountains and lakes. Also, **Lake Country.**

lake dweller, member of a prehistoric people who lived in lake dwellings.

lake dwelling, hut built on piles over water or marshland in prehistoric times.

lake trout, large trout, *Salvelinus namaycush,* grayish-green in color with pale spots, found in lakes of North America. Weight: usually 9 pounds or less.

Lake·wood (lāk′wood′) *n.* **1.** city in southern California, near Los Angeles. Pop. (1970), 82,973. **2.** city in northeastern Ohio, near Cleveland. Pop. (1970), 70,173.

lakh (lak) *lac².*

lam (lăm) *n. Slang.* **1. on the lam.** hiding or escaping, esp. from law enforcement officials. **2. to take it on the lam.** to escape or go into hiding, esp. from the law. [Of uncertain origin.]

Lam., Lamentations.

la·ma (lä′mə) *n.* priest or monk of Lamaism. [Tibetan *blama* priest.]

La·ma·ism (lä′mə ĭz′əm) *n.* religion centered in Tibet, Mongolia, and surrounding areas that is a mixture of Buddhism and the native religion, characterized by a strong organized hierarchy of monks. —**La′ma·ist,** *n.* —**La′ma·is′tic,** *adj.*

La·marck, Jean de (lə märk′; *French* zhäN də) 1744–1829, French naturalist.

La·marck·i·an (lə märk′ē ən) *adj.* of or relating to Lamarck or his theory. —*n.* supporter or follower of Lamarck or his theory.

La·marck·ism (lə märk′ĭz′əm) *n.* biological theory of Lamarck, now widely believed to be false, that characteristics acquired and developed by individuals in the struggle for life are passed on to their descendants.

La·mar·tine, Al·phonse de (lä mär tēn′; äl fôNs′) 1790–1869, French poet and statesman.

la·ma·ser·y (lä′mə sĕr′ē) *pl.,* **-ser·ies.** *n.* monastery of lamas.

Lamb, Charles (lăm) 1775–1834, English essayist and critic.

lamb (lăm) *n.* **1.** young sheep. **2.** meat from a lamb used as food. **3.** skin of a lamb. **4. the Lamb.** Jesus. **5.** one who is gentle, weak, or innocent. —*v.i.* to give birth to a lamb. [Old English *lamb* young of the sheep, innocent person.]

lam·baste (lăm bāst′, -băst′) **-bast·ed, -bast·ing.** *v.t. Slang.* **1.** to beat or thrash. **2.** to abuse verbally. [Probably from earlier *lam* to thrash (of Scandinavian origin) + BASTE³.]

lamb·da (lăm′də) *n.* **1.** eleventh letter (Λ, λ) of the Greek alphabet, corresponding to the English letter *L, l.* **2.** *Physics.* subatomic particle of the hyperon group. See **subatomic particle** for table.

lam·bent (lăm′bənt) *adj.* **1.** shining with a soft, clear light; softly radiant. **2.** (of a flame) flickering lightly over or on a surface. **3.** characterized by lightness and brilliance: *a lambent wit.* [Latin *lambēns,* present participle of *lambēre* to lick.]

lamb·kin (lăm′kĭn) *n.* **1.** little lamb. **2.** one who is dearly loved, esp. a young child.

Lamb of God, Jesus.

lam·bre·quin (lăm′brə kĭn, -bər-) *n.* drapery hanging from a shelf or covering the upper part of a window or door. [French *lambrequin* valance, going back to Middle Dutch *lamper* veil.]

lamb·skin (lăm′skĭn′) *n.* **1.** skin of a lamb, esp. when dressed with the wool left on it and used for clothing. **2.** leather made from the skin of a lamb. **3.** parchment made from this leather.

lame (lām) **lam·er, lam·est.** *adj.* **1.** unable to walk easily or properly; disabled in the leg or foot. **2.** stiff and painful: *a lame back.* **3.** poor or weak: *Chuck offered a lame excuse for his tardiness.* —*v.t.,* **lamed, lam·ing.** to make lame. [Old English *lama* disabled, infirm.] —**lame′ly,** *adv.* —**lame′ness,** *n.*

la·mé (la mā′, lä-) *n.* fabric woven with metallic threads or with threads which appear metallic. [French *lamé* spangled with gold or silver, from *lame* metal leaf, gold or silver wire, from Latin *lāmina* thin plate or leaf of metal or wood.]

lame duck 1. officeholder, esp. a U.S. Congressman, who has failed to win reelection but continues to hold office for a time after his defeat. **2.** one who is weak or disabled.

la·mel·la (lə mĕl′ə) *pl.,* **-mel·las** or **-mel·lae** (-mĕl′ē). *n.* **1.** thin plate, scale, sheet, or layer of bone or tissue. **2.** *Botany.* any of various thin

scales or scalelike parts of a plant, as a spore-bearing gill of a mushroom. [Latin *lāmella* small plate of metal, diminutive of *lāmina* thin plate or leaf of metal or wood.]

la·mel·lar (lə mel′ər, lam′ə lər) *adj.* lamellate.

lam·el·late (lam′ə lāt′, -lit, lə mel′āt, -it) *adj.* like, having, composed of, or arranged in lamellas.

la·mel·li·branch (lə mel′ə brank′) *n.* any mollusk of the class Pelecypoda, having a hinged bivalve shell, and comprising clams, oysters, and mussels. [Modern Latin *Lamellibranchia*, from Latin *lāmella* (see LAMELLA) + Greek *branchia* gills.]

la·ment (lə ment′) *v.t.* **1.** to feel or express deep sorrow or grief for or about: *to lament the loss of a friend.* **2.** to feel or express deep regret over: *to lament a mistake.* —*v.i.* to feel or express deep sorrow or grief. —*n.* **1.** expression of sorrow or grief. **2.** literary form, as a song or poem, that expresses sorrow or grief. **3.** expression of regret. [Latin *lāmentārī* to wail, bewail.]

lam·en·ta·ble (lam′ən tə bəl, lə men′-) *adj.* **1.** that is to be lamented: *a lamentable tragedy, a lamentable oversight.* **2.** expressing sorrow; mournful. —**lam′en·ta·bly,** *adv.*

lam·en·ta·tion (lam′ən tā′shən) *n.* **1.** act of lamenting. **2.** mournful outcry of sorrow or grief. **3. Lamentations,** book of the Old Testament attributed by some to Jeremiah.

lam·i·na (lam′ə nə) *pl.,* **-nae** (-nē) or **-nas.** *n.* **1.** thin plate, scale, or layer. **2.** *Botany.* flat or expanded part of a leaf or petal. [Latin *lāmina* thin plate or leaf of metal or wood.]

lam·i·nar (lam′ə nər) *adj.* **1.** like, having, composed of, or arranged in thin plates, scales, or layers. **2.** *Hydraulics.* moving in a smooth regular pattern, as air over or about an inert fluid. Opposed to *turbulent.*

lam·i·nate (*v.,* lam′ə nāt′; *n.,* lam′ə nit, -nāt′) **-nat·ed, -nat·ing.** *v.t.* **1.** to form by uniting or bonding different layers, as with glue or heat. **2.** to beat or roll (metal) into thin plates. **3.** to cover with thin sheets or layers. **4.** to split or separate into thin layers. —*n.* product formed by laminating, as safety glass or plywood. —**lam′i·na′tor,** *n.*

lam·i·nat·ed (lam′ə nā′tid) *adj.* manufactured or formed by laminating.

lam·i·na·tion (lam′ə nā′shən) *n.* **1.** process of laminating; being laminated. **2.** thin layer, esp. when bonded to something else: *A lamination of plastic makes the counter more durable.* **3.** laminated structure; arrangement in thin layers.

Lam·mas (lam′əs) *n.* harvest festival formerly celebrated in England and still observed in Scotland, during which newly baked loaves of bread are blessed at Mass. August 1. Also, **Lam′mas·tide′.**

lamp (lamp) *n.* **1.** portable or freestanding device by which light is produced by the use of a light bulb or by burning a substance, as gas or oil. **2.** electric bulb that gives off light or other radiation. **3.** source of knowledge or spiritual guidance. [Old French *lampe* device for lighting, from Latin *lampas* torch, light, from Greek *lampas.*]

lamp·black (lamp′blak′) *n.* black pigment, consisting of almost pure carbon soot, made by burning oil or gas in insufficient air.

lamp·light (lamp′līt′) *n.* light from a lamp or lamps.

lamp·light·er (lamp′līt′ər) *n.* formerly, one whose job was to light the gas or oil street lights at night.

lam·poon (lam pōōn′) *n.* piece of satirical writing, often scurrilous or malicious, directed against a person or an institution. —*v.t.* to satirize or attack in a lampoon. [French *lampon* usually satirical drinking song, probably from *lampons* let us drink (word often used in such songs), from *lamper* to drink; of imitative origin.] —**lam·poon′er, lam·poon′ist,** *n.*

lamp·post (lamp′pōst′) *n.* post supporting a lamp, esp. in a public place, as a street or a park.

lam·prey (lam′prē) *pl.,* **-preys.** *n.* any of a group of primitive, brown·or eel·like fish, family Petromyzontidae, found in salt and fresh water in temperate regions. The lamprey has a round mouth with a rasping tongue and sharp toothlike structures for attaching itself to food or game fish and feeding parasitically on their blood. Length: 6–40 inches. [Old French *lamproie,* from Medieval Latin *lampreda* lamprey, limpet; of uncertain origin.]

lamp shell, brachiopod.

la·nai (lä nī′, lə-) *n.* porch or veranda. [Hawaiian *lanai.*]

Lan·cas·ter (lang′kəs tər; *def.* 2 also lang′kas′tər) *n.* **1.** English royal house in rivalry with York, descended from John of Gaunt, whose kings were Henry IV, Henry V, and Henry VI. **2.** city in southeastern Pennsylvania. Pop. (1970), 57,690.

Lan·cas·tri·an (lang kas′trē ən) *adj.* of or relating to the house of Lancaster. —*n.* member or supporter of the house of Lancaster.

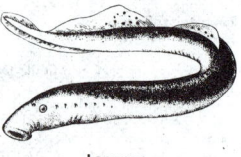

Lamprey

lance (lans) *n.* **1.** long spear, usually consisting of a wooden shaft with a sharp metal head, carried by mounted soldiers or knights. **2.** any spearlike weapon or instrument. **3.** soldier armed with a lance. **4.** lancet. —*v.t.,* **lanced, lanc·ing. 1.** to pierce with or as with a lancet. **2.** to open with or as with a lancet: *to lance and drain an abscess.* [Old French *lance* spear, from Latin *lancea* light spear; probably of Celtic origin.]

lance corporal 1. enlisted man in the U.S. Marine Corps ranking above a private first class and below a corporal. **2.** *British.* private acting as a corporal, without a pay increase.

Lan·ce·lot (lan′sə lot′) *n.* in Arthurian legend, important knight of the Round Table and lover of Guinevere.

lan·ce·o·late (lan′sē ə lāt′, -lit) *adj.* narrow and tapering toward each end, like the head of a lance. [Latin *lanceolātus* shaped like a small spear, from *lanceola* small spear, diminutive of *lancea* light spear. See LANCE.]

lanc·er (lan′sər) *n.* cavalry soldier armed with a lance, or one whose regiment was traditionally so armed.

lanc·ers (lan′sərz) *n.,pl.* **1.** dance that is a form of quadrille. **2.** music for such a dance. ▲ construed as singular.

lan·cet (lan′sit) *n.* short surgical knife having two sharp edges. [Old French *lancette* surgeon's lancet, little spear, diminutive of *lance* spear. See LANCE.]

lance·wood (lans′wood′) *n.* **1.** tough, straight-grained, elastic wood, used mainly for fishing rods and billiard cues. **2.** any of various tropical trees yielding this wood, found esp. in South America.

Lan·chow (län′jō′) *n.* city in northwestern China. Pop. (1957 est.), 699,000.

land (land) *n.* **1.a.** exposed, solid portion of the earth's surface, as distinguished from the submerged parts or the ocean: *to travel by land and by sea.* **b.** any similar surface on a planet or large natural satellite. **2.** ground or soil with reference to its qualities: *arable land, desert land, low land.* **3.** rural or agricultural areas as distinguished from urban areas. **4.** part of the earth's surface marked off by natural, political, or cultural boundaries; country; region: *China is a vast land.* **5.** people of such a region; nation: *The whole land rejoiced.* **6.** *also,* **lands.** real estate except for permanent buildings. **7.** natural resources in their original, undeveloped state, esp. as entering into the process of production along with labor and capital. —*v.i.* **1.a.** (of aircraft or spacecraft) to come down from the air or sky under control and alight on land, water, or any suitable surface. **b.** (of seagoing vessels) to come to land. **2.** to come to rest, as after a fall or flight: *Mary threw her glove, and it landed on the hall table.* **3.** to go or come ashore from a vessel; disembark. **4.** to arrive in a specific, esp. bad, point, place, or situation; end up: *to land in jail. The letter landed in the wrong office.* —*v.t.* **1.** to bring (a craft) down from the air or sky onto a suitable surface. **2.** to set ashore from a vessel; unload onto land: *to land a cargo, to land passengers.* **3.** to put in a specific, esp. bad, point, place, or situation: *Fishing without a license will land you in trouble.* **4.** to bring (a fish) to land or into a boat. **5.** *Informal.* to secure; win; get: *to land a good position.* **6.** *Informal.* to deliver (a blow). [Old English *land* solid part of the earth's surface, ground, nation.]

-land *combining form* place of; region of: *homeland, fairyland.*

lan·dau (lan′dou, -dô) *n.* **1.** four-wheeled, two-seated carriage with a top that opens in the center and can be folded down in the back and front. **2.** automobile with a similar collapsible top. [From *Landau,* German town where this carriage was first made.]

Landau

lan·dau·let (lan′dô let′) *also,* **lan·dau·lette** *n.* **1.** small landau, usually having only one seat. **2.** automobile with a collapsible top over the back section.

land breeze, breeze blowing toward the sea from the land.

land crab, any of various tropical crabs that live on beaches or mud flats.

land·ed (lan′did) *adj.* **1.** owning land: *landed gentry.* **2.** consisting of land: *landed property.*

land·fall (land′fôl′) *n.* **1.** act or instance of reaching or sighting land, as after a long voyage. **2.** land so reached or sighted.

land·form (land′fôrm′) *n.* feature on the earth's surface resulting from natural causes, as a valley or mountain range.

land grant, gift of public land by the government for a public purpose, as establishing a college.

land·grave (land′grāv′) *n.* in medieval Germany, count or prince, esp. one having authority over a large territory. [German *Landgraf* count²; literally, land count, from *Land* land + *Graf* count².]

land·hold·er (land'hōl'dər) *n.* one who owns land.

land·ing (lan'ding) *n.* **1.** act or process of one who or that which lands. **2.** space on a dock or pier for disembarking from or unloading a ship. **3.** platform at the end of or between flights of stairs.

landing field, area of land designed or suited for the takeoff and landing of aircraft.

landing gear, wheels, shock absorbers, and other structures on which an aircraft rests while it is on the land or water.

landing net, net to take a hooked fish from the water.

landing stage, floating platform, often built to rise and fall with the tide, used for loading and unloading people and goods at a landing.

landing strip, long, narrow area suitable for the landing and takeoff of aircraft.

land·la·dy (land'lā'dē) *pl.,* **-dies.** *n.* **1.** woman who owns houses or apartments occupied by tenants. **2.** landlord's wife. **3.** woman who runs an inn, boarding house, or lodging house.

land·less (land'lis) *adj.* owning no land: *landless tenant farmers.*

land·locked (land'lokt') *adj.* **1.** entirely or almost entirely surrounded by land, esp. having no harbor or seacoast: *a landlocked nation.* **2.** (of certain species of salmon) living out the entire life cycle in fresh water.

land·lord (land'lôrd') *n.* **1.** one, esp. a man, who owns houses or apartments occupied by tenants. **2.** landowner or lord of a manor, who exacts rent or service for the use of his land. **3.** one who runs an inn, boarding house, or lodging house.

land·lub·ber (land'lub'ər) *n.* one who is awkward or inexperienced on ships. ▲ often used in mild scorn by experienced sailors.

land·mark (land'märk') *n.* **1.** prominent feature of a landscape, often used to determine direction or location. **2.** historically important building or site: *The Civil War battlefield was declared a national landmark.* **3.** prominent or historically important fact or event: *The court decision was a landmark in civil rights.* **4.** object that marks a boundary line.

land·mass (land'mas') *n.* large area of land.

land mine, metal device with an explosive charge, concealed in the ground and set off esp. by the weight or proximity of troops or vehicles or by a timing mechanism.

land office, government office that handles and records transfers and sales of public lands.

land-office business, large amount or high rate of buying or selling.

Land of Promise, in the Old Testament, Canaan, the land promised by God to Abraham and his descendants.

Land of the Midnight Sun 1. Norway. **2.** part of the world above the Arctic Circle, where in the summer the sun does not set.

land·own·er (land'ō'nər) *n.* one who owns land. —**land'own'ing,** *adj.*

land·poor (land'poor') *adj.* owning much land, esp. nonproductive land, but without money available for taxes or other expenses.

land reform, redistribution of large holdings of agricultural land among small farmers, esp. as a government measure.

land·scape (land'skāp') *n.* **1.** view of natural inland scenery. **2.** picture representing a view of natural scenery or land. **3.** branch of painting, photography, or the like, dealing with natural scenery or land. —*v.t.,* **-scaped, -scap·ing.** to beautify or improve (a piece of land), as by planting trees and shrubs. —*v.i.* to engage in landscape architecture or gardening. [Dutch *landschap* province, painting of a land scene, from *land* land + *-schap* -ship.]

landscape architect, one whose profession is landscape architecture.

landscape architecture, art or profession of arranging or changing the natural scenery of a place for aesthetic effect or some desired purpose.

landscape gardener, one whose work is landscape gardening.

landscape gardening, 1. art or work of beautifying land, as the grounds around a house, by planting trees and other plants and designing gardens. **2.** result or example of this.

land·scap·ist (land'skā'pist) *n.* painter of landscapes.

land·slide (land'slīd') *n.* **1.** the sliding or falling of a mass of soil, rock, or debris down a slope. **2.** mass that slides down. **3.** overwhelming victory, esp. in an election.

land·slip (land'slip') *n. British.* landslide (*defs. 1, 2*).

lands·man (landz'mən) *pl.,* **-men.** *n.* one who lives or works on land.

land·ward (land'wərd) *adj.* lying or going toward the land. —*adv. also,* **landwards.** toward the land.

land wind, wind blowing toward the sea from the land.

lane (lān) *n.* **1.** narrow way or road, esp. in a rural area. **2.** any long, narrow way or passage between barriers. **3.** course or route bounded by definite lines: *a shipping lane, a traffic lane.* **4.** bowling alley (*def. 2*). [Old English *lane* narrow road.]

lang., language.

Lang·land, William (lang'lənd) c.1332–c.1400, English poet.

Lang·ley, Samuel Pier·pont (lang'lē; pēr'pont) 1834–1906, U.S. aeronautical pioneer and scientist.

lan·guage (lang'gwij) *n.* **1.** means of communication in which vocal sounds are combined into meaningful units to convey thoughts and feelings; human speech. **2.** written symbols representing these sounds. **3.** all the vocal sounds, and the written symbols representing them, that make up a system by which the members of a nation, tribe, or other group communicate with each other. **4.** any means of communication, as through gestures, signs, or symbols: *computer language. Algebra is a mathematical language.* **5.** the special vocabulary, uses, and forms characteristic of a particular group or profession: *military language, the language of medicine.* **6.** style or kind of language; manner of expression: *earthy language, flowery language, Milton's majestic language.* **7.** means of communication used by animals: *the language of dolphins.* **8.** *Law.* the exact wording of a document: *the language of a contract.* **9.** the study of language or languages; linguistics. [Old French *langage* speech of a country, expression of thought by words, from *langue* tongue, speech of a country, from Latin *lingua* tongue, speech.]

language laboratory, room specially equipped with tape recordings or records to enable students to listen to and practice speaking a foreign language that they are studying.

Langue·doc (läng dôk') *n.* historic region and former province of France, in the southern part of the country on the Mediterranean.

langue d'oc (läng dôk') any of a group of dialects spoken in southern France in the Middle Ages, from which modern Provençal is descended. [Old French *langue d'oc* language of *oc.* The two principal dialects of Old French took their names from *oc* and *oïl,* their different words for "yes." See LANGUE D'OÏL, LANGUAGE.]

langue d'oïl (läng dô ēl') any of a group of dialects spoken in northern France in the Middle Ages, from which modern French is descended. [Old French *langue d'oïl* language of *oïl.* See LANGUE D'OC.]

lan·guid (lang'gwid) *adj.* **1.** lacking or showing a lack of energy or force; weak; sluggish. **2.** lacking interest or spirited concern; indifferent. [Latin *languidus* weak, sluggish.]

lan·guish (lang'gwish) *v.i.* **1.** to grow weak or feeble; lose health or vitality. **2.** to live under conditions which lower the spirits: *The people languished under dictatorial rule.* **3.** to lose vigor or intensity. **4.** to suffer with desire; pine (with *for*): *She languished for her husband in the Army.* **5.** to assume a languid look or expression, as an indication of sorrowful or tender emotion. [Old French *languiss-,* a stem of *languir* to be listless, pine, going back to Latin *languēre* to be weak.] —**lan'guish·er, lan'guish·ment,** *n.*

lan·guish·ing (lang'gwi shing) *adj.* **1.** becoming weak or spiritless; pining away. **2.** indicating tender, sentimental emotion.

lan·guor (lang'gər) *n.* **1.** lack of vigor; weakness; fatigue. **2.** lack of activity; stagnation. **3.** tenderness or softness of mood or feeling. **4.** lack of spirit or interest; indifference. **5.** oppressive stillness. [Old French *languor* prolonged physical or emotional depression, from Latin *languor* faintness.]

lan·guor·ous (lang'gər əs) *adj.* **1.** languid. **2.** causing or tending to cause languor.

lan·gur (lung goor') *n.* any of various long-tailed monkeys, genus *Presbytis,* found in Asia, usually having a slender body and long limbs. [Hindi *langūr,* possibly from Sanskrit *lāngūlin* having a tail.]

lan·iard (lan'yərd) lanyard.

lank (langk) *adj.* **1.** long and lean; slender. **2.** (of hair) straight and flat. [Old English *hlanc* lean.] —**lank'ness,** *n.*

lank·y (lang'kē) lank·i·er, lank·i·est. ungracefully tall and thin: *the lanky giraffe.* —**lank'i·ly,** *adv.* —**lank'i·ness,** *n.*

lan·o·lin (lan'əl in) *also,* **lan·o·line** (lan'əl in, -ēn') *n.* fatty substance obtained from the wool of sheep, used in various ointments, cosmetics, and soaps. [Latin *lāna* wool + *oleum* oil + -IN[1].]

Lan·sing (lan'sing) *n.* capital of Michigan, in the south-central part of the state. Pop. (1970), 131,546.

lan·tern (lan'tərn) *n.* **1.** light, as a kerosene light, with a protective, partly transparent casing, usually made to be carried in the hand. **2.** casing or covering for a light, esp. a decorative paper covering. **3.** chamber at the top of a lighthouse in which the light is placed. **4.** *Architecture.* turret-shaped structure, esp. on the top of the roof, with windows or openings to admit light and air. **5.** *Archaic.* slide or motion-picture projector. [Old French *lanterne* box with transparent sides in which a light is enclosed for protection, from Latin *lanterna* torch, lamp, from Greek *lamptēr.*]

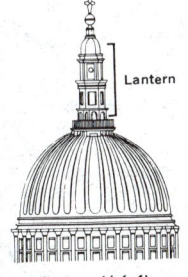

Lantern

Lantern (*def. 4*)

at; āpe; cär; end; mē; it; īce; hot; ōld; fôrk; wood; fōōl; oil; out; up; ūse; tu̇rn; sing; thin; this; zh in treasure; ə in ago, taken, pencil, lemon, circus.

575

lantern jaw, long, thin projecting jaw.

lantern slide *Archaic.* photographic slide.

lan·tha·num (lan'thə nəm) *n.* soft, white metallic element belonging to the rare-earth group, used esp. in the manufacture of electronic devices. Symbol: **La** See element in table. [Modern Latin *lanthanum,* from Greek *lanthanein* to escape notice; because it was difficult to isolate.]

lan·yard (lan'yərd) *also,* **lan·iard.** *n.* **1.** short rope or cord used on ships to fasten or tighten rigging. **2.** cord worn around the neck, from which to hang something, as a knife or whistle. **3.** cord with a small hook at one end, used in firing certain types of cannon. [Earlier *lanyer,* from Old French *laniere,* from *lasne* thong, from *lasne* thong, noose, possibly from blend of *las* noose (see LACE) + *nasle* string (of Germanic origin).]

La·oc·o·ön (lā ok'ō on') *n.* *Greek Legend.* Trojan priest who was killed with his two sons by two sea serpents after he warned the Trojans against the Trojan horse.

La·os (lā'ōs, lā'os) *n.* country in southeastern Asia, between Thailand and North Vietnam. Capital, Vientiane. Area, 91,428 sq. mi. Pop. (1969 est.), 2,893,000.

La·o·tian (lā ō'shən) *adj.* of or relating to Laos, its people, or their language. —*n.* native or inhabitant of Laos.

Lao-tse (lou'dzu') *also,* **Lao-tze, Lao-tsu.** *n.* born c.600 B.C., Chinese philosopher, reputed founder of Taoism.

lap¹ (lap) *n.* **1.** level area formed between the waist and the knees of a seated person. **2.** clothing that covers this area. **3.** area of responsibility or control: *Don't drop all your personal problems in my lap.* **4.** place or condition in which something is cared for; surrounding protection or care: *in the lap of luxury.* [Old English *læppa* flap (of a garment).]

lap² (lap) *lapped,* **lap·ping.** *v.i.* **1.** to lie partly over or beside another; overlap. **2.** to extend beyond something in space or time (with *over*): *One meeting lapped over into the next.* **3.** to wind, wrap, or fold something. —*v.t.* **1.** to wind, wrap, or fold about: *The mother lapped the child in a blanket.* **2.** to lay (something) partly over or beside another: *to lap one shingle over another.* **3.** to get a lap or more ahead of. **4.** to cut or polish with a lap. —*n.* **1.** act or fact of lapping over. **2.** part that extends partly over another. **3.** amount of overlapping. **4.** one circuit around a racetrack. **5.** revolving disk used to cut or polish, as glass or gems. [Probably from LAP¹.]

lap³ (lap) *lapped,* **lap·ping.** *v.t.* **1.** to drink (a liquid) by lifting it into the mouth with the tongue (often with *up*): *The cat lapped its milk.* **2.** to move or wash gently against with a splashing sound: *Waves lapped the dock.* —*v.i.* **1.** to drink a liquid by lifting it into the mouth with the tongue. **2.** to move or wash gently with a splashing sound. —*n.* **1.** act of lapping. **2.** gentle, splashing sound. [Old English *lapian* to take up liquid with the tongue.] —**lap'per,** *n.*

La Paz (lä päs') city in western Bolivia, in the Andes Mountains, the seat of the government and unofficial capital of the country. Pop. (1969 est.), 525,000.

lap·board (lap'bôrd') *n.* board held on the lap and used as a table.

lap dog, pet dog, small enough to be held easily on the lap.

la·pel (lə pel') *n.* part of the front of a coat or jacket folded back and forming a continuation of the collar. [From LAP¹.]

lap·ful (lap'fool') *pl.,* **-fuls.** *n.* as much as the lap can hold.

lap·i·dar·y (lap'ə der'ē) *pl.,* **-dar·ies.** *n.* one who engraves, cuts, or polishes precious stones. —*adj.* **1.** of or relating to the cutting or engraving of precious stones. **2.** engraved on stone, as an epitaph. [Latin *lapidārius* stonecutter, from *lapis* stone.]

lap·in (lap'in) *n.* rabbit fur, often dyed to resemble more valuable furs. [French *lapin* rabbit; possibly of Iberian origin.]

lap·is laz·u·li (lap'is laz'ū lē, lazh'-) **1.** translucent semiprecious stone used for carvings or jewelry, usually azure blue or violet blue. **2.** deep, violet-blue color. [Medieval Latin *lapis lazuli* stone of azure, from Latin *lapis* stone + Medieval Latin *lazuli,* genitive of *lazulum* a blue semiprecious stone, azure (from Arabic *lāzward*). See AZURE.]

La·place, Marquis Pierre Si·mon de (lä pläs', pyär sē mōn' də) 1749–1827, French mathematician and astronomer.

Lap·land (lap'land') *n.* region in northern Europe, including the northernmost sections of Norway, Sweden, and Finland, and the northwestern Soviet Union. Area, approx. 150,000 sq. mi.

Lap·land·er (lap'lan'dər) *n.* Lapp (def. 1).

La Pla·ta (lä plä'tə) port city in eastern Argentina. Pop. (1960), 337,060.

Lapp (lap) *n.* **1.** member of a people living in Lapland, formerly nomadic, now partly settled. **2.** language of the Lapps, a member of

the Ural-Altaic family of languages. [Possibly from Finnish *lapaan* nomad.]

lap robe, fur robe or blanket used to protect the legs from the cold, as when riding in an open carriage or sleigh.

lapse (laps) *n.* **1.** small error; mistake, esp. a trivial one: *a spelling lapse, a memory lapse.* **2.** period or interval: *The wanderer returned after a lapse of ten years.* **3.** slipping or falling away, as from a moral standard. **4.** fact of stopping, going out of effect, or falling into disuse. **5.** termination of a right or privilege through failure to use or renew it or to meet stated obligations. —*v.i.* **lapsed, laps·ing. 1.** to make an error or mistake, esp. by not doing what is moral or right. **2.** to slip or fall (with *into*): *to lapse into silence. The building lapsed into ruin.* **3.** (of time) to elapse. **4.** to stop, go out of effect, or fall into disuse. **5.** (of a right or privilege) to terminate or become void through failure to use or renew or to meet stated obligations. [Latin *lapsus* fall, slipping.]

lap·sus lin·guae (lap'səs ling'gwē) *Latin.* slip of the tongue.

lap·wing (lap'wing') *n.* any of various crested plovers, family Charadriidae, noted for its slow, irregular wing beat in flight and a shrill, wailing cry. Length: 10–16 inches. [Old English *hlēapewince,* from *hlēapan* to spring + *wincian* to blink; originally, to move from side to side; because it turns about when it flies.]

Lapwing

lar·board (lär'bôrd', -bərd) *n., adj. Nautical.* port². [Modification (influenced by STARBOARD) of earlier *ladeborde* literally, loading side, apparently from LADE + BOARD.]

lar·ce·ny (lär'sə nē) *pl.,* **-nies.** *n.* crime of unlawfully taking away another's property, with the intent of depriving him of it permanently. [Old French *larcin* theft, from Latin *latrōcinium* robbery.] —**lar'ce·nous,** *adj.*

larch (lärch) *n.* **1.** any of a group of tall hardwood trees, genus *Larix,* of the pine family, found in the cold regions of the Northern Hemisphere, bearing needle-shaped leaves that are shed annually. **2.** hard, strong, durable wood of this tree, used mainly in shipbuilding, for telephone poles, and for railroad ties. [German *Lärche* this tree, going back to Latin *larix.*]

lard (lärd) *n.* soft, white, edible fat obtained by rendering fatty tissue from the body of a hog, used in cooking and as a base for certain ointments. —*v.t.* **1.** to add lard to or cover with lard. **2.** to stuff or cover (poultry or meat) with pieces of fat before cooking. **3.** to add extra material to (speech or writing): *to lard a passage with quotations.* [Old French *lard* bacon, from Latin *lār(i)dum.*]

lar·der (lär'dər) *n.* **1.** place where food is kept; pantry. **2.** stock of provisions. [Anglo-Norman *larder* tub in which bacon is kept, from Old French *lard* bacon. See LARD.]

La·re·do (lə rā'dō) *n.* city in southern Texas, near the U. S.-Mexican border. Pop. (1970), 69,024.

lar·es and penates (lär'ēz) **1.** household gods of the ancient Romans. **2.** treasured possessions of a family or household. [Latin *lārēs et penātēs* household gods of the ancient Romans.]

large (lärj) **larg·er, larg·est.** *adj.* **1.** of considerable size or quantity; not small. **2.** exceeding the usual size or quantity: *a large ant.* **3.** wide in range or capacity: *The president's powers under the bill would be very large.* —*n.* **at large. 1.** at liberty; free: *The suspect is still at large.* **2.** of, by, or relating to an entire political unit, as a state: *Since the representatives were elected at large, they all had to campaign statewide.* **3.** as a whole; in general: *to talk about the world at large.* **4.** at length; in detail; fully: *to speak at large on a subject.* [Old French *large* broad, great, generous, from Latin *largus* abundant.] —**large'ness,** *n.* —Syn. *adj.* **2.** see **great.**

large-heart·ed (lärj'här'tid) *adj.* generous; liberal; kindly. —**large'-heart'ed·ness,** *n.*

large intestine, lower part of the intestines, between the small intestine and the anus, consisting of the cecum, colon, and rectum.

large·ly (lärj'lē) *adv.* to a great extent; mostly; mainly: *The buildings in this area are largely two-bedroom homes.*

large-scale (lärj'skāl') *adj.* **1.** of broad scope; extensive: *a large-scale strike.* **2.** drawn or made to a large scale: *a large-scale map, a large-scale graph.*

lar·gess (lär jes', lär'jis) *also,* **lar·gesse.** *n.* **1.** generous giving. **2.** gift or gifts so given. [Old French *largesse* bounty, going back to Latin *largus* abundant.]

lar·ghet·to (lär get'ō) *Music. adj., adv.* rather slow. —*n. pl.,* **-tos.** composition, movement, or part in such a tempo. [Italian *larghetto* somewhat slow, diminutive of *largo* slow, wide, from Latin *largus* abundant.]

larg·ish (lär'jish) *adj.* rather large.

lar·go (lär'gō) *Music. adj., adv.* very slow and dignified; stately.

at; āpe; cär; end; mē; it; īce; hot; ōld; fôrk; wood; fōōl; oil; out; up; ūse; turn; sing; thin; this; zh in treasure; ə in ago, taken, pencil, lemon, circus.

—*n. pl.*, **-gos.** largo composition, movement, or part. [Italian *largo* slow, wide, from Latin *largus* abundant.]

lar·i·at (lar′ē ət) *n.* **1.** long rope with a loop secured in a running knot at one end, used esp. for roping livestock; lasso. **2.** tether. [Spanish *la reata* the rope, *reata* rope, from *reatar* to tie again, going back to Latin *re-* again + *aptāre* to adjust.]

lark[1] (lärk) *n.* **1.** any of various small songbirds, family Alaudidae, usually having predominantly gray-brown plumage, as the skylark, *Alauda arvensis*, found in Europe, and the **horned lark**, *Eremophila alpestris*, the only North American lark. Length: 5–9 inches. **2.** any of various similar but unrelated birds, as the meadow lark. [Old English *lāwerce*.]

lark[2] (lärk) *n.* playful, frivolous adventure or antic; something done just for fun: *John jumped in the fountain for a lark.* —*v.i.* to do things just for fun. [Possibly modification of dialectal English *lake* to play, from Old Norse *leika*.]

lark·spur (lärk′spur′) *n.* delphinium. [LARK[1] + SPUR; because of its spur-shaped calyx.]

La Roche·fou·cauld, Fran·çois, Duc de (lä rōsh fōō kō′; frän-swä′; dook də) 1613–80, French author noted for his maxims.

lar·rup (lar′əp) **-ruped, -rup·ing.** *v.t. Informal.* to beat; flog; thrash. [Possibly from Dutch *larpen* to thrash.] —**lar′rup·er**, *n.*

lar·va (lär′və) *pl.*, **-vae** (-vē). *n.* **1.** early, usually wormlike, form of an insect, before it undergoes metamorphosis. The caterpillar is the larva of a butterfly. **2.** early form of any animal that undergoes metamorphosis. The tadpole is the larva of a frog. [Latin *lārva* ghost, mask; because this stage was thought to mask the final form of the insect.] —**lar′val**, *adj.*

la·ryn·ge·al (lə rin′jē əl) *adj.* of, relating to, or located in or on the larynx. —**la·ryn′ge·al·ly**, *adv.*

lar·yn·gi·tis (lar′ən jī′tis) *n.* inflammation of the voice box or larynx, often characterized by hoarseness of the voice. [Modern Latin *laryngitis*, from Greek *larynx* throat + -ITIS.] —**lar′yn·git·ic** (lar′ən-jit′ik), *adj.*

la·ryn·go·scope (lə ring′gə skōp′) *n.* tubular telescopic and reflecting instrument for examining the larynx, as during surgery. —**la·ryn·go·scop·ic** (lə ring′gə skop′ik); *also.* **la·ryn′go·scop′i·cal**, *adj.* —**la·ryn′go·scop′i·cal·ly**, *adv.*

lar·ynx (lar′ingks) *pl.*, **la·ryn·ges** (lə rin′jēz) or **lar·ynx·es.** *n.* **1.** triangular, boxlike chamber at the upper end of the human windpipe, containing the vocal cords and serving as the organ of speech. **2.** similar organ in most other mammals and some other animals. [Modern Latin *larynx*, from Greek *larynx* throat.]

la·sa·gne (lə zän′yə, lä-) *n.* **1.** baked dish usually consisting of alternating layers of wide noodles, chopped meat, tomato sauce, cheese, and seasonings. **2.** broad, flat noodle, sometimes having ruffled edges. [Italian *lasagne* (plural), going back to Latin *lasanum* cooking pot, from Greek *lasanon* chamber pot.]

La Salle, Re·né Ro·bert Ca·ve·lier, Sieur de (lə sal′; rə nā′ rō ber′ kä vəl yā′; sœr də) 1643–87, French explorer of Canada and the Great Lakes.

las·car (las′kər) *n.* East Indian sailor. [Hindi *lashkarī* sailor, soldier, going back to Persian *lashkar* army, from Arabic *al'askar* the army, possibly, through Greek, going back to Latin *exercitus* army.]

las·civ·i·ous (lə siv′ē əs) *adj.* **1.** feeling, showing, or characterized by lust. **2.** arousing lust. [Late Latin *lascīviōsus* lustful, from Latin *lascīvia* wantonness, playfulness.] —**las·civ′i·ous·ly**, *adv.* —**las·civ′i·ous·ness**, *n.*

la·ser (lā′zər) *n. Physics.* device that generates and amplifies light energy, producing an extremely powerful beam consisting of light waves which are of the same wavelength and are in phase. Also, **optical maser.** [Abbreviation of *l(ight) a(mplification by) s(timulated) e(mission of) r(adiation)*.]

lash[1] (lash) *n.* **1.** stroke or blow with a whip, scourge, thong, or the like: *The seaman was given ten lashes for insubordination.* **2.** flexible, often braided, part of a whip. **3.** eyelash. **4.** movement or impact like that of a whip: *the lash of the animal's tail.* **5.** anything that cuts or gives pain like a blow from a whip: *the lash of his conscience.* —*v.t.* **1.** to beat or strike with a whip, scourge, or other flexible object. **2.** to beat or strike with violence; dash forcefully against: *The rain lashed the windows.* **3.** to wave or move to and fro like a whip; switch angrily: *The tiger lashed its tail.* **4.** to attack violently; assail; hurt. **5.** to incite, as if by whipping: *The orator lashed the crowd into violent action.* —*v.i.* **1.** to dash violently; rush: *The waves lashed against the rocks.* **2.** to beat or strike with, or as with, a whip or scourge (with *at*). **3.** to strike out with sudden violence or abuse (with *out*): *The horse*

lashed out with his rear leg. The girl lashed out against her parents. [Possibly imitative.] —**lash′er**, *n.*

lash[2] (lash) *v.t.* to tie or fasten, as with a rope or cord: *The boys lashed logs together to make a raft.* [Old French *lachier* to tie with a lace, going back to Latin *laqueus* snare.]

lash·ing[1] (lash′ing) *n.* **1.** act or instance of whipping. **2.** sharp rebuke or scolding. [LASH[1] + -ING[1].]

lash·ing[2] (lash′ing) *n.* that which fastens or ties, as a rope or cord. [LASH[2] + -ING[1].]

Las Pal·mas (läs päl′mäs) port city in the Canary Islands. Pop. (1968), 229,868.

La Spe·zia (lä spät′syä) port city and naval base in northwestern Italy. Pop. (1968), 129,266.

lass (las) *n.* **1.** young woman; girl. **2.** sweetheart. [Of uncertain origin.]

las·sie (las′ē) *n.* young girl; lass.

las·si·tude (las′ə tōōd′, -tūd′) *n.* fatigue; weariness; weakness. [Latin *lassitūdō*.]

las·so (las′ō, la sōō′) *pl.*, **-sos** or **-soes.** *n.* long rope with a running knot at one end, used esp. for roping livestock. —*v.t.*, **las·soed, las·so·ing.** to rope with a lasso. [Spanish *lazo* slip knot, snare, going back to Latin *laqueus* snare.]

last[1] (last) *adj.* **1.** following or subsequent to all others, as in order, time, or occurrence; furthest from the first; final: *the last one in line, the last day of the month.* **2.** being the only one remaining: *The vendor sold his last balloon.* **3.** next before the present; most recent; latest: *last night.* **4.** conclusive; final: *Did you have the last word in the argument?* **5.** most probable: *She'd be the last person to go along with the scheme.* **6.** least important; ranking lowest: *the last prize.* **7.** belonging to the end of final stages, esp. of life: *His last days were spent in bed.* **8.** utmost; extreme: *to the last degree.* —*adv.* **1.** after all others in time or sequence; at the end: *Last came the clowns.* **2.** at a past time nearest to the present; most recently: *When did you last visit the dentist?* **3.** in conclusion; finally: *Last, I would like to summarize the points of my argument.* —*n.* **1.** one who or that which is last: *He is the last in line. This is the last of the milk.* **2.** end; conclusion: *He gave in at the last and told all he knew.* **3.** at last. finally. **4. to see** (or **hear**) **the last of.** to come in contact with for the last time; be rid of: *You will never hear the last of it. We haven't seen the last of him.* **5. to breathe one's last.** to die. [Old English *latost, lætest*, superlative of *læt* slow, tardy.]

Syn. *adj.* **1. Last, final, ultimate** mean occurring at the end of all others in a series. **Last** denotes occurring at the end of a series of things that are the same or similar in order of succession: *The quotation was taken from the last chapter of the book.* **Final** means relating to or occurring at the end of a progression or serving to complete and terminate a series decisively: *Election of a new executive committee was the final item on the agenda.* **Ultimate** refers to the final or the most remote stage of a long series or process: *The explorers discovered the ultimate source of the Nile.*

last[2] (last) *v.i.* **1.** to go on; continue: *The play lasted three hours.* **2.** to stay in good condition: *These colors won't last if exposed to the sun.* **3.** to be enough not to give out or be depleted: *The hiker hoped his strength would last until he reached the cabin.* [Old English *læstan* to follow, continue.] —**Syn. 1.** see **continue.**

last[3] (last) *n.* wood or metal form, shaped like a human foot, on which footwear is made or repaired. —*v.t.* to form (footwear) on a last. [Old English *læste* this wooden form, from *lāst* footprint.]

Las·tex (las′teks) *Trademark. n.* elastic yarn made with a core of rubber thread covered with any of various fibers, used for such items as bathing suits, girdles, and ski wear. [(E)LAST(IC) + TEX(TILE).]

last·ing (las′ting) *adj.* that lasts; permanent; enduring; durable. —**last′ing·ly**, *adv.*

Last Judgment, Judgment Day.

last·ly (last′lē) *adv.* in the last place; in conclusion.

last quarter, half moon that follows a full moon. See **moon** for illustration.

last rites, sacraments administered by a Roman Catholic priest to someone in danger of death, consisting of confession, the viaticum, and anointing of the sick.

last straw, that which finally makes something intolerable.

Last Supper, final meal of Jesus and the Apostles on the night before His Crucifixion.

last word 1. final remark, as in an argument. **2.** ultimate authority: *The congress is supposed to have the last word in declaring war.* **3.** *Informal.* most recent style or development: *She is wearing the last word in boots.*

Lasso

Larynx

Las Ve·gas (läs vā′gəs) city in southeastern Nevada, noted as a tourist resort and a gambling center. Pop. (1970), 125,787.

lat., latitude.

Lat., Latin.

latch (lach) n. any device for keeping a door, window, or gate closed, usually consisting of a bar that falls or slides into a notch, hole, or groove. —v.t. 1. to secure the latch of (something). —v.i. 1. to be equipped with a latch; close with a latch: *Do the cabinet doors latch?* 2. **to latch onto.** *Informal.* **a.** to attach oneself to; stick close to. **b.** to grasp or obtain. [Old English *læccan* to seize.]

latch·et (lach′it) n. *Archaic.* thong used to fasten a shoe; shoelace. [Dialectal Old French *lachet* thong, lacing, diminutive of Old French *las* noose. See LACE.]

Latch

latch·key (lach′kē′) n. key for opening the latch of a door or gate.

latch·string (lach′string′) n. string passing through a door, used to open a latch.

late (lāt) lat·er or lat·ter, lat·est or last. *adj.* 1. coming or appearing after the proper time: *I was late for our appointment.* 2. coming or being after the usual or customary time: *a late lunch.* 3.a. beginning or occurring at, or going on until, an advanced time, as of night: *to call at a late hour, a late movie.* **b.** of or relating to an advanced stage of history or development: *late Byzantine architecture.* 4. recent: *to fill someone in on the latest developments.* 5. recently but no longer holding office. 6. recently dead. —adv., lat·er, lat·est. 1. after the proper or agreed on time or the usual or customary time: *Wendy arrived late at the party. The mail was delivered late today.* 2. at or until an advanced time, as of night: *The children stayed up late.* 3. at or to an advanced stage or period. 4. **of late.** lately; recently. 5. *Archaic.* not long since; recently. [Old English *læt* slow, tardy.] —**late′ness,** n.

Syn. *adj.* 1. **Late, tardy** mean happening after the due or appointed time. **Late** means falling behind a schedule or the usual rate of progress: *The train was five minutes late.* **Tardy** means happening later than the prescribed time because of lack of punctuality, sluggishness, or delay: *Gwen was tardy this morning and missed the train.*

late·com·er (lāt′kum′ər) n. 1. one who arrives after the proper or agreed on time. 2. one who or that which has recently arrived; newcomer.

la·teen (la tēn′, lə-) *adj.* of, relating to, or having a sailing rig characterized by a triangular sail that is suspended from a long slanting yard and extends both fore and aft of the mast. —n. also, **la·teen′er,** ship having such a rig, common esp. in the Mediterranean Sea. [French (voile) *latine* Latin (sail), feminine of *latin* Latin, from Latin *Latīnus* (see LATIN); because of its use in the Mediterranean Sea.]

Lateen sails

Late Greek, form of the Greek language used from about A.D. 300 to 600.

Late Latin, form of the Latin language used from about A.D. 300 to 600.

late·ly (lāt′lē) adv. 1. within a recent time; not long ago: *Have you seen her lately?* 2. now and during a recent time; these days: *John isn't feeling well lately.* 3. *Archaic.* not long since.

la·tent (lāt′ənt) adj. present and actual, but not obvious, developed, or brought out; hidden: *the latent meaning of a ritual.* [Latin *latēns*, present participle of *latēre* to lie concealed.] —**la′ten·cy,** n.

Syn. Latent, dormant mean potential but inactive. **Latent** implies that something is not actualized but is capable of bursting into full activity under certain conditions: *Education can develop the latent talents of a child.* **Dormant** usually refers to things that were once active but are no longer so: *That volcano has been dormant for twenty years.*

latent image, image *(def. 6b).*

lat·er (lā′tər) a comparative of **late.**

lat·er·al (lat′ər əl) adj. 1. of or relating to the side; at, from, or toward the side. 2. *Phonetics.* articulated with the breath passing over the sides of the tongue. 3. descended from a brother or a sister of an ancestor: *a lateral relation.* —n. 1. lateral or side part, member, or object. 2. *Football.* pass thrown to the side or in a direction away from the opponent's goal, rather than forward. Also, **lateral pass.** 3. *Phonetics.* lateral consonant sound. In English, the only lateral is *l.* —v.i. *Football.* to throw a lateral. [Latin *laterālis* relating to the side, from *latus* side.] —**lat′er·al·ly,** adv.

Lat·er·an (lat′ər ən) n. 1. cathedral of the pope as bishop of Rome. 2. palace, formerly the official papal residence and now a museum, adjoining this church.

la·tex (lā′teks) pl., **la·tex·es** or **lat·i·ces** (lat′ə sēz′.) n. 1. milky liquid obtained from a rubber tree, esp. the tropical rubber tree, *Hevea brasiliensis,* that consists of small globules of pure rubber suspended in water. 2. similar milky liquid found in some other plants, as milkweeds and poppies. 3. liquid emulsion consisting of small globules of plastic or of synthetic rubber suspended in water, used esp. as a base for certain paints. [Latin *latex* liquid, probably from Greek *latax* wine lees.]

lath (lath) n. 1. one of the thin, narrow strips of wood used esp. to form a lining or a base for a coat of plaster or for tiles or slates, as on a roof. 2. sheet or sheets of building material, esp. metal mesh, used for a similar purpose. Also, **lath′ing.** —v.t. to build or line with laths. [Old English *lætt* thin, narrow strip of wood used as a base for plaster of a building or for lattice work.]

lathe (lāth) n. machine that holds a long piece of wood, metal, or other material at both ends and rotates it for shaping by a cutting tool. [Of Scandinavian origin.]

lath·er (lath′ər) n. 1. foam, froth, or suds made esp. from soap moistened with water. 2. foam caused by profuse sweating, esp. on a horse. 3. *Informal.* state of excitement or agitation. —v.i. 1. to form a lather. 2. to become covered with lather. —v.t. 1. to cover with lather. 2. *Informal.* to beat; thrash. [Old English *lēathor* foam from soap and water.]

lath·ing (lath′ing) n. 1. lath or laths. 2. act or process of putting laths in place for use.

Lat·in (lat′in) n. 1. language of the ancient Romans, a member of the Italic group of the Indo-European family of languages, the parent of the Romance languages. 2. member of any of the peoples, as Italians or Portuguese, whose languages are derived from Latin. 3. native or inhabitant of ancient Latium, which included Rome. 4. Roman Catholic of the Latin Rite. —adj. 1. of, relating to, or composed in Latin. 2. of or relating to the people or countries that use languages descended from Latin. 3. of or relating to Latium or its people. 4. of or relating to the Roman Catholic Church or its Latin Rite. [Latin *Latīnus* Roman, relating to Latium, from *Latium* the region in Italy in which ancient Rome was located.]

Latin America, geographical area in the Western Hemisphere, south of the United States, which includes many countries and foreign-owned territories in which the official language, as French, Spanish, or Portuguese, is of Latin origin. —**Latin American.**

Lat·in-A·mer·i·can (lat′in ə mer′i kən) adj. of or relating to Latin America.

Latin Church, the Roman Catholic Church.

Latin cross, cross formed by one short horizontal bar that intersects a longer vertical bar near the top, used as a sacred symbol, esp. in certain Christian religions. See **cross** for illustration.

Lat·in·ism (lat′in iz′əm) n. word, idiom, or expression borrowed from or modeled on Latin.

Lat·in·ist (lat′in ist) n. student of or expert in Latin.

La·tin·i·ty (lə tin′ə tē) n. use of Latin or its style or idioms.

Lat·in·ize (lat′in īz′) -ized, -iz·ing. v.t. 1. to translate into Latin. 2. to make (writings, customs, or rituals) conform to something Latin, as the Latin language. 3. to put into the Roman alphabet. —**Lat′in·i·za′tion,** n.

Latin Quarter, district in Paris, south of the Seine River, noted as a residence for students and artists. [Translation of French *Quartier Latin* section of Paris where, in the Middle Ages, Latin was spoken by those connected with the University of Paris, which was situated there. See QUARTER, LATIN.]

Latin Rite, liturgy of the Roman Catholic Church, formerly in the Latin language.

lat·ish (lā′tish) adj., adv. somewhat late.

lat·i·tude (lat′ə tōōd′, -tūd′) n. 1. distance north or south of the equator, expressed as degrees measured from the earth's center. All points of a given latitude form a circle running east and west and parallel to the equator. 2. place or region marked by parallels of latitude: *temperate latitudes.* 3. freedom from narrow restrictions: *The minor official was given little latitude to make decisions.* 4. *Astronomy.* projection of latitudes from a point, usually the center of the earth, onto the celestial sphere, measured as angular distance north or south of the celestial equator. [Latin *lātitūdō* breadth.]

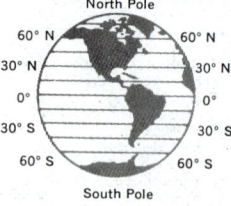

Lines of latitude

lat·i·tu·di·nal (lat′ə tōōd′ən əl, -tūd′-) adj. of or relating to latitude.

at; āpe; cär; end; mē; it; īce; hot; ōld; fôrk; wood; fōōl; oil; out; up; ūse; turn; sing; thin; this; zh in treasure; ə in ago, taken, pencil, lemon, circus.

lat·i·tu·di·nar·i·an (lat′ə tōōd′ən ār′ē ən, -tūd′-) *adj.* demanding, promoting, or allowing others much freedom in beliefs and conduct, esp. in religious matters. —*n.* one who is latitudinarian in thought and conduct.

La·ti·um (lā′shē əm) *n.* region in west-central Italy. In ancient times it was inhabited by the Latins and later taken over by the Romans. Area, 6642 sq. mi. Pop. (1961), 3,958,957.

la·trine (lə trēn′) *n.* toilet or privy, often temporary and without plumbing. [French *latrines* (plural) privies, from Latin *lātrīna* privy, bath, going back to *lavāre* to wash.]

lat·ter (lat′ər) *adj.* **1.** second of the two mentioned: *They looked up the areas of Texas and Alaska and found that the latter was larger.* Opposed to **former. 2.** nearer to the end or to the present time: *In the latter part of his career, the author turned to religious topics.* [Old English *lætra* slower, later, comparative of *læt* slow, tardy.]

Lat·ter-day Saint (lat′ər dā′) member of the Church of Jesus Christ of Latter-day Saints; Mormon.

lat·ter·ly (lat′ər lē) *adv.* at a late or recent time; lately.

lat·tice (lat′is) *n.* **1.** openwork structure of crossed or interlaced strips, as of wood or metal, spaced to form a regular pattern of openings. **2.** something having a lattice, as a window. **3.** anything having an orderly arrangement like a lattice, as the molecules of certain crystals. —*v.t.*, **-ticed, -tic·ing. 1.** to form into or arrange like a lattice. **2.** to furnish with a lattice. [Old French *lattis* lath work, from *latte* lath; of Germanic origin.]

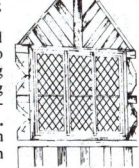

Lattice window

lattice work 1. lattice. **2.** structure made of lattices.

Lat·vi·a (lat′vē ə) *n.* republic of the Soviet Union, in the European part of the country, on the Baltic Sea. It was formerly an independent nation. Official name: Latvian Soviet Socialist Republic. Area, approx. 24,600 sq. mi. Pop. (1963 est.), 2,187,000.

Lat·vi·an (lat′vē ən) *n.* **1.** native or inhabitant of Latvia. **2.** language of the Latvians; Lett. —*adj.* of or relating to Latvia or its people, language, or culture.

laud (lôd) *v.t.* to praise; extol. —*n.* **1.** hymn or song of praise. **2. lauds.** second of the seven canonical hours, during which psalms and prayers of praise are recited with matins. [Latin *laudāre* to praise, from *laus* praise.]

Laud, William (lôd) 1573–1645, archbishop of Canterbury from 1633 to 1645, beheaded by the Puritans.

laud·a·ble (lô′də bəl) *adj.* praiseworthy; commendable. —**laud′a·bil′i·ty,** *n.* —**laud′a·bly,** *adv.*

lau·da·num (lôd′ən əm) *n.* medicinal solution of opium in alcohol.

lau·da·tion (lô dā′shən) *n.* act of lauding; praise.

laud·a·to·ry (lô′də tôr′ē) *adj.* containing or expressing praise.

laugh (laf) *v.i.* **1.** to make the inarticulate sounds and the associated facial and body movements that show any of several emotions, such as amusement, joy, or scorn. **2.** to feel amusement or joy; be happy. **3. to laugh at.** to deride, ridicule, or fail to take seriously. —*v.t.* **1.** to produce a specified effect upon by laughing: *to laugh oneself silly.* **2. to laugh off.** to reject, negate, or dismiss lightly: *The player received a bad bruise but laughed it off.* —*n.* **1.** act, sound, or manner of laughing. **2.** that which provokes or tends to provoke laughter. [Old English *hlæhhan, hliehhan* to indicate mirth by sound.] —**laugh′er,** *n.*

laugh·a·ble (laf′ə bəl) *adj.* provoking or tending to provoke laughter, esp. derisive laughter. —**laugh′a·ble·ness,** *n.* —**laugh′a·bly,** *adv.*

laugh·ing (laf′ing) *adj.* **1.** that laughs or seems to laugh: *a laughing brook.* **2.** laughable: *Your error is no laughing matter.* —*n.* laughter. —**laugh′ing·ly,** *adv.*

laughing gas, nitrous oxide.

laugh·ing-stock (laf′ing stok′) *n.* object of ridicule.

laugh·ter (laf′tər) *n.* action or sound of laughing. [Old English *hleahtor* action of laughing.]

launch¹ (lônch) *v.t.* **1.** to put (a boat or ship) into the water. **2.** to push or propel forcibly into motion, esp. outward into the air: *to launch a spear, to launch a rocket.* **3.** to start (someone or something) on a course or career: *He launched his son in business.* **4.** to put into operation; start: *The governor launched a new program.* —*v.i.* **1.** to throw oneself into or begin vigorously: *The journalist suddenly launched into intensive questioning.* **2.** to move outward into the water or air: *to launch into the blue.* —*n.* act or instance of launching. [Old French *lanc(h)ier* to throw, from *lance* spear. See LANCE.] —**launch′er,** *n.*

launch² (lônch) *n.* **1.** open or half-decked powerboat. **2.** formerly, the largest boat carried by a warship. [Spanish *lancha* pinnace, from Malay *lancharan* swift boat, from *lanchār* swift.]

launching pad, area or structure from which a rocket or missile is launched. Also, **launch pad.**

laun·der (lôn′dər) *v.t.* to wash or wash and iron (clothes or linens).

—*v.i.* **1.** to wash or wash and iron clothes or linens. **2.** to withstand washing or washing and ironing: *This material launders poorly.* [From Middle English *launder, lavender* one who washes (clothes), from Old French *lavandier,* going back to Latin *lavanda* things to be washed, from *lavāre* to wash.] —**laun′der·er,** *n.*

laun·dress (lôn′dris) *n.* woman employed to do laundering.

Laun·dro·mat (lôn′drə mat) *n. Trademark.* self-service laundry that has coin-operated washing machines and dryers.

laun·dry (lôn′drē) *pl.,* **-dries.** *n.* **1.** that which is to be, is being, or has been laundered recently. **2.** place where laundering is done.

laun·dry·man (lôn′drē mən) *pl.,* **-men.** *n.* **1.** man who works in or runs a laundry. **2.** man who collects and delivers laundry.

laun·dry·wom·an (lôn′drē woom′ən) *pl.,* **-wom·en.** *n.* laundress.

lau·re·ate (lôr′ē it) *n.* **1.** one singled out for special honor, esp. an honor relating to arts and sciences: *Nobel laureate.* **2.** poet laureate.

—*adj. Archaic.* crowned or decked with laurel as a mark of honor; greatly honored. [Latin *laureātus* crowned with laurel, from *laurea* laurel tree or crown; referring to the ancient Roman custom of crowning victorious athletes with a laurel wreath.]

Laurel flower and leaves

lau·rel (lôr′əl, lor′-) *n.* **1.** either of two medium-sized evergreen trees, genus *Laurus,* native to the Mediterranean area, bearing stiff lance-shaped leaves and clusters of tiny yellow flowers. **2.** any of various trees or shrubs of the same family, as the sassafras and avocado or the mountain laurel of the heath family. **3.** foliage of the laurel tree used as an emblem of victory or of distinction. **4. laurels.** honor; distinction. **5. to rest on one's laurels.** to be satisfied with what one has already achieved or accomplished. —*v.t.* **-reled, -rel·ing;** also, *British,* **-relled, -rel·ling.** to honor by or as by crowning with laurel. [Old French *laurier* laurel tree, going back to Latin *laurus.*]

Lau·ren·tian Mountains (lô ren′shən) low mountain range in eastern Canada, between Hudson Bay and the St. Lawrence River. Also, **Lau·ren′tians.**

Lau·sanne (lō zan′) *n.* city in western Switzerland, on Lake Geneva. Pop. (1969 est.), 138,300.

la·va (lä′və, lav′ə) *n.* **1.** molten material that flows from a volcano or a fissure in the earth's surface. **2.** volcanic rock of varied structure and texture formed by the cooling of such molten material. [Dialectal Italian *lava* torrent, avalanche, from Latin *lābēs* a fall.]

La·val (lə val′, -väl′) *n.* city in southern Quebec, Canada, near Montreal. Pop. (1969), 196,088.

lav·a·liere (lav′ə lēr′, lä′və-) *also,* **lav·a·lier.** *n.* ornamental pendant on a small chain, worn around the neck. [French *lavallière* loose necktie, from the Duchess of *La Vallière,* a mistress of King Louis XIV of France.]

lav·a·to·ry (lav′ə tôr′ē) *pl.,* **-ries.** *n.* **1.** room with toilets and facilities for washing the hands and face. **2.** toilet. **3.** bowl or basin for washing. [Late Latin *lavātōrium* place for washing, going back to Latin *lavāre* to wash. Doublet of LAVER.]

lave (lāv) **laved, lav·ing.** *v.t.* **1.** to wash or bathe. **2.** to flow along or against: *The waves laved the shore.* —*v.i.* to wash or bathe. [Old English *lafian* to wash, going back to Latin *lavāre* to wash.]

lav·en·der (lav′ən dər) *n.* **1.** pale reddish-purple color. **2.** any of a group of plants and shrubs, genus *Lavandula,* of the mint family, cultivated throughout the world, esp. the common lavender, *L. officinalis,* having narrow grayish leaves and spikes of fragrant pale-purple flowers which yield an oil used in perfumes. **3.** dried leaves and flowers of this plant, used mainly in sachets. [Anglo-Norman *lavendre* the plant, from Medieval Latin *lavendula,* possibly going back to Latin *lavāre* to wash; because of its use in perfuming laundered clothing and bath water.]

la·ver (lā′vər) *n. Archaic.* basin, bowl, or trough to wash in. [Old French *laveo(i)r* basin, from Late Latin *lavātōrium* place for washing, going back to Latin *lavāre* to wash. Doublet of LAVATORY.]

lav·ish (lav′ish) *adj.* **1.** given or done extravagantly, out of or as if out of great wealth or abundance; expensive or ostentatious: *a lavish gift.* **2.** more than necessary; profuse; abundant: *lavish amounts of cream.* —*v.t.* to give generously or profusely; shower: *to lavish gifts upon the grandchildren.* [From obsolete *lavish* profusion, from Old French *lavasse* abundant rain, from *laver* to wash, from Latin *lavāre* to wash, shower.] —**lav′ish·ly,** *adv.* —**lav′ish·ness,** *n.*

La·voi·sier, An·toine Lau·rent (lä vwä zyā′; äṉ twäṉ′ lō räṉ′) 1743–94, French chemist and physician.

law (lô) *n.* **1.** rule that forbids or requires certain conduct or activities, established by custom or by official adoption, as by a legislature, and applying to all members of a community: *to pass a new health-insurance law.* **2.** particular set of such rules: *international law, tribal law, Soviet law.* **3.** abstract principle that all such rules share; principle of regula-

tion of society by such rules: *respect for the law, the rule of law.*
4. agency or agency applying or enforcing such rules: *an officer of the law.* **5.** legal action as a means of redressing grievances or enforcing claims: *to resort to law.* **6.** department of knowledge dealing with these rules: *a student of law.* **7.** profession of being a lawyer: *to practice law.* **8.** governing principle that regulates a certain area: *the laws of right conduct, the law of the jungle.* **9.** statement in science concerning the relation between two or more factors or variables which is or was universally accepted because it is observed to be true under all circumstances. **10.** rule or principle that is applied throughout a body of mathematics or to all members of a set. **11.** something considered to be authoritative; that which must be obeyed: *His word is law.* **12.** divine commandment or precept. **13.** Law. Law of Moses. **14. to lay down the law.** to command in an authoritative manner. **15. to read law.** to study to become a lawyer by serving as an apprentice in a law office rather than attending a law school. [Old English *lagu* body of rules, a rule, custom; of Scandinavian origin.]

Syn. 1. Law, regulation, rule denote a principle controlling conduct. **Law** is an enactment made binding by the sanction of official authority: *The judge interpreted the law for the jury.* **Regulation** is an authoritative order: *Soldiers are governed by military regulations.* **Rule** denotes an instruction for enforcing discipline, uniformity, or order in relation to a specific individual, group, or activity: *Under the rules of the House of Representatives, the speaker is elected by a simple majority.*

law·a·bid·ing (lô′ə bī′ding) *adj.* obedient to the law.
law·break·er (lô′brā′kər) *n.* one who violates the law.
law·ful (lô′fəl) *adj.* **1.** allowed by or not contrary to law: *exercising their rights in a lawful manner.* **2.** according to or recognized by law: *a lawful marriage.* —**law′ful·ly,** *adv.* —**law′ful·ness,** *n.*

Syn. 2. Lawful, legal, legitimate mean recognized by or according to law. **Lawful** means deriving authority from law: *Charles is the lawful heir to that property.* **Legal** means strictly accordant with statute law and its requirements: *Gambling is legal in the state of Nevada.* **Legitimate** means recognized or authorized by law and custom as rightful, just, and proper: *Physical deformity is a legitimate ground for seeking exemption from military service.*

law·giv·er (lô′giv′ər) *n.* one who establishes a law or code of laws for a country or people.
law·less (lô′lis) *adj.* **1.** not following the law. **2.** not controlled by law: *lawless instincts.* **3.** without laws. —**law′less·ly,** *adv.* —**law′less·ness,** *n.*
law·mak·er (lô′mā′kər) *n.* one who makes laws; legislator.
lawn¹ (lôn) *n.* grassy area that is kept closely mowed, esp. around a house or building or in a park. [Old French *launde* heath; of Celtic origin.]
lawn² (lôn) *n.* lightweight, sheer cotton fabric, used esp. for blouses and handkerchiefs. [From *Laon,* French town famous for the manufacture of linen.]
lawn mower, any of various machines with revolving blades used for cutting grass.
lawn tennis, tennis (*def.* 1).
Law of Moses, first five books of the Old Testament: Genesis, Exodus, Leviticus, Numbers, and Deuteronomy. Also, **Pen′ta·teuch′, To′rah.**
Law·rence (lôr′əns, lor′-) *n.* **1. D**(avid) **H**(erbert). 1885–1930, English writer and poet. **2. T**(homas) **E**(dward). 1888–1935, English soldier, adventurer, and author, known as **Lawrence of Arabia. 3.** city in northeastern Massachusetts, near Boston. Pop. (1970), 66,915. **4.** city in eastern Kansas, near Topeka. Pop. (1970), 45,698.
law·ren·cium (lô ren′sē əm, lo-) *n.* short-lived, radioactive element produced by bombarding a californium target with boron ions. Symbol: **Lr** See **element** for table. [From E. O. *Lawrence,* 1901–58, U.S. physicist who invented the cyclotron.]
law·suit (lô′sōōt′) *n.* action instituted in a civil court or a court of equity.
Law·ton (lôt′ən) *n.* city in southwestern Oklahoma. Pop. (1970), 74,470.
law·yer (lô′yər, loi′ər) *n.* one whose profession is representing clients in lawsuits and advising them in other legal matters; attorney.

Syn. Lawyer, counselor, attorney mean a practitioner of law. **Lawyer** is the general term for a person versed in legal procedure who is admitted to the bar and authorized to practice law: *The lawyer asked the court for an adjournment of the case.* **Counselor** denotes a lawyer who conducts cases in court and gives advice on legal rights and problems: *The company retained a counselor to argue their case before the Supreme Court.* **Attorney** denotes a lawyer who serves as an agent who is appointed to transact legal business: *Robinson's attorney represented him before the probate court.*

lax (laks) *adj.* **1.** not careful or watchful enough; allowing too much latitude; negligent: *a lax inspection procedure that passes too many faulty cars.* **2.** not rigid, tense, or firm; slack. [Latin *laxus* loose.]
lax·a·tive (lak′sə tiv) *n.* drug that promotes the discharge of feces

from the bowels. [Medieval Latin *laxativus* loosening, going back to Latin *laxus* loose.]
lax·i·ty (lak′sə tē) *n.* state or quality of being lax.
lay¹ (lā) laid, lay·ing. *v.t.* **1.** to put or place in a reclining, prostrate, or down position; cause to lie: *to lay the plate on the table, to lay the baby in his crib.* **2.** to prepare for use; make ready; set: *to lay a trap, to lay plans, to lay a course for home.* **3.** to do the work of putting down and securing (something) in the required position: *to lay a pipeline through the swamp, to lay a floor.* **4.** to produce and deposit (an egg or eggs): *The robin laid three eggs in the nest.* **5.** to assign or attribute (with *to*): *The food shortage was laid to a lack of rain.* **6.** to place or allocate (with *on*): *The detective lays great stress on details.* **7.** to submit; present: *to lay a case before a judge.* **8.** to impose: *The Congress shall have power to lay and collect taxes, duties, imposts, and excises* (U.S. Constitution, 1787). **9.** to place (a bet); bet. **10.** to place in the setting or location of: *The novel is laid in Chicago around the turn of the century.* **11.** to cause to settle, subside, or be still: *The rain laid the dust on the dirt road.* **12.** to apply (one's strength) energetically (with *to* or *into*): *The soldiers laid their backs to the truck and moved it out of the mud.* **13.** to arrange dishes, silverware, and other items upon (a table) in preparation for a meal. **14.** to apply in layers: *to lay peanut butter and jelly on bread.* **15.** to make (rope) by twisting strands together. **16.** *Slang.* to tell or give (something) to (with *on*). —*v.i.* to lay eggs.
  to lay about. a. to strike out on all sides; deliver blows wildly. **b.** to begin energetically; act with vigor.
  to lay aside. a. to put out of the way; set or put down. **b.** to put away or save for future use; reserve: *The newsboy laid aside five dollars a week.* **c.** to do away with; abandon; discard: *Plans for the new building were laid aside.*
  to lay away. to reserve for safe keeping, future delivery, or later use, esp. to hold (an item) until all payments on it have been made.
  to lay bare. to expose or make known: *All the facts are laid bare in this special report.*
  to lay by. to put away; reserve; save: *to lay by part of one's income.*
  to lay down. a. to assert or declare, esp. officially, dogmatically, or authoritatively: *The regime laid down a ban on travel abroad.* **b.** to give up; sacrifice; relinquish: *to lay down one's life.* **c.** to bet; wager. **d.** to store away for future use: *to lay down wine in the cellar.*
  to lay for. to lie in wait to or as to attack.
  to lay in. to get and store for the future: *to lay in provisions.*
  to lay into. to make a vigorous physical or verbal attack on.
  to lay off. a. to mark off; fix: *to lay off boundaries.* **b.** to dismiss from employment: *Workers were laid off in several plants.* **c.** *Slang.* to stop: *The girl said to lay off teasing her kid brother.*
  to lay out. a. to spread out and arrange: *to lay out one's clothes for packing.* **b.** to arrange according to design; prepare: *to lay out the strategy for the campaign.* **c.** to prepare (a corpse) for burial. **d.** *Slang.* to spend: *She laid out twenty dollars for the gift.* **e.** *Slang.* to knock unconscious: *The ex-fighter laid him out with one blow.*
  to lay over. to stop temporarily in the course of a trip.
  to lay to. a. to apply oneself with vigor. **b.** to bring a boat or ship into the wind and maintain it in a stationary or nearly stationary position.
  to lay up. a. to store or put aside for future use. **b.** to confine or incapacitate, as from illness or injury. **c.** to take (a boat or ship) out of service and put it in dock, as for repairs.
  —*n.* manner, direction, or position in which something lies or is arranged: *the lay of the land.* [Old English *lecgan* to put, place.]
lay² (lā) past tense of **lie².**
lay³ (lā) *adj.* **1.** of or relating to those who are not members of the clergy. **2.** of or relating to those who are not in a certain profession: *The lay knowledge of a case is often incomplete.* [Old French *lai* secular, relating to the laity, from Latin *lāicus* relating to the people, from Greek *lāikos,* from *lāos* the people.]
lay⁴ (lā) *n.* **1.** short lyric or narrative poem originally intended to be sung. **2.** melody; song. [Old French *lai* type of poem; of Celtic origin.]
lay·er (lā′ər) *n.* **1.** single thickness laid on over something or forming one level of a stack or series: *a layer of ice on the street, a wedding cake with four layers.* **2.** one who or that which lays, esp. a chicken.
lay·ette (lā et′) *n.* complete outfit for a newborn baby, including clothes, toilet articles, and bedding. [French *layette* baby's garments, box, diminutive of Old French *laie* box, from Middle Dutch *laeye.*]
lay figure 1. jointed model of a human body, usually of wood, used esp. by artists to show the arrangement of drapery. **2.** one who lacks importance or individuality. [From obsolete *layman* jointed model of the body (from Dutch *leeman* literally, joint man, from Middle Dutch *led* joint + *man* man) + FIGURE.]
lay·man (lā′mən) *pl.,* **-men.** *n.* one not belonging to a certain profession, esp. one not belonging to the clergy. [LAY¹ + MAN.]
lay·off (lā′ôf′) *n.* **1.** act of firing or dismissing a relatively large number of employees. **2.** period of enforced unemployment or inactivity.

at; āpe; cär; end; mē; it; īce; hot; ōld; fôrk; wood; fŏŏl; oil; out; up; ūse; turn; sing; thin; this; zh in treasure; ə in ago, taken, pencil, lemon, circus.

lay·out (lā'out') *n.* **1.** act or process of laying out. **2.** way in which the various parts of something are located or arranged; design: *the layout of the building.* **3.** plan or design of material prepared for printing. **4.** establishment; situation. **5.** outfit or set, as of tools.

lay·o·ver (lā'ō'vər) *n.* temporary stop in the course of a trip.

laz·ar (laz'ər, lā'zər) *n.* *Archaic.* poor person afflicted with a loathsome disease, esp. leprosy. [Medieval Latin *lazarus* leper, from *Lazarus,* name of the beggar in Luke 16:20.]

laze (lāz) lazed, laz·ing. *v.i.* to be lazy; loaf. —*v.t.* to pass (time) lazily. [From LAZY.]

la·zy (lā'zē) la·zi·er, la·zi·est. *adj.* **1.** unwilling to work or exert oneself. **2.** moving slowly; sluggish: *a lazy river.* **3.** causing laziness: *a lazy summer day.* [Of uncertain origin.] —**la'zi·ly,** *adv.* —**la'zi·ness,** *n.*

la·zy·bones (lā'zē bōnz') *n.* *Informal.* lazy person.

lazy susan, revolving tray for food or condiments placed in the center of a dining table.

lb., pound; pounds. [Abbreviation of Latin *libra* pound¹, scales.]

lbs., pounds.

l.c., lower case.

l.c.m., least common multiple.

Ld., Lord.

-le *suffix* (used to form verbs) repeatedly: *fizzle.* [Old English *-lian.*]

lea (lē) *n.* meadow; pasture. [Old English *lēah* open ground.]

leach (lēch) *v.t.* **1.** to drain or wash by filtering with water or other liquid. **2.** to remove soluble or loose parts from (ashes, soils, ores, or other materials) by fire or by filtration with water. —*v.i.* to lose soluble or loose parts by the filtering through of water or other liquid. —*n.* **1.** material or container used to leach. **2.** act, instance, or result of leaching. [Old English *leccan* to wet.]

lead¹ (lēd) led, lead·ing. *v.t.* **1.** to show the way to, esp. by going first: *Our guide led us through the ruins of the ancient city.* **2.** to conduct or guide by pulling or other contact: *The Seeing Eye dog led the blind man across the street.* **3.** to be or mark out a route or way for: *This road leads you into town. The lights led him to the house.* **4.** to go or be ahead of: *Which state leads the others in auto safety?* **5.** to show, influence, or direct (others) what to do; exercise leadership or guidance over: *to lead the cleanup committee, to lead an orchestra.* **6.** to cause to come to or do; draw on; bring: *What led you to this conclusion? People's mispronunciations led him to change his name.* **7.** to have or experience (a life); live. **8.** to cause to proceed in; draw into: *The rabbit led the hounds a hard chase.* **9.** to aim or throw ahead of (a target) to allow for its motion: *The quarterback leads his receivers so they can catch his passes on the run.* **10.** *Informal.* to keep the interest of; entice; encourage (with *on*): *She led him on for four months.* **11.** *Card Games.* to begin a round with (a card). —*v.i.* **1.** to go or be first, ahead of all others: *The burro leads, and the horses follow. Food leads his list of necessities.* **2.** to be ahead of most others; be among the leaders: *Chile leads in copper production.* **3.** to show, influence, or direct others what to do; exercise leadership or guidance. **4.** to be a route or way, as to a place or conclusion: *Poor sanitation leads to disease. This hall leads to the bedroom.* **5.** to submit to being led: *Some horses lead more easily than others.* **6.** to make the first play in a round, as in a card game. **7.** *Boxing.* to jab first at an opponent: *Lead with your left.* **8. to lead off. a.** to take the initiative; begin; open. **b.** *Baseball.* to be the first man on a team to come to bat in an inning. —*n.* **1.** position of being ahead of all others. **2.** measure or extent of being ahead: *a lead of several years in space technology.* **3.** example or direction: *One woman sat down, and soon others followed her lead.* **4.** clue or indication that may serve to locate someone or obtain something: *to follow a lead on a missing person. I don't have an apartment yet, but I have several leads.* **5.** rope or leash, as for walking a dog. **6.** conductor of electricity, as a wire, esp. one connecting a piece of apparatus to an antenna or other source of signals or to a power source. **7.** *Theater.* **a.** principal part in a play, motion picture, or other theatrical presentation. **b.** one who plays such a part. **8.** introductory paragraph of a news story, usually giving a summary of the contents. **9.** *Baseball.* position or distance of a base runner away from his base. **10.** *Card Games.* **a.** act, obligation, or right of playing first in a round: *It is your lead.* **b.** card so played. **11.** open water channel through a field of ice. **12.** *Archaic.* leash. —*adj.* that is or goes first; leading: *The president rode in the lead car.* [Old English *lǣdan* to conduct, guide.]

Syn. *v.t.* **1. Lead, guide** mean to show the way. **Lead** means to conduct or show the way by going along with or in advance: *Can a blind man lead a blind man?* (Luke: 6:39). **Guide** means to escort and direct with the help of prior knowledge over an unknown and particularly difficult region: *The native guided the explorers over the mountains.*

lead² (led) *n.* **1.** heavy, soft, poisonous, silver-gray metallic element, used esp. in storage batteries and as a gasoline additive. Symbol: **Pb** See **element** for table. **2.** thin stick of graphite, as in a pencil. **3.** weight attached to a line used to determine the depth of water. **4.** bullets; shot. **5.** *Printing.* thin, metal strip used to widen the space between lines of

type. **6. leads. a.** *British.* sheets or strips of lead used to cover a roof. **b.** lead frames in which panes of glass are fixed. —*v.t.* **1.** *Printing.* to increase the space separating the lines of (print) by inserting leads. **2.** to cover, join, weight, or mix with lead. [Old English *lēad* the metallic element.]

lead·en (led'ən) *adj.* **1.** made of lead: *a leaden bucket.* **2.** dull-gray like lead: *a leaden sky.* **3.** heavy like lead. **4.** dull; depressed; gloomy.

lead·er (lē'dər) *n.* **1.** one who or that which is or goes first or is ahead of most others: *After the first lap, Scott was the leader. The community is a leader in preventing pollution.* **2.** one who influences others, or shows or directs others what to do: *a leader of the opposition in the House.* **3.** leading article. **4.** short length of material, now usually nylon, connecting the lure or hook to a fish line. **5.** horse or other draft animal at the front of a team. **6.** loss leader. **7. leaders.** row or rows of dots or dashes used to guide the eye horizontally across a printed page. —**lead'er·less,** *adj.*

lead·er·ship (lē'dər ship') *n.* **1.** position or function of a leader. **2.** ability to lead or guide others. **3.** act or fact of being a leader. **4.** leaders as a group: *the union leadership.*

lead glass (led) glass containing lead oxide and potassium oxide, used esp. in making fine glassware, optical lenses, and radio and television tubes.

lead·ing¹ (lē'ding) *adj.* **1.** chief; principal: *a leading cause of heart disease.* **2.** that is or goes first; forward; frontmost: *the leading edge of a cold front.* **3.** that plays a lead: *the leading man in the amateur production.* **4.** that directs or influences. —*n.* act of one who or that which leads. [From LEAD¹.]

lead·ing² (led'ing) *n.* **1.** frame or covering of lead. **2.** spacing created by using metal strips between lines of type. [From LEAD².]

lead·ing article (lē'ding) article that begins in the upper right-hand column of the first page of a newspaper or is the first article in a magazine.

lead·ing question (lē'ding) question worded so as to suggest the desired answer.

lead·ing strings (lē'ding) **1.** strings or straps by which to support a child learning to walk. **2.** excessive control or guidance.

lead-in wire, wire that connects or leads in, as one connecting a receiver or transmitter to an antenna.

lead line (led) *Nautical.* line with a weight on the end, used to find the depth of water.

lead·off (lēd'ôf') *n.* **1.** opening action; beginning. **2.** *Baseball.* first man on a team to come to bat in an inning. —*adj.* beginning; starting: *a leadoff batter.*

lead pencil (led) ordinary pencil, having a thin stick of graphite as its marking material.

leaf (lēf) *pl.,* **leaves.** *n.* **1.** one of the flattened, usually green parts that grow as extensions of a plant's stem and serve as the plant's food manufacturing organs by means of photosynthesis. **2.** sheet of paper, esp. in a book. **3.** very thin sheet of metal, esp. gold, used for decoration. **4.** strip or plate of strong metal that is a layer of a leaf spring. **5.** extra piece for extending a table, that drops out of place, slides in, or comes out when not in use. **6. to turn over a new leaf.** to adopt a different and better line of conduct. —*v.i.* **1.** to put forth leaves. **2.** to turn and glance at the pages of (with *through*): *to leaf through a book.* [Old English *lēaf* the part of a plant, sheet of paper.]

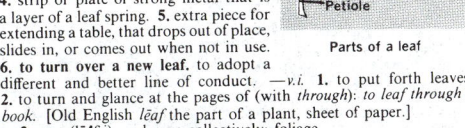

Parts of a leaf

leaf·age (lē'fij) *n.* leaves collectively; foliage.

leaf·less (lēf'lis) *adj.* without leaves.

leaf·let (lēf'lit) *n.* **1.** single sheet of printed matter, folded or unfolded, used in an information, advertising, or political campaign; handbill; flyer. **2.** small, unbound book; booklet: *This leaflet contains your operating instructions.* **3.** small or young leaf. **4.** *Botany.* one of the separate blades or divisions of a compound leaf.

leaf spring, spring made of layers of flexible metal strips.

leaf·stalk (lēf'stôk') *n.* petiole *(def. 1).*

leaf·y (lē'fē) leaf·i·er, leaf·i·est. *adj.* covered with, consisting of, or resembling leaves. —**leaf'i·ness,** *n.*

league¹ (lēg) *n.* **1.** association of individuals, groups, or countries formed to foster common interests. **2.** association of athletic teams who compete regularly among themselves. **3. in league with.** acting in cooperation with; associated with: *Anybody on the road might be a robber or in league with robbers* (Dickens, 1859). —*v.t., v.i.* to form, join, or band together into a league. [French *ligue* confederacy, from Italian *liga,* going back to Latin *ligāre* to bind.] —**Syn.** *n.* **1.** see **alliance.**

league² (lēg) *n.* measure of distance, used esp. for distances over the

sea, equal to three nautical miles. See **weights and measures** for table. [Late Latin *leuga* measure of distance; of Celtic origin.]

League of Nations, association of nations established in 1920 and dissolved in 1946, designed to settle international disputes and to promote world peace and cooperation.

lea·guer¹ (lē′gər) *Archaic. v.t.* to besiege; beleaguer. —*n.* **1.** seige. **2.** camp, esp. of a besieging army. [Dutch *leger* lair, camp.]

lea·guer² (lē′gər) *n.* member of a league. [LEAGUE¹ + -ER¹.]

Le·ah (lē′ə) *n.* in the Old Testament, Jacob's first wife.

leak (lēk) *n.* **1.** unwanted passage, as of water, air, or light, in or out through a hole, fissure, or other small opening: *to stop a leak in the roof. The tire went flat because of a slow leak.* **2.** hole or fissure itself: *Jack patched the leak in his rowboat.* **3.** process or condition by which withheld information becomes known: *A security leak ended all hopes of secrecy.* —*v.i.* **1.** to have a leak: *The water pipes leak.* **2.** to pass through a small opening (often with *out*): *All the gasoline leaked out during the night.* **3.** to become known (often with *out*): *News leaked out of a plot to overthrow the government.* —*v.t.* **1.** to permit the unwanted passage of (something) in or out through a small opening: *My fountain pen leaks ink.* **2.** to permit or cause (withheld information) to become known: *to leak a secret.* [Old Norse *leka* to drip.]

leak·age (lē′kij) *n.* **1.** act, process, or instance of leaking. **2.** that which leaks. **3.** amount that leaks. **4.** *Commerce.* allowance for loss by leaking, as of liquids in shipment.

leak·y (lē′kē) leak·i·er, leak·i·est. *adj.* having a leak or leaks. —**leak′i·ness,** *n.*

lean¹ (lēn) **leaned** or **leant, lean·ing.** *v.i.* **1.** to go or be at an angle from the upright: *The walls of the dilapidated shed lean outward.* **2.** (of a person) to bend or stretch: *The customer leaned over the counter. The barber leaned down to hear the child. Grandfather leaned back in his chair.* **3.** to rest on or against something for support: *to lean against a fence. Lean on my arm.* **4.** to depend on or use, as for support, background, or aid: *In evaluating applicants some colleges lean heavily on interviews.* **5.** to tend in favor or oppose (with *toward* or *against*); *to lean toward socialism.* —*v.t.* **1.** to cause to bend or stretch: *to lean one's body over a railing.* **2.** to cause to be or to rest at an angle from the upright: *Lean the fishing rod against the tree.* —*n.* act or condition of leaning; inclination. [Old English *hleonian* to recline, incline, bend.]

lean² (lēn) *adj.* **1.** with little or no extra flesh or fat: *The star center is tall and lean.* **2.** (of meat) containing little or no fat. **3.** lacking in substance, richness, or productiveness; poor; scanty: *a lean year for the farmers.* —*n.* part of meat containing little or no fat. [Old English *hlæne* thin.] —**lean′ness,** *n.*

Syn. *adj.* **1. Lean, thin, slender** mean having little flesh. **Lean** suggests a healthy and natural lack of fat: *Lincoln was a tall and lean person.* **Thin** suggests a gauntness or a lack of fullness, caused esp. by malnutrition, overwork, or age: *Grandpa was a thin and bony man with hollow cheeks.* **Slender** denotes a leanness without gawkiness or awkwardness and suggests a graceful, well-proportioned figure: *The model was proud of her slender figure.*

Le·an·der (lē an′dər) *n.* see **Hero.**

lean·ing (lē′ning) *n.* tendency to favor.

Leaning Tower of Pisa, bell tower at Pisa, Italy, that slants more than seventeen feet from the perpendicular.

leant (lent) a past tense and past participle of **lean¹.**

lean-to (lēn′tōō′) *pl.* **-tos.** *n.* **1.** shed or building having a roof which slopes in one direction, supported by the wall of an adjoining structure. **2.** crude, usually open shelter, consisting only of a sloping roof that extends to the ground.

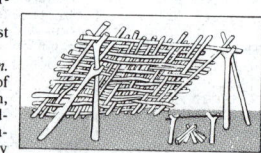

Lean-to

leap (lēp) **leaped** or **leapt, leap·ing.** *v.i.* **1.** to make a big, impressive, or spectacular jump: *The dancers leaped into the air.* **2.** to move eagerly or quickly: *to leap into battle.* —*v.t.* **1.** to make a big or spectacular jump over: *The horse leaped a wall.* **2.** to cause to make a big jump: *The rider leaped the horse.* —*n.* **1.** big, impressive, or spectacular jump: *a circus leap through a burning hoop.* **2.** distance covered in a leap. **3.** sudden transition. **4.** place for leaping. [Old English *hlēapan* to run, spring.] —**Syn.** *v.i.* **1.** see **jump.**

leap·frog (lēp′frôg′, -frog′) *n.* game in which players take turns jumping or vaulting, with legs spread apart, over the backs of the other players. —*v.i.* to leap or vault over in or as in a game of leapfrog.

leapt (lept, lēpt) a past tense and past participle of **leap.**

leap year, calendar year containing an extra day, February 29, incorporated in the Gregorian calendar to compensate for the difference between the ordinary calendar year of 365 days and the slightly longer

solar year. Leap years occur in every century year evenly divisible by 400, such as 1200, 1600, or 2000, and at four-year intervals thereafter.

Lear (lēr) *n.* legendary king of Britain, written of in early chronicles and histories and by Spenser in *The Faerie Queen,* and hero of Shakespeare's tragedy *King Lear.*

learn (lurn) **learned** or **learnt, learn·ing.** *v.t.* **1.** to acquire knowledge of or skill in (something) as a result of study, experience, or teaching: *to learn how to ski, to learn algebra, to learn the history of the Cherokee.* **2.** to memorize: *to learn the lines in a play.* **3.** to become informed of; find out: *to learn the truth at last.* —*v.i.* **1.** to acquire knowledge or skill: *Children learn at different rates.* **2.** to become informed: *to learn of a marriage.* [Old English *leornian* to acquire knowledge.] —**learn′er,** *n.*

learn·ed (lur′nid) *adj.* **1.** having or displaying much knowledge: *a learned person.* **2.** produced by or for someone with much knowledge: *a learned study.*

learn·ing (lur′ning) *n.* **1.** act of acquiring knowledge or skill. **2.** knowledge, esp. when acquired by systematic study.

learnt (lurnt) a past tense and past participle of **learn.**

lear·y (lēr′ē) leery.

lease (lēs) *n.* **1.** contract for the use of property for a specified period of time. **2.** period of time specified in such a contract. —*v.t.,* **leased, leas·ing. 1.** to take or hold a lease on: *They leased the property from the Smith family.* **2.** to grant possession or use of by a lease: *The Smith family leased the property to them.* —*v.i.* to be available for lease or require for lease: *The property leases for $5000 a year.* [Anglo-Norman *les* a letting, leaving, from *lesser* to let¹, leave¹, from Latin *laxāre* slacken.]

Syn. *v.t.* **2. Lease, rent¹, hire, charter** mean to grant the temporary use and enjoyment of something for a fixed payment. **Lease** means to grant or convey property, as land and buildings, for a specified period and payment under the terms of a written contract: *We leased our seaside cottage to a German family for the summer.* **Rent** means to grant the possession and occupancy of something in return for a fixed payment: *That hotel rents halls for conventions.* **Hire** means to grant or engage the temporary use or service of something for a stipulated sum: *That company hires delivery trucks for moving furniture.* **Charter** means to rent by contract: *The group chartered a bus for the excursion to the country.*

lease·hold (lēs′hōld′) *n.* **1.** tenure by lease. **2.** real estate held under a lease.

leash (lēsh) *n.* **1.** strap, chain, or other line fastened to a dog or other animal to control it. **2.** *Hunting.* group of three, as of hounds. —*v.t.* to control or hold with or as with a leash. [Old French *laisse* thong to hold an animal, from *laisser* to let¹, leave¹, loosen, from Latin *laxāre* to slacken, open.]

least (lēst) *adj.* smallest in size, degree, amount, or importance. —*n.* **1.** that which is least. **2. at (the) least. a.** at the lowest or minimum estimate: *At least twenty parents will come, probably more.* **b.** at any rate; in any event: *He should at least let us know where he is.* **3. in the least.** in the smallest degree; at all. —*adv.* in the smallest or lowest degree. [Old English *lǣst* smallest.]

least common denominator, smallest number that can be divided by each of the denominators of a given group of fractions without leaving a remainder.

least common multiple, smallest number that is an exact multiple of two or more given quantities. The least common multiple of 2, 3, and 4 is 12.

least·wise (lēst′wīz′) *also,* **least·ways.** *adv. Informal.* at least; at any rate.

leath·er (lethʹər) *n.* tough, resilient material made from animal skin or hide, usually with hair or fur removed, prepared for use by tanning or a similar process. —*adj.* of or made of leather. —*v.t.* **1.** to cover or furnish with leather. **2.** *Informal.* to beat with or as with a strap; thrash. [Old English *lether* hide², skin.]

Leath·er·ette (lethʹə ret′) *Trademark. n.* any of various plastics or fabrics that resemble leather in appearance.

leath·ern (lethʹərn) *adj.* **1.** made of leather. **2.** resembling leather.

leath·er·neck (lethʹər nek′) *n. Slang.* U.S. Marine. [From the stiff collars lined with *leather* on jackets worn by U.S. Marines in the mid-nineteenth century.]

leath·er·y (lethʹər ē) *adj.* resembling leather; tough like leather. —**leath′er·i·ness,** *n.*

leave¹ (lēv) **left, leav·ing.** *v.i.* **1.** to go to another place, after a stay in one place; go away: *I thought the guests would never leave.* **2.** to depart or set out: *Your plane leaves at 10:00. Joe left for college last week.* **3. to leave off.** to stop; cease. —*v.t.* **1.** to go away from: *Alice left the table after dinner.* **2.** to separate, withdraw, or depart from; quit: *to leave one occupation for another, to leave the United States. The country left the alliance.* **3.** to neglect to take along or remove; allow to stay: *Someone left the keys in the ignition.* **4.** to go away and allow to stay

at; āpe; cãr; end; mē; it; īce; hot; ōld; fôrk; wood; fōōl; oil; out; up; ūse; turn; sing; thin; this; zh in treasure; ə in ago, taken, pencil, lemon, circus.

in a particular state or condition: *Rose left the ironing undone and went bowling.* **5.** to place (something or someone) in the care of: *to leave the children with friends.* **6.** to let remain; not use: *The food was left on her plate. I have $300 left.* **7.** to allow to stay or continue as is, without interference: *When he is in a mood like this, we leave him alone.* **8.** to entrust, refer, or commit: *His future was left to fate. Her parents left her to choose her own friends.* **9.** to have remaining at death: *Private Jones leaves a wife and three children.* **10.** to transmit at death; give by will; bequeath: *How much property did he leave to the college?* **11.** to have remaining after subtraction: *10 minus 3 leaves 7.* **12. to leave off,** to refrain from using or wearing. **13. to leave out,** to omit or exclude. [Old English *lǣfan* to bequeath, to allow to remain.] —*Syn. v.t.* **2.** see **go¹.**

leave² (lēv) *n.* **1.** permission to do something. **2.** permission to be absent, esp. from military duty. **3.** period that the permission lasts. **4. on leave,** absent from duty with permission. **5. to take leave of,** to bid farewell or leave behind. [Old English *lēaf* permission.]

leave³ (lēv) *leaved, leav·ing. v.i.* to put forth leaves; leaf. [Middle English *leven,* from *lef* leaf. See LEAF.]

leav·en (lev′ən) *n.* **1.** substance, such as yeast or baking powder, that produces fermentation, esp. in dough or batter. **2.** small portion of fermented dough reserved for this purpose. **3.** pervasive and subtle influence that brings about significant change. —*v.t.* **1.** to produce fermentation in (dough) by means of a leaven; raise and make light. **2.** to influence pervasively and subtly. [Old French *levain* fermented substance that causes dough to rise, going back to Latin *levāmen* alleviation; literally, a raising.]

leav·en·ing (lev′ə ning) *n.* that which leavens.

Leav·en·worth (lev′ən wurth′) *n.* city in northeastern Kansas, site of a federal prison. Pop. (1970), 25,147.

leaves (lēvz) plural of **leaf.**

leave-tak·ing (lēv′tā′king) *n.* act of taking leave; bidding farewell.

leav·ings (lē′vingz) *n.,pl.* that which is left unused; remains; refuse: *The dogs ate the leavings from the table.*

Leb·a·non (leb′ə non) *n.* country in southwestern Asia, on the eastern shore of the Mediterranean Sea. Capital, Beirut. Area, 4000 sq. mi. Pop. (1967 est.), 2,520,000. —**Leb·a·nese** (leb′ə nēz′, -nēs′), *adj., n.* -

Le·bens·raum (lā′bəns roum′) *n.* additional territory, esp. that claimed by Nazi Germany, desired by a nation in order to accommodate the growth of its economy and population. [German *Lebensraum* living space, from *Leben* life + *Raum* space.]

lech·er (lech′ər) *n.* man given to or engaging in lechery. [Old French *lecheor* glutton, libertine; literally, one who licks, from *lechier* to lick; of Germanic origin.]

lech·er·ous (lech′ər əs) *adj.* given to, chosen by, or exhibiting lechery. —**lech′er·ous·ly,** *adv.* —**lech′er·ous·ness,** *n.*

lech·er·y (lech′ər ē) *n.* excessive preoccupation with or indulgence of sexual desires.

lec·tern (lek′tərn) *n.* **1.** stand with an inclined shelf for holding the written speech or other papers of a speaker. **2.** reading desk in a church, esp. one from which scripture lessons are read during services. [Old French *letrun* reading desk, going back to Late Latin *lēctrum* from Latin *legere* to read.]

lec·ture (lek′chər) *n.* **1.** prepared talk on a specific subject delivered before an audience for the purpose of instruction. **2.** lengthy reprimand or scolding: *Father gave Pete a lecture for driving too fast.* —*v.i.* -tured, -tur·ing. to give a lecture or lectures. —*v.t.* **1.** to give a lecture to; instruct by means of a lecture. **2.** to reprimand or scold at length. [Late Latin *lēctūra* a reading, from Latin *legere* to read.]

lec·tur·er (lek′chər ər) *n.* **1.** one who lectures. **2.** one who holds a temporary or permanent teaching position below professorial rank in a college or university.

led (led) past tense and past participle of **lead¹.**

Le·da (lē′də) *n. Greek Mythology.* mother of two mortals, Castor and Clytemnestra, and of two immortals, Pollux and Helen of Troy.

ledge (lej) *n.* **1.** narrow shelf or similar flat surface, projecting from a vertical plane. **2.** narrow, flat surface projecting from the side of a mountain or other natural formation. **3.** mineral-bearing vein or outcropping, usually of quartz. [Middle English *legge* bar, possibly going back to Old English *lecgan* to place.]

ledg·er (lej′ər) *n.* book in which all financial transactions of a business are recorded and classified by accounts. [Middle English *legger* record book, going back to Old English *lecgan* to place.]

ledger line, short line added above or below the musical staff for the placement of notes too high or too low to be put on the staff.

lee (lē) *n.* **1.** shelter or protection. **2.** side or part, esp. of a ship,

sheltered or turned away from the wind. **3.** direction toward which the wind is blowing. —*adj.* of, relating to, located on, or moving toward the side or direction toward which the wind blows. [Old English *hlēo* protection, shelter.]

Lee (lē) **1.** Henry. 1756–1818, U.S. soldier in the American Revolution and father of Robert E. Lee, best known as Light-Horse Harry Lee. **2.** Robert E. 1807–70, U.S. Army officer and Confederate general.

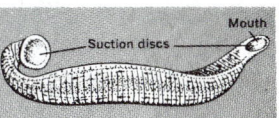

Leech

leech¹ (lēch) *n.* **1.** any of a group of bloodsucking parasitic worms, class Hirudinea, found in salt water, fresh water, and damp soil, which suck the blood of animals, esp. the **medicinal leech,** *Hirudo medicinalis,* once used by physicians to bleed their patients. Length: 1–4 inches. **2.** one who clings persistently to others for personal gain; parasite. **3.** *Archaic.* physician. —*v.t.* **1.** to bleed with leeches. **2.** *Archaic.* to cure; heal. [Old English *lǣce* bloodsucking worm, physician.]

leech² (lēch) *n.* **1.** either of the side edges of a square sail. **2.** the after edge of a fore-and-aft sail. [Probably from Middle Low German *līk* rope to which the sail is fastened.]

Leeds (lēdz) *n.* city in north-central England. Pop. (1968), 506,100.

leek (lēk) *n.* **1.** narrow flat leaves and stalk of a plant, *Allium porrum,* of the lily family, eaten as a vegetable. **2.** the plant itself, widely cultivated throughout the world, growing from a slender underground bulb and bearing clusters of small pinkish flowers. [Old English *lēac* the plant.]

leer (lēr) *n.* sly look or sidelong glance expressing cunning, lust, or malice. —*v.i.* to look with a leer. [Old English *hlēor* cheek, face, look.] —**leer′ing·ly,** *adv.*

leer·y (lēr′ē) *also,* **lear·y.** *adj. Informal.* wary; suspicious.

lees (lēz) *n.,pl.* sediment, esp. of wine; dregs. [Old French *lie;* of Celtic origin.]

lee shore, shore lying off the leeward side of a vessel, toward which the vessel may be driven by the wind.

lee·ward (lē′wərd, lōō′ərd) *adj.* located on or moving toward the side toward which the wind is blowing. —*n.* side or direction toward which the wind is blowing; lee. —*adv.* toward the lee. Opposed to **windward.**

Lee·ward Islands (lē′wərd) **1.** Caribbean island group forming the northern part of the Lesser Antilles. Land area, 1273 sq. mi. **2.** former British colony consisting of certain of these islands.

lee·way (lē′wā′) *n.* **1.** sideways drift of a boat or ship to leeward, off its course. **2.** safe margin for freedom or variation of movement or action provided by extra time, space, or the like: *My schedule isn't full; I have plenty of leeway to do what I want.*

left¹ (left) *adj.* **1.** of, for, relating to, designating, or situated on or toward the side that is to the west when one is facing north: *the left side of a road.* **2.** *also,* **Left.** relating to or having liberal or radical political views. —*n.* **1.** left side or direction: *Stuart was seated on my left. The car skidded to the left.* **2.** *also,* **Left.** party or group holding liberal or radical political views. Also, **left wing. 3.** blow delivered with the left hand, as in boxing. —*adv.* to or toward the left: *Walk three blocks and then turn left at the corner.* [Dialectal Old English *left* weak.]

left² (left) past tense and past participle of **leave¹.**

Left Bank, section of Paris bordering the south bank of the Seine, frequented by artists, students, and writers.

left field 1. *Baseball.* **a.** left section of the outfield when viewed from home plate. **b.** position of the player stationed in this area. **2. out in left field.** *Slang.* completely incorrect; wrong.

left-hand (left′hand′) *adj.* **1.** situated on or toward the left: *the top left-hand drawer of the desk.* **2.** of, for, relating to, or with the left hand: *a left-hand hitter in baseball.*

left-hand·ed (left′han′did) *adj.* **1.** using the left hand habitually and more easily than the right. **2.** done with the left hand. **3.** made to be held in or used by the left hand. **4.** turning or moving from right to left; counterclockwise. **5.** ambiguous; insincere: *His left-handed compliment was hardly flattering.* **6.** clumsy; awkward. —*adv.* with the left hand.

left·ist (lef′tist) *n.* one who has liberal or radical political views. —*adj.* of, relating to, or characterized by liberal or radical political views.

left·o·ver (left′ō′vər) *n. also,* **leftovers.** that which remains unused, esp. unconsumed food from a meal: *We ate leftovers for a week after Thanksgiving.* —*adj.* remaining; unused.

left-wing (left′wing′) *adj.* of, relating to, or belonging to the left wing. —**left′-wing′er,** *n.*

---

left wing 1. left *(def. 2)*. 2. portion of a political party or group characterized by a more liberal or radical outlook than the rest.

leg (leg) *n*. 1. one of the paired limbs or appendages in vertebrates and various other animals, used chiefly for supporting the body and for locomotion. 2. that part of such a limb, esp. in man, between the knee and the ankle. 3. something resembling a leg in shape, position, or function: *the leg of a chair.* 4. part of a garment, esp. of trousers, that covers a leg. 5. distinct portion or stage of a journey or course: *The first leg of the voyage took them to Australia.* 6. distance traveled by a sailing vessel on a single tack. 7. either of the sides of a triangle other than the base or, in a right triangle, the hypotenuse.
on one's last legs. *Informal.* close to death, collapse, or failure.
to give (someone) a leg up. to assist or aid by boosting or providing support.
to not have a leg to stand on. to have no defense or justification.
to pull one's leg. *Informal.* to trick or tease; make fun of.
to shake a leg. *Slang.* to make haste; hurry.
to stretch one's legs. to stand up or walk around, esp. after sitting for a long time.
—*v.i.*, **legged, leg·ging.** *Informal.* to walk or run (often with *it*): *We legged it home when the storm broke.* [Old Norse *leggr* this limb.]

leg. 1. legal. 2. legato. 3. legislative. 4. legislature.

leg·a·cy (leg′ə sē) *pl.*, **-cies.** *n.* 1. property bequeathed by will: *His uncle left Andrew a legacy of $5000.* 2. anything received from an ancestor, predecessor, or previous era: *Books are the legacies that a great genius leaves to mankind* (Addison, 1711). [Old French *legacie* office of a legate, going back to Latin *lēgāre* to appoint, bequeath.] —**Syn.** 2. see **heritage.**

le·gal (lē′gəl) *adj.* 1. of, relating to, or concerned with law: *to be in need of legal advice, to raise a legal objection.* 2. in conformity with or permitted by law; lawful: *the legal possession of firearms.* 3. established or authorized by law: *to know one's legal rights, to be the legal owner of the property.* 4. recognized or enforced by or under the jurisdiction of courts of law, rather than courts of equity. 5. of, relating to, or characteristic of lawyers or the practice of law: *legal ethics, a keen legal mind.* [Latin *lēgālis* relating to the law, from *lēx* law. Doublet of LOYAL.] —**le′gal·ly,** *adv.*

legal cap, thin, white writing paper, often ruled, usually measuring 8½ by 13 inches, and having a fold at the top.

legal holiday, holiday established by law on which the transaction of official business is restricted.

le·gal·ism (lē′gə liz′əm) *n.* strict, literal adherence to law, esp. excessive conformity to the letter rather than the spirit of the law. —**le′gal·ist,** *n.* —**le′gal·is′tic,** *adj.*

le·gal·i·ty (li gal′ə tē) *pl.*, **-ties.** *n.* 1. state or quality of being legal; lawfulness. 2. adherence to or observance of law.

le·gal·ize (lē′gə līz′) **-ized, -iz·ing.** *v.t.* to make legal or lawful. —**le′gal·i·za′tion,** *n.*

legal tender, coin or currency which, by law, must be accepted by a creditor when offered by the debtor in payment of his debt.

leg·ate (leg′it) *n.* 1. cardinal sent by the pope on a special diplomatic or ecclesiastical mission. 2. official envoy or representative. [Latin *lēgātus* envoy, ambassador, deputy.]

leg·a·tee (leg′ə tē′) *n.* one to whom a legacy is bequeathed.

le·ga·tion (li gā′shən) *n.* 1. diplomatic mission of a country, ranking below an embassy and consisting of a minister and his staff. 2. official residence and offices of such a mission in a foreign country where an embassy is not maintained. 3. office or rank of a legate. [Latin *lēgātio* embassy.]

le·ga·to (lə gä′tō, lā-) *Music. adj.* smooth and even, with no noticeable breaks between successive tones. —*adv.* in a legato manner. —*n. pl.,* **-tos.** legato style, performance, or passage. [Italian *legato* bound, past participle of *legare* to bind, from Latin *ligāre.*]

leg·end (lej′ənd) *n.* 1. unauthenticated story, handed down by tradition and popularly regarded as historical: *There are many legends about the exploits of Robin Hood.* 2. such stories collectively, esp. of a nation or culture. 3. popular, often fictitious or romanticized concept of a well-known person: *the legends surrounding a movie star.* 4. legendary figure: *Washington became a legend in his own time.* 5. inscription or motto, esp. on a coin, medal, or coat of arms. 6. explanatory description accompanying a chart, map, or other illustration. [Old French *legende* things to be read, from *legere* to read.]
Syn. 1. **Legend, myth** designate a fabulous story of unknown origin handed down from the past. **Legend** is a popularly accepted and highly romanticized story or tradition that has grown around a slight core of historical fact: *The story of Faust is a famous medieval legend.* **Myth** is a legend steeped in the religious imagination of ancient peoples that serves to explain natural or supernatural phenomena in fanciful and symbolic terms: *In Greek myths, Zeus was the ruler of gods and men.*

leg·end·ar·y (lej′ən der′ē) *adj.* 1. of, relating to, or characteristic of

a legend or legends: *a legendary account of a battle.* 2. celebrated or described in, or as if in, legend: *a legendary queen.*

leg·er·de·main (lej′ər də mān′) *n.* 1. sleight of hand. 2. artful trickery; deception. [Old French *legier de main* literally, light of hand, going back to Latin *levis* light + *dē* from + *manus* hand.]

-legged *combining form* having a specified kind or number of legs: *bowlegged, four-legged.*

leg·gings (leg′ingz) *n.,pl.* coverings of cloth or leather for the legs, usually extending to the ankle, for use out of doors.

leg·gy (leg′ē) **-gi·er, -gi·est.** *adj.* having disproportionately long, usually slender, legs.

Leg·horn (leg′hôrn′; *def. 2 also* leg′ərn) *n.* 1. port city on the western coast of Italy. Pop. (1968), 172,400. Also, *Italian,* **Li·vor′no.** 2. any of a breed of small, hardy domestic fowl, raised primarily for their white-shelled eggs. 3. leghorn. **a.** fine, braided wheat straw obtained principally from Italy and used in the manufacture of hats. **b.** hat made of this straw.

leg·i·ble (lej′ə bəl) *adj.* easily read or deciphered: *The address on the envelope was not legible.* [Late Latin *legibilis* readable, from Latin *legere* to read.] —**leg′i·bil′i·ty,** *n.* —**leg′i·bly,** *adv.*

le·gion (lē′jən) *n.* 1. military unit in the army of ancient Rome, varying from 3000 to 6000 infantrymen and from 300 to 700 cavalrymen. 2. any large military unit; army. 3. vast number of persons or things; multitude: *a legion of stars in the night sky.* ▲ sometimes used as a predicate adjective to mean "innumerable": *Their forces are legion.* [Old French *legion* a Roman legion, body of soldiers, from Latin *legiō,* from *legere* to gather, choose.] —**Syn.** 3. see **host²**.

le·gion·ar·y (lē′jə ner′ē) *adj.* 1. of or relating to a legion or army. 2. constituting a legion or multitude; innumerable. —*n. pl.,* **-ar·ies.** soldier of a legion.

le·gion·naire (lē′jə nãr′) *n.* 1. *also,* **Legionnaire.** member of any of various military or honorary national organizations, as the American Legion or the Foreign Legion. 2. legionary. [French *légionnaire* legionary, from Old French *legion.* See LEGION.]

Legion of Honor, French order of merit founded by Napoleon Bonaparte in 1802.

leg·is·late (lej′is lāt′) **-lat·ed, -lat·ing.** *v.i.* to make or enact a law or laws: *Parliament legislates for the United Kingdom.* —*v.t.* to cause, regulate, or bring about by passing laws: *Congress legislated increased benefits for veterans.* [From LEGISLATOR.]

leg·is·la·tion (lej′is lā′shən) *n.* 1. making or enacting of laws. 2. laws made or enacted. 3. proposed law that has been introduced in a legislative body for enactment.

leg·is·la·tive (lej′is lā′tiv) *adj.* 1. of or relating to legislation: *the legislative power of the king.* 2. having the power to make or enact laws: *Congress is a legislative body.* 3. of or relating to a legislature. —*n.* the legislative branch of a government. —**leg′is·la′tive·ly,** *adv.*

leg·is·la·tor (lej′is lā′tər) *n.* member of a legislative body, esp. a member of a state legislature or of the Congress. [Latin *lēgis lātor* proposer of a law.]

leg·is·la·ture (lej′is lā′chər) *n.* governmental body consisting of a group of persons invested with the power to make laws for a political unit, esp. for a state.

le·git (li jit′) *adj.* *Slang.* legitimate.

le·git·i·ma·cy (li jit′ə mə sē) *n.* quality or state of being legitimate.

le·git·i·mate (*adj.,* li jit′ə mit; *v.,* li jit′ə māt′) *adj.* 1. authorized or sanctioned by or conforming to law or rule: *The judge ruled that the claim was legitimate.* 2. logically correct or valid: *a legitimate argument.* 3. authentic; genuine: *a legitimate excuse.* 4. born of parents who are legally married to each other. 5. resting on or ruling by the principle of hereditary right: *the legitimate king of England.* 6. of, relating to, designating, or performing stage plays presented by professional actors before an audience, as distinguished from other media, as motion pictures, and, usually, from other forms of live performance, as vaudeville: *a legitimate play.* —*v.t.,* **-mat·ed, -mat·ing.** 1. to make or show to be lawful or legal: *The judge legitimated the use of the gun as evidence.* 2. to make (a child) legitimate, esp. by legal enactment. 3. to show to be justified; serve as justification for. [Medieval Latin *legitimatus,* past participle of *legitimare* to make lawful, from Latin *legitimus* lawful.] —**le·git′i·mate·ly,** *adv.* —**Syn.** *adj.* 1. see **lawful.**

le·git·i·mist (li jit′ə mist) *n.* supporter of legitimate authority, esp. of claims to rule based on the principle of hereditary right.

le·git·i·mize (li jit′ə mīz′) **-mized, -miz·ing.** *v.t.* to legitimate. —**le·git′i·mi·za′tion,** *n.*

leg·man (leg′man′) *pl.,* **-men.** *n.* 1. newspaperman who is assigned to gather information. 2. assistant who gathers information and runs errands for an office.

leg-of-mut·ton (leg′əv mut′ən) *adj.* tapering sharply from a wide end to a narrow end or point, as a sleeve or sail.

leg·ume (leg′ūm, li gūm′) *n.* 1. any of a large group of plants, family

at; āpe; cär; end;-mē; it; īce; hot; ōld; fôrk; wood; fo͞ol; oil; out; up; ūse; turn; sing; thin; this; zh in treasure; ə in ago, taken, pencil, lemon, circus.

Leguminosae, as peas, peanuts, and alfalfa. Legumes are cultivated as food crops, for fodder, and as natural fertilizers. **2.** seed pod characteristic of such a plant, usually having the seeds arranged in one or more rows along the pod. [French *légume* vegetable, from Latin *legūmen* bean, pulse².]

le·gu·mi·nous (li gū′mə nəs) *adj.* **1.** of or relating to plants of the legume family: *leguminous crops.* **2.** of, relating to, or consisting of the seed pods of these plants: *leguminous vegetables.*

leg·work (leg′wurk′) *n.* **1.** work of a leg man. **2.** any chores or errands performed by or as by walking.

Le Ha·vre (la hä′vrə, -vər, häv′) port city in northern France, at the mouth of the Seine. Pop. (1968), 199,509. Also, **Ha′vre.**

le·hu·a (lā hōō′ä) *n.* **1.** bright-red flower of a hardwood tree, *Metrosideros collina,* of the myrtle family, found in the Pacific islands. **2.** the tree itself. [Hawaiian *lehua* the tree.]

lei (lā) *pl.*, **leis.** *n.* garland of flowers, leaves, or other material, often worn about the neck in Hawaii. [Hawaiian *lei.*]

Leib·niz, Gott·fried Wil·helm von (līb′nits; got′frēd vil′helm) 1646–1716, German philosopher and mathematician.

Leices·ter (les′tər) *n.* city in central England. Pop. (1968) 280,300.

Leip·zig (līp′sig, -sik) *n.* city in southern East Germany. Pop. (1968 est.), 590,291.

lei·sure (lē′zhər, lezh′ər) *n.* **1.** time that one can spend as one pleases; free or unoccupied time: *After he retired, grandfather had the leisure to travel.* **2.** freedom from the demands of work or duty: *a life of leisure.* **3. at leisure. a.** having free time: *I am now at leisure to visit my friends.* **b.** without haste; slowly: *This new proposal must be considered at leisure.* **4. at one's leisure.** at one's ease or convenience. *—adj.* **1.** free or unoccupied: *Kathie spent her leisure hours playing the piano.* **2.** having much leisure: *the leisure classes.* [Old French *leisir* free time, from Latin *licēre* to be permitted.]

lei·sured (lē′zhərd, lezh′ərd) *adj.* characterized by or having leisure: *a leisured class of society.*

lei·sure·ly (lē′zhər lē, lezh′ər-) *adj.* characterized by leisure; unhurried; relaxed: *a leisurely drive in the country.* *—adv.* in a leisurely manner. *—lei′sure·li·ness, n.*

leit·mo·tif (līt′mō tēf′) *also,* **leit·mo·tiv.** *n.* **1.** short passage or theme recurring throughout a musical composition and associated with a certain person, situation, sentiment, or the like. **2.** any dominant, recurring theme, as in a literary work. [German *Leitmotiv* the musical passage or theme, from *leiten* to lead + *Motiv* theme (from French *motif*). See MOTIF.]

lek (lek) *n.* monetary unit of Albania.

lem·an (lem′ən, lē′mən) *n. Archaic.* sweetheart or lover. [Middle English *lemman,* from Old English *lēof* dear + *mann* human being.]

Le·man, Lake (lē′mən) Lake Geneva.

Le Mans (lə män′) city in northwestern France. Pop. (1968) 143,246.

Lem·berg (lem′burg′) *n. German.* Lvov.

lem·ming (lem′ing) *n.* any of various arctic rodents, family Cricetidae, having a stout body and long, predominantly yellowish-brown fur, esp. the **Norway lemming,** *Lemmus lemmus,* noted for their recurrent mass migrations which sometimes end in drowning when they reach the sea. Length: 3–6 inches. [Norwegian *lemming.*]

Lemming

lem·on (lem′ən) *n.* **1.** edible oval fruit of a citrus tree, *Citrus limon,* having a thick yellow rind and a juicy, sour pulp. **2.** thorny evergreen tree bearing this fruit, cultivated in warm climates. **3.** clear, brightyellow color characteristic of lemon. **4.** *Slang.* one who or that which is unsatisfactory, defective, or worthless: *My old car is a real lemon.* [Old French *limon* a sour citrus fruit, going back to Persian *līmūn* fruit of the lemon tree.]

lem·on·ade (lem′ə nād′) *n.* drink made from lemon juice, water, and, usually, sugar.

lem·pi·ra (lem pēr′ə) *n.* monetary unit and coin of Honduras, equal to 100 centavos. [From *Lempira,* Indian leader who opposed the Spaniards.]

le·mur (lē′mər) *n.* any of various monkeylike mammals, family Lemuridae, found chiefly in Madagascar, usually having a foxlike face, soft woolly fur, and a long tail. Length: to 3½ feet including the tail. [Latin *lemurēs* ghosts; with reference to the nocturnal habits of lemurs.]

Lemur

Le·na (lē′nə) *n.* river in Siberia flowing to the Arctic Ocean.

lend (lend) lent, lend·ing. *v.t.* **1.** to grant the use of (something) with the understanding that it, or its equivalent, will be returned: *I'll lend you my records for the party.* **2.** to give the temporary use of (money) on condition of repayment and at a specified date of interest. **3.** to furnish or impart: *Distance lends enchantment to the view.* **4.** to make available for aid or support: *to lend a hand.* **5.** to adapt or suit (itself or oneself) to a specific use or purpose: *This novel lends itself to various interpretations.* *—v.i.* to make a loan or loans. [Old English *lǣnan* to give, grant temporarily.] *—lend′er, n.*

lending library **1.** circulating library. **2.** small library operated by a store or other commercial establishment, which lends books for a minimal daily fee.

lend-lease (lend′lēs′) *n.* system under which goods and services were provided during World War II to foreign countries whose defense was deemed vital to the security of the United States. *—v.t.* **-leased, -leas·ing.** to supply with (goods and services) by lend-lease.

length (lengkh, length) *n.* **1.** linear extent of anything as measured from end to end, esp. the greater or greatest dimension: *The length of the football field is one hundred yards.* **2.** extent from beginning to end, esp. duration in time: *the length of a vacation, the length of a book.* **3.** state, quality, or fact of being long: *The length of the climb discouraged all but the professional mountaineers.* **4.** measurement of anything considered as a unit: *We parked one car's length away from the hydrant.* **5.** in racing, the extent from front to back of a competing animal, vehicle, or the like, used to describe distance: *The horse won the race by two-and-a-half lengths.* **6.** piece or portion of anything, esp. of a certain or standard size: *a length of silk.* **7.** long stretch or extent: *to drive down a length of highway.* **8. at full length.** fully extended; completely stretched out: *He lay at full length on the couch.* **9. at length. a.** in full; in detail: *We discussed the matter at length.* **b.** after a time; finally: *At length they reached their destination.* **10. to go to any (or great) length (or lengths).** to do whatever is necessary: *The politician would go to any length to win the election. Our hostess went to great lengths to make sure we were comfortable.* **11. to keep at arm's length.** to discourage from becoming too familiar. [Old English *lengthu* linear extent.]

length·en (lenk′thən, leng′-) *v.t., v.i.* to make or become longer: *to lengthen a dress. The shadows lengthened at dusk.*

length·wise (lengkth′wīz′, length′-) *also,* **length·ways.** *adj., adv.* in the direction of the length.

length·y (lenk′thē, leng′-) **length·i·er, length·i·est.** *adj.* unusually or unduly long, esp. in duration: *The crowd was bored by the lengthy speech.* *—length′i·ly, adv.* *—length′i·ness, n.*

len·i·en·cy (lē′nē ən sē, lēn′yən) *n.* quality or state of being lenient. Also, **len′i·ence.** *—Syn.* see mercy.

len·i·ent (lē′nē ənt, lēn′yənt) *adj.* not severe or harsh; merciful; tolerant: *a lenient judge, lenient laws.* [Latin *lēniēns,* present participle of *lēnīre* to soften.] *—len′i·ent·ly, adv.*

Len·in, Vlad·i·mir Il·yich (len′in; vlad′ə mir il′yich) 1870–1924, Russian revolutionary leader, political philosopher, and founder of the Soviet Union; born Vladimir Ilyich Ulyanov and also called Nikolai Lenin.

Len·in·grad (len′in grad′) *n.* historic city and former capital of Russia, in the northwestern Soviet Union, the chief Soviet port on the Baltic Sea. It was formerly known as St. Petersburg, and later as Petrograd. Pop. (1970 est.), 3,513,000.

Len·in·ism (len′in iz′əm) *n.* economic, political, and social theories and practices of Lenin, esp. the theory of dictatorship by the proletariat.

len·i·tive (len′ə tiv) *adj.* capable of alleviating pain or discomfort, as a medicine. *—n.* that which is lenitive.

len·i·ty (len′ə tē) *n.* leniency. [Latin *lēnitās* softness, mildness.]

lens (lenz) *pl.,* **lens·es.** *n.* **1.** piece of glass or other transparent material, having two nonparallel surfaces, either both curved, or one plane and one curved, which cause the light rays passing through them to either diverge or converge. **2.** any combination of such lenses. **3.** colorless, transparent body present in the eyes of all vertebrates, which focuses the image on the retina. **4.** device used to direct or focus radiation, as electro-magnetic radiation, electrons,

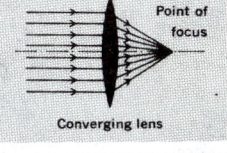

Point of focus

Converging lens

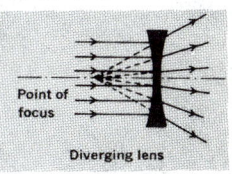

Point of focus

Diverging lens

Lenses

or other charged particles, or sound waves. [Latin *lēns* lentil; because the shape of a glass lens often resembles that of a lentil seed.]

lent (lent) past tense and past participle of **lend.**

Lent (lent) *n.* period of penitence and prayer observed in Christian churches beginning on Ash Wednesday and continuing for the forty weekdays before Easter. [Old English *lengten* spring, Lent, from *lang* long¹; probably with reference to the lengthening of the days in spring.]

Lent·en (lent′ən) *also,* **lent·en.** *adj.* **1.** of, relating to, or characteristic of Lent. **2.** suitable for Lent: *a Lenten diet.*

len·til (len′til) *n.* **1.** edible seed of a plant, *Lens culinaris,* of the pea family, cooked and eaten as a vegetable, esp. in soups and stews, ground into meal, or used as livestock feed. **2.** the plant itself, cultivated chiefly in Europe and Asia, bearing tiny white or pale-blue flowers that ripen into broad pods containing two seeds. [Old French *lentille,* from Latin *lenticula* small lentil, diminutive of *lēns* the plant.]

len·to (len′tō) *Music. adj.* slow. —*adv.* slowly. [Italian *lento* slow, from Latin *lentus.*]

l'en·voy (len′voi, län′-) *also,* **l'en·voi.** *n.* envoy². [Old French *l'envoy, l'envoi* the sending, the envoy². See ENVOY².]

Le·o (lē′ō) *n.* **1.** constellation in the northern sky, on the ecliptic, containing the bright star Regulus, conventionally depicted as a lion. **2.** fifth sign of the zodiac. See **zodiac** for illustration. [Latin *leō.* See LION.]

Leo I, Saint, A.D. c.400–461, pope from A.D. 440 to 461. Also, **Leo the Great.**

Leo III, Saint, A.D. c.750–816, pope from A.D. 795 to 816.

Leo X, 1475–1521, pope from 1513 to 1521.

Leo XIII, 1810–1903, pope from 1878 to 1903.

Le·ón (lā ōn′) *n.* **1.** region and former kingdom in northwestern Spain. **2.** city in central Mexico. Pop. (1969), 341,446.

Le·o·nar·do da Vin·ci (lā′ə när′dō də vin′chē) 1452–1519, Italian artist and scientist.

le·one (lē ōn′) *n.* standard monetary unit of Sierra Leone.

Le·o·nid (lē′ə nid) *n.* one of a shower of meteors, occurring on or about November 15, which appear to come from the constellation Leo.

le·o·nine (lē′ə nīn′) *adj.* relating to, characteristic of, or resembling a lion: *leonine courage.* [Latin *leōnīnus,* from *leō.* See LION.]

leop·ard (lep′ərd) *n.* **1.** carnivorous mammal, *Panthera pardus,* of the cat family, found in Africa, India, and eastern Asia, having either a tawny coat marked with black spots or a solid black coat.

Leopard

Length: to 9 feet including the tail. **2.** any of various similar related felines, as the cheetah, jaguar, and ounce. [Old French *leopard* the mammal *Panthera pardus,* from Late Latin *leopardus,* from Late Greek *leopardos,* from *leōn* lion + *pardos* panther; because it was thought to be the offspring of a lion and a panther.] —**leop′ard·ess,** *n.*

Le·o·pold·ville (lē′ə pōld vil′) *n.* see Kinshasa.

le·o·tard (lē′ə tärd′) *also,* **le·o·tards.** *n.* stretchable, close-fitting, one-piece garment extending from the neck or waist to the feet. [From Jules Léotard, nineteenth-century French aerialist who made it popular.]

lep·er (lep′ər) *n.* one who is afflicted with leprosy. [Old French *lepre* leprosy, from Latin *lepra,* from Greek *leprā,* from *lepros* scaly; because a leper's skin becomes scaly.]

lep·i·dop·ter·ous (lep′ə dop′tər əs) *adj.* of, relating to, or belonging to any of various insects of the order Lepidoptera, including butterflies and moths, which develop by complete metamorphosis and have four broad wings covered with small, usually colorful scales. [Modern Latin *Lepidoptera* (from Greek *lepid-,* stem of *lepis* scale + *pteron* wing) + -OUS.]

lep·re·chaun (lep′rə kon′, -kôn′) *n.* Irish Folklore. a mischievous fairy with the appearance of a little old man. [Old Irish *lupracān,* earlier *luchrupān* literally, very small body, from *lu* little + *corpān* small body (going back to Latin *corpus* body).]

lep·ro·sy (lep′rə sē) *n.* infectious disease caused by a bacterium and affecting the body tissues, esp. the skin, nerves, and mucous membranes. Also, Hansen's disease. [LEPROUS + -Y¹.]

lep·rous (lep′rəs) *adj.* **1.** afflicted with leprosy. **2.** of, relating to, or characteristic of leprosy. [Late Latin *leprōsus* having leprosy, from Latin *lepra* leprosy. See LEPER.] —**lep′rous·ly,** *adv.*

lep·ton (lep′ton) *n.* any of a group of subatomic particles including the electron, the muon, the electron's neutrino, and the muon's neutrino. See **subatomic particle** for table. [Greek *leptos* thin, fine + (I)ON.]

les·bi·an (lez′bē ən) *n.* female homosexual. —*adj.* of or relating to homosexuality between women. [From the supposed homosexuality of Sappho, a native of Lesbos.] —**les′bi·an·ism,** *n.*

Les·bos (lez′bos, -bōs) *n.* Greek island in the Aegean, near the western coast of Asia Minor. Area, approx. 629 sq. mi. Pop. (1961), 117,371.

lese-maj·es·ty (lēz′maj′is tē) *n.* **1.** *Law.* crime or offense against the sovereign power of a state or against the dignity of a ruler; treason. **2.** lack of respect for or an affront to the dignity of an institution, person, custom, or the like that is widely held in esteem. [French *lèse-majesté* high treason, from Latin *laesa mājestās* literally, violated majesty.]

le·sion (lē′zhən) *n.* injury; wound. [Latin *laesiō.*]

Le·so·tho (lə sō′tō) *n.* country in southern Africa, formerly the British possession of Basutoland. Capital, Maseru. Area, 11,716 sq. mi. Pop. (1967), 885,000.

less (les) *adj.* comparative of **little.** **1.** not so much or as great in quantity, extent, or degree: *less trouble, less time.* **2.** lower in rank, consequence, or importance: *No less a man than the king made the decree.* —*adv.* to a smaller extent or degree: *The movie was less funny than the book.* —*n.* a smaller amount or quantity: *I finished less of the work than I'd hoped.* —*prep.* with the subtraction of; minus: *Ten less seven is three.* [Old English *læssa* smaller, used as comparative of *little.*]

-less *suffix* **1.** (used to form adjectives from nouns) without; having no: *hopeless.* **2.** (used to form adjectives from verbs) that does not: *tireless.* **3.** (used to form adjectives from verbs) that cannot be: *numberless.* [Old English *-lēas* without.]

les·see (le sē′) *n.* one to whom a lease is granted.

less·en (les′ən) *v.i.* to become less; decrease: *The value of money lessens during inflation.* —*v.t.* **1.** to make less; diminish. **2.** to degrade; belittle.

less·er (les′ər) *adj.* smaller or less, as in quantity, quality, extent, degree, or importance: *the lesser of two evils.*

Lesser Antilles, island group of the West Indies southeast of Puerto Rico, consisting of the Leeward Islands, the Windward Islands, Barbados, Trinidad, Tobago, the Virgin Islands, and the small islands north of Venezuela.

lesser panda, panda (def. 2).

les·son (les′ən) *n.* **1.** period or unit of instruction devoted to a particular subject or skill: *a French lesson, a riding lesson.* **2.** that which is learned or studied, esp. material assigned, presented, or learned at one time: *Dwight didn't understand today's math lesson.* **3.** instructive event or experience serving to guide or warn: *Remember what happened and let it be a lesson to you.* **4.** selection from the Scriptures or other sacred writings read during a church service. **5.** rebuke; reprimand: *The judge read the prisoner a stern lesson.* —*v.t.* **1.** to give a lesson to. **2.** to rebuke; reprimand. [Old French *leçon* a reading, lecture, part of a church service, from Latin *lēctiō* a reading.]

les·sor (les′ôr, le sôr′) *n.* one who grants a lease.

lest (lest) *conj.* **1.** in order to prevent the possibility of; for fear that: *Let this be a reminder lest you forget.* **2.** that: *I feared lest he'd lose his life at sea.* [Old English *thy lǣs* literally, whereby less that.]

let¹ (let) *v.t.* **1.** to give permission, leave, or opportunity to; permit; not to prevent: *Father let me drive the car. A stroke of luck let us win the game.* **2.** to allow to pass, go, or come: *to let someone out of prison. The crowd wouldn't let him by.* **3.** to cause; make: *I'll let you know my decision. Let me hear from you.* **4.** used as an auxiliary verb, usually in the imperative, to indicate: **a.** a suggestion, command, or warning: *Let's take a walk. Let's go! Just let him try to win!* **b.** a supposition or assumption: *Let x + y = a + b.* **5.** to rent or lease, as a house or room: *to let a cottage to vacationers.* **6.** to assign or give out, as a contract for work. **7.** to allow or cause to flow, as blood. **8.** to let. to leave undisturbed; not interfere or tamper with: *When he's unhappy he wants people to let him be.* **9.** to let down. **a.** to fall or descend; lower: *to let down her hair, to let down a hem.* **b.** to fail to fulfill the hopes or expectations of; disappoint: *He let the team down by not trying hard enough.* **10.** to let off. **a.** to discharge or excuse temporarily, as from obligation or service: *He was let off for a week's vacation.* **b.** to emit or release, as from tension or pressure: *to let off anger.* **c.** *Informal.* to give little or no punishment; treat leniently: *The judge let him off with a warning.* **11.** to let out. **a.** to give vent to; emit: *to let out a scream, to let out one's anger on an innocent person.* **b.** to enlarge or extend (a garment or the like), as by releasing or unfastening: *to let out a hem. When Ruth gained weight, the dress had to be let out.* —*v.i.* **1.** to be rented: *The apartment lets on a yearly basis.* **2.** to let on. *Informal.* **a.** to allow something to be known: *The spy was too smart to let on about the plot.* **b.** to pretend: *Rob let on that he was richer than he really was.* **3.** to let out. to dismiss or be concluded: *School lets out at three o'clock.* **4.** to let up. *Informal.* to stop or abate: *The storm let up about noon.* **5.** to let up on. *Informal.* to treat less forcefully or severely; be more gentle with. [Old English *lǣtan* to allow, leave behind.]

at; āpe; cär; end; mē; it; īce; hot; ōld; fôrk; wood; fōōl; oil; out; up; ūse; turn; sing; thin; this; zh in treasure; ə in ago, taken, pencil, lemon, circus.

Syn. *v.t.* **1. Let, allow, permit** mean not to prevent or forbid. **Let** means to refrain from preventing through negligence or inability or lack of inclination to do otherwise: *The mother let her children stay up late.* **Allow** means to refrain from hindering or prohibiting but does not connote sanction or approval: *Smoking is allowed in this railroad car.* **Permit** implies formal or authoritative consent: *The law permits all citizens above a certain age to vote in elections.*

let² (let) *n.* **1.** in tennis, volleyball, and similar games, a service or other stroke that must be repeated because of interference, esp. a service which touches the net. **2.** *Archaic.* hindrance; obstacle; obstruction. —*v.t.,* **let·ted** or **let, let·ting.** *Archaic.* to prevent or hinder. [Old English *lettan* to hinder.]

-let *suffix* (used to form nouns) **1.** little: *booklet, kinglet.* **2.** article worn on or around (a specified part of the body): *anklet, wristlet.* [Old French *-elet,* from *-el,* noun ending (sometimes from Latin *ellus,* diminutive suffix; sometimes from Latin *-āle,* neuter of *-ālis* -AL¹) + -ET.]

let·down (let'doun') *n.* **1.** disappointment; disillusionment: *It was a real letdown when our plan failed.* **2.** letup. **3.** descent of an airplane from cruising altitude as it nears its destination.

le·thal (lē'thəl) *adj.* causing or capable of causing death; deadly: *a lethal wound, a lethal poison.* [Latin *lēt(h)ālis,* from *lētum* death.] —**Syn.** see **deadly.**

lethal gene, gene, usually recessive, that is capable of causing the premature death of an organism. Also, **lethal factor.**

le·thar·gic (li thär'jik) *adj.* **1.** feeling or exhibiting lethargy; sluggish; apathetic. **2.** causing lethargy. Also, **le·thar'gi·cal.** —**le·thar'gi·cal·ly,** *adv.*

leth·ar·gy (leth'ər jē) *pl.,* **-gies.** *n.* **1.** quality or state of sluggish indifference or inactivity; apathy. **2.** abnormal condition characterized by excessive drowsiness or by prolonged deep sleep. [Late Latin *lēthargia* drowsiness, from Greek *lēthargiā.*]

Le·the (lē'thē) *n.* **1.** *Classical Mythology.* a river in Hades, where spirits about to be reborn drank to forget their former existence. **2.** forgetfulness; oblivion. —**Le·the·an** (li thē'ən) *adj.*

Le·to (lē'tō) *n.* *Greek Mythology.* mother of Apollo and Artemis by Zeus.

let's (lets) let us.

Lett (let) *n.* **1.** member of a people living in Latvia and adjacent Baltic regions. **2.** their language, a member of the Baltic group of the Indo-European family of languages; Lettish.

let·ted (let'id) a past tense and past participle of **let².**

let·ter (let'ər) *n.* **1.** mark or character, usually printed or written, which represents one or more speech sounds; character of an alphabet. **2.** written or printed message, usually of a personal or business nature, sent by one person or organization to another. **3.** official or legal document granting a specific right, authority, or privilege to a person. **4.** literal meaning or exact wording of something, esp. as distinguished from the general meaning or interpretation: *The lawyer argued that the letter of the law was less important than the spirit.* **5. letters. a.** literary culture; literature: *a student of art and letters.* **b.** knowledge of or acquaintance with literature: *a man of letters.* **c.** literary profession. **6.** initial of a school or college awarded for superior achievement in a particular area, esp. a sport. **7.** *Printing.* **a.** one piece of type producing a single character. **b.** particular style of type: *The sign was printed in block letters.* **8. to the letter.** exactly as written or spoken; precisely; implicitly: *He followed the instructions to the letter.* —*v.t.* **1.** to mark or inscribe with letters: *to letter a sign.* **2.** to inscribe (a word or words) in letters: *The word "exit" was lettered on the door.* —*v.i.* to form letters. [Old French *lettre* letter of the alphabet, written message, from Latin *littera* letter of the alphabet (in plural: written document, literature).] —**let'ter·er,** *n.*

letter box, mailbox.

letter carrier, mailman.

let·tered (let'ərd) *adj.* **1.** able to read and write; literate. **2.** of, relating to, or characterized by learning or literary culture. **3.** marked or inscribed with letters.

let·ter·head (let'ər hed') *n.* **1.** information printed at the top of a sheet of paper, as the name and address of the sender. **2.** sheet of paper with such a heading.

let·ter·ing (let'ər ing) *n.* **1.** act or art of forming or inscribing letters, esp. by hand. **2.** letters so formed or inscribed.

let·ter·man (let'ər man') *pl.,* **-men.** *n.* *Informal.* athlete to whom a letter has been awarded for achievement.

letter of credit, letter issued by a bank, authorizing the person named to draw money or have credit established up to a specified amount at that bank, its branches, or a correspondent bank.

letter of marque *also,* **letters of marque.** formerly, documents issued by a government authorizing a private citizen to arm a ship for the purpose of capturing enemy ships and their cargo. Also, **letter of marque and reprisal.** [LETTER + OF + Old French *marque* arrest,

seizure, from Old Provençal *marca* reprisal; of Germanic origin.]

let·ter-per·fect (let'ər pur'fikt) *adj.* **1.** correct in every detail; completely accurate. **2.** knowing one's part or lesson perfectly, as an actor. —*adv.* perfectly.

let·ter·press (let'ər pres') *n.* printing produced from a plate on which the image to be reproduced is raised or in relief.

letters patent 1. formerly, in English law, a grant by a sovereign, conferring on a subject or subjects some right, property, franchise, or the like. **2.** *British.* patent (def. 1).

Let·tish (let'ish) *adj.* of or relating to the Letts, their culture, or their language. —*n.* Lett (def. 2).

let·tuce (let'is) *n.* **1.** large green leaves of a plant, *Lactuca sativa,* of the composite family, forming a round, oval, or long, loose head, eaten mainly as a raw vegetable in salads. **2.** the plant itself, widely cultivated in many parts of the world. [Old French *laitues,* plural of *laitue* this plant, from Latin *lactūca,* from *lac* milk; because of the plant's milky juice.]

let·up (let'up') *n.* *Informal.* lessening or slackening, as of pace, force, or intensity; lull or cessation.

leu·ke·mia (lo͞o kē'mē ə) *n.* disease characterized by the formation of abnormal numbers of white blood cells, for which no certain cure has yet been found. [Modern Latin *leukaemia,* from Greek *leukos* white + *haima* blood.]

leu·ko·cyte (lo͞o'kə sīt') *also,* **leu·co·cyte.** *n.* white blood cell. [Greek *leukos* white + *kytos* hollow container.]

Lev., Leviticus.

Le·vant (lə vant') *n.* region bordering the eastern shore of the Mediterranean Sea, comprising the present nations of Greece, Turkey, Syria, Lebanon, Israel, Egypt, and the islands in the eastern Mediterranean.

Le·van·tine (lev'ən tīn', -tēn', lə van'tin) *adj.* of, relating to, or characteristic of the Levant. —*n.* member or close descendant of the people of the Levant.

lev·ee¹ (lev'ē) *n.* **1.** wall of earth and other materials built along the banks of a river to prevent flooding. **2.** landing place, esp. on a river; pier; quay. [French *levée* raising, embankment, from *lever* to raise, from Latin *levāre.*]

lev·ee² (lev'ē, lə vē') *also,* **lev·ée.** *n.* reception held by one of high rank, esp. a sovereign, upon rising in the morning. [French *levé* rising, from *(se) lever* to rise, from Latin *levāre* to raise.]

lev·el (lev'əl) *adj.* **1.** having no part higher than another; having a surface with no irregularities in height; flat; even: *The steamroller made the road level.* **2.** parallel to the plane of the horizon; perpendicular to the line of gravity; horizontal. **3.** being or situated at the same height or on the same plane as something else: *The two paintings were level with the window.* **4.** having the surface even with the rim or edge of a container: *a level teaspoon of flour.* **5.** equal to someone or something, as in degree, importance, rank, or stage of development: *Educationally he is level with other children his age.* **6.** even or uniform, as in quality, tone, or style: *Even though he was getting angry, his voice remained level.* **7.** *Informal.* mentally well-balanced; sensible: *a level head. Tony was able to keep level and calm during the crisis.* **8. one's level best.** *Informal.* one's very best; the utmost one can do: *The runner did his level best to win.* —*n.* **1.** relative position or degree in any scale or order: *a low level of economic development.* **2.** horizontal surface, plane, or line, esp. as used to determine or measure the relative position of one or more points or surfaces: *The town is situated 200 feet above sea level.* **3.** height; depth; altitude: *Snow rose to a level of three feet.* **4.** relatively flat surface; horizontal area or expanse, as of land. **5.** area lying in a horizontal plane and constituting a floor or story of a structure: *The car is parked on the lower level of the garage.* **6.a.** any of various devices used to determine whether a surface is horizontal or to determine the degree of depar-

Level

ture from the horizontal, used esp. in surveying and carpentry. **b.** measurement of differences in height, elevation, or altitude with such an instrument. **7. to find one's** (or **its**) **level.** to reach an appropriate or natural position in relation to something else. **8. on the level.** *Informal.* honest; upright; fair. —*v.t.* **-eled, -el·ing;** *also, British,* **-elled, -el·ling. 1.** to make even, flat, or smooth: *The bulldozer leveled the mound of earth.* **2.** to bring to the level of the ground; destroy; raze: *The house was leveled by the fire.* **3.** *Informal.* to knock (someone) down, with or as with a blow: *The punch leveled him.* **4.** to reduce or bring to equality in degree, state, or condition; equalize: *to level the ranks of society.* **5.** to bring to, and aim and point in, a horizontal plane: *to level a gun.* **6.** to aim, direct, or point (something, as words): *to level an accusation at someone.* **7.** in surveying, to measure or determine differences in elevation or in (a plot of land) with

a level. —*v.i.* **1.** to bring people and things to a common level. **2.** to aim or point a weapon: *He leveled and fired.* **3.** *Slang.* to be candid and honest (often with *with*). **4. to level off. a.** to proceed on a horizontal course after gaining or losing altitude. **b.** to arrive at and maintain stability after a period of fluctuation: *Prices leveled off after the inflation ended.* [Old French *livel* carpenter's level, going back to Latin *lībella,* diminutive of *lībra* balance, scales.] —**lev'el·ness, lev'el·er,** *n.* —**lev'el·ly,** *adv.*

Syn. *adj.* **1.** Level, flat[1] relate to a uniform surface. **Level** describes a horizontal state or condition comparable to the surface of still water: *The billiard table has a level top.* **Flat** relates to a continuous, horizontal or sloping surface without observable inequalities, depressions, or projections: *Prairies are flat lands.*

lev·el·head·ed (lev'əl hed'id) *adj.* having or showing common sense and sound judgment; sensible. —**lev'el·head'ed·ness,** *n.*

lev·er (lev'ər, lē'vər) *n.* **1.** device consisting of a rigid body, such as a rod or bar, that transmits force or motion from one point to another as it rotates about a fixed point, the fulcrum. **2.** anything that operates in this way, as a crowbar or pry. **3.** means of exerting effective power: *The politician used his position as a lever for getting favors.* —*v.t.* to move or pry with or as if with a lever. —*v.i.* to use a lever. [Old French *levier* crowbar, from *lever* to raise, from Latin *levāre.*]

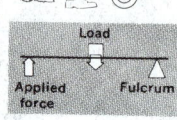

Lever

lev·er·age (lev'ər ij, lē'vər-) *n.* **1.** action of a lever. **2.** mechanical advantage or power gained by use of a lever. **3.** increased power to act or influence.

lev·er·et (lev'ər it) *n.* young hare, esp. one that is in its first year. [Anglo-Norman *leveret,* diminutive of *levre* hare, from Latin *lepus.*]

Le·vi (lē'vī) *n.* in the Old Testament, a son of Jacob and Leah and ancestor of the Levites.

le·vi·a·than (li vī'ə thən) *n.* **1.** in the Old Testament, a huge sea monster, variously thought to be a whale or a crocodile. **2.** anything of huge size, esp. a large ship. **3.** one who or that which has immense size or great power. [Late Latin *leviathan* sea monster, from Hebrew *livyāthān* dragon, sea monster, from *lāvāh* to twist; because it twisted itself into coils.]

le·vi's (lē'vīz) *n.,pl.* *Trademark.* close-fitting trousers, esp. of blue denim, reinforced at points of strain with copper rivets.

lev·i·tate (lev'ə tāt') *v.i.* to rise or float in the air due to, or as if due to, buoyancy or supernatural power. —*v.t.* to cause to rise or float in the air. [From LEVITY, on the model of English GRAVITATE.] —**lev'i·ta'tion, lev'i·ta'tor,** *n.*

Le·vite (lē'vīt) *n.* member of the tribe of Levi.

Le·vit·i·cal (lə vit'i kəl) *adj.* **1.** of or relating to the Levites. **2.** of or relating to the book of Leviticus or its laws.

Le·vit·i·cus (li vit'i kəs) *n.* third book of the Old Testament, containing the laws for the priests and Levites and the body of the Jewish ceremonial law.

lev·i·ty (lev'ə tē) *pl.,* **-ties.** *n.* **1.** attitude or behavior lacking seriousness; lightness. **2.** fickleness; inconstancy. [Latin *levitās* lightness.]

lev·u·lose (lev'yə lōs') *n.* fructose. [Latin *laevus* left; because the plane of polarization of polarized light passing through it is rotated to the left.]

lev·y (lev'ē) **lev·ied, lev·y·ing.** *v.t.* **1.** to impose or collect by force or authority: *to levy taxes.* **2.** to conscript (men) for military service. **3.** to prepare for, commence, or wage (war). —*v.i.* *Law.* to seize and dispose of property in order to satisfy unpaid debts. —*n. pl.,* **lev·ies. 1.** anything collected by authority, as troops or taxes. **2.** act of levying. [French *levée* raising, embankment, raising of money or soldiers. See LEVEE[1].]

lewd (lōōd) *adj.* obscene; bawdy; indecent. [Old English *lǣwede* lay[1], layman; originally, with reference to laymen as ignorant or of low class in comparison with churchmen.] —**lewd'ly,** *adv.* —**lewd'ness,** *n.*

Lew·is (lōō'is) **1.** John L(lewellyn). 1880–1969, U.S. labor leader. **2.** Mer·i·weth·er (mer'i weth'ər). 1774–1809, U.S. explorer. **3.** Sinclair. 1885–1951, U.S. novelist.

lex (leks) *pl.,* **le·ges** (lē'jēz). *n.* law. [Latin *lēx.*]

lex·i·cal (lek'si kəl) *adj.* **1.** of or relating to the words or vocabulary of a language. **2.** of or relating to a lexicon.

lex·i·cog·ra·pher (lek'sə kog'rə fər) *n.* one whose profession is writing or compiling a dictionary. [Greek *lexikographos* (from *lexikon* dictionary + *graphein* to write) + -ER[1].]

lex·i·cog·ra·phy (lek'sə kog'rə fē) *n.* process or profession of writ-

ing or compiling a dictionary. —**lex·i·co·graph·ic** (lek'si kə graf'ik), **lex'i·co·graph'i·cal,** *adj.*

lex·i·con (lek'sə kən, -kon') *n.* **1.** dictionary, esp. of Greek, Hebrew, Latin, or other ancient language. **2.** list of vocabulary belonging to a specific field, profession, activity, or the like. [Greek *lexikon* dictionary, from *lexikos* relating to words, from *lexis* word, speech.]

Lex·ing·ton (lek'sing tən) *n.* **1.** historic town in northeastern Massachusetts, site of the first battle of the American Revolution on April 19, 1775. Pop. (1970), 31,886. **2.** city in north-central Kentucky. Pop. (1970), 108,137.

Ley·den jar (līd'ən) device for storing an electric charge, consisting of a glass jar that is coated almost to the top with metal foil inside and outside. The two coatings are equivalent to the two plates of a capacitor. [From *Leiden,* city of the Netherlands where it was invented.]

Leyden jar

Ley·te (lā'tē, -tā) *n.* mountainous island in the south-central Philippines. Area, 2785 sq. mi. Pop. (1960), 1,177,440.

LG, Low German.

L.Gk., Late Greek.

Lha·sa (lä'sə, las'ə) *n.* capital of Tibet, in western China, the center of Lamaism. Pop. (1953), 70,000.

Lhasa ap·so (ap'sō) shaggy dog having short legs, a thick, solid-colored or parti-colored coat of long, straight hair, and a tail curving over the back. Height: 10 inches at the shoulder. [LHASA + Tibetan *apso* this dog.]

Lhasa apso

Li, lithium.

L.I., Long Island.

li·a·bil·i·ty (lī'ə bil'ə tē) *pl.,* **-ties.** *n.* **1.** state or condition of being liable. **2.** that for which one is liable, esp. a financial obligation or debt. **3.** something that works to one's disadvantage; handicap: *Lack of education was a liability in getting a job.* **4. liabilities.** in accounting, the debts or financial commitments of a business, as entered on a balance sheet or stated in an annual report. Opposed to **assets.**

li·a·ble (lī'ə bəl) *adj.* **1.** legally responsible; obligated by law: *He was liable for damages.* **2.** subject or susceptible (with *to*): *He is liable to heart trouble.* **3.** *Informal.* apt; likely. [French *lier* to bind (from Latin *ligāre*) + -ABLE.]

li·ai·son (lē'ə zon', lē ā'-) *n.* **1.** line of communication between military units, as a regiment and headquarters, used to ensure coordination of actions. **2.** agent or means of maintaining or improving communication. **3.** illicit love affair. **4.** in certain languages, esp. French, the pronunciation of a silent final consonant of a word as the first letter of a following word that begins with a vowel or mute *h.* Example: The pronunciation in French of the "s" in "les" in "les amis" (lā zä mē') or the "s" in "les" in "les hommes" (lā zōm'). [French *liaison,* from Late Latin *ligātiō* a binding, from Latin *ligāre* to bind.]

li·a·na (lē ä'nə, -an'ə) *also,* **li·ane** (lē än'). *n.* any of various climbing vines found in tropical forests, having woody stems that wind around the trunks of trees, often climbing from tree to tree before dropping to the ground. [French *liane,* probably from *lier* to bind. See LIABLE.]

li·ar (lī'ər) *n.* one who tells lies.

lib. 1. book. [Latin *liber.*] **2.** librarian. **3.** library.

li·ba·tion (lī bā'shən) *n.* **1.** ritual of pouring out wine or other liquid as an offering to a deity. **2.** liquid offered in this way. **3.** *Informal.* drink, esp. an alcoholic beverage. [Latin *lībātiō* liquid poured out as an offering to a deity.]

li·bel (lī'bəl) *n.* **1.** *Law.* act or crime of damaging a person's reputation by printing, writing, or representing in a picture false or malicious information about him. Distinguished from **slander. 2.** any false or malicious statement or picture. —*v.t.,* **-beled, -bel·ing;** *also, British.* **-belled, -bel·ling. 1.** to write or publish a libel about. **2.** to defame or misrepresent, as by libel. [Latin *libellus* little book, pamphlet, lampoon, diminutive of *liber* book; because of the use of pamphlets or "little books" to damage reputations in ancient Rome.]

li·bel·er (lī'bə lər) *also, British.* **li·bel·ler.** *n.* one who libels.

li·bel·ous (lī'bə ləs) *also, British.* **li·bel·lous.** *adj.* constituting or containing a libel. —**li'bel·ous·ly,** *adv.* —*also, British.* **li'bel·lous·ly,** *adv.*

lib·er·al (lib'ər əl, lib'rəl) *adj.* **1.** characterized by or inclining toward opinions favoring progress and reform, as in politics. **2.** free from prejudice; broad-minded; tolerant. **3.** characterized by generosity; bountiful: *He is liberal with his money.* **4.** ample or plentiful; abundant:

liberal spending. **5.** not literal or strict: *a liberal interpretation of the law.* —*n.* **1.** one who has liberal opinions or advocates progress and reform. **2. Liberal.** member of a Liberal Party, esp. in Great Britain, the United States, or Canada. [Latin *liberālis* befitting a free man, generous, from *liber* free.] —**lib′er·al·ly,** *adv.* —**lib′er·al·ness,** *n.*

liberal arts, subjects stressed in an academic curriculum, including literature, languages, history, sciences, psychology, and philosophy.

lib·er·al·ism (lib′ər ə liz′əm, lib′rə-) *n.* **1.** liberal principles and ideals; belief in progress and reform. **2.** *also,* **Liberalism.** principles and policies of a Liberal Party. —**lib′er·al·ist,** *adj., n.* —**lib′er·al·is′tic,** *adj.*

lib·er·al·i·ty (lib′ə ral′ə tē) *pl.,* **-ties.** *n.* **1.** generosity; magnanimity. **2.** tolerant beliefs or beliefs; broad-mindedness. **3.** generous gift.

lib·er·al·ize (lib′ər ə līz′, lib′rə-) **-ized, -iz·ing.** *v.t., v.i.* to make or become liberal. —**lib′er·al·i·za′tion, lib′er·al·iz′er,** *n.*

Liberal Party, political party, as in Great Britain, the United States, or Canada, that favors progress and reform.

lib·er·ate (lib′ə rāt′) **-at·ed, -at·ing.** *v.t.* **1.** to set free; release. **2.** *Chemistry.* to free (a gas) from combination, as by heating. [Latin *līberātus,* past participle of *līberāre* to set free.] —**lib′er·a′tion, lib′er·a′tor,** *n.*

Li·be·ri·a (lī bēr′ē ə) *n.* country on the west coast of Africa, first settled in 1822 by freed Negro slaves from the United States. Capital, Monrovia. Area, 43,000 sq. mi. Pop. (1969 est.), 1,200,000. —**Li·be′ri·an,** *adj., n.*

lib·er·tar·i·an (lib′ər tār′ē ən) *n.* **1.** one who advocates liberty, esp. of thought or conduct. **2.** one who believes in the doctrine of free will. —**lib′er·tar′i·an·ism,** *n.*

lib·er·tine (lib′ər tēn′, -tin) *n.* one who is lacking in moral restraint, esp. a dissolute man. —*adj.* dissolute; immoral. [Latin *libertīnus* freed slave, going back to *liber* free; with reference to the loose morals associated with former slaves of ancient Rome.] —**lib′er·tin·ism,** *n.*

lib·er·ty (lib′ər tē) *pl.,* **-ties.** *n.* **1.** freedom from tyranny or foreign domination; political independence. **2.** freedom from imprisonment, captivity, or other physical restraint: *The prisoner was finally given his liberty.* **3.** ability to act as one pleases; freedom of choice: *You have the liberty to say what you want.* **4.** freedom of thought and action possessed by the people of a state or nation, considered as a human right: *Freedom of speech is a precious liberty.* **5.** privilege or immunity possessed by individuals in a state or community: *civil liberties.* **6.** action or speech beyond the limits of propriety: *He embarrassed us by taking too many liberties.* **7.** permission to move freely within specified limits (with *of*): *The dog had the liberty of the entire house.* **8.** in the navy, time off granted to a sailor or seaman to go ashore or to be off the post for a short period. **9. at liberty. a.** free: *The captives were set at liberty.* **b.** permitted; allowed: *I am not at liberty to tell you.* **c.** not busy or engaged in activity, esp. without a job. [Old French *liberte* freedom, from Latin *libertās.*] —**Syn. 3.** see **freedom.**

Liberty Bell, bell rung on July 8, 1776 in Philadelphia to proclaim the signing of the Declaration of Independence by the Continental Congress.

li·bid·i·nous (li bid′ən əs) *adj.* characterized by or exhibiting excessive carnal desires; lustful. [Latin *libīdinōsus,* from *libīdō* lust.] —**li·bid′i·nous·ly,** *adv.* —**li·bid′i·nous·ness,** *n.*

li·bi·do (li bē′dō) *n.* **1.** sexual drive or instinct. **2.** in psychoanalysis, mental energy or impulse. At first it is associated only with the sexual instinct, but becomes directed toward a variety of objects as the person matures. [Latin *libīdō* lust, desire.] —**li·bid·i·nal** (li bid′ən əl), *adj.*

Li·bra (lī′brə, lē′-) *n.* **1.** small, dim constellation in the southern sky just south of the celestial equator, conventionally depicted as a pair of scales. **2.** seventh sign of the zodiac. See **zodiac** for illustration. [Latin *lībra* pound1, balance, scales.]

li·brar·i·an (lī brâr′ē ən) *n.* **1.** one who is in charge of a library. **2.** one who is trained for work in a library. [LIBRARY + -AN.]

li·brar·y (lī′brer′ē, -brər ē) *pl.,* **-brar·ies.** *n.* **1.** collection of books or other literary, artistic, or reference material. **2.** room or building containing such a collection. **3.** public or private institution that maintains and circulates such a collection. [Old French *librairie* collection of books, going back to Latin *librārius* relating to books, from *liber* book.]

Library of Congress, national library of the United States, in Washington, D.C.

li·bret·tist (li bret′ist) *n.* writer of a libretto.

li·bret·to (li bret′ō) *pl.,* **-bret·tos** or **-bret·ti** (-bret′ē). *n.* **1.** text of an opera or other long vocal composition. **2.** book or pamphlet containing such a text. [Italian *libretto,* diminutive of *libro* book, from Latin *liber.*]

Li·bre·ville (lē′brə vil′) *n.* capital, largest city, and chief seaport of Gabon, on the northwestern coast of the country. Pop. (1964 est.), 46,600.

Lib·y·a (lib′ē ə) *n.* **1.** country on the Mediterranean coast of northern Africa. Capitals, Tripoli and Benghazi. Area, 679,362 sq. mi. Pop. (1969 est.), 1,869,000. **2.** in ancient Greece and Rome, that part of Africa west of Egypt. —**Lib′y·an,** *adj., n.*

Libyan Desert, eastern part of the Sahara Desert, in northern Africa.

lice (līs) plural of **louse.**

li·cense (lī′səns) *n.* **1.** document, certificate, or metal object that indicates that the possessor has official permission to do something, as to drive a car, or to own something, such as a dog. **2.** permission given by law or a competent authority to do something. **3.** freedom of action permitted or conceded. **4.** undisciplined and excessive freedom; abuse of liberty. **5.** deviation from a rule or standard for the sake of effect. —*v.t.* **-censed, -cens·ing.** to grant a license to or for; permit or authorize. [Old French *licence* permission of action granted, unregulated freedom, from Latin *licentia.*] —**li′cens·a·ble,** *adj.* —**li′cens·er,** *n.*

li·cen·see (lī′sən sē′) *also,* **li·cen·cee.** *n.* one to whom a license has been granted.

li·cen·ti·ate (lī sen′shē it, -āt′) *n.* **1.** one who has a license, as from a board of examiners or a university, to practice a profession. **2.** in certain universities of Europe, a degree between bachelor and doctor, or the holder of such a degree.

li·cen·tious (lī sen′shəs) *adj.* **1.** lacking moral restraint; lewd. **2.** *Archaic.* disregarding commonly accepted rules. [Latin *licentiōsus* unrestrained, from *licentia* unrestrained liberty.] —**li·cen′tious·ly,** *adv.* —**li·cen′tious·ness,** *n.*

li·chee (lē′chē) litchi.

li·chen (lī′kən) *n.* any of a large group, Lichenes, of nonflowering plants found in all parts of the world, usually growing on tree trunks, rocks, or the ground. It consists of a fungus that usually forms the outer layer and an inner supporting network, and an alga that contains chlorophyll and manufactures food. [Latin *lichēn,* from Greek *leichēn.*] —**li′chen·ous,** *adj.*

lich gate (lich) *also,* **lych gate.** roofed gateway to a churchyard, sometimes used as a resting place for a bier. [Obsolete *lich* body (from Old English *līc*) + GATE.]

lic·it (lis′it) *adj.* lawful; permitted. [Latin *licitus,* past participle of *licēre* to be permitted.] —**lic′it·ly,** *adv.* —**lic′it·ness,** *n.*

Lich gate

lick (lik) *v.t.* **1.** to move the tongue over the surface of: *The kitten licked its paw. Jerry licked the envelope and sealed it.* **2.** to taste, eat, or remove by moving the tongue over: *to lick an ice-cream cone.* **3.** to move over or touch lightly or quickly: *Flames from the campfire licked the branches of the tree.* **4.** *Informal.* to hit forcefully; thrash: *The little boy was licked for being naughty.* **5.** *Informal.* to gain a victory over; defeat; overcome: *to lick a difficult problem.* **6. to lick (something) into shape.** *Informal.* to give proper or satisfactory form or appearance to: *to lick a report into shape.* **7. to lick one's chops.** *Slang.* to show delighted anticipation. **8. to lick one's wounds.** to recuperate after a defeat. —*n.* **1.** stroke of the tongue while licking. **2.** small quantity; bit: *Jack was too lazy to do even a lick of work.* **3.** salt lick. **4.** *Informal.* sharp blow: *He took his licks like a man.* **5.** *Slang.* chance or turn: *to take a lick at writing a book.* **6.** *Informal.* speed; rate: *The horse galloped at a fast lick.* **7. a lick and a promise.** *Informal.* hasty and superficial effort. **8. last licks.** *Informal.* final chance or turn, as in baseball. [Old English *liccian* to pass the tongue over, lap1.]

lick·er·ish (lik′ər ish) *adj.* *Archaic.* **1.** craving delicious food. **2.** lecherous. [Modification of obsolete *lickerous,* going back to Old French *licherous* lecherous, from *lecheor.* See LECHER.]

lick·e·ty-split (lik′ə tē split′) *adv.* *Informal.* at great speed.

lick·ing (lik′ing) *n.* **1.** act of one who or that which licks. **2.** *Informal.* thrashing; beating.

lick·spit·tle (lik′spit′əl) *n.* servile flatterer or admirer.

lic·o·rice (lik′ər is, -ish, lik′rish) *also,* **liqu·o·rice.** *n.* **1.** candy or other confection flavored with the sweet juice or extract obtained from the root of a plant, *Glycyrrhiza glabra,* of the pea family. **2.** plant yielding this juice or extract, widely cultivated in Europe and Asia, bearing spikes of pale-blue flowers. **3.** the sweet juice or extract itself, used esp. as a flavoring agent in candy, liquor, and tobacco. [Old French *licorece* licorice plant or extract, from late Latin *liquiritia,* going back to Greek *glykyrrhiza,* from *glykys* sweet + *rhiza* root.]

lic·tor (lik′tər) *n.* one of the officers or attendants who preceded the Roman magistrates and carried the fasces. [Latin *lictor.*]

lid (lid) *n.* **1.** hinged or removable cover placed over the opening of a receptacle: *Put the lid on the garbage can.* **2.** eyelid. **3.** *Informal.* anything that restrains, restricts, or covers up: *The police put the lid*

at; āpe; cär; end; mē; it; īce; hot; ōld; fôrk; wood; fōol; oil; out; up; ūse; turn; sing; thin; this; zh in treasure; ə in ago, taken, pencil, lemon, circus.

on gambling in the town. **4.** *Slang.* hat; cap. **5. to flip one's lid.** *Slang.* to lose one's temper, composure, or sanity. [Old English *hlid* cover.]

lid·less (lid'lis) *adj.* **1.** having no lid. **2.** *Archaic.* watchful; vigilant: *a lidless watcher of the public weal* (Tennyson, 1847).

lie¹ (lī) *n.* **1.** false statement made with the purpose of deceiving; falsehood. **2.** anything that is intended or serves to give a false impression: *Her smile was a lie that concealed her true feelings.* **3. to give the lie to. a.** to accuse of lying. **b.** to expose as false. —*v.i.,* **lied, ly·ing. 1.** to make a false statement or statements with the purpose of deceiving: *He lied about his reasons for being late.* **2.** to create or convey a false impression: *Mirrors don't lie.* **3. to lie in** (or **through**) **one's teeth.** to lie outrageously. —*v.t.* **1.** to put or bring into a specified condition by lying. [Old English *lēogan* to make a false statement.]

Syn. *n.* **1. Lie, falsehood, untruth, fib** denote a misrepresentation of the truth. **Lie** denotes a dishonest statement with the purpose of deceiving: *The district attorney proved that the witness's testimony was a lie.* **Falsehood** is a fictitious statement or prevarication that deviates from or distorts the truth but does not suggest an intent to deceive: *The witness was accused of telling a falsehood about the incident.* **Untruth** relates to an inaccurate or mendacious assertion resulting from ignorance or misunderstanding: *That biography is riddled with untruths.* **Fib** is a harmless and trivial lie: *That child is in the habit of telling fibs to her mother.*

lie² (lī) **lay, lain, ly·ing** *v.i.* **1.** to be or place oneself in a reclining or prostrate position: *to lie in bed.* **2.** to be placed upon or rest against a surface, esp. in a horizontal position: *The quilt is lying across the bed.* **3.** to remain in a specified state or condition: *The fields lay fallow throughout the winter.* **4.** to be situated; occupy a location: *Mexico lies to the south of Texas.* **5.** to extend or continue in a specific direction: *The long road lay in front of us. A great future lies before him.* **6.** to be; be found; exist: *His fate lies in the hands of the jury. The solution lies in social and political reform.* **7.** to be buried, as in a grave or tomb. **8.** *Archaic.* to reside temporarily; spend the night; lodge; sleep.

to lie in. to be confined for childbirth.

to lie in wait. to wait for in concealment so as to attack by surprise. *The hunter lay in wait for the lion.*

to lie low. *Slang.* **a.** to conceal oneself; hide: *The thief decided to lie low for a few days.* **b.** to refrain from action until the opportune moment.

to lie off. (of a vessel) to keep near the shore or nearly alongside another vessel.

to lie over. to be postponed: *Because of the weather our outing will have to lie over until next weekend.*

to lie to. to keep a vessel in a nearly stationary position by facing into the wind.

to lie with. a. to be dependent upon or up to; rest with: *The decision lies with the judge. The success of our plan lies with you.* **b.** *Archaic.* to have sexual intercourse with.

to take (something) lying down. *Informal.* to accept without protest; submit to: *Don't take that kind of insult lying down!*

—*n.* **1.** manner, direction, or position in which something lies; lay: *the lie of the land.* **2.** *Golf.* position in which a ball rests on the course. [Old English *licgan* to be in a prostrate position, to be placed in a horizontal position.]

Lie, Tryg·ve Halv·dan (lē; trig'və hälv'dän) 1896–1968, Norwegian statesman and first secretary-general of the United Nations.

Liech·ten·stein (lik'tən stīn'; *German* liKH'tən shtīn') *n.* small country in central Europe, between Austria and Switzerland. Capital, Vaduz. Area, 61 sq. mi. Pop. (1968 est.), 21,000.

Lie·der·kranz (lē'dər kränts', -krants') *Trademark. n.* creamy mild cheese with a pungent odor, similar to Limburger. [German *Liederkranz* literally, garland of songs.]

lie detector, instrument that detects certain bodily changes considered to occur when a person lies.

lief (lēf) *adv.* willingly; gladly: *I would as lief go there as anywhere* (Thackeray, 1852). —*adj. Archaic.* **1.** beloved; dear. **2.** willing. [Old English *lēof* dear.]

liege (lēj) *n.* **1.** feudal lord or sovereign entitled to the allegiance and service of his vassals or subjects. **2.** vassal or subject bound to give allegiance and service to a feudal lord or sovereign. —*adj.* **1.** entitled to the allegiance and service of vassals or subjects. **2.** bound to give allegiance and service to a feudal lord or sovereign. **3.** of, relating to, or designating the relationship or bond between vassal and lord. **4.** loyal; faithful. [Old French *liege* relating to a vassal bound to a lord, from Late Latin *laeticus* relating to a serf, from *laetus* serf; probably of Germanic origin.]

Li·ège (lē äzh') *n.* city in eastern Belgium. Pop. (1968 est.), 150,127.

liege·man (lēj'mən) *pl.,* **-men.** *n.* **1.** vassal. **2.** faithful follower or subject: *foes of God and liegemen of the Devil* (Parkman, 1865).

lien (lēn) *n.* legal claim placed on the property of another for payment of a debt. [French *lien* bond, tie, from Latin *ligāmen.*]

lieu (lōō) *n.* **1. in lieu of.** in place of; instead of: *The salesman received commissions in lieu of salary.* **2.** *Archaic.* place; stead. [Old French *lieu* place, from Latin *locus.*]

Lieut., Lieutenant.

lieu·ten·an·cy (lōō ten'ən sē) *pl.,* **-cies.** *n.* rank, status, or commission of a lieutenant.

lieu·ten·ant (lōō ten'ənt; *British* lef ten'ənt) *n.* **1.a.** first lieutenant. **b.** second lieutenant. **2.** officer in the U.S. Navy or Coast Guard ranking next below a lieutenant commander and above a lieutenant junior grade. **3.** one who acts in the place of a superior; deputy: *He had the trustiest of lieutenants in his brothers* (Freeman, 1869). [French *lieutenant* deputy, from *lieu* place (from Latin *locus*) + *tenant,* present participle of *tenir* to hold (going back to Latin *tenēre*); with reference to his taking the place of his superior.]

lieutenant colonel, officer in the U.S. Army, Air Force, and Marine Corps ranking next below a colonel and above a major.

lieutenant commander, officer in the U.S. Navy or Coast Guard ranking next below a commander and above a lieutenant.

lieutenant general, officer in the U.S. Army, Air Force, and Marine Corps ranking next below a general and above a major general.

lieutenant governor 1. second-ranking executive officer in thirty-eight U.S. states who succeeds to the governorship when that office is declared vacant and in certain states presides over the state senate. **2.** titular head of a district or province that is under the jurisdiction of a governor general.

lieutenant junior grade, officer in the U.S. Navy or Coast Guard ranking next below a lieutenant and above an ensign.

life (līf) *pl.,* **lives.** *n.* **1.** form or quality of existence that distinguishes animals and plants from inorganic or inanimate things. The characteristics of life that are shared by all living organisms are growth, reproduction, metabolism, and the capacity to respond to stimuli. **2.** state, condition, or fact of possessing this form or quality of existence: *to lose one's life.* **3.** spiritual existence regarded as transcending physical death. **4.** living organisms collectively: *No life has been found on the moon.* **5.** living being; person: *The firemen helped to save many lives.* **6.** period from birth to death; duration of existence: *a long and happy life, to achieve success early in life.* **7.** specific portion of this period: *adult life, later life.* **8.** particular aspect of existence: *one's private life.* **9.** period during which something lasts or remains useful or effective: *Minor accidents can shorten the life of a car.* **10.** human activities, relationships, or pursuits collectively: *a common occurrence of everyday life.* **11.** manner of existence, esp. characteristic activities of a group, location, time, or the like: *military life, city life.* **12.** written account of the history of an individual; biography. **13.** that which supports, sustains, shapes, or is essential to the existence of someone or something: *Tourism is the life of the island.* **14.** animation; spirit; vivacity: *jolly and full of life.* **15.** source of liveliness or vitality; animating force: *to be the life of the party.* **16.** living form or model: *The portrait was painted from life.*

a matter of life and (or **or**) **death.** something extremely important, urgent, or critical.

as big (or **large**) **as life.** in person: *I never expected to meet him, but there he was as big as life.*

for dear life. to or as if to save one's life; with great effort or urgency: *When the dog growled, Billy ran for dear life.*

for life. for the remaining period of one's life. *The murderer was imprisoned for life.*

for the life of one. *Informal.* under any circumstances; at all: *I can't for the life of me remember his name.*

not on your life. *Informal.* under no circumstances; never: *Are you going? Not on your life.*

to bring to life. a. to cause to regain consciousness; revive. **b.** to make animated or lively. **c.** to cause to appear to be alive or real; make lifelike: *A great actor can bring a fictional character to life.*

to come to life. a. to regain consciousness. **b.** to become animated or lively: *The city comes to life at night.* **c.** to appear to be alive or real; become lifelike.

to take (someone's) life. to kill (someone).

true to life. corresponding to reality; faithfully representing real life: *a novel that is true to life.*

[Old English *līf* quality of being alive, period from birth to death.]

life belt, life preserver in the form of a belt.

life-blood (līf'blud') *n.* **1.** blood necessary to life. **2.** *also,* **life's blood.** that which supports, sustains, or is essential to the existence of someone or something: *The participation of every citizen is the lifeblood of democracy.*

life-boat (līf'bōt') *n.* strong, buoyant boat, usually carried on a larger ship, constructed and equipped for saving lives at sea in case of shipwreck or other emergency.

life buoy, life preserver, often ring-shaped, used to keep afloat a person in danger of drowning.

at; āpe; cär; end; mē; it; īce; hot; ōld; fôrk; wood; fōōl; oil; out; up; ūse; turn; sing; thin; this; zh in treasure; ə in ago, taken, pencil, lemon, circus.

life cycle *Biology.* series of changes in form and function undergone by an organism from a particular stage in one generation to the development of the same stage in the next generation.

life expectancy, probable length of the life of an individual, determined statistically and affected by such factors as age, sex, physical condition, and occupation.

life·guard (līf'gärd') *n.* expert swimmer employed at a beach or a swimming pool to protect and aid swimmers.

Life Guards, two regiments of British cavalry which, together with the Royal Horse Guards, form the Household Cavalry, the personal guard of the sovereign.

life insurance 1. contract between an individual and an insurance company requiring the individual to pay regular premiums over a specified period of time and providing for cash payment to a designated beneficiary upon the death of the insured or to the insured himself when he reaches a certain age. **2.** sum specified in such a contract. **3.** premiums paid on such a contract.

life jacket, life preserver in the form of a jacket or vest.

life·less (līf'lis) *adj.* **1.** not having life; inanimate: *lifeless statues.* **2.** no longer alive; dead: *the lifeless form of the dead soldier.* **3.** lacking animation or vigor; dull: *lifeless speech.* **4.** devoid of living organisms: *a lifeless land.* —**life'less·ly,** *adv.* —**life'less·ness,** *n.* —**Syn.** 2. see **dead.**

life·like (līf'līk') *adj.* accurately resembling or imitating real life: *The doll was amazingly lifelike.* —**life'like'ness,** *n.*

life line 1. rope used for rescue or security, esp. one attached to a life preserver and thrown to a person in the water. **2.** route that is the only one over which vital supplies are transported to a place.

life·long (līf'lông') *adj.* lasting or continuing through a lifetime: *a lifelong struggle, a lifelong student of literature.*

life mask, cast, usually of plaster, made of the face of a living person.

life net, strong net or sheet of canvas, used to catch people falling or jumping from a great height, as from a burning building.

life preserver 1. buoyant device, esp. in the form of a belt, jacket, or circular tube. These devices are inflated with air or filled with cork or other buoyant material to be used by a person to keep afloat. **2.** *British.* blackjack, bludgeon, or similar weapon.

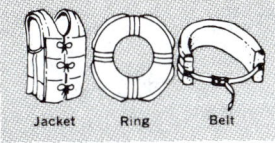

Jacket Ring Belt

Life preservers

lif·er (līf'fər) *n. Slang.* one sentenced to prison for life.

life raft, floating structure, esp. an inflatable rubber raft or boat, used to rescue people, as from a sinking ship.

life·sav·er (līf'sā'vər) *n.* **1.** one who saves another from death. **2.** lifeguard. **3.** *Informal.* one who or that which provides help in a time of need or crisis. **4.** life preserver in the form of a ring. —**life'sav'ing,** *adj., n.*

life's blood, lifeblood *(def. 2).*

life-size (līf'sīz') *adj.* of the same size as the thing portrayed: *a life-size portrait of the president.*

life·time (līf'tīm') *n.* duration of existence or effective functioning: *a lifetime devoted to learning, the lifetime of a television set.* —*adj.* lasting for such a period.

life·work (līf'wurk') *n.* principal or entire work of a lifetime: *Jim chose medicine as his lifework.*

lift (lift) *v.t.* **1.** to bring up into the air from a surface, as the ground; elevate: *to lift a heavy suitcase.* **2.** to direct or raise upward: *Good fortune lifted our spirits. The stranger lifted his eyebrows as we walked by.* **3.** to protect, display, or support in the air; hold up: *The castle lifted turrets toward the sky.* **4.** to raise in rank, condition, or estimation; exalt: *Richard's success lifted him in our eyes.* **5.** to project in a clear, loud tone: *The carolers lifted their voices in song.* **6.** to revoke or remove; cancel: *The ban on parking was lifted temporarily.* **7.** to put an end to (something, as a siege or blockade), esp. by removing forces. **8.** to pay off (an obligation, as a debt or mortgage). **9.** *Golf.* to pick up (a ball) from an unplayable position and place it in a more favorable position. **10.** to dig up (something, as a root or seedling) to prepare it for transplanting. **11.** *Informal.* to steal: *The burglars lifted three radios.* **12.** *Informal.* to plagiarize: *The author lifted the paragraph from someone else's work.* —*v.i.* **1.** to admit of being or becoming raised; go up: *This box is too heavy to lift.* **2.** to exert strain or effort in order to raise something. **3.** to rise or seem to rise and disperse; disappear: *The fog lifted.* **4.** to cease temporarily: *The storm lifted for a few hours.* **5.** to become better; improve: *His spirits lifted.* —*n.* **1.** act or instance of lifting or rising: *a lift of the eyebrow.* **2.** distance, height, or extent to which a thing is lifted or raised: *The canal lock has a lift of ten feet.* **3.** free ride given to a person: *to get a lift into town.* **4.** elevating influence or effect, esp. a content or happy feeling: *The compliment gave her a lift. The drink gave him a lift.* **5.** elevated manner of carriage, as of the head or neck: *the lift of the chin.* **6.** mechanical device or apparatus that lifts, conveys, or hoists. **7.** *British.* elevator. **8.** one of the layers of leather, rubber, or plastic at the bottom of the heel of a shoe. **9.** rise or elevation in ground. **10.** component of aerodynamic force that opposes the force of gravity on an airfoil, such as a plane wing, and causes an aircraft to stay aloft. [Old Norse *lypta* to raise.] —**lift'er,** *n.*

—**Syn.** *v.t.* **1.** **Lift, raise, elevate** mean to bring or move upward. **Lift** means to carry or move from a lower to a higher position or level by expending an effort sufficient to overcome its weight: *The man lifted the heavy baggage.* **Raise** means to bring something to a markedly higher or upright position for which it was naturally designed: *The soldier raised the flag to the top of the pole.* **Elevate** means to lift up in space or from an original position: *A hoist elevates men and materials to the top floor.*

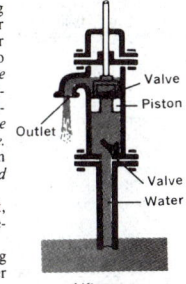

Valve
Piston
Outlet
Valve
Water

Lift pump

lift-off (lift'ôf') *n.* takeoff of an aircraft, esp. the initial motion of a rocket or spacecraft as it rises from its launching pad.

lift pump, pump that operates by lifting liquid on the top of a rising piston, rather than by forcing it up by downward movement of a piston.

lig·a·ment (lig'ə mənt) *n.* **1.** band of strong fibrous tissue that connects two bones or cartilages or supports muscles. **2.** connecting bond or tie. [Latin *ligāmentum* tie, bond.]

li·gate (lī'gāt) *-gat·ed, -gat·ing. v.t.* to bind up or tie off. [Latin *ligātus,* past participle of *ligāre* to bind, tie.] —**li·ga'tion,** *n.*

lig·a·ture (lig'ə choor', -chər) *n.* **1.** that which is used to bind, tie, or constrict, esp. thread, wire, or string used to tie off a blood vessel. **2.** act of binding up or tying off; ligation. **3.** *Music.* slur or a group of notes connected by a slur. **4.** *Printing.* two or more letters joined together to form one character. Œ is a ligature. —*v.t.,* **-tured, -tur·ing.** to bind up or tie off with a ligature; ligate.

Si — lent — night

Ligature

[Late Latin *ligātūra* bond, tie, from Latin *ligāre* to bind, tie.]

light¹ (līt) *n.* **1.a.** electromagnetic radiation that can be detected by the human eye and travels at a velocity of about 186,000 miles per second. **b.** invisible electromagnetic radiation, esp. ultraviolet or infrared radiation. **2.a.** medium or condition that makes vision possible; illumination: *Is there enough light to read?* **b.** particular instance of such illumination: *a strong light, a bright light.* **3.** sensation produced by stimulation of the organs of sight: *The light hurt his eyes when he walked from the dark room.* **4.** source of illumination or brightness, as a lamp or a traffic light: *Shut off the lights when you leave. Turn left at the light.* **5.** something that admits light, as a window or a windowpane. **6.** portion or quantity of light: *The heavy curtains reduced the light in the room.* **7.** illumination that comes from the sun in the day; daylight: *Plants grow rapidly when exposed to light.* **8.** dawn; daybreak. **9.** something, as a flame or spark, used to ignite a combustible substance: *Give me a light for my cigarette.* **10.** mental or spiritual comprehension; enlightenment: *The investigation shed new light on the mystery.* **11.** public observation or knowledge: *a political scandal that has recently come to light.* **12.** manner in which something is seen or judged; aspect: *to see her in a new light, in the light of all that has gone before.* **13.** outstanding or prominent person, esp. one serving as a model of excellence; luminary: *one of the leading lights in the field of medicine.* **14.** animated facial expression, esp. in the eyes. **15.** *Art.* **a.** representation of light, as in a painting. **b.** bright portion, as in a painting or statue. **16. to see the light (of day). a.** to come into existence; be born. **b.** to come to public notice; become widely known. **c.** to arrive at an understanding (about something); comprehend. —*adj.* **1.** having light; brightly illuminated; not dark: *The room was light in the morning than in the afternoon.* **2.** pale or whitish in color: *a light pink. She has a light complexion.* —*v.t.,* **light·ed** or **lit, light·ing. 1.** to cause to catch fire; kindle; ignite: *to light a fire.* **2.** to cause to emit light or illumination: *She lighted the lamp every evening at six.* **3.** to give light to; illuminate: *One large lamp lighted the room.* **4.** to make bright or animated: *Her face was lighted by happiness.* **5.** to show the way to by means of a light or lights; guide: *The beam lighted the ship into the harbor.* —*v.i.*

at; āpe; cär; end; mē; it; īce; hot; ōld; fôrk; wood; fōōl; oil; out; up; ūse; turn; sing; thin; this; zh in treasure; ə in ago, taken, pencil, lemon, circus.

591

1. to take fire; become ignited: *Wet wood doesn't light easily.* **2.** to become radiant or bright (often with *up*): *Sue's face lighted up when she heard the good news.* [Old English *lēoht* illumination, source of illumination, daylight.] —**Syn.** *v.t.* **1.** see kindle.

light² (līt) *adj.* **1.** having little weight; not heavy. **2.** possessing little weight in proportion to size or bulk; of low specific gravity: *Hydrogen is a light gas.* **3.** below the legal, standard, or usual weight: *a light coin.* **4.** having little pressure, momentum, or force: *a light wind.* **5.** of low density, amount, intensity, or degree: *a light fog.* **6.** not hard to bear; easily endurable: *light punishment.* **7.** easy to do or perform; not difficult: *light housework.* **8.** moving easily; nimble; agile: *to be light on one's feet.* **9.** buoyant; graceful: *a light step.* **10.** graceful in form or appearance; delicate; airy: *The church had a small, light spire.* **11.** happy; cheerful: *light and gay laughter.* **12.** free from care or worry; carefree: *a light heart, light spirits.* **13.** intended chiefly to entertain; not serious: *light reading, light comedy.* **14.** characterized by levity; not serious; trivial: *He took seriously what was only a light remark.* **15.** few or slight, as in number, quantity, or consequence: *The army sustained light casualties.* **16.** containing a comparatively small percentage of alcohol: *a light wine.* **17.** easily eaten or digested; not rich or fatty: *a diet of light foods.* **18.** having an airy or spongy consistency: *The cake is moist and light.* **19.** having a loose consistency; porous; sandy: *light soil.* **20.** designed for swiftness and easy maneuverability: *a light ship.* **21.** designating troops or units with relatively little heavy equipment: *light cavalry.* **22.** unstressed or unaccented, as a syllable or vowel. **23.** light in the head. **a.** dizzy; giddy. **b.** foolish. **24.** to make light of. to consider or treat as of little or no importance. —*adv.* lightly, esp. without unnecessary equipment: *to travel light.* [Old English *lēoht, līht* of little weight, gentle, unimportant, easy.]

light³ (līt) **light·ed** or **lit, light·ing.** *v.i.* **1.** to get down or descend; alight: *to light from a carriage.* **2.** to settle or come to rest, esp. from flight: *a bee lighted on his hand.* **3.** to come by chance; happen (with *on* or *upon*): *He lighted on a scheme.* **4.** to fall or strike suddenly, as a blow. **5. to light into.** *Slang.* **a.** to jump on or attack. **b.** to reprimand sharply; scold. **6. to light out.** *Slang.* to leave suddenly and hastily; take flight. [Old English *līhtan* to descend; literally, to make not heavy (with reference to removing the weight of a rider from a horse), from *līht* light².]

light·en¹ (līt'ən) *v.t.* **1.** to make lighter or brighter: *The painter lightened the color with white.* **2.** to make luminous; illuminate: *A shooting star lightened the sky.* —*v.i.* **1.** to grow or become light or bright: *When the storm ended the sky lightened.* **2.** to brighten or gleam. **3.** to flash with lightning. [LIGHT¹ + -EN¹.]

light·en² (līt'ən) *v.t.* **1.** to reduce the weight or load of; make less heavy. **2.** to make less oppressive or burdensome: *Machines lighten the work of laborers.* **3.** to relieve, as of care or distress; gladden; ease. [LIGHT² + -EN¹.]

light·er¹ (līt'tər) *n.* one who or that which causes something to ignite, esp. a mechanical device used to light cigarettes, cigars, or the like. [LIGHT¹ + -ER¹.]

light·er² (līt'tər) *n.* flat-bottomed barge usually used in a harbor for loading and unloading ships or for transporting goods for short distances. —*v.t., v.i.* to transport (goods) in a lighter. [Dutch *lichter* barge, from *lichten* to lighten, unload.]

light·er·age (līt'tər ij) *n.* **1.** act of loading and unloading ships, or transporting goods, by means of a lighter. **2.** charge made for this service.

light·er·than·air (līt'tər thən ār') *adj.* of a gas, having specific gravity less than that of air.

lighter·than·air craft, aircraft that maintains buoyancy by having compartments filled with a gas less dense than the air around it, as a blimp, balloon, or dirigible; airship.

light·face (līt'fās') *n.* type whose characters have thin, light lines.

light·fin·gered (līt'fing'gərd) *adj.* skillful at stealing, esp. at picking pockets.

light·foot·ed (līt'foot'id) *adj.* having a light and graceful step. Also, **light'-foot'.** —**light'-foot'ed·ly,** *adv.* —**light'-foot'ed·ness,** *n.*

light·head·ed (līt'hed'id) *adj.* **1.** somewhat faint or delirious; dizzy. **2.** frivolous in attitude or behavior; flighty; giddy. —**light'-head'ed·ly,** *adv.* —**light'-head'ed·ness,** *n.*

light·heart·ed (līt'här'tid) *adj.* free from care or anxiety; cheerful; gay. —**light'-heart'ed·ly,** *adv.* —**light'-heart'ed·ness,** *n.*

light heavyweight, athlete who competes in the second heaviest weight class in boxing, wrestling, and weightlifting.

light·house (līt'hous') *n.* tower or simi-

Lighthouse

lar structure equipped with a powerful light and other devices, erected as a warning and guide to ships near a place dangerous to navigation.

light·ing (līt'ting) *n.* **1.** act of lighting; being lighted; illumination. **2.** arrangement or system of lights. **3.** distribution of light and shadow, as in a painting.

light·ly (līt'lē) *adv.* **1.** with little weight or force; not heavily. **2.** in a small degree or amount: *to season food lightly.* **3.** with a light or buoyant motion. **4.** nimbly: *to step lightly.* **5.** in a carefree manner; cheerfully: *Don accepted his defeat lightly.* **6.** with little concern; frivolously; indifferently: *It is too serious a matter to be taken lightly.*

light meter *Photography.* device used to measure the intensity of light in a certain place and thus determine the correct exposure. Also, **exposure meter.**

light·mind·ed (līt'mīn'did) *adj.* characterized by a lack of seriousness; frivolous. —**light'-mind'ed·ly,** *adv.* —**light'-mind'ed·ness,** *n.*

light·ness¹ (līt'nis) *n.* **1.** quality or state of being light; brightness. **2.** paleness of color. [Old English *līhtnes* brightness, from *līht* bright + -*nes* -ness.]

light·ness² (līt'nis) *n.* **1.** quality or state of having relatively light weight, heaviness, force, or the like. **2.** quality of being nimble or graceful; agility. **3.** freedom from sorrow or care; gayness; blitheness. **4.** lack of seriousness. [LIGHT² + -NESS.]

light·ning (līt'ning) *n.* visible electrical discharge in the atmosphere, between two regions in the air or between the ground and a region in the air. [LIGHTEN¹ + -ING¹.]

lightning arrester, device for protecting radio, television, or other electric equipment from damage from lightning.

lightning bug, firefly.

lightning rod, metal conductor that is used to protect a building from damage by lightning by conducting the electricity to the ground.

light·proof (līt'proof') *adj.* that cannot be penetrated by light.

lights (līts) *n.,pl.* lungs of an animal, esp. a sheep or pig, used as food. [Because they weigh so little. See LIGHT².]

light·ship (līt'ship') *n.* vessel equipped with lights and signals, moored at a place dangerous to navigation as a warning and guide to ships.

light·some (līt'səm) *adj.* **1.** having the quality of agility or buoyancy; nimble. **2.** light-hearted; gay; cheerful. **3.** flighty; frivolous. —**light'-some·ly,** *adv.* —**light'some·ness,** *n.*

light·weight (līt'wāt') *n.* **1.** someone or something of less than average weight. **2.** athlete who competes in the fifth heaviest weight class in boxing and wrestling and the fourth heaviest weight class in weight lifting. **3.** *Informal.* one who has little intelligence, importance, or competence. —*adj.* **1.** light in weight. **2.** of or relating to a lightweight. **3.** not important.

light·year (līt'yēr') *n.* astronomical unit of distance equal to the distance that light travels through space in one year; approximately 5.878 trillion miles.

lig·ne·ous (lig'nē əs) *adj.* of or resembling wood; woody. [Latin *ligneus,* from *lignum* wood.]

lig·nite (lig'nīt) *n.* brownish-black, low-quality coal, denser and with more carbon than peat, in which the texture of the original wood can be seen. [French *lignite,* from Latin *lignum* wood; because of its woody texture and color.]

lig·num vi·tae (lig'nəm vī'tē) **1.** any of a small group of evergreen trees and shrubs, genus *Guaiacum,* found in Central America, Mexico, and the West Indies, bearing leathery leaves and small pale-purple flowers. **2.** hard, heavy wood of this tree, having a dark-brown color streaked with black and containing an oily resin. It is used mainly for propeller-shaft bearings of ships. [Modern Latin *lignum vitae,* from Late Latin *lignum vitae* literally, wood of life; because it was once thought to have medicinal value.]

li·gro·in (lī'grō in) *n.* petroleum derivative used as a solvent; benzine.

Li·gu·ri·a (li gyoor'ē ə) *n.* region in northwestern Italy. Area, 2091 sq. mi. Pop. (1965 est.), 1,846,400. —**Li·gu'ri·an,** *adj., n.*

lik·a·ble (lī'kə bəl) *also,* **like·a·ble.** *adj.* of a nature to be liked; pleasing; genial. —**lik'a·ble·ness,** *n.*

like¹ (līk) *prep.* **1.** having a close resemblance to; similar to: *She is like her sister. The house is exactly like the others on the street.* **2.** in the same manner as; with the characteristics of; similar to: *She walks like a cat. He runs like a streak of lightning.* **3.** corresponding in character to; typical of: *It was like him to forget her birthday.* **4.** such as: *fruit like apples, oranges, and grapes. He does well in subjects like math and chemistry.* **5.** mentally inclined to; desirous of: *I feel like taking a vacation. I feel like walking.* **6.** giving promise or indication of; indicative of: *It looks like a long, cold winter.* —*adj.* **1.** having identical or similar form, appearance, or characteristics; corresponding, as in kind, amount, or degree; similar. **2.** equal or equivalent: *to receive a like amount.* **3.** bearing a faithful resemblance to the original: *a like portrait.* **4.** *Archaic.* alike: *They are as like as twins.* **5.** *Archaic.* likely: *That horse is like to buck.* —*adv.* **1.** *Informal.* probably; likely: *Like enough she'll*

at; āpe; cär; end; mē; it; īce; hot; ōld; fôrk; wood; fōōl; oil; out; up; ūse; turn; sing; thin; this; zh in treasure; ə in ago, taken, pencil, lemon, circus.

arrive today. **2.** to some extent or degree; somewhat: *I'm tired like.* ▲ not used in standard English in def. 2. —*n.* **1.** one who or that which is considered equal, as in qualities or values, to another; match; counterpart: *I haven't seen his like in several years of teaching.* **2.** something of similar nature (preceded by *the*): *We bought chairs, tables, and the like.* —*conj.* **1.** in a similar way to that; as: *This doesn't taste like it should.* **2.** as if; as though: *It looks like I'll be late today.* ▲ not used as a conjunction in standard English. [Old English *(ge)līc* similar, alike, equal.]
Syn. *adj.* **1. Like, similar, comparable** describe things or persons that agree or correspond in details when matched together. **Like** relates to things or persons that agree or correspond so closely as to be almost indistinguishable: *The two brothers are of like disposition but have different interests.* **Similar** means having prominent characteristics in common without overall correspondence or identity: *Teenagers have similar tastes in dress.* **Comparable** means having enough like or parallel characteristics to afford and sustain an appropriate comparison: *The author's second novel is comparable to his first in quality.*
like² (līk) *v.t.* **1.** to take pleasure in; enjoy: *to like school.* **2.** to feel affection, tenderness, or fondness for: *I like her now that I know her better.* **3.** to wish or desire; prefer. —*v.i.* to have a desire or preference; choose; prefer: *Do what you like.* —*n.* usually, **likes.** inclination; preference: *She has strange likes and dislikes.* [Old English *līcian* to please.]
-like *suffix* (used to form adjectives from nouns) **1.** resembling or similar to: *catlike.* **2.** having the characteristics of: *childlike.* **3.** appropriate or fit for; suited to: *ladylike.* [From LIKE¹.]
like·a·ble (lī'kə bəl) *adj.* likable. —**like'a·ble·ness,** *n.*
like·li·hood (līk'lē hood') *n.* probability: *In all likelihood, I will leave tomorrow.*
like·ly (līk'lē) *-li·er, -li·est. adj.* **1.** apparently true; credible; probable: *a likely excuse.* **2.** having or showing a tendency or possibility: *He is likely to do something wrong.* **3.** suitable; appropriate: *a likely spot to build a house on.* **4.** promising: *likely young horses.* —*adv.* probably: *She's most likely very intelligent.* [Old Norse *līkligr* probable.]
lik·en (lī'kən) *v.t.* to represent as like; compare.
like·ness (līk'nis) *n.* **1.** state or quality of being alike; resemblance. **2.** representation or facsimile, esp. a portrait: *A likeness of her son hung above the mantel.* **3.** semblance or appearance; guise: *Zeus often took on the likeness of animals.*
like·wise (līk'wīz') *adv.* **1.** in a like manner; similarly: *I became angry, and he reacted likewise.* **2.** in addition; moreover.
lik·ing (lī'king) *n.* **1.** favorable regard; inclination; fondness: *Dick has a liking for eggs.* **2.** preference; taste: *Her humor is not much to my liking.* [Old English *līcung* pleasure.]
li·lac (lī'lak, -lak, -lok) *n.* **1.** purple, pink, or white flower cluster, composed of fragrant, tube-shaped flowers, borne by any of a group of plants, genus *Syringa,* of the olive family. **2.** shrub or small tree bearing this flower, widely cultivated throughout the world, having oval or lance-shaped leaves. **3.** pale pinkish-purple color characteristic of lilac blossoms. [Middle French *lilac,* through Spanish and Arabic, from Persian *līlak* bluish, going back to Sanskrit *nīla* dark blue.]

Lilac

Lille (lēl) *n.* city in northern France, a major textile center. Pop. (1968), 190,546. Also, **Lisle.**
Lil·li·put (lil'ə put') *n.* in Swift's *Gulliver's Travels,* an island inhabited by tiny people who are only six inches tall.
Lil·li·pu·tian (lil'ə pū'shən) *adj.* **1.** of or relating to the island of Lilliput or its inhabitants. **2.** lilliputian. **3.** of small size; tiny; dwarfed. —*n.* **1.** inhabitant of Lilliput. **2.** lilliputian. person of small size, intelligence, or importance.
lilt (lilt) *v.t., v.i.* to sing or play (music) with a light, graceful rhythm. —*n.* **1.** lively song or tune with a light, graceful rhythm. **2.** lively, buoyant quality of voice or movement. [Of uncertain origin.]
lil·y (lil'ē) *pl.* **-ies.** *n.* **1.** showy trumpet-shaped flower of any of a large group of plants, genus *Lilium,* growing singly or in clusters. Two of the best-known species are the Easter lily, *L. longiflorum,* variety *eximium,* having fragrant white flowers, and the tiger lily, *L. tigrinum,* having red flowers spotted with black. **2.** hardy plant bearing this flower, found both wild and cultivated throughout the northern temperate regions of the world, growing directly from an underground bulb and bearing narrow lance-shaped leaves. **3.** any of various other plants, as the calla lily or the water lily. **4.** *Heraldry.* fleur-de-lis, esp. as in

Lily

the royal coat of arms of France. —*adj.* resembling a lily, as in whiteness, delicacy, or beauty. [Old English *lilie* flower or plant of the genus *Lilium,* from Latin *lilium.*]
lil·y-liv·ered (lil'ē liv'ərd) *adj.* cowardly.
lily of the valley *pl.* **lilies of the valley. 1.** long cluster of small, fragrant, usually white, bell-shaped flowers that grow down one side of the stalk of either of two plants, genus *Convallaria,* of the lily family. **2.** plant bearing this flower, found both wild and cultivated in many parts of the world, having long oval leaves which grow directly from a rootstock.

Lily of the valley

Li·ma (def. 1., lē'mə; def. 2., lī'mə) *n.* **1.** capital and chief city of Peru, in the west-central part of the country. Pop. (1961), 1,436,231. **2.** city in northwestern Ohio. Pop. (1970), 53,734.
li·ma bean (lī'mə) **1.** pale-green kidney-shaped seed of a plant, *Phaseolus limensis,* of the pea family, cooked and eaten as a vegetable. **2.** the dwarf bush or stout climbing plant itself, widely cultivated in the tropics. [From LIMA, Peru; because it originally came from tropical America.]
limb¹ (lim) *n.* **1.** part of the body of an animal or human being distinct from the head and torso, used for support, locomotion, grasping, or the like, as an arm, leg, wing, or flipper. **2.** one of the large branches of a tree. **3.** extension or projecting part or member. **4.** one who or that which is regarded as a member, extension, or representative of a larger group: *An army is but the limb of a nation* (Kinglake, 1863). **5.** *Archaic.* mischievous child; rascal; imp. **6. out on a limb.** *Informal.* in a difficult, vulnerable, or precarious position: *The newsman went out on a limb by predicting the results of a close election.* [Old English *lim* the part of the body, branch of a tree.] —**Syn.** 2. see branch.
limb² (lim) *n.* **1.** apparent edge of a heavenly body: *the southern limb of the sun.* **2.** expanded upper part of a calyx or corolla. [Latin *limbus* border.]
lim·ber¹ (lim'bər) *adj.* **1.** bending or flexing easily; pliant: *The ballerina kept her legs limber by exercising.* **2.** able to bend or move easily; lithe; nimble. —*v.t.* to make limber: *The violinist limbered up his fingers.* —*v.i.* to become limber, esp. by exercising (with *up*): *The football player limbered up before the game.* [Of uncertain origin.] —**lim'ber·ness,** *n.* —**Syn.** *adj.* 1. see flexible.
lim·ber² (lim'bər) *n.* detachable front part of a gun or caisson, formerly used to hold boxes of ammunition. [Possibly from French *limonière* wagon with shafts, from *limon* shaft; probably of Celtic origin.]
lim·bo (lim'bō) *n.* **1.** also, **Limbo.** in Roman Catholic theology, the abode of souls not entitled to enter Heaven, but not condemned to the punishment of Hell, esp. those of infants who died before being baptized. **2.** place or condition of oblivion or neglect to which unwanted, useless, or forgotten people or things are relegated: *The hopes of his youth had been sent to the limbo of forgotten dreams.* **3.** any place of confinement, esp. a prison. [Medieval Latin *(in)limbo* (on) the border of hell, going back to Latin *in in + limbus* border.]
Lim·burg·er (lim'bur'gər) *n.* semisoft, white cheese having a strong odor and a mild flavor. Also, **Lim·burg cheese** (lim'burg'). [From *Limburg,* Belgian province where it was first made.]
lime¹ (līm) *n.* **1.** white powdery compound consisting largely of calcium oxide, usually prepared by burning limestone, and used in making cement and as a fertilizer. Also, **quick'lime'. 2.** *Archaic.* birdlime. —*v.t.* **limed, lim·ing. 1.** to treat with lime; apply lime to. **2.** *Archaic.* to smear with birdlime. **3.** *Archaic.* to catch with birdlime. [Old English *līm* birdlime, quicklime.]
lime² (līm) *n.* **1.** small oval or round fruit of a citrus tree, *Citrus aurantifolia,* having a thin rind and a juicy, tart pulp. **2.** thorny evergreen tree bearing this fruit, cultivated in many tropical and subtropical areas of the world, esp. in the West Indies and southern Florida. [French *lime* the fruit, through Provençal, from Arabic *līmah.*]
lime³ (līm) *n.* linden tree. [Earlier *line,* going back to Old English *lind* linden.]
lime-kiln (līm'kil', -kiln') *n.* kiln or furnace in which lime is made by burning limestone, shells, or other materials.
lime·light (līm'līt') *n.* **1.** conspicuous position before the public; center of interest: *The election victory put the candidate and his family in the limelight.* **2.** strong light used in the theater to illuminate a performer, part of the stage, or the like, originally produced by heating lime to incandescence.
lim·er·ick (lim'ər ik) *n.* humorous verse form consisting of five anapestic lines of which the first, second, and fifth have three accents and the third and fourth have two accents. It has a rhyme scheme of *aabba.* Example: *There was a young lady of Niger/ Who smiled as she rode on a tiger;/ They returned from the ride/ With the lady inside,/ And the smile on the face of the tiger* (Anon.). [From *Limerick,* Ireland;

---

at; āpe; cär; end; mē; it; īce; hot; ōld; fôrk; wood; fōōl; oil; out; up; ūse; turn; sing; thin; this; zh in treasure; ə in ago, taken, pencil, lemon, circus.

possibly with reference to the practice at certain social gatherings of singing the refrain "Will you come up to Limerick?" after each guest extemporized nonsense verse.]

lime·stone (līm′stōn′) *n.* sedimentary rock consisting chiefly of calcium carbonate, used for building, and yielding lime when burned.

lime·wa·ter (līm′wô′tər, -wot′ər) *n.* water solution of calcium hydroxide, used medicinally as an antacid and in the laboratory to test for the presence of carbon dioxide.

lim·ey (lī′mē) *pl.,* **-eys.** *n.* *Slang.* Englishman, esp. an English sailor. [From the use of *lime* juice in the British navy to prevent scurvy.]

lim·it (lim′it) *n.* **1.** furthest or utmost range, extent, or boundary; point at which something ends or must end: *the limit of patience, to exceed the speed limit.* **2.** *also,* **limits.** boundary of a specified area: *It is illegal to drive faster than twenty-five miles per hour within the city limits.* **3.** amount or quantity established as the maximum allowed, esp. in hunting or fishing: *They caught more than the limit of trout yesterday and had to throw some back.* **4.** in certain gambling games, maximum amount a player may bet at one time. **5.** *Mathematics.* finite quantity that the terms of a converging series progressively approach but never reach. **6.** **off limits.** prohibited or forbidden. **7.** **the limit.** *Slang.* one who or that which approaches or exceeds certain limits, as of credibility or tolerance. —*v.t.* to keep within or set a bound or bounds; restrict; confine. [Latin *limit-,* stem of *līmes* boundary.] —**lim′it·a·ble,** *adj.* —**lim′it·er,** *n.*

lim·i·ta·tion (lim′ə tā′shən) *n.* **1.** that which limits, esp. a restrictive weakness or lack of capacity; limiting condition or circumstance: *to know one's limitations.* **2.** act of limiting; being limited. **3.** *Law.* period of time, prescribed by statute, during which an action may be brought and after which no claim will be recognized.

lim·i·ta·tive (lim′ə tā′tiv) *adj.* limiting; restrictive.

lim·it·ed (lim′ə tid) *adj.* **1.** confined within or having a limit or limits; restricted: *The offer is good for a limited time only.* **2.** lacking imagination, independence, or originality; narrow: *a limited person with few interests.* **3.** having governing powers restricted, as by constitutional law: *a limited monarchy.* **4.** restricted in liability to the amount of capital invested by stockholders: *a limited company.* **5.** (of trains, buses, or other public conveyances) making a restricted number of stops and carrying no more than a specified number of passengers. —*n.* limited train, bus, or other public conveyance.

lim·it·less (lim′it lis) *adj.* having no limits; boundless.

limn (lim) *v.t.* *Archaic.* **1.** to paint or draw. **2.** to portray in words. [Form of earlier *lumine* to light up, illuminate (manuscripts), modification of Middle French *enluminer,* going back to Latin *illūmināre* to light up, embellish.] —**lim′ner** (lim′nər), *n.*

Li·moges (li mōzh′) *n.* **1.** city in west-central France. Pop. (1968), 132,935. **2.** variety of fine porcelain manufactured at Limoges.

li·mo·nite (lī′mə nīt′) *n.* hydrous iron oxide, dark-brown to black in color, formed by the oxidation and hydration of iron-bearing minerals. [German *Limonit* literally, meadow ore, from Greek *leimón* meadow.]

lim·ou·sine (lim′ə zēn′, lim′ə zēn′) *n.* **1.** large sedan with a glass partition between the front and back seats, often driven by a chauffeur. **2.** formerly, large automobile having a closed compartment for passengers, often with the roof extending out over an open driver's seat. **3.** large automobile used as a commercial passenger vehicle: *an airport limousine.* [French *limousine* originally, a cloak worn by the people of Limousin, former province of central France.]

limp¹ (limp) *v.i.* **1.** to walk lamely, esp. by favoring one leg. **2.** to move or proceed slowly or with difficulty: *The old train limped along the tracks.* —*n.* lame movement or walk. [Probably from obsolete *limphalt* lame, from Old English *lemphealt.*] —**limp′er,** *n.*

limp² (limp) *adj.* **1.** lacking stiffness or firmness; wilted: *After three days the flowers became limp.* **2.** without force or vigor; weak: *a limp argument.* [Possibly of Scandinavian origin.] —**limp′ly,** *adv.* —**limp′ness,** *n.*

lim·pet (lim′pit) *n.* any of a group of brownish-green, saltwater mollusks, order Prosobranchia, having a conical shell and a large muscular foot which acts as a suction cup, enabling the limpet to cling firmly to rocks. [Old English *lempedu,* from Medieval Latin *lampreda* lamprey, limpet; of uncertain origin.]

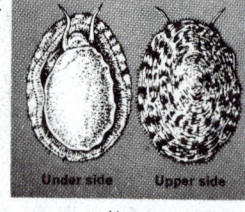

Under side   Upper side

Limpet

lim·pid (lim′pid) *adj.* **1.** clear; transparent: *pure and limpid crystal.* **2.** characterized by clarity or lucidity, as of style: *limpid prose.* [Latin *limpidus* clear.] —**lim·pid′i·ty, lim′pid·ness,** *n.* —**lim′pid·ly,** *adv.*

lim·y (lī′mē) **lim·i·er, lim·i·est.** *adj.* **1.** consisting of, containing, or resembling lime. **2.** smeared with or as with birdlime; sticky.

lin·age (lī′nij) *n.* **1.** number of lines in a piece of printed or written matter. **2.** payment for written work based on the number of such lines.

linch·pin (linch′pin′) *n.* pin passed through the end of an axle to keep the wheel in place. [Old English *lynis* axle + *pinn* peg.]

Lin·coln (ling′kən) *n.* **1.** Abraham. 1809–65, sixteenth president of the United States from 1861 to 1865. **2.** capital of Nebraska, in the southeastern part of the state. Pop. (1970), 149,518.

Lind·bergh, Charles A(ugustus) (lind′burg′, lin′-) 1902–74, U.S. aviator.

lin·den (lin′dən) *n.* any of a large group of tall trees, genus *Tilia,* grow throughout northern temperate regions of the world, bearing broad, usually heart-shaped, leaves and drooping clusters of small, fragrant, pale-yellow flowers. [Probably from Middle English *linden* made of the wood of the linden, from Old English *linden,* from *lind* linden.]

line¹ (līn) *n.* **1.** continuous mark or stroke, usually straight, having greater length than width, as that made by a writing implement or pointed tool: *White lines divided the lanes of the highway.* **2.** mark resembling such a mark, as a band of color, a furrow, or a wrinkle. **3.** outline, contour, or profile: *the sleek lines of a sports car.* **4.** limit or boundary, as between two areas; border: *The town is two miles from the state line.* **5.** division or demarcation between contrasting ideas, qualities, conditions, or the like: *the line between communism and democracy.* **6.** number of persons or things arranged in one continuous series; row: *We waited in a long line outside the movie theater.* **7.** continuous chronological succession of persons or things related by, or as by, direct descent: *Elizabeth I was the last ruler of the Tudor line.* **8.** row of words or letters printed or written between the margins of a page or column: *Each page has fifty lines of type.* **9.** short letter; note: *Jean dropped me a line thanking me for the gift.* **10.** series of words forming a single verse of poetry: *There are six lines in each stanza of the poem.* **11. lines.** spoken or sung parts of a theatrical presentation, esp. those for a single performer. **12.** course or direction of progress or movement: *An innocent bystander was caught in the line of fire.* **13.** course of action, conduct, or thought; method: *I couldn't follow the author's line of reasoning.* **14.** *also,* **lines.** general plan or concept, as of construction, action, or procedure: *The house was designed along very simple lines.* **15.** state of agreement, conformity, or accord: *His actions were not in line with his beliefs.* **16.** scope or field of interest, activity, ability, or the like: *Cooking just isn't my line.* **17.** particular business or activity: *to be in the banking line.* **18.** stock of merchandise of a particular or related type: *The department store is selling a new line of winter coats.* **19.a.** wire or series of wires connecting points or stations in a telegraph or telephone system. **b.** system of such connections. **c.** connection or contact established between two points by such a system: *to keep a line open. Hold the line, please.* **20.a.** system of transportation consisting of public conveyances traveling regularly over an established route: *a steamship line serving the Pacific.* **b.** one branch of such a system of transportation. **c.** group or company that owns or manages such a system. **21.** roadbed and track of a railroad: *to lay down a new line over the mountains.* **22.** piece of rope, cord, or wire: *to hang wet clothes on the line.* **23.a.** *Nautical.* any rope, cable, hawser, or the like used for a specific purpose. **b.** cord, wire, or tape used in surveying for taking measurements. **c.** cord with one or more hooks, used for fishing. **24.** channel, wire, pipe, or other means of conveyance that carries a substance, as gas, water, or electricity, from one point to another: *The electric lines were knocked down in the thunderstorm.* **25.** *Mathematics.* track thought of as having length but no thickness, as being generated by a moving point, and consisting of a set of points. It may be straight or curved. **26.** *Music.* one of the five parallel, horizontal lines that form the staff. **27.** *Art.* **a.** use of strokes and outlines as opposed to shading and color, as in a painting. **b.** distinctive form or contours of a work of art. **28.** *Football.* **a.** line of scrimmage. **b.** the row of players who are arranged along the line of scrimmage at the beginning of a play. **29. lines.** *Military.* arrangement of fighting forces in closest contact with the opposing forces: *He was captured behind enemy lines.* **30.** *Military.* **a.** formation in which the elements, as troops or ships, are arranged abreast. Distinguished from **column. b.** extended series of fortifications forming a front. **c.** formerly, military forces that do the actual fighting. **31.** *Informal.* glib, often insincere talk, esp. when used to make a good impression, ingratiate oneself, persuade, or sell: *He gave her a line about how pretty she is.*

all along the line. in every way or at every point; including everything: *His actions were accurate all along the line.*

in line for. in a deserving or promising position or course: *to be in line for a raise.*

on a line. aligned evenly; level.

on the line. a. in a vulnerable or hazardous position: *The senator put his reputation on the line by defending an unpopular cause.* **b.** paid immediately: *cash on the line.*

at; āpe; cär; end; mē; it; īce; hot; ōld; fôrk; wood; fōōl; oil; out; up; ūse; turn; sing; thin; this; zh in treasure; ə in ago, taken, pencil, lemon, circus.

out of line. not in conformity with certain accepted standards, as of behavior: *He was out of line for criticizing her publicly.*

to draw a (or **the**) **line.** to establish and not go beyond a certain limit.

to get (or **have**) **a line on.** *Informal.* to acquire information about.

to hold the line. to maintain a defense or opposition; remain firm or steadfast: *The government tried to hold the line against inflation.*

to read between the lines. to understand something that is implied but not actually stated. —*v.t.*, **lined, lin·ing. 1.** to mark or cover with lines: *to line paper. Wrinkles lined her face.* **2.** to place or arrange in a line; bring into alignment (often with *up*): *to line children up according to height.* **3.** to arrange or form a line along; border: *Trees lined the edge of the road.* **4.** *Baseball.* to hit (a ball) so that it travels through the air in an almost completely horizontal path. **5. to line up.** to obtain the use or services of; gather; procure: *to line up a speaker for the meeting.* —*v.i.* **1.** to form a line (often with *up*). **2. to line out.** *Baseball.* to make an out by hitting a line drive that is caught by a fielder. **3. to line up.** to get together or rally, as in support of something. [Partly from Old English *līne* cord, rope, row¹, from Latin *līnea* linen thread, thin continuous mark¹, line of descent; partly from Old French *ligne* cord, line of descent, row of words, from Latin *līnea.*]

line² (līn) **lined, lin·ing.** *v.t.* **1.** to cover the inner surface of: *The tailor lined the jacket with silk.* **2.** to supply or fill: *Line the cupboard with food.* **3.** to serve or be used as a lining for: *Family portraits lined the walls.* [From Middle English *line* flax, linen, from Old English *līn;* referring to the use of linen to line clothes.]

lin·e·age (lin'ē ij) *n.* **1.** direct descent from an ancestor; pedigree. **2.** those descended from a common ancestor collectively; family. [Old French *lignage* all those descended from the same line, from *ligne* line of descent. See LINE¹.]

lin·e·al (lin'ē əl) *adj.* **1.** being in the direct line of descent. **2.** of, relating to, or based upon direct descent; hereditary: *a lineal right to the title.* **3.** linear. [Late Latin *lineālis* relating to a line, from Latin *līnea* line¹, linen thread.] —**lin'e·al·ly,** *adv.*

lin·e·a·ment (lin'ē ə mənt) *n.* **1.** feature, detail, or contour of the face or body. **2.** distinctive feature or quality. [Latin *līneāmentum* feature, delineation, from *līneāre* to reduce to a straight line.]

lin·e·ar (lin'ē ər) *adj.* **1.** of or relating to a line or lines. **2.** consisting of or involving the use of lines. **3.** extended in a line or lines. **4.** extending in one dimension only; relating to length. **5.** resembling a line; long and narrow. [Latin *līneāris* relating to a line, from *līnea* line, linen thread, line¹.]

linear equation *Mathematics.* algebraic equation of the first degree whose graph is a straight line.

linear measure 1. measurement by length. **2.** unit or system of units for measuring length.

line drive *Baseball.* strongly hit ball that travels through the air in an almost completely horizontal path. Also, **lin'er.**

line·man (līn'mən) *pl.*, **-men.** *n.* **1.** *also,* **lines·man.** one who installs or repairs telegraph, telephone, or electric wires. **2.** one who inspects railroad tracks. **3.** *Football.* any of the players in the line. **4.** one who carries the line, tape, chain, or the like in surveying.

lin·en (lin'ən) *n.* **1.** usually lustrous, durable fabric woven from flax fibers, used for such items as dresses, suits, and tablecloths. **2.** household articles or garments made of linen or similar fabric: *table linen.* **3. to wash dirty linen in public.** to make information public that is usually kept confidential since it is unflattering to a group or individual. —*adj.* made of linen. [Old English *līnen* made of flax, from *līn* flax.]

line officer, officer of the armed forces who is assigned to a combat unit. Distinguished from **staff officer.**

line of force *Physics.* imaginary line in a field of force, indicating the direction of force of the field.

line of scrimmage, imaginary line running across a football field parallel to the goal lines, on which the ball is placed by the referee, a new line being established wherever the ball is ruled dead at the end of a play.

line of sight 1. imaginary line from an observer's eye to a distant object that he is viewing. **2.** *Electronics.* straight path, unobstructed by the horizon, between transmitting and receiving antennas.

lin·er (lī'nər) *n.* **1.** ship or airplane operated by a transportation line, esp. a transoceanic passenger ship. **2.** one who or that which makes lines. **3.** *Baseball.* line drive.

lines·man (līnz'mən) *pl.*, **-men.** *n.* **1.** lineman (*def. 1*). **2.a.** official in tennis who judges whether the ball falls inside or outside the lines marking the boundaries of the court. **b.** official in football who measures and marks the yardage gained or lost on a play and keeps count of the downs. **c.** official who assists the referee in certain other games, as hockey.

line·up (līn'up') *also,* **line-up.** *n.* **1.a.** arrangement of persons or things in or as in a line or row. **b.** number of suspects lined up by the police

for the purpose of identification by a victim or witness. **2.a.** players on a team actually participating in play at any given time during a game. **b.** list of the players on a team who will play at the start of a game. **c.** arrangement of the players, as in football, when in position for play.

ling (ling) *pl.*, **lings** or **ling.** *n.* **1.** saltwater fish, *Molva vulgaris*, found in the North Atlantic, the largest member of the cod family. Length: to 7 feet. **2.** any of various related fish, esp. the burbot. [Possibly of Low German origin.]

-ling¹ *suffix* (used to form nouns) **1.** little; unimportant: *duckling, princeling.* **2.** one who or that which belongs to or is related to, characterized by, or concerned with: *earthling, underling.* [Old English *-ling.*]

-ling² *suffix* (used to form adverbs) toward: *sideling.* [Old English *-ling.*]

lin·ger (ling'gər) *v.i.* **1.** to stay on as if reluctant to leave; delay leaving; tarry: *Children lingered outside the school in the afternoon.* **2.** to proceed at a slow pace; dawdle: *Mother told him not to linger on the way home.* **3.** to continue to exist; endure; persist: *The memory lingers on.* **4.** to continue living although very close to death: *She lingered several days after the accident.* **5.** to be tardy in action; hesitate; delay: *to linger in obeying an order.* [Middle English *lengeren* to tarry (from *lengen*, from Old English *lengan* to prolong) + -ER⁴.]

lin·ge·rie (län'zhə rā', -zhə rē', lan'-) *n.* women's underwear, nightgowns, robes, and similar garments. [French *lingerie* underclothes, from *linge* linen, going back to Latin *līnum* flax, linen.]

lin·go (ling'gō) *pl.*, **-goes.** *n.* *Slang.* **1.** language, esp. that which is unintelligible. **2.** terminology peculiar to a particular group, profession, or the like: *legal lingo, political lingo.* [Provençal *lingo, lengo* tongue, speech, from Latin *lingua.*]

Syn. 2. Lingo, slang, jargon designate a nonstandard style of speech. Lingo is a derogatory term applied to a speech, peculiar to a class or group, that sounds outlandish to outsiders: *School children speak their own lingo.* Slang designates colorful and uninhibited colloquial speech composed esp. of recently coined words that gain wide acceptance: *The slang of one generation often becomes the literary language of the next* (Weekley, 1920). Jargon is shop talk or technical and obscure terminology peculiar to a profession or social class: *Articles in scientific journals are usually written in technical jargon.*

lin·gua fran·ca (ling'gwə frang'kə) *pl.*, **lin·gua fran·cas** or **lin·guae fran·cae** (ling'gwē fran'sē). **1.** hybrid language, based on Italian, with elements of French, Spanish, Greek, and Arabic, formerly used in Mediterranean ports. **2.** any hybrid language used by people who speak different languages, esp. for the purpose of transacting business. [Italian *lingua franca* literally, language of the Franks: *lingua* language, from Latin *lingua* speech, tongue. See FRANK.]

lin·gual (ling'gwəl) *adj.* **1.** of or relating to the tongue. **2.** *Phonetics.* articulated chiefly with the tongue. **3.** of language or languages. —*n. Phonetics.* sound articulated chiefly with the tongue, as *l* or *t*. [Medieval Latin *lingualis* relating to the tongue, from Latin *lingua* tongue, speech.] —**lin'gual·ly,** *adv.*

lin·guist (ling'gwist) *n.* **1.** one who is fluent in several languages. **2.** student of or expert in linguistics. [Latin *lingua* tongue, speech + -IST.]

lin·guis·tic (ling gwis'tik) *adj.* of or relating to language or linguistics. —**lin·guis'ti·cal·ly,** *adv.*

linguistic form, unit of speech that has meaning, as an affix, word, phrase, or sentence.

lin·guis·tics (ling gwis'tiks) *n.* comparative study of languages, including their origins, development, and interrelationships; science of language. **a** treated as singular.

lin·i·ment (lin'ə mənt) *n.* liquid rubbed on the skin to relieve pain or stiffness, as from a bruise or sprain. [Late Latin *linimentum* ointment, from *linīre* to smear.]

lin·ing (lī'ning) *n.* **1.** surface, layer, or coating covering the inside of something: *the silk lining of a jacket.* **2.** material used or suitable for this purpose.

link¹ (lingk) *n.* **1.** one of the rings or loops of a chain. **2.** something resembling a link in a chain: *a link of sausage.* **3.** anything that serves to join or connect: *a link with the past.* **4.** single segment of an interrelated series: *the only weak link in his reasoning.* **5.a.** in surveying, single division of a chain used as a measure of length, equal to 7.92 inches. **b.** in engineering, single division of a chain used as a measure of length, equal to 1 foot. —*v.t., v.i.* to join or be joined by or as by a link or links; unite; connect. [Of Scandinavian origin.]

link² (lingk) *n.* *Archaic.* torch. [Possibly from Medieval Latin *linchinus,* form of *lichinus* candle, wick, from Greek *lychnos* lamp.]

link·age (ling'kij) *n.* **1.** act of linking; being linked. **2.** system of interconnected links or mechanical parts.

linking verb, verb that connects a subject with a predicate adjective or noun without expressing action; copula. *Appear, be,* and *seem* are linking verbs.

---

at; āpe; cär; end; mē; it; īce; hot; ōld; fôrk; wood; fōol; oil; out; up; ūse; turn; sing; thin; this; zh in treasure; ə in ago, taken, pencil, lemon, circus.   595

links (lingks) *n.,pl.* golf course. [Old English *hlinc* hill.]

Lin·nae·us, Car·o·lus (li nē′əs; kar′ə ləs) 1707–78, Swedish naturalist and botanist.

Lin·ne·an (li nē′ən) *also,* **Lin·nae·an.** *adj.* of or relating to Linnaeus or to his system of binomial nomenclature.

lin·net (lin′it) *n.* songbird, *Carduelis cannabina,* of Europe and Asia. [Old French *linette,* from *lin* flax, from Latin *līnum* flax, linen; because it eats flax seeds.]

li·no·le·um (li nō′lē əm) *n.* **1.** material used for covering floors, made into sheets or tiles from a mixture of linseed oil, finely ground cork or wood, resins, and pigments, that is applied to a fabric backing, as burlap, canvas, or felt. [Latin *līnum* flax, linen + *oleum* oil.]

li·no·type (lī′nə tīp′) *n. Trademark.* typesetting machine operated by a keyboard, which casts entire lines of type in one piece.

lin·seed (lin′sēd′) *n.* flaxseed, the source of linseed oil. [Old English *līnsēd,* from *līn* flax + *sēd* seed.]

linseed oil, yellow or brown oil obtained from the seed of certain flax plants, used in making such items as paints, varnish, printing ink, patent leather, and linoleum.

lin·sey-wool·sey (lin′zē wool′zē) *pl.,* **-wool·seys.** *n.* strong, coarse, loosely woven fabric of linen and wool or of cotton and wool. [From *Lindsey,* English town where it was first produced + WOOL.]

lint (lint) *n.* **1.** tiny bits of thread or fluff. **2.** soft, downy or fleecy material obtained by scraping linen fibers, formerly used as a dressing for wounds. [Latin *linteum* linen cloth, going back to *līnum* flax, linen.]

lin·tel (lint′əl) *n.* horizontal member spanning an opening, as of a door or window, and supporting the structure above it. [Old French *lintel,* going back to Latin *līmes* (stem *limit-*) boundary.]

Lintel

li·on (lī′ən) *n.* **1.** carnivorous mammal, *Panthera leo,* of the cat family, native to Africa and southern Asia, having a tawny coat of short, coarse hair and a tufted tail. The male has a shaggy mane encircling the neck, head, and shoulders. Length: up to 10 feet including the tail. **2.** any of various animals related or in some way similar to the lion, as the mountain lion and the sea lion. **3.** man of great strength or courage. **4.** famous person, esp. one much sought after socially; celebrity. **5.** to **beard the lion in his den.** to defy or confront a person on his own territory. [Old French *lion* the mammal *Panthera leo,* from Latin *leō* the mammal *Panthera leo,* courageous person, the constellation Leo, the sign of the zodiac Leo, from Greek *leōn.*]

Lion

Lioness

Lion and lioness

li·on·ess (lī′ə nis) *n.* female lion.

li·on-heart·ed (lī′ən här′tid) *adj.* brave; courageous.

li·on·ize (lī′ə nīz′) **-ized, -iz·ing.** *v.t.* to treat (someone or something) as very important. —**li′on·i·za′tion,** *n.*

lion's share, largest or best portion.

lip (lip) *n.* **1.** either of the two fleshy folds forming the opening of the mouth: *She has red lips.* **2.** any projecting part resembling this: *the flared lip of a bell.* **3.** edge or rim of any opening or cavity: *the lip of a crater, the lip of a glass.* **4.** position and adjustment of the lips and tongue in playing a wind instrument; embouchure. **5.** *Botany.* protruding part, occurring singly or paired, in an unequally divided calyx or corolla, as in a snapdragon or orchid. **6.** *Slang.* insolent talk; impudence: *Don't give me any of your lip.* **7. to button one's lip.** *Slang.* to stop talking. **8. to hang on the lips of.** to listen attentively to every word: *The audience hung on the lips of the speaker.* **9. to keep a stiff upper lip.** to face adversity with courage; show fortitude: *He kept a stiff upper lip during the crisis.* **10. to smack one's lips.** to show pleasure at the thought of something enjoyable. —*v.t.* **1.** to touch with the lips; apply the lips to: *to lip a glass.* **2.** *Archaic.* to utter softly; murmur. **3.** to use the lips in playing (a wind instrument). **4.** *Golf.* to hit the ball so that it stops at the edge of the hole (the hole). —*adj.* **1.** *Phonetics.* articulated primarily by the lips; labial: *a lip consonant.* **2.** of, relating

to, or for the lips. [Old English *lippa* fleshy fold around the mouth.]

li·pase (lī′pās, lip′ās) *n.* enzyme that aids in the breaking down of fats into glycerol and fatty acids. [Greek *lipos* fat + -ASE.]

lip·id (lip′id) *also,* **lip·ide** (lip′īd) *n.* any of a group of organic compounds that consist of the fats and other substances with similar properties, and constitute, with proteins and carbohydrates, the principal structural components of living cells. Lipids are insoluble in water, soluble in fat solvents, and greasy to the touch. [From Greek *lipos* fat.]

Lip·pi, Fra Fi·lip·po (lip′ē; frä fi lip′ō) c.1406–69, Florentine painter.

lip-read (lip′rēd′) **-read** (-red′), **-read·ing.** *v.i.* to interpret or understand speech by watching the movements of the speaker's lips, used esp. by the deaf.

lip reader, one who lip-reads.

lip reading, technique or practice of interpreting or understanding speech by watching the movements of the speaker's lips.

lip service, insincere expression of devotion, respect, loyalty, or the like.

lip·stick (lip′stik′) *n.* cosmetic preparation used to color the lips, consisting of wax, oil, coloring matter, and often perfume, usually contained in a small cylinder.

liq. 1. liquid. **2.** liquor.

liq·ue·fac·tion (lik′wə fak′shən) *n.* act or process of liquefying; being liquefied.

liq·ue·fy (lik′wə fī′) **-fied, -fy·ing.** *v.t., v.i.* to reduce to or become a liquid. [Middle French *liquefier* to make liquid, from Latin *liquefacere,* from *liquēre* to be fluid + *facere* to make.] —**liq′ue·fi′a·ble,** *adj.* —**liq′ue·fi′er,** *n.*

li·ques·cent (li kwes′ənt) *adj.* becoming or tending to become liquid; melting. [Latin *liquēscēns,* present participle of *liquēscere* to become liquid.] —**li·ques′cence, li·ques′cen·cy,** *n.*

li·queur (li kur′, -kyoor′) *n.* strong, sweet-flavored alcoholic beverage. Also, **cor′dial.** [French *liqueur* liquid, liqueur, from Latin *liquor* fluid, liquid. Doublet of LIQUOR.]

liq·uid (lik′wid) *n.* **1.** form of matter that is characterized by the ability of its atoms or molecules to move about freely within a restricted area, but not completely independently of the other atoms or molecules. A liquid can assume the shape of but not necessarily fill its container. Distinguished from **gas** and **solid. 2.** *Phonetics.* the consonant sound of *l* or *r.* —*adj.* **1.** in the form of, or having the properties of, a liquid; capable of flowing or being poured; fluid: *The medicine comes either in a pill or in liquid form.* **2.** clear or transparent; limpid: *The dark hazel eyes shine with a more liquid luster* (Kingsley, 1850). **3.** flowing musically and clearly: *the poet's liquid verses.* **4.** gracefully flowing and unconstrained: *the liquid motion of the ballerina's arms.* **5.** consisting of, or readily convertible into, cash: *liquid assets.* **6.** *Phonetics.* of a consonant, frictionless and like a vowel. [Latin *liquidus* fluid, clear.]

liquid air, bluish transparent or milky liquid mixture formed when air is subjected to great pressure and then cooled by its own expansion, used as a refrigerant.

liq·ui·date (lik′wə dāt′) **-dat·ed, -dat·ing.** *v.t.* **1.** to pay off or settle (a debt or obligation). **2.** to settle the accounts of (a business) by using the assets to pay off the liabilities, as in bankruptcy. **3.** to convert (assets) into cash. **4.** to do away with; dispose of: *Strong censorship helped liquidate oppposition to the regime.* **5.** to murder: *The gangster was liquidated by a rival mob.* [Late Latin *liquidātus,* past participle of *liquidāre* to make clear or liquid, from Latin *liquidus* fluid, clear.] —**liq′ui·da′tion,** *n.*

li·quid·i·ty (li kwid′ə tē) *n.* state or quality of being liquid.

liquid measure, system for measuring the volume of liquids.

liq·uor (lik′ər) *n.* **1.** any alcoholic beverage, esp. one produced by distillation rather than by fermentation. **2.** any liquid substance, as the natural liquid of certain shellfish or broth or juice produced in cooking. —*v.t. Slang.* to cause to become intoxicated with alcohol (with *up*). [Old French *lic(o)ur* fluid, liquid, from Latin *liquor.* Doublet of LIQUEUR.]

liq·uo·rice (lik′ər is, -ish, lik′rish) licorice.

li·ra (lēr′ə) *pl.* **li·re** (lēr′ā) or **li·ras.** *n.* **1.** monetary unit of Italy. **2.** monetary unit of Turkey. [Italian *lira* Italian monetary unit, from Latin *lībra* pound[1], scales.]

Lis·bon (liz′bən) *n.* capital, largest city, and chief seaport of Portugal, in the western part of the country. Pop. (1968), 828,000. Also, *Portuguese,* **Lis·bo·a** (lēzh bō′ə).

lisle (līl) *n.* **1.** fine, strong thread, usually of cotton fibers that have been tightly twisted and given a smooth finish, used principally for such knit items as socks, underwear, and gloves. **2.** knit fabric made of this thread. [From *Lisle* (now Lille), French town where it was first produced.]

Lisle (lēl) Lille.

lisp (lisp) *n.* **1.** speech defect or mannerism in which the sounds of *s* and *z* are mispronounced, as with the sounds of *th* in *think* and *them,*

respectively. **2.** act or habit of speaking with a lisp. **3.** sound resembling lisping: *with lisp of leaves and ripple of rain* (Swinburne, 1864). —*v.t., v.i.* **1.** to speak or pronounce with a lisp. **2.** to speak or pronounce imperfectly, as a child does. [Middle English *lispen* to speak with a lisp, going back to Old English *wlisp* lisping.] —**lisp′er,** *n.*

lis·some (lis′əm) *also,* **lis·som.** *adj.* **1.** bending easily; limber; supple. **2.** moving gracefully; nimble; agile. [Form of earlier *lithesome,* from LITHE + -SOME[1].] —**lis′some·ly,** *adv.* —**lis′some·ness,** *n.*

list[1] (list) *n.* itemized series of names, numbers, words, or the like; catalog; roll: *a list of addresses.* —*v.t.* **1.** to make a list of; itemize: *Mother listed the items she wanted to buy.* **2.** to enter or include in a list: *Natalie is listed in the telephone directory.* [French *liste* roll, catalog; of Germanic origin.]

Syn. *n.* **List, catalog, register** denote a definite series of items or names that serves as a record or reference. **List** is an item-by-item arrangement of related units: *The hostess drew up a list of her guests for the party.* **Catalog** is a systematized, complete, and descriptive presentation or enumeration of items in a particular order: *The museum has a printed catalog of its exhibits.* **Register** is a written, esp. an official record containing regular entries of names, transactions, and other particulars: *The county clerk maintains a register of births and deaths.*

list[2] (list) *n.* border, edging, or selvage of cloth. —*v.t.* to edge with list. [Old English *līste* border, strip[2].]

list[3] (list) *n.* inclination or leaning to one side; tilt. —*v.i., v.i.* to tilt or cause to tilt to one side: *The ship listed 15° in the storm.* [Of uncertain origin.]

list[4] (list) *Archaic. v.t.* to be pleasing to; please; gratify. —*v.i.* to be inclined; choose; wish. [Old English *lystan.*]

list[5] (list) *Archaic. v.i.* to listen. —*v.t.* to listen to; hear. [Old English *hlystan.*]

lis·ten (lis′ən) *v.i.* **1.** to give attention for the purpose of hearing; try to hear: *We listened for the sound of the bell.* **2.** to give heed; pay attention: *The child refused to listen to his mother and did as he pleased.* **3. to listen. in. a.** to listen to without participating, esp. to eavesdrop: *to listen in on a private conversation.* **b.** to listen to a broadcast. [Modification (influenced by LIST[5]) of Old English *hlysnan.*] —**lis′ten·er,** *n.* —**Syn. 1.** see **hear.**

list·er (lis′tər) *n.* plow equipped with a double moldboard that throws soil to both sides of the furrow. [From LIST[3].]

Lis·ter, Joseph (lis′tər) 1827–1912, English surgeon who developed antiseptic surgical techniques.

list·ing (lis′ting) *n.* **1.** act of making or entering in a list. **2.** entry in a list: *a new listing in the telephone directory.*

list·less (list′lis) *adj.* characterized by or exhibiting indifference or lack of energy; apathetic: *Agatha remained weak and listless for weeks after her illness.* [Archaic *list* desire (from LIST[4]) + -LESS.] —**list′less·ly,** *adv.* —**list′less·ness,** *n.*

list price, price of an item, as published in a catalog or price list, often subject to discounts.

lists (lists) *n.,pl.* **1.** field or area in which knights fought tournaments. **2.** barriers enclosing the field or area. **3.** any area or place of combat, controversy, or competition. **4. to enter the lists.** to enter a contest or controversy. [Plural of LIST[2]; influenced in meaning by Old French *lice* barrier (probably of Germanic origin).]

Liszt, Franz (list; *French:* fränts) 1811–86, Hungarian composer and pianist.

lit (lit) *a* past tense and past participle of **light**[1] and **light**[3].

lit. **1.** liter. **2.** literal; literally. **3.** literary; literature.

lit·a·ny (lit′ən ē) *pl., -*nies. *n.* **1.** form of prayer consisting of a series of petitions spoken by the minister to which the choir or the congregation makes fixed responses. **2.** long or repetitious series: *a litany of woes.* [Old French *litanie,* from Late Latin *litanīa* form of prayer, from Greek *litaneiā* entreaty, prayer.]

li·tchi (lē′chē) *also,* **li·chee.** *n.* **1.** small, round, edible fruit of a tree, *Litchi chinensis,* having a brittle red outer shell and juicy white flesh. Also, **litchi nut. 2.** tree bearing this fruit, widely cultivated in China. [Chinese (Mandarin) *li chih.*]

li·ter (lē′tər) *also, British,* **li·tre.** *n.* unit of capacity in the metric system, equal to one cubic decimeter, 1.05668 U.S. liquid quarts, or about 0.9080 U.S. dry quart. See **weights and measures** in table. [French *litre,* from obsolete *litron* measure of capacity, from Medieval Latin *litra,* from Greek *lītrā* pound[1].]

lit·er·a·cy (lit′ər ə sē) *n.* ability to read and write: *Proof of literacy was a requirement for voting.*

lit·er·al (lit′ər əl) *adj.* **1.** following the exact words: *The student prepared a literal translation of the German poem.* **2.** based on or following exactly; not figurative or metaphorical: *the literal sense of a word.* **3.** having a tendency to regard what is said in an exact and unimaginative manner: *a literal person.* **4.** factual; unexaggerated: *a literal description.* **5.** of, relating to, or expressed by letters. [Late Latin *litterālis* relating to a letter, from Latin *littera* letter of the alphabet.] —**lit′er·al·ness,** *n.*

lit·er·al·ism (lit′ər ə liz′əm) *n.* adherence to the exact meaning in a translation or interpretation. —**lit′er·al·ist,** *n.* —**lit′er·al·is′tic,** *adj.* —**lit′er·al·is′ti·cal·ly,** *adv.*

lit·er·al·ly (lit′ər ə lē) *adv.* **1.** in a literal manner or sense: *Don't take what he says about his fishing trip literally.* **2.** without exaggeration; actually; really: *The city was literally destroyed.* **3.** for all practical purposes; in effect; virtually. ▲ used loosely to make a statement more emphatic: *The spectators were literally glued to their seats as the game reached its exciting conclusion.* **4.** word for word: *He translated the story literally, without embellishments or changes.*

lit·er·ar·y (lit′ə rer′ē) *adj.* **1.** of or relating to literature: *literary history.* **2.** appropriate to literature: *literary effects.* **3.a.** well versed in or occupied with literature: *a literary family.* **b.** of or relating to literary people: *a literary society.* [Latin *litterārius* relating to reading and writing, from *littera* letter of the alphabet.]

lit·er·ate (lit′ər it) *adj.* **1.** able to read and write: *Only one half of the native population was literate.* **2.** well-read; cultured. —*n.* **1.** one who can read and write. **2.** one who is well-read. [Latin *litterātus* educated; literally, one who knows letters, from *littera* letter.] —**lit′er·ate·ly,** *adv.*

lit·e·ra·ti (lit′ə rä′tē, -rā′tē) *n.,pl.* persons who have achieved distinction as scholars or writers.

lit·e·ra·tim (lit′ə rā′tim) *adv.* letter for letter; literally. [Medieval Latin *litterātim* letter by letter, from Latin *littera* letter.]

lit·e·ra·ture (lit′ər ə chər, -choor′, lit′rə-) *n.* **1.** writings that have artistic merit rather than didactic or expository value; belles-lettres. **2.** body of writings, as of a particular period, country, language, or style: *children's literature, classical literature, French literature.* **3.** writings dealing with a particular subject: *the literature of science.* **4.** activity or profession of writing. **5.** printed matter of any kind: *The automobile salesman gave us some literature on the latest models.* [Latin *litterātūra* learning, writing, grammar, going back to *littera* letter.]

lith·arge (lith′ärj, li thärj′) *n.* red or yellow oxide of lead. Formula: PbO [Old French *litarge,* from Latin *lithargyrus,* from Greek *lithargyros,* from *lithos* stone + *argyros* silver.]

lithe (līth) *adj.* easily bent; flexible; pliant. Also, **lithe′some.** [Old English *līthe* soft, mild.] —**lithe′ly,** *adv.* —**lithe′ness,** *n.* —**Syn.** see **graceful.**

lith·i·a (lith′ē ə) *n.* white oxide of lithium. Formula: Li₂O [Modern Latin *lithia,* going back to Greek *lithos* stone.]

lith·ic (lith′ik) *adj.* **1.** of or relating to stone. **2.** of, relating to, or containing lithium. [Greek *lithikos* relating to stone, from *lithos* stone.]

lith·i·um (lith′ē əm) *n.* soft, silvery metallic element, lightest of the solid elements. Symbol: Li See **element** for table. [Modern Latin *lithium,* from LITHIA.]

lith·o·graph (lith′ə graf′) *n.* print made by lithography. —*v.t.* to produce or reproduce by lithography. [From LITHOGRAPHY.] —**lith′o·graph′ic;** *also,* **lith′o·graph′i·cal,** *adj.* —**lith′o·graph′i·cal·ly,** *adv.*

li·thog·ra·phy (li thog′rə fē) *n.* art or process of printing from a flat surface, as a smooth stone, on which a design has been drawn with a special grease crayon and to which water and then ink are applied. The ink adheres to the crayon image and is repelled by the moist areas. [Greek *lithos* stone + -GRAPHY.] —**li·thog′ra·pher,** *n.*

lith·o·sphere (lith′ə sfēr′) *n.* crust of the earth. [Greek *lithos* stone + SPHERE.]

Lith·u·a·ni·a (lith′ōō ā′nē ə) *n.* republic of the Soviet Union, in the northwestern part of the country, on the Baltic Sea. Official name: **Lithuanian Soviet Socialist Republic.** Area, 25,200 sq. mi. Pop. (1968 est.), 3,060,000.

Lith·u·a·ni·an (lith′ōō ā′nē ən) *adj.* of or relating to Lithuania, its people, or their language. —*n.* **1.** member or close descendant of the people of Lithuania. **2.** language belonging to the Baltic branch of the Indo-European language family.

lit·i·ga·ble (lit′i gə bəl) *adj.* capable of being made the subject of a lawsuit.

lit·i·gant (lit′i gənt) *n.* party to a lawsuit: *Neither litigant was pleased with the judge's ruling.* —*adj.* engaged in a lawsuit.

lit·i·gate (lit′i gāt′) *v.t.* to make the subject of a lawsuit. —*v.i.* to engage in a lawsuit. [Latin *lītigātus,* past participle of *lītigāre* to dispute, from *līs* lawsuit, quarrel + *agere* to drive.] —**lit′i·ga′tor,** *n.*

lit·i·ga·tion (lit′i gā′shən) *n.* **1.** act or process of engaging in a lawsuit. **2.** lawsuit.

li·ti·gious (li tij′əs) *adj.* **1.** of or relating to lawsuits. **2.** inclined to engage in lawsuits; fond of litigation. [Latin *lītigiōsus* contentious, from *lītigium* dispute.]

lit·mus (lit′məs) *n.* dye obtained from any of various lichens, which turns blue in alkaline solutions and red in acid solutions. [Old Norse *litmosi* herbs for dyeing, from *litr* color + *mosi* moss.]

litmus paper, paper impregnated with litmus, used as a chemical indicator.

li·tre (lē′tər) *British.* liter.

---

at; āpe; cär; end; mē; it; īce; hot; ōld; fôrk; wood; fōōl; oil; out; up; ūse; turn; sing; thin; this; zh in treasure; ə in ago, taken, pencil, lemon, circus.

lit·ter (lit'ər) *n.* **1.** accumulation of things scattered about carelessly; rubbish; mess. **2.** young produced by an animal at one birth. **3.** loose straw, hay, or similar material used as bedding for animals. **4.** vehicle consisting of a couch usually enclosed by curtains and carried on men's shoulders or by animals. **5.** stretcher for carrying a sick or injured person. —*v.t.* **1.** to make disordered or untidy by scattering things about carelessly: *to litter a park with bottles.* **2.** to scatter carelessly. **3.** to give birth to (young). **4.** to provide (animals) with litter for bedding. —*v.i.* **1.** to scatter things about carelessly. **2.** to give birth to a litter: *The cat littered last night in the garage.* [Old French *litiere* bed, material for bedding, going back to Latin *lectus* bed.]

Litter *(def. 4)*

lit·te·ra·teur (lit'ər ə tur') *also,* **lit·té·ra·teur.** *n.* literary man. [French *littérateur*, from Latin *litterātor* critic, grammarian.]

lit·ter·bug (lit'ər bug') *n.* one who litters public places.

lit·tle (lit'əl) less or less·er or lit·tler, least or lit·tlest. *adj.* **1.** small in size: *the little finger.* **2.** short in extent or duration; brief: *a little trip, a little while.* **3.** small in amount or degree; not much: *a little water.* **4.** not of great importance or interest; trivial: *Your problems seem very little.* **5.** lacking in force or intensity; weak: *The child had a plaintive little voice.* **6.** lacking in or having little power or influence: *the little people in society.* **7.** ignoble or petty in nature; mean; narrow: *They are bigoted men with pathetically little minds.* **8.** charming or endearing: *She had the sweetest little smile!* —*adv.,* less, least. **1.** to a small extent; not much; slightly: *He liked her very little.* **2.** not at all: *He little imagined the consequences.* ▲ used before a verb. —*n.* **1.** small amount: *I'll have a little.* **2.** short time or distance: *He walked a little down the road.* **3.** in little. on a small scale. **4.** by little. by slow degrees; gradually. **5. to make little of.** to treat as unimportant; disparage. **6. to think little of. a.** to regard as insignificant. **b.** to have no hesitation about. [Old English *lȳtel* small, few, trivial.] —**lit'tle·ness,** *n.*

Little Bighorn, river in northern Wyoming and southern Montana near the site of the battle in which General George Custer and his entire body of troops were killed by Indians in 1876.

Little Dipper, group of stars in the constellation Ursa Minor, which forms the outline of a dipper.

Little League, baseball league for boys under thirteen years of age.

lit·tle·neck (lit'əl nek') *n.* young of the quahog clam, *Venus mercenaria,* usually served on the half shell and eaten raw.

Little Rock, capital and largest city of Arkansas, in the central part of the state. Pop. (1970), 132,483.

little slam, winning of twelve tricks in a round of bridge.

little theater, amateur theater group established by a community or college for the production of live drama.

lit·to·ral (lit'ər əl) *adj.* of or relating to a shore. —*n.* region lying along the shore. [Latin *litorālis* relating to the seashore, from *litus* seashore.]

li·tur·gi·cal (li tur'ji kəl) *adj.* **1.** of or relating to liturgies. **2.** of or relating to the liturgy or communion service. Also, **li·tur'gic.** —**li·tur'gi·cal·ly,** *adv.*

lit·ur·gy (lit'ər jē) *pl.,* **-gies.** *n.* in various churches, the prescribed form of public worship, esp. the communion service. [Late Latin *litūrgia* the service of the Mass, from Greek *leitourgiā* public service, public worship.]

liv·a·ble (liv'ə bəl) *also,* **live·a·ble.** *adj.* **1.** fit to live in; habitable: *Now that the house is clean, it is livable again.* **2.** worth living; endurable.

live¹ (liv) lived, liv·ing. *v.i.* **1.** to be alive; have life: *His grandfather lived during the Civil War.* **2.** to continue to exist; remain alive: *to live through a famine.* **3.** to support oneself: *to live on one's income.* **4.** to subsist; feed: *to live on fruit.* **5.** to make one's abode: *to live in the city.* **6.** to pass or conduct one's life: *to live well.* **7.** to get the fullest enjoyment from life: *After his twenty-first birthday, he really began to live.* **8.** to persist in memory or remain in use: *These books will live throughout the ages.* **9. to live and let live.** to be tolerant, as of the behavior, customs, or beliefs of others. **10. to live in.** (of domestic help) to reside where one works. **11. to live out.** (of domestic help) to reside away from where one works. **12. to live up to.** to abide by: *She tries to live up to her ideals. He will live up to his end of the bargain.* **13. to live with.** to bear with; endure: *to live with one's mistakes.* —*v.t.* **1.** to pass (one's life): *The young heiress lived a life of luxury.* **2.** to practice or express in one's life: *to live one's philosophy.* **3. to live down.** to live so as to atone for or remove the effects of (a crime or mistake). **4. to live it up.** *Informal.* to have a very good time. [Old English *lifian, libban* to have life, pass life, maintain life.]

Syn. *v.i.* **1.** Live, exist mean to have being. Live means to have life and be capable of vital functions, as an animal or plant: *Man cannot live without oxygen.* Exist means to be real as an independent entity in the objective world of space and time: *Many forms of life exist in the ocean.*

live² (līv) *adj.* **1.** possessing life; living: *The hunter brought back a live elephant.* **2.a.** of or relating to the living state or a living being: *a live voice.* **b.** filled with life; energetic; lively: *She is a vital, live woman.* **3.** of present interest or importance; timely: *a live topic.* **4.** burning: *a live coal.* **5.** containing an explosive charge: *live ammunition.* **6.** carrying electrical current: *live wire.* **7.** seen or presented while actually occurring, as on the stage, or on radio or television: *a live performance, a live broadcast.* **8.** having or imparting movement: *a live pulley.* **9.** in the natural state, without having been quarried or mined: *live rock.* **10.** *Printing.* ready to be used, as type, plates, or copy. [Short for ALIVE.]

lived (līvd, livd) *adj.* having a life or lives. ▲ used in combination, as in *long-lived.*

live·li·hood (līv'lē hood') *n.* that which serves to maintain or support life: *Selling newspapers is his livelihood.* [Modification (influenced by LIVELY and -HOOD) of Middle English *livelode* course of life, maintenance, going back to Old English *līf* life + *lād* course.]

live·long (liv'lông') *adj.* whole; entire: *the livelong night.*

live·ly (līv'lē) -li·er, -li·est. *adj.* **1.** full of life, energy, or movement; vigorous; active: *a lively walk.* **2.** gay; sprightly: *a lively tune.* **3.** stimulating; exciting: *a lively debate.* **4.** characterized by or indicative of mental keenness, brilliance, or creativity: *a lively imagination.* **5.** intensely felt or perceived; vivid; striking: *a lively fear, lively colors.* **6.** fresh; invigorating: *a lively breeze.* **7.** springing back quickly; resilient: *a lively tennis ball.* —*adv.* in a lively manner; energetically; vigorously: *to step lively.* [Old English *līflīc* living, vital.] —**live'li·ness,** *n.*

liv·en (lī'vən) *v.t., v.i.* to make or become more cheerful, active, or exciting (usually with *up*).

live oak (līv) evergreen oak, *Quercus virginiana,* found in the southeastern United States.

liv·er¹ (liv'ər) *n.* **1.** large, reddish-brown gland that secretes bile and performs metabolic functions. It is the largest gland in the human body. **2.** liver of certain other vertebrate animals, used as food. [Old English *lifer.*]

liv·er² (liv'ər) *n.* one who lives in a certain manner: *a fast liver, an easy liver.* [LIVE¹ + -ER¹.]

liver fluke, any of various parasitic flatworms, esp. *Fasciola hepatica,* that invade the liver and bile ducts.

liv·er·ied (liv'ər ēd, liv'rēd) *adj.* dressed in livery.

Liv·er·pool (liv'ər pool') *n.* port city in western England. Pop. (1968), 688,000.

Liv·er·pud·li·an (liv'ər pud'lē ən) *n.* inhabitant or native of Liverpool.

liv·er·wort (liv'ər wurt') *n.* **1.** any of various primitive, mosslike plants, class Hepaticae, found throughout the world, growing mostly in damp, shady areas. **2.** hepatica.

liv·er·wurst (liv'ər wurst', -woorst') *n.* sausage made of or consisting mostly of liver, esp. pork liver. [Partial translation of German *Leberwurst,* from *Leber* liver + *Wurst* sausage.]

liv·er·y (liv'ər ē, liv'rē) *pl.,* **-er·ies.** *n.* **1.** uniform provided for male servants. **2.** any distinctive garb or uniform worn by members of a group or profession. **3.** characteristic dress or outward appearance. **4.** stabling and feeding of horses for pay. **5.** livery stable. [Old French *livree* something delivered (as a servant's clothes), from *livrer* to deliver, from Late Latin *līberāre* to give freely, from Latin *līberāre* to set free.]

liv·er·y·man (liv'ər ē mən, liv'rē-) *pl.,* **-men.** *n.* one who owns or works in a livery stable.

livery stable, stable where horses are cared for and let out for hire, with or without vehicles.

lives (līvz) plural of **life.**

live·stock (līv'stok') *n.* domestic animals raised or kept for use or profit, as cattle, sheep, or pigs. ▲ construed as either singular or plural.

live wire (līv) **1.** wire carrying electrical current. **2.** *Informal.* vigorously energetic, forceful, or alert person.

liv·id (liv'id) *adj.* **1.** having a pale coloration, as from strong emotion. **2.** furious; enraged. **3.** having a grayish-blue coloration from a contusion. [Latin *līvidus* bluish.] —**liv'id·ly,** *adv.* —**liv'id·ness,** *n.*

liv·ing (liv'ing) *adj.* **1.** having life; being alive. **2.** of or relating to life, or suitable for life: *Living conditions in the city are sometimes unbearable.* **3.** of or relating to persons now alive: *in living memory.* **4.** still valid, active, or in use: *a living faith, a living language.* **5.** relating to or sufficient for maintaining existence: *a living wage.* **6.** true to life; lifelike: *The boy is the living image of his father.* —*n.* **1.** fact or state

Diaphragm

Liver   Stomach
Small
intestine

Liver

of being alive. **2.** that which serves to maintain or support life; livelihood: *The old man earned his living by selling newspapers.* **3.** manner of life: *clean living, plain living.* **4.** *British.* benefice. **5. the living.** persons now alive.

liv·ing room, room in a home for general family use or for receiving guests.

Liv·ing·stone, David (liv′ing stən) 1813–73, Scottish missionary and explorer in Africa.

Li·vo·ni·a (li vō′nē ə) *n.* city in southeastern Michigan, a residential suburb of Detroit. Pop. (1970), 110,109.

Li·vor·no (lē vôr′nō) *n. Italian.* Leghorn.

li·vre (lē′vər, -vrə) *n.* former coin of France, replaced by the franc. [French *livre* pound¹, unit of money, from Latin *lībra* pound¹, scales.]

Liv·y (liv′ē) *n.* 59 B.C.–A.D. 17, Roman historian; born Titus Livius.

liz·ard (liz′ərd) *n.* any of a group of scaly reptiles, suborder Sauria, typically having a long, narrow body, four legs, and a tapering tail, found in tropical and temperate regions. [Old French *lesard*, from Latin *lacertus.*]

Lju·blja·na (lū′blä nä) *n.* city in northwestern Yugoslavia. Pop. (1965), 182,000.

ll., lines.

LL, Late Latin.

lla·ma (lä′mə) *pl.* **-mas** or **-ma.** *n.* cud-chewing, South American mammal, *Lama glama*, related to the camel, having a thick, woolly coat and used chiefly as a pack animal. Height: 4 feet at the shoulder. [Spanish *llama*; of Quechuan origin.]

Llama

lla·no (lä′nō) *pl.* **-nos.** *n.* level grassland or plain, found esp. in South America. [Spanish *llano* level field, level, from Latin *plānus* level.]

LL.B., Bachelor of Laws.

LL.D., Doctor of Laws.

Lloyd George, David (loid′ jôrj′) 1863–1945, British statesman.

lo (lō) *interj.* look; see: *Lo and behold!* [Old English *lā.*]

loach (lōch) *n.* any of a group of freshwater fish, family Cobitidae, found in inland waters of Europe and Asia. [Old French *loche;* of uncertain origin.]

Loach

load (lōd) *n.* **1.** something that is carried by a vehicle, as a truck, or borne by a man or animal. **2.** amount or quantity that can be carried by any of these means, taken as a unit of measure. **3.** something wearisome, oppressive, or grievous: *a load of sorrow, a load of guilt.* **4.** amount of work a person or machine is expected to do: *The secretary's typing load was twenty letters a day.* **5.** weight or pressure supported by a structure or part. **6.** charge for a firearm. **7.** external resistance overcome by an engine or other power source. **8. loads.** *Informal.* a great quantity or number: *My sister has loads of friends.* **9. to get a load of.** *Slang.* to look at or listen to. —*v.t.* **1.** to put a load on or in: *to load a shelf with books.* **2.** to place (something) on or in a conveyance: *to load cattle in a boxcar.* **3.** to weigh down; oppress: *The city council loaded the community with taxes.* **4.** to supply abundantly or in excess: *Relatives loaded him with gifts when he graduated.* **5.** to alter or add weight to, esp. in order to deceive or commit fraud: *The manufacturer loaded his product with inferior materials.* **6.** to slant so as to prejudice the response or outcome: *to load a question, to load evidence.* **7.a.** to place something, as film or a tape cartridge, into (an apparatus, as a camera or tape recorder). **b.** to place (something, as film or a tape cartridge) into: *He loaded the film into the camera.* **8.** to place a charge in (a firearm). —*v.i.* **1.** to put on or take on a load: *The workmen have finished loading. This camera loads easily.* **2.** to place a charge in a firearm: *The soldiers loaded and fired.* **3.** to enter: *The people loaded into the elevator.* [Old English *lād* way, journey, carrying.] —**load′er,** *n.*

Syn. *n.* **1. Load, freight, cargo** designate goods in transit. **Load** designates a burden carried by whatever means: *In some countries mules are used to transport loads.* **Freight** specifically applies to commodities and merchandise hauled over a long distance: *That truck is carrying freight from New York to San Francisco.* **Cargo** is restricted to freight or lading carried by ship or aircraft: *That ship is carrying a cargo of wheat to India.*

load·ed (lō′did) *adj.* **1.** carrying a load: *The cart was loaded with fruit.* **2.** holding something, as film or ammunition: *a loaded gun.* **3.** altered or weighted, as fraudulent dice. **4.** slanted so as to prejudice the response or outcome: *a loaded question.* **5.** *Slang.* intoxicated. **6.** *Slang.* extremely wealthy.

load·star (lōd′stär′) lodestar.

load·stone (lōd′stōn′) lodestone.

loaf¹ (lōf) *pl.*, **loaves.** *n.* **1.** bread molded and baked as one mass. **2.** any molded portion of food: *a meat loaf, a sugar loaf.* [Old English *hlāf* loaf or bread.]

loaf² (lōf) *v.i.* **1.** to spend time doing nothing; idle: *My lazy brother loafs all day.* **2.** to work lazily or inefficiently. —*v.t.* to spend (time) doing nothing (often with *away*): *The old man loafed the afternoon away.* [Possibly from LOAFER.]

loaf·er (lō′fər) *n.* **1.** one who loafs; idler. **2.** casual, moccasinlike shoe made to slip onto the foot easily. [Possibly shortened and modified form of German *Landläufer* vagabond.]

loam (lōm) *n.* **1.** soil that is a mixture of clay, sand, and silt. It often contains much organic matter. **2.** mixture of clay, sand, and straw used in making bricks and molds and in plastering walls. —*v.t.* to cover, fill, or coat with loam. [Old English *lām* clay, earth.] —**loam′i·ness,** *n.* —**loam′y,** *adj.*

loan (lōn) *n.* **1.** act or instance of lending. **2.** something lent, esp. a sum of money lent at interest. **3. on loan.** borrowed, as from a museum, for use or display at another location. —*v.t., v.i.* to lend. [Old Norse *lān* a lending.]

loan shark *Informal.* one who lends money at an excessive rate of interest.

loan word *also,* **loan-word, loan·word.** word taken into one language from another. *Pizza, blitz,* and *menu* are loan words. [Translation of German *Lehnwort.*]

loath (lōth, lō*th*) *also,* **loth.** *adj.* reluctant; unwilling: *The young man was loath to serve in the army.* [Old English *lāth* hateful, hostile.]

loathe (lō*th*) **loathed, loath·ing.** *v.t.* to regard with extreme disgust or hate; show repugnance for; detest. [Old English *lāthian* to be hateful.] —**Syn.** see hate.

loath·ing (lō′*th*ing) *n.* extreme disgust; repugnance; detestation. —**loath′ing·ly,** *adv.*

loath·ly¹ (lō*th*′lē, lōth′-) *adj.* loathsome. [Old English *lāthlīc.*]

loath·ly² (lō*th*′lē, lōth′-) *adv.* unwillingly. [Old English *lāthlīce* dreadfully, shockingly.]

loath·some (lō*th*′səm, lōth′-) *adj.* extremely disgusting; repulsive; offensive. —**loath′some·ly,** *adv.* —**loath′some·ness,** *n.*

loaves (lōvz) plural of **loaf¹.**

lob (lob) **lobbed, lob·bing.** *Tennis. v.t.* to hit (a ball) high and far to the back of the opponent's court. —*n.* ball hit in such a manner. [Possibly of Low German origin.]

lo·bar (lō′bər) *adj.* of or relating to a lobe, as of the lungs: *lobar pneumonia.*

lo·bate (lō′bāt) *adj.* having or resembling a lobe.

lo·ba·tion (lō bā′shən) *n.* lobe or lobate formation.

lob·by (lob′ē) *pl.,* **lob·bies.** *n.* **1.** entrance hall, as in an apartment house, hotel, or theater. **2.** person or group of persons who seek to influence legislators in their voting. —*v.i.* **lob·bied, lob·by·ing.** to try to influence legislators in their voting to favor some special group or interest. —*v.t.* to promote the passage of (legislation) by lobbying. [Medieval Latin *lobia* covered walk, portico; of Germanic origin.]

lob·by·ist (lob′ē ist) *n.* one who seeks to influence legislators in their voting to favor a special group or interest. —**lob′by·ism,** *n.*

lobe (lōb) *n.* rounded division or projection, as of a bodily organ, leaf, or external ear. [Late Latin *lobus* hull, pod, from Greek *lobos* lobe of the ear, liver¹, or lung.]

lobed (lōbd) *adj.* having a lobe or lobes.

lo·bel·ia (lō bēl′yə) *n.* any of a large group of plants, genus *Lobelia*, found in many parts of the world, having oval or lance-shaped leaves and showy, blue, red, white, or yellow flowers. [Modern Latin *Lobelia*, from Matthias de Lobel, 1538–1616, Flemish botanist.]

lob·lol·ly (lob′lol′ē) *pl.,* **-lies.** *n.* **1.** thick mud; mire; swamp. **2.** loblolly pine. [Of uncertain origin.]

loblolly pine **1.** evergreen tree, *Pinus taeda,* of the pine family, growing in the southern United States. **2.** the wood of this tree.

lo·bot·o·my (lō bot′ə mē) *pl.,* **-mies.** *n.* operation in which the nerve connections between one lobe of the brain and lower brain centers are cut.

lob·ster (lob′stər) *n.* **1.** any of several edible saltwater crustaceans having five pairs of walking legs, including one pair of large pincer claws, and a hard, mottled, dark-green body, esp. the American lobster, *Homarus americanus,* found in North Atlantic waters. **2.** spiny lobster. [Old English *loppestre* saltwater crustacean, from Latin *locusta* saltwater crustacean, locust.]

Lobster

lobster pot, slatted, wooden trap, with cord funnels baited at either end, used to catch lobsters.

lob·ule (lob′ūl) *n.* **1.** small lobe. **2.** subdivision of a lobe.

lo·cal (lō′kəl) *adj.* **1.** of or relating to a particular place: *the local newspaper, local politics.* **2.** limited or restricted; narrow: *The writer's fame is local rather than national.* **3.** (of a means of public transportation) stopping at all stations: *a local subway.* **4.** relating to or affecting a particular part or organ of the body: *a local inflammation, local anesthesia.* **5.** of or relating to position in space: *The poet's pen . . . gives to airy nothing a local habitation and a name* (Shakespeare, *A Midsummer Night's Dream*). —*n.* **1.** train, bus, or other means of public transportation that stops at all the stations along its route. **2.** branch or chapter of an organization, esp. a labor union. [Late Latin *locālis* relating to a place, from Latin *locus* place.] —**lo′cal·ly,** *adv.*

local color, character or atmosphere of a particular place or period, as found in works of literature.

lo·cale (lō kal′) *n.* a particular place, esp. with reference to events or circumstances connected with it. [French *local* place, relating to a place, from Late Latin *locālis.* See LOCAL.]

local government 1. control or authority over the local affairs of a county, town, or other small political unit held by its own people. **2.** elected officials of a county, town, or other small political unit.

lo·cal·ism (lō′kə liz′əm) *n.* **1.** word, idiom, or manner of speech peculiar to a particular place. **2.** provincialism.

lo·cal·i·ty (lō kal′ə tē) *pl.* **-ties.** *n.* place, region, or district and its surroundings.

lo·cal·ize (lō′kə līz′) **-ized, -iz·ing.** *v.t.* **1.** to restrict to a particular place: *to localize an inflammation.* **2.** to assign to a particular place; find the place of origin of: *to localize the folk song.* —**lo′cal·i·za′-tion,** *n.*

local option, right of a local government to allow or prohibit something, as the sale and distribution of liquor.

lo·cate (lō′kāt, lō kāt′) **-cat·ed, -cat·ing.** *v.t.* **1.** to discover the exact place of: *The police were able to locate the lost child.* **2.** to assign a particular place to; fix the position of: *The captain located the ship's position on the chart.* **3.** to establish in a particular place; settle: *The company located its branch office in the suburbs.* —*v.i.* to establish oneself in a particular place; settle. [Latin *locātus,* past participle of *locāre* to place, put.] —**lo·cat′a·ble,** *adj.* —**lo′cat·er,** *n.*

lo·ca·tion (lō kā′shən) *n.* **1.** act of locating; being located. **2.** exact position; place: *the location of the thief's hide-out.* **3.** place where something, as a store, factory, or home, might be established; site: *a perfect location for a drugstore.* **4.** place away from a motion-picture studio, used in filming.

loc·a·tive (lok′ə tiv) *n.* **1.** *Grammar.* case in Latin and certain other Indo-European languages that indicates the place in which someone or something is located. **2.** word or construction in this case. —*adj.* of, relating to, or designating this case. [From Latin *locus* place, on the model of VOCATIVE.]

loc. cit., in the place cited. [Abbreviation of Latin *locō citātō.*]

loch (lok, loкн) *n. Scottish.* **1.** lake. **2.** narrow arm of the sea, esp. one partially landlocked. [Gaelic *loch* lake.]

lo·ci (lō′sī) plural of **locus.**

lock¹ (lok) *n.* **1.** mechanical device used to fasten something, as a door. **2.** any device that fastens or secures something in place, as a brake to keep a wheel from turn-

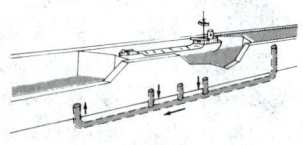

Lock¹ *(def. 3)*

ing. **3.** enclosure in a canal or other waterway with gates at each end, in which the water level can be changed to raise or lower vessels. **4.** mechanism in a gun that explodes the charge. **5.** any of several holds in wrestling. **6. lock, stock, and barrel.** *Informal.* entirely; completely. **7. under lock and key.** securely confined or put away. —*v.t.* **1.** to fasten or secure with a lock or locks: *Don't forget to lock the door.* **2.** to shut up or confine securely (often with *up*): *She locked herself in her room. The guards locked the prisoners up.* **3.** to join or link together firmly: *He locked his arm in hers.* **4.** to grip firmly, as in an embrace. **5. to lock out. a.** to shut out by or as if by locking. **b.** to keep (employees) from working by closing a plant or business. —*v.i.* **1.** to become fastened or secured with a lock or locks: *The house was locked up when we left.* **2.** to become joined or linked together firmly: *The bumpers of the two cars locked.* [Old English *loc* door fastener, bolt¹.]

lock² (lok) *n.* **1.** tuft or strand of hair; tress. **2. locks.** the hair of the head. **3.** tuft of wool, cotton, or flax. [Old English *locc* tress.]

lock·age (lok′ij) *n.* **1.** operation of a lock or locks in a canal during the passage of a vessel. **2.** toll for such passage.

Locke, John (lok) 1632–1704, English philosopher.

lock·er (lok′ər) *n.* **1.** enclosed compartment, as a cabinet or chest, that can be locked. **2.** refrigerated compartment used to store frozen foods. **3.** one who or that which locks.

locker room, room in a building, as in a gymnasium or clubhouse, equipped with lockers.

lock·et (lok′it) *n.* small case holding a picture, a lock of hair, or other keepsake, usually worn on a necklace. [Old French *loquet* door latch, diminutive of Old French *loc* latch; of Germanic origin.]

lock·jaw (lok′jô′) *n.* tetanus.

lock·out (lok′out′) *n.* closing of a plant or a business by an employer until certain conditions are met by employees.

lock·smith (lok′smith′) *n.* one who makes, installs, and repairs locks.

lock step, marching step in which each person follows exactly the step of the person ahead of him.

lock stitch, stitch made by a sewing machine in which two threads are interlocked at short intervals.

lock·up (lok′up′) *n.* **1.** jail. **2.** act of locking up; being locked up.

lo·co (lō′kō) *pl.* **-cos.** *n.* locoweed. —*adj. Informal.* crazy; insane. [Spanish *loco* insane; of uncertain origin.]

lo·co·mo·tion (lō′kə mō′shən) *n.* act or capability of moving from place to place. [Latin *locō,* ablative of *locus* place + MOTION.]

lo·co·mo·tive (lō′kə mō′tiv) *n.* self-propelled vehicle used to haul railroad cars. —*adj.* of, relating to, or capable of locomotion.

lo·co·mo·tor (lō′kə mō′tər) *adj.* of or relating to locomotion.

locomotor ataxia, disease of the spinal cord and other parts of the nervous system, usually caused by syphilis and characterized by loss of muscular control, atrophy of certain muscles and nerves, and sharp pains.

lo·co·weed (lō′kō wēd′) *n.* any of several plants of the pea family, genera *Astragalus* and *Oxytropis,* found in the Rocky Mountain and prairie regions of the western United States, containing a poison that is harmful to animals. Also, **lo′co.** [Spanish *loco* insane (of uncertain origin) + WEED¹.]

lo·cum te·nens (lō′kəm tē′nənz) *pl.* **lo·cum te·nen·tes** (lō′kəm tə nen′tēz). *n. British.* one who substitutes for another, esp. for a doctor or a clergyman. [Medieval Latin *locum tenens* deputy; literally, one holding the place (of another), going back to Latin *locus* place + *tenēre* to hold.]

lo·cus (lō′kəs) *pl.* **lo·ci.** *n.* **1.** place. **2.** *Mathematics.* any set of points that satisfies one or more specified conditions. [Latin *locus* place.]

lo·cust (lō′kəst) *n.* **1.** any of several short-horned grasshoppers, family Locustidae, often migrating in large swarms, which destroy much of the vegetation in their paths. **2.** any of certain cicadas, esp. the seventeen-year locust. **3.** any of a group of North American shrubs and trees, genus *Robinia,* having compound leaves and showy clusters of flowers. **4.** any of various related trees, as the honey locust. [Latin *locusta* grasshopper; locust.]

lo·cu·tion (lō kū′shən) *n.* **1.** form of verbal expression; phrase. **2.** style or manner of verbal expression; phraseology. [Latin *locūtiō* way of speaking, speech.]

lode (lōd) *n.* deposit containing valuable minerals, often found in a rock fissure. [Old English *lād* way, course.]

lode·star (lōd′stär′) *also,* **load·star.** *n.* **1.** star that serves as a guide to navigators. **2.** Polaris. **3.** focus of attention or hopes; guiding principle. [Middle English *lodesterre,* from *lode* way, course (from Old English *lād*) + *sterre* star. See STAR.]

lode·stone (lōd′stōn′) *also,* **load·stone.** *n.* variety of magnetite possessing the qualities of a magnet.

lodge (loj) *n.* **1.** small house, cabin, or hut, often secluded and of rustic appearance, used esp. as a temporary abode during a vacation or hunting trip. **2.** small house or cottage on the grounds of a park or estate: *caretaker's lodge.* **3.a.** branch of a fraternal or secret society. **b.** meeting place for such a branch. **4.** hut or dwelling of a North American Indian. **5.** den of certain wild animals, esp. beavers. —*v.t.* **lodged, lodg·ing. 1.** to provide with a temporary place to stay, as for the night. **2.** to rent a room or rooms to: *The widow lodged students in her home.* **3.** to bring formally to an authority: *to lodge a complaint in court.* **4.** to fix, settle, or embed: *to lodge an arrow in a tree.* **5.** to place for safekeeping: *to lodge money in a bank.* **6.** to confer (authority or power) on; vest (with *with* or *in*). —*v.i.* **1.** to have a temporary place to stay: *He lodged with friends for the night.* **2.** to occupy a rented room or rooms. **3.** to be deposited or embedded: *A pebble lodged in his shoe.* [Old French *loge* shed, small house; of Germanic origin.]

Lodge, Henry Cabot (loj) 1850–1924, U.S. statesman.

lodg·er (loj′ər) *n.* one who rents a room or rooms, as in a private home.

lodg·ing (loj′ing) *n.* **1.** temporary place to stay, as for the night. **2. lodgings.** rented room or rooms, as in a private home.

lodg·ment (loj′mənt) *also,* **lodge·ment.** *n.* **1.** act of lodging; being lodged. **2.** something deposited or embedded. **3.** *Military.* position gained from the enemy.

Lódź (looj) *n.* city in central Poland, southwest of Warsaw. Pop. (1968 est.), 747,700.

loess (les, lō′əs, lus) *n.* yellowish-brown, very fine-grained deposit of silt, commonly found in river valleys. [German *Löss*, from Swiss German *lösch* loose.]

Lo·fo·ten Islands (lō fōt′ən) group of Norwegian islands off the northwestern coast of Norway. Land area, approx. 475 sq. mi.

loft (lôft) *n.* **1.** upper story of a building, as a warehouse, often used as a storeroom or workroom. **2.** room or space directly beneath a roof; attic. **3.** gallery in a hall or church: *a choir loft.* **4.** hayloft. **5.** *Golf.* **a.** backward angle of a club's face that enables the golfer to hit the ball so that it rises in an arc. **b.** stroke that accomplishes this. —*v.t.* **1.** to hit (a golf ball) so that it rises in an arc. **2.** to store in a loft. —*v.i.* to hit a golf ball in an arc. [Old Norse *lopt* sky, upper room.]

loft·y (lôf′tē) loft·i·er, loft·i·est. *adj.* **1.** extending to a great height; towering: *We stood in awe of the lofty redwood trees.* **2.** exalted in dignity, rank, character, or quality: *lofty ideals.* **3.** having or showing excessive pride; haughty: *The lofty looks of man shall be humbled* (Isaiah 2:11). —**loft′i·ly,** *adv.* —**loft′i·ness,** *n.* —**Syn. 1.** see **high.**

log¹ (lôg, log) *n.* **1.** unhewn portion of wood cut from a tree. **2.a.** official daily record of the voyage of a ship. **b.** book in which such a record is kept. **3.** record of the flight of an aircraft. **4.** device for measuring the speed of a ship. —*v.t.,* **logged, log·ging. 1.** to cut down trees on (an area of land). **2.** to cut (trees) into logs. **3.** to record in a log. —*v.i.* **1.** to cut down trees, cut them into logs, and transport the logs to a sawmill. [Of uncertain origin.]

log² (lôg) *n.* logarithm.

lo·gan·ber·ry (lō′gən ber′ē) *pl.,* **-ries.** *n.* **1.** tart, reddish-purple fruit of the shrub *Rubus ursinus,* widely grown in the western United States. **2.** thorny shrub bearing this fruit. [From James H. *Logan,* 1841–1928, American judge who first grew this shrub.]

log·a·rithm (lô′gə rith′əm, log′ə-) *n.* exponent indicating the power to which a base must be raised in order to produce a given number. The logarithm of 9 to the base 3 is 2. [Modern Latin *logarithmus,* from Greek *logos* word, reckoning, ratio + *arithmos* number.]

log·a·rith·mic (lô′gə rith′mik, log′ə-) *adj.* of or relating to a logarithm or logarithms. Also, **log·a·rith′mi·cal.**

log·book (lôg′book′, log′-) *n.* log¹ *(def. 4).*

loge (lōzh) *n.* **1.** seating area in a theater, consisting of the first few rows of the lowest balcony. **2.** box in a theater. [French *loge* small house, box at a theater; of Germanic origin.]

log·ger (lô′gər, log′ər) *n.* **1.** one who logs; lumberjack. **2.** machine for handling logs.

log·ger·head (lô′gər hed′, log′ər-) *n.* **1.** large-headed saltwater turtle, genus *Caretta,* whose flesh and eggs are valued as food. It may weigh as much as 850 pounds and have a flipper spread of nine feet. Also, **loggerhead turtle. 2.** stupid person; blockhead. **3. at loggerheads.** engaged in a dispute. [Possibly from dialectal English *logger* block of wood used as a hobble for horses (from LOG¹) + HEAD.]

log·gia (loj′ə, loj′ē ə; *Italian* lōd′jä) *pl.,* **log·gias** or *(Italian)* **log·gie** (lōd′jä). *n.* open gallery whose roof is supported by an arcade or colonnade. [Italian *loggia,* from French *loge* small house; of Germanic origin.]

log·ging (lô′ging, log′ing) *n.* work of chopping down trees, cutting them into logs, and transporting the logs to a sawmill.

Loggia

log·ic (loj′ik) *n.* **1.** science of correct reasoning. **2.** system or method of reasoning: *the logic of Aristotle.* **3.** sound thinking; reason: *There is much logic in what he says.* **4.** agreement between parts or elements found in something, as in a series of events or in a work of art. [Late Latin *logica* art of reasoning, from Greek *logikē,* going back to *logos* word, reason.]

log·i·cal (loj′i kəl) *adj.* **1.** of, relating to, or in accordance with logic: *a logical inference, a logical explanation.* **2.** following as a natural consequence; reasonably expected: *a logical conclusion.* **3.** capable of reasoning correctly: *a logical mind.* —**log′i·cal·ly,** *adv.*

lo·gi·cian (lō jish′ən) *n.* one who is skilled in logic.

lo·gis·tic (lō jis′tik) *adj.* of or relating to logistics. Also, **lo·gis′ti·cal.**

lo·gis·tics (lō jis′tiks) *n.pl.* branch of military science concerned with the movement, procurement, and maintenance of equipment, facilities, and personnel. ▲ construed as singular. [French *logistique,* from *logis* lodging, from *loger* to lodge, from *loge* small house; with reference to finding quarters for soldiers. See LODGE.]

log·jam (lôg′jam′, log′-) *n.* **1.** mass of floating logs that have become so pressed together that they cannot move. **2.** blockage.

log·o·type (lō′gə tīp′, log′ə-) *n.* piece of type on which the letters of a word or syllable, as a trademark, are cast. [Greek *logos* word, speech + TYPE.]

log·roll (lôg′rōl′, log′-) *v.t.* to procure passage of (a bill) by logrolling. —*v.i.* to take part in logrolling. —**log′roll′er,** *n.*

log·roll·ing (lôg′rō′ling, log′-) *n.* **1.** political bargaining among legislators who trade favors. **2.** sport in which two men stand on and rotate a floating log, each trying to get the other off balance and into the water. **3.** act of rolling logs.

log·wood (lôg′wood′, log′-) *n.* **1.** spiny tropical evergreen tree, *Haematoxylon campechianum,* found esp. in Central America, having leaves composed of leaflets and bearing clusters of yellow flowers. **2.** wood of this tree, which yields a purplish-red dye.

lo·gy (lō′gē) -gi·er, -gi·est. *adj.* acting or moving slowly; heavy; sluggish. [Possibly from Dutch *log* heavy, cumbersome + -Y¹.]

-logy combining form **1.** study or science of: *astrology, theology, paleontology.* **2.** saying; speaking: *tautology.* [Greek *-logiā.*]

loin (loin) *n.* **1.** *usually,* **loins.** part of the body of man or a quadruped between the thorax and the pelvis. **2.** cut of meat from this part with the flank removed. See **beef** for illustration. **3. loins.** lower part of the abdomen and groin considered as the seat of physical strength or generative power. **4. to gird up one's loins.** to prepare for strenuous activity. [Old French *loigne* the part of the body, going back to Latin *lumbus.*]

loin·cloth (loin′klôth′) *n.* piece of cloth, skin, or other material worn around the hips and loins.

Loire (lwär) *n.* longest river of France, flowing from the south-central part of the country into the Bay of Biscay.

loi·ter (loi′tər) *v.i.* **1.** to linger idly or aimlessly about a place. **2.** to move sluggishly or with frequent pauses: *With weary steps I loiter on* (Tennyson, 1850). —*v.t.* to waste (time); dawdle (with *away*): *The young man loitered away the hours.* [Possibly from Middle Dutch *loteren* to delay.] —**loi′ter·er,** *n.*

Lo·ki (lō′kē) *n.* Norse Mythology. god of fire, strife, and evil, who provoked conflict among the gods.

loll (lol) *v.i.* **1.** to recline or lean in a careless, lazy, or relaxed manner: *The children lolled about on the park bench.* **2.** to hang down loosely; droop: *The weary animal's tongue lolled out.* —*v.t.* to allow to hang down; let droop. —*n.* act of lolling. [Possibly imitative.]

lol·li·pop (lol′ē pop′) *also,* **lol·ly·pop.** *n.* piece of candy placed on the end of a stick. [Possibly from dialectal English *lolly* tongue (of uncertain origin) + POP¹.]

Lom·bard (lom′bärd, -bərd, lum′-) *n.* **1.** member of a Germanic tribe that invaded Italy in the sixth century A.D. and founded the kingdom of Lombardy. **2.** native or inhabitant of Lombardy.

Lom·bar·dy (lom′bər dē, lum′-) *n.* leading industrial and commercial region of Italy, in the northern part of the country. Area, 9191 sq. mi. Pop. (1965 est.), 7,941,200.

Lombardy poplar, tall, slender, columnar or spire-shaped poplar, *Populus nigra,* variety *italica.*

Lo·mé (lō mā′) *n.* capital, largest city, and chief commercial center of Togo. Pop. (1968 est.), 90,600.

Lon·don (lun′dən) *n.* **1.** capital and leading city of the United Kingdom and of the Commonwealth of Nations, in southeastern England, on the Thames. Pop. (1968 est.), 7,763,800. **2. City of.** small section of London, on the north bank of the Thames, that is the financial and commercial center. Area, approx. 1 sq. mi. Pop. (1965), approx. 5000. Also, **the City. 3.** city in southeastern Canada, in Ontario. Pop. (1968), 194,416. **4. Jack.** 1876–1916, U.S. novelist and short-story writer.

London broil, flank steak that is broiled and thinly sliced.

Lon·don·der·ry (lun′dən der′ē) *n.* port city in northwestern Northern Ireland. Pop. (1966), 55,694.

Lon·don·er (lun′də nər) *n.* native or inhabitant of London.

lone (lōn) *adj.* **1.** without companions; alone; solitary: *a lone traveler.* **2.** standing apart from others; isolated: *a lone castle.* **3.** only; sole: *a lone request.* **4.** single or widowed: *lone women.* [Short for ALONE.] —**Syn. 1.** see **alone. 3.** see **only.**

lone·ly (lōn′lē) -li·er, -li·est. *adj.* **1.** without friendship or companionship; solitary; lone: *a lonely old man.* **2.a.** depressed from lack of friendship or companionship; lonesome: *The young boy felt very lonely in the new school.* **b.** causing such depression: *a lonely room, a lonely evening.* **3.** lacking people; unfrequented; deserted: *a lonely road.* —**lone′li·ness,** *n.*

lone·some (lōn′səm) *adj.* **1.** depressed from lack of friendship or companionship. **2.** causing such depression. **3.** unfrequented; deserted: *a lonesome road.*

long¹ (lông) long·er (lông′gər), long·est (lông′gist). *adj.* **1.** having great extension in space; of considerable length: *He has long arms.* **2.** having great duration: *That was a long performance.* **3.** having a specified dis-

tance or duration: *The road is only two blocks long. The program was an hour long.* **4.** containing many units or entries: *She prepared a long list of rules.* **5.** exceeding in quantity a standard or average, as a long dozen, containing thirteen rather than twelve. **6.** seemingly prolonged; dull; tedious: *It's been a long day.* **7.** having an abundant supply of (with on): *He was long on humorous anecdotes.* **8.** extending far into the past or future: *John has a long memory.* **9.** (of vowels) relatively prolonged in duration, as the *e* in *be.* **10.** *Finance.* holding large amounts of some commodity or stock in anticipation of a rise in prices. —*adv.* **1.** for an extended period: *He did not stay long.* **2.** throughout the length of; for the specified period of: *He works all day long.* **3.** far from the time indicated: *long after, long ago.* **4.** as long as. *See:* *I'll go as long as you are going too.* —*n.* **1.** a long time. **2.** long vowel. **3.** before long. soon. **4. the long and the short of.** the sum total; substance of. [Old English *lang, long* extended, not short.]

long² (lông) *v.i.* to have a strong or persistent desire; wish earnestly; yearn: *I long to see her again.* [Old English *langian.*]

long., longitude.

Long Beach, seaport and resort city in southwestern California, bordering Los Angeles. Pop. (1970 est.), 358,633.

long·boat (lông'bōt') *n.* largest boat carried by a sailing ship.

long·bow (lông'bō') *n.* large bow drawn by hand, used by the English during the Middle Ages as a major military weapon.

long-dis·tance (lông'dis'təns) *adj.* **1.** covering a long distance: *a long-distance runner, a long-distance mover.* **2.** connecting distant locations: *a long-distance call.* —*adv.* by long-distance telephone.

long distance, operator or exchange that handles long-distance telephone calls.

long-drawn (lông'drôn') *adj.* prolonged. Also, **long'-drawn'-out'**.

lon·gev·i·ty (lon jev'ə tē) *n.* long life. [Late Latin *longaevitās,* going back to Latin *longus* long + *aevum* age.]

Long·fel·low, Henry Wadsworth 1807–82, U.S. poet.

long·hair (lông'hâr') *Informal. adj.* **1.** of, relating to, or characteristic of an intellectual or his taste. **2.** of or relating to classical music. Also, **long'-haired'.** —*n.* an intellectual.

long·hand (lông'hand') *n.* writing by hand in which the words are written out in full. Opposed to **shorthand.**

long·head·ed (lông'hed'id) *adj.* **1.** *Anthropology.* having a long head. **2.** discerning; shrewd; far-sighted.

long·horn (lông'hôrn') *n.* one of a breed of long-horned cattle of Spanish origin, formerly widely raised in the southwestern United States.

long·house, communal dwelling of the Iroquois and certain other Indian tribes.

long·ing (lông'ing) *n.* strong or persistent desire; yearning. —*adj.* feeling or expressing such a desire. —**long'ing·ly,** *adv.*

long·ish (lông'ish) *adj.* somewhat long.

Long Island, long, narrow island in southeastern New York State, south of Connecticut. Area, 1682 sq. mi. Pop. (1970), 7,115,137.

Long Island Sound, arm of the North Atlantic separating Connecticut from Long Island.

lon·gi·tude (lon'jə tōōd', -tūd') *n.* **1.** distance on the earth's surface, measured in degrees east and west of the prime meridian and expressed by imaginary lines from the North Pole to the South Pole. **2.** *Astronomy.* distance measured eastward on the ecliptic from the vernal equinox. [Latin *longitūdō* length.]

lon·gi·tu·di·nal (lon'jə tōōd'-ən əl, -tūd'-) *adj.* **1.** of or relating to longitude. **2.** running lengthwise: *a longitudinal cross section.* —**lon'-gi·tu'di·nal·ly,** *adv.*

long-lived (lông'līvd', -livd') *adj.* living or lasting a long time: *a long-lived illness.*

Long Parliament, English Parliament that was formed under Charles I in 1640, dissolved by Oliver Cromwell in 1653, and restored from 1659 to 1660.

long-play·ing (lông'plā'ing) *adj.* of or relating to a phonograph record played at 33⅓ revolutions per minute.

long-range (lông'rānj') *adj.* **1.** for or involving the future: *long-range plans.* **2.** capable of firing over long distances: *long-range guns.*

long·shore·man (lông'shôr'mən) *pl.,* **-men.** a man employed in loading and unloading ships. [Short for ALONGSHORE + MAN.]

long shot 1. entry in a contest or race considered to have little chance of winning. **2.** venture promising great rewards but having little chance

of success. **3.** television or motion-picture shot taken at some distance from the subject.

long-stand·ing (lông'stan'ding) *adj.* lasting a long time: *a long-standing friendship.*

long-suf·fer·ing (lông'suf'ər ing) *adj.* enduring wrongs, trouble, or pain patiently for a long time. —*n.* long and patient endurance of wrongs, trouble, or pain.

long suit 1. largest suit held in a hand in card games. **2.** valuable quality or ability; that in which one excels.

long-term (lông'turm') *adj.* **1.** planned for or involving a long period of time, as a project. **2.** requiring payment after a long period of time, as a loan.

long ton, ton (def. 1b.).

long-wind·ed (lông'win'did) *adj.* **1.** speaking or writing at a great length: *The long-winded politician spoke for seven hours.* **2.** tediously long and wordy: *a long-winded speech.* **3.** capable of sustained effort or activity without loss of breath. —**long'-wind'ed·ly,** *adv.* —**long'-wind'ed·ness,** *n.*

long·wise (lông'wīz') *also,* **long·ways** (lông'wāz'). *adv.* lengthwise.

loo (lōō) *n.* card game in which each player who fails to win a trick must pay a specified number of chips into the next pool. [Short for earlier *lanterloo,* from French *lanturelu* originally, the refrain of a seventeenth-century French song.]

look (look) *v.i.* **1.** to exercise the power of sight; use one's eyes; see. **2.** to direct one's eyes: *She looked toward the window.* **3.** to use one's eyes in making a search or examination: *We helped him look for his wallet.* **4.** to gaze or glance in a meaningful way: *She looked lovingly at him.* **5.** to give the impression of being; seem: *She looks tired.* **6.** to turn one's attention or regard; take notice: *We look at this situation in a different light now.* **7.** to face in a certain direction or have a certain view: *The windows looked north. The porch looks onto the neighbor's yard.* —*v.t.* **1.** to have a fitting appearance: *The actor looks the part.* **2.** to direct one's eyes upon or toward: *He looked me straight in the face.* **3.** to express or suggest by one's glance or appearance: *Soft eyes looked love* (Byron, 1811).

to look after, to take care of.
to look back on. to recall.
to look down on. to consider beneath one; regard with contempt.
to look for. to expect: *I'll look for you on Sunday.*
to look forward to. to anticipate happily or eagerly.
to look in. to make a brief visit.
to look into. to make an examination of; investigate.
to look on. a. to be a spectator. **b.** to regard; consider.
to look oneself. to seem to be one's normal self.
to look out. to take care; watch out.
to look out for. to protect.
to look over. to examine, esp. hastily or superficially.
to look to. a. to attend to; take care of. **b.** to depend upon; rely on.
to look up. a. to locate: *He looked up the date in the encyclopedia.* **b.** to pay a visit to: *He looked her up when he got into town.* **c.** *Informal.* to improve: *Business is looking up.*
to look up to. to regard with respect.

—*n.* **1.** act or instance of looking; glance: *Take a look at this car.* **2.** air or appearance: *He has a cheerful look.* **4. looks.** outward appearance: *Charlotte is endowed with good looks.* [Old English *lōcian* to see, direct one's eyes.]

Syn. *v.t.* **2. Look, see¹, watch** mean to exercise the sense of sight. **Look** means to set one's eyes upon something or to direct one's eyes in a particular direction: *He looked me right in the eyes and lied.* **See** means to perceive by means of the eyes and to receive visual impressions: *The blind cannot see anything.* **Watch** means to look at steadily and observe attentively and persistently: *The audience watched the play.*

look·er (look'ər) *n.* **1.** one who looks. **2.** *Slang.* one who is very attractive: *She was a real looker.*

look·er-on (look'ər ôn', -on') *pl.,* **look·ers-on.** *n.* one who looks on; spectator.

looking glass, mirror.

look·out (look'out') *n.* **1.** act of looking out; watch. **2.** place where a watch is kept. **3.** person or group that keeps watch. **4.** *Informal.* matter of interest or concern: *How he solves the problem is his lookout.*

loom¹ (lōōm) *n.* machine for weaving thread into cloth. [Old English *gelōma* tool.]

loom² (lōōm) *v.i.* **1.** to have a large or indistinct appearance: *The tall building loomed in the distance.* **2.** to appear to the mind as large or ominous; stand out prominently or threateningly. [Of uncertain origin.]

loon¹ (lōōn) *n.* any of various web-footed diving birds, genus

Loon

at; āpe; cär; end; mē; it; īce; hot; ōld; fôrk; wood; fōōl; oil; out; up; ūse; turn; sing; thin; this; zh in treasure; ə in ago, taken, pencil, lemon, circus.

North Pole

180° 0°

South Pole

west

Lines of longitude

Gavia, of the Northern Hemisphere, having a slender pointed bill, small pointed wings, and short legs, esp. the **common loon,** *G. immer,* noted for its laughlike call. Length: 26–37½ inches. [Modification of earlier *loom,* from Old Norse *lōmr.*]

loon² (lōōn) *n.* crazy, stupid, or worthless person. [Of uncertain origin.]

loon·y (lōō′nē) **loon·i·er, loon·i·est.** *Informal. adj.* demented; crazy. —*n. pl.,* **loon·ies.** a lunatic. [Short for LUNATIC + -Y¹; influenced by LOON².]

loop (lōōp) *n.* **1.** portion of a string, wire, or other similar material that is doubled over itself, forming an elliptical or circular shape with an opening between the parts. **2.** anything resembling this: *the loop of a planetary orbit, the loop of a river.* **3.** round or bent piece of material, as metal or cord, serving as a hook or ornament: *a belt loop.* **4.** maneuver in which an airplane makes a complete turn in a vertical plane. **5.** closed electrical circuit. **6. the Loop.** commercial center of Chicago. —*v.t.* **1.** to form into a loop or loops. **2.** to furnish with a loop or loops: *The river loops the valley.* **3.** to fasten with by forming into a loop or loops (often with *up*): *to loop a curtain up.* **4.** to encircle with a loop: *He looped his finger with a string.* **5.** to fly (an airplane) in a loop or loops. **6. to loop the loop.** to make loops in the air. —*v.i.* to form a loop or loops. [Of uncertain origin.]

loop·hole (lōōp′hōl′) *n.* **1.** means or method of escape or evasion, esp. one provided by an ambiguity or omission in a law or contract. **2.** small opening in a wall, as the wall of a fortification, through which small arms may be fired or observations may be made. [Earlier *loop* opening (possibly from Middle Dutch *lupen* to watch) + HOLE.]

loose (lōōs) **loos·er, loos·est.** *adj.* **1.a.** not attached firmly or securely; not fastened: *There were several loose pages in the book.* **b.** not set tightly or firmly in position: *The diamond was loose in its setting.* **2.** free from physical restraint; not bound or confined; at liberty: *He got his arm loose from his assailant's grip.* **3.** not fitting tightly or snugly: *She wore loose garments in the summer.* **4.** not taut; slack: *loose reins.* **5.** not tied or joined together: *loose keys.* **6.** not contained in something, as a package or receptacle: *loose candy.* **7.** spread out or apart in arrangement or structure; not compact: *loose gravel, a fabric of loose texture.* **8.** not careful, accurate, or precise: *loose reasoning, a loose translation.* **9.** not under control; unrestrained: *a loose tongue, a loose temper.* **10.** characterized by a lack of moral restraint; dissolute: *a loose person, loose behavior.* —*adv.* in a loose manner. —*n.* **on the loose.** *Informal.* **a.** free from captivity or restraint. **b.** behaving in an unrestrained manner. —*v.t.* **loosed, loos·ing.** **1.** to set free, from bonds or physical restraint; set at liberty: *to loose an animal from a cage.* **2.** to untie; unfasten: *to loose a knot.* **3.** to make less tight; loosen. **4.** to shoot or let fly: *to loose a dart.* [Old Norse *lauss* free, immoral.] —**loose′ly,** *adv.* —**loose′ness,** *n.*

loose-joint·ed (lōōs′join′tid) *adj.* **1.** having joints that are loosely formed. **2.** having limber movement.

loose-leaf (lōōs′lēf′) *adj.* containing or designed to contain specially perforated sheets that may be bound or removed easily.

loos·en (lōō′sən) *v.t.* **1.** to make less tight: *to loosen a tie.* **2.** to detach by unfastening or by rendering loose: *to loosen a stone in a wall.* **3.** to spread out or separate elements of (a substance); make less compact: *to loosen the soil, to loosen the weave of a fabric.* **4.a.** to lessen or remove restraints upon: *to loosen the tongue.* **b.** to relax the severity or strictness of: *to loosen discipline.* —*v.i.* to become loose or looser. —**loos′en·er,** *n.*

loose-strife (lōōs′strīf′) *n.* any of various plants, genus *Lysimachia,* having flowers that are usually yellow or white. [Translation of Latin *lysimachia,* going back to Greek *Lysimachos* name of its discoverer, from *lysis* loosing + *machē* strife.]

loot (lōōt) *n.* **1.** valuables seized by thieves in a robbery. **2.** valuables taken from an enemy during a war; booty; plunder. —*v.t.* **1.** to rob by force, as during a war; plunder: *The soldiers looted the town.* **2.** to rob by fraud; expropriate; embezzle: *The politicians looted the city treasury.* **3.** to carry off as loot: *Robbers broke into John's apartment and looted all of his belongings.* —*v.i.* to engage in plunder; take booty: *The officers could not keep the soldiers from looting when they reached the city.* [Hindi *lūt* plunder, from Sanskrit *lōtra* booty.] —**loot′er,** *n.*

lop¹ (lop) **lopped, lop·ping.** *v.t.* **1.** to cut off or remove as unnecessary (often with *off*): *The woodsman lopped the dead branches from trees.* **2.** to cut off parts, as branches, from: *to lop trees.* [Of uncertain origin.]

lop² (lop) **lopped, lop·ping.** *v.t., v.i.* to hang or let hang loosely; droop. [Possibly imitative.]

lope (lōp) **loped, lop·ing.** *v.t., v.i.* to run or cause to run with a long, easy, often bounding stride: *The dog and his owner could be seen loping together in the park.* —*n.* long, easy, often bounding stride. [Old Norse *hlaupa* to leap.] —**lop′er,** *n.*

lop-eared (lop′ērd′) *adj.* having ears that hang down loosely.

lop-sid·ed (lop′sī′did) *adj.* **1.** larger or heavier on one side than the other; not symmetrical. **2.** leaning or slanting to one side. —**lop′-sid′ed·ly,** *adv.* —**lop′sid′ed·ness,** *n.*

lo·qua·cious (lō kwā′shəs) *adj.* characterized by or disposed to excessive talking; talkative. [Latin *loquāc-,* stem of *loquāx* talkative + -OUS.] —**lo·qua′cious·ly,** *adv.* —**lo·qua′cious·ness,** *n.* —Syn. see talkative.

lo·quac·i·ty (lō kwas′ə tē) *n.* act or instance of talking excessively; talkativeness.

lo·quat (lō′kwot, -kwat) *n.* **1.** yellow or orange plumlike fruit of a tree, *Eriobotrya japonica,* of the rose family, having a slightly acid taste and used esp. in preserves. **2.** small evergreen tree, native to Japan and China, cultivated for this fruit. [Chinese (Cantonese) *lō kwat* literally, rush orange.]

Lo·rain (lə rān′) *n.* port city in northern Ohio, on Lake Erie. Pop. (1970), 78,185.

lo·ran (lôr′ən) *n.* navigational system in which the geographical position of a ship or aircraft can be determined by the utilization of signals transmitted by three radio stations. [Abbreviation of *lo(ng) ra(nge) n(avigation).*]

lord (lôrd) *n.* **1.** one who has power or authority over others, as a feudal superior. **2.** *British.* titled nobleman or peer of the realm belonging to the House of Lords. **3. Lord.** *British.* **a.** title or form of address for any of various noblemen or peers of the realm. *The Earl of Arran* would be referred to informally as *Lord Arran.* **b.** title or form of address for certain high churchmen or officials: *Lord Mayor of London, Lord Archbishop of Canterbury.* **4. the Lord. a.** Supreme Being; God. **b.** Jesus Christ. **5. Lords.** House of Lords in the British Parliament. —*v.t.* **to lord it** (over). to behave in a grand, haughty, or domineering manner: *The arrogant man lorded it over everyone he met.* [Old English *hlāford* master, ruler, husband, from *hlāf* loaf + *weard* keeper; referring to the concept in earlier times of the master of a household as the keeper of the loaf of bread of his dependents. See LADY.]

lord·ling (lôrd′ling) *n.* little or insignificant lord.

lord·ly (lôrd′lē) **-li·er, -li·est.** *adj.* **1.** of, relating to, or suited for a lord. **2.** haughty, imperious, or insolent: *Michael's lordly manner and arrogant tone caused most people to dislike him instantly.* —*adv.* in a lordly manner. —**lord′li·ness,** *n.*

Lord's Day *also,* **Lord's day.** Sunday.

lord·ship (lôrd′ship′) *n.* **1.** *also,* **Lordship.** *British.* title used in addressing or referring to a judge or nobleman other than a duke (preceded by *his* or *your*). **2.** rank, power, or authority of a lord. **3.** territory over which a lord holds dominion.

Lord's Prayer, prayer given by Jesus to His Apostles, which begins "Our Father." Also, **Pa′ter·nos′ter.**

Lord's Supper. 1. Last Supper. **2.** Holy Communion; Eucharist.

lore (lôr) *n.* **1.** body of traditional or popular facts or beliefs on a particular subject: *nature lore.* **2.** learning; knowledge: *a man of lore.* [Old English *lār* teaching, doctrine.]

Lor·e·lei (lôr′ə lī′) *n.* *German Legend.* siren of the Rhine who by her song lured sailors to their deaths.

lor·gnette (lôrn yet′) *n.* **1.** pair of eyeglasses or opera glasses held by a short, usually ornate handle. [French *lorgnette* opera glasses, from *lorgner* to leer at, from *lorgne* squinting; of uncertain origin.]

lo·ris (lôr′is) *pl.,* **-ris.** *n.* small, tree-climbing mammal related to the lemur, having a small head, rounded ears, and large eyes. There are two kinds, the **slender loris,** *Loris,* and the **slow loris,** *Nycticebus,* both of Asia. Length: 5–18 inches. [French *loris,* probably from obsolete Dutch *loeris* clown.]

Loris

lorn (lôrn) *adj. Archaic.* bereft of; abandoned; lonely: *She might be despised by my lord's circle, and left lone and lorn* (Hardy, 1876). [Old English *loren,* past participle of *-lēosan* (used only in compounds) to lose.]

Lor·rain, Claude (lō raN′; klôd) 1600–82, French painter of landscapes; born Claude Gellée.

Lor·raine (lə rān′) *n.* region and former province in northeastern France, bordering on Belgium, Luxembourg, and West Germany.

lor·ry (lôr′ē, lor′ē) *pl.,* **-ries.** *n.* **1.** long flat wagon without sides, drawn by a horse. **2.** *British.* truck. [Possibly from dialectal English *lurry* to pull; of uncertain origin.]

lo·ry (lôr′ē) *pl.,* **-ries.** *n.* any of various brightly colored parrots of Australasia having a brushlike tip on the tongue, esp. **Swainson's lory,** *Trichoglossus haematodus.* [Malay *lūrī.*]

Los Al·a·mos (lôs al′ə mōs′) unincorporated community in north-central New Mexico, a major U.S. center for atomic research. Pop. (1970), 11,310.

Los An·ge·les (lôs an′jə ləs, -lēz, ang′gə-) chief port and largest city

---

at; āpe; cär; end; mē; it; īce; hot; ōld; fôrk; wood; fōōl; oil; out; up; ūse; turn; sing; thin; this; zh in treasure; ə in ago, taken, pencil, lemon, circus.   603

of California, in the southwestern part of the state. Pop. (1970 est.), 2,816,061.

lose (lo͞oz) lost, los·ing. *v.t.* **1.** to have no longer because of some act or mishap: *John lost his house in the flood.* **2.** to put in a place afterward forgotten; misplace: *Helen lost her car keys somewhere in her apartment.* **3.** to be deprived of by death: *Mary lost her brother in the war.* **4.** to fail to win: *The army lost the war.* **5.** to fail to preserve or maintain: *Don loses his temper easily.* **6.** to let pass unprofitably or wastefully; fail to take advantage of: *We lost valuable time waiting for him.* **7.** to fail to keep up with, esp. in order to understand or see: *I lost the sense of what he was saying.* **8.** to wander from: *The explorer lost the way in the darkness.* **9.** to allow (oneself) to be engrossed (with *in*): *The young girl lost herself in her reading.* **10.** to leave behind; outdistance: *The deer easily lost the hunters pursuing it.* **11.** to cause the loss of: *The young man's arrogance lost him his friends.* **12.** to be brought to destruction; perish: *The ship was lost in the hurricane.* ▲ used in the passive. —*v.i.* **1.** to suffer loss: *The investors lost heavily when the stock market declined.* **2.** to be defeated: *I usually lose when I play chess.* **3. to lose out.** to fail to get or achieve something contended for: *to lose out in the promotion, to lose out in the election.* **4. to lose out on.** to fail to take advantage of: *He lost out on the special sale because he did not read the advertisement announcing it.* [Old English *losian* to be lost, perish, escape.] —**los′er,** *n.* —**Syn.** *v.t.* **2.** see **misplace.**

los·ing (lo͞o′zing) *adj.* **1.** bringing about a loss: *a losing game.* **2.** that is defeated: *the losing team.* —*n., pl.* **losings.** losses, esp. gambling losses.

loss (lôs) *n.* **1.** act or fact of losing; being lost. **2.** that which is lost, as a person, thing, or amount: *The company's profits greatly outweighed its losses.* **3.** damage or disadvantage that results from losing something. **4. losses.** soldiers lost in action; casualties. **5. at a loss.** puzzled; confused; perplexed: *Her statement left me completely at a loss.* [Probably from *lost,* past participle of LOSE.]

loss leader, item offered for sale by a retail store at a loss to attract customers.

lost (lôst) past tense and past participle of **lose.** *adj.* **1.** that cannot be found; misplaced or missing: *a lost book, a lost dog.* **2.** no longer possessed or used: *a lost fortune, lost youth, lost art.* **3.** not won; defeated. **4.** not used effectively or profitably: *a lost opportunity, a lost weekend.* **5.** having gone astray: *We are lost in the woods.* **6.a.** harmed irreparably; ruined: *lost health, lost reputation.* **b.** utterly immoral; spiritually ruined: *a lost sinner.* **7.** confused; bewildered: *a lost expression.* **8.** engrossed; absorbed (with *in*): *lost in meditation, lost in one's work.* **9.** unable to help oneself: *The woman is lost without her maid.* **10. to be lost to. a.** to be no longer possessed by. **b.** to be no longer possible: *All chance of friendship was lost to him.* **c.** insensible to: *lost to shame.*

lot (lot) *n.* **1.** object used to determine something by chance: *to draw lots.* **2.** casting or drawing of such an object or objects as a means of determining: *to choose by lot.* **3.** choice resulting from this: *The lot fell on John to pay the bill.* **4.** that which one receives in this manner; portion or share. **5.** portion of land, esp. one set aside for a particular purpose: *a building lot.* **6.** motion-picture studio and its property. **7.** portion or way of life believed to be determined by fate: *the difficult lot of the poor.* **8.** item or items separated from others of the same kind for sale or auction: *The first three lots of furniture were sold this morning.* **9.** number of persons or things considered as a unit or group: *They were a sorry lot of workers. Our entire lot of tomatoes spoiled.* **10.** *Informal.* (of a person) a specific type; sort: *Mary's brother is a bad lot.* **11.a.** **lots.** *Informal.* considerable number or amount; great deal: *She bought lots of clothes in New York.* **12. to cast (or throw in) one's lot with.** to associate with and share the fortunes of. —*adv.* considerably; very much: *Hank is a lot taller than his brother.* Also, **lots.** —*v.t.* **lot·ted, lot·ting. 1.** to portion out; allot: *Her uncle's will lotted most of the estate to her.* **2.** to divide (something) into lots —*v.i.* to cast or draw lots. [Old English *hlot* share, object used to determine something by chance.] —**Syn.** *n.* **7.** see **fate.**

Lot (lot) *n.* in the Old Testament, a nephew of Abraham whose wife looked back at the destruction of Sodom and was changed into a pillar of salt.

loth (lōth, lōth) loath.

Lo·thar·i·o (lō thâr′ē ō′) *pl.,* **-thar·i·os.** *n.* libertine; rake. [From *Lothario,* a libertine in *The Fair Penitent,* a play by Nicholas Rowe, 1674–1718, English writer.]

lo·tion (lō′shən) *n.* liquid preparation containing medication or softening agents, used on the skin to heal, soothe, or cleanse. [Latin *lōtiō* a washing.]

lot·ter·y (lot′ər ē) *pl.,* **-ter·ies.** *n.* manner of raising money in which chances are sold and winners are decided by a drawing. [Italian *lotteria,* from *lotto* lot, share. See LOTTO.]

lot·to (lot′ō) *n.* game of chance in which a caller draws numbered disks or balls from a bag and the players cover squares on cards containing the corresponding numbers, the winner being the first player to cover a row of squares. [Italian *lotto* lot, share, from French *lot;* of Germanic origin.]

lo·tus (lō′təs) *pl.* **-tus·es.** *also,* **lo·tos.** *n.* **1.** large, showy flower of any of several plants of the water lily family. One of the best-known species is the **white lotus,** *Nymphaea lotus.* **2.** the plant bearing this flower, having leaves on the surface of water. **3.** any of a small group of shrubby plants, genus *Lotus,* of the pea family. **4.** fruit eaten by the lotus-eaters, thought to be the jujube (def. 2). [Latin *lōtus* name of several plants, from Greek *lōtos;* of Semitic origin.]

Lotus

lo·tus-eat·er (lō′təs ē′tər) *n.* **1.** *Greek Legend.* one of a race of men who ate lotus fruit and led lives of indolence and forgetfulness. **2.** one who leads a life of luxury and indolence.

loud (loud) *adj.* **1.** having great intensity of sound: *a loud cry, a loud noise.* **2.** producing great intensity of sound; resounding: *loud cymbals, a loud voice.* **3.** vehement or insistent: *loud denunciations, loud demands.* **4.** tastelessly bright; garish; flashy: *a loud red automobile.* **5.** obtrusive in appearance or manner: *Joe is a loud, vulgar person.* —*adv.* in a loud manner. [Old English *hlūd* sonorous, strongly audible.] —**loud′ly,** *adv.* —**loud′ness,** *n.*

loud-speak·er (loud′spē′kər) *also,* **loud-speak·er.** *n.* device that transforms a varying electrical signal into sound and amplifies the sound to the desired volume.

lough (lok, lоκн) *n. Irish.* **1.** lake. **2.** arm of the sea.

Lou·is IX (lo͞o′ē, lo͞o′is; *French* lwē) 1214–70, king of France from 1226 to 1270.

Louis XI, 1423–83, king of France from 1461 to 1483.

Louis XIII, 1601–43, king of France from 1610 to 1643.

Louis XIV, 1638–1715, king of France from 1643 to 1715. Also, **Louis the Great.**

Louis XV, 1710–74, king of France from 1715 to 1774.

Louis XVI, 1754–93, king of France from 1774 to 1792.

Louis XVIII, 1755–1824, king of France from 1814 to 1824, successor of Napoleon.

lou·is d'or (lo͞o′ē dôr′) former gold coin of France, used during the seventeenth and eighteenth centuries. Also, **lou′is.** [French *louis d'or* literally, louis of gold, from *Louis* XIII, in whose reign the coin was first issued.]

Lou·i·si·an·a (lo͞o ē′zē an′ə, lo͞o′ə zē-) *n.* state in the southern United States, on the Gulf of Mexico and the Mississippi River. Capital, Baton Rouge. Area, 48,523 sq. mi. Pop. (1970), 3,643,180. Abbreviation, **La.** —**Lou·i′si·an′an, Lou·i′si·an′i·an,** *adj., n.*

Louisiana Purchase, territory purchased by the United States from France in 1803, extending from the Mississippi River to the Rocky Mountains and from Canada to the Gulf of Mexico.

Louis Napoleon, Napoleon III.

Louis Phi·lippe (fi lēp′) 1773–1850, king of France from 1830 to 1848.

Lou·is·ville (lo͞o′ē vil′) *n.* largest city in Kentucky, a port in the northern part of the state, on the Ohio River. Pop. (1970), 361,472.

lounge (lounj) lounged, loung·ing. *v.i.* **1.** to lean, sit, or recline lazily; loll: *The young man lounged on the sofa and watched television.* **2.** to move lazily, listlessly, or unhurriedly: *The bored man lounged about the yard.* **3.** to spend time doing nothing; idle. —*v.t.* to pass (time) by lounging. —*n.* **1.** public room where one may lounge, smoke, relax, or wait, as in a hotel, restaurant, or club. **2.** sofa for reclining, provided with a headrest and sometimes having no back. [Of uncertain origin.] **loung′er,** *n.*

lour (lour) lower².

Lourdes (loord, loordz) *n.* town in southwestern France, site of a Roman Catholic shrine. Pop. (1962), 16,023.

louse (lous) *n. (def. 1)* **lice** or *(def. 2)* **lous·es.** *n.* **1.** any of a large number of tiny wingless insects that live as parasites on birds and mammals. They are divided into two groups, the **biting louse,** order Mallophaga, and the **sucking louse,** order Anoplura, which includes the human **body louse,** *Pediculus humanus.* **2.** *Slang.* a low, contemptible person. —*v.t.,* **loused, lous·ing. 1.** to delouse. **2. to louse up.** *Slang.* to make a mess or muddle of; spoil. [Old English *lūs* the insect.]

lous·y (lou′zē) lous·i·er, lous·i·est. *adj.* **1.** infested with lice. **2.** *Slang.* **a.** disgusting, contemptible: *a lousy trick.* **b.** of wretched quality; terrible: *This is lousy coffee.* **3. lousy with.** *Slang.* well provided with; loaded: *That guy is lousy with money.* —**lous′i·ly,** *adv.* —**lous′i·ness,** *n.*

lout (lout) *n.* awkward, stupid person; oaf. [Possibly from Old Norse *lūtr* bent down.]

at; āpe; cär; end; mē; it; īce; hot; ōld; fôrk; wood; fo͞ol; oil; out; up; ūse; turn; sing; thin; this; zh in treasure; ə in ago, taken, pencil, lemon, circus.

lout·ish (lou′tish) *adj.* resembling a lout; awkward; clumsy. —**lout′ish·ly,** *adv.* —**lout′ish·ness,** *n.*

lou·ver (lōō′vər) *n.* **1.** ventilator placed in a window or other opening, consisting of a series of horizontal slats fitted in a frame. **2.** in medieval architecture, a turret or turretlike structure, as on the roof of a church, that is provided with slanted slats for ventilation. **3.** any ventilating slit, as in the hood of an automobile. [Old French *lov(i)er* skylight; possibly of Germanic origin.]

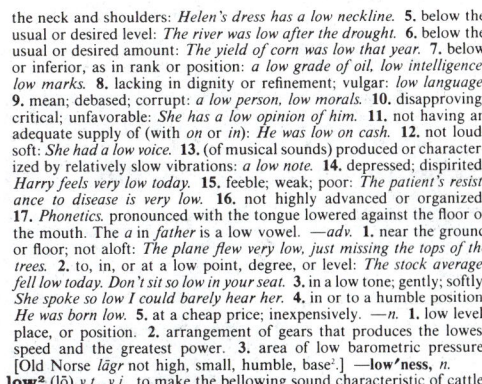

Louver

Lou·vre (lōō′vrə) *n.* art museum in Paris.

lov·a·ble (luv′ə bəl) *adj.* worthy of being loved; endearing. —**lov′a·bil′i·ty, lov′a·ble·ness,** *n.* —**lov′a·bly,** *adv.*

love (luv) *n.* **1.a.** profound affection and deep devotion between persons: *the love of a mother for her child, the love between friends.* **b.** passionate affection arising from sexual desire: *the love of a man for a woman.* **c.** compassion and concern for another or others: *love for one's neighbor, love for mankind.* **2.a.** benevolence and concern of God for His creation. **b.** man's devotion to God. **3.** beloved person; sweetheart. ▲ often used as a term of endearment. **4.** strong liking for: *a love of luxury, a love of traveling.* **5.** sexual relations. **6.** Love. Eros; Cupid. **7.** no points in tennis.
for love. as a favor; for nothing.
for love or money. by any means; at all: *I wouldn't go there for love or money.*
for the love of. for the sake of; in consideration of: *For the love of God, please stop arguing.*
in love. feeling love; enamored.
to fall in love. to become enamored.
to make love. a. to woo or embrace. **b.** to engage in sexual intercourse. —*v.t.,* **loved, lov·ing. 1.** to have a profound affection for and deep devotion to; cherish. **2.** to have a passionate affection for; be in love with. **3.** to have a strong liking for; take great pleasure or interest in: *She loved good books.* **4.** to show affection, as by embracing or caressing. **5.** to thrive upon or flourish in: *Plants love sunlight.* —*v.i.* to be in love. [Old English *lufu* profound affection, attachment.]

love affair, amorous episode or relationship between two lovers.
love apple, *Archaic.* tomato. [Probably a translation of French *pomme d'amour,* from Italian *pomo d'amoro,* alteration of *pomo dei Mori* apple of the Moors; referring to the introduction of the tomato into Italy by the Moors.]
love·bird (luv′burd′) *n.* any of several small parrots, genus *Agapornis,* having predominantly gray or green plumage. It is noted for its affectionate behavior with its mate.
love feast 1. among early Christians, a meal eaten together in token of brotherly love. **2.** religious service in imitation of this, practiced today by some Christians. **3.** banquet or other gathering held to honor someone or promote good will.
love knot, knot tied as a token of love and loyalty.
love·less (luv′lis) *adj.* **1.** untouched by love; void of love. **2.** feeling or expressing no love; unloving. **3.** not loved.
love-lies-bleed·ing (luv′līz′blē′ding) *n.* amaranth, *Amaranthus caudatus,* having spikes of showy, bright-red flowers.
love·lock (luv′lok′) *n.* lock of hair usually tied separately from the rest of the hair, esp. a curl formerly worn by courtiers.
love·lorn (luv′lôrn′) *adj.* abandoned or rejected by one's lover.
love·ly (luv′lē) **-li·er, -li·est.** *adj.* **1.** possessing beautiful qualities, as an attractive appearance or a pleasing personality. **2.** *Informal.* very delightful; enjoyable; pleasing: *What a lovely time!* —**love′li·ness,** *n.* —**Syn.** see beautiful.
love-mak·ing (luv′mā′king) *n.* act of making love.
lov·er (luv′ər) *n.* **1.** one who loves another. **2. lovers.** two people involved in a love affair. **3.** one who has a strong liking for or takes great pleasure or interest in. —**lov′er·ly,** *adj., adv.*
love seat, small sofa seating two persons.
love·sick (luv′sik′) *adj.* **1.** languishing with love. **2.** expressing such feeling: *a lovesick ballad.*
lov·ing (luv′ing) *adj.* feeling or expressing love; affectionate; fond. —**lov′ing·ly,** *adv.*
loving cup 1. large, often inscribed cup, usually with handles, presented as a prize, trophy, or memento. **2.** formerly, a large wine cup passed from person to person.
lov·ing-kind·ness (luv′ing kīnd′nis) *n.* affectionate tenderness and consideration arising from or expressing love.
low¹ (lō) *adj.* **1.** having little vertical extension; rising only slightly above the surface; not high: *A low hedge surrounds the yard.* **2.** located close to the ground or to some other base: *The piano bench was too low and had to be raised. The low branches of the tree were cut off.* **3.** lying below the average or natural level of the ground: *A low valley formed a depression in the otherwise flat plain.* **4.** cut so as to expose

the neck and shoulders: *Helen's dress has a low neckline.* **5.** below the usual or desired level: *The river was low after the drought.* **6.** below the usual or desired amount: *The yield of corn was low that year.* **7.** below or inferior, as in rank or position: *a low grade of oil, low intelligence, low marks.* **8.** lacking in dignity or refinement; vulgar: *low language.* **9.** mean; debased; corrupt: *a low person, low morals.* **10.** disapproving; critical; unfavorable: *She has a low opinion of him.* **11.** not having an adequate supply of (with *on* or *in*): *He was low on cash.* **12.** not loud; soft: *She had a low voice.* **13.** (of musical sounds) produced or characterized by relatively slow vibrations: *a low note.* —*adv.* **1.** near the ground or floor; not aloft: *The plane flew very low, just missing the tops of the trees.* **2.** to, in, or at a low point, degree, or level: *The stock averages fell low today. Don't sit so low in your seat.* **3.** in a low tone; gently; softly: *She spoke so low I could barely hear her.* **4.** in or to a humble position: *He was born low.* **5.** at a cheap price; inexpensively. —*n.* **1.** low level, place, or position. **2.** arrangement of gears that produces the lowest speed and the greatest power. **3.** area of low barometric pressure. [Old Norse *lāgr* not high, small, humble, base².] —**low′ness,** *n.*
low² (lō) *v.t., v.i.* to make the bellowing sound characteristic of cattle; moo. —*n.* such a sound. [Old English *hlōwan* to moo.]
low·born (lō′bôrn′) *adj.* of humble birth.
low·boy (lō′boi′) *n.* low chest of drawers on short legs.
low·bred (lō′bred′) *adj.* of poor breeding or inferior birth; vulgar.
low·brow (lō′brou′) *Informal. n.* one who lacks cultivated tastes or who avoids intellectual pursuits. —*adj.* of, relating to, or suitable for a lowbrow.
Low Church, group in the Anglican Church that minimizes the importance of church authority, liturgy, and sacraments.
low comedy, comedy relying on slapstick and broad humor rather than witty dialogue. Opposed to **high comedy.**
Low Countries, region of northwestern Europe consisting of the countries of the Netherlands, Belgium, and Luxembourg.
low-down (*n.,* lō′doun′; *adj.,* lō′doun′) *n. also,* **low-down.** *Slang.* bare facts; truth. —*adj. Informal.* mean; disgusting; contemptible.
Low·ell (lō′əl) *n.* **1.** James Russell. 1819–91, U.S. poet, essayist, and critic. **2.** city in northeastern Massachusetts. Pop. (1970), 94,239.
low·er¹ (lō′ər) *adj.* **1.** *also,* **Lower.** designating an earlier part of a geological period. **2.** *also,* **Lower.** constituting the branch of a bicameral legislature that is usually the larger and more representative branch, as the House of Commons in the British Parliament. —*v.t.* **1.** to take or bring down; let down: *to lower the flag, to lower a bucket into a well.* **2.** to reduce, as in height, amount, value, or degree: *to lower the water level, to lower prices.* **3.** to lessen the intensity of; diminish the volume of: *He lowered his voice.* **4.** to bring down in value or estimation: *He would be lowering himself if he did that.* **5.** to lessen the force or effectiveness of; weaken: *to lower one's resistance.* —*v.i.* to become lower.
low·er² (lou′ər) *also,* **lour.** *v.i.* **1.** to frown; scowl. **2.** to appear dark, gloomy, or threatening. —*n.* **1.** frown; scowl. **2.** dark, gloomy, or threatening appearance, as in the sky. [Of uncertain origin.]
Lower California, long narrow peninsula in northwestern Mexico, separating the Gulf of California from the Pacific Ocean. Area, 55,634 sq. mi. Also, **Baja California.**
low·er-case (lō′ər kās′) *adj.* of or relating to or printed in small letters. Distinguished from **upper-case.** —*v.t.,* **-cased, -cas·ing.** to set in or print with small letters.
lower case 1. small letters. **2.** type case holding small letters.
low·er-class (lō′ər clas′) *adj.* of or relating to the lower class.
lower class, portion of society, including the working class and the very poor, occupying a social and economic position below that of the middle class.
low·er·most (lō′ər mōst′) *adj.* lowest.
lower world, abode of the dead; Hades.
low frequency, any radio frequency between 30 and 300 kilocycles per second.
Low German 1. form of the German language spoken predominantly in the lowlands of northern Germany. **2.** group of Germanic languages, including Frisian, Dutch, and Flemish, spoken predominantly in the Low Countries.
low-keyed (lō′kēd′) *adj.* characterized by restraint; quiet. Also, **low′-key′.**
low·land (lō′lənd) *n.* land that is on a lower level than the surrounding land. —*adj.* **1.** of, relating to, or characteristic of such land. **2. Lowland.** of or relating to the Scottish Lowlands.
low·land·er (lō′lən dər) *n.* **1.** native or inhabitant of a lowland. **2. Lowlander.** inhabitant of the Lowlands of Scotland.
Low·lands (lō′ləndz) *n.* low region of central Scotland.

at; āpe; cär; end; mē; it; īce; hot; ōld; fôrk; wood; fōōl; oil; out; up; ūse; turn; sing; thin; this; zh in treasure; ə in ago, taken, pencil, lemon, circus.

605

low·ly (lō′lē) -li·er, -li·est. *adj.* **1.** humble in condition or quality; low in rank or importance: *a lowly birth, a lowly cottage, a lowly clerk.* **2.** humble in manner or spirit; meek: *He was a gentle, lowly, and unassuming man.* —*adv.* in a humble manner; humbly; meekly. —**low′·li·ness,** *n.*

Low Mass, simplified form of Mass that is said, not sung, by the celebrant, who is assisted by one or two servers. It is celebrated without the use of choir, music, or incense. Distinguished from **High Mass.**

low·mind·ed (lō′mīn′did) *adj.* having a base or vulgar mind or nature.

low·necked (lō′nekt′) *adj.* (of a garment) cut so as to expose the neck and shoulders; décolleté.

low·pitched (lō′picht′) *adj.* **1.** having a low tone: *The low-pitched, rumbling sound in the tunnel alerted the miners to impending disaster.* **2.** (of a roof) having little slope.

low·pres·sure (lō′presh′ər) *adj.* **1.** having, using, or indicating a low degree of pressure. **2.** having a low barometric pressure. **3.** calm and unhurried; relaxed.

low relief, bas-relief.

low·spir·it·ed (lō′spir′i tid) *adj.* depressed; dispirited.

low tide 1. tide at its lowest level. **2.** time when this level is reached. **3.** lowest point of anything.

low water 1. water that has reached the lowest level, as in a river or stream. **2.** low tide.

low·water mark 1. mark indicating the lowest level reached by a body of water. **2.** lowest point of anything, as a career.

lox¹ (loks) *n.* smoked, heavily cured salmon, usually served with cream cheese and bagels. [Yiddish *laks,* from German *Lachs* salmon.]

lox² (loks) *n.* liquid oxygen, esp. used as an oxidizer in many rocket engines. [Short for *l(iquid) ox(ygen).*]

loy·al (loi′əl) *adj.* **1.** steadfast in one's friendship, devotion, or regard; faithful to one's trust or duty: *He is a loyal friend. The workmen are loyal to their company.* **2.** constant in one's allegiance to one's sovereign, government, or country. **3.** characterized by or expressing loyalty: *a loyal declaration.* [French *loyal* faithful, lawful, from Latin *lēgālis* relating to the law, from *lēx* law. Doublet of LEGAL.] —**loy′al·ly,** *adv.* —**Syn. 1.** see faithful.

loy·al·ist (loi′ə list) *n.* **1.** one who supports the existing sovereign or government, esp. during times of war or revolution. **2.** *also,* **Loyalist.** colonist who remained loyal to the British government during the American Revolution. **3. Loyalist.** one who supported the Republic during the Spanish Civil War.

loy·al·ty (loi′əl tē) *pl.,* -ties. *n.* constant devotion or allegiance; faithful adherence: *loyalty to one's country.*

Syn. Loyalty, fidelity, allegiance denote faithfulness. **Loyalty** refers to devoted, steadfast, and deeply personal attachment or adherence that is secure against wavering and temptation: *The king rewarded the general's loyalty with knighthood.* **Fidelity** denotes faith that is kept against odds and suggests unswerving and tenacious observance of an obligation or trust: *Paul's fidelity to his word made him respected among his friends.* **Allegiance** applies to the compelling and supreme obligation to be faithful, as that of a citizen to a country: *All American citizens swear allegiance to the flag of the United States.*

Loy·o·la, Ignatius (loi ō′lə) Ignatius of Loyola.

loz·enge (loz′inj) *n.* **1.** small tablet of sugar and other flavoring, often containing medicine. **2.** figure having two acute and two oblique angles and four equal sides; diamond. [Old French *losenge* figure or object shaped like a diamond; probably of Celtic origin.]

LP *pl.,* **LPs** or **LP's.** *Trademark.* long-playing record.

LSD, psychedelic drug that produces hallucinations and temporary changes in personality. [Abbreviation of *l(y)s(ergic acid) d(iethylamide).*]

l.t. **1.** local time. **2.** long ton.

Lt., Lieutenant.

Ltd. *British.* limited. Also, **ltd.**

Lu, lutetium.

Lu·an·da (lōō an′də) *n.* port city on the southwestern coast of Africa, the capital and largest city of Angola. Pop. (1966), 225,000.

lu·au (lōō′ou′) *n.* Hawaiian feast. [Hawaiian *lu′au.*]

lub·ber (lub′ər) *n.* **1.** heavy, clumsy, stupid person. **2.** awkward or inexperienced sailor; landlubber. [Possibly of Scandinavian origin.] —**lub′ber·ly,** *adj., adv.*

Lub·bock (lub′ək) *n.* city in northwestern Texas. Pop. (1970), 149,-101.

Lü·beck (lü′bek) *n.* port city in northeastern West Germany. Pop. (1968), 242,427.

Lu·blin (lōō′blin, -blēn) *n.* city in eastern Poland. Pop. (1968), 234,-300.

lu·bri·cant (lōō′brə kənt) *n.* any substance, as oil or grease, used to reduce friction between moving parts of a machine. —*adj.* lubricating.

lu·bri·cate (lōō′brə kāt′) -cat·ed, -cat·ing. *v.t.* **1.** to apply oil, grease,

or other lubricant to the moving parts of a machine in order to reduce friction. **2.** to make slippery or smooth: *to lubricate the skin with oil.* —*v.i.* to act as a lubricant. [Latin *lūbricātus,* past participle of *lūbricāre* to make slippery.] —**lu′bri·ca′tion, lu′bri·ca′tor,** *n.* —**lu′bri·ca′tive,** *adj.*

lu·bric·i·ty (lōō bris′ə tē) *pl.,* -ties. *n.* **1.** state or quality of being slippery; oiliness; smoothness. **2.** elusiveness; instability. **3.** lewdness; lasciviousness. [Medieval Latin *lubricitas* lechery, from Late Latin *lūbricitās* slipperiness, from Latin *lūbricus* slippery.]

lu·bri·cous (lōō′bri kəs) *adj.* **1.** slippery; oily: *a lubricous surface.* **2.** elusive; unstable: *a lubricous mobility, lubricous proof.* **3.** lewd; lascivious. Also, **lu·bri·cious** (lōō brish′əs). [Latin *lūbricus* slippery.]

Lu·bum·ba·shi (lōō′bōōm bä′shē) *n.* city in the southeastern part of the Congo, formerly known as Elisabethville. Pop. (1966 est.), 233,-145.

Luc·ca (lōō′kä) *n.* city in north-central Italy, an artistic center during the Middle Ages and Renaissance. Pop. (1968 est.), 74,200.

lu·cent (lōō′sənt) *adj.* **1.** shining; bright; luminous. **2.** translucent. [Latin *lūcēns,* present participle of *lūcēre* to shine.] —**lu′cen·cy,** *n.* —**lu′cent·ly,** *adv.*

lu·cerne (lōō surn′) *n.* *British.* alfalfa. [French *luzerne,* from Provençal *luzerno* glowworm, going back to Latin *lucerna* lamp; referring to its shiny seeds.]

Lu·cerne (lōō surn′) *n.* **1.** resort city in central Switzerland. Pop. (1969), 73,000. Also, *German,* **Lu·zern′.** **2.** Lake of. large lake in central Switzerland.

Lu·cian (lōō′shən) *n.* A.D. c.120–180, Greek satirist.

lu·cid (lōō′sid) *adj.* **1.** easily understood; fully intelligible; clear: *a lucid explanation.* **2.** rational; sane: *a lucid person, lucid reasoning.* **3.** transparent: *the pure and lucid mountain air.* **4.** shining; bright; luminous. [Latin *lūcidus* bright, shining.] —**lu·cid′i·ty, lu′cid·ness,** *n.* —**lu′cid·ly,** *adv.*

Lu·ci·fer (lōō′sə fər) *n.* **1.** rebellious angel, identified with Satan, cast out of heaven with his followers. **2.** planet Venus when it appears as the morning star. **3. lucifer.** friction match. [Latin *lūcifer* light-bringing, the planet Venus, from *lūx* light + *ferre* to bring.]

Lu·cite (lōō′sīt) *n. Trademark.* transparent, acrylic resin available in solid or liquid form and having many uses, as in light fixtures. [Latin *lūc-,* stem of *lūx* + -ITE¹.]

luck (luk) *n.* **1.a.** unpredictable factor influencing events or circumstances for good or ill. **b.** events or circumstances so influenced: *His life has been filled with bad luck.* **2.** success: *She had no luck in finding her glasses.* **3. to be down on one's luck.** *Informal.* to experience bad luck. **4. to be in luck.** to have good luck. **5. to be out of luck.** to have bad luck. [Middle Dutch *luc* good fortune.] —**Syn. 1.a.** see chance.

luck·i·ly (luk′ə lē) *adv.* with or by a stroke of good luck.

luck·less (luk′lis) *adj.* not having good luck; unlucky.

Luck·now (luk′nou) *n.* city in north-central India. Pop. (1969), 763,-604.

luck·y (luk′ē) luck·i·er, luck·i·est. *adj.* **1.** having good luck; fortunate. **2.** occurring happily or fortunately. **3.** thought to bring good luck. —**luck′i·ness,** *n.*

lu·cra·tive (lōō′krə tiv) *adj.* yielding profit; profitable: *a lucrative business.* [Latin *lucrātīvus,* going back to *lucrum* gain.] —**lu′cra·tive·ly,** *adv.* —**lu′cra·tive·ness,** *n.*

lu·cre (lōō′kər) *n.* monetary gain. [Latin *lucrum.*]

Lu·cre·tius (lōō krē′shəs) *n.* 99–55 B.C., Roman poet.

lu·cu·brate (lōō′kyə brāt′) -brat·ed, -brat·ing. *v.i.* **1.** to write or study laboriously, esp. at night. **2.** to write in a learned or pedantic manner. [Latin *lūcubrātus,* past participle of *lūcubrāre* to work by lamplight at night.]

lu·cu·bra·tion (lōō′kyə brā′shən) *n.* **1.** laborious writing or study, esp. done late at night. **2.** elaborately written and pedantic literary work. [Latin *lūcubrātiō* a working at night.]

Lu·cul·lus (lōō kul′əs) *n.* c.117–c.56 B.C., Roman general known for his lavish banquets and his patronage of literature. —**Lu·cul′lan,** *adj.*

lu·di·crous (lōō′də krəs) *adj.* worthy of or arousing derisive laughter; laughable; ridiculous: *The old woman looked ludicrous dressed in her daughter's clothes.* [Latin *lūdicrus* sportive, playful, from *lūdus* sport, play.] —**lu′di·crous·ly,** *adv.* —**lu′di·crous·ness,** *n.*

luff (luf) *n.* **1.** sailing of a ship closer to the wind. **2.** forward edge of a fore-and-aft sail. —*v.i.* to turn the bow of a ship nearer to the wind, so that the sails flap and do not fill with air. [Old French *lof* device to change the course of a ship; of Germanic origin.]

Luft·waf·fe (lōōft′vä′fə) *n. German.* German air force under the Nazis.

lug¹ (lug) lugged, lug·ging. *v.t.* to pull or carry with effort: *John lugged the heavy trunk three blocks.* —*v.i.* to pull or tug. [Probably of Scandinavian origin.]

lug² (lug) *n.* **1.** projecting part by which something is gripped or held. **2.** heavy nut fitting over a large bolt, used esp. to attach a wheel to an

at; āpe; cär; end; mē; it; īce; hot; ōld; fôrk; wood; fōōl; oil; out; up; ūse; turn; sing; thin; this; zh in treasure; ə in ago, taken, pencil, lemon, circus.

automobile axle. Also, **lug nut. 3.** *Slang.* clumsy, doltish person. [Of uncertain origin.]

lug³ (lug) *n.* lugsail.

lug·gage (lug′ij) *n.* bags, boxes, trunks, or suitcases used by a traveler for transporting belongings. [LUG¹ + -AGE.]

lug·ger (lug′ər) *n.* small boat having two or three masts and rigged with lug-sails.

lug nut, lug² (*def. 2*).

lug·sail (lug′sāl′, -səl) *n.* four-sided sail without a boom, held by a yard that hangs obliquely to the mast. Also, **lug.** [Dialectal English *lug* pole (of uncertain origin) + SAIL.]

lu·gu·bri·ous (loo goo′brē əs, -gū′-) *adj.* excessively mournful or sorrowful. [Latin *lūgubris* mournful + -OUS.] —**lu·gu′bri·ous·ly,** *adv.* —**lu·gu′bri·ous·ness,** *n.*

Lugger

lug·worm (lug′wurm′) *n.* marine worm, genus *Arenicola,* having tufted gills in two rows on its back, that burrows in the sand along the seashore. [Of uncertain origin.]

Luke (look) *n.* **1.** one of the four Evangelists, a physician, a companion of the Apostle Paul, and the reputed author of Acts. **2.** third Gospel of the New Testament, attributed to him.

luke·warm (look′wôrm′) *adj.* **1.** moderately warm; tepid: *lukewarm bath water.* **2.** having or expressing little warmth or enthusiasm; lacking zeal; indifferent: *He is not an ardent reformer, but a lukewarm conformist.* [Dialectal English *luke* (of uncertain origin) + WARM.] —**luke′warm·ly,** —**luke′warm′ness,** *n.* —**Syn. 2.** see half-hearted.

lull (lul) *v.t.* **1.** to calm with soothing sounds or caresses: *The sound of the rain lulled me to sleep.* **2.** to calm by deception: *He was lulled into a false sense of security.* —*v.i.* to become calm; diminish in force gradually. —*n.* **1.** brief calm or period of quiet. **2.** brief lessening or cessation of activity: *There was a lull in business.* [Imitative.]

lul·la·by (lul′ə bī′) *pl.* **-bies.** *n.* song sung to lull a child to sleep.

lum·ba·go (lum bā′gō) *n.* pain in the region of the back between the chest cavity and the pelvis. [Late Latin *lumbāgō,* from Latin *lumbus* loin.]

lum·bar (lum′bər) *adj.* of, relating to, or near the loins. —*n.* lumbar vertebra, artery, nerve, or the like. [Modern Latin *lumbaris,* from Latin *lumbus* loin.]

lumb·er¹ (lum′bər) *n.* **1.** timber cut as planks and boards. **2.** useless articles, as old furniture or worn-out household items, taking up space. —*v.i.* to cut timber into lumber and prepare it for market. —*v.t.* **1.** to cut down the trees in: *to lumber a forest.* **2.** to cut down (trees) for lumber. **3.** to take up space or encumber (something, as a room) with useless articles. [Possibly from obsolete *lombard* pawnshop, from French *Lombard* a Lombard, through Late Latin; of Germanic origin; with reference to the importance of the Lombards as pawnbrokers and to their use of pawnshops as storage places for miscellaneous articles pledged for loans.]

lum·ber² (lum′bər) *v.i.* to move in a clumsy or noisy manner: *The old wagon lumbered down the dirt road.* [Possibly of Scandinavian origin.]

lum·ber·ing¹ (lum′bər ing) *n.* business of cutting down trees and cutting them into lumber for market. [LUMBER¹ + -ING¹.]

lum·ber·ing² (lum′bər ing) *adj.* moving in a clumsy or noisy manner. [LUMBER² + -ING².]

lum·ber·jack (lum′bər jak′) *n.* one who cuts down trees and prepares logs for transportation to the sawmill.

lum·ber·man (lum′bər man′) *pl.,* **-men.** *n.* **1.** lumberjack. **2.** one who works in or manages a lumberyard.

lum·ber·yard (lum′bər yärd′) *n.* business concern that sells lumber.

lu·men (loo′mən) *pl.,* **-mens** or **-mi·na** (-mə nə) *n.* unit of luminous flux equal to the amount of light falling on one square unit of surface area, of which each point is at a distance of one unit from a light source with an intensity of one candle. [Latin *lūmen* light.]

lu·mi·nar·y (loo′mə ner′ē) *pl.,* **-nar·ies.** *n.* **1.** one who is recognized as preeminent in his field or who is noted for high achievement, as in the world of affairs; notable: *A group of luminaries led the panel discussion.* **2.** light-giving body, esp. the sun or the moon. [Medieval Latin *luminarium* light, lamp, going back to Latin *lūmen* light.]

lu·mi·nes·cence (loo′mə nes′əns) *n.* **1.** emission of visible light without heat, as by means of some chemical reaction or some electrical action within or upon the emitting body. Phosphorescence and fluorescence are two forms of luminescence. **2.** light thus emitted. [Latin *lūmen* light + -ESCENCE.] —**lu′mi·nes′cent,** *adj.*

lu·mi·nif·er·ous (loo′mə nif′ər əs) *adj.* producing or transmitting light. [Latin *lūmen* light + -FEROUS.]

lu·mi·nos·i·ty (loo′mə nos′ə tē) *pl.,* **-ties.** *n.* **1.** quality or condition of being luminous. **2.** something luminous.

lu·mi·nous (loo′mə nəs) *adj.* **1.** emitting light; shining: *luminous flames.* **2.** full of light; bright; resplendent. **3.** clear to the mind; easily understood: *luminous prose.* [Latin *lūminōsus* full of light, from *lūmen* light.] —**lu′mi·nous·ly,** *adv.* —**lu′mi·nous·ness,** *n.* —**Syn. 2.** see bright.

luminous flux, rate of transmission of light energy.

lum·mox (lum′əks) *n.* clumsy, foolish person.

lump¹ (lump) *n.* **1.** solid, usually shapeless piece or mass: *a lump of iron ore, a lump of clay.* **2.** small cube: *a lump of sugar.* **3.** swelling; protuberance: *Jim had a lump on his neck.* **4.** heavy, often dull person. **5. lumps.** deserved rebuke or punishment. **6. a lump in one's throat.** feeling of tightness in the throat, as from emotion. —*adj.* formed or included in a lump. —*v.t.* **1.** to put or bring together, as in one pile or collection. **2.** to consider or deal with as a whole. —*v.i.* to form into lumps; become lumpy. [Of uncertain origin.]

lump² (lump) *v.t. Informal.* to endure despite one's displeasure: *If you don't like it, lump it.* [Of uncertain origin.]

lump·ish (lum′pish) *adj.* **1.** like a lump. **2.** heavy and awkward. **3.** stupid; dull.

lump·y (lum′pē) **lump·i·er, lump·i·est.** *adj.* **1.** covered or filled with lumps: *lumpy oatmeal.* **2.** heavy and awkward; lumpish. —**lump′i·ly,** *adv.* —**lump′i·ness,** *n.*

Lu·na (loo′nə) *n.* Roman goddess of the moon. Her Greek counterpart is Selene. [Latin *lūna* moon.]

lu·na·cy (loo′nə sē) *pl.,* **-cies.** *n.* **1.a.** madness; insanity. **b.** formerly, periodic insanity thought to be caused by changes of the moon. **2.** senseless or reckless conduct; utter folly. [LUNA(TIC) + -CY.]

lu·na moth (loo′nə) *also,* **Luna moth.** large green moth, *Actias luna,* having wings with transparent spots and, on the hind wings, graceful tail-like extensions.

lu·nar (loo′nər) *adj.* **1.** of or relating to the moon: *the lunar orbit.* **2.** measured by the revolutions of the moon. **3.** of, relating to, or containing silver: *lunar crystals.* [Latin *lūnāris* relating to the moon, from *lūna* moon.]

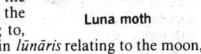

Luna moth

lunar eclipse, see eclipse (*def. 1*).

lunar month, month (*def. 4*).

lunar year, year (*def. 3*).

lu·nate (loo′nāt) *adj.* crescent-shaped. [Latin *lūnātus,* from *lūna* moon.]

lu·na·tic (loo′nə tik) *n.* **1.** insane person. **2.** senseless or reckless person. —*adj.* **1.** insane; crazy. **2.** of or for insane people. **3.** extremely senseless or reckless. [Late Latin *lūnāticus* insane, moonstruck, from *lūna* moon; with reference to the earlier belief that a form of insanity was related to changes of the moon.]

lunatic fringe, members of a movement or society, who express extremist views.

lunch (lunch) *n.* **1.** meal between breakfast and supper, usually eaten around noon. **2.** food prepared for such a meal. —*v.i.* to eat lunch. [Short for LUNCHEON.] —**lunch′er,** *n.*

lunch counter, area where light meals are served, consisting of a counter and a row of stools, found in some retail stores.

lunch·eon (lun′chən) *n.* lunch, esp. a formal one. [Possibly a modification of dialectal English *nuncheon* light noon snack, going back to Old English *nōn* (see NOON) + *scenc* a drink.]

lunch·eon·ette (lun′chə net′) *n.* small restaurant or lunch counter where light meals, esp. breakfast and lunch, are served.

lunch·room (lunch′room′, -room′) *n.* place where light meals are served, esp. a cafeteria in a school or factory.

lune (loon) *n.* crescent-shaped plane figure or figure on the surface of a sphere bounded by two arcs of circles. [Latin *lūna* moon.]

lu·nette (loo net′) *n.* **1.** curved or crescent-shaped window or other opening in a vaulted ceiling or dome. **2.** wall area bounded by the curve of a rounded or pointed arch, often decorated with paintings or sculpture. [French *lunette,* diminutive of *lune* moon, from Latin *lūna.*]

Trachea

Right lung   Cross section of left lung

Bronchial tubes

Lungs (exterior and interior)

lung (lung) *n.* **1.** in many vertebrates, one of a pair of spongy, cone-shaped organs of respiration that supply the blood with oxygen and rid the blood of carbon dioxide. **2.** similar organ in certain inverte-

brates, as the freshwater snail or the land snail. [Old English *lungen* the organ of respiration in vertebrates.]

lunge (lunj) *n.* **1.** any sudden forward movement. **2.** sudden forward thrust, as with a sword. —*v.i.* to make a sudden forward movement. —*v.t.* to thrust or cause to thrust. [Short for obsolete *allonge,* from French *allonger* to lengthen, going back to Latin *ad* to + *longus* extended; referring to the extension of the body when lunging.] —**lung′er,** *n.*

lung·fish (lung′fish′) *pl.* **-fish** or **-fish·es.** *n.* any of several air-breathing fish, order Dipnoi, that inhabit freshwater swamps and marshes in Africa, South America, and Australia, having paired lungs and a brown or tan body with two pairs of ribbonlike fins. Length: 2–4 feet.

lung·wort (lung′wurt′) *n.* any of a small group of plants, genus *Pulmonaria,* found in Europe and Asia, bearing clusters of large blue or purple, funnel-shaped flowers, esp. the **blue lungwort,** *P. officinalis,* grown as a garden plant.

Lu·per·ca·li·a (lōō′pər kā′lē ə) *n.* ancient Roman fertility festival celebrated on February 15.

lu·pine[1] (lōō′pin) *n.* any of a group of plants, genus *Lupinus,* of the pea family, bearing spikes of white, yellow, blue, or purple flowers. [Latin *lupīnum,* from *lupus* wolf; referring to the belief that the plant exhausts the soil.]

lu·pine[2] (lōō′pin) *adj.* **1.** related to the wolf. **2.** of or resembling a wolf; fierce; ravenous. [Latin *lupīnus,* from *lupus* wolf.]

lu·pus (lōō′pəs) *n.* tubercular disease of the skin and mucous membrane. [Latin *lupus* wolf; referring to the resemblance of its sores to wolf bites.]

lurch[1] (lurch) *n.* sudden rolling or swaying to one side or from side to side. —*v.i.* **1.** to move jerkily and unsteadily; stagger. **2.** to roll or sway suddenly to one side or from side to side. [Of uncertain origin.]

lurch[2] (lurch) *n.* **1. to leave in the lurch.** to leave (someone) in a difficult or embarrassing situation. **2.** situation of the loser at the end of various games when he fails to score or is far behind his opponent. [French *lourche* name of a game resembling backgammon; probably of Germanic origin.]

lurch·er (lur′chər) *n.* *Archaic.* petty thief; poacher.

lure (loor) *n.* **1.** powerful or irresistible attraction: *the lure of the unknown.* **2.** that which attracts. **3.** bait, as an artificial fly used in fishing. —*v.t.* to attract; tempt. [Old French *loirre* bait; of Germanic origin.]

lu·rid (loor′id) *adj.* **1.** terrible; sensational; shocking: *a lurid crime.* **2.** shining with a reddish glow or fiery glare: *a lurid fire.* [Latin *lūridus* pale yellow, wan.]

lurk (lurk) *v.i.* **1.** to lie hidden: *The thief lurked in the bushes.* **2.** to move about in a furtive manner; steal; sneak. [Middle English *lurken,* from *luren* to frown; of uncertain origin.]

Lu·sa·ka (lōō sä′kə) *n.* capital and largest city of Zambia, in the south-central part of the country. Pop. (1969), 238,200.

lus·cious (lush′əs) *adj.* **1.** sweet and pleasing to the taste or smell; delicious: *ripe, luscious fruit.* **2.** pleasing to the mind or to the senses. [Possibly a shortening and modification of DELICIOUS.] —**lus′cious·ly,** *adv.* —**lus′cious·ness,** *n.*

lush[1] (lush) *adj.* **1.** rich and abundant; luxuriant: *a lush growth, lush ferns.* **2.** characterized by or covered with luxuriant growth: *land lush with vegetation, lush forests.* **3.** luxurious; sumptuous; rich: *lush velvet wall hangings, a lush carpet.* [Possibly a form of obsolete *lash* soft, watery, from Old French *lasche* slack, loose, from Latin *laxus* loose.] —**lush′ly,** *adv.* —**lush′ness,** *n.*

lush[2] (lush) *n.* *Slang.* one who drinks alcoholic beverages often and to excess. [Of uncertain origin.]

Lu·si·ta·ni·a (lōō′sə tā′nē ə) *n.* ancient Roman province in the Iberian Peninsula, corresponding to most of modern Portugal.

lust (lust) *n.* **1.** intense sexual appetite or desire. **2.** any strong or excessive desire: *a lust for power.* —*v.i.* to have a strong or excessive desire, as a sexual desire (often with *for* or *after*): *to lust after power.* [Old English *lust* pleasure, desire.]

lus·ter (lus′tər) *also, British,* **lus·tre.** *n.* **1.** quality of shining by reflected light; luminous glow; sheen. **2.** radiance; brightness: *the luster of her countenance, the luster of her eyes.* **3.** splendor; glory; renown: *His deeds add much luster to his reputation.* **4.** shiny, often iridescent, metallic glazed surface, as on pottery. **5.** any of several substances, as a polish, used to give a glossy finish or appearance. **6.** fabric that has a glossy appearance. [French *lustre* brightness, from Italian *lustro,* from *lustrare* to illuminate, from Latin *lūstrāre.*]

Syn. 1. Luster, sheen, gloss[1] refer to the quality of being shiny or bright through reflected light. **Luster** refers to luminous brilliance: *Burnished brass has a beautiful luster.* **Sheen** is soft and subdued surface luster: *Her hair has a fine sheen.* **Gloss** is the superficial sheen or glistening brightness of a buffed, polished, or lacquered surface: *Newly waxed floors have a high gloss.*

lus·ter·ware (lus′tər wâr′) *n.* pottery having a shiny, often iridescent, glazed surface.

lust·ful (lust′fəl) *adj.* **1.** full of or characterized by lust. **2.** *Archaic.* lusty; vigorous. —**lust′ful·ly,** *adv.* —**lust′ful·ness,** *n.*

lus·tral (lus′trəl) *adj.* **1.** of, relating to, or used in rites of purification. **2.** occurring every five years. [Latin *lūstrālis,* from *lustrum* rites of purification performed in ancient Rome once in five years.]

lus·trate (lus′trāt) *-trat·ed, -trat·ing. v.t.* to purify by a rite or ceremony. [Latin *lūstrātus,* past participle of *lūstrāre* to illuminate, purify.] —**lus·tra′tion,** *n.*

lus·tre (lus′tər) *British.* luster.

lus·trous (lus′trəs) *adj.* having a glossy surface; shining: *lustrous hair, lustrous fabric.* —**lus′trous·ly,** *adv.*

lus·trum (lus′trəm) *pl.,* **-trums** or **-tra** (-trə) *n.* **1.** purification ceremony performed by the censors for the ancient Roman people every five years. **2.** period of five years. [Latin *lūstrum.*]

lust·y (lus′tē) *lust·i·er, lust·i·est. adj.* **1.** full of strength and vigor; healthy: *a lusty young man.* **2.** strong or abundant: *a lusty wine.* —**lust′i·ly,** *adv.* —**lust′i·ness,** *n.*

lute (lōōt) *n.* stringed musical instrument having a pear-shaped body and a long fretted neck, played with the fingers or a plectrum. [Old French *lëut,* going back to Arabic *al-′ūd* the wood, the lute.]

lu·te·ti·um (lōō tē′shē əm) *n.* heavy, silvery-white metallic element, one of the rare-earth elements. Symbol **Lu** See **element** for table. [Modern Latin *lutetium,* from Latin *Lūtētia* ancient name for Paris, the birthplace of Georges Urbain, 1872–1938, French chemist who discovered the element.]

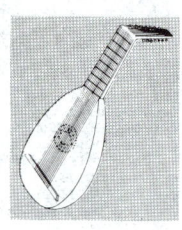

Lute

Lu·ther, Martin (lōō′thər) 1483–1546, German theologian and leader of the Protestant Reformation.

Lu·ther·an (lōō′thər ən) *adj.* of or relating to Luther, his doctrines, or one of the Protestant churches named after him. —*n.* member of a Lutheran Church. —**Lu′ther·an·ism,** *n.*

Lux·em·bourg (luk′səm burg′) *also,* **Lux·em·burg.** *n.* **1.** small country in western Europe, bordering France, Belgium, and West Germany. Capital, Luxembourg. Area, 998 sq. mi. Pop. (1969 est.), 337,-000. **2.** capital and chief city of Luxembourg, in the south-central part of the country. Pop. (1968), 77,458.

Lux·or (luk′sôr) *n.* town in Egypt, on the Nile River, noted for the ancient temples and burial grounds found nearby.

lux·u·ri·ance (lug zhoor′ē əns, luk shoor′-) *n.* state or quality of being luxuriant. Also, **lux·u′ri·an·cy.**

lux·u·ri·ant (lug zhoor′ē ənt, luk shoor′-) *adj.* **1.** thick or abundant: *luxuriant hair, a luxuriant growth.* **2.** rich or excessive: *a luxuriant imagination, luxuriant decoration.* **3.** producing in great abundance: *luxuriant soil.* [Latin *luxuriāns,* present participle of *luxuriāre* to abound.] —**lux·u′ri·ant·ly,** *adv.*

lux·u·ri·ate (lug zhoor′ē āt′, luk shoor′-) *-at·ed, -at·ing. v.i.* **1.a.** to indulge oneself in pleasure or luxury; live luxuriously. **b.** to take great delight (with *in* or *on*): *They luxuriated in their power.* **2.** to grow in great abundance: *The plants luxuriated in the warm, moist climate.* [Latin *luxuriātus,* past participle of *luxuriāre* to abound.]

lux·u·ri·ous (lug zhoor′ē əs, luk shoor′-) *adj.* **1.** given to pleasure or luxury: *a luxurious people, luxurious tastes.* **2.** characterized by luxury: *a luxurious mansion, luxurious decorations.* —**lux·u′ri·ous·ly,** *adv.* —**lux·u′ri·ous·ness,** *n.*

lux·u·ry (luk′shər ē, lug′zhər ē) *pl.,* **-ries.** *n.* **1.** that which is conducive to one's comfort or pleasure: *She filled her home with such luxuries as Persian carpets.* **2.** indulgence in that which gives comfort or pleasure. [Latin *luxuria* excess, abundance, extravagance.]

Lu·zern (lōō tsern′) *German.* Lucerne.

Lu·zon (lōō zon′) *n.* largest and northernmost island of the Philippines. Area, 40,420 sq. mi. Pop. (1960), 11,736,300.

Lvov (lə vôf′) *n.* city in the southwestern part of the Soviet Union, in the Ukraine. Pop. (1964 est.), 487,000. Also, *Polish,* **Lwów** (lvōōf); *German,* **Lem′berg.**

-ly[1] *suffix* (used to form adverbs) **1.** in a particular manner or to a particular extent: *gladly, greatly.* **2.** in a particular position or at a particular time: *secondly, hourly.* [Old English *-līce.*]

-ly[2] *suffix* (used to form adjectives) **1.** like, of the nature of, or suited to: *brotherly, princely.* **2.** occurring at specified periods of time: *weekly.* [Old English *-līc.*]

ly·can·thrope (lī′kən throp′, lī kan′throp) *n.* werewolf. [Greek *lykanthropos,* from *lykos* wolf + *anthropos* man.]

ly·cée (lē sā′) *pl.,* **-cées** (-sāz′, -sā′). *n.* preparatory school in France supported by the government. [French *lycée,* from Latin *Lyceum* gymnasium near Athens, where Aristotle taught, from Greek *Lykeion.* Doublet of LYCEUM.]

at; āpe; cär; end; mē; it; īce; hot; ōld; fôrk; wood; fōōl; oil; out; up; ūse; turn; sing; thin; this; zh in treasure; ə in ago, taken, pencil, lemon, circus.

ly·ce·um (lī sē′əm, lī′sē-) *n.* **1.** public hall in which educational programs, as concerts or lectures, are presented. **2.** any of a number of organizations devoted to such educational programs. [Latin *Lycēum* gymnasium near Athens, where Aristotle taught, from Greek *Lykeion.* Doublet of LYCÉE.]

lych gate (lich) lich gate.

Ly·ci·a (lish′ē ə) *n.* ancient district in southwestern Asia Minor.

ly·co·pod (lī′kə pod′) *n.* any of various small, green, creeping or erect, mosslike plants, as the club moss.

ly·co·po·di·um (lī′kə pō′dē əm) *n.* **1.** lycopod. **2.** yellow powder made from the spores of certain lycopods. [Modern Latin *Lycopodium,* from Greek *lykos* wolf + *pous* foot; referring to its claw-shaped root.]

lydd·ite (lid′īt) *n.* picric acid.

Lyd·i·a (lid′ē ə) *n.* ancient country in western Asia Minor.

Lyd·i·an (lid′ē ən) *n.* **1.** member of the people inhabiting Lydia. **2.** language spoken in Lydia. —*adj.* of or relating to Lydia, its people, their language, or culture.

lye (lī) *n.* **1.** commercial sodium hydroxide, used to make soap and detergents. **2.** solution obtained from leaching wood ashes, consisting mostly of potassium carbonate, used in making soap and glass. [Old English *lēag* strong alkaline solution.]

ly·ing[1] (lī′ing) *n.* act of telling lies: *I do not mind lying, but I hate inaccuracy* (Butler, 1912). —*adj.* untruthful or deceitful.

ly·ing[2] (lī′ing) present participle of **lie**[2].

ly·ing-in (lī′ing in′) *pl.,* **ly·ings-in** or **ly·ing-ins.** *n.* confinement of a woman while giving birth.

Lyl·y, John (lil′ē) c.1554–1606, English author.

lymph (limf) *n.* clear, colorless fluid, similar to blood in composition, that bathes the body cells, bringing nutrients and oxygen to the cells and carrying away wastes. [Latin *lympha* water.]

lym·phat·ic (lim fat′ik) *adj.* **1.** of, relating to, or containing lymph. **2.** dull; sluggish. —*n.* lymphatic vessel.

lymph gland, any of the small nodes or bodies in the lymphatic vessels that filter out harmful substances and produce lymphocytes. Also, **lymph node.**

lym·pho·cyte (lim′fə sīt′) *n.* one of the white blood cells formed in the lymph glands, having a role in the formation of antibodies. [Latin *lympha* water + Greek *kytos* hollow vessel.]

lym·phoid (lim′foid) *adj.* of, relating to, or resembling lymph or the tissue of the lymph glands.

lynch (linch) *v.t.* to seize by mob action and put to death, usually by hanging, without due process of law. [From LYNCH LAW.] —**lynch′er,** *n.*

lynch law, administration of punishment, usually death by hanging, without due process of law. [Earlier *Lynch's law,* possibly from Charles Lynch, a Virginia farmer who organized bands of patriots to punish British sympathizers during the American Revolution.]

Lynn (lin) *n.* port city in eastern Massachusetts, an industrial and commercial suburb of Boston. Pop. (1970), 90,294.

lynx (lingks) *pl.,* **lynx** or **lynx·es.** *n.* any of various wildcats, genus *Lynx,* characterized by long legs, a short tail, and usually tufted ears. [Latin *lynx,* from Greek *lynx.*]

lynx-eyed (lingks′īd′) *adj.* having sharp vision.

Ly·on (lē ôn′; *French* lyôN) *n.* city in east-central France. Pop. (1968), 527,800. Also, **Ly·ons** (lī′ənz).

ly·on·naise (lī′ə nāz′) *adj.* cooked with finely chopped onions: *lyonnaise potatoes.* [Probably short for French *à la lyonnaise* in the manner of LYON.]

Lynx

Ly·ra (lī′rə) *n.* constellation in the northern sky containing the bright star Vega. [Latin *lyra.* See LYRE.]

ly·rate (lī′rāt) *adj.* resembling a lyre in shape. Also, **ly′rat·ed.**

lyre (līr) *n.* stringed musical instrument, used by the ancient Greeks to accompany singing and recitation. [Old French *lyre,* from Latin *lyra,* from Greek *lyrā.*]

lyre·bird (līr′burd′) *n.* Australian bird, genus *Menura,* having predominantly brown plumage. The male has a long tail that is lyre-shaped when spread. There are two species: *M. superba* and *M. alberti.* Length: to 38 inches.

lyr·ic (lir′ik) *adj.* **1.** of or relating to a type of poetry characterized by poems that are direct, spontaneous expressions of strong personal emotion. **2.** characterized by or having a spontaneous emotional or rapturous style or manner: *a lyric quality, lyric prose.* **3.** intended to be sung. **4.** of, relating to, or adapted to the lyre. **5.** having a light, flexible singing voice: *a lyric soprano.* Also, **lyr′i·cal.** —*n.* **1.** lyric poem or lyric poetry. **2. lyrics.** words written for a song. [Latin *lyricus* relating to the lyre, from Greek *lyrikos,* from *lyrā* lyre; originally referring to songs or poems accompanied by the lyre.] —**lyr′i·cal·ly,** *adv.*

Lyrebird

ly·sin (lī′sin) *n.* antibody capable of bringing about the destruction of cells, tissues, or bacteria. [Greek *lysis* a releasing, dissolution + -IN[1].]

ly·sine (lī′sēn, -sin) *n.* essential amino acid produced by the hydrolysis of certain proteins, important for human growth. Formula: $C_6H_{14}N_2O_2$ [Greek *lysis* a releasing, dissolution + -INE[2].]

Ly·sol (lī′sôl) *n. Trademark.* oily liquid containing soap and cresols, used as an antiseptic and disinfectant. [Greek *lysis* a releasing + Latin *oleum* oil.]

Lyt·ton (lit′ən) see **Bulwer-Lytton.**

---

at; āpe; cär; end; mē; it; īce; hot; ōld; fôrk; wood; fōol; oil; out; up; ūse; turn; sing; thin; this; zh in treasure; ə in ago, taken, pencil, lemon, circus.

m, M (em) *pl.,* **m's, M's.** *n.* thirteenth letter of the English alphabet.
M, Roman numeral for 1000.
M'- *prefix* Mac-; Mc.
m. **1.** mile; miles. **2.** male; masculine. **3.** meter; meters. **4.** minute; minutes. **5.** month. **6.** married. **7.** meridian. **8.** morning. **9.** mass.
M. **1.** Monday. **2.** Master. **3.** Monsieur.
ma (mä) *n. Informal.* mother. [Short for MAMA.]
M.A., Master of Arts.
ma'am (mam; *unstressed* məm) *n. Informal.* madam (*def.* 1).
Mab, Queen (mab) *English and Celtic Folklore.* the queen of the fairies.
Mac- *also,* **Mc-, M'-.** *prefix* son of. ▲ used in certain Scottish and Irish family names. [Irish and Gaelic *mac* son.]
ma·ca·bre (mə kä′brə, -bər, -käb′) *adj.* suggesting the horror and gruesomeness associated with death; strange in a ghastly or ghoulish way: *macabre tales of witchcraft, a macabre sense of humor that enjoyed sick jokes.* [French *macabre* gruesome, ghastly (from the phrase *danse macabre* dance of death), possibly modification of Old French *Macabe* Maccabaeus; referring to the martyrdom of the Maccabees.]
mac·ad·am (mə kad′əm) *n.* **1.** pavement or road surface consisting largely or entirely of layers of crushed stone. **2.** crushed stone used in such pavements or roads. [From John L. *McAdam,* 1756–1836, Scottish engineer who introduced such roads.]
mac·ad·am·ize (mə kad′ə mīz′) **-ized, -iz·ing.** *v.t.* to construct or pave (a road) with macadam. —**mac·ad′am·i·za′tion,** *n.*
Ma·cao (mə kou′) *n.* **1.** Portuguese overseas province on the southern coast of China. Area, 6 sq. mi. Pop. (1967 est.), 261,000. **2.** seaport on this peninsula. Pop. (1960), 9753.
ma·caque (mə kak′, -käk′) *n.* any of various short-tailed monkeys, genus *Macaca,* having cheek pouches in which food is stored. Length: 15–30 inches without the tail. [French *macaque,* from Portuguese *macaco* monkey, macaque; of Bantu origin.]
mac·a·ro·ni (mak′ə rō′nē) *pl.,* **-nis** or **-nies.** *n.* **1.** food made from a wheat-flour paste or dough, usually in the shape of short, hollow tubes, prepared for eating by boiling. **2.** *Archaic.* affected fop or dandy of eighteenth-century England. [Dialectal Italian *maccaroni,* plural of *maccarone* dumpling, small cake, paste with cheese; of uncertain origin.]
mac·a·roon (mak′ə rōōn′) *n.* small cake or cookie made chiefly of ground almonds or coconut, egg whites, and sugar. [French *macaron,* from dialectal Italian *maccarone.* See MACARONI.]
Mac·Ar·thur, Douglas (mə kär′thər) 1880–1964, U.S. general.
Ma·cas·sar (mə kas′ər) *also,* **Ma·kas·sar.** *n.* largest city and chief port of Celebes, Indonesia. Pop. (1961 est.), 384,159.
Ma·cau·lay, Thomas Bab·ing·ton (mə kô′lē; bab′ing tən) 1800–59, English historian, essayist, statesman, and poet.
ma·caw (mə kô′) *n.* any of several long-tailed parrots, family Psittacidae, found in Central and South America, esp. genus *Ara,* which is brilliantly colored. Length: to 3 feet. [Portuguese *macau,* probably from *macaúba* a kind of palm tree, from Tupi-Guarani *macauba;* supposedly because it eats the fruit of this tree.]

Macaw

Mac·ca·bees (mak′ə bēz′) *n.,pl.* **1.** family of Jewish patriots, esp. Judas Maccabeus and his brothers, that led a revolt against Syrian domination and religious oppression and then ruled Judea in the second and first centuries B.C. **2.** four books dealing with Jewish history, legend, and law. The first two are the last Old Testament books of the Douay Bible.

Mac·ca·be·us, Judas (mak′ə bē′əs) *also,* **Mac·ca·bae·us.** died c.160 B.C., Jewish patriot and military leader.
mace¹ (mās) *n.* **1.** heavy war club, usually having a spiked metal head, used esp. in the Middle Ages for crushing armor. **2.** ornamental scepter or staff resembling such a club in shape, used as a ceremonial symbol of office or authority. [Old French *mace* large mallet, going back to Latin *matteola* mallet.]
mace² (mās) *n.* delicately flavored, aromatic spice made by grinding the dried outer covering of the seed of the nutmeg. [Old French *macis,* possibly going back to Latin *macir* red spicy bark from India, from Greek *makir* a spice from India.]

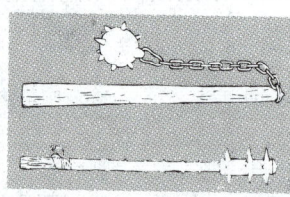

Maces

mace³ (mās) *n.* chemical mixture containing tear gas, used chiefly in riot control. Trademark: Chemical Mace. —*v.t.,* **maced, mac·ing.** to subject to mace; use mace against. [From MACE¹.]
mac·é·doine (mas′ā dwän′) *n.* **1.** mixture of raw or cooked vegetables or fruits, sometimes jellied. **2.** mixture; medley; hodgepodge. [French *macédoine* medley, hodgepodge, from Latin *Macedonia* Macedonia; referring to the mixture and variety of peoples living in Macedonia.]
Mac·e·do·ni·a (mas′ə dō′nē ə) *n.* **1.** ancient kingdom north of Greece, the center of the empire created by Alexander the Great. Also, **Mac·e·don** (mas′ə don′). **2.** historic region in southeastern Europe, including parts of Greece, Yugoslavia, and Bulgaria. —**Mac′e·do′ni·an,** *adj.,* *n.*
mac·er·ate (mas′ə rāt′) **-at·ed, -at·ing.** *v.t.* **1.** to soften or separate into constituent parts by or as by soaking in liquid. **2.** to cause to waste away or grow thin. —*v.i.* to become macerated. [Latin *mācerātus,* past participle of *mācerāre* to soften.] —**mac′er·a′tion,** *n.*
Mach (mäk, mak) *also,* **mach.** *n.* Mach number.
mach., machine; machinery; machinist.
ma·chet·e (mə shet′ē, -chet′ē) *n.* broad heavy knife used as a tool and weapon. [Spanish *machete,* from *macho* hammer, from Latin *marculus* small hammer.]
Mach·i·a·vel·li, Nic·co·lò (mak′ē ə vel′ē; nē′kō lō′) 1469–1527, Florentine author and statesman.
Mach·i·a·vel·li·an (mak′ē ə vel′ē ən) *adj.* **1.** characterized by subtle or sinister cunning, unscrupulous deception, and a tendency to do what is expedient rather than what is moral. **2.** acting in accordance with or characterized by the principles of government set forth by Machiavelli, whereby expediency is placed above morality and the use of unscrupulous means of acquiring and maintaining power is justified. **3.** of, relating to, or resembling Machiavelli or his political theories. —*n.* follower of the political methods and theories advocated by Machiavelli. —**Mach′i·a·vel′li·an·ism, Mach′i·a·vel′lism,** *n.*
ma·chic·o·la·tion (mə chik′ə lā′shən) *n.* **1.** opening, as in the base of a parapet or in the roof of a portal or entrance of a castle, through which missiles or molten lead could be dropped on attackers. **2.** projecting gallery or parapet supported on corbels, with or without such openings.

Machicolation

610   at; āpe; cär; end; mē; it; īce; hot; ōld; fôrk; wood; fōōl; oil; out; up; ūse; turn; sing; thin; <u>th</u>is; zh in treasure; ə in ago, taken, pencil, lemon, circus.

mach·i·nate (mak′ə nāt′) -nat·ed, -nat·ing. *v.t., v.i.* to scheme or contrive, esp. artfully or with evil purpose. [Latin *māchinātus,* past participle of *māchinārī* to contrive.] —**mach′i·na′tor,** *n.*

mach·i·na·tion (mak′ə nā′shən) *n.* artful, secret, or elaborate plot or scheme, often for some evil purpose.

ma·chine (mə shēn′) *n.* **1.** apparatus consisting of a number of integrated, usually moving, parts having specific functions, used in the performance of work, esp. a mechanical apparatus used to perform mechanical work. **2.** device, as a lever, pulley, or screw, that is used to perform work by directing, transmitting, or modifying force or motion. Also, **simple machine. 3.** complex system or organization coordinated to function efficiently and smoothly: *a nation that built up a powerful war machine.* **4.** political organization, usually headed by a boss or clique, that controls a political party in an area. **5.** one who behaves in a rigid or mechanical manner without emotion, thought, or will. **6.** one who performs a particular activity or functions within a particular area with great efficiency and precision: *a boxer who is the local fighting machine.* —*v.t.* **-chined, -chin·ing.** to make, shape, or finish with a machine. [French *machine* engine, contrivance, from Latin *māchina,* going back to Greek *mēchanē.*]

ma·chine-gun (mə shēn′gun′) **-gunned, -gun·ning.** *v.t.* to fire at or shoot with a machine gun.

machine gun, automatic weapon that uses small arms ammunition and fires continuously while pressure on the trigger is maintained.

ma·chin·er·y (mə shē′nər ē) *pl.,* **-er·ies.** *n.* **1.** machines or machine parts, collectively: *a factory equipped with the latest machinery. 2.* the working parts of a particular machine, collectively: *to repair the machinery of an elevator.* **3.** means or working parts by which something is kept in motion or a desired result is obtained: *the machinery of government.*

machine shop, workshop where metal or other material is cut, shaped, and finished with machine tools.

machine tool, power-driven, automatic or semiautomatic tool designed to cut, shape, and perform similar operations.

ma·chin·ist (mə shē′nist) *n.* **1.** one who is skilled in running and working with machine tools. **2.** one who designs, assembles, installs, or repairs machinery.

ma·chis·mo (mä chēz′mō) *n.* in Spanish cultures, institutionalized concept of male superiority and of the pride and assertiveness regarded as essential to masculinity. Also, **ma′cho.** [Spanish *machismo* virility, manhood, from *macho.* See MACHO.]

Mach·me·ter (mäk′mē′tər, mak′-) *also,* **mach·me·ter.** *n.* device that indicates the speed of an aircraft in relation to the speed of sound.

Mach number *also,* **mach number.** number expressing the ratio of the speed of a body in a given atmosphere to the speed of sound in the same atmosphere. Also, **Mach.** [From Ernst *Mach,* 1838–1916, Austrian physicist.]

ma·cho (mä′chō) *pl.,* **-chos.** *n.* **1.** in Spanish cultures, a strong, brave, and virile man. **2.** machismo. —*adj.* brave, virile; masculine. [Spanish *macho* male, going back to Latin *masculus.* See MASCULINE.]

mac·in·tosh (mak′in tosh′) *n.* mackintosh.

Mac·ken·zie (mə ken′zē) *n.* river in northwestern Canada, flowing into the Arctic Ocean.

mack·er·el (mak′ər əl, mak′rəl) *pl.,* **-els** *or* **-el.** *n.* any of a group of commercially important food and game fish, family Scombridae, related to the tuna, having a silvery body that is marked in metallic blue on its upper surface. [Old French *makerel, maquerel;* of uncertain origin.]

mackerel sky, sky covered with rows of small, white, fleecy clouds resembling the patterns on the back of a mackerel.

Mack·i·nac, Straits of (mak′ə nô′, -nak′) strait connecting Lake Michigan and Lake Huron.

mack·i·naw (mak′ə nô′) *n.* **1.** short coat made of a heavy woolen fabric that is usually napped on both sides and woven in a plaid. Also, **Mackinaw coat. 2.** thick blanket made of a heavy woolen fabric, often woven in wide bands of different colors. Also, **Mackinaw blanket.** [From *Mackinac* Island, Michigan, where these items were traded in the nineteenth century.]

mack·in·tosh (mak′in tosh′) *also,* **mac·in·tosh.** *n.* **1.** any raincoat. **2.** raincoat made of a waterproof, rubberized fabric. **3.** the waterproof fabric itself. [From Charles *Macintosh,* 1766–1843, Scottish chemist who invented the fabric.]

Mac·Leish, Ar·chi·bald (mak lēsh′, mək-) 1892—, U. S. poet, dramatist, and critic.

Mac·mil·lan, Har·old (mək mil′ən) 1894—, English statesman and prime minister of Great Britain from 1957 to 1963.

Ma·con (mā′kən) *n.* city in central Georgia. Pop. (1970), 122,423.

mac·ra·mé (mak′rə mā′, mak′rə mā′) *n.* coarse lacework made by knotting thread or cord, often in geometric patterns. [Turkish *makrama* towel, napkin, from Arabic *miqramah* striped cloth.]

macro- combining form large; long; great: *macrocosm, macroeconomics.* [Greek *makros.*]

mac·ro·bi·ot·ic (mak′rō bī ot′ik) *adj.* living a long time, as some seeds and certain microscopic organisms. [Greek *makrobiotos* long-lived (from *makros* long + *bios* life) + -IC.]

mac·ro·cosm (mak′rə koz′əm) *n.* **1.** a great complex regarded as reflecting on a large scale the nature or structure of one of its constituents. **2.** the whole world or universe, esp. in contrast to man. [French *macrocosme* universe, through Medieval Latin, from Greek *makros* large, long, great + *kosmos* world.]

mac·ro·ec·o·nom·ics (mak′rō ek′ə nom′iks, -ē′kə-) *n.,pl.* branch of economics concerned with the broad and general aspects of an economy, as the national income, and the relationship between various sectors of an economy. ▲ construed as singular.

mac·ro·mol·e·cule (mak′rō mol′ə kūl′) *n.* very large molecule, as that of a protein or rubber.

ma·cron (mā′kron, mak′ron) *n.* short horizontal line (ˉ) placed over a vowel to show that it has a long sound. [Greek *makron,* neuter of *makros* large, long, great.]

mac·ro·nu·cle·us (mak′rō nōō′klē əs, -nū′-) *n.* the larger of the two types of nuclei present in various ciliate protozoans, believed to control nutritional processes.

mac·ro·scop·ic (mak′rə skop′ik) *adj.* large enough to be visible to the naked eye. Also, **mac′ro·scop′i·cal.**

mad (mad) **mad·der, mad·dest.** *adj.* **1.** feeling or exhibiting anger, resentment, or irritation. **2.** suffering from or exhibiting mental disorder; insane. **3.** totally lacking in reason, prudence, or judgment; wildly foolish or rash: *You'd be mad to turn down that good an offer.* **4.** marked by confusion, agitation, or frantic activity: *Because all tickets were for general admission, there was a mad scramble for seats when the doors opened.* **5.** going beyond bounds or limits; violently unrestrained: *to have a mad passion for chocolate ice cream.* **6.** violently affected or moved; frantic: *mad with jealousy.* **7.** *Informal.* feeling or exhibiting intense eagerness, liking, and desire; wildly enthusiastic or fond (with *about, for,* or *over*): *to be mad about racing cars, to be mad about someone.* **8.** (of dogs and other animals) having rabies; rabid. **9.** (of animals) enraged to the point of being murderous; dangerously violent: *a mad bull.* **10. like mad.** *Informal.* with great speed, vigor, or energy; furiously: *The audience cheered like mad when he finished speaking.* —*n. Informal.* period or fit of anger or ill temper: *He's had a mad on all day.* [Old English *(ge)mǣded* maddened.]

Mad·a·gas·car (mad′ə gas′kər) *n.* large island in the Indian Ocean, comprising the major part of the Malagasy Republic. Area, 227,800 sq. mi. Pop. (1969 est.), 6,643,000.

mad·am (mad′əm) *pl., (def. 1)* **mes·dames** *or (def. 2)* **mad·ams.** *n.* **1.** lady; mistress. ▲ used as a form of respectful or polite address to a woman: *Madam Gandhi, Madam Chairman. Madam, may I help you?* **2.** woman who runs a brothel. [Old French *ma dame* my lady, going back to Latin *mea,* feminine of *meus* my + *domina* mistress, lady.]

mad·ame (mə dam′, ma-, mad′əm) *pl.,* **mes·dames.** *n.* Mrs. ▲ French form of address for a married woman; also used as a title of distinction. [French *madame,* from Old French *ma dame* my lady. See MADAM.]

mad·cap (mad′kap′) *adj.* wildly impulsive, reckless, or eccentric. —*n.* one who is madcap. [MAD + CAP.]

mad·den (mad′ən) *v.t.* **1.** to drive to frenzy or violent, uncontrollable rage. **2.** to cause to feel anger, resentment, or irritation. —*v.i.* to become maddened.

mad·den·ing (mad′ən ing) *adj.* **1.** tending to provoke anger, resentment, or irritation: *her maddening habit of cracking his knuckles.* **2.** tending to drive to frenzy, hysteria, or madness: *the continual, maddening throbbing of drums.* —**mad′den·ing·ly,** *adv.*

mad·der[1] (mad′ər) *n.* **1.** climbing plant, *Rubia tinctorum,* found in Asia and southern Europe, having long, fleshy red roots. **2.** red dye contained in the roots of this plant; alizarin. **3.** brilliant red color. [Old English *mædere* the plant.]

mad·der[2] (mad′ər) comparative of mad.

mad·ding (mad′ing) *adj. Archaic.* acting as if mad; frenzied: *far from the madding crowd's ignoble strife* (Gray, 1749).

made (mād) *v.* past tense and past participle of make. —*adj.* **1.** produced; constructed; shaped. ▲ often used in combination: *a well-made chair, a handmade sweater.* **2. to have it made.** *Informal.* to be assured of success.

Ma·dei·ra[1] (mə dēr′ə) *n.* **1.** Portuguese island group in the North Atlantic, off the coast of Morocco. Land area, approx. 308 sq. mi. Pop. (1960), 268,937. Also, **Madeira Islands. 2.** largest island in this group. Area, approx. 286 sq. mi. **3.** large river in northwestern Brazil, one of the principal tributaries of the Amazon.

Ma·dei·ra[2] (mə dēr′ə) *also,* **ma·dei·ra.** *n.* any of a group of white wines, many of them sweet, amber-colored wine originally made on the island of Madeira.

mad·e·moi·selle (mad′ə mə zel′, mad′mwə zel′) *pl.,* **mad·e·moi·selles** *or* **mes·de·moi·selles.** *n.* miss. ▲ French form of address

for an unmarried girl or woman. [French *mademoiselle* literally, my young lady, going back to Latin *mea*, feminine of *meus* my + *domina* mistress, lady.]

made-to-order (mād′tōō ôr′dər, -tə-) *adj.* **1.** made in accordance with specified instructions, measurements, or requirements; custom-made: *a made-to-order suit.* **2.** perfectly suited to tastes or requirements: *a house that is made-to-order.*

made-up (mād′up′) *adj.* **1.** not real or true; fictitious: *a made-up name.* **2.** having cosmetics or make-up applied: *a heavily made-up face.* **3.** put together; finished.

mad·house (mad′hous′) *n.* **1.** formerly, a hospital or asylum for the mentally ill. **2.** place or scene of wild uproar or confusion.

Ma·di·nat ash Sha'b (mad′ə noo′ ash shab′) capital of Southern Yemen, in the southern part of the country.

Mad·i·son (mad′ə sən) **1.** **Dol·ley** (dol′ē). *also,* **Dol·ly.** 1768–1849, wife of James Madison. **2.** **James.** 1751–1836. fourth president of the United States, from 1809 to 1817. **3.** capital of Wisconsin, in the south-central part of the state. Pop. (1970), 173,258.

Madison Avenue **1.** street in New York City where the offices of many advertising firms are located. **2.** the advertising industry or its practices, methods, and attitudes.

mad·ly (mad′lē) *adv.* **1.** in an insane or hysterical manner. **2.** with great speed, vigor, or energy; furiously: *The men worked madly to reinforce the dam in time.* **3.** to an excessive degree; in a violently unrestrained manner: *to be madly in love.* **4.** in a foolish or rash manner.

mad·man (mad′man′, -mən) *pl.* **-men.** *n.* man who is or acts as if insane. **—mad′wom′an,** *n.*

mad·ness (mad′nis) *n.* **1.** mental illness; insanity. **2.** extreme imprudence, foolishness, or rashness; utter folly. **3.** violent, frenzied, or uncontrollable rage. **4.** wild excitement or enthusiasm: *The madness of independence has spread from colony to colony* (Johnson, 1775).

Ma·don·na (mə don′ə) *n.* **1.** the Virgin Mary. **2.** representation of the Virgin Mary, as in painting or sculpture. [Italian *Madonna*, going back to Latin *mea*, feminine of *meus* my + *domina* mistress, lady.]

mad·ras (mad′rəs, mə dras′) *n.* cotton fabric usually having a plaid, checked, or striped pattern, often colored with dyes that will bleed in washing. [From MADRAS, where it was first produced.]

Ma·dras (mə dras′, mə dräs′) *n.* port city in southeastern India. Pop. (1969), 2,047,735.

Ma·drid (mə drid′) *n.* capital and largest city of Spain, in the central part of the country. Pop. (1968), 2,850,631.

mad·ri·gal (mad′ri gəl) *n.* **1.** short, lyric medieval poem suitable for setting to music. **2.** unaccompanied part song, usually with elaborate counterpoint and secular lyrics. **3.** any song, esp. a part song. [Italian *madrigale* the short lyric poem, from Medieval Latin *matricalis* simple, from Late Latin *mātricālis* relating to the womb, from Latin *mātrix* womb, source.]

mad·ri·lène (mad′rə lān′, -len′) *also,* **mad·ri·lene.** *n.* tomato-flavored consommé served hot or cold. [Short for French *consommé madrilène* literally, consommé of Madrid, from Spanish *madrileño* relating to Madrid, from MADRID.]

Ma·du·ra (mə door′ə) *n.* **1.** small Indonesian island off the northeastern coast of Java. Area, 1,726 sq. mi. Pop. (1961), 2,150,200. **2.** see **Madurai.**

Ma·du·rai (mad′ə rī′) *n.* city in southern India, formerly known as Madura. Pop. (1969), 436,000.

Mae·ce·nas (mi sē′nəs, mī-) **1.** **Gai·us Cil·ni·us** (gā′əs sil′nē əs). c.70–8 B.C., Roman statesman and literary patron. **2.** any generous patron, esp. of literature or art.

mael·strom (māl′strəm) *n.* **1.** violent or turbulent whirlpool. **2.** something resembling such a whirlpool in intensity, violence, or destructive force: *the maelstrom of battle.* **3.** **Maelstrom.** dangerous whirlpool located in a strait off the northwestern coast of Norway. [Obsolete Dutch *maelstrom* literally, grinding stream, from *malen* to grind + *strom* stream.]

mae·nad (mē′nad) *also,* **me·nad.** *n.* **1.** priestess or female worshiper of Dionysus, esp. one taking part in the frenzied, orgiastic rites that characterized his worship. **2.** any frenzied woman. [Latin *maenas*, from Greek *mainas.*]

mae·sto·so (mī stō′sō) *Music. adj.* majestic; stately. **—adv.** in a majestic, stately manner. [Italian *maestoso* majestic, stately, from *maesta* majesty, from Latin *mājestās* dignity, authority.]

maes·tro (mīs′trō) *pl.,* **-tros** *or* **-tri** (-trē). *n.* **1.** eminent conductor, composer, or teacher of music. **2.** eminent master of any art. [Italian *maestro* master, teacher, from Latin *magister.*]

Mae West (mā′west′) inflatable vestlike life jacket, used esp. by aviators. [From *Mae West,* 1892—, buxom U. S. actress.]

Ma·fi·a (mä′fē ə, -fē ä′) *also,* **Maf·fi·a.** *n.* **1.** secret criminal society in Sicily operating in opposition to legal and governmental authority. **2.** criminal organization or syndicate believed to be related to this society, thought to be active in the United States and other countries.

[Italian *mafia,* from dialectal Italian *mafia* boldness, possibly from Arabic *mahyah* boasting.]

mag. **1.** magazine. **2.** magnetism. **3.** magnitude.

mag·a·zine (mag′ə zēn′, mag′ə zēn′) *n.* **1.** periodical publication, often issued weekly or monthly, usually bound in a paper cover, containing articles, stories, pictures, or other features. **2.** building or place for storing ammunition and explosives, as a storeroom in a ship or fort. **3.** building or place for storing military supplies, as arms or provisions. **4.** metal container for holding bullets or cartridges so that they can be fed into the chamber of a gun for firing. **5.** supply chamber, as the receptacle for film in a camera. [French *magasin* storehouse, store, from Italian *magazzino* storehouse, from Arabic *makhzan.*]

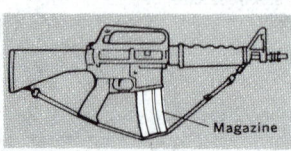
Magazine

Mag·da·lene (mag′də lēn′) *also,* **Mag·da·len** (mag′də lən). *n.* **1.** Mary Magdalene. **2.** **magdalene.** reformed and repentant prostitute.

Mag·de·burg (mag′də burg′) *n.* port city in west-central East Germany, on the Elbe River. Pop. (1968 est.), 268,269.

mage (māj) *n.* *Archaic.* magician. [Latin *magus.* See MAGI.]

Ma·gel·lan (mə jel′ən) **1.** **Ferdinand.** c.1480–1521, Portuguese explorer and navigator. **2.** **Strait of.** strait at the southern tip of mainland South America, linking the Atlantic and the Pacific.

Ma·gen Da·vid (mô′gən dô′vid, dä′vid) Star of David. [Hebrew *māgen Dāwid* literally, shield of David, Biblical king of Israel.]

ma·gen·ta (mə jen′tə) *n.* **1.** purplish-red color. **2.** fuchsin. [From the Battle of *Magenta,* 1859; because the dye fuchsin was discovered about that time.]

mag·got (mag′ət) *n.* **1.** wormlike larva of a fly, usually legless and having a thick body. **2.** odd or fantastic notion; whim. [Of Scandinavian origin.]

mag·got·y (mag′ə tē) *adj.* infested with maggots; rotten.

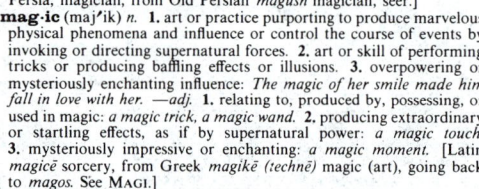
Maggot

Ma·gi (mā′jī, maj′ī) *sing.,* **Ma·gus.** *n.,pl.* **1.** in the New Testament, the three wise men from the East who brought gifts to the infant Jesus. **2.** priests of ancient Persia. [Latin *magī,* plural of *magus* magician, from Greek *magos* priest of ancient Persia, magician, from Old Persian *magush* magician, seer.]

mag·ic (maj′ik) *n.* **1.** art or practice purporting to produce marvelous physical phenomena and influence or control the course of events by invoking or directing supernatural forces. **2.** art or skill of performing tricks or producing baffling effects or illusions. **3.** overpowering or mysteriously enchanting influence: *The magic of her smile made him fall in love with her.* **—adj. 1.** relating to, produced by, possessing, or used in magic: *a magic trick, a magic wand.* **2.** producing extraordinary or startling effects, as if by supernatural power: *a magic touch.* **3.** mysteriously impressive or enchanting: *a magic moment.* [Latin *magicē* sorcery, from Greek *magikē (technē)* magic (art), going back to *magos.* See MAGI.]

Syn. *n.* **1.** Magic, sorcery, witchcraft mean an occult power or art. **Magic** is usually applied to the power or art of invoking the supernatural to perform miraculous acts: *Some primitive tribes believe that ritual magic can drive illness from the body.* **Sorcery** refers to the magic performed with the use of incantations and spells to harm and enthrall others: *The evil fairy used sorcery to transform the prince into a frog.* **Witchcraft** designates the power practiced by a person possessed of evil spirits: *Puritans in New England used to burn those accused of witchcraft.*

mag·i·cal (maj′i kəl) *adj.* of, relating to, or produced by or as if by magic. **—mag′i·cal·ly,** *adv.*

ma·gi·cian (mə jish′ən) *n.* **1.** entertainer who performs tricks of illusion or sleight of hand. **2.** one who uses, or is skilled in the use of, magic; sorcerer; wizard. **3.** one whose ability or skill is seemingly magical. [Old French *magicien* one skilled in magic, from *magique* sorcery, from Latin *magicē.* See MAGIC.]

magic lantern, early kind of projector for showing slides.

Ma·gi·not Line (mazh′ə nō′) system of French fortifications built along the eastern border of France in the 1930s as a defense against a future German invasion, outflanked by the Germans in May, 1940. [From André *Maginot,* 1877–1932, who was the French minister of war when its construction began.]

mag·is·te·ri·al (maj′is tēr′ē əl) *adj.* **1.** relating to or befitting a person in a position of authority; commanding. **2.** imperious; dictatorial. **3.** of or relating to a magistrate, his office, or his duties. [Medieval Latin

magisterialis relating to authority, going back to Latin *magister* master.]
—**mag·is·te′ri·al·ly,** *adv.*

mag·is·tra·cy (maj′is trə sē) *pl.,* **-cies.** *n.* **1.** office, duties, or term of a magistrate. **2.** magistrates collectively. **3.** district under the jurisdiction of a magistrate.

mag·is·trate (maj′is trāt′, -trit) *n.* **1.** government officer empowered to administer and enforce the law. **2.** judicial official having limited jurisdiction, empowered to try minor civil and criminal cases and issue marriage licenses and traffic summonses, as a justice of the peace. [Latin *magistrātus* civil office, public official, from *magister* master.]

mag·ma (mag′mə) *pl.,* **-mas** or **-ma·ta.** *n.* molten rock that exists beneath the surface of the earth and from which lava and igneous rocks are formed. [Latin *magma* the dregs of an unguent, from Greek *magma* thick unguent.]

Mag·na Car·ta (mag′nə kär′tə) *also,* **Mag·na Char·ta. 1.** great charter that King John of England was compelled to grant to his barons at Runnymede on June 15, 1215, defining the limits of an English king's power. **2.** any document guaranteeing or securing liberties and rights. [Medieval Latin *magna c(h)arta* literally, great charter, going back to Latin *magnus* great, large + *charta* paper. See CHART.]

mag·na cum lau·de (mag′nə koom lou′də, kum lô′dē) with high honors or praise. Distinguished from **cum laude** and **summa cum laude.** ▲ used to signify graduation with high honors from a university or college. [Modern Latin *magna cum laude.*]

mag·na·nim·i·ty (mag′nə nim′ə tē) *pl.,* **-ties.** *n.* **1.** quality of being magnanimous. **2.** magnanimous act.

mag·nan·i·mous (mag nan′ə məs) *adj.* **1.** generous and noble of mind and heart, esp. in forgiving insults or injuries; free from pettiness: *a magnanimous ruler.* **2.** characterized by or arising from magnanimity: *a magnanimous gesture of clemency.* [Latin *magnanimus* great-souled, high-minded, from *magnus* great, large + *animus* soul, mind.] —**mag·nan′i·mous·ly,** *adv.* —**mag·nan′i·mous·ness,** *n.*

mag·nate (mag′nāt) *n.* person of great power, importance, or wealth in a field of activity, esp. in business or industry: *a railroad magnate, a shipping magnate.* [Late Latin *magnās* (stem *magnāt-*) great man, from Latin *magnus* great, large.]

mag·ne·sia (mag nē′shə, -zhə) *n.* white powder compound used esp. in furnace linings and in laxatives and other pharmaceuticals; magnesium oxide. Formula: MgO [Modern Latin *magnesia (alba)* (white) magnesia, going back to Greek *(hē) Magnēsiā (lithos)* (the stone from) Magnesia, a region in Thessaly noted for metals.]

mag·ne·si·um (mag nē′zē əm, -zhəm) *n.* tough, very light, silverwhite metallic element used esp. in the production of lightweight alloys. Symbol: **Mg** **See element** for table. [Modern Latin *magnesium,* from MAGNESIA.]

mag·net (mag′nit) *n.* **1.** body made of iron, steel, or certain other materials that attracts iron, steel, and other materials and that both attracts and repels other magnetic bodies. **2.** one who or that which attracts. [Latin *magnet-,* stem of *magnēs* lodestone, from Greek *Magnētis lithos* stone from Magnesia (a region in Thessaly where it was first found by the ancient Greeks), lodestone.]

mag·net·ic (mag net′ik) *adj.* **1.** having the properties of a magnet; able to exert magnetism. **2.** of, relating to, producing, or caused by magnetism. **3.** capable of being magnetized or of being attracted or repelled by a magnet. **4.** of or relating to the magnetism of the earth. **5.** possessing power to attract, influence, or charm: *a magnetic leader.* Also, **mag·net′i·cal.** —**mag·net′i·cal·ly,** *adv.*

magnetic equator, imaginary line around the earth, encircling it nearly halfway between the magnetic poles, along which a magnetic needle does not dip. Also, **aclinic line.**

magnetic field, region around a magnet or an electric current, in which a magnetic force can be detected.

magnetic flux, total number of lines of force in a magnetic field. Also, **flux.**

magnetic induction, induction *(def. 3b).*

magnetic mine, underwater mine that is detonated by an electric current induced by the magnetic field of a passing ship.

magnetic needle, slender bar of magnetized steel, as in a compass, that points approximately toward the earth's North and South Magnetic Poles.

magnetic north, direction toward which the north-seeking end of a compass needle points, usually differing from true north.

magnetic pole 1. either of the two poles of a magnet, from which or toward which the lines of force of the magnet diverge or converge. **2.** either of two points on the earth's surface that are the poles of the earth's magnetic field and toward which a compass needle points. The **North Magnetic Pole** is at approximately 75 degrees North latitude and 101 degrees West longitude. The **South Magnetic Pole** is at approximately 69 degrees South latitude and 14 degrees East longitude.

magnetic storm, sudden and intense disturbance of the earth's magnetic field, caused by sunspots and other solar disturbances.

magnetic tape, thin tape coated with magnetically sensitive material, used to record sound or light patterns.

mag·net·ism (mag′nə tiz′əm) *n.* **1.** property of certain materials and of all electric currents enabling them to produce a magnetic field external to themselves, attract iron, steel, and other materials, and both attract and repel materials like themselves. **2.** branch of physics dealing with magnets, their fields of force, and their magnetic properties. Also, **mag·net′ics. 3.** extraordinary power to attract, influence, or charm.

mag·net·ite (mag′nə tīt′) *n.* black magnetic iron ore often found in igneous and metamorphic rocks. Formula: Fe_3O_4

mag·net·ize (mag′nə tīz′) **-ized, -iz·ing.** *v.t.* **1.** to give magnetic properties to; make into a magnet. **2.** to attract as if by a magnet; charm. —**mag′net·i·za′tion, mag′net·iz′er,** *n.*

mag·ne·to (mag nē′tō) *pl.,* **-tos.** *n.* small generator of alternating current, using permanent magnets rather than electromagnets. [Short for *magnetoelectric machine.*]

mag·ne·to·e·lec·tric (mag nē′tō i lek′trik) *adj.* of or relating to electricity produced by magnets.

mag·ne·tom·e·ter (mag′nə tom′ə tər) *n.* instrument for measuring the intensity of magnetic forces, esp. the earth's magnetic field.

mag·ne·to·sphere (mag nē′tə sfēr′) *n.* region around the earth in which charged particles are trapped by the earth's magnetic field. It contains the Van Allen radiation belt.

magni- *combining form* great; large: *magnify.* [Latin *magnus.*]

mag·nif·ic (mag nif′ik) *adj. Archaic.* **1.** magnificent. **2.** pompous. Also, **mag·nif′i·cal.** [Latin *magnificus* splendid, noble, from *magnus* great + *facere* to make, do.]

Mag·nif·i·cat (mag nif′i kat′, män yif′i kät′) *n.* **1.** hymn of the Virgin Mary, consisting of her words at the Visitation, beginning "My soul doth magnify the Lord." **2.** musical setting for this hymn. **3.** **magnificat.** any song or hymn of praise. [Latin *magnificat* it magnifies; the first word of the Latin form of the hymn of the Virgin Mary.]

mag·ni·fi·ca·tion (mag′nə fi kā′shən) *n.* **1.** act, process, or degree of magnifying. **2.** state of being magnified. **3.** something that has been magnified; enlarged copy or representation.

mag·nif·i·cence (mag nif′ə səns) *n.* state or quality of being magnificent. [Latin *magnificentia* splendor, nobleness.]

mag·nif·i·cent (mag nif′ə sənt) *adj.* **1.** presenting a breathtaking or imposing appearance; surpassingly beautiful or splendid: *a magnificent view of the valley, magnificent tapestries.* **2.** having a nobility or grandeur of character; inspiring: *a magnificent victory over a seemingly invincible enemy.* **3.** extraordinarily good; exceptional; outstanding: *a magnificent opportunity.* [Old French *magnificent* splendid, grand, from Latin *magnificentior,* comparative of *magnificus* splendid, noble. See MAGNIFIC.] —**mag·nif′i·cent·ly,** *adv.*

Syn. 1. Magnificent, splendid, sumptuous mean of surpassing beauty, excellence, or magnitude. **Magnificent** may be used to describe grandeur that overwhelms the senses: *The Capitol has a magnificent rotunda.* **Splendid** may be used to describe what is resplendent and glorious: *The queen looked splendid in her royal robes.* **Sumptuous** may be used to describe what is extravagantly rich in effects and lavish in luxury: *The room had a sumptuous appearance with damask hangings and chandeliers.*

mag·nif·i·co (mag nif′i kō′) *pl.,* **-coes.** *n.* **1.** formerly, a Venetian nobleman. **2.** person of high rank, great importance, or distinguished appearance. [Italian *magnifico* splendid, from Latin *magnificus* splendid, noble. See MAGNIFIC.]

mag·ni·fy (mag′nə fī′) **-fied, -fy·ing.** *v.t.* **1.** to increase the apparent size of, as by means of a lens: *This microscope magnifies by 1000 times the sample on the slides.* **2.** to cause to seem greater or more important than is really so; exaggerate: *to magnify the dangers.* **3.** to increase the size or extent of; add to; enlarge. **4.** *Archaic.* to praise; glorify. —*v.i.* to increase or have the power to increase the apparent size of an object, as a lens. [Latin *magnificāre* to make large, praise highly, going back to *magnus* great, large + *facere* to make, do.] —**mag′ni·fi′er,** *n.*

magnifying glass, lens or combination of lenses that increases the apparent size of an object seen through it.

mag·nil·o·quent (mag nil′ə kwənt) *adj.* lofty, pompous, or highflown in speech or style of expression. [Latin *magniloquus* pompous, lofty + -ENT.] —**mag·nil′o·quence,** *n.* —**mag·nil′o·quent·ly,** *adv.*

Mag·ni·to·gorsk (mag′ni tə górsk′) *n.* city in the west-central Soviet Union. Pop. (1970 est.), 364,000.

mag·ni·tude (mag′nə tōōd′, -tūd′) *n.* **1.** size or extent, esp. greatness of size or extent: *to determine the magnitude of an angle, a conflict of great magnitude.* **2.** greatness of significance; importance: *To intervene now would be a blunder of the first magnitude.* **3.** relative brightness of a star or other celestial body, as designated on a numerical scale. **Apparent magnitude** refers to the relative brightness of a body as observed from the earth. **Absolute magnitude** refers to the relative brightness of a body as it would appear at a distance of ten parsecs from the observer. [Latin *magnitūdō* greatness.]

mag·no·lia (mag nōl′yə, -nō′lē ə) n. 1. any of a group of ornamental trees and tall shrubs, genus *Magnolia*, often cultivated for their large, showy, fragrant flowers. 2. the flower itself, growing in white, rose, purple, or yellow. [Modern Latin *Magnolia*, from Pierre *Magnol*, 1638–1715, French botanist.]

mag·num (mag′nəm) n. 1. bottle for various wines, often holding two quarts or two-fifths of a gallon. 2. amount that such a bottle holds. [Latin *magnum*, neuter of *magnus* great, large.]

mag·num o·pus (mag′nəm ō′pəs) great work, esp. the greatest single work or achievement of a writer, artist, or composer; masterpiece. [Latin *magnum opus* great work.]

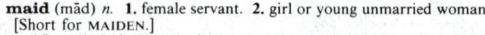

Magnolia

Ma·gog (mā′gog) see Gog and Magog.

mag·pie (mag′pī) n. 1. any of various noisy, long-tailed birds, family Corvidae, esp. genus *Pica*, having a stout black-and-white bill. The **black-billed magpie**, *P. pica*, has black-and-white plumage with iridescent patches of blue and green on the wings and tail. Also, **pie.** 2. one who chatters incessantly. [*Mag*, familiar form of *Margaret* female proper name + PIE².]

mag·uey (mag′wā) n. 1. any of several Mexican agave plants, some of which yield long, tough fibers used for making cord and rope. 2. fiber obtained from such a plant. [Spanish *maguey* the plant; of Taino origin.]

ma·gus (mā′gəs, mag′əs) pl., **ma·gi,** n. 1. also, **Magus.** one who practices magic or is knowledgeable about the stars or the occult; sorcerer; wizard. 2. **Magus.** one of the Magi of ancient Persia. [Latin *magus* magician. See MAGI.]

Magpie

Mag·yar (mag′yär) n. 1. member of a tribe of the Ural-Altaic language family that settled in Hungary in the ninth century. 2. Hungarian *(def. 2)*. —adj. of or relating to the Magyars or their language; Hungarian. [Magyar *Magyar* a Magyar.]

Ma·ha·bha·ra·ta (mə hä′bär′ə tə) n. one of the two great Sanskrit epic poems of ancient India. It is the longest poem in the world and contains the Bhagavad-Gita.

ma·ha·ra·jah (mä′hə rä′jə) also, **ma·ha·ra·ja.** n. any of certain sovereign princes in India. [Sanskrit *mahārājā* great king, from *mahā* great + *rājā* king.]

ma·ha·ra·ni (mä′hə rä′nē) also, **ma·ha·ra·nee.** n. 1. wife of a maharajah. 2. sovereign princess of India, holding the rank in her own right. [Hindi *mahārānī* great queen, from *mahā* great + *rānī* queen.]

ma·hat·ma (mə hät′mə, -hat′-) n. venerated wise and holy person. ▲ often used as a Hindu title of respect: *Mahatma Gandhi*. [Sanskrit *mahātman* great-souled, wise, from *mahā* great + *ātman* soul.]

Mah·di (mä′dē) pl., **-dis.** n. 1. In Islam, a messianic spiritual and temporal leader expected to lead the Muslims to salvation, convert mankind to Islam, and establish a reign of righteousness. 2. any of several persons who have claimed to be this leader. [Arabic *mahdīy* one who is guided aright.]

Ma·hi·can (mə hē′kən) pl. **-cans** or **-can.** n. member of a tribe of North American Indians of the Algonquian language family, formerly living in the area of the upper Hudson River. Also, **Mo·hi′can.**

mah jongg (mä′ jong′, zhong′) also, **mah-jongg, mah-jong.** 1. game of Chinese origin for from two to four players, played with 152 decorated tiles, the object being to obtain any of various winning combinations of tiles. 2. winning hand or combination in this game. [Chinese (Mandarin) *ma chiang* this game; literally, sparrow; referring to the bird depicted on some of the tiles used in the game.]

Mah·ler, Gus·tav (mä′lər; goos′täf) 1860–1911, Austrian composer and conductor.

ma·hog·a·ny (mə hog′ə nē) pl., **-nies.** n. 1.a. strong, hard, reddish-brown or yellowish wood of any of several tropical evergreen trees, genus *Swietenia*, widely used for making such items as furniture, cabinets, and musical instruments. b. tree yielding this wood. 2.a. similar wood of several other trees, as **African mahogany,** obtained from various trees of the genus *Khaya*. b. tree yielding this wood. 3. any of various reddish-brown colors, esp. a rich reddish brown. [Of uncertain origin.]

Ma·hom·et (mə hom′it) Muhammad.

Ma·hom·et·an (mə hom′ət ən) Muslim.

ma·hout (mə hout′) n. elephant driver or trainer. [Hindi *mahāwat*, from Sanskrit *mahāmātra* high official; literally, great in measure.]

maid (mād) n. 1. female servant. 2. girl or young unmarried woman. [Short for MAIDEN.]

maid·en (mād′ən) n. 1. girl or young unmarried woman. 2. a virgin. —adj. 1. of, relating to, or befitting a maiden. 2. unmarried: *a maiden lady*. 3. first or earliest: *maiden voyage, a maiden effort.* 4. untried; unused; fresh. [Old English *mægden* young unmarried woman, virgin.]

maid·en·hair (mād′ən hâr′) n. any of a large group of delicate ferns, genus *Adiantum*, having slender stems and feathery fronds.

maid·en·head (mād′ən hed′) n. hymen.

maid·en·hood (mād′ən hood′) n. state or time of being a maiden.

maid·en·ly (mād′ən lē) adj. of or befitting a maiden.

maiden name, surname that a woman had when she was not yet married.

maid-in-wait·ing (mād′in wā′ting) pl., **maids-in-wait·ing.** also, **maid in waiting.** n. unmarried woman, esp. a noblewoman, who attends a queen or princess.

maid of honor pl., **maids of honor. 1.** chief unmarried female attendant of the bride at a wedding. **2.** maid-in-waiting.

Maid of Orléans, Joan of Arc.

maid·ser·vant (mād′sur′vənt) n. female servant.

mail¹ (māl) n. **1.a.** letters, other written or printed matter, and packages, collectively, sent, distributed, or received by post. **b.** similar material sent, distributed, or received in a similar way: *interoffice mail.* **2.** such material as sent or delivered at a specific time: *His check should arrive in today's mail.* **3.** also, **mails.** system, usually operated by the national government, by which mail is collected, transported, and delivered; postal system. —v.t. to send by mail; deposit in a mailbox or at a post office. [Old French *male* bag; of Germanic origin; originally referring to the bag in which letters were carried.]

mail² (māl) n. **1.** armor made of interlinked rings of metal, usually iron or steel. **2.** any protective or defensive covering, as the shell of a turtle. —v.t. to cover or protect with or as with mail. [Old French *maille* link of metal, mesh, from Latin *macula* spot, mesh.]

mail·bag (māl′bag′) n. **1.** canvas or leather bag or pouch to be worn suspended from the shoulder, used by mailmen for carrying mail. **2.** large canvas bag or sack in which mail is transported.

mail·box (māl′boks′) n. **1.** box into which mail is deposited by the public for collection by the post office. **2.** box located at or near a dwelling, into which the occupants' mail is delivered.

mailed fist, use or threat of aggressive force, esp. between nations.

mail·gram (māl′gram) n. in the United States, a letter sent by telegraph to a local post office from which it is delivered with regular mail.

mailing list, list of people, businesses, or organizations to whom a business or organization mails advertisements and other literature.

mail·man (māl′man′) pl., **-men.** n. one who carries and delivers mail. Also, **post′man.**

mail order, order for merchandise that is received and filled by mail. —**mail′-order,** adj.

mail-order house, business that sells its merchandise primarily through the mail by filling mail orders received.

maim (mām) v.t. **1.** to injure or disfigure seriously and horribly; **2.** to render defective or less powerful; impair. [Old French *mahaignier* to wound; possibly of Germanic origin.]

Mai·mon·i·des, Moses (mī mon′ə dēz′) 1135–1204, Spanish-born Jewish philosopher and theologian; born Moses ben Maimon.

main (mān) adj. **1.** greatest or foremost in some capacity, as in size, extent, or importance; principal; chief: *the main branch of a library*. **2.** fully exerted; sheer: *by main force*. **3.** Nautical. of, near, or connected with the mainmast or mainsail. —n. **1.** principal pipe, duct, conduit, or cable for the passage of water, gas, sewage, or electricity. **2.** principal or chief part or point: *The main of life is composed of small incidents* (S. Johnson, 1750). **3.** open sea: *over the bounding main*. **4.** physical strength or effort; force; power. ▲ used chiefly in the phrase *with might and main*. **5.** Archaic. mainland. **6. in the main.** for the most part; on the whole; chiefly. [Partly from Old English *mægen* strength; partly from Old Norse *megn* strong.]

Syn. adj. **Main, chief, principal, primary** mean what is preeminent or leading. **Main** refers to the section or unit of a whole that is foremost in some capacity: *Dessert and coffee will follow the main course.* **Chief** applies to the leader of a division or group who outranks all others in importance, influence, or authority: *He was chief designer for the fashion house.* **Principal** refers to the person or thing which precedes, directs, or controls others: *The principal office of the company is in Chicago.* **Primary** refers to what is first in importance or is dominant in a system, structure, or progression: *The lotus is the primary motif in this design.*

main clause, independent clause.

Maine (mān) n. state in the northeastern United States, on the Atlantic. Capital, Augusta. Area, 33,215 sq. mi. Pop. (1970), 992,048. Abbreviation, **Me.**

at; āpe; cär; end; mē; it; īce; hot; ōld; fôrk; wood; fōōl; oil; out; up; ūse; turn; sing; thin; this; zh in treasure; ə in ago, taken, pencil, lemon, circus.

main·land (mān′land′, -lənd) *n.* body of land forming the principal or largest land mass of a region, country, or continent, as distinguished from an island or peninsula: *the mainland of Greece.*

main·line (mān′līn′) **-lined, -lin·ing.** *v.t., v.i. Slang.* to inject (a narcotic or other illegal drug) into a vein.

main·ly (mān′lē) *adv.* for the most part; chiefly. —**Syn.** see **especially.**

main·mast (mān′mast′, -məst) *n.* **1.** principal mast of a vessel, usually the second mast from the bow, as in a schooner or a brig. **2.** mast nearer the bow, as in a ketch or a yawl.

main·sail (mān′sāl′, -səl) *n.* **1.** in a fore-and-aft-rigged vessel, the principal sail set on the mainmast. **2.** in a square-rigged vessel, the sail bent to the main yard.

main·sheet (mān′shēt′) *n.* sheet or rope by which the mainsail is trimmed and secured.

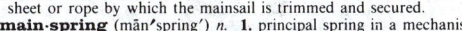

Mainmast

main·spring (mān′spring′) *n.* **1.** principal spring in a mechanism, esp. in a watch or clock. **2.** chief motivating force.

main·stay (mān′stā′) *n.* **1.** person or thing that is the chief support or part of something: *Fishing is the mainstay of their economy.* **2.** rope extending forward from the head of the mainmast, used to support and steady the mast.

main·stream (mān′strēm′) *n.* principal or prevailing direction or trend of development: *in the mainstream of American art.*

Main Street 1. principal street, esp. the main business street of a small American town. **2.** American middle-class attitudes, esp. those regarded as complacent, provincial, or conservative.

main·tain (mān tān′) *v.t.* **1.** to keep in existence or continuance; carry on, go on with, or persevere in: *Maintain this speed on the highway, but slow up when you approach the exit.* **2.** to have or hold or continue to have or hold; retain; preserve: *to maintain an open mind.* **3.** to keep in force, operation, or desirable or proper condition; keep from declining: *The city maintains public roads.* **4.** to keep, sustain, or hold on to against, or as if against, attack or opposition: *to maintain a position, to maintain one's ground.* **5.** to state positively or firmly; claim; declare: *No matter what he says, I still maintain he lied.* **6.** to insist on the truth of; uphold or assert against dispute: *to maintain one's innocence.* **7.** to provide for the support or upkeep of; bear the expenses of: *They maintain a house in the country as well as an apartment in the city.* [Old French *maintenir* to uphold, from Latin *manū tenēre* to hold by the hand.]

main·te·nance (mānt′ən əns) *n.* **1.** act of maintaining; being maintained. **2.** work of keeping something in desirable or proper condition. **3.** support or subsistence; livelihood.

main·top (mān′top′) *n.* platform at the head of the lower section of a mainmast.

main·top·gal·lant (mān′top′gal′ənt, -tə gal′-) *n.* mast, sail, or yard above the maintopmast.

main·top·mast (mān′top′mast′, -məst) *also,* **main·top·mast.** *n.* section of the mast next above the lower section of the mainmast.

main·top·sail (mān′top′sāl′, -səl) *n.* sail above the mainsail, set on the maintopmast.

main yard, lower yard on the mainmast.

Mainz (mīnts) *n.* port city in central West Germany, on the Rhine. Pop. (1968), 148,163.

maî·tre d' (mā′tər dē′, -trə) *pl.,* **maî·tre d's.** *Informal.* maître d'hôtel.

maî·tre d'hô·tel (mā′tər dō tel′, mā′trə) *pl.,* **mai·tres d'hô·tel. 1.** headwaiter. **2.** manager of a hotel. **3.** major-domo. [French *maître d'hôtel* headwaiter, butler; literally, master of the house, going back to Latin *magister* master + *dē* from + Medieval Latin *hospitale.* See HOTEL.]

maize (māz) *n.* **1.** corn (*defs. 1, 2*). **2.** color of ripe corn; deep yellow. [Spanish *maíz* Indian corn, from Taino *mahiz.*]

maj., major.

ma·jes·tic (mə jes′tik) *adj.* having or exhibiting majesty. Also, **ma·jes′ti·cal.** —**ma·jes′ti·cal·ly,** *adv.* —**Syn.** see **grand.**

maj·es·ty (maj′is tē) *pl.,* **-ties.** *n.* **1.** impressive or awesome dignity or splendor; stateliness; grandeur: *the majesty of the sea. The queen was seated on the throne in all her majesty.* **2.** sovereign power or authority. **3. Majesty,** used as a form of address for a sovereign and preceded by *His, Her,* or *Your.* [Old French *majeste,* from Latin *mājestās* dignity, authority.]

ma·jol·i·ca (mə jol′i kə, mə yol′-) *n.* **1.** glazed earthenware that is richly colored and decorated over a surface of opaque, white enamel, as that made in Renaissance Italy. **2.** pottery made in imitation of this.

[Italian *maiolica,* from *Majolica,* earlier name of Majorca, where such pottery was first made.]

ma·jor (mā′jər) *adj.* **1.** great or greater in extent, size, amount, or degree: *He spent the major part of a year abroad.* **2.** of great or comparatively great importance, value, or rank: *a major European author.* **3.** designating or relating to the academic subject or study specialized in by a degree candidate in a college or university: *His major field is economics.* **4.** of or relating to a majority. **5.** *Music.* **a.** of or relating to an interval equivalent to the distance between the tonic and the second or third or sixth or seventh degrees of a major scale. **b.** based on a major scale. **c.** of or relating to a triad in which the third tone above the fundamental is a whole step above the second tone. **6.** *Law.* having reached majority. —*n.* **1.** in the U.S. Army, Air Force, and Marine Corps, officer ranking below a lieutenant colonel and above a captain. **2.a.** subject or field of study in which a degree candidate in a college or university specializes or gives most emphasis in his studies. **b.** student concentrating on or specializing in such a subject or field of study. **3.** *Music.* major scale, key, mode, or interval. **4.** *Sports.* **majors.** major leagues collectively. **5.** *Law.* person who has reached majority. —*v.i.* to pursue studies in a major subject or field (often with *in*): *I majored in English.* [Latin *mājor* greater, comparative of *magnus* great. Doublet of MAYOR.]

Ma·jor·ca (mə jôr′kə, -yôr′-) *also,* **Mal·lor·ca.** *n.* largest of the Balearic Islands in the western Mediterranean. Area, 1405 sq. mi. Pop. (1960), 363,199. —**Ma·jor′can,** *adj., n.*

ma·jor·do·mo (mā′jər dō′mō) *pl.,* **-mos.** *n.* **1.** chief steward in a royal, noble, or great household. **2.** butler; steward. [Spanish *mayordomo,* from Medieval Latin *major domus* chief of the house, going back to Latin *mājor* greater + *domus* house.]

ma·jor·ette (mā′jə ret′) *n.* drum majorette.

major general, in the U.S. Army, Air Force, and Marine Corps, officer ranking below a lieutenant general and above a brigadier general.

ma·jor·i·ty (mə jôr′ə tē, -jor′-) *pl.,* **-ties.** *n.* **1.** number or group larger than another number or group with which it makes up a whole; portion constituting more than half of a total: *In the majority of cases, that does not hold true.* **2.** number of votes or of persons casting votes that are in agreement and compose more than half of a total number or group: *This measure received a majority.* **3.** number of votes cast for someone or something, over and above the total number of the rest of the votes. **4.** party, group, or faction with the most power, largest number of votes, or greatest representation. **5.** *Law.* age at which a person is legally entitled to manage his own affairs and has full legal rights and responsibilities. **6.** military rank or commission of a major. [French *majorité,* going back to Latin *mājor* greater. See MAJOR.]

majority leader, member of the party that holds a majority of seats in a legislative body, who organizes the members of his party regarding party tactics and measures to be voted on.

major league 1. either of the two main groups of professional baseball teams in the United States. **2.** any league of principal importance in certain other professional sports, as in ice hockey.

major premise, premise in a syllogism, usually the opening one, that is used as the predicate of the conclusion. See **syllogism.**

major scale, diatonic musical scale having half steps instead of whole steps after the third and seventh notes.

major term, term in a syllogism constituting the predicate of the conclusion. See **syllogism.**

Ma·kas·sar (mə kas′ər) Macassar.

make (māk) **made, mak·ing.** *v.t.* **1.** to form or bring into being by shaping, altering, or combining material or materials; construct; fashion: *The birds made a nest in the tree.* **2.** to cause to exist or occur; be the cause or occasion of; bring about: *to make a change in plans. Don't make a sound.* **3.** to produce, achieve, or accomplish, as through exertion or activity: *to make progress in peace talks.* **4.** to cause to appear; give shape or form to; form: *You don't make your capital letters large enough.* **5.** to bring to a particular state or condition; cause to be or become: *The smell of food made him hungry.* **6.** to cause to act or behave in a particular manner: *Peeling the onions made my eyes water.* **7.** to cause to seem or appear in a specified way: *That dress makes you look heavier than you are.* **8.** to constrain by or as by physical force; induce or compel (to do something): *You'll never make him talk.* **9.** to deliver verbally; utter; express: *to make an announcement.* **10.** to frame, hold, or arrive at in one's mind; entertain or formulate mentally: *to make plans, to make a decision.* **11.** to perform (an action); execute: *to make a phone call, to make a curtsy.* **12.** to carry out; engage in: *to make war, to make love.* **13.** to earn or gain, as through working, investing, or financial transactions: *We made a large profit on that deal. He makes $3.50 an hour.* **14.** to win, acquire, or obtain, as through one's behavior or actions: *He makes friends easily.* **15.** to prepare or put together, as a meal: *to make breakfast. Better make another pot of coffee.* **16.** to arrange or put into proper condition for use (often with *up*): *Make the beds before you leave.* **17.** to draw or set up; frame; enact; establish:

to make a will, to make rules. **18.** to cause to be available; allow provision for: *We'll make room for you in the back of the car.* **19.** to put forward or present: *to make friendly overtures, to make demands.* **20.** to put into a specified rank, position, or office; appoint; assign; elect: *They made him chairman.* **21.** to regard as or conclude as to the meaning or nature (with *of*): *What do you make of his last letter?* **22.** to fit or intend, as if by destiny or deliberate creation; be naturally fitted or destined: *He was made to be a writer.* **23.** to amount to; add up to; form as a total: *Five and five make ten. Twelve inches make one foot.* **24.** to constitute or be equivalent to in effect or significance: *This paragraph doesn't make sense.* **25.** to bring the total to; count as: *That makes the fourth time he's tried to get on the team.* **26.** to be sufficient to constitute; be the essential criterion, element, or determinant of: *Do clothes make the man?* **27.** to serve as; act as: *Nervous people make poor subjects in this type of experiment.* **28.** to have or turn out to have the necessary or essential qualities of: *She'll make a good wife.* **29.** to afford what is necessary for; be useful as: *Beef makes a good stew.* **30.** to cause or assure the success of: *His last novel made him. Her singing makes the show.* **31.** to appear in or on or succeed in getting recognition in or on: *Their breakthrough made the headlines.* **32.a.** *Informal.* to succeed in winning a place or position in or on; succeed in becoming a member of: *She made the cheerleading squad.* **b.** to achieve the rank or status of: *He made lieutenant.* **33.** to cause to be complete or totally satisfactory: *Just seeing her makes my day.* **34.** to judge or calculate to be; estimate: *I make the wall's height to be nine feet.* **35.** to arrive in time for: *They barely made the train.* **36.** to arrive at; reach: *We made the city in four hours.* **37.** to travel at the rate of: *This car can easily make eighty miles an hour on an open highway.* **38.** to cover by traveling; traverse: *We can make 300 miles before dark.* **39.** to close or complete (an electric circuit). **40.** to shuffle (a deck of cards). —*v.i.* **1.** to move or set out; proceed; head: *The ship made for shore.* **2.** to cause something or someone to be in some state or condition: *We made ready for battle.* **3.** to act or behave in a certain manner: *to make bold.* **4.** to start or appear to start to do something: *He made as if to throw the ball, then took a jump shot instead.*

to make do. to manage, function, or get along (with what is on hand, however unsatisfactory or inadequate): *I'll have to make do with my old coat this winter.*

to make for. a. to be conducive or favorable to; help promote or maintain; further: *Thoughtfulness makes for closer relationships.* **b.** to afford, provide, or constitute: *This book makes for very enjoyable reading.*

to make it. to succeed (in doing, achieving, or attaining something): *They'll never make it across the desert.*

to make off. to depart suddenly; run away.

to make off (or **away**) **with.** to carry off; steal.

to make out. a. to write out or fill out; complete or fill in by writing: *to make out a bill of sale, to make out a check.* **b.** to manage to see or read clearly; distinguish; discern: *I can't make out his handwriting.* **c.** to grasp the meaning, nature, or drift of (something); understand; comprehend. **d.** to get along; manage; succeed: *How did you make out at the interview?* **e.** to attempt to prove or show to be; represent or portray as being: *He's not the fool you make him out to be.* **f.** *Informal.* to neck.

to make over. a. to change or redo; renovate. **b.** to transfer title or ownership of: *to make over an account to someone.*

to make up. a. to be the parts or components of; constitute: *Nine players make up a team.* **b.** to put together or prepare from parts or ingredients; compose; assemble: *to make up a prescription.* **c.** to be reconciled, as after a dispute; resolve differences and become friendly or loving again. **d.** to create or devise in the mind; construct or concoct fictionally or falsely: *to make up an excuse.* **e.** to make suitable or equal return, payment, or amends for: *I promise I'll make it all up to you.* **f.** to supply an equivalent to or for: *What he lacks in good looks he makes up for in brains.* **g.** to supply what is lacking in; complete: *We need one more to make up the dozen.* **h.** to apply cosmetics to (the face): *to make up one's face heavily.* **i.** to take (an examination one has missed) at a later time. **j.** to take (a course or examination one has failed) again. **k.** *Printing.* to arrange type, illustrations, or other material into columns or pages for (a book or other publication).

to make up to. to try to win favor with by flattery or a show of affection, admiration, or friendliness.

—*n.* **1.a.** particular style or type of manufactured article with reference to the maker or identified by the maker's name or trademark; brand: *When it comes to watches, I wouldn't buy any other make.* **b.** such an article with reference to the original or place of manufacture: *a camera of Japanese make.* **2.** manner in which a thing is made: *I like the make of that dress.* **3.** physical, mental, or moral constitution; nature; character: *A man of his make is rare.* **4. on the make.** *a. Informal.* aggressively or eagerly intent on obtaining social or financial success, profit, or

advancement. **b.** *Slang.* in search of sexual relations. [Old English *macian* to fashion, frame, produce, cause.]

Syn. *v.t.* **1. Make, build, construct** mean to form or fashion. **Make** is commonly used in the sense of causing something to come into being by fashioning materials into a desired shape: *We make bricks out of clay.* **Build** may be preferred when one makes many parts or materials into a whole that has a well-defined base, design, and structure: *The boys built a tree house in the backyard.* **Construct** adds to *build* the distinct suggestion of a pattern or plan and implies skill in combining and designing materials: *There is a plan to construct a dam on this river.*

make-be·lieve (māk′bi lēv′) *n.* playful or fanciful pretense; imaginative belief or invention; fantasy: *Don't be afraid of the monster— the story's only make-believe.* —*adj.* resembling, involving, or produced by make-believe; imaginary.

mak·er (mā′kər) *n.* **1.** one who or that which makes something. ▲ often used in combination, as in *noisemaker, shoemaker, troublemaker.* **2. Maker.** God. **3. to meet one's Maker.** to die.

make-shift (māk′shift′) *n.* temporary or expedient substitute for the proper or desired thing. —*adj.* of the nature of or used as a makeshift: *That carton makes a good makeshift table.*

make-up (māk′up′) *also,* **make·up.** *n.* **1.** cosmetics collectively, esp. those applied to the face: *You're wearing too much eye make-up.* **2.** sum of cosmetics, wigs, or other articles used by a performer for the portrayal of a role. **3.** way in which something is put together or organized; composition: *The firm's make-up is complex and involves an elaborate hierarchy of management.* **4.** physical, mental, or moral constitution; nature: *Being nasty just isn't in his make-up.* **5.** *Printing.* arrangement of type, illustrations, or other material into columns or pages. **6.** *Informal.* examination to be taken by a student in substitution for a previous examination he has missed or failed.

make-weight (māk′wāt′) *n.* **1.** something placed on a scale to make the required weight. **2.** person or thing, often of insignificant value, used to make up a deficiency or fill a gap.

mak·ing (mā′king) *n.* **1.** act of one who or that which makes or the process of being made: *a dilemma not of his own making, to witness news in the making.* **2.** means or cause of improvement, advancement, or success: *Winning the case was the making of his career as a lawyer.* **3.** *usually,* **makings.** materials or qualities from which something can be made; components: *He had the makings of a great athlete.* **4.** quantity made at one time.

mal- *prefix* **1.** bad or badly; wrong or wrongly: *malpractice.* **2.** defective or defectively; inadequate or inadequately: *malformed.* **3.** not: *malcontent.* [French *mal-* badly, bad, from Latin *male* badly, ill and *malus* bad, evil.]

Mal·a·bar Coast (mal′ə bär′) region on the western coast of India.

Ma·lac·ca (mə lak′ə) *n.* stem of a rattan palm, used for making such items as canes and walking sticks. [From *Malacca,* a city and political subdivision in Malaysia.]

Mal·a·chi (mal′ə kī′) *n.* **1.** Hebrew prophet of the fifth century B.C. **2.** last book of the Protestant Old Testament, attributed to him. Also, in Douay Bible, **Mal·a·chi·as** (mal′ə kī′əs).

mal·a·chite (mal′ə kīt′) *n.* bright-green translucent copper ore used for making ornaments and jewelry. Formula: $Cu_2Co_3(OH)_2$ [Greek *malachē* mallow + -ITE¹; because its color is similar to that of the mallow's leaves.]

mal·ad·just·ed (mal′ə jus′tid) *adj.* poorly adjusted, esp. in relationship to the conditions or requirements of one's environment or the circumstances of one's life.

mal·ad·just·ment (mal′ə just′mənt) *n.* poor or faulty adjustment.

mal·ad·min·is·ter (mal′əd min′is tər) *v.t.* to administer or manage inefficiently or improperly. —**mal′ad·min′is·tra′tion,** *n.*

mal·a·droit (mal′ə droit′) *adj.* lacking in skill or dexterity; awkward; clumsy. [French *maladroit,* from *mal-* (see MAL-) + *adroit* skillful. See ADROIT.] —**mal′a·droit′ly,** *adv.* —**mal′a·droit′ness,** *n.*

mal·a·dy (mal′ə dē) *pl.,* **-dies.** *n.* **1.** sickness; illness. **2.** any disturbed or unwholesome condition: *social maladies.* [Old French *maladie* sickness, from *malade* sick, from Latin *male habitus* literally, badly kept.]

Mál·a·ga (mal′ə gə, mä′lə-) *n.* port city in southern Spain. Pop. (1968), 319,235.

Mal·a·ga (mal′ə gə) *n.* **1.** rich, sweet, white wine, originally made in Málaga, Spain. **2.** muscat (*def. 1*).

Mal·a·gas·y (mal′ə gas′ē) *pl.,* **-gas·y** or **-gas·ies.** *n.* **1.** native or inhabitant of Madagascar or of the Malagasy Republic. **2.** language belonging to the Malayo-Polynesian family of languages, spoken predominantly on Madagascar.

Malagasy Republic. island country in the Indian Ocean, consisting of Madagascar and some smaller islands. Capital, Tananarive. Land area, 226,658 sq. mi. Pop. (1969 est.), 6,643,000.

ma·laise (mə lāz′) *n.* **1.** indefinite feeling of ennui or dissatisfaction. **2.** vague feeling of physical discomfort, as at the onset of an illness. [French *malaise,* from *mal-* (see MAL-) + *aise* comfort. See EASE.]

ma·la·mute (mal'ə mūt') *also,* **ma·le·mute.** *n.* Alaskan malamute. [From *Malemute,* the Eskimo tribe that developed this dog.]

mal·a·pert (mal'ə purt') *Archaic. adj.* impudent; forward; bold. —*n.* impudent, bold person. [Old French *mal apert* insolent, from *mal-* (see MAL-) + *apert,* form of *espert* clever, from Latin *expertus* tested.]

mal·a·prop·ism (mal'ə prop iz'əm) *n.* **1.** humorously ridiculous misuse of words, esp. use of one word for another having a similar sound but a different meaning. **2.** instance of this, for example: *to reach new platitudes of achievement* instead of *to reach new plateaus of achievement.* [From Mrs. *Malaprop,* character who misused words in the play *The Rivals* (1775) by Richard Brinsley Sheridan; from MALAPROPOS.]

mal·ap·ro·pos (mal'ap rə pō') *adj.* out of place; inappropriate. —*adv.* inappropriately. [French *mal à propos* inappropriately, improperly, from *mal-* (see MAL-) + *à propos* to the purpose. See APROPOS.]

ma·lar·i·a (mə lâr'ē ə) *n.* disease characterized by recurring attacks of chills, high fever, and sweating, caused by microscopic parasites introduced into the bloodstream by the bite of female anopheles mosquitoes. [Italian *malaria,* from *mala aria* bad air, going back to Latin *malus* bad + *āēr* atmosphere; because it was once believed that the foul air of swamps caused this disease. See AIR.]

ma·lar·i·al (mə lâr'ē əl) *adj.* **1.** relating to or caused by malaria. **2.** having malaria. Also, **ma·lar'i·an, ma·lar'i·ous.**

ma·lar·key (mə lâr'kē) *also,* **ma·lar·ky.** *n. Informal.* insincere talk; nonsense. [Of uncertain origin.]

Ma·la·wi (mä'lä wē) *n.* country in southeastern Africa, formerly the British protectorate of Nyasaland. Capital, Zomba. Area, 45,483 sq. mi. Pop. (1970 est.), 4,530,000.

Ma·lay (mā'lā, mə lā') *n.* **1.** member of a people of southeastern Asia speaking a Malayo-Polynesian language, living in the Malay Peninsula, eastern Sumatra, parts of Borneo, Singapore, and some adjacent islands. **2.** language belonging to the Malayo-Polynesian family of languages, spoken predominantly in the Malay Peninsula and the East Indies. —*adj.* of or relating to the Malays, their culture, or their language.

Ma·lay·a (mə lā'ə) *n.* region of southeastern Asia, on the Malay Peninsula, part of Malaysia, known as West Malaysia. Area, 50,700 sq. mi. Pop. (1967 est.), 8,655,000.

Mal·a·ya·lam (mal'ə yä'ləm) *n.* language belonging to the Dravidian family of languages spoken predominantly in southwestern India.

Ma·lay·an (mə lā'ən) *adj.* Malay. —*n.* Malay (*def. 1*).

Malay Archipelago, large island group in the Pacific, between Australia and southeastern Asia. Also, **East Indies.**

Ma·lay·o·Pol·y·ne·sian (mə lā'ō pol'ə nē'zhən) *n.* family of languages spoken predominantly in the Pacific islands and some islands in the Indian Ocean. Also, **Aus'tro·ne'sian.**

Malay Peninsula, long, narrow peninsula in southeastern Asia, including Malaya and part of Thailand.

Ma·lay·sia (mə lā'zhə, -shə) *n.* **1.** country in southeastern Asia, divided by the South China Sea, comprising Malaya on the west and Sarawak and Sabah on the east. Capital, Kuala Lumpur. Land area, 128,430 sq. mi. Pop. (1967 est.), 10,071,000. **2.** Malay Archipelago. —**Ma·lay'sian,** *adj., n.*

Mal·colm X (mal'kəm) 1925–65, American civil rights leader; born Malcolm Little.

mal·con·tent (mal'kən tent') *adj.* discontented or dissatisfied, esp. with established or existing conditions. —*n.* one who is malcontent.

Mal·den (môl'dən) *n.* city in eastern Massachusetts, near Boston. Pop. (1970), 56,127.

Mal·dive, Republic of (mal'dīv) island country in the Indian Ocean. Capital, Male. Land area, 115 sq. mi. Pop. (1975 est.), 100,000.

male (māl) *adj.* **1.** of or relating to the sex that begets young or produces sperm. **2.** masculine (*def. 1*). **3.** of or relating to a plant that bears staminate flowers. **4.** (of an object or device) having a part designed to be inserted into a corresponding hollow part. —*n.* male person, animal, or plant. [Old French *ma(s)le* masculine, manly, from Latin *masculus,* diminutive of *mās* male creature.] —**male'ness,** *n.*

Ma·le (mä'lē) *n.* capital of the Maldive Islands. Pop. (1967), 11,760.

mal·e·dic·tion (mal'ə dik'shən) *n.* **1.** utterance of a curse against someone. **2.** malicious talk; slander. [Latin *maledictiō* abuse, curse, going back to *male* badly + *dīcere* to speak. Doublet of MALISON.]

mal·e·dic·to·ry (mal'ə dik'tər ē) *adj.* containing, expressing, or of the nature of a malediction.

mal·e·fac·tion (mal'ə fak'shən) *n.* evil deed; wrongdoing.

mal·e·fac·tor (mal'ə fak'tər) *n.* **1.** one who commits a crime; criminal. **2.** evildoer. [Latin *malefactor* evildoer, going back to *male* badly + *facere* to do.] —**mal'e·fac'tress,** *n.*

ma·lef·ic (mə lef'ik) *adj.* producing or causing evil. [Latin *maleficus* evildoing, wicked, going back to *male* badly + *facere* to do.]

ma·lef·i·cence (mə lef'ə səns) *n.* **1.** the doing of evil, mischief, or harm. **2.** state or quality of being maleficent. [Latin *maleficentia* evildoing, harm, going back to *male* badly + *facere* to do.]

ma·lef·i·cent (mə lef'ə sənt) *adj.* causing or doing evil, mischief, or harm. [From MALEFICENCE.]

ma·le·mute (mal'ə mūt') *n.* Alaskan malamute.

ma·lev·o·lence (mə lev'ə ləns) *n.* disposition to do or wish evil or harm to others.

ma·lev·o·lent (mə lev'ə lənt) *adj.* **1.** doing or desiring to do evil or harm to others. **2.** tending to exert an evil or harmful influence. [Latin *malevolēns* ill-disposed, envious, going back to *male* badly + *velle* to wish.] —**ma·lev'o·lent·ly,** *adv.*

mal·fea·sance (mal fē'zəns) *n. Law.* performance of a wrongful act, esp. by a public official; official misconduct. Distinguished from **misfeasance** and **nonfeasance.** [Old French *faire* to do, from Latin *facere.*] —**mal·fea'sant,** *adj., n.*

mal·for·ma·tion (mal'fôr mā'shən) *n.* irregular, defective, or abnormal formation or structure, esp. in an organism.

mal·formed (mal'fôrmd') *adj.* irregularly, defectively, or abnormally formed; misshapen.

mal·func·tion (mal fungk'shən) *n.* failure to function properly: *A malfunction in the carburetor caused the car to stall repeatedly.* —*v.i.* to fail to function properly.

Ma·li (mä'lē) *n.* large landlocked country in western Africa, formerly a French possession. Capital, Bamako. Area, 463,950 sq. mi. Pop. (1969 est.), 4,929,000.

mal·ic acid (mal'ik, mā'lik) organic acid found in apples and many other fruits. Formula: COOHCH₂CH(OH)COOH [French *(acide) malique* malic (acid), from Latin *mālum* apple, from dialectal Greek *mālon.*]

mal·ice (mal'is) *n.* **1.** desire to cause injury or pain to another; desire to take pleasure in the misfortune of another: *With malice toward none; with charity for all* (Lincoln, 1865). **2.** *Law.* willful, deliberate committing of an unlawful act, with the intent to inflict injury or under conditions that imply an evil intent. [Old French *malice* wickedness, from Latin *malitia.*]

ma·li·cious (mə lish'əs) *adj.* **1.** characterized by, showing, or resulting from malice: *a malicious person.* **2.** *Law.* involving or caused by malice. —**ma·li'cious·ly,** *adv.* —**ma·li'cious·ness,** *n.*

ma·lign (mə līn') *v.t.* to speak ill of or harmful untruths about; slander: *to malign someone's character.* —*adj.* **1.** having or showing an evil disposition toward others; malevolent. **2.** evil or harmful in nature or effect; injurious. [Late Latin *malignāre* to act maliciously, from Latin *malignus* malicious, wicked.]

ma·lig·nan·cy (mə lig'nən sē) *pl.,* **-cies.** *n.* **1.** state or quality of being malignant. Also, **ma·lig'nance.** **2.** any malignant disease, process, or conditon, esp. a cancerous tumor.

ma·lig·nant (mə lig'nənt) *adj.* **1.** *Medicine.* **a.** (of a growth or tumor) tending to grow and spread uncontrollably or to recur after removal. **b.** (of a disease) tending to become progressively worse and to result in death unless halted by treatment. **2.** viciously evil or harmful in nature, influence, or effect. **3.** feeling or showing great or vicious malevolence. [Late Latin *malignāns,* present participle of *malignāre.* See MALIGN.] —**ma·lig'nant·ly,** *adv.*

ma·lig·ni·ty (mə lig'nə tē) *pl.,* **-ties.** *n.* **1.** state or quality of being malign. **2.** something evil.

ma·lines (mə lēn') *also,* **ma·line.** *n.* **1.** Mechlin. **2.** very fine, stiff net, similar to tulle, used chiefly in millinery trimming. [French *malines* Mechlin, from *Malines,* the French name for Mechlin, the Belgian town where this lace was originally made.]

ma·lin·ger (mə ling'gər) *v.i.* to attempt to avoid or shirk work or duty, esp. by pretending to be sick or injured. [From French *malingre* sickly, possibly from *mal-* (see MAL-) + Old French *haingre* thin (probably of Germanic origin).] —**ma·lin'ger·er,** *n.*

mal·i·son (mal'ə sən, -zən) *n. Archaic.* malediction; curse. [Old French *maleison,* from Latin *maledictiō* abuse, curse, going back to *male* badly + *dīcere* to speak. Doublet of MALEDICTION.]

mall (môl, mal) *n.* **1.** walk or promenade, usually public and lined with trees. **2.** shopping area closed off to vehicles and often covered, enclosed, or partially underground. [Old French *mail* hammer, from Latin *malleus;* development of meaning from the hammer or mallet used to play the game pall-mall, to the alley in which the game was played, to an alley or lane.]

mal·lard (mal'ərd) *pl.,* **-lards** or **-lard.** *n.* wild duck, *Anas platyrhynchos,* of freshwater ponds and marshes throughout temperate northern regions. The male has a green head, a white band around the neck, a reddish-brown breast, and a grayish back. Length: 28 inches. [Old French *mallart* wild drake; of uncertain origin.]

Mallard

at; āpe; cär; end; mē; it; īce; hot; ōld; fôrk; wood; fōōl; oil; out; up; ūse; turn; sing; thin; this; zh in treasure; ə in ago, taken, pencil, lemon, circus.

617

mal·le·a·ble (mal′ē ə bəl) *adj.* **1.** capable of being hammered, pressed, or beaten into various shapes without breaking. **2.** capable of being molded, changed, or influenced; flexible: *a malleable personality.* [Old French *malleable* capable of being hammered, going back to Latin *malleus* hammer.] —**mal′le·a·bil′i·ty, mal′le·a·ble·ness,** *n.* —**mal′-le·a·bly,** *adv.* —**Syn. 1.** see **pliable.**

mal·let (mal′it) *n.* **1.** short-handled hammer with a heavy, cylindrical, usually wooden, head. **2.** long-handled wooden mallet used to strike the ball in certain games, as croquet or polo. [Old French *maillet* hammer, diminutive of *mail,* from Latin *malleus.*]

mal·le·us (mal′ē əs) *pl.,* **mal·le·i** (mal′ē ī′). *n.* one of the three bones of the middle ear; hammer. [Latin *malleus* hammer.]

Mal·lor·ca (mä lyôr′kä, -yôr′-) Majorca.

mal·low (mal′ō) *n.* **1.** any of a group of plants, genus *Malva,* having small pink or white flowers and lobed or cut leaves. **2.** any plant of the family Malvaceae, usually having large, showy flowers, as the hollyhock or okra. —*adj.* designating a family, Malvaceae, of herbs, shrubs, and trees found in temperate and tropical regions, with stamens united in a column and with pistils having many carpels. [Old English *mealewe* plant of the genus *Malva,* from Latin *malva.* Doublet of MAUVE.]

Mallow

malm·sey (mäm′zē) *n.* aromatic, sweet wine. [Medieval Latin *Malmasia* Monemvasia, Greek town near which this wine was first made, from Greek *Monembasiā.*]

mal·nu·tri·tion (mal′nōō trish′ən, -nū-) *n.* condition resulting from a lack of nutrients in the body tissues.

mal·oc·clu·sion (mal′ə klōō′zhən) *n.* condition in which the teeth of the upper and lower jaws do not meet properly.

mal·o·dor·ous (mal ō′dər əs) *adj.* having a disagreeable odor. —**mal·o′dor·ous·ly,** *adv.* —**mal·o′dor·ous·ness,** *n.*

Mal·o·ry, Sir Thomas (mal′ər ē) died 1471, English author noted esp. for his retelling of legends of King Arthur.

mal·prac·tice (mal prak′tis) *n.* **1.** injurious, improper, or culpably negligent treatment of a patient by a doctor. **2.** improper or unethical conduct in any professional or official position.

malt (môlt) *n.* **1.** cereal grain, esp. barley, steeped in warm water until it germinates and then kiln-dried, used chiefly in brewing and distilling. **2.** alcoholic beverage or liquor brewed from malt, as beer or ale. **3.** *Informal.* malted. —*v.t.* **1.** to cause (grain) to become malt. **2.** to treat or mix with malt. —*v.i.* to become malt. [Old English *mealt* barley or other grain specially prepared for brewing or distilling.]

Mal·ta (môl′tə) *n.* **1.** country consisting of an island group in the Mediterranean, south of Sicily. Capital, Valletta. Land area, 122 sq. mi. Pop. (1968 est.), 328,000. Also, **Maltese Islands. 2.** chief island of this country. Area, 95 sq. mi.

mal·ted (môl′tid) *n.* drink made by whipping milk, dried milk, malted cereals, and usually flavoring and ice cream.

malted milk 1. malted. **2.** powdered preparation consisting chiefly of dried milk and malted cereals, used esp. in making malteds.

Mal·tese (môl tēz′, -tēs′) *pl.,* **-tese. 1.** native or inhabitant of Malta. **2.** language of Malta, an Arabic dialect containing Italian elements. —*adj.* of or relating to Malta, its people, or their language.

Maltese cat, short-haired, bluish-gray domestic cat.

Maltese cross, eight-pointed cross resembling four arrowheads pointed inward and meeting at a central point.

Maltese Islands, Malta *(def. 1).*

malt extract, thick, sugary substance obtained by soaking malt in water.

Mal·thus, Thomas R. (mal′thəs) 1766–1834, English economist and clergyman.

Mal·thu·si·an (mal thōō′zē ən, -zhən) *adj.* of or relating to Malthus or his theory that population tends to increase at a faster rate than its means of subsistence unless it is checked by some natural disaster or a voluntary limitation of the birth rate. —*n.* believer in the theories of Malthus.

malt liquor, alcoholic liquor made by fermenting malt.

malt·ose (môl′tōs) *n.* colorless crystalline compound similar to sucrose, produced by the enzymatic action of diastase on starch, used esp. as a foodstuff and as a sweetening agent. Formula: $C_{12}H_{22}O_{11}·H_2O$ Also, **malt sugar.**

mal·treat (mal trēt′) *v.t.* to abuse. —**mal·treat′ment,** *n.*

ma·ma (mä′mə, mə mä′) *also,* **mam·ma.** *n. Informal.* mother. [Repetition of *ma,* a sound commonly uttered by infants.]

mam·bo (mäm′bō) *pl.,* **-bos.** *n.* **1.** social dance of Latin American origin resembling the rumba. **2.** music for this dance. —*v.i.* to dance the mambo. [Spanish *mambo* this dance, possibly from Haitian *mambo* voodoo priestess.]

Mam·e·luke (mam′ə lōōk′) *n.* member of a military class that ruled Egypt from about 1250 to 1517 and remained powerful until 1811.

mam·mal (mam′əl) *n.* any animal of a class, Mammalia, of warm-blooded vertebrates, the females of which have mammary glands, including humans, dogs, elephants, porcupines, and whales. Mammals are the only animals that have hair. [Modern Latin *Mammalia,* neuter plural of Latin *mammālis* relating to the breast, from Latin *mamma* breast; because this class of vertebrates feeds its young on milk produced by the mammary glands.] —**mam·ma·li·an** (mə mā′lē ən, -māl′yən), *adj. n.*

mam·mal·o·gy (mə mal′ə je) *n.* branch of zoology dealing with mammals. —**mam·mal′o·gist,** *n.*

mam·ma·ry (mam′ər ē) *adj.* of, relating to, or of the nature of a milk-secreting gland with which female mammals nourish their young.

mam·mil·la (ma mil′ə) *pl.,* **-mil·lae** (-mil′ē). *n.* **1.** nipple or teat. **2.** any nipple-shaped structure or protuberance. [Latin *mamilla* nipple, teat, diminutive of *mamma* breast.]

mam·mo·gram (mam′ə gram) *n.* X ray of the breast.

mam·mog·ra·phy (ma mog′rə fē) *n.* X ray examination of the breast.

Mam·mon (mam′ən) *n.* **1.** *also,* **mammon.** personification of riches and worldly gain, as a false god. **2.** *usually,* **mammon.** riches regarded as an evil influence or as an object of worship and greedy pursuit. [Latin *mammōna* riches, from Greek *mamōnās,* from Aramaic *māmōnā.*]

Mammoth

mam·moth (mam′əth) *n.* any of various extinct, prehistoric elephants, genus *Mammuthus,* that had long, upward-curving tusks and shaggy, blackish hair. Height: to 14 feet at the shoulder. —*adj.* of immense size; huge; gigantic. [Russian *mamont,* possibly going back to Yakut *mamma* earth; because mammoths were thought to burrow in the earth.]

mam·my (mam′ē) *pl.,* **-mies.** *also,* **mam·mie.** *n.* **1.** *Informal.* mother. **2.** formerly, esp. in the southern United States, a black woman serving as a nurse to white children. ▲ now usually considered offensive. [Dialectal form of MAMA.]

man (man) *pl.,* **men.** *n.* **1.** adult male human being: *He may still be a boy, but he has the physique of a man.* **2.** member of the human race; human being; person: *All men are created equal.* **3.** human beings collectively; the human race; mankind: *the study of man through the ages.* **4.** any of various extinct, prehistoric mammals, family Hominidae, that were the evolutionary ancestors of the modern human being, as Java man and Neanderthal man. **5.** male human being eminently endowed with or distinguished by qualities considered as manly, as strength and courage: *If you can keep your head when all about you are losing theirs and blaming it on you . . . you'll be a man, my son* (Kipling, 1910). **6.a.** male human being considered to be in some way under the control, supervision, or leadership of another: *Our platoon lost two officers and twenty men.* **b.** male employee; worker; hand: *The boss assigned four men to do the job.* **c.** male servant, esp. a valet: *My man Robert will lay out your clothes.* **d.** one of the members of a team; player: *The coach had to send a new man in after the first quarter.* **7.** one of the pieces used to play certain games, as chess and checkers. **8.** husband, lover, or sweetheart. ▲ now chiefly used informally, except in the phrase *man and wife.* **9.** *Slang.* fellow. ▲ used as a term of address: *Hey, man, how've you been?* **10.** as one man; in unison; unanimously: *They answered his question as one man.* **11. to a man,** without exception: *We all feel the same way on this issue to a man.* **12. to be one's own man.** to be one's own master; be independent. —*interj. Slang.* used to express surprise or excitement or to emphasize what is said: *Man, it's freezing out there!* —*v.t.,* **manned, man·ning. 1.** to supply with men, as for work or defense: *to man the fort.* **2.** to take one's place or station at for service: *Man the torpedoes.* **3.** to summon up strength or fortitude: *to man oneself for an ordeal.* [Old English *mann* human being, adult male.] —**Syn. n. 2.** see **human being.**

Man, Isle of (man) island in the Irish Sea, administered by the United Kingdom. Area, 227 sq. mi. Pop. (1961), 48,133.

man about town, sophisticated man who frequents fashionable places.

man·a·cle (man′ə kəl) *n.* **1.** *usually,* **manacles.** handcuff. **2.** anything that restrains or fetters. —*v.t.,* **-cled, -cling. 1.** to put manacles on. **2.** to restrain; hamper. [Old French *manicle* handcuff, from Latin *manicula* little hand, handle, diminutive of *manus* hand.]

man·age (man′ij) **-aged, -ag·ing.** *v.t.* **1.** to direct, guide, or control

the affairs or operation of: *to manage a department store, to manage a campaign.* **2.** to succeed in accomplishing somehow: *I'll manage to see you before I leave.* **3.** to exert control or influence over, so as or as if to make submissive or docile. **4.** to control the use, movement, or behavior of; handle: *Can you manage all those heavy bundles?* —*v.i.* **1.** to be able to get along; make out: *I don't know how we'll manage without her.* **2.** to direct, guide, or control affairs; carry on business; act as a manager. [Italian *maneggiare* to control (a horse), handle, from *mano* hand, from Latin *manus.*]
Syn. *v.t.* **1. Manage, direct, administer** mean to exercise authority to conduct affairs. **Manage** may be used when one supervises an organization with responsibility for results: *Henry manages a hotel.* **Direct** may be used when one issues general instructions and oversees the actions of subordinates: *David directed the advertising campaign.* **Administer** may be used when one performs executive duties directed toward the achievement of the objectives of an organization: *The chancellor administers the university.*
man·age·a·ble (man′i jə bəl) *adj.* capable of being managed. —**man′age·a·bil′i·ty, man′age·a·ble·ness,** *n.* —**man′age·a·bly,** *adv.*
man·age·ment (man′ij mənt) *n.* **1.** act, art, or practice of managing. **2.a.** person or persons who manage a business, institution, or other enterprise: *I'm going to complain to the management about the very poor service in this hotel.* **b.** such persons collectively, esp. in relation to workers or unions: *A strike was called because labor and management could not agree upon a settlement.*
man·ag·er (man′i jər) *n.* **1.** one who manages a business, institution, organization, or other enterprise. **2.** one who takes care of or who is in charge of the business or professional affairs of an entertainer, athlete, or similar client. **3.** one who is skilled in managing, as business, monetary, or household affairs. —**man′ag·er·ess, man′ag·er·ship′,** *n.*
man·a·ge·ri·al (man′ə jēr′ē əl) *adj.* of or relating to a manager or management: *managerial duties or position.* —**man′a·ge′ri·al·ly,** *adv.*
Ma·na·gua (mə nä′gwə) *n.* capital and largest city of Nicaragua, in the southwestern part of the country. Pop. (1965), 262,047.
ma·ña·na (mən yä′nə, mä nyä′nä) *adv.* at some indefinite future time; tomorrow: *We'll do all that work mañana.* —*n.* some indefinite future time; tomorrow. [Spanish *mañana* morning, tomorrow, going back to Latin *māne* in the morning.]
Ma·nas·sas (mə nas′əs) *n.* town in northeastern Virginia near which the two battles of Bull Run took place during the Civil War.
Ma·nas·seh (mə nas′ə) *n.* **1.** in the Old Testament, the elder son of Joseph. **2.** one of the twelve tribes of Israel, descended from him. **3.** king of Judah who ruled in the seventh century B.C.
man-at-arms (man′at ärmz′) *pl.,* **men-at-arms.** *n.* **1.** soldier. **2.** in the Middle Ages, heavily armed soldier, usually mounted.
man·a·tee (man′ə tē′) *n.* any of various aquatic mammals, genus *Trichechus,* having two broad front flippers and a flat, paddlelike tail, found in the warm coastal waters of the Atlantic. Length: 7 feet. [Spanish *manatí;* of Carib origin.]

Manatee

Man·ches·ter (man′ches′tər, -chis-) *n.* **1.** city in northwestern England. Pop. (1968), 602,800. **2.** city in southern New Hampshire, on the Merrimack River. Pop. (1970), 87,754.
Man·chu (man′chōō) *pl.,* **-chus** or **-chu.** *n.* **1.** member of a Mongolian people of the Tungus language family, living in Manchuria, who completed a conquest of China in 1644 and established a dynasty that ruled until 1912. **2.** language belonging to the Ural-Altaic family of languages, spoken predominantly in Manchuria. —*adj.* **1.** of or relating to the Manchus or their dynasty, language, or culture. **2.** of or relating to Manchuria, its people, or their language.
Man·chu·kuo (man′chōō′kwō′) *n.* puppet state consisting principally of Manchuria, established by Japan in 1932 and lasting until 1945.
Man·chu·ri·a (man chōor′ē ə) *n.* historic region in northeastern China. Area, approx. 310,000 sq. mi. Pop. (1962 est.), 57,000,000. —**Man·chu′ri·an,** *adj., n.*
man·ci·ple (man′sə pəl) *n.* officer or steward, as of a college or monastery, authorized to purchase provisions. [Old French *mancip(l)e* slave, from Latin *mancipium* legal purchase (as of a slave), slave, going back to *manus* hand + *capere* to take.]
Man·da·lay (mand′əl ā′, mand′əl ā′) *n.* city in central Burma, on the Irrawaddy River. Pop. (1962 est.), 200,000.
man·da·mus (man dā′məs) *n.* written order from a higher court to a lower court, or to an official or organization, commanding that an act be performed or not performed. [Latin *mandāmus* we command.]
man·da·rin (man′dər in) *n.* **1.** in imperial China, member of any of the nine ranks of high public officials. **2.** member of any elite or influen-

tial group, esp. one who is elderly or conservative or whose power seems unduly unrestricted. **3. Mandarin.** principal dialect of Chinese that is the official national language of mainland China. **4.** mandarin orange. —*adj.* of, relating to, or characteristic of a mandarin. [Portuguese *mandarim* high-ranking Chinese official, modification (influenced by Portuguese *mandar* to order) of Malay *mantrī* counselor, going back to Sanskrit *mantrin.*]
mandarin orange, small, sweet orange having a thin rind that is easy to peel.
man·da·tar·y (man′də ter′ē) *pl.,* **-tar·ies.** *also,* **man·da·to·ry.** *n.* person or nation holding or receiving a mandate.
man·date (man′dāt) *n.* **1.** instruction, authorization, or support given by an electorate to its representative in government, as regarding a program or policy, expressed or implied by the results of an election or vote. **2.** authoritative or official command, order, or charge. **3.a.** commission from the League of Nations to a member nation for the administration of a territory until the territory was ready for self-government. **b.** territory so administered. **4.** *Law.* order from a higher court or judicial officer directing that action be taken by a lower court or judicial officer. —*v.t.* **-dat·ed, -dat·ing.** to administer or assign (a territory) under a mandate. [Latin *mandātum* order, commission.]
man·da·tor (man dā′tər) *n.* one who gives a mandate.
man·da·to·ry (man′də tôr′ē) *adj.* **1.** required by or as if by a mandate; compulsory; obligatory. **2.** of, relating to, or conveying a mandate. **3.** holding a mandate over some territory. —*n.* mandatary.
man·di·ble (man′də bəl) *n.* **1.** bone of the lower jaw in vertebrates. **2.** either the upper or lower part of a bird's beak. **3.** one of a pair of jawlike parts used for seizing and biting, located on either side of the mouth opening in insects and other arthropods. [Latin *mandibula* jaw, from *mandere* to chew.]

Mandible *(def. 3)*
Eye · Mandible · Maxilla · Palpi

Man·din·go (man ding′gō) *pl.,* **-gos** or **-goes.** *n.* **1.** member of an African people of Negroid stock, living primarily in western Africa in the region of the Niger River. **2.** any of a group of languages spoken predominantly in western Africa, esp. in Liberia and Sierra Leone.
man·do·lin (mand′əl in′, mand′əl in′) *n.* lute-like musical instrument having a pear-shaped body, a fretted neck, and metal strings, usually played by plucking with a plectrum. [French *mandoline,* from Italian *mandolino,* diminutive of *mandola* lute, through Late Latin, from Greek *pandoura* three-stringed musical instrument.]

Mandolin

man·drake (man′drāk′) *n.* **1.** low-growing plant, *Mandragora officinarum,* of the nightshade family, having thick fleshy roots, wavy-edged oval leaves, and cup-shaped flowers. Also, **man·drag·o·ra** (man drag′ər ə). **2.** root of this plant, formerly believed to have magical powers. **3.** Mayapple. [Modification (probably influenced by obsolete *drake* dragon) of Old English *mandragora,* from Latin *mandragoras,* from Greek *mandragoras.*]
man·drel (man′dril) *also,* **man·dril.** *n.* **1.** shaft, spindle, or similar piece for holding material to be shaped or worked, as on a lathe. **2.** metal rod or core around which material may be shaped, cast, or bent. [Of uncertain origin.]
man·drill (man′dril) *n.* large ground-dwelling baboon, *Mandrillus sphinx,* of tropical western Africa, having a long, ridged nose, the male of which has a pale-blue nose with a red streak in the center, a black mask around the eyes, a scarlet rump shading into blue or black, and an olive-brown and gray body. Length: 3 feet. [MAN + DRILL⁴; because of its resemblance to *man.*]

Mandrake

mane (mān) *n.* **1.** long, heavy hair along the back of and around the neck of certain animals, as the horse and lion. **2.** long or abundant growth of hair on a person's head. [Old English *manu* mane of an animal.]
man-eat·ing (man′ē′ting) *adj.* likely to attack and eat human beings; that eats, or is said to eat, human flesh: *a man-eating tiger, man-eating sharks.* —**man′eat′er,** *n.*
ma·nège (ma nezh′, -näzh′, mə-) *also,* **ma·nege.** *n.* **1.** art or practice

of training, managing, or riding horses; horsemanship. **2.** movements or paces of a trained horse. **3.** school for training horses and teaching horsemanship. [French *manège*, from Italian *maneggio*, from *maneggiare* to control (a horse), handle. See MANAGE.]

ma·nes (mā′nēz) *also*, **Ma·nes.** *n.,pl.* **1.** among the ancient Romans, the good spirits of the dead, esp. of dead ancestors, regarded as gods. **2.** spirit or shade of a particular dead person. ▲ construed as singular in def. 2. [Latin *mānēs* the gods of the lower world, the deified souls of the dead.]

Ma·net, É·douard (ma nā′; ā dwär′) 1832–83, French painter who was a forerunner of impressionism.

ma·neu·ver (mə nōō′vər) *also*, *British*, **ma·noeu·vre.** *n.* **1.** *Military.* **a.** planned tactical or strategic movement, as of ships, troops, or firepower. **b.** *usually*, **maneuvers.** large-scale tactical exercise simulating combat. **2.** any skillful move, procedure, or stratagem, as one executed to gain a desired goal: *political maneuvers.* **3.** physical movement showing or marked by agility or skill. —*v.t.* to move or manage skillfully, as into a desired position or toward a desired goal: *I maneuvered my way through the crowded entrance.* —*v.i.* **1.** to perform a maneuver or maneuvers. **2.** to use skillful movements, procedures, or stratagems; craftily shift position, ground, or tactics: *to maneuver for a position of power.* [French *manœuvre* action, scheme; literally, a work with the hand, going back to Latin *manū operārī* to work with the hand.] —**ma·neu′ver·a·bil′i·ty, ma·neu′ver·er,** *n.* —**ma·neu′ver·a·ble,** *adj.*

man Friday **1.** dependable, faithful servant, aide, or follower. **2.** male employee, esp. in an office, with a wide variety of duties. [From *Friday*, the faithful servant and companion in the novel *Robinson Crusoe* (1719) by Daniel Defoe.]

man·ful (man′fəl) *adj.* having or showing manly spirit; brave; resolute. —**man′ful·ly,** *adv.* —**man′ful·ness,** *n.*

man·ga·nese (mang′gə nēz′, -nēs′) *n.* brittle, silver-gray, highly reactive metallic element, used esp. in the production of steel. Symbol: **Mn** See **element** for table.

mange (mānj) *n.* contagious skin disease of cattle, horses, dogs, and other domestic animals, caused by certain mites and marked by scaly pimples and often by a loss of hair. [Old French *manjue* itching, from *mangier* to eat, from Latin *mandūcāre.*]

man·gel-wur·zel (mang′gəl wur′zəl) *n.* large, sweet beet, *Beta vulgaris,* cultivated in Europe and western North America for its sweet, fleshy roots, used as food for livestock. [German *Mangoldwurzel* beet root, from *Mangold* beet + *Wurzel* root.]

man·ger (mān′jər) *n.* box or trough designed to hold feed, as for horses or cows. [Old French *mangeure,* from *mangier* to eat, from Latin *mandūcāre.*]

man·gle¹ (mang′gəl) -gled, -gling. *v.t.* **1.** to disfigure or mutilate, as by tearing or crushing. **2.** to render imperfect or mar in the making or performing; botch: *The inexperienced translator mangled the author's style.* [Anglo-Norman *mangler* to maim, from Old French *mahaignier.* See MAIM.]

man·gle² (mang′gəl) *n.* machine for pressing and smoothing cloth by passing it between rollers. —*v.t.*, -gled, -gling. to press or smooth with a mangle. [Dutch *mangel* roller, through Late Latin, from Greek *manganon* axis of a pulley.]

man·go (mang′gō) *pl.* -goes or -gos. *n.* **1.** yellowish-red, oval, edible fruit of any of a group of trees, genus *Mangifera,* of the cashew family, having a sweet, spicy taste. **2.** tropical evergreen tree bearing this fruit. [Portuguese *manga* this fruit, from Malay *maṅgā,* from Tamil *mān-kāy.*]

man·go·nel (mang′gə nel′) *n.* formerly, machine used in war to hurl large stones and other missiles at the enemy. [Old French *mangonel,* from Late Latin *mangonellus,* diminutive of *manganum,* from Greek *manganon* axis of a pulley, war engine.]

man·go·steen (mang′gə stēn′) *n.* **1.** reddish-purple edible fruit of a small tree, *Garcinia mangostana,* having a juicy white pulp. **2.** tree bearing this fruit, cultivated in tropical regions. [Malay *mangustan* this fruit.]

man·grove (mang′grōv′) *n.* **1.** any of several evergreen trees, genus *Rhizophora,* found in tropical marshy and coastal regions. **2.** any of various other trees, as the **black mangrove,** *Avicennia marina.* [Spanish *mangle* mangrove tree (of Taino origin) + GROVE.]

Mangrove

man·gy (mān′jē) -gi·er, -gi·est. *adj.* **1.** affected with, resembling, or caused by mange. **2.** worn, dirty, and squalid in appearance; shabby; seedy. —**man′gi·ly,** *adv.* —**man′gi·ness,** *n.*

man·han·dle (man′hand′əl) -dled, -dling. *v.t.* **1.** to use the hands on with gruff force; handle roughly: *The prisoner charged that the guards had manhandled him.* **2.** to accomplish by human strength alone, without mechanical aids.

Man·hat·tan (man hat′ən, mən-) *n.* **1.** island and borough of New York City, in southeastern New York, the financial, commercial, and cultural center of the city. Area, 22.6 sq. mi. Pop. (1970), 1,524,541. **2.** *also,* **man·hat·tan.** cocktail consisting of whiskey, vermouth, and, sometimes, bitters.

Manhattan Project, atomic research project established in the United States in August, 1942 that developed the first atomic bomb.

man·hole (man′hōl′) *n.* opening, usually with a removable cover, through which a sewer, steam boiler, or other structure may be entered, esp. for purposes of inspection or repair.

man·hood (man′hood′) *n.* **1.** state of being an adult male human being. **2.** character or qualities, as strength and courage, considered to be manly. **3.** men collectively: *The hero was a fine example of American manhood.* **4.** state of being human.

man-hour (man′our′, -ou′ər) *n.* amount of work that can be done by one man in one hour, used as a unit or standard of measurement.

man·hunt (man′hunt′) *n.* organized, large-scale, and intensive search for a man, usually a fugitive criminal.

ma·ni·a (mā′nē ə, mān′yə) *n.* **1.** enthusiasm or desire so excessive as to resemble madness: *a love for music that almost amounted to a mania.* **2.** wild insanity, esp. a mental disorder characterized by great excitability and disorganized, often violent behavior. [Latin *mania* madness, from Greek *maniā.*]

-mania *combining form* **1.** madness; insanity: *kleptomania, megalomania.* **2.** abnormally excessive or intense interest, desire, or liking: *Anglomania.* [Greek *maniā* madness.]

ma·ni·ac (mā′nē ak′) *n.* person who is or acts as if wildly or violently insane; madman. —*adj.* wildly or violently insane.

-maniac *combining form* one affected by a specified mania: *pyromaniac.* [Greek *maniakos* like a madman, from *maniā* madness.]

ma·ni·a·cal (mə nī′ə kəl) *adj.* of, relating to, or characteristic of mania or a maniac: *maniacal laughter.* —**ma·ni′a·cal·ly,** *adv.*

ma·nic (man′ik) *adj.* relating to, resembling, or affected by mania: *a manic personality, a manic mood.*

man·ic-de·pres·sive (man′ik di pres′iv) *adj.* designating a mental disorder in which periods of extreme excitement alternate with periods of extreme depression. —*n.* one who suffers from this disorder.

Man·i·chae·an (man′ə kē′ən) *also,* **Man·i·che·an.** *n.* follower of or believer in Manichaeism. Also, **Man′i·chee.** —*adj.* of or relating to Manichaeism.

Man·i·chae·ism (man′ə kē iz′əm) *also,* **Man·i·che·ism.** *n.* Oriental religious system originating in Persia in the third century A.D., whose basic doctrine was belief in a dualistic universe where spiritual forces of light and goodness were in conflict with material forces of darkness and evil. Also, **Man′i·chae′an·ism.**

man·i·cure (man′ə kyoor′) *n.* treatment for the hands chiefly consisting of cleaning, shaping, and polishing the nails. —*v.t.,* -cured, -cur·ing. **1.** to care for (the hands); clean, shape, and polish (the fingernails). **2.** to give a manicure to. **3.** *Informal.* to trim evenly, closely, or elaborately: *The gardener manicured the lawns of the estate.* [French *manicure* treatment for the care of the hands, from Latin *manus* hand + *cūra* care.] —**man′i·cur′ist,** *n.*

man·i·fest (man′ə fest′) *v.t.* **1.** to make obvious or clear; show plainly. **2.** to be evidence of; prove. —*adj.* plainly apparent; evident; obvious. —*n.* list of cargo or passengers for a ship or plane. [Latin *manifestus* evident.] —**man′i·fest′ly,** *adv.*

man·i·fes·ta·tion (man′ə fis tā′shən) *n.* **1.** act of manifesting; being manifested. **2.** that which manifests; indication; sign. **3.** public demonstration or display, as for political effect.

manifest destiny *also,* **Manifest Destiny.** nineteenth-century doctrine that the United States was inevitably destined to expand territorially from the Atlantic to the Pacific.

man·i·fes·to (man′ə fes′tō) *pl.,* -toes or -tos. *n.* public declaration of principles or objectives, as that issued by a political party. [Italian *manifesto,* going back to Latin *manifēstus* evident.]

man·i·fold (man′ə fōld′) *adj.* **1.** of many kinds or varieties; multiple; diverse. **2.** having many parts or features: *a manifold process.* **3.** consisting of or operating several things of one kind at once. —*n.* **1.** pipe fitting having several openings for connecting one pipe with others. **2.** copy made by manifolding. **3.** that which is manifold. —*v.t.* **1.** to make more than one copy of, as with carbon paper. **2.** to make manifold; multiply. [Old English *manigfeald* various, varied, numerous.]

man·i·kin (man′ə kin) *also,* **man·ni·kin.** *n.* **1.** little man; dwarf. **2.** anatomical model of the human body, as one used for teaching anatomy. **3.** mannequin. [Middle Dutch *manneken* little man, diminutive of *man* man.]

ma·nil·a (mə nil′ə) *also,* **Ma·nil·a, ma·nil·la.** *n.* **1.** Manila hemp. **2.** Manila paper. **3.** cheroot made in Manila.

Ma·nil·a (mə nil′ə) *n.* largest city of the Philippines, on the island of Luzon. Pop. (1968), 1,499,000.

Manila Bay, large inlet of the South China Sea, on the southwestern coast of the island of Luzon, site of an American naval victory during the Spanish-American War.

Manila hemp, fiber obtained from the leaves of the abaca, widely used in the manufacture of rope, cord, and paper.

Manila paper, strong, brown or yellow paper originally made from Manila hemp, used esp. for bags and file folders.

man in the street, average or ordinary person.

man·i·oc (man′ē ok′) *n.* cassava (*def.* 1).

man·i·ple (man′ə pəl) *n.* **1.** in ancient Rome, a legion, consisting of two centuries. **2.** silk band worn on the left arm as a Eucharistic vestment. [Old French *maniple* handful, handerkerchief, from Latin *manipulus* handful, bundle of hay serving as a standard, company of soldiers.]

ma·nip·u·late (mə nip′yə lāt′) -lat·ed, -lat·ing. *v.t.* **1.** to try to influence, adapt, or manage to one's own advantage: *to manipulate public opinion.* **2.** to manage or work with or as with the hands, esp. with dexterity or skill: *By manipulating a few wires, he repaired the lamp.* **3.** to change, falsify, or tamper with for one's own purpose or profit. [From MANIPULATION.] —**ma·nip′u·la′tive,** *adj.* —**ma·nip·u·la·to·ry** (mə-nip′yə lə tôr′ē), *adj.* —**ma·nip′u·la′tor,** *n.* —**Syn. 2.** see **handle.**

ma·nip·u·la·tion (mə nip′yə lā′shən) *n.* **1.** act of manipulating; being manipulated. **2.** fraudulent handling, clever trick, clever manipulation. [French *manipulation* handling, from Latin *manipulus* handful.]

Man·i·to·ba (man′ə tō′bə) *n.* province in south-central Canada. Area, 251,000 sq. mi. Pop. (1966), 963,066.

man·i·tou (man′ə tōō′) *also,* **man·i·to, man·i·tu.** *n.* among the Algonquian Indians, a spirit worshiped as a governing force of life and nature. [Algonquian *manito* spirit.]

man·kind (*def.* 1 man′kīnd′; *def.* 2 man′kīnd′) *n.* **1.** human beings collectively; the human race. **2.** men collectively.

man·like (man′līk′) *adj.* **1.** befitting a man; manly. **2.** resembling a man. **3.** resembling a human being: *manlike apes.*

man·ly (man′lē) -li·er, -li·est. *adj.* **1.** having the qualities generally attributed to or characteristic of men. **2.** relating to or appropriate for a man. —**man′li·ness,** *n.* —**Syn. 1.** see **masculine.**

man-made (man′mād′) *adj.* made by man, rather than by natural processes; synthetic; artificial: *man-made snow.*

Mann (*def.* 1 man; *def.* 2 män) **1.** Horace. 1796–1859, U.S. educator. **2.** Thomas. 1875–1955, German author.

man·na (man′ə) *n.* **1.** in the Old Testament, the food miraculously supplied to the Israelites during their flight from Egypt. **2.** anything that is badly needed and is unexpectedly or miraculously supplied. [Late Latin *manna* the food miraculously supplied to the Israelites, from Greek *manna,* from Aramaic *mannā,* from Hebrew *mān.*]

man·ne·quin (man′i kin) *also,* **man·i·kin.** *n.* **1.** full-sized, usually jointed model of a human figure, used esp. for displaying clothes. **2.** one who models clothing. **3.** person who seems devoid of animation, warmth, or spontaneity. [French *mannequin,* from Middle Dutch *manneken* little man. See MANIKIN.]

man·ner (man′ər) *n.* **1.** way in which something happens or is done; mode; fashion: *Fill out the form in the following manner.* **2.** customary or characteristic way of acting or behaving: *Her sarcastic manner actually frightens some people.* **3.** typical or characteristic way or style of doing something, esp. a distinctive style in the arts: *to study the manner of life in the eighteenth century.* **4. manners. a.** ways of behaving in society, esp. with reference to standards of politeness: *good manners.* **b.** polite or socially correct ways of behaving in society; etiquette. **c.** prevailing social conditions, customs, or rules of behavior: *a novel of manners.* **5.** kind; sort: *What manner of man is he?* **6. in a manner of speaking.** so to speak. [Anglo-Norman *manere* way of behaving, going back to Latin *manuārius* handy, relating to the hand, from *manus* hand.]

man·nered (man′ərd) *adj.* **1.** having (a specified kind of) manner or manners. ▲ used in combination: *mild-mannered.* **2.** having or marked by mannerisms, as in writing or speech; stilted.

man·ner·ism (man′ə riz′əm) *n.* **1.** characteristic manner of speaking or behaving; trait peculiar to a person: *She has many of her mother's mannerisms.* **2.** exaggerated or affected use of a particular manner or style, esp. in literature or art. **3.** *usually,* **Mannerism.** style of sixteenth-century European art that stressed emotional expression and boldly dramatic effects. —**man′ner·is′tic,** *adj.*

man·ner·ly (man′ər lē) *adj.* having or showing good manners; polite. —*adv.* with good manners; politely. —**man′ner·li·ness,** *n.*

Mann·heim (män′hīm′) *n.* port city in south-central West Germany, on the Rhine. Pop. (1968), 324,307.

man·ni·kin (man′i kin) *n.* manikin.

man·nish (man′ish) *adj.* **1.** of, for, or characteristic of a man. **2.** resembling a man. —**man′nish·ly,** *adv.* —**man′nish·ness,** *n.*

ma·noeu·vre (mə nōō′vər) *British. n.* maneuver. —*v.t., v.i.,* **-vred, -vring.** to maneuver.

man of God 1. clergyman. **2.** holy man, as a saint or prophet.

man of the world, worldly, sophisticated, cosmopolitan man.

man-of-war (man′əv wôr′) *pl.,* **men-of-war.** *n.* warship.

ma·nom·e·ter (mə nom′ə tər) *n.* instrument used to measure the pressure exerted by a gas. [French *manomètre,* from Greek *mānos* thin + *metron* measure.]

man·or (man′ər) *n.* **1.** under the feudal system, self-sufficient estate under the authority of a lord, in which part of the land was divided among serfs, who were bound to the estate. **2.** manor house. **3.** land unit or landed estate, as one largely farmed by tenants who pay rent to the owner. **4.** mansion, esp. the main house on an estate. [Old French *manoir* mansion, dwelling, from *manoir* to dwell, from Latin *manēre* to remain.] —**ma·no·ri·al** (mə nôr′ē əl) *adj.*

manor house, residence of the lord of a manor.

man-o′-war bird (man′ə wôr′) frigate bird.

man·power (man′pou′ər) *n.* **1.** number of persons available to serve, regarded as a labor force. **2.** *also,* **man power.** power or force supplied by the physical exertion of man.

man·qué (män kā′) *adj. French.* aspiring but unsuccessful. ▲ placed after the noun it modifies: *an author manqué.*

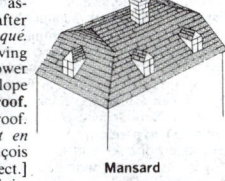

man·sard (man′särd) *n.* **1.** roof having two slopes on all sides, with the lower slope almost vertical and the upper slope almost horizontal. Also, **mansard roof.** **2.** room or story under such a roof. [French *mansarde* garret, and *toit en mansarde* mansard roof, from François Mansart, 1598–1666, French architect.]

Mansard

manse (mans) *n.* residence of a minister, esp. of a Presbyterian minister: parsonage. [Medieval Latin *mansus* farm, dwelling, from Latin *manēre* to remain.]

man·serv·ant (man′sur′vənt) *pl.,* **men·serv·ants.** *n.* male servant.

man·sion (man′shən) *n.* very large, stately, or imposing house. [Old French *mansion* dwelling, from Latin *mānsiō.*]

man-sized (man′sīzd′) *adj. Informal.* requiring a man's capabilities; large enough for a man: *a man-sized job.*

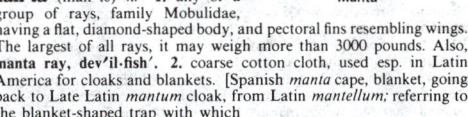

man·slaugh·ter (man′slô′tər) *n.* **1.** *Law.* unlawful killing of a human being, without malice or cold-blooded intent. **2.** the slaying of a human being by another.

man·ta (man′tə) *n.* **1.** any of a group of rays, family Mobulidae, having a flat, diamond-shaped body, and pectoral fins resembling wings. The largest of all rays, it may weigh more than 3000 pounds. Also, **manta ray, dev′il·fish′.** **2.** coarse cotton cloth, used esp. in Latin America for cloaks and blankets. [Spanish *manta* cape, blanket, going back to Late Latin *mantum* cloak, from Latin *mantellum;* referring to the blanket-shaped trap with which a manta ray is caught.]

Manta

man·tel (mant′əl) *also,* **man·tle.** *n.* **1.** structure of stone, brick, or other material, surrounding the opening of a fireplace. **2.** upper, horizontal portion of this, usually in the form of a projecting shelf.

Mantelpiece

man·tel·et (mant′əl et′, mant′lit) *n.* **1.** short cloak or mantle. **2.** movable shelter, screen, or shield, formerly used esp. to protect soldiers when besieging an enemy. Also (*def.* 2), **mant′let.**

man·tel·piece (mant′əl pēs′) *n.* upper, horizontal portion of a mantel.

man·til·la (man til′ə, -tē′ə) *n.* scarflike covering for the head worn by women, esp. in Spain and Latin America, usually made of black or white lace. [Spanish *mantilla,* going back to Latin *mantellum* cloak.]

Mantel

man·tis (man′tis) *pl.,* **-tis·es** or **-tes** (-tēz). *n.* praying mantis. [Modern Latin *mantis,* from Greek *mantis;* because it often holds its forelegs in a position suggesting hands folded in prayer.]

man·tis·sa (man tis′ə) *n.* the decimal part of a logarithm. [Latin *mantissa* makeweight; possibly of Etruscan origin.]

man·tle (mant′əl) n. 1. loose, usually sleeveless cloak. 2. something that covers or envelops: *under the mantle of night.* 3. mantel. 4. layer of the earth's interior between the crust and the core. 5. fleshy fold of tissue that encloses the internal organs and secretes the shell in mollusks. 6. plumage of the back and folded wings of a bird, esp. when differently colored from the rest of the body. 7. gas mantle. —*v.t.*, **-tled, -tling.** 1. to cover with or as with a mantle; conceal; envelop. —*v.i.* 1. to cover or spread over the surface of something. 2. to be or become covered with a coating or scum. 3. to blush. [Partly from Old French *mantel* cloak; partly from Old English *mentel* cloak; both from Latin *mantellum* cloak, napkin.]

mant·let (mant′lit) mantelet *(def. 2).*

man·tu·a (man′chōō ə) n. loose gown worn by women in the seventeenth and eighteenth centuries. [Modification of French *manteau* cloak, from Latin *mantellum.*]

man·u·al (man′yōō əl) adj. 1. relating to or done by the hands: *a manual operation.* 2. operated by hand: *a manual control.* 3. involving or requiring physical exertion or work with the hands: *manual labor.* —*n.* 1. concise book of instructions or other information on a particular subject. 2. prescribed drill in the handling of a weapon. Also, **manual of arms.** 3. organ keyboard played with the hands, as distinguished from one that is played with the feet. [Latin *manuālis* relating to the hand, from *manus* hand.] —**man′u·al·ly,** *adv.*

Syn. 1. **Manual, handbook, guide** mean a handy reference book. **Manual** is a book containing in concise form the principles and rules needed for mastering an art, science, or skill: *This book is a manual of golf.* **Handbook** is a concise book of ready reference covering a particular subject or occupational field: *The scientist consulted his handbook of geology.* **Guide** is a book of practical instructions and information in an unfamiliar field: *The tourist bought a guide to the city.*

manual alphabet, alphabet used to communicate with the deaf, consisting of a series of signs made with the fingers, each sign representing a letter of the written alphabet.

manual training, practical training in various manual crafts, as machine and tool operation, esp. as given in schools.

man·u·fac·to·ry (man′yə fak′tər ē) pl., **-ries.** n. *Archaic.* factory.

man·u·fac·ture (man′yə fak′chər) **-tured, -tur·ing.** *v.t.* 1. to make or produce (a product), esp. on a large scale by means of machinery and a division of labor. 2. to make or process, as a raw material, into a form or product suitable for use: *to manufacture wool into cloth.* 3. to make up or concoct; invent; fabricate: *to manufacture excuses.* 4. to produce or turn out, as a literary work, in a mechanical way, without evidence of originality or individuality. —*v.i.* to make, produce, or process something. —*n.* 1. act or process of manufacturing. 2. something manufactured; product. [French *manufacture* a making, workmanship, from Medieval Latin *manufactura* handiwork, going back to Latin *manū factūra* a making by hand.]

man·u·fac·tur·er (man′yə fak′chər ər) n. person or company whose business is manufacturing; owner of a factory.

man·u·mis·sion (man′yə mish′ən) n. liberation from slavery or bondage; emancipation. [Latin *manūmissiō* the freeing of a slave.]

man·u·mit (man′yə mit′) **-mit·ted, -mit·ting.** *v.t.* to release from slavery or bondage; emancipate; liberate. [Latin *manūmittere,* from *manū* from the hand + *mittere* to send.]

ma·nure (mə noor′, -nyoor′) n. any natural organic material, esp. the waste matter from domestic animals, used as fertilizer. —*v.t.*, **-nured, -nur·ing.** to put manure in or on. [Middle English *manouren* to till (land), from Old French *manouvrer* to work with the hands, going back to Latin *manū operārī.*]

man·u·script (man′yə skript′) n. 1. typewritten or handwritten version of a book, article, or other work, prepared for a publisher or printer. 2. book or document written by hand, esp. one written before the invention of printing. —*adj.* handwritten or typewritten; not printed. [Medieval Latin *manuscriptum* something written by hand, going back to Latin *manū scriptus* written by hand.]

Manx (mangks) n. 1. **the Manx.** people of the Isle of Man. 2. language belonging to the Celtic branch of the Indo-European family of languages, spoken on the Isle of Man. —*adj.* of or relating to the Isle of Man, its people, or their language.

Manx cat, short-haired domestic cat having long hind legs, a high, rounded rump, and, usually, no tail.

Manx·man (mangks′mən) pl., **-men.** n. native or inhabitant of the Isle of Man.

man·y (men′ē) more, most. adj. consisting of or amounting to a large number; numerous: *many complaints.* —*n.* 1. large number (of persons or things): *Many of the delegates vetoed the plan.* 2. **the many.** the majority of people. —*pron.* large number of persons or things: *Many are called, but few are chosen* (Matthew 22:14). [Old English *manig* a great number, numerous.]

man·y·plies (men′ē plīz′) n. omasum. [MANY + plies, plural of PLY².]

man·za·ni·ta (man′zə nē′tə) n. any of several evergreen shrubs or small trees, genus *Arctostaphylos,* of the heath family, that grow in western North America, bearing thick leaves and white or pink urn-shaped flowers. [Spanish *manzanita* little apple, diminutive of *manzana* apple, from Latin *Matiāna* (apples) of Matius; possibly from Caius *Matius* Calvena, a Roman who wrote a cookbook in the first century A.D.]

Mao·ism (mou′iz′əm) n. political theories, principles, and practices of Mao Tse-tung. —**Mao′ist,** *adj., n.*

Ma·o·ri (mä′ôr ē, mour′ē) pl., **-ris.** n. 1. member of an aboriginal people of New Zealand. 2. their language, a member of the Malayo-Polynesian family of languages. —*adj.* of or relating to the Maoris or their language.

Mao Tse-tung (mou′ tsə toong′, dzu doong′) 1893–1976, Chinese Communist leader.

map (map) n. 1. drawing or other representation of an area, as of the earth's surface, typically showing the relative position and size of the features or places represented. 2. **off the map.** out of existence; into oblivion: *The enemy threatened to wipe the region off the map.* 3. **to put on the map.** *Informal.* to make well-known: *The discovery of oil in the area will put this town on the map.* —*v.t.*, **mapped, map·ping.** 1. to make a map of; represent on a map. 2. to plan in detail (often with *out*): *to map out one's future.* [Medieval Latin *mappa (mundi)* map (of the world), from Latin *mappa* napkin, (painted) cloth; of Semitic origin.]

Syn. *v.t.* 1. **Map, chart, diagram** mean to represent graphically. **Map** emphasizes relative features, sizes, and positions: *The explorer mapped the new territory.* **Chart** suggests representation of data about variable conditions or facts, as by means of graphs or symbols: *The meteorologist charted the rainfall for the whole year.* **Diagram** suggests presentation by means of a drawing that shows the relationship of parts or explains the working of something: *The professor diagramed the circulatory system.*

ma·ple (mā′pəl) n. 1. any of a large group of trees, genus *Acer,* growing throughout the Northern Hemisphere, having lobed leaves and small winged fruits. 2. wood of this tree, used in the manufacture of furniture. 3. flavor of maple syrup or of maple sugar. [Old English *mapulder* the tree.]

Flowers   Fruit   Leaf

Maple

maple sugar, sugar made by boiling down maple syrup.

maple syrup, syrup obtained by boiling and concentrating the sap of the sugar maple or of any of several other maple trees.

map·ping (map′ing) n. *Mathematics.* the establishing of relationships between elements of one set and elements of another set.

mar (mär) **marred, mar·ring.** *v.t.* 1. to spoil the appearance of; deface; disfigure: *to mar a table top.* 2. to damage the quality or character of; impair: *It was an enjoyable time, but marred by your absence.* —*n.* something that mars. [Old English *merran.*] —**Syn.** 1. see deface.

Mar., March.

mar·a·bou (mar′ə bōō′) n. 1. any of several storks, genus *Leptoptilus,* of Africa, India, and southeastern Asia, having white, black, and gray plumage. Height: to 6 feet. Also, **adjutant bird.** 2. soft, downy feather from this bird, often used in millinery. 3. trimming or material made from such feathers. 4. lightweight fabric, woven with a white silk thread. [French *marabout,* through Portuguese, from Arabic *murābit* hermit; supposedly because the bird tends to be solitary.]

Marabou

ma·ra·ca (mə rä′kə) n. instrument made of a dried gourd or gourd-shaped rattle that contains seeds or pebbles, often played in pairs. [Portuguese *maracá* this instrument; probably from Tupi-Guarani.]

Mar·a·cai·bo (mar′ə kī′bō) n. 1. port city in northwest Venezuela, near the Caribbean Sea. Pop. (1969), 625,101. 2. **Lake.** lake in northwestern Venezuela.

mar·a·schi·no (mar′ə skē′nō, -shē′nō) n. sweet cordial or liqueur made from the fermented juice of certain cherries. [Italian *maraschino,* from *(a)marasca* a sour cherry, going back to Latin *amārus* bitter, sour.]

maraschino cherry, cherry preserved in real or imitation maraschino.

Ma·rat, Jean Paul (mä rä′; zhäɴ pōl) 1743–93, French revolutionary leader.

Ma·ra·thi (mə rä′tē, -rat′ē) *n.* Indo-Iranian language spoken chiefly in central and western India.

mar·a·thon (mar′ə thon′) *n.* **1.** foot race of 26 miles, 385 yards, run over an open course. **2.** any long-distance race or other competition testing the stamina of the participants; endurance contest: *dance marathon.* **3.** any activity of great length that tests or requires endurance. [From a Greek soldier's legendary run from MARATHON to Athens, about 25 miles, to announce his country's defeat of Persia at Marathon.]

Mar·a·thon (mar′ə thon′) *n.* plain in Attica, Greece, where the Athenians defeated the Persians in battle in 490 B.C.

ma·raud (mə rôd′) *v.i.* to rove in search of plunder; make raids for booty. —*v.t.* to plunder; raid. [French *marauder* to pilfer, from *maraud* rascal, vagabond; of uncertain origin.]

ma·raud·er (mə rô′dər) *n.* rover in search of booty or plunder, esp. one who is part of a wandering band of plunderers.

mar·ble (mär′bəl) *n.* **1.** metamorphosed limestone usually mottled or streaked with variously colored swirls, widely used in architecture and sculpture. **2.** piece, block, or slab of marble. **3.** piece of sculpture in marble. **4.** something resembling marble, as in hardness or smoothness. **5.** small hard ball of glass or other material, used in children's games. **6. marbles.** any of various games played with a number of these balls. ▲ construed as singular. **7. marbles.** *Slang.* common sense; wits. —*adj.* resembling marble, as in being hard or smooth. —*v.t.* **-bled, -bling.** to marbleize. [Old French *marbre* the limestone, from Latin *marmor,* from Greek *marmaros.*]

marble cake, cake made of dark and light batter mixed so as to give a streaked or marblelike appearance.

mar·ble·ize (mär′bə līz′) **-ized, -iz·ing.** *v.t.* to color, mottle, or streak in imitation of marble; give the appearance of marble to.

mar·ca·site (mär′kə sīt′) *n.* opaque yellow or white ore with a metallic luster. Formula: FeS₂ [French *marcassite,* through Spanish and Arabic; of Persian origin.]

mar·cel (mär sel′) *n.* series of deep, even waves put in the hair with a curling iron. —*v.t.,* **-celled, -cel·ling.** to put a series of deep, even waves in (the hair) with a curling iron. [From *Marcel* Grateau (died 1936), French hairdresser.]

march¹ (märch) *v.i.* **1.** to walk or move in time with regular, measured steps, esp. in a group or formation: *The soldiers marched by the reviewing stands.* **2.** to walk or move in a steady, deliberate, or solemn manner: *The children marched off to bed soon after supper.* **3.** to go or advance steadily; proceed with regularity: *Time marches on.* —*v.t.* to cause (someone) to march: *to march troops up and down.* —*n.* **1.** act of marching. **2.** distance covered by a march: *a twenty-mile march.* **3.** steady forward movement: *the march of time.* **4.** regular measured step, esp. of a body of soldiers. **5.** musical composition, usually in duple time, having a strong rhythmical accent and suitable for marching. **6. on the march.** moving or advancing at a steady pace. **7. to steal a march on.** to gain an advantage over (someone) stealthily or secretly. [French *marcher* to walk; originally, to trample, going back to Late Latin *marcus* hammer.] —**march′er,** *n.*

march² (märch) *n. Archaic.* marches. [Old French *marche* frontier, boundary; of Germanic origin.]

March (märch) *n.* third month of the year, containing thirty-one days. [Dialectal Old French *Marche,* from Latin *Martius* (*mēnsis*) (month) of MARS; referring to the ancient Roman practice of waging war during the month of March.]

march·es (mär′chiz) *n.,pl.* region along the border or frontier of a country.

mar·chion·ess (mär′shə nis) *n. British.* marquise *(defs. 1,2).* [Medieval Latin *marchionissa,* feminine of *marchio* marquis; literally, ruler of a march, from *marca* march²; of Germanic origin.]

march·pane (märch′pān′) *n.* marzipan.

Mar·co·ni, Gu·gliel·mo (mär kō′nē; gōōl yel′mō) 1874–1937, Italian electrical engineer who helped develop the wireless telegraph.

Mar·co Po·lo (mär′kō pō′lō) see **Polo, Marco.**

Mar·cus Au·re·li·us (mär′kəs ô rēl′yəs, -rē′lē əs) A.D. 121–180, Roman emperor and Stoic philosopher.

Mar·di Gras (mär′dē grä′) **1.** last day before Lent. Also, **Shrove Tuesday. 2.** celebration held in honor of this day, marked by parades and festivities. [French *mardi gras* Shrove Tuesday; literally, fat Tuesday, going back to Latin *Martis diēs* Tuesday (literally, day of Mars) + *crassus* fat, thick; supposedly referring to its being the last day of feasting before Lent.]

Mar·duk (mär′dook′) *n. Babylonian Mythology.* the chief god.

mare¹ (mâr) *n.* female of various equine animals, as the horse, donkey, or zebra. [Old English *mere,* feminine of *mearh* horse.]

ma·re² (mä′rā, mâr′ē) *pl.* **ma·ri·a.** *n.* any of various dark smooth lowlands on the moon's surface. [Latin *mare* sea; because Galileo thought they resembled seas.]

mare's-nest (mârz′nest′) *n.* **1.** discovery that seems to be great or important but turns out to be a hoax or mistake. **2.** confusing and disorderly situation.

mare's-tail (mârz′tāl′) *n.* **1.** long, feathery, cirrus cloud, resembling a horse's tail. **2.** water plant, *Hippuris vulgaris,* having whorls of narrow tapered leaves and tiny, pale-green flowers. **3.** horsetail *(def. 1).*

Mar·ga·ret of Anjou (mär′gər it, mär′grit) 1430–82, queen consort of Henry VI of England.

Margaret of Navarre, 1492–1549, queen of Navarre.

Margaret of Valois, 1553–1615, queen of France and Navarre.

mar·ga·rine (mär′jər in, -jə rēn′) *also,* **mar·ga·rin** (mär′jər in). *n.* food product made from animal or vegetable oil, milk, water, and salt, used as a substitute for butter. Also, **o'le·o·mar'ga·rine.** [French *margarine,* from Greek *margaron* pearl; referring to the pearl-like sheen of an acid found in some fats.]

marge (märj) *n. Archaic.* border; margin. [French *marge,* from Latin *margō.*]

mar·gin (mär′jin) *n.* **1.** blank space around the body of written or printed matter on a page. **2.** amount allowed or available in addition to what is necessary or needed: *a margin of error.* **3.** amount or degree of difference: *We won the game by a narrow margin.* **4.** edge; border: *the margin of a river.* **5.** difference between the cost and selling price of merchandise. **6.** minimum return necessary for an enterprise to continue to be profitable. **7.** percentage of the total purchase price of stocks and bonds that the purchaser has to pay in cash. **8. on margin.** with only a percentage of the total purchase price of stocks and bonds: *to buy on margin, to trade on margin.* —*v.t.* **1.** to provide with a margin; border. **2.** to enter in the margin of a page, as notes. [Latin *margin-,* stem of *margō* edge, border.]

mar·gin·al (mär′jin əl) *adj.* **1.** written or printed in the margin of a page: *marginal notes.* **2.** of, relating to, constituting, or situated near a margin: *a marginal piece of land.* **3.** barely adequate, acceptable, or desirable; minimal: *marginal ability.* **4.** close to the point below which an investment is considered unprofitable; making very little profit. —**mar′gin·al·ly,** *adv.*

mar·grave (mär′grāv′) *n.* **1.** formerly, a prince of any of certain states of the Holy Roman Empire and Germany. **2.** formerly, a military governor of a German border province. [Middle Dutch *markgrave* count of a march², from *mark* march² + *grave* count².]

mar·gra·vine (mär′grə vēn′) *n.* wife or widow of a margrave.

mar·gue·rite (mär′gə rēt′) *n.* **1.** common daisy, *Chrysanthemum leucanthemum,* bearing white petals and having a yellow center. **2.** any of several other plants bearing daisylike flower heads. [French *marguerite,* daisy, going back to Latin *margarīta* pearl, from Greek *margarītēs.*]

ma·ri·a (mä′rē ə, mâr′-) plural of **mare².**

Mar·i·an·a Islands (mar′ē an′ə) volcanic island group in the western Pacific administered by the United States. Land area, approx. 370 sq. mi. Pop. (1963 est.), 9,700. Also, **Mar′i·an′as.**

Ma·ri·a The·re·sa (mə rē′ə tə rē′sə) 1717–80, archduchess of Austria, queen of Hungary and Bohemia from 1740 to 1780.

Ma·rie An·toi·nette (mə rē′ an′twə net′) 1755–93, queen of France from 1774 to 1792.

Marie Lou·ise (lōō ēz′) 1791–1847, Austrian princess, the second wife of Napoleon I, and empress of France from 1810 to 1814.

mar·i·gold (mar′ə gōld′) *n.* **1.** fragrant yellow, orange, or red flower head of any of a group of plants, genus *Tagetes,* of the composite family, as the **African marigold,** *T. erecta.* **2.** plant bearing this flower head. **3.** any of various other plants, as the pot marigold and the marsh marigold. [MARY + GOLD; named after the Virgin Mary and referring to the gold-colored or yellow flowers of the plant.]

mar·i·jua·na (mar′ə wä′nə) *also,* **mar·i·hua·na.** *n.* **1.** drug obtained from the dried flowering tops of the hemp plant, *Cannabis sativa,* usually smoked in the form of cigarettes for its intoxicating effect. **2.** hemp plant yielding this drug. [Spanish *marihuana* kind of hemp with narcotic properties; of uncertain origin.]

ma·rim·ba (mə rim′bə) *n.* a musical percussion instrument resembling a large xylophone, consisting of a series of

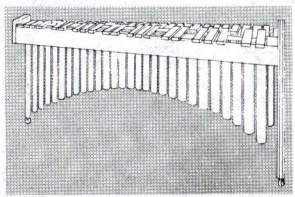

Mare's-tail

Marimba

at; āpe; cär; end; mē; it; īce; hot; ōld; fôrk; wood; fōōl; oil; out; up; ūse; turn; sing; thin; <u>th</u>is; zh in treasure; ə in ago, taken, pencil, lemon, circus.

623

wooden bars, usually mounted over resonators, played by striking the bars with hand-held hammers. [Of Bantu origin.]

ma·ri·na (mə rē′nə) n. dock or basin where slips, moorings, and, often, supplies, repairs, and other services are available for small boats. [Italian or Spanish *marina* seashore, going back to Latin *marīnus* relating to the sea, from *mare* sea.]

mar·i·nade (mar′ə nād′) n. mixture, usually containing vinegar or wine and various spices, in which food is soaked before cooking. —v.t., **-nad·ed, -nad·ing.** to marinate. [French *marinade* liquid used for marinating, something marinated in this liquid, from *mariner* to marinate, from *marin* relating to the sea, from Latin *marīnus.* See MARINE.]

mar·i·nate (mar′ə nāt′) -nat·ed, -nat·ing. v.t. to soak (food) in a marinade. [French *mariner* to marinate + -ATE¹. See MARINADE.]

ma·rine (mə rēn′) adj. 1. of or relating to the sea: *marine biology.* 2. existing in or formed by the sea: *marine life, marine shells.* 3. of, relating to, or used in sea navigation; nautical: *marine barometer.* 4. of or relating to commerce or shipping on the sea; maritime. 5. of or relating to the navy or naval affairs. —n. 1. **Marine.** member of the U.S. Marine Corps. 2. soldier serving on a ship. 3. seascape. [Old French *marin* relating to the sea, from Latin *marīnus,* from *mare* sea.]

Syn. adj. 1., 3. **Marine, maritime, nautical** mean of or relating to the sea. **Marine** is the general term: *He loved the marine life.* **Maritime** is used mainly in reference to shipping or commerce on the sea: *Ships at sea are governed by maritime laws.* **Nautical** applies to the art and practice of navigation: *That yachtsman has considerable nautical skills.*

Marine Corps, branch of the armed forces of the United States, under the Department of the Navy, that provides amphibious forces for overseas campaigns and detachments for other naval duties.

mar·i·ner (mar′ə nər) n. one who navigates or assists in navigating a ship; sailor. [Anglo-Norman *mariner,* from Medieval Latin *marinarius,* from Latin *marīnus* relating to the sea, from *mare* sea.]

mar·i·o·nette (mar′ē ə net′) n. small jointed figure, often of wood, manipulated by strings, wires, or rods held from above. [French *marionette,* diminutive of *Marion* Marian, from *Marie* Mary.]

Mar·i·po·sa lily (mar′ə pō′sə, -zə) 1. showy tulip-shaped flower of any of a group of plants, genus *Calochortus,* of the lily family, having white, violet, blue, or yellow petals. 2. plant bearing this flower, found in western North America. [Spanish *mariposa* butterfly (of uncertain origin) + LILY; referring to the resemblance of its multi-colored flowers to butterflies.]

Marionette

mar·ish (mar′ish) Archaic. n. marsh. —adj. marshy.

mar·i·tal (mar′it əl) adj. of or relating to marriage. [Latin *marītālis,* from *marītus* husband.] —**mar′i·tal·ly,** adv.

mar·i·time (mar′ə tīm′) adj. 1. bordering on, close to, or living near the sea: *a maritime town, a maritime people.* 2. of or relating to the sea or its navigation, commerce, or shipping: *maritime law.* [Latin *maritimus* relating to the sea, from *mare* sea.] —**Syn.** 2. see **marine.**

Maritime Alps, part of the Alps, on the border between France and Italy.

Maritime Provinces, Canadian provinces of New Brunswick, Nova Scotia, and Prince Edward Island, on the Atlantic Ocean.

Mar·i·us, Gai·us (mâr′ē əs; gā′əs) c.155–86 B.C., Roman general.

mar·jo·ram (mär′jər əm) n. 1. dried leaves of an aromatic plant, *Majorana hortensis,* of the mint family, used as a spice. 2. the plant itself, cultivated as a garden herb, bearing small, fuzzy, round leaves and clusters of tiny pink, white, or lilac flowers. Also, **sweet marjoram.** [Old French *majorane* the plant, from Medieval Latin *maiorana,* possibly through Latin from Greek *amārakos.*]

mark¹ (märk) n. 1. any visible trace left by a material object when it comes into contact with the surface of another. 2. any sign or symbol used in writing or printing. 3. cross or other sign made in place of a signature by a person who cannot write. 4. number, letter, or rating used to indicate the level, merit, or quality of performance, achievement, or conduct. 5. visible indication of some quality, feature, or characteristic: *a mark of intelligence.* 6. permanent or distinct impression: *It may safely be predicted that they will make their mark in the world* (Moore, 1893). 7. something, as a seal, label, or inscription, placed on or attached to an object, esp. to indicate ownership, origin, quality, or authenticity. 8. something, as a line or object, used as a guide, indicator, or point of reference. 9. target or other object aimed at: *The archer missed the mark.* 10. knot or piece of leather or colored cloth placed at measured intervals on a lead line to indicate fathoms of depth. 11. that which one desires or strives for; goal. 12. accepted standard or criterion, as of quality, performance, or propriety.

13. distinction; note; importance: *a fellow of no mark, nor likelihood* (Shakespeare, *Henry IV, Part I*). 14. in medieval Germany, tract of land held in common by a village community. 15. *Archaic.* boundary; frontier. 16. *Informal.* one who is easily fooled or victimized: *an easy mark for swindlers.* 17. **wide of** (or **beside**) **the mark. a.** missing that which is aimed at. **b.** not pertinent; irrelevant. 18. **to hit the mark. a.** to be accurate. **b.** to be successful; attain one's goal. —v.t. 1. to make or put a mark or marks on (a surface): *The children marked the sidewalk with chalk.* 2. to trace, form, or indicate the limits or boundaries of (often with *out* or *off*): *to mark off an area on a map.* 3. to indicate or represent, as by a sign or symbol: *The editor marked his corrections in green.* 4. to distinguish; characterize: *Solemnity marked the occasion.* 5. to give or assign a mark to: *The teacher marked the papers.* 6. to pay attention to; heed. 7. to write (often with *down*): *I marked down the date of the party on my calendar.* 8. to single out, designate, or select as if by marking; destine: *to be marked for death.* 9. to provide with a mark, as a label or tag, to indicate something, as price, content, or quality: *They marked all the merchandise before displaying it.* 10. in various games, to keep (the score): *to mark the score on a card.* 11. to make obvious or clear; manifest: *A smile marked her happiness.* 12. **to mark down.** to reduce the price of. 13. **to mark up.** to increase the price of. 14. **to mark time. a.** to move the feet as in marching, but without advancing. **b.** to perform the motions or actions of something without really accomplishing anything. **c.** to suspend progress or activity temporarily. [Old English *mearc* boundary, trace, sign.]

mark² (märk) n. 1. deutsche mark. 2. ostmark. 3. reichsmark. [Old English *marc* unit of weight, esp. for gold and silver; possibly of Scandinavian origin.]

Mark (märk) n. 1. one of the four Evangelists, a disciple of the Apostles Peter and Paul. 2. one of the four Gospels, the second book of the New Testament, attributed to him.

mark·down (märk′doun′) n. 1. amount subtracted from the cost of an item in determining the selling price. 2. reduction in price. 3. amount of reduction in price.

marked (märkt) adj. 1. very noticeable; obvious: *a marked similarity between the two dresses.* 2. singled out and watched as an object of suspicion, vengeance, punishment, or death: *a marked man.* 3. having a mark or marks. —**mark·ed·ly** (mär′kid lē), adv.

mark·er (mär′kər) n. 1. one who marks, esp. one who keeps score in a game or grades test papers. 2. that which marks, esp. a bookmark, milestone, or gravestone. 3. one who removes a target, marks the hits, and puts up a new target for the next round.

mar·ket (mär′kit) n. 1. open space or building where food products or goods are bought and sold; marketplace: *The farmer took his vegetables to the market every week.* 2. shop or store, esp. one where food products are sold: *a fish market.* 3. region or country where commodities can be bought and sold; area of demand for commodities: *the foreign market.* 4. trade and commerce, esp. in a specified service or commodity: *the grain market.* 5. demand (for a commodity): *There is very little market for such goods today.* 6. rate or value (of a stock or commodity): *What is the current market for utilities?* 7. state of trading: *an active market, a bull market.* 8. available supply of a specified service or commodity: *a large labor market.* 9. stock market. 10. **to be in the market for.** to be interested in buying: *He's in the market for a used car.* 11. **on the market.** available for purchase: *That company makes the cheapest television sets on the market.* 12. **to take** (or **pull**) **off the market.** to make unavailable for purchase. 13. **to play the market.** to speculate on the stock market. —v.i. 1. to buy food products and other household items in a market. 2. to deal in a market; buy and sell. —v.t. to sell or offer for sale. [Anglo-Norman *market* trade, bargain, place for commercial transactions, from Latin *mercātus* trade, market-place, going back to *merx* merchandise.]

mar·ket·a·ble (mär′kit ə bəl) adj. that can be sold; salable. —**mar′ket·a·bil′i·ty,** n.

mar·ket·place (mär′kit plās′) also, **market place.** n. place where food products or goods are bought and sold.

market price, current or prevailing price of goods, services, or securities on the open market.

market value, current value of goods, services, or securities as established by sales on the open market. Distinguished from **book value.**

mark·ing (mär′king) n. 1. mark or marks. 2. also, **markings.** arrangement of marks and colors on a plant or animal: *a bird with red markings.* 3. act of making a mark or marks on something.

mark·ka (mär′kä) n. standard monetary unit of Finland.

marks·man (märks′mən) pl., **-men.** n. 1. one skilled in shooting a gun or other weapon. 2.a. in the U.S. Armed Forces, lowest category of qualification in target shooting. b. one who has qualified in this category. —**marks′man·ship′,** n.

mark·up (märk′up′) n. 1. amount added to the cost of an item in determining the selling price. 2. increase in price. 3. amount of increase in price.

at; āpe; cär; end; mē; it; īce; hot; ōld; fôrk; wood; fōōl; oil; out; up; ūse; turn; sing; thin; this; zh in treasure; ə in ago, taken, pencil, lemon, circus.

marl (märl) *n.* **1.** clay containing calcium carbonate and, often, fragments of shells from mollusks, used in making portland cement and as a fertilizer. **2.** *Archaic.* earth. [Old French *marle* this clay, from Medieval Latin *margila,* diminutive of Latin *marga;* possibly of Celtic origin.]

Marl·bor·ough, Duke of (märl′bur′ō, -brə, môl′-) 1650–1722, English general; born John Churchill.

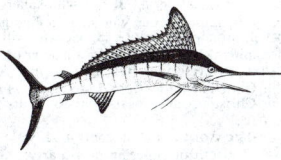

Marlin

mar·lin (mär′lin) *pl.,* **-lins** or **-lin.** *n.* any of a group of saltwater gamefish, genus *Makaira,* having a long spearlike bill. Length: to 14 feet. [Short for MARLINESPIKE; referring to the spearlike appearance of its upper jaw.]

mar·line (mär′lin) *n.* small cord of two strands loosely twisted together, used for winding around the ends of ropes or cables to prevent fraying. [Dutch *marlijn,* from *marren* to tie + *lijn* line (from French *ligne* cord). See LINE¹.]

mar·line·spike (mär′lin spīk′) *also,* **mar·lin·spike, mar·ling·spike** (mär′ling-spīk′). *n.* pointed iron pin used to separate strands of rope, as in splicing.

Mar·lowe, Christopher (mär′lō) 1564–93, English dramatist and poet.

Marlinespike

mar·ma·lade (mär′mə lād′) *n.* jam made by boiling the peel and flesh of fruit, usually citrus fruit, with sugar. [French *marmelade,* from Portuguese *marmelada* quince jelly, marmalade, from *marmelo* quince, through Latin, from Greek *melimēlon* apple grafted on a quince, from *meli* honey + *mēlon* apple; because this jam was originally made of quinces.]

Mar·ma·ra, Sea of (mär′mər ə) *also,* **Sea of Mar·mo·ra.** sea between the European and Asian parts of Turkey, connected with the Black Sea by the Bosporus and with the Mediterranean by the Dardanelles.

mar·mo·re·al (mär môr′ē əl) *adj.* made of, relating to, or like marble: *the cold, marmoreal beauty of a Greek statue.* Also, **mar·mo′re·an.** [Latin *marmoreus* (from *marmor* marble) + -AL¹. See MARBLE.]

mar·mo·set (mär′mə zet′) *n.* any of various tree-dwelling monkeys, family Callithricidae, of Central and South America, having shaggy or soft and fine fur, long, curved claws except on the big toe, and a long tail. Length: to 14 inches including tail. [Old French *marmoset* grotesque image; of uncertain origin.]

Marmoset

mar·mot (mär′mət) *n.* any of various plump, short-legged rodents, genus *Marmota,* having a gray or brown, thick, coarse coat and a short, bushy tail. Marmots, which hibernate during the cold months, are found in North America, Europe, and Asia. Length: to 30 inches. [French *marmotte,* possibly going back to Latin *mūs* (stem *mūr-*) mouse + *montānus* of the mountains.]

Marne (märn) *n.* river in east-central France.

ma·roon¹ (mə rōōn′) *n.* dark brownish-red color. [French *marron* chestnut, from Italian *marrone;* of uncertain origin.]

ma·roon² (mə rōōn′) *v.t.* **1.** to put ashore and leave on a desolate island or coast. **2.** to leave helpless and alone; abandon. —*n.* fugitive slave or his descendant living in the West Indies and Dutch Guiana in the seventeenth and eighteenth centuries. [French *marron* wild, runaway (slave), from Spanish *cimarrón* wild; of uncertain origin.]

Marmot

marque (märk) *n.* *Archaic.* letter of marque.

mar·quee (mär kē′) *n.* **1.** canopy or other rooflike shelter, as of metal or canvas, over an entrance, esp. to a theater. **2.** large tent. One put up for an outdoor party or reception. [French *marquise* (mistaken for plural) awning, large tent, probably from *marquise,* feminine of *marquis* (see MARQUIS); possibly referring to the use of a tent or awning to protect a lady of rank from bad weather.]

Mar·que·sas Islands (mär kā′səs) group of volcanic islands in

French Polynesia. Land area, approx. 409 sq. mi. Pop. (1962), 4837.

mar·quess (mär′kwis) marquis.

mar·que·try (mär′ki trē) *pl.,* **-tries.** *n.* inlaid work consisting of pieces of wood, often interspersed with other materials, as ivory or metal. [French *marqueterie,* from *marqueter* to inlay, from *marque* sign, mark¹; of Germanic origin.]

Mar·quette, Father Jacques (mär ket′; zhäk) 1637–75, French missionary and explorer.

mar·quis (mär′kwis, mär kē′) *pl.,* **-quis·es** or **-quis** (-kēz′). *also, British,* **mar·quess.** *n.* nobleman ranking next below a duke and above an earl or count. [Old French *marquis, marchis* originally, governor of a frontier, from *marche* frontier; of Germanic origin.]

mar·quis·ate (mär′kwi zit) *n.* status or rank of a marquis.

mar·quise (mär kēz′) *n.* **1.** wife or widow of a marquis. **2.** woman holding in her own right the rank equal to that of a marquis. Also *(defs. 1, 2), British,* **mar′chion·ess. 3.** pointed oval shape of gems, esp. diamonds. **4.** ring set with a pointed oval gem or a cluster of such gems. [French *marquise,* feminine of *marquis.* See MARQUIS.]

mar·qui·sette (mär kə zet′, -kwə-) *n.* sheer, lightweight, mesh fabric made of various fibers, used esp. for curtains. [French *marquisette,* diminutive of *marquise* awning, large tent. See MARQUEE.]

Mar·ra·kesh (mə rä′kish, mar′ə kesh) *also,* **Mar·ra·kech.** *n.* city in central Morocco. Pop. (1969), 295,000.

mar·riage (mar′ij) *n.* **1.a.** state of being married; wedlock. **b.** legal union of a man and woman. **2.a.** act of marrying. **b.** ceremony or procedure accompanying this; wedding. **3.** close union: *the marriage of minds.* **4.** in pinochle, a meld of the king and queen of the same suit. [Old French *mariage* the legal union of a man and a woman, from *marier* to wed. See MARRY¹.]

mar·riage·a·ble (mar′i jə bəl) *adj.* fit or suitable for marriage. —**mar′riage·a·bil′i·ty,** *n.*

mar·ried (mar′ēd) *adj.* **1.** joined in marriage. **2.** having a husband or wife. **3.** of or relating to marriage or married persons: *married life.* **4.** closely united.

mar·row (mar′ō) *n.* **1.** soft tissue that fills the cavities and spongy parts of bones. **2.** inmost, best, or vital part. [Old English *mearh, mærg* the tissue in the cavities of bones.]

mar·row·bone (mar′ō bōn′) *n.* **1.** bone containing edible marrow, used for making soups and stews. **2.** marrowbones. **a.** *Informal.* knees. **b.** crossbones.

mar·ry¹ (mar′ē) **-ried, -ry·ing.** *v.t.* **1.** to take as a husband or wife; wed: *He married a girl he had known for many years.* **2.** to join as husband and wife; unite in wedlock: *The judge will marry them in his office.* **3.** to give in marriage (often with *off*): *He married off his daughter.* **4.** to obtain or establish oneself with by marriage (often with *into*): *She married money.* **5.** to unite closely. —*v.i.* **1.** to take a husband or wife. **2.** to enter into a close union. [Old French *marier* to unite by marriage, wed, from Latin *marītāre* to wed, give in marriage, from *marītus* husband.]

mar·ry² (mar′ē) *interj.* *Archaic.* exclamation, as of anger, surprise, or indignation. [From the Virgin MARY (used as an exclamation).]

Mars (märz) *n.* **1.** Roman god of war. His Greek counterpart is Ares. **2.** seventh largest planet of the solar system and fourth in order of distance from the sun.

mar·seilles (mär sālz′) *also,* **mar·seille.** *n.* thick cotton cloth woven with raised figures or stripes, used esp. for bedspreads and quilts. [From *Marseilles,* where it was first made.]

Mar·seilles (mär sā′, -sālz′) *also,* **Mar·seille.** *n.* chief seaport of France, on the Mediterranean. Pop. (1968), 889,029.

marsh (märsh) *n.* tract of low, wet land covered with grasses and grasslike plants, as reeds. [Old English *mersc.*]

mar·shal (mär′shəl) *n.* **1.** officer of a federal court who is appointed to a judicial district to carry out orders and perform other duties similar to those of a sheriff. **2.** in some states, law officer of a city or borough having powers similar to those of a sheriff. **3.** head of a city police or fire department. **4.** field marshal. **5.** person in charge of arranging and regulating processions and ceremonies. **6.** high official of a royal household or court, esp. one in charge of protocol and official ceremonies. —*v.t.,* **-shaled, -shal·ing;** *also, British,* **-shalled, -shal·ling. 1.** to arrange in methodical order: *He marshaled his arguments for the debate.* **2.** to organize or place (soldiers) in proper order, as for battle. **3.** to usher; lead. [Old French *mareschal* high official; originally, groom, farrier, going back to Old High German *marah* horse + *scalc* servant. The medieval marshal's prestige grew with the rise in importance of the cavalry.] —**Syn.** *v.t.* **2.** see **muster.**

Marshall Islands, Pacific island group administered by the United States. Land area, approx. 70 sq. mi. Pop. (1962), 15,700.

Marshall Plan, U.S. plan for economic aid to western Europe after World War II. Also, **European Recovery Program.** [From George C. Marshall, 1880–1959, statesman who initiated the plan.]

marsh gas, methane.

at; āpe; cär; end; mē; it; īce; hot; ōld; fôrk; wood; fōōl; oil; out; up; ūse; turn; sing; thin; this; zh in treasure; ə in ago, taken, pencil, lemon, circus.

625

marsh·mal·low (märsh′mel′ō, -mal′ō) n. soft, usually white, spongy confection made from starch, sugar, gelatin, and corn syrup and covered with powdered sugar. [Because this confection was once made from the root of the marsh mallow.]

marsh mallow, tall, leafy plant, *Althaea officinalis*, found growing wild in eastern Europe and the eastern United States, bearing downy, oval or heart-shaped leaves and pink flowers. [Old English *merscmealwe*. See MARSH, MALLOW.]

marsh marigold, any of several fleshy plants, genus *Caltha*, bearing large heart- or kidney-shaped leaves and flowers resembling buttercups.

marsh·y (mär′shē) **marsh·i·er, marsh·i·est,** adj. **1.** like a marsh; swampy. **2.** of, relating to, or containing a marsh or marshes. **3.** growing or occurring in a marsh. —**marsh′i·ness,** n.

mar·su·pi·al (mär sōō′pē əl) n. any of various mammals, order Marsupialia, as kangaroos, the female of which has an abdominal pouch in which the young are carried after birth. —adj. **1.** of, relating to, or designating a marsupial. **2.** of, like, or relating to a marsupium.

mar·su·pi·um (mär sōō′pē əm) pl., **-pi·a** (-pē′ə). n. **1.** pouch on the abdomen of a female marsupial, used for carrying the newborn offspring. **2.** similar pouch on certain fish and crustaceans, used for carrying eggs or young. [Latin *marsūpium* pouch, from Greek *marsypion*, diminutive of *marsypos* pouch, purse.]

mart (märt) n. trading center; market: *a food mart.* [Obsolete Dutch *mart*, form of *markt* market.]

Mar·tel, Charles (mär tel′) A.D. c.688–741, Frankish ruler who defeated the Muslims at Tours in 732.

mar·ten (märt′ən) pl., **-tens** or **-ten.** n. **1.** any of various weasel-like mammals, genus *Martes*, having thick, soft fur ranging in color from golden brown to blackish-brown. Length: to 30 inches including the tail. **2.** its fur, made into coats, stoles, and trimmings; sable. [Old French *martrine* the fur of the marten, from *martre* marten (animal); of Germanic origin.]

Marten

Mar·tha (mär′thə) n. in the New Testament, the sister of Mary and follower of Jesus.

Martha's Vineyard, island off the Massachusetts coast. Land area, approx. 100 sq. mi. Pop. (1970 est.), 6000.

mar·tial (mär′shəl) adj. **1.** of, relating to, or suitable for war or military life: *martial music.* **2.** of or characteristic of a warrior; warlike. [Latin *mārtiālis* relating to Mars, from *Mārs* the Roman god of war; referring to the belief of ancient astrologers that people born under the influence of the planet Mars were warlike.] —**mar′tial·ly,** adv.

martial law, military rule or authority imposed on a civilian population when the civil authorities cannot maintain law and order, as in a time of war or during an emergency.

Mar·tian (mär′shən) adj. of or relating to the planet Mars. —n. supposed inhabitant of the planet Mars. [Latin *mārtius* relating to Mars (from *Mārs* Mars) + -AN.]

mar·tin (märt′ən, mär′tin) n. any of various dark-colored swallows widely distributed throughout the world, as the **sand martin,** *Riparia riparia*. [From *St. Martin;* supposedly referring to its migration around St. Martin's Day on November 11.]

Mar·tin, Saint (märt′ən, mär′tin) A.D. c.316–c.397, French bishop.

mar·ti·net (märt′ən et′) n. strict disciplinarian, esp. a military one. [From Jean *Martinet*, French general under King Louis XIV, who originated a system of military drill.]

mar·tin·gale (märt′ən gāl′, mär′ting-) n. **1.** strap of a horse's harness attached under the belly at one end to the girth, passing between the forelegs, and secured to the nose band. It prevents the horse from rearing or throwing back its head. See **girth** for illustration. **2.** *Nautical.* **a.** lower stay that supports the jib boom or flying jib boom. **b.** small spar projecting down from the end of the bowsprit, designed to spread such stays. ·Also, **dolphin striker.** [French *martingale*, supposedly going back to *Martigue*, a town in Provence; with reference to its inhabitants' practice of fastening trousers in the back.]

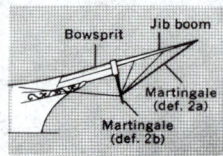

Martingales

mar·ti·ni (mär tē′nē) pl., **-nis.** n. cocktail consisting of gin or vodka and dry vermouth. [Possibly from *Martini* Italian proper name.]

Mar·ti·nique (mär′ti nēk′) n. French island in the Caribbean. Land area, approx. 425 sq. mi. Pop. (1969), 332,000.

Mar·tin·mas (märt′ən məs, mär′tin-) n. church festival held in honor of Saint Martin. November 11.

mar·tyr (mär′tər) n. **1.** one who suffers death rather than deny his religious faith. **2.** one who dies, suffers greatly, or sacrifices all for a belief, principle, or cause. **3.** one who willingly suffers greatly or sacrifices much. —v.t. **1.** to make a martyr of. **2.** to cause to suffer greatly; torture or persecute. [Old English *martyr* one who dies or suffers for the Christian faith, from Late Latin *martyr* one who, in dying for the Christian faith, bears witness to its truth, witness, from Greek *martys.*]

mar·tyr·dom (mär′tər dəm) n. **1.** state or condition of being a martyr. **2.** death or suffering of a martyr. **3.** extreme pain or suffering; torture; torment.

mar·vel (mär′vəl) n. wonderful or astonishing thing: *the marvels of modern medicine.* —v.i. **-veled, -vel·ing;** also, *British,* **-velled, -vel·ling.** to be or become filled with wonder or astonishment. [Old French *merveille* wonder, going back to Latin *mīrābilia* (plural) wonderful things.]

mar·vel·ous (mär′və ləs) also, *British,* **mar·vel·lous.** adj. **1.** causing or exciting wonder or astonishment: *marvelous and daring feats.* **2.** very good; splendid: *We had a marvelous vacation.* **3.** extremely improbable; incredible. —**mar′vel·ous·ly,** adv. —**mar′vel·ous·ness,** n.

Marx, Karl (märks; kärl) 1818–83, German economist and philosopher.

Marx·ism (märk′siz′əm) n. socialist theories of Karl Marx and Friedrich Engels.

Marx·ist (märk′sist) n. one who believes in or adheres to the theories of Marx and Engels. —adj. of or relating to Marxism. Also, **Marx′-i·an.**

Mar·y (mâr′ē) n. **1.** in the New Testament, the mother of Jesus. Also, **Blessed Virgin, Virgin Mary. 2.** in the New Testament, the sister of Martha, who lived in Bethany and was a follower of Jesus. [Latin *Maria*, from Greek *Mariā*, from Hebrew *Miryām* Miriam.]

Mary I, 1516–58, queen of England from 1553 to 1558 and wife of Philip II of Spain; known as Bloody Mary. Also, **Mary Tudor.**

Mary II, 1662–94, queen of England from 1689 to 1694.

Mar·y·land (mer′ə lənd) n. state in the eastern United States. Capital, Annapolis. Area, 10,577 sq. mi. Pop. (1970), 3,922,399. Abbreviation, **Md.**

Mary Magdalene, in the New Testament, a woman from whom Jesus cast out seven devils, often identified with the repentant sinner who anointed the feet of Jesus.

Mary, Queen of Scots, 1542–87, queen of Scotland. Also, **Mary Stuart.**

mar·zi·pan (mär′zə pan′) n. confection made of ground almonds, sugar, and egg whites, often molded into various forms. Also, **march′-pane′.** [German *Marzipan*, from Italian *marzapane* marzipan, container for sweets, from Arabic *martabān* container.]

masc., masculine.

mas·car·a (mas kar′ə) n. cosmetic preparation used to color the eyelashes and make them appear longer. [Spanish *máscara* mask, possibly from Arabic *maskharah* buffoon, person in masquerade.]

mas·con (mas′kon′) n. area of concentrated mass under the surface of the moon, believed to be responsible for uneven gravitational pull on spacecraft orbiting the moon. [Abbreviation of *ma(ss) con(centration).*]

mas·cot (mas′kot) n. animal, person, or thing supposed to bring good luck: *The school mascot was a bulldog.* [French *mascotte*, from Provençal *mascoto* sorcery, from *masco* witch; of uncertain origin.]

mas·cu·line (mas′kyə lin) adj. **1.** of, relating to, or characteristic of a man. **2.** having characteristics regarded as manly. **3.** (of a woman) mannish. **4.** *Grammar.* of the gender that includes words applying to things regarded as male. —n. *Grammar.* **1.** masculine gender. **2.** word or other element belonging to the masculine gender. [Latin *masculīnus* male, manly, from *masculus.* See MALE.] —**mas′cu·line·ly,** adv.

Syn. adj. **2. Masculine, manly, virile** mean belonging to or befitting a man. **Masculine** emphasizes the peculiar and distinctive characteristics of the male of the human species, esp. those attributes distinguishing men from women: *That opera singer has a deep, booming, masculine voice.* **Manly** accents those mental characteristics and virtues considered desirable in a man, as courage, independence, and determination: *He is an outstanding, manly boy.* **Virile** implies manifestation of sexual potency typical of manhood: *That actor exudes virile charm.*

masculine rhyme, rhyme consisting of a single stressed syllable, as *sakes* and *lakes* or *maroon* and *baboon.*

mas·cu·lin·i·ty (mas′kyə lin′ə tē) n. **1.** quality or state of being masculine: *He lacks masculinity.* **2.** mannishness.

Mase·field, John (mās′fēld′, māz′-) 1878–1967, English poet.

ma·ser (mā′zər) n. electronic device that produces or amplifies electromagnetic waves by use of the excess energy from an excited atomic

at; āpe; cär; end; mē; it; īce; hot; ōld; fôrk; wood; fōōl; oil; out; up; ūse; turn; sing; thin; this; zh in treasure; ə in ago, taken, pencil, lemon, circus.

or molecular system. [Abbreviation of *m(icrowave) a(mplification by) s(timulated) e(mission of) r(adiation).*]

Mas·e·ru (maz′ə rōō′) *n.* capital of the kingdom of Lesotho. Pop. (1966), 14,000.

mash (mash) *n.* **1.** feed that consists of a mixture of ground grains and is fed either wet or dry to livestock or poultry. **2.** ground or crushed malt or meal combined with water, used to make beer. **3.** any soft, pulpy mass or mixture. —*v.t.* **1.** to make into a soft, pulpy mass or mixture: *to mash potatoes.* **2.** to mix thoroughly (ground barley malt) with hot water to produce wort. **3.** to cause to be crushed or squeezed. [Old English *māsc*- malt mixed with hot water for brewing.] —**mash′er,** *n.*

Mash·had (mä shäd′) Meshed.

mash·ie (mash′ē) *pl.,* **mash·ies.** *also,* **mash·y.** *n.* golf club with a metal head having a short sloping face and giving a moderate amount of loft; number five iron.

mask (mask) *n.* **1.** covering worn over all or part of the face, used to conceal or disguise one's identity. **2.** covering, as of metal, plastic, wire, or gauze, worn on the face for protection, as in certain sports or occupations. **3.** covering worn over the face of an actor, as in ancient Greek or Roman drama. **4.** molded or sculptured likeness of a face, often made of plaster, clay, or papier-mâché. **5.** anything that hides or disguises something from view. **6.** distinctive marking on the face of certain animals, esp. dogs. **7.** gas mask. —*v.t.* **1.** to cover with a mask. **2.** to conceal or disguise, as from view: *A high stone wall masked the house from the road.* [French *masque* visor, disguise for the face, masked person, from Italian *maschera*, possibly from Arabic *mask-harah* buffoon, person in masquerade.]

Syn. *v.t.* **2. Mask, cloak, disguise** mean to conceal. **Mask** is used where the concealment is intended to mislead concerning the true identity, nature, or feelings: *His forced smile masked his disappointment.* **Cloak** is used where the deceptive pretense is intended to screen an ulterior design or true identity: *The naval exercises were cloaked in secrecy.* **Disguise** may be used where there is an intention to prevent recognition by altering or obscuring one's appearance or character or by assuming a counterfeit identity: *The duke disguised himself as a priest in order to leave the country.*

masked ball, ball at which masks, and often costumes, are worn by the guests.

masking tape, tape coated on one side with a sticky substance, used esp. to cover and protect surfaces, as during painting.

mas·o·chism (mas′ə kiz′əm) *n.* abnormal tendency to derive sexual pleasure from the infliction of pain or punishment on oneself by oneself or others. Distinguished from **sadism.** [From Leopold von Sacher-*Masoch,* 1836–95, Austrian novelist who described it.]

ma·son (mā′sən) *n.* **1.** one whose occupation is building with stone, brick, or concrete. **2. Mason.** Freemason. [Old French *masson* worker in stone; of Germanic origin.]

Ma·son-Dix·on line (mā′sən dik′sən) boundary line between Maryland and Pennsylvania, originally regarded as the dividing line between free and slave states, now the boundary between the North and the South.

Ma·son·ic (mə son′ik) *adj.* of, relating to, or characteristic of Freemasons or Freemasonry.

Ma·son·ite (mā′sə nīt′) *n. Trademark.* any of several fiberboards, used esp. for paneling or insulation.

Mason jar, glass jar with a screw top, used for home canning and preserving. [From John L. *Mason,* nineteenth-century American inventor who patented it.]

ma·son·ry (mā′sən rē) *pl.,* **-ries.** *n.* **1.** that which is built by a mason, esp. in stone. **2.** art, skill, or occupation of a mason. **3. Masonry.** Freemasonry.

masque (mask) *n.* **1.** form of dramatic entertainment popular in the sixteenth and seventeenth centuries, often using masks and based on allegory. **2.** literary work written for such a performance. **3.** masquerade *(def. 1).* [French *masque* visor, disguise for the face, masked person. See MASK.]

mas·quer·ade (mas′kə rād′) *n.* **1.** social gathering at which masks and fancy costumes are worn. **2.** false outward show; pretense. —*v.i.,* **-ad·ed, -ad·ing. 1.** to take part in a masquerade. **2.** to assume a false appearance or identity; disguise oneself; pose: *The poor girl masqueraded as an heiress.* [French *mascarade* band of masked persons, false pretense, from Italian *mascherata* band of masked persons, from *maschera* disguise for the face, masked person. See MASK.] —**mas′quer·ad′er,** *n.*

Roman mask   American Indian mask

Masks

mass (mas) *n.* **1.** coherent body of matter having an indefinite shape and a relatively large size: *a mass of snow.* **2.** large quantity, amount, or number: *a mass of people.* **3.** collection of individual parts or elements that together compose a single body: *a mass of rocks.* **4.** magnitude; bulk. **5.** main or greater part; majority. **6.** *Physics.* fundamental property of matter, measurable in terms of the inertia of a body, and used as a measure of the quantity of matter a body contains. **7. the masses.** the great body of the common people; the populace. —*v.t., v.i.* to form or gather into a mass; assemble. [Latin *massa* lump, from Greek *māza* lump, barley cake.]

Syn. **1. Mass, bulk** mean the body of substance that constitutes a thing. **Mass** relates to an aggregate, multitude, or expanse forming a large, unbroken, or solid body of indefinite size: *The Himalayas form the largest mountain mass in the world.* **Bulk** refers to an inordinately large or heavy body considered primarily as a mass of substance: *The hippopotamus is an animal of great bulk.*

Mass (mas) *also,* **mass.** *n.* **1.** main ceremony of worship in the Roman Catholic and parts of the Anglican churches. **2.** musical setting for certain parts of this service. [Old English *mæsse* celebration of the Eucharist, from Late Latin *missa,* from Latin *mittere* to send (away): supposedly from *Ite, missa est* Go, it is the dismissal (spoken at the end of the Mass).]

Mass., Massachusetts.

Mas·sa·chu·setts (mas′ə chōō′sits, -zits) *n.* state in the northeastern United States. Capital, Boston. Area, 8257 sq. mi. Pop. (1970), 5,689,170. Abbreviation, **Mass.**

Massachusetts Bay, inlet of the Atlantic, off of Massachusetts.

mas·sa·cre (mas′ə kər) *n.* **1.** brutal, indiscriminate slaughter, esp. of people. **2.** *Informal.* overwhelming defeat, as in sports. —*v.t.,* **-cred, -cring. 1.** to kill brutally and indiscriminately. **2.** *Informal.* to defeat overwhelmingly, as in sports. [French *massacre* slaughter; of uncertain origin.] —**mas·sa·crer** (mas′ə krər), *n.*

mas·sage (mə säzh′) *n.* manipulation of parts of the body, as by rubbing, esp. to increase circulation or relax muscles. —*v.t.,* **-saged, -sag·ing.** to give a massage to. [French *massage* manipulation of parts of the body, from *masser* to give a massage to, from Arabic *mass* to touch.]

Mas·sa·soit (mas′ə soit′) c.1580–1661, American Indian chief.

mass-en·er·gy equation (mas′en′ər jē) equation, $E = mc^2$, expressing the relation of mass and energy. In the equation, E = energy, m = mass, c = the velocity of light. Also, **Einstein's equation.**

mas·seur (mə sur′, ma-) *n.* man whose occupation is giving massages and other body-conditioning treatments. [French *masseur,* from *masser* to give a massage to. See MASSAGE.]

mas·seuse (mə sōōs′, -sōōz′) *n.* female masseur. [French *masseuse,* feminine of *masseur.* See MASSEUR.]

mas·sive (mas′iv) *adj.* **1.** consisting of or forming a large mass; having great size and weight: *The vault had massive steel doors.* **2.** imposing or exceedingly large, as in scope, scale, degree, or intensity: *a massive bombing raid.* [French *massif* bulky, heavy, going back to Latin *massa* lump. See MASS.] —**mas′sive·ly,** *adv.* —**mas′sive·ness,** *n.*

mass media, the various means of public communication, as television, newspapers, and magazines, that reach large audiences.

mass meeting, large public gathering of people to discuss, listen to discussion of, or act on some matter of common interest.

mass number, total number of protons and neutrons in the nucleus of an atom.

mass-pro·duce (mas′prə dōōs′, -düs′) **-duced, -duc·ing.** *v.t.* **1.** to manufacture or produce (goods) in large quantities, esp. by the use of machinery and assembly lines. **2.** to produce or turn out anything in large quantities.

mass production, act or process of mass-producing.

mass·y (mas′ē) **mass·i·er, mass·i·est.** *adj. Archaic.* massive.

mast¹ (mast) *n.* **1.** vertical pole set upright in a sailing boat or ship to support the yards, sails, and rigging. **2.** any upright pole, as of a crane. **3. before the mast.** as a common sailor: *to sail before the mast.* —*v.t.* to supply with a mast or masts. [Old English *mæst* the vertical pole of a ship.]

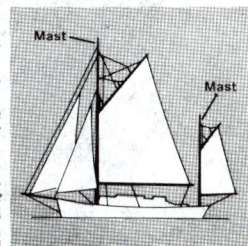

Mast   Mast

mast² (mast) *n.* fruit of certain trees, as the chestnut, esp. when used as food for animals. [Old English *mæst.*]

mas·tec·to·my (mas tek′tə mē) *pl.,* **-mies.** *n.* surgical removal of a breast. [Greek *mastos* breast + *ektomē* a cutting out.]

mas·ter (mas′tər) *n.* **1.** one who is in possession of, or has power,

control, or authority over, someone or something: *A dog should obey his master.* **2.** one who has great skill, ability, or knowledge in something; expert: *a master of deception.* **3.** one who possesses the power or ability to use, influence the course of, or dispose of something at will or to advantage: *He is the master of his emotions.* **4.** skilled craftsman or worker qualified to practice his craft or trade independently and to train apprentices. **5.** male teacher. **6.** great artist: *the Renaissance masters.* **7.** captain of a merchant ship. **8.** one who is a teacher or leader, as in religion or philosophy, and has followers or adherents. **9.** *also,* **Master.** one who has received a master's degree. **10. Master.** title of address appearing before the name of a youth or boy not considered old enough to be addressed as *Mister.* **11.** *also,* **Master.** one charged with the care, direction, or control of something specified. **12.** one who overcomes or defeats another; victor. **13.** one who is appointed as a representative of the court to assist the judge by hearing evidence in a dispute, as between labor and management. **14.** something, as a phonograph record, from which duplicates can be made. —*adj.* **1.** being a master in one's craft or trade: *a master plumber.* **2.** main; principal: *a master bedroom.* **3.** of, relating to, or characteristic of a master; skilled. **4.** designating a device or mechanism that controls, operates, or fits any of various similar devices or mechanisms: *a master switch.* —*v.t.* **1.** to gain control over; overcome; defeat: *to master one's fears.* **2.** to acquire complete knowledge or understanding of; become expert in: *to master French, to master a trade.* [Partly from Old English *mægister* chief, teacher; partly from Old French *maistre* one in charge, chief; both from Latin *magister* superior, chief, teacher.]

mas·ter-at-arms (mas′tər ət ärmz′) *pl.,* **mas·ters-at-arms.** *n.* member of a ship's crew who is responsible for maintaining order on a ship and performing duties of a disciplinary nature.

mas·ter·ful (mas′tər fəl) *adj.* **1.** forceful or authoritative. **2.** having or exhibiting mastery; expert. —**mas′ter·ful·ly,** *adv.*

master key, key designed to open all the locks of a certain type. Also, **pass′key′.**

mas·ter·ly (mas′tər lē) *adj.* characteristic of a master; expert. —*adv.* in a masterly manner. —**mas′ter·li·ness,** *n.*

mas·ter·mind (mas′tər mīnd′) *n.* one who has or displays great intelligence and ingenuity, esp. in devising or directing a course of action. —*v.t.* to devise or direct a course of action for (something): *to mastermind a robbery.*

Master of Arts 1. master's degree granted by a college or university to a person who has completed an advanced course of study in the arts or social sciences. **2.** person who has received this degree.

master of ceremonies, person who officiates at a formal gathering or entertainment and usually introduces the speakers or performers.

Master of Science 1. master's degree granted by a college or university to a person who has completed an advanced course of study in science or mathematics. **2.** person who has received this degree.

mas·ter·piece (mas′tər pēs′) *n.* **1.** something, as a work of art, that is outstanding in its field or superior to others of its kind. **2.** something regarded as a person's greatest achievement.

master's degree, graduate degree that usually represents one year of study beyond the bachelor's degree. The most commonly awarded forms of this degree are Master of Arts and Master of Science.

master sergeant, noncommissioned officer of the second highest rank in the U.S. Army and Marine Corps, and of the third highest rank in the U.S. Air Force.

mas·ter·ship (mas′tər ship′) *n.* **1.** office, status, or function of a master. **2.** state or condition of being a master; rule; control. **3.** skill, knowledge, or ability of a master.

master stroke, masterly or ingenious act or achievement.

mas·ter·y (mas′tər ē) *pl.,* **-ter·ies.** *n.* **1.** state of being master; rule; control. **2.** expert skill or knowledge. **3.** superiority or victory in competition; the upper hand. **4.** act of mastering something, as a craft or subject.

mast·head (mast′hed′) *n.* **1.** head or top of a ship's mast. **2.** notice printed in a newspaper or magazine giving the title, publisher's name, subscription rates, and other information.

mas·tic (mas′tik) *n.* **1.** thick yellowish resin obtained from an evergreen tree, *Pistacia lentiscus,* used to make dental cement, incense, and varnish. **2.** tree yielding this resin. **3.** any of various coal tar or asphalt mixtures used for setting windows, repairing roofs, or paving. [Old French *mastic* the resin, through Latin, from Greek *mastíchē.*]

mas·ti·cate (mas′tə kāt′) **-cat·ed, -cat·ing,** *v.t.* **1.** to chew. **2.** to grind, crush, or knead to a pulp, as rubber. [Late Latin *masticātus,* past participle of *masticāre* to chew, from Greek *mastíchān* to grind the teeth.] —**mas′ti·ca′tion,** *n.*

mas·ti·ca·tor (mas′tə kā′tər) *n.* **1.** one who or that which chews. **2.** machine for grinding or crushing something into pieces or pulp.

mas·ti·ca·to·ry (mas′tə kə tôr′ē) *adj.* **1.** of, relating to, or used in chewing. **2.** adapted for chewing. —*n. pl.,* **-ries.** substance chewed to increase salivation.

mas·tiff (mas′tif) *n.* large dog having a heavy head, a predominantly light-brown, short-haired coat, dark ears and muzzle, and a long, tapering tail. Height: 32 inches at the shoulder. [Modification (influenced in spelling by Old French *mestif* mongrel) of Old French *mastin,* going back to Latin *mānsuētus* tame.]

mas·to·don (mas′tə don′) *n.* any of various extinct, elephantlike mammals, genus *Mammut,* that originated in Africa and inhabited the Northern Hemisphere and South America. [Modern Latin *mastodon,* from Greek *mastos* breast + *odōn* tooth; referring to the nipple-shaped projections on its molars.]

mas·toid (mas′toid) *n.* that part of the skull bone behind and below each ear. —*adj.* of, relating to, designating, or near the mastoid or mastoid process. [Greek *mastoeidēs* like a breast, from *mastos* breast + *eidos* form.]

Mastiff

mas·toid·i·tis (mas′toi dī′tis) *n.* inflammation of the mastoid or mastoid process.

mastoid process, cone-shaped projection extending down from each mastoid just behind the lower part of the ear lobe.

mas·tur·bate (mas′tər bāt′) **-bat·ed, bat·ing.** *v.i.* to engage in masturbation.

mas·tur·ba·tion (mas′tər bā′shən) *n.* stimulation of the genital organs, usually by self-manipulation.

mat¹ (mat) *n.* **1.** small, flat piece of material, as rubber or woven straw, usually used as a floor covering or placed in front of a door. **2.** small, flat piece of material placed on a table under a vase or other object for protection or decoration. **3.** large, thick pad or covering placed on the floor to protect wrestlers, boxers, or gymnasts. **4.** any thick, tangled mass: *a mat of hair.* —*v.t.,* **mat·ted, mat·ting. 1.** to cover with or as with a mat or mats. **2.** to entangle or entwine into a thick mass. —*v.i.* to become entangled into a thick mass. [Old English *matt* piece of fabric made of rushes, from Late Latin *matta;* possibly of Semitic origin.]

mat² (mat) *n.* piece of cardboard or other material serving as a mount or frame for a picture, or as a border between a picture and its frame. Also, **matt.** —*v.t.,* **mat·ted, mat·ting.** to provide (a picture) with a mat. [French *mat* dull color, from *mat* dull, faded. See MAT³.]

mat³ (mat) *adj.* matte. —*n.* matte. —*v.t.,* **mat·ted, mat·ting.** to matte. [French *mat* dull, faded, from Old French *mat* conquered, from Late Latin *mattus* stupid, drunk.]

mat·a·dor (mat′ə dôr′) *n.* man who kills the bull in a bullfight. [Spanish *matador* killer, bullfighter who kills the bull, from Latin *mactātor* killer.]

match¹ (mach) *n.* **1.** short piece of wood, cardboard, or other material coated on one end with a substance, such as a compound of sulfur and phosphorous, that is easily ignited by friction. **2.** wick prepared to burn at a uniform rate, formerly used to fire guns and cannon. [Old French *mesche* wick of a candle or lamp, fuse, going back to Latin *myxa* nozzle of a lamp, from Greek *myxā.*]

match² (mach) *n.* **1.** one who or that which corresponds exactly to another; counterpart; facsimile: *I lost the match to this glove.* **2.** one who or that which can compete with or oppose another as an equal: *He has yet to meet his match.* **3.** one who or that which is similar to another in some respect. **4.a.** two persons or things that are like, or suitable for, each other: *The blue coat and the blue dress are a good match.* **b.** one who or that which is like, or suitable for, another: *The gloves are a good match for the bag.* **5.** game or contest between two or more persons, animals, or teams: *a wrestling match.* **6.** matrimonial agreement or union; marriage: *She made a bad match when she married him.* **7.** possible marriage partner. —*v.t.* **1.** to be like, suitable for, or a counterpart of: *The pattern on this material matches that of the sofa.* **2.a.** to find, select, or produce (things) that are equal to or suitable for one another: *to match socks.* **b.** to find, select, or produce something that is a counterpart of or is suitable for (another): *I'm trying to match this fabric.* **3.** to compete with or oppose as an equal; be a match for: *No one can match him in oratory.* **4.** to place in competition or opposition, esp. in order to determine superiority (often with *against*): *to match wits.* **5.** to cause to correspond: *I will match my donation to yours.* **6.a.** to flip (a coin or coins) and bet on or compare the faces that are revealed. **b.** to flip coins in this way with (another person). **7.** to join in marriage; marry. —*v.i.* to be equal or correspond. [Old English *gemæcca* companion, mate¹.]

match·less (mach′lis) *adj.* having no equal; peerless; unrivaled. —**match′less·ly,** *adv.* —**match′less·ness,** *n.*

match·lock (mach′lok′) *n.* formerly, a type of gun fired by igniting the powder with a slow-burning wick.

match·mak·er (mach′mā′kər) *n.* **1.** one who arranges or tries to arrange marriages for others. **2.** one who arranges sports contests, as

boxing matches. [MATCH² + MAKER.] —**match′mak′ing,** adj., n.

match play, method of scoring in golf in which the total number of holes won determines the winner. Distinguished from **medal play.**

match point, in certain games, the final point that is needed to win a match.

match·wood (mach′wood′) n. **1.** wood used or suitable for making matches. **2.** splinters.

mate¹ (māt) n. **1.** one of a pair: *the mate to a sock.* **2.** husband or wife. **3.** male or female of a pair of animals that have paired or been paired for propagation. **4.** officer on a merchant ship, ranking next below the captain. **5.** assistant to a warrant officer in the U.S. Navy. **6.** close associate; companion. —v.t., **mat·ed, mat·ing. 1.** to join together or match. **2.** to cause (animals) to produce offspring; pair. **3.** to join in marriage. —v.i. **1.** (of animals) to pair for propagation: *Birds mate in the spring.* **2.** to become joined in marriage. [Middle Low German *mate* companion.]

mate² (māt) **mat·ed, mat·ing.** *Chess.* v.t. to checkmate. —n. checkmate. [From Old French chess term *eschec et mat* literally, check and conquered. See CHECKMATE.]

ma·té (mä′tā, mat′ā) n. **1.** greenish tealike beverage made from the dried leaves of an evergreen shrub, *Ilex paraguariensis,* of the holly family, containing caffeine and having a slightly bitter taste. **2.** leaves and shoots used to make this beverage. **3.** the shrub itself, found in South America. [Spanish *mate* this tealike beverage, vessel in which maté is made, from Quechua *mati* calabash vessel.]

ma·ter (mā′tər) n. mother. ▲ often used as an affectation or in humorous contexts. [Latin *mater.*]

ma·te·ri·al (mə tēr′ē əl) n. **1.** substance or substances of which something is or may be made or composed. **2.** fabric. **3.** that which may be used, developed, or elaborated on, esp. in creating or making something: *The author is gathering material for his new novel.* **4.** one who or that which is especially suited for, or has great potential for succeeding in, a particular field or endeavor: *He is excellent executive material.* **5.** materials. things, as tools or implements, needed to make or do something: *writing materials.* —adj. **1.** of, relating to, or consisting of matter; physical: *a material object.* **2.** of or relating to the body or physical well-being: *material needs.* **3.** concerned with or caring primarily for the physical rather than the intellectual or spiritual things of life; materialistic. **4.** essential; important. **5.** *Law.* likely to influence the outcome of a case or the character of a document: *a material witness.* **6.** relevant; pertinent (with *to*). **7.** *Philosophy.* of or relating to matter or substance, as opposed to form. [Late Latin *materialis* relating to matter, from Latin *materia* wood, matter, topic.]

Syn. 1. Material, substance mean the stuff of which a thing is made. **Material** refers to the basic and tangible matter constituting a thing, esp. something made: *Brick and wood are building materials.* **Substance** relates to the specific type of matter that something is composed of and endows it with particular characteristics: *Tar is a viscous substance.* —adj. **1.** see **physical.**

ma·te·ri·al·ism (mə tēr′ē ə liz′əm) n. **1.** philosophical doctrine that everything that exists is either composed of matter or depends on matter for its existence. **2.** tendency to be unduly concerned with material rather than intellectual or spiritual things.

ma·te·ri·al·ist (mə tēr′ē ə list) n. **1.** believer in philosophical materialism. **2.** one who is unduly or solely concerned with the material rather than the intellectual or spiritual things of life. —**ma·te′ri·al·is′tic,** adj. —**ma·te′ri·al·is′ti·cal·ly,** adv.

ma·te·ri·al·ize (mə tēr′ē ə līz′) -ized, -iz·ing. v.i. **1.** to come into being; become actual fact; be realized: *His dreams of success failed to materialize.* **2.** to assume or appear in bodily or visible form: *During the séance, spirits seemed to materialize.* —v.t. to give material form or character to. —**ma·te′ri·al·i·za′tion,** n.

ma·te·ri·al·ly (mə tēr′ē ə lē) adv. **1.** with regard to material or physical things: *He was well-off materially.* **2.** considerably; substantially. **3.** *Philosophy.* in matter, content, or substance, not only in form.

ma·te·ri·a med·i·ca (mə tēr′ē ə med′i kə) n. **1.** drugs and similar substances used in the treatment of disease. **2.** branch of medicine that deals with the origin, preparation, and administration of drugs and similar substances. [Modern Latin *materia medica* healing matter.]

ma·té·ri·el (mə tēr′ē el′) n. **1.** equipment, apparatus, and supplies used by a military force. **2.** equipment, apparatus, and supplies of any organized body. [French *matériel* equipment, from Late Latin *materialis* relating to matter. See MATERIAL.]

ma·ter·nal (mə turn′əl) adj. **1.** of, relating to, or like a mother; motherly: *maternal instincts.* **2.** inherited or derived from one's mother. **3.** related through one's mother: *a maternal aunt.* [Latin *maternus* relating to a mother (from *mater* mother) + -AL¹.] —**ma·ter′nal·ly,** adv.

ma·ter·ni·ty (mə tur′nə tē) adj. **1.** for pregnant women: *a maternity dress.* **2.** designed for the care of newborn babies and women during and after childbirth: *a maternity ward.* —n. **1.** state of being a mother;

motherhood. **2.** qualities or characteristics of a mother; motherliness.

math (math) n. mathematics.

math·e·mat·i·cal (math′ə mat′i kəl) adj. **1.** of, relating to, of the nature of, or concerned with mathematics. **2.** rigorously exact; precise: *mathematical certainty.* Also, **math′e·mat′ic.** —**math·e·mat′i·cal·ly,** adv.

mathematical induction, induction (def. 4b).

math·e·ma·ti·cian (math′ə mə tish′ən) n. one who is an expert in or student of mathematics.

math·e·mat·ics (math′ə mat′iks) n.,pl. science dealing with the properties and the relations between quantities, sets, and operations. Mathematics includes arithmetic, algebra, geometry, and calculus. ▲ construed as singular. [Latin *mathematica,* from Greek *mathematike (techne)* mathematical (art), from *mathema* something learned, science.]

mat·i·nee (mat′ən ā′) also, **mat·i·née.** n. theatrical presentation performed in the afternoon. [French *matinee,* from *matin* morning; in medieval France, morning was considered to be from sunrise until three o'clock. See MATINS.]

ma·tins (mat′inz) n.,pl. **1.** first of the canonical hours in the breviary, usually recited with Lauds. **2.** in the Church of England, the morning service prescribed by the Book of Common Prayer. **3.** also, **matin.** *Archaic.* any morning song. [French *matins* morning prayer, from *matin* morning, from Latin *matutinum,* going back to *Matuta* ancient Roman goddess of dawn.]

Ma·tisse, Hen·ri (mä tēs′; äN rē′) 1869–1954, French painter.

ma·tri·arch (mā′trē ärk′) n. **1.** woman who is the head of a family or tribe. **2.** woman who dominates or has great authority in any group. [Latin *matr-,* stem of *mater* mother; on the model of PATRIARCH.]

ma·tri·ar·chal (mā′trē är′kəl) adj. **1.** relating to, of the nature of, or based on a matriarchy: *a matriarchal society.* **2.** of or relating to a matriarch.

ma·tri·ar·chy (mā′trē är′kē) pl., -chies. n. form of society in which the woman is the head of a family or tribe and descent is traced through the maternal line.

ma·tri·ces (mā′trə sēz′, mat′rə-) plural of **matrix.**

mat·ri·cid·al (mat′rə sīd′əl, mā′trə-) adj. of or relating to matricide or one who commits matricide.

mat·ri·cide¹ (mat′rə sīd′, mā′trə-) n. act of killing one's mother. [Latin *matricidium,* from *mater* mother + -cidium. See -CIDE¹.]

mat·ri·cide² (mat′rə sīd′, mā′trə-) n. one who kills his mother. [Latin *matricida,* from *mater* mother + -cida. See -CIDE².]

ma·tric·u·lant (mə trik′yə lənt) n. one who has matriculated or is a candidate for matriculation.

ma·tric·u·late (mə trik′yə lāt′) -lat·ed, -lat·ing. v.t., v.i. to admit or enroll in a college or university as a candidate for a degree. [Late Latin *matriculatus* past participle of *matriculare* to register, enroll, going back to Latin *matrix* womb, list, register.] —**ma·tric′u·la′tion,** n.

mat·ri·lin·e·al (mat′rə lin′ē əl, mā′trə-) adj. of, relating to, or tracing descent through the maternal line.

mat·ri·mo·ni·al (mat′rə mō′nē əl) adj. of or relating to marriage. —**mat′ri·mo′ni·al·ly,** adv.

mat·ri·mo·ny (mat′rə mō′nē) pl., -nies. n. **1.** state or condition of being married. **2.** rite or ceremony of marriage. [Latin *matrimonium* marriage, from *mater* mother.]

ma·trix (mā′triks, mat′riks) pl., -tri·ces or -trix·es. n. **1.** that in which something originates, develops, forms, or is contained. **2.** *Geology.* **a.** the grains of smaller size in a rock in which some grains are much larger than others. **b.** natural material in which something, as a fossil, pebble, crystal, or mineral, is embedded. **3.** *Biology.* intercellular substance of tissue. **4.** *Anatomy.* formative cells from which a structure, as a tooth or nail, grows. **5.** the womb. **6.** *Printing.* shallow mold, usually of paper, lead, or brass, in which typefaces are cast. [Latin *matrix* womb, source, from *mater* mother.]

ma·tron (mā′trən) n. **1.** married woman, esp. one who has children or is mature in age and manner. **2.** woman who supervises or guards the inmates of an institution, as a hospital or jail. **3.** female rest room attendant, as in a restaurant. [Old French *matrone* married woman, from Latin *matrona,* from *mater* mother.]

ma·tron·ly (mā′trən lē) adj. characteristic of, suitable for, or like a matron. —**ma′tron·li·ness,** n.

matron of honor, married woman who is the chief attendant of the bride at a wedding.

Mat·su (mat soo′, mat′soo) n. small island off the coast of the China mainland, held by the Republic of China. Area, approx. 10 sq. mi. Pop. (1955 est.), 10,500.

Matt., Matthew.

matte (mat) adj. having a dull, lusterless finish or surface. —n. dull, lusterless finish or surface, as on glass or paper. —v.t. **mat·ted, mat·ting.** to produce a dull, lusterless finish or surface on. [Form of MAT³.]

---

mat·ted (mat´id) *adj.* **1.** entangled or entwined in a thick mass: *Her wet hair was matted.* **2.** covered with a dense growth. **3.** covered with or made of matting. [MAT¹ + -ED².]

mat·ter (mat´ər) *n.* **1.** anything that occupies space and has weight. The three common states of matter are solid, liquid, and gaseous. **2.** specified kind or form of substance: *inorganic matter.* **3.** something that is the subject of discussion, concern, feeling, or action: *a legal matter. This matter does not concern us.* **4.** difficult, unpleasant, or unsatisfactory condition or circumstance; trouble; problem (with *the*): *What is the matter with my report?* **5.** importance; significance: *It's of no matter to me what you do.* **6.** instance in which something comes into play (with *of*): *a matter of opinion, a matter of preference.* **7.** material to be read in a book, advertisement, or the like, as distinguished from illustrative material: *reading matter.* **8.** substance of that which is written or spoken, as distinguished from the form, style, or manner in which it is conveyed. **9.** indefinite amount, quantity, or extent (with *of*): *The police arrived in a matter of minutes.* **10.** anything sent by mail: *third-class matter.* **11.** substance excreted by the body, as from a wound or abscess. **12.** *Printing.* type or plates set up or to be set up. **13.** **as a matter of fact.** actually; truthfully: *As a matter of fact, I do know her.* **14.** **no matter.** regardless of; despite: *No matter what you say, I still disagree with you.* —*v.i.* to be of importance. [Old French *mat(i)ere* substance, subject, pus, from Latin *māteria* wood, substance, subject.]

Mat·ter·horn (mat´ər hôrn´) *n.* steep, jagged mountain peak in the Alps, on the border between Switzerland and Italy.

mat·ter-of-course (mat´ər əv kôrs´) *n.* something to be expected as a natural or logical result.

mat·ter-of-fact (mat´ər əv fakt´) *adj.* **1.** dealing with facts; unimaginative; practical: *a matter-of-fact narrative.* **2.** having or exhibiting no emotion or feeling; disinterested. —**mat´ter-of-fact´ly,** *adv.* —**mat´ter-of-fact´ness,** *n.*

Mat·thew (math´ū) *n.* **1.** one of the four Evangelists chosen by Jesus as one of the twelve Apostles. **2.** one of the four Gospels, the first book of the New Testament, attributed to him.

mat·ting¹ (mat´ing) *n.* **1.** coarse, woven fabric of grass, straw, hemp, or other fiber, used esp. for making mats and as a packing material. **2.** mats collectively. [MAT¹ + -ING¹.]

mat·ting² (mat´ing) *mat².*

mat·ting³ (mat´ing) *n.* **1.** matte. **2.** act or process of producing a matte finish or surface on something. [MAT¹ + -ING¹.]

mat·tock (mat´ək) *n.* tool consisting of a handle and a two-headed head, used for loosening soil and cutting roots. [Old English *mattuc.*]

mat·tress (mat´ris) *n.* pad covered with strong cloth or other material and often stuffed with hair, cotton, batting, or rubber, designed to fit on the frame of a bed, esp. on top of a box spring. [Old French *materas* quilt to lie on, through Italian, from Arabic *matrah* place where something is thrown, cushion.]

Mattocks

mat·u·rate (mach´ə rāt´) *-rat·ed, -rat·ing.* *v.i.* to ripen; mature. —**mat´u·ra´tion,** *n.*

ma·ture (mə choor´, -tyoor´, -toor´) *adj.* **1.** having reached full growth or development: *mature fruit, a physically mature person.* **2.** having the qualities or characteristics of one who has reached full physical and mental development: *mature behavior, a mature attitude.* **3.** fully or thoroughly developed or thought out: *a mature scheme.* **4.** due for payment, as a loan or bond. **5.** having reached maximum development and form as produced by erosion: *a mature river.* —*v.i.* **-tured, -tur·ing.** **1.** to become fully grown or developed; reach maturity. **2.** to become due for payment: *This bond matures in five years.* —*v.t.* **1.** to bring to full growth or development. **2.** to develop or think out fully; complete. [Latin *mātūrus* ripe.] —**ma·ture´ly,** *adv.*

ma·tu·ri·ty (mə choor´ə tē, -tyoor´-, -toor´-) *pl.,* **-ties.** *n.* **1.** state or quality of being mature: *Accepting responsibility is a sign of maturity.* **2.a.** time at which something, as a bond, is due for payment. **b.** state of being due for payment.

ma·tu·ti·nal (mə toot´ən əl, -tūt´-) *adj.* of, relating to, or occurring in the morning; early in the day. [Late Latin *mātūtīnālis,* from Latin *mātūtīnus,* from *Mātūta.* See MATINS.]

mat·zoh (mät´sə, -sō) *also,* **mat·zo.** *n.* thin, flat piece of unleavened bread, traditionally eaten at Passover. [Hebrew *matztzāh.*]

maud·lin (môd´lin) *adj.* excessively and foolishly sentimental.

Maugham (William) Som·er·set (môm; sum´ər set´, -sit) 1874–1965, English writer.

Mau·i (mou´ē) *n.* second largest island of Hawaii. Area, 728 sq. mi. Pop. (1970), 46,156.

maul (môl) *n.* heavy mallet or hammer used for driving wedges, stakes, or piles. —*v.t.* **1.** to injure, as by beating, bruising, or knocking about.

2. to handle roughly or clumsily; abuse. **3.** to split (wood) with a maul and wedge. [Old French *mail* hammer, from Latin *malleus.*]

Mau Mau (mou´ mou´) *pl.,* **Mau Mau** or **Mau Maus.** **1.** former secret terrorist society organized by Kikuyu tribesmen of Kenya to drive out white settlers. **2.** member of this society.

Mau·na Lo·a (mou´nə lō´ə) largest known active volcano in the world, on the island of Hawaii.

maun·der (môn´dər) *v.i.* **1.** to talk in a rambling, incoherent manner. **2.** to move or act in an aimless, dreamy, and confused manner. [Of uncertain origin.]

Maun·dy Thursday (môn´dē) Thursday of Holy Week, commemorating the Last Supper, at which Christ washed the feet of the Apostles. Also, **Holy Thursday.** [Old French *mande* command (from Latin *mandātum*) + THURSDAY; referring to the first word, *mandātum,* of a Latin anthem sung on the Thursday before Good Friday.]

Mau·re·ta·ni·a (môr´ə tā´nē ə) *n.* ancient country in northwestern Africa.

Mau·ri·ta·ni·a (môr´ə tā´nē ə) *n.* country on the northwestern coast of Africa, formerly a possession of France. Capital, Nouakchott. Area, 397,955 sq. mi. Pop. (1968 est.), 1,120,000.

Mau·ri·tius (mô rish´əs) *n.* small island country in the western Indian Ocean, east of Madagascar, formerly a British possession. Capital, Port Louis. Area, 720 sq. mi. Pop. (1968 est.), 810,000.

mau·so·le·um (mô´sə lē´əm, -zə-) *pl.,* **-le·ums** or **-le·a** (-lē´ə). *n.* stately, often large, building housing a tomb or tombs. [Latin *mausōleum* magnificent tomb, from Greek *Mausōleion* the splendid tomb of *Mausolus,* king in ancient Asia Minor.]

mauve (mōv) *n.* any of various pale, purplish-blue or rose colors. [French *mauve* mallow, the color of the flower of the mallow, from Latin *malva* mallow. Doublet of MALLOW.]

mav·er·ick (mav´ər ik) *n.* **1.** unbranded animal, esp. a calf, traditionally belonging to the first person to find and brand it. **2.** *Informal.* one who takes an unorthodox stand, esp. in politics, independently of the group with which he is nominally aligned. [From Samuel A. *Maverick,* 1803–70, Texan who decided not to brand his calves because his ranch was on an island.]

ma·vis (mā´vis) *n.* song thrush. [Old French *mauvis;* of uncertain origin.]

ma·vour·neen (mə voor´nēn) *also,* **ma·vour·nin.** *n.* my darling. [Irish *mo* my + *muirnín* darling.]

maw (mô) *n.* **1.** jaws, mouth, throat, or gullet of any animal. **2.** stomach. [Old English *maga* stomach.]

mawk·ish (mô´kish) *adj.* **1.** excessively and foolishly sentimental. **2.** having a sickly, insipid flavor; nauseating. [Obsolete *mawk* maggot (from Old Norse *mathkr*) + -ISH.] —**mawk´ish·ly,** *adv.* —**mawk´ish·ness,** *n.*

max., maximum.

max·il·la (mak sil´ə) *pl.,* **max·il·lae** (mak sil´ē). *n.* **1.** bone of the upper jaw. **2.** in arthropods, either of a pair of appendages, just behind the mandibles, often modified to perform other functions, but usually acting as accessory jaws. [Latin *maxilla* jawbone, jaw.]

max·il·lar·y (mak´sə ler´ē) *adj.* of, relating to, or situated near the bone of the upper jaw: *maxillary artery.* —*n. pl.,* **-lar·ies.** maxilla.

max·im (mak´sim) *n.* concise statement expressing a general truth or doctrine; precept. [French *maxime,* from Late Latin *maxima (prōpositiō)* greatest (proposition), axiom, feminine of Latin *maximus* greatest. See MAXIMUM.] —**Syn.** see proverb.

max·i·mal (mak´sə məl) *adj.* of or being a maximum; greatest or highest possible.

Max·i·mil·ian (mak´sə mil´yən) 1832–67, archduke of Austria; emperor of Mexico from 1864 to 1867.

Maximilian I, 1459–1519, Holy Roman emperor from 1493 to 1519.

Maximilian II, 1527–76, Holy Roman emperor from 1564 to 1576.

max·i·mize (mak´sə mīz´) **-mized, -miz·ing.** *v.t.* to make as great as possible; raise or increase to the maximum.

max·i·mum (mak´sə məm) *pl.,* **-mums** or **-ma** (-mə). *n.* **1.** greatest possible amount, degree, or quantity: *It will take a maximum of three hours.* **2.** highest point, degree, or number reached or recorded: *It reached a maximum today of 90°.* —*adj.* greatest possible; highest: *The maximum speed on this road is sixty miles per hour.* [Latin *maximum,* neuter of *maximus* greatest, superlative of *magnus* great.]

may (mā) Present: *sing.,* first person, **may;** second, **may** or *(archaic)* **may·est** or **mayst;** third, **may;** *pl.,* **may.** Past: **might.** auxiliary verb (followed by an infinitive without *to* or elliptically with the infinitive understood) **1.** used to express permission: *You may leave the table.* ▲ see usage note under **can.** **2.** used to express possibility or likelihood: *It may snow.* **3.** used to express desire, hope, or wish: *May you have many happy years together.* **4.** used to express contingency, esp. in clauses expressing condition, concession, purpose, or result: *He is willing to be captured, so that we may escape.* [Old English *mæg* I can or may.]

May (mā) *n.* fifth month of the year, containing thirty-one days.

[Old French *Mai,* from Latin *Māius (mēnsis)* (month) of Maia, Roman earth goddess.]

Ma·ya (mä′yə) *pl.,* **Ma·yas** or **Ma·ya.** *n.* **1.** member of a tribe of highly civilized American Indians who lived in southern Mexico and parts of Central America at the time of the Spanish conquest in the sixteenth century. **2.** their language, a branch of the Mayan family of languages. —*adj.* of or relating to the Mayas, their language, culture, or civilization.

Ma·yan (mä′yən) *adj.* Maya. —*n.* **1.** a Maya. **2.** family of Central American Indian languages, including that of the Mayas.

May apple 1. small North American plant, *Podophyllum peltatum,* having a white cup-shaped flower that grows in the center of a forked stem. Also, **man′drake′. 2.** yellowish, egg-shaped fruit of this plant, used mainly to make preserves.

may·be (mā′bē) *adv.* possibly; perhaps.

May·day (mā′dā′) *n.* international radiotelephone signal word used by ships or aircraft as a call for help. [French *m'aidez* help me, going back to Latin *mē* me + *adjūtāre* to help.]

May Day, holiday traditionally celebrated as a spring festival. Some countries commemorate the growth of the international labor movement on this day with parades and other demonstrations. May 1.

may·est (mā′ist) *Archaic.* present indicative, second person singular of **may.**

may·flow·er (mā′flou′ər) *n.* **1.** any of various plants whose flowers blossom in May, as the trailing arbutus. **2. Mayflower.** ship on which the Pilgrims came to America in 1620.

may·fly (mā′flī′) *pl.,* **-flies.** *n.* any of a group of insects, order Ephemeroptera, having two pairs of finely veined wings, and tail-like filaments attached to the end of the body. Length: to 1 inch.

may·hap (mā′hap, mā′hap′) *adv. Archaic.* perhaps. [Shortened from the phrase *it may hap.*]

may·hem (mā′hem, mā′əm) *n.* **1.a.** crime of intentionally, unlawfully, and violently injuring or maiming a person's body so as to render him less able to defend himself or to annoy his adversary. **b.** commission of

Mayfly

such a crime. **2.** state of confusion and disorder, often noisy, and sometimes accompanied by violence and the destruction of property: *There was utter mayhem in the theater when the fire alarm sounded.* [Anglo-Norman *mahaym* injury, from Old French *mahaignier* to injure. See MAIM.]

may·n't (mā′ənt, mānt) may not.

may·on·naise (mā′ə nāz′, mā′ə nāz′) *n.* thick, creamy sauce made of egg yolks, olive oil, vinegar or lemon juice, and seasoning. [French *mayonnaise,* from *Mahón* chief town of Minorca; possibly in honor of the capture of *Mahón* by the French in 1756.]

may·or (mā′ər, mâr) *n.* official head of a municipal government. [Old French *maire,* from Latin *mājor* greater, comparative of *magnus* great. Doublet of MAJOR.]

may·or·al·ty (mā′ər əl tē, mâr′-) *pl.,* **-ties.** *n.* office or term of office of a mayor.

May·pole (mā′pōl′) *also,* **may·pole.** *n.* pole decorated with flowers and ribbons, around which people dance on May Day.

mayst (māst) *Archaic.* present indicative, second person singular of **may.**

May·time (mā′tīm′) *n.* month of May. Also, **May′tide′.**

Maz·a·rin, Jules (maz′ər in; *French* mä zä raN′; zhool) 1602–61, French statesman.

Maz·da·ism (maz′də iz′əm) *also,* **Maz·de·ism.** *n.* Zoroastrianism.

maze (māz) *n.* **1.** intricate, confusing network of paths or passageways, usually bordered by high walls or shrubs, through which it is difficult to find one's way. **2.** any intricate and confusing network or situation. **3.** state of bewilderment, indecision, or confusion. [From archaic *maze* to daze, confuse, form of AMAZE.]

ma·zur·ka (mə zur′kə, -zoor′-) *also,* **ma·zour·ka. n. 1.** lively Polish dance resembling the polka. **2.** music for such a dance. [Polish *mazurka* a Polish dance; literally, woman of *Mazovia,* a Polish province.]

maz·y (mā′zē) **maz·i·er, maz·i·est.** *adj.* like a maze.

Maz·zi·ni, Giu·sep·pe (mat sē′nē, mät-; jə zep′ē) 1805–72, Italian revolutionary and patriot.

M.B.A., Master of Business Administration.

Mba·ba·ne (mbä bä′nä) *n.* capital of Swaziland, in the western part of the country. Pop. (1968 est.), 13,800.

Mc- prefix son of. ▲ used in certain Irish and Scottish names.

M.C. 1. Master of Ceremonies. **2.** Member of Congress.

Mc·Clel·lan, George B. (mə klel′ən) 1826–85, Union general in the U.S. Civil War.

Mc·Cor·mick, Cy·rus Hall (mə kôr′mik; sī′rəs hôl) 1809–84, U.S. inventor of the reaping machine.

Mc·Coy (mə koi′) *n.* **the real McCoy.** genuine person or thing: *My dress is a copy, but hers is the real McCoy.* [Possibly the expression originated to distinguish the famous boxer Kid *McCoy* from a minor fighter having the same last name.]

Mc·Hen·ry, Fort (mək hen′rē, mə ken′-) former U.S. fort at the entrance to Baltimore harbor. During its bombardment by the British in 1814, Francis Scott Key wrote *The Star-Spangled Banner.*

Mc·In·tosh (mak′in tosh′) *n.* juicy red apple with white flesh. [From John *McIntosh,* Canadian who discovered it around 1796.]

Mc·Kin·ley (mə kin′lē) **1. William.** 1843–1901, twenty-fifth president of the United States from 1897 to 1901. **2. Mount.** highest mountain in North America, in south-central Alaska.

Md, mendelevium.

Md., Maryland.

M.D., Doctor of Medicine.

mdse., merchandise.

me (mē) *pron.* objective case of **I.**

Me., Maine.

ME, Middle English.

M.E. 1. Mechanical Engineer. **2.** Master of Education. **3.** Mining Engineer. **4.** Methodist Episcopal. **5.** Master of Engineering.

mead¹ (mēd) *n.* alcoholic drink made from fermented honey and water and flavored with herbs. [Old English *meodu.*]

mead² (mēd) *n. Archaic.* meadow. [Old English *mǣd.*]

mead·ow (med′ō) *n.* **1.** piece of grassy land, used as a pasture or for growing hay. **2.** tract of low, well-watered grassland, usually near a river or stream. [Old English *mǣdwe,* oblique case of *mǣd* grassy land used for growing hay.] —**mead′ow·y,** *adj.*

mead·ow·lark (med′ō lärk′) *n.* North American songbird, genus *Sturnella,* having a pointed, cone-shaped bill, predominantly mottled-brown plumage, and a yellow breast with a black crescent across it. There are two species: the **eastern meadowlark,** *S. magna,* and the **western meadowlark,** *S. neglecta.* Length: 8½–11 inches.

Meadowlark

mead·ow·sweet (med′ō swēt′) *n.* **1.** either of two North American shrubs, *Spiraea alba* or *Spiraea latifolia,* of the rose family, grown for their dense clusters of small, fragrant pink or white flowers. **2.** any of a group of tall, hardy plants, genus *Filipendula,* of the rose family, found in north temperate regions, grown for their showy clusters of small white, pink, or purple flowers.

mea·ger (mē′gər) *also,* **mea·gre.** *adj.* **1.** scarcely adequate in amount or quantity; insufficient. **2.** thin; lean. [Old French *maigre* thin, from Latin *mācer.*] —**mea′ger·ly,** *adv.* —**mea′ger·ness,** *n.*

Syn. 1. Meager, scanty, skimpy, sparse mean an insufficiency in some respect. **Meager** suggests being conspicuously deficient in amount, number, or quality necessary to achieve fullness, richness, and strength: *Jim could not support his family on his meager salary.* **Scanty** implies being barely adequate or inadequate in an amount essential to support an activity or come up to a standard: *The camp had only a scanty supply of food for the winter.* **Skimpy** implies being meager because of parsimony or penury: *Bob's father paid him a skimpy allowance every week.* **Sparse** implies being thinly spread in space or time and lacking in density or substance: *The ground was covered with sparse vegetation.*

meal¹ (mēl) *n.* **1.** food or drink served or eaten at one time. **2.** time or occasion during which such food or drink is regularly served or eaten. [Old English *mǣl* mealtime, measure.]

meal² (mēl) *n.* **1.** edible part of any grain, coarsely ground and unsifted. **2.** any similar ground substance. [Old English *melu* ground grain.]

meal ticket 1. ticket or card entitling the owner to meals at a specified restaurant or cafeteria, esp. at reduced prices. **2.** *Slang.* person or thing depended on as a source of livelihood.

meal·time (mēl′tīm′) *n.* customary time for a meal.

meal·y (mē′lē) **meal·i·er, meal·i·est.** *adj.* **1.** resembling meal; dry and powdery: *mealy potatoes.* **2.** of or containing meal. **3.** sprinkled or covered with or as with meal. **4.** pale: *a mealy complexion.* **5.** mealymouthed. —**meal′i·ness,** *n.*

meal·y·mouthed (mē′lē mouthd′, -moutht′) *adj.* unwilling to say plainly what is meant; not outspoken; insincere.

mean¹ (mēn) **meant, mean·ing.** *v.t.* **1.** to have in mind as a purpose or intention: *He did not mean to hurt you.* **2.** to intend to convey or indicate: *I do not know what you mean by that remark.* **3.** to have as

at; āpe; cär; end; mē; it; īce; hot; ōld; fôrk; wood; fōōl; oil; out; up; ūse; turn; sing; thin; **this**; zh in treasure; ə in ago, taken, pencil, lemon, circus.

631

a particular sense; be defined as: *These words mean exactly the same thing.* **4.** to intend or design for a particular person, purpose, use, destination, or end: *I think Fate meant us for each other* (Smith, 1884). **5.** to represent or serve as an indication or sign of: *Smoke usually means fire.* **6.** to bring about or have as a consequence: *Her promotion means a raise in salary.* —*v.i.* **1.** to be of or have a specified importance or value: *His friendship means a lot to her.* **2.** to have intentions of a particular kind; be disposed: *to mean well.* [Old English *mǣnan* to intend.]

mean² (mēn) *adj.* **1.** of low social position, origin, or rank; humble: *of mean birth.* **2.** miserly; stingy; penurious. **3.a.** lacking in kindness, compassion, or understanding: *She apologized for having been so mean to me.* **b.** full of or exhibiting malice; spiteful: *a mean look.* **4.** of little importance, worth, or consequence. **5.** poor in appearance; shabby. **6.** ignoble; base; petty. **7.** inferior in quality or grade; poor. **8.** dangerous or vicious: *a mean dog.* **9.** *Informal.* hard to cope with; difficult: *a mean curve in the road.* **10.** *Slang.* expert; excellent: *to play a mean game of tennis.* [Old English *(ge)mǣne* common.] —**mean′ly,** *adv.*

mean³ (mēn) *n.* **1.** something, as a point, state, or course of action, that is midway between two extremes. **2. means. a.** method, agency, or way by which something is or may be accomplished: *by devious means. By what means do you propose to achieve your goal?* **b.** money, property, or other resources; wealth: *a man of means.* **3.** *Mathematics.* **a.** number or algebraic expression having a value intermediate between the values of a set of other numbers or algebraic expressions. **b.** either the second or third term of a mathematical proportion of four terms. In *a/b = c/d, b* and *c* are the means. **4. by all means.** without fail or hesitation: *Go, by all means.* **5. not by any means.** not at all. **6. by means of.** with the help or use of: *He crossed by means of the bridge.* **7. by no means.** **a.** in no way; not at all. **b.** on no account: *By no means should he be left alone.* —*adj.* **1.** intermediate, as in size, quality, or degree. **2.** midway between two extremes. [Old French *meien* middle, from Latin *mediānus,* from *medius.*]

Syn. *n.* **1.** see **norm. 2.a. Means, agency, instrument** mean that by or with which something is brought about. **Means** applies to a person or concrete thing used as an instrument and to his or its activity and operation: *Camels are the principal means of transportation in the Arabian desert.* **Agency** implies the instrumentality or the means by which power is exerted and a desired result achieved: *He got his new job through the agency of his friends.* **Instrument** is a tool or person that is susceptible or responsive to manipulation and whereby something is achieved, performed, or furthered: *The prophet regarded himself as an instrument of God.* **1.** see **average.**

me·an·der (mē ăn′dər) *v.i.* **1.** to follow a winding course: *The stream meandered through the woods.* **2.** to wander aimlessly or idly: *I meandered slowly through the gardens.* —*n.* **1.** also, **meanders.** circuitous journey or movement; winding course. **2. meanders.** windings or turnings, as of a stream. **3.** ornamental geometric pattern of interlocking or crisscrossing lines. [Latin *maeander* a winding, winding pattern, from Greek *maiandros,* from *Maiandros* a river in Asia Minor proverbial for its unusually winding course.]

mean·ing (mē′ning) *n.* **1.** intention; purpose: *What is the meaning of this disgraceful behavior?* **2.** that which is to be expressed or understood by language: *What is the meaning of this word?* **3.** that which is intended to be or actually is conveyed or indicated; significance: *the meaning of a dream.* —*adj.* having meaning; expressive; significant: *a meaning smile.* —**mean′ing·ly,** *adv.*

Syn. *n.* **2. Meaning, sense, significance** denote the idea which something expresses or suggests to the mind. **Meaning** broadly applies to the total definition of a word, expression, action, or symbol when properly used, understood, or interpreted: *This dictionary gives the meanings of English words and idioms.* **Sense** stresses the specific meaning of a word as intended by a speaker or writer or as construed in a given context: *She is an angel in the figurative sense of the term.* **Significance** emphasizes the covert or subtle meaning of a word weighted with emotional or symbolic nuances and connotations as distinguished from the established meaning: *Can you explain the significance of these metaphors in the poem?*

mean·ing·ful (mē′ning fəl) *adj.* full of meaning; significant. —**mean′ing·ful·ly,** *adv.* —**Syn.** see **expressive.**

mean·ing·less (mē′ning lis) *adj.* without meaning or significance; senseless. —**mean′ing·less·ly,** *adv.* —**mean′ing·less·ness,** *n.*

mean·ness (mēn′nis) *n.* **1.** state or quality of being mean. **2.** mean or spiteful act.

meant (ment) past tense and past participle of **mean¹.**

mean·time (mēn′tīm′) *n.* intervening time. —*adv.* in or during the intervening time.

mean·while (mēn′hwīl′, -wīl′) *adv.* **1.** in or during the intervening time: *The train doesn't leave for an hour; meanwhile, I'm going to take a nap.* **2.** at the same time: *Mother went shopping; meanwhile, I cleaned the house.* —*n.* intervening time.

mea·sles (mē′zəlz) *n.,pl.* **1.** highly infectious virus disease characterized by cold symptoms, fever, and a rash. **2.** German measles. **3.** disease of hogs and cattle caused by the presence of parasitic tapeworm larvae in the muscle tissue. ▲ construed as singular in all meanings. [Probably from Middle Dutch *māsel* spot on the skin associated with measles; influenced by Middle English *mesel* leper, from Old French *mesel,* going back to Latin *miser* wretched.]

mea·sly (mēz′lē) **-sli·er, -sli·est.** *adj.* **1.** of, like, or having measles; spotted. **2.** *Slang.* contemptibly scanty; worthless: *He gave me a measly fifteen cents for mowing the lawn.*

meas·ur·a·ble (mezh′ər ə bəl) *adj.* that can be measured. —**meas′ur·a·bil′i·ty, meas′ur·a·ble·ness,** *n.* —**meas′ur·a·bly,** *adv.*

meas·ure (mezh′ər) **-ured, -ur·ing.** *v.t.* **1.** to ascertain the dimensions, weight, extent, duration, quantity, or capacity of (a person or thing), esp. by comparison with a fixed standard: *to measure one's height, to measure the speed of light, to measure someone for a dress.* **2.** to obtain the dimensions of, mark off, set apart, or allot by or as by measuring (often with *out* or *off*): *to measure out two cups of flour.* **3.** to bring into opposition, comparison, or competition (with *with* or *against*): *to measure one's strength against another's.* **4.** to serve as a standard or unit of measurement for: *Degrees measure temperature.* **5.** to estimate by comparison; judge; appraise: *to measure the difficulty of a task.* **6.a.** to adjust, proportion, or regulate by some standard. **b.** to think over carefully and choose: *to measure one's words.* **7.** *Archaic.* to travel over or through; traverse. **8. to measure swords. a.** to fight with swords. **b.** to fight or contend, as in an argument or duel. —*v.i.* **1.** to take measurements: *A carpenter must measure accurately.* **2.** to have a specific measurement of: *The room measures ten feet by twelve feet.* **3.** to admit of measurement. **4. to measure up.** to have the necessary or proper qualifications: *Does he measure up for the job?* **5. to measure up to.** to fulfill or meet, as a standard or expectation. —*n.* **1.** dimensions, weight, extent, duration, quantity, or capacity of anything as determined by measuring; measurement. **2.** act or process of measuring; measurement. **3.** unit or standard of measurement, as an inch, quart, or minute. **4.** any standard or basis of comparison, estimation, or judgment: *the measure of one's strength.* **5.** system of measurement. **6.** instrument, container, or other device used for measuring: *a gallon measure.* **7.** amount or degree that should not be exceeded; limit: *Her generosity knows no measure.* **8.** definite amount or degree: *The children were given a great measure of independence.* **9.** quantity, degree, or proportion: *to take a measure of pride in one's work.* **10.** also, **measures.** course of action or procedure taken or used as a means to an end: *to take drastic measures.* **11.** a legislative proposal or enactment. **12.** *Poetry.* **a.** rhythm; meter. **b.** metrical unit; foot. **13.** music contained between two bar lines; bar. **14. measures.** *Geology.* series of strata that share some common characteristic: *coal measures.* **15.** *Archaic.* dance or dance movement, esp. one that is slow and stately. **16. for good measure.** in addition to what is needed or called for. [Old French *mesure* dimensions, moderation, degree, from Latin *mēnsūra* quantity, degree, proportion, extent.]

meas·ured (mezh′ərd) *adj.* **1.** characterized by uniformity of movement or rhythm: *The bride walked down the aisle with measured steps.* **2.** carefully weighed and chosen; deliberate and restrained. **3.** regulated or determined by some standard.

meas·ure·less (mezh′ər lis) *adj.* that cannot be measured; immeasurable.

meas·ure·ment (mezh′ər mənt) *n.* **1.** act or process of measuring. **2.** that which is found or determined by measuring, as dimensions or quantity. **3.** system of measuring or of measures.

measuring worm, inchworm.

meat (mēt) *n.* **1.** parts of an animal used as food, esp. as distinguished from fish or fowl. **2.** edible part of anything: *the meat of a coconut.* **3.** main idea or most important part; substance: *the meat of a story.* **4.** anything eaten for nourishment: *meat and drink.* [Old English *mete* food.]

meat packing, business of slaughtering animals for food and processing, packing, and distributing meat and meat by-products.

me·a·tus (mē ā′təs) *pl.* **-tus·es** or **-tus.** *n.* passage or opening in the body. [Latin *meātus* path.]

meat·y (mē′tē) **meat·i·er, meat·i·est.** *adj.* **1.** of, relating to, or like meat. **2.** full of meat; fleshy; plump. **3.** full of substance or significance: *a meaty dialogue on a controversial topic.*

Mec·ca (mek′ə) also, **Mek·ka.** *n.* **1.** birthplace of Muhammad and holiest city of Islam, in western Saudi Arabia, near the Red Sea. Muslims face Mecca when praying and travel there on pilgrimages. Pop. (1965), 185,000. **2.** also, **mecca. a.** any place that is visited by many people or has a special attraction. **b.** goal of one's hopes.

me·chan·ic (mi kan′ik) *n.* **1.** one skilled in designing, repairing, or operating machinery: *auto mechanic.* **2.** *Archaic.* one skilled in working with tools. [Latin *mēchanicus* inventive, relating to machines, from Greek *mēchanikos,* from *mēchanē* device, contrivance.]

me·chan·i·cal (mi kan′i kəl) *adj.* **1.** of, relating to, or involving machinery or tools. **2.** produced or operated by a machine. **3.** lacking spontaneity or originality; automatic: *His movements were very mechanical.* **4.** of, relating to, or in accordance with the science of mechanics. —*n.* layout from which plates for printing are prepared, showing text and art copy as it will appear when printed. —**me·chan′i·cal·ly,** *adv.*

mechanical drawing **1.** drawing, usually of machinery or mechanical parts, done with the aid of rulers, scales, compasses, and similar instruments. **2.** art or process of making such a drawing.

me·chan·ics (mi kan′iks) *n.,pl.* **1.** branch of physics that deals with the conditions under which bodies and fluids move or remain at rest. **2.** body of knowledge dealing with the design, construction, operation, and care of machinery. **3.** mechanical or technical aspects of anything: *the mechanics of painting.* ▲ construed as singular in defs. 1 and 2, as plural in def. 3.

mech·a·nism (mek′ə niz′əm) *n.* **1.** working parts, or arrangement of parts, of a machine: *The jeweler fixed the broken mechanism of my pocket watch.* **2.** system of parts resembling those of a machine in structure or function: *the mechanism of speech, the mechanism of the nervous system.* **3.** agency, means, or process by which an effect is produced or a purpose accomplished. **4.** *Philosophy.* theory that the universe is like a great machine and that everything in it moves and changes in accordance with natural laws.

mech·a·nist (mek′ə nist) *n.* one who believes in philosophical mechanism.

mech·a·nis·tic (mek′ə nis′tik) *adj.* **1.** of or relating to mechanics. **2.** of or relating to philosophical mechanism.

mech·a·nize (mek′ə nīz′) -nized, -niz·ing. *v.t.* **1.** to equip with or convert to machinery as a means of production: *Much industry has been mechanized.* **2.** to equip (a military unit or army) with tanks, armored personnel carriers, and other vehicles. **3.** to give a mechanical character to; make automatic. —**mech′a·ni·za′tion,** *n.*

Mech·lin (mek′lin) *n.* lace with the pattern, often a floral design, clearly outlined by a fine, but distinct, thread, used for such items as scarfs and veilings. Also, **ma·lines′.**

Mechlin

med. **1.** medical. **2.** medicine. **3.** medieval. **4.** medium.

med·al (med′əl) *n.* flat piece of metal bearing a design or inscription, often given as an award in recognition of merit, achievement, or distinguished service. [French *médaille,* from Italian *medaglia,* going back to Latin *metallum* metal. See METAL.]

med·al·ist (med′əl ist) *also, British.* **med·al·list.** *n.* **1.** one who engraves, designs, or makes medals. **2.** one who has been awarded a medal.

me·dal·lion (mi dal′yən) *n.* **1.** large medal. **2.** anything resembling a medallion or medal, as an ornamental object or design. [French *médaillon* large medal, locket, from Italian *medaglione,* from *medaglia* medal. See MEDAL.]

Medal of Honor, highest U.S. military decoration, awarded by the president in the name of Congress to military personnel cited for conspicuous gallantry above and beyond the call of duty. Also, **Congressional Medal of Honor.**

medal play, method of scoring in golf in which the lowest total number of strokes determines the winner. Distinguished from **match play.**

Me·dan (me dän′) *n.* city on the northeast coast of Sumatra, Indonesia. Pop. (1961), 479,098.

med·dle (med′əl) -dled, -dling. *v.i.* **1.** to concern oneself with or intrude in the affairs of others without having been asked. **2.** to tamper: *Someone has meddled with the lock on this door.* [Old French *medler, mesler* to mix, going back to Latin *miscēre* to mix.] —**med′dler,** *n.* —**Syn.** see interfere.

med·dle·some (med′əl səm) *adj.* tending to meddle. —**med′dle·some·ness,** *n.*

Mede (mēd) *n.* member of the people who inhabited ancient Media.

Me·de·a (mi dē′ə) *n. Greek Legend.* an enchantress who helped Jason get the Golden Fleece in return for marrying her.

Me·del·lín (med′əl ēn′; *Spanish* mä′thä yēn′) *n.* city in west-central Colombia. Pop. (1969), 967,825.

Med·ford (med′fərd) *n.* city in eastern Massachusetts. Pop. (1970), 64,397.

me·di·a (mē′dē ə) plural of **medium.**

Me·di·a (mē′dē ə) *n.* ancient kingdom in northwestern Persia.

me·di·ae·val (mē′dē ē′vəl, mid′ē-, med′ē-, mid ē′vəl) medieval.

me·di·al (mē′dē əl) *adj.* **1.** of, relating to, or situated in the middle. **2.** of, relating to, or being a mathematical mean; average. [Late Latin *mediālis* middle, from Latin *medius.*] —**me′di·al·ly,** *adv.*

me·di·an (mē′dē ən) *n.* **1.** middle number in a set of numbers or, where there is no middle number, the average of the two middle numbers. **2.a.** line segment from a vertex of a triangle to the midpoint of the opposite side. **b.** line segment joining the midpoints of the nonparallel sides of a trapezoid. —*adj.* **1.** of, relating to, or situated in the middle; medial. [Latin *mediānus* middle, from *medius.*]

Me·di·an (mē′dē ən) *adj.* of or relating to ancient Media or the Medes. —*n.* Mede.

median strip, raised strip, usually landscaped or paved, that separates opposing lanes of traffic on some roads or highways.

Medians AD, BE, CF, and GH are medians.

me·di·ate (*v.,* mē′dē āt′; *adj.,* mē′dē it) -at·ed, -at·ing. *v.t.* **1.** to bring about by intervening between disputing or opposing parties: *He mediated a settlement between labor and management.* **2.** to settle (differences) by intervening between disputing or opposing parties. **3.** to serve as the medium for bringing about (a result) or for conveying (an object or information). —*v.i.* **1.** to act as a mediator in order to bring about an agreement or settlement. **2.** to occupy an intermediate place or position. —*adj.* acting through or involving an intermediate agency; indirect. [Latin *mediātus,* past participle of *mediāre* to halve, be in the middle, from *medius* middle.]

me·di·a·tion (mē′dē ā′shən) *n.* act of mediating; intervention.

me·di·a·tor (mē′dē ā′tər) *n.* person or group that comes between disputing or opposing parties in order to bring about a settlement.

me·di·a·to·ry (mē′dē ə tôr′ē) *adj.* **1.** of, relating to, or of the nature of mediation. **2.** serving to mediate. Also, **me·di·a·to′ri·al.**

med·ic¹ (med′ik) *n. Informal.* **1.** physician. **2.** medical student or intern. **3.** corpsman. [Latin *medicus* physician.]

med·ic² (med′ik) *also,* **med·ick.** *n.* any of a group of plants, genus *Medicago,* of the pea family, most of which bear purple or yellow cloverlike flower heads. [Latin *Mēdica* kind of clover, lucerne, from Greek *Mēdikē (poā)* Median (grass), lucerne.]

Med·i·caid (med′i kād′) *n.* U.S. government program of health insurance for persons of all ages within certain income limits, financed by local, state, and federal funds. [MEDIC(AL) + AID.]

med·i·cal (med′i kəl) *adj.* of or relating to doctors, medicine, or the study or practice of medicine. [Late Latin *medicālis* relating to a physician, from Latin *medicus* physician.] —**med′i·cal·ly,** *adv.*

me·dic·a·ment (mi dik′ə mənt, med′i kə-) *n.* substance used to treat disease or relieve pain; medicine. [Latin *medicāmentum.*]

Med·i·care (med′i kār′) *n.* U.S. federal program of health insurance for persons aged sixty-five and over. [MEDI(CAL) + CARE.]

med·i·cate (med′i kāt′) -cat·ed, -cat·ing. *v.t.* **1.** to treat with medicine. **2.** to impregnate with medicine. [Latin *medicātus,* past participle of *medicārī* to heal.]

med·i·ca·tion (med′i kā′shən) *n.* **1.** substance used to treat disease or relieve pain; medicine. **2.** act or process of medicating; being medicated.

Med·i·ci (med′i chē) **1.** Catherine de′. see, Catherine de Medici. **2.** Co·si·mo de′ (kō′zē mō). 1389-1464, ruler of Florence and first great patron of arts and letters of the Italian Renaissance. **3.** Cosimo I de′. 1519-74, ruler of Florence and grand duke of Tuscany. **4.** Lo·ren·zo de′ (lô ren′zō). 1449-92, ruler of Florence and patron of the arts. **5.** Marie de′. 1573-1642, queen of Henry IV of France, and regent of France after his death.

me·dic·i·nal (mi dis′ə nəl) *adj.* **1.** having the properites of medicine; healing, curative, or relieving. **2.** characteristic of or resembling medicine: *The hospital room had a medicinal smell.* —**me·dic′i·nal·ly,** *adv.*

med·i·cine (med′ə sin) *n.* **1.** drug or other substance used to treat disease or relieve pain. **2.** science that deals with the cause, prevention, and treatment of disease and the preservation of health. **3.** medical profession. **4.** among North American Indians, any object or ceremony thought to have magical or curative powers. **5. to take one's medicine.** to endure or accept something that is forthcoming, as punishment, esp. when it is a consequence of something one has done. [Latin *medicīna* healing art, remedy.]

medicine ball, large, heavy stuffed ball thrown from one person to another for exercise.

medicine man, among North American Indians, a person believed to possess magical powers through communication with supernatural beings; shaman.

me·di·e·val (mē′dē ē′vəl, mid′ē-, med′ē-, mid ē′vəl) *also,* **me·di·ae·val.** *adj.* of, relating to, belonging to, or characteristic of the Middle Ages. [Latin *medius* middle + *aevum* age + -AL¹; referring to its

occurrence in the middle of, or between, early and recent times.]
—me′di·e′val·ly, *adv.*

me·di·e·val·ism (mē′dē ē′və liz′əm, mid′ē-, med′ē-, mid ē′və-) *n.*
1. spirit, beliefs, customs, and practices of the Middle Ages. **2.** devotion
to or adoption of the beliefs, customs, and practices of the Middle Ages.
3. anything, as a belief or custom, surviving from the Middle Ages.

me·di·e·val·ist (mē′dē ē′və list, mid′ē-, med′ē-, mid ē′və-) *n.*
1. scholar of, or a specialist in, medieval history, literature, or art.
2. one devoted to the spirit, beliefs, and customs of the Middle Ages.

Medieval Latin, Latin, esp. as a literary language, from the eighth
to the fifteenth centuries A.D.

Me·di·na (mə dē′nə) *n.* one of the holiest cities of Islam, site of
Muhammad's tomb, in western Saudi Arabia. Pop. (1963 est.), 72,000.

me·di·o·cre (mē′dē ō′kər) *adj.* not exceptional; ordinary; commonplace. [French *médiocre* middling, from Latin *mediocris* literally, halfway up a mountain, from *medius* middle + *ocris* rugged mountain.]
—**Syn.** see ordinary.

me·di·oc·ri·ty (mē′dē ok′rə tē) *pl.,* **-ties.** *n.* **1.** state or quality of
being mediocre. **2.** mediocre ability, accomplishment, or performance.
3. person of mediocre talents or ability.

med·i·tate (med′ə tāt′) **-tat·ed, -tat·ing.** *v.i.* to think seriously and
carefully; reflect. —*v.t.* to consider; intend. [Latin *meditātus,* past participle of *meditārī* to consider, reflect.]
Syn. *v.i.* **Meditate, ponder, muse** mean to consider deliberately. **Meditate** may be used when one contemplates and dwells intently upon a
problem or concentrates one's attention in order to comprehend something in all its aspects: *The monk meditated on the sacred mysteries.*
Ponder may be used when one weighs and deliberates over a complex
problem soberly and deeply in an effort to comprehend its consequences: *The novelist pondered over the plot of his new novel.* **Muse** may
be used when one considers a problem casually and unhurriedly and
suggests a thoughtfulness that is not necessarily profound or productive:
On his way home, George mused on the events of the day.

med·i·ta·tion (med′ə tā′shən) *n.* serious and careful thought.

med·i·ta·tive (med′ə tā′tiv) *adj.* given to, expressing, or characterized by meditation: *meditative mood.* —**med′i·ta·tive·ly,** *adv.*

Med·i·ter·ra·ne·an (med′ə tə rā′nē ən) *n.* **1.** large, almost landlocked arm of the Atlantic between southern Europe, western Asia, and
northern Africa. Also, **Mediterranean Sea. 2. the Mediterranean.** region consisting of this sea and those countries in and around it.
—*adj.* of, relating to, or characteristic of the Mediterranean or the
nearby countries and their people.

me·di·um (mē′dē əm) *pl.,* **-di·ums** or **-di·a** (-dē ə). *n.* **1.** something
occupying an intermediate position between two extremes; mean.
2. enveloping substance in which something exists or functions; environment: *Most bacteria grow best in a slightly acid medium.* **3.** means or
form of communication or expression: *Television is a medium that
reaches a large audience.* **4.** substance, means, or agency through, in,
or by which something may act, be carried, or accomplished: *The
atmosphere is a medium for sound waves.* **5.** one through whom the
spirits of the dead allegedly communicate with the world of the living.
6. material or technique used as a means of artistic expression: *The
artist's medium is watercolor.* **7.** in painting, a liquid with which pigments are mixed and made sufficiently fluid for application. —*adj.*
intermediate, as in quantity, amount, or degree: *a girl of medium height.*
[Latin *medium* the midst, the middle.] —**Syn.** *adj.* see **average.**

med·lar (med′lər) *n.* thorny tree, *Mespilus germanica,* of the rose
family, bearing apple-shaped fruits that have an acid taste and are used
to make preserves or are eaten raw after they are somewhat decayed.
[Old French *medler, mesler,* from *mesle* the fruit of the medlar, through
Latin, from Greek *mespilon.*]

med·ley (med′lē) *pl.,* **-leys.** *n.* **1.** confused and disordered mass of
things; jumble; hodgepodge. **2.** musical composition made up of various
tunes or parts from other compositions. —*adj.* made up of varied parts.
[Old French *medlee, meslee* a mixing, mixture, fight, from *medler,
mesler* to mix, going back to Latin *miscēre.*]

me·dul·la (mi dul′ə) *pl.,* **-dul·lae**
(-dul′ē). *n.* **1.** medulla oblongata.
2. inner substance of an organ or
part. [Latin *medulla* marrow, pith.]

medulla ob·lon·ga·ta (ob′lông-
gä′tə) lowest and hindmost part of
the brain, connected with the top of
the spinal cord. [Modern Latin
medulla oblongata literally, oblong
marrow.]

med·ul·lar·y (med′əl er′ē, mej′-,
mi dul′ər ē) *adj.* of, relating to, or
like the medulla or the medulla
oblongata.

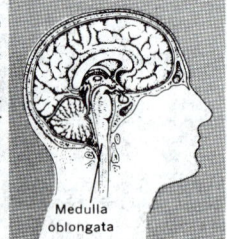

Medulla
oblongata

me·du·sa (mi dōō′sə, -zə, -dū′-) *pl.,* **-sas** or **-sae** (-sē or -zē). *n.*
jellyfish. [From MEDUSA; referring to the resemblance between some
types of jellyfish and a head with snakelike hair.]

Me·du·sa (mi dōō′sə, -zə, -dū′-) *pl.,* **-sas.** *n. Greek Mythology.* one
of the three Gorgons, slain by Perseus.

meed (mēd) *n. Archaic.* well-deserved recompense. [Old English
mēd.]

meek (mēk) *adj.* **1.** unduly submissive or lacking in spirit. **2.** patient
and mild in manner or disposition; gentle. [Old Norse *mjūkr* soft, mild.]
—**meek′ly,** *adv.* —**meek′ness,** *n.*

meer·schaum (mēr′shəm, -shôm′) *n.* **1.** soft, porous, light, white
clay mineral that is heat-resistant, used to make tobacco pipes.
2. tobacco pipe, the bowl of which is made of meerschaum. [German
Meerschaum this mineral; originally, a variety of coral; literally, sea
foam; supposedly because this coral was once believed to be sea foam
hardened into stone.]

meet[1] (mēt) **meet, meet·ing.** *v.t.* **1.** to come face to face with; come upon
or across: *I met her just as I was leaving.* **2.** to make the acquaintance
of; be introduced to: *Haven't I met you before?* **3.** to keep an appointment with: *I'll meet you by the information booth.* **4.** to go to or be
present at the arrival of: *He met my plane.* **5.** to satisfy, fulfill, or comply
with: *He didn't meet the qualifications.* **6.** to come into contact or
conjunction with: *The river meets the ocean at New York.* **7.** to come
into the presence or company of, as for a meeting: *The judge met the
lawyers in his chambers.* **8.** to come into the perception, observation,
or notice of: *Her eyes met mine.* **9.** to pay: *I couldn't meet my bills this
month.* **10.** to oppose or fight with, as in battle: *to meet an adversary.*
11. to deal or cope with effectively; confront: *He met their criticism with
indifference.* **12.** to experience: *to meet a cold reception.* —*v.i.*
1. to come face to face: *We met in the elevator.* **2.** to be introduced;
become acquainted: *We met at a party.* **3.** to come into contact, conjunction, or union; join: *Oh, East is East, and West is West, and never
the twain shall meet* (Kipling, 1892). **4.** to assemble, as for business or
worship: *The committee met for two hours.* **5.** to be opposed, as in battle:
to meet on the battlefield. **6. to meet with. a.** to receive: *Her suggestion
met with opposition.* **b.** to experience; undergo: *to meet with adversity.*
—*n.* assembly or gathering, esp. for an athletic contest: *a swimming
meet.* [Old English *mētan* to find.]
Syn. *v.t.* **1. Meet, face, encounter, confront** mean to approach someone
or something directly. **Meet** suggests coming across a person approaching from another direction by chance or design: *I met her on the way
to the grocer's store.* **Face** implies a direct meeting, esp. a bold or confident
one: *The negotiators faced each other across the table.* **Encounter**
conveys the sense of running into something hostile, difficult, or unexpected: *I encountered heavy traffic on the way home.* **Confront** is the
appropriate word when one meets what is unavoidable without flinching
and with the determination to clear up or settle a matter: *The accused
confronted his accuser in the court.*

meet[2] (mēt) *adj. Archaic.* suitable; proper. [Old English *(ge)mǣte.*]
—**meet′ly,** *adv.*

meet·ing (mē′ting) *n.* **1.a.** gathering or assembly of people: *The chairman of the committee adjourned the meeting for the day.* **b.** persons so
gathered: *The committee meeting set the date for the party.* **2.** act of
coming together: *a meeting of minds.* **3.** place or point where things
come together; junction: *meeting of two rivers.* **4.** assembly of people,
esp. Quakers, for worship.
Syn. 1. Meeting, assembly, gathering mean a group of people coming
together. **Meeting** is a company of persons collected in one place for
a social or business purpose: *There was a luncheon meeting at the club
today.* **Assembly** is a number of people meeting together as an organized
group united in discussion, action, worship, or entertainment: *A large
assembly celebrated the poet's birthday.* **Gathering** is a group of people
coming from far and wide and congregating in one place: *There is an
annual gathering of Scottish clans in Edinburgh.*

meeting house, building or house which is used for worship, esp.
by Quakers.

mega- *combining form* **1.** large; great: *megalith.* **2.** multiplied by a
million; a million of (a specified unit): *megacycle.* [Greek *megas* great,
large.]

meg·a·cy·cle (meg′ə sī′kəl) *n.* **1.** a million cycles per second, used
esp. in measuring frequency of radio waves and other electromagnetic
radiation. **2.** a million cycles. [MEGA- + CYCLE.]

meg·a·lith (meg′ə lith′) *n.* huge stone, esp. one used in prehistoric
monuments or in ancient constructive work. [MEGA- + Greek *lithos*
stone.]

megalo- *combining form* large, abnormally large, excessive, or exaggerated: *megalopolis, megalomania.* [Greek *megal-,* stem of *megas*
great, large.]

meg·a·lo·ma·ni·a (meg′ə lō mā′nē ə) *n.* **1.** mental disorder characterized by delusions of greatness, power, or wealth. **2.** tendency to
exaggerate. [MEGALO- + MANIA.] —**meg′a·lo·ma′ni·ac,** *adj., n.*

at; āpe; cär; end; mē; it; īce; hot; ōld; fôrk; wood; fōōl; oil; out; up; ūse; turn; sing; thin; this; zh in treasure; ə in ago, taken, pencil, lemon, circus.

meg·a·lop·o·lis (meg′ə lop′ə lis) *n.* urban complex made up of a number of adjoining metropolitan areas. [*Megalo-* + Greek *polis* city.]

meg·a·phone (meg′ə fōn′) *n.* funnel-shaped device used to amplify or direct the sound of the voice. [MEGA- + Greek *phōnē* sound, voice.]

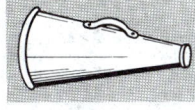
Megaphone

meg·a·ton (meg′ə tun′) *n.* unit used to measure the explosive force of nuclear bombs, equivalent to the force produced by the detonation of one million tons of TNT. [MEGA- + TON.]

me·grim (mē′grim) *n.* **1.** migraine. **2.** megrims, low spirits. **3.** *Archaic.* whim; fancy. [Old French *migraine* headache. See MIGRAINE.]

mei·o·sis (mī ō′sis) *n.* in organisms that reproduce sexually, the process of cell division by which the number of chromosomes in a sex cell are halved. [Greek *meiōsis* diminution, lessening.] —**mei·ot′ic**, *adj.*

Meis·ter·sing·er (mīs′tər sing′ər, -zing′-) *pl.*, **-sing·er.** *n.* member of one of the German guilds of the fifteenth and sixteenth centuries that specialized in the composition of poems and songs.

Mek·ka (mek′ə) Mecca.

Mek·nès (mek nes′) *n.* city in northwestern Morocco. Pop. (1969), 235,000.

Me·kong (mā′kong′) *n.* river in southeastern Asia flowing southeastward from western China into the South China Sea.

mel·a·mine (mel′ə mēn′) *n.* any of several amino resins used to make strong, chemical-resistant, thermosetting plastics for tableware and plywood adhesives.

mel·an·cho·li·a (mel′ən kō′lē ə) *n.* mental disorder characterized by severe depression and self-criticism. [Late Latin *melancholia* the humor thought to cause gloominess, a kind of madness, going back to Greek *melās* black + *cholē* bile. See HUMOR.]

mel·an·chol·ic (mel′ən kol′ik) *adj.* **1.** melancholy; sad; dejected. **2.** of, relating to, or suffering from melancholia.

mel·an·chol·y (mel′ən kol′ē) *n. pl.*, **-chol·ies. 1.** gloomy or depressed state of mind; sadness. **2.** sober thoughtfulness; pensiveness. [Old French *melancolie* gloominess, humor thought to cause gloominess, from Late Latin *melancholia.* See MELANCHOLY.] —*adj.* **1.** low in spirits; sad; depressed. **2.** suggestive of or causing sadness; depressing; dismal: *melancholy music.* **3.** soberly thoughtful; meditative; pensive. —*n. pl.*, **-chol·ies.**

Mel·a·ne·sia (mel′ə nē′zhə, -shə) *n.* one of the three major divisions of the Pacific islands, east of Australia.

Mel·a·ne·sian (mel′ə nē′zhən, -shən) *n.* **1.** member of a Negroid people living in Melanesia. **2.** subfamily of the Malayo-Polynesian family of languages, consisting of a number of languages, spoken predominantly in Melanesia. —*adj.* of or relating to Melanesia, its people, their languages, or their cultures.

mé·lange (mā länzh′) *n.* mixture; medley: *The furnishings were a mélange of antique and modern.* [French *mélange*, from *mêler* to mix, from Old French *mesler.* See MEDLEY.]

mel·a·nin (mel′ə nin) *n.* dark-brown pigment present in skin, hair, and other animal tissues, which helps to determine the color of the skin, hair, and eyes. [Greek *melan-*, stem of *melās* black + -IN¹.]

mel·a·nism (mel′ə niz′əm) *n.* excessive or abnormal pigmentation of the skin, hair, or other animal tissues. Also, **mel·a·no·sis** (mel′ə nō′sis). [Greek *melan-*, stem of *melās* black + -ISM.] —**mel′a·nis′tic**, *adj.*

mel·a·no·ma (mel′ə nō′mə) *n.* malignant tumor consisting of cells that contain melanin. [Modern Latin *melanoma*, from Greek *melan-*, stem of *melās* black.]

Mel·ba toast (mel′bə) very thin, dry slices of toast.

Mel·bourne (mel′bərn) *n.* port city in southeastern Australia, capital of Victoria. Pop. (1966), metropolitan area, 2,228,511.

meld (meld) *v.t., v.i.* in card games, to place (one or more cards) on the table in a set or on another set. —*n.* **1.** act of melding. **2.** cards melded. [German *melden* tell, inform.]

me·lee (mā′lā′, mā lā′) *also,* **mê·lée.** *n.* confused, hand-to-hand fight involving a number of people. [French *mêlée*, from *mêler* to mix from Old French *mesler*, going back to Latin *miscēre.*]

mel·io·rate (mēl′yə rāt′, mē′lē ə-) **-rat·ed, -rat·ing.** *v.t., v.i.* to make or become better; ameliorate. [Late Latin *meliōrātus*, past participle of *meliōrāre* to improve, from Latin *melior* better.] —**mel′io·ra′tion**, *n.* —**mel′io·ra′tive**, *adj.*

mel·lif·lu·ent (me lif′lōō ənt) *adj.* mellifluous. —**mel·lif′lu·ence**, *n.* —**mel·lif′lu·ent·ly**, *adv.*

mel·lif·lu·ous (me lif′lōō əs) *adj.* sweetly or smoothly flowing: *a mellifluous voice.* [Late Latin *mellifluus* flowing with honey, from Latin *mel* honey + *fluere* to flow.] —**mel·lif′lu·ous·ly**, *adv.*

mel·low (mel′ō) *adj.* **1.** (of fruit) soft, sweet, and juicy from ripeness. **2.** rich, delicate, and fully aged: *a mellow cheese.* **3.** softened and made wise, gentle, and understanding by age and experience. **4.** full, rich, and

soft: *a mellow color, a mellow tone.* **5.** (of soil) rich and loamy. —*v.t., v.i.* to make or become mellow. [Probably from Old English *melu* flour, meal².] —**mel′low·ly**, *adv.* —**mel′low·ness**, *n.*

me·lo·de·on (mi lō′dē ən) *n.* small reed organ. [From MELODY.]

me·lod·ic (mi lod′ik) *adj.* **1.** of, relating to, or containing melody. **2.** melodious *(def. 1).* —**me·lod′i·cal·ly**, *adv.*

me·lo·di·ous (mi lō′dē əs) *adj.* **1.** pleasant to hear; musical: *a melodious voice.* **2.** of, relating to, containing, or producing melody. —**me·lo′di·ous·ly**, *adv.* —**me·lo′di·ous·ness**, *n.*

mel·o·dra·ma (mel′ə drä′mə, -dram′ə) *n.* **1.a.** dramatic performance or play characterized by exaggerated appeal to the emotions, sensational or overly sentimental incidents, and usually having a happy ending. **b.** such plays collectively. **2.** sensational or overly emotional writing, speech, or behavior. [French *mélodrame* such a play, from Greek *melos* song + *drāma* play; referring to the inclusion of songs and music in the original melodramas.]

mel·o·dra·mat·ic (mel′ə drə mat′ik) *adj.* of, relating to, or characteristic of melodrama; exaggerated. —**mel′o·dra·mat′i·cal·ly**, *adv.*

mel·o·dra·mat·ics (mel′ə drə mat′iks) *n.,pl.* melodramatic behavior.

mel·o·dy (mel′ə dē) *pl.*, **-dies.** *n.* **1.** pleasing arrangement or succession of sounds. **2.** *Music.* **a.** succession of single tones constituting a complete phrase or idea; tune. **b.** principal part in a harmonized composition. [Late Latin *melōdia* pleasant song, from Greek *melōidiā* a singing, going back to *melos* song + *ōidē* song.]

mel·on (mel′ən) *n.* large, edible fruit of any of several leafy vines, having a sweet, soft, juicy pulp, as the watermelon. [Old French *melon*, through Latin, from Greek *mēlopepōn.*]

Mel·pom·e·ne (mel pom′ə nē) *n. Greek Mythology.* Muse of tragedy.

melt (melt) **melt·ed, melt·ed** or *(archaic)* **mol·ten, melt·ing.** *v.i.* **1.** to be changed from a solid to a liquid state, esp. by heating. **2.** to dissolve, as in water. **3.** to disappear gradually; disperse (often with *away*). **4.** to pass or change by gradual and imperceptible degrees; blend (with *into*): *The blue of the sky melted into the green landscape.* **5.** to become filled, as with love, compassion, or tenderness. —*v.t.* **1.** to change (something) from a solid to a liquid state, esp. by heating. **2.** to dissolve (something), as in water. **3.** to fill, as with love, compassion, or tenderness; make gentle or tender. **4.** to cause (something) to disappear gradually. **5.** to cause (something) to pass or change by gradual and imperceptible degrees. [Old English *meltan* to liquefy or become liquefied by heat, dissolve, be overwhelmed.] —**melt′a·ble**, *adj.* —**melt′er**, *n.*

melting point, temperature at which a given solid changes into a liquid. It is identical to its freezing point. Zero degrees centigrade is the melting point of ice and the freezing point of water.

melting pot, country, city, or region in which people of various races and nationalities are assimilated.

mel·ton (mel′tən) *n.* heavyweight woolen fabric having a close weave and napped on both sides, used esp. for overcoats and pea jackets. [From *Melton* Mowbray, English town famous for hunting; referring to Melton hunting jackets and their woolen cloth.]

Mel·ville, Herman (mel′vil) 1819–91, U.S. novelist.

mem·ber (mem′bər) *n.* **1.** one belonging to a group or organization: *The club has 200 members.* **2.** *also,* **Member.** representative of a legislative body: *a member of Congress.* **3.** *Mathematics.* **a.** either of the sides of an algebraic equation. **b.** one of the collection of objects comprising a set; element. **4.** part of a human or animal body, esp. a limb. **5.** constituent part of a whole. [Old French *membre* limb, from Latin *membrum* limb, part.]

mem·ber·ship (mem′bər ship′) *n.* **1.** state of being a member of a group or organization. **2.** members of a group or organization collectively: *The union membership voted to strike.* **3.** number of members in a group or organization.

mem·brane (mem′brān) *n.* thin layer of tissue that lines a cavity or passage in the body or covers a body surface. [Latin *membrāna.*]

mem·bra·nous (mem′brə nəs) *adj.* **1.** of, relating to, or resembling a membrane. **2.** characterized by the formation of a membrane.

me·men·to (mi men′tō) *pl.*, **-tos** or **-toes.** *n.* anything serving as a reminder of someone or something; keepsake; souvenir. [Latin *mementō* remember, imperative of *meminisse* to remember.] —**Syn.** see keepsake.

memento mo·ri (môr′ī) anything serving as a reminder of death, as a skull. [Latin *mementō mori* remember that you must die.]

Mem·non (mem′non) *n.* **1.** *Greek Legend.* Ethiopian king killed by Achilles in the Trojan War. **2.** colossal statue at Thebes, Egypt, said to give forth a musical sound when touched by the rays of the sun at dawn.

mem·o (mem′ō) *pl.*, **mem·os.** *n.* memorandum.

mem·oir (mem′wär, -wôr) *n.* **1.** *usually,* **memoirs. a.** record of facts and events concerning a particular subject or period, usually written

from the writer's personal knowledge, experiences, and observations: *a Confederate general's memoirs of the Civil War.* **b.** written account of the incidents and experiences of one's life; autobiography: *At the end of his career in politics, he retired and wrote his memoirs.* **2.** biography. **3. memoirs.** report of the proceedings of a learned society. **4.** report or dissertation on a scientific or scholarly subject; monograph. [French *mémoire* remembrance, record, from Latin *memoria* remembrance, historical account. Doublet of MEMORY.]

mem·o·ra·bil·i·a (mem'ər ə bil'ē ə) *n.,pl.* things worthy of remembrance or record. [Latin *memorābilia,* neuter plural of *memorābilis* worthy of remembrance. See MEMORABLE.]

mem·o·ra·ble (mem'ər ə bəl) *adj.* not to be forgotten; worthy of remembrance; notable. [Latin *memorābilis,* going back to *memor* mindful.] —**mem'o·ra·bly,** *adv.*

mem·o·ran·dum (mem'ə ran'dəm) *pl.,* **-dums** or **-da** (-də). *n.* **1.** brief note written as a reminder. **2.** informal letter, record, or communication, as that sent between persons in a business office. **3.** *Law.* short document stating the terms of a contract or transaction. **4.** in business, a statement of goods sent to the buyer by the seller. **5.** in diplomacy, brief statement, summary, or outline, as of a subject under discussion between governments. [Latin *memorandum* something to be remembered, neuter of *memorandus* to be remembered, gerundive of *memorāre* to remember.]

me·mo·ri·al (mi môr'ē əl) *n.* **1.** something, as a monument or plaque, serving as a remembrance of some person or event. **2.** written request or statement of facts sent to a government, legislative body, or other group in authority. —*adj.* serving as a memorial; commemorative: *a memorial plaque.* [Latin *memoriālis* relating to memory, from *memoria* ability to remember, remembrance, historical account.]

Memorial Day, a U.S. holiday usually celebrated on May 30, in memory of servicemen killed in all American wars. Some southern states celebrate it on April 26, May 10, or June 3. Also, **Decoration Day.**

me·mo·ri·al·ize (mi môr'ē ə līz') **-ized, -iz·ing.** *v.t.* **1.** to preserve or honor the memory of. **2.** to submit a memorial to; petition.

mem·o·rize (mem'ə rīz') **-rized, -riz·ing.** *v.t.* to commit to memory; learn by heart. [MEMORY + -IZE.] —**mem'o·ri·za'tion,** *n.* —**mem'o·riz'er,** *n.*

mem·o·ry (mem'ər ē) *pl.,* **-ries.** *n.* **1.** mental power or capacity to recall or reconstruct past experiences. **2.** all that one can or does recall: *to recite a poem from memory.* **3.** someone or something remembered: *The war is an unpleasant memory for him.* **4.** that which is remembered of a person or thing: *to honor the memory of those who died in war.* **5.** period of time during or within which someone or something can be or is remembered: *within the memory of man.* **6.** act of remembering; being remembered. **7.** component in an electronic computer in which information is stored. **8. in memory of.** in honor or commemoration of. [Latin *memoria* ability to remember, remembrance, time of remembrance, historical account. Doublet of MEMOIR.]

Syn. 1. Memory, recollection, remembrance mean conscious evocation of things past. **Memory** is the faculty and power of recalling the past and preserving what was previously known or experienced: *The old man's memory was failing him.* **Recollection** is the retrospective and effortful summoning up of things past that are half forgotten or not thought of for a long time: *Gene's recollection of his childhood in Brooklyn was tinged with nostalgia.* **Remembrance** is the act of bringing back to mind a particular event of the past: *The remembrance of that indignity made him furious.*

Mem·phis (mem'fis) *n.* **1.** largest city in Tennessee, in the southwestern part of the state. Pop. (1970), 623,530. **2.** city in ancient Egypt, on the west bank of the Nile.

mem·sa·hib (mem'sä'ib, -ēb) *n.* in colonial India, a European woman. ▲ formerly used as a term of address. [Hindi *memsāhib,* from *mem* lady (from English MA'AM) + *sāhib* master (from Arabic *sahib* master, friend).]

men (men) plural of **man.**

men·ace (men'is) *n.* **1.** one who or that which is a threat; danger. **2.** very annoying or troublesome person. —*v.t.* **-aced, -ac·ing.** to threaten; endanger. —*v.i.* to be or pose a threat. [Old French *menace* threat, from Latin *minācia.*] —**men'ac·ing·ly,** *adv.*

me·nad (mē'nad) maenad.

mé·nage (mā näzh') *also,* **me·nage.** *n.* **1.** domestic establishment; household. **2.** management of a household; housekeeping. [French *ménage,* going back to Latin *mānsiō* a staying, dwelling.]

me·nag·er·ie (mi naj'ər ē, -nazh'-) *n.* **1.** collection of wild or unusual animals kept in cages or other enclosures, usually for exhibition. **2.** enclosure where such animals are kept. [French *ménagerie* originally, place for keeping animals of a household, from *ménage* household, housekeeping. See MÉNAGE.]

Men·ci·us (men'shē əs) *n.* c.372–c.289 B.C., Chinese philosopher.

mend (mend) *v.t.* **1.** to restore to a sound condition or working order: *to mend a broken vase, to mend a torn curtain.* **2.** to reform, correct,

or improve (something): *The boy was warned to mend his ways.* —*v.i.* **1.** to knit, as a broken bone; heal. **2.** to regain one's health; recover. **3.** to improve: *Things will mend in time.* —*n.* **1.** mended place: *a mend in the sole of a shoe.* **2. on the mend.** getting better, esp. in health; improving. [Short for AMEND.]

Syn. *v.t.* **1. Mend, repair[1], fix** mean to restore to good condition that which was broken, damaged, or defective. **Mend** suggests removal of defects and restoration to former usefulness without actual replacement of materials: *Mother mended the torn dress.* **Repair** suggests restoration to former working order by replacement or rehabilitation of parts and suggests that skill is required: *The garage charged forty dollars to repair the car.* **Fix** is a rather informal word conveying the idea of making whole and serviceable what was torn, broken, or injured: *We called in the plumber to fix the drain.*

men·da·cious (men dā'shəs) *adj.* **1.** given to lying; untruthful: *a mendacious person.* **2.** false; untrue: *mendacious reports.* [Latin *mendāc-,* stem of *mendāx* lying + -OUS.] —**men·da'cious·ly,** *adv.*

men·dac·i·ty (men das'ə tē) *pl.,* **-ties.** *n.* **1.** quality of being mendacious; untruthfulness. **2.** falsehood; lie.

Men·del, Gre·gor (mend'əl; greg'ôr) 1822–84, Austrian monk and botanist.

men·de·le·vi·um (mend'əl ā'vē əm) *n.* radioactive, metallic element that does not occur in nature, produced by bombarding an isotope of einsteinium with helium ions. Symbol: **Md** See **element** for table. [From D. I. *Mendeleev,* 1834–1907, Russian chemist.]

Men·de·li·an (men dē'lē ən) *adj.* **1.** of or relating to Mendel. **2.** of, relating to, or in accordance with Mendel's laws.

Mendel's laws, laws that govern the transmission of characteristics from parents to offspring, forming the basis for modern genetic theory, discovered and formulated by Gregor Mendel.

Men·dels·sohn, Felix (mend'əl sən) 1809–47, German composer.

men·di·cant (men'di kənt) *adj.* **1.** given to or characterized by begging; living on alms. **2.** of, relating to, or characteristic of a religious order, as the Franciscans, that formerly lived on alms. —*n.* **1.** beggar. **2.** mendicant friar. [Latin *mendīcāns,* present participle of *mendīcāre* to beg.] —**men'di·can·cy, men·dic·i·ty** (men dis'ə tē), *n.*

Men·e·la·us (men'əl ā'əs) *n. Greek Legend.* king of Sparta whose wife, Helen, was carried off to Troy by Paris.

men·folk (men'fōk') *also,* **men·folks.** *n.,pl. Informal.* males collectively, esp. the male members of a group.

men·ha·den (men hād'ən) *pl.,* **-den.** *n.* saltwater fish, *Brevoortia tyrannus,* of the herring family,

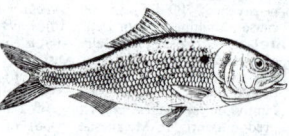

Menhaden

found in the western Atlantic from Nova Scotia to Brazil, used as a source of animal feed, fertilizer, and oil. [Modification of Narragansett *munnawhatteaûg,* from *munnawhat* fertilizer; referring to its use as a fertilizer by the Indians.]

men·hir (men'hir) *n.* prehistoric monument consisting of a single, tall, rough-hewn stone standing upright, either alone or in a group. [French *menhir,* going back to Breton *men* stone + *hir* long.]

me·ni·al (mē'nē əl, mēn'yəl) *adj.* **1.** degrading; servile: *menial tasks.* **2.** of, relating to, or suitable for a servant. —*n.* servant who performs very lowly or humble tasks. [Middle English *meineal* of a servant, servant, from *meine(e)* household, from Old French *mesnie, meinie,* going back to Latin *mānsiō* dwelling.] —**me'ni·al·ly,** *adv.*

me·nin·ges (mi ninʹjēz) *sing.,* **me·ninx** (mē'ningks). *n.,pl.* the three membranes that enclose and protect the brain and spinal cord. [Modern Latin *meninges,* plural of *meninx,* from Greek *mēninx* membrane.]

men·in·gi·tis (men'in jī'tis) *n.* serious illness characterized by inflammation of the meninges. [Modern Latin *meningitis,* from Greek *mēninx* membrane + -ITIS.]

me·nis·cus (mi nis'kəs) *pl.,* **-nis·cus·es** or **-nis·ci** (-nis'ī). *n.* **1.** crescent or crescent-shaped body. **2.** *Physics.* curved upper surface of a liquid in a container. Certain liquids, as water, have a concave meniscus; others, as mercury, have a convex meniscus. **3.** lens that is convex on one side and concave on the other. [Modern Latin *meniscus,* from Greek *mēniskos* crescent, diminutive of *mēnē* moon.]

Men·non·ite (men'ə nīt') *n.* member of a Protestant sect founded in Holland in the sixteenth century that rejects infant baptism, the taking of oaths, the holding of public office, and military service. [From *Menno* Simons, 1492–1559, religious reformer of Friesland who founded this sect + -ITE[1].]

men·o·pause (men'ə pôz') *n.* the cessation of menstruation. [Greek *mēn* month + *pausis* a stopping. See MENSES.]

Meniscus (def. 3)

at; āpe; cär; end; mē; it; īce; hot; ōld; fôrk; wood; fōōl; oil; out; up; ūse; turn; sing; thin; this; zh in treasure; ə in ago, taken, pencil, lemon, circus.

Me·nor·ca (me nôr′kä) *Spanish.* Minorca *(def. 1).*

men·ser·vants (men′sur′vənts) plural of **manservant.**

men·ses (men′sēz) *n.,pl.* menstruation. [Latin *mēnsēs*, plural of *mēnsis* month; because it follows a monthly cycle.]

Men·she·vik (men′shə vik′) *pl.*, **-viks** or **-vi·ki** (-vē′kē). *n.* member of the more moderate wing of the Russian Social Democratic Party that was opposed to the Bolsheviks. [Russian *menshevik* minority, from *menshe* less; because this wing was originally in the minority.]

men·stru·al (men′strōō əl) *adj.* **1.** of or relating to menstruation. **2.** monthly.

men·stru·ate (men′strōō āt′) *-at·ed, -at·ing. v.i.* to undergo menstruation. [Late Latin *mēnstruātus*, past participle of *mēnstruāre* to menstruate, going back to Latin *mēnsis* month. See MENSES.]

men·stru·a·tion (men′strōō ā′shən) *n.* **1.** the periodic discharge of blood and bloody fluid from the uterus through the genital tract, usually occurring every twenty-eight days. **2.** menstrual period.

men·stru·um (men′strōō əm) *pl.*, **-stru·ums** or **-stru·a** (-strōō ə). *n.* solvent *(def. 1).*

men·su·ra·bil·i·ty (men′shər ə bil′ə tē) *n.* state or quality of being mensurable.

men·su·ra·ble (men′shər ə bəl) *adj.* that can be measured; measurable.

men·su·ra·tion (men′shə rā′shən) *n.* **1.** act, art, or process of measuring. **2.** branch of mathematics dealing with the determination of lengths, areas, and volumes. [Late Latin *mēnsūrātio* act of measuring, going back to Latin *mēnsūra*. See MEASURE.]

-ment *suffix* (used to form nouns) **1.** act or process of: *accomplishment, abridgment.* **2.** state or condition of being: *merriment, amazement.* **3.** product or result of: *pavement, improvement.* **4.** means or instrument of: *inducement.* [Old French *-ment*, from Latin *-mentum.*]

men·tal (men′təl) *adj.* **1.** of or relating to the mind: *one's mental state, mental awareness.* **2.** carried on in, or performed by, the mind: *mental arithmetic.* **3.** mentally ill: *a mental patient.* **4.** for the care of the mentally ill: *a mental hospital.* [Late Latin *mentālis* relating to the mind, from Latin *mēns* mind.]

mental age, level of mental development as measured by performance on an intelligence test. A five-year-old child who performs as well on an intelligence test as an average ten-year-old child is said to have a mental age of ten.

mental deficiency, mental retardation.

men·tal·i·ty (men tal′ə tē) *pl.*, **-ties.** *n.* **1.** mental capacity or power. **2.** manner or way of thinking; outlook: *a ghetto mentality.*

men·tal·ly (ment′əl ē) *adv.* **1.** with regard to the mind: *mentally ill.* **2.** in or with the mind: *to add a column of figures mentally without pencil and paper.*

mental retardation, faulty development of intelligence characterized by difficulty in learning and adapting to the demands of society. The classifications of moron, imbecile, and idiot are now considered outdated.

men·thol (men′thôl) *n.* white, crystalline, organic alcohol derived from peppermint oil by freezing. Formula: $CH_3C_6H_9(C_3H_7)OH$ [Latin *ment(h)a* mint[1] + -OL. See MINT[1].]

men·tho·lat·ed (men′thə lā′tid) *adj.* containing menthol.

men·tion (men′shən) *v.t.* to speak about or refer to incidentally or briefly: *He mentioned you in his last letter.* —*n.* incidental or brief remark or reference. [Latin *mentiō* a calling to mind.]

Men·tor (men′tər) *n.* **1.** *Greek Mythology.* loyal friend of Odysseus, left in charge of Odysseus's household and son. **2. mentor.** wise and trusted counselor.

men·u (men′ū, mā′nū) *n.* **1.** list of the food served or available, as in a restaurant. **2.** the food served or available. [French *menu* minute detail, bill of fare, small, from Latin *minūtus* small.]

me·ow (mē ou′) *also,* **mi·aow, mi·aou.** *n.* cry of a cat. —*v.i.* to make such a sound. [Imitative.]

Meph·is·to·phe·le·an (mef′is tə fē′lē ən) *also,* **Meph·is·to·phe·li·an.** *adj.* of, relating to, or like Mephistopheles; fiendish and crafty.

Meph·i·stoph·e·les (mef′ə stof′ə lēz′) *n.* **1.** *German Legend.* the devil to whom Faust sold his soul. **2.** any crafty, evil person.

me·phit·ic (mi fit′ik) *adj.* **1.** having an offensive odor. **2.** noxious; poisonous. [Late Latin *mephīticus* pestilential, from Latin *mephītis* stench.]

me·phi·tis (mi fī′tis) *n.* **1.** offensive odor; stench. **2.** noxious or foul-smelling emanation from the earth. [Latin *mephītis* stench.]

mer·can·tile (mur′kən tēl′, -tīl′) *adj.* **1.** of, relating to, or characteristic of merchants or commerce; commercial. **2.** of or relating to mercantilism. [French *mercantile* commercial, from Italian *mercantile*, going back to Latin *mercārī* to trade.]

mer·can·til·ism (mur′kən tē liz′əm, -tī-) *n.* **1.** economic system developed in France and England in the sixteenth and seventeenth centuries that stressed strict government regulation of the national economy and believed that an excess of exports over imports was favorable because it brought in gold and silver from abroad. Also, **mercantile system. 2.** spirit or practice of a mercantile life; devotion to trade; commercialism. —**mer′can·til·ist,** *n., adj.*

Mer·ca·tor, Ger·har·dus (mər kā′tər; jər här′dəs) 1512–94, Flemish geographer, map maker, and mathematician.

Mercator projection, map projection developed in the sixteenth century in which the distances between parallels of latitude gradually increase, moving to the north and south away from the equator. Though distorting relative sizes of areas in the higher latitudes, it shows compass directions as straight lines and so is ideal for navigation over small areas. [From Gerhardus MERCATOR.]

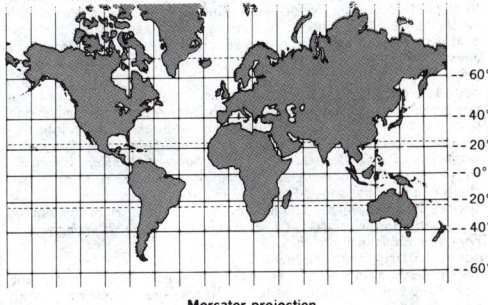

Mercator projection

mer·ce·nary (mur′sə ner′ē) *adj.* **1.** working or acting for money or material gain only. **2.** (of a soldier) serving in a foreign army for pay. —*n. pl.*, **-nar·ies.** mercenary soldier. [Latin *mercēnārius* hired for pay, from *mercēs* wages, reward.]

mer·cer (mur′sər) *n.* *British.* dealer in textiles. [Old French *mercier* trader, going back to Latin *merx* merchandise.]

mer·cer·ize (mur′sə rīz′) **-ized, -iz·ing.** *v.t.* to treat (cotton thread or fabric) by immersing under tension in a caustic soda solution so as to increase its luster, strength, and absorbency and make it more receptive to dyes. [From John *Mercer*, 1791–1866, English calico printer who developed the process + -IZE.]

mer·chan·dise (mur′chən dīz′; *n. also* mur′chən dīs′) *n.* articles bought and sold; commodities; wares. —*v.t.*, **-dised, -dis·ing. 1.** to buy and sell; trade. **2.** to promote the sale of, as through advertising. —*v.i.* to carry on commerce; trade. [Old French *marcheandise* goods, trading, from *marcheant* trader, going back to Latin *mercārī* to trade.] —**mer′chan·dis′er,** *n.*

mer·chan·dize (mur′chən dīz′) **-dized, -diz·ing.** *v.t., v.i.* to merchandise.

mer·chant (mur′chənt) *n.* **1.** one whose business is buying and selling merchandise for profit. **2.** one who owns or runs a retail store; storekeeper. —*adj.* **1.** of or relating to merchants or commerce. **2.** of or relating to the merchant marine. [Old French *marcheant* trader, shopkeeper, going back to Latin *mercārī* to trade.]

mer·chant·a·ble (mur′chən tə bəl) *adj.* marketable; salable.

mer·chant·man (mur′chənt mən) *pl.*, **-men.** *n.* ship used in commerce.

merchant marine, 1. all the commercial or trading ships of a nation collectively. **2.** officers and crew of such ships.

Mer·ci·a (mur′shē ə, -shə) *n.* ancient kingdom founded by the Angles in central England.

Mer·ci·an (mur′shē ən, -shən) *n.* **1.** member of the people that inhabited Mercia. **2.** Old English dialect spoken in Mercia. —*adj.* of or relating to Mercia, its people, or their dialect.

mer·ci·ful (mur′si fəl) *adj.* feeling, exhibiting, or characterized by mercy. —**mer′ci·ful·ly,** *adv.* —**mer′ci·ful·ness,** *n.*

mer·ci·less (mur′si lis) *adj.* without mercy; pitiless; unrelenting. —**mer′ci·less·ly,** *adv.* —**mer′ci·less·ness,** *n.*

mer·cu·ri·al (mər kyoor′ē əl) *adj.* **1.** erratic; changeable: *a mercurial personality.* **2.** of, relating to, containing, or caused by the action of mercury: *mercurial compounds, mercurial poisoning.* **3.** lively; quick. —**mer·cu′ri·al·ly,** *adv.*

mer·cu·ric (mər kyoor′ik) *adj.* (of compounds) containing mercury, esp. bivalent mercury.

Mer·cu·ro·chrome (mər kyoor′ə krōm′) *n. Trademark.* red antiseptic liquid solution containing mercury.

mer·cu·rous (mər kyoor′əs, mur′kyər əs) *adj.* (of compounds) containing mercury, esp. monovalent mercury.

mer·cu·ry (mur′kyər ē) *pl.*, **-ries.** *n.* **1.** heavy, shiny, silver-colored,

poisonous metallic element obtained by roasting cinnabar in air, used esp. in thermometers and barometers. Symbol: **Hg** See **element** for table. Also, **quick′sil′ver**. **2.** column of mercury in a thermometer or barometer, used as an indication of temperature: *The mercury rose today.* **3. Mercury.** smallest planet of the solar system and closest in order of distance to the sun. It is the fastest-moving planet, completing a full revolution in eighty-eight days. **4. Mercury.** Roman messenger of the gods and patron of commerce. His Greek counterpart is Hermes. [Latin *Mercurius* the Roman god.]

mer·cy (mur′sē) *pl.,* **-cies.** *n.* **1.** kindness, forbearance, or compassion toward another or others where severity is expected or merited; leniency: *The prisoner begged his captors for mercy.* **2.** disposition or power to be kind, forbearing, or forgiving: *The convicted man threw himself on the mercy of the court.* **3.** something to be thankful for; blessing. **4. at the mercy of.** wholly in the power of: *We were at the mercy of the enemy.* [Old French *merci* thanks, pity, from Latin *mercēs* wages, reward.]
Syn. 1. Mercy, clemency, leniency mean the quality or state of being kind and compassionate toward offenders. **Mercy** implies a compassion that goes beyond the requirements of justice in extending comfort to the defenseless: *Earthly power doth then show likest God's when mercy seasons justice* (Shakespeare, *The Merchant of Venice*). **Clemency** stresses the quality of being slow to punish and quick to forgive, esp. charity and mildness in judgment: *The judge showed clemency to the young offender.* **Leniency** emphasizes the absence of rigor, harshness, and severity in the exercise of justice: *The press blamed the increase in crimes on the leniency of the courts.*

mercy killing, euthanasia (*def. 1*).

mercy seat 1. in the Old Testament, the solid gold covering on the Ark of the Covenant, regarded by the Hebrews as the resting place of God. **2.** throne of God.

mere¹ (mēr) *superlative,* **mer·est.** *adj.* being nothing more or other than what is specified; only: *a mere trifle, a mere child.* [Latin *merus* pure, not mixed.]

mere² (mēr) *n. Archaic.* lake; pond. [Old English *mere* sea, lake.]

Mer·e·dith (mer′ə dith) **1. George.** 1828–1909, English novelist and poet. **2. Owen.** see **Bulwer-Lytton, Edward Robert.**

mere·ly (mēr′lē) *adv.* and nothing more; only: *His explanations were merely poor excuses.*

mer·e·tri·cious (mer′ə trish′əs) *adj.* attractive or plausible in a vulgar or deceitful way: *the meretricious excitement of a gambling casino.* [Latin *meretrīcius* relating to a harlot, from *meretrīx* harlot.] —**mer′-e·tri′cious·ly,** *adv.*

mer·gan·ser (mər gan′sər) *pl.,* **-sers** or **-ser.** *n.* any of several fish-eating diving ducks, native to the colder regions of the Northern Hemisphere, having a long, slender bill with saw-toothed edges and usually a crested head. [Modern Latin *merganser,* from Latin *mergus* diving bird + *anser* goose.]

merge (murj) **merged, merg·ing.** *v.i.* **1.** to be united so as to become one: *The two lanes merge going into the tunnel.* **2.** (of corporations) to be joined in a merger. —*v.t.* to unite so as to become one and lose individual identity: *The library merged the two collections into each other.* [Latin *mergere* to dip, plunge.]

merg·er (mur′jər) *n.* **1.** union of corporations in which one corporation continues to retain its identity while absorbing all the rights, privileges, franchises, and properties of another corporation or corporations. **2.** act of merging.

Mé·ri·da (mer′i də; *Spanish* mā′rē thä′) *n.* city in southeastern Mexico, on the Yucatán Peninsula. Pop. (1969), 200,889.

Mer·i·den (mer′əd ən) *n.* city in central Connecticut. Pop. (1970), 55,959.

me·rid·i·an (mə rid′ē ən) *n.* **1.a.** imaginary great circle on the earth's surface passing through the North and South poles. **b.** half of such a circle extending from pole to pole; line or parallel of longitude. **2.** great circle on the celestial sphere passing through the north and south celestial poles. **3.** highest or culminating point; zenith: *the moment at which the fortunes of Montague reached the meridian* (Macaulay, 1859). —*adj.* of or relating to a meridian. [Latin *merīdiānus* relating to midday, relating to the south, from *merīdiēs* midday, south.]

me·rid·i·o·nal (mə rid′ē ən əl) *adj.* **1.** of, relating to, or resembling a meridian. **2.** of, relating to, or characteristic of the south or the people inhabiting the south, esp. the south of France. **3.** situated in the south; southerly. —*n.* inhabitant of the south, esp. the south of France. [Late Late Latin *merīdiōnālis* relating to midday, southern, from *merīdiēs* midday, south.]

Mé·ri·mée, Pros·per (mā rē mā′; prōs per′) 1803–70, French author.

me·ringue (mə rang′) *n.* **1.** mixture of stiffly beaten egg whites and sugar, usually baked and used as a topping, as on cakes or pies. **2.** small cake or pastry shell made of this mixture. [French *meringue;* of uncertain origin.]

me·ri·no (mə rē′nō) *pl.,* **-nos.** *n.* **1.** sheep of a breed originally developed in Spain, having a light-colored fleece and a white face, raised for its wool. **2.** wool of this sheep. **3.** fine, soft yarn or fabric made from this wool, used for such items as suits or dresses. **4.** knitted fabric woven from a blend of cotton and wool fibers, used for such items as hosiery and underwear. [Spanish *merino;* probably from Berber *Benī Merīn* the Berber tribe that developed this sheep.]

Merino

mer·it (mer′it) *n.* **1.** quality, worth, or excellence: *The author's latest book is totally without merit.* **2.** also, **merits.** something deserving praise or reward; commendable quality: *You may not like him, but he has his merits.* **3. merits.** actual facts of a matter under consideration, whether good or bad or right or wrong: *He will judge the case solely on its merits.* —*v.t.* to be deserving of. [Latin *meritum* value, worth, desert', from *merēre* to earn, deserve.]
Syn. v.t. Merit, earn, deserve mean being worthy of or qualified for reward. **Merit** implies being entitled to a reward or liable for a punishment on the ground of intrinsic quality of character: *The judges decided that Paul's entry merited the first prize in the competition.* **Earn** stresses being entitled to an equitable reward on the basis of a corresponding effort: *After years of hard work, John had earned his promotion.* **Deserve** stresses being entitled to something whether or not such a claim is recognized: *Although Mary deserved a promotion, someone else got the position.*

mer·i·to·ri·ous (mer′ə tôr′ē əs) *adj.* worthy of reward or praise; having merit. —**mer′i·to′ri·ous·ly,** *adv.* —**mer′i·to′ri·ous·ness,** *n.*

merit system, in the U.S. Civil Service, system in which people are hired or promoted on the basis of competence.

merle (murl) *also,* **merl.** *n.* blackbird (*def. 2*). [Old French *merle* blackbird, from Latin *merula.*]

mer·lin (mur′lin) *n.* pigeon hawk. [Anglo-Norman *merilun,* from Old French *esmerillon;* of Germanic origin.]

Mer·lin (mur′lin) *n.* in Arthurian legend, wise magician who protected and counseled King Arthur.

mer·lon (mur′lən) *n.* solid part of a battlement between any two embrasures. See **battlement** for illustration. [French *merlon,* from Italian *merlone,* from *merlo* battlement; of uncertain origin.]

mer·maid (mur′mād′) *n.* in folklore, sea creature having the head and body of a beautiful woman and the tail of a fish instead of legs. [MERE² + MAID.]

mer·man (mur′man′) *pl.,* **-men.** *n.* in folklore, sea creature having the head and body of a man and the tail of a fish instead of legs. [MERE² + MAN.]

Mer·o·vin·gi·an (mer′ə vin′jē ən) *adj.* of, relating to, or designating the first Frankish dynasty, reigning from A.D. c.500–c.751. —*n.* one of the Merovingian kings.

Mer·ri·mac (mer′i mak′) *also,* **Mer·ri·mack.** *n.* U.S. steam-driven wooden frigate salvaged and converted to an ironclad by the Confederates and renamed the *Virginia.* It engaged in a historic battle with the *Monitor* at Hampton Roads, Virginia, on March 9, 1862.

mer·ri·ment (mer′i mənt) *n.* playfulness and gaiety; fun.

mer·ry (mer′ē) **-ri·er, -ri·est.** *adj.* **1.** festive and cheerful; full of merriment. **2.** characterized by festivity and rejoicing; joyous. **3.** *Archaic.* pleasant; delightful. **4. to make merry.** to be festive and jovial; engage in or have fun. [Old English *myrge* pleasant.] —**mer′ri·ly,** *adv.*

mer·ry-an·drew (mer′ē an′drōō) *n.* clown; buffoon.

mer·ry-go-round (mer′ē gō round′) *n.* **1.** revolving circular platform equipped with wooden animals, esp. horses, and often having benchlike seats, ridden for amusement. Also, **car′ou·sel′. 2.** circular platform that revolves when pushed, found in playgrounds. **3.** rapid round; whirl: *a merry-go-round of social activity.*

mer·ry·mak·ing (mer′ē māk′ing) *n.* **1.** act of engaging in or having fun; making merry. **2.** boisterous or gay festivity. —*adj.* full of joy and fun; gay and festive. —**mer′ry·mak′er,** *n.*

me·sa (mā′sə) *n.* flat-topped hill or mountain with steep sides descending to the plain below; high plateau. [Spanish *mesa,* going back to Latin *mēnsa* table.]

mé·sal·li·ance (mā zal′ē əns; *French* mā zál yäns′) *n.* marriage with a person of inferior social position. [French *mésalliance,* from *més-* + *alliance.* See MIS-, ALLIANCE.]

mes·cal (mes kal′) *n.* **1.** colorless alcoholic beverage distilled from the fermented juice of certain agave plants. **2.** peyote. [Spanish *mescal* the alcoholic beverage, from Nahuatl *mexcalli,* from *metl* maguey + *ixcalli* stew.]

mes·ca·line (mes′kə lēn′, -lin) *n.* crystalline drug that produces hal-

lucinations, derived from the dried tops of the peyote cactus. Formula: $C_{11}H_{17}NO_3$ [MESCAL + -INE².]

mes·dames (mā däm′) plural of **madame.**

mes·de·moi·selles (mād mwä zel′) plural of **mademoiselle.**

mes·en·ter·y (mes′ən ter′ē) pl., -ter·ies. n. fold of the peritoneum that attaches the small intestine and most of the large intestine to the abdominal wall. [Modern Latin *mesenterium,* from Greek *mesenterion* membrane connecting all the intestines, from *mesos* middle + *enteron* intestine.]

mesh (mesh) n. **1.** one of the open spaces between the cords, threads, or wires of a net or netting. **2. meshes.** cords, threads, or wires bounding such a space or spaces. **3.** open network consisting of interlaced cords, threads, or wires; netting. **4.** any of various fabrics consisting of an open network of interlaced threads. **5.** *also,* **meshes.** anything that entangles or ensnares. **6.** the interlocking or engagement of the teeth of a gear. **7. in mesh.** fitted together; in gear; interlocked. —v.t., v.i. **1.** to catch or be caught in or as in a net; enmesh or become enmeshed. **2.** to engage or become engaged, as the teeth of a gear; interlock. [Middle Dutch *maesche* net, opening of a net.]

Me·shed (mə shed′) n. city in northeastern Iran. Pop. (1969 est.), 409,616. Also, **Mash·had′.**

mes·mer·ism (mez′mə riz′əm, mes′-) n. hypnotism. [From F. A. *Mesmer,* 1734–1815, Austrian physician associated with hypnotism + -ISM.] —**mes·mer·ic** (mez mer′ik, mes-), adj. —**mes′mer·ist,** n.

mes·mer·ize (mez′mə rīz′, mes′-) -ized, -iz·ing. v.t. **1.** to hypnotize. **2.** to put as if into a trance; fascinate. —**mes′mer·i·za′tion, mes′mer·iz′er,** n.

mes·o·carp (mez′ə kärp′, mes′-) n. middle layer of the pericarp, as the fleshy part of certain fruits. [Greek *mesos* middle + *karpos* fruit.]

mes·o·derm (mez′ə durm′, mes′-) n. middle of the three primary germ layers of an animal embryo, from which the skeletal, muscular, connective, and reproductive tissues develop. [Greek *mesos* middle + *derma* skin.]

mes·o·morph (mez′ə môrf′, mes′-) n. person having a muscular, athetic body. Distinguished from **ectomorph** and **endomorph.** [Greek *mesos* middle + *morphē* form, shape.] —**mes′o·mor′phic,** adj.

mes·on (mez′on, mes′zon, mez′on, mē′son) n. any of a group of subatomic particles whose mass is greater than that of a muon but less than that of a proton. See **subatomic particle** for table. [Greek *mesos* middle + (ELECTR)ON.]

Mes·o·po·ta·mi·a (mes′ə pə tā′mē ə) n. historic region in southwestern Asia, between the Tigris and Euphrates rivers, an ancient center of civilization. —**Mes′o·po·ta′mi·an,** adj., n.

mes·o·sphere (mez′ə sfēr′) n. layer of the atmosphere above the stratosphere, from about thirty to about sixty miles above the earth's surface. [Greek *mesos* middle + SPHERE.]

Mes·o·zo·ic (mes′ə zō′ik) n. one of the major geological eras, comprising the Cretaceous, Jurassic, and Triassic periods; age of reptiles. See **geology** for table. —adj. of, relating to, or characteristic of this era. [Greek *mesos* middle + *zōē* life + -IC.]

mes·quite (mes kēt′, mes′kēt) n. small thorny tree, *Prosopis glandulosa,* of the pea family, that grows in desert regions from the southwestern United States to Chile, bearing pinnate leaves, small flowers, and slender seedpods containing beans used for forage. [Spanish *mezquite,* from Nahuatl *mizquitl.*]

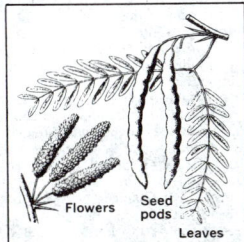

Flowers Seed pods

Leaves

Mesquite

mess (mes) n. **1.a.** untidy, disorderly, or dirty state or condition: *The closet is in a mess.* **b.** one who or that which is in such a state or condition: *The room was a mess after the party.* **2.** unpleasant, difficult, embarrassing, or confusing situation or state of affairs; muddle: *She made a mess of her life.* **3.** untidy or confused mass or collection; jumble: *a mess of newspapers on the floor.* **4.** indefinite amount: *to catch a mess of fish.* **5.a.** group of people who take meals together regularly, esp. in the army or navy. **b.** meal eaten by such a group. **c.** place where such a meal is eaten; mess hall. **6.** unappetizing or disagreeable concoction: *I can't eat this mess.* **7.** portion of soft, partly liquid food. —v.t. **1.** to make dirty or untidy (often with *up*): *to mess up a room.* **2.** to make a mess of; confuse or spoil (often with *up*): *Her late arrival messed up our plans.* **3.** to treat or handle roughly (often with *up*): *The thieves messed him up pretty badly.* **4.** *Military.* to provide with a meal or meals. —v.i. **1.** to interfere or tamper (often with *around*): *Don't mess with him when he's angry.* **2.** to waste time or busy oneself by

puttering (with *around* or *about*): *We messed around the house all day because it rained.* **3.** to take one's meals in a military mess. [Old French *mes* course of food, from Late Latin *missus,* from *mittere* to place, from Latin *mittere* to send.]

mes·sage (mes′ij) n. **1.** communication from one person or group transmitted to another. **2.** formal or official communication: *the president's message to Congress.* **3.** point of view or idea meant to be communicated: *a movie with a message.* [Old French *message* information transmitted orally or in writing, going back to Latin *missus,* past participle of *mittere* to send.]

mes·sa·line (mes′ə lēn′) n. soft, lightweight fabric woven of rayon or silk and having a satinlike finish. [Possibly from *Messalina* a wife of the Roman emperor Claudius.]

Mes·sei·gneurs (mā sen yœr′) plural of **Monseigneur.**

Mes·se·ne (mi sē′nē) n. ancient Greek city.

mes·sen·ger (mes′ən jər) n. **1.** one who picks up and delivers messages or runs errands. **2.** one employed to deliver telegrams, letters, or parcels. **3.** one whose work is carrying official dispatches. **4.** *Archaic.* harbinger; forerunner. [Old French *messag(i)er* bearer of a message, from *message.* See MESSAGE.]

Syn. 1. Messenger, courier, emissary mean an agent who carries messages in the line of duty. **Messenger** is a person who is employed to bear messages and to go on errands: *Laura's husband works as a messenger in a bank.* **Courier** suggests one who carries official information that has to be conveyed quickly or according to a regular schedule: *The courier from the foreign mission arrived by airplane.* **Emissary** is an agent empowered to act more or less independently and to convey a vital or secret message: *The mutineers sent an emissary to the captain with their demands.*

mess hall, place where a group of people take meals together regularly, esp. in the army or navy.

Mes·si·ah (mi sī′ə) n. **1.** in Judaism, the expected deliverer of the Jews promised by God. **2.** in Christianity, Jesus, regarded as the savior of mankind. **3.** *also,* **messiah.** any savior or deliverer. [Hebrew *māshīah* anointed.] —**mes·si·an·ic** (mes′ē an′ik); *also,* **Mes′si·an′ic,** adj.

mes·sieurs (mes′ərz; French mā syœ′) plural of **monsieur.**

Mes·si·na (mi sē′nə) n. **1.** port city in northeastern Sicily. Pop. (1968), 269,757. **2. Strait of.** narrow strait between Italy and Sicily.

mess kit, compactly arranged kit consisting of eating utensils and a metal container that opens to make two separate compartments, used by a soldier or camper.

mess·mate (mes′māt′) n. regular companion at meals, esp. in a ship's mess.

Messrs. (mes′ərz) Messieurs.

mess·y (mes′ē) mess·i·er, mess·i·est. adj. being in, characterized by, or causing a mess. —**mess′i·ness,** n.

mes·ti·zo (mes tē′zō) pl., -zos or -zoes. n. person of mixed blood, esp. one of Spanish and American Indian blood. [Spanish *mestizo* mongrel, from Late Latin *mixtīcius* of mixed race, from Latin *mixtus* mixed, past participle of *miscēre* to mix.]

met (met) past tense and past participle of **meet¹.**

met·a·bol·ic (met′ə bol′ik) adj. **1.** of, relating to, involving, or characterized by metabolism. **2.** of, relating to, or undergoing metamorphosis.

me·tab·o·lism (mi tab′ə liz′əm) n. total of all the biochemical processes that occur in a living organism. It is the means by which food is converted into protoplasm and by which the organism is provided with the energy necessary to carry on all basic life processes, as respiration, digestion, and cell division. [Greek *metabolē* change + -ISM.]

met·a·car·pal (met′ə kär′pəl) adj. of or relating to the metacarpus. —n. one of the bones of the metacarpus.

met·a·car·pus (met′ə kär′pəs) pl., -pi (-pī). n. **1.** part of the hand between the wrist and the fingers, having five bones. **2.** corresponding part of the forelimb of an animal. [Modern Latin *metacarpus,* going back to Greek *meta* between, after + *karpos* wrist.]

met·al (met′əl) n. **1.** any of a class of chemical elements, as iron, silver, copper, or lead, that exhibit certain typical properties, as luster, ductility, malleability, and conductivity of heat and electricity. **2.** mixture of such elements, as brass or bronze; alloy. **3.** broken stones or similar material, used for road surfaces and roadbeds. **4.** molten glass, esp. as used in making glass. **5.** intrinsic quality or substance; mettle. [Latin *metallum* mine², substance such as gold or copper, from Greek *metallon.*]

me·tal·lic (mi tal′ik) adj. **1.** of, relating to, or having the properties of metal. **2.** containing or yielding metal. **3.** resembling, characteristic of, or suggestive of metal: *a metallic sound.*

met·al·lif·er·ous (met′əl if′ər əs) adj. containing or yielding metal: *metalliferous deposits.* [Latin *metallifer* (from *metallum* metal + *ferre* to bear) + -OUS. See METAL.]

met·al·loid (met′əl oid′) n. any of a class of chemical elements that exhibit both metallic and nonmetallic properties. Also, **sem′i·met′al.**

—*adj.* **1.** of, relating to, or having the properties of a metalloid. **2.** resembling a metal. Also, **met′al·loi′dal.**

met·al·lur·gy (met′əl ur′jē) *n.* science and technology of separating metals from ores and preparing them for use, as by refining or fabricating. [Modern Latin *metallurgia,* from Greek *metallourgos* working in metals, from *metallon* metal + *ergon* work.] —**met′al·lur′gic;** *also,* **met′al·lur′gi·cal,** *adj.* —**met′al·lur′gist,** *n.*

met·al·work (met′əl wurk′) *n.* **1.** objects or structures made of metal. **2.** metalworking.

met·al·work·ing (met′əl wur′king) *n.* act, process, or business of making metal objects or structures. —**met′al·work′er,** *n.*

met·a·mor·phic (met′ə môr′fik) *adj.* **1.** of, relating to, or characterized by metamorphosis. **2.** *Geology.* of, relating to, exhibiting, or produced by metamorphism.

met·a·mor·phism (met′ə môr′fiz′əm) *n.* **1.** change in the texture, structure, and mineral composition of rock caused by processes operating beneath the surface of the earth. **2.** metamorphosis.

met·a·mor·phose (met′ə môr′fōz, -fōs) -**phosed,** -**phos·ing,** *v.t., v.i.* to undergo or cause to undergo metamorphosis or metamorphism.

met·a·mor·pho·sis (met′ə môr′fə sis) *pl.,* -**ses** (-sēz′). *n.* **1.** process by which certain animals undergo changes in form, structure, or function as they develop from an immature form at birth or hatching to an adult, as the change from a tadpole to a frog. **2.a.** change in form, shape, or structure; transformation, as by sorcery. **b.** one who or that which results from such a change. **3.** complete or marked change, as of appearance, character, or condition. [Latin *metamorphosis* transformation, from Greek *metamorphōsis.*]

met·a·phor (met′ə fôr′, -fər) *n.* **1.** figure of speech in which one object or idea is compared or identified with another in order to suggest a similarity between the two; for example: *He is a pillar of strength.* **2.** mixed metaphor. expression in

Egg
Larva
Pupa
Adult
Metamorphosis of a butterfly

which two or more metaphors are combined in an illogical and contradictory manner; for example: *to take arms against a sea of troubles* (Shakespeare, *Hamlet*). [Latin *metaphora* this figure of speech, from Greek *metaphorā* transference.] —**met·a·phor·ic** (met′ə fôr′ik, -for′-); *also,* **met′a·phor′i·cal,** *adj.* —**met′a·phor′i·cal·ly,** *adv.*

met·a·phys·i·cal (met′ə fiz′i kəl) *adj.* **1.** of, relating to, treated by, or characteristic of metaphysics. **2.** difficult to understand; highly abstract; abstruse. —**met′a·phys′i·cal·ly,** *adv.*

met·a·phy·si·cian (met′ə fi zish′ən) *n.* one who is skilled or expert in metaphysics.

met·a·phys·ics (met′ə fiz′iks) *n.,pl.* **1.** branch of philosophy that deals with the nature and meaning of existence and investigates such aspects of reality as the fundamental unity underlying all particular things, their nature and form, and their relationships. **2.** theoretical or speculative philosophy, esp. the principles underlying a branch of knowledge. **3.** any obscure or intricate speculation or discussion. ▲ construed as singular in all definitions. [Medieval Latin *metaphysica,* from Greek *ta meta ta physika* the (works) after the physics; because in one particular arrangement of the works of Aristotle, his works on abstract philosophy followed his works on physics. See PHYSICS.]

me·tas·ta·sis (mi tas′tə sis) *pl.,* -**ses** (-sēz′). *n.* spread of a disease, esp. a cancerous growth, from one part of the body to another. [Greek *metastasis* change, removal, transference.]

met·a·tar·sal (met′ə tär′səl) *adj.* of or relating to the metatarsus. —*n.* one of the bones of the metatarsus.

met·a·tar·sus (met′ə tär′səs) *pl.,* -**si** (-sī). *n.* **1.** part of the foot between the ankle and the toes, consisting of five bones. **2.a.** corresponding part of the hind foot of a quadruped. **b.** corresponding part of the foot of a bird. [Modern Latin *metatarsus,* from Greek *meta* between, after + *tarsos* flat of the foot, ankle.]

me·tath·e·sis (mi tath′ə sis) *pl.,* -**ses** (-sēz′). *n.* **1.** transposition of sounds or letters within a word. The Old English word *bridd* became *bird* in English through metathesis. **2.** any change or reversal. [Late Latin *metathesis* transposition of the letters of a word, from Greek *metathesis* change of position.]

met·a·zo·an (met′ə zō′ən) *n.* any animal, division Metazoa, whose body is composed of specialized cells grouped to form tissues and organs. All animals are metazoans except the protozoans and the sponges. —*adj.* of, relating to, or characteristic of the metazoans. Also, **met′a·zo′ic.** [Modern Latin *Metazoa* (from Greek *meta* after + *zōia,* plural of *zōion* animal) + -AN.]

mete[1] (mēt) **met·ed, met·ing.** *v.t.* **1.** to distribute by or as by measuring; apportion; allot (often with *out): to mete out punishment.* **2.** *Archaic.* to measure. [Old English *metan* to measure.]

mete[2] (mēt) *n.* boundary or limit: *to know the metes and bounds of one's abilities.* [Old French *mete,* from Latin *mēta* goal, boundary.]

me·tem·psy·cho·sis (mi temp′sə kō′sis, met′əm sī-) *pl.,* -**ses** (-sēz) *n.* the passage of the soul at death into a new body, either human or animal. [Greek *metempsychosis* transmigration of souls.]

me·te·or (mē′tē ər) *n.* body from space that enters the earth's atmosphere, where it is heated by friction until it burns with a bright light during its fall. Also, **shooting star.** [Modern Latin *meteorum,* from Greek *meteōron* thing in the air, from *meteōros* high in the air.]

me·te·or·ic (mē′tē ôr′ik, -or′ik) *adj.* **1.** of, relating to, or containing meteors. **2.** resembling a meteor; brilliant and swift: *a meteoric rise in politics.* **3.** of, relating to, or occurring in the earth's atmosphere: *meteoric phenomena.*

me·te·or·ite (mē′tē ə rīt′) *n.* meteor that has fallen to earth.

me·te·or·oid (mē′tē ə roid′) *n.* meteor that is still in space.

me·te·or·ol·o·gy (mē′tē ə rol′ə jē) *n.* science dealing with the study of the atmosphere and the changes that take place within it. One important branch of meteorology is the study of weather. [Greek *meteōrologiā,* from *meteōron* thing in the air + -*logiā* -logy. See METEOR, -LOGY.] —**me·te·or·o·log·ic** (mē′tē ər ə loj′ik); *also,* **me′te·or·o·log′i·cal,** *adj.* —**me′te·or·o·log′i·cal·ly,** *adv.* —**me′te·or·ol′o·gist,** *n.*

me·ter[1] (mē′tər) *also, British,* **me·tre.** *n.* fundamental unit of length in the metric system, equivalent to 3.28 feet. See **weights and measures** for table. [French *mètre,* from Greek *metron* measure, rule.]

me·ter[2] (mē′tər) *also, British,* **me·tre.** *n.* **1.** rhythmic arrangement of accented and unaccented or short and long syllables in a line of verse. **2.** basic rhythmic pattern of accented notes or beats in a musical composition: *duple meter, triple meter.* [Old English *mēter* poetic meter, from Latin *metrum* poetic meter, measure, from Greek *metron.*]

me·ter[3] (mē′tər) *n.* **1.** instrument or device for measuring and recording the amount of gas, water, or electricity used or the rate of flow. **2.** any of various similar instruments or devices for measuring and recording time, speed, distance, or degree of intensity. —*v.t.* to measure or record by means of a meter. [METE[1] + -ER.]

-meter *combining form* **1.** device for measuring: *speedometer.* **2.** having a specified amount of meters: *kilometer.* **3.** having a specified number of poetic feet: *tetrameter.* [Latin *metrum* measure, from Greek *metron.*]

me·ter·kil·o·gram·sec·ond (mē′tər kil′ə gram′sek′ənd) *adj.* of, relating to, or being a system of measurement in which the meter is the unit of length, the kilogram is the unit of mass, and the second is the unit of time.

Meth., Methodist.

meth·a·done (meth′ə dōn′) *n.* synthetic narcotic drug used as a pain-killer and as a substitute for heroin in the treatment of heroin addiction.

meth·ane (meth′ān) *n.* colorless, odorless, highly flammable gas of the alkane, or paraffin, series. Formula: CH_4 [METHYL + -ANE.]

meth·a·nol (meth′ə nôl′) *n.* clear, volatile, poisonous, liquid alcohol compound, used in antifreeze, shellac, and rocket fuel. Formula: CH_3OH Also, **methyl alcohol, wood alcohol.** [METHANE + -OL.]

me·theg·lin (mi theg′lin) *n.* alcoholic beverage made from fermented honey and water. [Welsh *meddyglyn,* from *meddyg* medicinal (from Latin *medicus* curative) + *llyn* liquor.]

me·thinks (mi thingks′) *past tense,* **me·thought.** *impersonal verb. Archaic.* it seems to me. [Old English *mē thynceth* to me it seems, from *mē,* dative of *ic* I + *thynceth,* third person singular present of *thyncan* to seem.]

meth·od (meth′əd) *n.* **1.** way, means, or manner of doing something, esp. so as to be systematic or orderly: *We didn't agree with his method of handling the situation.* **2.** orderliness and regularity in thought, action, or activity: *Your plan lacks method.* **3.** systematic and orderly arrangement, as of thoughts or topics: *His writings are totally without method.* **4.** principles and techniques applied in or characteristic of a particular field. **5.** the Method. introspective approach to acting in which an actor may draw on his own experiences in order to give a more truthful interpretation of a part. [Latin *methodus* way of proceeding, from Greek *methodos* pursuit, investigation, system.] —**Syn. 1.** see **process.**

me·thod·i·cal (mi thod′i kəl) *adj.* **1.** performed, arranged, or carried on in a systematic or orderly manner: *The police made a methodical search of the house.* **2.** characterized by systematic or

orderly habits or behavior. Also, **me·thod′ic.** —**me·thod′i·cal·ly,** *adv.* —**me·thod′i·cal·ness,** *n.* —**Syn. 1.** see **orderly.**

Meth·od·ism (meth′ə diz′əm) *n.* faith, doctrines, and practices of the Methodists.

Meth·od·ist (meth′ə dist) *n.* member of any of several branches of a Protestant denomination that had its origin in the teachings and work of John Wesley. —*adj.* of, relating to, or characteristic of the Methodists or Methodism.

meth·od·ize (meth′ə dīz′) **-ized, -iz·ing.** *v.t.* to reduce to or arrange according to a method; systematize.

meth·od·ol·o·gy (meth′ə dol′ə jē) *pl.,* **-gies.** *n.* **1.** orderly system of principles or methods of inquiry applied to a particular body of knowledge. **2.** branch of logic dealing with the examination and analysis of the principles or methods of inquiry as applied to a particular branch of knowledge. [Greek *methodos* pursuit, investigation, system + -LOGY.]

me·thought (mi thôt′) past tense of **methinks.**

Me·thu·se·lah (mə thoo′zə lə) *n.* **1.** Biblical patriarch who, according to Genesis, lived 969 years. **2.** any very old man.

meth·yl (meth′əl) *n.* organic group or radical formed from methane. Formula: CH₃ [French *méthyle,* going back to Greek *methy* wine + *hȳlē* wood, matter; supposedly because methyl alcohol is obtained by treating wood.]

methyl alcohol, methanol.

me·tic·u·lous (mi tik′yə ləs) *adj.* characterized by or exhibiting extreme or excessive concern about details; exacting: *a meticulous dresser.* [Latin *metīculōsus* full of fear, from *metus* fear.] —**me·tic′u·lous·ly,** *adv.* —**me·tic′u·lous·ness,** *n.* —**Syn.** see **careful.**

mé·tier (mā tyā′) *n.* **1.** trade, occupation, or profession. **2.** work or activity for which one is particularly suited. [French *métier* business, profession, going back to Latin *ministerium* service, occupation.]

met·o·nym (met′ə nim′) *n.* word used in metonymy.

met·o·nym·i·cal (met′ə nim′i kəl) *adj.* **1.** relating to or of the nature of metonymy. **2.** used in metonymy. Also, **met′o·nym′ic.** —**met′o·nym′i·cal·ly,** *adv.*

me·ton·y·my (mi ton′ə mē) *n.* use of the name of one thing for that of another associated with or related to it; for example: *crown* is a metonym for *monarch.* [Late Latin *metōnymia,* from Greek *metōnymia* literally, change of names.]

met·o·pe (met′ə pē, met′ōp) *n.* one of the square spaces, either sculptured or plain, between the triglyphs in a Doric frieze. [Greek *metopē,* from *meta* between + *opē* hole.]

me·tre¹ (mē′tər) *n.* British. meter¹.

me·tre² (mē′tər) *n.* British. meter².

met·ric¹ (met′rik) *adj.* of, relating to, or designating the metric system. [French *métrique,* from *mètre.* See METER¹.]

met·ric² (met′rik) *adj.* metrical.

met·ri·cal (met′ri kəl) *adj.* **1.** of, relating to, or used in measurement, or composed in poetic meter. [Latin *metricus* (from Greek *metrikos,* from *metron* measure, rule, poetic meter) + -AL¹.] —**met′ri·cal·ly,** *adv.*

metric system, a decimal system of measurement in which the meter is the fundamental unit of length, the kilogram is the fundamental unit of mass, and the second is the fundamental unit of time.

metric ton, measure of weight equal to 1000 kilograms or 2204.62 pounds avoirdupois.

met·ro (met′rō, mā′trō) *pl.,* **-ros.** *also,* **Met·ro.** *n.* subway system in any of several cities, as in Paris. [French *métro,* short for *(chemin de fer) métro(politain)* metropolitan railway.]

met·ro·nome (met′rə nōm′) *n.* mechanical device used for indicating the exact tempo to be maintained in music, usually having a reverse pendulum that can be adjusted to produce clicks at different tempos. [Greek *metron* measure + *nomos* law, rule.] —**met′ro·nom′ic,** *adj.*

me·trop·o·lis (mi trop′ə lis) *n.* **1.** large city, esp. one that is an important center of commerce, culture, or other activity. **2.** principal city of a particular country, state, or region, esp. one that is the capital or the largest city. **3.** city that is the seat of a metropolitan archbishop. [Late Latin *mētropolis* mother city (that established colonies), from Greek *mētropolis,* from *mētēr* mother + *polis* city.]

met·ro·pol·i·tan (met′rə pol′ə tən) *adj.* **1.** relating to, characteristic of, or belonging to a metropolis: *a metropolitan police force.* **2.** consisting of or constituting a metropolis and its surrounding regions: *the New York metropolitan area.* —*n.* in the Roman Catholic Church and certain Anglican and Orthodox churches, an archbishop who is the head of a church province.

-metry *combining form* art, science, or process of measuring: *geometry, optometry.* [Greek *-metriā* measurement, from *metron* measure.]

Met·ter·nich, Prince von (met′ər nik) 1773–1859, Austrian statesman.

met·tle (met′əl) *n.* **1.** spirit and courage. **2.** intrinsic value or substance, as of a person's character. **3. on one's mettle.** ready or eager to do one's best. [Form of METAL; difference in spelling developed to distinguish literal from figurative meaning.]

met·tle·some (met′əl səm) *adj.* full of mettle; spirited or courageous.

Metz (mets) *n.* city in northeastern France. Pop. (1968), 107,537.

Meuse (mūz; *French* mœz) *n.* river flowing from northeastern France through Belgium and the Netherlands.

Mev (mev) *n.* million electron volts.

mew¹ (mū) *n.* cry of a cat; meow. —*v.t.* to make such a sound. [Imitative.]

mew² (mū) *n.* gull, esp. the common gull, *Larus canus,* of Europe. Also, **sea mew.** [Old English *mæw.*]

mew³ (mū) *n.* cage for hawks, esp. when they are molting. —*v.t. Archaic.* to shut up in or as in a cage (often with *up*). [Old French *mue* cage for hawks, a molting, a change, from *muer* to molt, change, from Latin *mūtāre* to change.]

mewl (mūl) *v.i.* to cry feebly like a baby; whimper. [Imitative.]

mews (mūz) *n.,pl.* **1.** stables built around a court or alley, as in London, England. **2.** narrow street or alley, usually having houses that have been converted from stables. ▲ construed as singular and plural in both definitions. [Plural of MEW¹; because the royal stables in London were originally built on the site where the mews of the royal falcons were kept.]

Mex. 1. Mexico. **2.** Mexican.

Mex·i·can (mek′si kən) *n.* member or close descendant of the people of Mexico. —*adj.* of or relating to Mexico, its people, their language, or their culture.

Mexican-American War, war fought between the United States and Mexico from 1846 to 1848. Also, **Mexican War.**

Mexican jumping bean, jumping bean.

Mex·i·co (mek′si kō′) *n.* **1.** country in North America, south of and bordering the southwestern United States. Capital, Mexico City. Area, 761,604 sq. mi. Pop. (1969 est.), 48,933,000. **2. Gulf of.** arm of the Atlantic, between the United States and Mexico.

Mexico City, capital and largest city of Mexico, in the southern part of the country. Pop. (1969), 3,483,649.

me·zu·zah (mə zooz′ə, -zōō′zə) *pl.,* **-zu·zahs** or **-zu·zoth** (-zooz′ōt, -zōō′zōt). *also,* **me·zu·za.** *n.* in Judaism, small tubelike container containing parchment inscribed with Biblical passages, usually affixed to a doorpost or worn as an amulet. [Hebrew *mezūzāh* literally, doorpost; because affixed to doorposts.]

mez·za·nine (mez′ə nēn′) *n.* **1.** an intermediate story between two main floors of a building, usually just above the ground floor. **2.** lowest balcony in a theater or the first few rows of the balcony. [French *mezzanine* entresol, intermediate story, from Italian *mezzanino,* diminutive of *mezzano* middle, from Latin *mediānus.*]

mez·zo (met′sō, mez′ō) *Music. adj.* half; medium; moderate. —*adv.* moderately. [Italian *mezzo* middle, from Latin *medius.*]

mez·zo-so·pran·o (met′sō sə pran′ō, -prä′nō, mez′ō-) *pl.,* **-pran·os.** *n.* **1.** female voice intermediate between soprano and contralto. **2.** singer having such a voice. **3.** part composed for a mezzo-soprano. —*adj.* of or relating to a mezzo-soprano.

mez·zo·tint (met′sō tint′, mez′ō-) *n.* **1.** method of engraving in which the entire surface of a copper or steel plate is uniformly roughened and then partially scraped or burnished to produce effects of light and shade. **2.** print made from such a plate. —*v.t.* to engrave in mezzotint. [Italian *mezzotinto* half-tone, going back to Latin *medius* middle + *tinctus,* past participle of *tingere* to wet, dye.]

mf. *Music.* moderately loud. [Abbreviation of Italian *mezzo forte,* from Latin *mezzo* middle + *fortis* strong.]

mfg., manufacturing.

mfr., manufacture; manufacturer.

mg., milligram; milligrams.

Mg, magnesium.

Mgr. 1. Manager. **2.** Monseigneur. **3.** Monsignor.

MHG, Middle High German. Also, **M.H.G.**

mho (mō) *pl.,* **mhos.** *n.* unit for measuring the conductivity of a body whose resistance is one ohm. It is the reciprocal of ohm. [OHM spelled backward.]

mi (mē) *n.* third of the series of syllables used to name the eight tones of the diatonic scale. See *do²* for illustration. [See GAMUT.]

mi., mile; miles.

Mi·am·i (mī am′ē, -am′ə) *n.* resort and port city in southeastern Florida, the largest city in the state. Pop. (1970), 334,859.

Triglyphs

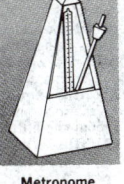

Metope

Metope

Metronome

at; āpe; cär; end; mē; it; īce; hot; ōld; fôrk; wood; fōōl; oil; out; up; ūse; turn; sing; thin; <u>th</u>is; zh in treasure; ə in ago, taken, pencil, lemon, circus.

641

Miami Beach, resort city in southeastern Florida, just east of Miami. Pop. (1970), 87,072.

mi·aow (mē ou′) *also,* **mi·aou.** meow.

mi·as·ma (mī az′mə, mē-) *pl.,* **-mas** or **-ma·ta** (-mə tə). *n.* **1.** noxious or poisonous emanations formerly believed to rise from the earth and decaying matter and pollute the air. **2.** any noxious or harmful influence, effect, or atmosphere. [Greek *miasma* pollution.]

mi·ca (mī′kə) *n.* any of a group of minerals that can be separated into thin sheets, often used as insulators in electric devices. Also, **i′sin·glass′.** [Latin *mīca* crumb; influenced by Latin *micāre* to shine.]

Mi·cah (mī′kə) *n.* **1.** in the Old Testament, a Hebrew prophet of the eighth century B.C. **2.** book of the Old Testament attributed to him.

mice (mīs) plural of **mouse.**

Mich., Michigan.

Mi·chael, Saint (mī′kəl) in the Bible, the archangel who cast Satan out of heaven.

Mich·ael·mas (mik′əl məs) *n.* church feast in honor of the archangel Michael. September 29.

Mi·che·as (mī kē′əs) *n.* in the Douay Bible, Micah.

Mi·chel·an·ge·lo (mī′kəl an′jə lō′) *n.* 1475–1564, Italian sculptor and painter; full name, Michelangelo Buonarroti.

Mich·i·gan (mish′ə gən) *n.* **1.** state in the north-central United States. Capital, Lansing. Area, 58,216 sq. mi. Pop. (1970), 8,875,083. Abbreviation, **Mich. 2.** Lake. third largest of the Great Lakes. It lies between Michigan and Wisconsin.

mick·le (mik′əl) *Archaic.* much. [Old English *micel.*]

Mic·mac (mik′mak′) *pl.,* **-macs** or **-mac.** *n.* **1.** member of a tribe of North American Indians of the Algonquian language family, living in Newfoundland, Nova Scotia, and New Brunswick. **2.** Algonquian language of this tribe. [Micmac *Migmac* literally, allies.]

mi·cra (mī′krə) a plural of **micron.**

micro- *combining form* **1.** very small; minute: *microorganism.* **2.** enlarging, magnifying, or amplifying: *microscope, microphone.* **3.** (of a science) relying on or using a microscope: *microbiology.* **4.** in systems of measurement, one millionth of a (specified unit): *microfarad.* [Greek *mīkros* small.]

mi·crobe (mī′krōb) *n.* microscopic living thing; microorganism, esp. one that causes disease. [MICRO- + *bios* life.]

mi·cro·bi·ol·o·gy (mī′krō bī ol′ə jē) *n.* branch of biology that studies microorganisms. [MICRO- + BIOLOGY.] —**mi′cro·bi′o·log′i·cal,** *adj.* —**mi′cro·bi·ol′o·gist,** *n.*

mi·cro·coc·cus (mī′krō kok′əs) *pl.,* **-coc·ci** (-kok′sī). *n.* any of several varieties of bacteria that are spherical or egg-shaped. [Modern Latin *micrococcus,* from MICRO- + COCCUS.]

mi·cro·cop·y (mī′krə kop′ē) *pl.,* **-cop·ies.** *n.* reduced photographic copy, as of a manuscript, picture, or letter.

mi·cro·cosm (mī′krə koz′əm) *n.* **1.** a little world; universe in miniature. **2.** anything thought of as being a miniature representation of a large whole: *The small town was a microcosm of all of society.* [French *microcosme,* through Late Latin, going back to Greek *mīkros* small + *kosmos* world.]

mi·cro·ec·o·nom·ics (mī′krō ek′ə nom′iks, -ē′kə-) *n.,pl.* branch of economics concerned with specific aspects of an economy, as the relative prices of a particular commodity. ▲ construed as singular.

mi·cro·far·ad (mī′krə far′əd, -ad) *n.* unit of electrical capacity equal to one-millionth of a farad. [MICRO- + FARAD.]

mi·cro·fiche (mī′krə fēsh′) *n.* plastic sheet containing microfilm on which images of pages of newspapers, books, and other printed matter are reproduced.

mi·cro·film (mī′krə film′) *n.* **1.** photographic film, usually thirty-five or sixteen millimeters wide, on which a newspaper or other printed matter is reproduced in miniature. **2.** reproduction made on such film. —*v.t.* to make a microfilm of.

mi·cro·groove (mī′krə grōōv′, -krō-) *n.* very fine, narrow groove on the surface of a long-playing phonograph record.

mi·cro·me·te·or·ite (mī′krō mē′tē ə rīt′) *n.* tiny meteorite that, because of its size, encounters no air resistance in falling to earth.

mi·crom·e·ter (mī krom′ə tər) *n.* **1.** any of a group of instruments that use a finely threaded screw, the head of which is divided into equal parts forming a scale, to measure very small dimensions, distances, or angles to a high degree of precision. **2.** micrometer caliper. [MICRO- + -METER.]

micrometer caliper, caliper having two jaws, one of which can be moved by turning a screw, used for making precise measurements.

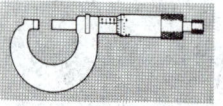

Micrometer caliper

mi·cron (mī′kron) *pl.,* **mi·crons** or **mi·cra** (mī′krə). *n.* unit of length equal to one-millionth of a meter. Symbol: μ. [Greek *mīkron,* neuter of *mīkros* small.]

Mi·cro·ne·sia (mī′krə nē′zhə, -shə) *n.* one of the three major divisions of the Pacific islands, north of Melanesia.

Mi·cro·ne·sian (mī′krə nē′zhən, -shən) *n.* **1.** member or recent descendant of the people living in Micronesia. **2.** subfamily of the Malayo-Polynesian family of languages, consisting of a number of languages, spoken predominantly in Micronesia. —*adj.* of or relating to Micronesia, its people, their languages, or their cultures.

mi·cro·nu·cle·us (mī′krō nōō′klē əs, -nū′-) *n.* the smaller of the two types of nuclei present in various ciliate protozoans, believed to control the process of reproduction.

mi·cro·or·gan·ism (mī′krō ôr′gə niz′əm) *n.* organism, as a virus, that is too small to be seen with the naked eye.

mi·cro·phone (mī′krə fōn′) *n.* device that converts sound waves to an electrical signal, used to record, transmit, or amplify sound. [MICRO- + Greek *phōnē* sound.]

mi·cro·scope (mī′krə skōp′) *n.* instrument with a lens or combination of lenses that give a clear magnified image of a small object viewed through it. [Modern Latin *microscopium,* from MICRO- + -SCOPE.]

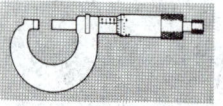

Microscope

mi·cro·scop·ic (mī′krə skop′ik) *adj.* **1.** so small as not to be seen without using a microscope; too small to be visible to the naked eye. **2.** extremely small; minute. **3.** of, relating to, or performed by a microscope: *a microscopic lens.* **4.** resembling, suggestive of, or functioning like a microscope: *a microscopic examination of the evidence.* Also, **mi′cro·scop′i·cal.** —**mi′cro·scop′i·cal·ly,** *adv.*

mi·cros·co·py (mī kros′kə pē, mī′krə skō′pē) *n.* **1.** process or technique of using a microscope. **2.** investigation with a microscope. —**mi·cros′co·pist,** *n.*

mi·cro·spore (mī′krə spôr′) *n. Botany.* small spore that develops into a male gametophyte.

mi·cro·wave (mī′krə wāv′) *n.* high-frequency electromagnetic wave having a wavelength in the range of from about one millimeter to thirty centimeters, used in radar and for such purposes as long-distance transmission of television signals through the air.

mid[1] (mid) *adj.* being at or near the middle: *the mid part of the year.* [Old English *mid* middle.]

mid[2] (mid) *also,* **'mid.** *prep. Archaic.* amid. [Short for AMID.]

mid- *combining form* **1.** middle part of: *mid-January, midbrain.* **2.** being in the middle or center: *midpoint.* [From MID.]

mid·air (mid′âr′) *n.* point or region high above the earth's surface.

Mi·das (mī′dəs) *n. Greek Legend.* a king of Phrygia to whom Dionysus gave the power of turning to gold all that he touched.

mid·brain (mid′brān′) *n.* middle part of the brain.

mid·day (mid′dā′) *n.* middle of the day; noon. —*adj.* of, relating to, or occurring during the middle part of the day: *midday heat.* [Old English *middæg* noon.]

mid·den (mid′ən) *n.* **1.** kitchen midden. **2.** dunghill or refuse heap. [Of Scandinavian origin.]

mid·dle (mid′əl) *adj.* **1.** equally distant from the sides, extremities, or exterior points: *The middle office is his. We sat in the middle row.* **2.** being or occurring halfway between two things, as in time, position, or amount: *the middle child, middle income.* **3.** average; medium: *She is of middle height.* —*n.* **1.** point, part, or area equally distant from the sides, extremities, or exterior points of anything: *He walked down the middle of the street.* **2.** part or portion approximately halfway between the beginning and the end: *We left in the middle of his speech.* **3.** middle part of the body; waist. [Old English *middel* midst, central part.]

middle age, time of life between youth and old age, usually thought of as being between forty and sixty.

mid·dle-aged (mid′əl ājd′) *adj.* **1.** in or of middle age. **2.** of, relating to, or characteristic of middle-aged persons.

Middle Ages, period of European history between the fall of the Western Roman Empire and the beginning of the Renaissance, from about the fifth century to the middle of the fifteenth century.

Middle Atlantic States, region of the eastern United States, usually considered to include New York, New Jersey, Pennsylvania, Delaware, Maryland, and the District of Columbia.

middle C *Music.* **1.** note written on the first ledger line below the treble staff and the first ledger line above the bass staff. **2.** corresponding tone or key.

middle class, part of society occupying an intermediate social and economic position. —**mid′dle-class′,** *adj.*

middle distance, area, as in a painting or photograph, between the foreground and the background. Also, **middle ground.**

Middle Dutch, Dutch language from the twelfth to the sixteenth centuries.

at; āpe; cär; end; mē; it; īce; hot; ōld; fôrk; wood; fōōl; oil; out; up; ūse; turn; sing; thin; this; zh in treasure; ə in ago, taken, pencil, lemon, circus.

middle ear, cavity between the eardrum and the inner ear, containing, in man, the hammer, anvil, and stirrup.

Middle East, region including the United Arab Republic and the Arab countries of southwestern Asia, as well as Israel, Turkey, and Iran, and sometimes including Algeria, Tunisia, Morocco, Libya, and Sudan. Also, **Mid′east′.** —**Middle Eastern.**

Middle English, English language from the twelfth to the sixteenth centuries.

Middle French, French language from the fourteenth to the sixteenth centuries.

Middle Greek, Greek language from the seventh to the fifteenth centuries.

Middle High German, High German from the twelfth to the sixteenth centuries.

Middle Latin, Medieval Latin.

Middle Low German, Low German from the twelfth to the sixteenth centuries.

mid·dle·man (mid′əl man′) *pl.* **-men.** *n.* **1.** one who buys goods directly from the producer and sells them to the retailer or consumer. **2.** any intermediary; go-between.

mid·dle·most (mid′əl mōst′) *adj.* being exactly in or nearest the middle.

mid·dle-of-the-road (mid′əl əv thə rōd′) *adj.* not taking or advocating any extreme position or side, as in matters of religion or politics; moderate. —**mid′dle-of-the-road′er,** *n.*

Mid·dles·brough (mid′əlz brə) *n.* city in northeastern England. Pop. (1968), 393,000.

middle term, term that appears in the major and minor premises of a syllogism but not in the conclusion.

mid·dle·weight (mid′əl wāt′) *n.* **1.** boxer, wrestler, or weight lifter weighing between 147 and 160 pounds. **2.** person or animal of average weight.

Middle West, region of the north-central United States, the major agricultural area of the country. Area, 765,530 sq. mi. Pop. (1965 est.), 54,021,000. Also, **Mid′west′.**

mid·dling (mid′ling) *adj.* medium, as in size, quality, or amount; average; ordinary. —*adv. Informal.* moderately; fairly. —*n. pl.* **middlings. 1.** products that are regarded as being average, as in size, quality, grade, or price. **2.** mixture of bran and coarsely ground particles of wheat, used esp. as a feed for poultry, hogs, and other livestock. [MID¹ + -LING.] —**Syn.** *adj.* see **average.**

mid·dy (mid′ē) *pl.* **-dies.** *n.* **1.** *Informal.* midshipman. **2.** middy blouse.

middy blouse, loosely fitting blouse designed to resemble a sailor's blouse.

Mid·east′ (mid′ēst′) *n.* Middle East.

midge (mij) *n.* **1.** any of various tiny flies that often gather in large swarms in cool, damp areas. Some midges can inflict a painful bite. **2.** very small person. [Old English *mycg(e)* gnatlike insect.]

Middy blouse

midg·et (mij′it) *n.* **1.** very small but well-proportioned person of normal intelligence. **2.** anything that is very small for its kind; dwarf. —*adj.* very small; diminutive. [MIDGE + -ET.]

Mi·di (mē dē′) *n.* the south of France.

Mid·i·an·ite (mid′ē ə nīt′) *n.* in the Old Testament, one of a wandering tribe of Arabs that warred with the Israelites.

mid·land (mid′lənd) *n.* central or interior part of a region or country. —*adj.* of, relating to, or situated in the midland.

Mid·land (mid′lənd) *n.* city in western Texas. Pop. (1970), 59,463.

mid·most (mid′mōst′) *adj.* being exactly in, or nearest the middle; middlemost. —*adv.* in the middle or midst.

mid·night (mid′nīt′) *n.* twelve o'clock at night; the middle of the night. —*adj.* **1.** of, relating to, or occurring at midnight: *a midnight train.* **2.** resembling midnight; very dark. **3. to burn the midnight oil,** to study or work late into the night.

midnight sun, sun seen at midnight during summer in the arctic and antarctic regions.

mid·point (mid′point′) *n.* point that is exactly in the middle of something, as a line.

mid·rib (mid′rib′) *n. Botany.* central vein of a leaf.

mid·riff (mid′rif′) *n.* **1.** that part of the body below the breast and above the waist. **2.** that part of a woman's garment that covers this part of the body. **3.** woman's blouse or blouselike garment that exposes this part of the body. **4.** diaphragm *(def. 1).* [Old English *midhrif,* from *midd* middle + *hrif* belly.]

mid·ship (mid′ship′) *adj.* of, relating to, or situated in or near the middle of a ship.

mid·ship·man (mid′ship′mən) *pl.* **-men.** *n.* **1.** in the U.S. Navy, a student in training at the U.S. Naval Academy for commission as an officer. **2.** *British.* second-year student in training on board ship for

commission as an officer. [MIDSHIP + MAN; with reference to the earlier stationing of cadets in the British Navy *amidships* when on duty.]

mid·ships (mid′ships′) *adv.* amidships.

midst¹ (midst) *n.* **1.** condition or position of being surrounded by, involved in, or beset by. ▲ used chiefly in the phrase *in the midst of.* **2.** gathering or association of people; company: *There is a traitor in our midst.* **3.** central or interior part: *Someone shouted in the midst of his speech.* [Partly from MID¹ + -EST; partly from Middle English *middes* middle, going back to Old English *(on) middan* (in) the middle.]

midst² (midst) *also,* **'midst.** *prep.* amid; amidst. [Form of AMIDST.]

mid·sum·mer (mid′sum′ər) *n.* **1.** middle of summer. **2.** the summer solstice, occurring about June 21. —*adj.* of, relating to, or occurring in the middle of summer.

mid·term (mid′turm′) *n.* **1.** middle of a school term or semester. **2.** examination taken during the middle of a school term or semester. —*adj.* taking place during the middle of a school term or semester.

mid·town (mid′toun′) *n.* central part of a city or town. —*adj.* relating to or located in midtown.

mid·Vic·to·ri·an (mid′vik tôr′ē ən) *adj.* **1.** of or relating to the middle period of Queen Victoria's reign in Great Britain, from about 1850 to 1880. **2.** relating to, resembling, or characteristic of the culture, fashions, ideas, and rigid moral and social standards of this period. —*n.* **1.** one who is prudish or old-fashioned, as in thinking or matters of morality. **2.** one who lived during the mid-Victorian period.

mid·way (mid′wā′) *adv., adj.* in or to the middle of the way or distance; halfway. —*n.* place where side shows and other amusements are located, as at a carnival, circus, or fair.

Midway Islands, small island group in the north-central Pacific, administered by the United States. Pop. (1960), 2356.

mid·week (mid′wēk′) *n.* **1.** middle of the week. **2. Midweek.** among the Quakers, Wednesday.

Mid·west (mid′west′) *n.* Middle West. —**Mid′west′ern,** *adj.* —**Mid′west′ern·er,** *n.*

mid·wife (mid′wīf′) *pl.* **-wives.** *n.* woman who assists women in childbirth. [Middle English *midwif,* from Old English *mid* with + *wif* woman.]

mid·wife·ry (mid′wī′fər ē, -wīf′rē) *n.* the assisting of women in childbirth.

mid·win·ter (mid′win′tər) *n.* **1.** middle of winter. **2.** the winter solstice, occurring around December 22. —*adj.* of, relating to, or occurring in the middle of winter.

mid·year (mid′yēr′) *n.* **1.** middle of the year. **2.** examination taken during the middle of a school year. —*adj.* taking place during the middle of a school or calendar year.

mien (mēn) *n.* person's manner or appearance, esp. as expressive of character or mood; bearing. [Modification (influenced by French *mine* appearance, look) of obsolete *demean* behavior, from DEMEAN².]

miff (mif) *v.t. Informal.* to cause to be offended or annoyed. [Of uncertain origin.]

MIG (mig) *also,* **Mig.** *n.* any of various jet fighters designed and built by the Soviet Union. [From *Mi(koyan)* and *G(urevich),* Soviet designers of airplanes.]

might¹ (mīt) past tense of **may.**

might² (mīt) *n.* **1.** great power, force, or influence: *the might of nations.* **2.** physical power or strength: *He slammed the door with all his might.* **3.** power or ability to do or accomplish something: *She tried with all her might not to cry.* [Old English *miht* power.]

might·i·ly (mī′tə lē) *adv.* **1.** with great force, power, or strength. **2.** to a great degree; very much; greatly.

might·y (mī′tē) **might·i·er, might·i·est.** *adj.* **1.** having or showing great power, strength, or ability: *a mighty foe.* **2.** very great in amount, degree, intensity, or extent: *a mighty task.* —*adv. Informal.* very; greatly: *It was mighty nice of them to call.* —**might′i·ness,** *n.*

mi·gnon (min yon′, min′yon) *adj.* delicately small and pretty. [French *mignon;* of uncertain origin.]

mi·gnon·ette (min′yə net′) *n.* any of various erect or trailing plants, genus *Reseda,* most of which are found in the Mediterranean region, bearing narrow spoon-shaped leaves and tiny yellowish-white or greenish-yellow flowers in long spikes or clusters. [French *mignonette* type of flower, diminutive of *mignon* delicate, pretty. See MIGNON.]

mi·graine (mī′grān) *n.* severe headache, usually affecting only one side of the head and tending to recur periodically. [Old French *migraine,* from Late Latin *hēmicrānia* pain on one side of the head, from Greek *hēmikrāniā,* from *hēmi* half + *kranion* skull.]

mi·grant (mī′grənt) *n.* one who or that which migrates. —*adj.* migrating; migratory: *a migrant worker.*

mi·grate (mī′grāt) **-grat·ed, -grat·ing.** *v.i.* **1.** to move from one country or region to another in order to settle there. **2.** to move seasonally or periodically from one region or climate to another, as certain birds, mammals, and fish. [Latin *migrātus,* past participle of *migrāre* to move from one place to another.]

---

mi·gra·tion (mī grā′shən) n. **1.** act or instance of migrating. **2.** group, as of people, animals, or fish, that migrate together. **3.** *Physics.* movement of particles from one place to another.

mi·gra·to·ry (mī′grə tôr′ē) adj. **1.** characterized by or given to migration; migrating: *migratory birds.* **2.** of or relating to migration. **3.** nomadic; wandering; roving.

mi·ka·do (mi kä′dō) pl. **-dos.** also, **Mi·ka·do.** n. **1.** emperor of Japan. [Japanese *mikado* literally, exalted gate, from *mi* exalted + *kado* gate.]

mike (mīk) n. *Informal.* microphone.

mil (mil) n. unit of length equal to one-thousandth of an inch, used in measuring the diameter of wires. [Short for Latin *millēsimus* thousandth, from *mille* thousand.]

mil. 1. military. **2.** mileage. **3.** militia.

mi·la·dy (mi lā′dē) also, **mi·la·di.** n. **1.** my lady. ▲ title of respect used in speaking or referring to an English gentlewoman or noblewoman. **2.** fashionable, well-dressed woman: *styles designed especially for milady.*

Mi·lan (mi lan′) n. city in northern Italy, the leading commercial and industrial center of the country. Pop. (1968), 1,687,264.

Mil·a·nese (mil′ə nēz′, -nēs′) adj. of or relating to Milan, its people, or their culture. —n. pl. **-nese.** native or inhabitant of Milan.

milch (milch) adj. (of a cow) giving milk. [Old English *-milce;* used in *thrimilce* month of May; literally, (month of) milking three times (a day).]

mild (mīld) adj. **1.** not extreme, harsh, or severe, as in intensity, degree, or effect; moderate: *a mild winter, a mild headache.* **2.** not sharp, strong, or bitter in taste or odor: *a mild cheese.* **3.** gentle or kind in disposition, manners, or behavior. [Old English *milde* kind, gentle.] —**mild′ly,** adv. —**mild′ness,** n. —Syn. **1.** see gentle.

mil·dew (mil′dōō, -dū′) n. **1.** any of various parasitic fungi that attack crop plants, appearing as a fine powder or fuzzy down and causing dwarfing, deformation, and loss of the affected parts of the plant. **2.** any of various fungi that appear as discolored areas on leather or other materials. —v.t., v.i. to affect or be affected with mildew. [Old English *meledēaw* honeydew; probably referring to the resemblance of certain blights to sticky honey.]

mile (mīl) n. unit of linear measure equal to 5280 feet or 1760 yards. Also, **statute mile.** See **weights and measures** for table. [Old English *mīl,* from Latin *mīlia (passuum),* plural of *mīlle (passuum)* Roman unit of measure; literally, one thousand (paces).]

mile·age (mī′lij) also, **mil·age.** n. **1.** total number of miles covered or traveled in a specified period of time: *We put a lot of mileage on the car during our vacation.* **2.** number of miles traveled, as by an automobile, on a certain amount of fuel. **3.** total length, extent, or distance, given or measured in miles. **4.** amount of use, service, or wear yielded by something, estimated according to miles traveled or used: *to get good mileage on a set of tires.* **5.** allowance for traveling expenses, estimated at a certain rate per mile. **6.** rate charged per mile, as for the use of a rented car. **7.** *Informal.* present or potential value or usefulness.

mile·post (mīl′pōst′) n. post set up, as on a highway, to mark the distance in miles to or from a specified place.

mile·stone (mīl′stōn′) n. **1.** stone set up, as on a highway, to mark the distance in miles to or from a certain place. **2.** important or significant event or development.

Mi·le·tus (mī lē′təs) n. ancient Greek city.

mil·foil (mil′foil′) n. yarrow. [Old French *milfoil,* from Latin *mīllefolium,* from *mīlle* thousand + *folium* leaf; referring to the many sections of its leaf.]

mi·lieu (mil yoo′, -yōō′, mēl-) n. surroundings or environment. [French *milieu* midst, environment; literally, middle place, going back to Latin *medius* middle + *locus* place.]

mil·i·tant (mil′ə tənt) adj. **1.** having or exhibiting a warlike or aggressive nature or tendency. **2.** engaged in war or fighting. —n. militant person. [Latin *mīlitāns,* present participle of *mīlitāre* to serve as a soldier, from *mīles* soldier.] —**mil′i·tan·cy,** n. —**mil′i·tant·ly,** adv.

mil·i·ta·rism (mil′ə tə riz′əm) n. **1.** glorification of war and the military class and its ideals and policies. **2.** national policy that emphasizes the power, influence, and predominance of the military. —**mil′i·ta·rist,** n. —**mil′i·ta·ris′tic,** adj.

mil·i·ta·rize (mil′ə tə rīz′) **-rized, -riz·ing.** v.t. **1.** to change to a military system or adapt for military use. **2.** to train and equip for war. **3.** to imbue with militarism. —**mil′i·ta·ri·za′tion,** n.

mil·i·tar·y (mil′ə ter′ē) adj. **1.** of, relating to, or involving armed forces, soldiers, or war: *military career.* **2.** composed of or for members of the armed forces: *a military uniform, a military unit.* —n. **1.** all the military forces of a country, taken as a whole. **2.** members of the military collectively, esp. officers. [Latin *mīlitāris* relating to a soldier or to war, from *mīles* soldier.] —**mil′i·tar′i·ly,** adv.

military police, members of the army assigned to police duties.

mil·i·tate (mil′ə tāt′) **-tat·ed, -tat·ing.** v.i. to act, operate, or have influence (often with *against*): *This testimony will militate against his*

acquittal. [Latin *mīlitātus,* past participle of *mīlitāre* to serve as a soldier, from *mīles* soldier.]

mi·li·tia (mi lish′ə) n. nonprofessional military force, as the National Guard, called for service in time of emergency. [Latin *mīlitia* troops, warfare, from *mīles* soldier.]

mi·li·tia·man (mi lish′ə mən) pl. **-men.** n. member of a militia.

milk (milk) n. **1.a.** white liquid secreted by the mammary glands of female mammals for the nourishment of their young. **b.** this liquid, esp. as secreted by cows, used as food by human beings. **2.** any liquid resembling this: *coconut milk.* —v.t. **1.** to draw milk from (a cow, goat, or other female mammal). **2.** to extract juice, poison, or other liquid from, by or as by milking: *to milk a snake.* **3.** to take advantage of for one's own benefit; exploit. **4.** to extract or take (something), as by milking: *to milk information from someone.* —v.i. **1.** to draw milk from a cow, goat, or other female mammal. **2.** to give or yield milk. [Old English *meolc* white liquid secreted by female mammals.]

milk·er (mil′kər) n. **1.** one who milks. **2.** machine that milks cows. **3.** cow or other animal that gives milk.

milk·ing (mil′king) n. **1.** act of one who draws milk from an animal, esp. a cow. **2.** amount of milk obtained at one time.

milk·maid (milk′mād′) n. woman or girl who milks cows or works in a dairy.

milk·man (milk′man′) pl. **-men.** n. man who sells or delivers milk.

milk of magnesia, milky white mixture of magnesium hydroxide in water, used as an antacid and laxative.

milk shake, frothy, cold drink made of milk, flavoring, and sometimes ice cream, shaken or whipped together.

milk snake, any of several yellowish-brown or pale-gray king snakes marked with red or reddish-brown blotches. It is harmless to man and feeds chiefly on other snakes and rodents, as mice or rats.

milk·sop (milk′sop′) n. unmanly or cowardly man or boy; sissy.

milk sugar, lactose.

milk tooth, in mammals, one of the temporary teeth that fall out and are replaced by permanent teeth.

milk·weed (milk′wēd′) n. any of a large group of plants, genus *Asclepias,* containing a milky juice and bearing large leaves and long, green pods containing many seeds.

milk-white (milk′hwīt′, -wīt′) adj. having the white or bluish-white color of milk.

milk·y (mil′kē) **milk·i·er, milk·i·est.** adj. **1.** resembling milk, esp. in color. **2.** containing or yielding milk or a milklike substance. **3.** insipid or timid. —**milk′i·ness,** n.

Milkweed

Milky Way, galaxy made up of more than 100 billion stars, appearing as a bright white path across the heavens. Also, **Gal′a·xy.**

mill¹ (mil) n. **1.a.** building or establishment containing machinery for grinding or crushing grain: *flour mill, corn mill.* **b.** machine or apparatus that grinds or crushes grain. **2.** any of various machines or devices for grinding or crushing substances: *a pepper mill, a coffee mill.* **3.** building or group of buildings containing machinery for manufacturing or processing materials: *a paper mill.* **4.** milling machine. **5.** establishment or process that operates in a routine or mechanical manner: *This school is a diploma mill.* **6.** through the mill. through a difficult and trying experience or period. —v.t. **1.** to subject to the mechanical operations performed by a mill, as grinding, stamping, pressing, or polishing. **2.a.** to stamp or cut a series of notches or ridges around the edge of (a coin or other piece of metal). **b.** to make a raised edge around (a coin or other piece of metal). —v.i. to move in an aimless or confused manner: *The crowd milled around after the game was over.* [Old English *myln* building containing machinery for grinding grain, going back to Latin *molīna* building containing millstones for grinding grain, from *mola* millstone.]

mill² (mil) n. unit of monetary value, equal to ¹/₁₀ of a cent. [Short for Latin *millēsimus* thousandth, from *mille* thousand.]

Mill, John Stuart (mil) 1806–73, English philosopher and economist.

Mil·lay, Edna St. Vincent (mi lā′) 1892–1950, U.S. poet.

mill·dam (mil′dam′) n. **1.** dam built across a stream to raise the water level sufficiently to supply water power for a mill. **2.** millpond.

mil·len·ni·al (mi len′ē əl) adj. **1.** of or relating to a thousand years. **2.** of, relating to, or suggestive of the millennium.

mil·len·ni·um (mi len′ē əm) pl. **mil·len·ni·ums** or **mil·len·ni·a** (mi len′ē ə) n. **1.** period of a thousand years. **2.** according to the New Testament, the period of a thousand years during which Christ will reign on earth. **3.** period of happiness, peace, and prosperity. [Modern Latin *millennium* period of a thousand years, from Latin *mīlle* thousand + *annus* year.]

at; āpe; cär; end; mē; it; īce; hot; ōld; fôrk; wood; fōōl; oil; out; up; ūse; turn; sing; thin; this; zh in treasure; ə in ago, taken, pencil, lemon, circus.

mil·le·pede (mil′ə pēd′) *also,* **mil·le·ped.** millipede.

mil·le·pore (mil′ə pôr′) *n.* any of a group of pink or yellow branching corals, genus *Millipora*, found in tropical reefs. [Modern Latin *Millepora*, from Latin *mille* thousand + *porus* pore¹; with reference to its many pores. See PORE¹.]

mill·er (mil′ər) *n.* **1.** one who owns or operates a mill, esp. one for grinding grain. **2.** any white or grayish moth whose wings look as if they were powdered with flour.

mill·er's-thumb (mil′ərz thum′) *n.* sculpin.

mil·les·i·mal (mi les′ə məl) *adj.* **1.** thousandth. **2.** of, relating to, or consisting of a thousandth. —*n.* a thousandth. [Latin *millēsimus* thousandth (from *mille* thousand) + -AL¹.]

mil·let (mil′it) *n.* **1.** any of several wheatlike grasses widely cultivated for their small, edible grains or as a forage crop, as **bread millet,** *Panicum miliaceum,* and **foxtail millet,** *Setaria italica.* **2.** small grain of any of these grasses. [Old French *millet,* diminutive of *mil,* from Latin *milium.*]

Mil·let, Jean Fran·çois (mi lā′; zhäN fräN swä′) 1814–75, French painter and etcher.

milli- *combining form* one-thousandth of (a specified unit): *milligram.* [Latin *mille* thousand.]

mil·li·am·pere (mil′ē am′pēr) *n.* one-thousandth of an ampere.

mil·liard (mil′yərd, -yärd′) *n. British.* a thousand millions; billion. [French *milliard,* from MILLION.]

Millet grain

mil·li·bar (mil′ə bär′) *n.* unit for measuring atmospheric pressure, equal to 1000 dynes per square centimeter.

mil·li·gram (mil′ə gram′) *also, British.* **mil·li·gramme.** *n.* metric unit of weight, equal to one-thousandth of a gram.

Mil·li·kan, Robert A. (mil′ə kən) 1868–1953, U.S. physicist.

mil·li·li·ter (mil′ə lē′tər) *also, British,* **mil·li·li·tre.** *n.* metric measure of capacity, equal to one-thousandth of a liter, 1.000027 cubic centimeters, or .061 cubic inch.

mil·li·me·ter (mil′ə mē′tər) *also, British,* **mil·li·me·tre.** *n.* metric measure of length, equal to one-thousandth of a meter, or .03937 inch.

mil·li·ner (mil′ə nər) *n.* one who designs, makes, trims, or sells women's hats. [Earlier *milaner* dealer in fancy wares, from *Milan,* Italian city famous for its fabrics, hats, gloves, and similar articles.]

mil·li·ner·y (mil′ə ner′ē, -nər ē) *n.* **1.** articles, esp. hats, sold by a milliner. **2.** business of a milliner.

mill·ing (mil′ing) *n.* **1.** act or process of subjecting to the mechanical operations performed by a mill. **2.a.** process of stamping or cutting notches or ridges around the edge of a piece of metal, as a coin. **b.** notches or ridges so produced.

milling machine, any of various machines that process materials by repeated simple operations, as stamping, pressing, or shaping.

mil·lion (mil′yən) *n.* **1.** the cardinal number that is one thousand times one thousand. **2.** symbol representing this number, 1,000,000. **3.** a million monetary units, or dollars: *He is worth three million.* **4.** indefinitely large number: *She has millions of hats.* —*adj.* numbering one million. [Old French *million* one thousand times one thousand, through Italian, from Latin *mille* thousand.]

mil·lion·aire (mil′yə nâr′) *n.* one who has a million or more units of a particular currency, as of dollars: *He was a millionaire by the time he was thirty.* [French *millionnaire* one who has more than a million francs, from *million.* See MILLION.]

mil·lionth (mil′yənth) *adj.* **1.** (the ordinal of million) being last in a series of one million. **2.** being one of a million equal parts. —*n.* **1.** that which is last in a series of one million. **2.** one of a million equal parts.

mil·li·pede (mil′ə pēd′) *also,* **mil·le·pede, mil·li·ped, mil·le·ped.** *n.* any of a group of wormlike arthropods, class Diplopoda, having as many as one hundred legs and feeding chiefly on decaying plant matter. [Latin *millepeda* wood louse; literally, thousand feet, from *mille* thousand + *ped-,* stem of *pēs* foot.]

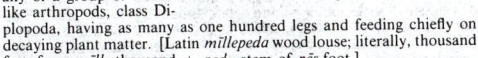

Millipede

mill·pond (mil′pond′) *n.* pond, usually formed by a dam, for supplying water power to a mill.

mill·race (mil′rās′) *n.* **1.** current of water leading into and driving a mill wheel. **2.** channel through which such a current runs.

mill·stone (mil′stōn′) *n.* **1.** either of a pair of circular stones between which grain or similar substances are placed for grinding. **2.** heavy burden: *a millstone of debt.*

mill·stream (mil′strēm′) *n.* **1.** stream whose water is used to run a mill. **2.** water in a millrace.

mill wheel, large wheel, usually turned by the force of falling water, that supplies mechanical power to run the machinery of a mill.

mill·work (mil′wurk′) *n.* **1.** ready-made products, esp. woodwork, finished or processed in a mill. **2.** work done in a mill.

mill·wright (mil′rīt′) *n.* one who designs or builds mills or installs and repairs machinery for mills.

mi·lord (mi lôrd′) *n.* my lord. ▲ title of respect used in speaking or referring to an English gentleman or nobleman.

milque·toast (milk′tōst′) *n.* weak, timid, apologetic person. [From Caspar *Milquetoast,* U.S. comic-strip character.]

milt (milt) *n.* in male fish, the sperm cells and the milky fluid containing them. [Probably from Middle Dutch *milte* milt of fish, spleen.]

Mil·ti·a·des (mil tī′ə dēz′) c.550–c.489 B.C., Athenian general who defeated the Persians at Marathon.

Mil·ton, John (milt′ən) 1608–74, English poet.

Mil·ton·ic (mil ton′ik) *adj.* **1.** of or relating to John Milton or his works. **2.** characteristic of Milton's literary style; lofty and majestic. Also, **Mil·to·ni·an** (mil tō′nē ən).

Mil·wau·kee (mil wô′kē) *n.* city in southeastern Wisconsin, on Lake Michigan. Pop. (1970), 717,099.

mime (mīm) *n.* **1.** performer who portrays characters or conveys an idea or story by body movements, facial expressions, and gestures rather than by the use of speech. **2.** art of pantomime. **3.a.** farcical drama popular among the ancient Greeks and Romans, in which actual persons and events were mimicked or ludicrously portrayed. **b.** actor in such a drama. **5.** *Archaic.* jester; buffoon. —*v.t.* **1.** **mimed, mim·ing.** to act out in mime; portray by pantomime. —*v.i.* to act or perform as a mime. [Latin *mīmus* actor, farce, from Greek *mīmos* imitator, actor, farce.] —**mim′er,** *n.*

mim·e·o·graph (mim′ē ə graf′) *n.* **1.** machine for printing copies of material written, typed, or drawn on a stencil. Trademark: Mimeograph. **2.** copy made by such a machine. —*v.t.* to make a copy on a mimeograph: *to mimeograph a financial report.* [Greek *mīmeisthai* to imitate + -GRAPH.]

mi·met·ic (mi met′ik, mī-) *adj.* **1.** relating to, characterized by, or exhibiting mimicry: *a mimetic portrayal, the mimetic coloration of certain insects.* **2.** make-believe; mimic. [Greek *mīmētikos* imitative, from *mīmeisthai* to imitate.]

mim·ic (mim′ik) *-icked, -ick·ing.* *v.t.* **1.** to imitate the speech, manners, or gestures of, esp. so as to ridicule. **2.** to copy closely or reproduce: *He could mimic the painter's style but never truly capture it.* **3.** to resemble closely, as in form or color; simulate: *The insect mimicked a dead twig.* —*n.* **1.** one who mimics; copy, a performer skilled in mime. **2.** something that is a copy; imitation. —*adj.* **1.** of the nature of or characterized by mimicry; imitative. **2.** make-believe; pretended; mock: *mimic rivalry.* [Latin *mimicus* farcical, from Greek *mīmikos* imitative, relating to farce, from *mīmos* actor, imitator, farce.] —**Syn.** *v.t.* **2.** see **imitate.**

mim·ic·ry (mim′ik rē) *pl.,* **-ries.** *n.* **1.** act, practice, art, or instance of mimicking. **2.** close external resemblance of one kind of animal to another or to an object in its natural environment for purposes of protection or concealment.

Mimosa

mi·mo·sa (mi mō′sə, -zə) *n.* any of a large group of plants, genus *Mimosa,* of the pea family, found esp. in tropical America, bearing fernlike leaves and dense heads or spikes of small white, pink, or purple flowers. [Modern Latin *Mimosa,* going back to Greek *mīmos* imitator, actor, farce; because in folding its leaves when touched, the mimosa mimics the reactions of animals.]

min. **1.** minute; minutes. **2.** minimum. **3.** mineralogical; mineralogy. **4.** mining.

mi·na¹ (mī′nə) *pl.,* **mi·nae** (mī′nē) or **mi·nas.** *n.* ancient unit of weight and money of varying amount and value. [Latin *mina* Greek unit of weight or money, from Greek *mnā;* of Semitic origin.]

mi·na² (mī′nə) *n.* myna.

mi·na·cious (mi nā′shəs) *adj.* menacing; threatening. [Latin *mināc-,* stem of *mināx* threatening + -OUS.]

min·a·ret (min′ə ret′) *n.* tall, slender tower attached to a mosque and having one or more projecting balconies. [Spanish *minarete,* from Arabic *manārat.*]

min·a·to·ry (min′ə tôr′ē) *adj.* expressing or uttering a threat; menacing. Also, **min′a·to′ri·al.** [Late Latin *minātōrius,* from Latin *minārī* to threaten.]

Minaret

mince (mins) *minced, minc-ing. v.t.* **1.** to cut or chop into very small, fine pieces: *to mince an onion.* **2.** to utter, express, or speak of in an indirect, restrained manner, esp. for the sake of politeness or decorum: *to mince words.* **3.** to utter or express with affected elegance, politeness, or refinement. —*v.i.* **1.** to walk with very short steps or affected daintiness. **2.** to act or speak with affected elegance, politeness, or refinement. —*n.* mincemeat. [Old French *mincier* to cut into small pieces, going back to Latin *minūtia* smallness.]

mince-meat (mins′mēt′) *n.* **1.** mixture of finely chopped apples, suet, raisins, currants, sugar, spices, and sometimes meat, used for pies. **2. to make mincemeat out of.** to destroy completely.

mince pie, pie made with mincemeat.

minc-ing (min′sing) *adj.* affectedly dainty, refined, or polite, as in speech or manner. —**minc′ing-ly,** *adv.*

mind (mīnd) *n.* **1.** totality of functions associated with or involving the brain and related nerve cells, that deal with the conscious and unconscious processes of thought, perception, memory, imagination, will, and reason. **2.** mind regarded as the source or repository of cognition and the intellectual aspects of consciousness. **3.** intellectual powers or mental ability: intelligence: *the mind of a five-year-old child.* **4.** sound or healthy mental state or condition; sanity. **5.** imagination: *It's all in his mind.* **6.** way of thinking or feeling; disposition: *He has an open mind on most issues.* **7.** what one thinks or feels; opinion or attitude: *She's a girl who knows her own mind.* **8.** memory; remembrance: *I'll keep it in mind for future reference.* **9.** attention: *I can't keep my mind on what I'm doing.* **10.** inclination, desire, intention, or wish: *I have a mind to visit them next week.* **11.** person regarded as having a highly developed intellect: *He is one of the great minds of the century.* **a piece of one's mind. a.** severe rebuke. **b.** one's harsh opinion. **on one's mind.** occupying one's thoughts, so as to be troublesome or worrisome: *She's always on his mind.* **to be of one mind.** to be in agreement. **to be of two minds.** to be undecided or uncertain. **to call to mind.** to serve as a reminder of. **to have a good mind.** to feel strongly inclined (to do something): *I have a good mind to go see her right now.* **to have in mind. a.** to be thinking of or about. **b.** to intend; plan: *What do you have in mind for us to do?* **to make up one's mind.** to come to a conclusion or judgment. **to slip one's mind.** to be forgotten. —*v.t.* **1.** to pay attention to; be concerned or careful about: *to mind one's manners. Don't mind what he says, he's just upset.* **2.** to take care of; look after; tend: *The babysitter will mind the children while I go shopping.* **3.** to obey: *The children always mind their mother.* **4.** to object to: *She doesn't mind eating alone.* **5.** to look or watch out for: *Mind the broken chair.* **6.** to be aware of; notice; perceive. **7.** *Archaic.* to remember. **8.** *Archaic.* to remind. —*v.i.* **1.** to object or care: *Do you mind if I call you later?* **2.** to pay attention; give heed: *Mind you, I'm not disputing what you say.* **3.** to be obedient: *My dog minds well.* **4.** to be careful or wary: *If you don't mind, you'll fall.* **5. never mind.** it is of no importance; disregard or forget it. [Old English *gemynd* memory, thought.]

Min-da-na-o (min′də nä′ō, -nou′) *n.* second-largest island of the Philippines. Area, 37,000 sq. mi. Pop. (1963 est.), 6,000,000.

mind-ed (mīn′did) *adj.* **1.** inclined; disposed: *Make those revisions if you are so minded.* **2.** having or marked by a (specified kind of) mind. ▲ used in combination, as in *open-minded, narrow-minded.*

mind-ful (mīnd′fəl) *adj.* conscious, aware, or careful (with *of*): *to be mindful of the risks involved.* —**mind′ful-ly,** *adv.* —**mind′ful-ness,** *n.*

mind-less (mīnd′lis) *adj.* **1.** lacking intelligence; stupid or foolish: *a mindless person.* **2.** without thought; heedless (with *of*): *He acted mindless of his responsibility.* —**mind′less-ly,** *adv.*

Min-do-ro (min dôr′ō) *n.* large island in the Philippines. Area, 3759 sq. mi. (1965 est.), 371,000 (including nearby islands).

mind reader, person who professes to have or is thought to have the ability to know or perceive the thoughts of others without normal or apparent communication.

mind's eye, imagination: *I can see it in my mind's eye.*

mine[1] (mīn) *pron.* **1.** belonging to me: *The red coat is mine.* **2.** the one or ones belonging to me: *Her daughter is three years old and mine is four.* **3. of mine.** belonging or relating to me: *a friend of mine.* —*adj. Archaic.* my. ▲ used before a word beginning with a vowel or *h,* or after a noun: *mine eyes, mine heart, mother mine.* [Old English *mīn* my, of me.]

mine[2] (mīn) *n.* **1.a.** large subterranean excavation from which coal, mineral ores, or other materials are extracted. **b.** site of such an excavation, including the buildings and equipment. **2.** deposit of coal, mineral ore, or other material that may be extracted from the earth. **3.** any abundant source or supply: *a mine of information.* **4.** encased explosive charge placed underground or in water and designed to be detonated, used to destroy enemy personnel or equipment. **5.** formerly,

tunnel beneath the walls of an enemy fortification, as for the placement of explosives. —*v.t.* *mined, min-ing.* **1.** to extract from the earth: *to mine coal.* **2.** to excavate (the earth), as for coal or mineral ores. **3.** to make by digging, as a tunnel. **4.** to place explosive mines in or under: *The enemy mined the harbor.* **5.** to dig a tunnel beneath the surface of, as for the placement of explosives. **6.** to attack, weaken, or destroy by gradual or secret means; undermine. **7.** to make use of in order to obtain something: *to mine a book for information.* —*v.i.* **1.** to excavate the earth, as for coal or precious stones; dig: *to mine for coal.* **2.** to work in a mine. **3.** to dig a tunnel or tunnels, as for the placement of explosives: *The enemy mined under the wall.* **4.** to place explosive mines underground or in water. [Old French *miner* to dig under, excavate, undermine; of Celtic origin.]

mine detector, electromagnetic device used for locating the position of explosive mines.

mine field, area in which explosive mines have been laid.

mine layer, ship equipped to place explosive mines in the water.

min-er (mī′nər) *n.* one who mines, esp. one whose occupation is excavating the earth for coal or other materials.

min-er-al (min′ər əl) *n.* **1.** any of various inorganic substances that occur in nature, having a characteristic chemical composition capable of being expressed by a chemical formula and found as individual crystals or distributed in rock. **2.** *Mining.* substance obtained by excavating the earth; ore. —*adj.* **1.** of, relating to, consisting of, or of the nature of a mineral or minerals: *mineral deposit, mineral ores.* **2.** impregnated with minerals. [Old French *mineral* substance that contains a metal, from *miniere* mind of metals, from *miner.* See MINE[2].]

min-er-al-ize (min′ər ə līz′) *-ized, -iz-ing. v.t.* **1.** to convert or transform (a metal or other substance) into a mineral. **2.** to impregnate or supply with minerals. —**min′er-al-i-za′tion,** *n.*

min-er-al-o-gist (min′ə rol′ə jist, -ral′-) *n.* one who is a specialist or expert in mineralogy.

min-er-al-o-gy (min′ə rol′ə jē, -ral′-) *n.* science or study of minerals, esp. with regard to their origin, structure, characteristics, and classification. —**min-er-a-log-i-cal** (min′ər ə loj′i kəl) *adj.* —**min′er-a-log′i-cal-ly,** *adv.*

mineral oil, any of a group of colorless, nearly odorless, and tasteless oils obtained as a by-product of petroleum refining, often used as a laxative.

mineral spring, spring that contains natural mineral water.

mineral water, water containing dissolved mineral salts and gases, used as a beverage and for medicinal purposes, esp. bathing.

mineral wool, fibrous material resembling wool, made by forcing air or steam through molten rock, glass, or slag, often used for thermal insulation and soundproofing in building construction.

Mi-ner-va (mi nûr′və) *n.* Roman goddess of wisdom, arts, crafts, and warfare. Her Greek counterpart is Athena.

min-e-stro-ne (min′ə strō′nē) *n.* thick soup containing vegetables, vermicelli, barley, and seasonings in a chicken or meat broth. [Italian *minestrone,* from *minestra* soup; literally, something served, going back to Latin *ministrāre* to serve.]

mine sweeper, ship or device used to detect, remove, or destroy marine mines.

Ming (ming) *n.* Chinese dynasty that ruled from 1368 to 1644, a period noted for artistic achievement, esp. in the making of porcelains. —*adj.* of or relating to this dynasty or the art of this period.

min-gle (ming′gəl) *-gled, -gling. v.i.* **1.** to be or become mixed or joined together. **2.** to associate, join in, or come into contact (often with *with*): *to mingle with the other guests at a party.* —*v.t.* to mix or join (something) together: *to mingle joy with sadness.* [Middle English *menglen* to join together, going back to Old English *mengan* to mix.]

mini- *combining form* smaller or shorter than usual: *miniskirt.* [Probably short for MINIATURE or MINIMUM.]

min-i-a-ture (min′ē ə chər, min′ə-) *adj.* existing or represented on a small or greatly reduced scale; diminutive: *miniature teacups.* —*n.* **1.** copy or representation on a small or greatly reduced scale: *a miniature of the Eiffel Tower.* **2.a.** painting, usually a portrait, done on a very small scale and in minute detail, as on ivory. **b.** art or technique of doing such paintings. **3.** small, highly detailed drawing or painting in an illuminated manuscript. **4. in miniature.** on a small scale; in a greatly reduced or condensed form. [Italian *miniatura* small picture, illumination of manuscripts, going back to Latin *miniāre* to paint with red lead, from *minium* red lead; referring to the decorating of medieval manuscripts with *minium* and to the small size of the illustrations so done. See MINIUM.]

min-i-a-tur-ize (min′ē ə chə rīz′, min′ə-) *-ized, -iz-ing. v.t.* to make or design in small or greatly reduced size; make very small and compact. —**min′i-a-tur-i-za′tion,** *n.*

min-im (min′im) *n.* **1.** very small liquid measure, equal to ¹⁄₆₀ of a fluid dram, or approximately one drop. **2.** very small or insignificant

portion or thing. **3.** *Music.* half note. [Latin *minimus* smallest, least.]

min·i·mal (min′ə məl) *adj.* of a minimum amount or degree; least possible or smallest; very small. —**min′i·mal·ly,** *adv.*

min·i·mize (min′ə mīz′) -mized, -miz·ing. *v.t.* **1.** to reduce to the smallest or least possible amount or degree; make as small as possible: *Hostility on both sides minimized the chance of reaching an agreement.* **2.** to represent or treat as being of small importance, value, amount, or degree. —**min′i·mi·za′tion, min′i·miz′er,** *n.*

min·i·mum (min′ə məm) *pl.,* -mums or -ma (-mə). *n.* **1.** least possible or smallest amount or degree: *We will need a minimum of one week to drive there.* **2.** lowest point, degree, or number reached or recorded: *The temperature was at its minimum this morning.* —*adj.* least possible; lowest; smallest. [Latin *minimum,* neuter of *minimus* smallest, least.]

minimum wage, lowest hourly wage, fixed by law, that an employer may pay an employee of a specified category.

min·ing (mī′ning) *n.* **1.** act, process, or business of excavating and working mines for coal, ores, gems, or other materials. **2.** act or process of laying explosive mines.

min·ion (min′yən) *n.* **1.** favorite, follower, or dependent, esp. one who acts servile. ▲ often used contemptuously. **2.** subordinate, as of an organization; minor official: *minions of the government.* **3.** *Printing.* 7-point type. [French *mignon* delicate, pretty; of uncertain origin.]

min·i·skirt (min′ē skurt′) *n.* short skirt, usually ending several inches above the knee. [MINI- + SKIRT.]

min·is·ter (min′is tər) *n.* **1.** one who is authorized to perform religious functions in a church, esp. in a Protestant church. **2.** one appointed to head an executive governmental department. **3.** diplomatic agent ranking below an ambassador and acting as his government's chief representative in a foreign country to which an ambassador is not sent. **4.** one who or that which acts as the agent or instrument of another person or thing. —*v.i.* to give aid, care, or attention (often with *to*): *to minister to someone's needs.* —*v.t.* **1.** to administer, apply, or dispose: *to minister a sacrament.* **2.** *Archaic.* to provide; furnish. [Latin *minister* attendant, servant.]

min·is·te·ri·al (min is tēr′ē əl) *adj.* **1.** of, relating to, or characteristic of religion or the ministry. **2.** of, relating to, or characteristic of a minister of state or executive functions of government. **3.** acting as an agent. —**min′is·te′ri·al·ly,** *adv.*

minister plenipotentiary *pl.,* **ministers plenipotentiary.** a plenipotentiary.

min·is·trant (min′is trənt) *adj.* serving as a minister. —*n.* one who ministers. [Latin *ministrāns,* present participle of *ministrāre* to serve.]

min·is·tra·tion (min′is trā′shən) *n.* **1.** act, process, or instance of giving aid. **2.** act of serving as a minister of religion.

min·is·try (min′is trē) *pl.,* -tries. *n.* **1.** profession, duties, functions, or time of service of a minister of religion. **2.** ministers of religion collectively; the clergy. **3.a.** governmental department headed by a minister. **b.** offices or building of such a department. **c.** governmental ministers collectively. **d.** duties, functions, or term of office of a governmental minister. **4.** act of ministering; ministration. [Latin *ministerium* service, office.]

min·i·um (min′ē əm) *n.* red lead. [Latin *minium;* probably of Iberian origin.]

min·i·ver (min′ə vər) *n.* fur, usually white or white mixed with gray or black, formerly used for trimming and lining garments. [Old French *menu vair* literally, small vair, going back to Latin *minūtus* small + *varius* of various colors. See VAIR.]

mink (mingk) *pl.,* **minks** or **mink.** *n.* **1.** weasel-like semiaquatic mammal, genus *Mustela,* native to woodlands near water, having soft, lustrous brown fur. There are two species: the **American mink,** *M. vison,* and the **European mink,** *M. lu-*

Mink

treola. Length: 2½ feet including the tail. **2.** valuable fur of this animal. [Probably from Swedish *mänk* the animal.]

Minn., Minnesota.

Min·ne·ap·o·lis (min′ē ap′ə lis) *n.* largest city in Minnesota, in the southeastern part of the state. Pop. (1970), 434,400.

min·ne·sing·er (min′i sing′ər) *n.* one of a group of poet-musicians of twelfth- to fourteenth-century Germany. [German *Minnesinger,* from *Minne* love + *Singer* singer; because love was the main theme of the poems and songs they composed.]

Min·ne·so·ta (min′ə sō′tə) *n.* state in the north-central United States. Capital, St. Paul. Area, 84,068 sq. mi. Pop. (1970), 3,805,069. Abbreviation, **Minn.** —**Min′ne·so′tan,** *n., adj.*

min·now (min′ō) *n.* **1.** any of a large number of freshwater fish, family Cyprinidae, found in temperate and tropical regions, widely used as bait. Length: to 9 feet. **2.** any very small fish. [Old English *myne* any of various small fish.]

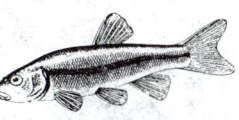

Minnow

Mi·no·an (mi nō′ən) *adj.* of or relating to the civilization of Crete from about 2500 B.C. to about 1100 B.C. —*n.* native or inhabitant of ancient Crete. [MINOS + -AN.]

mi·nor (mī′nər) *adj.* **1.** of small or comparatively small importance or rank: *minor details, one of Shakespeare's minor plays.* **2.** lesser in seriousness, risk, or danger: *minor injuries.* **3.** lesser or limited in extent, size, amount, or degree: *The scientist's inventions were ingenious but of only minor usefulness.* **4.** under legal age. **5.** *Music.* **a.** of or relating to an interval less by a half step than the corresponding major interval. **b.** based on a minor scale. **c.** of or relating to a triad in which the third tone above the fundamental is less by a half step than the corresponding major tone. —*n.* **1.** one who is under legal age. **2.a.** subject or field of study in which a college or university student takes a large number of courses or credits, but not enough to qualify that subject as a major. **b.** student studying a minor: *to be a philosophy minor.* **3.** *Music.* minor scale, key, mode, or interval. **4.** *Sports.* **a.** minor league. **b.** **minors.** minor leagues collectively. —*v.i.* **to minor** in. to take courses in a specified minor: *to minor in English literature.* [Latin *minor* less, smaller.]

Mi·nor·ca (mi nôr′kə) *n.* **1.** second largest of the Balearic Islands. Area, 271 sq. mi. Pop. (1960), 42,955. Also, *Spanish,* **Me·nor′ca.** **2.** one of a breed of black or white domestic fowl.

mi·nor·i·ty (mə nôr′ə tē, -nor′-, mī-) *pl.,* -ties. *n.* **1.** number or group smaller than another number or group with which it makes up a whole; portion constituting less than half of a total. Opposed to **majority.** **2.** racial, religious, political or other group differing in some way from the larger group of which it is a part. **3.** state or period of being under legal age. [Medieval Latin *minoritas* a being less, from Latin *minor* smaller, less.]

minority leader, member of the political party that holds a minority of seats in a legislative body, who organizes the members of his party regarding party tactics and measures to be voted on.

minor league, any league of professional sports clubs, esp. baseball, other than the major leagues.

minor premise, premise in a syllogism whose subject is used as the subject of the conclusion. See **syllogism.**

minor scale, diatonic scale consisting of eight tones. There are three minor scales: the **natural minor scale,** having half steps instead of whole steps after the second and fifth tones in ascending and the sixth and third in descending; the **melodic minor scale,** having half steps after the second and seventh in ascending and the sixth and third in descending; and the **harmonic minor scale,** having half steps after the second, fifth, and seventh in ascending and the eighth, sixth, and third in descending.

minor term, term of a syllogism constituting the subject of the conclusion. See **syllogism.**

Mi·nos (mī′nəs, -nos) *n.* *Greek Mythology.* **1.** king of Crete who became a judge of the dead in Hades. **2.** grandson of Minos and husband of Pasiphaë, who kept the Minotaur in a labyrinth.

Min·o·taur (min′ə tôr′) *n.* *Greek Mythology.* monster, half bull and half man, the offspring of Pasiphaë and a bull. It was confined by Minos in a labyrinth until killed by Theseus. [Latin *Mīnōtaurus,* from Greek *Mīnōtauros,* from *Mīnōs* (see MINOS) + *tauros* bull.]

Minsk (minsk) *n.* capital and largest city of Byelorussia. Pop. (1970), 907,000.

min·ster (min′stər) *n.* **1.** church attached to a monastery. **2.** cathedral or other large or important church, esp. in Great Britain. [Old English *mynster,* going back to Church Latin *monastērium* monastery, from Late Greek *monastērion,* from *monazein* to live alone. Doublet of MONASTERY.]

min·strel (min′strəl) *n.* **1.** in the Middle Ages, a traveling musician who sang or recited poems, usually to the accompaniment of a harp, lute, or similar instrument. **2.** any musician, singer, or lyric poet. **3.** performer in a minstrel show. [Old French *menestrel* entertainer, servant, from Late Latin *ministeriālis* official, servant, from Latin *ministerium* service.]

minstrel show, variety show popular in the United States during the nineteenth and early twentieth centuries, in which performers in blackface presented songs, dances, comic dialogues, and sketches.

min·strel·sy (min′strəl sē) *pl.,* -sies. *n.* **1.** art or occupation of a minstrel. **2.** collection of songs, lyrics, and ballads, as those sung by minstrels. **3.** company or group of minstrels.

mint¹ (mint) *n.* **1.** any of a large number of plants of the mint family,

---

at; āpe; cär; end; mē; it; īce; hot; ōld; fôrk; wood; fōōl; oil; out; up; ūse; turn; sing; thin; this; zh in treasure; ə in ago, taken, pencil, lemon, circus.

esp. those of the genus *Mentha*, as the peppermint or spearmint, used as a flavoring or scent. **2.** piece of candy flavored with mint. —*adj.* designating a family, Labiatae, of widely distributed herbs and shrubs, many of which are cultivated for their flavor or odor, as sage or thyme. [Old English *minte* the plant, going back to Latin *ment(h)a*, from Greek *minthē.*] —**mint′y,** *adj.*

mint² (mint) *n.* **1.** place where money is coined by authority of the government. **2.** very large amount, esp. of money: *Steve spent a mint getting his car repaired.* **3.** place where something is made or created. —*adj.* in its original condition; unused: *a mint stamp.* —*v.t.* **1.** to coin (money). **2.** to create or invent, esp. a phrase or word. [Old English *mynet* coin, from Latin *monēta* place for coining money, coin, from *Monēta,* epithet of Juno, in whose temple money was coined in ancient Rome. Doublet of MONEY.]

mint·age (min′tij) *n.* **1.** act or process of coining money. **2.** money manufactured by a mint. **3.** cost of, or charge for, minting or coining. **4.** impression stamped on a coin.

mint julep, alcoholic beverage usually made with bourbon, sugar, and ice, flavored with mint leaves. Also, **ju′lep.**

min·u·end (min′ū end′) *n.* number from which another is to be subtracted. In the equation 31 − 7 = 24, the minuend is 31. Distinguished from **subtrahend.** [Latin *minuendus* to be made smaller, gerundive of *minuere* to make smaller.]

min·u·et (min′ū et′) *n.* **1.** slow, stately dance for couples, introduced in seventeenth-century France. **2.** music for, or in the rhythm of, this dance. [French *menuet,* diminutive of *menu* small, from Latin *minūtus;* referring to the short steps characteristic of this dance.]

Min·u·it, Peter (min′ū it) c.1580–1638, Dutch colonial administrator in America, who bought Manhattan island from the Indians.

mi·nus (mī′nəs) *prep.* **1.** decreased by; less: *Ten minus seven is three.* **2.** without; lacking. —*adj.* **1.** negative. **2.** somewhat lower than; less than: *a grade of A minus.* —*n.* **1.** minus sign. **2.** negative quantity. **3.** deficiency or loss. [Latin *minus,* neuter of *minor* smaller, less.]

min·us·cule (min′əs kūl′, mi nus′kūl) *adj.* very small; tiny.

minus sign, symbol (−) used to indicate subtraction or a negative quantity.

min·ute¹ (min′it) *n.* **1.** unit of time equal to 1/60 of an hour; sixty seconds. **2.** short period of time; moment: *This phone call will just take a minute.* **3.** specific point in time: *I recognized Linda the minute she entered the room.* **4.** measure of distance in terms of the time needed to cover it: *The park is only a few minutes from my house.* **5. minutes.** official record of proceedings at a meeting or conference. **6.** unit of angular measurement equal to 1/60 of a degree. **7. up to the minute.** the very latest. [Old French *minute* 1/60 of an hour, short time, from Medieval Latin *minuta* 1/60 of an hour, 1/60 of a degree, going back to Latin *minūtus* small.]

mi·nute² (mī nōōt′, -nūt′, mi-) *adj.* **1.** very small; tiny: *minute grains of salt.* **2.** of small importance; trifling: *minute details.* **3.** characterized by close attention to details: *a minute examination.* [Latin *minūtus* small.] —**mi·nute′ness,** *n.*

minute hand (min′it) long hand of a clock or watch, indicating minutes.

min·ute·ly¹ (min′it lē) *adv.* every minute. [MINUTE¹ + -LY¹.]

mi·nute·ly² (mī nōōt′lē, -nūt′-, mi-) *adv.* in a minute manner or degree; in minute detail. [MINUTE² + -LY¹.]

min·ute·man (min′it man′) *pl.,* **-men.** *also,* **Min·ute·man.** *n.* volunteer militiaman during the American Revolution, ready to fight at a minute's notice.

minute steak, boneless, thin piece of beef that can be quickly cooked.

mi·nu·ti·ae (mi nōō′shē ē′, -nū′-) *sing..* **-ti·a** (-shē ə). *n.pl.* small or unimportant details. [Late Latin *minūtiae,* plural of Latin *minūtia* smallness.]

minx (mingks) *n.* pert or flirtatious girl. [Of uncertain origin.]

Mi·o·cene (mī′ə sēn′) *n.* **1.** fourth geological epoch of the Tertiary period of the Cenozoic era, during which grazing animals evolved and multiplied rapidly. **2.** strata formed in this epoch. See **geology** for table. —*adj.* of or relating to this epoch. [Greek *meiōn* less + *kainos* new, recent.]

Mir·a·beau, Comte de (mir′ə bō′) 1749–91, French revolutionary statesman; born Honoré Gabriel Riqueti.

mi·ra·bi·le dic·tu (mi rab′ə lē dik′tōō, -tū) *Latin.* wonderful to relate.

mir·a·cle (mir′ə kəl) *n.* **1.** event that cannot be explained scientifically and is therefore often attributed to a divine or supernatural power. **2.** amazing or marvelous occurrence or thing: *the miracle of childbirth.* **3.** outstanding or remarkable example: *a miracle of wisdom.* **4.** miracle play. [Old French *miracle* act of divine power contrary to the laws of nature, from Latin *mirāculum* wonderful thing, marvel, going back to *mīrus* wonderful.]

miracle play, religious drama popular in the Middle Ages, based on legends about the saints.

mi·rac·u·lous (mi rak′yə ləs) *adj.* **1.** beyond scientific explanation; of the nature of a miracle. **2.** amazing; extraordinary; incredible: *a miraculous escape.* **3.** working or having the power to work wonders. —**mi·rac′u·lous·ly,** *adv.* —**mi·rac′u·lous·ness,** *n.*

mi·rage (mi räzh′) *n.* **1.** optical illusion, as the appearance of a sheet of water on a highway, caused by the bending of light rays by layers of air having different densities and temperatures. **2.** something that seems real but is only illusory. [French *mirage,* from *mirer* to look at, from Late Latin *mīrāre* to behold, from Latin *mīrārī* to wonder at.]

mire (mīr) *n.* **1.** area of wet, soft ground; bog. **2.** deep, soft mud; muck. —*v.t.,* **mired, mir·ing. 1.** to cause to sink or get stuck in mire. **2.** to soil with mud or muck. **3.** to entangle or involve, as in difficulties. —*v.i.* to sink or get stuck in mire. [Old Norse *myrr* bog, swamp.]

Mir·i·am (mir′ē əm) *n.* in the Old Testament, sister of Moses and Aaron.

.mirk (murk) murk.

mirk·y (mur′kē) murky.

mir·ror (mir′ər) *n.* **1.** smooth reflecting surface, as of highly polished metal, that forms images by reflecting light, esp. such a surface made of glass that is coated on the back with a highly reflective material. **2.** that which gives a true representation, expression, or description: *Literature is a mirror of its time.* **3.** model; pattern. —*v.t.* to reflect in, or as if in, a mirror. [Old French *mireor* implement made of metal or glass and designed to reflect images, going back to Late Latin *mīrāre* to behold, from Latin *mīrārī* to wonder at.]

mirth (murth) *n.* merriment or gaiety. [Old English *myrgth.*]

mirth·ful (murth′fəl) *adj.* full of, expressing, or characterized by mirth; merry. —**mirth′ful·ly,** *adv.* —**mirth′ful·ness,** *n.*

mirth·less (murth′lis) *adj.* without mirth; joyless. —**mirth′less·ly,** *adv.* —**mirth′less·ness,** *n.*

MIRV (murv) *n.* long-range missile having several warheads that can be guided from beyond the atmosphere toward different enemy targets. [Short for *m(ultiple) i(ndependently-targeted) r(eentry) v(ehicle).*]

mis- *prefix* **1.** bad or wrong: *misconduct, misconception.* **2.** badly or wrongly: *mismanage, misquote.* **3.** lack of: *mistrust.* [Partly from Old English *mis-* bad, badly, wrong, wrongly; partly from Old French *mes-,* prefix with a disparaging or negative sense; of Germanic origin.]

mis·ad·ven·ture (mis′əd ven′chər) *n.* mishap; misfortune.

mis·ad·vise (mis′əd vīz′) **-vised, -vis·ing.** *v.t.* to give bad or wrong advice to; advise wrongly.

mis·al·li·ance (mis′ə lī′əns) *n.* improper or unsuitable alliance or association, esp. in marriage.

mis·an·thrope (mis′ən thrōp′, miz′-) *n.* one who hates or bitterly distrusts mankind. Also, **mis·an·thro·pist** (mis an′thrə pist, miz-). [Greek *mīsanthrōpos* hating mankind, from *mīsein* to hate + *anthrōpos* man.] —**mis·an·throp·ic** (mis′ən throp′ik, miz′-); *also,* **mis·an·throp′i·cal,** —**mis·an·throp′i·cal·ly,** *adv.*

mis·an·thro·py (mis an′thrə pē, miz-) *n.* hatred or bitter distrust of mankind.

mis·ap·ply (mis′ə plī′) **-plied, -ply·ing.** *v.t.* **1.** to apply or use incorrectly or badly: *to misapply a mathematical principle.* **2.** to apply or use illegally or dishonestly: *to misapply public money.* —**mis′ap·pli·ca′tion,** *n.*

mis·ap·pre·hend (mis′ap ri hend′) *v.t.* to misunderstand.

mis·ap·pre·hen·sion (mis′ap ri hen′shən) *n.* a misunderstanding.

mis·ap·pro·pri·ate (mis′ə prō′prē āt′) **-at·ed, -at·ing.** *v.t.* to take or use wrongly or dishonestly, esp. money with which one is entrusted. —**mis′ap·pro′pri·a′tion,** *n.*

mis·be·come (mis′bi kum′) **-came, -come, -com·ing.** *v.t.* to be inappropriate to; be unfit for.

mis·be·got·ten (mis′bi got′ən) *adj.* unlawfully or irregularly begotten, esp. illegitimate. Also, **mis′be·got′.**

mis·be·have (mis′bi hāv′) **-haved, -hav·ing.** *v.i.* to behave badly or improperly. —*v.t.* to conduct (oneself) badly or improperly.

mis·be·hav·ior (mis′bi hāv′yər) *also, British,* **mis·be·hav·iour.** *n.* bad or improper behavior.

mis·be·lief (mis′bi lēf′) *n.* **1.** false or erroneous belief or opinion. **2.** false, erroneous, or unorthodox religious belief.

mis·be·liev·er (mis′bi lēv′ər) *n.* one who holds or is regarded as holding a false, erroneous, or unorthodox belief, esp. in religion.

misc. **1.** miscellaneous. **2.** miscellany.

mis·cal·cu·late (mis kal′kyə lāt′) **-lat·ed, -lat·ing.** *v.t., v.i.* to calculate or estimate wrongly; misjudge. —**mis′cal·cu·la′tion,** *n.*

mis·call (mis kôl′) *v.t.* to call by a wrong name; misname.

mis·car·riage (mis kar′ij) *n.* **1.** failure to reach a proper, just, or desired end, often because of mismanagement: *The prisoner claimed he was innocent and had suffered a miscarriage of justice.* **2.** premature expulsion of a nonviable fetus.

mis·car·ry (mis kar′ē) **-ried, -ry·ing.** *v.i.* **1.** to fail to reach a proper, just, or desired end. **2.** to bring forth a nonviable fetus prematurely;

at; āpe; cär; end; mē; it; īce; hot; ōld; fôrk; wood; fōōl; oil; out; up; ūse; turn; sing; thin; this; zh in treasure; ə in ago, taken, pencil, lemon, circus.

suffer a miscarriage; abort. **3.** to fail to reach an intended destination; go astray or be lost in transit, as a letter or package.

mis·cast (mis kast′) -**cast,** -**cast·ing.** v.t. **1.** to cast (an actor) in a role not suited to him. **2.** to select an unsuitable actor or actors for (a role or a dramatic or theatrical production).

mis·ce·ge·na·tion (mis′ə jə nā′shən) n. interbreeding, marriage, or cohabitation between members of different races. [From Latin *miscēre* to mix + *genus* race, kind.]

mis·cel·la·ne·ous (mis′ə lā′nē əs) adj. **1.** of different kinds; having various characteristics or aspects: *miscellaneous items scattered all over the floor, miscellaneous arguments against the proposal.* **2.** composed of various things, elements, or members: *a miscellaneous assemblage.* **3.** dealing with a variety of subjects: *an elegant and miscellaneous author* (Browne, 1646). [Latin *miscellāneus* mixed, from *miscellus*.] —**mis′cel·la′ne·ous·ly,** adv. —**mis′cel·la′ne·ous·ness,** n.

Syn. 1. Miscellaneous, assorted mean composed of dissimilar or unrelated things. **Miscellaneous** implies a mixture of things that defy classification: *The family stored miscellaneous items in the closet in the basement.* **Assorted** describes a group of characteristically different elements within the same category: *This box contains assorted chocolates.*

mis·cel·la·ny (mis′ə lā′nē) pl., -**nies.** n. **1.** mixture of various things. **2.** volume containing a collection of literary pieces on various subjects. **3.** *also,* **miscellanies.** collection of various literary works brought together to form a book. [Latin *miscellānea* hodgepodge, various things, from *miscellāneus* mixed. See MISCELLANEOUS.]

mis·chance (mis chans′) n. bad luck or an instance of bad luck.

mis·chief (mis′chif′) n. **1.** act or conduct that is often playful but causes harm or annoyance: *The child was always involved in some mischief.* **2.** disposition to annoy, tease, or play pranks. **3.** harm, evil, or damage. **4.** cause or source of harm, annoyance, or trouble. [Old French *meschief* misfortune, damage, from *meschever* to be unfortunate, going back to *mes-* (see MIS-) + Latin *caput* head.]

mis·chie·vous (mis′chə vəs) adj. **1.** disposed to or characterized by conduct that is often playful but causes harm or annoyance. **2.** characteristic of or suggesting a disposition to such conduct; playful: *a mischievous practical joke.* **3.** harmful; damaging. —**mis′chie·vous·ly,** adv. —**mis′chie·vous·ness,** n.

mis·ci·ble (mis′ə bəl) adj. capable of being mixed: *Oil and water are not miscible.* [Latin *miscēre* to mix + -IBLE.] —**mis′ci·bil′i·ty,** n.

mis·con·ceive (mis′kən sēv′) -**ceived,** -**ceiv·ing.** v.t. to have a wrong conception of; misunderstand.

mis·con·cep·tion (mis′kən sep′shən) n. false or mistaken idea.

mis·con·duct (n., mis kon′dukt; v., mis kən dukt′) n. **1.** improper behavior. **2.** unlawful conduct, esp. by a public official. **3.** mismanagement: *misconduct of financial affairs.* —v.t. **1.** to behave (oneself) improperly. **2.** to mismanage.

mis·con·struc·tion (mis′kən struk′shən) n. false or incorrect interpretation; misunderstanding.

mis·con·strue (mis′kən strōō′) -**strued,** -**stru·ing.** v.t. to mistake the meaning or intention of; misinterpret.

mis·count (v., mis kount′; n., mis′kount′) v.t., v.i. to count incorrectly; miscalculate. —n. incorrect count.

mis·cre·ant (mis′krē ənt) n. **1.** villain; vile wretch. **2.** infidel; heretic. —adj. **1.** villainous; vile. **2.** infidel; heretical. [Old French *mescreant* disbelieving, infidel, present participle of *mescroire* to disbelieve, going back to *mes-* (see MIS-) + Latin *crēdere* to believe.]

mis·cue (mis kū′) n. **1.** stroke in pool or billiards in which the cue slips and glances off or misses the ball. **2.** mistake; error; slip. —v.i. -**cued,** -**cu·ing.** to make a miscue.

mis·deal (v., mis dēl′; n., mis′dēl′) -**dealt,** -**deal·ing.** Card Games. v.t., v.i. to deal (cards) incorrectly or improperly. —n. incorrect or improper deal.

mis·deed (mis dēd′) n. wicked, immoral, or criminal act.

mis·de·mean·or (mis′di mē′nər) also, British. **mis·de·mean·our.** n. **1.** illegal act less serious than a felony, usually punishable by a fine or a short term of imprisonment. **2.** misbehavior or an instance of it.

mis·di·rect (mis′di rekt′, -dī rekt′) v.t. to direct wrongly or badly: *to misdirect a traveler.* —**mis′di·rec′tion,** n.

mis·do (mis dōō′) -**did,** -**done,** -**do·ing.** v.t. to do (something) wrongly or improperly. [Old English *misdōn* to act wrongly.] —**mis·do′er,** n.

mis·doubt (mis dout′) v.t. **1.** to doubt; distrust. **2.** to fear; suspect. —n. doubt; suspicion.

mis·em·ploy (mis′em ploi′) v.t. to use wrongly or ineffectively; put to poor or improper use. —**mis′em·ploy′ment,** n.

mise en scène (mēz än′ sen′) French. **1.a.** scenery, properties, and other physical equipment used in staging a theatrical or dramatic production. **b.** arrangement of the actors, scenery, and properties. **2.** physical surroundings; environment.

mi·ser (mī′zər) n. one who greedily saves or hoards money. [Latin *miser* wretched.]

mis·er·a·ble (miz′ər ə bəl, miz′rə bəl) adj. **1.** very unhappy; wretched: *The girl felt so miserable she wanted to cry.* **2.** causing or marked by great discomfort or unhappiness: *a miserable toothache, miserable weather.* **3.** pitifully or pathetically poor, inadequate, or unfortunate: *the miserable starving children of a war-ravaged country.* **4.** of little or no value; of very poor quality: *The actor gave a miserable performance.* **5.** deserving contempt; deplorable; shameful. [Latin *miserābilis* pitiable, going back to *miser* wretched.] —**mis′er·a·ble·ness,** n. —**mis′er·a·bly,** adv.

Mis·e·re·re (miz′ə rār′ē, -rēr′ē) n. **1.** fifty-first Psalm in the Old Testament (the fiftieth in the Douay Bible). **2.** musical setting for this Psalm. [Latin *miserēre* have mercy (first word of this Psalm in the Vulgate), imperative of *miserērī* to have mercy.]

mi·ser·ly (mī′zər lē) adj. of, like, or characteristic of a miser; stingy. —**mi′ser·li·ness,** n.

mis·er·y (miz′ər ē) pl., -**er·ies.** n. **1.** state or condition of physical or mental suffering caused esp. by pain, privation, or extreme unhappiness; prolonged or intense distress. **2.** cause or source of such suffering. [Latin *miseria* wretchedness.] —**Syn. 1.** see **distress.**

mis·fea·sance (mis fē′zəns) n. Law. improper performance of a lawful act, as the wrongful exercise of lawful authority. Distinguished from **malfeasance** and **nonfeasance.** [Old French *mesfaisance* offense, misdemeanor, from *mesfaire* to do wrong, going back to *mes-* (see MIS-) + Latin *facere* to do.]

mis·file (mis fīl′) -**filed,** -**fil·ing.** v.t. to file (papers, documents, or the like) incorrectly.

mis·fire (mis fīr′) -**fired,** -**fir·ing.** v.i. **1.** to fail to fire, ignite, or explode at the proper time, as an internal-combustion engine. **2.** to fail to have the intended effect or result. —n. failure to fire, ignite, or explode at the proper time.

mis·fit (mis′fit′, mis fit′) n. **1.** something that does not fit properly, as a garment of the wrong size. **2.** one who is poorly adjusted to his environment or unable to fit in with his surroundings. **3.** act or condition of fitting improperly.

mis·for·tune (mis fôr′chən) n. **1.** bad luck; ill fortune. **2.** instance of this; unlucky accident; mishap.

mis·give (mis giv′) -**gave,** -**giv·en,** -**giv·ing.** v.t. to make doubtful, suspicious, or apprehensive. —v.i. to be doubtful, suspicious, or apprehensive.

mis·giv·ing (mis giv′ing) n. feeling of doubt, distrust, or apprehension.

mis·gov·ern (mis guv′ərn) v.t. to govern or manage badly. —**mis·gov′ern·ment,** n.

mis·guide (mis gīd′) -**guid·ed,** -**guid·ing.** v.t. to guide or direct wrongly; lead astray in action or thought. —**mis·guid′ance,** n.

mis·guid·ed (mis gī′did) adj. directed or influenced by or resulting from mistaken ideas or bad guidance: *He gave his friend some well-intentioned but misguided advice.* —**mis·guid′ed·ly,** adv.

mis·han·dle (mis hand′əl) -**dled,** -**dling.** v.t. to handle, treat, or manage badly.

mis·hap (mis′hap′, mis hap′) n. unfortunate accident.

mis·hear (mis hēr′) -**heard,** -**hear·ing.** v.t. to hear incorrectly or poorly.

mish·mash (mish′mash′, -mosh′) n. confused mixture; jumble. [Repetition of MASH with vowel change in the first syllable.]

Mish·nah (mish′nə) pl., **Mish·na·yoth** (mish′nə yōt′). *also,* **Mish·na.** n. **1.** first part of the Talmud, consisting of a collection of Jewish oral law and legal interpretations. **2.** a paragraph of this collection. [Hebrew *mishnāh* repetition, (oral) instruction.]

mis·in·form (mis′in fôrm′) v.t. to give false, inaccurate, or misleading information to. —**mis′in·for′ma·tion,** n.

mis·in·ter·pret (mis′in tur′prit) v.t. to interpret wrongly; explain or understand incorrectly: *Alice misinterpreted my compliment and felt insulted.* —**mis′in·ter′pre·ta′tion,** n.

mis·judge (mis juj′) -**judged,** -**judg·ing.** v.t., v.i. to judge incorrectly or unfairly: *to misjudge a person's character.* —**mis·judg′ment;** *also,* **mis·judge′ment,** n.

mis·la·bel (mis lā′bəl) -**beled,** -**bel·ing;** *also, British,* -**belled,** -**bel·ling.** v.t. to label incorrectly or deceptively.

mis·lay (mis lā′) -**laid,** -**lay·ing.** v.t. **1.** to put in a place afterward forgotten; lose temporarily. **2.** to lay or put down incorrectly, as a carpet. —**Syn. 1.** see **misplace.**

mis·lead (mis lēd′) -**led,** -**lead·ing.** v.t. **1.** to lead or guide in the wrong direction. **2.** to lead into error of thought, judgment, or action.

mis·lead·ing (mis lē′ding) adj. causing or tending to cause error of thought, judgment, or action: *a misleading speech, misleading instructions.* —**mis·lead′ing·ly,** adv.

Syn. Misleading, deceptive mean tending to delude. **Misleading** applies to what tends to lead astray, intentionally or otherwise, into a mistaken action or belief, esp. by misrepresenting the truth: *Misleading advertisements are prohibited by law.* **Deceptive** refers to what tends to deceive

or promote error and confusion by assuming false appearances with or without calculated intent: *That crook has a deceptive smile.*

mis·like (mis līk′) **-liked, -lik·ing.** *Archaic. v.t.* **1.** to dislike. **2.** to displease. —*n.* disapproval; dislike.

mis·man·age (mis man′ij) **-aged, -ag·ing.** *v.t.* to manage or handle badly or ineffectively. —**mis·man′age·ment,** *n.*

mis·match (mis mach′) *v.t.* to match badly or unsuitably. —*n.* bad or unsuitable match.

mis·mate (mis māt′) **-mat·ed, -mat·ing.** *v.t.* to mate unsuitably.

mis·name (mis nām′) **-named, -nam·ing.** *v.t.* to call by a wrong or inappropriate name.

mis·no·mer (mis nō′mər) *n.* **1.** name or designation incorrectly or unsuitably applied: *"Battleship" was a misnomer for the decrepit hulk.* **2.** error in naming a person or thing. [From Old French *mesnommer* to misname, going back to *mes-* (see MIS-) + Latin *nōmināre* to name.]

mi·sog·a·my (mi sog′ə mē) *n.* hatred of marriage. [Greek *mīsos* hatred + *gamos* marriage.] —**mi·sog′a·mist,** *n.*

mi·sog·y·ny (mi soj′ə nē) *n.* hatred of women. [Greek *mīsogyniā,* going back to *mīsos* hatred + *gynē* woman.] —**mi·sog′y·nist,** *n.* —**mis·og′y·nous,** *adj.*

mis·place (mis plās′) **-placed, -plac·ing.** *v.t.* **1.** to put in a place afterward forgotten; mislay. **2.** to put or locate in a wrong place: *to misplace an apostrophe.* **3.** to give to an unsuitable person or thing: *to misplace one's trust.* —**mis·place′ment,** *n.*

Syn. 1. Misplace, mislay, lose mean to be unable to find. **Misplace** may be used when one places a thing in a wrong or unaccustomed place or position: *The absent-minded clerk was always misplacing files.* **Mislay** implies placing something in a forgotten place so that there is no chance of immediate recovery: *Father mislaid his hat in the excitement.* **Lose** emphasizes loss of hope of recovery of something missing from one's possession or from its customary place: *Don't lose your wallet in the crowd.*

mis·play (mis plā′) *v.t.* to play (something) badly or incorrectly in a game or sport: *to misplay a poker hand.* —*n.* bad or incorrect play in a game or sport.

mis·print (*n.* mis′print′, mis print′; *v.* mis print′) *n.* error in printing. —*v.t.* to print incorrectly.

mis·pri·sion (mis prizh′ən) *n.* *Law.* wrongful action or conduct, esp. maladministration by a public official or failure of a citizen to report or try to prevent a crime. [Old French *mesprision* error, wrongdoing, from *mesprendre* to do wrong, going back to *mes-* (see MIS-) + Latin *prehendere* to seize, grasp.]

mis·prize (mis prīz′) **-prized, -priz·ing.** *v.t.* to undervalue; despise; scorn. [Old French *mesprisier,* from *mes-* (see MIS-) + *prisier* to value (going back to Latin *pretium* value).]

mis·pro·nounce (mis′prə nouns′) **-nounced, -nounc·ing.** *v.t., v.i.* to pronounce (words or sounds) incorrectly. —**mis′pro·nun′ci·a′tion,** *n.*

mis·quote (mis kwōt′) **-quot·ed, -quot·ing.** *v.t.* to quote incorrectly or inaccurately. —*n.* incorrect or inaccurate quotation. —**mis′quo·ta′tion,** *n.*

mis·read (mis rēd′) **-read, -read·ing.** *v.t.* to read, understand, or interpret incorrectly: *to misread a sign.*

mis·re·mem·ber (mis′ri mem′bər) *v.t., v.i.* to remember incorrectly.

mis·rep·re·sent (mis′rep ri zent′) *v.t.* **1.** to represent, describe, or portray falsely or inaccurately: *The company misrepresented its product in the advertisement.* **2.** to serve inadequately or improperly as the delegate or agent of: *a congressman who misrepresented his constituency.* —**mis′rep·re·sen·ta′tion,** *n.* —**mis′rep·re·sen′ta·tive,** *adj.*

mis·rule (mis rōōl′) *n.* **1.** bad, unjust, or unwise rule or government. **2.** disorder; tumult. —*v.t.* **-ruled, -rul·ing.** to rule or govern badly, unjustly, or unwisely.

miss¹ (mis) *v.t.* **1.** to fail to hit, reach, or land on: *The speeding car barely missed the pedestrian.* **2.** to fail to catch, meet, or get: *to miss a bus.* **3.** to fail to notice or find: *to miss a turnoff on a highway.* **4.** to fail to accomplish, attain, achieve, or obtain: *The golfer missed a short putt.* **5.** to fail to attend, perform, keep, or be present for: *to miss an appointment.* **6.** to fail to understand, perceive, or grasp: *You've missed the author's point.* **7.** to feel or regret the absence or loss of: *The mother missed her daughter who was away at college.* **8.** to discover or realize the absence or loss of: *It was a long time before the lady even missed her necklace.* **9.** to fail to take advantage of; let slip by: *to miss an opportunity.* **10.** to leave out; omit; skip: *to miss a name in calling attendance.* **11.** to escape; avoid: *to miss being struck by falling debris.* **12.** to be without; lack: *This coat is missing a button.* **13.** to do or answer incorrectly; get wrong: *to miss a question.* —*v.i.* **1.** to fail to hit something: *Several arrows were shot, but they all missed.* **2.** to be unsuccessful; fail: *Your ingenious plan can't miss.* **3.** to misfire. **4. to miss out.** to lose out on an opportunity: *If you don't get to the sale early, you'll miss out.* **5. to miss out on. a.** to fail to take advantage of: *to miss out*

on a great chance. **b.** to fail to get, have, or attain: *to miss out on a raise.* —*n.* failure to hit. [Old English *missan* to fail to hit.]

miss² (mis) *pl.,* **miss·es.** *n.* **1.** *also,* **Miss.** form of address used before, or in place of, the name of a girl or unmarried woman: *Miss Beck. May I help you, miss?* **2.** young unmarried woman; girl. [Short for MISTRESS.]

Miss., Mississippi.

mis·sal (mis′əl) *n.* book containing the prescribed prayers and liturgical form for celebrating Mass throughout the year. [Medieval Latin *missale,* from Late Latin *missa.* See MASS.]

mis·shape (mis shāp′) **-shaped, -shaped** or **-shap·en, -shap·ing.** *v.t.* to shape badly; deform.

mis·shap·en (mis shā′pən) *adj.* badly shaped or having an ugly or distorted shape; deformed.

mis·sile (mis′əl) *n.* **1.** object, esp. a weapon, designed to be thrown, shot, or otherwise projected or propelled, as a bullet, arrow, or stone; projectile. **2.** guided missile. **3.** ballistic missile. [Latin *missile* weapon that can be thrown, going back to *missus,* past participle of *mittere* to send, throw.]

mis·sil·ry (mis′əl rē) *also,* **mis·sil·ry.** *n.* science dealing with the construction and operation of missiles, esp. guided missiles.

miss·ing (mis′ing) *adj.* not present; lacking; lost: *a missing button, to report a missing person to the police.*

missing link 1. hypothetical primate thought to be a connecting link between the anthropoid apes and man in the evolutionary process. **2.** something lacking for the completion of a series.

mis·sion (mish′ən) *n.* **1.** group or number of persons sent or officially assigned to perform a specific function, task, or service, esp. a group of government representatives sent to a foreign country for diplomatic purposes, as to conduct negotiations. **2.** diplomatic office in a foreign country, usually permanent; embassy; legation. **3.** specific function, task, or service that a person or group of persons is sent or officially assigned to perform. **4.** military operation, task, or duty assigned to an individual or unit, esp. a combat flight by one or more aircraft: *a reconnaissance mission.* **5.** group of missionaries sent to do religious, humanitarian, or educational work, esp. in a foreign country. **6.** church, headquarters, or other place used by missionaries in the performance of their work. **7. missions.** organized missionary work or activities. **8.** organization or establishment set up to perform social services for the needy, as in a poor area of a large city. **9.** church or church district without its own priest or minister and served by a neighboring clergyman. **10.** special series of religious services for gaining converts or increasing the piety of believers. **11.** duty, function, or task that is self-imposed or that a person feels he is destined to perform. —*adj.* of, relating to, or resembling the style used in the early Spanish mission churches and buildings of the southwestern United States. [Latin *missiō* a sending.]

mis·sion·ar·y (mish′ə ner′ē) *pl.,* **-ar·ies.** *n.* **1.** one who is sent by his church to spread his religion among nonbelievers, esp. in a foreign country: *a Protestant missionary in India.* **2.** one who chooses or is sent to do humanitarian or educational work, esp. in a foreign country: *Albert Schweitzer served as a medical missionary in Africa.* **3.** one who advocates and works to gain support for some idea or cause. **4.** agent; envoy; emissary. —*adj.* of, relating to, or characteristic of missionaries or religious missions: *missionary zeal.*

mis·sis (mis′iz) *also,* **mis·sus.** *n.* *Informal.* **1.** wife. **2.** mistress of the household. [Modification of MISTRESS.]

Mis·sis·sip·pi (mis′ə sip′ē) *n.* **1.** principal river of the United States, flowing from northern Minnesota to the Gulf of Mexico. Also, **Mississippi River. 2.** state in the southern United States. Capital, Jackson. Area, 47,716 sq. mi. Pop. (1970), 2,216,912. Abbreviation, **Miss.**

Mis·sis·sip·pi·an (mis′ə sip′ē ən) *n.* **1.** native or inhabitant of Mississippi. **2.** earlier of the two geological subdivisions of the Carboniferous period, characterized by a tropical climate, and during which coal beds and extensive limestone deposits were formed. See **geology** for table. —*adj.* **1.** of or relating to Mississippi or the Mississippi River. **2.** of or relating to the earlier of the two subdivisions of the Carboniferous period.

mis·sive (mis′iv) *n.* written message; letter. [Middle French *missive,* short for *lettre missive* a letter sent, going back to Latin *missus,* past participle of *mittere* to send.]

Mis·sou·ri (mi zoor′ē, -zoor′ə) *n.* **1.** longest river in the United States, flowing from Montana to the Mississippi. Also, **Missouri River. 2.** state in the central United States. Capital, Jefferson City. Area, 69,686 sq. mi. Pop. (1970), 4,677,399. Abbreviation, **Mo. 3. from Missouri.** *Informal.* not convinced until given conclusive proof; skeptical. —**Mis·sour′i·an,** *adj., n.*

mis·spell (mis spel′) **-spelled** or **-spelt, -spell·ing.** *v.t., v.i.* to spell (a word) incorrectly.

mis·spell·ing (mis spel′ing) *n.* incorrect spelling.

mis·spend (mis spend′) **-spent, -spend·ing.** *v.t.* to spend or use wrongly or wastefully; squander.

at; āpe; cär; end; mē; it; īce; hot; ōld; fôrk; wood; fōōl; oil; out; up; ūse; turn; sing; thin; this; zh in treasure; ə in ago, taken, pencil, lemon, circus.

mis·state (mis stāt′) -stat·ed, -stat·ing. *v.t.* to state incorrectly or falsely. —**mis·state′ment**, *n.*

mis·step (mis step′) *n.* 1. wrong or careless step. 2. mistake in conduct; improper act.

mis·sus (mis′əz) *n. Informal.* missis.

miss·y (mis′ē) *pl.* **miss·ies.** *n. Informal.* miss.

mist (mist) *n.* 1. suspension of water in the air, at or near the earth's surface, consisting of tiny droplets that are finer than those occurring in fog and therefore permitting greater visibility. 2. water vapor condensed on and clouding a surface: *All the windows in the steamy room were covered with a thin mist.* 3. something resembling mist, as a thin cloud of smoke or a fine spray from a pressurized can. 4. cloudiness or filminess before the eyes that blurs the vision. 5. something that dims, clouds, or obscures: *times . . . half shrouded in the mist of legend* (Freeman, 1869). —*v.i.* 1. to be or become covered with or clouded by mist: *The young girl's eyes misted over with tears.* 2. to rain in very fine drops; drizzle. —*v.t.* to cover or cloud with mist. [Old English *mist* darkness.]

mis·tak·a·ble (mis tā′kə bəl) *adj.* capable of being mistaken or misunderstood. —**mis·tak′a·bly,** *adv.*

mis·take (mis tāk′) *n.* error in action, thought, judgment, or perception. —*v.t.,* -took, -tak·en, -tak·ing. 1. to regard, identify, or recognize (a person or thing) incorrectly; take (someone or something) to be another (often with *for*): *Tyrants often mistake fear for respect.* 2. to make an error in understanding or interpreting: *You must have mistaken my intentions.* —*v.i.* to make a mistake; err. [Old Norse *mistaka* to take in error.]

Syn. *n.* **Mistake, error, blunder** mean a wrong or inaccurate act or speech. **Mistake** is applied to a wrong action or statement arising from faulty judgment or inadequate knowledge: *The boy made a few mistakes in his first attempt to read the poem.* **Error** refers to an infraction of an accepted code, guide, or pattern arising from faulty reasoning or ignorance: *The typist has made several errors in copying the manuscript.* **Blunder** refers to a gross or stupid mistake resulting from mental confusion or lack of foresight and care: *The general's tactical blunder cost many lives.*

mis·tak·en (mis tā′kən) *adj.* 1. based on error or misjudgment; wrong: *a mistaken belief, a mistaken viewpoint.* 2. wrong in action, thought, judgment, or perception. —**mis·tak′en·ly,** *adv.*

mis·teach (mis tēch′) -taught, -teach·ing. *v.t.* to teach (a subject) poorly or incorrectly.

mis·ter (mis′tər) *n.* 1. **Mister.** form of address used before a man's name, usually written *Mr.: Mr. Smith, Mr. Chairman.* 2. *also,* **Mister.** form of address used in place of a man's name: *Want a paper, mister?* [Form of MASTER.]

mis·time (mis tīm′) -timed, -tim·ing. *v.t.* 1. to say or do at an inappropriate or wrong time. 2. to misjudge the time of.

mis·tle·toe (mis′əl tō′) *n.* 1. any of a large group of parasitic plants that live on the branches of various trees and have yellowish-green leaves and small, round fruits, as *Phoradendron flavescens,* the best-known U.S. species. 2. sprig of such a plant, often used for Christmas decoration. [Old English *misteltān* the plant.]

mis·took (mis took′) past tense of **mistake.**

mis·tral (mis′trəl, mis träl′) *n.* cold, dry wind, often of great intensity, that blows from the north or northwest toward the Mediterranean coast of France. [French *mistral,* from Provençal *mistral* literally, masterly wind, from Latin *magistrālis* relating to a master, from *magister* master.]

Mistletoe

mis·trans·late (mis′trans lāt′, -tranz-, mis trans′lāt, -tranz′-) -lat·ed, -lat·ing. *v.t.* to translate incorrectly. —**mis′trans·la′tion,** *n.*

mis·treat (mis trēt′) *v.t.* to treat badly or abusively. —**mis·treat′ment,** *n.*

mis·tress (mis′tris) *n.* 1. woman in a position of authority or control, as the head of a household or estate. 2. woman who owns an animal or, formerly, the female owner of a slave. 3. woman having complete control over something: *Her beauty made her mistress of men's hearts.* 4. *also,* **Mistress.** something that is thought of as female and has authority or control over something else: *England's mighty navy made her mistress of the high seas.* 5. woman who has a continued sexual relationship with a man to whom she is not married. 6. woman who has mastered an art or skill. 7. **Mistress.** *Archaic.* title of address used before the name of a woman. 8. *Archaic.* sweetheart. 9. *British.* female schoolteacher. [Old French *maistresse,* feminine of *maistre* one in charge, chief. See MASTER.]

mis·tri·al (mis trī′əl) *n. Law.* 1. trial that is invalid because of some error in the proceedings. 2. inconclusive trial in which the jury fails to agree on a verdict.

mis·trust (mis trust′) *n.* lack of trust or confidence. —*v.t.* to regard with suspicion or doubt. —*v.i.* to be suspicious or wary. —**mis·trust′ful,** *adj.*

mist·y (mis′tē) mist·i·er, mist·i·est. *adj.* 1. of, resembling, or characterized by mist: *a misty spring morning.* 2. clouded or obscured by or as by mist: *misty mountains in the distance.* 3. blurred or clouded with a mist of tears; tearful. 4. lacking clarity; vague; indistinct: *a misty recollection.* —**mist′i·ly,** *adv.* —**mist′i·ness,** *n.*

mis·un·der·stand (mis′un dər stand′) -stood, -stand·ing. *v.t., v.i.* to understand incorrectly or fail to understand; misinterpret.

mis·un·der·stand·ing (mis′un dər stan′ding) *n.* 1. failure to understand; error in interpretation. 2. disagreement; quarrel.

mis·un·der·stood (mis′un dər stood′) *adj.* 1. incorrectly understood. 2. not properly appreciated.

mis·us·age (mis ū′sij, -zij) *n.* 1. wrong or improper use or application, as of words. 2. bad treatment; abuse.

mis·use (*n.,* mis ūs′; *v.,* mis ūz′) *n.* wrong or improper use; misapplication: *the misuse of a word, misuse of funds.* —*v.t.,* -used, -us·ing. 1. to use wrongly or improperly; misapply. 2. to treat badly or abusively: *Who misuses a dog would misuse a child* (Tennyson, 1884).

mis·word (mis wurd′) *v.t.* to word incorrectly or poorly.

Mitch·ell, Mount (mich′əl) highest mountain in the eastern United States, in western North Carolina.

mite¹ (mīt) *n.* any of a group of tiny arachnids, order Acarina, having piercing, sucking mouth parts. Mites often damage stored foods or infest plants or animals. [Old English *mīte* any tiny insect.]

mite² (mīt) *n.* 1. very small amount, object, or creature. 2. very small sum of money or contribution. 3. coin of very small value. [Middle Dutch *mīte* coin of small value.]

mi·ter (mī′tər) *also,* **mi·tre.** *n.* 1. liturgical headdress worn by bishops and other prelates, consisting of a tall, peaked cap that can be folded flat, with two fringed strips of material hanging from the back. 2. official headdress of the ancient Jewish high priest, wrapped in folds around the head. 3. miter joint. 4. beveled edge on either of the pieces used to form a miter joint. —*v.t.* 1. to bestow a miter upon. 2. to join with a miter joint. 3. to cut or shape for forming a miter joint; cut to a miter. [Latin *mītra* cap, from Greek *mitra* headband.]

Miter

miter box, device with slotted sides used to guide a saw when making miter joints.

miter joint, joint formed by two pieces of wood or other material, whose joined edges have been beveled to form angles.

miter square, device having a blade set at a 45-degree angle or an adjustable blade, used to mark the angles of miter joints.

Mith·ra·ism (mith′rə iz′əm) *n.* ancient Persian religion based on the worship of Mithras. —**Mith·ra·ic** (mith rā′ik), **Mith′ra·is′tic,** *adj.* —**Mith′ra·ist,** *n., adj.*

Mith·ras (mith′ras) *also,* **Mith·ra** (mith′rə). *n.* Persian god of light and truth, associated with the sun.

Mith·ri·da·tes VI (mith′rə dā′tēz) c.132-63 B.C., king of Pontus from 120 to 63 B.C. and bitter opponent of Rome.

mit·i·gate (mit′ə gāt′) -gat·ed, -gat·ing. *v.t.* to make milder or less severe, intense, or painful: *to mitigate anger, to mitigate suffering.* [Latin *mītigātus,* past participle of *mītigāre* to make soft, calm.] —**mit′i·ga·ble** (mit′i gə bəl), *adj.* —**mit′i·ga′tion, mit′i·ga′tor,** *n.*

mit·i·ga·tive (mit′ə gā′tiv) *adj.* tending to mitigate. Also, **mit·i·ga·to·ry** (mit′i gə tôr′ē).

mi·to·chon·dri·a (mī′tə kon′drē ə, mit′ə-) *sing.* -dri·on (-drē ən) *n.,pl. Biology.* minute rods, filaments, or granules found in the cytoplasm of nearly all cells. They serve as centers of cellular respiration and the sites of energy production. [From Greek *mitos* thread + *chondrion* small grain.] —**mi′to·chon′dri·al,** *adj.*

mi·to·sis (mī tō′sis, mi-) *n.* process of cell division in which the nucleus of a cell normally divides into two identical nuclei, and the cell itself usually divides equally, separating into two new cells, each with the same number of chromosomes as the parent cell. [Modern Latin *mitosis,* from Greek *mitos* thread.] —**mi·tot·ic** (mī tot′ik), *adj.* —**mi·tot′i·cal·ly,** *adv.*

mi·tral (mī′trəl) *adj.* 1. of, relating to, or resembling a miter. 2. of or relating to a mitral valve.

mitral valve, heart valve consisting of two flaps, located between the left atrium and left ventricle.

mi·tre (mī′tər) *n.* —*v.t.,* **mi·tred, mi·tring.** to miter.

mitt (mit) *n.* 1. baseball glove, esp. that worn by the catcher. 2. mitten (*def.* 1). 3. woman's glove, often of lace, that may cover the

forearm, wrist, and part of the hand, but does not extend over the fingers. **4.** *Slang.* hand. [Short for MITTEN.]

mit·ten (mit′ən) *n.* **1.** covering for the hand enclosing the four fingers together and the thumb separately, esp. such a covering designed for protection, as against the cold. **2.** mitt *(def. 3).* [Old French *mitaine*, from *mite*; of uncertain origin.]

mitz·vah (mitz′və) *pl.,* **-voth** (-vōt) *or* **-vahs.** *also,* **mits·vah.** *n.* **1.** commandment or precept in Judaism. **2.** good or praiseworthy deed; act of kindness. [Hebrew *mitzwāh* commandment.]

mix (miks) *mixed* or *mixt,* **mix·ing.** *v.t.* **1.** to put together into one mass or compound so as to make the constituent parts indistinguishable: *to mix lemon juice, sugar, and water to make lemonade.* **2.** to make or prepare different ingredients together by mixing: *to mix up a martini, to mix up a batch of pancakes.* **3.** to put or add, as an ingredient: *to mix salt into a soup.* **4.** to stir or shake. **5.** to join or bring together: *to mix red and yellow roses in a bouquet.* **6.** to change the order or arrangement at random (often with *up*): *The man mixed up the ticket stubs and then drew the winning number.* **7.** to crossbreed. **8. to mix it up.** *Slang.* to fight. —*v.i.* **1.** to become mixed or be capable of being mixed into one mass or compound: *Oil and water will not mix.* **2.** to go or belong together: *Jack's plaid shirt didn't mix well with his striped trousers.* **3.** to associate, join in, or get along: *to mix with people from all walks of life.* **4.** to get involved; take part: *to mix in another person's affairs.* **5.** to crossbreed. **6. to mix up. a.** to confuse: *The files are all mixed up.* **b.** to involve: *The police suspected that some high official was mixed up in the crime.* —*n.* **1.** product, result, or act of mixing; mixture. **2.** mixture or combination of ingredients that is prepared and sold commercially: *a cake mix.* **3.** mixer *(def. 4).* [From obsolete *mixt* mixed, from Latin *mixtus,* past participle of *miscēre* to mingle.] —**mix′a·ble;** *also,* **mix′i·ble,** *adj.*

Syn. *v.t.* **1. Mix, blend, stir¹** mean to combine or merge different elements. **Mix** is the most inclusive and most widely applicable term and suggests a combination of different elements into a cohesive and stable mass or compound: *The workmen mixed sand, gravel, and cement to make concrete.* **Blend** may be used when one mixes ingredients smoothly and thoroughly into a uniform whole that combines the qualities of all its elements: *Laura blended the ingredients for a cake.* **Stir** may be used when one mixes by agitating with a circular movement: *Henry put the sugar in his coffee and stirred it with his spoon.*

mixed (mikst) *adj.* **1.** put together or formed by mixing; blended together into one mass or compound. **2.** of or composed of different or incongruous kinds, elements, or qualities: *to have mixed feelings about something.* **3.** made up of or involving persons of both sexes. **4.** made up of or involving persons of different race, religion, national origin, or social class: *a mixed marriage, a mixed neighborhood.*

mixed metaphor, metaphor *(def. 2).*

mixed number, number consisting of an integer and a proper fraction. The numbers $4\frac{7}{8}$ and $-7\frac{2}{3}$ are mixed numbers.

mixed-up (mikst′up′) *adj.* confused or disordered.

mix·er (mik′sər) *n.* **1.** one who or that which mixes, esp. a machine or device for mixing. **2.** person with regard to his ability to associate or get along with others: *Dan is a good mixer at parties.* **3.** dance, party, or other social gathering for the purpose of getting people acquainted. **4.** beverage, as soda or ginger ale, that is added to an alcoholic drink.

mixt (mikst) a past tense and past participle of **mix.**

mix·ture (miks′chər) *n.* **1.** product or result of mixing; combination; blend: *This batter is a mixture of milk, eggs, and flour. His first reaction was a strange mixture of joy and anger.* **2.** two or more substances that are put together but retain their individual properties and are not chemically combined. **3.** act or process of mixing; being mixed. [Latin *mixtūra* a mixing.]

mix-up (miks′up′) *n.* state or instance of confusion.

miz·zen (miz′ən) *also,* **miz·en.** *n.* **1.** fore-and-aft sail set on the mizzenmast. **2.** mizzenmast. —*adj.* of or relating to the mizzenmast. [Middle French *misaine* foresail, going back to Arabic *mazzān* mast.]

miz·zen·mast (miz′ən mast′, -mast) *also,* **miz·en·mast.** *n.* **1.** mast nearest the stern in a ship having two or three masts. **2.** third mast from the forward end of a ship having more than three masts.

mks, meter-kilogram-second.

mkt., market.

ml, milliliter; milliliters.

Mlle., Mademoiselle.

Mlles., Mesdemoiselles.

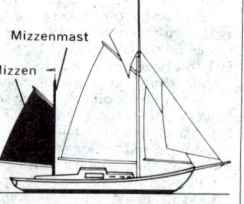
Mizzenmast
Mizzen —
Mizzen

mm, millimeter; millimeters.

MM., Messieurs.

Mme., Madame.

Mmes., Mesdames.

Mn, manganese.

mne·mon·ic (ni mon′ik) *adj.* **1.** aiding or intended to aid the memory. **2.** of or relating to memory. —*n.* device, as a formula or phrase, that aids one in remembering. [Greek *mnēmonikos* relating to memory, going back to *mnēmē* memory.] —**mne·mon′i·cal·ly,** *adv.*

mne·mon·ics (ni mon′iks) *n..pl.* technique or system for improving or developing the memory. ▲ construed as singular.

Mne·mos·y·ne (ni mos′ə nē) *n.* Greek goddess of memory.

Mo, molybdenum.

mo., month.

m.o., money order. Also, **M.O.**

Mo., Missouri.

mo·a (mō′ə) *n.* any of several extinct flightless birds resembling the ostrich, family Dinornithidae, once numerous in New Zealand. Height: 10 feet. [Of Maori origin.]

Mo·ab (mō′ab) *n.* ancient kingdom east of the Dead Sea, in what is now Jordan.

Mo·ab·ite (mō′ə bīt′) *n.* native or inhabitant of Moab. —*adj.* of or relating to Moab, its people, or their language or culture.

Moa

moan (mōn) *n.* **1.** low, prolonged, mournful sound, usually expressive of grief or pain. **2.** any sound resembling this: *the wind's eerie moan in the silent night.* **3.** *Archaic.* lamentation; complaint. —*v.i.* **1.** to utter or produce a moan or moans. —*v.t.* **1.** to utter or express with a moan or moans. **2.** to complain about; bemoan. [Probably from an unrecorded Old English word.]

moat (mōt) *n.* deep, wide ditch, usually filled with water, surrounding a castle, fortress, or town as a protection against assault. —*v.t.* to surround with or as with a moat. [Old French *mote* dike, mound; possibly of Celtic origin.]

mob (mob) *n.* **1.** disorderly, often menacing, crowd or throng. **2.** any crowd. **3.** common people collectively; the masses. **4.** *Informal.* organized group of gangsters. —*v.t.* **mobbed, mob·bing. 1.** to crowd around and jostle or annoy, as in curiosity: *Fans mobbed the actor wherever he went.* **2.** to crowd to capacity: *The store was mobbed by shoppers during the big sale.* **3.** to attack in or as in a mob. [Short for Latin *mōbile vulgus* fickle crowd.] —**Syn.** *n.* **1.** see **crowd.**

mob-cap (mob′kap′) *n.* large, loose, ruffled cap covering the hair and ears, formerly worn indoors by women. [Probably from Middle Dutch *mop* woman's cap + CAP.]

mo·bile (adj., mō′bəl, -bēl; n., mō′bēl) *adj.* **1.** capable of moving or being moved, esp. easily or readily movable: *Mobile radar units are used on the highways to catch speeders.* **2.** able or tending to change, respond, or adapt easily or quickly. **3.** flowing freely: *a mobile liquid.* **4.a.** capable of permitting movement from one social class or group to a higher one. **b.** characterized by the mixing of social groups. —*n.* construction or sculpture, as of metal, plastic, or cardboard, consisting of movable parts that are usually suspended from thin wires and can be set in motion, as by air currents. [Latin *mōbilis* movable, fickle, from *movēre* to move.] —**mo·bil·i·ty** (mō bil′ə tē), *n.*

Mo·bile (mō′bēl, mō bēl′) *n.* port city in southwestern Alabama, on Mobile Bay. Pop. (1970), 190,026.

Mobile Bay, shallow arm of the Gulf of Mexico, extending into southwestern Alabama.

mo·bi·lize (mō′bə līz′) **-lized, -liz·ing.** *v.t.* **1.** to summon, assemble, or prepare (armed forces) for active military service, or put into such service: *to mobilize the reserves in time of national emergency.* **2.** to prepare, organize, or adapt for use or action, or put into operation or active service, as for an emergency: *to mobilize backing for a political candidate.* —*v.i.* to become prepared, as for war or an emergency. [French *mobiliser* to prepare the military, economic, and governmental resources of a country for war, going back to Latin *mōbilis* movable. See MOBILE.] —**mo′bi·li·za′tion,** *n.*

Mö·bi·us strip (mœ′bē əs) surface having only one side and one edge, formed by turning one end of a rectangular strip 180 degrees and then attaching it to the other end. [From A. F. Möbius, 1790–1868, German mathematician who invented it.]

mob·ster (mob′stər) *n. Slang.* member of a criminal gang; gangster.

moc·ca·sin (mok′ə sin) *n.* **1.** shoe having a soft sole and no heel, generally constructed from one piece of leather, originally worn by American Indians. **2.** any shoe or slipper resembling an Indian moccasin. **3.** water moccasin. [Of Algonquian origin.]

moccasin flower, lady's-slipper.

at; āpe; cär; end; mē; it; īce; hot; ōld; fôrk; wood; fōōl; oil; out; up; ūse; turn; sing; thin; this; zh in treasure; ə in ago, taken, pencil, lemon, circus.

mo·cha (mō'kə) *n.* **1.** choice coffee originally grown in Arabia. **2.** flavoring made from an infusion of coffee or of a mixture of coffee and chocolate. **3.** soft leather made from sheepskin and processed to have a suede finish on both sides, used chiefly for gloves. —*adj.* flavored with coffee or with a mixture of coffee and chocolate. [From *Mocha*, a port in Yemen, from which this coffee was first obtained.]

mo·chi·la (mō chē'lə) *n.* saddle covering made of hide or leather. Mochilas equipped with pockets at each corner were used by pony express riders. [Spanish *mochila* cover for a horse, knapsack, from *mochil* errand boy, from Basque *motil* servant, youth, from Latin *mutilus* maimed, shortened (from the custom of cutting the hair of children).]

Mochila

mock (mok) *v.t.* **1.** to treat or address with ridicule or contempt; deride. **2.** to imitate or mimic, as in sport or derision. **3.** to treat or render meaningless; defy. **4.** to disappoint or deceive. —*v.i.* to express ridicule or contempt; scoff. —*adj.* not real; pretended; sham: *a mock battle, mock humility.* —*n.* **1.** act of mocking or ridicule; expression of mockery. **2.** one who or that which is or deserves to be mocked or ridiculed. **3.** imitation; counterfeit. [Old French *mocquer* to deride, scoff; possibly imitative.] —**mock'er,** *n.*

Syn. *v.t.* **1. Mock, ridicule, deride** mean to treat with contempt or scorn. **Mock** implies holding up to scorn and contempt, esp. by imitation: *The writings of Swift mocked the follies of his age.* **Ridicule** implies causing humiliation by making someone or something appear laughable: *Some contemporaries of Columbus ridiculed his idea of discovering a new route to the Indies.* **Deride** implies scoffing at something and making it the object of bitter contempt: *The opposition derided the government's handling of the problem.*

mock·er·y (mok'ər ē) *pl.* **-er·ies.** *n.* **1.** ridicule; contempt; derision. **2.** mocking or derisive speech or action. **3.** object of ridicule or contempt. **4.** false, ridiculous, or offensive imitation: *The trial was a mockery of justice.* **5.** something that is absurdly or offensively futile or unsuitable: *In her bitterness she felt that all rejoicing was mockery* (Eliot, 1863).

mock-he·ro·ic (mok'hi rō'ik) *adj.* satirizing or burlesquing heroic style, action, or character: *a mock-heroic poem, mock-heroic courage.* —*n.* satirical or burlesque imitation of something heroic, esp. a mock-heroic literary work. —**mock'·he·ro'i·cal·ly,** *adv.*

mock·ing·bird (mok'ing-burd') *n.* any of several North and South American birds, family Mimidae, usually having gray plumage, that can imitate the calls of other birds. Length: 9–11 inches.

Mockingbird

mock orange, any of a group of ornamental shrubs, genus *Philadelphus,* found throughout Europe, Asia, and North America, bearing showy, creamy white flowers. Also, **sy·rin'ga.**

mock turtle soup, soup made from calf's head or other meat and flavored to taste like green turtle soup.

mock-up (mok'up') *also,* **mock·up.** *n.* model, as of an airplane or machine, usually full-scale, used for study, testing, or display.

mod (mod) *adj. also,* **Mod.** *adj.* of or relating to a stylish, youth-oriented mode of dress first worn and popularized in England in the 1960s. [From MODERN.]

mod. 1. modern. **2.** moderato. **3.** moderate.

mo·dal (mōd'əl) *adj.* of or relating to mode or a mode. [Medieval Latin *modalis,* from Latin *modus* measure, manner.]

modal auxiliary, auxiliary verb used to indicate the mood of the verb with which it is used: *May, must,* and *would* are modal auxiliaries.

mo·dal·i·ty (mō dal'ə tē) *pl.* **-ties.** *n.* fact, quality, or state of being modal.

mode¹ (mōd) *n.* **1.a.** manner, way, or method of doing something or of acting: *to adopt a new mode of procedure.* **b.** particular form or variety: *Automobiles are a popular mode of transportation.* **2.** Grammar. mood². **3.** Music. **a.** any of various arrangements of the diatonic tones of an octave, derived by beginning on any one of the various tones of a given scale and proceeding through an octave. **b.** any of the eight, later twelve, scales thus derived, used in ancient and medieval music. **c.** either of the two forms, major and minor, of the modern diatonic scale. **4.** Statistics. value, number, or item occurring most often in a given series. [Latin *modus* measure, manner, melody.]

mode² (mōd) *n.* current or prevailing style or fashion, as of dress. [French *mode,* from Latin *modus* measure, manner.]

mod·el (mod'əl) *n.* **1.** representation or reproduction of something, usually constructed to scale or in miniature: *to build airplane models from kits, a working model of a new kind of engine.* **2.** image or figure in clay, wax, or plaster of something to be reproduced in a more durable material, as marble. **3.** one who or that which serves as an example or standard for imitation or comparison. **4.** one who or that which serves as the subject for an artist, photographer, or writer: *The painter's wife was the model for most of his portraits.* **5.** one who is employed to display merchandise, esp. a person employed to display or advertise clothing by wearing it. **6.** style, design, or type: *The car was a very old model.* —*v.t.,* **-eled, -el·ing;** *also, British,* **-elled, -el·ling. 1.** to fashion or plan according to or in imitation of a particular model, example, or pattern: *The painter modeled his style after that of Picasso.* **2.** to make or form or representation of: *to model a unicorn in wax.* **3.** to form or shape; make: *to model clay into a figure of a horse.* **4.** to display (clothing or other merchandise): *to model dresses.* **5.** to give a three-dimensional appearance to (a figure or object in painting or drawing), as by use of light and shadow. —*v.i.* **1.** to make or construct a model or models: *to model in plastic.* **2.** to serve, be employed, or pose as a model: *to model at a fashion show.* —*adj.* **1.** serving or used as a model. **2.** worthy of serving as a model: *a model husband.* [Middle French *modelle* pattern, mold¹, from Italian *modello,* going back to Latin *modulus* small measure, diminutive of *modus* measure, manner.] —**mod'el·er;** *also, British,* **mod'el·ler,** *n.*

Syn. *n.* **3. Model, Example** denote a person or thing worthy of imitation. **Model** suggests an ideal level of excellence and performance that one can strive to embody: *The U.S. Constitution is used as a model by governments of many new republics.* **Example** stresses the particular behavior which can serve as a guide for action and conduct: *The general set an example of courage for his men to follow.*

mod·el·ing (mod'əl ing) *also,* **mod·el·ling.** *n.* **1.** act or art of making or constructing a model or models. **2.** act or occupation of serving or posing as a model. **3.** rendering of three-dimensional form in painting or drawing, as by use of light and shadow. **4.** form or shape made by sculpture.

Model T *Trademark.* Ford automobile in production from 1908 to 1927.

Mo·de·na (mōd'ən ə) *n.* city in northern Italy. Pop. (1968), 163,262.

mod·er·ate (*adj., n.,* mod'ər it; *v.,* mod'ə rāt') *adj.* **1.** keeping or kept within reasonable or proper limits; not excessive or extreme: *a moderate price.* **2.** of medium or average amount, degree, or quality: *moderate traffic on the highway. She had only moderate success as an actress.* **3.** not violent or intense; mild; calm: *moderate weather.* **4.** having or characterized by a viewpoint that is not radical; opposed to extreme measures, esp. in politics: *Most of the moderate senators voted against the bill.* —*n.* one who holds moderate views, esp. in politics. —*v.t.,* **-at·ed, -at·ing. 1.** to make less excessive, extreme, violent, or intense: *The protesters were urged to moderate their demands.* **2.** to preside over: *to moderate a discussion.* —*v.i.* **1.** to become less excessive, violent, or intense. **2.** to act as a moderator; preside. [Latin *moderātus,* past participle of *moderārī* to regulate, control, from *modus* measure, limit.] —**mod'er·ate·ly,** *adv.* —**mod'er·ate·ness,** *n.*

mod·er·a·tion (mod'ə rā'shən) *n.* **1.** state or quality of being moderate; avoidance of excess or extremes. **2.** act of moderating. **3. in moderation,** within reasonable limits; without excess: *The physician advised him to exercise but in moderation.*

mo·de·ra·to (mod'ə rā'tō) *Music. adj.* in moderate tempo. —*adv.* at a moderate tempo. —*n.* moderato passage or movement. [Italian *moderato* restrained, from Latin *moderātus* controlled. See MODERATE.]

mod·er·a·tor (mod'ə rā'tər) *n.* **1.** one who or that which moderates, esp. one who presides, as over a meeting or discussion. **2.** arbitrator; mediator. **3.** *Physics.* graphite or other substance used in a nuclear reactor to slow down neutrons without absorbing them.

mod·ern (mod'ərn) *adj.* **1.** of, relating to, or characteristic of the present or recent time: *modern art, modern civilization.* **2.** up-to-date; not old-fashioned: *The kitchen had modern appliances.* —*n.* one who lives in modern times. **2.** one who has modern views or standards. [Late Latin *modernus* of the present, from Latin *modō* just now.] —**mod'ern·ly,** *adv.* —**mod'ern·ness,** *n.*

Syn. *adj.* **2. Modern, contemporary, current** mean of present or recent origin. **Modern** emphasizes the present or the immediate past, esp. as distinguished from the old and the traditional: *The medical students were taught modern techniques of surgery.* **Contemporary** refers to or examplifies up-to-date characteristics: *Jean was very contemporary in her outlook on marriage.* **Current** applies to what belongs to the immediate present or what is in vogue now: *Current English tends to be very informal.*

modern dance, dance of a form originating in the United States in

the early twentieth century, characterized by less formal steps and movements than those of classical ballet.

Modern English, English language from about 1500 to the present.

modern history, history from the latter part of the fifteenth century to the present.

mod·ern·ism (mod′ər niz′əm) *n.* **1.** modern character, thought, attitude, or manner of acting. **2.** something characteristic of modern times, as a newly introduced word or practice. **3.** *also,* **Modernism.** late nineteenth and early twentieth century movement in Christianity and Judaism to interpret religious doctrine in accordance with current ideas in philosophy and science, denounced as heretical by the Roman Catholic Church. —**mod′ern·ist,** *n., adj.* —**mod′ern·is′tic,** *adj.*

mo·der·ni·ty (mo dur′nə tē, mō-) *pl.,* **-ties.** *n.* quality or state of being modern.

mod·ern·ize (mod′ər nīz′) **-ized, -iz·ing.** *v.t.* to make modern, as in appearance, style, or character; change to suit present needs: *to modernize a hospital by installing the latest equipment.* —*v.i.* to become modern; adopt modern ways. —**mod′ern·i·za′tion,** *n.*

Modern Latin, Latin after 1500, used esp. in scientific terminology.

mod·est (mod′ist) *adj.* **1.** tending to avoid praise or credit; humble; unassuming. **2.** bashful and retiring; reserved: *a quiet, modest, diffident, questioning person* (Watson, 1901). **3.** having or showing a regard for propriety, esp. in behavior or dress: *Mistress Ford, the honest woman, the modest wife* (Shakespeare, *Merry Wives of Windsor*). **4.** not grand or showy; unpretentious; simple: *modest furnishings.* **5.** not excessive or extreme; moderate: *a modest sum of money.* [Latin *modestus* unassuming, moderate, keeping within bounds, from *modus* measure.] —**mod′est·ly,** *adv.* —**Syn. 1.** see **humble.**

Mo·des·to (mə des′tō) *n.* city in central California. Pop. (1970), 61,-712.

mod·es·ty (mod′is tē) *pl.,* **-ties.** *n.* quality or state of being modest.

mod·i·cum (mod′i kəm) *n.* small or moderate amount or portion. [Latin *modicum,* neuter of *modicus* moderate, from *modus* measure.]

mod·i·fi·ca·tion (mod′ə fi kā′shən) *n.* **1.** act of modifying; being modified. **2.** small or partial change, alteration, or adjustment: *The plan requires slight modification.* **3.** result of modifying; a modified form: *The law passed by Congress was a modification of the original bill.*

mod·i·fi·er (mod′ə fī′ər) *n.* **1.** *Grammar.* word, phrase, or clause that limits or qualifies the meaning of another word or group of words. Adjectives and adverbs are modifiers. **2.** one who or that which modifies.

mod·i·fy (mod′ə fī′) **-fied, -fy·ing.** *v.t.* **1.** to change or alter, as in form, usually to a small extent: *The inventor modified his original design to increase the machine's efficiency.* **2.** to make less severe or extreme; moderate: *The mediator attempted to get both sides to modify their positions.* **3.** *Grammar.* to limit or qualify the meaning of. In the phrase *a quiet evening,* the adjective *quiet* modifies the noun *evening.* —*v.i.* to be or become modified. [Old French *modifier* to change, moderate, from Latin *modificāre* to limit, control, from *modus* measure, limit + *facere* to make.] —**mod′i·fi′a·ble,** *adj.* —**Syn.** *v.t.* **1.** see **change.**

Mo·di·glia·ni, A·me·de·o (mō′dēl yä′nē; ä′mə dā′ō) 1884–1920, Italian painter and sculptor.

mod·ish (mō′dish) *adj.* fashionable. —**mod′ish·ly,** *adv.* —**mod′ish·ness,** *n.*

mo·diste (mō dēst′) *n.* one who makes or deals in women's fashions. [French *modiste* milliner, from *mode.* See MODE².]

Mo·dred (mō′drid) *also,* **Mor·dred.** *n.* in Arthurian legend, King Arthur's treacherous nephew.

mod·u·lar (moj′ə lər, mod′yə-) *adj.* of or relating to a module or modulus.

mod·u·late (moj′ə lāt′) **-lat·ed, -lat·ing.** *v.t.* **1.** to change or vary the tone, volume, or pitch of: *to modulate the voice.* **2.** to adjust, adapt, or regulate. **3.** to sing or intone, as a song or prayer. **4.** to vary some characteristic, as the amplitude or frequency, of (a carrier wave) for the transmission of a message. —*v.i. Music.* to pass from one key to another. [Latin *modulātus,* past participle of *modulārī* to measure off properly, to measure rhythmically, going back to *modus* measure.] —**mod′u·la·to·ry** (moj′ə lə tôr′ē), *adj.*

mod·u·la·tion (moj′ə lā′shən) *n.* **1.** act of modulating; being modulated. **2.** *Music.* passing from one key to another. **3.** process or result of the process of varying some characteristic of a carrier wave in accordance with another wave for the transmission of a message.

mod·u·la·tor (moj′ə lā′tər) *n.* **1.** device or circuit for modulating carrier waves. **2.** one who or that which modulates.

mod·ule (moj′ōōl, mod′ūl) *n.* **1.** standard or unit of measurement. **2.** *Architecture.* size of some part, as of a building, taken as a unit of measurement, used to regulate the proportion among the other parts. **3.** self-contained unit of a spacecraft, having a specific function. **4.** compact functional assembly used as a component part or unit, as in a computer. [Latin *modulus* small measure, diminutive of *modus* measure. Doublet of MOLD¹.]

mod·u·lus (moj′ə ləs) *pl.,* **-li** (lī′). *n.* **1.** *Physics.* quantity or number that is the measure of some function, property, force, or effect. **2.** *Mathematics.* integer that leaves the same remainder when divided into different numbers. [Modern Latin *modulus,* from Latin *modulus.* See MODULE.]

mo·dus o·pe·ran·di (mō′dəs op′ə ran′dī) *Latin.* manner of working; method of operation: *The police recognized the burgular by his modus operandi.*

mo·dus vi·ven·di (mō′dəs vi ven′dī) *Latin.* **1.** manner of living. **2.** temporary agreement between contending parties pending a final settlement of matters in debate.

Mo·ga·di·shu (mō′gə dē′shōō) *n.* capital of the Somali Republic, formerly known as Mogadiscio. Pop. (1967), 172,677.

Mo·gen Da·vid (mō′gən dō′vid, dā′-, mō′-) Star of David. [Form of MAGEN DAVID.]

mo·gul (mō′gul) *n.* bump or mound on a ski slope. [Possibly of Scandinavian origin.]

Mo·gul (mō′gul, -gəl) *n.* **1.** *also,* **Mu·ghul.** member or descendant of the Mongol conquerors of India who founded a Muslim empire that existed from 1526 to 1857. **2.** Mongol; Mongolian. **3.** *mogul.* powerful or important person: *The president of the studio was a mogul of the movie industry.*

mo·hair (mō′hâr′) *n.* **1.** long, silky hair of the Angora goat. **2.** woven fabric made from this hair, sometimes mixed with cotton. [Modification (influenced by English *hair*) of earlier *mocayare,* from Italian *moccaiaro* cloth of goat's hair, from Arabic *mukhayyer* literally, choice, select.]

Mo·ham·med (mō ham′id) Muhammad.

Mo·ham·med·an (mō ham′id ən) *adj., n.* Muslim.

Mo·ham·med·an·ism (mō ham′id ən iz′əm) *n.* Islam *(def. 1).*

Mo·ha·ve (mō hä′vē) *pl.,* **-ves** or **-ve.** *also,* **Mo·ja·ve.** *n.* member of a tribe of North American Indians of the Yuman language family, formerly living chiefly along the Colorado River.

Mohave Desert, Mojave Desert.

Mo·hawk (mō′hôk) *pl.,* **-hawks** or **-hawk.** *n.* **1.** member of a tribe of Iroquois Indians formerly living along the Mohawk River. **2.** river in central New York.

Mo·he·gan (mō hē′gən) *pl.,* **-gans** or **-gan.** *n.* member of a tribe of North American Indians of the Algonquian language family, originally a branch of the Mahicans, formerly living in Connecticut.

Mo·hi·can (mō hē′kən) *pl.,* **-cans** or **-can.** *n.* **1.** Mahican. **2.** Mohegan.

Mo·ho·ro·vi·čić discontinuity (mō′hō rō′və chich) boundary between the earth's two outer layers, the crust and the mantle, at a depth ranging from between twenty and twenty-five miles beneath the continents to between three and eight miles beneath the ocean floor. Also, **Mo·ho** (mō′hō). [From Andrija *Mohorovičić,* 1857–1936, Yugoslavian geologist who discovered it.]

Mohs scale (mōz) scale for judging the hardness of substances, esp. minerals, by comparing them with ten standard minerals arranged in order of increasing hardness from talc, with a value of 1, to diamond, with a value of 10. [From Friedrich *Mohs,* 1773–1839, German mineralogist who devised it.]

moi·dore (moi′dôr) *n.* former gold coin of Portugal or Brazil. [Portuguese *moeda d'ouro* literally, money of gold, going back to Latin *monēta* mint², coin + *dē* from, of + *aurum* gold.]

moi·e·ty (moi′ə tē) *pl.,* **-ties.** *n.* **1.** half. **2.** portion; part; share. [Old French *moitie* half, from Latin *medietās* half.]

moil (moil) *v.i.* to work hard; toil. —*n.* **1.** hard work; toil; drudgery. **2.** confusion; turmoil. [Middle English *moillen* to moisten, make dirty (with mud), from Old French *moillier* to moisten, going back to Latin *mollis* soft.]

moi·ré (mwä rā′, mō rā′) *n.* **1.** fabric having a wavy or rippling pattern. **2.** such a pattern, pressed into a fabric with engraved rollers. —*adj.* having a wavy or rippling appearance.

moist (moist) *adj.* **1.** slightly or moderately wet; damp: *a moist cloth.* **2.** characterized by or containing moisture: *moist air.* **3.** (of eyes) tearful. [Old French *moiste* wet, going back to a blend of Latin *mūcidus* moldy, musty, and *musteus* fresh, new.] —**moist′ly,** *adv.* —**moist′ness,** *n.*

moist·en (moi′sən) *v.t.* to make moist; wet slightly: *to moisten the lips.* —*v.i.* to become moist.

mois·ture (mois′chər) *n.* **1.** water or other liquid diffused in the air or condensed on a surface. **2.** dampness; slight wetness.

Mo·ja·ve (mō hä′vē) Mohave.

Mojave Desert *also,* **Mohave Desert.** large desert in southeastern California, covering about 15,000 square miles.

mol (mōl) mole⁴.

mo·lal (mō′lal) *adj.* (of a solution) containing one mole of solute per 1000 grams of solvent. [MOLE⁴ + -AL¹.] —**mo·lal·i·ty** (mō lal′ə tē), *n.*

at; āpe; cär; end; mē; it; īce; hot; ōld; fôrk; wood; fōōl; oil; out; up; ūse; turn; sing; thin; this; zh in treasure; ə in ago, taken, pencil, lemon, circus.

mo·lar¹ (mō′lər) *n.* in man and most mammals, any of the largest teeth in the mouth, having a broad, irregular surface for grinding food. In man there are twelve molars. —*adj.* **1.** used or adapted for grinding. **2.** of or relating to the molar teeth. [Latin *molāris* molar tooth, from *mola* millstone; referring to the similarity between the grinding action of molars and that of millstones.]

mo·lar² (mō′lər) *adj.* (of a solution) containing one mole of solute per liter of solution. [MOLE⁴ + -AR¹.] —**mo·lar·i·ty** (mō-lar′ə tē), *n.*

mo·las·ses (mə las′iz) *n.* sweet, thick, brownish syrup obtained from sugar cane as a by-product of the refining process. [Portuguese *melaço*, from Late Latin *mellāceum* must², from Latin *mel* honey.]

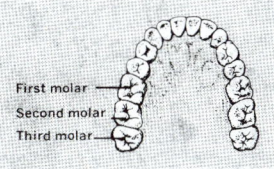

First molar
Second molar
Third molar

Molar¹

mold¹ (mōld) *also, British.* **mould.** *n.* **1.** hollow form or matrix for giving a particular shape to something in a fluid or plastic state. **2.** frame on or about which something is formed or made. **3.** that which is formed or made in or on a mold. **4.** shape given by a mold. **5.** general form; shape: *the mold of his face.* **6.** distinctive nature, character, or type: *brave men of rugged mold.* —*v.t.* **1.** to work into a particular shape; form: *to mold clay with the hands.* **2.** to form or make with or as with the use of a mold. **3.** to influence or direct: *to mold a personality.* [Old French *modle* hollow form for giving a particular shape to something, from Latin *modulus* small measure, diminutive of *modus* measure. Doublet of MODULE.] —**mold′er,** *n.*

mold² (mōld) *also, British.* **mould.** *n.* **1.** any of various woolly or furry growths that form on food and other oganic matter, caused by certain fungus plants. **2.** any of a number of fungus plants that cause such a growth. —*v.i.* to become covered with mold; grow moldy. [Possibly from Middle English *mouled*, past participle of *moulen* to grow moldy; of uncertain origin.]

mold³ (mōld) *also, British.* **mould.** *n.* **1.** loose soil that is rich in humus and suitable for plant growth. **2.** *Archaic.* ground; earth. [Old English *molde* soil¹, earth.]

Mol·da·vi·a (mol dā′vē ə, -dāv′yə) *n.* **1.** historic region of northeastern Romania. **2.** republic of the Soviet Union, in the European part of the country, bordering Romania. Official name: **Moldavian Soviet Socialist Republic.** Area, approx. 13,000 sq. mi. Pop. (1963 est.), 3,172,000. —**Mol·da′vi·an,** *adj., n.*

mold·board (mōld′bōrd′) *also, British.* **mould·board.** *n.* curved metal plate or board in a plow that turns over the soil as it is plowed.

mold·er (mōl′dər) *also, British.* **mould·er.** *v.i.* to turn to dust by natural decay; waste away; crumble. —*v.t.* to cause to crumble or decay. [MOLD² + -ER².]

mold·ing (mōl′ding) *also, British.* **mould·ing.** *n.* **1.** act or process of one who or that which molds. **2.** that which is formed or made by molding; molded object. **3.** shaped strip of wood, plaster, or other material, as

Moldings

along the upper part of a wall. **4.** decoratively molded surface, contour, or projection.

mold·y (mōl′dē) **mold·i·er, mold·i·est.** *also, British.* **mould·y.** *adj.* **1.** covered with or containing fungus mold: *old, moldy biscuits.* **2.** stale, as from age or decay; musty: *the moldy odor in an old house.* —**mold′i·ness,** *n.*

mole¹ (mōl) *n.* congenital brownish spot on the skin. [Old English *māl* spot, stain.]

mole² (mōl) *n.* any of various mammals, family Talpidae, of temperate regions of the Northern Hemisphere, that live in underground burrows. They have long claws used for digging, very small eyes, a pointed snout, and velvety fur. Length: 6–7 inches including the tail. [Possibly from Middle Dutch *mol.*]

Mole²

mole³ (mōl) *n.* **1.** massive structure, esp. of stone, that serves as a breakwater or pier. **2.** anchorage or harbor that is formed by such a structure. [Latin *mōlēs* mass, load, pier.]

mole⁴ (mōl) *also,* **mol.** *n. Chemistry.* quantity of an element or compound having a weight in grams numerically equal to the molecular weight. Also, **gram molecule, gram-molecular weight.** [German *Mol,* short for *Molekulargewicht* molecular weight.]

Mo·lech (mō′lek) Moloch.

mo·lec·u·lar (mə lek′yə lər) *adj.* relating to, caused by, or consisting of molecules.

molecular biology, branch of biology that deals with the molecular structure and basic chemical processes of living organisms.

molecular weight, sum of the atomic weights of the atoms in a molecule.

mol·e·cule (mol′ə kūl′) *n.* **1.** particle of matter consisting of two or more atoms joined by a covalent bond. **2.** any very small particle or bit. [Modern Latin *molecula,* diminutive of Latin *mōlēs* mass.]

mole·hill (mōl′hil′) *n.* **1.** small mound or ridge of earth formed by a mole burrowing under the ground. **2. to make a mountain out of a molehill,** to give too much importance or emphasis to something relatively insignificant.

mole·skin (mōl′skin′) *n.* **1.** soft, dark gray pelt of a mole, used as fur. **2.** strong, heavy, cotton fabric with a short nap on one side, used chiefly for work and sports clothes.

mo·lest (mə lest′) *v.t.* **1.** to annoy or disturb; bother. **2.** to make sexual advances to or force physical contact on (someone) indecently or illegally. [Latin *molestāre* to annoy, trouble.] —**mo·les·ta·tion** (mō′les tā′shən), —**mo·lest′er,** *n.*

Mo·lière (mōl yār′) *n.* 1622–73, French dramatist and comic actor; born Jean Baptiste Poquelin.

moll (mol) *n. Slang.* female companion or accomplice of a gangster. [From *Moll,* familiar form of MARY.]

mol·lie (mol′ē) *pl.,* **-lies.** *also,* **mol′ly.** *n.* any of a group of tropical fish, genus *Mollienesia,* that bear their young alive. [From Modern Latin *Molliensia,* from François N. Mollien, 1758–1850, French statesman.]

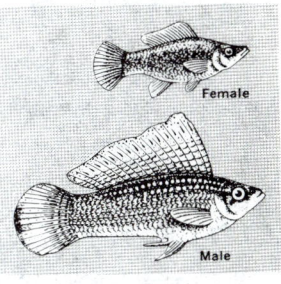

Female

Male

Mollies

mol·li·fy (mol′ə fī′) **-fied, -fy·ing.** *v.t.* **1.** to reduce the anger or strong feelings of; pacify: *to mollify an enraged person.* **2.** to reduce the intensity, severity, or harshness of: *to mollify someone's fury, to mollify demands.* [Latin *mollificāre* to soften, from *mollis* soft + *facere* to make.] —**mol′li·fi·ca′tion,** *n.*

mol·lusk (mol′əsk) *also, British.* **mol·lusc.** *n.* any of a large group of invertebrates, phylum Mollusca, found principally in salt water, including clams, oysters, and snails. Most mollusks have a hard, limy outer shell protecting a soft body, but some, as the squid and octopus, lack this type of shell. [Modern Latin *Mollusca,* neuter plural of Latin *molluscus* soft.]

mol·ly·co·dle (mol′ē kod′əl) *n.* man or boy of an unmanly or meek nature, who needs to be or has always been pampered. —*v.t.* **-dled, -dling.** to pamper; overprotect. [Obsolete *molly* milksop (from *Molly,* familiar form of MARY) + CODDLE.]

Mo·loch (mō′lok, mol′ək) *also,* **Mo·lech.** *n.* **1.** in the Old Testament, the chief god of the Ammonites to whom parents sacrificed their children by fire. **2.** anything regarded as requiring frightful sacrifice.

Mo·lo·kai (mō′lō kī′) *n.* one of the major islands of Hawaii, site of a leper colony. Area, 260 sq. mi. Pop. (1959 est.), 5230.

Mo·lo·tov (mol′ə tôf′, mō′lə-) **1. Vya·che·slav Mi·khai·lo·vich** (vyä′che släf′ mi khī′lə vich). 1890—, Soviet statesman and diplomat. **2.** See **Perm.**

Molotov cocktail, makeshift bomb consisting of a bottle filled with gasoline or other flammable liquid and a wick made of cloth or other material. [From Vyacheslav M. *Molotov.*]

molt (mōlt) *also, British.* **moult.** *v.i.* to shed the hair, feathers, skin, or shell previous to being replaced by a new growth. —*v.t.* to shed (an outer covering). —*n.* **1.** act or process of molting. **2.** that which is shed by molting. [Middle English *mouten* to shed feathers, through Old English, from Latin *mūtāre* to change.]

mol·ten (mōl′tən) *v. Archaic.* past participle of **melt.** —*adj.* **1.** melted or liquefied by heat: *Lava is molten rock.* **2.** made by melting and casting.

mol·to (mōl′tō) *adv. Music.* much; very. [Italian *molto,* from Latin *multum.*]

Mo·luc·cas (mə luk′əz, mō-) *n.,pl.* island group of Indonesia, for-

at; āpe; cär; end; mē; it; īce; hot; ōld; fôrk; wood; fōōl; oil; out; up; ūse; turn; sing; thin; this; zh in treasure; ə in ago, taken, pencil, lemon, circus.

merly known as the Spice Islands. Land area, approx. 20,000 sq. mi. Pop. (1961), 858,000. Also, **Molucca Islands.**

mo·ly (mō′lē) *pl.*, **-lies.** *n.* legendary herb with magical powers, having milk-white flowers and a black root, given to Odysseus by Hermes to counteract the spells of Circe. [Latin *mōly*, from Greek *mōly*.]

mo·lyb·de·nite (mə lib′də nīt′, mol′ib dē′nīt) *n.* soft, graphitelike molybdenum sulfide, the principal ore of molybdenum. Formula: MoS₂

mo·lyb·de·num (mə lib′də nəm, mol′ib dē′nəm) *n.* heavy, very hard, gray or black metallic element, used esp. to make high-strength alloys. Symbol: **Mo** See **element** for table. [Modern Latin *molybdenum*, through Latin, going back to Greek *molybdos* lead.]

mom (mom) *n. Informal.* mother.

Mom·ba·sa (mom bä′sə, -bas′ə) *n.* principal port city of Kenya, on the Indian Ocean. Pop. (1969), 246,000.

mo·ment (mō′mənt) *n.* **1.** short, indefinite period of time: *I'll be back in a moment.* **2.** particular point in time, esp. the present time: *Jerry's not here at the moment. The moment he spoke we recognized his voice.* **3.** particular period or stage, as in a course of events: *Democracy triumphed at that moment in the country's political development.* **4.** period or time distinguished by some quality, as excellence or enjoyment: *It was a pretty dull party, but it did have its moments.* **5.** importance; consequence: *This is a question of great moment.* **6.** *Physics.* turning effect of a force about a pivot point, measured as the product of the force and the distance between the point where the force is applied and the pivot point. [Latin *mōmentum* movement, motion, short period of time, importance.]

mo·men·tar·i·ly (mō′mən ter′ə lē) *adv.* **1.** for a moment: *Our train was momentarily delayed.* **2.** at any moment; very soon: *An announcement is expected momentarily.* **3.** from moment to moment; at every moment.

mo·men·tar·y (mō′mən ter′ē) *adj.* **1.** lasting only a very short time: *a momentary lull in the storm.* **2.** occurring at every moment. **3.** occurring at any moment. —**mo′men·tar′i·ness,** *n.*

mo·ment·ly (mō′mənt lē) *adv.* **1.** from moment to moment; every moment. **2.** for a moment. **3.** at any moment.

mo·men·tous (mō men′təs) *adj.* of great importance or consequence: *a momentous event.* —**mo·men′tous·ly,** *adv.* —**mo·men′tous·ness,** *n.*

mo·men·tum (mō men′təm) *pl.*, **-ta** (-tə) or **-tums.** *n.* **1.** *Physics.* property of a moving body, measured as the product of its mass and its velocity. **2.** force or speed resulting from motion; impetus. [Latin *mōmentum* movement, motion.]

mon-, form of **mono-** before vowels, as in *monandrous.*

Mon., Monday.

Mon·a·co (mon′ə kō′, mə nä′kō) *n.* **1.** small country in southwestern Europe, on the Mediterranean Sea. Capital, Monaco. Area, ⅓ sq. mi. Pop. (1969 est.), 23,000. **2.** capital of this country.

mon·ad (mon′ad, mō′nad) *n.* **1.** ultimate indivisible unit of existence; simplest living entity. According to the philosopher Leibniz, reality consists of an infinite number of these units. **2.** *Biology.* any single-celled organism. **3.** *Chemistry.* atom or element with a valence of one. [Late Latin *monad-,* stem of *monas* unit, from Greek *monas,* from *monos* alone.]

mo·nad·nock (mə nad′nok) *n.* isolated hill or mountain standing conspicuously above the surrounding country, left over by the process of erosion. [From Mt. *Monadnock,* in New Hampshire.]

mo·nan·drous (mə nan′drəs) *adj.* **1.** of, relating to, or characterized by the practice, custom, or condition of having only one husband at a time. **2.** *Botany.* having a single stamen, or bearing flowers that have a single stamen. [Greek *monandros* having only one husband, from *monos* alone + *anēr* (stem *andr-*) man.]

mo·nan·dry (mə nan′drē) *n.* **1.** practice, custom, or condition of having only one husband at a time. **2.** *Botany.* condition of being monandrous.

mon·arch (mon′ərk) *n.* **1.** hereditary, usually constitutional ruler, as a king or queen, having more or less limited powers. **2.** sole and absolute ruler of a state. **3.** someone or something suggesting, resembling, or of the nature of a monarch: *Mont Blanc is the monarch of mountains* (Byron, 1817). **4.** large orange and black butterfly, *Danaus plexippus,* that breeds

Monarch

in North America and is known for its fall migrations southward of several thousand miles. [Late Latin *monarcha* absolute ruler, from Greek *monarchēs* sole ruler, from *monos* alone + *archein* to rule.] —**mo·nar′chal** (mə när′kəl), **mo·nar′chi·al,** *adj.*

Syn. 2. Monarch, sovereign refer to a ruler of a state. **Monarch** refers to any hereditary ruler, as a king, queen, emperor, or empress: *French monarchs were noted for their patronage of the arts.* **Sovereign** applies esp. to a ruler who is invested with absolute powers and wields paramount authority: *Czars were the sovereigns of Russia.*

mo·nar·chi·cal (mə när′ki kəl) *adj.* **1.** of, relating to, or characteristic of a monarch or monarchy. **2.** ruled by or favoring a monarch or monarchy. Also, **mo·nar′chic.** —**mo·nar′chi·cal·ly,** *adv.*

mon·ar·chism (mon′ər kiz′əm) *n.* **1.** principles of monarchy. **2.** advocacy of or belief in monarchy as a form of government. —**mon′arch·ist,** *n., adj.* —**mon′ar·chis′tic,** *adj.*

mon·ar·chy (mon′ər kē) *pl.*, **-chies.** *n.* **1.** government by a monarch: *to favor monarchy over domocracy.* **2.** nation, state, or system of government ruled or headed by a monarch: *The United Kingdom is a monarchy.* [Late Latin *monarchia* absolute rule, from Greek *monarchia* government by one ruler, going back to *monas* alone + *archein* to rule.]

mon·as·te·ri·al (mon′əs tēr′ē əl) *adj.* of, relating to, or of the nature of a monastery or monastic life.

mon·as·ter·y (mon′əs ter′ē) *pl.*, **-ter·ies.** *n.* **1.** house or other place of residence occupied by a community of persons, esp. monks, living under religious vows and according to fixed rules. **2.** the community of persons living in such a place. [Church Latin *monastērium,* from Late Greek *monastērion,* from *monazein* to live alone. Doublet of MINSTER.] —**Syn. 1.** see **cloister.**

mo·nas·tic (mə nas′tik) *adj.* of, relating to, characteristic of, or of the nature of a monastery, its inhabitants, or their way of life: *monastic seclusion, monastic vows.* Also, **mo·nas′ti·cal.** —*n.* monk or other member of a religious order. [Late Latin *monasticus* solitary, from Late Greek *monastikos* living alone. going back to *monos* alone.]

mo·nas·ti·cism (mə nas′tə siz′əm) *n.* monastic system or way of life.

mon·a·tom·ic (mon′ə tom′ik) *adj.* (of a chemical element) occurring as a single atom rather than combined in a molecule.

mon·au·ral (mon ôr′əl) *adj.* of or relating to a system of sound reproduction in which the sound is heard from a single source. Also, **mon′o·phon′ic.** Distinguished from **stereophonic.**

Mon·dale, Walter Frederick (mon′dāl) 1928—, vice-president of the United States, since 1977.

Mon·day (mun′dē, -dā) *n.* second day of the week. [Old English *mōnandæg* literally, moon's day; translation of Latin *lūnae diēs.*]

Mo·nel metal (mō nel′) *Trademark.* silvery alloy consisting principally of nickel, copper, and iron. It is highly resistant to corrosion and is used to make equipment for the chemical industry.

Mo·net, Claude (mō nā′; klôd) 1840–1926, French impressionist painter.

mon·e·tar·y (mon′ə ter′ē, mun′-) *adj.* **1.** of or relating to the currency or coinage of a country: *The franc is the monetary unit of France.* **2.** of or relating to money: *monetary matters, a monetary gift.* [Late Latin *monētārius* relating to a mint², from Latin *monēta* mint², money. See MONEY.] —**mon′e·tar′i·ly,** *adv.*

mon·e·tize (mon′ə tīz′, mun′-) **-tized, -tiz·ing.** *v.t.* **1.** to establish as legal tender; legalize as money. **2.** to coin into money.

mon·ey (mun′ē) *pl.*, **mon·eys** or **mon·ies.** *n.* **1.** coins and paper currency issued by government authority to serve as a medium of exchange and a standard of value, generally used as payment for goods and services; legal tender. **2.** any article or substance used or serving as money, as checks. **3.** payment, gain, profit, or loss in terms of money: *The company made money on the deal.* **4.** wealth measured in terms of money, property, or possessions: *She tried to give the impression that her family had money.* **5.** sum of money, esp. a definite amount of money needed for something: *to give the landlord the rent money.* **6.** form or denomination of money. **7. in the money.** *Slang.* having a lot of money; wealthy. **8. to put** (or **place**) **money on.** to place a bet on: *to put money on the outcome of a race.* [Old French *moneie* coin, from Latin *monēta* place for coining money, coin, from *Monēta,* epithet of Juno, in whose temple money was coined in ancient Rome. Doublet of MINT².]

mon·ey·bag (mun′ē bag′) *n.* **1.** bag for holding money. **2. money-bags.** *Informal.* wealthy, often miserly person. ▲ construed as singular.

mon·ey·chang·er (mun′ē chān′jər) *n.* **1.** one whose business is exchanging money, usually that of one country for that of another. **2.** device that holds and dispenses coins.

mon·ey·eyed (mun′ēd) *also,* **mon·ied.** *adj.* **1.** having much money; wealthy. **2.** representing or derived from money or wealth: *the moneyed influence of the man of wealth* (Irving, 1825).

mon·ey·lend·er (mun′ē len′dər) *n.* one whose business is lending money at interest.

mon·ey·mak·ing (mun′ē mā′king) *adj.* **1.** designed or likely to earn money or successful in earning money: *a moneymaking scheme.* **2.** engaged in or intent on acquiring money or wealth: *a moneymaking spirit.* —*n.* acquisition of money or wealth. —**mon′ey·mak′er,** *n.*

at; āpe; cär; end; mē; it; īce; hot; ōld; fôrk; wood; fōōl; oil; out; up; ūse; turn; sing; thin; this; zh in treasure; ə in ago, taken, pencil, lemon, circus.

money of account, monetary denomination used in keeping accounts, esp. one not issued as a coin, as the U.S. mill.

money order, order for the payment of a specified sum of money, esp. one issued by one bank or post office and payable at another.

mon·ey·wise (mun′ē wīz′) *adv. Informal.* with reference to money.

mon·ger (mung′gər, mong′-) *n.* **1.** one who engages in or promotes something contemptible, discreditable, or harmful. ▲ usually used in combination, as in *scandalmonger, warmonger.* **2.** dealer in some commodity. ▲ usually used in combination, as in *fishmonger.* [Old English *mangere* dealer, going back to Latin *mangō.*]

mon·ger·ing (mung′gər ing, mong′-) *n.* promoting or dealing; peddling. ▲ usually used in combination, as in *warmongering.*

Mon·gol (mong′gəl, -gōl) *n.* **1.** member of the Mongolian-speaking nomadic tribes now living in the Mongolian People's Republic and nearby parts of China and southern Siberia. **2.** Mongolian *(defs. 1–3).* —*adj.* Mongolian *(def. 1).*

Mon·go·li·a (mong gō′lē ə) *n.* **1.** vast area in east-central Asia, extending from northern China to Siberia. Area, approx. 1,000,000 sq. mi. **2.** Mongolian People's Republic.

Mon·go·li·an (mong gō′lē ən) *n.* **1.** member or close descendant of the people of Mongolia. **2.** member of the Mongoloid division of the human race. **3.** subfamily of the Ural-Altaic family of languages, spoken predominantly in Mongolia and central Asia. —*adj.* **1.** of or relating to Mongolia. **2.** *also,* **mongolian.** of, relating to, or having mongolism.

Mongolian People's Republic, country in central Asia, bordered by the Soviet Union and China, formerly known as Outer Mongolia. Capital, Ulan Bator. Area, 604,250 sq. mi. Pop. (1967 est.), 1,170,000.

mon·gol·ism (mong′gə liz′əm) *also,* **Mon·gol·ism.** *n.* congenital abnormality in which a child is born mentally retarded with physical abnormalities, including slanting eyes and a broad, flattened skull.

Mon·gol·oid (mong′gə loid′) *adj.* **1.** of or relating to one of the ethnic divisions of the human race, usually characterized by yellowish skin, brown, slanted eyes, and straight, dark hair. The Mongoloid division includes the chief peoples of eastern Asia and Japan, the Eskimos, and the North American Indians. **2.** of, resembling, or characteristic of Mongols or Mongolians. **3.** of, relating to, or characteristic of mongolism. —*n.* **1.** member of the Mongoloid division of the human race. **2.** one who has mongolism.

mon·goose (mong′-gōōs′) *pl.,* **-goos·es.** *n.* slender, carnivorous mammal, family Viverridae, native to Africa, southern Asia, and parts of southern Europe, having a pointed face, a long tail, and rough, shaggy fur. It is noted for its ability to kill certain poisonous snakes, esp. cobras. Length: 1½–3½ feet including the tail. [Marathi *mangūs.*]

Mongoose

mon·grel (mung′grəl, mong′-) *n.* **1.** animal of mixed breed, esp. a dog. **2.** one who or that which is a mixture of different or incongruous elements. —*adj.* of mixed breed, origin, or nature. [From obsolete *mong* mixture, from Old English *gemang* a mingling.]

mon·ied (mun′ēd) moneyed.

mon·ies (mun′ēz) a plural of money.

mon·i·ker (mon′i kər) *also,* **mon·ick·er.** *n. Slang.* name or nickname. [Of uncertain origin.]

mon·ism (mon′iz′əm, mō′niz′-) *n.* philosophical theory that everything consists of or is reducible to one substance. Distinguished from **dualism** and **pluralism.** [Modern Latin *monismus,* from Greek *monos* single, alone.] —**mon′ist,** *n.*

mo·nis·tic (mə nis′tik, mō-) *adj.* of or relating to monism. Also, **mo·nis′ti·cal.**

mo·ni·tion (mə nish′ən) *n.* **1.** warning, admonition, or admonitory counsel. **2.** official, legal, or formal notice. [Latin *monitiō* a reminding, warning.]

mon·i·tor (mon′ə tər) *n.* **1.** student in school given a special duty or responsibility, as distributing materials or taking attendance. **2.** receiver used for checking, watching, or listening to transmissions, as those of television or radio. **3. Monitor.** Union ironclad warship with a low, flat deck and a revolving turret with two guns. It fought the Merrimac at Hampton Roads, Virginia in a historic Civil War battle on March 9, 1862. **4.** any of a group of large, mostly tropical lizards, genus *Varanus,*

Monitor *(def. 4)*

having a heavy, scaly, brown or black body, a thick, tapering tail, and strong legs with sharp claws. **5.** one who or that which warns, advises, or reminds. —*v.t.* **1.** to check, watch, or listen to (transmission) with a receiver. **2.** to keep track of with or as with an electronic device. **3.** to supervise; oversee. —*v.i.* to serve as a monitor, receiver, or supervisor. [Latin *monitor* admonisher, adviser, overseer.]

mon·i·to·ri·al (mon′ə tôr′ē əl) *adj.* **1.** of, relating to, or performed by a monitor or monitors. **2.** monitory.

mon·i·to·ry (mon′ə tôr′ē) *adj.* serving to warn or admonish. —*n. pl.,* **-ries.** letter of admonition, as from a religious superior.

monk (mungk) *n.* man who has entered a religious order devoted to prayer and contemplation and is bound by religious vows. [Old English *munuc,* going back to Late Latin *monachus,* from Late Greek *monachos,* from Greek *monos* alone.]

mon·key (mung′kē) *n.* **1.** any mammal of the order Primates, except man, lemurs, anthropoid apes, and tarsiers, of Asia, Africa, and North and South America, having long limbs and hands and feet adapted for grasping and climbing, as capuchins, marmosets, baboons, and rhesus monkeys. **2.** one who resembles a monkey in behavior or appearance, esp. a mischievous, playful, or imitative child. **3.** *Informal.* one who is made to appear foolish or ridiculous: *She really made a monkey out of me.* —*v.i.* **-keyed, -key·ing.** *Informal.* to play, fool, or meddle (often with *around* or *with*): *Don't monkey with the machinery.* —*v.t.* to imitate, mimic, or mock; ape. [Possibly from Middle Low German *Moneke,* name of an ape in medieval tales about Reynard the Fox.]

monkey bread 1. gourdlike fruit of the baobab tree. **2.** the tree itself.

monkey business *Informal.* playful, foolish, mischievous, or deceitful activity or behavior.

monkey jacket, short, close-fitting jacket, formerly worn by sailors. [Because it is like the jackets in which performing monkeys are dressed.]

mon·key·shines (mung′kē shīnz′) *n.,pl. Informal.* mischievous or playful acts; antics; pranks.

monkey suit *Slang.* man's formal dress suit. [Probably suggested by MONKEY JACKET.]

monkey wrench 1. wrench with an adjustable jaw and a fixed jaw, used on nuts and bolts of different sizes. **2.** something that disrupts or hinders: *This unexpected development threw a monkey wrench into our plans.*

Monkey wrench

monk·ish (mung′kish) *adj.* of, relating to, characteristic of, or like a monk or monks.

monks·hood (mungks′hood′) *n.* aconite *(def. 1).*

mo·no (mon′ō) *n. Informal.* infectious mononucleosis.

mono- *combining form* one; single; alone: *monogamy, monotheism.* [Greek *monos.*]

mon·o·ba·sic (mon′ə bā′sik) *adj.* (of an acid) yielding only one hydrogen ion.

mon·o·chord (mon′ə kôrd′) *n.* accoustical instrument for measuring and determining musical intervals, consisting of a sounding board over which is stretched a single string that can be divided at any point by a movable bridge. [Old French *monocorde,* through Medieval Latin, going back to Late Greek *monos* single + *chordē* string.]

mon·o·chro·mat·ic (mon′ə krō mat′ik, mon′ō krə-) *adj.* **1.** of or having only one color. **2.** consisting of or producing light of one wave length.

mon·o·chrome (mon′ə krōm′) *n.* **1.** painting or drawing done in a single color or in various shades of a single color. **2.** art or technique of producing such pictures. [Greek *monochrōmos* of one color, from *monos* single + *chrōma* color.]

mon·o·cle (mon′ə kəl) *n.* eyeglass for one eye. [French *monocle,* from Late Latin *monoculus* one-eyed, from Greek *monos* single + Latin *oculus* eye.]

mon·o·cled (mon′ə kəld) *adj.* wearing a monocle.

mon·o·cli·nous (mon′ə klī′nəs) *adj. Botany.* **1.** (of plants) having the stamens and pistils in the same flower. **2.** (of flowers) having both stamens and pistils. [Modern Latin *monoclinus,* from Greek *monos* single + *klinē* bed.]

Monocle

mon·o·cot·y·le·don (mon′ə kot′əl ēd′ən) *n.* any plant belonging to one of the two main divisions of flowering plants, characterized by having only one cotyledon in the embryo. Also, **mon′o·cot′.** —**mon′o·cot′y·le′don·ous,** *adj.*

mo·noc·u·lar (mə nok′yə lər) *adj.* **1.** having only one eye. **2.** of, relating to, using, or intended for use by one eye: *a monocular microscope.* [Late Latin *monoculus* one-eyed + -AR[1]. See MONOCLE.]

mon·o·cy·cle (mon′ə sī′kəl) *n.* unicycle.

mon·o·dy (mon′ə dē) *pl.,* **-dies.** *n.* **1.** in ancient Greek literature, an ode sung by a single voice, as in a tragedy, esp. a lament or dirge.

2. poem in which the poet laments someone's death. 3. *Music.*
a. homophonic style of composition. b. composition in this style.
[Greek *monōdidiā* solo, lament, going back to *monos* alone + *ōidē*
song.]

mo·noe·cious (mə nē′shəs) *also,* **mo·ne·cious.** *adj. Botany.* having
the stamens and the pistils in separate flowers on the same plant.
[MONO- + Greek *oikos* house + -OUS.]

mo·nog·a·mist (mə nog′ə mist) *n.* one who practices or believes in
monogamy.

mo·nog·a·mous (mə nog′ə məs) *adj.* of, relating to, or practicing monogamy. Also, **mon·o·gam·ic** (mon′ə gam′ik). —**mo·nog′-**
a·mous·ly, *adv.*

mo·nog·a·my (mə nog′ə mē) *n.* **1.** condition or practice of being
married to only one person at a time. **2.** *Zoology.* habit of having only
one mate. **3.** practice of marrying only one during life. [Late Latin
monogamia the marrying of only one wife, going back to Greek *monos*
single, alone + *gamos* marriage.]

mon·o·gram (mon′ə gram′) *n.* character consisting of two or more
letters, esp. the initials of one's name, combined or interlaced into one
design, used on clothing, stationery, and other items. —*v.t.* **-grammed**
or **-gramed, -gram·ming** or **-gram·ing.** to mark with a monogram.
[Late Latin *monogramma* character, consisting of several letters, from
Greek *monos* single, alone + *gramma* letter.] —**mon·o·gram·mat·ic**
(mon′ə grə mat′ik), *adj.*

mon·o·graph (mon′ə graf′) *n.* book, treatise, or article, usually of
a scholarly nature, written on a single subject or on a particular aspect
of a subject. —**mon′o·graph′ic,** *adj.*

mon·o·lith (mon′ə lith′) *n.* **1.** single, usually very large block of
stone, used in architecture and sculpture. **2.** monument or other structure formed of such a block of stone, as an obelisk. [Latin *monolithus*
made of one stone, from Greek *monolithos,* from *monos* single, alone
+ *lithos* stone.]

mon·o·lith·ic (mon′ə lith′ik) *adj.* **1.** formed of, relating to, or resembling a monolith. **2.** of the nature of a monolith; massive or uniform.

mon·o·logue (mon′ə lôg′, -log′) *also,* **mon·o·log.** *n.* **1.** long speech
made by one person, often monopolizing conversation. **2.** soliloquy.
3. dramatic or literary composition involving or performed by only one
speaker. **4.** entertainment consisting of a series of jokes, anecdotes, or
humorous stories presented by a single speaker. [French *monologue*
soliloquy, from Late Greek *monologos* speaking alone, from Greek
monos alone + *logos* word, discourse.] —**mon·o·log·ic** (mon′ə loj′ik);
also, **mon·o·log′i·cal,** *adj.* —**mo·nol·o·gist** (mə nol′ə jist), *n.*

mon·o·ma·ni·a (mon′ə mā′nē ə) *n.* **1.** mental disorder in which a
person has an obsession with one idea but otherwise appears sane.
2. excessive preoccupation with or enthusiasm for one idea or subject.
—**mon′o·ma′ni·ac,** *n.* —**mon·o·ma·ni·a·cal** (mon′ə mə nī′ə kəl), *adj.*

mon·o·mer (mon′ə mər) *n.* one of the small simple molecules making
up a polymer.

mon·o·met·al·lism (mon′ə met′əl iz′əm) *n.* theory or system of
using only one metal, usually gold, as the standard of currency.
—**mon·o·me·tal·lic** (mon′ə mi tal′ik), *adj.* —**mon′o·met′al·list,** *n.*

mo·no·mi·al (mə nō′mē əl, mō-) *adj.* consisting of a single term or
word. —*n.* monomial expression, quantity, or name. [MONO- +
(BIN)OMIAL.]

Mo·non·ga·he·la (mə nong′gə hē′lə) *n.* river in northern West Virginia and southwestern Pennsylvania joining the Allegheny at Pittsburgh to form the Ohio River.

mon·o·nu·cle·o·sis (mon′ə nōō′klē ō′sis, -nū′-) *n.* infectious
mononucleosis.

mon·o·phon·ic (mon′ə fon′ik) *adj.* **1.** *Music.* having a single melodic
line with no accompaniment. **2.** monaural.

Mo·noph·y·sit·ism (mō nof′ə sīt iz′əm) *n.* doctrine that the nature
of Christ was divine only, not both human and divine. This doctrine
is held by certain Eastern Christian churches, such as the Coptic Church.
—**Mo·noph′y·site** (mō nof′ə sīt′), *n.* —**Mon·o·phy·sit·ic** (mon′ə fi-
sit′ik), *adj.*

mon·o·plane (mon′ə plān′) *n.* airplane with only one main supporting surface or only one pair of wings.

mo·nop·o·list (mə nop′ə list) *n.* one who has a monopoly or favors
monopoly. —**mo·nop·o·lis′tic,** *adj.*

mo·nop·o·lize (mə nop′ə līz′) **-lized, -liz·ing.** *v.t.* **1.** to obtain or
exercise a monopoly of: *an attempt to monopolize the automobile industry.* **2.** to take or acquire exclusive control or possession of: *to
monopolize a conversation, to monopolize someone's time.* —**mo·nop′-**
o·li·za′tion, mo·nop′o·liz′er, *n.*

mo·nop·o·ly (mə nop′ə lē) *pl.,* **-lies.** *n.* **1.** exclusive control of a commodity or service in a particular market, or sufficient control to fix
prices and eliminate competition. **2.** right or privilege of such control
conferred by a government. A patent gives an inventor a monopoly over
his invention for a limited number of years. **3.** commodity or service
that is controlled by a monopoly. **4.** company or group that has a

monopoly. **5.** exclusive control or possession of something. [Latin
monopōlium privilege of exclusive dealing or sale, from Greek *monopō-
lion,* going back to *monos* single, alone + *pōlein* to sell.]

mon·o·rail (mon′ə rāl′) *n.* **1.** railway system of public transportation
in which the cars ride on a single rail, usually elevated above ground
traffic. Cars may either ride upon the rail or be suspended beneath it.
2. single rail for such a system.

mon·o·syl·lab·ic (mon′ə si lab′ik) *adj.* **1.** having only one syllable:
a monosyllabic suffix. **2.** consisting of or using monosyllables: *a curt,
monosyllabic reply.* —**mon′o·syl·lab′i·cal·ly,** *adv.*

mon·o·syl·la·ble (mon′ə sil′ə bəl) *n.* word of one syllable.

mon·o·the·ism (mon′ə thē iz′əm) *n.* doctrine or belief that there is
only one God. [MONO- + Greek *theos* god + -ISM.] —**mon′o·the′ist,**
n. —**mon′o·the·is′tic,** *adj.*

mon·o·tone (mon′ə tōn′) *n.* **1.** utterance of a succession of words or
sounds with no variation in pitch or key; single, unvaried tone in speaking, singing, or sound: *The lecturer spoke in a dull monotone.* **2.** sameness of style, manner, or color. —*adj.* **1.** monotonous. **2.** of, relating
to, or characterized by a sameness or lack of variation, as in color or
sound.

mo·not·o·nous (mə not′ən əs) *adj.* **1.** unvaried in tone, sound, or
cadence: *a monotonous voice, a monotonous rhythm.* **2.** tiresome or
uninteresting due to a lack of change or variety: *Steve quickly became
bored with the monotonous job.* —**mo·not′o·nous·ly,** *adv.* —**mo·**
not′o·nous·ness, *n.*

mo·not·o·ny (mə not′ən ē) *n.* **1.** tiresome sameness; lack of variety:
the monotony of prison life. **2.** lack of variation in tone, sound, or
cadence. [Greek *monotoniā* sameness of tone, going back to *monos*
single, alone + *tonos* sound.]

mon·o·treme (mon′ə trēm′) *n.* member of the most primitive order
of mammals, Monotremata, found chiefly in Australia, including the
platypus and echidna. Monotremes lay eggs but nurse their young.
[Modern Latin *Monotremata,* from MONO- + Greek *trēma* hole; referring to the single opening it has for its digestive, excretory, and reproductive organs.]

mon·o·type (mon′ə tīp′) *n.* **1.** machine consisting of a keyboard unit
and a typecasting unit, that casts and sets individual types for each
character and assembles them into lines of proper length. Trademark:
Monotype. **2.** type produced by such a machine: *The book was set in
monotype.* **3.** the sole representative of its group, as a single species that
constitutes a genus.

mon·o·va·lent (mon′ə vā′lənt) *adj.* having a valence of plus or
minus one; univalent. —**mon′o·va′lence, mon′o·va′len·cy,** *n.*

mon·ox·ide (mon ok′sīd, mə nok′-) *n.* oxide containing only one
atom of oxygen in each molecule.

Mon·roe (mən rō′) *n.* **1.** James. 1758–1831, fifth president of the
United States, from 1817 to 1825. **2.** city in northern Louisiana. Pop.
(1970), 56,374.

Monroe Doctrine, declaration of U.S. foreign policy made by President Monroe in 1823 that opposed further European colonization or
interference in the Western Hemisphere.

Mon·ro·vi·a (mon rō′vē ə) *n.* capital, chief port, and largest city of
Liberia, on the Atlantic Ocean. Pop. (1962 est.), 80,992.

Mon·sei·gneur (môN se nyœr′) *pl.,* **Mes·sei·gneurs.** *n.* **1.** French
title of honor given to men of eminence, as members of the higher
nobility, bishops, and cardinals. **2.** *also,* **monseigneur.** one who bears
this title. [French *monseigneur* my lord, from *mon* my (from Latin
meus) + *seigneur* lord (from Latin *senior* older).]

mon·sieur (mə syœ′) *pl.,* **mes·sieurs.** *n.* mister; sir. ▲ French form
of respectful or polite address for a man. [French *monsieur,* from *mon*
my (from Latin *meus*) + *sieur* lord (from Latin *senior* older).]

Mon·si·gnor (mon sēn′yər, môN′sēn yôr′) *pl.,* **Mon·si·gnors** or
Mon·si·gno·ri (môn′sēn yô′rē). *n.* **1.** title given to certain Roman
Catholic dignitaries, esp. those of the papal court and household.
2. *also,* **monsignor.** one who bears this title. [Italian *monsignore,* from
French *monseigneur.* See MONSEIGNEUR.]

mon·soon (mon sōōn′) *n.* **1.** seasonal wind of the Indian Ocean and
southern Asia, which blows from the southwest towards the land in
summer and from the northeast towards the ocean in winter. **2.** season
of the summer monsoon, characterized by heavy rains. **3.** any wind
system that seasonally reverses its direction. [Middle Dutch *monsoen*
periodic wind, from Portuguese *monção,* from Arabic *mausim* season.]

mon·ster (mon′stər) *n.* **1.** animal or plant that is abnormal in structure or appearance. **2.** imaginary creature that combines various animal
and human features, as a centaur or griffin. **3.** anything that is abnormal
or grotesque in shape or character. **4.** person or thing that is unusually
large. **5.** person whose behavior is inhumanly wicked, cruel, or immoral: *Hitler is a monster of wickedness, insatiable in his lust for blood*
(Churchill, 1941). —*adj.* enormous; gigantic. [Old French *monstre*
something abnormal in nature, from Latin *mōnstrum* portent, monstrosity, from *monēre* to warn.]

mon·strance (mon′strəns) *n.* vessel in which the consecrated Host is exposed for adoration, consisting of a glass receptacle surrounded by a frame of gold or silver rays. [Medieval Latin *monstrantia*, from Latin *mōnstrāre* to show.]

mon·stros·i·ty (mon stros′ə tē) *pl.* **-ties.** *n.* **1.** monstrous person or thing. **2.** quality or condition of being monstrous.

mon·strous (mon′strəs) *adj.* **1.** abnormal or grotesque in appearance or character. **2.** unusually large; enormous: *an error of monstrous proportions.* **3.** horrible; hideous; shocking: *monstrous lies.* —*adv. Archaic.* extremely. —**mon′strous·ly,** *adv.* —**mon′strous·ness,** *n.*

Mont., Montana.

mon·tage (mon tÄzh′) *n.* **1.** composite picture made by superimposing or combining several different pictorial elements. **2.** art or process of making such pictures. **3.** *Motion Pictures.* **a.** rapid succession of scenes or images, used esp. to create atmosphere or to illustrate a group of associated ideas. **b.** the revolving or flashing of images into focus or around a focused area. **4.** similar composite technique in radio, literature, music, and other arts. [French *montage* a putting together, from *monter* to put together, climb. See MOUNT[1].]

Mon·taigne, Mi·chel Ey·quem, Seigneur de (mon tän′; *French* môN ten′ye; mē shel′ e kem′) 1533–92, French essayist.

Mon·tan·a (mon tan′ə) *n.* state in the northwestern United States. Capital, Helena. Area, 147,138 sq. mi. Pop. (1970), 694,409. Abbreviation, **Mont.** —**Mon·tan′an,** *adj., n.*

Mont Blanc (mont blangk′; *French* môN blÄN′) highest mountain in the Alps, between France and Italy.

Mont·calm, Louis Jo·seph de (mont käm′; *French* môN kälm′; lwĕ zhô zef′) 1712–59, French general in the French and Indian War.

mon·te (mon′tē) *n.* card game of Spanish origin played with a special pack of forty cards, in which players bet against the dealer. Also, **monte bank.** [Spanish *monte* the game, pile of cards left after dealing, mountain, from Latin *mōns* heap, mountain.]

Mon·te Car·lo (mon′tē kär′lō) resort town in Monaco, on the Mediterranean, site of a world-famous gambling casino.

Mon·te·ne·gro (mon′tə nē′grō, -nÄ′-) *n.* constituent republic of Yugoslavia, on the Adriatic, formerly an independent kingdom. Area, approx. 5333 sq. mi. Pop. (1961), 471,894. —**Mon′te·ne′grin,** *adj., n.*

Mon·ter·rey (mon′tə rā′) city in northeastern Mexico. Pop. (1960), 596,939.

Mon·tes·so·ri, Maria (mon′tə sôr′ē) 1870–1952, Italian physician and educator.

Montessori method, method of preschool and primary education developed by Maria Montessori emphasizing sensory and motor training, individual expression, and the development of self-discipline and independence.

Mon·te·ver·di, Clau·dio (mon′tə vär′dē; klou′dyō) 1567–1643, Italian composer.

Mon·te·vi·de·o (mon′tə vi dā′ō, -vid′ē ō′) *n.* capital of Uruguay, in the southern part of the country, on the Plata River. Pop. (1964 est.), 1,200,000.

Mon·te·zu·ma II (mon′tə zōō′mə) c.1480–1520, emperor of the Aztecs.

Mont·gom·er·y (mont gum′ər ē, -gum′rē) *n.* capital of Alabama, in the central part of the state. Pop. (1970), 133,386.

month (munth) *n.* **1.** one of the twelve parts into which the calendar year is divided. Also, **calendar month. 2.** time from any day of one calendar month to the corresponding day of the next month. **3.** period of about four weeks or thirty days. **4.** period of a complete revolution of the moon around the earth, esp. the period from one new moon to the next, **synodic month,** or the period from a given star to the same star, **sidereal month.** Also, **lunar month. 5.** one-twelfth of the solar year. Also (*def.* 5), **solar month.** [Old English *mōnath.*]

month·ly (munth′lē) *adj.* **1.** done, happening, or appearing once a month. **2.** of or relating to a month. **3.** continuing or lasting a month. —*adv.* once a month; every month. —*n. pl.,* **-lies.** periodical published once a month.

Mont·mar·tre (môN mär′trə) *n.* district in Paris, formerly noted as a center for artists.

Mont·pel·ier (mont pēl′yər) *n.* capital of Vermont, in the central part of the state. Pop. (1970), 8609.

Mont·pel·lier (môN pel yā′) *n.* city in southern France. Pop. (1968), 161,910.

Mont·re·al (mon′trē ôl′) *n.* chief port and largest city of Canada, in southern Quebec, on the St. Lawrence River. Pop. (1968), 1,222,255.

Monstrance

Mont-Saint-Mi·chel (môN′saN mē shel′) *n.* islet in the English Channel off the coast of Normandy, noted for its Benedictine monastery.

mon·u·ment (mon′yə mənt) *n.* **1.** building, statue, arch, or other structure erected to commemorate a person or event. **2.** memorial stone or marker placed at a grave; tombstone. **3.** anything that serves as a memorial of a person, period, or event: *Shakespeare's plays remain as monuments to his genius.* **4.** work or achievement of enduring significance: *The discovery of penicillin was a monument in medical research.* **5.** area or site of special significance set aside and preserved by a government. **6.** marker or other object, either occurring naturally or placed by man, which indicates a boundary of real property. [Latin *monumentum* memorial, tomb.]

mon·u·men·tal (mon′yə ment′əl) *adj.* **1.** of enduring significance; notable: *a monumental decision of the U.S. Supreme Court.* **2.** of great size or scope; huge; colossal: *a monumental lie.* **3.** like a monument; imposing: *a monumental structure.* **4.** of, for, or serving as a monument. —**mon′u·men′tal·ly,** *adv.*

moo (mōō) *n.* sound made by a cow. —*v.i.,* mooed, moo·ing. to make such a sound. [Imitative.]

mooch (mōōch) *Slang. v.t.* **1.** to get without paying; beg: *to mooch a cigarette.* **2.** to steal; pilfer. —*v.i.* **1.** to get things without paying. **2.** to sneak; skulk. [Possibly from Old French *muchier* to hide, skulk; possibly of Celtic origin.] —**mooch′er,** *n.*

mood[1] (mōōd) *n.* **1.** state or frame of mind at a particular time: *He was in a happy mood.* **2.** state of mind disposing one to action: *Some artists work only when they are in the mood.* **3.** **moods.** fits of bad temper, sudden anger, or depression. [Old English *mōd* mind, spirit, feeling.]

mood[2] (mōōd) *n. Grammar.* the form of a verb that shows whether the speaker thinks of the statement as fact, command, wish, or possibility. There are three moods in English: indicative, imperative, and subjunctive. Also, **mode.** [Modification (influenced by *mood[1]*) of MODE[1].]

mood·y (mōō′dē) **mood·i·er, mood·i·est.** *adj.* **1.** given to or governed by changing moods, esp. gloomy or sullen moods. **2.** characterized by or expressing a gloomy mood: *a moody face, a moody film.* —**mood′i·ly,** *adv.* —**mood′i·ness,** *n.*

Syn. 1. Moody, temperamental mean extremely changeable in nature. **Moody** characterizes sudden, impulsive, and sharply varying states of mind, often subjecting one to fits of moroseness, gloom, and depression: *As grandpa grew older, he became very moody.* **Temperamental** characterizes erratic, unpredictable, and capricious changes in behavior arising from a high-strung, excitable, and volatile nature: *The director found it difficult to work with such a temperamental actress.*

moon (mōōn) *n.* **1.** the earth's natural satellite, visible by the sun's reflected light, orbiting the earth from west to east once in about 29½ days with reference to the sun and in about 27⅓ days with reference to the stars at a mean distance of about 238,857 miles. The moon has a mean diameter of 2160 miles or about ¼ that of the earth. Its mass is about $\frac{1}{81}$ and its volume, about $\frac{1}{49}$ that of the earth. **2.** any one of the phases of the moon. **3.** anything resembling the moon in any of its phases, as a crescent. **4.** satellite of any other planet: *Mars has two small moons.* **5.** month, esp. a lunar month. **6.** moonlight: *White in the moon the long road lies* (Houseman, 1896). —*v.i.* to move or look about dreamily or aimlessly. [Old English *mōna* satellite of the earth.]

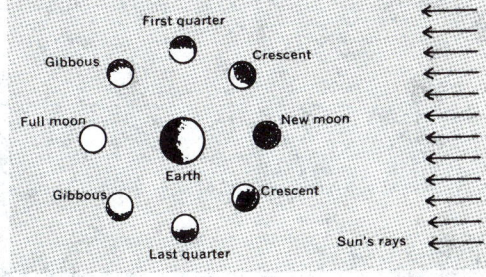

First quarter

Gibbous

Crescent

Full moon

New moon

Earth

Gibbous

Crescent

Last quarter

Sun's rays

Phases of the moon

moon·beam (mōōn′bēm′) *n.* ray of light from the moon.

moon·calf (mōōn′caf′) *pl.,* **-calves.** *n.* **1.** one who is born deformed. **2.** idiot. [From a belief that the influence of the moon can have a harmful effect.]

moon·light (mōōn′līt′) *n.* light shining from the moon. —*adj.* **1.** illuminated by the moon; moonlit. **2.** occurring or performed by the

light of the moon: *a moonlight raid.* —*v.i.* to work at a second job, esp. at night, in addition to one's regular job. —**moon′light′er,** *n.*

moon·lit (mōōn′lit′) *adj.* lighted by the moon.

moon·scape (mōōn′skāp′) *n.* picture or view of the moon's surface with the horizon in the background.

moon·shine (mōōn′shīn′) *n.* **1.** moonlight. **2.** empty talk or ideas; nonsense. **3.** liquor distilled secretly and illegally. —*v.t., v.i.,* **-shined, -shin·ing.** to distill (liquor) illegally. —**moon′shin′er,** *n.*

moon·stone (mōōn′stōn′) *n.* pearly, opalescent gem stone, an ornamental variety of feldspar containing either albite or orthoclase.

moon·struck (mōōn′struk′) *adj.* romantically dazed or slightly crazy because of the supposed influence of the moon.

moon·y (mōō′nē) **moon·i·er, moon·i·est.** *adj.* **1.** dreamy; moonstruck. **2.** of, relating to, or like the moon.

moor[1] (moor) *v.t.* to secure (a ship or other craft) in place, as at a dock or berth. —*v.i.* **1.** to secure or anchor a ship or other craft. **2.** to be secured, as by ropes and anchors. [Probably from Middle Low German *moren* to tie.]

moor[2] (moor) *n.* tract of open, rolling, wild land, often covered with heath, and having bogs and marshes. [Old English *mōr.*]

Moor (moor) *n.* **1.** member of a people of mixed Arab and Berber descent living in northern Africa. **2.** member of this people that invaded and conquered Spain in the eighth century A.D. [Old French *More,* from Latin *Maurus* inhabitant of Mauretania, from Greek *Mauros.*]

moor·age (moor′ij) *n.* **1.** place for mooring. **2.** act of mooring; being moored. **3.** charge for the use of moorings.

moor cock, male of the moorfowl.

Moore, Thomas (moor, môr) 1779–1852, Irish poet.

moor·fowl (moor′foul′) *n.* red grouse.

moor·hen (moor′hen′) *n.* **1.** female of the moorfowl. **2.** common gallinule.

moor·ing (moor′ing) *n.* **1.** act of a person or thing that moors. **2.** device, such as a cable line or anchor, by which a ship is moored. **3.** place where a boat or a ship can be moored. **4. moorings.** elements of one's life, as beliefs and habits, that make one feel stable and secure.

Moor·ish (moor′ish) *adj.* **1.** of or relating to the Moors. **2.** characteristic of the artistic style of the Moors.

moor·land (moor′land′, -lənd) *n. British.* tract of land consisting of moors.

moose (mōōs) *pl.* **moose.** *n.* **1.** large, heavily built mammal, *Alces alces,* the largest member of the deer family, native to the northern forests of North America, having a massive head, a short neck, humped shoulders, and a blackish-brown coat with gray markings. The male has enormous broad antlers which may measure more than 6½ feet across. Height: to 6 feet at the shoulder. **2.** elk (def. 2). [Of Algonquian origin.]

Moose

moot (mōōt) *adj.* **1.** subject to dispute or discussion; debatable: *a moot observation.* **2.** without practical significance or value; purely academic. —*v.t.* **1.** to bring up for discussion or debate. **2.** to make purely academic or unimportant. —*n.* in Anglo-Saxon England, an assembly of freemen to administer justice and discuss local problems. [Old English *mōt* assembly, discussion.]

moot court, teaching court in which law students plead imaginary cases and instructors evaluate their legal knowledge and abilities.

mop (mop) *n.* **1.** cleaning device consisting of a bundle of coarse yarn, cloth, sponge, or other absorbent material, fastened at the end of a handle. **2.** any thick, tangled mass resembling this, as a head of hair. —*v.t.,* **mopped, mop·ping. 1.** to clean with or as with a mop. **2. to mop up, a.** to finish a project. **b.** *Military.* to clear out remaining enemy troops from (a captured area). [Possibly from Old French *mappe* napkin, from Latin *mappa.*]

mope (mōp) **moped, mop·ing.** *v.i.* to be gloomy, apathetic, and sad. —*n.* one who mopes or is inclined to mope. [Of uncertain origin.] —**mop′er,** *n.* —**mop′ing·ly,** *adv.*

mo·ped (mō′ped) *n.* heavily built bicycle with a low-powered motor. [From *mo(tor)* and *ped(al).*]

mop·pet (mop′it) *n.* child, esp. a little girl. [Obsolete English *mop* fool, child (of uncertain origin) + -ET.]

mop-up (mop′up′) *n.* act or instance of mopping up.

mo·quette (mō ket′) *n.* fabric having a thick velvety pile, used for upholstery or carpeting. [French *moquette* Wilton carpet, modification of earlier *moucade* imitation velvet; of uncertain origin.]

mo·raine (mə rān′) *n.* raised land form consisting of accumulated rock debris deposited by a melting glacier. [French *moraine,* from dialectal French *morêna;* of uncertain origin.]

mor·al (môr′əl, mor′-) *adj.* **1.** being good according to a standard of right and wrong: *a moral person.* **2.** conforming to a standard of right conduct: *the moral thing to do.* **3.** of, relating to, or concerned with a standard of right conduct: *the moral climate of a university.* **4.** that promotes, aids, or is on the side of right conduct: *moral teachings.* **5.** acting on or relating to feelings or character: *moral support.* **6.** probable although not supported by evidence: *a moral certainty.* **7.** capable of conforming to a standard of right conduct: *Animals are not moral beings.* —*n.* **1.** lesson or inner meaning taught by a fable, a story, or an event. **2. morals.** principles or standards in regard to right or wrong conduct, esp. sexual conduct. [Latin *mōrālis* relating to manners, from *mōs* custom, manner.] —**mor′al·ly,** *adv.*

Syn. *adj.* **2. Moral, ethical** mean conforming to right conduct. **Moral** emphasizes the distinction between right and wrong as dictated by one's conscience: *The statesman stood up to his moral convictions even though his views made him unpopular.* **Ethical** relates to objectively defined principles governing ideal human conduct, esp. as embodied in a professional code laying down standards of honesty, integrity, and fairness: *As an ethical lawyer, Mr. Jackson refused to betray the confidence of his client.*

mo·rale (mə ral′) *n.* attitude or condition of an individual or group with respect to such qualities as courage, confidence, and high spirits: *Scoring a run boosted the team's morale.* [Modification of French *moral* spirit (as of troops), going back to Latin *mōrālis* relating to manners. See MORAL.]

mor·al·ism (môr′ə liz′əm, mor′-) *n.* adherence to or advocacy of strict moral standards, esp. in the form of common sayings or maxims.

mor·al·ist (môr′ə list, mor′-) *n.* **1.** one who teaches or writes on morality. **2.** one who is characterized by moralism.

mor·al·is·tic (môr′ə lis′tik, mor′-) *adj.* characterized by moralism, esp. tending to preach or urge morality.

mo·ral·i·ty (mə ral′ə tē) *pl.,* **-ties.** *n.* **1.** state or quality of being moral. **2.** moral conduct: *There may be morality where there is no religion* (R. W. Dale, 1878). **3.** system of conduct embodying principles of right and wrong; ethics: *Victorian morality.* **4.** discourse or instruction intended to teach a lesson in right conduct or ethics. **5.** morality play.

morality play, any of a group of moralistic dramatic works popular during the fifteenth and sixteenth centuries, in which the characters represent abstract qualities, such as envy or fortitude.

mor·al·ize (môr′ə līz′, mor′-) **-ized, -iz·ing.** *v.i.* to make judgments on matters of right and wrong, esp. to tell people what to do in a moralistic fashion. —*v.t.* **1.** to explain or interpret the lesson or moral of. **2.** to improve the morals of. —**mor′al·iz′er,** *n.*

moral philosophy, ethics.

moral victory, defeat that is felt to be a victory, esp. because of hopeful circumstances accompanying it.

mo·rass (mə ras′) *n.* **1.** piece of low, soft, wet ground; marsh; swamp. **2.** any state or situation that is entangling, perplexing, or hindering: *the morasses and fogs of doubt* (Gladstone, 1884). [Dutch *moeras* marsh, from Old French *mareis;* of Germanic origin.]

mor·a·to·ri·um (môr′ə tôr′ē əm, mor′-) *pl.,* **-to·ri·ums** or **-to·ri·a** (-tôr′ē ə). *n.* **1.** suspension for a specified period of time of the obligations of a debtor or debtors. **2.** period of such a suspension. **3.** any authorized temporary suspension or cessation of some activity. [Modern Latin *moratorium,* going back to Latin *morārī* to delay.]

Mo·ra·vi·a (mô rā′vē ə) *n.* historic region in central Czechoslovakia.

Mo·ra·vi·an (mô rā′vē ən) *adj.* **1.** of or relating to Moravia or its inhabitants. **2.** of or relating to the Moravian Church. —*n.* **1.** native or inhabitant of Moravia. **2.** member of the Moravian Church.

Moravian Church, Protestant denomination that originated in Germany in the eighteenth century among followers of John Huss.

mo·ray (môr′ā, mô rā′) *n.* any of various, often brilliantly colored saltwater eels, family Muraenidae, found in warm waters and feared by divers because of its vicious bite. Also, **moray eel.** [Portuguese *moreia* eel, from Latin *mūrena,* from Greek *myraina.*]

mor·bid (môr′bid) *adj.* **1.** overly sensitive to, or dwelling upon, death, disease, decay, and the like; not cheerful or wholesome. **2.** of or relating to death, disease, decay, and the like; gruesome; grisly: *a morbid graveyard scene.* **3.** relating to, caused by, or characteristic of disease: *a morbid condition of the liver.* [Latin *morbidus* sickly, from *morbus* disease.] —**mor′bid·ly,** *adv.* —**mor′bid·ness,** *n.*

mor·bid·i·ty (môr bid′ə tē) *n.* **1.** quality or state of being morbid. **2.** rate of disease or proportion of diseased persons in a given geographical area.

mor·da·cious (môr dā′shəs) *adj.* **1.** given to biting; biting. **2.** sarcastic; caustic. [Latin *mordāc-,* stem of *mordāx* biting + -OUS.] —**mor·da′cious·ly,** *adv.* —**mor·dac·i·ty** (môr das′ə tē), *n.*

mor·dan·cy (môrd′ən sē) *n.* quality of being sarcastic or biting.

mor·dant (môrd′ənt) *adj.* **1.** caustic, cutting, or sarcastic. **2.** that acts as a color fixative in dyeing. —*n.* **1.** any substance, as tannin, that when combined with a dye serves to fix the color in the cloth. **2.** acid or other

corrosive used in etching to eat into metal. [Old French *mordant* biting, present participle of *mordre* to bite, going back to Latin *mordēre*.]

Mor·de·cai (môr′də kī′) *n.* in the Old Testament, the cousin of Esther, who helped her save the Jews from the massacre planned by Haman.

mor·dent (môr′dənt, môr dent′) *n. Music.* quick alternation of a principal tone with a tone below it; downward trill. [Italian *mordente* literally, a bite, from *mordere* to bite, from Latin *mordēre*; with reference to the sharp manner of its playing.]

Mor·dred (môr′drid) *n.* Modred.

more (môr) *adj.* comparative of **much** or **many. 1.** greater in number, quantity, intensity, or degree: *more cars, more flour.* **2.** being an additional amount; further: *one more time. I'll have a minute more.* —*adv.* comparative of **much. 1.** in or to a greater extent or degree: *Be more careful. He exercises more regularly than I do.* **2.** in addition; further; again: *He fell once more.* **3. more or less. a.** in or to a greater or lesser degree or extent: *His condition has more or less improved.* **b.** just about; approximately: *He paid me more or less in time.* —*n.* **1.** greater number, quantity, amount, or degree: *The more I work, the more I accomplish.* **2.** an additional amount: *Say no more.* [Old English *māra* greater, larger.]

More, Sir Thomas (môr) 1478–1535, English statesman, writer, and saint.

Mo·re·a (mô rē′ə) *n.* Peloponnesus.

mo·reen (mə rēn′) *n.* medium-to-heavy wool or cotton fabric, woven with a lengthwise rib and given a moiré finish, used esp. for upholstery and men's suits.

mo·rel (mə rel′) *n.* any of a group of edible mushrooms, genus *Morchella,* having a brittle hollow stalk and a spongelike cap, esp. *M. esculenta.* [French *morille;* of Germanic origin.]

more·o·ver (môr ō′vər, môr′ō′vər) *adv.* in addition to what has been said; also: *The day was dark and cold, and moreover it was raining.*

mo·res (môr′āz, -ēz) *n.,pl.* customs that are considered essential for the preservation of a social system, such as particular standards of moral behavior. [Latin *mōrēs,* plural of *mōs* custom, manner.]

Mo·resque (mə resk′) *adj.* Moorish.

Mor·gan (môr′gən) **1. Sir Henry.** c.1635–88, English privateer. **2. J(ohn) P(ierpont).** 1837–1913, U.S. financier.

Mor·gan (môr′gən) *n.* light horse of a breed originally developed in New England, having short legs and powerful shoulders, and noted for its stamina and gentle disposition. [From Justin *Morgan,* 1747–98, U.S. owner of the horse that was the sire of the breed.]

mor·ga·nat·ic (môr′gə nat′ik) *adj.* of or designating a form of marriage between a person of royal or noble rank and a commoner in which the person of lower rank and any children of the marriage do not share in the titles and estates of the person of higher rank. [Modern Latin *morgenatica* morning gift (from Medieval Latin *matrimonium ad morganaticum* marriage with morning gift), going back to Old High German *morgan* morning; referring to the traditional gift given by a husband to a wife of lower rank on the morning after their wedding with the understanding that this gift was to be her sole share in her husband's estate.]

Mor·gan le Fay (môr′gən lə fā′) *Arthurian Legend.* a fairy, the evil half sister of King Arthur.

morgue (môrg) *n.* **1.** place, often run by the police, in which the bodies of persons who were the victims of accidents or violence or who were found dead are kept for identification. **2.** reference library, as in a newspaper office, in which old clippings and other sources of information are stored. [French *morgue* place where unknown dead persons are kept for identification; of uncertain origin.]

mor·i·bund (môr′ə bund′, mor′-) *adj.* in a dying state; nearly lifeless or outmoded: *a moribund empire.* [Latin *moribundus* dying, from *morī* to die.] —**mor′i·bun′di·ty,** *n.* —**mor′i·bund′ly,** *adv.*

mo·ri·on (môr′ē on′) *n.* metal helmet with a brim that comes to a peak in the front and back and has no visor or other part to protect the face, worn esp. by European soldiers of the sixteenth and seventeenth centuries. [French *morion,* from Spanish *morrión,* from *morra* crown of the head; of uncertain origin.]

Mor·mon (môr′mən) *n.* member of the Church of Jesus Christ of Latter-day Saints, a Christian denomination founded in 1830 in New York by Joseph Smith. One of the holy books of the Mormons is the Book of Mormon, an account of some ancient Hebrew peoples who supposedly were the ancestors of American Indians. —*adj.* of or relating to the Mormons, their beliefs, or their church.

morn (môrn) *n.* morning. [Old English *morgen.*]

morn·ing (môr′ning) *n.* **1.** first part of the day, beginning at midnight or daybreak and ending at noon. **2.** daybreak; dawn: *Morning began to streak the sky.* **3.** first part of anything; beginning: *the morning of creation.* —*adj.* of, relating to, or occurring in the morning: *morning chill, morning coffee.* [Middle English *morwening* beginning of morn, from *morwen* morning, from Old English *morgen.*]

morning glory *n.* **1.** trumpet-shaped flower of any of a large group of vines, shrubs, or trees, genus *Ipomoea,* growing mainly in purple, pink, yellow, or white. **2.** plant, esp. a twining vine, bearing this flower, widely cultivated in gardens and having oval or heart-shaped leaves.

morning star, planet, esp. Venus, visible in the eastern sky before sunrise.

Mo·ro (môr′ō) *pl.* **Mo·ros.** *n.* **1.** member of any of the various Muslim Malay tribes living in the southern Philippine Islands. **2.** language of these people, belonging to the Malayo-Polynesian language family. [Spanish *Moro* Moor, Muslim, from Latin *Maurus.* See MOOR.]

Mo·roc·can (mə rok′ən) *adj.* of or relating to Morocco, its people, or culture. —*n.* native or inhabitant of Morocco.

Morning glory

mo·roc·co (mə rok′ō) *pl.* **-cos.** *n.* **1.** leather that originally came from Morocco, made from goatskin tanned with sumac. It is often used for the bindings of fine books. **2.** leather finished in imitation of this. [From MOROCCO.]

Mo·roc·co (mə rok′ō) *n.* country in northwestern Africa, on the Atlantic and the Mediterranean, formerly governed by France and Spain. Capital, Rabat. Area, 171,835 sq. mi. Pop. (1969 est.), 15,050,000.

mo·ron (môr′on) *n.* **1.** one who is mentally retarded, having a mental age of up to 12 years. See **mental retardation. 2.** very foolish or stupid person. [Greek *mōron,* neuter of *mōros* dull, stupid.]

mo·rose (mə rōs′) *adj.* bad-tempered, gloomy, and withdrawn. [Latin *mōrōsus* peevish, particular, from *mōs* manner, custom.] —**mo·rose′ly,** *adv.* —**mo·rose′ness,** *n.*

mor·pheme (môr′fēm) *n.* smallest meaningful unit of language. A morpheme can be a word, a word element, or an affix. *Tri-, angle-,* and *-s* are the three morphemes in the word *triangles.* [French *morphème,* from Greek *morphē* shape, form.]

Mor·phe·us (môr′fē əs, -fūs) *n. Classical Mythology.* god of dreams, son of Hypnos.

mor·phine (môr′fēn) *n.* powerful, addicting drug derived from opium, valuable as a painkiller. Also, **mor·phi·a** (môr′fē ə). [German *Morphin,* from *Morphcus* god of dreams; because it causes sleep.]

mor·phin·ism (môr′fi niz′əm) *n.* **1.** pathological condition caused by habitual misuse of morphine. **2.** morphine addiction.

mor·pho·gen·e·sis (môr′fə gen′ə sis) *n. Biology.* evolutionary changes in the structure of an organism or part. [Greek *morphē* shape, form + GENESIS.] —**mor·pho·ge·net·ic** (môr′fō jə net′ik), **mor′pho·gen′ic,** *adj.*

mor·pho·log·i·cal (môr′fə loj′i kəl) *adj.* of, relating to, or part of morphology. Also, **mor′pho·log′ic.** —**mor′pho·log′i·cal·ly,** *adv.*

mor·phol·o·gy (môr fol′ə jē) *n.* **1.** biological study of the structure of animals and plants. **2.** structure of an organism considered as a whole. **3.** branch of linguistics which studies how groups of sounds are joined together to make words. [Greek *morphē* shape, form + -LOGY.]

mor·ris (môr′is, mor′-) *n.* vigorous English dance performed in fancy costumes, often representing Robin Hood and his men. Also, **morris dance.** [Form of MOORISH.]

Mor·ris (môr′is, mor′-) **1. Gouv·er·neur** (guv′ər nēr′). 1752–1816, U.S. statesman. **2. William.** 1834–96, English artist, poet, and social reformer.

Morris chair, easy chair with cushions and an adjustable back. [From William *Morris,* who designed it.]

mor·row (môr′ō, mor′ō) *n.* **1.** tomorrow: *I shall say good night till it be morrow* (Shakespeare, *Romeo and Juliet*). **2.** *Archaic.* morning. [Middle English *morwe,* form of *morwen* morning. See MORNING.]

Morse, Samuel F(inley) B(reese) (môrs) 1791–1872, U.S. inventor and artist.

Morse code, code used in telegraphy in which combinations of dots and dashes are used to represent the letters of the alphabet, numerals, and punctuation marks. [From Samuel F. B. *Morse,* who invented it.]

mor·sel (môr′səl) *n.* **1.** small bite or portion, as of food. **2.** small quantity or piece; fragment. [Old French *morsel* a small bite, diminutive of *mors* a bite, from Latin *morsus.*]

mor·tal (môr′tl) *adj.* **1.** subject to death; destined to die: *All things that live are mortal.* **2.** that causes death; fatal: *a mortal blow, a mortal disease.* **3.** that precedes, accompanies, or brings death: *a man in his last mortal agonies.* **4.** fought, pursued, or existing to the death; relentless; implacable: *engaged in mortal combat.* **5.** very great or intense: *He quaked in mortal fear of the spider.* **6.** limited and human; earthly. **7.** possible; conceivable: *What mortal reason can he have for saying that?* **8.** *Informal.* excessive or extremely great in some respect. **9.** *Informal.* long and tedious: *He worked on that car for three mortal hours.* **10.** (of sin) causing estrangement from God. Distinguished from **venial.** —*n.* human being; person. [Latin *mortālis* subject to death, from *mors* death.] —**mor′tal·ly,** *adv.* —**Syn.** *adj.* **2.** see **deadly.**

mor·tal·i·ty (môr tal′ə tē) *n.* **1.** state or condition of being subject to death. **2.** number of deaths in a given time in a given place. **3.** large-scale death or destruction, as from war. **4.** humanity; mankind.

mor·tar¹ (môr′tər) *n.* mixture of sand and water with lime which hardens as it dries, used esp. for binding bricks or stones together, as in a wall. [Old French *mortier* cement, from Latin *mortārium* vessel in which substances are pounded, pounded material.]

mor·tar² (môr′tər) *n.* **1.** thick bowl, as of marble, in which substances are crushed to a powder by means of a pestle. **2.** muzzle-loading, smooth-bored cannon for firing shells in a high trajectory. [French *mortier* mortar¹, vessel in which substances are pounded, type of cannon resembling this vessel, from Latin *mortārium*. See MORTAR¹.]

mor·tar·board (môr′tər bôrd′) *n.* **1.** square, flat plate of wood or metal with a centered handle, used by masons to hold mortar. **2.** skullcap attached to a square, cloth-covered piece of wood or cardboard, worn at graduations and other academic exercises by teachers and students.

mort·gage (môr′gij) *n.* **1.** right to claim real property, given as security for the payment of a debt or for the performance of some obligation. **2.** document proving that such security has been given. —*v.t.*, **-gaged, -gag·ing. 1.** to pledge (real property) as security for the payment of a debt or for the performance of some obligation. **2.** to give up or pledge in advance. [Old French *mortgage* literally, dead pledge (because the pledge is lost or "dead" to the mortgager if he fails to meet the conditions of the contract), from *mort* dead (from Latin *mortuus*) + *gage* pledge (of Germanic origin).]

mort·ga·gee (môr′gi jē′) *n.* one to whom property is mortgaged.

mort·ga·gor (môr′gi jər) *also,* **mort·gag·er.** *n.* one who mortgages his property.

mor·tice (môr′tis) *n.* mortise. —*v.t.*, **-ticed, -tic·ing.** to mortise.

mor·ti·cian (môr tish′ən) *n.* undertaker (*def. 1*). [From Latin *mors* (stem *mort-*) death, on the model of English *physician.*]

mor·ti·fi·ca·tion (môr′tə fi kā′shən) *n.* **1.** feeling of shame, humiliation, or embarrassment. **2.** anything causing such feelings. **3.** *Religion.* practice of suppressing desires and passions, as by austere living or self-infliction of pain. **4.** death and decay of one part of a living animal organism; gangrene.

mor·ti·fy (môr′tə fī′) **-fied, -fy·ing.** *v.t.* **1.** to subject to shame, humiliation, or embarrassment. **2.** *Religion.* to subject to mortification: *to mortify the desires of the flesh.* —*v.i.* to become gangrenous; decay. [Old French *mortifier* to torment the body by austerities, put to death, from Late Latin *mortificāre* to kill, from Latin *mors* death + *facere* to make.] —**mor′ti·fi′er,** *n.*

mor·tise (môr′tis) *n.* shaped hole, as in a piece of wood, to receive a tenon or projecting part of a second piece so as to form a tight joint. —*v.t.* **-tised, -tis·ing. 1.** to join or fasten securely, esp. by a tenon and mortise. **2.** to cut or make a mortise in. [Middle French *mortaise* hole in a piece of timber to receive the tenon, going back to Arabic *murtazz* fixed in.]

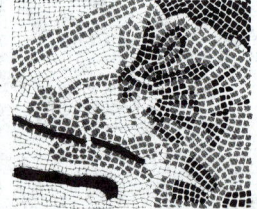
Mortise

mort·main (môrt′mān′) *n.* transfer of real property to any corporate body, as a religious order, in perpetuity. [Old French *mortemain* the state of being inalienable; literally, dead hand, from Medieval Latin *mortua manus* dead hand; probably because the property could not be disposed of.]

mor·tu·ar·y (môr′chōō er′ē) *pl.,* **-ies.** *n.* place where corpses are prepared, as by embalming, and kept until burial or cremation. —*adj.* of or relating to death or burial. [Late Latin *mortuārius* relating to the dead, from Latin *mortuus* dead.]

mos., months.

mo·sa·ic (mō zā′ik) *n.* **1.** inlaid surface decoration composed of variously colored bits of stone, glass, or other hard material forming a picture or design. **2.** technique or process of making such designs. **3.** anything that is similar to a mosaic: *The novelist's life was a mosaic of varying experiences.* [French *mosaïque* the inlaid surface decoration, through Italian and Medieval Latin, from Late Latin *mūsīvum,* from Latin *Mūsa.* See MUSE.]

Mo·sa·ic (mō zā′ik) *adj.* of or relating to Moses or the writings or laws ascribed to him.

Mosaic

Mosaic law 1. ancient civil and ceremonial law of the Hebrews, ascribed to Moses. **2.** the first five books of the Old Testament, containing these laws; the Pentateuch.

Mos·cow (mos′kou, -kō) *n.* capital and leading city of the Soviet Union and capital of the Russian Republic, in the western part of the country. (1970), 6,942,000.

Mo·selle (mō zel′) *n.* **1.** river rising in northeastern France, flowing past Luxembourg and into West Germany, where it joins the Rhine. **2.** light, dry, white wine produced in the valley along the Moselle River in Germany.

Mo·ses (mō′ziz, -zis) *n.* in the Old Testament, the great prophet and lawgiver of the Israelites who led them out of Egypt, regarded as the founder of Judaism.

Mosque

mo·sey (mō′zē) **-seyed, -sey·ing.** *v.i. Informal.* to shuffle along or move in a leisurely way. [Of uncertain origin.]

Mos·lem (moz′ləm, mos′-) *adj.* Muslim. —*n. pl.,* **-lems.** Muslim.

mosque (mosk) *n.* Muslim temple or place of worship. [French *mosquée,* through Italian and Spanish, from Arabic *masjid* temple, place of worship.]

mos·qui·to (məs kē′tō) *pl.,* **-toes** *or* **-tos.** *n.* any of a group of flies, family Culicidae, having a long proboscis that is used by the female to pierce the skin of vertebrates, including man, and suck their blood. The resulting bite causes itching and can transmit such diseases as malaria and yellow fever. [Spanish *mosquito,* diminutive of *mosca* fly, from Latin *musca.*]

mosquito net, screen or covering of gauzelike material that keeps out mosquitoes.

moss (môs) *n.* **1.** any of a large group of primitive, nonflowering plants, division Bryophyta, that grows in colonies and often forms soft dense mats. Mosses are found throughout the world, growing mostly in damp shady places, as on rocks, next to streams, on tree trunks, and on the ground. **2.** any of various other plants that resemble moss, as the club moss or the Iceland moss.

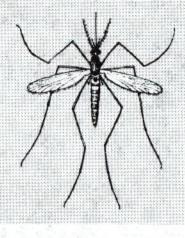
Mosquito

moss·back (môs′bak′) *n. Informal.* one who is extremely old-fashioned or conservative.

moss rose, widely cultivated rose, *Rosa centifolia,* variety *muscosa,* having mosslike hair on the stem and buds.

moss·y (mô′sē) **moss·i·er, moss·i·est.** *adj.* **1.** covered with or having much moss. **2.** resembling moss. —**moss′i·ness,** *n.*

most (mōst) *adj.* superlative of **much** and **many. 1.** greatest in number, quantity, or degree: *Who picked the most apples?* **2.** greatest part or number of; majority of: *Most American boys like to play baseball.* **3. for the most part.** in general; mainly: *Things have been quiet here, for the most part.* —*n.* **1.** greatest number, quantity, or degree: *That is the most I can do.* **2.** the greatest part or number of persons: *James did more to help than most would.* **3. at (the) most.** at or to the greatest extent or degree; not more than: *At most, I'll be away two days.* **4. to make the most of.** to employ to the best advantage: *Make the most of each opportunity.* —*adv.* superlative of **much. 1.** very: *a most gracious hostess. You are most convincing.* **2.** in or to the greatest extent or degree. **3.** *Informal.* almost; nearly: *He's most all tuckered out.* [Old English *mǣst* greatest.]

-most *suffix* (used to form adjectives in the superlative degree) most or closest to: *topmost.* [Old English *-mest.*]

most·ly (mōst′lē) *adv.* for the most part; mainly; chiefly: *Our weather has been mostly warm.*

mot (mō) *n.* brief, witty saying. [French *mot* word, going back to Latin *muttum* grunt, mutter.]

mote (mōt) *n.* particle or speck, as of dust. [Old English *mot.*]

mo·tel (mō tel′) *n.* hotel for motorists, usually situated near a main road or highway, with parking space convenient to the guest rooms. [Blend of MOTOR and HOTEL.]

mo·tet (mō tet′) *n. Music.* solo or choral vocal composition, often with no written accompaniment, usually meant to be sung in church. [Old French *motet,* diminutive of *mot* word. See MOT.]

moth (môth) *pl.,* **moths** (môthz, môths). *n.* **1.** any of a group of broad-

winged insects, order Lepidoptera, found throughout the world. Moths are distinguished from butterflies by flying mostly at night, by being less brightly colored with stouter bodies, and, in the male, by having comb-like antennae. **2.** clothes moth. [Old English *moththe* clothes moth.]

moth·ball (môth′bôl′) *n.* small ball of naphthalene or camphor, used to repel clothes moths from fabrics and furs.

moth·eat·en (môth′ēt′ən) *adj.* **1.** eaten away or damaged by clothes moths. **2.** worn-out or old-fashioned.

moth·er¹ (muth′ər) *n.* **1.** female that has given birth to an offspring. **2.** female that adopts or principally cares for a child or offspring. **3.** that which has given birth to or nurtures something; origin; source. **4.** woman who has a role like that of a mother. **5.** qualities characteristic of a mother, such as affection, concern, or protectiveness: *It brings out the mother in her.* **6.** mother superior. **7.** elderly woman. ▲ used as a respectful term of address. —*adj.* **1.** that is a mother: *a mother hen.* **2.** relating to or characteristic of a mother: *mother love.* **3.** native. **4.** bearing a relationship like that of a mother: *He was raised in the mother church.* —*v.t.* **1.** to be mother of. **2.** to treat in a motherly way, esp. by being too protective toward. [Old English *mōdor* female parent.] —**moth′er·less,** *adj.*

moth·er² (muth′ər) *n.* mother of vinegar.

Mother Car·ey's chicken (kâr′ēz) storm petrel.

mother country **1.** one's native country. **2.** country in relation to its colonies: *The American colonies rose against their mother country.*

Mother Goose, imaginary author of a collection of fairy tales and nursery rhymes.

moth·er·hood (muth′ər hood′) *n.* **1.** state or role of being a mother. **2.** mothers collectively.

Mother Hub·bard (hub′ərd) **1.** main character in an old nursery rhyme. **2.** *also,* **mother hubbard.** full, loose gown worn by women.

mother-in-law (muth′ər in lô′) *pl.,* **moth·ers-in-law.** *n.* mother of one's husband or wife.

mother lode, principal, broad vein of ore that runs through a district or particular section of country.

moth·er·ly (muth′ər lē) *adj.* characteristic of or befitting a mother: *motherly concern.* —*adv.* in the manner of a mother. —**moth′er·li·ness,** *n.*

Mother Nature, nature in a pure or unspoiled condition, including the earth, seas, atmosphere, and organic life, esp. when thought of as a source of generation.

moth·er-of-pearl (muth′ər əv purl′) *n.* hard, rainbow-colored layer lining the shells of pearl oysters, abalone, and certain other mollusks, used for making buttons and ornaments. Also, **na′cre.**

mother of vinegar, filmy layer on the surface of fermenting vinegar, wine, or cider formed of yeast cells and bacteria. [Possibly because the substance appeared to be a product of the "mother" liquid.]

Mother's Day, day set aside in honor of mothers, observed annually on the second Sunday of May.

mother superior, nun who is head of a female religious community.

mother tongue **1.** one's native language. **2.** language from which other languages are derived: *Latin is the mother tongue of the Romance languages.*

moth·proof (môth′prōōf′) *v.t.* to make resistant to clothes moths, as by treatment with insecticide: *The storage closet has been mothproofed.* —*adj.* resistant to clothes moths: *a mothproof sweater.*

moth·y (môth′ē) **moth·i·er, moth·i·est.** *adj.* containing or damaged by moths.

mo·tif (mō tēf′) *n.* **1.** idea, situation, incident, problem, or the like that serves as a major, and usually repeated, theme or subject in a work of art, literature, or drama. **2.** distinctive, usually repeated, figure, design, or color, as in a decoration or printed pattern: *The wallpaper has a floral motif.* **3.** *Music.* short and easily recognizable fragment of music which may be associated with a particular character or idea. [French *motif* theme, cause, from Medieval Latin *motivum* that which causes an action. See MOTIVE.]

mo·tile (mō′təl) *adj. Biology.* that which has the power to move itself: *a motile flagellum.* [Latin *mōtus,* past participle of *movēre* to set in motion + -ILE.] —**mo·til·i·ty** (mō til′ə tē), *n.*

mo·tion (mō′shən) *n.* **1.** fact or process of changing position or place or of not staying still: *the continual motion of the sea, the forward motion of a car.* **2.** act of moving the body or one of its parts, esp. in a meaningful manner: *The policeman signaled with a motion of his hand.* **3.** formal proposal or suggestion made in a law court or other meeting or assembly: *John made a motion to take a vote.* —*v.i.* to make a significant or meaningful movement of a part of the body: *The guide motioned to me to be silent.* —*v.t.* to direct with a movement or gesture: *The hostess motioned me to a seat.* [Latin *mōtio* movement, moving.]

mo·tion·less (mō′shən lis) *adj.* that does not or cannot move; not moving.

motion picture **1.** presentation or show created by projecting a sequence of still photographs onto a white screen or the like at high

speed, thus producing the illusion of movement or reproducing the movement originally photographed. **2.** specific story or other subject matter photographed as a motion picture. Also, **moving picture.**

motion sickness, disorder that results from being subjected to a swinging or rotary motion, as in a car, ship, or aircraft, characterized by nausea, vomiting, and dizziness.

mo·ti·vate (mō′tə vāt′) **-vat·ed, -vat·ing.** *v.t.* to provide with a motive; move to effort or action.

mo·ti·va·tion (mō′tə vā′shən) *n.* **1.** act or process of motivating; being motivated. **2.** that which motivates.

mo·tive (mō′tiv) *n.* **1.** mental state, internal need, or outward goal which causes one to act; motivation: *The motive for the attack was a fear of being attacked.* **2.** motif. —*adj.* of, relating to, or producing motion: *Wind is a motive power.* [Medieval Latin *motivum* that which causes an action, from *motivus* moving, from Latin *movēre* to set in motion.] —**Syn.** *n.* **1.** see **reason.**

mot juste (mō zhoost′) *pl.,* **mots justes** (mō zhoost′). *French.* word or phrase that is exactly appropriate to the situation.

mot·ley (mot′lē) *adj.* **1.** made up of diverse or varied elements; heterogeneous: *a motley blend of images, a motley group of people on a train.* **2.** of different colors; mottled: *the motley hues of autumn leaves.* —*n.* **1.** suit or costume of many different colors, esp. one worn by a clown or court jester. **2.** mixture of incongruous or varied elements. [Of uncertain origin.]

mo·tor (mō′tər) *n.* **1.** small engine, esp. an internal-combustion engine. **2.** *British.* automobile. **3.** that which causes or imparts motion. —*adj.* **1.** producing or imparting motion: *motor power.* **2.** equipped with or driven by a motor. **3.** of, relating to, used, or designed for motor vehicles. **4.** *Physiology.* of or relating to that part of the nervous system that sends out impulses to control the functioning, coordination, and behavior of the various muscles in the body: *motor control.* —*v.i.* to ride in or travel by motor vehicle, esp. by automobile. [Latin *mōtor* mover.]

mo·tor·bike (mō′tər bīk′) *n.* **1.** bicycle powered by a small motor. **2.** motorcycle.

mo·tor·boat (mō′tər bōt′) *n.* boat powered by a motor, esp. a small, open boat with an outboard motor.

mo·tor·bus (mō′tər bus′) *n.* bus.

mo·tor·cade (mō′tər kād′) *n.* procession of automobiles. [MOTOR + (CAVAL)CADE.]

mo·tor·car (mō′tər kär′) *n.* automobile.

motor court, motel.

mo·tor·cy·cle (mō′tər sī′kal) *n.* two-wheeled, motorized vehicle, built like a bicycle though larger and heavier, propelled by an internal-combustion engine. —**mo′tor·cy′clist,** *n.*

Motorcycle

mo·tor·ist (mō′tər ist) *n.* one who drives a car.

mo·tor·ize (mō′tə rīz′) **-ized, -iz·ing.** *v.t.* **1.** to equip or furnish with a motor; *to motorize a wheelchair.* **2.** to supply with motor-driven vehicles in place of horses and horse-drawn vehicles: *to motorize farms.* —**mo′tor·i·za′tion,** *n.*

mo·tor·man (mō′tər mən) *pl.,* **-men.** *n.* one who drives or operates a subway train, streetcar, or similar vehicle.

motor scooter, two-wheeled motorized vehicle similar to a child's scooter.

motor vehicle, any wheeled conveyance, as a truck, bus, automobile, or motorcycle, powered by a motor for use on roads and highways.

mot·tle (mot′əl) **-tled, -tling.** *v.t.* to mark or cover with irregular spots or streaks of different colors. —*n.* mottled coloring or pattern. [Probably from MOTLEY.]

mot·to (mot′ō) *pl.,* **-toes** or **-tos.** *n.* **1.** maxim or proverb that expresses a principle: *My motto is "Nothing ventured, nothing gained."* **2.** short, appropriate statement added to something to express or symbolize its content or nature. [Italian *motto* word, saying, going back to Latin *muttum* grunt, mutter.]

moue (mōō) *n.* pouting grimace. [French *moue*; of Germanic origin.]

mouf·lon (mōōf′lon) *also,* **mouf·flon.** *n.* wild sheep, *Ovis musimon,* native to Corsica and Sardinia, having a dark reddish-brown coat, and large curving horns in the male. Height: 27 inches at the shoulder. [French *mouflon,* from Italian *mufflone,* going back to Late Latin *mufrō* wild sheep; of uncertain origin.]

mould (mōld) *British.* mold.

mould·board (mōld′bôrd′) *British.* moldboard.

mould·er (mōl′dər) *British.* molder.

mould·ing (mōl′ding) *British.* molding.

mould·y (mōl′dē) **mould·i·er, mould·i·est.** *adj. British.* moldy. —**mould′i·ness**, *n.*

moult (mōlt) *British.* molt.

mound (mound) *n.* **1.** artificial elevation or bank of earth or stones: *a fortress surrounded by mounds and trenches.* **2.** any heap or pile: *a mound of leaves, a mound of garbage.* **3.** small, natural elevation; hillock. **4.** *Baseball.* slightly raised area in the center of the diamond from which the pitcher pitches. —*v.t.* **1.** to fortify or enclose with a mound. **2.** to heap up in a mound. [Possibly from Middle Dutch *mond* protection.]

Mound Builders (mound) various early Indian peoples of southeastern North America who built burial mounds and fortifications.

mount[1] (mount) *v.t.* **1.** to go up; climb: *to mount a small hill.* **2.** to get up on top of: *to mount a horse.* **3.** to place on or attach to a stable support or stand: *to mount a camera on a tripod.* **4.** to set in place, as for display: *to mount stamps in an album.* **5.** to prepare and begin to carry out: *The candidate mounted an attack on his rival's high campaign spending.* **6.** to provide (a theatrical presentation) with the accessories or equipment of production, as scenery, costumes, and lighting. **7.** to furnish with a horse or other animal for riding. **8.** *Military.* **a.** to have or carry (armaments): *A ship that mounts two fifty-caliber machine guns.* **b.** to post (someone) as a guard. —*v.i.* **1.** to increase or accumulate (often with *up*): *Tension mounts up.* **2.** to get up on something, as the back of a horse: *The cowboys mounted and rode off.* **3.** to rise; ascend. —*n.* **1.** horse or other animal for riding. **2.** that in which or on which anything is mounted; mounting. [Old French *monter* to go up, climb, going back to Latin *mōns* mountain, heap.] —**Syn.** *v.t.* **1.** see **climb.**

mount[2] (mount) *n.* **1.** mountain. ▲ now poetic except before a proper name: *Mount Rushmore.* [Old English *munt* mountain, hill, from Latin *mōns* mountain, heap; influenced by Old French *mont* mountain, hill.]

moun·tain (mount′ən) *n.* **1.** mass of land rising considerably above the surrounding country, usually to a peak, and produced by movements of the earth's crust, volcanic action, erosion of elevated land areas, or a combination of these processes. **2.** huge heap or pile; towering mass: *a mountain of ice.* **3.** great quantity or amount: *a mountain of trouble.* [Old French *montaigne* high hill, going back to Latin *montānus* relating to mountains, from *mōns* high hill, heap.]

mountain ash, any of a group of trees or tall shrubs, genus *Sorbus,* of the rose family, bearing foul-smelling white flowers and red or orange berrylike fruits, as the rowan.

mountain chain, series of mountains whose bases are continuous, making a sharply rising, clearly distinguished formation longer than it is broad.

moun·tain·eer (mount′ən ēr′) *n.* **1.** one who lives in or is part of the culture of a mountainous region. **2.** one who is skilled at mountain climbing. —*v.i.* to climb mountains.

mountain goat, Rocky Mountain goat.

mountain laurel, ornamental North American evergreen shrub, *Kalmia latifolia,* of the heath family, having glossy oblong leaves and large clusters of flowers in white or shades of rose.

mountain lion, cougar.

moun·tain·ous (mount′ən əs) *adj.* **1.** having many mountains. **2.** huge; enormous: *a mountainous pile of old cars.*

Mountain laurel

mountain range, ridge or series of ridges of mountains, usually alike in origin, geologic age, and form.

Mountain Standard Time, the local civil time of the 105th meridian west of Greenwich, England, used in the west-central United States. It is seven hours earlier than Greenwich Time.

mountain system, number of adjacent mountain ranges, usually parallel to each other.

moun·tain·top (mount′ən top′) *n.* top of a mountain.

moun·te·bank (moun′tə bank′) *n.* one who is deceitful or unscrupulous; trickster; charlatan. [Italian *montambanco* quack[2], short for *monta in banco* literally, climb on a fence (in order to address an audience), from *montare* to climb (going back to Latin *mōns* mountain) + *in* in + *banco.* See BANK[2].]

mount·ed (moun′tid) *adj.* **1.** seated or riding on a mount or mounts: *The huntsmen were mounted and ready.* **2.** serving on mounts, esp. horses: *mounted police.* **3.** in or on a stable support or stand: *The guns are mounted on the truck.* **4.** set in place, as for display: *an ashtray with mounted stones, a lamp mounted on a brass base, stamps mounted in an album.*

Moun·tie (moun′tē) *n. Informal.* member of the Royal Canadian Mounted Police.

mount·ing (moun′ting) *n.* **1.** anything that serves as a support or

setting: *The rifle is in its mounting on the wall.* **2.** act or process of one who or that which mounts.

Mount Ver·non (vur′nən) **1.** home and burial place of George Washington, on the Potomac in Virginia, near Washington, D.C. **2.** city in southeastern New York. Pop. (1970), 72,778.

mourn (môrn) *v.i.* **1.** to feel sorrow or grief: *We mourn for our fallen comrades.* **2.** to lament the death of someone, esp. by exhibiting conventional signs of grief. —*v.t.* **1.** to feel or express sorrow or grief over (someone's death): *We all mourn his passing.* **2.** to feel or express grief or sadness at; complain about or bemoan: *He mourned his great misfortunes.* [Old English *murnan* to feel sorrow, lament.]

mourn·er (môr′nər) *n.* one who mourns, esp. one attending a funeral: *The mourners walked slowly from the graveside.*

mourners' bench, front row of seats at a revival meeting, reserved for those who are repenting their sins.

mourn·ful (môrn′fəl) *adj.* **1.** feeling grief or sorrow: *the mournful widow.* **2.** expressing or filled with sadness or sorrow: *a mournful song, a mournful face.* —**mourn′ful·ly,** *adv.* —**mourn′ful·ness,** *n.*

mourn·ing (môr′ning) *n.* **1.** act of one who mourns; state of feeling sorrow or grief. **2.** conventional display of sorrow over a person's death, esp. the wearing of black. **3.** customary clothes, draperies, and other furnishings worn or used to express such sorrow: *a widow dressed in mourning.* **4.** period during which such garments or furnishings are worn or displayed: *The family is still in mourning.*

mourning dove, wild North American pigeon, *Zenaidura macroura,* having a mournful, cooing call. Length: 12 inches.

Mourning dove

mouse (*n.,* mous; *v.,* mouz) *pl.,* **mice** (mīs). *n.* **1.** any of numerous small rodents, families Muridae and Cricetidae, usually having pointed snouts, relatively small ears, and thin tails with little or no hair. **2.** one who is quiet or timid. **3.** *Slang.* bruise under the eye, usually from a punch; black eye. **4.** *Nautical.* act of mousing. —*v.i.,* **moused, mous·ing.** to hunt for or catch mice. —*v.t. Nautical.* to secure (a hook) with a mousing. [Old English *mūs* the small rodent.]

mous·er (mou′zər) *n.* animal, esp. a cat, that is good at catching mice.

mous·ing (mou′zing) *n. Nautical.* several turns of thin rope or cord fixed around the shank and point of a hook to prevent a load from unhooking.

mousse (mōōs) *n.* **1.** dessert consisting of whipped cream or beaten egg whites combined with a flavoring and chilled. **2.** dish made of finely chopped or pureed meat, poultry, or fish and stock and chilled in a mold until jelled. [French *mousse* froth, foam; probably of Germanic origin.]

Mousing

mousse·line (mōōs lēn′) *n. French.* fine, lightweight muslin.

mousseline de laine (də len′) *French.* lightweight woolen fabric that is often made with a printed pattern.

mousseline de soie (də swä′) *French.* thin silk muslin fabric, similar to but crisper than silk chiffon.

mous·tache (məs tash′, mus′tash) mustache.

mous·y (mou′sē) **mous·i·er, mous·i·est.** *adj.* **1.** of, resembling, or suggesting a mouse, esp. in color; drab or dirty: *mousy brown hair.* **2.** timid and quiet as a mouse. **3.** infested with mice.

mouth (*n.,* mouth; *v.,* mouth) *pl.,* **mouths** (mouthz). *n.* **1.a.** opening through which an animal takes in food. **b.** cavity bounded in front by the lips and teeth and in the back by the pharynx which, in higher vertebrates, encloses the teeth, gums, and tongue and through which sounds are uttered. **2.** parts of this outwardly visible on the face, esp. the lips. **3.** opening resembling a mouth: *the mouth of a jar, the mouth of a volcano.* **4.** living thing considered as needing food: *many mouths to feed.* **5.** power, quality, or manner of speech. **6.** part of a river where it empties into another body of water. **7.** *Archaic.* disapproving or derisive expression; grimace. **8. down in** (or **at**) **the mouth.** *Informal.* dejected; depressed: *down in the mouth because of defeat.* —*v.t.* **1.** to pronounce or speak without believing or understanding; say or repeat automatically: *to mouth opinions.* **2.** to appear to sing or speak (something) by silently moving the lips: *Some choir members never sing but only mouth their parts.* **3.** to speak or say (something) in a pompous, affected manner: *If you mouth it, as many of your players do, I had as lief the town-crier spoke my lines* (Shakespeare, *Hamlet*). **4.** to mumble or garble (one's speech). **5.** to take, grasp, or touch with the mouth. [Old English *mūth* body opening for the functions of eating and speaking.]

mouth·ful (mouth′fōōl′) *pl.,* **-fuls.** *n.* **1.** amount, as of food, that is or can be held in the mouth at one time. **2.** word or phrase that is

at; āpe; cär; end; mē; it; īce; hot; ōld; fôrk; wood; fōōl; oil; out; up; ūse; turn; sing; thin; this; zh in treasure; ə in ago, taken, pencil, lemon, circus.

difficult to pronounce: *That name is quite a mouthful.* **3. to say a mouthful.** to say something important, perceptive, or revealing.
mouth organ 1. harmonica. **2.** Panpipe.
mouth·piece (mouth′pēs′) *n.* **1.** piece or part, as of a musical instrument, telephone, or cigarette, that is placed between or applied to the lips. **2.** one who acts as a spokesman for an individual or group. **3.** *Slang.* criminal lawyer.
mouth·wash (mouth′wŏsh′) *n.* liquid preparation used to clean the mouth or to sweeten the breath.
mouth·y (mou′thē, -thē) **mouth·i·er, mouth·i·est.** *adj.* ranting or railing; bombastic: *the mouthy old fool.*
mov·a·ble (mōō′və bəl) *also,* **move·a·ble.** *adj.* **1.** that can be moved. **2.** that changes from one date to another in different years: *Thanksgiving is a movable holiday.* **3.** that can be broken down and reused: *movable type.* —*n.* **1.** any furnishing or piece of furniture that can be moved. **2. movables.** personal property. —**mov′a·bil′i·ty, mov′a·ble·ness,** *n.* —**mov′a·bly,** *adv.*
move (mōōv) **moved, mov·ing.** *v.i.* **1.** to change posture, position, or direction: *to move from your seat. The frightened deer didn't move.* **2.a.** to change the location of a residence or business: *to move downtown.* **b.** to take up residence (with *in*): *to move in next door.* **3.** to go forward; advance; progress: *The book moves slowly. Time moves quickly.* **4.** to live or circulate; have associations: *The crime reporter moved in a world of courts, prisons, hospitals, and police stations.* **5.** to go into action: *to move on an issue.* **6.** (of merchandise) to be sold. **7.** to make a formal motion, as in a court or legislative assembly: *to move for adjournment.* **8.** to be alive with activity: *The pressroom is really moving to get out the extra.* **9.** *Games.* to change the position of a playing piece: *Each player must move within two minutes.* —*v.t.* **1.** to change the location, position, or direction of: *Move the light away from your eyes.* **2.** to put or keep in motion: *Water moves the waterwheel.* **3.** to cause or urge: *He was moved by curiosity to open the box.* **4.** to affect with emotion; stir the feelings of: *The simple speech moved us deeply.* **5.** to put forward (a motion). **6.** to cause (the bowels) to evacuate. **7.** to sell (merchandise). —*n.* **1.** action calculated to secure a result; piece of strategy: *A wise move was to remain silent.* **2.** *Games.* **a.** act of moving a playing piece: *The wrong move of a pawn cost him the game.* **b.** turn to move a playing piece. **3.** act of changing one's posture or position, esp. in an accomplished or controlled way: *All the moves of the ballerina were graceful.* **4.** change of location of a business or residence. **5. on the move. a.** not staying in any one place very long; moving about. **b.** progressing; advancing: *Science is always on the move.* **6. to get a move on.** to hurry up; get started. [Anglo-Norman *mover* to set in motion, change the place of, cause, excite, propose, from Latin *movēre* to set in motion, cause.]
move·a·ble (mōō′və bəl) *adj.* movable. —**move′a·bil′i·ty, move′a·ble·ness,** *n.* —**move′a·bly,** *adv.*
move·ment (mōōv′mənt) *n.* **1.** act, process, or instance of moving. **2.** mechanism consisting of many closely associated moving parts, as in a watch. **3.** *Music.* one of the principal divisions or sections of a sonata, symphony, or other extended musical composition. **4.** group of people working together to achieve some specific end, or all their endeavors and actions together: *a civil rights movement.* **5.** course or tendency in a particular field; trend: *movement toward greater liberalism in education.* **6.** act of elimination through the bowels, or the matter so eliminated. **7.** *Music.* **a.** tempo. **b.** rhythm.
mov·er (mōō′vər) *n.* **1.** one who or that which moves. **2.** one whose work is moving furniture and belongings of others from one place to another, as from a former residence or office to a new one.
mov·ie (mōō′vē) *n. Informal.* **1.** motion picture. **2.** *usually,* **movies.** motion-picture theater: *We went to the movies up the street.* **3. movies.** the motion-picture industry: *to go to work in the movies.* [Short for MOVING PICTURE.]
mov·ing (mōō′ving) *adj.* **1.** that moves: *a moving target.* **2.** that causes or produces action or motion: *the moving force behind the revolution.* **3.** stirring or affecting the emotions, esp. evoking tender feelings; touching: *The mother made a moving plea for her son's life.* **4.** that is used or hired to move a residence or business: *a moving van, a moving company.* —**Syn. 3.** see **touching.**
moving picture, motion picture.
mow¹ (mō) **mowed, mowed** or **mown, mow·ing.** *v.t.* **1.** to cut (grass, hay, grain, or the like) with a scythe or machine. **2.** to cut the grass, grain, or hay from: *The gardener mowed the lawn.* **3.** to kill or destroy with or as with a single sweeping stroke; cut down (with *down*): *The outlaw drew first, but the marshal mowed him down.* —*v.i.* **1.** to cut grass, grain, hay, or the like. [Old English *māwan* to cut down crops with a scythe.] —**mow′er,** *n.*
mow² (mou) *n.* **1.** part of a barn where hay and grain are stored. **2.** pile or stack of hay or grain. [Old English *mūga* heap, stack.]
mow³ (mō, mou) *Archaic.* *n.* grimace. —*v.i.* to grimace. [Old French *moe* mouth, grimace; of Germanic origin.]

mox·ie (mok′sē) *n. Slang.* a combination of courage and audacity; nerve. [From *Moxie,* trademark for a U.S. soft drink.]
Mo·zam·bique (mō′zəm bēk′) *n.* Portuguese possession in southeastern Africa. Area, 302,329 sq. mi. Pop. (1969 est.), 7,376,000.
Mo·zart, Wolf·gang A·ma·de·us (mōt′särt; woolf′gäng′ ä′mə dā′əs) 1756–91, Austrian composer.
moz·za·rel·la (mot′sə rel′ə, mōt′-) *n.* soft, white cheese having a slightly acid, walnut flavor.
m.p. 1. military police. **2.** mounted police. **3.** melting point.
MP, Member of Parliament.
mph, miles per hour.
Mr. (mis′tər) *pl.,* **Messrs.** Mister. ▲ form of address used before a man's name, as in *Mr. Simpson,* or in polite address, as in *Mr. Chairman.*
Mrs. (mis′iz, miz′-) *pl.,* **Mmes.** form of address used before a married woman's name: *Mrs. Simpson.*
Ms., (miz, em′es′) *pl.,* **Mses.** form of address used before a woman's name: *Ms. Simpson.*
MS *pl.,* **MSS** manuscript.
M.S. 1. Master of Science. Also, **M.Sc. 2.** Master of Surgery.
Msgr., Monsignor.
MST., Mountain Standard Time.
Mt. 1. Mount. **2.** *also,* **Mtn.** mountain.
mu (mū, mōō) *n.* twelfth letter of the Greek alphabet (M, μ), corresponding to the English letter *M, m.*
much (much) **more, most.** *adj.* great in quantity, amount, or degree: *much trouble, not much power.* —*adv.,* **more, most. 1.** to a great extent or degree: *much the worse for wear.* **2.** just about; nearly; largely: *to leave something much as you found it.* —*n.* **1.** a great deal: *Much has been said.* **2.** a good, noteworthy, or impressive example: *not much of a speech.* **3.** *Informal.* one who or that which is impressive or important: *I visited the place last year, and it's not much.* **4. to make much of.** to treat, represent, or regard as noteworthy or of great importance: *to make much of trivial details.* [Middle English *muche(l)* great, great quantity of, from Old English *micel.*]
mu·ci·lage (mū′sə lij) *n.* **1.** clear, brownish glue used esp. on paper and cardboard and usually sold in a bottle topped with a rubber applicator. **2.** any of several sticky adhesive substances produced by certain plants, as the Irish moss. [Late Latin *mūcilāgō* musty juice, from Latin *mūcus* mucus.]
mu·ci·lag·i·nous (mū′sə laj′ə nəs) *adj.* **1.** of or like mucilage. **2.** producing or containing mucilage.
muck (muk) *n.* **1.** any dirty, moist, sticky or slimy substance, as mud or manure. **2.** *Informal.* anything messy or disgusting. **3.** *Informal.* unclean or untidy condition; mess. **4.** black humus consisting chiefly of highly decomposed plant matter. —*v.t.* **1.** to soil, make dirty, or cover with or as with muck (often with *up*). **2.** *Informal.* to make a mess of; ruin or spoil (with *up*): *The director mucked the film up by changing the ending.* —*v.i.* **to muck about** (or **around**). *British. Slang.* to fool around; idle; putter. [Of Scandinavian origin.]
muck·rake (muk′rāk′) **-raked, -rak·ing.** *v.i.* to search for and expose, as in the newspapers, real or alleged corruption in government or society. [From Theodore Roosevelt's reference to the man with the *muck rake* in John Bunyan's allegory *Pilgrim's Progress.*] —**muck′rak′er,** *n.*
muck·y (muk′ē) **muck·i·er, muck·i·est.** *adj.* of, containing, or like muck: *a mucky river bottom.*
mu·cous (mū′kəs) *adj.* **1.** containing or secreting mucus. **2.** of or like mucus. [Latin *mūcōsus* slimy, from *mūcus* mucus of the nose.]
mucous membrane, membrane secreting mucus, that lines body passages and cavities open to the outside, esp. the respiratory and digestive tracts.
mu·cus (mū′kəs) *n.* viscous fluid secreted by the mucous membranes, which serves as a lubricant and protective coating. [Latin *mūcus* mucus of the nose.]
mud (mud) *n.* **1.** soft, wet, sticky clay or dirt. **2.** this mixture after it has dried and hardened: *a house of mud and straw.* **3.** disgrace or scandalous charges: *to drag someone's name through the mud.* [Probably of Low German origin.]
mud·dle (mud′əl) *n.* cause or condition of bewilderment or confusion. —*v.t.,* **-dled, -dling. 1.** to bring into a state of confusion; mix up; bungle. **2.** to make bewildered or confused, as with liquor; befuddle. **3.** to mix; stir. —*v.i.* **to muddle through.** to achieve an objective despite bungling or incompetence. [MUD + -LE.] —**mud′dler,** *n.*
mud·dle·head·ed (mud′əl hed′did) *adj.* bungling or confused.
mud·dy (mud′ē) **-di·er, -di·est.** *adj.* **1.** covered or spattered with mud; full of mud: *a muddy raincoat, a muddy road.* **2.** of or resembling mud: *a muddy consistency.* **3.** clouded or dull with or as if with mud; not clear or pure: *a muddy pond.* **4.** vague or unclear; muddled: *a muddy prose style.* —*v.t.,* **-died, -dy·ing. 1.** to cover or spatter with mud; get mud on: *Don't muddy your new shoes.* **2.** to make confusing or bewildering: *to muddy an issue.* **3.** to make cloudy or dull: *to muddy the waters of a stream.* —**mud′died,** *adj.* —**mud′di·ness,** *n.*

---

at; āpe; cär; end; mē; it; īce; hot; ōld; fôrk; wood; fōōl; oil; out; up; ūse; turn; sing; thin; **this**; zh in treasure; ə in ago, taken, pencil, lemon, circus.

mud·guard (mud′gärd′) n. **1.** loose flap, as of rubber, hung so as to deflect mud thrown up by a wheel, as of a bicycle or truck. **2.** fender *(def. 1).*

mud hen, any of various marsh-dwelling water birds, as the coot or gallinule.

mud puppy, salamander, *Necturus maculosus,* found in fresh waters of North America, having three pairs of red, external gills. Length: to 17 inches.

mud·sill (mud′sil′) n. lowest sill, block, or timber of a structure, usually placed even with the ground.

mud·sling·er (mud′sling′ər) n. one who makes malicious charges, esp. against a political rival.

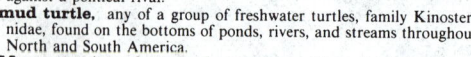

Mud puppy

mud turtle, any of a group of freshwater turtles, family Kinosternidae, found on the bottoms of ponds, rivers, and streams throughout North and South America.

Muen·ster (moon′stər, mun′-, min′-) n. mild, semi-soft cheese having a creamy-yellow color and smooth texture. [From *Munster,* French city where it was first made.]

mu·ez·zin (mū ez′in, moō-) n. in Muslim communities, the public crier who announces the hours of prayer from the minaret of a mosque. [Arabic *mu'adhdhin.*]

muff (muf) n. **1.** fluffy cylinder of fur or other material, designed so that one hand can be slipped in at each end for warmth. **2.** mistake or missed opportunity. —v.t. to fail at or miss: *You had your chance, and you muffed it.* —v.i. to make a mistake or miss an opportunity. [Dutch *mof* covering for the hands, from Middle Dutch *moffel* mitten, thick glove, from Medieval Latin *muffula* fur-lined glove; of uncertain origin.]

muf·fin (muf′in) n. light bread made of batter containing eggs, baked in individual portions, and usually served with butter. [Of uncertain origin.]

muf·fle (muf′əl) -fled, -fling. v.t. **1.** to deaden or soften (a sound): *to muffle a cry.* **2.** to deaden or soften the sound of (something) by or as if by wrapping it up in thick, heavy material: *to muffle the oars with wool for slipping by the sentry.* **3.** to deaden, repress, or cut off; muzzle: *to muffle criticism.* **4.** to wrap up or cover for protection or warmth; bundle (with *up*): *a child all muffled up in a sweater, scarf, and heavy blankets.* —n. **1.** cover or wrap used to deaden sound or for protection or warmth. **2.** oven or furnace in which objects, as pottery, can be heated without direct contact with the source of heat. [Possibly short for Old French *enmoufler* to wrap up, from *moufle* thick glove, from Medieval Latin *muffula* fur-lined glove. See MUFF.]

muf·fler (muf′lər) n. **1.** scarf, as of wool, worn around the neck for warmth. **2.** device that reduces the noise from an engine exhaust, as in an automobile, by gradually reducing the pressure of the escaping gases.

muf·ti (muf′tē) n. street dress or plain clothes, esp. when worn by a person who usually wears a uniform. [Arabic *muftī* Muslim interpreter of religious law; possibly because of the civil, rather than military, status of a Muslim mufti.]

mug (mug) n. **1.** large, heavy drinking cup. **2.** contents of a mug; as much as a mug holds: *a mug of cocoa.* **3.** *Slang.* face. **4.** *Slang.* person, esp. a hoodlum. —v.t., **mugged, mug·ging. 1.** to assault (a person) with intent to rob. **2.** to photograph the face of (a suspect or criminal) for police files. —v.i. to make faces or exaggerated expressions; grimace: *to mug for the camera.* [Probably of Scandinavian origin.]

mug·ger (mug′ər) n. **1.** one who assaults someone with intent to rob. **2.** one who makes faces or exaggerated expressions.

mug·ging (mug′ing) n. crime in which someone is assaulted and robbed.

mug·gy (mug′ē) -gi·er, -gi·est. adj. warm, humid, and stifling: *a hot, muggy day with no breeze.* [Dialectal English *mug* drizzle (of Scandinavian origin) + -y¹.] —**mug′gi·ness,** n.

Mu·ghul (moō′gəl) n. Mogul *(def. 1).*

mug shot *Slang.* police photograph of the face of a suspect or criminal.

mug·wump (mug′wump′) n. **1.** in U.S. politics, person who leaves his party in order to support an opposition candidate. **2.** any of the Republicans who refused to support the party ticket in 1884. [Algonquian *mugkuomp* great chief.]

Mu·ham·mad (moo ham′əd) *also,* **Mo·ham·med, Ma·hom·et,** n. c.570–632, Arab religious teacher and political and military leader; founder of Islam. —**Mu·ham′mad·an,** adj., n. —**Mu·ham′mad·an·ism,** n.

mu·jik (moō zhēk′, moō′zhik) muzhik.

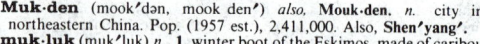

Muk·den (mook′dən, mook den′) *also,* **Mouk·den.** n. city in northeastern China. Pop. (1957 est.), 2,411,000. Also, **Shen′yang′.**

muk·luk (muk′luk) n. **1.** winter boot of the Eskimos, made of caribou or sealskin with waterproof seams and sole. **2.** any similar soft boot or slipper. [Eskimo *muklok* large seal¹.]

mu·lat·to (mə lat′ō, myoo-) pl., -toes. n. **1.** one who is of mixed white and Negro ancestry. **2.** one who has one white and one Negro parent. [Spanish *mulato* one of mixed race, from *mulo* mule (because it is a hybrid animal), from Latin *mūlus.*]

mul·ber·ry (mul′ber′ē) pl., -ries. n. **1.** any of various trees, genus *Morus,* of the mulberry family, as the **white mulberry,** *M. alba,* having thin, oval leaves which are fed to silkworms, and the **black mulberry,** *M. nigra,* bearing black fruits used to make preserves and wines. **2.** sweet, edible fruit of the black mulberry, similar to a blackberry. **3.** dark reddish-purple color. [Old English *mōrberie* the fruit, from Latin *mōrum* + Old English *berie* berry.]

mulch (mulch) n. any of various loose, porous materials, as straw, leaves, grass, or manure, spread around plants to protect them against loss of moisture or sharp changes in temperature, to help prevent soil erosion, and to slow the growth of weeds. —v.t., v.i. to cover (plants) with mulch. [From obsolete *mulch* soft, from Old English *myl(i)sc* mellow.]

mulct (mulkt) v.t. **1.** to punish by a fine or penalty. **2.** to swindle (someone) out of something. —n. any fine or penalty. [Latin *mulc(t)a* penalty, fine².]

mule¹ (mūl) n. **1.** large-eared domestic animal produced by cross-breeding a female horse with a male donkey. Mules are frequently used as pack animals and for farm work and are usually barren. Height: to 6 feet at the shoulder. **2.** *Informal.* one who is very stubborn. **3.** machine that spins fiber into yarn or thread and winds it on spindles. **4.** small tractor or engine. [Old French *mul* this animal, from Latin *mūlus.*]

Mule

mule² (mūl) n. slipper that leaves the back of the heel uncovered. [Middle French *mule* slipper, from Latin *mulleus* red shoe worn by high magistrates.]

mule deer, deer, *Odocoileus hemionus,* native to North America, having a tawny-gray coat and large ears. Height: 42 inches at the shoulder.

mule skinner *Informal.* one who drives mules.

mu·le·teer (mū′lə tēr′) n. one who is in charge of mules. [French *muletier,* from *mulet* mule¹, diminutive of Old French *mul.* See MULE¹.]

Mul·house (moo looz′) n. city in eastern France. Pop. (1968), 116,336. Also, *German,* **Mül·hau·sen** (mool hou′zən).

mul·ish (mū′lish) adj. stubborn; obstinate.

mull¹ (mul) v.t. to think about or reflect on; ponder (often with *over*): *The witness mulled the question over in his mind.* [Possibly form of MUDDLE.]

mull² (mul) v.t. to sweeten, heat, and add spices to (a beverage, as wine or cider). [Of uncertain origin.]

mull³ (mul) n. soft, sheer fabric woven of silk, cotton, and other fibers, used esp. for dresses and millinery. [Short for earlier *mulmul* muslin, from Hindi *malmal.*]

mul·lah (mul′ə, mool′ə) n. Muslim religious leader, esp. one versed in religious law. [Turkish, Persian, and Urdu *mullā,* from Arabic *maulā* judge, master.]

mul·lein (mul′in) *also,* **mul·len.** n. any of several tall plants with velvety, gray-green coarsely toothed leaves that are oblong or oval, as the **common mullein,** *Verbascum thapsus,* a widespread weed that bears yellow flowers. [Anglo-Norman *moleine,* probably from Old French *mol* soft, from Latin *mollis;* because of the soft down on its leaves.]

mul·let (mul′it) pl., -lets or -let. n. any of a group of saltwater and freshwater food fish, family Mugilidae, found throughout tropical and temperate regions, having a gray, red, or striped torpedo-shaped body with a spiny dorsal fin. [Old French *mulet,* from Latin *mullus.*]

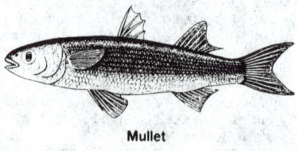

Mullet

mul·li·gan stew (mul′i gən) stew of fish, poultry, or meat and vegetables, often put together from leftovers. Also, **mul′li·gan.** [Possibly from the proper name *Mulligan.*]

at; āpe; cär; end; mē; it; īce; hot; ōld; fôrk; wood; foōl; oil; out; up; ūse; turn; sing; thin; this; zh in treasure; ə in ago, taken, pencil, lemon, circus.

mul·lion (mul′yən) *n.* vertical bar dividing panels, as of windows, doors, or screens. [Modification of obsolete *monial*, from Old French *moinel* middle, from *moien, meien.* See MEAN[1].]

multi- *prefix* **1.** more than one or two; many: *a multicolored cloak.* **2.** many times over: *a multi-million-dollar lawsuit.* [Latin *multus* much, many.]

mul·ti·cel·lu·lar (mul′ti sel′yə lər) *adj.* composed of several cells; many-celled.

mul·ti·col·ored (mul′ti kul′ərd) *adj.* of many or various colors. Also, **mul′ti·col′or.**

mul·ti·far·i·ous (mul′tə fâr′ē əs) *adj.* varied; diversified. [Latin *multifārius* manifold, various.] **—mul′ti·far′i·ous·ness,** *n.*

mul·ti·form (mul′tə fôrm′) *adj.* having many different forms or appearances.

Mul·ti·graph (mul′tə graf′) *n.* Trademark. machine with a rotary drum that reproduces typewritten material by means of metal type.

Mullions

mul·ti·lat·er·al (mul′ti lat′ər əl) *adj.* **1.** involving or participated in by three or more nations or governments: *a multilateral treaty.* **2.** many-sided.

Mul·ti·lith (mul′ti lith′) *n.* Trademark. small offset printing press.

mul·ti·mil·lion·aire (mul′ti mil′yə nâr′) *n.* one who has holdings worth several millions of some unit of currency, esp. dollars.

mul·tip·a·rous (mul tip′ər əs) *adj.* **1.** that produces more than one offspring at one time. **2.** (of a woman) having previously given birth at least once. [Modern Latin *multiparus,* from Latin *multus* much, many + *parere* to bring forth.]

mul·ti·ple (mul′tə pəl) *adj.* consisting of or characterized by many or by more than one part or individual: *multiple fractures, a multiple birth.* **—n.** number or algebraic expression that is a product of a given number or algebraic expression. The number 16 is a multiple of 8; $4x^2y$ is a multiple of *xy.* [French *multiple,* from Late Latin *multiplus* manifold, from Latin *multus* much, many.]

mul·ti·ple-choice (mul′tə pəl chois′) *adj.* that has a variety of answers given, from which the correct one or ones are to be chosen: *a multiple-choice exam, a multiple-choice question.*

multiple sclerosis, disease of the nervous system characterized by destruction of small areas of the brain and spinal cord, leading to eventual paralysis.

mul·ti·plex (mul′tə pleks′) *adj.* **1.** manifold; multiple: *brief and scattered letters out of the multiplex correspondence* (Farrar, 1879). **2.** of or relating to an electronic communication line which can carry several messages at once. [Latin *multiplex* manifold.]

mul·ti·pli·cand (mul′tə plə kand′) *n.* number or algebraic expression that is to be multiplied by another. [Latin *multiplicandus* to be increased, gerundive of *multiplicāre* to increase, multiply (in arithmetic).]

mul·ti·pli·ca·tion (mul′tə pli kā′shən) *n.* **1.** process of adding a number to itself a certain number of times. **2.** act or process of multiplying or increasing. **—mul′ti·pli·ca′tive,** *adj.*

mul·ti·plic·i·ty (mul′tə plis′ə tē) *pl.,* **-ties.** *n.* great number or variety. [Late Latin *multiplicitās,* from Latin *multiplex* manifold.]

mul·ti·pli·er (mul′tə plī′ər) *n.* **1.** number or algebraic expression by which another is to be multiplied. **2.** one who or that which multiplies or causes an increase.

mul·ti·ply (mul′tə plī′) **-plied, -ply·ing.** *v.i.* **1.** to perform multiplication. **2.** to reproduce: *Rabbits multiply rapidly.* **3.** to grow in number, quantity, or extent; increase: *In a few months the guerrilla army had multiplied tenfold.* **—v.t. 1.** to perform multiplication with (numbers or algebraic expressions): *to multiply the height by the width to determine the area.* **2.** to cause to increase in number, quantity, or extent: *The Indian wars greatly multiplied the dangers of frontier life.* [Old French *multiplier,* from Latin *multiplicāre.*]

mul·ti·stage (mul′ti stāj′) *adj.* (of a rocket or guided missile) having more than one stage.

mul·ti·tude (mul′tə tōōd′, -tūd′) *n.* **1.** great number, as of people or things, esp. when collected together in one place or regarded collectively: *A multitude listened silently to the speech. He had a multitude of problems.* **2. the multitude,** the masses; populace. [Latin *multitūdō* a great number.] **—Syn. 1.** see host[2].

mul·ti·tu·di·nous (mul′tə tōōd′n əs, -tūd′-) *adj.* of, like, or being a multitude: *so multitudinous and so various a host of personages* (Ward, 1882). **—mul′ti·tu′di·nous·ly,** *adv.*

mul·ti·va·lent (mul′ti vā′lənt, mul tiv′ə lənt) *adj.* showing more than one valence number. **—mul′ti·va′lence,** *n.*

mum[1] (mum) *adj.* silent; quiet. [Probably imitative.]

mum[2] (mum) *n. Informal.* chrysanthemum.

mum·ble (mum′bəl) **-bled, -bling.** *v.t., v.i.* **1.** to speak (words) softly and indistinctly, with or as with the mouth closed: *The shy boy mumbled his words.* **2.** *Archaic.* to chew or bite (something, as food) with or as if with toothless gums. **—n.** soft, indistinct sound, esp. of speech. [Middle English *momelen* to speak indistinctly, from *mom* inarticulate sound; of imitative origin.] **—mum′bler, mum′bling,** *n.* **—Syn.** *v.t.* **1.** see **murmur.**

mum·ble·ty-peg (mum′bəl tē peg′) *also,* **mum·ble·dy-peg** (mum′bəl dē peg′). *n.* game played by one or more persons, consisting of throwing or dropping a knife from various positions in such a way that it sticks in the ground. Also, **mum′bly-peg′.** [Because the loser formerly had to MUMBLE *the peg,* which had been driven into the ground, removing it from the ground with his teeth.]

mum·bo jum·bo (mum′bō jum′bō) **1.** meaningless, ritualistic words or actions; gibberish: *the secretive mumbo jumbo of an initiation ceremony.* **2.** *also,* **Mumbo Jumbo.** idol or image superstitiously worshiped or feared. [Modification of Mandingo *Mama Dyumbo* a tribal deity.]

mum·mer (mum′ər) *n.* **1.** one who wears a mask or costume, as for a parade or celebration. **2.** *Archaic.* actor. [Old French *momeur* masker, mountebank, from *momer* to go in a mask; of uncertain origin.]

mum·mer·y (mum′ər ē) *pl.,* **-mer·ies.** *n.* **1.** any ridiculous or hypocritical ritual or ceremony. **2.** performance or action of a mummer. [Old French *mommerie* masquerade, from Old French *momeur* masker. See MUMMER.]

mum·mi·fy (mum′ə fī′) **-fied, -fy·ing.** *v.t.* **1.** to make into a mummy by embalming. **2.** to preserve in a rigid, dead, or lifeless state. **—v.i.** to dry, shrivel up, or become lifeless like a mummy. **—mum′mi·fi·ca′tion,** *n.*

mum·my (mum′ē) *pl.,* **-mies.** *n.* dead body embalmed and dried for preservation, esp. in the manner of the ancient Egyptians. [Old French *momie,* going back to Arabic *mūmiyā,* from Persian *mūm* wax (used for embalming).]

mumps (mumps) *n.* contagious disease caused by a virus, characterized by painful swelling of the salivary glands at the side of the face. [Plural of obsolete *mump* grimace; of imitative origin.]

munch (munch) *v.t., v.i.* to chew or eat: *to munch on a sandwich, to munch a carrot.* [Imitative.]

Mun·cie (mun′sē) *n.* city in east-central Indiana. Pop. (1970), 69,080.

mun·dane (mun dān′, mun′dān) *adj.* **1.** of or relating to what is common, ordinary, or usual; prosaic: *Sam was bored by the mundane life he led.* **2.** of this world; earthly. [Late Latin *mundānus* relating to the world, from Latin *mundus* world.] **—mun·dane′ly,** *adv.* **—mun·dane′ness,** *n.*

Mu·nich (mū′nik) *n.* city in southern West Germany. Pop. (1968 est.), 1,260,553. Also, *German,* **Mün·chen** (moon′кнən).

Munich Pact, agreement signed at Munich in September, 1938, in which France and Great Britain sought to appease Germany by allowing Germany to annex the Sudetenland in Czechoslovakia.

mu·nic·i·pal (mū nis′ə pəl) *adj.* **1.** of or relating to the local government or affairs of a city, town, or other community: *a municipal transportation commission.* **2.** having municipal self-government. [Latin *mūnicipālis* relating to a township, going back to *mūnia* official duties + *capere* to take.] **—mu·nic′i·pal·ly,** *adv.*

mu·nic·i·pal·i·ty (mū nis′ə pal′ə tē) *pl.,* **-ties.** *n.* incorporated city, town, or other community.

mu·nic·i·pal·ize (mū nis′ə pə līz′) **-ized, -iz·ing.** *v.t.* **1.** to bring under municipal ownership or control: *to municipalize bus service.* **2.** to give (a city or town) municipal institutions. **—mu·nic′i·pal·i·za′tion,** *n.*

mu·nif·i·cent (mū nif′ə sənt) *adj.* **1.** very lavish and generous in giving: *a munificent benefactor.* **2.** showing or indicating lavish generosity: *Donating a new library to the school was a munificent gesture.* [Latin *mūnificēns,* going back to *mūnus* duty, gift + *facere* to make.] **—mu·nif′i·cence,** *n.*

mu·ni·ments (mū′nə mənts) *n.,pl.* documents, as deeds, by which an owner of property is enabled to defend his title. [Medieval Latin *mūnimentum* title deed, document, from Latin *mūnīmentum* defense, from *mūnīre* to fortify.]

mu·ni·tion (mū nish′ən) *n. usually,* **munitions.** military supplies, as guns, ammunition, or bombs. **—v.t.** to provide with munitions. [French *munition* provision, military supply, from Latin *mūnītiō* fortification, defense.]

Mün·ster (moon′stər) *n.* city in northwestern West Germany. Pop. (1968 est.), 202,752.

mu·on (mū′on) *n.* Physics. subatomic particle whose mass is greater than that of an electron but less than that of a meson. See **subatomic particle** for table. [MU + (MES)ON.]

mu·ral (myŏŏr′əl) *n.* picture painted directly on a wall or ceiling. **—adj.** **1.** placed, fixed, or executed on or in a wall. **2.** of, relating to, or resembling a wall. [French *mural* relating to a wall, from Latin *mūrālis,* from *mūrus* wall.]

mu·ral·ist (myŏŏr′ə list) *n.* artist who executes murals.

at; āpe; cär; end; mē; it; īce; hot; ōld; fôrk; wood; fōōl; oil; out; up; ūse; turn; sing; thin; this; zh in treasure; ə in ago, taken, pencil, lemon, circus.

Mu·rat, Jo·a·chim (moo rä′; zhō ä kĕm′) 1767–1815, French cavalry officer and king of Naples from 1808 to 1815.

mur·der (mur′dər) *n.* **1.** the unlawful and intentional killing of a human being. **2.** *Informal.* one who or that which is very difficult, trying, or dangerous: *It was murder to travel on the overcrowded trains.* **3. to get away with murder,** to be allowed to do something wrong without being punished. —*v.t.* **1.** to kill (a human being) unlawfully and intentionally. **2.** to kill or slaughter, esp. in a brutal manner. **3.** to abuse, mangle, or mar: *to murder the English language.* **4.** *Informal.* to defeat decisively; trounce: *We murdered them 65–0.* **5.** *Informal.* to impress (someone, esp. an audience) greatly. —*v.i.* to commit murder. [Old English *morthor* willful homicide.] —**mur′der·er, mur′der·ess,** *n.* —**Syn.** *v.t.* **1.** see **kill**[1].

mur·der·ous (mur′dər əs) *adj.* **1.** of, relating to, or characterized by murder: *a murderous sneak attack.* **2.** capable of or threatening murder: *a murderous gleam in the captor's eyes, a murderous tyrant.* **3.** very difficult, trying, or dangerous: *a murderous descent of several miles to the valley below.*

mu·rex (myoor′iks) *n.* marine gastropod, genus *Murex,* having a spiny shell, living in tropical seas, and yielding a purple dye. [Modern Latin *Murex,* from Latin *mūrex* a shellfish yielding a purple dye.]

mu·ri·at·ic acid (myoor′ē at′ik) commercial hydrochloric acid. [Latin *muriāticus* pickled in brine, from *muria* brine.]

murk (murk) *n.* darkness; gloom. —*adj. Archaic.* murky. [Probably from Old Norse *myrkr.*]

murk·y (mur′kē) **murk·i·er, murk·i·est.** *adj.* **1.** dark, obscured, or gloomy: *the murky waters of the muddy river.* **2.** dark and obscure to the mind; hard to understand. —**murk′i·ness,** *n.*

Mur·mansk (moor mänsk′) *n.* port city in the northwestern Soviet Union. Pop. (1970), 309,000.

mur·mur (mur′mər) *n.* **1.** low, continuous, rising and falling sound: *the murmur of the wind in the trees.* **2.** soft, low, nearly indistinct voice or speech: *She gave a murmur of approval.* **3.** abnormal rumbling or blowing sound in the heart, lungs, or arteries, that indicates some malfunction. **4.** expression of discontent; complaint; protest: *to accept a rebuke without a murmur.* —*v.i.* **1.** to make a murmur. **2.** to complain or protest. —*v.t.* to say in a soft, low, nearly indistinct voice. [Latin *murmur* a humming, rumbling, crashing.] —**mur′mur·er,** *n.* **Syn.** *v.t.* **Murmur, mutter, mumble** mean to make indistinct sounds. **Murmur** may be used when one utters a low, continuous, half-suppressed sound slightly above a whisper: *The shy girl murmured her thanks.* **Mutter** may be used when one murmurs angrily and complainingly: *The dissatisfied workman muttered a threat.* **Mumble** may be used when one utters a muted and half-articulated sound with lips half closed: *The old woman mumbled her prayers.*

mur·rain (mur′in) *n.* infectious disease of cattle, usually fatal, that is caused by a tick. [Old French *morine,* from *morir* to die, going back to Latin *mori.*]

mus. 1. museum. **2.** music; musician.

mus·ca·dine (mus′kə din, -dīn′) *n.* grape, *Vitis rotundifolia,* found growing in the southeastern United States.

mus·cat (mus′kat, -kət) *n.* large pale-green grape having seeds, used esp. to make raisins and muscatel. [French *muscat* this grape, wine from this grape, going back to Old Provençal *muscat* musky, going back to Late Latin *muscus* musk. See **MUSK.**]

Mus·cat (mus′kat) *n.* capital of Oman, in the northern part of the country. Pop. (1962 est.), 6,000.

Muscat and O·man (ō män′) independent sultanate on the southeastern coast of the Arabian peninsula, now officially known as Oman.

mus·ca·tel (mus′kə tel′) *n.* rich, sweet wine made from the muscat grape.

mus·cle (mus′əl) *n.* **1.** body tissue composed of bundles of cells, capable of contracting upon stimulation to produce motion. **2.** one of the organs of the body composed of these tissues, esp. one that is attached by tendons to bones and that functions to move part of the body. **3.** strength or force, esp. bodily strength. —*v.i.,* **-cled, -cling.** *Informal.* to force one's way into an activity or organization against resistance, by or as by sheer physical strength or power (with *in* or *into*): *Racketeers muscled in on the business.* [Latin *mūsculus* little mouse, the organ of the body, diminutive of *mūs* mouse; because certain muscles supposedly resemble a mouse in form and action.]

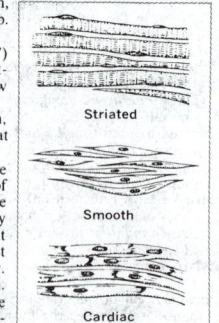

Striated

Smooth

Cardiac

Types of muscles

mus·cle-bound (mus′əl bound′) *adj.* having tight or overdeveloped muscles, as from too much exercise.

mus·co·vite (mus′kə vīt′) *n.* light yellow, brown, green, red, or colorless mineral that is the most common form of mica.

Mus·co·vite (mus′kə vīt′) *n.* native or resident of Moscow or, formerly, of Russia.

Mus·co·vy (mus′kə vē) *n. Archaic.* Russia.

Muscovy duck, duck, *Cairina moschata,* usually having black-and-white plumage, native to Mexico and Central and South America, now widely raised for its meat. Length: 28–30 inches.

mus·cu·lar (mus′kyə lər) *adj.* **1.** of, relating to, or involving muscles: *muscular coordination.* **2.** having well-developed muscles; strong: *a muscular young man.* **3.** composed or consisting of muscle: *the muscular system.*

muscular dys·tro·phy (dis′trə fē) disease, probably inherited, characterized by progressive weakening and wasting of the skeletal muscles. It usually begins in early childhood and is usually fatal.

mus·cu·lar·i·ty (mus′kyə lar′ə tē) *n.* strength, development, or condition of the muscles.

mus·cu·la·ture (mus′kyə lə chər) *n.* arrangement of the muscles in the body or in a particular part of the body. [French *musculature,* from Latin *mūsculus* muscle of the body. See **MUSCLE.**]

muse (mūz) **mused, mus·ing.** *v.i.* to think, reflect, or meditate, esp. in an idle or detached manner: *to muse on the events of the past day.* —*v.t.* to say or think in a reflective or detached manner. [Old French *muser* to ponder, linger, from *muse* snout of an animal (suggesting a dog's sniffing about); of uncertain origin.] —**mus′er,** *n.* —**Syn.** *v.i.* see **meditate.**

Muse (mūz) *n.* **1.** *Greek Mythology.* one of the nine goddesses who presided over the arts and sciences and were daughters of Zeus and Mnemosyne: Calliope, Clio, Erato, Euterpe, Melpomene, Polyhymnia, Terpsichore, Thalia, or Urania. **2. muse.** spirit or other source of genius or artistic inspiration. [Latin *Mūsa* one of these nine goddesses, from Greek *Mousa.*]

mu·se·um (mū zē′əm) *n.* building or place where a collection of objects of value or interest, as in the fields of art, science, history, or natural history, is preserved and displayed. [Latin *mūseum* library, study, museum, from Greek *mouseion* shrine of the Muses, philosophical school and library, from *Mousa* any of the nine ancient Greek Muses.]

mush[1] (mush) *n.* **1.** thick porridge made by boiling corn meal. **2.** any soft, thick, or pulpy mass. **3.** *Informal.* anything overly sentimental or romantic. [Form of **MASH.**]

mush[2] (mush) *interj.* go or go faster. ▲ said as an order to a team of dogs pulling a sled. —*v.i.* to travel on foot with a dog sled over snow. [Possibly from French *moucher* to go fast, from *mouche* fly, from Latin *musca.*] —**mush′er,** *n.*

mush·room (mush′rŏŏm, -room′) *n.* **1.** any of various fungus plants, shaped like an umbrella, a sponge, or a ball. There are poisonous and nonpoisonous mushrooms. **2.** anything resembling a mushroom, esp. in shape or rapid growth. —*v.i.* **1.** to spring up or grow suddenly and rapidly: *Buildings mushroomed all over the area.* **2.** to spread out or flatten at one end into the shape of a mushroom: *The cloud of smoke mushroomed in the sky.* [Middle French *moucheron* the fungus plant; of uncertain origin.]

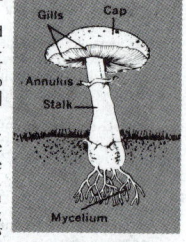

Gills

Cap

Annulus

Stalk

Mycelium

Mushroom

mushroom cloud, mushroom-shaped cloud resulting from an explosion, esp. of a nuclear weapon, either on the ground or at a low altitude.

mush·y (mush′ē) **mush·i·er, mush·i·est.** *adj.* **1.** having a soft and pulpy consistency like mush. **2.** *Informal.* overly sentimental or romantic. —**mush′i·ness,** *n.*

mu·sic (mū′zik) *n.* **1.** pleasing or harmonious succession or combination of sounds. **2.** art or science of producing and arranging aesthetically pleasing and emotionally expressive combinations of sounds, usually according to principles of rhythm, melody, harmony, tonality, and dynamics. **3.** musical composition as represented by graphic symbols, or the written or printed score of a musical composition: *music for a popular song. Can you read music?* **4.** any pleasant sound or series of sounds: *Her words of welcome were music to his ear.* **5. to face the music.** to face consequences bravely, no matter what they are. [Latin *mūsica* art of music, from Greek *mousikē* any art over which the Muses preside. See **MUSE.**]

mu·si·cal (mū′zi kəl) *adj.* **1.** of, relating to, or producing music. **2.** set to or accompanied by music: *a musical show.* **3.** similar to music in beauty or expression: *the musical sounds of a child's laughter.*

4. fond of or gifted in the performance of music: *Bach came from a very musical family.* —*n.* musical comedy or other musical play. —**mu·si·cal·i·ty** (mū′zi kal′ə tē), **mu′si·cal·ness,** *n.* —**mu′si·cal·ly,** *adv.*

musical chairs, children's game in which the players march to music around a row of chairs containing one chair fewer than the number of players. When the music being played suddenly stops, the players rush to sit down, and the one who cannot find a seat is eliminated. The game continues until only one player is left.

musical comedy, theatrical work combining songs, dances, and spoken dialogue, usually based on a rather slight plot.

mu·si·cale (mū′zi kal′), *n.* party or other social gathering featuring musical entertainment. [French (*soirée*) *musicale* musical (evening), from *musique* art of music, from Latin *mūsica*. See MUSIC.]

music box, box or case containing a device that produces a tune mechanically.

music hall **1.** auditorium or hall for musical performances. **2.** *British.* vaudeville theater.

mu·si·cian (mū zish′ən) *n.* one skilled in or professionally engaged in the performance or composition of music. —**mu·si′cian·ship′,** *n.*

mu·si·col·o·gy (mū′zi kol′ə jē) *n.* study of the history, theory, and forms of music. —**mu′si·col′o·gist,** *n.*

mu·sing (mū′zing) *n.* meditation; reflection. —*adj.* meditative. —**mu′sing·ly,** *adv.*

musk (musk) *n.* **1.** oily, strong-smelling substance secreted by an abdominal gland in the male musk deer, used in making perfumes, medicine, and soaps. **2.** any similar substance made synthetically or processed from secretions of muskrat, musk ox, or civet cat. **3.** odor of musk. [Late Latin *muscus* the substance obtained from the musk deer, through Persian, from Sanskrit *muskah* testicle similar in shape to the bag of the musk deer containing musk.]

musk deer, hornless deer, *Moschus moschiferous,* of central and eastern Asia, the male of which has a gland secreting musk.

mus·kel·lunge (mus′-kə lunj′) *pl.* **-lunge.** *n.* large greenish-brown freshwater game fish, *Esox masquinongy,* of the pike family, found esp. in

Muskellunge

the Great Lakes. Length: to 5 feet. Weight: to 70 pounds. Also, **mus·kie** (mus′kē). [Algonquian *maskinonge* large pike.]

mus·ket (mus′kit) *n.* any of several types of guns fired from the shoulder, esp. one having a smooth bore, used before the general adoption of rifles. [Middle French *mousquet,* from Italian *moschetto* musket; earlier, arrow for a crossbow, from *mosca* fly, from Latin *musca.*]

mus·ket·eer (mus′ki tēr′) *n.* **1.** soldier armed with a musket, or one whose regiment was traditionally so armed. **2.** member of the king's guard in seventeenth-century France.

mus·ket·ry (mus′ki trē) *n.* **1.** art or science of firing muskets. **2.** muskets collectively. **3.** musketeers: *to call out the musketry.*

musk·mel·on (musk′mel′ən) *n.* **1.** any of several large, edible fruits, as the cantaloupe, having a hard rind, sweet juicy flesh, and small flat seeds in the center. **2.** any of several trailing or climbing vines, *Cucumis melo,* of the gourd family, native to Central and North America and Europe and bearing these fruits.

Mus·ko·ge·an (mus kō′gē ən, -jē-) *n.* family of American Indian languages, including Chickasaw, Choctaw, and Seminole, spoken predominantly in the southern United States.

Musk ox

musk ox, buffalolike mammal, *Ovibos moschatus,* native to the tundra of northern Canada and Greenland, having a shaggy dark-brown or black coat. It gives off a musky odor during the mating season. Height: 4–6 feet at the shoulder.

musk·rat (musk′rat′) *pl.* **-rat** or **-rats.** *n.* **1.** any of various North American aquatic rodents, genus *Ondatra,* having webbed hind feet, a flat tail, a musky odor, and a thick, soft coat of glossy, dark-brown fur. Length: to 15 inches, including the tail. **2.** its fur.

musk·y (mus′kē) **musk·i·er, musk·i·est.** *adj.* of, relating to, resembling, or smelling like musk.

Muskrat

Mus·lim (muz′lim, mooz′-, moos′-) *also,* **Mus·lem, Mos·lem.** *adj.* of, relating to, or characteristic of Islam or its culture. —*n.* follower of Islam. Also, **Mo·ham′me·dan, Ma·ho′me·tan.** [Arabic *muslim* follower of Islam, one who has submitted (to God).]

mus·lin (muz′lin) *n.* any of a large group of cotton fabrics, varying from lightweight, sheer materials used for such items as blouses to heavyweight materials used for sheets and pillowcases. [French *mousseline* thin fine cotton cloth, from Italian *mussolino,* from *Mosul,* city in Iraq where it was first produced.]

muss (mus) *Informal. v.t.* to make disordered or untidy; rumple (often with *up*): *The wind mussed up her hair.* —*n.* disorder; mess. [Probably modification of MESS.]

mus·sel (mus′əl) *n.* **1.** any saltwater bivalve mollusk of the family Mytilidae, having a soft body encased in a bluish-black shell, esp. the common mussel, *Mytilus edulis,* found along the coasts of Europe and North America, which is used as food. Length: to 14 inches. **2.** any of the related freshwater mollusks of the family Unionidae, found in lakes and streams of the central United States. [Old English *muscle* saltwater mollusk, going back to Latin *mūsculus* a saltwater mollusk, muscle of the body. See MUSCLE.]

Mus·set, Alfred de (moo sā′) 1810–57, French poet, dramatist, and writer.

Mus·so·li·ni, Be·ni·to (moos′ə lē′nē, mōō′sə-; bə nē′tō) 1883–1945, Italian Fascist dictator.

Mus·sul·man (mus′əl mən) *pl.* **-mans.** *n. Archaic.* Muslim. [Persian *musulmān,* from Arabic *muslim.* See MUSLIM.]

muss·y (mus′ē) **muss·i·er, muss·i·est.** *adj. Informal.* disordered; untidy; rumpled.

must[1] (must) *auxiliary verb* (followed by an infinitive without *to*) **1.** to be obliged or bound: *I must return his call today.* **2.** to be forced or required by necessity, compulsion, or command: *An animal in the wilds must fight to survive.* **3.** to be reasonably or certainly expected: *You must be the new teacher.* —*n. Informal.* anything vital, necessary, or essential: *A dinner jacket is a must here.* —*adj. Informal.* vital, essential, or necessary: *a must movie for movie fans.* [Old English *mōste,* past tense of *mōtan* to have to, be permitted to, be able to.]

Syn. *auxiliary verb* **1. Must, ought**[1]**, should** mean to be obliged or bound to. **Must** expresses necessity or determination: *I must finish my work today.* **Ought** stresses duty or obligation: *She ought to be ashamed of herself.* **Should** stresses fitness, propriety, expediency, or natural expectation: *You should not make that mistake again.*

must[2] (must) *n.* unfermented or not completely fermented juice of fruit, esp. grapes, before it becomes wine. [Old English *must,* from Latin *mustum,* from *mustus* fresh, new.]

must[3] (must) *n.* mold; mustiness. [From MUSTY.]

mus·tache (mus′tash, məs tash′) *also,* **mous·tache.** *n.* **1.** *also,* **mus·taches.** growth of hair on the upper lip. **2.** growth of hairs or bristles around the mouth of certain animals. [French *moustache,* from Italian *mostaccio* ugly face, snout (in plural, hair on upper lip), going back to Greek *mystax* upper lip, hair on upper lip.]

mus·ta·chio (məs tash′ō, -tash′ē ō′) *pl.* **-chios.** *n.* mustache.

mus·tang (mus′tang) *n.* wild horse of the American plains, believed to be descended from stock brought by the Spanish. [Spanish *mestengo* stray, from *mesta* company of owners of cattle who disposed of strays, from Medieval Latin *mixta* (*animalia*) mixed (animals), including both stray and herd animals, from Latin *miscēre* to mix.]

mus·tard (mus′tərd) *n.* **1.** pungent, yellowish paste or powder made from the seeds of any of various plants, genus *Brassica,* used as a spice or medicinally as a stimulant and emetic. **2.** the plant itself, esp. the **black mustard,** *B. nigra* and the **white mustard,** *B. hirta.* **3.** *adj.* designating a family, Cruciferae, of plants growing in temperate parts of the world, including many common vegetables, as the broccoli, cabbage, radish, and turnip and plants with ornamental flowers, as the candytuft and wallflower. [Old French *mostarde* the plant of the genus *Brassica,* going back to Latin *mustum* must[2]; because must was once an ingredient of mustard paste.]

mustard gas, deadly poison gas that burns and blisters the skin and eyes and damages the bronchial tubes and lungs, made from ethylene or from hydrogen chloride and produced for chemical warfare and for the chemical industry.

mustard plaster, poultice made of a cloth covered with a mixture of mustard, flour, and water, used as a counterirritant.

mus·ter (mus′tər) *v.t.* **1.** to find and gather together; collect or summon: *to muster strength, to muster arguments in defense of a theory.* **2.** to gather or call (troops) together. **3.** to dismiss or discharge (someone), esp. from military service (with *out*): *They mustered John out last winter, and he still hasn't found a job.* —*v.i.* to gather together in a group; assemble: *The platoon mustered for roll call.* —*n.* **1.** act of assembling men or troops for military inspection or service. **2.** list of those so assembled. Also, **muster roll. 3.** any assembly or collection. [Old French *monstrer* to show, from Latin *mōnstrāre.*]

at; āpe; cär; end; mē; it; īce; hot; ōld; fôrk; wood; fōōl; oil; out; up; ūse; turn; sing; thin; ᵺis; zh in treasure; ə in ago, taken, pencil, lemon, circus.

669

Syn. *v.t.* **2. Muster, marshal** mean to assemble men or troops. **Muster** may be appropriately used when a body or company of persons is summoned for inspection or action or for exhibition and display: *The captain mustered all hands on deck for a review.* **Marshal** emphasizes the rigorously disciplined manner of the gathering or its arrangement in a particular order: *The general marshaled his troops for battle.*

must·n't (mus′ənt) must not.

mus·ty (mus′tē) **-ti·er, -ti·est.** *adj.* **1.** having a stale or moldy odor or taste: *a damp cellar with decaying furniture and cases of musty books.* **2.** old-fashioned; antiquated: *musty conventions that do not fit modern times.* [Possibly from obsolete *moisty* wet, damp, from MOIST.] —**mus′ti·ness,** *n.*

mu·ta·ble (mū′tə bəl) *adj.* that is liable or subject to change or alteration; variable; changeable. [Latin *mūtābilis,* from *mūtāre* to change.] —**mu′ta·bil′i·ty,** *n.*

mu·tant (mū′tənt) *n.* mutation *(def. 2).*

mu·tate (mū′tāt) **-tat·ed, -tat·ing.** *v.i.* to undergo change, esp. by mutation. —*v.t.* **1.** to cause to undergo change, esp. by mutation. **2.** *Linguistics.* to change (a vowel) by use of an umlaut.

mu·ta·tion (mū tā′shən) *n.* **1.** sudden change in a gene which affects the form or qualities of offspring and is inheritable. **2.** individual or species resulting from such a change. **3.** any act or process of changing in form or qualities; change. **4.** umlaut. [Latin *mūtātiō* change.]

mu·ta·tis mu·tan·dis (mū tā′tis mū tan′dis) *Latin.* with the necessary changes.

mute (mūt) *adj.* **1.** that cannot or does not speak as a result of an inborn defect or an injury. **2.** refusing to speak; not speaking: *The prisoner sat mute, offering nothing in his own defense.* **3.** that gives out or is accompanied by no sound or direct statement; silent: *The rows of graves were a mute reminder of the true effects of war.* **4.** *Linguistics.* not pronounced; silent. The *b* in *lamb* is mute. —*n.* **1.** one who is unable to speak, as because of an inborn defect or an injury. **2.** device inserted in or put on a musical instrument, e.g. a brass instrument, to muffle or soften the tone. **3.** silent letter, as the *e* in *mate.* —*v.t.,* **mut·ed, mut·ing.** **1.** to muffle or soften the sound of (a musical instrument). **2.** to make less brilliant, strident, or strong; restrain; soften: *to mute criticism. The artist muted the colors.* [Latin *mūtus* dumb.] —**mute′ly,** *adv.* —**mute′ness,** *n.*

mu·ti·late (mūt′əl āt′) **-lat·ed, -lat·ing.** *v.t.* **1.** to deform or injure seriously, as by the loss of a limb or member; maim. **2.** to damage or disfigure; mar: *The desk was mutilated by deep scratches.* **3.** to make incomplete, imperfect, or less effective by removing an important part or parts: *to mutilate a play by cutting out important scenes.* [Latin *mutilātus,* past participle of *mutilāre* to maim.] —**mu′ti·la′tion,** *n.*

mu·ti·neer (mūt′ə nēr′) *n.* one who is guilty of mutiny. [Middle French *mutinier,* from *mutin* rebellious, unruly. See MUTINY.]

mu·ti·nous (mūt′ən əs) *adj.* **1.** engaged in or disposed to engage in mutiny: *The mutinous sailors were seized and thrown into the brig.* **2.** of, relating to, or characterized by something like mutiny; rebellious: *a mutinous spirit among the students.* —**mu′ti·nous·ly,** *adv.* —**mu′ti·nous·ness,** *n.*

mu·ti·ny (mūt′ə nē) *pl.* **-nies.** *n.* forcible or open rebellion against authority, esp. by sailors or soldiers against their commanding officers. —*v.i.* **-nied, -ny·ing.** to engage in mutiny; revolt against authority. [From obsolete *mutine* rebellion, from French *mutin* rebellious, from Old French *muete* revolt, going back to Latin *movēre* to move.]

mutt (mut) *n. Informal.* dog, esp. a mongrel.

mut·ter (mut′ər) *v.i.* **1.** to speak in low, indistinct tones with the mouth nearly closed: *The old woman muttered to herself.* **2.** to complain; grumble: *The soldiers muttered angrily when they heard that all leaves had been canceled.* —*v.t.* to utter (words) in low, indistinct tones. —*n.* low, indistinct utterance. [Middle English *moteren* to speak low and indistinctly; probably imitative.] —**mut′ter·er,** *n.* —**Syn.** *v.t.* see **mur·mur.**

mut·ton (mut′ən) *n.* flesh from a sheep, esp. a sheep between one and two years of age, used as food. [Old French *moton* ram; of Celtic origin.]

mutton chop, piece of mutton from the rib or loin, usually for broiling.

mut·ton·chops (mut′ən chops′) *n.,pl.* side whiskers that are narrow at the temples and broad and rounded at the bottom, worn often with a mustache but not with a beard.

Muttonchops

mu·tu·al (mū′chŏŏ əl) *adj.* **1.** done, felt, or expressed by each of two toward the other; reciprocal: *Bill disliked the man immediately, and the feeling was mutual.* **2.** affecting or involving all parties: *mutual defense, mutual benefits.* **3.** shared; common: *They met each other through a mutual friend.* **4.** of or relating to a kind of insurance in which the policyholders form

the membership of the insurance company and indemnify one another against loss. [Old French *mutuel* reciprocal, from Latin *mūtuus.*] —**mu′tu·al′i·ty,** *n.* —**mu′tu·al·ly,** *adv.*

Syn. 1. Mutual, reciprocal mean done, said, or felt in common. **Mutual** stresses giving and receiving in equal measure, having the same feelings one for the other, and sharing and enjoying in common: *The two friends had a mutual enthusiasm for music.* **Reciprocal** emphasizes returning to another something similar or comparable to what has been received: *Each club extended reciprocal privileges to members of the other.*

mutual fund, investment company that sells an unlimited number of shares to the public and invests the proceeds in a variety of securities.

mu·tu·al·ism (mū′chŏŏ ə liz′əm) *n. Biology.* relationship in which two different kinds of organisms live together in a condition of symbiosis that benefits both of them.

mu·zhik (mōō zhik′, mōō′zhik) *also,* **mu·jik.** *n.* peasant in Russia under the czars. [Russian *muzhik,* diminutive of *muzh* man.]

muz·zle (muz′əl) *n.* **1.** projecting part of the head of an animal, including the nose, mouth, and jaws; snout. **2.** device usually made of straps or wires, which is put over an animal's mouth to keep it from biting or eating. **3.** opening at the front end of a gun, out of which the bullet or other projectile leaves the weapon. **4.** anything that discourages or restrains comments or spoken opinions, esp. of subordinates: *to put a muzzle on criticism.* —*v.t.,* **-zled, -zling. 1.** to put a muzzle on. **2.** to restrain or discourage (someone) from speaking; silence. [Old French *musel* snout, nose of an animal, from *muse* snout; of uncertain origin.] —**muz′zler,** *n.*

muz·zle·load·er (muz′əl lō′dər) *n.* gun loaded through the muzzle. —**muz′zle·load′ing,** *adj.*

muzzle velocity, speed at which a projectile, as a bullet, leaves the muzzle of a gun.

MVD, secret police of the USSR.

my (mī) *adj.* of or belonging to me: *my wife, my good fortune, my raincoat.* [Old English *mīn.*]

my·ce·li·um (mī sē′lē əm) *pl.,* **-li·a** (-lē ə). *n.* part of a fungus, consisting of a network of many thin threadlike fibers. [Modern Latin *mycelium,* from Greek *mykēs* fungus + *hēlos* nail, wart.]

My·ce·nae (mī sē′nē) *n.* ancient Greek city in the eastern Peloponnesus.

My·ce·nae·an (mī′sə nē′ən) *adj.* of or relating to the ancient civilization located at Mycenae.

my·col·o·gy (mī kol′ə jē) *n.* branch of botany that studies fungi. [Greek *mykēs* fungus + -LOGY.] —**my·col′o·gist,** *n.*

my·e·lin (mī′ə lin) *n.* white, fatty substance forming a sheath around certain nerve fibers. [Greek *myelos* marrow + -IN¹.]

my·na (mī′nə) *also,* **my·nah, mi·na.** *n.* any of several black or brown starlings, family Sturnidae, native to Asia, esp. the **hill myna,** *Gracula religiosa,* of India and Ceylon, which is very skillful at mimicking the human voice. [Hindi *mainā.*]

Myn·heer (mīn hār′, -hēr′) *n.* Mister; Sir. ▲ Dutch form of address for a man. [Dutch *mijnheer,* from *mijn* my + *heer* lord.]

my·o·pi·a (mī ō′pē ə) *n.* inability to see things that are far away; nearsightedness. [Modern Latin *myopia,* from Greek *myōpiā,* going back to *myein* to shut + *ops* eye.] —**my·op·ic** (mī op′ik), *adj.*

myr·i·ad (mir′ē əd) *n.* **1.** great or countless number: *Myriads of tiny creatures swarmed in the pond water. There are myriads of mistakes on your paper.* —*adj.* of indefinitely large number; countless; innumerable: *myriad possibilities.* [Greek *myriad-,* stem of *myrias* ten thousand, from *myrios* countless.]

myr·i·a·pod (mir′ē ə pod′) *n.* any of a group of arthropods, class Myriapoda, including centipedes and millipedes, having a wormlike, segmented body and many legs. [Modern Latin *Myriapoda,* from Greek *myrias* ten thousand + *pod-,* stem of *pous* foot.]

Myr·mi·don (mur′mə don′) *n.* **1.** *Greek Legend.* one of a group of warriors from ancient Thessaly who formed the army of Achilles in the Trojan War. **2. myrmidon.** any blindly faithful follower.

myrrh (mur) *n.* fragrant, yellowish-brown resin obtained from any of several tropical trees, esp. *Commiphora myrrha,* having a bitter taste and used esp. in the manufacture of dentifrices and perfumes. [Old English *myrra,* from Latin *myrrha,* from Greek *myrrā;* of Semitic origin.]

myr·tle (murt′əl) *n.* **1.** any of a group of fragrant evergreen shrubs and trees, genus *Myrtus,* widely grown for ornament, bearing shiny oval or lance-shaped leaves and white or pink flowers. **2.** common periwinkle, *Vinca minor.* [Old French *myrtille* myrtle berry, going back to Latin *myrtus* myrtle tree, from Greek *myrtos;* of Semitic origin.]

Myrtle

at; āpe; cär; end; mē; it; īce; hot; ōld; fôrk; wood; fōōl; oil; out; up; ūse; turn; sing; thin; this; zh in treasure; ə in ago, taken, pencil, lemon, circus.

my·self (mī self′) *pl.,* **our·selves.** *pron.* **1.** emphatic form of **me** and **I**: *I will do this myself.* **2.** reflexive form of **me** and **I**: *I don't pamper myself.* **3.** my usual, normal, or true self: *I haven't been myself since the accident.*

My·sore (mī sôr′) *n.* city in southern India. Pop. (1969), 262,136.

mys·te·ri·ous (mis tēr′ē əs) *adj.* full of, shrouded in, or suggesting mystery; impossible or difficult to explain or understand; puzzling; obscure: *a mysterious smile.* —**mys·te′ri·ous·ly,** *adv.* —**mys·te′ri·ous·ness,** *n.*

mys·ter·y (mis′tər ē) *pl.,* **-ter·ies.** *n.* **1.** something that is not or cannot be known, explained, or understood: *The identity of the thief is still a mystery.* **2.** thing or event that arouses curiosity or suspense because it is not fully explained or revealed: *It is a mystery to me how he can live so well on such a small salary.* **3.** book, play, motion picture, or the like involving a mysterious crime, esp. a narrative that gradually leads to the discovery of the criminal. **4.** mysterious, obscure, or secret character or quality: *An air of mystery surrounded the events leading up to his resignation.* **5.** religious doctrine or truth that cannot be understood by reason and can be known only through divine revelation. **6.** *usually,* **mysteries. a.** any of various ancient religious cults practicing secret rites to which uninitiated persons were not admitted. **b.** secret rite practiced by such a group. **7.a.** sacrament of the Christian religion, esp. the Eucharist. **b.** any of fifteen events connected with the lives of Christ and the Virgin Mary that serves as a subject for meditation during recitation of the rosary. **8.** mystery play. [Latin *mystērium* secret worship, from Greek *mystērion* secret rite, going back to *mȳein* to close (lips and eyes).]

mystery play, medieval religious drama based on events in the Bible, esp. in the life of Christ, often performed by trade guilds.

mys·tic (mis′tik) *adj.* **1.** of or relating to beliefs or practices that have hidden or secret meanings, as the ancient religious mysteries: *mystic rites.* **2.** having hidden or secret meaning or character; mysterious; enigmatic: *the mystic prophecies of the Delphic oracle.* **3.** of or relating to mystics or mysticism. **4.** mystical *(def. 1).* —*n.* one who seeks to achieve an intimate knowledge of God or absolute truth through personal spiritual experience. [Latin *mysticus* relating to secret rites, from Greek *mystikos,* from *mystēs* person who is initiated.]

mys·ti·cal (mis′ti kəl) *adj.* **1.** having a spiritual meaning that is beyond human knowledge or understanding. **2.** of or relating to a direct knowledge of God or absolute truth achieved through personal spiritual experience: *a mystical philosophy.* **3.** mystic *(defs. 1, 2).* —**mys′ti·cal·ly,** *adv.*

mys·ti·cism (mis′tə siz′əm) *n.* **1.** doctrines, beliefs, or ideas of mystics. **2.** doctrine that knowledge of God or absolute truth may be achieved through personal spiritual experience, esp. by contemplation. **3.** vague, confused, or illogical thinking.

mys·ti·fy (mis′tə fī′) **-fied, -fy·ing,** *v.t.* **1.** to bewilder or confuse, esp. intentionally: *The banker's sudden disappearance mystified the police.* **2.** to make obscure or difficult to understand; involve in mystery. [French *mystifier* to hoax, going back to Latin *mysticus* relating to secret rites + *facere* to make. See MYSTIC.] —**mys′ti·fi·ca′tion,** *n.*

myth (mith) *n.* **1.** traditional story of unknown authorship that expresses a belief of a particular people, usually involving gods and heroes. A myth is an attempt to explain a phenomenon of nature, an event in history, or the origin of a particular custom, practice, or religious belief. **2.** such accounts or stories collectively; mythology. **3.** any imaginary or fictitious person, story, or thing: *His prowess as a hunter is pure myth.* **4.** opinion, belief, or ideal that has no basis in truth or fact, esp. one uncritically held by the members of a group. [Late Latin *mȳthos* fable, from Greek *mȳthos* word, fable, story.] —**Syn. 1.** see **legend.**

myth·i·cal (mith′i kəl) *adj.* **1.** of, resembling, based on, or existing only in myths: *King Arthur's mythical kingdom.* **2.** imaginary; fictitious: *a purely mythical account of his early life.* Also, **myth′ic.** —**myth′i·cal·ly,** *adv.*

myth·o·log·i·cal (mith′ə loj′i kəl) *adj.* of, relating to, or found in mythology: *a mythological being.* —**myth′o·log′i·cal·ly,** *adv.*

my·thol·o·gist (mi thol′ə jist) *n.* **1.** one who collects or records myths. **2.** one who studies or is an expert in mythology.

my·thol·o·gy (mi thol′ə jē) *pl.,* **-gies.** *n.* **1.** myths and legends collectively, esp. a body of myths belonging to a specific ancient religion or culture or relating to a particular hero or event: *Egyptian mythology.* **2.** study and interpretation of myths and legends. [Late Latin *mȳthologia,* from Greek *mȳthologiā* legend, storytelling, from *mȳthos* word, fable, story + *logos* word, discourse.]

Myt·i·le·ne (mit′ə lē′nē) *n.* Lesbos.

myx·e·de·ma (mik′sə dē′mə) *n.* condition resulting from decreased activity of the thyroid gland, characterized by swelling, esp. of the hands and face, dryness of hair and skin, and sluggishness.

---

at; āpe; cär; end; mē; it; īce; hot; ōld; fôrk; wood; fōōl; oil; out; up; ūse; turn; sing; thin; this; zh in treasure; ə in ago, taken, pencil, lemon, circus.

n, N (en) *pl.*, **n's, N's.** *n.* fourteenth letter of the English alphabet.
n (en) *n.* any indefinite number.
N, nitrogen.
N **1.** North. **2.** Northern.
n. **1.** name. **2.** noun. **3.** neuter. **4.** nominative. **5.** north. **6.** northern. **7.** noon. **8.** born. **9.** new. **10.** number.
N. **1.** North. **2.** Northern. **3.** New. **4.** November. **5.** Navy. **6.** Norse. **7.** Noon. **8.** Nationalist.
Na, sodium. [Abbreviation of Modern Latin *natrium*.]
N.A., North America.
NAACP, National Association for the Advancement of Colored People.
nab (nab) **nabbed, nab·bing.** *v.t. Informal.* **1.** to capture or arrest: *The police nabbed the thief before he could escape.* **2.** to snatch or steal. [Probably of Scandinavian origin.]
Na·both (nā′both′) *n.* in the Old Testament, the owner of a vineyard that Ahab coveted. After Jezebel brought about Naboth's death, Ahab seized the vineyard.
na·celle (nə sel′) *n.* separate, enclosed part of an aircraft that carries the engines and sometimes the crew. [French *nacelle* nacelle, little boat, from Late Latin *navicella* little boat, diminutive of Latin *nāvis* ship.]
na·cre (nā′kər) *n.* mother-of-pearl. [French *nacre*, going back to Arabic *naqrah* cavity (as of a shell).] —**na·cre·ous** (nā′krē əs), *adj.*
na·dir (nā′dər, -dēr) *n.* **1.** point on the celestial sphere directly below the position of the observer. Opposed to **zenith.** **2.** lowest point: *The loss of the election marked the nadir of his political career.* [Arabic *nadir* opposite to (as to the zenith).]
nae (nā) *adj., adv.* Scottish. no.
nae·vus (nē′vəs) *n.* nevus —**nae′void,** *adj.*
nag¹ (nag) **nagged, nag·ging.** *v.t.* **1.** to annoy (someone) with repeated urging or complaining; badger: *His mother was constantly nagging him about his homework.* **2.** to cause continual discomfort or worry to; trouble: *His conscience nagged him.* —*v.i.* **1.** to annoy with continual urging or complaining. **2.** to be a persistent source of discomfort or worry (often with *at*): *The pain nagged at him.* —*n.* one who nags. [Probably of Scandinavian origin.] —**nag′ger,** *n.*
nag² (nag) *n.* **1.** old, broken-down horse. **2.** *Informal.* any horse. [Of uncertain origin.]
Na·ga·sa·ki (nä′gə sä′kē) *n.* city on the western coast of Kyushu, Japan. On August 9, 1945, the second atomic bomb used in World War II was dropped on this city. Pop. (1968), 422,000.
Na·go·ya (nä gô′yə) *n.* city in Japan, on the southern coast of central Honshu. Pop. (1968), 1,996,000.
Nag·pur (näg′poor) *n.* city in central India. Pop. (1969), 876,020.
Na·hua·tl (nä′wät′əl) *n.* language belonging to the Uto-Aztecan language family, spoken predominantly in central Mexico and parts of Central America by various Indian tribes. Also, **Az′tec.**
Na·hum (nā′əm, -həm) *n.* **1.** in the Old Testament, a Hebrew prophet of the seventh century B.C. **2.** book of the Old Testament containing his prophecies.
nai·ad (nā′ad, nī′-) *pl.* **-ads** or **-a·des** (-ə dēz′). *n.* Greek Mythology. water nymph living in a fountain, spring, or brook.
nail (nāl) *n.* **1.** slender piece of metal, usually pointed at one end and enlarged at the other, used chiefly as a peg or to penetrate wood and other materials so as to hold or fasten parts together. **2.a.** hard, horny structure that grows on the upper side at the end of a finger or toe in man and other primates. **b.** similar or corresponding structure in other animals, as a claw or talon. **3. hard as nails. a.** showing little or no

emotion; unfeeling; cold. **b.** in good physical condition; rugged; tough. **4. to hit the nail on the head.** to say or do something exactly right. —*v.t.* **1.** to fasten, attach, or close with a nail or nails. **2.** to hold fast or keep fixed: *Fear nailed him to the spot.* **3.** *Informal.* **a.** to catch or capture: *The police nailed the car thief.* **b.** to intercept and delay: *Reporters nailed the mayor on his way in.* **4.** *Informal.* to overcome in a fight. **5. to nail down.** to make certain of; secure: *to nail down a job. to nail down someone's opinions.* [Old English *naegel* metal spike, horny structure growing at the end of a finger or toe.]

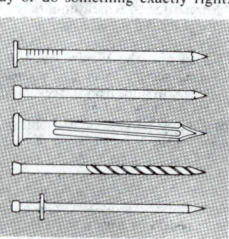

Nails

nail·set (nāl′set′) *also.* **nail set.** *n.* tool in the shape of a short rod, used for driving nails flush with or below a surface.
nain·sook (nān′sook′, nan′-) *n.* soft, lightweight cotton fabric, used for such items as infants' wear, blouses, and lingerie. [Hindustani *nainsukh* literally, pleasure to the eye, from *nain* eye + *sukh* pleasure.]
Nai·ro·bi (nī rō′bē) *n.* capital of Kenya, in the southern part of the country. Pop. (1969), 478,000.
na·ive (nä ēv′) *also.* **na·ïve.** *adj.* lacking knowledge of the ways of the world; unsophisticated; innocent: *She was naive to trust them.* [French *naïve*, feminine of *naïf* natural, from Latin *nātīvus* innate, natural. Doublet of NATIVE.] —**na·ive′ly;** *also,* **na·ïve′ly,** *adv.* —**na·ive′ness;** *also,* **na·ïve′ness,** *n.*
na·ive·té (nī ēv′tā′) *also.* **na·ïve·té.** *n.* **1.** quality or condition of being naive. **2.** naive remark or action. [French *naïveté* artlessness, from *naïf* natural. See NAIVE.]
na·ive·ty (nī ēv′tē, -ē′və tē) *pl.* **-ties.** *also.* **na·ïve·ty,** *n.* naiveté.
na·ked (nā′kid) *adj.* **1.** without clothing or similar covering; nude. **2.** devoid or stripped, as of vegetation, furnishings, or decoration; bare: *a naked room, a naked branch.* **3.** not covered or encased; exposed: *a naked light bulb, a naked wire, a naked sword.* **4.** without addition or concealment; plain: *the naked truth, naked jealousy.* **5.** without protection; vulnerable: *The west wall of the castle lay naked to attack.* [Old English *nacod* bare, unclothed.] —**na′ked·ly,** *adv.* —**na′ked·ness,** *n.* —**Syn. 1.** see **bare′.**
naked eye, eye unaided by a magnifying glass, telescope, or microscope: *The ameba was not visible to the naked eye.*
NAM, National Association of Manufacturers.
nam·by-pam·by (nam′bē pam′bē) *adj.* **1.** foolishly sentimental; wishy-washy; insipid. **2.** weak and indecisive. —*n. pl.* **-bies.** **1.** namby-pamby person. **2.** namby-pamby speech or writing. [Modification of *Ambrose Philips*, eighteenth-century English poet, whose sentimental poems and style were mocked by Alexander Pope and others.]
name (nām) *n.* **1.** word or group of words by which a person, animal, place, thing, or the like is known or referred to: *My brother's first name is Michael. The name of the city is New Orleans.* **2.** word or phrase, usually derogative, used to describe or characterize a person or thing: *to call someone names.* **3.a.** reputation; character: *His actions had given him a bad name.* **b.** distinguished reputation; fame; eminence: *Harry had earned a name as a fine singer.* **4.** mere semblance or representation, as opposed to fact or reality: *Theirs was a repressive society that was a democracy in name only.* **5.** one who or that which is famous or outstanding in some way: *one of the big names in the theater.* **6.** person or group of persons bearing the same appellation; family; clan: *all the clans hostile to the name of Campbell* (Macaulay, 1849). **7. in the name of. a.** with appeal or reference to: *What in the name of heaven are you*

at; āpe; cär; end; mē; it; īce; hot; ōld; fôrk; wood; fōŏl; oil; out; up; ūse; turn; sing; thin; this; zh in treasure; ə in ago, taken, pencil, lemon, circus.

doing here? **b.** on behalf of; for the sake of: *The ambassadors met in the name of peace.* **c.** by the authority or as the representative of: *The prime minister spoke in the name of the king.* **8.** to one's name. in one's possession; belonging to one: *I don't have a cent to my name.* —v.t., **named, nam·ing. 1.** to give a name or names to; designate by a particular appellation or epithet: *They named their son Anthony. The islands were named after their discoverer.* **2.** to mention or cite by name; refer to by name: *She refused to name the man who insulted her.* **3.** to identify correctly; call by the name: *Can you name all the presidents of the United States?* **4.** to speak of; mention: *Name a few things you'd like for Christmas.* **5.** to specify; fix: *Name the time and I'll meet you.* **6.** to nominate, appoint, or assign (a person) to some duty, position, or the like: *The president named him to head the commission.* [Old English *nama* specific designation.] —**nam′er,** *n.*

name·a·ble (nā′mə bəl) *also,* **nam·a·ble.** *adj.* **1.** that can be named. **2.** worthy of being mentioned; memorable.

name-drop·ping (nām′drop′ing) *n. Informal.* act or practice of attempting to impress others by frequently referring to famous or important people in a casual and familiar manner. —**name′-drop′per,** *n.*

name·less (nām′lis) *adj.* **1.** not identified by a name; without a name: *a nameless tomb. The newborn baby was still nameless.* **2.** not known or mentioned by name; anonymous: *a nameless benefactor. The culprit shall remain nameless.* **3.** not known to fame; obscure: *a nameless inventor.* **4.** that cannot be identified or described; inexpressible: *nameless fears.* **5.** too horrible to be mentioned or described: *nameless atrocities.* —**name′less·ly,** *adv.* —**name′less·ness,** *n.*

name·ly (nām′lē) *adv.* that is to say.

name·plate (nām′plāt′) *n.* strip of metal, plastic, or wood on which a name is printed.

name·sake (nām′sāk′) *n.* one named after or having the same name as another.

Nan·chang (nän′chäng′) *n.* city in southeastern China. Pop. (1957 est.), 508,000.

Nan·cy (nan′sē) *n.* city in northeastern France. Pop. (1968), 123,428.

nan·keen (nan kēn′) *also,* **nan·kin.** *n.* **1.** durable brownish-yellow or buff cotton fabric, formerly used for trousers and other articles of clothing. **2.** nankeens. trousers made of this fabric. [Modification of NANKING, where the cloth was originally produced.]

Nan·king (nan′king′) *n.* city in eastern China, on the Yangtze River, formerly the capital of the country. Pop. (1957 est.), 1,419,000.

nan·ny goat (nan′ē) *Informal.* female goat.

Nan·sen, Fridt·jof (nän′sən; frit′yof) 1861–1930, Norwegian arctic explorer, scientist, and statesman.

Nantes (nants; *French* nänt) *n.* **1.** port city in western France, in the region of Brittany. Pop. (1968), 259,208. **2. Edict of.** proclamation granting a substantial amount of religious freedom and political equality to French Protestants, issued in 1598 by Henry IV and revoked in 1685 by Louis XIV.

Nan·tuck·et (nan tuk′it) *n.* island off the southern coast of Cape Cod. Area, 49.53 sq. mi. Pop. (1970), 3774.

Na·o·mi (nā ō′mē, nā′ō mē′) *n.* in the Old Testament, the mother-in-law of Ruth.

nap¹ (nap) *n.* short sleep. —v.i. **napped, nap·ping. 1.** to sleep for a short time. **2.** to be off guard or unprepared. [Old English *hnappian* to sleep for a short time.]

nap² (nap) *n.* downy or fuzzy finish on fabric, formed by short fibers that are raised on the surface. —v.t., **napped, nap·ping.** to raise a nap on (fabric). [Middle Dutch *noppe* the downy finish on fabric.]

na·palm (nā′päm) *n.* **1.** aluminum soap compound used to thicken and jell gasoline. **2.** gasoline that has been thickened and jelled with napalm, used in incendiary bombs that break on impact and spread the flaming contents in all directions. —v.t. to attack with napalm.

nape (nāp, nap) *n.* the back of the neck. [Of uncertain origin.]

na·per·y (nā′pər ē) *n.* household linens, esp. tablecloths, napkins, and other table linens. [Old French *naperie* table linen, from *nappe* linen, going back to Latin *mappa* cloth, napkin; of Semitic origin.]

Naph·ta·li (naf′tə lī′) *n.* **1.** in the Old Testament, a son of Jacob. **2.** one of the twelve tribes of Israel, descended from him.

naph·tha (naf′thə, nap′-) *n.* any of several liquids made from petroleum or coal tar, whose boiling points are higher than gasoline but lower than kerosene. Naphtha is used in cleaning fluid, fuel mixtures, and solvents, and in the manufacture of rubber, paints, and varnishes. [Latin *naphtha*, from Greek *naphtha*; of Persian origin.]

naph·tha·lene (naf′thə lēn′, nap′-) *also,* **naph·tha·line.** *n.* white, crystalline compound with a strong coal-tar odor, used in making moth balls. Formula: $C_{10}H_8$. [NAPHTHA + -ENE.]

naph·thol (naf′thôl, nap′-) *n.* either of two crystalline substances obtained from naphthalene and caustic soda, used esp. in making dyes. Formula: $C_{10}H_7OH$. [NAPHTH(ALENE) + -OL.]

Na·pi·er, John (nā′pē ər) 1550–1617, Scottish mathematician, inventor of logarithms.

nap·kin (nap′kin) *n.* piece of cloth or paper, usually square, used at meals for protecting one's clothing or for wiping the lips, hands, or fingers. [Diminutive of Old French *nappe* linen. See NAPERY.]

Na·ples (nā′pəlz) *n.* **1.** port city in southern Italy, on the Bay of Naples. Pop. (1968), 1,267,073. **2. Bay of.** inlet of the Tyrrhenian Sea, on the southwestern coast of Italy.

na·po·le·on (nə pō′lē ən, -pōl′yən) *n.* **1.** former French gold coin equivalent to twenty francs. **2.** rich pastry, usually rectangular in shape, having cream or custard between layers of pastry dough, and frequently iced. [From NAPOLEON I.]

Na·po·le·on I (nə pō′lē ən, -pōl′yən) 1769–1821, French military leader and conqueror, emperor of France from 1804 to 1815; full name, Napoleon Bonaparte.

Napoleon III, 1808–73, nephew of Napoleon I; emperor of France from 1852 to 1870; born Charles Louis Napoleon Bonaparte.

Na·po·le·on·ic (nə pō′lē on′ik) *adj.* of, relating to, or characteristic of Napoleon I or his reign.

nar·cis·sism (när′si siz′əm) *n.* **1.** excessive admiration for or fascination with oneself; self-love. **2.** *Psychoanalysis.* arresting of development at, or regression to, the infantile stage of development in which one's own body is the object of one's erotic interest. —**nar′cis·sist,** *n.* —**nar′cis·sis′tic,** *adj.*

nar·cis·sus (när sis′əs) *pl.,* **-cis·sus·es** *or* **-cis·si** (-sis′ī). *n.* **1.** showy yellow or white flower of any of several plants, genus *Narcissus,* consisting of a star of petals around a central tube. **2.** plant bearing this flower, having long slender leaves that grow directly from an underground bulb. [Latin *narcissus,* from Greek *narkissos,* from *narkē* numbness; because of its narcotic effect.]

Nar·cis·sus (när sis′əs) *n. Greek Mythology.* handsome youth who scorned all women and was made to fall in love with his own reflection in a pool by the goddess of love, Aphrodite.

nar·co·sis (när kō′sis) *n.* deep stupor produced by a drug. [Modern Latin *narcosis,* from Greek *narkōsis* a benumbing, going back to *narkē* numbness.]

nar·cot·ic (när kot′ik) *n.* drug, as opium or morphine, that dulls the senses, produces sleep or unconsciousness, relieves pain, and, with prolonged use, usually becomes addictive. —*adj.* **1.** of, relating to, or caused by a narcotic or narcotics: *narcotic addiction, a narcotic stupor.* **2.** relating to, of the nature of, or inducing narcosis. **3.** having the properties of a narcotic. [Old French *narcotique* benumbing, from Greek *narkōtikos,* going back to *narkē* numbness.]

nard (närd) *n.* spikenard *(def. 2).* [Latin *nardus,* from Greek *nardos;* of Semitic origin.]

nar·es (nār′ēz) *sing.,* **nar·is** (nār′is). *n.,pl.* nostrils or nasal passages. [Latin *nārēs,* plural of *nāris* nostril.]

nar·ghi·le (när′gə lē, -lā′) *also,* **nar·gi·le.** *n.* Oriental pipe with a long flexible tube through which smoke passes and is cooled by water contained in a bowl or similar receptacle. [From Persian *nārgil* coconut (from which the bowls of these pipes were once made).]

Nar·ra·gan·sett (nar′ə gan′sit) *n.* **1.** member of a North American Indian tribe of the Algonquian language family, formerly living in the western woodlands of Rhode Island. **2.** Algonquian language of this tribe.

Narragansett Bay, large inlet of the Atlantic, on the eastern coast of Rhode Island.

nar·rate (nar′āt, na rāt′) **-rat·ed, -rat·ing.** *v.t., v.i.* **1.** to tell or relate (something), as a story, sequence of events, or experience. **2.** to speak in accompaniment to (a motion picture or the like) in order to relate certain facts or details. [Latin *narrātus,* past participle of *narrāre* to tell, relate.] —**nar′ra·tor;** *also,* **nar·ra·ter,** *n.*

nar·ra·tion (na rā′shən) *n.* **1.** act of narrating. **2.** that which is narrated; narrative. **3.** literary form, as fiction or history, relating a story or sequence of events.

nar·ra·tive (nar′ə tiv) *n.* **1.** story or account, as of an experience or sequence of events. **2.** act, art, or process of narrating. —*adj.* of, relating to, or containing narration: *narrative skill, a narrative poem.*

nar·row (nar′ō) *adj.* **1.** having little width; not broad: *a narrow aisle. We jumped across the narrow stream.* **2.** limited in extent; restricted: *Don has a narrow range of interests.* **3.** lacking tolerance, imagination, or breadth of view; limited; narrow-minded: *He is a poorly educated man with a narrow outlook on life.* **4.** barely successful or adequate; with little margin: *a narrow escape, a narrow victory.* **5.** with careful attention to detail; thorough; close: *a narrow search.* **6.** limited in income or other resources; straitened: *narrow circumstances.* **7.** *Phonetics.* articulated with muscular tension of the vocal organs. —*v.t., v.i.* to make or become smaller in width or extent: *We've narrowed the choices down to three. The river narrows at the bridge.* —*n. also,* **narrows.** narrow part, as of a body of water or a mountain pass: *A bridge was built across the narrows.* [Old English *nearu* having little width, small.] —**nar′row·ly,** *adv.* —**nar′row·ness,** *n.*

nar·row-gauge (nar′ō gāj′) *adj.* **1.** (of railroad track) having a

width less than the standard gauge of 56½ inches. **2.** designed for use on a narrow-gauge railroad track.

nar·row gauge, narrow-gauge railroad, locomotive, or car.

nar·row-mind·ed (nar′ō mīn′did) *adj.* having or showing a restricted and prejudiced outlook; illiberal. —**nar′row-mind′ed·ly,** *adv.* —**nar′row-mind′ed·ness,** *n.*

nar·thex (när′theks) *n.* **1.** in early Christian and Byzantine churches, a vestibule or portico extending across the ends of the nave and side aisles, forming an entrance. **2.** any vestibule leading to the nave of a church. [Late Greek *narthēx* portico, from Greek *narthēx* fennel; supposedly because the porch resembled the hollow stem of fennel.]

Narwhal

nar·whal (när′wəl) *n.* toothed whale, *Monodon monoceros,* native to the Arctic and North Atlantic oceans, having shiny, black skin with pale-yellow spots, the male of which has a twisted tusk that may be as long as nine feet. It is widely hunted by Eskimos for food and oil. Length: 12–15 feet. [Probably from Danish *narhval,* going back to Old Norse *nār* corpse + *hvalr* whale; because of its coloration.]

nar·y (när′ē) *adj. Informal.* not one (often with *a*): *There's nary a hope that they'll be found.* [Modification of earlier *ne'er a* never a.]

NASA (nas′ə) National Aeronautics and Space Administration.

na·sal (nā′zəl) *adj.* **1.** of, from, or relating to the nose: *nasal passage.* **2.** *Phonetics.* pronounced with the sound passing through the nose, as in the sounds of *m, n,* and *ng.* **3.** characterized by or resembling such a sound: *the nasal drone of a bagpipe.* —*n.* nasal sound or letter. [French *nasal* relating to the nose, from Latin *nāsus* nose.] —**na·sal·i·ty** (nā zal′ə tē), *n.* —**na′sal·ly,** *adv.*

na·sal·ize (nā′zə līz′) **-ized, -iz·ing,** *v.t.* to pronounce with a nasal tone quality. —*v.i.* to speak through the nose. —**na′sal·i·za′tion,** *n.*

nas·cent (nas′ənt, nā′sənt) *adj.* in the process of coming into being; beginning to exist or develop. [Latin *nāscēns,* present participle of *nāsci* to be born.] —**nas′cence, nas′cen·cy,** *n.*

Nash, Ogden (nash; og′dən) 1902–71, U.S. poet.

Nash·ville (nash′vil′) *n.* capital of Tennessee, in the central part of the state. Pop. (1970), 447,877.

Nas·sau (nas′ô) *n.* **1.** capital and largest city of the Bahamas. Pop. (1967), 100,000. **2.** royal family of the Netherlands that has ruled since 1815.

Nas·ser, Ga·mal Ab·del (nä′sər, nas′ər; gə mäl′ ab′del) 1918–70, Egyptian political leader and first president of the United Arab Republic.

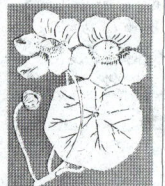

Nasturtium

na·stur·tium (nə stur′shəm) *n.* **1.** showy funnel-shaped flower of any of a small group of plants, genus *Tropaeolum,* growing in a variety of colors and often spotted or striped. It has sharp-tasting buds and seeds that are sometimes used in pickling. **2.** the climbing plant bearing this flower, having rounded or lobed leaves with heavy veins branching out from the center. [Latin *nasturtium* a kind of cress, from *nāsus* nose + *torquēre* to twist; because its strong odor irritates the nose.]

nas·ty (nas′tē) **-ti·er, -ti·est.** *adj.* **1.** malicious; spiteful: *a nasty rumor.* **2.** disagreeable or annoying; unpleasant: *Susan has a nasty habit of slamming the door.* **3.** seriously harmful; severe: *a nasty fall.* **4.** morally offensive; obscene; indecent: *nasty language.* **5.** repulsive to taste or smell; nauseating: *a nasty odor, a nasty medicine.* **6.** physically dirty; filthy. [Of uncertain origin.] —**nas′ti·ly,** *adv.* —**nas′ti·ness,** *n.*

nat. **1.** national. **2.** native. **3.** natural. **4.** naturalist.

na·tal (nāt′əl) *adj.* **1.** of, relating to, or dating from one's birth. **2.** *Archaic.* native: *He sought his natal mountain-peaks divine* (Shelley, 1820). [Latin *nātālis* relating to one's birth, from *nātus,* past participle of *nāsci* to be born.]

na·tal·i·ty (nā tal′ə tē) *pl.* **-ties.** *n.* birthrate.

na·tant (nāt′ənt) *adj.* swimming or floating. [Latin *natāns,* present participle of *natāre* to swim, float.]

na·ta·tion (nā tā′shən) *n.* act or art of swimming.

na·ta·to·ri·al (nā′tə tôr′ē əl) *adj.* of, relating to, characterized by, or adapted for swimming. Also, **na′ta·to′ry.** [Late Latin *natātōrius* relating to swimming (from Latin *natāre* to swim) + AL¹.]

na·ta·to·ri·um (nā′tə tôr′ē əm) *pl.* **-to·ri·ums** or **-to·ri·a** (-tôr′ē ə). *n.* swimming pool. [Late Latin *natātōrium,* from Latin *natāre* to swim.]

Natch·ez (nach′iz) *n.* member of a tribe of North American Indians of the Muskogean language family, formerly living in southwestern Mississippi.

na·tes (nā′tēz) *n.,pl.* the buttocks. [Latin *natēs,* plural of *natis* rump.]

Na·than (nā′thən) *n.* in the Old Testament, the prophet who rebuked David for the death of Uriah.

Na·than·a·el (nə than′ē əl, -than′yəl) *n.* in the New Testament, one of the disciples of Jesus, often identified with Bartholomew.

nathe·less (nāth′lis, nath′-) *adj.* **nath·less.** *Archaic. adv.* nevertheless. —*prep.* notwithstanding. [Old English *nā thē læs* not the less.]

na·tion (nā′shən) *n.* **1.a.** people occupying a defined territory and united under one political system, esp. people sharing a common ethnic origin and historical and cultural traditions. **b.** territory occupied by a nation; country: *He traveled through the nation.* **2.** group of people having a common origin, language, and history: *a member of the Irish nation.* **3.** tribe or federation of tribes, esp. of North American Indians. [Latin *nātiō* race, people.]

na·tion·al (nash′ən əl) *adj.* **1.** of, belonging to, involving, or affecting a nation as a whole: *the national welfare, a national political convention.* **2.** characteristic of or peculiar to a particular nation: *a national language, a national costume.* **3.** established or maintained by the central government. —*n.* one who is a member of a nation and is entitled to its protection; citizen or subject. —**na′tion·al·ly,** *adv.* —**Syn.** *n.* see **citizen.**

national bank **1.** in the United States, a commercial bank chartered by the federal government. **2.** bank associated with the finances of a nation, as the Federal Reserve Bank.

national debt, total amount owed by a national government. The United States Department of the Treasury finances the national debt by selling securities backed by the credit of the government.

National Guard, reserve component of the U.S. Army, constituting the military forces of the individual states. It is under the control of each governor, but may be put under federal control by the president in time of war or national emergency.

national income, total income of a nation, including rent from property, wages and salaries, interest from loans, and business profits earned during a specified period.

na·tion·al·ism (nash′ən əl iz′əm) *n.* **1.** devotion, often extreme or chauvinistic, to one's nation and its interests, heritage, welfare, and traditions. **2.** beliefs and policies stressing the different interests of different nations and opposed to international cooperation. **3.** desire or movement for national independence. —**na′tion·al·ist,** *n.* —**na′tion·al·is′tic,** *adj.* —**na′tion·al·is′ti·cal·ly,** *adv.*

Nationalist China, China (def. 2).

na·tion·al·i·ty (nash′ə nal′ə tē) *pl.* **-ties.** *n.* **1.** fact or state of belonging to a particular nation, esp. by birth: *His nationality is Australian.* **2.** group of people sharing a common origin, language, and history; nation: *Various nationalities were represented at the conference.* **3.** condition of being a politically independent nation: *Many small countries are fighting to achieve nationality.*

na·tion·al·ize (nash′ən əl īz′) **-ized, -iz·ing,** *v.t.* **1.** to place (something, as an industry) under the control or ownership of a national government. **2.** to extend throughout a nation; make nationwide: *to nationalize a television network.* —**na′tion·al·i·za′tion,** *n.*

national monument, natural formation, place of historic interest, or specially erected structure maintained by the federal government.

national park, area of land maintained by the federal government for public use.

National Security Council, group consisting of certain high officials of the executive branch of the U.S. Government, that advises the president on integrating domestic, foreign, and military policies for more effective national security.

National Socialism, political doctrine of racism, totalitarianism, and extreme militarism and nationalism of the Nazis in Germany prior to and during World War II. Also, **Na′zi·ism.**

na·tion·wide (nā′shən wīd′) *also,* **na·tion-wide.** *adj.* extending throughout the nation.

na·tive (nā′tiv) *n.* **1.** one who was born in a particular place or country: *a native of France, a native of Cleveland.* **2.** original inhabitant of a region or country, as distinguished from a foreigner, settler, or the like: *Missionaries were sent to try to convert the natives.* **3.** animal or plant indigenous or peculiar to a place: *That bird is a native of South Carolina.* **4.** one who has been a lifelong resident of a place, country, or region. —*adj.* **1.** belonging to a particular place or country, esp. by birth: *a native New Yorker, a native Londoner.* **2.** connected with or belonging to one by birth in a particular place, time, or circumstance: *French is not my native tongue.* **3.** inherent; innate; natural: *native intelligence.* **4.** originating, grown, or produced in a particular place; indigenous: *Cactus is native to desert regions.* **5.** of, relating to, or characteristic of the original inhabitants of a country or region or their descendants, esp. those regarded as primitive: *native tribal dances.* **6.** of, relating to, or characteristic of a region or its inhabitants: *native New England humor.* **7.** natural; simple; unaffected: *native sweetness.* **8.** occurring in nature in an uncombined or pure state: *Native silver is*

very soft. **9.** found in a natural state; not produced artificially: *Native coal is processed for use as a fuel.* **10. to go native.** to adopt the manner and style of living of a particular area, esp. to become more relaxed in dress and behavior. [Latin *nātīvus* born, innate, natural. Doublet of NAIVE.] **—na′tive·ly,** *adv.* **—na′tive·ness,** *n.*
Syn. *adj.* **1. Native, indigenous** mean belonging to a particular place by birth or origin. **Native** refers to persons or things having birth or origin in a particular place or locality: *The president of the United States must be a native American.* **Indigenous** is used in the sense of being prevalent or living naturally in an area and is usually applied to species and races inhabiting a large region rather than to individuals: *Kangaroos are indigenous to Australia.*

na·tive-born (nā′tiv bôrn′) *adj.* born in the place or country specified or understood: *a native-born Australian.*
na·tiv·i·ty (nə tiv′ə tē, nā-) *pl.* **-ties.** *n.* **1. Nativity. a.** birth of Christ. **b.** a representation of the birth of Christ, as in painting. **c.** Christmas; December 25. **2.** birth. **3.** position of the stars at the date of one's birth; horoscope. [Old French *nativite* birth, from Latin *nātīvitās.*]
natl., national.
NATO (nā′tō) North Atlantic Treaty Organization, established in 1949, a military alliance of fifteen Western nations.
nat·ty (nat′ē) **-ti·er, -ti·est.** *adj.* neat, trim, and stylish: *a natty new uniform.* [Possibly form of NEAT¹ + -Y¹.] **—nat′ti·ly,** *adv.*
nat·u·ral (nach′ər əl, nach′rəl) *adj.* **1.** produced by or existing in nature; not artificial: *a natural rock formation.* **2.** based on or derived from nature: *a natural growth process, the natural beauty of the Rocky Mountains.* **3.a.** of, relating to, or involving nature or its study. **b.** occupied or concerned with the study of natural science: *a natural scientist.* **4.** belonging to or existing in one as a result of birth; innate: *a girl with natural beauty.* **5.** being such by certain inherent qualities or abilities; born: *John is a natural athlete who plays many sports well.* **6.** happening in the ordinary course of things; unexceptional; normal: *to die from natural causes.* **7.** normally associated with, derived from, or pertaining to the essence of a person or thing; reasonable; expected: *Anger was a natural reaction to the insult.* **8.** exactly as created by or in nature: *Is blond her natural hair color?* **9.** closely imitating or resembling nature; realistic; lifelike: *a natural portrait, to assume a natural pose.* **10.** free from artificiality, affectation, or constraint; easy: *to walk at a natural gait, to speak in a natural voice.* **11.** based on the innate moral feeling of mankind; instinctively felt to be right and fair: *natural justice, natural rights.* **12.** based on what is observable in nature or has physical existence, rather than on faith or revelation: *natural religion.* **13.** illegitimate: *The natural child of the king could not succeed to the throne.* **14.** being related by birth rather than by adoption: *The adopted child never knew his natural parents.* **15.** *Music.* **a.** having neither sharps nor flats; without accidentals: *the natural scale of C major.* **b.** neither sharp nor flat: *She played F sharp instead of F natural.* **c.** having the pitch changed by the sign ♮. **—n. 1.** that which is natural or occurs in the normal course of things: *the natural and the supernatural.* **2.** *Music.* **a.** sign (♮) used to cancel the effect of a preceding sharp or flat. **b.** tone or note altered by this sign. **c.** in keyboard instruments, a white key. **3.** *Informal.* **a.** person who is endowed with a specific talent: *Some people have studied acting, but he's a natural.* **b.** person who seems exceptionally qualified or well-suited: *a natural for the job.* **c.** person or thing that seems highly likely to succeed. [Latin *nātūrālis* by birth, in accordance with nature, from *nātūra* character, disposition, course of things, the world.] **—nat′u·ral·ness,** *n.* **—Syn.** *adj.* **7.** see **typical.**
natural area, area, as of forest land, left to develop naturally, usually for the purpose of study and research.
natural childbirth, manner of giving birth to a baby using a minimum of drugs and anesthetics, in which the mother remains conscious and assists throughout labor and delivery of the baby. Exercises and training prepare expectant mothers for natural childbirth.
natural gas 1. mixture of the gaseous hydrocarbons (methane, ethane, propane, and butane) with other gases, found in underground deposits. **2.** commercial natural gas used as fuel, consisting mainly of methane.
natural history, observation and study of natural organisms, objects, and processes.
nat·u·ral·ism (nach′ər ə liz′əm, nach′rə-) *n.* **1.** in art and literature, faithful representation of or close adherence to nature or reality. **2.** principles and style of fiction writing developed in the mid-nineteenth century, in which environment, which is considered to be the strongest force in shaping a character's existence, is depicted realistically and in great detail. **3.** action or moral system based on or arising from natural instincts. **4.** philosophical view that the real world is that of nature as studied by science, and governed by natural mechanical laws and forces, rather than by supernatural ones. **5.** doctrine that all religious truth can be derived from the study of nature without the aid of divine revelation.

nat·u·ral·ist (nach′ər ə list, nach′rə-) *n.* **1.** one who studies natural science, esp. a botanist or zoologist. **2.** adherent of or believer in naturalism, esp. in art or in literature.
nat·u·ral·is·tic (nach′ər ə lis′tik, nach′rə-) *adj.* **1.** of, relating to, or characteristic of naturalism, esp. in art or literature. **2.** imitating or closely resembling nature: *The lighting on the stage set produced a naturalistic effect.*
nat·u·ral·ize (nach′ər ə līz′, nach′rə-) **-ized, -iz·ing.** *v.t.* **1.** to admit (an alien) to citizenship. **2.** to assimilate (something, as a foreign word or custom) into common use. **3.** to adapt (an animal or plant) to another environment; acclimate. **4.** to make lifelike; free from artificiality: *The photographer asked her to naturalize her pose.* **—v.i.** to adapt oneself to a place; become like a native: *The ambassador tried to naturalize in his new country.* **—nat′u·ral·i·za′tion,** *n.*
natural logarithm, logarithm that has *e* (2.7182818 . . .) as its base.
nat·u·ral·ly (nach′ər ə lē, nach′rə-) *adv.* **1.** as would be expected; of course: *Naturally I'll help you.* **2.** by nature; inherently: *Dan was naturally shy.* **3.** without affectation or artificiality: *She was too nervous to act naturally.* **4.** by natural processes: *Coconuts grow naturally on the island. He didn't die naturally—he was murdered.*
natural number, the number one or any number produced by repeatedly adding one to this number. 1, 4, 37, and 592 are natural numbers.
natural philosophy *Archaic.* physical sciences collectively, esp. physics.
natural resources, naturally occurring materials that are useful to man or necessary for his survival, as water, forests, and minerals.
natural science, any or all of the sciences concerned with the physical universe, including biology, chemistry, and geology.
natural selection, evolutionary process by which those animals and plants having characteristics best adapted to their environment tend to survive and pass those characteristics on to their progeny.
na·ture (nā′chər) *n.* **1.** essential properties, attributes, or qualities of a thing; inherent character: *What is the nature of your request? It is the nature of fire to burn.* **2.** *also,* **Nature.** sum total of the forces or processes which appear to create and regulate all things throughout the universe: *the laws of nature. Nature abhors a vacuum.* **3.** the entire physical universe with all its phenomena: *the beauties of nature.* **4.** fundamental inclination, disposition, or character of a person or animal: *a generous nature.* **5.a.** particular disposition or character; temperament: *a gentle nature.* **b.** person of a particular character: *He is a strange nature.* **6.** *also,* **Nature.** inherent power or impulse that determines, directs, or controls the actions and behavior of a person or thing; instinct. **7.** sort; kind; variety: *A story of this nature should not be published.* **8.** original state or condition of mankind before social organization, esp. regarded as primitive or uncivilized: *to live in the state of nature, to go back to nature.* **9.** natural plant and animal life: *a walk through the woods to observe nature.* **10.** vital functions, forces, and activities of an organism. **11.** *Theology.* state of man's soul without divine grace. **12. by nature.** as a result of the essential character of a person or thing; innately: *She is by nature a happy person.* **13. of** (or **in**) **the nature of.** having the nature, character, or qualities of; being; like. [Latin *nātūra* character, disposition, course of things, the world.]
nature study, elementary study of plant and animal life, esp. through field trips.
nature trail, path maintained in a park or other area, along which trees, plants, rocks, and other natural features are often marked for study.
na·tur·op·a·thy (nā′chə rop′ə thē, nach′ə-) *n.* method of medical treatment that avoids using drugs or surgery and depends only on natural healing agents, such as sunshine and water. **—na·tur·o·path** (nā′chər ə path′), *n.* **—na′tur·o·path′ic,** *adj.*
naught (nôt) *also,* **nought.** *n.* **1.** nothing: *All our plans came to naught.* **2.** zero: *Five plus naught equals five.* [Old English *nāwiht* mischief, nothing, from *nā* no + *wiht* thing.]
naugh·ty (nô′tē) **-ti·er, -ti·est.** *adj.* **1.** mischievous; disobedient. **2.** in bad taste; improper: *a naughty word.* [NAUGHT + -Y¹.] **—naugh′ti·ly,** *adv.* **—naugh′ti·ness,** *n.*
Na·u·ru (nä ōō′rōō) *n.* small island country in the central Pacific Ocean, northeast of Australia. Area, approx. 8 sq. mi. Pop. (1969 est.), 7000.
nau·se·a (nô′zē ə, -shə, -shē ə) *n.* **1.** sick feeling in the stomach that one is going to vomit. **2.** extreme disgust; revulsion. [Latin *nausea* seasickness, vomiting, from Greek *nausiā* seasickness, disgust, from *naus* ship.]
nau·se·ate (nô′zē āt′, -shē-) **-at·ed, -at·ing.** *v.t.* to produce nausea in: *The rolling of the ship nauseated the passengers.* **—v.i.** to become affected with nausea (often with *at*). [Latin *nauseātus,* past participle of *nauseāre* to be seasick, vomit, from *nausea* seasickness. See NAUSEA.] **—nau′se·at′ing·ly,** *adv.* **—nau′se·a′tion,** *n.*

---

at; āpe; cär; end; mē; it; īce; hot; ōld; fôrk; wood; fōol; oil; out; up; ūse; turn; sing; thin; this; zh in treasure; ə in ago, taken, pencil, lemon, circus.

nau·seous (nô′shəs, -zē əs) *adj.* **1.** sickened; nauseated: *to feel nauseous during an automobile ride.* **2.** repulsive to the taste or smell. [Latin *nauseōsus* that produces nausea, from *nausea* seasickness. See NAUSEA.] —**nau′seous·ly,** *adv.* —**nau′seous·ness,** *n.*

Nau·sic·a·ä (nô sik′ē ə, -ā ə) *n. Greek Mythology.* maiden who aided the shipwrecked Ulysses by taking him to her father's palace.

naut., nautical.

nautch (nôch) *n.* in India, an exhibition of dancing performed by professional dancing girls. [Hindi *nāch* a dance, from Prakrit *nachcha* dancing, from Sanskrit *nritja.*]

nau·ti·cal (nô′ti kəl) *adj.* of or relating to ships, seamen, or navigation. [Latin *nauticus* (from Greek *nautikos,* going back to *naus* ship) + -AL¹.] —**nau′ti·cal·ly,** *adv.* —**Syn.** see **marine.**

nautical mile, unit of distance officially fixed at 6080 feet in Great Britain and at 6080.2 feet in the United States. See **weights and measures** for table.

nau·ti·lus (nô′tl əs) *pl.,* **nau·ti·lus·es** or **nau·ti·li** (nô′tl ī′). *n.* any of a small group of saltwater cephalopods found in tropical waters, having a flattened spiral shell divided into chambers. The nautilus lives in the outermost chamber of its shell. **2.** paper nautilus. [Latin *nautilus,* from Greek *nautilos* nautilus, sailor, going back to *naus* ship; because it was once thought to use its shell as a sail.]

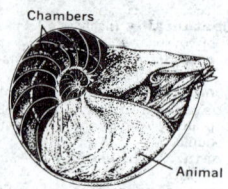

Chambers

Animal

Cutaway view of nautilus

nav. 1. naval. **2.** navigation.

Nav·a·ho (nav′ə hō′) *pl.,* **-hos** or **-hoes** or **-ho.** *n.* member of the largest tribe of North American Indians of the Athapascan language family, living in New Mexico, Arizona, and Utah. The Navahos are noted for their skill in weaving.

Nav·a·jo (nav′ə hō′) *pl.,* **-jos** or **-joes** or **-jo.** *n.* Navaho.

na·val (nā′vəl) *adj.* **1.** of or relating to warships: *naval maneuvers.* **2.** of or relating to a navy: *naval supplies, naval discipline.* **3.** of or relating to ships: *naval engineering.* **4.** possessing or based on the possession of a navy: *naval strength, a great naval power.* [Latin *nāvālis* relating to ships, from *nāvis* ship.] —**na′val·ly,** *adv.*

Na·varre (nə vär′) *n.* historic region and former kingdom located in the western Pyrenees, that included parts of southwestern France and northern Spain.

nave¹ (nāv) *n.* main body of a church situated between the side aisles and extending from the main entrance to the chancel or transepts. [Medieval Latin *navis,* from Latin *nāvis* ship; referring to the old comparison of the Christian church to a storm-tossed ship.]

nave² (nāv) *n.* hub of a wheel. [Old English *nafu.*]

na·vel (nā′vəl) *n.* rounded depression or scar in the middle of the surface of the abdomen that remains after the umbilical cord is cut; umbilicus. [Old English *nafela.*]

navel orange, large, usually seedless, sweet orange, having a navel-like formation at one end that contains a small undeveloped secondary fruit.

nav·i·ga·ble (nav′i gə bəl) *adj.* **1.** able to be traveled on or through by ships or other water vessels: *This stream is navigable by small boats only.* **2.** capable of being steered. —**nav′i·ga·bil′i·ty,** *n.*

nav·i·gate (nav′i gāt′) *-gat·ed, -gat·ing. v.t.* **1.** to direct the course of or operate (a water vessel or aircraft); pilot. **2.** to plan or direct the course of (a voyage, flight, or the like). **3.** to sail on or across (a body of water). **4.** to move through, on, or over: *It was impossible to navigate the snow-covered highway until a snowplow cleared a path.* —*v.i.* **1.** to direct the course of or operate a water vessel or aircraft. **2.** to plan or direct the course of a voyage, flight, or the like. **3.** to travel over the water; sail. [Latin *nāvigātus,* past participle of *nāvigāre* to sail, from *nāvis* ship + *agere* to drive.]

nav·i·ga·tion (nav′i gā′shən) *n.* **1.** act or practice of navigating a ship or aircraft. **2.** art or science of determining and directing the position and course of ships and aircraft. **3.** commerce by ship; shipping. —**nav′i·ga′tion·al,** *adj.*

navigation satellite, earth satellite intended to provide navigational data for ships or aircraft.

nav·i·ga·tor (nav′i gā′tər) *n.* **1.** one who navigates. **2.** one who has skill in or practices navigation, esp. of a ship or aircraft. **3.** formerly, one who explores the seas. [Latin *nāvigātor* sailor, from *nāvigāre* to sail. See NAVIGATE.]

nav·vy (nav′ē) *pl.,* **-vies.** *n. British.* unskilled laborer, esp. one who works on railways, roads, or the like. [Short for NAVIGATOR; referring to a laborer who worked on (dialectal English) *navigations* or canals.]

Chancel

Transept

Nave

Nave¹

na·vy (nā′vē) *pl.,* **-vies.** *n.* **1.** all the warships of a country, collectively. **2.a.** *also,* **Navy.** entire military sea force of a country, including ships, land bases, equipment, and personnel. **b.** department of government in charge of this. **3.** navy blue. **4.** *Archaic.* any large group of ships. [Old French *navie* ships, fleet, going back to Latin *nāvis* ship.]

navy bean, small, dried white bean related to the kidney bean and grown for its edible seeds.

navy blue, very dark-blue color.

navy yard, land base with docking facilities and drydocks where naval vessels are built, fitted out, and repaired.

nay (nā) *adv.* **1.** *Archaic.* no. **2.** not only that, but even: *She was disappointed, nay, heartbroken by the news.* —*n.* **1.** negative vote or voter. **2.** refusal, denial, or prohibition. [Old Norse *nei* no, from *ne* not + *ei* ever.]

Naz·a·rene (naz′ə rēn′, naz′ə rēn′) *n.* **1.** native or inhabitant of Nazareth. **2.** member of a sect of early Christians who observed the Mosaic Law. **3. the Nazarene.** Jesus.

Naz·a·reth (naz′ər əth) *n.* town in Galilee, in northern Israel, where Jesus spent his youth.

Naz·a·rite (naz′ə rīt′) *also,* **Naz·i·rite.** *n.* in the Old Testament, one of a group of Israelites who took certain strict religious vows as a symbol of service to God.

Na·zi (nät′sē, nat′-) *pl.,* **Na·zis.** *n.* **1.** member or follower of the party that controlled Germany under the leadership of Adolf Hitler from 1933 to 1945. **2.** one holding views similar to those of the German Nazis. —*adj.* of, relating to, or characteristic of the Nazis.

Na·zi·ism (nät′sē iz′əm, nat′-) *also,* **Na·zism** (nät′siz′əm, nat′-). *n.* National Socialism.

Nb, niobium.

N.B. 1. note well. [Latin *notā bene.*] **2.** New Brunswick.

N.C., North Carolina.

NCAA, National Collegiate Athletic Association.

N.C.O., noncommissioned officer.

Nd, neodymium.

N.D. 1. no date. **2.** North Dakota.

N. Dak., North Dakota.

Ne, neon.

NE 1. northeast. **2.** northeastern.

N.E., New England.

NEA, National Education Association.

Ne·an·der·thal (nē an′dər thôl′, -täl′) *adj.* of, relating to, or characteristic of Neanderthal man. —*n.* Neanderthal man.

Neanderthal man, any of a highly diversified, extinct species of prehistoric man, *Homo neanderthalensis,* that lived during the early Stone Age. [From the *Neanderthal* Valley of the Neander River in Germany, where bones of this prehistoric man were found.]

Ne·a·pol·i·tan (nē′ə pol′it ən) *adj.* **1.** of, relating to, or characteristic of Naples. **2.** having layers of different colors and flavors, as ice cream. —*n.* native or inhabitant of Naples.

neap tide (nēp) tide occurring at the first and third quarters of the moon, when there is the least difference between the levels of high and low tide. [Old English *nēp,* possibly meaning "lacking", "scanty" + TIDE.]

near (nēr) *adv.* **1.** to, within, or at a short distance; not far in time, place, or degree: *Night is drawing near.* **2.** almost; nearly: *We were near hysterical with worry.* **3.** intimately; closely. —*adj.* **1.** not distant in time, place, or degree: *Will we see you in the near future?* **2.** achieved or avoided by only a slight margin: *a near disaster, a near miss.* **3.** closely related or associated by or as by blood: *John is very near and dear to us.* **4.** closely resembling or approximating an original. **5.** short and direct: *the near route into the city.* **6.** stingy; miserly. **7.** left: *to pass on the near side of a car.* Opposed to **off.** —*prep.* close to or by: *Don't stand so near the train. The building is near completion.* —*v.t.* to come or draw near to; approach. —*v.i.* to come or draw near or nearer. [Old English *nēar* closer, nearer, comparative of *nēah* nigh.] —**near′ness,** *n.*

Syn. *adj.* **1. Near, close** mean in proximity. **Near** stresses being within a short distance or interval in space, time, degree, or relation: *The museum is quite near, less than two blocks away.* **Close** emphasizes being so contiguous and adjacent as to be almost in contact and joined together with only a slight interval in space, time, degree, or relation: *The tree was close to the house.* —*v.t.* see **approach.**

near·by (nēr′bī′) *adj., adv.* a short distance away; not far off: *a nearby town. We'll stop nearby for lunch.*

Near East, region usually regarded as including the countries of southwestern Asia, northeastern Africa, and sometimes the Balkans.

near·ly (nēr′lē) *adv.* **1.** all but; practically: *I nearly forgot your birthday. It's nearly midnight.* **2.** closely, as in time, degree, similarity, or the like: *She resembles her mother very nearly.* —**Syn. 1.** see **almost.**

near·sight·ed (nēr′sī′tid) *adj.* having a defect in vision in which near

at; āpe; cär; end; mē; it; īce; hot; ōld; fôrk; wood; fōōl; oil; out; up; ūse; turn; sing; thin; this; zh in treasure; ə in ago, taken, pencil, lemon, circus.

objects are seen clearly but those farther away appear blurred; myopic. Distinguished from **farsighted.** —**near′sight′ed·ly,** adv. —**near′-sight′ed·ness,** n.

neat¹ (nēt) adj. **1.** arranged in a clean and orderly manner; tidy: to keep a room neat. **2.** inclined to keep oneself or one's things in an orderly and clean manner: John is a neat dresser. **3.** clever; ingenious; adroit: a neat accomplishment. **4.** well-shaped or well-proportioned: a neat profile. **5.** without anything mixed in it, as an alcoholic beverage. **6.** (of money) remaining after deductions; net: a neat profit. **7.** Informal. wonderful; fine; swell: We had a neat time at the party. [Old French net clean, pure, from Latin nitidus shining, clear, elegant.] —**neat′ly,** adv. —**neat′ness,** n.

neat² (nēt) pl., **neat.** n. Archaic. cattle. [Old English nēat.]

neat·en (nēt′ən) v.t. Informal. to make neat; tidy (usually with up): Neaten up the room before you leave.

neath (nēth) also, **'neath.** prep. Archaic. beneath.

neat·herd (nēt′hûrd′) n. Archaic. cowherd.

neat's-foot oil (nēts′fo͝ot′) yellow oil obtained by boiling the feet and shinbones of cattle, used chiefly to soften leather.

neb (neb) n. Scottish. **1.** bill or beak, as of a bird. **2.** snout of an animal. **3.** nose or mouth of a person. **4.** tip or point of anything, esp. of a pen. [Old English nebb beak, nose.]

Neb., Nebraska.

Ne·bo, Mount (nē′bō) in the Old Testament, mountain from which Moses saw the Promised Land before his death.

Nebr., Nebraska.

Ne·bras·ka (ni bras′kə) n. state in the central United States. Capital, Lincoln. Area, 77,227 sq. mi. Pop. (1970), 1,483,791. Abbreviations, **Nebr., Neb.** —**Ne·bras′kan,** adj., n.

Neb·u·chad·nez·zar (neb′ə kəd nez′ər, neb′yə-) n. died 562 B.C., king of Babylon from 605 to 562 B.C.

neb·u·la (neb′yə lə) pl., **-lae** (-lē′) or **-las.** n. **1.** bright, cloudlike mass visible in the night sky, composed of dust and gases. **2.** galaxy (def.1). [Latin nebula mist, cloud.] —**neb′u·lar,** adj.

nebular hypothesis, any of various theories of the origin of the solar system stating that it condensed from a rotating nebula.

neb·u·lize (neb′yə līz′) v.t. -**lized, -liz·ing.** to reduce (a liquid) to a misty spray; atomize. —**neb′u·li·za′tion, neb′u·liz′er,** n.

neb·u·los·i·ty (neb′yə los′ə tē) pl., **-ties.** n. **1.** state or quality of being nebulous. **2.** nebula.

neb·u·lous (neb′yə ləs) adj. **1.** vague or confused; indistinct; unclear: nebulous theories. **2.** like a cloud or clouds; cloudy. **3.** resembling or characterized by the presence of a nebula or nebulae. [Latin nebulōsus misty, cloudy, from nebula mist, cloud.] —**neb′u·lous·ly,** adv. —**neb′u·lous·ness,** n.

nec·es·sar·i·ly (nes′ə ser′ə lē) adv. **1.** as an inevitable consequence: Tall, strong persons are not necessarily good athletes. **2.** because of necessity: You don't necessarily have to leave now.

nec·es·sar·y (nes′ə ser′ē) adj. **1.** needed for the achievement, existence, or continuance of something. **2.** being of such a nature that it must exist or occur; unavoidable: a necessary evil. **3.** that must result from the circumstances; that cannot logically be denied: He drew the necessary conclusions. **4.** resulting from, acting under, or required by obligation or compulsion. —n. pl., **-sar·ies.** that which cannot be done without; necessity; essential. [Latin necessārius unavoidable, needful, from necesse unavoidable.]

Syn. adj. **1. Necessary, indispensable, essential** mean urgently required. **Necessary** is applied chiefly to an urgent and compelling need to fill a want but falls short of suggesting that it is absolutely required or cannot be done without: Boots are necessary for walking through snow and slush. **Indispensable** suggests that a thing is a requisite adjunct and cannot be done without, set aside, or neglected: This book is an indispensable manual for doctors. **Essential** characterizes an absolute and vital requirement whose urgency is intrinsic and functional rather than external: Oxygen is essential to life.

ne·ces·si·tar·i·an (ni ses′ə tār′ē ən) adj. of, relating to, or advocating necessitarianism. —n. one who accepts or advocates necessitarianism.

ne·ces·si·tar·i·an·ism (ni ses′ə tār′ē ə niz′əm) n. philosophical belief that all events are determined by a fixed sequence of antecedent causes.

ne·ces·si·tate (ni ses′ə tāt′) -**tat·ed, -tat·ing.** v.t. to cause (something) to be needed or unavoidable; make necessary: His crime necessitated punishment. Your reasoning necessitates certain conclusions. **2.** to force or compel (someone) to do something. —**ne·ces′si·ta′tion,** n.

ne·ces·si·tous (ni ses′ə təs) adj. **1.** poverty-stricken; poor; needy. **2.** urgent; demanding; compelling. —**ne·ces′si·tous·ly,** adv. —**ne·ces′si·tous·ness,** n.

ne·ces·si·ty (ni ses′ə tē) pl., **-ties.** n. **1.** that which cannot be done without; requirement: Sturdy shoes are a necessity for hiking. He could

afford only the basic necessities. **2.** fact, quality, or condition of being necessary or indispensable. **3.** fact or state of extreme or urgent need; exigency: Necessity is the mother of invention (Franck, 1694). **4.** circumstances making a certain course of action compulsory: I went only out of necessity. **5.** that which is unavoidable, as because of natural or logical conditions. **6.** condition of poverty; neediness. **7. of necessity.** necessarily. [Latin necessitās inevitability, destiny.]

neck (nek) n. **1.** part of the body of a man or animal connecting the head and the trunk. **2.** part of a garment that fits around or encircles the neck. **3.** narrow portion of certain organs or parts of the body: the neck of the bladder. **4.** upper part of a bottle, vase, or other vessel that is narrower than the base. **5.** narrow strip of land extending into the water, as a cape or peninsula. **6.** narrow body of water, as a channel or inlet. **7.** part of a stringed musical instrument, as a violin or guitar, extending from the main body and carrying the fingerboard, strings, and tuning pegs. **8.** upper part of the shaft of a column, just below the capital. **9.** part of a tooth between the crown and the root. **10.** Informal. one's well-being and interests: He risked his neck for his friend. **11. neck and neck.** at an equal pace, as in a competition; even: A survey of voters showed the two candidates running neck and neck. **12. neck of the woods.** Informal. area; neighborhood: That song is very popular in my neck of the woods. **13. to stick (one's) neck out.** Informal. to risk one's well-being and interests, esp. by making a commitment. —v.i. Informal. to make love by kissing and caressing. [Old English hnecca part of the bone connecting the head and the trunk.]

neck·band (nek′band′) n. **1.** band of material around the neck of a shirt or other garment, to which a collar may be attached. **2.** band worn around the neck.

neck·cloth (nek′klôth′) n. piece of cloth worn around the neck, as a cravat.

neck·er·chief (nek′ər chif) n. scarf or kerchief worn around the neck.

neck·lace (nek′lis) n. ornament worn around the neck, as a string or chain of beads, gems, gold, or silver.

neck·line (nek′līn′) n. line or contour formed by the upper edge of a garment at or near the neck: This dress has a scalloped neckline.

Neckerchief

neck·tie (nek′tī′) n. strip of fabric designed to be worn around the neck, usually under the collar, and knotted in front. Also, **tie.**

neck·wear (nek′wâr′) n. any of various articles that are worn around the neck, as scarfs and neckties.

ne·crol·o·gy (ni krol′ə jē, ne-) pl., **-gies.** n. **1.** list of persons who have died, as at a given time or place. **2.** notice of a person's death; obituary. [Greek nekros corpse + -LOGY.]

nec·ro·man·cy (nek′rə man′sē) n. **1.** act or practice of predicting the future by communicating with the dead. **2.** black magic; sorcery. [Late Latin necromantía prophecy by invoking the dead, from Greek nekromanteiã, from nekros corpse + manteiã prophecy.] —**nec′ro·man′cer,** n.

ne·crop·o·lis (ni krop′ə lis, ne-) pl., **-lis·es.** n. cemetery. [Greek nekropolis literally, city of the dead, from nekros corpse + polis city.]

ne·cro·sis (ni krō′sis, ne-) pl., **-ses** (-sēz). n. death or decay of plant or animal cells or tissue. [Greek nekrōsis state of death, going back to nekros corpse.]

nec·tar (nek′tər) n. **1.** Greek Mythology. drink of the gods that made immortal all who drank it. **2.** thick, undiluted juice from any of various fruits, as peaches, pears, or apricots. **3.** sweet liquid secreted by the nectaries and glands of plants, used by bees in the making of honey. **4.** any sweet and delicious drink. [Latin nectar the drink of the gods, from Greek nektar.] —**nec′tar·ous,** adj.

nec·tar·ine (nek′tə rēn′) n. edible peach, Prunus persica, having a smooth, downless skin and firm pulp. [NECTAR + -INE¹.]

nec·ta·ry (nek′tər ē) pl., **-ries.** n. nectar-secreting part or organ of a plant.

née (nā) also, **nee.** adj. French. born. ▲ used chiefly in designating the maiden name of a married woman.

need (nēd) n. **1.** lack or absence of something necessary, useful, or desired (often with for): There is a need for college graduates in the industry. **2.** reason or obligation: There is no need to stay any longer. **3.** intense desire for something: a need for recognition, a need for love. **4.** something necessary, useful, or desired: What are your basic needs? **5.** poverty or hardship: His need led him to crime. **6.** time or condition of difficulty or trouble; exigency: a friend in need. **7. if need be.** if necessary: If need be, help him to do it. **8. to have need to.** to be required to: He has need to exercise daily. —v.t. to have need of; lack; require: to need shoes, to need a room for the night. —v.i. **1.** to be under a necessity or obligation: Need he do it at all. **2.** to be in want: Those who need are often reluctant to speak. **3.** Archaic. to be necessary. [Old English nēd necessity, distress.]

Syn. *v.t.* **Need, require, want** indicate a lack of something necessary. Need may be preferred when indicating that something is essential for existence: *Plants need water.* Require heightens the implication of a pressing need for a given task or purpose: *The victim required immediate medical attention.* Want suggests not so much a necessity as a desire: *Everyone wants peace.* —*n.* **1.** see **lack.**

need·ful (nēd′fəl) *adj.* needed; required; necessary. —**need′ful·ly,** *adv.*

need·i·ness (nē′dē nis) *n.* quality or condition of being needy.

nee·dle (nēd′əl) *n.* **1.** thin, pointed instrument, usually of steel, with a hole at one end through which thread is passed, used in sewing. **2.** thin pointer, as on a compass or dial. **3.** sharp, hollow tube attached to a hypodermic syringe to puncture the skin. **4.a.** slender rod tapered at one or both ends, used in knitting. **b.** slender rod with a hook at one end, used in crocheting. **5.** slender instrument of steel, diamond, sapphire, or other hard material, mounted in a cartridge at the end of the tone arm of a phonograph, that rides the grooves of a phonograph record and transmits sound vibrations. **6.** fine-pointed instrument used in etching, esp. dry point. **7.** slender rod used to control the opening of a valve. **8.** something resembling a needle in shape, as an obelisk or pinnacle. **9.** *Botany.* needle-shaped leaf of a fir, pine, or other conifer. See **pine** for illustration. —*v.t.,* **-dled, -dling.** *Informal.* to annoy, as by teasing repeatedly: *His friends were needling him about his girlfriend.* [Old English *nǣdl* pointed instrument used in sewing.]

nee·dle·point (nēd′əl point′) *n.* **1.** embroidery done on canvas, often used as upholstery fabric. **2.** lace made entirely with a sewing needle and worked with a buttonhole stitch over a paper pattern. Also (*def.* 2), **point lace, point.**

need·less (nēd′lis) *adj.* not needed; unnecessary. —**need′less·ly,** *adv.* —**need′less·ness,** *n.*

needle valve, valve with a narrow opening controlled by a conical or needle-shaped plug, used esp. to control the flow of a gas.

nee·dle·wom·an (nēd′əl woom′ən) *pl.* **-wom·en.** *n.* seamstress.

nee·dle·work (nēd′əl wurk′) *n.* **1.** work done with a needle, as embroidery. **2.** occupation or process of sewing, embroidering, or the like: *She is very skilled at needlework.*

need·n't (nēd′ənt) need not.

needs (nēdz) *adv.* Archaic. of necessity; necessarily (with *must*): *We must needs be leaving now.* [Old English *nēdes,* genitive of *nēd* necessity.]

need·y (nē′dē) **need·i·er, need·i·est.** *adj.* being in need, want, or poverty: *She gave clothes to needy families.*

ne'er (nâr) *adv.* Archaic. **1.** never: *ne'er was flattery lost on poet's ear* (Scott, 1805). **2.** not; nary (with *a*): *ne'er a one.*

ne'er-do-well (nâr′doo wel′) *n.* worthless person; good-for-nothing. —*adj.* worthless; good-for-nothing.

ne·far·i·ous (ni fâr′ē əs) *adj.* wicked; evil; villainous: *nefarious deeds, a nefarious scoundrel.* [Latin *nefārius,* going back to *ne-* not + *fās* divine law.] —**ne·far′i·ous·ly,** *adv.* —**ne·far′i·ous·ness,** *n.*

neg., negative.

ne·gate (ni gāt′) **-gat·ed, -gat·ing.** *v.t.* **1.** to render ineffective; nullify: *That one mistake negated all his efforts.* **2.** to deny the validity of. [Latin *negātus,* past participle of *negāre* to deny, refuse.]

ne·ga·tion (ni gā′shən) *n.* **1.** act of negating. **2.** that which negates; denial. **3.** absence or opposite of that which is positive: *A lie is the negation of truth.* **4.** something characterized by the absence of that which is positive. [Latin *negātiō* denial.]

neg·a·tive (neg′ə tiv) *adj.* **1.** expressing, containing, or implying negation, denial, or refusal: *a negative reply to the request.* **2.** characterized by the omission or absence of that which is positive: *The positive evidence of actually finding a substance is always more conclusive than the negative one, of not finding it* (Priestley, 1788). **3.** less than zero: *a negative number.* **4.** *Electricity.* of a lower electric potential than others in the same system: *a negative electrode.* **5.** *Physics.* (of ions) having more electrons than protons. **6.** *Photography.* having the areas that were light in the original subject dark, and those that were dark, light. **7.** not indicating the presence of a given condition, disease, or the like: *The tests for tuberculosis were negative.* —*n.* **1.** negative image on a photographic plate or film from which prints can be made. **2.** word or phrase that expresses negation, denial, or refusal: *"No" and "not" are negatives.* **3.** side or position that denies, as in an argument or debate. **4.** negative number or algebraic expression. **5.** *Electricity.* plate or element in an electric cell having the lower electric potential. **6.** *Archaic.* right to veto. **7. in the negative. a.** by or with an expression of negation, refusal, or denial: *to answer in the negative.* **b.** in negation, denial, or refusal of a proposal, suggestion, or the like: *to be resolved in the negative.* [Late Latin *negātīvus* that denies, from Latin *negāre* to deny.] —**neg′a·tive·ly,** *adv.* —**neg′a·tive·ness, neg′a·tiv′i·ty,** *n.*

neg·a·tiv·ism (neg′ə ti viz′əm) *n.* **1.** tendency to deny, contradict, or oppose. **2.** inclination to doubt or deny traditional beliefs; skepticism. —**neg′a·tiv·ist,** *adj., n.* —**neg′a·tiv·is′tic,** *adj.*

Neg·ev (neg′ev) *n.* desert region of southern Israel. Area, approx. 4000 sq. mi.

neg·lect (ni glekt′) *v.t.* **1.** to fail to give proper attention to: *to neglect one's duties. The public neglected his poetry.* **2.** to fail to take proper care of; leave uncared for: *to neglect one's appearance.* **3.** to fail to do or perform, esp. through forgetfulness or carelessness: *You've neglected to mention an important fact.* —*n.* **1.** act or instance of neglecting; negligence: *He was accused of neglect of his duties.* **2.** condition of being neglected: *The old house fell into neglect.* [Latin *neglectus,* past participle of *negligere* to disregard.] —**neg·lect′er,** *n.* —**Syn.** *v.t.* see **ignore.**

neg·lect·ful (ni glekt′fəl) *adj.* characterized by or indicating neglect: *She was neglectful of her clothing.* —**neg·lect′ful·ly,** *adv.* —**neg·lect′ful·ness,** *n.*

neg·li·gee (neg′lə zhā′) *n.* **1.** woman's loose, flowing nightgown or robe. **2.** free, informal, or careless dress. [French *négligée,* feminine past participle of *négliger* to be careless of, disregard, from Latin *negligere* to disregard.]

neg·li·gence (neg′li jəns) *n.* **1.** state or quality of being negligent. **2.** act or instance of being negligent. [Latin *negligentia* carelessness, neglect.]

neg·li·gent (neg′li jənt) *adj.* **1.** habitually neglecting to do what ought to be done; neglectful. **2.** marked by carelessness or indifference: *negligent attire.* [Latin *negligēns,* present participle of *negligere* to disregard.] —**neg′li·gent·ly,** *adv.*

neg·li·gi·ble (neg′li jə bəl) *adj.* not worth considering; that can be disregarded: *His contribution to the effort was negligible.* —**neg′li·gi·bil′i·ty,** *n.* —**neg′li·gi·bly,** *adv.*

ne·go·tia·ble (ni gō′shə bəl, -shē ə bəl) *adj.* **1.** that can be sold, transferred, or converted, as a bond. **2.** open to discussion, as a dispute: *a negotiable demand.* **3.** able to be traveled on or over; navigable. —**ne·go′tia·bil′i·ty,** *n.*

ne·go·ti·ate (ni gō′shē āt′) **-at·ed, -at·ing.** *v.t.* **1.** to bring about or arrange the terms of through negotiation: *to negotiate a strike settlement, to negotiate a loan.* **2.** to sell, transfer, or convert, as a bill or security. **3.** to conduct, manage, or carry out. **4.** to succeed in traveling over or on: *Snow tires helped the car to negotiate the icy road.* —*v.i.* to confer in order to bring about an agreement. [Latin *negōtiātus,* past participle of *negōtiārī* to carry on business, from *negōtium* business.] —**ne·go′ti·a′tor,** *n.* —**ne·go′ti·a·to·ry** (ni gō′shē ə tôr′ē), *adj.*

ne·go·ti·a·tion (ni gō′shē ā′shən) *n.* discussion for the purpose of bringing about an agreement or transaction.

Ne·gri·to (ni grē′tō) *pl.* **-tos** or **-toes.** *n.* member of one of the Pygmy peoples of southeastern Asia, esp. those of the Philippine and Andaman islands and the Malay Peninsula. [Spanish *negrito* young or small Negro, diminutive of *negro* black. See NEGRO.]

Ne·gro (nē′grō) *pl.* **-groes.** *n.* **1.** member of the Negroid division of the human race, including the chief peoples of southern and central Africa and Oceania. **2.** one who is of Negro ancestry. —*adj.* of, relating to, or characteristic of a Negro or Negroes. [Spanish *negro* black man, black, from Latin *niger* black.] —**Ne′gress,** *n.*

Ne·groid (nē′groid) *adj.* of, relating to, resembling, or belonging to one of the major ethnic divisions of the human race whose members are characterized by dark skin, tightly curled hair, and broad features. —*n.* member of the Negroid race.

Ne·gros (nā′grōs) *n.* one of the central islands of the Philippines. Area, 4905 sq. mi. Pop. (1960 est.), 2,000,000.

ne·gus (nē′gəs) *n.* drink made of wine, hot water, sugar, lemon juice, and spices. [From Colonel Francis *Negus,* died 1732, who originated it.]

Neh., Nehemiah.

Ne·he·mi·ah (nē′ə mī′ə) *n.* **1.** Hebrew leader of the fifth century B.C. who rebuilt the walls of Jerusalem. **2.** book of the Old Testament that tells his story.

Ne·he·mi·as (nē′ə mī′əs) *n.* in the Douay Bible, Nehemiah.

Neh·ru, Ja·wa·har·lal (nā′rōō; jə wä′hər läl′) 1889–1964, Indian statesman.

neigh (nā) *n.* characteristic cry of a horse. —*v.i.* to utter a neigh; whinny. [Old English *hnǣgan* to utter a neigh.]

neigh·bor (nā′bər) *also, British.* **neigh·bour.** *n.* **1.** one who lives near another, esp. one who lives in the house adjacent to one's own. **2.** one who or that which is situated next to another. **3.** fellow human being; brother: *Thou shalt love thy neighbor as thyself* (Mark 12:31). —*v.t.* to be located near to (an object, person, or place). —*v.i.* to associate with neighbors in a friendly way. —*adj.* living nearby. [Old English *nēahgebūr* one who lives near another.]

neigh·bor·hood (nā′bər hood′) *n.* **1.** comparatively small, populated district, often possessing characteristics that distinguish it from other districts: *an Irish-American neighborhood, a tough neighborhood.* **2.** people living in the same district: *The whole neighborhood is talking about it.* **3.** *Archaic.* neighborly relations or feelings. **4. in the neighbor-**

at; āpe; cär; end; mē; it; īce; hot; ōld; fôrk; wood; fŏŏl; oil; out; up; ūse; turn; sing; thin; this; zh in treasure; ə in ago, taken, pencil, lemon, circus.

hood of. somewhere near; about; approximately: *The dinner cost in the neighborhood of ten dollars.*

neigh·bor·ing (nā′bər ing) *adj.* living or situated near; bordering on or nearby; adjacent: *My friend comes from the neighboring town.*

neigh·bor·ly (nā′bər lē) *adj.* characteristic of a congenial neighbor; friendly; sociable. **—neigh′bor·li·ness,** *n.*

nei·ther (nē′thər, nī′-) *conj.* **1.** not either: *When I was sick, I could neither eat nor drink.* ▲ used with **nor** to introduce two or more negative alternatives. **2.** nor: *He cannot speak, neither can he hear.* **—adj.** not the one nor the other; not either: *Neither girl bought the dress.* **—pron.** not either one: *I tried on two dresses, but neither fit me.* [Middle English *neither* not either, from *ne* not (from Old English *ne*) + EITHER.]

nel·son (nel′sən) *n.* any of several wrestling holds, as the half nelson. [Of uncertain origin.]

Nel·son, Ho·ra·ti·o (nel′sən; hə rā′-shē ō′) 1758–1805, English admiral.

ne·ma·to·cyst (nem′ə tō sist′) *n.* stinging cell, as on the tentacles of jellyfish and other coelenterates, that ejects a poisonous thread when triggered. [Greek *nēmat-,* stem of *nēma* thread + CYST.]

nem·a·tode (nem′ə tōd′) *adj.* of or relating to a large group of worms, phylum Nematoda, having a cylindrical body tapering to a point at each end, including many crop pests and parasites, as the hookworm. **—n.** a nematode worm. [Modern Latin *Nematoda,* from *nēmat-,* stem of Greek *nēma* thread + *-ōdēs* like.]

Nem·bu·tal (nem′byə tôl′) *n.* *Trademark.* drug derived from barbituric acid, used as a sedative, esp. prior to anesthesia.

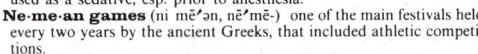

Nematocyst

(Labels on illustration: Trigger; Stinging capsule)

Ne·me·an games (ni mē′ən, nē′mē-) one of the main festivals held every two years by the ancient Greeks, that included athletic competitions.

Nemean lion, lion strangled by Hercules as the first of his twelve labors.

Nem·e·sis (nem′ə sis) *pl.,* **-ses** (-sēz) *n.* **1.** Greek goddess of vengeance who represented the gods' fury at injustice and arrogance. **2. nemesis. a.** one who or that which inflicts punishment; agent of retribution. **b.** principle or instance of just punishment; retributive justice. [Greek *nemesis* retribution.]

neo- *combining form* new; recent: *neoplasm, neoclassicism.* [Greek *neos.*]

ne·o·clas·si·cal (nē′ō klas′i kəl) *also,* **Ne·o·clas·si·cal.** *adj.* of or relating to neoclassicism. Also, **ne′o·clas′sic, Ne′o·clas′sic.**

ne·o·clas·si·cism (nē′ō klas′i siz′əm) *also,* **Ne·o·clas·si·cism.** *n.* revival of classical style in art, music, literature, or architecture, esp. that in Europe in the late seventeenth and eighteenth centuries. [NEO- + CLASSICISM.]

ne·o·dym·i·um (nē′ō dim′ē əm) *n.* yellowish metallic element of the rare-earth group, used esp. to make lavender-colored glass for use in lasers. Symbol: **Nd** See element for table. [Modern Latin *neodymium,* from NEO- + (DI)DYMIUM.]

ne·o·lith (nē′ə lith′) *n.* neolithic stone tool or implement.

ne·o·lith·ic (nē′ə lith′ik) *adj.* of, relating to, or characteristic of the last period of the Stone Age, that was marked by the development of agriculture, the domestication of animals for food and clothing, and the use of tools and implements made from shaped and polished stone. [NEO- + Greek *lithos* stone + -IC.]

ne·ol·o·gism (nē ol′ə jiz′əm) *n.* **1.** new word or new meaning of a word. **2.** use of such words or meanings. [French *néologisme* new word, going back to Greek *neos* new + *logos* word.]

ne·o·my·cin (nē′ō mī′sin) *n.* antibiotic drug used esp. to treat skin and eye infections. [NEO- + Greek *mykēs* fungus + -IN[1].]

ne·on (nē′on) *n.* colorless, odorless, non-metallic element that is inert and makes up a very small percentage of the air. Gaseous neon is used in lights, and liquid neon is used as a refrigerant. Symbol: **Ne** See element for table. [Modern Latin *neon* literally, the new (element), from Greek *neon,* neuter of *neos* new.]

ne·o·Na·zi·ism (nē′ō nät′sē iz′əm) *also,* **ne·o·Na·zism.** *n.* present-day movement to restore the theories and beliefs of National Socialism.

ne·o·phyte (nē′ə fīt′) *n.* **1.** one recently admitted to a religious denomination; new convert. **2.** beginner in any area; novice. [Church Latin *neophytus* new convert, newly planted, from Greek *neophytos,* from *neos* new + *phyton* plant.]

ne·o·plasm (nē′ə plaz′əm) *n.* any new growth in the body, as a tumor. [NEO- + -PLASM.]

Ne·o·pla·to·nism (nē′ō plāt′ən iz′əm) *n.* mystical philosophy of the third century A.D., which combined Platonic ideas with Oriental mysticism and greatly influenced early Christian theology. **—Ne·o·pla·ton·ic** (nē′ō plə ton′ik), *adj.* **—Ne′o·pla′to·nist,** *n.*

ne·o·prene (nē′ə prēn′) *n.* polymer compound made up of chloroprene units, used as a substitute for rubber where resistance to oil, chemicals, sunlight, or oxygen is needed.

Ne·o·Scho·las·ti·cism (nē′ō skə las′tə siz′əm) *n.* revival of Scholasticism begun in the late nineteenth century under Pope Leo XIII, emphasizing Thomism and the application of Scholastic thought to contemporary problems. **—Ne′o·Scho·las′tic,** *adj., n.*

Ne·o·zo·ic (nē′ə zō′ik) *adj.* Cenozoic. [NEO- + Greek *zōē* life + -IC.]

NEP, New Economic Policy. Also, **Nep.**

Ne·pal (nə pôl′, -päl′) *n.* country in central Asia, bounded by India and Tibet. Capital, Katmandu. Area, 54,000 sq. mi. Pop. (1969 est.), 10,845,000.

Ne·pa·li (nə pô′lē, -pä′-) *n.* language belonging to the Indo-Iranian branch of the Indo-European language family, spoken predominantly in Nepal.

ne·pen·the (ni pen′thē) *n.* **1.** drug that was thought by the ancient Greeks to bring forgetfulness of pain or sorrow. **2.** anything bringing forgetfulness of pain or sorrow. [Greek *nēpenthes,* neuter of *nēpenthēs* free from sorrow.]

neph·ew (nef′ū, nev′ū) *n.* **1.** son of one's brother or sister. **2.** son of one's brother-in-law or sister-in-law. [Old French *neveu,* from Latin *nepōs* nephew, grandson.]

ne·phrid·i·um (ni frid′ē əm) *pl.,* **-phrid·i·a** (-frid′ē ə). *n.* tubular excretory organ in mollusks, crustaceans, flatworms, and various other invertebrates.

neph·rite (nef′rīt) *n.* mineral that is a variety of jade, ranging in color from green to white and having a glassy luster. [German *Nephrit,* going back to Greek *nephros* kidney; because formerly believed to be a remedy for kidney diseases.]

ne·phrit·ic (ni frit′ik) *adj.* **1.** of, relating to, or suffering from nephritis. **2.** of or relating to the kidney or kidneys.

ne·phri·tis (ni frī′tis) *n.* inflammation of the kidneys. [Late Latin *nephrītis,* from Greek *nephrītis,* from *nephros* kidney.]

ne plus ultra (nē plus ul′trə) *Latin.* extreme or utmost point attainable; height of excellence.

nep·o·tism (nep′ə tiz′əm) *n.* appointment to a desirable position or the granting of privileges on the basis of family relationships; patronage towards relatives. [French *népotisme,* from Italian *nepotismo,* from *nepote* nephew, grandson, from Latin *nepōs.*] **—nep·ot·ic** (ni pot′ik), *adj.* **—nep′o·tist,** *n.*

Nep·tune (nep′tōōn, -tūn) *n.* **1.** Roman god of the sea and brother of Jupiter. His Greek counterpart is Poseidon. **2.** third-largest planet of the solar system and eighth in order of distance from the sun. It is invisible to the naked eye, but appears green when viewed through a telescope. [Latin *Neptūnus* the Roman god.]

nep·tu·ni·um (nep tōō′nē əm, -tū′-) *n.* silvery, man-made, radioactive metallic element similar chemically to uranium, produced by bombarding uranium with neutrons. Symbol: **Np** See element for table. [Modern Latin *neptunium,* from the planet *Neptune;* because it follows uranium in the periodic table and the planet Neptune comes after Uranus, after which uranium was named, in the solar system.]

Ne·re·id (nēr′ē id) *n.* Greek Mythology. water nymph living in the sea.

Ne·re·us (nēr′ē əs, nēr′oos) *n.* Greek sea god, father of the Nereids.

ne·rit·ic (ni rit′ik) *adj.* of, relating to, or inhabiting the waters of a shoreline. [Greek *nēritēs* a sea snail (from *Nēreus* Nereus) + -IC.]

Ne·ro (nēr′ō) *n.* A.D. 37–68, Roman emperor from A.D. 54–68.

ner·o·li (ner′ə lē, nēr′-) *n.* oil distilled from orange blossoms, used esp. in making perfume. Also, **neroli oil.** [From the Princess of *Neroli* who brought it to France in the late seventeenth century.]

ner·va·tion (nur vā′shən) *n.* venation.

nerve (nurv) *n.* **1.** bundle of fibers carrying impulses between the brain and spinal cord and other parts of the body. **2.** courage; bravery: *Jim didn't have the nerve to jump off the high diving board.* **3. nerves.** nervous system considered as the source of composure: *unsteady nerves. This work is very trying on the nerves.* **4.** *Informal.* brazen forwardness; presumption; audacity: *You've got a lot of nerve to ask such a personal question!* **5.** *Informal.* source of sensitivity, as a painful subject. **6. nerves.** emotional or physical tension; nervousness: *a bad case of nerves.* **7. to get on one's nerves.** to annoy; irritate. **8. to strain every nerve.** to make the greatest possible physical effort. **—v.t. nerved, nerv·ing,** to give courage or strength to: *The boxer nerved himself for the fight.* [Latin *nervus* sinew, bowstring, strength.]

nerve cell, neuron.

nerve center, group of neurons closely connected with one another and acting together in the performance of some specific function, as hearing or breathing.

at; āpe; cär; end; mē; it; īce; hot; ōld; fôrk; wood; fōōl; out; up; ūse; turn; sing; thin; this; zh in treasure; ə in ago, taken, pencil, lemon, circus.

nerve fiber, any of the threadlike fibers that constitute neurons; axon or dendrite.

nerve gas, in chemical warfare, any of several poisonous, gaseous compounds that attack the involuntary nervous system, often causing convulsions and death.

nerve impulse, electrochemical discharge produced and transmitted by nerve fibers.

nerve·less (nerv′lis) *adj.* **1.** lacking courage or determination; spineless. **2.** lacking energy or strength; feeble; weak. **3.** controlled and calm; not easily unnerved; poised. **4.** *Anatomy.* having no nerves. —**nerve′less·ly,** *adv.* —**nerve′less·ness,** *n.*

nerve-rack·ing (nurv′rak′ing) *also,* **nerve-wrack·ing,** *adj.* extremely irritating, upsetting, or frustrating: *a nerve-racking experience.*

ner·vine (nur′vēn, -vīn) *adj.* **1.** of or relating to the nerves. **2.** capable of calming the nerves. —*n.* any medicine that calms the nerves.

nerv·ous (nur′vəs) *adj.* **1.** characterized by or suffering from emotional or physical tension; restless; jumpy: *Music makes him nervous when he's trying to work.* **2.** apprehensive or timid: *I'm very nervous about taking that exam.* **3.** of, affecting, or originating in the nerves or nervous system: *a nervous disorder.* **4.** *Archaic.* vigorous; muscular; powerful. [Latin *nervōsus* sinewy, vigorous, from *nervus* sinew, strength.] —**nerv′ous·ly,** *adv.* —**nerv′ous·ness,** *n.*

nervous breakdown, any severe mental or emotional disturbance, usually requiring hospitalization.

nervous system, system of nerve tissue and nerve cells which, in vertebrates, includes the brain, spinal cord, ganglia, nerves, and nerve centers. The nervous system controls and coordinates all the activities of the body.

nerv·y (nur′vē) **nerv·i·er, nerv·i·est.** *adj.* **1.** brazenly forward; presumptuous; impudent. **2.** without fear; courageous; brave. **3.** *Archaic.* vigorous and powerful; strong; sinewy. **4.** *British. Informal.* nervous. —**nerv′i·ness,** *n.*

nes·cience (nesh′əns, -ē əns) *n.* **1.** ignorance. **2.** agnosticism. [Late Latin *nescientia* ignorance, from Latin *nescīre* to be ignorant, from *ne-* not + *scīre* to know.] —**nes′cient,** *adj.*

-ness *suffix* **1.** quality, state, or condition of being: *wilderness, lightness.* **2.** act or instance of being: *kindness.* [Old English *-nes(s).*]

nes·sel·rode (nes′əl rōd′) *n.* mixture of cream or custard, preserved fruits, and nuts, eaten as a pudding or used as a pie filling. [From Count Karl *Nesselrode,* 1780–1862, Russian statesman, whose chef supposedly invented it.]

nest (nest) *n.* **1.** structure or place in which birds lay their eggs and raise their young. **2.** place or structure used by insects, fish, turtles, mice, or other animals for depositing eggs or raising young: *a hornet's nest.* **3.** group of birds, animals, insects, or the like living in a nest. **4.** cozy dwelling or retreat. **5.a.** place where something dangerous, bad, or illegal flourishes or is fostered: *a smuggler's nest.* **b.** occupants of such a place. **6.** set of similar objects designed so that they can be stacked together, esp. so that each fits into the next largest one: *a nest of tables.* —*v.i.* to build or occupy a nest: *The birds nested in the oak tree.* —*v.t.* **1.** to settle or house in or as in a nest. **2.** to arrange (objects) in a stack, esp. with each fitting into the next largest one. [Old English *nest* bird's nest.]

Bird's nest   Wasp's nest
Nests

nest egg 1. reserve of money saved up, as for an emergency or retirement. **2.** *Agriculture.* natural or artificial egg left in a nest to induce a hen to continue laying eggs in the nest.

nes·tle (nes′əl) **-tled, -tling.** *v.i.* **1.** to press close, as in affection; cuddle: *The baby nestled in his mother's arms.* **2.** to settle oneself snugly and cozily: *to nestle by the fire.* **3.** to be situated in a snug and sheltered spot: *The cabin nestled among the hills.* —*v.t.* **1.** to hold or press closely, as in affection; snuggle: *Ruth nestled the kitten in her arms. She nestled her face against his collar.* **2.** to give protection to; shelter: *The thick forest nestled the family of deer.* [Old English *nestlian* to make a nest.] —**nes′tler,** *n.*

nest·ling (nest′ling) *n.* **1.** bird too young to leave the nest. **2.** baby or young child.

Nes·tor (nes′tər) *n. Greek Mythology.* oldest and wisest of the Greek chieftains in the Trojan war.

net¹ (net) *n.* **1.** any of various fabrics, as of thread or rope, knotted, twisted, or woven into an open, crisscross pattern. **2.** something made of such fabric, used to catch, hold, or protect: *a butterfly net. The fishermen caught fish in their nets. She put a net on her hair.* **3.** that which captures or entangles, as a scheme. **4.** fine, openwork fabric, used for such items as veils and as the foundation for various laces.

5. anything forming an open, crisscross pattern; network: *a net of veins.* **6.** net ball. —*v.t.* **net·ted, net·ting. 1.** to catch with or as with a net. **2.** to make into net. **3.** to protect or hold with a net. **4.** to hit (a ball) into the net. [Old English *net(t)* openwork fabric, snare.]

net² (net) *adj.* **1.** remaining after all deductions or allowances have been made: *net profit, net weight.* **2.** basic; final: *net results.* —*v.t.* **net·ted, net·ting.** to produce or earn as a final yield or profit: *After taxes he nets $7500 per year.* —*n.* that which remains after all deductions or allowances have been made. [French *net* remaining after all deductions, clean. See NEAT.]

net ball, in racket games, a ball hit into the net.

Neth., Netherlands.

neth·er (neth′ər) *adj.* lower: *the nether world.* [Old English *neothera,* from *nither* downward.]

Neth·er·lands, the (neth′ər ləndz) *n.* small country in northwestern Europe, on the North Sea. Capital, Amsterdam. Seat of Government, The Hague. Area, 12,950 sq. mi. Pop. (1970 est.), 13,033,000. Also, **Hol′land.** —**Neth·er·land·er** (neth′ər lan′dər), *n.*

Netherlands Antilles, Dutch island group in the southern Caribbean. Land area, 371 sq. mi. Pop. (1968 est.), 216,000.

Netherlands East Indies, islands off the southeastern coast of Asia, formerly controlled by the Netherlands, now part of Indonesia.

Netherlands Guiana, see **Surinam.**

Netherlands New Guinea, see **West Irian.**

neth·er·most (neth′ər mōst′) *adj.* lowest.

net·ting (net′ing) *n.* netted material, as fabric or wire.

net·tle (net′əl) *n.* any of a group of weedy plants, genus *Urtica,* whose leaves are covered with tiny hairs which, when touched, secrete a substance that irritates the skin. —*v.t.* **-tled, -tling.** to annoy; irritate; rile. [Old English *netele* the plant.]

net·work (net′wurk′) *n.* **1.** interlaced structure, as of lines or channels: *a network of branches, a network of tunnels.* **2.** interconnected organization or system: *a network of spies.* **3.** openwork material; net; netting. **4.a.** group of radio or television stations connected by transmission lines or coaxial cables so that they may all broadcast the same program. **b.** company that broadcasts programs for such a group, usually during certain specified hours. **6.** any interconnected system of electrical elements.

Neuf·châ·tel (nöö′shə tel′, nü′-) *n.* soft, white, uncured cheese similar to cream cheese, made from usually sweet, skim or whole milk, to which cream is added. [From *Neufchâtel,* French town where it is made.]

neur-, form of **neuro-** before vowels, as in **neurasthenia.**

neu·ral (noor′əl, nyoor′-) *adj.* of or relating to a nerve, neuron, or nervous system. [Greek *neuron* nerve + -AL¹.]

neu·ral·gia (noo ral′jə, nyoo ral′-) *n.* recurrent sharp pain along the path of a nerve. [NEURO- + Greek *algos* pain.] —**neu·ral′gic,** *adj.*

neu·ras·the·ni·a (noor′əs thē′nē ə, nyoor′-) *n.* condition characterized by excessive tiredness, depression, weakness, and inability to concentrate and remember. [NEURO- + Greek *astheneia* weakness.] —**neu·ras·then·ic** (noor′əs then′ik, nyoor′-) *adj., n.*

neu·ri·tis (noo rī′tis, nyoo-) *n.* inflammation of a nerve or nerves. [NEURO- + -ITIS.]

neuro- *combining form* nerve: *neurology, neurosis.* [Greek *neuron* sinew, nerve.]

neu·rog·li·a (noo rog′lē ə, nyoo-) *n.* connective tissue that supports the essential elements of nervous tissue in the central nervous system.

neu·rol·o·gy (noo rol′ə jē, nyoo-) *n.* branch of medicine concerned with the nervous system and its disorders. [NEURO- + -LOGY.] —**neu·rol′o·gist,** *n.*

neu·ro·ma (noo rō′mə, nyoo-) *pl.,* **-ma·ta** (-mə tə). *n.* tumor formed from nerve tissue.

neu·ron (noor′on, nyoor′-) *also,* **neu·rone** (noor′ōn, nyoor′-). *n.* basic structural unit of the nervous system, consisting of a cell body and its fibers, that receives nerve impulses and conveys them to other cells. Also, **nerve cell.** [Greek *neuron* sinew, nerve.]

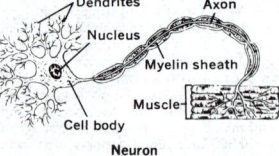
Dendrites   Axon
Nucleus
Myelin sheath
Muscle
Cell body
Neuron

neu·ro·sis (noo rō′sis, nyoo-) *pl.,* **-ses** (-sēz). *n.* emotional disorder brought on and characterized by frustration and emotional conflicts. [NEURO- + -OSIS.]

neu·rot·ic (noo rot′ik, nyoo-) *adj.* characteristic of or suffering from neurosis: *neurotic symptoms, a neurotic person.* —*n.* one who is neurotic.

neut., neuter.

neu·ter (nöö′tər, nü′-) *n.* **1.** *Grammar.* of or designating the gender

at; āpe; cär; end; mē; it; īce; hot; ōld; fôrk; wood; fōōl; out; up; ūse; turn; sing; thin; this; zh in treasure; ə in ago, taken, pencil, lemon, circus.

that includes words applying to things regarded as neither masculine nor feminine. **2.** having no sex organs or having sex organs that are undeveloped or nonfunctioning, as certain insects or castrated animals. **3.** *Archaic.* taking no side; neutral. —*n.* neuter animal or plant. **2.** neuter gender. **3.** word or other element belonging to the neuter gender. [Latin *neuter* neither, from *ne-* not + *uter* either.]

neu·tral (nōō′trəl, nū′-) *adj.* **1.** not participating in or not taking the part of either side in a conflict, controversy, or war. **2.** belonging to no side, as in a conflict or war: *a neutral zone. The leaders met on neutral ground.* **3.** having no particular shade or tint: *a neutral color.* **4.** falling into no particular category; having no marked characteristics. **5.** *Chemistry.* neither acid nor base. **6.** *Electricity.* neither positive nor negative. **7.** neuter (*def. 2*) —*n.* **1.** one who or that which is neutral. **2.** position of gears when they are not engaged and do not transmit motion from the engine to working parts, as the wheels. [Latin *neutrālis* neuter, from *neuter* neither. See NEUTER.] —**neu′tral·ly,** *adv.*

neu·tral·ism (nōō′trə liz′əm, nū′-) *n.* policy or advocacy of remaining neutral, esp. in foreign affairs. —**neu′tral·ist,** *adj., n.*

neu·tral·i·ty (nōō tral′ə tē, nū-) *n.* quality or state of being neutral, esp. impartiality or nonalignment in a conflict or war.

neu·tral·ize (nōō′trə līz′, nū′-) **-ized, -iz·ing,** *v.t.* **1.** to destroy or render ineffective by counteracting the force of. **2.** to exclude (a nation, territory, or the like) from the sphere of warlike operations; declare neutral. **3.** *Chemistry.* to make neutral. An acid and a base neutralize each other and form a salt and water. **4.** *Electricity.* to make neutral by balancing the positive and negative charges. —**neu′tral·i·za′tion, neu′tral·iz′er,** *n.*

neutral spirits, ethyl alcohol of at least 190 proof, frequently used in alcoholic beverage blends.

neutral vowel, schwa.

neu·tri·no (nōō trē′nō, nū-) *pl.,* **-nos.** *n.* either of two stable subatomic particles in the lepton group, having no mass or electric charge. See **subatomic particle** for table.

neu·tron (nōō′tron, nū′-) *n.* subatomic particle having no electric charge and constituting a part of the atomic nucleus. See **subatomic particle** for table. [NEUTR(AL) + *-on,* as in ELECTRON, ION.]

neutron bomb, hypothetical variation of the hydrogen bomb, that would produce an intense burst of radiation consisting chiefly of neutrons, but would cause little blast or fire damage and only slight fallout.

Nev., Nevada.

Ne·vad·a (nə vad′ə, -vä′də) *n.* state in the western United States. Capital, Carson City. Area, 110,540 sq. mi. Pop. (1970), 488,738. Abbreviation, **Nev.** —**Ne·vad′an,** *adj., n.*

né·vé (nā vā′) *n.* mass of accumulated snow partly converted to ice, forming the upper part of a glacier. [French *névé,* going back to Latin *nix* (stem *niv-*) snow.]

nev·er (nev′ər) *adv.* **1.** at no time; not ever: *I have never been to Australia.* **2.** in no way or degree; not at all: *This kind of behavior will never do.* [Old English *næfre* at no time, from *ne* not + *æfre* always.]

nev·er·more (nev′ər mōr′) *adv.* never again.

nev·er·the·less (nev′ər thə les′) *adv.* in spite of all; however; yet: *They thought it might rain; nevertheless, they went to the beach.*

ne·vus (nē′vəs) *pl.,* **-vi** (-vī) *n.* also, **nae·vus.** *n.* birthmark or mole. [Latin *naevus* mole[1], wart.] —**ne′void,** *adj.*

new (nōō, nū) *adj.* **1.** having existed only a short time; recently made, produced, invented, or the like: *There is a new movie playing this week.* **2.** made or brought into existence for the first time; not existing before; original: *The scientist developed a new synthetic fiber.* **3.** recognized, observed, discovered, or experienced for the first time, although existing before: *John found a new way to get to your house.* **4.** *also,* **New.** being or designating the more or most recent form, period, or development of something, as a language. **5.** unfamiliar, strange: *There were many new faces at the party.* **6.** not yet accustomed or experienced: *He made mistakes because he was new on the job.* **7.** having recently come into a certain state, position, relationship, or the like: *a new bride.* **8.** replacing another of its kind: *I'll need a new pair of shoes when these wear out.* **9.** not yet used or worn out: *The store sells both new and used furniture.* **10.** further; additional: *The police found new evidence.* **11.** coming as a resumption or repetition of some previous act or thing: *The defendant was granted a new trial.* **12.** physically or mentally changed, esp. in a positive manner: *After his vacation he felt like a new man.* **13.** modern; fashionable: *She followed all the new fads.* —*adv.* newly; recently; freshly. ▲ usually used in compounds: *new-fallen snow, a new-found friend.* —*n.* that which is new: *The design of the house combines both the old and the new.* [Old English *nīwe* not existing before, starting afresh, of recent origin.] —**new′ness,** *n.*

Syn. *adj.* **1. New, novel[2], original** mean having recently come into knowledge, existence, or use. **New** stresses being of recent origin, not having existed before or been known before, or having existed for only a short time: *The Joneses have a new baby.* **Novel** adds to *new* the idea of being so strikingly unusual and different from anything known before that it

challenges curiosity: *Clever advertising people think up novel ideas to sell products.* **Original** refers to what is not only new but also the first of its kind in conception and style or what has no known precedent or is not secondary, derivative, or imitative: *The film deals with a very original theme.*

New Amsterdam, Dutch colonial town and capital of New Netherland, on the lower tip of Manhattan, taken by the British in 1664 and renamed New York.

New·ark (nōō′ərk, nū′-) *n.* city in northeastern New Jersey, near New York City. Pop. (1970), 382,417.

New Bed·ford (bed′fərd) port city in southeastern Massachusetts. Pop. (1970), 101,777.

new·born (nōō′bôrn′, nū′-) *adj.* **1.** born very recently: *The parents took their newborn baby home from the hospital.* **2.** born again; regenerated.

New Britain, **1.** largest island in the Bismarck Archipelago. Area, approx. 14,100 sq. mi. Pop. (1966 est.), 148,817. **2.** city in central Connecticut. Pop. (1970), 83,441.

New Bruns·wick (brunz′wik) province of Canada, in the eastern part of the country. Area, 28,354 sq. mi. Pop. (1966), 616,788.

New Cal·e·do·nia (kal′ə dō′nē ə, -dōn′yə) French island in the South Pacific, northeast of Brisbane, Australia. Area, approx. 6200 sq. mi. Pop. (1965 est.), 92,000.

New·cas·tle (nōō′kas′əl, nū′-) *n.* **1.** port city in northeastern England, noted for its coal and shipbuilding industries. Pop. (1968 est.), 244,900. Also, **New·cas·tle-u·pon-Tyne** (nōō′kas′əl ə pon′tīn′, nū′-). **2. to carry** (or **bring**) **coals to Newcastle.** to supply something where it is already abundant. **3.** port city in southeastern Australia. Pop. (1968 est.), 144,450.

new·com·er (nōō′kum′ər, nū′-) *n.* one who has recently arrived: *a newcomer in our town, a newcomer to the craft of fiction.*

New Deal, domestic program of President Franklin D. Roosevelt during the 1930s that included immediate welfare measures and long-range social and economic reforms.

New Del·hi (del′ē) capital of India, in the north-central part of the country. Pop. (1967), 324,283.

New Economic Policy, policy adopted by the Soviet government under Lenin from 1921 to 1928 that permitted limited capitalistic practices.

new·el (nōō′əl, nū′-) *n.* **1.** post at the head or foot of a flight of stairs supporting the handrail. **2.** central upright pillar of a spiral staircase, newel post. [Old French *nouel* stone of a fruit, newel (because it is the center of a spiral staircase as a fruit stone is of its fruit), from Late Latin *nucālis* like a nut, from Latin *nux* nut.]

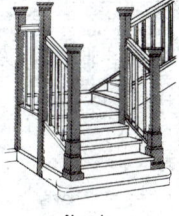

Newels

New England, region of the northeastern United States that includes Maine, New Hampshire, Vermont, Massachusetts, Rhode Island, and Connecticut. —**New Englander.**

new·fan·gled (nōō′fang′gəld, nū′-) *adj.* recently come into fashion; modern: *a newfangled invention.* ▲ used derogatorily. [From Middle English *newefangel* fond of novelty, going back to Old English *nīwe* new + *fangen,* past participle of *fōn* to take.]

new-fash·ioned (nōō′fash′ənd, nū′-) *adj.* of or in a new fashion; recently come into style.

New·found·land (nōō′fənd lənd, -land′, nū′-, nōō found′lənd, nū-) *n.* **1.** island off the east coast of Canada, part of Newfoundland and Labrador. Area, 43,359 sq. mi. **2.** Newfoundland and Labrador. **3.** large, heavily built dog of a breed developed in Newfoundland for pulling sleds and carrying packs, having a massive head and a dense, usually black, coat. Height: 28 inches at the shoulder.

Newfoundland and Labrador, easternmost province of Canada, composed of Newfoundland and Labrador. Area, 156,185 sq. mi. Pop. (1966), 493,-396.

Newfoundland

New France, former territory in North America explored and settled by the French from 1609 to 1763.

New Frontier, program of President John F. Kennedy in the early 1960s that emphasized a youthful, activist approach to meeting the problems and challenges of the period.

New·gate (nōō′gāt′, nū′-) *n.* prison in London, torn down in 1902.

New Granada **1.** Spanish province and later viceroyalty in northwestern South America from 1549 to 1810 which, at its greatest extent, included present-day Colombia, Panama, Venezuela, and Ecuador.

2. former republic in Latin America, formed from parts of this province in 1831, that included present-day Colombia and Panama.

New Guin·ea (gĭn′ē) **1.** second largest island in the world, in the western Pacific, north of Australia, divided into West Irian and the Territory of New Guinea. Area, 342,075 sq. mi. Pop. (1966 est.), 2,983,000. Also, **Pap′u·a. 2. Territory of.** Australian trust territory including northeastern New Guinea, the Bismarck Archipelago, and the Solomon Islands.

New Hamp·shire (hamp′shər, -shēr) state in the northeastern United States. Capital, Concord. Area, 9304 sq. mi. Pop. (1970), 737,-681. Abbreviation, **N.H.**

New Ha·ven (hā′vən) city in southern Connecticut. Pop. (1970), 137,707.

New Heb·ri·des (hĕb′rə dēz′) island group in the Pacific, east of Australia, under joint French and British sovereignty. Land area, 5700 sq. mi. Pop. (1969 est.), 80,000.

New Jer·sey (jûr′zē) state in the eastern United States. Capital, Trenton. Area, 7836 sq. mi. Pop. (1970), 7,168,164. Abbreviation, **N.J.** —New Jer′sey·ite′.

New Jerusalem, in the New Testament, heaven.

New Latin, Modern Latin.

New Left, diffuse political movement beginning in the late 1960s, involving radical leftist groups, composed chiefly of young people opposed to militarism, racism, and war, esp. the war in Vietnam.

new·ly (nōō′lē, nū′-) *adv.* **1.** lately; recently: *the newly elected senator.* **2.** in a new or different way; anew: *an old idea newly applied.* **3.** again; once more: *The house was newly painted.*

new·ly·wed (nōō′lē wĕd′, nū′-) *n.* one recently married.

New·man, John Henry (nōō′mən, nū′-) 1801–90, English theologian, philosopher, and cardinal of the Roman Catholic Church.

new mathematics, modern method of teaching mathematics that uses set theory and stresses understanding of basic mathematical concepts.

New Mexico, state in the southwestern United States. Capital, Santa Fe. Area, 121,666 sq. mi. Pop. (1970), 1,016,000. Abbreviations, **N. Mex., N.M.** —New Mexican.

new moon 1. moon when it is not visible or when, after two or three days, it reappears as a thin crescent with the hollow side on the right. **2.** period during which the new moon appears.

New Netherland, former Dutch colony in North America from 1624 to 1664, that consisted of parts of present-day New York, New Jersey, and Connecticut.

New Or·le·ans (ôr′lē ənz, -lənz, ôr lēnz′) city in southeastern Louisiana, on the Mississippi. Pop. (1970), 593,471.

New·port (nōō′pôrt′, nū′-) *n.* city in southeastern Rhode Island, at the mouth of Narragansett Bay. Pop. (1970), 34,562.

Newport News, port city in southeastern Virginia. Pop. (1970), 138,177.

New Ro·chelle (rə shĕl′, rō-) city in southeastern New York, near New York City. Pop. (1970), 75,385.

news (nōōz, nūz) *n.* **1.** report or information of a recent event, development, or the like, esp. when unusual or notable: *There's no news from home.* **2.** information recently discovered or disclosed: *That's news to me!* **3.** recent event or events: *a report of the news.* **4.** newscast: *We watch the news on television every night.* [Plural of NEW.]

news agency, organization that gathers and supplies news to subscribing newspapers, television stations, or the like. Also, **news service.**

news·boy (nōōz′boi′, nūz′-) *n.* boy who sells or delivers newspapers.

news·cast (nōōz′kăst′, nūz′-) *n.* radio or television program on which news items are broadcast. —news′cast′er, *n.*

news·deal·er (nōōz′dē′lər, nūz′-) *n.* one who sells newspapers and magazines.

news·let·ter (nōōz′lĕt′ər, nūz′-) *n.* printed report of news, usually published periodically and relating to a particular field of interest: *The university sent out a newsletter to all alumni.*

news·man (nōōz′măn′, nūz′-) *pl.,* **-men.** *n.* newspaper, magazine, radio, or television news reporter.

news·mon·ger (nōōz′mŭng′gər, -mŏng′-, nūz′-) *n.* gossip.

New South Wales, political subdivision of Australia, in the southeastern part of the country. Area, 309,433 sq. mi. Pop. (1969 est.), 4,474,800.

news·pa·per (nōōz′pā′pər, nūz′-) *n.* printed medium of communication, issued at regular intervals and providing diversified information on current events, opinions and commentary on these events, various types of feature columns, and advertising.

news·pa·per·man (nōōz′pā′pər man′, nūz′-) *pl.,* **-men.** *n.* reporter for, or owner or editor of, a newspaper.

news·print (nōōz′prĭnt′, nūz′-) *n.* thin paper made chiefly from wood pulp, on which newspapers are usually printed.

news·reel (nōōz′rēl′, nūz′-) *n.* short motion picture dealing with current events, usually shown in a motion-picture theater.

news service, news agency.

news·stand (nōōz′stand′, nūz′-) *n.* stand where newspapers, and often magazines and books, are sold.

New Style, method of calculating the months and days of the year according to the Gregorian calendar.

news·wor·thy (nōōz′wûr′thē, nūz′-) *adj.* significant or interesting enough to be reported in a newscast or newspaper.

news·y (nōō′zē, nū′-) **news·i·er, news·i·est.** *adj. Informal.* chatty and full of news; gossipy: *to receive a newsy letter from home.*

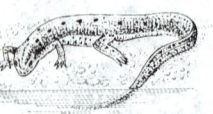

Newt

newt (nōōt, nūt) *n.* any of various small, brightly colored salamanders, family Salamandridae, found living in or around water in the Northern Hemisphere. Length: to 6 inches, including tail. [From the incorrect division of Middle English *an ewt(e)* (from Old English *efeta*) into *a newt(e).*]

New Testament, second part of the Bible, containing the life and teachings of Christ and His disciples, including the Gospels, the Acts, the Epistles, and Revelation.

new·ton (nōōt′ən, nūt′-) *n.* basic unit of force in the meter-kilogram-second system. It is equal to the amount of force that must be applied to a mass of one kilogram to produce an acceleration of one meter per second per second. [From Sir Isaac *Newton.*]

New·ton (nōōt′ən, nūt′-) *n.* **1.** Sir Isaac. 1642–1727, English physicist and mathematician. **2.** city in eastern Massachusetts. Pop. (1970), 91,-066.

New·to·ni·an (nōō tō′nē ən, nū-) *adj.* of, relating to, or in accordance with Isaac Newton or his theories or discoveries. —n. follower of Isaac Newton or his theories or discoveries.

New Windsor, Windsor *(def. 3).*

New World, the Western Hemisphere.

New Year's Day, first day of the calendar year, usually observed as a legal holiday. January 1. Also, **New Year, New Year's.**

New Year's Eve, night of December 31, the night before New Year's Day.

New York 1. state in the eastern United States. Capital, Albany. Area, 49,576 sq. mi. Pop. (1970), 18,190,740. Abbreviation, **N.Y.** Also, **New York State. 2.** largest city and a major port of the United States, in southeastern New York, at the mouth of the Hudson. Pop. (1970), 7,867,760. Also *(def. 2),* **New York City.**

New York Bay, bay of the Atlantic, south of New York City, at the mouth of the Hudson.

New York·er (yôr′kər) native or resident of New York, esp. of New York City.

New York State Barge Canal, toll-free system of canals in New York. It links the Hudson with lakes Ontario, Erie, and Champlain.

New Zea·land (zē′lənd) island country in the South Pacific, east of Australia. Capital, Wellington. Land area, 103,736 sq. mi. Pop. (1969 est.), 2,809,000. —New Zea′land·er.

next (nĕkst) *adj.* immediately succeeding or nearest in time, space, or order: *in the next room.* —adv. **1.** immediately afterward; subsequently. **2.** on the first subsequent occasion: *when next we meet.* **3. next door. a.** that is adjacent: *She lives in the house next door.* **b.** in, at, or to the adjacent building, apartment, or the like: *Let's go next door.* **4. next door to. a.** in or at the adjacent building, apartment, or the like: *He lives next door to me.* **b.** very close to: *Lying is next door to fraud.* **5. next to. a.** almost; nearly: *It was next to impossible to do.* **b.** beside: *We were standing next to them.* —prep. closest to or beside. [Old English *nēhst* nearest in time, place, or order, superlative of *nēah* nigh.]

next of kin 1. one's nearest relative or relatives. **2.** *Law.* nearest relative or relatives of a deceased person who died intestate, who are entitled to share in his estate.

nex·us (nĕk′səs) *pl.,* **-us** or **-us·es.** *n.* **1.** means of connection between two or more members of a group or series; bond; link. **2.** connected group or series. [Latin *nexus* a binding together.]

Nez Percé (nĕz′ pûrs′; *French* nā per sā′) *pl.,* **Nez Per·cés** (nĕz′ pur′siz; *French* nā per sā′). member of a North American Indian tribe formerly living in parts of what are now Idaho, Oregon, and Washington, now living primarily in Idaho. [French *nez percé* pierced nose, going back to Latin *nāsus* nose + *pertundere* to make a hole in; supposedly because of their custom of piercing noses.]

NF, Norman French.

Nfld., Newfoundland.

N.G. 1. New Guinea. **2.** National Guard. **3.** no good.

N.H., New Hampshire.

Ni, nickel.

N.I., Northern Ireland.

ni·a·cin (nī′ə sin) *n.* vitamin of the vitamin B complex occurring esp. in liver, yeast, beans, and grains, that helps to prevent and cure pellagra. Also, **nicotinic acid.** [NI(COTINIC) AC(ID) + -IN¹.]

Ni·ag·a·ra (nī ag′ər ə, -ag′rə) *n.* **1.** short river on which the Niagara Falls is located, flowing from Lake Erie into Lake Ontario. **2.** Niagara Falls.

Niagara Falls 1. waterfall on the Niagara River between the United States and Canada. **2.** city in western New York, noted as a tourist center. Pop. (1970), 85,615. **3.** city in southern Ontario, Canada, opposite Niagara Falls, New York. Pop. (1966), 56,891.

Ni·a·mey (nyä′mā) *n.* capital and largest city of Niger. Pop. (1968 est.), 78,991.

nib (nib) *n.* **1.** tip or point of a pen, esp. a fountain pen. **2.** projecting point of anything. **3.** bird's bill or beak. —*v.t.,* **nibbed, nib·bing. 1.** to furnish with a nib. **2.** to sharpen or repair the nib of. [Form of NEB.]

nib·ble (nib′əl) -**bled, -bling.** *v.t.* **1.** to eat by taking small, quick bites: *She was nibbling her food like a rabbit.* **2.** to take small, gentle bites on; bite softly: *The deer nibbled her finger.* **3.** *Informal.* to snack on: *He's been nibbling candy all day.* —*v.i.* **1.** to take small, gentle bites (often with *at* or *on*): *He nibbled on the end of his pencil.* **2.** to take small, quick bites (often with *at* or *on*): *He nibbled on the apple.* **3.** *Informal.* to snack. —*n.* **1.** small, quick bite, as that taken by a fish at bait. **2.** small piece; morsel: *There's not even a nibble left.* **3.** *Informal.* small bite; snack. [Of uncertain origin.] —**nib′bler,** *n.*

Ni·be·lung (nē′bə loong′) *n.* *Teutonic Mythology.* **1.** one of a family of evil dwarfs who possessed a treasure and a magic ring which were stolen from them by the hero Siegfried. **2.** any of the followers of Siegfried. **3.** any of the Burgundian kings in the *Nibelungenlied.*

Ni·be·lung·en·lied (nē′bə loong′ən lēt′) *n.* medieval German epic poem of unknown authorship, probably written in the early thirteenth century, relating stories of Siegfried, Kriemhild, and the Burgundian kings.

nib·lick (nib′lik) *n.* golf club having a metal head with a short sloping face and giving much loft; number nine iron. [Of uncertain origin.]

nibs (nibz) *n..pl.* one who is excessively demanding or dictatorial. ▲ construed as singular. Used with the possessive pronouns *his, her,* or *your,* frequently expressing mock admiration. [Of uncertain origin.]

Ni·cae·a (nī sē′ə) *n.* ancient town in Asia Minor, the site of two church councils.

Nic·a·ra·gua (nik′ə räg′wə) *n.* largest country of Central America. Capital, Managua. Area, 50,193 sq. mi. Pop. (1970 est.), 1,984,000. —**Nic′a·ra′guan,** *adj., n.*

nice (nīs) **nic·er, nic·est.** *adj.* **1.** agreeable; pleasant: *It's a nice day.* **2.** kind; considerate: *It was not nice of Harry to forget to call.* **3.** highly satisfactory; good: *Our company showed a nice profit last year. We had a nice turnout at the dance.* **4.** characterized by, exhibiting, or requiring discrimination, accuracy, skill, or delicacy: *a nice distinction.* **5.** suitable; appropriate: *That is not a particularly nice book for children to read.* **6.** respectable or well-bred: *nice society. There are many nice families in town.* **7.** *Archaic.* virtuous; pure. **8.** *Archaic.* particular; fastidious; fussy. **9. nice and.** perfectly: *nice and easy. He looks nice and healthy.* [Old French *nice* simple, foolish, from Latin *nescius* ignorant.] —**nice′ly,** *adv.* —**nice′ness,** *n.*

Nice (nēs) *n.* resort city in southeastern France, on the Mediterranean. Pop. (1968), 322,442.

Ni·cene (nī sēn′, nī′sēn) *adj.* of or relating to Nicaea.

Nicene Council, either of two general church councils held at Nicaea in A.D. 325 and 787, esp. the first, which condemned the Arian heresy.

Nicene Creed, formal statement of the chief tenets of Christian belief, an expanded form of the one adopted by the first Nicene Council, and generally accepted in varying beliefs throughout Christendom.

ni·ce·ty (nī′sə tē) *pl.* **-ties.** *n.* **1.** *also,* **niceties.** elegant or refined feature: *Having a chauffeur is one of the niceties of life.* **2.** *also,* **niceties.** minute or subtle detail; fine point: *She is very skilled in the niceties of etiquette.* **3.** quality of requiring delicacy, subtlety, or accuracy: *The nicety of the problem was a challenge.* **4.** exactness; accuracy; precision. **5.** quality of being particular; fastidiousness. **6. to a nicety.** exactly; perfectly. [Old French *nicete* simplicity, foolishness, from *nice* foolish, simple. See NICE.]

niche (nich) *n.* **1.** ornamental, usually arch-shaped recess in a wall, often used as a setting for statuary or other ornaments, as vases or glassware. **2.** place, position, or situation for which one is especially suited: *He quickly found his niche in the new school.* —*v.t.,* **niched, nich·ing.** to place in

a niche. [French *niche* recess, corner, going back to Latin *nīdus* nest.]

Nich·o·las, Saint (nik′ə ləs) bishop in Asia Minor in the fourth century A.D., the patron saint of children, often identified with Santa Claus.

Nicholas I, 1796–1855, czar of Russia from 1825 to 1855.

Nicholas II, 1868–1918, czar of Russia from 1894 to 1917.

nick (nik) *n.* **1.** place on a surface or edge that has been cut or chipped: *a nick on the skin. The table top was full of nicks.* **2. in the nick of time.** at the last critical moment; just in time: *They stopped him in the nick of time.* —*v.t.* to make a nick or nicks in or on. [Of uncertain origin.]

nick·el (nik′əl) *n.* **1.** hard, silvery, metallic element, used esp. as a constituent of alloys because of its strength and resistance to corrosion. Symbol: Ni See **element** for table. **2.** coin of the United States equal to five cents, or one-twentieth of a dollar. [Swedish *nickel* the metallic element, short for German *Kupfernickel* copper nickel; literally, copper devil (because the ore yielding nickel is copper-colored but contains no copper).]

nick·el·o·de·on (nik′ə lō′dē ən) *n.* **1.** formerly, a motion picture theater charging an admission price of five cents. **2.** formerly, a player piano or juke box. [NICKEL + (MEL)ODEON.]

nick·el-plate (nik′əl plāt′) -**plat·ed, -plat·ing.** *v.t.* to coat with nickel by electroplating.

nickel plate, thin coating of nickel deposited on a metal surface by electroplating, used esp. to prevent corrosion or improve appearance.

nickel silver, any of a group of silver-colored alloys of copper, nickel, and zinc that have low electrical conductivity and good resistance to corrosion. Also, **German silver.**

nick·er (nik′ər) *n.* neigh. —*v.i.* to neigh. [Probably imitative.]

nick·nack (nik′nak′) *n.* knickknack.

nick·name (nik′nām′) *n.* **1.** descriptive word or phrase used in addition to or instead of a name: *Katherine's nickname is Fatty.* **2.** familiar, usually shortened form of a name: *Dick is a nickname for Richard.* —*v.t.,* **-named, -nam·ing.** to give a nickname to: *He was nicknamed Rusty because he has red hair.* [From the incorrect division into *a nekename* of Middle English *an ekename* literally, an additional name (going back to Old English *ēaca* addition + *nama* name).]

Nic·o·bar Islands (nik′ə bär′) Andaman and Nicobar Islands.

Nic·o·si·a (nik′ə sē′ə) *n.* capital of Cyprus, in the north-central part of the country. Pop. (1968 est.), 112,000.

nic·o·tine (nik′ə tēn′) *n.* poisonous, oily alkaloid found in the leaves, roots, and seeds of the tobacco plant.

nic·o·tin·ic acid (nik′ə tin′ik) niacin. [NICOTINE + -IC; because obtained by the oxidation of nicotine.]

niece (nēs) *n.* **1.** daughter of one's brother or sister. **2.** daughter of one's brother-in-law or sister-in-law. [Old French *n(i)ece,* going back to Latin *neptis* niece, granddaughter.]

Nie·tzsche, Frie·drich Wil·helm (nē′chə, -chē; frē′driKH vil′helm) 1844–1900, German philosopher.

nif·ty (nif′tē) -**ti·er, -ti·est.** *adj.* *Informal.* **1.** fine; dandy; neat: *a nifty idea, a nifty party.* **2.** fashionable; stylish. [Possibly from MAGNIFICENT.]

Ni·ger (nī′jər) *n.* **1.** country in western Africa. Capital, Niamey. Area, 489,192 sq. mi. Pop. (1970 est.), 4,016,000. **2.** river flowing from western Africa into the Gulf of Guinea.

Ni·ge·ri·a (nī jēr′ē ə) *n.* country in western Africa, on the Gulf of Guinea. Capital, Lagos. Area, 356,669 sq. mi. Pop. (1967 est.), 61,-450,000. —**Ni·ge′ri·an,** *adj., n.*

nig·gard (nig′ərd) *n.* stingy person; skinflint. —*adj.* niggardly. [Of Scandinavian origin.]

nig·gard·ly (nig′ərd lē) *adj.* **1.** miserly; tight-fisted; penurious. **2.** scanty; paltry; meager: *a niggardly amount.* —*adv.* in a niggardly manner; stingily. —**nig′gard·li·ness,** *n.*

nigh (nī) *Archaic.* adv. **1.** near; close: *The carriage drew nigh.* **2.** practically; almost: *It's nigh onto midnight.* —*adj.,* **nigh·er, nigh·est** or **next;** near. —*v.i.* close: *the hour is nigh* (Scott, 1823). —*prep.* near; close to. [Old English *nēah* near.]

night (nīt) *n.* **1.** period of darkness between the setting and the rising of the sun; time from sunset to sunrise. **2.** beginning of night; nightfall. **3.** the darkness of night; the dark; darkness. **4.** state or time of mental or spiritual darkness: *In the real dark night of the soul it is always three o'clock in the morning* (Fitzgerald, 1936). [Old English *niht* period of darkness between evening and morning.]

night blindness, inability to see normally in dim light, often caused by a deficiency of vitamin A.

night-bloom·ing cereus (nīt′blōō′ming) any of several American cactuses bearing large, fragrant, usually white flowers that open at night.

night·cap (nīt′kap′) *n.* **1.** soft, cloth cap worn esp. in bed. **2.** *Informal.* alcoholic drink taken just before going to bed. **3.** *Informal.* the last event in a sports program, esp. the second game in a baseball doubleheader.

Niche

night·clothes (nīt′klōz′, -klōthz) *also,* **night clothes.** *n.* garments worn in bed, as pajamas.

night·club (nīt′klub′) *also,* **night club.** *n.* place of entertainment open until late at night, usually serving food and drink and offering a floor show.

night crawler, any large earthworm, esp. one that appears at night.

night·dress (nīt′dres′) *n.* **1.** nightgown. **2.** nightclothes.

night·fall (nīt′fôl′) *n.* end of the day; beginning of night.

night·gown (nīt′goun′) *n.* **1.** loose gown worn in bed by women or children. **2.** nightshirt.

Nighthawk

night·hawk (nīt′hôk′) *n.* **1.** any of various American birds, genus *Chordeiles,* related to and resembling the whippoorwill, and having mottled, predominantly gray plumage. Length: 10 inches. **2.** night owl.

night·in·gale (nīt′ən gāl′, nī′ting-) *n.* small European thrush, *Luscinia megarhyncha,* having predominantly reddish-brown plumage and a whitish breast, and noted for the rich, melodious song of the male. Length: 6½ inches. [Old English *nihtegale,* from *niht* night + *galan* to sing.]

Nightingale

Night·in·gale, Florence (nīt′ən gāl′, nī′ting-) 1820–1910, English nurse, regarded as the founder of modern nursing.

night·jar (nīt′jär′) *n.* any of various mostly nocturnal, insect-eating birds, family Caprimulgidae, found in temperate and tropical regions throughout the world, having plumage that is a mixture of buff, gray, black, and white. Length: 7½–11½ inches. Also, **goat′suck′er.** [NIGHT + JAR²; because the male makes a jarring noise.]

night latch, spring latch opened from the inside by a knob and from the outside only by a key.

night letter, telegram sent at night at a reduced rate and delivered the following morning.

night·long (nīt′lông′) *adj.* lasting through the whole night: *a nightlong vigil.* —*adv.* through the whole night.

night·ly (nīt′lē) *adj.* done, occurring, or appearing at night or every night. —*adv.* at night or every night.

night·mare (nīt′mâre′) *n.* **1.** bad dream producing feelings of great anxiety or intense fear. **2.** any experience or condition resembling a nightmare; something horrible or frightening. **3.** evil spirit formerly thought to oppress people during sleep. [NIGHT + obsolete *mare* horrible dream, from Old English *mare.*] —**night′mar′ish,** *n.*

night owl *Informal.* one who often stays up late at night.

night·rid·er (nīt′rī′dər) *n.* member of any of various vigilante groups that perform acts of violence at night for the purpose of intimidation, terrorizing, or revenge, esp. in the southern United States.

night school, school held in the evening, esp. for those unable to attend during the day.

night·shade (nīt′shād′) *n.* any of various plants, genus *Solanum,* having lobed leaves and small five-petaled flowers of various colors. —*adj.* designating a family, Solanaceae, of herbs, trees, and shrubs of warm regions, including the potato, tomato, petunia, morning glory, tobacco, and belladonna. [Old English *nihtscada* literally, shade of night; probably because it was used to induce sleep.]

night·shirt (nīt′shurt′) *n.* long shirt worn in bed by a man or boy.

night·stick (nīt′stik′) *n.* long, slender club carried by a policeman. Also, **bil′ly, billy club.**

night·time (nīt′tīme′) *n.* period of time between dusk and dawn.

night·walk·er (nīt′wô′kər) *n.* one who roves about during the night, esp. for criminal purposes.

night watch 1. watch or guard kept during the night. **2.** one who keeps such a watch. **3.** period of watch at night.

ni·hil·ism (nī′ə liz′əm) *n.* **1.** total rejection of all existing political and social institutions and traditional religious and moral values. **2.** *also,* **Nihilism.** revolutionary movement in Russia in the late nineteenth century that opposed existing social and political institutions and advocated the use of assassination and terrorism. **3.** any violent revolutionary movement advocating terrorism or anarchy. **4.** *Philosophy.* **a.** doctrine that nothing exists. **b.** doctrine that there is no basis for knowledge or truth. [Latin *nihil* nothing + -ISM.] —**ni′hil·ist,** *n.* —**ni′hil·is′tic,** *adj.*

Ni·jin·sky, Vas·lav (ni zhin′skē, -jin′-; väts läf′) 1890–1950, Russian ballet dancer.

-nik *suffix* (used to form nouns) one who is, has to do with, or advocates: *beatnik, peacenik.* [Russian *-nik.*]

Ni·ke (nī′kē) *n.* Greek goddess of victory, usually represented as a winged figure.

nil (nil) *n.* nothing; zero. [Latin *nil,* contraction of *nihil* nothing.]

Nile (nīl) *n.* longest river in the world, in east-central and northeastern Africa, flowing about 4150 miles to the Mediterranean.

nim·ble (nim′bal) **-bler, -blest.** *adj.* **1.** light and quick in movement. **2.** quick to perceive, understand, or respond: *a nimble mind.* [Middle English *nymel* quick, agile, going back to Old English *niman* to take.] —**nim′ble·ness,** *n.* —**nim′bly,** *adv.*

nim·bo·stra·tus (nim′bō strā′təs, -strat′əs) *pl.,* **-tus.** *n.* low, darkgray, shapeless cloud layer, usually bringing rain or snow.

nim·bus (nim′bəs) *pl.,* **-bus·es** or **-bi** (-bī). *n.* **1.** disk or ring of light surrounding the head of a deity, saint, or other sacred person in a painting or other artistic representation. **2.** bright cloud thought to surround a deity when on earth. **3.** aura of splendor or glory surrounding a person or thing. **4.** nimbostratus. [Latin *nimbus* cloud.]

Nîmes (nēm) *n.* city in southeastern France, the site of ancient Roman ruins. Pop. (1968), 123,292.

Nim·itz, Chester (nim′its) 1885–1966, U.S. admiral.

Nim·rod (nim′rod) *n.* **1.** in the Old Testament, a mighty hunter, the great-grandson of Noah. **2.** *also,* **nimrod.** a great hunter.

Ni·ña (nēn′yə) *n.* one of the three ships of Columbus on his first voyage to the New World, in 1492.

nin·com·poop (nin′kəm pōōp′, ning′-) *n. Informal.* silly or stupid person; fool; blockhead.

nine (nīn) *n.* **1.** the cardinal number that is one more than eight. **2.** symbol representing this number, as 9 or IX. **3.** something having this many units or members, as a playing card or a baseball team. —*adj.* numbering one more than eight. [Old English *nigon.*]

nine days' wonder, something that creates great excitement or interest for a short time.

nine·fold (nīn′fōld′) *adj.* **1.** nine times as great or numerous. **2.** having or consisting of nine parts. —*adv.* so as to be nine times greater or more numerous.

nine·pin (nīn′pin′) *n.* **1. ninepins.** bowling game using nine bottle-shaped wooden pins and a large ball. ▲ construed as singular. **2.** pin used in this game.

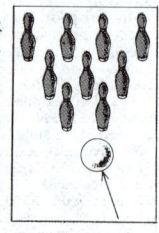

Ninepins

nine·teen (nīn′tēn′) *n.* **1.** the cardinal number that is nine more than ten. **2.** symbol representing this number, as 19 or XIX. **3.** something having this many units or members. —*adj.* numbering nine more than ten. [Old English *nigontyne.*]

nine·teenth (nīn′tēnth′) *adj.* **1.** (the ordinal of nineteen) next after the eighteenth. **2.** being one of nineteen equal parts. —*n.* **1.** that which is next after the eighteenth. **2.** one of nineteen equal parts; 1/19.

nine·ti·eth (nīn′tē ith) *adj.* **1.** (the ordinal of ninety) next after the eighty-ninth. **2.** being one of ninety equal parts. —*n.* **1.** that which is next after the eighty-ninth. **2.** one of ninety equal parts; 1/90.

nine·ty (nīn′tē) *n.* **1.** the cardinal number that is nine times ten. **2.** symbol representing this number, as 90 or XC. **3. the nineties.** number series from ninety through ninety-nine. ▲ used esp. in reference to the ninth decade of a century or of a person's life. —*adj.* numbering nine times ten. [Old English *nigontig.*]

Nin·e·veh (nin′ə və) *n.* capital of the ancient Assyrian empire. It lay on the east bank of the Tigris River, in what is now northern Iraq.

nin·ny (nin′ē) *pl.,* **-nies.** *n.* fool; simpleton.

ninth (nīnth) *adj.* **1.** (the ordinal of nine) next after the eighth. **2.** being one of nine equal parts. —*n.* **1.** that which is next after the eighth. **2.** one of nine equal parts; 1/9.

Ni·o·be (nī′ō bē′) *n. Greek Legend.* a queen of Thebes who angered the gods by boasting of the number and beauty of her children. Apollo and Artemis killed her children, causing her to weep unceasingly. She was then turned into a stone from which tears continued to flow.

ni·o·bi·um (nī ō′bē əm) *n.* steel-gray or silvery-white metallic element that is used as a constituent of various alloys. Symbol: **Nb** See element for table. [Modern Latin *niobium,* from *Niobe,* who was the daughter of Tantalus; referring to the element's similarity to tantalum.]

nip¹ (nip) **nipped, nip·ping.** *v.t.* **1.** to seize, as between two surfaces, and pinch or bite: *The parrot nipped her finger.* **2.** to sever by pinching, cutting, or biting (usually with *off* or *out*): *The gardener nipped the leaves off the bush with his fingers.* **3.** to cause (something) to smart or sting: *The cold night air nipped his fingers.* **4.** to check or destroy the development or growth of: *The late frost nipped the fruit trees. We nipped the rumor before it spread.* —*n.* **1.** act or instance of nipping. **2.** small portion or quantity; little bit. **3.** sharp, biting cold; chill: *There is a nip in the air today.* **4.** sharp or pungent flavor; tang. **5. nip and tuck.** *Informal.* so close or even as to leave the outcome in doubt; neck and neck. [Probably of Low German origin.]

nip² (nip) *n.* little drink; sip: *a nip of brandy.* —*v.t., v.i.,* **nipped, nip·ping.** to drink (liquor) in nips. [Short for obsolete *nipperkin* small vessel for measuring liquors; of uncertain origin.]

nip·per (nip′ər) *n.* **1.** one who or that which nips. **2. nippers.** any of various tools that seize and hold or cut, as pincers or pliers. **3.** one of the large claws of a crustacean. **4.** one of the incisors of a horse. **5.** *Informal.* small boy.

nip·ple (nip′əl) *n.* **1.** small conical projection at the center of the breast or udder that, in the female, contains the opening of the milk ducts. **2.** rubber mouthpiece of a baby's bottle. **3.** anything resembling a nipple in shape or function, as a short piece of pipe threaded at each end for use as a coupling. [Possibly diminutive of NIB, NEB.]

Nip·pon (ni pon′, nip′on) *n.* Japan.

Nip·pon·ese (nip′ə nēz′, -nēs′) *pl.,* **-ese.** *n.* Japanese. —*adj.* of or relating to Japan or its people.

nip·py (nip′ē) *adj.* **-pi·er, -pi·est.** *adj.* **1.** cold or chilling in a sharp, biting way: *The air is a bit nippy tonight.* **2.** tending or likely to nip.

nir·va·na (nir vä′nə, -van′ə) *also,* **Nir·va·na.** *n.* **1.** highest attainable state of bliss in Buddhism, in which all desire and suffering are extinguished and the soul is absorbed into the supreme universal soul. **2.** any place or condition free from care or pain. [Sanskrit *nirvāna* extinction.]

Ni·sei (nē′sā′) *pl.,* **-sei.** *n.* one who is born and educated in the United States or Canada and whose parents were immigrants from Japan. [Japanese *nisei* literally, second generation, from *ni* second + *sei* generation.]

nit (nit) *n.* egg or young of a parasitic insect, as a louse. [Old English *hnitu.*]

ni·ter (nī′tər) *also,* **ni·tre.** *n.* **1.** potassium nitrate. **2.** sodium nitrate. [French *nitre* saltpeter, from Latin *nitrum* natron, from Greek *nitron,* possibly from Hebrew *netr.*]

nit·pick (nit′pik′) *v.i.* *Slang.* to be overly concerned with minor faults or unimportant details. —**nit′-pick′er,** *n.*

ni·trate (nī′trāt) *n.* **1.** salt or ester of nitric acid. **2.** sodium nitrate or potassium nitrate used as a fertilizer. —*v.t.,* **-trat·ed, -trat·ing.** to treat or combine with nitric acid or a nitrate. —**ni·tra′tion,** *n.*

ni·tric (nī′trik) *adj.* of or containing nitrogen, esp. of a higher valence. [French *nitrique,* from *nitre* saltpeter. See NITER.]

nitric acid, colorless, highly corrosive liquid compound that is one of the strongest known oxidizing agents, used in the manufacturing of explosives, nitrate fertilizers, and dyes. Formula: HNO_3.

ni·tride (nī′trīd, -trid) *n.* compound of nitrogen with another element that is more electropositive, as calcium, boron, or lithium.

ni·tri·fi·ca·tion (nī′trə fi kā′shən) *n.* oxidation of ammonia into nitrites or nitrates, esp. by the action of bacteria in the soil.

ni·tri·fy (nī′trə fī′) **-fied, -fy·ing.** *v.t.* **1.** to oxidize into nitrites or nitrates, esp. by the action of bacteria in the soil. **2.** to cause to be permeated with nitrates. —**ni′tri·fi′er,** *n.*

ni·trite (nī′trīt) *n.* salt or ester of nitrous acid.

ni·tro·bac·te·ri·a (nī′trō bak tēr′ē ə) *n.* any of various soil bacteria that are involved in nitrification.

ni·tro·ben·zene (nī′trō ben′zēn, -ben zēn′) *n.* poisonous, yellow liquid compound, used esp. to make aniline. Formula: $C_6H_5NO_2$.

ni·tro·cel·lu·lose (nī′trə sel′yə lōs′) *n.* any of a number of flammable organic compounds produced by adding a mixture of concentrated sulfuric and nitric acids to cellulose, used in the manufacture of plastics, lacquers, and explosives. Also, **cellulose nitrate.**

ni·tro·gen (nī′trə jən) *n.* colorless, odorless, nonmetallic element that makes up about 78 percent of the volume of the air at sea level. Symbol: **N** See **element** for table. [French *nitrogène,* from Greek *nitron* (see NATRON) + *-genēs* (see -GEN).] —**ni·trog·e·nous** (nī troj′ə nəs), *adj.*

nitrogen cycle, continuous series of chemical changes by which nitrogen circulates between air, soil, and living organisms. Free nitrogen in the atmosphere passes into the soil, where it is converted by bacteria into soluble compounds for use by plants and animals. When the plant and animal matter decays, nitrogen is released to the atmosphere, completing the cycle.

nitrogen fixation 1. conversion of free nitrogen in the atmosphere into nitrogenous compounds that can be utilized by plants, through the action of certain bacteria living in soil or on the roots of such plants as peas or beans. **2.** conversion of free nitrogen to useful nitrogen compounds by any of various other processes, esp. by chemical means in the production of industrial products.

ni·tro·glyc·er·in (nī′trə glis′ər in) *also,* **ni·tro·glyc·er·ine.** *n.* colorless, oily, liquid organic compound that is poisonous and very explosive. Weak alcohol solutions of nitroglycerin are used to treat heart disease. Formula: $C_3H_5(ONO_2)_3$.

ni·trous (nī′trəs) *adj.* **1.** of or containing nitrogen, esp. of a lower valence. **2.** of or containing niter. [Latin *nitrōsus* full of natron, from *nitrum* natron. See NITER.]

nitrous acid, unstable compound of nitrogen occurring only in solution or in the form of its salts. Formula: HNO_2.

nitrous oxide, gas with a sweetish odor and taste that produces an exhilarating effect when breathed in small amounts; laughing gas. It is used as an anesthetic.

nit·wit (nit′wit′) *n.* stupid person. [Dialectal German *nit,* form of *nicht* not + WIT¹.]

nix¹ (niks) *Slang.* *n.* nothing. —*adv.* no. —*interj.* watch out! stop! —*v.t.* to reject or put a stop to: *They nixed our proposals.* [German *nix,* informal form of *nichts* nothing.]

nix² (niks) *pl.,* **nix·es.** *n.* *German Mythology.* a water sprite who can change shape at will, appearing at times as part fish and part human. [German *Nix.*]

Nix·on, Richard Mil·hous (nik′sən; mil′hous′) 1913—, thirty-seventh president of the United States, from 1968.

Nizh·ni Nov·go·rod (nizh′nē nôv′gə rod) see **Gorki.**

N.J., New Jersey.

NLRB, National Labor Relations Board.

N. Mex., New Mexico. Also, **N.M.**

NNE, north-northeast.

NNW, north-northwest.

no¹ (nō) *adv.* **1.** certainly not; not so. ▲ used to express denial, disagreement, dissent, or refusal: *No, I don't want to do it. No, that's not right.* Opposed to **yes. 2.** not at all. ▲ used with a comparative: *He is no worse than the others.* **3.** not: *whether or no.* —*interj.* used to express amazement, bewilderment, or skepticism. —*n. pl.,* **noes. 1.** utterance of the word "no"; negative response; refusal; denial. Opposed to **yes. 2.** negative vote or voter: *The noes have it.* [Old English *nā* never, from *ne* not + *ā* ever.]

no² (nō) *adj.* **1.** not any: *no mistakes. They've had no food all day.* **2.** not a: *He is no financial expert.* [Form of NONE.]

No, nobelium.

No. 1. north. **2.** northern. **3.** number. Also, **no.**

No·ah (nō′ə) *n.* in the Old Testament, a patriarch chosen by God to build an ark, in which he, his family, and a pair of every kind of animal survived the flood.

No·bel, Alfred Bern·hard (nō bel′; ber′närd) 1833–96, Swedish chemist and industrialist who established the Nobel prizes.

no·be·li·um (nō bē′lē əm) *n.* artificial radioactive metallic element produced by bombarding curium. Symbol: **No** See **element** for table. [Modern Latin *nobelium,* from Alfred B. *Nobel.*]

Nobel prize, any of the prizes established by Alfred B. Nobel to be awarded annually for accomplishments in the fields of physics, chemistry, medicine, economics, and literature, and for the promotion of peace.

no·bil·i·ty (nō bil′ə tē) *pl.,* **-ties.** *n.* **1.** class of people in a society having hereditary title, rank, and privileges: *A duke is a member of the nobility.* **2.** rank or quality of being distinguished by superior birth or rank. **3.** state or quality of being lofty in character. [Latin *nōbilitās.*]

no·ble (nō′bəl) **-bler, -blest.** *adj.* **1.** distinguished by superior birth, rank, or title; aristocratic. **2.** lofty in character: *a noble mind.* **3.** having superior merit; worthy: *noble sentiments, a noble cause, noble conduct.* **4.** impressive in appearance; splendid; magnificent: *a noble oak tree.* **5.** chemically inert or inactive. —*n.* **1.** one who is distinguished by superior birth, rank, or title; nobleman or noblewoman. **2.** former English gold coin. [Old French *noble* relating to the upper classes, superior in dignity and merit, from Latin *nōbilis* famous, of noble birth.] —**no′ble·ness,** *n.* —**no′bly,** *adv.*

no·ble·man (nō′bəl mən) *pl.,* **-men.** *n.* man of noble birth or rank.

no·blesse o·blige (nō bles′ ō blēzh′) obligation of those of noble birth or rank to behave nobly toward others. [French *noblesse oblige* literally, rank is under an obligation, going back to Latin *nōbilis* (see NOBLE) + *obligāre* (see OBLIGATE).]

no·ble·wom·an (nō′bəl woom′ən) *pl.,* **-wom·en.** *n.* woman of noble birth or rank.

no·bod·y (nō′bod′ē, -bə dē) *pron.* no person; no one. —*n. pl.,* **-bod·ies.** person of no importance, authority, or social position.

nock (nok) *n.* **1.** notch at either end of a bow that holds the bowstring. **2.** notch at the end of an arrow for receiving the bowstring. —*v.t.* **1.** to put a notch in (an arrow or bow). **2.** to fit (an arrow) to the bowstring ready for shooting. [Middle Dutch *nocke* notch.]

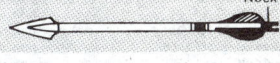

Nock *(def. 2)*

noc·tur·nal (nok turn′əl) *adj.* **1.** of or occurring at night: *nocturnal sounds, a nocturnal walk.* **2.** active at night: *The raccoon is a nocturnal animal.* **3.** (of a flower) opening at night and closing during the day. [Late Latin *nocturnālis* for night use, from Latin *nocturnus* relating to night, from *nox* night.] —**noc·tur′nal·ly,** *adv.*

---

at; āpe; cär; end; mē; it; īce; hot; ōld; fôrk; wood; fōōl; oil; out; up; ūse; turn; sing; thin; this; zh in treasure; ə in ago, taken, pencil, lemon, circus.

noc·turne (nok′turn′) *n.* **1.** musical composition of a dreamy, pensive, or romantic character appropriate to the evening. **2.** painting of a night scene. [French *nocturne,* from Latin *nocturnus* relating to night, from *nox* night.]

nod (nod) *nod·ded, nod·ding. v.i.* **1.** to lower briefly and then raise the head, as in greeting, acknowledgment, or assent. **2.** to let the head fall forward with a quick, involuntary motion, as when sleepy: *The student sat nodding over the dull book.* **3.** to bend forward with a swaying motion: *The grasses nodded as the breeze swept over the field.* **4.** to be careless or inattentive; make a slip. —*v.t.* **1.** to lower briefly and then raise (the head), as in greeting, acknowledgment, or assent. **2.** to signify or express by nodding: *He nodded approval.* **3.** to summon, invite, or send away by nodding. —*n.* lowering and raising of the head, as in greeting, acknowledgment, or assent. [Of uncertain origin.] —**nod′der,** *n.*

nod·dy (nod′ē) *pl.* **-dies.** *n.* **1.** fool; simpleton. **2.** any of several tropical terns, genus *Anous,* having dark-brown plumage and a short tail. [Of uncertain origin.]

node (nōd) *n.* **1.** knot, knob, or swelling. **2.** point of a stem from which a leaf or branch grows; joint. **3.** *Physics.* point, line, or plane in a vibrating body where there is no motion. **4.** either of two points at which the orbit of a celestial body intersects the ecliptic. [Latin *nōdus* knot.] —**nod′al,** *adj.*

Node

nod·ule (noj′ool) *n.* **1.** small knot, swelling, or growth, as on plant or animal tissue. **2.** small, rounded mass or lump, as of some mineral substance. [Latin *nōdulus* little knot, diminutive of *nōdus* knot.] —**nod·u·lar** (noj′ə lər), *adj.*

no·ël (nō el′) *n.* **1.** a Christmas carol. **2.** **Noël.** Christmas. [French *noël,* going back to Latin *nātālis* relating to one's birth (with reference to the birthday of Christ), from *nāsci* to be born.]

no-fault (nō′fôlt′) *adj.* of or pertaining to a form of insurance under which a person injured in an accident is compensated by his or her own insurance company regardless of whether or not he or she was responsible for the accident.

nog·gin (nog′in) *n.* **1.** small mug or cup. **2.** small quantity of drink. **3.** *Informal.* a person's head. [Of uncertain origin.]

no·how (nō′hou′) *adv.* *Slang.* in no way; not at all.

noise (noiz) *n.* **1.** sound that is loud, discordant, harsh, or unpleasant: *The noise of the traffic made it difficult to sleep.* **2.** any sound: *I heard a noise outside the window.* **3.** loud outcry or shouting; uproar; disturbance. **4.** unwanted electrical interference, as in a radio signal. —*v.t.* **noised, nois·ing.** to spread by rumor or report (usually with *abroad* or *about*). [Old French *noise* uproar, outcry, from Latin *nausea* seasickness, from Greek *nausia,* from *naus* ship.]

noise·less (noiz′lis) *adj.* making no noise; silent; quiet: *noiseless movements, a noiseless fan.* —**noise′less·ly,** *adv.* —**noise′less·ness,** *n.*

noise·mak·er (noiz′mā′kər) *n.* that which makes noise, esp. a horn, rattle, or other device used to make noise at a celebration.

noi·some (noi′səm) *adj.* **1.** offensive, esp. to the smell. **2.** harmful; injurious: *noisome fumes.* [Obsolete *noy* to vex (short for ANNOY) + -SOME.] —**noi′some·ly,** *adv.* —**noi′some·ness,** *n.*

nois·y (noi′zē) **nois·i·er, nois·i·est.** *adj.* making noise: *noisy children.* **2.** full of or characterized by noise: *a noisy argument. This city is too noisy for me.* —**nois′i·ly,** *adv.* —**nois′i·ness,** *n.*

nom., nominative.

no·mad (nō′mad, nom′ad) *n.* **1.** member of a group or tribe that has no permanent home and moves from place to place in search of food. **2.** any person who wanders from place to place. —*adj.* nomadic. [Latin *nomad-,* stem of *nomas* wanderer, from Greek *nomas* wandering, as in search of pasture, from *nomos* pasture.] —**no′mad·ism,** *n.*

no·mad·ic (nō mad′ik) *adj.* of, relating to, or resembling nomads; wandering: *nomadic gypsies.* —**no·mad′i·cal·ly,** *adv.*

no man's land **1.** tract of unowned or barren land. **2.** land between two opposing armies, not controlled by either one. **3.** area of thought or activity that is indefinite or uncertain.

nom de guerre (nôN də ger′) *French.* pseudonym.

nom de plume (nom′ də ploom′) pen name. [Translation into French of English *pen name.*]

Nome (nōm) *n.* port city in western Alaska. Pop. (1970), 2488.

no·men·cla·ture (nō′mən klā′chər, nō men′klə-) *n.* system of names, esp. in an art or science: *the nomenclature of biology.* [Latin *nōmenclātūra* calling by name, going back to *nōmen* name + *calāre* to call.]

nom·i·nal (nom′ən əl) *adj.* **1.** being so in name but not in fact; not real or actual: *a nominal peace. The queen of England is a nominal ruler.* **2.** small compared with the actual value: *a nominal cost.* **3.** of, relating to, or containing a name or names: *a nominal list, a nominal account.* **4.** *Grammar.* of, relating to, or used as a noun: *a nominal adjective.* [Latin *nōminālis* relating to a name, from *nōmen* name.] —**nom′i·nal·ly,** *adv.*

nom·i·nate (nom′ə nāt′) **-nat·ed, -nat·ing.** *v.t.* **1.** to propose as a candidate for an office or honor. **2.** to appoint to an office or duty: *The mayor nominated him as police chief.* [Latin *nōminātus,* past participle of *nōmināre* to name, from *nōmen* name.] —**nom′i·na′tor,** *n.*

nom·i·na·tion (nom′ə nā′shun) *n.* **1.** act or instance of nominating. **2.** state of being nominated: *His name was placed in nomination.*

nom·i·na·tive (nom′ə nə tiv, nom′nə-) *Grammar. adj.* of, relating to, or designating the case of the subject of a verb or of words agreeing with the subject. —*n.* **1.** nominative case. **2.** word in the nominative case. *I, they,* and *who* are nominatives. [Latin *nōminātīvus (cāsus)* nominative (case), from *nōmināre* to name.]

nom·i·nee (nom′ə nē′) *n.* one who is named, esp. as a candidate for office. —**Syn.** see candidate.

non- *prefix* failure or lack of; not. [Latin *nōn* not.] ▲ The meaning of a word in the lists at the bottom of this and the following pages can be understood by combining *non-* with the root word.

non·age (non′ij, nō′nij) *n.* **1.** period of legal minority. **2.** any period of immaturity. [Old French *nonage* state of being under age, going back to Latin *nōn* not + *aetās* age.]

non·a·ge·nar·i·an (non′ə jə nār′ē ən, nō′nə-) *n.* one who is ninety or between ninety and one-hundred years old. —*adj.* being ninety or between ninety and one-hundred years old. [Latin *nōnāgēnārius* containing ninety (going back to *nōnāginta* ninety) + -AN.]

non·a·gon (non′ə gon′) *n.* polygon with nine sides and nine angles. [Latin *nōnus* ninth + Greek *gōniā* angle.]

non·a·ligned (non′ə līnd′) *adj.* not allied with or following any major power in foreign affairs; committed to neutrality as a foreign policy. —**non′a·lign′ment,** *n.*

non·ap·pear·ance (non′ə pēr′əns) *n.* failure to appear, esp. in court as a witness or party to a suit.

nonce (nons) *n.* particular purpose or occasion. ▲ used chiefly in the phrase *for the nonce.* [From the incorrect division of Middle English *(for then) ones* literally, (for the) once, into *(for the) nones.* See ONCE.]

nonce word, word coined and used for a particular purpose or occasion.

non·cha·lance (non′shə läns′, -chə-) *n.* state of being nonchalant.

non·cha·lant (non′shə länt′, -chə) *adj.* characterized by or showing a lack of interest or enthusiasm; casually indifferent: *a nonchalant response.* [French *nonchalant* careless, going back to Latin *nōn* not + *calēre* to be warm.] —**non′cha·lant′ly,** *adv.*

non·com (non′kom′) *n. Informal.* noncommissioned officer.

non·com·bat·ant (non′ə kəm bat′ənt, non kom′bat ənt) *n.* **1.** member of the armed forces whose normal duties do not include fighting, as a doctor or chaplain. **2.** civilian in wartime.

non·com·mis·sioned officer (non′kə mish′ənd) enlisted man of the armed forces promoted to any of several grades, as corporal.

non′a·bra′sive	non′a·dult′	non′at·tend′ance	non′charge·a·ble
non′ab·sorb′ent	non′af·fil′i·at·ed	non′au·thor′i·ta′tive	non-Chris′tian
non′ac·a·dem′ic	non′ag·gres′sion	non′au·to·mat′ic	non′cit′i·zen
non′ac·cept′ance	non′ag·gres′sive	non·ba′sic	non·clin′i·cal
non·ac′tive	non′a·gree′ment	non·be′ing	non′co·he′sive
non′a·dapt′ive	non′ag·ri·cul′tur·al	non′be·liev′er	non′col·laps′a·ble
non′ad·dict′ing	non′al·co·hol′ic	non′be·liev′ing	non′col·laps′i·ble
non′ad·dict′ive	non′al·ler·gen′ic	non′bel·lig′er·ent	non′col·lect′a·ble
non′ad·her′ence	non′al·ler′gic	non′break′a·ble	non′col·lect′i·ble
non′ad·he′sive	non′a·quat′ic	non·cak′ing	non′col·le′giate
non′ad·ja′cent	non·as′pi·rat′ed	non·cal′or·ic	non·com′bat
non′ad·just′a·ble	non·as·ser′tive	non′car·bo·nat′ed	non′com·bus′ti·ble
non′ad·min′is·tra′tive	non·as·sess′a·ble	non′car·niv′o·rous	non′com·mer′cial
non′ad·mis′sion	non′ath·let′ic	non·cel′lu·lar	non′com·mis′sioned

at; āpe; cär; end; mē; it; īce; hot; ōld; fôrk; wood; fōōl; oil; out; up; ūse; turn; sing; thin; **this**; zh in treasure; ə in ago, taken, pencil, lemon, circus.

non·com·mit·tal (non′kə mit′əl) *adj.* not involving or expressing commitment to a particular opinion, view, or course of action: *The politician made a noncommittal statement urging further study of discrimination.* —**non′com·mit′tal·ly,** *adv.*

non·com·pli·ance (non′kəm plī′əns) *n.* failure or refusal to comply: *Noncompliance with the terms of the agreement resulted in court action.* —**non′com·pli′ant,** *adj., n.*

non com·pos men·tis (non′ kom′pəs men′tis) not mentally competent to manage one's affairs; of unsound mind. [Latin *nōn compos mentis* literally, not having control of the mind.]

non·con·duc·tor (non′kən duk′tər) *n.* substance that does not readily conduct some form of energy, as heat or electricity. —**non′con·duct′ing,** *adj.*

non·con·form·ist (non′kən fôr′mist) *n.* **1.** one who does not conform in thought, action, or belief to the pattern followed or approved by the majority of society; unconventional person. **2.** *also,* **Nonconformist.** in English history, any Protestant who is not a member of the Church of England.

non·con·form·i·ty (non′kən fôr′mə tē) *n.* **1.** refusal to conform to conventional thought, action, or belief; lack of conformity. **2.** *also,* **Nonconformity.** in English history, refusal to conform to the principles and requirements of the Church of England.

non·co·op·er·a·tion (non′kō op′ə rā′shən) *also,* **non·co·op·er·a·tion.** *n.* **1.** failure or refusal to cooperate. **2.** resistance to government through civil disobedience and a refusal to pay taxes or perform other civic duties. —**non′co·op′er·a′tion·ist, non′co·op′er·a′tor,** *n.* —**non′co·op′er·a′tive,** *adj.*

non·de·script (non′di skript′) *adj.* lacking liveliness or distinctive character; failing to make a distinct impression; colorless: *a nondescript dress, a nondescript personality, a nondescript performance.* —*n.* nondescript person or thing. [NON- + Latin *dēscrīptus,* past participle of *dēscrībere* to write down, represent.]

none (nun) *pron.* **1.** no one; not one: *Several senators criticized the bill, but none voted against it.* **2.** not any: *None of the money was ever recovered.* **3.** no part; nothing: *He has none of his brother's selfishness.* **▲** Because *none* originally meant "no one," it has traditionally been construed as singular: *None of his friends has ever been to Paris.* However, since the word is usually used with a plural noun, in current usage it is more often considered to be plural: *None of the passengers were aware of the danger.* —*adv.* by no means; not at all; to no extent: *Help came none too soon.* [Old English *nān* no one, not any, from *ne* not + *ān* one.]

non·en·ti·ty (non en′tə tē) *pl.,* **-ties.** *n.* **1.** person or thing of little

or no significance or individuality. **2.** something that does not exist or exists only as a figment of the imagination, as a mermaid or unicorn.

nones¹ (nōnz) *n.,pl.* in the ancient Roman calendar, the seventh day of March, May, July, or October, and the fifth day of the other months. **▲** construed as singular. [Latin *nōnae,* originally feminine plural of *nōnus* ninth, from *novem* nine; because it was the ninth day before the ides.]

nones² (nōnz) *also,* **Nones.** *n.,pl.* fifth of the seven canonical hours, or the service for it. [From Latin *nōna hōra* ninth hour (after sunrise).]

none·such (nun′such′) *also,* **non·such.** *n.* one who or that which has no equal or is beyond comparison; paragon.

none·the·less (nun′ṯhə les′) *adv.* nevertheless; however.

non·ex·ist·ent (non′ig zis′tənt) *adj.* not existing in reality; unreal: *a nonexistent problem, a nonexistent place.* —**non′ex·ist′ence,** *n.*

non·fat (non′fat′) *adj.* (of food) having fat or fat solids removed; containing no fats: *nonfat dry milk.*

non·fat·ten·ing (non′fat′ən ing) *adj.* (of food) relatively low in carbohydrates or fats.

non·fea·sance (non fē′zəns) *n.* *Law.* failure, esp. by a public official, to perform some act required by law or official duty. Distinguished from **malfeasance** and **misfeasance.**

non·fer·rous (non fer′əs) *adj.* **1.** (of a metal) containing little or no iron. **2.** relating to or designating metals other than iron or steel, as copper or tin.

non·fic·tion (non fik′shən) *n.* prose literature other than fiction, as essays or biographies, dealing with real or historical characters, circumstances, or events. —**non·fic′tion·al,** *adj.*

non·flam·ma·ble (non flam′ə bəl) *adj.* not likely to catch fire easily; not flammable.

no·nil·lion (nō nil′yən) *n.* **1.** in the United States and France, the cardinal number that is represented by 1 followed by thirty zeros. **2.** in Great Britain and Germany, the cardinal number that is represented by 1 followed by fifty-four zeros. —*adj.* numbering one nonillion. —**no·nil′lionth,** *adj., n.* [French *nonillion* one followed by thirty zeros (from Latin *nōnus* ninth), on the model of *million.* See MILLION.]

non·in·ter·ven·tion (non′in tər ven′shən) *n.* failure or refusal to intervene, esp. the systematic practice of noninterference by a nation in the affairs of other nations. —**non′in·ter·ven′tion·ist,** *adj., n.*

non·ju·ror (non joor′ər) *n.* **1.** one who refuses to take an oath, as of allegiance. **2.** *usually,* **Nonjuror.** one of the body of clergymen of the Church of England who refused to swear allegiance to William III and Mary II after their accession in 1688.

---

non′com·mu′ni·ca·ble	non′de·duct′i·ble	non-Eng′lish	non′he·red′i·tar·y
non′com·mu′ni·ca′tive	non′de·fer′a·ble	non-En′glish-speak′ing	non′his·tor′ic
non′com·mu·nist	non′de·fer′ra·ble	non′en·tan′gle·ment	non′his·tor′i·cal
non′com·pet′i·tive	non′de·liv′er·y	non′es·sen′tial	non-hu′man
non′com·plai′sant	non′dem·o·crat′ic	non′Es·tab′lish·ment	non′i·den′ti·cal
non′con·cil′i·a·to′ry	non′de·nom′i·na′tion·al	non′eth′i·cal	non′i·den′ti·ty
non′con·cur′rence	non′de·part·men′tal	non′-Eu·clid′e·an	non′i·de·o·log′i·cal
non′con·cur′rent	non′de·scrip′tive	non′-Eu·ro·pe′an	non′id·i·o·mat′ic
non′con·dens′ing	non′de·struc′tive	non′ex·change′a·ble	non′im·mu′ni·ty
non′con·duct′ing	non′de·tach′a·ble	non′ex·clu′sive	non′in·clu′sive
non′con·duc′tive	non′det′o·nat′ing	non′ex·empt′	non′in·de·pen′dent
non′con·fi·den′tial	non′dic·ta·to′ri·al	non′ex·pend′a·ble	non′in·dict′a·ble
non′con·flict′ing	non′dif·fer·en′ti·a′tion	non′ex·per′i·men′tal	non′in·dus′tri·al
non′con·form′ing	non′dip·lo·mat′ic	non′ex·plo′sive	non′in·fec′tious
non′con·gen′i·tal	non′di·rec′tion·al	non′ex·port′a·ble	non′in·flam′ma·ble
non′con·sec′u·tive	non′di·rec′tive	non·fac′tu·al	non′in·fla′tion·a·ry
non′con·serv′a·tive	non′dis·crim′i·na·to′ry	non·fad′ing	non′in·stan·ta′ne·ous
non′con·strain′ing	non′dis·tinc′tive	non·fa′tal	non′in·stinc′tu·al
non′con·struc′tive	non·doc′tri·nal	non′fed·er·at′ed	non′in·sti·tu′tion·al
non′con·sump′tion	non′dog·mat′ic	non·fil′ter·a·ble	non′in·tel·lec′tu·al
non′con·ta′gious	non′dra·mat′ic	non·fi′nite	non′in·ter·change′a·ble
non′con·tem′po·rar′y	non·drink′er	non·fis′cal	non′in·ter·course′
non′con·tin′u·ous	non·dry′ing	non·fis′sion·a·ble	non′in·ter′fer·ence
non′con·trib′u·ting	non′ec·cle′si·as′ti·cal	non·flex′i·ble	non′in·tox′i·cant
non′con·trib′u·to′ry	non·ed′i·ble	non·flow′er·ing	non′in·tox′i·cat′ing
non′con·trol′ling	non′ed·u·ca′tion·al	non·flu′id	non·ir′ri·tant
non′con·tro·ver′sial	non′ef·fer·ves′cent	non·fly′ing	non′-Jew′
non′con·ver′sant	non′e·lec′tion	non·freez′ing	non-Jew′ish
non′con·ver′sant	non′e·lec′tric	non′ful·fill′ment	non-ko′sher
non′con·vert′i·ble	non′e·lec′tri·cal	non·func′tion·al	non-lam′i·nat′ed
non′cor·ro′sive	non′el·i·gi·ble	non·fu′si·ble	non-le′thal
non′cre·a′tive	non′e·mu′la·tive	non·gas′e·ous	non·lin′e·ar
non′crim′i·nal	non′e·mo′tion·al	non′gov·ern·men′tal	non·liq′uid
non·crys′tal·line	non′em·pir′i·cal	non·gran′u·lar	non·lit′er·ar·y
non′cy′clic	non′en·force′a·ble	non·haz′ard·ous	non′li·tur′gi·cal
non′cy′cli·cal	non′en·force′ment		non·liv′ing
non′de·cid′u·ous			non·lu′mi·nous

---

at; āpe; cär; end; mē; it; īce; hot; ōld; fôrk; wood; fōōl; oil; out; up; ūse; turn; sing; thin; this; zh in treasure; ə in ago, taken, pencil, lemon, circus. 687

non·met·al (non met′əl) *n.* chemical element not having the character of a metal, esp. an element which tends to gain electrons and form negatively charged ions.

non·me·tal·lic (non′mi tal′ik) *adj.* **1.** not of or like metal. **2.** *Chemistry.* of or relating to a nonmetal.

non·mor·al (non môr′əl, -mor′-) *adj.* not relating to or involving morality or moral judgments; neither moral nor immoral; amoral.

non·ob·jec·tive (non′əb jek′tiv) *adj.* nonrepresentational; abstract.

non·pa·reil (non′pə rel′) *adj.* having no equal; incomparable; matchless. —*n.* **1.** one who or that which has no equal; paragon. **2.** small disk of chocolate candy covered with white pellets of sugar. **3.** 6-point blank space between lines of print. [French *nonpareil* matchless, from *non* not (from Latin *nōn*) + *pareil* equal (going back to Latin *pār*).]

non·par·ti·san (non pär′ti zən) *also,* **non·par·ti·zan.** *adj.* **1.** not supporting, affiliated with, or influenced by any single political party or its interests: *a nonpartisan ticket, a nonpartisan effort.* **2.** not partisan; objective; disinterested: *a nonpartisan judge of the community's needs.* —**non·par′ti·san·ship′**; *also,* **non·par′ti·zan·ship′,** *n.*

non·plus (non plus′) **-plused, -plus·ing;** *also,* **-plussed, -plus·sing.** *v.t.* to put at a loss for what to say, think, or do; bewilder; perplex: *to be nonplused by directions, to be nonplused by an outburst of profanity.* —*n.* state of bewilderment or perplexity. [Latin *nōn plūs* no more, no further.]

non·pro·duc·tive (non′prə duk′tiv) *adj.* **1.** not involved directly in the production of goods, as managerial or sales personnel. **2.** producing or yielding little or nothing. —**non′pro·duc′tive·ly,** *adv.* —**non′pro·duc′tive·ness,** *n.*

non·prof·it (non prof′it) *adj.* not operated for profit: *a nonprofit organization.*

non·rep·re·sen·ta·tion·al (non′rep ri zen tā′shən əl, -zen-) *adj.* characteristic of or designating a style of art that does not depict figures or objects as they appear in nature; abstract.

non·res·i·dent (non rez′ə dənt) *adj.* not residing in a particular place, esp. not residing permanently where one works, attends school, or owns property, as for tax or voting purposes. —*n.* one who is nonresident. —**non·res′i·dence, non·res′i·den·cy,** *n.*

non·re·sist·ance (non′ri zis′təns) *n.* **1.** policy or practice of refusing to resist authority however unjust or arbitrary. **2.** policy or practice of refusing to use force or violence even in self-defense. —**non′re·sist′ant,** *adj., n.*

non·re·stric·tive (non′ri strik′tiv) *adj.* *Grammar.* designating a

word, clause, or phrase that describes a modified element without limiting or changing the essential meaning of the sentence. In the sentence *Mr. Bridges, who is a captain in the army, was sent to Japan,* the clause *who is a captain in the army* is nonrestrictive. Opposed to **restrictive.**

non·sec·tar·i·an (non′sek târ′ē ən) *adj.* not restricted to or affiliated with any specific religious denomination or sect: *a nonsectarian service, a nonsectarian college.*

non·sense (non′sens, -səns) *n.* **1.** that which makes or has no sense, esp. language or behavior that is meaningless; absurdity: *The poor idiot in the play babbled nonsense.* **2.** language or conduct that is annoying, evasive, or otherwise lacking in good sense; foolishness: *I won't put up with any more of your nonsense—now get down to work!* **3.** things of no importance or value; trifles. [NON- + SENSE.]

non·sen·si·cal (non sen′si kəl) *adj.* having or making no sense or no good sense; foolish; absurd. —**non·sen′si·cal·ly,** *adv.*

non seq., non sequitur.

non se·qui·tur (non sek′wi tər) statement or conclusion that has no relevance to or does not follow from the statements or premises advanced, for example: *Why is the sky blue? Because it rains more in February than July.* [Latin *nōn sequitur* it does not follow.]

non·skid (non′skid′) *adj.* made or designed to prevent skidding: *nonskid tires, nonskid floor wax.*

non·stan·dard (non stan′dərd) *adj.* **1.** designating or belonging to those usages or varieties of a language that are not considered acceptable by educated users of the language. **2.** varying from the standard; not standard.

non·stop (non′stop′) *adj.* not making or scheduled to make any stops en route: *a nonstop flight.* —*adv.* without stops en route.

non·such (nun′such′) nonesuch.

non·suit (non′sōōt′) *n.* *Law.* judgment given against a plaintiff who fails to prosecute or provide sufficient evidence for a case. —*v.t.* to subject to a nonsuit.

non·sup·port (non′sə pôrt′) *n.* *Law.* failure to provide financial support for a legal dependent.

non trop·po (non trop′ō, -trō′pō, nōn-) *Music.* not too much; moderately. ▲ used to modify a direction: *allegro non troppo.* [Italian *non troppo,* from *non* not (from Latin *nōn*) + *troppo* too much (of Germanic origin).]

non·un·ion (non ūn′yən) *adj.* **1.** not employing union members; not recognizing any trade unions: *a nonunion shop.* **2.** not belonging to or affiliated with a trade or labor union: *nonunion electricians, a nonunion*

non·mag·net′ic	non′par·tic′i·pat′ing	non′re·deem′a·ble	non′spe·cif′ic
non·ma·lig′nant	non′par·tic′i·pa′tion	non′re·duc′i·ble	non·spec′u·la′tive
non·mal′le·a·ble	non′pa·ter′ni·ty	non′re·duc′ing	non·spir′i·tu·al
non·mar′ket·a·ble	non·pay′ing	non′re·fill′a·ble	non·stain′ing
non·mar′ry·ing	non·pay′ment	non′re·flec′tive	non′stan′dard·ized′
non·ma·te′ri·al·is′tic	non′per·for′mance	non·re·li′gious	non·start′er
non·math·e·mat′i·cal	non′per·form′er	non′re·mu′ner·a′tive	non·start′ing
non·mech·a·nis′tic	non′per·form′ing	non′re·new′a·ble	non′sta·tis′ti·cal
non·me·lo′di·ous	non′per·ish·a·ble	non′rep·re·sent′a·tive	non·stra·te′gic
non·mem′ber	non′per·ish·a·bles	non′res·i·den′tial	non·strik′er
non·mem′ber·ship′	non·per′ma·nent	non′re·strict′ed	non·struc′tur·al
non·met′ri·cal	non′phys′i·cal	non′ret·ro·ac′tive	non′sub·scrib′er
non·mi′gra·to′ry	non′phys·i·o·log′i·cal	non′re·turn′a·ble	non′suc·cess′
non·mil′i·tant	non·poi′son·ous	non′re·vers′i·ble	non′sup·port′er
non·mil′i·ta′ry	non′po·lit′i·cal	non·ru′ral	non′sup·port′ing
non′min·is·te′ri·al	non·po′rous	non·rust′ing	non·sur′gi·cal
non·mo′tile	non′pos·ses′sion	non·sal′a·ble	non′sus·tain′ing
non′mu·nic′i·pal	non·pred′i·ca′tive	non·sal′a·ried	non′sym·bol′ic
non·myth′i·cal	non′pre·scrip′tive	non·sched′uled	non·sym·met′ri·cal
non·nav′i·ga·ble	non′pro·duc′er	non·scho·las′tic	non′sym·pa·thiz′er
non·ne·go′ti·a·ble	non′pro·fes′sion·al	non′sci·en·tif′ic	non′sys·tem·at′ic
non·ob·serv′ance	non′pro·gres′sive	non·sea′son·al	non′sys·tem·at′i·cal
non·oc·cur′rence	non′pro·por′tion·al	non′sec·re·tar′i·al	non·tar′nish·a·ble
non·o′dor·ous	non′pro·pri′e·tar′y	non′seg′re·gat′ed	non·tax′a·ble
non·of·fi′cial	non′rab·bin′ic	non′se·lec′tive	non·tech′ni·cal
non·oil′y	non′rab·bin′i·cal	non′self·gov′ern·ing	non′tem′po·ral
non·op′er·a·ble	non·ra′cial	non·sen′su·al	non′ter·ri·to′ri·al
non·op′er·a′tive	non·rad′i·cal	non·sen′su·ous	non′the·at′ri·cal
non·or·gan′ic	non·ra′di·o·ac′tive	non·sex′u·al	non·tit′u·lar
non·or′tho·dox′	non·ra′tion·al	non·shrink′a·ble	non·tox′ic
non·own′er	non·re·ac′tive	non·skilled′	non′tra·di′tion·al
non·pal′a·tal	non·read′er	non·smok′er	non′trans·fer′a·ble
non·pal·a·tal·i·za′tion	non′re·al·is′tic	non·smok′ing	non′trans·par′ent
non·par′al·lel′	non′re·al′i·ty	non·so′cial	non·trop′i·cal
non·par·a·sit′ic	non′re·cip′ro·cal	non·sol′u·ble	non·typ′i·cal
non·par·lia·men′ta·ry	non′rec·og·ni′tion	non·speak′ing	non′ty·ran′ni·cal
non·pa·ro′chi·al	non′re·cov′er·a·ble	non·spe′cial·ist	non·ul′cer·ous
non′par·tic′i·pant	non′re·cur′rent	non·spe′cial·ized′	non·u′ni·form′
	non′re·cur′ring		non·us′er

at; āpe; cär; end; mē; it; īce; hot; ōld; fôrk; wood; fōōl; oil; out; up; ūse; turn; sing; thin; this; zh in treasure; ə in ago, taken, pencil, lemon, circus.

profession. **3.** not made or maintained by union labor or according to union regulations.

non·vi·a·ble (non vī′ə bəl) *adj.* not able to live or survive: *a nonviable fetus.*

non·vi·o·lence (non vī′ə ləns) *n.* philosophy or practice of opposing the use of all physical force or violence. —**non·vi′o·lent,** *adj.* —**non·vi′o·lent·ly,** *adv.*

non·white (non hwīt′, -wīt′) *n.* person who is not a member of the white race. —*adj.* of, designating, or relating to a nonwhite or non-whites.

noo·dle¹ (nōōd′əl) *n.* narrow, flat, or cylindrical strip of dried dough made from a mixture of flour, water, and eggs. [German *Nudel.*]

noo·dle² (nōōd′əl) *n.* **1.** silly or stupid person; fool. **2.** *Slang.* the head. [Of uncertain origin.]

nook (nook) *n.* **1.** any small recess or corner: *a breakfast nook.* **2.** secluded or sheltered place: *He found a shady nook in the woods.* [Of uncertain origin.]

noon (nōōn) *n.* **1.** twelve o'clock in the daytime; the middle of the day. **2.** highest point: *in the bright wisdom of youth's breathless noon* (Shelley, 1817). [Old English *nōn* ninth hour after sunrise, from Latin *nōna* (*hōra*) ninth (hour), feminine of *nōnus* ninth, from *novem* nine. When the time of the nones was changed from three P.M. to midday, the word *noon* also came to mean midday.]

noon·day (nōōn′dā′) *n.* noon. —*adj.* of or occurring at noon.

no one, nobody.

noon·time (nōōn′tīm′) *n.* noon. Also, **noon′tide′.**

noose (nōōs) *n.* **1.** loop of rope with a slip knot that allows the loop to tighten when the end of the rope is pulled. **2.** trap or snare. —*v.t.,* **noosed, noos·ing. 1.** to capture with a noose; entrap. **2.** to tie a noose with or in. [Provençal *nous* knot, from Latin *nōdus.*]

nor (nôr; *unstressed* nər) *conj.* **1.** used with a preceding *neither* or other negative to introduce another element in a series: *Neither she nor I have seen it.* **2.** used in place of *and . . . not* to continue the force of a negative: *He was not at work today, nor will he be there tomorrow.* [Contraction of obsolete *nother,* form of NEITHER; influenced in spelling by OR.]

Nor. 1. Norman. **2.** North. **3.** Norway; Norwegian.

Nor·dic (nôr′dik) *adj.* of or relating to one of the divisions of the Caucasoid people, characterized by tall stature, long heads, fair skin, and blond hair, and living mainly in northern Europe, esp. Scandinavia. —*n.* member of the Nordic people. [French *nordique* relating to the north, from *nord* north, going back to Old English *north.*]

Nor·folk (nôr′fək) *n.* largest city in Virginia, in the southeastern part of the state. Pop. (1970), 307,951.

Norfolk jacket, single-breasted, belted men's jacket that extends to the hips.

norm (nôrm) *n.* **1.** rule, standard, or pattern, as of behavior: *cultural norms.* **2.** average derived from the organization and analysis of data: *statistical norms.* [Latin *nōrma* carpenter's square, rule, pattern.] **Syn. 2.** Norm, **mean³, average** mean a point midway between two extremes. **Norm** implies a level of performance or achievement that can be accepted as a standard for guidance or as a pattern to be followed: *That child is above the norm for his age in arithmetic.* **Mean** suggests a quality, state, or degree intermediate between two extremes: *The speech struck a happy mean between overconfidence and despair.* **Average,** when applied to a class, group, or series of like but unequal things, refers to the typical value each item would have if all were equal: *Peter earned an average of C in his high school course.*

nor·mal (nôr′məl) *adj.* **1.** conforming to or constituting an accepted standard, model, or pattern; usual; standard; typical: *This heavy traffic is normal for this time of day.* **2.** having or demonstrating average intellectual or emotional development, as at a particular age: *According to various tests, Jack is normal for his age.* **3.** free from mental or emotional disturbance. **4.** *Mathematics.* perpendicular. **5.** of a solution, containing one gram equivalent weight of solute per liter. —*n.* **1.** anything that is normal. **2.** usual or standard condition or level: *His temperature was two degrees above normal.* **3.** *Mathematics.* line or

plane that is perpendicular to another. [Late Latin *nōrmālis* in conformity with rule, going back to Latin *nōrma* carpenter's square, rule, pattern.] —**Syn.** *adj.* **1.** see **typical.**

nor·mal·cy (nôr′məl sē) *n.* normality.

nor·mal·i·ty (nôr mal′ə tē) *n.* state or quality of being normal.

nor·mal·ize (nôr′mə līz′) -**ized, -iz·ing.** *v.t.* to cause to conform to the usual or standard condition; make normal. —**nor′mal·i·za′tion, nor′mal·iz′er,** *n.*

nor·mal·ly (nôr′mə lē) *adv.* **1.** under normal circumstances; ordinarily; usually: *Normally the train takes twenty minutes to reach the next town.* **2.** in a normal manner.

normal school, school that trains high school graduates to be teachers. [Partial translation of French *école normale* training school, going back to Late Latin *normālis* (see NORMAL) + Latin *schola* (see SCHOOL).]

Nor·man (nôr′mən) *n.* **1.** member of the Scandinavian people who invaded and conquered Normandy in the tenth century A.D. **2.** one of the descendants of these people and the French who conquered England in 1066. **3.** native or inhabitant of Normandy. **4.** Norman French. —*adj.* **1.** of or relating to Normandy or the Normans. **2.** relating to or designating a style of architecture that developed in Normandy and England in the eleventh and twelfth centuries, characterized by massive construction with short, heavy columns supported by semicircular arches.

Norman Conquest, conquest of England by the Normans under William the Conqueror, in 1066.

Nor·man·dy (nôr′mən dē) *n.* historic region and former province in northwestern France, bordering the English Channel. Area, approx. 11,820 sq. mi.

Norman French, dialect of French spoken by the people of Normandy in the Middle Ages. —**Nor′man-French′,** *adj.*

Norse (nôrs) *adj.* **1.** of or relating to ancient Scandinavia, its people, or their language. **2.** Norwegian. —*n.* **1. the Norse. a.** ancient Scandinavians. **b.** Norwegians. **2.** Old Norse. **3.** language of Norway; Norwegian. [Dutch *Noorsch* Scandinavian, from *noord* north.]

Norse·man (nôrs′mən) *pl.,* **-men.** *n.* member of the people of ancient Scandinavia; Northman.

north (nôrth) *n.* **1.** direction to one's right as one faces the sunset. **2.** one of the four cardinal points of the compass, directly opposite south, and at zero degrees. **3.** *also,* North. any region situated toward this direction in relation to a specified point of reference. **4. the North.** region of the United States north of Maryland, the Ohio River, and Missouri, esp. the Northern states that fought against the Confederacy in the Civil War. —*adj.* **1.** toward or in the north. **2.** coming from the north: *the north wind.* —*adv.* toward the north: *He walked north.* [Old English *north* toward the region farthest from sun at noon.]

North America, third largest continent, comprising all the land between the Atlantic and Pacific oceans north of the Panama-Colombia border, including Mexico, the continental United States, and Canada. Land area, approx. 9,362,000 sq. mi. Pop. (1966 est.), 299,000,000. —**North American.**

North·amp·ton (nôr thamp′tən, nôrth hamp′-) *n.* city in central England. Pop. (1968), 123,700.

north·bound (nôrth′bound′) *adj.* going northward: *northbound traffic.*

North Carolina, state in the southeastern United States, on the Atlantic. Capital, Raleigh. Area, 52,712 sq. mi. Pop. (1970), 5,082,059. Abbreviation, **N.C.** —**North Carolinian.**

North Dakota, state in the north-central United States. Capital, Bismarck. Area, 70,665 sq. mi. Pop. (1970), 617,761. Abbreviations, **N. Dak., N.D.** —**North Dakotan.**

north·east (nôrth′ēst′) *n.* **1.** direction halfway between north and east. **2.** point of the compass indicating this direction. **3.** region or place in this direction. **4. the Northeast.** northeastern part of the United States, esp. New England and New York. —*adj.* **1.** toward or in the northeast; northeastern. **2.** coming from the northeast: *the northeast wind.* —*adv.* toward the northeast.

north·east·er (nôrth′ēs′tər) *n.* strong wind or storm from the northeast.

north·east·er·ly (nôrth′ēs′tər lē) *adj., adv.* **1.** toward the northeast. **2.** from the northeast.

north·east·ern (nôrth′ēs′tərn) *adj.* **1.** to, toward, or in the northeast. **2.** *also,* Northeastern. of, relating to, or characteristic of the northeast or Northeast. **3.** coming from the northeast. —**North′east′ern·er,** *n.*

north·east·ward (nôrth′ēst′wərd) *adv. also,* **north·east·wards.** to-

non·vas′cu·lar	non·vi′bra·to·ry	non′vo·cal	non·vot′er
non·ven′om·ous	non′vint′age	non′vo·ca′tion·al	non·vot′ing
non·ver′bal	non′vi·o·la′tion	non′vo·la·tile	non·work′er
non·ver′i·fi′a·ble	non·vis′cous	non′vol·can′ic	non·work′ing
non·ver′ti·cal	non·vis′u·al	non′vol·un·tar′y	non·wo′ven

ward the northeast. —*adj.* toward or in the northeast. —*n.* northeastward direction, point, or part.

north·east·ward·ly (nôrth'ēst'wərd lē) *adj., adv.* **1.** toward the northeast. **2.** from the northeast.

north·er (nôr'thər) *n.* strong wind or storm from the north.

north·er·ly (nôr'thər lē) *adj., adv.* **1.** toward the north. **2.** from the north.

north·ern (nôr'thərn) *adj.* **1.** to, toward, or in the north. **2.** *also,* **Northern.** of, relating to, or characteristic of the north or North. **3.** coming from the north.

north·ern·er (nôr'thər nər) *n.* **1.** one who was born or lives in the north. **2.** *usually,* **Northerner.** one who was born or lives in the northern part of the United States.

Northern Hemisphere, the half of the earth north of the equator.

Northern Ireland, political division of the United Kingdom, occupying the northeast corner of the island of Ireland. Capital, Belfast. Area, approx. 5459 sq. mi. Pop. (1964 est.), 1,458,000.

northern lights, aurora borealis.

north·ern·most (nôr'thərn mōst') *adj.* farthest north.

Northern Rhodesia, Zambia.

North Island, smaller of the two main islands of New Zealand. Area, 44,281 sq. mi.

North Korea, country occupying the northern part of the Korean peninsula. Capital, Pyongyang. Area, 46,540 sq. mi. Pop. (1967 est.), 12,700,000.

north·land (nôrth'lənd) *n.* **1.** land in the north, as the northern region of a country. **2. Northland.** Scandinavia. —**north'land·er,** *n.*

North Little Rock, city in central Arkansas, near Little Rock. Pop. (1970), 60,040.

North·man (nôrth'mən) *pl.,* **-men.** *n.* Norseman.

north-north·east (nôrth'nôrth'ēst') *n.* point on the compass halfway between north and northeast. —*adj., adv.* toward the northnortheast.

north-north·west (nôrth'nôrth'west') *n.* point on the compass halfway between north and northwest. —*adj., adv.* toward the northnorthwest.

North Pole 1. northernmost point on earth; the northern end of the earth's axis. **2. north pole.** pole of a magnet that points to the north when the magnet swings freely.

North Sea, large arm of the Atlantic, between Great Britain and continental Europe.

North Star, Polaris.

North·um·bri·a (nôr thum'brē ə) *n.* ancient kingdom founded by the Angles in northern England.

North·um·bri·an (nôr thum'brē ən) *adj.* of or relating to Northumbria, its people, or their dialect. —*n.* **1.** member of the people inhabiting ancient Northumbria. **2.** Old English dialect spoken in Northumbria.

North Vietnam, country in southeastern Asia, bordering China on the north and South Vietnam on the south. Capital, Hanoi. Area, 61,294 sq. mi. Pop. (1967 est.), 20,100,000.

north·ward (nôrth'wərd) *adv. also,* **north·wards.** toward the north. —*adj.* toward or in the north. —*n.* northward direction, point, or part.

north·west (nôrth'west') *n.* **1.** direction halfway between north and west. **2.** point of the compass indicating this direction. **3.** region or place in this direction. **4. the Northwest.** northwestern part of the United States, esp. Idaho, Oregon, and Washington. —*adj.* **1.** toward or in the northwest; northwestern. **2.** coming from the northwest: *the northwest wind.* —*adv.* toward the northwest.

north·west·er (nôrth'wes'tər) *n.* strong wind or storm from the northwest.

north·west·er·ly (nôrth'wes'tər lē) *adj., adv.* **1.** toward the northwest. **2.** from the northwest.

north·west·ern (nôrth'wes'tərn) *adj.* **1.** to, toward, or in the northwest. **2.** *also,* **Northwestern.** of, relating to, or characteristic of the northwest or Northwest. **3.** coming from the northwest. —**North'west'ern·er,** *n.*

Northwest Passage, sea route along the north coast of North America connecting the Atlantic and Pacific.

Northwest Territories, administrative division of Canada, in the northern part of the country. Area, 1,304,903 sq. mi. Pop. (1966), 28,738.

Northwest Territory, territory organized in 1787, consisting of land between the Ohio and Mississippi rivers that now forms the states of Illinois, Indiana, Michigan, Ohio, Wisconsin, and part of Minnesota.

north·west·ward (nôrth'west'wərd) *adv. also,* **north·west·wards.** toward the northwest. —*adj.* toward or in the northwest. —*n.* northwestward direction, point, or part.

north·west·ward·ly (nôrth'west'wərd lē) *adj., adv.* **1.** toward the northwest. **2.** from the northwest.

Nor·walk (nôr'wôk) *n.* **1.** city in southern California, near Los

Angeles. Pop. (1970), 91,827. **2.** city in southwestern Connecticut. Pop. (1970), 79,113.

Nor·way (nôr'wā) *n.* country in northern Europe occupying part of the Scandinavian peninsula. Capital, Oslo. Area, 125,181 sq. mi. Pop. (1969 est.), 3,851,000.

Nor·we·gian (nôr wē'jən) *n.* **1.** member or recent descendant of the people of Norway. **2.** language belonging to the Germanic branch of the Germanic language family, spoken predominantly in Norway. —*adj.* of or relating to Norway, its people, or their language.

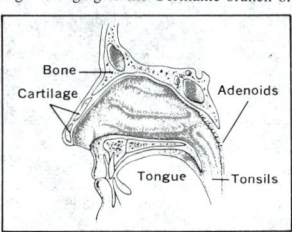
Nose

nose (nōz) *n.* **1.** part of the human face that contains the organ of smell and the breathing passages. **2.** corresponding part of the head in other animals. **3.** sense of smell. **4.** prominent or projecting part of something, as a ship or airplane.

5. ability to perceive or detect: *a reporter with a nose for news.* **6.** *Informal.* nose considered as a means of interfering or meddling: *Keep your nose out of this.*

by a nose. by a small margin.

to count noses. to determine the number of people present.

to follow one's nose. a. to go straight ahead. **b.** to be guided by instinct.

to lead by the nose. to be completely dominant over; control absolutely.

to look down one's nose at. *Informal.* to hold a superior attitude toward; disdain.

to pay through the nose. to pay an excessive amount.

to put (someone's) nose out of joint. to displease or disconcert (someone).

to turn up one's nose at. to express scorn or contempt for; show disdain toward.

under one's nose. within one's immediate view; plainly or easily visible.

—*v.t.,* **nosed, nos·ing. 1.** to discover or notice by smell (often with out): *The dog nosed out the scent.* **2.** to touch or rub with the nose; nuzzle. **3.** to push slowly or gently with or as with the nose: *Tugboats nosed the ship into the dock.* **4. to nose out.** to defeat by a small margin. —*v.i.* **1.** to sniff: *The puppy nosed at my arm.* **2.** to move forward, esp. with caution: *The ship slowly nosed through the narrow channel.* **3.** to pry or meddle: *to nose around for information.* [Old English *nosu* this part of the face.]

nose·band (nōz'band') *n.* strap on a bridle or halter that passes over the animal's nose. See **harness** for illustration.

nose·bleed (nōz'blēd') *n.* bleeding from the nose.

nose cone, conical front section of a rocket that carries the payload and is often equipped with a heat shield.

nose-dive (nōz'dīv') **-dived** or **-dove, -diving.** *v.i.* to take a rapid or abrupt plunge downward.

nose dive 1. rapid plunge downward by an aircraft, with the nose pointing toward the earth. **2.** rapid or abrupt plunge downward, as in prices or profits.

nose·gay (nōz'gā') *n.* small bunch of flowers; bouquet. [NOSE + obsolete *gay* ornament (from GAY).]

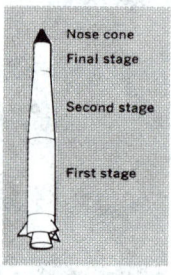
Nose cone Final stage Second stage First stage

Nose cone of a rocket

nose·piece (nōz'pēs') *n.* **1.** part of a helmet that protects the nose. **2.** part of a microscope, often rotatable, on which the objective lens or lenses are mounted. **3.** noseband.

nos·tal·gia (nos tal'jə, nəs-) *n.* **1.** sentimental longing for what is past or far away: *The faded mementos filled the old woman with nostalgia.* **2.** homesickness. [Modern Latin *nostalgia,* from Greek *nostos* return home + *algos* pain.] —**nos·tal'gic,** *adj.* —**nos·tal'gi·cal·ly,** *adv.*

nos·tril (nos'trəl) *n.* either of the two external openings of the nose. [Old English *nosthyrl,* from *nosu* nose + *thyrel* hole.]

nos·trum (nos'trəm) *n.* **1.** patent medicine, esp. one that is a quack remedy. **2.** pet scheme or favorite remedy, as for curing social ills. [Latin *nostrum,* neuter of *noster* our, ours; referring to the former use of the label *nostrum* (suggesting medicines of "our own preparation") for quack medicines.]

at; āpe; cär; end; mē; it; īce; hot; ōld; fôrk; wood; fōol; oil; out; up; ūse; turn; sing; thin; this; zh in treasure; ə in ago, taken, pencil, lemon, circus.

nos·y (nō′zē) **nos·i·er, nos·i·est.** also, **nos·ey.** adj. Informal. unduly curious; prying. —**nos′i·ly,** adv. —**nos′i·ness,** n.

not (not) adv. at no time; in no way. ▲ used to express negation, denial, refusal, or prohibition: She is not home. You may not go. [Contraction of NAUGHT, NOUGHT.]

no·ta be·ne (nō′tə bē′nē) Latin. note well; take notice.

no·ta·bil·i·ty (nō′tə bil′ə tē) pl., **-ties.** n. state or quality of being notable.

no·ta·ble (nō′tə bəl) adj. worthy of notice; noteworthy; remarkable: The novelist's first book was a notable achievement. —n. one who is worthy of notice; person of eminence or distinction. [Latin notābilis remarkable, from notāre to mark.] —**no′ta·ble·ness,** n. —**no′ta·bly,** adv.

no·tar·i·al (nō tār′ē əl) adj. of, relating to, or executed by a notary public.

no·ta·rize (nō′tə rīz′) **-rized, -riz·ing.** v.t. to certify (a document) as authentic; attest to as a notary public: to notarize a will. —**no′ta·ri·za′tion,** n.

no·ta·ry (nō′tər ē) pl., **-ries.** n. notary public. [Latin notārius stenographer, clerk, from nota mark.]

notary public, public officer authorized to administer oaths, certify documents as authentic, and take affidavits.

no·ta·tion (nō tā′shən) n. **1.** system of signs or symbols used to represent values, quantities, or other facts or information: musical notations, chemical notations. **2.** act or process of using such signs or symbols. **3.** brief note, as in the margin of a book. **4.** act of making notes in writing. [Latin notātiō designation, shorthand, from notāre to mark.] —**no·ta′tion·al,** adj.

notch (noch) n. **1.** wedge-shaped nick or other indentation cut into the surface or along the edge of something. **2.** narrow pass between mountains. **3.** Informal. step or degree: Harold has come down several notches in my estimation. —v.t. **1.** to cut a notch or notches in. **2.** to record by or as if by cutting notches. [Probably from the incorrect division into a notch of an otch, from Old French osche a nick, cut, from Old French oschier to nick, cut; of uncertain origin.]

note (nōt) n. **1.** usually, **notes.** brief record, as of a lecture, written down to assist the memory: He took notes in class. The professor spoke without notes. **2.** explanatory or critical comment added to a text, as at the bottom of a page. **3.** brief message or letter: The teacher sent a note to the boy's mother. **4.** formal, written diplomatic communication. **5.** careful notice; regard: John's opinions are worthy of note. **6.** distinction; importance; significance: The judge is a man of note. **7.** indication or suggestion, as of an emotion: He detected a note of bitterness in her voice. **8.** promissory note. **9.** piece of paper currency or a certificate of payment issued by a government or bank, serving as legal tender: a one-pound note. **10.** Music. **a.** tone of definite pitch. **b.** sign representing such a tone and indicating its pitch and duration. **c.** key of a piano or other similar instrument. **11.** Archaic. melody; tune; song. **12. to compare notes.** to exchange points of view or ideas. **13. to strike the right note.** to do or say what is appropriate. —v.t., **not·ed, not·ing. 1.** to set down in writing; make a note of: He noted her phone number in his address book. **2.** to take careful notice of; regard: Please note the enclosed instructions. **3.** to mention specially; remark about: The critic noted several of the young artist's paintings in his review. [Latin nota mark, sign, musical note.] —**not′er,** n.

note·book (nōt′book′) n. book containing blank pages for notes.

not·ed (nō′tid) adj. famous; celebrated; distinguished: Several noted authors attended the reception.

note·pa·per (nōt′pā′pər) n. paper used for writing notes.

note·wor·thy (nōt′wur′thē) adj. worthy of notice or special attention. —**note′wor′thi·ly,** adv. —**note′wor′thi·ness,** n.

noth·ing (nuth′ing) n. **1.** no thing; not anything: He had nothing to say about the matter. We bought nothing at the store. **2.** no part or share: His uncle left him nothing in the will. **3.** obscurity or insignificance: He rose from nothing to a position of power. **4.** one who or that which is of no value or significance. **5.** absence of matter or existence; nothingness. **6.** zero. **7. nothing doing.** Informal. absolutely not. —adv. in no way; not at all. [NO + THING.]

noth·ing·ness (nuth′ing nis) n. **1.a.** absence of matter; empty space; emptiness. **b.** absence of existence; nonexistence. **c.** absence of consciousness; unconsciousness or death. **2.** insignificance or worthlessness. **3.** thing of no value or significance.

no·tice (nō′tis) n. **1.** act of observing; being observed: to take notice, to escape notice, to bring something to notice, to attract notice. **2.** announcement, information, or warning: to attack without notice, to serve notice. **3.** printed

announcement: There were notices posted all over town about the sale. **4.** formal announcement, as of the end of an agreement: He gave his employer two weeks' notice. **5.** review: The play received very poor notices. **6. to serve notice.** to give warning or information; announce. —v.t., **-ticed, -tic·ing.** to become aware of visually; take notice of; observe: I noticed Fred's car parked outside. She noticed the changes in her friend's personality. [Middle French notice acquaintance, from Latin nōtitia knowledge, acquaintance, information.]

no·tice·a·ble (nō′ti sə bəl) adj. easily noticed: There is a noticeable difference in her appearance today. —**no′tice·a·bly,** adv.

no·ti·fi·ca·tion (nō′tə fi kā′shən) n. **1.** act of notifying; being notified. **2.** written or printed notice.

no·ti·fy (nō′tə fī′) **-fied, -fy·ing.** v.t. to give notice to; inform: to notify the police of an accident, to notify customers of a sale. [Old French notifier to make known, from Latin nōtificāre, from nōtus known + facere to make.] —**no′ti·fi′er,** n.

no·tion (nō′shən) n. **1.** mental image; conception; idea: She hasn't the faintest notion of what he meant by that remark. **2.** theory, belief, or opinion: She has the superstitious notion that breaking a mirror causes seven years' bad luck. **3.** intention or whim; desire: He had a sudden notion to leave. **4. notions.** small useful items, as ribbons, pins, needles, and thread. [Latin nōtiō becoming acquainted, idea.] —**no′tion·al,** adj.

no·to·chord (nō′tə kôrd′) n. stiff supporting rod that extends lengthwise below the spinal cord in lower chordates and is present during the early stages in the development of higher vertebrates. [Greek nōtos back + CHORD².]

no·to·ri·e·ty (nō′tə rī′ə tē) pl., **-ties.** n. quality or state of being notorious.

no·to·ri·ous (nō tôr′ē əs) adj. well-known for something bad; widely and unfavorably known: a notorious criminal, a notorious affair. [Medieval Latin notorius well-known, from Latin nōtus known.] —**no·to′ri·ous·ly,** adv. —**no·to′ri·ous·ness,** n.

no-trump (nō′trump′) n. **1.** bid in bridge in which no suit is named as trump. **2.** hand played without a trump suit. —adj. of or designating such a bid or hand.

Not·ting·ham (not′ing əm) n. city in central England. Pop. (1968), 305,100.

not·with·stand·ing (not′with stan′ding, -with-) prep. in spite of: The match was completed notwithstanding the bad weather. —adv. all the same; nevertheless. —conj. in spite of the fact that; although.

Nouak·chott (nwäk shot′) n. capital of Mauritania, in the western part of the country. Pop. (1965), 15,000.

nou·gat (nōō′gət) n. confection made mainly of sugar or honey and nuts. [French nougat, through Provençal, going back to Latin nux nut.]

nought (nôt) n. naught.

noun (noun) n. word that names or denotes something, as a person, animal, place, thing, action, or quality, and functions as the subject or object of a verb or the object of a preposition. Most English nouns have a plural formed by adding -s or -es and many have a possessive formed by adding -'s. [Anglo-Norman noun name, noun, going back to Latin nōmen.]

nour·ish (nur′ish) v.t. **1.** to sustain by furnishing with food and other substances necessary to life and growth. **2.** to promote the development of; foster: The young man nourished a deep affection for her. [Old French noris-, a stem of norir to bring up, nurture, from Latin nūtrīre to bring up, feed.]

nour·ish·ment (nur′ish mənt) n. **1.** that which nourishes; sustenance. **2.** act of nourishing; being nourished.

nou·veau riche (nōō′vō rēsh′) pl., **nou·veaux riches** (nōō′vō rēsh′). one who has recently become rich, esp. one who is vulgarly ostentatious in displaying his wealth. [French nouveau riche literally, new rich, from nouveau new (going back to Latin novus) + riche rich (of Germanic origin).]

Nov., November.

no·va (nō′və) pl., **no·vae** (nō′vē) or **no·vas.** n. star that rapidly increases in brightness and then gradually fades to its original magnitude. [Modern Latin nova (stella) new (star), from Latin novus new.]

No·va Sco·tia (nō′və skō′shə) province of Canada, in the southeastern part of the country. Area, 21,425 sq. mi. Pop. (1966), 756,039.

nov·el¹ (nov′əl) n. **1.** fictional prose narrative, usually of considerable length and containing detailed treatment of character and plot. **2.** literary form represented by this type of fiction: He read mostly essays on the novel. [Italian novella short story, news, from Latin novella (narrātiō) new kind of (narrative), feminine of novellus new. See NOVEL².]

nov·el² (nov′əl) adj. new and unusual: a novel idea, a novel technique. [Latin novellus new, young, diminutive of novus new.] —**Syn.** see **new.**

nov·el·ette (nov′ə let′) n. short novel.

nov·el·ist (nov′ə list) n. one who writes novels.

nov·el·is·tic (nov′ə lis′tik) adj. of, relating to, or characteristic of novels. —**nov′el·is′ti·cal·ly,** adv.

Musical notes

Whole note	𝅝
Half note	𝅗𝅥
Quarter note	𝅘𝅥
Eighth note	𝅘𝅥𝅮
Sixteenth note	𝅘𝅥𝅯

no·vel·la (nō vel′ə) pl., **-vel·las** or **-vel·le** (-vel′ā). n. short prose narrative of the type developed by Boccaccio, usually moral or satiric. **2.** short novel; novelette. [Italian *novella* short story, news. See NOVEL¹.]

nov·el·ty (nov′əl tē) pl., **-ties.** n. **1.** quality of being new; newness. **2.** that which is new or unusual, as a thing or event. **3. novelties.** small, inexpensive, manufactured articles, as small ornaments or toys. [Old French *novelete* something new, innovation, change, from Late Latin *novellitās* newness, from Latin *novellus* new. See NOVEL².]

No·vem·ber (nō vem′bər) n. eleventh month of the year, containing thirty days. [Latin *November* ninth month in the early Roman calendar (in which March was the first month), from *novem* nine.]

no·ve·na (nō vē′nə) pl., **-nas** or **-nae** (-nē). n. Roman Catholic devotion consisting of prayers said for nine consecutive days. [Medieval Latin *novena*, going back to Latin *novem* nine.]

nov·ice (nov′is) n. **1.** one who is new to an occupation, activity, or the like; beginner. **2.** one who is admitted into a religious order for a probationary period before taking vows. [Old French *novice*, going back to Latin *novīcius* new, from *novus.*]

no·vi·ti·ate (nō vish′ē it, -āt′) *also,* **no·vi·ci·ate.** n. **1.** state or period of being a novice. **2.** novice; beginner. **3.** quarters housing novices in a religious order. [Medieval Latin *novitiatus* the state of being a novice, going back to Latin *novus* new.]

No·vo·cain (nō′və kān′) n. *Trademark.* procaine. [Latin *novus* new + (CO)CAINE.]

No·vo·kuz·netsk (nō′və kooz netsk′) n. city in the south-central Soviet Union, in the Russian Republic. Pop. (1970 est.), 499,000.

No·vo·si·birsk (nō′və si bērsk′) n. city in the south-central Soviet Union, in the Russian Republic. Pop. (1970 est.), 1,161,000.

now (nou) *adv.* **1.** at the present time: *He is now living in London.* **2.** without delay; at once; immediately: *She must leave now.* **3.** a very short while ago: *He arrived just now, while you were out.* **4.** in a moment; shortly: *She is going to read now.* **5.** under the present circumstances: *Since Helen lost her keys, she must now wait until her brother comes home.* **6.** at the point of time referred to; then: *The war was now over, and the soldier could return to his family.* **7. now and again** or **now and then,** from time to time; occasionally. —*conj.* since (usually with *that*): *Now that we are alone, we can speak freely.* —*n.* present time; present: *The time to act is now.* —*interj.* used to express warning, sympathy, or reproach. [Old English *nū* at the present time, immediately.]

now·a·days (nou′ə dāz′) *adv.* at the present time; during these days.

no·way (nō′wā′) *also,* **no·ways.** *adv.* in no way; not at all.

no·where (nō′hwâr′, -wâr′) *adv.* **1.** to, in, or at no place; not anywhere. **2. to get nowhere,** to make absolutely no progress; fail completely. **3. nowhere near.** *Informal.* not nearly. —*n.* **1.** no place. **2.** place or state of obscurity or insignificance. [Old English *nāhwǣr* in no place.]

no·wise (nō′wīz′) *adv.* in no way; noway.

nox·ious (nok′shəs) *adj.* **1.** very harmful to the health; injurious: *noxious gases.* **2.** morally harmful. [Latin *noxius* injurious, from *noxa* harm, hurt.] —**nox′ious·ly,** *adv.* —**nox′ious·ness,** *n.*

Noyes, Alfred (noiz) 1880–1958, English poet.

noz·zle (noz′əl) n. projecting, often adjustable, spout at the end of a hose, pipe, or the like that serves as an outlet for a liquid or gas. [Diminutive of NOSE.]

Np, neptunium.

N.P., Notary Public.

N.S. 1. New Style. **2.** Nova Scotia.

N.S.P.C.A., National Society for the Prevention of Cruelty to Animals.

N.T., New Testament.

nth (enth) *adj.* **1.** relating to or denoting an indefinitely large or small number or value. **2. to the nth degree** (or **power**). **a.** to any degree or power, usually a high one. **b.** to the greatest extreme; to the utmost.

nt. wt., net weight.

nu (nōō, nū) n. thirteenth letter of the Greek alphabet (N, ν), corresponding to the English letter *N, n.*

nu·ance (nōō′äns, nū′-, nōō äns′, nū-) n. slight or delicate shade, as of tone, expression, or meaning. [French *nuance*, from *nuer* to shade, cloud, from *nue* cloud, going back to Latin *nūbēs.*]

nub (nub) n. **1.** knob or protuberance. **2.** small piece or lump: *a nub of a pencil, a nub of coal.* **3.** *Informal.* point or gist, as of a story. [Form of dialectal English *knub* small lump, swelling, from Middle Low German *knubbe* knot of a tree, knob.]

nub·bin (nub′in) n. **1.** small or imperfect ear of corn. **2.** any small or imperfect fruit. [Diminutive of NUB.]

Nu·bi·a (nōō′bē ə, nū′-) n. ancient country in what is now southern Egypt and the northern Sudan.

Nu·bi·an (nōō′bē ən, nū′-) n. **1.** member of the people of Nubia. **2.** language spoken in Nubia. —*adj.* of or relating to Nubia, its people, or their language.

Nu·bi·an Desert (nōō′bē ən, nū′-) desert region in the northeastern part of the Sudan, extending from the Red Sea to the Nile.

nu·bile (nōō′bil, -bīl, nū′-) *adj.* of an age suitable for marriage; marriageable. [Latin *nūbilis,* from *nūbere* to marry.] —**nu·bil′i·ty,** *n.*

nu·cle·ar (nōō′klē ər, nū′-) *adj.* **1.** of, relating to, or forming a nucleus. **2.** of, relating to, or involving the use of atomic nuclei.

nuclear energy, energy obtained from the nucleus of the atom.

nuclear fission, fission *(def. 2).*

nuclear fusion, fusion *(def. 5).*

nuclear physics, branch of physics that deals with the structure and properties of atomic nuclei.

nuclear reactor, device in which a nuclear chain reaction can be initiated, sustained, and controlled, used for generating heat or producing radiation.

nu·cle·ate (nōō′klē it, -āt′, nū′-) **-at·ed, -at·ing.** *v.t.* to form into a nucleus. —*v.i.* to form a nucleus. —*adj.* having a nucleus. [Late Latin *nucleātus,* past participle of *nucleāre* to become like a kernel, from Latin *nucleus* kernel, nut, diminutive of *nux* nut.] —**nu′cle·a′tion,** **nu′cle·a′tor,** *n.*

nu·cle·ic acid (nōō klē′ik, nū-) group of complex organic compounds found in all living cells, consisting of a combination of phosphoric acid, a sugar, and a nitrogenous base derived from purine or pyrimidine. The two main types of nucleic acid are DNA and RNA.

nu·cle·o·lus (nōō klē′ə ləs, nū-) n. small round body in the nucleus of a cell. [Latin *nucleolus* little nut, diminutive of *nucleus* nut, kernel, diminutive of *nux* nut.]

nu·cle·on (nōō′klē on′, nū′-) n. proton or neutron, esp. one constituting a part of the atomic nucleus. See **subatomic particle** for table.

nu·cle·on·ics (nōō′klē on′iks, nū-) n. branch of science or technology that deals with atomic nuclei, esp. with the production and application of nuclear energy.

nu·cle·o·tide (nōō′klē ə tīd′, nū′-) n. any of various organic compounds consisting of phosphoric acid, a sugar, and a purine or pyrimidine base. Nucleotides are the fundamental unit of nucleic acid.

nu·cle·us (nōō′klē əs, nū′-) pl., **-cle·i** (-klē ′ī′) or **-cle·us·es.** n. **1.** central or essential part around which other parts are grouped or collected; core: *The nucleus of the building is a large open court. There is a nucleus of truth in his story.* **2.** basis for further growth and development: *These volumes form the nucleus of a fine library.* **3.** small, dense, usually round or oval body located near the center of a plant or animal cell, surrounded by a delicate membrane and containing most of the cell's hereditary material. The nucleus is essential to growth, reproduction, metabolism, and other vital activities. **4.** positively charged central portion of an atom, containing most of the atom's mass and consisting of protons and neutrons, except in hydrogen, which consists of one proton only. **5.** central portion of the head of a comet. [Latin *nucleus* kernel, nut, diminutive of *nux* nut.]

nude (nōōd, nūd) *adj.* without clothing or other covering; unclothed; bare. —*n.* **1.** unclothed human figure, esp. one represented in a painting or other work of art. **2.** state of being unclothed: *in the nude.* [Latin *nūdus* naked.] —**nude′ly,** *adv.* —**nude′ness,** *n.* —**Syn.** *adj.* see **bare¹.**

nudge (nuj) **nudged, nudg·ing.** *v.t.* to push gently or touch, esp. to attract attention: *He nudged me with his elbow.* —*n.* gentle push or touch. [Of uncertain origin.]

nud·ism (nōō′diz′əm, nū′-) n. belief in or practice of living in the nude.

nud·ist (nōō′dist, nū′-) n. one who believes in or practices nudism. —*adj.* of or relating to nudism or nudists.

nu·di·ty (nōō′də tē, nū′-) pl., **-ties.** n. **1.** state of being nude; nakedness. **2.** something nude.

nu·ga·to·ry (nōō′gə tôr′ē, nū′-) *adj.* **1.** of little importance; insignificant; trifling: *He wasted time making nugatory comments.* **2.** without force or authority; ineffective; invalid. [Latin *nūgātōrius* trifling, going back to *nūgae* trifles.]

nug·get (nug′it) n. lump, esp. a lump of native gold. [Possibly from dialectal English *nug* lump; of uncertain origin.]

nui·sance (nōō′səns, nū′-) n. **1.** one who or that which annoys or offends. **2.** *Law.* that which annoys or offends another or others, as by

Nucleus (protons and neutrons)

Electrons

Nucleus of an atom

Nozzle

obstructing the use of property or by violating the laws of decency. [Old French *nuisance* offense, hurt, from *nuire* to harm, from Latin *nocēre.*]

nuisance tax, tax collected in small amounts from the consumer.

Nu·ku·a·lo·fa (noo'koō ə lō'fə) *n.* capital and chief port of Tonga. Pop. (1966 est.), 15,545.

null (nul) *adj.* **1.** without force or authority; not binding; invalid. **2.** insignificant; ineffective: *He based his argument on proofs that were considered null.* **3.** amounting to nothing; nonexistent. **4.** *Mathematics.* of or relating to a set that contains no elements or members. **5. null and void.** without legal force; invalid. [Latin *nūllus* not any, from *ne* not + *ūllus* any.]

nul·li·fi·ca·tion (nul'ə fi kā'shən) *n.* **1.** act of nullifying; being nullified. **2.** refusal of a state to recognize or enforce a federal law within its borders.

nul·li·fy (nul'ə fī') -fied, -fy·ing. *v.t.* **1.** to make void; declare invalid; annul; to *nullify a law.* **2.** to make useless; destroy. [Late Latin *nūllificāre* to despise, from Latin *nūllus* not any + *facere* to make.] —**nul'li·fi'er,** *n.*

nul·li·ty (nul'ə tē) *pl.,* **-ties.** *n.* **1.** quality or state of being null; nothingness. **2.** that which is null. [Medieval Latin *nullitas* nothingness, invalidity, from Latin *nūllus* not any.]

Num., Numbers.

numb (num) *adj.* deprived of sensation or movement: *to be numb with cold. He was numb with fear.* —*v.t.* to make numb. [Middle English *nomen,* past participle of *nimen* to take, seize, from Old English *niman.*] —**numb'ly,** *adv.* —**numb'ness,** *n.*

num·ber (num'bər) *n.* **1.a.** mathematical concept that indicates how many units or objects are contained in a certain group; that which tells how many members there are in a set. **b.** word or symbol, or group of words or symbols, representing such a concept; numeral. **2.** specified amount, as of persons or things; total; sum: *The hostess increased the number of invited guests to thirty.* **3.** unspecified amount, as of persons or things; quantity: *A number of people gathered in front of the display. He had read a number of books on the subject.* **4.** numeral given to or denoting a person or thing: *What is the number of his room?* **5.** one of a series that has been given numbers: *The football team was rated number one in all the polls.* **6.** one of the songs or other musical compositions on a program. **7.** single issue of a newspaper or periodical. **8.** *Informal.* one who or that which arouses interest, as an attractive girl. **9.** *Grammar.* form or property of a word that indicates whether the word is singular or plural. **10. numbers. a.** numerical superiority: *The army overpowered the invaders by force of numbers.* **b.** arithmetic. **c.** metrical lines; poetry. **d.** numbers racket. **11. to get** (or **have**) **one's number.** *Informal.* to discover or know one's true motives or character. **12. without number,** too many to be counted. —*v.t.* **1.** to ascertain the number of; count. **2.** to give a number or numbers to. **3.** to amount to or include: *The freshman class numbers over a thousand students.* **4.** to limit the number of: *The sands are numbered that make up my life* (Shakespeare, *Henry VI*). —*v.i.* **1.** to amount to a group or total: *The contest winners numbered in the hundreds.* **2.** to list or recite numbers: *Number from one to ten on your papers.* [Old French *nombre* unit (in counting), indefinite quantity, from Latin *numerus.*] —**num'ber·er,** *n.*

num·ber·less (num'bər lis) *adj.* **1.** too numerous to be counted; innumerable. **2.** without a number.

number line, line on which points are identified with real numbers.

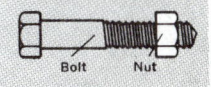
Number line

number one *Informal.* oneself: *In the future he's only going to look after number one and no one else.*

Num·bers (num'bərz) *n.* fourth book of the Old Testament, containing the census of the Israelites after their escape from Egyptian bondage. ▲ construed as singular.

numbers racket, illegal lottery in which bets are made that a particular number will appear in an unpredictable statistical total, as the amount of money wagered at a race track in a single day. Also, **numbers game, pol'i·cy.**

number theory, branch of mathematics dealing with the properties and relations of integers.

numb·skull (num'skul') numskull.

nu·mer·a·ble (noo'mər ə bəl, nū'-) *adj.* capable of being counted.

nu·mer·al (noo'mər əl, nū'-) *n.* **1.** symbol or a group of symbols representing a number, as 7 or VII. **2.** word standing for such a symbol, as *seven.* **3. numerals.** cloth numbers, usually the last two numbers of a student's year of graduation, awarded by a school for excellence in some sport. —*adj.* of, relating to, or representing a number or numbers. [Late Latin *numerālis* relating to number, from Latin *numerus* unit (in counting), quantity.]

nu·mer·ate (noo'mə rāt', nū'-) -at·ed, -at·ing. *v.i.* to number; count.

[Latin *numerātus,* past participle of *numerāre* to count, *numerus* unit (in counting), quantity.]

nu·mer·a·tion (noo'mə rā'shən, nū'-) *n.* **1.** act or process of numbering: *a numeration of the town's inhabitants.* **2.** system of representing numbers by symbols.

nu·mer·a·tor (noo'mə rā'tər, nū'-) *n.* **1.** number above or to the left of the line in a fraction, indicating the number of equal parts that are being considered; dividend. In the fraction ½, *1* is the numerator. **2.** one who or that which numbers. [Late Latin *numerātor* one who numbers, from Latin *numerāre* to count, number.]

nu·mer·i·cal (noo mer'i kəl, nū-) *adj.* of, relating to, or represented by numbers. Also, **nu·mer'ic. —nu·mer'i·cal·ly,** *adv.*

nu·mer·ol·o·gy (noo'mə rol'ə jē) *n.* study of the occult significance of numbers and of their supposed influence on the course of events. —**nu'mer·ol'o·gist,** *n.*

nu·mer·ous (noo'mər əs, nū'-) *adj.* **1.** forming a large number; many: *We visited them on numerous occasions.* **2.** containing a large number; abundant: *She has a numerous collection of antiques.* [Latin *numerōsus* plentiful, from *numerus* unit (in counting), quantity.] —**nu'mer·ous·ly,** *adv.* —**nu'mer·ous·ness,** *n.*

Nu·mid·i·a (noo mid'ē ə, nū-) *n.* ancient country in northwestern Africa, roughly comprising what is now Algeria. —**Nu·mid'i·an,** *adj.*

nu·mis·mat·ics (noo'miz mat'iks, -mis-, nū'-) *n.* collection or study of coins, paper money, or medals. [French *numismatique* numismatics, from Latin *numisma* coin, from Greek *nomisma* custom, coin.] —**nu'mis·mat'ic,** *adj.* —**nu·mis·ma·tist** (noo miz'mə tist, -mis'-, nū-), *n.*

num·skull (num'skul') *also,* **numb·skull.** *n.* stupid person; blockhead. [NUMB + SKULL.]

nun (nun) *n.* member of a religious order for women, living under vows in a convent and leading a life of prayer and good works. [Old English *nunne,* from Late Latin *nonna,* feminine of *nonnus* monk.]

nun·ci·o (nun'shē ō') *pl.,* **-ci·os.** *n.* permanent ambassador representing the pope. [Obsolete Italian *nuncio* ambassador, from Latin *nūntius* messenger.]

nun·ner·y (nun'ər ē) *pl.,* **-ner·ies.** *n.* residence of a society of nuns.

nup·tial (nup'shəl) *adj.* **1.** of or relating to marriage or the marriage ceremony: *nuptial bliss, the nuptial feast.* —*n.* usually, **nuptials.** marriage ceremony; wedding. [Latin *nuptiālis* relating to a wedding, from *nuptiae* wedding.]

Nu·rem·berg (noor'əm burg', nyoor'-) *n.* city in southern West Germany, where Nazis were placed on trial after World War II. Pop. (1968 est.), 466,668. Also, *German,* **Nürn·berg** (noorn'berk').

nurse (nurs) *n.* **1.** one who is trained to attend the sick or injured, usually under the direction of a physician. **2.** woman employed to attend children; nursemaid. **3.** woman employed to feed babies by suckling; wet nurse. —*v.t.,* **nursed, nurs·ing. 1.** to attend (the sick or injured); act as a nurse for. **2.** to feed (a baby) from the breast; suckle. **3.** to try to cure or heal (an illness or injury): *to nurse a sore throat with aspirin and plenty of rest.* **4.** to handle or use with care: *He nursed his weak knee by limping slightly.* **5.** to promote the growth or development of; foster: *to nurse a small tree, to nurse a talent.* **6.** to keep in the mind; harbor: *to nurse an idea, to nurse a grudge.* **7.** to consume slowly: *to nurse a drink.* —*v.i.* **1.** to be employed or work as a nurse. **2.** to suckle a baby. **3.** to be fed from the breast. [Old French *nurrice* one who nurses an infant or takes care of a child, from Late Latin *nūtrīcia* governess, wet nurse, going back to Latin *nūtrīx* wet nurse, nourisher.]

nurse·maid (nurs'mād') *n.* woman employed to attend children.

nurs·er·y (nur'sər ē) *pl.,* **-er·ies.** *n.* **1.** room set apart for small children, esp. a baby's bedroom. **2.** place where plants, esp. trees and shrubs, are raised for sale.

nurs·er·y·man (nur'sər ē mən) *pl.,* **-men.** *n.* one who owns or works in a nursery that raises and sells plants.

nursery rhyme, short, rhymed verse for young children.

nursery school, school for children too young for kindergarten.

nurs·ling (nurs'ling) *n.* **1.** one who is nursed, as a baby. **2.** one who or that which receives careful and loving attention.

nur·ture (nur'chər) -tured, -tur·ing. *v.t.* **1.** to nourish; feed. **2.** to educate or foster. —*n.* **1.** that which nourishes; food. **2.** act or instance of educating or fostering. [Anglo-Norman *nurture* nourishment, from Late Latin *nūtrītūra* a nursing, suckling, from *nūtrīre* to feed, bring up.] —**nur'tur·er,** *n.*

nut (nut) *n.* **1.** dry fruit of a plant, containing one or more kernels and having a hard, woody shell. **2.** kernel of such a fruit. **3.** block of metal or wood with a screw thread around a central opening into which the threaded end of a bolt fits. **4.** *Slang.* eccentric or crazy person.

Bolt · Nut

Nut (def. 3)

5. *Slang.* enthusiast; devotee; buff. **6. hard** (or **tough**) **nut to crack.** *Informal.* one who or that which is difficult to understand or deal with. —*v.i.,* **nut·ted, nut·ting.** to hunt for or gather nuts. [Middle English *note* this fruit, from Old English *hnutu.*]

nut·crack·er (nut′krak′ər) *n.* **1.** utensil for cracking nuts. **2.** any of various birds, genus *Nucifraga,* of the crow family, found in northern evergreen forests, having a long, pointed bill, and feeding on pine seeds and nuts.

nut·gall (nut′gôl′) *n.* nutlike gall, esp. on oaks. Also, **gall′nut′.**

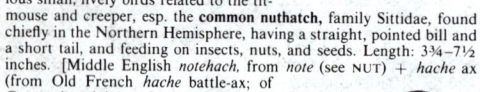

Nutcracker

nut·hatch (nut′hach′) *n.* any of various small, lively birds related to the titmouse and creeper, esp. the **common nuthatch,** family Sittidae, found chiefly in the Northern Hemisphere, having a straight, pointed bill and a short tail, and feeding on insects, nuts, and seeds. Length: 3¾–7½ inches. [Middle English *notehach,* from *note* (see NUT) + *hache* ax (from Old French *hache* battle-ax; of Germanic origin); referring to the way it hacks nuts open for food.]

nut·meat (nut′mēt′) *n.* edible kernel of a nut.

nut·meg (nut′meg′) *n.* **1.** hard, aromatic seed of an evergreen tree, *Myristica fragrans,* dried and ground or grated and used as a spice. **2.** tree from which this seed is derived, bearing light-green or yellowish-green leaves and yellow flowers. [Partial translation and modification of Old French *nois muguete* nutmeg seed; literally, nut with the smell of musk, going back to Latin *nux* nut + *muscus* (see MUSK).]

Nuthatch

nu·tri·a (nōō′trē ə, nū′-) *n.* **1.** coypu. **2.** soft, thick, velvety fur of the coypu, often dyed to resemble beaver. [Spanish *nutria* otter, from Latin *lutra.*]

nu·tri·ent (nōō′trē ənt, nū′-) *adj.* providing nourishment; nutritious. —*n.* nutritious substance that is essential for body functioning. Proteins, fats, carbohydrates, minerals, and vitamins are all sources of nutrients. [Latin *nŭtriēns,* present participle of *nŭtrīre* to feed, bring up.]

nu·tri·ment (nōō′trə mənt, nū′-) *n.* anything that nourishes; food. [Latin *nŭtrīmentum,* from *nŭtrīre* to feed, bring up.]

nu·tri·tion (nōō trish′ən, nū-) *n.* **1.** process by which essential nutrients are taken and absorbed into body tissues. **2.** nourishment: *Slum children often lack proper nutrition.* [Late Latin *nŭtrītiō* nourishment, from Latin *nŭtrīre* to feed.] —**nu·tri′tion·al,** *adj.* —**nu·tri′tion·al·ly,** *adv.*

nu·tri·tion·ist (nōō trish′ə nist, nū-) *n.* one who specializes in the study of nutrition.

nu·tri·tious (nōō trish′əs, nū-) *adj.* containing or giving nourishment; nourishing. [Latin *nŭtrītius,* going back to *nŭtrīre* to feed, bring up.] —**nu·tri′tious·ly,** *adv.* —**nu·tri′tious·ness,** *n.*

nu·tri·tive (nōō′tri tiv, nū′-) *adj.* **1.** giving nourishment; nutritious: *a nutritive diet.* **2.** of or relating to nutrition: *the nutritive functions.* —**nu′tri·tive·ly,** *adv.*

nuts (nuts) *adj. Slang.* **1.** eccentric or crazy. **2.** in love with or very enthusiastic about.

nut·shell (nut′shel′) *n.* **1.** hard shell of a nut. **2. in a nutshell.** in a few words.

nut·ty (nut′ē) **-ti·er, -ti·est.** *adj.* **1.** filled with or producing nuts. **2.** having the flavor of nuts. **3.** *Slang.* eccentric or crazy; nuts. —**nut′ti·ly,** *adv.* —**nut′ti·ness,** *n.*

nux vom·i·ca (nuks vom′i kə) **1.** drug obtained from the seed of an Indian tree, *Strychnos nux-vomica,* containing strychnine and other alkaloids, used in medicine. **2.** the tree itself. [Modern Latin *nux vomica* literally, vomiting nut, going back to Latin *nux* nut + *vomere* to vomit.]

nuz·zle (nuz′əl) **-zled, -zling.** *v.t., v.i.* **1.** to touch or rub with the nose: *The dog nuzzled his master.* **2.** to press or lie close; nestle; cuddle. [NOSE + -LE.]

NW, northwest; northwestern.

N.W.T., Northwest Territories.

N.Y., New York.

Ny·as·a, Lake (nyä′sə, nī as′ə) large lake in southeastern Africa.

Ny·as·a·land (nyä′sə land′, nī as′ə-) *n.* Malawi.

N.Y.C., New York City.

ny·lon (nī′lon) *n.* **1.** any of a group of strong, durable, synthetic substances that are used esp. to make thread for fabric, bristles for brushes, and automobile tires, tool handles, and other products. **2.** fabric woven with threads made from this substance. **3. nylons.** stockings made of nylon.

nymph (nimf) *n.* **1.** *Classical Mythology.* any of various female deities living esp. in forests, hills, or rivers, and usually represented as beautiful maidens. **2.** beautiful young woman; damsel. **3.** insect in the larval stage in incomplete metamorphosis. [Latin *nympha,* from Greek *nymphē.*]

N.Z., New Zealand.

---

at; āpe; cär; end; mē; it; īce; hot; ōld; fôrk; wood; fōōl; oil; out; up; ūse; turn; sing; thin; **this**; zh in treasure; ə in ago, taken, pencil, lemon, circus.

o, O (ō) pl. **o's, O's.** n. **1.** fifteenth letter of the English alphabet. **2.** shape of this letter or something having such a shape. **3.** zero.

O (ō) interj. **1.** used in direct address, esp. to express earnestness or solemnity: *O heart, how fares it with thee now?* (Tennyson, 1850). **2.** oh.

O, oxygen.

o' (ə, ō) prep. **1.** of: *man-o'-war.* **2.** Archaic. on.

o-, form of **ob,** before *m,* as in *omit.*

oaf (ōf) pl., **oafs.** n. stupid, clumsy person. [Old Norse *ālfr* elf.] —**oaf'ish,** adj.

O·a·hu (ō ä'hōō) n. one of the principal islands of Hawaii. Area, 595 sq. mi. Pop. (1970), 629,176.

oak (ōk) n. **1.** any of a large group of trees or shrubs, genus *Quercus,* of the beech family, bearing acorns and found esp. in northern temperate regions. **2.** hard, sturdy wood of this tree, finest of all timber woods. [Old English *āc* the tree.]

oak·en (ō'kən) adj. made of oak.

oak gall, boil-like swelling that occurs on the leaves and stems of oak trees, caused by injury or insects. Also, **oak apple.**

Oak·land (ōk'lənd) n. city in western California opposite San Francisco, on San Francisco Bay. Pop. (1970), 361,561.

oak leaf cluster, small bronze decoration awarded to members of the U.S. armed forces who already hold a decoration but merit another award of the same type, pinned to the face of the previous decoration.

Oak·ley, Annie (ōk'lē) 1860–1926, U.S. markswoman; full name, Phoebe Anne Oakley Mozee.

Oak Ridge, city in eastern Tennessee, a major atomic research and production center. Pop. (1970), 28,319.

oa·kum (ō'kəm) n. loose fiber obtained by untwisting and picking apart old ropes, often used for filling up seams and cracks in a boat or ship. [Old English *ācumba* tow²; literally, off combing; referring to *combing* the tow out of the flax before spinning.]

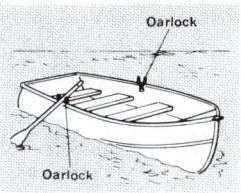

Oarlock

Oarlock

oar (ôr) n. **1.** long, usually wooden, pole with a flat or curved blade at one end, used to propel or steer a boat. **2.** one who rows a boat; oarsman. —*v.t.* to propel with or as with oars; row. —*v.i.* to advance by or as by rowing. [Old English *ār* implement for propelling a boat.]

oar·lock (ôr'lok') n. device, usually U-shaped, for holding an oar in place while rowing. Also, **row'·lock'.** [Old English *ārloc.*]

oars·man (ôrz'mən) pl., **-men.** n. one who rows a boat.

OAS, Organization of American States.

o·a·sis (ō ā'sis, ō'ə sis) pl., **-ses** (-sēz) n. place in the desert made fertile by a permanent or nearly permanent supply of water. [Late Latin *oasis* name of fertile spots in the Libyan desert, from Greek *oasis;* of Egyptian origin.]

oat (ōt) n. **1.** also, **oats.** cereal grain of the plant, *Avena sativa,* of the grass family, enclosed in a thick hull, cultivated mainly for animal feed. **2.** also, **oats.** the plant itself, having flat grasslike leaves or bluish green. **3.** any of various related grasses, as the wild oat. **4. to feel one's oats.** *Informal.* **a.** to be lively, high-spirited, or frisky. **b.** to feel self-assured or important and act accordingly. [Old English *āte* grain of a cereal plant.]

oat·cake (ōt'kāk') n. thin, hard oatmeal cake.

Oat

oat·en (ōt'ən) adj. relating to, containing, or made of oats, oatmeal, or oat straw.

oath (ōth) pl., **oaths** (ōthz, ōths). n. **1.** formal declaration bound by an appeal to God or a person or thing considered sacred to witness the truth of a statement or the binding character of a promise. **2.** careless or irreverent use of the name of God or a person or thing considered sacred to add emphasis or express anger. **3.** profane expression or utterance; swearword. [Old English *āth* formal statement bound by an appeal to God or something held sacred.]

oat·meal (ōt'mēl') n. **1.** meal made from oats; ground or rolled oats. **2.** porridge prepared from this.

ob- prefix **1.** in opposition to; against: *obstruct.* **2.** over; upon: *obscure.* **3.** toward; to: *obtrude.* **4.** completely: *obsolete.* **5.** contrary to the usual position; inversely: *oblate.* [Latin *ob* toward, against.]

ob., obiit.

O·ba·di·ah (ō'bə dī'ə) n. **1.** Hebrew prophet of the sixth century B.C. **2.** book of Old Testament prophecies, the shortest book of the Bible, attributed to him. Also, in Douay Bible, **Ab·di·as.**

ob·bli·ga·to (ob'li gä'tō) also, **ob·li·ga·to.** *Music. adj.* (of an accompaniment or part) essential to the performance of a composition. —*n. pl.* **-tos.** accompaniment or part of independent importance, esp. an instrumental solo accompanying a vocal piece. [Italian *obbligato* obligatory, past participle of *obbligare* to compel, bind, from Latin *obligāre* to bind; referring to music essential to a performance, such as an accompaniment.]

ob·du·ra·cy (ob'dər ə sē, ob'dyər-) n. state or quality of being obdurate.

ob·du·rate (ob'dər it, ob'dyər-) adj. **1.** stubborn; unyielding; obstinate. **2.** unmoved by feelings of pity or regret; hardhearted: *an obdurate murderer.* [Latin *obdūrātus,* past participle of *obdūrāre* to harden.] —**ob'du·rate·ly,** adv. —**ob'du·rate·ness,** n.

o·be·di·ence (ō bē'dē əns) n. act of obeying; being obedient.

o·be·di·ent (ō bē'dē ənt) adj. tending or willing to obey or comply with something, as a rule, order, or law; submissive to authority. [Old French *obedient,* from Latin *obēdiēns,* present participle of *obēdīre* to hearken, serve.] —**o·be'di·ent·ly,** adv.

Syn. **Obedient, compliant, submissive** mean yielding to the will and guidance of another. **Obedient** may be used when one yields dutifully to the restraints and commands of a superior person whose authority one recognizes: *Joan was a very obedient child who never disregarded her parents' wishes.* **Compliant** may be used when one consistently bends to the demands of another meekly and unquestioningly: *Four years of army life had made Nat compliant.* **Submissive** may be used when one is subject and subservient to the control of another and humbly obedient to his orders through an innate incapacity to assert one's own will: *After many years of harsh rule, the people had become submissive.*

o·bei·sance (ō bā'səns, ō bē'-) n. **1.** bodily movement or gesture, as a bow or curtsy, indicating or expressing obedience or respect. **2.** deference, respect, or reverent regard given or shown; homage. [Old French *obeissance* obedience, from *obeir* to obey, from Latin *obēdīre* to hearken, yield, serve.]

ob·e·lisk (ob'ə lisk') n. four-sided, usually monolithic, stone pillar that tapers as it rises and terminates in a pyramid, often used as a monument in ancient Egypt. [Latin *obeliscus* small spit², obelisk, from Greek *obeliskos,* diminutive of *obelos* a spit², obelisk.]

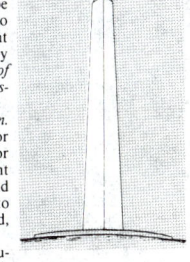

Obelisk

at; āpe; cär; end; mē; it; īce; hot; ōld; fôrk; wood; fōōl; oil; out; up; ūse; turn; sing; thin; this; zh in treasure; ə in ago, taken, pencil, lemon, circus.

695

O·ber·am·mer·gau (ō′bə rä′mər gou′) *n.* village in southern West Germany, noted for the Passion play performed there every ten years. Pop. (1961 est.), 4600.

O·ber·hau·sen (ō′bər hou′zən) *n.* city in northwestern West Germany. Pop. (1968 est.), 250,953.

O·ber·on (ō′bə ron′) *n.* *Medieval Legend and Literature.* king of the fairies and husband of Titania.

o·bese (ō bēs′) *adj.* extremely fat or fleshy. [Latin *obēsus* fat; literally, that has eaten himself fat, past participle of *obedere* to eat, eat away.] **—o·bese′ness,** *n.*

o·bes·i·ty (ō bē′sə tē) *n.* condition of being obese.

o·bey (ō bā′) *v.t.* **1.** to comply with or carry out the orders, commands, requests, or instructions of: *The child obeyed his parents.* **2.** to comply with or carry out: *to obey the law, to obey orders.* **3.** to be guided, controlled, or actuated by: *to obey one's conscience.* *—v.i.* to be obedient. [Old French *obeir,* from Latin *obēdīre* to hearken, yield, serve.]

ob·fus·cate (ob fus′kāt, ob′fəs kāt′) **-cat·ed, -cat·ing.** *v.t.* **1.** to make unclear; confuse; muddle. **2.** to make obscure or indistinct; darken. [Late Latin *obfuscātus,* past participle of *obfuscāre* to darken, going back to Latin *ob-* (see OB-) + *fuscus* dark.] **—ob′fus·ca′tion,** *n.*

Obi

o·bi (ō′bē) *n.* broad sash worn by women with traditional Japanese dress. [Japanese *obi.*]

o·bi·it (ō′bē it, ob′ē-) *Latin.* he (or she) died.

o·bit (ō′bit, ob′it) *n.* *Informal.* obituary.

ob·i·ter dic·tum (ob′i tər dik′təm) *pl.,* **ob·i·ter dic·ta** (dik′tə). **1.** opinion expressed by a judge, not directly related to the case in question and therefore not binding. **2.** any incidental statement or remark. [Latin *obiter dictum* something said in passing.]

o·bit·u·ar·y (ō bich′o͞o er′ē) *pl.,* **-ar·ies.** *n.* notice of a death, esp. in a newspaper, often including a short biography of the deceased. *—adj.* relating to or recording a death. [Medieval Latin *obituarius* record of a death, relating to death, from Latin *obitus* death.]

obj. 1. object. **2.** objection. **3.** objective.

ob·ject (*n.,* ob′jikt, -jekt; *v.,* əb jekt′) *n.* **1.** anything that can be seen or touched; material thing. **2.** one who or that which is the focus of feeling, thought, or action. **3.** thing aimed at; goal: *The object of his visit was not clear.* **4.a.** word or group of words that receive or are affected by the action of the verb. **b.** word or group of words expressing a relationship to a preposition. **5.** *Philosophy.* anything that is conceived of or apprehended by the mind. *—v.i.* **1.** to offer a reason or argument against; have or raise an objection (with *to*): *The defense lawyer objected to the prosecution's badgering of the witness.* **2.** to express or feel disapproval: *Mother objected to his rudeness.* *—v.t.* to bring forward or offer in opposition or criticism; state as an objection. [Latin *objectus* a casting before, something presented to the sight, from *obicere* to cast before or in the way of, oppose.] **—ob·jec′tor,** *n.*

ob·jec·ti·fy (əb jek′tə fī′) **-fied, -fy·ing.** *v.t.* to express in concrete form; make objective; externalize.

ob·jec·tion (əb jek′shən) *n.* **1.** cause or reason for opposing, disliking, or disapproving of something: *Mother's only objection to our going out was that it was too late.* **2.** statement or feeling of opposition, dislike, or disapproval: *He showed his objection to our presence by stalking out of the room.* **3.** act of objecting.

ob·jec·tion·a·ble (əb jek′shə nə bəl) *adj.* deserving of or arousing dislike or disapproval; offensive: *a highly objectionable decision.* **—ob·jec′tion·a·bly,** *adv.*

ob·jec·tive (əb jek′tiv) *adj.* **1.** unaffected by personal feelings or prejudices; without emotional or intellectual bias; detached: *The writer tried to be as objective as possible in evaluating his latest work.* **2.** concerned with or emphasizing external or observable phenomena rather than personal thoughts or feelings. **3.** having actual existence independent of the mind; real: *the objective universe.* **4.** designating the case of the object of a transitive verb or preposition. **5.** being the object toward which effort is directed: *The walled city was the army's objective point.* *—n.* **1.** that toward which effort is directed; aim. **2.a.** objective case. **b.** word in this case; object. **3.** lens or lenses nearest to the object being observed through an optical instrument, as a telescope, microscope, or camera. [Medieval Latin *objectivus* relating to an object, from Latin *objectus* object. See OBJECT.] **—ob·jec′tive·ly,** *adv.* **—ob·jec′tive·ness,** *n.*

Syn. *n.* **1. Objective, goal, end** mean the purpose of one's acts. **Objective** may be used to designate a concrete and clearly formulated purpose toward which one's efforts are directed: *The objective of the new organization was to provide free legal aid to the poor.* **Goal** may be used to designate the ideal aim which one strives for against odds and to the attainment of which one's ambitions and energies are totally committed: *The senator's goal was nothing less than the presidency.* **End** may be used to designate the outcome or result and suggests remoteness, finality, and a course of action planned in advance: *The end does not always justify the means.*

ob·jec·tiv·i·ty (ob′jek tiv′ə tē) *n.* **1.** state or quality of being objective. **2.** external or material reality.

object lesson, act or incident that demonstrates or exemplifies some moral or principle.

ob·jet d'art (ōb zhā där′) *pl.,* **ob·jets d'art** (ōb zhā där′). *French.* something, as a vase, that has artistic value.

ob·jur·gate (ob′jər gāt′, əb jur′gāt) **-gat·ed, -gat·ing.** *v.t.* to rebuke severely; scold harshly. [Latin *objurgātus,* past participle of *objurgāre* to scold.] **—ob′jur·ga′tion,** *n.*

ob·jur·ga·to·ry (əb jur′gə tôr′ē) *adj.* conveying or containing a sharp rebuke.

ob·late (ob′lāt, ob lāt′) *adj.* (of a spheroid) flattened at the poles. [Modern Latin *oblatus* stretched, from Latin *ob-* (see OB-) + *lātus* carried, past participle of *ferre* to bring, carry.]

ob·la·tion (ob lā′shən) *n.* **1.** act of offering a gift, sacrifice, or worship to God or another sacred being, esp. the offering of bread and wine in the Holy Communion service. **2.** anything offered as a gift or sacrifice, esp. the bread and wine of Holy Communion. [Late Latin *oblātiō* offering, from Latin *oblātus,* past participle of *offerre* to present, bring before, from *ob* toward + *ferre* to bring, carry.]

ob·li·gate (ob′lə gāt′) **-gat·ed, -gat·ing.** *v.t.* to bind morally or legally, as by a contract, promise, or sense of duty. [Latin *obligātus,* past participle of *obligāre* to bind.]

ob·li·ga·tion (ob′lə gā′shən) *n.* **1.** binding or constraining power, as of a law, promise, or sense of duty: *We are under no obligation to him.* **2.** that which one is morally or legally bound to do: *It is the obligation of all citizens to vote.* **3.** fact, state, or condition of being morally or legally bound to do something. **4.** fact, state, or condition of being grateful or indebted to another for something received, as a favor or service. **5.** that by which one is bound, as a promise or sense of duty or responsibility: *to discharge an obligation.* **6.** that which is owed in payment or return for something, as a favor or service received: *to repay an obligation.* **7.** something, as a benefit or service, for which one is obligated. **8.** *Law.* **a.** binding agreement acknowledging indebtedness or promising to perform some act. **b.** document containing the terms of such agreement. **—Syn. 5.** see **duty.**

ob·li·ga·to (ob′li gä′tō) obbligato.

ob·lig·a·to·ry (ə blig′ə tôr′ē, ob′li gə-) *adj.* of the nature of or constituting an obligation; mandatory; compulsory: *Serving in the armed forces is not obligatory for women.*

o·blige (ə blīj′) **o·bliged, o·blig·ing.** *v.t.* **1.** to bind, compel, or constrain, as by moral or legal force. **2.** to place under an obligation, as for a favor or service; make indebted or grateful (with *to*): *I'm obliged to you for all you've done for us.* **3.** to do a favor or service for: *Please oblige me by keeping quiet during the lecture.* [Old French *obliger* to bind, tie, from Latin *obligāre* to bind, make liable, pledge.] **—o·blig′er,** *n.* **—Syn. 1.** see **force.**

ob·li·gee (ob′lə jē′) *n.* **1.** *Law.* person to whom one is obligated by contract or bond. **2.** person who is under obligation to another.

o·blig·ing (ə blī′jing) *adj.* willing to do favors or to be of service; helpful. **—o·blig′ing·ly,** *adv.* **—o·blig′ing·ness,** *n.*

ob·lique (ə blēk′, ō blēk′) *adj.* **1.** having a slanting or sloping direction, position, or course; inclined. **2.** not straightforward or direct: *She gave an oblique answer to my question.* **3.** neither perpendicular nor parallel. *—n.* something that is oblique, as a line. *—v.i.,* **-liqued, -liqu·ing.** to deviate from the perpendicular; slant. [Latin *oblīquus* slanting, indirect.] **—ob·lique′ly,** *adv.*

oblique angle, angle that is not a right angle; acute or obtuse angle.

oblique case, any case of declension other than the nominative and vocative.

ob·liq·ui·ty (ə blik′wə tē) *pl.,* **-ties.** *n.* **1.** state, quality, or condition of being oblique. **2.a.** inclination from a vertical or horizontal line, plane, or position. **b.** amount of such inclination. **3.** deviation from accepted standards of morality or sound thinking.

ob·lit·er·ate (ə blit′e rāt′) **-at·ed, -at·ing.** *v.t.* **1.** to destroy completely; remove all traces of. **2.** to blot or rub out, as writing; erase. [Latin *oblīterātus,* past participle of *oblītarāre* to strike out, erase, from *ob* over + *littera* letter.] **—ob·lit′er·a′tion, ob·lit′er·a′tor,** *n.* **—ob·lit′er·a′tive,** *adj.*

ob·liv·ion (ə bliv′ē ən) *n.* **1.** state or condition of being entirely forgotten. **2.** state or condition of forgetting completely; forgetfulness. [Old French *oblivion* forgetfulness, from Latin *oblīviō.*]

ob·liv·i·ous (ə bliv′ē əs) *adj.* **1.** not aware or conscious; unmindful (with *of* or *to*): *The child ran into the street, oblivious of the dangers involved.* **2.** lacking memory; forgetful (with *of*). [Latin *oblīviōsus* forgetful, from *oblīviō* forgetfulness.] **—ob·liv′i·ous·ly,** *adv.* **—ob·liv′i·ous·ness,** *n.*

ob·long (ob′lông′) *adj.* having greater length than width, as an ellipse and certain rectangles. *—n.* oblong figure. [Latin *oblongus* rather long.]

ob·lo·quy (ob′lə kwē) *pl.,* **-quies.** *n.* 1. abusive, slanderous language addressed to or aimed at another, esp. by a large number of people. 2. disgrace or shame resulting from such abuse. [Late Latin *obloquium* contradiction, from Latin *obloquī* to speak against.]

ob·nox·ious (ob nok′shəs) *adj.* 1. extremely annoying and offensive: *an obnoxious person.* 2. extremely disagreeable; odious; repugnant: *an obnoxious smell.* [Latin *obnoxius* liable to injury, from *ob-* (see OB-) + *noxa* injury.] —**ob·nox′ious·ly,** *adv.* —**ob·nox′ious·ness,** *n.* —**Syn.** 2. see hateful.

o·boe (ō′bō) *n.* double-reed woodwind instrument having a high, penetrating tone and a range of three octaves. [Italian *oboe,* from French *hautbois.* See HAUTBOY.]

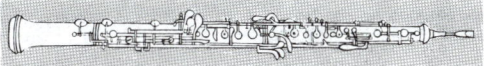

Oboe

ob·o·lus (ob′ə ləs) *pl.,* **-li** (-lī′). *n.* monetary unit and silver coin of ancient Greece. Also, **ob·ol** (ob′əl). [Latin *obolus,* from Greek *obolos.*]

obs. 1. obsolete. 2. observatory.

ob·scene (əb sēn′) *adj.* offensive to accepted standards of modesty or decency; indecent. [Latin *obscēnus* of bad omen, repulsive.] —**ob·scene′ly,** *adv.*

ob·scen·i·ty (əb sen′ə tē, -sē′nə-) *pl.,* **-ties.** *n.* 1. state or quality of being obscene; indecency. 2. something obscene, as an act, expression, or word.

ob·scur·ant (əb skyoor′ənt) *n.* one who opposes and tries to prevent inquiry, enlightenment, reform, and the advancement of knowledge. —*adj.* of, relating to, or characteristic of an obscurant. [Latin *obscūrāns,* present participle of *obscūrāre* to darken.]

ob·scur·ant·ism (əb skyoor′ən tiz′əm) *n.* opposition to inquiry, enlightenment, reform, and the advancement of knowledge; principles or practices of obscurants. —**ob·scur′ant·ist,** *n.*

ob·scu·ra·tion (ob′skyə rā′shən) *n.* act of obscuring; being obscured.

ob·scure (əb skyoor′) **-scur·er, -scur·est.** *adj.* 1. not clearly expressed; difficult to understand: *an obscure explanation.* 2. not clear or distinct; barely perceived by the senses: *an obscure figure.* 3. not well known; undistinguished: *an obscure writer.* 4. not easily seen or discovered; remote; hidden: *an obscure mountain village.* 5. having little or no light; dark; dim: *an obscure corner of the attic.* —*v.t.* **-scured, -scur·ing.** 1. to hide from view; darken or conceal: *Fog obscured the stars.* 2. to lessen the glory of; overshadow. 3. to make unintelligible or difficult to understand. [Old French *o(b)scur* dark, sinister, from Latin *obscūrus* dark, indistinct, from *ob-* over + *-scūrus* covered.] —**ob·scure′ly,** *adv.* —**ob·scure′ness,** *n.* —**Syn.** *adj.* 1. see vague.

ob·scu·ri·ty (əb skyoor′ə tē) *pl.,* **-ties.** *n.* 1. state or quality of being obscure. 2. one who or that which is obscure.

ob·se·quies (ob′sə kwēz) *sing.,* **-quy** (-kwē). *n.,pl.* funeral rites or ceremonies. [Anglo-Norman *obsequie(s),* from Late Latin *obsequiae* (plural), modification (influenced by Latin *obsequium* service) of Latin *exsequiae.*]

ob·se·qui·ous (əb sē′kwē əs) *adj.* too ready or eager to serve, please, or obey; fawning. [Latin *obsequiōsus* full of compliance, from *obsequium* compliance, service.] —**ob·se′qui·ous·ly,** *adv.* —**ob·se′qui·ous·ness,** *n.*

ob·serv·a·ble (əb zur′və bəl) *adj.* 1. that can be observed; perceptible: *an observable difference in attitude.* 2. that may or must be observed, celebrated, followed, or kept: *the formalities observable in a court of law.* —**ob·serv′a·bly,** *adv.*

ob·serv·ance (əb zur′vəns) *n.* 1. act or practice of following, adhering to, or complying with something, as a rule or law. 2. act or practice of keeping or celebrating a customary rite, ceremony, or holiday: *the observance of Easter.* 3. customary rite, ceremony, or celebration. 4. act of noticing or perceiving; observation.

ob·serv·ant (əb zur′vənt) *adj.* 1. quick to notice or perceive; alert. 2. carefully attentive in observing anything required or prescribed, as a rule, law, or custom (often with *of*): *observant of the laws.* [Latin *observāns,* present participle of *observāre* to watch, note, guard.] —**ob·serv′ant·ly,** *adv.*

ob·ser·va·tion (ob′zər vā′shən) *n.* 1.a. act, practice, or faculty of noticing or perceiving. b. fact of being observed; notice: *The thief escaped observation.* 2.a. act of examining, noting, and recording facts or phenomena, esp. for scientific study. b. record or data resulting from this. 3. remark or comment in reference to something that has been noticed or perceived.

ob·ser·va·tion·al (ob′zər vā′shən əl) *adj.* of, relating to, resulting from, or based on observation.

ob·serv·a·to·ry (əb zur′və tôr′ē) *pl.,* **-ries.** *n.* 1.a. place or building furnished with instruments and facilities for observing, studying, and collecting information on astronomical phenomena. b. institution in which such work is carried on. 2. similarly equipped place for observing other natural phenomena. 3. any place or structure affording an extensive view.

ob·serve (əb zurv′) **-served, -serv·ing.** *v.t.* 1. to notice or perceive. 2. to watch carefully; regard with attention. 3. to make a careful observation of, esp. for a scientific purpose: *The scientist observed the behavior of the mice after they were given the drug.* 4. to follow or comply with, as a rule or law. 5. to keep or celebrate according to custom, as a holiday. 6. to comment; remark. —*v.i.* 1. to attend or watch without taking an active role, as at a meeting. 2. to take notice. 3. to make a comment (often with *on* or *upon*). [Old French *observer* examine, keep, from Latin *observāre* to watch, note, guard.]

ob·serv·er (əb zur′vər) *n.* 1. one who observes. 2. one who attends a meeting, assembly, or convention to observe and report on the proceedings, rather than to participate as an official delegate. 3. member of an airplane crew who maintains observation during flight. —**Syn.** 1. see spectator.

ob·sess (əb ses′) *v.t.* to occupy or trouble the mind of excessively, esp. as a fixed idea: *The idea that someone was trying to kill him obsessed him.* [Latin *obsessus,* past participle of *obsidēre* to sit at, besiege.]

ob·ses·sion (əb sesh′ən) *n.* 1. that which obsesses, as a fixed idea or desire: *Proving the existence of unicorns became an obsession with the old man.* 2. act of obsessing; being obsessed.

ob·sid·i·an (əb sid′ē ən, ob-) *n.* hard, glassy igneous rock, usually black, formed when molten lava cools. [Latin *obsidiānus (lapis)* manuscript error for *obsiānus (lapis)* (stone) of Obsius, who is said to have found a similar stone in Ethiopia.]

ob·so·les·cent (ob′sə les′ənt) *adj.* going out of use or date; becoming obsolete. [Latin *obsolēscēns,* present participle of *obsolēscere* to grow old, fall into disuse.] —**ob·so·les′cence,** *n.*

ob·so·lete (ob′sə lēt′, ob′sə lēt′) *adj.* 1. no longer in use or practice: *an obsolete custom. Stagecoaches are obsolete.* 2. out-of-date; outmoded. [Latin *obsolētus,* past participle of *obsolēscere* to grow old, fall into disuse, from *ob* (see OB-) + *solēre* to be accustomed.]

ob·sta·cle (ob′stə kəl) *n.* one who or that which opposes, stands in the way of, or blocks progress. [Old French *o(b)stacle,* from Latin *obstāculum,* from *obstāre* to stand in the way.]

Syn. **Obstacle, obstruction, impediment** mean a hindrance to progress. **Obstacle** is usually applied to an object or condition which hinders one's progress by standing in the way and which must be removed or circumvented before resuming progress: *Her parents' opposition was a serious obstacle to their marriage.* **Obstruction** refers to an object or condition that blocks or physically interferes with a passage or way so as to make it impassable: *The guerrillas placed many obstructions on the road to the city.* **Impediment** applies to an object or condition that hinders or delays the normal function of something: *Pierre's foreign accent was an impediment to effective speech.*

ob·stet·ric (ob stet′rik) *adj.* of or relating to obstetrics and childbirth. Also, **ob·stet′ri·cal.**

ob·ste·tri·cian (ob′stə trish′ən) *n.* physician specializing in obstetrics.

ob·stet·rics (ob stet′riks) *n.,pl.* branch of medicine that deals with the care of women from the detection of pregnancy until a few weeks after delivery. ▲ construed as singular. [Plural of *obstetric,* from Modern Latin *obstetricus* relating to a midwife, from Latin *obstētrīx* midwife; literally, she who stands by.]

ob·sti·na·cy (ob′stə nə sē′) *pl.,* **-cies.** *n.* 1. state or quality of being obstinate. 2. act or instance of this.

ob·sti·nate (ob′stə nit) *adj.* 1. not yielding to argument, persuasion, or reason; inflexible. 2. difficult to overcome, control, or cure. [Latin *obstinātus* stubborn, past participle of *obstināre* to persist.] —**ob′sti·nate·ly,** *adv.*

ob·strep·er·ous (əb strep′ər əs) *adj.* noisy, boisterous, or unruly, esp. in resisting control. [Latin *obstreperus* clamorous.] —**ob·strep′er·ous·ly,** *adv.* —**ob·strep′er·ous·ness,** *n.*

ob·struct (əb strukt′) *v.t.* 1. to block or fill with obstacles or impediments that prevent passage: *Large boulders obstructed the entrance to the cave.* 2. to be or come in the way of: *The woman's hat obstructed my view of the stage.* 3. to interrupt, interfere with, or retard the action, passage, course, or progress of: *to obstruct justice.* [Latin *obstructus,* past participle of *obstruere* to block up, hinder, from *ob* against + *struere* to build up.] —**ob·struc′tive,** *adj.* —**Syn.** 3. see hinder[1].

ob·struc·tion (əb struk′shən) *n.* 1. that which obstructs. 2. act of obstructing; being obstructed. —**Syn.** 1. see obstacle.

ob·struc·tion·ist (əb struk′shə nist) *n.* one who systematically obstructs or impedes work or progress, esp. in a legislative body. —**ob·struc′tion·ism,** *n.*

ob·tain (əb tān′) *v.t.* to gain possession of, esp. as a result of effort;

acquire. —*v.i.* to be prevalent, established, or customary: *The custom still obtains in many parts of the country.* [Old French *obtenir* to acquire, succeed in getting, going back to Latin *obtinēre* to take hold of.] —**ob·tain′a·ble,** *adj.* —**Syn.** *v.t.* see **gain.**

ob·trude (əb trōōd′) **-trud·ed, -trud·ing.** *v.t.* **1.** to force or thrust, as an opinion or oneself, upon another or others in a rude or bold manner. **2.** to push out; thrust forward. —*v.i.* to force oneself upon another or others. [Latin *obtrūdere* to thrust against, from *ob* against + *trūdere* to thrust.] —**ob·trud′er,** *n.*

ob·tru·sion (əb trōō′zhən) *n.* **1.** act of obtruding. **2.** something obtruded.

ob·tru·sive (əb trōō′siv) *adj.* tending to obtrude; forward. —**ob·tru′sive·ly,** *adv.* —**ob·tru′sive·ness,** *n.*

ob·tuse (əb tōōs′, -tūs′) *adj.* **1.** slow in understanding or perceiving; lacking in sensitivity. **2.** not sharp or pointed; blunt: *an obtuse leaf.* **3.** indistinctly felt or perceived; not intense; dull: *an obtuse pain.* [Latin *obtūsus* blunted, past participle of *obtundere* to beat against, blunt.] —**ob·tuse′ly,** *adv.* —**ob·tuse′ness,** *n.*

obtuse angle, angle that is greater than 90 degrees but less than 180 degrees.

ob·verse (*n.,* ob′vurs; *adj.,* ob-vurs′, ob′vurs) *n.* **1.** side of a coin or medal that bears the principal design. Opposed to **reverse.** **2.** front or principal surface of anything. **3.** counterpart. **4.** *Logic.* proposition that is logically equivalent to another proposition from which it is formed by changing a positive predicate to a negative and vice versa, for example: *No men are immortal* is the obverse of *All men are immortal.* —*adj.* **1.** turned toward or facing the observer. **2.** narrower at the base than at the top: *an obverse leaf.* **3.** serving as or being a counterpart. [Latin *obversus,* past participle of *obvertere* to turn toward or against.] —**ob·verse′ly,** *adv.*

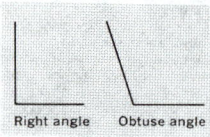

Right angle   Obtuse angle

Obtuse angle

ob·ver·sion (ob vur′zhən, -shən) *n.* **1.** act of obverting; being obverted. **2.** that which results from obverting.

ob·vert (ob vurt′) *v.t.* **1.** *Logic.* to derive or state the obverse of (a proposition). **2.** to turn (something) so as to show another surface. [Latin *obvertere* to turn toward or against.]

ob·vi·ate (ob′vē āt′) **-at·ed, -at·ing.** *v.t.* to prevent or remove by anticipatory measures; anticipate and dispose of: *to obviate the risks involved in shipping explosives.* [Late Latin *obviātus,* past participle of *obviāre* to meet, prevent, going back to Latin *ob* (see OB-) + *via* way.] —**ob′vi·a′tion,** *n.*

ob·vi·ous (ob′vē əs) *adj.* **1.** easily seen or understood; clearly evident: *She made it obvious that she didn't want to go.* **2.** lacking in subtlety; without pretense: *He was very obvious in his distrust of us.* [Latin *obvius* in the way, at hand, from *ob* (see OB-) + *via* way.] —**ob′vi·ous·ly,** *adv.* —**ob′vi·ous·ness,** *n.*

oc-, form of **ob-** before *c,* as in *occasion.*

oc·a·ri·na (ok′ə rē′nə) *n.* musical wind instrument having ten finger holes and producing a whistlelike tone when air is blown through the mouthpiece. [Italian *ocarina,* diminutive of *oca* goose (because of its shape), going back to Latin *avis* bird.]

Ocarina

O'Ca·sey, Sean (ō kā′sē; shôn) 1880–1964, Irish dramatist.

oc·ca·sion (ə kā′zhən) *n.* **1.** particular time at which something occurs: *I can't recall the occasion, but I've met her before.* **2.** event or occurrence: *on the occasion of her marriage.* **3.** event or function regarded as being special or significant: *My parents' fiftieth wedding anniversary was a very happy occasion.* **4.** favorable or suitable time; opportunity: *I don't have many occasions to talk to him.* **5.** immediate cause or reason: *His departure was the occasion of much sadness.* **6.** need or requirement: *I never had occasion to reprimand him.* **7. on occasion.** now and then; as opportunity or need arises. —*v.t.* to be the cause of; bring about. [Latin *occāsio* opportunity, going back to Latin *oc-* for *ob* (see OB-) + *cadere* to fall.] —**Syn. 4.** see **opportunity.**

oc·ca·sion·al (ə kā′zhən əl) *adj.* **1.** happening or appearing now and then; infrequent: *an occasional visitor, an occasional smile.* **2.** produced, intended, or used for some special occasion or event: *occasional verse.* **3.** (of furniture) not part of a set: *an occasional chair.*

oc·ca·sion·al·ly (ə kā′zhən əl ē) *adv.* once in a while; at times.

Oc·ci·dent (ok′sə dənt) *n.* countries of Europe and the Western Hemisphere. Distinguished from **Orient.** [Latin *occidēns* quarter of the setting sun, west.]

Oc·ci·den·tal (ok′sə dent′əl) *also,* **oc·ci·den·tal.** *adj.* of, relating to, or characteristic of the Occident. Distinguished from **Oriental.** —*n.* member or close descendant of a people native to the Occident.

oc·cip·i·tal (ok sip′ət əl) *adj.* of or relating to the occiput. —*n.* occipital bone.

occipital bone, bone located at the back of the skull.

oc·ci·put (ok′sə pət) *pl.* **oc·cip·i·ta** (ok sip′ə tə). *n.* back part of the head. [Latin *occiput,* from *ob* (see OB-) + *caput* head.]

oc·clude (o klōōd′) **-clud·ed, -clud·ing.** *v.t.* **1.** to stop up, close, or block, as a passage or pore. **2.** to shut in, out, or off. **3.** (of a chemical compound) to absorb and retain (another compound). **4.** (of a mass of cold air) to force (warm air) upward from the surface of the earth. —*v.i.* (of the teeth in the upper and lower jaws) to meet closely. [Latin *occlūdere* to shut up.]

occluded front, air mass formed when a cold air mass occludes a warm air mass.

oc·clu·sion (o klōō′zhən) *n.* **1.** act or process of occluding; being occluded. **2.** occluded front.

oc·cult (o kult′, ok′ult) *adj.* **1.** of, relating to, or concerned with certain mystical arts or practices, as astrology or alchemy. **2.** beyond the realm of human understanding; mysterious. **3.** communicated only to the initiated; secret. —*n.* occult arts or practices. ▲ usually preceded by *the: a follower of the occult.* —*v.t.* **1.** to conceal from view; hide. **2.** *Astronomy.* to conceal by occultation. —*v.i.* to become concealed from view. [Latin *occultus* hidden, past participle of *occulere* to cover up, hide.]

oc·cul·ta·tion (ok′ul tā′shən) *n.* **1.** eclipse of one celestial body by the passing of another between it and the observer. **2.** act of occulting; being occulted. **3.** disappearance from view or notice.

oc·cult·ism (ə kul′tiz′əm, ok′əl-) *n.* **1.** belief in the existence of mysterious or hidden spiritual powers. **2.** study or practice of occult arts.

oc·cu·pan·cy (ok′yə pən sē) *pl.* **-cies.** *n.* **1.** act of occupying; being occupied. **2.** period of time during which something is occupied. **3.** condition of being an occupant or tenant. **4.** *Law.* act of taking possession of ownerless property with the intention of acquiring right of ownership to it.

oc·cu·pant (ok′yə pənt) *n.* **1.** one who occupies a place or position. **2.** person, group, or organization having legal control or possession of a property, as a house, office building, or apartment; tenant or owner. [Latin *occupāns,* present participle of *occupāre* to seize.]

oc·cu·pa·tion (ok′yə pā′shən) *n.* **1.** trade, work, or activity pursued as the source of one's livelihood. **2.** act of occupying; being occupied. **3.** act or process of seizing and maintaining control of enemy territory by a military force. [Latin *occupātiō* a seizing, employment.]

oc·cu·pa·tion·al (ok′yə pā′shən əl) *adj.* of, relating to, or resulting from one's occupation.

occupational therapy, rehabilitation of mentally and physically disabled persons by teaching them a skill or providing them with creative activity, as arts and crafts.

oc·cu·py (ok′yə pī′) **-pied, -py·ing.** *v.t.* **1.** to take up (time or space): *Running errands occupied most of the morning.* **2.** to seize and maintain control of by military force. **3.** to inhabit; live in. **4.** to be the main consideration or interest of, as of the mind or thoughts. **5.** to have and retain possession; hold, as an office or position. [Old French *occuper* to keep busy, take possession of, from Latin *occupāre* to seize.] —**oc′cu·pi′er,** *n.*

oc·cur (ə kur′) **-curred, -cur·ring.** *v.i.* **1.** to take place; come to pass. **2.** to appear or be found: *The same theme occurs in much of his work.* **3.** to come into mind; suggest itself: *It did not occur to me to mention it.* [Latin *occurrere* to run to meet, present itself.] —**Syn. 1.** see **happen.**

oc·cur·rence (ə kur′əns) *n.* **1.** act or fact of occurring. **2.** something that occurs; incident: *an everyday occurrence.*

Syn. 2. Occurrence, happening mean that which takes place. **Occurrence** is the general term for an event or incident that comes to pass unexpectedly and without design: *A snowstorm is an unusual occurrence at this time of year.* **Happening** is an event, situation, or circumstance that comes into being either by design or by accident: *Her diary records all the happenings of the day.*

o·cean (ō′shən) *n.* **1.** the whole body of salt water that covers nearly three-fourths of the earth's surface. **2.** any one of the four major subdivisions of this body of water; the Atlantic, Pacific, Indian, or Arctic ocean. **3.** vast expanse or quantity: *an ocean of light.* **4.** mare². [Latin *ōceanus* the great sea around the earth, from Greek *ōkeanos.*]

ocean current, large-scale movement of ocean water flowing continuously in approximately the same path, as the Gulf Stream.

O·ce·an·i·a (ō′shē an′ē ə) *n.* islands of the Pacific, including Melanesia, Micronesia, and Polynesia, and sometimes including Australia, New Zealand, and the Malay Archipelago. Also, **O·ce·an·i·ca** (ō′shē an′i kə). —**O′ce·an′i·an,** *adj., n.*

o·ce·an·ic (ō′shē an′ik) *adj.* **1.** of, relating to, or inhabiting the ocean. **2.** resembling the ocean; vast.

O·ce·a·nid (ō sē′ə nid) *n.* *Greek Mythology.* any one of the ocean nymphs who were the daughters of Oceanus.

o·cean·og·ra·phy (ō′shə nog′rə fē) *n.* science of the sea, dealing with the structure of the ocean basins, composition and movement of the waters, and oceanic life.
—**o′cean·og′ra·pher,** *n.* —**o·cean·o·graph·ic** (ō′shə nə graf′ik); *also,* **o′cean·o·graph′i·cal,** *adj.*

ocean sunfish, large fish, *Mola mola,* found in temperate and tropical seas, having a flattened oval body and weighing up to 2000 pounds. Length: to 11 feet.

O·ce·a·nus (ō sē′ə nəs) *n. Greek Mythology.* Titan who was the father of the Oceanids and the ruler of the great river that surrounded the earth.

o·cel·lus (ō sel′əs) *pl.,* **o·cel·li** (ō sel′ī). *n.* **1.** in certain invertebrates, a simple eye consisting of sensory cells, pigment-containing cells, and sometimes a lens that can concentrate light rays. **2.** eyelike spot, as on a peacock feather. [Latin *ocellus* little eye, diminutive of *oculus* eye.]

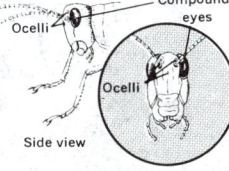

Ocelli of a grasshopper

o·ce·lot (os′ə lot′, ō′sə-) *n.* cat, *Felis pardalis,* native to Central and South America, having a yellowish coat marked with black spots, rings, and stripes. Height: 16 inches at the shoulder. [French *ocelot,* from Nahuatl *ocelotl* tiger, jaguar.]

o·cher (ō′kər) *also,* **o·chre.** *n.* **1.** any of several mixtures of clay and iron oxides used as pigments. Yellow or brown ochers consist of limonite; red ochers consist of hematite. **2.** reddish- or brownish-yellow color. [Old French *ocre* friable clay (yellow or red) used as a pigment, from Latin *ōchra* yellow ocher, from Greek *ōchrā,* from *ōchros* pale yellow.]

Ocelot

o'clock (ə klok′) *adv.* **1.** of or according to the clock: *two o'clock.* **2.** according to a direction measured from an observer, with reference to an imaginary point in a horizontal plane with the observer at the center of the clock facing or heading toward twelve o'clock. To such an observer someone behind him would be at six o'clock. [Contraction of *of the clock.*]

oct-, form of **octa-** or **octo-** before vowels.

Oct., October.

octa- *combining form* eight: *octahedron.* [Greek *oktō*.]

oc·ta·gon (ok′tə gon′, -gən) *n.* polygon having eight sides and eight angles. [Latin *octagōnum,* from Greek *oktagōnon,* going back to *oktō* eight + *gōniā* angle, corner.]

oc·tag·o·nal (ok tag′ən əl) *adj.* having the geometric properties of an octagon.

oc·ta·he·dral (ok′tə hē′drəl) *adj.* having the geometric properties of an octahedron.

oc·ta·he·dron (ok′tə hē′drən) *pl.,* **-drons** or **-dra** (-drə). *n.* polyhedron having eight faces. [Greek *oktaedron,* from *oktō* eight + *hedra* seat, base.]

oc·tane (ok′tān) *n.* colorless, liquid hydrocarbon of the alkane, or paraffin, series. Formula: C_8H_{18} [Greek *oktō* eight + -ANE.]

octane number, number indicating the extent to which a motor fuel resists engine knocking.

Octahedron

oc·tant (ok′tənt) *n.* **1.** aircraft navigation instrument used to measure the angle of elevation of heavenly bodies up to eighty degrees above the horizon. **2.** any of the eight parts into which space is divided by three mutually perpendicular planes having a common point of intersection. **3.** eighth of a circle or its circumference. [Late Latin *octāns* eighth part of a circle, from Latin *octō* eight.]

oc·tave (ok′tiv, -tāv) *n.* **1.a.** interval between a given tone or note and another that is eight diatonic degrees above or below it. **b.** tone or note at this interval having twice or half as many vibrations per second as the one below or above it. **c.** harmonic combination of two tones or notes at this interval sounded together. **d.** series of tones or notes or of keys of an instrument contained within this interval: *The singer's vocal range is two octaves.* **e.** organ stop giving tones an octave above those corresponding to the keys used. **2.a.** group or stanza of eight lines of verse, esp. the ottava rima. **b.** first two quatrains or first eight lines of a sonnet. Also, **oc·tet′. 3.a.** major religious feast and the week after it, totaling eight days. **b.** last of the eight days of such a period. **4.** any group of eight. [Latin *octāva,* feminine of *octāvus* eighth, from *octō* eight.]

Oc·ta·vi·an (ok tā′vē ən) *n.* Augustus.

oc·ta·vo (ok tā′vō, -tä′-) *pl.,* **-vos.** *n.* **1.** page or paper size, as of a book,

usually measuring from 5 by 8 inches to 6 by 9½ inches, formerly ⅛ of a whole printer's sheet. **2.** book having pages this size. [Latin *octāvō,* ablative of *octāvus* eighth. See OCTAVE.]

oc·tet (ok tet′) *also,* **oc·tette.** *n.* **1.a.** musical composition for eight voices or instruments. **b.** musical ensemble of eight performers. **2.** any group or set of eight persons or things. **3.** octave (*def.* 2). [Latin *octō* eight, on the model of DUET.]

oc·til·lion (ok til′yən) *n.* **1.** in the United States and France, the cardinal number that is represented by 1 followed by twenty-seven zeros. **2.** in Great Britain and Germany, the cardinal number that is represented by 1 followed by forty-eight zeros. —*adj.* numbering one octillion. [French *octillion* unit followed by twenty-seven zeros (from Latin *octō* eight), on the model of *million.* See MILLION.] —**oc·til′lionth,** *adj., n.*

octo- *combining form* eight: *octopus.* [Greek *oktō* or Latin *octō*.]

Oc·to·ber (ok tō′bər) *n.* tenth month of the year, containing thirty-one days. [Latin *October* eighth month in the early Roman calendar, in which March was the first month, from *octō* eight.]

oc·to·ge·nar·i·an (ok′tə jə när′ē ən) *n.* one who is eighty or between eighty and ninety years old. —*adj.* being eighty or between eighty and ninety years old. [Latin *octōgēnārius* containing eighty (going back to *octōgintā* eighty) + -AN.]

oc·to·pus (ok′tə pəs) *n.* **1.** any of a widespread group of saltwater cephalopods, family Octopodidae, having a soft, rounded body and eight tentacles that bear suckers and are used to move along the ocean bottom and to capture prey. **2.** corporation or other organization having much power and far-reaching influence. [Modern Latin *octopus,* from Greek *oktōpous* eight-footed, from *oktō* eight + *pous* foot.]

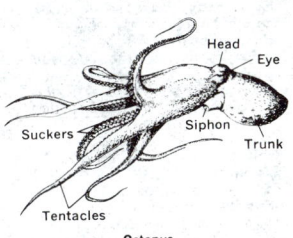

Octopus

oc·to·roon (ok′tə rōōn′) *n.* one who is one-eighth Negro. [OCTO- + (QUAD)ROON.]

oc·u·lar (ok′yə lər) *adj.* **1.** of, relating to, or like the eye or eyesight. **2.** seen by the eye; visual. —*n.* eyepiece of a telescope, microscope, or other optical instrument. [Late Latin *oculāris* relating to the eye, from Latin *oculus* eye.]

oc·u·list (ok′yə list) *n.* ophthalmologist. [French *oculiste,* from Latin *oculus* eye.]

O.D. 1. officer of the day. **2.** olive drab. **3.** overdraft. **4.** overdrawn.

o·da·lisque (ō′də lisk′) *also,* **o·da·lisk.** *n.* female slave or concubine in a harem. [French *odalisque,* from Turkish *ōdalīq* chambermaid, from *ōdah* chamber in a harem.]

odd (od) *adj.* **1.** differing from the usual or ordinary, as in appearance or behavior; strange; peculiar. **2.** not belonging or relating to any particular total, set, or group; mixed; miscellaneous: *odd bits of information.* **3.** being one of a pair or set of which the rest is missing: *an odd shoe, an odd glove.* **4.** differing from or in addition to the routine, habitual, or planned; irregular; occasional: *I often think of her at odd moments.* **5.** having a remainder of one when divided by two. **6.** with an indefinite amount in addition to a specified round number; plus a few more. ▲ often connected to a numerical adjective by a hyphen: *I have 400-odd dollars in the bank. He was born some forty-odd years ago.* **7.** left over; extra: *He was the odd man on the team.* [Old Norse *oddi* triangle, third or odd number.] —**odd′ly,** *adv.* —**odd′ness,** *n.* —**Syn. 1.** see **strange.**

odd·ball (od′bôl′) *Informal. n.* one whose behavior or way of thinking is odd; eccentric. —*adj.* eccentric or outlandish: *an oddball idea.*

odd·i·ty (od′ə tē) *pl.,* **-ties.** *n.* **1.** one who or that which is odd or peculiar: *His motorcycle was an oddity in his neighborhood.* **2.** odd characteristic or trait; peculiarity: *the oddities of his personality.* **3.** state or quality of being odd; strangeness: *The oddity of the situation bewildered us.*

odd·ment (od′mənt) *n. usually,* **oddments.** that which remains; leftover; remnant: *some oddments that didn't fit in the trunk.*

odds (odz) *n.,pl.* **1.** probability in favor of or against something being true or happening, often stated in the form of a ratio: *The odds are ten to one against your winning.* **2.** allowance or advantage given to the weaker opponent in a contest in order to equalize the competitors. **3.** difference that favors one side and is against another; advantage: *In a contest where strength is important, the odds are with him.* **4.** *Archaic.* unequal matters or conditions; inequalities. ▲ usually construed as plural in all definitions. **5. at odds.** quarreling; disagreeing. [From ODD.]

at; āpe; cär; end; mē; it; īce; hot; ōld; fôrk; wood; fōōl; oil; out; up; ūse; turn; sing; thin; this; zh in treasure; ə in ago, taken, pencil, lemon, circus.

699

odds and ends. miscellaneous or leftover articles, items, or matters: *I bought a few odds and ends at the hardware store.*

ode (ōd) *n.* **1.** lyric poem, usually rhymed, often in the form of an address, and usually dignified or lofty in subject, feeling, and style. **2.** formerly, a lyric poem intended or adapted to be sung. [French *ode,* from Late Latin *ōdē* song, from Greek *ōidē.*]

-ode *combining form* way; path: *cathode.* [Greek *hodos.*]

O·der (ō′dər) *n.* river flowing into the Baltic Sea, forming part of the boundary between Poland and East Germany.

O·des·sa (ō des′ə) *n.* **1.** port city in the southwestern Soviet Union, in the Ukraine, on the Black Sea. Pop. (1970 est.), 892,000. **2.** city in western Texas. Pop. (1970), 78,380.

O·din (ō′din) *n. Norse Mythology.* king of the gods and god of wisdom and war. His Teutonic counterpart is Woden.

o·di·ous (ō′dē əs) *adj.* causing hate, disgust, or repugnance; detestable: *the most pernicious race of little odious vermin* (Swift, 1726). [Latin *odiōsus,* from *odium* hatred.] —**o′di·ous·ly,** *adv.* —**o′di·ous·ness,** *n.* —**Syn.** see **hateful.**

o·di·um (ō′dē əm) *n.* **1.** extreme hatred, disgust, or repugnance; detestation: *the odium with which we view cruelty to others.* **2.** reproach, shame, or stigma attached to something hateful: *the odium of being a slave trader.* **3.** state or quality of being odious. [Latin *odium* hatred.]

o·dom·e·ter (ō dom′ə tər) *n.* device for measuring the distance traveled by a vehicle. [French *odomètre* pedometer, going back to Greek *hodos* way, path + *metron* measure.]

o·don·tol·o·gy (ō′don tol′ə jē) *n.* branch of science dealing with the structure, growth, and diseases of the teeth. [Greek *odont-,* stem of *odōn* tooth + -LOGY.]

o·dor (ō′dər) *also, British,* **o·dour.** *n.* **1.** that property of a thing or substance that makes it perceptible to the sense of smell; scent. **2.** reputation or estimation. [Old French *odeur* smell, from Latin *odor.*] —**Syn. 1.** see **smell.**

o·dor·if·er·ous (ō′də rif′ər əs) *adj.* having or emitting an odor, esp. a pleasant one. [Latin *odōrifer* fragrant, bringing odors (from *odor* smell + *ferre* to bear) + -OUS.] —**o′dor·if′er·ous·ly,** *adv.* —**o′dor·if′er·ous·ness,** *n.*

o·dor·ous (ō′dər əs) *adj.* having or emitting an odor, esp. a pleasant one. [Latin *odōrus* fragrant, from *odor* smell.] —**o′dor·ous·ly,** *adv.* —**o′dor·ous·ness,** *n.*

O·dys·se·us (ō dis′ē əs, ō dis′ūs) *n.* Ulysses.

od·ys·sey (od′ə sē) *pl.,* **-seys.** *n.* long, adventurous journey. [Referring to the long, adventurous journey of Odysseus on his way home after the Trojan War, described in the *Odyssey,* an epic poem by Homer.]

OE, Old English.

oec·u·men·i·cal (ek′yə men′i kəl) *British.* ecumenical.

Oed·i·pus (ed′ə pəs, ē′də-) *n. Greek Legend.* king who fulfilled a prophecy by unknowingly killing his father and marrying his mother.

Oedipus complex *Psychology.* strong, unconscious sexual attraction of a son toward his mother, characterized by feelings of jealousy and hostility toward his father.

Oe·no·ne (ē nō′nē) *n. Greek Mythology.* nymph who was the wife of Paris and was later deserted by him for Helen of Troy.

o'er (ôr) *prep., adv. Archaic.* over.

oe·soph·a·gus (i sof′ə gəs) *pl.,* **-gi** (-jī′). *n.* esophagus.

of (ov, uv; *unstressed* əv) *prep.* **1.** belonging to or possessed by: *the cover of a book, the leg of a chair.* **2.** descended or coming from: *a man of noble lineage, a citizen of France.* **3.** away or at a distance from: *within a yard of the finish line.* **4.** that is or are called; specified as: *the city of New York.* **5.** having a quality or attribute; characterized by: *news of importance.* **6.** in or with regard to; concerning: *to be in fear of one's life, to be innocent of a crime.* **7.** as a result of; caused by: *to die of suffocation.* **8.** having; possessing: *a family of wealth.* **9.** filled with or containing: *a book of poetry, a pitcher of milk.* **10.** from the whole number, amount, or group comprising: *Three members of the class were absent. He always gave freely of his time.* **11.** associated with as a member or adherent: *He is of the same background as you. They are of our faith.* **12.** made, created, or produced by; emanating from: *the novels of Dickens, the sweet fragrance of the flowers.* **13.** made from or with: *a ring of diamonds and emeralds.* **14.** so as to be without or separated from: *to be cured of a cold, to be robbed of one's money.* **15.** situated at or in: *the deserts of Arabia.* **16.** focused upon or directed toward; for: *a day of rest.* **17.** set aside for; devoted to: *an evening of music, a day of meditation.* **18.** on the part of: *It was kind of you to help him.* **19.** in, on, or during the time or occasion specified: *Your poor father and I have suffered very much of late* (Goldsmith, 1766). **20.** before. ▲ used in telling time: *We are meeting at five minutes of twelve.* **21.** *Archaic.* by: *beloved of the Lord.* [Old English *of* belonging to, made from, from, by, about, out of.]

of-. form of ob- before *f,* as in *offer.*

OF, Old French.

off (ôf) *prep.* **1.** so as to be removed, separated, or disconnected from: *to take a book off a shelf, to jump off a horse.* **2.** not engaged in or occupied with; free from: *to be off duty.* **3.** deviating from or less than the usual or normal: *to be off one's game, to be off balance.* **4.a.** by eating or consuming: *The prisoners lived off bread and water for many days.* **b.** on or with that which is provided by: *to live off the land.* **5.** branching or leading out or away from: *The house is on a road a couple of miles off the main highway.* **6.** abstaining from: *He's been off liquor since his illness.* **7.** *Informal.* from the hands, charge, or possession of; from: *She bought the book off me.* **8.** seaward of: *The submarine was a mile off the coast.* —*adv.* **1.** so as to be separated, removed, or detached: *to break off a piece of bread, to take off one's coat.* **2.** so as to be no longer operating, continuing, or functioning: *to break off negotiations, to turn the motor off.* **3.** at or to a distance; away: *The dog scared the intruder off.* **4.** to or at a (specified) distance in time or space: *The party was put off for a week. The house is three miles off in the opposite direction.* **5.** so as to be smaller, fewer, or diminished in amount or degree: *Business dropped off during the winter.* **6.** so as to exhaust, eliminate, or finish: *The dictator killed off all those who opposed him.* **7.** so as to be away from or deprived of work or duty: *to take the day off.* **8.** so as to divide, set apart, or delineate: *to mark off an area on a map.* **9.** so as not to hesitate or falter: *to rattle off a list of dates.* **10.** on the way: *to start off on a trip.* **11. to take off.** to depart; go away. **12. off and on.** now and then; intermittently. **13. off with (something).** remove: *Off with their heads.* ▲ used as an imperative. —*adj.* **1.** no longer in operation, existence, or effect: *Their engagement is off. The motor is off.* **2.** not occupied with work or duty: *She was off for the holidays.* **3.** in a specified state or condition: *to be well off financially.* **4.** inaccurate or incorrect: *He was off by three cents.* **5.** on the way; going: *The children are off to bed.* **6.** not up to the usual or normal level or standard; below average: *an off year for grapes.* **7.** unlikely; slight; remote: *an off chance.* **8.** right: *He mounted the horse on the off side.* Opposed to **near.** **9.** farther from the shore; seaward: *the off side of the ship.* [Old English of away, away from, from.]

off. **1.** office. **2.** officer. **3.** official.

of·fal (ô′fəl, of′əl) *n.* **1.** waste parts of a butchered animal. **2.** garbage; refuse. [OFF + FALL; originally referring to the fact that a butcher, when cutting up an animal, would cut off and throw away the refuse parts.]

off·beat (*adj.,* ôf′bēt′; *n.,* ôf′bēt′) *adj. Informal.* not conforming to the usual or ordinary; strange; unconventional: *an off-beat movie, an off-beat sense of humor.* —*n. Music.* any weak or unaccented beat in a measure.

off-Broad·way (ôf′brôd′wā′) *adj.* **1.** located outside of the Broadway theater district: *an off-Broadway theater.* **2.** of, relating to, or designating theatrical productions, often experimental or low-budget, produced in theaters outside of the Broadway theater district. —*n.* theatrical productions produced in off-Broadway theaters or as off-Broadway presentations.

off-color (ôf′kul′ər) *adj.* **1.** slightly improper; risqué: *an off-color joke.* **2.** without the usual or desired color.

Of·fen·bach, Jacques Le·vy (ô′fən bäk′; zhäk lā vē′) 1819–80, French composer born in Germany.

of·fend (ə fend′) *v.t.* **1.** to cause or arouse resentment, anger, or hostility in; insult. **2.** to be displeasing, disagreeable, or repugnant to: *His crudeness offended my sense of modesty.* —*v.i.* **1.** to cause resentment, anger, or displeasure. **2.** to commit an offense; do wrong. [Old French *offendre* to hurt, from Latin *offendere* to strike against, hurt, commit a fault.] —**of·fend′er,** *n.*

Syn. *v.t.* **1. Offend, affront, insult** mean to cause resentment or damage to self-respect. **Offend** may be appropriately used when one outrages another by hurting his feelings and violates his sense of honor, pride, and propriety: *We were offended by his vulgar language.* **Affront** is a more formal and polite word than *offend;* it may be preferred to express indignation when one humiliates and mortifies a person by open and deliberate display of contempt and discourtesy: *The upstart's arrogance affronted the whole community.* **Insult** may be used when one excessively offends another by word or action intended to rankle and humiliate: *Fred insulted Joe by calling him a liar in public.*

of·fense (*defs. 1–5* ə fens′; *defs. 6, 7* ô′fens, of′ens) *also, British,* **of·fence.** *n.* **1.** act of breaking or violating a moral or social code of conduct. **2.a.** act of breaking the law. **b.** criminal act; crime. **3.** act of causing or arousing resentment, anger, or displeasure. **4.** that which offends. **5.** act of attacking or assaulting. **6.** *Sports.* side, team, or players in possession of the ball or puck, as in basketball or hockey. **7. to give offense.** to cause resentment, anger, or displeasure. **8. to take offense.** to feel resentment, anger, or displeasure. [Old French *offense* injury by word or deed, from Latin *offēnsa* a striking against, wrong, displeasure.]

of·fense·less (ə fens′lis) *adj.* **1.** harmless. **2.** incapable of offense or attack.

at; āpe; cär; end; mē; it; īce; hot; ōld; fôrk; wood; fōol; oil; out; up; ūse; turn; sing; thin; this; zh in treasure; ə in ago, taken, pencil, lemon, circus.

of·fen·sive (ə fen′siv) *adj.* **1.** causing resentment, anger, or displeasure; giving offense. **2.** unpleasant to the senses; repugnant; disagreeable: *an offensive smell.* **3.** relating to, characterized by, or used for attack: *an offensive team, offensive tactics.* —*n.* position, attitude, or course of attack: *to assume the offensive.* —**of·fen′sive·ly,** *adv.* —**of·fen′sive·ness,** *n.* —**Syn.** *adj.* **1.** see hateful.

of·fer (ô′fər, of′ər) *v.t.* **1.** to present for acceptance or rejection: *to offer an apology.* **2.** to express one's willingness or readiness (to do or give something); volunteer: *She offered her help.* **3.** to put forth or propose for consideration. **4.** to attempt or make a show of: *to offer resistance.* **5.** to suggest or propose as payment: *We offered ten dollars for the book.* **6.** to present for sale: *He offered the car for a good price.* **7.** to present as an act of religious worship or devotion (often with *up*): *to offer prayers in thanksgiving, to offer up morning devotions.* —*v.i.* **1.** to present itself; occur: *He travels whenever the opportunity offers.* **2.** to make an offering in religious worship or devotion. —*n.* **1.** act of offering. **2.** that which is offered, as a suggestion, bid, or opinion. [Old English *offrian* to present a sacrifice or offering, from Latin *offerre* to bring before, present, from *of-* for *ob* (see OB-) + *ferre* to bring.]

of·fer·ing (ô′fər ing, of′ər-) *n.* **1.** contribution or gift, as at a religious service. **2.** that which is offered or presented, esp. in religious worship or devotion. **3.** act of making an offer.

of·fer·to·ry (ô′fər tôr′ē, of′ər-) *pl.,* **-ries.** *n.* **1.** that part of the Mass or Communion service at which the unconsecrated bread and wine are offered to God. **2.** collection of the congregation's offerings at a religious service. **3.** verses said by the celebrant or sung by the choir during the offerings at Mass or other religious services. [Church Latin *offertōrium* place to which offerings were brought, going back to Latin *offerre* to bring before, present.]

off·hand (ôf′hand′) *adv.* without previous thought or preparation: *She could not say offhand when she would arrive.* —*adj.* **1.** done, made, or said offhand: *offhand comments.* **2.** casual; informal: *an offhand manner.*

off·hand·ed (ôf′han′did) *adj.* offhand. —**off′hand′ed·ly,** *adv.* —**off′hand′ed·ness,** *n.*

of·fice (ô′fis, of′is) *n.* **1.a.** place in which business, professional services, or clerical duties are carried on. **b.** all the people who work in such a place: *The office is having a Christmas party.* **2.** position or post of authority, trust, or responsibility, esp. in a government or corporation: *the office of vice-president.* **3.** duty, service, or charge undertaken by or assigned to someone: *He exercises the offices of teacher and counselor.* **4.** *also,* **Office.** administrative unit or branch of a government. **5.** *also,* **offices.** something done for another; kindness, service, or favor: *We got the information we needed through his good offices.* **6.** *also,* **Office.** prescribed religious ceremony or service for a particular occasion or purpose, esp. the canonical hours. **7.** **offices.** *British.* rooms or buildings of a house or estate devoted to household or farm duties. [Old French *office* duty, position, religious service, from Latin *officium* duty, service, ceremony, kindness.]

office boy, man or boy hired to run errands and do odd jobs in a business office.

of·fice·hold·er (ô′fis hōl′dər, of′is-) *n.* one who holds a public office.

office hours **1.** hours during which an office is normally open for business. **2.** number of hours spent at work in an office.

of·fi·cer (ô′fə sər, of′ə-) *n.* **1.** person appointed to a particular rank and position of authority in a military service, esp. one holding a commission. **2.** person appointed or elected to a position or post of authority, trust, or responsibility. **3.** captain or any of his chief assistants on a boat or ship. **4.** policeman or constable. **5.** person holding the lowest rank in some honorary societies. [Old French *officier* one who has an office or employment, from Medieval Latin *officiarius* one who performs an office, from Latin *officium* service, duty.]

officer of the day, military officer who is in charge, for a specified period of time, of the buildings, equipment, and personnel, esp. the guards, of a unit.

of·fi·cial (ə fish′əl) *n.* one who holds an office or position. —*adj.* **1.** of or relating to an office or position of authority: *official duties.* **2.** coming from or authorized by a proper authority: *an official statement.* **3.** authorized to carry out some specific function: *an official scorekeeper.* **4.** characteristic of or befitting a person of authority; formal. [Late Latin *officiālis* relating to service, public servant, from Latin *officium* duty, service.] —**of·fi′cial·ly,** *adv.*

of·fi·cial·dom (ə fish′əl dəm) *n.* **1.** officials collectively. **2.** officialism.

of·fi·cial·ism (ə fish′ə liz′əm) *n.* attitudes and practices characteristic of officials, esp. excessive adherence to regulations and routine.

of·fi·ci·ate (ə fish′ē āt′) **-at·ed, -at·ing.** *v.i.* **1.** to perform the duties and functions of an office or position: *The governor officiated at the opening of the new school.* **2.** to perform the duties of a clergyman, esp. at a religious service. **3.** to act as umpire or referee in any of various

sports. [Medieval Latin *officiatus,* past participle of *officiare* to perform a religious service, from Latin *officium* service.]

of·fic·i·nal (ə fis′ən əl) *adj.* (of drugs) available or sold without prescription. —*n.* officinal drug. [Medieval Latin *officinalis* relating to a workshop (as of an apothecary), from Latin *officina* workshop, laboratory.]

of·fi·cious (ə fish′əs) *adj.* too forward in offering services or advice to others; meddlesome. [Latin *officiōsus* dutiful, obliging, from *officium* service, duty.] —**of·fi′cious·ly,** *adv.* —**of·fi′cious·ness,** *n.*

off·ing (ô′fing, of′ing) *n.* **1.** that part of the visible sea lying between the shore and the horizon. **2.** position at a distance from the shore. **3. in the offing. a.** in the near future. **b.** at a distance but within sight.

off·ish (ô′fish) *adj. Informal.* inclined to keep aloof; distant or cool in manner; reserved. —**off′ish·ness,** *n.*

off·set (*v.,* ôf′set′; *n.,* ôf′set′) **-set, -set·ting.** *v.t.* **1.** to balance or make up for: *Her virtues offset her faults.* **2.** to reproduce (something) by offset printing. —*v.i.* to develop or project as a branch or shoot. —*n.* **1.** that which balances or makes up for something else; compensation. **2.** shoot or branch that grows or develops from a root or main stem near the ground and can take root as a new plant. **3.** offshoot (def. 2). **4.a.** offset printing. **b.** image or impression made by offset printing. **c.** accidental smudge produced on a clean sheet of paper that is in contact with a freshly inked or printed page. **5.** ledge formed on a wall by narrowing the thickness above. **6.** bend or angle made in a pipe or bar to enable it to bypass an obstacle.

offset printing, printing process in which an inked impression is transferred from a coated zinc or aluminum plate to a cylinder covered with rubber, which in turn places it on paper.

off·shoot (ôf′shoot′) *n.* **1.** shoot that grows from the main stem of a plant. **2.** anything that develops, derives, or branches off from something else.

off·shore (ôf′shôr′) *adj.* **1.** moving or directed away from the shore: *an offshore storm.* **2.** situated, existing, or operating at a distance from the shore: *offshore fishermen.* **3.** *U.S.* operated outside the United States: *an off-shore business.* —*adv.* **1.** in a direction away from the shore: *The wind was moving offshore.* **2.** at a distance from the shore.

off·side (ôf′sīd′) *also,* **off·side.** *adj.* **1.** in football, illegally ahead of the ball before a play begins. **2.** in certain games, esp. ice hockey, illegally ahead of the puck or ball in an attacking zone or area. —*adv.* in or to a position that is offside. —*n.* act or instance of being offside.

off·spring (ôf′spring′) *pl.,* **-spring** or **-springs.** *n.* **1.** living organism born or produced as a result of the reproductive process. **2.** result; product. [Old English *ofspring* progeny.]

off·stage (ôf′stāj′) *adj.* located in or coming from that part of the stage that is not visible to the audience: *an off-stage voice.* —*adv.* away from that part of the stage that is visible to the audience: *to go off-stage.*

off-the-cuff (ôf′thə cuf′) *adj. Informal.* spontaneous; unplanned.

oft (ôft) *adv. Archaic.* often. ▲ sometimes used in combination, as in *oft-repeated.* [Old English *oft.*]

of·ten (ô′fən) *adv.* many times; repeatedly; frequently. [Middle English *often,* from *oft.* See OFT.]

of·ten·times (ô′fən tīmz′) *adv.* often. Also, **oft·times** (ôft′tīmz′).

Og·den (og′dən) *n.* city in northern Utah. Pop. (1970), 69,478.

o·gee (ō′jē) *n.* **1.** S-shaped curve or line. **2.** molding having an S-shaped curve in profile. **3.** ogee arch. [French *ogive* pointed arch; of uncertain origin.]

ogee arch, pointed arch each side of which is formed by a convex curve on the bottom and a concave curve on the top.

Ogee

o·gle (ō′gəl) **o·gled, o·gling.** *v.t.* **1.** to look or stare at in a leering manner or with desire. —*v.i.* to look or stare in a leering or amorous manner. —*n.* leering or amorous look. [Probably from Low German *oegeln,* from *oegen* to look at, from *oog* eye.] —**o′gler,** *n.*

OGPU (og′poo) former secret police of the Soviet Union. Also, **GPU.**

o·gre (ō′gər) *n.* **1.** in fairy tales and legends, fearsome man-eating giant or monster. **2.** any person or thing that is cruel, brutal, or dreaded. [French *ogre* the giant, possibly going back to Latin *Orcus* Roman god of the lower world, Pluto.] —**o′gre·ish,** *adj.* —**o′gress,** *n.*

oh (ō) *also,* **O.** *interj.* used to express an emotion or feeling, as of

Ogee arch

surprise, joy, grief, or pain. —*n. pl.,* **oh's** or **ohs.** the exclamation "oh" or an instance of it.

O. Henry (ō hen′rē) 1862–1910, U.S. short-story writer; born William Sidney Porter.

OHG, Old High German

O·hi·o (ō hī′ō) *n.* **1.** state in the north-central United States. Capital, Columbus. Area, 41,222 sq. mi. Pop. (1970), 10,652,017. **2.** river in the east-central United States, flowing from Pittsburgh southwest into the Mississippi. —**O·hi′o·an,** *adj., n.*

ohm (ōm) *n.* unit of electrical resistance equal to the resistance of a conductor in which a potential difference of one volt produces a current of one ampere. [From Georg S. *Ohm*, 1787–1854, German physicist.] —**ohm′ic,** *adj.*

o·ho (ō hō′) *interj.* used to express surprise, astonishment, or exultation.

-oid *suffix* (used to form adjectives from nouns) having the form, nature, or appearance of; like or resembling: *spheroid, planetoid.* [Greek *-oeidēs,* from *eidos* form, shape, sometimes through French *-oïde* and Latin *-oïdēs.*]

oil (oil) *n.* **1.** any of a large group of greasy substances that are insoluble in water but soluble in ether, and that are liquid at normal temperatures or liquefy readily when warmed. **2.** petroleum. **3.** oil paint. **4.** an oil painting. **5.** any of various substances having an oily consistency. **6. to strike oil.** to come upon a source of profit suddenly. **7. to burn the midnight oil.** to work or study until very late at night. **8. to pour oil on troubled waters.** to settle differences or a dispute, or calm a disturbance; pacify. —*v.t.* **1.** to cover, smear, lubricate, supply, or polish with oil: *to oil a hinge, to oil furniture.* **2.** to bribe or flatter. [Old French *huile* the greasy substance, from Latin *oleum* olive oil, oily substance, from Greek *elaion.*]

oil burner, furnace or heating unit that burns fuel oil.

oil cake, livestock feed consisting of a mass of seeds, as linseed, from which most of the oil has been pressed out.

oil·can (oil′kan′) *n.* can with a long spout, used for applying lubricating oil, as to machinery.

oil·cloth (oil′klôth′) *n.* waterproof fabric made by coating cloth with oil or a similar substance, used for such items as tablecloths, shelf lining, and cushion covers.

oil color, oil paint.

oil·er (oi′lər) *n.* **1.** one who or that which oils, esp. one who oils machinery and engines. **2.** oilcan.

oil field, area where subterranean deposits of petroleum of economic value have been found.

oil of turpentine, turpentine *(def. 2).* Also, **spirits of turpentine.**

oil of vitriol, sulfuric acid.

oil paint, paint that is made of pigment ground in linseed or other oil.

oil painting 1. painting done in oil paints. **2.** art of painting in oil paints.

oil·skin (oil′skin′) *n.* **1.** fabric that has been treated with oil or a similar substance to make it waterproof, used esp. for rainwear. **2.** garment made of this fabric.

oil slick, film of oil floating on the surface of water.

oil·stone (oil′stōn′) *n.* smooth, fine-grained stone treated with oil, used for sharpening blades.

oil well, well that is dug or drilled in the earth to obtain petroleum.

oil·y (oi′lē) *oil·i·er, oil·i·est. adj.* **1.** of, relating to, or containing oil. **2.** covered, smeared, or soaked with oil; greasy. **3.** too smooth or suave in speech or manner; disagreeably unctuous. —**oil′i·ness,** *n.*

oint·ment (oint′mənt) *n.* soft, unctuous substance, often medicated, applied to the skin to soothe, protect, or heal it; salve. [Old French *oignement,* going back to Latin *unguentum.*]

O·jib·wa (ō jib′wä′) *pl.,* **-wa** or **-was.** *also,* **O·jib·way.** *n.* **1.** member of a large tribe of North American Indians formerly living in the Great Lakes region, now living primarily in Minnesota, Wisconsin, and North Dakota. **2.** language of this tribe, belonging to the Algonquian language family. Also, **Chip′pe·wa′.**

OK (ō′kā′) *also,* **o·kay.** *Informal. adj.,adv.,interj.* all right. ▲ used to express endorsement, approval, or agreement. —*n.* endorsement, agreement, or approval. —*v.t.* to endorse, approve, or agree to, esp. by signing with an OK.

O·ka (ō kä′) *n.* river in the western Soviet Union.

o·ka·pi (ō kä′pē) *pl.,* **-pis** or **-pi.** *n.* rare African mammal, *Okapia johnstoni,* related to the giraffe, native to the forests of the Congo, with buff markings on the face and zebralike black and white

stripes on the upper legs and hindquarters. Height: to 6 feet at the shoulder. [From a Central African language.]

o·kay (ō′kā′) *Informal. adj.,adv.,interj.* OK. —*n. pl.,* **o·kays.** OK. —*v.t.,* **o·kayed, o·kay·ing.** to OK. [Form of ок.]

O·kie (ō′kē) *n. Informal.* migrant farm worker. [Referring originally to farmers from *Oklahoma* who had to leave their farms because of the depression of the 1930s.]

O·ki·na·wa (ō′kə nä′wə) *n.* Japanese island in the Pacific, formerly administered by the United States. It was the site of a major battle of World War II in 1945. Area, 454 sq. mi. Pop. (1965), 758,777.

Okla., Oklahoma.

O·kla·ho·ma (ō′klə hō′mə) *n.* state in the south-central United States. Capital, Oklahoma City. Area, 69,919 sq. mi. Pop. (1970), 2,559,253. Abbreviation, **Okla.** —**O′kla·ho′man,** *adj., n.*

Oklahoma City, capital of Oklahoma, in the central part of the state. Pop. (1970), 366,481.

o·kra (ō′krə) *n.* **1.** soft green pods of a plant, *Hibiscus esculentus,* having a waxy texture, eaten as a vegetable either cooked or pickled. **2.** the plant itself, cultivated in warm regions of the world, having broad oval leaves with coarsely toothed edges and bearing bell-shaped flowers. Also, **gum′bo.** [From a West African language.]

-ol *suffix* (used in chemistry to form nouns) alcohol: *glycerol.* [From (ALCOH)OL.]

OL, Old Latin.

O·laf II, Saint (ō′läf) A.D. 995–1030, king of Norway from 1016 to 1028.

Olaf V, 1903—, king of Norway since 1957.

old (ōld) *old·er* or *eld·er, old·est* or *eld·est. adj.* **1.** having lived or existed for a long time: *an old man.* **2.** of a specified age or length of existence: *Our car is three years old.* **3.** not new, recent, or current; made, produced, or created in the past: *an old song, an old joke.* **4.** familiar through having been acquainted with, known, or used in the past or for a long time: *the same old story. We're old friends.* **5.** of or belonging to antiquity or the remote past; ancient. **6.** former: *an old boyfriend.* **7.** worn with age or use; worn-out: *I gave away all my old dresses.* **8.** possessing or exhibiting the characteristics of age or aged persons: *Suffering made her old before her time.* **9.** of, relating to, or belonging to the latter part of life: *He married at a ripe old age.* **10.** experienced, skilled, or practiced: *He's an old hand at making speeches.* **11.** *Informal.* cherished; dear: *It's a grand old flag.* ▲ used as a term of affection or endearment. **12.** *Informal.* excellent; fine: *We had a grand old time at the party.* ▲ used as an intensifier. —*n.* former times: *the knights of old.* [Old English *eald, eald* having existed long, of a specified age, of the past, earlier.] —**Syn.** *adj.* **1.** see **aged.**

old country, country, esp. one in Europe, from which a person has emigrated.

Old Delhi, Delhi.

old·en (ōld′ən) *adj. Archaic.* old; ancient.

Old English 1. West Germanic language of the Indo-European family, spoken by the Anglo-Saxon people until about A.D. 1100. Also, **An′glo-Sax′on.** **2.** elaborate, angular type face, used esp. in printing formal documents or invitations.

𝕬𝕭𝕮𝕯𝕰𝕱𝕲𝕳
𝖓𝖔𝖕𝖖𝖗𝖘𝖙𝖚𝖛𝖜𝖝𝖞𝖟

Old English letters

Old English sheepdog, large dog having a long, shaggy, gray or bluish gray coat with white markings. Height: 2 feet at the shoulder.

old-fash·ioned (ōld′fash′ənd) *adj.* **1.** keeping to or favoring old ways, ideas, or customs. **2.** of, relating to, or characteristic of former times; out-of-date.

old fo·gy (fō′gē) *also,* **old fo·gey.** one who is old-fashioned and very conservative.

old-fo·gy·ish (ōld′fō′gē ish) *also,* **old-fo·gey·ish.** *adj.* of, like, or characteristic of an old fogy; behind the times.

Old French, French language from the ninth to the thirteenth centuries A.D.

Old Glory, flag of the United States.

Old Guard 1. select group of soldiers serving Napoleon I. **2. old guard.** conservative element, as of a political party, country, or community.

Old·ham (ōl′dəm) *n.* city in central England, near Manchester. Pop. (1968 est.), 109,100.

old hat *Informal.* out-of-date; old-fashioned.

Old High German, German language of southern Germany from the eighth to the twelfth centuries A.D. Modern standard German is descended from Old High German.

Old Icelandic, Icelandic from the ninth century to the thirteenth century A.D.

Okapi

Old English sheepdog

at; āpe; cär; end; mē; it; īce; hot; ōld; fôrk; wood; fōōl; oil; out; up; ūse; turn; sing; thin; <u>th</u>is; zh in treasure; ə in ago, taken, pencil, lemon, circus.

Old Irish, Irish from the seventh to the thirteenth centuries A.D.
old·ish (ōl′dish) *adj.* somewhat old.
Old Latin, Latin before the second century B.C.
old-line (ōld′līn′) *adj.* **1.** conservative or traditional in one's actions or way of thinking. **2.** firmly established; traditional.
old maid 1. woman who remains single considerably beyond the ordinary marrying age. **2.** *Informal.* one who is prim, fussy, and prudish. **3.** card game in which two or more players discard matched pairs of cards and the one holding the odd queen at the end is the loser. —**old′-maid′ish,** *adj.*
old master 1. any of the great painters, esp. of Italy and the Low Countries, who lived between the thirteenth and sixteenth centuries. **2.** painting by such a painter.
old moon, moon when seen as a thin crescent before the appearance of the new moon.
Old Nick, the Devil; Satan.
Old Norse, North Germanic language of Scandinavia from the eighth to the fourteenth centuries A.D., esp. in its Norwegian and Icelandic forms.
Old North French, any of several dialects of Old French that were spoken in the northern provinces of France, esp. Normandy and Picardy.
Old Persian, earliest form of the Persian language, found in inscriptions dating from the sixth century B.C.
Old Provençal, form of Provençal from the tenth to the thirteenth centuries A.D.
Old Saxon, dialect of Low German written and spoken by the Saxons in northwestern Germany from the ninth to the twelfth centuries A.D.
old school, any group of people regarded as having or clinging to conservative or traditional ideas, methods, or points of view.
Old Slavonic, language belonging to the southern group of the Slavic branch of the Indo-European language family, extinct as a vernacular but used in the liturgy of certain Orthodox churches.
old·ster (ōld′stər) *n.* *Informal.* old or elderly person.
Old Style 1. method of reckoning time according to the Julian calendar. **2. old style.** style of printing type characterized by slanting, rounded serifs and uniformly thick strokes.
Old Testament, collection of writings that makes up the first part of the Christian Bible and is the Jewish Bible. It contains an account of creation and early man, the sacred agreement between God and the Hebrews, and the laws, prophecies, and religious literature of the Hebrew nation up to the second century B.C.
old-time (ōld′tīm′) *adj.* belonging to, or characteristic of former times.
old-tim·er (ōld′tī′mər) *n.* *Informal.* **1.** one who has been a member of a group or organization for a long time. **2.** one who is old or elderly.
old wives' tale, belief not founded on fact; superstition.
Old-World (ōld′wurld′) *adj.* **1.** of, relating to, or belonging to the Old World: *Old-World customs. Old-World monkeys.* **2. old-world.** belonging to or characteristic of former times.
Old World, Eastern Hemisphere, including Europe, Asia, and Africa.
o·lé (ō lā′) *interj.* well done; bravo. —*n.* shout of "olé." [Spanish *olé;* probably imitative.]
o·le·ag·i·nous (ō′lē aj′ə nəs) *adj.* **1.** of, relating to, or containing oil: *oleaginous juices.* **2.** too smooth in speech or manner; oily; unctuous. [Latin *oleāginus* relating to the olive or olive tree, from *olea* olive, olive tree, from Greek *elaiā*.]
o·le·an·der (ō′lē an′-dər) *n.* extremely poisonous evergreen shrub, *Nerium oleander,* cultivated throughout the world, bearing narrow, lance-shaped leaves and clusters of fragrant funnel-shaped red, purple, or white flowers. [Medieval Latin *oleander,* possibly modification (influenced by Latin *olea* olive tree) of Late Latin *lōrandrum,* possibly modification of Latin *rhododendron* oleander. See RHODODENDRON.]

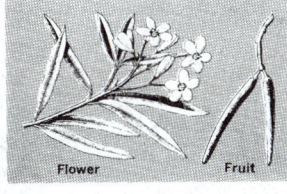

Flower Fruit
Oleander

o·le·ate (ō′lē āt′) *n.* salt or ester of oleic acid.
o·le·fin (ō′lə fin) *n.* *also,* **o·le·fine** (ō′lə fin, -fēn′). *n.* any member of the series of hydrocarbons having the general formula C$_n$H$_{2n}$; alkene. —**o′le·fin′ic,** *adj.*
o·le·ic acid (ō lē′ik, ō′lē ik) oily liquid compound that swells like lard and is derived from animal fat and vegetable oil by hydrolysis, used as a basis for soaps and ointments. Formula: C$_{17}$H$_{33}$COOH [Latin *oleum* (see OIL) + -IC + ACID.]

o·le·in (ō′lē in) *also,* **o·le·ine** (ō′lē in, -ēn′). *n.* oily, yellow liquid compound found in most oils and fats; glycerin ester of oleic acid. Formula: C$_3$H$_5$(C$_{17}$H$_{33}$COO)$_3$ [French *oléine,* from Latin *oleum* (see OIL).]
o·le·o·mar·ga·rine (ō′lē ō mär′jər in, -jə rēn′) *also,* **o·le·o·mar·ga·rin.** *n.* margarine. Also, **o′le·o′.** [Latin *oleum* (see OIL) + MARGARINE.]
o·le·o·res·in (ō′lē ō rez′in) *n.* naturally occurring mixture of a resin and an oil, as turpentine. [Latin *oleum* (see OIL) + RESIN.]
ol·fac·tion (ol fak′shən) *n.* **1.** act or process of smelling. **2.** sense of smell. [Latin *olfactus,* past participle of *olfacere* to smell + -ION.]
ol·fac·to·ry (ol fak′tər ē) *adj.* of or relating to the sense of smell. —*n. pl.,* **-ries.** olfactory organ. ▲ usually used in the plural.
ol·i·garch (ol′ə gärk′) *n.* any of the rulers in an oligarchy.
ol·i·gar·chic (ol′ə gär′kik) *adj.* of, relating to, or governed by an oligarchy. Also, **ol′i·gar′chi·cal.**
ol·i·gar·chy (ol′ə gär′kē) *pl.,* **-chies.** *n.* **1.** form of government in which power is held by only a few people. **2.** state having such a government. **3.** body of persons composing such a government. [Greek *oligarchiā* government by a few, going back to *oligos* few + *archein* to rule.]
Ol·i·go·cene (ol′ə gō sēn′) *n.* third geological epoch of the Tertiary period, during which time the first monkeys and apes appeared. See **geology** for table. —*adj.* of, relating to, or characteristic of this epoch. [Greek *oligos* few, little + *kainos* new.]
ol·ive (ol′iv) *n.* **1.** small, oily, edible fruit of any of a group of evergreen shrubs and trees, genus *Olea,* having a single hard seed and firm flesh, esp. the fruit of the common olive, *Olea europaea,* often eaten pickled and widely used as a source of edible oil. **2.** shrub or tree bearing this fruit, esp. the common olive, cultivated in warm regions, having gray-green leaves and clusters of fragrant white flowers. **3.** dull yellowish-green color. Also *(def. 3).* **olive green.** [Old French *olive* the tree, the fruit, from Latin *olīva,* from Greek *elaiā*.]
olive branch 1. branch of the olive tree regarded as a symbol of peace. **2.** anything offered as a token of peace or good will.
olive drab 1. dull greenish-brown color. **2.** woolen fabric of this color. **3.** *also,* **olive drabs.** military uniform made of this fabric.
olive oil, clear yellow or greenish-yellow oil obtained by pressing olives, widely used as a salad and cooking oil.
Ol·ives, Mount of (ol′ivz) mountain east of Jerusalem, thought to be the site of Jesus' ascension. The garden of Gethsemane is at the foot of this mountain. Also, **Ol·i·vet** (ol′i vet′).
ol·i·vine (ol′ə vēn′, ol′ə vēn′) *n.* transparent to translucent rock-forming silicate mineral ranging from olive to brown in color and containing varying amounts of magnesium and iron. It is found in dark rocks, as basalt. Formula: (Mg, Fe)$_2$SiO$_4$ [German *Olivin,* from Latin *olīva* (see OLIVE); referring to its color.]
ol·la (ol′ə) *n.* wide-mouthed earthenware jar or pot, used esp. for holding water or cooking. [Spanish *olla,* from Latin *ōlla*.]
ol·o·gy (ol′ə jē) *pl.,* **-gies.** *n.* *Informal.* any science or branch of knowledge. [From *-ology,* as in BIOLOGY, SOCIOLOGY. See -LOGY.]
O·lym·pi·a (ō lim′pē ə) *n.* **1.** plain in the northwestern Peloponnesus, site of the Olympic games in ancient Greece. **2.** capital of Washington, in the western part of the state. Pop. (1970), 23,111.
O·lym·pi·ad (ō lim′pē ad′) *n.* **1.** period of four years from one celebration of the Olympic games to another, by which the ancient Greeks computed time. **2.** celebration of the modern Olympic games.
O·lym·pi·an (ō lim′pē ən) *adj.* **1.** of or relating to Mount Olympus or the gods who, in Greek mythology, lived there. **2.** of or relating to Olympia or the Olympic games. Also, **O·lym′pic. 3.** like a god; majestic; exalted. —*n.* **1.** one of the twelve major Greek gods who lived on Mount Olympus. **2.** one who takes part in the Olympic games.
O·lym·pic games (ō lim′pik) **1.** in ancient Greece, Panhellenic festival consisting of a series of competitions in athletics, poetry, music, and oratory, held every four years at Olympia in honor of Zeus. Also, **Olympian games. 2.** modern international athletic contests modeled on the ancient Greek games, held every four years in a different country.
Olympic Mountains, mountain range in northwestern Washington.
O·lym·pics (ō lim′piks) *n.* Olympic games *(def. 2).*
O·lym·pus, Mount (ō lim′pəs) mountain in northeastern Greece that, in Greek mythology, was regarded as the home of the major gods.
O·man (ō män′) *n.* country on the southeastern coast of the Arabian peninsula, formerly Muscat and Oman. Capital, Muscat. Area, 82,000 sq. mi. Pop. (1975 est.), 800,000.
O·ma·ha (ō′mə hô′, -hä′) *n.* **1.** city in eastern Nebraska. Pop. (1970), 347,328. **2.** member of a tribe of North American Indians of the Siouan language family, formerly living in Nebraska and Iowa, now living in Nebraska.
O·mar Khay·yám (ō′mär kī yäm′, -yam′) died c.1123, Persian poet, astronomer, and mathematician.

o·ma·sum (ō mā′səm) *pl.*, **-sa** (-sə). *n.* third stomach of a cud-chewing animal. Also, **man′y·plies′**. [Latin *omāsum* tripe of a bullock; probably of Celtic origin.]

om·buds·man (om budz′mən) *pl.*, **-men.** *n.* official who investigates complaints by private citizens against government officials and agencies. [Swedish *ombudsman* commissioner, attorney.]

o·meg·a (ō meg′ə, ō mē′gə, ō mā′-) *n.* **1.** twenty-fourth and last letter of the Greek alphabet (Ω, ω), corresponding to the English long *o.* **2.** last in a group or series; end. **3.** subatomic particle of the baryon group. See **subatomic particle** for table. [Greek *ō mega* literally, great *o.*]

om·e·let (om′ə lit, om′lit) *also,* **om·e·lette.** *n.* dish consisting of eggs beaten with milk, cooked in a pan, and folded over, often having a filling, as of cheese or meat. [French *omelette*, going back to Latin *lāmella* thin metal plate; supposedly referring to its resemblance to a thin flat plate.]

o·men (ō′mən) *n.* sign or occurrence supposed to portend good or bad luck: *Breaking a mirror is considered a bad omen.* —*v.t.* to be an omen of; portend. [Latin *ōmen* sign of a future happening.]

om·i·cron (om′ə kron′, ō′mə-) *n.* fifteenth letter of the Greek alphabet (O, o), corresponding to the English short *o.* [Greek *o micron* literally, small *o.*]

om·i·nous (om′ə nəs) *adj.* like an evil omen; foreboding evil; threatening. [Latin *ōminōsus,* from *ōmen* omen.] —**om′i·nous·ly,** *adv.* —**om′i·nous·ness,** *n.*

o·mis·si·ble (ō mis′ə bəl) *adj.* that can be omitted.

o·mis·sion (ō mish′ən) *n.* **1.** act of omitting; being omitted. **2.** that which is omitted.

o·mit (ō mit′) **o·mit·ted, o·mit·ting.** *v.t.* **1.** to leave out; fail to include: *to omit an item on a shopping list.* **2.** to fail to do or perform; neglect: *He omitted telling me about the party.* [Latin *ōmittere* to let go, neglect.] —**Syn. 1.** see **exclude.**

omni- *combining form* all; totally; everywhere: *omnifarious.* [Latin *omnis* all, every.]

om·ni·bus (om′nə bus′) *n.* **1.** public motor vehicle having rows of seats to accommodate passengers and sometimes having two decks, used esp. along a fixed, regular route; bus. **2.** collection of works written by the same author or of writings relating to the same subject. —*adj.* including or covering a number of different items, cases, or instances: *an omnibus bill in a legislature.* [French *omnibus* public vehicle, from Latin *omnibus* for all, dative plural of *omnis* all; because the vehicle was intended for all classes of society.]

om·ni·far·i·ous (om′nə fãr′ē əs) *adj.* of all forms, varieties, or kinds. [Late Latin *omnifārius,* from Latin *omnis* all + *-fārius* -fold.]

om·nip·o·tence (om nip′ət əns) *n.* **1.** infinite or unlimited power or authority. **2. Omnipotence.** God.

om·nip·o·tent (om nip′ət ənt) *adj.* having infinite or unlimited power or authority; all-powerful. —*n.* **the Omnipotent.** God. [Latin *omnipotēns* almighty, from *omnis* all + *potēns* powerful.] —**om·nip′o·tent·ly,** *adv.*

om·ni·pres·ent (om′nə prez′ənt) *adj.* present in all places at the same time. [Medieval Latin *omnipraesens,* from Latin *omnis* all, every + *praesēns* that is before one.] —**om′ni·pres′ence,** *n.*

om·nis·cience (om nish′əns) *n.* **1.** infinite or unlimited knowledge. **2. Omniscience.** God. [Medieval Latin *omniscientia* infinite knowledge, from Latin *omnis* all, every + *scientia* knowledge.]

om·nis·cient (om nish′ənt) *adj.* having infinite or unlimited knowledge; knowing everything. —*n.* **the Omniscient.** God. —**om·nis′cient·ly,** *adv.*

om·ni·um-gath·er·um (om′nē əm gath′ər əm) *n.* miscellaneous collection; confused mixture. [Latin *omnium* of all (genitive of *omnis* all) + *gatherum,* Latinized form based on English *gather.*]

om·niv·o·rous (om niv′ər əs) *adj.* **1.** eating both animal and vegetable food. **2.** taking in or assimilating everything: *an omnivorous reader.* **3.** eating all kinds of food indiscriminately. [Latin *omnivorus* all-devouring, from *omnis* + *vorāre* to devour.] —**om·niv′o·rous·ly,** *adv.* —**om·niv′o·rous·ness,** *n.*

Om·pha·le (om′fə lē) *n. Greek Legend.* queen of Lydia whom Hercules voluntarily served as a slave to atone for having murdered a friend.

Omsk (omsk) *n.* city in the central Soviet Union. Pop. (1970 est.), 821,000.

on (ôn, on) *prep.* **1.** in a position above and supported by; above and in contact with: *The coats are on the bed.* **2.** so as to be in contact with any surface, regardless of position: *Please put butter on both sides of the bread.* **3.** fastened to or suspended from: *a watch on a chain, a chandelier on the ceiling.* **4.** in a position at, near, or adjacent to: *Their cabin is on the lake.* **5.** in the direction of; toward: *Our house is on the left.* **6.** directed toward, esp. in the way of attack; against: *to make war on one's enemies. His attacker pulled a knife on him.* **7.** in the state, condition, or process of: *I bought the dress on sale.* **8.** in regard to; about; concerning: *The lecture was on the fall of the Roman Empire.*

9. during the time, course, or occasion of: *We left on Thursday.* **10.** at the precise point or moment of: *The chimes ring every hour on the hour.* **11.** connected or associated with as a member: *Mr. Jones is on the board of trustees.* **12.** by means or use of: *He left on the last train.* **13.** so as to use as a source or means of support or sustenance: *You can never depend on him to keep a secret.* **14.** bound by: *on one's honor.* **15.** in such a position as to be supported or borne by: *to stand on one's toes.* **16.** for the purpose of: *He went away on business.* **17.** engaged in; occupied with: *He was on duty all day.* **18.** as a result or consequence of: *He made money on the deal.* **19.** available by means of: *The doctor is on call twenty-four hours a day.* **20.** coming after; following. **21.** in addition to. **22.** *Informal.* in the possession of; with: *Do you have a match on you?* **23.** *Informal.* at the expense of: *The joke's on me.* **24. to have something on (someone).** *Informal.* to possess damaging or unfavorable information about or evidence against (someone). —*adv.* **1.** in or into a position in contact with, attached to, supported by, or covering something: *to put one's shoes on.* **2.** in the direction of; toward. **3.** forward, in space or time; onward: *to move on. Time marches on.* **4.** in a continuous course; without stop: *The party went on until midnight.* **5.** in or into action, operation, or movement: *to turn the water on.* **6.** in or at the present place or position: *If you don't hang on, you'll fall.* **7.** in or into place or position for use or action: *The star of the show went on despite his injury. Bring on the food.* **8.** *Baseball.* on base. **9. and so on.** and more of the same; and so forth. **10. on and off.** from time to time; intermittently. **11. on and on.** without stopping; continuously. **12. to be on to.** *Informal.* to have knowledge of or information on. —*adj.* **1.** taking place; happening: *The war is still on.* **2.** operating: *The radio is on.* **3.** *Informal.* planned; scheduled: *What's on for tonight?* [Old English *on, an* above, upon, touching, near, toward.]

ON, Old Norse.

once (wuns) *adv.* **1.** one time: *John has a piano lesson once every two weeks. I saw him once and never again.* **2.** in time past; previously: *She was once a beautiful woman.* **3.** at any time; ever: *If we once lose sight of him, he'll disappear for the rest of the day.* **4. once (and) for all.** finally or for the last time. **5. once in a while.** occasionally. **6. once or twice.** a few times. **7. once upon a time.** at some time in the past; long ago. —*n.* **1.** one single time. **2. all at once. a.** suddenly: *All at once, I remembered.* **b.** all at the same time; simultaneously: *He tried to do everything all at once.* **3. at once. a.** without delay. **b.** at the same time; simultaneously: *Everything happened at once.* —*adj.* former. —*conj.* as soon as; when; whenever: *It's easy, once you learn the basic rules.* [Middle English *ōnes, ānes,* one time only, ever, formerly, genitive of *ōn, ān* one, from Old English *ān.* See **ONE.**]

once-o·ver (wuns′ō′vər) *n. Slang.* **1.** quick look or examination. **2.** quick, superficial cleaning or putting in order: *I gave the room a once-over.*

on·com·ing (ôn′kum′ing, on′-) *adj.* approaching: *an oncoming train.* —*n.* approach.

one (wun) *n.* **1.** the first and lowest cardinal number. **2.** symbol representing this number, as 1 or I. **3.** single person or thing. **4. at one.** in harmony or agreement. **5. one by one.** one at a time in succession. —*adj.* **1.** being a single object, unit, or individual: *one loaf of bread, one important point. One girl was left.* **2.** being a specific person, thing, or group, as contrasted with another or others: *The child ran from one side of the room to the other.* **3.** some: *She will probably marry one day.* **4.** single in kind; the same: *all the children of one family.* **5.** characterized by harmony, unity, or agreement: *They were of one mind.* **6.** a certain: *The thief was one Allen Jones.* **7. all one.** the same, as in thought or opinion; united: *Then we are all one on the matter?* —*pron.* **1.** specific person or thing: *One of the boys was left behind. I'll take that one.* **2.** any person or thing: *One could see that he was very upset.* **3.** the same thing: *He didn't know that water and H₂O are one.* **4. one another.** each other. ▲ see usage note under **each.** [Old English *ān* the lowest cardinal number, a single.]

-one *suffix* designating a ketone or related compound: *acetone.*

one-horse (wun′hôrs′) *adj.* **1.** drawn by or made for one horse: *a one-horse buggy.* **2.** *Informal.* of little significance, importance, or interest: *a one-horse town.*

O·nei·da (ō nī′də) *pl.,* **-das** or **-da.** *n.* member of a tribe of Iroquois Indians formerly living in central New York, now living primarily in Wisconsin and New York.

O'Neill, Eugene (Gladstone) (ō nēl′) 1888–1953, U.S. dramatist.

one·ness (wun′nis) *n.* **1.** state or quality of being one; singleness or sameness. **2.** agreement; harmony.

one-night stand (wun′nīt′) **1.** performance given in a specific place on one night only. **2.** place in which such a performance is given.

on·er·ous (on′ər əs) *adj.* difficult to bear; burdensome; oppressive. [Latin *onerōsus,* from *onus* burden.] —**on′er·ous·ly,** *adv.* —**on′er·ous·ness,** *n.*

one·self (wun self′) *also,* **one's self.** *pron.* **1.** reflexive form of **one:**

at; āpe; cär; end; mē; it; īce; hot; ōld; fôrk; wood; fōol; oil; out; up; ūse; turn; sing; thin; this; zh in treasure; ə in ago, taken, pencil, lemon, circus.

Seeing oneself on television is exciting. **2.** one's normal, average, or true self.

one-sid·ed (wun′sī′did) *adj.* **1.** favoring, dealing with, or presenting only one side; biased; partial. **2.** unequal or uneven. **3.** having, involving, or on one side only.

one-step (wun′step′) *n.* **1.** ballroom dance consisting of a series of rapid walking steps. **2.** music for such a dance. —*v.i.* **-stepped, -step·ping.** to dance the one-step.

one-time (wun′tīm′) *adj.* former: *his one-time associate.*

one-to-one (wun′tə wun′) *adj.* **1.** proportionately equal on both sides: *a one-to-one correspondence.* **2.** relating to the pairing of each element of one set with one and only one element from another set.

one-track (wun′trak′) *adj.* **1.** obsessed with or limited to one idea or purpose: *a one-track mind.* **2.** having one track.

one-way (wun′wā′) *adj.* **1.** moving or allowing movement in one direction only: *one-way traffic, a one-way street.* **2.** allowing travel in one direction only: *a one-way ticket.* **3.** one-sided: *a one-way conversation.*

on·go·ing (ôn′gō′ing, on′-) *adj.* continuing.

on·ion (un′yən) *n.* **1.** bulb of a plant, *Allium cepa,* having a pungent taste and smell, eaten as a vegetable either raw or cooked. **2.** the plant itself, widely cultivated, having clusters of pink or white bell-shaped flowers. [Old French *oignon* the plant, from Latin *ūniō* oneness, type of onion plant; because it forms a united whole despite its many layers.]

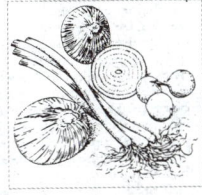

Onions

on·ion·skin (un′yən skin′) *n.* a thin, strong, translucent paper.

on-line (ôn′līn′, on′-) *adj.* operating under the direct control of the main computer: *an on-line airline seat reservations system.*

on·look·er (ôn′look′ər, on′-) *n.* one who looks on; spectator. —*Syn.* see **spectator.**

on·look·ing (ôn′look′ing, on′-) *adj.* looking on; watching; observing.

on·ly (ōn′lē) *adj.* **1.** alone of its kind or class; without others; solitary: *an only child. He was the only person present. My only concern is for your safety.* **2.** being a single individual, object, or method: *She is the only person for the job.* —*adv.* **1.** no more than; nothing but: *I have only two dollars. It's only a minor error.* **2.** no one or nothing other than: *Only she remembered that it was my birthday.* **3.** exclusively; solely: *This bus runs only on weekends.* —*conj.* except that; but: *I would have come, only it was raining.* [Old English *ānlic* unique, solitary, from *ān* one + *-līc* (see -LY²).]

Syn. *adj.* **1.** **Only, lone, sole²** mean one and no more. **Only** implies a restriction to the one that is specified and denotes no one else and nothing more: *This is the only copy of the book in the library.* **Lone** emphasizes the idea of exclusivity and denotes being by oneself or being considered apart from and without reference to anyone or anything else: *That lone incident baffled the police.* **Sole** stresses the idea of being the only one without another or others to share the specified condition: *Phil is the sole heir to all that property.*

on·o·mat·o·poe·ia (on′ə mat′ə pē′ə, -mä′tə-) *n.* **1.** formation of a name or word by imitating the natural sound associated with the thing designated. *Crackle, roar,* and *sizzle* are examples of onomatopoeia. **2.** word formed in this way. **3.** use of such words, as in poetry or rhetoric. [Greek *onomatopoiiā* formation of a word in imitation of a sound, from *onoma* name + *poiein* to make.]

on·o·mat·o·po·et·ic (on′ə mat′ə pō et′ik, -mä′tə-) *adj.* of, relating to, of the nature of, or characterized by onomatopoeia. Also, **on·o·mat·o·poe·ic** (on′ə mat′ə pē′ik, -mä′tə-).

On·on·da·ga (on′ən dô′gə, -dä′gə) *pl.,* **-gas** or **-ga.** *n.* member of a tribe of Iroquois Indians formerly living in central New York, now living primarily in Canada.

on·rush (ôn′rush′, on′-) *n.* rapid or violent forward flow or rush.

on·set (ôn′set′, on′-) *n.* **1.** beginning; start. **2.** attack; assault.

on·shore (ôn′shôr′, on′-) *adv., adj.* on or toward the shore.

on·side (ôn′sīd′, on′-) *adj., adv.* in various sports, not offside.

on·slaught (ôn′slôt′, on′-) *n.* vigorous or destructive attack.

Ont. Ontario.

On·tar·i·o (on tār′ē ō′) *n.* **1.** Lake. smallest and easternmost of the five Great Lakes, between New York and Canada. **2.** province of Canada, in the southeastern part of the country, north of the Great Lakes. Area, 412,582 sq. mi. Pop. (1966), 6,960,870. **3.** city in southern California, near Los Angeles. Pop. (1970), 64,118. —**On·tar′i·an,** *adj., n.*

on·to (ôn′tōō, -tə, on′-) *prep.* **1.** to a position on: *The door opens onto the street.* **2.** aware of: *I'm onto your tricks.*

on·tog·e·ny (on toj′ə nē) *pl.,* **-nies.** *n.* history of the development of an individual organism from fertilization to hatching or birth. [Greek *ont-,* stem of *ōn* being + *-geneia* birth.]

on·tol·o·gy (on tol′ə jē) *n.* branch of philosophy that deals with the nature of being. [Modern Latin *ontologia,* from Greek *ont-,* stem of *ōn* being + -LOGY.]

o·nus (ō′nəs) *n.* burden; responsibility. [Latin *onus.*]

on·ward (ôn′wərd, on′-) *adv. also,* **onwards.** toward a point in front; that is ahead or in front. —*adj.* moving or directed toward a point in front; forward: *an onward course.* —*Syn. adj.* see **forward.**

on·yx (on′iks) *n.* variety of quartz consisting of different colored layers, esp. white, yellow, black, or red. [Latin *onyx,* from Greek *onyx.*]

oo·dles (ōōd′əlz) *n.,pl. Informal.* large amount; a lot. [Of uncertain origin.]

o·o·lite (ō′ə līt′) *n.* **1.** pin-head sized sphere consisting of concentric layers of calcium carbonate, silica, or iron, often surrounding a particle of sand or some other substance. **2.** rock composed of such spheres. [Modern Latin *oōlites,* from Greek *ōion* egg + *lithos* stone.]

oo·long (ōō′lông′) *n.* variety of black tea prepared from leaves that were partially fermented before being dried. [Chinese (Mandarin) *wu lung* literally, black dragon.]

oomph (ōōmf) *n. Slang.* vitality or energy. [Imitative.]

ooze¹ (ōōz) *oozed, ooz·ing. v.i.* **1.** to pass out slowly through or as through small openings; seep. **2.** to disappear slowly or imperceptibly: *His enthusiasm oozed away.* **3.** to exude moisture or a liquid. —*v.t.* to emit or give off slowly or gradually. —*n.* **1.** slow, gradual leak or flow. **2.** something that oozes. [Old English *wōs* juice, sap².] —*Syn. v.i.* **1.** see **drip.**

ooze² (ōōz) *n.* soft, wet mud or slime, esp. at the bottom of a body of water. [Old English *wāse.*]

oo·zy¹ (ōō′zē) **-zi·er, -zi·est.** *adj.* slowly leaking; dripping. [OOZE¹ + -Y¹.]

oo·zy² (ōō′zē) **-zi·er, -zi·est.** *adj.* composed of or resembling ooze; slimy. [Middle English *wosie,* from *wose* mud, from Old English *wāse.*] —**oo′zi·ness,** *n.*

op-, form of **ob-** before *p,* as in *oppose.*

op. **1.** opera. **2.** operation. **3.** opposite. **4.** opus.

o·pac·i·ty (ō pas′ə tē) *pl.,* **-ties.** *n.* **1.** state or quality of being opaque. **2.** that which is opaque. [Latin *opācitās* shadiness.]

o·pal (ō′pəl) *n.* transparent to translucent mineral, an amorphous form of silica, found in igneous and sedimentary rocks and in deposits from hot springs. Iridescent white, milky blue, yellow, or black varieties are used as gems. Formula: SiO₂·nH₂O [Latin *opalus,* through Greek, from Sanskrit *upala* precious stone.]

o·pal·esce (ō′pə les′) **-esced, -esc·ing.** *v.i.* to exhibit an iridescent play of colors like that of the opal. [From OPALESCENT.]

o·pal·es·cence (ō′pə les′əns) *n.* iridescent play of colors like that of the opal.

o·pal·es·cent (ō′pə les′ənt) *adj.* exhibiting opalescence; having a milky iridescence. [OPAL + -ESCENT.]

o·pal·ine (ō′pə lin, -līn′) *adj.* of or resembling an opal.

o·paque (ō pāk′) *adj.* **1.** not letting light through; not transparent or translucent. **2.** not shining or lustrous; dull. **3.** difficult to understand; obscure. **4.** impervious to reason; unintelligent; obtuse. —*n.* that which is opaque. [Latin *opācus* shady, dark.] —**o·paque′ly,** *adv.* —**o·paque′ness,** *n.*

op art, style of abstract art in which geometrical patterns and other devices are used to create various optical illusions. [From OPTICAL.]

op. cit., in the work cited. [Latin *opere citātō.*]

ope (ōp) *oped, op·ing. v.t., v.i. Archaic.* to open.

o·pen (ō′pən) *adj.* **1.** affording free passage in and out; not shut: *an open door.* **2.** not sealed, wrapped, or otherwise done up: *an open letter.* **3.** having no surrounding barriers or obstructions; unenclosed: *an open meadow.* **4.** having no lid or other covering: *an open manhole.* **5.** free from obstructions or hindrances: *Only one lane is open because of the accident.* **6.** having spaces, holes, or gaps between the component parts or elements: *an open weave, an open formation of troops.* **7.** not drawn, folded, or rolled together; spread out; expanded: *an open hand, an open flower.* **8.** liable or subject to something; exposed (with *to*): *open to attack.* **9.** that can be availed (often with *to*): *There are two courses open to us.* **10.** not yet taken; unfilled: *The doctor has two appointments open.* **11.a.** receptive, as to new ideas, facts, or views; agreeable (often with *to*): *open to suggestions.* **b.** holding no preconceived biases; unprejudiced: *an open mind.* **12.** unreserved in expressing one's thoughts or feelings; outspoken; candid: *She was very open with me.* **13.** exposed to general view or knowledge; not secret or hidden: *open defiance.* **14.** ready or prepared to do business: *The store is not open after lunch.* **15.** accessible to the general public: *an open meeting.* **16.** not settled or decided; undetermined: *an open question.* **17.** having no prohibition or restriction: *open season on ducks.* **18.** generous; liberal: *to give with an open hand.* **19.a.** (of a vowel) articulated with the tongue held relatively low in the mouth. The *a* in *calm* is an open vowel. **b.** (of a syllable) ending in a vowel or diphthong. **20.** *Nautical.* free from fog, mist, or haze. **21.** *Informal.* characterized by ineffective or unen-

at; āpe; cär; end; mē; it; īce; hot; ōld; fôrk; wood; fōōl; oil; out; up; ūse; turn; sing; thin; this; zh in treasure; ə in ago, taken, pencil, lemon, circus.

705

forced legal restrictions, as on gambling or drinking: *an open town.* —*v.t.* **1.** to cause to be open; move from a closed position: *to open a door, to open a drawer, to open one's mouth.* **2.a.** to remove a lid or other covering from: *to open a jar.* **b.** to unwrap, unseal, or otherwise reveal: *to open one's mail. When are you going to open your presents?* **3.** to disclose the secrets of; lay bare: *to open one's heart.* **4.** to make more receptive, as to new ideas: *to open one's mind.* **5.** to unfold or unroll so as to expose that which is contained within: *to open a map.* **6.** to clear of obstructions or hindrances; make passable: *After the landslide, the road was not opened for three days.* **7.** to make or render accessible or available to the general public, as for use or settlement: *The city parks department opened the pool today.* **8.** to establish or set into operation: *to open a new office, to open an account.* **9.** to begin (something); start: *to open negotiations. He opened the meeting with a prayer.* **10.** to expand or spread out the component parts or elements of so as to leave spaces, holes, or gaps: *to open the ranks.* **11.** to cause to separate, burst open, or otherwise come apart: *to open a wound.* **12.** to make or form (a passage, hole, or other opening). —*v.i.* **1.** to become open: *The door opened.* **2.** to afford access or view; have an opening facing or towards: *The rooms open onto the pool.* **3.** to become ready to do business; begin operations: *The new store opens next week.* **4.** to become accessible or available to the general public, as for use. **5.** to begin; commence: *The exhibition opens tomorrow.* **6.** to spread apart; expand: *The flowers open in the spring.* **7.** to separate or burst open: *The wound opened when she fell.* **8.** to begin to appear; become disclosed or revealed. **9. to open up.** to disclose one's innermost thoughts or feelings: *She opened up to him.* —*n.* **1.** athletic contest, esp. a golf tournament, in which both amateurs and professionals may participate. **2. the open. a.** any clear or unenclosed space or area. **b.** public or general knowledge: *Her secret is now in the open.* [Old English *open* not shut, not closed, in, not secret, exposed.] —**o′pen·ly,** *adv.* —**o′pen·ness,** *n.*

o·pen-air (ō′pən âr′) *adj.* outdoor.

open air, outdoors.

o·pen-and-shut (ō′pən ən shut′) *adj.* that can be easily settled or decided; obvious: *an open-and-shut case.*

o·pen-door policy (ō′pən dôr′) policy of guaranteeing all nations equal trading and industrial rights in a particular region or area.

open-end investment company (ō′pən end′) mutual fund.

o·pen·er (ō′pə nər) *n.* **1.** any of various instruments or devices for opening tightly closed or sealed containers, as cans or bottles. **2.** first item or introductory part in any series. **3.** one who or that which opens.

o·pen-eyed (ō′pən īd′) *adj.* having eyes wide open, as in amazement.

open-hand·ed (ō′pən han′did) *adj.* liberal in giving; generous. —**o′pen·hand′ed·ly,** *adv.* —**o′pen·hand′ed·ness,** *n.*

o·pen-heart·ed (ō′pən här′tid) *adj.* **1.** candid; frank. **2.** generous. —**o′pen·heart′ed·ly,** *adv.* —**o′pen·heart′ed·ness,** *n.*

o·pen-hearth (ō′pən härth′) *adj.* **1.** relating to, designating, or used in a process for making steel, in which a furnace reflects heat from a low roof onto the raw material and in which brickwork on either side of the furnace retains heat that is then reutilized. **2.** of or relating to steel made by this process.

open house 1. party that is open to all who wish to come. **2.** occasion when an institution, school, or the like is open to visitors.

o·pen·ing (ō′pə ning) *n.* **1.** vacant or empty space: *an opening in the fence.* **2.** initial steps or stage; first part; beginning: *the opening of a legislative assembly.* **3.** unfilled position; job vacancy. **4.** first performance or occasion, as of a play. **5.** act of becoming open or of causing to open. **6.** clearing or open space in the forest. **7.** favorable opportunity.

open letter, statement of protest, appeal, or belief written in the form of a personal letter but intended for the public and published, as in a newspaper or magazine.

open market, market that is open or accessible to all buyers and sellers.

o·pen-mind·ed (ō′pən mīn′did) *adj.* having a mind that is receptive to new facts, ideas, views, or convictions; impartial; unprejudiced. —**o′pen-mind′ed·ly,** *adv.* —**o′pen-mind′ed·ness,** *n.*

o·pen-mouthed (ō′pən mouthd′, -mouth′) *adj.* **1.** having the mouth open, as in wonder, amazement, or surprise; gaping. **2.** greedy; ravenous. **3.** noisy; vociferous; clamorous.

open sesame, any miraculous, swift, or unfailing means of attaining a desired result: *They believed that money was the open sesame to happiness.* [From *open sesame,* the magic words used by Ali Baba to open the door of a robbers' cave in a story of the *Arabian Nights.*]

open shop 1. factory or other establishment in which belonging to or becoming a member of a union is not a requirement for employment. **2.** establishment that employs only nonunion labor. Distinguished from **closed shop.** —**open union shop** in both definitions.

o·pen·work (ō′pən wurk′) *n.* any ornamental work, as of metal, wood, or cloth, containing numerous small openings.

op·er·a[1] (op′ər ə, op′rə) *n.* **1.** play having all or most of its text sung, usually performed by solo voices, chorus, and orchestra, and presented with costumes, scenery, acting, and, often, dancing. **2.** branch of musical and dramatic art represented by such plays: *He prefers opera to symphonic music.* **3.** score or libretto of an opera. **4.** performance of an opera: *We went to the opera last night.* **5.** opera house. [Italian *opera* work, musical drama, short for *opera in musica* work set to music, from Latin *opera* work, labor.]

op·er·a[2] (op′ər ə, op′rə) plural of **opus.**

op·er·a·ble (op′ər ə bəl) *adj.* **1.** that can be done, carried out, or used. **2.** that can be treated by a surgical operation.

o·pé·ra bouffe (op′ər ə bōōf′, op′rə) *French.* comic opera, usually dealing with average human beings in farcical situations. Also, *Italian,* **o·pe·ra buf·fa** (op′ər ə bōō′fə, op′rə).

o·pé·ra co·mique (op′ər ə ko mēk′, kō mēk′, op′rə) *French.* opera having spoken dialogue.

opera glasses, small, low-power binoculars for use at theatrical entertainments, as operas, plays, or concerts.

opera hat, silk, top hat with a collapsible crown, worn by a man in formal dress.

opera house, theater esp. designed for the performance of operas.

Opera glasses

op·er·ate (op′ə rāt′) -at·ed, -at·ing. *v.i.* **1.** to perform or be at work: *They operate well as a unit.* **2.** to produce the intended or proper effect: *The antibiotic operated at once.* **3.** to perform a surgical operation: *The surgeon operated on Bob to remove his appendix.* **4.** to carry on military operations: *to operate behind enemy lines.* —*v.t.* **1.** to cause to perform or work: *to operate a machine.* **2.** to manage or direct the affairs of: *to operate a business.* **3.** to bring about; accomplish; produce. [Latin *operātus,* past participle of *operārī* to work.]

op·er·at·ic (op′ə rat′ik) *adj.* of, relating to, or like the opera. —**op′er·at′i·cal·ly,** *adv.*

op·er·a·tion (op′ə rā′shən) *n.* **1.** act or process of performing or being at work. **2.** way in which something operates. **3.** state or condition of performing or being at work: *The machine is in operation.* **4.** surgical procedure performed on the body for the purpose of relieving, removing, or repairing some diseased or malfunctioning part. **5.** specific act or process, esp. one that is part of a series. **6.** military movement, attack, or campaign. **7.** something done to one or more numbers or algebraic expressions to produce a single number or algebraic expression. Addition, subtraction, multiplication, and division are binary operations. [Latin *operātiō* a working.]

op·er·a·tive (op′ər ə tiv, op′rə-, op′ə rā′tiv) *adj.* **1.** functioning or producing effects. **2.** concerned with practical or physical work. **3.** of, resulting from, or relating to a surgical operation. —*n.* private or secret agent or investigator.

op·er·a·tor (op′ə rā′tər) *n.* **1.** one who operates a machine or other mechanical device. **2.** one who owns or runs a business or other enterprise. **3.** *Informal.* one who is shrewd, crafty, and often unscrupulous in obtaining what he wants.

o·per·cu·lar (ō pur′kyə lər) *adj.* of, relating to, or of the nature of an operculum.

o·per·cu·late (ō pur′kyə lit) *adj.* having an operculum. Also, **o·per·cu·lat·ed** (ō pur′kyə lā′tid).

o·per·cu·lum (ō pur′kyə ləm) *pl.,* **-la** (-lə) or **-lums.** *n.* any flaplike part or organ over an opening, esp. a bony, protective covering over the gills of bony fish. [Latin *operculum* cover, lid, from *operīre* to cover.]

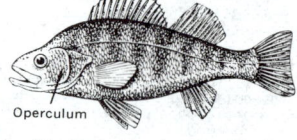

Operculum

op·er·et·ta (op′ə ret′ə) *pl.,* **-tas.** *n.* short opera, usually of a light and frivolous character, in which music and song are combined with spoken dialogue and dancing. [Italian *operetta,* diminutive of *opera.* See OPERA.]

o·phid·i·an (ō fid′ē ən) *adj.* of, relating to, or belonging to either of two reptilian suborders, Ophidia or Serpentes, that include all snakes. —*n.* member of either of these suborders; snake. [Modern Latin *Ophidia* (from Greek *ophis* snake) + AN.]

O·phir (ō′fər) *n.* in the Old Testament, a region famous for its gold and other valuable products.

oph·thal·mi·a (of thal′mē ə, op-) *n.* severe inflammation of the eye or the membrane that surrounds the eye and lines the eyelids. [Late Latin *ophthalmia,* from Greek *ophthalmiā,* from *ophthalmos* eye.]

oph·thal·mic (of thal′mik, op-) *adj.* **1.** of or relating to the eye or eyes. **2.** relating to or affected with ophthalmia.

at; āpe; cär; end; mē; it; īce; hot; ōld; fôrk; wood; fōōl; oil; out; up; ūse; turn; sing; thin; this; zh in treasure; ə in ago, taken, pencil, lemon, circus.

oph·thal·mol·o·gist (of'thal mol'ə jist, -thə mol'-, op'-) *n.* doctor who specializes in ophthalmology. Also, **oc'u·list.**

oph·thal·mol·o·gy (of'thal mol'ə jē, -thə mol'-, op'-) *n.* branch of medicine that deals with the treatment of diseases and disorders of the eye and includes eye surgery. [Greek *ophthalmos* eye + -LOGY.]

oph·thal·mo·scope (of thal'mə skōp', op-) *n.* instrument for examining the interior of the eye, esp. the retina. [Greek *ophthalmos* eye + -SCOPE.]

o·pi·ate (ō'pē it, -āt') *n.* **1.** drug that contains or is prepared from opium. **2.** anything that soothes, quiets, pacifies, or induces sleep. —*adj.* **1.** made with or containing opium. **2.** inducing sleep or relaxation. [Medieval Latin *opiātus* bringing sleep, from Latin *opium.* See OPIUM.]

o·pine (ō pīn') **o·pined, o·pin·ing.** *v.t., v.i.* Archaic. to hold or express as an opinion; think. [French *opiner,* from Latin *opīnārī.*]

o·pin·ion (ə pin'yən) *n.* **1.** belief or conclusion based on what one thinks rather than on what is proven or known to be true. **2.** impression, evaluation, or estimation formed of a person or thing with reference to worth, excellence, or quality. **3.** formal conclusion or estimation given by an expert or professional. [Old French *opinion* belief, from Latin *opīniō.*]

Syn. 1. Opinion, view, belief mean a judgment or conception which one holds to be true or valid. **Opinion** applies to a more or less clearly formulated judgment or settled conclusion concerning a debatable subject based on a subjective interpretation of facts and falling short of absolute certainty or positive knowledge: *The editorial expressed the paper's opinion on the election.* **View** applies to an overall opinion or set of opinions more or less colored by personal sentiment, bias, or intellectual makeup: *The elderly speaker aired his conservative views on the younger generation.* **Belief** emphasizes the intellectual acceptance and adoption of a doctrine or proposition not immediately susceptible to rigorous proof but sanctioned by a tradition or authority to which one subscribes strongly: *Karl has an unshakeable belief in reincarnation.*

o·pin·ion·at·ed (ə pin'yə nā'tid) *adj.* stubbornly holding to one's opinions; dogmatic.

o·pin·ion·a·tive (ə pin'yə nā'tiv) *adj.* **1.** opinionated. **2.** relating to or of the nature of opinion.

o·pi·um (ō'pē əm) *n.* powerful drug obtained from the white fluid contained in the unripe seed capsules of a poppy, *Papaver somniferum.* Opium and its derivatives, including morphine and codeine, are valuable for relieving pain and inducing sleep, but they are addictive. [Latin *opium,* from Greek *opion,* diminutive of *opos* juice.]

O·por·to (ō pôr'tō) *n.* port city in northwestern Portugal. Pop. (1968), 324,400.

o·pos·sum (ə pos'əm) *n.* any of various marsupials, family Didelphidae, native to North, Central, and South America, having a white, pointed snout, a hairless, ratlike tail, and long, coarse, usually gray-and-white fur. When frightened, the

Opossum

opossum suffers temporary paralysis and lies motionless, as if it were dead. Length: 3–15 inches. [Algonquian *ápasúm* literally, white animal.]

op·po·nent (ə pō'nənt) *n.* **1.** one who opposes, fights, or competes with another, as in a game or discussion. **2.** any of several muscles, esp. in the hand, that counteract the actions of other muscles. —*adj.* acting or behaving in opposition; antagonistic. [Latin *oppōnēns,* present participle of *oppōnere* to set or place against.]

Syn. n. 1. Opponent, antagonist, adversary mean one who contends with or opposes another. **Opponent** suggests one who is on the opposing side of a struggle, contest, or controversy: *Opponents of civil rights defeated the amendment.* **Antagonist** stresses the hostility that underlies one's opposition to another and motivates a desire for supremacy and control: *At last the two antagonists met on the battlefield.* **Adversary** suggests a determined and implacable opponent who manifests active hostility and animosity: *The old political bosses found a formidable adversary in the young lawyer.*

op·por·tune (op'ər tōōn', -tūn') *adj.* **1.** suitable or appropriate for a particular purpose. **2.** well-timed; timely. [Latin *opportūnus* convenient; literally, toward the harbor (referring to favorable winds) from *ob* (see OB-) + *portus* harbor.] —**op'por·tune'ly,** *adv.* —**op'por·tune'ness,** *n.*

op·por·tun·ist (op'ər tōō'nist, -tū'-) *n.* one who takes advantage of every opportunity in furthering his own interests or achieving some end, regardless of the consequences or of moral principles. —**op'por·tun'ism,** *n.* —**op'por·tun·is'tic,** *adj.*

op·por·tu·ni·ty (op'ər tōō'nə tē, -tū'-) *pl.* **-ties.** *n.* **1.** time or circumstance that is favorable for the achievement of some

purpose. **2.** good chance, as to advance oneself: *a job with many opportunities.*

Syn. 1. Opportunity, occasion, chance mean a combination of favorable circumstances. **Opportunity** is an advantageous combination of circumstances suitable or propitious for a particular activity in accord with one's ambitions or desires: *The hunter was waiting for an opportunity to shoot the tiger.* **Occasion** is a timely and convenient moment that offers not merely an opportunity but a pretext or excuse for some specific action: *Nat's visit to the library gave him the occasion to consult the encyclopedia.* **Chance** refers to an opportune juncture offering, seemingly by luck or accident, an opportunity for something to take place: *The scholarship gave Sam the chance to go abroad.*

op·pos·a·ble (ə pō'zə bəl) *adj.* **1.** that can be opposed. **2.** that can be placed opposite or in opposition to something else, as the human thumb.

op·pose (ə pōz') **-posed, -pos·ing.** *v.t.* **1.** to be or struggle against; offer resistance to: *to oppose change.* **2.** to place in opposition; contrast: *Evil is opposed to good.* —*v.i.* to act or be in opposition to something. [Old French *opposer* to cause to face, put in the way of, modification (influenced by French *poser* to put, place) of Latin *oppōnere* to set or place against.] —**op'pos'er,** *n.* —**Syn.** *v.t.* **1.** see withstand.

op·po·site (op'ə zit, -sit) *adj.* **1.** situated face to face with, against, or on the other side of an intervening space or thing. **2.** turned or moving the other way: *in opposite directions.* **3.** of a totally or radically different nature, character, or tendency: *Hot is opposite to cold.* **4.** growing in opposite directions from one node, as leaves. —*n.* one who or that which is opposite or contrary to another. —*prep.* across from or facing: *opposite the drugstore.* [Old French *opposite* placed facing, contrary, from Latin *oppositus,* past participle of *oppōnere* to set or place against.] —**op'po·site·ly,** *adv.* —**op'po·site·ness,** *n.*

op·po·si·tion (op'ə zish'ən) *n.* **1.** act of being or struggling against. **2.** state of being opposed or opposite. **3.** contrary or hostile action or feeling: *Our plan met with fierce opposition.* **4.** position that is opposite to another. **5.** *also,* **Opposition.** political party opposed to the party in power. **6.** Astronomy. situation of a planet when its celestial longitude differs by 180° from that of the sun. [Latin *oppositiō* an opposing.]

op·press (ə pres') *v.t.* **1.** to control or govern by the cruel and unjust use of force or authority; tyrannize. **2.** to affect with a feeling of pressure, constraint, or distress; weigh heavily on. [Old French *oppresser* to torment, harass, from Medieval Latin *oppressāre* to bear down on, suppress, from Latin *opprimere* to press against; suppress.]

Syn. 1. Oppress, suppress, repress mean to control by the use of force. To **oppress** is to burden, trample, and harass with cruel and unjust impositions so as to subjugate: *The people were oppressed by the dictator's secret police.* To **suppress** is to subdue or hold back effectively a person or thing that seeks an expression or outlet: *The army suppressed the revolt in the provinces.* To **repress** is to check, restrain, and stifle by strict force or control: *The captain quickly repressed the mutiny.*

op·pres·sion (ə presh'ən) *n.* **1.** act of oppressing; being oppressed. **2.** something that causes difficulty, pain, or suffering; hardship; burden. **3.** feeling of being mentally or physically weighed down.

op·pres·sive (ə pres'iv) *adj.* **1.** cruel and unjust; tyrannical: *an oppressive law.* **2.** producing a state or feeling of oppression. —**op·pres'sive·ly,** *adv.* —**op·pres'sive·ness,** *n.*

op·pres·sor (ə pres'ər) *n.* one who oppresses; tyrant.

op·pro·bri·ous (ə prō'brē əs) *adj.* **1.** expressing or conveying reproach, disapproval, or disgrace; abusive: *an opprobrious epithet.* **2.** deserving reproach or disapproval; disgraceful: *opprobrious conduct.* [Late Latin *opprobriōsus* full of reproach, from Latin *opprobrium* reproach, disgrace.] —**op·pro'bri·ous·ly,** *adv.*

op·pro·bri·um (ə prō'brē əm) *n.* **1.** disgrace or reproach arising from conduct considered shameful. **2.** cause, object, or occasion of disgrace or reproach. **3.** reproach or contempt. [Latin *opprobrium* reproach, disgrace.]

op·so·nin (op'sə nin) *n.* any of various antibodies in the blood serum that cause bacteria to be less resistant to the action of white blood cells. [Latin *opsōnium* victuals (from Greek *opsōnion* prepared food) + -IN[1].]

op·ta·tive (op'tə tiv) *adj.* of or relating to the verbal mood in certain languages, as Greek, that expresses a wish. —*n.* **1.** optative mood. **2.** verb or construction in this mood. [Late Latin *optātīvus* expressing a wish, from Latin *optāre* to wish.]

op·tic (op'tik) *adj.* of or relating to vision or the eye. [Old French *optique* relating to vision, from Greek *optikos.*]

op·ti·cal (op'ti kəl) *adj.* **1.** of or relating to vision. **2.** designed to aid vision. **3.** of or relating to the science of optics. —**op'ti·cal·ly,** *adv.*

optical fiber, transparent glass or plastic fiber, surrounded by a less refractive material, that conducts light by repeatedly reflecting light waves along its inner surface, used in groups to transmit entire images.

optical maser, laser.

op·ti·cian (op tish'ən) *n.* one who fills prescriptions for, and special-

izes in fitting and adjusting, eyeglasses and contact lenses. He may make or sell binoculars, magnifying glasses, and other optical instruments as well. [French *opticien*, from Medieval Latin *optica* optics, from Greek *ta optika*.]

optic nerve, nerve that carries impulses from the eye to the brain.

op·tics (op′tiks) *n.,pl.* branch of physics dealing with the nature and behavior of light. ▲ construed as singular.

op·ti·mal (op′tə məl) *adj.* best or most favorable.

op·ti·mism (op′tə miz′əm) *n.* **1.** belief that things will turn out for the best and are not hopeless: *Before the meeting, both parties expressed optimism about an eventual solution.* **2.** tendency or disposition to hope for or expect the best or to look on the bright side of things: *His optimism blinded him to many problems.* **3.** philosophical view, as stated by Leibniz, that the existing world is the best of all possible worlds. [French *optimisme*, from Latin *optimum* the best.] —**op′ti·mist**, *n.* —**op′ti·mis′tic**, *adj.* —**op′ti·mis′ti·cal·ly**, *adv.*

op·ti·mum (op′tə məm) *pl.*, **-mums** or **-ma** (-mə). *n.* best, highest possible, or most favorable point or level: *at an optimum.* —*adj.* best, highest possible, or most favorable: *In wartime, industries work at optimum efficiency.* [Latin *optimum* the best.]

op·tion (op′shən) *n.* **1.** ability or opportunity to choose: *You have the option of leaving or staying.* **2.** act of choosing or course of action chosen: *My option is to stay.* **3.** extra feature, esp. on an automobile, that is added at the buyer's request: *Additional options, such as airconditioning and bucket seats, made it an expensive car.* **4.** negotiable right to buy, sell, rent, or use something for a specified price within a stated period of time: *The new owner obtained an option to sell back the business if it didn't make money.* [Latin *optiō* choice.] —**Syn. 1.** see **choice.**

op·tion·al (op′shən əl) *adj.* that depends on choice; not required or automatic: *Ice cream on your pie is optional.* —**op′tion·al·ly**, *adv.*

op·tom·e·trist (op tom′ə trist′) *n.* one licensed to practice optometry.

op·tom·e·try (op tom′ə trē) *n.* practice or profession of testing the eyes for defects of vision and prescribing corrective lenses. [Greek *optos* seen, visible + -METRY.]

op·u·lent (op′yə lənt) *adj.* **1.** having much wealth; wealthy; affluent. **2.** indicating or showing wealth or affluence: *an opulent gift, an opulent apartment.* **3.** rich; profuse; luxuriant: *opulent tresses.* [Latin *opulentus* rich, from *ops* might, riches, aid.] —**op′u·lence**, *n.*

o·pus (ō′pəs) *pl.*, **op·er·a** or **o·pus·es.** *n.* work or composition. ▲ used with numbers to identify a composer's musical works according to the order in which they were composed or published. [Latin *opus* work, labor.]

or[1] (ôr; *unstressed* ər) *conj.* **1.** used to introduce an alternative of two or more: *hot or cold, red, blue, or green ink.* **2.** used to introduce the second of two alternatives when the first is introduced by *either* or *whether: Either write or phone me. We didn't know whether to stay or leave.* **3.** used to introduce a word meaning the same thing: *aeronautics or the science of flight.* **4.** otherwise: *You had better eat lunch or you will be hungry.* [Shortened from Middle English *other*, modification of Old English *oththe.*]

or[2] (ôr) *n. Heraldry.* gold or yellow, represented in engraving by small dots powdered over a plain field. [Old French *or* gold, from Latin *aurum.*]

-or *suffix* **1.** (used to form nouns from verbs) one who or that which performs the action of: *inventor, governor, elevator.* **2.** (used to form nouns) state, condition, or quality: *stupor, color, tremor.* [Latin *-or.*]

o·ra (ô′rə) plural of os[2].

or·a·cle (ôr′ə kəl, or′-) *n.* **1.** divinely inspired priest, priestess, or other medium through whom certain ancient gods, as Apollo, answered the questions of their worshipers. **2.** shrine or temple of a god, as that at Delphi, where answers were given. **3.** answer given by a medium at such a shrine, often having a vague or hidden meaning. **4.** one who or that which has, pretends to have, or is believed to have great knowledge, wisdom, or authority: *That newspaper is his oracle.* [Old French *oracle* divine announcement, place where a divine announcement is given, from Latin *ōrāculum*, from *ōrāre* to speak, pray.]

o·rac·u·lar (ô rak′yə lər) *adj.* **1.** of, relating to, or like an oracle. **2.** with vague or hidden meaning: *an author whose writings are mysterious and oracular.* —**o·rac′u·lar·ly**, *adv.*

o·ral (ôr′əl) *adj.* **1.** uttered or communicated in words; spoken: *oral teachings that were not recorded.* **2.** of or relating to the mouth: *oral surgery.* **3.** taken into the body through the mouth: *an oral vaccine.* **4.** *Phonetics.* produced by the mouth without the nasal passage. —*n.* school examination taken and administered orally. [Latin *ōr-*, stem of *ōs* mouth + -AL[1].] —**o′ral·ly**, *adv.*

Syn. *adj.* **1. Oral, verbal** mean of or in words. **Oral** refers to what is uttered by word of mouth as opposed to written communication: *The manager gave oral instructions to his staff.* **Verbal** relates to the use of words as a medium of communication and may apply indifferently to

what is written or spoken: *Visual images appeal to children more than verbal ones.*

O·ran (ō ran′, ô ran′) *n.* port city in northwestern Algeria, on the Mediterranean Sea. Pop. (1966 est.), 327,493.

or·ange (ôr′inj, or′-) *n.* **1.** round, edible fruit of a citrus tree having a thick orange or yellow rind and a juicy, sweetish or acid pulp. **2.** tropical evergreen tree, genus *Citrus*, bearing this fruit, having waxy white flowers. **3.** any of various other fruits or trees, as the trifoliate orange, *Poncirus trifoliata.* **4.** reddish-yellow color. —*adj.* **1.** reddish-yellow. **2.** made from or flavored with oranges: *orange juice, orange icing.* **3.** of, relating to, or containing oranges: *an orange grove.* [Old French *orenge* the citrus fruit, through Arabic, from Persian *nārang*, from Sanskrit *nāranga* the tree of the genus *Citrus.*]

Or·ange (ôr′inj, or′-) *n.* **1.** city in southern California, near Los Angeles. Pop. (1970), 77,374. **2.** princely family of Europe, now the royal family of the Netherlands.

or·ange·ade (ôr′in jād′, or′-) *n.* drink of orange juice and water, sweetened with sugar.

O·range·man (ôr′inj mən, or′-) *pl.*, **-men.** *n.* member of a secret political and religious society formed in the north of Ireland in 1795 to oppose Roman Catholicism and support Protestant control of Ireland.

orange pekoe, fine quality black tea processed from small leaves.

o·rang·u·tan (ə rang′oo tan′, ô rang′-) *also,* **o·rang·u·tan, o·rang·ou·tang** (ə rang′oo tang′, ô rang′-). *n.* tree-dwelling anthropoid ape, *Pongo pygmaeus*, native to the forests of Borneo and Sumatra, having very long powerful arms, short legs, and a shaggy coat of reddish-brown hair. Height: 4½ feet. [Malay *ōrang ūtan* wild man, from *ōrang* man + *ūtan* wild; applied by Malayans to savages, but by Europeans to a species of ape.]

Orang-utan

o·rate (ô rāt′, ôr′āt) *v.i.* to speak in a grandiose, pompous, or formal manner. [From ORATION.]

o·ra·tion (ô rā′shən) *n.* long, elaborate, formal speech, usually prepared for delivery before a large audience. [Latin *ōrātiō* speech, prayer. Doublet of ORISON.]

or·a·tor (ôr′ə tər, or′-) *n.* one who delivers orations or an oration. [Latin *ōrātor.*]

or·a·tor·i·cal (ôr′ə tôr′i kəl, or′ə tor′-) *adj.* **1.** overly pompous, grandiose, or formal like oratory. **2.** of or relating to orators or oratory. —**or′a·tor′i·cal·ly**, *adv.*

or·a·to·ri·o (ôr′ə tôr′ē ō′, or′-) *pl.*, **-ri·os.** *n.* dramatic musical composition, usually set to a religious text and performed by solo voices, chorus, and orchestra, without action, costumes, or scenery. [Italian *oratorio* oratorio, oratory[2], from Church Latin *ōrātōrium* place of prayer; because oratorios were introduced in the *Oratory* of St. Philip Neri in Rome.]

or·a·to·ry[1] (ôr′ə tôr′ē, or′-) *n.* **1.** eloquent or grandiose public speaking, often in an artificial style, designed to persuade or edify an audience: *campaign oratory.* **2.** art of public speaking. [Latin *(ars) ōrātōria* (art) of public speaking, from *ōrātor* speaker.]

or·a·to·ry[2] (ôr′ə tôr′ē, or′-) *pl.*, **-ries.** *n.* place set aside for prayer, as a room in a convent. [Church Latin *ōrātōrium* place of prayer.]

orb (ôrb) *Archaic. n.* something round, as a sphere, globe, planet, eyeball, or orb. —*v.t.* to form (something) into a circle or sphere, or encircle or surround (something). [Latin *orbis* circle, disk.]

or·bic·u·lar (ôr bik′yə lər) *adj.* round; rounded. Also, **or·bic·u·late** (ôr bik′yə lit, -lāt′). [Late Latin *orbiculāris* circular, from Latin *orbiculus* small disk, diminutive of *orbis* circle, disk.]

or·bit (ôr′bit) *n.* **1.** path of a celestial body as it revolves in a closed curve about another body. **2.** one complete trip of a spacecraft or artificial satellite along such a path, measured without regard to the speed or direction of the other body. Distinguished from **revolution. 3.** orbital. **4.** range of one's life, activities, or knowledge: *one's intellectual orbit.* **5.** either of the bony hollows or cavities in the skull in which the eyeballs are located; eye socket. —*v.t.* **1.** to move in an orbit around: *Mercury orbits the sun.* **2.** to put (a spacecraft or satellite) into an orbit. —*v.i.* to move in an orbit. [Latin *orbita* path, track made by a wheel, from *orbis* circle, disk.]

or·bit·al (ôr′bit əl) *adj.* of, relating to, in, or required for an orbit: *orbital docking, orbital velocity.* —*n.* area of space or fixed path through which an electron moves about the nucleus of an atom.

or·chard (ôr′chərd) *n.* **1.** area where fruit or nut trees are grown. **2.** the trees themselves. [Old English *ortgeard* garden, from Latin *hortus* garden + Old English *geard* yard[1].]

or·ches·tra (ôr′kis trə) *n.* **1.** comparatively large group of instrumen-

at; āpe; cär; end; mē; it; īce; hot; ōld; fôrk; wood; fo͞ol; oil; out; up; ūse; turn; sing; thin; this; zh in treasure; ə in ago, taken, pencil, lemon, circus.

talists performing as an organized unit under the direction of a conductor. **2.** instruments played by such a group, usually including strings, woodwinds, brasses, and percussion instruments. **3.** main floor of a theater. **4.** usually lowered or sunken area just in front of a stage, in which the orchestra plays at the performance of an opera, ballet, or other musical show. Also (*def. 4*), **orchestra pit.** [Latin *orchestra* place where the Senate sat in the theater, from Greek *orchēstrā* space in the Greek theater where the chorus danced; literally, dancing place, from *orcheisthai* to dance.]

or·ches·tral (ôr kes′trəl) *adj.* of, relating to, composed for, or performed by an orchestra. **—or·ches′tral·ly,** *adv.*

or·ches·trate (ôr′kis trāt′) *-trat·ed, -trat·ing. v.t.* **1.** to compose or arrange (music) for an orchestra, esp. to decide which instruments are to play each part. **2.** to combine harmoniously, like instruments in an orchestra. **—or′ches·tra′tion, or′ches·tra′tor;** also, **or′ches·trat′er,** *n.*

or·chid (ôr′kid) *n.* **1.** any of various flowers, often pale purple or white, having three petal-like sepals, two similar outer petals, and an inner petal or lip. **2.** any of various plants, family Orchidaceae, bearing this flower. **3.** bluish or rosy purple color. [From Modern Latin *Orchideae,* from Latin *orchis* the plant, from Greek *orchis* the plant, testicle; because of the shape of the root.]

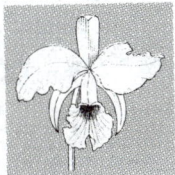

Orchid

or·dain (ôr dān′) *v.t.* **1.** to fix, decide, or command by or as by decree or authority: *Fate ordained that they would meet again.* **2.** to appoint to or formally introduce into a ministerial or other religious office. [Anglo-Norman *ordeiner,* from Latin *ordināre* to set in order.]

or·deal (ôr dēl′, ôr′dēl) *n.* **1.** circumstance or experience that is painful or difficult to endure. **2.** formerly, subjection of an accused person to some danger, as poison or fire. If the person was unharmed, it was believed to be proof of his innocence. [Old English *ordāl* form of trial in which the accused is forced to take a test of a dangerous nature.]

or·der (ôr′dər) *n.* **1.** *also,* **orders.** statement that tells someone what to do, esp. one backed by force or authority; command or direction: *orders from headquarters.* **2.** command or direction of a court or judge entered or made in writing, but not included in a judgment: *to obtain a court order releasing the prisoner from solitary confinement.* **3.** arrangement of things; position in a series: *You will pass a school, a church, and a bus station, in that order.* **4.** any fixed, lawful, or logical system, scheme, or condition: *the order of the universe.* **5.** set of established, usual, or normal practices, institutions, activities, or rules: *to destroy the old order of society, to restore order after a riot.* **6.** condition of being right, expected, or allowed according to prescribed or understood standards, as for conducting a meeting: *The motion to adjourn was out of order. An apology was in order.* **7.** clean, neat, proper, or manageable condition: *to put a room in order, to put one's life in order.* **8.** condition of functioning or working properly: *The telephone is out of order.* **9.** request for something, as food: *Has the waitress brought your order?* **10.** amount requested at one time; single portion: *two orders of French fried potatoes.* **11.** kind; type; sort: *an old bed sheet or something of that order to use as a tourniquet.* **12.** rank, level, relative extent, or approximate scale. **13.** *Biology.* category in the classification of plants and animals that ranks higher than a family but lower than a class; for example, the order Carnivora includes the cat, dog, bear, and other families, and is included in the class of mammals. **14.a.** any of the grades or ranks of the Christian clergy: *He was a member of the order of deacons.* **15.** body of persons living under the same regulations, esp. a religious group. **16.** honorary institution or society. **17.** body of persons united by some special interest or purpose; fraternal organization. **18.** decoration, as a medal or badge, awarded to persons admitted into an order. **19.a.** any one of the three major styles of classical Greek architecture, Doric, Ionic, or Corinthian, usually distinguished from each other by the general character of the columns, including proportion and capital types. **b.** column with its entablature forming the basic unit of a style. **20.** *Algebra.* degree. **21.** *also,* **orders.** rite of ordination. **22.** prescribed form for the performance of a religious service: *the order for the consecration of a bishop.* **23. to be in** (or **take**) **orders.** to be (or become) a member of the ordained clergy. **24. in order to** (or **that**). for the purpose that; so as to: *to stand on a chair in order to reach the shelf.* **25. in short order.** quickly; without delay. **26. made to order. a.** made according to the purchaser's specifications. **b.** ideally suited; just right: *a day made to order for a picnic.* **27. on order.** having been requested but not yet made or delivered. **—v.t. 1.** to command or direct (someone) to do something, esp. with force or authority: *to order the soldiers to retreat.* **2.** to give an order that (something) be done: *to order that the flag be flown at half-mast.* **3.** to place an order for; request: *to order wine with dinner.* **4.** to put into a fixed, logical, or proper order; give order to: *Here all things in their place remain, as all were ordered, ages*

since (Tennyson, 1842). **5.** *Archaic.* to ordain. **6. to order (someone) about** (or **around**). to treat (someone) as a subordinate; dominate. **7. to order arms.** to put one's rifle vertically, butt down, on the ground on the right side of the body. **—v.i.** to place or give an order or orders. [Old French *ordre* regular disposition of things, grade in the hierarchy of the church, each of a group making up a classification, from Latin *ordō* row[1], methodical arrangement, rank[1].] **—Syn.** *v.t.* **1.** see **command.**

ordered pair, *Mathematics.* pair of numbers or elements for which the order is specified. The ordered pair one, two is written (1,2). Also, **ordered couple.**

or·der·ly (ôr′dər lē) *adj.* **1.** that is in a certain order or has order: *to march in an orderly line, an orderly room.* **2.** free from disturbances or violence: *an orderly demonstration.* **3.** relating to or concerned with the execution of orders, as military orders. **—n.** *pl.,* **-lies. 1.** soldier assigned to an officer or officers for the purpose of carrying messages and performing various other tasks. **2.** male hospital attendant. **—or′der·li·ness,** *n.*

Syn. *adj.* **1. Orderly, methodical, systematic** mean following closely in a particular arrangement. **Orderly** suggests neatness of arrangement and freedom from confusion: *The officer maintained his records in an orderly fashion.* **Methodical** emphasizes following closely and regularly a logical or definite plan: *The detective searched for clues in a methodical manner.* **Systematic** is very close to *methodical* in meaning but adds to it the idea of thoroughness and elaborateness: *The school offered a systematic course in reading.*

Order of the Garter, oldest and most important order of knighthood in England, founded about 1350.

or·di·nal (ôrd′ən əl) *adj.* **1.** of, relating to, or indicating order or position in a series. **2.** of or relating to an order of animals or plants. **—n. 1.** ordinal number. **2.** book containing the directions for the performance of various ceremonies, esp. ordinations. [Late Latin *ōrdinālis* denoting an order of succession, from Latin *ōrdō* row[1], methodical arrangement, rank[1].]

ordinal number, number that shows sequence or position in a set or collection, as first, second, third, and so forth. ▲ see usage note under **cardinal number.**

or·di·nance (ôrd′ən əns) *n.* **1.** regulation or law, esp. that of a municipal body. **2.** prescribed religious ceremony. [Old French *ordinance* rule, government, going back to Latin *ōrdināre* to set in order.]

or·di·nar·i·ly (ôrd′ən er′ə lē) *adv.* **1.** in most cases; usually; commonly: *Ordinarily, the museum is open on Sundays.* **2.** in a usual or normal way: *ordinarily clothed.*

or·di·nar·y (ôrd′ən er′ē) *adj.* **1.** commonly used; habitual or regular; usual: *Betsy's ordinary tone of voice is very loud.* **2.** not distinguished in any way from others; not outstanding or exceptional: *an ordinary, routine performance.* **—n.** *pl.,* **-nar·ies. 1.** one who has power and jurisdiction attached directly to his position, esp. a bishop. **2.** prescribed form for saying Mass, esp. the prayers that do not change from day to day. **3. in ordinary.** in regular, steady service. **4. out of the ordinary.** unusual; exceptional. [Latin *ōrdinārius* usual, regular, from *ōrdō* row[1], rank[1], methodical arrangement.]

Syn. *adj.* **1.** see **common.** **2. Ordinary, mediocre, commonplace** mean lacking distinction and excellence. **Ordinary** may be applied to what is common, usual, and of everyday occurrence: *The book describes the way of life of the ordinary people of Mexico.* **Mediocre** may be applied to what lacks exceptional qualities and is merely average: *The audience was disappointed by the mediocre performance of the troupe.* **Commonplace** may be used to describe what is unworthy of special notice due to a lack of originality, individuality, or freshness: *Many movies deal with commonplace themes.*

ordinary seaman, seaman who is not yet qualified to be an able-bodied seaman.

or·di·nate (ôrd′ən it, -āt′) *n.* **1.** on a line graph, distance of a point from the horizontal axis measured parallel to the vertical axis, used to define the point in the system of Cartesian coordinates. Distinguished from **abscissa. 2.** line, number, or algebraic expression representing this distance. [Latin *ōrdinātus,* past participle of *ōrdināre* to set in order.]

Abscissa (5)

Ordinate (3)

Ordinate

or·di·na·tion (ôrd′ən ā′shən) *n.* **1.** ceremony of ordaining. **2.** state of being ordained. [Latin *ōrdinātiō* a setting in order, appointing to office.]

ord·nance (ôrd′nəns) *n.* **1.** military weapons and equipment. **2.** artillery. **3.** branch of a military service which procures, stores, and issues ammunition. [Form of ORDNANCE.]

Or·do·vi·cian (ôr′də vish′ən) *n.* second geological period of the Paleozoic era, when the first vertebrates, the fish, appeared. See **geology**

at; āpe; cär; end; mē; it; īce; hot; ōld; fôrk; wood; fōol; oil; out; up; ūse; turn; sing; thin; this; zh in treasure; ə in ago, taken, pencil, lemon, circus.

709

for table. —*adj.* of, relating to, or characteristic of this period. [Latin *Ordovicēs* an ancient Celtic tribe of Wales + -IAN; because this period was studied intensively in Wales.]

or·dure (ôr′jər, -dyər) *n.* filth; dung; excrement. [Old French *ordure* filth, from *ord* filthy, from Latin *horridus* rough, frightful.]

Or·dzho·ni·kid·ze (ôr′jō ni kēd′zə) *n.* city in the southwestern Soviet Union. Pop. (1970 est.), 236,000.

ore (ôr) *n.* substance in the earth that can be profitably mined for its content of metals or useful minerals. [Old English *ōra* crude metal.]

ö·re (œ′rə) *pl.*, **ö·re.** 1. one-hundredth of a krona and krone in Scandinavian currency. [Danish and Norwegian *øre* and Swedish *öre*, all going back to Latin *aureus* gold coin.]

Ore., Oregon.

o·re·ad (ôr′ē ad′) *n.* Greek Mythology. nymph who lived in a mountain or grotto. [Latin *Orēas*, from Greek *Oreias*, from *oros* mountain.]

Oreg., Oregon.

o·reg·a·no (ə reg′ə nō′, ô reg′-) *n.* any of various plants, genus *Origanum*, of the mint family, whose fragrant leaves are used for seasoning.

Or·e·gon (ôr′ə gon′, -gən, or′-) *n.* state in the northwestern United States, on the Pacific. Capital, Salem. Area, 96,981 sq. mi. Pop. (1970), 2,091,385. Abbreviations, **Oreg., Ore.** —**Or·e·go·ni·an** (ôr′ə gō′nē ən, or′-) *adj.*, *n.*

O·res·tes (ô res′tēz) *n.* Greek Mythology. brother of Electra, who killed his mother Clytemnestra and her lover because they had murdered his father Agamemnon.

or·gan (ôr′gən) *n.* 1. musical instrument in which tones are produced by compressed air, consisting of ranks of pipes of varied length, keyboards, or manuals, a pedalboard, and stops which regulate the volume and quality of the tone. Also, **pipe organ.** 2. similar instrument whose tones are produced and amplified electrically. 3. harmonium or reed organ. 4. barrel organ or hand organ. 5. mouth organ; harmonica. 6. *Biology.* any specialized structure, as a kidney, composed of several kinds of tissues, which performs a specific function or functions. Organs are present in all higher plants and animals. 4. medium of communication or of expression of opinion, as a newspaper or magazine for the employees of a company. 5. means or instrument by which something is performed or accomplished, esp. a government institution. [Latin *organum* implement, musical instrument, from Greek *organon.*]

or·gan·dy (ôr′gən dē) *pl.*, **-dies.** also, **or·gan·die.** *n.* sheer, lightweight fabric, usually made of cotton and given a crisp finish, used esp. for dresses and curtains. [French *organdi*; of uncertain origin.]

organ grinder, street musician, often accompanied by a monkey, who plays a hand organ.

or·gan·ic (ôr gan′ik) *adj.* 1. of, relating to, or including living things studied in biology: *organic nature.* 2. of or relating to a body organ. 3. of, using, or produced by methods that avoid the use of inorganic substances, as chemical fertilizers or insecticides: *organic farming, organic foods.* 4. that exists or operates on a deep level; not accidental or superficial; inherent; basic: *art that has an organic connection with religious faith.* 5. made up of interconnected and related parts: *The life of the pond formed an organic whole because each creature performed a function necessary to support the others.* 6. of, relating to, or belonging to a class of chemical compounds including most of the compounds of carbon. 7. *Archaic.* (of a chemical compound) produced only by living things or organisms. [Latin *organicus* relating to implements, going back to Greek *organon* implement.] —**or·gan′i·cal·ly,** *adv.*

organic chemistry, branch of chemistry that deals with organic compounds.

or·gan·ism (ôr′gə niz′əm) *n.* 1. living animal or plant having organs that function together to maintain vital activities. 2. something comparable to a living thing in having parts that function together to form a whole: *the economic organism.*

or·gan·ist (ôr′gə nist) *n.* one who plays the organ.

or·gan·i·za·tion (ôr′gə ni zā′shən) *n.* 1. act or process of organizing. 2. state or manner of being organized: *the organization of books by subject matter or by author.* 3. group composed of individuals united or organized for a particular purpose: *a labor organization.*

Organization of American States, regional organization composed of twenty-two Latin American countries and the United States, established in 1948 to provide collective security, economic cooperation, and peaceful settlement of disputes.

or·gan·ize (ôr′gə nīz′) **-ized, -iz·ing.** *v.t.* 1. to arrange in an orderly, systematic fashion: *to organize files.* 2. to put or bring together; bring into being; create: *to organize an amateur theater group.* 3. to cause (employees) to form or join a labor union: *to organize shop workers.* 4. to cause employees of (a business or an industry) to form or join a labor union: *to organize a factory.* —*v.i.* to form or join a labor union or other organization. [Medieval Latin *organizare* to arrange, form, from Latin *organum* implement. See ORGAN.] —**or′gan·iz′a·ble,** *adj.* —**or′gan·iz′er,** *n.*

organized labor, all the members of labor unions, considered collectively.

or·gan·za (ôr gan′zə) *n.* transparent, lightweight fabric that resembles organdy, usually made of rayon and given a stiff finish, used esp. for dresses, blouses, and trimmings.

or·gasm (ôr′gaz′əm) *n.* climax or point of highest excitement of sexual intercourse. [French *orgasme*, from Greek *orgasmos*, from *organ* to swell (with lust).]

or·gi·as·tic (ôr′jē as′tik) *adj.* of, relating to, or resembling an orgy: *orgiastic abandon, orgiastic rites.*

or·gy (ôr′jē) *pl.*, **-gies.** *n.* 1. wild, drunken, unrestrained revelry or party. 2. any excessive or unbridled indulgence: *an orgy of sentiment.* 3. **orgies.** in ancient Greece and Rome, secret rites or ceremonies dedicated to certain gods, as Bacchus or Ceres, accompanied by drunkenness, dancing, and singing. [Latin *orgia* wild rites connected esp. with the worship of Bacchus, secret, frantic revels, from Greek *orgia* secret rites.]

o·ri·el (ôr′ē əl) *n.* bay window built outward from a wall, resting on corbels or brackets. [Old French *oriol* porch, corridor; of uncertain origin.]

Oriel

o·ri·ent (*n., adj.,* ôr′ē ənt, -ent′; *v.,* ôr′ē ent′) *n.* 1. **Orient.** countries of Asia, esp. the Far East. Distinguished from **Occident.** —*v.t.* 1. to make familiar with new surroundings or circumstances or a situation: *The freshman took a while to orient himself.* 2. to get or fix the location or bearings of: *The explorer climbed a tree in order to orient himself.* 3. to fix so as to be pointed or directed: *to orient a tennis court north and south, to orient fashions toward youthful buyers.* 4. to place so as to face the east: *to orient a church.* —*adj. Archaic.* 1. eastern; oriental. 2. glowing; radiant; shining. 3. rising; ascending: *the orient moon of Islam* (Shelley, 1822). [Old French *orient* east, countries of Asia, from Latin *oriēns* rising sun, east, from *orīrī* to rise.]

O·ri·en·tal (ôr′ē ent′əl) *also,* **o·ri·en·tal.** *adj.* of, relating to, or characteristic of, the Orient. Distinguished from **Occidental.** —*n.* 1. *also,* **o·ri·en·tal.** member or close descendant of a people native to the Orient. 2. **oriental.** amethyst *(def. 2).*

O·ri·en·tal·ism (ôr′ē ent′əl iz′əm) *also,* **o·ri·en·tal·ism.** *n.* 1. any quality, characteristic, custom, or the like associated with people of the Orient. 2. knowledge of Oriental languages, literature, history, and culture. —**O′ri·en′tal·ist,** *n.*

oriental rug, handwoven rug or carpet having a geometric or floral design, made in the Orient.

o·ri·en·tate (ôr′ē en tāt′) **-tat·ed, -tat·ing.** *v.t., v.i.* to orient or become oriented.

o·ri·en·ta·tion (ôr′ē ən tā′shən) *n.* 1. act or process of orienting. 2. state or manner of being oriented: *an east-west orientation.* 3. introduction or familiarization with new surroundings or circumstances: *to provide an orientation for college freshmen.* 4. *Psychology.* awareness of one's surroundings or environment with reference to time, place, and people.

or·i·fice (ôr′ə fis, or′-) *n.* passage or opening, esp. in the body; aperture: *The ears, nose, and mouth are orifices.* [Old French *orifice*, from Late Latin *ōrificium* opening, from Latin *ōr-*, stem of *ōs* mouth + *facere* to make.]

or·i·flamme (ôr′ə flam′, or′-) *n.* 1. sacred banner of red silk carried in war by the early kings of France. 2. banner or symbol for any struggle or enterprise. [Old French *oriflambe* old banner of France, going back to Latin *aurum* gold + *flamma* blaze; because it was originally a red banner attached to a gilded pole.]

or·i·ga·mi (ôr′i gä′mē) *n.* Japanese art of folding paper into the form of an animal, flower, or other object. [Japanese *origami*, going back to *ori* a folding + *kami* paper.]

or·i·gin (ôr′ə jin, or′-) *n.* 1. source from which something begins or derives; root or cause: *The basement was the place of origin of the fire. What is the origin of the rumor?* 2. act or process of beginning existence: *The earth was here long before the origin of the human species.* 3. parentage; ancestry; extraction: *Sean is of Irish origin.* 4. *Mathematics.* point of intersection of the x-axis and the y-axis of a Cartesian coordinate system, with coordinates (0,0). 5. *Anatomy.* point of attachment of a muscle to a bone, that serves as a relatively fixed basis of movement. [Latin *orīgō* beginning, source.]

Syn. 1. **Origin, source** mean the point at which something comes into being. **Origin** applies to the point of time or space at which something rises, begins its course, or comes into existence: *Etymologists study the origin of words.* **Source** refers to the primary and ultimate point of beginning: *The sun is the source of all energy on earth.*

o·rig·i·nal (ə rij′ən əl) *adj.* 1. that has not been made, done, thought of, or used before; new or unusual: *an original suggestion, original*

research. **2.** capable of producing, doing, or thinking of something new or unusual; inventive; creative: *an original thinker.* **3.** of, relating to, or belonging to the origin or beginning of something; first; starting: *The original owner still lives in the house.* **4.** being that from which copies are made: *an original birth certificate.* **5.** that is not a copy, imitation, or translation: *an original painting by Van Gogh.* —*n.* **1.** that which is original and not a print, copy, imitation, or translation: *The original hangs in a Leningrad museum.* **2.** first form or type from which variations develop or derive: *The eohippus is the original of the horse.* **3.** one who is unusual or eccentric. **4.** *Archaic.* origin: *the true original of government.* —**Syn.** *adj.* **1.** see **new.**

o·rig·i·nal·i·ty (ə rij'ə nal'ə tē) *n.* **1.** quality of being original. **2.** ability to be inventive or creative.

o·rig·i·nal·ly (ə rij'ən əl ē) *adv.* **1.** at or from the start; at first; initially. **2.** with originality.

original sin, in Christian theology, an innate tendency in mankind toward evil, inherited from Adam as a result of his sin. Some Christians, esp. Roman Catholics, believe that original sin deprives man of divine grace, unless removed by baptism or other means.

o·rig·i·nate (ə rij'ə nāt') *-nat·ed, -nat·ing.* *v.i.* to start or bring into existence. —*v.i.* to come into existence; begin. —**o·rig'i·na'tion,** **o·rig'i·na'tor,** *n.* —**o·rig'i·na'tive,** *adj.*

O·ri·no·co (ôr'ə nō'kō) *n.* large river in South America, flowing through Venezuela into the Atlantic.

o·ri·ole (ôr'ē ōl') *n.* **1.** any of various songbirds, family Oriolidae, related to crows, of Eurasia, Africa, the East Indies, and Australia. The male is usually bright orange or yellow and has black markings on the head, wings, and tail, while the female is dull greenish-yellow. Length: 6–12 inches. **2.** any of various similar songbirds, family Icteridae, of North, Central, and South America, as the Baltimore oriole. [Old French *oriol* European bird with golden feathers, from Latin *aureolus* golden, going back to *aurum* gold; referring to the color of its plumage.]

Oriole

O·ri·on (ō rī'ən) *n.* constellation on the celestial equator containing the bright star Betelgeuse, conventionally depicted as a hunter wearing a belt with a sword at his side.

o·ri·son (ôr'i zən, or'-) *n.* prayer. [Old French *orison,* from Latin *ōrātiō* speech. Doublet of ORATION.]

O·ri·za·ba, Mount (ôr'ə zä'bə) extinct volcano southeast of Mexico City that is the tallest mountain in Mexico.

Or·lan·do (ôr lan'dō) *n.* city in east-central Florida. Pop. (1970), 99,006.

Or·lé·ans (ôr'lē ənz; *French* ôr lā äN') *n.* **1.** historic city in north-central France, on the Loire, that was saved by Joan of Arc from an English seige in 1429, during the Hundred Years' War. **2. Louis Philippe Jo·seph, Duc d'** (lwē fē lēp' zhō zef') 1747–93, French revolutionary leader.

Or·lon (ôr'lon) *n.* *Trademark.* synthetic acrylic fiber that resists stretching, mildew, acids, and moths, does not absorb water, and is not discolored by sunlight, widely used in the manufacture of clothing, bedding, and other textile products.

Or·mazd (ôr'mazd) *n.* Ahura Mazda.

or·mo·lu (ôr'mə lōō') *n.* alloy of copper, zinc, and tin that looks like gold, used for gilding articles and making inexpensive jewelry. [French *or moulu* literally, ground gold, going back to Latin *aurum* gold + *molere* to grind.]

or·na·ment (*n.,* ôr'nə mənt; *v.,* ôr'nə ment') *n.* **1.** small, often brightly colored or shiny, decorative object, as a colored ball for decorating a Christmas tree. **2.** one who adds grace, dignity, or luster to his time, sphere, or group: *He is an ornament of his profession.* **3.** ornamentation. **4.** *Music.* extra notes, as a trill or a cadenza, added to the notes of a simple melody for interest or expressiveness. **5.** any accessory used in church services, as the organ, vestments, or the altar. —*v.t.* **1.** to add an ornament or ornaments to: *to ornament a Christmas tree.* **2.** to be an ornament to: *A clock ornamented the mantelpiece.* [Old French *ornement* adornment, from Latin *ōrnāmentum* decoration, trinket.]

or·na·men·tal (ôr'nə ment'əl) *adj.* **1.** of, relating to, or being an ornament: *an ornamental design on a blouse.* **2.** serving more for beauty and adornment than for any practical use. —*n.* ornamental object, as a tree or shrub cultivated and used for decoration. —**or'na·men'tal·ly,** *adv.*

or·na·men·ta·tion (ôr'nə men tā'shən) *n.* **1.** act of ornamenting; being ornamented. **2.** ornaments collectively.

or·nate (ôr nāt') *adj.* having much ornamentation: *an ornate way of speaking, an ornate room.* [Latin *ōrnātus,* past participle of *ōrnāre* to adorn.] —**or·nate'ly,** *adv.* —**or·nate'ness,** *n.*

Syn. Ornate, florid, flamboyant mean extravagantly decorated or de-

signed. **Ornate** applies to anything overadorned: *The rococo is an ornate style of architecture.* **Florid** applies to what is excessively rich in pretentious flourishes and details: *Some medieval illuminated manuscripts have florid designs.* **Flamboyant** refers to things that are strikingly bold and showy: *That actor always wears flamboyant clothes.*

or·ner·y (ôr'nər ē) *adj.* **1.** stubborn and difficult to control; unruly: *an ornery mule.* **2.** mean or ugly in temperament. **3.** inferior. [Modification of ORDINARY.] —**or'ner·i·ness,** *n.*

or·ni·thol·o·gist (ôr'nə thol'ə jist) *n.* one who is a student of or expert in ornithology.

or·ni·thol·o·gy (ôr'nə thol'ə jē) *n.* branch of zoology that deals with birds. [Modern Latin *ornithologia,* from Greek *ornith-,* stem of *ornis* bird + -LOGY.] —**or·ni·tho·log·i·cal** (ôr'ni thə loj'i kəl), *adj.*

o·ro·tund (ôr'ə tund') *adj.* **1.** (of the voice) strong, full, resonant, and mellow. **2.** pompous; bombastic: *an orotund speech.* [Modification of Latin phrase *ōre rotundō* with polished speech; literally, with round mouth.]

or·phan (ôr'fən) *n.* child whose natural parents are absent or dead and who must be brought up in an orphanage or by foster parents. —*v.t.* to make an orphan of: *to be orphaned at the age of six.* [Late Latin *orphanus* child without parents, from Greek *orphanos* without parents, fatherless.]

or·phan·age (ôr'fə nij) *n.* **1.** institution that takes in and cares for orphans. **2.** state of being an orphan. [ORPHAN + -AGE.]

Or·phe·us (ôr'fē əs, ôr'fūs) *n.* *Greek Mythology.* musician renowned for his beautiful lyre playing which enchanted trees and stones and tamed wild beasts.

Or·phic (ôr'fik) *adj.* **1.** of, relating to, attributed to, or like Orpheus or his music. **2.** of or relating to mystical religious cults, esp. in ancient Greece and Rome, based on poems supposedly written by Orpheus. **3.** *also,* **orphic.** mystical or oracular.

or·ris (ôr'is, or'-) *n.* any of several varieties of iris having a fragrant root. [Form of IRIS.]

or·ris·root (ôr'is rōōt', -root', or'-) *n.* violet-scented root of the orris, dried and powered for use in perfume, sachets, and toothpowder.

Or·te·ga y Gas·set, Jo·sé (ôr tā'gə ē gä set', hō sā') 1883–1955, Spanish author, philosopher, and critic.

ortho- *combining form* straight, upright, right, or correct. [Greek *orthos.*]

or·tho·clase (ôr'thə klās', -klāz') *n.* hard mineral, a silicate of potassium and aluminum, characterized by a tendency to split along right-angled planes, used as a gemstone and in the manufacture of porcelain and glass. [German *Orthoklas,* from Greek *orthos* (see ORTHO-) + *klasis* a breaking.]

or·tho·don·tics (ôr'thə don'tiks) *also,* **or·tho·don·tia.** *n.,pl.* branch of dentistry that deals with the correction and prevention of abnormalities in the growth or position of the teeth and jaws. ▲ construed as singular. [Modern Latin *orthodontia* (from ORTHO- + Greek *odont-,* stem of *odōn* tooth) + -ICS.]

or·tho·don·tist (ôr'thə don'tist) *n.* dentist who specializes in orthodontics.

or·tho·dox (ôr'thə doks') *adj.* **1.** that is or adheres to whatever is established or accepted as the correct interpretation or opinion in theology or other intellectual matters: *orthodox doctrine, an orthodox economic theory, an orthodox Marxist.* **2.** marked by or limited to widely used or already proven methods or practices: *an orthodox approach to education.* **3. Orthodox. a.** of, relating to, or characteristic of the Orthodox Church. **b.** of, relating to, or designating the branch of Judaism that adheres to a strict interpretation and observance of the Torah. [Late Latin *orthodoxus* having the right faith, from Greek *orthodoxos* having the right opinion, from *orthos* straight, right + *doxa* opinion.]

Orthodox Church, group of Christian churches derived from the church of the Byzantine Empire. The Orthodox Church does not recognize the supremacy of the pope and accords special honor to the patriarch of Constantinople. Also, **Eastern Orthodox Church, Greek Orthodox Church.**

or·tho·dox·y (ôr'thə dok'sē) *pl.,* **-dox·ies.** *n.* **1.** quality or character of being orthodox. **2.** orthodox interpretation or opinion: *The omnipotence of God is an orthodoxy in several religions.*

or·tho·e·pist (ôr thō'ə pist) *n.* one who is a student of or an expert in orthoepy.

or·tho·e·py (ôr thō'ə pē) *n.* **1.** branch of grammar dealing with pronunciation of words. **2.** standard or customary pronunciation of a word. [Greek *orthoepeia* correctness of diction, from *orthos* straight, right + *epos* word.]

or·tho·gen·e·sis (ôr'thō jen'ə sis) *n.* theory in biology or sociology that all species, forms, and cultures evolve or develop along single straight lines that are predetermined, without disruption or alteration by random mutations or by any independent outside forces or conditions. [ORTHO- + GENESIS.]

or·thog·o·nal (ôr thog'ən əl) *adj.* of, relating to, composed of, or

employing right angles or perpendicular lines. [Latin *orthogōnius* rectangular, (from Greek *orthogōnios*, from *orthos* right + *gōniā* angle) + -AL.]

or·thog·ra·pher (ôr thog′rə fər) *n.* student of or expert in orthography.

or·tho·graph·ic (ôr′thə graf′ik) *adj.* **1.** of or relating to orthography. **2.** correct in spelling. Also, **or′tho·graph′i·cal.** —**or′tho·graph′i·cal·ly,** *adv.*

orthographic projection 1. technique of mechanical drawing in which each principal face of an object is isolated and drawn separately, showing the exact outlines but no depth, as though each face were projected onto a transparent surface. **2.** any drawing produced in this way. Also, **orthogonal projection.**

or·thog·ra·phy (ôr thog′rə fē) *pl.,* **-phies.** *n.* **1.** manner of representing the sounds of a language by written or printed symbols. **2.** spelling of words according to an accepted standard of correctness. **3.** study of letters and spelling. [Latin *orthographia* writing correctly, from Greek *orthographia,* going back to *orthos* right + *graphein* to write.]

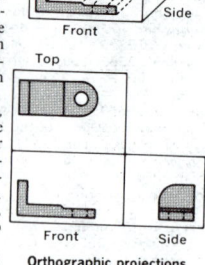

Top / Side / Front / Top / Front / Side

Orthographic projections

or·tho·pe·dic (ôr′thə pē′dik) *adj.* of, relating to, or used in orthopedics.

or·tho·pe·dics (ôr′thə pē′diks) *n.,pl.* branch of medicine that deals with injuries, disorders, and diseases of bones, tendons, ligaments, muscles, and joints. ▲ construed as singular. [ORTHO- + Greek *paid-,* stem of *pais* child + -ICS.]

or·tho·pe·dist (ôr′thə pē′dist) *n.* physician who specializes in orthopedics.

or·thop·ter·ous (ôr thop′tər əs) *adj.* of, relating to, or belonging to a group of insects, order Orthoptera, including the grasshopper, roach, and praying mantis, characterized by incomplete metamorphosis, biting mouth parts, and two pairs of wings, the thicker, narrower forewings held folded over the hind wings when at rest. [Modern Latin *Orthoptera* literally, straight wings (from ORTHO- + Greek *pteron* wing) + -OUS.]

or·tho·rhom·bic (ôr′thə rom′bik) *adj.* (of crystals) having three unequal axes at right angles to one another.

or·to·lan (ôrt′əl ən) *n.* **1.** European bunting, *Emberiza hortulana,* having predominantly blue-gray and brown plumage, valued for its meat, which is considered a delicacy. **2.** bobolink. [French *ortolan* the bunting, from Provençal *ortolan* gardener, going back to Latin *hortus* garden; because it is found in gardens.]

Or·well, George (ôr′wel′, -wəl) 1903–50, English novelist and essayist, born in India. His real name was Eric Blair. —**Or·well′i·an,** *adj.*

-ory *suffix* **1.** (used to form adjectives from verbs or from nouns that end in *-ion*) **a.** of, relating to, or doing, as in *contradictory.* **b.** serving to or characterized by: *illusory, compulsory, contributory.* **2.** (used to form nouns from verbs or from nouns) place or instrument for: *observatory, purgatory.* [Latin *-ōrius, -oria, -orium.*]

o·ryx (ôr′iks) *pl.,* **o·ryx·es** or **o·ryx.** *n.* any of several straight-horned antelopes, genera *Oryx* and *Aegoryx,* of desert regions of Africa and Arabia, having a gray or brown coat with striking black or brown markings. Height: to 7 feet at the shoulder. [Latin *oryx* gazelle, from Greek *oryx* pickax, antelope; because of its pointed horns.]

os¹ (os) *pl.,* **os·sa** (os′ə). *n.* bone. [Latin *os.*]

os² (os) *pl.,* **o·ra.** *n.* mouth or opening. [Latin *ōs.*]

Os, osmium.

O.S., Old Style.

O·sage (ō′sāj, ō sāj′) *n.* **1.** member of a tribe of North American Indians, originally inhabiting parts of Kansas, Missouri, and Illinois, now living in Oklahoma. **2.** their language, a member of the Siouan language family. —*adj.* of or relating to these people or their language.

Osage orange 1. thorny American shrub or tree, *Maclura pomifera,* of the mulberry family, widely cultivated as a hedge and for its strong wood that yields a yellowish-orange dye. **2.** yellow, inedible fruit of this shrub or tree, having a green, pebbly outer covering.

O·sa·ka (ō sä′kə) *n.* port city on the southwestern coast of Honshu, Japan. Pop. (1968) 3,078,000.

Os·car (os′kər) *n.* any of the gold statuettes awarded annually for

Osage orange

achievement in acting, direction, cinematography, and other areas of film production. [Supposedly from the comment, "It looks just like my Uncle Oscar," made by a member of the awarding society when shown one of the statuettes.]

os·cil·late (os′ə lāt′) -**lat·ed,** -**lat·ing.** *v.i.* **1.** to vibrate, fluctuate, or move back and forth between two points: *The flame of the candle oscillates. The compass needle oscillates between east and north.* **2.** *Physics.* to produce oscillation. [Latin *ōscillātus,* past participle of *ōscillāre* to swing, probably from *ōscillum* small mask of Bacchus hung from a tree and made to swing by the wind.]

os·cil·la·tion (os′ə lā′shən) *n.* **1.** act, condition, or process of oscillating. **2.** single movement from one point, limit, or extreme to another. **3.** *Physics.* **a.** periodic fluctuation between two extremes of a quantity, as voltage, or two extreme positions, as in a vibrating tuning fork. **b.** one complete cycle in which a vibrating object or particle starts at any given point, passes through maximum and minimum positions, and returns to the starting point.

os·cil·la·tor (os′ə lā′tər) *n.* **1.** one who or that which oscillates. **2.** device that produces electrical oscillations, or alternating current, used in radio and television transmitters and receivers. —**os·cil·la·to·ry** (os′ə lə tôr′ē), *adj.*

os·cil·lo·scope (ə sil′ə skōp′) *n.* electronic instrument that produces, on the fluorescent screen of a cathode-ray tube, a visible wave pattern corresponding to the electric signals fed into it. [Latin *ōscillāre* to swing + -SCOPE.]

os·cine (os′in, -īn) *adj.* of or relating to a large suborder of birds, Oscines, including those having the most highly developed vocal organs, as finches, thrushes, sparrows, and larks. —*n.* oscine bird. [From Modern Latin *Oscinēs,* from Latin *oscinēs,* plural of *oscen* a singing bird.]

os·cu·late (os′kyə lāt′) -**lat·ed,** -**lat·ing.** *v.i., v.t.* to kiss. [Latin *osculātus,* past participle of *osculārī* to kiss, going back to *ōs* mouth.] —**os′cu·la′tion,** *n.*

-ose¹ *suffix* (used to form adjectives) full of, given to, or like: *grandiose, bellicose.* [Latin *-ōsus* full of.]

-ose² *suffix* (used in chemistry to indicate a carbohydrate: *dextrose, sucrose.* [From *-ose,* last syllable of GLUCOSE.]

Osh·kosh (osh′kosh′) *n.* city in eastern Wisconsin. Pop. (1970), 53,221.

o·sier (ō′zhər) *n.* **1.** any of various species of willow, having pliable twigs and branches that are used in making baskets and wicker furniture. **2.** twig of such a willow. **3.** any of several varieties of dogwood. [Old French *osier* willow, from Medieval Latin *auseria* bed of willows; of uncertain origin.]

O·si·ris (ō sī′ris) *n. Egyptian Mythology.* god of the lower world and judge of the dead, husband and brother of Isis.

-osis *suffix* (used to form nouns) process or pathological condition of: *metamorphosis, tuberculosis.* [Greek *-ōsis.*]

Os·lo (os′lō, oz′-) *n.* capital and principal city of Norway, in the southeastern part of the country, formerly known as Christiania. Pop. (1970), 487,916.

Os·man·li (oz man′lē, os-) *pl.,* -**lis.** *n.* **1.** Ottoman Turk. **2.** language of the Ottoman Turks, belonging to the Ural-Altaic language family, spoken predominantly in Turkey. —*adj.* Ottoman.

os·mi·um (oz′mē əm) *n.* very hard, heavy, bluish-white metallic element, used to make alloys for pen points and electrical contacts. Symbol: **Os** See **element** for table. [Modern Latin *osmium,* from Greek *osmē* odor; because one of its oxides has a strong smell.]

os·mo·sis (oz mō′sis, os-) *n.* **1.** movement of a fluid through a semipermeable membrane into a solution that contains the same fluid; movement of a more-concentrated solution toward a less-concentrated one, thereby equalizing the pressure on both sides of a membrane. **2.** any gradual process of assimilation that seems to occur without conscious effort: *Young children learn their native language by osmosis.* [Modern Latin *osmosis,* from Greek *ōsmos* thrust + -OSIS.] —**os·mot·ic** (oz·mot′ik, os-), *adj.*

os·prey (os′prē) *pl.,* -**preys.** *n.* fish-eating hawk, *Pandion haliaetus,* having brownish plumage with a white head and undersides. Wingspan: 5½ feet. Also, **fish hawk.** [From an unrecorded Old French form, from Latin *ossifraga* osprey; literally, bone-breaking, from *os* bone + *frangere* to break; referring to the bird's great strength.]

Osprey

os·se·ous (os′ē əs) *adj.* made of, containing, or resembling bone; bony. [Latin *osseus,* from *os* bone.]

os·si·fi·ca·tion (os′ə fi kā′shən) *n.* **1.** abnormal hardening, as of muscle or other soft tissue, into bonelike tissue. **2.** normal process of bone formation. **3.** fact or process of becoming overly rigid, conservative, or conventional.

os·si·fy (os′ə fī′) **-fied, -fy·ing.** *v.i., v.t.* to undergo ossification or cause ossification in. [Latin *os* bone + -FY.]

os·ten·si·ble (os ten′sə bəl) *adj.* exhibited or put forth as actual; declared or apparent: *an ostensible victory that was in fact a defeat.* [French *ostensible* open, aboveboard, going back to Latin *ostendere* to show.] —**os·ten′si·bly,** *adv.*

os·ten·sive (os ten′siv) *adj.* directly pointing out; clearly demonstrative.

os·ten·ta·tion (os′tən tā′shən) *n.* showy, excessive, or overly ceremonial display: *the ostentation of an emperor's entry into a conquered city.* [Middle French *ostentation* display, from Latin *ostentātio.*]

os·ten·ta·tious (os′tən tā′shəs) *adj.* **1.** done with the intent of attracting notice; showy: *ostentatious contempt of the law.* **2.** characterized or marked by ostentation: *an ostentatious mansion.* —**os′ten·ta′tious·ly,** *adv.* —**os·ten·ta′tious·ness,** *n.*

osteo- *combining form* of or relating to bone: *osteopathy.* [Greek *osteon* bone.]

os·te·ol·o·gy (os′tē ol′ə jē) *n.* branch of anatomy dealing with bones and bone structure. [OSTEO- + -LOGY.]

os·te·o·my·e·li·tis (os′tē ō mī′ə lī′tis) *n.* infection of the bone, esp. the marrow, usually caused by a bacterium.

os·te·o·path (os′tē ə path′) *n.* one who is trained to practice osteopathy. Also, **os·te·o·path·ist** (os′tē op′ə thist).

os·te·op·a·thy (os′tē op′ə thē) *n.* system of treating patients by manipulating the bones and muscles, on the theory that abnormalities in the muscular and skeletal systems are the cause of disease and abnormal physiological functioning. [OSTEO- + -PATHY.] —**os·te·o·path·ic** (os′tē ə path′ik), *adj.*

Os·ti·a (os′tē ə) *n.* seaport of ancient Rome, at the mouth of the Tiber.

os·tler (os′lər) hostler.

ost·mark (ôst′märk′, ost′-) *n.* monetary unit of East Germany, equal to 100 pfennigs. [German *Ostmark,* from *Ost* east + *Mark* mark².]

os·tra·cism (os′trə siz′əm) *n.* **1.** act of ostracizing; being ostracized. **2.** in ancient Greece, temporary banishment by vote of the people.

os·tra·cize (os′trə sīz′) **-cized, -ciz·ing.** *v.t.* **1.** to cut off or exclude from a group or clique. **2.** to banish from society; exile. **3.** in ancient Greece, to banish temporarily by vote of the people. [Greek *ostrakizein* to banish through a vote recorded on potsherds, from *ostrakon* tile, potsherd.]

os·trich (ôs′trich, os′-) *n.* two-toed, flightless bird, *Struthio camelus,* of central Africa, the largest of all living birds. It has a long neck, long, powerful legs, a small, flat head, and, in the male, large, white plumes on the wings and tail that are used for ornamenting women's apparel. Height: 8 feet. [Old French *ostruce,* going back to Latin *avis* bird + Greek *strouthiōn* ostrich.]

Os·tro·goth (os′trə goth′) *n.* member of the eastern branch of the Goths, who controlled Italy from A.D. 493 to 554. [Late Latin *Ostrogothus;* of Germanic origin.] —**Os′tro·goth′ic,** *adj.*

O.T., Old Testament.

O·thel·lo (ə thel′ō) *n.* principal character of Shakespeare's tragedy *Othello,* who, driven to suspicion and jealousy by Iago's insinuations and lies, murders his faithful wife.

oth·er (uth′ər) *adj.* **1.** different from the one or ones already mentioned or implied; not the same: *If James won't do it, some other person will.* **2.a.** indicating the remaining one of two or more: *the other ear.* **b.** indicating the remaining ones of several: *The other guests have not arrived yet.* ▲ used with a plural subject. **3.** additional; further: *He has no other choice.* **4.** different in kind or quality: *I cannot be other than I am.* **5.** recently past (with *the*): *the other morning, the other night.* —*pron.* **1.** different or additional person or thing: *No other has a key to the vault.* **2.** remaining one of two or more: *If the first store is closed, we'll try the other.* **b.** remaining ones of several: *The others will join us later.* —*adv.* otherwise (with *than*): *I could not feel other than surprised.* [Old English *ōther* remaining, additional, different.]

oth·er·wise (uth′ər wīz′) *adv.* **1.** apart from that; in other respects: *The food ran out early, but otherwise the party was a success.* **2.** under any different circumstances; if not for that: *The sailors would have otherwise fallen into the sea.* **3.** in a different way or in any other way: *The door cannot be opened otherwise than with a key.* —*adj.* different; other: *This story sounds reasonable, but the facts are otherwise.* —*conj.* because if not; or else: *The shingles must be fixed; otherwise, the roof will leak.* [Old English *(on) ōthre wīsan* (in) other manner. See OTHER, WISE².]

oth·er·world·ly (uth′ər wurld′lē) *adj.* **1.** of, belonging to, or preoccupied with a future life, with heaven, or with an ideal world, while neglecting or discrediting the actual world: *an otherworldly religion.* **2.** not of this world or of life in this world; unearthly; strange: *music that is eerie and otherworldly.* —**oth′er·world′li·ness,** *n.*

o·ti·ose (ō′shē ōs′, ō′tē-) *adj.* that performs no work, has no effect, or serves no useful purpose. [Latin *ōtiōsus* at leisure, idle, from *ōtium* leisure.]

o·to·lar·yn·gol·o·gy (ō′tō lar′ing gol′ə jē) *n.* branch of medicine that deals with diseases of the ear, nose, and throat.

o·tol·o·gy (ō tol′ə jē) *n.* branch of medicine that deals with diseases of the ear.

ot·ta·va ri·ma (ō tä′və rē′mə) stanza form of Italian origin, consisting of eight lines of ten or eleven syllables each, having the rhyme scheme *abababcc.* [Italian *ottava rima* the stanza; literally, eighth rhyme, going back to Latin *octāvus* eighth + Old High German *rīm* series, row, number.]

Ot·ta·wa (ot′ə wə) *n.* **1.** capital of Canada, in the southeastern part of the country, in Ontario. Pop. (1968), 290,741. **2.** member of a tribe of Algonquian Indians who lived near the Great Lakes in what is now Michigan.

Otter

ot·ter (ot′ər) *pl.,* **-ters** or **-ter.** *n.* **1.** any of various web-footed, aquatic mammals, family Mustelidae, esp. genus *Lutra,* related to and resembling the weasel and mink, and having a long, slightly flattened tail. Length: 32–64 inches, including tail. **2.** its valuable brown, glossy fur, used in making coats and trimmings. [Old English *otor* the animal.]

Ot·to I (ot′ō) A.D. 912–973, emperor of the Holy Roman Empire. Also, **Otto the Great.**

Ot·to·man (ot′ə mən) *pl.,* **-mans.** *n.* **1.** Turk, esp. a member of the tribe whose ruling family founded and ruled the Ottoman Empire. **2. ottoman.** a. low, boxlike, upholstered seat or footstool resembling a hassock. **b.** couch or sofa, esp. one without back or arms. **3. ottoman.** medium- to heavy-weight fabric woven with a broad, flat, rib effect, used for such items as coats and upholstery. —*adj.* Turkish.

Ottoman Empire, Turkish empire that lasted from 1289 to 1922 and included part of eastern Europe, the Near East, Asia Minor, northern Africa, and the eastern Mediterranean.

Oua·ga·dou·gou (wä′gə doō′goō) *n.* capital of Upper Volta, in the central part of the country. Pop. (1966), 77,500.

ou·bli·ette (oō′blē et′) *n.* secret dungeon with a trap door at the top as the only opening. [French *oubliette,* from *oublier* to forget, going back to Latin *oblīvīscī.*]

ouch (ouch) *interj.* used to express pain or sympathy for being hurt.

ought¹ (ôt) *auxiliary verb* (followed by an infinitive with *to*) **1.** to be bound by a promise or duty or by values of right and wrong: *You ought to go to the funeral.* **2.** to be expected or likely: *I put in new batteries, so the radio ought to work.* **3.** to be prudent or well-advised: *You ought to take care of your cold.* **4.** to be bound by desirability: *You ought to read this book; it is very good.* [Old English *ahte,* past tense of *āgan* to own, owe.] —**Syn. 1.** see **must¹.**

ought² (ôt) *aught¹.*

ought³ (ôt) *n. Informal.* zero. [Form of NOUGHT, with incorrect division of *a nought* into *an ought.* See ADDER.]

oui·ja (wē′jə, -jē) *n.* board used in spiritualism, printed with letters, numbers, and other signs that are used to form messages as indicated by a special pointing device or planchette. Trademark: Ouija. [French *oui* yes + German *ja* yes.]

ounce¹ (ouns) *n.* **1.** unit of weight equal to ¹⁄₁₆ pound avoirdupois, or ¹⁄₁₂ pound troy. **2.** in liquid measure, fluid ounce. See **weights and measures** for table. **3.** small quantity: *The dancers didn't have an ounce of energy left.* [Old French *once, unce* unit of weight, from Latin *uncia* a twelfth part. Doublet of INCH.]

ounce² (ouns) *n.* snow leopard. [Old French *once,* form of *lonce,* going back to Latin *lynx* lynx, from Greek *lynx.*]

our (our, är) *adj.* possessive form of **we:** *our house.* [Old English *ūre* of us (genitive plural of first personal pronoun), belonging to us.]

Our Father, Lord's Prayer.

Our Lady, the Virgin Mary.

ours (ourz, ärz) *pron.* one or ones belonging to us: *Their dog is larger than ours. Ours is a miniature poodle.*

our·self (our self′, är-) *pron.* myself. ▲ used with *we* when *we* is singular: *"We declare ourself opposed," the congressman announced.*

our·selves (our selvz′, är-) *pron.,pl.* **1.** emphatic form of **we** or **us:**

at; āpe; cär; end; mē; it; īce; hot; ōld; fôrk; wood; foōl; oil; out; up; ūse; turn; sing; thin; this; zh in treasure; ə in ago, taken, pencil, lemon, circus.

713

We ourselves decided to go. **2.** reflexive form of **us:** *We took it upon ourselves to tell you.* **3.** our normal, average, or true state: *We haven't been ourselves since the accident.*

-ous *suffix* **1.** (used to form adjectives from nouns) of, full of, characterized by, like, or having: *religious, dangerous, bulbous, famous.* **2.** used in chemistry to indicate a lower valence than that indicated by *-ic: cuprous.* [Latin *-ōsus* full of (often through Old French *-ous, -eus*); also representing adjectival endings *-us* in Latin and *-os* in Greek.]

ou·sel (oo′zəl) ouzel.

oust (oust) *v.t.* to force or drive out; expel; dispossess. [Anglo-Norman *ouster* to remove, take away, going back to Latin *obstāre* to oppose, hinder.]

oust·er (ous′tər) *n.* **1.** act or instance of ousting. **2.** state of being ousted.

out (out) *adv.* **1.** from within or the inside; away from the center: *The road branched out. The water rushed out.* **2.** away from one's home or business: *The doctor went out on a call.* **3.** into the open air; outdoors: *The children went out to play.* **4.** from a source or receptacle: *to draw out a sword, to pour out wine.* **5.** so as to project or extend: *to stretch out one's hand. The rocks jutted out into the sea.* **6.** to an end or conclusion: *to fight it out, to hear someone out. We played the game out.* **7.** into a condition of inactivity or extinction: *That style went out a year ago. The firemen put out the flames.* **8.** so as to be exhausted or consumed: *The supplies gave out.* **9.** completely or thoroughly: *to fit out for a camping trip. Write your name out.* **10.** into existence or a state of activity: *Riots broke out. An epidemic of flu broke out.* **11.** into or within view, public notice, or circulation: *The sun came out. The book came out last week. The secret was out.* **12.** from a proper or usual place or position: *He put out his shoulder at football practice.* **13.** aloud, esp. with power or force: *The sergeant called out the names of the men. The bells rang out.* **14.** to others: *to deal out cards, to rent out rooms. The farmer parceled out his land.* **15.** from among others: *He picked out a new car.* **16.** from a state of composure or agreement into a state of annoyance or dispute: *She felt put out because the train was so late. The two friends fell out.* **17.** on strike: *The longshoremen went out for higher wages.* **18.** *Baseball.* in such a way as to cause a batter or base runner to be unsuccessful in reaching a base: *The batter struck out.* **19. out and away.** by far: *This car goes faster than that one out and away.* **20. out from under.** *Informal.* beyond (a difficult situation): *out from under debts.* **21. out of. a.** from within: *He looked out of the window. She went out of the room.* **b.** beyond the limits, scope, reach, range, or influence of: *The airplane flew out of sight. I called to him but he was out of hearing.* **c.** without: *out of breath. I'm out of butter.* **d.** so as to deprive or be deprived of: *to be swindled out of $500.* **e.** from, as material: *That house is built out of brick.* **f.** from among: *to choose one out of three.* **g.** because of; as a result of: *She cried out of sympathy. He did it out of kindness.* **h.** (of horses) born of: *a foal out of a good mare.* —*adj.* **1.** not in control or power: *He was out because he was defeated in the election.* **2.** beyond the usual or normal: *an out size.* **3.** at a financial loss: *I am out five dollars.* **4.** bared or threadbare: *His sweater is out at the elbow.* **5.** no longer skillful because of lack of practice: *His backhand is out.* **6.** in error; wrong: *He was out in his estimate.* **7.** not in working order or condition: *That road is out because of the flood.* **8.** considered unacceptable or impossible: *That plan is out.* **9.** directed outward: *an out train. Put your letter in the out box.* **10.** external; exterior; outer: *the out edge.* **11.** outlying: *out islands.* **12.** (in sports) beyond the prescribed playing area: *The ball is out at the forty-yard line.* **13.** *Baseball.* (of a batter or base runner) unsuccessful in reaching a base. **14. out for.** trying hard to get or do: *He is out for a raise in salary.* **15. out to.** trying hard to: *He is out to have a good time.* —*prep.* **1.** from within; out from: *She looked out the window.* **2.** outward on; out along: *Drive out the dirt road until you come to the highway.* —*n.* **1.** one who or that which is out. **2.** way or means of escaping or avoiding: *She didn't want to go, but she couldn't think of an out.* **3.** act or instance of putting out a player in baseball. **4.** serve or return that falls outside the court, as in tennis or squash. **5. outs.** (in politics) people out of office. **6.** *Printing.* omission of a word or words. **b.** word or words omitted. **7. on the** (or **at**) **outs.** in disagreement; quarreling. —*v.i.* to be disclosed or revealed; come out: *The truth will out.* —*v.t.* to put out. —*interj.* away; begone. [Old English *ūt, ūte* forth, away, into the open air, from the usual place or condition, into activity.]

out- *prefix* **1.** external, outside, or outward: *outline, outcry.* **2.** more than or better than: *outgrow, outshine, outshoot.* [From OUT.]

out-and-out (out′ən out′, -ənd-) *adj.* **1.** thorough; complete: *an out-and-out liar.* **2.** obvious; unconcealed: *an out-and-out fraud.*

out·back (out′bak′) *n.* wild, undeveloped part of Australia.

out·bid (out′bid′) **-bid, -bid** or **-bid·den, -bid·ding.** *v.t.* to offer a higher price than (someone else) or in or as in an auction.

out·board (out′bôrd′) *adj.* outside the hull or farther away from the center of a ship or boat.

outboard motor, gasoline engine and propeller externally mounted on the stern of a small boat.

out·bound (out′bound′) *adj.* outward bound: *trains outbound for Detroit.*

out·break (out′brāk′) *n.* sudden occurrence or eruption: *an outbreak of malaria, the outbreak of World War II.*

out·build·ing (out′bil′ding) *n.* separate building associated with a main building, as a woodshed, barn, or garage.

out·burst (out′bûrst′) *n.* outpouring or explosion: *an outburst of flames, a violent person given to sudden outbursts.*

out·cast (out′kast′) *n.* one who is rejected or forced out of a group.

out·class (out′klas′) *v.t.* to surpass in rank or skill.

out·come (out′kum′) *n.* result; consequence; issue.

out·crop (*n.,* out′krop′; *v.,* out′krop′) *n.* **1.** *Geology.* part of a rock layer that comes out to the surface of the ground so as to be visible or easily mined. **2.** process or fact of so coming out. —*v.i.* to form into an outcrop.

out·cry (out′krī′) *pl.,* **-cries.** *n.* **1.** strong objection or complaint, esp. of many people: *The proposed tax caused an outcry.* **2.** cry: *We heard a shot and then the outcry of a wounded animal.*

out·dat·ed (out′dā′tid) *adj.* obsolete; out-of-date.

out·dis·tance (out′dis′təns) **-tanced, -tanc·ing.** *v.t.* to leave behind in or as in a race: *Emily outdistanced her sister in beauty.*

out·do (out′dōō′) **-did, -done, -do·ing.** *v.t.* **1.** to be superior to; surpass; exceed. **2. to outdo oneself.** to perform beyond the usual: *The hostess outdid herself in planning this party.* —**Syn. 1.** see **excel.**

out·door (out′dôr′) *adj.* performed, located, or intended for use out in the open rather than inside a building: *outdoor furniture.*

out·doors (out′dôrz′) *adv.* not in a house or other building; out under the sky: *to take a walk outdoors.* —*n.* area that is not within a house or other building.

out·er (ou′tər) *adj.* **1.** far away from the center: *the outer reaches of the universe.* **2.** external: *outer garments.* —**Syn. 2.** see **exterior.**

Outer Mongolia, historic region in north-central Asia, now the Mongolian People's Republic.

out·er·most (ou′tər mōst′) *adj.* most distant or external or farthest out: *the outermost layer of an onion, the outermost island.*

outer space, space beyond the outermost layer of the earth's atmosphere; interplanetary and interstellar space.

out·face (out′fās′) **-faced, -fac·ing.** *v.t.* **1.** to stare down or overcome. **2.** to confront boldly; defy.

out·field (out′fēld′) *n.* *Baseball.* **1.** part of the field beyond the base lines between first and second, and second and third. **2.** players who play in this area.

out·fielder (out′fēl′dər) *n.* *Baseball.* player who plays a position in the outfield.

out·fit (out′fit′) *n.* **1.** set of different articles or equipment for doing something: *a camping outfit.* **2.** set of clothes; ensemble. **3.** *Informal.* group or team, as a business office or military unit. —*v.t.* to provide with articles or equipment: *to outfit an expedition to the North Pole.* —**out′fit′ter,** *n.*

out·flank (out′flangk′) *v.t.* **1.** to outmaneuver (an opposing army) by getting around its side. **2.** to get the better of (an opponent), esp. by outmaneuvering him and avoiding a direct assault.

out·flow (out′flō′) *n.* **1.** process or fact of flowing out: *an outflow of lava from a volcano.* **2.** that which flows out.

out·fox (out′foks′) *v.t.* to trick or outsmart (someone).

out·gen·er·al (out′jen′ər əl) **-aled, -al·ing;** *also,* **-alled, -al·ling.** *v.t.* to outmaneuver, esp. by superior military skill.

out·go (out′gō′) *pl.,* **-goes.** *n.* that which goes out, esp. money spent.

out·go·ing (out′gō′ing) *adj.* **1.** sociable, open, and talkative; not withdrawn or private: *an outgoing person who makes friends quickly.* **2.** going out or departing: *an outgoing president.*

out·grow (out′grō′) **-grew, -grown, -grow·ing.** *v.t.* **1.** to grow too large for: *to outgrow one's clothing.* **2.** to leave behind or lose in the process of developing or maturing: *to outgrow a fear of the dark.* **3.** to surpass in growth; grow taller than: *James outgrew his older brother by four inches.*

out·growth (out′grōth′) *n.* **1.** product or result: *The author's pacifism is a natural outgrowth of his wartime experiences.* **2.** that which grows out; growth.

out·guess (out′ges′) *v.t.* **1.** to guess correctly the plans of; outwit. **2.** to be smarter or more clever than.

out·house (out′hous′) *n.* **1.** small shed or stall outdoors that is used as a toilet. **2.** outbuilding.

out·ing (ou′ting) *n.* **1.** short pleasure trip; excursion. **2.** outing flannel.

outing flannel, soft, cotton fabric, napped on one or both sides, used chiefly for infant's wear.

out·land (out′land′) *also,* **out·lands.** *n.* outlying land or area.

out·land·er (out′lan′dər) *n.* stranger or foreigner.

out·land·ish (out lan′dish) *adj.* strange, unfamiliar, or bizarre.

at; āpe; cär; end; mē; it; īce; hot; ōld; fôrk; wood; fōōl; oil; out; up; ūse; turn; sing; thin; this; zh in treasure; ə in ago, taken, pencil, lemon, circus.

out·last (out′last′) *v.t.* to last longer than. —*Syn.* see **outlive**.

out·law (out′lô′) *n.* **1.** one who habitually breaks or defies the law; criminal. **2.** formerly, one who has been deprived of the benefits and protection of the law; fugitive or exile. —*v.t.* **1.** to make illegal; prohibit: *to outlaw the sale of certain drugs.* **2.** to declare (someone) an outlaw. **3.** to deprive (a debt or contract) of legal force, as because of the statute of limitations. [Old English *ūtlaga* one put outside of the law, going back to Old Norse *ūtlagr* banished.]

out·law·ry (out′lô′rē) *pl.,* **-ries.** *n.* **1.** constant defiance or disregard of the law. **2.** act of outlawing; being outlawed: *the outlawry of alcoholic beverages during Prohibition.* **3.** former practice of putting a person beyond the protection of the law, esp. as a punishment.

out·lay (*n.,* out′lā′; *v.,* out′lā′) *n.* **1.** investment or expenditure of money: *For a small initial outlay, they began a doughnut shop.* **2.** any expenditure, as of time or effort. —*v.t.,* **-laid, -lay·ing.** to expend.

out·let (out′let′, -lit) *n.* **1.** place at which something escapes or comes out: *the outlet of a swimming pool.* **2.** means of expression or gratification: *Sports are a good outlet for a young boy's energy.* **3.** place in an electrical wiring system having a female fitting, where appliances can be plugged in and the current tapped. **4.** place where products are sold, esp. a store which sells goods, often of a single manufacturer, at a discount.

out·line (out′līn′) *n.* **1.** *also,* **outlines.** shape or contour of an object formed by following or tracing along its outer edges: *Through the fog they saw the barely visible outline of a passing ship.* **2.** *also,* **outlines.** description without precise details; general idea: *to give a rough outline of your expenses for next year.* **3.** summary, often with separate parts marked off with Roman numerals and alphabet letters, that organizes the contents of a story, composition, or speech. **4.** style of drawing in which an object or scene is represented merely by lines of contour without shading: *to show a bridge in outline.* —*v.t.,* **-lined, -lin·ing.** **1.** to set off, make visible, or mark the outlines of: *Skyscrapers were outlined against the sky.* **2.** to summarize or give a general description of: *to outline travel plans.* **3.** to draw the outline of.

out·live (out′liv′) **-lived, -liv·ing.** *v.t.* **1.** to live longer than. **2.** to live through; survive; endure: *to outlive a serious automobile accident.*

Syn. 1. Outlive, outlast mean to live on or remain in existence beyond an implied point. **Outlive** implies keeping alive against odds and is appropriately used to stress a capacity for enduring competition, difficulty, and adversity: *Not marble, nor the gilded monuments of princes, shall outlive this powerful rhyme* (Shakespeare, Sonnet 55). **Outlast** may be used interchangeably with *outlive* without loss of meaning but is more commonly used with reference to things and stresses the fact of survival or duration rather than the capacity for endurance: *The Pyramids have outlasted many civilizations.*

out·look (out′look′) *n.* **1.** view into the future; expectation: *The outlook for a good corn crop is favorable.* **2.** point of view or set of opinions: *persons of different religious outlooks.* **3.a.** place from which a view is obtained; lookout. **b.** view from such a place: *the dreary outlook of chimney tops and smoke* (Kingsley, 1850). —*Syn.* **1.** see **prospect**.

out·ly·ing (out′lī′ing) *adj.* located far from the center of something, as a city.

out·ma·neu·ver (out′mə nōō′vər) **-vered, -ver·ing.** *v.t.* to maneuver better than or defeat by maneuvering.

out·mod·ed (out′mō′did) *adj.* no longer in style or no longer suitable or useful: *an outmoded refrigerator.*

out·most (out′mōst′) *adj.* farthest out; outermost.

out·num·ber (out′num′bər) *v.t.* to exceed in number; be greater in number than.

out-of-bounds (out′əv boundz′) *adv.* outside the legal area of play: *the ball went out-of-bounds.* —*adj.* outside the legal area of play.

out-of-date (out′əv dāt′) *adj.* no longer fashionable or being used; belonging to a former time.

out-of-doors (out′əv dôrz′) *adj. also,* **out-of-door.** outdoor. —*n.* outdoors. —*adv.* outdoors.

out-of-the-way (out′əv thə wā′) *adj.* **1.** not easily accessible; off the beaten track: *an out-of-the-way spot that is ideal for a honeymoon.* **2.** not usually met with; little known or unusual: *a few minor, out-of-the-way facts of history.*

out·pa·tient (out′pā′shənt) *n.* patient who receives care or treatment from a hospital, clinic, or similar institution without being confined or kept in a bed there.

out·play (out′plā′) *v.t.* to play better than.

out·point (out′point′) *v.t.* **1.** to score more points than. **2.** to sail closer to the wind than (another vessel).

out·post (out′pōst′) *n.* **1.** small military installation, usually at some distance from the main force, established to maintain control over the area and to guard against attack. **2.** military personnel assigned to such an installation. **3.** any settlement lying outside a border or boundary. **4.** anything beyond a border, far off, or in advance.

out·pour·ing (out′pôr′ing) *n.* act of pouring out something, esp. thoughts or feelings: *A great outpouring of emotion accompanied the end of the war.*

out·put (out′poot′) *n.* **1.** anything put or taken out. **2.** amount produced. **3.** information made available by a computer or any other storage and retrieval system.

out·rage (out′rāj′) *n.* **1.** act of extreme violence, viciousness, or excessive cruelty. **2.** great anger or rage: *The peasants felt outrage at the attacks on their villages.* **3.** deeply felt insult, indignity, or offense. —*v.t.,* **-raged, -rag·ing.** **1.** to cause great anger in: *The attacks outraged the peasants.* **2.** to subject to an outrage; abuse or injure greatly. **3.** to rape. [Old French *outrage* excess, presumption, going back to Latin *ultrā* beyond.]

out·ra·geous (out rā′jəs) *adj.* **1.** exceeding proper limits; unconventional or immoderate: *an outrageous request, outrageous behavior.* **2.** of or resembling an outrage.

out·rank (out′rangk′) *v.t.* to be of a higher rank than: *A major outranks a captain.*

ou·tré (ōō trā′) *adj.* French. beyond the bounds of what is usual or considered proper; eccentric; bizarre.

out·reach (out′rēch′) *v.t.* to reach further than; exceed.

out·rid·er (out′rī′dər) *n.* **1.** one who rides out or forth, esp. a guide or escort. **2.** cowboy who rides on the edge of a moving herd of cattle. **3.** mounted servant or attendant who goes in advance of or beside a vehicle, as a carriage.

Outrigger

out·rig·ger (out′rig′ər) *n.* **1.** extra float and its supporting frame that can be fixed to the side of a canoe to extend out into the water and prevent capsizing. **2.** any projecting support. **3.** bracket projecting outward from either side of a rowboat or racing shell to support an oarlock and provide greater leverage in rowing.

out·right (out′rīt′) *adj.* not qualified or changed by the addition or lack of anything: *outright viciousness, an outright lie.* —*adv.* **1.** without modification or qualification: *to say outright what you mean.* **2.** to buy (or sell) outright. to buy (or sell) completely and all at once: *Rather than lease the farm, the old man sold it outright for a large amount of cash.* **3.** to kill outright. to kill right away.

out·run (out′run′) **-ran, -run, -run·ning.** *v.t.* **1.** to run farther or faster than. **2.** to go beyond the limits of; exceed: *to allow zeal to outrun discretion.*

out·sell (out′sel′) **-sold, -sel·ling.** *v.t.* **1.** to sell more merchandise than: *to outsell the other salesmen.* **2.** to be sold in greater quantities than: *The red shoes outsell the others.*

out·set (out′set′) *n.* beginning; start: *the outset of a journey.*

out·shine (out′shīn′) **-shone, -shin·ing.** *v.t.* **1.** to shine more brightly than. **2.** to be more brilliant or excellent than.

out·shoot (*v.,* out′shōōt′; *n.,* out′shōōt′) **-shot, -shoot·ing.** *v.t.* **1.** to shoot beyond. **2.** to surpass in shooting. —*n.* that which shoots out; projection or protrusion: *an outshoot of rock.*

out·side (out′sīd′, out′sīd′) *n.* **1.** outer side, surface, or part; exterior: *The hamburger was burned on the outside. The outside of the house was painted white.* **2.** aspect, part, or side that is external, superficial, or able to be seen easily: *Although Alice was angry inside, she didn't show it on the outside.* **3.** *Informal.* area or world beyond the walls or boundaries of an enclosure, as a prison. **4. at the outside.** at most: *The repairman guessed the job would take two hours at the outside.* —*adj.* **1.** situated on the outside; outer: *The outside layer of paint was peeling.* **2.** coming from or acting from without; not originating or situated within: *outside influences, an outside observer.* **3.** directed or going outward: *an outside call, an outside line.* **4.** extremely slight; remote: *an outside chance.* **5.** reaching the utmost limit possible: *It is an outside estimate of expenses and the actual amount will probably be much less.* **6.** *Baseball.* (of a pitch) passing between the center of the plate and the side of the plate away from the batter. —*adv.* **1.** on, to, or toward the outside. **2.** outdoors: *The children played outside all day.* —*prep.* **1.** beyond the walls, surfaces, or boundaries of: *They live just outside Philadelphia.* **2.** beyond the space or limits of: *The matter falls outside the jurisdiction of this court.* **3.** *Informal.* with the exception of; besides. **4. outside of.** outside. —*Syn. adj.* **1.** see **exterior**.

out·sid·er (out′sī′dər) *n.* **1.** one who is not a member, as of a given group, society, or organization. **2.** one who has no special interest in or who is not acquainted with a particular matter: *We had to call in an outsider to settle the dispute.*

out·size (out′sīz′) *adj. also,* **out·sized.** irregularly or unusually large: *an outsize head, outsize shoes.* —*n.* irregular size, esp. an unusually large size.

out·skirts (out′skurts′) *n..pl.* regions or sections surrounding or at the edge of a specified area, as a city.

---

out·smart (out′smärt′) *v.t.* to get the better of (someone) by cunning or cleverness.

out·spo·ken (out′spō′kən) *adj.* **1.** open or unreserved in speech: *The young lady was very outspoken about her wish to be married.* **2.** expressed without reserve or evasion: *outspoken disapproval.* —**out′spo′ken·ness,** *n.* —**Syn. 1.** see **frank¹.**

out·spread (out′spred′) *adj.* spread out; extended: *outspread arms.*

out·stand·ing (out′stan′ding) *adj.* **1.** so excellent as to stand out from others of its kind: *an outstanding surgeon, an outstanding example.* **2.** that remains to be done, settled, or paid: *an outstanding obligation, an outstanding check.*

out·stay (out′stā′) *v.t.* to remain longer than or beyond the time or duration of: *to outstay one's welcome.*

out·stretch (out′strech′) *v.t.* **1.** to stretch out; extend. **2.** to stretch beyond.

out·strip (out′strip′) **-stripped, -strip·ping.** *v.t.* **1.** to surpass; excel: *to outstrip other nations in coal production.* **2.** to run farther or faster than, as in a race.

out·talk (out tôk′) *v.t.* to talk louder or with more skill than.

out·vote (out vōt′) **-vot·ed, -vot·ing.** *v.t.* to overcome or defeat in voting: *The proposal was outvoted.*

out·ward (out′wərd) *adv. also,* **out·wards.** from the inside to or toward the outside; away; out. —*adj.* **1.** of or relating to the outside, the visible, the apparent, or the external: *a serene man unaffected by outward things. There were outward changes, but the city remained essentially the same.* **2.** directed, turned, or proceeding toward the outside: *an outward flow of goods.* [Old English *ūteweard* outer, on the outside.] —**out′ward·ness,** *n.*

out·ward·ly (out′wərd lē) *adv.* **1.** on or toward the outside or outer surface: *The secret door was not outwardly visible.* **2.** in appearance or outward manifestation; seemingly: *outwardly happy.*

out·wear (out wâr′) **-wore, -worn, -wear·ing.** *v.t.* **1.** to last longer or wear better than: *This fabric outwears most other materials.* **2.** to wear out or exhaust.

out·weigh (out wā′) *v.t.* **1.** to be greater in weight than. **2.** to mean more than or be more important than; exceed in value or significance: *The advantages of the new system outweigh the disadvantages.*

out·wit (out·wit′) **-wit·ted, -wit·ting.** *v.t.* to get the better of (someone) by being smarter, more ingenious, or more clever: *The fox outwitted the pursuing hounds and escaped safely.*

out·work (*v.,* out′work′; *n.,* out′wurk′) *v.t.* to work better or faster than; outdo in working. —*n.* part of a castle, fortress, or stockade that is beyond the walls or parapet.

out·worn (out′wôrn′) *adj.* **1.** worn out: *an outworn coat.* **2.** no longer in use; out-of-date: *an outworn political slogan.*

ou·zel (ōō′zəl) *also,* **ou·sel.** *n.* **1.** any of various European thrushes, as the blackbird or the **ring ouzel,** *Turdus torquatus,* which is black with a white band on the neck and breast. **2.** water ouzel. [Old English *ōsle* blackbird.]

o·va (ō′və) plural of **ovum.**

o·val (ō′vəl) *adj.* **1.** shaped like an egg. **2.** shaped like an ellipse. —*n.* something having an oval shape. [Modern Latin *ovalis,* from Latin *ōvum* egg.]

o·var·i·an (ō vâr′ē ən) *adj.* of, relating to, or affecting an ovary.

o·va·ry (ō′vər ē) *pl.,* **-ries.** *n.* **1.** female reproductive organ that produces eggs and, in mammals, certain hormones. **2.** *Botany.* enlarged, saclike part of a pistil that encloses the ovule and later develops into the fruit. See **flower** for illustration. [Modern Latin *ovarium,* from Latin *ōvum* egg.]

o·vate (ō′vāt) *adj.* having an oval shape: *an ovate leaf.* [Latin *ōvātus* egg-shaped, from *ōvum* egg.]

Ovate leaf

o·va·tion (ō vā′shən) *n.* enthusiastic burst of applause or other demonstration of public acclaim: *The pianist received a standing ovation* honoring a victorious general; literally, rejoicing.] [Latin *ōvātiō* celebration

ov·en (uv′ən) *n.* enclosed chamber, as in a stove, that is used to heat, bake, roast, or dry objects placed within. [Old English *ofen.*]

ov·en·bird (uv′ən burd′) *n.* **1.** brownish warbler, *Seiurus aurocapillus,* of North America, that builds an ovenlike, domed nest on the ground. **2.** any of numerous Central and South American birds, family Furnariidae, esp. genus *Furnarius,* generally having brownish plumage, that build a fortified, often dome-shaped, nest.

ov·en·ware (uv′ən wâr′) *n.* heat-resistant containers of glass, ceramics, or metal, suitable for use in a hot oven.

o·ver (ō′vər) *prep.* **1.** in a place or position higher than; above: *Clouds hung over the lake. The roof jutted over the street.* **2.** upon so as to cover or close: *to put a blanket over a sleeping child. Put the lid over the jar.* **3.** on the surface of: *to spread butter over bread.* **4.** to the other side of; across: *The horse jumped over the fence. They walked over the bridge.* **5.** forward and down from: *to fall over a precipice.* **6.** from one end of to the other; along: *to walk over a path, to drive over an expressway.* **7.** on the other side of; beyond: *That city is over the border.* **8.** on or in all parts of; everywhere on: *Corn is raised over the Middle West.* **9.** from place to place on or in; to and fro upon: *to travel over the country.* **10.** through every part of; all through: *He pored over his notes.* **11.** until the end of: *School is closed over the holidays.* **12.** all through; during: *Payment may be made over a number of months.* **13.** at or up to a higher level than: *The water came over the tops of his shoes.* **14.** above in authority, power, or rank: *They need a strong leader over them.* **15.** above or beyond in degree, amount, quality, or extent: *She spent over twenty dollars on groceries.* **16.** in preference to: *He was chosen over all other candidates.* **17.** upon, as an effect or influence: *A sudden change came over him.* **18.** while engaged in or occupied with: *They discussed the plan over dinner.* **19.** with reference to; concerning; about: *to worry over details.* **20.** through the medium of; by means of: *The news came over the radio.* **21. over and above.** besides; in addition to: *We asked for a second estimate over and above the original one.* —*adv.* **1.** above; at a place that projects over. **2.** down or forward and down: *The ball rolled to the edge of the cliff and fell over.* **3.** above and beyond the top, brim, or edge: *The water boiled over.* **4.** from an erect or upright position: *The cat knocked the vase over.* **5.** so as to cover or be covered: *The lake froze over.* **6.** from one side to the other; across any intervening space: *Come over for a cup of coffee.* **7.** on or at the other side of some intervening space; at some distance: *He stayed over in Spain for three months.* **8.** from one opinion, attitude, or side to another: *He was won over by their arguments.* **9.** from one person to another: *He willed his property over to his sons.* **10.** so as to show the other or a different side: *Turn the baby over on his back.* **11.** once more; again: *He did his work over.* **12.** in repetition or succession: *three times over.* **13.** in all parts or directions; throughout: *to travel the whole world over.* **14.** from beginning to end; through: *He read the document over.* **15.** beyond a period of time: *Stay over through the weekend.* **16.** in excess; in addition; remaining: *Four goes into ten twice with two left over.* **17. over again.** once more: *I will do the job over again.* **18. over and above.** in addition to; more than; beyond. **19. over and over.** repeatedly. **20. over with.** finished. —*adj.* **1.** ended. **2.** upper or higher. [Old English *ofer* above, to or on the other side, exceeding in quantity.]

over- *prefix* **1.** too much; too highly; or too: *overload, overrate, overdeveloped.* **2.** above; higher: *overhead.* **3.** around, covering, or on top: *overgrowth, overcoat, overshoe.* **4.** from above to below; down: *overthrow, overturn.* [Old English *ofer-.*] ▲ The meaning of a word in the list at the bottom of this and the following pages can be understood by combining *over-* with the root word.

o·ver·a·bun·dant (ō′vər ə bun′dənt) *adj.* too abundant; excessive. —**o′ver·a·bun′dance,** *n.*

o·ver·a·chieve (ō′vər ə chēv′) **-chieved, -chiev·ing.** *v.i.* to do more or better than one is thought capable of. —**o′ver·a·chiev′er,** *n.*

o·ver·act (ō′vər akt′) *v.i.,v.t.* to act (a role or part) too emotionally or unrealistically; exaggerate in acting.

o·ver·ac·tive (ō′vər ak′tiv) *adj.* excessively or abnormally active: *an overactive child.* —**o′ver·ac′tive·ly,** *adv.*

o·ver·age¹ (ō′vər āj′) *adj.* **1.** too old. **2.** beyond the usual or normal age.

o·ver·age² (ō′vər ij) *n.* portion that is over the requested amount, as in weighing.

o·ver·all (ō′vər ôl′) *adj.* **1.** general or total: *The overall picture was favorable.* **2.** from one end to the other: *the overall length of a car.* —*adv.* as a whole; generally.

o·ver·alls (ō′vər ôlz′) *n.,pl.* loose-fitting trousers, often with a chest piece and suspenders attached, worn esp. by farmers and workmen.

Overalls

o·ver·anx·ious (ō′vər angk′shəs) *adj.* excessively anxious.

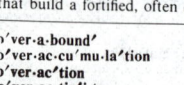

o′ver·a·bound′	o′ver·ad·vanced′	o′ver·an′a·lyt′i·cal
o′ver·ac·cu′mu·la′tion	o′ver·ad·vanc′ing	o′ver·an′a·lyze′
o′ver·ac′tion	o′ver·af·fect′	o′ver·an′a·lyzed′
o′ver·ac·tiv′i·ty	o′ver·ag·gres′sive	o′ver·an′a·lyz′ing
o′ver·a·dorned′	o′ver·am·bi′tious	o′ver·an′i·mat′ed
o′ver·ad·vance′	o′ver·am·bi′tious·ly	o′ver·an′i·mat′ed·ly

o′ver·ap·praise′
o′ver·ap·pre′ci·a′tion
o′ver·ap·pre′ci·a′tive
o′ver·ap′pre·hen′sive
o′ver·ap′pre·hen′sive·ness

o·ver·arch (ō′vər ärch′) v.t., v.i. to form an arch over (something).

o·ver·arm (ō′vər ärm′) adj., adv. with the arm raised above the shoulder.

o·ver·awe (ō′vər ô′) -awed, -aw·ing. v.t. to overcome, subdue, or restrain by inspiring awe.

o·ver·bal·ance (ō′vər bal′əns) -anced, -anc·ing. v.t. 1. to cause to lose balance. 2. to be greater than in weight or importance.

o·ver·bear (ō′vər bār′) -bore, -borne, -bear·ing. v.t. to oppress or drive down, as by weight or power.

o·ver·bear·ing (ō′vər bār′ing) adj. that oppresses, drives down, or overrules others; arrogantly superior. —o′ver·bear′ing·ly, adv.

o·ver·bid (ō′vər bid′) -bid, -bid or -bid·den, -bid·ding. v.t. 1. to bid higher than (a person); outbid. 2. to bid higher than the value of (a thing). —v.i. to bid too high. —n. a higher or excessive bid.

o·ver·bite (ō′vər bīt′) n. condition in which the upper front teeth project out abnormally over the lower.

o·ver·blown (ō′vər blōn′) adj. 1. blown up or inflated, as with vanity or conceit; bombastic: overblown rhetoric. 2. (of flowers or blossoms) past the stage of full bloom; withered.

o·ver·board (ō′vər bôrd′) adv. 1. over the side of a ship into the water: to fall overboard. He threw the net overboard. 2. to go overboard. to go to extremes, esp. because of enthusiasm or affection: The critic went overboard in his praise for the new play. 3. to throw overboard. to cast into abandonment or disuse; discard: All their hopes were thrown overboard when the news came.

o·ver·build (ō′vər bild′) -built, -build·ing. v.t., v.i. to build too many houses or buildings in (an area).

o·ver·bur·den (ō′vər burd′ən) v.t. to put too great a weight or burden on; overload. —n. 1. too great a burden. 2. layer of rock, earth, or other material lying over a useful mineral deposit.

o·ver·cap·i·tal·ize (ō′vər kap′it əl īz′) -ized, -iz·ing. v.t. 1. to invest more capital in (a company) than is warranted by actual prospects. 2. to fix the nominal value of the capital of a (corporation) higher than is justified by legal limits or by actual market value. 3. to overestimate the capital value of (a property or company). —o′ver·cap′i·tal·i·za′tion, n.

o·ver·cast (ō′vər kast′) adj. 1. clouded over; cloudy; dark; gloomy: an overcast sky. 2. sewn with overcasting. —v.t., v.i. -cast, -cast·ing. 1. to make or become clouded over. 2. to sew (fabric, esp. raw edges of fabric) over and over with long stitches to prevent unraveling —n. 1. covering of clouds. 2. stitch sewn with overcasting.

o·ver·cau·tious (ō′vər kô′shəs) adj. too cautious.

o·ver·charge (v., ō′vər chärj′; n., ō′vər chärj′) -charged, -charg·ing. v.t. 1. to charge (someone) more than the established, usual, or proper price. 2. to load, supply, or fill to excess: to overcharge an electric battery. —n. act, instance, or amount of overcharging.

o·ver·cloud (ō′vər kloud′) v.t. to cover with or as with clouds.

o·ver·coat (ō′vər kōt′) n. man's heavy outer coat worn over a suit or other clothing for added warmth.

o·ver·come (ō′vər kum′) -came, -come, -com·ing. v.t. 1. to get the better of, as in a contest or conflict; conquer: The army overcame all opposition in its march to the sea. 2. to rise above or get over: He overcame his fear of heights. 3. to exhaust, overwhelm, or make helpless: Many in the crowd were overcome by the heat. —v.i. to be victorious; conquer. [Old English ofercuman.] —Syn. v.t. 1. see defeat.

o·ver·com·pen·sate (ō′vər kom′pən sāt′) -sat·ed, -sat·ing. v.i. to engage in overcompensation. —v.t. to give excessive compensation to.

o·ver·com·pen·sa·tion (ō′vər kom′pən sā′shən) n. 1. Psychology. process of reacting to a feeling of inferiority by an exaggerated or excessive drive to compensate for it. Overcompensation may make a person who is self-conscious about his short stature engage in bragging and aggressive or arrogant behavior. 2. any process of excessive compensation.

o·ver·con·fi·dent (ō′vər kon′fə dənt) adj. too confident. —o′ver·con′fi·dence, n.

o·ver·cook (ō′vər kook′) v.t. to cook (something) too much or too long.

o·ver·crowd·ed (ō′vər krou′did) adj. having too many people or things; too crowded.

o·ver·de·vel·op (ō′vər di vel′əp) v.t. 1. to develop too much. 2. to submerge (a photographic film or plate) in developing solution too long, so that it becomes too dark. —o′ver·de·vel′op·ment, n.

o·ver·do (ō′vər doō′) -did, -done, -do·ing. v.t. 1. to do or use too much or carry too far: The writer overdid his criticism and made us feel sorry for the subject of his attacks. 2. to cook (food) too much. —v.i. to do too much or go too far.

o·ver·dose (ō′vər dōs′) n. too large a dose, as of a drug. —v.t., -dosed, -dos·ing. to give too large a dose to.

o·ver·draft (ō′vər draft′) n. 1. act or instance of overdrawing a bank account. 2. amount of the shortage in an overdrawn account.

o·ver·draw (ō′vər drô′) -drew, -drawn, -draw·ing. v.t. 1. to write a check against (a bank account) that is larger than the account's balance or credit. 2. to exaggerate, as in drawing or describing: The fisherman's description of the fish he nearly caught was very overdrawn.

o·ver·dress (ō′vər dres′) v.i., v.t. to dress in clothes that are too formal or fancy for the occasion.

o·ver·drive (ō′vər drīv′) n. additional set of gears in some motor vehicles that enables the driveshaft to turn faster than the engine or crankshaft, as at high cruising speeds.

o·ver·due (ō′vər doō′, -dū′) adj. 1. remaining unpaid past the assigned date of payment: an overdue bill. 2. that has not yet happened or arrived, though the expected or scheduled time is past: The train is overdue. 3. that should have happened sooner: An apology from him is long overdue.

o·ver·eat (ō′vər ēt′) -ate, -eat·en, -eat·ing. v.i. to eat too much.

o·ver·em·pha·size (ō′vər em′fə sīz′) -sized, -siz·ing. v.t. to place too much emphasis on; stress too much: That college overemphasizes athletics. —o′ver·em′pha·sis, n.

o·ver·es·ti·mate (v., ō′vər es′tə māt′; n., ō′vər es′tə mit) -mat·ed, -mat·ing. v.t. to make too high an estimate of: to overestimate a person's ability, to overestimate the cost of a project. —n. estimate that is too high. —o′ver·es′ti·ma′tion, n.

o·ver·ex·cite (ō′vər ik sīt′) -cit·ed, -cit·ing. v.t. to excite excessively. —o′ver·ex·cite′ment, n.

o·ver·ex·pose (ō′vər iks pōz′) -posed, -pos·ing. v.t. 1. to display or expose (someone or something) too much. 2. to expose (a photographic film or plate) for too long a time. —o′ver·ex·po′sure, n.

o·ver·ex·tend (ō′vər iks tend′) v.t. to extend (something) beyond what is safe, reasonable, or prudent.

o′ver·ar′gu·men′ta·tive	o′ver·con′cen·trat′ed	o′ver·de·pend′ent	o′ver·e·lab′o·rate
o′ver·as·sess′ment	o′ver·con′cen·trat′ing	o′ver·de·sir′ous	o′ver·e·lat′ed
o′ver·as·sured′	o′ver·con′cen·tra′tion	o′ver·de·struc′tive	o′ver·em·bel′lish
o′ver·at·tached′	o′ver·con·cern′	o′ver·de·struc′tive·ness	o′ver·em·broi′der
o′ver·at·ten′tive	o′ver·con·sci·en′tious	o′ver·de·tailed′	o′ver·e·mo′tion·al
o′ver·at·ten′tive·ly	o′ver·con·serv′a·tive	o′ver·de·vot′ed	o′ver·e·mo′tion·al·ize′
o′ver·at·ten′tive·ness	o′ver·con·sid′er·ate	o′ver·dil′i·gent	o′ver·e·mo′tion·al·ized′
o′ver·big′	o′ver·con·sump′tion	o′ver·dil′i·gent·ly	o′ver·e·mo′tion·al·iz′ing
o′ver·bold′	o′ver·cool′	o′ver·di·lute′	o′ver·em·phat′ic
o′ver·boun′te·ous	o′ver·count′	o′ver·di·lut′ed	o′ver·en·rich′
o′ver·bright′	o′ver·cour′te·ous	o′ver·di·lut′ing	o′ver·en·thu′si·as′tic
o′ver·bul′ky	o′ver·coy′	o′ver·dis′tant	o′ver·ex·act′ing
o′ver·bus′y	o′ver·crit′i·cal	o′ver·di′ver·si·fi·ca′tion	o′ver·ex′er·cise′
o′ver·care′ful	o′ver·cul′ti·vate′	o′ver·di·ver′si·fy′	o′ver·ex′er·cised′
o′ver·care′less	o′ver·cul′ti·vat′ed	o′ver·di·ver′si·fied′	o′ver·ex′er·cis′ing
o′ver·cas′u·al	o′ver·cul′ti·vat′ing	o′ver·di·ver′si·fy′ing	o′ver·ex·ert′
o′ver·char′i·ta·ble	o′ver·cun′ning	o′ver·dog·mat′ic	o′ver·ex·er′tion
o′ver·chill′	o′ver·cu′ri·ous	o′ver·dra·mat′ic	o′ver·ex·pand′
o′ver·civ′il	o′ver·dec′o·rate′	o′ver·drink′	o′ver·ex·pan′sion
o′ver·clean′	o′ver·dec′o·rat′ed	o′ver·ea′ger	o′ver·ex·pect′ant
o′ver·col′or	o′ver·dec′o·rat′ing	o′ver·ea′sy	o′ver·ex·plic′it
o′ver·com·pet′i·tive	o′ver·de·fen′sive	o′ver·ed′u·cate′	o′ver·ex·pres′sive
o′ver·com·plex′	o′ver·def′er·en′tial	o′ver·ed′u·cat′ed	o′ver·ex·pres′sive·ly
o′ver·com·pli′ant	o′ver·del′i·cate	o′ver·ed′u·cat′ing	o′ver·ex·pres′sive·ness
o′ver·con′cen·trate′	o′ver·de·mand′	o′ver·ef·fu′sive	o′ver·ex·u′ber·ant

o·ver·feed (ō′vər fēd′) *-fed, -feed·ing. v.t.* to feed to excess.

o·ver·flight (ō′vər flīt′) *n.* passage of an aircraft over an area without landing, as for spying.

o·ver·flow (*v.,* ō′vər flō′; *n.,* ō′vər flō′) *-flowed, -flown, -flow·ing. v.i.* **1.** to flow beyond the usual limits: *Water from the kitchen sink overflowed onto the floor.* **2.** to be so full that the contents flow over: *The bathtub overflowed.* **3.** to be full or more than full: *a heart overflowing with love.* —*v.t.* **1.** to flow over the top edge or rim of: *The river overflowed its banks.* **2.** to flow or spread over; flood. **3.** to cause to overflow; fill too full: *Don't overflow the bathtub.* —*n.* **1.** act or process of overflowing. **2.** that which overflows. **3.** outlet for excess liquid.

o·ver·grow (ō′vər grō′) *-grew, -grown, -grow·ing. v.t.* **1.** to cover with growth; grow over: *Weeds overgrew the yard.* **2.** to grow too large for; outgrow. —*v.i.* to grow too much or too fast.

o·ver·grown (ō′vər grōn′) *adj.* **1.** grown too large or beyond normal size. **2.** covered with foliage.

o·ver·growth (ō′vər grōth′) *n.* **1.** excessive growth. **2.** growth over-spreading or covering something.

o·ver·hand (ō′vər hand′) *adj.* **1.** performed with the hand raised above the elbow or the arm raised above the shoulder: *an overhand pitch.* Also, **o′ver·hand′ed.** **2.** sewn with closely spaced over-and-over stitches, as in joining finished edges: *an overhand seam.* —*adv.* in an overhand style or manner: *to throw overhand.* Also, **o′ver·hand′ed.** —*v.t.* to sew with overhand stitches. —*n.* overhand stroke or delivery, as in tennis.

overhand knot, knot made by forming a loop and passing the end of the rope or other material through it.

o·ver·hang (*v.,* ō′vər hang′; *n.,* ō′vər hang′) *-hung, -hang·ing. v.t.* **1.** to hang out over (something): *Tall bushes overhung the walk.* **2.** to loom over threateningly; menace. —*v.i.* to hang or project over something. —*n.* **1.** part or section that overhangs; projection. **2.** extent or amount of projection.

o·ver·haul (ō′vər hôl′) *v.t.* **1.** to examine thoroughly and make needed repairs or adjustments in: *to overhaul an engine.* **2.** to investigate thoroughly and make far-reaching changes in: *to overhaul the prison system.* **3.** to catch up with; overtake: *The coast guard cutter quickly overhauled the fishing boat.* —*n.* act or process of overhauling.

o·ver·head (*adv.,* ō′vər hed′; *n., adj.,* ō′vər hed′) *adv.* above the level of the head: *a light burning overhead, birds flying overhead.* —*n.* **1.** general operating expenses of a business, as rent, taxes, heating, lighting, and repair, as opposed to costs of materials and labor. **2.** stroke made above the level of the head in tennis and other racket games. —*adj.* **1.** situated, operating, or moving overhead: *overhead lights.* **2.** of or relating to overhead in business: *overhead expenses.*

o·ver·hear (ō′vər hēr′) *-heard, -hear·ing. v.t.* to hear without the speaker's intention or knowledge.

o·ver·heat (ō′vər hēt′) *v.t., v.i.* to make or become too hot.

o·ver·in·dulge (ō′vər in dulj′) *-dulged, -dulg·ing. v.t., v.i.* to indulge too much. —**o′ver·in·dul′gence,** *n.* —**o′ver·in·dul′gent,** *adj.*

o·ver·joy (ō′vər joi′) *v.t.* to make very joyful.

o·ver·joyed (ō′vər joid′) *adj.* very happy or joyful.

o·ver·kill (ō′vər kil′) *n.* **1.** capacity to kill more of an enemy or inflict greater damage than is necessary for victory, esp. by using nuclear weapons. **2.** *Informal.* any excessively powerful or heavy-handed measures. —*v.t.* to destroy by greater force than is necessary.

o·ver·land (ō′vər land′, -lənd) *adv., adj.* by, on, or across land: *to travel overland, an overland mail route.*

o·ver·lap (*v.,* ō′vər lap′; *n.,* ō′vər lap′) *-lapped, -lap·ping. v.t., v.i.* **1.** to rest on top of (something) and partially cover it up; lap over: *One feather overlaps another on a bird's wing.* **2.** to coincide partly with or have something in common: *The Renaissance overlapped the later Middle Ages.* —*n.* **1.** instance of overlapping. **2.** part that overlaps. **3.** extent or amount of overlapping.

o·ver·lay (*v.,* ō′vər lā′; *n.,* ō′vər lā′) *-laid, -lay·ing. v.t.* **1.** to place over or on each other; to overlay shingles. **2.** to cover or spread with something, as a layer of protective or decorative material: *to overlay painted wood with shellac.* —*n.* **1.** decorative or protective layer: *an overlay of gold.* **2.** any added, superficial front or veneer: *a violent society with an overlay of civility.* **3.** *Printing.* mostly transparent piece or sheet placed over art work to be printed, in order to add letters, lines, or other elements or to modify color or shading.

o·ver·leap (ō′vər lēp′) *-leaped or -leapt, -leap·ing. v.t.* **1.** to leap over or across. **2.** to overreach oneself by leaping too far. **3.** to pass over; ignore.

o·ver·lie (ō′vər lī′) *-lay, -lain, -ly·ing. v.t.* **1.** to lie over or upon: *The Cenozoic layer of rocks overlies the Paleozoic layers.* **2.** to smother (a baby) by lying on it.

o·ver·load (*v.,* ō′vər lōd′; *n.,* ō′vər lōd′) *v.t.* to put an excessive load or burden in or upon: *to overload a car.* —*n.* excessive load or burden.

o·ver·long (ō′vər lông′) *adj., adv.* too long.

o·ver·look (ō′vər look′) *v.t.* **1.** to fail to see, observe, or think of: *The robbers overlooked the possibility of the alarm system sounding.* **2.** to regard (something) as never having happened; disregard; ignore: *to overlook an insult.* **3.** to pass over indulgently; excuse: *to overlook a person's faults.* **4.a.** to look over or down upon from a higher place or position: *She overlooked the vast expanse from the tower.* **b.** to offer a view of: *The house on the hill overlooks the valley.*

o·ver·lord (ō′vər lôrd′) *n.* one who is the lord of other lords or rulers.

o·ver·ly (ō′vər lē) *adv.* excessively; too: *overly generous.*

o·ver·mas·ter (ō′vər mas′tər) *v.t.* to overcome; overpower; subdue.

o·ver·match (ō′vər mach′) *v.t.* **1.** to be more than a match for; surpass or defeat. **2.** to match with a superior opponent.

o·ver·much (ō′vər much′) *adj., adv., n.* too much.

o·ver·night (ō′vər nīt′) *adv.* **1.** during or through the night: *to keep watch overnight.* **2.** very quickly; suddenly: *The houses sprang up overnight.* **3.** in the space of one night: *to move a camp overnight.* —*adj.* **1.** for one night: *an overnight guest.* **2.** of, lasting through, or occurring during the night: *an overnight storm, an overnight attack of the flu.* **3.** suitable, used, or made for short trips: *an overnight bag.*

o·ver·pass (*n.,* ō′vər pas′; *v.,* ō′vər pas′) *n.* bridge, road, or other passage that crosses above another roadway or thoroughfare. —*v.t.* **1.** to pass over, across, or through. **2.** to disregard; ignore. **3.** to exceed; surpass.

o·ver·pay (ō′vər pā′) *-paid, -pay·ing. v.t.* **1.** to pay too highly. **2.** to pay more than (the amount required or due). —**o′ver·pay′ment,** *n.*

o·ver·play (ō′vər plā′) *v.t.* **1.** to treat as too strong or too certain; rely on or use too much. **2.** to play (a part or role) in an exaggerated manner; overact.

o·ver·plus (ō′vər plus′) *n.* excess; surplus.

o·ver·pop·u·late (ō′vər pop′yə lāt′) *-lat·ed, -lat·ing. v.t.* to fill with too many people. —**o′ver·pop′u·la′tion,** *n.*

o·ver·pow·er (ō′vər pou′ər) *v.t.* **1.** to overcome by greater strength or power. **2.** to make helpless or ineffective; overcome. **3.** to supply with too much power.

o·ver·praise (ō′vər prāz′) *-praised, prais·ing. v.t.* to praise too highly.

o′ver·fa·mil′iar	o′ver·grasp′ing	o′ver·in·flat′ing	o′ver·live′ly
o′ver·far′	o′ver·hard′	o′ver·in′flu·ence	o′ver·loud′
o′ver·fast′	o′ver·harsh′	o′ver·in′flu·enced	o′ver·lux·u′ri·ant
o′ver·fas·tid′i·ous	o′ver·hast′i·ly	o′ver·in·flu·enc′ing	o′ver·lux·u′ri·ous
o′ver·fat′	o′ver·hast′i·ness	o′ver·in·flu·en′tial	o′ver·mag·ni·fi·ca′tion
o′ver·fear′ful	o′ver·hast′y	o′ver·in·sis′tent	o′ver·mag′ni·fied′
o′ver·fill′	o′ver·high′	o′ver·in·sis′tent·ly	o′ver·mag′ni·fy′
o′ver·flour′ish	o′ver·hot′	o′ver·in·sure′	o′ver·mag′ni·fy′ing
o′ver·fond′	o′ver·i·de·al·is′tic	o′ver·in·sured′	o′ver·mod′est
o′ver·fool′ish	o′ver·i·de′al·ize′	o′ver·in·sur′ing	o′ver·mod′est·ly
o′ver·for′ward	o′ver·i·de′al·ized′	o′ver·in·tense′	o′ver·moist′
o′ver·frag′ile	o′ver·i·de′al·iz′ing	o′ver·in·tense′ly	o′ver·mourn′ful
o′ver·frail′	o′ver·im·ag′i·na′tive	o′ver·in·vest′	o′ver·nar′row
o′ver·frank′	o′ver·im·pres′sion·a·ble	o′ver·jeal′ous	o′ver·neat′
o′ver·fraught′	o′ver·in·cline′	o′ver·keen′	o′ver·nice′
o′ver·fre′quent	o′ver·in·clined′	o′ver·kind′	o′ver·of·fen′sive
o′ver·full′	o′ver·in·clin′ing	o′ver·large′	o′ver·op′ti·mis′tic
o′ver·gen·er·al·i·za′tion	o′ver·in·dus′tri·al·ize′	o′ver·late′	o′ver·or′na·ment′ed
o′ver·gen′er·al·ize′	o′ver·in·dus′tri·al·ized′	o′ver·laud′a·to′ry	o′ver·par·tic′u·lar
o′ver·gen′er·al·ized′	o′ver·in·dus′tri·al·iz′ing	o′ver·lav′ish	o′ver·pas′sion·ate
o′ver·gen′er·al·iz′ing	o′ver·in·flate′	o′ver·lax′	o′ver·pes′si·mis′tic
o′ver·gen′er·ous	o′ver·in·flat′ed	o′ver·lib′er·al	o′ver·pre·cise′

at; āpe; cär; end; mē; it; īce; hot; ōld; fôrk; wood; fōōl; oil; out; up; ūse; turn; sing; thin; this; zh in treasure; ə in ago, taken, pencil, lemon, circus.

o·ver·price (ō′vər prīs′) **-priced, -pric·ing.** *v.t.* to set too high a price or value upon.

o·ver·pro·duce (ō′vər prə dōōs′, -dūs′) **-duced, -duc·ing.** *v.t., v.i.* to produce (goods) in excess of demand. —**o′ver·pro·duc′tion,** *n.*

o·ver·pro·tect (ō′vər prə tekt′) *v.t.* to protect or shelter to too great a degree: *The mother overprotected her child.* —**o′ver·pro·tec′tive,** *adj.*

o·ver·rate (ō′vər rāt′) **-rat·ed, -rat·ing.** *v.t.* to rate, value, or estimate at too high a level: *The general overrated his army's ability to achieve a quick victory.*

o·ver·reach (ō′vər rēch′) *v.t.* **1.** to reach or extend over or beyond. **2.** to get the better of by cunning. **3. to overreach oneself.** to fail because of trying to do something beyond one's ability. —*v.i.* to reach too far. —**o′ver·reach′er,** *n.*

o·ver·ride (ō′vər rīd′) **-rode, -rid·den, -rid·ing.** *v.t.* **1.** to set aside (something), as by superior authority; cancel (an action or decision): *The legislature overrode the governor's veto and the bill became law.* **2.** to prevail over; supersede: *This problem overrides all other matters.* **3.** to ride (a horse or other animal) until it becomes exhausted. **4.** to ride over or across: *The flood waters overrode the valley.* **5.** to trample down. **6.** to extend or pass over.

o·ver·ripe (ō′vər rīp′) *adj.* past the peak of ripeness; becoming rotten.

o·ver·rule (ō′vər rōōl′) **-ruled, -rul·ing.** *v.t.* **1.** to invalidate or rule against by virtue of higher authority: *The Supreme Court overruled the decision of the lower court.* **2.** to decide against or put down: *Albert said we should stay, but he was overruled by the rest of the group.*

o·ver·run (*v.,* ō′vər run′; *n.,* ō′vər run′) **-ran, -run, -run·ning.** *v.t.* **1.** to swarm or spread over or throughout, esp. with harmful intent or effects: *Invaders overran the countryside. Poison ivy overran the park grounds.* **2.** to flow over: *The river overran its banks.* **3.** to run beyond: *He overran second base.* **4.** to go beyond or exceed (a limit): *The actual costs overran the budget by a large amount.* —*v.i.* **1.** to exceed a limit. **2.** to overflow; run over. —*n.* **1.** act or instance of overrunning. **2.** amount by which something overruns: *an overrun of two million dollars in the cost of building a new airplane.*

o·ver·seas (ō′vər sēz′) *also,* **o·ver·sea.** *adv.* over, across, or beyond the sea; abroad: *to travel overseas.* —*adj.* **1.** employed, situated, or serving overseas: *a company's overseas representative.* **2.** of or relating to countries across the sea; foreign: *overseas trade.*

o·ver·see (ō′vər sē′) **-saw, -seen, -see·ing.** *v.t.* to watch over and manage; have charge of; direct: *to oversee the building of a canal.*

o·ver·se·er (ō′vər sē′ər) *n.* one who oversees, esp. a person who supervises the work of laborers.

o·ver·sell (ō′vər sel′) **-sold, -sell·ing.** *v.t.* **1.** to take orders for or sell more of than is available. **2.** to try to sell (something) too aggressively. **3.** to try to promote (something or someone) excessively; praise too highly.

o·ver·set (*v.,* ō′vər set′; *n.,* ō′vər set′) **-set, -set·ting.** *v.t.* **1.** to overturn or overthrow. **2.** to overcome or upset. **3.** *Printing.* to set too much type or copy for (a given space). —*n.* act or fact of oversetting.

o·ver·shad·ow (ō′vər shad′ō) *v.t.* **1.** to be more important or significant than: *The continuing war overshadowed all the country's other problems.* **2.** to cast a shadow over; obscure; darken: *Dark clouds overshadowed the sun.*

o·ver·shoe (ō′vər shōō′) *n.* protective shoe or boot, usually made of rubber, worn over an ordinary shoe to protect against cold, snow, water, or mud.

o·ver·shoot (ō′vər shōōt′) **-shot, -shoot·ing.** *v.t.* **1.** to go or pass over, above, or beyond (a target, mark, or goal): *The aircraft overshot the landing field.* **2.** to shoot or project (something) over or beyond a target or goal. —*v.i.* to shoot or go too far.

o·ver·shot (ō′vər shot′) *adj.* **1.** having the upper jaw projecting beyond the lower. **2.** (of a water wheel) driven by water falling down from above, rather than by water flowing past.

o·ver·sight (ō′vər sīt′) *n.* **1.** careless, unintentional mistake: *The omission of your name from the guest list was an oversight.* **2.** watchful care or management; supervision.

o·ver·sim·pli·fy (ō′vər sim′plə fī′) **-fied, -fy·ing.** *v.t., v.i.* to make (something) appear to be much simpler than it really is. —**o′ver·sim′pli·fi·ca′tion,** *n.*

o·ver·size (ō′vər sīz′) *adj.* also, **o′ver·sized′.** larger than the normal or usual size. —*n.* **1.** size larger than the normal or usual size. **2.** something that is oversize.

o·ver·skirt (ō′vər skurt′) *n.* skirt worn over another skirt.

o·ver·sleep (ō′vər slēp′) **-slept, -sleep·ing.** *v.i.* to sleep beyond one's intended or usual time for waking up. —*v.t.* to sleep beyond (a particular time or event).

o·ver·spread (ō′vər spred′) **-spread, -spread·ing.** *v.t.* to spread or extend over: *Trees overspread the tiny cabin.*

o·ver·state (ō′vər stāt′) **-stat·ed, -stat·ing.** *v.t.* to state too strongly; exaggerate. —**o′ver·state′ment,** *n.*

o·ver·stay (ō′vər stā′) *v.t.* to stay beyond the time or limit of: *to overstay a visa.*

Overshot waterwheel

o·ver·step (ō′vər step′) **-stepped, -step·ping.** *v.t.* to go over or beyond (a limit); exceed: *to overstep one's authority.*

o·ver·stock (ō′vər stok′) *v.t.* **1.** to supply with too great a stock of. **2.** to stock (a commodity) to excess. —*n.* too large a stock or supply.

o·ver·strung (ō′vər strung′) *adj.* too highly strung; too tense.

o·ver·stuff (ō′vər stuf′) *v.t.* to stuff to excess.

o·ver·stuffed (ō′vər stuft′) *adj.* **1.** stuffed to excess. **2.** (of furniture) having the frame covered over with a thick padding or large amount of stuffing.

o·ver·sub·scribe (ō′vər səb skrīb′) **-scribed, -scrib·ing.** *v.t., v.i.* to subscribe for more of (something) than is available or necessary. —**o′ver·sub·scrip′tion,** *n.*

o·ver·sup·ply (*v.,* ō′vər sə plī′; *n.,* ō′vər sə plī′) **-plied, -ply·ing.** *v.t.* to supply in excess. —*n. pl.,* **-plies.** excessive supply.

o·vert (ō vurt′) *adj.* not hidden or concealed; easily observed; not secret. [Old French *overt,* past participle of *ovrir* to open, going back to Latin *aperīre.*] —**o·vert′ly,** *adv.*

o·ver·take (ō′vər tāk′) **-took, -tak·en, -tak·ing.** *v.t.* **1.a.** to catch up with: *The jaguar overtook the fleeing deer.* **b.** to catch up with and then pass: *Japan has overtaken West Germany in industrial production.* **2.** to come upon unexpectedly or suddenly.

o·ver·tax (ō′vər taks′) *v.t.* **1.** to place too heavy a burden on or draw too much from: *The country's resources were overtaxed by years of war.* **2.** to charge too great a tax on. —**o′ver·tax·a′tion,** *n.*

o·ver-the-coun·ter (ō′vər thə koun′tər) *adj.* **1.** of or relating to the buying and selling of securities that are not listed on an organized stock exchange and are not sold on the floor of an exchange. **2.** that may be sold legally without a doctor's prescription: *over-the-counter drugs.*

o·ver·throw (*v.,* ō′vər thrō′; *n.,* ō′vər thrō′) **-threw, -thrown, -throw·ing.** *v.t.* **1.** to remove from power or dominance, esp. by force or struggle: *to overthrow a government.* **2.** to throw or knock down; overturn; upset: *to overthrow a table in rage.* **3.** to throw something, as a baseball, beyond (the intended place). —*n.* **1.** act of overthrowing; fact of being overthrown. **2.** throw that goes beyond the intended place.

o·ver·time (*n., adv., adj.,* ō′vər tīm′; *v.,* ō′vər tīm′) *n.* **1.** time worked beyond the regular working hours. **2.** pay for such extra time. **3.** *Sports.* extra period of play, after regulation time has expired, to decide the winner of a contest that has ended in a tie. —*adv., adj.* of, for, or during overtime: *to work overtime, overtime pay.* —*v.,* **-timed, -tim·ing.** to allow too much time for: *to overtime a photographic exposure.*

o·ver·tone (ō′vər tōn′) *n.* **1.** fainter and higher tone heard along with the fundamental tone produced by a musical instrument; harmonic.

o′ver·prom′i·nent	o′ver·rig′or·ous	o′ver·small′	o′ver·stretch′
o′ver·pub′li·cize′	o′ver·ro·man′ti·cize′	o′ver·sol′emn	o′ver·strict′
o′ver·pub′li·cized′	o′ver·ro·man′ti·cized′	o′ver·so·lic′i·tous	o′ver·stu′di·ous
o′ver·pub′li·ciz′ing	o′ver·ro·man′ti·ciz′ing	o′ver·spe′cial·i·za′tion	o′ver·suf·fi′cient
o′ver·quick′	o′ver·rough′	o′ver·spe′cial·ize′	o′ver·sus·pi′cious
o′ver·qui′et	o′ver·salt′	o′ver·spe′cial·ized′	o′ver·sweet′
o′ver·rank′	o′ver·sen′si·tive	o′ver·spe′cial·iz′ing	o′ver·sys′tem·at′ic
o′ver·rash′	o′ver·sen′su·al	o′ver·spend′	o′ver·tech′ni·cal
o′ver·ra′tion·al·ize′	o′ver·sen′ti·men′tal	o′ver·spend′ing	o′ver·thick′
o′ver·ra′tion·al·ized′	o′ver·se′ri·ous	o′ver·spent′	o′ver·tight′
o′ver·ra′tion·al·iz′ing	o′ver·sharp′	o′ver·squeam′ish	o′ver·tire′
o′ver·re·fine′	o′ver·short′	o′ver·stim′u·late′	o′ver·tired′
o′ver·rich′	o′ver·skep′ti·cal	o′ver·stim′u·lat′ed	o′ver·tir′ing
o′ver·rig′id		o′ver·stim′u·lat′ing	

at; āpe; cär; end; mē; it; īce; hot; ōld; fôrk; wood; fōōl; oil; out; up; ūse; turn; sing; thin; <u>th</u>is; zh in treasure; ə in ago, taken, pencil, lemon, circus.   719

2. secondary or implicit meaning or quality; suggestion; hint: *His congratulatory remarks to his friend carried an overtone of jealousy.*

o·ver·top (ō′vər top′) **-topped, -top·ping.** *v.t.* **1.** to rise over or above the top of; be higher than: *The new building overtops the highest of the existing structures.* **2.** to surpass; excel.

o·ver·train (ō′vər trān′) *v.t., v.i.* to train beyond the point of best condition or readiness.

o·ver·trick (ō′vər trik′) *n.* card trick taken in excess of the number bid.

o·ver·trump (ō′vər trump′) *v.t., v.i.* to play a trump higher than one previously played.

o·ver·ture (ō′vər choor′, -chər) *n.* **1.** orchestral musical composition serving as a prelude, preview, or introduction to a larger, usually dramatic, musical work, as an opera. **2.** suggestion or proposal meant to lead to some new action; offer to begin something: *backward and delicate ladies who can die rather than make the first overture* (Fielding, 1752). [Old French *overture* opening, beginning, going back to Latin *apertūra* opening. Doublet of APERTURE.]

o·ver·turn (ō′vər turn′) *v.t.* **1.** to turn or throw over; upset: *Heavy winds overturned the sailboat.* **2.** to overthrow, defeat, or destroy. —*v.i.* to be or become turned over: *The car overturned on the sharp curve.*

o·ver·use (*v.,* ō′vər ūz′; *n.,* ō′vər ūs′) **-used, -us·ing.** *v.t.* to use too much. —*n.* too heavy or too frequent use: *The composer's overuse of the same theme became tiresome.*

o·ver·val·ue (ō′vər val′yoo) **-val·ued, -val·u·ing.** *v.t.* to place too high a value on.

o·ver·view (ō′vər vū′) *n.* broad, general view or survey.

o·ver·ween·ing (ō′vər wē′ning) *adj.* having or showing exaggerated arrogance, conceit, or self-importance. [Present participle of *overween* to be conceited, from Old English *oferwenian* to become insolent.]

o·ver·weigh (ō′vər wā′) *v.t.* **1.** to be greater in weight than; outweigh. **2.** to weigh down; burden; oppress.

o·ver·weight (ō′vər wāt′) *adj.* above the normal, desirable, or allowed weight. —*n.* more weight than is normal, desirable, or allowed. —*v.t.* **1.** to give too much emphasis or importance to. **2.** to weigh down; burden.

o·ver·whelm (ō′vər hwelm′, -welm′) *v.t.* **1.** to overcome completely; make helpless; overpower or crush: *The enemy forces overwhelmed the camp. He was overwhelmed by the death of his father.* **2.** to cover or bury completely: *Pompeii was overwhelmed by a vast accumulation of dust and ashes* (Huxley, 1878). [OVER- + WHELM.] —**o′ver·whelm′ing·ly,** *adv.*

o·ver·work (*v.,* ō′vər wurk′; *n.,* ō′vər wurk′) **-worked** or **-wrought, -work·ing.** *v.t.* **1.** to cause to work too hard; weary or exhaust with work. **2.** to use too often; make excessive use of: *to overwork a literary theme.* **3.** to work too hard or too long on: *to overwork a speech.* —*n.* more work than one should do or can be expected to do.

o·ver·write (ō′vər rīt′) **-wrote, -writ·ten, writ·ing.** *v.t., v.i.* to write too much about (a subject); write in too elaborate or pretentious a style.

o·ver·wrought (ō′vər rôt′) *adj.* **1.** worked up to an unhealthy excess of excitement or nervousness: *a bride overwrought with anticipation.* **2.** decorated or worked all over: *a dress overwrought with embroidered flowers.* **3.** to elaborate; overdone.

Ov·id (ov′id) *n.* 43 B.C.–A.D. c.17, Roman poet; born Publius Ovidius Naso.

o·vi·duct (ō′və dukt′) *n.* tube through which the egg cell passes from the ovary. [Modern Latin *oviductus,* from Latin *ōvum* egg + *ductus* a leading.]

o·vi·form (ō′və fôrm′) *adj.* egg-shaped. [Latin *ōvum* egg + -FORM.]

o·vip·a·rous (ō vip′ər əs) *adj.* producing eggs that hatch after leaving the body of the female. All birds and most fish and reptiles are oviparous. Distinguished from ovoviviparous, viviparous. [Latin *ōviparus,* from *ōvum* egg + *parere* to bring forth.]

o·vi·pos·i·tor (ō′və poz′i tər) *n.* organ at the end of the abdomen of the female of certain insects, by which eggs are deposited. [Latin *ōvum* egg + *positor* placer.]

Ovipositor

o·void (ō′void) *adj.* egg-shaped. —*n.* something shaped like an egg. [Modern Latin *ovoides,* from Latin *ōvum* egg.]

o·vo·vi·vip·a·rous (ō′vō vī vip′ər əs) *adj.* producing eggs that develop inside the body of the female and hatch either inside the mother or soon after they are laid. Certain reptiles and fish and many insects are ovoviviparous. Distinguished from **oviparous, viviparous.** [Latin *ōvum* egg + VIVIPAROUS.]

o·vu·late (ō′vyə lāt′) **-lat·ed, -lat·ing.** *v.i.* to produce egg cells or discharge them from the ovary. —**o′vu·la′tion,** *n.*

o·vule (ō′vūl) *n.* **1.** small egg, esp. one in an early stage of growth. **2.** part of a plant that develops into a seed after fertilization. [Modern Latin *ovulum,* diminutive of Latin *ōvum* egg.] —**o·vu·lar** (ō′vyə lər), *adj.*

o·vum (ō′vəm) *pl.,* **o·va.** *n.* egg (def. 3).

owe (ō) **owed, ow·ing.** *v.t.* **1.** to be under obligation to pay or repay (money): *to owe ten dollars to a friend, to owe the landlord two months' rent.* **2.** to be under obligation to offer or give: *to owe someone an apology.* **3.** to attribute or lay (something) to a cause or source: *To what do I owe the honor of your visit? We owe the general theory of relativity to Einstein.* —*v.i.* to be in debt. [Old English *āgan* to have to pay, possess, own.]

Ow·en, Robert (ō′in) 1771–1858, Welsh social reformer and founder of cooperative communities.

O·wens·bor·o (ō′inz bur′ō) *n.* city in northwestern Kentucky. Pop. (1970), 50,329.

ow·ing (ō′ing) *adj.* **1.** due to be paid; unpaid; owed. **2. owing to.** because of: *Owing to bad weather, today's game was postponed.*

owl (oul) *n.* any of numerous birds of prey, order Strigiformes, having a rounded head with large staring eyes and a hooked bill, a short, square tail, rounded wings, and soft, downy plumage. Owls usually hunt at night and feed chiefly on rodents and other small mammals. Height: 5½–27 inches. [Old English *ūle.*]

Owl

owl·et (ou′lit) *n.* **1.** young owl. **2.** small species of owl.

owl·ish (ou′lish) *adj.* resembling the features or characteristics of an owl. —**owl′ish·ly,** *adv.* —**owl′ish·ness,** *n.*

own (ōn) *adj.* of, relating to, or belonging to oneself or itself: *It was her own fault. His own brother testified against him.* ▲ used to intensify a possessive pronoun. —*n.* **1.** that which belongs exclusively to oneself or itself: *My time isn't my own.* **2.** one's own. belonging exclusively to oneself. **3. on one's own. a.** relying only on oneself for support or success. **b.** through one's personal efforts or initiative: *He got the job on his own.* **4. to come into one's own.** to receive that which rightfully belongs to one, esp. success or recognition. **5. to hold one's own.** to maintain one's standing, as against opposition or competition. —*v.t.* **1.** to have as one's property; have ownership of: *We own all the land between here and the river.* **2.** to acknowledge or admit: *I own that the mistake was my fault.* —*v.i.* **1.** to confess; admit (with *to*): *He owned to having lied.* **2. to own up.** to confess frankly and fully: *He owned up to his part in the crime.* [Old English *āgen* possessed, originally past participle of *āgan* to possess, have, owe.]

Syn. *v.t.* **1. Own, possess** mean to have something as one's property. **Own** stresses one's natural right to have personal property to use or dispose of at will: *Mr. North owns this company.* **Possess** stresses exclusive title to something and may refer to intangibles as well as property: *The museum possesses rare art treasures.*

own·er (ō′nər) *n.* one who owns something.

own·er·ship (ō′nər ship′) *n.* **1.** state of being an owner. **2.** legal title or right to something, esp. property.

ox (oks) *pl.,* **ox·en.** *n.* **1.** domesticated cow or bull, esp. a castrated adult male used as a draft animal or for beef. **2.** any bovine mammal, as a buffalo, bison, or yak. [Old English *oxa.*]

ox·a·late (ok′sə lāt′) *n.* salt or ester of oxalic acid.

ox·al·ic acid (ok sal′ik) poisonous organic acid that occurs in plants but is usually prepared synthetically, used as a stain, ink, and rust remover, and as a bleaching agent. Formula: $C_2H_2O_4$. [French *oxalique* extracted from sorrel[1] (from Latin *oxālis* sorrel[1]) + ACID; because it is found in the sorrel plant. See OXALIS.]

ox·al·is (ok sal′is, ok′sə lis) *n.* any of a large group of plants, genus *Oxalis,* having an acid juice and bearing small, round, pink, red, white, or yellow flowers and cloverlike leaves that fold up at night. [Latin *oxālis* sorrel[1], from Greek *oxalis,* from *oxys* sharp, acid, sour.]

ox·blood (oks′blud′) *n.* deep red color.

ox·bow (oks′bō′) *n.* **1.** wooden, U-shaped part of a yoke, placed as a collar under and around the neck of an ox. **2.** U-shaped bend in a river.

ox·cart (oks′kärt′) *n.* cart pulled by an ox or oxen.

at; āpe; cär; end; mē; it; īce; hot; ōld; fôrk; wood; fōōl; oil; out; up; ūse; turn; sing; thin; this; zh in treasure; ə in ago, taken, pencil, lemon, circus.

ox·en (ok′sən) plural of **ox.**

ox·eye (oks′ī′) *n.* any of several plants of the composite family, having showy yellow flower heads.

oxeye daisy, see **daisy.**

ox·ford (oks′fərd) *n.* **1.** shoe that comes up to just below the ankle and laces over the instep. Also, **oxford shoe. 2.** soft, medium-weight cotton fabric, used chiefly for shirts and blouses. Also, **oxford cloth.** [From *Oxford*, England.]

Oxfords

Ox·ford (oks′fərd) *n.* **1.** city in south-central England, on the Thames. Pop. (1968 est.), 110,100. **2.** noted university located there, established in the twelfth century.

Oxford gray, very dark gray color.

Oxford movement, movement in the Church of England during the middle of the nineteenth century, led by men at Oxford University, that stressed episcopal authority and a return to ceremonial worship.

ox·i·da·tion (oks′ə dā′shən) *n.* act of oxidizing; being oxidized.

oxidation number, number that expresses the degree to which a chemical element is or can be oxidized.

ox·ide (ok′sīd) *n.* compound of one other element with oxygen. [French *oxide* (now *oxyde*), from *ox(ygène)* (see OXYGEN) + *(ac)ide* acid (from Latin *acidus* sour).]

ox·i·dize (oks′ə dīz′) *-dized, -diz·ing. v.t.* **1.** to cause the atoms of (a chemical substance) to lose electrons, increasing the valence or oxidation number. **2.** to combine (a chemical substance) with oxygen; make into an oxide. —*v.i.* to become oxidized. [OXIDE + -IZE.]

ox·i·diz·er (oks′ə dī′zər) *n.* **1.** substance that yields oxygen for the burning of rocket fuel or a propellant, as nitric acid or liquid oxygen. **2.** any substance that causes oxidation.

ox·lip (oks′lip′) *n.* any of a species of primrose, *Primula elatior*, bearing clusters of yellow flowers and resembling the cowslip. [Old English *oxanslyppe*, from *oxan* ox's + *slyppe* slime.]

Ox·nard (oks′närd) *n.* city in southern California, near Los Angeles. Pop. (1970), 71,225.

Ox·o·ni·an (ok sō′nē ən) *adj.* of or relating to Oxford University or Oxford, England. —*n.* **1.** member or graduate of Oxford University. **2.** native or inhabitant of Oxford, England. [Medieval Latin *Oxonia* Oxford (from Old English *Oxenaford* literally, ford of oxen) + -AN.]

Ox·us (ok′səs) see **Amu Darya.**

ox·y·a·cet·y·lene torch (ok′sē ə set′əl ēn′) metal cutting and welding torch that burns a mixture of oxygen and acetylene and can produce temperatures of more than 4000 degrees centigrade.

ox·y·gen (ok′sə jən) *n.* colorless, odorless, nonmetallic element that makes up about one-fifth of the air and, in compounds, about one-half the weight of the earth's crust. Oxygen is essential to life. Symbol: **O** See **element** for table. [French *oxygène* oxygen; literally, producing acids, from Greek *oxys* sharp, acid + *-genēs* (see -GEN).]

ox·y·gen·ate (ok′sə jə nāt′) *-at·ed, -at·ing. v.t.* to treat, supply with, or mix with oxygen. —**ox′y·gen·a′tion,** *n.*

oxygen mask, device worn over the nose and mouth, through which oxygen is supplied from a storage container.

oxygen tent, tentlike structure, usually of a clear plastic material, placed over a patient's head and supplied with a flow of oxygen to assist breathing.

ox·y·he·mo·glo·bin (ok′sē hē′mə glō′bin) *n.* bright-red substance consisting of hemoglobin combined with oxygen, carried to tissues by the arteries.

ox·y·hy·dro·gen torch (ok′sē hī′drə jən) metal cutting and welding torch that burns a mixture of oxygen and hydrogen.

ox·y·mo·ron (ok′si môr′on) *pl.,* **-mo·ra** (-môr′ə). *n.* figure of speech in which contradictory or incongruous terms are combined, usually for emphasis, as in "bitterly happy" and "idiotic wisdom." [Greek *oxymōron* witty paradoxical saying, from *oxys* sharp + *mōros* foolish.]

o·yez (ō′yes, ō′yez, ō′yā) *interj.* hear ye! ▲ used to announce that court is in session and to ask for silence. [Anglo-Norman *oyez*, imperative plural of *oyer* to hear, from Latin *audīre*.]

oys·ter (ois′tər) *n.* any of a group of commercially important mollusks, family Ostreidae, widely found in shallow coastal waters, having a soft body enclosed in two irregular ear-shaped shells hinged at the narrow end. Oysters of the genus *Ostrea* are highly valued as food, while those of the genus *Pinctada* are raised for the fine pearls they produce. [Old French *oistre*, from Latin *ostrea*, from Greek *ostreon*.]

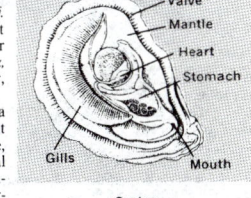

Oyster

oyster bed, area on the bottom of shallow coastal waters where oysters breed or are cultivated.

oyster crab, any of a group of small crabs, family Pinnotheridae, often living in a commensal relationship with a live oyster, inside the oyster's shell.

oyster cracker, small, salted cracker usually served with shellfish dishes, as oysters, or with soup.

oyster farm, place where oyster beds are seeded and maintained for commercial purposes.

oys·ter·man (ois′tər mən) *pl.,* **-men.** *n.* one who gathers, raises, or sells oysters.

oyster plant, salsify.

oz. *pl.,* **ozs.** ounce.

O·zark Mountains (ō′zärk) low, hilly area in southern Missouri, northern Arkansas, and northeastern Oklahoma. Also, **O′zarks.**

o·zone (ō′zōn) *n.* **1.** pale-blue gas with a distinctive odor, formed when an electric discharge passes through the air. Ozone is an allotropic form of oxygen. It is used esp. as a bleach, disinfectant, and deodorant. Symbol: O_3 **2.** *Informal.* pure, refreshing air. [German *Ozon* the gas, from Greek *ozōn* smelling, present participle of *ozein* to smell.]

o·zo·nif·er·ous (ō′zə nif′ər əs) *adj.* containing ozone.

o·zon·o·sphere (ō zon′ə sfēr′) *n.* layer of the stratosphere containing a high concentration of ozone, serving to absorb much ultraviolet radiation from the sun.

at; āpe; cär; end; mē; it; īce; hot; ōld; fôrk; wood; fōōl; oil; out; up; ūse; turn; sing; thin; this; zh in treasure; ə in ago, taken, pencil, lemon, circus.

p, P (pē) *pl.*, **p's, P's. 1.** sixteenth letter of the English alphabet. **2. to mind one's P's and Q's.** to be careful, esp. of one's behavior.
p 1. *Music.* piano. **2.** *Baseball.* pitcher.
P 1. phosphorus. **2.** *Chess.* pawn. **3.** *Physics.* pressure.
p. 1. page. **2.** part. **3.** participle. **4.** past. **5.** penny. **6.** per. **7.** pint. **8.** population. **9.** post.
P. 1. pastor. **2.** president. **3.** priest. **4.** prince.
pa (pä) *n. Informal.* father; papa.
Pa, protactinium. [P(ROTO-) + A(CTINIUM).]
p.a. 1. participial adjective. **2.** per annum.
Pa., Pennsylvania.
PA 1. press agent. **2.** public-address (system).
pab·lum (pab′ləm) *n.* **1.** soft, bland cereal used as food for infants. Trademark: Pablum. **2.** speaking or writing that is oversimplified; bland, dull language or ideas: *The politician's speech was nothing but pablum.* [Contraction of PABULUM.]
pab·u·lum (pab′yə ləm) *n.* **1.** substance that gives nourishment; food. **2.** pablum *(def. 2).* [Latin *pābulum.*]
Pac., Pacific.
pace (pās) *n.* **1.** single movement made by the leg in walking; step. **2.** distance covered in a step, often used as a variable measure of length averaging from 2½ to 3½ feet. **3.a.** rate of speed in walking or running: *to quicken one's pace.* **b.** rate of speed in any movement, activity, or progression: *They worked at a hectic pace to meet the deadline.* **4.** manner of stepping, as in walking or running; gait. **5.** gait, esp. of a horse, in which both feet on the same side are lifted and put down together. **6. to keep pace with. a.** to maintain the same speed of movement as: *The child ran along, trying to keep pace with the adults.* **b.** to maintain the same rate of progress as. **7. to put (someone) through his paces.** to test or exhibit the talents or abilities of: *The animals were put through their paces for the judges.* **8. to set the pace. a.** to set the speed for others to maintain or go beyond. **b.** to be an example for others to follow: *Our store set the pace in book sales.* —*v.t.,* **paced, pac·ing. 1.** to walk back and forth across, esp. with a slow, steady gait: *He paced the room while he waited.* **2.** to measure by paces (often with *off*): *They paced off twenty feet.* **3.** to set the rate of speed for. **4.** to train (a horse) to move at a certain gait, esp. the pace. —*v.i.* **1.** to walk with slow, steady steps. **2.** (of a horse) to move with the gait of the pace. [Old French *pas* step, rate, from Latin *passus* step.]
pace·mak·er (pās′mā′kər) *n.* **1.** one who sets the pace in a race. **2.** one who leads a trend or sets an example for others. **3.** any of several small electrical devices that control the rhythm of the heart, used in the treatment of heart disorders.
pac·er (pā′sər) *n.* **1.** one who paces or measures by paces. **2.** horse that paces, esp. one whose natural gait is a pace. **3.** pacemaker.
pace·set·ter (pās′set′ər) *n.* pacemaker *(defs. 1, 2).*
pa·cha (pä shä′, pash′ə, pä′shə) pasha.
pach·y·derm (pak′ə durm′) *n.* **1.** any of several large, thick-skinned, hoofed mammals, as the elephant or rhinoceros. **2.** stolid, thick-skinned, insensitive person. [French *pachyderme* the animal, from Greek *pachydermos* thick-skinned.]
pach·y·san·dra (pak′ə san′drə) *n.* any of various plants, genus *Pachysandra,* of the boxwood family, esp. *P. terminalis,* cultivated as a ground cover. [Modern Latin *Pachysandra* literally, having thick stamens, going back to Greek *pachys* thick + *andr-,* stem of *anēr* man.]
pa·cif·ic (pə sif′ik) *adj.* **1.** making or tending to make peace; conciliatory: *pacific gestures.* **2.** calm; tranquil: *pacific waters.* [Latin *pācificus* peacemaking.] —**pa·cif′i·cal·ly,** *adv.*
Pa·cif·ic (pə sif′ik) *n.* ocean bordered by North and South America on the east and by Asia and Australia on the west, the largest body of water in the world. Also, **Pacific Ocean.** —*adj.* **1.** of, relating to, or designating the Pacific. **2.** on, along, or near the coast of the Pacific.
pac·i·fi·ca·tion (pas′ə fi kā′shən) *n.* act of pacifying; being pacified.

pac·i·fi·ca·to·ry (pə sif′ə kə tôr′ē) *adj.* tending to make peace; conciliatory. —**pa·cif·i·ca·tor** (pə sif′ə kā′tər), *n.*
Pacific Standard Time, the local civil time of the 120th meridian west of Greenwich, England, used in the western coastal region of the United States. It is eight hours earlier than Greenwich Time.
pac·i·fi·er (pas′ə fī′ər) *n.* **1.** one who or that which pacifies. **2.** rubber nipple or similar object for babies to suck on.
pac·i·fism (pas′ə fiz′əm) *n.* principle of opposition to war or other violence; belief that peaceful methods should be used to settle differences among nations.
pac·i·fist (pas′ə fist) *n.* one who opposes war or other violence; person who believes in pacifism. —**pac′i·fis′tic,** *adj.*
pac·i·fy (pas′ə fī′) **-fied, -fy·ing.** *v.t.* **1.** to allay the anger, excitement, or agitation of; calm; quiet. **2.** to bring peace; end the fighting in: *It was evident that more troops were needed to pacify the area.* **3.** to make submissive; subdue. [Latin *pācificāre* to make peace.] —**Syn. 1.** see **appease.**
pack¹ (pak) *n.* **1.** collection of things enclosed in wrapping or tied together, esp. for carrying on the back. **2.a.** package containing a standard number of similar things: *a pack of matches, a pack of gum.* **b.** manner in which something is packaged. **3.** set or group of similar persons or things: *a pack of cards.* **4.** large quantity; heap: *a pack of lies.* **5.** group of animals living or hunting together: *a pack of wolves.* **6.** total amount of something, as fruits or vegetables, processed at one time, esp. in one season. **7.** absorbent material, as a cloth or sheet, soaked in water or medicinal liquid and applied to the body as a treatment. **8.** thick preparation applied in a layer to the skin, esp. the face, for cosmetic purposes. —*v.t.* **1.** to place in a receptacle for storing or carrying: *We packed the books in boxes.* **2.** to fill (something) with objects: *to pack a suitcase.* **3.** to make into a compact bundle or pack. **4.** to compress tightly; crowd closely together: *The child packed the sand down with his shovel.* **5.** to fill by crowding or pressing together: *Capacity crowds packed the hall.* **6.** to prepare and put into a suitable container to be marketed or stored: *to pack beans for consumer use.* **7.** to fill or surround tightly with something in order to make airtight, leak-proof, or impervious to damage. **8.** to load (an animal) with a pack. **9.** *Informal.* to carry or wear on one's person regularly: *to pack a gun.* **10.** *Informal.* to deliver or be able to deliver: *to pack a wallop.* **11.** to send or drive away; get rid of (with *off*): *They packed her off to her aunt's house.* —*v.i.* **1.** to place articles in a receptacle, as a suitcase or trunk, for carrying or storing. **2.** to admit of being placed into a receptacle; be stored: *This dress packs beautifully.* **3.** to compress into a compact mass. **4.** to press tightly; crowd together: *People packed into the subway car.* **5.** to go away quickly; depart hastily (with *off*). **6. to send packing.** to send away summarily. [Middle Dutch and Middle Low German *pak* bundle.]
pack² (pak) *v.t.* to select, arrange, or manipulate fraudulently or to one's own advantage: *to pack a jury.* [Possibly from PACT.]
pack·age (pak′ij) *n.* **1.** thing or group of things packed, wrapped up, or bound; parcel. **2.** box, case, or other receptacle in which things are packed. **3.** act or process of packing. **4.** group of items considered as a unit; offer composed of such a group: *The package offered by management included an increase in overtime pay.* Also *(def. 4).* **package deal.** —*v.t.,* **-aged, -ag·ing.** to make or put into a package, as for storage, transportation, or marketing. —**pack′ag·er,** *n.* —**Syn. 1.** see **bundle.**
package store, store that sells bottled or canned alcoholic beverages for consumption off the premises.
pack animal, animal, as a horse or mule, used for carrying loads.
pack·er (pak′ər) *n.* one who or that which packs, esp. one who owns or is employed in a business where produce or products are processed and packaged for sale: *a meat packer.*
pack·et (pak′it) *n.* **1.** small package or parcel: *a packet of letters.* **2.** packet boat. [PACK¹ + -ET.]

at; āpe; cär; end; mē; it; īce; hot; ōld; fôrk; wood; fōōl; oil; out; up; ūse; turn; sing; thin; this; zh in treasure; ə in ago, taken, pencil, lemon, circus.

packet boat, boat that conveys mail, passengers, and freight at fixed times over a regular route, esp. along a coast or river.

pack ice, large, uneven layer of floating ice formed by pieces of ice that are pressed together and frozen into a single mass. Also, **ice pack.**

pack·ing (pak′ing) n. **1.** act or work of one who or that which packs. **2.** processing and packaging of meat, vegetables, fruit, or other produce and products. **3.** material used to make something airtight, watertight, or otherwise secure.

packing house, establishment where produce or products are processed and packaged for sale. Also, **packing plant.**

pack rat, small, squirrel-like North American rodent, genus *Neotoma*, noted for its habit of collecting small shiny objects and leaving other objects, as nuts or pine cones, in exchange.

Pack rat

pack·sad·dle (pak′sad′əl) n. saddle designed to carry the load transported by a pack animal.

pack·thread (pak′thred′) n. strong thread or twine used for tying up packages.

pact (pakt) n. agreement; compact: *a nonaggression pact, a silent pact between friends.* [Latin *pactum.*]

pad¹ (pad) n. **1.** soft piece of dense or stuffed material, used as a filling or covering for the purpose of protection or comfort: *a gauze pad. The football player wore a pad on his knee.* **2.** number of sheets of paper fastened together along one edge; tablet: *a sketch pad.* **3.** one of the cushionlike parts on the underside of the toes of dogs, foxes, and certain other animals. **4.** foot of a dog, fox, or certain other animals. **5.** small ink-soaked block of cloth or other material, used to ink a rubber stamp. **6.** large floating leaf of a water plant. **7.** launching pad. **8.** soft, cushionlike saddle. **9.** *Slang.* place where one lives, as a room or apartment. —v.t., **pad·ded, pad·ding. 1.** to cover, fill, or line with a pad or padding. **2.** to lengthen (a speech or piece of writing) by adding unnecessary material (often with *out*): *The critic padded out the review with quotes from the author.* **3.** to add to dishonestly: *to pad an expense account.* [Possibly of Low German origin.]

pad² (pad) **pad·ded, pad·ding.** v.i. to move with dull, muffled, barely audible steps: *We took our shoes off and padded across the room.* —n. **1.** dull, muffled sound, as of a footstep. **2.** slow-paced horse used for riding on roads. [Possibly imitative.]

pad·ding (pad′ing) n. **1.** material, as cotton or foam rubber, used to make a pad. **2.** extraneous matter used to expand a speech or written material. **3.** act of one who or that which pads.

pad·dle¹ (pad′əl) n. **1.** short oar with a blade at one or both ends, used to propel a canoe or other small boat. **2.** round or rectangular board with a short handle, used to strike the ball in table tennis and similar games. **3.** flat, wooden board used for inflicting punishment by spanking. **4.** flat, wooden instrument used for beating clothes while washing them by hand, as in a stream. **5.** any of various paddle-shaped instruments used for stirring or mixing in industrial processes, as glassmaking or metal-working. **6.** one of the broad boards set on the circumference of a paddle wheel or water wheel. **7.** act of paddling. —v.t., **-dled, -dling. 1.** to propel (a canoe or other small boat) by means of a paddle or paddles. **2.** to convey by paddling: *The trappers paddled supplies to their camp further up the river.* **3.** to strike with or as with a paddle. **4.** to stir, beat, or mix with a paddle. —v.i. **1.** to propel a canoe or other small boat by means of a paddle. **2.** to row lightly or gently. [Of uncertain origin.] —**pad′dler,** n.

Paddle¹ *(def. 6)*

pad·dle² (pad′əl) v.i. **-dled, -dling. 1.** to move about or splash in shallow water; wade. **2.** to toddle. [Possibly PAD² + -LE.]

paddle boat, boat propelled by a paddle wheel or paddle wheels.

pad·dle·fish (pad′əl fish′) pl., **-fish** or **-fish·es.** n. any of several large-mouthed, grayish fish, family Polyodontidae, having a long, paddlelike snout. Length: to 12 feet including the snout.

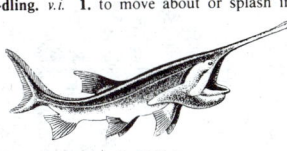

Paddlefish

paddle wheel, wheel having projecting floats or paddles around its circumference, used to propel a steamboat.

pad·dock (pad′ək) n. **1.** small field or enclosure in which an animal can graze and exercise. **2.** area at a race track in which the horses are saddled and mounted. [Modification of dialectal English *parrock*, from Old English *pearroc* enclosure.]

pad·dy (pad′ē) pl., **-dies.** n. rice, esp. in the husk. **2.** field where rice is grown. [Malay *pādī* rice in the husk.]

Pad·dy (pad′ē) pl., **-dies.** n. *Informal.* Irishman. ▲ used as a nickname. [Familiar form of *Patrick*, masculine proper name.]

paddy wagon. *Slang.* patrol wagon. [Probably from PADDY.]

Pad·e·rew·ski, Ig·nace Jan (pad′ə ref′skē, -rev′-; ēn yäs′ yän) 1860–1941, Polish pianist, composer, and statesman.

pad·lock (pad′lok′) n. detachable lock with a curved bar that is passed through an opening. —v.t. to fasten with or as with a padlock.

pa·dre (pä′drā) n. **1.** father. ▲ used in addressing or referring to a priest, esp. in Italy, Spain, Portugal, or Latin America. **2.** *Informal.* military chaplain. [Italian, Spanish, or Portuguese *padre* father, from Latin *pater*.]

pa·dro·ne (pə drō′nē, -nā) n. **1.** master; boss. **2.** one who employs or contracts Italian immigrants to work as laborers. [Italian *padrone*, from Latin *patrōnus* protector.]

Pad·u·a (paj′ōō ə, pad′ū ə) n. city in northeastern Italy. Pop. (1968), 222,832.

pae·an (pē′ən) *also,* **pe·an.** n. song of praise, joy, thanksgiving, or triumph. [Latin *paeān*, from Greek *paiān* hymn to Apollo (one of whose names was *Paiān*).]

pa·gan (pā′gən) n. **1.** one who is not a Christian, Jew, or Muslim. **2.** formerly, one who was not a Christian. **3.** irreligious person. —adj. **1.** of or relating to those who are not Christian, Jewish, or Muslim. **2.** irreligious; idolatrous. [Latin *pāgānus* villager, civilian (from the early Christian concept of heathens as civilians and members of the faith as soldiers of Christ), from *pāgus* village.] —**pa′gan·dom,** n.

Syn. 1. Pagan, heathen, infidel mean a person who is not a Christian, Jew, or Muslim. **Pagan** refers esp. to a person who worships many gods, esp. one who lived before the spread of monotheistic religion: *The ancient Greeks and Romans were pagans.* **Heathen** refers to a person who worships idols and who is regarded as primitive or uncivilized: *Missionaries went to Africa in the nineteenth century to convert heathens to the Christian faith.* **Infidel** refers esp. to a person who is thought to be unenlightened because he believes in a religion opposed to one's own: *The Crusaders considered the Turks as infidels.*

Pag·a·ni·ni, Ni·co·lò (pag′ə nē′nē; nē′kō lō′) 1782–1840, Italian violinist and composer.

pa·gan·ism (pā′gə niz′əm) n. **1.** beliefs, practices, and customs of pagans. **2.** state of being a pagan.

page¹ (pāj) n. **1.a.** one side of a leaf of a book, letter, or similar article: *to fill up the pages of a diary.* **b.** entire leaf. **2.** print, writing, or type used on one side of a leaf: *to read six pages of a diary.* **3.** record: *in the pages of medical science.* **4.** event, series of events, or period of time worthy of recording: *The Civil War was a tragic page in American history.* —v.t., **paged, pag·ing.** to number the pages of; paginate. [Old French *page* side of a leaf (of a book), from Latin *pāgina* leaf for writing.]

page² (pāj) n. **1.** male servant or attendant, esp. a boy who attends a person of rank, as in a royal household. **2.** young person employed to serve as an attendant to members of Congress or other legislatures while in session. **3.** boy employed to run errands or carry messages. **4.** formerly, a boy in training for knighthood. —v.t., **paged, pag·ing.** to seek or summon (someone) by repeatedly calling out his name. [Old French *page* young boy, valet, going back to Greek *paidíon* young boy, diminutive of *pais* child.]

pag·eant (paj′ənt) n. **1.** elaborate theatrical presentation, esp. one that celebrates historical events. **2.** brilliant spectacle, procession, or parade. [Medieval Latin *pagina* scene of a play, stage, from Latin *pāgina* leaf for writing.]

pag·eant·ry (paj′ən trē) pl., **-ries.** n. **1.** pageants collectively. **2.** ceremonial splendor or spectacular display.

page·boy (pāj′boi′) n. style of wearing hair with the ends curled inward into a roll.

pag·i·nal (paj′ən əl) adj. **1.** of, relating to, or consisting of pages. **2.** page for page: *a paginal reprint.*

pag·i·nate (paj′ə nāt′) **-nat·ed, -nat·ing.** v.t. to number the pages of (a book or other writing).

pag·i·na·tion (paj′ə nā′shən) n. **1.** numbers or figures with which pages are marked. **2.** arrangement or sequence of such figures or marks. **3.** act of paginating; being paginated.

at; āpe; cär; end; mē; it; īce; hot; ōld; fôrk; wood; fōōl; oil; out; up; ūse; turn; sing; thin; this; zh in treasure; ə in ago, taken, pencil, lemon, circus.

pa·go·da (pə gō′də) *n.* **1.** in the Far East, a temple or memorial tower, usually pyramidal in form, often with a series of boldly projecting roofs. **2.** any building resembling this, as an ornamental structure in a formal garden. [Portuguese *pagode* temple, probably going back to Persian *butkada* temple of idols.]

Pa·go Pa·go (päng′ō päng′ō, pä′gō pä′gō) capital of American Samoa, on the southeastern coast of Tutuila Island. Pop. (1960), 1251. Also, **Pango Pango.**

paid (pād) past tense and past participle of **pay¹**.

pail (pāl) *n.* **1.** open cylindrical container, usually with a handle, used for carrying liquid, sand, or other materials. **2.** pailful. [Partly from Old English *pægel*², wine measure; partly from Old French *paelle* pan, liquid measure, from Latin *patella* small pan¹. See PATELLA.]

pail·ful (pāl′fool′) *pl.,* **-fuls.** *n.* capacity of a pail.

pain (pān) *n.* **1.** unpleasant physical sensation resulting from or accompanying injury, illness, or other physical disorder. **2.** emotional distress or suffering; anxiety; grief: *the pain of loneliness.* **3. pains.** great care or trouble: *The hostess took pains with the table arrangements.* **4. pains.** pangs or labor of childbirth. **5.** *Informal.* nuisance; annoyance. **6. on** or **upon** or **under) pain of.** at the risk of or subject to (a specified punishment). —*v.t.* to cause pain to; make suffer: *My knee pains me on damp days.* —*v.i.* to be the cause of pain. [Old French *peine* punishment, suffering, from Latin *poena,* from Greek *poinē* punishment.]

Syn. *n.* **1. Pain, ache** mean an unpleasant bodily sensation causing suffering. **Pain** often refers to an acute and unpleasant sensation arising from bodily injury or disease: *The pain in his back was alleviated after three days of complete rest.* **Ache** is usually applied to a dull but steady pain in an organ or part of the body: *Although the ache in his shoulder persisted, he was still able to play baseball.*

Paine, Thomas (pān) 1737–1809, U.S. patriot, writer, and political theorist born in England.

pained (pānd) *adj.* **1.** affected with pain; hurt or distressed. **2.** showing pain: *a pained expression on his face.*

pain·ful (pān′fəl) *adj.* **1.** causing physical or mental pain; distressing: *a painful wound, a painful subject.* **2.** affected with pain; hurting: *a painful knee.* **3.** requiring effort or care; laborious; irksome. —**pain′ful·ly,** *adv.* —**pain′ful·ness,** *n.*

pain·kill·er (pān′kil′ər) *n.* substance, as a drug, that relieves pain.

pain·less (pān′lis) *adj.* free from pain; causing no pain: *a painless operation.* —**pain′less·ly,** *adv.* —**pain′less·ness,** *n.*

pains·tak·ing (pānz′tā′king) *adj.* characterized by or requiring close, careful labor or attention: *painstaking work.* —*n.* act of taking pains; careful effort; diligence. —**pains′tak′ing·ly,** *adv.*

paint (pānt) *n.* **1.a.** liquid coloring material consisting of one or more solid pigments mixed with a liquid such as oil or water, that dries to form a hard layer or film when applied to surfaces, and is used as a protective or decorative coating. **b.** layer or coating of such a material. **c.** the solid pigment alone. **2.** cosmetic, esp. one used to add color. —*v.t.* **1.** to represent on a surface with paints: *to paint a landscape.* **2.** to make, as a picture, by applying paints: *He painted four large canvases in two days.* **3.** to cover the surface of or decorate with paint: *to paint a house.* **4.** to depict or describe vividly in words. **5.** to color with cosmetics; apply cosmetics to. **6.** to apply with a brush or swab. —*v.i.* **1.** to practice the art of painting; make pictures: *He paints well.* **2.** to use cosmetics, esp. on the face. [Old French *peint,* past participle of *peindre* to color, represent pictorially, from Latin *pingere.*]

paint·brush (pānt′brush′) *n.* brush for applying paint.

paint·ed (pān′tid) *adj.* **1.** covered or adorned with or as with paint. **2.** represented in paint. **3.** wearing too much or highly colored make-up. **4.** having no reality; artificial; sham: *their painted expressions.*

Painted Desert, arid region in northeastern Arizona, noted for its multicolored rock formations.

paint·er¹ (pān′tər) *n.* **1.** artist who paints pictures. **2.** one who paints surfaces, esp. a person whose work is painting the interiors or exteriors of houses. [Old French *peintour,* going back to Latin *pictor.*]

paint·er² (pān′tər) *n.* rope attached to the bow of a boat for securing it to something. [Possibly from Old French *pentoir* rope for hanging things, from *pendre* to hang, from Latin *pendēre.*]

paint·er³ (pān′tər) *n.* cougar. [Form of PANTHER.]

paint·ing (pān′ting) *n.* **1.** act of covering with paint. **2.** art of applying paints to a surface in order to create an image or effect. **3.** picture or image produced in paint.

pair (pār) *pl.,* **pairs** or **pair.** *n.* **1.** set of two identical, similar, or corresponding things intended for use together or associated in some way: *a pair of slippers, a pair of oars.* **2.** a single thing consisting of two identical or similar connected parts: *a pair of pliers, a pair of glasses.* **3.** two persons who have something in common or are associated together: *a pair of policemen. He and his brother are a friendly pair.* **4.** married or engaged couple. **5.a.** two animals mated together. **b.** two animals working together. **6.a.** two members of a legislative body who, because they would vote differently and offset each other, arrange not to vote on a certain issue or issues. **b.** the arrangement thus made. **7.** in some card games, esp. poker, two cards of the same denomination: *a pair of aces.* —*v.t.* **1.** to join or match (two persons or things) in a pair: *They paired John and Marsha for the dance.* **2.** to arrange in pairs. **3. to pair off. a.** to join or match (two persons or things) in a pair. **b.** to separate into pairs. —*v.i.* **1.** to form a pair or pairs; separate into sets of two. **2.** to join in marriage or to produce offspring. **3. to pair off.** to form a pair or pairs. [Old French *paire* a set of two, from Latin *paria,* neuter plural of *pār* like¹, equal.]

pais·ley (pāz′lē) *n.* **1.** distinctive, usually colorful design that incorporates curved forms on a patterned background. **2.** soft woolen fabric having such a design. —*adj.* **1.** made of or resembling such fabric. **2.** designating or having the characteristic design of paisley. [From *Paisley,* city in Scotland once famous for woolen shawls in this pattern.]

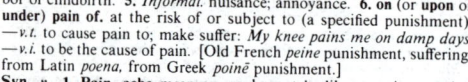

Paisley design

Pai·ute (pī oot′) *n.* **1.** member of any of a group of North American Indian tribes formerly living in Arizona, California, Nevada, and Utah. **2.** their language, belonging to the Shoshonean language family.

pa·ja·mas (pə jä′məz, -jam′əz) *also, British,* **py·ja·mas.** *n.,pl.* **1.** loose-fitting two-piece garment for sleeping or informal wear, consisting of a jacketlike top and trousers. **2.** loose trousers worn by men and women in Oriental countries. [Urdu *pāē jāmah* trousers; literally, leg garment, from Persian *pāē* leg + *jāmah* garment.]

Pak·i·stan (pak′i stan′, pä′ki stän′) *n.* country in southern Asia. Capital, Islamabad. Area, 310,724 sq. mi. Pop. (1975 est.), 70,600,000.

Pak·i·stan·i (pak′i stan′ē, pä′ki stä′nē) *pl.,* **-stan·i** or **-stan·is.** *n.* native or inhabitant of Pakistan. —*adj.* of or relating to Pakistan or its people.

pal (pal) *Informal. n.* close friend: *My pal and I went hunting together.* —*v.i.,* **palled, pal·ling.** to associate as pals. [Gypsy *pal* brother, going back to Sanskrit *bhrātar.*]

pal·ace (pal′is) *n.* **1.** official residence of a sovereign, member of royalty, or high dignitary, as a bishop. **2.** any large, splendid residence or building. **3.** large, often ornate, public building, esp. one used for exhibitions or entertainment: *a movie palace.* [Old French *palais* royal residence, from Latin *palātium,* from *Palātium* Palatine Hill in Rome, site of the first imperial palace of Rome, which was built by the emperor Augustus.]

pal·a·din (pal′ə din) *n.* **1.** *Medieval Legend.* one of the twelve peers or famous warriors who accompanied Charlemagne. **2.** any heroic champion. [French *paladin,* from Italian *paladino,* from Latin *palātīnus* officer of the palace. See PALATINE.]

pa·laes·tra (pə les′trə) palestra.

pal·an·quin (pal′ən kēn′) *also,* **pal·an·keen.** *n.* covered litter, usually for one person, carried on the shoulders of two or more men by means of poles, used esp. in Eastern countries. [Portuguese *palanquim,* going back to Sanskrit *palyanka* couch.]

pal·at·a·ble (pal′ə tə bəl) *adj.* **1.** agreeable to the taste or palate; savory. **2.** agreeable to the mind or feelings; acceptable: *The mediator's proposal was palatable to both labor and management.* —**pal′at·a·bil′i·ty,** *n.* —**pal′at·a·bly,** *adv.*

pal·a·tal (pal′ə təl) *adj.* **1.** of or relating to the palate. **2.** (of a speech sound) articulated with the tongue close to or touching the hard palate, as the *y* in *young.* —*n.* palatal sound.

pal·a·tal·ize (pal′ə təl īz′) **-ized, -iz·ing.** *v.t.* to pronounce as a palatal sound. —**pal′a·tal·i·za′tion,** *n.*

pal·ate (pal′it) *n.* **1.** roof of the mouth, consisting of the bony hard palate in the front of the mouth and the fleshy soft palate in the back of the mouth. **2.** sense of taste: *a food that is pleasing to the palate.* **3.** intellectual taste; liking. [Latin *palātum* roof of the mouth.]

pa·la·tial (pə lā′shəl) *adj.* **1.** of, resembling, or befitting a palace: *a palatial home.* [Latin *palātium* palace + -AL¹. See PALACE.] —**pa·la′tial·ly,** *adv.*

Pa·lat·i·nate (pə lat′ən āt′, -it) *n.* **1.** region in Germany, formerly part of Bavaria, now an administrative unit in the West German Federal Republic. **2.** palatinate. territory under the jurisdiction of a palatine.

pal·a·tine (pal′ə tīn′, -tin) *adj.* **1.** having royal privileges and prerogatives: *a count palatine.* **2.** of or relating to a palatine or palatinate. **3.** of or relating to a palace; palatial. **4. Palatine.** of or relating to the

at; āpe; cär; end; mē; it; īce; hot; ōld; fôrk; wood; fōol; oil; out; up; ūse; turn; sing; thin; this; zh in treasure; ə in ago, taken, pencil, lemon, circus.

Palatinate. —*n.* **1.** lord having royal privileges and prerogatives on his own territory. **2. Palatine.** native or inhabitant of the Palatinate. **3. Palatine.** Palatine Hill. [Latin *palātīnus* officer of the palace, relating to the imperial palace, from *palātium* palace. See PALACE.]

Palatine Hill, one of the seven hills on which ancient Rome was built.

Pa·lau (pä lou′) *n.* group of islands in the western Pacific, a part of the Caroline group. Pop. (1968 est.), 11,904.

pa·lav·er (pə lav′ər, -lä′vər) *n.* **1.** idle talk; chatter. **2.** parley or conference, esp. one between explorers or traders and native inhabitants. —*v.i.* to talk idly and profusely. [Portuguese *palavra* word, talk, from Latin *parabola* comparison, parable, from Greek *parabolē.* Doublet of PARABLE, PAROLE.]

Pa·la·wan (pä lä′wän) *n.* island in the southwestern Philippines.

pale¹ (pāl) **pal·er, pal·est.** *adj.* **1.** lacking natural or healthy color; pallid: *a pale complexion.* **2.** lacking intensity or depth of color: *pale green.* **3.** lacking in brightness or brilliance of light; dim: *pale moonlight.* **4.** feeble; weak: *a pale imitation.* —*v.t., v.i.,* **paled, pal·ing.** to make or turn pale. [Old French *pale* lacking color, from Latin *pallidus.* Doublet of PALLID.] —**pale′ly,** *adv.* —**pale′ness,** *n.*

Syn. *adj.* **Pale, pallid, wan¹** mean deficient in natural or healthy color. **Pale** describes a relative absence of natural color and a lack of healthy brightness and intensity: *That Spaniard has a pale complexion.* **Pallid,** chiefly restricted to the human face, suggests abnormal lack of color: *The lone survivor looked pallid as he left the scene of the accident.* **Wan** suggests the unnatural blanching frequently associated with emotional or physical disorders and stresses emaciation and sickness more than lack of color: *The patient looked wan after the operation.*

pale² (pāl) *n.* **1.** pointed narrow piece of wood; stake; picket. **2.** place, district, or territory enclosed within bounds. **3.** any boundary, barrier, or limit: *His behavior was beyond the pale of recognized propriety.* **4.** heraldic device consisting of a vertical strip through the middle of the shield, occupying one-third of its area. —*v.t.,* **paled, pal·ing.** to enclose with pales; fence in. [Old French *pal* stake, from Latin *pālus.*]

pale·face (pāl′fās′) *n.* white person. ▲ supposedly first used by North American Indians.

Pa·lem·bang (pä′lem bäng′) *n.* city in Indonesia, in southern Sumatra. Pop. (1961), 474,971.

paleo- *combining form* ancient; old: *paleography.* [Greek *palaios.*]

Pa·le·o·cene (pā′lē ə sēn′) *n.* earliest geological epoch of the Tertiary period of the Cenozoic era. See **geology** for table. —*adj.* of or relating to this epoch. [PALEO- + Greek *kainos* new.]

pa·le·og·ra·pher (pā′lē og′rə fər) *n.* one who studies or is an expert in paleography.

pa·le·og·ra·phy (pā′lē og′rə fē) *n.* **1.** ancient forms of writing or ancient writings collectively. **2.** study of ancient writings and inscriptions. [PALEO- + -GRAPHY.] —**pa·le·o·graph·ic** (pā′lē ə graf′ik), *adj.*

Pa·le·o·lith·ic (pā′lē ə lith′ik) *adj.* of, relating to, or designating the earliest part of the Stone Age, roughly corresponding to the Ice Age, characterized by tools made of crudely chipped stone. [PALEO- + Greek *lithos* stone + -IC.]

pa·le·on·tol·o·gy (pā′lē on tol′ə jē) *n.* science that deals with fossils and extinct forms of life. [PALEO- + Greek *ont-,* stem of *ōn* being + -LOGY.] —**pa·le·on·tol′o·gist,** *n.*

Pa·le·o·zo·ic (pā′lē ə zō′ik) *n.* geological era extending from the Cambrian to the Permian periods, characterized by the appearance of land plants, marine invertebrates, fish, amphibians, and reptiles. See **geology** for table. —*adj.* of, relating to, or characteristic of this era. [PALEO- + Greek *zōē* life + -IC.]

Pa·ler·mo (pä lār′mō, -lur′-) *n.* capital and largest city of Sicily, a port in the northwestern part of the island. Pop. (1968), 652,380.

Pal·es·tine (pal′is tīn′) *n.* **1.** region in southwestern Asia between the Mediterranean Sea and the Jordan River. In Biblical times it was the land of the Jews. **2.** former country in this region, under a British mandate following World War I, divided into Israel and part of Jordan in 1947. Israel has occupied the Jordanian part of Palestine since 1967. Also, **Holy Land.** —**Pal·es·tin·i·an** (pal′is tin′ē ən), *n., adj.*

pa·les·tra (pə les′trə) *also,* **pa·laes·tra.** *n.* school in ancient Greece for exercise and physical training, esp. in wrestling. [Latin *palaestra,* from Greek *palaistrā.*]

Pal·es·tri·na, Gio·van·ni Pier·lu·i·gi da (pal′is trē′nə; jō-vä′nē pyer′lōō ē′jē dä) c.1526–94, Italian composer.

pal·ette (pal′it) *n.* **1.** thin board or tablet, usually having a hole for the thumb, on which artists place and mix their paints. **2.** range or system of colors characteristic of a particular artist, painting, or school of painting. [French *palette,* going back to Latin *pāla* spade¹.]

pal·frey (pôl′frē) *pl.,* **-freys.** *n.* *Archaic.* saddle horse, esp. one for a woman. [Old French *palefrei,* going back to Late Latin *paraverēdus* post horse, from Latin *para* beside + Late Latin *verēdus* post horse (of Celtic origin).]

pal·imp·sest (pal′imp sest′) *n.* parchment or other writing material written upon two or more times, the earlier writing having been erased partially or completely to make room for the next. [Latin *palimpsēstus,* from Greek *palimpsēstos* scraped again.]

pal·in·drome (pal′in drōm′) *n.* word, verse, phrase, or sentence that reads the same forward and backward. "Otto" and "Was it a cat I saw?" are palindromes. [Greek *palindromos* running back again.]

pal·ing (pā′ling) *n.* **1.** fence made of pales. **2.** pales collectively. **3.** one of the pales forming a fence.

pal·i·sade (pal′i sād′) *n.* **1.** fence of strong, pointed stakes placed closely together and set firmly in the ground, used for defense or protection. **2.** one of the long, pointed stakes used in such a fence. **3. palisades.** line of steep, columnar cliffs, usually rising along the edge of a body of water. —*v.t.,* **-sad·ed, -sad·ing.** to enclose or fortify with a palisade. [French *palissade* fence of stakes, going back to Latin *pālus.*]

Pal·i·sades (pal′i sādz′) *n.,pl.* series of high, columnar cliffs along the western bank of the lower Hudson River in New Jersey and New York.

pall¹ (pôl) *n.* **1.** heavy covering of soft black or purple cloth, laid over a bier, coffin, hearse, or tomb. **2.** that which covers or conceals with an atmosphere of darkness and gloom: *A pall fell over the room when the news of the accident was announced.* —*v.t.* to cover with or as with a pall. [Old English *pæll* robe, cloak, purple cloth, from Latin *pallium* cloak, covering.]

pall² (pôl) *v.i.* **1.** to become insipid or boring to the interest or appetite. **2.** to have a cloying or displeasing effect (with *on*). —*v.t.* to satiate; cloy: *to pall the senses.* [Short for APPALL.]

pal·la·di·um (pə lā′dē əm) *n.* heavy, silver-white metallic element of the platinum family, used esp. as a catalyst in hydrogenation processes. Symbol: Pd See **element** for table. [Modern Latin *palladium,* from the asteroid *Pallas.*]

Pal·la·di·um (pə lā′dē əm) *pl.,* **-di·a** (-dē ə). *n.* **1.** in ancient Greece and Rome, a statue of Pallas Athena, esp. one in Troy on which the preservation of the city was supposed to depend. **2. palladium.** anything regarded as essential to the safety or preservation of a community or institution. [Latin *Palladium* statue of Pallas in Troy, from Greek *Palladion,* from *Pallas* Pallas.]

Pal·las (pal′əs) *n.* **1.** *Greek Mythology.* Athena. Also, **Pallas Athena.** **2.** one of the asteroids.

pall·bear·er (pôl′bâr′ər) *n.* one who carries or escorts the coffin at a funeral.

pal·let¹ (pal′it) *n.* **1.** straw bed or mattress. **2.** any small, hard, or temporary bed, often on the floor. [Anglo-Norman *paillete* straw, diminutive of *paille,* from Latin *palea.*]

pal·let² (pal′it) *n.* **1.** wooden tool with a flat blade and a handle, esp. one used by potters for mixing and shaping clay. **2.** palette *(def.* 1). **3.** movable platform for storing and transporting goods, as in a warehouse. **4.** projection on a pawl that engages the teeth of a ratchet wheel. See **pawl** for illustration. [Old French *palete* small shovel, diminutive of *pale,* shovel, spade¹, from Latin *pāla* spade¹.]

pal·li·ate (pal′ē āt′) **-at·ed, -at·ing.** *v.t.* **1.** to make (an offense or fault) appear less serious; extenuate. **2.** to alleviate the symptoms or effects of (a disease) without curing it. [Latin *palliātus* covered with a cloak, from *pallium* cloak.] —**pal′li·a′tion,** *n.*

pal·li·a·tive (pal′ē ā′tiv) *adj.* serving or tending to palliate: *palliative drugs, a palliative influence.* —*n.* that which palliates.

pal·lid (pal′id) *adj.* lacking natural or healthy color; pale. [Latin *pallidus.* Doublet of PALE¹.] —**Syn.** see **pale¹.**

pall-mall (pel′mel′) *n.* **1.** game formerly played in England, in which a ball was struck by a mallet and hit through a ring hung at the end of an alley. **2.** alley in which this game was played. [Middle French *pallemaille* the game, from Italian *pallamaglio,* from *palla* ball (of Germanic origin) + *maglio* mallet (from Latin *malleus* hammer).]

pal·lor (pal′ər) *n.* lack of natural or healthy color; paleness: *a pallor of fright.* [Latin *pallor.*]

palm¹ (päm) *n.* **1.** flexible inner surface of the hand, extending from the wrist to the base of the fingers. **2.** measure of length equivalent either to the width of a hand (three to four inches) or the length of a hand (about 8½ inches). **3.** part of a glove or mitten covering the palm. **4.** anything resembling or corresponding to the palm, as the blade of a paddle. **5. to grease the palm of.** to bribe. —*v.t.* **1.** to conceal in or about the palm or hand: *to palm cards.* **2.** to hold or handle with the palm of the hand. **3. to palm off.** to pass off or dispose of by deceit or fraud. [Old French *paume* the inner surface of the hand, from Latin *palma.* See PALM².]

Palm tree

palm² (päm) *n.* **1.** any of a large group of tropical and subtropical trees,

at; āpe; cär; end; mē; it; īce; hot; ōld; fôrk; wood; fōōl; oil; out; up; ūse; turn; sing; thin; this; zh in treasure; ə in ago, taken, pencil, lemon, circus.

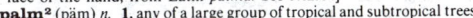

725

shrubs, or vines, family Palmae, usually having large, featherlike or fan-shaped leaves growing in a cluster at the top of a tall, branchless trunk. **2.** leaf or branch of such a tree, esp. when considered or used as a symbol of victory or success. **3.** anything awarded as a symbol of superiority or victory. **4.** victory; triumph. **5. to bear** (or **carry**) **off the palm.** to be the winner. [Old English *palm* the tree, from Latin *palma* palm tree and leaf, palm of the hand (from the resemblance of the palm leaf to the outspread palm of the hand).]

pal·mate (pal'māt) *adj.* **1.** resembling a hand with the fingers spread or extended: *the palmate antlers of the reindeer.* **2.** (of a compound leaf) composed of leaflets that originate from a common point. **3.** webbed, as the toes of a bird. [Latin *palmātus* shaped like the palm of the hand, from *palma* palm of the hand. See PALM¹.]

Palmate compound leaf

Palm Beach, resort in southeastern Florida. Pop. (1970), 9086.

palm·er (pä'mər, päl'-) *n.* **1.** in the Middle Ages, a pilgrim who went to the Holy Land and brought back a palm branch as a token of his pilgrimage. **2.** any pilgrim. [Anglo-Norman *palmer* pilgrim returning from the Holy Land, going back to Latin *palma* palm tree, palm leaf.]

Palm·er·ston, Viscount (pä'mər stən) 1784–1865, British statesman, prime minister from 1855 to 1858 and from 1859 to 1865; born Henry John Temple.

pal·met·to (pal met'ō) *pl.,* **-tos** or **-toes.** *n.* any of a group of hardy palms, genus *Sabal,* widely cultivated as ornamentals in the southern United States. [Spanish *palmito,* diminutive of *palma* palm tree, from Latin *palma.*]

palm·ist (pä'mist) *n.* one who practices palmistry.

palm·is·try (pä'mis trē) *n.* art or practice of telling fortunes and describing personal character by examining the lines and configurations in the palm of the hand. [Middle English *pawmestry,* possibly from *palme* palm of the hand (see PALM¹) + *mestry* mastery (from Old French *maistrie,* from *maistre* one in charge). See MASTER.]

palm oil, yellowish butterlike oil obtained from the fruit of several species of palm, used in the manufacture of many products, as soap, candles, and cosmetics.

Palm Sunday, Sunday before Easter Sunday, commemorating Christ's entry into Jerusalem, when people spread palm branches before Him.

palm·y (pä'mē) **palm·i·er, palm·i·est.** *adj.* **1.** full of or producing palm trees. **2.** flourishing; prosperous: *the palmy days of his career.* **3.** of like a palm.

Pal·my·ra (pal mī'rə) *n.* ancient city in Syria, now in ruins.

Pal·o Al·to (pal'ō al'tō) city in western California, on San Francisco Bay. Pop. (1970), 55,966.

pal·o·mi·no (pal'ə mē'nō) *pl.,* **-nos.** *n.* light-tan or golden horse having a cream-colored or white mane and tail. [Spanish *palomino* dovecolored, going back to Latin *palumbes* dove.]

palp (palp) *n.* palpus.

pal·pa·ble (pal'pə bəl) *adj.* **1.** capable of being touched or felt; tangible. **2.** easily perceived by the senses or mind; obvious; noticeable: *a palpable lie, a palpable error.* [Late Latin *palpābilis* capable of being touched, from Latin *palpāre* to touch.] —**pal'pa·bil'i·ty,** *n.* —**pal'pa·bly,** *adv.*

pal·pate (pal'pāt) **-pat·ed, -pat·ing.** *v.t.* to examine by touching, esp. for medical diagnosis. [Latin *palpātus,* past participle of *palpāre* to touch.] —**pal·pa'tion,** *n.*

pal·pi·tate (pal'pə tāt') **-tat·ed, -tat·ing.** *v.i.* **1.** to beat irregularly or at an abnormally rapid rate: *His heart palpitated from overexertion.* **2.** to quiver, tremble, or vibrate. [Latin *palpitātus,* past participle of *palpitāre* to throb.]

pal·pi·ta·tion (pal'pə tā'shən) *n.* **1.** abnormally rapid and often irregular beating of the heart. **2.** quivering, trembling, or vibrating motion.

pal·pus (pal'pəs) *pl.,* **-pi** (-pī) *n.* jointed organ of touch or taste attached to the mouth of insects and some other arthropods. [Modern Latin *palpus,* from Latin *palpāre* to touch.]

pal·sied (pol'zēd) *adj.* **1.** paralyzed. **2.** trembling; shaking.

pal·sy (pol'zē) *pl.,* **-sies.** *n.* **1.** paralysis. **2.** any impairment of the power to feel or to control movement of any part of the body, usually characterized by trembling. —*v.t.,* **-sied, -sy·ing. 1.** to paralyze. **2.** to make helpless or cause to tremble, as

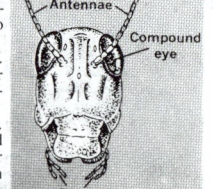

Palpi of a grasshopper

from fear. [Old French *paralysie* paralysis, from Latin *paralysis,* from Greek *paralysis* paralysis, disabling of the nerves. Doublet of PARALYSIS.]

pal·ter (pôl'tər) *v.i.* **1.** to talk or act insincerely; equivocate; lie. **2.** to deal carelessly or capriciously; trifle. **3.** to haggle; quibble. [Of uncertain origin.]

pal·try (pôl'trē) **-tri·er, -tri·est.** *adj.* **1.** having little or no value; insignificant: *a paltry sum.* **2.** contemptible; mean; petty: *a paltry, hypocritical group.* [Possibly from dialectal English *palt* trash; possibly of Low German origin.] —**pal'tri·ness,** *n.*

Syn. 1. Paltry, trifling mean small and insignificant. **Paltry** is chiefly applied to what is ridiculously or contemptibly petty or insufficient and suggests a certain shabby and unfeeling neglect of human dignity: *Pat was paid only a paltry salary as a clerk.* **Trifling** is usually applied to what is so unimportant, small, and insignificant as to be practically negligible: *The accountant made only a trifling error in calculation.*

Pa·mirs (pä mērz') *also,* **Pa·mir.** *n.* mountainous region in central Asia, lying principally in the Soviet Union but extending into Afghanistan and China.

Pam·li·co Sound (pam'li kō') shallow inlet of the Atlantic Ocean, lying between the coast of North Carolina and its chain of offshore islands.

pam·pas (pam'pəz) *also,* **pam·pa.** *n.,pl.* vast, treeless plain extending from the Atlantic Ocean to the Andes Mountains in Argentina and other areas of South America. [Spanish *pampas,* plural of *pampa* plain, from Quechua *pampa.*]

pam·per (pam'pər) *v.t.* to treat with extreme indulgence or care; cater to the needs or desires of; coddle: *to pamper one's children.* [Probably of Flemish origin.] —**pam'per·er,** *n.* —**Syn.** see humor.

pam·phlet (pam'flit) *n.* **1.** printed publication stitched or fastened together but not bound, usually enclosed in a paper cover: *political pamphlets.* **2.** short essay or treatise, usually on a current or controversial issue, published in this form. [Medieval Latin (in England) *panfletus* a little book, from Old French *Pamphilet,* popular name of *Pamphilus seu de Amore* Pamphilus or About Love, a medieval Latin poem that was first published as a small booklet containing a few pages.]

pam·phlet·eer (pam'fli tēr') *n.* one who writes or publishes pamphlets. —*v.i.* to write or issue pamphlets.

Pam·plo·na (pam plō'nə) *n.* city in northern Spain. Pop. (1968), 122,005.

pan¹ (pan) *n.* **1.** broad, shallow container, usually made of metal and without a cover, used for cooking, holding liquids, and other household purposes. **2.** any similar vessel or receptacle, as the container used to separate precious minerals from gravel by washing with water, or either of the two dishes for holding objects on a pair of scales. **3.** layer of hard subsoil; hardpan. **4.** hollow depression in the ground. —*v.t.,* **panned, pan·ning. 1.** to cook in a pan. **2.** *Informal.* to give an unfavorable review to; criticize harshly: *to pan a musical comedy.* **3.** to separate (gold or other precious minerals) from gravel by washing in a pan. **4.** to wash (earth, gravel, or other material) in a pan to separate the gold or other precious minerals. —*v.i.* **1.** to wash earth or gravel in a pan in search for gold or other precious minerals. **2.** (of gravel) to yield gold or other precious minerals when washed in a pan. **3. to pan out.** *Informal.* to turn out well; succeed. [Old English *panne* the container, possibly going back to Latin *patina* broad, shallow dish, from Greek *patanē* flat dish.]

pan² (pan) **panned, pan·ning.** *v.i., v.t.* (of a motion picture or television camera) to move or be moved so as to take in a wide area or follow a moving object. [From PANORAMA.]

Pan (pan) *n.* Greek god of forests, fields, flocks, and shepherds, characteristically depicted as a man with the horns, ears, legs, and tail of a goat.

pan- *combining form* **1.** all; every: *panchromatic.* **2.a.** *usually,* **Pan-.** of, including, or applying to all (members of a specified group or area): *Pan-American, Panhellenic.* **b.** advocating or designating the cooperation or union of all (members of a specified group or area): *Pan-Americanism.* [Greek *pān,* neuter of *pâs* all, every.]

pan·a·ce·a (pan'ə sē'ə) *n.* remedy for all diseases or evils; cure-all. [Latin *panacēa,* from Greek *panakeia.*]

pa·nache (pə nash', -näsh') *n.* dashing or flamboyant manner; flair. [French *panache* plume, swagger, going back to Latin *penna* wing, feather.]

pan·a·ma (pan'ə mä') *also,* **Pan·a·ma.** *n.* hat, esp. for men, made from the young leaves of a palmlike tropical American plant.

Pan·a·ma (pan'ə mä') *n.* **1. Isthmus of.** narrow strip of land connecting North and South America. **2.** country on the Isthmus of Panama, on either side of the Canal Zone. Capital, Panama City. Area, 29,209 sq. mi. Pop. (1969 est.), 1,417,000. **3.** capital and port city of this nation, on the Pacific coast. Pop. (1969), 389,000. Also (def. 3), **Panama City.**

Panama Canal, ship canal across the Isthmus of Panama connecting

at; āpe; cär; end; mē; it; īce; hot; ōld; fôrk; wood; fōol; oil; out; up; ūse; turn; sing; thin; this; zh in treasure; ə in ago, taken, pencil, lemon, circus.

the Atlantic and Pacific, built and administered by the United States.

Panama Canal Zone, Canal Zone.

Pan·a·ma·ni·an (pan′ə mā′nē ən) *adj.* of or relating to Panama or its inhabitants. —*n.* native or inhabitant of Panama.

Pan-A·mer·i·can (pan′ə mer′i kən) *adj.* including or relating to all the countries or people of North, Central, and South America.

Pan-A·mer·i·can·ism (pan′ə mer′i kə niz′əm) *n.* political movement for cooperation in social, cultural, economic, and peace-keeping activities among nations of the Western Hemisphere.

Pan American Union, secretariat of the Organization of American States, located in Washington, D.C.

Pa·nay (pä nī′) *n.* island in the central Philippines. Area, 4445 sq. mi. Pop. (1960 est.), 1,746,700.

pan-broil (pan′broil′) **-broiled, -broil·ing.** *v.t.* to cook in a skillet over direct heat, using little or no fat.

pan·cake (pan′kāk′) *n.* **1.** thin, flat cake of batter, cooked in a pan or on a griddle; flapjack. **2.** landing in which an airplane levels off in the air and drops flat on to the landing surface. —*v.i.* **-caked, -cak·ing.** (of an airplane) to make a pancake landing. —*v.t.* to cause (an airplane) to make a pancake landing.

pan·chro·mat·ic (pan′krō mat′ik) *adj.* sensitive to light of all colors, as a photographic film.

pan·cre·as (pan′krē əs) *n.* long, narrow gland below the stomach that secretes enzymes into the small intestine and the hormone insulin into the bloodstream. [Modern Latin *pancreas,* from Greek *pankreas,* from *pān-* (see PAN-) + *kreas* flesh; because it is all meat without bone.] —**pan′cre·at′ic,** *adj.*

pan·cre·at·ic juice (pan′krē at′ik) clear, watery fluid containing the digestive enzymes secreted by the pancreas.

pan·da (pan′də) *n.* **1.** bearlike mammal, *Ailuropoda melanoleuca,* native to the bamboo forests of the mountains of southwestern China, having a shaggy white coat with black markings. Length: 5 feet. Also, **giant panda. 2.** reddish-brown, raccoonlike mammal, *Ailurus fulgens,* native to the Himalayas, having short legs, a long, bushy, ringed tail, and a white face. Length: 3 feet, including tail. Also, **lesser panda.** [From a Nepali word for the animal.]

pan·dect (pan′dekt) *n.* **1.** complete body of laws. **2.** any comprehensive digest. **3. Pandects.** digest of Roman civil law made by order of the Emperor Justinian in the sixth century A.D., consisting of fifty books. [Late Latin *pandectēs* Pandects, going back to Greek *pandektēs* comprehensive.]

pan·dem·ic (pan dem′ik) *adj.* (of a disease) epidemic over a large area and affecting all or a majority of a population. [Greek *pandēmos* relating to all the people + -IC.]

pan·de·mo·ni·um (pan′də mō′nē əm) *n.* **1.** wild disorder or uproar. **2.** place or gathering of wild disorder or uproar. **3.** also, **Pandemonium. a.** abode of all the demons. **b.** hell. [Modern Latin *Pandemonium,* from Greek *pan-* (see PAN-) + *daimōn* demon; coined by John Milton as the name for the capitol of hell.]

pan·der (pan′dər) *n.* **1.** go-between in sexual intrigues; procurer; pimp. **2.** one who indulges or exploits the baser desires, feelings, or prejudices of others. —*v.i.* to act as a pander: *That writer panders to the public taste for violent stories.* [From *Pandarus,* a character in medieval legend who procured Cressida for Troilus.]

Pan·do·ra (pan dôr′ə) *n.* Greek Mythology. the first mortal woman, sent to earth as a punishment to man for Prometheus' theft of fire from the gods. Her curiosity led her to open a box into which Zeus had put all human evils and miseries, thus allowing them to escape into the world.

Pandora's box, source of many unforeseen troubles.

pan·dow·dy (pan dou′dē) *pl.* **-dies.** *n.* deep pie or pudding having only a top crust: *apple pandowdy.* [Of uncertain origin.]

pane (pān) *n.* **1.** one of the divisions of a window or door, filled with a sheet of glass or similar material. **2.** sheet of glass or similar material for such a division. **3.** panel, as in a door or ceiling. [Old French *pan* piece, panel, from Latin *pannus* piece of cloth, rag.]

pan·e·gyr·ic (pan′ə jir′ik, -jī′rik) *n.* **1.** formal oration or writing eulogizing a person or thing. **2.** elaborate praise; laudation. [Latin *panēgyricus* public eulogy, from Greek *panēgyrikos* relating to public assembly, praising, going back to *pān-* (see PAN-) + *agyris* assembly.] —Syn. see eulogy.

pan·e·gyr·ist (pan′ə jir′ist, -jī′rist) *n.* one who speaks or writes panegyrics.

pan·el (pan′əl) *n.* **1.** section of a surface, as of a door or cabinet, distinguished from the surrounding surface by being raised, recessed, or bordered. **2.** flat piece of material, as of wood or plastic, made to be joined with others. **3.** lengthwise section of fabric in a garment. **4.a.** thin wooden board used as the surface for an oil painting. **b.** painting on such a board. **c.** any picture or photograph much longer than it is wide. **5.** board or other surface on which controls, instruments, or dials are mounted. **6.** group of persons selected for some purpose, as to hold a discussion or participate in something as a team: *a panel of experts.* **7.a.** list of persons summoned for jury duty on a single case. **b.** members of a jury. —*v.t.* to furnish or decorate with panels: *The walls of the living room were paneled with dark mahogany.* [Old French *panel* piece, piece of cloth, going back to Latin *pannus* piece of cloth, rag.]

panel discussion, discussion of a specific topic by a selected group of speakers, usually before an audience.

pan·el·ing (pan′əl ing) *n.* **1.** wood or other material used to make panels. **2.** panels collectively.

pan·el·ist (pan′əl ist) *n.* one who serves on a panel or participates in a panel discussion.

panel truck, small truck with a fully enclosed body, used esp. for delivery service.

pang (pang) *n.* **1.** sudden, sharp pain: *pangs of hunger.* **2.** sharp feeling of mental distress: *He felt pangs of guilt after lying to his friend.* [Of uncertain origin.]

pan·go·lin (pang gō′lin) *n.* any of several scale-covered, toothless mammals, order Pholidota, native to Asia, Africa, and certain Pacific islands, having sharp claws, a long extensile tongue, and usually a long tail. Length: 3–6 feet. Also, **scaly anteater.** [Malay *peng-gōling* roller; referring to its habit of rolling itself into a ball.]

Pang·o Pang·o (pang′ō pang′ō) Pago Pago.

pan·han·dle¹ (pan′han′dl) *n.* **1.** handle of a pan. **2.** also, **Panhandle.** narrow strip of projecting land that is attached to a larger land mass: *the Texas Panhandle.*

pan·han·dle² (pan′han′dl) **-dled, -dling.** *v.i.* Informal. to beg, esp. in the streets: *The old man panhandled a dime for a cup of coffee.* [Of uncertain origin.] —**pan′han′dler,** *n.*

Pan·hel·len·ic (pan′hə len′ik) also, **pan·hel·len·ic.** *adj.* **1.** of or relating to all Greek people. **2.** of or relating to all Greek-letter fraternities and sororities.

pan·ic (pan′ik) *n.* **1.** sudden, overpowering fear, esp. when affecting a number of persons at once. **2.** instance of such fear: *There was a panic when the fire broke out.* **3.** sudden and widespread financial crisis caused by a collapse of public confidence, as in banks, the stock market, or foreign currencies. **4.** Slang. person who is very amusing. —*v.i.* **-icked, -ick·ing.** to become affected with panic: *The children panicked when they realized they were lost.* —*v.t.* **1.** to affect with panic. **2.** Slang. to amuse greatly. —*adj.* of the nature of or resulting from panic; showing panic. [French *panique* sudden fear, from Greek *Pānikos* relating to Pan, who was said to inspire unreasoning fear by unexpected appearances.] —**pan′ick·y,** *adj.* —Syn. *n.* **1.** see terror.

pan·i·cle (pan′i kəl) *n.* bushy flower cluster consisting of tiny stalked flowers that grow from secondary stems off the main stem. [Latin *pānicula,* diminutive of *pānus* thread wound round a bobbin.]

pan·ic-strick·en (pan′ik strik′ən) *adj.* overcome by panic.

pa·nic·u·late (pə nik′yə lāt′, -lit) *adj.* (of flowers) growing in a panicle.

pan·ni·er (pan′ē ər) *n.* **1.** large basket for carrying goods, esp. one of a connected pair designed to be slung across the back of a pack animal. **2.** framework of hoops formerly used to give fullness to the sides of a woman's skirt. **3.** drapery gathered at the sides of a skirt. [Old French *panier* basket, from Latin *pānārium* breadbasket, from *pānis* bread.]

pa·no·cha (pə nō′chə) *n.* **1.** coarse Mexican sugar. **2.** penuche. [Spanish *panocha,* diminutive of *pan* bread, from Latin *pānis;* because they come in chunks that resemble small loaves of bread.]

pan·o·ply (pan′ə plē) *pl.* **-plies.** *n.* **1.** complete suit of armor. **2.** any magnificent array or covering: *The lakes were surrounded by a panoply of mountains.* [Greek *panopliā* complete suit of armor, from *pān-* (see PAN-) + *hopla* arms.] —**pan′o·plied,** *adj.*

Panicle

Pancreas (illustration labels: Stomach, Gall bladder, Pancreatic duct, Pancreas, Duodenum)

Panda

at; āpe; cär; end; mē; it; īce; hot; ōld; fôrk; wood; fōol; oil; out; up; ūse; turn; sing; thin; this; zh in treasure; ə in ago, taken, pencil, lemon, circus.

727

pan·o·ram·a (pan′ə ram′ə, -rä′mə) *n.* **1.** complete or unbroken view of an area in every direction: *A vast panorama of the valley lay before us.* **2.** complete and comprehensive survey or presentation of a subject: *a panorama of the current political scene.* **3.** picture or series of pictures representing a continuous scene, unrolled and passed continuously before the spectators. **4.** continuously passing or changing scene. [PAN- + Greek *horāma* view.] —**pan′o·ram′ic,** *adj.* —**pan′o·ram′i·cal·ly,** *adv.*

pan·pipe (pan′pīp′) *also,* **Pan·pipe.** *n.* primitive wind instrument consisting of a graduated series of reeds or tubes bound together.

Panpipe

pan·sy (pan′zē) *pl.,* **-sies.** *n.* **1.** velvety flower of a common garden plant, *Viola tricolor,* of the violet family, having five flat overlapping petals and growing in a variety of colors. **2.** plant bearing this flower, having many branching stems. [Old French *pensee* the flower, thought, from *penser* to think, from Latin *pēnsāre* to consider.]

pant (pant) *v.i.* **1.** to breathe quickly, spasmodically, or heavily; gasp for breath: *He panted after running up the stairs.* **2.** to emit steam, smoke, or the like in loud puffs. **3.** to desire breathlessly; long eagerly; yearn (with *for* or *after*). **4.** to throb or pulsate rapidly. —*v.t.* to utter breathlessly: *He panted out his story to his friends.* —*n.* **1.** short or labored breath; gasp. **2.** puff, as from an engine. **3.** throb or pulsation, as of the heart. [Probably from Old French *pantaisier* to gasp, through an unrecorded Vulgar Latin word meaning "to gasp from a nightmare," going back to Greek *phantasiā* imagination, appearance.]

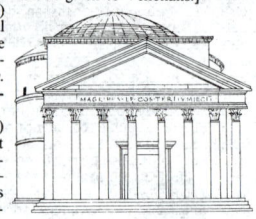

Pansies

pan·ta·lets (pant′əl ets′) *also,* **pan·ta·lettes.** *n.,pl.* long ruffled drawers formerly worn by women and girls. [Diminutive of PANTALOON.]

pan·ta·loon (pant′əl ōon′) *n.* **1. pantaloons.** tight-fitting trousers formerly worn by men. **2. Pantaloon.** stock character in sixteenth-century Italian commedia dell'arte, usually a foolish old man wearing pantaloons and slippers. **3.** similar stock character in modern pantomime, usually the object of the clown's jokes. [French *pantalon* the trousers, from Italian *Pantalone* Pantaloon, who represented Venetians, from *Pantaleone* Venetian saint and nickname given to Venetians.]

pan·the·ism (pan′thē iz′əm) *n.* **1.** religious and philosophical theory that God and the universe are identical. **2.** belief in and worship of all gods. —**pan′the·ist,** *n.* —**pan′the·is′tic,** *adj.* —**pan′the·is′ti·cal·ly,** *adv.*

pan·the·on (pan′thē on′, -ən) *n.* **1. Pantheon.** temple built at Rome by Agrippa in 27 B.C., rebuilt by Hadrian in A.D. 120–124 and, since A.D. 609, used as a Christian church. **2.** any temple dedicated to all the gods. **3.** all the gods of a people collectively. **4.** public building serving as a memorial or mausoleum for the famous people of a nation. [Latin *Panthēon* the Roman temple, going back to Greek *pantheios* common to all the gods, from *pān-* (see PAN-) + *theos* a god.]

Pantheon

pan·ther (pan′thər) *pl.,* **-thers** or **-ther.** *n.* **1.** leopard, esp. one having a black coat. **2.** cougar. **3.** jaguar. [Old French *panthere* large wild animal of the cat family with spotted skin, from Latin *panthēra,* from Greek *panthēr.*]

pant·ies (pan′tēz) *also,* **pant·ie, pant·y.** *n.,pl.* short underpants worn by girls and women. [From PANTS.]

pan·to·graph (pan′tə graf′) *n.* instrument used for copying plane figures on any scale desired. It has a framework of four rods jointed in parallelogram form. [Greek *pant-,* stem of *pās* all + -GRAPH.]

pan·to·mime (pan′tə mīm′) *n.* **1.** technique of conveying meaning or a story without speech, through the use of gestures, body movements, and facial expressions. **2.** dramatic performance using this technique. **3.** traditional English Christmas entertainment using stock characters, originally without speech, but later expanded to include dialogue. —*v.t., v.i.,* **-mimed, -mim·ing.** to act or express in pantomime. [Latin *pantomīmus* pantomimic actor, from Greek *pantomīmos,* from *pant-,* stem of *pās* all + *mīmos* imitator.] —**pan·to·mim·ic** (pan′tə mim′ik), *adj.* —**pan′to·mim′ist,** *n.*

pan·to·then·ic acid (pan′tə then′ik) yellow oily compound of the vitamin B complex required for obtaining energy from carbohydrates

in the body, found esp. in eggs and liver. [Greek *pantothen* on every side (from *pant-,* stem of *pās* all) + -IC + ACID.]

pan·try (pan′trē) *pl.,* **-tries.** *n.* room or closet in which food and articles connected with the preparation and serving of food are kept. [Old French *paneterie* place where bread is kept, from Medieval Latin *panetaria* place where bread is made, going back to Latin *pānis* bread.]

pants (pants) *n.,pl.* **1.** trousers. **2.** underpants. [Short for *pantaloons,* plural of PANTALOON.]

pan·ty·waist (pan′tē wāst′) *n.* **1.** child's two-piece undergarment buttoning at the waist. **2.** *Informal.* weak or effeminate man or boy.

pan·zer (pan′zər) *adj.* of, relating to, or designating an armored military unit: *a panzer division.* [German *Panzer* armor, from Old French *panciere* coat of mail; literally, piece for the belly, from Latin *pantex* belly.]

pap (pap) *n.* **1.** soft or semiliquid food for infants or invalids. **2.** ideas, speech, or writing without real substance or value: *That magazine contains nothing but worthless pap.* **3.** money or favors given as political patronage. [Probably imitative of baby talk.]

pa·pa (pä′pə, pə pä′) *n.* father. [French *papa,* from Latin *pāpa.*]

pa·pa·cy (pā′pə sē) *pl.,* **-cies.** *n.* **1.** office or authority of the pope. **2.** tenure of a pope's reign. **3.** line of the popes; popes collectively. **4.** system of governing the Roman Catholic Church in which the Pope is supreme ruler. [Medieval Latin *papatia* dignity or authority of the pope, from Late Latin *pāpa.* See POPE.]

pa·pal (pā′pəl) *adj.* **1.** of or relating to the pope or the papacy: *papal influence, papal reforms.* **2.** of or relating to the Roman Catholic Church. [Medieval Latin *papalis* relating to the pope, from Late Latin *pāpa.* See POPE.]

Papal States, territory in central Italy ruled by the popes from 755 to 1870. Also, **States of the Church.**

pa·paw (pə pô′, pô′pô) *also,* **paw·paw.** *n.* **1.** strong-smelling, edible oblong fruit of a tree, *Asimina triloba,* having yellow flesh and a bananalike taste. **2.** tree bearing this fruit, growing mainly in the central United States. Also *(defs. 1, 2),* **custard apple.** **3.** papaya. [Spanish *papaya* the fruit; of Carib origin.]

pa·pa·ya (pə pä′yə) *n.* **1.** edible yellowish-orange fruit of an evergreen tree, *Carica papaya,* having a thick rind, many small black seeds, and a fleshy pulp with a sweet musky flavor. **2.** tree bearing this fruit, raised in warm regions, having a trunk crowned by a cluster of seven-lobed leaves. [Spanish *papaya* the fruit; of Carib origin.]

Pa·pe·e·te (pä′pē ā′tā) *n.* capital of French Polynesia, a port on the island of Tahiti. Pop. (1967), 22,278.

Papaya tree

pa·per (pā′pər) *n.* **1.** material made from matted fibers, as those obtained from wood pulp, rags, and certain grasses, usually formed in thin flexible sheets, used for writing, printing, wrapping, and many other purposes. **2.** piece or sheet of this material: *He wrote his name at the top of the paper.* **3.** sheet or sheets of this material bearing writing or printing; document. **4.** written discourse, report, or essay: *to present a paper at a medical conference.* **5.** written piece of schoolwork, as an essay or examination: *His paper on the Civil War is overdue.* **6.** newspaper. **7. papers.** collection of letters, journals, or other writings, esp. of one person: *the Churchill papers.* **8. papers.** collection of documents that identify a person; credentials. **9.** negotiable written or printed note, as a check or promissory note. **10.** paper money. **11.** card or sheet of paper holding something: *a paper of pins.* **12.** wallpaper. **13.** on paper. **a.** in written or printed form. **b.** in theory: *The idea looked good on paper, but it never worked out.* —*v.t.* to cover or decorate with paper, esp. wallpaper: *to paper a room.* —*adj.* **1.** made or consisting of paper: *paper flowers.* **2.** like paper in thinness; flimsy: *These apartments have paper walls.* **3.** existing only in writing; never realized in actuality: *paper promises.* [Old French *papier* the material made from matted fibers, sheet for writing, from Latin *papȳrus* paper made of papyrus, papyrus plant, from Greek *papȳros* papyrus plant. Doublet of PAPYRUS.] —**pa′per·er,** *n.* —**pa′per·y,** *adj.* —**Syn.** *n.* **4.** see *essay.*

pa·per·back (pā′pər bak′) *n.* book bound in paper. —*adj.* paperbound.

pa·per·bound (pā′pər bound′) *adj.* (of a book) bound in paper.

paper boy, boy who sells or delivers newspapers, esp. to the home.

pa·per·hang·er (pā′pər hang′ər) *n.* one whose work is hanging wallpaper.

paper knife, thin, dull knife used for cutting open sealed envelopes.

paper money, currency printed on paper, issued by a government or authorized banks.

at; āpe; cär; end; mē; it; īce; hot; ōld; fôrk; wood; fōol; oil; out; up; ūse; turn; sing; thin; this; zh in treasure; ə in ago, taken, pencil, lemon, circus.

paper nautilus, any of a group of eight-armed marine mollusks, family Argonautidae, related to the octopus, the female of which secretes a delicate shell-like cradle in which her eggs are hatched.

paper profit, profit that could be realized if a stock were sold.

pa·per·weight (pā′pər wāt′) *n.* small, heavy object, often ornamental, placed on top of papers to hold them down.

pa·per·work (pā′pər wurk′) *n.* routine clerical work, esp. when considered to be incidental to some more important task.

pa·pier-mâ·ché (pā′pər mə shā′) *n.* substance made of paper mixed with glue and other materials, which can be molded when moist and which hardens when dry. [French *papier-mâché* literally, chewed paper, going back to Latin *papyrus* (see PAPYRUS) + Late Latin *masticātus,* past participle of *masticāre.* See MASTICATE.]

pa·pil·la (pə pil′ə) *pl.* **-pil·lae** (-pil′ē). *n.* **1.** small knoblike projection of a hair follicle, containing tiny blood vessels that nourish the root of the hair. **2.** any of certain small protuberances located in or on the surface of various parts of the body. Many are connected with the senses of touch, taste, or smell. **3.** any small, nipplelike projection. [Latin *papilla* nipple.] **—pap·il·lar·y** (pap′ə ler′ē) *adj.*

pa·pist (pā′pist) *n., adj.* Roman Catholic. ▲ used disparagingly. [Modern Latin *papista,* from Late Latin *pāpa.* See POPE.] **—pa′·pist·ry,** *n.*

pa·poose (pa pōōs′) *also,* **pap·poose.** *n.* North American Indian baby or small child. [Algonquian *papoos* child.]

pap·py (pap′ē) *pl.* **-pies.** *n. Informal.* father. [Diminutive of PAPA.]

pap·ri·ka (pə prē′kə, pa-, pap′ri kə) *n.* orange-red spice made from the powdered fruits of the sweet red pepper. [German *Paprika* red pepper, through Magyar and Serbo-Croatian, from Greek *peperi* pepper. See PEPPER.]

Pap·u·a (pap′ū ə) *n.* **1.** New Guinea. **2. Territory of.** Australian possession in the southeastern part of New Guinea. Area, 86,100 sq. mi. Pop. (1966), 600,597.

Pap·u·an (pap′ū ən) *adj.* of or relating to Papua, its native inhabitants, or their languages. **—***n.* **1.** member of any of the dark-skinned peoples inhabiting New Guinea, Papua, and adjacent islands. **2.** any of a number of languages spoken predominantly in the southwest Pacific islands, constituting a separate language family.

pa·py·rus (pə pī′rəs) *pl.* **-ri** (-rī). *n.* **1.** stiff grasslike plant, *Cyperus papyrus,* found growing in swamps and along rivers in northern Africa and southern Europe, having dark-green hollow stalks. **2.** writing material made from the stems of this plant by the ancient Egyptians and other peoples. **3.** manuscript or document written on this material. [Latin *papyrus* the plant and the paper, from Greek *papyros* the plant. Doublet of PAPER.]

par (pär) *n.* **1.** average or normal, as in amount, degree, quality, or condition: *His performance is above par.* **2.** equal or common level: *Your work is on a par with his.* **3.** state of equality between the face value and the market value of bonds, shares of stock, and other financial instruments. If a stock is selling at par, it is selling at the value actually printed on the stock certificate. **4.** ratio of the monetary unit of one country to the monetary unit of another country, based on the same standard of value. **5.** *Golf.* number of strokes set as a standard minimum of skillful play for a hole or course. **—***adj.* **1.** average; normal. **2.** in commerce, of or at par. [Latin *pār* equal.]

par-, form of **para-¹** before vowels and *h,* as in *parody, parhelion.*

par. **1.** paragraph. **2.** parallel. **3.** parenthesis. **4.** parish.

para-¹ *prefix* **1.** beside; near; along with: *parallel, paraphrase, parasympathetic.* **2.** beyond; aside from: *paradox.* **3.** disordered; abnormal; malfunctioning: *paranoia, paraplegia.* **4.** similar to; resembling: *paratyphoid.* **5.** subordinate to: *paraprofessional.* [Greek *para* beside, beyond.]

para-² *combining form* **1.** protection against: *parachute, parasol.* **2.** using a parachute: *paratroops.* [French *para-* guarding against, from Italian *para* ward off, imperative of *parare* to ward off, from Latin *parāre* to make ready.]

par·a·ble (par′ə bəl) *n.* short allegorical story illustrating some truth or moral lesson. [Latin *parabola* allegory, comparison, proverb, from Greek *parabolē* comparison, proverb; literally, a throwing beside, from *para* beside + *ballein* to throw. Doublet of PALAVER, PAROLE.]

pa·rab·o·la (pə rab′ə lə) *n., pl.* **-las.** *n.* open curve consisting of a set of points in a plane that lie at equal distances from a fixed point, or focus, and a fixed line, or directrix; conic section formed by the intersection of a cone and a plane parallel to a side of the cone. [Modern Latin *parabola,* from Greek *parabolē* juxtaposition, comparison. See PARABLE.]

Parabola

par·a·bol·ic¹ (par′ə bol′ik) *adj.* of, resembling, or expressed in a parable. [Late Latin *parabolicus.* from Late Greek *parabolikos* figurative, from *parabolē.* See PARABLE.]

par·a·bol·ic² (par′ə bol′ik) *adj.* of, relating to, or having the form of a parabola. [PARABOLA + -IC.]

Par·a·cel·sus, Phi·lip·pus Au·re·o·lus (par′ə sel′səs; fi lip′əs ō rē′ə ləs) 1493–1541, Swiss physician and alchemist; born Theophrastus Bombastus von Hohenheim.

par·a·chute (par′ə shōōt′) *n.* **1.** umbrellalike device for retarding the speed of a body falling through the air, used primarily to drop a person or object safely to the ground from an aircraft. **2.** any similar device for retarding speed, as of an aircraft in landing. **—***v.i.* **-chut·ed, -chut·ing.** to descend by parachute: *The soldiers parachuted into the war zone.* **—***v.t.* to drop, as troops or supplies, by parachute. [French *parachute* the device, from *para-* guarding against (see PARA-²) + *chute* fall. See CHUTE.]

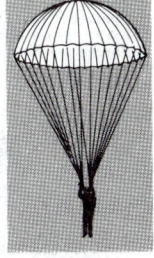

Parachute

par·a·chut·ist (par′ə shōō′tist) *n.* one who is skilled in parachuting.

pa·rade (pə rād′) *n.* **1.** organized, often ceremonial march or procession in honor of a person or special occasion: *a circus parade, a Memorial Day parade.* **2.** a long line or succession; array: *a parade of suitors.* **3.** pretentious display; exhibition: *He made a parade of his loyalty to the cause.* **4.** public place where people promenade. **5.** the people who promenade. **6.** procession or assembly of troops for inspection, display, or review. **7. on parade.** on display; in review. **—***v.i.* **-rad·ed, -rad·ing. 1.** to march formally in an organized procession. **2.** to walk about to show off oneself. **3.** to march or assemble for military review or inspection. **—***v.t.* **1.** to walk through or down, as in an organized procession. **2.** to display ostentatiously; make a show of: *He liked to parade his medals for new guests.* **3.** to cause (troops) to march in review or assemble for inspection. [French *parade* military review, display, through Spanish, going back to Latin *parāre* to make ready.] **—pa·rad′er,** *n.*

parade rest, in military drill, formal position of rest in which the feet are placed twelve inches apart, the hands are clasped behind the back, and the head faces forward and is held motionless.

par·a·digm (par′ə dīm′, -dim′) *n.* **1.** pattern or example. **2.** *Grammar.* list of all the inflectional forms of a word. [Late Latin *paradigma* example, from Greek *paradeigma* example, model.]

par·a·dise (par′ə dīs′) *n.* **1.** the abode of God, the angels, and those who are saved; heaven. **2.** any place of extreme beauty or delight. **3.** state of supreme happiness or bliss: *Comfort seems to many Englishmen the only real paradise* (Fairbairn, 1902). **4. Paradise.** garden of Eden. [Late Latin *paradīsus* heaven, garden of Eden, park, from Greek *paradeisos;* of Persian origin.]

par·a·dox (par′ə doks′) *n.* **1.** statement that seems to be contradictory or absurd, but in fact may be true: *the legal paradox, that a libel may be the more a libel for being true* (Coleridge, 1810). **2.** statement that is in fact self-contradictory and therefore false. **3.** any seemingly inconsistent or contradictory person or thing. [Latin *paradoxum* something unexpected, from Greek *paradoxos* contrary to or beyond expectation, incredible.] **—par′a·dox′i·cal,** *adj.* **—par′a·dox′i·cal·ly,** *adv.*

par·af·fin (par′ə fin) *n.* **1.** solid, waxy, white substance obtained from petroleum and used esp. in the making of candles, waxed paper, and cosmetics. **2.** any member of the series of hydrocarbons having the general formula C_nH_{2n+2}; alkane. **—***v.t.* to treat or saturate with paraffin. [German *Paraffin* the waxy substance, from Latin *parum* too little + *affīnis* related; because it has little affinity for other materials.]

par·a·gon (par′ə gon′) *n.* model or pattern of excellence or perfection: *a paragon of virtue.* [Obsolete French *paragon,* from Italian *paragone* touchstone, going back to Greek *para* beside + *akonē* whetstone.]

par·a·graph (par′ə graf′) *n.* **1.** distinct unified section of a chapter, article, or other written matter, usually consisting of a number of sentences on one particular point or idea, and begun on a new, usually indented, line. **2.** brief article or item, as in a newspaper. **3.** mark (¶) used in printing and writing to indicate the beginning of a paragraph or to refer to other material, as a footnote or appendix. **—***v.t.* **1.** to arrange in or divide into paragraphs. **2.** to write about or express in a paragraph. [Medieval Latin *paragraphus* mark indicating a section of writing, from Greek *paragraphos* line in the margin (indicating a break in sense), from *para* beside + *graphein* to write.] **—par′a·graph′er,** *n.*

Par·a·guay (par′ə gwā′, -gwī′) *n.* **1.** country in south-central South America. Capital, Asunción. Area, 157,048 sq. mi. Pop. (1969 est.), 2,303,000. **2.** principal river of this country, flowing south from Brazil through Paraguay into the Paraná River. **—Par′a·guay′an,** *adj., n.*

par·a·keet (par′ə kēt′) *also,* **par·a·quet, par·e·quet, par·ra·keet.** *n.* any of various small parrots, usually having brightly colored plumage, often kept as cage birds. Length: 7–12 inches. [Old French *paroquet* parrot, possibly modification of *Perrot,* diminutive of *Pierre* Peter. See PARROT.]

Par·a·li·pom·e·non (par′ə li pom′ə non′) *n.* in the Douay Bible, either of two books of the Old Testament corresponding to I and II Chronicles.

par·al·lac·tic (par′ə lak′tik) *adj.* of or relating to a parallax.

par·al·lax (par′ə laks′) *n.* apparent shift in the position of an object, relative to its background, that occurs when an observer changes his position. In astronomy parallax is used to determine the distances of nearby stars. [Greek *parallaxis* alternation, change.]

par·al·lel (par′ə lel′, -ləl) *adj.* **1.** extending in the same direction and always the same distance apart at every point, so as never to meet, as lines or planes: *The rails of a railroad track are parallel.* **2.** similar or corresponding, as in direction, meaning, or development: *He cited parallel passages in both books.* **3.** having statements expressed in the same grammatical form. **4.** of or designating an electrical circuit that is connected in parallel. —*n.* **1.** parallel line, plane, or surface. **2.** close similarity or correspondence: *We can find many parallels in the customs of those two tribes.* **3.** one who or that which closely resembles or corresponds to another; counterpart. **4.** comparison to show similarity or correspondence. **5.a.** any of the imaginary lines that circle the earth parallel to the equator, designating degrees of latitude. **b.** marking on a map, globe, or chart representing such a line. **6. in parallel.** (of electric circuits) connected so as to form separate paths between the positive and negative terminals of the current source for each object, as each light, in the circuit. —*v.t.,* **-leled, -lel·ing;** *also, British,* **-lelled, -lel·ling. 1.** to be or lie in a direction parallel to. **2.** to cause to be or lie in a parallel direction; make parallel. **3.** to be similar or equal to; correspond to. **4.** to show, find, or furnish a parallel or equal for. **5.** to compare in order to show similarity of; liken. —*adv.* in a parallel manner or direction (often with *to* or *with*). [Latin *parallēlus* extending in the same direction and equidistant, from Greek *parallēlos* side by side.]

parallel bars, two poles, as of wood, set parallel to each other and supported by adjustable uprights, used in gymnastics.

par·al·lel·e·pi·ped (par′ə lel′ə pī′ped) *n.* polyhedron with six faces that are all parallelograms. Also, **par·al·lel·e·pip·e·don** (par′ə lel′ə pip′ə don′). [Greek *parall-ēlepipedon* body with parallel surfaces, from *parallēlos* side by side + *epipedon* plane surface.]

par·al·lel·ism (par′ə lel′ iz′əm) *n.* **1.** state or condition of being parallel. **2.** close similarity or resemblance; correspondence. **3.** similarity in grammatical form of the elements of a phrase or sentence.

par·al·lel·o·gram (par′ə lel′ə gram′) *n.* polygon with four sides whose opposite sides are parallel and equal in length. [Greek *parallēlogrammon,* from *parallēlos* side by side + *grammē* line.]

pa·ral·y·sis (pə ral′ə sis) *pl.,* **-ses** (-sēz′). *n.* **1.** loss of the power of motion or sensation in a muscle due to disease of, or an injury to, the nervous system. **2.** cessation of normal functioning or movement. [Latin *paralysis* the medical condition, from Greek *paralysis* disabling of the nerves. Doublet of PALSY.]

par·a·lyt·ic (par′ə lit′ik) *adj.* **1.** of, relating to, or characteristic of paralysis. **2.** having paralysis. —*n.* one who has paralysis.

par·a·lyze (par′ə līz′) **-lyzed, -lyz·ing.** *v.t.* **1.** to affect with paralysis; make paralytic. **2.** to make helpless, powerless, or ineffective: *The bus strike paralyzed the city.*

Par·a·mar·i·bo (par′ə-mar′ə bō′) *n.* capital of Surinam, a port in the northern part of the territory. Pop. (1967 est.), 123,000.

par·a·me·ci·um (par′ə-mē′shē əm, -sē əm) *pl.,*

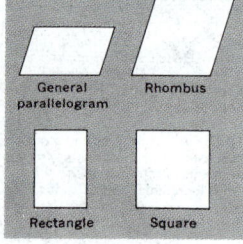

Parakeet

Parallelograms

General parallelogram | Rhombus

Rectangle | Square

Contractile vacuole | Macronucleus

Micronucleus

Cilia

Food vacuole | Cytoplasm

Paramecium

-ci·a (-shē ə, -sē ə). *n.* slipper-shaped freshwater protozoan, genus *Paramecium,* having cilia that provide locomotion and help to sweep food into its mouth. [Modern Latin *paramecium,* from Greek *paramēkēs* oblong.]

pa·ram·e·ter (pə ram′ə tər) *n.* **1.** quantity in a mathematical expression that is constant in a particular case under consideration but varies in different cases. In the equation for a circle, $x^2 + y^2 = a^2$, the quantity a^2 is a parameter determining the radius and varies with the size of the circle. **2.** any constant in a given situation that determines or limits other conditions of that situation. [PARA-¹ + Greek *metron* measure.]

par·a·mount (par′ə mount′) *adj.* above all others, as in influence or importance; preeminent; supreme: *The children's welfare was her paramount consideration.* [Anglo-Norman *par amont* at the top, above, going back to Latin *per* through, beyond + *ad montem* to a mountain, upward.] —**Syn.** see **dominant.**

par·a·mour (par′ə moor′) *n.* lover, esp. an illicit lover of one who is married. [Old French *par amour* by love, from Latin *per* by + *amor* love.]

Pa·ra·ná (par′ə nä′) *n.* river in South America, flowing south through Brazil, Paraguay, and Argentina into the Plata River.

par·a·noi·a (par′ə noi′ə) *n.* **1.** psychotic condition marked by feelings of grandeur or persecution. **2.** tendency to distrust others and to regard everyone as an enemy. [Modern Latin *paranoia,* Greek *paranoia* derangement, going back to *para* beyond + *nous* mind.]

par·a·noid (par′ə noid′) *adj.* relating to, characteristic of, or affected with paranoia. *n.* one who is affected with paranoia. Also, **par·a·noi·ac** (par′ə noi′ak).

par·a·pet (par′ə pit, -pet′) *n.* **1.** low wall of earth or stone, esp. on a rampart, to protect troops from observation or fire. **2.** low wall or railing around the edge of a balcony, roof, or other structure. [Italian *parapetto* breast-high wall, from *para* (see PARA-²) + *petto* breast (from Latin *pectus*).] —**par′a·pet·ed,** *adj.*

par·a·pher·nal·ia (par′ə fər näl′yə) *n.,pl.* **1.** personal belongings. **2.** any group of articles, esp. those used in a particular activity; equipment; gear. [Medieval Latin *paraphernalia* (goods) of a bride in addition to her dowry, through Latin, from Greek *parapherna,* from *para* beyond, beside + *phernē* dowry.]

Parapet

par·a·phrase (par′ə frāz′) *n.* restatement of the meaning of a work or passage. —*v.t., v.i.,* **-phrased, -phras·ing.** to express in or make a paraphrase. [Latin *paraphrasis* restatement of the meaning of a passage, from Greek *paraphrasis.*]

par·a·ple·gi·a (par′ə plē′jē ə) *n.* paralysis of both legs and all or part of the trunk. [Modern Latin *paraplegia,* from Greek *paraplēgia* paralysis of one side (of the body).] —**par′a·ple′gic,** *n., adj.*

par·a·pro·fes·sion·al (par′ə prə fesh′ən əl) *n.* one who works with and assists a professional in a subsidiary capacity.

par·a·psy·chol·o·gy (par′ə sī kol′ə jē) *n.* study of extrasensory perception and other psychic phenomena.

par·a·quet (par′ə kēt′) *n.* parakeet.

par·a·sang (par′ə sang′) *n.* ancient Persian measure of length, varying from two to four miles. [Latin *parasanga,* from Greek *parasangēs;* of Persian origin.]

par·a·site (par′ə sīt′) *n.* **1.** animal or plant that lives on or in another organism of a different species and obtains all or part of its food from that organism while contributing nothing to its survival. **2.** one who lives off another or who associates with another for personal gain while providing nothing in return. [Latin *parasitus* one who lives off another, from Greek *parasītos* one who eats at the table of another, from *para* beside + *sitos* food; with reference to the men in ancient Greece and Rome who offered flattery in return for food or support.] —**par′a·sit′ism,** *n.*

par·a·sit·ic (par′ə sit′ik) *adj.* **1.** of or relating to a parasite. **2.** caused by a parasite: *a parasitic disease.* Also, **par′a·sit′i·cal.** —**par′a·sit′i·cal·ly,** *adv.*

par·a·sol (par′ə sôl′, -sol′) *n.* small, light decorative umbrella, used esp. by women for protection from the sun. [French *parasol,* from Italian *parasole,* from *para* (see PARA-²) + *sole* sun (from Latin *sōl*).]

par·a·sym·pa·thet·ic (par′ə sim′pə thet′ik) *adj.* of, relating to, or designating that part of the autonomic nervous system that helps to regulate the functions of the body's internal organs. Distinguished from **sympathetic.**

par·a·thy·roid glands (par′ə thī′roid) small endocrine glands behind the thyroid glands, producing a hormone that regulates the body's use of calcium and phosphorus.

par·a·troop (par′ə trōōp′) *adj.* of or relating to paratroops.

par·a·troop·er (par′ə trōō′pər) *n.* member of the paratroops. [PARA(CHUTE) + TROOPER.]

par·a·troops (par′ə trōōps′) *n.,pl.* group of soldiers trained to parachute from airplanes into the area of their objective.

par·boil (pär′boil′) *v.t.* to cook partially by boiling, usually for a short time. [Old French *parboillir* to cook thoroughly, from Late Latin *perbullire*, from Latin *per* through + *bullire* to boil; meaning influenced by association with PART.]

Par·cae (pär′sē) *n.,pl. Roman Mythology.* the three Fates.

par·cel (pär′səl) *n.* **1.** thing or group of things packed together; package; bundle. **2.** distinct portion of land. **3.** group of similar persons or things; pack; bunch: *a parcel of fools.* **4.** quantity of merchandise put up for sale. —*v.t.,* **-celed** or **-celled, -cel·ing** or **-cel·ling.** to divide into sections or distribute in portions: *to parcel up land.* [Old French *parcelle* small part, going back to Latin *particula,* diminutive of *pars* portion.] —**Syn.** *n.* **1.** see **bundle.**

parcel post **1.** classification of mailable matter, used esp. for packages weighing sixteen ounces or more. **2.** branch of the postal service handling such mail. **3.** mail handled by this service.

parch (pärch) *v.t.* **1.** to make very dry or shriveled, as by exposure to heat. **2.** to make very thirsty. **3.** to dry by roasting slightly. —*v.i.* **1.** to become very dry or hot, as by exposure to heat. **2.** to become very thirsty. [Of uncertain origin.]

Par·chee·si (pär chē′zē) *n. Trademark.* board game in which each player tries to be the first to move his tokens into a home square, with the moves governed by throws of the dice.

parch·ment (pärch′mənt) *n.* **1.** skin of sheep, goats, or other animals, prepared for writing or painting upon. **2.** manuscript or document written on this material. **3.** any of several types of paper made to resemble this material. [Old French *parchemin* such skin, modification (influenced by Latin *Parthica pellis* Parthian leather) of Latin *pergamīna,* from Greek *pergamēnē,* from *Pergamon,* city in Asia Minor where it was first produced.]

pard[1] (pärd) *n. Archaic.* leopard; panther. [Latin *pardus* male panther, from Greek *pardos.*]

pard[2] (pärd) *n. Slang.* close friend; partner. [Short for PARDNER.]

pard·ner (pärd′nər) *n. Slang.* close friend; chum. [Modification of PARTNER.]

par·don (pärd′ən) *v.t.* **1.** to release (a person) from punishment for an offense: *The governor pardoned the condemned prisoner.* **2.** to pass over (an offense) without exacting penalty or placing blame; forgive. **3.a.** to overlook as a courtesy: *Please pardon my manners.* **b.** to grant courteous tolerance to: *Please pardon me if I hurt your feelings.* —*n.* **1.** release from punishment for an offense. **2.** document or official warrant granting such a release. **3.** polite forebearance, as for a discourtesy. **4.** act of passing over without exacting penalty or placing blame: *You have my pardon for your recent actions.* **5.** in the Roman Catholic Church, a release from temporal punishment due to sin; indulgence. [Old French *pardonner* to forgive, bestow, from Late Latin *perdōnāre* to remit, give wholeheartedly, from Latin *per* through + *dōnāre* to give.] —**par′don·a·ble,** *adj.* —**par′don·a·bly,** *adv.* —**Syn.** *v.t.* **2.** see **excuse.**

par·don·er (pärd′ən ər, pärd′nər) *n.* **1.** in the Middle Ages, one who was authorized to grant ecclesiastical indulgences. **2.** one who pardons.

pare (pār) *v.t.,* **pared, par·ing.** *v.t.* **1.** to cut or peel off the outer layer or skin of: *to pare an apple.* **2.** to cut, trim, or shave off (an outer layer or part). **3.** to reduce or lessen: *to pare down an essay for publication.* [Old French *parer* to trim, from Latin *parāre* to make ready.]

par·e·gor·ic (par′ə gôr′ik, par′ə gor′ik) *n.* medicine containing opium and camphor, used primarily to treat diarrhea. [Late Latin *parēgoricus* assuaging, from Greek *parēgorikos* soothing, going back to *para* beside + *agorā* public assembly.]

paren., parenthesis.

pa·ren·chy·ma (pə reng′kə mə) *n.* **1.** basic tissue in plants, consisting of unspecialized thin-walled cells that are able to differentiate into other specialized types of cells. **2.** basic tissue of an animal organ, contained in and supported by connective tissue. [Modern Latin *parenchyma,* from Greek *parenchyma* tissue of internal organs, from *parenchein* to pour in beside; referring to the belief that the tissues of these organs were poured in by their blood vessels.]

par·ent (pār′ənt) *n.* **1.** person who produces offspring; father or mother. **2.** one who performs the functions of a father or mother. **3.** any organism that produces offspring. **4.** anything regarded as a cause; origin or source: *Virtue is the parent of good deeds.* —*adj.* **1.** of or designating a predecessor or original: *a parent group.* **2.** of or designating a corporation in relation to a subsidiary: *a parent company.* [Latin *parēns* father or mother.]

par·ent·age (pār′ən tij) *n.* **1.** descent from parents; origin: *a man of humble parentage.* **2.** state of being a parent; parenthood.

pa·ren·tal (pə ren′əl) *adj.* of, relating to, or characteristic of a parent: *parental duties.* —**pa·ren′tal·ly,** *adv.*

pa·ren·the·sis (pə ren′thə sis) *pl.* **-ses** (-sēz′). *n.* **1.** word, phrase, or clause inserted as an explanation or qualification in a sentence that would be grammatically complete without it, usually set off by curved marks. **2.** either of the curved marks ( ) used to set off such material, or to enclose symbols or numbers to be considered as a single entity. **3.** remark or comment that digresses from a main theme. **4.** episode that is a break in continuity. [Medieval Latin *parenthesis* insertion, from Greek *parenthesis.*]

pa·ren·the·size (pə ren′thə sīz′) **-sized, -siz·ing.** *v.t.* **1.** to enclose within marks of parentheses. **2.** to insert or express as a parenthesis. **3.** to insert a parenthesis in.

par·en·thet·i·cal (par′ən thet′i kəl) *adj.* **1.** inserted as qualifying or explanatory material: *a parenthetical remark.* **2.** using or containing parentheses: *a parenthetical style.* Also, **par′en·thet′ic.** —**par′en·thet′i·cal·ly,** *adv.*

par·ent·hood (pār′ənt hood′) *n.* state of being a parent.

pa·re·sis (pə rē′sis, par′ə sis) *n.* **1.** partial paralysis in which movement, but not sensation, is impaired. **2.** general paresis. [Modern Latin *paresis,* from Greek *paresis* a letting go.]

pa·ret·ic (pə ret′ik) *adj.* relating to, affected with, or caused by a paresis. —*n.* one who is affected with a paresis.

par ex·cel·lence (pär′ ek′sə läns′) in the highest degree; beyond comparison: *a musician par excellence.* [French *par excellence* literally, by way of excellence, going back to Latin *per* through + *excellentia* excellence.]

par ex·em·ple (pär eg zän′plə) *French.* for example.

par·fait (pär fā′) *n.* **1.** dessert made of layers of ice cream, syrup, and sometimes fruit, usually served in a tall slender glass. **2.** dessert made of custard or whipped cream and syrup frozen together. [French *parfait* perfect, going back to Latin *perficere* to finish.]

par·he·lion (pär hēl′yən) *pl.* **-he·lia** (-hēl′yə). *n.* bright spot resembling the sun, seen on a solar halo. [Latin *parēlion,* from Greek *parēlion,* from *para* beside + *hēlios* sun.]

pa·ri·ah (pə rī′ə) *n.* **1.** one who is shunned or despised by others; outcast. **2.** *also,* **Pariah.** member of a low caste in India and Burma, traditionally considered untouchable by some Hindus. [Tamil *paraiyan* member of a low caste, from *parai* drum; with reference to the traditional task of drumbeating performed by this caste.]

Par·i·an (pār′ē ən) *adj.* **1.** of or relating to Paros or the white marble found there. **2.** pertaining to or designating a coarse, unglazed porcelain resembling the marble of Paros. —*n.* **1.** native or inhabitant of Paros. **2.** coarse, unglazed, ivory-colored porcelain resembling the marble of Paros, used esp. for making statuettes.

pa·ri·e·tal (pə rī′ət əl) *adj.* of or relating to the wall of any body cavity. —*n.* either of a pair of bones that form part of the sides and top of the skull, lying between the frontal and the occipital bones. [Late Latin *parietālis* relating to a wall, from Latin *paries* wall.]

Parietal · Frontal

Occipital

Parietal

par·i·mu·tu·el (par′i mū′chōō əl) *n.* **1.** system of betting in which the odds are automatically adjusted according to the betting and in which the winners share the total amount wagered minus a percentage for the operators of the contests and for the state. **2.** computer for recording and showing the odds of such bets. Also, **to′tal·i·za′tor.** [French *pari mutuel* literally, mutual bet, going back to Latin *pār* equal + *mūtuus* reciprocal.]

par·ing (pār′ing) *n.* **1.** that which has been pared off: *carrot parings.* **2.** act of one who pares.

pa·ri pas·su (par′ē pas′ōō) *Latin.* at the same rate; equally.

Par·is (par′is) *n.* capital and largest city of France, in the north-central part of the country, on the Seine. Pop. (1968), 2,590,771.

Par·is (par′is) *n. Greek Legend.* son of Priam, whose abduction of Helen brought on the Trojan War, in which he himself was killed.

Paris green, extremely poisonous, emerald-green copper compound containing arsenic, used as a pigment and in insecticides.

par·ish (par′ish) *n.* **1.** in the Anglican, Roman Catholic, and some other churches, a district having its own church and one or more resident clergymen. **2.** in Louisiana, a civil district corresponding to a county. **3.** in Great Britain, a civil district that is a subdivision of a county. **4.** people of a parish. [Old French *paroisse* ecclesiastical district, from Late Latin *parochia,* from Greek *paroikiā,* going back to *para* beside + *oikos* house.]

pa·rish·ion·er (pə rish′ə nər) *n.* member of a parish.

Pa·ri·sian (pə rē′zhən, -rizh′ən) *adj.* of, relating to, or characteristic of the city of Paris or its people. —*n.* native or inhabitant of Paris.

par·i·ty (par′ə tē) *n.* **1.** state or quality of being equal or equivalent, as in power, position, value, or degree: *The two countries reached parity in military strength.* **2.** equivalence in value between farmers' present purchasing power and their purchasing power at a given base period,

maintained by government price supports. **3.** equivalence in value of one kind of currency or security with respect to another currency or security. [Latin *paritās* equality.]

park (pärk) *n.* **1.** area of land set apart for the pleasure and use of the public, as a small area in a city with paths, benches, and playgrounds or a large expanse of scenic land preserved in its natural state. **2.** spacious grounds of a country estate, often having woods, lakes, and fields. **3.** stadium and surrounding facilities, used esp. for athletic contests. —*v.t.* **1.** to leave or situate (a vehicle) in a certain place where it may remain temporarily. **2.** *Informal.* to place, leave, or situate: *The guards parked themselves at the entrance to the hall.* —*v.i.* to leave or situate a vehicle temporarily. [Old French *parc* enclosure, from Medieval Latin *parricus;* of uncertain origin.]

par·ka (pär′kə) *n.* **1.** hooded fur outer garment worn by Eskimos. **2.** any similar hooded garment for outdoor wear.

parking lot, area set aside for cars to be parked.
parking meter, timer mounted on a pole, into which coins are inserted to pay for the use of a parking space by a motor vehicle for a limited period of time.

Parka (def. 2)

Par·kin·son's disease (pär′kin sənz) disease characterized by rhythmic tremor, stiffness of the muscles, and slowing of movement, caused by damage to certain brain cells. [From James *Parkinson*, 1755–1824, English physician who first described it.]

Park·man, Francis (pärk′mən) 1823–93, U.S. historian.

park·way (pärk′wā′) *n.* highway or wide thoroughfare divided by or bordered with landscaped trees, bushes, or grass. —**Syn.** see **road.**

par·lance (pär′ləns) *n.* manner of speech; type of talk: *medical parlance.* [Old French *parlance,* from *parler* to speak. See **PARLEY.**]

par·lay (pär′lā, -lē) *v.t.* **1.** to bet (the money from a first bet plus the winnings) on one or more succeeding races or contests. **2.** to exploit, utilize, or increase (an asset or talent) successfully: *He parlayed his small inheritance into a fortune.* —*n.* bet made by parlaying. [French *paroli* double stake, from dialectal Italian *paroli,* from *paro* equal, pair, from Latin *pār* equal.]

par·ley (pär′lē) *pl.* **-leys.** *n.* conference, esp. one between enemies on the terms of a truce or agreement. —*v.i.* **leyed, -ley·ing.** to hold a conference, esp. to discuss terms with an enemy. [Old French *parlee* conversation, from *parler* to speak, from Late Latin *parabolāre,* from Latin *parabola* comparison, allegory. See **PARABLE.**]

par·lia·ment (pär′lə mənt) *n.* **1. Parliament.** legislature of Great Britain, consisting of the House of Commons, the House of Lords, and the monarch. **2.** any legislature based on the British system, in which political power rests with the legislature and is not shared with a president or other authority. **3.** any formal assembly or conference dealing with governmental affairs. [Old French *parlement* a speaking, conference, from *parler* to speak. See **PARLEY.**]

par·lia·men·tar·i·an (pär′lə men târ′ē ən) *n.* **1.** one versed in parliamentary procedure or debate. **2. Parliamentarian.** one who supported the Long Parliament during the reign of Charles I in England.

par·lia·men·ta·ry (pär′lə men′tər ē, -ment′rē) *adj.* **1.** of, relating to, or characteristic of a parliament. **2.** according to the rules of a parliament or other deliberative body: *parliamentary procedure.* **3.** enacted or issued by a parliament: *a parliamentary act.* **4.** having or governed by a parliament: *a parliamentary democracy.*

par·lor (pär′lər) *also, British,* **par·lour.** *n.* **1.** room in a home in which visitors are received and entertained. **2.** small, semiprivate sitting room for relaxation or conversation in a hotel, club, or other public facility. **3.** business establishment, often having special equipment or decor to suggest the intimacy of a private sitting room: *a funeral parlor, ice cream parlor.* [Old French *parleor* reception room; literally, place for conversation, from *parler* to speak. See **PARLEY.**]

parlor car, railroad passenger car equipped with individual chairs and other equipment, affording more comfort than ordinary passenger cars.

par·lous (pär′ləs) *Archaic. adj.* perilous; dangerous. —*adv.* exceedingly; extremely. [Form of **PERILOUS.**] —**par′lous·ly,** *adv.*

Par·ma (pär′mə) *n.* **1.** city in north-central Italy. Pop. (1968), 169,-128. **2.** city in northeast Ohio. Pop. (1970), 100,216.

Par·men·i·des (pär men′ə dēz) *n.* Greek philosopher of the fifth century B.C.

Par·me·san cheese (pär′mə zän′, -zan′, -zən) *n.* pale-yellow, hard, dry Italian cheese made from skim milk, usually grated and used in soups, sauces, and other dishes. [French *parmesan,* from Italian *parmegiano* relating to Parma, from *Parma,* Italy, where it is made.]

Par·nas·sus (pär nas′əs) *n.* **1. Mount.** mountain in southern Greece, held to be sacred to Apollo and the Muses in Greek mythology. **2.** any center of poetic or literary activity. —**Par·nas′si·an,** *adj.*

Par·nell, Charles Stewart (pär nel′, pärn′əl) 1846–91, Irish political leader.

pa·ro·chi·al (pə rō′kē əl) *adj.* **1.** of, relating to, or supported by a parish. **2.** restricted to a narrow area or scope; narrow; provincial: *parochial ideas.* [Late Latin *parochiālis* relating to a parish, from *parochia* parish. See **PARISH.**] —**pa·ro′chi·al·ly,** *adv.*

pa·ro·chi·al·ism (pə rō′kē ə liz′əm) *n.* quality of being parochial in thinking; narrowness of viewpoint; provincialism.

parochial school, school maintained and controlled by a church or other religious organization.

par·o·dy (par′ə dē) *pl.* **-dies.** *n.* **1.** imitation of something serious, as a literary or artistic work, a style of composition, or a way of life, presented for comic effect or ridicule. **2.** poor or weak imitation: *The dress was a parody of the latest fashions.* —*v.t.* **-died, -dy·ing.** to make a parody of. [Greek *parōidiā* burlesque poem.] —**par′o·dist,** *n.* —**Syn.** *n.* **1.** see **caricature.**

pa·role (pə rōl′) *n.* **1.** *Law.* **a.** conditional release of a prisoner before the expiration of his full sentence. **b.** period of such conditional release. **2.** conditional freedom granted instead of imprisonment. **3.** word of honor, esp. the pledge of a prisoner of war to his captors to refrain from escape attempts. **4. on parole.** out of prison on the conditions of parole. —*v.t.* **-roled, -rol·ing.** to release (a prisoner) on the conditions of parole. [Old French *parole* word, promise, going back to Latin *parabola* comparison, allegory, proverb, from Greek *parabolē* comparison, proverb. Doublet of **PALAVER, PARABLE.**]

pa·ro·lee (pə rō′lē′, pə rō′lē′) *n.* one who is released from prison on parole.

par·o·quet (par′ə ket′) parakeet.

Par·os (par′os) *n.* Greek island in the Aegean Sea, one of the Cyclades.

pa·rot·id (pə rot′id) *adj.* **1.** of or designating one of the paired salivary glands situated below and in front of each ear. **2.** situated near the ear. —*n.* parotid gland. [Modern Latin *parotis,* from Latin *parōtis,* tumor near the ear, from Greek *parōtis.*]

par·ox·ysm (par′ək siz′əm) *n.* **1.** sudden outburst or fit, as of laughter or rage. **2.** sudden attack or intensification of a disease or a symptom, usually of a recurring nature: *He suffers paroxysms of malaria every few years.* [Medieval Latin *paroxysmus* irritation, from Greek *paroxysmos* irritation, fit (of a disease).] —**par′ox·ys′mal,** *adj.*

par·quet (pär kā′, -ket′) *n.* **1.** flooring made of parquetry. **2.** main floor of a theater, esp. the section from the orchestra pit to the parquet circle; orchestra. —*adj.* made of parquetry: *parquet floors.* —*v.t.* **-queted, -quet·ing.** to make or furnish with parquetry. [French *parquet* wooden floor; earlier, small enclosure, from Old French *parc* enclosure. See **PARK.**]

parquet circle, the part of the main floor of a theater at the rear of the parquet and under the balcony.

par·quet·ry (pär′kit rē) *pl.* **-ries.** *n.* inlaid mosaic of wood, usually in geometric patterns, used esp. for floors. [French *parqueterie* inlaid floor, from *parquet* wooden floor. See **PARQUET.**]

Parquetry

parr (pär) *pl.* **parrs** or **parr.** *n.* young salmon before it is mature enough to begin its migration downstream to the sea. [Of uncertain origin.]

par·ra·keet (par′ə ket′) parakeet.

par·ri·cide¹ (par′ə sīd′) *n.* murder of a parent or other close relative. [Latin *parricīdium.* See **-CIDE¹.**] —**par′ri·cid′al,** *adj.*

par·ri·cide² (par′ə sīd′) *n.* one who murders a parent or other close relative. [Latin *parricīda.* See **-CIDE².**]

par·rot (par′ət) *n.* any of numerous hook-billed birds, family Psittacidae, found throughout the Southern Hemisphere and in warmer parts of the Northern Hemisphere, having a large head and glossy, usually brightly colored plumage, capable of imitating speech and other sounds, and popular as a pet. Length: 3½–39 inches. **2.** one who repeats or imitates the words or actions of others without thinking. —*v.t.* to repeat or imitate without thinking. [Obsolete French *Perrot* man's proper name, diminutive of *Pierre* Peter, from Latin *Petrus,* from Greek *Petros.*]

Parrot

par·ry (par′ē) **-ried, -ry·ing.** *v.t., v.i.* **1.** to stop or deflect (the opponent's attack) or to parry, as with the side of one's own sword. **2.** to ward off or divert (any attack or threatened danger): *The speaker deftly parried the questions from the audience.* —*n. pl.* **-ries.** act or

at; āpe; cär; end; mē; it; īce; hot; ōld; fôrk; wood; fo͞ol; oil; out; up; ūse; turn; sing; thin; this; zh in treasure; ə in ago, taken, pencil, lemon, circus.

instance of parrying. [French *parez,* imperative of *parer* to defend, from Latin *parāre* to make ready.]

parse (pärs) **parsed, pars·ing.** *v.t.* **1.** to analyze (a sentence) grammatically, describing the parts of speech, their functions, and their relation to each other. **2.** to analyze (a word in a sentence) by stating its part of speech, its function, and its relation to the other words in the sentence. [Latin *pars (ōrātiōnis)* part (of speech).]

par·sec (pär′sek) *n.* unit of measure used in astronomy to express the distance between stars, equal to 19.2 trillion miles, or 3.26 light years. It corresponds to the distance at which an object has a parallax of one second of arc in one year. [PAR(ALLAX) + SEC(OND).]

Par·see (pär′sē) *also,* **Par·si.** *n.* member of a Zoroastrian sect located chiefly in India, descended from Persians who fled from Muslim persecution in the eighth century A.D. [Persian *Pārsī* Persian, from *Pārs* Persia.]

par·si·mo·ni·ous (pär′sə mō′nē əs) *adj.* extremely cautious with money; stingy. —**par′si·mo′ni·ous·ly,** *adv.* —**par′si·mo′ni·ous·ness,** *n.*

par·si·mo·ny (pär′sə mō′nē) *n.* extreme cautiousness with money; excessive frugality; stinginess. [Latin *parsimōnia.*]

pars·ley (pärs′lē) *pl.* **-leys.** *n.* low-branching plant, *Petroselinum crispum,* having finely divided, fragrant leaves used to flavor and garnish food. —*adj.* designating a large family of plants, Umbelliferae, grown throughout most parts of the world, bearing tiny flowers in round, mostly flat-topped clusters, and including vegetables, as celery, carrots, and parsnips, and many herbs, as caraway, dill, and parsley. [Old French *peresil* the plant parsley, going back to Latin *petroselīnum,* from Greek *petroselīnon.*]

pars·nip (pärs′nip) *n.* **1.** thick, white, edible root of a plant, *Pastinaca sativa,* of the parsley family, having a sweet flavor, cooked and eaten as a vegetable, and used in making wine and as feed for livestock. **2.** the plant itself, having a hollow grooved stem and clusters of greenish flowers. [Modification (influenced by Middle English *nepe* turnip) of Old French *pasnaie* the plant parsnip, from Latin *pastināca.*]

par·son (pär′sən) *n.* **1.** clergyman in charge of a parish; pastor; rector. **2.** any clergyman, esp. a Protestant minister. [Medieval Latin *persona* parish priest, from Latin *persōna* mask, character, personage, probably from Etruscan *phersu* mask. Doublet of PERSON.]

par·son·age (pär′sə nij) *n.* residence of a parson or clergyman, usually provided by the church.

part (pärt) *n.* **1.** portion constituting a whole or into which a whole can be divided; something less than the whole: *He ate part of his dinner. The second part of his argument was very convincing.* **2.** *Mathematics.* one of several equal portions or quantities into which a whole may be divided; aliquot: *An inch is a twelfth part of a foot.* **3.** component of a machine or other system, esp. one that can be separated: *automobile parts.* **4.** portion of assigned or assumed responsibility; share: *I'll do my part to make it work.* **5.** participation; interest; concern: *I had no part in it.* **6.** one of the sides in a contest, dispute, or question. **7.** line made by separating one's hair: *She always wears a center part.* **8.** *usually,* **parts.** region; area; place: *to travel to parts unknown.* **9.** *usually,* **parts.** ability; accomplishments; talent: *a man of many parts.* **10.a.** role in a film, play, opera, or other dramatic presentation. **b.** lines or actions assigned to a character in a dramatic presentation. **11.** *Music.* **a.** one of the voices or instruments in concerted music. **b.** melody or melodic line for such a voice or instrument. **c.** written or printed musical score for such a voice or instrument.

for one's part. as far as one is concerned.

for the most part. to the greatest extent; generally.

in good part. in a friendly or good-natured way.

in part. to some extent; partly.

part and parcel. essential part: *That sentence is the part and parcel of the essay.*

to take part. to have a share; join (usually with *in*): *He refused to take part in the disciplinary procedures.*

to take someone's part. to support someone in an argument or dispute. —*v.t.* **1.** to separate by coming between; draw or hold apart: *The referee parted the fighters.* **2.** to comb (the hair) so as to make a part. **3.** to divide into two or more portions or sections. **4. to part company.** to dissolve or end a relationship. —*v.i.* **1.** to become separated or divided into two or more pieces: *The shirt parted at the seams.* **2.** to go in different directions; go apart from one another: *They parted at the corner. The paths parted at the river.* **3.** to depart; leave. **4. to part from.** to separate from; go away from; leave. **5. to part with.** to give up; surrender: *to part with one's money.* —*adv.* in part; partly. —*adj.* not full or complete; partial. [Latin *part-,* stem of *pars* portion, share.]

Syn. 1. Part, portion, piece mean something less than a whole. **Part** is the most general term and designates any of the divisions which, when assembled, compose a whole: *This is the best part of the story.* **Portion** is usually applied to a well-defined part of a whole considered primarily as the measure of an allotment or share: *The millionaire's widow received*

the major portion of the estate. **Piece** implies a distinct, often detached, unit formed by or as if by cutting and dividing a mass: *Give him two pieces of cake.*

part. **1.** participle. **2.** particular.

par·take (pär tāk′) **-took** or **-tak·en, -tak·ing.** *v.i.* **1.** to take part; participate (with *in*): *She partook in the festivities.* **2.** to take or have a portion: *The meal was ready, but he refused to partake.* **3. to partake of. a.** to take or have a portion of: *to partake of one's generosity.* **b.** to have the character or quality of; resemble: *His wild acts partake of madness.* —**par·tak′er,** *n.*

par·terre (pär târ′) *n.* **1.** section of a theater under the balcony and behind the parquet. **2.** flower garden having the beds separated by paths and arranged in patterns. [French *parterre,* from *par terre* along the ground, going back to Latin *per* through + *terra* earth.]

par·the·no·gen·e·sis (pär′thə nō jen′ə sis) *n.* reproduction in which a new organism develops from an egg cell without fertilization. [Greek *parthenos* virgin + GENESIS.]

Parthenon

Par·the·non (pär′thə-non′) *n.* temple of Athena on the Acropolis in Athens, built in the fifth century B.C. It is considered the finest existing example of Greek Doric architecture. [Latin *Parthenon,* from Greek *Parthenōn,* from *parthenos* virgin (because Athena was a virgin).]

Par·thi·a (pär′thē ə) *n.* ancient country in Asia southeast of the Caspian Sea, now a part of Iran. —**Par′thi·an,** *n., adj.*

Parthian shot, remark or attack made in parting or fleeing. [From the custom of the Parthian cavalry of shooting arrows as it was fleeing.]

par·tial (pär′shəl) *adj.* **1.** not complete or total; of or involving a part only: *a partial recovery.* **2.** favoring one side, person, or group more than another; prejudiced; biased. **3. partial to.** having a strong liking for; fond of: *Our whole family is partial to sweets.* [Middle French *partial* biased, incomplete, from Late Latin *partiālis* relating to a part, incomplete, from Latin *pars* share, portion.] —**par′tial·ly,** *adv.*

par·ti·al·i·ty (pär′shē al′ə tē, pär shal′-) *pl.* **-ties.** *n.* **1.** quality or state of favoring one side, person, or group more than another; bias; prejudice. **2.** strong liking or fondness.

Syn. 1. Partiality, prejudice, bias mean a mental attitude that interferes with fair judgment. **Partiality** suggests an unfair favoritism toward a particular person or thing: *The officer showed partiality in promoting his old friend to the post.* **Prejudice** suggests a preconceived and unreasonable attitude often characterized by suspicion against a person or thing: *The family revealed their prejudice when they refused to associate with their new neighbor.* **Bias** suggests distorted judgment owing to the influence of prejudice or partiality: *Bias in the recruitment of employees is illegal.*

par·tic·i·pant (pär tis′ə pənt) *n.* one who participates. —*adj.* taking part; participating.

par·tic·i·pate (pär tis′ə pāt′) **-pat·ed, -pat·ing.** *v.i.* to take part or have a share with others, as in an activity or quality: *to participate in sports.* [Latin *participātus,* past participle of *participāre* to take part in, going back to *pars* share + *capere* to take.] —**par·tic′i·pa′tor,** *n.* —**Syn. see share[1].**

par·tic·i·pa·tion (pär tis′ə pā′shən) *n.* act or condition of taking part or sharing.

par·ti·cip·i·al (pär′tə sip′ē əl) *adj.* of, based on, or used as a participle. —**par′ti·cip′i·al·ly,** *adv.*

par·ti·ci·ple (pär′tə sip′əl) *n.* verb form used as an adjective and possessing certain qualities of both verbs and adjectives. Participles are like verbs in that they may take an object *(leaving his books behind him),* they may be modified by adverbs *(having quickly used up his supplies),* and that they are formed in tenses. The present participle ends in *-ing (speaking),* the past participle in *-ed, -en,* or other forms *(spoken),* and the perfect participle is formed by adding *having* before the past participle *(having spoken).* Participles may also function as pure adjectives *(a broken dish).* [Old French *participle,* form of *participe,* from Latin *participium* a sharing, participle (from its sharing of the uses of a noun).]

par·ti·cle (pär′ti kəl) *n.* **1.** very small bit or minute amount; trace; speck: *a particle of soot, a particle of truth.* **2.** subatomic particle. **3.a.** short, indeclinable part of speech, as a preposition, conjunction, or article. **b.** prefix or suffix. [Latin *particula* small part, diminutive of *pars* share, portion.] —**Syn. 1.** see bit[2].

particle accelerator, accelerator (def. 2).

par·ti-col·ored (pär′ti kul′ərd) *also,* **par·ty-col·ored.** *adj.* **1.** having different colors in different parts. **2.** characterized by variation or diver-

sity: *parti-colored fancies.* [Old French *parti* divided, past participle of *partir* to divide (from Latin *partīre*) + COLORED. See COLOR.]

par·tic·u·lar (pər tik′yə lər) *adj.* **1.** distinct or separate from others; individual: *This particular suitcase is too small.* **2.** belonging to or characteristic of a single specified person or thing: *His particular strength is in science.* **3.** special in some way; exceptional; noteworthy: *a news item of particular interest.* **4.** attentive to details; careful or exacting; fastidious: *to be particular about one's clothes.* **5.** precise or detailed, as a description. **6.** *Logic.* of or relating to a proposition which includes or treats its predicate in part or with qualification. *Some horses are ponies* is a particular proposition. Opposed to **universal.** —*n.* **1.** single and distinct instance or fact; individual case: *to generalize from particulars, to go into particulars to prove a point.* **2.** specific item of information; detail: *a paper that is faulty in every particular.* **3. in particular.** specifically; especially. [Old French *particuler* characteristic, special, from Late Latin *particulāris* relating to a small part, partial, from Latin *particula* small part. See PARTICLE.]

Syn. 1. Particular, individual, specific mean relating or belonging to one thing or class distinct or separate from all others. **Particular** is usually applied to one definite thing or quality when considered apart from all others of the same kind: *This particular hobby has always fascinated me.* **Individual** usually refers to a single, separate entity exhibiting certain attributes peculiar to itself: *Each individual member of the club must contribute his share.* **Specific** suggests an explicit restriction to a special and well-defined category or individual: *This sum was allotted in the budget for the specific purpose of providing housing for the poor.*

par·tic·u·lar·i·ty (pər tik′yə lar′ə tē) *pl.*, **-ties.** *n.* **1.** quality or condition of being distinct from others; individuality. **2.** attentiveness to details; carefulness; fastidiousness. **3.** precision or exactitude of detail, as in description. **4.** distinctive, individual quality or trait. **5.** individual item or detail; particular.

par·tic·u·lar·ize (pər tik′yə lə rīz′) -ized, -iz·ing. *v.t.* **1.** to state in detail; treat individually; specify. —*v.i.* to give particulars; go into detail. —**par·tic′u·lar·i·za′tion,** *n.*

par·tic·u·lar·ly (pər tik′yə lər lē) *adv.* **1.** to an unusual degree; especially: *a particularly hot day. He is particularly suited for this job.* **2.** in a precise manner; item by item; in detail: *to discuss issues particularly.* —**Syn. 1.** see **especially.**

part·ing (pär′ting) *n.* **1.** departure or leave-taking. **2.** act of separating or state of being separated: *the parting of the Red Sea.* **3.** line, point, or place of division or separation: *the parting of the ways.* **4.** death. —*adj.* **1.** given, spoken, or performed at parting: *a parting warning.* **2.** leaving; departing: *The parting train disappeared down the track.* **3.** serving to separate or divide: *a parting layer of rock.*

par·ti·san (pär′tə zən) *also,* **par·ti·zan.** *n.* **1.** one who strongly supports a person, idea; cause, or side, esp. one who is an overly zealous adherent. **2.** member of a body of irregular soldiers usually engaged in resistance work within enemy lines; guerrilla. —*adj.* **1.** of, relating to, or characteristic of a partisan or partisans: *to take a partisan stand on an issue, an attack of partisan troops.* **2.** composed of, proposed by, or controlled by one party, faction, or group: *partisan politics.* [Middle French *partisan* supporter of a side, from Italian *partigiano* protector, partner, from *parte* part, faction, from Latin *pars* portion.] —**par′ti·san·ship′,** *n.*

par·ti·tion (pär tish′ən) *n.* **1.** a dividing or being divided into shares or distinct parts; division and distribution of portions: *the partition of territory between rival states.* **2.** section or part into which a thing is divided. **3.** that which divides, as an interior wall separating parts of a room. —*v.t.* **1.** to divide into shares or distinct parts: *to partition land for sale, to partition office space into small cubicles.* **2.** to separate by a partition (with *off*): *to partition off a space for storage.* [Latin *partītiō* division.]

par·ti·tive (pär′tə tiv) *Grammar. n.* word that expresses part of a collective whole. —*adj.* denoting or used as part of a whole. —**par′-ti·tive·ly,** *adv.*

part·ly (pärt′lē) *adv.* in some degree; not wholly or completely.

part·ner (pärt′nər) *n.* **1.** one who joins or associates with another or others in some action or enterprise; sharer: *partners in crime.* **2.** member of a business partnership. **3.** player on the same side in a game, usually when there are only two players on a side, as in bridge or tennis. **4.** either of two persons dancing together. **5.** wife or husband. **6.** one of the timbers used to strengthen and support a ship's deck at the place where a mast, capstan, pump, or other structure passes through the deck. —*v.t.* **1.** to make a partner; join or associate: *Jim and Sue were partnered for the dance.* **2.** to be or act as the partner of: *Bob partnered his father well at the tournament.* [Modification (influenced by *part*) of earlier *parcener,* from Old French *parçoner* one who shares, from Medieval Latin *partionarius* one who has a share, going back to Latin *partītiō* sharing, division.]

part·ner·ship (pärt′nər ship′) *n.* **1.** state of being a partner; associa-

tion. **2.a.** form of business organization in which two or more persons are associated in carrying on commercial or professional activities, usually sharing the profits and losses in specified proportions. **b.** contract creating such an association. **c.** persons so associated.

part of speech, one of the major classes into which words of a language can be divided. The traditional parts of speech for English are noun, pronoun, adjective, verb, adverb, preposition, conjunction, and interjection.

par·took (pär took′) past tense of **par·take.**

par·tridge (pär′trij) *pl.,* **-tridg·es** or **-tridge.** *n.* **1.** any of several plump-bodied game birds, family Phasianidae, native to temperate regions of Europe, Asia, and Africa, having plumage patterned with gray, brown, and white markings. Length: 12–14 inches. **2.** any of various similar or related birds, esp. the ruffed grouse and the bobwhite. [Old French *perdris* the game bird, going back to Latin *perdīx,* from Greek *perdīx.*]

Partridge

par·tridge·ber·ry (pär′trij ber′ē) *pl.,* **-ries.** *n.* **1.** trailing evergreen plant, *Mitchella repens,* found in North America, having round, dark-green leaves, white flowers, and bright red berries. **2.** the edible berry itself.

part song, song having two or more voice parts, esp. one without an accompaniment.

part-time (pärt′tīm′) *adj.* for or during part of the normal time: *a part-time job.* —*adv.* on a part-time basis: *to work part-time.*

par·tu·ri·ent (pär toor′ē ənt, -tyoor′-) *adj.* **1.** giving birth or about to give birth to young. **2.** of or relating to parturition.

par·tu·ri·tion (pär′tə rish′ən, pär′chə-) *n.* act of giving birth; childbirth. [Late Latin *parturītiō,* from Latin *parturīre* to be in labor.]

par·ty (pär′tē) *pl.,* **-ties.** *n.* **1.** social gathering or entertainment: *a cocktail party, a garden party.* **2.** group of people gathered together for a specific purpose or engaged in a common activity: *a search party.* **3.** group of people organized to gain control of or influence the government, esp. through the election of its candidates. **4.** one who takes part in or is involved with an action or plan: *He refused to be a party to such underhanded schemes.* **5.** person or organization directly participating in a lawsuit, contract dispute, or other legal matter. **6.** person: *Certain unnamed parties have informed us of your plan.* —*adj.* **1.** of, for, or relating to a social party: *party hats.* **2.** of, relating to, or characteristic of a political party: *party politics.* [Old French *partie* side, contract, share, from *partir* to divide, from Latin *partīre.*] —**Syn. n. 2.** see **company.**

par·ty-col·ored (pär′tē kul′ərd) parti-colored.

party line 1. single telephone circuit with two or more subscribers on it, arranged so that only one call at a time can be made or received. **2.** official views and policies of a political party, esp. the Communist Party.

party wall, common wall between adjoining properties or structures, in which each owner has a partial right of use.

par value, value printed on the face of a stock, bond, or other financial instrument; nominal or face value.

par·ve·nu (pär′və nōō′, -nū′) *n.* one who has recently or suddenly attained wealth or importance and is not yet fit for his new position; upstart. [French *parvenu,* from *parvenir* to arrive, from Latin *perve-nīre.*]

pas (pä) *pl.,* **pas.** *n.* **1.** dance step or series of steps. **2.** dance. **3.** right of precedence. [French *pas,* from Latin *passus* step.]

Pas·a·de·na (pas′ə dē′nə) *n.* **1.** city in southern California, near Los Angeles. Pop. (1970), 113,327. **2.** city in southeastern Texas, an industrial suburb of adjacent Houston. Pop. (1970), 89,277.

Pas·cal, Blaise (pas kal′, pas′kəl; blez) 1623–62, French philosopher, mathematician, physicist, and inventor.

pas·chal (pas′kəl) *adj.* **1.** of or relating to the Passover. **2.** of or relating to Easter. [Old French *pascal,* from Late Latin *paschālis,* from Latin *pascha* Passover, Easter, from Greek *paschā* Passover, going back to Hebrew *pesakh.*]

paschal lamb 1. in ancient times, the lamb eaten at the Passover. **2. Paschal Lamb. a.** Jesus Christ. **b.** Agnus Dei *(def. 3).*

pa·sha (pə shä′, pash′ə, pä′shə) *also,* **pa·cha.** *n.* title formerly placed after the name of high-ranking Turkish civil or military officials. Also, **ba·shaw′.** [Turkish *pasa.*]

Push·to (push′tō) *also,* **Push·tu.** *n.* official language of Afghanistan. Also, **Af′ghan.**

Pa·siph·a·ë (pə sif′ə ē′) *n. Greek Mythology.* wife of Minos and mother of the Minotaur by a white bull.

pasque·flow·er (pask′flou′ər) *n.* either of two early-blooming plants, the **American pasqueflower,** *Anemone patens,* and the **European**

at; āpe; cär; end; mē; it; īce; hot; ōld; fôrk; wood; fōōl; oil; out; up; ūse; turn; sing; thin; this; zh in treasure; ə in ago, taken, pencil, lemon, circus.

pasqueflower, *A. pulsatilla*, that bear purple or reddish bell-shaped flowers and fan-shaped leaves. [Modification (influenced by Middle French *Pasque* Easter, from Latin *pascha* Easter, Passover) of French *passe-fleur* an anemone, from *passer* to move on, surpass + *fleur* flower (from Old French *flo(u)r*); referring to its blooming around Easter. See PASS, FLOWER, PASCHAL.]

pas·quin·ade (pas'kwə nād') *n.* satire or lampoon posted in a public place. —*v.t.*, **-ad·ed, -ad·ing.** to attack or satirize in a pasquinade; lampoon. [French *pasquinade* a lampoon, from Italian *pasquinata*, from *Pasquino* a statue in Rome to which lampoons were once attached.]

pass (pas) *v.i.* **1.** to go or move; proceed: *The waitress passed from table to table. Several thoughts passed through my mind.* **2.** to go or move by: *A flock of birds passed overhead.* **3.** to make or force one's way with difficulty: *The politician passed wearily through the throng of reporters.* **4.** to extend; run; lead: *The new subway passes under the park.* **5.** to elapse; go by (often with *away*): *The hours passed slowly.* **6.** to get away; slip by: *You let a good opportunity pass.* **7.** to come to an end; cease (often with *away*): *As time went on, his sorrow passed.* **8.** to die (often with *on* or *away*). **9.** to undergo transition, as from one state or form to another: *A thing of beauty is a joy forever; . . . it will never pass into nothingness* (Keats, 1818). **10.** to get through or complete an examination, trial, or course of study successfully or satisfactorily: *to pass by five points.* **11.** to be accepted or taken (with *for* or *as*): *She was seventeen years old but could pass for twenty-one.* **12.** to be approved or ratified: *The bill passed easily in the Senate.* **13.** to go without censure, challenge, or notice: *It was a thoughtless remark to make, but we let it pass.* **14.** to be exchanged or transacted, as between two persons: *Angry words passed between them.* **15.** to take place; happen; occur: *We had no idea of what had passed at the meeting.* **16.** to go or be handed about; circulate: *The story passed from person to person.* **17.** to be transferred to another, as by a will. **18.a.** to pronounce or express a judgment, opinion, or sentence (with *on* or *upon*): *The judge could not pass on the matter without more facts.* **b.** to sit in inquest or judgment (with *on* or *upon*): *A jury will be selected to pass upon this question.* **19.** *Sports.* to transfer the ball or puck to a teammate. **20.** *Card Games.* to decline to bid. **21. to come to pass.** to happen; come about. **22. to pass out.** to lose consciousness; faint. —*v.t.* **1.** to go or move by (something): *David passes my house on the way to school.* **2.a.** to get through or complete (an examination, trial, or course of study) successfully or satisfactorily: *to pass a physical, to pass a spelling test.* **b.** to cause or allow to get through or complete successfully or satisfactorily: *The teacher passed all the students in English.* **3.** to transfer, hand about or over, or spread (something) from one person or place to another: *Please pass the salt. Did you pass the word?* **4.** to give out, issue, or distribute (often with *out* or *around*): *to pass bad checks, to pass leaflets to go.* **5.** to cause or allow (something) to move or go in a specified way: *to pass thread through the eye of a needle.* **6.** to cause to go or march by: *to pass soldiers in review.* **7.** to go beyond; exceed; surpass: *This year's attendance may pass that of last year.* **8.** to go through, across, or over: *harsh language . . . pass'd my lips* (Fletcher, c.1622). **9.** to cause or allow to elapse; spend (often with *away*): *to pass the summer traveling.* **10.** to undergo; experience; endure: *Natalie passed a sleepless night in the old house.* **11.** to disregard or leave unnoticed or unmentioned; overlook (often with *over, by,* or *up*): *to pass over a chapter in a book.* **12.a.** to approve or ratify: *Congress passed the resolution.* **b.** to be approved or ratified by: *The bill passed the Senate by three votes.* **13.** to pronounce or express: *to pass judgment on someone. The judge passed sentence.* **14.** to discharge (waste) from the body; excrete. **15.** to omit payment of (a dividend). **16.** *Sports.* to transfer (the ball or puck) to a teammate. **17.** *Baseball.* to walk (a batter) intentionally. **18. to bring to pass.** to cause to happen; bring about. **19. to pass off.** to cause to be accepted, regarded, or received, esp. by deception: *The man tried to pass the fur off as mink.* **20. to pass up.** to reject or allow to get away: *to pass up a chance to be famous.* —*n.* **1.a.** permit or written authorization to come, go, or move about freely: *No one was allowed to enter the government building without showing a pass.* **b.** ticket, usually free, entitling the holder to admission or transportation: *two free passes to a baseball game. Bus passes go on sale Thursday.* **c.** written authorization to be absent from military duty, esp. for a specified period of time. **2.** way or opening through which one can go or move, esp. a narrow gap in or passage through a mountain range or ridge. **3.** condition or situation; state of affairs: *Events had been brought to a critical pass.* **4.** sweep or dive made by an aircraft at a particular target. **5.** thrusting or lunging movement, as in fencing: *The knight drew his sword and made a pass at the man.* **6.** movement of the hand or hands over or along anything, esp. such a motion as used in magic or hypnotism. **7.** act of passing; passage. **8.** *Sports.* transfer of the ball or puck to a teammate. **9.** *Baseball.* walk, esp. an intentional walk. **10.** *Card Games.* act of declining to bid. **11.** *Informal.* flirtatious or sexually inviting action, overture, or gesture: *Several men made*

passes at the attractive woman. [Old French *passer* to go across, go beyond, spend (time), ratify, going back to Latin *passus* step.]

pass. 1. passive. **2.** passenger. **3.** passage.

pass·a·ble (pas'ə bəl) *adj.* **1.** fairly good; adequate; acceptable: *She speaks passable French.* **2.** capable of being traveled through, across, or over: *The dense jungle was barely passable.* **3.** acceptable as currency. [Old French *passable* capable of being traversed, from *passer* to move on, walk, cross. See PASS.]

pass·a·bly (pas'ə blē) *adv.* fairly well; adequately.

pas·sa·ca·glia (pä'sə käl'yə) *n.* musical composition having one theme, usually in the bass, that is repeated over and over. [Italian *passacaglia*, through Spanish, going back to Latin *passus* step + *callis* street; because frequently played in the street.]

pas·sage (pas'ij) *n.* **1.a.** portion, usually short, of a written work or speech: *The author read a passage from his latest novel.* **b.** *Music.* phrase or other short section of a composition. **2.** route, path, or other way through or by which someone or something may pass, go, or move: *air passages, a mountain passage.* **3.** passageway in a building; corridor. **4.** right, permission, or liberty to pass, go, or travel: *The king granted them passage through his realm.* **5.** journey, esp. by sea or air: *Her passage across the Pacific was uneventful.* **6.** privilege of conveyance as a passenger, esp. on a ship; passenger accommodations: *to book passage on an ocean liner.* **7.** course, progress, or advance: *the passage of time.* **8.** act or process of passing, moving, or changing, as from one place or state to another. **9.** approval or enactment by a legislative body: *Congressional passage of such a resolution seemed unlikely.* **10.** *Archaic.* exchange between persons, as of blows or words. [Old French *passage* a going across, portion of a speech or book, from *passer* to move on, walk, cross. See PASS.]

Syn. 2. see route. **3. Passage, corridor, aisle** mean a way connecting rooms or sections of a building. **Passage** is a narrow hallway or gallery for passing through or for gaining access to different rooms or parts of a building: *Don't get lost in the long passages of the building.* **Corridor** is a passageway leading from one part of a building to another and into which rooms or compartments open: *The sleeping car had a long corridor.* **Aisle** is a long passageway flanked by a row of seats, as in an auditorium: *The ushers were escorting the wedding guests up the aisle of the church.*

pas·sage·way (pas'ij wā') *n.* way through or by which someone or something can pass, go, or move, as a corridor or alley; passage.

Pas·sa·ic (pə sā'ik) *n.* city in northeastern New Jersey. Pop. (1970), 55,124.

pas·sant (pas'ənt) *adj. Heraldry.* (of a beast) walking and looking to the right side with the right forepaw raised. [Old French *passant*, present participle of *passer* to move on, walk. See PASS.]

pass·book (pas'book') *n.* bankbook.

pas·sé (pa sā') *adj.* no longer in style; out-of-date. [French *passé*, past participle of *passer* to go, fade, expire. See PASS.]

passed ball *Baseball.* pitch that gets away from the catcher even though it was within his reach, allowing one or more base runners to advance.

pas·sel (pas'əl) *n. Informal.* large number; group: *a passel of troubles.* [Modification of PARCEL.]

passe·men·terie (pas men'trē) *n.* heavy ornamental trimming, as of beads, braid, or cord.

pas·sen·ger (pas'ən jər) *n.* one who travels in an automobile, train, airplane, or other conveyance. [Old French *passager* passenger on a ship, passing, from *passage* a going across. See PASSAGE.]

passenger pigeon, extinct wild pigeon, *Ectopistes migratorius*, having chiefly blue-gray plumage and a wine-colored breast.

passe-par·tout (pas'pär tōō') *n.* **1.** picture frame usually consisting of a pasteboard back and a piece of glass, often with a plain or ornamented mat, held together by strips of gummed paper attached to the backing. **2.** gummed paper used for this purpose. **3.** mat used for mounting a picture. **4.** something that enables one to pass, enter, or go everywhere, esp. a master key. [French *passe-partout* a frame; literally, pass everywhere, from *passer* to go, move on + *partout* everywhere (going back to Latin *per* through + *tōtus* all). See PASS.]

Passenger pigeon

pass·er·by (pas'ər bī') *pl.* **pass·ers·by.** *also,* **pass·er·by.** *n.* one who passes or goes by.

pas·ser·ine (pas'ər in, -ə rīn') *adj.* of, belonging to, or relating to an order of perching birds, Passeriformes, including all songbirds and more than half of all living birds. —*n.* passerine bird. [Latin *passerīnus* relating to the sparrow, from *passer* sparrow.]

pas·sim (pas'im) *adv. Latin.* here and there; in different places. ▲ used

as a reference note to indicate the occurrence of something, as a phrase, in various places throughout a book.

pass·ing (pas'ing) *adj.* **1.** going or moving by: *Linda grew wiser with the passing years.* **2.** of brief duration; transitory: *a passing fancy.* **3.** cursory; casual: *a passing glance.* **4.** allowing one to pass an examination, trial, or course of study; satisfactory: *to receive a passing grade in English.* —*n.* **1.** act of one who or that which passes. **2.** means or place of passing or crossing; way through, across, or over. **3.** death; dying. **4. in passing,** in the course of proceeding; incidentally. —*adv. Archaic.* exceedingly; very: *strange, passing strange indeed* (Disraeli, 1837).

pas·sion (pash'ən) *n.* **1.** strong or intense feeling, as love, hate, or anger, esp. when overwhelming or violent. **2.** strong or ardent liking, desire, or enthusiasm: *a passion for ice cream.* **3.** object of strong feeling, liking, desire, or enthusiasm: *Painting was the artist's only passion.* **4.** amorous feeling; love. **5.** sexual desire. **6.** outburst or fit of strong or violent feeling, esp. of rage: *to fly into a passion.* **7.** *also,* **Passion. a.** sufferings of Jesus Christ following the Last Supper and ending with the Crucifixion. **b.** chapters in the Gospels that relate these sufferings. [Old French *passion* suffering, from Late Latin *passiō* suffering, affection, from Latin *patī* to suffer.]
Syn. 1. Passion, fervor, ardor mean an intense and vehement emotion. **Passion** suggests an overpowering or violent emotion and may be applied indiscriminately to an excess of any feeling, as love, anger, grief, hate, or hope: *Give me the man that is not passion's slave* (Shakespeare, *Hamlet*). **Fervor** is evocative of a steady passion that is sustained over a long period: *His spiritual fervor gained him many disciples.* **Ardor** is commonly interchangeable with *fervor* but is more evocative of an emotion that is wavering and restless: *The ardor of his patriotism moved his listeners to tears.* See also **feeling.**

pas·sion·ate (pash'ə nit) *adj.* **1.** characterized by or tending to display strong or intense feeling; ardent: *a passionate defender of religious freedom.* **2.** expressing, revealing, or arising from such feeling: *a passionate plea for his client's life.* **3.** (of an emotion) overwhelming; vehement. **4.** easily angered; hot-tempered. [Medieval Latin *passionatus* enraged, having strong feelings, from Late Latin *passiō* suffering, affection. See PASSION.] —**pas'sion·ate·ly,** *adv.*

pas·sion·flow·er (pash'ən flou'ər) *n.* **1.** large showy flower of any of a group of climbing vines, genus *Passiflora,* esp. the **wild passionflower,** *P. incarnata,* having white petals and a pinkish crown. **2.** vine that bears this flower. [Because parts of the flower supposedly resemble the instruments of the crucifixion of Christ.]

Passionflower

passion fruit, edible fruit of the passionflower.

pas·sion·less (pash'ən lis) *adj.* without feeling; unemotional.
Passion play *also,* **passion play.** dramatic representation of the Passion, death, and Resurrection of Jesus Christ.
Passion Sunday, second Sunday before Easter and fifth Sunday in Lent.
Passion Week, fifth week in Lent, beginning with Passion Sunday.

pas·sive (pas'iv) *adj.* **1.** acted upon or tending to be acted upon without responding or reacting: *a meek and passive person who could be talked into anything.* **2.** submitting without opposition or resistance; submissive: *passive endurance of adversity.* **3.** not taking part, acting, or operating: *a passive observer.* **4.** relating to or designating the voice of a verb whose subject is represented as receiving the action expressed by the verb. In the sentence *The boy was bitten by a dog, was bitten* is in the passive voice. Opposed to **active.** —*n.* **1.** the passive voice. **2.** verb form or construction in this voice. [Latin *passivus* capable of suffering.] —**pas'sive·ly,** *adv.* —**pas'sive·ness, pas·siv'i·ty,** *n.*
passive resistance, method of resisting authority or protesting against some law or act by nonviolent means, as by refusing to comply or by staging a sit-in.
pass·key (pas'kē') *n.* **1.** master key. **2.** any of various other keys, as a skeleton key or latchkey.
Pass·o·ver (pas'ō'vər) *n.* annual Jewish feast commemorating the Exodus of the Jews from Egypt. [From the phrase PASS OVER; referring to the episode in the Bible in which God *passed over* the houses of the Jews in Egypt when he killed the first-born children of the Egyptians.]
pass·port (pas'pôrt') *n.* **1.** document issued by the government of a citizen's own country, certifying his citizenship and identity and granting him permission to travel abroad. **2.** that which enables one to gain acceptance or admission or achieve an end: *A clever mind was his passport to success.* [French *passeport* from the document, from *passer* to move on, go + *port* harbor. See PASS, PORT¹.]
pass·word (pas'wurd') *n.* secret word or phrase that identifies the speaker or allows him to pass a guard.
past (past) *adj.* **1.** gone by; ended; over: *The days of his youth are past.*

2. having occurred or existed in or belonging to time gone by: *to learn from past mistakes.* **3.** gone by immediately before the present time; just passed: *She's been on the phone for the past hour.* **4.** having served formerly: *a past mayor.* **5.** *Grammar.* indicating a state or action in time gone by. —*n.* **1.** time that has gone by: *Cavemen lived in the remote past.* **2.** that which was done or has happened in the past. **3.** past life, career, history, or reputation, esp. if concealed, questionable, or regarded as disreputable. **4.** *Grammar.* past tense or a verb in the past tense. —*prep.* **1.** beyond in place; farther than: *John threw the ball past the catcher.* **2.** beyond in time; after: *It's past your bedtime.* **3.** beyond the power, scope, limits, or reach of: *His poetry is past comprehension.* **4.** beyond in amount, number, or degree: *Donna looks young but is past forty.* —*adv.* so as to pass or go by: *We watched the old wagon rumble past.* [Middle English *past,* past participle of *passen* to pass. See PASS.]
pas·ta (päs'tə) *n.* **1.** paste or dough made with semolina and flour, used to make macaroni, ravioli, and similar food products. **2.** dish or food product consisting of cooked pasta. [Italian *pasta,* from Late Latin *pasta* dough. See PASTE.]
paste (pāst) *n.* **1.** mixture, as of flour and water, used as an adhesive. **2.** any similar soft, smooth, often moist substance. **3.** soft, creamy food preparation: *anchovy paste.* **4.** dough, esp. that made with butter or lard and used for pastry. **5.a.** hard glasslike material used to make artificial or imitation gems. **b.** gem made of this material. **6.** moistened clay mixture used in making pottery and porcelain. —*v.t.,* **past·ed, past·ing. 1.** to fasten with or as with paste. **2.** to cover or fill with something that is pasted on: *The wall was pasted with posters.* **3.** *Slang.* to strike with a hard blow; punch. [Old French *paste* dough, from Late Latin *pasta,* from Greek *pasta* barley porridge.]
paste·board (pāst'bôrd') *n.* **1.** stiff material made of sheets of paper pasted together or of paper pulp pressed together. **2.** *Informal.* any of various cards made of such material, as a playing card, calling card, or ticket. —*adj.* **1.** made of pasteboard. **2.** unsubstantial; flimsy; sham.
pas·tel (pas tel', pas'tel) *n.* **1.** crayon consisting of dried paste made by mixing ground pigment with resin, gum, or a similar binding material. **2.** picture drawn with such crayons. **3.** art or process of drawing with such crayons. **4.** any pale, soft shade of color. —*adj.* **1.** of, relating to, or drawn with pastels. **2.** (of a color) having a pale, soft shade. [French *pastel* crayon, from Italian *pastello,* from Late Latin *pastellus* woad, diminutive of *pasta* dough; referring to the paste for pigment made from woad. See PASTE.]
pas·tern (pas'tərn) *n.* part of a horse's foot between the fetlock and the hoof. [Old French *pasturon,* from *pasture* tether (tied around the pastern of a horse at pasture), pasture, food, from Late Latin *pāstūra* feeding. See PASTURE.]

Pastern

Pas·teur, Lou·is (pas tur'; lŏō'ē) 1822–95, French chemist and bacteriologist.
pas·teur·ize (pas'chə rīz', pas'tə-) **-ized, -iz·ing.** *v.t.* to subject (milk or other food) to a temperature high enough to destroy disease-producing bacteria and organisms that cause food spoilage. [From Louis *Pasteur,* who discovered this process + -IZE.] —**pas'teur·i·za'tion,** *n.*
pas·tiche (pas tēsh') *n.* artistic, literary, or musical work composed of excerpts from various sources, often intended to satirize other artists. [French *pastiche,* from Italian *pasticcio* hodgepodge, pasty², going back to Late Latin *pasta.* See PASTE.]
pas·tille (pas tēl') *also,* **pas·til** (pas'til). *n.* **1.** lozenge; troche. **2.** small roll or cone of benzoin or other aromatic paste, burned as a disinfectant or deodorizer. [French *pastille* lozenge, from Latin *pastillus* little roll or loaf, lozenge, diminutive of *pānis* bread.]
pas·time (pas'tīm') *n.* something that serves to make time pass pleasantly; diversion. [PASS + TIME.] —**Syn.** see **amusement.**
past master, one who is highly skilled or thoroughly experienced in something, as an art or profession; expert.
pas·tor (pas'tər) *n.* clergyman in charge of a parish or congregation. [Latin *pāstor* shepherd; literally, feeder, from *pāscere* to feed.]
pas·tor·al (pas'tər əl) *adj.* **1.** of, relating to, or portraying rural life, esp. idealized rural life: *pastoral poetry.* **2.** of or relating to shepherds or herdsmen or their way of life: *a pastoral tribe.* **3.** having the simplicity, peacefulness, charm, and other qualities usually associated with idealized rural life or the country: *pastoral scenery.* **4.** of or relating to a pastor or his duties. —*n.* **1.** literary work, esp. a poem or play, that deals with rural life, usually in an idealized or artificial manner. **2.** picture or scene depicting rural life. **3.** pastorale. **4.** [Latin *pāstōrālis* relating to shepherds, from *pāstor* shepherd. See PASTOR.] —**pas'tor·al·ly,** *adv.*
pas·to·rale (pas'tə ral', -räl') *pl.,* **-rales** or **-ra·li** (-rä'lē). *n.* musical

at; āpe; cär; end; mē; it; īce; hot; ōld; fôrk; wood; fōol; oil; out; up; ūse; turn; sing; thin; this; zh in treasure; ə in ago, taken, pencil, lemon, circus.

composition, as an opera, based on or suggestive of a pastoral theme or subject. [Italian *pastorale* pastoral, from Latin *pāstōrālis*. See PASTORAL.]

pas·tor·ate (pas′tər it) *n.* **1.** office, position, or jurisdiction of a pastor. **2.** tenure of service of a pastor with one parish or congregation. **3.** pastors collectively.

past participle, participle expressing a past action or state, used esp. in English with auxiliary verbs to form perfect tenses of the active voice and all tenses of the passive voice. In the sentence *The decision was made in haste,* the word *made* is a past participle.

past perfect 1. verb tense expressing past action completed before another past action or before a specified past time. In the sentence *Steve had returned by the time Frieda arrived,* the phrase *had returned* is in the past perfect. **2.** verb in this tense. Also, **plu·per′fect.**

pas·tra·mi (pəs trä′mē) *n.* cut of beef, especially a shoulder cut, smoked and highly seasoned.

pas·try (pās′trē) *pl.,* **-tries.** *n.* **1.** any of several flour doughs used in making pie crusts, tarts, and other items. **2.** baked foods made with such a dough, collectively. **3.** any sweet, baked food. [PASTE + -RY.]

past tense 1. verb tense expressing an action or state that occurred in the past. In the sentence *The bird flew away,* the word *flew* is in the past tense. **2.** verb in this tense.

pas·tur·age (pas′chər ij) *n.* **1.** growing grass and other herbage that animals feed on. **2.** land used or suitable for grazing livestock. **3.** action or business of grazing livestock. [Old French *pasturage* food, from *pasture.* See PASTURE.]

pas·ture (pas′chər) *n.* **1.** field or other tract of land suitable for the grazing of cattle, sheep, or other animals. **2.** grass and other herbage that animals feed on. —*v.t.,* **-tured, -tur·ing.** **1.** to put (animals) into a pasture to graze. —*v.i.* **2.** to graze. [Old French *pasture* food, grass, from Late Latin *pāstūra* feeding, from Latin *pāscere* to feed.]

past·y¹ (pās′tē) **past·i·er, past·i·est.** *adj.* **1.** resembling paste, as in consistency. **2.** pale and sickly: *a pasty complexion.* [PASTE + -Y¹.] —**past′i·ness,** *n.*

pas·ty² (pas′tē) *pl.,* **-ties.** *n.* small pie with a filling usually of meat. [Old French *pastee,* from *paste* dough. See PASTE.]

pat¹ (pat) **pat·ted, pat·ting.** *v.t.* **1.** to stroke or tap gently, usually with the hand, esp. in affection or approval. **2.** to shape or smooth by striking gently with a flat surface. —*n.* **1.** gentle tap or stroke. **2.** sound made by such a tap or stroke. **3.** small slice or molded mass of butter. **4. pat on the back.** *Informal.* gesture or expression of approval. [Imitative.]

pat² (pat) *adj.* **1.** glib; contrived; insincere: *They were the same pat compliments he gave to every pretty girl.* **2.** exactly suitable for the purpose or occasion; fitting. **3.** needing no change: *a pat hand in poker.* —*adv.* **1.** perfectly; completely; thoroughly: *I have the information down pat.* **2.** unchanging; firm: *to stand pat on an issue.* **3.** aptly; suitably. [From PAT¹.]

pat., patent; patented.

pa·ta·gi·um (pə tā′jē əm) *n.* web of skin between the body and wing of a bird. [Modern Latin *patagium,* from *patagium* gold border on a tunic, from Greek *patageion.*]

Pat·a·go·ni·a (pat′ə gō′nē ə) *n.* region in southern Argentina, between the Andes and the Atlantic. Area, approx. 300,000 sq. mi. —**Pat′a·go′ni·an,** *adj., n.*

patch (pach) *n.* **1.** piece of material used to mend or cover a hole, strengthen a worn spot, or ornament a garment. **2.** pad, piece of material, or other covering worn or put over a wound or injured part, usually for protection: *an eye patch.* **3.** any of the pieces of material used in making patchwork. **4.** small piece of black silk or court plaster formerly worn on the face or neck to enhance beauty or cover a blemish. **5.** small area, as of a surface, that differs or stands out from the whole: *Only a tiny patch of blue was visible in the cloudy sky.* **6.** small piece or section of ground, esp. one in which a specific kind of plant is grown: *a lettuce patch.* **7.** small scrap, piece, or area of anything. —*v.t.* **1.** to put a patch or patches of material on, esp. to mend, cover, strengthen, or ornament (often with *up*): *to patch up a torn pair of dungarees.* **2.** to fix, repair, or put together, esp. in a hasty, poor, or makeshift way (often with *up* or *together*): *The man patched up the broken vase before his wife noticed it.* **3.** to make by joining pieces together: *to patch a quilt.* **4.** to smooth over; settle (often with *up*): *to patch up a quarrel.* [Possibly from Old French *pieche,* form of *piece* part of a whole, period of time. See PIECE.]

patch·ou·li (pach′oo lē, pə choo′lē) *also,* **patch·ou·ly.** *n.* **1.** either of two East Indian plants, *Pogostemon heyneanus* and *P. cablin,* of the mint family. **2.** strong perfume derived from the dried leaves of either of these plants. [Tamil *pacculi* the plant, from *paccu* green + *ilai* leaf.]

patch test, any of several skin tests used chiefly for determining susceptibility to or the presence of disease or allergy.

patch·work (pach′wurk′) *n.* **1.** needlework consisting of pieces of material, usually of varying colors or shapes, that are sewed together. **2.** any surface divided into sections of varying colors or shapes. **3.** something composed of miscellaneous or incongruous parts; jumble: *a patchwork of three languages.*

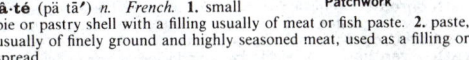

Patchwork

patch·y (pach′ē) **patch·i·er, patch·i·est.** *adj.* **1.** made up of, marked by, or occurring in patches: *patchy fog.* **2.** lacking uniformity, consistency, or completeness: *Only patchy reports were received from the battle front.* —**patch′i·ly,** *adv.* —**patch′i·ness,** *n.*

patd., patented.

pate (pāt) *n.* head, esp. the crown of the head.

pâ·té (pä tā′) *n. French.* **1.** small pie or pastry shell with a filling usually of meat or fish paste. **2.** paste, usually of finely ground and highly seasoned meat, used as a filling or spread.

pâ·té de foie gras (pä tā′ də fwä grä′) *French.* paste made from livers of specially fattened geese, often with truffles added.

pa·tel·la (pə tel′ə) *pl.,* **-tel·lae** (-tel′ē) or **-tel·las.** *n.* **1.** kneecap. **2.** in ancient Rome, a small pan or dish. [Latin *patella* small pan¹ or dish, diminutive of *patina* pan¹, dish. See PATEN.] —**pa·tel′lar,** *adj.*

pa·tel·li·form (pə tel′ə fôrm′) *adj.* having the shape of a pan or saucer. [PATELLA + -FORM.]

pat·en (pat′ən) *n.* **1.** plate, esp. the small circular plate, usually of gold or silver, on which the bread is placed during the celebration of the Eucharist. **2.** metal disk. [Latin *patina, patena* dish, pan¹, from Greek *patanē* flat dish.]

pa·ten·cy (pāt′ən sē) *n.* state or quality of being obvious or evident.

pat·ent (pat′ənt, pāt′ənt) *n.* **1.** government grant to an individual or organization conferring, for a certain period of time, the exclusive right of making, using, or selling a new invention. **2.** invention that is protected by such a grant. **3.** official document granting a right or privilege: *a patent of nobility.* **4.a.** grant of public land by a government to an individual. **b.** land so granted. **5.** any exclusive right or privilege. —*adj.* **1.** conferred or protected by a patent. **2.** obvious; evident; clear: *patent arrogance, a patent lie.* **3.** open to or suited for an invention); protect with a patent. [Latin *patēns* open, present participle of *patēre* to lie open; because the official document granting a patent was open to public inspection.] —**pat′ent·a·ble,** *adj.*

pat·ent·ee (pat′ən tē′) *n.* one to whom a patent is granted.

patent leather (pat′ənt) smooth, soft leather that is finished to a very high gloss.

pat·ent·ly (pāt′ənt lē, pat′-) *adv.* obviously; evidently.

patent medicine, medicine that is patented and can be purchased without a prescription.

Patent Office, U.S. government office that issues patents and administers federal patent and trademark laws.

pat·en·tor (pat′ən tər) *n.* one who grants a patent.

pa·ter (pā′tər) *n.* father. ▲ often used as an affectation or in humorous contexts. [Latin *pater.*]

pa·ter·fa·mil·i·as (pā′tər fə mil′ē əs) *n.* father or head of a family or household. [Latin *paterfamiliās,* from *pater* father + *familiās,* archaic genitive of *familia* household.]

pa·ter·nal (pə turn′əl) *adj.* **1.** of, relating to, or like a father; fatherly: *paternal affection.* **2.** related through one's father: *a paternal grandmother.* **3.** inherited or derived from one's father. [Latin *paternālis* relating to a father, going back to Latin *pater* father.] —**pa·ter′nal·ly,** *adv.*

pa·ter·nal·ism (pə turn′əl iz′əm) *n.* principle or practice of regulating the life and supplying the needs of a country or group of people in a way suggestive of a father handling his children. —**pa·ter′nal·is′tic,** *adj.*

pa·ter·ni·ty (pə tur′nə tē) *n.* **1.** state of being a father. **2.** paternal origin. [Late Latin *paternitās,* going back to Latin *pater* father.]

pat·er·nos·ter (pā′tər nos′tər, pat′ər-) *n.* **1.** *also,* Paternoster, Pater Noster, the Lord's Prayer, esp. the Latin version. **2.** one of several beads of a rosary, often distinct in size, shape, or spacing from the other beads, on which the Lord's Prayer is said. [Latin *pater noster* our father (the first two words of the Latin version of the Lord's Prayer).]

Pat·er·son (pat′ər sən) *n.* city in northeastern New Jersey. Pop. (1970), 144,824.

path (path) *pl.,* **paths** (pathz). *n.* **1.** trail or way that has been trodden or worn, as through a forest. **2.** way or road constructed for a specific purpose: *to shovel a path through the snow.* **3.** route along which something or someone travels: *the path of a projectile. A black cat crossed his path.* **4.** way or line of action, behavior, or procedure: *a path to fame.* [Old English *paeth.*]

at; āpe; cär; end; mē; it; īce; hot; ōld; fôrk; wood; fōōl; oil; out; up; ūse; turn; sing; thin; this; zh in treasure; ə in ago, taken, pencil, lemon, circus.

737

path., pathology; pathological.

Pa·than (pə tän′, pət hän′) *n.* **1.** member of any of various peoples living in West Pakistan. **2.** Afghan.

pa·thet·ic (pə thet′ik) *adj.* **1.** arousing or expressing pity, sadness, or compassion: *a pathetic tale of misery and death.* **2.** extremely or pitifully inadequate or ineffective: *the actor's pathetic attempt to portray Julius Caesar.* Also, **pa·thet′i·cal.** [Late Latin *pathēticus* full of pathos, from Greek *pathētikos* capable of emotion, going back to *pathein* to suffer.] —**pa·thet′i·cal·ly,** *adv.*

pathetic fallacy, attribution of human feelings or characteristics to nature or inanimate objects; for example: *an angry sea.*

path·find·er (path′fīn′dər) *n.* one who discovers or leads the way, as through an unknown region.

path·o·gen (path′ə jən) *also,* **path·o·gene** (path′ə jēn′). *n.* any disease-causing microorganism or the toxic secretion of such a microorganism. [Greek *pathos* suffering + -GEN.]

path·o·gen·e·sis (path′ə jen′ə sis) *n.* origin and development of a disease. Also, **pa·thog·e·ny** (pə thoj′ə nē). [Modern Latin *pathogenesis,* from Greek *pathos* suffering + GENESIS.]

path·o·gen·ic (path′ə jen′ik) *adj.* producing disease or relating to the production of disease. Also, **path·o·ge·net·ic** (path′ə ji net′ik).

pathol., pathology; pathological.

path·o·log·i·cal (path′ə loj′i kəl) *adj.* of, relating to, or concerned with pathology. **2.** characteristic of, caused by, or accompanying disease. Also, **path′o·log′ic.** —**path′o·log′i·cal·ly,** *adv.*

pa·thol·o·gy (pə thol′ə jē) *pl.,* **-gies.** *n.* **1.** science that deals with the nature, cause, and development of disease. **2.** abnormal condition and bodily change resulting from a disease. [Modern Latin *pathologia,* from Greek *pathos* suffering, emotion + -LOGY.] —**pa·thol′o·gist,** *n.*

pa·thos (pā′thos) *n.* quality, as in an event or work of art, that arouses a feeling of pity, sadness, or compassion. [Greek *pathos* suffering, emotion.]

path·way (path′wā′) *n.* path.

-pathy *combining form* **1.** feeling: *sympathy, empathy.* **2.** disease: *psychopathy.* **3.** treatment of disease: *osteopathy.* [Greek *-patheia* suffering, feeling.]

pa·tience (pā′shəns) *n.* **1.** quality, state, or fact of being patient or the ability to be patient. **2.** solitaire *(def. 1).*

pa·tient (pā′shənt) *adj.* **1.** capable of waiting calmly or without complaint: *We must be patient until our turn comes.* **2.** able to endure annoyance, hardship, or difficulty without complaining or losing one's composure: *to be resign'd when ills betide, patient when favours are denied* (Cotton, 1751). **3.** exhibiting or characterized by such an ability to wait or endure: *with patient heart to . . . hope and wait* (Morris, 1869). **4.** calm and sympathetic; understanding: *It was a difficult lesson, but the professor was very patient with the class.* **5.** persevering; diligent: *Whatever I have done is due to patient thought* (Newton, 1727). —*n.* one who is undergoing medical care or treatment. [Old French *patient* waiting, enduring troubles, one who is undergoing medical treatment, from Latin *patiēns* suffering, present participle of *patī* to suffer.] —**pa′tient·ly,** *adv.*

pat·i·na (pat′ən ə) *n.* **1.** green film or incrustation produced by oxidation on the surface of bronze. **2.** surface appearance, as a dull finish, usually produced gradually by age and use, as on wood. [Italian *patina* incrustation, coating, from Latin *patina* dish, pan[1]. See PATEN.]

pat·i·o (pat′ē ō′) *pl.,* **-i·os.** *n.* **1.** terrace *(def. 2).* **2.** inner court open to the sky, as in a Spanish or Spanish-American house. [Spanish *patio* courtyard, possibly going back to Latin *patēre* to lie open.]

pa·tis·se·rie (pə tis′ə rē) *n.* store that sells, and usually makes, baked goods, esp. pastries.

Pat·na (pat′nə) *n.* city in eastern India, on the Ganges. Pop. (1969), 449,471.

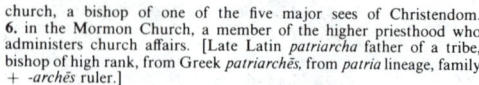

Patio (def. 2)

pat·ois (pat′wä) *pl.,* **pat·ois** (pat′wäz). *n.* dialect, esp. a substandard form of a language, spoken by the common people of a district. [French *patois* rustic speech, from *patte* paw (of uncertain origin); referring to the clumsy style of the speakers.]

pat. pend., patent pending.

pa·tri·arch (pā′trē ärk′) *n.* **1.** paternal head of a family or tribe. **2.** one who is regarded as the founder or father of something, as a philosophy, religion, or order. **3.** old man who is venerated by a group and whose opinions have great influence or authority. **4.** in the Roman Catholic, Orthodox, and various other Christian churches in the Middle East, a prelate who exercises the highest authority over all archbishops, bishops, clergy, and laity of his territory. **5.** in the early Christian

church, a bishop of one of the five major sees of Christendom. **6.** in the Mormon Church, a member of the higher priesthood who administers church affairs. [Late Latin *patriarcha* father of a tribe, bishop of high rank, from Greek *patriarchēs,* from *patria* lineage, family + *-archēs* ruler.]

pa·tri·ar·chal (pā′trē är′kəl) *adj.* **1.** of, relating to, or characteristic of a patriarch: *patriarchal authority.* **2.** of, relating to, or of the nature of a patriarchy: *the patriarchal form of government.* **3.** ruled by a patriarch: *a patriarchal see.*

pa·tri·ar·chate (pā′trē är′kit, -kāt) *n.* **1.** office, jurisdiction, or territory of an ecclesiastical patriarch. **2.** patriarchy.

pa·tri·ar·chy (pā′trē är′kē) *pl.,* **-chies.** *n.* **1.** system of social organization in which the father or eldest male is head of the family or tribe and descent is traced through the paternal line. **2.** government of a family, tribe, or the like by men.

pa·tri·cian (pə trish′ən) *n.* **1.** member of one of the aristocratic families in ancient Rome who were descended from the original settlers of the city. **2.** one who is of high birth or social status; aristocrat. —*adj.* **1.** of or relating to aristocracy, esp. that of ancient Rome. **2.** aristocratic; noble. [Latin *patricius* noble, of senatorial rank (from *patrēs* senators, fathers, plural of *pater* father) + -AN.]

pat·ri·ci·dal (pat′rə sīd′əl) *adj.* of or relating to patricide or one who commits patricide.

pat·ri·cide[1] (pat′rə sīd′) *n.* act of killing one's father. [Latin *pater* father + *-cīdium* (see -CIDE[1]).]

pat·ri·cide[2] (pat′rə sīd′) *n.* one who kills his father. [Latin *pater* father + *-cīda* -CIDE[2].]

Pat·rick, Saint (pat′rik) A.D. c.389–c.461, Christian missionary and patron saint of Ireland.

pat·ri·lin·e·al (pat′rə lin′ē əl, pā′trə-) *adj.* of, relating to, or tracing descent through the paternal line.

pat·ri·mo·ny (pat′rə mō′nē) *pl.,* **-nies.** *n.* **1.** inheritance from one's father or ancestors. **2.** anything inherited; heritage. **3.** property or endowment of a church or other religious institution. [Old French *patrimoine* inheritance, from Latin *patrimōnium,* from *pater* father.] —**pat′ri·mo′ni·al,** *adj.* —**Syn.** 2. see **heritage.**

pa·tri·ot (pā′trē ət) *n.* one who loves and enthusiastically supports his country. [Middle French *patriote,* from Late Latin *patriōta* fellow countryman, from Greek *patriōtēs.*]

pa·tri·ot·ic (pā′trē ot′ik) *adj.* characterized by, displaying, or inspired by patriotism. —**pa′tri·ot′i·cal·ly,** *adv.*

pa·tri·ot·ism (pā′trē ə tiz′əm) *n.* love for and enthusiastic support of one's country.

pa·tris·tic (pə tris′tik) *adj.* of or relating to the fathers of the early Christian church or to their doctrines or writings. Also, **pa·tris′ti·cal.**

Pa·tro·clus (pə trō′kləs) *n.* Greek Legend. a friend of Achilles. When Patroclus took Achilles' place in battle, he was killed by Hector.

pa·trol (pə trōl′) **-trolled, -trol·ling.** *v.t., v.i.* to go through or around (an area or place) for the purpose of guarding or inspecting: *Several police cars patrolled the neighborhood.* —*n.* **1.** one or more persons who patrol or are assigned to patrol. **2.** detachment of ground, sea, or air forces sent out for reconnaissance, combat, or some other purpose: *All the soldiers in the patrol returned safely.* **3.** act of patrolling: *Sentries maintained an all-night patrol.* **4.** unit of a Boy or Girl Scout troop usually consisting of eight scouts. [French *patrouiller* to paddle in mud (because sentries often had to walk back and forth in mud), from *patte* paw; of uncertain origin.]

patrol car, squad car.

pa·trol·man (pə trōl′mən) *pl.,* **-men.** *n.* policeman assigned to patrol a certain area.

patrol wagon, specially equipped truck used by the police for conveying prisoners.

pa·tron (pā′trən) *n.* **1.** one who supports, promotes, or protects a person, cause, organization, or undertaking by the use of his money or influence: *a patron of the arts.* **2.** regular customer. **3.** patron saint. [Old French *patron* protector, from Latin *patrōnus,* from *pater* father.] —**pa′tron·al,** *adj.* —**pa′tron·ess,** *n.*

Syn. 1. Patron, sponsor mean one who supports another person or fosters an activity. **Patron** designates a wealthy and influential supporter, esp. a benefactor of the arts or social causes: *That millionaire is a patron of the arts.* **Sponsor** designates a person or agency that assumes certain public responsibilities in behalf of another, as a promoter, backer, or endorser: *That foundation was the sponsor of this study on urban life.*

pa·tron·age (pā′trə nij, pat′rə-) *n.* **1.** support or assistance provided by a patron. **2.** financial support given to a commercial establishment by customers. **3.** condescending manner or treatment. **4.a.** in the public service, power, right, or system of distributing jobs or favors. **b.** jobs or favors so distributed.

pa·tron·ize (pā′trə nīz′, pat′rə-) **-ized, -iz·ing.** *v.t.* **1.** to be a customer of (a commerical establishment), esp. on a regular basis. **2.** to treat in

a condescending manner. **3.** to give support or assistance to; act as a patron toward.

patron saint, saint chosen as the special guardian or protector of a person, place, organization, or the like.

pat·ro·nym·ic (pat′rə nim′ik) *n.* name derived from the name of one's father or other male ancestor, esp. by the addition of a prefix or suffix, as *Ericson,* son of Eric. —*adj.* **1.** relating to or derived from the name of one's father or other male ancestor: *a patronymic surname.* **2.** indicating such descent: *a patronymic suffix.* [Late Latin *patrōnymicus* derived from the name of a father, from Greek *patrōnymicos,* from *patēr* father + (dialectal) *onyma* name, word.]

pa·troon (pə trōōn′) *n.* proprietor of a feudal estate in the former Dutch colony of New Netherland. [Dutch *patroon* employer, master, from Latin *patrōnus* protector.]

pat·sy (pat′sē) *pl.,* **-sies.** *n. Slang.* one who has been tricked, taken advantage of, or made a fool of. [Of uncertain origin.]

pat·ten (pat′ən) *n.* any of various types of footwear, including shoes, overshoes, and sandals, having thick, often wooden soles and formerly worn to protect the feet from dampness. [Old French *patin* a clog, wooden shoe, from *patte* paw, foot; of uncertain origin.]

pat·ter¹ (pat′ər) *v.i.* **1.** to make a rapid succession of soft taps: *the sound of raindrops as they patter on the roof.* **2.** to move with soft, rapid steps: *We heard the children pattering down the stairs.* —*n.* rapid succession of soft taps. [PAT¹ + -ER¹.]

pat·ter² (pat′ər) *n.* **1.** any rapid, glib speech, esp. the fast, fluent talk of a salesman, barker, or the like. **2.** jargon of a particular class or group; cant. —*v.t., v.i.* to speak rapidly, glibly, or mechanically. [Short for PATERNOSTER; referring to the effect of the rapid repetition of the *paternoster* by priests in earlier times.]

pat·tern (pat′ərn) *n.* **1.** decorative or artistic design: *the pretty flower pattern of a dress.* **2.** any natural or accidental arrangement or design of colors, shapes, or lines: *The trees cast an intricate pattern of shadows on the ground.* **3.** something designed or used as a guide, esp. in the making of some article: *to follow a dress pattern.* **4.** example worthy of or proposed for imitation; model. **5.** set of habitual or representative actions or characteristics: *to examine a child's behavior pattern.* **6.** style or form, as of a literary or musical work. **7.** representative sample, specimen, or instance. —*v.t.* **1.** to make or fashion according to or in imitation of a particular pattern, guide, or example: *The young man patterned his life after that of his hero.* **2.** to mark or decorate with a pattern or design. [Old French *patron* protector, model, from Latin *patrōnus* protector.]

pat·ty (pat′ē) *pl.,* **-ties.** *n.* **1.** small, round, flattened cake of ground or chopped food: *a hamburger patty.* **2.** small pie. **3.** small, flat piece, esp. of candy. [French *pâté* pie, pastry, from Old French *pastee* pie, from *paste* dough. See PASTE.]

patty shell, small shell of puff paste, used to serve creamed meat, fish, vegetables, or fruit.

pau·ci·ty (pô′sə tē) *n.* **1.** smallness of number; fewness: *this theory's paucity of supporters.* **2.** scarcity; insufficiency: *a paucity of evidence.* [Latin *paucitās.*]

Paul, Saint (pôl) died A.D. c.68, Apostle to the Gentiles.

Paul III, 1468–1549, pope from 1534 to 1549.

Paul VI, 1897—, pope since 1963.

Paul Bunyan, in American folklore, giant lumberjack credited with superhuman feats.

Paul·ine (pô′līn) *adj.* of or relating to Saint Paul or to his doctrines or writings.

paunch (pônch, pänch) *n.* **1.** belly, esp. when large and protruding. **2.** first stomach of a cud-chewing animal; rumen. [Dialectal Old French *panche* belly, from Latin *pantex.*]

paunch·y (pôn′chē, pän′-) **-chi·er, -chi·est.** *adj.* having a large, protruding belly. —**paunch′i·ness,** *n.*

pau·per (pô′pər) *n.* very poor person, esp. one supported by charity. [Latin *pauper.* Doublet of POOR.]

pau·per·ism (pô′pə riz′əm) *n.* poverty.

pau·per·ize (pô′pə rīz′) **-ized, -iz·ing.** *v.t.* to make a pauper of. —**pau′per·i·za′tion,** *n.*

pause (pôz) **paused, paus·ing.** *v.i.* to stop for a short time. —*n.* **1.** brief or temporary stop, hesitation, or delay: *After a pause, the game continued.* **2.** brief stop or break in speaking, reading, or writing, esp. to clarify meaning or add expression. **3.** *Music.* sign (⌒ or ⌄) placed above or below a note or rest to indicate that it is to be prolonged. **4.** cause or reason to stop or hesitate: *For in that sleep of death what dreams may come, . . . must give us pause* (Shakespeare, *Hamlet*). [Latin *pausa* a stop, ceasing, from Greek *pausis.*]

pa·vane (pə vän′, -van′) *also,* **pav·an** (pav′ən) *n.* **1.** slow, stately dance of the sixteenth century. **2.** music for this dance.

pave (pāv) **paved, pav·ing.** *v.t.* **1.** to cover (a road or other surface) with pavement: *to pave a driveway with concrete.* **2.** to cover as if with pavement. **3. to pave the way.** to prepare or lead the way. [Old French

paver to cover ground with paving stones, going back to Latin *pavīre* to strike, tread down.]

pave·ment (pāv′mənt) *n.* **1.** covering or surface of concrete, asphalt, brick, or similar material, as for a road or sidewalk. **2.** material used to make such a covering or surface. **3.** sidewalk. [Old French *pavement* floor, going back to Latin *pavīmentum* hard floor.]

pa·vil·ion (pə vil′yən) *n.* **1.** ornamental, often open building, as in a park or public garden, used for exhibition, entertainment, recreation, or shelter. **2.** large, often ornate tent. **3.** one of a group of related buildings or an extension of a main building, as of a hospital. **4.** projecting part of a building, often elaborately decorated. —*v.t.* to shelter or enclose in or as if in a pavilion. [Old French *pavillon* tent, canopy, from Latin *pāpiliō* butterfly, tent; because it resembles a butterfly with outspread wings.]

pav·ing (pā′ving) *n.* **1.** act of laying a pavement. **2.** paved surface; pavement. **3.** material used for pavement.

Pav·lov, Ivan (pav′lov; i vän′) 1849–1936, Russian physiologist.

Pav·lo·va, Anna (päv lō′və, pav′lə vä) 1882–1931, Russian ballerina.

paw (pô) *n.* **1.** foot of an animal having nails or claws. **2.** *Informal.* human hand. —*v.t.* **1.** to strike or scrape (something) with the paws or hooves: *The angry bull pawed the ground.* **2.** to touch or handle roughly, clumsily, or in too familiar a manner. —*v.i.* **1.** to strike or scrape something with the paws or hooves: *The dog pawed at the spot where the bone had been buried.* **2.** to make rough or clumsy movements with the hands. [Old French *powe* foot of an animal or bird; claw; possibly of Germanic origin.]

pawl (pôl) *n.* catch or bar on a pivot that engages the teeth of a ratchet, permitting the wheel to revolve in only one direction. [Possibly modification of Dutch *pal.*]

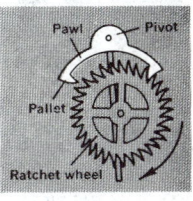

Pawl

pawn¹ (pôn) *v.t.* **1.** to deposit as security for a loan, esp. with a pawnbroker. **2.** to risk or wager; pledge: *I will pawn my life for her* (Richardson, 1741). —*n.* **1.** condition of being held as security, as for a loan. **2.** one who or that which is given or held as security, as for a loan. [Old French *pan* pledge, security; of Germanic origin.] —**pawn′er;** *also,* **paw′nor,** *n.*

pawn² (pôn) *n.* **1.** *Chess.* any of the sixteen chess pieces of lowest value, eight to each player, that is usually able to move only one square forward at a time and captures by moving one square diagonally. **2.** one who or that which is manipulated by another, esp. a person who is exploited or used for another's purposes or personal gain. [Old French *paon, peon* chess piece, from Medieval Latin *pedo* foot soldier, from Latin *pēs* foot. Doublet of PEON.]

pawn·bro·ker (pôn′brō′kər) *n.* one licensed to lend money at interest on articles of personal property left as security for a loan.

Pawn

Paw·nee (pô nē′) *pl.,* **-nees** *or* **-nee.** *n.* **1.** member of any of a group of North American Indian tribes formerly living in the valley of the Platte River in Nebraska, now living in Oklahoma. **2.** language of the Pawnees.

pawn·shop (pôn′shop′) *n.* pawnbroker's shop.

paw-paw (pô′pô′) papaw.

Paw·tuck·et (pô tuk′it) *n.* city in northeastern Rhode Island. Pop. (1970), 76,984.

pax (paks) *n.* **1.** small metal or wooden tablet bearing a representation of the Crucifixion or other sacred object, formerly kissed by the priest and congregation at Mass. **2.** in a High Mass, an embrace symbolic of brotherly love, exchanged between the celebrant and his assistants. [Latin *pāx* peace.]

pax vo·bis·cum (paks′ vō bis′kəm) *Latin.* peace be with you.

pay¹ (pā) **paid** *or (for def. 11b)* **payed, pay·ing.** *v.t.* **1.** to give (a person, company, or organization) what is due for services rendered or goods received. **2.** to give (money) in return for goods or services or to settle a debt. **3.** to give, provide, or hand over the amount or cost of: *to pay a bill.* **4.** to yield as return or recompense: *This job pays ninety dollars a week.* **5.** to be profitable to or worthwhile for: *It will pay you to plan now for the future.* **6.** to make return, recompense, or retaliation for or to; requite (often with *back* or *off*): *to pay back a favor, to pay off an old score.* **7.** to give, render, or bestow: *to pay a compliment.* **8.** to make (a visit or call). **9.** to undergo; suffer; bear: *It's Jerry's error, and he'll pay the consequences.* **10. to pay off. a.** to pay all that is owed; pay in full: *to pay off a bet.* **b.** to bribe. **11. to pay one's way.** to pay one's own share of expenses. **12. to pay out. a.** to expend; disburse.

b. to let out by slackening, as a rope or line. —*v.i.* **1.** to give something, esp. money, as in making a purchase or settling a debt or obligation; make payment: *Can I pay by check?* **2.** to be profitable or worthwhile: *It pays to get a good education.* **3.** to undergo suffering; be punished. **4. to pay off.** to yield favorable or desired results; to be profitable: *His hard work paid off when he got the promotion.* **5. to pay up.** to pay what is due; pay in full: *The landlord demanded that the man pay up or go to jail.* —*n.* **1.** something given in return or recompense, esp. money given for work done: *The workers demanded higher pay.* **2.** paid employment: *in the pay of the government.* —*adj.* **1.** (of earth) yielding valuable minerals in mining: *a pay lode.* **2.** operated by or made available for use by the deposit of a coin or coins: *a pay toilet, a pay telephone.* [Old French *paier* to appease, satisfy (as with money), discharge a debt, from Latin *pācāre* to appease, pacify.]
Syn. *n.* **1. Pay, wage, salary** mean an amount that an employee is paid for his services. **Pay** is the general term for the amount of money earned by an employee: *Paul's pay goes up by $200 every year.* **Wage** usually refers to the compensation paid to a worker at weekly, daily, or hourly rate, often for menial, mechanical, or manual labor: *The miners demanded higher wages.* **Salary** refers to a fixed compensation paid regularly at intervals longer than a week at a monthly or annual rate for professional or managerial services requiring special training and abilities: *The president's salary is $200,000 a year.*
pay² (pā) **payed** or **paid, pay·ing.** *v.t.* to cover with tar, pitch, or other waterproof material, as the seams of a boat or ship. [Old French *peier* to cover with pitch, from Latin *picāre.*]
pay·a·ble (pā′ə bəl) *adj.* **1.** to be paid; due: *The bill is payable within ninety days.* **2.** capable of being paid; that can be paid: *I made the check payable to the manager.* **3.** profitable, as a mine.
pay·day (pā′dā′) *n.* day on which wages are paid.
pay dirt **1.** earth, ore, or similar material containing enough valuable metal to make mining profitable. **2.** any source of profit or success: *We really hit pay dirt with this idea.*
pay·ee (pā′ē′) *n.* one to whom money has been or is to be paid.
pay·er (pā′ər) *n.* one who pays or is responsible for paying, as a bill.
pay·load (pā′lōd′) *n.* **1.** cargo or part of a cargo transported, as on a ship or truck, that produces profit. **2.** in a rocket, aircraft, or spacecraft, anything carried in addition to what is essential to the operation of the craft, as scientific instruments for collecting data. **3.** warhead of a guided or ballistic missile.
pay·mas·ter (pā′mas′tər) *n.* one in charge of paying wages.
pay·ment (pā′mənt) *n.* **1.** act of paying: *The company required that payment be made on time.* **2.** that which is paid: *The man received little payment for his services.* **3.** reward or punishment; requital: *The harsh sentence was just payment for his crime.*
pay·nim (pā′nim) *n. Archaic.* **1.** heathen. **2.** non-Christian, esp. a Muslim. [Old French *paienisme* heathendom, from Late Latin *pāgānismus,* from Latin *pāgānus* heathen, villager, civilian. See PAGAN.]
pay·off (pā′ôf′) *n.* **1.** payment, as of wages. **2.** *Informal.* climax or outcome, as of a narrative or series of events. **3.** *Informal.* bribe.
pay·o·la (pā ō′lə) *n. Informal.* payment made as a bribe, esp. for illegal favors. [From PAY¹.]
pay·roll (pā′rōl′) *also,* **pay roll.** *n.* **1.** list of employees to be paid, with the amounts to which each is entitled. **2.** total amount of money to be paid to employees.
payt., payment.
Pb, lead. [Latin *plumbum.*]
PBB, polybrominated biphenyl.
pc., piece.
p.c. **1.** percent. **2.** post card. **3.** petty cash.
P.C., Privy Council.
PCB, polychlorinated biphenyl.
pct., percent.
pd., paid.
p.d., per diem.
Pd, palladium.
P.D., Police Department.
P.E., Protestant Episcopal.
pea (pē) *n.* **peas** or *(archaic)* **pease.** *n.* **1.** round, usually green seed of a pod-bearing plant, *Pisum sativum,* eaten as a vegetable, either raw or cooked. **2.** the plant itself, having oval or oblong leaflets and white flowers with winglike petals. **3.** any of various pod-bearing plants or their seeds, as the cowpea. [Taken as singular of earlier *pease* pea, mistakenly thought to be plural. See PEASE.]
peace (pēs) *n.* **1.** freedom from or cessation of war or hostilities: *A day will come when wars will cease—a day of calm, a time of peace.* **2.** agreement, treaty, or settlement to end a war or hostilities. **3.** public order and security: *Law officers were assigned to keep the peace.* **4.** absence of or freedom from disturbance or agitation: *the peace and quiet of the country.* **5.** mental, emotional, or spiritual tranquillity or contentment: *to find inner peace through meditation.* **6. to hold** (or

keep) **one's peace.** to be or remain silent. **7. to make one's peace with.** to make a reconciliation with. —*interj.* **1.** be quiet; keep silent. **2.** peace be with you. [Old French *pais* untroubled state, absence of war, end war, from Latin *pāx.*]
peace·a·ble (pē′sə bəl) *adj.* **1.** inclined to avoid strife and disturbance; disposed to peace: *The villagers were a simple, peaceable people.* **2.** characterized by peace; peaceful: *The king had a short but peaceable reign.* —**peace′a·ble·ness,** *n.* —**peace′a·bly,** *adv.*
Peace Corps, U.S. government agency that trains and sends volunteer workers to aid people of underdeveloped countries.
peace·ful (pēs′fəl) *adj.* **1.** free from war, strife, or other disturbance. **2.** not violent, warlike, or quarrelsome: *to change society by peaceful means.* **3.** tranquil; serene; calm. —**peace′ful·ly,** *adv.* —**peace′ful·ness,** *n.*
peace·mak·er (pēs′mā′kər) *n.* one who brings about or tries to bring about a reconciliation between warring or disputing parties. —**peace′mak′ing** *n., adj.*
peace offering **1.** offering, as a gift, made to appease anger or bring about reconciliation or peace. **2.** in the Old Testament, an offering of thanksgiving to God, prescribed by Levitical law.
peace officer, civil officer, as a sheriff or policeman, whose duty is the preservation of public order and security.
peace pipe, tobacco pipe with a long ornamented stem, used by North American Indians on ceremonial occasions as a symbol of peace. Also, **cal′u·met′.**
peace·time (pēs′tīm′) *n.* period when a nation is not involved in war: *The soldier had been a teacher in peacetime.* —*adj.* of, for, or characteristic of such a period: *a peacetime army.*
peach¹ (pēch) *n.* **1.** sweet, juicy fruit of a tree, *Prunus persica,* of the rose family, having a large rough stone or pit, thick fleshy pulp, and a velvety yellow or yellow-red skin. **2.** tree bearing this fruit, having pink flowers, widely cultivated in temperate climates. **3.** yellowish-pink color. **4.** *Slang.* exceptionally beautiful, pleasing, or excellent person or thing. [Old French *pesche* the fruit, from Latin *Persicum* literally, Persian; referring to the Romans' importing of peaches from Persia.]
peach² (pēch) *v.i. Slang.* to inform on an accomplice; turn informer. [Short for obsolete *appeach* to accuse, from Anglo-Norman *apecher,* form of Old French *empecher* to hinder. See IMPEACH.]
peach·glow (pēch′glō′) *n.* pale pinkish-purple glaze used on some Chinese porcelain. Also, **peach·bloom** (pēch′blōōm′).
peach·y (pē′chē) **peach·i·er, peach·i·est.** *adj.* **1.** resembling a peach, esp. in color or texture. **2.** *Informal.* fine; great; dandy. —**peach′i·ness,** *n.*
pea·coat (pē′kōt′) *also,* **pea coat.** *n.* pea jacket.
pea·cock (pē′kok′) *n.* **1.** male of the peafowl, native to India and Ceylon, having a fan-shaped crest, shiny blue plumage on the head, neck, and body, and a train of bright metallic-green feathers covered with large eyelike spots. When the train is raised and spread, it is fan-shaped. Length: to 92 inches, including train. **2.** any peafowl. **3.** vain and ostentatious person. [Old English *pēa, pāwa* peafowl (from Latin *pāvō*) + *cocc* (see COCK¹).]

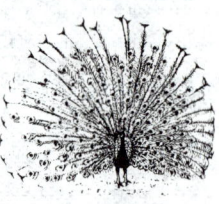

Peacock

peacock blue, bright greenish-blue.
pea·fowl (pē′foul′) *pl.* **-fowls** or **-fowl.** *n.* any of several pheasants, family Phasianidae, esp. genus *Pavo,* native to Asia and Africa, noted for the brilliant ornamental feathers of the male. The male is called a peacock and the female a peahen. [PEA(COCK) + FOWL.]
pea green, medium yellowish-green.
pea·hen (pē′hen′) *n.* female peafowl.
pea jacket, short, double-breasted coat of thick woolen cloth, worn esp. by sailors. Also, **pea′coat′.** [Modification of Dutch *pijjekker,* from *pij* thick cloth + *jekker* jacket (going back to Old French *jaque*). See JACKET.]
peak (pēk) *n.* **1.** pointed top of a mountain. **2.** mountain having a pointed summit. **3.** sharp, tapering, or projecting point or end: *the peak of a skyscraper.* **4.** maximum point or greatest level, as of development or intensity: *Traffic reaches its peak during rush hour.* **5.** projecting brim of a cap. **6.** narrow part of a ship's hull at the bow or stern. **7.** upper after corner of a fore-and-aft sail that is attached to a gaff. —*adj.* of, relating to, or constituting the maximum: *the peak hours of production.* —*v.i.* to reach the maximum point or greatest level: *Sales peak during this time of year.* [Form of PIKE².]
Syn. *n.* **4. Peak, summit, pinnacle** mean the highest point. **Peak** implies the highest point or maximum degree in an ascending course of development: *This year the stock market reached its peak in September.* **Summit** implies the highest level attainable by effort or the final and ultimate

stage of one's aspirations: *The presidency was the summit of his career.*
Pinnacle intensifies the idea of height and implies a dizzying and precarious eminence that culminates a spectacular series of achievements: *In his early thirties, the actor had reached the pinnacle of success.*

peaked¹ (pēkt, pē′kid) *adj.* having or ending in a peak; pointed. [PEAK + -ED².]

peak·ed² (pē′kid) *adj.* pale and emaciated; sickly: *Les has looked rather peaked since his illness.* [From earlier *peak* to look wan, fade (of uncertain origin) + -ED².]

peal (pēl) *n.* **1.** loud, sonorous, often prolonged sound or succession of sounds, as of a bell or laughter. **2.** set of bells tuned to one another. —*v.t., v.i.* to sound or give forth in a peal or peals. [Short for APPEAL.]

pe·an (pē′ən) paean.

pea·nut (pē′nut′) *n.* **1.** edible nutlike seeds of a plant, *Arachis hypogaea,* of the pea family, that develops in an underground pod and has a thin brownish skin. **2.** such a pod, usually containing two of these seeds. **3.** the bush or runner-type plant bearing these pods, widely cultivated in warm climates, having short-lived yellow flowers. **4.** peanuts. *Slang.* small or insignificant sum of money. [PEA + NUT.]

Peanut plant

peanut brittle, hard candy containing peanuts.

peanut butter, soft, creamy food made by grinding blanched, roasted peanuts with salt and vegetable oil, usually used as a spread.

peanut oil, oil extracted from peanuts by pressing or by means of solvents, used in cooking and in the manufacture of margarine.

pear (pâr) *n.* **1.** sweet, bell-shaped, edible fruit of any of a group of trees, genus *Pyrus,* of the rose family, having a firm, juicy sandy-textured flesh and a smooth yellow, brown, or reddish skin. **2.** tree bearing this fruit. [Old English *pere* the fruit, going back to Latin *pirum.*]

Pear

pearl (purl) *n.* **1.** lustrous, rounded, usually white or cream-colored gem formed from a secretion around a foreign substance inside the shell of a mollusk, esp. an oyster of the genus *Pinctada.* A cultured pearl is one that forms when the foreign body is introduced by man rather than entering naturally. **2.** something resembling a pearl in appearance, as a drop of water. **3.** one who or that which is choice, precious, or the finest example of something: *a pearl of a girl, pearls of wisdom.* **4.** mother-of-pearl. **5.** pearl gray. **6. to cast pearls before swine.** to offer or give something of great value to someone who cannot appreciate it and may defile or abuse it. —*adj.* **1.** relating to, consisting of, or adorned or set with a pearl or pearls. **2.** of the color or shape of a pearl. —*v.i.* **1.** to form drops or beads resembling pearls. **2.** to dive or fish for pearls. [Old French *perle* the gem, a very fine example, going back to Latin *perna* ham, a sea mussel (in which pearls were sometimes found).] —**pearl′er,** *n.*

pearl gray, clear, pale, bluish-gray color.

Pearl Harbor, principal U.S. naval base in the Pacific, near Honolulu on the island of Oahu, Hawaii. The bombing of Pearl Harbor by the Japanese on December 7, 1941, caused the United States to enter World War II.

pearl·y (pur′lē) *adj.* **pearl·i·er, pearl·i·est.* **1.** resembling a pearl or pearls. **2.** adorned with pearls or mother-of-pearl.

pearly nautilus, chambered nautilus.

Pea·ry, Robert Edwin (pēr′ē) 1856–1920, U.S. Arctic explorer.

peas·ant (pez′ənt) *n.* **1.** member of the working class, as in Europe, who makes his living as a farmer or farm laborer. **2.** unsophisticated, boorish, or lowbred person. [Old French *païsant* native, dweller in rural areas, from *païs* country, district, going back to Latin *pāgus* village, district.]

peas·ant·ry (pez′ən trē) *n.* **1.** peasants considered collectively or as a social class. **2.** rank, condition, or behavior of a peasant.

pease (pēz) *n. Archaic.* plural of **pea.** [Old English *pise* pea plant or its seed, from Latin *pīsum,* from Greek *pison.*]

pease·cod (pēz′kod′) *also,* **peas·cod.** *n. Archaic.* pod of the pea plant.

pea·shoot·er (pē′shōō′tər) *n.* toy consisting of a tube through which small pellets may be blown.

peat (pēt) *n.* deposit of decomposed plant matter that accumulates in bogs and similar poorly drained areas, used as a plant covering or dried and burned as fuel. [Medieval Latin (in England) *peta;* possibly of Celtic origin.]

peat moss 1. any of a group of pale-green mosses, genus *Sphagnum,*

that grow in swamps and bogs and are the major source of peat. **2.** residue of such mosses, used as a mulch.

pea·vey (pē′vē) *pl.,* **-veys.** *n.* heavy pole having a strong metal spike at the tip and a hinged hook near the end, used by lumberjacks to handle logs. [From Joseph *Peavey,* nineteenth-century American blacksmith, who supposedly invented it.]

pea·vy (pē′vē) *pl.,* **-vies.** *n.* peavey.

peb·ble (peb′əl) *n.* **1.** small, usually round, stone that is worn or eroded by the action of water or sand. **2.** rough, irregular surface, as on leather or paper. —*v.t.* **-bled, -bling.** to impart a rough, irregular surface to (leather). [Old English *papol(stān)* small stone.] —**peb′bly,** *adj.*

pe·can (pi kän′, -kan′) *n.* **1.** sweet, edible nut of a large North American tree, *Carya illinoensis,* of the walnut family, having a thin, brittle shell and an outer husk. **2.** tree producing this nut, having a deeply ridged gray or brown bark, hard, strong wood, and leaves composed of many leaflets. [Algonquian *pakan* hard-shelled nut.]

pec·ca·dil·lo (pek′ə dil′ō) *pl.,* **-loes** or **-los.** *n.* slight fault or sin. [Spanish *pecadillo,* diminutive of *pecado* sin, from Latin *peccātum.*]

pec·cant (pek′ənt) *adj.* **1.** guilty, esp. of a moral offense; sinning. **2.** violating a rule or principle; faulty. [Latin *peccāns,* present participle of *peccāre* to sin.] —**pec′can·cy,** *n.* —**pec′cant·ly,** *adv.*

pec·ca·ry (pek′ər ē) *pl.,* **-ries.** *n.* wild, piglike mammal, genus *Tayassu,* native to brush and forest country from the southern United States to Argentina, having coarse, bristly hair and straight tusks that point downward. Length: 3 feet. [Carib *pakira.*]

Peccary

peck¹ (pek) *n.* **1.** unit of dry measure, equal to eight quarts or one-fourth of a bushel. See **weights and measures** for table. **2.** vessel for measuring or holding a peck. **3.** *Informal.* great deal; considerable amount: *The little boy got himself into a peck of trouble.* [Old French *pek* unit of measure for oats; of uncertain origin.]

peck² (pek) *v.t.* **1.** to strike (something) with the beak in a short, rapid movement: *The parakeet pecked the bars of his cage.* **2.** to make by striking with the beak: *to peck a hole.* **3.** to strike at and pick up, as food, with the beak: *to peck seeds.* —*v.i.* **1.** to strike or try to strike with the beak in a short, rapid movement (often with *at*). **2.** to eat in small amounts, esp. without appetite or interest (with *at*). —*n.* **1.** short, rapid stroke made with the beak. **2.** hole or mark made by such a stroke. **3.** *Informal.* quick, light kiss: *He greeted her with a peck on the cheek.* [Possibly form of PICK¹.]

pecking order 1. social hierarchy within a flock of birds composed of a single species, esp. of poultry, in which each member is able to peck at and dominate weaker members and is in turn pecked and dominated by those stronger than he. **2.** any similar social hierarchy. Also, **peck order.**

Pe·cos Bill (pā′kəs, -kōs) in American folklore, cowboy hero known for his superhuman exploits.

Pecos River, river flowing from northern New Mexico southeast through Texas into the Rio Grande.

pec·ten (pek′tən) *pl.,* **pec·ti·nes** (-tə nēz′). *n.* comblike part, esp. a fan-shaped membrane in the eyes of birds and reptiles, that has folds resembling the teeth of a comb. [Latin *pecten* comb.]

pec·tin (pek′tin) *n.* any of several gelatinous substances found esp. in certain ripe fruits and used to gel jams and jellies. [Greek *pēktos* congealed, curdled + -IN¹.]

pec·to·ral (pek′tər əl) *adj.* **1.** of, relating to, or situated in or on the chest. **2.** worn on the chest or breast: *a pectoral cross.* —*n.* **1.** pectoral fin. **2.** medicine to cause coughing; expectorant. **3.** pectoral organ, as a muscle. **4.** something worn on the breast. [Latin *pectorālis* relating to the breast, from *pectus* breast.]

pectoral fin, in fish, one of a pair of fins behind the head, corresponding to the forelimbs of higher vertebrates.

pectoral girdle 1. in vertebrates, the ring of bones to which the forelimbs or arms are attached. **2.** in man, the bony structure to which the arms are attached, consisting of the shoulder blades, collarbone, and top of the breastbone. Also, **pectoral arch.**

pec·u·late (pek′yə lāt′) *-lat·ed, -lat·ing.* *v.t., v.i.* to steal (money or property entrusted to one, esp. public funds); embezzle. [Latin *pecūlātus,* past participle of *pecūlāri* to embezzle public money, going back to *pecu* money, cattle (because wealth in ancient times was often thought of in terms of cattle).] —**pec′u·la′tion, pec′u·la′tor,** *n.*

pe·cu·liar (pi kūl′yər) *adj.* **1.** strange; odd; unusual: *a peculiar habit.* **2.** belonging exclusively to a certain person, group, place, or thing: *a brand of hypocrisy peculiar to politicians.* **3.** distinct from others; special; particular: *This discovery is of peculiar interest to students of Greek history.* [Latin *pecūliāris* one's own, from *pecūlium* property

at; āpe; cär; end; mē; it; īce; hot; ōld; fôrk; wood; fōōl; oil; out; up; ūse; turn; sing; thin; this; zh in treasure; ə in ago, taken, pencil, lemon, circus.

741

(in cattle), private property, from *pecu.* See PECULATE.] —pe·cul′-iar·ly, *adv.* —Syn. 1. see strange.

pe·cu·li·ar·i·ty (pi kū′lē ar′ə tē) *pl.*, -ties. *n.* 1. strange or unusual feature or characteristic: *Sam's preoccupation with voodoo is only one of his peculiarities.* 2. special or particular characteristic. 3. quality or state of being peculiar: *The peculiarity of her behavior puzzled everyone.*

pe·cu·ni·ar·y (pi kū′nē er′ē) *adj.* 1. of, relating to, or consisting of money: *a pecuniary reward.* 2. (of a legal offense) entailing a fine. [Latin *pecūniārius* relating to money, from *pecūnia* money, from *pecu* money, cattle. See PECULATE.]

-ped, form of -pede, as in *biped.*

ped·a·gog·ic (ped′ə goj′ik, -gō′jik) *adj.* of, relating to, or characteristic of a pedagogue or pedagogy. Also, ped′a·gog′i·cal. —ped′a·gog′i·cal·ly, *adv.*

ped·a·gog·ics (ped′ə goj′iks, -gō′jiks) *n.,pl.* pedagogy. ▲ construed as singular.

ped·a·gogue (ped′ə gog′, -gôg′) *also*, ped·a·gog. *n.* teacher, esp. one who is pedantic and narrow-minded. [Latin *paedagōgus* slave who led a boy to school, teacher, from Greek *paidagōgos*, from *pais* boy + *agōgos* leader.]

ped·a·go·gy (ped′ə goj′ē, -gō′jē) *n.* art, science, or profession of teaching.

ped·al (ped′əl) *n.* 1. foot-operated part or lever that activates or controls a machine or part of a machine, as in a bicycle or automobile. 2. similar part or lever worked by the foot that modifies the sound of a musical instrument, as in a piano. —*v.t.*, -aled, -al·ing; *also*, British, -alled, -al·ling. to work the pedals of; operate by working pedals. —*v.i.* to work or use a pedal or pedals. —*adj.* 1. of or relating to a foot or the feet. 2. of, relating to, or operated by a pedal or pedals. [Latin *pedālis* relating to the foot, from *pēs* foot.]

ped·al·board (ped′əl bôrd′) *n.* organ keyboard played with the feet.

pedal point *Music.* note or tone sustained, usually in the bass, while the other parts progress harmonically and melodically.

pedal pushers, women's slacks that extend to, or just below, the knee.

ped·ant (ped′ənt) *n.* one who presents his knowledge in an ostentatious, dogmatic, or dull manner, often placing excessive emphasis on trivial details and formal rules. [Italian *pedante* schoolmaster, teacher; of uncertain origin.]

pe·dan·tic (pi dan′tik) *adj.* of, like, characteristic of, or of the nature of a pedant or pedantry. —pe·dan′ti·cal·ly, *adv.*

ped·ant·ry (ped′ən trē) *pl.*, -ries. *n.* 1. qualities, characteristics, manner, or practices of a pedant, esp. ostentatious display of knowledge or overemphasis on trivial details and formal rules. 2. instance of being pedantic.

ped·ate (ped′āt) *adj.* 1. having feet: *pedate animals.* 2. resembling or serving as a foot or feet; footlike. 3. *Botany.* having the two lateral lobes divided into smaller segments: *a pedate leaf.* [Latin *pedātus*, past participle of *pedāre* to furnish with feet, from *pēs* foot.]

ped·dle (ped′əl) -dled, -dling. *v.t.* 1. to sell (merchandise), usually in small quantities, esp. by traveling from place to place. 2. to dispense, deal out, or distribute: *to peddle rumors.* —*v.i.* to travel from place to place offering merchandise for sale. [From PEDDLER.]

ped·dler (ped′lər) *also*, ped·lar. *n.* one who peddles. [Modification of obsolete *pedder*, from (dialectal) *ped* basket; of uncertain origin.]

-pede *combining form* foot; feet: *centipede.* [Latin *pēs*, stem of *pēs* foot.]

ped·er·ast (ped′ə rast′) *n.* man who engages in pederasty.

ped·er·as·ty (ped′ə ras′tē) *n.* sexual relations between males, esp. between a man and a boy. [Greek *paiderastiā* love of boys, going back to *pais* boy + *erān* to love.]

ped·es·tal (ped′əst əl) *n.* 1. architectural support for a column, statue, or similar upright structure. 2. any base or supporting structure, as for a bust, sculpture, or urn. 3. on a pedestal, in a position or state of high, often excessive or exaggerated regard or estimation: *The little boy put his father on a pedestal.* —*v.t.*, -taled, -tal·ing; *also*, British, -talled, -tal·ling. to place on or support with a pedestal. [French *piédestal* support, from Italian *piedistallo* base[1], support, from *pie* foot (from Latin *pēs*) + *di* (from Latin *dē* from) + *stallo* stall (of Germanic origin).]

pe·des·tri·an (pə des′trē ən) *n.* one who travels on foot, esp. as opposed to a motorist; walker. —*adj.* 1. traveling on foot; walking. 2. lacking originality, imagination, or excitement; commonplace or dull: *a pedestrian literary style.* [Latin *pedester* (from *pēs* foot) + -IAN.]

pedi- *combining form* foot; feet: *pedicure.* [Latin *ped-*, stem of *pēs* foot.]

pe·di·a·tri·cian (pē′dē ə trish′ən) *n.* doctor specializing in pediatrics. Also, pe·di·at·rist (pē′dē ə trist′).

pe·di·at·rics (pē′dē at′riks) *n.,pl.* branch of medical science that

deals with the care of babies and children and the treatment of their diseases. ▲ construed as singular. [Greek *paid-*, stem of *pais* child + *iātreiā* medical treatment + -ICS.] —pe′di·at′ric, *adj.*

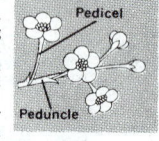

ped·i·cel (ped′i səl) *also*, ped·i·cle (ped′i kəl). *n.* 1. *Botany.* small stem, esp. one supporting a single flower in a flower cluster. 2. *Zoology.* small foot or footlike part or organ. [Modern Latin *pedicellus*, from Latin *pedīculus* footstalk, diminutive of *pēs* foot.]

pe·dic·u·lo·sis (pi dik′yə lō′sis) *n.* state or condition of being infested with lice. [Modern Latin *pediculosis*, from Latin *pedīculus* louse, diminutive of *pedis.*]

Pedicel

ped·i·cure (ped′i kyoor′) *n.* cosmetic treatment of the feet, esp. trimming and polishing of the toenails. [French *pédicure*, from Latin *pēs* foot + *cūra* care.]

ped·i·gree (ped′i grē′) *n.* 1. line of ancestors; descent; lineage. 2. detailed record or list of ancestry or descent, esp. of an animal. 3. distinguished or pure descent. [Probably from Middle French *pie de grue* foot of a crane (from Latin *pēs* foot + *dē* from + *grūs* crane); referring to the resemblance to a crane's foot of a mark used to indicate descent in genealogies.]

ped·i·greed (ped′ə grēd′) *adj.* having a recorded or known pedigree, esp. one that is distinguished.

ped·i·ment (ped′ə mənt) *n.* 1. low-pitched, triangular, gablelike part on the front of a building, as over a portico. 2. similar decorative member, not necessarily triangular in shape, as over a door, screen, or window. [Earlier *periment*, probably a modification of PYRAMID.]

Pediment

ped·lar (ped′lər) peddler.

pe·dol·o·gy (pi dol′ə jē) *n.* science that deals with the origin, nature, and classification of soils. [Greek *pedon* soil[1] + -LOGY.] —pe·do·log·i·cal (pē′də loj′i kəl), *adj.* —pe·dol′o·gist, *n.*

pe·dom·e·ter (pi dom′ə tər) *n.* instrument that measures the distance covered in walking by counting the number of steps taken and multiplying by the length of a single step. [French *pédomètre*, from Latin *pēs* foot + Greek *metron* measure.]

pe·dun·cle (pi dung′kəl) *n.* 1. *Botany.* stem, esp. one supporting a flower cluster. 2. *Zoology.* stemlike part or structure. 3. *Anatomy.* one of several bundles of nerve fibers connecting parts of the central nervous system. [Modern Latin *pedunculus*, diminutive of Latin *pēs* foot.] —pe·dun·cu·lar (pi dung′kyə lər), pe·dun′cled, *adj.*

pe·dun·cu·late (pi dung′kyə lit) *adj.* growing on or having a peduncle. Also, pe·dun·cu·lat·ed (pi dung′kyə lā′tid).

peek (pēk) *v.i.* to look quickly, furtively, or cautiously. —*n.* quick, furtive, or cautious look. [Of uncertain origin.]

peel¹ (pēl) *n.* skin or outer covering that has been or can be removed from certain fruits and vegetables: *a banana peel.* —*v.t.* 1. to remove the skin or outer covering from: *to peel a potato.* 2. to remove or strip off (an outer covering): *to peel a stamp off an envelope.* —*v.i.* 1. to come off, as in pieces or strips: *The paint is peeling off the walls.* 2. to lose or shed an outer covering or layer, as of skin: *Gary's sunburned back was already peeling.* 3. *Slang.* to undress. 4. to keep one's eye(s) peeled. *Informal.* to be watchful; keep alert: *Keep your eyes peeled for any sign of trouble.* 5. to peel off. (of aircraft) to veer off from a flight formation, esp. in order to make a dive. [Old French *peler* to strip off, as skin, from Latin *pilāre* to deprive of hair, from *pilus* hair.]

peel² (pēl) *n.* long-handled, shovel-like implement used by bakers to put bread or other items into an oven or remove them. [Old French *pele* shovel, from Latin *pāla* shovel, spade[1].]

Peel, Sir Robert (pēl) 1788–1850, English statesman.

peel·er (pē′lər) *n.* device for peeling the skin or outer covering from certain fruits and vegetables: *a potato peeler.*

peel·ing (pē′ling) *n.* something that has or has been peeled off: *paint peelings.*

peen (pēn) *n.* cone-shaped, hemispherical, or ball-shaped end of the head of a hammer opposite the face. [Probably of Scandinavian origin.]

peep¹ (pēp) *v.i.* 1. to look furtively or cautiously, as through a narrow opening or from a concealed place; peek: *to peep through a crack in a wall.* 2. to come gradually or partially into view: *The moon peeped through the clouds.* —*v.i.* to cause to become visible; put forth. —*n.* 1. furtive, cautious, or quick look. 2. first appearance: *the peep of dawn.* [Possibly form of PEEK.]

peep² (pēp) *n.* 1. short, sharp sound, as that made by a young bird; cheep. 2. utterance; sound: *Not another peep out of you!* —*v.i.* to utter

one or more short, sharp sounds, like those of a young bird; chirp. [Imitative.]

peep·er¹ (pē′pər) n. 1. one who peeps or spies. 2. *Informal.* eye. [PEEP¹ + -ER¹.]

peep·er² (pē′pər) n. any of several tree frogs, family Hylidae, that make a shrill, peeping noise, esp. the **spring peeper,** *H. crucifer,* found in the United States and Canada. [PEEP² + -ER¹.]

peep·hole (pēp′hōl′) n. small hole or opening through which one may look, esp. in a door.

peep·ing Tom (pē′ping) *also,* **Peep·ing Tom.** one who spies on others, esp. in order to derive sexual pleasure. [From *Peeping Tom,* a tailor who attempted to look at the naked Lady Godiva during her ride through Coventry and was instantly struck blind.]

peep show *also,* **peep′show′.** exhibition of pictures or objects viewed through a small opening that is usually fitted with a magnifying glass.

peer¹ (pēr) n. 1. one who is equal to another, as in status, social class, or ability; equal: *to be tried by a jury of one's peers. As an orator, he had few peers.* 2. titled nobleman, esp. in Great Britain, a member of one of the five degrees of nobility: duke, marquis, earl, viscount, or baron. [Old French *per* one of equal rank, from Latin *pār* equal.]

peer² (pēr) v.i. 1. to look closely or searchingly, as in an effort to see clearly: *to try to peer through the darkness, to peer at the small print in a newspaper.* 2. to come into view; be partially visible. [Possibly short for APPEAR.]

peer·age (pēr′ij) n. 1. rank or dignity of a peer or nobleman. 2. peers or noblemen of a country collectively: *The peerage controlled the wealth of the country.* 3. book containing a list of the peers of a country and their genealogies.

peer·ess (pēr′is) n. 1. wife or widow of a peer or nobleman. 2. woman who holds the rank of a peer in her own right.

peer·less (pēr′lis) adj. without equal; matchless: *We were awed by the building's peerless grandeur.* —**peer′less·ly,** adv. —**peer′less·ness,** n.

peeve (pēv) peeved, peev·ing. v.t. to annoy; irritate; vex. —n. cause of annoyance; grievance. [From PEEVISH.]

pee·vish (pē′vish) adj. 1. irritable and ill-tempered; cranky: *Rick always gets very peevish when he doesn't feel well.* 2. displaying or marked by annoyance or irritation: *a peevish expression.* [Of uncertain origin.] —**pee′vish·ly,** adv. —**pee′vish·ness,** n.

pee·wee (pē′wē′) n. *Informal.* unusually small person or thing.

peg (peg) n. 1. piece of wood, metal, or other hard substance, usually cylindrical and tapered, that can be fitted or driven into a surface, as to fasten parts together, hang something on, or serve as a marker. 2. wooden, plastic, or metal pin in a stringed instrument that secures and regulates the tension of a string. 3. step; degree: *You've come down a peg in my estimation.* 4. reason; pretext; basis: *a peg to hang a grievance upon* (Surtees). 5. alcoholic drink, esp. brandy and soda or whiskey and soda. 6. *Informal.* throw, esp. a fast and accurate throw in baseball. 7. **to take down a peg.** to lower the self-opinion of; humble. —v.t., **pegged, peg·ging.** 1. to fasten or mark with a peg or pegs. 2. to fix the price of, as a stock, by keeping it at or close to a certain figure. 3. *Informal.* to throw. 4. *Informal.* to recognize or classify; identify: *I had him pegged as a scoundrel from the very beginning.* —v.i. *Informal.* to work hard and persistently (often with *away*). [Possibly from Middle Dutch *pegge* little wooden pin for fastening.]

Peg·a·sus (peg′ə səs) n. 1. *Greek Mythology.* winged horse that sprang from the blood of Medusa when she was killed by Perseus. 2. constellation in the northern sky, conventionally depicted as a winged horse.

peg·board (peg′bôrd′) n. board having holes into which pegs or hooks can be inserted, as for keeping score.

peg leg *Informal.* 1. artificial leg, esp. one made of wood. 2. person having such a leg.

peg·ma·tite (peg′mə tīt′) n. coarse-grained granite rock often found in dikes, the source of many rare elements. [Greek *pēgmat-,* stem of *pēgma* framework + -ITE¹.]

peg-top (peg′top′) adj. wide or full at the top and tapering towards the bottom: *peg-top trousers.*

P.E.I. Prince Edward Island.

peign·oir (pān wär′, pen-, pān′wär, pen′-) n. woman's dressing gown or negligee. [French *peignoir,* from *peigner* to comb the hair, from Latin *pectināre* to comb.]

Pei·ping (pā′ping′, bā′-) see Peking.

pe·jo·ra·tion (pej′ə rā′shən, pē′jə-) n. worsening; deterioration.

pe·jo·ra·tive (pi jôr′ə tiv, -jor′-, pej′ə rā′tiv) adj. having a derogatory meaning or effect; disparaging: *to use a word in its pejorative sense.* [Latin *pejōrātus,* past participle of *pejōrāre* to make worse + -IVE.] —**pe·jo′ra·tive·ly,** adv.

Pe·king (pē′king′) n. capital of the People's Republic of China, in the northeastern part of the country, formerly known as Peiping. Pop. (1958 est.), 3,500,000.

Pe·king·ese (pē′kə nēz′, -nēs′, pē′king ēz′, -ēs′) pl., **-ese.** *also,* **Pe·kin·ese** (pē′kə nēz′, -nēs′). n. 1. small dog having a wrinkled, flat face, bulging eyes, and a long, silky coat. Height: 6 inches at the shoulder. 2. member or close descendant of the people of Peking. 3. Chinese dialect spoken in Peking. —adj. of or relating to Peking or its people.

Peking man. extinct primitive man whose fossil remains were found near Peking, China. First classified as *Sinanthropus pekinensis,* it is now generally classified with Java man as *Homo erectus.*

Pekingese

pe·koe (pē′kō) n. superior grade of black tea from India, Ceylon, and Java, made from the smallest tea leaves. [Chinese *pek-ho* white down²; because only the young tea leaves that still have down are picked.]

pel·age (pel′ij) n. hair, fur, wool, or other soft covering of a mammal. [French *pelage* coat of an animal, from Old French *pel* hair, from Latin *pilus.*]

pe·lag·ic (pə laj′ik) adj. of, relating to, or inhabiting the open sea, usually near the surface of the water. [Latin *pelagicus* relating to the sea, from Greek *pelagikos,* from *pelagos* sea.]

Pe·lée, Mount (pə lā′) volcano on the island of Martinique in the West Indies.

pel·er·ine (pel′ə rēn′) n. waist-length cape, usually having long ends hanging down in front, worn by women in the seventeenth and eighteenth centuries. [French *pèlerine,* from *pèlerin* pilgrim. See PILGRIM.]

pelf (pelf) n. money; wealth. ▲ usually used disparagingly. [Old French *pelfre* booty; of uncertain origin.]

pel·i·can (pel′i kən) n. any of various web-footed water birds, genus *Pelecanus,* having predominantly white plumage and a large, distensible pouch beneath the bill that is used for storing fish. Length: 4–6 feet. [Late Latin *pelicānus,* from Greek *pelekan,* from *pelekys* ax; referring to the appearance of its large bill.]

Pelican

pe·lisse (pə lēs′) n. woman's coat or cloak, usually lined or trimmed with fur, worn in the eighteenth and nineteenth centuries. [Old French *pelisse* fur, fur coat, going back to Late Latin *pelliceus* made of skins, from Latin *pellis* skin, pelt².]

pel·lag·ra (pə lag′rə, -lā′grə) n. disease characterized by digestive disturbances, skin eruptions, and nervous disorders. It is caused by a niacin deficiency in the diet. [Italian *pellagra,* from *pelle* skin, from Latin *pellis.*]

pel·let (pel′it) n. 1. small ball, as of food, medicine, or paper. 2. bullet or piece of shot. 3. ball usually of stone, formerly used as a missile, as in a cannon. [Old French *pelote* small ball, going back to Latin *pila* ball.]

pel·li·cle (pel′i kəl) n. thin skin or film, as on the surface of a liquid. [Latin *pellicula* small skin, diminutive of *pellis* skin.]

pell-mell (pel′mel′) *also,* **pell·mell.** adv. 1. in great, often disorderly haste; headlong. 2. in a jumbled or confused manner; without order. —adj. disorderly; hasty; confused; tumultuous. —n. confused mixture; jumble; disorder. [French *pêle-mêle* disorder, confusedly, earlier *pesle-mesle* (rhyming repetition with change of consonant of *mesle,* imperative of *mesler* to mix, going back to Latin *miscēre*).]

pel·lu·cid (pə lōō′sid) adj. 1. transparent or translucent, as glass. 2. easy to understand; lucid: *a pellucid writing style.* [Latin *pellūcidus* transparent, going back to *per* through + *lūcēre* to shine.] —**pel·lu·cid·i·ty** (pel′yə sid′ə tē), **pel·lu′cid·ness,** n. —**pel·lu′cid·ly,** adv.

Peloponnesian War. war fought between Athens and Sparta from 431 to 404 B.C., ending in a victory for Sparta.

Pel·o·pon·ne·sus (pel′ə pə nē′səs) *also,* **Pel·o·pon·ne·sos.** n. peninsula in southern Greece between the Ionian and Aegean seas, formerly known as Morea. —**Pel·o·pon·ne·sian** (pel′ə pə nē′zhən, -shən), adj.

Pe·lops (pē′lops) n. *Greek Mythology.* son of Tantalus, served to the gods as food by his father but later restored to life by them.

pe·lo·ta (pe lō′tə) n. jai alai. [Spanish *pelota* ball, going back to Latin *pila* ball.]

pelt¹ (pelt) v.t. 1. to attack or strike repeatedly with or as if with something thrown: *The children pelted each other with snowballs.* 2. to beat against continuously or repeatedly: *A shower of hail pelted the roof.* 3. to throw or hurl (missiles). —v.i. to beat or strike heavily or continuously. —n. 1. hard blow, as from something thrown.

2. full pelt. maximum speed: *The horse galloped away at full pelt.* [Of uncertain origin.]

pelt² (pelt) *n.* skin of an animal with its fur or hair, esp. when removed to be used for making garments or other items. [Possibly from PELTRY.]

pelt·ry (pel′trē) *n.* pelts collectively. [Anglo-Norman *pelterie,* going back to Old French *pel* skin, from Latin *pellis* skin.]

pel·vic (pel′vik) *adj.* of or relating to the pelvis.

pelvic fin, in fish, one of a pair of hind fins, corresponding to the hind limbs of higher vertebrates.

pelvic girdle 1. in vertebrates, the bony arch to which the hind limbs are attached. **2.** in man, the arch by which the lower limbs are attached. Also, **pelvic arch.**

pel·vis (pel′vis) *pl.,* **-vis·es** or **-ves** (-vēz) *n.* **1.** large, basin-shaped ring of bone that protects and supports the organs in the lower abdomen, consisting, in humans, of the sacrum, the coccyx, and the hipbones. **2.** similar structure in many vertebrates. [Latin *pēlvis* basin; referring to its resemblance to a basin.]

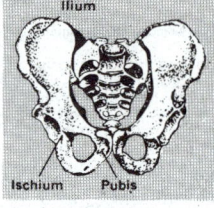
Pelvis

Ilium / Ischium / Pubis

Pem·ba (pem′bə) *n.* island in the Indian Ocean, off the eastern coast of Africa, part of Tanzania. Area, approx. 380 sq. mi. Pop. (1967), 164,243.

pem·mi·can (pem′i kən) *also,* **pem·i·can.** *n.* **1.** food preparation consisting of lean meat that is dried, pounded, and mixed with melted fat to form a paste and pressed into cakes. **2.** similar concentrated food preparation made of dried meat, dried fruit, flour, and sugar, used as emergency rations. [Cree *pimecan* the food preparation of lean meat, from *pime* fat.]

pen¹ (pen) *n.* **1.** any of various instruments for writing or drawing with ink. **2.** detachable metal point of certain pens. **3.** fountain pen. **4.** ball-point pen. **5.** pen regarded as a means of expression or instrument of authorship: *The pen is mightier than the sword* (Bulwer-Lytton, 1839). **6.** writing style or ability: *the author's scathing pen.* **7.** profession of writing: *men of the pen.* **8.** writer; author. —*v.t.,* **penned, pen·ning.** to write with or as with a pen: *to pen a letter.* [Old French *penne* quill, feather pen for writing, from Latin *penna* feather; because the earliest pens were made from feathers.]

pen² (pen) *n.* **1.** small enclosure used to confine animals. **2.** animals confined in such an enclosure. **3.** any of various small or relatively small enclosures, as a playpen or a bull pen. —*v.t.,* **penned** or **pent, pen·ning.** to confine in or as in a pen. [Old English *penn* fold².]

pen³ (pen) *n. Slang.* penitentiary.

pen⁴ (pen) *n.* female swan. [Of uncertain origin.]

pen., peninsula.

pe·nal (pēn′əl) *adj.* **1.** of, relating to, or prescribing punishment, esp. legal punishment: *penal laws.* **2.** for or constituting punishment: *penal servitude.* **3.** liable to punishment; punishable: *a penal offense.* [Latin *poenalis* relating to punishment, from *poena* punishment, from Greek *poinē* penalty.]

pe·nal·ize (pēn′əl īz′) -ized, -iz·ing. *v.t.* **1.** to subject to a penalty or punishment: *Team members will be penalized for lateness.* **2.** to declare (an action) liable to penalty or punishment: *That type of violation is penalized in all sports.* **3.** to put at a disadvantage; handicap: *His lack of education penalized him in the business world.* —**pe′nal·i·za′tion,** *n.*

pen·al·ty (pen′əl tē) *pl.,* **-ties.** *n.* **1.** punishment established or imposed for violating a law or regulation. **2.** sum of money required to be paid as punishment for a violation committed; fine. **3.** unpleasant or painful consequence of an action or condition: *His foolishness had earned him the penalty he'd now have to suffer.* **4.** *Sports.* disadvantage or punishment imposed on a player or side for an infraction of the rules. [Medieval Latin *poenalitas* punishment, from Latin *poenalis* relating to punishment. See PENAL.]

pen·ance (pen′əns) *n.* **1.** punishment, usually self-inflicted, undergone to express or demonstrate repentance for a sin or offense. **2.** in some Christian churches, a sacrament administered by a priest that includes sorrow for and confession of sin, acceptance of prescribed penalties, and absolution. **3. to do penance.** to express or demonstrate repentance by undergoing punishment. [Old French *peneance,* from Latin *paenitentia* repentance. Doublet of PENITENCE.]

Pe·nang (pi nang′) *n.* **1.** island off the western coast of the Malay Peninsula. Area, 108 sq. mi. Pop. (1962 est.), 671,300. **2.** port city on this island, formerly known as George Town. Pop. (1957), 234,930.

pe·na·tes (pə nā′tēz) *n.,pl.* household gods of the ancient Romans. [Latin *Penātēs.*]

pence (pens) *British.* plural of **penny.**

pen·chant (pen′chənt) *n.* strong liking or inclination: *a penchant for*

gardening. [French *penchant* inclination, from *pencher* to lean, incline, going back to Latin *pendēre* to hang.]

pen·cil (pen′səl) *n.* **1.** marking, drawing, or writing implement usually consisting of a stick of graphite, chalk, or similar substance enclosed in a case of wood, metal, or plastic. **2.** something like a pencil in shape or use, esp. an implement or stick having a cosmetic or medicinal use, as a styptic pencil. **3.** style, ability, or technique in drawing or writing. —*v.t.,* **-ciled, -cil·ing;** *also, British,* **-cilled, -cil·ling.** to write, draw, mark, or color with or as if with a pencil. [Old French *pincel* painter's brush, going back to Latin *penicillus* little tail, painter's brush (which resembled a little tail), diminutive of *pēnis* tail.]

pend·ant (pen′dənt) *n.* **1.** piece of jewelry or other ornamental object that is suspended, as from a necklace or bracelet. **2.** ornament or fixture, often elaborately decorated, hanging down, as from a roof or ceiling. **3.** match, parallel, companion, or addition: *The narrative of the historian forms a fitting pendant to that of the satirist* (Merivale, 1862). —*adj.* pendent. [Old French *pendant,* present participle of *pendre* to hang, going back to Latin *pendēre* to hang.]

pend·ent (pen′dənt) *adj.* **1.** suspended; hanging. **2.** jutting out; overhanging. **3.** undecided or unsettled; pending. —*n.* pendant. [Latin *pendēns,* present participle of *pendēre* to hang.] —**pen′dent·ly,** *adv.*

pen·den·tive (pen den′tiv) *n.* spherical triangular member between each pair of arches supporting a dome. [French *pendentif,* from Latin *pendēns.* See PENDENT.]

pend·ing (pen′ding) *adj.* **1.** awaiting decision or settlement; remaining undecided: *The issue in question is still pending.* **2.** impending; imminent. —*prep.* **1.** while awaiting; until: *We postponed our picnic pending a change in the weather.* **2.** during. [Obsolete *pend* to hang (going back to Latin *pendēre*) + -ING².]

pen·drag·on (pen drag′ən) *n.* in ancient Britain, supreme leader or chief. [Welsh *pendragon* supreme leader in war, from *pen* chief + *dragon* dragon, leader in war (from Latin *dracō* dragon); referring to the dragon on the leader's banner. See DRAGON.]

pen·du·lous (pen′jə ləs, -dyə ləs, pend′jə əs) *adj.* **1.** hanging, esp. in a loose or drooping manner. **2.** swinging: *a pendulous motion.* **3.** wavering; vacillating. [Latin *pendulus* hanging, from *pendēre* to hang.] —**pen′du·lous·ly,** *adv.* —**pen′du·lous·ness,** *n.*

pen·du·lum (pen′jə ləm, -dyə ləm, pend′əl əm) *n.* **1.** suspended body that can be set in motion to swing back and forth or oscillate about a fixed point. **2.** such a device used to regulate the movement of a clock. [Modern Latin *pendulum,* from Latin *pendulus* hanging. See PENDULOUS.]

Pendentives

Pe·nel·o·pe (pə nel′ə pē) *n. Classical Legend.* wife of Ulysses, noted for her faithfulness during her husband's long absence.

pe·ne·plain (pē′nə plān′) *also,* **pe·ne·plane.** *n.* land surface reduced by erosion to an almost flat plain. [Latin *paene* almost + PLAIN¹.]

pen·e·tra·ble (pen′ə trə bəl) *adj.* capable of being penetrated. [Latin *penetrābilis,* from *penetrāre* to enter, pierce.] —**pen′e·tra·bil′i·ty,** *n.*

pen·e·trate (pen′ə trāt′) -trat·ed, -trat·ing. *v.t.* **1.** to pass into or through, esp. by force or with difficulty: *to penetrate enemy lines. The lance penetrated the knight's shield.* **2.** to seep or spread through; permeate: *The rain penetrated my jacket.* **3.** to discover the meaning of; understand: *Science endeavors to penetrate the mysteries of nature.* **4.** to have a strong effect on; affect deeply. —*v.i.* **1.** to pass or force a way into or through something. **2.** to have a strong effect on someone. [Latin *penetrātus,* past participle of *penetrāre* to enter, pierce.] —**Syn.** *v.t.* **2.** see permeate.

pen·e·trat·ing (pen′ə trā′ting) *adj.* **1.** having a strong effect, as on the senses or emotions; piercing: *a penetrating wind, a penetrating stare.* **2.** discerning; acute: *a penetrating analysis.* —**pen′e·trat′ing·ly,** *adv.*

pen·e·tra·tion (pen′ə trā′shən) *n.* **1.** act, power, or extent of penetrating or making a way into or through something. **2.** mental acuteness; insight; discernment.

pen·e·tra·tive (pen′ə trā′tiv) *adj.* tending or able to penetrate. —**pen′e·tra′tive·ly,** *adv.* —**pen′e·tra′tive·ness,** *n.*

pen·guin (pen′gwin, peng′-) *n.* any of various flightless sea birds, family Spheniscidae, native to Antarctica and to coastlines of southern continents, having webbed feet, flipperlike wings

Penguin

used for swimming, and dense plumage that is typically black or gray on the back and white on the chest, stomach, and legs. Height: to 4 feet. [Possibly from Welsh *pen* head + *gwyn* white; name originally applied by sailors to the great auk, now extinct, a flightless bird with a white patch on its face, and later applied to the penguin, also flightless, but usually having a black head.]

pen·i·cil·lin (pen′ə sil′in) *n.* powerful antibiotic made from certain penicillium molds, used in the treatment of a wide variety of bacterial infections. [From PENICILLIUM.]

pen·i·cil·li·um (pen′ə sil′ē əm) *pl.*, **-cil·li·ums** or **-cil·li·a** (-sil′ē ə). *n.* any of a group of fungi, class Ascomycetes, commonly found as a blue-green mold on bread, cheese, and other foods. Certain penicillium molds are a source of the drug penicillin. [Modern Latin *penicillium,* from Latin *pēnicillus* painter's brush; referring to its brushlike spore case. See PENCIL.]

pen·in·su·la (pə nin′sə lə, -syə lə) *n.* body of land almost entirely surrounded by water, usually connected with the mainland by an isthmus. [Latin *paeninsula,* from *paene* almost + *īnsula* island.] —**pen·in′su·lar,** *adj.*

pe·nis (pē′nis) *pl.,* **-nis·es** or **-nes** (-nēz). *n.* male organ of urination and copulation. [Latin *pēnis* penis, tail.] —**pe·ni·al** (pē′nē əl), **pe·nile** (pē′nīl), *adj.*

pen·i·tence (pen′ə təns) *n.* state of being penitent; repentance; contrition. [Old French *penitence,* from Latin *paenitentia.* Doublet of PENANCE.]

Syn. Penitence, repentance, contrition mean sincere sorrow or remorse for sin or wrongdoing. **Penitence** suggests humble sorrow for one's wrongdoing: *Tom's father forgave him after he expressed his true penitence.* **Repentance** implies the complete realization of one's sinfulness and the sincere will to reform: *I came not to call the righteous, but sinners to repentance* (Luke 5:32). **Contrition** suggests repentance as expressed through outward signs of pain, grief, and self-abasement: *Tears of contrition fell down her cheek.*

pen·i·tent (pen′ə tənt) *adj.* feeling or expressing sorrow or regret for sin or wrongdoing and resolved on atonement; repentant: *She wrote me several penitent letters acknowledging her crime* (Defoe, 1723). —*n.* **1.** one who is penitent. **2.** one who repents of sin and receives the sacrament of penance. [Latin *paenitēns,* present participle of *paenitēre* to repent.] —**pen′i·tent·ly,** *adv.*

pen·i·ten·tial (pen′ə ten′shəl) *adj.* **1.** of, relating to, or expressing penitence or repentance. **2.** of or relating to penance. —**pen′i·ten′tial·ly,** *adv.*

pen·i·ten·ti·a·ry (pen′ə ten′shər ē) *pl.,* **-ries.** *n.* **1.** institution, esp. a state or federal institution, for the confinement of persons convicted of major crimes. **2.** in the Roman Catholic Church, a tribunal of the Holy See, headed by a cardinal, that is concerned with special dispensations, problems of conscience, and certain other matters. —*adj.* **1.** (of an offense) punishable by imprisonment in a penitentiary. **2.** relating to or used for imprisonment, punishment, discipline, or reformation. **3.** of or relating to penance.

pen·knife (pen′nīf′) *pl.,* **-knives.** *n.* small pocketknife, originally used for making or sharpening quill pens.

pen·man (pen′mən) *pl.,* **-men.** *n.* **1.** writer; author. **2.** one skilled in penmanship.

pen·man·ship (pen′mən ship′) *n.* **1.** style or quality of handwriting. **2.** art or skill of handwriting.

Penn, William (pen) 1644–1718, English Quaker and founder of Pennsylvania.

Penn., Pennsylvania. Also, **Penna.**

pen name, assumed name under which an author writes; pseudonym; nom de plume. —**Syn.** see **pseudonym.**

pen·nant (pen′ənt) *n.* **1.** long flag, usually triangular, used esp. as a school or team emblem or, on a ship, for signaling or identification. **2.** championship in one of the professional baseball leagues, symbolized by such a flag awarded to the winning team. [Blend of PENNON and PENDANT.]

pen·nate (pen′āt) *adj.* having wings or feathers. Also, **pen′nat·ed.** [Latin *pennātus* winged, from *penna* feather, wing.]

pen·ni·less (pen′ē lis) *adj.* having no money; extremely poor.

pen·non (pen′ən) *n.* **1.** long, triangular or swallow-tailed flag or streamer borne on the head of a knight's lance in the Middle Ages. **2.** any flag or banner. **3.** *Archaic.* wing. [Middle French *penon* flag, streamer, from *pene* feather, wing, from Latin *penna.*]

Penn·syl·va·nia (pen′səl vān′yə, -vā′nē ə) *n.* state in the eastern United States, the country's leading center of iron and steel production. Capital, Harrisburg. Area, 45,333 sq. mi. Pop. (1970), 11,793,909. Abbreviations, **Pa., Penn.**

Pennsylvania Dutch 1. descendants of German immigrants who settled in southeastern Pennsylvania in the seventeenth and eighteenth centuries. **2.** High German dialect heavily mixed with English, spoken by these people.

Penn·syl·va·nian (pen′səl vān′yən, -vā′nē ən) *n.* **1.** native or inhabitant of Pennsylvania. **2.** later of the two geological subdivisions of the Carboniferous period, during which insects were abundant and the first reptiles appeared. See **geology** for table. —*adj.* **1.** of or relating to Pennsylvania. **2.** of or relating to the later of the two geological subdivisions of the Carboniferous period.

pen·ny (pen′ē) *pl.,* **pen·nies** or (*def. 2*) **pence. 1.** coin of the United States and Canada, equal to one cent. **2.** coin of the United Kingdom equal to 1/100 of a pound, formerly equal to 1/12 of a shilling. **3.** sum of money. **4. a pretty penny.** *Informal.* a large sum of money. [Old English *pening* British coin equal to one-twelfth of a shilling.]

penny ante 1. poker game having very low stakes. **2.** *Informal.* any transaction of little significance.

penny arcade, place or area, as in an amusement park, made up principally of coin-operated games and entertainment devices.

penny pincher, stingy or miserly person. —**pen′ny-pinch′ing,** *adj., n.*

pen·ny·roy·al (pen′ē roi′əl) *n.* any of several fragrant plants of the mint family, esp. the **Eurasian pennyroyal,** *Mentha pulegium,* that yields an aromatic oil used chiefly in making soaps, and the **American pennyroyal,** *Hedeoma pulegioides,* a common weed bearing aromatic leaves used in cooking. [Modification of earlier *puliol real* from Old French *puliol* pennyroyal (going back to Latin *pūlēium*) + *real* kingly (going back to Latin *rēgālis* relating to a king). See ROYAL.]

pen·ny·weight (pen′ē wāt′) *n.* measure of weight equal to twenty-four grains or 1/20 of a troy ounce.

pen·ny·wise (pen′ē wīz′) *adj.* prudent or thrifty in small matters: *to be penny-wise and pound-foolish.*

pen·ny·worth (pen′ē wurth′) *n.* **1.** as much as can be bought for a penny. **2.** small amount. **3.** bargain.

Pe·nob·scot (pə nob′skot) *n.* member of an American Indian tribe of the Algonquian language family, formerly living in central Maine.

pe·nol·o·gy (pē nol′ə jē) *n.* study of the punishment and rehabilitation of criminals and the management of prisons. [Greek *poinē* punishment + -LOGY.] —**pe·no·log·i·cal** (pē′nə loj′i kəl), *adj.* —**pe·nol′o·gist,** *n.*

pen pal, person with whom one exchanges letters, esp. without ever having met or when living so far apart that a personal meeting is not possible.

Pen·sa·co·la (pen′sə kō′lə) *n.* port city in northwestern Florida, on the Gulf of Mexico. Pop. (1970), 59,507.

pen·sile (pen′sil, -sīl) *adj.* **1.** hanging; suspended. **2.** (of birds) building a hanging nest. [Latin *pēnsilis* hanging down, from *pendēre* to hang.]

pen·sion[1] (pen′shən) *n.* periodic payment, other than wages, made to a retired or disabled person who has fulfilled certain requirements or conditions, by a former employer. —*v.t.* **1.** to grant a pension to. **2.** to retire or dismiss with a pension (with *off*). [Old French *pension* payment, from Latin *pēnsiō.*]

pen·sion[2] (päN syōN′) *n.* in France and other European countries, a boarding house or boarding school. [French *pension,* from Latin *pēnsiō* payment.]

pen·sion·er (pen′shə nər) *n.* **1.** one who receives a pension. **2.** hireling.

pen·sive (pen′siv) *adj.* **1.** engaged in deep and serious thought, often concerning matters of a sad nature: *The old man sat on the curb silently pensive.* **2.** marked by or expressing deep, often sad thoughtfulness: *a pensive look, a pensive mood.* [Old French *pensif* preoccupied by thought, from *penser* to think, from Latin *pēnsāre* to weigh, ponder.] —**pen′sive·ly,** *adv.* —**pen′sive·ness,** *n.*

pent (pent) *v.* a past tense and past participle of **pen**[2]. —*adj.* closely confined; shut up.

penta- *combining form* five: *pentagon, pentameter.* [Greek *pente* five.]

pen·ta·cle (pen′tə kəl) *n.* star with five points, used as a symbolic figure in magic. Also, **pen′ta·gram.** [Medieval Latin *pentaculum,* from Greek *pente* five.]

pen·ta·gon (pen′tə gon′) *n.* **1.** polygon with five sides and five angles. **2.a.** the **Pentagon,** five-sided building in Arlington, Virginia, that is the headquarters of the U.S. Department of Defense. **b.** power and influence of the military as represented by this building; the U.S. military establishment. [Late Latin *pentagōnum* the polygon, from Greek *pentagōnon,* from *pente* five + *gōnia* angle.]

pen·tag·o·nal (pen tag′ən əl) *adj.* having the geometric properties of a pentagon.

pen·ta·gram (pen′tə gram′) *n.* pentacle.

pen·ta·he·dron (pen′tə hē′drən) *pl.,* **-drons** or **-dra** (-drə). *n.* polyhedron with five faces. [Modern Latin *pentahedron,* Greek *pente* five + *hedra* base[1], seat.]

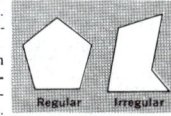

Pentagons

Regular   Irregular

pen·tam·e·ter (pen tam′ə tər) *n.* **1.** line of verse consisting of five metrical feet. **2.** verse composed of such lines. —*adj.* consisting of five metrical feet. [Latin *pentameter*, from Greek *pentametros*, from *pente* five + *metron* measure.]

pen·tane (pen′tān) *n.* colorless, volatile hydrocarbon of the alkane series, used as an anesthetic and to make ice. Formula: C₅H₁₂ [Greek *pente* five + -ANE; referring to the *five* carbon atoms in its molecule.]

Pen·ta·teuch (pen′tə tōōk′, -tūk′) *n.* first five books of the Old Testament collectively, ascribed to Moses, and consisting of Genesis, Exodus, Leviticus, Numbers, and Deuteronomy. In Judaism this group is called the Torah.

pen·tath·lon (pen tath′lən) *n.* athletic contest in which each contestant participates in five different events. [Greek *pentathlon*, from *pente* five + *āthlon* contest.]

pen·ta·ton·ic (pen′tə ton′ik) *adj.* of, designating, or relating to a musical scale consisting of only five tones.

Pen·te·cost (pen′tə kŏst′, kost′) *n.* **1.** Christian feast observed on the seventh Sunday after Easter, commemorating the descent of the Holy Ghost upon the Apostles. Also, **Whit′sun′day. 2.** shavuoth. [Latin *pentēcostē*, from Greek *pentēkostē (hēmera)* fiftieth (day).] —**pen′te·cos′tal,** *adj.*

pent·house (pent′hous′) *n.* **1.** apartment or dwelling on the roof of a building. **2.** shed, sloping roof, or similar structure attached to a wall or building. [Modification (influenced by English *house*) of earlier *pentice,* from Old French *apentis* shed with sloping roof forming part of a building, from Late Latin *appendicium* appendage, from Latin *appendēre* to hang on something.]

Pen·to·thal Sodium (pen′tə thŏl′) *n. Trademark.* sodium pentothal.

pent-up (pent′up′) *adj.* not expressed or released; restrained; held in: *pent-up feelings, pent-up hostility.*

pe·nu·che (pi nōō′chē) *n.* candy, resembling fudge, usually made of brown sugar, milk or cream, butter, and nuts. Also, **pa·no′cha.** [Form of PANOCHA.]

pe·nult (pē′nult, pi nult′) *n.* second to last syllable in a word. Also, **pe·nul·ti·ma** (pi nul′tə mə). [Latin *paenultima (syllaba)* last (syllable) but one, from *paene* almost + *ultimus* last.]

pe·nul·ti·mate (pi nul′tə mit) *adj.* **1.** next to the last. **2.** of, relating to, or occurring on the penult of a word. —*n.* the second to last.

pe·num·bra (pi num′brə) *pl.* **-brae** (-brē) or **-bras.** *n.* **1.** *Astronomy.* **a.** in an eclipse, the partial shadow between the region of total eclipse and the region of complete illumination. **b.** diverging cone of partial shadow cast by a nonradiant body, as a planet, in the direction away from the sun. **c.** grayish fringe around the dark central portion of a sunspot. **2.** partially darkened region surrounding the completely dark central region of a shadow. Distinguished from **umbra** in all definitions. [Modern Latin *penumbra*, from Latin *paene* almost + *umbra* shadow.]

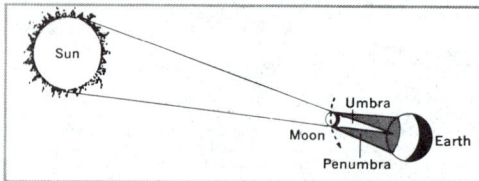

Penumbra

pe·nu·ri·ous (pi noor′ē əs, -nyoor′-) *adj.* **1.** greatly reluctant to spend or part with money; miserly. **2.** extremely poor; poverty-stricken. **3.** scanty; barren. —**pe·nu′ri·ous·ly,** *adv.* —**pe·nu′ri·ous·ness,** *n.*

pen·u·ry (pen′yər ē) *n.* extreme poverty. [Latin *pēnūria* want.]

pe·on (pē′on, -ən) *n.* unskilled worker or farm laborer in Latin America or the southwestern United States, esp. one who is forced to work in exchange for the payment of debts. [Spanish *peon* foot soldier, day laborer, from Medieval Latin *pedō* foot soldier, going back to Latin *pēs* foot. Doublet of PAWN².]

pe·on·age (pē′ə nij) *n.* **1.** condition of being a peon. **2.** practice of forcing people to work in exchange for the payment of debts.

pe·o·ny (pē′ə nē) *pl.* **-nies.** *n.* **1.** large, showy, pink, red, or white flower of any of a group of hardy plants, genus *Paeonia.* **2.** plant bearing this flower, widely cultivated in gardens. [Old English *peonie,* from Latin *paeōnia,* from Greek *paiōniā,* from *Paiōn* physician of the Greek gods who supposedly discovered the plant.]

peo·ple (pē′pəl) *pl.* **-ple** or *(def. 2)* **-ples.** *n.* **1.** persons, esp. when considered indefinitely or collectively: *She's afraid of what people might say. This theater can seat 500 people.* **2.** body of persons comprising a

nation, race, tribe, or community: *the Israeli people, primitive peoples, the peoples of Asia.* **3.** body of persons considered as or comprising a distinct group: *rich people, thin people, people of New England.* **4.** body of citizens of a state or other political unit: *Congressmen are elected by the people.* **5.** body or mass of common persons as distinguished from persons of some special group or class: *the everyday language of the people.* **6.** persons in relation to a superior, as the subjects of a ruler: *The king was loved by his people.* **7.** human beings as distinguished from animals: *Distemper is not a disease affecting people.* **8.** *Informal.* one's family; relatives. **9. the little** (or **good) people.** leprechauns; fairies. —*v.t.,* **-pled, -pling.** to fill with inhabitants; populate: *the myriad of human beings who people the earth.* [Old French *pueple* body of persons, nation, the public, from Latin *populus.*]

People's Party, Populist Party.

Pe·o·ri·a (pē ôr′ē ə) *n.* city in north-central Illinois. Pop. (1970), 126,963.

pep (pep) *n.* liveliness and high spirits; energy: *Mom's always full of pep in the morning.* —*v.t.* **pepped, pep·ping.** to make lively or cheerful; fill with energy (with *up*): *The good news pepped him up.* [Short for PEPPER.]

pep·los (pep′ləs) *also,* **pep·lus.** *n.* garment resembling a shawl, draped over the upper part of the body by women of ancient Greece. [Greek *peplos.*]

pep·lum (pep′ləm) *pl.* **-lums** or **-la** (-lə). *n.* **1.** short overskirt or ruffle attached at the waistline and extending over the hips. **2.** peplos. [Latin *peplum* upper garment, from Greek *peplos* upper garment, mantle.]

pe·po (pē′pō) *pl.* **-pos.** *n.* fruit, usually containing numerous seeds, that resembles the berry in structure but has a hard rind, as the watermelon, cucumber, or squash. [Latin *pepō* melon, from Greek *pepōn.*]

pep·per (pep′ər) *n.* **1.a.** hot, pungent spice consisting of the berries, either whole or ground, of the plant, *Piper nigrum.* **Black pepper** is prepared from entire dried berries that are ground. **White pepper** consists of the dried seeds of the berries with the outer coat and pulp removed. **b.** any plant of the genus *Piper,* family Piperaceae. **2.a.** red or green, sweet or hot, edible fruit of the plant *Capsicum frutescens.* **b.** plant bearing this fruit. **c.** any plant of the genus *Capsicum.* **3.** cayenne. —*v.t.* **1.** to sprinkle or season with pepper. **2.** to cover or sprinkle, as with pepper: *The tweed was peppered with flecks of red and blue.* **3.** to shower or pelt with bullets or other small missiles. **4.** to add spice or variety to: *He peppered his writing with humorous expressions.* [Old English *pipor* the spice, from Latin *piper* the plant, from Greek *peperi,* from Sanskrit *pippali* berry, peppercorn.]

pep·per-and-salt (pep′ər ən sôlt′) *adj.* composed of a fine mixture of black and white: *a pepper-and-salt tweed.* Also, **salt′-and-pep′per.**

pep·per·corn (pep′ər kôrn′) *n.* dried fruit of the black pepper, *Piper nigrum,* used as a spice, either whole or ground.

pep·per·grass (pep′ər gras′) *n.* any of a large group of plants, genus *Lepidium,* of the mustard family, whose leaves have a pungent flavor.

pepper mill, utensil used to grind peppercorns.

pep·per·mint (pep′ər mint′) *n.* **1.** fragrant plant, *Mentha piperita,* of the mint family, having small purple or white flowers and toothedged leaves. **2.** pungent oil obtained from this plant, having a minty aroma and taste and used as a flavoring, esp. in candy, chewing gum, and toothpaste. **3.** candy or lozenge flavored with peppermint oil.

pepper tree, either of two evergreen trees of tropical America, the **California peppertree,** *Schinus molle,* and the **Brazilian peppertree,** *S. terebinthifolius,* bearing clusters of small white or yellowish flowers and red or rose-colored berries.

Peppermint plant

pep·per·y (pep′ər ē) *adj.* **1.** of, like, or relating to pepper; pungent: *a peppery taste.* **2.** (of speech or writing) biting; sharp; stinging. **3.** hot-tempered; testy. —**pep′per·i·ness,** *n.*

pep pill *Informal.* tablet or capsule containing a stimulant, esp. amphetamine.

pep·py (pep′ē) **-pi·er, -pi·est.** *adj. Informal.* full of pep or energy; lively. —**pep′pi·ness,** *n.*

pep·sin (pep′sin) *n.* **1.** enzyme produced in the stomach that aids in the digestion of proteins. **2.** medicine used to relieve indigestion, containing pepsin taken from the stomach of certain animals. [German *Pepsin,* from Greek *pepsin* digestion.]

pep talk, speech given to an individual or group for the purpose of increasing enthusiasm or confidence or bolstering morale.

pep·tic (pep′tik) *adj.* **1.** of, relating to, or promoting digestion; diges-

at; āpe; cär; end; mē; it; īce; hot; ōld; fôrk; wood; fōōl; out; up; ūse; turn; sing; thin; this; zh in treasure; ə in ago, taken, pencil, lemon, circus.

tive. **2.** of or relating to pepsin or other digestive secretions or resulting from their action: *a peptic ulcer.* —*n.* substance that promotes digestion. [Greek *peptikos* able to digest, from *peptein* to digest, cook.]

pep·tide (pep′tīd) *n.* complex protein formed by the linking together of amino acids into a long chain by bonds composed of one atom each of nitrogen, hydrogen, carbon, and oxygen. [PEPT(ONE) + -IDE.]

pep·tone (pep′tōn) *n.* any of a class of soluble substances derived from proteins during the process of digestion. [German *Pepton*, going back to Greek *peptein* to cook, digest.]

Pepys, Samuel (pēps) 1633–1703, English diarist and naval administrator.

Pe·quot (pē′kwot) *n.* member of a tribe of Algonquian Indians formerly living in Connecticut.

per (pur; *unstressed* pər) *prep.* **1.** for each: *The speed limit is forty miles per hour. He earns $120 per week.* **2.** by means of; by; through: *a message sent per my representative.* **3.** according to: *as per instructions.* [Latin *per* through, by.]

per- *prefix* **1.** through; throughout: *perforate, perfume.* **2.** thoroughly; completely: *perfect, perceive.* **3.** *Chemistry.* containing a relatively large or the largest possible proportion of a specified element: *hydrogen peroxide.* [Latin *per* through, by.]

per·ad·ven·ture (pur′əd ven′chər) *Archaic.* *adv.* perhaps; perchance. —*n.* chance or uncertainty; doubt; question. [Old French *par aventure* perchance, perhaps, from *par* by (from Latin *per* through, by) + *aventure* chance. See ADVENTURE.]

per·am·bu·late (pər am′byə lāt′) -lat·ed, -lat·ing. *v.t.* **1.** to walk through, around, or about (a place). **2.** to walk around or through so as to survey, inspect, or examine: *The lord perambulated his estate.* —*v.i.* to walk about; stroll: *He perambulated aimlessly about the park.* [Latin *perambulātus*, past participle of *perambulāre* to ramble through.] —**per·am′bu·la′tion**, *n.*

per·am·bu·la·tor (pər am′byə lā′tər) *n.* **1.** baby carriage. **2.** one who perambulates.

per an·num (pər an′əm) for each year; per year; annually: *His income exceeds $12,000 per annum.* [Latin *per annum.*]

per·cale (pər kāl′) *n.* closely woven, lightweight cotton fabric with a smooth, dull finish, used esp. for sheets, pajamas, and shirts. [French *percale*, back to Persian *pargālah* shred, scrap.]

per cap·i·ta (pər kap′i tə) for, from, or by each person: *The per capita income in the city has risen this year to over $1,500.* [Latin *per capita* literally, by heads.]

per·ceive (pər sēv′) -ceived, -ceiv·ing. *v.t.* **1.** to be or become aware of through the senses; see, hear, taste, smell, or feel: *to perceive a change in the temperature.* **2.** to take in or grasp mentally; comprehend: *I perceived that it would be a long struggle.* [Old French *perceivre*, from Latin *percipere* to take possession of, observe.] —**Syn. 2.** see discern.

per·cent (pər sent′) *also,* **per cent.** *n.* number of parts in or to every hundred. Two percent of 50 is ²⁄₁₀₀ × 50, or 1. ▲ the symbol for percent (%) is often used with figures, as in *6% interest.* [Latin *per centum* by the hundred.]

per·cent·age (pər sen′tij) *n.* **1.** rate or proportion of to every hundred: *What percentage of registered voters actually voted?* **2.** part or proportion in regard to the whole: *A great percentage of our pilots retire early.* **3.** amount calculated by percent, as an allowance, commission, or rate of interest. **4.** *Informal.* advantage; profit: *There's no percentage in fighting.*

per·cen·tile (pər sen′tīl, -til) *n.* any value in a series of values on a scale found by dividing a group into a hundred equal parts. A person with a percentile of eighty on a test has done as well or better than eighty percent of the people taking the test.

per centum, percent.

per·cept (pur′sept) *n.* **1.** that which is perceived. **2.** knowledge or understanding that results from perceiving. [From PERCEPTION.]

per·cep·ti·ble (pər sep′tə bəl) *adj.* that can be perceived; noticeable: *There has been a perceptible change in his behavior lately.* —**per·cep′ti·bil′i·ty,** *n.* —**per·cep′ti·bly,** *adv.*

per·cep·tion (pər sep′shən) *n.* **1.** act or process of perceiving. **2.** result or product of perceiving; percept. **3.** awareness, insight, or information gained by perceiving. **4.** faculty of perceiving: *His perception of colors is poor.* [Latin *perceptiō* collecting, comprehending.]

per·cep·tive (pər sep′tiv) *adj.* **1.** capable of or characterized by keen perception: *a perceptive judge of human nature, perceptive and intelligent advice.* **2.** having the power of perceiving. **3.** of or relating to perception. —**per·cep′tive·ly,** *adv.* —**per·cep·tiv′i·ty, per·cep′tive·ness,** *n.*

Per·ce·val (pur′sə vəl) *also,* **Per·ci·val** or **Per·ci·vale.** *n.* *Arthurian Legend.* knight of the Round Table who, along with Galahad, sought the Holy Grail.

perch¹ (purch) *n.* **1.** anything on which a bird can alight or come to rest, esp. a horizontal bar or branch. **2.** any elevated place or position, esp. for sitting or standing: *The lifeguard watched the swimmers from*

his perch above the pool. **3.** measure of length equal to one rod; 5½ yards. **4.** measure of area equal to one square rod; 30¼ square yards. **5.** measure of volume for stone, usually equal to 24¾ cubic feet. —*v.i.* to alight or rest on; sit on or as on a perch; settle: *Spectators perched on the fence.* —*v.t.* to set or place on or as on a perch: *The cat perched himself on the bookcase.* [Old French *perche* place where a bird alights, long piece of wood, from Latin *pertica* pole¹, bar.]

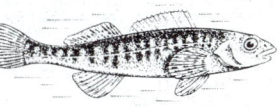

perch² (purch) *pl.,* **perches** or **perch.** *n.* any of a large group of commercial and freshwater food and game fish, family Percidae, as the **yellow perch,** *Perca flavescens,* found in shallow lakes and slow-moving streams of

Perch

North America, and having a yellow body marked with blackish bands. Length: 4–15 inches. [Old French *perche* a small freshwater fish, from Latin *perca,* from Greek *perkē.*]

per·chance (pər chans′) *adv.* by chance; possibly; perhaps. [Old French *par* by (from Latin *per* through, by) + *ch(e)ance* a falling. See CHANCE.]

perch·er (pur′chər) *n.* **1.** one who or that which perches. **2.** bird whose feet are adapted for perching.

Per·che·ron (pur′chə ron′, -shə-) *n.* one of a breed of strong, very heavy draft horses, usually having a gray or black coat. [French *Percheron* horse or mare, from *Le Perche,* region in France noted for its horses.]

per·cip·i·ent (pər sip′ē ənt) *adj.* having the faculty of perception; perceiving; discerning: *the percipient mind of a philosopher.* —*n.* one who perceives. [Latin *percipiēns,* present participle of *percipere* to take possession of, observe.]

Per·ci·val (pur′sə vəl) *also,* **Per·ci·vale.** Perceval.

per·co·late (pur′kə lāt′) -lat·ed, -lat·ing. *v.t., v.i.* to drip, filter, or cause to filter through spaces or small holes, as a liquid in a porous substance: *to percolate coffee.* [Latin *percōlātus,* past participle of *percōlāre* to strain through.] —**per′co·la′tion,** *n.*

per·co·la·tor (pur′kə lā′tər) *n.* kind of coffee pot in which boiling water rises through a tube to a perforated basket containing ground coffee, and then filters back down to the bottom. **2.** that which percolates.

per·cuss (pər kus′) *v.t.* *Medicine.* to tap (a part of the body) with the finger or an instrument for diagnostic or therapeutic purposes.

per·cus·sion (pər kush′ən) *n.* **1.** striking of one body with or against another with great force; collision. **2.** shock or impact resulting from such a collision. **3.** striking of sound waves upon the ear. **4.** act of striking the percussion cap of a firearm. **5.** *Medicine.* the tapping of a part of the body with the finger or an instrument. **6.** percussion instruments collectively. [Latin *percussiō* a striking.]

percussion cap, small cap, formerly of iron or pewter, now made of copper, containing a small amount of powder in a cavity at the bottom, covered with a layer of tinfoil and sealed with shellac. It explodes to set off a larger charge when it is struck by a sharp blow, as from the hammer of a gun.

percussion instrument, any of various musical instruments in which tones are produced by shaking or by a blow or stroke from a hammer or similar implement. The drum, cymbal, xylophone, tambourine, and piano are percussion instruments.

per·cus·sion·ist (pər kush′ə nist) *n.* musician who plays a percussion instrument.

per·cus·sive (pər kus′iv) *adj.* of, relating to, or characterized by percussion. —**per·cus′sive·ly,** *adv.* —**per·cus′sive·ness,** *n.*

per di·em (pər dē′əm, dī′əm) **1.** for each day; per day; daily. **2.** daily allowance for expenses. [Latin *per diem* daily.]

per·di·tion (pər dish′ən) *n.* **1.** loss of one's soul and of heavenly salvation; eternal damnation. **2.** hell. **3.** utter ruin; complete destruction. [Latin *perditiō* destruction, ruin, from Latin *perdere* to destroy.]

per·e·gri·nate (per′ə grə nāt′) -nat·ed, -nat·ing. *v.t., v.i.* to travel; journey. [Latin *peregrīnātus,* past participle of *peregrīnārī* to travel abroad.] —**per′e·gri·na′tion, per′e·gri·na′tor,** *n.*

per·e·grine (per′ə grin, -grēn′, -grīn′) *also,* **per·e·grin** (per′ə grin). *n.* falcon, *Falco peregrinus,* having predominantly bluish-gray plumage and formerly much used in falconry. Length: to 19 inches. Also, **peregrine falcon, peregrin falcon.** —*adj.* **1.** of or coming from another country; alien; foreign. **2.** wandering; migratory. [Latin *peregrīnus* foreign, going back to *per* through, beyond + *ager* (*Rōmānus*) (Roman) territory.]

Peregrine

per·emp·to·ry (pə remp′tər ē) *adj.* **1.** absolutely settled or determined; unconditional; final: *a peremptory court action.* **2.** allowing no denial or refusal; imperative: *The orders of the president were peremptory.* **3.** imperious; dictatorial; dogmatic: *a peremptory and self-appointed expert on everything.* [Latin *peremptōrius* destructive, decisive.] —**per·emp′to·ri·ly,** *adv.* —**per·emp′to·ri·ness,** *n.*

per·en·ni·al (pə ren′ē əl) *adj.* **1.** lasting or continuing through the year or many years. **2.** lasting for a long time; enduring: *the perennial optimism of youth.* **3.** *Botany.* living more than two years. —*n.* perennial plant. [Latin *perennis* lasting through the year (from *per* through + *annus* year) + -AL¹.] —**per·en′ni·al·ly,** *adv.*

perf. 1. perfect **2.** perforated.

per·fect (*adj., n.,* pur′fikt; *v.,* pər fekt′) *adj.* **1.** free from any defect or imperfection; faultless: *perfect weather for a picnic, a poem with perfect meter. Her examination paper was perfect except for one spelling mistake.* **2.** having all the proper or essential qualities or characteristics; fully developed, formed, or done; complete: *He had found perfect happiness.* **3.** corresponding exactly to the original; accurate; correct: *That photo is a perfect likeness of you.* **4.** highly trained or skilled; accomplished: *a perfect marksman.* **5.** very great; absolute; utter: *He made a perfect fool of himself!* **6.** *Grammar.* of, relating to, or designating the verbal tenses that express action completed in the past or at the time of speaking. There are three perfect tenses in English: present perfect, past perfect (or pluperfect), and future perfect. —*n. Grammar.* **1.** perfect tense. **2.** verb form in such a tense. —*v.t.* **1.** to make perfect or flawless; *to perfect a new surgical technique.* **2.** to make (someone) skilled or expert in: *He has perfected himself in every facet of his job.* [Latin *perfectus* completed, excellent, past participle of *perficere* to complete, do thoroughly.]
Syn. *adj.* **1. Perfect, ideal, flawless** mean excellent beyond improvement. **Perfect** suggests not only the presence of all desirable qualities but also that each quality is complete and unimpaired in itself: *This cathedral is a perfect example of Gothic architecture.* **Ideal** implies perfection exceeding what is normally possible in reality and corresponding to a vision or standard of excellence: *Helen of Troy was an ideal beauty.* **Flawless** suggests a state of absolute and unqualified excellence in which no flaws or defects can be detected: *The maestro's techniques were flawless.*

per·fect·i·ble (pər fek′tə bəl) *adj.* capable of becoming or being made perfect: *Some philosophers argue that man is perfectible.* —**per·fect′i·bil′i·ty,** *n.*

per·fec·tion (pər fek′shən) *n.* **1.** quality or state of being perfect or faultless; excellence: *He is an idealist who always strives for perfection.* **2.** one who or that which is the embodiment of excellence: *The novelist's most recent book is really perfection.* **3.** act or process of perfecting: *The perfection of the violinist's technique took years of practice.* **4. to perfection.** perfectly; completely: *The kitchen was cleaned to perfection.*

per·fec·tion·ism (pər fek′shə niz′əm) *n.* **1.** belief that moral perfection is possible and that man should strive for it. **2.** practice of setting extremely high standards for oneself and others.

per·fec·tion·ist (pər fek′shə nist) *n.* **1.** one who sets extremely high standards and goals for himself and others; person who demands perfection. **2.** one who believes in perfectionism. —*adj. also,* **per·fec′tion·is′tic.** relating to or characteristic of a perfectionist or perfectionism.

per·fect·ly (pur′fikt lē) *adv.* **1.** in a perfect manner; faultlessly: *This dress fits perfectly.* **2.** completely; entirely: *a perfectly awful day. You are perfectly correct.*

perfect number, number that is equal to the sum of its divisors, not including the number itself. 28, which can be divided by 1, 2, 4, 7, and 14, is a perfect number.

per·fec·to (pər fek′tō) *pl.,* **-tos.** *n.* thick, medium-length cigar tapering almost to a point at both ends. [Spanish *perfecto* complete, faultless, from Latin *perfectus* completed. See PERFECT.]

perfect participle, participle that denotes action completed prior to the time of the main verb. In the sentence *Having seen the body, she fainted, having seen* is a perfect participle.

per·fer·vid (pər fur′vid) *adj.* very fervid; ardent: *a perfervid reformer.*

per·fid·i·ous (pər fid′ē əs) *adj.* given to or characterized by perfidy; faithless; treacherous. —**per·fid′i·ous·ly,** *adv.* —**per·fid′i·ous·ness,** *n.*
per·fi·dy (pur′fi dē) *pl.,* **-dies.** *n.* deliberate breach of faith; base treachery; faithlessness. [Latin *perfidia* treachery.]

per·fo·li·ate (pər fō′lē it, -āt′) *adj.* (of a leaf) growing around the stem so that the stem appears to pass through it. [Modern Latin *perfoliatus,* from Latin *per* + *folium* leaf.]

Perfoliate leaf

per·fo·rate (*v.,* pur′fə rāt′; *adj.,* pur′fər it, -fə rāt′) **-rat·ed, -rat·ing.** *v.t.* **1.** to make a hole or holes through; pierce: *He perforated his*

opponent's shield with his lance. **2.** to make a row or series of small holes through (something): *The edge of the order blank in the catalog was perforated so that it could be torn out easily.* —*adj.* pierced with a hole or holes; perforated. [Latin *perforātus,* past participle of *perforāre* to pierce through.] —**per′fo·ra′tor,** *n.* —**Syn.** *v. t.* **1.** see **pierce.**

per·fo·ra·tion (pur′fə rā′shən) *n.* **1.** act or process of perforating; being perforated. **2.** hole made by boring or piercing through something: *perforations in a sheet of postage stamps.*

per·force (pər fôrs′) *adv. Archaic.* of or by necessity; necessarily: *The reader must perforce . . . make his own inferences* (Edwards, 1868). [Old French *par force* by force, from *par* by (from Latin *per*) + *force.* See FORCE.]

per·form (pər fôrm′) *v.t.* **1.** to begin and carry out to completion; execute; do: *A noted surgeon performed the operation.* **2.** to act in accordance with the requirements of; fulfill; discharge: *to perform one's duty.* **3.** to give a performance of; render or enact: *to perform a play by Shakespeare, to perform the role of the king.* —*v.i.* **1.** to carry out or execute an undertaking; function: *He performs well under pressure.* **2.** to give a performance: *The singer had never performed in New York before.* [Anglo-Norman *parformer* to accomplish, form of Old French *parfournir,* from *par* thoroughly (from Latin *per* through) + *fournir* to provide (of Germanic origin).]
Syn. *v.t.* **1. Perform, execute** mean to carry out a task or assignment. **Perform** is used when one carries out skillfully a process or task according to an established routine or procedure: *The mathematician performed calculations at lightning speed.* **Execute** is used when one carries out or accomplishes a plan or program according to a prescribed design: *The general executed the maneuver boldly and speedily.*

per·for·mance (pər fôr′məns) *n.* **1.** public presentation, as of a play, musical program, or other entertainment: *The show closed after ten performances.* **2.** act or manner of performing; being performed: *The first American performance of this opera was in 1926.* **3.** thing performed; action; deed.

per·form·er (pər fôr′mər) *n.* one who performs, esp. one who gives or takes part in public entertainment.

per·fume (*n.,* pur′fūm′, pər fūm′; *v.,* pər fūm′) *n.* **1.** solution with a pleasing fragrance, used for personal adornment and to give a pleasing odor to various products. **2.** sweet or pleasant odor; fragrance: *the perfume of a flower garden.* —*v.t.,* **-fumed, -fum·ing.** to fill or scent with a sweet or pleasant odor. [French *parfumer* to fill with a pleasant odor, fumigate, through Italian, going back to Latin *per* through + *fūmāre* to smoke.]

per·fum·er (pər fū′mər) *n.* one who makes or sells perfumes.

per·fum·er·y (pər fū′mər ē) *pl.,* **-er·ies.** *n.* **1.** art of making perfumes or the business of selling them. **2.** place where perfumes are made or sold. **3.** perfume or perfumes collectively.

per·func·to·ry (pər fungk′tər ē) *adj.* **1.** done merely for the sake of requirements or routine; mechanical; superficial: *He was too busy to give it more than a perfunctory inspection.* **2.** acting in such a manner; half-hearted; indifferent. [Late Latin *perfunctōrius* careless, done superficially, from Latin *perfungī* to perform.] —**per·func′to·ri·ly,** *adv.* —**per·func′to·ri·ness,** *n.*

per·fuse (pər fūz′) **-fused, -fus·ing.** *v.t.* to permeate, suffuse, or sprinkle with (something, as liquid, color, or light). **2.** to spread or pour (a liquid) over or through something. [Latin *perfūsus,* past participle of *perfundere* to pour over.] —**per·fu′sion,** *n.* —**per·fu·sive** (pər fū′siv), *adj.*

per·go·la (pur′gə lə) *n.* structure resting on columns or other supports and having an open roof, used esp. as a trellis for vines. [Italian *pergola,* from Latin *pergula* vine arbor, shed.]

per·haps (pər haps′) *adv.* possibly but not certainly; maybe: *Perhaps your friend would like to join us.* [PER- + *haps,* plural of HAP.]

pe·ri (pēr′ē) *n. Persian Mythology.* an evil demon descended from fallen angels and excluded from paradise until penance has been done. [Persian *parī* fairy.]

per·i·anth (per′ē anth′) *n.* external part or envelope of a flower, including the calyx and the corolla. [Modern Latin *perianthium,* Greek *peri* around + *anthos* flower.]

per·i·car·di·al (per′ə kär′dē əl) *adj.* of, relating to, or affecting the pericardium. Also, **per′i·car′di·ac.**

per·i·car·di·tis (per′ə kär dī′tis) *n.* inflammation of the pericardium.

per·i·car·di·um (per′ə kär′dē əm) *pl.,* **-di·a** (-dē ə). *n.* thin membranous sac that surrounds and protects the heart. [Modern Latin *pericardium,* from Greek *perikardion,* neuter of *perikardios* around the heart, from *peri* around + *kardiā* heart.]

per·i·carp (per′ə karp′) *n.* wall of a ripened ovary, sometimes consisting of three layers, the epicarp, mesocarp, and endocarp; seedcase. [Greek *perikarpion* shell, husk, from *peri* around + *karpos* fruit.]

Per·i·cles (per′ə klēz′) *n.* c.495–429 B.C., Athenian statesman, orator, and general.

per·i·cra·ni·um (per′ə krā′nē əm) *pl.,* **-ni·a** (-nē ə). *n.* membrane covering the external surface of the skull. [Modern Latin *pericranium,* Greek *perikrānion,* neuter of *perikrānios* around the skull, from *peri* around + *krānion* skull.]

per·i·gee (per′ə jē) *n.* point in the orbit of the moon or an artificial satellite at which it is closest to the earth. [French *périgée,* from Modern Latin *perigēum,* from Late Greek *perigeion,* going back to Greek *peri* around, near + *gē* earth.]

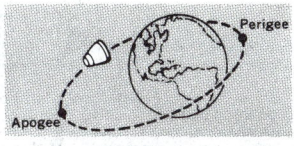
Perigee

per·i·he·li·on (per′ə hē′lē ən, -hēl′yən) *pl.,* **-he·li·a** (-hē′lē ə, -hēl′yə). *n.* point in the orbit of a planet or other heavenly body at which it is closest to the sun. [Modification of Modern Latin *perihelium,* from Greek *peri* around, near + *hēlios* sun.]

per·il (per′əl) *n.* **1.** chance or risk of injury, loss, or destruction; danger: *He commanded the army during a time of peril.* **2.** something that may cause injury or damage: *Icy roads are a peril to motorists.* —*v.t.,* **-iled, -il·ing;** *also, British,* **-illed, -il·ling.** to expose to danger; imperil. [Old French *peril* danger, from Latin *perīculum.*] —**Syn.** *n.* **1.** see **danger.**

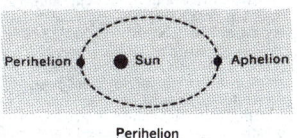
Perihelion

per·il·ous (per′ə ləs) *adj.* full of or involving peril; hazardous; dangerous: *a perilous journey.* [Old French *perillous,* from Latin *perīculōsus,* from *perīculum* danger.] —**per′il·ous·ly,** *adv.* —**per′il·ous·ness,** *n.*

per·im·e·ter (pə rim′ə tər) *n.* **1.** boundary of an area or a closed plane figure. **2.** measure or length of such a boundary. [Latin *perimetros,* from Greek *perimetros,* from *peri* around + *metron* measure.]

per·i·ne·um (per′ə nē′əm) *pl.,* **-ne·a** (-nē′ə). *n.* region of the body between the thighs, extending from the anus to the genitals. [Modern Latin *perineum,* going back to Greek *perineos.*] —**per′i·ne′al,** *adj.*

pe·ri·od (pēr′ē əd) *n.* **1.** portion of time characterized or defined by certain conditions, events, or the like: *a period of relatively mild weather. His driver's license was revoked for a period of three months.* **2.** portion of time regarded as a phase of evolution or development; stage: *This painting is from the artist's last period.* **3.** portion of time marked off by some recurring action or event: *The tides of the ocean . . . flow in periods* (McCosh, 1850). **4.** *Physics.* time of one complete cycle of an oscillation or other recurring motion or phenomenon. **5.** time that it takes a planet or satellite to make one complete revolution. **6.** timed portion of certain games and sports: *The goal was scored in the second period of the hockey game.* **7.** one of the divisions of time in a school day. **8.** fundamental unit of the standard geologic time scale, a major subdivision of an era, characterized by certain kinds of rock formations and usually named for the place where such formations were discovered or are particularly prominent. **9.** menstruation (*def. 2*). **10.** duration or stage in the duration of a disease. **11.** mark of punctuation (.) indicating the end of a declarative sentence or an abbreviation. **12.** pause at the end of a sentence. **13.** complete sentence, esp. one consisting of several clauses. **14.** end, completion, or conclusion. —*adj.* of, relating to, or characteristic of a certain era or time: *The actors in the tragedy were all dressed in period costumes. This book is a period piece.* [Latin *periodus* sentence, cycle, from Greek *periodos.*] —**Syn.** *n.* **1.** see **era.**

pe·ri·od·ic (pēr′ē od′ik) *adj.* **1.** happening on occasion; intermittent: *periodic shifts in public opinion.* **2.** appearing or occurring at regular intervals; recurrent: *periodic audits of the bank's records.* **3.** of or relating to a period or cycle; cyclical: *the periodic rise and fall of the tide.* —**pe·ri·od′i·cal·ly,** *adv.*

Syn. 1. Periodic, sporadic, intermittent mean occurring in interrupted sequence. **Periodic** usually describes something that happens at more or less regular intervals and is therefore fairly predictable: *The state law requires periodic inspection of motor vehicles.* **Sporadic** implies that something takes place at widely scattered, unpredictable intervals of time or space: *Even after the truce, there was sporadic firing on the battlefront.* **Intermittent** suggests an irregular succession of happenings and stresses lack of continuity: *I was distracted by the intermittent buzzing.*

pe·ri·od·i·cal (pēr′ē od′i kəl) *n.* publication issued at regular intervals, but less often than daily. —*adj.* **1.** of or relating to periodicals. —**Syn.** *n.* see **journal.**

pe·ri·o·dic·i·ty (pēr′ē ə dis′ə tē) *pl.,* **-ties.** *n.* **1.** tendency to appear

or occur at regular intervals. **2.** tendency of the chemical elements to exhibit the same or similar properties at regular intervals when arranged in order of increasing atomic numbers.

periodic law, statement that the properties of the chemical elements vary at regular intervals with their atomic numbers.

periodic sentence, sentence so constructed that its meaning and grammatical structure are not complete until the very end, for example: *The jury, after much deliberation, found the defendant in the case to be not guilty.*

periodic table, table in which the chemical elements are arranged in order of increasing atomic numbers, with elements having similar properties arranged in vertical columns. See **element** for table.

per·i·os·te·um (per′ē os′tē əm) *pl.,* **-te·a** (-tē ə). *n.* dense, fibrous membrane consisting of two layers, that covers the surface of bones except at the joints and supplies the bones with blood vessels and nerves. [Modern Latin *periosteum,* going back to Greek *periosteon,* neuter of *periosteos* around the bones.]

per·i·pa·tet·ic (per′ə pə tet′ik) *adj.* **1.** walking or traveling from place to place; rambling; itinerant: *a peripatetic peddler.* **2. Peripatetic.** of, relating to, or adhering to the philosophy of Aristotle, who taught while walking in the Lyceum of ancient Athens. —*n.* **1.** one who walks or travels from place to place; itinerant. **2. Peripatetic.** one of Aristotle's followers. [Latin *peripatēticus* relating to the philosophy of Aristotle, from Greek *peripatētikos* given to walking about.]

pe·riph·er·al (pə rif′ər əl) *adj.* **1.** relating to, situated at, or forming a periphery: *peripheral vision, peripheral expansion.* **2.** of or relating to that part of the nervous system that connects the central nervous system to the rest of the body, consisting of the cranial and spinal nerves, which serve the voluntary muscles, sense organs, and skin, and the autonomic nerves, which regulate the internal organs. —**pe·riph′er·al·ly,** *adv.*

pe·riph·er·y (pə rif′ər ē) *pl.,* **-er·ies.** *n.* **1.** external boundary or surface of an area or object. **2.** surrounding area or region; environs. [Late Latin *peripheria,* from Greek *periphereia* circumference of a circle.]

pe·riph·ra·sis (pə rif′rə sis) *pl.,* **-ses** (-sēz). *n.* **1.** roundabout or unnecessarily wordy way of expressing an idea; circumlocution. **2.** instance of this. Also, **per·i·phrase** (per′ə frāz′). [Latin *periphrasis,* from Greek *periphrasis.*]

per·i·phras·tic (per′ə fras′tik) *adj.* **1.** of, characterized by, or expressed by periphrasis. **2.** *Grammar.* denoting a construction using an auxiliary word rather than an inflectional form, as *more rich* rather than *richer* or *Mary* rather than *Mary's.* —**per′i·phras′ti·cal·ly,** *adv.*

per·i·scope (per′ə skōp′) *n.* optical instrument, as in a submarine or tank, for viewing objects not directly in the observer's line of sight, consisting of a tube with an arrangement of prisms or mirrors that reflect the images through the tube to the eye of the observer. [Greek *peri* around + -SCOPE.]

per·i·scop·ic (per′ə skop′ik) *adj.* **1.** *Optics.* denoting a special type of lens permitting oblique or peripheral vision as well as vision in a direct line. **2.** of or relating to a periscope.

per·ish (per′ish) *v.i.* **1.** to die, esp. in a violent or untimely way: *Many people perished when the ship sank.* **2.** to pass from existence; disappear: *Government of the people, by the people, and for the people, shall not perish from the earth* (Lincoln, 1863). [Old French *periss-,* a stem of *perir* to die, from Latin *perīre.*]

per·ish·a·ble (per′i shə bəl) *adj.* subject to destruction or decay: *Perishable foods should be refrigerated.* —*n.* **perishables.** something liable to decay, esp. unprocessed or unpreserved foods. —**per′ish·a·bil′i·ty, per′ish·a·ble·ness,** *n.*

per·i·stal·sis (per′ə stôl′sis, -stal′-) *pl.,* **-ses** (-sēz). *n.* successive waves of contractions in the walls of the intestine or another tubular organ, that propel the contents of the organ onward. [Modern Latin *peristalsis,* from Greek *peri* around + *stalsis* checking.] —**per′i·stal′tic,** *adj.*

per·i·style (per′ə stīl′) *n.* **1.** row of columns surrounding an area, as a temple, building, or court. **2.** area so enclosed. [French *péristyle,* from Latin *peristylum,* from Greek *peristylon,* from *peri* around + *stylos* pillar.]

Peristyle

per·i·to·ne·um (per′i tə nē′əm) *pl.,* **-ne·a** or **-nae·a** (-nē′ə). *also,* **per·i·to·nae·um.** *n.* transparent serous membrane that lines the walls of the abdominal cavity and covers the organs in it. [Late Latin *peritonaeum,* from Greek *peritonaion,* going back to *peri* around + *teinein* to stretch.] —**per′i·to·ne′al,** *adj.*

per·i·to·ni·tis (per′i tə nī′tis) *n.* inflammation of the peritoneum. [Modern Latin *peritonitis,* from Greek *peritonaion* peritoneum + -*itis* -ITIS.

per·i·wig (per′i wig′) *n.* wig or peruke. [Modification of PERUKE.]

per·i·win·kle¹ (per′i wing′kəl) *n.* any of a group of erect or trailing plants, genus *Vinca,* esp. the **common periwinkle,** *V. minor,* having lilac-blue flowers and oval leaves. [Latin *pervinca.*]

Periwig

per·i·win·kle² (per′i wing′kəl) *n.* any of a group of small sea snails, genus *Littorina,* found in shallow waters along the coasts of Europe and northeastern North America, esp. the **common periwinkle,** *L. littorea,* having a cone-shaped spiral shell that is usually olive green, sometimes banded with red or brown. Length: ¾ inch. [Of uncertain origin.]

per·jure (pur′jər) **-jured, -jur·ing.** *v.t.* to make (oneself) guilty of perjury: *The district attorney proved that the witness had perjured himself.* [Old French *parjurer,* from Latin *perjūrāre.*] **—per′jur·er,** *n.*

per·ju·ry (pur′jər ē) *pl.,* **-ries.** *n.* act or instance of swearing under oath to the truth of something one knows to be untrue. [Anglo-Norman *perjurie,* from Latin *perjūrium.*]

perk (purk) *v.i.* **1.** to recover one's liveliness and vigor (usually with *up*): *My sick friend perked up.* **2.** to move or lift one's head and carry oneself in a jaunty manner. *—v.t.* **1.** to raise smartly or briskly: *The fox perked his ears up.* **2.** to make spruce, trim, or smart (often with *up* or *out*). [Dialectal Old French *perquer* to perch, from *perque* perch, from Latin *pertica* pole, bar.]

Periwinkle²

perk·y (pur′kē) **perk·i·er, perk·i·est.** *adj.* **1.** brisk and lively; smart; jaunty; pert. **2.** spirited; self-assured. **—perk′i·ly,** *adv.* **—perk′i·ness,** *n.*

Perm (perm) *n.* city in the west-central Soviet Union, in the Russian Republic, formerly known as Molotov. Pop. (1970 est.), 850,000.

perm·a·frost (pur′mə frôst′, -frost′) *n.* layer of permanently frozen earth found in arctic regions.

per·ma·nence (pur′mə nəns) *n.* durability; endurance.

per·ma·nen·cy (pur′mə nən sē) *n.* permanence.

per·ma·nent (pur′mə nənt) *adj.* continuing or intended to last indefinitely without change; lasting; enduring: *a permanent dye, permanent employment.* *—n.* permanent wave. [Latin *permanēns,* present participle of *permanēre* to endure, continue.] **—per′ma·nent·ly,** *adv.*

permanent magnet, magnet that retains its magnetism after the magnetic force has been removed.

permanent press, (of a fabric or garment) finished in such a manner that little or no ironing is required after washing.

permanent wave, curl lasting several months, set in the hair with a chemical solution or with heat.

per·me·a·bil·i·ty (pur′mē ə bil′ə tē) *n.* **1.** quality or state of being permeable. **2.** *Physics.* measure of the ability of a liquid or gas to pass through a given substance or medium. **3.** measure of the ability of a substance to conduct magnetic lines of force.

per·me·a·ble (pur′mē ə bəl) *adj.* capable of being permeated: *a permeable membrane.* *The enemy's defenses are permeable at several points.* [Late Latin *permeābilis,* from Latin *permeāre* to pass through.]

per·me·ate (pur′mē āt′) **-at·ed, -at·ing.** *v.t.* **1.** to pass through the pores, openings, or interstices of: *Water can permeate sand.* **2.** to spread throughout; pervade: *Grief permeated her whole being.* *—v.i.* to spread or diffuse itself: *Fear permeated throughout the entire community.* [Latin *permeātus,* past participle of *permeāre* to pass through.] **—per′me·a′tion,** *n.*

Syn. *v.t.* **1. Permeate, penetrate, pervade** mean to spread through and be present throughout a substance or thing. **Permeate** emphasizes diffusion throughout a substance, solid, or gas in such a way that no part is left untouched or unaffected: *The odor of incense permeated the air.* **Penetrate** emphasizes the entry of something that goes deep and spreads extensively: *The chill morning air penetrated the room.* **Pervade** shifts the accent from entry to effect and suggests a spreading diffusion throughout the open spaces of a chamber: *A smell of jasmine pervaded the living room.*

Per·mi·an (pur′mē ən) *n.* seventh and last geological period of the Paleozoic era, when mammal-like reptiles and the ancestors of coniferous trees appeared. See **geology** for table. *—adj.* of, relating to, or characteristic of the Permian. [From *Perm,* area in the Ural Mountains of the Soviet Union.]

per·mis·si·ble (pər mis′ə bəl) *adj.* that may be permitted; allowable. **—per·mis′si·bly,** *adv.*

per·mis·sion (pər mish′ən) *n.* **1.** act of permitting. **2.** formal consent; authorization; leave: *Do I have your permission to go?* [Latin *permissiō* a giving up, leave.]

per·mis·sive (pər mis′iv) *adj.* **1.** allowing much freedom; not strict; lenient: *a permissive parent.* **2.** granting permission; permitting; allowing: *a permissive proclamation.* **3.** permitted; optional: *permissive legislative powers.* **—per·mis′sive·ly,** *adv.* **—per·mis′sive·ness,** *n.*

per·mit (*v.,* pər mit′; *n.,* pur′mit, pər mit′) **-mit·ted, -mit·ting.** *v.t.* **1.** to allow (a person) to do something; give leave to: *Permit me to be of assistance to you.* **2.** to allow (something) to be done; give consent to: *This state permits the sale of alcoholic beverages.* **3.** to afford an opportunity for; admit of: *The large window permitted a panoramic view of the land.* *—v.i.* to afford an opportunity; allow: *I'll call you today if time permits.* *—n.* **1.** *Law.* written order or license issued by a competent authority, granting permission to a party to perform some action not allowed without such permission. **2.** permission, esp. in written form. [Latin *permittere* to allow.] **—Syn.** *v.t.* **1.** see **let¹.**

per·mu·ta·tion (pur′mū tā′shən) *n.* **1.** act of rearranging; alteration. **2.** *Mathematics.* **a.** change in the order of sequence of a set of objects. **b.** any ordered arrangement of the elements of a set of objects. The sequences *abc, acb, bac,* and *cab* are permutations of *a, b,* and *c.* [Latin *permūtātiō* a changing.]

per·mute (pər mūt′) **-mut·ed, -mut·ing.** *v.t.* to subject to permutation, esp. to alter by changing the order of.

per·ni·cious (pər nish′əs) *adj.* **1.** destructive; malicious; harmful: *Pernicious gossip ruined his reputation.* **2.** fatal: *a pernicious disease.* [Latin *perniciosus* destructive, from *perniciēs* destruction.] **—per·ni′cious·ly,** *adv.* **—per·ni′cious·ness,** *n.*

pernicious anemia, severe anemia caused by an inability of the system to absorb vitamin B_{12}, characterized by weakness, shortness of breath, and a greatly decreased number of red corpuscles in the blood.

per·nick·e·ty (pər nik′ə tē) *adj.* persnickety.

per·o·rate (per′ə rāt′) **-rat·ed, -rat·ing.** *v.i.* **1.** to speak at length; make a speech. **2.** to deliver a peroration. [Latin *perōrātus,* past participle of *perōrāre* to speak from beginning to end.]

per·o·ra·tion (per′ə rā′shən) *n.* concluding part of a speech or oration, reiterating and summing up what has been said. [Latin *perōrātiō.*]

per·ox·ide (pə rok′sīd) *n.* **1.** compound of a metal and oxygen, whose formula contains one more oxygen atom than the corresponding oxide or dioxide. In peroxides, the oxygen atoms form a weak bond with each other. **2.** oxide containing the highest possible proportion of oxygen. **3.** hydrogen peroxide. *—v.t.,* **-id·ed, -id·ing.** to bleach (hair) using hydrogen peroxide. [PER- + OXIDE.]

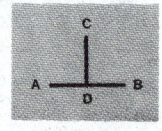

Perpendicular lines

per·pen·dic·u·lar (pur′pən dik′yə lər) *adj.* **1.** at right angles to the plane of the horizon; upright; vertical. **2.** *Mathematics.* at right angles to a given line, plane, or surface. The sides of a square are perpendicular to the base. *—n.* **1.** perpendicular line or plane. **2.** perpendicular position. [Latin *perpendicularis* vertical, from *perpendiculum* plumb line.]

per·pe·trate (pur′pə trāt′) **-trat·ed, -trat·ing.** *v.t.* to do, perform, or commit (a crime, trick, or the like): *They perpetrated a hoax that fooled even the newspapermen.* [Latin *perpetrātus,* past participle of *perpetrāre* to perform, accomplish.] **—per′pe·tra′tion, per′pe·tra′tor,** *n.*

per·pet·u·al (pər pech′ŏŏ əl) *adj.* **1.** lasting or enduring forever; eternal: *a mountaintop enveloped in perpetual snow.* **2.** continuing throughout one's lifetime; permanent: *perpetual vows, a perpetual annuity.* **3.** continuing without interruption; unceasing: *the perpetual ebb and flow of the tide.* **4.** *Botany.* continuously blooming throughout the growing season or year. [Latin *perpetuālis* permanent, from *perpetuus* continuous.] **—per·pet′u·al·ly,** *adv.*

perpetual motion, constant motion, esp. that of a hypothetical machine that, once set into motion, would continue moving indefinitely without any additional energy being supplied to it.

per·pet·u·ate (pər pech′ōō āt′) **-at·ed, -at·ing.** *v.t.* to preserve in fact or existence forever: *History perpetuates the deeds of our forefathers.* [Latin *perpetuātus,* past participle of *perpetuāre* to make perpetual.] **—per·pet′u·a′tion, per·pet′u·a′tor,** *n.*

per·pe·tu·i·ty (pur′pə tōō′ə tē, -tū′-) *pl.,* **-ties.** *n.* **1.** quality or state of being perpetual; endless existence or duration. **2.** something perpetual. **3.** *Law.* **a.** condition or limitation under which property is inalienable for the duration of a certain period of time. **b.** property so limited. **4. in perpetuity,** forever. [Latin *perpetuitās* continuity.]

per·plex (pər pleks′) *v.t.* **1.** to trouble with doubt or uncertainty: *Contradictory news reports perplexed the public.* **2.** to make (something) intricate, complex, or difficult to understand; complicate; muddle. [Latin *perplexus* involved, confused, entangled.] **—Syn.** **1.** see **puzzle.**

per·plex·i·ty (pər plek′sə tē) *pl.,* **-ties.** *n.* **1.** state or condition of being perplexed; bewilderment; confusion: *her continual perplexity with the simplest problems.* **2.** perplexing situation or circumstances. **3.** quality or state of being involved or complicated; intricacy.

per·qui·site (pur′kwə zit) *n.* **1.** any incidental or additional profit or benefit received for work besides regular salary: *Free room and board*

was one of the perquisites of the job. **2.** special privilege or advantage expected or due by right of one's position or office; prerogative. [Medieval Latin *perquisitum* acquisition, from Latin *perquirere* to search diligently.]

Per·ry (per′ē) **1.** Oliver Haz·ard (haz′ərd). 1785–1819, U.S. naval commander. **2.** Matthew C. 1794–1858, his brother; U.S. naval officer.

per se (pər sā′, sē′) *Latin.* by or in itself; intrinsically.

per·se·cute (pur′sə kūt′) -cut·ed, -cut·ing. *v.t.* **1.** to persistently subject to cruel, harmful, or oppressive treatment: *a minority group that was persecuted for centuries. The heretic was persecuted for his beliefs.* **2.** to constantly harass, vex, or annoy: *A salesman persecuted me with telephone calls.* [Old French *persecuter,* going back to Latin *persequī* to follow after, prosecute.] —**per′se·cu′tor,** *n.*

per·se·cu·tion (pur′sə kū′shən) *n.* act of persecuting; being persecuted. [Latin *persecūtiō* pursuit, prosecution.]

Per·seph·o·ne (pər sef′ə nē) *n. Greek Mythology.* goddess of vegetation and of death. She was the daughter of Zeus and Demeter and wife of Hades, the god of the underworld. Her Roman counterpart is Proserpina.

Per·sep·o·lis (pər sep′ə lis) *n.* ruined city in central Iran, the capital of ancient Persia.

Per·se·us (pur′sē əs, pur′sūs) *n.* **1.** *Greek Mythology.* hero who killed Medusa and rescued Andromeda from a sea monster. **2.** constellation in the northern celestial hemisphere, between Taurus and Cassiopeia.

per·se·ver·ance (pur′sə vēr′əns) *n.* act or quality of persevering; persistence. —**Syn.** see **persistence.**

per·se·vere (pur′sə vēr′) -vered, -ver·ing. *v.i.* to continue steadfastly in a course of action or pursuit in spite of difficulties or obstacles; persist: *Despite the failure of his early experiments, the scientist persevered in his research.* [Old French *perseverer,* from Latin *persevērāre.*] —**per′·se·ver′ing·ly,** *adv.*

Per·shing, John Joseph (pur′shing) 1860–1948, U.S. general.

Per·sia (pur′zhə) *n.* **1.** great ancient empire of southwestern Asia, extending from Egypt to the Indus River. It was conquered by Alexander the Great in the fourth century B.C. Also, **Persian Empire. 2.** former name of Iran.

Per·sian (pur′zhən) *adj.* of or relating to Persia, its people, their language, or their culture. —*n.* **1.** native or inhabitant of ancient Persia or Iran. **2.** language of Persia, belonging to the Indo-Iranian branch of the Indo-European language family.

Persian cat, cat of a breed having a round head and long, silky fur.

Persian Gulf, shallow body of water between Iran and Arabia.

Persian lamb, tightly curled fur from newborn karakul lambs.

per·si·flage (pur′sə fläzh′) *n.* light, flippant speech or writing; banter. [French *persiflage,* from *persifler* to jeer, going back to Latin *per* through + *sibilāre* to hiss.]

per·sim·mon (pər sim′ən) *n.* **1.** fleshy, edible berry of any of a group of trees and shrubs, genus *Diospyros,* having thin orange or yellow skin and containing from one to ten flat seeds. **2.** tropical tree or shrub bearing this berry. [Algonquian *pasimenan* dried fruit.]

Fruit and leaves

Halved fruit

Persimmons

per·sist (pər sist′, -zist′) *v.i.* **1.** to continue firmly and steadily, esp. in the face of opposition or difficulty; persevere: *If you persist in misbehaving, you will be punished.* **2.** to be insistent, as in repeating a statement: *"But I'm innocent," she persisted.* **3.** to continue to exist; endure. [Latin *persistere* to continue steadfastly.]

per·sist·ence (pər sis′təns, -zis′-) *n.* **1.** act of persisting; stubborn or resolute continuance. **2.** quality or state of being persistent; tenacity. **3.** continued occurrence or existence, as of an effect after its cause is removed; endurance: *the persistence of a sensory impression.* Also, **per·sist′en·cy.**

Syn. 1. Persistence, perseverance mean continuing a course of action despite difficulties or obstacles. **Persistence** may refer to a determined effort to achieve something against odds, but more often it suggests a stubborn and unreasonable adherence to a purpose or belief: *The salesman's persistence annoyed the old lady, but finally she gave in.* **Perseverance** is always used favorably, and stresses patience and courage in pursuit of a goal: *Great works are performed not by strength but by perseverance* (Johnson, 1759).

per·sist·ent (pər sis′tənt, -zis′-) *adj.* **1.** persisting in the face of difficulty or opposition; persevering or stubborn in a course of action: *a persistent suitor.* **2.** enduring; continual: *persistent interruptions, a persistent cough.* **3.** (of plant or animal structures) not shed or modified in maturation; retained permanently. —**per·sist′ent·ly,** *adv.*

per·snick·e·ty (pər snik′ə tē) *also,* **per·nick·e·ty.** *Informal. adj.* **1.** excessively fastidious; exacting; fussy. **2.** requiring minute care and strict attention to detail.

per·son (pur′sən) *n.* **1.** man, woman, or child; human being; individual. **2.a.** living body of a human being. **b.** bodily appearance. **3.** *Grammar.* **a.** any of three categories of personal pronouns or verb inflections indicating the person speaking (first person), the person spoken to (second person), or the person or thing spoken of (third person). **b.** any of the pronoun forms or verb inflections giving such indication. **4.** *Law.* any individual or corporation having certain legal rights and duties. **5.** *also,* **Person.** one of the three modes of being in the Trinity. The Father is the First Person, the Son is the Second Person, and the Holy Spirit is the Third Person. **6. in person.** in the flesh; physically present: *The movie star looked old when I saw him in person.* [Old French *persone* human being, creature, from Latin *persōna* mask used by an actor, character, personage, probably from Etruscan *phersu* mask. Doublet of PARSON.] —**Syn. 1.** see **human being.**

per·so·na (pər sō′nə) *pl.,* **-nae** (-nē). *n.* character in a drama, novel, or the like. [Latin *persōna* mask used by an actor, character.]

per·son·a·ble (pur′sə nə bəl) *adj.* having a pleasing or attractive appearance and manner: *a personable, fair-haired young man.* —**per′son·a·ble·ness,** *n.* —**per′son·a·bly,** *adv.*

per·son·age (pur′sə nij) *n.* **1.** person of distinction or importance. **2.** any person; individual. **3.** persona. [Old French *personage* person, from *persone.* See PERSON.]

per·so·na gra·ta (pər sō′nə grä′tə, grat′ə) person who is acceptable or welcome. [Latin *persōna grāta.*]

per·son·al (pur′sən əl) *adj.* **1.** of or relating to a particular person; individual; private: *a personal matter that shouldn't be discussed in public.* **2.** done, made, or performed in person; carried on directly between persons: *a personal interview. The actress made a personal appearance at the premiere.* **3.** of or relating to the body or physical appearance: *personal adornments.* **4.** making or inclined to make remarks about or inquiries into private matters: *a reporter who often becomes personal in his comments about celebrities.* **5.** relating or directed to a particular person or persons, esp. in a disparaging or offensive sense or manner: *a personal insult, a personal attack.* **6.** of, relating to, or having the characteristics of a person considered as a self-conscious, rational being, as opposed to a thing or abstraction: *a personal God.* **7.** *Law.* relating to or designating temporary or movable things. Distinguished from **real. 8.** *Grammar.* indicating person. —*n.* short paragraph or item in a newspaper relating to a particular person or persons, or to private matters: *The request for information was put in a personal.* [Late Latin *persōnālis* relating to a person, from Latin *persōna* mask, character, personage.]

personal equation, individual tendency for deviation or error in observation, judgment, or calculation for which allowance must be made.

personal foul, any of various infractions of the rules in certain team sports, as basketball, usually involving body contact.

per·son·al·i·ty (pur′sə nal′ə tē) *pl.,* **-ties.** *n.* **1.** the sum of the traits, habits, and behavior of an individual that differentiates that individual from all others. **2.** distinctive personal characteristics or attributes, esp. those that are pleasing socially: *Her personality, not her beauty, made her popular.* **3.** well-known or distinguished person; celebrity: *a stage and screen personality.* **4.** quality, fact, or condition of being a person, not a thing; personal existence; identity. **5.** remark or reference, often disparaging, made about or to some person: *a gossip who frequently indulged in personalities.*

per·son·al·ize (pur′sən əl īz′) -ized, -iz·ing. *v.t.* **1.** to make personal. **2.** to personify. **3.** to mark (property or possessions) with the name or initials of a person: *Vera's stationary was personalized with her monogram.*

per·son·al·ly (pur′sən əl ē) *adv.* **1.** not by the aid of or through others; in person: *The senator visited the war zone personally.* **2.** as far as oneself is concerned; for oneself: *Personally, I am in favor of the new policy.* **3.** as an individual: *He is a respected author but is very unpopular personally.* **4.** as though directed toward or intended for one as a person: *Bill took Pam's remarks personally and felt insulted.*

personal pronoun, one of a group of pronouns indicating the speaker, the person or persons addressed, or any other persons, places, or things spoken about, as *I, you, she, it,* or *they.*

personal property, movable property, as clothes, money, or furniture, as distinguished from real property, as land or buildings.

per·son·al·ty (pur′sən əl tē) *pl.,* **-ties.** *n.* personal property.

per·so·na non gra·ta (pər sō′nə non grä′tə, grat′ə) person who is not acceptable or welcome. [Latin *persōna nōn grāta.*]

per·son·ate (pur′sə nāt′) -at·ed, -at·ing. *v.t.* **1.** to act the part of (a character in a play or the like). **2.** *Law.* to impersonate or assume the identity of (someone) with intent to deceive. [Latin *persōnātus* masked, pretended, from *persōna* mask, character.] —**per′son·a′tor,** or **per′son·a′tion,** *n.*

per·son·i·fi·ca·tion (pər son′ə fi kā′shən) *n.* **1.** figure of speech in which human characteristics are attributed to an animal, inanimate

at; āpe; cär; end; mē; it; īce; hot; ōld; fôrk; wood; fōōl; oil; out; up; ūse; turn; sing; thin; this; zh in treasure; ə in ago, taken, pencil, lemon, circus.

751

object, or quality; for example: *The sun smiled down on the green meadows.* **2.** person or thing that typifies a specified quality or idea; embodiment: *a hero who is the personification of bravery.* **3.** imaginary or ideal person or creature conceived as representing a thing or abstraction: *Neptune was the personification of the sea.*

per·son·i·fy (pər son'ə fī') **-fied, -fy·ing.** *v.t.* **1.** to regard or represent as having human characteristics. **2.** to be an embodiment of; typify: *a literary character that personifies goodness.* **3.** to represent or conceive as representing a thing or an abstraction: *Satan personifies evil.*

per·son·nel (pur'sə nel') *n.* **1.** persons employed in any business, service, or public institution: *doctors, nurses, and all the rest of the personnel of the hospital.* **2.** department in a business or other organization that hires the employees, maintains their records, and handles most aspects of employee relations. [French *personnel* persons employed in an organization, going back to Late Latin *persōnālis* relating to a person. See PERSONAL.]

per·spec·tive (pər spek'tiv) *n.* **1.** art or theory of representing three-dimensional objects on a flat surface in such a way as to

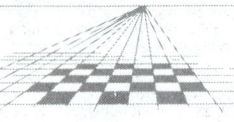

Perspective

give the appearance of depth and distance. **2.** effect of distance on the appearance of objects by means of which spatial relations are perceived. **3.** appearance, relationship, or relative importance of events from a specific point of view: *That battle is of great significance when viewed in the perspective of the progress of the war.* **4.** appropriate relation of parts to one another and to the whole view, subject, or the like; proper proportion: *We must keep these minor details in perspective and not waste too much time on them.* **5.** view from a distance; vista. —*adj.* of, relating to, seen, or represented according to the art or theory of perspective: *a perspective drawing.* [Medieval Latin *perspectiva (ars)* optical (science), from Late Latin *perspectīvus* optical, from Latin *perspicere* to see through, look at closely.]

per·spi·ca·cious (pur'spi kā'shəs) *adj.* having keen powers of observation and judgment; discerning. [Latin *perspicāc-*, stem of *perspicāx* sharp-sighted, acute + -OUS.] —**per'spi·ca'cious·ly**, *adv.* —**per'spi·ca'cious·ness**, *n.*

per·spi·cac·i·ty (pur'spə kas'ə tē) *n.* keenness in observation and judgment; discernment.

per·spi·cu·i·ty (pur'spə kū'ə tē) *n.* quality of being perspicuous; lucidity.

per·spic·u·ous (pər spik'ū əs) *adj.* clearly expressed; easily understood; lucid: *a long but perspicuous speech.* [Latin *perspicuus* transparent, clear.] —**per·spic'u·ous·ly**, *adv.* —**per·spic'u·ous·ness**, *n.*

per·spi·ra·tion (pur'spə rā'shən) *n.* **1.** action of excreting moisture through the pores of the skin; sweating. **2.** that which is so excreted; sweat: *There were beads of perspiration on the runner's brow.*

per·spire (pər spīr') **-spired, -spir·ing.** *v.i.* to give off perspiration; sweat. —*v.t.* to give off or expel through the pores; exude. [Latin *perspīrāre* literally, to breathe through.]

per·suade (pər swād') **-suad·ed, -suad·ing.** *v.t.* **1.** to induce (someone) to do or believe something, as by argument, entreaty, or reasoning: *The salesman persuaded us to buy his product.* **2.** to lead to believe; convince: *I am thoroughly persuaded of his loyalty.* [Latin *persuādēre.*] —**per·suad'er**, *n.*

Syn. 1. see **induce. 2.** Persuade, convince mean to prevail on another person to do or believe something. **Persuade** suggests winning over a person by an overt appeal addressed primarily to his emotions: *The governor's wife persuaded him not to run for a second term.* **Convince** suggests demonstrating to another the truth of something with the aid of arguments and logical proof: *He convinced his employer that he was right by citing many pertinent facts and figures.*

per·sua·si·ble (pər swā'sə bəl) *adj.* capable of being persuaded; open to persuasion. Also, **per·suad·a·ble** (pər swā'də bəl).

per·sua·sion (pər swā'zhən) *n.* **1.** act of persuading: *He won their support by persuasion, not force.* **2.** power or ability to persuade; persuasiveness. **3.** state or fact of being persuaded; firm belief; conviction. **4.** religious belief; creed. **5.** religious sect or denomination: *a clergyman of the Lutheran persuasion.* [Latin *persuāsiō* act of persuading, belief.]

per·sua·sive (pər swā'siv, -ziv) *adj.* able or tending to persuade: *The lawyer presented a persuasive argument for the acquittal of his client.* —**per·sua'sive·ly**, *adv.* —**per·sua'sive·ness**, *n.*

pert (purt) *adj.* **1.** disrespectfully forward or free in speech or behavior; saucy; impudent: *The fresh young girl made a pert reply to the teacher's question.* **2.** Informal. in good health or spirits; lively; vivacious. [Short for Old French *apert* open, from Latin *apertus*; partly also from Old French *aspert* able, from Latin *expertus* experienced.] —**pert'ly**, *adv.* —**pert'ness**, *n.*

per·tain (pər tān') *v.i.* **1.** to have reference; refer; relate: *The president*

and his advisors discussed matters that pertained to the war. **2.** to belong or be connected as an adjunct, accessory, or the like: *The duke's son inherits his title and all that pertains to it.* **3.** to be fitting or appropriate: *all the good will pertaining to the Christmas season.* [Old French *partenir* to belong, from Latin *pertinēre* to belong, concern.]

Perth (purth) *n.* city in southwestern Australia, near the Indian Ocean. Pop. (1968), 96,800.

per·ti·na·cious (purt'ən ā'shəs) *adj.* resolute in holding to a purpose, action, or opinion; stubbornly persistent. [Latin *pertināc-*, stem of *pertināx* tenacious, steadfast + -OUS.] —**per'ti·na'cious·ly**, *adv.*

per·ti·nac·i·ty (purt'ən as'ə tē) *n.* quality or state of being pertinacious.

per·ti·nence (purt'ən əns) *n.* quality or state of being pertinent. Also, **per'ti·nen·cy**.

per·ti·nent (purt'ən ənt) *adj.* belonging, relating, or appropriate to the matter at hand; relevant: *The commentator made a number of pertinent observations on the senator's speech.* [Latin *pertinēns*, present participle of *pertinēre* to belong, concern.] —**per'ti·nent·ly**, *adv.*

Syn. Pertinent, relevant, germane mean relating to or bearing on the matter at hand. **Pertinent** suggests something that contributes to the understanding of the subject under consideration: *Some literary critics feel that the details of an author's life are not pertinent to a criticism of his works.* **Relevant** implies a necessary and logical connection that lends significance and appropriateness: *The judge ruled that the evidence was not relevant to the case.* **Germane** stresses a true or natural relation and a closeness in spirit, tone, or origin that reinforces the fitness of the association: *A feeling of curiosity is germane to any scientific investigation.*

per·turb (pər turb') *v.t.* to disturb or disquiet greatly; make uneasy or anxious; trouble: *The dictator was perturbed by reports of unrest among the people.* [Latin *perturbāre.*] —**Syn.** see **disturb.**

per·tur·ba·tion (pur'tar bā'shən) *n.* **1.** act of perturbing; being perturbed. **2.** that which causes disquiet or anxiety. **3.** deviation from the regular orbit of a celestial body, caused by the gravitational attraction of other celestial bodies.

Pe·ru (pə rōō') *n.* country on the western coast of South America. Capital, Lima. Area, 496,224 sq. mi. Pop. (1970 est.), 13,586,000.

Pe·ru·gi·no (per'ə jē'nō) *n.* c.1446–1523, Italian painter; born Pietro di Cristoforo Vannucci.

pe·ruke (pə rōōk') *n.* wig, esp. of the type worn by men in the seventeenth and eighteenth centuries. [French *perruque*, from Italian *parrucca;* of uncertain origin.]

pe·rus·al (pə rōō'zəl) *n.* act or process of perusing; reading through or examining carefully; thorough scrutiny: *A careful perusal of the documents revealed inconsistencies.*

pe·ruse (pə rōōz') **-rused, -rus·ing.** *v.t.* **1.** to read through or examine carefully; scrutinize thoroughly: *Cindy perused Dan's letters for signs of his affection for her.* **2.** to read: *to peruse the newspaper before dinner.* [Middle English *perusen* to use up, from PER- + *usen* to use. See USE.]

Pe·ru·vi·an (pə rōō'vē ən) *adj.* of or relating to Peru, its people, their language, or their culture. —*n.* native or inhabitant of Peru.

Peruvian bark, cinchona *(def. 2).*

per·vade (pər vād') **-vad·ed, -vad·ing.** *v.t.* to spread or diffuse through every part of: *The odor of jasmine pervaded the room. A strong sense of patriotism pervades his writings.* [Latin *pervādere* to go through.] —**per·va'sion**, *n.* —**Syn.** see **permeate.**

per·va·sive (pər vā'siv) *adj.* having the power of or tending to pervade; thoroughly penetrative. —**per·va'sive·ly**, *adv.* —**per·va'sive·ness**, *n.*

per·verse (pər vurs') *adj.* **1.** willfully determined or disposed to go counter to what is reasonable, expected, or required; contrary: *a perverse child who refused to obey anyone.* **2.** characterized by or arising from such a disposition. **3.** obstinate or persistent in what is wrong; stubborn: *perverse disbelief in the face of positive proof.* **4.** morally wrong or erring; wicked; corrupt. [Latin *perversus*, past participle of *pervertere* to turn around, corrupt.] —**per·verse'ly**, *adv.* —**per·verse'ness**, *n.*

per·ver·sion (pər vur'zhən, -shən) *n.* **1.** act of perverting; being perverted. **2.** any perverted form, act, or practice.

per·ver·si·ty (pər vur'sə tē) *pl.* **-ties.** *n.* **1.** quality or state of being perverse. **2.** instance of this.

per·vert (*v.*, pər vurt'; *n.*, pur'vurt) *v.t.* **1.** to lead or turn from what is considered right or moral; lead astray; corrupt. **2.** to distort the meaning of; misconstrue: *to pervert the truth.* **3.** to divert from proper purposes; misuse. **4.** to bring into a worse or inferior condition; debase. —*n.* one who is perverted or given to perversion, esp. sexual perversion. [Latin *pervertere* to turn around, corrupt.] —**per·vert'er**, *n.*

per·vi·ous (pur'vē əs) *adj.* **1.** allowing passage or entrance; capable of being penetrated; permeable: *a fiber pervious to heat.* **2.** open to influence, reasoning, or argument: *He is narrow-minded and not pervious to our suggestions.* [Latin *pervius* passable.]

at; āpe; cär; end; mē; it; īce; hot; ōld; fôrk; wood; fōōl; oil; out; up; ūse; turn; sing; thin; this; zh in treasure; ə in ago, taken, pencil, lemon, circus.

pe·se·ta (pə sā′tə) *n.* monetary unit of Spain. [Spanish *peseta*, diminutive of *pesa* weight, from Latin *pēnsa*, plural of *pēnsum* weight.]

Pe·sha·war (pe shä′wər) *n.* city in northwestern West Pakistan, near the Khyber Pass. Pop. (1969), 296,000.

pes·ky (pes′kē) -ki·er, -ki·est. *adj. Informal.* troublesome; annoying. [Modification of PEST + -Yⁱ.]

pe·so (pā′sō) *pl.*, **-sos.** *n.* monetary unit of Mexico, several South and Central American countries, Cuba, the Dominican Republic, and the Philippines. [Spanish *peso* weight, Latin-American monetary unit, from Latin *pēnsum* weight.]

pes·si·mism (pes′ə miz′əm) *n.* **1.** disposition or tendency to take a gloomy or cynical view of or see the worst aspect of things. **2.** doctrine or belief that everything naturally tends to evil and that this is the worst possible world. [Latin *pessimus* worst + -ISM.] —**pes′si·mist**, *n.* —**pes′si·mis′tic**, *adj.* —**pes′si·mis′ti·cal·ly**, *adv.*

pest (pest) *n.* **1.** person or thing that is troublesome, annoying, or destructive; nuisance: *Locusts, gnats, and mosquitos are insect pests. He made a pest of himself by repeatedly asking personal questions.* **2.** epidemic disease; pestilence. [Latin *pestis* plague.]

pes·ter (pes′tər) *v.t.* to trouble repeatedly with petty annoyances; bother; annoy: *The children were always pestering her with demands.* [Short for Middle French *empestrer* to hobble, entangle, tether a horse at pasture, going back to Latin *in* in + Medieval Latin *pastōrium* clog (for a horse at pasture), from Latin *pastus* pasture, food.]

Syn. Pester, plague, harass mean to worry and annoy. **Pester** may be used when one annoys another with repeated and trivial importunities, sometimes goading him past endurance: *Beggars pestered the tourists at the resort.* **Plague** may be used when one torments another persistently and suggests that one has no control over one's tormentor: *Misfortunes continued to plague Joan throughout her youth.* **Harass** may be used when one persecutes another systematically with demands and exactions that drain his physical and mental powers: *The new administration was harassed by opposition at home and abroad.* See also **bait.**

pest·house (pest′hous′) *n. Archaic.* hospital for those suffering from an epidemic disease.

pes·ti·cide (pes′tə sīd′) *n.* chemical or other substance used to destroy harmful plants or animals. —**pes′ti·ci′dal**, *adj.*

pes·tif·er·ous (pes tif′ər əs) *adj.* **1.** producing or carrying disease or plague: *a pestiferous tropical climate.* **2.** morally corrupting; evil: *the pestiferous example of a dope seller.* **3.** *Informal.* mischievous; troublesome; annoying: *a pestiferous young prankster.* [Latin *pestiferus* bringing pestilence, destructive, from *pestis* plague + *ferre* to bring.]

pes·ti·lence (pes′tə ləns) *n.* any highly infectious, epidemic disease, esp. bubonic plague.

pes·ti·lent (pes′tə lənt) *adj.* **1.** producing or tending to produce infectious disease. **2.** harmful or destructive to peace, morals, or the like: *pestilent ambition that knew no bounds.* **3.** troublesome; annoying. [Latin *pestilēns* unhealthy.]

pes·ti·len·tial (pes′tə len′shəl) *adj.* **1.** of, relating to, causing, or resembling a pestilence. **2.** harmful; pernicious. **3.** troublesome; annoying. —**pes′ti·len′tial·ly**, *adv.*

pes·tle (pes′əl, pes′-) *n.* blunt tool for pounding, grinding, or mixing substances in a mortar. —*v.t., v.i.*, **-tled, -tling.** to pound, grind, or mix with or as if with a pestle. [Old French *pestel* the tool, from Latin *pistillum*, going back to *pinsere* to pound.]

pet¹ (pet) *n.* **1.** tame animal that is kept chiefly for amusement and companionship, as a dog or cat. **2.** any person who is indulged or treated with special favor or kindness; favorite: *That boy is the teacher's pet.* —*adj.* **1.** kept or treated as a pet: *a pet frog.* **2.** expressing fondness or familiarity; affectionate: *a pet name.* **3.** favorite; cherished: *Getting up early is my pet peeve.* —*v.t.*, **pet·ted, pet·ting.** to stroke, pat, or caress: *The cat purred when she was petted.* —*v.i. Informal.* to make love by kissing and caressing. [Of uncertain origin.]

pet² (pet) *n.* fit of peevishness or ill humor; discontent. [Of uncertain origin.]

pet·al (pet′əl) *n.* one of the usually colored divisions or leaflike parts of the corolla of a flower. [Modern Latin *petalum*, from Greek *petalon* leaf, from *petalos* spread out.] —**pet′aled;** *also,* **pet′alled,** *adj.*

pe·tard (pi tärd′) *n.* **1.** formerly, an explosive device used to blow in a door or gate or to make a breach in a wall, consisting of a bell-shaped or boxlike structure fastened against the surface of the obstacle and ignited by a fuse. **2.** hoisted by (or with) one's own petard, caught or victimized by one's own actions. [French *pétard*, from *péter* to break wind, from *pet* a breaking wind, from Latin *pēditum*.]

pet·cock (pet′kok′) *n.* small valve or faucet.

pe·ter (pē′tər) *v.i. Informal.* to diminish gradually and disappear (usu-

ally with *out*): *The vein of silver petered out.* [Of uncertain origin.]

Pe·ter (pē′tər) *n.* **1.** died A.D. c.67, one of the twelve Apostles. Also, **Simon Peter.** **2.** either of two Epistles of the New Testament attributed to him.

Peter I, 1672–1725, czar of Russia, from 1682 to 1725. Also, **Peter the Great.**

pet·i·o·late (pet′ē ə lāt′) *adj.* having a petiole. Also, **pet′i·o·lat′ed.**

pet·i·ole (pet′ē ōl′) *n.* **1.** slender stalk that attaches a leaf to a stem. Also, **leaf′stalk′.** **2.** slender, stalklike structure, as the waist of an ant or wasp connecting the thorax and abdomen. [Late Latin *petiolus* stalk of fruits, diminutive of Latin *pēs* foot.]

Petiole

Def. 1   Def. 2

Petioles

pet·it (pet′ē) *also,* **pet·ty.** *adj. Law.* small; lesser; minor. [Old French *petit;* of uncertain origin.]

pe·tite (pə tēt′) *adj.* of small size; little; tiny. ▲ said especially of a woman or girl. [French *petite*, feminine of *petit;* of uncertain origin.]

pet·it four (pet′ē fōr′) *pl.*, **pet·its fours** (pet′ē fōrz′). small cake covered with icing. [French *petit four* literally, small oven, from *petit* small (of uncertain origin) + *four* oven (from Latin *furnus*).]

pe·ti·tion (pə tish′ən) *n.* **1.** formal request to a superior or one in authority for some favor, privilege, redress of a grievance, or the like: *We signed a petition asking our senator to support the proposed legislation.* **2.** prayer or entreaty; supplication. **3.** that which is formally requested or entreated. **4.** *Law.* written application made to a court requesting the court to take some action. —*v.t.* **1.** to make a petition to. **2.** to pray or beg for; request. —*v.i.* to make a petition: *The defendant's lawyer petitioned for a new trial.* [Latin *petītiō* request, solicitation.] —**pe·ti′tion·ar′y**, *adj.* —**pe·ti′tion·er**, *n.*

pet·it jury (pet′ē) *also,* **petty jury.** jury, usually composed of twelve persons, selected to hear a civil or criminal case in a court of law.

pet·it larceny (pet′ē) *also,* **petty larceny.** larceny in which the goods stolen do not exceed a specified statutory value. Distinguished from **grand larceny.**

pe·tit mal (pə tē′ mäl′, mal′) form of epilepsy, characterized by brief attacks of unconsciousness and often by mild twitching. [French *petit mal* literally, small sickness, from *petit* small (of uncertain origin) + *mal* sickness (going back to Latin *malus* bad).]

pet·it point (pet′ē) **1.** small stitch used in needlepoint. **2.** work done with this stitch.

Pe·trarch (pē′trärk) *n.* 1304–74, Italian poet and scholar.

Pe·trar·chan sonnet (pi trär′kən) sonnet form developed by Petrarch, consisting of an eight-line stanza rhyming *abbaabba* and a six-line stanza often rhyming *cdecde.* Also, **Italian sonnet.**

pet·rel (pet′rəl) *n.* any of various hook-billed sea birds, order Procellariiformes, usually having blackish or brownish plumage with white markings. There are three families of petrels, the best known being the storm petrels. [Possibly diminutive of St. *Peter;* because it seems to walk on water like St. Peter.]

pet·ri·fac·tion (pet′rə fak′shən) *n.* **1.** act or process of petrifying; being petrified. **2.** that which is petrified. Also, **pet·ri·fi·ca·tion** (pet′rə fi kā′shən).

pet·ri·fy (pet′rə fī′) **-fied, -fy·ing.** *v.t.* **1.** to convert (organic material) into stone or a stony substance. **2.** to paralyze with fear, astonishment, or horror. **3.** to harden or stiffen; deaden. —*v.i.* **1.** to become stone or like stone. [French *pétrifier* to turn into stone, amaze, from Latin *petra* rock (from Greek *pétrā*) + *facere* to make.]

pet·ro·dol·lars (pet′rō dol′ərz) *n..pl.* U.S. dollars earned by countries rich in oil from their increased oil revenues, usually invested in the industries of large, highly developed countries. [PETRO(L) + DOLLAR.]

Pet·ro·grad (pet′rə grad′) *n.* see **Leningrad.**

pe·trog·ra·phy (pi trog′rə fē) *n.* branch of geology that deals with the systematic classification and description of rocks. [Greek *petrā* rock + -GRAPHY.] —**pe·trog′raph·er**, *n.*

pet·rol (pet′rəl) *n. British.* gasoline. [French *pétrole* petroleum, oil, from Medieval Latin *petroleum.* See PETROLEUM.]

pet·ro·la·tum (pet′rə lā′təm) *n.* jellylike substance obtained from petroleum, used esp. in ointments and dressings. [Modern Latin *petrolatum*, from English PETROLEUM.]

pe·tro·le·um (pi trō′lē əm) *n.* viscous, flammable liquid, occurring naturally, usually beneath the earth's surface, consisting of a mixture of hydrocarbons, with traces of organic sulfur, nitrogen, and oxygen compounds. Petroleum yields various products, as gasoline, diesel fuel, and lubricants, and many derivatives used in the manufacture of various products. [Medieval Latin *petroleum* literally, rock oil, from Latin

petra rock (from Greek *petrā*) + *oleum* oil (from Greek *elaion*).]

pe·trol·o·gy (pi trol′ə jē) *n.* branch of geology that deals with the study of the origin, structure, and characteristics of rocks. [Greek *petrā* rock + -LOGY.] —**pet·ro·log·ic** (pet′rə loj′ik); *also,* **pet′ro·log′i·cal,** *adj.* —**pe·trol′o·gist,** *n.*

pet·rous (pet′rəs, pē′trəs) *adj.* **1.** of or like rock; stony; rocky. **2.** of or relating to the part of the temporal bone that contains the inner ear.

pet·ti·coat (pet′ē kōt′) *n.* **1.** skirtlike undergarment, esp. one designed to be worn under and add fullness to a skirt. **2.** formerly, a skirt. **3.** *Slang.* woman; girl. —*adj.* of, relating to, or influenced by women: *to be engaged in petticoat politics.* [Earlier PETTY COAT literally, little coat; because it originally was a short coat for men worn under armor or a doublet.]

pet·ti·fog (pet′ē fôg′, -fog′) **-fogged, -fog·ging.** *v.i.* to act like a pettifogger.

pet·ti·fog·ger (pet′ē fô′gər, -fog′ər) *n.* **1.** inferior lawyer, esp. one who is involved in insignificant matters or employs devious or unethical methods. **2.** one who quibbles over trivialities. [PETTY + obsolete *fogger* pettifogger; of uncertain origin.] —**pet′ti·fog′ger·y,** *n.*

pet·tish (pet′ish) *adj.* ill-tempered; cross; peevish. [PET² + -ISH.] —**pet′tish·ly,** *adv.*

pet·ty (pet′ē) **-ti·er, -ti·est.** *adj.* **1.** of little value or importance; insignificant: *a petty complaint.* **2.** mean; spiteful. **3.** minor; inferior; subordinate: *a petty government official.* **4.** having or marked by a small range of interests or sympathies; narrow-minded. **5.** *Law.* petit. [Old French *petit* small, little; of uncertain origin.] —**pet′ti·ly,** *adv.* —**pet′ti·ness,** *n.*

Syn. 1. Petty, trivial mean little and insignificant. **Petty** may be applied to what is the smallest in size or the least important among others of the same kind: *It was only a petty problem and they soon solved it.* **Trivial** may be applied to what is so commonplace and ordinary that it is unworthy of serious consideration or interest: *Agnes spends most of her time spreading trivial gossip.*

petty cash, small cash fund kept on hand to pay minor or incidental expenses, as in a business office: *The secretary took money for postage stamps and mailing envelopes out of petty cash.*

petty jury, petit jury.

petty larceny, petit larceny.

petty officer, any enlisted man in the U.S. Navy or Coast Guard of a rank corresponding to any of the noncommissioned ranks in the U.S. Army.

pet·u·lance (pech′ə ləns) *n.* quality or state of being petulant; peevishness. Also, **pet′u·lan·cy.**

pet·u·lant (pech′ə lənt) *adj.* having or showing a tendency to be easily or unpredictably angered. [Latin *petulāns* pert, saucy.] —**pet′u·lant·ly,** *adv.*

pe·tu·nia (pi tōōn′yə, -tūn′-) *n.* **1.** funnel-shaped white, pink, or purple flower of any of a group of plants, genus *Petunia,* of the nightshade family, sometimes having fringed or ruffled petals. **2.** plant bearing this flower, widely cultivated in the United States, having hairy branches and smooth, soft leaves. [Modern Latin *Petunia,* from French *petun* tobacco plant, through Portuguese, from Tupi-Guarani *petyn* tobacco.]

Petunias

pew (pū) *n.* any of the fixed benches with a back in a church. [Old French *puie* elevated place, from Latin *podia,* plural of *podium* elevated place. See PODIUM.]

pe·wee (pē′wē′) *n.* any of various small flycatchers, family Tyrannidae, that is native to the temperate and tropical regions of the Western Hemisphere, having dull olive-brown or gray plumage. [Imitative.]

pe·wit (pē′wit′, pū′it) *n.* any of several birds with a shrill cry, esp. the lapwing. [Imitative.]

pew·ter (pū′tər) *n.* **1.** alloy, formerly made of tin, lead, and copper, now made of ninety to ninety-five percent tin, and antimony, used to make tableware, utensils, and ornamental objects. **2.** articles made of this alloy. —*adj.* made of pewter. [Old French *peautre* tin; of uncertain origin.]

pey·o·te (pā ō′tē) *n.* **1.** small cactus, *Lophophora williamsii,* grown in dry regions from Texas to Central America. Also, **mes·cal′.** **2.** mescaline. [Spanish *peyote* the cactus, from Nahuatl *peyotl* caterpillar; referring to the plant's hairy center.]

pf. 1. pfennig. **2.** preferred.

pfc, private first class. Also, **Pfc.**

pfen·nig (pfen′ig) *pl.* **pfen·nigs** or **pfen·ni·ge** (pfen′i gə). *n.* small bronze coin of East and West Germany. [German *Pfennig.*]

pfg., pfennig.

Pg. 1. Portugal. **2.** Portuguese.

Phae·dra (fē′drə, fā′-) *n. Greek Mythology.* daughter of Minos and wife of Theseus, king of Athens. She fell in love with her stepson Hippolytus, but he resisted her advances. She falsely accused him of seducing her and hanged herself.

Pha·ë·thon (fā′ə thon′, -thən) *n. Greek Mythology.* mortal son of Helios, god of the sun. He tried to drive the chariot of the sun across the sky, but couldn't control it and scorched the earth before Zeus could stop him with a deadly thunderbolt.

pha·e·ton (fā′ət ən) *n.* **1.** light, low, open, four-wheeled carriage. **2.** open automobile whose body resembles that of the phaeton carriage. [French *phaéton* light, open carriage, from PHAËTHON.]

Phaeton *(def. 1)*

-phage *combining form* one who or that which eats, devours, or consumes: *bacteriophage.* [Greek *phagein* to eat.]

phag·o·cyte (fag′ə sīt′) *n.* any cell, esp. a white blood cell, or leucocyte, that can absorb and destroy bacteria and other harmful material. [Greek *phagos* eating + *kytos* hollow vessel.]

pha·lan·ger (fə lan′jər) *n.* any of various arboreal, nocturnal marsupials, family Phalangeridae, native to Australia, having small round ears and a long bushy tail. [Modern Latin *phalanger,* from Greek *phalanx* bone between two joints of the fingers or toes; with reference to the formation of its toes.]

pha·lanx (fā′langks, fal′angks) *pl.,* **pha·lanx·es** or **pha·lan·ges** (fə-lan′jēz). *n.* **1.** in ancient Greek and Macedonian armies, a battle formation of infantry standing in close ranks with their shields and long spears overlapping each other. **2.** compact body of persons, animals, or things, massed together, as for attack or for defense: *A phalanx of police held back the crowd.* **3.** number of persons united for a common purpose, esp. in support of some cause. **4.** any of the bones in the fingers or toes. [Latin *phalanx* multitude, battalion, battle array, from Greek *phalanx* line of battle, battle array, bone between two joints of the fingers or toes.]

phal·lus (fal′əs) *pl.,* **-li** (-lī) or **-lus·es.** *n.* **1.** representation of the male sexual organs, symbolizing in certain religions the generative power in nature. **2.** penis. [Late Latin *phallus,* from Greek *phallos.*] —**phal′lic,** *adj.*

phan·tasm (fan′taz′əm) *n.* **1.** thing seen in the imagination; unreal or fantastic idea or fancy: *the bizarre phantasms of a nightmare.* **2.** ghost; phantom; apparition. [Latin *phantasma* apparition, from Greek *phantasma.* Doublet of PHANTOM.]

phan·tas·ma·go·ri·a (fan taz′mə gôr′ē ə) *n.* **1.** shifting series or succession of imaginary figures, as those seen in a dream: *Milton's genius has filled the atmosphere with a brilliant phantasmagoria of contending angels* (White, 1875). **2.** formerly, an exhibition of optical illusions produced by a magic lantern. [French *fantasmagorie,* from Greek *phantasma* apparition + *agora* assembly.] —**phan·tas·ma·gor·ic** (fan-taz′mə gôr′ik, -gor′-); *also,* **phan·tas′ma·gor′i·cal,** *adj.*

phan·tas·mal (fan taz′məl) *adj.* of or like a phantasm; unreal; imaginary.

phan·ta·sy (fan′tə sē, -zē) *pl.,* **-sies.** *n.* fantasy.

phan·tom (fan′təm) *n.* **1.** something apparent to the sight or other sense, but having no material substance or physical reality; ghost; apparition. **2.** something existing only as an image in the mind; illusion. **3.** mere show or appearance lacking force or substance: *The king had only the phantom of authority.* —*adj.* resembling a phantom; unreal; illusive: *A phantom army roamed the battlefield.* [Old French *fanto(s)me* ghost, from Latin *phantasma* apparition, from Greek *phantasma.* Doublet of PHANTASM.]

Phar·aoh (fâr′ō) *n.* title of the kings of ancient Egypt. [Late Latin *Pharaô,* through Greek and Hebrew, from Egyptian *per-o* literally, great house.]

Phar·i·sa·ic (far′ə sā′ik) *adj.* **1.** of or relating to the Pharisees. **2. pharisaic. a.** emphasizing strict outward observance of religious or moral laws and principles without regard for their essence or real meaning. **b.** assuming a moral superiority; self-righteous; hypocritical. —**Phar′i·sa′i·cal·ly;** *also,* **phar′i·sa′i·cal·ly,** *adv.*

Phar·i·sa·ism (far′ə sā iz′əm) *n.* **1.** doctrines and practices of the Pharisees. **2. pharisaism.** character or behavior of a pharisee; rigid formalism, hypocrisy, or self-righteousness.

Phar·i·see (far′ə sē) *n.* **1.** member of an ancient Jewish sect that was very strict in observing both the written law and the oral tradition of Judaism. **2. pharisee.** one who emphasizes strict outward observance of religious or moral laws and principles without regard for their essence or real meaning. **b.** one who is self-righteous or hypocritical.

phar·ma·ceu·ti·cal (fär′mə sōō′ti kəl) *adj.* of or relating to phar-

---

at; āpe; cär; end; mē; it; īce; hot; ōld; fôrk; wood; fōōl; out; up; ūse; turn; sing; thin; this; zh in treasure; ə in ago, taken, pencil, lemon, circus.

macy or drugs. Also, **phar′ma·ceu′tic**. [Late Latin *pharmaceuticus* (from Greek *pharmakeutikos*, going back to *pharmakon* drug) + -AL¹.]

phar·ma·ceu·tics (fär′mə soo′tiks) *n.,pl.* pharmacy *(def. 2).* ▲ construed as singular.

phar·ma·cist (fär′mə sist) *n.* one who is licensed to prepare drugs and fill prescriptions.

phar·ma·col·o·gist (fär′mə kol′ə jist) *n.* one who is skilled or an expert in pharmacology.

phar·ma·col·o·gy (fär′mə kol′ə jē) *n.* branch of science that deals with the sources, qualities, preparation, uses, and esp. the effects of drugs. [Greek *pharmakon* drug + -LOGY.]

phar·ma·co·poe·ia (fär′mə kə pē′ə) *n.* **1.** book that lists and describes drugs, their sources, qualities, and uses, esp. one published by a government agency. **2.** stock of drugs. [Modern Latin *pharmacopoeia*, from Greek *pharmakopoiiā* preparation of drugs, from *pharmakon* drug + *poiein* to make.]

phar·ma·cy (fär′mə sē) *pl.,* **-cies.** *n.* **1.** drugstore. **2.** science, practice, or profession of preparing and dispensing drugs. Also *(def. 2),* **phar′ma·ceu′tics.** [Old French *pharmacie* treatment with drugs or medicines, through Late Latin, from Greek *pharmakeiā* use of drugs, from *pharmakon* drug.]

Phar·os (fār′os) *n.* huge lighthouse constructed on an island in the harbor of Alexandria, Egypt, in the third century B.C.

pha·ryn·ge·al (fə rin′jē əl, -jəl, far′in jē′əl) *adj.* of, relating to, or affecting the pharynx.

phar·yn·gi·tis (far′in jī′tis) *n.* inflammation of the mucous membrane of the pharynx. [Modern Latin *pharyngitis*, from Greek *pharynx* throat + -ITIS.]

phar·ynx (far′ingks) *n.,* **pharynx·es** or **pha·ryn·ges** (fə rin′jēz) *n.* short, muscular tube that connects the mouth and nasal cavity with the esophagus and windpipe. [Modern Latin *pharynx*, from Greek *pharynx* throat.]

Adenoids

Eustachian tube

Tonsils

Pharynx

Esophagus

Windpipe

Pharynx

phase (fāz) *n.* **1.** state or stage of development of a person or thing: *Digging the foundation is the first phase of our building project. The child went through a phase during which he was completely rebellious.* **2.** one side, view, or aspect of a subject or phenomenon: *The president received a report covering all phases of the program.* **3.** *Astronomy.* one of the recurring variations in the appearance of the illuminated visible portion of the moon or of a planet. **4.** *Chemistry.* distinct homogeneous part of a heterogeneous system that is mechanically separable from the other parts: *the solid, liquid, and gaseous phases of water.* **5.** *Physics.* any stage or point in a periodic motion, as a sound wave, usually reckoned with reference to an arbitrarily fixed starting point or moment of starting. **6. in phase.** *Physics.* being at the same point or stage, thereby reinforcing one another, as two or more sound waves. **7. out of phase.** *Physics.* being at different points or stages, thereby weakening or neutralizing one another, as two or more sound waves. —*v.t.,* **phased, phas·ing. 1. to phase in.** to introduce in stages: *The company is phasing in new production plans.* **2. to phase out.** to eliminate in stages: *The army plans to phase out the equipment as it becomes obsolete.* [Modern Latin *phasis*, from Greek *phasis* appearance, phase of the moon.]

Ph.B., Bachelor of Philosophy.

Ph.C., pharmaceutical chemist.

Ph.D., Doctor of Philosophy.

pheas·ant (fez′ənt) *pl.,* **-ants** or **-ant.** *n.* **1.** any of various long-tailed birds, family Phasianidae, originally native to Asia and now found in most parts of the world, the male of which often has brilliantly colored and patterned plumage, while the female is generally brownish. Length: 1½–8 feet including tail. **2.** any of various similar birds, esp. the ruffed grouse. [Anglo-Norman *fesaunt*, from Latin *phasiāna*, from Greek *phasianos* literally, of *Phasis*, a river in Colchis associated with the Asian bird.]

phe·nix (fē′niks) phoenix.

phe·no·bar·bi·tal (fē′nō bär′bə tôl′) *n.* soluble white powder derived from barbituric acid, used as a sedative.

phe·nol (fē′nôl) *n.* **1.** poisonous crystalline organic compound used

Pheasant

in plastics, explosives, weed killers, and pharmaceuticals. It was formerly used as an antiseptic and disinfectant. Formula: C_6H_5OH Also, **carbolic acid. 2.** any compound that contains one or more hydroxyl groups attached to a benzene ring. [Greek *phainein* to show, shine + -OL.]

phe·nol·phthal·e·in (fē′nôl thal′ē in, -thal′ēn) *n.* pale-yellow, crystalline, powdery organic compound, used esp. in alcohol solution as an indicator to test whether a substance is acid or base. Formula: $C_{20}H_{14}O_4$

phe·nom·e·nal (fə nom′ən əl) *adj.* **1.** of or relating to a phenomenon. **2.** remarkable; extraordinary; prodigious: *Herman has phenomenal strength for such a small man.* **3.** *Philosophy.* that can be perceived by the senses. —**phe·nom′e·nal·ly,** *adv.*

phe·nom·e·non (fə nom′ə non′, -nən) *pl.,* **-na** (-nə) or **-nons.** *n.* **1.** fact, event, or condition that can be perceived by the senses: *Rain and snow are phenomena of the weather.* **2.** one who or that which is extraordinary or remarkable: *Harry's rapid success made him a phenomenon in the business world.* **3.** *Philosophy.* that which is perceived by the senses. [Late Latin *phaenomenon* appearance, from Greek *phainomenon*, neuter present participle of *phainesthai* to appear.]

phe·no·type (fē′nə tīp′) *n.* physical characteristics exhibited by an organism which result from environmental influences. Opposed to **genotype.** [PHENO(MENON) + TYPE.]

phen·yl (fen′əl, fēn′-) *n.* radical or group left when one atom of hydrogen is taken away from benzene. Formula: C_6H_5 [Greek *phainein* to show, shine + -YL.]

phew (fū, whū) *interj.* used to express disgust, weariness, or surprise.

phi (fī, fē) *n.* twenty-first letter of the Greek alphabet (Φ, φ), corresponding to English *Ph, ph,* and *F, f.*

phi·al (fī′əl) *n.* vial.

Phi Beta Kappa, American honor society founded in 1776 for college and university students and graduates of high academic achievement and scholarship in the liberal arts or sciences. [From the initial letters of the society's Greek motto *philosophia biou kubernētēs* philosophy the guide of life.]

Phid·i·an (fid′ē ən) *adj.* of, relating to, or following the style of Phidias.

Phid·i·as (fid′ē əs) *n.* c.490–c.432 B.C., Greek sculptor.

Phil. 1. Philippians. **2.** Philippine.

Phila., Philadelphia.

Phil·a·del·phi·a (fil′ə del′fē ə) *n.* city in southeastern Pennsylvania, on the Delaware River. Pop. (1970), 1,948,609.

phi·lan·der (fi lan′dər) *v.i.* (of a man) to make love without serious intentions. [From the use of *Philander* as the name of a lover in plays and romances, from Greek *philandros* loving men, from *philos* loving + *anēr* man.] —**phi·lan′der·er,** *n.*

phi·lan·thro·py (fi lan′thrə pē) *pl.,* **-pies.** *n.* **1.** love of mankind expressed in practical efforts to promote the happiness and well-being of humanity. **2.** philanthropic action, service, or agency. [Late Latin *philanthrōpia* benevolence, from Greek *philanthrōpia*, going back to *philos* loving + *anthrōpos* man.] —**phil·an·throp·ic** (fil′ən throp′ik); *also,* **phil′an·throp′i·cal,** *adj.* —**phil′an·throp′i·cal·ly,** *adv.* —**phi·lan′thro·pist,** *n.* —Syn. 2. see charity.

phi·lat·e·ly (fə lat′əl ē) *n.* the collecting, arranging, and studying of postage stamps and related items, as stamped envelopes, post cards, or revenue stamps, esp. as a hobby. [French *philatélie*, from Greek *philos* loving + *ateleiā* freedom from taxes; because the postage stamp freed the letter writers from paying the mailing costs.] —**phil·a·tel·ic** (fil′ə tel′ik); *also,* **phil·a·tel′i·cal,** *adj.* —**phi·lat′e·list,** *n.*

-phile *combining form* one who has a strong liking or love for: *Anglophile.* [Greek *philos* friend, loving, dear.]

Phi·le·mon (fi lē′mən) *n.* **1.** New Testament Epistle written by Paul. **2.** *Classical Mythology.* husband of Baucis.

phil·har·mon·ic (fil′här mon′ik, fil′ər-) *adj.* **1.** fond of or devoted to music. **2.** of, relating to, or presented by a musical society or an orchestra, esp. a symphony orchestra: *a philharmonic concert.* —*n.* philharmonic orchestra, concert, or society. [French *philharmonique* loving music, through Italian, from Greek *philos* loving + *harmonia* music.]

Phil·ip (fil′əp) *n.* one of the twelve Apostles of Christ.

Philip II 1. 382–336 B.C., king of Macedonia, from 359 to 336 B.C. and the father of Alexander the Great; known as Philip of Macedon. **2.** 1165–1223, king of France, from 1180 to 1223. Also, **Philip Augustus. 3.** 1527–98, king of Spain, from 1556 to 1598.

Phi·lip·pi (fə lip′ī) *n.* ancient city in Macedonia where, in 42 B.C., Octavian and Mark Antony defeated Brutus and Cassius. St. Paul later founded a Christian church there.

Phi·lip·pi·ans (fi lip′ē ənz) *n.* New Testament Epistle written by Paul to the Christians of Philippi.

Phi·lip·pic (fi lip′ik) *n.* **1.** any of a series of orations by Demosthenes against King Philip of Macedon warning the Athenians of Philip's

at; āpe; cär; end; mē; it; īce; hot; ōld; fôrk; wood; fōōl; oil; out; up; ūse; turn; sing; thin; this; zh in treasure; ə in ago, taken, pencil, lemon, circus.

755

growing power and of his threat to Athenian political freedom. **2. philippic.** bitter verbal denunciation or attack; invective.

Phil·ip·pine (fil'ə pēn') *adj.* of or relating to the Philippines or their inhabitants. Also, **Fil'i·pi'no.**

Phil·ip·pines (fil'ə pēnz') *n.* island country in the western Pacific, southeast of China. Capital, Quezon City. Land area, 115,831 sq. mi. Pop. (1970 est.), 38,613,000. Also, **Philippine Islands.**

Phi·lis·ti·a (fə lis'tē ə) *n.* land of the ancient Philistines, on the southwestern coast of Palestine.

Phil·is·tine (fil'is tēn', fi lis'tin, -tēn) *n.* **1.** in the Bible, member of an ancient people of Philistia, often mentioned in the Old Testament as enemies of the Israelites. **2.** *also,* **philistine.** one who is ignorant, uncultured, or smugly conventional in ideas and tastes. —*adj.* **1.** of or relating to the Philistines. **2.** *also,* **philistine.** lacking culture and refinement. —**Phil'is·tin'ism,** *n.*

phil·o·den·dron (fil'ə den'drən) *n.* any of various tropical American plants, family Araceae, often with heart-shaped, glossy leaves.

phi·lol·o·gy (fi lol'ə jē) *n.* **1.** study, criticism, and interpretation of literature and other written records. **2.** linguistics. [Latin *philologia* love of learning, love of letters, from Greek *philologiā,* going back to *philos* loving + *logos* word.] —**phil·o·log·i·cal** (fil'ə loj'i kəl), *adj.* —**phi·lol'o·gist,** *n.*

phil·o·mel (fil'ə mel') *also,* **Phil·o·mel.** *n. Archaic.* nightingale. [Latin *philomēla,* from PHILOMEL A.]

Phil·o·me·la (fil'ə mē'lə) *n.* **1.** *Classical Mythology.* princess of Athens who was raped by her sister Procne's husband, the king of Thrace, who then tore out her tongue. In revenge the two sisters murdered his son, and when the enraged king threatened to kill them, they were changed by the gods into birds, Philomela into a nightingale and Procne into a sparrow. **2. philomela.** philomel.

phi·los·o·pher (fi los'ə fər) *n.* **1.** one who studies or is an expert in philosophy. **2.** one who advocates or lives according to a particular system of philosophy. **3.** one who accepts life and its difficulties and uncertainties with serenity and composure. [Anglo-Norman *philosofre* one who studies philosophy, from Latin *philosophus,* from Greek *philosophos* lover of wisdom, one who speculates on philosophical subjects, from *philos* loving + *sophos* wise.]

philosophers' stone, imaginary substance believed by the alchemists to have the power to transmute elements, esp. to change base metals into gold or silver.

phil·o·soph·i·cal (phil'ə sof'i kəl) *adj.* **1.** of or relating to philosophy: *a philosophical treatise.* **2.** of, relating to, or characteristic of a philosopher: *a philosophical mind.* **3.** accepting life and its difficulties and uncertainties with composure and serenity. Also, **phil'o·soph'ic.** —**phil'o·soph'i·cal·ly,** *adv.*

phi·los·o·phize (fi los'ə fīz') *-phized, -phiz·ing. v.i.* to think or reason as a philosopher does, esp. to speculate about fundamental concepts. —**phi·los'o·phiz'er,** *n.*

phi·los·o·phy (fə los'ə fē) *pl.,* **-phies.** *n.* **1.** study of or search for the fundamental nature, function, and purpose of man, the universe, and life itself, as well as most general causes and principles of the universe. **2.** system of thought of a particular school or philosopher: *the philosophy of Plato.* **3.** study of the fundamental principles of a particular branch of knowledge, an activity, or a field of experience: *the philosophy of history.* **4.** system for guiding life or conduct, esp. personal principles and beliefs: *My philosophy is "live and let live."* **5.** calm, philosophical attitude. [Latin *philosophia* study of wisdom, from Greek *philosophiā* love of study, love of wisdom.]

phil·ter (fil'tər) *also,* **phil·tre.** *n.* **1.** magic drug or potion supposed to arouse sexual passion. **2.** any magic drug or potion. [French *philtre* love potion, from Latin *philtrum,* from Greek *philtron.*]

phle·bi·tis (fli bī'tis) *n.* inflammation of a vein, frequently accompanied by the formation of a blood clot. [Modern Latin *phlebitis,* from Greek *phleps* vein + -ITIS.]

phle·bot·o·my (fli bot'ə mē) *n.* the practice of opening a vein in order to draw blood, used as a therapeutic measure. [Late Latin *phlebotomia,* from Greek *phlebotomiā,* from *phleps* vein + *tomos* a cutting.] —**phle·bot'o·mist,** *n.*

phlegm (flem) *n.* **1.** mucus, esp. in the nose or throat during a respiratory infection. **2.** sluggish, unexcitable disposition; indifference. **3.** calm; equanimity. [Old French *fleume,* from Late Latin *phlegma* clammy humor of the body, from Greek *phlegma* the humor thought to cause sluggishness. See HUMOR.]

phleg·mat·ic (fleg mat'ik) *n.* **1.** sluggish; unexcitable; indifferent. **2.** calm; self-possessed. Also, **phleg·mat'i·cal.** [Late Latin *phlegmaticus* full of phlegm, from Greek *phlegmatikos,* from *phlegma* the humor thought to cause sluggishness. See HUMOR.] —**phleg·mat'i·cal·ly,** *adv.*

phlo·em (flō'em) *n.* layer of plant tissue that conducts food made in the leaves down to the other parts of the plant. In woody plants, it lies just under the hard, outer bark. Also, **bast.** [German *Phloem,* from Greek *phloos* bark.]

phlo·gis·ton (flō jis'tən) *n.* basic substance which, according to a theory of combustion held in the seventeenth and eighteenth centuries, was present in all combustible materials and given off by them when they burned. [Modern Latin *phlogiston,* from Greek *phlogiston,* neuter of *phlogistos* inflammable, going back to *phlox* flame.]

phlox (floks) *n.* any of a group of erect or trailing plants, genus *Phlox,* bearing showy clusters of small tubular flowers that are white or various shades of red, pink, violet, or blue. [Latin *phlox,* from Greek *phlox.*]

Phnom Penh (pə nôm' pen') *also,* **Pnom·penh.** capital, largest, and leading city of Cambodia, an inland port in the south-central part of the country. Pop. (1962 est.), 403,500.

Phlox

-phobe *suffix* (used to form nouns) one who fears or dreads: *Anglophobe.* [Greek *-phobos* fearing, from *phobos* panic fear.]

pho·bi·a (fō'bē ə) *n.* an excessive or unnatural dread or fear, esp. of a specific object, situation, phenomenon, or the like. [Greek *-phobiā* (from *phobos* panic fear), often through Latin *-phobia.*]

phoe·be (fē'bē) *n.* any of several small flycatchers, family Tyrannidae, native to tropical and temperate regions of the Western Hemisphere, as the **eastern phoebe,** *Sayornis phoebe,* having gray-brown plumage with white underparts. Length: 7 inches. [Imitative, but influenced by the proper name *Phoebe.*]

Phoe·be (fē'bē) *n.* **1.** *Greek Mythology.* Artemis, esp. as goddess of the moon. **2.** *Archaic.* the moon.

Phoe·bus (fē'bəs) *n.* **1.** *Greek Mythology.* Apollo, esp. as god of the sun. Also, **Phoebus Apollo. 2.** *Archaic.* the sun.

Phoe·ni·cia (fə nish'ə, -nē'shə) *n.* ancient district on the eastern Mediterranean coast, in the area that is now Lebanon.

Phoe·ni·cian (fə nish'ən, -nē'shən) *adj.* of or relating to Phoenicia, its people, their language, or culture. —*n.* **1.** member of the people inhabiting Phoenicia. **2.** extinct language of Phoenicia, belonging to the Semito-Hamitic language family.

phoe·nix (fē'niks) *also,* **phe·nix.** *n. Egyptian and Greek Mythology.* a miraculous bird with a life span of 500 years. At the end of this time it built a great funeral pyre and died in the flames, a new phoenix arising from the ashes. [Latin *phoenix,* from Greek *phoinīx.*]

Phoe·nix (fē'niks) *n.* capital, largest city, and principal industrial and commercial center of Arizona, in the south-central part of the state. Pop. (1970), 581,562.

phone¹ (fōn) *n. Informal.* telephone. [Short for TELEPHONE.]

phone² (fōn) *n. Phonetics.* a single speech sound. [Greek *phōnē* sound.]

pho·neme (fō'nēm) *n. Phonetics.* a number of sounds recognized as a single sound unit by the users of a language. The *t* of *tip* and the *t* of *stop* are different allophones because of the influence of the adjacent sounds, but belong to the same phoneme *t.* [Greek *phōnēma* sound.]

pho·net·ic (fə net'ik) *adj.* **1.** of or relating to speech sounds or phonetics. **2.** representing or corresponding to speech sounds, esp. representing such sounds with a set of characters or symbols, each of which stands for a distinct speech sound: *a phonetic alphabet, phonetic spelling.* Also, **pho·net'i·cal.** [Modern Latin *phoneticus,* from Greek *phōnētikos* relating to speaking, going back to *phōnē* sound.] —**pho·net'i·cal·ly,** *adv.*

pho·ne·ti·cian (fō'nə tish'ən) *n.* one who studies or is an expert in phonetics. Also, **pho·net'i·cist** (fə net'ə sist).

pho·net·ics (fə net'iks) *n.,pl.* **1.** branch of linguistics that deals with speech sounds and their use in communication and the production, transmission, and perception of speech. **2.** system of speech sounds of a particular language. ▲ construed as singular in both definitions.

phon·ic (fon'ik, fō'nik) *adj.* of, relating to, or of the nature of sound, esp. speech sound. [Greek *phōnē* sound + -IC.]

phon·ics (fon'iks, fō'niks) *n.,pl.* **1.** any of various methods employing phonetics in the teaching of reading. **2.** acoustics *(def. 2).* ▲ construed as singular in both definitions. [Greek *phōnē* sound + -ICS.]

pho·no·gram (fō'nə gram') *n.* symbol that represents a single speech sound, syllable, or word, esp. one used in shorthand. [Greek *phōnē* sound + -GRAM¹.]

pho·no·graph (fō'nə graf') *n.* device that reproduces sounds recorded on a disc of plastic or other material. [Greek *phōnē* sound + -GRAPH.]

pho·no·graph·ic (fō'nə graf'ik) *adj.* **1.** of, relating to, or produced by a phonograph. **2.** of, relating to, or written in phonography. —**pho·nog'raph'i·cal·ly,** *adv.*

pho·nog·ra·phy (fə nog'rə fē) *n.* **1.** spelling based on sound or pronunciation; phonetic spelling or transcription. **2.** any system of shorthand that uses symbols to represent letters, syllables, and words. —**pho·nog'ra·pher, pho·nog'ra·phist,** *n.*

at; āpe; cär; end; mē; it; īce; hot; ōld; fôrk; wood; fōōl; oil; out; up; ūse; turn; sing; thin; this; zh in treasure; ə in ago, taken, pencil, lemon, circus.

pho·nol·o·gist (fŏ nol′ə jist) *n.* one who studies or is an expert in phonology.

pho·nol·o·gy (fŏ nol′ə jē) *n.* **1.** system of speech sounds of a language. **2.** science that studies the special sounds of a language. [Greek *phōnē* sound + -LOGY.]

pho·ny (fŏ′nē) -ni·er, -ni·est. *Informal. adj.* not genuine; spurious; counterfeit; fake: *a phony diamond.* —*n. pl.,* -nies. **1.** that which is not genuine; fake. **2.** one who pretends or tries to be what he is not. [Of uncertain origin.] —**pho′ni·ness,** *n.*

phos·gene (fos′jēn) *n.* colorless, lethal poison gas that acts on the respiratory system, used in chemical warfare. Formula: $COCl_2$ [Greek *phōs* light + -*genēs* born, produced.]

phos·phate (fos′fāt) *n.* **1.** any salt of phosphoric acid. **2.** fertilizer having a high phosphorus content. **3.** beverage made with carbonated water and fruit syrup. [PHOSPH(ORUS) + -ATE².]

phos·phide (fos′fīd) *n.* compound of phosphorus and a single metallic element.

phos·phite (fos′fīt) *n.* salt of phosphorous acid.

phos·phor (fos′fər) *n.* substance that emits light when stimulated by an electronic beam. [French *phosphore* phosphorus, from Modern Latin *phosphorus.* See PHOSPHORUS.]

Phos·phor (fos′fər) *n. Archaic.* the morning star, esp. Venus.

phos·pho·resce (fos′fə res′) -resced, -resc·ing. *v.i.* to give off faint light without noticeable heat.

phos·pho·res·cence (fos′fə res′əns) *n.* **1.** emission of light from a substance that is absorbing radiant energy and, after a time delay, emitting it as visible light. It continues after the source of energy is removed. Distinguished from **fluorescence. 2.** light so produced.

phos·pho·res·cent (fos′fə res′ənt) *adj.* exhibiting phosphorescence.

phos·phor·et·ed (fos′fə ret′id) *also,* **phos·phor·et·ted, phos·phu·ret·ed, phos·phu·ret·ted.** *adj.* combined with phosphorus.

phos·phor·ic (fos fôr′ik, -for′-) *adj.* of, relating to, or containing phosphorus, esp. in a higher oxidation state than in phosphorous compounds.

phosphoric acid, any of three acids containing phosphorus. Formulas: HPO_3; H_3PO_4; $H_4P_2O_7$

phos·pho·rous (fos′fər əs, fos fôr′-) *adj.* of, relating to, or containing phosphorus, esp. in a lower oxidation state than in phosphoric compounds.

phosphorous acid, crystalline acid, used as a reducing agent and to make phosphites. Formula: H_3PO_3

phos·pho·rus (fos′fər əs) *n.* nonmetallic element existing in three allotropic forms. **Yellow phosphorus** is a poisonous, waxy solid that glows faintly in the dark. **Red phosphorus** is a less-reactive, reddish-brown crystalline powder. **Black phosphorus** is prepared by heating yellow phosphorus under very high pressure. Symbol: **P** See **element** for table. [Modern Latin *phosphorus,* from Greek *phōsphoros* bringing light; because it glows in the dark.]

phos·phu·ret·ed (fos′fyə ret′id) *also,* **phos·phu·ret·ted.** *adj.* phosphoreted.

pho·to (fŏ′tō) *pl.,* -tos. *n. Informal.* photograph.

photo- *combining form* **1.** of, relating to, or produced by light: *photosynthesis, photometry.* **2.** of, relating to, or produced by photography; photographic: *photogravure, photomechanical.* [Greek *phōt-,* stem of *phōs* light.]

pho·to·chem·is·try (fŏ′tō kem′is trē) *n.* branch of science that deals with the chemical changes brought about by the action of electromagnetic radiation, esp. visible light and ultraviolet radiation, on matter. —**pho′to·chem′i·cal,** *adj.* —**pho′to·chem′i·cal·ly,** *adv.* —**pho′·to·chem′ist,** *n.*

pho·to·cop·y (fŏ′tō cop′ē) -cop·ied, -cop·y·ing. *v.t., v.i.* to make copies of (printed matter or the like) by a photographic process. —*n. pl.,* -cop·ies. copy produced by such a process. —**pho′to·cop′i·er,** *n.*

pho·to·e·lec·tric (fŏ′tō i lek′trik) *adj.* of or relating to the emission of electrons from a surface due to the action of light.

photoelectric cell, electric device that is sensitive to light or other electromagnetic radiation, used esp. in electric eyes, television cameras, and light meters. Also, **pho′to·cell′.**

pho·to·en·grav·ing (fŏ′tō en grā′ving) *n.* **1.** process by which engraved plates for relief printing are produced from photographs of illustrations. **2.** plate or print so produced. **3.** print or engraving made from this.

photo finish 1. in horse racing, finish so close that a photograph of the horses as they cross the finish line is required to decide which one is the winner. **2.** finish of any contest which is extremely close or not decided until the last minute.

pho·to·flood lamp (fŏ′tō flud′) floodlight used for taking pictures.

pho·to·gen·ic (fŏ′tə jen′ik) *adj.* **1.** suitable for or being a good subject for photographing: *a photogenic person.* **2.** *Biology.* emitting light; luminescent; phosphorescent. [PHOTO- + -GEN + -IC.]

pho·to·gram·me·try (fŏ′tə gram′i trē) *n.* science of using measurements taken from photographs for map making or for architectural and engineering construction work.

pho·to·graph (fŏ′tə graf′) *n.* picture or reproduction made by photography. —*v.t.* to take a photograph of. —*v.i.* **1.** to take photographs. **2.** to appear or look in a photograph: *an actress who always photographs well.*

pho·tog·ra·pher (fə tog′rə fər) *n.* one who takes photographs, esp. as a profession.

pho·to·graph·ic (fŏ′tə graf′ik) *adj.* **1.** used in or produced by photography: *photographic equipment.* **2.** relating to or resembling photography: *a photographic style of painting.* Also, **pho′to·graph′i·cal.** —**pho′to·graph′i·cal·ly,** *adv.*

pho·tog·ra·phy (fə tog′rə fē) *n.* **1.** technique of recording the image of a given area or object at a point in time by the photochemical action of light on a light-sensitive surface. **2.** art of taking photographs.

pho·to·gra·vure (fŏ′tə gra vyoor′) *n.* **1.** photoengraving process in which a printing plate is made by transferring the photographic negative of the image to be reproduced to the metal plate and then etching the image into it. **2.** plate or picture produced by this method. Also, **gra·vure′.**

pho·to·jour·nal·ism (fŏ′tō jurn′əl iz′əm) *n.* journalism in which photographic presentation of the news is more important than the written account of it. —**pho′to·jour′nal·ist,** *n.*

pho·to·me·chan·i·cal (fŏ′tō mi kan′i kəl) *adj.* of or relating to any process by which printed material is produced from a photograph.

pho·tom·e·ter (fŏ tom′ə tər) *n.* any device for determining the intensity of a light source by comparing it to a source of known intensity.

pho·to·met·ric (fŏ′tə met′rik) *adj.* of or relating to photometry or a photometer. —**pho′to·met′ri·cal·ly,** *adv.*

pho·tom·e·try (fŏ tom′ə trē) *n.* branch of physics that deals with the measurement of the intensity of light.

pho·to·mi·cro·graph (fŏ′tə mī′krə graf′) *n.* photograph taken through a microscope. —**pho·to·mi·crog·ra·phy** (fŏ′tə mī krog′-rə fē), *n.*

pho·ton (fŏ′ton) *n.* basic quantum, or unit, of light or other electromagnetic radiant energy, considered a discrete particle. See **subatomic particle** for table. [PHOTO- + (ELECTR)ON.]

pho·to·play (fŏ′tə plā′) *n.* script for a motion picture; screenplay.

pho·to·sphere (fŏ′tə sfēr′) *n.* **1.** visible surface of the sun consisting of a layer of hot gases about 250 miles thick. **2.** similar surface on any star.

Pho·to·stat (fŏ′tə stat′) *n.* **1.** *Trademark.* device for making photographic copies of graphic matter directly on specially prepared paper. **2.** *also,* **photostat.** copy made by Photostat. —*v.t. also,* **photostat.** to make a photostat of. [PHOTO- + Greek -*statēs* that causes to stand, that stands.]

pho·to·syn·the·sis (fŏ′tə sin′thə sis) *n.* manufacture of organic compounds, as sugar and starch, from inorganic substances, including water and carbon dioxide, by living plant cells, using the energy of light absorbed by the plant pigment, chlorophyll. —**pho·to·syn·thet·ic** (fŏ′tə sin thet′ik), *adj.* —**pho′to·syn·thet′i·cal·ly,** *adv.*

pho·to·te·leg·ra·phy (fŏ′tə tə leg′rə fē) *n.* facsimile (def. 2).

pho·tot·ro·pism (fŏ tot′rə piz′əm) *n.* tendency of a plant or plant part to turn toward light. [PHOTO- + TROPISM.] —**pho·to·trop·ic** (fŏ′tə trop′ik), *adj.*

pho·to·type (fŏ′tə tīp′) *n. Printing.* **1.** plate with a relief surface for printing produced by photography. **2.** process for making such a plate. **3.** picture printed from such a plate.

phras·al (frā′zəl) *adj.* of, like, or consisting of a phrase or phrases.

phrase (frāz) *n.* **1.** one or more words in combination, preceded and followed by pauses. **2.** sequence of grammatically related words conveying a single thought, but not containing a subject and predicate. In the sentence *To achieve success is his goal, To achieve success* is a phrase. **3.** particular or characteristic expression; terse, often striking, slogan. **4.** short, distinct division of a musical composition, forming an independent unit of melody. **5.** series of movements regarded as a complete unit in a dance pattern. —*v.t.,* **phrased, phras·ing. 1.** to express in a particular or distinctive way: *The defense attorney phrased his summation very carefully.* **2.** to designate by or divide into phrases. **3.** to divide or mark off (a melody, musical composition, or the like) into phrases, esp. in performance. [Latin *phrasis* diction, from Greek *phrasis* speech, expression.]

phra·se·ol·o·gy (frā′zē ol′ə jē) *pl.,* -gies. *n.* particular style or manner of expression; choice and arrangement of words: *a document written in complex legal phraseology.*

phras·ing (frā′zing) *n.* **1.** phraseology. **2.** way of marking off musical phrases.

phra·try (frā′trē) *pl.,* -tries. *n.* **1.** subdivision of an ancient Greek phyle. **2.** any similar tribal subdivision, as a clan, among primitive peoples. [Greek *phrātriā* tribe, clan.]

phre·net·ic (fri net′ik) frenetic. [Latin *phrenēticus* mad, from Greek *phrenētikos*, from *phrēnītis* delirium.]

phre·nol·o·gy (fri nol′ə jē) *n.* system of judging a person's character and intelligence by feeling the bumps and depressions on his skull. [Greek *phrēn* mind + -LOGY.] —**phren·o·log·i·cal** (fren′ə loj′i kəl), *adj.* —**phre·nol′o·gist,** *n.*

Phryg·i·a (frij′ē ə) *n.* ancient country in west-central Asia Minor, in what is now central Turkey. —**Phryg′i·an,** *adj., n.*

phthis·ic (tiz′ik) *n.* phthisis. —*adj.* phthisical.

phthis·i·cal (tiz′i kəl) *adj.* of, relating to, or suffering from phthisis.

phthi·sis (thī′sis) *n.* atrophy of any part of the body, esp. tuberculosis of the lungs. [Latin *phthisis* consumption, from Greek *phthisis* consumption, a wasting away.]

phy·lac·ter·y (fi lak′tər ē) *pl.*, **-ter·ies.** *n.* **1.** small leather case with straps attached, containing texts from the Old Testament. Orthodox Jews fasten one around the forehead and one around the left arm during prayer as a reminder to them to keep the Mosaic law. **2.** charm worn as a protection or safeguard; amulet. [Late Latin *phylactērium* amulet, from Greek *phylaktērion* amulet, safeguard.]

phyle (fīl) *n.* largest political subdivision in ancient Athens. [Greek *phylē* tribe.]

phyl·lox·e·ra (fil′ək sēr′ə, fi lok′sir ə) *n.* any of a group of destructive plant lice, genus *Phylloxera*, esp. *P. vitifoliae*, which attacks the roots and leaves of European grape vines. [Modern Latin *phylloxera*, from Greek *phyllon* leaf + *xēros* dry.]

phy·log·e·ny (fī loj′ə nē) *pl.*, **-nies.** *n.* history of the evolution of a species or group. Also, **phy·lo·gen·e·sis** (fī′lə jen′ə sis). [Greek *phylon* tribe, race + *-geneia* birth, origin.] —**phy·lo·ge·net·ic** (fī′lə ji net′ik), **phy′lo·gen′ic,** *adj.*

phy·lum (fī′ləm) *pl.*, **-la** (-lə). *n.* primary classification of the animal kingdom. Phylum is sometimes used to denote a division, a similar classification in the plant kingdom. [Modern Latin *phylum*, from Greek *phylon* class, tribe, race.]

phys·ic (fiz′ik) *n.* **1.** any medicine, esp. one that purges. **2.** *Archaic.* science, practice, or profession of medicine. —*v.t.,* **-icked, -ick·ing.** *Archaic.* to treat with or as with a physic; relieve; cure. [Medieval Latin *physica* medical science, from Latin *physica* natural science, from Greek *physikē*, going back to *physis* nature.]

phys·i·cal (fiz′i kəl) *adj.* **1.** of or relating to the body: *physical strength.* **2.** of, relating to, or containing matter. **3.** of or relating to matter and energy or the relationship between them. **4.** of or relating to physics. —*n.* physical examination. —**phys′i·cal·ly,** *adv.*
Syn. *adj.* 2, **Physical, material, corporeal** mean of or relating to matter. **Physical** relates especially to the form and structure of all things constituting the natural world that can be perceived and identified by the senses: *All living things are influenced by their physical environment.* **Material** relates to whatever is composed of matter or forms the basis of an objective phenomenon that occupies space and lends itself to physical handling: *An archaeologist studies the material remains of ancient cultures.* **Corporeal** refers more specifically to a thing that has physical existence as a tangible body or entity: *A chair is a corporeal thing.*

physical education, instruction in physical activities and hygiene, designed to promote the growth and development of the human body.

physical examination, medical examination to determine one's general state of health or one's fitness, as for an activity.

physical geography, study of the physical features of the earth, as land formation, climate, and vegetation. Also, **phys′i·og′ra·phy.**

physical science, any science concerned with matter that is nonliving, as physics, chemistry, or astronomy.

physical therapy, treatment of disease or injury by physical methods, as heat, massage, or exercise. Also, **phys′i·o·ther′a·py.**

phy·si·cian (fi zish′ən) *n.* one who is licensed to practice medicine, as a general practitioner. [Old French *fisicien*, from *fisique* medicine, from Latin *physica* natural science. See PHYSIC.]

phys·i·cist (fiz′ə sist) *n.* one who is a student of or expert in physics.

phys·ics (fiz′iks) *n.,pl.* **1.** science concerned with matter and energy or the relationships between them, encompassing the fields of mechanics, light, heat, sound, optics, and electricity and magnetism. **2.** physical properties or processes: *the physics of space flight.* ▲ construed as singular. [Plural of PHYSIC (to represent neuter plural of Latin *physica,* from Greek *ta physika,* title given to Aristotle's works on physics).]

phys·i·og·no·my (fiz′ē og′nə mē, -on′ə mē) *pl.*, **-mies.** *n.* **1.** features or appearance of the face, esp. when considered as an indication of character. **2.** art of judging character from the features or appearance of the face. **3.** general appearance of something: *the physiognomy of the land.* [Old French *phisonomie* art of judging character by the features, through Medieval Latin, going back to Greek *physiognōmoniā,* going back to *physis* nature + *gnōmōn* interpreter.] —**phys·i·og·nom·ic** (fiz′ē og nom′ik, fiz′ē ə-); also, **phys′i·og·nom′i·cal,** *adj.* —**phys′i·og′no·mist,** *n.*

phys·i·og·ra·phy (fiz′ē og′rə fē) *n.* physical geography. [Greek *physis* nature + -GRAPHY.] —**phys′i·og′ra·pher,** *n.* —**phys·i·o·graph·ic** (fiz′ē ə graf′ik); also, **phys′i·o·graph′i·cal,** *adj.*

phys·i·o·log·i·cal (fiz′ē ə loj′i kəl) *adj.* **1.** of or relating to physiology. **2.** characteristic of or promoting the normal functioning of an organism. Also, **phys′i·o·log′ic.** —**phys′i·o·log′i·cal·ly,** *adv.*

phys·i·ol·o·gy (fiz′ē ol′ə jē) *n.* **1.** science concerned with the functions and processes of living organisms. **2.** functions or processes of an organism or of any of its parts: *the physiology of the frog, the physiology of respiration.* [Latin *physiologia* study of nature, from Greek *physiologiā.*] —**phys′i·ol′o·gist,** *n.*

phys·i·o·ther·a·py (fiz′ē ō ther′ə pē) *n.* physical therapy. [Greek *physis* nature + THERAPY.]

phy·sique (fi zēk′) *n.* structure, development, or appearance of the body: *a muscular physique.* [French *physique* physical, from Latin *physicus* natural, from Greek *physikos,* from *physis* nature.]

-phyte *combining form.* plant, esp. one having a specified environment or nature: *saprophyte, zoophyte.* [Greek *phyton* plant.]

pi¹ (pī) *pl.*, **pis.** *n.* **1.** sixteenth letter of the Greek alphabet (Π, π), corresponding to the English letter *P, p.* **2.** ratio of the circumference of a circle to its diameter, denoted by the Greek letter π. Pi is approximately 3.1415926. [Middle Greek *pi* sixteenth letter of the Greek alphabet, from Greek *peî;* of Semitic origin.]

pi² (pī) *also,* **pie.** *n. Printing.* type that has been mixed together. —*v.t.,* **pied, pi·ing.** to mix or jumble up (type). [Of uncertain origin.]

P.I., Philippine Islands.

pi·a ma·ter (pī′ə mā′tər) *n.* thin, delicate membrane, the innermost of the three coverings of the brain and spinal cord. [Medieval Latin *pia mater (cerebri)* literally, pious mother (of the brain).]

Grand piano

Upright piano

Pianos

pi·a·nis·si·mo (pē′ə nis′i mō′, pyä-) *Music. adj.* very soft. —*adv.* very softly. —*n. pl.*, **-mos.** very soft passage of music. [Italian *pianissimo* very softly, superlative of *piano* softly. See PIANO².]

pi·an·ist (pē an′ist, pyan′-, pē′ə nist) *n.* one who plays the piano.

pi·an·o¹ (pē an′ō, pyan′ō) *pl.*, **-an·os.** *n.* stringed musical instrument that produces tones when felt-covered hammers, operated by a keyboard, strike the strings. Also, **pi·an′o·for′te.** [Short for PIANOFORTE.]

pi·a·no² (pē ä′nō, pyä′-) *Music. adj.* soft. —*adv.* softly. —*n. pl.*, **-nos.** soft passage of music. [Italian *piano* softly, from Late Latin *plānus* smooth, from Latin *plānus* flat, level.]

pi·an·o·for·te (pē an′ə fôr′tē, -tä, pyan′-) *n.* piano¹. [Italian *pianoforte,* from *piano* (see PIANO²) + *forte* loud (from Latin *fortis* strong); referring to the ability of the instrument to produce both soft and loud sounds.]

pi·as·ter (pē as′tər) *also,* **pi·as·tre.** *n.* **1.** monetary unit of certain Middle Eastern countries, as Libya, Turkey, and the United Arab Republic, equal to ¹⁄₁₀₀ of a pound. **2.** monetary unit of South Vietnam. [French *piastre,* from Italian *piastra* metal plate, coin, going back to Latin *emplastrum* medical plaster. See PLASTER.]

pi·az·za (pē az′ə, -ä′zə, -ät′sə) *n.* **1.** public square in a town, esp. in Italy. **2.** veranda. [Italian *piazza* marketplace, square, from Latin *platēa* broad way, from Greek *plateia (hodos)* broad (way). Doublet of PLACE, PLAZA.]

pi·broch (pē′brok) *n.* musical composition originating in the Scottish Highlands, performed on the bagpipe and consisting of variations on a basic, usually martial or dirgelike theme. [Scottish Gaelic *piobaireachd,* going back to *piob* pipe, bagpipe.]

pi·ca¹ (pī′kə) *n.* **1.** unit of measure used in printing, equal to twelve points, or about ⅙ inch. **2.** size of type for typewriters, providing ten characters to the linear inch. [Medieval Latin *pica* book of rules regarding religious services (said to have been written in *pica* lettering), from Latin *pica* magpie; because the black lettering on white paper recalled the colors of the magpie.]

pi·ca² (pī′kə) *n.* craving for or compulsive eating of nonfood substances, as clay, paint, or starch. [Modern Latin *pica,* from Latin *pica* magpie; because of its omnivorous eating habits.]

pic·a·dor (pik′ə dôr′) *n.* any of the horsemen who pricks the neck of the bull with a lance in a bullfight in order to weaken the bull's neck muscles. [Spanish *picador* literally, pricker, from *picar* to prick, probably going back to Latin *pīcus* woodpecker.]

at; āpe; cär; end; mē; it; īce; hot; ōld; fôrk; wood; fōōl; oil; out; up; ūse; turn; sing; thin; this; zh in treasure; ə in ago, taken, pencil, lemon, circus.

Pic·ar·dy (pik′ər dē) *n.* historic region and former province of northern France.

pic·a·resque (pik′ə resk′) *adj.* of or relating to rogues and their adventures, esp. as described in fiction. [Spanish *picaresco* roguish, from *picaro* rogue, from *picar* to prick. See PICADOR.]

pic·a·roon (pik′ə rōōn′) *n.* **1.** rogue; scoundrel; adventurer. **2.** pirate. [Spanish *picarón* great rogue, villain, from *picaro* rogue. See PICARESQUE.]

Pi·cas·so, Pa·blo (pi kä′sō; pä′blō) 1881–1973, Spanish painter and sculptor.

pic·a·yune (pik′ə ūn′) *adj.* **1.** of little value or significance; paltry: *a picayune sum.* **2.** narrow-minded; mean; petty: *That was a picayune thing to do.* —*n.* one who or that which is insignificant. [French *picaillon* copper coin of small value, from Provençal *picaioun;* of uncertain origin.]

Pic·ca·dil·ly (pik′ə dil′ē) *n.* fashionable street in London.

pic·ca·lil·li (pik′ə lil′ē) *pl.,* **-lis.** *n.* relish made of chopped vegetables, sugar, hot spices, and vinegar. [Modification (possibly influenced by CHILI) of PICKLE.]

pic·co·lo (pik′ə lō′) *pl.,* **-los.** *n.* small flute pitched one octave higher than the ordinary flute. [Italian *piccolo* small, small flute; of uncertain origin.]

pick¹ (pik) *v.t.* **1.** to select from a number; choose (often with *out*): *The city picked the site for the new museum. Have you picked out the movie you want to see?* **2.** to gather with the fingers; pluck: *She picked flowers in the garden.* **3.a.** to use the fingers or something pointed in order to remove a part or other matter from (something): *to pick one's teeth.* **b.** to remove bit by bit with the fingers or something pointed: *to pick the meat from a bone.* **4.** to prepare by removing feathers, hulls, leaves, or other parts: *to pick a chicken.* **5.** to pierce, dig into, or break up the (surface of anything) with something pointed: *to pick frozen ground.* **6.** to make or form (a hole) with something pointed. **7.** to pull apart or to pieces, as rags or fibers. **8.** (of birds) to take up (food) with the beak or bill. **9.a.** to pluck with the fingers or a plectrum, as the strings of a guitar. **b.** to play (a stringed instrument) by plucking the strings with the fingers or a plectrum. **10.** to provoke deliberately: *He picked a fight with his older brother.* **11.** to look for critically and point out: *He picked many flaws in the plan.* **12.** to steal the contents of: *The thief picked the man's pocket.* **13.** to open (a lock) with a pointed instrument or wire instead of a key. **14. to pick off. a.** to shoot one by one after taking careful aim: *The hunters picked off the ducks as they flew above the pond.* **b.** *Baseball.* to tag (a base runner) out after he has taken a lead off a base. **15. to pick out. a.** to distinguish (something) from its surroundings or from among a group: *He picked out a friend's face in the crowd.* **b.** to make out or gather (the sense or meaning); discern. **c.** to play (a tune) by ear or note by note. **16. to pick over.** to examine (a group of things) in order to make a selection: *She picked over the pears to find the ripest ones.* **17. to pick up. a.** to take up; lift up: *The campers picked up sticks for firewood.* **b.** to take (someone or something) into a vehicle or ship: *He picked up a hitchhiker. The shipwrecked sailors were picked up by a passing liner.* **c.** to acquire casually or by chance: *He picked up a few dollars by doing odd jobs. He picks up languages easily.* **d.** to bring into range of sight or hearing: *He picked up London on his short wave radio.* **e.** *Informal.* to become acquainted without being introduced and take out on a date. **f.** to arrange neatly; tidy up: *This room must be picked up before the guests arrive.* **g.** *Slang.* to take into custody: *He was picked up for vagrancy.* **h.** to accelerate: *The car picked up speed on the downgrade.* —*v.i.* **1.** to use or work with something pointed. **2.** to eat sparingly or without appetite (often with *at*): *to pick at one's food. Why don't you eat a full meal rather than pick?* **3.** to select, esp. very fastidiously and carefully: *to pick and choose.* **4. to pick at. a.** to pull on; toy with; handle: *She picked at her necklace nervously.* **b.** *Informal.* to find fault with constantly; nag: *Mother constantly picked at her for being sloppy.* **5. to pick on. a.** *Informal.* to find fault with; criticize: *He picked on the plan from every angle.* **b.** *Informal.* to annoy; harass: *The older boys picked on the younger ones.* **6. to pick up. a.** *Informal.* to improve; recover: *Business picked up after the depression. His spirits picked up after we told him the good news.* **b.** to go faster; accelerate: *The tempo of the orchestra picked up.* —*n.* **1.** act or right of selecting; choice: *Take your pick of these books.* **2.** one who or that which is selected: *He is my pick for class treasurer.* **3.** best or choicest part or example: *That puppy is the pick of the litter.* **4.** quantity of a crop gathered by hand at one time: *This pick of corn is the largest in several years.* **5.** stroke with something pointed. **6.** plectrum. [Possibly from Middle French *piquer* to prick, strike. See PIKE¹.] —**Syn.** 1 *see* CHOOSE.

pick² (pik) *n.* **1.** chipping or breaking tool that has a metal head, usually with one or two tips sharpened to a point, attached to a wooden handle. **2.** any of various sharp-pointed tools without a head, as an ice pick. [Form of PIKE².]

pick·a·back (pik′ə bak′) *adv., adj.* piggyback.

pick·a·nin·ny (pik′ə nin′ē) *pl.,* **-nies.** *n.* Negro child. ▲ usually considered offensive. [Probably from Portuguese *pequenino* very small, diminutive of *pequeno* small; of uncertain origin.]

pick·ax (pik′aks′) *also,* **pick·axe.** *n.* pick² (def. 1). [Modification (influenced by AX) of Middle English *pikois,* from Old French *picois,* from *pic,* probably going back to Latin *picus* woodpecker.]

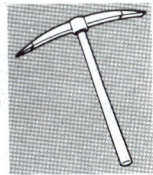

Pickax

picked (pikt) *adj.* **1.** specially selected: *picked men.* **2.** cleaned or cleared, as of matter.

pick·er·el (pik′ər əl, pik′rəl) *pl.,* **-els** or **-el.** *n.* any of several freshwater game and food fish related to the pike, genus *Esox,* found in North America, having a slender body and long snout. Length: to 2 feet. [Diminutive of PIKE¹.]

pick·er·el·weed (pik′ər əl wēd′, pik′rəl-) *n.* North American water plant, *Pontederia cordata,* found in the shallow waters of ponds or streams, having a single, heart-shaped leaf and dense spikes of funnel-shaped, violet-blue flowers with two yellow and white spots.

pick·et (pik′it) *n.* **1.** pointed stake or slat usually driven into the ground to secure something, as a tent, or to build something, as a stockade. **2.** one who is stationed outside an establishment, as a place of business or government office, to draw attention to a grievance or prevent workers or customers from entering, as in a labor dispute, or to protest against something, as in a political demonstration. **3.** *Military.* guard or body of troops stationed ahead of an army or outside a camp, to watch for and give warning of the enemy's approach. —*v.t.*

Pickerel

1. to act as or station a picket or pickets outside (an establishment): *to picket a store, to picket an embassy.* **2.** to guard with a picket or pickets. **3.** to post as a picket. **4.** to fasten to a picket, as a horse. **5.** to enclose or fortify with pickets. —*v.i.* to act as a picket. [Partly from French *piquet* pointed stake, diminutive of *pic* pickax, going back to Latin *picus* woodpecker; partly from French *piquer* to prick. See PIKE¹.] —**pick′et·er,** *n.*

picket fence, fence made of upright slats attached to horizontal rails.

picket line, line of people picketing an establishment.

pick·ing (pik′ing) *n.* **1.** act of one who picks. **2. pickings.** that which is left over to be picked; scraps: *the pickings of a turkey.* **3.** *usually,* **pickings.** that which is acquired dishonestly.

pick·le (pik′əl) *n.* **1.** any food, esp. a cucumber, that has been preserved in a solution of salt water or vinegar. **2.** solution of salt water or vinegar used to preserve or flavor food. **3.** acid solution for removing oxides from the surfaces of metal. **4.** *Informal.* difficult or disagreeable situation. —*v.t.,* **-led, -ling. 1.** to preserve or flavor in a solution of salt water or vinegar. **2.** to remove oxides from (metal) by means of an acid solution. [Middle Dutch *pekel* solution for preserving food, food preserved in such a solution.]

pick·pock·et (pik′pok′it) *n.* thief who steals from the pockets or purses of others.

pick·up (pik′up′) *n.* **1.** act or instance of picking up. **2.** capacity for quick acceleration: *The old car doesn't have much pickup.* **3.** device that holds a phonograph needle and transforms its vibrations into a weak electric current; cartridge. **4.** in radio and television, reception of sound or light waves by the transmitter for conversion into electric waves. **5.** small truck with an open body. Also, **pickup truck. 6.** *Baseball.* act or instance of fielding a ball that has just bounced. **7.** *Informal.* **a.** casual acquaintance with a stranger, esp. for the purpose of making love. **b.** one with whom such an acquaintance is made. **8.** *Informal.* increase or improvement, as in activity or business.

pick·y (pik′ē) **-i·er, -i·est.** *adj.* hard to please; finicky; fussy.

pic·nic (pik′nik) *n.* **1.** outing that includes a meal eaten out-of-doors. **2.** *Slang.* pleasant experience or easy job. —*v.i.* **-nicked, -nick·ing.** to go on or have a picnic: *We picnicked in the park.* [French *piquenique* meal taken on the grass out-of-doors, from *piquer* to forage, prick (see PIKE¹) + Old French *nique* thing without value (of uncertain origin).] —**pic′nick·er,** *n.*

pi·cot (pē′kō) *n.* one of a series of small loops forming part of an ornamental edging on a piece of material, as ribbon or lace. —*v.t.* to finish or ornament with such loops. [French *picot* literally, small point, diminutive of *pic* point, pickax. See PICKAX.]

pic·ric acid (pik′rik) poisonous, very bitter, organic acid, used esp. in explosives. Formula: $C_6H_2(NO_2)_3OH$ [Greek *pikros* bitter + -IC + ACID.]

Picot trim

at; āpe; cär; end; mē; īce; hot; ōld; fôrk; wood; fōōl; oil; out; up; ūse; turn; sing; thin; <u>this</u>; zh in treasure; ə in ago, taken, pencil, lemon, circus.

759

Pict (pikt) *n.* member of an ancient people formerly living in northern and central Scotland.

Pict·ish (pik'tish) *n.* language spoken by the Picts. —*adj.* of or relating to the Picts, their language, or culture.

pic·to·graph (pik'tə graf') *n.* **1.** picture of an object or pictorial symbol used as part of a system of picture writing. **2.** diagram, graph, or chart using pictures to represent data. [Latin *pictus,* past participle of *pingere* to paint + -GRAPH.] —**pic'to·graph'ic,** *adj.* —**pic'to·graph'i·cal·ly,** *adv.*

Pictograph meaning "No bicycle riding"

pic·to·ri·al (pik tôr'ē əl) *adj.* **1.** of, relating to, or of the nature of pictures: *pictorial art, pictorial writing.* **2.** illustrated by or containing pictures: *The school subscribes to several pictorial publications.* **3.** vividly descriptive; graphic. —*n.* periodical containing many illustrations. [Late Latin *pictōrius* relating to painters (from Latin *pictor* painter) + -AL[1].] —**pic·to'ri·al·ly,** *adv.*

pic·ture (pik'chər) *n.* **1.** representation of something on a two-dimensional surface, as a drawing, painting, or photograph. **2.** something presented to the eye, as a fleeting image on a television or television screen: *She gets a very bright picture on her television set.* **3.a.** vivid or graphic description in words: *The lecturer gave an excellent picture of living conditions in China.* **b.** impression or idea: *He already had a mental picture of how she looked.* **4.** typical example; embodiment: *He looks the picture of health.* **5.** one who closely resembles another; counterpart; likeness: *John is the picture of his grandfather.* **6.** motion picture. **7.** situation: *Here's the economic picture as I see it.* —*v.t.,* -**tured,** -**tur·ing. 1.** to represent something visually, as in a drawing or painting; depict. **2.** to give a vivid or graphic description of; describe. **3.** to form an impression or idea of: *Picture yourself in that suit.* [Latin *pictūra* art of painting, a painting.]

pic·tur·esque (pik'chə resk') *adj.* **1.** having pleasing visual qualities suitable for a picture: *a picturesque cottage.* **2.** strikingly graphic or vivid: *picturesque speech.* [French *pittoresque,* from Italian *pittoresco* in the style of a painter, from *pittore* painter, form Latin *pictor;* influenced by PICTURE.] —**pic'tur·esque'ly,** *adv.* —**pic'tur·esque'ness,** *n.* —**Syn. 2.** see **graphic.**

picture tube, cathode-ray tube with a phosphor coating at one end, that serves as the screen of a television receiver. Also, **kin'e·scope'.**

picture window, large window that frames an outside view.

picture writing 1. use of pictures or pictorial symbols in writing, esp. by primitive peoples. **2.** pictures so used.

pid·dle (pid'əl) -**dled, -dling.** *v.i.* to dawdle; trifle. —*v.t.* to waste (usually with *away*): *to piddle away time.* [Of uncertain origin.]

pid·dling (pid'ling) *adj.* trivial; insignificant; petty.

pid·gin (pij'ən) *n.* any hybrid language composed of the reduced and modified vocabularies of two or more languages and a simplified grammar of one of these languages. [Chinese modification of BUSINESS.]

pidgin English, pidgin resulting from the contact of English with certain other languages, as Chinese or Melanesian.

pie[1] (pī) *n.* baked dish composed of pastry with a filling of meat, fruit, fish, or other food. [Possibly from PIE[2]; referring to the magpie's habit of collecting odds and ends (which the contents of a pie resemble) in its nest.]

pie[2] (pī) *n.* magpie. [Old French *pie,* from Latin *pīca.*]

pie[3] (pī) *n.* pi[2]. [Of uncertain origin.]

pie·bald (pī'bôld') *adj.* having spots or patches, esp. of black and white. —*n.* piebald animal, esp. a horse. [PIE[2] + BALD; referring to the variegated coloring of the magpie.]

piece (pēs) *n.* **1.** separated or detached part; fragment: *a piece of broken glass.* **2.** part of something forming a single unit or whole: *a piece of a machine.* **3.** single object belonging to a set or group: *a piece of luggage, a piece of china.* **4.** artistic composition or production: *a piece of music, a literary piece.* **5.** particular quantity or amount, as of fabric sold or work done. **6.** instance; example; specimen: *a piece of impudence, a piece of trash.* **7.** coin: *a ten-cent piece.* **8.** any of the small objects, as disks or chessmen, used in playing checkers, chess, or other board games. **9.** gun or cannon. **10. of a piece.** of the same sort; alike. —*v.t.,* **pieced, piec·ing. 1.** to join the pieces of in order to construct or mend (usually with *together*): *to piece together a quilt, to piece a story together from scattered information, to piece together a broken flowerpot.* **2.** to complete or mend by adding a piece or pieces; patch: *to piece a dress.* [Old French *piece* part of a whole; of Celtic origin.] —**Syn. 2.** see **part.**

pièce de ré·sis·tance (pyes' də rä zēs täns') *French.* **1.** main dish of a meal. **2.** main or most important event, incident, item, or accomplishment, as in a series.

piece·meal (pēs'mēl') *adv.* **1.** piece by piece; by degrees: *The book was written piecemeal over a long period of time.* **2.** *Archaic.* into pieces or fragments: *to be torn piecemeal.* —*adj.* made or done piece by piece:

The legislators offered only piecemeal reform. [Middle English *pecemele* piece by piece, from *pece* piece + Old English *mǣlum,* dative plural of *mǣl* measure. See PIECE.]

piece of eight, former old Spanish coin equal to eight reals.

piece·work (pēs'wurk') *n.* work done and paid for by the piece rather than by the hour or the day —**piece'work'er,** *n.*

pied (pīd) *adj.* having large spots of different colors; mottled. [PIE[2] + -ED[2]; originally referring to the variegated coloring of the magpie.]

Pied·mont (pēd'mont) *n.* **1.** highly productive agricultural and industrial area in northwestern Italy, bordering France and Switzerland. **2.** region of the eastern United States extending from northeastern New Jersey to central Alabama and sloping seaward from the Appalachian Mountains to the Atlantic coastal plain.

pie·plant (pī'plant') *n.* rhubarb.

pier (pēr) *n.* **1.** structure secured by piles over the water, used esp. as a landing place for boats or ships. **2.** any solid support on which an arch rests, as in an arcade. **3.** solid part of a wall between openings, as windows. [Medieval Latin (in England) *pera* (of a bridge); of uncertain origin.]

Pier

pierce (pērs) **pierced, pierc·ing.** *v.t.* **1.** to penetrate or pass into or through, as with a sharp-pointed instrument: *to pierce the skin.* **2.** to make a hole or opening into or through; perforate: *to pierce the ice.* **3.** to make (a hole or opening) as by perforating: *to pierce a hole in the ice.* **4.** to force or break a way into or through: *The enemy's offensive pierced our army's line.* **5.** to perceive visually or mentally; see into or through; discern: *to pierce the fallacy of an argument.* **6.** to affect the emotions keenly; touch or move deeply: *to pierce the heart.* **7.** to penetrate with a sharp sound: *A shout pierced the stillness of the room.* —*v.i.* to penetrate or pass into or through: *The knife did not pierce very deeply.* [Old French *perc(i)er* to make a hole in, going back to Latin *pertūsus,* past participle of *pertundere* to bore through.] —**pierc'er,** *n.* —**pierc'ing·ly,** *adv.*

Syn. *v.t.* **1. Pierce, perforate, puncture** mean to make a hole in or through something. **Pierce** may be preferred when one thrusts a sharp, pointed instrument, cutting through the entire thickness to the other side: *The bayonet pierced the soldier's leg.* **Perforate** is used chiefly to characterize the action of a machine or instrument that makes a series of incisions or small round holes for a definite purpose: *The box was perforated to let in air and allow the cat to breathe.* **Puncture** suggests the entry of a sharp, pointed instrument or object into a substance or material, often causing it to deflate or collapse: *The nail punctured the tire, and it went flat.*

Pierce, Franklin (pērs) 1804–69, fourteenth president of the United States, from 1853 to 1857.

Pi·e·ri·an spring (pī ēr'ē ən) fountain sacred to the Muses, considered a source of poetic inspiration.

Pierre (pēr) *n.* capital of South Dakota, in the central part of the state. Pop. (1970), 9699.

Pi·er·rot (pē'ə rō') *n.* buffoon in French pantomime, usually costumed in loose white pantaloons and jacket. [French *Pierrot,* diminutive of *Pierre* Peter.]

Pie·tà (pē'ä tä', pyä tä') *also,* **pie·tà.** *n.* representation in a work of art, as a painting or sculpture, of the Virgin Mary holding the dead body of Jesus. [Italian *pietà* compassion, piety, from Latin *pietās.* See PIETY.]

pi·e·tism (pī'ə tiz'əm) *n.* **1.** religious devotion or godliness; piety. **2.** affectation of piety. **3. Pietism.** reform movement of the Lutheran Church in Germany, begun in the late seventeenth century. [German *Pietismus* form of evangelical devotional piety, from Latin *pietās* dutiful conduct, devotion.] —**pi'e·tist,** *n.* —**pi·e·tis'tic;** *also,* **pi'e·tis'ti·cal,** *adj.* —**pi'e·tis'ti·cal·ly,** *adv.*

pi·e·ty (pī'ə tē) *pl.,* **-ties.** *n.* **1.** reverance for God; religious devoutness; godliness. **2.** loyalty and obedience, as to one's parents. **3.** pious act or belief. [Old French *piete* dutiful conduct, compassion, from Latin *pietās* dutiful conduct, devotion, kindness. Doublet of PITY.]

pi·e·zo·e·lec·tric·i·ty (pī ē'zō i lek'tris'ə tē) *n.* electricity produced on the opposite faces of certain crystals when they are subjected to pressure. [Greek *piezein* to squeeze, press[1] + ELECTRICITY.] —**pi·e'zo·e·lec'tric,** *adj.* —**pi·e'zo·e·lec'tri·cal·ly,** *adv.*

pif·fle (pif'əl) *n. Informal.* foolish talk; nonsense. —*v.i.* -**fled, -fling.** to talk or act in a foolish way. [Of uncertain origin.]

pig (pig) *n.* **1.** hoofed mammal, genus *Sus,* esp. one of various breeds widely raised for food, typically having a stout, roundish body, short legs, and a blunt snout. Length: to 4 feet. **2.** young swine, esp. one weighing less than 120 pounds. **3.** flesh of a pig used as food; pork. **4.a.** oblong mass of metal, esp. iron from a blast furnace, that has been

at; āpe; cär; end; mē; it; īce; hot; ōld; fôrk; wood; fōōl; oil; out; up; ūse; turn; sing; thin; this; zh in treasure; ə in ago, taken, pencil, lemon, circus.

found by casting molten metal in a mold. **b.** any mold used for casting such metal. **c.** pig iron. **5.** guinea pig. **6.** *Informal.* one who is dirty, greedy, or excessively fat. **7. pig in a poke.** that which is offered for sale or bought without the buyer seeing it or knowing its real value. [Probably from an unrecorded Old English word.]

Pig

pi·geon (pij′ən) *n.* **1.a.** any of numerous wild or domesticated birds, family Columbidae, native to temperate or tropical regions throughout the world, having a stout body, a small head, and thick, soft plumage. Certain smaller or medium-sized birds of this family are called doves. **b.** blue and gray domesticated bird of this family, a variety of *Columba livia,* found commonly in cities and sometimes raised for food. **2.** *Slang.* one who is easily cheated or fooled; dupe. [Old French *pijon* young bird, from Late Latin *pīpiō* squab, young chirping bird, from Latin *pīpīre* to chirp.]

pigeon hawk, falcon, *Falco columbarius,* that feeds on small birds. Also, **mer′lin.**

pi·geon·heart·ed (pij′ən här′tid) *adj.* easily frightened; timid.

pi·geon·hole (pij′ən hōl′) *n.* **1.** small compartment, as in a cabinet or desk, for holding papers or other articles. **2.** small hole or place for pigeons to nest in. —*v.t.,* **-holed, -hol·ing. 1.** to put in a small compartment; file: *to pigeonhole the mail.* **2.** to lay aside or put away and forget: *The committee pigeonholed the project permanently.* **3.** to lay aside for future consideration. **4.** to arrange in categories or classify.

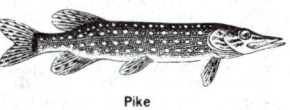

Pigeon

pi·geon·toed (pij′ən tōd′) *adj.* having the toes or feet turned inward.

pig·ger·y (pig′ər ē) *pl.,* **-ger·ies.** *n. British.* pigpen.

pig·gish (pig′ish) *adj.* piglike in habits or manners, esp. greedy. —**pig′gish·ly,** *adv.* —**pig′gish·ness,** *n.*

pig·gy·back (pig′ē bak′) *adv., adj.* on the back or shoulders. Also, **pick′a·back′.**

piggy bank, small bank, often in the shape of a pig, used esp. by children for saving coins.

pig·head·ed (pig′hed′id) *adj.* unreasonably obstinate; stubborn. —**pig′·head′ed·ly,** *adv.* —**pig′·head′ed·ness,** *n.*

pig iron, iron from which the impurities have been removed in a blast furnace, used to make commercial iron or steel.

pig Latin, code language used esp. by children, in which the first consonant is placed at the end of the word and followed by *-ay,* as *irlgay* for *girl.*

pig·ment (pig′mənt) *n.* **1.** substance used for coloring, esp. a powdered substance that is mixed with a liquid to produce a paint or dye. **2.** any substance, as melanin or chlorophyll, that is the coloring matter of animal or plant tissues. [Latin *pigmentum* substance used for coloring, paint. Doublet of PIMENTO.] —**pig′men·tar′y,** *adj.*

pig·men·ta·tion (pig′men tā′shən) *n.* **1.** coloration in plant or animal tissues caused by pigment. **2.** deposition of pigment in plant or animal tissues.

pig·my (pig′mē) pygmy.

pig·nut (pig′nut′) *n.* **1.** small brown nut of a North American hickory tree, *Carya glabra.* **2.** tree that produces this nut, having a strong, tough wood, used in making tool handles, as a fuel, and for smoking meats. **3.** edible tuberous root of an herb, *Conopodium denudatum,* of the parsley family.

Pignut fruit and leaves

pig·pen (pig′pen′) *n.* **1.** pen for pigs. **2.** dirty place.

pig·skin (pig′skin′) *n.* **1.** skin of a pig. **2.** leather made of this. **3.** *Informal.* football.

pig·sty (pig′stī′) *pl.,* **-sties.** *n.* pigpen.

pig·tail (pig′tāl′) *n.* **1.** braid of hair hanging down the back. **2.** tobacco twisted into a thin rope.

pig·weed (pig′wēd′) *n.* **1.** goosefoot. **2.** any of several weedy plants, genus *Amaranthus,* sometimes used as salad greens.

pi·ka (pī′kə) *n.* any of various rabbitlike mammals, genus *Ochotona,* native to mountain ranges of western North America and Eurasia, having a gray or buff-colored coat. Length: 6 inches. Also, **co′ny.**

pike¹ (pīk) *n.* weapon consisting of a long wooden shaft with a pointed tip of iron or steel, formerly used by foot soldiers. [Old French *pique,*

from *piquer* to prick, pierce, probably going back to Latin *pīcus* woodpecker.]

pike² (pīk) *n.* sharp point, as the tip of a spear. [Old English *pīc;* possibly of Celtic origin.]

pike³ (pīk) *n.* **1.** large carnivorous freshwater game and food fish, *Esox lucius,* found in Europe, Asia, and northern North America, having a slim, tapering olive-green body, with a duck-billed snout and many sharp teeth. Length: to over 4 feet. **2.** any of several similar or related fish. [Possibly from PIKE²; referring to the pointed shape of the head.]

Pike

pike⁴ (pīk) *n.* turnpike.

pike·man (pīk′mən) *pl.,* **-men,** *n.* soldier armed with a pike.

pik·er (pī′kər) *n. Slang.* one who is miserly, overly cautious, or petty, esp. in his dealings with others. [Of uncertain origin.]

Pike's Peak (pīks) mountain of the Rocky Mountains, in central Colorado.

pike·staff (pīk′staf′) *pl.,* **-staves** (-stāvz′). *n.* **1.** shaft of a pike. **2.** walking stick with a metal tip at the lower end, used by walkers.

pi·laf (pi läf′, pē′läf) *also,* **pi·laff.** *n.* dish of Middle Eastern origin that consists mainly of rice boiled with meat or fish and is flavored with spices. Also, **pi·lau** (pi lô′). [Persian *pilāw.*]

pi·las·ter (pi las′tər) *n.* rectangular flat column projecting from a wall or pier. [French *pilastre,* from Italian *pilastro,* going back to Latin *pīla* pillar.]

Pi·late, Pon·tius (pī′lət; pon′shəs, -tē əs) Roman governor of Judea from A.D. 26 to 36.

pil·chard (pil′chərd) *n.* small herringlike fish of the family Clupeidae, found in oceans of the temperate zone, as the **Pacific pilchard,** *Sardinops caerulea.* [Of uncertain origin.]

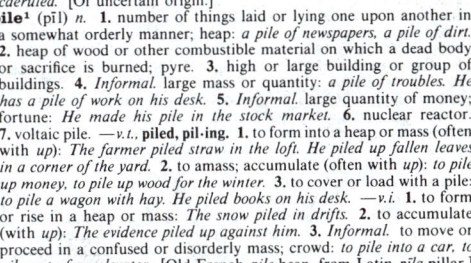

Pilasters

pile¹ (pīl) *n.* **1.** number of things laid or lying one upon another in a somewhat orderly manner; heap: *a pile of newspapers, a pile of dirt.* **2.** heap of wood or other combustible material on which a dead body or sacrifice is burned; pyre. **3.** high or large building or group of buildings. **4.** *Informal.* large mass or quantity: *a pile of troubles. He has a pile of work on his desk.* **5.** *Informal.* large quantity of money; fortune: *He made his pile in the stock market.* **6.** nuclear reactor. **7.** voltaic pile. —*v.t.,* **piled, pil·ing. 1.** to form into a heap or mass (often with *up*): *The farmer piled straw in the loft. He piled up fallen leaves in a corner of the yard.* **2.** to amass; accumulate (often with *up*): *to pile up money, to pile up wood for the winter.* **3.** to cover or load with a pile: *to pile a wagon with hay. He piled books on his desk.* —*v.i.* **1.** to form or rise in a heap or mass: *The snow piled in drifts.* **2.** to accumulate (with *up*): *The evidence piled up against him.* **3.** *Informal.* to move or proceed in a confused or disorderly mass; crowd: *to pile into a car, to pile out of an elevator.* [Old French *pile* heap, from Latin *pīla* pillar.]

pile² (pīl) *n.* strong, slender beam of wood, steel, or concrete, driven vertically into the ground to support a structure, as a bridge or wharf. —*v.t.,* **piled, pil·ing. 1.** to furnish or support with piles. **2.** to drive piles into. [Old English *pīl* pointed stick, from Latin *pīlum* javelin.]

pile³ (pīl) *n.* **1.** raised cut or uncut loops that form the surface of a fabric, as velvet, or a carpet. **2.** fine hair or fiber. [Latin *pilus* hair.]

pile driver, machine for driving piles into the ground, usually consisting of a frame in which a heavy weight is suspended and then dropped on the pile.

piles (pīlz) *n.,pl.* hemorrhoids. [Latin *pila* ball; referring to the shape.]

pil·fer (pil′fər) *v.t., v.i.* to steal in small quantities. [Old French *pelfrer,* from *pelfre* booty. See PELF.] —**pil′fer·age, pil′fer·er,** *n.* —**Syn.** see **steal.**

pil·grim (pil′grəm) *n.* **1.** one who journeys to a sacred place for a religious purpose, as for penance or devotion. **2.** traveler. **3. Pilgrim.** one of the group of English religious dissenters who founded Plymouth Colony in 1620. [Old French *peligrin, pelerin* one who travels to a sacred place for penance or religious devotion, going back to Latin *peregrīnus* foreigner, foreign; with reference to a pilgrim's wandering away from home.]

pil·grim·age (pil′grə mij) *n.* **1.** journey to a sacred place for a religious purpose, as for penance or devotion. **2.** long journey for a special purpose: *to make a pilgrimage to the museums of Europe.*

pil·ing (pī′ling) *n.* piles collectively or a structure composed of piles.

pill (pil) *n.* **1.** pellet of medicine that is swallowed whole or chewed.

at; āpe; cär; end; mē; it; īce; hot; ōld; fôrk; wood; fōͨol; oil; out; up; ūse; turn; sing; thin; this; zh in treasure; ə in ago, taken, pencil, lemon, circus.

761

2. that which is disagreeable but must be endured: *The loss of the election was a bitter pill for him to swallow.* **3.** *Slang.* one who is disagreeable or boring. **4. the pill.** oral contraceptive. —*v.t.* to dose with pills. —*v.i.* to form into balls, as fuzz on a sweater; ball. [Latin *pilula* small ball, pellet of medicine, diminutive of *pila* ball.]

pil·lage (pil′ij) **-laged, -lag·ing.** *v.t.* **1.** to rob by force, as during a war; plunder: *to pillage a town.* **2.** to carry off as booty: *to pillage valuables.* —*v.i.* to take booty. —*n.* **1.** act of plundering. **2.** that which is carried off as booty; plunder. [Old French *pillage* plunder, from *piller* to plunder, going back to Late Latin *pilleus* rag, from Latin *pilleus* cap of felt.] —**pil′lag·er,** *n.*

pil·lar (pil′ər) *n.* **1.** detached, upright structure, usually of stone, wood, or metal, that serves as a support for a building or stands alone as a monument. **2.** something resembling a pillar in shape or function. **3.** one who is a chief supporter of something, as an institution: *a pillar of society.* **4. from pillar to post.** from one place, person, or resource to another. [Old French *pil(i)er* column, vertical support for a building, going back to Latin *pīla* column.]

Pillars of Hercules, two promontories, the Rock of Gibraltar and the mountain of Jebel Musa, on opposite sides of the eastern end of the Strait of Gibraltar.

pill·box (pil′boks′) *n.* **1.** small box for pills. **2.** small, low, concrete gun emplacement. **3.** woman's small round hat without a brim and with a flat top.

pil·lion (pil′yən) *n.* pad or cushion attached behind the saddle of a horse or the seat of a motorcycle for another rider. [Scottish Gaelic *pillean* cushion, diminutive of *peall* skin, from Latin *pellis*.]

pil·lo·ry (pil′ər ē) *pl.,* **-ries.** *n.* **1.** wooden frame fitted with openings to hold the head and hands of an offender. **2.** exposure to public ridicule or abuse. —*v.t.,* **-ried, -ry·ing. 1.** to put in a pillory. **2.** to expose to public ridicule or abuse. [Old French *pilori* the wooden frame; of uncertain origin.]

pil·low (pil′ō) *n.* **1.** bag or casing filled with soft or resilient material, as feathers, down, or foam rubber, used to support the head during sleep or for decoration. **2.** something resembling a pillow in shape or function, as a pad on which bobbin lace is made. —*v.t.* **1.** to rest on or as on a pillow: *John pillowed his head on his hand.* **2.** to be or serve as a pillow for: *Mary's arm pillowed the baby's head.* [Old English *pyle, pylu* cushion for the head, going back to Latin *pulvīnus.*] —**pil′low·y,** *adj.*

pil·low·case (pil′ō kās′) *n.* removable cover, usually of cloth, for a pillow. Also, **pil·low·slip** (pil′ō slip′).

pillow lace, bobbin lace.

pi·lose (pī′lōs) *adj.* covered with fine or soft hair. [Latin *pilōsus* hairy, from *pilus* hair.]

pi·lot (pī′lət) *n.* **1.** one who operates the flight controls of an aircraft or spacecraft. **2.** one who steers a ship, esp. in coastal waters or into or out of a harbor. **3.** one who directs another in his conduct or course of action; guide. **4.** pilot light. **5.** pilot film. **6.** cowcatcher. —*v.t.* **1.** to act as the pilot of; steer. **2.** to guide. —*adj.* preliminary, trial, or sample: *a pilot study.* [French *pilote* steersman, from Italian *pilota,* form of obsolete Italian *pedota,* going back to Greek *pēdon* rudder.]

pi·lot·age (pī′lə tij) *n.* **1.** act of piloting. **2.** fee paid to a pilot. **3.** navigation of a ship or aircraft by observation of landmarks.

pilot biscuit, hardtack. Also, **pilot bread.**

pilot film, sample program of a proposed television series.

pilot fish, small fish, *Naucrates ductor,* found in temperate seas, that usually swims along with sharks or other large fish.

pi·lot·house (pī′lət hous′) *n.* enclosed structure on the deck of a ship that shelters the steering equipment and the pilot. Also, **wheel′·house′.**

pilot lamp, small lamp that indicates that a circuit or motor is in operation.

pilot light **1.** small flame kept burning so as to light a gas burner when it is turned on, as in a gas stove. **2.** pilot lamp.

Pilt·down man (pilt′doun′) early species of man who was presumed to have existed from remains that were discovered in Sussex, England, and in 1953 shown to have been a hoax.

Pi·ma (pē′mə) *pl.,* **-mas** or **-ma.** *n.* **1.** member of a tribe of North American Indians living in southern Arizona. **2.** language belonging to the Uto-Aztecan language family spoken by the Pimas. —**Pi′man,** *adj.*

Pima cotton, variety of strong, fine cotton developed from Egyptian cotton.

pi·men·to (pi men′tō) *pl.,* **-tos.** *n.* **1.** evergreen tree, *Pimenta officinalis,* of the myrtle family, from which allspice is derived. **2.** pimiento.

[Spanish *pimiento* capsicum, from Medieval Latin *pigmentum* spice, from Late Latin *pigmentum* juice of plants, from Latin *pigmentum* substance used for coloring. Doublet of PIGMENT.]

pi meson, pion.

pi·mien·to (pi myen′tō, -men′tō) *pl.,* **-tos.** *also,* **pi·men·to.** *n.* mild, sweet red pepper used as a garnish or as a stuffing for olives. [Spanish *pimiento* capsicum. See PIMENTO.]

pimp (pimp) *n.* one who procures for a prostitute; procurer. —*v.i.* to act as a pimp. [Of uncertain origin.]

pim·per·nel (pim′pər nel′, -pərn əl) *n.* **1.** small, bell-shaped, scarlet, purple, or white flower of any of a group of plants, genus *Anagallis,* of the primrose family, esp. the **scarlet pimpernel,** *A. arvensis.* **2.** plant bearing this flower. [Old French *pimpernelle* the plant, going back to Latin *piper* pepper plant; referring to the resemblance of its fruit to that of the pepper plant. See PEPPER.]

pim·ple (pim′pəl) *n.* small, inflamed swelling of the skin, often containing pus. [Of uncertain origin.] —**pim′pled, pim′ply,** *adj.*

pin (pin) *n.* **1.** short, straight, stiff piece of wire with a point at one end and a head at the other, used to fasten things together. **2.** ornament or emblem that has a pin or clasp for attaching it to clothing: *a fraternity pin.* **3.** peg, usually made of wood or metal, used for various purposes, as to fasten things together, hold a thing in place, or hang something on. **4.** anything like a pin in form or use, as a safety pin, a clothespin, hairpin, bobby pin, or cotter pin. **5.** long, thin piece of metal used to join the ends of a broken bone. **6.** *Bowling.* any of the usually bottle-shaped pieces of wood of varying sizes, set up as a target in tenpins, duckpins, and other bowling games. **7.** *Wrestling.* act of forcing an opponent's shoulder to the mat for a specified length of time. **8.a.** *Nautical.* thole. **b.** belaying pin. **9.** *Music.* peg *(def. 2).* **10.** *Golf.* staff of the pennant that marks the hole on a green. **11.** something very small or of little value or significance; trifle: *That ring is not worth a pin. He doesn't care a pin for her.* **12.** pins. *Informal.* legs. **13. to be on pins and needles.** to be nervous, anxious, or uneasy. —*v.t.,* **pinned, pin·ning. 1.** to fasten or attach with or as with a pin or pins: *She pinned the pattern to the material. He pinned his hopes on going to college.* **2.** to seize and hold fast in one spot or position: *The fighter pinned his opponent against the ropes.* **3.** to hold or bind strictly, as to a course of action or to a promise (often with *down*): *I tried to pin him down to a definite answer.* **4.** *Slang.* to place the blame or responsibility for: *They tried to pin the robbery on him.* **5.** *Wrestling.* to force the shoulders of (an opponent) to touch the mat for a specified length of time. [Old English *pinn* peg.]

pin·a·fore (pin′ə fôr′) *n.* apron, or garment resembling an apron, covering most of a dress, worn esp. by young girls. [PIN + AFORE; referring to the fact that it was formerly pinned on the front of a dress.]

pin·ball (pin′bôl′) *n.* game in which a steel ball is driven by a plunger onto a slanted board and against pins or into holes that record the score electronically.

pinball machine, machine in which pinball is played, often used for gambling.

pince-nez (pans′nā′, pins′-) *pl.,* **pince·nez.** *n.* eyeglasses held on the nose by a spring. [French *pince-nez,* from *pincer* to nip (of uncertain origin) + *nez* nose (from Latin *nāsus*).]

pin·cers (pin′sərz, -chərz) *also,* **pinch·ers.** *n.,pl.* **1.** gripping implement having a pair of jaws and handles that are fastened on a pivot. **2.** grasping claw resembling this, as of a crab or lobster. [From an unrecorded Old French word, from Old French *pincier* to nip. See PINCH.]

pinch (pinch) *v.t.* **1.** to squeeze between two surfaces or edges, as between the forefinger and thumb. **2.** to compress painfully: *John's new shoes pinched his toes.* **3.** to afflict with physical or mental hardship: *to be pinched by poverty.* **4.** to make haggard or wrinkled: *Grief pinched the woman's face.* **5.** to subject to severe restrictions; limit greatly: *Paying all our debts pinched us for a while.* **6.** *Slang.* to steal. **7.** *Slang.* to arrest. **8. to pinch pennies.** to be frugal; manage economically. —*v.i.* **1.** to compress painfully; hurt. **2.** to be frugal or miserly. —*n.* **1.** act of pinching. **2.** quantity that can be taken up between the forefinger and thumb; very small amount: *Add a pinch of salt.* **3.** physical or mental hardship: *Everyone felt the pinch of the new taxes.* **4.** time of stress or need; emergency: *I can loan you money in a pinch.* **5.** *Slang.* theft. **6.** *Slang.* arrest. [Old French *pincier* to nip; of uncertain origin.]

pinch·beck (pinch′bek′) *n.* **1.** alloy of zinc and copper, used in cheap imitation gold. **2.** something spurious or imitative. —*adj.* **1.** made of pinchbeck. **2.** not genuine; spurious; imitative. [From Christopher Pinchbeck, died 1732, English watchmaker who invented the alloy.]

pinch·er (pin′chər) *n.* **1.** one who or that which pinches. **2.** pinchers. pincers.

pinch-hit (pinch′hit′) **-hit, -hit·ting.** *v.i.* **1.** *Baseball.* to bat in place of another player, esp. when a hit is needed. **2.** to take someone's place; be a substitute;

at; āpe; cär; end; mē; it; īce; hot; ōld; fôrk; wood; fōol; oil; out; up; ūse; turn; sing; thin; this; zh in treasure; ə in ago, taken, pencil, lemon, circus.

pinch hitter, one who pinch-hits.

pin·cush·ion (pin'koosh'ən) *n.* small cushion into which pins are stuck until needed.

Pin·dar (pin'dər) *n.* c.518–438 B.C., Greek lyric poet.

Pin·dar·ic (pin dar'ik) *adj.* of, relating to, or characteristic of the style of Pindar.

Pindaric ode, ode composed in a series of triads, each triad consisting of three stanzas, the strophe, antistrophe, and epode.

pine[1] (pīn) *n.* **1.** any of a large group of evergreen trees, genus *Pinus,* found in all temperate regions of the world, bearing cones and needlelike leaves. **2.** wood of this tree, widely used in building and as a source of turpentine. [Old English *pīn* the tree, from Latin *pīnus.*]

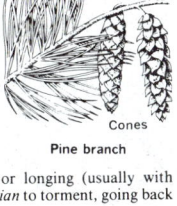
Needles
Cones
Pine branch

pine[2] (pīn) *pined, pin·ing. v.i.* **1.** to long intensely; wish earnestly; yearn (usually with *for*): *to pine for a loved one.* **2.** to become weak or unhealthy, as from grief or longing (usually with *away*): *to pine away and die.* [Old English *pīnian* to torment, going back to Latin *poena* penalty, from Greek *poinē*.]

pin·e·al (pin'ē əl) *adj.* **1.** shaped like a pine cone. **2.** of or relating to the pineal body.

pineal body, small organ whose function is not fully known, found in the brain of vertebrates. Also, **pineal gland.**

pine·ap·ple (pīn'ap'əl) *n.* **1.** large, oval, edible fruit of a tropical American plant, *Ananas comosus,* having firm, juicy, yellow flesh and a hard, scaly, reddish outer covering with a crown of stiff, narrow leaves. **2.** plant bearing this fruit, having jaggededged leaves and clusters of reddish or violet flowers.

Pineapple

Pine Bluff, city in south-central Arkansas. Pop. (1970), 57,389.

pine needle, slender, usually very small needlelike leaf of a pine tree.

pine tar, substance prepared from the destructive distillation of pine wood, used in paints and varnishes and in medicines for treating skin diseases.

pin·e·y (pī'nē) **pin·i·er, pin·i·est.** *adj.* piny.

pin·feath·er (pin'feth'ər) *n.* undeveloped feather, esp. one that is just beginning to break through the skin.

pin·fold (pin'fōld') *n.* place in which stray animals, as cattle or sheep, are kept. —*v.t.* to confine in or as in a pinfold. [Old English *pundfald* pound[1].]

ping (ping) *n.* sudden, high-pitched sound, as of a bullet striking a metal surface. —*v.i.* to produce a ping. [Imitative.]

Ping-Pong (ping'pong', -pông') *n. Trademark.* table tennis. [Imitative.]

pin·head (pin'hed') *n.* **1.** head of a pin. **2.** something of very small size or value. **3.** *Informal.* stupid person.

pin·hole (pin'hōl') *n.* small hole made by or as by a pin.

pin·ion[1] (pin'yən) *n.* **1.** last segment of a bird's wing, including the carpus, metacarpus, and phalanges. **2.** wing of a bird. **3.** feather; quill. —*v.t.* **1.** to prevent (a bird) from flying by cutting off or binding the pinions. **2.** to cut off or bind (the pinions). **3.** to bind or hold firmly: *to pinion someone's arms behind him.* [Old French *pignon* feather, wing, going back to Latin *pinna.*]

pin·ion[2] (pin'yən) *n.* small cogwheel that engages a larger cogwheel or rack and transmits motion to it. [French *pignon* cogwheel; earlier, battlement, going back to Latin *pinna* wing, pinnacle.]

Pinion[1]
Pinion[2]

pink[1] (pingk) *n.* **1.** light red color. **2.** most perfect condition or highest degree: *He is in the pink of health.* **3.** showy fragrant flower of any of a group of plants, genus *Dianthus,* having five or more petals that are often fringed, as the carnation. **4.** plant bearing this flower, having grayish-green leaves. **5.** *Informal.* one who holds radical leftist political or economic views. —*adj.* **1.** of the color pink: *a pink dress.* **2.** *Informal.* holding radical leftist views, esp. political or economic. **3.** designating a family, Caryophyllaceae, of widely distributed plants, many of which are cultivated for their flowers, as the carnation, sweet william, and baby's breath. [Of uncertain origin.]

pink[2] (pingk) *v.t.* **1.** to pierce slightly or stab with a sharp, pointed weapon, as a sword. **2.** to cut and finish the edge of (fabric) with a series of small notches. **3.** to ornament (material) with a pattern of small holes. [Possibly of Low German origin.]

pink·eye (pingk'ī') *n. Medicine.* contagious inflammation of the tissue that covers the white of the eyeball and lines the lower and upper lids; conjunctivitis.

pink·ie (pingk'kē) *pl.*, **pink·ies.** *also,* **pink·y.** *n. Informal.* smallest finger.

pinking shears, scissors having notched blades, used to pink fabric.

pink·ish (pingk'ish) *adj.* somewhat pink: *The sky took on a pinkish hue at sunset.*

pink·o (pingk'kō) *pl.*, **-os** or **-oes.** *n. Slang.* pink[1] (def. 5).

pin money, small sum of money for minor expenditures, esp. an allowance given by a man to his wife for her personal expenses.

pin·na (pin'ə) *pl.*, **pin·nae** (pin'ē) or **pin·nas.** *n.* **1.** feather, wing, fin, or winglike part. **2.** external ear. **3.** one of the primary divisions of a pinnate leaf; leaflet. [Latin *pinna* feather, wing, fin.]

pin·nace (pin'is) *n.* **1.** small boat, usually schoonerrigged with two masts, formerly attending a larger vessel. **2.** any of various ship's boats. [French *pinasse* small boat, from Italian *pinaccia,* going back to Latin *pīnus* pine[1]; because it was originally made of pine wood.]

pin·na·cle (pin'ə kəl) *n.* **1.** high, pointed formation, as a mountain peak. **2.** highest point; acme: *the pinnacle of success.* **3.** *Architecture.* small, vertical structure, usually set above a buttress or parapet. —*v.t.* **-cled, -cling. 1.** to put on or as on a pinnacle. **2.** to furnish with a pinnacle or pinnacles. [Late Latin *pinnāculum* peak of a building, diminutive of *pinna* peak, from Latin *pinna* feather, wing.] —**Syn. 2.** see peak.

Pinnacle
(def. 3)

pin·nate (pin'āt) *adj.* **1.** resembling a feather in shape or structure. **2.** of a compound leaf, having leaflets on opposite sides of a stalk. [Latin *pinnātus* feathered, winged, from *pinna* feather, wing.] —**pin'nate·ly,** *adv.*

pi·noch·le (pē'nuk'əl, -nok'-) *also,* **pi·noc·le.** *n.* **1.** game played usually by four persons with two special decks of forty-eight cards each, in which points are scored by melding. **2.** meld of the jack of diamonds and the queen of spades in this game. [Of uncertain origin.]

Pinnate leaf

pi·ñon (pin'yon, -yōn) *pl.*, **pi·ñons** or **pi·ño·nes** (pin yō'nēz) *n.* **1.** any of several small, evergreen pine trees, genus *Pinus,* found in the southwestern United States. **2.** edible nut of this tree. [Spanish *piñon* pine nut, from *piña* pine nut, pine cone, from Latin *pīnea.*]

pin·point (pin'point') *v.t.* **1.** to locate or identify precisely: *to pinpoint the trouble.* **2.** to aim at with great accuracy: *to pinpoint a target.* —*adj.* strict; exact: *pinpoint accuracy.* —*n.* something very small or insignificant.

pin·stripe (pin'strīp') *n.* very narrow stripe on a fabric.

pint (pīnt) *n.* **1.** unit of liquid measure equal to half of a quart or one-eighth of a gallon. **2.** unit of dry measure equal to half of a quart or one-sixteenth of a peck. See **weights and measures** for table. **3.** container that holds a pint. [Old French *pinte* old measure of capacity; of uncertain origin.]

pin·ta (pin'tə) *n.* disease found predominantly in Latin America, characterized by sores and patches of discoloration on the skin. [Spanish *pinta* spot, mark, going back to Latin *picta,* feminine of *pictus.* See PINTO.]

pin·tail (pin'tāl') *pl.*, **-tails** or **-tail.** *n.* **1.** long-necked duck, *Anas acuta,* having long, pointed central tail feathers. Length: 25–30 inches, including tail. **2.** North American grouse, *Pedioecetes phasianellus,* having a long, pointed tail.

pin·to (pin'tō) *adj.* having spots or patches, esp. of two colors; mottled; piebald. —*n. pl.*, **-tos. 1.** pinto horse or pony. **2.** pinto bean. [Obsolete Spanish *pinto* spotted, going back to Latin *pictus,* past participle of *pingere* to paint.]

pinto bean, a variety of kidney bean noted for its mottled seeds, found in several western states.

pin·up (pin'up') *n.* **1.** picture pinned up on a wall, esp. of a very attractive girl. **2.** girl pictured in a pinup. —*adj.* **1.** of or relating to a pinup: *a pinup girl.* **2.** designed to be fastened to a wall: *a pinup lamp.*

pin·wheel (pin'hwēl', -wēl') *n.* **1.** toy made of colored paper or plastic pinned to a stick so as to revolve when spun by hand or blown upon. **2.** firework supported by a pin upon which it revolves when lighted.

pin·worm (pin'wurm') *n.* small, white, threadlike roundworm, *Enterobius vermicularis,* infesting the lower intestinal tract, esp. of children.

pin·y (pī'nē) **pin·i·er, pin·i·est.** *also,* **pin·e·y.** *adj.* **1.** of, relating to, or suggestive of pine trees. **2.** covered with or abounding in pine trees.

at; āpe; cär; end; mē; it; īce; hot; ōld; fôrk; wood; fōōl; oil; out; up; ūse; turn; sing; thin; this; zh in treasure; ə in ago, taken, pencil, lemon, circus.

763

pi·on (pī'on) *n.* subatomic particle of the meson group. Also, **pi meson.** See **subatomic particle** for table. [Contraction of PI MESON.]

pi·o·neer (pī'ə nēr') *n.* **1.** one who is first or among the first to explore or settle a region. **2.** one who is first or among the first to open up or develop an area of thought, inquiry, or endeavor: *He was a pioneer in modern medical practice.* —*v.t.* **1.** to explore or settle: *They pioneered the Northwest Territory.* **2.** to open up or develop. —*v.i.* to be a pioneer. [French *pionnier* settler of previously unsettled land, soldier who goes ahead to clear the way for an army, from Old French *peon* foot soldier, from Medieval Latin *pedo,* from Latin *pēs* foot.]

pi·ous (pī'əs) *adj.* **1.** having reverence for God; devoutly religious: *a pious woman.* **2.** of, relating to, or proceeding from religious devotion: *pious writings.* **3.** characterized by a false or hypocritical religious devoutness. **4.** *Archaic.* respectful or dutiful to one's parents. [Latin *pius* devout, dutiful.] —**pi'ous·ly,** *adv.* —**pi'ous·ness,** *n.*
Syn. 1. Pious, devout, religious mean showing fervor in the practice of religion. **Pious** emphasizes the zealous performance of one's religious duties and obligations, or those involving outward acts or worship not necessarily reflecting a genuine reverence for God: *The pious man attended Mass every day.* **Devout** stresses a state of mind deeply imbued with an inward love of God and a sincere attachment to the tenets of one's faith: *I was often devout, my eyes filling with tears at the thought of God* (Yeats, 1923). **Religious** implies a formal faith in a particular religion and a constant adherence to a way of life sanctioned by that religion: *The old woman led a religious life.*

pip¹ (pip) *n.* **1.** seed of a fruit, as an apple or orange. **2.** *Slang.* one who or that which is remarkable or excellent: *He sure is a pip!* [Short for PIPPIN.]

pip² (pip) *n.* **1.** contagious disease of poultry and other birds, characterized by the secretion of thick mucus in the mouth and throat or the formation of a scale on the tongue. **2.** *Informal.* any of various minor illnesses in man. [Middle Dutch *pippe* the disease of birds, slime, going back to Latin *pītuīta* phlegm.]

pip³ (pip) *n.* **1.** any of the spots or marks on dominoes, dice, or playing cards. **2.** rhizome of various flowering plants, esp. the lily-of-the-valley. **3.** one of the small, diamond-shaped segments on the surface of a pineapple. [Of uncertain origin.]

pip⁴ (pip) *v.* **pipped, pip·ping.** —*v.i.* to peep. —*v.t.* to break through an eggshell, as a chick. [Form of PEEP¹.]

pipe (pīp) *n.* **1.** hollow cylinder for the conveyance of a gas or liquid; tube. **2.a.** implement for smoking tobacco, consisting of a tube with a bowl at one end, that is usually made of briar or clay. **b.** amount of tobacco that fills the bowl of a pipe. **3.a.** wind instrument, as a flute. **b.** one of the tubes in an organ in which tones are produced. **4. pipes. a.** instrument consisting of a series of tubes bound together; panpipe. **b.** bagpipe. **5.a.** *also,* **pipes.** sound of the voice, esp. when singing. **b.** song or note of a bird. **6.** any natural formation resembling a tube, as a cylindrical passage opening into the crater of a volcano. **7.** boatswain's whistle. **8.a.** cask for wine holding 126 gallons. **b.** unit of measure equivalent to this. —*v.t.* **1.** to convey by means of a pipe or pipes: *to pipe water.* **2.** to supply with pipes: *to pipe a new house for gas.* **3.** to play (music) on a pipe. **4.** to utter in a loud, shrill voice: *The child piped his objections.* **5.** to summon by sounding a boatswain's whistle: *The boatswain piped all hands on deck.* **6.** to finish or trim (fabric) with piping. —*v.i.* **1.** to make a loud, shrill sound. **2.** to play on a pipe. **3.** to summon the crew or give orders by sounding a boatswain's whistle. **4. to pipe down.** *Slang.* to be quiet. **5. to pipe up.** to begin to play, sing, or speak, esp. in a loud, shrill voice. [Old English *pīpe* tube, musical wind instrument, going back to Latin *pīpāre* to chirp.]

pipe cleaner, tufted wire used esp. to clean the stem of a tobacco pipe.

pipe dream, fanciful notion or wish.

pipe·ful (pīp'fool') *pl.,* **-fuls.** *n.* amount of tobacco sufficient to fill the bowl of a pipe.

pipe·line (pīp'līn') *n.* **1.** line of pipes for the conveyance of gas or liquid. **2.** route by which privileged or secret information is conveyed: *The businessman has a direct pipeline to the governor's office.*

pipe organ, organ (def. 1).

pip·er (pī'pər) *n.* **1.** one who plays on a pipe, esp. the bagpipes. **2. to pay the piper.** to bear the responsibility or endure the consequences of one's actions.

pipe·stem (pīp'stem') *n.* stem of a tobacco pipe.

pi·pette (pī pet') *n.* slender glass tube, usually marked with gradations, for transferring or measuring liquids. [French *pipette,* diminutive of *pipe* pipe, going back to Latin *pīpāre* to chirp.]

pip·ing (pī'ping) *n.* **1.** system of pipes. **2.** music of a pipe or pipes: *the piping of a flute.* **3.** loud, shrill sound: *the piping of a bird.* **4.** thin strip of material used for trimming items made of fabric, as garments or cushions, along the seams or edges. —*adj.* **1.** shrill: *The old man had a thin, piping voice.* **2. piping hot.** very hot.

pip·it (pip'it) *n.* any of various small, sparrowlike birds, genus *Anthus,*

having a thin bill and predominantly brown plumage. Also, **tit'lark'.** [Imitative.]

pip·kin (pip'kin) *n.* small earthenware pot. [Probably PIPE (cask) + -KIN.]

pip·pin (pip'in) *n.* any of various kinds of apple. [Old French *pepin* seed of a fruit; of uncertain origin.]

pip·sis·se·wa (pip sis'ə wə) *n.* woody, evergreen herb, *Chimaphila umbellata,* found in Europe, Asia, and North America, bearing white or pinkish flowers and leaves, used in medicine as a diuretic or tonic. [Cree *pipisisikweu* literally, it separates (a bladder stone) into small particles; referring to its use by American Indians as a medicine to treat gall stones.]

pi·quant (pē'kənt) *adj.* **1.** agreeably sharp to the taste; pungent; tart: *a piquant sauce.* **2.** stimulating; provocative; charming: *piquant comments, a piquant face.* [French *piquant,* present participle of *piquer* to prick, pierce, sting. See PIKE¹.] —**pi'quan·cy, pi'quant·ness,** *n.* —**pi'quant·ly,** *adv.*

pique (pēk) *n.* feeling of anger or resentment resulting from wounded pride: *Helen gave back the engagement ring in a fit of pique.* —*v.t.,* **piqued, pi·quing. 1.** to arouse a feeling of anger or resentment in; wound the vanity of; offend: *She was piqued by his thoughtless remark.* **2.** to stimulate; arouse; excite: *The remark piqued my curiosity.* **3.** *Archaic.* to pride (oneself) (with *on* or *upon*). [French *piquer* to prick, pierce, sting. See PIKE¹.]

pi·qué (pi kā', pē-) *n.* fabric usually made of cotton, woven with narrow, lengthwise ribs. [French *piqué* quilting, from *piquer* to prick, quilt, stitch. See PIKE¹.]

pi·quet (pi kā', -ket') *n.* card game played by two people, requiring a deck of thirty-two cards with no cards below the seven. [French *piquet* the card game, peg, diminutive of *pic* pickax, probably going back to Latin *pīcus* woodpecker.]

pi·ra·cy (pī'rə sē) *pl.,* **-cies.** *n.* **1.** robbery on the high seas. **2.** unauthorized publication, reproduction, or use of another's work, invention, or ideas, esp. in violation of a copyright. [Medieval Latin *piratia* robbery on the high seas, from Late Greek *peirāteiā,* from Greek *peirātēs* pirate.]

Pi·rae·us (pī rē'əs, pi rā'əs) *n.* principal seaport and leading industrial center of Greece, and port of nearby Athens, in the eastern part of the country. Pop. (1961), 183,877.

pi·ra·gua (pi räg'wə) *n.* **1.** large canoe made by hollowing out the trunk of a tree. **2.** flat-bottomed sailing vessel with two masts. [Spanish *piragua* canoe; of Carib origin.]

Pi·ran·del·lo, Lu·i·gi (pir'ən del'ō; loō ē'jē) 1867–1936, Italian playwright, short-story writer, novelist, and poet.

pi·ra·nha (pi ran'yə, -rän'-) *n.* any of several voracious fish, genus *Serrasalmus,* found in the rivers and streams of tropical South America, which travel in schools and feed on other fish. Piranhas will also attack large animals, including man. Average length: less than 1 foot. [Portuguese *piranha,* from Tupi-Guarani *piranha* literally, toothed fish, from *pirá* fish + *sainha* tooth.]

Piranha

pi·rate (pī'rit) *n.* **1.** one who robs on the high seas or plunders in coastal regions. **2.** sailing vessel used by pirates. **3.** one who appropriates the work, invention, or ideas of another without permission or authorization. —*v.t.,* **-rat·ed, -rat·ing. 1.** to rob on the high seas. **2.** to publish, reproduce, or use (another's work, invention, or ideas) without permission or authorization. —*v.i.* to practice piracy. [Latin *pīrāta* robber on the high seas, from Greek *peirātēs* one who attacks, adventurer, robber on the high seas.] —**pi·rat·ic** (pi rat'ik); *also,* **pi·rat'i·cal,** *adj.* —**pi·rat'i·cal·ly,** *adv.*

pir·ou·ette (pir'oo et') *n.* rapid turning about on the toes. —*v.i.,* **-et·ted, -et·ting.** to perform a pirouette. [French *pirouette* spinning top, a whirling about; of uncertain origin.]

Pi·sa (pē'zə) *n.* city in central Italy. Pop. (1968), 102,326.

pis·ca·to·ry (pis'kə tôr'ē) *adj.* **1.** of or relating to fish or fishing. **2.** employed in or devoted to fishing: *piscatory tribes.* Also, **pis'ca·to'ri·al.** [Latin *piscātōrius* relating to fishermen or fishing, going back to *piscis* fish.]

Pis·ces (pī'sēz, pis'ēz) *n.* **1.** constellation in the northern sky, conventionally depicted as two fish. **2.** twelfth sign of the zodiac. See **zodiac** for illustration. [Latin *Piscēs* literally, the Fish, plural of *piscis* fish.]

Pis·gah, Mount (piz'gə) mountain ridge in Jordan that includes Mount Nebo.

pis·ta·chi·o (pis tash'ē ō', -tash'ō) *pl.,* **-chi·os.** *n.* **1.** small, edible, greenish nut of a tree, *Pistacia vera,* of the cashew family, having a thin purple skin and covered by a hard gray shell. **2.** small tree bearing this nut. **3.** flavor of the nut. **4.** light yellowish-green color. [Italian *pis-*

at; āpe; cär; end; mē; it; īce; hot; ōld; fôrk; wood; fōōl; oil; out; up; ūse; turn; sing; thin; this; zh in treasure; ə in ago, taken, pencil, lemon, circus.

tacchio the nut, the tree, from Latin *pistācium* the nut, from Greek *pistakion,* from Persian *pistah.*]

pis·til (pist′əl) *n.* part of a flower where seeds are produced, consisting of the ovary, style, and stigma. See **flower** for illustration. [Latin *pistillum* pestle; referring to its shape.]

pis·til·late (pist′əl āt′) *adj.* having a pistil or pistils, esp. having pistils but no stamens.

pis·tol (pist′əl) *n.* small firearm designed to be held and fired with one hand. [French *pistole,* from German *Pistole,* from Czech *pišt'al* tube, firearm.]

pis·tole (pis tōl′) *n.* any of various old European gold coins, esp. one of Spain. [French *pistole* coin, pistol. See PISTOL.]

pis·ton (pis′tən) *n.* **1.** disk or cylinder that fits closely inside a sleeve or hollow cylinder, where it moves back and forth. **2.** in a brass instrument, a sliding valve used to change the pitch of tones. [French *piston,* from Italian *pistone,* from *pistare* to pound[2], going back to Latin *pistus,* past participle of *pīnsere.*]

piston ring, metal ring that encircles a piston and seals off the gap between the piston and the surrounding cylinder.

piston rod, rod by which power is imparted to a piston or by which it imparts power to another part.

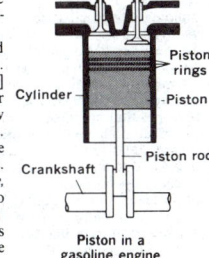

Piston in a gasoline engine

pit[1] (pit) *n.* **1.** hole or cavity in the ground, either natural or man-made. **2.a.** very small indentation or scar on a surface, as a pockmark on the skin. **b.** natural hollow or depression in the body: *the pit of the stomach.* **3.** sunken or enclosed area for fights between animals. **4.** sunken area in front of the stage of a theater for the orchestra. **5.a.** abyss; depth: *the pit of despair.* **b.** hell; the fiery pit. **6.** area of an exchange where a particular commodity is traded: *the wheat pit.* —*v.t.,* **pit·ted, pit·ting. 1.** to make small holes or indentations in; mark with pits: *to pit glass with pebbles.* **2.** to place in opposition or rivalry; match (often with *against*): *to pit the challenger against the champion.* [Old English *pytt* hole in the ground, well, from Latin *puteus* well, shaft.]

pit[2] (pit) *n.* hard stone of a fruit, as of a peach or cherry. —*v.t.,* **pit·ted, pit·ting.** to remove stones from (fruit). [Dutch *pit* kernel.]

pit·a·pat (pit′ə pat′) *adv.* with a quick succession of beats or taps: *Mary's heart went pitapat.* —*n.* sound made by this. —*v.i.,* **-pat·ted, -pat·ting.** to go pitapat. [Imitative.]

pitch[1] (pich) *v.t.* **1.** to throw, hurl, or toss: *to pitch horseshoes, to pitch pennies.* **2.** *Baseball.* **a.** to throw (the ball) to the batter. **b.** to be the pitcher in (a game or part of one). **3.** to fix or set firmly in the ground, as a peg or stake. **4.** to set up; erect: *to pitch a camp in the mountains. The campers pitched their tent by the lake.* **5.** to put in a fixed or definite place or position: *The painter pitched the ladder against the house.* **6.** to set at a particular point, degree, or level: *The carpenters pitched the roof steeply. He pitched his hopes of success too high.* **7.** *Music.* to set or determine the key of, as a tune, the voice, or an instrument. —*v.i.* **1.** to fall or plunge forward or headlong: *The window washer lost his balance and pitched off the ladder.* **2.** to incline or slope downward: *The vein of ore pitched at a 45° angle.* **3.** to settle temporarily; encamp. **4.** to stagger around; lurch. **5.** to throw or toss anything. **6.** *Baseball.* **a.** to throw the ball to the batter. **b.** to play the position of pitcher. **7.a.** (of a boat or ship) to plunge with alternate rise and fall of bow and stern. **b.** (of an aircraft or spacecraft) to turn about a lateral axis so that the nose rises and falls. **8.** to choose or select more or less casually (with *on* or *upon*): *They pitched on his idea at once.* **9. to pitch in.** *Informal.* **a.** to set to work with promptness and energy: *There was so much to do that we all pitched in.* **b.** to contribute to a common goal or purpose; cooperate: *We all pitched in to rent a boat.* **10. to pitch into.** *Informal.* to attack verbally or physically: *His boss pitched into him for being late.* —*n.* **1.** throw; hurl; toss. **2.** point, degree, or level: *a high pitch of excitement.* **3.** highest point or degree: *the pitch of happiness.* **4.** height: *the pitch of an arch.* **5.** downward slope or inclination: *The road takes a pitch around the bend.* **6.** amount of slope or inclination. **7.** that which is pitched: *a pitch of hay.* **8.** *Baseball.* **a.** act or manner of pitching the ball to the batter. **b.** ball so pitched. **9.** act or manner of pitching. **10.** highness or lowness of a sound or musical tone, depending on the relative rapidity of the vibrations by which it is produced. A high pitch results from rapid vibrations and a low pitch, from slow vibrations. **11.** alternate rise and fall of the bow and stern of a ship in a rough sea. **12.** movement of the lateral axis of an aircraft or spacecraft up or down from the horizontal plane. **13.** the theoretical distance that a propeller would move forward in one revolution. **14.a.** distance between corresponding points of two adjacent gear teeth. **b.** distance between any two adjacent things in a machine, as the threads of a screw. **15.** *Slang.* talk intended to persuade, usually using high-pressure tactics:

a sales pitch. [Possibly from an unrecorded Old English word.] —Syn. *v.t.* **1.** see throw.

pitch[2] (pich) *n.* **1.** dark, thick, sticky substance obtained by the distillation of such substances as petroleum, coal tar, or wood tar, used for waterproofing, insulating, or paving. **2.** resin from pines. —*v.t.* to cover or smear with or as with pitch. [Old English *pic* dark resinous substance, from Latin *pix.*]

pitch-black (pich′blak′) *adj.* extremely black.

pitch·blende (pich′blend′) *n.* massive, black, lumpy variety of uraninite. [German *Pechblende,* from *Pech* pitch[2] (from Latin *pix*) + *Blende.* See BLENDE.]

pitch-dark (pich′därk′) *adj.* extremely dark.

pitched battle 1. battle in which the troops have been specially positioned in advance. **2.** any heatedly fought battle.

pitch·er[1] (pich′ər) *n.* **1.** vessel with a handle and a lip or spout, used chiefly for holding and pouring liquids. **2.** amount contained by a pitcher. **3.** leaf of a pitcher plant. [Old French *pichier* container for liquids, going back to Late Latin *bīcārium* goblet, possibly from Greek *bīkos* jar.]

pitch·er[2] (pich′ər) *n.* **1.** one who pitches. **2.** player on a baseball team who throws the ball to the batter. [PITCH[1] + -ER[1].]

Pitcher plant

pitcher plant, any of several plants, genus *Sarracenia* or *Darlingtonia,* shaped like a pitcher, that capture insects, esp. *S. purpura,* found in North America, bearing long, drooping yellow or purple flowers.

pitch·fork (pich′fôrk′) *n.* long-handled tool with projecting prongs, used esp. to lift and pitch hay. —*v.t.* to lift and pitch with or as with a pitchfork.

pitch·out (pich′out′) *n.* **1.** pitch in baseball intentionally thrown too wide of home plate for the batter to hit, done to make it easier for the catcher to throw out a base runner attempting to steal. **2.** lateral pass in football behind the line of scrimmage, usually from the quarterback to another back.

pitch pipe, small pipe that has a fixed note, used to give the pitch to a singer or instrumentalist.

pitch·y (pich′ē) **pitch·i·er, pitch·i·est.** *adj.* **1.** full of or covered with pitch: *a pitchy roadbed.* **2.** resembling pitch, as in color or consistency.

pit·e·ous (pit′ē əs) *adj.* deserving or arousing pity; pitiable; pathetic. [Old French *pitos, piteus,* going back to Latin *pietās* dutiful conduct, kindness.] —**pit′e·ous·ly,** *adv.* —**pit′e·ous·ness,** *n.*

Pitchfork

pit·fall (pit′fôl′) *n.* **1.** trap dug into the ground and hidden, used to catch animals. **2.** any hidden danger or unforeseen difficulty.

pith (pith) *n.* **1.** soft, spongy tissue in the center of the stems of certain plants. **2.** soft tissue resembling this: *the pith of a grapefruit.* **3.** important or essential part; essence; substance: *the pith of an essay.* [Old English *pitha* medulla of plants, essential part.]

Pith·e·can·thro·pus (pith′ə kan′thrə pəs, -kan thrō′pəs) *pl.* **-pi** (-pī). *n.* Java man. [Modern Latin *pithecanthropus,* from Greek *pithēkos* ape + *anthrōpos* man.]

pith·y (pith′ē) **pith·i·er, pith·i·est.** *adj.* **1.** of, like, or full of pith. **2.** concise and full of substance. —**pith′i·ly,** *adv.* —**pith′i·ness,** *n.*

pit·i·a·ble (pit′ē ə bəl) *adj.* **1.** deserving or arousing pity; lamentable. **2.** deserving or arousing contempt; mean. —**pit′i·a·ble·ness,** *n.* —**pit′i·a·bly,** *adv.*

pit·i·ful (pit′i fəl) *adj.* **1.** arousing pity: *a pitiful look.* **2.** arousing contempt; paltry. **3.** *Archaic.* full of pity; compassionate. —**pit′i·ful·ly,** *adv.* —**pit′i·ful·ness,** *n.*

pit·i·less (pit′i lis) *adj.* without pity; showing no mercy: *a pitiless attack.* —**pit′i·less·ly,** *adv.* —**pit′i·less·ness,** *n.*

Pitt (pit) **1. William.** 1708–78, first Earl of Chatham, English statesman. **2. William.** 1759–1806, his son; English statesman and prime minister from 1783 to 1801 and 1804 to 1806.

pit·tance (pit′əns) *n.* small or meager amount or allowance, as of money. [Old French *pi(e)tance* allowance of food, pity, going back to Latin *pietās* dutiful conduct, kindness.]

pit·ter-pat·ter (pit′ər pat′ər) *n.* quick succession of light taps or beats: *the pitter-patter of footsteps.* —*adv.* with a quick succession of light taps or beats. [Imitative.]

Pitts·burgh (pits′bûrg′) *n.* city in southwestern Pennsylvania, the leading center of U.S. iron and steel production. Pop. (1970), 520,117.

Pitts·field (pits′fēld′) *n.* city in western Massachusetts. Pop. (1970), 57,020.

pi·tu·i·tar·y (pi tōō′ə ter′ē, -tū′-) *n.* **1.** pituitary gland. **2.** extract from the pituitary glands of certain animals. —*adj.* of or relating to the pituitary gland. [Latin *pītuītārius* relating to or secreting phlegm, from *pītuīta* phlegm, slime.]

---

at; āpe; cär; end; mē; it; īce; hot; ōld; fôrk; wood; fōōl; oil; out; up; ūse; turn; sing; thin; this; zh in treasure; ə in ago, taken, pencil, lemon, circus.

pituitary gland, small, oval endocrine gland located beneath the brain, which secretes hormones that regulate the functions of other body organs. Also, **pituitary body.**

pit viper, any of several poisonous snakes, family Crotalidae, including the bushmaster, copperhead, and water moccasin, having a deep heat-sensitive pit on each side of the head.

pit·y (pit′ē) *pl.,* **pit·ies.** *n.* **1.** feeling of profound sympathy aroused by the unhappiness or suffering of another; commiseration. **2.** cause for sympathy or regret: *What a pity you can't go.* **3. to have** (or **take**) **pity on.** to be merciful to. —*v.t.,* **pit·ied, pit·y·ing.** to feel sympathy for. [Old French *pite* dutifulness, compassion, from Latin *pietās* dutiful conduct, devotion, kindness. Doublet of PIETY.] —**pit′y·ing·ly,** *adv.*

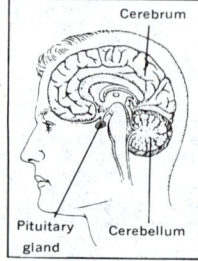

Cerebrum

Pituitary gland

Cerebellum

Pituitary gland

Syn. *n.* **1. Pity, sympathy, compassion** mean deep sorrow excited by the suffering and misfortunes of others. **Pity** has strong emotional overtones and suggests an attitude of heartfelt distress and concern induced by a contemplation of another's plight and unhappiness, sometimes tinged with contempt for his weakness and inferiority: *A retarded child needs help, not pity.* **Sympathy** ranges in its implications from emotional identification with one stricken by afflictions to keen sorrow at another's misfortunes and profound sensitivity to his unhappiness: *Dick was touched by the sympathy he received from his friends during his illness.* **Compassion** stresses a deep consciousness of the personal tragedies of others accompanied by a willingness to understand and share in their suffering: *Dr. Albert Schweitzer was a man of great compassion.*

Pi·us IX (pī′ əs) 1792–1878, pope from ·1846 to 1878.

Pius X, 1835–1914, pope from 1902 to 1914.

Pius XI, 1857–1939, pope from 1922 to 1939.

Pius XII, 1876–1958, pope from 1939 to 1958.

piv·ot (piv′ət) *n.* **1.** shaft or pin about which something turns. **2.** person or thing of importance on which something hinges or depends. **3.** act of turning on or as on a pivot. —*v.t.* to place on or furnish with a pivot. —*v.i.* to turn on or as on a pivot. [French *pivot* hinge, pin; of uncertain origin.]

piv·ot·al (piv′ət əl) *adj.* **1.** of, relating to, or serving as a pivot. **2.** of central or vital importance; crucial: *a pivotal matter.* —**piv′ot·al·ly,** *adv.*

pix·y (pik′sē) *pl.,* **pix·ies.** *Also,* **pix·ie.** *n.* imaginary small or mischievous being; fairy; elf. [Of uncertain origin.]

Pi·zar·ro, Fran·cis·co (pi zär′ō; fran sis′kō) c.1471–1541, Spanish conqueror of Peru.

piz·za (pēt′sə) *n.* open pie with a breadlike crust topped with tomatoes, cheese, and sometimes other ingredients, as sausages or mushrooms. [Italian *pizza,* possibly from *pizza* edge, point; of uncertain origin.]

piz·ze·ri·a (pēt′sə rē′ə) *n.* place where pizzas are prepared and sold.

piz·zi·ca·to (pit′si kä′tō) *Music. adj.* (of a stringed instrument, as a violin) played by plucking the strings with the finger. —*n. pl.,* **-ca·ti** (-kä′tē). note or passage played in this way. [Italian *pizzicato* plucked, past participle of *pizzicare* to pluck, pinch, from *pizzare* to prick, sting, from *pizza* edge, point; of uncertain origin.]

pk. *pl.,* **pks. 1.** pack. **2.** park. **3.** peak. **4.** peck.

pkg. *pl.,* **pkgs.** package.

pl. 1. place. **2.** plate. **3.** plural.

PL/1, computer coding system oriented toward solving both scientific and business problems. [Short for *p(rogramming) l(anguage)/one*.]

plac·a·ble (plak′ə bəl, plā′kə-) *adj.* easily placated; forgiving. [Latin *plācābilis,* from *plācāre* to appease.] —**plac′a·bil′i·ty, plac′a·ble·ness,** *n.*

plac·ard (plak′ärd, -ərd) *n.* large, usually printed paper or cardboard sign or notice to be displayed in a public place. —*v.t.* **1.** to display placards on or in: *to placard the wall of the building.* **2.** to make known by means of placards. **3.** to display as a placard. [French *placard* poster, from *plaquer* to stick on, plaster, from Middle Dutch *placken* to patch, plaster.]

pla·cate (plā′kāt, plak′āt) **-cat·ed, -cat·ing.** *v.t.* to allay the hostility or anger of; pacify: *He tried to placate the indignant woman.* [Latin *plācātus,* past participle of *plācāre* to appease.] —**pla′cat′er, pla·ca′tion,** *n.;* **pla′ca·tive, plac·a·tor·y** (plak′ə tôr′ē), *adj.*

place (plās) *n.* **1.** portion of space actually occupied by a person or thing: *The vase has a place on the shelf.* **2.** particular part of space, of defined or undefined extent, but of definite position. **3.** space in general: *time and place.* **4.** portion of space in which people live together, as a city, town, or village: *I don't know the name of this place.* **5.** building, part of a building, or location set apart for any purpose: *a place of*

worship, *a place of amusement.* **6.** house, dwelling, or residence: *We have a place in the country.* **7.** particular part or spot in a body or on a surface: *a sore place, a wet place on the floor.* **8.** particular part, passage, or other point in a book or other writing: *She looked up from her book and lost her place.* **9.** space or seat for one person, as in a train or theater, or at a table: *Save a place for me at the movies.* **10.** right or appropriate position, time, or location: *A crowded bus is not the place for a private conversation.* **11.** situation or circumstances: *If I were in your place, I wouldn't go out on such a rainy night.* **12.a.** position or standing in a social scale or in any order of merit: *In the Middle Ages, a lord and a serf had very different places in life.* **b.** high rank or dignity: *That author has a place in the history of English literature.* **13.** job, position, or employment, esp. an official position: *She found a place as a salesgirl.* **14.** duty or business: *It is not your place to criticize.* **15.** step or point in the order of progression: *in the first place.* **16.a.** position among the first three leaders at the finish of a race or competition. **b.** second position at the end of a horse race. **17.** *Mathematics.* relative position of a figure in a series, as in decimal notation. In .347, *4* is the second decimal place. **18.** short street. **19.** position customarily occupied by another; stead: *Will you go in my place?* **20. in place.** in the original, proper, or natural place or position: *The books were in place on the shelves.* **21. in place of.** instead of: *Use cream in place of milk in the recipe.* **22. out of place. a.** not in the original, proper, or natural place or position. **b.** not proper; unsuitable. **23. to go places.** *Slang.* to become increasingly successful. **24. to take place.** to come to pass; come about: *The opening of the play will take place tomorrow night.* —*v.t.* **placed, plac·ing. 1.** to put or set in a particular place or position: *to place the fork to the left of the plate.* **2.** to put in the proper relation, position, or order; arrange: *Place the books in alphabetical order.* **3.** to arrange or make provision for: *to place an order, to place a bet.* **4.** to identify by connecting with the proper location, set of circumstances, or time: *I finally placed him as an old school friend.* **5.** to put in office or a position of authority: *He was placed on the president's cabinet.* **6.** to find employment or a home for: *The child was placed in an orphanage.* —*v.i.* **1.** to finish among the first three in a race or competition. **2.** to finish second in a horse race. Distinguished from **show** and **win.** [Old French *place* space occupied by a person or thing, spot, room, court, rank, going back to Latin *platēa* broad way, from Greek *plateia (hodos)* broad (way). Doublet of PIAZZA, PLAZA.]

Syn. *n.* **1. Place, position, situation** mean a particular portion of space occupied by a person or thing. **Place** is the most general of these terms and may be applied loosely to any limited and not always clearly defined portion of space that is occupied by a person or thing: *At the end of the game we changed places.* **Position** chiefly refers to a definite point or area in space actually occupied by an object as its natural or proper location in relation to others or something else: *He took his position at the head of the procession.* **Situation** is a little more specific regarding the kind of location or site in which something is placed or built: *Its situation on a hill made the fort impregnable.* —*v.t.* **1.** see **put.**

pla·ce·bo (plə sē′bō) *pl.,* **-bos** or **-boes.** *n.* preparation having no medicinal value, given to soothe or humor a patient or used as a control in an experiment. [Latin *placēbō* I shall please.]

place-kick (plās′kik′) *v.t., v.i.* to give a place kick (to).

place kick, kick in which a football is placed or held nearly upright on the ground, as in kicking off or attempting a field goal.

place mat, small piece of material, as linen or plastic, placed on a table under a table setting and dish for protection or decoration.

place·ment (plās′mənt) *n.* **1.** act or instance of putting or setting in a particular place or position: *the placement of furniture.* **2.** act or instance of finding employment or a home for: *placement in a job.* **3.** placing of the ball in football for a place kick.

pla·cen·ta (plə sen′tə) *pl.,* **-tae** (-tē) or **-tas.** *n.* **1.** organ attached to the wall of the uterus and to the umbilical cord through which the embryo receives food and oxygen and gives off waste. **2.** *Botany.* place in the ovary of a flowering plant where ovules are borne. [Latin *placenta* cake, from Greek *plakoenta,* accusative of *plakoeis* flat cake; referring to the shape.] —**pla·cen′tal,** *adj.*

plac·er (plas′ər) *n.* alluvial or glacial deposit, as of gravel or sand, which contains particles of gold or other valuable minerals. [Spanish *placer* mass or ridge of sand, from *plaza* square, market, from Latin *plātea* broad way. See PLACE.]

plac·er mining (plas′ər) mining in which gravel or sand is washed to sort out gold or other valuable minerals.

plac·id (plas′id) *adj.* calm or peaceful; undisturbed: *a placid temperament.* [Latin *placidus* gentle, pleasing.] —**pla·cid′i·ty, plac′id·ness,** *n.* —**plac′id·ly,** *adv.*

plack·et (plak′it) *n.* **1.** usually concealed opening or slit at the top of a garment, as at the neckline or wrists, that makes it easy to put the garment on or take it off. **2.** *Archaic.* pocket in a woman's skirt. [Possibly a form of PLACARD.]

at; āpe; cär; end; mē; it; īce; hot; ōld; fôrk; wood; fool; oil; out; up; ūse; turn; sing; thin; this; zh in treasure; ə in ago, taken, pencil, lemon, circus.

pla·gia·rism (plā′jə riz′əm) *n.* **1.** act or instance of taking and passing off as one's own someone else's work or ideas. **2.** work or ideas taken and passed off as one's own. [Earlier *plagiary* plagiarist, plagiarism (from Latin *plagiārius* kidnaper, literary thief) + -ISM.] —**pla′gia·rist,** *n.* —**pla′gia·ris′tic,** *adj.*

pla·gia·rize (plā′jə rīz′) **-rized, -riz·ing.** *v.t.* **1.** to take and pass off as one's own (someone else's work or ideas): *to plagiarize a passage from an essay by Emerson.* **2.** to take and pass off as one's own the work or ideas of: *to plagiarize an author.* —*v.i.* to commit plagiarism. —**pla′gia·riz′er,** *n.*

plague (plāg) *n.* **1.** highly infectious, often fatal disease that occurs in several forms and is characterized by high fever and the swelling of the lymph glands, esp. the bubonic plague. **2.** great affliction, calamity, or evil: *The land was ravaged by a plague of locusts.* **3.** one who or that which causes trouble or annoyance: *A plague of bill collectors hounded the widow.* —*v.t.,* **plagued, plagu·ing. 1.** to afflict with or as with a plague. **2.** to trouble or annoy. [Latin *plāga* blow[1], pestilence.] —**Syn.** *v.t.* **2.** see **pester.**

pla·guy (plā′gē) *also,* **pla·guey.** *adj. Informal.* troubling or annoying.

plaice (plās) *pl.,* **plaic·es** *or* **plaice.** *n.* **1.** European flatfish, *Pleuronectes platessa,* found in the North Atlantic. **2.** any of various American flatfish. [Old French *plaïs* the European flatfish, going back to Late Latin *platessa,* possibly from Greek *platys* flat.]

plaid (plad) *n.* **1.** pattern consisting of alternating narrow and wide stripes of varying colors that cross one another at right angles. **2.** shawl having such a pattern. It is part of the traditional Scottish Highland dress. See **kilt** for illustration. **3.** fabric made with such a pattern. —*adj.* having such a pattern. [Scottish Gaelic *plaide* blanket.] —**plaid′ed,** *adj.*

plain[1] (plān) *adj.* **1.** clearly seen or heard; distinct: *It was in plain sight.* **2.** clearly understood; evident; obvious: *He made it plain that he would not change his mind.* **3.** downright; sheer; unqualified: *That's just plain nonsense!* **4.** straightforward or direct; outspoken; frank: *I will be plain with you and tell you the truth.* **5.** not intricate or complicated; simple; easy: *plain sewing.* **6.** without ornament or embellishment; unadorned: *a plain black dress.* **7.** without pattern, figure, or special weave: *plain sheets, plain dishes.* **8.** not rich or highly seasoned: *plain bread and butter, a plain diet.* **9.** without position or pretensions; unsophisticated or ordinary: *plain people, a plain town.* **10.** not beautiful or striking in appearance; homely: *a plain face and figure.* **11.** *Archaic.* flat or level, as land. —*n.* expanse of level or nearly level land. —*adv.* in a plain manner; clearly; distinctly. [Old French *plain* flat, level, from Latin *plānus.*] —**plain′ly,** *adv.* —**plain′ness,** *n.*

plain[2] (plān) *v.i. Archaic.* to complain. [Old French *plaindre* to mourn, from Latin *plangere* to lament aloud, beat (the breast).]

plain·chant (plān′chant′) *n.* plainsong.

plain·clothes man (plān′klōz′, -klōthz′) *also,* **plain·clothes·man.** policeman who wears civilian clothes while on duty.

plain sailing, easy progress, as in an endeavor.

Plains Indian, member of any of various American Indian tribes who formerly inhabited the Great Plains.

plains·man (plānz′mən) *pl.,* **-men.** *n.* inhabitant of the plains.

plain·song (plān′sông′) *n.* vocal music used in the Roman Catholic liturgical services, having a simple melody that is not divided into measures and an irregular rhythm that depends on the accentuation of the words. It is sung in unison without accompaniment. Also, *Gregorian chant,* **plain′chant′.**

plain-spo·ken (plān′spō′kən) *adj.* open or unreserved in speech; outspoken; frank.

plaint (plānt) *n.* **1.** complaint. **2.** *Archaic.* lament. [Old French *plaint,* from Latin *planctus* lamentation.]

plain·tiff (plān′tif) *n.* party that brings a suit into a court of law. [Old French *plaintif,* from *plaintif* complaining, lamenting. See PLAINTIVE.]

plain·tive (plān′tiv) *adj.* expressing sorrow; mournful; sad: *a plaintive face.* [Old French *plaintif* lamenting, complaining, going back to Latin *planctus* lamentation.] —**plain′tive·ly,** *adv.* —**plain′tive·ness,** *n.*

plait (plāt, plat) *n.* **1.** braid, as of hair. **2.** pleat. —*v.t.* **1.** to braid. **2.** to make by braiding: *The two women plaited a rug.* **3.** to pleat. [Old French *pleit* fold, going back to Latin *plicitus,* past participle of *plicāre* to fold[1].]

plan (plan) *n.* **1.** method or program, as of action: *The general's plan of attack was poorly conceived.* **2.** that which one intends to do: *My plans for the weekend are still tentative.* **3.** outline or system; arrangement: *The author drew up a plan for his new novel.* **4.** drawing or

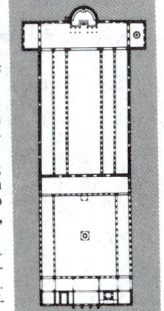

Plan (def. 4)
Floor plan of a basilica

diagram, often made to scale, that shows the relative position of parts, as of a building or a section of land. —*v.t.,* **planned, plan·ning. 1.** to prepare a method, program, or outline for. **2.** to have in mind as a purpose; intend: *She plans to do it tomorrow.* **3.** to make a drawing or diagram of; design: *The architect planned a house for us.* —*v.i.* to make a plan or plans. [French *plan* ground plan (drawn on a flat surface), design, scheme, going back to Latin *plānus* flat, level.] —**plan′ner,** *n.*

Syn. *n.* **1. Plan, scheme** mean a proposed method of achieving a given end. **Plan** refers to a tentative formulation of a program of action worked out in detail rendering systematically the steps and procedures necessary to achieve the objective: *The committee discussed the plan for the reorganization of the department.* **Scheme** refers to an outline of a planned undertaking and is often used to indicate a plan that may be somewhat dishonest: *Most of his schemes were never carried out for lack of money.*

pla·nar (plā′nər, -när) *adj.* **1.** of or relating to a plane. **2.** flat. [Late Latin *plānāris* flat, from Latin *plānum.* See PLANE[1].]

pla·nar·i·an (plə nâr′ē ən) *n.* any of various small free-swimming flatworms of the order Tricladida that inhabits freshwater lakes, streams, or ponds. It has the power of regenerating injured body parts. Length: to 4 inches. [Modern Latin *Planaria,* going back to Latin *plānus* flat.]

plan·chette (plan shet′) *n.* small wooden, three-cornered or heart-shaped board supported by a pencil and two short legs resting on casters, used in divination. A modified planchette is used as the pointing device on a ouija board. [French *planchette* planchette, small board, diminutive of *planche* board, from Latin *planca.*]

Planck, Max (plängk) 1858–1947, German physicist who formulated the quantum theory.

plane[1] (plān) *n.* **1.** flat or level surface. **2.** level or degree, as of development, character, or existence: *a high plane of achievement.* **3.** airplane or hydroplane. **4.** flat or curved supporting surface of an airplane wing. **5.** *Geometry.* flat surface that wholly contains every line connecting any two points on it. —*adj.* **1.** level; flat. **2.** of, relating to, or designating a plane or planes, or a figure contained in a plane: *a plane curve.* —*v.i.,* **planed, plan·ing. 1.** to glide or soar. **2.** to ride in an airplane. **3.** to rise partly out of the water when moving at a high speed, as a motor boat. [Latin *plānum* level surface.]

plane[2] (plān) *n.* hand tool with an adjustable, inclined blade that projects from the bottom, used for leveling or smoothing wood. —*v.t.,* **planed, planing. 1.** to level or smooth with or as with a plane. **2.** to remove with or as with a plane: *to plane the rough edges of a plank.* —*v.i.* **1.** to work with a plane. **2.** to do the work of a plane: *A knife will not plane adequately.* [Old French *plane* the tool, going back to Late Latin *plāna,* from Latin *plānāre* to level.]

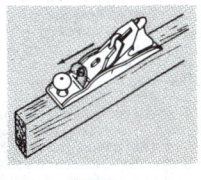

Plane[2]

plane[3] (plān) *n.* plane tree. [Old French *plane,* from Latin *platanus,* from Greek *platanos,* from *platys* broad; referring to its broad leaves.]

plane geometry, branch of geometry that deals with plane figures.

plan·er (plā′nər) *n.* **1.** one who planes. **2.** machine that planes.

plan·et (plan′it) *n.* **1.** any one of the nine massive, spherical bodies that revolve around the sun and shine by reflected light. The planets in order of their distance from the sun are Mercury, Venus, Earth, Mars, Jupiter, Saturn, Uranus, Neptune, and Pluto. **2.** *Astrology.* a heavenly body supposed to influence people and events. [Late Latin *planēta* wandering star (as it appeared to the ancient astronomers), from Greek *planētēs* wanderer, wandering star.]

plan·e·tar·i·um (plan′ə târ′ē əm) *pl.,* **-i·a** (-ē ə) *or* **-i·ums.** *n.* **1.** apparatus designed to display the positions and motions of celestial bodies by projecting their images on the inside of a hemispherical dome. **2.** room or building housing such an apparatus. **3.** model or apparatus that represents the solar system. [Modern Latin *planetarium,* going back to Latin *planēta* wandering star. See PLANET.]

plan·e·tar·y (plan′ə ter′ē) *adj.* **1.** of, relating to, or resembling a planet. **2.** wandering; erratic: *a planetary life.* **3.** terrestrial; global: *of planetary importance.* **4.** of, relating to, or designating a gear train consisting of several gears placed around and meshed with a central gear, as in the automatic transmission of an automobile.

plan·e·tes·i·mal (plan′ə tes′ə mal) *adj.* of or relating to minute solid bodies in space. —*n.* one of these minute bodies. [PLANET + (INFINIT)ESIMAL.]

planetesimal hypothesis, hypothesis that planetesimals gradually came together to form the planets and the satellites of the solar system.

plan·et·oid (plan′ə toid′) *n.* asteroid. [PLANET + -OID.]

plane tree, any of a group of trees, genus *Platanus,* esp. *P. orientalis,* found in parts of Europe and Asia, and *P. occidentalis,* found in North America, having smooth, brown bark that flakes off in thin layers and bearing dense, round clusters of tiny flowers at the ends of the branches. The plane tree of North America is also called the sycamore.

Bark

Leaves   Fruit

Plane tree

plank (plangk) *n.* **1.** long, flat piece of sawed wood thicker than a board. **2.** item forming part of the platform of a political party, as a statement of policy on an issue. **3. to walk the plank,** to walk blindfolded off a plank extending over the water from the side of a ship, as did prisoners of pirates. —*v.t.* **1.** to cover or lay with planks. **2.** to cook and serve (steak or fish) on a board. **3.** *Informal.* to put or set down forcefully. **4.** *Informal.* to pay quickly or at once (usually with *down* or *out): John planked down his share of the bill.* [Dialectal Old French *planke* board, from Latin *planca.*]

plank·ing (plang′king) *n.* **1.** planks collectively: *the planking on a floor.* **2.** act of covering or laying with planks.

plank·ton (plangk′tən) *n.* minute plants and animals that drift or float in a body of water. Plankton is the basic source of food for all aquatic animals. [German *Plankton,* from Greek *plankton,* neuter of *planktos* wandering; referring to their wandering or drifting habits.] —**plank·ton·ic** (plangk ton′ik), *adj.*

pla·no·con·cave (plā′nō kon′kāv) *adj.* flat on one side and concave on the other, as a lens. [Latin *plānus* flat, level + CONCAVE.]

pla·no·con·vex (plā′nō kon′veks) *adj.* flat on one side and convex on the other, as a lens. [Latin *plānus* flat, level + CONVEX.]

plant (plant) *n.* **1.** any living organism that characteristically lacks locomotive power and sensory organs, has cellulose cell walls, and grows by photosynthesis. **2.** small plant having a soft stem, as distinguished from a tree or shrub. **3.** young tree, vine, shrub, or herb recently planted or ready for planting. **4.** buildings, machinery, tools, apparatus, and the like needed to carry on an industrial or manufacturing operation or process: *an automobile plant.* **5.** apparatus or equipment for a mechanical operation or process: *a heating plant for an office building.* **6.** buildings, equipment, and grounds of an institution: *a university plant.* **7.** person placed in an audience and rehearsed to react in a seemingly spontaneous way to the action of a play or show. **8.** *Slang.* scheme to deceive or trap. —*v.t.* **1.** to set or place in the ground to take root and grow. **2.** to furnish or stock (land) with growing plants. **3.** to introduce (a breed of animals) into a country. **4.** to deposit, as spawn or oysters, in a body of water. **5.** to implant, introduce, or establish, as principles or ideas: *to plant doubt in their minds.* **6.** to place or set firmly in position: *to plant a signpost. He planted his feet on the ground.* **7.** *Slang.* to deliver, as a blow. **8.** to establish or found, as a colony, city, or church. **9.** *Slang.* to hide or conceal, as something stolen: *to plant stolen jewels under a house.* **10.** *Slang.* to place (someone or something) in order to deceive or trick: *to plant fake evidence.* [Old English *plante* young tree or shrub ready for planting or recently planted, from Latin *planta* sprout, shoot (for planting).]

Plan·tag·e·net (plan taj′ə nit) *n.* family that ruled England from 1154 to 1399. The kings from Henry II through Richard II were Plantagenets. Also, **An′ge·vin.** —*adj.* of or relating to this royal family or to the period of their rule.

plan·tain[1] (plant′ən) *n.* **1.** large greenish-yellow fruit of a tropical plant, *Musa paradisiaca,* resembling a banana. **2.** plant bearing this fruit. [Spanish *plantano* the plant, going back to Latin *platanus* plane tree. See PLANE[1].]

plan·tain[2] (plant′ən) *n.* any of a group of plants, genus *Plantago,* found as a common weed in Europe, Asia, and North America, bearing clusters of tiny flowers on slender spikes and large, heavily ribbed leaves. [Old French *plantain,* from Latin *plantāgō,* from *planta* sole of the foot; referring to the appearance of its leaves, which are broad and flat.]

plan·ta·tion (plan tā′shən) *n.* **1.** large estate or farm where usually a single crop, as cotton, tobacco, or sugar, is grown. **2.** group of plants, as rubber trees, that has been planted. **3.** formerly, newly established colony or settlement. [Latin *plantātiō* planting.]

plant·er (plan′tər) *n.* **1.a.** one who plants. **b.** any of various mechanical devices used for planting. **2.** one who owns or manages a plantation. **3.** decorative container for growing plants. **4.** formerly, a colonist.

plan·ti·grade (plan′tə grād′) *adj.* walking on the entire sole of the foot. —*n.* plantigrade animal, as man or a bear. [French *plantigrade,* from Latin *planta* sole of the foot + *gradī* to walk.]

plant louse, aphid.

plaque (plak) *n.* **1.a.** flat plate, slab, or disk of a hard material, as porcelain, wood, or metal, that is ornamented or engraved for mounting, as on a wall. **b.** flat, inscribed tablet mounted on the side of a building or monument for identification or commemoration. **2.** platelike ornament worn as a badge. [French *plaque,* from Dutch *plak* tablet.]

plash (plash) *n.* splash. —*v.t., v.i.* to splash. [Old English *plæsc* puddle, pool.]

-plasm *combining form* molded or formed cellular material: *cytoplasm.* [Greek *plasma* something molded or formed.]

plas·ma (plaz′mə) *n.* **1.** clear yellow liquid that forms the fluid portion of blood. **2.** thin liquid that forms the fluid portion of milk; whey. **3.** protoplasm. **4.** gaseous mixture of electrons, ions, and atoms or molecules, considered electrically to be the fourth state of matter. [Late Latin *plasma* mold[1], image, from Greek *plasma* something molded or formed.]

plas·ter (plas′tər) *n.* **1.** mixture of lime, sand, and water that becomes a hard, smooth material when dry, used for coating walls, ceilings, or partitions. **2.** plaster of Paris. **3.** medical preparation that is spread on cloth and then applied to the body for healing purposes. —*v.t.* **1.** to cover or coat with plaster. **2.** to cover as if with plaster: *The men plastered the fence with posters.* **3.** to spread thickly or abundantly. **4.** to cause to adhere or lay flat: *He plastered his cowlick down with hair tonic.* [Old English *plaster* medical plaster, going back to Latin *emplastrum,* from Greek *emplastron,* from *emplassein* to daub on.] —**plas′ter·er,** *n.*

plas·ter·board (plas′tər bôrd′) *n.* thin, firm board composed of layers of paper and plaster, used for walls or partitions.

plaster cast 1. cast or copy, as of a work of art, made with plaster of Paris. **2.** rigid form made of plaster of Paris and gauze, used to immobilize a broken bone or badly sprained muscle.

plaster of Paris, powdered gypsum that is mixed with water to form a paste, which dries rapidly into a hard, solid mass. It is used for making molds, casts, or reproductions of works of art. [Middle English *plaster of paris;* referring to the fact that in the Middle Ages the highest grade of gypsum for making plaster came from *Paris.*]

plas·tic (plas′tik) *n.* any of a group of man-made organic materials that can be molded or shaped when softened. Most plastics are poor conductors of electricity and heat, resist chemical attack, and are waterproof. —*adj.* **1.** capable of being molded or shaped: *a plastic material.* **2.** of or relating to molding or shaping: *the plastic arts.* **3.** made of plastic. **4.** capable of molding or shaping material; creative: *a plastic artist.* **5.** easily changed, modified, or influenced; impressionable; adaptable. [Latin *plasticus* relating to molding or forming, from Greek *plastikos,* going back to *plassein* to mold[1], form.] —**plas′ti·cal·ly,** *adv.*

plas·ti·ciz·er (plas′tə sī′zər) *n.* any of a group of substances that is added to a plastic to make it softer or more flexible.

plastic surgery, branch of surgery concerned with the repairing or restoring of injured or malformed parts of the body.

plas·tron (plas′trən) *n.* **1.** protective pad worn over the chest in fencing. **2.** metal breastplate worn under a coat of mail. **3.** shell that covers the belly of a turtle or tortoise. [French *plastron* breastplate, fencer's chest pad, from Italian *piastrone,* from *piastra* breastplate, metal plate, from Latin *emplastrum* medical plaster. See PLASTER.]

Plastron

plat[1] (plat) *n.* **1.** small piece of ground; plot. **2.** map, chart, or plan. —*v.t.,* **plat·ted, plat·ting.** to make a plat of. [Partly a form of PLOT; partly from Old French *plat* flat, going back to Greek *platys* flat, broad.]

plat[2] (plat) *n.* plait. —*v.t.,* **plat·ted, plat·ting.** to plait. [Form of PLAIT.]

plate (plāt) *n.* **1.** dish from which food is served or eaten. **2.** contents of such a dish. **3.a.** food and service for one person at a meal: *The banquet cost twelve dollars a plate.* **4.** entire course served on one plate: *to order the luncheon plate.* **4.** dish passed to take collections, as in a church. **5.a.** dishes and table utensils coated with a thin layer of silver or gold. **b.** dishes and table utensils made of silver or gold. **6.a.** flat, comparatively thin sheet of metal of uniform thickness and even surface: *a plate of steel.* **b.** armor made of such pieces of metal. **7.** piece of metal, usually thin and flat, on which something is or can be engraved. **8.** print made from an engraved piece of metal, as an illustration in a book. **9.** *Printing.* cast of a page of type to be printed from, as an electrotype or a stereotype. **10.** *Photography.* thin sheet of glass, metal, or other material coated with a substance sensitive to light, used to take photographs. **11.** *Baseball.* home plate. **12.** *Biology.* platelike part,

at; āpe; cär; end; mē; it; īce; hot; ōld; fôrk; wood; fōōl; oil; out; up; ūse; turn; sing; thin; this; zh in treasure; ə in ago, taken, pencil, lemon, circus.

organ, or structure, as the bony plates protecting the armadillo. **13.** piece of metal, plastic, or similar material implanted with a set of artificial teeth, fitted to the gums to replace missing natural teeth. **14.** thin cut of beef from the lower end of the breast or brisket. **15.** anode in a vacuum tube toward which electrons flow because of its positive charge. **16.** horizontal timber supporting the ends of other timbers, as one of the wall supports for a girder or roof. —*v.t.* **plated, plat·ing. 1.** to coat with a thin layer of metal, as silver, gold, or chromium. **2.** to cover with metal plates for protection. **3.** *Printing.* to make an electrotype or stereotype from (type). [Old French *plate* sheet of metal, from *plat* flat, going back to Greek *platys* flat, broad.]

pla·teau (pla tō′) *pl.,* **-teaus** or **-teaux** (-tōz′). *n.* **1.** elevated, relatively flat land area. **2.** relatively stable or inactive period or stage: *to reach a new plateau in one's development.* [French *plateau* tableland, from Old French *plat* flat. See PLATE.]

plate·ful (plāt′fool′) *pl.,* **-fuls.** *n.* as much as a plate will hold, esp. a large amount.

plate glass, highly transparent, strong glass used for windowpanes or mirrors.

plate·let (plāt′lit) *n.* blood platelet.

plat·en (plat′ən) *n.* **1.** flat metal plate in a printing press that presses the paper against the inked type to make an impression. **2.** roller of a typewriter. [Old French *platine* flat plate, from *plat* flat. See PLATE.]

plat·form (plat′fôrm′) *n.* **1.** raised, flat structure or flooring at the end of an auditorium or for a speaker. **2.** raised area alongside the tracks at a railroad or subway station. **3.** declaration of the principles of a group or individual, esp. a public statement of the principles and policies of a political party. [French *plateforme,* from *plat* flat + *forme* form, shape. See PLATE, FORM.]

platform car, flatcar.

plat·ing (plā′ting) *n.* **1.** thin coating or layer of metal, esp. of a precious metal, as gold or silver. **2.** external layer or sheath of metal plates.

plat·i·num (plat′ən əm) *n.* heavy, soft, silvery-white metallic element, used esp. in jewelry and as a catalyst in chemical processes. Symbol: Pt See **element** for table. [Modern Latin *platinum* (referring to its silvery color), going back to Spanish *plata* silver, from Old French *plate* sheet of metal. See PLATE.]

plat·i·tude (plat′ə tōōd′, -tūd′) *n.* **1.** dull, trite, or commonplace remark, esp. one meant to sound original or important. **2.** state or quality of being dull, trite, or commonplace. [French *platitude,* from *plat* flat. See PLATE.] —**Syn. 1.** see truism.

plat·i·tu·di·nous (plat′ə tōōd′ən əs, -tūd′-) *adj.* **1.** of, relating to, or having the nature of a platitude; trite. **2.** given to or full of platitudes. —**plat·i·tu′di·nous·ly,** *adv.*

Pla·to (plā′tō) c.428–c.347 B.C., Greek philosopher.

Pla·ton·ic (plə ton′ik) *adj.* **1.** of or relating to Plato or his philosophy. **2.** *also,* **platonic.** of or designating a relationship between a man and woman that is spiritual rather than sensual. —**Pla·ton′i·cal·ly,** *adv.*

Pla·to·nism (plāt′ən iz′əm) *n.* **1.** philosophy of Plato or his followers. **2.** a Platonic doctrine or saying. **3.** *also,* **platonism.** doctrine or practice of Platonic love.

Pla·to·nist (plāt′ən ist) *n.* **1.** follower of Plato or of his philosophy. **2.** one whose thinking or method tends to be intuitive or idealistic rather than deductive or empirical.

pla·toon (plə tōōn′) *n.* **1.** military unit forming part of a company, usually commanded by a lieutenant. **2.** group of people working together. **3.** group of football players who specialize in either offensive or defensive play and enter or leave the game as a unit. [French *peloton* group, little ball, from *pelote* ball. See PELLET.]

Platte (plat) *n.* river flowing from central Nebraska into the Missouri River.

plat·ter (plat′ər) *n.* **1.** large, usually oval dish for holding or serving food. **2.** food served on a platter: *a platter of roast beef.* **3.** *Slang.* phonograph record. [Anglo-Norman *plater* dish, from Old French *plat,* from *plat* flat. See PLATE.]

plat·y·pus (plat′ə pəs) *pl.,* **-pus·es** or **-pi** (-pī′). *n.* primitive, egg-laying mammal, *Ornithorhynchus anatinus,* native to Australia and Tasmania,

Platypus

having a flat, wide bill, webbed feet, a beaverlike tail, and soft brown fur. Length: to 2 feet, including tail. Also, **duck′bill′.** [Greek *platypous* flat-footed.]

plau·dit (plô′dit) *usually,* **plau·dits.** *n.* expression of praise or approval, as enthusiastic applause. [Latin *plaudite* applaud, plural imper-

ative of *plaudere* to applaud (request for applause made by ancient Roman actors at the end of a performance).]

plau·si·ble (plô′zə bəl) *adj.* **1.** apparently true or acceptable; likely: *What he says is plausible.* **2.** seemingly or deceptively honest or worthy of confidence. [Latin *plausibilis* praiseworthy, from *plausus,* past participle of *plaudere* to applaud.] —**plau′si·bil′i·ty, plau′si·ble·ness,** *n.* —**plau′si·bly,** *adv.*

Plau·tus (plô′təs) *n.* c.251–184 B.C., Roman dramatist.

play (plā) *n.* **1.** exercise or action done for recreation, pleasure, or amusement: *children at play.* **2.a.** act of carrying on a game. **b.** manner or style of carrying on a game: *There was some rough play in that hockey game.* **3.** turn to move or act in a game: *It's your play.* **4.a.** literary composition in the form of dialogue, adapted for performance on a stage with appropriate action; drama. **b.** performance of such a composition. **5.** action of a specified kind: *fair play.* **6.** action; operation; working: *a play of fancy. The engine was in full play.* **7.** rapid, light, often irregular movement or change, esp. of light or color: *the play of shadows on a wall.* **8.** free or unimpeded motion or action: *the play of a wheel, the play of muscles.* **9.** space or room for movement, as of a part of a mechanism. **10.** gambling. **11. in play. a.** *Sports.* in a state of being in legitimate or active use or motion. **b.** as a jest or joke: *I said it only in play.* **12. out of play.** *Sports.* out of a state of being in legitimate or active use or motion: *The ball is out of play on the 45 yard line.* —*v.i.* **1.** to engage in exercise or action for recreation, pleasure, or amusement: *The boys played in the backyard.* **2.** to act or deal carelessly (usually with *with*): *Don't play with a loaded gun.* **3.** to do something that is not to be taken seriously. **4.** to perform on or as on a stage: *to play in a comedy.* **5.** to act or behave (in a specified way): *to play dead, to play false.* **6.** to perform on a musical instrument: *to play in an orchestra.* **7.** to give out sound, esp. musical sound: *The band is playing. Is the phonograph playing?* **8.** to move lightly or rapidly, esp. with irregular motion: *A smile played on her lips. The wind played among the leaves.* **9.** to operate with continuous or repeated action: *The hose played on the fire.* **10.** to engage in a game: *They played for three innings.* **11.** to gamble: *to play at the races.* **12.** to lend itself to performance: *The third act plays well.* **13.** to be performed: *What's playing at the movies?* **14. to play at. a.** to take part in; participate in: *to play at cards.* **b.** to do half-heartedly: *to play at being an actress.* **15. to play into the hands of.** to act in such a way as to give the advantage to, as an opponent. **16. to play off.** to play one or more games, rounds, or matches in order to settle a tie. **17. to play on** (or **upon**). to make use of unfairly or unscrupulously; take advantage of: *to play on a person's sympathies.* **18. to play up to.** *Informal.* to try to gain one's favor, as by flattery: *to play up to one's boss.* —*v.t.* **1.** to act the part of in a dramatic performance: *to play an old man.* **2.** to behave like; act as: *to play the fool, to play the hostess.* **3.** to perform on the stage: *to play a comedy.* **4.** to give performances in: *They will play New York next week.* **5.** to represent or imitate, as for amusement: *to play astronauts.* **6.** to do; perform, esp. in fun or to deceive: *to play a trick on someone.* **7.** to operate or cause to operate with or as with continuous or repeated action: *to play a hose on a burning building.* **8.** to cause to move lightly or rapidly: *to play lights on a fountain.* **9.** to bet on: *to play the horses.* **10.** to engage in (a game or other activity): *to play a round of golf, to play baseball.* **11.** to contend in a game against: *New York played Chicago for the baseball championship.* **12.** to occupy or perform in (a specified position) in a game: *Smith will play first base.* **13.** to use in a game or sport: *Play Smith at center. Play your jack of clubs.* **14.** to perform or produce (music) on an instrument. **15.** to perform on (a musical instrument): *to play the piano.* **16.** to give out sound, esp. of music: *to play a phonograph.* **17.** to let (a hooked fish) tire itself by pulling on the line. **18. to play down.** to treat as of little importance or significance; depreciate. **19. to play out.** to pay or reel out, as a fishing line or rope. **20. to play up.** to emphasize the importance of. [Old English *pleg(i)an* to sport, play (a game), amuse oneself.] —**play′a·ble,** *adj.*

Syn. *n.* **1. Play, sport, game[1]** mean recreational activity or exercise. **Play** has a broad range of application and implies undirected and spontaneous recreational activity: *The children spent the whole afternoon in play.* **Sport** is more often applied to outdoor physical activity with a body of organized rules requiring skill and stamina on the part of participants and affording diversion and amusement to spectators: *Baseball is my favorite sport.* **Game** emphasizes the competitive nature of an athletic or recreational activity in which participants play in direct opposition to each other with the specific object of winning: *Chess is a popular game throughout the world.*

play·back (plā′bak′) *n.* act or process of playing a recording again, esp. a tape recording that has just been made.

play·bill (plā′bil′) *n.* announcement or program of a play.

play·boy (plā′boi′) *n.* wealthy man who spends much of his time seeking pleasure.

play·er (plā′ər) *n.* **1.** one who engages in a sport or game: *a baseball*

at; āpe; cär; end; mē; it; īce; hot; ōld; fôrk; wood; fōōl; oil; out; up; ūse; turn; sing; thin; this; zh in treasure; ə in ago, taken, pencil, lemon, circus.

769

player, a chess player. **2.** one who performs on the stage in a theater; actor. **3.** one who performs upon a musical instrument; musician: *a piano player.* **4.** that which causes something to operate or give out a sound, as a mechanical device on a player piano. **5.** record player.
play·er piano, piano played by a mechanical device.
play·fel·low (plā′fel′ō) *n.* playmate.
play·ful (plā′fəl) *adj.* **1.** spirited and full of fun; lively; frolicsome: *a playful puppy.* **2.** humorous; joking: *a playful remark.* —**play′ful·ly,** *adv.* —**play′ful·ness,** *n.*
play·go·er (plā′gō′ər) *n.* one who attends the theater often.
play·ground (plā′ground′) *n.* area used for outdoor recreation, esp. by children.
play·house (plā′hous′) *n.* **1.** theater. **2.** small house for children to play in. [Old English *pleghūs* theater.]
playing card, card belonging to a deck of cards, esp. a deck divided into four suits and consisting of face cards and cards numbered from one to ten, used for playing games.
play·mate (plā′māt′) *n.* companion in recreation or amusement.
play·off (plā′ôf′) *n.* **1.** game played to break a tie. **2.** one or more games played to decide a championship.
play·pen (plā′pen′) *n.* small, portable enclosure in which a baby may play.
play·room (plā′rōōm′, -room′) *n.* room used for recreation or amusement.
play·thing (plā′thing′) *n.* thing to play with; toy.
play·time (plā′tīm′) *n.* time for recreation or amusement.
play·wright (plā′rīt′) *n.* one who writes plays.
pla·za (plä′zə, plaz′ə) *n.* public square or open space in a city or town. [Spanish *plaza,* going back to Latin *platēa* broad way, from Greek *plateia (hodos)* broad (way). Doublet of PLACE, PIAZZA.]
plea (plē) *n.* **1.** earnest or urgent request or appeal: *a plea for help.* **2.** excuse; justification; pretext. **3.** *Law.* answer which the defendant in a criminal or civil action makes to the charge or allegation against him. [Old French *plaid* lawsuit, discussion, from Medieval Latin *placitum* lawsuit, from Latin *placitum* opinion, from *placēre* to be pleasing.]
plea bargaining, practice in which the prosecuting attorney in a criminal case allows the defendant to plead guilty to a lesser charge, usually so as to get his or her cooperation in testifying against a defendant in another criminal action.
pleach (plēch) *v.t.* to interlace, as growing vines; interweave. [Old French *plessier,* going back to Latin *plectere* to weave, plait.]
plead (plēd) **plead·ed** or **pled, plead·ing.** *v.i.* **1.** to make an earnest or urgent appeal; beg: *to plead for mercy.* **2.** to furnish or act as an appeal or argument: *His youth and inexperience plead for him.* **3.** to answer to a charge or allegation in a court of law: *to plead not guilty.* **4.** to conduct or argue a case in a court of law. —*v.t.* **1.** to give as an excuse or justification: *to plead illness to get out of an engagement.* **2.** to argue or present (a case or cause) in or as in a court of law. **3.** to present by way of an answer to a charge or allegation in a court of law. [Old French *plaidier* to argue a case in court, from *plaid* lawsuit, discussion. See PLEA.] —**Syn.** *v.i.* **1.** see appeal.
plead·ing (plē′ding) *n.* **1.** act of one who pleads. **2.** *Law.* a. science and system of rules governing the presentation of the formal statements in a legal proceeding. **b. pleadings.** formal statements by the parties to an action of their claims and defenses.
pleas·ant (plez′ənt) *adj.* **1.** to one's liking; agreeable: *pleasant surroundings.* **2.** having or characterized by pleasing or amiable manners or behavior. [Old French *plaisant* pleasing, present participle of *plaisir* to be agreeable to, delight. See PLEASE.] —**pleas′ant·ly,** *adv.* —**pleas′ant·ness,** *n.*
pleas·ant·ry (plez′ən trē) *pl.,* **-ries.** *n.* **1.** pleasant, courteous remark. **2.** good-naturedly humorous or playful remark or action.
please (plēz) **pleased, pleas·ing.** *v.t.* **1.** to give pleasure or satisfaction to; be agreeable to. **2.** to be so kind or obliging as to. ▲ used in the imperative to indicate a request or politely expressed command: *No smoking, please.* **3.** to be the will or pleasure of: *May it please Your Honor.* —*v.i.* **1.** to give pleasure or satisfaction; be agreeable. **2.** to have the will or desire; choose: *You may leave whenever you please.* [Old French *plaisir* to be agreeable to, delight, from Latin *placēre* to be pleasing.]
Syn. *v.t.* **1. Please, gratify, delight** mean to make happy. **Please** is applicable to a conscious attempt to give pleasure or satisfaction to another: *Our host's warm welcome pleased us.* **Gratify** stresses even more strongly an actual and positive satisfaction that answers a deep need, expectation, or desire: *The president was gratified with the results of the election.* **Delight** stresses the emotional content of the happiness and pleasure that is keenly felt and often openly expressed: *The man's attentions and flattery delighted the girl.*
pleas·ing (plē′zing) *adj.* giving pleasure or satisfaction; agreeable. —**pleas′ing·ly,** *adv.* —**pleas′ing·ness,** *n.*
pleas·ur·a·ble (plezh′ər ə bəl) *adj.* giving or producing pleasure

or enjoyment: *a pleasurable experience, a pleasurable sensation.* —**pleas′ur·a·ble·ness,** *n.* —**pleas′ur·a·bly,** *adv.*
pleas·ure (plezh′ər) *n.* **1.** enjoyable or delightful sensation or emotion, as that arising from gratification or good. **2.** that which is the source or cause of such a sensation or emotion: *It was a pleasure to see you again.* **3.** worldly or sensual amusement or gratification. **4.** that which one desires or chooses: *It is His Majesty's pleasure that you join him.* [Old French *plaisir,* noun use of *plaisir* to be agreeable to, delight. See PLEASE.]

Box pleats   Knife pleats
Pleat

pleat (plēt) *n.* lengthwise fold in cloth or other material, made by doubling the material upon itself and then pressing, stitching, or otherwise fastening into place. —*v.t.* to make a pleat or pleats in; arrange in pleats. [Form of PLAIT.]
plebe (plēb) *n.* member of the freshman class at the U.S. Military Academy at West Point or the Naval Academy at Annapolis. [Short for PLEBEIAN.]
ple·be·ian (pli bē′ən) *n.* **1.** member of the common people in ancient Rome. **2.** one of the common people. **3.** person who is coarse, common, or vulgar. —*adj.* **1.** of or relating to the common people of ancient Rome. **2.** relating to, belonging to, or characteristic of the common people. **3.** coarse; vulgar. [Latin *plēbēius* relating to the common people (from *plēbs* the common people) + -AN.]
pleb·i·scite (pleb′ə sīt′, -sit) *n.* direct vote by the people of a country or territory on a specific question submitted to them, usually concerning national self-determination or a choice of government or ruler. [Latin *plēbiscītum* decree of the people, from *plēbs* the common people + *scītum* decree.]
plebs (plebz) *pl.,* **ple·bes** (plē′bēz). *n.* **1.** the common people of ancient Rome. **2.** the common people. [Latin *plēbs* the common people.]
plec·trum (plek′trəm) *pl.,* **-trums** or **-tra** (-trə). *also,* **plec·tron** (plek′tron). *n.* small, thin implement of horn, plastic, or other material, used for plucking the strings of a guitar or similar instrument. Also, **pick.** [Latin *plectrum,* from Greek *plēktron.*]
pled (pled) a past tense and past participle of **plead.**
pledge (plej) *n.* **1.** binding assurance of the fulfillment or performance of some act, agreement, or duty; promise. **2.** something given or held as security to guarantee fulfillment of an agreement or obligation, or payment of a debt. **3.** state of being given or held as security. **4.** something given as a sign of affection or favor or as an assurance of something to come; token. **5.** person who is undergoing a trial period before attaining full membership in a fraternity or similar organization. **6.** expression or assurance of allegiance or good will conveyed by drinking a person's health; toast. **7. to take the pledge.** to promise not to drink alcoholic beverages. —*v.t.,* **pledged, pledg·ing.** **1.** to offer or guarantee with a pledge; promise solemnly or formally. **2.** to bind or commit by or as by a pledge: *We were all pledged to secrecy.* **3.** to give (something) as security or guarantee, as for the payment of a debt. **4.** to drink a toast to: *The knights pledged their lord's health.* **5.** to undergo a trial period before attaining full membership in (a fraternity or similar organization). [Old French *plege* surety, security, from Late Latin *plebium* security, of Germanic origin.] —**Syn.** *v.t.* **1.** see promise.
Ple·ia·des (plē′ə dēz′) *sing.* **Ple·iad** (plē′əd). *n.,pl.* **1.** *Greek Mythology.* seven daughters of Atlas, who were placed in the sky as stars by Zeus. **2.** group of approximately 200 stars in the constellation Taurus that, to the naked eye, appears to number six or seven stars.
Plei·o·cene (plī′ə sēn′) *n.* Pliocene.
Pleis·to·cene (plīs′tə sēn′) *n.* first geological epoch of the Quaternary period of the Cenozoic era, during which glaciers advanced and receded over large areas of North and South America, Europe, and Asia and during which man appeared. Also, **Ice Age.** See geology for table. —*adj.* of, relating to, or belonging to this epoch. [Greek *pleistos* most + *kainos* new.]
ple·na·ry (plē′nər ē, plen′ər ē) *adj.* **1.** attended by all qualified members: *a plenary session of a legislative assembly.* **2.** complete; absolute; perfect: *plenary goodness.* [Late Latin *plēnārius,* from Latin *plēnus* full.]
plen·i·po·ten·ti·ar·y (plen′i pə ten′chər ē, -chē er′ē) *pl.,* **-ar·ies.** *n.* ambassador or other diplomatic agent having full power in representing his government and negotiating with other countries. —*adj.* having or bestowing full power. [Medieval Latin *plenipotentiarius,* from Latin *plēnus* full + *potentia* power.]
plen·i·tude (plen′i tōōd′, -tūd′) *n.* **1.** plentiful amount; abundance. **2.** quality or state of being full. [Latin *plēnitūdō.*]

at; āpe; cär; end; mē; it; īce; hot; ōld; fôrk; wood; fōōl; oil; out; up; ūse; turn; sing; thin; this; zh in treasure; ə in ago, taken, pencil, lemon, circus.

plen·te·ous (plen′tē əs) *adj.* plentiful. **—plen′te·ous·ly,** *adv.* **—plen′te·ous·ness,** *n.*

plen·ti·ful (plen′ti fəl) *adj.* **1.** existing in great quantity; abundant; ample. **2.** providing or yielding an abundance: *a plentiful harvest.* **—plen′ti·ful·ly,** *adv.* **—plen′ti·ful·ness,** *n.* **—Syn. 1.** see **abundant.**

plen·ty (plen′tē) *pl.,* **-ties.** *n.* **1.** full or totally sufficient supply or amount; more than enough: *There's plenty of food for everybody.* **2.** quality or state of being plentiful; abundance: *Resources in plenty can be found in this territory.* **3.** abundance of the necessities and comforts of life: *an era of peace and plenty.* **—adj.** more than enough; plentiful; abundant: *Half a watermelon is plenty for me.* **—adv.** *Informal.* with some to spare; quite; very: *He'll be plenty mad when he finds out.* [Old French *plente* abundance, from Latin *plēnitās* fullness.]

ple·o·nasm (plē′ə naz′əm) *n.* **1.** use of more words than are necessary to express an idea; redundancy. **2.** instance of this. [Late Latin *pleonasmus,* from Greek *pleonasmos* excess, surplus.] **—ple·o·nas·tic** (plē′ə nas′tik), *adj.* **—ple′o·nas′ti·cal·ly,** *adv.*

ple·si·o·saur (plē′sē ə sôr′) *n.* any of a group of extinct water-dwelling dinosaurs, suborder Plesiosauria, of the Mesozoic era, having a small head, long neck, and four paddlelike limbs. Also, **ple′si·o·sau′rus.** [Greek *plēsios* near + *sauros* lizard.]

pleth·o·ra (pleth′ər ə) *n.* **1.** excess; superabundance. **2.** *Medicine.* excess of any body fluid, esp. an increase in the quantity of blood. [Modern Latin *plēthōra,* from Greek *plēthōrē.*]

ple·thor·ic (ple thôr′ik, -thor′-, pleth′ər ik) *adj.* **1.** excessively full; inflated; turgid. **2.** *Medicine.* relating to, characteristic of, or affected by plethora.

pleu·ra (ploor′ə) *pl.,* **pleu·rae** (ploor′ē). *n.* thin, serous membrane enclosing the lungs and lining the inner walls of the chest cavity. [Modern Latin *pleura,* from Greek *pleurā* side, rib.] **—pleu′ral,** *adj.*

pleu·ri·sy (ploor′ə sē) *n.* inflammation of the pleura, often accompanied by fever, difficulty in breathing, and a painful cough. Also, **pleu·ri·tis** (ploo rī′tis). [Old French *pleurisie,* from Late Latin *pleurisis,* going back to Greek *pleurītis,* from *pleurā* side, rib.] **—pleu·rit·ic** (ploo rit′ik), *adj.*

Plex·i·glas (plek′si glas′) *n. Trademark.* transparent, thermoplastic, acrylic resin used for such items as canopies and windows in aircraft.

plex·us (plek′səs) *pl.,* **-us·es** or **-us.** *n.* network or interlacing, as of nerves or blood vessels. [Latin *plexus* a twining.]

pli·a·ble (plī′ə bəl) *adj.* **1.** readily yielding to force or pressure without breaking; flexible. **2.** easily influenced or persuaded; yielding: *a pliable clay.* **3.** readily adjusting to change; adaptable. [French *pliable,* from *plier* to bend, fold, from Latin *plicāre* to fold.] **—pli′a·bil′i·ty, pli′a·ble·ness,** *n.* **—pli′a·bly,** *adv.*

Syn. 1. Pliable, ductile, malleable mean capable of being fashioned easily into a different shape or form. **Pliable** suggests being flexible enough to be easily bent or twisted: *The young tree's branches were pliable.* **Ductile** suggests the quality of being soft and pliant enough to be molded into any desired shape: *The art class heated wax to make it ductile and then molded it into shapes.* **Malleable** suggests a capacity for being hammered, beaten, or pressed into any shape: *The malleable metal was beaten into thin sheets.*

pli·an·cy (plī′ən sē) *n.* quality or state of being pliant.

pli·ant (plī′ənt) *adj.* **1.** capable of being bent with ease; supple. **2.** easily influenced or controlled; yielding; docile. [Old French *pliant,* present participle of *plier* to bend, fold.] **—Syn. 1.** see **PLIABLE.** **—pli′ant·ly,** *adv.*

pli·cate (plī′kāt) *adj.* folded like a fan; pleated. [Latin *plicātus,* past participle of *plicāre* to fold.]

pli·ers (plī′ərz) *n.,pl.* small pincers with parallel, often toothed jaws, used chiefly for gripping or bending objects. ▲ usually construed as plural, but sometimes construed as singular: *The pliers are in the drawer. The pliers is on the table.* [From PLY.]

Pliers

plight[1] (plīt) *n.* unfortunate, distressing, or dangerous situation or condition. [Anglo-Norman *plit* a fold, going back to Latin *plicitus,* past participle of *plicāre* to fold.]

plight[2] (plīt) *v.t.* **1.** to bind by a pledge; pledge; promise. **2. to plight one's troth.** to promise oneself in marriage. [Old English *plihtan* to endanger, from *pliht* danger.]

plink (plingk) *n.* light, sharp, high sound, as that made on a piano. **—v.i.** to make such a sound. **—v.t.** to cause to make such a sound: *to plink a banjo.* [Imitative.]

plinth (plinth) *n.* **1.** slab, block, stone, or other projecting member,

Plinth

usually square, forming the lowest part of a base upon which a column, pedestal, or the like rests. **2.** horizontal projecting course of masonry at the base of a wall or building. [Latin *plinthus* base of a column, from Greek *plinthos* brick.]

Plin·y (plin′ē) **1. the Elder.** A.D. 23–79, Roman author, scholar, and naturalist; born Gaius Plinius Secundus. **2. the Younger.** A.D. 62–c.113, his nephew; Roman writer and orator; born Gaius Plinius Caecilius Secundus.

Pli·o·cene (plī′ə sēn′) *also,* **Plei·o·cene.** *n.* fifth and last geological epoch of the Tertiary period of the Cenozoic era, during which most of the major mountain ranges were uplifted and herbaceous plants appeared. See **geology** for table. **—adj.** of, relating to, or belonging to this epoch. [Greek *pleion* more + *kainos* new, recent.]

Pli·o·film (plī′ə film′) *n. Trademark.* transparent, pliant plastic used to make raincoats and for wrappings.

plod (plod) **plod·ded, plod·ding.** *v.i.* **1.** to walk or move slowly and laboriously; trudge: *The tired patrol silently plodded through the snowdrifts.* **2.** to work or proceed slowly, laboriously, and with stolid perseverance: *to plod through a difficult book.* **—v.t.** to trudge slowly and heavily along, over, or through. **—n.** act of walking or moving slowly and laboriously. [Imitative.] **—plod′der,** *n.*

plop (plop) **plopped, plop·ping.** *v.i.* **1.** to drop or fall heavily, with or as with a sound like that of an object dropping into water: *She plopped on the bed and kicked off her shoes.* **—v.t.** to drop or let fall so as to make such a sound. **—n.** act or sound of plopping. **—adv.** with a plop: *He fell plop into the puddle.* [Imitative.]

plo·sive (plō′siv, -ziv) *Phonetics. adj.* pronounced with a sudden letting go of breath, as the consonants *p, b, d,* and *k.* **—n.** plosive speech sound. Also, **ex·plo′sive.**

plot (plot) *n.* **1.** secret, underhanded, or devious plan, esp. to accomplish some evil or illegal purpose: *a plot to take over the government.* **2.** main story or order of incidents in a play, novel, or other literary work. **3.** small piece of ground, usually used for a specific purpose: *a cemetery plot.* **4.** chart, diagram, or map, as of a building or estate. **—v.t. plot·ted, plot·ting. 1.** to devise a plot for: *to plot the downfall of a regime.* **2.** to make a diagram or map of; chart: *to plot a ship's course.* **3.** to mark the position of or show on a diagram or map: *All the fireboxes are plotted on this map of the city.* **4.** *Mathematics.* **a.** to locate and mark (a point or set of points) in a plane or in space by means of coordinates. **b.** to draw (a curve) by joining points so marked. **c.** to represent (an equation) by drawing such a curve. **—v.i.** to form or devise a plot; scheme. [Partly from Old English *plot* piece of ground; partly short for earlier *complot* secret plan (from Old French *complot;* of uncertain origin); partly modification of PLAT[1].] **—plot′ter,** *n.*

Syn. n. 1. Plot, intrigue, conspiracy mean a secret plan devised to accomplish an evil end. **Plot** suggests a treacherous plan that has been carefully constructed: *A plot to assassinate the president was uncovered by government agents.* **Intrigue** suggests a more complex scheme that may be far-reaching and involve many people: *The king was not aware of the intrigues of his ministers.* **Conspiracy** is a more sinister word to suggest a plot involving two or more persons who plan together to commit a serious crime: *The commission found no evidence to suggest a conspiracy to assassinate the president.*

Plov·div (plôv′dif′ -div′) *n.* city in south-central Bulgaria. Pop. (1968 est.), 234,-547.

plo·ver (pluv′ər, plō′vər) *n.* any of various shore birds, family Charadriidae, having a straight, pointed bill. Length: 6–16 inches. [Anglo-Norman *plover,* going back to Latin *pluvia* rain; because it was thought to be seen most often during a rainy season.]

Plover

plow (plou) *also,* **plough.** *n.* **1.** farm implement for turning over or breaking up the soil in preparation for sowing or planting, usually drawn by animals or a tractor. **2.** any of various devices resembling a plow in shape or function, as a snowplow. **—v.t. 1.** to break and turn up the surface of (soil) with a plow: *to plow a field.* **2.** to form or make with or as if with a plow: *We plowed our way through the crowd in front of the theater.* **3.** to furrow, tear, or gash with or as with a plow (often with *up*): *The plane plowed up the airstrip during its forced landing.* **4.** to dig out, remove, or expose with or as with a plow (often with *up*): *Farmers occasionally plow up old Indian relics.* **5.** to cleave the surface of or move through (water) like a plow. **6.** to clear the snow from with a snowplow or similar device: *to plow a driveway.* **7. to plow back.** to put back in the same business or enterprise: *All the profits were plowed back into the farm.* **8. to plow under. a.** to cover or bury, as crops, by plowing. **b.** *Informal.* to overwhelm: *We are plowed under with work.* **—v.i. 1.** to break and turn up soil with a plow.

at; āpe; cär; end; mē; it; īce; hot; ōld; fôrk; wood; fōol; oil; out; up; ūse; turn; sing; thin; this; zh in treasure; ə in ago, taken, pencil, lemon, circus.

771

2. to undergo plowing; admit of being plowed: *Hard earth doesn't plow well.* **3.a.** to advance forcefully and often with difficulty, through or as through hindrances; move, as a plow does. **b.** to proceed steadily, laboriously, or doggedly: *He plowed through the assigned books in one evening.* **4.** *Informal.* to crash into with violent, jarring force: *The bus went out of control and plowed into a truck.* [Old English *plōg* area of land that can be tilled by eight oxen in a year, from Old Norse *plōgr* the farm implement.]

plow·boy (plou′boi′) *also,* **plough·boy.** *n.* **1.** boy who leads or guides the animal or animals drawing a plow. **2.** country boy.

plow·man (plou′mən) *pl.,* **-men.** *also,* **plough·man.** *n.* **1.** man who guides or operates a plow. **2.** farmer; rustic.

plow·share (plou′shâr′) *also,* **plough·share.** *n.* leading edge or blade of a plow, which cuts the soil.

ploy (ploi) *n.* tricky maneuver or piece of strategy: *Her tears are only a ploy to gain attention.* [Scottish *ploy* enterprise, trick, possibly short for EMPLOY.]

pluck (pluk) *v.t.* **1.** to pull out or off; pick: *to pluck the feathers from a chicken.* **2.** to remove something, as feathers, from (something) by plucking: *to pluck one's eyebrows.* **3.a.** to pull with sudden force or with a jerk; snatch: *He plucked the letter from her hands.* **b.** to pull, grasp, or tug at: *to pluck someone's sleeve.* **4.** to pull on and quickly release (the strings of a musical instrument), causing them to sound. **5.** *Slang.* to rob; swindle; cheat. —*v.i.* **1.** to give a pull; grasp; tug (with *at*): *The prisoner plucked at the king's robe and begged for mercy.* **2. to pluck up.** to summon or gather up; rouse: *to pluck up one's courage.* —*n.* **1.** courage, spirit, and determination, esp. as shown in the face of danger or difficulty. **2.** act of pulling; tug; jerk. [Old English *pluccian* to pull off, pick'.]

pluck·y (pluk′ē) **pluck·i·er, pluck·i·est.** *adj.* having or showing courage, spirit, and determination, esp. in the face of danger or difficulty. —**pluck′i·ly,** *adv.* —**pluck′i·ness,** *n.*

plug (plug) *n.* **1.** piece of wood, rubber, or other material used to stop up a hole or fill a gap. **2.** male fitting with two or three prongs, attached to the end of a wire or cable and inserted into a female outlet or receptacle to make an electrical connection. **3.** cake of pressed or twisted tobacco, or a piece of it cut off for chewing. **4.** spark plug (*def. 1*). **5.** fireplug. **6.** *Informal.* favorable mention of or piece of publicity about a product, person, or enterprise, esp. one that is unrelated to the subject at hand: *He managed to sneak in a plug for his new movie during the interview.* **7.** *Slang.* old, worn-out, or inferior horse. —*v.t.,* **plugged, plug·ging. 1.** to stop or fill with or as if with a plug (often with *up*): *The coffee grains plugged up the kitchen drain.* **2.** to insert the plug of (an electrically powered device) into an outlet or receptacle to make an electrical connection (with *in*): *Plug in the toaster.* **3.** *Informal.* **a.** to insert a plug for; make favorable public mention of. **b.** to publicize frequently or insistently, as by repeated exposure or advertisements: *This disc jockey keeps plugging his wife's latest record.* **4.** *Slang.* to hit with a bullet; shoot. —*v.i. Informal.* to work doggedly or persistently: *Keep on plugging for that raise.* [Middle Dutch *plugge* wooden peg.] —**plug′ger,** *n.*

plug·ug·ly (plug′ug′lē) *pl.,* **-lies.** *n. Slang.* hoodlum; thug.

plum (plum) *n.* **1.** edible round or oval fruit of a tree, genus *Prunus,* of the rose family, having a flattened pit, soft, juicy flesh, and smooth skin that may be purple, red, yellow, or green. **2.** tree bearing this fruit, having oval leaves and small white or pink flowers. **3.** something choice or desirable, as a fine job or position: *The supporter was given a political plum for his contributions to the campaign.* **4.** dark, reddish-purple or bluish-red color. **5.** raisin, when added to a pudding or other dish. **6.** sugarplum. [Old English *plūme* the fruit, going back to Latin *prūnum,* from Greek *proumnon.* Doublet of PRUNE.]

plum·age (plŏŏ′mij) *n.* feathers of a bird collectively. [Old French *plumage,* from *plume* feather. See PLUME.]

plumb (plum) *v.t.* **1.** to test or adjust by a plumb line. **2.** to measure the depth of (a body of water) with or as with a plumb line; sound: *They plumbed the river to mark a channel for ships.* **3.** to discover or examine closely the dimensions, nature, or contents of: *to plumb a mystery.* **4.** to make vertical; straighten (often with *up*). **5.** to seal with lead. —*adj.* **1.** vertical. **2.** *Informal.* complete; absolute: *He's a plumb fool. That's plumb nonsense.* —*adv.* **1.** in a vertical direction or line; vertically: *The wall must run plumb.* **2.** *Informal.* completely; absolutely: *She's plumb crazy.* —*n.* **1.** plumb bob. **2. out of** (or **off**) **plumb.** not vertical. [Old French *plomb* lead, plumb bob, from Latin *plumbum* lead.]

plum·ba·go (plum bā′gō) *n.* graphite. [Latin *plumbāgō* lead ore, from *plumbum* lead.]

plumb bob, weight, often pointed, at the end of a plumb line. Also, **plumb, plum′met.**

plumb·er (plum′ər) *n.* one who installs and repairs plumbing. [Old French *plommier,* from Latin *plumbārius,* from *plumbum* lead; because plumbers originally worked with lead.]

plumb·ing (plum′ing) *n.* **1.** pipes, fixtures, and other apparatus involved in the use of water and the disposal of sewage in a building or other structure. **2.** work or trade of a plumber.

plumb line, line from which a weight is suspended, used to measure depths, as of excavations or bodies of water, or to determine whether something is vertical. Also, **plum′met.**

plume (plŏŏm) *n.* **1.** large, fluffy, showy feather. **2.** ornament consisting of a plume or cluster of plumes, or of a feathery tuft of fluffy material. **3.** something resembling a plume: *a plume of smoke.* —*v.t.,* **plumed, plum·ing. 1.** to adorn or furnish with or as with a plume or plumes. **2.** (of a bird) to smooth or dress (itself) with the beak; preen. [Old French *plume* feather, from Latin *plūma.*]

plum·met (plum′it) *v.i.* **1.** to fall or drop straight downward; plunge. —*n.* **1.** plumb bob. **2.** plumb line. [Old French *plommet* plumb bob, diminutive of *plomb* lead. See PLUMB.]

plu·mose (plŏŏ′mōs) *adj.* **1.** having feathers or plumes. **2.** like a plume or feather; feathery. [Latin *plūmōsus* full of feathers, from *plūma* feather.]

plump¹ (plump) *adj.* having a full or rounded form; somewhat fat or well filled out: *a plump child, a plump cushion.* —*v.t.* to make plump (often with *up* or *out*): *She plumped up the pillows on the couch.* —*v.i.* to become plump (with *up* or *out*). [Possibly from Middle Dutch *plomp* blunt, stupid.] —**plump′ly,** *adv.* —**plump′ness,** *n.*

plump² (plump) *v.i.* **1.** to fall or drop heavily, suddenly, or with abrupt impact: *He plumped down onto the sofa.* **2.** to support someone or something completely and enthusiastically (with *for*): *to plump for the election of a candidate.* —*v.t.* to throw, put, or let fall heavily or abruptly. —*adv.* **1.** directly; exactly; straight: *The shed was built plump in the middle of the oil field.* **2.** with an abrupt impact; heavily; suddenly: *He fell plump on the bed.* **3.** with no qualifications; bluntly. —*adj.* downright; blunt: *a plump denial.* —*n.* **1.** heavy or abrupt fall. **2.** sound made by such a fall. [Imitative.]

plum pudding, boiled or steamed pudding containing flour, suet, eggs, raisins, currants, and spices.

plu·mule (plŏŏ′mūl) *n.* **1.** small downy feather. **2.** bud that is part of the embryo in a seed and that develops into the first growing shoot of the plant. [Latin *plūmula* little feather, diminutive of *plūma* feather.]

plum·y (plŏŏ′mē) *adj.* **1.** covered or adorned with feathers or plumes. **2.** like a plume; feathery.

plun·der (plun′dər) *v.t.* **1.** to ravage or rob by open force, as during a war: *to plunder a town.* **2.** to take wrongfully or by force; steal: *to plunder goods.* —*v.i.* to engage in plundering. —*n.* **1.** that which is taken by plundering; booty; loot. **2.** act of plundering. [German *plündern* to pillage, from Middle High German *plunder* household effects.] —**plun′der·er,** *n.*

plunge (plunj) **plunged, plung·ing.** *v.t.* **1.** to put, cast, or insert forcefully or suddenly; thrust: *to plunge one's hand into water.* **2.** to force or place abruptly or forcibly into some condition, state, or course of action: *A power failure plunged the room into darkness.* —*v.i.* **1.** to dive, fall, or otherwise move suddenly or sharply in a downward direction: *The elevator plunged three stories when the cable snapped.* **2.** to move quickly, suddenly, or with a headlong lunge: *The thief plunged into the crowd and disappeared from sight.* **3.** to enter or fall headlong into some condition, state, or course of action: *to plunge into war.* **4.** to descend, dip, or extend downward suddenly: *The road plunges toward the beach.* —*n.* act or motion of plunging. [Old French *plongier* going back to Latin *plumbum* lead.] —**Syn.** *v.t.* **1.** see **dip.**

plung·er (plun′jər) *n.* **1.** device consisting of a rubber suction cup attached to the end of a long handle, used to unclog toilets and drains. **2.** any device or machine that works with a plunging or thrusting motion, esp. a piston when it is part of a pump. **3.** one who or that which plunges.

plunk (plungk) *Informal. v.t.* **1.** to pluck or strum the strings of (a musical instrument). **2.** to throw or put heavily or abruptly (often with *down*): *He plunked down all his change.* —*v.i.* **1.** to drop or fall heavily or abruptly. **2.** to give out a twanging sound, as a banjo. —*n.* **1.** act or sound of plunking. **2.** heavy, direct blow. —*adv.* **1.** directly; exactly: *The arrow hit plunk in the center of the target.* **2.** with a plop or a twanging or thudding sound. [Imitative.]

Plunger

plu·per·fect (plŏŏ pur′fikt) *Grammar. n.* the past perfect. —*adj.* of, relating to, or designating the past perfect. [Short for Latin *(tempus) plūs quam perfectum* more than perfect (tense).]

plupf., pluperfect.

plur., plural.

plu·ral (plŏŏr′əl) *adj.* **1.** containing, consisting of, or relating to more than one. **2.** of or relating to a grammatical form that denotes more than one. —*n.* form of a word denoting more than one. *Doors* is the

at; āpe; cär; end; mē; it; īce; hot; ōld; fôrk; wood; fŏŏl; oil; out; up; ūse; turn; sing; thin; this; zh in treasure; ə in ago, taken, pencil, lemon, circus.

plural of *door*, and *women* is the plural of *woman*. [Latin *plūrālis* relating to more than one, from *plūs* more.] —**plu′ral·ly,** *adv.*

plu·ral·ism (ploor′ə liz′əm) *n.* **1.** existence within a nation or society of a number of different ethnic, religious, racial, or social groups, who have individual interests and who often form diverse institutions and organizations representing these respective interests. **2.** quality or state of being plural. **3.** *Philosophy.* theory that reality or the universe has many basic elements or aspects. Distinguished from **dualism** and **monism.** —**plu′ral·ist,** *n., adj.* —**plu′ral·is′tic,** *adj.*

plu·ral·i·ty (ploo ral′ə tē) *pl.* **-ties.** *n.* **1.a.** number of votes that a winning candidate receives over and above the number cast for his nearest opponent. **b.** number of votes cast for any one candidate in a contest of more than two candidates, that is greater than the number cast for anyone else, but not greater than one-half of the total votes cast. **2.** state or fact of being plural.

plus (plus) *prep.* **1.** increased by; added to: *Two plus two is four.* **2.** with the addition of; together with: *The set consists of a table plus chairs.* —*adj.* **1.** somewhat higher than: *a grade of C plus.* **2.** involving or characterized by advantage or desirability: *a big plus factor that outweighs other considerations.* **3.** *Mathematics.* of, relating to, or denoting a quantity that is greater than zero; positive. **4.** *Electricity.* positive. **5.** *Informal.* and more: *a girl with personality plus.* —*n. pl.,* **plus·es.** **1.** plus sign. **2.** added, favorable, or advantageous factor or quality: *His good record is a plus in his favor.* **3.** positive quantity. [Latin *plūs* more.]

plus fours, loose knickers that extend below the knee, formerly worn for sports activities, as golf.

plush (plush) *adj.* exhibiting or characteristic of an abundance of wealth; luxurious: *a plush hotel.* —*n.* fabric similar to but having a deeper pile than velvet, used esp. for upholstery. [French *peluche* the fabric, going back to Latin *pilus* hair.] —**plush′y,** *adj.*

plus sign, symbol (+) used to indicate addition or a positive quantity.

Plu·tarch (plōō′tärk) *n.* A.D. c.46–c.120, Greek essayist and biographer.

Plu·to (plōō′tō) *n.* **1.** Greek god of the dead and ruler of the underworld. His Roman counterpart is Dis. Also, **Ha′des. 2.** planet furthest and ninth in order of distance from the sun.

plu·toc·ra·cy (plōō tok′rə sē) *pl.* **-cies.** *n.* **1.** government by the wealthy. **2.** government or state in which the wealthy rule. **3.** controlling or influential class of wealthy persons, esp. a wealthy class that rules such a government or state. [Greek *ploutokratiā* government by the wealthy, from *ploutos* wealth + *-kratiā* power, rule.]

plu·to·crat (plōō′tə krat′) *n.* **1.** one who has power or influence because of his wealth. **2.** wealthy person.

plu·to·crat·ic (plōō′tə krat′ik) *adj.* of, relating to, or resembling plutocrats or plutocracy. Also, **plu′to·crat′i·cal.** —**plu′to·crat′i·cal·ly,** *adv.*

Plu·to·ni·an (plōō tō′nē ən) *adj.* of, relating to, or suggesting Pluto or the underworld.

plu·ton·ic (plōō ton′ik) *adj.* **1.** (of igneous rocks) formed and crystallized far beneath the earth's crust. **2.** *also,* **Plutonic.** of or relating to the theory that much of the rock in the earth's crust was formed by the cooling of molten material from deep within the earth. **3. Plutonic.** Plutonian. [From *Pluto* Greek god of the underworld.]

plu·to·ni·um (plōō tō′nē əm) *n.* silvery, radioactive, metallic element with several isotopes, important as a fuel in nuclear reactors and as the fission material in atomic bombs. Symbol: **Pu** See **element** for table. [Modern Latin *plutonium,* from *Pluto* the planet.]

Plu·tus (plōō′təs) *n.* *Classical Mythology.* the god of wealth, blinded by Zeus so he would distribute riches without regard to merit.

plu·vi·al (plōō′vē əl) *adj.* **1.** of or relating to rain. **2.** caused by the action of rain. [Latin *pluviālis* rainy, from *pluvia* rain.]

plu·vi·om·e·ter (plōō′vē om′ə tər) *n.* rain gauge. [Latin *pluvia* rain + -METER.]

plu·vi·ous (plōō′vē əs) *adj.* of or characterized by rain; rainy.

ply[1] (plī) **plied, ply·ing.** *v.t.* **1.** to use, wield, or apply diligently or vigorously: *The crew plied their oars.* **2.** to work at or pursue steadily; practice: *to ply one's trade.* **3.** to act upon; work on: *to ply clay with potter's tools.* **4.** to provide frequently or persistently, as if attempting to cajole or persuade: *to ply someone with liquor.* **5.** to address or harass repeatedly in a pressing way: *The lawyer plied the witness with questions.* **6.** to travel or traverse regularly: *The boat plies the route from the island to the mainland.* —*v.i.* **1.** to travel or traverse the same course regularly. **2.** to work busily or steadily. [Short for APPLY.]

ply[2] (plī) *pl.* **plies.** *n.* **1.** fold or layer, as of cloth or wood. **2.** one of the strands twisted together to make yarn, rope, or similar material. ▲ Both noun defs. are used in combination to indicate a specified number of layers or strands: *two-ply tissues, three-ply yarn.* [Old French *pli* a fold[1], bend, from *plier* to fold[1], bend, from Latin *plicāre* to fold[1].]

Plym·outh (plim′əth) *n.* **1.** town in southeastern Massachusetts, on the Atlantic, settled in 1620 by the Pilgrims. Pop. (1970), 18,606.

2. seaport in southwestern England, on the English Channel. Pop. (1968), 246,300.

Plymouth Colony, first English settlement in New England, founded by the Pilgrims at Plymouth, Massachusetts, in 1620.

Plymouth Rock 1. rock at Plymouth, Massachusetts, on which the Pilgrims, according to tradition, first set foot in America in 1620. **2.** one of an American breed of domestic fowl, having white, buff, or blue plumage sometimes barred with gray.

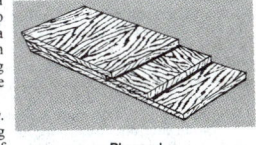

Plywood

ply·wood (plī′wood′) *n.* construction material consisting of a number of thin layers of wood glued together, with the grain of one layer at right angles to the grain of the next. [PLY[2] + WOOD.]

Pm, promethium.

p.m. 1. post meridiem. **2.** post-mortem.

P.M. 1. post meridiem. **2.** Prime Minister. **3.** Postmaster.

pneu·mat·ic (nōō mat′ik, nū-) *adj.* **1.** operated by or using the force of compressed air: *a pneumatic drill.* **2.** containing or filled with air, esp. compressed air: *a pneumatic tire.* **3.** of or relating to air or other gases or to pneumatics. [Latin *pneumaticus* relating to air or wind, from Greek *pneumatikos,* from *pneuma* air, wind.] —**pneu·mat′i·cal·ly,** *adv.*

pneu·mat·ics (nōō mat′iks, nū-) *n.,pl.* branch of physics that deals with the physical properties of air and other gases and with their action on stationary objects. ▲ construed as singular.

pneu·mo·ni·a (nōō mōn′ya, nū-) *n.* any of several diseases characterized by inflammation of the lungs, resulting esp. from a bacterial or viral infection. [Modern Latin *pneumonia,* from Greek *pneumoniā,* from *pneumōn* lung.]

Pnom·penh (pə nom′pen′) *also,* **Pnom-Penh.** *n.* Phnom Penh.

Po (pō) *n.* largest and longest river in Italy, in the northern part of the country, flowing into the Adriatic.

Po, polonium.

P.O., post office.

poach[1] (pōch) *v.t.* **1.** to cook (an egg) unbroken and without the shell in simmering water or in a receptacle placed above simmering water. **2.** to cook in simmering liquid: *to poach fish.* [Old French *pochier* originally, to put in a bag, from *poche* pocket, bag; of Germanic origin; because the white of the egg forms a pouchlike bag around the yolk.]

poach[2] (pōch) *v.i.* **1.** to hunt or fish illegally, as on another's property. **2.** to trespass for the purpose of taking game or fish. —*v.t.* **1.** to take (game or fish) illegally. **2.** to trespass on (property) for hunting or fishing. [Middle French *pocher* to encroach on, gouge; of Germanic origin.]

Po·ca·hon·tas (pō′kə hon′təs) *n.* c.1595–1617, American Indian princess, reputed to have saved the life of Captain John Smith.

pock (pok) *n.* **1.** pustule on the skin, caused by such diseases as smallpox and acne. **2.** scar or pit left by such a pustule. —*v.t.* to mark with or as if with pocks. [Old English *pocc* pustule.]

pock·et (pok′it) *n.* **1.** pouchlike compartment sewn into or on a garment, used esp. as a receptacle for small articles. **2.** something resembling a pocket in shape or function: *There are pockets inside the briefcase for loose notes.* **3.** isolated, usually small area or group, distinguished or different in some manner from a surrounding area or group: *a poverty pocket.* **4.** financial means or resources: *Inflation becomes a drain on everyone's pocket.* **5.** any of the pouches at the corners and sides of a pool or billiard table, into which the balls are driven. **6.** air pocket. **7.a.** cavity in the earth containing ore. **b.** small body or deposit of ore. —*adj.* adapted or intended to be carried in a pocket: *a pocket radio.* —*v.t.* **1.** to put in or as if in a pocket: *He pocketed his change and left.* **2.** to take possession of for one's own, esp. dishonestly. **3.** to confine or enclose, as in a pocket. **4.** to give no indication of, as emotions; suppress. **5.** to accept meekly or without protest, as an insult. **6.** to hit (a ball) into a pocket, as in pool. **7.** to exercise a pocket veto. [Anglo-Norman *pokete* little bag, diminutive of *poke* bag, sack; of Germanic origin.]

pocket billiards, pool[2] (def. 1).

pock·et·book (pok′it book′) *n.* **1.** bag or case, as of leather, used by women for carrying small articles. **2.** financial means, resources, or interests: *The company's failure will affect every stockholder's pocketbook.* **3.** *also,* **pocket book.** book, usually paperbound, small enough to be carried in a pocket.

pock·et·ful (pok′it fool′) *pl.* **-fuls.** *n.* amount that a pocket holds.

pocket gopher, gopher (def. 1).

pock·et·knife (pok′it nīf′) *pl.* **-knives.** *n.* knife with one or more blades that fold into the handle.

pocket money, spending money.

---

at; āpe; cär; end; mē; it; īce; hot; ōld; fôrk; wood; fōōl; out; up; ūse; turn; sing; thin; this; zh in treasure; ə in ago, taken, pencil, lemon, circus.

pocket veto 1. power of the president of the United States to veto a bill passed by Congress during the last ten days of a session by simply retaining the bill unsigned until Congress adjourns. **2.** similar power exercised by a chief executive, as a state governor.

pock·mark (pok′märk′) *n.* pit or scar left on the skin, as by smallpox or acne. —*v.t.* to mark with or as with pockmarks.

pod (pod) *n.* **1.** seed vessel, esp. of a leguminous plant, as a pea, that usually splits along two seams when it is ripe. **2.** container or covering resembling this, as a cocoon. **3.** separate enclosure on an aircraft, usually located beneath a wing, for housing fuel, an engine, cargo, or weapons. —*v.i.,* **pod·ded, pod·ding. 1.** to produce pods. **2.** to swell out into or as if into a pod. [Of uncertain origin.]

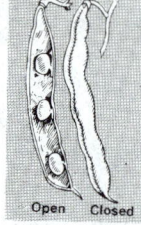

Open   Closed

Pods

pod- *combining form* **1.** foot: *podiatry.* **2.** having a specified number or kind of feet: *arthropod.* [Greek *pod-,* stem of *pous* foot.]

po·di·a·trist (pə dī′ə trist) *n.* one who is trained in and licensed to practice podiatry. Also, **chi·rop′o·dist.**

po·di·a·try (pə dī′ə trē) *n.* medical specialty that includes the diagnosis and treatment of diseases and injuries of the foot. Also, **chi·rop′o·dy.** [Greek *pod-,* stem of *pous* foot + *iātreiā* art of healing.]

po·di·um (pō′dē əm) *pl.* **-di·a** (-dē ə) or **-di·ums.** *n.* **1.** raised platform from which a conductor leads an orchestra. **2.** place or structure from which to address a group; lectern; rostrum. **3.** *Zoology & Anatomy.* foot or any structure serving as or resembling a foot. [Latin *podium* elevated place, from Greek *podion,* diminutive of *pous* foot.]

Po·dunk (pō′dungk′) *n. Informal.* any small, backward, or insignificant town.

Poe, Edgar Allan (pō) 1809–49, U.S. writer, poet, and critic.

po·em (pō′əm) *n.* **1.** composition usually designed to convey a complex, emotive, and intense sense of experience, written in some rhythmic scheme, and characterized by language regarded as more condensed and vivid than that of prose, often employing such devices as rhyme, meter, and metaphor. **2.** any literary composition written with an intensity or lyricism of language thought to be more characteristic of poetry than of prose. **3.** something having qualities or effects similar or likened to those of poetry. [Latin *poēma* composition in verse, from Greek *poiēma* a work, composition in verse.]

po·e·sy (pō′ə sē, -zē) *n. Archaic.* **1.** poems collectively; poetry. **2.** art of writing poetry. [Old French *poësie* poetry, going back to Latin *poēsis,* from Greek *poiēsis* a making, poetry.]

po·et (pō′it) *n.* **1.** one who writes poetry. **2.** person who is greatly sensitive to beauty and who expresses himself with imagination and lyricism. [Latin *poēta* maker, composer of verse, from Greek *poiētēs.*] —**po′et·ess,** *n.*

po·et·as·ter (pō′it as′tər) *n.* one who writes poor poetry; inferior poet. [Modern Latin *poetaster,* from Latin *poēta* poet + *-aster* (suffix indicating inferiority).]

po·et·ic (pō et′ik) *adj.* **1.** of or relating to poetry: *poetic genius, poetic works.* **2.** having a quality or style characteristic of poetry: *a poetic description.* **3.** characteristic of or showing the qualities of a poet. Also, **po·et′i·cal.** —**po·et′i·cal·ly,** *adv.*

poetic justice, ideal or appropriate distribution of reward and punishment as often represented in literature.

poetic license, deviation from a rule, standard, or fact for the sake of effect, as in works of literature.

po·et·ics (pō et′iks) *n.,pl.* branch of literary criticism that deals with the theory, nature, and forms of poetry. ▲ construed as singular.

poet laureate *pl.,* **poets laureate** or **poet laureates. 1.** in Great Britain, poet appointed for life by the sovereign as official poet of the royal household, and whose duties formerly included writing verses to commemorate state occasions. **2.** poet acclaimed as the most eminent of a locality or group.

po·et·ry (pō′i trē) *n.* **1.** poems collectively: *a volume of poetry.* **2.** writing or language characteristic of poems. **3.** art of writing poems. **4.** quality or effect considered characteristic of poetry: *the poetry of the ballerina's movements.* **5.** something having such quality or effect. [Medieval Latin *poetria* poetic art, from Latin *poēta.* See POET.]

po·go stick (pō′gō) stiltlike device consisting of a stick with footrests and a spring at its base, on which a person may move along by propelling himself in a series of bounds.

po·grom (pō grom′, pō′grəm) *n.* organized, often officially initiated persecution and massacre of a minority group, esp. of Jews. [Russian *pogrom* devastation.]

poi (poi) *n.* food of Hawaiian origin, made from taro root which is cooked, pounded into a paste, and fermented. [Hawaiian *poi.*]

poign·ant (poin′yənt) *adj.* **1.** evoking emotions, esp. sadness or melancholy; touching: *a poignant story of a son leaving for the war.* **2.** sharply felt; severe: *a poignant sense of loss.* **3.** sharp; penetrating. **4.** sharp or biting to the taste or smell; pungent. [Old French *poignant,* present participle of *poindre* to prick, from Latin *pungere.*] —**poign′-ance, poign′an·cy,** *n.* —**poign′ant·ly,** *adv.* —**Syn. 1.** see **touching.**

poin·ci·a·na (poin′sē an′ə) *n.* any of several tropical trees or shrubs, genus *Poinciana,* that bears clusters of large red, yellow, or orange flowers. [Modern Latin *Poinciana,* from M. de *Poinci,* a seventeenth-century governor of the French West Indies.]

poin·set·ti·a (poin set′ē ə, -set′ə) *n.* tropical American shrub, *Euphorbia pulcherrima,* bearing oval-shaped leaves and small flowers surrounded by showy red, pink, or white leaflike parts that resemble flower petals, widely used as a Christmas decoration. [Modern Latin *poinsettia,* from J. R. *Poinsett,* 1779–1851, U.S. diplomat who discovered it in Mexico.]

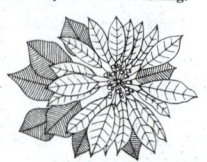

Poinsettia

point (point) *n.* **1.** sharp or tapering end: *the point of a pencil, the point of a knife.* **2.** something that has a sharp or tapering end, as a sword. **3.** tapering projection of land; cape; promontory. **4.** dot or other small mark used in writing or printing. **5.** punctuation mark, esp. a period. **6.** decimal point. **7.** *Geometry.* something having position, but no length, width, or height: *to draw a line between two points.* **8.** definite position; place; spot: *We stopped at all the points of interest.* **9.** definite position in or as in a scale: *the point at which a metal melts. She worked to the point of exhaustion.* **10.** particular moment or time, as when something happens or is about to happen: *At that point, he got up and left the room.* **11.** essential or important thing: *to keep to the point in a discussion.* **12.** main or most important idea: *the point of a story.* **13.** impressive or effective fact, idea, or argument: *You've got a point there.* **14.** object; purpose: *What's the point in telling her again?* **15.** item; detail: *He explained the plan point by point.* **16.a.** distinguishing mark or quality; trait; characteristic: *Being on time is not his strong point.* **b.** physical characteristic of an animal, esp. one by which the excellence or purity of the breed is judged. **17.** unit of count in a game: *Our team won by ten points.* **18.** unit equal to one dollar, used to quote current prices of stocks and commodities. **19.** unit of academic credit, equal to a certain number of hours of class work. **20.** *Printing.* unit for measuring type, approximately ¹/₇₂ inch. **21.a.** one of the thirty-two marks showing direction on a compass card. **b.** interval between any two such marks, equal to 11 degrees 15 minutes. **22.** needlepoint (def. 2). **23.** *British.* railroad switch. **24.** either of two electrical contacts that make or break the flow of current in a distributor, as in an automobile. **25.** branch of a deer's antler. **26.** small group that goes ahead of an advance unit in a military maneuver. **27. in point.** pertinent; apt: *a case in point.* **28. in point of.** as regards; with respect to: *In point of place the two stories of the accident agree.* **29. to make a point of.** to be resolved to; insist upon: *He always made a point of being on time.* **30. to stretch a point. a.** to make an exception or concession: *I'll stretch a point in your case and let you leave work early.* **b.** to exceed the reasonable limit: *You're stretching a point when you try to apply the rule to all the cases under discussion.* **31. to the point.** pertinent; apt: *His argument was short and to the point.* —*v.t.* **1.** to direct or aim, as a finger or weapon: *to point a gun at game.* **2.** to indicate with or as with the finger; direct attention to (usually with *out*): *to point her mistakes out to her, to point the way.* **3.** to give a point to; sharpen, as a pencil. **4.** to mark or separate with points or dots; punctuate: *to point a sentence.* **5.** to separate (figures) with points or dots (with *off*): *to point off two decimal places.* **6.** to give force or emphasis to (often with *up*): *to point one's remarks, to point up a moral.* **7.** (of a hunting dog) to indicate the presence and position of (game) by freezing in a rigid stance with the nose and body facing the quarry. **8.** to fill the joints of (brickwork) with mortar. —*v.i.* **1.** to indicate position or direction; direct attention with or as with the finger: *to point at a house.* **2.** to direct the mind or thought in a certain direction: *All the evidence points to his guilt.* **3.** to have a specified direction: *The house points toward the bay.* **4.** (of a hunting dog) to point game. **5.** (of a ship) to sail close to the wind. [Old French *point* mark, a pricking, and *pointe* something pointed, both going back to Latin *pungere* to prick.]

point-blank (point′blangk′) *adv.* **1.** from so close a range that missing a target is unlikely or impossible: *to fire point-blank at a target.* **2.** without hesitation or qualification; plainly and bluntly; flatly: *They asked him point-blank if he'd stolen the money.* —*adj.* **1.** pointed or aimed directly or straight at the mark. **2.** esp. from close range: *to be exposed to point-blank fire.* **2.** so close that missing a target is unlikely or impossible: *point-blank range.* **3.** plain and blunt: *a point-blank denial.*

at; āpe; cär; end; mē; it; īce; hot; ōld; fôrk; wood; fōōl; oil; out; up; ūse; turn; sing; thin; this; zh in treasure; ə in ago, taken, pencil, lemon, circus.

point·ed (poin'tid) *adj.* **1.** having or coming to a point or points: *a clown's pointed cap.* **2.** to the point; pertinent and incisive; cutting: *a pointed question.* **3.** clearly or particularly aimed at or referring to a person, group, or thing: *a pointed comment.* **4.** clearly evident; conspicuous; marked. —**point'ed·ly,** *adv.* —**point'-ed·ness,** *n.*

point·er (poin'tər) *n.* **1.** long, tapered stick used to point out things, as on a blackboard, chart, or map. **2.** short-haired dog having long ears, a long, tapering tail, and a smooth, solid-color or spotted coat. It hunts game birds by scent and points to their location. Height: 25 inches at the shoulder. **3.** needle, hand, or similar device, as on a scale or meter, indicating a recording or measurement; indicator. **4.** *Informal.* useful or instructive piece of information or advice; hint; suggestion. **5.** one who or that which points.

Pointer

poin·til·lism (pwänt'əl iz'əm, pwän'tē iz'əm, point'əl-) *n.* technique in painting originating in France during the 1880s and 1890s, consisting of applying to canvas or a similar surface small dots or dashes of pure, unmixed colors, the dots blending into recognizable forms and patterns through the optical processes of the spectator. [French *pointillisme,* from *pointiller* to dot, from *point* a dot, a mark. See POINT.]

point lace, needlepoint (*def. 2*).

point·less (point'lis) *adj.* **1.** without force, purpose, or concrete result; useless; ineffective: *a pointless attempt.* **2.** without meaning or relevance; inane: *a pointless remark, a pointless joke.* **3.** without a point or sharp or tapering end. —**point'less·ly,** *adv.* —**point'less·ness,** *n.*

point of honor, matter regarded as vitally affecting or relating to one's honor, reputation, or principles.

point of order, question raised as to whether the correct or appropriate parliamentary procedure is being observed.

point of view, **1.** manner of thinking, feeling, or acting; attitude. **2.** position from which something is considered or evaluated.

poise (poiz) *n.* **1.** relaxed and self-possessed composure, assurance, and dignity, esp. as expressed in one's manner or bearing. **2.** balance; equilibrium. —*v.t.,* **poised, pois·ing.** to place, carry, or hold in equilibrium: *The diver poised himself at the edge of the board.* —*v.i.* to be balanced, suspended, or held in equilibrium. [Old French *poiser, peser* to weigh, going back to Latin *pēnsāre* to weigh out.]

poised (poizd) *adj.* **1.** having a relaxed assurance and dignity of manner or bearing; composed; self-possessed. **2.** suspended, balanced, or hovering in or as in midair: *an eagle poised in flight.* **3.** being in a state of balance or equilibrium: *a diver poised on the edge of the pool.*

poi·son (poi'zən) *n.* **1.** any substance dangerous to life and health and causing serious injury, illness, or death by its chemical action on an organism. **2.** something to be detested or shunned as harmful, corrupting, or destructive: *a speaker who maintained that narcotics are poison.* —*v.t.* **1.** to administer poison to; injure or kill with poison. **2.** to put poison in, on, or into; cause to become harmful or deadly: *These minerals have poisoned the water.* **3.** to have a harmful, corrupting, or destructive effect on: *She poisoned his mind with ideas of hate and revenge.* —*adj.* poisonous. [Old French *poison* magic potion, poisonous drink, drink, from Latin *pōtiō.* Doublet of POTION.] —**poi'son·er,** *n.*

poison ivy, **1.** woody vine, *Rhus radicans,* of North America, having shiny leaves composed of three jagged oval leaflets and containing an oil in the stems, leaves, and roots that causes a rash when it comes in contact with the skin. **2.** rash caused by contact with any of these plants.

poison oak, **1.** slender woody plant, *Rhus toxicodendron,* growing in dry barrens and sandy regions of North America, related to poison ivy and causing a similar rash, and having leaves composed of three usually oval, often lobed, leaflets. **2.** rash caused by contact with this plant.

Poison ivy

Poison oak

Poison sumac

Poison oak

poi·son·ous (poi'zə nəs) *adj.* **1.** full of, containing, or constituting a poison: *a poisonous snake.* **2.** having a harmful, corrupting, or destructive effect: *a poisonous influence.* **3.** full of malice, spite, or ill will; malevolent: *a poisonous glance.* —**poi'son·ous·ly,** *adv.* —**poi'son·ous·ness,** *n.*

poison sumac, **1.** shrub or small tree, *Rhus vernix,* growing in swamps of eastern North America, related to poison ivy and causing a similar rash, and having leaves that consist of from seven to thirteen oblong or oval leaflets. **2.** rash caused by contact with this plant.

poke[1] (pōk) **poked, pok·ing.** *v.t.* **1.** to push into or against, as with something pointed; prod: *He poked the frog with a stick to make it jump.* **2.** to push; thrust: *She poked her head out of the window.* **3.** to make by or as if by pushing or thrusting: *The stick poked a hole in the drum.* **4.** *Informal.* to hit with the fist; strike; punch. —*v.i.* **1.** to make a pushing, thrusting, or prodding movement. **2.** to thrust forward or stick out; protrude; appear: *A tall tree trunk poked up out of the water.* **3.** to look, search, or investigate stealthily or curiously (often with *around* or *about*). **4.** to intrude or meddle; pry: *to poke into someone else's business.* **5.** to move or proceed slowly or lazily; dawdle: *We'll be late if you don't stop poking along.* —*n.* **1.** pushing, thrusting, or prodding movement. **2.** *Informal.* blow with the fist; punch. [Possibly from Middle Dutch *poken* to thrust, stick[2].]

poke[2] (pōk) *n.* bag; sack. [Dialectal Old French *poque;* of Germanic origin.]

poke·ber·ry (pōk'ber'ē) *pl.,* **-ries.** *n.* **1.** berry of the pokeweed. **2.** the pokeweed itself.

poke bonnet, bonnet having a large, deep, projecting brim in front.

Poke bonnet

pok·er[1] (pō'kər) *n.* metal rod for stirring a fire. **2.** one who or that which pokes. [POKE[1] + -ER[1].]

pok·er[2] (pō'kər) *n.* any of several card games in which the players bet on the value of their hands, the winner being the player having the hand of highest value of those who have stayed in the game. [Possibly from German *Pochspiel* a card game similar to poker, from *pochen* to brag.]

poker face, *Informal.* face held expressionless, as that of an expert poker player who does not want to reveal the nature of his hand.

poke·weed (pōk'wēd') *n.* coarse, strong-smelling weed, *Phytolacca americana,* found in eastern North America, having edible shoots, poisonous seeds, and fleshy roots and bearing pale-green flowers that ripen into juicy, deep-purple berries. Also, **poke'ber'ry, ink'ber'ry.**

po·key (pō'kē) *pl.,* **-keys.** *n. Slang.* jail.

pok·y (pō'kē) **pok·i·er, pok·i·est.** *also,* **pok·ey.** *adj.* extremely slow; dawdling. [POKE[1] + -Y[1].]

Pol., Poland; Polish.

Po·land (pō'lənd) *n.* country in central Europe, on the Baltic Sea. Capital, Warsaw. Area, 120,360 sq. mi. Pop. (1969 est.), 32,555,000.

Poland China, one of a breed of black-and-white hogs having white markings on the feet, face, and tail.

po·lar (pō'lər) *adj.* **1.** of or relating to a pole or poles, as of a magnet, battery, or sphere. **2.** relating to, near, or coming from the North or South Pole: *the polar icecap, a polar expedition.* **3.** directly opposite in character, action, or tendency. **4.** resembling a pole around which all other things revolve; central; pivotal. **5.** serving to guide or direct, as a polestar. [Modern Latin *polaris,* from Latin *polus* end of an axis. See POLE[2].]

polar bear, large white bear, *Thalarctos maritimus,* native to arctic regions. Length: to 9 feet.

Polar bear

polar body, one of the minute bodies or cells cast off during the maturation of an ovum.

polar circle, either of two parallels of latitude each at a distance of about 23 degrees 27 minutes from a pole of the earth; Arctic Circle or Antarctic Circle.

polar coordinates, *Mathematics.* either of two coordinates locating a point in a plane, one being the distance of the point from a fixed point on a fixed line and the other being the angle made by this fixed line with the line connecting the two points.

Po·lar·is (pō lar'is) *n.* star of the second magnitude, located very near the north celestial pole. It is the outermost star in the handle of the Little Dipper. Also, **North Star, pole'star'.**

po·lar·i·scope (pō lar'ə skōp') *n.* instrument for measuring or exhibiting the polarization of light, or for studying substances in polarized light.

po·lar·i·ty (pō lar'ə tē) *n.* **1.** possession by a body of two poles at opposite extremities, the properties of one pole being of an opposite or contrasting nature to the other, as in a magnet. **2.** condition of being either positive or negative with respect to electric or magnetic poles. **3.** condition of having or showing two opposite principles, tendencies, or qualities: *political polarity.*

po·lar·i·za·tion (pō'lər i zā'shən) *n.* **1.** *Optics.* condition, or the

production of a condition, in which the vibrations of light waves assume a definite form, esp. one in which the vibrations are confined to a single plane or direction. **2.** increase in the internal resistance of an electric cell, resulting in a drop in voltage. Polarization is usually caused by the deposit of gases produced during electrolysis on the electrodes of the cell. **3.** state of having polarity; act of producing polarity, as the concentration of groups or forces about two opposing positions.

po·lar·ize (pō′lə rīz′) **-ized, -iz·ing.** *v.t.* **1.** to cause polarization in; give polarity to: *to polarize light.* **2.** to cause to separate into opposing groups: *Disagreement over the government's policies threatened to polarize the country.* —*v.i.* to become polarized. [French *polariser* to cause polarization, from Modern Latin *polaris.* See POLAR.]

Po·lar·oid (pō′lə roid′) *n. Trademark.* **1.** transparent plastic material capable of polarizing light, used esp. in lamps and eyeglasses to reduce glare. **2.** portable camera that produces a finished print within seconds after exposure. Also (*def.* 2), **Polaroid Land Camera.**

pol·der (pōl′dər, pol′-) *n.* area of low land reclaimed from the sea or another body of water and protected by dikes, esp. in the Netherlands. [Dutch *polder.*]

pole¹ (pōl) *n.* **1.** long, slender, usually cylindrical piece of wood, metal, or other material: *a fishing pole.* **2.a.** unit of length equal to 5½ yards; rod. **b.** unit of area equal to 30¼ square yards; square rod. —*v.t.,* **poled, pol·ing.** to propel, push, or strike with a pole: *to pole a boat down a river.* [Old English *pāl* stake, from Latin *pālus.*]

pole² (pōl) *n.* **1.a.** either end of the earth's axis; North Pole or South Pole. **b.** one of the two points where the axis of any rotating sphere intersects the surface of the sphere. **c.** celestial pole. **2.** either of two regions or parts at which opposite forces are concentrated or appear to originate, as the ends of a magnet or the terminals of an electric battery. **3.** *Biology.* either end of the main axis of a nucleus, cell, or ovum, at or near which certain parts are symmetrically arranged. **4.** *Mathematics.* the point of origin, or fixed point, in a system of polar coordinates. **5.** any fixed point of reference or guidance. **6.** either of two directly opposed opinions, principles, or ideas: *Their political beliefs are at opposite poles.* **7. poles apart.** wholly or completely opposite in nature, opinions, beliefs, or values: *The two candidates are poles apart on many of the issues.* [Latin *polus* end of an axis, from Greek *polos* pivot, axis.]

Pole (pōl) *n.* member or close descendant of the people of Poland.

pole·ax (pōl′aks′) *also,* **pole·axe.** *n.* battle-ax having a long handle, esp. one with a hook, spike, or hammer opposite the blade. [Middle English *pollax* literally, head ax, from *pol* head (see POLL) + *ax.* See AX.]

pole bean, any of various cultivated climbing beans having long vine-like stems that twine around poles or other supports.

pole·cat (pōl′kat′) *n.* **1.** small, carnivorous European mammal, *Mustela putorius,* closely related to the weasel and ferret and having long, soft, buff-gray fur. It sprays a foul-smelling liquid when attacked or frightened. Length: to 30 inches including tail. **2.** skunk. [Middle English *polcat,* possibly from Old French *po(u)le* hen (going back to Latin *pullus* young fowl) + CAT; possibly because it steals chickens.]

po·lem·ic (pə lem′ik) *n.* **1.** argument or controversial discussion, esp. a refutation of or attack on a particular opinion, doctrine, or theory. **2. polemics.** art or practice of disputation or controversy. ▲ construed as singular. **3.** one who engages in controversy or argument. —*adj. also,* **po·lem′i·cal,** of or relating to controversy or dispute. [Greek *polemikos* warlike, from *polemos* war.] —**po·lem′i·cal·ly,** *adv.*

po·lem·i·cist (pə lem′ə sist) *n.* one who is skilled or engaged in polemics.

pole·star (pōl′stär′) *n.* **1.** Polaris. **2.** something that guides or directs; guiding principle.

pole·vault (pōl′vôlt′) *v.i.* to make a pole vault.

pole vault 1. athletic field event in which the contestant jumps for height from a running start, vaulting over a horizontal bar with the aid of a long pole. **2.** such a vault.

po·lice (pə lēs′) *n.* **1.** official force or department established and empowered, usually by a local government, to prevent and detect crime, enforce the law, and maintain public order, peace, and safety. **2.** members of such a force collectively. ▲ construed as plural. **3.** any group officially employed to enforce regulations or maintain order and safety: *campus police.* —*v.t.,* **-liced, -lic·ing.** to patrol, regulate, or maintain order in by or as by means of police. [Middle French *police* civil administration, from Late Latin *politīa* government, from Latin *politīa* the state, from Greek *politeiā* citizenship, government.]

police dog, German shepherd dog.

po·lice·man (pə lēs′mən) *pl.,* **-men.** *n.* member of the police. —**po·lice′wom′an,** *n.*

police state, country or other political unit in which the government exercises repressive control over political, social, and economic activity, esp. by means of a secret police force.

police station, headquarters of a local or district police force.

pol·i·cy¹ (pol′ə sē) *pl.,* **-cies.** *n.* **1.** guiding principle, course, or method of action followed or adhered to habitually or consistently: *a nation's foreign policy.* **2.** prudence, sagacity, or shrewdness in the management of affairs. [Old French *policie* government, administration, from Late Latin *politīa.* See POLICE.]

pol·i·cy² (pol′ə sē) *pl.,* **-cies.** *n.* **1.** written contract of insurance between an insurance company and the party or parties insured. **2.** numbers racket. Also (*def.* 2), **policy racket.** [French *police* contract, through Italian and Latin, from Greek *apodeixis* proof.]

pol·i·cy·hold·er (pol′ə sē hōl′dər) *n.* one who holds a policy of insurance.

po·li·o (pō′lē ō′) *n.* poliomyelitis.

po·li·o·my·e·li·tis (pō′lē ō mī′ə lī′tis) *n.* highly contagious disease caused by a virus and occurring mainly in children, that, in its mild forms, is characterized by headache, sore throat, and fever, and, in its severe forms, attacks the central nervous system and is characterized by the destruction of nervous tissue, muscular weakness, and paralysis. Also, **infantile paralysis.** [Modern Latin *poliomyelitis,* from Greek *polios* gray + *myelos* marrow + -ITIS.]

po·lis (pō′lis) *pl.,* **-leis** (-līs). *n.* city-state of ancient Greece. [Greek *polis* city, state.]

pol·ish (pol′ish) *n.* **1.** smoothness or glossiness of surface or finish, as that produced by rubbing or by the application of a special preparation; bright, shiny appearance; luster: *He buffed the floor to a high polish.* **2.** preparation or substance used to shine, clean, or smooth a surface: *shoe polish.* **3.** smooth elegance of manner or style; refinement: *a man with polish and poise.* —*v.t.* **1.** to shine, clean, or smooth, as by rubbing or applying a special preparation: *to polish silverware.* **2.** to make more finished or complete; free from imperfections; improve (often with *up*): *Polish up that speech a bit.* **3.** to make more elegant; refine: *to polish one's manners.* **4. to polish off. a.** to finish completely and quickly: *to polish off a meal, to polish off an assignment.* **b.** to subdue, overcome, or eliminate quickly: *to polish off an opponent.* —*v.i.* to become smooth or glossy. [Old French *poliss-,* a stem of *polir* to make smooth, make elegant, from Latin *polīre* to make smooth.] —**pol′ish·er,** *n.*

Pol·ish (pō′lish) *adj.* of or relating to Poland, its people, their language, or their culture. —*n.* language belonging to the western division of the Slavic branch of the Indo-European language family, spoken predominantly in Poland.

Polish Corridor, narrow strip of land taken from Germany and given to Poland after World War I to give Poland access to the Baltic Sea.

pol·ished (pol′isht) *adj.* **1.** elegant; cultured; refined: *polished manners.* **2.** free from flaws or imperfections: *a polished performance.* **3.** having a smooth, glossy, shiny surface.

Po·lit·bu·ro (pol′it byoor′ō, pə lit′-) *n.* highest policy-making and executive committee of a Communist Party.

po·lite (pə līt′) *adj.* **1.** having or exhibiting good manners, a tactful consideration for others, and a regard for correct social behavior; courteous. **2.** characterized by correct social behavior; refined: *polite society.* **3.** showing or characterized by cultivation or refined taste: *polite letters.* [Latin *politus,* past participle of *polīre* to make smooth.] —**po·lite′ly,** *adv.* —**po·lite′ness,** *n.*

Syn. 1. Polite, courteous mean showing good manners in social intercourse. **Polite** suggests observance of correct social usage characterized by habitual tact and a desire not to offend others by rudeness and roughness: *Bob was polite even to his opponents.* **Courteous** stresses thoughtfulness and regard for the feelings and dignity of others: *The courteous policeman helped the old lady across the street.*

pol·i·tic (pol′ə tik) *adj.* **1.** characterized by prudence or shrewd good judgment; skillfully or judiciously contrived. **2.** having or using a shrewd awareness of what is expedient or advantageous; artful. **3.** scheming; crafty; cunning. [Middle French *politique* political, from Latin *politicus* relating to the state, from Greek *politikos* civic, civil, going back to *polis* city, state.]

po·lit·i·cal (pə lit′i kəl) *adj.* **1.** of, relating to, or concerned with the science or activities of government or the administering of governmental affairs. **2.** of, relating to, or involved in politics. **3.** of, relating to, or characteristic of politicians. **4.** relating to or characterized by opposition to a government. **5.** having a definite, organized system of government. —**po·lit′i·cal·ly,** *adv.*

political science, study of the origin, organization, principles, and manner of operation of government.

pol·i·ti·cian (pol′ə tish′ən) *n.* **1.** one who is active in politics, esp. one holding public office. **2.** one who is skilled in political maneuvering. —**Syn. 1.** see **statesman.**

pol·i·tick (pol′ə tik) *v.i. Informal.* to engage in campaigning or other political activity.

po·lit·i·co (pə lit′i kō′) *pl.,* **-cos.** *n.* one active in or shrewdly knowledgeable about politics; politician.

---

at; āpe; cär; end; mē; it; īce; hot; ōld; fôrk; wood; fōōl; oil; out; up; ūse; turn; sing; thin; this; zh in treasure; ə in ago, taken, pencil, lemon, circus.

pol·i·tics (pol′ə tiks) *n., pl.* **1.** activities or affairs involved in the administering of a government or relating to governmental or state matters. **2.** dealings, methods, or maneuvers involved in controlling, administering, or seeking to control a government. **3.** science or art of government or of the management of state or public affairs. **4.** political opinions, convictions, or affiliations. **5.** factional scheming or intrigues for positions or power within a group: *office politics.* ▲ usually construed as singular or plural in defs. 1, 2, 3, 5, as plural in def. 4.

pol·i·ty (pol′ə tē) *pl.,* **-ties.** *n.* **1.** form, system, or method of government. **2.** any community living under some form or system of government. [Late Latin *polītīa* government. See POLICE.]

Polk, James Knox (pōk) 1795–1849, eleventh president of the United States from 1845 to 1849.

pol·ka (pōl′kə, pō′kə) *n.* **1.** lively dance of Bohemian origin that is danced in couples and whose basic movement consists of three steps and a hop in duple time. **2.** music for this dance. —*v.i.* **-kaed, -ka·ing.** to dance the polka. [French *polka* the dance, the music, from Czech *pulka* half step, from *pul* half.]

pol·ka dot (pō′kə) **1.** one of a series of round dots spaced to form a pattern on fabric or other materials. **2.** pattern or material with such dots.

poll (pōl) *n.* **1.** survey of public opinion on a given subject, usually obtained by questioning a sample group of people. **2.** the casting and recording of votes in an election. **3.** total number of votes cast or recorded. **4. polls.** place where votes are cast and recorded. **5.** list of persons, esp. of eligible voters. **6.** the head, esp. that part of it on which the hair grows. **7.** blunt or flat end of certain tools, as a hammer or ax. —*v.t.* **1.** to receive (a given number of votes) in an election: *The winner polled twice as many votes as his opponent.* **2.** to question or canvass (a sample group of people) to obtain a survey of public opinion. **3.** to record or register the votes of: *to poll a district.* **4.** to cut off, trim, or crop, as hair or horns. **5.** to cut off, trim, or crop the hair, horns, branches, or other growth of. —*v.i.* to cast one's vote in an election. [Middle English *pol(le)* head, possibly from Middle Dutch *pol(le);* referring to the counting of heads.]

pol·lack (pol′ək) *also,* **pol·lock.** *n.* commercially important food and game fish, *Pollachius virens,* related to the cod, found in coastal waters of the northern Atlantic and having a body that is greenish-brown on top and gray underneath. Length: to over 40 inches. [Of uncertain origin.]

pol·len (pol′ən) *n.* fine, yellowish, powderlike material produced in the anthers of flowering plants that acts as a fertilizing element in plant reproduction. [Latin *pollen* fine flour.]

pol·li·nate (pol′ə nāt′) **-nat·ed, -nat·ing.** *v.t.* to carry or transfer pollen from an anther to a stigma of (a flower or plant).

pol·li·na·tion (pol′ə nā′shən) *n.* transfer of pollen from the anther of a flower to the stigma of the same or another flower, which is followed by fertilization.

pol·li·wog (pol′ē wog′) *also,* **pol·ly·wog.** *n.* tadpole. [Middle English *polywygle,* from *pol* head (see POLL) + *wigelen* to move to and fro. See WIGGLE.]

pol·lock (pol′ək) pollack.

Pol·lock, Jackson (pol′ək) 1912–56, U.S. painter.

poll·ster (pōl′stər) *n.* one whose work is conducting public opinion polls.

poll tax, tax levied on persons, rather than on property or transactions, often payable as a prerequisite to voting in state or local elections in some states.

pol·lut·ant (pə loōt′ənt) *n.* something that pollutes, esp. industrial waste or other material that contaminates air, water, or soil.

pol·lute (pə loōt′) **-lut·ed, -lut·ing.** *v.t.* **1.** to contaminate or make impure or foul, as with industrial waste, esp. to a degree disturbing or harmful to plant or animal life. **2.** to destroy the purity of; sully; corrupt. [Latin *pollūtus,* past participle of *polluere* to defile.]
Syn. 1. Pollute, defile′, contaminate mean to make dirty or unclean. Pollute stresses the completion of the process of making physically filthy or noxious what once was or ideally should be clean, bright, and clear: *Garbage pollutes our rivers and streams.* Defile may be preferred when suggesting willful pollution of something that is by its nature clean: *Litter defiled the park.* Contaminate specifically suggests the introduction, presence, or influence of an external agent that infects, taints, or makes unwholesome: *Flies contaminate food.*

pol·lu·tion (pə loō′shən) *n.* **1.** act or process of polluting; being polluted. **2.** that which pollutes, esp. that which contaminates air, water, or soil.

Pol·lux (pol′əks) *n.* see **Castor and Pollux.**

Pol·ly·an·na (pol′ē an′ə) *n.* excessively or blindly optimistic person who tends to find good in everything. [From *Pollyanna,* the young heroine of *Pollyanna,* a novel by Eleanor H. Porter, 1868–1920, U.S. writer.]

pol·ly·wog (pol′ē wog′) *n.* tadpole.

po·lo (pō′lō) *n.* **1.** game played on horseback by two teams of four men each, using long-handled mallets, with which they attempt to hit a wooden ball through the opponent's goal posts. **2.** water polo. [Probably from dialectal Tibetan *polo* ball.]

Po·lo, Mar·co (pō′lō; mär′kō) c.1254–1324, Italian traveler.

pol·o·naise (pol′ə nāz′, pō′lə-) *n.* **1.** stately, majestic dance of Polish origin, in three-quarter time, characterized by slow, gliding steps. **2.** music for this dance. **3.** woman's dress popular in the eighteenth century, having a fitted bodice and a full skirt, worn over a separate skirt and open in the front so that the sides could be looped up to form three panels. [French *polonaise,* feminine of *polonais* Polish, from Medieval Latin *Polonia* Poland, from Polish *Polanie.*]

po·lo·ni·um (pə lō′nē əm) *n.* heavy, radioactive, metallic element, the first radioactive element to be discovered. It occurs naturally as a decay product of pitchblende. Symbol: **Po** See **element** for table. [Modern Latin *polonium,* from Medieval Latin *Polonia* Poland; because one of its discoverers, Marie Curie, was born in Poland. See POLONAISE.]

Polonaise

polo shirt, pullover sport shirt of knitted cotton, usually close-fitting.

Pol·ta·va (pəl tä′və) *n.* city in the southwestern Soviet Union, in the Ukraine. Pop. (1970), 220,000.

pol·ter·geist (pōl′tər gīst′) *n.* ghost or supernatural presence, traditionally regarded as mischievous, that supposedly makes its presence known by unexplained sounds and by moving inanimate objects. [German *Poltergeist,* from *poltern* to make a noise + *Geist* ghost.]

pol·troon (pol troōn′) *n.* contemptible, spiritless coward. [French *poltron,* from Italian *poltrone,* from *poltro* colt, going back to Latin *pullus* young animal.]

poly- *combining form* more than one; many; much: *polychrome, polygon.* [Greek *polys* much, many.]

pol·y·an·drous (pol′ē an′drəs) *adj.* **1.** of, relating to, or characterized by the practice, custom, or condition of having more than one husband at a time. **2.** *Botany.* marked by or having many stamens.

pol·y·an·dry (pol′ē an′drē) *n.* **1.** practice, custom, or condition of having more than one husband at a time. **2.** *Botany.* condition of being polyandrous. [Greek *polyandriā* condition of having many men, going back to *polys* much, many + *anēr* (stem *andr-*) man, husband.]

pol·y·an·thus (pol′ē an′thəs) *pl.,* **-thus·es.** *n.* **1.** hardy primrose, *Primula polyantha,* that bears flowers of many colors. **2.** widely cultivated narcissus, *Narcissus tazetta,* that bears small clusters of fragrant white flowers. [Modern Latin *polyanthus,* from Greek *polyanthos* having many flowers, from *polys* much, many + *anthos* flower.]

pol·y·bro·mi·nat·ed bi·phen·yl (pol′ē brō′mə nāt′əd; bī fen′əl) any one of a group of poisonous chemicals related to the polychlorinated biphenyls, used in industry and regarded as dangerous to the environment. Also, **PBB.**

pol·y·car·pous (pol′ē kär′pəs) *adj.* having two or more carpels.

pol·y·chlo·ri·nat·ed bi·phen·yl (pol′ē klôr′ə nāt′əd; bī fen′əl) any of several compounds that are made by replacing hydrogen atoms with chlorine. They are used in industry and are poisonous pollutants of the environment. Also, **PCB.**

pol·y·chro·mat·ic (pol′ē krō mat′ik) *adj.* having or showing several colors or changes of color. Also, **pol·y·chro·mic** (pol′ē krō′mik).

pol·y·chrome (pol′ē krōm′) *adj.* having several colors. —*n.* work of art executed or decorated in several colors. [French *polychrome* of many colors, from Greek *polys* much, many + *chrōma* color.]

pol·y·clin·ic (pol′ē klin′ik) *n.* clinic or hospital for the study and treatment of a wide variety of diseases.

pol·y·es·ter (pol′ē es′tər) *n.* any of several thermosetting polymeric resins, used esp. in making textile fibers. [POLY(MER) + ESTER.]

pol·y·eth·yl·ene (pol′ē eth′ə lēn′) *n.* any of several thermoplastic resins produced by the polymerization of ethylene, used esp. in making bags, containers, and insulation. [POLY(MER) + ETHYLENE.]

po·lyg·a·mous (pə lig′ə məs) *adj.* **1.** of, relating to, or practicing polygamy. **2.** *Botany.* bearing unisexual and monoclinous flowers on the same plant. —**po·lyg′a·mist,** *n.* —**po·lyg′a·mous·ly,** *adv.*

po·lyg·a·my (pə lig′ə mē) *n.* practice, custom, or condition of having more than one spouse or mate at a time. [Greek *polygamiā,* from *polys* much, many + *gamos* marriage.]

pol·y·glot (pol′ē glot′) *n.* **1.** one who speaks, understands, or writes several languages. **2.** book containing versions of the same text in several different languages. **3.** mixture of several languages. —*adj.* **1.** speaking, understanding, or writing several languages. **2.** of, composed of, or expressed in several languages. [Greek *polyglōttos* speaking many languages, from *polys* much, many + *glōtta* tongue, language.]

at; āpe; cär; end; mē; it; īce; hot; ōld; fôrk; wood; foōl; oil; out; up; ūse; turn; sing; thin; this; zh in treasure; ə ago, taken, pencil, lemon, circus.

pol·y·gon (pol′ē gon′) *n.* closed plane figure consisting of joined line segments, each two adjoining line segments having a common end point. [Late Latin *polygōnum,* from Greek *polygōnon,* from *polys* much, many + *gōniā* angle.] —**po·lyg·o·nal** (pə lig′ən əl), *adj.*

pol·y·graph (pol′ē graf′) *n.* instrument that simultaneously measures and records changes in heartbeat, blood pressure, respiration, and other physiological processes, used esp. as a lie detector. [Greek *polygraphos* writing much.]

po·lyg·y·ny (pə lij′ə nē) *n.* practice, custom, or condition of having more than one wife at a time. [POLY- + Greek *gynē* woman.] —**po·lyg′y·nous,** *adj.*

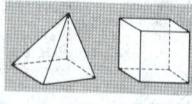

Polyhedrons

pol·y·he·dron (pol′ē hē′drən) *pl.,* **-drons** or **-dra** (-drə). *n.* closed solid figure that is the union of plane polygons, each two adjoining polygons having a common edge. [Greek *polyedron,* neuter of *polyedros* having many bases or sides, from *polys* much, many + *hedrā* base¹, side.] —**pol′y·he′dral,** *adj.*

Pol·y·hym·ni·a (pol′ē him′nē ə) *n.* Greek Mythology. the Muse of sacred poetry. [Latin *Polyhymnia,* from Greek *Polymnia,* going back to *polys* much, many + *hymnos* hymn.]

pol·y·mer (pol′i mər) *n.* **1.** any large molecule formed of smaller simple molecules linked together in long chains of repeating units. The number of molecules that unite to form a polymer may vary from a few to thousands. **2.** substance made of polymers. [Greek *polymerēs* having many parts, from *polys* much, many + *meros* part.]

pol·y·mer·ic (pol′i mer′ik) *adj.* of, relating to, or consisting of a polymer.

po·lym·er·i·za·tion (pə lim′ər i zā′shən, pol′i mər ə-) *n.* the uniting of two or more monomers to form a polymer.

po·lym·er·ize (pə lim′ə rīz′, pol′i mə-) **-ized, -iz·ing.** *v.t., v.i.* to subject to or undergo polymerization.

pol·y·mor·phism (pol′ē môr′fiz′əm) *n.* **1.** state or quality of being polymorphous. **2.** *Chemistry.* (of a substance with a single chemical composition, as sulphur) occurrence in two or more different crystalline forms.

pol·y·mor·phous (pol′ē môr′fəs) *adj.* having, assuming, or occurring in many or various forms, stages, or characters. Also, **pol·y·mor′phic.** [Greek *polymorphos* multiform, from *polys* much, many + *morphē* form, shape.]

Pol·y·ne·sia (pol′i nē′zhə, -shə) *n.* one of the three main divisions of the Pacific islands, in the central and southern part of the Pacific, east of Melanesia and Micronesia.

Pol·y·ne·sian (pol′i nē′zhən, -shən) *n.* **1.** member or close descendant of the people inhabiting Polynesia. **2.** subfamily of the Malayo-Polynesian family of languages, spoken predominantly in Polynesia and including Hawaiian, Maori, and Tahitian. —*adj.* of or relating to Polynesia, its people, their languages, or their culture.

pol·y·no·mi·al (pol′ē nō′mē əl) *n. Mathematics.* expression consisting of two or more terms. —*adj.* consisting of or characterized by two or more names or terms. [POLY- + (BI)NOMIAL.]

pol·yp (pol′ip) *n.* **1.** any small aquatic coelenterate with a cup-shaped or saclike body, having a mouth opening located at one end of the body and surrounded by numerous tentacles studded with stinging cells. **2.** *Medicine.* any mass of projecting tissue, esp. a growth on a mucous or serous surface. [French *polype,* from Latin *polypus* octopus, from Greek *polypous* literally, many-footed, from *polys* much, many + *pous* foot.]

Pol·y·phe·mus (pol′i fē′məs) *n. Greek Mythology.* Cyclops who imprisoned Ulysses and his men in a cave until Ulysses blinded him and finally escaped with his companions.

pol·y·phon·ic (pol′ē fon′ik) *adj.* **1.** consisting of or producing many sounds or voices. **2.** *Music.* of, relating to, or composed of the simultaneous combination of two or more independent, melodic voices or parts, with harmonious effect; contrapuntal. Opposed to **homophonic.**

po·lyph·o·ny (pə lif′ə nē) *pl.* **-nies.** *n.* **1.** multiplicity of sounds or voices, as in an echo. **2.** *Music.* polyphonic composition or music; counterpoint. [Greek *polyphōniā* variety of tones, from *polys* much, many + *phōnē* sound, voice.]

pol·y·syl·lab·ic (pol′ē si lab′ik) *adj.* **1.** consisting of three or more syllables. **2.** characterized by words of three or more syllables.

pol·y·syl·la·ble (pol′ē sil′ə bəl) *n.* word of three or more syllables.

pol·y·tech·nic (pol′ē tek′nik) *adj.* of, relating to, or devoted to many arts or sciences and their practical application. Also, **pol′y·tech′ni·cal.** —*n.* school offering instruction and training in applied science and technology. [French *polytechnique,* going back to Greek *polys* many, much + *technē* art.]

pol·y·the·ism (pol′ē thē iz′əm) *n.* belief in or worship of more than one god. [French *polythéisme,* going back to Greek *polys* many, much + *theos* god.] —**pol′y·the′ist,** *n.* —**pol′y·the·is′tic,** *adj.*

pol·y·un·sat·u·rat·ed (pol′ē un sach′ə rā′tid) *adj.* containing more than two double or triple bonds in a molecule, as certain vegetable and animal fats and oils.

pol·y·wa·ter (pol′ē wô′tər, -wot′ər) *n.* rare, polymeric form of water whose freezing point is lower than that of ordinary water and whose boiling point is higher than that of ordinary water.

pom·ace (pum′is) *n.* **1.** residue of fruit and plant parts after the juice has been extracted, esp. the crushed pulp of apples, used for making cider. **2.** any similar pulpy material. [Medieval Latin *pomacium* cider, from Latin *pōmum* apple, fruit.]

po·ma·ceous (pə mā′shəs) *adj.* **1.** of or relating to a pome or a plant bearing a pome, as the apple. **2.** of, relating to, or consisting of apples. [Modern Latin *pomaceus,* from Latin *pōmum* apple, fruit.]

po·made (po mād′, -mäd′, pə-) *n.* perfumed ointment, esp. one for dressing the hair. —*v.t.* **-mad·ed, -mad·ing.** to anoint or dress with pomade. [French *pommade* ointment, from Italian *pomata,* from *pomo* apple, from Latin *pōmum* apple, fruit; because formerly made with the pulp of apples.]

po·man·der (pə man′dər, pō′man′-) *n.* mixture of aromatic substances, often shaped into a ball, that gives off a pleasing scent, formerly worn esp. as a guard against infection but now placed in closets and dresser drawers. [Middle French *pome d'ambre* apple or ball of amber. See POME, AMBER.]

pome (pōm) *n.* fleshy, firm, edible fruit having several seeds rather than a stone, as the apple or pear. [Old French *pome* apple, going back to Latin *pōmum* apple, fruit.]

pome·gran·ate (pom′gran′it, pom′ə-, pum′-) *n.* **1.** round edible fruit of a shrub or small tree, *Punica granatum,* having a golden-red leathery rind and containing many small seeds, each of which is enclosed by a juicy reddish pulp. **2.** shrub or tree bearing this fruit, having red or orange trumpet-shaped flowers. [Old French *pome grenate* the fruit, going back to Latin *pōmum* apple, fruit + *grānātum,* neuter of *grānātus* having many grains.]

pom·e·lo (pom′ə lō′) *pl.,* **-los.** *n.* grapefruit (def. 1).

Pomeranian

Pom·er·a·ni·a (pom′ə rā′nē ə) *n.* historic region of north-central Europe, in northwestern Poland and southeastern East Germany, along the Baltic Sea.

Pom·er·a·ni·an (pom′ə rā′nē ən) *n.* **1.** native or inhabitant of Pomerania. **2.** small, long-haired dog having a fox-like head and a bushy tail that lies flat on the back. Height: 7 inches at the shoulder. —*adj.* of or relating to Pomerania, its people, their language, or their culture.

pom·mel (pum′əl, pom′-) *n.* **1.** upward-projecting front part of a saddle, consisting of a knob that is used chiefly as a grip. **2.** rounded knob on the hilt of a sword, dagger, or similar weapon. —*v.t.* to pummel. [Old French *pomel* knob on the hilt of a sword; literally, small apple, going back to Latin *pōmum* apple, fruit.]

po·mol·o·gy (pō mol′ə jē) *n.* branch of botany that deals with fruits and their cultivation. [Modern Latin *pomologia,* from Latin *pōmum* apple, fruit + -LOGY.]

Po·mo·na (pə mō′nə) *n.* **1.** Roman goddess of fruit trees. **2.** city in southwestern California, near Los Angeles. Pop. (1970), 87,384.

pomp (pomp) *n.* **1.** stately and splendid ceremony or display; splendor; pageantry: *the pomp and ritual of the Queen's coronation.* **2.** vain, ostentatious show or display. [Latin *pompa* procession, display, from Greek *pompē.*]

pom·pa·dour (pom′pə dôr′, -door′) *n.* **1.** man's hair style in which the hair is combed up high from the forehead. **2.** woman's hair style in which the hair is combed back from the forehead and puffed high in front, often over a pad. [From the Marquise de *Pompadour.*]

Pom·pa·dour, Marquise de (pom′pə dôr′, -door′) 1721–64, mistress of Louis XV of France.

pom·pa·no (pom′pə nō′) *pl.,* **-nos.** *n.* any of several food and game fish, family Carangidae, found in temperate and tropical waters of the Americas, having a flattened roundish or oval body that is usually silver in color. Length: to 18 inches. [Spanish *pampano* a kind of fish, tendril of a vine, from Latin *pampinus* tendril of a vine.]

Pom·pe·ii (pom pā′, -pā′ē) *n.* partially excavated ancient city in southwestern Italy, near Naples, buried by the eruption of Mount Vesuvius in A.D. 79. —**Pom·pei′an,** *adj., n.*

Pom·pey (pom′pē) *n.* 106–48 B.C., Roman general, statesman, and triumvir; born Gnaeus Pompeius.

pom·pom (pom′pom′) also, **pom-pom, pom·pon** (pom′pon′). **1.** ornamental ball or tuft of wool or other material, used esp. as a decoration on clothing. **2.** globe-shaped, usually small, flower, as a chrysanthemum. [French *pompon* ornamental tuft; of uncertain origin.]

pom·pos·i·ty (pom pos′ə tē) *pl.,* **-ties.** *n.* **1.** state or quality of being

pompous. 2. instance of being pompous; pompous action, remark, or display.

pom·pous (pom′pəs) *adj.* **1.** exhibiting or characterized by an exaggerated or complacent sense of dignity or self-importance. **2.** excessively lofty or ornate, as language. **3.** characterized by or full of pomp or stately ceremony. [Late Latin *pompōsus* stately, from Latin *pompa* procession, display. See POMP.] **—pom′pous·ly,** *adv.* **—pom′pous·ness,** *n.*

Ponce de Le·ón, Juan (pons′ də lē′ən, pon′sə dā lā′ōn; *hwän*) c.1460–1521, Spanish explorer and discoverer of Florida.

pon·cho (pon′chō) *pl.,* **-chos.** *n.* **1.** cloaklike garment consisting of a piece of cloth with a slit or hole in the middle so that it can be slipped over the head. **2.** waterproof garment resembling this, worn chiefly as a raincoat. [Spanish *poncho,* from Araucanian *pontho* woolen cloth.]

pond (pond) *n.* body of still or standing water, usually smaller than a lake. [Form of POUND¹.]

pon·der (pon′dər) *v.t.* to weigh in the mind; consider or think over carefully: *They pondered the fate awaiting them.* *—v.i.* to think or deliberate; muse; reflect: *to ponder over a problem.* [Latin *ponderāre.*] **—Syn.** *v.i.* see **meditate.**

pon·der·a·ble (pon′dər ə bəl) *adj.* capable of being weighed or evaluated; appreciable.

pon·der·ous (pon′dər əs) *adj.* **1.** having great weight or bulk; heavy; unwieldy: *The ponderous old cart lumbered down the road.* **2.** clumsy, slow, or labored, as if because of weight: *ponderous movements.* **3.** lacking grace or interest; tedious: *a ponderous style of writing.* [Latin *ponderōsus* heavy, weighty, from *pondus* weight.] **—pon′der·os′i·ty** (pon′də ros′ə tē), **pon′der·ous·ness,** *n.* **—pon′der·ous·ly,** *adv.* **—Syn.** 1. see **heavy.**

pond lily, any of a group of water plants, genus *Nuphar,* of the water lily family, usually having yellowish flowers that grow above the water.

pond·weed (pond′wēd′) *n.* any of a large group of water plants, genus *Potamogeton,* found growing in large numbers in ponds and streams, bearing dense spikes of tiny flowers just above the water's surface.

pone (pōn) *n.* corn pone. [Of Algonquian origin.]

pon·gee (pon jē′) *n.* brownish-yellow, lightweight fabric having an uneven surface, originally woven by hand in China from silk. [Dialectal Chinese *pun-chī* own loom.]

pon·iard (pon′yərd) *n.* dagger. *—v.t.* to stab with a poniard. [French *poignard* dagger, from *poing* fist, from Latin *pugnus.*]

pons (ponz) *pl.,* **pon·tes** (pon′tēz). *n.* band of nerve fibers in the brain connecting the cerebellum, cerebrum, and medulla oblongata. [Latin *pōns* bridge.]

Pon·ti·ac (pon′tē ak′) *n.* **1.** c.1720–69, Ottawa Indian chief. **2.** city in southeastern Michigan. Pop. (1970), 85,279.

pon·ti·fex (pon′ti feks′) *pl.,* **pon·tif·i·ces** (pon tif′ə sēz′). *n.* in ancient Rome, a member of the principal college of priests in charge of the state religion. [Latin *pontifex.*]

pon·tiff (pon′tif) *n.* **1.** pope. **2.** any high priest. **3.** *Archaic.* any bishop. [French *pontif* high priest of ancient Rome, ecclesiastical dignitary, from Latin *pontifex* high priest of Rome.]

pon·tif·i·cal (pon tif′i kəl) *adj.* **1.** of, relating to, or suitable for a pope; papal. **2.** of or relating to a bishop. **3.** characterized by a haughty and pompous sense of self-importance or authority. *—n.* **pontificals.** vestments and insignia of office worn by bishops, cardinals, and the Pope at certain ecclesiastical ceremonies. **—pon·tif′i·cal·ly,** *adv.*

pon·tif·i·cate (*v.,* pon tif′i kāt′; *n.,* pon tif′i kit, -kāt′). **-cat·ed, -cat·ing.** *v.i.* **1.** to speak or act with haughty, pompous self-importance or authority. **2.** to discharge the duties or officiate in the capacity of a pontiff, esp. of a pope. *—n.* office or term of office of a pontiff, esp. of a pope.

pon·toon (pon tōōn′) *n.* **1.** flat-bottomed boat or similar floating structure used as a support, as in the construction of floating bridges over water or in the raising of submerged vessels. **2.** float of a seaplane. [French *ponton* bridge of boats, low flat boat, from Latin *pontō,* from *pōns* bridge.]

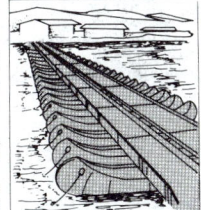

Pontoon bridge

pontoon bridge, bridge, often temporary, that is supported in the water by pontoons.

Pon·tus (pon′təs) *n.* ancient kingdom in northeastern Asia Minor, on the Black Sea, later a Roman province.

Pon·tus Eu·xin·us (pon′təs ūk·sī′nəs) see **Black Sea.**

po·ny (pō′nē) *pl.,* **-nies.** *n.* **1.** horse of any of various small breeds, esp. one not more than fourteen hands high at the shoulder. **2.** any horse, esp. one small in size. **3.** *Informal.* synopsis of a literary work, or any other prepared text or aid, esp. a literal translation of a work in a foreign

language, used by students, usually illicitly, in doing schoolwork or in preparing for an exam. Also, **trot.** **4.** *Informal.* **a.** small glass for liquor. **b.** amount such a glass will hold. [Old French *poulenet* little colt, diminutive of *poulain* colt, going back to Latin *pullus* young animal.]

pony express, rapid postal service in which mail was carried in relays by riders mounted on fast horses, in operation between Missouri and California from 1860 to 1861.

po·ny·tail (pō′nē tāl′) *also,* **pony tail.** *n.* woman's hair style in which the hair is drawn tightly back from the face and fastened at the back of the head, so as to hang down like a pony's tail.

pooch (pōōch) *n.* *Slang.* dog. [Of uncertain origin.]

pood (pōōd) *n.* unit of weight used in Russia, equal to approximately thirty-six pounds. [Russian *pood,* going back to Latin *pondō* by weight.]

poo·dle (pōōd′əl) *n.* curly-haired dog having a dense, usually solid-colored coat that is often clipped in elaborate styles. There are three varieties which differ only in size: the **toy poodle,** to 10 inches at the shoulder; the **miniature poodle,** 10 to 15 inches at the shoulder; and the **standard poodle,** over 15 inches.

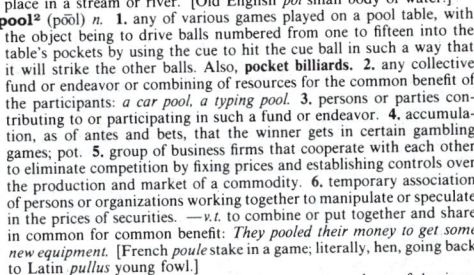

Poodle

[German *Pudel,* from *pudeln* to splash in water; because the poodle was originally used in hunting to retrieve waterfowl.]

pooh (pōō) *interj.* used to express disbelief, disdain, or impatience. [Imitative.]

pooh-pooh (pōō′pōō′) *v.t.* to express contempt or disdain for. [Repetition of POOH.]

pool¹ (pōōl) *n.* **1.** small body of still or standing water, usually fresh. **2.** indoor or outdoor tank designed for swimming, often rectangular in shape and usually built of concrete and furnished with water-filtering equipment. Also, **swimming pool. 3.** small, shallow body or accumulation of liquid on a surface: *a pool of blood, a pool of sweat.* **4.** still, deep place in a stream or river. [Old English *pōl* small body of water.]

pool² (pōōl) *n.* **1.** any of various games played on a pool table, with the object being to drive balls numbered from one to fifteen into the table's pockets by using the cue to hit the cue ball in such a way that it will strike the other balls. Also, **pocket billiards. 2.** any collective fund or endeavor or combining of resources for the common benefit of the participants: *a car pool, a typing pool.* **3.** persons or parties contributing to or participating in such a fund or endeavor. **4.** accumulation, as of antes and bets, that the winner gets in certain gambling games; pot. **5.** group of business firms that cooperate with each other to eliminate competition by fixing prices and establishing controls over the production and market of a commodity. **6.** temporary association of persons or organizations working together to manipulate or speculate in the prices of securities. *—v.t.* to combine or put together and share in common for common benefit: *They pooled their money to get some new equipment.* [French *poule* stake in a game; literally, hen, going back to Latin *pullus* young fowl.]

pool·room (pōōl′rōōm′, -room′) *n.* room or place of business equipped for the playing of pool or billiards. Also, **pool hall.**

pool table, rectangular table used in playing pool, having a felt-covered slate surface and six pockets, one in each of the four corners and one in the center of each of the sides.

Poo·na (pōō′nə) *n.* city in western India, southeast of Bombay. Pop. (1969), 718,270.

poop¹ (pōōp) *n.* poop deck. *—v.t.* **1.** (of a wave) to break over the stern of (a boat or ship). **2.** (of a boat or ship) to receive (a wave) over the stern. [French *poupe* stern of a ship, going back to Latin *puppis.*]

poop² (pōōp) *v.t.* *Slang.* to cause to become exhausted or thoroughly fatigued. [Of uncertain origin.]

poop deck, short deck above the main deck at the stern of a boat or ship, often forming the roof of a cabin.

poor (poor) *adj.* **1.** lacking wealth, material possessions, or means of subsistence; having little or no money; needy: *a poor family who struggled to make ends meet.* **2.** characterized by or indicating such a lack: *a poor neighborhood.* **3.** lacking or deficient in proper, necessary, or desirable qualities; inferior in quality or value: *poor health.* **4.** being less than wanted, needed, or expected; scanty; insufficient: *a poor wheat crop.* **5.** lacking skill, ability, or proficiency; not capable or talented: *a poor writer, a poor student.* **6.** arousing or deserving pity or compassion; unhappy: *The poor man has lived alone for years.* *—n.* **the poor,** poor or needy persons collectively. [Old French *povre* needy man, needy, from Latin *pauper.* Doublet of PAUPER.] **—poor′ness,** *n.*

Syn. *adj.* **1. Poor, destitute, indigent** mean having little or no money or material possessions. **Poor** admits of widest use in suggesting a lack of resources or means of subsistence that deprives one of most of the

necessities and all of the luxuries of life: *His parents were poor immigrants from Europe.* **Destitute** suggests an abject poverty that deprives one of the basic necessities of life, as clothing, food, and shelter: *The death of her husband left Maria penniless and destitute.* **Indigent** is a more literary word to suggest an urgent need for money: *The state provides scholarships for indigent students.*

poor·house (poor'hous') *n.* establishment or institution maintained at public expense to shelter and aid poor people.

poor law, law providing for public relief or support of the poor.

poor·ly (poor'lē) *adv.* in a poor manner; badly: *He has performed rather poorly this term.* —*adj. Informal.* somewhat ill; ailing; indisposed: *She's been feeling poorly lately.*

poor-spir·it·ed (poor'spir'i tid) *adj.* lacking spirit or courage; cowardly.

poor white, white person, esp. in the southern United States, of very low social and economic status and having little educational or cultural background. ▲ usually considered offensive.

pop[1] (pop) **popped, pop·ping.** *v.i.* **1.** to make a short, sharp, explosive sound: *The champagne cork popped when the bottle was opened.* **2.** to burst open or explode with such a sound: *The corn popped quickly.* **3.** to move, go, appear, or come quickly, suddenly, or unexpectedly: *to pop out of bed. She popped in to see us yesterday.* **4.** (of the eyes) to open wide, esp. suddenly, so as to protrude or start from the sockets: *Their eyes popped when they heard the news.* **5.** to shoot a firearm. **6.** *Baseball.* to hit a pop fly (often with *out* or *up*). —*v.t.* **1.** to cause to burst with a short, sharp, explosive sound. **2.** to put or thrust quickly, suddenly, or unexpectedly: *She popped the bread into the oven. He popped his head out the window.* **3.** *Baseball.* to hit (the ball) high into the air into or near the infield, in such a manner that an opposing player can catch it before it touches the ground. **4. to pop the question.** *Informal.* to propose marriage, esp. suddenly or unexpectedly. —*n.* **1.** short, sharp, explosive sound. **2.** flavored, nonalcoholic, carbonated beverage; soda. —*adv.* **1.** with a pop. **2.** suddenly; unexpectedly. [Imitative.]

pop[2] (pop) *adj. Informal.* of, relating to, or designating popular music: *a pop singer, a pop concert.* [Short for POPULAR.]

pop. **1.** population. **2.** popular; popularly.

pop art, art movement whose subjects, image, themes, and techniques are taken from advertising, comic strips, motion pictures, and other forms of popular culture. [Short for *popular art;* because it deals with subjects taken from popular culture.]

pop·corn (pop'kôrn') *n.* **1.** variety of corn, *Zea mays everta,* having small, hard kernels that, when heated, burst open and puff out to form white, fluffy masses. **2.** white, fluffy mass so formed, eaten as a snack.

pope (pōp) *also,* **Pope.** *n.* bishop of Rome and supreme head of the Roman Catholic Church, who, according to Catholic doctrine, derives his authority from, and acts as vicar of, Christ. [Old English *pāpa,* from Church Latin *pāpa* pope, bishop, from Latin *pāpa* father, from Greek *papās* bishop, father.]

Pope, Alexander (pōp) 1688–1744, English poet and satirist.

pop·er·y (pō'pər ē) *n.* doctrines and practices of the Roman Catholic Church. ▲ usually considered offensive.

pop fly *Baseball.* high fly ball hit into or near the infield in such a manner that an opposing player can catch it before it touches the ground. Also, **pop′-up′.**

pop·gun (pop'gun') *n.* any toy gun that produces a loud pop when fired, esp. one that fires pellets or corks by means of air compressed in the barrel.

pop·in·jay (pop'in jā') *n.* vain, foppish person given to unthinking chatter. [Old French *popingay, papegai* parrot, from Arabic *babaghā;* influenced by JAY.]

pop·ish (pō'pish) *adj.* of or relating to popes or the Roman Catholic Church. ▲ usually considered offensive. —**pop′ish·ly,** *adv.* —**pop′ish·ness,** *n.*

pop·lar (pop'lər) *n.* **1.** any of a small group of fast-growing trees, genus *Populus,* of the willow family, found throughout the Northern Hemisphere, having pale ridged bark and broad leaves and widely cultivated as ornamentals and windbreaks. **2.** soft

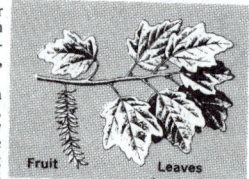

Fruit — Leaves

Poplar

white wood of this tree, often used to make shipping boxes and pulp. [Old French *poplier* the tree, going back to Latin *pōpulus.*]

pop·lin (pop'lin) *n.* durable fabric woven with a pronounced crosswise rib, often made of cotton, and used for such items as shirts, dresses, curtains, and pajamas. [Obsolete French *papeline,* possibly from *Poperinge,* a Flemish city famous for its fabrics in the Middle Ages.]

Po·po·cat·e·petl (pō'pō kə tā'pet'əl, -kat'ə pet'əl) *n.* volcano in south-central Mexico.

pop·o·ver (pop'ō'vər) *n.* very light muffin, made of flour, eggs, milk, and shortening, that puffs up and becomes hollow when baked. [POP[1] + OVER; because it *pops* up *over* the edge of the pan while baking.]

pop·per (pop'ər) *n.* **1.** device used for popping popcorn, usually a covered wire basket or metal pan. **2.** one who or that which pops.

pop·pet (pop'it) *n.* intake or exhaust valve that works by being lifted up and down, rather than by turning or pivoting. Also, **poppet valve.** [Form of PUPPET.]

pop·py (pop'ē) *pl.,* **-pies.** *n.* **1.** round showy flower of any of a small group of plants, genus *Papaver,* often cultivated as a garden flower. **2.** plant bearing this flower, containing a milky juice. One species, *P. somniferum,* is the source of the drug opium. **3.** any of various other plants related to the poppy, as the **California poppy,** *Eschscholtzia californica.* **4.** bright orange-red color. [Old English *popæg* the plant and flower of the genus *Papaver,* going back to Latin *papāver.*]

pop·py·cock (pop'ē kok') *n.* utterly foolish or empty talk; nonsense. [Dialectal Dutch *pappekak* literally, soft dung.]

Pop·si·cle (pop'si kəl) *n. Trademark.* frozen confection consisting of a bar of flavored ice or ice cream on a stick.

pop·u·lace (pop'yə lis) *n.* **1.** all the inhabitants of a place; population. **2.** the common people, as distinguished from the higher classes; the masses. [French *populace* the common people, from Italian *popolaccio,* going back to Latin *populus* the people.]

pop·u·lar (pop'yə lər) *adj.* **1.** pleasing to or favored by very many or most people: *a popular actor.* **2.** having many friends and acquaintances; generally liked, admired, or beloved by others; well-liked: *My brother was voted the most popular boy in his class.* **3.** of, relating to, representing, or carried on by the common people or the people at large: *a popular election, popular government.* **4.** accepted or widespread among the people in general; common; prevalent: *a popular misconception.* **5.** suited to or intended for the taste and intelligence of the average person or the general public: *popular music.* **6.** suited to or within the means of ordinary people; moderate: *This model is now available at popular prices.* **7.** arising from or originating among the common people: *an old legend of popular origin.* [Latin *populāris* relating to the people, from *populus* the people.] —**pop′u·lar·ly,** *adv.*

popular front, coalition of communist, socialist, and moderate political groups behind a common platform opposed to fascism.

pop·u·lar·i·ty (pop'yə lar'ə tē) *n.* quality or state of being widely liked, admired, or favored.

pop·u·lar·ize (pop'yə lə rīz') **-ized, -iz·ing.** *v.t.* to make popular, esp. to cause to become intelligible to the general public or widely known or accepted: *a writer who popularized the use of many new words.* —**pop′u·lar·i·za′tion, pop′u·lar·iz′er,** *n.*

pop·u·late (pop'yə lāt') **-lat·ed, -lat·ing.** *v.t.* **1.** to inhabit. **2.** to furnish with inhabitants, as by colonization; people. [Medieval Latin *populatus,* past participle of *populāre* to people, going back to Latin *populus* the people.]

pop·u·la·tion (pop'yə lā'shən) *n.* **1.** total number of people living in a particular area or place: *The population of that state has doubled in the past decade.* **2.** the people themselves: *The entire population was up in arms about the tax increase.* **3.** segment of such people considered as a distinct group or distinguished in some way from the rest: *the French-speaking population of Montreal.* **4.** all the organisms living in a given area. **5.** act or process of populating; furnishing with inhabitants. **6.** *Statistics.* group of individuals or items to be studied. [Late Latin *populātiō* the people, from Latin *populus.*]

Pop·u·list (pop'yə list) *adj.* of, relating to, or characteristic of the Populist Party. —*n.* member or supporter of the Populist Party. —**Pop′u·lism,** *n.* —**Pop′u·lis′tic,** *adj.*

Populist Party, profarmer and prolabor political party active in the United States in the 1890s, chiefly advocating a graduated income tax, public ownership of railroads, direct election of senators, and free coinage of silver to increase the amount of currency in circulation. Also, **People's Party.**

pop·u·lous (pop'yə ləs) *adj.* having many inhabitants; heavily populated. [Latin *populōsus* full of people, from *populus* the people.] —**pop′u·lous·ly,** *adv.* —**pop′u·lous·ness,** *n.*

pop-up (pop'up') *n.* pop fly.

por·ce·lain (pôr'sə lin, pôrs'lin) *n.* **1.** fine ceramic ware that is hard, white, translucent, and nonporous. **2.** objects made of this, collectively. [French *porcelaine* china, a kind of shell whose polished surface resembled that of china, from Italian *porcellana,* going back to Latin *porcus* pig; because the shell supposedly resembled a pig's back.]

porch (pôrch) *n.* **1.** roofed, sometimes partly or totally enclosed area attached to and extending along and outward from the outside of a house. **2.** structure forming an entrance to a building, often covered. [Old French *porche,* from Latin *porticus* arcade, colonnade. Doublet of PORTICO.]

por·cine (pôr'sīn) *adj.* **1.** of or relating to pigs. **2.** resembling a pig or pigs. [Latin *porcīnus* relating to a pig, from *porcus* pig.]

por·cu·pine (pôr′kyə pīn′) *n.* any of various rodents, families Erethizontidae and Hystricidae, whose body and tail are covered with spines or quills which serve as protection. Length: to 3 feet. [Old French *pore espin* literally, thorny pig, going back to Latin *porcus* pig + *spīna* thorn.]

Porcupine

pore¹ (pôr) *n.* very small opening, as in the skin of an animal, serving as an outlet for perspiration, or as in the surface of a leaf, serving as a means of absorption. [Old French *pore*, from Latin *porus*, from Greek *poros*.]

pore² (pôr) *pored, por·ing. v.i.* 1. to read or study with great attention, application, care, or absorption (with *over*): *She pored over her notes while awaiting her turn to speak.* 2. to meditate or ponder. 3. to gaze earnestly or steadily. [Of uncertain origin.]

por·gy (pôr′gē) *pl.,* **-gies** or **-gy.** *n.* any of a group of commercially important food and game fish, family Sparidae, found chiefly in coastal waters of the Atlantic Ocean, having a flattened, oval, usually silvery-gray body with a stiff, spined dorsal fin. Length: 1–2½ feet. [Modification of earlier *pargo*, from Spanish *pargo*, from Latin *pagarus* sea bream, from Greek *phagros*.]

pork (pôrk) *n.* 1. meat of a pig or hog used as food. 2. *Informal.* government funds, jobs, or favors that benefit or enrich only one local district, given to gain political advantage for the representative of the district. [Old French *pore* pig, meat of a pig, from Latin *porcus* pig.]

pork-bar·rel (pôrk′bar′əl) *adj. Informal.* designating a government project or appropriation favoring one locality, meant to ingratiate the representative of that area with his constituents.

pork barrel *Informal.* pork-barrel project or appropriation or any appropriation of public money for local projects that are considered unnecessary or extravagant.

pork·er (pôr′kər) *n.* pig or hog, esp. one fattened for slaughter.

pork·pie (pôrk′pī′) *n.* man's hat having a low, flat crown. Also, **porkpie hat.**

por·nog·ra·phy (pôr nog′rə fē) *n.* material, as pictures or writings, intended to arouse sexual desires or excitement. [Greek *pornographos* writing about harlots (from *pornē* harlot + *-graphos* writing) + -Y¹.] —**por·nog′ra·pher,** *n.* —**por·no·graph·ic** (pôr′nə graf′ik), *adj.*

po·ros·i·ty (pô rôs′ə tē) *pl.,* **-ties.** *n.* 1. quality or condition of being porous. 2. pore or similar opening.

po·rous (pôr′əs) *adj.* 1. having or full of pores. 2. permeable by liquids, air, or light. —**po′rous·ness,** *n.*

por·phy·ry (pôr′fər ē) *pl.,* **-ries.** *n.* volcanic rock composed of two or more minerals, one of which, usually a feldspar mineral, occurs in much larger crystals than the other mineral or minerals. [Old French *porfire* a purple stone, through Latin, going back to Greek *porphyrītēs,* from *porphyra* a shellfish from which a purple dye was obtained.]

Porpoise

por·poise (pôr′pəs) *pl.,* **-pois·es** or **-poise.** *n.* 1. any of various fishlike mammals, family Phocaenidae, closely related to and resembling the dolphin, inhabiting all oceans except those in polar regions, having a torpedo-shaped body that is usually black with white undersides or with a large white patch on the side. Unlike most dolphins, most porpoises have a rounded head without a beak. Length: 4–6 feet. [Old French *porpeis, porpois,* going back to Latin *porcus* pig + *piscis* fish.]

por·ridge (pôr′ij, por′-) *n.* soft food made by boiling oatmeal or other meal in water or milk until thickened, usually used as a breakfast dish. [Form of POTTAGE.]

por·rin·ger (pôr′in jər, por′-) *n.* small, shallow bowl, usually with a short handle, for holding porridge, soup, or other food, esp. such a bowl of silver or other material used by children. [Modification of earlier *pottinger,* going back to Old French *potager* relating to pottage, from *potage.* See POTTAGE.]

port¹ (pôrt) *n.* 1. place where boats or ships can anchor and be protected from storms; harbor. 2. place with facilities for loading and unloading boats or ships; city or town with a harbor. [Old English *port,* from Latin *portus* harbor.] —**Syn.** 1. see **harbor.**

port² (pôrt) *n.* left side of a boat or ship as one faces forward. Opposed to **starboard.** —*adj.* of, relating to, or located on the left side of a boat or ship. —*v.t., v.i.* to turn or shift to the port side. [Possibly once referring to the side of the ship facing the harbor or *port.*]

port³ (pôrt) *n.* strong, sweet wine, usually dark red in color.

[From *Oporto,* a Portuguese city from which this wine was shipped.]

port⁴ (pôrt) *n.* 1. porthole. 2. covering for a porthole. 3. opening in a piece of machinery for the passage of fluids, often controlled by a valve. [Old French *porte* grate, from Latin *porta.*]

port⁵ (pôrt) *v.t. Military.* to bring (a rifle, sword, or other weapon) to a diagonal position in front of the chest and close to the body, with the muzzle or blade near the left shoulder. —*n.* 1. *Military.* position of a rifle or other weapon when ported. 2. manner in which one carries oneself; bearing. [Old French *port* carriage, demeanor, from *porter* to carry, from Latin *portāre* to carry.]

Port., Portugal; Portuguese.

port·a·ble (pôr′tə bəl) *adj.* capable of being carried, esp. easily carried, as in or with the hand: *a portable radio, a portable phonograph.* —*n.* something that is portable, as a lightweight typewriter. [Late Latin *portābilis* capable of being carried, from *portāre* to carry.]

por·tage (pôr′tij) *n.* 1. act of transporting boats or goods overland between navigable waters. 2. route or place over which this is done. 3. act or work of carrying or transporting. 4. cost or charge for this. —*v.t., v.i.* **-taged, -tag·ing.** to carry (boats or goods) over a portage. [French *portage* act of carrying, going back to Latin *portāre* to carry.]

por·tal (pôr′təl) *n.* door, gate, or entrance, esp. a large and imposing one. [Medieval Latin *portale,* from *portalis* relating to a gate, from Latin *porta* gate.]

por·tal-to-por·tal pay (pôr′təl tə pôr′təl) wages computed from the time an employee enters the door of his employer's place of business to begin work until he passes through the door after he has stopped work.

portal vein, large vein that carries blood from the pancreas, spleen, stomach, and intestines to the liver.

Port Arthur 1. naval base and port city in eastern China. Pop. (1953), 126,000. 2. port city in southeastern Texas. Pop. (1970), 57,371.

Port-au-Prince (pôrt′ō prins′) *n.* capital, principal city, and chief port of Haiti, in the southwestern part of the country, on the Caribbean. Pop. (1961 est.), 250,000.

port authority, commission charged with regulating and administering the transportation facilities and the water, rail, and other traffic of a port.

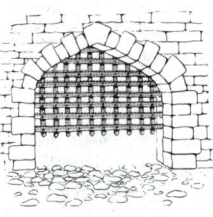

Portcullis

port·cul·lis (pôrt kul′is) *n.* heavy grating constructed so as to slide up and down in grooves cut in the sides of the gateway of a castle or fortress, capable of being lowered quickly as a defense against assault. [Anglo-Norman *porte colice* literally, sliding gate, going back to Latin *porta* gate + *colāre* to strain, filter.]

Porte (pôrt) *n.* formerly, the government of the Ottoman Empire. The Porte fell in 1923.

porte-co·chere (pôrt′kō shār′) *also,* **porte-co·chère.** *n.* 1. covered passage or entrance for carriages or other vehicles, leading into a courtyard. 2. large porch at the entrance of a building, extending over the driveway, for sheltering persons entering or leaving vehicles. [French *porte-cochère* carriage entrance, from *porte* gate + *cochère* for carriages (from *coche* carriage). See PORT⁴, COACH.]

Port Elizabeth, port city on the southern coast of the Republic of South Africa. Pop. (1967), 374,066.

por·tend (pôr tend′) *v.t.* to be a warning, sign, or indication of; indicate beforehand; forebode. [Latin *portendere* to predict.]

por·tent (pôr′tent) *n.* 1. warning or indication of what is to come, esp. of something momentous or calamitous; omen. 2. ominous or prophetic significance. [Latin *portentum* sign, omen.]

por·ten·tous (pôr ten′təs) *adj.* 1. of the nature of or constituting a portent; ominous; threatening. 2. exciting or causing wonder or awe: *a portentous era in our history.* —**por·ten′tous·ly,** *adv.* —**por·ten′tous·ness,** *n.*

por·ter¹ (pôr′tər) *n.* 1. one who is employed to carry baggage at a transportation terminal, as a railroad station, or in a hotel. 2. attendant in the parlor car of a train. [Old French *porteur* bearer, from Late Latin *portātor,* from Latin *portāre* to carry.]

por·ter² (pôr′tər) *n.* 1. one employed to do cleaning and maintenance work in a building or establishment, as in an apartment house; janitor. 2. doorkeeper; gatekeeper. [Old French *portier* gatekeeper, from Late Latin *portārius* doorkeeper, from Latin *porta* gate, door.]

por·ter³ (pôr′tər) *n.* dark-brown, heavy, bitter beer brewed from partly charred malt. [Short for *porter's ale;* supposedly because this beer was popular among porters.]

Por·ter, William Sydney (pôr′tər) see **O. Henry.**

por·ter·house (pôr′tər hous′) *n.* choice cut of beef taken from the loin, including a large part of the tenderloin. Also, **porterhouse steak.**

at; āpe; cär; end; mē; it; īce; hot; ōld; fôrk; wood; fōol; oil; out; up; ūse; turn; sing; thin; this; zh in treasure; ə in ago, taken, pencil, lemon, circus.

[Supposedly from earlier *porterhouse* a place where porter and other malt beverages were sold and where steaks were also served.]

port·fo·li·o (pôrt fō′lē ō′) *pl.*, **-li·os.** *n.* **1.** portable case for holding or carrying loose papers, drawings, documents, and similar materials. **2.** office, position, and duties of a cabinet member or a minister of state in charge of a department. **3.** list or group of security holdings of a bank, investment company, or other investor. [Italian *portafoglio* wallet, office of a cabinet minister, going back to Latin *portāre* to carry + *folium* leaf, leaf of paper.]

port·hole (pôrt′hōl′) *n.* **1.** small, usually circular opening in the side of a boat or ship, chiefly for admitting air and light. **2.** opening in a wall, as of a fort, through which to shoot; embrasure.

por·ti·co (pôr′ti kō′) *pl.*, **-coes** or **-cos.** *n.* roofed structure forming a covered walk, which is usually attached to a building, supported by columns or piers, and open on at least one side. [Italian *portico*, from Latin *porticus* arcade, colonnade. Doublet of PORCH.]

Portico

por·tiere (pôr tyār′) *also*, **por·tière.** *n.* curtain hung at a doorway, used either instead of a door or as a decoration. [French *portière*, from *porte* door, gate, from Latin *porta*.]

por·tion (pôr′shən) *n.* **1.** limited amount, piece, or segment of something. **2.** segment of a whole that is allotted or belongs to one person or group; share. **3.** quantity of food served to or for one person. **4.** share of an estate received through inheritance or by gift. **5.** dowry brought by a woman to her husband at the time of their marriage. **6.** that which is allotted to a person or group by providence; lot; fate; destiny. —*v.t.* **1.** to divide into portions or shares; distribute; parcel (often with *out*). **2.** to furnish with a share, inheritance, or dowry. [Old French *portion* share, from Latin *portiō*.] —**Syn.** *n.* **1.** see **part.**

Port·land (pôrt′lənd) *n.* **1.** largest city, chief port, and principal industrial and commercial center of Maine, in the southwestern part of the state. Pop. (1970), 65,116. **2.** chief port and largest and principal city of Oregon, in the northwestern part of the state. Pop. (1970), 382,619.

port·land cement (pôrt′lənd) *also*, **Portland cement.** bluish-gray construction cement composed chiefly of silicon and aluminum compounds of calcium, that, when mixed with sand or gravel, forms concrete that will harden under water as well as in the air. [From its resemblance to *Portland* stone, a limestone quarried on the Isle of *Portland*, a peninsula of southern England.]

Port Louis, capital, chief port, and largest city of Mauritius, on the northwestern coast of the island. Pop. (1967 est.), 136,200.

port·ly (pôrt′lē) *pl.*, **-li·er, -li·est.** *adj.* **1.** having a heavy or stout but usually dignified appearance. **2.** *Archaic.* stately or imposing, esp. in bearing. [PORT⁴ + -LY².] —**port′li·ness,** *n.* —**Syn.** **1.** see **fat.**

port·man·teau (pôrt man′tō) *pl.*, **-teaus** or **-teaux** (-tōz). *n.* suitcase or traveling bag, esp. a stiff leather one hinged at the back so as to open like a book into two compartments. [French *portemanteau* suitcase; literally, cloak bearer (originally, the official who carried the king's cloak or mantle in a case), from *porter* to carry + *manteau* cloak (from Latin *mantellum* cloak). See PORT⁵, MANTLE.]

Pôr·to A·le·gre (pôr′tō ə lā′grə) inland port city in southern Brazil. Pop. (1968), 932,801.

port of call, port where vessels stop in the course of voyages to obtain supplies, undergo repairs, or take on or discharge cargo or passengers.

port of entry, place, designated by law, at which persons or goods may enter or leave a country under official supervision of customs or other authorities.

Port-of-Spain (pôrt′əv spān′) *also*, **Port of Spain.** *n.* capital and chief port of Trinidad and Tobago, in the northwestern part of the island of Trinidad. Pop. (1960), 93,954.

Por·to-No·vo (pôr′tō nō′vō) *n.* capital of Benin, in the southeastern part of the country. Pop. (1975 est.), 91,000.

Por·to Ri·co (pôr′tō rē′kō) Puerto Rico.

por·trait (pôr′trit, -trāt) *n.* **1.** painting, photograph, or other visual representation of a person or group of persons, usually drawn or otherwise produced from life, often showing the face and upper body only. **2.** verbal picture or description, esp. of a person. [French *portrait*, from Old French *portraire* to draw, depict. See PORTRAY.]

por·trait·ist (pôr′tri tist, -trā-) *n.* one who makes portraits; portrait painter or photographer.

por·trai·ture (pôr′trə choor′, -chər) *n.* **1.** art or practice of making portraits. **2.** portrait. **3.** portraits collectively. [Old French *portraiture* likeness, representation, from *portrait*, from *portraire*. See PORTRAY.]

por·tray (pôr trā′) *v.t.* **1.** to set forth a picture of in words; describe. **2.** to make a visual likeness or representation of. **3.** to play the part of, as on the stage. [Old French *portraire*, from Late Latin *prōtrahere* to depict, from Latin *prōtrahere* to draw forth.] —**por·tray′er,** *n.*

Syn. 2. Portray, delineate, depict mean to present a visual image. **Portray** suggests a detailed representation of something in its most characteristic and revealing aspect: *The painting portrays Cortez as a ruthless conqueror.* **Delineate** emphasizes sharpness, accuracy, and minute attention to details: *The artist delineated the face of the old man with great compassion.* **Depict** may suggest a faithful representation of a broader subject: *The mural depicts rural America.*

por·tray·al (pôr trā′əl) *n.* **1.** act or process of portraying. **2.** that which is portrayed; representation.

Port Sa·id (sä ēd′) port city in northeastern Egypt, at the Mediterranean end of the Suez Canal. Pop. (1966), 283,400.

Ports·mouth (pôrts′məth) *n.* **1.** port city and naval base in southeastern Virginia. Pop. (1965 est.), 118,000. **2.** port city in southern England, on the English Channel. Pop. (1965 est.), 216,300.

Por·tu·gal (pôr′chə gəl) *n.* country in southwestern Europe, in the western part of the Iberian Peninsula, on the Atlantic. Capital, Lisbon. Area, 35,340 sq. mi. Pop. (1969 est.), 9,560,000.

Por·tu·guese (pôr′chə gēz′, -gēs′) *pl.*, **-guese.** *n.* **1.** member or close descendant of the people of Portugal. **2.** Romance language of the Indo-European language family, spoken predominantly in Portugal and Brazil. —*adj.* of or relating to Portugal, its people, their language, or their culture.

Portuguese East Africa, former Portuguese possession in southeastern Africa, now Mozambique.

Portuguese Guinea, former Portuguese possession in western Africa, now Guinea (Bissau).

Portuguese man-of-war, floating colony of sea animals, *Physalia pelagica,* found in warm waters of the Atlantic Ocean, in which one individual much larger than the others forms a gas-filled, floating sac and other individuals bearing stinging cells for stunning and holding its prey.

Portuguese man-of-war

Portuguese West Africa, former Portuguese province on the west coast of Africa, now Angola.

por·tu·lac·a (pôr′chə lak′ə) *n.* any of a group of plants, genus *Portulaca,* bearing clusters of showy flowers that have notched petals and that open only in full sunlight. [Modern Latin *Portulaca,* from Latin *portūlāca* purslane, going back to *porta* gate; because the covering on its capsule opens like a gate.]

pose¹ (pōz) *n.* **1.** position of the body or of part of the body, esp. such a position held for or depicted by an artist or photographer. **2.** attitude assumed for effect; pretense. —*v.i.*, **posed, pos·ing. 1.** to assume or hold a particular position or attitude, as for a photograph. **2.** to assume a false appearance or identity: *to pose as a member of the nobility.* —*v.t.* **1.** to place in a particular position. **2.** to cause or put forward: *to pose a question. His reluctance to cooperate poses a problem.* [Old French *poser* to place, put, halt, from Late Latin *pausāre* to cease, cause to rest, from Latin *pausa* cessation; influenced in meaning by Latin *pōnere* (past participle *positus*) to place. See PAUSE.]

Syn. *n.* **2. Pose, air, affectation** mean an artificial manner of speech or behavior. **Pose** is always used disapprovingly and implies a contrived attitude or studied pretense deliberately assumed in order to impress or deceive others: *The senator's concern for the poor is a mere pose.* **Air,** especially in the plural, implies the intention to give an appearance of good breeding or superiority: *Paul's insufferable airs made him very unpopular.* **Affectation** usually refers to a specific instance of artificial speech or behavior intended to impress others: *His British accent is an affectation; he was born in Ohio.*

pose² (pōz) *v.t.*, **posed, pos·ing.** to puzzle or confuse, as with a difficult question; perplex. [Short for obsolete *appose,* form of OPPOSE; meaning influenced by Latin *appōnere* to put to.]

Po·sei·don (pə sīd′ən) *n.* Greek god of the sea and brother of Zeus and Pluto. His Roman counterpart is Neptune.

Po·sen (pō′zən) German. Poznań.

pos·er¹ (pō′zər) *n.* one who poses. [POSE¹ + -ER¹.]

pos·er² (pō′zər) *n.* puzzling question or problem. [POSE² + -ER¹.]

po·seur (pō zœr′) *n.* one who assumes a particular attitude, manner, or role in order to deceive or impress others. [French *poseur,* from *poser* to place, put. See POSE¹.]

posh (posh) *adj. Informal.* extremely fashionable, luxurious, or elegant. [Possibly from obsolete *posh* a dandy; of uncertain origin.]

pos·it (poz′it) *v.t.* **1.** to propose or assume as a fact or basis of argument. **2.** to place in position. [Latin *positus,* past participle of *pōnere* to place.]

po·si·tion (pə zish′ən) *n.* **1.** place occupied by a person or thing: *I*

can't see the door from this position. **2.a.** manner in which something is placed or arranged: *If you change the position of the chairs around the table, there will be more room.* **b.** arrangement of the body or of its parts: *an uncomfortable position, to lie in a horizontal position.* **3.** proper or appropriate place: *The members of the band were in position.* **4.** way in which one looks upon or views a particular issue or subject; point of view: *Before the debate, both sides made their positions clear.* **5.** social standing or rank. **6.** work in which one engages or is employed; post of employment: *He has held the same position with the company for three years.* **7.** state or situation in relation to circumstances: *His request for a loan put me in an awkward position. I'm not in a position to pass judgment.* —*v.t.* to put in a particular location or arrangement. [Latin *positiō* a placing, situation.] —**po·si′tion·er**, *n.* —**Syn.** *n.* **1.** see **place.** **5.** see **rank**[1].

pos·i·tive (poz′ə tiv) *adj.* **1.a.** admitting of no question or doubt; undeniable: *positive proof.* **b.** clearly expressed or stated; definite; emphatic. **2.a.** confident in opinion or assertion; fully assured; convinced: *Are you positive that you saw him?* **b.** overconfident; opinionated. **3.** expressing, containing, or implying affirmation or acceptance; of an affirmative nature: *a positive reply.* **4.** constructive or practical: *He made a positive contribution to the discussion.* **5.** tending or moving in a direction considered to be one of increase, improvement, progress, or forward motion: *There was a positive change in his behavior.* **6.** possessing or characterized by the presence of real or particular qualities. **7.** *Mathematics.* of or relating to a quantity that is greater than zero. **8.** *Medicine.* indicating the presence of a particular disease, germ, or other abnormality. **9.** *Physics.* of (of ions) having more protons than electrons. **10.** *Electricity.* of or having the kind of electricity exhibited by a glass rod when rubbed with silk; having a deficiency of electrons. **11.** *Photography.* showing light and shade as they appear in the original. Opposed to **negative.** **12.** *Grammar.* designating the simple form or degree of an adjective or adverb. *Fast* is the positive degree of the adjective *fast.* Distinguished from **comparative** and **superlative.** **13.** *Informal.* out-and-out; downright: *He is a positive idiot.* —*n.* **1.** positive photographic print or transparency. **2.** positive form or degree of an adjective or adverb. [Latin *positīvus* settled by agreement, from *positus,* past participle of *pōnere* to place.] —**pos′i·tive·ly,** *adv.* —**pos′i·tive·ness,** *n.* —**Syn.** *adj.* **2.a.** see **sure.**

pos·i·tiv·ism (poz′ə ti viz′əm) *n.* **1.** philosophical view formulated in the 1800s, holding that all knowledge should be limited to the simple observation of phenomena, rather than metaphysical speculations for which no definite proof can be obtained. **2.** certainty; dogmatism. —**pos′i·tiv·ist,** *n.* —**pos′i·tiv·is′tic,** *adj.*

pos·i·tron (poz′ə tron′) *n.* antiparticle of the electron. [POSI(TIVE) + (ELEC)TRON.]

poss. **1.** possessive. **2.** possession.

pos·se (pos′ē) *n.* **1.** group of men summoned by a sheriff to assist him, as in capturing a criminal. **2.** group of people temporarily organized to make a search. [Medieval Latin *posse* power, from Latin *posse* to be able.]

pos·sess (pə zes′) *v.t.* **1.** to hold as property; own: *He possesses great wealth.* **2.** to have a quality, characteristic, or attribute: *She possesses much talent.* **3.** to exert an overwhelming power or influence over: *What possessed you to buy that hat? A need for revenge possessed him.* **4.** to put in possession; make master or owner (with *of*): *He possessed himself of the gold.* [Latin *possessus,* past participle of *possidēre* to own.] —**pos·ses′sor,** *n.* —**Syn.** **1.** see **own.**

pos·sessed (pə zest′) *adj.* **1.** in possession of; having (with *of*): *possessed of a quick temper.* **2.** controlled by or as by an evil spirit or demon: *Many thought the old woman was possessed.*

pos·ses·sion (pə zesh′ən) *n.* **1.** act or fact of holding or owning. **2.** state of being possessed; ownership. **3.** that which is held or owned. **4.** possessions. wealth or property. **5.** territory under the rule of a foreign country but not participating in its government. **6.** domination by or as by an evil spirit or demon. **7.** self-control; composure.

pos·ses·sive (pə zes′iv) *adj.* **1.** characterized by or displaying a strong desire to own, keep, or dominate: *He's very possessive about his books.* **2.** denoting, or in a grammatical case that expresses, possession. —*n.* **1.** possessive case. **2.** possessive form or construction. In the sentence *I met Karen's brother, Karen's* is a possessive. —**pos·ses′sive·ly,** *adv.* —**pos·ses′sive·ness,** *n.*

possessive adjective, adjective that shows possession, formed from a personal pronoun. In the sentence *This is your book, your* is a possessive adjective.

possessive pronoun, pronoun that shows possession, derived from a personal pronoun. In the sentence *This book is mine, mine* is a possessive pronoun.

pos·set (pos′it) *n.* hot drink made of milk curdled with ale or wine and usually spiced. [Of uncertain origin.]

pos·si·bil·i·ty (pos′ə bil′ə tē) *pl.* **-ties.** *n.* **1.** state or condition of being possible; likelihood. **2.** something possible.

pos·si·ble (pos′ə bəl) *adj.* **1.** capable of existing, happening, being done, or being proven true: *It's possible that he's lying. It is possible that she will agree to our plan.* **2.** that can be used, chosen, or considered; potential: *The senator is a possible candidate for the presidency.* [Latin *possibilis* that may be done, from *posse* to be able.]

pos·si·bly (pos′ə blē) *adv.* **1.** by any possibility: *Our plan can't possibly succeed.* **2.** by some possibility: *I'll see you today, or possibly tomorrow.*

pos·sum (pos′əm) *n. Informal.* **1.** opossum. **2. to play possum.** to pretend to be dead or asleep. [Form of OPOSSUM.]

post[1] (pōst) *n.* **1.** upright piece of wood, stone, or other solid material, used esp. as a support or marker. **2.** point at which a horse race begins. —*v.t.* **1.** to put up (an announcement or notice), esp. in a public place. **2.** to announce by or as by putting up a notice: *to post a reward. The teacher posted the grades on the door.* **3.** to put up signs or notices warning against trespassing on (property). **4.** to enter the name of on a list. [Old English *post* piece of timber used as a support, from Latin *postis* doorpost.]

post[2] (pōst) *n.* **1.** place where someone, as a soldier or policeman, is stationed or assigned for duty: *The sentry was ordered not to leave his post except in an emergency.* **2.a.** place where one or more military units are stationed. **b.** buildings and grounds of such a place. **3.** position of employment, esp. a public office to which one is appointed. **4.** trading post. **5.** local unit or chapter of a veterans' organization. —*v.t.* to station at or assign to a post. [French *poste* station, from Italian *posto,* going back to Latin *positum,* neuter past participle of *pōnere* to place.]

post[3] (pōst) *n.* **1.** system by which mail is collected, transported, and delivered, usually operated by a national government. **2.** *British.* **a.** single delivery of mail. **b.** mail delivered. **c.** mailbox. **d.** post office. **3.a.** formerly, one of a series of stations furnishing relays of men and horses for the carrying and delivery of mail; postrider. **b.** rider who carries and delivers mail on such a route; postrider. —*v.t.* **1.** to deposit in a mailbox or at a post office; transmit by mail. **2.** *Informal.* to supply with information or the latest news; inform: *Keep me posted on what happens while I'm away.* **3.** *Bookkeeping.* **a.** to transfer (accounts or items) from a journal to the ledger. **b.** to make the proper or necessary entries in (a ledger). —*v.i.* **1.** to travel with speed or haste; hurry. **2.** to travel with post horses. **3.** to rise and fall in the saddle in rhythm with the horse's gait when trotting. —*adv. Archaic.* posthaste. [Middle French *poste* relay station, courier, from Italian *posta,* going back to Latin *posita,* feminine past participle of *pōnere* to place; referring to the early transporting of mail by *posts,* or relay stations with couriers.]

post- prefix coming after in time or order; later: *postlude.* [Latin *post* behind, after.]

post·age (pōs′tij) *n.* amount charged for sending something by mail.

postage meter, machine that prints labels indicating the amount of postage paid on each piece of mail.

postage stamp, official stamp issued and sold by a national government, affixed to mail to show payment of postage.

post·al (pōst′əl) *adj.* of, relating to, or involving mail or the way in which it is collected, transported, and delivered. —*n.* postal card *(def.* 1*).*

postal card **1.** card issued and sold by a government and bearing an official, imprinted postage stamp. It can be sent through the mail without an envelope. **2.** post card *(def.* 1*).*

post·bel·lum (pōst bel′əm) *adj.* occurring after a war, esp. the U.S. Civil War. [Latin *post* after + *bellum* war.]

post card **1.** card, usually with a picture on one side, that can be sent through the mail without an envelope. **2.** postal card *(def.* 1*).*

post chaise, four-wheeled carriage drawn by post horses, used to carry mail and passengers from station to station.

post·date (pōst′dāt′) **-dat·ed, -dat·ing.** *v.t.* **1.** to date (a check, letter, or the like) with a date that is later than the actual one. **2.** to occur later than; follow in time.

post·er (pōs′tər) *n.* **1.** large, usually printed sheet of paper bearing words, pictures, or a combination of both, usually displayed in some public place as an advertisement or public notice. **2.** one who posts bills, advertisements, or notices.

pos·te·ri·or (pos tēr′ē ər, pōs-) *adj.* **1.** situated at or toward the back; rear. **2.** coming after in a series. —*n.* buttocks. [Latin *posterior,* comparative of *posterus* coming after.]

pos·ter·i·ty (pos ter′ə tē) *n.* **1.** generations of the future collectively. **2.** all of one's descendants collectively. [Latin *posteritās.*]

pos·tern (pōs′tərn, pos′-) *n.* back door or gate, esp. in a castle or fortification. —*adj.* located at the back or side: *a postern door.* [Old French *posterne* back door to a fort, going back to Latin *posterus* coming after.]

post exchange, nonprofit government store at a military installation that sells tax-free goods to military personnel, their families, and to civilian employees.

post·grad·u·ate (pōst′graj′o̅o̅ it) *adj.* of, relating to, or taking a

course of study after graduation from a college or university, esp. after receiving a bachelor's degree. —*n.* postgraduate student.

post·haste (pōst'hāst') *adv.* as quickly as possible; with utmost haste. [POST¹ + HASTE.]

post horse, horse kept for use by postriders or for hire to travelers.

post·hu·mous (pos'chə məs) *adj.* **1.** published after the death of the author. **2.** arising or occurring after one's death: *a posthumous award, posthumous fame.* **3.** (of a child) born after the death of the father. [Latin *posthumus,* modification of *postumus* last, superlative of *post* after; *h* of *posthumus* due to incorrect association with *humus* ground (as if *post humum* after (burial in) the ground).] —**post'hu·mous·ly,** *adv.*

post·hyp·not·ic (pōst'hip not'ik) *adj.* of or relating to the time following a hypnotic trance.

pos·til·ion (pōs til'yən, pos-) *also,* **pos·til·lion.** *n.* one who guides the team of a horse-drawn carriage by riding the left lead horse. [French *postillon,* from Italian *postiglione,* from *posta* messenger, relay station. See POST¹.]

post·im·pres·sion·ism (pōst'im presh'ə niz'əm) *n.* period in French painting, beginning in the late nineteenth century and lasting until the early twentieth century, exemplified by such painters as Vincent Van Gogh and Paul Cézanne, and characterized by an emphasis on the emotional content of subject matter, the expression of intensely personal views, and the free use of many colors. —**post'·im·pres'sion·ist,** *n., adj.* —**post'im·pres'sion·is'tic,** *adj.*

post·lude (pōst'lōōd') *n.* concluding musical piece or movement, as that played at the end of a religious service. [POST- + (PRE)LUDE.]

post·man (pōst'mən) *pl.,* **-men.** *n.* mailman.

post·mark (pōst'märk') *n.* official mark stamped on mail to cancel the postage stamp and to show the place and date of mailing. —*v.t.* to stamp with a postmark.

post·mas·ter (pōst'mas'tər) *n.* official in charge of a post office. —**post'mis'tress,** *n.*

postmaster general *pl.,* **postmasters general. 1.** head of the postal service of a country. **2. Postmaster General.** head of the postal service of the United States, appointed by the president with the approval of the Senate.

post·me·rid·i·an (pōst'mə rid'ē ən) *adj.* of, relating to, or occurring during the afternoon.

post me·rid·i·em (pōst'mə rid'ē əm) between noon and midnight. [Latin *post merīdiem* after midday.]

post·mor·tem (pōst'môr'təm) *adj.* **1.** taking place or done after a person's death. **2.** of or relating to an autopsy. **3.** following and concerned with an event, esp. something unpleasant: *The candidate's advisers held a post-mortem discussion of his defeat.* —*n.* **1.** post-mortem examination; autopsy. **2.** review discussion of something that has been done or accomplished. [Latin *post mortem* after death.]

post·na·sal (pōst'nā'zəl) *adj.* situated or occurring behind the nose.

post·na·tal (pōst'nāt'əl) *adj.* occurring after birth; subsequent to birth: *postnatal care.*

post·o·bit (pōst'ō'bit, -ob'it) *n.* written agreement by which a borrower promises to repay a debt upon the death of a specified person from whom he expects to inherit. Also, **post-obit bond.** —*adj.* made or taking effect after a person's death. [Latin *post obitum* after death.]

post office 1. department of a national government in charge of handling mail. **2.** local branch of such a department, responsible for the collection, sorting, and distribution of mail.

post·op·er·a·tive (pōst'op'ər ə tiv) *adj.* occurring after a surgical operation.

post·paid (pōst'pād') *adj.* having the postage prepaid.

post·pone (pōst pōn') **-poned, -pon·ing.** *v.t.* to put off to a later time: *The game was postponed until next week because of rain.* [Latin *postpōnere* to put after.] —**post·pone'ment,** *n.* —**Syn.** see delay.

post·pran·di·al (pōst pran'dē əl) *adj.* after a meal, esp. after dinner. [POST- + PRANDIAL.]

post·rid·er (pōst'rī'dər) *n.* one who carries and delivers mail on horseback over a fixed route.

post road, road over which mail is or was carried, esp. one having post stations.

post·script (pōst'skript') *n.* **1.** message or note added to a letter after the closing signature. **2.** supplement or appendix of any composition or literary work. [Latin *postscrīptum,* neuter past participle of *postscrībere* to write after.]

pos·tu·lant (pos'chə lənt) *n.* one who is a candidate, esp. for admission as a novice to a religious order. [Latin *postulāns,* present participle of *postulāre* to demand, request.]

pos·tu·late (*n.,* pos'chə lit; *v.,* pos'chə lāt') *v.t.* **1.** statement or principle accepted as true without proof; self-evident or universally accepted truth. **2.** fundamental principle. **3.** necessary condition; prerequisite. —*v.t.* **-lat·ed, -lat·ing. 1.** to accept (something) as true without proof; take for granted. **2.** to require, demand, or claim. **3.** to claim the truth

or existence of. [Latin *postulātus,* past participle of *postulāre* to demand, request.] —**pos'tu·la'tion,** *n.*

pos·ture (pos'chər) *n.* **1.** manner of carrying or holding the head and body; carriage. **2.a.** position of the body or of parts of the body. **b.** such a position assumed, as in posing for an artist. **3.** relative state or condition; situation: *the posture of public affairs.* **4.** mental or spiritual attitude; frame of mind. —*v.i.,* **-tured, -tur·ing.** to take or assume a certain bodily position, esp. for effect. —*v.t.* to put in a certain position; pose. [French *posture* attitude, situation, from Italian *postura* attitude, position, from Latin *positūra* position.] —**pos'tur·al,** *adj.* —**Syn.** *n.* see bearing.

post·vo·cal·ic (pōst'vō kal'ik) *adj.* following immediately after a vowel.

post·war (pōst'wôr') *adj.* after a war.

po·sy (pō'zē) *pl.,* **-sies.** *n.* **1.** a single flower. **2.** bouquet of flowers; nosegay. **3.** *Archaic.* motto or inscription engraved on a ring, knife, or the like. [Form of POESY.]

pot (pot) *n.* **1.** container of metal, earthenware, or other material, usually round and having one or two handles, used esp. in cooking. **2.a.** pot and its contents. **b.** amount contained in a pot; potful. **3.** stakes in a card game, esp. poker. **4.** lobster pot. **5.** *Informal.* large sum of money. **6.** *Slang.* marijuana. **7. to go to pot.** to go to ruin; deteriorate. —*v.t.,* **pot·ted, pot·ting. 1.** to put into a flowerpot: *to pot a plant.* **2.** to preserve (food) in a pot or jar. **3.** to cook in a pot; stew: *to pot beef.* **4.** to shoot (game) for food rather than for sport. **5.** *Informal.* to win, seize, or capture; bag. [Old English *pott* round, deep container.]

po·ta·ble (pō'tə bəl) *adj.* fit or suitable for drinking. —*n.* also, **potables.** something drinkable; drink. [Late Latin *pōtābilis* drinkable, from Latin *pōtāre* to drink.]

pot·ash (pot'ash') *n.* **1.** potassium carbonate. **2.** any of various commercial compounds, as fertilizers, that contain potassium, used esp. in fertilizers, soaps, and in making glass. [Earlier *pot ashes,* translation of obsolete Dutch *potasschen* literally, pot ashes; because it was formerly obtained from the ashes of vegetable substances burned in iron pots.]

potash alum, alum (*def. 2*).

po·tas·si·um (pə tas'ē əm) *n.* very soft, light, silver-white metallic element whose compounds include some of the most important fertilizers and industrial chemicals. Symbol: **K** See **element** for table. [Modern Latin *potassium,* from *potassa,* from POTASH.]

potassium bi·tar·trate (bī tär'trāt) cream of tartar.

potassium carbonate, white compound obtained from potassium chloride, used esp. as a fertilizer and in the manufacture of explosives, chemicals, glass, soap, textiles, and ceramics. Formula: K_2CO, Also, **pot'ash'.**

potassium chlorate, poisonous crystalline substance obtained from potassium carbonate, used in the manufacture of explosives, fireworks, and matches. Formula: $KClO$,

potassium chloride, crystalline compound that is the principal source of potassium for other compounds and is used esp. as a fertilizer. Formula: KCl

potassium cyanide, extremely poisonous, solid compound that smells like bitter almonds, used in electroplating and in the extraction of gold and silver from their ores. Formula: KCN

potassium hydroxide, white, caustic compound used esp. in the manufacture of soap. Formula: KOH

potassium nitrate, colorless crystalline compound, used in gunpowder and explosives and as an oxidizing agent in solid rocket fuels. Formula: KNO, Also, **ni'ter, salt'pe'ter.**

potassium permanganate, dark-purple crystalline compound, used as a disinfectant, an oxidizing agent to purify water and air, and a bleaching agent. Formula: $KMnO_4$

po·ta·tion (pō tā'shən) *n.* **1.** act of drinking. **2.** drink, or glass of liquor. [Latin *pōtātiō* a drinking.]

po·ta·to (pə tā'tō) *pl.,* **-toes.** *n.* **1.** edible tuber of a leafy low-growing plant, *Solanum tuberosum,* originally grown in South America. It is a basic food in Europe, America, and other parts of the world, and is used to make a wide variety of products, as starch, flour, and vodka. **2.** the plant itself, having dull-green leaves and white, blue, or purple flowers. **3.** sweet potato. [Spanish *patata,* from Taino *batata* sweet potato.]

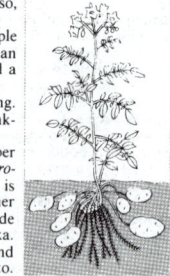

Potato plant

potato beetle, Colorado potato beetle. Also, **potato bug.**

potato chip, very thin slice of potato, fried crisp and usually salted.

pot·bel·ly (pot'bel'ē) *pl.,* **-lies.** *n.* **1.** large or protuberant belly. **2.** person who has such a belly. —**pot'bel'lied,** *adj.*

at; āpe; cär; end; mē; it; īce; hot; ōld; fôrk; wood; fōōl; oil; out; up; ūse; turn; sing; thin; this; zh in treasure; ə in ago, taken, pencil, lemon, circus.

potbelly stove, stove having bulging, rounded sides, that burns coal or wood. Also, **potbellied stove.**

pot·boil·er (pot′boi′lər) *n. Informal.* work of literature or art, usually inferior, produced merely to earn money.

pot cheese, cottage cheese, esp. a form having large curds and a dry consistency.

po·ten·cy (pōt′ən sē) *pl.,* **-cies.** *n.* **1.** state or quality of being potent. **2.** degree of this. **3.** capacity for development; potentiality. [Latin *potentia* power.]

po·tent (pōt′ənt) *adj.* **1.** having force, effectiveness, strength, or power: *a potent medicine, a potent argument.* **2.** (of males) capable of engaging in sexual intercourse. [Latin *potēns* powerful, present participle of *posse* to be able.] —**po′tent·ly,** *adv.*

po·ten·tate (pōt′ən tāt′) *n.* one who has great power or authority; a monarch or ruler. [Late Latin *potentātus,* from Latin *potentātus* power, rule.]

Potbelly stove

po·ten·tial (pə ten′shəl) *adj.* **1.** capable of being or becoming; possible but not actual: *a potential leader, a potential criminal, a potential source of trouble.* **2.** denoting that aspect of the subjunctive mood that expresses possibility by the use of such auxiliary verbs as *may, might,* and *can.* —*n.* **1.** inherent quality or ability capable of being developed or advanced: *a novelist with great potential.* **2.** that aspect of the subjunctive mood that expresses possibility. **3.** amount of electrification of a point with reference to some standard, such as the earth. [Late Latin *potentiālis* possessing power, from Latin *potentia* power.] —**po·ten′tial·ly,** *adv.*

potential difference, amount of work, measured in volts, required to move a unit charge of electricity between two points.

potential energy, energy possessed by a body due to its position or form. Distinguished from *kinetic energy.*

po·ten·ti·al·i·ty (pə ten′shē al′ə tē) *pl.,* **-ties.** *n.* **1.** inherent quality or ability capable of being developed or advanced; potential. **2.** something potential; possibility.

po·ten·ti·om·e·ter (pə ten′shē om′ə tər) *n.* device used to divide a given input voltage in a specified manner and to measure unknown voltages by comparing them with voltages of standard sources. [POTENTI(AL) + -METER.]

pot·ful (pot′fool′) *pl.,* **-fuls.** *n.* amount that a pot can hold.

poth·er (poth′ər) *n.* **1.** confused or excited state; commotion; uproar. **2.** choking cloud of dust or smoke. —*v.t., v.i.* to worry· or bother. [Of uncertain origin.]

pot·herb (pot′ûrb′, -hûrb′) *n.* any plant whose leaves, stems, or flowers are cooked and eaten as a vegetable, as spinach, or used as a seasoning, as sage or thyme.

pot·hole (pot′hōl′) *n.* **1.** deep hole worn in the rock bed of a river or stream by stones and gravel whirled around by the force of the current. **2.** any deep hole, esp. in the surface of a road.

pot·hook (pot′hook′) *n.* **1.** hook used to hang a pot over an open fire. **2.** iron rod with a hook at the end, used to lift hot pots, irons, or stove lids. **3.** S-shaped stroke in writing.

pot·hunt·er (pot′hun′tər) *n.* **1.** one who hunts primarily for food rather than for sport. **2.** one who takes part in a contest merely for the sake of winning a prize.

po·tion (pō′shən) *n.* drink, esp. one supposedly having magical properties. [Latin *pōtiō.* Doublet of POISON.]

pot liquor, liquid left in a pot after meat and vegetables have been cooked in it.

pot·luck (pot′luk′) *n.* whatever food may be available for a meal for which no special preparation was made: *If you come for dinner tonight, you'll have to take potluck.*

pot marigold, a showy yellow or orange flower head of a group of plants, *Calendula officinalis,* of the composite family, formerly used for seasoning. **2.** plant bearing this flower head, having thick oblong leaves.

Po·to·mac (pə tō′mak) *n.* river in the eastern United States, flowing through West Virginia, Virginia, and Maryland.

pot·pie (pot′pī′) *n.* **1.** pie filled with meat or poultry and usually vegetables, encased in a pastry dough and baked in a deep dish. **2.** meat stew with dumplings.

pot·pour·ri (pō′poo rē′, pot poor′ē) *n.* **1.** medley or anthology, as of music or literature. **2.** mixture of dried flower petals and spices, kept in a jar and used for fragrance. **3.** any mixture or collection of miscellaneous things. [French *potpourri* hodgepodge, medley; literally, rotten pot, translation of Spanish *olla podrida* dish of meat and vegetables; literally, rotten pot (because cooked till "rotten"), going back to Latin *ōlla* pot + *pūtridus* rotten.]

pot roast, meat, usually beef, browned in a pot, covered, and cooked slowly in a small amount of water, often with vegetables.

Pots·dam (pots′dam′) *n.* city in central East Germany, site of a meeting of the heads of the three major Allied governments after World War II. Pop. (1963 est.), 115,100.

pot·sherd (pot′shurd′) *also,* **pot·shard** (pot′shärd′). *n.* fragment of pottery, esp. one found at the site of an archaeological expedition. [POT + *sherd,* form of SHARD.]

pot shot 1. shot fired at random or without careful aim from close range. **2.** shot fired to kill game for food, with little or no regard to the rules of sport.

pot·tage (pot′ij) *n.* thick soup or broth with vegetables and sometimes meat. [Old French *potage,* from *pot* pot; of Germanic origin.]

pot·ted (pot′id) *adj.* **1.** put or kept in a pot: *a potted plant.* **2.** cooked or preserved in a pot or can: *potted meat.* **3.** *Slang.* intoxicated; drunk.

pot·ter[1] (pot′ər) *n.* one who makes pottery. [Old English *pottere,* from *pott* pot.]

pot·ter[2] (pot′ər) *v.i., v.t.* to putter. [Dialectal English *pote* to poke (from Old English *potian* to push) + -ER[1].] —**pot′ter·er,** *n.*

potter's field, piece of ground used as a burial place for the poor and the unknown.

potter's wheel, rotating level disk that is turned by a motor or by pumping with the foot, used by a potter to make objects from soft clay.

pot·ter·y (pot′ər ē) *pl.,* **-ter·ies.** *n.* **1.** pots, vases, and other objects made from soft clay and hardened by heat. **2.** art or technique of making pottery. **3.** place where pottery is made. [Old French *poterie,* from *potier* potter[1], from *pot* pot; of Germanic origin.]

pouch (pouch) *n.* **1.** bag, sack, or other receptacle, usually made of a soft, flexible material, as leather. **2.** anything resembling this. **3.** mailbag. **4.** baglike structure on the abdomen of female marsupials, in which the young are carried after birth. **5.** any baglike cavity or part. [Old French *po(u)che,* pocket; of Germanic origin.]

poul·ter·er (pōl′tər ər) *n.* one who deals in poultry. [Obsolete *poulter* (from Old French *pouletier,* from *poulet* young chicken) + -ER[1]. See POULTRY.]

poul·tice (pōl′tis) *n.* soft, moist mass of an absorbent substance, as mustard, heated and applied to a part of the body as a medicine for soreness or inflammation. —*v.t.* **-ticed, -tic·ing.** to apply a poultice to. [Earlier *pultes,* from Latin *pultes,* plural of *puls* thick pap, pottage.]

poul·try (pōl′trē) *n.* any domestic fowl, as chickens, turkeys, geese, and ducks, usually raised for their meat or eggs. [Old French *pouleterie,* from *poulet* young chicken, diminutive of *poule* hen, going back to Latin *pullus* young fowl, young animal.]

pounce[1] (pouns) *v.i.* **pounced, pounc·ing.** **1.** to swoop down, or leap suddenly in or as in attack (with *on, upon,* or *at*). **2.** to attack in such a way. —*n.* **1.** act of pouncing. **2.** claw or talon of a bird of prey. [Probably from Middle English *ponson* sharp tool, from Old French *poinçon, poinchon.* See PUNCHEON[2].]

pounce[2] (pouns) *n.* **1.** fine powder, as of cuttlebone, formerly used to soak up excess ink in writing or to prepare a surface, as of parchment, for writing. **2.** fine powder, as of charcoal, dusted over a stencil to transfer the design to the surface beneath. —*v.t.* **pounced, pounc·ing.** **1.** to trace or transfer (a design) with pounce. **2.** to sprinkle, smooth, or rub with pounce. [French *ponce* pumice stone, going back to Latin *pūmex.*]

pound[1] (pound) *pl.,* **pounds** or **pound.** *n.* **1.** unit of weight equal to 16 ounces avoirdupois or 12 ounces troy, or 5760 grains apothecaries' weight. See **weights and measures** for table. **2.** basic monetary unit of the United Kingdom, equal to 100 pence, formerly equal to twenty shillings. Also, **pound sterling. 3.** monetary unit of varying value in various other countries, as in Ireland, Egypt, Ghana, Israel, Lebanon, Libya, and Turkey. [Old English *pund* a measure of weight, an English monetary unit, from Latin *pondō* by weight.]

pound[2] (pound) *v.t.* **1.** to strike or hit with heavy, repeated blows: *to pound a nail into a wall.* **2.** to reduce to a powder or pulp by pounding; pulverize: *to pound garlic into paste.* **3.** to force or cause to give way by beating or hitting (often with *down*): *The angry mob pounded down the door.* **4.** to instill or implant by repetition or drill: *The teacher pounded the multiplication tables into her students.* **5.** to produce by or as by hitting or thumping (often with *out*): *The secretary pounded out the letter on her typewriter.* —*v.i.* **1.** to strike heavy, repeated blows (often with *on, upon,* or *against*): *to pound on a door.* **2.** to beat heavily: *He could feel his heart pounding against his chest.* **3.** to walk or move with heavy steps; plod: *The boys pounded into the house.* —*n.* **1.a.** heavy blow. **b.** sound of this; thump; thud. **2.** act of pounding. [Old English *pūnian* to bruise, pulverize.] —**Syn.** *v.t.* **1.** see **beat.**

pound[3] (pound) *n.* **1.** enclosure for confining animals, esp. stray dogs. **2.** place of confinement, as for prisoners. **3.** compartment or net for catching or confining fish. [Old English *pund* enclosure.]

Pound, Ezra (Loo·mis) (pound; lōo′mis) 1885–1972, U.S. poet, critic, and translator.

pound·age (poun′dij) *n.* tax, commission, rate, or the like calculated per pound sterling or per pound weight.

at; āpe; cär; end; mē; it; īce; hot; ōld; fôrk; wood; fōol; oil; out; up; ūse; turn; sing; thin; this; zh in treasure; ə in ago, taken, pencil, lemon, circus.

pound·al (pound′əl) *n.* amount of force that gives an acceleration of one foot per second per second to a mass of one pound.

pound cake, rich cake made with whole eggs and originally containing equal amounts of butter, sugar, and flour.

pound·er[1] (poun′dər) *n.* one who or that which pounds. [POUND[2] + -ER[1].]

pound·er[2] (poun′dər) *n.* one who or that which weighs or is worth a certain number of pounds. ▲ used in combination: *This fish is a three-pounder.* [POUND[1] + -ER[1].]

pound-fool·ish (pound′foo′lish) *adj.* unwise or careless about spending large sums of money.

pound sterling, pound[1] (*def.* 2).

pour (pôr) *v.t.* **1.** to cause to flow in a continuous stream: *to pour water from a bucket.* **2.** to send forth, emit, or utter rapidly or in profusion: *to pour out one's fury.* —*v.i.* **1.** to flow in a continuous stream: *The stream poured into the river.* **2.** to rain hard. **3.** to move or come forth in great numbers; swarm: *The people poured out of the train.* **4.** to act as hostess by pouring beverages for guests. —*n.* heavy rainfall; downpour. [Of uncertain origin.] —**pour′er,** *n.*

pour·boire (poor bwär′) *n. French.* tip; gratuity.

pout[1] (pout) *v.i.* **1.** to thrust out the lips, as in displeasure or sullenness. **2.** to be sullen; sulk. **3.** to swell out; protrude. —*v.t.* to thrust out or protrude. —*n.* **1.** protrusion of the lips, as when displeased. **2.** fit of sullenness. [Of uncertain origin.] —**pout′y,** *adj.*

pout[2] (pout) *n.* any of various catfish, as the eelpout. [Old English -pūte, as in ælepūte eelpout.]

pout·er (pou′tər) *n.* **1.** one who pouts. **2.** any of a breed of domestic pigeons having an enlarged esophagus and crop that can be inflated with air and puffed out.

pov·er·ty (pov′ər tē) *n.* **1.** state or condition of being poor: *to live in poverty.* **2.** deficiency or lack of necessary or desirable qualities: *the poverty of the soil in a desert area.* **3.** smallness of amount; scarcity; dearth. [Old French *poverte* state of being poor, need, from Latin *paupertās.*]

pov·er·ty-strick·en (pov′ər tē strik′ən) *adj.* very poor; destitute.

POW, prisoner of war.

pow·der (pou′dər) *n.* **1.** fine, minute particles produced by grinding, crushing, pounding, or crumbling a dry substance. **2.** any of various preparations or substances in such a form: *soap powder.* **3.** gunpowder. **4.** **to take a powder.** *Slang.* to run away; leave quickly. —*v.t.* **1.** to reduce to powder; pulverize. **2.** to sprinkle or cover with or as with powder: *She powdered the rolling pin with flour.* **3.** to use or apply powder as a cosmetic on (the face or body). —*v.i.* **1.** to be reduced to powder. **2.** to apply cosmetic powder to the face or body. [Old French *poudre,* earlier *pol(d)re* dust, solid substance reduced to fine particles, explosive, from Latin *pulvis* dust.]

powder blue, pale-blue color.

powder flask, flask, usually of leather or metal, used for carrying gunpowder.

powder horn, horn of a cow or other animal, used for carrying gunpowder.

powder magazine, room or compartment where gunpowder and other explosives are stored.

powder puff, soft pad for applying powder to the skin.

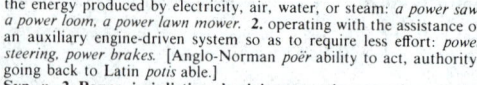

Powder flask

pow·der·y (pou′dər ē) *adj.* **1.** consisting of or resembling powder. **2.** sprinkled or covered with or as with powder. **3.** capable of being easily reduced to powder; friable.

pow·er (pou′ər) *n.* **1.** ability to do or effect something: *It is not in his power to help you.* **2.** ability or right to command, control, or make decisions; authority: *A struggle for power took place within the company.* **3.** *also,* **powers,** particular mental or physical ability or faculty: *He lost his power of speech.* **4.** one who or that which possesses or exercises influence, control, or authority over others: *The United States is a major world power.* **5.** political or military strength of a nation, government, or similar organization. **6.** legal ability or authority to do or act: *The president has the power to veto bills.* **7.** physical strength; force: *There was no power behind his punch.* **8.a.** number of times, indicated by an exponent, that a given number or algebraic expression is multiplied by itself. The power of 4^3 is 3. **b.** product found by multiplying a number or algebraic expression by itself a given number or times as indicated by an exponent. The second power of 5 is 25 since $5^2 = 5 \times 5 = 25.$ **9.** energy or force that can do work, esp. electrical energy. **10.** rate at which work is done or energy is used. The power of a source is equal to the force exerted, multiplied by the distance through which it acts, divided by the time during which it acts. **11.** capacity of a lens or a combination of lenses to magnify the apparent size of an object. **12.** **powers,** member of the sixth of the nine orders of angels. **13.** *Informal.* large number or quantity. —*v.t.* to provide with power, esp. mechanical power. —*adj.* **1.** operated or driven by a motor or by

the energy produced by electricity, air, water, or steam: *a power saw, a power loom, a power lawn mower.* **2.** operating with the assistance of an auxiliary engine-driven system so as to require less effort: *power steering, power brakes.* [Anglo-Norman *poër* ability to act, authority, going back to Latin *potis* able.]

Syn. *n.* **2. Power, jurisdiction, dominion** mean the possession or exercise of the right or ability to rule. **Power** suggests the capacity to command inherent in an office or rank and stresses the ability to compel obedience, make decisions, and wield influence: *In ancient times kings had absolute power over their subjects.* **Jurisdiction** suggests a legal right to exercise certain functions within a specified area: *A circuit court has jurisdiction over a number of states.* **Dominion** suggests ultimate supremacy: *Though lovers be lost love shall not; and death shall have no dominion* (Thomas, 1943).

pow·er·boat (pou′ər bōt′) *n.* motorboat.

power dive, dive of an airplane accelerated by the power of its engine or engines.

pow·er·ful (pou′ər fəl) *adj.* **1.** having great strength or force: *a powerful machine, a powerful athlete.* **2.** having great influence or effect: *a powerful argument.* **3.** having or showing great power, authority, or control over others: *a powerful nation.* —*adv. Informal.* very: *He was powerful hungry.* —**pow′er·ful·ly,** *adv.*

pow·er·house (pou′ər hous′) *n.* **1.** power plant. **2.** *Informal.* person possessing a great deal of strength or energy.

pow·er·less (pou′ər lis) *adj.* **1.** lacking the ability or authority to do or effect something. **2.** lacking power or strength; weak. —**pow′er·less·ly,** *adv.* —**pow′er·less·ness,** *n.*

power of attorney 1. written document authorizing one person to act as the attorney or legal agent for another. **2.** legal authority granted by such a document.

power pack, electrical unit used to convert the voltage of a power supply to a voltage suitable for an electric or electronic device.

power plant 1. generating station for electrical power. Also, **power station. 2.** any system that produces mechanical or electrical energy in useful form from fuels or other sources.

power play, play in hockey in which a team having more players on the ice than the opposition concentrates its men in the offensive zone in an attempt to score a goal.

power politics, use of or the threatened use of force by countries in order to strengthen their positions and increase their power.

Pow·ha·tan (pou′ə tan′, pou hat′ən) *n.* c.1550–1618, Algonquian Indian chief.

pow·wow (pou′wou′) *n.* **1.** conference of or with North American Indians. **2.** North American Indian ceremony characterized by feasting, dancing, and rites performed by a medicine man, esp. for the cure of disease or success in war or hunting. **3.** North American Indian medicine man or priest. **4.** *Informal.* any conference or meeting. —*v.i.* to hold a powwow. [Algonquian *powwaw* magician; literally, he dreams.]

pox (poks) *n.* **1.** any of several diseases characterized by skin eruptions, as chickenpox or smallpox. **2.** syphilis. [Form of earlier *pocks,* plural of POCK.]

Poz·nań (pôz′nän, -nän′ya) *n.* city in western Poland. Pop. (1968 est.), 455,500. Also, *German,* **Po′sen.**

pp., pianissimo.

pp. 1. pages. **2.** past participle.

p.p. 1. parcel post. Also, **P.P. 2.** past participle. **3.** postpaid.

ppd. 1. postpaid. **2.** prepaid.

ppr., present participle. Also, **p.pr.**

Pr, praseodymium.

pr. 1. pair; pairs. **2.** price. **3.** present. **4.** power. **5.** pronoun.

PR, Public Relations.

P.R., Puerto Rico.

prac·ti·ca·ble (prak′ti kə bəl) *adj.* **1.** that can be put into practice; feasible: *a practicable plan.* **2.** that can be used: *a practicable road.* [Modification (influenced by earlier *practic* practice) of French *praticable,* going back to Middle French *pratique* practice, through Latin, from Greek *praktikē* practical (as opposed to theoretical) science.] —**prac′ti·ca·bil′i·ty, prac′ti·ca·ble·ness,** *n.* —**prac′ti·ca·bly,** *adv.*

prac·ti·cal (prak′ti kal) *adj.* **1.** of, relating to, or derived from experience, action, or use rather than from theory or speculation: *practical knowledge.* **2.** that can be done, used, or carried out: *a practical method of solving a problem.* **3.a.** capable of applying or utilizing actual knowledge or experience. **b.** tending or preferring to act rather than to theorize or speculate. **4.** to all intents and purposes; virtual. **5.** actively engaged in the practice of a profession or occupation: *a practical psychologist.* [Late Latin *practicus* relating to action (from Greek *prāktikos,* from *prāssein* to do, accomplish) + -AL[1].] —**prac·ti·cal·i·ty** (prak′tə kal′ə tē), **prac′ti·cal·ness,** *n.*

practical joke, prank, trick, or other joke played on someone, esp. in order to cause him embarrassment.

at; āpe; cär; end; mē; it; īce; hot; ōld; fôrk; wood; fōol; oil; out; up; ūse; turn; sing; thin; this; zh in treasure; ə in ago, taken, pencil, lemon, circus.

prac·ti·cal·ly (prak′tik lē) *adv.* **1.** to all intents or purposes; virtually. **2.** nearly; almost: *The work is practically finished.* **3.** in a practical manner; through actual experience or use. —**Syn. 1.** see **virtually. 2.** see **almost.**

practical nurse, one who has training and experience in performing certain nursing duties, but lacks the training and education of a registered nurse.

prac·tice (prak′tis) *also, British,* **prac·tise.** *n.* **1.a.** repeated or continuous performance or exercise of an action in order to attain knowledge, skill, or proficiency: *Practice makes perfect.* **b.** session during which such an action is performed: *If we don't hurry, we'll be late for football practice.* **c.** condition of being skilled or proficient through repeated or continuous performance or exercise of an action: *to be out of practice.* **2.** act or process of doing, using, or carrying out something; execution: *The idea is not good in practice.* **3.** habitual or usual action; habit: *He makes a practice of calling whenever he's going to be late.* **4.** usual or established way of doing something: *It is the army's practice to play taps every night.* **5.** regular exercise or pursuit of a profession or occupation: *the practice of medicine.* **6.** professional business, esp. of a doctor or lawyer: *The doctor has a lucrative practice.* **7.** established method of conducting legal proceedings. **8. practices.** schemes or plots. —*v.t.,* **-ticed, -tic·ing. 1.** to perform (something) repeatedly or continuously in order to attain knowledge, skill, or proficiency: *to practice playing the violin. The golfer practiced putting.* **2.** to carry out in action; put into practice: *Practice what you preach.* **3.** to do or observe habitually or frequently; make a habit or custom of: *to practice caution, to practice a religion.* **4.** to work at or pursue as a profession or occupation: *to practice law.* **5.** to train or instruct by practice. —*v.i.* **1.** to perform something repeatedly or continuously in order to acquire knowledge, skill, or proficiency. **2.** to work at or pursue a profession or occupation: *The doctor practiced in New York City.* [Old French *practiser* to do often, exercise, going back to Late Latin *pràcticus* relating to action. See PRACTICAL.] —**prac′tic·er,** *n.*
Syn. *n.* **1. Practice, exercise, drill¹** mean a set of activities undertaken for training and proficiency. **Practice** suggests a systematic and disciplined mental or physical activity, repeated performance of which helps one to learn or improve a skill: *Long hours of practice enabled the pianist to perfect his technique.* **Exercise** is commonly applied to activities directed toward maintaining or achieving physical health, strength, or vigor: *The boxer keeps in shape by doing exercises every day.* **Drill** suggests an activity aimed at perfecting a skill in a specific area by repeated training procedures: *The boy improved his pronunciation after a few drills.* **3.** see **habit.**

prac·ticed (prak′tist) *also, British,* **prac·tised.** *adj.* **1.** proficient through practice; experienced: *a practiced craftsman.* **2.** learned or perfected through practice: *a practiced art.*

prac·tise (prak′tis) *British. v.* **practice.** —*v.t., v.i.,* **-tised, -tis·ing.** to practice.

prac·ti·tion·er (prak tish′ə nər) *n.* **1.** one who practices a profession. **2.** in Christian Science, one who is authorized to heal.

prae·fect (prē′fekt) *prefect.*

prae·no·men (prē nō′mən) *pl.,* **-nom·i·na** (-nom′i nə). *n.* first name of an ancient Roman citizen. [Latin *praenōmen.*]

prae·tor (prē′tər) *also,* **pre·tor.** *n.* in ancient Rome, an elected magistrate or judge subordinate to and performing some duties of a consul. [Latin *praetor.*]

prae·to·ri·an (prē tôr′ē ən) *also,* **pre·to·ri·an.** *adj.* **1.** of or relating to a praetor. **2. Praetorian.** of, relating to, or constituting the Praetorian Guard. —*n.* **1.** praetor or ex-praetor. **2. Praetorian.** member of the Praetorian Guard.

Praetorian Guard 1. bodyguard of the ancient Roman emperors or military commanders. **2.** member of this bodyguard.

prag·mat·ic (prag mat′ik) *adj.* **1.** concerned with practical results or values rather than theory or speculation: *From a pragmatic point of view, this idea is ridiculous.* **2.** of or relating to philosophical pragmatism. Also, **prag·mat′i·cal.** [Latin *prāgmaticus* skilled in business, from Greek *prāgmatikos* businesslike, statesmanlike, from *prāgma* deed, affair.] —**prag·mat′i·cal·ly,** *adv.*

pragmatic sanction, edict or decree issued by a sovereign and having the force of a fundamental law.

prag·ma·tism (prag′mə tiz′əm) *n.* **1.** philosophical view set forth in the late nineteenth century by William James and Charles S. Peirce and further developed by John Dewey, holding that the validity of an idea should be evaluated in terms of its practical consequences. **2.** pragmatic quality or character. —**prag′ma·tist,** *n.*

Prague (präg) *n.* capital and largest city of Czechoslovakia, in the western part of the country. Pop. (1967 est.) 1,031,870.

prai·rie (prâr′ē) *n.* vast, level or gently rolling treeless grassland. [French *prairie* meadow, going back to Latin *prātum.*]

prairie chicken, henlike grouse, genus *Tympanuchus,* of the prairies of North America, having brownish plumage heavily barred with black, and, in the male, inflatable air sacs on each side of the neck. The **greater prairie chicken,** *T. cupido,* has orange air sacs, and the **lesser prairie chicken,** *T. pallidicinctus,* has red air sacs. Also, **prairie hen.**

prairie dog, any of various burrowing rodents, genus *Cynomys,* having a plump body, a short tail, and a coarse buff-colored coat. Length: to 15 inches including tail.

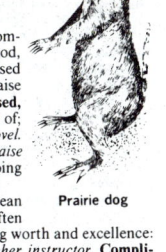

Prairie dog

prairie schooner, covered wagon, smaller and more compact than the Conestoga wagon, used by pioneers in crossing the prairies westward to the Pacific coast.

prairie wolf, coyote.

praise (prāz) *n.* **1.** expression of admiration, commendation, or approval. **2.** glorification of a god, ruler, or hero, esp. worship of God when expressed in words or song. **3. to sing the praises of.** to praise highly or with enthusiasm; extol. —*v.t.,* **praised, prais·ing. 1.** to express admiration or approval of; commend: *The critics praised his latest novel.* **2.** to worship or glorify in words or song: *to praise God.* [Old French *preisier* to price, value, going back to Latin *pretium* price.] —**prais′er,** *n.*
Syn. *n.* **1. Praise, compliment, acclamation** mean an expression of esteem or approval. **Praise** often implies the judgment of a superior in recognizing worth and excellence: *The girl's piano recital won great praise from her instructor.* **Compliment** suggests warm admiration or appreciation of a specific act: *Before leaving, he paid the hostess a compliment for her graciousness.* **Acclamation** usually describes an enthusiastic public demonstration of approval: *The candidate acknowledged the acclamation of his supporters.*

praise·wor·thy (prāz′wur′thē) *adj.* worthy of praise; commendable. —**praise′wor′thi·ly,** *adv.* —**praise′wor′thi·ness,** *n.*

Pra·krit (prä′krit) *n.* any of the various ancient or medieval Indic dialects spoken predominantly in northern and central India. Many languages and dialects spoken in modern India developed from them. [Sanskrit *prākṛta* natural, vulgar.]

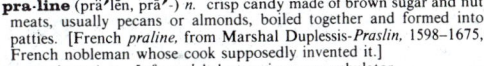

Prairie schooner

pra·line (prä′lēn, prā′-) *n.* crisp candy made of brown sugar and nut meats, usually pecans or almonds, boiled together and formed into patties. [French *praline,* from Marshal Duplessis-*Praslin,* 1598–1675, French nobleman whose cook supposedly invented it.]

pram (pram) *n. Informal.* baby carriage; perambulator.

prance (prans) *pranced, pranc·ing. v.i.* **1.** to move in a proud, elated, or arrogant manner; strut; swagger: *The drum major pranced across the football field.* **2.** (of a horse) **a.** to spring forward from the hind legs. **b.** to move by a succession of such springs. **3.** to ride on a horse that is prancing. **4.** to run, leap, or skip about in play; gambol. —*n.* act of prancing or a prancing movement. [Of uncertain origin.]

pran·di·al (pran′dē əl) *adj.* of or relating to a meal, esp. dinner. [Latin *prandium* lunch, meal′ + -AL¹.]

prank¹ (prangk) *n.* something done to provoke laughter or amusement; mischievous or playful act. [Of uncertain origin.] —**prank′-ster,** *n.*
Syn. Prank, caper², antic mean a playful and mischievous act or trick. **Prank** suggests a practical joke or trick that is frivolous rather than malicious: *On the first of April some people play pranks on others.* **Caper** is usually applied to a carefree, reckless, or harebrained escapade: *The boy's capers amused his friends but irritated his parents.* **Antic** stresses ludicrous or grotesque actions rather than a spirit of mischievousness: *The clowns' hilarious antics kept the audience laughing through the entire show.*

prank² (prangk) *v.t.* to dress or adorn in a showy way; decorate. —*v.i.* to make an ostentatious show or display. [Possibly from Dutch *pronken* to show off.]

pra·se·o·dym·i·um (prā′zē ō dim′ē əm) *n.* soft, slightly yellowish, rare-earth metallic element, used in small amounts to color glass, enamel, and synthetic emeralds. Symbol: **Pr** See **element** for table.

prate (prāt) *prat·ed, prat·ing. v.i.* to talk at length and to little purpose; chatter; babble. —*v.t.* to utter in an idle or foolish manner. —*n.* idle or foolish talk; prattle. [Middle Dutch *praten* to chatter; probably of imitative origin.] —**prat′er,** *n.* —**prat′ing·ly,** *adv.*

prat·fall (prat′fôl′) *n.* a fall on the buttocks.

prat·tle (prat′əl) **-tled, -tling.** *v.i.* to talk childishly or foolishly; babble. —*v.t.* to utter or tell in a childish or foolish manner. —*n.* **1.** idle or simple talk. **2.** sound that is suggestive of baby talk. [Middle Low German *pratelen* to chatter, from *praten.*] —**prat′tler,** *n.*

---

prawn (prôn) *n.* any of various edible, shrimplike shellfish found in salt and fresh waters throughout warm and temperate regions of the world. [Of uncertain origin.]

Prax·it·e·les (prak sit′əl ēz′) *n.* c.390–c.330 B.C., Greek sculptor.

pray (prā) *v.i.* **1.** to enter into spiritual communion with God, esp. for the purposes of adoration, contrition, petition, or thanksgiving. **2.** to make supplication to God or to another object of worship or veneration: *to pray for divine guidance.* —*v.t.* **1.** to ask earnestly; beg; entreat: *I pray you to stay.* **2.** to ask by entreaty; implore: *I know not how to pray your patience* (Shakespeare, *Much Ado About Nothing*). **3.** to get or bring about by praying. **4.** to be so kind or obliging as to. ▲ used in the imperative to indicate a request or politely expressed command: *Pray don't do that.* [Old French *prier* to worship God, ask earnestly (for), from Latin *precārī* to entreat, call upon.]

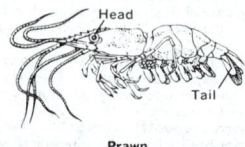

Head

Tail

Prawn

pray·er¹ (prā′ər) *n.* one who prays. [PRAY + -ER¹.]

prayer² (prār) *n.* **1.** act of praying, esp. to God. **2.** something prayed for: *Their prayers were granted.* **3.** set form of words used in praying: *a book of prayers.* **4.** *also,* **prayers.** form of worship consisting entirely or mainly of prayers: *morning prayers.* **5.** earnest request; supplication; entreaty. [Old French *priere* act of worshiping God, earnest request, going back to Latin *precārius* obtained by entreaty. See PRECARIOUS.]

prayer book (prār) **1.** book of formal prayers and other forms of religious devotion. **2.** *also,* **Prayer Book.** Book of Common Prayer.

prayer·ful (prār′fəl) *adj.* given to prayer; devout. —**prayer′ful·ly,** *adv.* —**prayer′ful·ness,** *n.*

prayer meeting (prār) Protestant service of prayer and worship, often held on a weekday night.

praying mantis, any of a group of brown or green insects, family Mantidae, related to the grasshopper, most numerous in the tropics, having stout, spiny forelegs for grasping its prey. Length: 1–5 inches. Also, **man′tis.** [See MANTIS.]

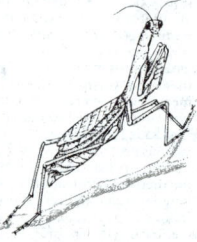

Praying mantis

pre- *prefix* **1.** before in place, time, order, position, or rank: *prewar, pretest, prehistoric.* **2.** in preparation for; preliminary to: *preschool.* [Latin *prae* before, often through French *pré-.*]

preach (prēch) *v.i.* **1.** to speak publicly on a religious subject, as a Scriptural text; deliver a sermon. **2.** to give advice, esp. in an officious or sanctimonious way. —*v.t.* **1.** to set forth or proclaim by preaching: *to preach the word of God.* **2.** to deliver (a sermon or other religious discourse). **3.** to advocate or recommend strongly: *to preach legislative reform.* [Old French *prechier* to make known or teach the word of God, exhort, from Latin *praedicāre* to declare publicly, proclaim.]

preach·er (prē′chər) *n.* one who preaches, esp. a Protestant clergyman.

preach·i·fy (prē′chə fī′) -fied, -fy·ing. *v.i. Informal.* to preach or moralize in a tedious or tiresome way.

preach·ment (prēch′mənt) *n.* **1.** act of preaching. **2.** sermon or speech, esp. a tedious or tiresome one.

preach·y (prē′chē) preach·i·er, preach·i·est. *adj. Informal.* given to or suggestive of preaching. —**preach′i·ness,** *n.*

pre·am·ble (prē′am′bəl) *n.* **1.** preliminary statement or introduction, esp. one stating reasons or purposes, as in a statute. **2.** introductory fact or circumstance. [Old French *preambule* preface, going back to Late Latin *praeambulus* walking in front, from Latin *prae* before + *ambulāre* to walk.]

pre·am·pli·fi·er (prē am′plə fī′ər) *n.* device in a sound reproduction system that contains the volume, tone, and other controls, and amplifies and directs signals to the main amplifier.

pre·ar·range (prē′ə rānj′) -ranged, -rang·ing. *v.t.* to arrange beforehand. —**pre′ar·range′ment,** *n.*

pre·a·tom·ic (prē′ə tom′ik) *adj.* of or relating to the time before the first use of atomic energy.

preb·end (preb′ənd) *n.* **1.** part of the income of a cathedral church given as a stipend to a clergyman serving that church. **2.** church property or tax that supplies the money for this stipend. **3.** prebendary. [Medieval Latin *praebenda* church living, from Late Latin *praebenda* pension, allowance, going back to Latin *praebēre* to furnish.]

preb·en·dar·y (preb′ən der′ē) *pl.,* -dar·ies. *n.* clergyman who receives a prebend.

Pre·cam·bri·an (prē kam′brē ən) *n.* geological era during which

the earliest animals appeared, and bacteria and algae were the only forms of plant life. See **geology** for table. —*adj.* of, relating to, or characteristic of the Precambrian.

pre·car·i·ous (pri kâr′ē əs) *adj.* **1.** involving or dependent on chance or circumstance; uncertain; insecure: *a precarious investment.* **2.** exposed to danger; hazardous; perilous: *a precarious position on a cliff.* **3.** based on insufficient or doubtful evidence; unfounded: *a precarious theory.* [Latin *precārius* obtained by entreaty, doubtful, going back to *prex* prayer, entreaty.] —**pre·car′i·ous·ly,** *adv.* —**pre·car′i·ous·ness,** *n.*

pre·cau·tion (pri kô′shən) *n.* **1.** measure taken beforehand to avoid danger, failure, loss, or harm: *to take precautions against burglary.* **2.** caution or care taken beforehand; foresight. [Late Latin *praecautiō,* from Latin *praecavēre* to guard against beforehand.]

pre·cau·tion·ar·y (pri kô′shə ner′ē) *adj.* relating to, advising, or using precaution.

pre·cede (pri sēd′) -ced·ed, -ced·ing. *v.t.* **1.** to go or come before or ahead of, as in time, order, or importance. **2.** to introduce, as with a preface. —*v.i.* to go or come before. [Latin *praecēdere* to go before.]

prec·e·dence (pres′ə dəns, pri sēd′əns) *n.* **1.** act, right, or fact of preceding, as in time, rank, or order. **2.** superiority of rank or position, esp. at ceremonial or formal occasions: *the precedence of a senator over a representative.* —**Syn. 2.** see **priority.**

prec·e·dent (*n.,* pres′ə dənt; *adj.,* pri sēd′ənt, pres′ə dənt) *n.* **1.** act or instance that may serve as an example, pattern, or rule for similar future actions. **2.** decision or ruling of a court of law that serves as an example for deciding future similar cases. —*adj.* preceding. [Latin *praecēdēns,* present participle of *praecēdere* to go before.]

pre·ced·ing (pri sē′ding) *adj.* that precedes; previous.

pre·cen·tor (pri sen′tər) *n.* one who directs the singing of a church choir or congregation, esp. a clergyman in charge of a cathedral choir. [Late Latin *praecentor,* going back to Latin *prae* before + *canere* to sing.]

pre·cept (prē′sept) *n.* **1.** rule intended as a guide for conduct or action. **2.** maxim. [Latin *praeceptum* rule, maxim, direction.]

pre·cep·tor (pri sep′tər, prē′sep′-) *n.* teacher; instructor. [Latin *praeceptor.*] —**pre·cep·to·ri·al** (prē′sep tôr′ē əl), *adj.* —**pre·cep′tress,** *n.*

pre·ces·sion (prē sesh′ən) *n.* **1.** act or fact of preceding; precedence. **2.** wobbling motion of a spinning body, as a top, whose axis of rotation has been shifted by an external force. **3.** precession of the equinoxes. [Late Latin *praecessiō* a going before, from Latin *praecēdere* to go before.]

pre·ces·sion·al (prē sesh′ən əl) *adj.* of, relating to, or resulting from the precession of the equinoxes.

precession of the equinoxes, earlier occurrence of the equinoxes in each successive sidereal year, caused by the gradual westward movement of the equinoxes as a result of the slight wobbling of the earth as it rotates on its axis. It takes about 26,000 years for the equinoxes to move westward through 360 degrees and return to their starting points.

pre·cinct (prē′singkt′) *n.* **1.** subdivision or district of a city or town, esp. such a district under the jurisdiction of a particular police station or one whose residents all vote in one polling place. **2.** police station in such a district. Also, **precinct house.** **3.** enclosed or bounded space. **4.** precincts. neighborhood; environs. [Medieval Latin *praecinctum* boundary, originally neuter past participle of Latin *praecingere* to enclose.]

pre·ci·os·i·ty (presh′ē os′ə tē) *pl.,* -ties. *n.* fastidious or affected refinement, as in taste or the use of language. [French *préciosité* affectation, from Latin *pretiōsitās* preciousness.]

pre·cious (presh′əs) *adj.* **1.** having great cost or value; costly. **2.** held in high esteem; cherished: *Justice, which is a treasure far more precious than gold* (Jowett, 1875). **3.** beloved; dear. **4.** affecting or displaying fastidious delicacy or refinement: *precious manners.* **5.** *Informal.* very great. —*adv.* extremely; very: *They had precious little food remaining.* —*n.* loved one; dear; darling. [Old French *precios* expensive, from Latin *pretiōsus* valuable, from *pretium* price, value.] —**pre′cious·ly,** *adv.* —**pre′cious·ness,** *n.* —**Syn.** *adj.* **1.** see **valuable.**

precious stone, rare, valuable gem, as a diamond or emerald.

prec·i·pice (pres′ə pis) *n.* **1.** high, steep, often vertical or overhanging face of rock. **2.** brink of a hazardous or perilous situation. [Latin *praecipitium* a steep place.]

pre·cip·i·tance (pri sip′ə təns) *n.* quality of being precipitant. Also, **pre·cip′i·tan·cy.**

pre·cip·i·tant (pri sip′ə tənt) *adj.* **1.** falling or rushing rapidly or headlong. **2.** acting hastily or rashly; impetuous. **3.** very sudden or unexpected; abrupt. —*n.* chemical substance that reacts with ions of a dissolved element in a solution to form a solid, insoluble compound. [Latin *praecipitāns,* present participle of *praecipitāre* to throw down headlong.] —**pre·cip′i·tant·ly,** *adv.*

pre·cip·i·tate (*v.,* pri sip′ə tāt′; *n., adj.,* pri sip′ə tit, -tāt′) -tat·ed,

at; āpe; cär; end; mē; it; īce; hot; ōld; fôrk; wood; fōōl; oil; out; up; ūse; turn; sing; thin; this; zh in treasure; ə in ago, taken, pencil, lemon, circus.

-tat·ing. *v.t.* **1.** to bring on or hasten the occurrence of; cause to happen before expected, needed, or desired: *to precipitate an argument, to precipitate a politician's resignation.* **2.** to throw down violently from or as from a height; hurl downward. **3.** *Chemistry.* to cause (a substance in a solution) to combine to form a solid, insoluble substance. —*v.i.* **1.** (of vapor) to be condensed and fall, as in the form of rain, snow, or dew. **2.** *Chemistry.* to be precipitated. **3.** to fall headlong. —*n.* solid, insoluble chemical compound formed in a solution by the reaction of ions of a dissolved compound or element with ions of a compound or element added to the solution. —*adj.* **1.** falling or rushing rapidly or headlong. **2.** acting or done without deliberation; hasty; rash. **3.** coming on suddenly or unexpectedly; abrupt: *a precipitate change in the weather.* [Latin *praecipitātus,* past participle of *praecipitāre* to throw down headlong.] —**pre·cip′i·tate·ly,** *adv.* —**pre·cip′i·ta′tor,** *n.*

pre·cip·i·ta·tion (pri sip′ə tā′shən) *n.* **1.a.** any form of water, as rain, hail, or snow, that falls to earth. **b.** depositing of such moisture on the earth. **c.** amount, as of rain or snow, deposited. **2.** chemical process of forming solid substances in a solution. **3.** act of precipitating; being precipitated. **4.** rash or sudden haste.

pre·cip·i·tous (pri sip′ə təs) *adj.* **1.** of the nature of or having a precipice or precipices; very steep: *precipitous cliffs.* **2.** precipitate; hasty; rash. —**pre·cip′i·tous·ly,** *adv.* —**pre·cip′i·tous·ness,** *n.*

pré·cis (prā′sē, prā sē′) *pl., -cis.* *n.* concise summary, as of a book or article; abstract. [French *précis,* from Latin *praecīsus* cut off, brief, past participle of *praecīdere* to cut off in front.] —**Syn.** see **summary.**

pre·cise (pri sīs′) *adj.* **1.** strictly accurate or clearly defined; exact; definite: *His instructions were not very precise.* **2.** being exactly what is called for or needed; neither more nor less: *a precise amount.* **3.** distinguished from others; particular; very: *At that precise moment he entered the room.* **4.** strictly or scrupulously observant, as of rules or standards: *a rigid, precise person.* [Latin *praecīsus* cut off, brief, past participle of *praecīdere* to cut off in front.] —**pre·cise′ly,** *adv.* —**pre·cise′ness,** *n.* —**Syn. 1.** see **correct.**

pre·ci·sion (pri sizh′ən) *n.* state or quality of being precise; accuracy; exactness. —*adj.* marked by or designed for a high degree of fineness or accuracy: *a precision tool.*

pre·clude (pri klōōd′) *-clud·ed, -clud·ing.* *v.t.* to make impossible by previous action; prevent. [Latin *praeclūdere* to close, shut off, hinder from access.] —**pre·clu·sion** (pri klōō′zhən), *n.* —**pre·clu·sive** (pri klōō′siv, -ziv), *adj.* —**pre·clu′sive·ly,** *adv.*

pre·co·cious (pri kō′shəs) *adj.* **1.** developed or matured earlier than usual; displaying maturity at an unusually early age: *a precocious child.* **2.** characterized by displaying premature development. [Latin *praecocx-,* stem of *praecox* ripe before its time + -OUS.] —**pre·co′cious·ly,** *adv.* —**pre·co′cious·ness,** *precocity* (pri kos′ə tē), *n.*

pre·cog·ni·tion (prē′kog nish′ən) *n.* **1.** prior knowledge of specific future events. **2.** ability to predict specific future events without any rational means of such prediction.

pre·con·ceive (prē′kən sēv′) *-ceived, -ceiv·ing.* *v.t.* to form an idea or opinion of beforehand.

pre·con·cep·tion (prē′kən sep′shən) *n.* **1.** idea or opinion formed beforehand. **2.** act of preconceiving.

pre·con·cert (prē′kən surt′) *v.t.* to arrange by previous agreement.

pre·cur·sor (pri kur′sər, prē-) *n.* one who or that which precedes and announces or indicates the approach of another; forerunner. [Latin *praecursor.*]

pre·cur·so·ry (pri kur′sər ē) *adj.* indicative of something to follow; preliminary or introductory. Also, **pre·cur′sive.**

pred., predicate.

pre·da·cious (pri dā′shəs) *also,* **pre·da·ceous.** *adj.* predatory. [From Latin *praedārī* to plunder.]

pre·date (prē dāt′) *-dat·ed, -dat·ing.* *v.t.* **1.** to give a date earlier than the correct one: *to predate a check.* **2.** to be or occur earlier than; precede in time.

pred·a·tor (pred′ə tər) *n.* **1.** animal that lives by preying on other animals, as a wolf, lion, or hawk. **2.** predatory person.

pred·a·to·ry (pred′ə tôr′ē) *adj.* **1.** living by preying on other animals. **2.** addicted to or living by plundering, robbing, or exploiting others: *a predatory person.* **3.** of, relating to, or characterized by plundering or pillage: *predatory instincts.* [Latin *praedātōrius* plundering, going back to *praedārī* to plunder.]

pred·e·ces·sor (pred′ə ses′ər) *n.* **1.** one who precedes another person in time, esp. in an office or position. **2.** that which precedes another thing; ancestor. [Late Latin *praedēcessor* forerunner in office, from Latin *prae* before + *dēcessor* retiring official.]

pre·des·ti·nate (*v.,* prē des′tə nāt′; *adj.,* prē des′tə nit, -nāt′) *-nat·ed, -nat·ing.* *v.t.* **1.** to foreordain by divine decree or purpose. **2.** predestine. —*adj.* predestined. [Latin *praedestinātus,* past participle of *praedestināre* to determine beforehand.]

pre·des·ti·na·tion (prē des′tə nā′shən) *n.* **1.** act of predestining; being predestined. **2.a.** doctrine held by certain Christian churches that

God has ordained from all eternity the salvation or damnation of each soul. **b.** divine decree wherein God has ordained for all eternity whatever is to happen.

pre·des·tine (prē des′tin) *-tined, -tin·ing.* *v.t.* to determine, decree, or decide beforehand; foreordain.

pre·de·ter·mine (prē′di tur′min) *-mined, -min·ing.* *v.t.* **1.** to determine, decree, or decide beforehand; predestine. **2.** to give direction to or influence beforehand; prejudice. —**pre′de·ter′mi·na′tion,** *n.*

pred·i·ca·ble (pred′i kə bəl) *adj.* capable of being predicated or affirmed. —*n.* that which is predicable. —**pred′i·ca·bil′i·ty, pred′i·ca·ble·ness,** *n.* —**pred′i·ca·bly,** *adv.*

pre·dic·a·ment (pri dik′ə mənt) *n.* **1.** unpleasant, trying, or difficult situation. **2.** that which can be predicated; attribute. [Late Latin *praedicāmentum* category, quality, from Latin *praedicāre* to proclaim.]

pred·i·cate (*n., adj.,* pred′i kit; *v.,* pred′i kāt′) *n.* **1.** that part of a sentence or clause, consisting of the verb with its objects and modifiers, that expresses what is said about the subject, as *laughed* in *He laughed, ran home* in *The dog ran home,* or *is of the essence* in *Time is of the essence.* **2.** *Logic.* that which is stated about the subject in a proposition. *Mortal* is the predicate in the proposition *Socrates is mortal.* —*v.t.* *-cat·ed, -cat·ing.* **1.** to found or base (something, as an action or statement): *to predicate a belief on one's experiences.* **2.** to affirm or assert as an attribute, quality, or property of something. **3.** to involve in direct association; connote; imply. **4.** to assert or affirm. —*adj.* *Grammar.* of or belonging to the predicate: *a predicate noun.* [Latin *praedicātus,* past participle of *praedicāre* to declare publicly; proclaim.] —**pred′i·ca′tive,** *adj.* —**pred′i·ca′tive·ly,** *adv.*

predicate adjective, adjective that follows a linking verb and refers to the subject of the verb. In the sentence *The woods are lovely, lovely* is a predicate adjective.

predicate nominative, noun or pronoun that follows a linking verb and refers to the subject of the verb. In the sentence *No man is an island, island* is a predicate nominative.

pred·i·ca·tion (pred′ə kā′shən) *n.* **1.** act of predicating. **2.** *Logic.* predicate.

pre·dict (pri dikt′) *v.t.* to announce or declare beforehand; prophesy. —*v.i.* to make a prediction. [Latin *praedictus,* past participle of *praedīcere* to foretell.] —**pre·dict′a·bil′i·ty,** *n.* —**pre·dict′a·ble,** *adj.* —**pre·dict′a·bly,** *adv.*

Syn. *v.t.* **Predict, forecast** mean to state beforehand what is going to happen. **Predict** implies scientific method in arriving at what is foretold: *The surgeon predicted that the patient would be walking again in a week.* **Forecast** implies arranging possibilities and probabilities and deducing what the future holds by carefully examining them: *Most financial experts forecast an extended period of inflation.*

pre·dic·tion (pri dik′shən) *n.* **1.** act of predicting. **2.** something predicted; prophecy. —**pre·dic′tive,** *adj.* —**pre·dic′tive·ly,** *adv.*

pre·di·lec·tion (pred′əl ek′shən, prēd′-) *n.* preference or partiality (with *for*): *She has a predilection for jazz.* [French *prédilection,* going back to Latin *prae* before + *dīligere* to choose, love.]

pre·dis·pose (prē′dis pōz′) *-posed, -pos·ing.* *v.t.* **1.** to make susceptible, liable, or subject to. **2.** to give an inclination to; influence: *His openness predisposed me to like him.*

pre·dis·po·si·tion (prē′dis pə zish′ən) *n.* state or condition of being predisposed; tendency; inclination: *He has a predisposition to suspect everyone of trying to harm him.*

pre·dom·i·nance (pri dom′ə nəns) *n.* state or quality of being predominant. Also, **pre·dom′i·nan·cy.**

pre·dom·i·nant (pri dom′ə nənt) *adj.* **1.** having or exerting superior power, authority, or influence over others. **2.** more frequent, common, or noticeable: *Red is the predominant color in that painting.* —**pre·dom′i·nant·ly,** *adv.* —**Syn. 1.** see **dominant.**

pre·dom·i·nate (pri dom′ə nāt′) *-nat·ed, -nat·ing.* *v.i.* **1.** to exert power, authority, or influence; have control (often with *over*). **2.** to surpass others, as in power, influence, or amount; prevail. —**pre·dom′i·na′tion,** *n.*

pre·em·i·nent (prē em′ə nənt) *also,* **pre-em·i·nent.** *adj.* superior to or surpassing others; outstanding. [Latin *praeēminēns,* present participle of *praeēminēre* to excel.] —**pre·em′i·nence;** *also,* **pre·em′i·nence,** *n.* —**pre·em′i·nent·ly;** *also,* **pre·em′i·nent·ly,** *adv.*

pre·empt (prē empt′) *also,* **pre-empt.** *v.t.* **1.** to acquire or take possession of before others. **2.** to settle on (land) with the right to purchase it in preference to others. **3.** (of a radio or television program) to be presented in the place of (another): *The football game preempted the regularly scheduled program.* **4.** to cause (a radio or television program) to be canceled and present another in its place. [From PREEMPTION.] —**pre·empt′or;** *also,* **pre·empt′or,** *n.*

pre·emp·tion (prē emp′shən) *also,* **pre-emp·tion.** *n.* right of the actual settler of public land to purchase such land at a fixed price to the exclusion of any other prospective purchasers. [PRE- + Latin *emptiō* a buying.]

pre·emp·tive (pri emp′tiv) *also.* **pre-emp·tive.** *adj.* of, relating to, or capable of preemption.

preen (prēn) *v.t.* **1.** (of birds) to clean and smooth (feathers) with the beak. **2.** to dress or adorn (oneself) carefully; primp. **3.** to take or display pride or satisfaction in (with *on*): *He preens himself on having made the honor roll.* —*v.i.* to primp. [Possibly form of archaic *prune* to preen; of uncertain origin; influenced by dialectal *preen* to pierce, going back to Old English *prēon* pin (referring to a bird's use of its beak to preen its feathers).]

pre·ex·ist (prē′ig zist′) *also,* **pre-e·xist.** *v.t., v.i.* to exist beforehand. —**pre′ex·ist′ence;** *also,* **pre′-ex·ist′ence,** *n.* —**pre′ex·ist′ent;** *also,* **pre′-ex·ist′ent,** *adj.*

pref. **1.** preface. **2.** prefix. **3.** preferred.

pre·fab (prē fab′, prē′fab′) *n.* prefabricated building, esp. a house.

pre·fab·ri·cate (prē fab′rə kāt′) **-cat·ed, -cat·ing.** *v.t.* **1.** to construct or manufacture in standardized parts for easy and rapid assembly, and often, low cost. **2.** to fabricate or produce beforehand: *to prefabricate an excuse for being late.* —**pre′fab·ri·ca′tion,** *n.*

pref·ace (pref′is) *n.* **1.** introduction to a speech, book, or other literary work, often written by the author. **2.** anything introductory or preliminary. —*v.t.,* **-faced, -fac·ing. 1.** to introduce or furnish with a preface. **2.** to serve as a preface to: *A short documentary prefaced the featured movie.* [Old French *preface* introduction to a book, going back to Latin *praefātiō* introduction to a speech or to writing, a saying beforehand.] —**Syn.** *n.* **1.** see **introduction.**

pref·a·to·ry (pref′ə tôr′ē) *adj.* relating to, of the nature of, or serving as a preface; introductory: *prefatory remarks.*

pre·fect (prē′fekt) *also,* **prae·fect.** *n.* **1.** in ancient Rome, any of various high-ranking military or civil officials. **2.a.** head administrative official of one of the departments of France. **b.** police chief of Paris. [Latin *praefectus* commander, overseer, director.]

pre·fec·ture (prē′fek′chər) *n.* **1.** office, district, or authority of a prefect. **2.** official residence of a prefect. [Latin *praefectūra* office of an overseer.]

pre·fer (pri fur′) **-ferred, -fer·ring.** *v.t.* **1.** to like better; choose above others: *I prefer tea to coffee.* **2.** to put forward or offer for consideration or decision before a court of law or other legal authority: *We didn't prefer charges, since the stolen articles were returned.* **3.** to advance or promote, as in rank or office. [Latin *praeferre* to carry in front, set before.] —**pre·fer′rer,** *n.*

pref·er·a·ble (pref′ər ə bəl, pref′rə-) *adj.* worthy of being chosen; more desirable. —**pref′er·a·bly,** *adv.*

pref·er·ence (pref′ər əns, pref′rəns) *n.* **1.** act of choosing one over others; being so chosen. **2.** right or opportunity of so choosing. **3.** one who or that which is preferred; first choice. **4.** granting of rights or priorities to one over others, as to one country or group of countries with regard to international trade.

pref·er·en·tial (pref′ə ren′chəl) *adj.* **1.** of, giving, or receiving preference. **2.** arising from or indicating preference: *a preferential tariff.* —**pref′er·en′tial·ly,** *adv.*

preferential shop, establishment in which union members are given special privileges, as in hiring.

pre·fer·ment (pri fur′mənt) *n.* **1.** advancement, as to higher rank; promotion. **2.** position or office to which one is advanced, esp. one having prestige, honor, or financial profit.

preferred stock, stock on which dividends must be paid before they can be paid on common stock. Preferred stock usually also has preference in the event of dissolution of the corporation. Distinguished from **common stock.**

pre·fig·u·ra·tion (prē′fig yə rā′shən) *n.* **1.** act of prefiguring. **2.** that which prefigures; prototype.

pre·fig·ure (prē fig′yər) **-ured, -ur·ing.** *v.t.* **1.** to show, indicate, or suggest beforehand; foreshadow. **2.** to picture or imagine to oneself beforehand. [Late Latin *praefigūrāre* to represent beforehand, from Latin *prae* before + *figūrare* to form.] —**pre·fig′ure·ment,** *n.*

pre·fix (*n.,* prē′fiks′; *v.,* prē fiks′) *n.* syllable or group of syllables attached to the beginning of a word, root, or stem so as to alter or modify its meaning or to form a new word. In the word *postwar, post-* is a prefix. —*v.t.* to put before or at the beginning: *to prefix a title to a name.* [Modern Latin *praefixum,* from Latin *praefīxus,* past participle of *praefīgere* to fix in front.]

preg·na·ble (preg′nə bəl) *adj.* capable of being taken by force; open to attack. [Middle French *prenable,* from *prendre* to take, seize, from Latin *prehendere.*]

preg·nan·cy (preg′nən sē) *pl.,* **-cies.** *n.* condition or quality of being pregnant: *a woman in the sixth month of pregnancy.*

preg·nant (preg′nənt) *adj.* **1.** (of a female animal) having one or more unborn offspring in the uterus; being with child or young. **2.** full of significance or importance; having meaning: *a pregnant statement.* **3.** filled; replete; abounding: *a remark that is pregnant with meaning.* **4.** abounding with ideas; inventive; imaginative: *a pregnant mind.*

5. having results; productive; fruitful. [Latin *praegnāns* being with child or with young.] —**preg′nant·ly,** *adv.*

pre·heat (prē hēt′) *v.t.* to heat before using, as an oven.

pre·hen·sile (prē hen′sil, -sīl) *adj.* adapted for grasping or holding, esp. by wrapping around: *A monkey has a prehensile tail.* [French *préhensile,* from Latin *prehēnsus,* past participle of *prehendere* to grasp, seize.]

pre·his·tor·ic (prē′his tôr′ik, -tor′ik) *adj.* of, relating to, or belonging to the period before recorded history: *prehistoric peoples.* Also, **pre′his·tor′i·cal.** —**pre′his·tor′i·cal·ly,** *adv.*

pre·judge (prē juj′) **-judged, -judg·ing.** *v.t.* to judge beforehand or without sufficient inquiry or investigation. —**pre·judg′ment;** *also,* **pre·judge′ment,** *n.*

prej·u·dice (prej′ə dis) *n.* **1.a.** opinion or judgment, esp. an unfavorable one, formed beforehand or without sufficient knowledge or just grounds. **b.** act or state of holding such an opinion. **2.** hatred or intolerance of a particular group, as a race or religion. **3.** injury or damage resulting from an unfair or hasty judgment or action by another or others. —*v.t.,* **-diced, -dic·ing. 1.** to cause to have a prejudice. **2.** to damage or injure, as by an unfair opinion or action. [Old French *prejudice* act of deciding beforehand, from Latin *praejūdicium* a preceding judgment, disadvantage.] —**Syn. 1.a.** see **partiality.**

prej·u·di·cial (prej′ə dish′əl) *adj.* causing prejudice or injury; detrimental. —**prej′u·di′cial·ly,** *adv.*

prel·a·cy (prel′ə sē) *pl.,* **-cies.** *n.* **1.** rank or dignity of a prelate. **2.** prelates collectively. **3.** system of church government by prelates.

prel·ate (prel′it) *n.* clergyman of high rank, esp. one with authority over other clergymen. Bishops, archbishops, and cardinals are prelates. [Old French *prelat,* going back to Latin *praelātus,* past participle of *praeferre* to set before, carry in front.]

prelim., preliminary.

pre·lim·i·nar·y (pri lim′ə ner′ē) *adj.* preceding and leading up to the main event, subject, or action: *preliminary arrangements, a preliminary statement.* —*n. pl.,* **-nar·ies. 1.** preliminary step or action. **2.** contest or match preceding the main one. [French *préliminaire,* going back to Latin *prae-* before + *līmen* threshold.] —**pre·lim′i·nar′i·ly,** *adv.*

pre·lit·er·ate (prē lit′ər it) *adj.* (of a society of culture) not having a written language.

prel·ude (prel′ūd, prā′lōōd) *n.* **1.** preliminary or introductory event, action, or performance. **2.a.** musical composition or movement preceding or introducing another, as that played before a religious service or a fugue. **b.** short, independent musical composition in a free style, often written for a keyboard instrument or an orchestra. —*v.t.,* **-ud·ed, -ud·ing. 1.** to serve as a prelude to. **2.** to introduce with a prelude. —*v.i.* to serve as a prelude. [French *prélude* introduction, introduction to a piece of music, going back to Latin *praelūdere* to play beforehand.]

pre·ma·ture (prē′mə choor′, -tyoor′, -toor′) *adj.* arriving, occurring, or existing before the usual or proper time: *a premature baby, a premature decision.* [Latin *praemātūrus,* from *prae* before + *mātūrus* ripe.] —**pre′ma·ture′ly,** *adv.* —**pre′ma·ture′ness,** *pre′ma·tur′i·ty,* *n.*

pre·med (prē′med′) *Informal. adj.* premedical. —*n.* premedical student.

pre·med·i·cal (prē med′i kəl) *adj.* of, relating to, or preparing for the study of medicine.

pre·med·i·tate (prē med′ə tāt′) **-tat·ed, -tat·ing.** *v.t.* to consider, think out, or plan beforehand: *to premeditate a crime.* [Latin *prae-meditātus,* past participle of *praemeditārī* to think over beforehand.]

pre·med·i·ta·tion (prē′med ə tā′shən) *n.* **1.** act of premeditating. **2.** planning and deliberation of a crime in advance, showing intent to commit the crime.

pre·mier (pri mēr′, prim yēr′) *n.* prime minister in certain European countries, as France and Italy. —*adj.* **1.** first in position, rank, or authority; chief. **2.** first in order of time; earliest. [French *premier* first, from Latin *prīmārius* of the first rank, chief, from *prīmus* first.]

pre·miere (pri mēr′, prim yār′) *n.* first formal public performance or presentation, as of a play or motion picture. —*v.t., v.i.,* **-miered, -mier·ing.** to present or appear for the first time. [French *première,* from *premier* first. See **PREMIER.**]

prem·ise (prem′is) *n.* **1.** statement or principle accepted as true without proof; self-evident or universally accepted truth from which a conclusion is drawn. **2. premises. a.** land and the buildings on it. **b.** building or part of a building. **3.** *Logic.* one of the initial statements in a syllogism, asserted as true, from which the conclusion is drawn. **4. premises.** *Law.* **a.** matters previously stated, as a description of the property or the names of the parties concerned in a deed or contract. **b.** property that is the subject of a conveyance. —*v.t., v.i.,* **-mised, -mis·ing. 1.** to mention beforehand as an introduction or explanation. **2.** to state or assume as a premise in an argument. [Medieval Latin *praemissa (propositio)* literally, (proposition) put before, from Latin *praemissus,* past participle of *praemittere* to send or put before.]

at; āpe; cär; end; mē; it; īce; hot; ōld; fôrk; wood; fōōl; oil; out; up; ūse; turn; sing; thin; this; zh in treasure; ə in ago, taken, pencil, lemon, circus.

pre·mi·um (prē′mē əm) *n.* **1.** something offered free or at a lower price as an inducement, esp. to buy something else. **2.** amount paid by an insured party for insurance. **3.** high or unusual value: *to put a premium on virtue.* **4.** amount paid in addition to the regular or usual price, wage, or other fixed amount. **5.** value of one form of money in excess of another of the same nominal value. **6.** reward or prize given for a specific act. **7. at a premium. a.** in great demand; valuable. **b.** at more than the nominal or usual price or value; above par. [Latin *praemium* reward, booty, profit.]

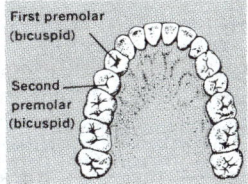

First premolar (bicuspid)

Second premolar (bicuspid)

Premolars

pre·mo·lar (prē mō′lər) *n.* any of eight permanent human teeth, having double-pointed crowns and situated between the molars and the cuspids; bicuspid. —*adj.* of or relating to the premolars.

pre·mo·ni·tion (prē′mə nish′ən, prem′ə-) *n.* **1.** feeling that something is about to happen. **2.** warning or sign of something to come. [Late Latin *praemonitiō* forewarning, from Latin *praemonēre* to forewarn.] —**pre·mon·i·to·ry** (prē mon′ə tôr′ē), *adj.* —**pre·mon·i·to′·ri·ly,** *adv.*

pre·na·tal (prē nāt′əl) *adj.* of or relating to the period prior to birth.

pren·tice (pren′tis) *n. Archaic.* apprentice.

pre·oc·cu·pa·tion (prē ok′yə pā′shən) *n.* **1.** state or condition of being preoccupied; engrossment; absorption. **2.** anything that engrosses the mind or attention: *Reading is his main preoccupation.* **3.** act of occupying beforehand or before others. Also, **pre·oc′cu·pan·cy.**

pre·oc·cu·pied (prē ok′yə pīd′) *adj.* **1.** absorbed in thought; engrossed. **2.** previously occupied.

pre·oc·cu·py (prē ok′yə pī′) **-pied, -py·ing.** *v.t.* **1.** to engage all the attention of; engross. **2.** to occupy or take possession of beforehand or before others.

pre·or·dain (prē′ôr dān′) *v.t.* to ordain or appoint beforehand; predestine. —**pre·or·di·na·tion** (prē ôrd′ən ā′shən), *n.*

prep (prep) *Informal. adj.* preparatory: *prep school.* —*v.i.* **prepped, prep·ping. 1.** to attend preparatory school. **2.** to prepare oneself, as by study. —*v.t.* to prepare: *to prep a person for an operation.*

prep. 1. preposition. **2.** preparatory.

prep·a·ra·tion (prep′ə rā′shən) *n.* **1.** act or process of preparing. **2.** state of being prepared or in readiness. **3.** measure or provision needed or taken to prepare for something: *Mary took care of the preparations for our party.* **4.** something prepared for a specific purpose, as a medicine or food.

pre·par·a·tive (pri par′ə tiv) *adj.* preparatory. —*n.* something preparatory.

pre·par·a·to·ry (pri par′ə tôr′ē, prep′ər ə-) *adj.* **1.** serving to prepare; preliminary: *a preparatory course.* **2.** undergoing preparation, as for college: *a preparatory student.* —*adv.* **preparatory to.** in preparation for.

preparatory school, school, esp. one that is private, that prepares students for college.

pre·pare (pri pâr′) **-pared, -par·ing.** *v.t.* **1.** to make ready or fit, as for a particular purpose, event, or undertaking. **2.** to put together by combining various ingredients or parts: *to prepare a meal, to prepare a medicine, to prepare a speech.* **3.** to provide with whatever is necessary for an event or undertaking. —*v.i.* to get ready: *to prepare for college, to prepare for a party.* [Latin *praeparāre* to make ready beforehand.] —**pre·par′er,** *n.*

pre·par·ed·ness (pri pâr′id nis) *n.* state or condition of being prepared, esp. for war.

pre·pay (prē pā′) **-paid, -pay·ing.** *v.t.* to pay or pay for in advance. —**pre·pay′ment,** *n.*

pre·pense (pri pens′) *adj.* planned or considered beforehand; premeditated. ▲ used chiefly in the phrase *malice prepense.* [Modification of earlier *purpensed,* from Old French *purpense,* past participle of *purpenser* to premeditate, going back to Latin *prō* before + *pēnsāre* to weigh, ponder.]

pre·pon·der·ance (pri pon′dər əns) *n.* superiority, as in quantity, weight, power, or influence. Also, **pre·pon′der·an·cy.**

pre·pon·der·ant (pri pon′dər ənt) *adj.* superior, as in quantity, weight, power, or influence; predominant. —**pre·pon′der·ant·ly,** *adv.* —**Syn.** see **dominant.**

pre·pon·der·ate (pri pon′də rāt′) **-at·ed, -at·ing.** *v.i.* **1.** to be superior, as in quantity, power, influence, or importance; predominate: *Which party will preponderate in the election?* **2.** to be greater in weight. **3.** to descend or incline downward, as one end of a balance. [Latin

praeponderātus, past participle of *praeponderāre* to outweigh.] —**pre·pon′der·a′tion,** *n.*

prep·o·si·tion (prep′ə zish′ən) *n.* word belonging to the part of speech that shows the relationship between a noun or pronoun and another word, as a verb or another noun. *By, into,* and *on* are prepositions in English. [Latin *praepositiō* a putting before, preposition.]

prep·o·si·tion·al (prep′ə zish′ən əl) *adj.* relating to, functioning as, or having a preposition: *a prepositional phrase.* —**prep′o·si′tion·al·ly,** *adv.*

pre·pos·sess (prē′pə zes′) *v.t.* **1.** to preoccupy the mind of to the exclusion of other thoughts, feelings, or ideas. **2.** to impress or influence beforehand or immediately, esp. in a favorable manner. **3.** to influence for or against; prejudice; bias.

pre·pos·sess·ing (prē′pə zes′ing) *adj.* making a favorable impression; pleasing: *a prepossessing manner.*

pre·pos·ses·sion (prē′pə zesh′ən) *n.* **1.** opinion formed beforehand; prejudice. **2.** state of being preoccupied, as with thoughts or feelings.

pre·pos·ter·ous (pri pos′tər əs, -trəs) *adj.* contrary to truth, reason, or common sense; absurd; ridiculous: *a preposterous idea.* [Latin *praeposterus* reversed, absurd; literally, before coming after.] —**pre·pos′ter·ous·ly,** *adv.* —**pre·pos′ter·ous·ness,** *n.*

pre·puce (prē′pūs) *n.* fold of skin that covers the end of the penis or clitoris. Also, **fore′skin′.** [Latin *praepūtium.*]

Pre-Raph·a·el·ite (prē raf′ē ə līt′) *n.* **1.** one of a group of nineteenth-century English artists and poets organized by Dante Gabriel Rossetti, whose works reflected a nostalgia for the medieval and early Renaissance periods. **2.** any modern artist with similar aims. **3.** any Italian painter who preceded Raphael. —*adj.* of, relating to, or characteristic of the Pre-Raphaelites, their principles, or style.

pre·re·cord (prē′ri kôrd′) *v.t.* to record beforehand for later broadcast or telecast.

pre·req·ui·site (prē rek′wə zit) *n.* something required or necessary beforehand for something that follows: *a prerequisite for college entrance.* —*adj.* required or necessary beforehand: *a prerequisite course.*

pre·rog·a·tive (pri rog′ə tiv) *n.* **1.** right or privilege belonging to a particular person, class, or group of persons, esp. a hereditary or official right. **2.** any distinguishing and exclusive right or privilege: *He feels it is his prerogative to raise his child as he sees fit.* —*adj.* of, relating to, or having a prerogative. [Latin *praerogātīva* privilege, preference, previous choice, from *praerogātīvus* asked for an opinion ahead of others.]

pres., present.

Pres., President.

pres·age (*n.,* pres′ij; *v.,* pres′ij, pri sāj′) *n.* **1.** sign or warning of a future event; omen; portent. **2.** prophetic feeling; premonition; presentiment. **3.** prophetic significance or import of something. —*v.t.,* **-aged, -ag·ing. 1.** to give or be a sign or warning of; portend. **2.** to have a presentiment of. **3.** to give a prophecy of; predict; foretell. —*v.i.* to make a prediction. [Latin *praesāgium* foreboding.]

pres·by·ter (prez′bə tər, pres′-) *n.* **1.** in the early Christian church, an elder who belonged to a council that governed a congregation. **2.** minister in the Presbyterian church. **3.** lay elder in the Presbyterian church who belongs to a board that rules a local church. **4.** minister or priest in churches having hierarchies. [Church Latin *presbyter* an elder, from Greek *presbýteros,* comparative of *presbys* old. Doublet of PRIEST.]

Pres·by·te·ri·an (prez′bə tēr′ē ən, pres′-) *adj.* of or relating to any of various Calvinistic Protestant denominations, esp. those of English or Scottish origin. —*n.* **1.** one who believes in Presbyterianism, esp. a member of a Presbyterian church. **2.** doctrines, beliefs, and practices of the Presbyterian churches, characterized by Calvinistic theology and simple religious services.

Pres·by·te·ri·an·ism (prez′bə tēr′ē ə niz′əm, pres′-) *n.* system of church government by ministers or elders of equal rank.

pres·by·ter·y (prez′bə tēr′ē, pres′-) *pl.,* **-ter·ies.** *n.* **1.** in Presbyterianism, a church court having jurisdiction over the congregations in a certain area, composed of all the ministers and certain of the elders of the congregations. **2.** congregations under the jurisdiction of such a court, collectively. **3.** part of a church, in or near the sanctuary, reserved for the clergy. [Church Latin *presbyterium* council of elders, from Greek *presbyterion,* from *presbýteros* elder. See PRESBYTER.]

pre·school (prē′skool′) *adj.* of, relating to, or for a child past infancy but younger than school age, usually between the ages of two and five.

pre·sci·ence (prē′shē əns, presh′ē-) *n.* knowledge of something before it exists or occurs; foreknowledge. [Church Latin *praescientia,* from Latin *praesciēns,* present participle of *praescīre* to foreknow.] —**pre′sci·ent,** *adj.*

Pres·cott, William Hick·ling (pres′kət; hik′ling) 1796–1859, U.S. historian.

pre·scribe (pri skrīb′) **-scribed, -scrib·ing.** *v.t.* **1.** to set down or give as a rule or direction to be followed. **2.** to order or recommend for use

at; āpe; cär; end; mē; it; īce; hot; ōld; fôrk; wood; fōōl; oil; out; up; ūse; turn; sing; thin; this; zh in treasure; ə in ago, taken, pencil, lemon, circus.

791

as a remedy or treatment. —*v.i.* **1.** to set down or give rules or directions; dictate. **2.** to give medical advice or a prescription. [Latin *praescrībere* to write before, order, appoint.]

pre·script (*n.* prē′skript′; *adj.* pri skript′, prē′skript′) *n.* something prescribed; rule or direction. —*adj.* prescribed. [Latin *praescrīptum* order, rule, from *praescrībere* to write before, order, appoint.]

pre·scrip·tion (pri skrip′shən) *n.* **1.a.** formula written by a physician for the preparation and use of a medicine or other remedy. **b.** medicine or remedy prescribed. **2.** act of prescribing. **3.** that which is prescribed; rule or direction. **4.a.** process of acquiring right or title to property by virtue of having used or possessed it from time immemorial or for a long period of time. **b.** title or right so acquired. [Latin *praescrīptiō* a writing before, order, from *praescrībere*. See PRESCRIBE.]

pre·scrip·tive (pri skrip′tiv) *adj.* **1.** giving or setting down strict rules, laws, or directions. **2.** arising from established use or custom. **3.** acquired by or based on legal prescription.

pres·ence (prez′əns) *n.* **1.** state or fact of being in a specific place at a given time: *His presence in the room made me uneasy.* **2.** area or vicinity immediately surrounding a person or thing; close proximity: *Please don't speak of him in my presence.* **3.** immediate vicinity of a person of very high rank, esp. a sovereign. **4.** appearance, carriage, or bearing of a person, esp. when dignified or impressive: *a stately presence.* **5.** spiritual being or invisible influence felt to be present. [Old French *presence* a being at hand, bearing, from Latin *praesentia* a being at hand.]

presence chamber, reception room in which a king or other person of rank receives guests.

presence of mind, ability to maintain one's self-control and act intelligently in an emergency or other difficult situation.

pres·ent¹ (prez′ənt) *adj.* **1.** in a specific place at a given time; at hand: *We were not present when he arrived.* **2.** existing or going on at this time: *the present generation.* **3.** being dealt with, written, discussed, or considered; in mind: *the present question.* **4.** to be found; existing: *Lead is present in some gasolines.* **5.** *Grammar.* indicating an action now taking place or a state of being now existing. —*n.* **1.** present time; time now passing: *He is not working at present.* **2.** *Grammar.* present tense or a verb in the present tense. **3.** *Law.* **presents,** documents at hand. [Latin *praesēns* that is before one or at hand.] —**Syn.** *adj.* **2.** see **current.**

pre·sent² (*v.,* pri zent′; *n.,* prez′ənt) *v.t.* **1.a.** to bring into the formal acquaintance of another or others; introduce: *May I present you to my husband?* **b.** to bring (oneself) into the presence of another or others or into a particular place. **2.** to make a gift, offer, or donation of; bestow: *The principal will present the diplomas. Please present my compliments to the chef.* **3.** to put in the possession of something (with *with*): *He presented me with a copy of his latest book.* **4.** to suggest, put forward, or bring up for consideration: *This latest development presents a problem.* **5.** to expose to view or notice, esp. before the public; display; show: *The gallery will present the works of a new artist.* **6.** to hand or send in; submit, as a bill or petition. **7.** to point, aim, or turn in the direction of. **8.** *Archaic.* to represent on the stage; act. **9. to present arms,** to salute by bringing a weapon, as a rifle, to a vertical position in front of the body with the muzzle up and the trigger facing out. —*n.* something presented; gift or donation. [Old French *presenter* to offer, from Latin *praesentāre* to place before, hold out.] —**Syn.** *v.t.* **1.a.** see **introduce. 2.** see **give.** *n.* see **gift.** *adj.* see **current.**

pre·sent·a·ble (pri zen′tə bəl) *adj.* **1.** suitable to be present in company, as in appearance or attire; fit to be seen. **2.** capable of being offered, given, or shown. —**pre·sent′a·bil′i·ty,** *n.* —**pre·sent′a·bly,** *adv.*

pres·en·ta·tion (prez′ən tā′shən, prē′zən-) *n.* **1.** act of presenting; being presented. **2.** exhibition or showing, as of a play. **3.** something presented; gift or donation.

pres·ent-day (prez′ənt dā′) *adj.* of, belonging to, or occurring at the present time; current.

pre·sen·ti·ment (pri zen′tə mənt) *n.* a feeling that something is about to happen; premonition. [Obsolete French *presentement,* going back to Latin *praesentīre* to perceive beforehand.]

pres·ent·ly (prez′ənt lē) *adv.* **1.** in a little while; shortly: *They will arrive presently.* **2.** at the present time; currently: *We are presently working out a new filing system.* —**Syn. 1.** see **shortly.**

pre·sent·ment (pri zent′mənt) *n.* **1.** act of presenting. **2.** something presented; exhibition; showing. **3.** written statement by a grand jury concerning an offense, based on the jury's own knowledge or observation and presented without an indictment. **4.** presentation of a note, bill of exchange, or the like for acceptance or payment. [Old French *presentement* act of presenting, from *presenter* to offer. See PRESENT².]

present participle, participle expressing a present action or state, formed with the suffix *-ing* and used esp. to form the progressive tenses and as an adjective or noun. In the sentence *I am awaiting your reply,* the word *awaiting* is a present participle.

present perfect 1. verb tense expressing action completed at the time of speaking. In the sentence *Bill has seen that science fiction movie three times,* the phrase *has seen* is in the present perfect. **2.** verb in this tense.

present tense 1. verb tense expressing an action or state that is occurring or exists at the present time. In the sentence *He plays the bugle well,* the word *plays* is in the present tense. **2.** verb in this tense.

pre·serv·a·tive (pri zur′və tiv) *n.* anything that preserves, esp. a chemical substance added to foods to prevent or retard spoilage. —*adj.* tending or serving to preserve.

pre·serve (pri zurv′) **-served, -serv·ing.** *v.t.* **1.** to maintain or keep intact; make lasting: *She dieted constantly in order to preserve her youthful figure.* **2.** to prepare (food) for future use, as by salting, smoking, or pickling. **3.** to protect from harm or danger; keep in safety; save. **4.** to keep from spoiling or decomposing, as with chemical substances. —*n.* **1.** *usually,* **preserves.** fruit that has been boiled with sugar and stored in airtight containers to prevent spoilage or fermentation. **2.a.** area set aside for the protection of plant and animal life or other natural resources. **b.** area set aside for restricted or private hunting or fishing. [Medieval Latin *praeservāre* to guard, from Late Latin *praeservāre* to observe, from Latin *prae* before + *servāre* to keep, protect.] —**pres·er·va·tion** (prez′ər vā′shən), **pre·serv′er,** *n.* —**pre·serv′a·ble,** *adj.*

Syn. *v.t.* **1. Preserve, conserve** mean to keep something intact or safe from loss. **Preserve** emphasizes the use of adequate measures to keep something unchanged, safe, and entire by protecting its integrity and individuality: *A commission was set up to preserve historical houses in the city.* **Conserve** emphasizes the wise use or utilization of a valuable asset that will be difficult to replace once used up: *It is everyone's duty to help conserve our natural resources.*

pre·shrunk (prē′shrungk′) *adj.* (of a fabric) shrunk during manufacture to minimize subsequent shrinkage during cleaning or washing.

pre·side (pri zīd′) **-sid·ed, -sid·ing.** *v.i.* **1.** to occupy the place of authority, as at a meeting; act as president or chairman. **2.** to exercise authority, direction, or control. [Latin *praesidēre* to sit before, watch, guard.] —**pre·sid′er,** *n.*

pres·i·den·cy (prez′ə dən sē) *pl.,* **-cies.** *n.* **1.** office or function of president. **2.** time during which a president holds office. **3.** *also,* **Presidency.** office of President of the United States.

pres·i·dent (prez′ə dənt) *n.* **1.** *also,* **President.** chief executive of a republic, esp. of the United States. **2.** chief officer, as of a company, college, or organization. [Latin *praesidēns* ruler, director, from *praesidēre* to sit before, watch, guard.] —**pres·i·den·tial** (prez′ə den′shəl), *adj.*

pres·i·dent-e·lect (prez′ə dənt i lekt′) *n.* one who has been elected president but has not yet been inaugurated.

pre·sid·i·um (pri sid′ē əm) *n.* **1.** any of various political or governmental committees in the Soviet Union empowered to act for a larger governing body between its sessions. **2. Presidium.** such a committee empowered to act for the Supreme Soviet. [Russian *prezidium,* from Latin *praesidium* a presiding over, defense.]

press¹ (pres) *v.t.* **1.** to act upon or against with steady force or weight; exert continuous pressure on: *to press a button, to press one's nose against a window.* **2.a.** to extract by pressure; squeeze out: *to press juice from grapes.* **b.** to compress or exert pressure on to extract juice from: *to press grapes.* **3.** to give a particular shape, consistency, smoothness, or thickness to by means of pressure. **4.** to iron: *to press a suit.* **5.** to hold close; embrace; hug: *She pressed herself against him.* **6.** to urge strongly and persistently; entreat; importune: *They pressed her to go with them.* **7.** to cause difficulties for; harass: *Please help us; we are being sorely pressed.* **8.a.** to lay stress on; emphasize: *to press a point.* **b.** to insist on; urge strongly: *to press a claim, to press charges against someone.* **9.** to constrain; compel; force. **10.** to urge onward; cause to hasten. —*v.i.* **1.** to exert pressure. **2.** to push or strain forward; advance with force, haste, or eagerness: *to press through a crowd. They pressed on in spite of the storm.* **3.** to demand or seek urgently: *to press for reforms.* **4.** to crowd; throng. **5.** to iron clothes. **6.** to be capable of taking or holding an ironing: *This dress presses well.* **7.** to weigh heavily or bear down, as upon the mind. —*n.* **1.** act or fact of pressing; push. **2.** crowding or thronging forward or together: *the press of the people in the square.* **3.** urgency; hurry; pressure: *the press of events. He felt the press of business daily.* **4.** any of various instruments or machines for exerting pressure, as to stamp or compress materials or to extract juice from fruits or vegetables. **5.** printing press. **6.** establishment for printing or publishing. **7.** business, process, or art of printing. **8.a.** media used for collection and dissemination of news, as newspapers and periodicals. **b.** people who collect, write, or distribute news, as reporters or journalists. **c.** news media in general or collectively. **9.** that which appears in newspapers or magazines, as comment or criticism: *His campaign tactics got a bad press.* **10.** condition of being ironed: *This fabric holds a press nicely.* **11.** large, usually shelved cup-

at; āpe; cär; end; mē; it; īce; hot; ōld; fôrk; wood; fōol; oil; out; up; ūse; turn; sing; thin; this; zh in treasure; ə in ago, taken, pencil, lemon, circus.

board, as for linen. **12. to go to press.** to begin to be printed. [Old French *presser* to strain, crush, urge strongly, going back to Latin *premere* to bear down upon, burden, force.]

press² (pres) *v.t.* **1.** to force into military service; impress. **2.** to use in a manner different from the ordinary or intended. —*n.* impressment into military service. [Modification of obsolete *prest* to enlist by giving earnest money, from obsolete *prest* earnest money, from Old French *prest*, from *prester* to lend, from Latin *praestāre* to become surety for, furnish; formerly, recruits in England were given *prest* or earnest money, but later the forcing of men into military service became associated with PRESS¹ in the sense of "force."]

press agent, one who manages publicity or public relations for an individual or organization, as an actor or motion picture studio.

press conference, interview granted to an assembly of newsmen, as by a public official or celebrity.

press gang, formerly, a group of men employed to impress others into military service.

press·ing (pres′ing) *adj.* demanding or calling for immediate action or attention. —**press′ing·ly,** *adv.* —**Syn.** see urgent.

press·man (pres′mən) *pl.,* -**men.** *n.* one who operates or has charge of a printing press.

press release, information formally issued or released to the press for broadcast or publication after a specified time.

pres·sure (presh′ər) *n.* **1.** force exerted by one body upon another with which it is in contact. **2.** compelling or constraining force or influence: *social pressure, to put pressure on someone.* **3.** urgent and stressing demands on one's time or energy: *He works well under pressure.* **4.** burden or oppression, as of something difficult to bear: *the pressure of grief.* **5.** *Physics.* amount of force exerted on a unit of area. **6.** electromotive force. —*v.t.* **-sured, -sur·ing.** to apply compelling or constraining force or influence on. [Latin *pressūra* a pressing, burden, oppression.] —**Syn.** n. **3.** see stress.

pressure cooker, airtight metal pot for quick cooking by steam pressure at a temperature above the boiling point of water.

pressure gauge, device for measuring the pressure of a fluid.

pressure group, any group of persons that share a common interest and try by lobbying and propaganda to influence public opinion and legislators or other government officials for the benefit of that interest.

pressure point, any of various points on the body, close to major arteries, where pressure may be applied in order to stop the flow of blood from a wound.

pressure suit, inflatable suit worn, as by an aviator, to maintain normal atmospheric pressure while flying at high altitudes.

pres·sur·ize (presh′ə rīz′) **-ized, -iz·ing.** *v.t.* **1.** to maintain a certain atmospheric pressure in the interior of (something, as an airplane, spacecraft, or diving apparatus). **2.** to subject to or keep under high pressure, as the contents of an aerosol bomb.

press·work (pres′wurk′) *n.* **1.** working or management of a printing press. **2.** work done by a printing press.

Pres·ter John (pres′tər) in medieval legend, a rich and powerful Christian priest-king who was believed to rule a great kingdom somewhere in Asia.

pres·ti·dig·i·ta·tion (pres′tə dij′ə tā′shən) *n.* sleight of hand; legerdemain. [French *prestidigitation,* going back to Latin *praestō* ready, at hand + *digitus* finger.] —**pres′ti·dig′i·ta′tor,** *n.*

pres·tige (pres tēzh′, -tēj′, pres′tij) *n.* **1.** power, influence, or authority based on prior success, reputation, or achievements. **2.** power to command the respect or admiration of others. [French *prestige* influence, magic spell, illusion, from Latin *praestīgium* trick, illusion.]

pres·tis·si·mo (pres tis′i mō′) *Music. adv.* in a very rapid tempo. —*adj.* very rapid. *n.* prestissimo passage, movement, or piece. [Italian *prestissimo* very quickly, superlative of *presto* quickly. See PRESTO.]

pres·to (pres′tō) *adv.* **1.** at once; immediately. **2.** *Music.* in a rapid tempo. —*adj. Music.* rapid; quick. —*n. Music.* presto passage, movement, or piece. [Italian *presto* quick, quickly, going back to Latin *praestō* ready, at hand.]

pre·sum·a·ble (pri zōō′mə bəl) *adj.* capable of being presumed or taken for granted; likely; probable. —**pre·sum′a·bly,** *adv.*

pre·sume (pri zōōm′) **-sumed, -sum·ing.** *v.t.* **1.** to accept as true until proven otherwise; take for granted; suppose: *I presume that you know what you're talking about.* **2.** to take upon oneself without permission or authority; dare: *Do you presume to tell me how to raise my child?* **3.** to appear to be evidence or proof of. —*v.i.* **1.** to be presumptuous; take liberties. **2.** to take unfair advantage of something (with *on* or *upon*): *to presume on a person's good nature.* [Late Latin *praesūmere* to assume, from Latin *praesūmere* to take beforehand, anticipate.] —**pre·sum·ed·ly** (pri zōō′mid lē), **pre·sum′ing·ly,** *adv.* —**pre·sum′er,** *n.*

pre·sump·tion (pri zump′shən) *n.* **1.** act of presuming. **2.** something taken for granted; supposition; assumption: *He went to the party*

on the presumption that we would be there. **3.** ground or reason for presuming; evidence leading to a probability. **4.** excessive boldness or arrogance in thought or conduct; effrontery. **5.** inference of a fact, based on its connection with another or proven facts. [Late Latin *praesumptiō* boldness, from Latin *praesumptiō* a taking beforehand, supposition.]

pre·sump·tive (pri zump′tiv) *adj.* **1.** giving reasonable grounds for acceptance or belief: *presumptive evidence.* **2.** based on presumption or inference; presumed. —**pre·sump′tive·ly,** *adv.*

pre·sump·tu·ous (pri zump′chōō əs, -shəs) *adj.* excessively bold or arrogant; taking liberties; impertinent. [Late Latin *praesūmptuōsus,* from *praesumptiō* boldness. See PRESUMPTION.] —**pre·sump′tu·ous·ly,** *adv.* —**pre·sump′tu·ous·ness,** *n.*

pre·sup·pose (prē′sə pōz′) **-posed, -pos·ing.** *v.t.* **1.** to take for granted; assume beforehand. **2.** to involve or imply as a necessary antecedent or condition: *A good performance presupposes much rehearsal.*

pre·sup·po·si·tion (prē′sup ə zish′ən) *n.* **1.** act of presupposing. **2.** that which is presupposed.

pret., preterit.

pre·tend (pri tend′) *v.t.* **1.** to allege or claim, esp. falsely or insincerely: *He does not pretend to be an expert.* **2.** to give a false show or appearance of; feign: *to pretend to play in play; make believe: The little boy pretended he was a soldier.* **4.** to presume; venture; attempt. —*v.i.* **1.** to act out in play: *Children love to pretend.* **2.** to give a false appearance in order to deceive: *His parents knew he wasn't ill, only pretending.* **3.** to lay claim (with *to*): *to pretend to a high office.* [Latin *praetendere* to stretch forth, allege, simulate.]

Syn. *v.t.* **2. Pretend, feign, simulate** mean to assume a false appearance. **Pretend** suggests a passive evasion to mislead others and to avoid involvement and responsibility for oneself: *He pretends ignorance of the affair.* **Feign** is often used pejoratively and suggests an active and hypocritical deception to make oneself acceptable or to accomplish one's ends: *The plant owner feigned indignation before the public, while secretly permitting the dangerous experimentation to continue.* **Simulate** suggests that one goes to greater lengths to consciously imitate something that is often more favorable or desirable under certain circumstances: *The wounded soldier simulated death on the battlefield to avoid being captured by the enemy.*

pre·tend·ed (pri ten′did) *adj.* **1.** alleged or claimed, esp. falsely or insincerely: *pretended allegiance.* **2.** not genuine; false: *a pretended friend.* —**pre·tend′ed·ly,** *adv.*

pre·tend·er (pri ten′dər) *n.* **1.** one who makes false or insincere claims or presents a false appearance. **2.** claimant or aspirant, esp. to a throne.

pre·tense (prē′tens, pri tens′) *also,* **pre·tence.** *n.* **1.** pretext or false show or appearance, esp. for the purpose of deception: *The boy used any pretense to avoid school.* **2.** claim made or implied, esp. one that is false or insincere. **3.** falseness, affectation, or ostentation. **4.** acting out in play; fantasy. [Anglo-Norman *pretense* claim, affectation, going back to Late Latin *pratēnsus,* past participle of Latin *praetendere* to stretch forth, allege.]

pre·ten·sion (pri ten′shən) *n.* **1.** claim or assertion of a claim (often with *to*): *pretensions to greatness.* **2.** false display; affectation; ostentation. **3.** allegation; assertion.

pre·ten·tious (pri ten′shəs) *adj.* **1.** making claims to, or presenting a false or exaggerated display of, some distinction or quality: *a talented but pretentious writer.* **2.** intended to show off or attract attention. [French *prétentieux,* going back to Latin *praetentus,* past participle of *praetendere* to stretch forth, allege.] —**pre·ten′tious·ly,** *adv.* —**pre·ten′tious·ness,** *n.*

preter-, prefix more than; beyond; past: *preternatural.*

pret·er·it (pret′ər it) *also,* **pret·er·ite.** *Grammar. n.* past tense or a verb in the past tense. —*adj.* expressing past time or action: *the preterit tense.* [Latin *praeteritus,* by past, past participle of *praeterīre* to go by.]

pre·ter·nat·u·ral (prē′tər nach′ər əl) *adj.* **1.** going beyond or differing from the natural or ordinary; abnormal. **2.** supernatural. [Medieval Latin *praeternaturalis* that is beyond nature, going back to Latin *praeter* beyond + *nātūra* nature, character, order of things, world.] —**pre′ter·nat′u·ral·ly,** *adv.*

pre·test (prē′test′) *n.* **1.** preliminary test designed to give practice in certain school work or to determine readiness for this work: *a spelling pretest.* **2.** test given to certain merchandise prior to public sale. —*v.t.* to give a pretest to.

pre·text (prē′tekst′) *n.* false reason or excuse given to conceal a true reason or motive: *He returned to her house on the pretext of having forgotten something.* [Latin *praetextum,* from *praetexere* to allege; literally, to weave in front.]

pre·tor (prē′tər) praetor.

Pre·to·ri·a (pri tôr′ē ə) *n.* administrative capital of the Republic of South Africa, in the northeastern part of the country. Pop. (1967), 479,739.

pre·to·ri·an (pri tôr′ē ən) praetorian.

pret·ti·fy (prit′ə fī′) **-fied, -fy·ing.** *v.t.* to make pretty. ▲ often used pejoratively. —**pret′ti·fi·ca′tion,** *n.*

pret·ty (prit′ē) **-ti·er, -ti·est** *adj.* **1.** pleasing or attractive to the eye, esp. in a feminine, childlike, graceful, or dainty way: *a pretty girl, a pretty flower.* **2.** pleasant; charming: *a pretty poem, a pretty thought.* **3.** fine; nice. ▲ usually used ironically: *Richard certainly got us into a pretty mess this time.* **4.** *Informal.* fairly large in amount; considerable: *a pretty sum of money.* **5.** foppish. —*adv.* **1.** fairly; rather; quite: *It was raining pretty hard when we left.* **2. sitting pretty.** *Informal.* in a good or favorable condition or position; well-off. —*n. pl.,* **-ties.** one who or that which is pleasing or attractive. —*v.t.,* **-tied, -ty·ing.** *Informal.* to make pretty, attractive, or pleasant (often with *up*): *to pretty up a room.* [Old English *praettig* crafty, tricky.] —**pret′ti·ly,** *adv.* —**pret′ti·ness,** *n.* —**Syn.** *adj.* **1.** see **beautiful.**

pret·zel (pret′səl) *n.* slender roll of dough that is baked in any of various forms, esp. a loose knot or a short stick, and usually salted on the outside. [German *Brezel,* going back to Latin *bracchium* arm; possibly because it resembles a pair of folded arms. See **BRACE.**]

pre·vail (pri vāl′) *v.i.* **1.** to be superior in power or influence; be victorious; triumph (often with *over* or *against*): *Good will prevail over evil in the end.* **2.** to prove successful; be effective; succeed: *If words do not prevail, we must use force.* **3.** to be widespread; persist: *Violence still prevails in our cities.* **4.** to be the most usual; be predominant: *Warm weather prevails in that region.* **5.** to use persuasion successfully (with *on* or *upon*): *They prevailed upon me to remain a little longer.* [Latin *praevalēre* to have greater power.]

pre·vail·ing (pri vā′ling) *adj.* **1.** most common or frequent: *prevailing winds.* **2.** having superior power or influence. —**pre·vail′ing·ly,** *adv.*

prev·a·lent (prev′ə lənt) *adj.* of common or general occurrence, use, or acceptance; widespread: *a prevalent belief.* [Latin *praevalēns,* present participle of *praevalēre* to have greater power.] —**prev′a·lence,** *n.* —**prev′a·lent·ly,** *adv.*

pre·var·i·cate (pri var′ə kāt′) **-cat·ed, -cat·ing.** *v.i.* to speak falsely, deceptively, or ambiguously; evade the truth; lie. [Latin *praevāricātus,* present participle of *praevāricārī* to walk crookedly, collude.] —**pre·var′i·ca′tion, pre·var′i·ca′tor,** *n.*

pre·vent (pri vent′) *v.t.* **1.** to keep from happening or developing: *to prevent forest fires.* **2.** to keep from doing something (often with *from*): *We must prevent them from leaving.* —*v.i.* to interpose a hindrance or obstacle. [Latin *praeventus,* past participle of *praevenīre* to go before, hinder.] —**pre·vent′a·ble;** *also,* **pre·vent′i·ble,** *adj.*

pre·ven·tion (pri ven′shən) *n.* **1.** act of preventing. **2.** that which prevents.

pre·ven·tive (pri ven′tiv) *adj.* serving or intended to prevent something; concerned with prevention: *to take preventive measures against disease.* —*n.* **1.** that which prevents; means of preventing. **2.** drug or other agent used to prevent disease. Also, **pre·vent·a·tive** (pri ven′tə tiv). —**pre·ven′tive·ly,** *adv.* —**pre·ven′tive·ness,** *n.*

preventive medicine, branch of medicine that studies the origins of disease, how disease spreads, and methods of preserving health.

pre·view (prē′vū) *also,* **pre·vue.** *n.* **1.** advance presentation of a motion picture, play, or exhibition before its formal presentation to the public. **2.** advance showing of scenes from a motion picture or television program for the purpose of advertisement. **3.** advance view, indication, or survey: *a preview of the term's work.* —*v.t.* to present or view in advance.

pre·vi·ous (prē′vē əs) *adj.* **1.** that came or was made before; earlier: *the previous day, a previous appointment.* **2.** *Informal.* premature; hasty. **3. previous to,** before: *She became ill previous to her visit.* [Latin *praevius* going before.] —**pre′vi·ous·ly,** *adv.*

previous question, motion in a parliamentary body that the main question be brought to a vote without further debate.

pre·vi·sion (prə vizh′ən) *n.* **1.** knowledge of the future; prescience; foreknowledge. **2.** prophetic or anticipatory vision or perception. —**pre·vi′sion·al,** *adj.*

pre·war (prē′wôr′) *adj.* occurring or existing before a war. [PRE- + WAR.]

prey (prā) *n.* **1.** any animal hunted or killed for food. **2.** victim: *The old man was the prey of a mugger.* **3.** act or habit of hunting or killing for food: *a beast of prey.* —*v.i.* **1.** to hunt or kill for food (often with *on* or *upon*): *Owls prey on rodents and other small mammals.* **2.** to take advantage of; victimize (often with *on* or *upon*): *confidence men who prey on the public.* **3.** to have a harmful or wearing effect (with *on* or *upon*): *Feelings of guilt preyed on his mind.* **4.** to plunder; pillage (with *on* or *upon*). [Old French *preie* animal seized by carnivorous animals for food, booty, from Latin *praeda* booty.] —**Syn.** *n.* **2.** see **victim.**

Pri·am (prī′əm) *n. Greek Legend.* King of Troy during the Trojan War and father of Hector and Paris.

price (prīs) *n.* **1.** amount of money or its equivalent for which something is bought or sold: *The price of milk may go up next year.*

2. cost at which something is obtained: *victory at the price of honor.* **3.** amount of money, or other consideration, necessary or sufficient for a bribe: *Every man has his price.* **4.** reward offered for the capture or killing of a person. **5.** value; worth. **6. beyond** (or **without**) **price.** invaluable; priceless. —*v.t.,* **priced, pric·ing. 1.** to set a price on; fix the price of: *These meats are priced much too high.* **2.** to find out the price of. [Old French *pris* value, from Latin *pretium* value, reward.] **Syn.** *n.* **1. Price, charge, cost** mean the outlay of money for which something is bought or sold. **Price** applies to the sum of money asked by a seller for an item of merchandise offered for sale: *What is the price of this hat?* **Charge** is usually restricted to the expenditure or expense incurred for a specified service: *There is a nominal charge for the delivery.* **Cost** is applied to the price at which something is actually obtained apart from its worth: *The shopkeeper sold us the wristwatch below cost.*

price·less (prīs′lis) *adj.* **1.** of greater value than can be measured; invaluable: *a priceless painting.* **2.** wonderfully or uniquely memorable or endearing: *That remark was priceless.*

prick (prik) *v.t.* **1.** to pierce slightly with a sharp point: *She pricked her finger with a pin.* **2.** to cause sharp mental or emotional pain to; sting: *His conscience pricks him.* **3.** to mark, trace, or outline with punctures. **4.** *Archaic.* to urge on with or as with a spur or other sharp point. **5. to prick up one's ears. a.** to raise the ears to an erect position. **b.** to listen closely or with sudden interest. —*v.i.* **1.** to have a sensation of being pricked with a sharp point. **2.** *Archaic.* to ride fast. **3. to prick up.** to stand erect or rise to an erect position. —*n.* **1.** act of piercing or pricking or the sensation produced by this. **2.** sharp mental or emotional pain: *a sudden prick of sorrow.* **3.** mark or opening made by a sharp point; puncture. **4.** pointed object or instrument, as a thorn. [Old English *prica* point.]

prick·le (prik′əl) *n.* **1.** small, sharp point, as a thorn. **2.** stinging or tingling sensation, as of being pricked. —*v.t.,* **-led, -ling** to cause a stinging or tingling sensation in, as by pricking. —*v.i.* to sting or tingle. [Old English *pricel* a goad.]

prick·ly (prik′lē) **-li·er, -li·est.** *adj.* **1.** having prickles. **2.** stinging; tingling. **3.** difficult; troublesome: *a prickly situation.* —**prick′li·ness,** *n.*

prickly heat, skin rash characterized by redness and itching, caused by inflammation of the sweat glands.

prickly pear 1. edible, red or purple pear-shaped fruit of any of a large group of cacti, genus *Opuntia,* found in North and South America. **2.** spiny plant bearing this fruit.

Prickly pear

pride (prīd) *n.* **1.** sense of one's personal worth or dignity; self-respect: *Despite years of poverty, the man had maintained his pride.* **2.** exaggerated or unreasonable sense of one's worth or importance: *Ken knew he was wrong, but his foolish pride kept him from apologizing.* **3.** pleasure or satisfaction resulting as from an achievement or possession. **4.** one who or that which causes such pleasure or satisfaction: *The child was his mother's pride and joy.* **5.** best or most flourishing part or time; prime. **6.** company of lions. —*v.t.,* **prid·ed, prid·ing.** to take pride, pleasure, or satisfaction in (oneself) for (with *on* or *upon*): *The man prided himself on his financial success.* [Old English *prȳte* great self-esteem.]

pride·ful (prīd′fəl) *adj.* full of pride; haughty. —**pride′ful·ly,** *adv.*

prie-dieu (prē dyoo′) *pl.,* **prie-dieus** or **prie-dieux** (prē dyooz′). *n.* small desk having a shelf for a prayer book and a platform for kneeling in prayer. [French *prie-Dieu,* from *prier* to pray (from Latin *precārī* to ask) + *Dieu* God (from Latin *deus* a god).]

Prie-dieu

priest (prēst) *n.* **1.** in the Roman Catholic, Orthodox, and Anglican churches, a clergyman ranking next below a bishop, who has taken holy orders that empower him to celebrate the Eucharist, administer sacraments, and pronounce absolution. **2.** any clergyman of a Christian church. **3.** one empowered to perform the rites of a religion, esp. one who performs sacrificial rites or other public religious acts. [Old English *prēost* Christian clergyman, modification of Church Latin *presbyter* an elder, from Greek *presbyteros,* comparative of *presbys* old (referring to the respect for the elders of a community). Doublet of **PRESBYTER.**]

priest·ess (prēs′tis) *n.* female priest, esp. in a pagan religion.

priest·hood (prēst′hood′) *n.* **1.** office or dignity of a priest. **2.** priests collectively.

at; āpe; cär; end; mē; it; īce; hot; ōld; fôrk; wood; fōōl; oil; out; up; ūse; turn; sing; thin; this; zh in treasure; ə in ago, taken, pencil, lemon, circus.

priest·ly (prēst′lē) -li·er, -li·est. adj. **1.** of or relating to a priest or the priesthood. **2.** like, characteristic of, or befitting a priest. —**priest′li·ness,** n.

prig (prig) n. smug, self-righteous person whose rigid adherence to propriety or morality often annoys others. [Of uncertain origin.] —**prig′ger·y,** —**prig′gish·ness,** n. —**prig′gish,** adj.

prim (prim) **prim·mer, prim·mest.** adj. stiffly or excessively formal, neat, or precise; proper. [Old French prim fine, delicate, from Latin prīmus first.] —**prim′ly,** adv. —**prim′ness,** n.

prim. 1. primary. **2.** primitive.

pri·ma ballerina (prē′mə) pl., **pri·ma ballerinas.** leading female dancer in a ballet company. [Italian prima ballerina, from prima first (going back to Latin prīmus) + ballerina. See BALLERINA.]

pri·ma·cy (prī′mə sē) pl., **-cies.** n. **1.** state of being first, as in rank or importance. **2.** rank or dignity of an ecclesiastical primate. **3.** in the Roman Catholic Church, the jurisdiction and supreme authority of the pope. [Medieval Latin primatia first place or rank, from Late Latin prīmās one of the first, chief. See PRIMATE.]

pri·ma don·na (prē′mə don′ə) pl., **pri·ma don·nas. 1.** principal female singer in an opera company. **2.** temperamental or vain person. [Italian prima donna literally, first lady, going back to Latin prīmus first + domina lady.]

pri·ma-fa·ci·e (prī′mə fā′shē ē′, -shē) adj. Law. sufficient to establish a fact or facts unless rebutted or contradicted: prima-facie evidence.

pri·ma fa·ci·e (prī′mə fā′shē ē′, fā′shē) at first sight; before further investigation. [Latin prīmā faciē.]

pri·mal (prī′məl) adj. **1.** original; first; primitive. **2.** of first importance; fundamental. [Medieval Latin primalis principal, excellent, from Latin prīmus first.]

pri·ma·ri·ly (prī mer′ə lē) adv. **1.** chiefly; principally. **2.** in the first place; originally.

pri·ma·ry (prī′mer′ē, -mər ē) adj. **1.** first or greatest in importance or degree; principal: Your safety is my primary concern. **2.** first in order, as in a series, sequence, or grouping: the primary grades in school. **3.** first or earliest in time; primitive; elementary: the primary phase of development. **4.** basic; fundamental; elemental: a primary structural unit. **5.** not derived from something else; original; direct: We consulted only primary sources in our research. **6.** relating to the induction circuit, coil, or current in an electrically powered machine. —n. pl., **-ries. 1.** election in which contenders from the same party oppose each other for the party's nomination or for the right to run for office with the party's support. Also, **primary election. 2.** one of the primary colors. [Latin prīmārius of the first rank, chief, from prīmus first.] —**Syn.** adj. **1.** see **main.**

primary accent 1. principal stress in the pronunciation of a word. **2.** mark (′) used to indicate this stress.

primary colors, any of several groups of colors from which all other colors are considered to be derived. The primary colors produced by directing light through a prism are orange-red, green, and blue; those used in mixing pigments are red, yellow, and blue.

primary school, school providing instruction for very young pupils, comprising the first three or four grades of elementary school.

pri·mate (prī′māt, -mit) n. **1.** in the Roman Catholic, Orthodox, and Anglican churches, an archbishop whose see ranks above all others in a country or church province. **2.** any member of the highest order of mammals, including man, apes, monkeys, lemurs, and tarsiers. [Late Latin prīmāt-, stem of prīmās of the first rank, archbishop, from Latin prīmus first.]

prime (prīm) adj. **1.** first in importance or value; main; chief: Her welfare was his prime concern. **2.** first in rank, dignity, influence, or authority: the prime statesman of our time. **3.** of the best quality; excellent: a prime cut of beef. **4.** first in order of time or development: in the prime period of history. **5.** Mathematics. **a.** relating to or designating a prime number. **b.** having no common divisor except 1. —n. **1.** best or most flourishing stage or condition: The trees were cut down before they had reached their prime. **2.** most flourishing time (of a person's life): He was still in his prime at forty. **3.** the best or most desirable part: He always expects to be given the prime. **4.** beginning or first part; earliest stage. **5.** spring; springtime: in the prime of the year. **6.** second of the seven canonical hours or service for it. **7.** prime number. **8.a.** one of the parts, usually sixty, into which a unit, as a degree, may be divided. **b.** mark (′) indicating this. —v.t., **primed, prim·ing. 1.** to make ready or prepare by filling or charging with something, as a car's carburetor with gasoline. **2.** to pour water into (a pump) so as to make it ready for operation. **3.** to prepare for painting, as by applying a base coat: to prime a wall. **4.** to instruct or prepare (a person) beforehand in what he is to say or do: The lawyer primed the witness. **5.** to prepare (a gun or mine) for firing by supplying a charge of gunpowder or a primer. [Partly from Latin prīmus first; partly from Old English prīm first hour of the day of the Church (originally beginning at 6 A.M.), from Latin prīma (hōra) first (hour).] —**prime′ness,** n.

prime meridian, meridian that passes through Greenwich, England, designated as zero degrees longitude, and from which longitude east and west is measured.

prime minister, highest-ranking member of a body of executive administrators or of a council of ministers, esp. in a parliamentary government, as that of Great Britain.

prime mover 1. original or principal force in an undertaking. **2.** initial force that puts a machine in motion. **3.** machine that converts the energy of a natural force into work.

prime number, number that can be divided without a remainder only by itself and by 1, as 2, 3, 7, 13, 29, or 41.

prim·er¹ (prim′ər) n. **1.** elementary book for teaching children to read. **2.** elementary or introductory book on any subject. [Medieval Latin primarius (liber) basic (book), from Latin prīmārius of the first rank, chief. See PRIMARY.]

prim·er² (prī′mər) n. **1.** flat disk or other device that is filled with a small quantity of explosive and used to detonate the main charge in a cartridge, shell, or the like. **2.** substance put on a surface in preparation for painting, esp. a first coat of paint applied as a base. **3.** one who or that which primes. [PRIME + -ER¹.]

pri·me·val (prī mē′vəl) adj. of, relating to, or belonging to the first or earliest age or ages, esp. of the world; primitive. [Latin prīmaevus in the first period of life (from prīmus first + aevum age) + -AL¹.] —**pri·me′val·ly,** adv.

prim·ing (prī′ming) n. **1.** powder or other material used to ignite a charge. **2.** primer².

prim·i·tive (prim′ə tiv) adj. **1.** of, relating to, or characteristic of an early or original stage, esp. in the development of something: primitive life forms. **2.** of, relating to, or characteristic of the earlier stages in the development of man or human civilization or culture: an exhibit of primitive art. **3.** crude or simple; unsophisticated: primitive adobe huts. **4.** not derived; original; basic. —n. **1.** artist, often self-taught, whose work is characterized by a certain naive or simple quality. **2.** artist active in the early stage of a movement or in an early artistic period. **3.** work of art, esp. a painting, by such an artist. **4.** member of a primitive people; person living in primitive times. [Latin prīmitīvus earliest of its kind, from prīmus first.] —**prim′i·tive·ly,** adv. —**prim′i·tive·ness,** n.

pri·mo·gen·i·tor (prī′mə jen′ə tər) n. earliest ancestor; forefather. [Late Latin prīmōgenitor, going back to Latin prīmus first + genitor father.]

pri·mo·gen·i·ture (prī′mə jen′ə choor′, -chər) n. **1.** state or fact of being the first-born child of the same parents. **2.** right of the eldest son to inherit his father's entire estate. [Late Latin prīmōgenitūra first birth, going back to Latin prīmus first + genitūra birth.]

pri·mor·di·al (prī môr′dē əl) adj. **1.** of, relating to, or existing at or from the very beginning; first in time or order. **2.** fundamental; basic. [Late Latin prīmōrdiālis original, from Latin prīmōrdium origin.] —**pri·mor′di·al·ly,** adv.

primp (primp) v.t., v.i. to dress, groom, or adorn, esp. with excessive or vain attention to detail: Iris would primp for hours before leaving the house. [Of uncertain origin.]

Primrose

prim·rose (prim′rōz′) n. **1.** trumpet-shaped flower of any of a large group of plants, genus Primula, cultivated as a garden flower. **2.** plant bearing this flower. **3.** pale greenish-yellow. —adj. designating a family, Primulaceae, of widely distributed plants growing mainly in the Northern Hemisphere, having flowers with petals united in a tube that flares out at the end, including the pimpernel, shooting star, and primrose. [Medieval Latin prima rosa first rose, going back to Latin prīmus first + rosa rose (flower and bush).]

primrose path 1. way of life characterized by ease and pleasure: the primrose path of dalliance (Shakespeare, Hamlet). **2.** course of action that appears easy but may prove disastrous.

prin. 1. principal. **2.** principle.

prince (prins) n. **1.** male member of a royal family other than the sovereign, esp. a son or grandson in the paternal line of a British sovereign. **2.** male sovereign; monarch. **3.** ruler of a small state or territory. **4.** high-ranking nobleman in certain countries. **5.** one who or that which is preeminent in a group, class, or profession: the prince of thieves. **6.** Informal. fine, decent, or admirable person. [Old French prince sovereign, member of a royal house, the best of a group, from Latin prīnceps first man, leader.]

Prince Albert, long, double-breasted frock coat. [Probably from Prince Albert (later EDWARD VII), who popularized it.]

at; āpe; cär; end; mē; it; īce; hot; ōld; fôrk; wood; fōōl; oil; out; up; ūse; turn; sing; thin; this; zh in treasure; ə in ago, taken, pencil, lemon, circus.

795

prince consort, husband of a female sovereign.
prince·dom (prins′dəm) *n.* **1.** state or territory ruled by a prince; principality. **2.** rank or dignity of a prince.
Prince Edward Island, smallest province of Canada, consisting of an island in the Gulf of St. Lawrence. Area, 2184 sq. mi. Pop. (1966), 108,535.
prince·ly (prins′lē) -li·er, -li·est. *adj.* **1.** of, relating to, resembling, or befitting a prince. **2.** lavish; sumptuous; magnificent: *a princely sum of money.* —**prince′li·ness,** *n.*
Prince of Darkness, the Devil; Satan.
Prince of Wales, the male heir apparent to the British throne, a title usually given to the sovereign's eldest son.
prince royal, eldest son and heir apparent of a sovereign.
prin·cess (prin′sis, -ses) *n.* **1.** any female member of a royal family other than the sovereign, esp. a daughter or granddaughter in the paternal line of a British sovereign. **2.** wife of a prince. **3.** female sovereign, esp. a female ruler of a principality. [French *princesse,* feminine of *prince.* See PRINCE.]
prin·cesse (prin ses′) *also,* **prin·cess.** *adj.* (of a woman's dress, coat, or similar garment) designed to fit closely and fall in an unbroken line from the shoulders to the hem. [French *princesse.* See PRINCESS.]
princess royal, eldest daughter of a sovereign.
prin·ci·pal (prin′sə pəl) *adj.* greatest or first, as in importance, rank, or value; chief: *The striking workers made higher pay their principal demand.* —*n.* **1.** administrative head of an elementary or secondary school. **2.** one who takes a leading part or plays the main role in some activity. **3.** original sum of money borrowed or invested, exclusive of interest charged or income earned. **4.** main body of an estate, as distinguished from income. **5.** *Law.* person directly responsible for a crime. **6.** *Law.* one who authorizes another to act for him. **7.** person primarily responsible for legal obligations. [Latin *prīncipālis* chief, first, from *prīnceps* first man, leader.]
Syn. 1. Principal, headmaster, dean mean the executive officer of an educational institution. **Principal** is the head or the chief administrative officer of a public school: *Mrs. Wallace is the principal of our school.* **Headmaster** is the head of the teaching staff of a private school for boys, having some teaching duties but mainly concerned with administration, discipline, and counseling: *Mr. Black was popular with the teachers and the boys during his ten years as headmaster.* **Dean** is the head of one of the faculties or schools of a college or university having, in some cases, disciplinary and administrative powers: *Lisa went to the dean of the school for help and advice.* —*adj.* see **main.**
prin·ci·pal·i·ty (prin′sə pal′ə tē) *pl.,* -ties. *n.* **1.** state or territory ruled by a prince or from which a prince takes his title. **2.** position or jurisdiction of a prince. **3. principalities.** seventh of the nine orders of angels.
prin·ci·pal·ly (prin′sə plē, -sip lē) *adv.* for the most part; mainly; chiefly. —Syn. see **especially.**
principal parts, those forms of a verb from which all other inflected forms can be derived, consisting, in English, of the present infinitive, the past tense, and the past participle.
prin·cip·i·um (prin sip′ē əm) *pl.,* -cip·i·a (-sip′ē ə). *n.* basic principle.
prin·ci·ple (prin′sə pəl) *n.* **1.** fundamental truth, law, belief, or doctrine: *a government based on the principle that all men are equal.* **2.** rule of personal conduct: *Hold faithfulness and sincerity as first principles* (Confucius). **3.** adherence to moral or ethical standards; sense of right or honorable action; integrity: *Thus my pride, not my principle . . . kept me honest* (Defoe, 1721). **4.** ethical or moral consideration. **5.** scientific rule or law concerned with or explaining the operation of a mechanical process or natural phenomenon: *to understand the principles of inertia.* **6.** line of reasoning or mode of operation used as a basis for or guide to action. [Modification of Latin *prīncipium* beginning, origin.]
prin·ci·pled (prin′sə pəld) *adj.* having, characterized by, or based on ethical or moral principles. ▲ often used in combination, as in *high-principled.*
prink (pringk) *v.t., v.i.* to dress in a showy manner; primp. [Possibly form of PRANK².]
print (print) *v.t.* **1.** to reproduce (a text, picture, or design) on a surface, as paper, by applying inked type, plates, or blocks. **2.** to reproduce a text, picture, or design on (a surface) by applying inked type, plates, or blocks. **3.** to cause to be printed; publish: *That newspaper printed the whole story.* **4.** to write in letters like those used in print: *Please print your name on the application.* **5.** to mark or indent by pressing or stamping: *to print butter with a trademark.* **6.** to produce, as a mark or indentation, by pressing or stamping: *The king printed his seal in the wax.* **7.** to impress or fix, as upon the mind or memory. **8.** to produce (a photograph) by transmission of light through a negative onto a sensitized surface. **9. print out.** (of a computer) to produce (print-out). —*v.i.* **1.** to take an impression from or as from type, as in a

printing press. **2.** to write in letters like those used in print. **3.** to produce something in print. **4.** to practice the trade of a printer. —*n.* **1.** printed lettering: *large print, clear print.* **2.** mark or indentation made by pressing or stamping: *the print of a foot in the sand.* **3.** device which produces a mark or figure by pressing or stamping, as a die, seal, or stamp. **4.** something that has been marked or formed by pressing or stamping: *a print of butter.* **5.** picture or design printed from a block or plate. **6.** photograph made from a negative. **7.** printed publication, esp. a newspaper or periodical. **8.a.** cloth with a design printed on it by means of dyes on engraved rollers, woodblocks, or screens. **b.** article made of such cloth. **9. in print. a.** in a printed form or state; published: *She finally saw her novel in print.* **b.** (of a book) still being printed and available for purchase from the publisher. **10. out of print.** (of a book) no longer available for purchase from the publisher. [Old French *preinte* impression, stamp, from *preindre* to impress, stamp, from Latin *premere* to bear down upon.]
print·a·ble (prin′tə bəl) *adj.* **1.** suitable for publication. **2.** capable of being printed or being printed from.
printed circuit, electrical circuit consisting of a pattern of conducting material deposited on a flat plate or base of insulating material, widely used in electronic equipment.
print·er (prin′tər) *n.* **1.** one who or that which prints, esp. a person or company whose business is printing. **2.** part of a computer that delivers output data in printed form.
printer's devil, devil (*def.* 8).
print·ing (prin′ting) *n.* **1.** process, business, or art of producing printed matter, esp. by means of a printing press. **2.** that which is printed; printed matter. **3.** all the copies of a book or other matter printed at one time. **4.** writing that resembles printed matter.
printing press, machine for producing copies by transferring ink from a metal plate, typeface, or similar device to paper or other material.
print-out (print′out′) *also,* **print-out.** *n.* printed output of a computer.
pri·or¹ (prī′ər) *adj.* **1.** preceding in time, order, or importance: *a prior commitment.* **2. prior to.** before. [Latin *prior* sooner, former, superior.]
pri·or² (prī′ər) *n.* monk who ranks next below an abbot in a monastery or who is the superior of a priory. [Old English *prior* superior of a priory, from Late Latin *prior* administrator, superior, from Latin *prior* former, sooner, superior.]
pri·or·ess (prī′ər is) *n.* nun who ranks next below an abbess in an abbey or who is the superior of a priory.
pri·or·i·ty (prī ôr′ə tē, -or′-) *pl.,* -ties. *n.* **1.** precedence, as in order or importance. **2.** acknowledged or established right to precedence or preferential treatment: *Military personnel often have priority over civilians.* **3.** matter or consideration deserving or receiving chief emphasis or attention: *Buying a new car was first on my list of priorities.*
Syn. 1. Priority, precedence mean an arrangement in which one goes before another. **Priority** is usually used in the sense of being first and implies a sense of urgency: *The problems requiring immediate solution will be given priority at the meeting.* **Precedence** implies being ahead of someone or something because of particular circumstances: *Her dental appointment took precedence over her club meeting that afternoon.*
pri·o·ry (prī′ər ē) *pl.,* -ries. *n.* religious house ranking next below an abbey, governed by a prior or prioress. [Medieval Latin *prioria,* from Late Latin *prior* superior, administrator. See PRIOR².]
prise (prīz) **prised, pris·ing.** *v.t.* to prize⁴. —*n.* to prize⁴.
prism (priz′əm) *n.* **1.** polyhedron with two congruent and parallel faces, and whose other faces are parallelograms. **2.** transparent solid having this shape, used for dispersing light or for breaking it up into its component colors. [Late Latin *prisma* the polyhedron, from Greek *prisma* literally, something sawed, from *priein* to saw¹.]

Prism

pris·mat·ic (priz mat′ik) *adj.* **1.** of, relating to, or like a prism. **2.** formed by or as by a transparent prism. **3.** of varied colors; brilliant. Also, **pris·mat′i·cal.** —**pris·mat′i·cal·ly,** *adv.*
prismatic colors, the seven colors, red, orange, yellow, green, blue, indigo, and violet, that are produced when white light is passed through a prism.
pris·on (priz′ən) *n.* **1.** building or institution in which persons convicted or accused of crimes are confined. **2.** any place of confinement. **3.** imprisonment. —*v.t.* to imprison. [Old French *prison* building for the confinement of criminals, from Latin *prēnsiō,* form of *prehēnsiō* a seizing.]
pris·on·er (priz′ə nər) *n.* **1.** person confined in a prison. **2.** one who is arrested or taken into custody. **3.** one who or that which is forcibly restrained, deprived of freedom, or held in captivity. **4.** prisoner of war.
Syn. 2. Prisoner, captive mean one who is deprived of liberty and held under constraint. **Prisoner** is the general term but is usually applied

specifically to one held under arrest in a prison or under guard while on trial or serving a prison sentence: *The prisoner was released on parole.* **Captive** is restricted to prisoners captured and held by an enemy during war or for ransom and suggests a state of complete subjugation rather than imprisonment: *The downed airman was held as a captive by the enemy for six months.*

prisoner of war, person captured or held by the enemy in war.

pris·sy (pris′ē) **-si·er, -si·est.** *adj.* very prim, fussy, or prudish. [Blend of PRIM and SISSY.]

pris·tine (pris′tēn) *adj.* **1.** of or relating to the earliest time, period, or condition; original; primitive. **2.** pure; uncorrupted; unspoiled: *the pristine beauty of freshly fallen snow.* [Latin *pristinus* former, primitive.]

prith·ee (prith′ē) *interj. Archaic.* I pray thee; please.

pri·va·cy (prī′və sē) *pl.,* **-cies.** *n.* **1.** state or condition of being private, secluded, or isolated: *The writer needed privacy to finish his novel.* **2.** right to be free from interference with one's private affairs: *Opening someone else's mail is an invasion of privacy.* **3.** secrecy. —**Syn.** 1. see **solitude.**

pri·vate (prī′vit) *adj.* **1.** belonging or restricted to or reserved for a particular person or persons: *a private driveway, private property.* **2.** personal; individual; primitive. **3.** not intended for general or public knowledge; confidential: *a private conversation.* **4.** not holding public office or having an official position: *a private citizen.* **5.** not supported or managed by or connected with the government: *an agency under private control.* **6.** secluded; isolated. —*n.* **1.** in the U.S. Army and Marine Corps, an enlisted man of the lowest rank. **2.** privates. external sex organs; genitals. Also, **private parts. 3. in private.** confidentially or secretly; privately. [Latin *privatus* apart from the state, belonging to an individual. Doublet of PRIVY.] —**pri′vate·ly,** *adv.* —**pri′vate·ness,** *n.*

private detective, detective who is employed by a private person or group rather than a police force or government agency. Also, **private investigator.**

private enterprise, free enterprise.

pri·va·teer (prī′və tēr′) *n.* **1.** privately owned armed ship commissioned by a government to attack enemy ships, esp. merchant ships. **2.** commander or a member of the crew of such a ship. —*v.i.* to sail on or as a privateer.

private eye *Informal.* private detective.

private first class 1. in the U.S. Army, an enlisted man ranking below a corporal and above a private. **2.** in the U.S. Marine Corps, an enlisted man ranking below a lance corporal and above a private.

private school, school that is supported and managed by a private group rather than by the government.

pri·va·tion (prī vā′shən) *n.* **1.** lack of the comforts or necessities of life or the condition resulting from such a lack. **2.** act of depriving; being deprived. [Latin *privatio* a taking away.]

priv·a·tive (priv′ə tiv) *adj.* **1.** causing deprivation or loss. **2.** *Grammar.* altering the meaning of a word from positive to negative, as by means of a prefix. —*n. Grammar.* privative prefix or suffix. [Latin *privativus* denoting privation, negative, from *privare* to deprive, rob.]

priv·et (priv′it) *n.* any of a group of evergreen shrubs or small trees, genus *Ligustrum,* widely used for hedges, usually having white flowers and black berries. [Of uncertain origin.]

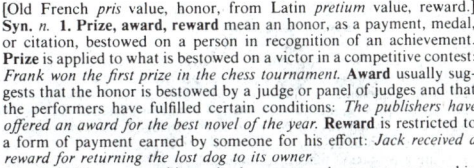

Flowers

Fruit

Leaves

Privet

priv·i·lege (priv′ə lij, priv′lij) *n.* special right, advantage, benefit, or immunity granted to or enjoyed by a certain person, group, or class. —*v.t.,* **-leged, -leg·ing.** to grant a privilege to. [Latin *privilegium* law for or against an individual, from *privus* one's own, individual + *lex* law.]

priv·i·leged (priv′ə lijd, priv′lijd) *adj.* **1.** having or enjoying a privilege or privileges. **2.** confidential; restricted: *privileged information.*

priv·i·ly (priv′ə lē) *adv.* privately; secretly.

priv·y (priv′ē) *adj.* **1.** participating in the knowledge of something secret or private (with *to*): *Only three people were privy to the plot.* **2.** *Archaic.* secret; concealed. **3.** *Archaic.* private; personal. —*n. pl.,* **priv·ies.** outhouse *(def. 1).* [Old French *prive* intimate, private, from Latin *privatus* belonging to an individual. Doublet of PRIVATE.]

Privy Council, honorary body appointed by the British sovereign, having about 300 members.

privy seal, in Great Britain, seal affixed to certain documents.

prize¹ (prīz) *n.* **1.** that which is offered or won as a reward, esp. for winning in a competition or in a game of chance. **2.** anything worth striving for. —*adj.* **1.** that has won or is likely to win a prize. **2.** offered or given as a prize. **3.** worthy of a prize; outstanding.

[Old French *pris* value, honor, from Latin *pretium* value, reward.] **Syn.** *n.* **1. Prize, award, reward** mean an honor, as a payment, medal, or citation, bestowed on a person in recognition of an achievement. **Prize** is applied to what is bestowed on a victor in a competitive contest: *Frank won the first prize in the chess tournament.* **Award** usually suggests that the honor is bestowed by a judge or panel of judges and that the performers have fulfilled certain conditions: *The publishers have offered an award for the best novel of the year.* **Reward** is restricted to a form of payment earned by someone for his effort: *Jack received a reward for returning the lost dog to its owner.*

prize² (prīz) *n.* something seized or captured, esp. an enemy ship captured at sea during wartime. [Old French *prise* seizure, booty, from *prendre* to take, from Latin *prehendere* to seize.]

prize³ (prīz) **prized, priz·ing.** *v.t.* **1.** to value or esteem highly: *to prize a friend's advice.* **2.** to estimate the value of; appraise: *a man who prizes his honor above his life.* [Old French *pr(e)isier* to value, esteem, from Late Latin *pretiare* to value, from Latin *pretium* value.]

prize⁴ (prīz) **prized, priz·ing.** *v.t. also,* **prise.** *v.t.* **1.** to raise or force with a lever; pry. —*n.* **1.** instrument used for prying; lever. **2.** leverage. [From PRIZE².]

prize·fight (prīz′fīt′) *n.* boxing match between professional boxers. —**prize′fight′er,** *n.*

prize ring, rope-enclosed area, usually on a raised platform, in which boxers fight.

pro¹ (prō) *adv.* in favor of; for. —*n. pl.,* **pros.** reason, argument, or person in favor of something: *The chairman listed all the pros and cons of the proposal.* [Latin *pro* in favor of, for.]

pro² (prō) *n. pl.,* **pros.** *Informal. n.* professional; expert. —*adj.* professional. [Short for PROFESSIONAL.]

pro-¹ *prefix* **1.** in favor of; supporting; in behalf of: *proslavery.* **2.** forward; forth; out: *progress, project.* **3.** in place of; acting as; substituting for: *pronoun.* [Latin *pro* in favor of, for, before, instead of.]

pro-² *prefix* before in time or place: *prognosis.* [Greek *pro.*]

pro·a (prō′ə) *n.* swift Malay boat having a triangular sail and a single outrigger. [Malay *prau.*]

Proa

prob. 1. problem. **2.** probable; probably.

prob·a·bil·i·ty (prob′ə bil′ə tē) *pl.,* **-ties.** *n.* **1.** quality or state of being probable; likelihood: *A willingness to negotiate increased the probability of an early settlement.* **2.** something probable or likely. **3.** *Mathematics.* ratio of the number of chances favoring the occurrence of an event to the total number of possible occurrences. **4. in all probability.** most probably; very likely.

prob·a·ble (prob′ə bəl) *adj.* **1.** likely to occur or to be true but not certain; that can reasonably be expected or believed: *The experts all agreed on the probable outcome of the boxing match.* **2.** rendering something likely but not certain. [Latin *probabilis* provable, likely, from *probare* to try, test, approve, demonstrate.]

prob·a·bly (prob′ə blē) *adv.* most likely; in all likelihood.

pro·bate (prō′bāt) *n.* act or process of legally proving a will. —*adj.* of or relating to a probate court or to probate. —*v.t.* **-bat·ed, -bat·ing.** to establish the authenticity or validity of (a will). [Latin *probatum* thing proved or approved, from *probare* to test, demonstrate, approve.]

probate court, court having jurisdiction over the probate of wills and over the administration of the property of deceased persons.

pro·ba·tion (prō bā′shən) *n.* **1.** testing or trial of the ability, qualifications, or suitability of a person, as a new employee, usually for a specified period of time. **2.** *Law.* action or practice of allowing a person convicted of a minor or first offense to go free under close supervision and on the condition that his behavior be exemplary. **3.** period of being on probation or the status of one on probation. [Latin *probatio* a proving, approval.] —**pro·ba′tion·al, pro·ba′tion·ar′y,** *adj.*

pro·ba·tion·er (prō bā′shən nər) *n.* one who is on probation.

probation officer, officer appointed to supervise a probationer.

pro·ba·tive (prō′bə tiv) *adj.* **1.** affording proof or evidence. **2.** serving or designed to test. Also, **pro′ba·to′ry.**

probe (prōb) *n.* **1.** thorough investigation or examination: *The court case led to a Senate probe into prison conditions.* **2.** slender surgical instrument for exploring a body cavity, wound, or similar opening. **3.** device, mechanism, or object used for investigation or exploration, esp. a space probe. —*v.t.* **probed, prob·ing. 1.** to investigate, examine, or explore thoroughly: *The psychiatrist probed the patient's subconscious in discussing the dream.* **2.** to examine or explore with a surgical probe. —*v.i.* to conduct a thorough investigation or examination: *Scientists probed into the nature of the phenomenon.* [Medieval Latin *proba* ex-

amination, from Late Latin *proba* proof, from Latin *probāre* to test, demonstrate.] —**Syn.** *n.* **1.** see **inquiry.**

pro·bi·ty (prō′bə tē, prob′ə-) *n.* moral excellence; integrity. [Latin *probitās* honesty, goodness.] —**Syn.** see **honesty.**

prob·lem (prob′ləm) *n.* **1.** question, situation, or condition that is difficult, perplexing, or unresolved: *Air pollution is a major problem facing our cities.* **2.** person who is troublesome or causes difficulty: *The oldest boy at camp was a problem to his counselor.* **3.** question proposed for consideration, discussion, or solution: *a physics problem.* —*adj.* **1.** being a problem; difficult to handle: *a problem child.* **2.** concerned with or presenting a moral or social problem. [Latin *problēma* question proposed for solution, from Greek *problēma* something put forward (as for discussion).]

prob·lem·at·ic (prob′lə mat′ik) *adj.* constituting, presenting, or involving a problem; uncertain. Also, **prob′lem·at′i·cal.** —**prob′lem·at′i·cal·ly,** *adv.*

pro bo·no pu·bli·co (prō bō′nō pub′li kō′) Latin. for the public good.

pro·bos·cis (prō bos′is) *pl.* **-bos·cis·es** or **-bos·ci·des** (-bos′i dēz′). *n.* **1.** trunk of an elephant. **2.** long, flexible snout, as of a tapir. **3.** long, tubular mouth parts of certain insects, as mosquitoes and butterflies, adapted for sucking. **4.** human nose. ▲ used humorously in def. 4. [Latin *proboscis* elephant's trunk, snout, from Greek *proboskis* elephant's trunk, from *pro-* before + *boskein* to feed.]

pro·caine (prō′kān) *n.* synthetic drug widely used as a local anesthetic in dentistry and medicine. [PRO-¹ + (CO)CAINE.]

pro·ce·dure (prə sē′jər) *n.* **1.** particular accepted or prescribed course of action, esp. one that follows a definite order of steps: *What is the proper procedure for leaving the building in case of fire?* **2.** customary or established way of conducting legal, parliamentary, or similar business. **3.** manner of proceeding or acting. [French *procédure,* from *procéder* to come, go on, originate (from), from Latin *prōcēdere* to go forward.] —**pro·ce′du·ral,** *adj.* —**Syn.** **1.** see **process.**

pro·ceed (prə sēd′) *v.i.* **1.** to continue, esp. after a stop or interruption: *The politician waited for the applause to die down and then proceeded with his speech.* **2.** to begin or undertake some action or process: *The mechanic jacked up the car and then proceeded to change the tire.* **3.** to move on or forward. **4.** to be carried on or put into action: *The experiment is proceeding as planned.* **5.** to come or originate (with *from*): *Kate's ambition to become a nurse proceeded from a desire to help others.* **6.** to institute and carry on a legal action (often with *against*). [Latin *prōcēdere* to go forward.] —**Syn.** **1.** see **advance.**

pro·ceed·ing (prə sē′ding) *n.* **1.** action or course of action; procedure. **2.** proceedings. series of actions or events; happenings. **3.** proceedings. record of business transacted at a meeting of a society or similar organization. **4.** Law. **a. proceedings.** legal action: *contempt proceedings.* **b.** instituting and carrying on of legal action.

pro·ceeds (prō′sēdz) *n.,pl.* money or profit derived from a commercial undertaking, esp. money raised for a particular cause.

proc·ess (pros′es, prō′ses) *n.* **1.** series of operations in the production of something: *the process of making butter.* **2.** series of continuous changes or actions leading to a specified end: *the process of growth.* **3.** course or lapse: *In the process of time the job will be done.* **4.** course of being done or going on: *The house is in the process of being built.* **5.** Law. **a.** writ or summons by which a person is ordered to appear in court in a legal action. **b.** all of the proceedings in a legal action. **6.** Biology. outgrowth or protruding part: *a bony process.* —*v.t.* **1.** to handle by routine procedures: *to process draftees.* **2.** to treat, make, or prepare, as by special method: *to process cheese.* **3.** Law. **a.** to institute legal action against. **b.** to serve a writ or summons on. —*adj.* made or prepared by some special method: *process cheese.* [Old French *proces* legal proceedings, progress, from Latin *prōcessus* a going forward.]

Syn. *n.* **1. Process, procedure, method** mean a series of actions by which something is made or done. **Process** generally involves a number of distinct but interdependent steps or stages: *The scientist explained the chemical process to the students.* **Procedure** emphasizes the sequence of steps to be followed in carrying through a process or performing a duty: *The chairman was quite familiar with the procedure for conducting a meeting.* **Method** suggests a systematic plan spelling out the techniques to be followed: *He introduced better methods of management in this company.*

pro·ces·sion (prə sesh′ən) *n.* **1.** continuous or steady forward movement or progression, esp. in a formal, orderly, or ceremonious manner. **2.** group of persons or things moving along in this way, often in a long line: *The wedding procession moved slowly down the aisle.* **3.** continuous course or succession: *the endless procession of day and night.* —*v.i.* Archaic. to move in procession. [Late Latin *prōcessiō* religious procession, from Latin *prōcessiō* a marching forward.]

pro·ces·sion·al (prə sesh′ən əl) *adj.* of, relating to, or moving in a procession. —*n.* **1.** music accompanying or designed for a procession.

2. book containing the hymns, prayers, and ritual to be used in religious processions.

pro·claim (prə klām′) *v.t.* **1.** to announce officially; declare publicly: *to proclaim a truce.* **2.** to make clear; reveal: *The youth's harsh retort proclaimed his bitter anger.* [Latin *prōclāmāre* to cry out, call out.] —**Syn.** see **declare.**

proc·la·ma·tion (prok′lə mā′shən) *n.* **1.** that which is proclaimed, esp. an official public announcement. **2.** act of proclaiming.

pro·cliv·i·ty (prō kliv′ə tē) *pl.* **-ties.** *n.* tendency or inclination; propensity: *a proclivity to complain.* [Latin *prōclīvitās* tendency, steep descent.]

Proc·ne (prok′nē) *n.* see **Philomela.**

pro·con·sul (prō kon′səl) *n.* **1.** governor or military commander of an ancient Roman province. **2.** administrator of a colony, dependency, or occupied country, usually having extensive power. [Latin *prōcōnsul* the Roman governor, from *prō cōnsule* for the consul.] —**pro·con′su·lar,** *adj.* —**pro·con·su·late** (prō kon′sə lit), **pro·con′sul·ship′,** *n.*

pro·cras·ti·nate (prō kras′tə nāt′) **-nat·ed, -nat·ing.** *v.i.* to put off doing something until a future time, esp. to do this habitually. —*v.t.* to postpone; defer. [Latin *prōcrāstinātus,* past participle of *prōcrāstināre* to delay, going back to *prō-* forward + *crās* tomorrow.] —**pro·cras′ti·na′tion, pro·cras′ti·na′tor,** *n.*

pro·cre·ate (prō′krē āt′) **-at·ed, -at·ing.** *v.t.* to produce or beget (offspring). —*v.i.* to produce offspring. [Latin *prōcreātus,* past participle of *prōcreāre* to produce.] —**pro′cre·a′tion, pro′cre·a′tor,** *n.*

pro·cre·a·tive (prō′krē ā′tiv) *adj.* **1.** capable of procreating. **2.** of or relating to procreation.

Pro·crus·te·an (prō krus′tē ən) *also,* **pro·crus·te·an.** *adj.* **1.** of, relating to, or characteristic of Procrustes. **2.** producing conformity.

Pro·crus·tes (prō krus′tēz) *n.* Greek Legend. robber who stretched or mutilated his victims to make them fit the length of his bed.

proc·tol·o·gy (prok tol′ə jē) *n.* branch of medicine dealing with the structure and diseases of the rectum and anus. [Greek *prōktos* anus + -LOGY.] —**proc·tol′o·gist,** *n.*

proc·tor (prok′tər) *n.* **1.** one appointed to maintain order and supervise students during an examination at a college or university. **2.** one appointed to manage another's affairs or to represent another in a court of law. —*v.t.* to act as proctor for (an examination); supervise. [Contraction of PROCURATOR.] —**proc·to·ri·al** (prok tôr′ē əl), *adj.*

pro·cum·bent (prō kum′bənt) *adj.* **1.** lying face down; prostrate; prone. **2.** Botany. lying along the ground but not taking root. [Latin *prōcumbēns,* present participle of *prōcumbere* to fall forward.]

proc·u·ra·tor (prok′yə rā′tər) *n.* **1.** one who manages the affairs of another or is authorized to act in another's behalf, as an agent or attorney. **2.** chief financial agent or chief administrator of a province or district in the Roman Empire. [Latin *prōcūrātor.*]

pro·cure (prə kyoor′) **-cured, -cur·ing.** *v.t.* **1.** to acquire or obtain, esp. with effort. **2.** to bring about; effect; cause. **3.** to obtain (women) for the purpose of prostitution. —*v.i.* to procure women. [Late Latin *prōcūrāre* to obtain, from Latin *prōcūrāre* to take care of, manage.] —**pro·cur′a·ble,** *adj.* —**pro·cure′ment, pro·cur′er,** *n.*

Pro·cy·on (prō′sē on′) *n.* double star, one of the twenty brightest stars, and brightest in the constellation Canis Minor.

prod (prod) **prod·ded, prod·ding.** *v.t.* **1.** to push or jab, as with a pointed instrument. **2.** to stir to action; rouse. —*n.* **1.** push; jab. **2.** pointed instrument ·used for prodding, as a goad. [Of uncertain origin.] —**prod′der,** *n.*

prod. 1. produced. **2.** product.

prod·i·gal (prod′i gəl) *adj.* **1.** recklessly extravagant; wasteful: *The man's prodigal spending habits had brought him close to bankruptcy.* **2.** lavish, generous, or profuse; abundant (often with *of*). —*n.* one who is recklessly extravagant. [Late Latin *prōdigālis* wasteful, from Latin *prōdigus.*] —**prod·i·gal·i·ty** (prod′ə gal′ə tē), *n.* —**prod′i·gal·ly,** *adv.* —**Syn.** *adj.* **1.** see **extravagant.**

pro·di·gious (prə dij′əs) *adj.* **1.** huge or extraordinary in size, number, or degree; enormous: *The jagged peaks rose to a prodigious height.* **2.** causing amazement; marvelous: *a prodigious feat of strength.* [Latin *prōdigiōsus* strange, marvelous, from *prōdigium* portent, omen.] —**pro·di′gious·ly,** *adv.* —**pro·di′gious·ness,** *n.*

prod·i·gy (prod′ə jē) *pl.* **-gies.** *n.* **1.** extraordinarily gifted or talented person, esp. a child. **2.** something that causes wonder or amazement; marvel. **3.** Archaic. omen; portent. [Latin *prōdigium.*]

pro·duce (*v.,* prə dōōs′, -dūs′; *n.,* prod′ōōs, -ūs, prō′dōōs, -dūs) **-duced, -duc·ing.** *v.t.* **1.** to make or bring into being, esp. by means of machinery and on a large scale; manufacture: *a company that produces steel.* **2.** to bring forth; yield; bear: *A cow produces milk.* **3.** to bring into existence by mental or artistic effort; create: *a playwright who produced some of the greatest works of his time.* **4.** to give rise to; cause: *the ability of an actor to produce a reaction from his audience.* **5.** to bring forward or present; show; furnish: *The lawyer could not produce any convincing evidence.* **6.** to prepare (a motion picture or

at; āpe; cär; end; mē; it; īce; hot; ōld; fôrk; wood; fōōl; oil; out; up; ūse; turn; sing; thin; this; zh in treasure; ə in ago, taken, pencil, lemon, circus.

similar form of entertainment) for public presentation, as by securing financial backing and hiring performers. **7.** to lengthen or extend, as a line. —*v.i.* to bring forth or make something: *These workers produce at a very fast rate.* —*n.* **1.** that which is produced. **2.** farm products, esp. fresh fruit and vegetables. [Latin *prōdūcere* to bring forward, bring forth.] —**pro·duc′i·ble,** *adj.*

pro·duc·er (prə dōō′sər, -dū′-) *n.* **1.** one who or that which produces. **2.** one who uses basic resources, as land or raw materials, to produce goods or services for consumer use. **3.** person in charge of producing a play, motion picture, or similar entertainment.

pro·duct (prod′əkt) *n.* **1.** anything that is produced: *dairy products.* **2.** result; consequence. **3.** number or algebraic expression obtained by multiplication. [Latin *prōductum* something produced, from *prōdūcere* to bring forward, bring forth.]

pro·duc·tion (prə duk′shən) *n.* **1.** act or process of producing. **2.** that which is produced, esp. a play, motion picture, or similar form of entertainment presented to the public. **3.** amount produced.

pro·duc·tive (prə duk′tiv) *adj.* **1.** producing abundantly; fertile or prolific: *productive land, a productive author.* **2.** having favorable, useful, or positive results; fruitful; effective: *Talks to end the strike had not been very productive.* **3.** yielding some product at a profit: *a productive business.* **4.** producing, tending to produce, or capable of producing (often with *of*): *Heav′n would sure grow weary of a world productive only of a race like ours* (Cowper, 1785). **5.** having as a result or consequence; causing (with *of*): *a set of circumstances inevitably productive of violence.* —**pro·duc′tive·ly,** *adv.* —**pro·duc′tive·ness, pro·duc·tiv·i·ty** (prō′duk tiv′ə tē, prod′ak-), *n.*

pro·em (prō′em) *n.* introductory statement or comment, as in a book; preface. [Latin *prooemium,* from Greek *prooimion,* from *pro* before + *oimos* way, path.]

prof (prof) *n. Informal.* professor.

Prof., professor.

prof·a·na·tion (prof′ə nā′shən, prō′fə-) *n.* act or instance of profaning.

pro·fane (prō fān′, prə-) *adj.* **1.** showing or characterized by irreverence, disrespect, or contempt for God or sacred things; blasphemous. **2.** not concerned with or relating to religion or religious matters; secular. **3.** vulgar; coarse; obscene: *profane language.* —*v.t.,* **-faned, -faning. 1.** to treat (something sacred) with irreverence, disrespect, or contempt; desecrate: *You have been guilty of profaning the Lord's day* (Defoe, 1715). **2.** to put to wrong, degrading, or unworthy use; debase; abuse: *so idly to profane the precious time* (Shakespeare, *Henry IV*). [Latin *profānus* not sacred, unholy, from *prō* before (outside) + *fānum* temple.] —**pro·fan·a·to·ry** (prə fan′ə tôr′ē, prō-), *adj.* —**pro·fane′ly,** *adv.* —**pro·fane′ness,** *n.*

pro·fan·i·ty (prō fan′ə tē, prə-) *pl.,* **-ties.** *n.* **1.** profane language or act. **2.** use of profane or vulgar language. **3.** quality or state of being profane.

pro·fess (prə fes′) *v.t.* **1.** to claim, esp. falsely or insincerely: *Jack professes to know everything about sculpture.* **2.** to declare openly; affirm: *We profess ourselves to be the slaves of chance* (Shakespeare, *The Winter's Tale*). **3.** to affirm one's faith in: *to profess Judaism.* **4.** to claim knowledge of or skill in; have as one's profession: *to profess law.* —*v.i.* to make a declaration or affirmation. [From PROFESSED.]

pro·fessed (prə fest′) *adj.* **1.** alleged; pretended: *His professed ignorance is only a façade.* **2.** openly declared; affirmed: *a professed enemy.* **3.** having taken the vows of a religious order: *a professed nun.* [Latin *professus* manifest, confessed, past participle of *prōfitērī* to declare publicly + -ED².]

pro·fess·ed·ly (prə fes′id lē) *adv.* **1.** avowedly. **2.** allegedly.

pro·fes·sion (prə fesh′ən) *n.* **1.** occupation that requires special education and training, as law, medicine, or theology. **2.** body of persons following such an occupation: *The young doctor was already a leading member of the medical profession.* **3.** any activity considered as a profession. **4.** act or instance of professing or declaring: *The emperor questioned his guard's profession of loyalty.* **5.** affirmation of faith in a religion. **6.** professed or avowed religion or faith. **7.** act of taking vows of a religious order following the period of novitiate. [Latin *professiō* declaration, a business.]

pro·fes·sion·al (prə fesh′ən əl) *adj.* **1.** of, relating to, characteristic of, or suitable for a profession or a person engaged in a profession: *a doctor's fee for professional services.* **2.** engaged in a profession: *The party was restricted to professional people in the publishing industry.* **3.** having as the source of one's livelihood an activity or occupation not usually pursued for gain, as a sport: *a professional golfer.* **4.** engaged in by professionals as opposed to amateurs: *professional basketball.* **5.** engaged in a certain activity as if it were a profession: *a professional revolutionary, a professional student.* —*n.* **1.** person engaged in a profession. **2.** person having as the source of his livelihood an activity or occupation not usually pursued for gain, esp. a professional athlete. **3.** one whose ability or status as a professional is unquestionable or quite

evident: *His calm manner made it obvious that he was no common gunman, but a professional.* —**pro·fes′sion·al·ly,** *adv.*

pro·fes·sion·al·ism (prə fesh′ən əl iz′əm) *n.* professional methods, spirit, character, or status.

pro·fes·sor (prə fes′ər) *n.* **1.** teacher of the highest rank in a college, university, or other institution of higher education. **2.** *Informal.* any teacher. **3.** one who professes skill in or teaches some sport or art. **4.** one who professes, esp. one who affirms his faith in a religion. [Latin *professor* teacher, from *prōfitērī* to declare publicly.] —**pro·fes·so·ri·al** (prō′fə sôr′ē əl, prof′ə-), *adj.* —**pro′fes·so′ri·al·ly,** *adv.*

pro·fes·sor·ate (prə fes′ər it) *n.* office, position, or term of office of a professor.

pro·fes·sor·ship (prə fes′ər ship′) *n.* position or duties of a professor.

prof·fer (prof′ər) *v.t.* to present for acceptance; offer. —*n.* offer. [Anglo-Norman *proffer* to offer, going back to Latin *prō* before + *offerre* to bring before, present.]

pro·fi·cien·cy (prə fish′ən sē) *pl.,* **-cies.** *n.* state or quality of being proficient; skill.

pro·fi·cient (prə fish′ənt) *adj.* highly skilled; expert; adept: *Years of practice had made Steve proficient in playing the flute.* —*n. Archaic.* expert. [Latin *prōficiēns,* present participle of *prōficere* to advance, accomplish.] —**pro·fi′cient·ly,** *adv.* —**Syn.** *adj.* see **expert.**

pro·file (prō′fīl′) *n.* **1.a.** a side view, esp. of a human face or head. **b.** outline of this, or a drawing or other representation of such an outline. **2.** any outline or representation of an outline: *The mountain's jagged profile stood out against the darkening sky.* **3.** brief biographical sketch. **4.** analysis, usually represented by means of a graph or diagram, of some person, process, or thing: *a personality profile, a vote profile.* **5.** representation of a cutaway side view or vertical section of an architectural structure or geologic feature. —*v.t.,* **-filed, -fil·ing.** to make, draw, or write a profile of. [Italian *profilo* outline, side view, going back to Latin *prō* before + *fīlum* thread.]

Profile

Syn. *n.* **1. Profile, silhouette, contour** mean the outline of a body or mass. **Profile** is the outline or representation of a side view of a face showing the outline of the head from the top to the chin: *The actor was proud of his handsome profile.* **Silhouette** is a likeness or drawing of a head or body having its outlines filled in with black against a light background without any details: *The children saw only the man's dark silhouette against the wall.* **Contour** suggests the form or shape of an object as determined by its outline, esp. the curving lines suggestive of grace or fullness: *The drawing accented the swanlike contour of her neck.*

prof·it (prof′it) *n.* **1.** *also,* **profits.** amount remaining after all the costs of a business or business transaction have been paid. **2.** *also,* **profits.** financial gain, esp. return or income received from investment or property. **3.** difference between the initial cost of an item and its selling price. **4.** benefit or advantage; gain. —*v.i.* **1.** to derive benefit or profit; gain: *to profit from an experience.* **2.** to be of advantage, use, or benefit. —*v.t.* to be of advantage, use, or benefit to. [Old French *profit* advantage, gain from property, from Latin *prōfectus* advance, progress.] —**Syn.** *n.* **4.** see **advantage.**

prof·it·a·ble (prof′i tə bəl) *adj.* **1.** yielding a financial profit: *a profitable business.* **2.** beneficial; useful: *a profitable experience.* —**prof′it·a·ble·ness,** *n.* —**prof′it·a·bly,** *adv.*

prof·it·eer (prof′ə tēr′) *n.* one who makes or seeks to make excessive profits, esp. by selling goods at exorbitant prices during a time of shortage. —*v.i.* to act as a profiteer.

profit sharing, system by which employees are given a share of the profits of a business in addition to their regular salary or wages.

prof·li·gate (prof′lə git) *adj.* **1.** totally corrupt with regard to one's morals; thoroughly immoral; dissolute. **2.** recklessly extravagant or wasteful. —*n.* profligate person. [Latin *prōflīgātus* wretched, dissolute, past participle of *prōflīgāre* to dash to the ground, ruin.] —**prof′li·ga·cy,** *n.* —**prof′li·gate·ly,** *adv.*

pro·found (prə found′) *adj.* **1.** showing or characterized by great understanding, knowledge, or insight: *a profound idea, a profound literary work.* **2.** coming from or penetrating to the depth of one's being; intensely felt: *We experienced a profound sorrow upon hearing of his death.* **3.** significant; far-reaching; extensive: *The doctor's discovery will have a profound influence on mankind.* **4.** absolute; complete; thorough: *a profound silence.* **5.** situated or extending far beneath the surface; of great depth: *for all . . . the profound sea hides in unknown fathoms* (Shakespeare, *The Winter's Tale*). [Old French *profond* deep, from Latin *prōfundus.*] —**pro·found′ly,** *adv.* —**pro·found′ness,** *n.*

pro·fun·di·ty (prə fun′də tē) *pl.,* **-ties.** *n.* **1.** quality or being

profound; depth. **2.** profound or abstruse statement, idea, or matter. [Late Latin *prŏfunditās* depth, from Latin *prŏfundus* deep.]

pro·fuse (prə fūs') *adj.* **1.** great or abundant in amount; plentiful: *profuse undergrowth, profuse bleeding.* **2.** given or giving freely, often to excess; lavish: *profuse expressions of praise.* [Latin *prŏfūsus* spread out, lavish, past participle of *prŏfundere* to pour out.] —**pro·fuse′ly,** *adv.* —**pro·fuse′ness,** *n.*

pro·fu·sion (prə fū′zhən) *n.* **1.** plentiful amount; abundance. **2.** extravagance; lavishness.

pro·gen·i·tor (prō jen′ə tər) *n.* **1.** ancestor from whom lineal descent is traced; forefather. **2.** precursor; originator. [Latin *prŏgenitor* ancestor.]

prog·e·ny (proj′ə nē) *pl.* **-nies.** *n.* offspring, descendants, or children collectively. [Old French *progenie,* from Latin *prŏgeniēs* lineage, descent; offspring.]

pro·ges·ter·one (prō jes′tə rōn′) *n.* female sex hormone that functions with estrogen to prepare the uterus for receiving and nourishing a fertilized egg. It also helps maintain pregnancy by keeping the uterus in a suitable condition for the embryo. [PRO-¹ + GE(STATION) + ST(EROL) + -ONE.]

prog·na·thous (prog′nə thəs) *adj.* having or characterized by jaws that project beyond the upper part of the face. Also, **prog·nath·ic** (prog nath′ik). [PRO-² + Greek *gnathos* jaw + -OUS.] —**prog·na·thism** (prog′nə thiz′əm), *n.*

prog·no·sis (prog nō′sis) *pl.* **-ses** (-sēz). *n.* **1.** prediction of the probable course and outcome of a disease. **2.** any prediction or forecast. [Late Latin *prognōsis* foreknowledge, prediction of the course of a disease, from Greek *prognōsis.*]

prog·nos·tic (prog nos′tik) *adj.* **1.** of, relating to, or serving as a basis for a prognosis. **2.** foretelling; predictive. —*n.* **1.** sign or indication of some future occurrence. **2.** prediction or forecast. [Latin *prognōsticon* sign of the future, from Greek *prognōstikon.*]

prog·nos·ti·cate (prog nos′tə kāt′) **-cat·ed, -cat·ing.** *v.t.* **1.** to predict on the basis of present indications; forecast; prophesy. **2.** to foreshadow; presage. —**prog·nos′ti·ca′tion,** **prog·nos′ti·ca′tor,** *n.*

pro·gram (prō′gram, -grəm) *also, British,* **pro·gramme.** *n.* **1.** list or printed announcement, esp. for some public presentation, as a play or concert, usually indicating what is to be presented and in what order and who will participate. **2.** presentation or performance, esp. a television or radio show. **3.** schedule or procedure: *The Senate committee formulated a new crime-prevention program.* **4.** set of organized activities or other offerings planned by or available at a particular place or institution: *Our school runs a good weekend youth program. This university has an excellent English program.* **5.** schedule of classes of an individual student or teacher in an educational institution. **6.a.** series of steps specified for the solution of a particular problem, to be coded for use in a computer. **b.** sequence of coded instructions used to direct a computer in the solution of such a problem. **7.** material to be taught through programmed instruction, structured and presented according to a definite sequential method. —*v.t.,* **-gramed, -gram·ing;** *also, British,* **-grammed, -gram·ming.** **1.** to arrange or include in a program or schedule. **2.** to make up or work out a program for. **3.** to write a program for (a computer) or provide with such a program. [Late Latin *programma* proclamation, from Greek *programma* public notice.]

Syn. *n.* **3.** **Program, agenda** mean a schedule of things to be done in a certain order. **Program** is a brief schedule listing things to be done or to take place and their time limits: *What is your program for tomorrow?* **Agenda** denotes the order of business to be discussed or transacted at a meeting: *The agenda was circulated among all members.*

programmed instruction, self-teaching with the aid of a textbook or teaching machine that presents material structured in a logical sequence. Programmed instruction allows the student to check his answer immediately for correctness.

programmed learning, learning by means of programmed instruction.

pro·gram·mer (prō′gram′ər) *also,* **pro·gram·er.** *n.* one who programs, esp. one who programs computers.

prog·ress (*n.,* prog′rəs, -res; *British* prō′gres; *v.,* prə gres′) *n.* **1.** forward movement in space: *Heavy rains hindered the explorer's progress through the jungle.* **2.** movement toward a goal or toward completion: *Are you making any progress with your report?* **3.** movement toward the resolution of a dispute: *Negotiators for both sides reported that no progress had been made in the talks.* **4.** development to a better or higher state; improvement: *a patient's progress toward recovery.* **5.** journey, esp. a royal or official tour. —*v.i.* **1.** to move forward or onward; proceed: *The author's argument progresses logically from one step to the next.* **2.** to move toward a goal or toward completion: *Construction of the new hospital is progressing according to schedule.* **3.** to develop to a better or higher state; improve. [Latin *prŏgressus* an advance, going forward.] —**Syn.** *v.i.* **1.** see **advance.**

pro·gres·sion (prə gresh′ən) *n.* **1.** act of progressing; advance.

2. sequence of numbers or algebraic expressions in which the same relation holds between each quantity and the one succeeding it; arithmetic or geometric progression. **3.** sequence or succession, as of events. **4.** *Music.* **a.** movement from one tone or chord to another. **b.** succession of tones or chords.

pro·gres·sive (prə gres′iv) *adj.* **1.** moving forward; advancing. **2.** proceeding steadily or step by step. **3.** favoring, advocating, or characterized by progress, reform, or improvement, esp. in political or social matters. **4.** (of a disease) advancing steadily in severity or extent. **5.** designating or relating to a tax that increases in rate as the amount taxed increases. **6.** of or relating to a theory of education emphasizing each child's individual needs and capacities and favoring a more informal classroom situation. **7.** **Progressive.** of, relating to, or belonging to a Progressive Party. **8.** *Grammar.* denoting action in progress. —*n.* **1.** one who favors or advocates progress or reform, as in political, social, or educational matters. **2.** **Progressive.** member of a Progressive Party. —**pro·gres′sive·ly,** *adv.* —**pro·gres′sive·ness,** *n.*

Progressive Party 1. political party formed by liberal Republicans in 1912 to back the candidacy of Theodore Roosevelt for president. It advocated direct election of senators, woman suffrage, and adoption of the initiative, referendum, and recall. **2.** political party that was formed in 1924 and was supported by farmer, labor, and Socialist groups. **3.** political party that was formed in 1948 and backed Henry A. Wallace for president.

pro·hib·it (prō hib′it) *v.t.* **1.** to forbid by authority: *Smoking is prohibited in this building.* **2.** to prevent; hinder. [Latin *prōhibitus,* past participle of *prōhibēre* to forbid, prevent.] —**Syn. 1.** see **forbid.**

pro·hi·bi·tion (prō′ə bish′ən) *n.* **1.** act of prohibiting. **2.** law, order, or rule that forbids something. **3.a.** the forbidding by law of the manufacture, transportation, and sale of alcoholic beverages. **b. Prohibition.** period from 1920 to 1933 during which alcoholic beverages were prohibited by federal law in the United States.

pro·hi·bi·tion·ist (prō′ə bish′ə nist) *n.* **1.** one who favors the prohibition of alcoholic beverages. **2.** member of the Prohibition Party.

Prohibition Party, minor U.S. political party organized in 1869, advocating the prohibition of the manufacture, sale, and consumption of alcoholic beverages.

pro·hib·i·tive (prō hib′ə tiv) *adj.* **1.** so high or expensive as to make difficult or impossible the purchase, use, or payment of something: *merchandise sold at an almost prohibitive price.* **2.** prohibiting or tending to prohibit. Also, **pro·hib·i·to·ry** (prō hib′ə tôr′ē).

proj·ect (*n.,* proj′ekt; *v.,* prə jekt′) *n.* **1.** plan; scheme; proposal. **2.** task or activity that is to be done; undertaking. **3.** housing complex, usually made up of apartment buildings, esp. such a complex supported by the government to provide housing for low-income families. —*v.t.* **1.** to throw, shoot, or hurl forward: *The catapult projected stones into the air.* **2.** to cause (a shadow, light, or image) to fall on a surface: *The strange figure projected a frightening shadow on the wall.* **3.** to cause (one's voice) to be heard distinctly at a distance. **4.** to visualize or conceive by using one's imagination: *to project oneself into the future.* **5.** to predict on the basis of certain given or known information: *to project the winner of an election by using a computer.* **6.** to attribute unconsciously (one's own feelings, thoughts, or qualities) to another. **7.** to plan; propose. **8.** to cause to stick out. **9.** *Geometry.* to represent (a given figure) on a plane or curved surface by means of a correspondence between the points of the two figures. —*v.i.* **1.** to stick out; protrude: *A narrow promontory projected into the sea.* **2.** to cause one's voice to be heard distinctly at a distance. **3.** to attribute unconsciously one's own feelings, thoughts, or qualities to another. [Latin *prōjectus,* past participle of *prōicere* to throw forth.]

Syn. *n.* **2.** **Project, enterprise, undertaking** mean a systematically planned venture. **Project** implies a venture organized for a specific goal and ending once it has been accomplished; although it may require money and equipment, it stresses the complicated organization and the joint efforts of several persons which make it possible: *For the term project, the committee built a model city and presented a panel discussion on urban planning.* **Enterprise** implies a more tentative and risky venture, and stresses individual effort and initiative and a pioneering and competitive spirit, rather than cooperation: *The enterprise had been a failure, but it paved the way for future explorations.* **Undertaking** implies a more carefully planned effort, often one of great significance and seriousness, that implies a great burden of responsibility on those involved: *The general considered the review of military strategy to be a solemn undertaking.*

pro·jec·tile (prə jek′til, -tīl) *n.* object that is designed to be shot or otherwise projected, as a bullet. —*adj.* **1.** capable of being thrown, shot, or hurled forward. **2.** impelling or driving forward.

pro·jec·tion (prə jek′shən) *n.* **1.** act of projecting. **2.** something that sticks out or projects; protruding part. **3.a.** process of projecting images, as from a film or printed page, onto a screen or other surface. **b.** image so projected. **4.** prediction based on certain given or known

at; āpe; cär; end; mē; it; īce; hot; ōld; fôrk; wood; fŏŏl; oil; out; up; ūse; turn; sing; thin; this; zh in treasure; ə in ago, taken, pencil, lemon, circus.

information: *a computer projection of an election's outcome.* **5.** act, process, or instance of unconsciously attributing one's own feelings, thoughts, or qualities to another. **6.** forming of a plan. **7.** representation on a plane surface, as in a map, of all or part of the earth's surface or of the celestial sphere. **8.** *Geometry.* result or process of representing a given figure on a plane or curved surface by means of a correspondence between the points of the two figures.

pro·jec·tion·ist (prə jek′shə nist) *n.* one who operates a motion-picture or slide projector.

projective geometry, study of those properties of geometric figures that do not vary under projection.

projective test, any of various psychological personality tests, as the Rorschach test.

pro·jec·tor (prə jek′tər) *n.* **1.** apparatus that projects images, as from a film or printed page, onto a screen or other surface. **2.** one who devises projects or plans.

Pro·kof·iev, Ser·gei Ser·ge·ye·vich (prə kô′fē ef′, -kôf′yef; ser gā′ ser gā′-yə vich) 1891–1953, Russian composer.

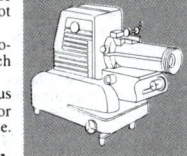

Projector

pro·lac·tin (prō lak′tin) *n.* pituitary hormone that promotes lactation.

pro·late (prō′lāt) *adj.* lengthened in the direction of the polar diameter, as a spheroid formed by the revolution of an ellipse about its longer axis. [Latin *prōlātus* extended, past participle of *prōferre* to bring forward, extend.]

pro·le·tar·i·an (prō′lə tãr′ē ən) *adj.* of, relating to, or characteristic of the proletariat. —*n.* member of the proletariat. [Latin *prōlētārius* Roman citizen of the lowest class who was so poor that he was able to serve the state only by having children (from *prōlēs* offspring) + -AN.]

pro·le·tar·i·at (prō′lə tãr′ē ət) *n.* **1.a.** the working class, esp. in Marxist theory. **b.** lowest and poorest class, owning no means of production. **2.** in ancient Rome, the lowest class. [French *prolétariat* the working class, from Latin *prōlētārius* Roman citizen of the lowest class. See PROLETARIAN.]

pro·lif·er·ate (prō lif′ə rāt′) -at·ed, -at·ing. *v.i.* to multiply, reproduce, or grow rapidly, as cells. —*v.t.* to cause to spread, increase, or reproduce: *to proliferate radical ideas.* [Medieval Latin *prolifer* bearing offspring (from Latin *prōlēs* offspring + *ferre* to bear¹) + -ATE¹.] —**pro·lif′er·a′tion,** *n.*

pro·lif·ic (prə lif′ik) *adj.* **1.** producing abundantly through creative or artistic effort; highly productive: *a prolific novelist.* **2.** producing offspring or fruit in abundance; fertile: *a prolific apple tree.* [Medieval Latin *prolificus* fertile, from Latin *prōlēs* offspring + *facere* to make.] —**pro·lif·i·ca·cy** (prə lif′i kə sē), **pro·lif′ic·ness,** *n.* —**pro·lif′i·cal·ly,** *adv.*

pro·lix (prō liks′, prō′liks′) *adj.* **1.** so long and wordy as to be tedious: *a prolix sermon.* **2.** inclined to speak or write in a tediously long and wordy manner. [Latin *prōlixus* extended.] —**pro·lix′i·ty,** *n.* —**pro·lix′ly,** *adv.*

pro·logue (prō′lôg′, -log′) *also,* **pro·log.** *n.* **1.** introduction to a play, poem, discourse, or other literary work. **2.** any introductory or preliminary act or event. [Latin *prōlogus* introduction to a play, from Greek *prologos* introduction to a play or speech.] —**Syn. 1.** see **introduction.**

pro·long (prə lông′) *v.t.* to lengthen, esp. in time or duration; extend: *Judy prolonged the suspense by not telling us what had happened until the next day.* [Late Latin *prōlongāre,* from Latin *prō* forward + *longus* not short, lengthy.]

pro·lon·gate (prə lông′gāt) -gat·ed, -gat·ing. *v.t.* to prolong.

pro·lon·ga·tion (prō′lông gā′shən) *n.* **1.** act of prolonging; being prolonged. **2.** something that prolongs or is prolonged.

prom (prom) *n. Informal.* formal school or college dance. [Short for PROMENADE.]

prom·e·nade (prom′ə nād′, -näd′) *n.* **1.** leisurely walk, esp. one taken in a public place for pleasure or display. **2.** place or area for such walking. **3.a.** formal dance; ball. **b.** ceremonious march of the guests at the opening of a formal dance. **4.** march of dancers in a square dance. —*v.i.,* -nad·ed, -nad·ing. **1.** to go on a promenade or leisurely walk. **2.** to execute a promenade in a square dance. —*v.t.* **1.** to take a leisurely walk through or on. **2.** to display on or as if on a promenade; parade. [French *promenade* act of walking, place for walking, from Old French *promener* to walk, from Late Latin *prōmināre* to drive forward, going back to Latin *prō* forward + *minārī* to threaten.]

promenade deck, upper deck of a passenger ship, or an open area of a deck, where passengers can walk.

Pro·me·the·an (prə mē′thē ən) *adj.* **1.** of, relating to, or like Prometheus. **2.** daringly creative or original. —*n.* one who is Promethean in spirit or actions.

Pro·me·the·us (prə mē′thē əs, -thūs) *n. Greek Mythology.* Titan who stole fire from the gods and brought it to man. Zeus punished him by chaining him to a rock where an eagle ate away at his liver every day.

pro·me·thi·um (prə mē′thē əm) *n.* man-made, radioactive, metallic element, one of the rare-earth elements. Symbol: **Pm** See **element** for table. [Modern Latin *promethium,* from PROMETHEUS.]

prom·i·nence (prom′ə nəns) *n.* **1.** state or quality of being prominent. **2.** something prominent; projection.

prom·i·nent (prom′ə nənt) *adj.* **1.** well-known or important; notable: *a prominent member of the community.* **2.** very noticeable; conspicuous: *One decrepit shack was the landscape's only prominent feature.* **3.** sticking out from a surface; projecting. [Latin *prōminēns,* present participle of *prōminēre* to project.] —**prom′i·nent·ly,** *adv.*

prom·is·cu·i·ty (prom′ə skū′ə tē) *n.* **1.** promiscuous sexual relations or behavior. **2.** state or quality of being promiscuous. **3.** indiscriminate mixture.

pro·mis·cu·ous (prə mis′kū əs) *adj.* **1.** indiscriminate, esp. engaging in sexual relations indiscriminately or with many persons. **2.** made up of varied and unrelated things, parts, or individuals. [Latin *prōmiscuus.*] —**pro·mis′cu·ous·ly,** *adv.* —**pro·mis′cu·ous·ness,** *n.*

prom·ise (prom′is) *n.* **1.** assurance or pledge given that one will do or refrain from doing some act or that something will or will not occur: *Many people began to lose faith in the president's promises of coming prosperity.* **2.a.** indication of or reasonable basis for expectation of future excellence, success, or progress: *a drug that shows promise in treating a disease.* **b.** indication of something that may occur or develop. —*v.t.,* -ised, -is·ing. **1.** to declare or guarantee with a promise. ▲ used with an infinitive or clause: *The boss promised to give everyone a raise.* **2.** to make a promise of (something): *Politicians often promise improvements that will never take place.* **3.** to give reason to expect or anticipate (something): *The clear skies promised a nice day.* ▲ often used with an infinitive: *This promises to be an interesting evening.* —*v.i.* **1.** to make a promise. **2.** to give reason for expectation. [Latin *prōmissum* assurance given regarding the future, expectation.]

Syn. *v.t.* **1. Promise, pledge, vow** mean to give one's word to act in a certain way. **Promise** expresses intention but does not guarantee what the outcome will be: *He promised his wife a mink coat for her birthday.* **Pledge** is often used in the context of a business agreement or other transaction and implies a solemn and formal guarantee backed up by a person's honor, integrity, or reputation: *The knight pledged allegiance to the king.* **Vow** emphasizes the emotional character of a promise, suggesting a religious intensity and steadfastness: *The lovers vowed eternal devotion.*

Promised Land 1. in the Old Testament, the land of Canaan, promised by God to Abraham and his descendants. **2. promised land.** any place where final happiness is hoped or expected to be found. **3.** heaven.

prom·is·ing (prom′i sing) *adj.* showing promise for the future: *The young man's sharp wit made him one of the most promising new playwrights.* —**prom′is·ing·ly,** *adv.* —**Syn.** see **favorable.**

prom·is·so·ry (prom′ə sôr′ē) *adj.* containing or conveying a promise: *a promissory pact.*

promissory note, written promise to pay a specified sum of money to a certain party at a future time or on demand.

prom·on·to·ry (prom′ən tôr′ē) *pl.,* -ries. *n.* elevated portion of land extending out into a body of water; headland. [Latin *prōmonturium.*]

pro·mote (prə mōt′) -mot·ed, -mot·ing. *v.t.* **1.** to raise in rank, position, or honor: *Several instructors were promoted to assistant professor this year.* **2.** to aid in or contribute to the growth, development, or progress of: *Certain foods promote tooth decay.* **3.** to work for; advocate: *to promote the passage of a bill.* **4.** to advance (a student) to the next higher grade. **5.** to try to sell, increase the popularity of, or obtain the necessary capital for (a product, business undertaking, or the like), as by advertising. [Latin *prōmōtus,* past participle of *prōmovēre* to move forward.]

pro·mot·er (prə mō′tər) *n.* **1.** one who or that which promotes, advances, or furthers something. **2.** one who organizes or promotes a business undertaking or commercial enterprise, esp. one who arranges for the presentation of a sports event.

pro·mo·tion (prə mō′shən) *n.* **1.** advancement in rank, position, honor, or grade. **2.** furtherance of a product or commercial enterprise. **3.** act of promoting. —**pro·mo′tion·al,** *adj.*

Syn. 1. Promotion, advancement mean the act of raising a person in rank or position. **Promotion** implies raising a person to a higher or better position with greater privileges and salary, esp. when done according to a fixed and normal gradation or after tests evaluating professional competence: *Jack worked hard and received quick promotions.* **Advancement** suggests elevation to a position of greater personal dignity and importance from among the ranks of contenders and may be preferred when a gain in professional standing is to be implied: *At sixty he had no further hope of advancement.* **2.** see **publicity.**

at; āpe; cär; end; mē; it; īce; hot; ōld; fôrk; wood; fōōl; oil; out; up; ūse; turn; sing; thin; this; zh in treasure; ə in ago, taken, pencil, lemon, circus.

prompt (prompt) *adj.* **1.** acting or occurring at the proper time; on time; punctual: *Henry is usually prompt in arriving.* **2.** done or given without delay: *a repair shop known for its prompt service.* **3.** quick to act; ready: *Jane is always prompt to voice some criticism.* —*v.t.* **1.** to move to action; incite: *An odd sense of foreboding prompted me to return home.* **2.** to give rise to; inspire: *The scandal prompted a senate investigation.* **3.** to remind, advise, or direct, esp. to supply (a performer or speaker) with words he has forgotten or a cue he has missed. [Latin *promptus* ready, at hand, past participle of *prōmere* to bring forth. Doublet of PRONTO.] —**prompt′ly,** *adv.* —**prompt′ness,** *n.*

prompt·er (promp′tər) *n.* one who or that which prompts, esp. a person whose task is to prompt the actors in a theatrical production.

promp·ti·tude (promp′tə tōōd′) *n.* quality or habit of being prompt; promptness.

prom·ul·gate (prom′əl gāt′, prō mul′gāt) **-gat·ed, -gat·ing.** *v.t.* **1.** to make known or put into effect formally and officially, esp. by public declaration; proclaim: *to promulgate a law.* **2.** to make widespread; disseminate. [Latin *prōmulgātus,* past participle of *prōmulgāre* to make known, publish.] —**prom′ul·ga′tion, prom′ul·ga′tor,** *n.*

pron. **1.** pronoun. **2.** pronounced; pronunciation.

prone (prōn) *adj.* **1.** lying with the face or front downward; prostrate. **2.** naturally inclined; disposed (often with *to*): *Some people are prone to distrust strangers.* [Latin *prōnus* leaning forward, inclined.] —**prone′ly,** *adv.* —**prone′ness,** *n.*

prong (prông, prong) *n.* **1.** sharply pointed end of a tool or implement, as of a fork. **2.** any sharply pointed projection, as of an antler. —*v.t.* to pierce or stab with or as with a prong. [Of uncertain origin.]

pronged (prôngd, prongd) *adj.* having prongs.

prong·horn (prông′hôrn′, prong′-) *pl.,* **-horns** or **-horn.** *n.* cud-chewing mammal, *Antilocapra americana,* resembling an antelope, found chiefly on the Rocky Mountain plains, and having slender, pronged horns. Height: 3 feet at the shoulder.

Pronghorn

pro·nom·i·nal (prō nom′in əl) *adj.* of, relating to, or having the nature or function of a pronoun. [Late Latin *prōnōmenālis,* from Latin *prōnōmen* pronoun.] —**pro·nom′i·nal·ly,** *adv.*

pro·noun (prō′noun′) *n.* word used as a substitute for a noun, denoting a person, place, or thing without naming it as, *I, you, he, who, what, this.* [Latin *prōnōmen,* from *prō nōmine* instead of a noun.]

pro·nounce (prə nouns′) **-nounced, -nounc·ing.** *v.t.* **1.** to utter (a word or sound). **2.a.** to utter (a word or sound) in a particular way, esp. with a certain accent or according to an accepted standard: *She knows a lot of Spanish words but pronounces them incorrectly.* **b.** to indicate the correct manner of uttering (a word) with phonetic symbols. **3.** to declare or state, esp. officially, formally, or solemnly: *The judge pronounced the man not guilty.* —*v.i.* **1.** to state an opinion, judgment, or decision; make a pronouncement. **2.** to utter or pronounce words. [Old French *proncier* to articulate, declare formally, from Latin *prōnūntiāre* to announce, recite, tell.] —**pro·nounce′a·ble,** *adj.*

pro·nounced (prə nounst′) *adj.* clearly recognizable; strongly defined; decided: *Kurt's foreign accent becomes less pronounced the longer he remains in this country.* —**pro·nounc·ed·ly** (prə noun′sid lē, -nounst′lē), *adv.*

pro·nounce·ment (prə nouns′mənt) *n.* **1.** formal or authoritative declaration or statement. **2.** opinion, judgment, or decision.

pron·to (pron′tō) *adv. Informal.* quickly; promptly; immediately. [Spanish *pronto* quick, quickly, from Latin *promptus* ready, at hand, past participle of *prōmere* to bring forth. Doublet of PROMPT.]

pro·nun·ci·a·men·to (prə nun′sē ə men′tō) *pl.,* **-tos.** *n.* proclamation; manifesto. [Spanish *pronunciamiento,* going back to Latin *prōnuntiāre* to announce, recite, tell.]

pro·nun·ci·a·tion (prə nun′sē ā′shən) *n.* **1.** act or manner of pronouncing words: *to make one's pronunciation more distinct.* **2.a.** accepted or standard way of pronouncing a word: *There are many words that have more than one pronunciation.* **b.** phonetic transcription of a word indicating the way it is pronounced. [Latin *prōnūntiātiō* public declaration, delivery (of a speech).]

Syn. 1. Pronunciation, enunciation, articulation mean the way of uttering speech sounds. Pronunciation considers speech in terms of a particular pattern of accent, stress, and inflection, esp. that accepted as standard: *This dictionary gives the American pronunciation of English words.* Enunciation considers speech in terms of clarity and the listener's ease of understanding: *We could not understand what the drunk man*

said because his enunciation was slurred. Articulation emphasizes the process and technique of manipulating vocal organs so that sounds have maximum intelligibility and distinctness: *The deaf are trained in the articulation of syllables.*

proof (prōōf) *n.* **1.** evidence sufficient to establish a fact or induce belief. **2.** test or trial, as of the truth, quality, or strength of something. **3.** establishment of the validity or truth of something; conclusive demonstration: *The philosopher used simple logic in the proof of his assertion.* **4.** *Law.* evidence serving to determine a judgment or verdict. **5.** sequence of logical steps serving to demonstrate or establish a proposition. **6.a.** standard alcoholic content and strength of a liquor. **b.** strength with reference to this standard. **7.** *Printing.* trial impression taken from type, blocks, or plates for the purpose of checking and making corrections or changes before printing. **8.** *Etching and Engraving.* trial impression taken from an engraved stone, plate, or block for the purpose of examination. **9.** *Photography.* trial print from a photographic negative. —*adj.* **1.** firmly or successfully resistant to; impervious to (with *against*): *to be proof against temptation.* **2.** used in proving, testing, or correcting. **3.** of standard alcoholic strength. —*v.t.* **1.** to make resistant or impervious to. ▲ used in combination: *to waterproof a garment.* **2.** to make a proof of. [Old French *prueve* that which establishes the truth of something, from Late Latin *proba* test, evidence, from Latin *probāre* to test, demonstrate.] —**Syn.** *n.* **1.** see **evidence.**

-proof *combining form* **1.** impervious or resistant to: *waterproof, fireproof.* **2.** safe from; protected against: *foolproof.* [From PROOF.]

proof·read (prōōf′rēd′) **-read** (-red′), **-read·ing.** *v.t., v.i.* to read (written material, esp. printers' proofs) for the purpose of detecting and correcting errors. —**proof′read′er,** *n.*

prop[1] (prop) **propped, prop·ping.** *v.t.* **1.** to support, hold up, or hold in place by placing something under or against (often with *up*): *The man propped up the sagging roof with some pieces of lumber.* **2.** to sustain; support; bolster. —*n.* **1.** that which serves to prop up something or hold something in place; support. **2.** one who or that which props or sustains. [Possibly from Middle Dutch *proppe* a support.]

prop[2] (prop) *n.* property *(def. 6).*

prop[3] (prop) *n. Informal.* propeller.

prop. **1.** property. **2.** proposition. **3.** proprietor.

prop·a·gan·da (prop′ə gan′də) *n.* **1.** body of doctrines, ideas, or attitudes of a particular group promoted, often through public allegation and in a distorted or biased form, in order to influence the point of view of others, gain supporters, or damage an opposing group. **2.** systematic promotion or dissemination of such doctrines, ideas, or attitudes. **3.** Propaganda. congregation of the Curia, composed of a committee of cardinals charged with the care of foreign missions and the training of missionaries. [Modern Latin *(congregatio de) propaganda (fide)* (congregation for) propagating (the faith).]

prop·a·gan·dism (prop′ə gan′diz′əm) *n.* act or practice of using propaganda. —**prop′a·gan′dist,** *n., adj.* —**prop′a·gan·dis′tic,** *adj.* —**prop′a·gan·dis′ti·cal·ly,** *adv.*

prop·a·gan·dize (prop′ə gan′dīz) **-dized, -diz·ing.** *v.t.* **1.** to spread by means of propaganda. **2.** to subject to propaganda. —*v.i.* to spread or carry on propaganda.

prop·a·gate (prop′ə gāt′) **-gat·ed, -gat·ing.** *v.i.* to multiply by reproduction; breed. —*v.t.* **1.** to cause (animals or plants) to reproduce; breed or raise. **2.** (of an animal or plant) to reproduce (itself). **3.** to transmit (characteristics) to one's offspring. **4.** to spread or transmit from person to person, as information; disseminate: *to propagate false rumors.* **5.** to transmit, as light or sound, through a medium: *to propagate radio waves over a great distance.* [Latin *prōpāgātus,* past participle of *prōpāgāre* to plant slips, beget, increase, extend.] —**prop′a·ga′tive,** *adj.* —**prop′a·ga′tor,** *n.*

prop·a·ga·tion (prop′ə gā′shən) *n.* **1.** multiplication by reproduction. **2.** dissemination, as of a belief; spread. **3.** act or process of propagating; being propagated.

pro·pane (prō′pān) *n.* colorless gas found in petroleum and natural gas, widely used as a heating fuel. Formula: C₃H₈.

pro·pel (prə pel′) **-pelled, -pel·ling.** *v.t.* **1.** to cause to move forward or onward; put or sustain in motion: *to propel an aircraft by jet engines.* **2.** to urge onward: *He was propelled not only by the desire of glory, but by the urgent necessity of money* (Bevan, 1902). [Latin *prōpellere* to drive forward.]

pro·pel·lant (prə pel′ənt) *also,* **pro·pel·lent.** *n.* propelling agent or substance, esp. a fuel for propelling a rocket.

pro·pel·lent (prə pel′ənt) *adj.* propelling or capable of propelling. —*n.* propellant.

pro·pel·ler (prə pel′ər) *n.* device consisting of a hub having blades mounted at an angle. When the hub revolves, the action of the blades creates a driving force that can be used to propel a boat or aircraft. Also, **screw propeller, screw.**

Propeller

pro·pen·si·ty (prə pen′sə tē) *pl.,* **-ties.** *n.* nat-

ural tendency; inclination. [Latin *prōpēnsus* inclined, past participle of *prōpendēre* to be inclined + -ITY.]

prop·er (prop′ər) *adj.* **1.** suitable, appropriate, or correct: *To do good work, one must have the proper tools.* **2.** conforming to a particular or the accepted standard, as of behavior or precedure: *to be given a proper burial.* **3.** strictly formal, neat, or respectable; decorous; prim: *a lady so proper that she was unwilling to defy the slightest convention.* **4.** understood or considered in a precise or strict sense: *Despite its proximity, the town is not really part of Boston proper.* **5.** belonging to or characteristic of (with *to*): *weather conditions proper to that region of the world.* **6.** *Grammar.* designating or derived from a particular person, place, or thing. **7.** *Archaic.* handsome; attractive. **8.** *Informal.* thorough; complete; out-and-out: *a proper rogue.* **9.** *Informal.* fine; excellent. [Old French *propre* suitable, characteristic of a person or thing, from Latin *proprius* one's own.]
Syn. 1. Proper, appropriate, fitting mean suitable for a purpose, need, or condition. **Proper** suggests something that complies with an absolute standard, whether of an ethical, physical, or functional nature: *This is the proper way to iron a shirt.* **Appropriate** implies a relative standard of judgment, suggesting how something may be changed or affected by a particular circumstance or occasion: *I didn't think it was appropriate to question the boy in front of all those people.* **Fitting** places the greatest emphasis on the special harmony between means and ends: *The inauguration was celebrated with fitting pomp and ceremony.*

proper fraction, fraction in which the numerator is less or of lower degree than the denominator, as ⅝ or *a*/*a*².

prop·er·ly (prop′ər lē) *adv.* **1.** in a suitable, appropriate, or correct manner: *to be properly equipped for a fishing trip.* **2.** in accordance with a particular or the accepted standard, as of behavior or precedure: *to be properly married.* **3.** with precision or accuracy; exactly; strictly: *Properly speaking, this work is not a novel.* **4.** with good reason; justifiably. **5.** *Informal.* thoroughly; completely.

proper noun, noun that denotes a particular person, place, or thing and, in English, is always capitalized when written. *Elizabeth, Geneva,* and *Saturday* are proper nouns. Distinguished from **common noun.**

proper subset, set that contains fewer members than the set of which it is a subset. The proper subsets of the set [a,b] are [a], [b], and [o].

prop·er·tied (prop′ər tēd) *adj.* owning property.

prop·er·ty (prop′ər tē) *pl.,* **-ties.** *n.* **1.** that which one has or may have as a possession: *The statue was considered town property.* **2.** piece of real estate: *expensive waterfront property.* **3.** anything, as a literary work, in which one has or may have a legal interest. **4.** right to the possession, use, or disposal of a thing or things; ownership. **5.** special attribute or quality belonging to a person or thing: *a metal with heat-resistant properties.* **6.** any movable article, except scenery and costumes, used on the set of a theatrical production. [Old French *propriete* possession(s), special quality, from Latin *prōprietās* ownership, quality. Doublet of PROPRIETY.]

property man, one who is in charge of theatrical properties. Also, **prop man.**

proph·e·cy (prof′ə sē) *pl.,* **-cies.** *n.* **1.** act of telling beforehand what is to come; foretelling of the future. **2.** that which is foretold; prediction. **3.** divinely inspired utterance or revelation. **4.** power or ability to foretell the future. [Old French *prophecie,* form of *prophetie* prediction, revelation of a prophet, from Late Latin *prophētīa* prediction, from Greek *prophēteiā.*]

proph·e·sy (prof′ə sī′) **-sied, -sy·ing.** *v.t.* to tell beforehand (what is to come); foretell; predict: *The oracle prophesied that the king would have a long and prosperous reign.* —*v.i.* **1.** to foretell the future; make predictions. **2.** to speak as a prophet. —**proph′e·si′er,** *n.* —**Syn.** *v.t.* see **foretell.**

proph·et (prof′it) *n.* **1.** one who speaks or claims to speak by divine inspiration or as the interpreter of divine will, esp. a religious teacher or leader professing or considered to be divinely inspired. **2.** one who foretells the future. **3.** spokesman, as for a cause or movement. **4. the Prophet. a.** Muhammad. **b.** Joseph Smith, founder of the Mormon Church. **5. the Prophets.** those books of the Old Testament either written by prophets or composed mainly of prophecies. [Late Latin *prophēta* person who predicts, soothsayer, from Greek *prophētēs* person who predicts, interpreter of divine will.] —**proph′et·ess,** *n.*

pro·phet·ic (prə fet′ik) *adj.* **1.** containing or of the nature of prophecy. **2.** of, relating to, or belonging to a prophet. Also, **pro·phet′i·cal.** —**pro·phet′i·cal·ly,** *adv.*

pro·phy·lac·tic (prō′fi lak′tik, prof′i-) *adj.* serving to protect against or prevent something, esp. disease. —*n.* prophylactic device, medicine, or treatment. [Greek *prophylaktikos* guarding from, going back to *pro* before + *phylassein* to guard.]

pro·phy·lax·is (prō′fi lak′sis, prof′i-) *pl.,* **-lax·es** (-lak′sēz). *n.* **1.** protection against or prevention of disease. **2.** drugs, treatment, or other measure used to prevent disease. [Modern Latin *prophylaxis,* from Greek *pro* before + *phylaxis* guarding.]

pro·pin·qui·ty (prō ping′kwə tē) *n.* **1.** nearness in time or place; proximity. **2.** nearness of relation; kinship. [Latin *propinquitās.*]

pro·pi·ti·ate (prə pish′ē āt′) -at·ed, -at·ing. *v.t.* to win over, as someone who has been offended; appease; conciliate: *The natives thought they could propitiate the angry gods with a human sacrifice.* [Latin *propitiātus,* past participle of *propitiāre* to render favorable.] —**pro·pi′ti·a′tion,** **pro·pi′ti·a′tor,** *n.*

pro·pi·ti·a·to·ry (prə pish′ē ə tôr′ē) *adj.* serving, tending, or intended to propitiate: *a propitiatory sacrifice.*

pro·pi·tious (prə pish′əs) *adj.* **1.** favorably disposed; gracious. **2.** of favorable import; boding well. **3.** presenting or attended by favorable or suitable conditions: *It seemed to be a propitious time for such a voyage.* [Latin *propitius* favorable; literally, falling or flying forward (possibly referring to the interpretation of the flight of birds in the ancient art of augury).] —**pro·pi′tious·ly,** *adv.* —**pro·pi′tious·ness,** *n.*

prop man, property man.

pro·po·nent (prə pō′nənt) *n.* **1.** one who favors or supports something, as a cause; advocate: *The senator is a leading proponent of the new tax-reform program.* **2.** one who proposes or propounds something. [Latin *prōpōnēns,* present participle of *prōpōnere* to set forth.]

pro·por·tion (prə pôr′shən) *n.* **1.** relation of one thing to another with respect to size, number, amount, or degree; ratio: *the proportion of men to women in a profession.* **2.** proper or balanced relation between parts; harmony; symmetry: *The length and height of the room were in proportion.* **3.** part or share, esp. in relation to the whole: *A proportion of the profits was allotted to each partner in the company.* **4.** relative size, degree, or extent: *a collection of paintings of considerable proportion.* **5. proportions.** dimensions: *the proportions of a room.* **6.** relation between two ratios in which the first of four quantities divided by the second is equal to the third divided by the fourth: *8 is to 4, as 6 is to 3.* —*v.t.* **1.** to cause to be in a proper or balanced relation to something else with respect to size or extent: *to proportion the width of a building to its height, to proportion expenditure to income.* **2.** to form the parts of (a whole) so as to be in harmonious or symmetrical relation. [Latin *prōportiō* analogy, comparative relation, from *prōportiōne* relatively.] —**pro·por′tion·ment,** *n.*

pro·por·tion·a·ble (prə pôr′shə nə bəl) *adj.* in proper proportion; proportional. —**pro·por′tion·a·bly,** *adv.*

pro·por·tion·al (prə pôr′shən əl) *adj.* **1.** in or having proportion: *Achievement is usually proportional to effort expended.* **2.** of, relating to, or based on proportion; relative: *a proportional scale of values.* **3.** *Mathematics.* having the same or a constant ratio. —*n.* one of the terms of a mathematical proportion. —**pro·por′tion·al·ly,** *adv.*

proportional representation, system of voting under which seats in the legislative body are distributed in proportion to the vote cast for the various parties.

pro·por·tion·ate (*adj.,* prə pôr′shə nit; *v.,* prə pôr′shə nāt′) *adj.* in proper proportion; proportional: *Our reward was proportionate to the time we spent.* —*v.t.,* -at·ed, -at·ing. to make proportionate. —**pro·por′tion·ate·ly,** *adv.*

pro·pos·al (prə pō′zəl) *n.* **1.** something put forward for consideration, discussion, or acceptance, as a plan or a course of action. **2.** offer of marriage. **3.** act of proposing.

pro·pose (prə pōz′) **-posed, -pos·ing.** *v.t.* **1.** to put forward for consideration, discussion, or acceptance: *The mayor proposed a new plan for settling the wage dispute.* **2.** to suggest or present (someone), as for a position or office. **3.** to intend; plan: *The general proposes to attack the city at dawn.* **4.** to suggest (a toast). —*v.i.* to make an offer of marriage. [Old French *proposer* to put forth, make a formal proposal, modification (influenced by Old French *poser* to place, put) of Latin *prōpōnere* to set forth. See POSE¹.] —**pro·pos′er,** *n.*

prop·o·si·tion (prop′ə zish′ən) *n.* **1.** something proposed for consideration or acceptance; proposal, offer, or suggestion: *The business proposition was rejected as impractical.* **2.** *Informal.* matter, undertaking, or situation: *Finding a buyer for this old car is not an easy proposition.* **3.** statement or subject to be discussed: *The two teams prepared to debate the given proposition.* **4.** *Logic.* statement in which something (the predicate) is affirmed or denied in relation to something else (the subject). **5.** *Mathematics.* statement of a theorem to be demonstrated or a problem to be solved. **6.** *Informal.* thought, idea, or possibility: *The proposition of working all night was quite depressing.* —*v.t.* to make a proposal or offer to, esp. to suggest sexual intercourse to. [Latin *prōpositiō* a setting forth, statement.] —**prop′o·si′tion·al,** *adj.*

pro·pound (prə pound′) *v.t.* to put forward for consideration, as a theory; set forth. [Earlier *propone,* from Latin *prōpōnere* to set forth.]

pro·prae·tor (prō prē′tər) *also,* **pro·pre·tor.** *n.* official sent to govern an ancient Roman province after having served as praetor in Rome. [Latin *prōprāetor,* from *prō praetōre* for the praetor.]

pro·pri·e·tar·y (prə prī′ə ter′ē) *adj.* **1.** of, relating to, or characteristic of a proprietor or proprietors. **2.** made and sold by exclusive legal

right, as a medicine. **3.** privately owned and operated: *a proprietary hospital.* —*n. pl.,* **-tar·ies. 1.** proprietor. **2.** group of proprietors. **3.** ownership; proprietorship. **4.** a proprietary medicine. [Late Latin *proprietārius* owner, belonging to someone as property, from Latin *proprietās* ownership, property.]

proprietary colony, any of certain early American colonies granted by the British Crown to an individual or small group of individuals vested with full governing power.

pro·pri·e·tor (prə prī′ə tər) *n.* **1.** one who has legal title or right to something, esp. to property; an owner. **2.** owner or operator of a small business establishment. **3.** individual granted a proprietary colony. [Modification of PROPRIETARY.] —**pro·pri′e·tor·ship′, pro·pri′e·tress,** *n.*

pro·pri·e·ty (prə prī′ə tē) *pl.,* **-ties.** *n.* **1.** quality of being proper or appropriate; suitability. **2.** conformity with what is proper, esp. with socially accepted standards of manners and conduct. **3. the proprieties.** standards of manners and conduct approved by polite society. [Latin *proprietās* proper signification of words, quality, ownership. Doublet of PROPERTY.]

pro·pri·o·cep·tive (prō′prē ə sep′tiv) *adj.* of, relating to, or being stimuli that arise within the organism. [Latin *proprius* one's own + (RE)CEPTIVE.]

pro·pri·o·cep·tor (prō′prē ə sep′tər) *n.* sensory receptor, as in a muscle, tendon, or joint, that is responsive to stimuli arising from bodily movement. [Latin *proprius* one's own + (RE)CEPTOR.]

pro·pul·sion (prə pul′shən) *n.* **1.** act or process of driving forward or propelling. **2.** something that propels; propelling force. [Latin *prōpulsus,* past participle of *prōpellere* to drive forward + -ION.]

pro·pul·sive (prə pul′siv) *adj.* serving to propel or capable of propelling: *a propulsive force.*

pro·pyl·ene (prō′pə lēn′) *n.* colorless, extremely flammable gas of the alkene, or olefin, series, used in the manufacture of artificial rubber. Formula: C_3H_6.

pro ra·ta (prō rā′tə, rä′tə) in proportion; proportionately. [Latin *prō ratā (parte)* according to a calculated (portion), in proportion.]

pro·rate (prō rāt′, prō′rāt′) **-rat·ed, -rat·ing.** *v.t.* *v.i.* to distribute, divide, or assess proportionately. [From PRO RATA.] —**pro·ra′tion,** *n.*

pro·rogue (prō rōg′) **-rogued, -rogu·ing.** *v.t.* to discontinue or suspend a session of (a lawmaking assembly), esp. by authority of a monarch. [Latin *prōrogāre* to extend, defer.] —**pro·ro·ga·tion** (prō′rə-gā′shən), *n.*

pro·sa·ic (prō zā′ik) *adj.* **1.** imaginative; commonplace; ordinary. **2.** of or like prose. [Late Latin *prōsaicus* in prose (as opposed to verse), from Latin *prōsa (ōrātiō)* straightforward (speech).] —**pro·sa′i·cal·ly,** *adv.* —**pro·sa′ic·ness,** *n.*

pro·sce·ni·um (prō sē′nē əm) *pl.,* **-ni·a (-nē ə).** *n.* **1.** the part of the stage in front of the curtain. **2.** structure that frames the stage opening, usually arch-shaped. Also, **proscenium arch. 3.** stage in an ancient theater. [Latin *proscēnium* stage, from Greek *proskēnion,* from *pro* before + *skēnē* tent, booth (in which actors dressed and before which they performed in the early Greek theater).]

Proscenium

pro·scribe (prō skrīb′) **-scribed, -scrib·ing.** *v.t.* **1.** to prohibit or condemn (something); interdict. **2.** to outlaw (someone); banish. [Latin *prōscrībere* to publish in writing, outlaw.] —**pro·scrib′er,** *n.*

pro·scrip·tion (prō skrip′shən) *n.* **1.** act of proscribing; being proscribed. **2.** law or order that proscribes; prohibition. —**pro·scrip′tive,** *adj.* —**pro·scrip′tive·ly,** *adv.*

prose (prōz) *n.* **1.** written or spoken language without metrical structure, as distinguished from poetry. **2.** dull, commonplace discourse, expression, or quality. —*adj.* **1.** of, relating to, or prose. **2.** commonplace; unimaginative. —*v.t.* *v.i.,* **prosed, pros·ing.** to write or speak in prose. [Old French *prose* form of language without metrical structure (as opposed to poetry), from Latin *prōsa (ōrātiō)* straightforward (speech).]

pros·e·cute (pros′ə kūt′) **-cut·ed, -cut·ing.** *v.t.* **1.** to institute and conduct legal proceedings against (a person, corporation, or institution) in a court of law. **2.** to seek to obtain or enforce by legal process: *to prosecute a claim for damages.* **3.** to follow up or pursue (something) to completion or conclusion: *to prosecute an investigation.* **4.** to engage in; carry on. —*v.i.* **1.** to institute and conduct legal proceedings. **2.** to act as prosecutor. [Latin *prōsecūtus,* past participle of *prōsequī* to pursue.]

prosecuting attorney, attorney empowered to represent the government in instituting and conducting criminal prosecutions.

pros·e·cu·tion (pros′ə kū′shən) *n.* **1.a.** act or process of instituting and conducting legal proceedings in a court of law. **b.** party or parties

instituting and conducting such proceedings. **2.** act or process of prosecuting.

pros·e·cu·tor (pros′ə kū′tər) *n.* **1.** prosecuting attorney. **2.** one who institutes and conducts a legal action, esp. criminal proceedings. **3.** one who prosecutes.

pros·e·lyte (pros′ə līt′) *n.* one who has been brought over from one point of view, belief, or party to another, esp. a new convert to a religion. —*v.t.,* *v.i.,* **-lyt·ed, -lyt·ing.** to proselytize. [Late Latin *prosēlytus* stranger, religious convert, from Greek *prosēlytos.*]

pros·e·lyt·ism (pros′ə li tiz′əm, -lī-) *n.* **1.** act or practice of proselytizing. **2.** state of being or act of becoming a proselyte.

pros·e·lyt·ize (pros′ə li tīz′, -lī-) **-ized, -iz·ing.** *v.t.* *v.i.* to convert or attempt to convert, as from one religion or point of view to another.

Pro·ser·pi·na (prō sur′pə nə) *also,* **Pro·ser·pi·ne** (prō sur′pə nē). *n. Roman Mythology.* daughter of Jupiter and Ceres, whose uncle, Pluto, carried her off and made her queen of the underworld. She was allowed to revisit the earth for part of each year, and her return was accompanied by the coming of spring. Her Greek counterpart is Persephone.

pro·sit (prō′sit, -zit) *interj.* to your health. ▲ used as a drinking toast, as in Germany. [Latin *prōsit* may it be profitable.]

pro·slav·er·y (prō slā′vər ē) *adj.* favoring slavery, esp., in U.S. history, supporting the institution of Negro slavery.

pros·o·dist (pros′ə dist) *n.* one skilled in prosody.

pros·o·dy (pros′ə dē) *n.* **1.** study or art of versification. **2.** particular system of versification. [Latin *prosōdia* tone or accent of a syllable, from Greek *prosōidía* song sung to instrumental music, pronunciation, accent.] —**pro·sod·ic** (prə sod′ik); *also,* **pro·sod′i·cal,** *adj.* —**pro·sod′i·cal·ly,** *adv.*

pros·pect (pros′pekt) *n.* **1.** mental vision of a future possibility or probability: *John was excited by the prospect of owning his own boat.* **2.** act of looking forward to something; anticipation. **3.** *usually,* **prospects.** chance for future success: *good prospects.* **4.** one who shows promise of some kind, as a possible customer or a potential winner in a political or athletic contest. **5.** scene spread out before the eye; view. —*v.t.* *v.i.* to search or explore: *to prospect an area for minerals, to prospect for gold.* [Latin *prōspectus* lookout, view.]

Syn. *n.* **1.** Prospect, outlook mean a mental picture of future probabilities based on an analysis of the present. **Prospect** implies a projection or vision of what the future, esp. the near future, holds in store in terms of personal hopes, desires, and chances: *Bert enjoyed the prospect of a weekend in the country.* **Outlook** suggests a projection of the future indicating remote as well as immediate probabilities: *The weather bureau said that the outlook for the next week is warm and sunny.*

pro·spec·tive (prə spek′tiv) *adj.* **1.** probable or expected; future: *a prospective buyer, a prospective bride.* **2.** of, relating to, or in the future: *prospective laws.* —**pro·spec′tive·ly,** *adv.*

pros·pec·tor (pros′pek tər, prə spek′-) *n.* one who explores an area for minerals, as gold.

pro·spec·tus (prə spek′təs) *pl.,* **-tus·es.** *n.* printed statement describing a proposed enterprise, undertaking, or work. [Latin *prōspectus* lookout, view.]

pros·per (pros′pər) *v.i.* to be prosperous; flourish. [Latin *prosperāre* to make happy.]

Syn. Prosper, thrive, flourish mean to grow and advance to success. **Prosper** implies an increasing and continued success marked esp. by a gain in wealth and material possessions: *He came to America as a poor immigrant but soon prospered as a merchant.* **Thrive** is usually applied to living things and implies vigorous physical growth because of certain conditions: *Plants thrive in sunshine.* **Flourish** suggests reaching a high level of development and sustaining that level over a period of time: *The arts flourished in Athens under Pericles.*

pros·per·i·ty (pros per′ə tē) *pl.,* **-ties.** *n.* state or condition of being prosperous, esp. economic well-being.

pros·per·ous (pros′pər əs) *adj.* **1.** having success, wealth, or good fortune. **2.** conducive to success; favorable; propitious. [Latin *prosperus* favorable, from *prō* for + *spēs* hope.] —**pros′per·ous·ly,** *adv.* —**pros′per·ous·ness,** *n.*

pros·tate (pros′tāt) *n.* chestnut-shaped gland present in male mammals, lying below the bladder and surrounding the urethra. Also, **prostate gland.** —*adj.* of, relating to, or affecting this gland. [Modern Latin *prostata,* from Greek *prostatēs* one who stands before, guardian.]

pros·the·sis (pros thē′sis, pros′thə-) *pl.,* **-ses** (-sēz). *n.* **1.** replacement of a missing part of the body by a mechanical or other artificial device. **2.** device so used, as an artificial leg, arm, or eye. [Late Latin *prosthesis* prefixing a letter or syllable to a word, from Greek *prosthesis* addition.]

pros·ti·tute (pros′tə tōōt′, -tūt′) *n.* **1.** woman who engages in sexual acts for money. **2.** one who puts himself or his abilities to an unworthy use, esp. for money. —*v.t.,* **-tut·ed, -tut·ing. 1.** to sell (oneself or another) for sexual purposes. **2.** to put (oneself or one's abilities) to an unworthy use, esp. for money. [Latin *prōstitūtus,* past participle of *prōstituere* to expose publicly, dishonor.]

pros·ti·tu·tion (pros′tə tōō′shən, -tū′-) *n.* **1.** act or practice of engaging in sexual acts for money. **2.** act of putting (someone or something) to an unworthy use.

pros·trate (pros′trāt) **-trat·ed, -trat·ing.** *v.t.* **1.** to lay or throw (oneself) face downward on the ground in humility, adoration, or submission. **2.** to lay or throw down on the ground; flatten: *With a single blow he prostrated his assailant.* **3.** to weaken or make helpless: *The disease prostrated him.* —*adj.* **1.** lying face downward on the ground in humility, adoration, or submission. **2.** lying or thrown down. **3.** completely exhausted, helpless, or overcome: *The country was left prostrate by the war.* [Latin *prōstrātus,* past participle of *prōsternere* to throw before one, throw down.]

pros·tra·tion (pros trā′shən) *n.* **1.** act of prostrating; being prostrated. **2.** extreme mental or physical exhaustion.

pros·y (prō′zē) **pros·i·er, pros·i·est.** *adj.* **1.** like prose; prosaic: *a prosy statement.* **2.** wearisome; tedious: *a prosy speaker.* —**pros′i·ly,** *adv.* —**pros′i·ness,** *n.*

Prot., Protestant.

prot·ac·tin·i·um (prōt′ak tin′ē əm) *n.* rare radioactive metallic element. Symbol: **Pa** See **element** for table. [PROTO- + ACTINIUM.]

pro·tag·o·nist (prō tag′ə nist) *n.* **1.** leading character or hero in a novel, play, or other work of literature. **2.** central figure, leader, or champion in an event, cause, or undertaking. [Greek *prōtagōnistēs* chief actor in a drama, going back to *prōtos* first + *agōn* contest.]

Pro·tag·o·ras (prō tag′ər əs) *n.* c.481–c.411 B.C., Greek philosopher.

pro·te·an (prō′tē ən, prō tē′-) *adj.* readily assuming different shapes; variable. [PROTEUS + -AN.]

pro·tect (prə tekt′) *v.t.* **1.** to defend or shield from harm; keep safe: *A football player wears a helmet to protect his head.* **2.** to guard or promote the development of (a domestic industry) by means of a protective tariff. [Latin *prōtectus,* past participle of *prōtegere* to cover in front, shield from danger.] —**pro·tect′ing·ly,** *adv.* —**Syn. 1.** see **defend.**

pro·tec·tion (prə tek′shən) *n.* **1.** act of protecting; being protected. **2.** one who or that which protects. **3.** system of guarding or promoting the development of a domestic industry by means of a protective tariff. **4.** *Informal.* money paid to gangsters for freedom from violence.

pro·tec·tion·ism (prə tek′shə niz′əm) *n.* economic system or theory of guarding or promoting the development of domestic industries by means of protective tariffs. —**pro·tec′tion·ist,** *n., adj.*

pro·tec·tive (prə tek′tiv) *adj.* protecting or intended to protect: *a protective shell, protective measures.* —**pro·tec′tive·ly,** *adv.* —**pro·tec′tive·ness,** *n.*

protective coloration, any inherited coloration or pattern of coloration that helps to conceal an animal in its natural surroundings, enabling it to escape the notice of predators.

protective tariff, tariff for the protection of domestic industry against foreign competition rather than for revenue.

pro·tec·tor (prə tek′tər) *n.* one who or that which protects; guardian; defender. —**pro·tec′tress,** *n.*

pro·tec·tor·ate (prə tek′tər it) *n.* **1.** relationship of protection and partial control assumed by a strong country over a weaker one. **2.** country that surrenders part of its sovereignty to another country in such a relationship.

pro·té·gé (prō′tə zhā′, prō′tə zhā′) *n.* one who is under the care, guidance, or patronage of an influential or prominent person. [French *protégé* favorite, dependent, from *protéger* to shield, guard, from Latin *protegere* to shield from danger.]

pro·tein (prō′tēn, -tē in) *n.* any of a large group of organic compounds containing nitrogen, carbon, hydrogen, and oxygen, whose complex molecules are formed of chains of amino acids. Proteins are present in all living cells. Also, **pro·teid** (prō′tēd, -tē id). [German *Protein,* from Greek *prōteios* primary; because it is the *primary* material in the composition of animal and plant tissue.]

pro tem (prō tem′) pro tempore.

pro tem·po·re (prō tem′pər ē) *Latin.* for the time being; temporarily.

Prot·er·o·zo·ic (prot′ər ə zō′ik, prō′tər-) *n.* geological division of the Precambrian era, during which the earliest animals appeared, and algae and bacteria were the only forms of plant life. —*adj.* of, relating to, or characteristic of the Proterozoic. [Greek *proteros* former + *zōē* life + -IC.]

pro·test (*n.,* prō′test; *v.,* prə test′) *n.* **1.** strong expression or declaration of disapproval or dissent: *The demonstration was a protest against the proposed new highway.* **2.** solemn declaration or affirmation: *She scorned his protests of love.* **3.** formal declaration in writing, prepared by a notary public, that a check, note, or other similar written order has been presented for payment or acceptance and has been refused. —*v.i.* **1.** to express strong disapproval or dissent: *The group protested against the country's foreign policy.* **2.** to make a solemn declaration. —*v.t.* **1.** to express strong disapproval of; object to: *The committee*

protested the budget cuts. **2.** to declare solemnly: *The young man, accused of the crime, protested his innocence.* **3.** to declare with a notarial certificate that (a check, note, or other similar written order) has been refused. [Middle French *protester* to declare in public, object, from Latin *prōtestārī* to declare in public, testify.] —**pro·test′ing·ly,** *adv.*

Prot·es·tant (prot′is tənt) *n.* **1.** member of any of various Christian churches that are distinct from the Roman Catholic Church or the Orthodox Church. **2. protestant,** one who protests. —*adj.* of or relating to Protestants or Protestantism. [Latin *prōtestāns,* present participle of *prōtestārī* to declare in public, testify.]

Protestant Episcopal Church, church in the United States that agrees in doctrine, beliefs, and practices with the Church of England.

Prot·es·tant·ism (prot′is tən tiz′əm) *n.* **1.** doctrines, beliefs, and practices of Protestants. **2.** Protestants or the Protestant churches collectively.

prot·es·ta·tion (prot′is tā′shən, prō′tes-) *n.* **1.** act of protesting. **2.** solemn declaration or affirmation: *protestations of loyalty.* **3.** strong expression of disapproval or dissent; protest.

Pro·te·us (prō′tē əs) *n. Classical Legend.* sea god who had the power of prophecy and of assuming many different shapes.

pro·thal·lus (prō thal′əs) *pl.* **-thal·li** (-thal′ī). *n.* gametophyte of a fern or related plant. [Modern Latin *prothallus,* from Greek *pro-* before + *thallos* young shoot.]

pro·tist (prō′tist) *n.* any of a group of single-celled microscopic organisms, including bacteria, some algae, and some viruses. [Modern Latin *Protista,* from Greek *prōtistos* the very first, superlative of *prōtos* first.]

proto- *combining form* first in time; earliest; original: *protozoan, prototype.* [Greek *prōtos* first.]

pro·to·col (prō′tə kôl′, -kol′) *n.* **1.** customs and regulations of diplomatic conduct. **2.** first draft, original copy, or record of a document, as a treaty. **3.** first draft, original copy of a contract or deed, through Medieval Latin, from Late Greek *prōtokollon* first sheet glued to a manuscript containing its date and the author's name, from Greek *prōtos* first + *kolla* glue.]

pro·ton (prō′ton) *n.* subatomic particle found in the nucleus of all atoms, having a positive electric charge equal to the negative charge of an electron. The atomic number of an atom is equal to the number of protons in its nucleus. See **subatomic particle** for table. [Greek *prōton,* neuter of *prōtos* first.]

pro·to·plasm (prō′tə plaz′əm) *n.* jellylike substance that is the living matter of every plant and animal cell, consisting of water, proteins, sugars, fats, acids, and salts. [German *Protoplasma,* from Greek *prōtos* first + *plasma* something molded.] —**pro′to·plas′mal, pro′to·plas·mat′ic, pro′to·plas′mic,** *adj.*

pro·to·type (prō′tə tīp′) *n.* **1.** original or model from which something is derived or on which something is based. **2.** typical example: *That character is the prototype of the romantic hero.* [Modern Latin *prototypon,* going back to Greek *prōtotypos* original, primitive, from *prōtos* first + *typos* model.]

pro·to·zo·an (prō′tə zō′ən) *n.* any of a large group of single-celled microscopic animals of the phylum Protozoa, as the ameba. —*adj.* of or relating to protozoans. [Modern Latin *Protozoa* (from Greek *prōtos* first + *zōia* animals) + -AN; because they were the first animals of the earth.]

pro·tract (prō trakt′) *v.t.* **1.** to lengthen in time; prolong: *to protract a speech.* **2.** to draw (lines) with a scale and protractor. **3.** *Anatomy.* to extend or protrude. [Latin *prōtractus,* past participle of *prōtrahere* to draw forth, prolong.]

pro·trac·tile (prō trak′til, -tīl) *adj.* capable of being extended or protruded: *a protractile tongue.*

pro·trac·tion (prō trak′shən) *n.* **1.** act of protracting; being protracted. **2.** that which has been protracted.

pro·trac·tor (prō trak′tər) *n.* **1.** instrument in the form of a semicircle marked off in degrees, used for measuring or drawing angles. **2.** one who or that which protracts.

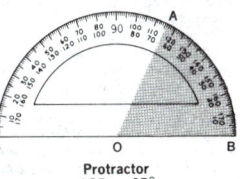

Protractor
AOB = 65°

pro·trude (prō trōōd′) **-trud·ed, -trud·ing.** *v.i.* to stick out; project: *Rocks protruded from the snow.* —*v.t.* to cause to stick out: *The snail protruded its horns.* [Latin *prōtrūdere* to thrust forward.]

pro·tru·sion (prō trōō′zhən) *n.* **1.** act of protruding; being protruded. **2.** that which protrudes.

pro·tru·sive (prō trōō′siv) *adj.* protruding; projecting: *a protrusive chin.*

pro·tu·ber·ance (prō tōō′bər əns, -tū′-) *n.* **1.** that which sticks out, as a swelling or bulge. **2.** state or condition of being protuberant.

---

at; āpe; cär; end; mē; it; īce; hot; ōld; fôrk; wood; fōōl; oil; out; up; ūse; turn; sing; thin; <u>th</u>is; zh in treasure; ə in ago, taken, pencil, lemon, circus.

pro·tu·ber·ant (prō tōō′bər ənt, -tū′-) *adj.* sticking out; bulging.
—**pro·tu′ber·ant·ly,** *adv.*

proud (proud) *adj.* **1.** taking great personal satisfaction in something or someone: *John was proud of his father's achievements. She was proud of her son.* **2.** having a sense of one's personal worth or dignity: *He is too proud to beg.* **3.** having an exaggerated or unreasonable sense of one's worth or dignity; haughty: *Harold is a proud, vain man.* **4.** causing pleasure or satisfaction: *Winning the award was her proudest moment.* **5.** noble or majestic; magnificent. **6.** arising from or caused by pride: *He had a proud, contemptuous look.* [Old English *prūd* valuing oneself highly, from Old French *prud, prod* valiant, brave, from Late Latin *prōde* useful, from Latin *prōdesse* to be useful or profitable.] —**proud′ly,** *adv.* —**proud′ness,** *n.*

Syn. 3. Proud, haughty, arrogant mean having an exaggerated sense of superiority. **Proud** suggests both a sense of one's own importance and a corresponding lack of humility: *The young man was too proud to admit publicly that he had made a mistake.* **Haughty** implies a strong, often exaggerated, consciousness of one's high birth or social standing that is shown in contempt for others considered to be inferior: *The girl's haughty attitude made her unpopular among her classmates.* **Arrogant** suggests a domineering and overbearing attitude toward others: *The dictator had an arrogant disregard for public opinion.*

proud flesh, swollen, irregular surface of flesh formed around the edges of a healing wound.

Proust, Mar·cel (prōost; mar sel′) 1871–1922, French novelist.

Prov. 1. Provençal. **2.** Proverbs.

prove (prōov) *proved, proved* or *prov·en, prov·ing.* *v.t.* **1.** to show convincingly the truth or genuineness of: *The lawyer proved the innocence of his client.* **2.** to test the worth or qualities of: *to prove oneself, to prove a new rifle.* **3.** to confirm the authenticity or validity of: *The probate judge proved the will.* **4.** *Mathematics.* to verify the correctness of: *to prove an equation.* —*v.i.* to turn out: *The play proved to be very good.* [Old French *prover* to try, approve, verify, from Latin *probāre* to test, try, approve, demonstrate.] —**prov′a·ble,** *adj.*

Pro·ven·çal (prov′ən säl′, prō′vən-) *adj.* of or relating to Provence, its people, or their language. —*n.* **1.** native or inhabitant of Provence. **2.** Romance language of Provence.

Pro·vence (prō väns′) *n.* historic region and former province in southeastern France, bordering the Mediterranean Sea.

prov·en·der (prov′ən dər) *n.* **1.** dry food for livestock. **2.** *Informal.* food; provisions. [Old French *provend(r)e,* going back to Late Latin *praebenda* allowance. See PREBEND.]

prov·erb (prov′ərb) *n.* short, pithy saying expressing popular wisdom. [Latin *prōverbium.*]

Syn. Proverb, adage, maxim, aphorism mean a concise expression of a universal truth. A **proverb** is a traditional truth expressed in homely language, as *A rolling stone gathers no moss.* **Adage** is applied to a proverb that is time-honored, widely accepted, and often repeated, as *Where there's smoke, there's fire.* A **maxim** is a general truth or rule of behavior drawn from practical experience, as *Neither a borrower, nor a lender be.* An **aphorism** is usually of known authorship and of distinct literary quality, characteristically cloaking a profound and thought-provoking idea in a pithy and well-turned phrase, as *Where ignorance is bliss, 'tis folly to be wise.*

pro·ver·bi·al (prə vur′bē əl) *adj.* **1.** of, relating to, or characteristic of a proverb. **2.** expressed in a proverb. **3.** commonly spoken of; well-known: *the proverbial ingenuity of American pioneers.* —**pro·ver′bi·al·ly,** *adv.*

Prov·erbs (prov′ərbz) *n.,pl.* book of the Old Testament containing practical advice and moral instruction. ▲ construed as singular.

pro·vide (prə vīd′) *vid·ed, vid·ing.* *v.t.* **1.** to fit out with what is needed or desired; furnish: *John's parents provided him with food and equipment for the camping trip.* **2.** to give; yield: *Trees provide shelter from the sun.* **3.** to specify as a condition; stipulate: *The law provides that a person is innocent until proven guilty.* —*v.i.* **1.** to make adequate preparation for a future need (with *for* or *against*). **2.** to make provision for present need (with *for*): *He provided for his family by working in a mill.* [Latin *prōvidēre* to foresee, look after, act with foresight. Doublet of PURVEY.] —**pro·vid′er,** *n.* —**Syn.** *v.t.* **1.** see **furnish.**

pro·vid·ed (prə vī′did) *conj.* on the condition that; with the stipulation that; if: *I'll lend you my saw, provided you return it by next week.*

prov·i·dence (prov′ə dəns) *n.* **1.** God's care, control, or guidance. **2.** prudent regard for the future; foresight. **3.** Providence. God.

Prov·i·dence (prov′ə dəns) *n.* capital and largest city of Rhode Island, in the eastern part of the state. Pop. (1970), 179,213.

prov·i·dent (prov′ə dənt) *adj.* **1.** having a prudent regard for the future. **2.** economical; frugal. [Latin *prōvidēns,* present participle of *prōvidēre* to foresee, look after.] —**prov′i·dent·ly,** *adv.*

prov·i·den·tial (prov′ə den′shəl) *adj.* **1.** of, relating to, or proceeding from divine providence. **2.** coming about as if through divine intervention; fortunate: *A providential rain put out the fire.*

pro·vid·ing (prə vī′ding) *conj.* provided.

prov·ince (prov′ins) *n.* **1.** political division of a country. **2.** sphere of activity or authority: *Judging the legality of the ordinance is within the province of the courts.* **3.** territory outside Italy ruled by ancient Rome. **4. the provinces.** regions of a country outside the capital or cultural center. [Old French *province* the political division, from Latin *prōvincia* such a Roman territory, official duty.]

pro·vin·cial (prə vin′shəl) *adj.* **1.** of or relating to a province: *a provincial government, a provincial dialect.* **2.** characteristic of the inhabitants of a province, esp. unsophisticated or unfashionable: *provincial manners.* **3.** having or showing a limited point of view; narrow-minded: *provincial attitudes.* —*n.* **1.** native or inhabitant of a province. **2.** one who is provincial, esp. in manner, speech, or point of view. —**pro·vin′cial·ly,** *adv.*

pro·vin·cial·ism (prə vin′shəl liz′əm) *n.* **1.** state or quality of being provincial, in manner, speech, or point of view. **2.** that which is provincial, as a particular word, expression, or way of pronunciation.

pro·vin·ci·al·i·ty (prə vin′shē al′ə tē) *pl.,* **-ties.** *n.* **1.** state or quality of being provincial. **2.** that which is provincial.

proving ground, place for testing new devices or theories, esp. a tract of land for testing military weapons and equipment.

pro·vi·sion (prə vizh′ən) *n.* **1.** act of giving or supplying: *The foreman supervised the provision of equipment to the workers.* **2.** preparation made for a future need: *There was little provision for adequate housing of the urban poor.* **3.** that which is given or supplied; stock: *We brought along a provision of gasoline.* **4.** that which is specified as a condition; stipulation: *A provision in the labor agreement called for a retroactive pay increase.* **5. provisions.** supply of food. —*v.t.* to supply with provisions. [Latin *prōvīsiō* foresight.]

pro·vi·sion·al (prə vizh′ən əl) *adj.* provided for a present or temporary need; for the time being: *a provisional government.* —**pro·vi′sion·al·ly,** *adv.*

pro·vi·so (prə vī′zō) *pl.,* **-sos** or **-soes.** *n.* **1.** clause that specifies a condition: *a proviso in a contract.* **2.** stipulation; condition: *He agreed to be interviewed with the proviso that he be allowed to choose the questions to be asked.* [Medieval Latin *proviso (quod)* it being provided (that), going back to Latin *prōvidēre* to foresee, look after.]

pro·vi·so·ry (prə vī′zər ē) *adj.* **1.** subject to or containing a proviso; conditional. **2.** provisional.

pro·vi·ta·min (prō vī′tə min) *n.* any of various substances that can be converted into a vitamin by the body, as carotene.

prov·o·ca·tion (prov′ə kā′shən) *n.* **1.** act of angering or inciting. **2.** that which angers or incites: *He often loses his temper without any provocation.* [Latin *prōvocātiō* summoning, challenging.]

pro·voc·a·tive (prə vok′ə tiv) *adj.* tending to provoke, esp. by arousing anger, interest, or desire: *a provocative glance, a provocative newspaper editorial.* —**pro·voc′a·tive·ly,** *adv.* —**pro·voc′a·tive·ness,** *n.*

pro·voke (prə vōk′) *-voked, -vok·ing.* *v.t.* **1.** to anger or enrage; irritate greatly. **2.** to stir up (a person) to some action or emotion; incite; arouse: *to provoke someone to anger.* **3.** to cause by inciting; bring about deliberately: *to provoke a fight, to provoke gossip.* **4.** to call forth or bring out; elicit: *to provoke interest.* [Latin *prōvocāre* to call forth, challenge.] —**pro·vok′ing·ly,** *adv.* —**Syn. 2.** see **incite.**

prov·ost (prov′əst, prō′vəst) *n.* **1.** head of a college or university. **2.** chief magistrate of a Scottish town or city. **3.** chief dignitary of a cathedral or collegiate church. [Old English *prōfost* ecclesiastical dignitary, one placed in charge, going back to Latin *praepositus* overseer.]

provost marshal, officer in the army or navy who performs police duties.

prow (prou) *n.* **1.** forward part of a boat or ship; bow. **2.** something resembling the prow of a ship, as the front end of an airplane. [Old French *prouë* forward part of a ship, through Italian and Latin, from Greek *prōira.*]

prow·ess (prou′is) *n.* **1.** great valor, strength, or daring, esp. in battle. **2.** great ability or skill: *athletic prowess.* [Old French *proesce* bravery, from *prod* brave. See PROUD.]

prowl (proul) *v.i.* to rove about furtively, esp. in search of prey: *The tiger prowled through the jungle.* —*v.t.* to roam over or through furtively: *The thug prowled the streets at night.* —*n.* act of prowling. [Of uncertain origin.] —**prowl′er,** *n.*

prowl car, squad car.

prox·i·mal (prok′sə məl) *adj.* **1.** located closest to the body or to the place or point of attachment, as a limb or bone. Opposed to **distal.** **2.** proximate. [Latin *proximus* nearest + -AL¹.]

prox·i·mate (prok′sə mit) *adj.* **1.** nearest in sequence, space, time, or degree; next. **2.** approximate. [Latin *proximātus,* past participle of *proximāre* to approach.] —**prox′i·mate·ly,** *adv.*

prox·im·i·ty (prok sim′ə tē) *n.* state or condition of being nearest in sequence, space, time, or degree; nearness. [Latin *proximitās.*]

proximity fuse, fuse designed to detonate a charge when it approaches within a certain distance of the target.

at; āpe; cär; end; mē; it; īce; hot; ōld; fôrk; wood; fōol; oil; out; up; ūse; turn; sing; thin; this; zh in treasure; ə in ago, taken, pencil, lemon, circus.

prox·i·mo (prok′sə mō′) *adv.* in or of the next month: *on the twelfth proximo.* [Latin *proximō (mense)* in the next (month).]

prox·y (prok′sē) *pl.,* **prox·ies.** *n.* **1.** one authorized to act for another; substitute. **2.** act or instance of authorizing such a person: *to vote by proxy.* **3.** document authorizing a person to act for another. [Modification of Middle English *procuracie* management or action for another, deputy, from Medieval Latin *procuratia* management, from Latin *prōcūrātiō*.] —**Syn. 1.** see **substitute.**

prude (prōod) *n.* one who is excessively modest or proper in behavior, dress, and speech. [French *prude,* short for *prudefemme* respectable woman, going back to Late Latin *prōde* useful + Latin *dē* from + *fēmina* woman. See **PROUD.**]

pru·dence (prōod′əns) *n.* **1.** state or quality of being prudent; circumspection. **2.** careful or frugal management; economy.

pru·dent (prōod′ənt) *adj.* **1.** having or exercising good judgment; wise: *a prudent leader.* **2.** proceeding with caution; circumspect: *a prudent investor.* **3.** marked by or resulting from good judgment or caution: *a prudent policy, a prudent act.* **4.** economical; frugal: *a prudent use of one's money.* [Latin *prūdēns* foreseeing, skilled.] —**pru′dent·ly,** *adv.*

pru·den·tial (prōo den′shəl) *adj.* **1.** of, characterized by, or resulting from good judgment or caution. **2.** exercising good judgment or caution. —**pru·den′tial·ly,** *adv.*

prud·er·y (prōod′ər ē) *pl.,* **-er·ies.** *n.* **1.** excessive concern with modesty or propriety. **2.** instance of prudish talk or behavior.

prud·ish (prōod′ish) *adj.* characterized by an excessive concern with modesty or propriety: *Suzanne's prudish attitude was the result of an overly strict upbringing.* —**prud′ish·ly,** *adv.* —**prud′ish·ness,** *n.*

prune[1] (prōon) *n.* **1.** dried fruit of certain varieties of the plum. **2.** any of various kinds of plums that can be dried without spoiling. [Old French *prune* plum, going back to Latin *prūnum,* from Greek *proumnon.* Doublet of **PLUM.**]

prune[2] (prōon) **pruned, prun·ing.** *v.t.* **1.** to cut off (branches, twigs, or roots). **2.** to cut off unwanted twigs, branches, or roots from (a plant), usually to improve growth or appearance. **3.** to remove unnecessary or unwanted parts from: *to prune a manuscript.* [Old French *proignier* to trim (vines or trees); of uncertain origin.] —**prun′er,** *n.*

pru·ri·ent (proor′ē ənt) *adj.* characterized by, having, or arousing lewd or indecent thoughts. [Latin *prūriēns,* present participle of *prūrīre* to itch; be wanton.] —**pru′ri·ence,** *n.* —**pru′ri·ent·ly,** *adv.*

Prus·sia (prush′ə) *n.* former state in northern Germany, formally dissolved in 1947 and divided among East and West Germany, Poland, and the Soviet Union.

Prus·sian (prush′ən) *adj.* **1.** of or relating to Prussia or its people. **2.** characteristic of or resembling the Junkers of Prussia; militaristic: *Prussian discipline.* —*n.* native or inhabitant of Prussia.

Prussian blue, dark-blue pigment, used esp. in painting, consisting of cyanide and ferric iron.

prus·sic acid (prus′ik) hydrocyanic acid.

pry[1] (prī) **pried, pry·ing.** *v.i.* to look closely or curiously; peer or search inquisitively: *to pry into another person's affairs.* [Of uncertain origin.]

pry[2] (prī) **pried, pry·ing.** *v.t.* **1.** to move, raise, or pull by force of a lever: *to pry off the top of a box.* **2.** to get with much effort; extract: *to pry information from someone.* —*n. pl.,* **pries.** anything used as a lever for prying, as a crowbar. [From **PRIZE**[4].]

pry·ing (prī′ing) *adj.* unduly curious.

Ps., Psalm; Psalms.

P.S. 1. postscript. **2.** public school.

psalm (säm, sälm) *n.* **1.** sacred poem, song, or hymn. **2.** **Psalm.** any one of the sacred, lyric poems that form the Book of Psalms in the Old Testament. [Old English *psalm, sealm* sacred song, especially one of those in the Old Testament, from Late Latin *psalmus,* from Greek *psalmos* a plucking of the harp; hence, song accompanied by the harp.]

psalm·ist (sä′mist, säl′mist) *n.* **1.** writer or composer of sacred poems, songs, or hymns. **2.** **the Psalmist.** King David.

psalm·o·dy (sä′mə dē, säl′mə-) *pl.,* **-dies.** *n.* **1.** act, practice, or art of singing psalms, esp. in public worship. **2.** collection of psalms. [Late Latin *psalmōdia,* from Greek *psalmōidia* singing to the harp, from *psalmos* song accompanied by the harp + *ōidē* song.]

Psalms (sämz) *n.,pl.* book of sacred, lyric poetry in the Old Testament. ▲ construed as singular.

Psal·ter (sôl′tər) *n.* **1.** the Book of Psalms. **2.** version of all or part of the Psalms arranged for liturgical or devotional use. [Old English *(p)saltere,* from Church Latin *psaltērium* the Psalms of David in the Old Testament, from Latin *psaltērium* stringed instrument. See **PSALTERY.**]

psal·ter·y (sôl′tər ē, -trē) *pl.,* **-ter·ies.** *n.* ancient musical instrument having a flat sounding board and a variable number of strings, played by plucking. [Latin *psaltērium,* from Greek *psaltērion.*]

pseu·do (sōo′dō) *adj.* false; pretended; spurious: *a pseudo intellectual.* [From **PSEUDO-**.]

pseudo- *combining form* **1.** false; pretended: *pseudonym.* **2.** closely or deceptively resembling: *pseudopod.* [Greek *pseudēs* false.]

pseu·do·carp (sōo′də kärp′) *n.* fruit consisting of other parts in addition to the ovary and its contents, as the apple.

pseu·do·nym (sōod′ən im) *n.* fictitious name, esp. one used by an author to conceal his true identity. [Greek *pseudōnymon,* from *pseudēs* false + (dialectal) *onyma* name, word.]

Syn. Pseudonym, alias, pen name mean a fictitious name. **Pseudonym** is the general term for a fictitious name, assumed typically by well-known persons, as entertainers, writers, or prizefighters, for the sake of anonymity or from a desire to be known by a name with more popular appeal: *The movie star registered at the hotel under the pseudonym of "John Smith" to avoid attracting attention to his visit.* **Alias** is associated with violators of the law, and describes a name assumed to conceal one's identity or to disguise the stigma of a criminal record: *The swindler was known by many aliases.* **Pen name** is specifically applied to a fictitious name used by a writer: *The novelist published books under his real name as well as under a pen name.*

pseu·do·pod (sōo′də pod′) *n.* temporary tongue-shaped projection sent out from an ameba as a means of locomotion and to capture food.

pseu·do·po·di·um (sōo′də pō′dē əm) *pl.,* **-di·a** (-dē ə). *n.* pseudopod.

pshaw (shô) *interj.* used to express disdain, impatience, or disapproval.

psi (sī, psē) *n.* twenty-third letter of the Greek alphabet (Ψ, ψ).

psit·ta·co·sis (sit′ə kō′sis) *n.* infectious disease of certain birds, esp. parrots, that can be transmitted to man, in whom it produces a form of pneumonia. [Modern Latin *psittacosis,* from Greek *psittakos* parrot + -OSIS.]

pso·ri·a·sis (sə rī′ə sis) *n.* chronic skin disease characterized by dry, reddish patches covered with silvery scales. [Modern Latin *psoriasis,* going back to Greek *psōrā* itch, mange.]

PST, Pacific Standard Time.

psych-, form of **psycho-** before certain vowels.

Psy·che (sī′kē) *n.* **1.** *Classical Mythology.* a beautiful princess who fell in love with Eros. She is considered the personification of the human soul. **2.** **psyche.** human soul or mind. **3.** **psyche.** *Psychiatry.* the mind in its capacity to perform psychological functions or acts. [Latin *Psychē* the mythological character, from Greek *Psychē,* from *psychē* soul, mind.]

psy·che·del·ic (sī′kə del′ik) *adj.* **1.** of, characterized by, or promoting hallucinations, intensified perceptions, or a trancelike state. **2.** of or relating to psychedelic drugs. —*n.* psychedelic drug. [Greek *psychē* soul, mind + *dēlos* clear + -IC.]

psy·chi·at·ric (sī′kē at′rik) *adj.* of or relating to psychiatry. Also, **psy′chi·at′ri·cal.** —**psy′chi·at′ri·cal·ly,** *adv.*

psy·chi·a·trist (si kī′ə trist, sī-) *n.* physician who specializes in the diagnosis and treatment of emotional and mental disorders.

psy·chi·a·try (si kī′ə trē, sī-) *n.* branch of medicine that deals with the diagnosis and treatment of emotional and mental disorders. [PSYCHO- + Greek *iātreiā* art of healing.]

psy·chic (sī′kik) *adj.* **1.** of or relating to the human soul or mind; spiritual or mental. **2.** of, relating to, designating, or caused by extrasensory, nonphysical, or supernatural influences or forces. **3.** sensitive to such influences or forces. Also, **psy′chi·cal.** —*n.* one who is sensitive to extrasensory, nonphysical, or supernatural influences or forces. [Greek *psychikos* relating to the soul, from *psyche* soul, mind.]

psycho- *combining form* mind or mental processes: *psychology, psychotherapy.* [Greek *psyche* soul, mind.]

psy·cho·a·nal·y·sis (sī′kō ə nal′ə sis) *n.* **1.** theory of psychology, set forth by Sigmund Freud, that seeks to explore the unconscious mind and its relationship to the conscious mind. **2.** therapeutic procedure used to explore the unconscious mind and treat emotional and mental disorders. —**psy·cho·an·a·lyt·ic** (sī′kō an′əl it′ik); *also,* **psy′cho·an′a·lyt′i·cal,** *adj.* —**psy′cho·an′a·lyt′i·cal·ly,** *adv.*

psy·cho·an·a·lyst (sī′kō an′əl ist) *n.* one who practices psychoanalysis. Also, **an′a·lyst.**

psy·cho·an·a·lyze (sī′kō an′əl īz′) **-lyzed, -lyz·ing.** *v.t.* to treat by psychoanalysis.

psy·cho·dra·ma (sī′kə drä′mə, -dram′ə) *n.* technique of psychotherapy in which patients enact roles and incidents.

psy·cho·log·i·cal (sī′kə loj′i kəl) *adj.* **1.** of or relating to psychology. **2.** of or relating to the mind or mental processes. Also, **psy′cho·log′ic.** —**psy′cho·log′i·cal·ly,** *adv.*

psychological moment, most favorable or critical moment for producing a desired effect.

psy·chol·o·gist (si kol′ə jist) *n.* one who is trained or who specializes in psychology.

psy·chol·o·gy (si kol′ə jē) *pl.,* **-gies.** *n.* **1.** study of the mind and of mental and emotional processes and human behavior. **2.** mental, emotional, or behavioral processes characteristic of a person or group, or

at; āpe; cär; end; mē; it; īce; hot; ōld; fôrk; wood; fōōl; oil; out; up; ūse; turn; sing; thin; this; zh in treasure; ə in ago, taken, pencil, lemon, circus.

807

relating to an experience: *the psychology of the artist, the psychology of the criminal, the psychology of defeat.* [Modern Latin *psychologia,* from PSYCHO- + -LOGY.]

psy·cho·met·rics (sī′kə met′riks) *n.,pl.* branch of psychology dealing with the measurement of mental abilities and processes. ▲ construed as singular. Also, **psy·chom·e·try** (sī kom′ə trē).

psy·cho·neu·ro·sis (sī′kō noo rō′sis, -nyoo-) *pl.,* **-ses** (-sēz). *n.* neurosis.

psy·cho·path (sī′kə path′) *n.* one who is mentally unbalanced, esp. one who exhibits antisocial or criminal behavior. Also, **psychopathic personality.** —**psy′cho·path′ic,** *adj.*

psy·chop·a·thy (sī kop′ə thē) *n.* mental disorder.

psy·cho·phys·ics (sī′kō fiz′iks) *n.* branch of psychology that deals with the interrelation of mental and physical phenomena.

psy·cho·sis (sī kō′sis) *pl.,* **-ses** (-sēz). *n.* severe mental disorder involving loss of contact with reality. [Late Greek *psychōsis* animation, principle of life, from Greek *psychoun* to give life to.]

psy·cho·so·mat·ic (sī′kō sə mat′ik) *adj.* **1.** of or relating to the interrelation of mind and body. **2.** of or relating to physical symptoms and changes in the body that are the result of emotional or mental conditions: *a psychosomatic illness, psychosomatic medicine.*

psy·cho·ther·a·py (sī′kō ther′ə pē) *n.* treatment of emotional or mental disorders by psychological means, as by psychoanalysis and group therapy. —**psy′cho·ther′a·pist,** *n.*

psy·chot·ic (sī kot′ik) *n.* one afflicted with a psychosis. —*adj.* of, relating to, suffering from, or caused by a psychosis.

Pt, platinum.

pt. **1.** part. **2.** payment. **3.** pint. **4.** point. **5.** port.

PTA, Parent-Teacher Association.

ptar·mi·gan (tär′mi gən) *pl.,* **-gans** or **-gan.** *n.* any of various grouse, genus *Lagopus,* of arctic or subarctic regions, having brownish plumage and feathered legs and feet. [Modification of Scottish Gaelic *tarmachan.*]

Ptarmigan

PT boat, small, fast, and highly maneuverable boat used extensively in the Pacific Ocean during World War II. [Abbreviation of *p(atrol) t(orpedo) boat.*]

pte·rid·o·phyte (tə rid′ə fīt′, ter′ə dō-) *n.* any of a group of seedless, flowerless plants, as club mosses or ferns. [Modern Latin *Pteridophyta,* from Greek *pteris* fern + *phyta* plants.]

pter·o·dac·tyl (ter′ə dak′til) *n.* any of a group of extinct flying reptiles, order Pterosauria, having greatly enlarged fourth fingers supporting featherless, leathery wing membranes. [Greek *pteron* feather, wing + *daktylos* finger, toe; referring to the long finger to which the wing was attached.]

Pterodactyl

Ptol·e·ma·ic (tol′ə mā′ik) *adj.* **1.** of or relating to the astronomer Ptolemy. **2.** of or relating to the Ptolemies or to their rule in Egypt from 323 B.C. to 30 B.C.

Ptolemaic system, theory advanced by the astronomer Ptolemy, maintaining that the earth was the center of the universe and that the sun, moon, and all the planets moved about it.

Ptol·e·my (tol′ə mē) *n.* **1.** Claudius. Greek astronomer, geographer, and mathematician who lived in the second century A.D. **2.** any member of a Greek dynasty that ruled Egypt from 323 B.C. to 30 B.C.

Ptolemy I, c.367–283 B.C., Greek general and king of Egypt from 323 B.C. to 285 B.C.

pto·maine (tō′mān, tō mān′) *also,* **pto·main.** *n.* any of various, often poisonous, substances formed by the decomposition of proteins. [Italian *ptomaina,* from Greek *ptōma* corpse.]

ptomaine poisoning, food poisoning.

pty·a·lin (tī′ə lin) *n.* enzyme in the saliva that converts starch into dextrin and maltose. [Greek *ptyalon* saliva + -IN¹.]

Pu, plutonium.

pub (pub) *n. Informal.* tavern or inn. [Short for PUBLIC HOUSE.]

pu·ber·ty (pū′bər tē) *n.* age at which a person becomes physically capable of reproducing offspring, occurring at about fourteen for boys and twelve for girls. [Latin *pūbertās* age of maturity.]

pu·bes·cence (pū bes′əns) *n.* **1.** state or quality of being pubescent. **2.** covering of soft down that grows on certain plants or insects.

pu·bes·cent (pū bes′ənt) *adj.* **1.** attaining or having attained puberty.

2. covered with soft down: *a pubescent leaf.* [Latin *pūbēscēns,* present participle of *pūbēscere* to reach puberty.]

pu·bic (pū′bik) *adj.* of, relating to, or near the pubis.

pu·bis (pū′bis) *pl.,* **-bes** (-bēz). *n.* portion of the hipbone that forms the front of the pelvis. [Shortened from Modern Latin *os pubis* bone of the groin, from Latin *ōs* bone + *pūbis,* genitive of *pūbēs* groin.]

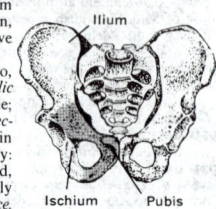

Ilium

Ischium   Pubis

Pubis

pub·lic (pub′lik) *adj.* **1.** of, relating to, or affecting the people as a whole: *public welfare.* **2.** for the use of all the people; open to all: *a public park, a public lecture.* **3.** of, relating to, or engaged in the affairs of the community or country: *a public servant.* **4.** existing, performed, or conducted in the open; generally known: *a public denial, a public disgrace.* —*n.* **1.** the people as a whole; all the inhabitants of a community, state, or country. **2.** group of people having similar interests or tastes: *the reading public, a movie star's public.* **3. in public,** not in private; openly. [Latin *pūblicus* relating to the people or the state, going back to *populus* body of persons.]

pub·lic-ad·dress system (pub′lik ə dres′) electrical apparatus for amplifying sound out-of-doors or in an auditorium.

pub·li·can (pub′li kən) *n.* **1.** *British.* keeper of a public house. **2.** tax collector in ancient Rome. [Latin *pūblicānus* the tax collector, from *pūblicum* public revenue.]

pub·li·ca·tion (pub′li kā′shən) *n.* **1.** act of publishing: *The manuscript is ready for publication.* **2.** that which has been published, as a book, magazine, or newspaper. **3.** public notification or announcement: *These comments are not for publication.* [Late Latin *pūblicātiō* a making known, publishing, going back to Latin *pūblicus.* See PUBLIC.]

public defender, attorney employed at public expense to defend accused persons who cannot afford to hire their own attorney.

public domain **1.** lands owned by the government. **2.** status of an invention or work no longer protected by a patent or copyright.

public enemy, one who is a serious menace to the public, as a criminal.

public house *British.* tavern; saloon.

pub·li·cist (pub′lə sist) *n.* **1.** one who is skilled in or writes on law or public affairs. **2.** press agent.

pub·lic·i·ty (pu blis′ə tē) *n.* **1.** information about someone or something brought to the public's attention. **2.** public notice, attention, or notoriety resulting from such information. **3.** means used to achieve such public notice. **4.** state or condition of being public.
    Syn. **3. Publicity, promotion, advertising** mean a systematic effort to influence public opinion in favor of something. **Publicity** may be applied to the activity of disseminating information in order to generate and sustain public interest in one's products or ideas: *The movie was released in a blaze of publicity.* **Promotion** may be applied to the efforts to gain advance publicity for a new product in order to persuade the public to accept it: *Heavy promotion helped to make that novel a best-seller.* **Advertising** emphasizes the desirable qualities of one's products in order to stimulate sales: *The company relies mainly on television advertising.*

pub·li·cize (pub′lə sīz′) **-cized, -ciz·ing.** *v.t.* to give publicity to; bring to public attention.

pub·lic·ly (pub′lik lē) *adv.* **1.** in a public manner. **2.** by or in the name of the public, or with public consent.

public opinion, opinion of a majority of the people.

public relations, act, process, or method of promoting good will for an individual or organization.

public school **1.** elementary or secondary school supported and administered by state and local officials. **2.** in Great Britain, a private boarding school, esp. for boys, that prepares students for the university.

public servant, one who serves the public by holding an elective or appointive government office.

public speaking, act or art of making a speech before an audience.

pub·lic-spir·it·ed (pub′lik spir′ə tid) *adj.* promoting or showing a concern for the welfare of the community.

public television, television that broadcasts cultural and educational programs for the public and is supported by donated funds rather than by revenues from commercial advertising.

public utility, utility *(def. 2).*

public works, projects financed and constructed by a government for public use, as roads, dams, or sewers.

pub·lish (pub′lish) *v.t.* **1.a.** to produce and issue (printed material, as a book) for sale to the public. **b.** to produce and issue in printed form the works of (an author) for sale to the public: *The same company published both Hemingway and Fitzgerald.* **2.** to make known publicly; promulgate. —*v.i.* **1.** to produce and issue printed material for sale to

the public. **2.** to have one's works issued in printed form: *The young writer hasn't published yet.* [Old French *publiss*, a stem of *publier* to make public, from Latin *pūblicāre.*] —**pub'lish·a·ble,** *adj.*

pub·lish·er (pub'li shər) *n.* one who or that which publishes, esp. a business that publishes printed material.

Puc·ci·ni, Gia·co·mo (pōō chē'nē; jä'kō mō) 1858–1924, Italian composer of operas.

puce (pūs) *n.* purplish- or reddish-brown color. [French *puce* flea, having the color of a flea, from Latin *pūlex* flea.]

puck¹ (puk) *n.* black disk of rubber or other hard material used in playing ice hockey. [From dialectal English *puck* to strike, form of POKE¹.]

puck² (puk) *n.* **1.** mischievous spirit; elf. **2. Puck,** a mischievous fairy or sprite in English folklore. Also, **Robin Goodfellow.** [Old English *pūca* goblin.]

puck·er (puk'ər) *v.t.* to gather into irregular folds or wrinkles: *to pucker the sleeves, to pucker the lips.* —*v.i.* to become gathered into wrinkles. —*n.* irregular fold or wrinkle. [POKE¹ + -ER⁴.]

puck·ish (puk'ish) *adj.* mischievous; impish: *the boy's puckish smile.* —**puck'ish·ly,** *adv.*

pud·ding (pood'ing) *n.* **1.** sweet dessert, usually having a soft consistency, that is cooked by being boiled, baked, or steamed. **2.** similar preparation that is served as a main dish or as part of a main course: *corn pudding.* [Of uncertain origin.]

pud·dle (pud'əl) *n.* **1.** small, shallow pool, esp. of muddy water. **2.** small, shallow pool of any liquid. **3.** mixture of clay, sand, and water, used to make something watertight. —*v.t.,* **-dled, -dling. 1.** to make muddy. **2.** to make (clay, sand, and water) into a watertight mixture. **3.** to convert (pig iron) into wrought iron. [Middle English *podel* small pool of muddy water, diminutive of Old English *pudd* ditch.] —**pud'dly,** *adj.*

pud·dling (pud'ling) *n.* process of converting pig iron into wrought iron by removing the impurities and excess carbon in a furnace.

pu·den·cy (pū'dən sē) *n.* modesty; prudishness; shame. [Late Latin *pudentia* shame, from Latin *pudēns,* present participle of *pudēre* to make or feel ashamed.]

pudg·y (puj'ē) **pudg·i·er, pudg·i·est.** *adj.* short and fat. [Of uncertain origin.] —**pudg'i·ness,** *n.*

Pueb·la (pweb'lä) *n.* city in central Mexico. Pop. (1969), 383,879.

pueb·lo (pweb'lō) *pl.,* **-los.** *n.* **1.** Indian village consisting of adobe and stone houses, found esp. in the southwestern United States. **2. Pueblo,** member of any of several Indian tribes that live in such villages, as the Hopi. [Spanish *pueblo* population, village, from Latin *populus* body of persons.]

Pueb·lo (pweb'lō) *n.* city in south-central Colorado. Pop. (1970), 97,453.

puer·ile (pyoor'il, -īl) *adj.* **1.** childish; silly: *puerile pranks.* **2.** of or relating to boyhood or childhood. [Latin *puerīlis* childish, from *puer* boy, child.]

puer·il·i·ty (pyoo ril'ə tē) *pl.,* **-ties.** *n.* **1.** state or quality of being puerile; childishness. **2.** childish act, idea, or remark.

pu·er·per·al (pū ur'pər əl) *adj.* of, relating to, or accompanying childbirth. [Latin *puerpera* woman in childbirth (from *puer* child + *parere* to bring forth) + -AL¹.]

Puer·to Ri·co (pwer'tō rē'kō, pôr'-) island in the West Indies, a commonwealth of the United States. Capital, San Juan. Area, 3435 sq. mi. Pop. (1969 est.), 2,804,000. —**Puerto Rican.**

puff (puf) *n.* **1.** short, forceful emission or blast, as of breath, air, or smoke. **2.** amount of air, smoke, or other material emitted at one time: *Puffs of smoke were rising.* **3.** act of drawing in and blowing out smoke, as from a cigarette or pipe. **4.** something that looks soft and fluffy: *puffs of hair drawn back in a bow. Puffs of clouds filled the skies.* **5.** powder puff. **6.** light pastry shell, usually having a filling, as of whipped cream. **7.** portion of fabric that is gathered and held down at the edges but left full and fluffy in the middle, as on dresses and blouses. **8.** slight swelling; protuberance. **9.** excessive praise, as in a newspaper or advertisement. —*v.i.* **1.** to blow with a puff or puffs: *Smoke puffed out of the chimney.* **2.** to breathe hard, as from physical exertion. **3.** to emit or give forth puffs, as of steam or smoke: *The locomotive puffed.* **4.** to move while giving out puffs: *The car puffed up the hill.* **5.** to take puffs, as on a cigar, cigarette, or pipe. **6.** to swell or inflate, as with air or a liquid (usually with *up*): *His eye puffed up.* **7.** to become filled with pride (usually with *up*). —*v.t.* **1.** to emit, blow, or send forth in a puff or puffs: *The engine puffed smoke.* **2.** to smoke (a cigar, cigarette, or pipe). **3.** to inflate, swell, or make fluffy: *to puff a pillow. The wind puffed out the ship's sails.* **4.** to swell with pride or conceit (usually with *up*): *His recent successes puffed him up.* **5.** to praise excessively. [Old English *pyffan* to puff.]

puff adder 1. poisonous snake, *Bitis arietans,* of Africa, having a brown or gray body with crescent-shaped yellow markings. Length: 3–5 feet. **2.** hognose snake.

puff·ball (puf'bôl') *n.* any of a group of round, edible mushroomlike fungi, order Lycoperdales, that emit cloudlike mists of spores when mature.

puff·er (puf'ər) *n.* **1.** one who or that which puffs. **2.** globefish.

puf·fin (puf'in) *n.* any of various stout-bodied sea birds, genera *Fratercula* and *Lunda,* found chiefly around the edges of the Arctic Ocean and on the northern coasts of North America and Europe, having a large triangular bill, webbed feet, and black plumage with white or grayish feathers on the cheeks, breast, and underparts. Length: 12–15 inches. [Of uncertain origin.]

Puffin

puff paste, dough of flour, salt, and ice water, rolled into very thin sheets that puff up during baking, used to make very light, flaky pastries.

puff·y (puf'ē) **puff·i·er, puff·i·est.** *adj.* **1.** puffed up; swollen: *a puffy face.* **2.** blowing in puffs: *puffy wind.* —**puff'i·ness,** *n.*

pug¹ (pug) *n.* **1.** short-haired dog resembling a small bulldog, having a black, silver, or fawn-colored glossy coat. Height: 11 inches at the shoulder. **2.** pug nose. [Of uncertain origin.]

pug² (pug) *n.* *Slang.* pugilist; boxer. [Short for PUGILIST.]

Pu·get Sound (pū'jit) inlet of the Pacific extending into the northwestern part of the state of Washington.

pu·gi·lism (pū'jə liz'əm) *n.* art or practice of fighting with the fists; boxing. [Latin *pūgil* boxer + -ISM.]

pu·gi·list (pū'jə list) *n.* one who fights with the fists, esp. a professional boxer. —**pu'gi·lis'tic,** *adj.*

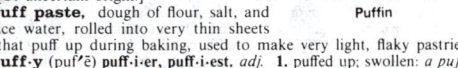

Pug¹

pug·na·cious (pug na'shəs) *adj.* disposed to fight; quarrelsome. [Latin *pūgnāci-,* stem of *pūgnāx* combative (from *pūgnāre* to fight) + -OUS.] —**pug·na'cious·ly,** *adv.* —**pug·na'cious·ness, pug·nac·i·ty** (pug nas'ə tē), *n.*

pug nose, short, broad, turned-up nose. —**pug'-nosed',** *adj.*

puis·sance (pwis'əns, pū'i səns) *n.* power; strength; might.

puis·sant (pwis'ənt, pū'i sənt) *adj.* powerful; mighty. [Old French *puissant,* going back to Latin *posse* to be able.] —**puis'sant·ly,** *adv.*

puke (pūk) *v.* **puked, puk·ing.** *Informal. v.t., v.i.* to vomit. —*n.* vomit. [Possibly imitative.]

puk·ka (puk'ə) *adj.* first-rate, genuine, or good. [Hindi *pakka* mature, from Sanskrit *pakva.*]

Pu·las·ki, Count Cas·i·mir (poo las'kē, pə-; kaz'ə mir) 1748–79, Polish nobleman and general in the American Revolutionary army.

pul·chri·tude (pul'krə tōod', -tūd') *n.* physical beauty. [Latin *pulchritūdō.*]

pule (pūl) *v.i.* **puled, pul·ing.** *v.i.* to cry in a weak voice; whimper; whine. [Probably imitative.] —**pul'er,** *n.*

Pu·litz·er, Joseph (pool'it sər, pū'lit-) 1847–1911, U.S. journalist and newspaper publisher.

Pulitzer Prize, any of a group of annual prizes in journalism, literature, and music, established by Joseph Pulitzer.

pull (pool) *v.t.* **1.** to exert force upon so as to cause or tend to cause motion toward the force: *Two black horses pulled the wagon.* **2.** to exert a force upon as in snatching or grabbing: *She pulled his sleeve to get his attention.* **3.** to rip or tear by or as by exerting such a force: *The puppy pulled the blanket to pieces.* **4.** to take, tear, or remove from a fixed position by exerting such a force: *to pull a tooth, to pull a branch from a tree.* **5.** to bring or cause to come into a particular state, condition, or position: *When he realized how late it was, he pulled his clothes on and ran out.* **6.** to injure or weaken by overexertion or excessive stretching; strain: *to pull a muscle in one's shoulder.* **7.** to exert an influence on; impel. **8.** to withdraw or remove (often with *out*): *Seeing the speed of the enemy's advance, the captain pulled out his troops.* **9.** *Informal.* to carry out or bring about; perform; accomplish (often with *off*): *He was suspected of pulling the holdup.* **10.** *Informal.* to draw or attract: *His performances always pull a large crowd.* **11.** to draw (a weapon) out so as to use: *to pull a gun.* **12.** to take (an impression or proof) from or as from type. **13. a.** to operate (an oar) in rowing. **b.** to be rowed with: *a boat that pulls four oars.* **14.** to hit (a ball) so that it moves to the side opposite that from which one hits, as when a right-handed batter hits a baseball to left field.

to pull apart, to criticize mercilessly or in detail.

to pull down, to tear down, demolish, or overthrow: *to pull down a house, to pull down a government.*

to pull in. *Slang.* to arrest and bring to police headquarters.

to pull oneself together. to compose oneself; regain one's self-control or self-possession.

to pull through. to bring through a difficult situation or period successfully: *Her belief that he was safe was what pulled her through the years they were separated.*

to pull up. to cause to come or bring to a halt; stop: *He pulled the car up at the curb.*
—*v.i.* **1.** to perform the action of pulling: *She pulled on the reins to slow the horse up.* **2.** to move, go, or proceed: *The car pulled into the driveway. He pulled ahead of the other runner.* **3.** to exert a sucking or drawing force; drink or puff deeply (often with *on* or *at*): *to pull on a cigarette.* **4.** to row: *They pulled toward the bank of the river.*

to pull for. to hope for the success of; support or encourage.

to pull in. to arrive.

to pull out. a. to depart; leave. **b.** to retreat or withdraw, as from an undertaking: *They pulled out of the deal at the last minute.*

to pull through. to get through a difficult situation or period successfully: *He was very ill for a time, but he managed to pull through.*

to pull together. to work in harmony; cooperate.

to pull up. to come to a halt; stop: *A car pulled up in front of the house.*
—*n.* **1.** act or instance of pulling or exerting force in snatching, grabbing, or moving something toward one: *He gave the tablecloth a pull, and all the dishes went flying.* **2.** force or effort expended in pulling. **3.** effort expended in moving forward; arduous, continuous effort: *It was a long hard pull for him to get to the top of his profession.* **4.** any instrument or device for pulling, as a handle, knob, or rope. **5.** *Informal.* hold or claim on those who are powerful; means of gaining special consideration or treatment; influence: *He got the job through his pull with our manager.* **6.** *Informal.* ability to draw or attract; appeal; allure: *a star with great box-office pull.* **7.** act of exerting a sucking or drawing force; deep swallow or puff. **8.** *Sports.* act or instance of pulling a ball. [Old English *pullian* to draw with force, pluck.]

Syn. *v.t.* **1. Pull, drag, draw** mean to cause something to move in the direction from which force is exerted. **Pull** is the general word to imply a forward movement caused by a person or thing exerting physical force: *She pulled the door open.* **Drag** suggests hauling something slowly and heavily over the ground and stresses resistance on the part of the thing dragged and great effort on the part of the agent exerting force: *The lumberjack dragged the logs down to the river.* **Draw** is used when something is pulled forward or toward the person or thing that exerts force and suggests a steady, smooth motion: *The children rode in a cart that was drawn by a pony.*

pull·back (pool'bak') *n.* **1.** act of pulling back, esp. an orderly military retreat. **2.** that which pulls back, as a device.

pul·let (pool'it) *n.* young hen less than a year old. [Old French *poulette* young hen, diminutive of *poule* hen, going back to Latin *pullus* young fowl or animal.]

pul·ley (pool'ē) *pl.* **-leys.** *n.* **1.** grooved wheel on which a rope or chain is pulled, used to lift heavy loads or change the direction of an applied force. **2.** simple machine consisting of such a wheel or set of such wheels mounted in a casing; block. [Old French *po(u)lie* the grooved wheel, going back to Greek *polos* pivot, axis.]

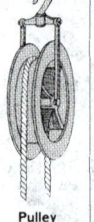

Pulley

Pull·man (pool'mən) *n.* railroad car with sleeping accommodations. [From George M. *Pullman,* 1831–97, American industrialist who designed it.]

pull·out (pool'out') *n.* **1.** act of pulling out, esp. an orderly military retreat. **2.** that which is pulled out or intended to be pulled out. **3.** maneuver in which an airplane is pulled out of a dive or spin and returned to level flight.

pull·o·ver (pool'ō'vər) *n.* garment, as a shirt or sweater, that is put on by being pulled over the head. —*adj.* that is put on by being pulled over the head.

pul·lu·late (pul'yə lāt') **-lat·ed, -lat·ing.** *v.i.* **1.** to put forth buds; germinate. **2.** to spring up abundantly; abound; teem. [Latin *pullulātus,* past participle of *pullulāre* to put forth, sprout.] —**pul'lu·la'tion,** *n.*

pul·mo·nar·y (pool'mə ner'ē, pul'-) *adj.* **1.** of, relating to, or affecting the lungs: *the pulmonary organs, a pulmonary disease.* **2.** having lungs or lunglike organs. [Latin *pulmōnārius* relating to the lungs, from *pulmō* lung.]

pulmonary artery, artery that carries blood from the heart to the lungs.

pulmonary vein, one of four veins that returns oxygenated blood from the lungs to the heart.

Pul·mo·tor (pool'mō'tər, pul'-) *n.* *Trademark.* machine for producing artificial respiration that forces oxygen into the lungs of persons experiencing suffocation. [Latin *pul(mō)* lung + MOTOR.]

pulp (pulp) *n.* **1.** soft, juicy part of a fruit. **2.** inner part of a tooth containing soft tissue, blood vessels, and nerves. **3.** any soft, moist, formless mass, as the mixture of matted fibers of wood used in making

paper. **4.** magazine printed on a cheap grade of paper made from wood pulp, usually containing sensational stories or articles. —*v.t.* **1.** to make into pulp; reduce to pulp. **2.** to remove the pulp from. —*v.i.* to become pulp. [Latin *pulpa* fleshy part of animal bodies and fruit.]

pul·pit (pool'pit, pul'-) *n.* **1.** raised structure, often elaborately carved, from which a minister delivers a sermon or conducts a worship service. **2.** ministers collectively; the clergy. **3.** ministry. [Latin *pulpitum* scaffold, platform.]

pulp·wood (pulp'wood') *n.* wood used to make paper, esp. softwood, as pine, fir, or spruce.

pulp·y (pul'pē) **pulp·i·er, pulp·i·est.** *adj.* of or resembling pulp; soft or fleshy. —**pulp'i·ly,** *adv.* —**pulp'i·ness,** *n.*

pul·que (pool'kā, -kē) *n.* fermented drink made from the juice of the maguey plant in Mexico.

pul·sar (pul'sär) *n.* any of a number of astronomical objects that emit intense pulses of electromagnetic energy at regular intervals.

Pulpit

pul·sate (pul'sāt) **-sat·ed, -sat·ing.** *v.i.* **1.** to expand and contract rhythmically: *The heart pulsates.* **2.** to vibrate; quiver. [Latin *pulsātus,* past participle of *pulsāre* to beat, strike.]

pul·sa·tion (pul sā'shən) *n.* **1.** act of pulsating. **2.** single beat or vibration.

pulse¹ (puls) *n.* **1.** rhythmic expansion and contraction of the arteries caused by the pulsation of the heart. **2.** any regular, rhythmical beating or vibrating. **3.** sentiment, feeling, or opinion of a group. —*v.i.* **pulsed, puls·ing.** to beat or vibrate; pulsate. [Latin *pulsus* a beating.]

pulse² (puls) *n.* **1.** edible seeds of such plants as peas, beans, or lentils. **2.** any plant yielding such seeds. [Latin *puls* thick pottage made of pulse.]

pulse-jet (puls'jet') *n.* type of jet engine that operates by means of a series of short, separate combustions.

pul·ver·ize (pul'və rīz') **-ized, -iz·ing.** *v.t.* **1.** to reduce to powder or dust, as by pounding or grinding. **2.** to smash or destroy completely. —*v.i.* to become powder or dust. [Late Latin *pulverizāre* to reduce to dust, from Latin *pulvis* dust.] —**pul'ver·iz'a·ble,** *adj.* —**pul'ver·i·za'tion, pul'ver·iz'er,** *n.*

pu·ma (pū'mə) *n.* cougar. [Spanish *puma,* from Quechua *puma.*]

pum·ice (pum'is) *n.* light, porous volcanic rock used in powdered form, as for smoothing or polishing. Also, **pumice stone.** —*v.t.* **-iced, -ic·ing.** to clean, smooth, or polish with pumice. [Old French *pomis* the rock, going back to Latin *pūmex.*]

pum·mel (pum'əl) **-meled, -mel·ing;** *also, British.* **-melled, -mel·ling.** *also,* **pom·mel.** *v.t.* to strike repeatedly with the fists: *The two boys pummeled one another.* [Form of POMMEL.]

pump¹ (pump) *n.* device for moving fluids or gases from one place to another. —*v.t.* **1.** to move (a fluid) from one place to another by means of a pump. **2.** to remove fluid from (often with *out*): *to pump out a flooded basement.* **3.** to fill with a gas, esp. with air, by means of a pump (often with *up*). **4.** to move or operate by forcing up and down or back and forth repeatedly: *to pump an accelerator.* **5.a.** to obtain or attempt to obtain information from, esp. by persistent questioning. **b.** to obtain (information), esp. by persistent questioning. —*v.i.* **1.** to make a fluid move from place to place by means of a pump. **2.** to move up and down or back and forth repeatedly. [Possibly from Middle Dutch *pompe* pipe of wood or metal, from Spanish *bomba* pumping device; imitative.] —**pump'er,** *n.*

pump² (pump) *n.* low-cut shoe without laces or other fasteners. [Of uncertain origin.]

pum·per·nick·el (pum'pər nik'əl) *n.* coarse black or dark-brown bread made of unsifted rye flour. [German *Pumpernickel.*]

pump·kin (pump'kin, pum'-, pung'-) *n.* **1.** large orange or yellow-orange fruit of a plant, *Cucurbita pepo,* having a soft pulp containing many seeds and a firm outer rind. **2.** trailing, coarse vine bearing this fruit. [Modification of earlier *pumpion,* from Middle French *pompon* pumpkin, melon, going back to Latin *pepō,* from Greek *pepōn* large melon.]

pump·kin·seed (pump'kin sēd', pum'-, pung'-) *n.* **1.** seed of a pumpkin. **2.** freshwater sunfish, *Lepomis gibbosus,* found in lakes and ponds of eastern North America. Length: to 8 inches.

pun (pun) *n.* play on words in which a double meaning is applied to the same word or to two words having the same sound. —*v.i.* **punned, pun·ning.** to make a pun or puns. [Possibly short for Italian *puntiglio* a fine point. See PUNCTILIO.]

punch¹ (punch) *v.t.* **1.** to hit (someone or something), esp. with the fist. **2.** to operate by pressing: *to punch a time clock.* **3.** *Informal.* to drive (cattle). —*v.i.* to hit, esp. with the fist. —*n.* **1.** blow made, esp.

with the fist. **2.** *Informal.* force; vitality: *to put punch in one's words.* **3. to pull one's punches.** *Informal.* to refrain from speaking or acting with bluntness. [Possibly form of POUNCE¹.] —**punch′er,** *n.*

punch² (punch) *n.* tool for making holes, stamping, or impressing a design in or on a surface. —*v.t.* to make holes, stamp, or impress a design in or on (a surface) with a punch. —*v.i.* to use a punch. [Short for PUNCHEON².]

punch³ (punch) *n.* drink made from various ingredients, usually fruit juice and an alcoholic or carbonated beverage, often sweetened and spiced. [Hindi *pānch* five, from Sanskrit *pānchan;* referring to the five ingredients originally used to make it.]

Punch (punch) *n.* **1.** ill-tempered, humpbacked hero of the puppet show *Punch and Judy.* **2. pleased as Punch.** extremely pleased; delighted. [Short for PUNCHINELLO.]

Punch-and-Ju·dy show (punch′ən jōō′dē) puppet show noted for its broad humor and satirical dialogue, having as its main characters Punch and his wife Judy.

punch card, card with holes punched in specific positions to provide instructions or information for a data processing machine.

punch-drunk (punch′drungk′) *adj.* **1.** having a dazed mental condition brought about by repeated blows on the head in prize fighting. **2.** *Informal.* dazed or confused.

pun·cheon¹ (pun′chən) *n.* **1.** large cask of varying capacity, holding from 70 to 120 gallons. **2.** amount contained in a puncheon. [Old French *po(i)nchon* wine cask; of uncertain origin.]

pun·cheon² (pun′chən) *n.* **1.** broad, heavy piece of timber roughly dressed on one side. **2.** short upright piece of timber used as support in a wooden framing. **3.** punch². [Old French *poinchon* pointed tool, from Latin *pūnctiō* a piercing.]

Pun·chi·nel·lo (pun′chə nel′ō) *pl.,* **-los** or **-loes.** *n.* humpbacked, doltish character in an Italian puppet show. [Modification of Italian *Pulcinella,* diminutive of *pulcino* young chicken, going back to Latin *pullus* young fowl or animal.]

punching bag, inflated or stuffed leather or canvas bag, usually suspended, punched for exercise or training in boxing.

punch line, last sentence or phrase of a joke or story, that gives it humor or meaning.

punch·y (pun′chē) **punch·i·er, punch·i·est.** *adj. Informal.* dizzy or groggy.

Punching bag

punc·til·i·o (pungk til′ē ō′) *pl.,* **-os.** *n.* **1.** fine point of proper or polite behavior. **2.** strict or meticulous observance of such fine points. [Italian *puntiglio* fine point, diminutive of *punto* point, from Latin *pūnctum.*]

punc·til·i·ous (pungk til′ē əs) *adj.* **1.** strictly attentive to the fine points of proper or polite behavior. **2.** very careful and exact. —**punc·til′i·ous·ly,** *adv.* —**punc·til′i·ous·ness,** *n.* —**Syn. 2.** see **careful.**

punc·tu·al (pungk′chōō əl) *adj.* **1.** acting or happening at the correct or appointed time; prompt. **2.** paid at the correct or appointed time: *a punctual payment.* [Medieval Latin *punctualis* relating to a point, from Latin *pūnctum* point.] —**punc·tu·al·i·ty** (pungk′chōō al′ə tē), **punc′tu·al·ness,** *n.* —**punc′tu·al·ly,** *adv.*

punc·tu·ate (pungk′chōō āt′) **-at·ed, -at·ing.** *v.t.* **1.** to mark (written material) with punctuation marks. **2.** to interrupt from time to time: *a speech punctuated by cheers.* **3.** to give emphasis to. —*v.i.* to use punctuation marks. [Medieval Latin *punctuatus,* past participle of *punctuare* to prick, mark by points, from Latin *pūnctum* point.]

punc·tu·a·tion (pungk′chōō ā′shən) *n.* **1.** use, practice, or system of marking written material with punctuation marks for clarity of meaning. **2.** punctuation mark or marks.

punctuation mark, any of various marks, as the comma, semicolon, or period, used to clarify the meaning of written material.

punc·ture (pungk′chər) **-tured, -tur·ing.** *v.t.* **1.** to make a hole in (something) with a sharp or pointed object. **2.** to make (a hole) by piercing. **3.** to reduce in importance; deflate: *Her ridicule punctured his ego.* —*v.i.* to become punctured. —*n.* **1.** hole made by a sharp or pointed object. **2.** act of puncturing. [Latin *pūnctūra* a pricking.] —**Syn. 1.** see **pierce.**

pun·dit (pun′dit) *n.* **1.** learned Brahmin, esp. one versed in the laws, language, or religion of India. **2.** learned person, esp. one who is an expert in a particular field: *a political pundit.* [Hindi *pandit* learned Brahmin, from Sanskrit *pandita* learned.]

pun·gent (pun′jənt) *adj.* **1.** sharply affecting the senses of taste or smell. **2.** sharply expressive, stinging, or severe: *a pungent wit, pungent criticism.* [Latin *pungēns,* present participle of *pungere* to prick.] —**pun′gen·cy,** *n.* —**pun′gent·ly,** *adv.*

Pu·nic (pū′nik) *adj.* of or relating to Carthage, its people, or their language. —*n.* Semitic language of ancient Carthage.

pun·ish (pun′ish) *v.t.* **1.** to cause (someone) to suffer for an offense; subject to a penalty. **2.** to impose a penalty for (an offense). **3.** to treat severely; handle roughly. [Old French *puniss-,* a stem of *punir* to inflict punishment on, from Latin *pūnīre.*] —**pun′ish·a·ble,** *adj.* —**pun′ish·er,** *n.*

pun·ish·ment (pun′ish mənt) *n.* **1.** act of punishing; being punished. **2.** penalty imposed for an offense. **3.** severe treatment; rough handling: *The car took a lot of punishment on the dirt road.*

pu·ni·tive (pū′nə tiv) *adj.* involving or inflicting punishment; punishing: *a punitive law, a punitive action.* Also, **pu·ni·to·ry** (pū′nə tôr′ē). [French *punitif,* going back to Latin *pūnītus,* past participle of *pūnīre* to punish.] —**pu′ni·tive·ly,** *adv.* —**pu′ni·tive·ness,** *n.*

Pun·jab (pun jäb′, pun′jäb′) *n.* region and former province in northern India, now divided between India and Pakistan.

punk¹ (pungk) *n.* **1.** dry substance that burns slowly without a flame, used esp. to light fireworks. **2.** dry, decayed wood, used esp. as tinder. [Possibly from Algonquian *punk* smoldering ashes.]

punk² (pungk) *Slang.* *n.* young or inexperienced person, esp. a young hoodlum. —*adj.* of poor quality; worthless. [Of uncertain origin.]

pun·kah (pung′kə) *n.* large fan that hangs from the ceiling and is kept in motion by a servant or by machinery, used esp. in India. [Hindi *pankhā,* from Sanskrit *pakshaka.*]

pun·ster (pun′stər) *n.* one who frequently makes puns.

punt¹ (punt) *n.* flat-bottomed boat with square ends, usually propelled by a long pole. —*v.t.* **1.** to propel (a boat) with a long pole. **2.** to carry in a punt. —*v.i.* to go or travel in a punt.

Punt¹

[Old English *punt* such a boat, from Latin *pontō.*] —**punt′er,** *n.*

punt² (punt) *n.* kick in which a football is dropped from the hands and kicked before it reaches the ground. —*v.t.* to kick (a football) before it reaches the ground. —*v.i.* to punt a football. [Of uncertain origin.] —**punt′er,** *n.*

punt³ (punt) *v.i.* to bet against the bank in a game of chance. [French *ponter* to gamble, from *ponte* one who punts, ace in cards, from Spanish *punto* point, pip on cards, from Latin *pūnctum* point.]

pu·ny (pū′nē) **-ni·er, -ni·est.** *adj.* inferior in size, strength, or importance; weak. [Anglo-Norman *pune, puisne* born after, younger, going back to Latin *post nātus* born after.] —**pu′ni·ness,** *n.*

pup (pup) *n.* **1.** young dog; puppy. **2.** young of various other animals, as the fox, wolf, or seal. [From PUPPY.]

pu·pa (pū′pə) *pl.,* **-pae** (-pē) or **-pas.** *n.* insect in the intermediate stage of complete metamorphosis, coming after the larval and before the adult stage. See **metamorphosis** for illustration. [Modern Latin *pupa,* from Latin *pūpa* girl, doll.] —**pu′pal,** *adj.*

pu·pil¹ (pū′pəl) *n.* one who studies under the direction of an instructor; student. [Latin *pūpillus* orphan, ward, diminutive of *pūpus* boy.]

pu·pil² (pū′pəl) *n.* opening in the center of the iris through which light enters the eye. [Latin *pūpilla* little girl, pupil of the eye, diminutive of *pūpa* girl, doll; referring to the small images that can be seen reflected in the pupil of the eye.]

pup·pet (pup′it) *n.* **1.** small, usually jointed, figure representing a person or animal and manipulated by the hand or by strings, wires, or rods. **2.** small doll. **3.** one who or that which is under the complete domination of another, as a government. [Old French *poupette* little doll, going back to Latin *pūpa* girl, doll.]

pup·pet·eer (pup′ə tēr′) *n.* one who manipulates puppets for entertainment.

pup·pet·ry (pup′i trē) *n.* art of making puppets or producing puppet shows.

Puppet

pup·py (pup′ē) *pl.,* **-pies.** *n.* **1.** young dog. **2.** silly, conceited, or foppish young man. [Middle French *poupée* doll, toy, going back to Latin *pūpa* girl, doll.] —**pup′py·hood′,** *n.* —**pup′py·ish′,** *adj.*

pup tent, small two-man tent in two pieces that button or fasten together. Also, **shelter tent.**

pur·blind (pur′blīnd′) *adj.* **1.** partially or nearly blind. **2.** lacking in understanding; obtuse; dull. [Earlier *pure blind* completely blind. See PURE, BLIND.] —**pur′blind′ly,** *adv.* —**pur′blind′ness,** *n.*

Pur·cell, Henry (pur′səl) 1659–95, English composer.

pur·chas·a·ble (pur′chə sə bəl) *adj.* **1.** that can be purchased: *a purchasable commodity.* **2.** that can be bribed; corrupt; venal.

pur·chase (pur′chəs) **-chased, -chas·ing.** *v.t.* **1.** to obtain by paying money or its equivalent; buy. **2.** to obtain by hardship, sacrifice, or suffering: *a military victory purchased at great cost of life.* **3.** to raise,

move, or hold by mechanical power: *to purchase an anchor.* —*n.*
1. act or instance of purchasing. **2.** something purchased. **3.** mechanical
advantage or power; leverage: *The horse had no purchase for its feet on
the smooth pavement.* **4.** device for obtaining such mechanical advantage or power. [Anglo-Norman *purchacer* to pursue, procure, going
back to Latin *prō* before, for + *captāre* to try to catch, pursue.]
—**pur′chas·er,** *n.* —**Syn.** *v.t.* **1.** see **buy.**

pur·dah (pur′də) *n.* **1.** curtain, screen, or concealing garment used
by some Hindus and Muslims to hide women from the gaze of men or
strangers. **2.** practice or system of such concealment of women.
[Urdu *pardah* veil, from Persian *pardah*.]

pure (pyoor) *adj.* **pur·er, pur·est.** *adj.* **1.** having the same components or
character throughout; not mixed with anything else; unadulterated: *a
scarf of pure silk.* **2.** not stained, spotted, or contaminated; clean: *pure
water.* **3.** free from moral corruption, evil intent, or guilt: *a pure heart.*
4. virtuous; chaste. **5.** free from foreign or incongruous elements: *She
speaks pure Italian.* **6.** of unmixed descent: *That cat is pure Siamese.*
7. nothing but; sheer; utter: *Your explanation of what happened is pure
speculation.* **8.** theoretical or abstract: *pure science.* [Old French *pur*
unmixed, mere, from Latin *pūrus* clean, unmixed, chaste.] —**pure′-
ness,** *n.*

pure·bred (pyoor′bred′) *adj.* descended from ancestors of unmixed
stock: *Joan's horse is a purebred Arabian stallion.*

pu·ree (pyoo rā′, -rē′) *n.* **1.** raw or cooked food that is put through
a sieve, food mill, or blender and made into a thick, moist mass.
2. smooth, thick soup. —*v.t.* **-reed, -re·ing.** to make (raw or cooked
food) into a puree. [French *purée* thick soup, from *purer* to strain, from
Latin *pūrāre* to cleanse.]

pure·ly (pyoor′lē) *adv.* **1.** entirely; simply: *What happened is purely
coincidental.* **2.** in a pure manner. **3.** virtuously; chastely.

pur·ga·tion (pur gā′shən) *n.* act of purging.

pur·ga·tive (pur′gə tiv) *n.* medicine that causes the bowels to empty;
strong laxative; cathartic. —*adj.* tending to purge. [Late Latin
pūrgātīvus cathartic, from Latin *pūrgāre* to cleanse, purify.]

pur·ga·to·ri·al (pur′gə tôr′ē əl) *adj.* **1.** of or relating to purgatory.
2. serving to purge from sin; expiatory.

pur·ga·to·ry (pur′gə tôr′ē) *pl.,* **-ries.** *n.* **1.** in Roman Catholic doctrine, a temporary place of purification, where souls are purged of
unrepented minor sins or of major sins that have been forgiven but not
wholly punished. **2.** any place or condition of temporary punishment
or suffering. [Medieval Latin *purgatorium* a means of cleansing, going
back to Latin *pūrgāre* to cleanse.]

purge (purj) purged, purg·ing. *v.t.* **1.** to cleanse or rid of whatever is
unclean or undesirable. **2.** to remove by cleansing (with *away* or *off*).
3. to eliminate persons from (a political party, government, or other
organization). **4.** to eliminate (a person or persons) from a political
party, government, or other organization. **5.** to free of sin or guilt.
6. to cause (the bowels) to empty. —*v.i.* **1.** to become clean or pure.
2. to undergo a purging of the bowels. —*n.* **1.** act or process of purging.
2. elimination, esp. by expulsion or death, of persons from a political
party, government, or other organization. **3.** purgative medicine; cathartic. [Old French *purg(i)er* to cleanse, purify, from Latin *pūrgāre.*]

pu·ri·fi·ca·tion (pyoo′ə fi kā′shən) *n.* act or process of purifying;
being purified.

pu·ri·fy (pyoor′ə fī′) **-fied, -fy·ing.** *v.t., v.i.* to make or become pure
or clean. [Old French *purifier* to make pure, from Latin *pūrificāre.*]
—**pu′ri·fi′er,** *n.*

Pu·rim (poor′im, poo rim′) *n.* annual Jewish holiday observed in
February or March, commemorating the deliverance of the Jews by
Queen Esther from a massacre plotted by Haman. [Hebrew *pūrīm,*
plural of *pūr* lot.]

pu·rine (pyoor′ēn) *n.* **1.** colorless, crystalline organic compound, the
parent substance of a group of nitrogenous compounds that serve
as the fundamental base of many biochemical substances. Formula:
$C_5H_4N_4$ **2.** any of these compounds, such as uric acid.

pur·ism (pyoor′iz′əm) *n.* strict adherence to or insistence upon
purity, as in language.

pur·ist (pyoor′ist) *n.* one who advocates, practices, or insists upon
strict adherence to purity, as of language or artistic style. —**pu·ris′tic,**
adj.

Pu·ri·tan (pyoor′it ən) *n.* **1.** one of a sect of English Protestants in
the sixteenth and seventeenth centuries who advocated simplified religious ceremonies and high standards of morality. **2.** puritan, one who
is scrupulously or excessively strict in matters of morality or religion.
—*adj.* **1.** of, relating to, or characteristic of the Puritans or Puritanism.
2. puritan. of, relating to, or characteristic of a puritan. [Late Latin
pūritās cleanliness + -AN. See PURITY.]

pu·ri·tan·i·cal (pyoor′i tan′i kəl) *adj.* **1.** scrupulously or excessively strict in matters of morality or religion: *a puritanical attitude.*
2. Puritanical. of, relating to, or characteristic of Puritans or Puritan-

ism. Also, **pu·ri·tan′ic.** —**pu·ri·tan′i·cal·ly,** *adv.* —**pu·ri·tan′i·cal·
ness,** *n.*

Pu·ri·tan·ism (pyoor′it ən iz′əm) *n.* **1.** beliefs and practices of the
Puritans. **2. puritanism.** scrupulous or excessive strictness in matters
of morality or religion.

pu·ri·ty (pyoor′ə tē) *n.* **1.** state or quality of being pure; freedom from
extraneous matter or contamination. **2.** freedom from moral corruption, evil intent, or guilt. **3.** freedom from foreign or incongruous elements: *purity of language.* [Late Latin *pūritās* cleanliness, from Latin
pūrus clean, unmixed, chaste.]

purl[1] (purl) *v.i.* to flow, ripple, or swirl, esp. with a murmuring sound.
—*n.* murmuring sound made by a shallow stream or brook. [Possibly
imitative.]

purl[2] (purl) *v.t., v.i.* **1.** to knit with inverted stitches. **2.** to decorate
or finish with small loops. —*n.* **1.** small loop, or chain of small loops,
used to decorate or finish the edge of lace or other fabric; picot.
2. thread of twisted gold or silver wire, used in embroidery. [Of uncertain origin.]

pur·lieu (pur′loo, purl′ū) *n.* **1.** neighboring or outlying area.
2. purlieus. outskirts. **3.** area that one knows well or frequents.
[Modification (influenced by French *lieu* place) of Anglo-Norman *pu-
ralee* perambulation, from Old French *po(u)raler* to traverse, going back
to Latin *prō* before, for + *ambulāre* to walk.]

pur·lin (pur′lin) *also,* **pur·line.** *n.* one of the horizontal timbers supporting the rafters of a roof. [Of uncertain origin.]

pur·loin (pur loin′) *v.t., v.i.* to steal. [Anglo-Norman *purloigner* to
delay, remove, going back to Latin *prō* before, forth + *longē* far.]
—**pur·loin′er,** *n.*

pur·ple (pur′pəl) *n.* **1.** color between crimson and violet, formed by
mixing red and blue. **2.** cloth or garment of this color, esp. as worn
as a symbol of royalty or high rank. —*adj.* **1.** of the color purple.
2. full of exaggerated or florid literary devices or effects: *purple passages.*
[Old English *purple* of the color purple, going back to Latin *purpura*
a shellfish yielding a purple dye, this dye, from Greek *porphýrā.*]

Purple Heart, U.S. military award given to a member of the armed
forces who is wounded while in action against the enemy.

purple martin, North American swallow, *Progne subis,* the male of
which has glossy, blue-black plumage. Length: 8 inches.

pur·plish (pur′plish) *adj.* somewhat purple.

pur·port (*v.,* pər pôrt′; *n.,* pur′pôrt′) *v.t.* **1.** to claim or profess, often
falsely: *He purports to be an expert on automobiles.* **2.** to intend; mean.
—*n.* meaning or substance: *Her letter gives the purport of our conversation.* [Anglo-Norman *purporter* to intend, contain, going back to Latin
prō forth + *portāre* to carry.]

pur·pose (pur′pəs) *n.* **1.** result or goal that is desired; object to which
effort is directed; intention. **2.** object or reason for which something
is made or exists; function or use. **3.** act or result of determining;
resolution. **4. on purpose.** not by accident; intentionally. —*v.t.* **-posed,
-pos·ing.** to intend, resolve, or propose. [Old French *purpos* resolution,
from *purposer* to intend, propose, modification (influenced by Old
French *poser* to place, put) of Latin *prōpōnere* to set forth. See POSE[1].]
Syn. *n.* **1. Purpose, aim, intention** mean what one hopes to achieve by
doing something. **Purpose** emphasizes a determination in striving toward a specific goal: *I have a purpose in making this trip to Europe.* **Aim**
emphasizes the general direction one takes in accomplishing an ultimate
end: *His aim in life was to create good will between the races.* **Intention**
emphasizes personal desire, esp. as contrasted with the actual outcome:
It wasn't my intention to hurt her feelings.

pur·pose·ful (pur′pəs fəl) *adj.* **1.** having a purpose or meaning; intentional. **2.** having or showing determination: *a purposeful man.*
—**pur′pose·ful·ly,** *adv.* —**pur′pose·ful·ness,** *n.*

pur·pose·less (pur′pəs lis) *adj.* without purpose or meaning.
—**pur′pose·less·ly,** *adv.* —**pur′pose·less·ness,** *n.*

pur·pose·ly (pur′pəs lē) *adv.* on purpose; intentionally; deliberately.

purr (pur) *n.* **1.** soft, murmuring sound made by a cat when pleased
or contented. **2.** any similar sound. —*v.i.* to make a soft, murmuring
sound. —*v.t.* to express by making a soft, murmuring sound. [Imita-
tive.]

purse (purs) *n.* **1.** woman's handbag. **2.** small bag, pouch, or case for
carrying money. **3.** anything resembling this, as in shape or use.
4. available money; funds. **5.** sum of money offered as a prize or given
as a gift. —*v.t.* **pursed, purs·ing.** to draw together into wrinkles or
folds; pucker. [Old English *purs* small bag for carrying money, from
Late Latin *bursa* leather bag, wallet, from Greek *byrsā* hide[2], skin (used
to make purses). Doublet of BOURSE, BURSA.]

purs·er (pur′sər) *n.* officer who has charge of financial matters on
board a ship.

purs·lane (purs′lin, -lān) *n.* trailing plant, *Portulaca oleracea,* having
bright yellow flowers and fleshy stems and leaves, sometimes used as
a salad green. [Old French *porcelaine,* modification of Latin *porcilāca,*
form of *portulāca.* See PORTULACA.]

at; āpe; cär; end; mē; it; īce; hot; ōld; fôrk; wood; fo̅o̅l; oil; out; up; ūse; turn; sing; thin; this; zh in treasure; ə in ago, taken, pencil, lemon, circus.

pur·su·ance (pər sōō′əns) *n.* a carrying out; prosecution: *In pursuance of their plan, the young couple bought the house.*

pur·su·ant (pər sōō′ənt) *adj.* going in pursuit; pursuing. —*adv.* in accordance with (often with *to*): *I loaned him the money, pursuant to our agreement.*

pur·sue (pər sōō′) -**sued, -su·ing.** *v.t.* **1.** to follow in order to overtake, capture, or kill: *The hounds pursued the fox.* **2.** to proceed along or hold to the course of; follow: *to pursue a plan of action.* **3.** to endeavor to attain; strive for; seek: *to pursue pleasure, to pursue a goal.* **4.** to continue or follow through; continue: *to pursue the study of Spanish.* **5.** to continue to distress, disturb, or trouble; plague; harass. —*v.i.* **1.** to go in pursuit; follow. **2.** to go on; continue. [Anglo-Norman *pursuer* to follow up or closely, going back to Latin *prōsequī* to follow after.] —**pur·su′a·ble,** *adj.* —**pur·su′er,** *n.* —**Syn.** *v.t.* **1.** see **hunt.**

pur·suit (pər sōōt′) *n.* **1.** act of following in order to overtake: *the pursuit of a bandit.* **2.** act of seeking: *the pursuit of wealth.* **3.** any occupation, pastime, or interest.

pur·sui·vant (pur′swi vənt) *n.* **1.** heraldic official ranking below a herald. **2.** *Archaic.* attendant; follower. [Old French *pursivant* follower, from *pursivre* to pursue, going back to Latin *prōsequī.*]

pu·ru·lence (pyoor′ə ləns, pyoor′yə-) *n.* **1.** condition of forming, containing, or discharging pus; suppuration. **2.** pus. Also, **pu′ru·len·cy.**

pu·ru·lent (pyoor′ə lənt, pyoor′yə-) *adj.* forming, containing, or discharging pus; suppurating. [Latin *pūrulentus* festering, from *pūs* pus.]

pur·vey (pur vā′) *v.t.* to supply (something, as food or provisions). [Anglo-Norman *purveier* to provide, from Latin *prōvidēre* to foresee, provide. Doublet of *provide.*] —**pur·vey′ance,** *n.*

pur·vey·or (pur vā′ər) *n.* one who supplies something, esp. food or provisions.

pur·view (pur′vū) *n.* **1.** range or scope of authority, activity, or concern. **2.** range of vision or comprehension. **3.** *Law.* body of a statute, containing its purpose, scope, or limit. [Anglo-Norman *purveu* provided (as in the phrases *purveu est* it is provided, and *purveu que* provided that), past participle of *purveier* to provide. See PURVEY.]

pus (pus) *n.* thick, yellowish fluid that collects in abscesses and other infections in the body, and contains bacteria and dead white blood cells. [Latin *pūs.*]

Pu·san (pōō′sän′) *n.* chief port of South Korea, on the southeastern coast of the country. Pop. (1966 est.), 1,425,703.

push (poosh) *v.t.* **1.** to exert force upon or against so as to cause or tend to cause motion away from the force: *He pushed the door with his shoulder but couldn't seem to budge it.* **2.** to move by such exertion of force: *She pushed the baby carriage up the hill. He impatiently pushed the hair out of his eyes.* **3.** to urge with vigor and persistence the adoption or advancement of; recommend or advocate strongly: *a legislator who consistently pushes reform in government.* **4.** to make with effort or force, as against opposition or difficulty: *They pushed their way through the underbrush.* **5.** to put forcibly into some condition, situation, or position: *Increased demand has pushed prices up.* **6.** to advance or expand by or as by persistent or diligent effort; extend: *The settlers pushed the frontier farther west.* **7.** to put under pressure or stress; bear hard upon; press: *She always pushed her son to become a doctor.* **8.** to carry on, prosecute, or follow up with energy: *to push a claim.* **9.** *Informal.* to be close to, as in time; near; approach: *He's pushing fifty, but he looks younger.* **10.** *Slang.* to advertise persistently and otherwise make a determined effort to sell: *The company is really pushing their new brand of soap.* **11.** *Slang.* to sell (narcotic or hallucinogenic drugs) illegally. **12. to push around.** *Informal.* to deal roughly with; abuse; mistreat. —*v.i.* **1.** to exert force upon or against something so as or as if to move it: *If you push against the fence, it'll give way.* **2.** to move, advance, or proceed with effort or vigor or as against opposition: *The guards pushed through the crowd to get to the platform.* **3.** to put forth vigorous or persistent effort (often with *for*): *a group pushing for the adoption of the proposed bill.* —*n.* **1.** act of pushing or exerting force so as or as if to move something: *to give someone a push and knock him down.* **2.** vigorous or determined effort, attempt, or drive: *The troops made one last push to take the town.* **3.** something that stimulates or provokes; inducement or stimulus, as to action: *The economy has been lagging for months and needs a push of some kind.* **4.** case or time of stress or urgency; emergency. **5.** *Informal.* persevering energy or enterprise: *He doesn't have enough push to get ahead.* [Old French *pousser* to thrust, from Latin *pulsāre* to beat, strike, thrust.]

push·ball (poosh′bôl′) *n.* **1.** game in which players of two opposing teams try to push a large, inflated ball, usually six feet in diameter, across a goal line. **2.** ball used in this game.

push·but·ton (poosh′but′ən) *adj.* using or controlled by or as by automatic or remote-control mechanisms: *push-button warfare.*

push button, small button or knob pushed to open or close an electric circuit.

push·cart (poosh′kärt′) *n.* small cart pushed by hand, used esp. by a peddler.

push·er (poosh′ər) *n.* **1.** one who or that which pushes. **2.** airplane with its propeller or propellers located behind the wings. **3.** *Slang.* one who sells narcotic or hallucinogenic drugs illegally.

Push·kin, Alexander Ser·ge·ye·vich (poosh′kin; ser gā′yə vich) 1799–1837, Russian poet and dramatist.

push·o·ver (poosh′ō′vər) *n.* *Slang.* **1.** one who is easily defeated or imposed upon. **2.** anything easily done.

Push·tu (push′tōō) Pashto.

push-up (poosh′up′) *n.* exercise in which a person lies prone and, keeping his body straight, alternately raises and lowers himself by straightening and bending his arms.

push·y (poosh′ē) **push·i·er, push·i·est.** *adj. Informal.* self-assertive or aggressive in an offensive manner. —**push′i·ly,** *adv.* —**push′i·ness,** *n.*

pu·sil·la·nim·i·ty (pū′sə lə nim′ə tē) *n.* state or quality of being cowardly; cowardliness; faintheartedness.

pu·sil·lan·i·mous (pū′sə lan′ə məs) *adj.* lacking courage; fainthearted; cowardly. [Late Latin *pūsillanimis* (from Latin *pūsillus* very small + *animus* mind, soul) + -OUS.] —**pu′sil·lan′i·mous·ly,** *adv.*

puss[1] (poos) *n.* **1.** cat. **2.** girl or woman. [Possibly imitative of the spitting of a cat.]

puss[2] (poos) *n. Slang.* the face or mouth. [Irish *pus* lip, mouth.]

puss·y[1] (poos′ē) *pl.* **puss·ies.** *n.* cat. [PUSS[1] + -Y[2].]

pus·sy[2] (pus′ē) -**si·er, -si·est.** *adj.* forming, containing, or resembling pus. [PUS + -Y[1].]

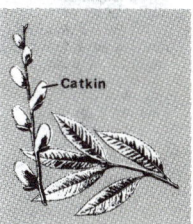
Catkin

puss·y·foot (poos′ē foot′) *v.i.* **1.** to move quietly, cautiously, or stealthily. **2.** to act in a cautious or timid manner; be unwilling to commit oneself, as on a political issue.

pussy willow, shrub or small tree, *Salix discolor,* growing in moist regions of eastern North America, bearing furry silvery-gray catkins.

Pussy willow

pus·tu·lant (pus′chə lənt) *adj.* causing pustules to form. —*n.* medicine or agent that causes pustules to form.

pus·tu·lar (pus′chə lər) *adj.* of, resembling, or characterized by pustules.

pus·tu·la·tion (pus′chə lā′shən) *n.* formation of pustules.

pus·tule (pus′chōōl) *n.* **1.** small, inflamed swelling of the skin containing pus. **2.** any similar swelling. [Latin *pustula* pimple, blister.]

put (poot) *v.t.* **put, put·ting.** *v.t.* **1.** to cause to be in a specified place or position; place; set; lay: *Put the package on the table. He put another log on the fire.* **2.** to cause to be in a specified condition: *Her smile put him at ease. Our troops put the enemy to flight.* **3.** to cause to undergo; subject: *to put a prisoner to death.* **4.** to set at a certain point or amount; estimate as being: *to put the value of a car at five hundred dollars.* **5.** to assign; ascribe; attribute: *The report put the blame on him.* **6.** to throw or cast with an overhand pushing motion: *to put the shot.* **7.** to propose for consideration or judgment: *to put a question to a person.* **8.** to express; state: *To put it mildly, we were surprised by his actions.* **9.** to render into another language or form of expression; translate: *to put a poem to music.* **11.** to bring to bear; apply: *to put one's knowledge to use.* **12.** to impose: *to put a tax on cigarettes.* **13.** to bet: *to put two dollars on a race horse.* **14.** to invest: *to put all one's money into stocks.* —*v.i.* to direct one's course; go; proceed: *to put out to sea.*

to put about. a. to put (a ship) on the opposite tack; cause to change direction. **b.** to change direction, as a ship.

to put across. *Informal.* **a.** to cause to be understood or accepted. **b.** to carry out with success.

to put aside (or **by).** to reserve for later use; save.

to put away. a. to reserve for later use; save. **b.** *Informal.* to consume by eating or drinking. **c.** *Informal.* to confine in a mental institution or jail. **d.** to give up; discard; abandon. **e.** *Informal.* to kill.

to put down. a. to put an end to by force or authority; suppress; crush: *to put down a rebellion.* **b.** to set down in writing. **c.** *Informal.* to treat in a disparaging or slighting manner; belittle, embarrass, or snub.

to put forth. a. to send out; sprout; grow: *The tree put forth leaves.* **b.** to exert: *to put forth great effort.* **c.** to propose; present: *to put forth several ideas.* **d.** to set out; start on one's way, as to sea.

to put forward. to propose; present: *to put forward a new theory.*

to put in. a. (of a ship) to enter port. **b.** *Informal.* to spend (time) in a specified manner: *to put in a day at the office.* **c.** to present or submit (a request, offer, claim, or the like). **d.** to interpose; insert: *He put in a good word for him.*

to put in for. to make an application or request for: *The soldier put in for a transfer.*

to put off. a. to postpone or delay: *to put off a trip, to put off making a decision.* **b.** to cause (someone) to wait until a later time. **c.** to get rid of by delay or evasion. **d.** to rid oneself of; take off; discard.

to put on. a. to clothe oneself with; don: *He put on his jacket.* **b.** to assume or adopt an affectation: *to put on airs.* **c.** to pretend; feign: *to put on a display of concern.* **d.** to stage, present, or perform: *to put on a play.* **e.** to apply: *The driver put on the brakes.* **f.** *Slang.* to tease or fool (a person); deceive playfully; poke fun at.

to put one (or **something**) **over on.** *Informal.* to deceive or trick.

to put out. a. to extinguish: *to put out a fire.* **b.** to disconcert; embarrass. **c.** to annoy; irritate; vex: *She was easily put out by little things.* **d.** to inconvenience: *Will it put you out to pick up the package for me?* **e.** to eject; expel. **f.** to publish; issue: *to put out a new edition of a book.* **g.** *Baseball.* to cause (a batter or base runner) to be out.

to put over. *Informal.* to complete (something) successfully.

to put through. 1. to have a successful conclusion. **2.** to cause to undergo or do: *to put a horse through exercises.*

to put to it. to place in a difficult situation: *He was put to it to keep up his grades.*

to put up. a. to erect; build. **b.** to preserve (food). **c.** to provide or obtain lodgings: *We put up for the night at a farmhouse.* **d.** to make available; provide: *to put up money for a project.* **e.** to stake; wager: *to put up two dollars on a racehorse.* **f.** to propose or nominate: *to put up a candidate for office.* **g.** to offer for public sale. **h.** to carry on: *to put up a struggle.* **i.** to show: *He put up a calm front when he was frightened.*

to put upon. to take advantage of; treat unfairly.

to put up to. *Informal.* to provoke to; incite to: *He put the other boys up to that prank.*

to put up with. to bear patiently; tolerate; endure.
—*n.* act of putting the shot. —*adj.* immobile; in place; fixed; settled: *The restless child would not stay put.* [From an unrecorded Old English word parallel to Old English *potian* to thrust.]

Syn. *v.t.* **1. Put, place** mean to bring or take an object to a certain location or position and leave it there. **Put** is the common word and stresses the action of placing an object: *Put the book down.* **Place** stresses a considered intent that is lacking in *put* and implies putting an object in a particular location: *Joan placed the dishes carefully on the table.*

pu·ta·tive (pū′tə tiv) *adj.* generally considered or supposed; reputed. [Late Latin *putātīvus* imaginary, from Latin *putāre* to think.]

put-down (poot′doun′) *n. Slang.* remark or action intended to belittle, embarrass, or reject someone.

put-on (*adj.*, poot′ŏn′, -ôn′; *n.*, poot′ŏn′, -ôn′) *adj.* pretended; assumed: *a put-on display of grief.* —*n.* **1.** act or instance of deceiving someone with a falsehood or practical joke. **2.** falsehood or practical joke: *The whole story was an elaborate put-on.*

put·out (poot′out′) *n. Baseball.* act or instance of putting out a batter or base runner.

pu·tre·fac·tion (pū′trə fak′shən) *n.* act or process of rotting; being rotten.

pu·tre·fac·tive (pū′trə fak′tiv) *adj.* **1.** causing putrefaction. **2.** of, relating to, or characterized by putrefaction.

pu·tre·fy (pū′trə fī′) -fied, -fy·ing. *v.t.* to cause to rot; make putrid. —*v.i.* to rot. [Latin *putrefacere* to make rotten, from *puter* rotten + *facere* to make.] —**Syn.** *v.i.* see **decay.**

pu·tres·cent (pū tres′ənt) *adj.* **1.** becoming rotten; decaying. **2.** of or relating to putrefaction. [Latin *putrēscēns,* present participle of *putrēscere* to grow rotten.] —**pu·tres′cence,** *n.*

pu·trid (pū′trid) *adj.* **1.** being in a decayed, foul-smelling state; rotten. **2.** characteristic of or produced by putrefaction. **3.** extremely bad; terrible; vile: *a putrid situation, a putrid place.* [Latin *putridus* rotten, corrupt.] —**pu·trid′i·ty, pu·trid′ness,** *n.* —**pu·trid′ly,** *adv.*

putsch (pooch) *also,* **Putsch.** *n.* armed uprising or revolt. [German *Putsch.*]

putt (put) *n. Golf.* light stroke made on a putting green in an attempt to send the ball into the cup. —*v.t., v.i.* to hit (a ball) with such a stroke. [Form of PUT.]

put·tee (put′ē, pu tē′) *n.* long, narrow strip of cloth wound round the leg from ankle to knee, worn as a protection and support to the leg. [Hindi *paṭṭī* bandage, band².]

put·ter¹ (put′ər) *also,* **pot·ter.** *v.i.* to work, act, or proceed in a trifling or aimless way. —*v.t.* to waste (time) in puttering (with *away*). [Form of POTTER².] —**put′ter·er,** *n.*

putt·er² (put′ər) *n.* **1.** golf club with a short shaft and a metal head having little or no loft, used in putting. **2.** one who putts. [PUTT + -ER.]

putting green, green (def. 4).

put·ty (put′ē) *pl.,* **-ties.** *n.* soft, doughlike mixture of whiting and linseed oil, used esp. for filling cracks or attaching panes of glass.
—*v.t.,* **-tied, -ty·ing.** to fill, fasten, or cover with putty. [French *potée* loam for molding; originally, potful, from *pot* pot, jug; of Germanic origin.]

put-up (poot′up′) *adj. Informal.* devised or arranged beforehand in a secret or underhand manner: *a put-up job.*

puz·zle (puz′əl) *n.* **1.** problem, game, or toy designed to challenge one's skill and ingenuity. **2.** one who or that which perplexes or confuses. **3.** state of perplexity or difficulty; quandary; dilemma. —*v.t.,* **-zled, -zling. 1.** to perplex; bewilder: *His recent behavior puzzles me.* **2.** to solve or arrive at an understanding of, esp. by persistent effort (with *out*). —*v.i.* to be perplexed: *I'm puzzled about this situation.* **2. to puzzle over.** to endeavor to understand or solve; ponder. [Of uncertain origin.] —**puz′zler,** *n.*

Syn. *v.t.* **1. Puzzle, perplex, bewilder** mean to confuse or disturb mentally. **Puzzle** emphasizes mild frustration when faced with a problem that is difficult to solve or understand: *The boy's unusual behavior puzzled the doctor.* **Perplex** suggests a deeper feeling of confusion: *The attitudes and behavior of the younger generation perplexed the old man.* **Bewilder** stresses the sense of confusion to the degree where one is unable to think clearly or act coherently: *The contradictory orders from the captain bewildered the crew.*

puz·zle·ment (puz′əl mənt) *n.* state of being puzzled; perplexity; confusion.

Pvt., Private.

PWA, Public Works Administration.

pwt., pennyweight.

PX, Post Exchange.

py·e·mi·a (pī ē′mē ə) *also,* **py·ae·mi·a.** *n.* disease caused by the releasing of pus into the bloodstream. [Modern Latin *pyaemia,* from Greek *pyon* pus + *haima* blood.]

Pyg·ma·lion (pig māl′yən, -mā′lē ən) *n. Greek Legend.* sculptor and King of Cyprus who fell in love with the statue of a maiden he had carved. Aphrodite brought the statue, called Galatea, to life in response to Pygmalion's prayers.

Pyg·my (pig′mē) *pl.,* **-mies.** *also,* **Pig·my.** *n.* **1.a.** member of a dark-skinned people of small stature living in the tropical rain forests of Africa. **b.** member of a group of small stature living in southeastern Asia. Also, **Ne·gri′to. 2. pygmy.** very small or insignificant person or thing. —*adj.* **1.** of or relating to the Pygmies. **2. pygmy.** very small or insignificant. [Latin *pygmaeus* dwarfish, from Greek *pygmaios* literally, as tall as a *pygmē,* from *pygmē* fist, cubit.]

py·ja·mas (pə jä′məz, -jam′əz) *n.pl. British.* pajamas.

py·lon (pī′lon) *n.* **1.** monumental gateway, esp. to an Egyptian temple. **2.** tower for guiding aviators, esp. in a race. **3.** tall steel tower that supports high-tension wires. [Greek *pylōn* gateway.]

py·lo·rus (pī lôr′əs) *pl.,* **-lo·ri** (-lôr′ī). *n.* opening between the stomach and the duodenum. [Late Latin *pylōrus,* from Greek *pylōros* gatekeeper, pylorus; because it was thought of as the gatekeeper to the intestines.] —**py·lor′ic,** *adj.*

Pym, John (pim) 1584–1643, English statesman.

Pyong·yang (pyung′yäng′) *n.* capital of North Korea, in the west-central part of the country. Pop. (1960 est.), 653,100.

py·or·rhe·a (pī′ə rē′ə) *also,* **py·or·rhoe·a.** *n.* inflammation of the gums and other soft tissues that surround the teeth, resulting in the loosening of the teeth. [Modern Latin *pyorrhoea,* from Greek *pyon* pus + *rhoia* flow, flux.]

pyr-, form of pyro- before *h* and certain vowels.

pyr·a·mid (pir′ə mid′) *n.* **1.a.** massive structure of masonry, usually having a square base and four triangular sides that slope upward to an apex, built esp. in ancient Egypt. **b. Pyramids.** three such structures built as royal tombs, including the Great Pyramid, located at Giza,

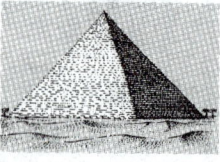

Pyramid

Egypt. **2.** solid figure having a polygonal base and triangular sides intersecting at a point. **3.** anything resembling a pyramid in form or structure: *The acrobats formed a human pyramid.* —*v.t.* to arrange or raise in or as in the shape of a pyramid. —*v.i.* **1.** to assume the shape of a pyramid. **2.** to rise or increase, esp. on a progressively broader base, as prices or wages: *The cost of food has pyramided in recent years.* [Latin *pȳramis* the geometric figure, Egyptian tomb shaped like such a figure, from Greek *pȳramis;* possibly of Egyptian origin.]

py·ram·i·dal (pi ram′əd əl) *adj.* of, relating to, or resembling a pyramid. Also, **pyr·a·mid·ic** (pir′ə mid′ik), **pyr·a·mid′i·cal.** —**py·ram′i·dal·ly,** *adv.*

Pyr·a·mus and Thisbe (pir′ə məs) *Classical Mythology.* two young lovers of Babylon. Believing Thisbe slain by a lion, Pyramus took his own life, and Thisbe, upon finding his body, killed herself.

at; āpe; cär; end; mē; it; īce; hot; ōld; fôrk; wood; fōōl; oil; out; up; ūse; turn; sing; thin; this; zh in treasure; ə in ago, taken, pencil, lemon, circus.

pyre (pīr) *n.* pile of wood or other combustible material, used esp. for burning a dead body. [Latin *pyra* funeral pyre, from Greek *pyrá*.]

Pyr·e·nees (pir′ə nēz′) *n.,pl.* mountain range in southwestern Europe extending along the border of France and Spain from the Bay of Biscay to the Mediterranean Sea. —**Pyr′e·ne′an,** *adj.*

py·re·thrum (pī rē′thrəm) *n.* **1.** any of several chrysanthemums, as *Chrysanthemum cinerariaefolium,* whose dried flowers are ground and used as an insecticide. **2.** insecticide made from the dried flowers of these chrysanthemums. [Modern Latin *Pyrethrum,* going back to Greek *pyrethron* feverfew, possibly from *pyretos* fever.]

py·ret·ic (pī ret′ik) *adj.* relating to, causing, or affected with fever; febrile. [Modern Latin *pyreticus,* from Greek *pyretos* fever, from *pȳr* fire.]

Py·rex (pī′reks) *n. Trademark.* heat-resistant glass used in ovenware, laboratory glassware, and telescope mirrors.

pyr·i·dox·ine (pir′ə dok′sēn, -sin) *n.* water-soluble vitamin of the vitamin B complex, found esp. in whole-grain cereals, yeast, and liver; vitamin B₆. Formula: $C_8H_{11}NO_3$.

py·rim·i·dine (pī rim′ə dēn′, pi-) *n.* **1.** colorless, liquid or crystalline organic compound, the fundamental form of a group of nitrogenous bases that are constituents of nucleic acid and other biochemical substances. Formula: $C_4H_4N_2$. **2.** any of these bases, as cytosine, thymine, or uracil.

py·rite (pī′rīt) *n.* hard, shiny, yellow iron disulfide often mistaken for gold, used in the manufacture of sulfuric acid. Formula: FeS_2. Also, **fool's gold.** [Latin *pyrītēs.* See PYRITES.]

py·ri·tes (pī rī′tēz, pi-, pī′rīts) *n.,pl.* any of various compounds of sulfur and a metal, as marcasite or chalcopyrite. [Latin *pyrītēs* flint, from Greek *pyrītēs* flint, relating to fire, from *pȳr* fire.]

pyro- *combining form* fire or heat, or resulting from fire or heat: *pyromania, pyrotechnic, pyroelectric.* [Greek *pȳr* fire.]

py·ro·e·lec·tric (pī′rō i lek′trik) *adj.* of, relating to, or exhibiting pyroelectricity. —*n.* pyroelectric substance.

py·ro·e·lec·tric·i·ty (pī′rō i lek′tris′ə tē) *n.* polarized charges of electricity that occur on certain crystals when the temperature of the crystals is changed.

py·ro·gen·ic (pī′rō jen′ik) *adj.* **1.** producing or produced by fever or heat. **2.** *Geology.* igneous.

py·rog·ra·phy (pī rog′rə fē) *n.* art or process of burning designs on material, as on wood or leather. —**py·ro·graph** (pī′rə graf′), **py·rog′ra·pher,** *n.* —**py·ro·graph′ic,** *adj.*

py·ro·ma·ni·a (pī′rə mā′nē ə) *n.* uncontrollable desire to set fire to something. [PYRO- + -MANIA.] —**py′ro·ma′ni·ac,** *adj., n.* —**py·ro·ma·ni·a·cal** (pī′rō mə nī′ə kəl), *adj.*

py·rom·e·ter (pī rom′ə tər) *n.* device designed to measure high temperature.

py·ro·tech·nic (pī′rə tek′nik) *adj.* **1.** of or relating to fireworks. **2.** resembling or suggesting fireworks; brilliant: *a pyrotechnic display of wit.* Also, **py′ro·tech′ni·cal.** [PYRO- + TECHNIC.] —**py′ro·tech′ni·cal·ly,** *adv.*

py·ro·tech·nics (pī′rə tek′niks) *n.,pl.* **1.** manufacture or use of fireworks. Also, **py′ro·tech′ny. 2.** display of fireworks. **3.** brilliant, dazzling, or sensational display, as of wit, eloquence, or musical ability. ▲ construed as singular in def. 1 and as singular or plural in defs. 2 and 3. —**py′ro·tech′nist,** *n.*

py·rox·y·lin (pī rok′sə lin) *also,* **py·rox·y·line** (pī rok′sə lēn′, -lin). *n.* very flammable substance made by the limited nitration of cellulose, used in the manufacture of such products as collodion and artificial leather. [PYRO- + Greek *xylon* wood + -IN¹; referring to its very flammable nature.]

Pyr·rha (pir′ə) *n. Greek Mythology.* wife of Deucalion.

Pyrrhic victory, victory won at an excessive or ruinous cost. [From *Pyrrhus,* who sustained extremely heavy losses in defeating the Romans in 279 B.C.]

Pyr·rhus (pir′əs) *n.* c.318–272 B.C., king of Epirus.

py·ru·vic acid (pī rōō′vik) colorless, organic acid that is an important intermediate in the metabolism of carbohydrates and proteins. Formula: $CH_3COCOOH$ [PYRO- + Latin *ūva* grape + -IC + ACID.]

Py·thag·o·ras (pi thag′ər əs) *n.* c.580–c.500 B.C., Greek mathematician and philosopher.

Py·thag·o·re·an (pi thag′ə rē′ən) *adj.* of or relating to Pythagoras, his doctrines, or his followers. —*n.* follower of Pythagoras.

Pythagorean theorem, theorem that the square of the length of the hypotenuse of a right triangle is equal to the sum of the squares of the lengths of the sides.

Pyth·i·an (pith′ē ən) *adj.* **1.** of or relating to Apollo, Delphi, or the Delphic oracle. **2.** of or relating to the Pythian games. [Latin *Pythius* relating to Delphi or Apollo (from Greek *Pythios* relating to Delphi, from *Pythō* earlier name of Delphi) + -AN.]

Pythian games, national festival in ancient Greece, held every four years at Delphi in honor of Apollo.

Pyth·i·as (pith′ē əs) *see* **Damon and Pythias.**

py·thon (pī′thon, -thən) *n.* any of a small group of nonpoisonous snakes, genus *Python,* found in tropical regions of Asia, Africa, the East Indies, and Australia, that coil around and suffocate or crush their prey. Length: 3–30 feet. [Latin *Pȳthōn* serpent killed by Apollo near Delphi, from Greek *Pȳthōn,* from *Pȳthō* earlier name of Delphi.]

py·tho·ness (pī′thə nis) *n.* **1.** priestess of Apollo at Delphi. **2.** prophetess. [Late Greek *pȳthōn* spirit of divination + -ESS.]

pyx (piks) *n.* **1.** container made of precious metal in which the consecrated Host is kept, esp. a small, flat box for carrying the Host to the sick. **2.** box or chest at a mint in which sample coins are deposited and held for testing. [Latin *pyxis* box¹, from Greek *pyxis* box¹ (originally made of boxwood), from *pyxos* boxwood.]

pyx·id·i·um (pik sid′ē əm) *pl.,* **-i·a** (-ē ə). *n.* seed vessel having an upper portion that acts as a lid by splitting open. [Modern Latin *pyxidium,* from Greek *pyxidion* little box, diminutive of *pyxis* box¹. See PYX.]

Pyxidium

---

at; āpe; cär; end; mē; it; īce; hot; ōld; fôrk; wood; fōol; oil; out; up; ūse; turn; sing; thin; this; zh in treasure; ə in ago, taken, pencil, lemon, circus.

q, Q (kū) *pl.,* **q's, Q's.** *n.* seventeenth letter of the English alphabet.
q. **1.** quart. **2.** quarter; quarterly. **3.** quarto. **4.** query. **5.** question. **6.** quire¹.
Q., Queen.
Qa·tar (kä′tər) *n.* country, an independent sheikdom, in southwestern Asia, on the Persian Gulf coast of Arabia. Capital, Doha. Area, 8500 sq. mi. Pop. (1975 est.), 100,000.
Q.E.D., which was to be proved or demonstrated. [Abbreviation of Latin *quod erat demonstrandum.*]
QM, quartermaster.
QMG, Quartermaster General.
qr. **1.** quarter; quarterly. **2.** quire¹.
qt. **1.** quart; quarts. **2.** quantity.
q.t. *Slang.* **1.** quiet. **2. on the q.t.** in secret.
qty., quantity.
quack¹ (kwak) *n.* harsh, flat sound made by a duck. —*v.i.* to make such a sound. [Imitative.]
quack² (kwak) *n.* **1.a.** unqualified person who falsely practices as a doctor. **b.** any incompetent, poorly qualified doctor. **2.** one with little knowledge or skill who poses as an expert; charlatan. —*adj.* **1.** of, relating to, or characteristic of a quack or quackery; fake: *quack medicine, a quack solution.* [Short for earlier *quacksalver* charlatan, from obsolete Dutch *quacksalver* literally, one who prattles about his ointments, from *quacken* to prattle + *salf* ointment.]
quack·er·y (kwak′ər ē) *pl.,* **-er·ies.** *n.* practices or methods of a quack; fakery.
quack grass, grassy weed, *Agropyron repens,* having a white creeping stem, that spreads easily in cultivated ground. Also, **couch grass, quitch, quitch grass.**
quad¹ (kwod) *n. Informal.* quadrangle or courtyard, esp. one at a college.
quad² (kwod) *n. Informal.* quadruplet.
quad³ (kwod) *n.* quadrat.
Quad·ra·ges·i·ma (kwod′rə jes′ə mə) *n.* **1.** first Sunday in Lent. Also, **Quadragesima Sunday. 2.** formerly, the forty days of Lent. [Latin *quadrāgēsima (diēs)* literally, fortieth, fortieth (day); reckoned approximately as the fortieth day before Easter and therefore applied to the forty days of Lent.]
quad·ran·gle (kwod′rang′gəl) *n.* **1.** polygon having four angles and four sides; quadrilateral. **2.a.** square or oblong space, esp. a courtyard, partially or totally surrounded by a building or buildings. **b.** building or buildings surrounding such a space. [Late Latin *quadrangulum* square, going back to Latin *quadrus* square, fourfold + *angulus* corner, angle.] —**quad·ran′gu·lar,** *adj.*
quad·rant (kwod′rənt) *n.* **1.** quarter of a circle, or an arc of 90 degrees. **2.** instrument consisting of an arc divided into 90 degrees, used in navigation and astronomy for measuring altitude or angular distance above the horizon. **3.** any of the four parts into which a plane is divided by perpendicular coordinate axes. [Latin *quadrāns* a fourth part, quarter.]

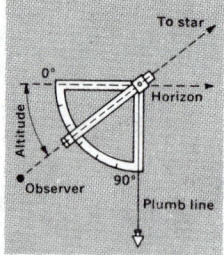

Quadrant (def. 2)

quad·rat (kwod′rət) *n.* blank piece of type, lower than the face of type, used in printing for spacing, filling out ends of lines, or indentations. [Form of QUADRATE.]
quad·rate (*adj., n.,* kwod′rāt, -rit; *v.,* kwod′rāt) *adj.* square or rectangular. —*n.* square or rectangular object or area. —*v.i.* **-rat·ed, -rat·ing.**

to agree, correspond, or conform (with *with*). [Latin *quadrātus* squared, past participle of *quadrāre* to make square.]
quad·rat·ic (kwod rat′ik) *adj. Algebra.* of, relating to, or involving a quantity or quantities that are squared but none that are raised to a higher power. $x^2 + 4x + 3 = 15$ is a quadratic equation. —*n.* quadratic equation or expression. [QUADRATE + -IC.]
quad·ra·ture (kwod′rə choor′, -chər) *n.* **1.** process of finding a square equal in area to the surface of a given geometrical figure. **2.** an angular distance of 90 degrees between two celestial bodies as measured from a third celestial body. **3.** the first or the third quarter of the moon. [Latin *quadrātūra* a squaring.]
quad·ren·ni·al (kwod ren′ē əl) *adj.* **1.** occurring every four years. **2.** lasting four years. [Latin *quadrennium* period of four years (from *quadrus* fourfold, square + *annus* year) + -AL¹.] —**quad·ren′ni·al·ly,** *adv.*
quad·ri·lat·er·al (kwod′rə lat′ər əl) *adj.* having four sides. —*n.* polygon with four sides and four angles. [Latin *quadrilaterus* four-sided (from *quadrus* fourfold, square + *latus* side) + -AL¹.]
qua·drille (kwä dril′, kwə-) *n.* **1.** square dance popular in the nineteenth century, performed by two to four couples and consisting of five figures or parts. **2.** music for such a dance. [French *quadrille* square dance with four couples, small troop of cavalry, from Spanish *cuadrilla* troop, from *cuadra* a square, from Latin *quadra.*]

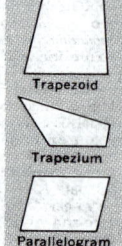

Quadrilaterals

quad·ril·lion (kwod ril′yən) *n.* **1.** in the United States and France, the cardinal number that is represented by 1 followed by fifteen zeros. **2.** in Great Britain and Germany, the cardinal number that is represented by 1 followed by twenty-four zeros. —*adj.* numbering one quadrillion. [Latin *quadrus* fourfold, square + (M)ILLION.] —**quad·ril′lionth,** *adj., n.*
quad·ri·no·mi·al (kwod′rə nō′mē əl) *n.* polynomial with four terms. [Latin *quadrus* fourfold, square + (BI)NOMIAL.]
quad·riv·i·um (kwod riv′ē əm) *n.* four sciences, arithmetic, geometry, astronomy, and music, that composed the more advanced group of the seven liberal arts in medieval universities. Distinguished from **trivium.** [Late Latin *quadrivium* from Latin *quadrivium* crossroads, from *quadrus* fourfold, square + *via* way, road.]
quad·roon (kwod rōōn′) *n.* one who has one Negro grandparent. [Spanish *cuarterón,* from *cuarto* a fourth part, from Latin *quartus* fourth.]
quad·ru·ped (kwod′rə ped′) *n.* any animal, esp. a mammal, having four feet. —*adj.* having four feet. [Latin *quadrupēs* having four feet, from *quadrus* fourfold, square + *pēs* foot.]
quad·ru·ple (kwo drōō′pəl, -drup′əl, kwod′rə pəl) *adj.* **1.** consisting of four parts or members: *a quadruple alliance made up of four western European nations.* **2.** four times as great or as many: *The value of the painting is quadruple what it was a hundred years ago.* **3.** *Music.* having four beats in each measure, the first and third being accented: *quadruple meter, quadruple time.* —*v.t., v.i.,* **-pled, -pling.** to make or become four times as great or as many; multiply by four. —*n.* number or amount four times as great as another. [Latin *quadruplus* fourfold.]
quad·rup·let (kwo drup′lit, -drōō′plit, kwod′rə plit) *n.* **1.a.** one of four offspring born at one birth. **b. quadruplets.** four offspring born at one birth. **2.** any set or combination of four. [QUADRUPLE + -ET.]
qua·dru·pli·cate (*adj., n.,* kwo drōō′plə kit; *v.,* kwo drōō′plə kāt′) *adj.* four times as great or as many; quadruple. —*v.t.* **-cat·ed, -cat·ing.** to multiply by four; quadruple. —*n.* one of four identical things, esp. copies of printed matter. [Latin *quadruplicātus,* past participle of *quadruplicāre* to multiply by four.] —**quad·ru′pli·ca′tion,** *n.*

at; āpe; cär; end; mē; it; īce; hot; ōld; fôrk; wood; fōōl; oil; out; up; ūse; turn; sing; thin; this; zh in treasure; ə in ago, taken, pencil, lemon, circus.

quaes·tor (kwes′tər, kwĕs′-) *n.* **1.** in ancient Rome, any of various officials who were in charge of the public taxes and expenditures. **2.** in ancient Rome, public prosecutor in serious criminal cases. [Latin *quaestor.*] —**quaes′tor·ship′,** *n.*

quaff (kwăf, kwäf) *v.t., v.i.* to drink heartily and deeply. —*n.* hearty drink. [Of uncertain origin.]

quag (kwag, kwog) *n.* quagmire; marsh. [Of uncertain origin.]

quag·ga (kwag′ə) *n.* extinct southern African zebra, *Equus quagga,* which had a reddish-brown coat with white stripes on the head, neck, and shoulders. [Probably of Bantu origin.]

quag·gy (kwag′ē, kwog′ē) *-gi·er, -gi·est. adj.* soft and muddy; marshy. [QUAG + -Y¹.]

quag·mire ((kwag′mīr′, kwog′-) *n.* **1.** soft, muddy ground that yields under the foot. **2.** position or situation from which extrication is difficult: *to be caught in a quagmire of debts.* [QUAG + -MIRE.]

Quagga

qua·hog (kwô′hôg′, -hog′) *n.* roundish hard-shelled clam, *Venus mercenaria,* found in shallow waters along the Atlantic coast of North America. [Short for Algonquian *poquaŭhock,* from *pokhemi* closed + *hogki* shell.]

quail¹ (kwāl) *pl.* **quails** or **quail.** *n.* any of various game birds, family Phasianidae, usually having gray or brown plumage that is often speckled with white, as the **European quail,** *Coturnix coturnix.* Length: 7–12 inches. [Old French *quaille,* from Medieval Latin *quaccula* quail; of imitative origin.]

quail² (kwāl) *v.i.* to recoil or shrink back in fear. [Of uncertain origin.]

quaint (kwānt) *adj.* **1.** charming or attractive in an old-fashioned way: *the quaint, narrow streets of the old town.* **2.** pleasingly unusual or odd: *He found Nanette's French accent quaint and attractive.* [Old French *queinte, cointe* neat, fine, from Latin *cognitus* known, past participle of *cognōscere* to know.] —**quaint′ly,** *adv.* —**quaint′ness,** *n.*

European quail

quake (kwāk) **quaked, quak·ing.** *v.i.* to shake, tremble. —*n.* **1.** trembling or shuddering. **2.** earthquake. [Old English *cwacian* to shake, tremble.] —**Syn.** *v.i.* see **shake.**

Quak·er (kwā′kər) *n.* member of the Society of Friends, a Christian denomination founded in the seventeenth century. Also, **Friend.** [QUAKE + -ER¹; supposedly because the society's founder, George Fox, urged people to *quake* at the word of God.] —**Quak′er·ess,** *n.*

Quak·er·ism (kwā′kə riz′əm) *n.* doctrines and practices of the Quakers.

Quak·er·la·dies (kwā′kər lā′dēz) *n.,pl.* bluet.

qual·i·fi·ca·tion (kwol′ə fi kā′shən) *n.* **1.** act of qualifying; being qualified. **2.** any ability, accomplishment, or the like that makes a person suitable for, or is a requirement for, a certain position, privilege, office, or other function. **3.** restriction or modification: *He is, without qualification, the finest man I've ever known.*

qual·i·fied (kwol′ə fīd′) *adj.* **1.a.** having the necessary abilities, accomplishments, or requirements for something, as a position, privilege, office, or other function: *John is not qualified to teach on the college level.* **b.** eligible by law or custom: *a qualified voter.* **2.** limited; restricted: *The play was at best a qualified success.*

qual·i·fi·er (kwol′ə fī′ər) *n.* **1.** one who or that which qualifies. **2.** word that modifies another word, as an adjective or adverb.

qual·i·fy (kwol′ə fī′) **-fied, -fy·ing.** *v.t.* **1.** to make capable or suitable, as for a certain position, privilege, office, or other function. **2.** to make legally capable; give the legal power to. **3.** to limit; restrict; modify: *His statement was too general and should have been qualified with the phrase "in most cases."* **4.** to describe or designate in a particular way; name or characterize: *The theologian's beliefs were qualified as heretical.* **5.** Grammar. to modify the meaning of (a word or phrase). —*v.i.* to meet the necessary standards or requirements: *He expects to qualify for the job.* [Medieval Latin *qualificare* to provide with a quality, from Latin *quālis* of what sort + *facere* to make.] —**qual′i·fi′a·ble,** *adj.* —**qual′i·fi′er,** *n.*

qual·i·ta·tive (kwol′ə tā′tiv) *adj.* of or relating to quality. Distinguished from **quantitative.** —**qual′i·ta′tive·ly,** *adv.*

qualitative analysis, procedure for identifying the constituents in a chemical substance by employing both physical and chemical tests. Distinguished from **quantitative analysis.**

qual·i·ty (kwol′ə tē) *pl.* **-ties.** *n.* **1.** that which defines something or makes it what it is. **2.** distinguishing or inherent feature: *He has all the qualities of a successful businessman.* **3.** degree of excellence; grade: *Our butcher sells only meat that is of a very high quality.* **4.** excellence; superiority: *The store prides itself on the quality of its wines.* **5.** *Music.* timbre of a tone, voice, or musical instrument. **6.** high social position: *people of quality.* [Latin *quálitās* nature, property.]

Syn. 2. Quality, trait, attribute mean some identifying aspect of a thing. **Quality** usually implies a judgment about some distinguishing feature: *Generosity is one of his good qualities.* **Trait** and **attribute** are more neutral terms. **Trait** is usually restricted to persons or types: *Red hair and freckles are traits in Jim's family.* **Attribute** is a quality essential to the nature of a person or thing: *Omniscience is an attribute of God.*

qualm (kwäm) *n.* **1.** twinge of conscience; compunction: *to have qualms about cheating.* **2.** sudden feeling of apprehension or doubt; misgiving. **3.** sudden, but quickly passing, feeling of faintness, nausea, or the like. [Of uncertain origin.] —**qualm′ish,** *adj.*

quan·da·ry (kwon′dər ē, -drē) *pl.* **-ries.** *n.* state of difficulty or uncertainty; predicament. [Of uncertain origin.]

quan·ti·fy (kwan′tə fī′) **-fied, -fy·ing.** *v.t.* to calculate or express the quantity of.

quan·ti·ta·tive (kwon′tə tā′tiv) *adj.* of or relating to quantity. Distinguished from **qualitative.** —**quan′ti·ta′tive·ly,** *adv.*

quantitative analysis, procedure for determining the amounts of each constituent of a chemical substance, as by measuring weights and volumes. Distinguished from **qualitative analysis.**

quan·ti·ty (kwon′tə tē) *pl.* **-ties.** *n.* **1.** specified or indefinite number or amount: *The recipe calls for a small quantity of water.* **2.** large or considerable amount or number: *It is often less expensive to buy goods in quantity.* **3.** property of a thing that is determinable by measurement. **4.** amount, number, or algebraic expression representing a value. **5.** relative length or brevity of a vowel sound or syllable in pronunciation or prosody. **6.** relative duration of a note or tone. [Latin *quantitās* greatness, amount.]

Syn. 1. Quantity, amount mean a measure of extent, duration, volume, magnitude, or value. **Quantity** is used chiefly of things measured or measurable in bulk: *This hotel buys a vast quantity of meat every day.* **Amount** is usually applied to things that are divisible into units admitting of exact measurement and designates the sum total or aggregate of all the units viewed as a whole: *The amount of the fine is ten dollars.*

quan·tum (kwon′təm) *pl.* **-ta** (-tə) *n. Physics.* small, separate amount, or packet, of energy. [Latin *quantum,* neuter of *quantus* how much.]

quantum theory, theory, formulated by Max Planck in 1900, stating that radiant energy is emitted and absorbed in quanta, rather than in a continuous manner.

quar·an·tine (kwôr′ən tēn′, kwor′-) *n.* **1.** isolation imposed on a person, animal, place, or object affected with, or considered to be a carrier of, an infectious disease, in order to prevent the spread of the disease. **2.** place where such isolation is imposed. **3.** any enforced isolation. —*v.t.* **1.** to impose isolation on in order to prevent the spreading of a disease; put in quarantine. **2.** to isolate or exclude from normal relations, as for political, social, or economic reasons: *The country was quarantined after its unprovoked attack on its neighbor.* [Italian *quarantina* isolation to prevent the spread of disease (referring to the period of forty days during which ships from regions noted for contagious diseases were formerly isolated), from *quaranta* forty, from Latin *quadrāginta.*]

quark (kwôrk) *n. Nuclear Physics.* one of three hypothetical particles that are thought to be the basic constituents of all known atomic particles. [Named by Murray Gell-Mann, 1929–, American physicist, from a word coined by James Joyce in *Finnegans Wake.*]

quar·rel (kwôr′əl, kwor′-) *n.* **1.** conflict or difference of opinion that leads to the suspension of friendly relations. **2.** cause for such a conflict or difference of opinion. —*v.i.* **-reled, -rel·ing;** *also, British,* **-relled, -rel·ling. 1.** to engage in a quarrel: *The children quarreled about who would ride the bicycle first.* **2.** to find fault; complain (with): *We quarreled with his methods, not with his goals.* [Old French *querele* dispute, from Latin *querēla* complaint.] —**quar′rel·er;** *also, British,* **quar′rel·ler,** *n.*

quar·rel·some (kwôr′əl səm, kwor′-) *adj.* inclined and ready to quarrel, esp. in a petty manner. —**quar′rel·some·ly,** *adv.* —**quar′rel·some·ness,** *n.*

quar·ry¹ (kwôr′ē, kwor′ē) *n.,* **-ries.** *n.* excavation from which stone is cut or blasted for use in building, road construction, or the like. —*v.t.,* **-ried, -ry·ing. 1.** to obtain from or as from a quarry: *to quarry marble.* **2.** to make a quarry in: *to quarry a hillside.* [Old French *quarriere* quarry of stone, from Late Latin *quadrāria* quarry for squared stones, going back to Latin *quadrus* square.] —**quar′ri·er,** *n.*

quar·ry² (kwôr′ē, kwor′ē) *n.,* **-ries.** *n.* **1.** animal hunted or pursued; prey. **2.** anything hunted or pursued. [Modification of Old French *cuiree,* originally, parts of a slain animal wrapped in a skin and given

to the hounds after a hunt, from *cuir* skin, from Latin *corium*.] —**Syn. 2.** see **victim.**

quart (kwôrt) *n.* **1.** unit of liquid measure equal to one-fourth of a gallon, or two pints. **2.** unit of dry measure equal to one-eighth of a peck. See **weights and measures** for table. **3.** container that holds a quart. [Old French *quarte* measure of capacity, from Latin *quárta (pars)* a fourth (part).]

quar·tan (kwôr′tən) *adj.* recurring every seventy-two hours, or every fourth day, counting inclusively. —*n.* malarial fever which recurs every fourth day, counting each recurrence on the first and the last day of a cycle. [Old French *quartaine* fever recurring every fourth day, from Latin *quártāna (febris)* (fever) occurring every fourth day, going back to *quártus* fourth.]

quar·ter (kwôr′tər) *n.* **1.** one of four equal or corresponding parts into which anything is or may be divided; one fourth. **2.** coin of the United States and Canada worth twenty-five cents, or one-quarter of a dollar. **3.** one-fourth of an hour; fifteen minutes or the moment marking the beginning or the end of this period. **4.** one-fourth of a year; three months. **5.** part of an academic year, usually lasting three months. **6.** *Astronomy.* **a.** fourth part of the period of the moon's revolution around the earth, lasting about seven days. **b.** either of the two phases of the moon when one-half of its disk is illuminated as seen from earth. **7.** *Sports.* one of the four equal time periods into which certain games, as football or basketball, are divided. **8.** one-fourth of a yard; nine inches; span. **9.** one-fourth of a hundredweight, in the United States, equal to twenty-five pounds, and in Great Britain, twenty-eight pounds. **10.** one of the four principal divisions of the compass. **11.** rear part of a ship's side. **12.** in slaughtering, one of the four parts into which an animal's carcass is divided; half of a side. **13.** *Heraldry.* **a.** one of four or more divisions of a shield made by perpendicular lines. **b.** charge that occupies such a division, esp. one in the upper right fourth of a shield. **14.** part of a boot or shoe above the heel that extends from the center of the back to the vamp on both sides. **15.** particular section or district, as of a city or town: *Sightseers are delighted with the quaint French quarter.* **16.** person, place, or group, esp. one that is unspecified: *The ruling came from the right quarters. The marchers came from all quarters.* **17.a. quarters.** place of residence; living accommodations: *winter quarters.* **b.** proper or assigned position or station, as on a warship. **18.** forequarters or hindquarters of a quadruped, esp. of a horse. **19.** mercy, esp. when granted to a defeated enemy. **20. at close quarters,** at close range; very close together; nearby. —*v.t.* **1.** to divide into four equal parts. **2.** to divide into several parts or pieces. **3.** to provide with living accommodations; lodge: *to quarter the troops for the night.* **4.** to cut the body of (an executed person) into four parts. **5.** to place or bear (several coats of arms) upon one shield. —*v.i.* **1.** to have or be assigned living accommodations; lodge. **2.** (of wind) to blow on a ship's quarter. —*adj.* **1.** being one of four equal parts. **2.** constituting one-fourth of a standard value. [Old French *quartier* a fourth part, district, from Latin *quártárius* a fourth part, from *quártus* fourth.]

quar·ter·back (kwôr′tər bak′) *n. Football.* **1.** player whose position is directly behind the center, and who directs the team and calls signals for the offense. **2.** position played by such a player.

quarter day, any of the four days of the year, regarded as the beginning of a new quarter, when quarterly payments usually are due.

quar·ter·deck (kwôr′tər dek′) *n.* part of the upper deck of a ship extending between the stern and mainmast, reserved esp. for officers.

quar·ter·hour (kwôr′tər our′) *also,* **quarter hour.** *n.* **1.** fifteen minutes. **2.** point on a clock fifteen minutes before or after an hour.

quar·ter·ly (kwôr′tər lē) *adj.* occurring at intervals of three months: *the quarterly interest on a savings account.* —*n. pl.,* **-lies.** publication issued four times a year, or once every three months. —*adv.* once every three months: *The payments were made quarterly.*

quar·ter·mas·ter (kwôr′tər mas′tər) *n.* **1.** military officer responsible for providing quarters, clothing, food, equipment, and the like for troops. **2.** in the U.S. Navy, petty officer on a ship who is in charge of navigation and certain equipment, as compasses and signals.

quar·tern (kwôr′tərn) *n.* quarter, or fourth part, of certain weights and units of measure, as a peck or a pound. [Old French *quarteron* quarter (of a pound), from *quartier* a fourth part. See QUARTER.]

quarter note *Music.* note having one-fourth the time value of a whole note. Also, *British,* **crotch′et.**

quar·ter·saw (kwôr′tər sô′) **-sawed, -sawed** or **-sawn, -saw·ing.** *v.t.* to saw (a log) lengthwise into quarters.

quarter section, tract of land, usually square, containing 160 acres, or one-fourth of a square mile.

quarter sessions, any of various courts of law held quarterly in Great Britain and certain states of the United States.

Quartered arms

quar·ter·staff (kwôr′tər staf′) *pl.,* **-staves.** *n.* stout pole six to eight feet long, having iron tips, formerly used in England as a weapon.

quar·tet (kwôr tet′) *also,* **quar·tette.** *n.* **1.** musical composition for four voices or instruments. **2.** four musicians who perform such a composition. **3.** any group of four persons or things. [Italian *quartetto,* from *quarto* fourth, from Latin *quártus.*]

quar·to (kwôr′tō) *pl.,* **-tos.** *n.* **1.** page size obtained by folding one sheet of paper into four parts, each usually about nine by twelve inches. **2.** book composed of pages of this size. [Short for Modern Latin *in quarto* in a fourth (part of a sheet of paper), going back to Latin *in* in + *quártus* fourth.]

quartz (kwôrts) *n.* very hard form of silica that occurs in crystals or in a single mass and is colorless and transparent in its pure state. Certain impure colored varieties, as amethyst, are used as semiprecious stones. Quartz is the most common of all minerals and the principal constituent of sand. Formula: SiO_2 [German *Quarz;* of uncertain origin.]

quartz·ite (kwôrt′sīt) *n.* granular metamorphic rock consisting chiefly of quartz.

qua·sar (kwā′sär) *n.* any of various starlike bodies that are extremely powerful emitters of radio waves, light, and other electromagnetic radiation. [Short for *quas(i-stell)ar (radio source).* See QUASI, STELLAR.]

quash[1] (kwosh) *v.t.* to put down or suppress forcibly and quickly: *The dictator was quick to quash the insurrection.* [Old French *quasser* to break, from Latin *quassāre* to shake.]

quash[2] (kwosh) *v.t.* to nullify, make void, or set aside, as a law, decision, election, or indictment. [Old French *quasser* to annul, from Latin *quassāre* to shake; influenced by Late Latin *cassāre* to annul, from Latin *cassus* empty.]

qua·si (kwā′zī, -sī, kwä′zē, -sē) *adj.* resembling or similar to, but not the same as. —*adv.* seemingly, but not really; almost or somewhat. ▲ usually used in combination: *a quasi-success, quasi-religious fervor.* [Latin *quási* as if.]

quas·sia (kwosh′ə) *n.* **1.** drug obtained from the wood of a tropical American tree, *Quassia amara,* used as a bitter tonic. **2.** any of a small group of shrubs and trees, genus *Quassia,* found in Central and South America, bearing clusters of scarlet flowers. [From Graman *Quassi,* Surinam Negro who discovered the value of the Surinam quassia for medicinal purposes about 1730.]

Qua·ter·na·ry (kwä′tər ner′ē, kwə tur′nər ē) *n.* second geological period of the Cenozoic era, including the Pleistocene and Recent epochs. See **geology** for table. —*adj.* of, relating to, or characteristic of this period. [Latin *quaternárius* consisting of four each, from *quaterní* four each.]

quat·rain (kwot′rān) *n.* stanza or poem of four lines, esp. one with alternately rhyming lines. [French *quatrain,* from *quatre* four, from Latin *quattuor.*]

quat·re·foil (kat′ər foil′, kat′rə-) *n.* **1.** leaf having four leaflets or a flower having four petals. **2.** ornament in architecture consisting of four foils or arcs joined by cusps. [Old French *quatre* four (from Latin *quattuor*) + *foil* leaf (from Latin *folium*).]

Quatrefoils

qua·ver (kwā′vər) *v.i.* **1.** to tremble or shake, as the voice. **2.** to perform or produce trill in singing or in playing a musical instrument. —*n.* **1.** shaking or trembling, esp. of the voice. **2.** trill produced or performed in singing or in playing a musical instrument. **3.** *Music.* eighth note. [Obsolete *quave* to tremble (possibly imitative) + -ER[1].] —**qua′ver·ing·ly,** *adv.* —**qua′ver·y** *adj.*

quay (kē) *n.* artifical landing place, usually made of stone, lying along or projecting into navigable water, as for loading and unloading ships. [Modification (influenced by French *quai*) of Old French *cai;* of Celtic origin.]

Quay

Que., Quebec.

quean (kwēn) *n.* brazen, impudent, or disreputable girl or woman. [Old English *cwene* woman, prostitute.]

quea·sy (kwē′zē) **-si·er, -si·est.** *adj.* **1.** nauseated: *The boat trip made her queasy.* **2.** causing or tending to cause nausea. **3.** uneasy; uncomfortable: *Cindy had a queasy feeling that something was wrong.* **4.** squeamish; fastidious; qualmish. [Of uncertain origin.] —**quea′si·ly,** *adv.* —**quea′si·ness,** *n.*

Que·bec (kwi bek′) *n.* **1.** largest province of Canada, in the eastern part of the country. Area, 594,860 sq. mi. Pop. (1966), 5,780,845.

at; āpe; cär; end; mē; it; īce; hot; ōld; fôrk; wood; fōōl; oil; out; up; ūse; turn; sing; thin; this; zh in treasure; ə in ago, taken, pencil, lemon, circus.

2. capital of this province, a port city in southeastern Canada, on the St. Lawrence River. Pop. (1968), 166,984.

que·bra·cho (kä brä′chō) *n.* **1.** any of several tropical American trees having very hard wood, as the **red quebracho**, *Schinopsis lorentzii*, whose wood yields tannin. **2.** hard wood or bark of any of these trees. [Spanish *quebracho* this tree; literally, ax-breaker, from *quebrar* to break (from Latin *crepitāre* to crack) + *hacha* ax (of Germanic origin); because of the hardness of the wood.]

Quech·u·a (kech′ōō ə, kə chōō′ə) *n.* **1.** one of a tribe of South American Indians that dominated the Incan empire before the Spanish conquest. **2.** South American Indian language, formerly spoken by the Incas, now spoken predominantly in Peru, Ecuador, and parts of Bolivia and Argentina. —**Quech′u·an,** *adj., n.*

queen (kwēn) *n.* **1.** wife or widow of a king. **2.** female sovereign of a kingdom who rules in her own right. **3.** woman, or something construed as female, that is supreme or preeminent, as in a given field or activity: *The new ocean liner is the queen of the seas.* **4.** fully developed, mated female in a colony of social insects, as bees or ants, whose function is to lay eggs. **5.** playing card bearing a picture of a queen. **6.** *Chess.* most powerful piece, able to move any number of spaces in any straight or diagonal line. —*v.i.* to reign as or act like a queen. —*v.t.* to make (a woman) a queen. [Old English *cwēn* king's wife, female sovereign of a kingdom, outstanding woman.]

Queen (def. 6)

Queen Anne's lace, wild carrot.

queen consort, wife of a reigning king, esp. one who does not share his sovereignty.

queen dowager, widow of a king.

queen·ly (kwēn′lē) -li·er, -li·est, *adj.* characteristic of, resembling, or suitable for a queen. —*adv.* in a queenly manner. —**queen′li·ness,** *n.*

queen mother, queen dowager who is also the mother of the reigning sovereign.

queen post, one of two vertical posts in a roof truss or the like, supporting the rafters and resting on the tie beam.

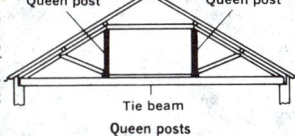

Queen post   Queen post

Tie beam

Queen posts

queen regent 1. queen ruling in place of a king who is absent, incapacitated, or too young. **2.** queen regnant.

queen regnant, queen ruling in her own right.

Queens (kwēnz) *n.* largest borough of New York City, east of Manhattan. Area, 114.7 sq. mi. Pop. (1970), 1,973,708.

Queens·land (kwēnz′land) *n.* political subdivision of Australia, in the northeastern part of the country. Area, 667,000 sq. mi. Pop. (1969 est.), 1,768,000.

queer (kwēr) *adj.* **1.** differing from what is normal or expected; strange; eccentric: *a queer sense of humor.* **2.** questionable; suspicious: *a queer request.* **3.** physically unwell; faint; giddy. **4.** *Informal.* slightly unbalanced mentally. **5.** *Slang.* not genuine or authentic; counterfeit. —*v.t. Slang.* to spoil; ruin. [German *quer* perverse, cross, oblique.] —**queer′ly,** *adv.* —**queer′ness,** *n.*

quell (kwel) *v.t.* **1.** to put down; crush; suppress: *to quell a mutiny.* **2.** to put an end to; allay; quiet: *Medicine quelled the pain.* [Old English *cwellan* to kill.]

Que·moy (ki moi′) *n.* heavily fortified island off the coast of the mainland of China, held by the Republic of China. Area, 68 sq. mi. Pop. (1962 est.), 49,345.

quench (kwench) *v.t.* **1.** to satisfy; slake: *We quenched our thirst with a cold glass of lemonade.* **2.** to put out or extinguish, as a fire. **3.** to put an end to; suppress. **4.** to cool suddenly, as hot iron or steel, by plunging into a liquid. [Old English *ācwencan* to extinguish.] —**quench′a·ble,** *adj.*

quern (kwurn) *n.* hand-operated mill for grinding grain, usually consisting of two circular stones. [Old English *cweorn.*]

quer·u·lous (kwer′ə ləs, kwer′yə-) *adj.* **1.** disposed to complain or find fault: *The querulous old man was dissatisfied with everything.* **2.** characterized by or indicating a disposition to complain or find fault. [Latin *querulus,* from *querī* to complain.] —**quer′u·lous·ly,** *adv.* —**quer′u·lous·ness,** *n.*

que·ry (kwēr′ē) *pl.,* -ries. *n.* **1.** that which is asked; question. **2.** mental reservation; doubt. **3.** question mark, esp. when used to express doubt regarding the correctness or validity of written or printed matter: *The proofreader wrote a query next to what he thought was a misspelling.* —*v.t.,* -ried, -ry·ing. **1.** to inquire into; ask about. **2.** to ask a question or questions of. **3.** to express doubt about the correctness or validity of, as by marking with a question mark.

[Modification of Latin *quaere* inquire, imperative of *quaerere* to inquire, seek.] —**Syn.** *v.* **1.** see **question.** —*v.t.* **1.** see **ask.**

quest (kwest) *n.* **1.** search or pursuit made in order to secure an object or achieve a goal: *the quest for peace of mind. The explorer's quest for gold was in vain.* **2.** in the Middle Ages, expedition or adventure undertaken by a knight or knights, esp. one made in order to achieve some feat. **3.** knight or knights on such an expedition or adventure. —*v.i.* to go on a quest. [Old French *queste* search, going back to Latin *quaesīta* thing sought, from *quaerere* to seek, inquire.]

ques·tion (kwes′chən) *n.* **1.** expression of a desire to know something, inviting or calling for a reply; that which is asked: *Alice refused to answer so personal a question.* **2.** matter receiving or requiring deliberation or discussion; issue: *The law dealt with the question of civil rights.* **3.** subject of dispute or doubt; controversy: *A question arose as to who was the legal heir.* **4.** possibility of disagreement or uncertainty; doubt: *He is, without question, the smartest man I know. I'm right, and there's no question about it!* **5.** proposal brought up for consideration in a meeting or legislative assembly or placed on a ballot to be voted on by the electorate. **6. in question,** under consideration or discussion: *Congress debated the matter in question.* **7. out of the question,** not considered or thought of; impossible: *Without a passport, leaving the country is out of the question.* **8. to call into question,** to be unconvinced or uncertain about; doubt. —*v.t.* **1.** to ask a question or questions of: *to question an applicant. The police questioned the suspect.* **2.** to ask questions about: *Tom questioned everything he didn't understand.* **3.** to challenge; doubt: *Experts questioned the authenticity of the painting.* —*v.i.* to ask a question or questions: *The best way to learn is to question.* [Old French *question* that which is asked, from Latin *quaestiō* a seeking, inquiry.] —**ques′tion·er,** *n.* —**ques′tion·ing·ly,** *adv.*

Syn. *n.* **1.** **Question, query** mean an interrogative sentence calling for an answer. **Question** is usually applied to an interrogative sentence addressed to someone and designed to elicit definite information in reply or to test a person's knowledge: *Answer me directly unto this question that I ask* (Shakespeare, *Henry IV*). **Query** is restricted to a formal inquiry posed to someone capable of providing authoritative information for resolving a problem: *All queries should be addressed to the author.* —*v.t.* **1.** see **ask.**

ques·tion·a·ble (kwes′chə nə bəl) *adj.* **1.** of dubious character, propriety, honesty, respectability, or the like: *questionable motives.* **2.** open to question or dispute; doubtful; uncertain. —**ques′tion·a·bly,** *adv.*

question mark, punctuation mark (?) used to indicate that the sentence that it closes is a direct question. Also, **interrogation point.**

ques·tion·naire (kwes′chə nâr′) *n.* written or printed form consisting of a series of questions, esp. one submitted to a number of persons for the purpose of obtaining statistically useful data. [French *questionnaire* list of questions, from *question* interrogation, query. See QUESTION.]

quet·zal (ket säl′) *n.* **1.** Central American bird, *Pharomachrus mocino,* having an iridescent green body and bright red underparts, and the male of which has a feathery chest and four long tail feathers. Length: to 4 feet including tail. **2.** standard monetary unit of Guatemala. [Spanish *quetzal,* from Nahuatl *quetzaltototl* this bird, from *quetzalli* beautiful tail feather + *tototl* bird.]

queue (kū) *n.* **1.** braid of hair made at the back of the head. **2.** line of people, vehicles, or the like. —*v.i.,* queued, queu·ing. to form, stand, or wait in a line (often with *up*): *People queued up to buy tickets for the play.* [French *queue* tail, going back to Latin *cauda.*]

Que·zon, Ma·nuel Lu·is (kā′zon; män wel′ lōō ēs′) 1878–1944, Philippine independence leader and first president of the Philippine Commonwealth.

Que·zon City (kā′zon) capital of the Philippines, a residential suburb of Manila. Quezon City replaced Manila as the country's capital in 1948. Pop. (1968), 545,500.

quib·ble (kwib′əl) -bled, -bling. *v.i.* to make petty objections or criticism. —*n.* petty objection or criticism. [Diminutive of obsolete *quib* quip, probably from Latin *quibus,* dative or ablative plural of *quī* who, which (much used in legal documents).] —**quib′bler,** *n.*

quick (kwik) *adj.* **1.** done or occurring with promptness or within a very short time: *a quick glance at the clock, the quick return of a loan.* **2.** moving, acting, or responding with considerable speed: *She was quick to criticize others. The secretary is a quick typist.* **3.** understanding, thinking, learning, or responding readily or rapidly: *a quick wit. John did not have as quick a mind as his precocious little brother.* **4.** easily provoked or stirred: *a quick temper.* **5.** responding or perceiving keenly; sensitive: *The quick ear of the conductor detected a wrong note.*

Quetzal

6. readily convertible into cash: *quick assets.* **7.** *Archaic.* having life; living; alive. —*n.* **1.** tender, sensitive flesh, esp. that beneath a fingernail or toenail. **2.** living persons. ▲ used chiefly in the phrase *the quick and the dead.* **3. to cut (someone) to the quick.** to cause acute mental or emotional pain; hurt deeply: *Her tactless remarks cut him to the quick.* —*adv.* quickly: *He runs as quick as a deer.* [Old English *cwic* living, alive.] —**quick′ness,** *n.*

Syn. *adj.* **1. Quick, fast[1], rapid** mean moving with great speed. **Quick** stresses an act that is sudden and of brief duration: *The tiger took a quick leap at the hunter.* **Fast** stresses swiftness and constant speed: *A fast train can cover the distance in two hours.* **Rapid** may refer to overall movement that is considered swift but whose speed may not be constant: *The growth of industry has been rapid in recent years.*

quick·en (kwik′ən) *v.t.* **1.** to cause to go or move more rapidly; hasten or accelerate: *He quickened his steps. Fear quickened her pulse.* **2.** to restore life to, cause to revive: *to quicken the dying embers.* **3.** to enliven; excite; stimulate: *to quicken the mind.* —*v.i.* **1.** to go or move more rapidly. **2.** to return to life; revive. **3.** to begin to show signs of life, as a fetus. **4.** (of a female) to reach the stage of pregnancy at which the child shows signs of life.

Syn. *v.t.* **1. Quicken, accelerate, expedite** mean to cause to move faster. **Quicken** conveys the idea of a perceptible increase in the rate of activity, motion, growth, or tempo and stresses vigor and animation in the performance of a task and shorter time for its accomplishment: *The troops quickened their steps when they approached the city.* **Accelerate** lays stress on a hastening of an ordinary progress or development without necessarily implying speed: *The death of the king accelerated the decline of the empire.* **Expedite** blends the ideas of speed and efficiency and may be appropriately applied to an official process carried through with dispatch with a minimum of waste and bungling: *The officer expedited the grant of the loan.*

quick-freeze (kwik′frēz′) **-froze, -fro·zen, -freez·ing.** *v.t.* to freeze food so rapidly that it retains its flavor and is able to undergo prolonged storage at low temperatures.

quick·ie (kwik′ē) *n. Slang.* something, as a book or motion picture, done or produced cheaply or in haste.

quick·lime (kwik′līm′) *n.* lime[1] (*def. 1*).

quick·ly (kwik′lē) *adv.* with speed or haste; rapidly.

quick·sand (kwik′sand′) *n.* bed of loose, wet sand, usually of considerable depth, that readily engulfs any heavy object that rests or moves upon it.

quick·set (kwik′set′) *n.* **1.** cuttings of a plant, esp. hawthorn, set to grow in a hedge. **2.** hedge grown from such cuttings.

quick-sil·ver (kwik′sil′vər) *n.* mercury (*def. 1*). [Old English *cwicseolfor* literally, living silver, translation of Latin *argentum vīvum*; because the silver-colored metal is liquid and moves about as if alive. See QUICK, SILVER.]

quick-step (kwik′step′) *n.* march music composed in a rapid tempo.

quick-tem·pered (kwik′tem′pərd) *adj.* easily angered.

quick time *Military.* normal marching rate, consisting of 120 thirty-inch steps per minute.

quick-wit·ted (kwik′wit′id) *adj.* having or showing a quick or ready wit; mentally alert or keen.

quid[1] (kwid) *n.* piece of something to be chewed, esp. tobacco. [Old English *cwidu* what is chewed, cud.]

quid[2] (kwid) *pl.,* **quid,** *n. British. Slang.* one pound sterling or twenty shillings. [Of uncertain origin.]

quid·nunc (kwid′nungk′) *n.* inquisitive, nosy person. [Latin *quid nunc?* what now?]

quid pro quo (kwid′ prō kwō′) *Latin.* one thing given or taken in return for another; equal exchange; substitution.

qui·es·cent (kwī es′ənt) *adj.* in a state of inactivity or repose. [Latin *quiēscēns,* present participle of *quiēscere* to rest.] —**qui·es′cence,** *n.* —**qui·es′cent·ly,** *adv.*

qui·et (kwī′it) *adj.* **1.** making little or no noise: *The children were quiet while the teacher taught.* **2.** with or characterized by little or no noise: *It was hard to concentrate when the library wasn't quiet.* **3.** with or characterized by little or no motion; still. **4.** free from excessive activity, turmoil, disturbance, or the like; uneventful; peaceful: *to lead a quiet life in the country, a quiet day when there weren't many customers in the store.* **5.** not showy, pretentious, or brash; unobtrusive: *an anonymous, quiet gesture of charity.* **6.** restful or soothing, as to the eye: *The room was decorated in beige and other quiet colors.* —*n.* quality or state of being quiet. —*v.t.* to make or become quiet (often with *down*). [Latin *quiētus* at rest, calm. Doublet of COY.] —**qui′et·er, qui′et·ness,** *n.* —**qui′et·ly,** *adv.*

Syn. *adj.* **3. Quiet, still** mean little or no sound resulting from a lack of movement. **Quiet** may refer to an atmosphere of calm, relatively free from agitation: *The sea was quiet before the storm struck.* **Still** characterizes what is silent and absolutely tranquil: *The forest was eerily still at night.*

qui·e·tude (kwī′i tōōd′, -tūd′) *n.* state or condition of calmness or tranquility. [Late Latin *quiētūdō,* from Latin *quiētus* at rest, calm.]

qui·e·tus (kwī ē′təs) *n.* **1.** that which serves to suppress, check, eliminate, or settle something. **2.** release from life; death: *if an unlucky bullet should carry a quietus with it* (Sheridan, 1775). **3.** final discharge, as of a debt. [Short for Medieval Latin *quietus est* he is acquitted, from Latin *quiētus est* he is at rest.]

quill (kwil) *n.* **1.a.** feather, esp. a large, stiff feather from the tail or wing. **b.** hard, hollow stem of a feather. **2.** pen, esp. one made from the hollow stem of a feather. **3.** one of the sharp spines of the porcupine or hedgehog. **4.** any of various devices, as a toothpick or plectrum, made from or as from the hollow stem of a feather. [Possibly of Low German origin.]

quilt (kwilt) *n.* **1.** bed cover consisting of two pieces of cloth filled with soft stuffing material, as feathers or cotton batting, and held together by lines of stitching, usually in a pattern, across the entire surface. **2.** something quilted or resembling a quilt. —*v.t.* to make a quilt or quilted article. —*v.i.* **1.** to stitch together (two pieces of cloth) with a soft lining between. **2.** to stitch (cloth) in lines or patterns that resemble those used in making quilts. [Old French *cuilte* mattress, from Latin *culcita* cushion, mattress.]

quilt·ing (kwil′ting) *n.* **1.** act or process of making quilts or quilted work. **2.** material used in making quilts.

quilting bee, social gathering of women to make quilts.

quince (kwins) *n.* **1.** pear-shaped yellow fruit of a small Asian tree, *Cydonia oblonga,* of the rose family, used esp. in preserves. **2.** tree bearing this fruit, having round white or pale-pink flowers. [Originally plural of obsolete *quince* this fruit, from Old French *coin,* through Latin, going back to Greek *kydōnion mēlon* literally, apple of Cydonia (ancient Cretan city).]

Quince branch

Quin·cy (kwin′zē) *n.* city in eastern Massachusetts, on the Atlantic, just south of Boston. Pop. (1970), 87,966.

qui·nine (kwī′nīn) *also,* **quin·in.** *n.* bitter, colorless, crystalline drug obtained from the bark of the cinchona tree. Its medicinal preparations are used to treat malaria and other illnesses. [Spanish *quina* bark of cinchona (from Quechua *kina* bark) + -INE[2].]

Quin·qua·ges·i·ma (kwing′kwə jes′i mə) *n.* the last Sunday before Lent, immediately preceding Shrove Tuesday and Ash Wednesday. [Latin *quīnquāgēsima (diēs)* literally, fiftieth (day); reckoned approximately as the fiftieth day before Easter.]

quin·quen·ni·al (kwing kwen′ē əl) *adj.* **1.** of or for five years. **2.** occurring every five years. [Latin *quīnquennis* (from *quinque* five + *annus* year) + -AL[1].]

quin·sy (kwin′zē) *n.* acute inflammation of the tonsils and throat, often followed by the formation of an abscess. [Old French *quinancie* very sore throat, from Late Latin *cynanchē,* from Greek *kynanchē,* from *kyōn* dog + *anchein* to strangle; because a sensation of strangling accompanies this disease.]

quint (kwint) *n. Informal.* quintuplet.

quin·tal (kwint′əl) *n.* **1.** in the United States, a measure of weight equal to 100 pounds; hundredweight. **2.** metric measure of weight equal to 100 kilograms, or 220.46 pounds avoirdupois. [Old French *quintal* weight of one hundred pounds, from Arabic *qintār,* going back to Latin *centēnārius* consisting of one hundred.]

quin·tes·sence (kwin tes′əns) *n.* **1.** purest, most essential part or form of something: *This chapter contains the quintessence of the author's thought.* **2.** most perfect example or manifestation of something: *His behavior was the quintessence of generosity.* [Modification of Medieval Latin *quinta essentia* fifth essence or element (which in ancient and medieval philosophy was aether), going back to Latin *quīntus* fifth + *essentia* essence, being.] —**quin·tes·sen·tial** (kwin′tə sen′shəl), *adj.*

quin·tet (kwin tet′) *n.* **1.** musical composition for five voices or instruments. **2.** five musicians who perform such a composition. **3.** any group or set of five. [Italian *quintetto,* from *quinto* fifth, from Latin *quīntus.*]

Quin·til·ian (kwin til′yən) *n.* A.D. c.35–95, Roman writer and orator.

quin·til·lion (kwin til′yən) *n.* **1.** in the United States and France, the cardinal number represented by 1 followed by eighteen zeros. **2.** in Great Britain and Germany, the cardinal number represented by 1 followed by thirty zeros. —*adj.* numbering one quintillion. [Latin *quīntus* fifth + (M)ILLION.]

quin·tu·ple (kwin tōō′pəl, -tū′-, kwin′tə pəl) *adj.* **1.** consisting of five parts. **2.** five times as great or as many. —*v.t., v.i.* **-pled, -pling.** to make or become five times as great or as many. —*n.* number or amount five times as great as another. [French *quintuple* fivefold, going back to Latin *quīntus* fifth.]

at; āpe; cär; end; mē; it; īce; hot; ōld; fôrk; wood; fōōl; oil; out; up; ūse; turn; sing; thin; this; zh in treasure; ə in ago, taken, pencil, lemon, circus.

quin·tu·plet (kwin tup′lit, -tūp′-, kwin′təp-) *n.* **1.a.** one of five offspring born at one birth. **b. quintuplets.** five offspring born at one birth. **2.** any set or combination of five. [QUINTUPLE + -ET.]

quip (kwip) *n.* **1.** clever or witty remark or saying, usually made on the spur of the moment. **2.** sharp or sarcastic remark or retort; taunt; gibe. —*v.i.* **quipped, quip·ping.** to make a quip or quips. [Form of obsolete *quippy* clever or sarcastic remark, possibly from Latin *quippe* forsooth, indeed (used sarcastically).]

quire[1] (kwīr) *n.* twenty-four or twenty-five uniform sheets of paper. [Old French *quaier* group of four sheets, going back to Latin *quāternī* four each, four at a time, from *quattuor* four.]

quire[2] (kwīr) *n. Archaic.* choir.

Quir·i·nal (kwir′in əl) *n.* **1.** one of the seven hills on which ancient Rome was built. **2.** palace built on this hill, formerly the residence of popes and kings, now the official residence of the president of Italy. Also, **Quirinal Palace.** **3.** civil or royal government of Italy, as distinguished from the Vatican.

quirk (kwurk) *n.* **1.** personal peculiarity or mannerism; idiosyncrasy. **2.** sudden or unexpected twist or turn: *a quirk of fate.* [Of uncertain origin.]

quirt (kwurt) *n.* flexible whip made of knotted rawhide thongs and having a short handle. [Possibly from Spanish *cuerda* rope, from Latin *c(h)orda* gut, rope, from Greek *chordē* gut, string of gut.]

quis·ling (kwiz′ling) *n.* traitor who collaborates with an invading enemy, esp. by serving in a puppet government. [From Major Vidkun *Quisling,* Norwegian who collaborated with the Nazi invaders of Norway during World War II.]

quit (kwit) **quit** or **quit·ted, quit·ting.** *v.t.* **1.** to stop; cease; discontinue: *He quit studying to take a walk. It was hard to quit smoking.* **2.** to give up, abandon, or resign; renounce: *to quit a job.* **3.** to go away from; leave: *The guard did not quit his post all night long.* **4.** *Archaic.* to acquit or conduct (oneself). —*v.i.* **1.** to stop, cease, or discontinue doing something. **2.** to resign from a position of employment: *Kate quit because her salary was too low.* **3.** to give up or stop trying, as in defeat or discouragement: *Steve quit when he realized he could not win.* —*adj.* free, clear, or rid of, as an obligation: *quit of all debts.* [Old French *quite* discharged, freed, clear, going back to Latin *quiētus* at rest, calm.]

quitch (kwich) *n.* quack grass. Also, **quitch grass.** [Old English *cwice.*]

quit·claim (kwit′klām′) *Law. n.* giving up of one's claim, title, or right of action. —*v.t.* to release or give up claim or title to or right of action on. [Anglo-Norman *quiteclamer* to declare free, going back to Latin *quiētus* at rest + *clāmāre* to call, proclaim.]

quite (kwīt) *adv.* **1.** completely; entirely; wholly: *left quite alone, quite the opposite.* **2.** actually; really: *quite an accomplishment.* **3.** to a considerable extent or degree; rather: *The weather is quite warm for November.* [Middle English *quite* completely, from *quite* free, clear, from Old French *quite* freed. See QUIT.]

Qui·to (kē′tō) *n.* capital and chief cultural center of Ecuador, in the north-central part of the country, in the Andes. Pop. (1969), 496,410.

quit·rent (kwit′rent′) *n.* formerly, rent paid in lieu of services owed to a feudal lord. [QUIT + RENT[1].]

quits (kwits) *adj.* **1.** on even terms by means of repayment or retaliation: *After the last payment was made, we were quits.* **2. to call it quits.** to discontinue something, as an activity or relationship. [Medieval Latin *quittus* at rest, free, from Latin *quiētus* at rest, calm.]

quit·tance (kwit′əns) *n. Law.* **1.** discharge or release, as from debt or obligation. **2.** document or receipt certifying this. **3.** recompense; repayment. [Old French *quitance* acquittance, from *quiter* to release, going back to Latin *quiētus* at rest.]

quit·ter (kwit′ər) *n.* one who gives up easily.

quiv·er[1] (kwiv′ər) *v.t., v.i.* to shake with a slight but rapid vibration; shiver; tremble. —*n.* act or motion of quivering. [Possibly imitative.]

quiv·er[2] (kwiv′ər) *n.* case for holding arrows. [Old French *quivre;* probably of Germanic origin.]

qui vive (kē vēv′) **1.** who goes there? **2. on the qui vive.** on the alert; watchful. [French *Qui vive?* literally, (long) live who? (used as a sentinel's challenge), going back to Latin *quī* who + *vīvere* to live.]

Qui·xo·te, Don (ki hō′tē, kwik′sət) see **Don Quixote.**

quix·ot·ic (kwik sot′ik) *adj.* ridiculously or excessively chivalrous or romantic; idealistic in an impractical degree. [From DON QUIXOTE.] —**quix·ot′i·cal·ly,** *adv.*

quiz (kwiz) *pl.* **quiz·zes.** *n.* informal written or oral examination of an individual or class. —*v.t.* **quizzed, quiz·zing.** to question; examine: *The police quizzed the suspect. The students were quizzed on last week's work.* [Of uncertain origin.] —**quiz′zer,** *n.*

quiz show, radio or television show in which contestants try to answer questions put to them by a master of ceremonies. Also, **quiz program.**

quiz·zi·cal (kwiz′i kəl) *adj.* **1.** questioning; uncertain; puzzled: *The child looked quizzical because he didn't understand what we meant.* **2.** teasing; mocking; bantering: *George took her quizzical remark too seriously.* —**quiz′zi·cal·ly,** *adv.*

Qum·ran Valley (koom rän′) site in northwestern Jordan, near the Dead Sea, where the Dead Sea Scrolls were found in 1947.

quoin (koin, kwoin) *n.* **1.** external angle of a wall or building. **2.** one of the stones forming such an angle. **3.** wedge or wedge-shaped piece of material, as wood or metal, used for various purposes, as in printing to lock type in a galley. [Form of COIN.]

quoit (kwoit) *n.* **1. quoits.** game played by throwing a flattened metal or rope ring in an attempt to encircle or come as close as possible to a peg stuck in the ground. ▲ construed as singular. **2.** flattened metal or rope ring used in this game. [Of uncertain origin.]

quon·dam (kwon′dəm) *adj.* that once was; former. [Latin *quondam* formerly.]

Quon·set hut (kwon′sit) *Trademark.* prefabricated structure made of corrugated metal, having a semicircular roof whose sides curve down to form the walls. [From *Quonset* Point, Rhode Island, where it was first produced.]

Quonset hut

quo·rum (kwôr′əm) *n.* minimum number or proportion of members of a committee, organization, deliberative assembly, or the like, whose presence at a meeting is necessary if the meeting is to make binding decisions. [Latin *quōrum* of whom (word occurring in earlier designations of the number of justices of the peace whose presence was necessary at certain court sessions in England).]

quot., quotation.

quo·ta (kwō′tə) *n.* **1.** fixed amount, or a share of a total, due to or required of a given person, group, state, or the like: *Each soldier received his daily quota of rations. The salesman failed to sell his quota of shoes.* **2.** fixed or maximum number or proportion of a certain group or category of people allowed or admitted, as to enter a country or school: *The government set a quota on the annual number of immigrants from Italy.* [Medieval Latin *quota* share, short for Latin *quota pars* how great a part.]

quot·a·ble (kwō′tə bəl) *adj.* suitable for quoting: *The reporters found nothing quotable in the senator's speech.*

quo·ta·tion (kwō tā′shən) *n.* **1.** words quoted: *The book contained quotations from obscure authors.* **2.** act of quoting. **3.a.** statement of the current prices offered or bid for stocks, bonds, commodities, and the like. **b.** the price so stated.

quotation mark, one of a pair of punctuation marks (" ") used chiefly to indicate the beginning and end of a quotation. Single quotation marks (' ') are usually used to indicate a quotation within another quotation.

quote (kwōt) **quot·ed, quot·ing.** *v.t.* **1.** to repeat or reproduce the exact words of: *The newspapers quoted the president's speech. The author frequently quoted Shakespeare.* **2.** to bring forward or refer to (something, as a rule, book, or the like) as evidence, substantiation, or illustration: *The driving instructor quoted the statistics on accidents to his pupil.* **3.** to state (a price) for something, as securities or goods. **4.** to enclose in quotation marks. —*v.i.* to repeat or reproduce the exact words of another: *If you're going to quote, give credit to the author.* —*n. Informal.* **1.** quotation (def. 1). **2.** quotation mark. [Medieval Latin *quotare* to number, mark references by numbers, from Latin *quot* how many.] —**quot′er,** *n.*

quoth (kwōth) *v. Archaic.* said or spoke. [Past tense of obsolete *quethe* to speak, say, from Old English *cwethan.*]

quoth·a (kwōth′ə) *interj. Archaic.* forsooth; indeed. ▲ usually used to express sarcasm or surprise. [Contraction of *quoth he.*]

quo·tid·i·an (kwō tid′ē ən) *adj.* recurring or occurring every day; daily. —*n.* malarial fever that occurs daily. [Latin *quotīdiānus* daily.]

quo·tient (kwō′shənt) *n.* number or algebraic expression found by dividing one number or algebraic expression by another. In 12 ÷ 4 = 3, 3 is the quotient. [Latin *quotiēns* how many times.]

quo war·ran·to (kwō wə ran′tō) *n.* **1.** legal proceeding begun to prevent the continued exercise by a person of unlawfully asserted authority. **2.** formerly, writ in English law calling upon a person to show by what authority or warrant he claimed or exercised an office or franchise. [Medieval Latin *quo warranto* by what warrant, from *quo,* ablative of Latin *quod* what + *warranto,* ablative of *warrantum* warrant (of Germanic origin).]

q.v., which see. [Abbreviation of Latin *quod vide.*]

at; āpe; cär; end; mē; it; īce; hot; ōld; fôrk; wood; fo͞od; oil; out; up; ūse; turn; sing; thin; this; zh in treasure; ə in ago, taken, pencil, lemon, circus.

R

r, R (är) *pl.,* **r's, R's.** *n.* **1.** eighteenth letter of the English alphabet. **2. the three R's.** the basics of elementary education, esp. reading, writing, and arithmetic (humorously spelled *reading,* '*riting,* and '*rithmetic*).

r **1.** *Electricity.* resistance. **2.** roentgen.

r. **1.** radius. **2.** rod (measure of length). **3.** road. **4.** railroad. **5.** railway. **6.** *Baseball.* run; runs. **7.** received. **8.** residence. **9.** rare. **10.** ruble. **11.** rupee.

R. **1.** river. **2.** Republican. **3.** rabbi. **4.** road. **5.** *Baseball.* run; runs. **6.** royal. **7.** railroad. **8.** railway.

R **1.** *Chemistry.* radical. **2.** *Electricity.* resistance.

Ra (rä) *n.* a hawk-headed sun god of ancient Egypt, the chief official deity under the early dynasties. Also, **Re.**

Ra, radium.

R.A. **1.** rear admiral. **2.** Royal Academy.

Ra·bat (rə bät′) *n.* capital of Morocco, in the northern part of the country. Pop. (1966), 370,000.

rab·bet (rab′it) *n.* **1.** cut or groove made on the edge of a board to receive the edge of another board similarly cut or grooved, to form a joint. **2.** joint so formed. —*v.t.* **1.** to cut a rabbet in. **2.** to join with a rabbet or rabbets. [Old French *rabat* recess, from *rabattre* to beat down. See REBATE.]

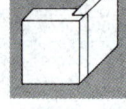

Rabbet *(def. 2)*

rab·bi (rab′ī) *pl.,* **-bis** or **-bies.** *n.* teacher of the Jewish religion who has completed a prescribed course of study and is usually the leader of a Jewish congregation. [Hebrew *rabbī* my master.]

rab·bin·ate (rab′ə nit, -nāt′) *n.* **1.** position or term of office of a rabbi. **2.** rabbis collectively.

Rab·bin·ic (rə bin′ik) *n.* Hebrew language as used in medieval rabbinical writings.

rab·bin·i·cal (rə bin′i kəl) *adj.* of or relating to rabbis, their language, views, or writings. Also, **rab·bin′ic.**

rab·bit (rab′it) *n.* **1.** any of various burrowing mammals, family Leporidae, having long ears and a short tail, as the cottontail. Length: 5–29 inches. **2.** its fur. **3.** loosely, hare. **4.** Welsh rabbit. [Middle English *rabet* the animal, possibly from Walloon *robete,* diminutive of Middle Dutch *robbe.*]

rabbit fever, tularemia.

rab·ble (rab′əl) *n.* **1.** disorderly crowd; mob. **2. the rabble.** mass of people. ▲ used contemptuously. [Of uncertain origin.]

rab·ble-rous·er (rab′əl rou′zər) *n.* one who tries to stir up masses of people by exciting their emotions, prejudices, or passions.

Rab·e·lais, Fran·çois (rab′ə lā′; frän swä′) 1494–1553, French satirist and humorist.

Rab·e·lai·si·an (rab′ə lā′zē ən, -zhən) *adj.* of, relating to, or suggesting Rabelais or his broad, lusty humor.

rab·id (rab′id) *adj.* **1.** unreasonably extreme in beliefs or actions; fanatical. **2.** violent; raging; furious: *rabid hunger.* **3.** of or affected with rabies; mad. [Latin *rabidus* raving.]
—**rab′id·ly,** *adv.* —**rab′id·ness,** *n.*

ra·bies (rā′bēz) *n.* infectious virus disease of warm-blooded animals that attacks the central nervous system and is usually transmitted by the bite of a rabid animal. Also, **hy′dro·pho′bi·a.** [Latin *rabiēs* rage, madness.]

rac·coon (ra kōōn′) *also,* **ra·coon.** *n.* **1.** small tree-dwelling mammal, *Procyon lotor,* of North and Central America, having brownish-gray fur with black masklike facial markings and a ringed tail. Length: 2½ feet, including tail. **2.** its fur. Also, **coon.** [Algonquian *ärähkun* the animal.]

Raccoon

race¹ (rās) *n.* **1.a.** contest of speed, as in running or riding. **b. races.** series of such contests, esp. horse races, run at a fixed time over the same course. **2.** any contest or competition. **3.a.** strong or swift current of water. **b.** channel for such a current. **4.** artificial channel transporting water to or from a point where its energy is utilized. **5.** track or groove in a machine in which a part slides or rolls. **6.** onward movement or course, as of time or life. —*v.i.,* **raced, rac·ing.** **1.** to take part in a contest of speed. **2.** to run, move, or go rapidly. **3.** (of machinery) to run too fast, as when the load is reduced while the power remains constant. —*v.t.* **1.** to contend against in a contest of speed. **2.** to cause to race. [Old Norse *rās* running.]

race² (rās) *n.* **1.** subdivision of the human species based on distinguishing physical characteristics that are passed on to succeeding generations. **2.** group of persons sharing a common ancestry, history, nationality, or area of origin. **3.** lineage; ancestry. **4.** group of people sharing similar characteristics, interests, or habits: *the race of statesmen.* **5.** group of animals or plants having distinguishing characteristics that are passed on to succeeding generations; variety. **6.** mankind. [French *race* lineage, family, breed, from Italian *razza* breed, kind², possibly from Arabic *rā's* origin.]

race·horse (rās′hôrs′) *n.* horse bred and trained for racing.

ra·ceme (rā sēm′, rə sēm′) *n.* simple inflorescence in which the flowers are arranged on short stalks arising from the main stem. Doublet of RAISIN. [Latin *racēmus* cluster of grapes. Doublet of RAISIN.]

rac·er (rā′sər) *n.* **1.** one who or that which races or takes part in a race or is capable of great speed. **2.** any of various swift American snakes, esp. the blacksnake.

race·track (rās′trak′) *n.* area of ground, usually oval, laid out for racing, esp. for horse racing. Also, **race′course′.**

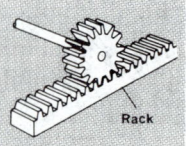

Raceme of a lily of the valley

Ra·chel (rā′chəl) *n.* in the Old Testament, the second and favorite wife of Jacob and the mother of Joseph and Benjamin.

ra·chis (rā′kis, rak′is) *pl.,* **ra·chis·es** or **rach·i·des** (rak′ə dēz, rā′kə-). *n.* **1.** elongated axis of an inflorescence. **2.** shaft of a feather, esp. the part bearing the barbs. **3.** spinal column. [Modern Latin *rachis,* from Greek *rhachis* spine.]

ra·chi·tis (rə kī′tis) *n.* rickets. [Modern Latin *rachitis,* from Greek *rhachitis* disease of the spine, from *rhachis* spine + *-itis.* See -ITIS.] —**ra·chit·ic** (rə kit′ik), *adj.*

Rach·ma·ni·noff, Ser·gei (räk mä′ni nôf′; ser gā′) 1873–1943, Russian composer and pianist.

ra·cial (rā′shəl) *adj.* **1.** of, relating to, or characteristic of a race. **2.** of, relating to, or arising from relations between races. —**ra′cial·ly,** *adv.*

Ra·cine (*def. 1* rä sēn′; *def. 2* rə sēn′) **1. Jean Bap·tiste** (zhän ba tēst′) 1639–99, French dramatist. **2.** city in southeastern Wisconsin, on Lake Michigan. Pop. (1970), 95,162.

rac·ism (rā′siz′əm) *n.* **1.** doctrine or belief that inherent differences make one race, esp. one's own, superior to another. **2.** political policy or social system based on such a doctrine or belief. Also, **ra′cial·ism.** —**rac′ist,** *adj., n.*

rack¹ (rak) *n.* **1.** framework or stand for hanging, displaying, or storing things. **2.** hayrack. **3.** former instrument of torture used to stretch or pull a victim's body in different directions. **4.** *Pool.* tri-

Rack

Rack¹ *(def. 5)*

at; āpe; cär; end; mē; it; īce; hot; ōld; fôrk; wood; fōōl; oil; out; up; ūse; turn; sing; thin; this; zh in treasure; ə in ago, taken, pencil, lemon, circus.

angular frame in which the balls are set before the opening shot. **5.** bar with teeth on one surface that meshes with a toothed gear or wheel. **6.** state or cause of acute mental or physical suffering. **7.** strain: *a tree bent by the rack of storms.* **8. on the rack.** suffering acute pain, tension, or anxiety. —*v.t.* **1.** to cause to suffer mentally or physically; torment: *a body racked with pain.* **2.** to put pressure on; strain: *to rack one's brains.* **3.** to torture on a rack. **4.** *Pool.* to arrange (the balls) in the rack. **5. to rack up.** *Informal.* to score or achieve, esp. impressively: *to rack up points.* [Possibly from Middle Dutch *rec* framework.]

rack² (rak) *n.* **1.** destruction. **2. to go to rack and ruin.** to deteriorate; fall apart. [Form of WRACK.]

rack³ (rak) *n.* either of two gaits of a horse, pace or single-foot. —*v.i.* (of a horse) to move at either of these gaits. [Possibly form of ROCK².]

rack⁴ (rak) *n.* mass of thin or broken clouds driven by the wind. [Probably from Scandinavian origin.]

rack·et¹ (rak'it) *n.* **1.** loud or confusing noise; clamor. **2.** *Informal.* dishonest or illegal scheme or activity, esp. one for getting money by the use of bribery, extortion, fraud, or threats of violence. **3.** *Slang.* occupation; job. [Possibly imitative.]

rack·et² (rak'it) *also,* **rac·quet.** *n.* **1.a.** round or oval frame strung with a network, usually of gut or nylon, and having a handle of various lengths, used to strike a ball, as in tennis. **b.** paddle¹ *(def. 2).* **2. rackets.** racquets. [French *raquette* the frame; earlier, *rachette* palm of the hand, going back to Arabic *rāha.*]

rack·et·eer (rak'ə tēr') *n.* one engaged in a dishonest or illegal scheme or activity for getting money. —*v.i.* to engage in a racket. —**rack'et·eer'ing,** *n.*

rac·on·teur (rak'on tur') *n.* one skilled in telling stories. [French *raconteur,* from *raconter* to narrate. See RECOUNT.]

ra·coon (ra kōōn') *n.* raccoon.

rac·quets (rak'its) *n.,pl.* game resembling tennis, played in a walled court. ▲ construed as singular.

rac·y (rā'sē) *rac·i·er, rac·i·est. adj.* **1.** suggestive or risqué. **2.** having a distinctive or characteristic flavor or quality. [From RACE² (referring to that which is characteristic or distinctive) + -Y¹.] —**rac'i·ly,** *adv.* —**rac'i·ness,** *n.*

ra·dar (rā'där) *n.* device or system for detecting the position and direction of a distant object by sending out high-frequency radio waves and measuring the time taken for them to be reflected back from the object. [Short for *ra(dio) d(etecting) a(nd) r(anging).*]

radar beacon, radar system that transmits or reflects radio waves in a narrow beam as navigational aid to ships and aircraft.

ra·dar·scope (rā'där skōp') *n.* the viewing screen of a radar receiver.

ra·di·al (rā'dē əl) *adj.* **1.** of, relating to, or arranged like rays or radii. **2.** having parts extending from a common center. **3.** being or moving in the direction of a radius. **4.** arranged uniformly around a central axis, as the arms of a starfish. **5.** of, relating to, or near the radius bone. —**ra'di·al·ly,** *adv.*

radial engine, internal-combustion engine with radially arranged cylinders, used esp. in airplanes.

ra·di·an (rā'dē ən) *n.* angle at the center of a circle subtended by an arc of the circle equal in length to the radius. One radian is approximately 57.2958 degrees. [RADIUS + -AN.]

ra·di·ance (rā'dē əns) *n.* quality or state of being radiant. Also, **ra'di·an·cy.**

ra·di·ant (rā'dē ənt) *adj.* **1.** shining brightly; beaming. **2.** beaming, as with joy, contentment, or love: *a radiant smile upon her face.* **3.** emitting rays, as of light or heat. **4.** emitted or transmitted by radiation. —*n.* point or object from which rays are emitted. [Latin *radiāns,* present participle of *radiāre* to emit beams.] —**ra'di·ant·ly,** *adv.* —**Syn.** *adj.* **1.** see **bright.**

radiant energy, energy transmitted by waves, esp. electromagnetic waves.

radiant heating, system of heating a room or building by wall, ceiling, or floor panels that are heated by electric coils or hot-air or hot-water pipes.

ra·di·ate (rā'dē āt') *-at·ed, -at·ing. v.i.* **1.** to emit rays, as of light or heat. **2.** to issue in rays. **3.** to move or spread outward from a center: *Several narrow streets radiated from the town's main square.* —*v.t.* **1.** to emit in rays: *The sun radiates light.* **2.** to show, as joy, contentment, pleasure, or love. **3.** to spread outward from a center. —*adj.* **1.** having rays spreading outward from a center: *a radiate flower.* **2.** radiating from a center. **3.** *Zoology.* having radial symmetry of parts. [Latin *radiātus,* past participle of *radiāre* to emit beams.]

ra·di·a·tion (rā'dē ā'shən) *n.* **1.a.** process of emitting radiant energy in waves or particles. **b.** process in which radiant energy is emitted, transmitted, and absorbed. **c.** radiant energy emitted in the form of waves or particles. **2.** act or process of radiating.

radiation sickness, reaction to an overexposure to the ionizing forms of radiation given off by X rays and radioactive materials, charac-

terized by nausea, diarrhea, internal bleeding, and changes in tissue structure.

ra·di·a·tor (rā'dē ā'tər) *n.* **1.** heating device consisting of a series of pipes or coils through which steam or hot water circulates. **2.** cooling device through which water or other fluid circulates, as in an automobile engine. **3.** one who or that which radiates.

rad·i·cal (rad'i kəl) *adj.* **1.** to the fullest extent; thoroughgoing; extreme: *a radical change of attitude.* **2.** advocating extreme change in political, social, and economic institutions. **3.** going to or coming from the root or the origin; fundamental; basic. —*n.* **1.** one who advocates extreme change, as in political, social, and economic institutions. **2.** group of atoms remaining connected and acting as a unit, often in the form of an ion, in chemical reactions. **3.** *Mathematics.* **a.** root of a quantity. **b.** radical sign. **4.** *Linguistics.* root¹. [Late Latin *rādicālis* having roots, from Latin *rādix* root.] —**rad'i·cal·ly,** *adv.* —**rad'i·cal·ness,** *n.*

rad·i·cal·ism (rad'i kə liz'əm) *n.* advocacy of extreme change in political, social, and economic institutions.

radical sign *Mathematics.* the sign ($\sqrt{\ }$) placed before a number or an algebraic expression to indicate that its root is to be extracted.

rad·i·cand (rad'i kand') *n.* quantity under a radical sign: *9 is the radicand of* $\sqrt{9}$.

rad·i·ces (rad'ə sēz, rā'də-) a plural of radix.

rad·i·cle (rad'i kəl) *n.* **1.** part of the embryo of a plant that develops into the root. **2.** *Anatomy.* small rootlike part, as the beginning of a nerve or vein. [Latin *rādicula* small root, diminutive of *rādix* root.]

Radicle

ra·di·i (rā'dē ī') a plural of radius.

ra·di·o (rā'dē ō') *pl. -di·os. n.* **1.** wireless means of communication in which sound signals are changed into electromagnetic waves and transmitted to a receiver, where they are changed back into sounds. **2.** apparatus for receiving radio broadcasts, or for sending and receiving radio messages. **3.** radio broadcasting as an industry or entertainment form. **4.** message sent by radio. —*adj.* **1.** of, relating to, used in, or sent by radio. **2.** of or relating to radio frequency. —*v.t., -di·oed, -di·o·ing.* **1.** to transmit (a message) by radio. **2.** to send a radio message to. —*v.i.* to transmit by radio. [Short for RADIOTELEGRAPHY.]

radio- *combining form* **1.** radio: *radiotelephone.* **2.** radioactive: *radiocarbon.* **3.** radiation: *radiometer.* [Latin *radius* ray¹.]

ra·di·o·ac·tive (rā'dē ō ak'tiv) *adj.* of, relating to, caused by, or exhibiting radioactivity.

radioactive disintegration series, sequence of radioactive elements, each of which decays to form the next until a stable form, usually lead, is formed.

ra·di·o·ac·tiv·i·ty (rā'dē ō ak tiv'ə tē) *n.* emission of alpha and beta particles and gamma rays from the nuclei of atoms during a process of decay or disintegration in which atoms of one element are transformed into atoms of another element.

radio astronomy, branch of astronomy that studies celestial objects by means of the radio waves they emit.

radio beacon, radio transmitter that sends out special signals to assist ships and aircraft in determining their position and course.

ra·di·o·car·bon (rā'dē ō kär'bən) *n.* radioactive carbon, esp. carbon 14.

radio frequency, electromagnetic frequency from about ten kilocycles per second to several thousand megacycles per second, used esp. in sending radio and television signals.

ra·di·o·gram (rā'dē ō gram') *n.* **1.** message transmitted by radiotelegraphy. **2.** radiograph.

ra·di·o·graph (rā'dē ō graf') *n.* picture produced on a sensitive surface by radiation other than visible light, esp. by X rays. —*v.t.* to make a radiograph of.

ra·di·o·i·so·tope (rā'dē ō ī'sə tōp') *n.* radioactive isotope.

ra·di·o·lar·i·an (rā'dē ō lâr'ē ən) *n.* any of a group of one-celled marine protozoans, order Radiolaria, having skeletons made of silica and small spines radiating from their bodies. [Modern Latin *Radiolaria,* from Late Latin *radiolus,* diminutive of *radius* ray¹.]

ra·di·ol·o·gy (rā'dē ol'ə jē) *n.* branch of medicine dealing with the use of radiant energy in the diagnosis and treatment of diseases. [RADIO- + -LOGY.] —**ra'di·ol'o·gist,** *n.*

Radiometer

ra·di·om·e·ter (rā'dē om'ə tər) *n.* instrument for detecting and measuring radiant energy, consisting of a glass bulb enclosing a partial vacuum and containing four thin pieces of metal

that rotate when exposed to sunlight or other radiant energy. [RADIO- + -METER.]

ra·di·o·phone (rā′dē ō fōn′) *n.* radiotelephone.

ra·di·o·sonde (rā′dē ō sond′) *n.* instrument that is carried aloft by a balloon to radio back information about meteorological conditions at high altitudes. [RADIO- + French *sonde* sounding line (probably of Germanic origin).]

ra·di·o·tel·e·graph (rā′dē ō tel′ə graf′) *n.* sending of messages by radiotelegraphy.

ra·di·o·te·leg·ra·phy (rā′dē ō tə leg′rə fē) *n.* wireless telegraphy. [RADIO- + TELEGRAPHY.]

ra·di·o·tel·e·phone (rā′dē ō tel′ə fōn′) *n.* telephone that uses radio waves to transmit sound.

ra·di·o·tel·e·scope (rā′dē ō tel′ə skōp′) *n.* telescope that detects radio waves that come from various cosmic sources, consisting of a reflector to focus the waves and a sensitive radio receiver.

ra·di·o·ther·a·py (rā′dē ō ther′ə pē) *n.* treatment of disease by means of X rays or radioactive substances.

radio tube, vacuum tube used in radio sets.

radio wave, electromagnetic wave having a radio frequency.

rad·ish (rad′ish) *n.* **1.** edible fleshy root of a plant, *Raphanus sativus,* of the mustard family, usually white or red and having a pungent taste. **2.** the plant itself. [Old English *rædic,* from Latin *rādīx* root; influenced by French *radis* the plant, through Italian, from Latin *rādīx.* Doublet of RADIX.]

ra·di·um (rā′dē əm) *n.* white, highly radioactive metallic element found in pitchblende and other uranium ores that is formed as part of the uranium radioactive disintegration series. Symbol: **Ra** See **element** for table. [Modern Latin *radium,* from Latin *radius* ray¹; because it gives off radiation.]

ra·di·us (rā′dē əs) *pl.,* **-di·i** (-dē ī′) or **-di·us·es.** *n.* **1.a.** line joining the center of a circle or sphere and any point on the circumference or surface. **b.** length of such a line. **c.** circular area defined by such a line or its circumference. **2.** range or scope, as of activity or influence. **3.** radial part. **4.a.** shorter and thicker of the two bones of the forearm, extending from the humerus to the wrist on the thumb side of the arm. **b.** similar bone in the forelimb of other vertebrates. [Latin *radius* rod, ray¹. Doublet of RAY¹.]

ra·dix (rā′diks) *pl.,* **rad·i·ces** (rad′ə sēz, rā′də-) or **ra·dix·es.** *n.* **1.** *Linguistics.* root¹. **2.** root of a plant. **3.** *Mathematics.* number taken as the base of a system of numbers. [Latin *rādīx* root. Doublet of RADISH.]

Ra·dom (rä′dōm) *n.* city in east-central Poland, south of Warsaw. Pop. (1968), 152,500.

ra·dome (rā′dōm′) *n.* dome-shaped protective housing for a radar antenna. [RA(DAR) + DOME.]

ra·don (rā′don) *n.* colorless, radioactive gaseous element given off in the radioactive disintegration of radium, used in the treatment of cancer. Symbol: **Rn** See **element** for table. [From RADIUM.]

rad·u·la (raj′ə lə) *pl.,* **-lae** (-lē) or **-las.** *n.* flexible, filelike organ in most mollusks, bearing rows of small, horny teeth, used to tear up food. [Latin *rādula* scraper.]

RAF, Royal Air Force.

raf·fi·a (raf′ē ə) *n.* **1.** strong fiber obtained from the leaves of an evergreen palm tree, *Rafia farinifera,* used to make matting and baskets. **2.** the tree itself, found in Madagascar, having long featherlike leaves. [Of Malagasy origin.]

raf·fi·nose (raf′ə nōs′) *n.* crystalline sugar, $C_{18}H_{32}O_{16}·5H_2O$, occurring in sugar beets and cottonseed meal.

raf·fish (raf′ish) *adj.* **1.** vulgar in a flashy way; tawdry. **2.** disreputable; rakish. —**raf′fish·ly,** *adv.* —**raf′fish·ness,** *n.*

raf·fle (raf′əl) *n.* lottery in which chances are sold for a prize. —*v.t.,* **-fled, -fling.** to dispose of by a raffle (often with *off*). —*v.i.* to conduct or take part in a raffle. [Middle French *rafle* a gambling game with dice; of Germanic origin.]

raf·fle·sia (rə flē′zhə, -zhē ə) *n.* any of a group of malodorous, parasitic plants, genus *Rafflesia,* of the Malay Archipelago, having very large flowers and no leaves.

raft¹ (raft) *n.* **1.** flat, floating platform, as of logs or planks fastened together, used for transportation on water. **2.** life raft. —*v.t.* **1.** to transport or carry on a raft. **2.** to make into a raft. —*v.i.* to travel on a raft. [Old Norse *raptr* rafter.]

raft² (raft) *n.* *Informal.* large collection or quantity. [Form of dialectal English *raff* abundance; of uncertain origin.]

raft·er (raf′tər) *n.* one of the sloping beams that supports a roof. [Old English *ræfter.*]

Rafters

rag¹ (rag) *n.* **1.** small piece of cloth, esp. a torn or worn one. **2. rags.** old, worn, tattered clothing. **3.** fragment or shred of anything, esp. something of no value. **4.** cotton or linen cloth remnants used in making paper. [Middle English *ragge* small piece of cloth, going back to Old Norse *rögg* tuft of fur.]

rag² (rag) **ragged, rag·ging.** *v.t. Slang.* **1.** to tease. **2.** to scold. **3.** *British.* to play practical jokes upon. [Of uncertain origin.]

rag·a·muf·fin (rag′ə muf′in) *n.* ragged, unkempt person, esp. a ragged, dirty child. [From *Ragamoffyn,* name of a demon in the medieval poem *Piers Plowman.*]

rage (rāj) *n.* **1.** violent or uncontrolled anger; fury: *His eyes flashed with rage.* **2.** fit of violent anger: *He was in a rage.* **3.** intense force or violence, as of a disease or storm. **4.** great enthusiasm; ardent desire. **5.** fad; fashion; craze. —*v.i.,* **raged, rag·ing. 1.** to feel or show violent anger; be in a rage. **2.** to act or move with great violence: *a hurricane raging from the south.* **3.** to spread or prevail without control. [Old French *rage* violent anger, madness, going back to Latin *rabiēs.*]

rag·ged (rag′id) *adj.* **1.** worn into rags; tattered; frayed. **2.** wearing tattered clothing. **3.** shaggy; unkempt: *ragged fur.* **4.** having rough or uneven projections; jagged: *ragged cliffs.* **5.** irregular or imperfect. **6.** harsh; discordant, as a sound. —**rag′ged·ly,** *adv.* —**rag′ged·ness,** *n.*

rag·lan (rag′lən) *n.* **1.** sleeve that extends over the shoulder to the collar. Also, **raglan sleeve. 2.** loose overcoat having such sleeves. —*adj.* of or having such sleeves. [From Lord *Raglan,* 1788–1855, British general, who is said to have designed such an overcoat.]

Raglan sleeves on a sweater

rag·man (rag′man′) *pl.,* **-men.** *n.* one who collects and deals in rags and junk. Also, **rag′pick·er.**

ra·gout (ra gōo′) *n.* highly seasoned meat and vegetable stew. [French *ragoût,* from *ragoûter* to restore the appetite, going back to Latin *re-* again, back + *ad* to + *gustus* taste.]

rag·time (rag′tīm′) *n.* **1.** kind of music originating in the United States in the nineteenth century, written primarily for the piano and characterized by steady, marchlike rhythm in the bass and syncopation in the treble. **2.** syncopated rhythm of such music. [Possibly from RAGGED + TIME; referring to the syncopated beat.]

rag·weed (rag′wēd′) *n.* **1.** any of several weeds, genus *Ambrosia,* of the composite family, whose pollen is one of the major causes of hay fever. **2.** *British.* ragwort. [RAG¹ + WEED¹; referring to the ragged appearance of its leaves.]

rag·wort (rag′wurt′) *n.* any of several plants, genus *Senecio,* of the composite family, having yellow flowers. [RAG¹ + WORT; referring to the ragged appearance of its leaves.]

rah (rä) *interj.,* *n.* hurrah. [Short for HURRAH.]

raid (rād) *n.* **1.** sudden, surprise invasion, as by police. **2.** sudden attack, esp. by a small force for military purposes. —*v.t.* to make a raid on. —*v.i.* to take part in or conduct a raid. [Scottish form of ROAD.] —**raid′er,** *n.* —**Syn. 2.** see **invasion.**

rail¹ (rāl) *n.* **1.** long, narrow bar, as of wood or metal, resting horizontally on posts, used as a guard or support. **2.** fence or railing. **3.** one of a pair of metal bars that make up a railroad track. **4.** railroad as a means of transportation. —*v.t.* to furnish or enclose with a rail or rails. [Old French *reille* bar, from Latin *rēgula* rod. Doublet of RULE.]

rail² (rāl) *v.i.* to use abusive language; scold or complain bitterly (with *at* or *against*): *to rail at fate.* [French *railler* to jest, mock, through Provençal, going back to Late Latin *ragere* to neigh; possibly imitative.] —**rail′er,** *n.*

rail³ (rāl) *n.* any of numerous small birds, family Rallidae, that have short wings, strong legs, long toes, and a harsh cry and are found in marshy areas in most parts of the world. [Old French *raale,* from *raaler* to screech; probably of imitative origin.]

Rail³

rail·ing (rā′ling) *n.* **1.** fence or barrier made of a rail and its supports. **2.** rails collectively.

rail·ler·y (rā′lər ē) *n.* good-natured teasing or ridicule; banter. [French *raillerie* jesting, bantering, from *railler.* See RAIL².]

rail·road (rāl′rōd′) *n.* **1.** permanent road laid with parallel metal rails fixed by ties and providing a track for trains and other rolling stock. **2.a.** entire system of such roads, including stations, rolling stock, and land. **b.** company of persons who own or manage such a system. —*v.t.* **1.** to transport by railroad. **2.** *Informal.* **a.** to rush or push through with great haste, esp. without proper consideration: *to railroad a bill through Congress.* **b.** to cause to be imprisoned on false charges or without a fair trial. —*v.i.* to work on a railroad.

rail·road·ing (rāl′rō′ding) *n.* construction or operation of railroads.

rail·way (rāl′wā′) *n.* **1.** railroad, esp. one operating within a small area. **2.** any line or set of rails for wheels.

rai·ment (rā′mənt) *n.* clothing; attire. [Short for obsolete *arrayment,* from Anglo-Norman *araiement,* from *arayer* to array. See ARRAY.]

rain (rān) *n.* **1.** water condensed from vapor in the atmosphere, falling in drops from the sky to the earth. **2.** fall of rain; rainstorm or shower. **3.** rainy weather. **4.** heavy or rapid fall of anything. **5. the rains.** rainy season, as in tropical climates. —*v.i.* **1.** (of rain) to fall: *It's raining hard.* —*v.t.* **1.** to pour or send down like rain: *to rain confetti.* **2.** to give abundantly. **3. to rain out.** to cause (an outdoor event) to be canceled or postponed because of rain. [Old English *regn* precipitation in the form of water.]

rain·bow (rān′bō′) *n.* **1.** arc of spectral colors seen in the sky opposite the sun and caused by the reflection and refraction of the sun's rays by water droplets in the air. **2.** any similar arc. [Old English *regnboga* the rainbow seen in the sky.]

rain check **1.** ticket stub on an outdoor event entitling the holder to admission at a future date if the original event is canceled or postponed because of rain. **2.** postponement of an invitation until a future date.

rain·coat (rān′kōt′) *n.* waterproof or water-resistant coat.

rain·drop (rān′drop′) *n.* drop of rain.

rain·fall (rān′fôl′) *n.* **1.** fall or shower of rain. **2.** total amount of water falling in the form of rain, snow, sleet, or hail in a given area within a given time.

rain gauge, instrument for measuring the depth of rainfall. Also, **plu′vi·om′e·ter, u·dom′e·ter.**

Rai·nier, Mount (rə nēr′, rā-) mountain in west-central Washington.

rain·mak·er (rān′mā′kər) *n.* **1.** (esp. among American Indians) one who tries to cause rain by incantation or supernatural means. **2.** *Informal.* one who tries to cause rain artificially by using scientific techniques.

rain·proof (rān′prōōf′) *adj.* not letting rain in; shedding rain.

rain·storm (rān′stôrm′) *n.* storm with rain.

rain water, water that has fallen as rain.

rain·y (rā′nē) **rain·i·er, rain·i·est.** *adj.* **1.** characterized by or full of rain: *rainy weather.* **2.** bringing rain: *rainy clouds.* **3.** wet with rain: *rainy streets.* —**rain′i·ness,** *n.*

rainy day, time or possible time of need.

raise (rāz) **raised, rais·ing.** *v.t.* **1.** to move or cause to move to a higher level or position; lift. **2.** to set upright or in a standing position. **3.** to build; construct. **4.** to cause to rise or appear: *The bee sting raised a bump on his arm.* **5.** to move to a higher rank, position, or dignity. **6.** to increase in amount, size, or value: *to raise taxes.* **7.** to increase in degree, intensity, strength, or pitch: *to raise one's voice.* **8.** to gather together; collect: *to raise money.* **9.a.** to breed or grow: *to raise wheat.* **b.** to bring up; rear: *to raise a family.* **10.** to bring up for consideration or discussion. **11.** to stir up; arouse: *to raise a commotion.* **12.** to cause to come about; provoke: *The joke raised a laugh.* **13.** to bring back from or as if from death. **14.** to utter, esp. with a loud voice: *to raise a cry.* **15.** to make light: *to raise bread with yeast.* **16.** to bet more than (a preceding bet or better in poker). **17.** to increase the bid of (one's bridge partner). **18.** *Nautical.* to cause to appear above the horizon by coming nearer. **19.** to end (a siege) by withdrawing troops or by forcing the enemy to withdraw its troops. —*v.i.* **1.** to increase a bet in poker. —*n.* **1.** act or instance of raising. **2.** increase in amount. [Old Norse *reisa* to cause to rise.] —**rais′er,** *n.* —**Syn.** *v.t.* **1.** see LIFT.

rai·sin (rā′zin) *n.* sweet grape of any of various kinds, dried in the sun or artificially. [Old French *raisin* grape, from Latin *racēmus* cluster of grapes. Doublet of RACEME.]

rai·son d'ê·tre (rā′zōn det′rə) *French.* justification for existing.

raj (räj) *n.* (in India) rule; reign. [Hindi *rāj.*]

ra·jah (rä′jə) *also,* **ra·ja.** *n.* ruler or prince in India and the East Indies. [Hindi *rājā,* from Sanskrit *rājan* king.]

Raj·put (räj′pŏŏt′) *also,* **Raj·poot.** *n.* member of a Hindu ruling caste supposedly descended from ancient warriors.

rake¹ (rāk) *n.* **1.** long-handled tool with teeth, used as to gather fallen leaves. **2.** any of various similar tools. —*v.t.,* **raked, rak·ing. 1.** to gather, scrape, loosen, or smooth with or as with a rake. **2.** to search carefully and thoroughly: *to rake the files for a lost document.* **4.** to bring to

renewed attention; uncover facts about (with *up*): *to rake up an old scandal.* **5.** to direct gunfire along the length of. —*v.i.* to use a rake. [Old English *raca* the long-handled tool with teeth.]

rake² (rāk) *n.* dissolute person; roué; libertine. [Short for archaic *rakehell,* from RAKE¹ + HELL, from the idea that one would have to *rake* hell to find such a person.]

rake³ (rāk) *n.* slope or inclination, as of the mast of a ship. —*v.i.,* **raked, rak·ing.** to slope or incline. [Of uncertain origin.]

rake-off (rāk′ôf′) *n. Slang.* share or rebate, esp. one that is illegitimate.

rak·ish¹ (rā′kish) *adj.* **1.** dashing; jaunty: *a rakish outfit.* **2.** having a streamlined appearance suggesting speed, as a boat. [RAKE³ + -ISH.]

rak·ish² (rā′kish) *adj.* like a rake; dissolute. [RAKE² + -ISH.]

Ra·leigh (rô′lē) **1. Sir Walter.** c.1552–1618, English courtier, colonizer, statesman, and author. **2.** capital of North Carolina, in the central part of the state. Pop. (1970), 121,577.

rall. rallentando.

ral·len·tan·do (rä′len tän′dō) *adj., adv. Music.* gradually slower. [Italian *rallentando,* present participle of *rallentare* to slow down, slacken, going back to Latin re- again + *ad* to + *lentus* slow.]

ral·ly¹ (ral′ē) **-lied, -ly·ing.** *v.t.* **1.** to bring together so as to restore order: *to rally scattered troops.* **2.** to bring together for a common purpose; assemble. **3.** to pull together; revive or arouse: *to rally one's strength.* —*v.i.* **1.** to come together and into order again. **2.** to unite or come together for a common purpose. **3.** to come to aid or support a cause or person: *to rally around a political candidate.* **4.** to recover normal strength, vigor, or energy. **5.** (in tennis and similar games) to exchange a series of strokes before a point is made. —*n. pl.,* **-lies. 1.** act of rallying. **2.** mass meeting for a common purpose: *a political rally.* **3.** (in tennis and similar games) series of strokes exchanged before a point is made. **4.** long-distance automobile race over public highways. [French *rallier* to assemble, going back to Latin re- again + *ad* to + *ligāre* to bind.]

ral·ly² (ral′ē) **-lied, -ly·ing.** *v.t., v.i.* to tease good-naturedly; banter. [French *railler* to jest, mock. See RAIL².]

ram (ram) *n.* **1.** male sheep. **2.** any of various devices used to batter, crush, or force something by impact, as a battering ram. **3.** plunger of a force pump. **4.** hydraulic ram. **5.a.** projection on the bow of a warship, used to batter and crush an enemy ship. **b.** warship with such a projection. —*v.t.,* **rammed, ram·ming. 1.** to batter or strike against with great force; butt against. **2.** to force or drive down or into place. **3.** to stuff or cram. [Old English *ram(m)* male sheep, battering ram.] —**ram′mer,** *n.*

Ra·ma (rä′mə) *n.* any of three incarnations of Vishnu who were heroes of Hindu mythology, esp. the hero of the Ramayana.

Ram·a·dan (ram′ə dän′) *n.* **1.** ninth month of the Islamic year, observed as a fast from sunrise to sunset for thirty days. **2.** the daily fasting itself.

Ra·ma·ya·na (rä mä′yə nə) *n.* Hindu epic, written in Sanskrit, recounting the adventures of Rama.

ram·ble (ram′bəl) **-bled, -bling.** *v.i.* **1.** to go about or move about aimlessly or in a leisurely manner; roam. **2.** to talk or write aimlessly and at length, esp. without a logical sequence of ideas. **3.** to grow or spread irregularly or without definite direction, as a vine. —*n.* aimless or leisurely walk. [Possibly ROAM + -LE.] —**Syn.** *v.i.* see ROAM.

ram·bler (ram′blər) *n.* **1.** one who or that which rambles. **2.** any of various climbing roses.

ram·bunc·tious (ram bungk′shəs) *adj.* wild and boisterous. [Possibly modification of earlier *robustious* strong, boisterous, from RO-BUST.]

ram·e·kin (ram′ə kin) *also,* **ram·e·quin.** *n.* **1.** individual baking dish, esp. of earthenware. **2.** portion of food, esp. a cheese mixture with bread crumbs and eggs, cooked or served in such a dish. [French *ramequin;* of Germanic origin.]

Ram·ses (ram′ə sēz) *n.* any of eleven kings reigning in Egypt from c.1320 B.C. to c.1090 B.C., esp. **Rameses II,** who died c.1234 B.C., believed to be the pharaoh who oppressed the Hebrews. Also, **Ram′ses.**

ram·ie (ram′ē) *n.* **1.** Asian shrub, *Boehmeria nivea,* whose stems yield a fiber used to make fabrics and other products. **2.** the fiber itself. [Malay *rāmī* the plant.]

ram·i·fi·ca·tion (ram′ə fi kā′shən) *n.* **1.** act or process of dividing or spreading into branches or branchlike parts. **2.** branch, as of an artery. **3.** result or consequence developing from a situation or statement: *the ramifications of a problem.*

ram·i·fy (ram′ə fī′) **-fied, -fy·ing.** *v.i.* to divide or spread into or as into branches or branchlike parts. [Old French *ramifier* to branch, going back to Latin *rāmus* branch + *facere* to make.]

ram·jet (ram′jet′) *n.* jet engine in which the fuel is ignited along with air compressed by the high forward speed of the aircraft.

ra·mose (rā′mōs) *adj.* having many branches; branching. [Latin *rāmōsus,* from *rāmus* branch.]

at; āpe; cär; end; mē; it; īce; hot; ōld; fôrk; wood; fōōl; oil; out; up; ūse; turn; sing; thin; this; zh in treasure; ə in ago, taken, pencil, lemon, circus.

825

ra·mous (rā′məs) *adj.* **1.** ramose. **2.** of or like a branch.

ramp¹ (ramp) *n.* **1.** sloping passageway or roadway connecting different levels, as of a building or road. **2.** movable staircase for entering or leaving an airplane. **3.** short concave bend or slope where a handrail or coping changes direction. [French *rampe* slope, from *ramper* to climb. See RAMP².]

ramp² (ramp) *v.i.* **1.** to act menacingly or violently; rampage. **2.** to stand in a rampant position, as a lion in heraldry. **3.** to leap or rush with fury. [Old French *ramper* to creep, climb; of Germanic origin.]

ram·page (*n.,* ram′pāj′; *v.,* ram·pāj′, ram pāj′) *n.* course of violent or reckless behavior or action. —*v.i.* **-paged, -pag·ing.** to behave in a violent or reckless manner; rage. [RAMP² + -AGE.]

ramp·an·cy (ram′pən sē) *n.* quality or state of being rampant.

ramp·ant (ram′pənt) *adj.* **1.** growing profusely; luxuriant: *a rampant growth of weeds.* **2.** going beyond usual limits; unchecked; unrestrained. **3.** *Heraldry.* (of an animal) rising on the left hind leg, with the other legs and tail raised and the head and body in profile. **4.** violent in behavior or action. [Old French *rampant,* present participle of *ramper* to creep, climb. See RAMP².] —**ramp′ant·ly,** *adv.*

ram·part (ram′pärt′, -pərt) *n.* **1.** embankment built for defense, esp. around a castle. **2.** anything that serves as a defense or protection. [French *rempart* from *remparer* to fortify, going back to Latin *re-* back + *ante* before + *parāre* to make ready.]

ram·rod (ram′rod′) *n.* **1.** rod used for ramming the charge down the barrel of a muzzleloading firearm. **2.** rod used to clean the barrel of a rifle or other firearm.

Ram·ses (ram′sēs) Rameses.

ram·shack·le (ram′shak′əl) *adj.* likely to collapse; dilapidated; rickety. [From earlier *ramshackled,* originally past participle of obsolete *rans(h)ackle* to ransack, from RANSACK + -LE.]

ran (ran) past tense of **run.**

Ran (rän) *n.* Norse sea goddess.

ranch (ranch) *n.* **1.** large farm, esp. in the western United States, used to raise large herds of livestock. **2.** any farm devoted to raising a particular crop or animal. **3.** persons employed or living on a ranch. **4.** ranch house. —*v.i.* to manage or work on a ranch. [Spanish *rancho* small farm, group of people who eat together, from Old High German *hring* circle.]

ranch·er (ran′chər) *n.* one who owns or works on a ranch.

ranch house **1.** main building of a ranch, esp. the owner's house. **2.** long, low house with all the rooms on one floor.

ranch·man (ranch′mən) *pl.,* **-men.** *n.* rancher.

ran·cid (ran′sid) *adj.* having the unpleasant odor or taste of a spoiled oily substance: *rancid butter.* [Latin *rancidus* stinking.] —**ran·cid′i·ty, ran′cid·ness,** *n.*

ran·cor (rang′kər) *also, British,* **ran·cour.** *n.* bitter or rankling malice or resentment; deep spite. [Old French *rancour* hatred, from Latin *rancor* grudge, rancidity.]

ran·cor·ous (rang′kər əs) *adj.* bitterly malicious; deeply spiteful. —**ran′cor·ous·ly,** *adv.* —**ran′cor·ous·ness,** *n.*

rand (rand) *n.* monetary unit of South Africa, Botswana, Swaziland, and Lesotho equal to 100 cents. [Afrikaans *rand;* originally, shield, from Dutch *rand* edge.]

ran·dom (ran′dəm) *adj.* lacking definite aim, pattern, or purpose; haphazard: *He made a random choice.* —*n.* **at random.** with no definite aim, pattern, or purpose. [Old French *randon* impetuosity, from *randir* to run impetuously; of Germanic origin.] —**ran′dom·ly,** *adv.* —**ran′dom·ness,** *n.*

Syn. *adj.* **Random, haphazard** mean a lack of plan or direction. **Random** is often used neutrally to describe that which is done or occurs by chance but also suggests that one is receptive to the possibilities of the unexpected: *His random walk led him to a beautiful view of the town.* **Haphazard** implies a certain careless or reckless disregard for the results of an action: *She hung the pictures in a haphazard fashion.*

random sample *Statistics.* sample drawn from a whole in which each individual has an equal chance of being drawn.

ra·nee (rä′nē) *also,* **ra·ni.** *n.* **1.** wife of a rajah. **2.** reigning Hindu queen or princess. [Hindi *rānī* queen, from Sanskrit *rājñī.*]

rang (rang) past tense of **ring².**

range (rānj) *n.* **1.** extent to which or limits between which something varies: *a wide range of prices.* **2.** extent or area of operation or action: *range of vision.* **3.a.** maximum effective distance a projectile, as a bullet, can be propelled. **b.** distance of a weapon from a target: *to shoot at close range.* **4.** maximum distance that an aircraft, ship, or vehicle can travel without refueling. **5.a.** place or area set aside for shooting practice. **b.** area set aside for the testing of rockets and missiles. **6.** extent of variation in pitch of a singing voice or musical instrument. **7.** large area of open land over which livestock roam and graze. **8.** row, line, or series, esp. of mountains. **9.** large stove having burners and an oven. **10.** region in which a certain kind of plant or animal normally lives or grows. **11.** rank, class, or order. **12.** *Mathematics.* set of values that the dependent variable in a function may have. **13.** act of wandering around. —*v.t.,* **ranged, rang·ing. 1.** to place in a particular order, esp. in rows or lines; arrange: *to range books on the shelf.* **2.** to place in a particular position, company, or category; classify. **3.** to move or wander over (an area), as in exploration: *Cattle ranged the prairie.* **4.** to put (livestock) to graze on a range. **5.** to align (a gun or telescope) with a target. **6.** to obtain the range of, as a target. —*v.i.* **1.** to vary within specified limits: *The quality of food ranges from good to excellent.* **2.** to move over or explore an area: *My eye ranged over the crowded room, seeking a familiar face.* **3.** to wander or roam over: *to range through the woods.* **4.** to stretch out in or as in a line; extend: *Trees ranged along the road.* **5.** (of plants and animals) to live or grow in a given region. [Old French *ranger* to array, rank, from *reng* rank¹, row¹. See RANK¹.] —**Syn.** *n.* **2.** see **scope.**

range finder, any of various instruments for determining the distance of an object.

rang·er (rān′jər) *n.* **1.** forest ranger. **2.** member of a body of armed men who patrol a region to maintain law and order. **3. Ranger.** soldier in the U.S. Army specially trained to carry out raids on enemy positions; commando. **4.** one who or that which ranges.

Ran·goon (rang gōōn′) *n.* capital and chief port of Burma, in the southern part of the country. Pop. (1967 est.), 1,616,948.

rang·y (rān′jē) **rang·i·er, rang·i·est.** *adj.* **1.** suited for ranging or running, as an animal. **2.** slender and long-limbed. **3.** having or permitting wide range; roomy.

ra·ni (rä′nē) ranee.

rank¹ (rangk) *n.* **1.a.** relative position, standing, or class: *men of all ranks.* **b.** official position or grade: *the rank of captain.* **c.** high position, standing, or class: *a doctor of rank.* **2.** line of persons, animals, or things placed side by side. **3.** row of soldiers standing side by side in close order. Distinguished from **file. 3. ranks. a.** common soldiers of an army, as opposed to the officers. **b.** army. **4.** *Chess.* any row of squares running across the board. See **chessboard** for illustration. **5. to pull** (one's) **rank.** *Slang.* to exert authority in order to overcome opposition, esp. in an imperious manner (often with *on*). —*v.t.* **1.** to arrange in a row or rows: *to rank soldiers.* **2.** to assign a position to; classify: *to rank students according to their grades.* **3.** to take precedence over; outrank: *Lieutenants rank sergeants.* —*v.i.* **1.** to have a certain rank or position, esp. in relation to others: *He who ranks high in his class.* **2.** to form in a row or rows. [Old French *reng, renc* row¹, row; of Germanic origin.]

Syn. *n.* **1. Rank, position, standing** mean status or class. **Rank** emphasizes a recognized or established sequence and suggests that honor is derived from the title and ceremony associated with a hierarchy, such as that of the military or the aristocracy: *He has achieved high rank in the army.* **Position** suggests a high but less definite status than rank: *I have my position in society to consider.* **Standing** is often used of things as well as persons to emphasize the requirements which must be met for a particular status: *Now that he's paid his fine, he's a member in good standing at the fraternity.*

rank² (rangk) *adj.* **1.** growing profusely or luxuriantly, as vegetation. **2.** producing profuse growth, as land. **3.** having a strong, foul smell or taste; rancid. **4.** utter or complete; extreme: *a rank liar.* **5.** vulgar, gross, or indecent. [Old English *ranc* strong.] —**rank′ly,** *adv.* —**rank′ness,** *n.*

rank and file **1.** common soldiers of an army, as distinguished from the officers. **2.** people who constitute the body of a group, as distinguished from the leaders.

ran·kle (rang′kəl) **-kled, -kling.** *v.t., v.i.* to irritate or anger (someone) continuously. [Old French *rancler,* form of *draoncler* to fester, from *draoncle* ulcer, going back to Late Latin *dracunculus* literally, little dragon, diminutive of Latin *dracō* serpent, reptile monster. See DRAGON.]

ran·sack (ran′sak′) *v.t.* **1.** to search thoroughly: *to ransack a drawer for a missing glove.* **2.** to search through for plunder; pillage. [Old Norse *rannsaka* to search a house.]

ran·som (ran′səm) *n.* **1.** release of a captive or captured property for a price. **2.** price paid or demanded. **3.** redemption from sin and its consequences. —*v.t.* **1.** to obtain the release of by paying a certain price. **2.** to release upon receiving payment of ransom. **3.** to redeem from sin and its consequences. [Old French *raençon* price paid for the release of a captive, from Latin *redēmptiō* a buying back. Doublet of REDEMPTION.]

rant (rant) *v.i.* to speak extravagantly, violently, or loudly; rave. —*n.* extravagant, violent, and loud speech or language. [Obsolete Dutch *ranten* to rave.] —**rant′er,** *n.*

rap¹ (rap) *n.* **1.** quick, sharp, or light blow or knock. **2.** *Slang.* punishment or blame, esp. a prison sentence: *to take the rap for stealing.* **3.** *Slang.* discussion. —*v.i.,* **rapped, rap·ping. 1.** to knock or rap sharply: *to rap at the door.* **2.** *Slang.* to have a discussion (with *with*).

at; āpe; cär; end; mē; it; īce; hot; ōld; fôrk; wood; fōōl; oil; out; up; ūse; turn; sing; thin; this; zh in treasure; ə in ago, taken, pencil, lemon, circus.

—*v.t.* **1.** to knock or hit sharply: *to rap a person's knuckles.* **2.** to say sharply (with *out*): *to rap out a reply.* [Imitative.]

rap² (răp) *n. Informal.* the least bit: *He doesn't care a rap about sports.* [Of uncertain origin.]

ra·pa·cious (rə pā′shəs) *adj.* **1.** grasping; greedy. **2.** (of animals) living on live prey; predatory. **3.** given to taking by force; plundering. [Latin *rapāci-,* stem of *rapāx* grasping + -OUS.] —**ra·pa′cious·ly,** *adv.* —**ra·pa′cious·ness,** *n.*

ra·pac·i·ty (rə pas′ə tē) *n.* quality of being rapacious.

rape¹ (rāp) *n.* **1.a.** crime of forcing a woman to have sexual intercourse against her will. **b.** statutory rape. **2.** seizing and carrying off by force. —*v.t.,* **raped, rap·ing. 1.** to have sexual intercourse with forcibly. **2.** *Archaic.* to seize and carry off by force. **3.** to plunder, as a city. [Latin *rapere* to seize.]

rape² (rāp) *n.* leafy branching plant, *Brassica napus,* whose leaves are used as fodder and whose seeds yield an oil. Also, **cole.** [Latin *rāpa* turnip.]

rape³ (rāp) *n.* refuse of grapes after the juice has been extracted, used in making vinegar. [French *râpe* grape stalk; of Germanic origin.]

rape oil, oil obtained from rapeseed, used in cooking and as a lubricant. Also, **rapeseed oil, col′za.**

rape·seed (rāp′sēd′) *n.* seed of the rape plant. Also, **col′za.**

Raph·a·el (raf′ē əl, rä′fē-, rä′fī el′) *n.* **1.** 1483–1520, Italian painter. **2.** one of the archangels.

rap·id (rap′id) *adj.* moving, acting, or happening with speed; swift: *rapid development.* —*n. usually,* **rapids.** part of a river where the current is swift, caused by a steep descent of the riverbed. [Latin *rapidus* swift.] —**rap′id·ly,** *adv.* —**rap′id·ness,** *n.* —**Syn.** *adj.* see **quick.**

rap·id-fire (rap′id fīr′) *adj.* **1.** (of guns) firing or capable of firing shots in quick succession. **2.** characterized by or occurring in quick succession: *rapid-fire questions.*

ra·pid·i·ty (rə pid′ə tē) *n.* state or quality of being rapid; quickness.

rapid transit, system of rapid passenger transportation in an urban area, as a subway system.

ra·pi·er (rā′pē ər) *n.* **1.** long, slender sword with a two-edged blade, used during the sixteenth and seventeenth centuries. **2.** light sword of the eighteenth century, having a sharp point and no cutting edge, used only for thrusting. [French *rapière;* earlier, in phrase *espee rapiere* rapier sword; of uncertain origin.]

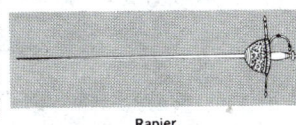

Rapier

rap·ine (rap′in) *n.* act of seizing and carrying off; plunder; pillage. [Latin *rapīna.*]

rap·port (ra pôr′) *n.* relationship or connection, esp. one that is characterized by harmony or close agreement: *The professor had good rapport with his students.* [French *rapport,* from *rapporter* to bring back, going back to Latin *re-* back + *ad* to + *portāre* to carry.]

rap·proche·ment (ra prōsh mäN′) *n.* establishment or reestablishment of friendly relations, as between nations. [French *rapprochement* a bringing together, from *rapprocher* to bring together, going back to Latin *re-* again + *ad* to + *prope* near.]

rap·scal·lion (rap skal′yən) *n.* rascal; rogue; scamp. [Earlier *rascallion,* from RASCAL.]

rapt (rapt) *adj.* **1.** carried away with strong emotion, as with joy or delight; enraptured. **2.** deeply absorbed; engrossed: *rapt attention.* **3.** showing or caused by rapture: *a rapt smile.* [Latin *raptus,* past participle of *rapere* to seize.]

rap·to·ri·al (rap tôr′ē əl) *adj.* **1.** of or relating to birds of prey. **2.** adapted for seizing prey: *raptorial talons.* **3.** predatory. [Latin *raptor* one who seizes by force + -IAL.]

rap·ture (rap′chər) *n.* **1.** state of being carried away by strong emotion, as joy or love. **2.** *also,* **raptures.** expression of great joy.

rap·tur·ous (rap′chər əs) *adj.* showing or feeling rapture. —**rap′-tur·ous·ly,** *adv.*

ra·ra a·vis (râr′ə ā′vis) *pl.,* **ra·ra a·vis·es** or **ra·rae a·ves** (râr′ē ā′vēz). rare person or thing. [Latin *rāre avis* rare bird.]

rare¹ (râr) **rar·er, rar·est.** *adj.* **1.** seldom occurring, seen, or found; unusual; uncommon: *It was rare to find him at home.* **2.** unusually excellent; remarkably good or fine, esp. because of uncommonness: *a rare gem, a rare talent.* **3.** of thin consistency; not dense: *The air is rare at high altitudes.* [Latin *rārus* uncommon, thin.] —**rare′ness,** *n.* —**Syn. 1.** see **uncommon.**

rare² (râr) **rar·er, rar·est.** *adj.* (of meat) cooked for a brief period of time. [Old English *hrēr* underdone.]

rare·bit (râr′bit) *n.* Welsh rabbit.

rare earth, 1. oxide of any of the rare-earth elements. **2.** any rare-earth element.

rare-earth element, any of a group of metallic elements of atomic numbers 57 through 71. Also, **rare-earth metal.**

rar·e·fac·tion (râr′ə fak′shən) *n.* **1.** act of rarefying. **2.** state of being rarefied.

rar·e·fy (râr′ə fī′) **-fied, -fy·ing.** *v.t.* **1.** to make thinner or less dense: *to rarefy air.* **2.** to refine or purify. —*v.i.* to become thinner or less dense. [Latin *rārefacere* to make thin, from *rārus* thin + *facere* to make.]

rare·ly (râr′lē) *adv.* **1.** not often; seldom; infrequently. **2.** in an unusual degree; exceptionally: *He is rarely handsome.* **3.** remarkably well; excellently: *a rarely written novel.*

rar·i·ty (râr′ə tē) *pl.,* **-ties.** *n.* **1.** one who or which is rare: *Rain is a rarity in the desert.* **2.** quality, state, or fact of being rare: *the rarity of the air at high altitudes.*

ras·cal (ras′kəl) *n.* **1.** mischievous, playful person; scamp. **2.** low, mean, dishonest person; scoundrel. [Old French *rascaille* outcasts, from *rasche* filth. See RASH².] —**Syn.** see **rogue.**

ras·cal·i·ty (ras kal′ə tē) *pl.,* **-ties.** *n.* **1.** character or behavior of a rascal. **2.** act of a rascal.

ras·cal·ly (ras′kə lē) *adj.* of or characteristic of a rascal. —*adv.* in a rascally manner.

rash¹ (rash) *adj.* **1.** acting too hastily or with lack of thought: *a rash young man.* **2.** characterized by too great haste or lack of thought: *a rash decision.* [Probably from an unrecorded Old English word.] —**rash′ly,** *adv.* —**rash′ness,** *n.*

Syn. 2. Rash, reckless indicate something done or made without forethought or preparation. Rash emphasizes the tendency to go to extremes, esp. when acting under pressure: *It was a rash statement made in the heat of anger and later regretted.* Reckless stresses the dangerous and destructive consequences of an act: *A reckless squandering of our natural resources characterized much of the period of western settlement.*

rash² (rash) *n.* **1.** eruption of red spots on the skin. **2.** outbreak of many instances within a short time: *a rash of burglaries.* [Old French *rasche* scurf, filth, going back to Latin *rāsus,* past participle of *rādere* to scrape, scratch.]

rash·er (rash′ər) *n.* **1.** slice of bacon for frying or broiling. **2.** serving of such slices. [Of uncertain origin.]

rasp (rasp) *v.t.* **1.** to scrape or grate with or as with a rough instrument. **2.** to grate upon; irritate: *The loud noise rasped his nerves.* **3.** to utter in a rough, grating voice. —*v.i.* **1.** to scrape or grate. **2.** to make a rough, grating sound. —*n.* **1.** rough, grating sound. **2.** coarse file with raised, pointed projections, used esp. on wood. **3.** act of rasping. [Old French *rasper* to scrape, scratch; of Germanic origin.]

rasp·ber·ry (raz′ber′ē) *pl.,* **-ries.** *n.* **1.** edible, thimble-shaped fruit of any of several plants, genus *Rubus,* of the rose family, consisting of a cluster of red or black drupelets. **2.** prickly plant that bears this fruit. **3.** *Slang.* sound of disapproval or contempt made with the tongue vibrating between the lips. [Obsolete *raspis* the fruit and plant (of uncertain origin) + BERRY.]

Raspberries

Ras·pu·tin, Gri·go·ri Ye·fi·mo·vich (ras pū′tin, -pōō′-; gri-gôr′ē ye fē′mo vich) c.1871–1916, Russian courtier and monk who had great influence in the court of Czar Nicholas II.

rat (rat) *n.* **1.** any of a great variety of rodents, genus *Rattus,* found throughout most of the world, resembling, but larger than, a mouse. Length: 5–12 inches, without the tail. **2.** *Slang.* sneaky, contemptible person, esp. one who deserts or betrays his associates. **3.** pad worn under hair to make it look thicker. **4.** to smell a rat. to suspect something underhanded. —*v.i.* **rat·ted, rat·ting. 1.** to hunt for rats. **2.** *Slang.* to desert or betray one's associates. [Old English *ræt* the rodent.]

rat·a·ble (rā′tə bəl) *also,* **rate·a·ble.** *adj.* **1.** capable of being rated or estimated. **2.** *British.* taxable.

ra·tan (ra tan′) *n.* rattan.

ratch·et (rach′it) *n.* **1.** mechanism consisting of a wheel or bar whose slanted teeth engage a catch or pawl which permits motion in one direction only. **2.** pawl, wheel, or bar of such a mechanism. [French *rochet,* earlier *rocquet* blunt head of a lance (referring to the resemblance between the head of a lance and the teeth of a ratchet); of Germanic origin.]

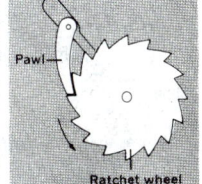

Pawl

Ratchet wheel

Ratchet

rate¹ (rāt) *n.* **1.** amount or number of one thing in relation to a certain

at; āpe; cär; end; mē; it; īce; hot; ōld; fôrk; wood; fōōl; oil; out; up; ūse; turn; sing; thin; this; zh in treasure; ə in ago, taken, pencil, lemon, circus.

827

amount or number of something else: *rate of speed per hour.* **2.** price or charge, as of a commodity or service, fixed according to a standard, scale, or ratio: *telephone rates.* **3.** relative quality or rank; class: *a movie of the first rate.* **4.** degree of speed of working, moving, or acting: *to build at a rapid rate.* **5.** *British.* local tax on property. **6. at any rate.** in any case; at least. —*v.t.* **rat·ed, rat·ing. 1.** to estimate the value of; appraise: *to rate a house for tax purposes.* **2.** to place in a certain class or rank: *to rate a ship.* **3.** to consider; regard: *Historians rate him as one of the greatest statesmen of his time.* **4.** to fix or set a rate for. **5.** *Informal.* to deserve; merit: *to rate a raise in salary.* —*v.i.* **1.** to have rank or class. **2.** to have value or standing: *He rates among the best novelists.* [Old French *rate* price, value, from Medieval Latin *rata* fixed amount, from Latin *rata,* feminine past participle of *rērī* to reckon, think.] —**Syn.** *v.t.* **1.** see **estimate.**

rate² (rāt) **rat·ed, rat·ing.** *v.t., v.i.* to scold. [Possibly of Scandinavian origin.]

ra·tel (rāt′əl, rāt′-) *n.* badgerlike mammal, genus *Mellivora,* of Africa and parts of Asia. Length: 2½ feet including tail.

rate of exchange, ratio at which the currency of one country is converted into the equivalent currency of another country.

rath·er (rath′ər, rä′thər) *adv.* **1.** more readily or willingly: *I would rather stay home tonight than go out.* **2.** more properly; with better reason or ground: *I rather deserve a promotion than he does.* **3.** more correctly or precisely: *The airplane is arriving at noon or, rather, 12:15.* **4.** to some degree; somewhat: *It is rather cold out.* **5.** on the contrary: *He is not happy; rather, he is sad.* —*interj. British.* certainly. [Old English *hrathor* more readily, comparative of *hræthe* quickly.]

raths·kel·ler (rät′skel′ər, rath′-) *n.* **1.** cellar of a German town hall, often used as a restaurant or beer hall. **2.** restaurant or bar, modeled after such a cellar. [German *Ratskeller,* from *Rat(haus)* town hall + *Keller* cellar.]

rat·i·fi·ca·tion (rat′ə fi kā′shən) *n.* act of ratifying; being ratified.

rat·i·fy (rat′ə fī′) **-fied, -fy·ing.** *v.t.* to validate by giving formal consent, approval, or sanction; confirm. [Old French *ratifier* to confirm, going back to Latin *ratus* fixed, past participle of *rērī* to reckon, think + *facere* to make.] —**rat′i·fi′er,** *n.*

rat·ing (rā′ting) *n.* **1.** classification according to a relative measure or standard; rank; grade: *a television show with a high rating.* **2.** position in a specific classification. **3.** an amount fixed as a rate. **4.** estimate of the financial status of an individual, business, or security. **5.** operating capacity of a piece of electrical machinery expressed as in horsepower or kilowatts.

ra·ti·o (rā′shē ō′, rā′shō) *pl.* **-ti·os.** *n.* **1.** comparison in quantity, amount, or size between two things. **2.** *Mathematics.* indicated quotient of two numbers or algebraic expressions. The ratio of 3 to 7 is written 3:7 or ³⁄₇. [Latin *ratiō* calculation, relation. Doublet of RATION, REASON.]

ra·ti·oc·i·nate (rash′ē os′ə nāt′) **-nat·ed, -nat·ing.** *v.i.* to reason. [Latin *ratiōcinātus,* past participle of *ratiōcinārī* to calculate, consider.] —**ra′ti·oc·i·na′tion,** *n.*

ra·tion (rash′ən, rā′shən) *n.* **1.** fixed portion or share. **2.** fixed daily food allowance, as for a soldier. **3. rations.** food. —*v.t.* **1.** to distribute in fixed portions: *During the blizzard, meat was rationed until new deliveries could be made.* **2.** to supply with rations, as an army. **3.** to restrict to fixed portions: *People were rationed to a quart of milk a week during the war.* [French *ration* allowance, from Latin *ratiō* calculation, relation. Doublet of RATIO, REASON.]

ra·tion·al (rash′ən əl) *adj.* **1.** conformable to reason; sensible: *Although the arguments were rational, he was not convinced.* **2.** sane: *The old man was perfectly rational when he made out his will.* **3.** endowed with the ability to reason: *He did not behave as a rational being but acted on emotion alone.* **4.** of, relating to, or based on reason. **5.** *Mathematics.* of or relating to a rational number or to an algebraic expression without radicals. [Latin *ratiōnālis* relating to reason, from *ratiō* reason, calculation, relation.] —**ra′tion·al·ly,** *adv.* —**Syn. 3.** see **reasonable.**

ra·tion·ale (rash′ə nal′) *n.* underlying reason; rational or logical basis: *The rationale of the war was not clearly stated.* [Latin *ratiōnāle* rational thing, neuter of *ratiōnālis* relating to reason. See RATIONAL.]

ra·tion·al·ism (rash′ən əl iz′əm) *n.* reliance on reason alone as the supreme authority in matters of opinion, belief, or conduct. —**ra′tion·al·ist,** *n., adj.* —**ra′tion·al·is′tic,** *adj.* —**ra′tion·al·is′ti·cal·ly,** *adv.*

ra·tion·al·i·ty (rash′ə nal′ə tē) *n.* quality or state of being rational.

ra·tion·al·ize (rash′ən əl īz′) **-ized, -iz·ing.** *v.t.* **1.** to explain (one's behavior) in a manner that is reasonable or plausible but unrelated to actual motivation: *He rationalized his cheating by saying that everyone else cheated.* **2.** to explain or interpret so as to appear reasonable. **3.** to make rational. —*v.i.* to devise plausible but inaccurate explanations for behavior. —**ra′tion·al·i·za′tion, ra′tion·al·iz′er,** *n.*

rational number, real number that can be expressed as a quotient of two integers or as an integer. ¾ is a rational number.

rat·line (rat′lin) *also,* **rat·lin.** *n.* **1.** one of the small ropes stretching horizontally across the shrouds of a ship, used as a ladder for going aloft. **2.** rope so used. [Of uncertain origin.]

rat race *Informal.* any frantic, senseless, endless, and usually competitive round of activity.

rat·tan (ra tan′) *also,* **ra·tan.** *n.* **1.** long thin stems of any of several tropical climbing palms, genus *Calamus,* used for mats, baskets, chairs, and other products. **2.** plant having these stems, found in southern Asia and the East Indies. **3.** cane or switch made from the rattan stem. [Malay *rōtan* the plant.]

rat·ter (rat′ər) *n.* animal, as a dog or cat, that catches rats.

rat·tle (rat′əl) **-tled, -tling.** *v.i.* **1.** to make a rapid succession of short, sharp sounds, as of small, hard objects colliding. **2.** to move with such sounds; clatter: *The old car rattled over the cobblestones.* **3.** to talk quickly and aimlessly; chatter (often with *on*): *She rattled on, unaware of her listeners.* —*v.t.* **1.** to cause to rattle. **2.** to say rapidly and fluently (usually with *off*): *She rattled off her answers.* **3.** to confuse; embarrass: *He was rattled by the insult.* —*n.* **1.** rapid succession of short, sharp sounds. **2.** sealed container, esp. a baby's toy, with small pellets or stones inside, which move around and make a rattling noise when the container is shaken. **3.** rattling sound caused by mucus in the throat, supposedly heard just before death. **4.** series of interlocking rings of horny tissue at the end of a rattlesnake's tail. [Imitative.]

rat·tle·brain (rat′əl brān′) *n.* empty-headed, talkative person.

rat·tler (rat′lər) *n.* **1.** one who or that which rattles. **2.** rattlesnake.

rat·tle·snake (rat′əl snāk′) *n.* any of a group of venomous snakes, genera *Crotalus* and *Sistrurus,* having a series of interlocking rings of horny tissue at the end of its tail which rattle when shaken. Length: from 15 inches to over 8 feet.

rat·tle·trap (rat′əl trap′) *n.* anything old and rattling, esp. an old car.

rat·ty (rat′ē) **-ti·er, -ti·est.** *adj.* **1.** of or relating to rats. **2.** infested with rats. **3.** disheveled; shabby.

rau·cous (rô′kəs) *adj.* **1.** harsh; grating: *His raucous voice made his singing unbearable.* **2.** disorderly; rowdy: *The raucous party left the house in shambles.* [Latin *raucus* hoarse.] —**rau′cous·ly,** *adv.* —**rau′cous·ness,** *n.*

rav·age (rav′ij) **-aged, -ag·ing.** *v.t.* to lay waste to; destroy. —*v.i.* to lay waste; be destructive. —*n.* destructive or ruinous action or its result: *The ravages of time left their marks on the old woman's face.* [Old French *ravage* havoc, from *ravir* to carry away, seize, going back to Latin *rapere*.] —**rav′ag·er,** *n.*

rave (rāv) **raved, rav·ing.** *v.i.* **1.** to talk wildly or irrationally. **2.** to talk with extravagant enthusiasm: *She raved about the new movie.* **3.** to roar; rage: *The storm raved along the coast.* —*n.* **1.** act of raving. **2.** extravagantly enthusiastic approval or recommendation. —*adj.* extravagantly enthusiastic or approving: *The new show received rave reviews.* [Old French *raver, resver* to wander, be delirious; of uncertain origin.]

rav·el (rav′əl) **-eled, -el·ing;** *also, British,* **-elled, -el·ling.** *v.t.* **1.** to cause (cloth or rope) to separate into loose threads; fray. **2.** to make plain or clear; unravel. **3.** to entangle, confuse, or perplex. —*v.i.* **1.** to become raveled; fray. **2.** to become entangled, confused, or perplexing. —*n.* loose thread or raveled part. [Middle Dutch *ravelen* to entangle, fray.]

Ra·vel, Mau·rice Joseph (rə vel′, ra-; mô rēs′) 1875–1937, French composer.

rav·el·ing (rav′ə ling) *also, British,* **rav·el·ling.** *n.* loose thread; ravel.

ra·ven¹ (rā′vən) *n.* any of several large birds, family Corvidae, having glossy black plumage and a harsh cry. Length: to 27 inches. —*adj.* glossy black. [Old English *hræfn* the bird.]

rav·en² (rav′ən) *v.i.* **1.** to eat voraciously; feed greedily. **2.** to seek plunder or prey voraciously. —*v.t.* to devour voraciously. [Old French *raviner* to ravage, going back to Latin *rapīna* plunder.] —**rav′en·er,** *n.*

Ra·ven·na (rə ven′ə) *n.* city in northeastern Italy. Pop. (1968), 129,-508.

Ratlines

Rattlesnake

Raven

at; āpe; cär; end; mē; it; īce; hot; ōld; fôrk; wood; fōōl; oil; out; up; ūse; turn; sing; thin; this; zh in treasure; ə in ago, taken, pencil, lemon, circus.

rav·en·ous (rav′ə nəs) *adj.* **1.** extremely hungry; famished; voracious. **2.** greedy; rapacious: *The ravenous mob pillaged the town.* **3.** very eager, as for satisfaction or gratification: *to be ravenous for attention.* [Old French *ravineux* violent, from *raviner* to ravage. See RAVEN².] —**rav′en·ous·ly,** *adv.* —**rav′en·ous·ness,** *n.*

ra·vine (rə vēn′) *n.* deep, narrow valley, esp. one eroded by running water. [French *ravine*; earlier, violent rush, as of water, from Latin *rapina* violence, plunder.]

rav·ing (rā′ving) *adj.* **1.** wild; frenzied. **2.** *Informal.* outstanding; extraordinary: *a raving success, a raving beauty.* —*n.* wild, irrational talk.

rav·i·o·li (rav′ē ō′lē) *n.,pl.* small envelopes of dough containing various fillings, such as chopped meat or cheese, which are boiled and served with a tomato sauce. ▲ construed as singular or plural. [Italian *ravioli,* plural of dialectal Italian *raviolo* little turnip, diminutive of *rava* turnip, from Latin *rāpa.*]

rav·ish (rav′ish) *v.t.* **1.** to seize and carry off by force. **2.** to rape. **3.** to carry away with joy; enrapture; enchant. [Old French *raviss-,* a stem of *ravir.* See RAVAGE.] —**rav′ish·er,** **rav′ish·ment,** *n.*

rav·ish·ing (rav′i shing) *adj.* enchanting; delightful. —**rav′ish·ing·ly,** *adv.*

raw (rô) *adj.* **1.** uncooked. **2.** not refined, manufactured, or processed; in a natural state: *raw cotton, raw milk.* **3.** having the skin off, as a wound. **4.** inexperienced or untrained: *a raw recruit.* **5.** piercingly damp and cold, as the weather. **6.** brutally frank or vulgar: *raw humor, a raw account of the accident.* **7.** severe or unfair: *a raw deal.* —*n.* **in the raw. 1.** in the natural or crude state: *nature in the raw.* **2.** naked. [Old English *hrēaw* uncooked.] —**raw′ly,** *adv.* —**raw′ness,** *n.*

Ra·wal·pin·di (rä′wəl pin′dē) *n.* city in northeastern West Pakistan, formerly the capital of Pakistan. Pop. (1961), 197,370.

raw·boned (rô′bōnd′) *adj.* having little flesh; gaunt.

raw·hide (rô′hīd′) *n.* **1.** untanned hide of cattle or other animals. **2.** rope or whip made of such hide. —*v.t.,* **-hid·ed, -hid·ing.** to whip with or as with a rawhide.

raw material, material not yet refined, manufactured, or processed: *Wood is the raw material of paper.*

ray¹ (rā) *n.* **1.** narrow beam of light. **2.** hint; trace: *a ray of hope.* **3.** *Mathematics.* **a.** raylike line, esp. one of a group of lines coming out from a common center. **b.** straight line that extends from a point. **4.** *Physics.* **a.** thin beam of radiant energy. **b.** stream of particles moving in the same line. **5.** *Zoology.* **a.** one of the radiating arms of a radiate animal, as a starfish. **b.** one of the bony rods supporting a fish's fin membrane. **6.** *Botany.* **a.** one of the flower stalks of an umbel. **b.** ray flower. —*v.i.* to send forth in rays; radiate. [Old French *rai* beam of light, from Latin *radius* rod, beam of light. Doublet of RADIUS.] —**Syn.** *n.* **1.** see **beam.**

ray² (rā) *n.* any of a number of horizontally flat fish, order Rajiformes, having a skeleton of cartilage rather than bone. Length: 1–22 feet. Weight: to 3500 pounds. [Old French *raie,* from Latin *raia.*]

ray flower, one of the marginal flowers around the flower head of certain composite plants, as the daisy. Also, **ray floret.**

ray·on (rā′on) *n.* any of a group of synthetic textile fibers made by pressing chemically treated cellulose through very fine holes and solidifying the resulting filaments. [From RAY¹; referring to the fiber's shine.]

raze (rāz) *razed, raz·ing. v.t.* to tear down; demolish. [Old French *raser* to shave, demolish, going back to Latin *rāsus,* past participle of *rādere* to scrape, scratch.] —**Syn.** see **demolish.**

ra·zor (rā′zər) *n.* **1.** sharp-edged instrument used for shaving off or cutting hair. **2.** electrically driven clipper used for the same purpose. [Old French *rasor,* from *raser* to shave. See RAZE.]

ra·zor·back (rā′zər bak′) *n.* **1.** wild or partly wild hog common in the southern United States, having a thin body, long legs, and a ridged back. **2.** finback.

razz (raz) *Slang. v.t.* to make fun of; ridicule. —*n.* raspberry *(def. 3).* [From RASPBERRY.]

raz·zle-daz·zle (raz′əl daz′əl) *n. Informal.* confusing, gaudy, or showy action or display.

Rb, rubidium.

R.C. 1. Red Cross. **2.** Roman Catholic.

rd, rod; rods.

Rd., road. Also, **rd.**

R.D., rural delivery.

re¹ (rā) *n.* second of the series of syllables used to name the eight tones of the diatonic scale. See **do²** for illustration. [See GAMUT.]

re² (rē) *prep.* about; concerning. [Latin *rē* (in) the matter, ablative of *rēs* thing, matter.]

Re (rā) Ra.

Re, rhenium.

re- *prefix* **1.** again: *re-count.* **2.** back: *repel.* [Latin *re-* again, back; often through French *re-.*] ▲ The meaning of a word in the lists at the bottom of this and the following pages can be understood by combining *re-* with the root word.

reach (rēch) *v.t.* **1.** to arrive at; get as far as; come to: *to reach a conclusion.* **2.** to touch or grasp by something extended: *to reach a book on a shelf.* **3.** to stretch or extend: *He reached out his arms to greet me.* **4.** *Informal.* to hold out and give by or as by the outstretched hand; pass: *Will you reach me the sugar?* **5.** to communicate with; contact: *I reached him by telephone.* **6.** to affect or influence: *He tried to reach her with presents.* **7.** to amount to: *The profit reached over a thousand dollars.* —*v.i.* **1.** to stretch, as with the arm or hand: *He reached to touch the ceiling.* **2.** to try to grasp something: *to reach for a book.* **3.** to stretch or extend in space, time, or influence: *The king's decree reached to the furthest corners of the empire.* **4.** to carry; penetrate: *How far can his voice reach?* **5.** to sail with the wind just forward of, on, or just behind the beam. —*n.* **1.** act of reaching or stretching out. **2.** extent or distance covered in reaching: *One would need a long reach to be able to touch the ceiling.* **3.** power or extent of comprehension, influence, or accomplishment; range: *Choose a goal within your reach.* **4.** continuous stretch or course; expanse: *a reach of level ground, a reach of water.* **5.** stretch of a river or channel between bends. **6.** tack sailed with the wind forward of, on, or just behind the beam. [Old English *rǣcan* to stretch out, succeed in touching.]

re·act (rē akt′) *v.i.* **1.** to respond, as to a stimulus: *The press reacted to the demand for censorship with angry editorials.* **2.** to act in opposition (usually with *against*): *He reacted against his parents' strictness.* **3.** to act in return or reciprocally. **4.** to act in a reverse way, esp. as to return to a former condition. **5.** to undergo a chemical reaction.

re·act (rē akt′) *v.t.* to act again.

re·ac·tance (rē ak′təns) *n. Electricity.* opposition to an alternating current in a circuit, caused by capacitance and inductance.

re·ac·tant (rē ak′tənt) *n.* any substance in a chemical reaction.

re·ac·tion (rē ak′shən) *n.* **1.** response, as to a stimulus: *What was the critic's reaction to the book?* **2.** reversing or opposing action. **3.** movement or a tendency to return to a former condition, esp. one of extreme political and social conservatism. **4.** *Chemistry.* process in which substances are changed chemically into new substances. **5.** *Physics.* force equal to but opposing the force which produces it. **6.** process that involves change in atomic nuclei.

re·ac·tion·ar·y (rē ak′shə ner′ē) *adj.* of, relating to, characterized by, or favoring political and social reaction. —*n. pl.,* **-ar·ies,** one who favors or tends toward political and social reaction.

re·ac·ti·vate (rē ak′tə vāt′) *-vat·ed, -vat·ing. v.t.* to make active again. —**re·ac′ti·va′tion,** *n.*

re·ac·tive (rē ak′tiv) *adj.* **1.** tending to react. **2.** relating to or characterized by reaction.

re·ac·tor (rē ak′tər) *n.* nuclear reactor.

read¹ (rēd) *read* (red), *read·ing. v.t.* **1.** to understand the meaning of (something written, printed, or stamped): *to read a magazine.* **2.** to utter aloud (something written or printed): *The mother read bedtime stories to her children.* **3.** to understand letters or symbols in (a foreign language): *to read French.* **4.** to understand, as by interpreting outward signs: *She read his thoughts.* **5.** to explain the meaning of; interpret: *There are two ways of reading his behavior.* **6.** to infer (often with *into*): *He read love into her casual friendliness.* **7.** to bring (to a certain state) by reading: *The mother read the child to sleep.* **8.** to have or give as the wording in a particular passage: *The book reads "effect" for "affect."* **9.** to indicate or register: *The speedometer read sixty miles per hour.* **10.** to foretell; predict: *to read the future.* **11.** to lip-read. **12.** *British.* to study: *to read classics.* **13.** (of a computer) to convert (information) from the form supplied, as punch cards, to a form suitable for computation or storage. **14.** *to read out of.* to expel from (a political party or other group). —*v.i.* **1.** to understand something written, printed, or stamped. **2.** to utter aloud something written or printed. **3.** to learn by reading (with *of* or *about*): *I read about the incident in the newspaper.* **4.** to have or produce a particular impression when read: *The novelist's prose reads well like poetry.* **5.** to have a specific wording: *These two editions read differently.* **6.** to admit of interpretation: *The law reads two ways.* **7.** to give a public reading or recital. **8.** (of a computer) to read information. **9. to read out.** to provide a display of information stored in or produced by a computer. **10. to read up on.** to study. [Old English *rǣdan* to guess, interpret, understand writing; referring originally to the interpretation of magic runes scratched on pieces of wood.]

read² (red) *adj.* informed by reading. [Past participle of READ¹.]

read·a·ble (rē′də bəl) *adj.* **1.** easy or interesting to read. **2.** capable of being read; legible. —**read′a·bil′i·ty, read′a·ble·ness,** *n.*

| re′ab·sorb′ | re·ac′cli·mate′ | re′ac·cus′tom | re′ac·quire′ |
| re′ab·sorp′tion | re′ac·cuse′ | re′ac·quaint′ | re′a·dapt′ |

read·er (rē′dər) *n.* **1.** one who reads. **2.** schoolbook with exercises for learning and practicing reading. **3.** one employed to read manuscripts submitted to a publisher and to evaluate their fitness for publication. **4.** professor's assistant who reads and grades examinations and papers. **5.** proofreader. **6.** *British.* lecturer or instructor in a university. **7.** one authorized to read the lessons or other parts of the service in a church.

read·er·ship (rē′dər ship′) *n.* **1.** readers of a newspaper or magazine. **2.** *British.* position or office of a reader.

read·i·ly (red′ə lē) *adv.* **1.** willingly: *The boy readily followed his friend's advice.* **2.** easily: *The poem could not be readily understood.* **3.** quickly.

read·i·ness (red′ē nis) *n.* **1.** quality or state of being ready. **2.** quickness. **3.** willingness; inclination. **4.** ease; facility.

read·ing (rē′ding) *n.* **1.** act or practice of one who reads. **2.** act or instance of uttering aloud, esp. publicly, something written or printed. **3.** material read or to be read: *This book is good reading.* **4.** extent to which one has read; literary knowledge. **5.** form in which a given word, sentence, or passage appears in a particular text. **6.** personal or particular interpretation: *a fine reading of Bach.* **7.** information indicated or registered, as on a meter, dial, or graduated instrument. —*adj.* **1.** inclined to read: *the reading public.* **2.** made or used for reading: *reading glasses.*

Read·ing (red′ing) *n.* **1.** city in southeastern Pennsylvania. Pop. (1970), 87,643. **2.** city in southern England, near London. Pop. (1968), 127,300.

reading room, room for reading, as in a library or club.

read·out (rēd′out′) *n.* display of information stored in or produced by a computer.

read·y (red′ē) **read·i·er, read·i·est.** *adj.* **1.** prepared or fit for use or action: *We are ready to go.* **2.** mentally prepared; willing: *He was ready to take any job in order to pay for a college education.* **3.** apt; inclined; disposed: *to be too ready to criticize others.* **4.** immediately liable or likely: *The dynamite is ready to explode.* **5.** quick or prompt: *a ready answer.* **6.** quick or prompt in action or thought: *a ready mind.* **7.** immediately available: *ready cash.* —*v.t.* **read·ied, read·y·ing.** to make ready; prepare: *to ready a runway for the takeoff of a jet.* [Old English *ræde* prepared, prompt, swift.]

read·y-made (red′ē mād′) *adj.* **1.** made for immediate use by any purchaser; not made-to-order: *a rack of ready-made dresses.* **2.** unoriginal or commonplace, as an idea.

re·a·gent (rē ā′jənt) *n.* any substance used in a chemical reaction for the purpose of detecting, measuring, examining, or producing other substances.

re·al¹ (rē′əl, rēl) *adj.* **1.** occurring as a fact; not imagined or fictitious; actual or true: *He preferred literature to real life.* **2.** not artificial; genuine; authentic: *real pearls.* **3.** not pretended or pretending: *real grief.* **4.** *Law.* relating to or designating permanent or immovable things, as lands or buildings: *real property.* Distinguished from **personal.** **5.** *Mathematics.* of or relating to a real number. —*adv. Informal.* very; extremely: *He was real sorry.* [Late Latin *reālis* actual, relating to a thing, from Latin *rēs* thing, matter.] —**re′al·ness,** *n.*
Syn. *adj.* **1. Real, actual, true** indicate something that matches fact. **Real** implies that something is what it seems or is said to be, suggesting the concrete, measurable, or even intractable nature of things: *We need real help, not just promises.* **Actual** is a more neutral term that emphasizes circumstantial reality, what occurs as distinguished from what is possible or ideal: *The car performs well under actual road conditions.* **True** emphasizes the subjective reality, a product of personal or ethical standards: *Although we have the facts, we'll never know the true story.*

re·al² (rā äl′) *pl.* **re·als** or **re·a·les** (rā ä′lās). *n.* former coin and monetary unit of Spain and various Latin American countries. [Spanish *real,* going back to Latin *rēgālis* royal, from *rēx* king.]

real estate, land together with the permanent buildings, trees, water, or mineral deposits on it.

real focus, focus *(def. 1a).*

real image, image *(def. 7a).*

re·al·ism (rē′ə liz′əm) *n.* **1.** concern with and preference for what is actual or practical, as opposed to what is imaginary or visionary. **2.** artistic and literary style that emphasizes an accurate and objective representation of life. **3.** *Philosophy.* **a.** view that ideas, esp. universal concepts, have a real existence independent of the material world and man's consciousness of them. **b.** view that the world of material objects has a real existence both independent of and proven by man's consciousness of it.

re·al·ist (rē′ə list) *n.* **1.** one who is concerned with and prefers what is actual or practical, as opposed to what is imaginary or visionary. **2.** artist or writer whose work is characterized by realism. **3.** *Philosophy.* one who believes in realism.

re·al·is·tic (rē′ə lis′tik) *adj.* **1.** accurate and objective, as in literary or artistic representation; of, relating to, or characterized by artistic or literary realism. **2.** not visionary or idealistic; concerned with what is actual or practical: *a realistic appraisal of a situation.* **3.** *Philosophy.* of or relating to realists or realism. —**re′al·is′ti·cal·ly,** *adv.*

re·al·i·ty (rē al′ə tē) *pl.* **-ties.** *n.* **1.** state or quality of being real. **2.** real object, fact, or event. **3.** *Philosophy.* **a.** that which has real existence. **b.** totality of real objects, facts, and events. **4. in reality,** in fact; really: *The child thought he was being helpful, but in reality he was a nuisance.*

re·al·i·za·tion (rē′ə li zā′shən) *n.* **1.** act of realizing; being realized. **2.** something realized.

re·al·ize (rē′ə līz′) **-ized, -iz·ing.** *v.t.* **1.** to understand completely; comprehend clearly. **2.** to make real, as an idea or emotion: *His hopes were never realized.* **3.** to cause to seem real, as a character in a play. **4.** to gain (a sum of money), as by selling property or investing capital. **5.** to bring (a certain sum of money), as from a sale.

re·al·ly (rē′ə lē, rē′lē) *adv.* **1.** in fact; actually: *The witness wrote an account of how the accident really happened.* **2.** indeed: *Really, that was a terrible mistake.* ▲ used for emphasis. **3.** truly; genuinely: *We spent a really pleasant day in the park.*

realm (relm) *n.* **1.** kingdom. **2.** sphere or province, as of knowledge, power, or influence: *the realm of science, the realm of fantasy.* [Old French *realme* kingdom, going back to Latin *regimen* government; influenced by Old French *reial* royal, from Latin *rēgālis.*]

real number *Mathematics.* any rational or irrational number.

Re·al·tor (rē′əl tər) *n.* **1.** real estate agent or broker who is a member of the National Association of Real Estate Boards. **2.** realtor. *Informal.* real estate agent or broker.

re·al·ty (rē′əl tē) *n.* real estate. [REAL¹ + -TY².]

ream¹ (rēm) *n.* quantity of paper of uniform size and quality, varying from 480 to 500 sheets, depending on grade. [Old French *raime,* from Arabic *rizmah* bundle.]

ream² (rēm) *v.t.* **1.** to create or enlarge (a hole). **2.** to remove, as a defect or extraneous material, with a reamer. [Old French *rēman* to open up.]

ream·er (rē′mər) *n.* **1.** cylindrical steel tool with lengthwise blades or cutting edges, turned in a drilled hole to enlarge or shape it. **2.** utensil used for extracting juice from oranges, lemons, and other fruit; juicer. **3.** one who or that which reams.

reap (rēp) *v.t.* **1.** to cut down and gather (grain). **2.** to obtain or gather (a crop) by reaping. **3.** to cut down or harvest the crop or produce from: *to reap fields.* **4.** to receive, esp. as a reward: *The child's good behavior reaped praise.* —*v.i.* to receive in return for something done. [Old English *repan* to cut grain.]

reap·er (rē′pər) *n.* **1.** one who reaps. **2.** harvesting machine formerly used to cut and collect grain.

re·ap·pear (rē′ə pēr′) *v.i.* to appear again. —**re′ap·pear′ance,** *n.*

rear¹ (rēr) *n.* **1.** part, position, or space which is behind or in the back; back. **2.** part of a military force farthest from the fighting area; the last elements in a column or line of march. **3.** the buttocks. —*adj.* pertaining to or situated at or in the back, behind, from Old French *arere* backward. See ARREARS.]

rear² (rēr) *v.t.* **1.** to help bring to maturity; raise, esp. a child. **2.** to construct; build: *They reared the building in 1941.* **3.** to bring to an upright position; lift up: *to rear one's head from a pillow.* —*v.i.* (of an animal) to rise on the hind legs. [Old English *ræran* to raise.]

rear admiral, officer in the U.S. Navy ranking below a vice admiral and above a captain.

rear guard, body of troops assigned to bring up the rear and guard it from attack, esp. during a retreat.

re·arm (rē ärm′) *v.t.* to arm again, esp. with new or better weapons. —**re·ar′ma·ment,** *n.*

rear·most (rēr′mōst′) *adj.* farthest in the rear; last.

re·add′	re·ad·mit′	re′al·lo·ca′tion	re′ap·ply′
re′ad·dress′	re·ad·mit′tance	re·al′ter	re′ap·point′
re′ad·journ′	re′a·dopt′	re′a·nal′y·sis	re′ap·point′ment
re′ad·journ′ment	re·af·firm′	re·an′a·lyze′	re′ap·por′tion
re′ad·just′	re′af·fir·ma′tion	re·an′i·mate′	re′ap·por′tion·ment
re′ad·just′a·ble	re·a·lign′	re·an′nex′	re′ap·prais′al
re′ad·just′ment	re′a·lign′ment	re′an·nex·a′tion	re′ap·praise′
re′ad·mis′sion	re·al′lo·cate′	re′ap·pli·ca′tion	re·ar′gue

re·ar·range (rē′ə rānj′) -ranged, -rang·ing. *v.t.* to arrange again, esp. in a different way. —**re′ar·range′ment,** *n.*

rear-view mirror (rēr′vū′) mirror, esp. in a motor vehicle, placed so that the driver can see what is behind him while still facing forward.

rear·ward (rēr′wərd) *adj.* situated in or directed toward the rear. —*adv. also,* **rear·wards.** in, at, or toward the rear.

rea·son (rē′zən) *n.* **1.** something, as a fact or circumstance, which serves as a ground, motive, or cause: *There is no reason to doubt his word.* **2.** statement used to justify, prove, or explain: *He could give no reason for his beliefs.* **3.** power or faculty to think logically, draw conclusions, or make inferences. **4.** sensible view; good judgment: *His actions showed a lack of reason.* **5.** sanity: *The shock caused him to lose all reason.* **6. by reason of.** due to the fact that; because of. **7. in (or within) reason.** conforming to that which is sensible, just, or proper; reasonable. **8. to stand to reason.** to be logical to assume: *It stands to reason that he won't be able to meet us.* —*v.i.* **1.** to make inferences or draw conclusions; think rationally or logically: *His primary aim was to teach his students to reason.* **2.** to try to persuade or influence someone by logical argument (with *with*): *Reasoning with him was useless.* **3.** *Archaic.* to engage in discussion; dispute; argue: *Let us reason together.* —*v.t.* **1.** to think about carefully in a logical manner; analyze (with *out*): *He reasoned the problem out and came to a conclusion.* **2.** to give reasons for; support by argument. [Old French *raison* understanding, act of reasoning, from Latin *ratiō* calculation, relation, understanding, cause. Doublet of RATIO, RATION.] —**rea′son·er,** *n.*

Syn. *n.* **1. Reason, motive** mean factors that explain action. **Reason** suggests a rational or abstract explanation offered in support of a particular course of action and evaluated according to standards of merit, value, or usefulness: *His reasons for closing down the plant were outlined in a detailed memo.* **Motive** suggests a psychological factor that underlies behavior, and which must be determined by an observer because it is not often expressed: *The police suggested that the motive for the crime was jealousy.*

rea·son·a·ble (rē′zə nə bəl, rēz′nə-) *adj.* **1.** according to or conforming with reason; not foolish; sensible: *A reasonable assumption could be made if we knew all the facts.* **2.** not excessive or extravagant; moderate; fair: *a reasonable request.* **3.** worth the price asked for. **4.** having the ability to reason. —**rea′son·a·ble·ness,** *n.* —**rea′son·a·bly,** *adv.*

Syn. **4. Reasonable, rational** indicate the presence of thought in making decisions. **Reasonable** stresses moderation, flexibility, and wisdom, esp. in applying reason: *The reasonable man adapts himself to the world* (Shaw, 1903). **Rational** stresses logical and systematic thought as an exclusive means of solving problems: *As a purely rational man, he failed to recognize the human need for love.*

rea·son·ing (rē′zə ning, rēz′ning) *n.* **1.** mental process employed to draw conclusions from facts. **2.** that which is used in this process, as arguments or evidence.

re·as·sur·ance (rē′ə shoor′əns) *n.* **1.** repeated or fresh assurance. **2.** restoration of courage or confidence. **3.** reinsurance.

re·as·sure (rē′ə shoor′) -sured, -sur·ing. *v.t.* **1.** to restore confidence or courage in: *to reassure a frightened child.* **2.** to assure again: *Reassure him that we shall go.* **3.** to insure again. —**re′as·sur′ing·ly,** *adv.*

reave (rēv) reaved *or* reft, reav·ing. *v.t. Archaic.* to take or deprive of forcibly; carry away; rob. [Old English *rēafian.*]

re·bate (rē′bāt, ri bāt′) *n.* sum of money which is deducted or returned, as a discount. —*v.t.,* **-bat·ed, -bat·ing.** to make a rebate of. [Old French *rebattre* to beat down again, from *re-* (see RE-) + *abat(t)re* to beat down. See ABATE.]

re·bec (rē′bek) *also,* **re·beck.** *n.* medieval musical instrument resembling a violin and usually having three strings. [Old French *rebec,* form of *rebebe,* from Arabic *rabāb.*]

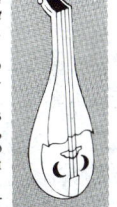

Rebec

Re·bec·ca (ri bek′ə) *n.* in the Old Testament, the wife of Isaac and the mother of Esau and Jacob.

reb·el (*n., adj.,* reb′əl; *v.,* ri bel′) *n.* **1.** one who resists or refuses to obey law, authority, or control of any kind. **2. Rebel.** one who fought on the side of the Confederacy in the Civil War. —*adj.* of a rebel or rebels: *rebel forces, a rebel victory.* —*v.i.* **1. re·belled, re·bel·ling. 1.** to resist or disobey law or authority (often with *against*). **2.** to feel or show anger or repugnance. [Old French *rebeller* to revolt, from Latin *rebellāre* from *re-* again + *bellāre* to make war. Doublet of REVEL.]

re·bel·lion (ri bel′yən) *n.* **1.** organized armed resistance against a legal government; insurrection. **2.** resistance or defiance against any control or authority. [Old French *rebellion* act of revolting, from Latin *rebelliō* revolt.] —**Syn. 1.** see **revolt.**

re·bel·lious (ri bel′yəs) *adj.* **1.** behaving or disposed to be like a rebel. **2.** characteristic of or marked by rebels or rebellion: *a rebellious period in history.* **3.** hard to manage or treat; refractory. —**re·bel′lious·ly,** *adv.* —**re·bel′lious·ness,** *n.*

re·birth (rē burth′, rē′burth′) *n.* **1.** second birth; reincarnation. **2.** revival; renaissance.

re·born (rē bôrn′) *adj.* born again.

re·bound (*v.,* ri bound′; *n.,* rē′bound′, ri bound′) *v.i.* to bound back, as from force of impact; spring back. —*n.* **1.** act of springing back; recoil. **2. on the rebound.** *Informal.* as a result of an emotional reaction to rejection or disappointment, esp. in love. [Old French *rebondir* to leap back, from *re-* (see RE-) + *bondir* to leap. See BOUND².]

re·broad·cast (rē brôd′kast′) -cast *or* -cast·ed, -cast·ing. *v.t.* **1.** to broadcast (a program) again at a later time from the same station. **2.** to broadcast a program relayed from another station). —*n.* program that is or was rebroadcast.

re·buff (ri buf′) *n.* **1.** blunt or sudden rejection, as of a person's advances; snub. **2.** sudden check, as to further action or progress; repulse. —*v.t.* **1.** to reject bluntly or suddenly; snub. **2.** to check suddenly; repulse. [Italian *ribuffo* check, scolding, from *ri-* back (from Latin *re-*) + *buffo* puff (imitative).]

re·build (rē bild′) -built, -build·ing. *v.t.* **1.** to build (something) again. **2.** to make extensive changes in; repair or remodel. —*v.i.* to build again.

re·buke (ri būk′) -buked, -buk·ing. *v.t.* to chide sharply; reprimand. —*n.* sharp chiding; reprimand; reproof. [Anglo-Norman *rebuker* to repel, going back to Old French *re-* (see RE-) + *buschier* to strike, cut wood (from *busche* log; of Germanic origin).] —**re·buk′er,** *n.* —**Syn.** *v.t.* see **reprove.**

re·bus (rē′bəs) *pl.,* -bus·es. *n.* representation of a syllable, word, or phrase by pictures or symbols whose names sound like the intended syllable or words. A picture of an eye followed by one of a tin can is a rebus for "I can." [Latin *rēbus* by means of things (because things or pictures are used in a rebus), ablative plural of *rēs* thing.]

re·but (ri but′) -but·ted, -but·ting. *v.t.* to disprove, as by counterargument; refute. [Old French *reboter* to repulse, from *re-* (see RE-) + *boter* to push (of Germanic origin).] —**re·but′ter,** *n.*

re·but·tal (ri but′əl) *n.* act of rebutting, esp. in law; refutation.

rec. **1.** receipt. **2.** recipe. **3.** record. **4.** recorder.

re·cal·ci·trant (ri kal′sə trant) *adj.* obstinately defiant; unmanageable; refractory. —*n.* recalcitrant person. [Latin *recalcitrāns,* present participle of *recalcitrāre* to kick back, going back to *re-* back + *calx* heel.] —**re·cal′ci·trance,** *or* **re·cal′ci·tran·cy,** *n.*

re·call (*v.,* ri kôl′; *n.,* ri kôl′, rē′kôl′) *v.t.* **1.** to call or bring back to mind; remember: *I don't recall his name.* **2.** to call back; summon back: *He was recalled home when his mother died.* **3.** to take back; revoke: *The chess player's careless move could not be recalled.* **4.** to bring back; restore: *The invalid could not be recalled to his former vitality.* —*n.* **1.** remembrance, as of events or learning: *He had total recall of the book.* **2.** a calling back; summoning back: *The recall of the ambassador was embarrassing for the country.* **3.** revocation, as of an order. **4.** process of removal, or right of removal, of a public official from office before his term is over, by direct popular vote. **5.** signal, as a bugle call or flag, used to call back soldiers or ships.

re·cant (ri kant′) *v.t.* to withdraw formally or publicly, as a statement or opinion; renounce; retract. —*v.i.* to renounce or retract a previously held opinion or allegiance. [Latin *recantāre* to sing again, revoke.] —**re·can·ta·tion** (rē′kan tā′shən), *n.*

re·cap¹ (rē′kap′) -capped, -cap·ping. *v.t.* to cement and vulcanize a

at; āpe; cär; end; mē; it; īce; hot; ōld; fôrk; wood; fool; oil; out; up; ūse; turn; sing; thin; this; zh in treasure; ə in ago, taken, pencil, lemon, circus.

strip of rubber on the worn surface of the tread of a pneumatic tire. —*n.* recapped tire. [RE- + CAP.]

re·cap² (rē′kap′) **-capped, -cap·ping.** *Informal. v.t., v.i.* to recapitulate. —*n.* recapitulation. [Short for RECAPITULATE.]

re·ca·pit·u·late (rē′kə pich′ə lāt′) **-lat·ed, -lat·ing.** *v.t., v.i.* to restate briefly; summarize. [Late Latin *recapitulātus,* past participle of *recapitulāre* to summarize, going back to Latin *re-* again + *capitulum* chapter of a book. See CHAPTER.] —**re′ca·pit′u·la′tion,** *n.*

re·cast (*v.,* rē kast′; *n.,* rē′kast′) **-cast, -cast·ing.** *v.t.* **1.** to cast again or anew. **2.** to fashion again; remodel; reconstruct. —*n.* something recast.

recd., recvd. received. Also, **rec'd.**

re·cede (ri sēd′) **-ced·ed, -ced·ing.** *v.i.* **1.** to move back or away: *The waves receded.* **2.** to become, or seem to become, more distant: *The houses receded as we drove by.* **3.** to slope or appear to slope backward: *The man's hairline receded.* **4.** to withdraw, as from a promise, position, or bargain. [Latin *recēdere* to retreat, go back.]

re·ceipt (ri sēt′) *n.* **1.** written acknowledgment that something, as money, goods, or mail, has been received. **2.** receipts. amount or quantity received, esp. of money. **3.** act of receiving; being received. **4.** recipe. —*v.t.* **1.** to write a receipt for (money, goods, or mail). **2.** to mark (an account) as paid. [Old Norman French *receite* money or value received, going back to Latin *recepta* thing received, from *recipere* to take back, accept.]

re·ceiv·a·ble (ri sē′və bəl) *adj.* **1.** capable of being received; acceptable. **2.** awaiting receipt of payment; due. Accounts receivable are unpaid accounts held by a creditor, rather than a debtor.

re·ceive (ri sēv′) **-ceived, -ceiv·ing.** *v.t.* **1.** to take (something) into one's hands or possession; acquire; get: *to receive a letter.* **2.** to take in or acquire mentally; learn; comprehend: *to receive instructions.* **3.a.** to meet with; experience: *to receive a shock.* **b.** to be subjected to; suffer: *He received a broken jaw.* **4.** to greet or welcome: *The host received his guests at the door.* **5.** to allow to enter; admit: *He was received at the club.* **6.** to listen to: *to receive a confession.* **7.** to take the impact or force of; bear: *He received her entire weight when she fell.* **8.** to have capacity for; hold: *The car was too little to receive all the passengers.* **9.** to accept as authentic or valid; believe: *an axiom universally received.* **10.** to have (something) bestowed or conferred, as a title, honor, or office: *to receive a knighthood.* —*v.i.* **1.** to take, acquire, or get something; be a recipient: *Be grateful for what you receive.* **2.** to greet and entertain visitors. **3.** to convert incoming radio or television signals into sound or pictures. [Old French *receivre* to accept, going back to Latin *recipere.*]
Syn. *v.t.* **1. Receive, accept** mean retaining something offered or given. **Receive** suggests no special effort to obtain something but rather a passive taking of what is presented: *He received a watch on his birthday.* **Accept** implies an active response, although often of an undiscriminating nature: *He accepted the long-distance call.*

re·ceiv·er (ri sē′vər) *n.* **1.** one who or that which receives. **2.** one who knowingly receives or buys stolen goods; fence. **3.** one appointed by a court of law to take charge of and administer the property or business of others pending the outcome of litigation, as when a company becomes bankrupt. **4.a.** device that receives electrical impulses or radio waves and converts them into pictures or sound, as the part of a telephone held to the ear. **b.** television or radio receiving set.

re·ceiv·er·ship (ri sē′vər ship′) *n.* **1.** condition of being in the hands of a receiver. **2.** position and functions of a receiver.

receiving set, apparatus for receiving electromagnetic waves and converting them into pictures or sounds, as in radio or television reception; set.

re·cen·sion (ri sen′shən) *n.* **1.** critical or careful revision or editing of a text. **2.** text resulting from such revision.

re·cent (rē′sənt) *adj.* **1.** done, happening, or made just before the present: *What is the most recent news?* **2.** of or belonging to a period of time not far removed; modern: *a recent period in history.* **3. Recent.** of, relating to, or characteristic of the Recent geological epoch. Also (*def.* 3), **Hol′o·cene.** —*n.* **Recent.** present geological epoch, the second of the Quaternary period, during which the climate has become warmer, glaciers have melted, and modern man has flourished. Also, **Hol′o·cene.** [Latin *recēns* fresh, new.] —**re′cent·ly,** *adv.* —**re′cent·ness,** *n.*

re·cep·ta·cle (ri sep′tə kəl) *n.* **1.** object or place which receives and holds something, as a box or bag. **2.** swollen tip of the stem of a flower, which bears the sepals, the petals, the stamens, and the carpels. [Latin *receptāculum* place to receive things.]

re·cep·tion (ri sep′shən) *n.* **1.** act of receiving or fact of being received. **2.** way in which someone or something is accepted or received: *a cordial reception.* **3.** social gathering, esp. one of a formal or ceremo-

nious nature. **4.** conversion of radio or television signals into sound or pictures, esp. with reference to quality. [Latin *receptiō* a receiving.]

re·cep·tion·ist (ri sep′shə nist) *n.* one who is employed in an office to receive callers, make appointments, and give general information.

re·cep·tive (ri sep′tiv) *adj.* able or disposed to receive, as suggestions or impressions. —**re·cep′tive·ly,** *adv.* —**re·cep′tive·ness, re·cep·tiv·i·ty** (rē′sep tiv′ə tē), *n.*

re·cep·tor (ri sep′tər) *n.* cell or group of cells connected to one or more nerve cells, which, when stimulated, cause nerve impulses to be relayed to the brain. [Latin *receptor* receiver.]

re·cess (rē′ses, ri ses′) *n.* **1.** period of cessation, as from usual work. **2.** part in a wall that is depressed or indented from the rest; niche. **3.** remote or secret spot or part; quiet, hidden place: *the recesses of one's heart.* —*v.t.* **1.** to place in or as in a recess; set back or away. **2.** to make a recess in. —*v.i.* to take a recess. [Latin *recessus* a going back, retreat.]

re·ces·sion¹ (ri sesh′ən) *n.* **1.** act of receding; withdrawal. **2.** period of decline in business activity, less severe than a depression, occurring esp. after a period of relative economic prosperity. [Latin *recessiō* a going back, receding.]

re·ces·sion² (ri sesh′ən) *n.* ceding back of territory to the country or government previously owning it. [RE- + CESSION.]

re·ces·sion·al (ri sesh′ən əl) *adj.* of, relating to, or occurring at the end of a church service: *a recessional hymn.* —*n.* **1.** recessional hymn or music. **2.** procession at the end of a ceremony, as of the clergy returning to the sacristy from the sanctuary.

re·ces·sive (ri ses′iv) *adj.* **1.** tending to go back; receding. **2.** relating to or designating one of a pair of hereditary characteristics appearing in an organism, that is prevailed over by another when both are present in a genetic make-up. Opposed to **dominant.** —*n. Genetics.* **1.** recessive hereditary characteristic. **2.** organism having one or more recessive characteristics.

re·cher·ché (rə shār′shā, -shär shā′) *adj.* **1.** carefully sought out; choice. **2.** refined; elegant. **3.** overrefined; strained. [French *recherché,* from *rechercher* to seek. See RESEARCH.]

re·cid·i·vism (ri sid′ə viz′əm) *n.* habitual relapse into previous behavior or activity, esp. undesirable or criminal behavior. —**re·cid′i·vist,** *n.* —**re·cid′i·vis′tic, re·cid′i·vous,** *adj.*

rec·i·pe (res′ə pē′) *n.* **1.** list of ingredients and directions for the preparation of food or drink. **2.** method or formula for attaining an end. **3.** formerly, medical prescription. [Latin *recipe* take (imperative of *recipere* to take); originally, an order to the pharmacist to "take" certain drugs and fill a doctor's prescription.]

re·cip·i·ent (ri sip′ē ənt) *n.* one who or that which receives. —*adj.* receiving or able to receive; receptive. [Latin *recipiēns,* present participle of *recipere* to take, receive.]

re·cip·ro·cal (ri sip′rə kəl) *adj.* **1.** existing on both sides: *reciprocal respect, reciprocal acts of hostility.* **2.** given, felt, or shown in return: *reciprocal aid.* **3.** denoting a pronoun that expresses mutual action or relation. *One another* is a reciprocal pronoun. **4.** *Mathematics.* of or relating to a reciprocal. —*n. Mathematics.* number or algebraic expression by which a given number or an algebraic expression is multiplied to produce one. The reciprocal of ⅗ is ⁵⁄₃, since ⅗ × ⁵⁄₃ = 1. [Latin *reciprocus* returning, alternating + -AL¹.] —**re·cip′ro·cal·ly,** *adv.* —**Syn.** *adj.* **2.** see **mutual.**

re·cip·ro·cate (ri sip′rə kāt′) **-cat·ed, -cat·ing.** *v.t.* **1.** to return: *to reciprocate love.* **2.** to give and return mutually; interchange: *to reciprocate favors.* —*v.i.* **1.** to act or feel something in return: *I loved him, but he did not reciprocate.* [Latin *reciprocātus,* past participle of *reciprocāre* to move backwards and forwards.] —**re·cip′ro·ca′tion,** *n.*

reciprocating engine, any engine in which mechanical power is produced by the backward and forward motion of pistons in cylinders.

rec·i·proc·i·ty (res′ə pros′ə tē) *n.* **1.** quality or state of being reciprocal. **2.** mutual interchange between or recognition by countries, states, or organizations, as the exchange of trading advantages or the honoring of one another's licenses.

re·cit·al (ri sīt′əl) *n.* **1.** performance or concert of music or dance, often given by a single performer or devoted to the works of a single composer. **2.** act of repeating or reading something aloud in public: *a poetry recital.*

rec·i·ta·tion (res′ə tā′shən) *n.* **1.** act of repeating or reading something aloud in public; recital. **2.a.** act of reciting a lesson. **b.** class meeting in which students participate, as in a college. **3.** material recited.

rec·i·ta·tive (res′ə tə tēv′) *n.* **1.** style of vocal music intermediate between speaking and singing, esp. found in the narrative parts and dialogue of operas and oratorios. **2.** passage, part, or composition in

re·cat′a·log′	re·chal′lenge	re·chart′	re·chris′ten
re·cel′e·brate′	re·chan′nel	re·char′ter	re·cir′cle
re·cer′ti·fy′	re·charge′	re·check′	re·cir′cu·late′

at; āpe; cär; end; mē; it; īce; hot; ōld; fôrk; wood; fo͞ol; oil; out; up; ūse; turn; sing; thin; this; zh in treasure; ə in ago, taken, pencil, lemon, circus.

this style. [Italian *recitativo*, from *recitare* to repeat, perform, from Latin *recitāre* to read aloud.]

re·cite (ri sīt′) **-cit·ed, -cit·ing.** *v.t.* **1.** to repeat from, or as from, memory, esp. in a formal way. **2.** to give an account of; narrate: *to recite one's life story.* **3.** to enumerate. —*v.i.* **1.** to repeat something memorized, esp. before an audience. **2.** to repeat a lesson or answer questions in class. [Latin *recitāre* to read aloud, repeat from memory.] —**re·cit′er,** *n.*

reck (rek) *v.t., v.i.* *Archaic.* **1.** to take or have care; heed. **2.** to concern or interest (one); be important; matter. [Old English *reccan* to heed.]

reck·less (rek′lis) *adj.* **1.** heedless; careless, as of danger. **2.** characterized or distinguished by such heedlessness; irresponsible: *reckless driving.* [Old English *reccelēas* heedless.] —**reck′less·ly,** *adv.* —**reck′less·ness,** *n.* —**Syn. 2.** see **rash**[1].

reck·on (rek′ən) *v.t.* **1.** to compute; calculate: *Interest is reckoned from day of deposit to day of withdrawal.* **2.** to consider; regard; suppose to be: *They reckon her a beauty.* **3.** *Informal.* to suppose: *I reckon that he'll come.* —*v.i.* **1.** to count, depend, or rely (with *on*). **2.** to make a calculation; count or figure. **3.** *Informal.* to suppose; guess. **4.** to **reckon with. a.** to take into account or consideration. **b.** to go over or settle accounts. [Old English (*ge*)*recenian* to explain.] —**reck′on·er,** *n.* —**Syn.** *v.t.* **1.** see **calculate.**

reck·on·ing (rek′ən ing) *n.* **1.** act of calculating; calculation. **2.** settlement of accounts. **3.** bill, as at an inn or hotel. **4.** dead reckoning.

re·claim (ri klām′) *v.t.* **1.** to render useful or restore to a useful state or condition: *to reclaim land.* **2.** to obtain or recover from old or waste products: *to reclaim copper from a copper alloy coin.* **3.** to recall from error or improper behavior; reform. [Old French *reclamer* to call back, invoke, going back to Latin *re-* back + *clāmāre* to call.] —**re·claim′a·ble,** *adj.* —**re·claim′er,** *n.*

re·claim (rē klām′) *v.t.* to get or attempt to get back.

rec·la·ma·tion (rek′lə mā′shən) *n.* act of reclaiming; being reclaimed; restoration.

re·cline (ri klīn′) **-clined, -clin·ing.** *v.t., v.i.* to assume or cause to assume a recumbent position; lie back or down. [Latin *reclīnāre* to lean back.]

re·cluse (rek′lōōs, ri klōōs′) *n.* one who lives in solitude or seclusion. —*adj.* characterized by seclusion; solitary. [Old French *reclus*, past participle of *reclure* to shut up, from Late Latin *reclūdere*, from Latin *reclūdere* to open.]

rec·og·ni·tion (rek′əg nish′ən) *n.* **1.** act of recognizing; being recognized. **2.** acknowledgment of something, esp. as true or valid: *There was no recognition of their claim of citizenship.* **3.** favorable attention or notice; acceptance: *The doctor gained recognition for his work.* **4.** formal acknowledgment conveying approval or sanction, esp. of one government by another. [Latin *recognitiō* a recognizing, reviewing.]

re·cog·ni·zance (ri kog′nə zəns, -kon′ə-) *n.* *Law.* **1.a.** bond or obligation by which a person promises to perform a particular act, as to appear for a hearing or trial. **b.** amount of such a bond, to be forfeited if the act is not performed. **2.** on (one's) own recognizance. without bail; in consideration of one's promise to appear for hearing or trial: *The prisoner was released on his own recognizance.* [Old French *recoigni- sance* a recognizing, acknowledgment, from *reconoistre* to recognize, from Latin *recognōscere.*]

rec·og·nize (rek′əg nīz′) **-nized, -niz·ing.** *v.t.* **1.** to perceive to be identical to something previously known; know again. **2.** to identify, as from a description or distinctive feature: *to recognize a bird by its coloring.* **3.** to perceive clearly; realize: *to recognize a fact.* **4.** to acknowledge; admit: *to recognize one's obligations.* **5.** to take notice of, esp. as a way of granting permission to speak. **6.** to indicate appreciation of: *The president recognized the employees' worth by giving them a bonus.* **7.** to acknowledge the existence of (another nation) by a proclamation or formal diplomatic exchange. [RECOGN(ITION) + -IZE.] —**rec′og·niz′a·ble,** *adj.* —**rec′og·niz′a·bly,** *adv.* —**Syn. 2.** see **discern.**

re·coil (*v.,* ri koil′, *n.,* ri koil′, rē′koil′) *v.i.* **1.** to draw or shrink back, as in fear, horror, or surprise. **2.** to fly back, as from force of impact or discharge; spring back. **3.** to return to or as to or against a starting point or source; react: *The good or evil we confer on others, very often*

. . . *recoils on ourselves* (Fielding, 1749). —*n.* **1.** act of recoiling. **2.** the backward movement of a firearm when discharged. [Old French *reculer* to go back, retire, going back to Latin *re-* back + *cūlus* rump.]

rec·ol·lect (rek′ə lekt′) *v.t.* to recall to mind; remember. —*v.i.* to have a recollection; remember. [Medieval Latin *recollectus*, past participle of *recolligere* to recall, from Latin *recolligere* to gather again.]

re·col·lect (rē′kə lekt′) *v.t.* **1.** to collect or gather again, as things scattered. **2.** to recover control of (oneself); compose (oneself).

rec·ol·lec·tion (rek′ə lek′shən) *n.* **1.** act or power of recalling to mind; remembrance. **2.** thing remembered; memory. —**Syn. 1.** see **memory.**

rec·om·mend (rek′ə mend′) *v.t.* **1.** to speak of or present favorably: *to recommend a movie.* **2.** to advise: *to recommend going to the doctor.* **3.** to make acceptable, pleasing, or attractive: *The boy's consideration for others recommended him to the group.* **4.** to commit; entrust: *I recommend him to your care,* from Latin *re-* again + *commendāre* to entrust, obtain a favor for, from Latin *re-* again + *commendāre* to entrust.]

rec·om·men·da·tion (rek′ə mən dā′shən, -men-) *n.* **1.** act of recommending. **2.** anything, as a letter, that recommends.

rec·om·men·da·to·ry (rek′ə men′də tôr′ē) *adj.* recommending or serving to recommend.

re·com·mit (rē′kə mit′) **-mit·ted, -mit·ting.** *v.t.* **1.** to commit again. **2.** to refer again to a committee, as a legislative bill. —**re′com·mit′al, re′com·mit′ment,** *n.*

rec·om·pense (rek′əm pens′) **-pensed, -pens·ing.** *v.t.* **1.** to pay or repay (someone), as for something done or given; reward. **2.** to make up for, as a loss; give compensation for. —*n.* **1.** payment, as for something done or given; reward. **2.** compensation, as for loss or injury. [Late Latin *recompēnsāre* to reward, make amends, from Latin *re-* back + *compēnsāre* to weigh together.]

rec·on·cile (rek′ən sīl′) **-ciled, -cil·ing.** *v.t.* **1.** to restore to friendship or good relations, as after an estrangement: *to reconcile quarreling friends.* **2.** to make (someone) content with; bring to acceptance of: *The boy could not reconcile himself to failure.* **3.** to settle, as a controversy, difference, or disagreement. **4.** to make harmonious or congruous: *to reconcile the different accounts of the accident.* [Latin *reconciliāre* to bring together again.] —**rec′on·cil′a·bil′i·ty, rec′on·cile′ment, rec′- on·cil′er,** *n.* —**rec′on·cil′a·ble,** *adj.*

rec·on·cil·i·a·tion (rek′ən sil′ē ā′shən) *n.* **1.** act of reconciling; being reconciled. **2.** process of making harmonious or congruous. —**rec′on·cil′i·a·to·ry,** *adj.*

rec·on·dite (rek′ən dīt′, ri kon′dīt) *adj.* **1.** difficult to understand; profound; abstruse. **2.** dealing with difficult or abstruse matters. **3.** little known; obscure. [Latin *reconditus*, past participle of *recondere* to put away, hide.]

re·con·di·tion (rē′kən dish′ən) *v.t.* to restore to good condition, as by repairing or cleaning.

re·con·nais·sance (ri kon′ə səns) *n.* examination or survey to obtain information, esp. military information about an enemy. [French *reconnaisance*, from *reconnaître* to recognize, from Latin *recognōscere.*]

rec·on·noi·ter (rē′kə noi′tər, rek′ə-) *v.t.* to inspect, examine, or survey (an area) in order to secure information, as for military, engineering, or geological purposes. —*v.i.* to make a reconnaissance. [Obsolete French *reconnoître* to recognize, from Latin *recognōscere.*] —**re′con·noi′ter·er,** *n.*

rec·on·noi·tre (rē′kə noi′tər, rek′ə-) **-tred, -tring,** *v.t., v.i. British.* to reconnoiter.

re·con·sid·er (rē′kən sid′ər) *v.t.* to consider again, esp. with a view to revise or reverse an action or decision. —*v.i.* to consider an action or decision again. —**re′con·sid′er·a′tion,** *n.*

re·con·sti·tute (rē′kən stə tōōt′, -tūt′) **-tut·ed, -tut·ing.** *v.t.* **1.** to constitute or form again. **2.** to restore to a former condition: *to reconstitute powdered milk by adding water.*

re·con·struct (rē′kən strukt′) *v.t.* **1.** to construct again; rebuild. **2.** to recreate (what happened or existed) in the mind from available evidence or information: *to reconstruct a crime.*

re·con·struc·tion (rē′kən struk′shən) *n.* **1.** act of reconstructing; being reconstructed. **2.** something reconstructed. **3. Reconstruction.**

re·clasp′	re′com·bine′	re′con·den·sa′tion	re′con·se·cra′tion
re·class′i·fi·ca′tion	re′com·dense′	re′con·sign′	re′con·sign′
re·class′i·fy′	re′com·mence′	re′con·duct′	re′con·sign′ment
re·clean′	re′com·mence′ment	re′con·fine′	re′con·sol′i·date
re·cod′i·fy′	re′com·mis′sion	re′con·firm′	re′con·sult′
re′col·o·ni·za′tion	re′com·pile′	re′con·fir·ma′tion	re·con′tact
re·col′o·nize′	re′com·pound′	re′con·nect′	re′con·tam′i·nate′
re·col′or	re′com·pu·ta′tion	re·con′quer	re′con·tam′i·na′tion
re·comb′	re′com·pute′	re·con′quest	re′con·tract′
re′com·bi·na′tion	re′con·cen·trate′	re′con·se·crate′	re′con·vene′

at; āpe; cär; end; mē; it; īce; hot; ōld; fôrk; wood; fōōl; oil; out; up; ūse; turn; sing; thin; this; zh in treasure; ə in ago, taken, pencil, lemon, circus.

a. process for restoring the former Confederate States to the Union after the Civil War. **b.** period during which this process took place, from 1867 to 1877. —**re′con·struc′tive,** *adj.*

rec·ord (*n., adj.* rek′ərd; *v.,* ri kôrd′) *n.* **1.** account preserved in writing or other permanent form: *health records.* **2.** known facts about activity or achievement: *His political record was outstanding.* **3.** performance surpassing all others of its kind, as in sports: *a track record.* **4.** disk on which sounds are recorded to be played back on a phonograph. **5.** history of criminal behavior. **6.** official written account of public acts or proceedings: *a record of a town meeting.* **7. to break a record,** to surpass all previous performances. **8. off the record. a.** not for quotation, publication, or identification: *His remarks were off the record.* **b.** unofficial or unofficially: *The president said it off the record.* **9.** on record. set down; recorded. —*adj.* surpassing all others of its kind: *a record attendance.* —*v.t.* **1.** to set down in permanent form, as in writing: *to record history.* **2.** to indicate; register: *The dial on the left records speed.* **3.a.** to convert (sound) by electrical or mechanical means into a form that can be registered permanently, as on a phonograph record or magnetic tape. **b.** to make a recording of: *to record Beethoven's Fifth Symphony.* —*v.i.* **1.** to record something: *The singer recorded in the morning.* **2.** to admit of being recorded or of being used to record: *Does this machine record well?* [Old French *recorder* to call to mind, remember, from Latin *recordārī,* from *re-* back, again + *cor* mind, heart; referring to the fact that records were originally learned by heart or memorized before writing became common.]

record changer, device that holds a stack of phonograph records above a turntable and automatically drops each one on the turntable to be played after the preceding record has finished.

re·cord·er (ri kôr′dər) *n.* **1.** one who is employed to take notes and keep records. **2.** machine that records sounds, as on magnetic tape. **3.** in certain cities, a judge. **4.** any of several musical instruments of the woodwind family, having eight finger holes to regulate pitch, and producing a tone similar to a flute's.

re·cord·ing (ri kôr′ding) *n.* **1.** phonograph record or magnetic tape. **2.** sound registered on a phonograph record or magnetic tape.

record player, instrument that reproduces the sound on a phonograph record; phonograph.

re·count (ri kount′) *v.t.* **1.** to tell in detail; narrate. **2.** to tell in order; enumerate. [Dialectal Old French *reconter* to narrate, from *re-* (see RE-) + *conter* to tell, reckon. See COUNT¹.]

re·count (*v.,* rē kount′; *n.,* rē′kount′, rē kount′) *v.t.* to count again. —*n.* second count, esp. of votes in an election. [RE- + COUNT¹.]

re·coup (ri kōōp′) *v.t.* **1.** to make up for; return the equivalent of, as a loss. **2.** to reimburse; repay, as for a loss. [Old French *recouper* to cut back or again, from *re-* (see RE-) + *couper* to cut (from *coup* blow, stroke). See COUP.]

re·course (rē′kôrs, ri kôrs′) *n.* **1.** appeal or resort for help or protection. **2.** one who or that which is appealed to; resort. **3.** right to demand payment from the maker or endorser of a negotiable commercial paper. [Old French *recours* appeal, resort, from Latin *recursus* a running back, retreat.]

re·cov·er (ri kuv′ər) *v.t.* **1.** to get back (something lost or stolen); regain. **2.** to make up for, as a loss or damage. **3.** to restore (oneself) to a normal position or condition. **4.** to reclaim, as land. **5.** to obtain or obtain again by legal process: *to recover damages.* **6.** *Sports.* to bring (oneself or one's equipment) back to a beginning position in preparation for the next move. —*v.i.* **1.** to get back to a normal position or condition. **2.** to be successful in a lawsuit. **3.** *Sports.* to bring oneself or one's equipment back to a beginning position in preparation for the next move. [Old French *recoverer* to get again, from Latin *recuperāre.*]

re·cov·er (rē kuv′ər) *v.t.* to cover again.

re·cov·er·y (ri kuv′ər ē) *pl.* **-er·ies.** *n.* **1.** act of recovering or being recovered. **2.** restoration of a person to a healthy or normal condition.

recovery room, hospital room, usually in close proximity to the operating room, where patients are temporarily placed after an operation for special care and observation.

rec·re·ant (rek′rē ənt) *adj.* **1.** unfaithful; disloyal. **2.** craven; cowardly. —*n.* **1.** deserter; traitor. **2.** coward. [Old French *recreant,* present participle of *recroire* to surrender, from Medieval Latin *recredere,* from Latin *re-* again + *crēdere* to believe.] —**rec′re·ance, rec′re·an·cy,** *n.*

rec·re·ate (rek′rē āt′) **-at·ed, -at·ing.** *v.t.* to refresh or enliven, as with some form of amusement or relaxation, esp. after work; amuse; entertain. —*v.i.* to take recreation. [Latin *recreātus,* past participle of *recreāre* to restore, refresh.]

re·cre·ate (rē′krē āt′) **-at·ed, -at·ing.** *v.t.* to create anew.

rec·re·a·tion (rek′rē ā′shən) *n.* **1.** refreshment by means of some form of amusement or relaxation; diversion. **2.** any form of amuse-

ment or relaxation. —**rec′re·a′tion·al,** *adj.* —Syn. **1.** see amusement.

re·crim·i·nate (ri krim′ə nāt′) **-nat·ed, -nat·ing.** *v.i.* to make a counter accusation. —*v.t.* to accuse (someone) in return; make a counter accusation against. [Medieval Latin *recriminatus,* past participle of *recriminari* to make charges against, from Latin *re-* again + *criminārī* to accuse of crime.] —**re·crim′i·na′tion,** *n.* —**re·crim′i·na′tive, re·crim·i·na·to·ry** (ri krim′ə nə tôr′ē), *adj.*

re·cru·desce (rē′krōō des′) **-desced, -desc·ing.** *v.i.* to break out or appear again, as a disease. [Latin *recrūdēscere.*]

re·cru·des·cence (rē′krōō des′əns) *n.* new outbreak; reappearance. [Latin *recrūdēscere* to break out again + -ENCE.] —**re′cru·des′cent,** *adj.*

re·cruit (ri krōōt′) *n.* **1.** newly enlisted member of the armed forces. **2.** new member of any group or organization. —*v.t.* **1.** to get (someone) to join the armed forces; enlist (someone) for military service. **2.** to raise, make up, or fill up the number of by getting new members: *to recruit a new baseball team.* **3.** to hire or otherwise obtain the services of: *to recruit teachers for a school system.* **4.** to secure the support or allegiance of, as for some cause or position. —*v.i.* to persuade people to join; enlist new members or employees. [French *recruter* to levy troops, going back to *recroître* to grow again, from Latin *recrēscere.*] —**re·cruit′er, re·cruit′ment,** *n.*

rect-, form of **recti-** before vowels, as in *rectangle.*

rect. **1.** receipt. **2.** rector; rectory. **3.** rectangle; rectangular. **4.** rectified.

rec·tal (rekt′əl) *adj.* relating to, affecting, or near the rectum.

rec·tan·gle (rek′tang′gəl) *n.* parallelogram having four right angles. [Medieval Latin *rectangulus* having a right angle, from Latin *rēctus* straight, right + *angulus* angle¹, corner.]

rec·tan·gu·lar (rek tang′gyə lər) *adj.* **1.** shaped like a rectangle. **2.** having a base or section in the form of a rectangle: *a rectangular pyramid.* **3.** having one or more right angles. —**rec·tan′gu·lar′i·ty,** *n.* —**rec·tan′gu·lar·ly,** *adv.*

Rectangles

recti- *combining form* straight; right: *rectilinear.* [Latin *rēctus.*]

rec·ti·fi·er (rek′tə fī′ər) *n.* **1.** one who or that which rectifies. **2.** *Electronics.* **a.** device for changing alternating current into direct current. **b.** device for changing radio frequency into audio frequency.

rec·ti·fy (rek′tə fī′) **-fied, -fy·ing.** *v.t.* **1.** to set or make right; amend; correct: *to rectify an error.* **2.** to put or set right by adjustment or calculation; adjust: *to rectify a telescope.* **3.** *Electronics.* **a.** to change (an alternating current) into a direct current. **b.** to change (radio frequency) into audio frequency. **4.** *Mathematics.* to determine the length of (the arc of a curve). **5.** *Chemistry.* to refine or purify (liquids) by repeated distillation. [Late Latin *rēctificāre* to make right, from Latin *rēctus* right + *facere* to make.] —**rec′ti·fi·a·ble,** *adj.* —**rec′ti·fi·ca′tion,** *n.*

rec·ti·lin·e·ar (rek′tə lin′ē ər) *adj.* **1.** moving in or forming a straight line or lines. **2.** consisting of or bounded by a straight line or lines. [Late Latin *rēctilīneus* having straight lines, arranged in straight lines (from Latin *rēctus* straight + *līnea* linen thread, stroke¹) + -AR¹.]

rec·ti·tude (rek′tə tōōd′, -tūd′) *n.* uprightness of moral character. [Late Latin *rēctitūdō* straightness, uprightness, from Latin *rēctus* straight, right.]

rec·tor (rek′tər) *n.* **1.** Anglican or Episcopalian clergyman who has charge of a parish, esp., in England, one who receives the parish income. **2.** priest in the Roman Catholic Church, esp. in the Jesuit order, in charge of a seminary, college, or religious house. **3.** in certain schools, colleges, or universities, the chief administrator. [Latin *rēctor* ruler.]

rec·to·ry (rek′tər ē) *pl.* **-ries.** *n.* **1.** rector's dwelling. **2.** in England, benefice held by a rector.

rec·tum (rek′təm) *n.* terminal part of the large intestine, connecting the colon to the anus. [Modern Latin *rectum,* short for Latin *intestīnum rēctum* the straight intestine.]

re·cum·bent (ri kum′bənt) *adj.* lying down; reclining; leaning. [Latin *recumbēns,* present participle of *recumbere* to recline.] —**re·cum′ben·cy, re·cum′bence,** *n.* —**re·cum′bent·ly,** *adv.*

re·cu·per·ate (ri kōō′pə rāt′, -kū′-) **-at·ed, -at·ing.** *v.i.* to regain health or strength; recover. [Latin *recuperātus,* past participle of *recuperāre* to get back again, regain.] —**re·cu′per·a′tion,** *n.*

re·cu·per·a·tive (ri kōō′pə rā′tiv, -pər ə tiv, -kū′-) *adj.* relating to, assisting in, or promoting recuperation. Also, **re·cu·per·a·to·ry** (ri kōō′pər ə tôr′ē, -kū′-).

re·cur (ri kur′) **-curred, -cur·ring.** *v.i.* **1.** to take place, come up, or appear again: *His fever recurred after two days.* **2.** to come back or

re·cop′y	re·crate′	re·cross′	re·crys′tal·ize′
re·cou′ple	re·crit′i·cize′	re·crown′	re·crys′tal·li·za′tion

at; āpe; cär; end; mē; it; īce; hot; ōld; fôrk; wood; fōōl; oil; out; up; ūse; turn; sing; thin; this; zh in treasure; ə in ago, taken, pencil, lemon, circus.

return to the mind or memory: *Thoughts of home and family recurred to the lonely traveler.* **3.** to go back or return in thought or discourse: *to recur to a subject.* [Latin *recurrere* to run back, return.] —**re·cur′rence,** *n.*

re·cur·rent (ri kûr′ənt) *adj.* **1.** happening or appearing again, esp. repeatedly or periodically. **2.** *Anatomy.* turning back in the opposite direction, as a nerve. [Latin *recurrēns,* present participle of *recurrere.* See RECUR.] —**re·cur′rent·ly,** *adv.*

re·cy·cle (rē sī′kəl) -**cy·cled, -cy·cling.** *v.t.* **1.** to render (refuse) suitable for reuse. **2.** to set a new or different cycle in, as a machine or process. **3.** to reset a cycle in, as a machine or process.

red (red) *n.* **1.** color appearing at the lower end of the spectrum opposite violet. **2.** something that imparts this color, as a dye or paint. **3.** *also,* **Red.** *Informal.* **a.** political leftist, radical, or revolutionary; esp. a communist. **b.** inhabitant of a country governed or dominated by a Communist party, as the Soviet Union. **4. in the red.** losing or owing money. Opposed to **in the black. 5. to see red.** *Informal.* to be or become extremely angry. —*adj.* **red′der, red′dest. 1.** having the color red. **2.** florid; blushing; flushed: *to be red with embarrassment.* **3.** inflamed or bloodshot, as the eyes. **4.** *also,* **Red.** *Informal.* **a.** politically leftist, radical, or revolutionary, esp. communist. **b.** of or relating to a country governed or dominated by a Communist party, as the Soviet Union. [Old English *rēad* having the color red.]

re·dact (ri dakt′) *v.t.* **1.** to draw up or frame, as a statement or a decree. **2.** to put into proper literary form; prepare for publication; edit. [Latin *redāctus.* See REDACTION.]

re·dac·tion (ri dak′shən) *n.* **1.** act or process of preparing literary matter for publication. **2.** result of such a process, esp. a new edition; revision. [French *rédaction* editing, from Latin *redāctus,* past participle of *redigere* to bring back, reduce.]

re·dan (ri dan′) *n.* simple fortification consisting of two walls forming an angle that resembles a V with the point projecting outward. [French *redan,* going back to Latin *re-* back + *dēns* tooth.]

red·bird (red′bûrd′) *n.* any of several birds, as the cardinal, bullfinch, or scarlet tanager, having predominantly red plumage.

red blood cell, one of the cells found in the blood of man and other vertebrates, having no nucleus, containing hemoglobin, and functioning chiefly to carry oxygen to the cells and tissues and carbon dioxide back to the respiratory organs. Also, **e·ryth′ro·cyte′.**

red-blood·ed (red′blud′id) *adj.* full of vitality; vigorous.

red·breast (red′brest′) *n.* **1.** any of various birds having a red breast, esp. a robin. **2.** freshwater sunfish, *Lepomis auritus,* of the eastern United States, having a reddish belly.

red·bud (red′bud′) *n.* any of a group of shrubs or small trees, genus *Cercis,* of the pea family, having clusters of red or pink budlike flowers and heart-shaped leaves. Also, **Judas Tree.**

red·cap (red′kap′) *n.* porter who handles baggage, esp. at a railroad station. [From the *red cap* often worn by such a porter.]

red carpet, display of elaborate or deferential courtesy, hospitality, or welcome. [From the traditional practice of laying down a strip of *red carpet* for a distinguished visitor to walk upon.]

red cent *Informal.* very small or insignificant amount; least bit: *His advice isn't worth a red cent.*

Red China, China (def. 1).

red clover, clover, *Trifolium pratense,* of a type having large, round, red flower heads, cultivated for forage.

red·coat (red′kōt′) *n.* British soldier of a time when the British uniform included a red coat, as at the time of the American Revolution and War of 1812.

Red Cross 1. international humanitarian organization founded in 1864, having as its main purpose the care and relief of victims of war and natural disasters, as floods, fires, or earthquakes. **2.** any national branch of this organization. **3. red cross.** a red Greek cross on a white ground, emblem of this organization.

Red deer

red deer 1. reddish-brown deer, *Cervus elaphus,* native to the forests of Europe, Asia, and northern Africa, having a yellowish patch of fur on the rump. Height: 4 feet at the

shoulder. **2.** the white-tailed deer in summer, when its coat turns reddish-brown.

red·den (red′ən) *v.i.* **1.** to become red. **2.** to blush or flush, as from embarrassment or anger. —*v.t.* to make red.

red·dish (red′ish) *adj.* mixed or tinged with red; somewhat red.

re·deem (ri dēm′) *v.t.* **1.** to recover ownership of, as something pawned or lost through foreclosure, by payment. **2.** to pay off, as a promissory note. **3.** to exchange, as trading stamps, for money or merchandise. **4.** to get or win back; regain; recover: *to redeem one's good name.* **5.** to offset or make up for; compensate for: *The play's witty dialogue does nothing to redeem the absurdity of its plot.* **6.** to make good or fulfill (a pledge or promise). **7.** to set free, as from captivity; rescue; ransom. **8.** *Religion.* to deliver from a state of sinfulness and its penalties. [Latin *redimere* to buy back.] —**re·deem′a·ble,** *adj.*

re·deem·er (ri dē′mər) *n.* **1.** one who redeems or rescues another. **2. Redeemer.** Jesus Christ.

re·deem·ing (ri dē′ming) *adj.* that offsets or compensates for what is faulty, weak, or lacking.

re·demp·tion (ri demp′shən, -dem′-) *n.* **1.** act or instance of redeeming; being redeemed. **2.** *Religion.* deliverance or salvation from sin through the Atonement of Jesus Christ. [Late Latin *redemptiō* deliverance from sin, from Latin *redemptiō* a buying back. Doublet of RANSOM.] —**re·demp′tive,** *adj.*

red fox, any of various foxes, genus *Vulpes,* often having reddish fur, as *V. fulva,* of the United States, Canada, and Iceland.

red grouse, brown ptarmigan, *Lagopus scoticus,* native to England and Ireland. Also, **moor′fowl′.**

red-hand·ed (red′han′did) *adj.* in the act of doing, or having just done, something, esp. something wrong.

red·head (red′hed′) *n.* **1.** person having red hair. **2.** freshwater diving duck, *Aythya americana,* native to North America and Mexico, the male of which has a reddish-brown head. Length: 18–22 inches.

red heat 1. temperature at which a substance, as a metal, turns red with heat. **2.** state or condition of being red with heat.

red herring 1. herring dried and smoked to a reddish color. **2.** something intended to divert attention from the problem at hand.

red-hot (red′hot′) *adj.* **1.** red or glowing with heat; very hot. **2.** marked by or showing great intensity, as of anger, enthusiasm, or violence. **3.** fresh from a source; new.

red·in·gote (red′ing gōt′) *n.* **1.** man's double-breasted, full-skirted overcoat, popular in the eighteenth and early nineteenth centuries. **2.** belted dress or overcoat worn by women during this period, open down the front to show a dress or petticoat beneath. [French *redingote,* modification of English *riding coat.*]

re·di·rect (rē′di rekt′, -dī rekt′) *v.t.* to change the direction or course of: *to redirect traffic.* —*n. Law.* questioning or examination of a witness, after cross-examination, by the lawyer who originally questioned him. —*adj. Law.* of or relating to such questioning. —**re′di·rec′tion,** *n.*

re·dis·trict (rē dis′trikt) *v.t.* to revise or rearrange the boundaries of, esp. electoral or administrative districts.

red lead, bright red, powdery oxide of lead, used chiefly in rust-preventive paints and as a pigment in red pencils and rubber. Formula: Pb_3O_4. Also, **min′i·um.**

red-let·ter (red′let′ər) *adj.* especially significant or happy; memorable: *a red-letter day.* [From the practice of marking holidays with *red letters* on church calendars.]

red light 1. red traffic signal indicating a directive to stop. **2.** red warning or danger signal.

red·lin·ing (red′līn′ing) *n.* practice by banks of charging higher rates or of refusing to grant loans or mortgages in urban areas that are potential slums.

red oak 1. any of several oaks having brown or ruddy bark. **2.** wood of such a tree.

red ocher, red, earthy hematite, used as a pigment.

red·o·lent (red′əl ənt) *adj.* **1.** having or giving off a pleasant odor; fragrant. **2.** giving off a certain odor; smelling (with *of*): *a garden redolent of roses.* **3.** permeated; suggestive; reminiscent (with *of* or *with*): *a custom redolent of superstition.* [Latin *redolēns,* present participle of *redolēre* to emit a scent.] —**red′o·lence, red′o·len·cy,** *n.* —**red′o·lent·ly,** *adv.*

re·dou·ble (rē dub′əl) -**bled, -bling.** *v.t.* to increase greatly or renew with great vigor; intensify: *He redoubled his efforts to finish the work*

re·dec′o·rate′	re·dem′on·strate′	re·de·vel′op	re·dis·solve′
re·dec·o·ra′tion	re·de·ploy′	re·de·vel′op·er	re·dis·till′
re·ded′i·cate′	re·de·ploy′ment	re·de·vel′op·ment	re·dis·till·a′tion
re·ded·i·ca′tion	re·de·pos′it	re·di·gest′	re·dis·trib′ute
re·de·fine′	re·de·scend′	re·di·ges′tion	re·dis·tri·bu′tion
re·def·i·ni′tion	re·de·scribe′	re·dis′count	re·di·vide′
re·de·liv′er	re·de·sign′	re·dis·cov′er	re·do′
re·de·liv′er·y	re·de·ter′mine	re·dis·cov′er·y	re·dock′

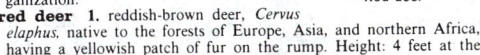

at; āpe; cär; end; mē; it; īce; hot; ōld; fôrk; wood; fōol; oil; out; up; ūse; turn; sing; thin; this; zh in treasure; ə in ago, taken, pencil, lemon, circus.

on time. —*v.i.* **1.** to be increased; become intensified: *The horse's pace redoubled as he entered the home stretch.* **2.** to turn back; double back (with *on*). **3.** *Bridge.* to double an opponent's bid of a double. **4.** *Archaic.* to echo; resound.

re·doubt (ri dout′) *n.* **1.** small enclosed fortification, either natural or man-made, esp. one used for temporary defense. **2.** refuge; retreat; stronghold. [French *redoute* the small fortification, through Italian, going back to Latin *reductus*, past participle of *redūcere* to bring back, withdraw.]

re·doubt·a·ble (ri dou′tə bəl) *adj.* **1.** inspiring or causing fear; formidable; awesome. **2.** deserving or commanding respect, trust, or deference. [Old French *redoutable* formidable, from *redouter* to fear, going back to Latin *re-* back + *dubitāre* to be uncertain.] —**re·doubt′a·ble·ness,** *n.* —**re·doubt′a·bly,** *adv.*

re·dound (ri dound′) *v.i.* **1.** to be a contributing factor; become transferred or added. **2.** to come or be reflected back. [Old French *redonder* to overflow, abound, from Latin *redundāre*, going back to *re-* back, again + *unda* wave.]

red pepper 1. edible podlike fruit of any of a group of pepper plants, *Capsicum frutescens*, esp. variety *longum*, the hot pepper, or variety *grossum*, the sweet pepper. **2.** cayenne.

re·dress (*v.*, ri dres′; *n.*, rē′dres, ri dres′) *v.t.* **1.** to correct and compensate for; set right; rectify; remedy: *to redress a grievance.* **2.** to make reparation or amends to; compensate. —*n.* **1.** compensation, as for injury suffered or wrong done; reparation; satisfaction. **2.** act or instance of redressing. [Middle French *redresser* to straighten, going back to Latin *re-* back, again + *dīrēctus* straight, just.]

re·dress (rē dres′) *v.t., v.i.* to dress again.

Red River, river flowing from southwestern Oklahoma, across the southern United States, into the Mississippi.

Red Sea, narrow sea between the Arabian peninsula and northeastern Africa, opening into the Gulf of Aden and the Arabian Sea.

red·skin (red′skin′) *n. Informal.* North American Indian. ▲ considered offensive.

red squirrel, North American squirrel, genus *Tamiasciurus*, having reddish fur. Length: 12–14 inches including the tail. Also, **chick′a·ree.**

red·start (red′stärt′) *n.* **1.** European singing bird, genus *Phoenicurus*, having a reddish tail. Length: 6 inches. **2.** flycatching warbler, *Setophaga ruticilla*, of eastern North America, the male of which is black with orange or red patches. Length: 5 inches. [RED + obsolete *start* tail (from Old English *steort*).]

Redstart

red tape, attention to or following of official rules, forms, and procedures, esp. as involving inaction and delay. [From the practice that began in the seventeenth century in England of using *red tape* to tie official documents.]

red·top (red′top′) *n.* grass of a kind widely used for pasture and as hay in the northern United States.

re·duce (ri dōōs′, -dūs′) -**duced,** -**duc·ing.** *v.t.* **1.** to make less or smaller, as in size, number, or degree; decrease; diminish: *to reduce the speed of an automobile, to reduce the price of an item.* **2.** to bring from a higher to a lower position or condition; degrade: *The colonel reduced the sergeant to private.* **3.a.** to bring to a particular state, form, or condition: *The fire reduced the forest to ashes.* **b.** to compel or force, as by want or need, into some act or condition: *Hunger reduced them to stealing.* **4.** to bring under control or into submission; conquer; subdue: *to reduce a town by a siege.* **5.** to break down or bring to a systematic or simpler form or character: *to reduce an argument to its basic propositions.* **6.** *Mathematics.* to change (an expression) to an equivalent but more elementary form: *to reduce ⅜ to ½.* **7.** *Chemistry.* **a.** to add electrons to (the atom of an element) so that its oxidation number is decreased. **b.** to remove oxygen from (a compound). **8.** *Medicine.* to restore (a fractured or displaced body part) to normal position or condition. —*v.i.* **1.** to lose weight, as by dieting. **2.** to become reduced. [Latin *redūcere* to bring back, withdraw.] —**re·duc′er,** *n.* —**re·duc′i·ble,** *adj.*

reducing agent, any chemical substance that reduces the oxidation number of or gives up electrons to a substance that reacts with it.

re·duc·ti·o ad ab·sur·dum (ri duk′shē ō′ ad ab sur′dəm) disproof of a proposition by showing that it leads to an absurd proposition when it is carried to its logical conclusion. [Latin *reductiō ad absurdum* literally, a bringing back or reduction to absurdity.]

re·duc·tion (ri duk′shən) *n.* **1.** act or process of reducing; being

reduced. **2.** amount by which something is reduced. **3.** that which results from reducing, as a copy of something that is smaller than the original. [Latin *reductiō.*] —**re·duc′tion·al, re·duc′tive,** *adj.*

re·dun·dan·cy (ri dun′dən sē) *pl.,* -**cies.** *n.* **1.a.** use of more words than are necessary to convey an idea; needless repetition. **b.** instance of this, for example: *He does it every sixty minutes on the hour.* **2.** excessive amount; superfluity. Also, **re·dun′dance.**

re·dun·dant (ri dun′dənt) *adj.* **1.** using more words than are necessary; characterized by wordiness or repetition. **2.** unnecessary; superfluous. [Latin *redundāns,* present participle of *redundāre* to overflow, abound. See REDOUND.] —**re·dun′dant·ly,** *adv.*

red-winged blackbird (red′wingd′) *also,* **redwing blackbird.** American blackbird, *Agelaius phoeniceus*, the male of which has a scarlet patch edged with yellow or white at the shoulder of each wing. Also, **red′wing′.**

red·wood (red′wŏŏd′) *n.* **1.** tall evergreen tree, *Sequoia sempervirens*, having a thick reddish-brown bark, found only along the western coast of North America. Redwoods may grow from 300 to 340 feet tall and some are probably more than 2000 years old. **2.** soft, light wood of this tree, strong and highly resistant to decay.

Red·wood City (red′wŏŏd′) city in western California, south of San Francisco. Pop. (1970), 55,686.

re·ech·o (rē ek′ō) -**echoed,** -**ech·o·ing.** *also,* **re·ech·o.** *v.i.* to repeat or send back an echo; reverberate; resound: *The voices reechoed through the vast cave.* —*v.t.* to repeat the sound of: *The hall reechoed the children's singing.* —*n. pl.,* -**ech·oes.** something reechoed.

reed (rēd) *n.* **1.** any of a number of tall grasses, having long narrow leaves and slender, often hollow, stems, growing chiefly around marshes and other wet areas. **2.** stem of such grass. **3.** musical pipe made from a reed or from some other hollow stalk or stem. **4.** *Music.* **a.** thin tongue of wood, reed, or other flexible material, used in the mouthpiece of certain wind instruments and the pipes of certain organs, which, when caused to vibrate by a current of air, produces a musical sound. **b.** musical wind instrument, as of the clarinet or oboe family, whose tone is produced by the vibration of a single or double reed. Also (*def. 4b*), **reed instrument.** [Old English *hrēod* stalk of such a grass.]

Reed, Walter (rēd) 1851–1902, U.S. army surgeon and microbiologist who proved that yellow fever is transmitted by mosquitoes.

reed·bird (rēd′burd′) *n.* bobolink.

reed organ, keyboard musical instrument whose tones are produced by currents of air vibrating small metal reeds. Also, **har·mo′ni·um.**

reed pipe, organ pipe whose tone is produced by currents of air vibrating small metal reeds.

reed·y (rē′dē) reed·i·er, reed·i·est. *adj.* **1.** having a sound like a reed instrument: *reedy voices.* **2.** resembling a reed or reeds: *reedy legs.* **3.** full of reeds. —**reed′i·ness,** *n.*

reef[1] (rēf) *n.* ridge of sand, rock, or coral, that lies at or near the surface of a sea or other body of water. [Dutch *rif* ridge, from Old Norse *rif* ridge, rib.]

reef[2] (rēf) *n.* portion of a sail that can be rolled up or let out in order to regulate the area of the sail exposed to the wind. —*v.t.* **1.** to reduce the area of (a sail) by rolling or folding up a portion and securing it. **2.** to reduce the length of, as a topmast or bowsprit. [Old Norse *rif* foldable portion of a sail, rib.]

reef·er[1] (rē′fər) *n.* **1.** short, usually double-breasted, coat or jacket of heavy fabric, often worn by sailors and fishermen. **2.** one who reefs. [REEF[2] + -ER[1].]

reef·er[2] (rē′fər) *n. Slang.* marijuana cigarette. [Probably from REEF[2], in the sense of to roll up.]

reef knot, square knot.

reek (rēk) *v.i.* **1.** to give off or be permeated by a strong, offensive odor; smell strongly and unpleasantly: *The lot reeks from the garbage dumped there.* **2.** to evince, give an impression of, or be pervaded with something offensive (often with *of* or *with*): *Those political appointments reek of corruption.* **3.** to give off smoke or vapor; steam; fume. —*v.t.* to give off or exude, as fumes or an odor. —*n.* strong, offensive odor. [Old English *rēc* vapor.]

re·draft′	re·drive′	re·dye′	re·ed′it
re·draw′	re·dry′	re·ed·i·fi·ca′tion	re·ed′u·cate′
re·drawn′	re·dust′	re·ed′i·fy′	re·ed·u·ca′tion

at; āpe; cär; end; mē; it; īce; hot; ōld; fôrk; wood; fōōl; oil; out; up; ūse; turn; sing; thin; this; zh in treasure; ə in ago, taken, pencil, lemon, circus.

reel¹ (rēl) *n.* **1.** spool, cylindrical frame, or other device, usually turning on an axle, on which long strips or strands, as of rope, fish line, or tape, can be wound for convenient use and storage. **2.a.** reel and that which is wound on it, as wire. **b.** quantity of material wound on a reel. —*v.t.* **1.** to draw or pull in by or as by winding a line on a reel (often with *in*): *to reel in a bass.* **2.** to say or write quickly, easily, or fluently (with *off*): *He reeled off the answers.* **3.** to wind on a reel. [Old English *hrēol* device for winding thread or silk.]

reel² (rēl) *v.i.* **1.** to recoil, fall back, or be thrown off balance, as from a blow; stagger. **2.** to walk or move unsteadily, as from drunkenness; totter; lurch. **3.** to be dizzy or in confusion, as from sickness or shock. **4.** to turn or seem to turn round and round; whirl. —*v.t.* to cause to reel. —*n.* reeling movement. [Possibly from REEL¹.]

Reel¹ (fishing reel)

reel³ (rēl) *n.* **1.** lively folk dance, performed by two or more couples, in which the dancers form two lines facing each other. **2.** music for such a dance. [From REEL¹.]

re·en·force (rē´en fôrs´) -**forced,** -**forc·ing.** *also,* **re·en·force.** *v.t.* to reinforce. —**re´en·force´ment,** *n.*

re·en·ter (rē en´tər) *also,* **re·en·ter.** *v.t., v.i.* to enter again. —**re·en´trance,** *n.*

re·en·try (rē en´trē) *pl.,* -**tries.** *also,* **re·en·try.** *n.* **1.** act or instance of entering again. **2.** passage of a missile or spacecraft back into the earth's atmosphere. **3.** act of reclaiming possession of real property by entering or setting foot on it.

reeve¹ (rēv) *n.* in the feudal system, the overseer of an estate; steward; bailiff. [Old English *(ge)rēfa* officer.]

reeve² (rēv) **reeved** or **rove, reev·ing.** *v.t. Nautical.* **1.** to pass (a rope or line) through an opening or pulley block. **2.** to pass a rope or line through (an opening or pulley block). **3.** to fasten by reeving. [Of uncertain origin.]

re·ex·am·ine (rē´ig zam´in) -**ined,** -**in·ing.** *also,* **re·ex·am·ine.** *v.t.* **1.** to examine again. **2.** *Law.* to question (a witness) again after cross-examination.

ref. **1.** referee. **2.** reference; referred. **3.** reformed. **4.** refund.

re·fec·tion (ri fek´shən) *n.* **1.** refreshment, esp. with food or drink. **2.** light meal; repast. [Latin *refectiō* a restoring.]

re·fec·to·ry (ri fek´tər ē) *pl.,* -**ries.** *n.* dining hall, as in a school, monastery, or other institution. [Late Latin *refectōrium* dining hall in a monastery, going back to Latin *reficere* to restore.]

re·fer (ri fur´) -**ferred,** -**fer·ring.** *v.t.* **1.** to send or direct (someone), as for information or aid: *The doctor referred the patient to a specialist.* **2.** to submit or turn over, as a problem, for consideration or for a recommendation or decision: *Management referred the labor dispute to arbitration.* **3.** to assign to a cause or source; attribute. —*v.i.* **1.** to call or direct attention; make reference; allude (with *to*): *The speaker referred to him as an up-and-coming politician.* **2.** to use as a source, as of information or aid (with *to*): *to refer to notes while speaking.* **3.** to be restricted; pertain; relate; apply (with *to*). [Latin *referre* to carry back.] —**re·fer´a·ble,** *adj.* —**re·fer´ral, re·fer´rer,** *n.*

ref·er·ee (ref´ə rē´) *n.* **1.** official in certain sports and games, often the chief official, who interprets and enforces the rules and sometimes keeps score. **2.** one to whom a matter or question in dispute is referred for decision or settlement. —*v.t., v.i.* -**reed,** -**fer·ee·ing.** to act as referee in. —*v.i.* to act as referee.

ref·er·ence (ref´ər əns) *n.* **1.** act of referring. **2.** a direction of attention; mention; allusion: *a disparaging reference to his past.* **3.** relation; respect; regard (with *to*): *in reference to your letter of November 5.* **4.** one who or that which is referred to; source, as of information or aid. **5.** statement attesting to a person's character or ability. **6.** one to whom another is referred for such a statement. **7.a.** note referring a reader to or acknowledging the use of another source or authority. **b.** mark or sign, as a number or asterisk, designating such a note. —*adj.* used for information or aid: *a reference book.*

ref·er·en·dum (ref´ə ren´dəm) *pl.,* -**dums** or -**da** (-də). *n.* **1.** direct popular vote on a public measure. **2.** procedure by which public measures are submitted to such a vote. [Latin *referendum* that which must be carried back, neuter gerundive of *referre* to carry back.]

re·fill (*v.,* rē fil´; *n.,* rē´fil´) *v.t.* to fill again. —*n.* supply of a product, as lipstick or lead, replacing material that filled the original container and has been used up. —**re·fill´a·ble,** *adj.*

re·fine (ri fīn´) -**fined,** -**fin·ing.** *v.t.* **1.** to make fine or pure; free from impurities or other unwanted matter: *to refine crude oil.* **2.** to free from imperfections or defects. **3.** to free from coarseness; imbue with culture, polish, or delicate sensibilities. **4.** to take or remove by purifying (with *out* or *away*): *They refined the gold out of the ore.* —*v.i.* **1.** to become free of impurities or other unwanted matter. **2.** to use overly fine distinctions in thought or speech. **3.** **to refine on** (or **upon**). to improve by adding subtleties or fine distinctions. [RE- + earlier *fine* to make fine, from FINE¹.] —**re·fin´er,** *n.*

re·fined (ri fīnd´) *adj.* **1.** free from coarseness, commonness, or vulgarity. **2.** free from impurities or other unwanted matter. **3.** precise or subtle to a fine degree.

re·fine·ment (ri fīn´mənt) *n.* **1.** freedom from coarseness, commonness, and vulgarity. **2.** act or process of refining. **3.** change or addition intended to improve or perfect; improvement.

re·fin·er·y (ri fī´nər ē) *pl.,* -**ies.** *n.* place or establishment where some crude substance, as petroleum, sugar, or grain, is broken down and its usable components are extracted in pure form.

re·fit (rē fit´) -**fit·ted,** -**fit·ting.** *v.t., v.i.* to make or be made fit for use again, as by the adjustment or repair of machinery or material or the provision of new supplies.

re·flect (ri flekt´) *v.t.* **1.** to turn or throw back, as waves of light, heat, or sound. **2.** to give back an image of; mirror. **3.** to be a truthful representation of: *That choice reflects your good taste.* **4.** to bring or give back as a result; cast (with *on* or *upon*). **5.** to ponder or realize: *He reflected that he hadn't seen her in some time.* —*v.i.* **1.** to think seriously or carefully; ponder: *to reflect on the question.* **2.** to bring blame or discredit (with *on* or *upon*): *His cowardice reflects on his character.* [Latin *reflectere* to turn or bend back.]

re·flec·tance (ri flek´təns) *n. Physics.* ratio of radiant energy reflected from a given surface to the total energy falling on the surface.

reflecting telescope, telescope having at the objective a concave mirror which reflects light toward the eyepiece. Also, **re·flec´tor.**

re·flec·tion (ri flek´shən) *also, British,* **re·flex·ion.** *n.* **1.** image given back by a reflecting surface. **2.** something reflected or produced by reflection: *The reflection of the sun on the windshield was blinding.* **3.** serious or careful thinking; consideration. **4.** observation or statement that results from such thinking. **5.** the turning back of waves, as light, heat, or sound waves, at the boundary of a material. **6.** that which represents or exhibits something else: *His smile was a reflection of his happiness.* **7.** that which brings or incurs blame or discredit. **8.** blame; discredit. **9.** act of reflecting; being reflected.

re·flec·tive (ri flek´tiv) *adj.* **1.** given to or showing serious or careful thinking; thoughtful; pensive. **2.** that throws back waves of light, heat, sound, or the like; reflecting. **3.** of, relating to, or produced by reflection. —**re·flec´tive·ly,** *adv.* —**re·flec´tive·ness, re·flec·tiv·i·ty** (rē´flek tiv´ə tē), *n.*

re·flec·tor (ri flek´tər) *n.* **1.** that which reflects. **2.** surface or device designed to reflect or direct light, heat, sound, or the like. **3.** telescope that reflects light to form an image; reflecting telescope.

re·flex (*n.,* rē´fleks; *v.,* ri fleks´) *n.* **1.** involuntary response to a stimulus, as the contraction of a muscle or the secretion by a gland. **2. reflexes.** capacity to react with speed and accuracy. **3.** *Archaic.* reflection, or image produced by reflection. —*adj.* **1.** relating to, produced by, or designating an involuntary response to a stimulus. The immediate withdrawal of one's hand from a hot surface is a reflex response. **2.** bent or turned back, as by a surface or boundary. **3.** (of an angle) between 180 and 360 degrees. —*v.t.* to bend or turn back. [Latin *reflexus,* past participle of *reflectere* to bend or turn back.]

reflex arc, path traveled by the neural impulses involved in a reflex action.

re´e·lect´	re´em·pha·size´	re´e·quip´	re´ex·press´
re´e·lec´tion	re´em·ploy´	re´es·tab´lish	re·face´
re·el´i·gi·ble	re´em·ploy´ment	re´es·tab´lish·ment	re·fash´ion
re´em·bark´	re´en·act´	re´e·val´u·ate´	re·fas´ten
re´em·bod´i·ment	re´en·ac´tion	re´e·val´u·a´tion	re·fight´
re´em·bod´y	re´en·act´ment	re´e·voke´	re·fig´ure
re´em·brace´	re´en·gage´	re´ex·am´i·na´tion	re·film´
re´e·merge´	re´en·gage´ment	re´ex·change´	re·fil´ter
re´e·mer´gence	re´en·list´	re´ex·hib´it	re·fi´nance
re´e·mer´gent	re´en·list´ment	re´ex·pe´ri·ence	re·fin´ish
re·em´i·grate´	re´en·slave´	re´ex·plain´	re·fire´
re´em·pha´sis		re´ex·port´	re·fix´

at; āpe; cär; end; mē; it; īce; hot; ōld; fôrk; wood; fōōl; oil; out; up; ūse; turn; sing; thin; this; zh in treasure; ə in ago, taken, pencil, lemon, circus.

re·flex·ive (ri flek′siv) *adj.* **1.** *Grammar.* relating to, expressing, or denoting an action directed back upon the subject or agent and having a subject or agent and an object that are identical. In the sentence *He washed himself, himself* is a reflexive pronoun and *washed* is a reflexive verb. **2.** of, relating to, or capable of a reflex. —*n.* reflexive verb or pronoun. —**re·flex′ive·ly,** *adv.* —**re·flex′ive·ness, re·flex·iv·i·ty** (rē′flek siv′ə tē), *n.*

ref·lu·ent (ref′lōō ənt) *adj.* flowing back; ebbing. [Latin *refluēns,* present participle of *refluere* to flow back.] —**ref′lu·ence,** *n.*

re·flux (rē′fluks′) *n.* a flowing back; ebb. [RE- + FLUX.]

re·for·est (rē fôr′ist, -for′-) *v.t., v.i.* to reseed or replant (an area) with trees. —**re′for·est·a′tion,** *n.*

re·form (ri fôrm′) *v.t.* **1.** to make a change for the better in; correct what is wrong with (something), esp. by removing defects or abuses: *a movement to reform the postal system.* **2.** to cause (someone) to change for the better; rehabilitate: *to reform a drunkard.* —*v.i.* to become changed for the better. —*n.* **1.** change for the better: *reform of the prison system.* **2.** change for the better in conduct or character, esp. a giving up of wrongdoing or irresponsible ways. —*adj.* **1.** of or relating to reform or correction. **2. Reform.** of, relating to, or designating the branch of Judaism that deemphasizes strict observance of traditional law and ritual and retains only those elements of tradition considered relevant in the modern world. [Latin *reformāre* to shape again, change.] —**re·form′a·ble, re·form′a·tive,** *adj.* —**re·form′er, re·form′ist,** *n.*

re-form (rē fôrm′) *v.t., v.i.* to form again.

ref·or·ma·tion (ref′ər mā′shən) *n.* **1.** act of reforming; being re-formed. **2. Reformation.** religious movement in sixteenth-century Europe, led by Martin Luther, that began as an attempt to reform the Catholic Church and resulted in the establishment of Protestant churches.

re·form·a·to·ry (ri fôr′mə tôr′ē) *pl.,* **-ries.** *n.* penal institution to which youthful or certain first offenders are sent and which emphasizes rehabilitation rather than punishment. —*adj.* serving or intended to reform.

re·formed (ri fôrmd′) *adj.* **1.** improved in character, conduct, or morals: *a reformed gambler.* **2.** freed of defects or abuses; corrected. **3. Reformed.** of, relating to, or designating those Protestant churches deriving their beliefs and practices from the teachings of Huldreich Zwingli and John Calvin.

reform school, reformatory.

re·fract (ri frakt′) *v.t.* to cause to undergo refraction. [Latin *refractus,* past participle of *refringere* to break up.]

refracting telescope, telescope having at the objective a concave lens which refracts light toward the eyepiece. Also, **re·frac′tor.**

re·frac·tion (ri frak′shən) *n.* the bending of waves, esp. light waves, as they pass from a substance in which they travel at one velocity to a substance in which they travel at another, or as they pass through a substance whose density is not uniform.

re·frac·tive (ri frak′tiv) *adj.* of, relating to, or resulting from refraction; having the capacity to refract. —**re·frac′tive·ly,** *adv.* —**re·frac′tive·ness, re·frac·tiv·i·ty** (rē′frak tiv′ə tē), *n.*

refractive index, index of refraction.

re·frac·tor (ri frak′tər) *n.* **1.** something that refracts. **2.** telescope that refracts light to form an image; refracting telescope.

re·frac·to·ry (ri frak′tər ē) *adj.* **1.** difficult to control or manage; rebellious; obstinate. **2.** resisting treatment, as a disease. **3.** resistant to heat, fusion, or reduction, as firebrick and certain ores or metals. [Earlier *refractary,* from Latin *refrāctārius* stubborn.] —**re·frac′to·ri·ly,** *adv.* —**re·frac′to·ri·ness,** *n.*

re·frain¹ (ri frān′) *v.i.* to hold oneself back; restrain oneself: *She could scarcely refrain from laughing.* [Old French *refrener* to bridle, from Latin *refrēnāre,* from *re-* back + *frēnum* a bridle, curb.]

re·frain² (ri frān′) *n.* **1.** phrase or verse in a song, poem, or the like, recurring regularly, esp. at the end of each stanza; chorus. **2.** musical setting for this. **3.** saying or utterance that is frequently repeated. [Old French *refrain* repeated phrase or verse (of a ballad), from *refraindre* to sing a refrain, break, going back to Latin *refringere* to break up; because it breaks the flow of the melody or poem.]

re·fran·gi·ble (ri fran′jə bəl) *adj.* capable of being refracted, as light waves. [RE- + FRANGIBLE.] —**re·fran·gi·bil′i·ty,** *n.*

re·fresh (ri fresh′) *v.t.* **1.** to restore strength or vitality to, as through food or rest; revive. **2.** to cause to recollect; prompt (the memory). **3.** to replenish; refill. **4.** to impart freshness to, as by wetting or cooling. [Old French *refreschir* to restore, revive, from *re-* (see RE-) + *fresche,* feminine of *fres* fresh (of Germanic origin).]

.re·fresh·er (ri fresh′ər) *n.* **1.** one who or that which refreshes. **2.** refresher course.

refresher course, course of instruction reviewing material previously studied, often providing instruction in recent developments in a professional field.

re·fresh·ing (ri fresh′ing) *adj.* **1.** pleasingly novel or unusual. **2.** that refreshes. —**re·fresh′ing·ly,** *adv.*

re·fresh·ment (ri fresh′mənt) *n.* **1. refreshments.** food or drink, as snacks or a light meal. **2.** that which refreshes. **3.** act of refreshing; being refreshed.

re·frig·er·ant (ri frij′ər ənt) *n.* **1.** any substance, as ammonia, capable of absorbing heat when changing from one form to another, as from a liquid to a gas, used as an agent in cooling or refrigeration. **2.** medication or other substance, as ice, used to reduce fever. —*adj.* **1.** cooling or freezing; refrigerating. **2.** reducing fever, as a medication.

re·frig·er·ate (ri frij′ə rāt′) **·at·ed, ·at·ing.** *v.t.* to make or keep cold or cool, esp. to chill or freeze (food) for preservative purposes. [Latin *refrigerātus,* past participle of *refrigerāre* to make cool.]

re·frig·er·a·tion (ri frij′ə rā′shən) *n.* **1.** process or system of maintaining cool or freezing temperatures in an enclosed area, as through compression and expansion of a refrigerant or by thermoelectricity. **2.** state of being refrigerated.

re·frig·er·a·tor (ri frij′ə rā′tər) *n.* **1.** insulated, boxlike appliance, esp. one equipped with a cooling apparatus, in which cool temperatures are maintained, used for the preservation of food and other perishables. **2.** any enclosed area, as a room or railroad car, that is kept cool by refrigeration.

reft (reft) a past tense and past participle of **reave.**

re·fu·el (rē fū′əl) **-eled, -el·ing;** *also, British.* **-elled, -el·ling.** *v.t.* to supply again with fuel. —*v.i.* to take on a fresh supply of fuel.

ref·uge (ref′ūj) *n.* **1.** shelter or protection, as from danger, trouble, or hardship. **2.** place providing shelter, protection, or safety; asylum; haven. **3.** source of safety, aid, or relief. [Old French *refuge,* from Latin *refugium.*] —**Syn. 2.** see **shelter.**

ref·u·gee (ref′ū jē′) *n.* one who flees to safety or refuge, esp. one who leaves his home or homeland because of persecution, war, or danger and seeks safety in another place. [French *réfugié,* going back to Latin *refugium* refuge.]

re·ful·gent (ri ful′jənt) *adj.* shining brightly; radiant. [Latin *refulgēns,* present participle of *refulgēre* to flash back, glitter.] —**re·ful′gence, re·ful′gen·cy,** *n.* —**re·ful′gent·ly,** *adv.*

re·fund¹ (*v.,* ri fund′; *n.,* rē′fund) *v.t.* to give or pay back: *We'll refund your deposit if you decide not to buy.* —*n.* **1.** sum refunded. **2.** act of refunding. [Latin *refundere* to pour back.]

re·fund² (rē fund′) *v.t.* **1.** to allocate funds for again or anew: *to refund a child-care program.* **2.** to replace (a security about to fall due) with a new security. [RE- + FUND.]

re·fur·bish (ri fur′bish) *v.t.* to brighten or freshen up.

re·fus·al (ri fū′zəl) *n.* **1.** act of refusing. **2.** opportunity or privilege of rejecting or accepting before others may; option.

re·fuse¹ (ri fūz′) **-fused, -fus·ing.** *v.t.* **1.** to withhold acceptance of; turn down; reject: *to refuse a bribe.* **2.** to withhold the giving or granting of; deny: *to refuse permission.* **3.** to be determined not to (do something); be unwilling: *You always refuse to see my point of view.* **4.** (of a horse) to stop short at (an obstacle) instead of leaping. —*v.i.* to withhold acceptance, consent, or compliance: *He can't refuse if you ask politely.* [Old French *refuser* to push back, repudiate, recoil, possibly going back to Latin *recūsāre* to reject, be unwilling to do something; influenced by *refūtāre* to repel, rebut.]

Syn. *v.t.* **1. Refuse, reject, decline** mean saying no to. **Refuse** implies that something definite is turned down, esp. a request: *He refused all further interviews.* **Reject** is more absolute, implying the casting off of something that is judged not to meet certain specified standards: *They rejected his application for membership.* **Decline** is the mildest term, suggesting gentility and a regard for social form: *He declined the offer of candy with thanks.*

ref·use² (ref′ūs, -ūz) *n.* anything discarded as useless or worthless; waste; rubbish. —*adj.* discarded or rejected as useless or worthless. [Middle French *refus* rejection, remains, from Old French *refuser* to push back, repudiate, recoil. See REFUSE¹.]

re·fu·tal (ri fūt′əl) *n.* refutation.

ref·u·ta·tion (ref′yoo tā′shən) *n.* **1.** act of refuting. **2.** that which refutes or disproves, as evidence or an argument.

re·fute (ri fūt′) **-fut·ed, -fut·ing.** *v.t.* **1.** to prove, as a statement or argument, to be false or incorrect. **2.** to prove (someone) to be wrong. [Latin *refūtāre* to repel, rebut.] —**re·fut′a·ble,** *adj.* —**re·fut′a·bly,** *adv.* —**re·fut′er,** *n.*

reg. **1.** register; registered. **2.** registrar. **3.** registry. **4.** regular; regularly. **5.** regulation. **6.** regent. **7.** regiment.

re·float′	re·forge′	re·for′ti·fi·ca′tion	re·freeze′
re·fo′cus	re·for′mu·late′	re·for′ti·fy′	re·fry′
re·fold′	re·for′mu·la′tion	re·frame′	re·fur′nish

at; āpe; cär; end; mē; it; īce; hot; ōld; fôrk; wood; fōol; oil; out; up; ūse; turn; sing; thin; this; zh in treasure; ə in ago, taken, pencil, lemon, circus.

re·gain (rē gān′) v.t. **1.** to get possession of again; get back; recover. **2.** to reach again; get back to.

re·gal (rē′gəl) adj. **1.** resembling, befitting, or characteristic of a king or other sovereign; stately; splendid; dignified: *a regal bearing.* **2.** of or belonging to a king or other sovereign; royal. [Latin *rēgālis* royal, from *rēx* king.] —**re·gal·i·ty** (ri gal′ə tē), n. —**re′gal·ly,** adv. —**Syn. 2.** see royal.

re·gale (ri gāl′) -galed, -gal·ing. v.t. **1.** to delight or entertain; give great pleasure to: *She regaled us with stories of her childhood.* **2.** to provide a feast for. —v.i. to feast. [French *régaler* to entertain, going back to Old French *gale* pleasure, from Middle Dutch *wale* wealth.] —**re·gale′ment,** n.

re·ga·li·a (ri gā′lē ə, -gāl′yə) n.,pl. **1.** insignia of royalty, including crowns, scepters, and ceremonial swords. **2.** symbols, insignia, or decorations of any rank, office, society, or order. **3.** splendid or fancy clothes; finery. [Latin *rēgālia* literally, royal things, neuter plural of *rēgālis* royal. See REGAL.]

re·gard (ri gärd′) v.t. **1.** to look upon or think of; consider: *He regards that candidate as the best man for the job.* **2.** to look at attentively; observe closely: *The sentry regarded us suspiciously.* **3.** to show respect or consideration for: *to regard the rights of others.* **4.** to have relation or pertinence to; have to do with; concern. **5.** to pay attention to or take into account; heed: *He did not regard their warnings.* —n. **1.** careful thought, notice, or attention; heed; consideration: *No regard was given to the needs of the people.* **2.** esteem; affection: *I know no one for whom I have more regard.* **3.** reference; relation: *I'll write you later in regard to this matter.* **4. regards,** best wishes: *Give my regards to your family.* **5.** particular respect; matter: *I agree with you in that regard.* **6.** Archaic. look; gaze. [French *regarder* to look at, see, from RE- (see RE-) + *garder* to keep, watch over (of Germanic origin).] —**Syn. 1.** see respect.

re·gard·ful (ri gärd′fəl) adj. **1.** heedful; observant; mindful. **2.** respectful.

re·gard·ing (ri gär′ding) prep. in reference to; concerning.

re·gard·less (ri gärd′lis) adj. having or showing no regard or consideration; heedless; unmindful. —adv. in spite of everything; anyway. —**re·gard′less·ly,** adv.

re·gat·ta (ri gat′ə, -gä′tə) n. boat race or a series of boat races. [Dialectal Italian *regatta* gondola race; literally, contention for victory; of uncertain origin.]

re·gen·cy (rē′jən sē) pl., -cies. n. **1.** office, government, or power of a regent or body of regents. **2.** period during which a regent or body of regents governs. **3.** body of regents. **4.** district or territory under the rule of a regent or body of regents. **5. Regency. a.** in English history, the period from 1811 to 1820. **b.** in French history, the period from 1715 to 1723. —adj. also, **Regency.** of, relating to, or characteristic of the Regency in French or English history, or to the styles of furniture prevalent during those periods.

re·gen·er·a·cy (ri jen′ər ə sē) n. state of being regenerate or regenerated.

re·gen·er·ate (v., ri jen′ə rāt′; adj., ri jen′ər it) -at·ed, -at·ing. v.t. **1.** to cause to be morally or spiritually renewed. **2.** to form, produce, or create anew. **3.** to reproduce or grow anew, as a new limb or new tissue, in order to replace something lost or damaged. —v.i. **1.** to become formed anew; be reproduced. **2.** to be spiritually renewed or morally improved. —adj. **1.** morally or spiritually renewed. **2.** restored to a better state; renewed. [Latin *regenerātus,* past participle of *regenerāre* to bring forth again.] —**re·gen′er·a′tion, re·gen′er·a′tor,** n. —**re·gen′er·a·tive,** adj.

re·gent (rē′jənt) n. **1.** one who exercises royal or ruling authority in place of a monarch who is absent, incapacitated, or too young. **2.** member of a governing board, esp. of a state college or university or a state educational system. —adj. acting as a regent: *a prince regent.* [Latin *regēns* ruler, from *regere* to keep straight, guide, rule.]

reg·i·cide¹ (rej′ə sīd′) n. act of killing a king or sovereign. [Latin *rēgi-,* stem of *rēx* king + -CIDE¹.]

reg·i·cide² (rej′ə sīd′) n. one who kills or helps to kill a king or sovereign. [Latin *rēgi-,* stem of *rēx* king + -CIDE².]

re·gime (rə zhēm′, rā-) also, **ré·gime.** n. **1.** prevailing administration or system of government: *a dictatorial regime.* **2.** social pattern or system. **3.** regimen (def. 1). [French *régime,* from Latin *regimen* rule, government. Doublet of REGIMEN.]

reg·i·men (rej′ə mən, -men′) n. **1.** systematic, regulated course or schedule, as for diet, exercise, sleep, or study, intended to improve health or to have some specific result. Also, **ré·gime.** **2.** government; control; rule. [Latin *regimen* rule, government. Doublet of REGIME.]

reg·i·ment (n., rej′ə mənt; v., rej′ə ment′) n. military unit usually commanded by a colonel, composed of three battalions and a headquar-

ters, and forming part of a division. —v.t. **1.** to force arbitrary or rigid uniformity upon; exert strict control over: *The company regiments its workers.* **2.** to form into an organized group. **3.** to organize or put into definite order or into a rigid pattern or system, esp. to achieve regulation and control: *to regiment one's thinking.* **4.** to assign to a regiment or group. [Late Latin *regimentum* rule, government, from Latin *regere* to rule.] —**reg′i·men′tal,** adj. —**reg′i·men·ta′tion,** n.

reg·i·men·tals (rej′ə men′təlz) n.,pl. **1.** uniform of a regiment. **2.** any military uniform.

Re·gi·na (ri jī′nə) n. city in southern Canada, capital of Saskatchewan. Pop. (1968), 137,000.

re·gion (rē′jən) n. **1.** geographic area having one or more unifying characteristics, as particular topographic features, cultural factors, or economic activities, that set it apart from other areas: *an industrial region.* **2.** extensive or indefinite portion of territory, space, or a surface: *the upper regions of the atmosphere.* **3.** any indefinite space, area, or portion: *the dark unknown regions of the mind.* **4.** division or part of the body: *the abdominal region.* **5.** sphere of interest or activity; field; realm; domain: *the region of philosophy.* [Latin *regiō* line¹, direction, district.]

re·gion·al (rē′jən əl) adj. **1.** of or relating to a particular region; local; sectional. **2.** of or relating to an entire region, esp. a geographic one. —**re′gion·al·ly,** adv.

reg·is·ter (rej′is tər) n. **1.a.** formal or official record, as of names, data, or transactions: *a register of volunteers.* **b.** book or system for such records, as for public or official purposes: *a hotel register.* **c.** single entry in such a book or record. **2.** registration; registry; enrollment. **3.** registrar. **4.** automatic recording or counting device, as a cash register. **5.** device in a heating or ventilating system, esp. a closable grille over an opening in a wall or floor, used to regulate the passage of air into a room. **6.** Music. **a.** range of a voice or instrument, esp. a particular portion of the range in which all the tones are produced in the same manner or are of similar timbre. **b.** set of organ pipes controlled by one stop. **7.** Printing. proper alignment of various plates, stones, or screens to assure clear and accurate reproduction, as of color: *in register, off register.* —v.t. **1.** to enter or have entered in or as in a register; record: *to register the names of absent students, to register a complaint.* **2.** to enroll formally or officially, as a voter or student. **3.** to indicate or record, as on a scale: *The thermometer registered fifty degrees.* **4.** to show or express: *His face registered disappointment.* **5.** to cause, as mail, to be officially recorded by payment of a fee, so as to insure against loss, theft, or damage. —v.i. **1.** to enter one's name or cause it to be entered in a register: *to register at a hotel.* **2.** to record formally or officially. **3.** *Informal.* to make an impression. [Medieval Latin *registrum,* form of *regestum* book for records, going back to Latin *regestus,* past participle of *regerere* to record, carry back.] —**reg′is·tra·ble,** adj. —**Syn. 1.** see list¹.

reg·is·tered (rej′is tərd) adj. **1.** recorded in a register, esp. officially recorded to insure against loss, theft, damage, or fraud. **2.** enrolled and certified as having met certain technical or legal qualifications.

registered nurse, nurse licensed by the state in which she practices after completing established training and education requirements.

reg·is·trar (rej′is trär′, rej′is trär′) n. administrative official, esp. at a college or university, in charge of keeping records. [REGISTER + -AR³.]

reg·is·tra·tion (rej′is trā′shən) n. **1.** act or instance of registering or being registered. **2.** document verifying this: *car registration.* **3.** entry in a register. **4.** number of people registered; total enrollment, esp. at a college or university.

reg·is·try (rej′is trē) pl., -tries. n. **1.** act of registering. **2.** place where registering is kept; office of registration. **3.** register (def. 1).

reg·nant (reg′nənt) adj. **1.** exercising rule; ruling; reigning. **2.** exercising authority, sway, or influence; predominant. **3.** prevalent; widespread. [Latin *regnāns,* present participle of *regnāre* to reign, rule.] —**reg′nan·cy,** n.

re·gress (v., ri gres′; n., rē′gres) v.i. to go back or return to an earlier or less advanced form or state; revert. —n. **1.** act of going back; return. **2.** power or right of returning. **3.** backward movement; retrograde motion. [Latin *regressus,* past participle of *regredī* to go back, return.]

re·gres·sion (ri gresh′ən) n. **1.** reversion to a less advanced form or behavioral pattern. **2.** lessening of the symptoms of a disease. **3.** backward movement; retrograde motion.

re·gres·sive (ri gres′iv) adj. **1.** regressing or tending to regress. **2.** of or characterized by regression. **3.** designating or relating to a tax that decreases in rate as the amount taxed increases. —**re·gres′sive·ly,** adv. —**re·gres′sive·ness,** n.

re·gret (ri gret′) -gret·ted, -gret·ting. v.t. **1.** to feel sorry or distressed about: *I regret the loss of her friendship.* **2.** to remember with a sense

re·gath′er	re·gear′	re·glaze′	re·grade′
re·gauge′	re·gild′	re·glue′	re·graft′

of loss: *I regret my lost youth.* —*n.* **1.** feeling of distress, misgiving, or being sorry. **2.** sense of loss or longing. **3. regrets.** apology offered for one's absence, esp. a polite refusal of an invitation: *to send one's regrets.* **4.** expression of sorrow, distress, or disappointment. [Old French *regreter* to bewail (the dead), probably from *re-* (see RE-) + Old Norse *grāta* to lament.] —**re·gret′ta·ble,** *adj.* —**re·gret′ta·bly,** *adv.* —**re·gret′ter,** *n.*

Syn. *n.* **2. Regret, remorse, compunction** mean qualms felt. **Regret** suggests distress over being unable to do something, rather than doing something wrong: *My only regret is that I could not devote more time to this worthy cause.* **Remorse** implies a sincere, profound, long-lasting sense of sorrow that arises from guilt and works to prevent future misdeeds or wrongdoings: *His remorse about taking the book was sufficient punishment.* **Compunction** suggests a momentary mental reservation that is easily overcome, rather than a deep sense of guilt: *Although he felt some compunction, the senator voted against the bill.*

re·gret·ful (ri gret′fəl) *adj.* full of regret; feeling or expressing regret. —**re·gret′ful·ly,** *adv.* —**re·gret′ful·ness,** *n.*

Regt. **1.** regent. **2.** regiment.

reg·u·lar (reg′yə lər) *adj.* **1.** conforming to or fixed by the ordinary or customary course of events; normal; usual: *Our regular teacher was absent today.* **2.** occurring at fixed or uniform intervals; unvarying; steady: *regular train departures.* **3.** conforming in form or arrangement to a type or standard; evenly or uniformly arranged: *regular teeth.* **4.** habitual; consistent: *a regular customer.* **5.** conforming to some established or prescribed rule or usage. **6.** orderly; methodical; well-ordered. **7.** of, designating, or adhering to an official party leadership, organization, and program: *a regular Republican.* **8.** belonging to, designating, or constituting a permanent or standing armed service. **9.** *Grammar.* using the usual or most common inflectional endings in conjugations and declensions. **10.** *Mathematics.* having all angles equal and all sides equal in length: *a regular polygon.* **11.** *Religion.* belonging to a religious order or bound by its rule, as a monk or nun. **12.** (of a flower) having symmetrical parts that are identical in shape, size, or structure. **13.** *Informal.* **a.** unmitigated; thorough; out-and-out: *a regular nuisance.* **b.** nice; decent; pleasant: *a regular guy.* —*n.* **1.** soldier belonging to a permanent or standing armed service. **2.** member of a political party who can generally be relied upon to vote for and support its candidates or position. **3.** one who belongs to a religious order bound by certain rules. **4.** *Informal.* one who or that which is regular. [Late Latin *rēgulāris* usual, containing rules, from Late Latin *rēgulāris* relating to a rule or ruler, from *rēgula* rule, ruler, model.] —**reg·u·lar·i·ty** (reg′yə lar′ə tē) and **reg′u·lar·ness,** *n.* —**reg′u·lar·ly,** *adv.*

reg·u·lar·ize (reg′yə lə rīz′) -ized, -iz·ing. *v.t.* to make regular; standardize. —**reg′u·la·ri·za′tion,** *n.*

reg·u·late (reg′yə lāt′) -lat·ed, -lat·ing. *v.t.* **1.** to manage or control according to rule, principle, or system: *to regulate the economy.* **2.** to adjust for accurate functioning: *to regulate the clock.* **3.** to maintain in conformity with a certain standard or requirement, as of degree, rate, or amount; keep constant: *a valve that regulates the intake of air.* **4.** to put or keep in good or proper order. [Late Latin *rēgulātus,* past participle of *rēgulāre* to direct, from Latin *rēgula* rule, ruler, model.] —**reg′u·la·tive, reg′u·la·to′ry,** *adj.*

reg·u·la·tion (reg′yə lā′shən) *n.* **1.** authoritative directive or order intended to control behavior or procedure; governing rule or law: *customs regulations.* **2.** act of regulating; being regulated. —*adj.* **1.** required by or in accordance with regulation: *a regulation size.* **2.** usual; ordinary. —**Syn.** *n.* **1.** see **law.**

reg·u·la·tor (reg′yə lā′tər) *n.* **1.** one who or that which regulates. **2.** device used to adjust the speed of the balance wheel of a clock or watch. **3.** very precise clock used as a standard of time, by which other clocks are set or automatically controlled. **4.** any of several mechanical or electrical devices for controlling or keeping something constant under changing conditions, as the flow of liquids, gases, or electric current.

re·gur·gi·tate (rē gur′jə tāt′) -tat·ed, -tat·ing. *v.t.* **1.** to vomit. **2.** *Informal.* to give back or cast forth that which has not been assimilated. —*v.i.* to rush, surge, or flow back, as liquids, gases, or undigested food. [Medieval Latin *regurgitatus,* past participle of *regurgitare* to engulf, going back to Latin *re-* back, again + *gurges* whirlpool, gulf.] —**re·gur′gi·ta′tion,** *n.*

re·ha·bil·i·tate (rē′hə bil′ə tāt′) -tat·ed, -tat·ing. *v.t.* **1.** to restore or bring to a state of health or useful and purposeful activity, as through

training or therapy. **2.** to restore to a good condition; renovate. **3.** to restore the former rank, privileges, or good name of; reinstate. [Medieval Latin *rehabilitatus,* past participle of *rehabilitare* to restore, going back to Latin *re-* again + *habilis* fit.] —**re′ha·bil′i·ta′tion,** *n.*

re·hash (*v.,* rē hash′; *n.,* rē′hash′) *v.t.* to review or rework without significantly changing or improving (old material). —*n.* **1.** work or thought that is not original or creative. **2.** act of rehashing.

re·hears·al (ri hur′səl) *n.* **1.** practice session or performance in preparation for a public or official performance: *dance rehearsal.* **2.** act of rehearsing.

re·hearse (ri hurs′) -hearsed, -hears·ing. *v.t.* **1.** to practice, as a play, song, or role, in preparation for a public or official performance. **2.** to instruct or prepare by repetition or practice. **3.** to relate in detail; enumerate. —*v.i.* to take part in a rehearsal. [Old French *rehercier* to harrow over again, repeat, from *re-* (see RE-) + *hercier* to harrow (going back to Latin *hirpex* harrow, rake). See HEARSE.]

Reich (rīk; *German* rīKH) *n.* empire. [German *Reich.*]

reichs·mark (rīks′märk′) *pl.,* -marks or -mark. *n.* former monetary unit of Germany. [German *Reichsmark.*]

reign (rān) *n.* **1.** period of rule of a monarch or ruler. **2.** supreme power or rule, as of a monarch; sovereignty. **3.** pervasive or dominant influence: *the reign of reason.* —*v.i.* **1.** to hold or exercise the power of a monarch or other ruler. **2.** to have a pervasive influence; hold sway; prevail: *Famine reigns over the countryside.* [Old French *regne* kingdom, from Latin *rēgnum* kingdom, rule.] —**Syn.** *v.i.* **1.** see **rule.**

Reign of Terror, period of the French Revolution, from about May 1793 to July 1794, during which thousands of persons were imprisoned or guillotined.

re·im·burse (rē′im burs′) -bursed, -burs·ing. *v.t.* to pay back for what has been spent, used, or lost; recompense. [RE- + obsolete *imburse* to put into a purse, from Medieval Latin *imbursare,* from Latin *in* in + Late Latin *bursa* leather bag; influenced by French *rembourser* to repay. See PURSE.] —**re′im·burse′ment,** *n.*

Reims (rēmz; *French* raNs) *also,* **Rheims.** *n.* historic city in northern France, northeast of Paris. Pop. (1968), 152,967.

rein (rān) *n.* **1.** one of two or more long, narrow straps attached to a bit at either side of the mouth and used to control a horse or other draft animal. **2.** any means of guidance, restraint, or control; check: *Keep a tight rein on your temper.* **3. to give (free) rein to.** to give complete freedom to; free from restraint: *to give one's imagination free rein.* —*v.t.* to guide, control, or check with or as with reins. —*v.i.* to slow down or stop a horse or other animal by means of reins (with *in* or *up*). [Old French *rene* strap of a bridle, going back to Latin *retinēre* to hold back.]

re·in·car·nate (rē′in kär′nāt) -nat·ed, -nat·ing. *v.t.* to cause to undergo reincarnation.

re·in·car·na·tion (rē′in kär nā′shən) *n.* **1.** passage of a soul at death into another body; transmigration. **2.** belief that the soul undergoes such a passage, as in Buddhism or Hinduism. **3.** new incarnation or embodiment.

rein·deer (rān′dēr′) *pl.,* -deer. *n.* caribou, *Rangifer tarandus,* native to Lapland and Greenland, and introduced into other northern regions, having a white, gray, or brown coat, and branched antlers in both sexes, domesticated for use as a beast of burden and as a source of meat, milk, and hides. Reindeer skins are used to make shoes,

Reindeer

parkas, trousers, and other articles of clothing. Height: 3½–4½ feet at the shoulder. [Old Norse *hreindýri.*]

re·in·force (rē′in fôrs′) -forced, -forc·ing. *also,* **re·in·force, re·en·force.** *v.t.* **1.** to strengthen by repairing or replenishing or by adding some extra support, part, or material: *to reinforce a dam with sandbags.* **2.** to strengthen, esp. a military or naval force, with additional men, supplies, or other equipment. **3.** to make stronger or more forceful or effective. **4.** *Psychology.* to provide usually immediate and repeated reward or punishment for (behavior) in order to encourage the retention of learning or the reappearance of a particular response. [RE- + *inforce,* form of ENFORCE.]

reinforced concrete, concrete poured around or over metal, usu-

re·grind′	re·hard′en	re·hire′	re·im·pris′on·ment
re·group′	re·har′ness	re·hos′pi·tal·ize′	re·in·cor′po·rate
re·grow′	re·hear′	re·house′	re·in′cur′
re·growth′	re·hear′ing	re′ig·nite′	re·in·fect′
re·ham′mer	re·heat′	re′im·pose′	re·in·fec′tion
re·han′dle	re·heel′	re′im·po·si′tion	re·in·flame′
re·hang′	re·hem′	re′im·pris′on	re·in·flate′

at; āpe; cär; end; mē; it; īce; hot; ōld; fôrk; wood; fōōl; oil; out; up; ūse; turn; sing; thin; **this;** zh in treasure; ə in ago, taken, pencil, lemon, circus.

ally steel bars or mesh, and used where extra strength is needed to support heavy weight, as in buildings, bridges, and highways.

re·in·force·ment (rē′in fôrs′mənt) *also,* **re·in·force·ment, re·en·force·ment.** *n.* **1.** act of reinforcing; being reinforced. **2.** that which reinforces. **3. reinforcements.** troops, vessels, or other supplies added to those originally committed to a military action.

re·in·state (rē′in stāt′) **-stat·ed, -stat·ing.** *v.t.* to restore to a former position or condition. —**re′in·state′ment,** *n.*

re·in·vest (rē′in vest′) *also,* **re·in·vest.** *v.t.* to invest (money) again, esp. to invest income from previous investments. —**re′in·vest′·ment,** *n.*

re·is·sue (rē ish′oo) *n.* a reprinting or subsequent issue, as of books or stamps. —*v.t.,* **-sued, -su·ing.** to issue again.

re·it·er·ate (rē it′ə rāt′) **-at·ed, -at·ing.** *v.t.* to say or do again or repeatedly; repeat. [Late Latin *reiterātus,* past participle of *reiterāre* to repeat, going back to Latin *re-* again + *iterum* again.] —**re·it′er·a′tion,** *n.* —**re·it′er·a′tive,** *adj.*

re·ject (*v.,* ri jekt′; *n.,* rē′jekt) *v.t.* **1.** to refuse to accept, believe, grant, or approve: *The union rejected the company's offer.* **2.** to refuse (someone) acceptance, recognition, or consideration. **3.** to throw away, set aside, or discard as worthless or defective. **4.** to be unable to incorporate or assimilate, as food; expel: *The patient's body rejected the heart transplant.* —*n.* one who or that which is rejected. [Latin *rejectus,* past participle of *reicere* to throw back, scorn.] —**re·ject′er;** *also,* **re·jec′tor, re·jec′tion,** *n.* —**Syn.** *v.t.* **1.** see **refuse¹.**

re·joice (ri jois′) **-joiced, -joic·ing.** *v.i.* to express great joy or be filled with joy. —*v.t.* to fill with joy; gladden. [Old French *re(s)joïss-,* a stem of *re(s)joïr* to gladden, going back to Latin *re-* again + *gaudēre* to be glad.]

re·join¹ (rē join′) *v.t.* **1.** to join the company of again. **2.** to join together again. —*v.i.* to join again. [RE- + JOIN.]

re·join² (ri join′) *v.t., v.i.* to answer; reply. [Old French *rejoindre* to join again, reunite, going back to Latin *re-* again + *jungere* to unite.]

re·join·der (ri join′dər) *n.* reply, or retort, esp. an answer to a reply.

re·ju·ve·nate (ri joo′və nāt′) **-nat·ed, -nat·ing.** *v.t.* to make young or vigorous again. [RE- + Latin *juvenis* young + ATE¹.] —**re·ju′ve·na′tion, re·ju′ve·na′tor,** *n.*

rel. 1. relating. **2.** relative; relatively. **3.** religion; religious. **4.** released.

re·lapse (*n.,* rē′laps′; *v.,* ri laps′) *n.* act or instance of falling or slipping back into a former condition, esp. the recurrence of an illness after partial recovery. —*v.i.* **-lapsed, -laps·ing.** to have a relapse. [Latin *relapsus,* past participle of *relābī* to slide back.]

re·late (ri lāt′) **-lat·ed, -lat·ing.** *v.t.* **1.** to report the events or details of; narrate; tell: *The witness related the facts.* **2.** to show as having to do with; bring into relation; link. —*v.i.* **1.** to have connection, reference, or relation; apply; pertain (with *to*): *How does this evidence relate to the case?* **2.** to establish rapport; feel empathy (often with *to*): *to relate well to children.* [Latin *relātus,* past participle of *referre* to carry back, report.] —**re·lat′er;** *also,* **re·la′tor,** *n.* —**Syn.** *v.t.* **1.** see **tell.**

re·lat·ed (ri lā′tid) *adj.* **1.** having relation; connected: *related problems.* **2.** allied by blood, marriage, or common origin: *The zebra is related to the horse.* —**re·lat′ed·ness,** *n.*

re·la·tion (ri lā′shən) *n.* **1.** fact or condition of involving, affecting, or having to do with; association between two or more things: *the relation of crime to poverty.* **2.** position of one person or thing with respect to another: *the relation of the individual to society.* **3. relations.** conditions or associations that bring one person or thing in contact with another; affairs; dealings: *business relations.* **4.** relative formed by blood, marriage, or common origin. **5.** a relative. **6.** reference; regard: *to spend in relation to one's income.* **7.a.** act or instance of narrating or telling. **b.** that which is narrated or told; narrative; account. [Latin *relātiō* a carrying back, report.]

re·la·tion·ship (ri lā′shən ship′) *n.* **1.** connection; link: *the relationship between supply and demand.* **2.** state of emotional interaction. **3.** condition of being allied by blood, marriage, or common origin; kinship.

rel·a·tive (rel′ə tiv) *adj.* **1.** resulting from or determined by comparison; comparative: *He retired and lived in relative isolation.* **2.** existing or having significance only in relation to something else, as the terms *right* and *left.* **3. relative to.** having relation, reference, or application

to; pertinent to; concerning: *Relative to its size, the city is sparsely populated.* **4.** *Grammar.* modifying or referring to an antecedent. —*n.* **1.a.** person allied with another by blood or marriage. **b.** animal or plant allied with another by common origin or descent. **2.** *Grammar.* relative word or term, esp. a relative pronoun. [Late Latin *relātīvus* having reference to, from Latin *relātus,* past participle of *referre* to carry back, report.] —**rel′a·tive·ly,** *adv.* —**rel′a·tive·ness,** *n.* —**Syn.** *adj.* **1.** see **comparative.**

relative clause, dependent clause introduced by a relative pronoun or adverb. In the sentence *He who laughs last laughs best,* the phrase *who laughs last* is a relative clause.

relative humidity, humidity (*def.*2).

relative pronoun, pronoun that connects a dependent clause to a main clause and refers to a substantive in the main clause. In the sentence *He who laughs last laughs best,* the word *who* is a relative pronoun.

rel·a·tiv·ism (rel′ə ti viz′əm) *n.* *Philosophy.* theory that truth and standards of judgment are relative and may vary according to the individual, time, or place.

rel·a·tiv·i·ty (rel′ə tiv′ə tē) *n.* **1.** quality, state, or fact of being relative. **2.** theory of the interdependent nature of space, time, energy, and gravitation, developed by Albert Einstein. The **special theory of relativity** discusses the behavior of matter, energy, and light as experienced by observers who are moving in a straight line at a constant speed with respect to some other object, and states that there is no absolute motion, only motion relative to some other object. The **general theory of relativity** extends this theory to explain the forces of gravity acting on the motion of celestial bodies.

re·lax (ri laks′) *v.t.* **1.** to make less rigid or tense; loosen: *to relax one's grip.* **2.** to make less strict, severe, or harsh: *to relax a law.* **3.** to reduce in intensity; lessen; slacken: *to relax one's attention.* **4.** to provide release from tension or strain: *He needed a good book to relax him.* —*v.i.* **1.** to become less rigid or tense. **2.** to become less strict, severe, or harsh. **3.** to become less formal, distant, or constrained; unwind. **4.** to avoid or be relieved from work, effort, or strain; rest. [Latin *relaxāre* to loosen. Doublet of RELEASE.]

re·lax·a·tion (rē′lak sā′shən) *n.* **1.** act of relaxing; being relaxed. **2.** that which relaxes.

re·lay (*n.,* rē′lā; *v.,* rē′lā, ri lā′) *n.* **1.** fresh set or team, as of men or animals, prepared to replace or relieve another. **2.a.** relay race. **b.** one lap or portion of a relay race. **3.** electric switch that opens or closes in response to changes in the condition of an electric current or to mechanical forces. —*v.t.* **1.** to carry forward or pass along by or as by relays. **2.** to provide with relays. **3.** to transmit or redirect by an electrical relay. [Middle French *relais* set of fresh horses or dogs (as for a hunt), going back to Old French *re-* (see RE-) + *laier* to leave (going back to Latin *laxāre* to loosen).]

re·lay (rē lā′) **-laid, -lay·ing.** *v.t.* to lay again: *to re-lay rugs after cleaning.* [RE- + LAY¹.]

relay race (rē′lā′) race between two or more teams in which each team member in turn runs a portion of the total course and is then relieved by a teammate.

re·lease (ri lēs′) **-leased, -leas·ing.** *v.t.* **1.** to set free or loose from restraint, confinement, or bondage: *to release pent-up emotions, to release a hostage.* **2.** to let go or cause to be free from something that holds or fastens: *to release a brake.* **3.** to relieve from obligation or from something that burdens or oppresses: *to release someone from a promise.* **4.** to authorize or permit the publication, circulation, sale, or use of: *to release a movie for distribution.* **5.** to surrender, as a right, privilege, or claim. —*n.* **1.** act of releasing; being released. **2.** that which offers deli   nce or relief, as from work or tension. **3.** written discharge, as from obligation or responsibility: *You can't use those files without obtaining a release.* **4.** that which is formally issued or released to the public, as a printed statement or a movie: *a news release.* **5.** device, as a catch or button, that activates or releases a mechanism. **6.** surrender, as of a right, privilege, or claim, to another. [Old French *relaissier* to leave behind, abandon, from Latin *relaxāre* to loosen. Doublet of RELAX.]

re·lease (rē lēs′) **-leased, -leas·ing.** *v.t.* to lease again.

rel·e·gate (rel′ə gāt′) **-gat·ed, -gat·ing.** *v.t.* **1.** to send away or remove,

re′in·hab′it	re′in·stall′	re′in·ter′ment	re′in·vig′or·a′tion
re′in·ject′	re′in·stal·la′tion	re′in·ter′pret	re′in·vite′
re′in·jure′	re′in·stall′ment	re′in·ter′pre·ta′tion	re′in·voke′
re′in·oc′u·late′	re′in·stal′ment	re′in·ter′ro·gate′	re·judge′
re′in·oc′u·la′tion	re′in·sti·tute′	re′in·ter′ro·ga′tion	re·kin′dle
re′in·sert′	re′in·sti·tu′tion	re′in·tro·duce′	re·knit′
re′in·ser′tion	re′in·struct′	re′in·tro·duc′tion	re·la′bel
re′in·spect′	re·in′te·grate′	re′in·ves′ti·gate′	re·launch′
re′in·spec′tion	re·in′te·gra′tion	re′in·ves′ti·ga′tion	re·laun′der
re′in·spire′	re′in·ter′	re′in·vig′or·ate′	re·learn′

at; āpe; cär; end; mē; it; īce; hot; ōld; fôrk; wood; fōōl; oil; out; up; ūse; turn; sing; thin; this; zh in treasure; ə in ago, taken, pencil, lemon, circus.

esp. to an inferior position or obscure place: *We relegated those old toys to the junk pile.* **2.** to turn over or refer (a matter or task) to another. [Latin *relegātus*, past participle of *relegāre* to send away.] —**rel′e·ga′tion,** *n.*

re·lent (ri lent′) *v.i.* to become less harsh, severe, or persistent; soften; yield. [Possibly from RE- + Latin *lentus* flexible, slow.]

re·lent·less (ri lent′lis) *adj.* **1.** pitiless; unyielding; harsh. **2.** steady and persistent; unremitting; ceaseless. —**re·lent′less·ly,** *adv.* —**re·lent′less·ness,** *n.*

rel·e·vant (rel′ə vənt) *adj.* bearing upon or connected with the matter in hand; appropriate; pertinent: *a relevant question.* [French *relevant,* present participle of *relever* to raise up, help, from Latin *relevāre.*] —**rel′e·vance, rel′e·van·cy,** *n.* —**Syn.** see **pertinent.**

re·li·a·ble (ri lī′ə bəl) *adj.* that can be depended on with confidence; trustworthy: *a reliable firm.* —**re·li·a·bil′i·ty, re·li′a·ble·ness,** *n.* —**re·li′a·bly,** *adv.*

re·li·ance (ri lī′əns) *n.* **1.** act of relying. **2.** confidence or dependence. **3.** person or thing relied on; mainstay. —**Syn. 2.** see **trust.**

re·li·ant (ri lī′ənt) *adj.* having or showing reliance.

rel·ic (rel′ik) *n.* **1.** remaining portion or fragment that has survived decay, destruction, or the passage of time; remnant: *relics of the Roman civilization.* **2.** surviving trace, as of some past or outmoded custom, institution, or belief. **3.** body or part of the body of a saint, martyr, or other venerated person, or some object associated with him, often enshrined as a memorial. **4.** that which is cherished for its age or sentimental associations; memento; keepsake. **5.** *Informal.* any person or thing of great age. **6.** *Archaic.* corpse; remains. [Old French *reliques* remains of a saint after death, remains (as of a meal), from Latin *reliquiae* remains.]

re·lief¹ (ri lēf′) *n.* **1.** the freeing from or alleviating of physical or mental discomfort: *We sought relief from the heat in the air-conditioned room.* **2.** that which so frees or alleviates. **3.** financial assistance from government funds to those in poverty or need: *to go on relief.* **4.** aid or assistance, as to those in poverty or need: *relief for flood victims.* **5.** release from a post or duty, as by the substitution of a person or persons for another. **6.** person or persons so substituting for another. [Old French *relief* reparation, act of restoring, from *relever.* See RELIEVE.]

re·lief² (ri lēf′) *n.* **1.** distinctness or prominence resulting from contrast: *The gnarled tree stood in bold relief against the clear sky.* **2.** variation in elevations of an area of the earth's surface, esp. as depicted by a contour line on a map. **3.a.** projection of a figure or design from a flat surface or ground, as in sculpture or architecture. **b.** art or process of projecting a figure or design from such a surface, as by cutting, engraving, or sculpting. **c.** work executed by this process. **4.** illusion of depth created in a painting or drawing by the apparent projection of a figure or object from the surface, obtained by the use of line, shading, or color. [French *relief,* from Italian *rilievo* projection; literally, a raising, going back to Latin *relevāre* to raise again.]

Relief carving

relief map, map that shows the relative elevations and other physical features of an area of the earth's surface by means of contour lines, shading, color, or molding.

re·lieve (ri lēv′) -**lieved, -liev·ing.** *v.t.* **1.** to remove or make less or easier to bear; reduce: *This lotion relieves itching.* **2.** to free from pain, anxiety, discomfort, or the like. **3.** to free from a post or duty by providing or serving as a substitute: *The corporal will relieve the sentry in an hour.* **4.** to furnish aid to. **5.** to break the monotony through contrast or variety. **6.** to **relieve of.** to rid or take from: *The doorman relieved me of my packages.* [Old French *relever* to raise again, revive, restore, from Latin *relevāre* to raise again.]

re·lie·vo (ri lē′vō) *pl.,* -**vos.** *n.* relief² *(def. 3).* [Italian *rilievo* projection, from *rilevare* to raise, protrude, from Latin *relevāre* to raise again.]

re·li·gion (ri lij′ən) *n.* **1.** belief in, reverence for, or worship of a deity or deities, often thought of as having created or as governing the universe. **2.** system, esp. an institutionalized one, of such belief and worship, often involving the observance of particular doctrines and practices. **3.** any object attended to with devotion or conscientiousness. [Latin *religiō* reverence for the gods.]

re·li·gi·os·i·ty (ri lij′ē os′ə tē) *n.* religious feeling or sentiment, esp. excessive or affected piety.

re·li·gious (ri lij′əs) *adj.* **1.** imbued with or adhering to religion or a religion; showing devotion to a religion; pious. **2.** of or relating to religion: *religious instruction.* **3.** scrupulously careful and exact; conscientious; strict: *to pay religious attention to details.* **4.** of, relating to, or belonging to an order or community bound by monastic vows. —*n. pl.* -**gious. 1.** one bound by monastic vows, as a monk or nun. **2.** such persons collectively. [Latin *religiōsus* pious, from *religiō* reverence for the gods.] —**re·li′gious·ly,** *adv.* —**re·li′gious·ness,** *n.* —**Syn.** *adj.* **1.** see **pious.**

re·lin·quish (ri ling′kwish) *v.t.* **1.** to give over possession or control of; surrender; yield: *to relinquish territory.* **2.** to put aside or give up; abandon: *to relinquish a plan.* **3.** to let go, as a grasp; release: *to relinquish one's hold.* [Old French *relinquiss-,* a stem of *relinquir* to abandon, leave, from Latin *relinquere* to leave behind.] —**re·lin′quish·ment,** *n.*

rel·i·quar·y (rel′ə kwer′ē) *pl.* -**quar·ies.** *n.* receptacle, often of precious metal and richly decorated, for a religious relic or relics. [Old French *reliquaire,* going back to Latin *reliquiae* remains.]

rel·ish (rel′ish) *n.* **1.a.** mixture of spices and chopped vegetables, pickles, or other food, used chiefly as a condiment or as a side dish. **b.** food, as celery, olives, or pickles, to be eaten with other food as a garnish or appetizer or to add flavor. **2.** appetite; enjoyment; appreciation: *to eat with great relish.* **3.** anything that lends pleasure, zest, or interest; attractive quality. **4.** zestful, pleasing, or appetizing flavor. **5.** trace or suggestion, as of a quality or characteristic. —*v.t.* **1.** to take pleasure in; savor; enjoy: *to relish a meal.* **2.** to give a pleasant flavor to. [Old French *reles* remainder, from *relaissier* to leave behind (referring to the good taste that is left behind). See RELEASE.]

re·live (rē liv′) -**lived, -liv·ing.** *v.t.* to live over again, esp. in the mind: *to relive one's childhood.*

re·lo·cate (rē lō′kāt) -**cat·ed, -cat·ing.** *v.t.* to move, as a business, to another place. —*v.i.* to move to another place.

re·luc·tance (ri luk′təns) *n.* state of being reluctant; lack of eagerness; hesitation; unwillingness. Also, **re·luc′tan·cy.**

re·luc·tant (ri luk′tənt) *adj.* **1.** feeling hesitation; unwilling; averse: *I was reluctant to lend him my books.* **2.** marked by unwillingness or hesitation. [Latin *reluctāns,* present participle of *reluctārī* to struggle against, going back to *re-* back + *lucta* wrestling.] —**re·luc′tant·ly,** *adv.*

Syn. 1. Reluctant, unwilling indicate reservations about something. **Reluctant** suggests that one acts or becomes involved despite vague, often inarticulate misgivings which make one uncomfortable: *She was reluctant to go to the doctor but made the appointment anyway.* **Unwilling** suggests that one may refuse to do or approve something because of a strong opposition that can be forcefully expressed: *She was unwilling to lend the book to him because he never returned things.*

re·ly (ri lī′) -**lied, -ly·ing.** *v.i.* to have confidence; trust; depend (with *on* or *upon*): *Rely on him to be prompt.* [Old French *relier* to bind together, from Latin *religāre* to bind fast.]

rem (rem) *n.* unit for measuring quantities of biologically absorbed radiation, equivalent to one roentgen of X rays.

re·main (ri mān′) *v.i.* **1.** to continue in the same place; stay behind; abide: *You should've remained at home.* **2.** to continue unchanged or in the same state; go on being: *We remained fast friends for years.* **3.** to be left, as after the removal, departure, or destruction of all else: *Take three apples from five apples and two remain.* **4.** to be still to be dealt with: *That remains to be seen.* [Old French *remaindre* to stay behind, from Latin *remanēre.*] —**Syn. 1.** see **stay¹.**

re·main·der (ri mān′dər) *n.* **1.** that which remains or is left; remaining part: *the remainder of the day.* **2.** *Mathematics.* **a.** number found when one number is subtracted from another; for example: ten subtracted from twelve leaves a remainder of two. **b.** number remaining when one number is divided by another; for example: seven divided by three gives two and a remainder of one. **3.** copy of a book remaining with a publisher, esp. after the demand for it has fallen off. —*v.t.* to dispose of or sell, usually at a reduced price, as a book or clothing. —**Syn.** *n.* **1.** see **balance.**

re·mains (ri mānz′) *n.,pl.* **1.** that which remains or is left: *the remains of ancient Rome.* **2.** dead body; corpse.

re·make (*n.* rē′māk′; *v.* rē māk′) *n.* something made again or anew: *a remake of an old motion picture.* —*v.t.,* -**made, -mak·ing.** to make again or anew.

re·mand (ri mand′) *v.t.* **1.** to send, call, or order back: *to remand a soldier to his post.* **2.** *Law.* **a.** to return (a prisoner or an accused person) to custody. **b.** to send (a case) back to a lower court for further proceedings. —*n.* act of remanding; being remanded. [Late Latin *remandāre*

re·let′	re·light′	re·lo·ca′tion	re·mail′
re·let′ter	re·line′	re·lock′	re′man·u·fac′ture
re·li′cense	re·load′	re·low′er	re·map′

at; āpe; cär; end; mē; it; īce; hot; ōld; fôrk; wood; fōōl; oil; out; up; ūse; turn; sing; thin; this; zh in treasure; ə in ago, taken, pencil, lemon, circus.

to send back word, from Latin re- back + *mandāre* to order, consign.]

re·mark (ri märk′) *n.* **1.** oral or written statement or observation, esp. a brief or casual comment. **2.** act of taking notice or observing; notice: *a development worthy of remark.* —*v.t.* **1.** to express as an opinion or observation. **2.** to take notice of; observe; perceive. —*v.i.* to make remarks (with *on* or *upon*). [French *remarquer* to note, heed, from *re-* (see RE-) + *marquer* to mark (of Germanic origin).]

re·mark·a·ble (ri mär′kə bəl) *adj.* **1.** having unusual qualities; extraordinary; uncommon. **2.** worthy of notice or likely to be noticed. —re·mark′a·ble·ness, *n.* —re·mark′a·bly, *adv.* —**Syn. 1.** see extraordinary.

Rem·brandt (rem′brant) *n.* 1606–69, Dutch painter and etcher; full name Rembrandt Harmenszoon van Rijn.

re·me·di·a·ble (ri mē′dē ə bəl) *adj.* capable of being remedied or cured. —re·me′di·a·bly, *adv.*

re·me·di·al (ri mē′dē əl) *adj.* providing or intending to provide a remedy: *a remedial reading program.* [Late Latin *remediālis* healing, from Latin *remedium.* See REMEDY.] —re·me′di·al·ly, *adv.*

rem·e·dy (rem′ə dē) *pl.,* **-dies.** *n.* **1.** something, as a medicine or treatment, that relieves or is intended to relieve a disease, disorder, or the like: *a headache remedy.* **2.** that which corrects, counteracts, or eliminates an evil: *a remedy for air pollution.* —*v.t.,* **-died, -dy·ing. 1.** to relieve or cause to heal or improve (a disease or disorder), as by medicinal treatment. **2.** to set or make right; correct: *to remedy conditions in the slums.* [Latin *remedium,* cure.] —**Syn.** *v.t.* **1.** see cure.

re·mem·ber (ri mem′bər) *v.t.* **1.** to bring back or recall to the mind or memory; recollect: *Do you remember where you put the keys?* **2.** to keep in mind carefully: *to remember an appointment.* **3.** to think of or keep in mind as worthy of affection, regard, or recognition: *I′ll always remember you for your kindness.* **4.** to reward or present with a gift, as a legacy or tip. **5.** to convey greetings from (with *to*): *Remember me to your parents.* —*v.i.* to have or use the faculty of memory. [Old French *remembrer* to recall, from Late Latin *rememorārī,* going back to Latin *re-* again + *memor* mindful.]

re·mem·brance (ri mem′brəns) *n.* **1.** that which is remembered; recollection. **2.** act or power of remembering; being remembered. **3.** object, as a gift, serving to bring to or keep in mind something or someone; memento; keepsake. **4.** length of time over which one′s memory extends: *It′s the coldest winter in my remembrance.* —**Syn. 2.** see memory.

re·mind (ri mīnd′) *v.t.* to bring to mind or cause to remember; make (someone) think of (something or someone). —re·mind′er, *n.*

rem·i·nisce (rem′ə nis′) *v.i.,* **-nisced, -nisc·ing.** *v.i.* to recollect or tell of past experiences or events: *We reminisced about home.*

rem·i·nis·cence (rem′ə nis′əns) *n.* **1.** recollection of past experiences or events. **2.** *also,* **reminiscences.** narration or account of past experiences or events. **3.** that which recalls, suggests, or is a reminder of something else. **4.** something remembered; memory. [Late Latin *reminiscentia* remembrance, from Latin *reminiscī* to remember.]

rem·i·nis·cent (rem′ə nis′ənt) *adj.* **1.** reminding or suggestive (of). **2.** marked by or given to reminiscence.

re·miss (ri mis′) *adj.* **1.** careless or negligent, as in attending to duty; lax. **2.** characterized by a lack of earnestness, energy, or attention. [Latin *remissus,* past participle of *remittere* to send back, slacken.] —re·miss′ly, *adv.* —re·miss′ness, *n.*

re·mis·si·ble (ri mis′ə bəl) *adj.* capable of being remitted or pardoned, as a sin.

re·mis·sion (ri mish′ən) *n.* **1.** act of remitting; being remitted. **2.** release from penalty or guilt; pardon. **3.** abatement, esp. a temporary one, of pain or the symptoms of a disease. **4.** lessening of degree or intensity. **5.** cancellation, as of a debt.

re·mit (ri mit′) *v.t.,* **-mit·ted, -mit·ting.** *v.t.* **1.** to send (money), as in payment. **2.** to release from the penalty or guilt of; pardon; forgive, as a sin or offense. **3.** to refrain from exacting or inflicting; cancel: *to remit punishment.* **4.** to allow to slacken or abate, as vigilance: *to remit one′s efforts.* **5.** to submit or refer for consideration, decision, or action, esp. to one in authority. **6.** *Law.* to send (a case) back to a lower court for further proceedings. —*v.i.* **1.** to send money, as in payment. **2.** to become less; abate; diminish: *His fever remitted.* [Latin *remittere* to send back, slacken, forgive.] —re·mit′ta·ble, *adj.* —re·mit′ter, *n.*

re·mit·tal (ri mit′əl) *n.* remission.

re·mit·tance (ri mit′əns) *n.* **1.** sending of money or its equivalent. **2.** the money or its equivalent sent.

re·mit·tent (ri mit′ənt) *adj.* characterized by abatements in severity: *a remittent heat wave.*

rem·nant (rem′nənt) *n.* **1.a.** remaining quantity, part, or piece; remainder; fragment: *remnants of a meal.* **b.** surviving trace or vestige, as of a former time or condition. **2.** odd piece of cloth, as at the end of a bolt, left over from the cutting of a larger piece, often sold at a reduced price. [Old French *remanant* residue, from *remanoir* to stay behind, from Latin *remanēre.*]

re·mod·el (rē mod′əl) **-eled, -el·ing;** *also, British,* **-elled, -el·ling.** *v.t.* to make over or anew, as with a new structure; reconstruct; renovate.

re·mon·strance (ri mon′strəns) *n.* act or instance of remonstrating; protest.

re·mon·strant (ri mon′strənt) *adj.* that remonstrates.

re·mon·strate (ri mon′strāt) **-strat·ed, -strat·ing.** *v.t.* to say or plead in protest, opposition, or disapproval. —*v.i.* to present reasons in complaint or objection; plead or argue in protest. [Medieval Latin *remonstratus,* past participle of *remonstrare* to demonstrate, going back to Latin *re-* again, back + *mōnstrāre* to show.] —re·mon·stra·tion (rē′mən strā′shən), re·mon′stra·tor, *n.* —re·mon·stra·tive (ri mon′stra tiv), *adj.*

re·morse (ri môrs′) *n.* deep, painful feeling of guilt, sorrow, or distress for wrongdoing or past misdeeds. —re·morse′ful, *adj.* —re·morse′ful·ly, *adv.* —re·morse′ful·ness, *n.* —**Syn.** see regret.

re·morse·less (ri môrs′lis) *adj.* having no pity or compassion; merciless. —re·morse′less·ly, *adv.* —re·morse′less·ness, *n.*

re·mote (ri mōt′) **-mot·er, -mot·est.** *adj.* **1.** situated at a distance; not near; far away or off: *remote regions.* **2.** located out of the way; secluded: *a remote house.* **3.** far removed from the present; distant in time: *the remote past.* **4.** small in degree; slight; faint: *a remote possibility.* **5.** having no close or immediate connection or bearing: *a question remote from the topic under consideration.* **6.** not closely related by blood or marriage: *a remote ancestor.* **7.** lacking warmth and friendliness; aloof and cool; reserved. [Latin *remōtus* far off, past participle of *removēre* to move back.] —re·mote′ly, *adv.* —re·mote′ness, *n.*

remote control, control from a distance of a machine or apparatus, as a guided missile or television, esp. by means of radio signals.

re·mov·al (ri mōō′vəl) *n.* **1.** act of removing; being removed. **2.** changing of place or relocation, as of a business. **3.** dismissal, as from an office or position.

re·move (ri mōōv′) **-moved, -mov·ing.** *v.t.* **1.** to take or move away, as from one place or position to another: *to remove dishes from a table.* **2.** to take off or shed, as an article of clothing. **3.** to do away with; eliminate: *to remove all cause for alarm.* **4.** to dismiss from an office or position. **5.** to take or withdraw; separate; extract (with *from*): *to remove a mineral from an ore.* **6.** to assassinate; murder. —*v.i.* to change one′s place of residence or business; move. —*n.* **1.** distance or interval separating one person or thing from another. **2.** step, as in a graded scale. **3.** act of removing; removal. [Old French *removoir* to take away, from Latin *removēre* to move back, take away.] —re·mov′a·ble, *adj.* —re·mov′er, *n.*

re·moved (ri mōōvd′) *adj.* **1.** separated by a degree in relationship: *He′s my cousin once removed.* **2.** distant; remote.

re·mu·ner·ate (ri mū′nə rāt′) **-at·ed, -at·ing.** *v.t.* **1.** to pay an equivalent to (someone) for any service, loss, or expense; reward; repay. **2.** to compensate for. [Latin *remūnerātus,* past participle of *remūnerāre* to reward, repay.] —re·mu′ner·a′tion, *n.*

re·mu·ner·a·tive (ri mū′nə rā′tiv, -nər ə tiv) *adj.* **1.** tending to be well remunerated; lucrative; profitable. **2.** that remunerates.

Re·mus (rē′məs) see **Romulus.**

ren·ais·sance (ren′ə säns′, -zäns′, ren′ə säns′, -zäns′, ri nā′səns) *also,* **re·nas·cence.** *n.* **1.** renewal of activity, interest, or enthusiasm concerning something; rebirth; revival. **2. Renaissance. a.** movement thought to have originated in Italy in the fourteenth century, marked by a growth of interest in classical literature and art, concern with individualism, and intellectual, scientific, and artistic activity. **b.** period of European history during which this occurred, extending from the fourteenth through the sixteenth century. **c.** style of art, as painting, sculpture, and architecture, developed during and characteristic of this period. **3.** *also,* **Renaissance.** any movement or period of flourishing artistic and intellectual activity. —*adj.* of, characteristic of, or in the style of the Renaissance. [French *renaissance* rebirth, renewal, from *renaître* to be born again, from Latin *renāscī.*]

re·nal (rēn′əl) *adj.* of, relating to, or near the kidneys. [Late Latin *rēnālis,* from Latin *rēn* kidney.]

re·nas·cence (ri nas′əns, -nā′səns) renaissance.

re·nas·cent (ri nas′ənt, -nā′sənt) *adj.* showing renewed growth or vigor; being born again; resurgent. [Latin *renāscēns,* present participle of *renāscī* to be born again.]

re·mar′riage	re·meas′ure	re·mil′i·ta·rize′	re·mold′
re·mar′ry	re·melt′	re·mix′	re·mort′gage
re·mar′shal	re·mi′grate	re·mo′bi·lize′	re·mul′ti·ply′
re·match′	re·mil′i·ta·ri·za′tion	re·mod′i·fy	re·name′

at; āpe; cär; end; mē; it; īce; hot; ōld; fôrk; wood; fōol; oil; out; up; ūse; turn; sing; thin; this; zh in treasure; ə in ago, taken, pencil, lemon, circus.

rend (rend) *rent* or *rend·ed, rend·ing. v.t.* **1.** to split or tear apart or into pieces forcibly or violently: *The gale rent the sails.* **2.** to divide or split into parts as if by tearing: *Racial strife rent the community.* **3.** to remove forcibly, as from a place or position; wrest. **4.** to pass through or disturb suddenly or sharply; pierce: *Her screams rent the stillness.* **5.** to distress violently or painfully. —*v.i.* to become split or torn; come apart. [Old English *rendan* to tear.] —**Syn.** *v.t.* **1.** see **tear¹**.

ren·der (ren′dər) *v.t.* **1.** to cause to be or become; make: *to render someone speechless.* **2.** to give or pay as something owed or due: *to render an apology.* **3.** to give or make available; furnish; provide: *to render aid to the needy.* **4.** to give in return or requital. **5.** to perform; do; execute. **6.** to represent or depict, as in painting. **7.** to present and interpret in performance, as a concert. **8.** to deliver or state formally: *The jury rendered a verdict of not guilty.* **9.** to reproduce or express in another language; translate. **10.** to offer or submit, as for consideration, approval, or payment: *to render a bill.* **11.** to give up; surrender; yield (often with *up*). **12.** to separate, clarify, or extract by melting: *to render fat.* [Old French *rendre* to give back, yield, going back to Latin *reddere*; influenced by Latin *prendere* to take.]

ren·dez·vous (rän′də vŏŏ′, -dā-) *pl.* **-vous** (-vŏŏz′). *n.* **1.** appointment to meet at a fixed place or time. **2.** place appointed for such a meeting. **3.** any meeting or gathering place. —*v.t., v.i.,* **-voused** (-vŏŏd′), **-vous·ing** (-vŏŏ′ing). to meet or cause to meet by arrangement. [French *rendezvous* appointment, place of meeting, from *rendez-vous,* imperative of *se rendre* to betake oneself, yield. See RENDER.] —**Syn.** *n.* **1.** see **appointment**.

ren·di·tion (ren dish′ən) *n.* **1a.** interpretation given by a performer to an artistic, dramatic, or musical composition. **b.** performance of such a composition. **2.** interpretation or version of a text; translation. **3.** act of rendering. [Obsolete French *rendition* a giving back, from Old French *rendre* to give back. See RENDER.]

ren·e·gade (ren′ə gād′) *n.* **1.** one who abandons, rejects, or turns against his group, religion, cause, or allegiance, often in favor of another; turncoat; apostate. **2.** outlaw. —*adj.* that is a renegade: *a renegade soldier.* [Spanish *renegado* apostate, from Medieval Latin *renegatus,* past participle of *renegare* to deny, from Latin *re-* again + *negāre* to deny.]

re·nege (ri nig′, -neg′, -nēg′) *-neged, -neg·ing. v.i.* **1.** to fail to fulfill a promise or commitment: *to renege on a business deal.* **2.** *Card Games.* to fail to play a card of the suit led when the rules require such play and the player is able to make such a play. —*n. Card Games.* act of reneging. [Medieval Latin *renegare* to deny. See RENEGADE.] —**re·neg′er,** *n.*

re·new (ri nŏŏ′, -nū′) *v.t.* **1.** to make new or as if new again; restore to a previous or sound condition; revive: *to renew one's spirits.* **2.** to begin again or start over; take up again; resume: *to renew a discussion.* **3.** to cause to continue in effect: *to renew a subscription.* **4.** to say again, as if to reaffirm; repeat: *to renew an oath.* **5.** to bring back into use or existence; reestablish. **6.** to replace with something new of the same sort; fill again; replenish: *The ship renewed its provisions.* **7.** to make new spiritually; regenerate. —*v.i.* **1.** to become new or as if new again. **2.** to begin anew or start over; resume.

re·new·al (ri nŏŏ′əl, -nū′-) *n.* **1.** act of renewing; being renewed. **2.** something renewed.

ren·i·form (ren′ə fôrm′, rē′nə-) *adj.* having the form of a kidney; kidney-shaped. [Latin *rēn* kidney + -FORM.]

Rennes (ren) *n.* city in northwestern France. Pop. (1968), 180,943.

ren·net (ren′it) *n.* curdling agent containing rennin, obtained from the stomachs of young calves and added to milk to make cheese. [Possibly from an unrecorded Old English word.]

ren·nin (ren′in) *n.* enzyme present in the gastric juice of certain mammals, esp. infants and calves, that curdles milk into a pulpy mass. [RENNET + -IN¹.]

Re·no (rē′nō) *n.* city in western Nevada. Pop. (1970), 72,863.

Re·noir, Pierre Au·guste (ren′wär, rə nwär′; pyer ō goost′) 1841–1919, French painter.

re·nounce (ri nouns′) *-nounced, -nounc·ing. v.t.* **1.** to give up, abandon, or resign, esp. by formal declaration: *to renounce a claim.* **2.** to refuse to recognize as one's own; repudiate; disown. [Old French *renoncer* to abandon entirely, from Latin *renūntiāre* to report, disclaim.] —**re·nounce′ment,** *n.*

ren·o·vate (ren′ə vāt′) *-vat·ed, -vat·ing. v.t.* to make new or like new, esp. by extensive repair or alteration: *to renovate a building.* [Latin *renovātus,* past participle of *renovāre* to renew.] —**ren′o·va′tion, ren′o·va′tor,** *n.*

re·nown (ri noun′) *n.* widespread reputation; fame. [Anglo-Norman *renoun,* going back to Latin *re-* again + *nōmen* name.]

re·nowned (ri nound′) *adj.* having renown; famous. —**Syn.** see **famous**.

rent¹ (rent) *n.* **1.** payment for the use or occupation of property, esp. such payment made periodically by a tenant to a landlord or owner. **2. for rent.** available for use or occupancy in return for the paying of rent. —*v.t.* **1.** to obtain the right to use or occupy (property) in return for the paying of rent: *to rent a car.* **2.** to grant the use or occupancy of (property) in return for the paying of rent (often with *out*): *a store that rents out bicycles.* **3.** to be for rent: *The apartment rents for $100 a month.* [Old French *rente* revenue, income, going back to Latin *reddita,* feminine past participle of *reddere* to give back.] —**Syn.** *v.t.* **2.** see **lease**.

rent² (rent) *v.* a past tense and past participle of **rend**. —*n.* **1.** opening or hole made by rending or tearing; gap; slit: *a rent in a dress, a rent in a wall.* **2.** sharp division or split, as in an organized group or between persons: *a rent in a political party.* [From dialectal English *rent* to tear, form of REND.]

rent·al (rent′əl) *n.* **1.** amount charged, paid, or collected as rent. **2.** act of renting. **3.** property rented or available for renting. —*adj.* of, for, or relating to rent or renting: *a car rental agency.*

re·nun·ci·a·tion (ri nun′sē ā′shən) *n.* act of renouncing. [Latin *renūntiātiō.*] —**re·nun′ci·a′tive, re·nun·ci·a·to·ry** (ri nun′sē ə tôr′ē), *adj.*

re·o·pen (rē ō′pən) *v.t., v.i.* **1.** to open again. **2.** to begin again; resume: *to reopen discussion.*

re·or·der (rē ôr′dər) *v.t.* **1.** to order or organize in a new or different way; rearrange. **2.** to order again. **3.** to restore to proper or original order; put back in order. —*n.* second or repeated order, as for goods or materials.

re·or·gan·i·za·tion (rē′ôr gə ni zā′shən) *n.* **1.** act or process of reorganizing; being reorganized. **2.** thorough reconstruction of a business corporation, as after bankruptcy, involving a change in capital structure.

re·or·gan·ize (rē ôr′gə nīz′) *-ized, -iz·ing. v.t., v.i.* to organize again or anew.

rep (rep) *also,* **repp.** *n.* any of various fabrics, esp. one made of cotton, having alternating large and small ribs and used for such items as upholstery and drapes. [French *reps;* of uncertain origin.]

rep. **1.** report; reporter. **2.** representative. **3.** republic.

Rep. Republican.

re·paid (ri pād′) past tense and past participle of **repay**.

re·pair¹ (ri pâr′) *v.t.* **1.** to restore to a sound condition or working order, as by replacing parts or putting together what has broken; fix; mend: *The road crew repaired the highway.* **2.** to correct or eliminate by repairing something. **3.** to bring back to a sound or healthy state; renew: *to repair damaged body tissues.* **4.** to make good; set right; remedy. **5.** to give satisfaction for or make amends for; make up for; compensate for. —*n.* **1.** act or process of repairing: *The roof is beyond repair.* **2.** instance or result of repairing: *The repair in the rug is hardly noticeable.* **3.** condition with respect to soundness or need of repairing: *The barn is in good repair.* **4.** state of being in good or sound condition: *Our car is out of repair.* [Latin *reparāre* to get back, restore.] —**re·pair′er,** *n.* —**Syn.** *v.t.* **1.** see **mend**.

re·pair² (ri pâr′) *v.i.* to betake oneself; go: *to repair to bed.* —*n.* **1.** act of repairing. **2.** place to which one repairs, esp. frequently or habitually. [Old French *repair(i)er* to return, stay, from Late Latin *repatriāre* to return to one's country, from Latin *re-* back + *patria* native land.]

re·pair·man (ri pâr′man′, -mən) *pl.* **-men.** *n.* one whose occupation is making repairs: *a television repairman.*

rep·a·ra·ble (rep′ər ə bəl) *also,* **re·pair·a·ble** (ri pâr′ə bəl). *adj.* capable of being repaired.

rep·a·ra·tion (rep′ə rā′shən) *n.* **1.** act of giving satisfaction or making amends, as for a wrong or injury. **2.** something done or given as satisfaction or amends. **3. reparations.** money or material given in compensation for damage or loss sustained in war, esp. that given by a defeated nation to a victorious one. **4.** act of repairing; being repaired. [Late Latin *reparātiō* restoration, from Latin *reparāre.* See REPAIR¹.] —**re·par·a·tive** (ri par′ə tiv), *adj.*

Reniform leaf

---

re·nom′i·nate′	re·oc·cur′	re·or·ches·trate′	re·pack′age
re′nom·i·na′tion	re′oc·cur′rence	re·or′i·ent	re·paint′
re·num′ber	re·of′fer	re′or·i·en·tate′	re·pan′el
re′oc·cu·pa′tion	re·oil′	re′or·i·en·ta′tion	re·pa′per
re·oc′cu·py′	re·op′er·ate′	re·pack′	re·park′

---

at; āpe; cär; end; mē; it; īce; hot; ōld; fôrk; wood; fŏŏl; oil; out; up; ūse; turn; sing; thin; this; zh in treasure; ə in ago, taken, pencil, lemon, circus.

rep·ar·tee (rep'ər tē', -tā', rep'är-) *n.* **1.** spirited exchange of quick, witty replies. **2.** skill or quickness in making such replies. **3.** quick, witty reply. [French *repartie* retort, reply, from *repartir* to reply, going back to Latin *re-* again, back + *pars* part.]

re·past (ri past') *n.* meal, or the food and drink eaten or provided at a meal. [Old French *repast,* going back to Latin *re-* again + *pāscere* to feed.]

re·pa·tri·ate (*v.,* rē pā'trē āt', -pat'rē-; *n.,* rē pā'trē it, -pat'rē-) **-at·ed, -at·ing.** *v.t.* to return (someone) to his country of origin or citizenship, as a prisoner of war or refugee. —*n.* one who has been repatriated. [Late Latin *repatriātus,* past participle of *repatriāre* to return to one's country, from Latin *re-* back + *patria* native land.] —**re·pa'tri·a'tion,** *n.*

re·pay (ri pā') **-paid, -pay·ing.** *v.t.* **1.** to pay or give back, as money: *to repay a loan.* **2.** to pay or give something back to (someone); make return to: *I'll never be able to repay you for your help.* **3.** to give or make some return or recompense for. **4.** to give, make, or do in return. —**re·pay'a·ble,** *adj.* —**re·pay'ment,** *n.*

re·peal (ri pēl') *v.t.* to withdraw or cancel formally or officially; annul; revoke; to repeal a law. —*n.* act of repealing: *the repeal of a constitutional amendment.* [Anglo-Norman *repeler* to revoke, going back to Latin *re-* back + *appellāre* to call upon.]

re·peat (ri pēt') *v.t.* **1.** to say or utter (something already said) again; reiterate: *Joe loudly repeated his question.* **2.** to say (exactly what someone else or oneself has said): *Excuse me if I'm repeating myself.* **3.** to tell or divulge to another or others: *Don't repeat a word of what I'm about to tell you.* **4.** to say again or recite from memory. **5.** to do, make, or perform again: *The player repeated the serve.* **6.** to undergo or go through again. **7.** to present again; cause to appear again. **8.** to occur again in the same form: *History repeats itself.* —*v.i.* **1.** to say or do something again. **2.** to vote fraudulently more than once in a single election. —*n.* **1.** act of repeating. **2.** something repeated; repetition. **3.** rebroadcast, esp. of a television program. **4.** *Music.* **a.** passage, section, or movement that is to be repeated. **b.** any of several signs indicating this, esp. double bar lines with two dots, placed at the end (:||), and usually also at the beginning (||:) of such a passage. [Latin *repetere* to do again, say again.]

re·peat·ed (ri pē'tid) *adj.* said, done, or occurring again and again. —**re·peat'ed·ly,** *adv.*

re·peat·er (ri pē'tər) *n.* **1.** repeating firearm. **2.** student who repeats a course, usually one that he has previously failed. **3.** one who has been arrested or convicted more than once for violating the law. **4.** one who or that which repeats. **5.** timepiece, esp. a watch, having a spring or lever that, when pressed, causes it to strike again the hour or part of the hour last struck.

repeating decimal, decimal in which a particular digit or series of digits is repeated indefinitely, for example: 0.666 . . . and 0.1232323 . . . are repeating decimals.

repeating firearm, rifle or pistol that can be fired more than once without reloading.

re·pel (ri pel') **-pelled, -pel·ling.** *v.t.* **1.** to drive back or away: *to repel an attack.* **2.** to cause to feel dislike, aversion, or disgust: *Every aspect of war repelled him.* **3.** to be resistant or impervious to: *This material will repel heat and moisture.* **4.** to refuse to accept or consider; reject: *to repel an offer.* **5.** to push away or force apart: *The negative poles of two magnets will repel each other.* —*v.i.* **1.** to cause dislike, aversion, or disgust. **2.** to act so as to drive or push something away. [Latin *repellere* to drive back, from *re-* back + *pellere* to drive.]

re·pel·lent (ri pel'ənt) *adj.* **1.** causing dislike, aversion, or disgust; repugnant. **2.** resistant or impervious to something. ▲ usually used in combination, as in *a water-repellent coat.* **3.** serving or tending to drive away. —*n.* something that repels: *a mosquito repellent.*

re·pent (ri pent') *v.i.* **1.** to feel such abhorrence of or contrition for one's sins as to reject sinful ways and reform one's life. **2.a.** to feel sorrow, deep regret, or compunction for something one has done or failed to do. **b.** to change one's mind regarding past action or conduct, as through dissatisfaction with it or its consequences (often with *of*). —*v.t.* to feel sorrow or compunction for: *David later repented his misdeeds and resolved to make amends.* [Old French *repentir,* going back to Latin *re-* again + *paenitēre* to cause to be sorry.]

re·pent·ance (ri pent'əns) *n.* **1.** sorrow, deep regret, or compunction, as for sin or wrongdoing. **2.** act or process of repenting. —**Syn.** **1.** see penitence.

re·pent·ant (ri pent'ənt) *adj.* feeling, showing, or characterized by repentance; penitent. —**re·pent'ant·ly,** *adv.*

re·per·cus·sion (rē'pər kush'ən) *n.* **1.** effect or result, often indirect, of an action or event; consequence. **2.** echo; reverberation. **3.** rebound or recoil after impact. [Latin *repercussiō* a rebounding.] —**re'per·cus'sive,** *adj.*

rep·er·toire (rep'ər twär') *n.* **1.** stock of artistic works, as plays, operas, or songs, that a performer or group of performers has learned. **2.** list of such works. **3.** range of skills, abilities, or devices possessed by a person or group. [French *répertoire* list, from Late Latin *repertōrium* inventory, from Latin *reperīre* to find again. Doublet of REPERTORY.]

rep·er·to·ry (rep'ər tôr'ē) *pl.* **-ries.** *n.* **1.** repertoire. **2.** store or collection. **3.** storehouse. **4.** repertory theater. [Late Latin *repertōrium* inventory, from Latin *reperīre* to find again. Doublet of REPERTOIRE.]

repertory theater, theatrical organization in which a permanent acting company alternates performances of its productions.

rep·e·ti·tion (rep'ə tish'ən) *n.* **1.** act of repeating. **2.** that which is repeated. [Latin *repetītiō.*]

rep·e·ti·tious (rep'ə tish'əs) *adj.* full of, characterized by, or containing repetition, esp. unnecessary or tiresome repetition: *a repetitious speaker.* —**rep'e·ti'tious·ly,** *adv.* —**rep'e·ti'tious·ness,** *n.*

re·pet·i·tive (ri pet'ə tiv) *adj.* characterized by or relating to repetition. —**re·pet'i·tive·ly,** *adv.* —**re·pet'i·tive·ness,** *n.*

re·phrase (rē frāz') **-phrased, -phras·ing.** *v.t.* to phrase again, esp. to express in a different way: *to rephrase a question.*

re·pine (ri pīn') **-pined, -pin·ing.** *v.i.* to feel or express discontent or unhappiness; fret; complain. [RE- + PINE².]

re·place (ri plās') **-placed, -plac·ing.** *v.t.* **1.** to take or fill the place of: *Richard will replace John as club president.* **2.** to provide or procure a substitute or equivalent for: *The car battery is defective and should be replaced.* **3.** to restore or return to the original or proper place; put back: *He replaced the magazine in the rack.* **4.** to repay or make good; return. —**re·place'a·ble,** *adj.*

re·place·ment (ri plās'mənt) *n.* **1.** one who or that which replaces. **2.** act of replacing; being replaced.

re·plen·ish (ri plen'ish) *v.t.* **1.** to bring back to a state of fullness or completeness, as by replacing what is lacking or has been used: *to replenish one's food supplies.* **2.** to provide a new supply for: *to replenish a cupboard.* [Old French *repleniss-,* a stem of *replenir* to fill up again, going back to Latin *re-* again + *plēnus* full.] —**re·plen'ish·ment,** *n.*

re·plete (ri plēt') *adj.* **1.** filled or abundantly supplied; overflowing; abounding (with *with*): *a garden replete with brightly colored flowers.* **2.** filled to satisfaction or capacity with food or drink; gorged; sated. [Latin *replētus* filled up, past participle of *replēre* to fill up.] —**re·plete'ness,** *n.*

re·ple·tion (ri plē'shən) *n.* **1.** state or condition of being replete: *to eat to repletion.* **2.** satisfaction or fulfillment.

rep·li·ca (rep'li kə) *n.* **1.** close or exact copy or reproduction, esp. one done on a smaller scale than the original: *a replica of a battleship.* **2.** copy or reproduction of a work of art, esp. one made by the original artist. [Italian *replica,* from *replicare* to duplicate, repeat, from Late Latin *replicāre.* See REPLY.] —**Syn.** **1.** see duplicate.

rep·li·cate (rep'lə kāt') **-cat·ed, -cat·ing.** *v.t.* **1.** to make a replica of. **2.** to fold over or bend back. [Late Latin *replicātus,* past participle of *replicāre.* See REPLY.]

rep·li·ca·tion (rep'lə kā'shən) *n.* **1.** act or process of replicating or reproducing. **2.** copy or reproduction. **3.** reply or rejoinder; response. **4.** reverberation or echo. **5.** *Law.* plaintiff's reply to a defendant's counterclaim or defense. **6.** *Biology.* process occurring during the division of cells, in which the DNA present in a cell duplicates itself, thus insuring that all new cells are exactly like the original.

re·ply (ri plī') **-plied, -ply·ing.** *v.i.* **1.** to respond orally or in writing; answer: *He did not reply to the accusation.* **2.** to make return or response by some action; react: *The girl replied only with a smile.* **3.** to echo; resound. —*v.t.* to say in response; give as a response. —*n. pl.* **-plies.** something said, written, or done in response. [Old French *replier* to fold back, answer back, from Late Latin *replicāre* to repeat, from Latin *replicāre* to unfold.] —**Syn.** **1.** see answer.

re·port (ri pôrt') *n.* **1.a.** account, statement, or announcement: *scattered reports of flying saucer landings.* **b.** formal or official account or statement, esp. an analysis or presentation of facts based on investigation: *a news and weather report.* **2.** explosive sound or noise, esp. that made by a rifle or pistol when fired. **3.** record, often formal and detailed, of the proceedings, as of a meeting or legislative assembly. **4.** common talk; rumor; gossip. **5.** reputation; repute: *a man of good report.* **6.** *also,* **reports.** collection of volumes published periodically, containing accounts of cases heard in state and federal courts and the decisions handed down. —*v.t.* **1.** to make or give an account or statement of, often formally or officially. **2.** to make known; relate. **3.** to bring back, repeat, or deliver, as a message; convey. **4.** to bring charges of wrongdo-

at; āpe; cär; end; mē; it; īce; hot; ōld; fôrk; wood; fōōl; oil; out; up; ūse; turn; sing; thin; this; zh in treasure; ə in ago, taken, pencil, lemon, circus.

ing or misconduct against; denounce or complain about, as to someone in authority: *to report a rude salesperson to the manager.* **5.** of a legislative committee, to send on (a bill) to the entire legislative body, usually with a recommendation for passage (often with *out*). —*v.i.* **1.** to make a report: *to report on slum conditions.* **2.** to work or act as a reporter. **3.** to present oneself: *He reported for work at noon.* [Old French *reporter* to carry back, bring news, denounce, from Latin *reportāre* to carry back.] —**re·port′a·ble,** *adj.* —**Syn.** *n.* **1.** see **account.**

report card, periodic written report of a pupil's grades and conduct.

re·port·ed·ly (ri pôr′tid lē) *adv.* according to report.

re·port·er (ri pôr′tər) *n.* **1.** one employed to gather and report news, as for a newspaper, magazine, or television network. **2.** one who takes down and transcribes proceedings: *a court reporter.* **3.** one who reports. —**rep·or·to·ri·al** (rep′ər tôr′ē əl), *adj.*

re·pose¹ (ri pōz′) *n.* **1.** relaxation, as after exertion or activity; rest; sleep. **2.** peace and quiet; tranquility: *the beauty and repose of the forest.* **3.** absence of animation or movement; undisturbed condition: *Her face in repose was somber.* **4.** calmness or ease, as of manner; composure. —*v.i.* **-posed, -pos·ing. 1.** to lie or be at rest; rest; sleep. **2.** to be supported; rest; lie. **3.** to lie dead. **4.** to depend or rely (with *on, upon,* or *in*). —*v.t.* to lay in a position of rest. [Old French *reposer* to rest, going back to Latin *re-* again + Late Latin *pausāre* to cause to rest. See POSE¹.]

re·pose² (ri pōz′) **-posed, -pos·ing.** *v.t.* to place, as confidence or hope (with *in*). [RE- + POSE¹.]

re·pose·ful (ri pōz′fəl) *adj.* full of repose; calm; quiet.

re·pos·i·to·ry (ri poz′ə tôr′ē) *pl.* **-ries.** *n.* **1.** place or receptacle in which something is or may be stored or deposited. **2.** person to whom something, as a secret, is confided or entrusted. **3.** burial vault; sepulcher. [Latin *repositōrium* storehouse.]

re·pos·sess (rē′pə zes′) *v.t.* **1.** to possess again; regain possession of. **2.** to resume possession of (something bought on installments or credit) for failure of the buyer to make due payment: *to repossess a car.* **3.** to put (someone) again in possession of something; return possession to. —**re′pos·ses′sion,** *n.*

re·pous·sé (rə pōō sā′) *adj.* **1.** formed in relief, as by hammering a thin piece of metal on the reverse side: *a repoussé design.* **2.** ornamented or shaped with designs or figures formed in relief: *a repoussé box.* [French *repoussé,* from *repousser* to thrust back, from *re-* back (from Latin *re-*) + *pousser* to thrust. See PUSH.]

repp (rep) rep.

rep·re·hend (rep′ri hend′) *v.t.* to criticize sharply; reprove; censure. [Latin *reprehendere* to hold back, blame.]

rep·re·hen·si·ble (rep′ri hen′sə bəl) *adj.* deserving sharp criticism or reproof. —**rep′re·hen′si·bil′i·ty, rep′re·hen′si·ble·ness,** *n.* —**rep′re·hen′si·bly,** *adv.*

rep·re·hen·sion (rep′ri hen′shən) *n.* act of reprehending; criticism; reproof. [Latin *reprehensiō.*] —**rep′re·hen′sive,** *adj.*

rep·re·sent (rep′ri zent′) *v.t.* **1.** to serve as a symbol, sign, or expression of; stand for; signify; symbolize: *In this story the sorcerer represents evil.* **2.** to express or designate by some symbol, character, sign, or the like: *to represent speech sounds by letters.* **3.** to speak or act for; serve as the delegate or agent of: *Two senators represent each state.* **4.** to present an image or likeness of; portray or depict, as in painting or sculpture. **5.** to set forth or point out in words; describe; explain. **6.** to be tantamount to; amount to; constitute: *Their actions represent a violation of the agreement.* **7.** to serve as an example, specimen, or instance of; exemplify; typify. **8.** to present or picture to the mind. **9.** to act the part or role of. **10.** to perform or produce, as on the stage; present, as a play. [Latin *raepraesentāre* to show, exhibit.]

rep·re·sen·ta·tion (rep′ri zen tā′shən, -zən-) *n.* **1.** act of representing; being represented. **2.** account, statement, or description. **3.** that which represents, as a picture or other likeness. **4.** state, fact, or right of being represented in a legislative or deliberative assembly. **5.** body or number of representatives. **6.** dramatic performance or presentation. **7.** statement of arguments, esp. one made in protest or intended to influence action or opinion. —**re′pre·sen·ta′tion·al,** *adj.*

rep·re·sent·a·tive (rep′ri zen′tə tiv) *n.* **1.** one who is chosen or authorized to represent another or others; delegate; agent: *The company had a representative in Rome.* **2.** person or thing serving to exemplify or typify a group, kind, or class. **3.** elected member of a legislative assembly, esp. a member of the lower house of Congress or of a state legislature. —*adj.* **1.** exemplifying or typifying a group, kind, or class; typical; characteristic. **2.** acting for or authorized to act for another or others. **3.** composed of representatives or based on or relating to political representation: *a representative government.* **4.** serving to represent, portray, or symbolize. —**rep′re·sen′ta·tive·ly,** *adv.* —**rep′re·sen′ta·tive·ness,** *n.* —**Syn.** *n.* **1.** see **agent.**

re·press (ri pres′) *v.t.* **1.** to hold back or keep under control or in check; restrain: *to repress a smile.* **2.** to put down or put a stop to, esp. by force; subdue; quell: *to repress an uprising.* **3.** to prevent the natural development or expression of: *His creative talents had been repressed for too long.* **4.** to relegate to the unconscious mind, as painful memories or disturbing desires. Distinguished from **suppress.** [Latin *repressus,* past participle of *reprimere* to press back, check.] —**re·press′er;** *also,* **re·pres′sor,** *n.* —**Syn.** **1.** see **oppress.**

re·pres·sion (ri presh′ən) *n.* **1.** act or instance of repressing; being repressed. **2.** psychological process by which painful memories or disturbing desires are relegated to the unconscious mind. Distinguished from **suppression.**

re·pres·sive (ri pres′iv) *adj.* tending or serving to repress; capable of repressing. —**re·pres′sive·ly,** *adv.* —**re·pres′sive·ness,** *n.*

re·prieve (ri prēv′) *n.* **1.** *Law.* a. official postponement of the carrying out of a sentence, esp. a delay in the execution of a condemned person. b. document ordering such a postponement. **2.** respite or temporary relief or escape, as from something unpleasant or difficult. —*v.t.* **-prieved, -priev·ing. 1.** to grant a reprieve to (someone), esp. to delay the execution of (a condemned person) for a specified period of time. **2.** to free temporarily, as from something unpleasant or difficult. [Middle English *repreven,* form of *reproven* to reprove; literally, to test again. See REPROVE.]

rep·ri·mand (rep′rə mand′) *v.t.* to reprove sharply or formally. —*n.* sharp reproof, esp. one formally or officially given. [French *réprimande* reproof, check, from Latin *reprimenda* (thing) to be checked, feminine gerundive of *reprimere* to press back, check.] —**Syn.** *v.t.* see **reprove.**

re·print (*n.* rē′print′; *v.* rē print′) *n.* **1.** new edition of a work previously published. **2.** separately printed excerpt, as of an article printed in a magazine. —*v.t.* to print a new edition or copy of; print again.

re·pris·al (ri prī′zəl) *n.* **1.** retaliation against an enemy for injuries or losses suffered, with the intent of inflicting equal or greater injury. **2.** act or instance of retaliating. **3.** *also,* **reprisals.** something given or paid in restitution; compensation. [Anglo-Norman *reprisaille* a seizing on, from Old French *repris,* past participle of *reprendre* to reprove, seize again, from Latin *reprehendere* to hold back.]

re·prise (ri prīz′, -prēz′) *n. Music.* repetition of a song that has been sung previously or of an earlier section of a composition. [Old French *reprise* a taking back, from *reprendre* to take back, seize again, from Latin *reprehendere* to hold back.]

re·proach (ri prōch′) *v.t.* to charge with or blame for a fault or wrongdoing; chide; reprove: *He reproached the typist for her carelessness.* —*n.* **1.** act of reproaching; blame; reproof. **2.** expression of this. **3.** cause, object, or occasion of blame or disgrace: *These slums are a reproach to our city.* **4.** discredit; disgrace. [Old French *reprochier* to blame, accuse, going back to Latin *re-* again + *prope* near.] —**Syn.** *v.t.* see **blame.**

re·proach·ful (ri prōch′fəl) *adj.* full of or expressing reproach. —**re·proach′ful·ly,** *adv.* —**re·proach′ful·ness,** *n.*

rep·ro·bate (rep′rə bāt′) *n.* depraved, unprincipled, or profligate person. —*adj.* given to immorality; profligate. —*v.t.* **-bat·ed, -bat·ing.** to condemn. [Late Latin *reprobātus,* past participle of *reprobāre* to disapprove, condemn, from Latin *re-* again + *probāre* to test, try.]

rep·ro·ba·tion (rep′rə bā′shən) *n.* condemnation; censure.

re·pro·duce (rē′prə dōōs′, -dūs′) **-duced, -duc·ing.** *v.t.* **1.** to produce, form, or bring about again or anew; re-create: *The movie reproduced the grandeur of ancient Greece.* **2.** to make a duplicate, counterpart, or representation of: *to reproduce a picture.* **3.** to give rise to or produce (offspring or others of the same kind) by sexual or asexual means. **4.** to foster or bring about the generation of (plants or animals). **5.** to replace, as a lost or damaged limb, by regeneration. —*v.i.* **1.** to give rise to or produce offspring or others of the same kind. **2.** to undergo reproduction.

re·pro·duc·tion (rē′prə duk′shən) *n.* **1.** process by which living organisms give rise to or produce offspring or others of their kind. **2.** that which is reproduced. **3.** act or process of reproducing; being reproduced.

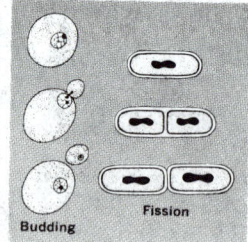

Budding

Fission

Asexual reproduction

re·pro·duc·tive (rē′prə duk′tiv) *adj.* of, employed in, or relating to

---

re·por′tion
re·pos′tu·late′

re′pos·tu·la′tion
re·pot′

re·pour′
re·prac′tice

re·price′
re·proc′ess

at; āpe; cär; end; mē; it; īce; hot; ōld; fôrk; wood; fōōl; oil; out; up; ūse; turn; sing; thin; this; zh in treasure; ə in ago, taken, pencil, lemon, circus.

reproduction. —**re′pro·duc′tive·ly,** *adv.* —**re′pro·duc′tive·ness,** *n.*

re·proof (ri prŏŏf′) *n.* **1.** act of reproving. **2.** expression of censure; rebuke. [Old French *reproche* reproach, from *reprover.* See REPROVE.]

re·prove (ri prŏŏv′) **-proved, -prov·ing.** *v.t.* to blame, censure, or find fault with; scold; rebuke. [Old French *reprover* to reproach, from Late Latin *reprobāre* to disapprove, condemn, from Latin *re-* again + *probāre* to test, try (suggesting testing again and condemning).] —**re·prov′a·ble,** *adj.*
Syn. Reprove, rebuke, reprimand mean the expression of criticism or blame. **Reprove** suggests a direct attempt, esp. a kindly effort, to instruct or to correct a fault: *The director reproved the star for missing his cue.* **Rebuke** implies a severe and biting warning, esp. in public: *The premier rebuked those nations that had supported the rebels.* **Reprimand** is usually less intense and personal and suggests sharp official, public, and formal reproof by a superior: *The principal reprimanded the student for his chronic lateness.*

rep·tile (rep′til, -tīl) *n.* **1.** any of a group of cold-blooded vertebrates, class Reptilia, including lizards, snakes, crocodiles, and turtles, having dry, usually scaly skin and often reproducing by laying eggs. **2.** groveling, treacherous, or despicable person. —*adj.* reptilian. [Late Latin *rēptile* creeping creature, neuter of *rēptilis* creeping, from Latin *rēpere* to creep, crawl.]

rep·til·i·an (rep til′ē ən, -til′yən) *adj.* **1.** of, relating to, or characteristic of a reptile or reptiles. **2.** like a reptile; treacherous; despicable. —*n.* a reptile.

Repub. 1. Republic. **2.** Republican.

re·pub·lic (ri pub′lik) *n.* **1.** form of government in which the final authority of the state rests with voting citizens and is exercised by elected officials, rather than by a hereditary monarch. **2.** nation or state that has such a form of government. [Latin *rēspublica* state; literally, public thing.]

re·pub·li·can (ri pub′li kən) *adj.* **1.** of, characteristic of, or like a republic. **2.** Republican. of, relating to, or characteristic of the Republican Party. **3.** supporting or advocating a republic as a form of government. —*n.* **1.** Republican. member of the Republican Party. **2.** one who believes in or advocates a republic as a form of government.

re·pub·li·can·ism (ri pub′li kə niz′əm) *n.* **1.** system or principles of government used by republics. **2.** belief in or advocacy of such principles. **3.** Republicanism. principles or policies of the Republican Party.

Republican Party, one of the two major political parties in the United States.

re·pu·di·ate (ri pū′dē āt′) **-at·ed, -at·ing.** *v.t.* **1.** to refuse to accept as valid; reject as unjust or untrue: *to repudiate an accusation.* **2.** to refuse to have anything to do with; cast off; disown: *to repudiate a wife, to repudiate a son.* **3.** to refuse to acknowledge or pay, as a debt. [Latin *repudiātus,* past participle of *repudiāre* to put away, reject, from *repudium* divorce, a casting off.] —**re·pu′di·a′tion, re·pu′di·a′tor,** *n.*

re·pug·nance (ri pung′nəns) *n.* extreme dislike or aversion; disgust. Also, **re·pug′nan·cy.**

re·pug·nant (ri pug′nənt) *adj.* **1.** causing extreme dislike or aversion; highly distasteful; offensive; repulsive: *a repugnant odor.* **2.** contrary or opposed; antagonistic. [Latin *repugnāns,* present participle of *re·pugnāre* to resist, oppose.]

re·pulse (ri puls′) **-pulsed, -puls·ing.** *v.t.* **1.** to beat or drive back; repel, as with force: *Our army repulsed the enemy's advance.* **2.** to refuse to accept; reject, as by discourtesy or coldness; rebuff: *She repulsed his attentions.* —*n.* **1.** act of repulsing or driving back; being repulsed. **2.** rejection; rebuff. [Latin *repulsus,* past participle of *repellere* to drive back.]

re·pul·sion (ri pul′shən) *n.* **1.** extreme dislike, aversion, or disgust. **2.** act of repelling; being repelled.

re·pul·sive (ri pul′siv) *adj.* **1.** causing extreme dislike, disgust, or aversion; highly distasteful or offensive. **2.** tending to repel. —**re·pul′sive·ly,** *adv.* —**re·pul′sive·ness,** *n.*

rep·u·ta·ble (rep′yə tə bəl) *adj.* having a good reputation; trustworthy; respectable. —**rep′u·ta·bil′i·ty,** *n.* —**rep′u·ta·bly,** *adv.*

rep·u·ta·tion (rep′yə tā′shən) *n.* **1.** general or public estimation of something or someone: *a judge who has a reputation for fair-mindedness.* **2.** state of being highly regarded or esteemed: *to ruin one's reputation.* [Latin *reputātiō* consideration, from *reputāre.* See REPUTE.]

re·pute (ri pūt′) *n.* **1.** general or public estimation of something or someone. **2.** state of being highly regarded or esteemed. —*v.t.,* **-put·ed, -put·ing.** to consider to be; suppose. [Latin *reputāre* to think over, esteem.]

re·put·ed (ri pū′tid) *adj.* generally considered or supposed. —**re·put′ed·ly,** *adv.*

re·quest (ri kwest′) *v.t.* **1.** to express a wish or desire for; ask for, esp. politely or formally: *He requested a raise.* **2.** to express a wish or desire to; ask. —*n.* **1.** act or instance of requesting: *Our firm will mail you a catalogue upon request.* **2.** that which is requested: *to grant a request.* **3.** state of being so desired or esteemed as to be sought after or in demand. [Old French *requeste* petition, probably from *request,* past participle of *requerre* to ask, ask for, going back to Latin *requīrere* to ask, seek again.]

Req·ui·em (rek′wē əm, rē′kwē-) *n.* **1.** Mass offered for the eternal rest of the soul or souls of one or more deceased persons, esp. as part of a funeral. **2.** *also,* **requiem.** musical setting for this. **3.** **requiem.** any musical composition, hymn, or service in honor of the dead. [Latin *requiem,* accusative of *requiēs* rest; the first word of the introit of the Mass for the dead.]

re·qui·es·cat (rek′wē es′kat) *n.* wish or prayer for the repose of the dead. [Latin, first word of REQUIESCAT IN PACE.]

requiescat in pa·ce (pä′chā) *Latin.* may he rest in peace.

re·quire (ri kwīr′) **-quired, -quir·ing.** *v.t.* **1.** to have need of: *His arm requires medical attention.* **2.** to impose as an obligation or condition: *Knitting requires much patience.* **3.** to order or compel (someone) to do something: *The border police required the traveler to unlock his luggage.* —*v.i.* to request or demand. [Latin *requīrere* to ask for, need.] —**Syn.** *v.t.* **1.** see need. **3.** see demand.

re·quire·ment (ri kwīr′mənt) *n.* **1.** that which is imposed as an obligation or condition. **2.** that which is needed.

req·ui·site (rek′wə zit) *adj.* required; necessary; indispensable: *The camper found the requisite ferns and branches and built a lean-to.* —*n.* that which cannot be done without; essential. [Latin *requīsītus,* past participle of *requīrere* to ask for, need.] —**req′ui·site·ly,** *adv.* —**req′ui·site·ness,** *n.*

req·ui·si·tion (rek′wə zish′ən) *n.* **1.a.** official written request or application, as for new equipment. **b.** act of putting through such a request. **c.** form on which such a request is made. **2.** act of taking, as through assertion of authority: *The army's requisition of food brought hardship to the people.* —*v.t.* **1.** to put through a requisition for. **2.** to take, as through assertion of authority. **3.** to make a requisition of: *We requisitioned the storeroom for a few supplies.*

re·quit·al (ri kwīt′əl) *n.* **1.** act of requiting. **2.** that which is given or done in return: *a proper requital for his insults.*

re·quite (ri kwīt′) **-quit·ed, -quit·ing.** *v.t.* **1.** to give or pay back in kind; return: *He requited her love.* **2.** to repay or reward. [RE- + obsolete *quite* to repay, form of QUIT.]

rere·dos (rēr′dos, rēr′ə-, rār′ə-) *n.* screen or ornamental work covering the wall behind an altar. [Short for Old French *areredos,* going back to Latin *ad* to + *retrō* backward + *dorsum* back.]

re·route (rē rŏŏt′, -rout′) **-rout·ed, -rout·ing.** *v.t.* to send by a new or different route.

re·run (*n.* rē′run′; *v.* rē run′) *n.* **1.a.** showing of a filmed or taped performance, as a motion picture, after its original showing. **b.** filmed or taped performance itself. **2.** act or instance of running again. —*v.t.* **-ran, -run·ning. 1.** to show as a rerun. **2.** to run again, as a race.

re·sale (rē′sāl′, rē sāl′) *n.* act of selling what one has bought.

re·scind (ri sind′) *v.t.* to make void, as a law; annul; cancel. [Latin *rescindere* to cut off, annul.]

re·scis·sion (ri sizh′ən) *n.* act of rescinding. [Late Latin *rescissiō,* from Latin *rescindere* to cut off, annul.]

re·script (rē′skript′) *n.* **1.** formal written reply, as from a pope, to a written question or petition. **2.** official edict, decree, or announcement. **3.** act or product of rewriting. [Late Latin *rescriptum* emperor's decision, reply (to a letter), from Latin *rescribere* to write in reply.]

res·cue (res′kū) **-cued, -cu·ing.** *v.t.* **1.** to save or free, as from danger. **2.** *Law.* to free (someone or something) forcibly and knowingly from legal custody. —*n.* act of rescuing. [Old French *rescourre* to save, going back to Latin *re-* back, again + *excutere* to drive away (suggesting driving danger away).] —**res′cu·er,** *n.* —**Syn.** *v.t.* **1.** see save[1].

re·search (ri surch′, rē′surch′) *n.* systematic study or investigation in a particular field, usually as a basis for new facts and interpretations. —*v.t.* to make a systematic study or investigation of or for: *to research a topic, to research a term paper.* [Middle French *recerche* a diligent search, from *recercher* to seek, from Old French *re-* (see RE-) + *cerchier* to seek. See SEARCH.] —**re·search′er,** *n.*

Reredos

re′pub·li·ca′tion	re·read′	re·sad′dle	re·screen′
re·pub′lish	re′re·cord′	re·sched′ule	re·seal′
re′pur·sue′	re·roll′	re·score′	re·seal′a·ble

at; āpe; cär; end; mē; it; īce; hot; ōld; fôrk; wood; fŏŏl; oil; out; up; ūse; turn; sing; thin; <u>th</u>is; zh in treasure; ə in ago, taken, pencil, lemon, circus.

re·seat (rē sēt′) *v.t.* **1.** to seat again. **2.** to assign to a new or different seat. **3.** to install in office again; reelect. **4.** to put a new seat on or in, as a chair or pair of pants.

re·sem·blance (ri zem′bləns) *n.* **1.** similarity, as of physical detail; likeness: *a close resemblance between the two brothers.* **2.** someone or something similar. [Anglo-Norman *resemblance* likeness, from Old French *resembler* to be like.]

re·sem·ble (ri zem′bəl) **-bled, -bling.** *v.t.* to be like, as in appearance or nature. [Old French *resembler,* going back to Latin *re-* again + *simulāre* to imitate, make like.]

re·sent (ri zent′) *v.t.* to feel resentment at or toward: *John resented Steve because of his successes.* [French *ressentir,* going back to Latin *re-* back, again + *sentīre* to feel.]

re·sent·ful (ri zent′fəl) *adj.* characterized by or inclined toward resentment. —**re·sent′ful·ly,** *adv.* —**re·sent′ful·ness,** *n.*

re·sent·ment (ri zent′mənt) *n.* indignation, anger, or bitterness resulting from a real or imagined offense or injury.

res·er·va·tion (rez′ər vā′shən) *n.* **1.a.** arrangement whereby something, as a theater seat or hotel room, is reserved. **b.** that which is reserved: *Our reservation is in the main dining room.* **c.** assurance of this, usually in writing: *Our hotel reservations came today.* **2.a.** tract of land set aside by the U.S. government for an Indian tribe or group to live on. **b.** tract of land set aside by the government, as for military purposes or as a wildlife preserve. **3.** doubt; misgiving: *She had some reservations about her new job.* **4.** expressed or tacit qualification: *We approved the plan without a single reservation.* **5.** act or instance of withholding, saving, or keeping for oneself.

re·serve (ri zurv′) **-served, -serv·ing.** *v.t.* **1.** to set aside or have set aside, as for a particular person or purpose or for future use: *He reserved a table for two. Our grandmother reserved an hour each afternoon for a nap.* **2.** to withhold or save, esp. until a later time: *The athlete reserved his strength for the race. I will reserve my opinion at this time.* **3.** to keep for oneself: *I reserve the right to make my own decisions.* —*n.* **1.** that which is set aside, as for a special purpose or future use; store; supply: *The old man keeps a large reserve of firewood for cold weather.* **2.** state or condition of being set aside or saved: *There was food in reserve for emergencies. The books were on reserve.* **3.** tract of land set aside by the government for a special purpose; preserve. **4.** self-control or restraint, as in speech or behavior. **5.** tendency or habit of keeping silent, esp. as to one's feelings or thoughts; taciturnity: *The man's icy reserve offended us.* **6.** *Finance.* amount of capital or gold held back, as from investment, to meet emergencies or special demands. **7.** *also,* **reserves.** part of the armed forces not on active duty but available for service in an emergency. **8. reserves.** part of a fighting force withheld from action until needed. —*adj.* kept in reserve; constituting a reserve. [Latin *reservāre* to keep back, save up.] —**Syn.** *n.* **1.** see **stock.**

re·serve (rē surv′) **-served, -serv·ing.** *v.t., v.i.* to serve again.

reserve bank, Federal Reserve Bank.

re·served (ri zurvd′) *adj.* **1.** set aside, as for a particular person or purpose or for future use: *This table is reserved.* **2.** characterized by reserve in speech and behavior. —**re·serv·ed·ly** (ri zur′vid lē) *adv.* —**re·serv′ed·ness,** *n.*

Reserve Officers' Training Corps, see ROTC.

re·serv·ist (ri zurv′ist) *n.* member of a military reserve.

res·er·voir (rez′ər vwär′, -vôr′, rez′ə-) *n.* **1.** natural or man-made place used for the storage of water. **2.** receptacle or part used for the storage of a liquid or gas. **3.** place where anything is collected and stored: *Great literature is a reservoir of wisdom.* **4.** reserve; store; supply: *This book contains a reservoir of facts.* [French *réservoir,* going back to Latin *reservāre* to keep back, save up.]

re·set (*v.,* rē set′; *n.,* rē′set′) **-set, -set·ting.** *v.t.* **1.** to set again: *to reset the clock.* **2.** to set in a different place or position: *He reset the shrubs behind the house.* —*n.* **1.** act of resetting. **2.** that which is reset.

re·shape (rē shāp′) **-shaped, -shap·ing.** *v.t.* to give a new or different shape to.

re·ship (rē ship′) **-shipped, -ship·ping.** *v.t.* **1.** to transport again, as by ship, rail, or truck; ship again. **2.** to transfer to another ship. —*v.i.* **1.** to sign up for another voyage as a crew member: *He reshipped on the vessel the day before it sailed.* **2.** to board a ship again; reembark.

re·ship·ment (rē ship′mənt) *n.* **1.** act of transporting again, as by ship. **2.** that which is transported again.

re·side (ri zīd′) **-sid·ed, -sid·ing.** *v.i.* **1.** to make one's home permanently or for a considerable time: *The woman resides with her mother.* **2.** to be vested (with *in* or *with*): *The power of veto resides with the president.* **3.** to be present or inherent (with *in*): *Much goodness resides in him.* [Latin *residēre* to remain behind, abide.] —**re·sid′er,** *n.*

res·i·dence (rez′ə dəns) *n.* **1.** place where one resides. **2.** act or state of residing, esp. to satisfy legal requirements or to discharge some duty: *His residence in the town enabled him to vote.* **3.** period of time spent residing in a place: *After ten years' residence, he left the community.* —**Syn. 1.** see **home.**

res·i·den·cy (rez′ə dən sē) *pl.,* **-cies.** *n.* **1.** period during which a physician receives advanced, specialized clinical training. **2.** residence.

res·i·dent (rez′ə dənt) *n.* **1.** one who resides in a particular place. **2.** physician serving a residency. —*adj.* **1.** residing in a particular place. **2.** residing in a place in connection with work or duty: *a resident surgeon.*

res·i·den·tial (rez′ə den′shəl) *adj.* **1.** of or relating to residence: *He met the residential requirement for voting.* **2.** characterized by, restricted to, or suitable for residences: *a residential neighborhood.*

re·sid·u·al (ri zij′ōō əl) *adj.* of, relating to, or constituting a residue; remaining. —*n.* **1.** *also,* **residuals.** accrual of payments made to a performer for the repeated use or showing of a film in which he appears. **2.** remaining quantity or substance.

re·sid·u·ar·y (ri zij′ōō er′ē) *adj.* of, relating to, or entitled to that part of an estate not otherwise disposed of by bequests.

res·i·due (rez′ə dōō, -dū′) *n.* **1.** substance remaining at the end of a separating process, such as evaporation, combustion, or filtration. **2.** anything that remains, as after a main part is taken away. [Middle French *residu* surplus, remainder, from Latin *residuum,* neuter of *residuus* remaining.] —**Syn. 2.** see **balance.**

re·sid·u·um (ri zij′ōō əm) *pl.,* **-sid·u·a** (-zij′ōō ə). *n.* residue.

re·sign (ri zīn′) *v.i.* to give up voluntarily, as a job, position, or office: *The president of the club resigned today.* —*v.t.* **1.** to give up (a position or responsibility) voluntarily: *The general resigned his commission.* **2.** to make (oneself) accept (with *to*): *to resign oneself to the facts.* **3.** *Archaic.* to relinquish; surrender. [Old French *resigner* to give up, from Latin *resignāre* to unseal, annul.]

res·ig·na·tion (rez′ig nā′shən) *n.* **1.** act of resigning. **2.** formal, usually written, notice that one is resigning. **3.** unresisting acceptance; acquiescence; submission.

re·signed (ri zīnd′) *adj.* characterized by resignation; acquiescent. —**re·sign·ed·ly** (ri zī′nid lē), *adv.* —**re·sign′ed·ness,** *n.*

re·sil·ience (ri zil′yəns, -zil′ē əns) *n.* power or quality of being resilient. Also, **re·sil′ien·cy.**

re·sil·ient (ri zil′yənt, -zil′ē ənt) *adj.* **1.** capable of springing back to the original size, shape, or position after being bent, compressed, or stretched. **2.** capable of recovering quickly or easily, as from depression or adversity. [Latin *resiliēns,* present participle of *resilīre* to leap back, rebound.]

res·in (rez′in) *n.* **1.** any of various translucent yellow or brown sticky substances secreted by certain trees, as pine and balsam trees, used esp. in the improvement of paints and plastics and in the manufacture of linoleum, adhesives, and rubber. **2.** any of various similar synthetic materials that are the main constituents of plastics. **3.** rosin (*def.* 1). [Latin *rēsīna* resin from trees, from Greek *rhētīnē* resin from the pine.]

res·in·ous (rez′ə nəs) *adj.* **1.** of, relating to, or resembling resin. **2.** obtained from or containing resin. Also, **res′in·y.**

re·sist (ri zist′) *v.t.* **1.** to refrain from yielding to; abstain from: *She found it difficult to resist his charms.* **2.** to repel or oppose: *The nation was unable to resist the invasion.* **3.** to withstand the action or effect of: *This metal resists corrosion.* —*v.i.* to act in opposition. [Latin *resistere* to withstand.] —**re·sist′er,** *n.* —**Syn.** *v.t.* see **withstand.**

re·sist·ance (ri zis′təns) *n.* **1.** act of resisting. **2.** capacity to resist something, esp. disease: *Her resistance is low.* **3.** underground group that works against or opposes an occupying or oppressive power, esp. by noncooperation or guerrilla tactics. **4.** force that opposes or hinders the motion of another: *Cars are streamlined to overcome air resistance.* **5.** characteristic of a current-carrying medium that opposes the flow of current and produces heat. A good conductor, such as silver, has low resistance. A superconductor, when cold enough, has no resistance. **6.** resistor.

resistance coil, resistor in the form of a coil of wire.

re·sist·ant (ri zis′tənt) *adj.* offering resistance; resisting.

re·sist·i·ble (ri zis′tə bəl) *adj.* capable of being resisted. —**re·sist′i·bil′i·ty,** *n.* —**re·sist′i·bly,** *adv.*

re·sist·less (ri zist′lis) *adj.* **1.** that cannot be resisted. **2.** that does not or cannot resist.

re·sis·tor (ri zis′tər) *n.* electric element whose primary effect in a circuit is due to its resistance, often used to limit the flow of current or to produce heat, as in a toaster.

re·sole (rē sōl′) **-soled, -sol·ing.** *v.t.* to put a new sole on.

re·seed′	re·sen′tence	re·sharp′en	re·sil′ver
re·seize′	re·set′tle	re·shine′	re·sit′u·ate′
re·sei′zure	re·set′tle·ment	re·shoe′	re·sketch′
re·sell′	re·sew′	re·shuf′fle	re·sol′der

at; āpe; cär; end; mē; it; īce; hot; ōld; fôrk; wood; fŏŏl; oil; out; up; ūse; turn; sing; thin; this; zh in treasure; ə in ago, taken, pencil, lemon, circus.

re·sol·u·ble (ri zol′yə bəl) *adj.* capable of being resolved.

res·o·lute (rez′ə lŏŏt′) *adj.* having or characterized by steadfast determination. [Latin *resolūtus*, past participle of *resolvere* to untie, separate.] —**res′o·lute′ly**, *adv.* —**res′o·lute′ness**, *n.*

res·o·lu·tion (rez′ə lŏŏ′shən) *n.* **1.** act or process of resolving or determining. **2.** that which is resolved upon; vow: *He made a New Year's resolution to give up smoking.* **3.** formal statement of a decision, opinion, or course of action, presented to or adopted by an assembly. **4.** state or quality of being resolute. **5.** act or result of settling, explaining, or solving. **6.** act or process of breaking or transforming into separate or simpler parts.

re·solv·a·ble (ri zol′və bəl) *adj.* capable of being settled, explained, or solved.

re·solve (ri zolv′) **-solved, -solv·ing.** *v.t.* **1.** to decide (to do something); determine: *He resolved not to go to the party.* **2.** to settle, explain, or solve, as a mystery, problem, or dispute. **3.** to formally express a decision or opinion by vote, as in a legislative assembly. **4.** to dispel, as a doubt or fear. **5.** to break or transform into simpler or separate parts by or as by dissolution: *The prism resolved the light into the colors of the spectrum.* —*v.i.* **1.** to come to a decision; decide (often with *on* or *upon*): *He resolved on the pie for dessert.* **2.** to be broken or transformed into simpler or separate parts by or as by dissolution. —*n.* **1.** steadfast determination or firmness of purpose. **2.** something resolved upon; resolution. [Latin *resolvere* to untie, separate, disclose.] —**re·solv′er**, *n.* —**Syn.** *v.t.* **1.** see **decide.** **2.** see **solve.**

re·solved (ri zolvd′) *adj.* resolute; determined. —**re·solv·ed·ly** (ri·zol′vid lē), *adv.*

res·o·nance (rez′ə nəns) *n.* **1.** quality or state of being resonant; fullness and richness of sound: *the resonance of a piano.* **2.** *Physics.* **a.** state of a mechanical or electrical system characterized by a vibration or oscillation of large amplitude, occurring when an external force is applied at a frequency equal or nearly equal to one of the natural frequencies of the system. Because of resonance, a swing will rise to a great height if it is given a regular series of pushes at the same frequency at which it swings. **b.** the vibration produced in such a state. **3.** the reinforcement and prolongation of sound by the sympathetic vibration of another object, as when the tone produced by the strings of a violin is enhanced by vibrations of the body of the instrument. **4.** *Chemistry.* property of a molecule of being intermediate in structure between two or more theoretically possible forms that differ only in the distribution of their electrons. **5.** *Phonetics.* the intensification of a vocal sound caused by its vibration in a resonating cavity, as the mouth or the nose.

res·o·nant (rez′ə nənt) *adj.* **1.** continuing to sound; echoing. **2.** capable of increasing or prolonging sounds: *the resonant wood of the guitar.* **3.** having a full, rich sound: *a resonant voice.* [Latin *resonāns*, present participle of *resonāre* to sound again, reecho.] —**res′o·nant·ly**, *adv.*

res·o·nate (rez′ə nāt′) **-nat·ed, -nat·ing.** *v.i.* to exhibit or produce resonance. [Latin *resonātus*, past participle of *resonāre* to sound again, reecho.]

res·o·na·tor (rez′ə nā′tər) *n.* device that produces resonance or increases sound by means of resonance. [Modern Latin *resonator*, from Latin *resonāre* to sound again, reecho.]

res·or·cin·ol (rez ôr′sə nôl′, ri zôr′-) *n.* white, crystalline substance made from benzene, used esp. in medicine and in making dyes. Formula: $C_6H_4(OH)_2$. Also, **res·or′cin.**

re·sort (ri zôrt′) *v.i.* **1.** to make use of or appeal to for aid, relief, protection, or support (with *to*): *John resorts to lying whenever he's in trouble.* **2.** to go frequently or customarily, as for recreation. —*n.* **1.** place where people go, esp. for recreation or relaxation: *The ski resort provided instruction for beginners.* **2.** one who or that which one makes use of or appeals to, as for protection or support: *He turned to his family only as a last resort.* **3.** use of or appeal to, as for protection or support: *to have resort to friends in an emergency.* **4.** act of gathering at a place frequently or customarily. [Old French *resortir* to go out again, repair[2], from RE- + *sortir* to go out (of uncertain origin).]

re·sort (rē sôrt′) *v.t., v.i.* to sort (something) again.

re·sound (ri zound′) *v.i.* **1.** to be filled with sound: *The hills resound with music.* **2.** to produce a loud, echoing, or prolonged sound: *The rocket resounded as it blasted off the launching pad.* **3.** (of sounds) to be echoed; ring: *The shouts resounded in our ears.* **4.** *Archaic.* to be much talked about, esp. with praise; be extolled or celebrated: *His name will resound through the ages.* —*v.t.* **1.** to give back (sound); echo. **2.** *Archaic.* to extol or celebrate. [Old French *reson(n)er* to give back sound, give forth sound, from Latin *resonāre* to sound again, reecho.]

re·source (rē′sôrs′, ri sôrs′) *n.* **1.** that which is appealed to or made use of, as for aid or support. **2.** *usually*, **resources.** actual wealth of a country or its means of producing wealth: *Oil is one of our largest natural resources.* **3.** skill and ingenuity in dealing with circumstances.

4. action or means resorted to in an emergency or difficult situation; expedient: *When caught, his only resource is to lie.* [French *ressource* resort, expedient, from Old French *resourdre* to rise again, from Latin *resurgere.*]

re·source·ful (ri sôrs′fəl) *adj.* capable of or skilled in coping with new or difficult situations. —**re·source′ful·ly**, *adv.* —**re·source′ful·ness**, *n.*

re·spect (ri spekt′) *n.* **1.a.** regard for or appreciation of the fundamental worth or value of someone or something: *respect for life.* **b.** recognition of superiority, as in force or wisdom; awesome regard: *The chief had the respect of everyone in the village.* **2.** courteous regard; considerateness: *to show respect for one's elders.* **3.** specific aspect or manner; particular detail. **4.** relation; reference: *an improvement with respect to wages.* **5. respects.** courteous expressions of regard and esteem: *Please send my respects to your family.* **6. to pay (one's) respects.** to express one's regard and esteem for someone, as by a visit. **7. to pay (one's) last respects.** to attend a funeral or interment. —*v.t.* **1.** to have or feel respect for. **2.** to show consideration for; act so as not to interfere with: *I respect his privacy.* **3.** to relate or refer to; concern. [Latin *respectus* a looking about, regard.] —**re·spect′er**, *n.*

Syn. *n.* **2. Respect, regard, consideration** mean care for or courtesy to others. **Respect** suggests compliance with social form or a moral code of behavior: *He showed his respect by doffing his hat to the lady.* **Regard** implies a sympathetic good will as the reason for courtesy: *He refrained from criticism out of regard for her feelings.* **Consideration** implies that emotional sensitivity is reinforced by a conscious awareness of the effects of one's actions: *He showed her every consideration in her time of grief.*

re·spect·a·bil·i·ty (ri spek′tə bil′ə tē) *n.* state, quality, or condition of being respectable, esp. of having proper or approved standards of conduct and a good reputation.

re·spect·a·ble (ri spek′tə bəl) *adj.* **1.** having or showing proper or approved standards of conduct; honest and decent. **2.** well thought of; accepted: *Respectable authorities differ on the question.* **3.** fit to be seen or used; presentable: *a respectable suit of clothes.* **4.** considerable in size or quantity; substantial: *There was a respectable turnout for the church supper.* **5.** better than average; reasonably good: *The amateur drama group put on a respectable performance.* —**re·spect′a·bly**, *adv.*

re·spect·ful (ri spekt′fəl) *adj.* full of, characterized by, or showing respect, esp. courteousness. —**re·spect′ful·ly**, *adv.* —**re·spect′ful·ness**, *n.*

re·spect·ing (ri spek′ting) *prep.* with respect to; concerning.

re·spec·tive (ri spek′tiv) *adj.* relating severally to each of two or more persons or things under consideration; particular: *the respective advantages of each method.*

re·spec·tive·ly (ri spek′tiv lē) *adv.* with respect to each of two or more in the order considered: *Jones and Edwards are, respectively, the producer and director of the film.*

res·pi·ra·tion (res′pə rā′shən) *n.* **1.** breathing in and out. **2.** the totality of physical and chemical processes by which living things obtain energy from food. These processes include the breathing of gases in and out and a series of chemical reactions within cells.

res·pi·ra·tor (res′pə rā′tər) *n.* **1.** device with compressed air or oxygen, used in giving artificial respiration. **2.** device worn over the mouth or the nose and mouth to prevent the breathing in of fumes, dust, or the like.

res·pi·ra·to·ry (res′pər ə tôr′ē, ri spīr′ə-) *adj.* of or relating to respiration or to organs used in respiration: *a respiratory disease.*

re·spire (ri spīr′) **-spired, -spir·ing.** *v.t., v.i.* to inhale and exhale; breathe. [Latin *respīrāre.*]

res·pite (res′pit) *n.* **1.** interval of rest or relief, as from work or unpleasantness: *The cowboys enjoyed their short respite from the dust of the trail.* **2.** delay or extension of time granted, as in carrying out a sentence of death. [Old French *respit* delay, from Latin *respectus* a looking about.]

re·splen·dence (ri splen′dəns) *n.* state or quality of gleaming splendor; lustrous brilliance. Also, **re·splen′den·cy.**

re·splen·dent (ri splen′dənt) *adj.* full of splendor; gleaming; brilliant. [Latin *resplendēns*, present participle of *resplendēre* to shine brightly.] —**re·splend′ent·ly**, *adv.*

re·spond (ri spond′) *v.i.* **1.** to give an answer: *Would you respond to my question?* **2.** to act in return; react: *She responded to the sudden light by blinking her eyes.* **3.** to be improved or positively affected by: *The patient responded to treatment.* —*v.t.* to answer by saying. [Latin *respondēre* to answer, promise in return.]

re·spond·ent (ri spon′dənt) *adj.* answering; responding. —*n.* **1.** defendant, esp. in an equity, admiralty, or divorce case. **2.** one who responds.

re·sponse (ri spons′) *n.* **1.** act of responding. **2.** that which is re-

re·sol′id·i·fy′	re·sow′	re·spell′	re·spread′

at; āpe; cär; end; mē; it; īce; hot; ōld; fôrk; wood; fŏŏl; oil; out; up; ūse; turn; sing; thin; this; zh in treasure; ə in ago, taken, pencil, lemon, circus.

sponded, esp. something said in answer. **3.** behavior resulting from an external influence or stimulus. **4.** words said or sung by the congregation or choir in answer to a short sentence said or sung by the officiating clergyman. [Latin *respōnsum* answer, reply.] **—Syn. 2.** see **answer.**

re·spon·si·bil·i·ty (ri spon′sə bil′ə tē) *pl.,* **-ties.** *n.* **1.** state, quality, or condition of being responsible. **2.** job, duty, or area of concern: *Opening the mail is your responsibility.*

re·spon·si·ble (ri spon′sə bəl) *adj.* **1.** having as a job, duty, or area of concern: *The government is responsible for the nation's welfare.* **2.** faithful to obligations; trustworthy; reliable: *Alice is a very responsible baby-sitter.* **3.** being the primary cause: *The freezing weather is responsible for the cracks in the pavement.* **4.a.** carefully and thoroughly considered, esp. as to consequences; prudent: *a responsible action.* **b.** kept within prescribed bounds; temperate: *responsible criticism.* **5.** involving obligations or duties, as a job or position. **6.** deserving blame or condemnation: *to be responsible for one's actions.* **7.** under the supervision of; answerable to (with *to*): *The foreman is responsible to the manager.* [Latin *responsus,* past participle of *respondēre* to answer + -IBLE.] **—re·spon′si·ble·ness,** *n.* **—re·spon′si·bly,** *adv.*

re·spon·sive (ri spon′siv) *adj.* **1.** readily reacting in sympathy or harmony: *She was responsive to her friend's misery.* **2.** answering as called for by the question; not evasive: *a responsive answer by the witness.* **3.** of, relating to, or conveying an answer: *a responsive gesture.* **4.** characterized by or made up of responses: *a responsive chant.* **—re·spon′sive·ly,** *adv.* **—re·spon′sive·ness,** *n.*

Whole Quarter Sixteenth
Half Eighth

Rest¹ *(def. 8b)*

rest¹ (rest) *n.* **1.** period of inactivity, relaxation, or refreshment, esp. after work or physical exertion: *The workmen had a short rest after working all morning.* **2.** freedom from exertion, distress, or disturbance; quiet; ease: *a day of rest.* **3.** sleep: *He does not get enough rest at night.* **4.** state of being motionless: *The plane came to rest in the field.* **5.** something that serves as a stand or support: *a book rest, a gun rest.* **6.** temporary lodging place: *a travelers' rest.* **7.** death. **8.** *Music.* **a.** interval of silence between tones, corresponding in duration to a note of the same name: *half rest, whole rest.* **b.** any of the various characters indicating such a pause. **9.** pause or break in a line of verse; caesura. **10.** *Military.* command to soldiers in formation, permitting them to relax and talk while keeping the right foot in place. **—v.i. 1.** to relax or refresh oneself, esp. after work or physical exertion: *The children rested on the porch after the ball game.* **2.** to be quiet or at ease: *She wouldn't rest until she knew that her son was safe.* **3.** to come to rest; cease activity: *After skidding ten feet, the car finally rested in a ditch.* **4.** to sleep: *I did not rest at all last night.* **5.** to be supported, as by leaning or lying: *Her hands rested in her lap.* **6.** to be fixed or directed (with *on* or *upon*): *His curious gaze rested on the strange woman.* **7.** to remain without change or further action; stand: *If only we could let the matter rest.* **8.a.** to be dependent; rely (with *on* or *upon*): *The outcome rests on your decision.* **b.** to be founded (with *on* or *upon*): *The burden of proof rests on him.* **10.** to be or lie in a specified place: *The trouble rests with him.* **11.** to lie in death: *May he rest in peace.* **12.** *Law.* to cease presenting evidence in a case voluntarily. **—v.t. 1.** to give rest to. **2.** to put, lay, or lean (something), as for support: *He rested his arm on the table.* **3.** to direct or fix, as the eyes. **4.** to base; ground: *He rested his theory on years of research.* **5.** *Law.* to cease presenting evidence in (a case) voluntarily. [Old English *rest* quiet, repose, bed.]

rest² (rest) *n.* **1.** that which remains; remainder. **2.** those remaining; others: *The rest are to wait for us.* ▲ construed as plural in def. 2. **—v.i.** to continue to be; remain: *You may rest assured that I'll be there.* [Old French *reste* remainder, from *rester* to remain, from Latin *restāre* to stand still, remain.] **—Syn.** *n.* **1.** see **balance.**

re·state (rē stāt′) **-stat·ed, -stat·ing.** *v.t.* to state again or in a new or different way. **—re·state′ment,** *n.*

res·tau·rant (res′tər ənt, -tə ränt′) *n.* establishment where food is prepared and served to customers at tables by a waiter or waitress. [French *restaurant,* from *restaurer* to restore, refresh, from Latin *restaurāre* to restore, renew.]

res·tau·ra·teur (res′tər ə tur′) *n.* one who owns or manages a restaurant. [French *restaurateur,* from *restaurer.* See RESTAURANT.]

rest cure, treatment for certain types of nervous disorders, consisting

of complete rest combined with a special diet and various types of therapy.

rest·ful (rest′fəl) *adj.* **1.** full of or giving rest: *a restful vacation.* **2.** being at rest; quiet; tranquil: *a restful manner, the restful landscape.* **—rest′ful·ly,** *adv.* **—rest′ful·ness,** *n.*

res·ti·tu·tion (res′tə tōō′shən, -tū′-) *n.* **1.** act of restoring something that has been lost or taken away. **2.** compensation for any loss or damage; reparation. [Latin *restitūtiō* a restoring.]

res·tive (res′tiv) *adj.* **1.** unable to rest; restless; fretful. **2.** stubborn and difficult to manage; unruly. **3.** refusing to move; balky: *a restive horse.* [Old French *restif* stubborn, refusing to go forward, from *rester* to remain. See REST².] **—res′tive·ly,** *adv.* **—res′tive·ness,** *n.*

rest·less (rest′lis) *adj.* **1.** agitated in mind or body; unable to rest. **2.** characterized by lack of rest; not restful: *a restless night.* **3.** constantly in motion; never still: *the restless wind, the restless sea.* **4.** constantly shifting or changing from one thing to another: *a restless mind.* **—rest′less·ly,** *adv.* **—rest′less·ness,** *n.*

res·to·ra·tion (res′tə rā′shən) *n.* **1.** act of restoring; being restored. **2.** that which is or has been restored. **3. Restoration. a.** reestablishment of the English monarchy in 1660 under Charles II. **b.** period following this, including the reign of Charles II, from 1660 to 1685, and sometimes also the reign of James II, from 1685 to 1688.

re·stor·a·tive (ri stôr′ə tiv) *adj.* **1.** capable of restoring: *a restorative medicine.* **2.** of or relating to restoration: *They have almost completed the restorative work on the building.* **—n.** that which restores, esp. that which restores health or strength.

re·store (ri stôr′) **-stored, -stor·ing.** *v.t.* **1.** to bring back; reestablish: *The monarchy was restored.* **2.** to bring back to a former or original state or conditon: *The cathedral was restored during the early eighteenth century.* **3.** to return (something lost, taken, or stolen). [Old French *restorer,* from Latin *restaurāre* to repair¹, renew.] **—re·stor′er,** *n.*

re·strain (ri strān′) *v.t.* **1.** to hold in; keep in check: *He tried to restrain his laughter.* **2.** to prevent from acting; hold back: *We restrained him from breaking the window.* **3.** to deprive of liberty, as by confinement in prison. [Old French *restraindre* to confine, bind, from Latin *restringere* to bind back, tighten.] **—re·strain′a·ble,** *adj.* **—re·strain·ed·ly** (ri strā′nid lē), *adv.*

re·straint (ri strānt′) *n.* **1.** act of restraining; being restrained. **2.** that which restrains. **3.** holding back; reserve.

restraint of trade, interference with the free movement of goods or services or the reduction or prevention of free competition.

re·strict (ri strikt′) *v.t.* to keep within prescribed limits; confine: *Use of the pool is restricted to club members.* [Latin *restrictus,* past participle of *restringere* to bind back, tighten.]

re·stric·tion (ri strik′shən) *n.* **1.** that which restricts, as a rule or limitation. **2.** act of restricting; being restricted.

re·stric·tive (ri strik′tiv) *adj.* **1.** serving or tending to restrict: *The students decided the rules were too restrictive.* **2.** *Grammar.* designating a word, clause, or phrase that limits the meaning of its antecedent and is usually not set off by commas. In the sentence *Anyone who stands up to that bully will be a neighborhood hero,* the clause *who stands up to that bully* is restrictive. Opposed to **nonrestrictive. —re·stric′tive·ly,** *adv.* **—re·stric′tive·ness,** *n.*

rest room, toilet in a public building; washroom.

re·sult (ri zult′) *n.* that which occurs or is brought about because of an earlier action, process, or condition; effect. **—v.i. 1.** to be a result (with *from*). **2.** to have as a result; terminate (with *in*). [Medieval Latin *resultare* to happen, proceed from, from Latin *resultāre* to spring back, rebound.] **—Syn.** *n.* see **effect.**

re·sult·ant (ri zul′tənt) *adj.* occurring or brought about as a result. **—n. 1.** result. **2.** *Physics.* force that is the equivalent and result of, and has the same effect as, two or more forces acting together.

re·sume (ri zōōm′) **-sumed, -sum·ing.** *v.t.* **1.** to proceed after interruption: *The violinist resumed playing after intermission.* **2.** to take or occupy again: *He resumed his former position with the company.* [Latin *resūmere* to take up again.] **—re·sum′a·ble,** *adj.*

ré·su·mé (rez′oo mā′, rez′oo mā′) *also,* **re·su·me.** *n.* **1.** statement of one's qualifications and work record, used in applying for employment. **2.** summary: *The professor gave a résumé of the major points of his lecture.* [French *résumé* summary, from *résumer* to sum up, from Latin *resūmere* to take up again.]

re·sump·tion (ri zump′shən) *n.* act or instance of resuming.

re·sur·gence (ri sur′jəns) *n.* a rising again; revival.

re·sur·gent (ri sur′jənt) *adj.* rising or tending to rise again. [Latin *resurgēns,* present participle of *resurgere* to rise again.]

re·stack′	re·stitch′	re·struc′ture	re′sub·mit′
re·staff′	re·stock′	re·stud′y	re′sub·scribe′
re·stage′	re·straight′en	re·stuff′	re·sum′mon
re·start′	re·strike′	re·style′	re′sup·ply′
re·ster′i·lize′	re·string′	re′sub·mis′sion	re·sur′face

at; āpe; cär; end; mē; it; īce; hot; ōld; fôrk; wood; fōōl; oil; out; up; ūse; turn; sing; thin; this; zh in treasure; ə in ago, taken, pencil, lemon, circus.

res·ur·rect (rez′ə rekt′) *v.t.* **1.** to raise (a person) from the dead; restore to life. **2.** to restore (something) after disuse or neglect: *The new owners hope to resurrect the old house.* —*v.i.* to rise from the dead. [From RESURRECTION.]

res·ur·rec·tion (rez′ə rek′shən) *n.* **1.** act of rising from the dead. **2.** state of those having risen from the dead. **3.** restoration of something after disuse or neglect; revival. **4. Resurrection.** the rising again of Christ after His death and burial. [Late Latin *resurrēctiō* a rising again from the dead, from Latin *resurgere* to rise again.]

re·sus·ci·tate (ri sus′ə tāt′) *-tat·ed, -tat·ing.* *v.t.* **1.** to bring or come back to life or consciousness. [Latin *resuscitātus,* past participle of *resuscitāre* to raise up again.] —**re·sus′ci·ta′tion,** *n.* —**re·sus′ci·ta′tive,** *adj.*

re·sus·ci·ta·tor (ri sus′ə tā′tər) *n.* **1.** one who or that which resuscitates. **2.** machine or other device that resuscitates by forcing oxygen into the lungs.

ret (ret) **ret·ted, ret·ting.** *v.t.* to dampen, as flax or hemp, and cause partial rotting in order to soften and separate the fibers. [Middle Dutch *reten.*]

re·tail (rē′tāl; *v.t., def. 2 also* ri tāl′) *n.* sale of goods or articles individually or in small quantities, directly to the consumer. Distinguished from **wholesale.** —*adj.* of, relating to, or engaged in the selling of goods at retail: *a retail store.* —*adv.* in a retail quantity or at a retail price: *to buy something retail.* —*v.t.* **1.** to sell (goods) individually or in small quantity directly to the consumer: *to retail clothing.* **2.** to repeat or retell: *to retail gossip.* —*v.i.* to be sold at retail: *This shirt retails for eight dollars.* [Old French *retaille* a shred, paring, going back to Latin *re-* again + *tālea* rod, cutting; with reference to selling things in small amounts.]

re·tail·er (rē′tā′lər) *n.* retail merchant or dealer: *a retailer of children's clothing.*

re·tain (ri tān′) *v.t.* **1.** to have or hold or continue to have or hold; maintain or preserve. **2.** to hold back or contain: *The cracked jar would not retain water.* **3.** to keep in mind; remember. **4.** to employ by the payment of an advance fee: *He retained a lawyer to represent him.* [Old French *retenir* to hold back, keep, going back to Latin *retinēre* to hold back.] —**Syn.** see **keep.**

re·tain·er[1] (ri tā′nər) *n.* attendant or servant, esp. one who is liveried. [RETAIN + -ER¹.]

re·tain·er[2] (ri tā′nər) *n.* **1.** fee paid to obtain services, esp. of an attorney. **2.** fee paid to an attorney for a specified period of time to insure that his services are constantly available to his client. [Middle French *retenir,* noun use of the infinitive *retenir* to hold back, retain. See RETAIN.]

retaining wall, wall for securing a bank as of earth or slag.

re·take (*v.,* rē tāk′; *n.,* rē′tāk′) **-took, -tak·en, -tak·ing.** *v.t.* **1.** to take again: *He retook the test.* **2.** to take back: *We retook possession of our property.* **3.** to recapture. **4.** to film or photograph again. —*n.* **1.** act of filming or photographing again. **2.** result of this: *The retake was more in focus than the first shot.*

re·tal·i·ate (ri tal′ē āt′) **-at·ed, -at·ing.** *v.i.* to return like for like, esp. to return evil for evil. —*v.t.* to repay (an injury or wrong) with the like. [Latin *retāliātus,* past participle of *retāliāre* to requite.] —**re·tal′i·a′tive, re·tal′i·a·to′ry,** *adj.*

re·tal·i·a·tion (ri tal′ē ā′shən) *n.* act of retaliating; reprisal. —**Syn.** see **vengeance.**

re·tard (ri tärd′) *v.t.* to delay the progress of (an action or process); hinder: *Her severe illness retarded her growth.* —*v.i.* to be delayed. [Latin *retardāre* to delay.] —**re·tard′er,** *n.*

re·tar·da·tion (rē′tär dā′shən) *n.* **1.** act of retarding; being retarded. **2.** that which retards; impediment; hindrance. **3.** mental retardation.

re·tard·ed (ri tär′did) *adj.* suffering from or characterized by mental retardation.

retch (rech) *v.i.* to make an effort to vomit. [Old English *hrǣcan* to clear the throat.]

retd., returned.

re·ten·tion (ri ten′shən) *n.* **1.** act of retaining; being retained. **2.** capacity or power to retain. **3.** faculty of remembering. [Latin *retentiō* a holding back.]

re·ten·tive (ri ten′tiv) *adj.* having the ability or capacity to retain: *The mind is the retentive faculty.* —**re·ten′tive·ness,** *n.*

ret·i·cence (ret′ə səns) *n.* restraint or reserve, esp. in speech.

ret·i·cent (ret′ə sənt) *adj.* restrained or reserved, esp. in speech. [Latin *reticēns,* present participle of *reticēre* to be silent.] —**ret′i·cent·ly,** *adv.*

re·tic·u·lar (ri tik′yə lər) *adj.* **1.** of or resembling a net. **2.** entangled; intricate; complicated.

re·tic·u·late (*v.,* ri tik′yə lāt′; *adj.,* ri tik′yə lit, -lāt′) **-lat·ed, -lat·ing.** *v.t.* to form into, cover, or mark with a network. —*v.i.* to form a network. —*adj.* covered with or resembling a network. [Latin *rēticulātus* netlike, going back to *rēte* net.]

re·tic·u·la·tion (ri tik′yə lā′shən) *n.* reticulated structure or arrangement; netlike formation. [RETICULATE + -ION.]

ret·i·cule (ret′ə kūl′) *n.* small handbag, esp. one made of woven material or net, formerly used by women. [French *réticule,* from Latin *rēticulum* little net, network bag, diminutive of *rēte* net. Doublet of RETICULUM.]

re·tic·u·lum (ri tik′yə ləm) *pl.,* **-la** (-lə). *n.* **1.** any reticulated system or structure; network. **2.** second stomach of cud-chewing animals. [Latin *rēticulum* little net, network bag, diminutive of *rēte* net. Doublet of RETICULE.]

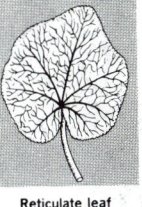

Reticulate leaf

ret·i·na (ret′ən ə) *pl.,* **ret·i·nas** or **ret·i·nae** (ret′ən ē′). *n.* inner membrane of the eyeball, consisting of several layers of cells sensitive to light that transmit the images entering the eye to the optic nerve. [Medieval Latin *retina,* probably from Latin *rēte* net; because it resembles a network.] —**ret′i·nal,** *adj.*

ret·i·nue (ret′ən ōō′, -ən ū′) *n.* body of retainers accompanying a person of rank or authority. [Old French *retenue,* from *retenir* to hold back, keep. See RETAIN.]

re·tire (ri tīr′) **-tired, -tir·ing.** *v.i.* **1.** to withdraw oneself from business, public life, or active service. **2.** to go to bed. **3.** to go away, as for seclusion or rest. **4.** to retreat, as from battle or danger; fall back. **5.** to move back or away, or appear to do so. —*v.t.* **1.** to remove from an office, position, or active service. **2.** to cause to withdraw from action. **3.a.** to pay off and cancel an obligation, as bonds or notes, before or on the date of maturity. **b.** to take (money) out of circulation. **4.** to put out (a batter or side), as in baseball. [Old French *retirer* to withdraw, from *re-* (see RE-) + *tirer* to draw, pull (of uncertain origin).]

re·tire·ment (ri tīr′mənt) *n.* **1.** act of retiring. **2.** state or condition of being retired. **3.** place of seclusion or privacy.

re·tir·ing (ri tīr′ing) *adj.* avoiding society or publicity; reserved; shy.

re·tort[1] (ri tôrt′) *v.i.* to make a reply, esp. in a quick, witty, or sharp manner. —*v.t.* **1.** to reply in kind, esp. in a quick, witty, or sharp manner: *to retort an argument.* **2.** to return in kind, as an insult or injury; pay back. —*n.* **1.** quick, witty, or sharp reply. **2.** act of retorting. [Latin *retortus,* past participle of *retorquēre* to twist back.]

re·tort[2] (ri tôrt′, rē′tôrt′) *n.* container, usually consisting of a glass globe with a long tube extending downward, in which chemists distill or decompose substances by heat. [Medieval Latin *retorta* container with a bent neck; literally, twisted back, from Latin *retorta,* feminine past participle of *retorquēre* to twist back.]

Retort

re·touch (rē tuch′) *v.t.* **1.** to improve, as a painting, by additional touches or slight changes. **2.** to change (a photographic negative or print) by eliminating or adding details, often with an air brush or brush and ink. —*n.* additional touch, as to a painting or photograph, for improvement or change.

re·trace (rē trās′) **-traced, -trac·ing.** *v.t.* **1.** to go back over; trace backward: *to retrace one's steps.* **2.** to trace back to a source or origin: *to retrace one's ancestors.* [French *retracer* to trace again, from *re-* (see RE-) + *tracer* to trace (going back to Latin *tractus,* past participle of *trahere* to draw).] —**re·trace′a·ble,** *adj.*

re·trace (rē trās′) **-traced, -trac·ing.** *v.t.* also **re·trace.** *v.t.* to trace over again, as a drawing. [RE- + *trace.*]

re·tract (ri trakt′) *v.t.* **1.** to withdraw or recant (something); take back: *The politician retracted his earlier statement.* **2.** to draw (something) back or in: *No longer frightened, the cat retracted her claws.* —*v.i.* to withdraw or recant: *When confronted with the facts, he retracted.* [Latin *retractāre.*] —**re·tract′a·ble;** also, **re·tract′i·ble,** *adj.*

re·trac·tile (ri trak′til) *adj.* capable of being drawn back or in, as the head of a turtle.

re·trac·tion (ri trak′shən) *n.* **1.** act of retracting; being retracted. **2.** statement that retracts: *a printed retraction.*

re·trac·tor (ri trak′tər) *n.* **1.** one who or that which retracts. **2.** muscle that retracts an organ or protruded part. **3.** surgical instrument for holding back the edges of a wound or incision.

re′sur·vey′	re·teach′	re·test′	re·thought′
re·swal′low	re·tell′	re·tes′ti·fy′	re·tie′
re·tape′	re·tel′e·vise′	re·think′	re·ti′tle

re·tread (v., rē tred'; n., rē'tred') -tread·ed, -tread·ing. v.t. to put a new tread on (a tire casing). —n. a retreaded tire casing.

re·tread (rē tred') -trod, -trod·den, -tread·ing. also, re·tread. v.t. to tread again.

re·treat (ri trēt') v.i. to withdraw, as from battle or an untenable situation; draw back. —n. 1. act of retreating. 2. retirement to a quiet or private place: a retreat from public life. 3. place of retirement, rest, or relaxation: a summer retreat. 4. retirement for religious study, contemplation, and prayer; period of such retirement: a youth retreat. 5. signal for a military retreat. 6. Military. a. flag-lowering ceremony at sunset. b. signal, as on a bugle, played at this ceremony. 7. to beat a retreat. to run away; flee. [Old French retraite place of refuge, from retraire to withdraw, from Latin retrahere to draw back.]

re·trench (ri trench') v.t. 1. to cut down (expenditures). 2. to put an end to or remove: The military regime gradually retrenched their freedoms. —v.i. to reduce expeditures; economize. [Middle French retrencher to cut off, curtail, from re- (see RE-) + Old French trencher to cut (going back to Latin truncāre to cut off).]

re·trench·ment (ri trench'mənt) n. act or instance of retrenching.

re·tri·al (rē'trī'əl, -trīl') n. second trial, as of a judicial case.

ret·ri·bu·tion (ret'rə bū'shən) n. 1. act of paying back for past deeds, esp. for evil committed. 2. that which is done or given in repayment, as punishment. [Latin retribūtiō repayment.] —Syn. 2. see vengeance.

re·trib·u·tive (ri trib'yə tiv) adj. serving as or characterized by retribution. Also, re·trib'u·to·ry.

re·triev·al (ri trē'vəl) n. 1. act or process of retrieving. 2. possibility of recovery or restoration.

re·trieve (ri trēv') -trieved, -triev·ing. v.t. 1. to recover; regain: He retrieved the golf ball from the lake. 2. to bring back to a former condition; restore: Nothing could retrieve his spirits. 3. to make amends for; make good: He attempted to retrieve his debts. 4. to recall to mind. 5. to locate and fetch (wounded or dead game). [Old French retreuv-, a stem of retrover to find again, from re- (see RE-) + trover to find (of uncertain origin).] —re·triev'a·ble, adj.

re·triev·er (ri trē'vər) n. 1. dog of any of various breeds, as a Labrador retriever, trained to retrieve game for a hunter. 2. any dog trained or used for retrieving game.

retro- prefix backward, back, or behind: retrograde. [Latin retrō.]

ret·ro·act (ret'rō akt') v.i. 1. to act in return; react. 2. to affect past events or conditions. —ret'ro·ac'tion, n.

ret·ro·ac·tive (ret'rō ak'tiv) adj. affecting that which has taken place prior to the time of enactment, as of a law or tax.

ret·ro·cede¹ (ret'rə sēd') -ced·ed, -ced·ing. v.i. to go back; recede. [Latin retrōcēdere.]

ret·ro·cede² (ret'rə sēd') -ced·ed, -ced·ing. v.t. to cede back (territory). [RETRO- + CEDE.]

ret·ro·fire (ret'rō fīr') n. fire of a retrorocket.

ret·ro·flex (ret'rə fleks') adj. 1. bent backward. 2. articulated with the tip of the tongue bent backward toward the soft palate. [Latin retrōflexus, past participle of retrōflectere to bend back.]

ret·ro·flex·ion (ret'rə flek'shən) also, ret·ro·flec·tion. n. act of bending backward; being bent backward.

ret·ro·grade (ret'rə grād') adj. 1. moving backward; reversed: Numbers in a countdown are given in retrograde order. 2. becoming worse; deteriorating: There are retrograde conditions in the older buildings. 3. moving from east to west, said esp. of the apparent motion of a planet relative to the motion of the earth or with respect to the stars. —v.i. -grad·ed, -grad·ing. 1. to move backward; reverse. 2. to become worse; deteriorate. [Latin retrōgradus going backward, going back to retrō backward + gradī to go.]

ret·ro·gress (ret'rə gres', ret'rə gres') v.i. to move or go backward, esp. to a worse or a less advanced condition. [Latin retrōgressus, past participle of retrōgradī to go backward.]

ret·ro·gres·sion (ret'rə gresh'ən) n. act or process of retrogressing.

ret·ro·gres·sive (ret'rə gres'iv) adj. of or characterized by retrogression.

ret·ro·rock·et (ret'rō rok'it) n. spacecraft that produces thrust opposed to forward motion to reduce speed, to make mid-course corrections, or to separate a section of a spacecraft.

ret·ro·spect (ret'rə spekt') n. contemplative view or survey of past events: In retrospect, it seems to have been a mistake. [Latin retrōspectus, past participle of retrōspicere to look back.]

ret·ro·spec·tion (ret'rə spek'shən) n. act of contemplating or surveying past events.

ret·ro·spec·tive (ret'rə spek'tiv) adj. 1. looking back on or thinking about past events. 2. presenting or containing things from the past. —ret'ro·spec'tive·ly, adv.

ret·rous·sé (ret'roo sā') adj. turned up: a retroussé nose. [French retroussé, past participle of retrousser to turn up, from re- (see RE-) + trousser to pack¹ (of uncertain origin).]

re·try (rē trī') -tried, -try·ing. v.t. to try (a defendant or case) again.

ret·ting (ret'ing) n. process of soaking the stems of certain plants, as flax or hemp, until they decay in order to separate the fibers. [RET + -ING¹.]

re·turn (ri turn') v.i. 1. to come or go back, as to a former place or condition: to return to consciousness, to return home. 2. to come or go back in thought or speech: The speaker finally returned to the topic. 3. to occur again or reappear: The patient's madness returned in a new guise. 4. to answer or reply. —v.t. 1. to take, bring, send, give, or put back: Alice returned what she had taken. 2. to give or pay back in kind: The enemy returned our fire. 3. to reciprocate or repay: The selfish child returned his parent's love with contempt. 4. to report officially; render: to return a verdict. 5. to elect: For the first time, the district returned a Laborite. 6. to yield, as in income or profit: The new taxes returned only fifty percent of the estimated amount. 7. to carry (a football) in a runback. 8. in certain games, as tennis or badminton, to hit or throw (a ball or shuttlecock) back to an opponent. —n. 1. act, fact, or process of coming or going back: a slow return to health. 2. recurrence or reappearance: The return of winter brought hardship. 3. act of taking, bringing, sending, giving, or putting back. 4. act of giving or paying back in kind: Your prompt return of my call was unexpected. 5. reciprocation; repayment: Francis didn't expect any return for his generosity. 6. official or formal report, esp. of tabulated statistics: a tax return, election returns. 7. also, returns. income or profit, as from land, labor, or an investment. 8. answer. 9. Football. runback. 10.a. act of returning a ball or shuttlecock. b. ball or shuttlecock so returned. —adj. 1. of, relating to, or for coming or going back: a return ticket, a return route. 2. given or done in return for something: a return visit. 3. played, performed, or presented again: a return match. [Old French retorner to turn back, give back, come back, from re- (see RE-) + tourner to cause to revolve, go around (from Latin tornāre to turn on a lathe). See TURN.]

re·turn·a·ble (ri tur'nə bəl) adj. 1. capable of being, or meant to be, returned. 2. required to be returned, as on a certain day.

re·tuse (ri tōōs', -tūs') adj. (of a leaf) having a blunt, rounded end with a shallow notch or depression. [Latin retūsus, past participle of retundere to beat back.]

Reu·ben (rōō'bən) n. 1. in the Old Testament, the oldest son of Jacob and Leah. 2. one of the twelve tribes of Israel, descended from him.

re·un·ion (rē ūn'yən) n. 1. act of reuniting. 2. social gathering of friends, classmates, or relatives after separation or absence.

Ré·u·nion (rē ūn'yən; French rā ūn nyōn') n. mountainous French island in the Indian Ocean, east of Madagascar. Area, 970 sq. mi. Pop. (1969), 430,000.

re·u·nite (rē'ū nīt') -nit·ed, -nit·ing. v.t., v.i. to bring or come together again.

Reu·ther, Wal·ter (rōō'thər) 1907–70, U.S. labor leader.

rev (rev) revved, rev·ving. v.t. to increase the speed of (often with up): Archie revved up the car's engine.

rev. 1. revenue. 2. reverse. 3. review. 4. revised; revision. 5. revolution.

Rev. 1. Reverend. 2. Revelation.

re·val·u·ate (rē val'ū āt') -at·ed, -at·ing. v.t. to make a new valuation of, as currency.

re·val·u·a·tion (rē val'ū ā'shən) n. 1. act or process of revaluating. 2. result of this.

re·vamp (rē vamp') v.t. 1. to repair or replace the vamp of (a shoe). 2. to patch up, renovate, or revise: The author revamped his novel.

re·vanche (ri vänch') n. policy of government that advocates or supports wars against other countries to regain lost territory. Also, re·vanch'ism. [French revanche return, revenge, from revancher to take vengeance, from Old French revengier. See REVENGE.] —re·vanch'ist, n.

re·veal (ri vēl') v.t. 1. to make known; divulge. 2. to expose to view; display; show. [Latin revēlāre to unveil, disclose.] —re·veal'a·ble, adj. —re·veal'er, n.

Syn. 1. Reveal, disclose, divulge mean making known something previously hidden or unknown. Reveal may be used to suggest an unintentional exposure, esp. of the truth: His letter revealed his ignorance of

Retuse leaf

re'trans·late'	re·tune'	re'up·hol'ster	re·vac'cin·ate'
re'trans·mit'	re·turf'	re·us'a·ble	re·val'ue
re·try'	re·type'	re·use'	re·var'nish

at; āpe; cär; end; mē; it; īce; hot; ōld; fôrk; wood; fōōl; oil; out; up; ūse; turn; sing; thin; this; zh in treasure; ə in ago, taken, pencil, lemon, circus.

his grandmother's serious illness. **Disclose** implies a deliberate decision to end suspense and expose something intentionally concealed to the scrutiny of a wide public: *The newspaper refused to disclose the names of its informants.* **Divulge** also suggests something intentionally concealed that is impulsively expressed to another person or small group: *He divulged his feelings about the girl to his friends.*

rev·eil·le (rev′ə lē) *n. Military.* **1.** first formation of the day at which roll call is taken. **2.** signal, as on a bugle, calling for this formation. [French *réveillez* wake up, imperative of *réveiller* to awaken, going back to Latin *re-* again + *vigilāre* to keep watch.]

rev·el (rev′əl) -eled, -el·ing; *also, British,* -elled, -el·ling. *v.i.* **1.** to take great pleasure (with *in*): *They reveled in their unaccustomed wealth.* **2.** to participate in boisterous festivities; make merry. —*n.* boisterous festivity; merrymaking. [Old French *reveler* to revolt, make merry noisily, from Latin *rebellāre* to revolt, from *re-* again + *bellāre* to make war. Doublet of REBEL.] —rev′el·er; *also, British,* rev′el·ler, *n.*

rev·e·la·tion (rev′ə lā′shən) *n.* **1.** act of divulging; disclosure. **2.** that which is divulged. **3.a.** disclosure or communication of divine truth, esp. by supernatural means. **b.** that which has been so disclosed. **4. Revelation.** last book of the New Testament, attributed to Saint John. Also, **A·poc′a·lypse.** [Church Latin *revēlātiō* uncovering, the Book of Revelation, from Latin *revēlāre* to unveil, disclose.]

rev·el·ry (rev′əl rē) *pl.,* -ries. *n.* boisterous festivity; merrymaking.

re·venge (ri venj′) *n.* **1.** opportunity to retaliate in return for an injury, wrong, or offense: *The dead man's brother will get his revenge.* **2.** desire for vengeance; vindictiveness: *Revenge was his one consuming passion.* **3.** act of retaliating in return for an injury or wrong. **4.** that which is done in return for an injury or wrong; vengeance. —*v.t.,* -venged, -veng·ing. **1.** to inflict injury, harm, or punishment in return for: *to revenge an insult.* **2.** to take vengeance on behalf of. [Old French *revengier* to take vengeance, going back to Latin *re-* again + *vindicāre* to avenge.]

Syn. *v.t.* **2. Revenge, avenge** mean damage or injury done another in return for a wrong. **Revenge** suggests personal rancor and spite as a motive for retaliation, esp. for a wrong committed against oneself: *He revenged himself on his neighbors by selling his land to a commercial contractor.* **Avenge** implies a primitive code of justice according to which punishment is justly meted out, esp. for a wrong committed against another: *By murdering the king, Hamlet avenged his father.*

re·venge·ful (ri venj′fəl) *adj.* full of or showing revenge; vindictive. —re·venge′ful·ly, *adv.* —re·venge′ful·ness, *n.*

rev·e·nue (rev′ə nōō′, -nū′) *n.* **1.** income from property or other investments. **2.** annual or current income of a municipal, state, or federal government that is derived from taxation and other sources. **3.** item or source of income. [Old French *revenue* rent, income, from *revenir* to return, from Latin *revenīre.*]

revenue stamp, stamp indicating that tax has been paid to the government, as for liquor, cigarettes, or hunting licenses.

re·ver·ber·ant (ri vur′bər ənt) *adj.* reverberating; resonant.

re·ver·ber·ate (ri vur′bə rāt′) -at·ed, -at·ing. *v.i.* **1.** to be echoed; resound: *The sounds reverberated through the empty house.* **2.** to be reflected, as light or heat. **3.** (of heat) to be bent back or deflected in a reverberatory furnace. —*v.t.* **1.** to reecho (sound). **2.** to reflect, as light or heat. **3.** to bend back or deflect (heat) in a reverberatory furnace. **4.** to subject or expose (something) to heat in a reverberatory furnace. [Latin *reverberātus,* past participle of *reverberāre* to strike back, going back to *re-* back + *verber* whip, blow¹.] —re·ver′ber·a′tive, *adj.* —re·ver′ber·a′tor, *n.*

re·ver·ber·a·tion (ri vur′bə rā′shən) *n.* **1.** act or process of reverberating. **2.** that which is reverberated, as sound or heat.

re·ver·ber·a·to·ry (ri vur′bər ə tôr′ē) *adj.* characterized or produced by reverberations. —*n. pl.,* -ries. reverberatory furnace.

reverberatory furnace, furnace or kiln that treats substances by means of heat deflected downward from the ceiling.

re·vere (ri vēr′) -vered, -ver·ing. *v.t.* to hold in deepest respect and affection; venerate. [Latin *reverēri* to stand in awe of, respect.] —Syn. see **worship.**

Re·vere, Paul (ri vēr′) 1735–1818, American patriot and craftsman.

rev·er·ence (rev′ər əns, rev′rəns) *n.* **1.** feeling of deepest respect and affection; veneration. **2.** gesture of respect; obeisance. **3.** state of being revered. **4. Reverence.** a used as a form of address in speaking of or in referring to a Roman Catholic priest, as in *Your Reverence.* —*v.t.,* -enced, -enc·ing. to regard with reverence. [Latin *reverentia* awe, respect.]

rev·er·end (rev′ər ənd, rev′rənd) *adj.* **1.** worthy of reverence. **2. Reverend.** a used as a form of address in speaking or referring to a clergyman, as in *Reverend Moore.* —*n. Informal.* clergyman. [Latin *reverendus* to be respected, gerundive of *reverēri* to respect.]

rev·er·ent (rev′ər ənt, rev′rənt) *adj.* feeling or showing reverence.

[Latin *reverēns,* present participle of *reverēri* to respect.] —rev′er·ent·ly, *adv.*

rev·er·en·tial (rev′ə ren′shəl) *adj.* feeling or showing reverence; reverent. —rev′er·en·tial·ly, *adv.*

rev·er·ie (rev′ər ē) *also,* rev·er·y, *n.* **1.** fanciful musing, esp. of happy, pleasant things. **2.** daydream. [French *rêverie* dreaming, musing, from *rêver* to dream, muse, from Old French *resver* to be delirious, wander; of uncertain origin.]

re·ver·sal (ri vur′səl) *n.* **1.** change of fortune from good to bad. **2.** act of reversing; being reversed.

re·verse (ri vurs′) *n.* **1.** that which is the direct opposite of something else; contrary. **2.** position of gears in a machine that makes them transmit force or cause movement in a direction opposite to that which is usual. **3.** back side: *the reverse of the record.* **4.** side of a coin or medal that does not bear the principal design. Opposed to **obverse.** **5.** change of fortune from good to bad; setback: *The army suffered many reverses.* —*adj.* **1.** opposite, as in position, direction, or, order. **2.** acting or moving in a manner or direction opposite to that which is usual: *The reverse rotation of the blender indicated that it was broken.* **3.** transmitting force or causing movement in a direction opposite to that which is usual: *in reverse gear.* —*v.t.* -versed, -vers·ing. **1.** to turn (something) around, upside down, or inside out. **2.** to exchange: *The two men reversed roles.* **3.** to change to the opposite: *The government reversed its policy.* **4.** to turn or cause to turn or move in a direction opposite to that which is usual. **5.** to invert the order or sequence of: *to reverse a process.* **6.** to set aside, as a judgment; annul; revoke. —*v.i.* to move or turn in the opposite direction, as in dancing. [Latin *reversus,* past participle of *revertere* to turn back, come back.] —re·verse′ly, *adv.* —re·vers′er, *n.*

re·vers·i·ble (ri vur′sə bəl) *adj.* **1.** capable of reversing or being reversed. **2.** made so as to be worn or used on either side, as a jacket or fabric. —*n.* garment worn with either side out. —re·vers′i·bil′i·ty, re·vers′i·ble·ness, *n.* —re·vers′i·bly, *adv.*

re·ver·sion (ri vur′zhən, -shən) *n.* **1.** return, as to a prior condition, practice, or belief. **2.** act of reversing; being reversed. **3.** atavism. **4. Law. a.** return of an estate to the grantor or his heirs after the period or term of the grant has expired. **b.** estate so returned. **c.** right of possession and future enjoyment of an estate presently in the possession of another. [Latin *reversiō* a turning back, returning.]

re·ver·sion·ar·y (ri vur′zhə ner′ē, -shə-) *adj.* of, relating to, or involving reversion. Also, **re·ver′sion·al.**

re·vert (ri vurt′) *v.i.* **1.** to return, as to a prior condition, practice, or belief. **2. Law.** to return to the grantor or his heirs. [Latin *revertere* to turn back, come back.]

rev·er·y (rev′ər ē) *pl.,* -er·ies. *n.* reverie.

re·vet (ri vet′) re·vet·ted, re·vet·ting. *v.t.* to provide a revetment for (an embankment, rock, or other exposed surface). [French *revêtir,* going back to Latin *re-* again + *vestīre* to clothe.]

re·vet·ment (ri vet′mənt) *n.* any wall or covering, as of concrete or grass, that protects an exposed surface from erosion by the elements. [French *revêtement,* from *revêtir.* See REVET.]

re·view (ri vū′) *v.t.* **1.** to examine, study, or go over again: *In preparing for the exam, John reviewed his notes.* **2.** to restate or present a summary of: *The lawyer reviewed his client's case for the benefit of the jury.* **3.** to write or give a summary and critical evaluation of: *A famous critic was asked to review the play in the newspaper.* **4.** to go over in one's mind; look back upon: *Phyllis reviewed the day's events with a smile.* **5.** to consider or examine (a court action) again for constitutionality, legality, or points of law. **6.** to make formal or official inspection of: *The general reviewed the troops.* **7.** *Archaic.* to view or see again. —*n.* **1.** act of examining, studying, or going over again. **2.** summary or survey: *The speaker presented a review of recent developments in the Middle East.* **3.** summary and critical evaluation of an artistic work, as a book or play. **4.** periodical containing articles of criticism, esp. relating to a particular field of interest: *classics review, literary review.* **5.** reexamination by a higher court of an action of a lower court for constitutionality, legality, or points of law. **6.** formal or official inspection, as of troops. **7.** revue. [French *revue* survey, critical article, magazine, from *revoir* to see again, going back to Latin *re-* again + *vidēre* to see.] —Syn. *n.* **3.** see **criticism.**

re·view·er (ri vū′ər) *n.* **1.** one who summarizes and critically evaluates an artistic work, as a book or play. **2.** one who reviews.

re·vile (ri vīl′) -viled, -vil·ing. *v.t.* to attack with abusive, contemptuous language; abuse verbally. —*v.i.* to use abusive, contemptuous language. [Old French *reviler* to regard as vile, going back to Latin *re-* again + *vilis* cheap, base.] —re·vile′ment, *n.*

re·vise (ri vīz′) -vised, -vis·ing. *v.t.* **1.** to change in order to correct, improve, or update: *to revise a manuscript.* **2.** to make different; alter: *to revise an opinion.* —*n.* proof sheet embodying corrections made on

---

| re′ver·i·fi·ca′tion | re·ver′i·fy′ | re·vin′di·cate′ | re′vin·di·ca′tion |

---

a former proof sheet. [Latin *revīsere* to look back, revisit, going back to *re-* again + *vidēre* to see.] —**re·vis′er,** *n.*

Revised Version, revised form of the King James Version of the Bible prepared by a commission of British and American scholars. The New Testament was published in 1881 and the Old Testament in 1885.

re·vi·sion (ri vizh′ən) *n.* **1.** act or process of revising. **2.** that which is revised.

re·vi·sion·ist (ri vizh′ə nist) *n.* one who follows or develops a revised and weakened version of a doctrine or creed, esp. one who revises Marxist doctrine by holding that socialism may be established by slow, peaceful means rather than by revolution.

re·viv·al (ri vī′vəl) *n.* **1.** act, instance, or process of reviving; being revived. **2.** awakening or increase of interest in religion in a church, community, or denomination. **3.** special service held to increase interest in religion.

re·viv·al·ist (ri vī′və list) *n.* one who holds or promotes religious revivals.

re·vive (ri vīv′) **-vived, -viv·ing.** *v.t.* **1.** to bring back to consciousness: *The child seemed dead, but the firemen revived her.* **2.** to bring back into existence, use, currency, or awareness. **3.** to give new strength, vitality, or freshness to. —*v.i.* **1.** to come back to consciousness. **2.** to show new strength, vitality, or freshness: *John's spirits revived when he heard the good news.* [Latin *revīvere* to live again.] —**re·viv′er,** *n.*

re·viv·i·fy (rē viv′ə fī′) **-fied, -fy·ing.** *v.t.* to restore to consciousness or give new strength, vitality, or freshness to. —**re·viv′i·fi·ca′tion,** *n.*

rev·o·ca·ble (rev′ə kə bəl) *also,* **re·vok·a·ble** (ri vō′kə bəl). *adj.* capable of being revoked.

rev·o·ca·tion (rev′ə kā′shən) *n.* act or fact of revoking; being revoked.

re·voke (ri vōk′) **-voked, -vok·ing.** *v.t.* to cancel or make no longer valid: *The license bureau revoked his driver's permit.* —*v.i.* to renege (def. 2). —*n.* renege. [Latin *revocāre* to call back, recall.]

re·volt (ri vōlt′) *n.* **1.** uprising or rebellion against existing governmental authority. **2.** any rebellion against or refusal to submit to authority or established practice. **3.** state of a person or persons who rebel: *The people are in revolt.* —*v.i.* **1.** to rebel, esp. by beginning a revolution. **2.** to be disgusted or repelled. —*v.t.* to repel; disgust: *The idea revolted her.* [French *révolter* to cause to rebel, disgust, from Italian *rivoltare* to overthrow, disgust, going back to Latin *revolvere* to roll back, revolve.]

Syn. *n.* **1. Revolt, rebellion, revolution** mean an armed and active effort to overthrow a government. All these terms presume the presence of great discontent and real grievances in the face of unresponsive, corrupt, or dictatorial power. **Revolt** is the broadest term and implies sharp and immediate action, esp. as a reaction to increasing oppression: *The revolt of the American colonies was caused by the arbitrary levy of taxes.* **Rebellion** applies to open, organized, and widespread defiance that usually fails: *All those connected with the rebellion were shot.* **Revolution,** in contrast, is usually conducted by an influential minority but is almost always successful in replacing one authority with another, and thus implies great change: *The Cuban revolution brought the Communists to power, beginning a new era in Latin American politics.* See also **uprising.**

re·volt·ing (ri vōl′ting) *adj.* disgusting; repellent.

rev·o·lute (rev′ə lōōt′) *adj.* rolled backward, as the edges of a leaf. [Latin *revolūtus,* past participle of *revolvere* to roll back.]

rev·o·lu·tion (rev′ə lōō′shən) *n.* **1.** overthrow of an existing political system or form of government by those governed, usually through the use of force, and the establishment of a new or different system of government. **2.** any sudden, far-reaching, or radical change: *a revolution in education.* **3.** movement in a closed curve around a central point or object. **4.a.** a spinning or turning around an axis; rotation. **b.** one complete turn of a rotating body: *The crankshaft of this engine makes up to 5000 revolutions per minute.* **5.a.** movement of one celestial body in an orbit around another, esp. the movement of the planets about the sun. **b.** one complete course of such a body. **c.** such a course considered to be complete when the first body has passed twice over a particular point on the second, rather than when it has completed a circuit in space. Distinguished from **orbit.** **6.** cycle of successive events: *the revolution of the seasons.* [Late Latin *revolūtiō* return, a rolling back, from Latin *revolvere* to roll back, revolve.] —**Syn. 1.** see **revolt.**

rev·o·lu·tion·ar·y (rev′ə lōō′shə ner′ē) *adj.* **1.** relating to, of the nature of, or tending to promote a revolution. **2. Revolutionary.** of or relating to the American Revolution. —*n. pl.,* **-ar·ies.** one who is dedicated to or takes part in a revolution.

Revolutionary War, American Revolution.

rev·o·lu·tion·ist (rev′ə lōō′shə nist) *n.* revolutionary.

rev·o·lu·tion·ize (rev′ə lōō′shə nīz′) **-ized, -iz·ing.** *v.t.* to produce a far-reaching or radical change in: *The young directors revolutionized film making.*

re·volve (ri volv′) **-volved, -volv·ing.** *v.i.* **1.** to move in a closed curve around a central point or object; move in a circle: *The planets revolve around the sun.* **2.** to spin or turn around on an axis; rotate: *Wheels revolve when in motion.* **3.** to proceed or occur in a cycle; recur periodically, as the seasons. —*v.t.* **1.** to cause to move in a closed curve. **2.** to cause to rotate. **3.** to think about; ponder; consider. **4.** to depend upon as a central force or element (with *around* or *about*): *His whole life revolves around his work.* [Latin *revolvere* to roll back.] —**re·volv′a·ble,** *adj.*

re·volv·er (ri vol′vər) *n.* pistol fitted with a cylinder that holds the bullets and revolves with each shot, thus enabling the weapon to be fired several times without reloading.

re·vue (ri vū′) *also,* **re·view.** *n.* theatrical presentation usually consisting of songs, satirical skits, and one-line jokes. [French *revue,* from *revoir* to see again. See REVIEW.]

Revolver

re·vul·sion (ri vul′shən) *n.* **1.** aversion aroused by something offensive; disgust; repugnance. **2.** act of drawing back or away; withdrawal. [Latin *revulsiō* a tearing away.]

Rev. Ver., Revised Version.

re·ward (ri wôrd′) *n.* **1.** something given or received in return, as for service or merit; recompense. **2.** money offered or given, as for the recovery of lost property or the capture of criminals. —*v.t.* **1.** to give a reward to. **2.** to give a reward for; recompense. **3.** to be a reward for: *Success rewarded his efforts.* [Anglo-Norman *rewarder,* form of Old French *regarder* to look at (suggesting looking at and judging to be worthy of reward). See REGARD.] —**re·ward′a·ble,** *adj.* —**re·ward′er,** *n.* —**Syn.** *n.* **1.** see **prize**[1].

re·write (*v.* rē rīt′; *n.,* rē′rīt′) **-wrote, -writ·ten, -writ·ing.** *v.t.* **1.** to write again, esp. in a different form. **2.** *Journalism.* to write a news story, based on a reporter's story or notes, in a form suitable for publication. —*n.* act or result of rewriting.

Rey·kja·vik (rā′kyə vēk′) *n.* capital and largest city of Iceland, in the southwestern part of the country. Pop. (1968 est.), 81,026.

Reyn·ard (ren′ərd, rā′närd) *n.* in medieval fables, the clever fox who outwits other animals. [Old French *renard* fox; originally, the name of the fox in the medieval story of *Reynard the Fox,* from Old High German *Reginhart* literally, strong in counsel; referring to the wiliness of the fox.]

Rey·nolds, Sir Joshua (ren′əldz) 1723–92, English painter.

r.f. **1.** radio frequency. **2.** rapid-fire. Also, **R.F.**

RFD, Rural Free Delivery. Also, **R.F.D.**

Rh, rhodium.

R.H., Royal Highness.

rhap·so·dize (rap′sə dīz′) **-dized, -diz·ing.** *v.i.* to speak or write with intense or excessive emotion: *The critics rhapsodized about the new play.*

rhap·so·dy (rap′sə dē) *pl.,* **-dies.** *n.* **1.** speech or writing characterized by or expressing intense or excessive emotion. **2.** instrumental musical composition that is irregular in form and suggestive of improvisation. [Latin *rhapsōdia* part of an epic poem, from Greek *rhapsōidiā* epic poem, reciting of an epic poem.] —**rhap·sod′ic** (rap sod′ik); *also,* **rhap·sod′i·cal,** *adj.* —**rhap·sod′i·cal·ly,** *adv.*

rhe·a (rē′ə) *n.* flightless South American bird, genera *Rhea* and *Pterocnemia,* resembling, but smaller than, the ostrich and having predominantly brownish plumage. Height: 3½–4½ feet. [Unexplained use of RHEA.]

Rhe·a (rē′ə) *n. Greek Mythology.* wife and sister of Cronus and mother of Zeus, Hera, Poseidon, Pluto, Demeter, and Hestia.

Rhea

Rheims (rēmz; French raNs) *n.* Reims.

Rhine·gold (rīn′gōld′) *also,* **Rhine·gold.** *n. Germanic Legend.* a hoard of gold kept at the bottom of the Rhine river, which gives its possessor magical powers.

Rhen·ish (ren′ish) *adj.* of or relating to the river Rhine or the regions bordering it. —*n.* Rhine wine. [Latin *Rhēn(us)* Rhine + -ISH.]

re·vis′it	re·wak′en	re·wed′	re·word′
re·vi′tal·ize′	re·warm′	re·weigh′	re·work′
re·vote′	re·wash′	re·weld′	re·wrap′
re·wake′	re·weave′	re·wind′	re·zone′

rhe·ni·um (rē′nē əm) *n.* soft, heavy, silver-white element, used esp. to make electrical contacts. Symbol: **Re** See **element** for table. [Modern Latin *rhenium*, from Latin *Rhēnus* Rhine.]

rhe·o·stat (rē′ə stat′) *n.* electrical device for varying the resistance of a circuit, used esp. in switches that slowly dim lights. [Greek *rheos* stream + *statos* standing.]

rhe·sus monkey (rē′səs) yellowish-brown monkey, *Macaca mulata,* native to northern India, used extensively in biological experiments. [Unexplained use of the name *Rhesus,* a mythical king of Thrace.]

Rhesus factor, Rh factor.

rhet·o·ric (ret′ər ik) *n.* **1.** art or skill of speaking or writing effectively, esp. for the purpose of persuasion. **2.** study of the rules and principles of literary composition and oratory. **3.** pretentious, inflated language in speech or writing; bombast; grandiloquence: *The politician's speech was mere rhetoric.* [Latin *rhētorica* art of oratory, from Greek *rhētorikē (technē)* rhetorical (art), from *rhētōr* orator.]

rhe·tor·i·cal (ri tôr′i kəl, -tor′-) *adj.* **1.** of the nature of or relating to rhetoric. **2.** using rhetoric. —**rhe·tor′i·cal·ly,** *adv.* —**rhe·tor′i·cal·ness,** *n.*

rhetorical question, question asked only for effect, with no answer expected.

rhet·o·ri·cian (ret′ə rish′ən) *n.* **1.** one who is skilled in or teaches rhetoric. **2.** one who writes or speaks in a grandiloquent manner.

rheum (rōōm) *n.* **1.** watery discharge from mucous membranes, as in the nose. **2.** *Archaic.* catarrh; cold. [Old French *reume* catarrh, from Late Latin *rheuma* flow, catarrh, from Greek *rheuma* stream, discharge from the body.]

rheu·mat·ic (rōō mat′ik) *adj.* **1.** of, relating to, or caused by rheumatism. **2.** subject to or affected with rheumatism. —*n.* one who is subject to or affected with rheumatism. [Latin *rheumaticus* troubled with rheum, from Greek *rheumatikos,* from *rheuma.* See RHEUM.]

rheumatic fever, inflammatory disease of unknown origin, most frequently occurring in childhood, characterized esp. by inflammation in the connective tissues and often resulting in serious damage to the heart.

rheu·ma·tism (rōō′mə tiz′əm) *n.* any of several diseases characterized by inflammation, swelling, and stiffness of the muscles and joints. [Latin *rheumatismus* catarrh, from Greek *rheumatismos* discharge from the body, going back to RHEUM.]

rheu·ma·toid arthritis (rōō′mə toid′) chronic progressive disease of unknown origin affecting the joints and characterized by inflammation, swelling, and deformity of the affected joints.

Rh factor, substance often found in the blood of humans and certain other mammals. Blood containing this substance, **Rh positive,** often causes severe reactions when combined with blood lacking it, **Rh negative,** as in transfusions. Also, **Rhesus factor.** [In reference to its discovery in the blood of the *rh*esus monkey.]

rhi·nal (rī′nəl) *adj.* of or relating to the nose; nasal. [Greek *rhīn-,* stem of *rhīs* nose + -AL¹.]

Rhine (rīn) *n.* river flowing from eastern Switzerland through West Germany and the Netherlands.

Rhine·gold (rīn′gōld′) Rheingold.

Rhine·land (rīn′land′, -lənd) *n.* region in the westernmost part of West Germany, along the Rhine.

rhine·stone (rīn′stōn′) *n.* colorless, cut gem made of quartz or glass paste, used to imitate diamonds. [Translation of French *caillou du Rhin* literally, pebble of the Rhine; because first made at Strasbourg (located on the Rhine).]

Rhine wine 1. any of several light-bodied wines, usually white, produced in the vicinity of the Rhine valley. **2.** any of various light white wines produced elsewhere.

rhi·ni·tis (rī nī′tis) *n.* inflammation of the mucous membranes of the nose. [Greek *rhīn-,* stem of *rhīs* nose + -ITIS.]

rhi·no (rī′nō) *pl.,* **-nos.** *n.* rhinoceros.

rhi·noc·er·os (rī nos′ər əs) *pl.,* **-os·es** or **-os.** *n.* any of several thick-skinned mammals, family Rhinocerotidae, native to Africa and Asia, having a large, rotund body, a massive head, and one or two horns rising from the snout.

Rhinoceros

Height: 4½–6½ feet at the shoulder. [Latin *rhīnocerōs,* from Greek *rhīnokerōs,* from *rhīs* nose + *keras* horn; in reference to the horn(s) on its snout.]

rhi·zoid (rī′zoid) *adj.* rootlike. —*n.* rootlike filament of certain plants, as liverwort and moss, that attaches the plant to the subsoil. [Greek *rhīza* root¹ + -OID.]

rhi·zome (rī′zōm) *n.* fleshy underground stem, usually growing paral-lel to the surface of the ground, containing stored food materials and bearing many nodes that can give rise to new plants. [Greek *rhizōma* mass of roots of a tree, going back to *rhizā* root¹.]

rhi·zo·pod (rī′zə pod′) *n.* any of a group of one-celled animals, class Rhizopoda, including amebas, that form temporary projections of protoplasm for locomotion and for taking in food. [Modern Latin *Rhizopoda* literally, having rootlike feet, from Greek *rhizā* root¹ + -POD.]

rho (rō) *n.* seventeenth letter of the Greek alphabet (P,ρ), corresponding to English *R, r.*

Rhode Island (rōd) state in the northeastern United States, the smallest state in the country. Capital, Providence. Area, 1214 sq. mi. Pop. (1970), 949,723. Abbreviation, **R.I.**

Rhode Island Red, any of an American breed of domestic fowl having dark-red plumage marked with black on the wings and tail.

Rhodes (rōdz) *n.* **1.** Greek island in the southeastern Aegean Sea, off the coast of Turkey. Area, 542 sq. mi. Pop. (1961), 63,951. **2.** port city and capital of this island. The Colossus of Rhodes stood by the entrance to its harbor during the third century B.C. Pop. (1961), 27,393.

Rho·de·sia (rō dē′zhə) *n.* country in south-central Africa, formerly known as Southern Rhodesia. Capital, Salisbury. Area, 150,333 sq. mi. Pop. (1969 est.), 5,090,000. —**Rho·de′sian,** *adj., n.*

Rhodesian man, extinct primitive man, *Homo rhodesiensis,* the remains of which were first discovered in Northern Rhodesia.

rho·di·um (rō′dē əm) *n.* heavy, silver-white, metallic element, often used in alloys with platinum for making high-temperature laboratory equipment. Symbol: **Rh** See **element** for table. [Modern Latin *rhodium,* from Greek *rhodon* rose¹; because its salts are rose-colored.]

rho·do·den·dron (rō′də den′drən) *n.* any of a large group of shrubs and trees, genus *Rhododendron,* bearing clusters of usually bell-shaped flowers. [Latin *rhododendron* oleander, from Greek *rhododendron* literally, rose tree, from *rhodon* rose¹ + *dendron* tree.]

rhomb (rom, romb) *n.* rhombus. **rhom·bic** (rom′bik) *adj.* relating to or having the form of a rhombus. Also, **rhom′bi·cal.**

rhom·boid (rom′boid) *n.* oblique-angled parallelogram with unequal adjacent sides. —*adj.* **1.** having the shape of a rhomboid. **2.** having a shape similar to that of a rhombus. [Late Latin *rhomboīdēs* the geometric figure, from Greek *rhomboeidēs* shaped like a rhombus, from *rhombos.* See RHOMBUS.] —**rhom·boi′dal,** *adj.*

rhom·bus (rom′bəs) *pl.,* **-bus·es** or **-bi** (-bī). *n.* equilateral parallelogram having two obtuse angles and two acute angles. [Latin *rhombus,* from Greek *rhombos* magic wheel, lozenge.]

Rhombus

Rhône (rōn) *n.* river flowing generally southwest-ward from central Switzerland through southeastern France into the Mediterranean.

rhu·barb (rōō′bärb) *n.* **1.** Asian plant, *Rheum rhaponticum,* cultivated in North America for its edible reddish leafstalks, which have a slight acidic taste. Also, **pie′plant′. 2.** leafstalks of this plant, cooked in pies, sauces, and other dishes. **3.** medicine made from certain species of rhubarb, used as an astringent, tonic, and laxative. **4.** *Slang.* heated dispute or squabble. [Old French *reubarbe* this plant, its stalks used as food, from Medieval Latin *rheubarbarum* the plant, going back to Greek *rhēon barbaron* literally, foreign rhubarb.]

rhyme (rīm) *also,* **rime.** *n.* **1.** correspondence of sounds in words, esp. at the ends of lines of verse. **2.** word corresponding in sound with another. *Tried* is a rhyme for *side.* **3.** verse or poetry whose lines have a correspondence of terminal sounds. —*v.i.* **rhymed, rhym·ing. 1.** to form or make a rhyme: *to make the last two lines of a poem rhyme.* **2.** to compose rhyme or verse. —*v.t.* **1.** to put into rhyme. **2.** to use (a word) as a rhyme. [Old French *rime* correspondence of the final sounds of words or lines of verse; of Germanic origin; confused with English *rhythm.*] —**rhym′er,** *n.*

rhyme royal, in poetry, a stanza of seven lines in iambic pentameter in which the first and third lines rhyme, the second, fourth, and fifth lines rhyme, and the sixth and seventh lines rhyme: *ababbcc.* It was first used in English by Chaucer.

rhyme·ster (rīm′stər) *also,* **rime·ster.** *n.* writer of doggerel.

rhythm (rith′əm) *n.* **1.** regular repetition or orderly recurrence of elements, as sounds or movements: *the rhythm of the drumbeats.* **2.** movement marked by such regular repetition or orderly recurrence of elements. **3.** *Poetry.* meter. **4.** *Music.* **a.** repetition or recurrence of regular or irregular pulses according to the relative stress and duration of tones. **b.** specific or characteristic form of this: *tango rhythm.* [Latin *rhythmus* measure in music or speech, from Greek *rhythmos* measured motion, time, proportion.]

rhyth·mi·cal (rith′mi kəl) *adj.* of, relating to, or characterized by rhythm. Also, **rhyth′mic.** —**rhyth′mi·cal·ly,** *adv.*

R.I., Rhode Island.

at; āpe; cär; end; mē; it; īce; hot; ōld; fôrk; wood; fōōl; oil; out; up; ūse; turn; sing; thin; this; zh in treasure; ə in ago, taken, pencil, lemon, circus.

ri·al (rē′əl) *n.* monetary unit and silver coin of Iran. [Persian *rial,* from Arabic *riyāl* Arab coin, from Spanish *real* royal, from Latin *rēgalis,* from *rēx* king.]

ri·al·to (rē al′tō, -äl′tō) *pl.* **-tos.** *n.* any bustling, centrally located district in a large city, esp. a commercial or a theater district.

rib (rib) *n.* 1. in most vertebrates, one of the series of curved bones attached in pairs to the backbone and enclosing and protecting the upper part of the torso. 2. cut of meat including one or more ribs. 3. any long, stiff structural part, as an exposed timber in an arched roof or a thin rod in the fabric of an umbrella. 4. raised ridge, as in a knitted sweater or sock. 5. primary vein or any prominent vein of a leaf or leaflike organ. —*v.t.* **ribbed, rib·bing.** 1. *Informal.* to poke fun at; tease. 2. to strengthen or support with ribs. 3. to make raised ridges in. [Old English *ribb* the bone.] —**rib′ber,** *n.*

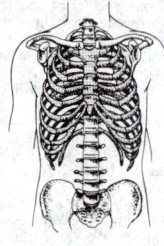

Ribs

rib·ald (rib′əld) *adj.* vulgar; coarse: *ribald humor.* [Old French *ribauld* ruffian, from *riber* to be licentious; of Germanic origin.]

rib·ald·ry (rib′əld rē) *n.* ribald behavior or language.

rib·and (rib′ənd) *also,* **rib·band.** *n. Archaic.* ribbon.

rib·bing (rib′ing) *n.* 1. *Informal.* teasing. 2. ribs collectively.

rib·bon (rib′ən) *n.* 1. band of fabric, paper, or other material used for decoration, as in trimming garments or tying packages. 2. any similar band of a flexible material: *a typewriter ribbon.* 3. strip: *The road was a ribbon of concrete across the desert.* 4. *Military.* small strip of cloth of one or more colors worn on the left breast of a uniform or other garment to indicate that the wearer has been awarded a particular medal or other honor or has served in a particular theater of operations or in a certain war. 5. **to cut** (or **tear**) **to ribbons,** to destroy or demolish. [Old French *riban, ruban* the band of fabric; of Germanic origin.]

rib·bon·fish (rib′ən fish′) *pl.* **-fish** or **-fish·es.** *n.* any of various snake-like fish, family Trachipteridae, inhabiting deep seas throughout the world, having a single fin that begins at the head and runs the length of the body. Length: 8–20 feet.

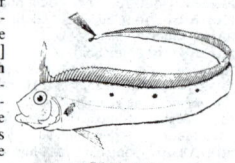

Ribbonfish

ri·bo·fla·vin (rī′bə flā′vin) *n.* orange-yellow, water-soluble vitamin of the vitamin B complex, required for growth and the utilization of carbohydrates, and found in liver, eggs, milk, and lean meats. Also, **lac′to·fla′vin, vitamin B₂,** vitamin G.

ri·bo·nu·cle·ic acid (rī′bō nōō klē′ik, -nū-) see RNA.

ri·bose (rī′bōs) *n.* simple sugar that is a component of ribonucleic acid. Formula: $C_5H_{10}O_5$.

rice (rīs) *n.* 1. the edible grains of a cereal grass, *Oryza sativa,* grown in many warm regions. 2. the plant itself. —*v.t.* **riced, ric·ing.** to reduce to small grains resembling rice: *to rice potatoes.* [Old French *ris* the grain and the plant, from Italian *riso,* through Latin, from Greek *rȳza;* probably of Persian origin.]

rice·bird (rīs′bûrd′) *n.* bobolink.

rice paper 1. thin paper made from the stems of rice plants. 2. similar thin paper made from certain other plants.

ric·er (rī′sər) *n.* kitchen utensil used to rice vegetables, such as potatoes, by forcing them through small perforations.

rich (rich) *adj.* 1. having great wealth: *a rich industrialist.* 2. well-supplied with something: *The old house was rich in memories.* 3. productive; fertile: *a rich harvest, a rich imagination.* 4. deep; full; warm: *a rich brown color.* 5. (of foods) having a heavy, strong flavor or containing concentrated amounts of nutritious, sugary, or creamy ingredients: *a rich sauce.* 6. not thin or diluted. 7. elegant; sumptuous; extravagant: *rich ornamentation.* 8. *Informal.* amusing; ridiculous. [Old English *rīce* powerful, wealthy; of Celtic origin.] —**rich′ness,** *n.*

Rich·ard I (rich′ərd) 1157–99, king of England from 1189 to 1199. Also, **Richard the Lion-Hearted, Richard Coeur de Li·on** (kur′ də lē′ən).

Richard II, 1367–1400, king of England from 1377 to 1399.

Richard III, 1452–85, king of England from 1483 to 1485.

Rich·ard·son, Samuel (rich′ərd sən) 1689–1761, English novelist.

Rich·e·lieu, Cardinal (rish′ə lyōō′; *French* rēsh lyœ′) 1585–1642, French statesman; full name, Armand Jean du Plessis de Richelieu.

rich·es (rich′iz) *n.,pl.* abundance of valuable possessions; wealth. [Old French *richece,* from *riche* powerful, wealthy; of Germanic origin.]

rich·ly (rich′lē) *adv.* 1. amply; fully: *rewards richly merited.* 2. in a rich manner: *a richly decorated snuff box.*

Rich·mond (rich′mənd) *n.* 1. capital of Virginia, a port city in the eastern part of the state. Pop. (1970), 249,621. 2. port city in western California. Pop. (1970), 79,043. 3. borough of New York City comprising Staten Island. Area, 60.9 sq. mi. Pop. (1970), 295,443.

Rich·ter scale (rik′tər) scale for measuring the magnitude of earthquakes and other seismic disturbances, having graded steps from 1 to 10. Each successive number stands for an earthquake about ten times stronger than the one represented by the preceding number. For example, an earthquake of magnitude 6 (moderately destructive) releases about one hundred times more energy than an earthquake of magnitude 4 (slight damage). [From Charles F. *Richter,* 1900–, American seismologist who devised this scale.]

rick (rik) *n.* stack of hay, straw, or grain. —*v.t.* to form into a rick or ricks. [Old English *hrēac* heap.]

rick·ets (rik′its) *n.* disease occurring in infants and children, usually caused by lack of vitamin D, characterized by softening, and sometimes bending, of the bones and enlargement of the liver and spleen. Also, **ra·chi′tis.** [Of uncertain origin.]

rick·et·y (rik′ə tē) *adj.* 1. liable to fall; tottering; shaky. 2. affected with, subject to, or like rickets. 3. feeble in the joints; infirm. —**rick′et·i·ness,** *n.*

rick·sha (rik′shô′) *also,* **rick·shaw.** *n.* two-wheeled carriage with retractable hood, drawn by one or two men, used originally in the Orient. Also, **jin·rick′sha, jin·rik′i·sha.** [Short for JINRICKSHA.]

Ricksha

ric·o·chet (rik′ə shā′; *British* rik′ə shet′) *n.* skipping or glancing of an object off a surface, esp. a flat surface. —*v.i.* **-cheted** (-shād′), **-chet·ing** (-shā′ing); to skip or glance off a surface. [French *ricochet* rebound, succession; of uncertain origin.]

ri·cot·ta (ri kot′ə, -kō′tə) *n.* soft, moist uncured cheese resembling cottage cheese, made from whole milk or whey. [Italian *ricotta,* from Latin *recocta,* feminine past participle of *recoquere* to cook again.]

rid¹ (rid) rid or **rid·ded, rid·ding.** *v.t.* to clear or free, as from something unpleasant (often with *of*). [Old Norse *rythja* to clear, empty.]

rid² (rid) *Archaic.* a past tense and past participle of **ride.**

rid·dance (rid′əns) *n.* 1. act of ridding; being rid. 2. **good riddance,** welcome release, as from someone or something burdensome.

rid·den (rid′ən) a past participle of **ride.**

-ridden *combining form* dominated, oppressed, or burdened with or by: *hagridden, guilt-ridden.* [From RIDDEN.]

rid·dle¹ (rid′əl) *n.* 1. puzzling problem or question so worded as to test one's ingenuity in solving or answering it. 2. one who or that which is difficult to understand; enigma. —*v.i.* **-dled, -dling.** to speak in riddles. —*v.t.* to solve or explain (a riddle). [Old English *rǣdels* enigma.]

rid·dle² (rid′əl) **-dled, -dling.** *v.t.* 1. to pierce in many places with holes. 2. to penetrate throughout in a harmful manner. 3. to sift through a coarse sieve. —*n.* coarse sieve. [Old English *hrīddel* coarse sieve.]

ride (rīd) rode or *(archaic)* rid, **rid·den** or *(archaic)* rid, **rid·ing.** *v.i.* 1.a. to sit on and be carried by a horse or other animal in motion, esp. while controlling its movement. b. to sit on and be carried by something in motion, as a bicycle, and control its movement. 2. to travel or be carried on or in something, as a vehicle or other conveyance: *We rode through the countryside on the train.* 3. to proceed or be carried along, as if riding. 4. to be carried or supported while moving: *While making the turn, the car rode on two wheels.* 5. to move or float or appear to move or float: *The ship rode over the waves.* 6. to carry or support a rider in a certain manner: *The car rides smoothly.* 7. to move or work upward out of place (with *up*). 8. to depend (with *on*): *The outcome will ride on his decision.* 9. *Nautical.* to be moored: *The ship rode at anchor in the harbor.* 10. *Informal.* to continue unchanged or without interruption: *Let the matter ride until further notice.* —*v.t.* 1. to sit on and be carried by (something) in motion, esp. while controlling its movement. 2. to travel or be carried on or in (something). 3. to cause to proceed or be carried. 4. to ride over or along: *The cowboy rides the range.* 5. to accomplish or perform by riding. 6. *Nautical.* to be moored by. 7. *Informal.* to harass or tease: *The youth's friends rode him about his girlfriend.* 8. **to ride down.** a. to collide with and knock down while riding. b. to overtake by riding. 9. **to ride out,** to withstand (something) without damage; endure or survive: *The ship rode out the hurricane.* —*n.* 1. short trip by any means of conveyance. 2. any of various vehicles or devices, as a merry-go-round or ferris wheel, which people can ride on or in for amusement. 3. manner in which something, esp. a vehicle, moves: *a smooth ride.* [Old English *rīdan* to be carried by a horse, to sail on the water.] —**Syn.** *v.t.* 7. see **bait.**

rid·er (rī′dər) *n.* 1. one who or that which rides. 2. amendment or addition, as to a contract or legislative bill.

at; āpe; cär; end; mē; it; īce; hot; ōld; fôrk; wood; fōōl; oil; out; up; ūse; turn; sing; thin; this; zh in treasure; ə in ago, taken, pencil, lemon, circus.

ridge (rij) *n.* **1.** long and narrow upper part or crest of something. **2.** any raised narrow strip, as on fabric. **3.** long and narrow elevation of land, or a chain of hills or mountains. **4.** horizontal line formed by the juncture of two sloping sides: *the ridge of a roof.* **5.** back or backbone of an animal. —*v.t.*, **ridged, ridg·ing. 1.** to form or make into ridges. **2.** to mark or cover with ridges. —*v.i.* to form a ridge or ridges. [Old English *hrycg* back of a man or an animal, crest.]

ridge·pole (rij´pōl´) *n.* horizontal timber along the top of a roof or tent to which sloping beams are fastened.

ridg·y (rij´ē) *adj.* rising in a ridge or ridges; ridged.

rid·i·cule (rid´ə kūl´) -culed, -cul·ing. *v.t.* to make (someone or something) appear foolish; expose to laughter. —*n.* words or actions intended to ridicule someone or something. [French *ridicule* something laughable, from Latin *rīdiculum.*] —**Syn.** *v.t.* see **mock.**

ri·dic·u·lous (ri dik´yə ləs) *adj.* deserving or arousing ridicule; laughable; silly. [Latin *rīdiculus.*] —**ri·dic´u·lous·ly,** *adv.* —**ri·dic´u·lous·ness,** *n.*

rid·ing habit (rī´ding) any of various outfits designed to be worn while horseback riding, usually consisting of jodhpurs, a jacket, boots, and hat.

Rif (rif) *also,* **Riff.** *n.* mountain range in northern Morocco, along the Mediterranean.

rife (rīf) *adj.* **1.** occurring commonly or frequently; widespread: *Discontent is rife throughout the land.* **2.** large in number or quantity; abundant; plentiful. **3.** filled; abounding (with *with*). [Old English *rȳfe* abundant, probably from Old Norse *rīfr.*]

riff (rif) *n.* *Music.* in jazz music, a melodic phrase played repeatedly, serving as the main theme or background. [Probably shortened and altered from REFRAIN[1].]

rif·fle (rif´əl) *n.* **1.** shallow place in the bed of a river or stream over which water moves swiftly so that the surface is broken into ripples. **2.** ripple. **3.** act or method of shuffling cards by separating them into two piles and bending and releasing the edges of the cards so that the two piles mix. **4.** *Mining.* groove or indentation in the bottom of a trough or sluice to trap gold in sand or gravel. —*v.t.* **-fled, -fling. 1.** to cause ripples on (the surface of water): *The breeze riffled the lake.* **2.** to leaf or thumb through (something) hurriedly: *The student riffled the pages of the book.* **3.** to shuffle (cards). [Possibly blend of RIPPLE[1] and RUFFLE[1].]

riff·raff (rif´raf´) *n.* **1.** low, disreputable, or worthless persons. **2.** trash; rubbish. [Old French *rif et raf* one and all, completely, from *rifler* to plunder (of uncertain origin) + *et* and (from Latin *et*) + *raffler* to snatch away (of Germanic origin).]

ri·fle[1] (rī´fəl) *n.* **1.** firearm, designed to be fired from the shoulder, having spiral grooves cut into its bore to cause the bullet to spin as it is fired. **2.** rifles. formerly, military unit equipped with rifles. —*v.t.* **-fled, -fling.** to cut spiral grooves in (the bore of a firearm). [From earlier *rifle* to form spiral grooves in (from French *rifler* to file, plane[2]; of uncertain origin) + GUN.]

ri·fle[2] (rī´fəl) **-fled, -fling.** *v.t.* **1.** to search through (something) thoroughly and rob; ransack: *The thief rifled the wall safe.* **2.** to seize and carry off as plunder. **3.** to strip (something) bare; despoil (often with *of*): *The thieves rifled the house of its contents.* —*v.i.* to search thoroughly and rob. [Old French *rif(f)ler* to plunder; of uncertain origin.] —**ri´fler,** *n.*

rifle range, area set aside for target practice with a rifle or other firearms.

ri·fling (rī´fling) *n.* **1.** act or process of cutting spiral grooves in the bore of a firearm. **2.** spiral grooves of a firearm collectively.

rift (rift) *n.* **1.** opening made by splitting; break; fissure. **2.** breach in a relationship, as between friends; quarrel. —*v.t.*, *v.i.* to cleave; split. [Of Scandinavian origin.]

rig[1] (rig) **rigged, rig·ging.** *v.t.* **1.** to fit (a boat or ship) with masts, sails, spars, lines, and the like. **2.** to fit (sails, spars, lines, and the like), as to their respective masts or yards. **3.** to fit out; equip. **4.** to make or build hurriedly or as a makeshift (often with *up*): *The youth rigged up a hi-fi set from old radio parts.* **5.** *Informal.* to dress, as with costumes (often with *out* or *up*). —*n.* **1.** arrangement of masts, sails, spars, lines, and the like on a boat or ship. **2.** apparatus or equipment used for drilling an oil well. **3.** any apparatus or equipment used for a particular purpose: *fishing rig.* **4.** *Informal.* dress; costume. **5.** *Informal.* carriage or cart with its horse or horses. [Probably of Scandinavian origin.]

rig[2] (rig) **rigged, rig·ging.** *v.t.* to manipulate, control, or fix (something) fraudulently, as for personal gain: *to rig an election.* [From earlier *rig* scheme, trick; of uncertain origin.]

Ri·ga (rē´gə) *n.* **1.** port city in the western Soviet Union on the Baltic,

capital of Latvia. Pop. (1968 est.), 694,000. **2. Gulf of.** arm of the eastern Baltic Sea bordering Estonia and Latvia.

rig·a·ma·role (rig´ə mə rōl´) rigmarole.

rig·ger (rig´ər) *n.* **1.** one who rigs. **2.** one who installs and repairs the rigging and hoisting gear of sailboats or ships.

rig·ging (rig´ing) *n.* **1.** all the lines of a boat or ship, as the ropes, chains, and wires, used for supporting the masts or working the sails. **2.** apparatus or equipment used for a special purpose, as drilling an oil well.

right (rīt) *adj.* **1.** conforming to truth, fact, or reason; correct; accurate. **2.** in accordance with that which is regarded as just, moral, or good. **3.** of, for, relating to, designating, or situated on or toward the side of the body that is to the east when one is looking or facing north. **4.** appropriate; suitable; proper. **5.** with or having the side or surface meant to be seen: *the right side of cloth.* **6.** *also,* **Right.** relating to or having conservative or reactionary political views. **7.** in a normal or proper state; in good order. **8.** healthy; sound. **9.** having its axis perpendicular to the base: *a right cone.* **10.** straight: *a right line.* —*n.* **1.** that which is just, moral, or good: *the triumph of right over wrong.* **2.** *also,* **rights.** just, legal, or moral claim or power. **3.** right side or direction: *to drive on the right.* **4.** *also,* **Right.** party or group holding conservative or reactionary political views. Also, **right wing. 5.** blow delivered with the right hand, as in boxing. **6.a.** privilege held by a stockholder of subscribing for additional shares of stock, usually at a price lower than the market value. **b.** negotiable certificate entitling a stockholder to such a privilege. **7. in the right.** not wrong, mistaken, or at fault. **8. to rights.** *Informal.* in or into a proper or orderly condition. —*adv.* **1.** according to truth, fact, or reason; correctly: *John didn't spell my name right.* **2.** according to that which is just, moral, or good. **3.** in a proper or suitable manner: *This telephone doesn't work right.* **4.** exactly; precisely: *right here.* **5.** without delay or pause; immediately: *Let's leave right now.* **6.** satisfactorily; favorably. **7.** in a straight line; directly: *The arrow went right to the mark.* **8.** to or toward the right: *to lean right.* **9.** *Informal.* extremely; very: *We had a right good time at the party.* ▲ appearing also in formal usage as part of certain titles: *The Right Reverend O'Grady.* **10.** completely: *She turned right around.* **11. right away** (or **off**). without delay; immediately. —*v.t.* **1.** to make reparation for; redress or avenge: *to right a wrong.* **2.** to make right; correct. **3.** to restore to an upright or normal position. **4.** to do justice to (someone). —*v.i.* to recover an upright or normal position: *The capsized boat righted.* [Old English *riht* straight, good, true, correct, proper.]

right angle, angle of 90 degrees, formed by two lines perpendicular to each other.

right-an·gled (rīt´ang´gəld) *adj.* containing one or more right angles.

right ascension, angular distance of a celestial body measured along the celestial equator east of the vernal equinox.

right·eous (rī´chəs) *adj.* **1.** doing what is right; virtuous. **2.** proceeding from a sense of what is right; justifiable: *righteous indignation.* [Old English *rihtwīs,* from *riht* good + *wīs(e)* way, manner.] —**right´eous·ly,** *adv.* —**right´eous·ness,** *n.*

right field *Baseball.* **1.** right section of the outfield when viewed from home plate. **2.** position of the player stationed in this area.

right·ful (rīt´fəl) *adj.* **1.** having a just legal or moral claim: *The young prince is the rightful heir to the throne.* **2.** owned or held by such claim: *rightful property.* **3.** appropriate; proper. —**right´ful·ly,** *adv.* —**right´ful·ness,** *n.*

right-hand (rīt´hand´) *adj.* **1.** situated on or to the right: *to drive on the right-hand side.* **2.** of, relating to, for, or with the right hand. **3.** *right-hand man.* most trusted and useful assistant.

right-hand·ed (rīt´han´did) *adj.* **1.** using the right hand habitually and more easily than the left. **2.** done with the right hand. **3.** made to be held in or used by the right hand. **4.** turning or moving from left to right: *a right-handed spiral.* —*adv.* with the right hand: *to pitch right-handed.*

right·ist (rī´tist) *n.* one who has conservative or reactionary political views. —*adj.* of, relating to, or characterized by conservative or reactionary political views.

Rifle

North celestial pole

Star

Earth

Right ascension

Celestial equator

South celestial pole

Vernal equinox

Right ascension

at; āpe; cär; end; mē; it; īce; hot; ōld; fôrk; wood; fŏŏl; oil; out; up; ūse; turn; sing; thin; this; zh in treasure; ə in ago, taken, pencil, lemon, circus.

right·ly (rīt′lē) *adv.* **1.** correctly; accurately. **2.** properly; suitably. **3.** justly or honestly. [Old English *rihtlīce.*]

right of way **1.** right of someone or something to proceed first or cross in front of another or others: *A pedestrian in a crosswalk has the right of way.* **2.** legal right to go across property belonging to another; path or route used in doing this. **3.** strip of land set aside for a specific purpose, as for railroad tracks, public roads, or power lines.

right-to-die (rīt′tə dī′) *adj.* opposed to employing artificial or extreme means to prolong the life of a person who is incurably sick or injured.

right-to-life (rīt′tə līf′) *adj.* opposed to laws making induced abortion or euthanasia legal.

right triangle, triangle with a right angle.

right-wing (rīt′wing′) *adj.* of, relating to, or belonging to the right wing. —**right′-wing′er,** *n.*

right wing, portion of a party, group, or political spectrum characterized by a more conservative or reactionary outlook than the rest.

rig·id (rij′id) *adj.* **1.** not yielding or bending; stiff: *Rigid steel girders made up the frame of the building.* **2.** strict; severe: *a rigid disciplinarian.* **3.** unchanging and inflexible; fixed. **4.** scrupulously exact, as in method or procedure. [Latin *rigidus* stiff, stern.] —**ri·gid′i·ty, rig′id·ness,** *n.* —**rig′id·ly,** *adv.* —**Syn. 1.** see **stiff.**

rig·ma·role (rig′mə rōl′) *n.* **1.** complicated and often foolish or unnecessary procedure. **2.** disjointed and incoherent statements; nonsense. Also, **rig′a·ma·role′.** [Modification of obsolete *ragman roll* list, catalogue, from *ragman* (of uncertain origin) + ROLL.]

rig·or (rig′ər) *also, British,* **rig·our.** *n.* **1.** strictness or inflexibility: *the rigor of the law.* **2.** severity; inclemency: *the rigor of winter.* **3.** harsh, oppressive, or cruel act: *Millions have suffered under the rigors of tyranny.* **4.** exactness, as in an intellectual endeavor. **5.** chill preceding fever or caused by cold or shock. [Latin *rigor* stiffness, hardness.]

rig·or mor·tis (rig′ər môr′tis) temporary stiffening of the muscles that begins shortly after death and persists until the onset of decomposition. [Latin *rigor mortis* stiffness of death.]

rig·or·ous (rig′ər əs) *adj.* **1.** very strict or inflexible: *rigorous interpretation of the law.* **2.** severe; inclement: *The cold climate was rigorous.* **3.** very exact or precise. —**rig′or·ous·ly,** *adv.* —**rig′or·ous·ness,** *n.*

Rig-Ve·da (rig vā′də, -vē′də) oldest and most important of the sacred Hindu books, written in Sanskrit.

Ri·je·ka (rē ek′ə) *n.* port city in northwestern Yugoslavia, on the Adriatic. Pop. 100,989.

rile (rīl) riled, ril·ing. *v.t. Informal.* **1.** to irritate or annoy; provoke. **2.** to roil (liquid). [Form of ROIL.]

rill (ril) *n.* tiny stream or brook. [Low German *rille.*]

rim (rim) *n.* **1.** outer edge or border of or around something: *the rim of a glass.* **2.** strip of metal on an automobile wheel on which the tire is fastened. —*v.t.* **rimmed, rim·ming. 1.** to form a rim around: *The mountains rimmed the valley.* **2.** to roll around the rim of (something) without going in: *The basketball rimmed the basket and bounced out.* [Old English *rima* border, coast.] —**Syn. 1.** see **edge.**

rime¹ (rīm) rhyme.

rime² (rīm) *n.* hoarfrost. —*v.t.,* rimed, rim·ing. to cover with rime. [Old English *hrīm* hoarfrost.]

rime·ster (rīm′stər) rhymster.

Rim·ski-Kor·sa·kov, Ni·ko·lai (rim′skē kôr′sə kôf′; nē kə lī′) 1844–1908, Russian composer.

rind (rīnd) *n.* firm outer covering or skin, as of fruit or cheese. [Old English *rind(e)* bark of a tree, crust.]

rin·der·pest (rin′dər pest′) *n.* acute, usually fatal, infectious disease of cattle and sometimes sheep and goats. [German *Rinderpest,* from *Rinder,* plural of *Rind* ox + *Pest* plague (from Latin *pestis*).]

ring¹ (ring) *n.* **1.** circular configuration; circle: *The teacher drew a ring around the error.* **2.** circular band, often of precious metal, worn on the finger. **3.** any circular band, as of metal, wood, or plastic, used esp. for holding or carrying something: *a napkin ring, curtain rings.* **4.** circular course: *The danced in a ring around the fire.* **5.** group of persons or things forming a circle: *The president was surrounded by a ring of bodyguards.* **6.a.** circular, usually enclosed, area used for circus performances, exhibitions, or athletic events. **b.** square or rectangular, usually enclosed, area used for boxing matches. **c.** boxing; prize fighting. **7.** group of persons working together, esp. for an illicit or criminal purpose: *a ring of car thieves.* **8.** any of a series of concentric layers of wood produced annually in the trunk of a tree. **9.** *Chemistry.* closed chain of atoms. —*v.t.,* ringed, ring·ing. **1.** to enclose with a ring; encircle. **2.** to form into a ring or rings. **3.** to provide with a ring. **4.** in certain games, to throw something, as a horseshoe or ring, over (a stake or pin). —*v.i.* to move in a ring or spiral. [Old English *hring* circle of metal, circular group.]

ring² (ring) rang or rung, rung, ring·ing. *v.i.* **1.** to make a clear, resonant sound, as a bell when struck. **2.** to cause a bell or bells to sound, esp. as a signal or summons: *She rang for the maid.* **3.** to resound loudly and clearly; reverberate; echo: *The room rang with laughter.* **4.** to be filled with talk or rumor: *The school rang with praise for the team.* **5.** to appear to be of a certain quality: *His promises rang false to me.* **6.** to have a sensation, as of echoing sound or buzzing: *My ears rang from the shrill noise.* —*v.t.* **1.** to cause (something) to ring: *The visitors rang the doorbell.* **2.** to announce or proclaim by the ringing of bells: *The chimes rang the hour.* **3.** to usher by or as by the ringing of bells (often with *in* or *out*): *to ring out the old year.* **4.** to call on the telephone (often with *up*). **5.** to make (a sound) by or as by ringing. **6. to ring up the curtain.** to signal for a theater curtain to be raised. **7. to ring down the curtain.** to signal for a theater curtain to be lowered. **8. to ring up the curtain on.** to begin (something). **9. to ring down the curtain on.** to conclude (something). —*n.* **1.** act of ringing something, esp. a bell. **2.** clear, resonant sound, as that made by a bell when struck. **3.** sound expressing a certain quality; tone. **4.** *Informal.* telephone call. [Old English *hringan* to clash, make a clear, resonant sound.]

ring·bolt (ring′bōlt′) *n.* bolt with a ring fitted into an eye in its head.

ring·er¹ (ring′ər) *n.* **1.** one who or that which rings or encircles. **2.** horseshoe or quoit thrown so as to encircle a stake or pin. [RING¹ + -ER¹.]

ring·er² (ring′ər) *n.* **1.** one who or that which rings a bell, chime, or the like. **2.** *Slang.* horse or athlete fraudulently entered in a contest, as by the falsification of name or age. **3.** *Slang.* one who or that which closely resembles another: *He is a dead ringer for his uncle.* [RING² + -ER².]

Ringbolt

ring·lead·er (ring′lē′dər) *n.* one who leads others, esp. in unlawful acts or enterprises. [From the earlier phrase *to lead the ring* to take the lead.]

ring·let (ring′lit) *n.* **1.** coiled or curved lock of hair. **2.** *Archaic.* small ring.

ring·mas·ter (ring′mas′tər) *n.* one who introduces the acts in a circus.

ring·side (ring′sīd′) *n.* **1.** area just outside the ring, as that containing the first row of seats at a prize fight. **2.** any area affording a close view.

ring·worm (ring′wurm′) *n.* any of several contagious fungus infections of the skin, including athlete's foot, characterized by ring-shaped patches.

rink (ringk) *n.* **1.** building, part of a building, or area containing a surface for ice skating or roller skating. **2.** the surface itself. [Possibly from Old French *renc* range, row¹, circle; of Germanic origin.]

rinse (rins) rinsed, rins·ing. *v.t.* **1.** to remove (soap or impurities) by washing with clear water (often with *out* or *off*): *He rinsed the soap off his hands.* **2.** to remove soap or impurities from (something) by washing with clear water: *to rinse clothes.* **3.** to cleanse or wash lightly (often with *out* or *off*): *She rinsed her hair with vinegar after shampooing.* —*n.* **1.** act of rinsing. **2.** water or other liquid used for rinsing. **3.** liquid preparation that is applied to the hair to tint or condition it. [Old French *raincier* to cleanse with water; of uncertain origin.]

Ri·o (rē′ō) *n. Informal.* Rio de Janeiro.

Ri·o de Ja·nei·ro (rē′ō dā zhə när′ō, dē jə nēr′ō) port city in southeastern Brazil, formerly the capital. It is one of the ten largest cities of the world. Pop. (1968) 4,207,322.

Ri·o Grande (rē′ō grand′, gran′dē) river flowing from southwestern Colorado into the Gulf of Mexico and forming the border between Texas and Mexico.

ri·ot (rī′ət) *n.* **1.** disorderly, often violent, disturbance or outbreak by a large group of people assembled together. **2.** *Law.* disturbance of the peace by three or more persons assembled together. **3.** bright, lavish display. **4.** *Archaic.* wanton behavior; wild revelry. **5.** *Slang.* someone or something that is extremely amusing. **6. to run riot. a.** to behave or move wildly and without restraint. **b.** to grow profusely, uncontrollably, or luxuriantly. —*v.i.* **1.** to engage in a disorderly, often violent, disturbance. **2.** *Archaic.* to engage in debauchery or wild revelry. [Old French *riote* dispute, brawling, from *rihoter* to make a disturbance; of uncertain origin.] —**ri′ot·er,** *n.*

Riot Act **1.** English law of 1715 providing for the dispersal or punishment of any group of twelve or more persons who disturb the peace. **2. to read the riot act to.** to rebuke severely.

ri·ot·ous (rī′ə təs) *adj.* **1.** of, relating to, or engaging in a disorderly, often violent, disturbance. **2.** boisterous; uproarious: *riotous laughter.* **3.** loose; wanton: *riotous living.* —**ri′ot·ous·ly,** *adv.* —**ri′ot·ous·ness,** *n.*

rip¹ (rip) ripped, rip·ping. *v.t.* **1.** to tear (something); rend: *The boy ripped his trousers on the fence.* **2.** to make by ripping: *The nail ripped a hole in her dress.* **3.** to tear or cut into pieces (with *up*). **4.** to remove (something) by tearing or pulling (often with *off, out,* or *away*): *to rip out a seam.* **5.** to saw or split (wood) along the grain. —*v.i.* **1.** to become torn apart. **2. to rip into.** *Informal.* to set upon vigorously;

at; āpe; cär; end; mē; it; īce; hot; ōld; fôrk; wood; fōōl; out; up; ūse; turn; sing; thin; this; zh in treasure; ə in ago, taken, pencil, lemon, circus.

last night. **b.** to exploit financially. —*v.i.* **1.** to become torn apart. **2. to rip into.** *Informal.* to set upon vigorously; attack. —*n.* torn place; tear. [Of uncertain origin.] —**Syn.** *v.t.* **1.** see **tear¹.**

rip² (rip) *n.* **1.** stretch of rough water made turbulent by the meeting of opposing currents. **2.** riptide. [Possibly from RIP¹.]

R.I.P., requiescat in pace.

ri·par·i·an (ri pâr′ē ən, rī-) *adj.* of, relating to, or on the bank, as of a river. [Latin *rīpārius* (from *rīpa* bank¹, shore) + -AN.]

rip cord, cord with a handle that opens a parachute when pulled.

ripe (rīp) **rip·er, rip·est.** *adj.* **1.** fully grown and ready to be gathered and used as food: *The tomatoes were not ripe yet.* **2.** matured or aged sufficiently for use: *The tobacco is not yet ripe.* **3.** advanced: *Our grandmother lived to a ripe old age.* **4.** fully prepared to do or undergo something; on the verge: *The country was ripe for revolution.* **5.** (of time) favorable or suitable. **6.** healthy, ruddy, and full. [Old English *rīpe* ready for reaping.] —**ripe′ly,** *adv.* —**ripe′ness,** *n.*

rip·en (rī′pən) *v.t., v.i.* to make or become ripe; mature.

rip-off (rip′ôf′) *n.* *U.S. slang.* **1.** act or instance of exploiting financially. **2.** robbery.

ri·poste (ri pōst′) *also,* **ri·post.** *n.* **1.** *Fencing.* quick thrust made after successfully parrying an opponent's lunge. **2.** quick, witty, or sharp reply; retort. —*v.i.* **-post·ed, -post·ing.** to make a riposte. [French *riposte* thrust in fencing, retort, from Italian *risposta* response, from *rispondere* to answer, from Latin *respondēre*.]

rip·ping (rip′ing) *British. Slang. adj.* excellent; splendid; first-rate. —*adv.* very.

rip·ple (rip′əl) *n.* **1.** very small wave on the surface of a liquid, as water. **2.** anything resembling this. **3.** sound resembling that made by the flowing of very small waves: *a ripple of applause.* —*v.i.* **-pled, -pling. 1.** to form or have very small waves on the surface. **2.** to flow with such waves. **3.** to make a sound resembling that made by the flowing of very small waves. —*v.t.* to cause very small waves on the flowing of very small waves. —*v.t.* to cause very small waves on.

rip·ply (rip′lē) *adj.* marked or characterized by ripples.

rip·rap (rip′rap′) *n.* **1.** layer of large stones or rocks used as a cover to protect earth or soft rock from being washed away or as the foundation for a breakwater. —*v.t.* **-rapped, -rap·ping.** to make a riprap in or on. [Repetition of RAP¹, with vowel change in the first syllable.]

rip·roar·ing (rip′rôr′ing) *adj.* *Informal.* noisy and lively: *a riproaring fight.*

rip·saw (rip′sô′) *n.* handsaw with squared, chisel-like cutting edges on its teeth, used properly to cut wood with the grain, not across it. See **saw¹** for illustration. [RIP¹ + SAW¹.]

rip·tide (rip′tīd′) *n.* strong seaward movement of water which returns water brought shoreward by waves. Also, **rip.**

Rip·u·ar·i·an (rip′ū âr′ē ən) *adj.* of, relating to, or designating a tribe of Franks settled along the Rhine near Cologne in the fourth century A.D. —*n.* Ripuarian Frank.

Rip Van Win·kle (rip′ van wing′kəl) hero of a story by Washington Irving, who slept for twenty years and awakened to find his wife dead and his village and country changed completely.

rise (rīz) **rose, ris·en, ris·ing.** *v.i.* **1.** to assume an upright posture or position; get up; stand up. **2.** to move from a lower to a higher place or position; go upward: *Smoke rose from the chimney.* **3.** to get out of bed: *The farmer always rises early.* **4.** (of the sun and other heavenly bodies) to appear above the horizon. **5.** to incline or slope upward: *The land rises at this point to a steep cliff.* **6.** to have elevation or altitude; extend upward: *The monument rises above the trees.* **7.** to increase, as in amount, value, degree, or intensity: *The cost of living rose last year.* **8.** to advance, as in rank, position, or influence. **9.** to reach a higher level; increase in height: *The river rose two feet.* **10.** to be built or erected: *New apartment buildings rose on the site.* **11.** to expand and become lighter: *The cake will rise.* **12.** to increase in pitch or become louder, as the voice. **13.** to become more animated or vigorous: *The army's morale rose with the ending of winter.* **14.** to revolt; rebel (often with *up*): *The oppressed people rose up against the tyrant.* **15.** to emanate or originate: *A loud roar rose from the crowd.* **16.** to emerge; appear: *A blister rose on his hand.* **17.** to come to pass; happen. **18.** to come back from death or the grave; return to life. **19. to rise above.** to free oneself from the limitations of. **20. to rise to.** to be or become equal to the demands of: *to rise to the challenge.* —*n.* **1.** upward movement; ascent: *the rise of water in a tank.* **2.** increase, as in amount, value, degree, or intensity. **3.** upward slope or direction. **4.** piece of rising ground; hill. **5.** advance or advance, as in rank, fortune, power, or influence: *the rise of modern science.* **6.** increase in loudness or pitch. **7.** appearance of a heavenly body above the horizon. **8.** origin; beginning; source: *Where do these problems have their rise?* **9.** vertical height, as of a step, landing, or arch. **10.** *Informal.* emotional reaction, esp. of anger or resentment: *I can't get a rise out of him.* **11. to give rise to.** to cause; originate: *The depression gave rise to widespread unemployment.* [Old English *rīsan* to go up; ascend.]

ris·en (riz′ən) past participle of **rise.**

ris·er (rī′zər) *n.* **1.** one who or that which rises: *Because of the nature of his work, the farmer had to be an early riser.* **2.** vertical part of a step.

ris·i·ble (riz′ə bəl) *adj.* **1.** able or disposed to laugh. **2.** exciting laughter; amusing; laughable. [Late Latin *rīsibilis* laughable, from Latin *rīdēre* to laugh.] —**ris′i·bil′i·ty,** *n.*

ris·ing (rī′zing) *n.* **1.** act of one who or that which rises. **2.** uprising; insurrection. —*adj.* that rises.

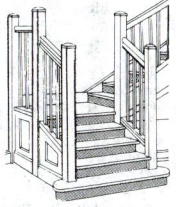

Risers

risk (risk) *n.* **1.** exposure to loss or harm: *There is great risk involved in that plan.* **2.** person or thing with reference to the probability of loss from insuring or relying on him or it: *a bad risk.* —*v.t.* **1.** to expose to loss or harm. **2.** to take the risk of: *They risked losing everything.* [French *risque* peril, from Italian *risico,* from *risicare* to venture; of uncertain origin.] —**Syn.** *n.* **1.** see **danger.** *v.t.* **1.** see **venture.**

risk·y (ris′kē) **risk·i·er, risk·i·est.** *adj.* attended with risk; dangerous. —**risk′i·ness,** *n.*

ris·qué (ris kā′) *adj.* slightly improper; suggestive. [French *risqué,* past participle of *risquer* to venture, from Italian *rischiare;* of uncertain origin.]

rit., ritardando. Also, **ritard.**

ri·tar·dan·do (rē′tär dän′dō) *Music. adj.* becoming gradually slower. —*n.* gradual slowing of tempo. [Italian *ritardando,* present participle of *ritardare* to be slow, delay, from Latin *retardāre* to hinder, delay.]

rite (rīt) *n.* **1.** formal act or set of acts prescribed by ritual or tradition: *marriage rites.* **2.** form or procedure prescribed for the performance of this: *the rite of baptism.* **3.** *also,* **Rite.** specific form of public worship, esp. the communion service; liturgy. [Latin *rītus* religious ceremony, custom.] —**Syn. 1.** see **ceremony.**

rit·u·al (rich′ōō əl) *n.* **1.** set form or procedure governing the performance of a religious or solemn rite. **2.** system or body of rites. **3.** observance of such a system or body of rites. **4.** routine faithfully followed, often in a pretentious or elaborate manner. —*adj.* of, relating to, or performed as a ritual. [Latin *rītuālis* relating to religious ceremonies, from *rītus* religious ceremony, custom.] —**rit′u·al·ly,** *adv.* —**Syn. 1.** see **ceremony.**

rit·u·al·ism (rich′ōō ə liz′əm) *n.* **1.** strict observance of or adherence to ritual. **2.** study of religious ritual.

rit·u·al·ist (rich′ōō ə list) *n.* **1.** one who practices or advocates ritualism. **2.** one who studies religious ritual.

rit·u·al·is·tic (rich′ōō ə lis′tik) *adj.* **1.** of or relating to ritual or ritualism. **2.** fond of or advocating ritual.

ritz·y (rit′sē) **ritz·i·er, ritz·i·est.** *adj.* *Informal.* very elegant or luxurious; posh. [From the *Ritz* hotels known for their elegance, established by the Swiss entrepreneur César Ritz, 1850–1918.]

riv., river.

ri·val (rī′vəl) *n.* **1.** one who competes with another to achieve the same thing or tries to equal or surpass another; competitor. **2.** one who or that which compares favorably with or equals another: *The imposing interior of the cathedral has few rivals.* —*v.t.* **-valed, -val·ing;** *also,* British. **-valled, -val·ling. 1.** to try to equal or surpass; compete with. **2.** to compare favorably with or be the equal of. —*adj.* being a rival; competing. [Latin *rīvālis* competitor, neighbor, one getting water from the same brook as another, from *rīvus* brook.]

ri·val·ry (rī′vəl rē) *pl.,* **-ries.** *n.* **1.** act of rivaling; competition. **2.** state of being rivals. —**Syn. 1.** see **emulation.**

rive (rīv) **rived, rived or riv·en** (riv′ən), **riv·ing.** *v.t.* **1.** to split; cleave. **2.** to rend or distress (the heart, soul, or spirit). [Old Norse *rīfa* to tear, break.]

riv·er¹ (riv′ər) *n.* **1.** large stream of water within a definite course or channel, usually larger than a creek. **2.** anything resembling a river, as in quantity or flow. [Anglo-Norman *rivere* stream, going back to Latin *rīpārius* relating to the bank of a stream, from *rīpa* bank of a stream.]

riv·er² (rī′vər) *n.* one who or that which rives. [RIVE + -ER¹.]

Ri·ve·ra, Die·go (ri vâr′ə; dyā′gō) 1886–1957, Mexican painter.

riv·er·bank (riv′ər bangk′) *n.* ground bordering a river.

river basin, land area drained by a river and its tributaries.

riv·er·bed (riv′ər bed′) *n.* bottom of the channel through which a river flows or formerly flowed.

riv·er·boat (riv′ər bōt′) *n.* boat used for river travel, esp. a large paddle-wheel boat used on the southern and midwestern rivers of the United States during the nineteenth and early twentieth centuries.

riv·er·head (riv′ər hed′) *n.* source of a river.

river horse, hippopotamus.

riv·er·ine (riv′ə rēn′, -rin) *adj.* **1.** of, like, or relating to a river. **2.** situated or living on the banks of a river.

riv·er·side (riv′ər sīd′) *n.* area along the edge or the bank of a river.

Riv·er·side (riv′ər sīd′) *n.* city in southwestern California. Pop. (1970), 140,089.

riv·et (riv′it) *n.* threadless metal bolt used to make permanent fastenings, esp. in metalwork and leatherwork. The shaft of the rivet is put through aligned holes in materials to be joined; then the headless end is flattened to make a tight connection.

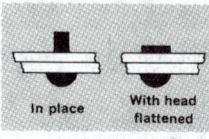

In place   With head flattened

Rivets

—*v.t.* **1.** to fasten with a rivet or rivets. —**2.** to fasten or hold firmly: *The sudden movement riveted the bird dog to the ground. John's complete attention was riveted on the football game.* **3.** to flatten the headless end of (a bolt, pin, or rod), esp. to secure it in place. [Old French *rivet* small bolt, from *river* to fasten, fix; of uncertain origin.] —**riv′et·er**, *n.*

Riv·i·er·a (riv′ē ār′ə) *n.* narrow strip of land along the Mediterranean coasts of Italy, France, and Monaco.

riv·u·let (riv′yə lət) *n.* **1.** any tiny stream; trickle. **2.** small brook. [Italian *rivoletto*, diminutive of *rivolo* brook, going back to Latin *rīvus.*]

rix-dol·lar (riks′dol′ər) *n.* any of several silver coins formerly used in the Netherlands, Denmark, Germany, Sweden, and Austria. [Obsolete Dutch *rijcksdaler*, from *rijck* realm + *daler* dollar. See DOL-LAR.]

Ri·yadh (rē yäd′) *n.* capital of Saudi Arabia, in the east-central part of the country. Pop. (1965), 225,000.

rm. **1.** room. **2.** ream.

RM, reichsmark; reichsmarks.

Rn, radon.

RN **1.** registered nurse. **2.** Royal Navy.

RNA, any of various nucleic acids found in the cytoplasm and nucleus of all living cells, consisting of a long strand made up of alternating units of sugar and phosphate connected by a nitrogen base. One form of this acid, **messenger RNA,** carries the genetic information contained in DNA from the cell nucleus to the cytoplasm. Another form, **transfer RNA,** arranges amino acids so that protein is produced in the manner directed by DNA. [Abbreviation of *r(ibo)n(ucleic) a(cid).*]

roach¹ (rōch) *n.* cockroach.

roach² (rōch) *pl.* **roach·es** or **roach.** *n.* **1.** freshwater fish, *Rutilus rutilus,* related to the carp and found in lakes and rivers in northern Europe. **2.** any of several similar fish found in North America. [Old French *roche* the European fish; of uncertain origin.]

road (rōd) *n.* **1.** strip of pavement or cleared, packed ground used for traveling between places; open way for the passage of vehicles, persons, or animals. **2.** any means of advancing or progressing toward a specific end: *the road to power, the road to heaven.* **3.** protected area near the shore where ships can ride at anchor, less sheltered than a harbor. **4.** railroad. **5. on the road. a.** traveling for professional or business reasons, as a salesman or member of a theatrical company. **b.** living the life of a wanderer or vagabond. [Old English *rād* journey, a riding.] **Syn. 1. Road, highway, thoroughfare, parkway** indicate a passage for vehicles. **Road** is the general term: *a dirt road. The road was widened to accommodate extra traffic.* **Highway** denotes a principal public road of special construction: *The number of trucks on the highways increases every year.* A **thoroughfare** is a principal road, street, or highway that connects with other roads at both ends: *We spent our vacation in a small town far from the traveled thoroughfares.* A **parkway** has carefully landscaped greenery on either side of the road and also, usually, between opposing traffic lanes: *That parkway is a pleasant route for a drive.*

road agent, highwayman, esp. one who robbed stagecoaches in the western United States.

road·bed (rōd′bed′) *n.* **1.** foundation or bed for the ties and rails of a railroad. **2.** foundation or surface of a road.

road·block (rōd′blok′) *n.* **1.** blockade to stop traffic on a road, as that used by the police to stop criminals. **2.** anything that hinders progress.

road hog *Informal.* driver who obstructs traffic by allowing his vehicle to occupy more than one lane of the road.

road·house (rōd′hous′) *n.* tavern, night club, or similar establishment located on a highway, usually outside city limits.

road metal, broken stone, cinders, and similar materials used in making and repairing roads and roadbeds.

road·run·ner (rōd′run′ər) *n.* ground-dwelling cuckoo, *Geococcyx californianus,* native to flat, barren

Roadrunner

country from the southwestern United States to central Mexico, having brownish-black streaked plumage, a long, white-tipped tail, and a shaggy crest. Length: 20–24 inches.

road·side (rōd′sīd′) *n.* area along the side of a road. —*adj.* along the side of a road.

road·stead (rōd′sted′) *n.* road (*def.* 3).

road·ster (rōd′stər) *n.* open automobile with a single seat for two or more people, often with a rumble seat or luggage compartment in the rear.

road test, test of a vehicle or any of its parts under actual driving conditions.

road·way (rōd′wā′) *n.* road, esp. that part over which vehicles travel.

road·work (rōd′wurk′) *n.* physical exercise or training consisting of long runs over a road or path.

roam (rōm) *v.i.* to go about without a specific purpose or destination, esp. over a large area; wander. —*v.t.* to wander over or through (a place): *Hungry wolves roamed the forest in search of food.* [Of uncertain origin.] —**roam′er**, *n.*
Syn. *v.i.* **Roam, rove′, ramble** indicate leisurely or lengthy wandering. **Roam** implies pleasure obtained from the freedom to go wherever one desires: *He roamed about the old section of the city.* **Rove** suggests a more energetic ranging over a wide area, often with some purpose but with no particular destination: *They roved through the hill country searching for antiques.* **Ramble** implies walking aimlessly and leisurely: *The park's twisting paths were designed for those who love to ramble.*

roan (rōn) *n.* **1.** reddish-brown mixed with gray or white. **2.** horse of this color. [Old French *roan* the color, from Spanish *roane;* of uncertain origin.]

Ro·a·noke (rō′ə nōk′) *n.* city in southwestern Virginia. Pop. (1970), 92,115.

roar (rôr) *v.i.* **1.** to utter a loud, deep sound or cry. **2.** to resound loudly and deeply, as a motor or gun. **3.** to move with a loud, deep noise: *The plane roared up the runway.* **4.** to laugh loudly. —*v.t.* to shout or express in a roar: *He roared his displeasure.* —*n.* **1.** loud, deep sound or cry, as of a man or animal. **2.** loud, resounding noise: *the roar of the ocean waves.* [Old English *rārian* to shout, yell.] —**roar′er**, *n.*

roast (rōst) *v.t.* **1.** to cook in a dry oven or by exposure to an open fire or hot coals: *to roast a chicken, to roast chestnuts.* **2.** to dry and brown by exposure to heat: *to roast coffee beans.* **3.** *Informal.* to criticize or ridicule severely. **4.** to make warm or excessively hot. **5.** *Metallurgy.* to heat (ore) with exposure to air so as to purify, dehydrate, or oxidize. —*v.i.* **1.** to be cooked in a dry oven or by exposure to an open fire or hot coals. **2.** to be uncomfortably hot: *I'm roasting in this heavy coat.* —*n.* **1.** cut of meat that has been roasted or is prepared to be roasted. **2.** outdoor gathering at which food is cooked over an open fire or hot coals. —*adj.* roasted: *a roast chicken.* [Old French *rostir* to cook before a fire; of Germanic origin.]

roast·er (rōs′tər) *n.* **1.** pan or appliance used for roasting. **2.** animal suitable for roasting, esp. a chicken or a young pig. **3.** one who roasts.

rob (rob) **robbed, rob·bing.** *v.t.* **1.** to take property from (a person, place, or thing) by illegal means, esp. with the threat or use of violence; commit robbery upon: *They robbed the jewelry store in broad daylight.* **2.** to deprive of something deserved or rightfully due, esp. by unjust or deceitful means: *to be robbed of one's dignity.* **3.** to take away (property) by illegal means; steal. —*v.i.* to commit robbery. [Old French *rob(b)er* to steal; literally, to strip; of Germanic origin.]

rob·ber (rob′ər) *n.* one who robs.

rob·ber·y (rob′ər ē) *pl.* **-ber·ies.** *n.* act of unlawfully taking another's property, esp. the felonious taking of someone's property from his person or in his presence with the threat or use of violence. [French *roberie,* from *rob*. See ROB.]

robe (rōb) *n.* **1.** loose outer garment, esp. one worn at home or on informal occasions: *a beach robe.* **2.** garment worn to show office, profession, or rank, as by a judge or a member of the clergy. **3.** blanket or other covering, as for use by spectators at outdoor sporting events: *a lap robe.* —*v.t.,* **robed, rob·ing.** to put a robe on; dress. —*v.i.* to put on a robe; dress. [Old French *robe* garment, booty (because booty in medieval times often consisted of clothing); of Germanic origin.]

Rob·ert I (rob′ərt) see Bruce, Robert the.

Robes·pierre, Max·i·mi·lien Ma·rie I·si·dore (rōbz′pēr, -pē är′; mäk sē mēl yän′ mä rē′ ē zē dōr′) 1758–94, one of the leaders of the French Revolution and of the Reign of Terror.

rob·in (rob′in) *n.* **1.** North American thrush, *Turdus migratorius,* having a reddish-orange breast and a black head and tail. Length: 10 inches. **2.** plump-bodied thrush, *Erithacus rubecula,* native to Europe and

Robin

at; āpe; cär; end; mē; it; īce; hot; ōld; fôrk; wood; fōōl; oil; out; up; ūse; turn; sing; thin; this; zh in treasure; ə in ago, taken, pencil, lemon, circus.

parts of Asia and Africa, having a brown back, a white underside, and a reddish-brown breast and forehead. Length: 6 inches. Also, **robin redbreast.** [Old French *Robin,* familiar form of *Robert,* man's proper name.]

Rob·in Good·fel·low (rob'in good'fel'ō) Puck.

Robin Hood *English Legend.* medieval outlaw who lived in Sherwood Forest with his band of men and robbed the rich to help the poor.

rob·in's-egg blue (rob'inz eg') greenish-blue color.

Rob·in·son, Edwin Arlington (rob'in sən) 1869–1935, U.S. poet.

Robinson Cru·soe (krōō'sō) hero of Daniel Defoe's novel of the same name, published in 1719.

ro·bot (rō'bot, -bət) *n.* **1.** machine somewhat resembling a man that can perform some human functions. **2.** one who performs or acts in a mechanical way. **3.** any device, as a chess-playing computer, that performs complex tasks automatically. [Czech *robot* the machine, from *robota* compulsory labor, coined by Karel Čapek, 1890–1938, Czech playwright, for his play *R.U.R.*]

robot bomb, buzz bomb.

ro·bust (rō bust', rō'bust) *adj.* **1.** having strength and vigor; in good health; hardy: *a robust young athlete.* **2.** requiring strength and vigor: *the robust life of a forest ranger.* **3.** rich and full-bodied: *a robust flavor.* **4.** coarse; boisterous: *robust humor.* [Latin *rōbustus* oaken, strong, from *rōbur* oak, strength.] **—ro·bust'ly,** *adv.* **—ro·bust'ness,** *n.*

roc (rok) *n. Arabian Legend.* an enormous and fearsome bird of prey. [Arabic *rukhkh;* of Persian origin.]

Ro·cham·beau, Count de (rō'shäm bō', -sham-) 1725–1807, commander of the French forces that fought with the American army during the Revolutionary War.

Ro·chelle salt (rō shel') salt of tartaric acid, used in crystalline form for phonograph pickups and microphones, and in powdered form as a laxative; potassium sodium tartrate. Formula: $KNaC_4H_4O_6 \cdot 4H_2O$ [From *(La) Rochelle,* a French seaport.]

Roch·es·ter (roch'es'tər, -is tər) *n.* **1.** city in western New York, on Lake Ontario. Pop. (1970), 296,233. **2.** city in southeastern Minnesota. Pop. (1970), 53,766.

roch·et (roch'it) *n.* knee-length vestment of white linen with close-fitting sleeves, worn by bishops and other church dignitaries. [Old French *rochet;* of Germanic origin.]

rock¹ (rok) *n.* **1.** fragment or piece of stone: *The angry mob began to throw rocks at the speaker.* **2.** large mass of stone forming a cliff or peak: *The ship was dashed violently against the rocks.* **3.** *Geology.* **a.** extensive, naturally formed uniform mass of mineral matter that forms part of the crust of the earth. **b.** particular kind of such matter, as igneous, sedimentary, or metamorphic. **4.** something resembling a rock in firmness, esp. a source of strength or support. **5.** *Informal.* large gem, esp. a diamond. **6. on the rocks.** *Informal.* **a.** served over ice cubes, as an alcoholic beverage. **b.** in a state of destruction or ruin. **c.** without money; bankrupt. [Old French *rocque, roche* mass of hard stone; of uncertain origin.]

rock² (rok) *v.t.* **1.** to move back and forth or from side to side gently: *She rocked the baby in her arms.* **2.** to move or shake violently: *The hurricane rocked the house.* **3.** to upset or unnerve: *The news of his illness rocked the student body.* *—v.i.* **1.** to be moved back and forth or from side to side gently: *The porch chair rocked in the breeze.* **2.** to be shaken violently: *The ship rocked in the squall.* *—n.* **1.** rocking motion. **2.a.** rock 'n' roll. **b.** form of popular music that evolved from rock 'n' roll, influenced by folk and country-and-western music and characterized esp. by the use of amplified instruments and by generally more complex lyrics and arrangements than rock 'n' roll. [Old English *roccian* to move to and fro.]

rock-and-roll (rok'ən rōl') *n.* rock 'n' roll.

rock bottom, lowest level; very bottom: *The stock market hit rock bottom.* **—rock'-bot'tom,** *adj.*

rock-bound (rok'bound') *adj.* hemmed in or surrounded by rocks: *the rock-bound coast of Maine.*

rock candy, clear, hard crystals of pure sugar.

rock crystal, clear, colorless variety of quartz, used to make optical devices, jewelry, vases, and other ornaments.

Rock·e·fel·ler (rok'ə fel'ər) **1. John D.** 1839–1937, U.S. industrialist and philanthropist. **2. John D., Jr.** 1874–1960, his son; U.S. philanthropist. **3. Nelson A.** 1908–, American political leader, son of John D. Rockefeller, Jr.

rock·er (rok'ər) *n.* **1.** rocking chair. **2.** one of the two curved pieces on which a cradle, rocking chair, or other object rocks. **3. off one's rocker.** *Slang.* not in one's right mind; crazy.

rock·et (rok'it) *n.* **1.** device that is propelled by a jet of hot gases ejected in a direction opposite to the direction of motion and does not require air from the outside for its operation. **2.** vehicle, missile, or projectile propelled by such a device. *—v.i.* to move or rise swiftly. [Italian *rocchetta* a firework, bobbin, diminutive of *rocca* distaff; of

Germanic origin; because the shape of this kind of firework resembles that of a bobbin or distaff.]

rock·et·eer (rok'ə tēr') *n.* one who works with rockets, esp. an expert in rocketry.

rock·et·ry (rok'it rē) *n.* science of rocket design, construction, and flight.

rock·fish (rok'fish') *pl.,* **-fish** or **-fish·es.** *n.* any of several food and game fish, family Scorpaenidae, having a number of sharp, strong spines projecting from the top and bottom fins. Length: 1½ feet.

Rock·ford (rok'fərd) *n.* city in northern Illinois. Pop. (1970), 147,-370.

rock garden, garden arranged with flowers and plants on rocky ground or among rocks.

Rock·ies (rok'ēz) *n.* Rocky Mountains.

rocking chair, chair mounted on rockers or springs.

rocking horse, toy horse mounted on rockers, large enough for a child to ride. Also, **hob'by·horse'.**

Rock Island, city in northwestern Illinois. Pop. (1970), 50,166.

rock lobster, spiny lobster.

rock 'n' roll (rok'ən rōl') form of popular music derived from the blues, gospel music, and jazz, characterized esp. by a strong, persistent beat and relatively simple lyrics and arrangements.

rock-ribbed (rok'ribd') *adj.* **1.** marked by rows or ridges of rock. **·2.** unyielding in feeling, belief, or position.

rock salt, common salt occurring in solid form, esp. in large crystals.

rock·weed (rok'wēd') *n.* any of various seaweeds that grow on rocks.

rock wool, fibrous, fireproof insulating material produced by blowing steam or hot air through a molten mass of rock, as limestone.

rock·y¹ (rok'ē) **rock·i·er, rock·i·est.** *adj.* **1.** composed of or abounding in rocks. **2.** resembling rock; hard; unyielding. [ROCK¹ + -Y¹.] **—rock'i·ness,** *n.*

rock·y² (rok'ē) **rock·i·er, rock·i·est.** *adj.* **1.** inclined to sway or totter; shaky. **2.** *Informal.* physically weak or unsteady. [ROCK² + -Y¹.] **—rock'i·ness,** *n.*

Rocky Mountain goat, goat-like, cud-chewing mammal, *Oreamnos americanus,* native to mountain ranges of western North America, having black horns and a thick coat of long, white hair. Height: 3½ feet at the shoulder. Also, **mountain goat.**

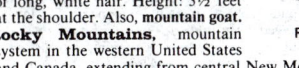
Rocky Mountain goat

Rocky Mountains, mountain system in the western United States and Canada, extending from central New Mexico to northern Alaska. Also, **Rock'ies.**

Rocky Mountain sheep, bighorn.

Rocky Mountain spotted fever, infectious disease caused by a microorganism and transmitted by the bite of a tick, characterized by high fever, headache, generalized pain, and a red or purple rash.

ro·co·co (rə kō'kō, rō'kō kō') *n.* style of interior decoration, architecture, and painting that originated in France and northern Italy and flourished during the eighteenth century, characterized esp. by the use of curved and asymmetrical forms based on objects from nature, such as shells, flowers, and branches of leaves. *—adj.* **1.** of, relating to, or in this style. **2.** excessively elaborate or ornate; florid: *rococo notions of Imperial glory* (Jenkins, 1878). [French *rococo,* modified form of *rocaille* shellwork, from *roc* rock¹; of uncertain origin; from the use of shell patterns in this style of decoration.]

rod (rod) *n.* **1.** thin, straight, usually cylindrical piece of metal, wood, or other material: *a curtain rod, a connecting rod in an automobile engine.* **2.** slender straight stick cut from or growing on a tree or bush. **3.** fishing rod. **4.a.** stick or bundle of sticks used to beat or punish. **b. the rod.** punishment; discipline: *Spare the rod and spoil the child* (Butler, 1664). **5.** unit of linear measurement equal to 5½ yards or 16½ feet. See **weights and measures** for table. **6.** stick or bar used for measuring. **7.** *Slang.* pistol or revolver. **8.** one of the rod-shaped cells on the retina of the eye that are sensitive to dim light. **9.** scepter, staff, or similar object carried or viewed as a symbol of office, power, or authority. [Old English *rodd* thin, straight stick, pole¹.]

rode (rōd) past tense of **ride.**

ro·dent (rōd'ənt) *n.* any of numerous mammals constituting the order Rodentia, having a pair of chisel-like front teeth adapted for gnawing. Rats, mice, squirrels, guinea pigs, porcupines, and beavers are rodents. *—adj.* **1.** gnawing: *the rodent teeth of a beaver.* **2.** of, relating to, or characteristic of a rodent. [Latin *rōdēns,* present participle of *rōdere* to gnaw.]

ro·de·o (rō'dē ō', rō dā'ō) *pl.,* **-de·os.** *n.* **1.** show in which cowboys compete in various events, as horseback and bull riding, calf roping, and steer wrestling, often for cash prizes. **2.** cattle roundup. [Spanish

rodeo roundup, from *rodear* to go around, from *rueda* wheel, from Latin *rota*.]

Ro·din, Au·guste (rō dan′, -daN′; ō goost′) 1840–1917, French sculptor.

rod·o·mon·tade (rod′ə mon tād′, -täd′) *n.* vain boasting; bluster. [French *rodomontade,* from Italian *rodomontata,* from *Rodomonte* boastful character in Ariosto's epic poem *Orlando Furioso.*]

roe[1] (rō) *n.* eggs of fish or crustaceans, some of which are eaten as a delicacy, either raw or cooked. [Possibly from Old Norse *hrogn*.]

roe[2] (rō) *pl.* **roes** or **roe.** *n.* small deer, *Capreolus capreolus,* native to the forests of Europe and northern Asia, having a coarse, reddish-brown coat with a white patch over the rump. Height: 30 inches at the shoulder. Also, **roe deer.** [Old English *rāha, rā.*]

Roe[2]

roe·buck (rō′buk′) *n.* male of the roe deer.

roent·gen (rent′gən, runt′-) *n.* international unit for measuring the intensity of X rays or gamma rays. [From W. K. *Roentgen.*]

Roent·gen, Wil·helm Kon·rad (rent′gən, runt′-; wil′helm kon′rad) *also,* **Rönt·gen.** 1845–1923, German physicist who discovered X rays.

roent·gen·ol·o·gy (rent′gə nol′ə jē, runt′-) *n.* science that deals with the use, properties, and effects of X rays. —**roent′gen·ol′o·gist,** *n.*

Roentgen ray, X ray. [From W. K. *Roentgen.*]

ro·ga·tion (rō gā′shən) *n.* a solemn prayer of supplication, esp. the litanies chanted on the Monday, Tuesday, and Wednesday preceding Ascension Day. [Latin *rogātiō* supplication.]

rog·er (roj′ər) *interj.* **1.** in radio communications, message received and understood. **2.** *Informal.* all right or okay. [From *Roger,* proper name used in communications for *r,* the first letter of received.]

rogue (rōg) *n.* **1.** one who is dishonest and deceitful; scoundrel. **2.** one who is mischievous and playful. **3.** wild animal, esp. an elephant, of a dangerous or savage nature, driven away or living apart from the herd. [Of uncertain origin.]
Syn. 1. Rogue, rascal, scoundrel refer to persons of a low, unprincipled, tricky nature. **Rogue** implies lack of restraint or concern for law or custom: *The rogue had staged forty robberies in broad daylight in the last two months.* **Rascal** suggests a cleverness in carrying out dishonest schemes: *The rascal got away before we discovered that the home sites we bought were actually on swampland.* **Scoundrel** implies a complete lack of principles and a baseness bordering on the vicious: *The scoundrels deliberately contaminated the town's water supply.*

ro·guer·y (rō′gər ē) *pl.* **-guer·ies.** *n.* **1.** behavior or act characterized by dishonesty and trickery. **2.** playfully mischievous act or conduct.

rogues' gallery, collection of photographs of known criminals and suspects kept by police to aid in making identifications.

ro·guish (rō′gish) *adj.* **1.** dishonest and deceitful; unscrupulous. **2.** playfully mischievous. —**ro′guish·ly,** *adv.* —**ro′guish·ness,** *n.*

roil (roil) *v.t.* **1.** to make (liquid) muddy or unsettled by stirring up sediment. **2.** to disturb or vex (someone). [Of uncertain origin.]

rois·ter (rois′tər) *v.i.* to behave or frolic in a loud and riotous manner. [Old French *ru(i)stre* ruffian, form of *ruste* a rustic, from Latin *rūsticus* peasant, rustic.] —**rois′ter·er,** *n.*

Ro·land (rō′lənd) *n.* in French and Italian literature, a historical hero who fought under Charlemagne and, according to legend, was killed by the Saracens in 778.

role (rōl) *also,* **rôle.** *n.* **1.** character or part played by an actor. **2.** part played by anyone or anything; position or function: *the role of the press in determining public opinion. He assumed the role of interpreter for the group.* [French *rôle* actor's part; originally, roll of paper containing such a part, going back to Latin *rotula* little wheel. See ROLL.]

roll (rōl) *v.i.* **1.** to move by rotating on an axis or by turning over and over: *The ball rolled down the hill.* **2.** to move or be moved on rollers or wheels: *The truck rolled along the highway.* **3.** to turn over many times in succession: *The child rolled in the mud.* **4.** to move in a smooth, rising and falling manner: *The fog rolled in from the water.* **5.** to extend in gentle rises and dips: *The hills rolled toward the horizon.* **6.** to pass or elapse (with *by* or *on*): *The years roll on.* **7.** to form a ball or cylinder when turned over and over: *Cardboard won't roll without creasing.* **8.** to turn around wholly or partially: *His eyes rolled in amazement.* **9.** to rock from side to side; sway: *The ship rolled violently in the storm.* **10.** to walk with a swaying motion. **11.** to make a deep, continuous sound; rumble: *The drums rolled.* **12.** to become spread out or flattened

under a roller: *This paint rolls on easily.* **13.** *Informal.* to make progress or start: *Let's get this project rolling.* **14.** (of a celestial body) to perform a periodical revolution. **15.** to recur periodically (with *around*): *Winter has rolled around again.* **16. to roll in. a.** to arrive, esp. in large numbers or amounts: *The train rolled in two hours late. Orders rolled in faster than they could be filled.* **b.** *Informal.* to luxuriate or abound in: *to be rolling in money.* —*v.t.* **1.** to cause to move by rotating on an axis or by turning over and over: *to roll a hoop.* **2.** to move by means of rollers or wheels: *to roll a bed against the wall.* **3.** to wrap (something) around on itself or on something else; shape into a cylinder or a ball: *to roll a cigarette, to roll up a blanket.* **4.** to enfold or wrap, as in a covering. **5.** to drive or impel with a sweeping motion: *The wind rolled the waves onto the shore.* **6.** to spread out, flatten, or make smooth with a roller: *to roll metal into sheets, to roll out dough for cookies.* **7.** to cause to rock from side to side. **8.** to beat (a drum) with quick continuous blows. **9.** to pronounce (a speech sound) with a trill, esp. the sound of *r.* **10.** to emit with a prolonged deep sound. **11.** to turn (the eyes) around, wholly or partially. **12.** to cast (dice), as in craps. **13.** *Slang.* to rob (a drunk or unconscious person). **14. to roll back.** to reduce (something, as prices or wages) to a previous lower level. **15. to roll up.** to accumulate: *We rolled up a large score against the visiting team.* —*n.* **1.** cylinder formed by winding something round and round; something rolled up: *a roll of stamps, a roll of wallpaper.* **2.** quantity of something rolled up, usually considered as a standard measure. **3.** list of names of people belonging to a group: *a class roll.* **4.** catalogue, list, or record. **5.** mass of something that is somewhat rounded or cylindrical: *a roll of fat around a person's waist.* **6.a.** individual piece of baked bread dough. **b.** any food, as meat or cake, that is rolled up. **7.** rolling or swaying motion: *The roll of the boat was making us dizzy.* **8.** rapid, uniform, continuous series of short sounds, as those made by beating on a drum. **9.** deep, loud reverberation: *the roll of thunder.* **10.** gentle rising and falling: *the roll of the terrain.* **11.** roller. **12.** act or instance of rolling. **13.** *Slang.* money, esp. a wad of paper money. **14.** change in the position of an aircraft around a front to back axis, so that one wing rises and the other drops. [Old French *roller, rouler* to move by turning over and over, wind on a cylinder, going back to Latin *rotula* little wheel, diminutive of *rota* wheel.]

roll·back (rōl′bak′) *n.* reduction of prices or wages to a previous lower level, as by a governmental order.

roll call **1.** act of calling a list of names, as those registered in a class, to determine who is present. **2.** signal or time at which this is done.

roll·er (rō′lər) *n.* **1.** cylinder on which something is wound up: *the roller of a window shade.* **2.** cylinder that smooths, spreads out, flattens, or crushes: *a paint roller.* **3.** small wheel, as that of a roller skate or caster, on which something is rolled: *We had to put the piano on rollers before we could move it.* **4.** any of various cylindrical devices over which something is moved. **5.** hollow cylinder of wire mesh, metal, or plastic on which hair is rolled up. **6.** long, swelling wave breaking on a shoreline. **7.** any of various jaylike birds, family Coraciidae, native to Africa, Eurasia, the East Indies, and Australia, having brightly colored plumage and noted for the tumbling and rolling flight of the male during courtship. Length: 9½–18 inches. **8.** canary having a rolling, or trilling, song. **9.** one who rolls.

roller bearing, bearing used esp. for heavy loads, in which the friction-reducing parts are cylindrical or cone-shaped rollers.

roller coaster, amusement ride consisting of a series of open, attached cars that move at high speeds over a track having sharp turns and steep inclines and dips.

roll·er-skate (rō′lər skāt′) **-skat·ed, -skat·ing.** *v.i.* to skate on roller skates.

roller skate, skate having small wheels on the bottom instead of a runner, used for skating on a flat surface, as a floor or sidewalk.

Roller skates

rol·lick (rol′ik) *v.i.* to behave in a carefree, joyous manner; frolic. [Possibly blend of ROMP and FROLIC.]

rol·lick·ing (rol′i king) *adj.* jovial and carefree; merry; frolicking.

roll·ing (rō′ling) *adj.* **1.** moving by turning over and over: *a rolling snowball.* **2.** moving on wheels: *a rolling teacart.* **3.** extending in gentle rises and falls: *rolling plains.* **4.** moving in swells or undulations: *the rolling sea.* **5.** moving from side to side; swaying: *a rolling gait.* **6.** deep and resounding; reverberating: *rolling thunder.* **7.** folded over as if on a cylinder: *a rolling collar.* —*n.* act of a person or thing that rolls or is rolling.

rolling mill **1.** factory where metal is made into sheets, bars, or plates by being passed between heavy rollers. **2.** machine with rollers for doing this.

at; āpe; cär; end; mē; it; īce; hot; ōld; fôrk; wood; fōōl; oil; out; up; ūse; turn; sing; thin; this; zh in treasure; ə in ago, taken, pencil, lemon, circus.

rolling pin, smooth cylinder with a handle at each end, used to roll out dough.
rolling stock, locomotives, cars, and other wheeled vehicles of a railroad.
roll-top desk (rōl′top′) writing desk with a slatted movable top that can be rolled back.
ro·ly-po·ly (rō′lē pō′lē) *adj.* short and plump; pudgy: *a roly-poly child.* —*n. pl.,* **-lies. 1.** short, plump person or thing. **2.** *British.* cakelike pudding made of seasoned jam or fruit spread on dough, rolled up, and cooked in any of various ways.
Rom. 1. Roman. **2.** Romans (New Testament). **3.** Romance (languages).
Ro·ma·ic (rō mā′ik) *n.* vernacular of modern Greece. —*adj.* relating to this speech or to those who use it.
ro·maine (rō mān′) *n.* **1.** narrow crisp leaves of a lettuce plant, variety *longifolia,* forming a long loose head. **2.** the plant itself. [French *romaine,* from *romain* Roman (with reference to its having come from Avignon when Avignon was the papal residence), from Latin *Rōmānus* relating to Rome.]
Ro·man (rō′mən) *adj.* **1.** of or relating to ancient or modern Rome, its people, or their culture. **2.** of or relating to the Roman Catholic Church or its members. **3.** *usually,* **roman.** of or designating the most widely used style of type or lettering, characterized by upright letters. This sentence is in roman type. **4.** of or designating a style of architecture used in ancient Rome, characterized esp. by the arch, vault, and dome and by the use of brick and concrete. —*n.* **1.** native, inhabitant, or citizen of ancient or modern Rome. **2.** *usually,* **roman.** roman type or lettering. [Latin *Rōmānus* relating to Rome, from *Rōma* Rome.]
ro·man à clef (rô mäN′ ä klā′) *pl.,* **romans à clef** (rô mäNz′ ä klā′). novel in which real people and events are depicted in disguised form. [French *roman à clef* literally, novel with a key, going back to Latin *Rōmānus* (see ROMAN) + *ad* to, at + *clāvis* key. See ROMANCE.]
Roman candle, firework consisting of a long tube that shoots out balls of fire and different kinds of sparks.
Roman Catholic 1. of, relating to, or characteristic of the Roman Catholic Church. **2.** member of the Roman Catholic Church.
Roman Catholic Church, Christian church that recognizes the pope as its supreme head.
Roman Catholicism, beliefs, practices, and system of government of the Roman Catholic Church.
ro·mance (rō mans′, rō′mans) *n.* **1.** love affair. **2.** quality or appearance of love, excitement, mystery, or adventure: *the romance of the sea. The dim lights lent an air of romance to the room.* **3.** interest in or tendency toward that which is exciting, adventurous, mysterious, or amorous. **4.** work of literature primarily concerned with a love story. **5.** narrative in prose or verse dealing with heroes and their deeds, esp. one about knights and chivalry: *Arthurian romance.* **6.** any narrative, esp. a novel, emphasizing adventure, mysterious events, or exotic settings: *Gothic romance.* **7.** fanciful or exaggerated account. —*v.i.,* **-manced, -manc·ing. 1.** to behave or speak in a romantic way. **2.** to compose or relate fanciful stories. —*v.t. Informal.* to make love to; court; woo. [Old French *romanz* (later, *roman*) work written in a Romance language, from Late Latin *Rōmānicē* in a Romance language, from Latin *Rōmānus* relating to Rome.] —**ro·manc′er,** *n.*
Romance languages, languages descended from Latin, including French, Italian, Spanish, Portuguese, Romanian, Catalan, and Provençal.
Roman Empire, empire of ancient Rome ranging from Britain to North Africa to the Persian Gulf, begun under the Emperor Augustus in 27 B.C., reaching its greatest extent under Trajan by A.D. 117, and continuing until A.D. 395, when it was divided into the Eastern Roman Empire and the Western Roman Empire.
Ro·man·esque (rō′mə nesk′) *adj.* **1.** of, relating to, or designating the style of architecture that flourished in western Europe during the eleventh and twelfth centuries, characterized by massive stone construction, rounded arches and vaults, and elaborate ornamentation. **2.** of or designating a corresponding style of art or sculpture. —*n.* Romanesque style of architecture, art, or sculpture.
Ro·ma·ni·a (rō mā′nē ə) *also,* **Rou·ma·ni·a, Ru·ma·ni·a.** *n.* country in southeastern Europe, in the northeastern part of the Balkan Peninsula. Capital, Bucharest. Area, 91,700 sq. mi. Pop. (1969 est.), 20,-010,000.
Ro·ma·ni·an (rō mā′nē ən) *also,* **Rou·ma·ni·an, Ru·ma·ni·an.** *adj.* of or relating to Romania, its people, or their language. —*n.* **1.** native or inhabitant of Romania. **2.** Romance language containing words borrowed from Slavic and other languages, spoken predominantly in Romania and parts of the southwestern Soviet Union.
Ro·man·ism (rō′mə niz′əm) *n.* Roman Catholicism. ▲ used in a derogatory manner. —**Ro′man·ist,** *n.*
Roman nose, nose with a jutting or prominent bridge.
Roman numeral, any of the numerals I, V, X, L, C, D, M or any

combination of these, used in the ancient Roman system of notation. I = 1, V = 5, X = 10, L = 50, C = 100, D = 500, and M = 1000. The value of any combination of numerals is their sum, except when one is preceded by another of smaller value. In this case the smaller is subtracted from the larger. VI = 6, but IV = 4.
Ro·ma·no cheese (rō mä′nō) sharp, hard cheese having a blackgreen rind, grated and served over food, esp. spaghetti and other pasta. [Italian *romano* Roman, from Latin *Rōmānus.*]
Ro·ma·nov (rō′mə nôf′, -nof′, rō mä′nəf) *also,* **Ro·ma·noff. 1.** dynasty that ruled Russia from 1613 to 1917. **2. Mi·kha·il Feo·do·ro·vich** (mi KHī ēl′ fyô′dər ə vich). 1596–1645, czar of Russia from 1613 to 1645, founder of this dynasty.
Ro·mans (rō′mənz) *n.,pl.* book of the New Testament, a letter from Saint Paul to the Christians of Rome. ▲ construed as singular.
ro·man·tic (rō man′tik) *adj.* **1.** relating to, characterized by, or having thoughts and feelings of love. **2.** of or relating to the quality or appearance of adventure, excitement, or mystery: *the romantic life of Robin Hood.* **3.** suitable for or conducive to love or romance: *a romantic setting.* **4.** not practical or real; visionary; idealized: *romantic notions.* **5.** *also,* **Romantic.** of or relating to romanticism in art, literature, or music. —*n.* **1.** romantic person. **2.** romanticist. [French *romantique* emotional, relating to romanticism, from Middle French *romant* tale in a Roman language, from Late Latin *Rōmānicē* in a Romance language. See ROMANCE.] —**ro·man′ti·cal·ly,** *adv.*
ro·man·ti·cism (rō man′tə siz′əm) *n.* **1.** *also,* **Romanticism.** style that prevailed in literature, music, and art during the last part of the eighteenth century and the first half of the nineteenth century, characterized typically by spontaneous feeling, appreciation of nature, and disregard of rules and forms. **2.** spirit, quality, or feeling of romance.
ro·man·ti·cist (rō man′tə sist) *n.* adherent of romanticism in literature, music, or art.
ro·man·ti·cize (rō man′tə sīz′) *-cized, -ciz·ing. v.t.* to invest with a romantic spirit or character; make romantic. —*v.i.* to act, talk, or think romantically.
Romantic Movement, romanticism in literature, music, and art in the late eighteenth century and early nineteenth century in Europe and America.
Rom·a·ny (rom′ə nē, rō′mə-) *pl.,* **-nies.** *n.* **1.** Gypsy. **2.** language of the Gypsies, belonging to the Indo-Iranian branch of the Indo-European language family. —*adj.* of or relating to the Gypsies or their language.
Rome (rōm) *n.* **1.** capital of Italy, on the Tiber, and former capital and center of the ancient Roman republic and the Roman Empire. It is the site of Vatican City, the headquarters of the pope and the Roman Catholic Church. Pop. (1968 est.), 2,656,104. **2.** the ancient Roman republic. **3.** Roman Empire. **4.** Roman Catholic Church: *Henry VIII of England broke completely from Rome in 1534.* **5.** city in central New York. Pop. (1970), 50,148.
Ro·me·o (rō′mē ō′) *n.* **1.** hero of Shakespeare's tragedy *Romeo and Juliet.* **2.** a male lover.
Rom·ney, George (rom′nē, rum′-) 1734–1802, English painter.
romp (romp) *v.i.* to play or frolic in a lively or boisterous way. —*n.* lively or boisterous play; frolic: *The boy and his dog went for a romp in the woods.* [Form of RAMP².]
romp·er (rom′pər) *n.* **1.** rompers. loose one-piece garment combining trousers and a top, worn by young children. **2.** one who romps.
Rom·u·lus and Remus (rom′yə ləs) *Roman Mythology.* twin sons of Mars and the founders of the city of Rome, who were abandoned as infants and raised by wolves.
ron·deau (ron′dō, ron dō′) *pl.,* **ron·deaux** (ron′dōz, ron dōz′). *n.* poem consisting of ten or thirteen lines, using two rhymes, with the opening words used in the middle and at the end as a refrain. [French *rondeau,* form of Old French *rondel* form of lyric poem (in which the first two lines are repeated or come round), from *rond* circular, from Latin *rotundus.*]
ron·do (ron′dō, ron dō′) *pl.,* **-dos.** *n.* musical composition or movement having a principal theme that is stated at least three times in the same key and in which return is made after the introduction of each subordinate theme. [Italian *rondo,* from French *rondeau* rondeau. See RONDEAU.]
Rönt·gen (rent′gən) Roentgen.
rood (rōōd) *n.* **1.** unit of land measure equal to 40 square rods; one-fourth of an acre. **2.** cross or crucifix, esp. a large crucifix over an altar. [Old English *rōd* pole¹, cross, measure of land.]
roof (rōōf, roof) *n.* **1.** external covering of the top of a building. **2.** something resembling a roof in position or function, as the upper part of the mouth or the top of a car. **3.** house or home. —*v.t.* to provide or cover with a roof. [Old English *hrōf* external covering of the top of a building.]
roof·er (rōō′fər, roof′ər) *n.* one who constructs or repairs roofs.
roof·ing (rōō′fing, roof′ing) *n.* material used to construct roofs.

roof·less (rōōf′lis, roof′lis) *adj.* **1.** having no roof. **2.** having no shelter; homeless.

roof·tree (rōōf′trē′, roof′-) *n.* ridgepole of a roof.

rook[1] (rook) *n.* **1.** Eurasian bird, *Corvus frugilegus,* closely related to and resembling the crow. Length: 18 inches. **2.** one who cheats, esp. at dice or cards. —*v.t.* to cheat; swindle. [Old English *hrōc* the bird.]

rook[2] (rook) *n.* any of the four chess pieces, two to each player, that may move any number of spaces parallel to the sides of the board. Also, **cas′tle.** [Old French *roc,* from Persian *rukh.*]

Rook[2]

rook·er·y (rook′ər ē) *pl.,* **-er·ies.** *n.* **1.** breeding place or colony of rooks. **2.** breeding place or colony of other birds or of animals, as penguins and seals.

rook·ie (rook′ē) *n. Informal.* **1.** inexperienced recruit. **2.** inexperienced athlete, esp. a professional player in his first year with a major league team. **3.** any novice. [Modification (influenced by ROOK[1]) of RECRUIT.]

room (rōōm, room) *n.* **1.** area that is or may be occupied by something; space: *Is there enough room in the corner to put the desk there? We have room for one more in the car.* **2.** interior area divided by walls or partitions from the rest of the structure in which it is found: *a house with seven rooms.* **3.** people in such an area: *The whole room stared as she walked by.* **4.** suitable scope; opportunity: *There is room for improvement in your work.* **5. rooms.** living quarters; lodgings: *The student took rooms near the campus.* —*v.i.* to live in a room or rooms; lodge: *We roomed together at college.* [Old English *rūm* space.]

room and board, lodging and meals.

room·er (rōō′mər, room′ər) *n.* one who occupies a rented room or rooms in another's house; lodger.

room·ette (rōō met′, room-) *n.* small private compartment on a railroad sleeping car.

room·ful (rōōm′fool′, room′-) *pl.,* **-fuls.** *n.* **1.** as much or as many as a room will hold. **2.** people or objects in a room.

rooming house, house with furnished rooms for rent.

room·mate (rōōm′māt′, room′-) *n.* person, or one of the persons, with whom one shares a room or rooms.

room·y (rōō′mē, room′ē) **room·i·er, room·i·est.** *adj.* having ample room; large; spacious. —**room′i·ness,** *n.*

Roo·se·velt (rō′zə velt′, -volt) **1. (Anna)** Eleanor. 1884–1962, U.S. humanitarian, writer, and diplomat; wife of Franklin D. Roosevelt. **2.** Franklin Del·a·no (del′ə nō′). 1882–1945, thirty-second president of the United States, from 1933 to 1945. **3.** Theodore. 1858–1919, twenty-sixth president of the United States from 1901 to 1909.

roost (rōōst) *n.* **1.** perch on which birds, esp. domestic fowl, rest or sleep. **2.** place for birds to rest or sleep for the night. **3.** place in which people rest, stay, or congregate. **4. to rule the roost.** to have unchallenged control; dominate. **5. to come home to roost.** to have repercussions on the originator, esp. unpleasant ones: *A crime often comes home to roost.* —*v.i.* **1.** to rest or sleep on or as on a roost. **2.** to settle or lodge, esp. for the night. [Old English *hrōst* resting place for birds.]

roost·er (rōōs′tər) *n.* male of the domestic fowl. Also, **cock.**

root[1] (rōōt, root) *n.* **1.** lower part of a plant that grows downward, serving to anchor the plant in the soil. Roots absorb water and dissolved nutrients from the soil and store food. **2.** any of various underground plant parts, as a tuber or rhizome. **3.** attached or embedded part of an organ or structure: *the root of a tooth, the root of a hair.* **4.** that from which anything derives; origin; source: *to trace the roots of a revolution.* **5.** basic part; essence; core: *We must get to the root of the problem.* **6. roots.** condition or feeling of being settled and having ties to a particular place, society, or tradition: *He had moved so often that he had no roots anywhere.* **7.** *Linguistics.* basic word to which affixes are added to form other words. *Faith* is the root of *faithful, faithless,* and *unfaithful.* **8.** *Mathematics.* **a.** quantity that, when multiplied by itself a specified number of times, will produce a given quantity. 3 is the square root of 9 and the cube root of 27. **b.** quantity that, when substituted for an unknown quantity in an equation, will satisfy the equation. **9.** *Music.* **a.** tone from whose overtones a chord is constructed. **b.** lowest tone of a chord. **10. to take root. a.** to develop roots and begin to grow. **b.** to become firmly settled or established. —*v.i.* **1.** to develop roots and begin to grow: *These plants will not root in such arid soil.* **2.** to be or become firmly settled or established. —*v.t.* **1.** to fix or implant by or as by roots. **2.** to pull, tear, or dig by or as by the roots; remove completely (with *up* or *out*): *to root up a weed, to root out an informer.* [Old Norse *rōt* underground part of a plant.]

root[2] (rōōt, root) *v.i.* **1.** to turn up or dig in the earth or as with the snout or nose. **2.** to search for something; rummage. —*v.t.* **1.** to turn up or dig with or as with the snout or nose. [Old English *wrōtan* to turn up with the snout.] —**root′er,** *n.*

root[3] (rōōt, root) *v.i.* **1.** to give encouragement to a contestant or team, as by applauding or shouting; cheer (with *for*). **2.** to lend support or

wish success to someone or something: *We're all rooting for you to win the scholarship.* [Possibly a form of earlier *rout* to make a loud noise; probably of Scandinavian origin.] —**root′er,** *n.*

Root, El·i·hu (rōōt; el′ə hū′) 1845–1937, U.S. lawyer and statesman.

root beer, nonalcoholic beverage made from the extracted juice of the roots of various plants, as sarsaparilla or sassafras.

root hair, thin, hairlike projection of a plant root that absorbs water and dissolved minerals from the soil.

root·less (rōōt′lis, root′-) *adj.* **1.** without ties to a particular place, society, or tradition. **2.** having no roots. —**root′less·ness,** *n.*

root·let (rōōt′lit, root′-) *n.* small root.

root·stock (rōōt′stok′, root′-) *n.* **1.** rhizome. **2.** source; origin.

rope (rōp) *n.* **1.** strong cord made of twisted or intertwined strands of fiber, wire, or similar material. **2.** string of things joined together by twisting, twining, or threading: *a rope of pearls.* **3.** hangman's noose. **4.** execution or death by hanging. **5.** lasso. **6.** sticky, threadlike formation, as in a liquid. **7. to know the ropes.** *Informal.* to be familiar with all aspects of an activity. **8. the end of one's rope.** *Informal.* to be at the end of one's strength, patience, or resources. —*v.t.,* **roped, rop·ing. 1.** to tie, bind, or fasten with or as with a rope. **2.** to separate or enclose with a rope: *to rope off a street for a parade.* **3.** to catch with a lasso. **4. to rope in.** *Informal.* to persuade or involve by deceit; take in. —*v.i.* to form threadlike, sticky strands. [Old English *rāp* strong, twisted cord.] —**rop′er,** *n.*

rope·danc·er (rōp′dan′sər) *n.* one who dances, walks, or does stunts on the tightrope.

rope·walk (rōp′wôk′) *n.* long, narrow area, as a covered path or building, where ropes are made.

rope·walk·er (rōp′wô′kər) *n.* ropedancer.

rop·y (rō′pē) **rop·i·er, rop·i·est.** *adj.* **1.** forming or having sticky threads, as some liquids. **2.** like a rope or cord. —**rop′i·ness,** *n.*

roque (rōk) *n.* difficult form of croquet played on a hard-surfaced court. [Modification of CROQUET.]

Roque·fort cheese (rōk′fərt) cream-colored cheese veined with a blue mold. It is pungent in taste, and often crumbly in texture. [From *Roquefort,* a town in France where it was originally made.]

ror·qual (rôr′kwəl) *n.* finback. [French *rorqual,* from Norwegian *röyrkval* literally, red whale (with reference to its red streaks).]

Ror·schach test (rôr′shäk) psychological test of personality in which a subject interprets each of a series of ink blots. [From Hermann *Rorschach,* 1884–1922, Swiss psychiatrist who developed it.]

ro·sa·ceous (rō zā′shəs) *adj.* **1.** of or relating to the rose family. **2.** resembling a rose. [Latin *rosāceus,* from *rosa* rose[1].]

Ro·sa·ri·o (rō zär′ē ō′, -sär′-) *n.* port city in east-central Argentina, on the Paraná. Pop. (1960), 591,428.

ro·sa·ry (rō′zər ē) *pl.,* **-ries.** *n.* **1.a.** in the Roman Catholic Church, a string of beads used for counting in the recitation of prayers. **b.** series of prayers said with these beads, commonly consisting of fifteen decades of Ave Marias, each decade preceded by a paternoster and followed by a Gloria Patri. **2.** string of beads used similarly in other religions. [Medieval Latin *rosarium,* from Latin *rosā·rium* rose garden, from *rosa* rose[1].]

rose[1] (rōz) *n.* **1.** fragrant flower of any of a large group of plants, genus *Rosa,* usually having from three to nine toothed leaflets and growing in a variety of colors. Roses are among the most widely cultivated of all garden flowers. **2.** woody plant bearing this flower, having thorny stems that are usually erect and stout, but which sometimes trail or climb. **3.** pinkish-red color. **4.** something resembling a rose in shape or form. **5.** rosette. **6.** round, perforated nozzle on a pipe or watering can. **7.** compass card. **8.** type of gem cut characterized by a flat base and a many-faceted top. —*adj.* designating a large family, Rosaceae, of flowering plants, shrubs, and trees that grow in temperate parts of the world. Many plants of the family are cultivated for their fruits and flowers, as apple and cherry trees and strawberry and rose bushes. [Old English *rose* the flower and plant, from Latin *rosa.*]

rose[2] (rōz) past tense of **rise.**

ro·sé (rō zā′) *n.* pink, usually dry, table wine made from red grapes whose skins are removed early in the fermentation process. [French *rosé* this wine, pink, from *rose* rose[1], from Latin *rosa.*]

ro·se·ate (rō′zē it, -āt′) *adj.* **1.** rose-colored; rosy. **2.** optimistic; promising.

Tea rose   Shrub rose

Hybrid perpetual rose

Roses

rose·bud (rōz′bud′) *n.* bud of a rose.
rose·bush (rōz′boosh′) *n.* plant bearing roses.
rose-col·ored (rōz′kul′ərd) *adj.* **1.** pinkish-red. **2.** seeing or viewed with optimism; optimistic.
Rose·crans, William Starke (rōz′krans; stärk) 1819–98, Union general in the Civil War.
rose fever, form of hay fever believed to be caused by the pollen of roses.
rose·fish (rōz′fish′) *pl.* **-fish** or **-fish·es.** *n.* orange-red food fish, *Sebastes marinus,* found in the North Atlantic.
rose geranium, geranium, *Pelargonium odoratissimum,* having fragrant, narrowly divided leaves and yielding an oil used in the manufacture of perfume and soap.
rose mallow, any of a large group of plants, genus *Hibiscus,* of the mallow family, esp. *H. moscheutos,* a hairy marsh herb, widely cultivated for its pink or white flowers.
rose·mar·y (rōz′mâr′ē) *pl.* **-mar·ies.** *n.* **1.** fragrant lance-shaped leaves of an evergreen shrub, *Rosmarinus officinalis,* of the mint family, used as an herb. **2.** shrub bearing these leaves, having pale-blue tubular flowers borne in clusters. The leaves and flowers yield an oil that is used in the manufacture of perfume, soap, and other products. [Modification (influenced by ROSE[1] and MARY) of obsolete *rosmarine,* from Latin *rōs marīnus* literally, dew of the sea.]
rose of Sharon, Asian shrub, *Hibiscus syriacus,* of the mallow family, bearing oval or lobed leaves and cultivated for its bell-shaped flowers which may be red, purple, violet, or white.
Ro·set·ta stone (rō zet′ə) basalt slab inscribed with a decree written in 196 B.C., found in 1799 near Rosetta, Egypt. Written in hieroglyphics, demotic characters, and Greek, it provided the key to deciphering ancient Egyptian writing.
ro·sette (rō zet′) *n.* **1.** ornament, usually made of gathered or pleated ribbon in the shape of a rose, used as a decoration or as a badge of honor or office. **2.** any object, structure, or arrangement shaped like a rose, as a circular carved or molded architectural ornament, or a circlet of leaves radiating from a central point. [French *rosette* rose-shaped object, small rose, diminutive of *rose* rose[1], from Latin *rosa.*]
rose water, preparation made either by distilling oil of roses or rose petals with water, used in cosmetics and in cooking.
rose window, circular window, usually made up of stained glass sections that radiate from a center.
rose·wood (rōz′wood′) *n.* **1.** hard, strongly grained, dark-red wood of any of several tropical evergreen trees of the pea family, widely used to make furniture, sporting goods, and other products. **2.** tree yielding such wood.

Rose window

Rosh Ha·sha·nah (rōsh′ hə shä′nə) the Jewish New Year, occurring in September or early October. [Hebrew *rōsh hashshānāh* literally, head of the year.]
Ro·si·cru·cian (rō′zə krōō′shən) *n.* **1.** member of an international fraternal society devoted to the improvement of mankind through the application of secret mystical doctrines. **2.** member of any of several similar secret societies prominent in the seventeenth and eighteenth centuries. —*adj.* of, relating to, or characteristic of the Rosicrucians. [From the Latinized form (*rosa crucis* rose of the cross) of the German name of the alleged founder of this society, Christian *Rosenkranz* literally, rosy cross.] —**Ro′si·cru′cian·ism,** *n.*
ros·in (roz′in) *n.* **1.** hard, brittle substance obtained by heating crude turpentine from pine trees in copper stills and removing the surface oil. It is used in the manufacture of paints and other products and is rubbed on the surface of certain items, as violin bows and dancers' shoes, to make them less slippery. **2.** resin (*def.* 1). —*v.t.* to rub or cover with rosin. [Form of RESIN.]
Ross (rôs) **1. Betsy.** 1752–1836, American woman reputed to have made the first American flag; born Elizabeth Griscom. **2. Sir James.** 1800–62, British polar explorer.
Ros·set·ti (rō zet′ē, -set′ē) **1. Christina Georgiana** 1830–94, English poet. **2. Dante Gabriel.** 1828–82, her brother; English poet and painter.
Ros·si·ni, Gio·ac·chi·no An·to·nio (rō sē′nē; jō′ä kē′nō än-tōn′yō) 1792–1868, Italian operatic composer.
Ross Sea, large inlet of the Pacific, on the coast of Antarctica.
Ros·tand, Edmond (rôs taN′) 1868–1918, French dramatist.
ros·ter (ros′tər) *n.* **1.** list of names. **2.** list of military officers and men enrolled for duty. [Dutch *rooster* gridiron, list (referring to the resemblance of a paper with ruled lines to a gridiron), from *roosten* to roast.]
Ros·tov (ros tôf′, ros′tov) *n.* port city in the southwestern Soviet Union, on the Don River. Pop. (1970 est.), 789,000. Also, **Ros·tov-on-Don** (ros tôf′on don′).

ros·trum (ros′trəm) *pl.,* **-trums** or **-tra** (-trə). *n.* **1.** raised area, as a platform or pulpit, used for public speaking. **2.** projection on the bow of a ship, esp. one on an ancient Roman warship used for ramming. **3.** *Biology.* beaklike part or projection. [Latin *rōstrum* beak; with reference to the platform for speakers (that was adorned with the *beaks* of captured ships) in the Roman forum.] —**ros′tral,** *adj.*
ros·y (rō′zē) **ros·i·er, ros·i·est.** *adj.* **1.** of the color rose; pinkish-red; blushing: *The baby's cheeks were rosy from the cold.* **2.** full of hope or optimism; bright; promising: *a rosy outlook on life.* —**ros′i·ly,** *adv.* —**ros′i·ness,** *n.*
rot (rot) **rot·ted, rot·ting.** *v.i.* **1.** to become damaged or ruined by breaking down in composition, as through the action of bacteria or disease: *The apples rotted on the tree.* **2.** to deteriorate, as by decay or idleness: *A man's mind can rot in prison.* **3.** to become morally corrupt; degenerate. —*v.t.* **1.** to cause to become damaged or ruined by breaking down in composition. **2.** to ret (flax or hemp). —*n.* **1.** process of rotting. **2.** that which is rotting or rotted. **3.** disease of plants caused by any of various fungi or bacteria, characterized by breakdown of tissue. **4.** any of various parasitic diseases of animals, characterized by tissue loss. **5.** *Informal.* nonsense; rubbish; trash. —*interj.* used to express disgust, disdain, or impatience. [Old English *rotian* to decay, putrefy.]
Ro·tar·i·an (rō târ′ē ən) *n.* member of a Rotary Club.
ro·ta·ry (rō′tər ē) *adj.* **1.** turning or designed to turn around an axis; rotating. **2.** characterized by or occurring with a rotating movement. **3.** having a part or parts that rotate: *a rotary plow.* —*n. pl.,* **-ta·ries.** **1.** traffic circle. **2.** rotary machine, device, or part. [Latin *rota* wheel + -ARY[1].]
Rotary Club, local club belonging to Rotary International.
rotary engine 1. internal-combustion engine in which circularly arranged cylinders revolve about a fixed crankshaft, used esp. in airplanes. **2.** any engine, as a turbine, that produces rotation or torque directly rather than by back-and-forth movement.
Rotary International, international service organization of business and professional men, founded in Chicago in 1905.
ro·tate (rō′tāt) **-tat·ed, -tat·ing.** *v.t., v.i.* **1.** to turn or cause to turn around on or as on an axis. **2.** to change or cause to change in sequence; alternate regularly: *to rotate crops. The guards will rotate every four hours.* [Latin *rotātus,* past participle of *rotāre* to turn around, revolve.]
ro·ta·tion (rō tā′shən) *n.* **1.** act or process of turning on or as on an axis. **2.** one complete turn of such movement: *The rotation of the earth takes twenty-four hours.* **3.** change or alternation in sequence: *rotation of assignments among the reporters on a newspaper.* —**ro·ta′tion·al,** *adj.*
rotation of crops, systematic alternation of the crops grown in a given field from one year to the next, esp. to prevent the loss of soil fertility or to control plant disease.
ro·ta·tor (rō′tā tər) *n.* one who or that which rotates, as a muscle that serves to rotate a part of the body. [Latin *rotātor.*]
ro·ta·to·ry (rō′tə tôr′ē) *adj.* **1.** of, relating to, or characterized by rotation. **2.** causing rotation.
ROTC, Reserve Officers' Training Corps, a U.S. military corps in which college and high school students are trained to become officers in the armed services.
rote (rōt) *n.* **1.** mechanical routine. **2. by rote.** in a mechanical way, without reference to meaning or thought: *to learn by rote, to recite by rote.* [Of uncertain origin.]
Roth·schild (rôth′chīld′, rôths′-) **1. Mey·er Am·schel** (mī′ər am′shəl). 1743–1812, German banker who founded the **House of Rothschild,** an international banking firm. **2. Nathan Meyer.** 1777–1836, his son; British banker who founded the London branch of the firm.
ro·ti·fer (rō′tə fər) *n.* any of a group of many-celled, microscopic aquatic animals, phylum Rotifer, commonly found in ponds and puddles, having a ring of cilia at one end of the body that is used for locomotion and feeding, and which resembles a rotating wheel when in motion. [Modern Latin *Rotifera,* from Latin *rota* wheel + *ferre* to carry.]
ro·tis·se·rie (rō tis′ər ē) *n.* cooking device or appliance having a rotating spit on which food is roasted.

Rotifer

ro·to·gra·vure (rō′tə grə vyoor′, -grāv′yər) *n.* **1.** printing process in which the image to be printed is reproduced on a copper surface in a pattern of depressions. These depressions are then filled with ink and the pattern is transferred under pressure to the surface to be printed. **2.** picture or print made by this process. **3.** pictorial section of a newspaper, esp. one containing pictures printed by this process. [Latin *rota* wheel + GRAVURE.]
ro·tor (rō′tər) *n.* **1.** rotating part of a motor or other machine.

2. set of large, revolving blades that lifts and moves an aircraft, as a helicopter. [Short for ROTATOR.]

rot·ten (rot′ən) *adj.* **1.** damaged or ruined by having undergone a breakdown in composition; putrid: *a rotten apple. This meat smells rotten.* **2.** unsound, as if from rotting; not safe; weak: *rotten timbers.* **3.** very bad; disagreeable; contemptible: *a rotten cold, a rotten way to act.* **4.** corrupt, dishonest, or depraved: *Something is rotten in the State of Denmark* (Shakespeare, *Hamlet*). [Old Norse *rotinn* putrid.] —**rot′ten·ly,** *adv.* —**rot′ten·ness,** *n.*

rotten borough 1. borough in England having only a few voters, but still entitled to send a representative to Parliament, abolished by reform legislation in 1832. **2.** any election district having greater representation than is warranted by its population.

Rot·ter·dam (rot′ər dam′) *n.* port city in the southwestern Netherlands, near the North Sea. Pop. (1968 est.), 704,858.

ro·tund (rō tund′) *adj.* **1.** rounded; plump: *A rotund little man waddled into the room.* **2.** full-toned; sonorous: *a rotund delivery of a speech.* [Latin *rotundus* circular. Doublet of ROUND.] —**ro·tund′ly,** *adv.* —**ro·tund′ness,** *n.*

ro·tun·da (rō tun′də) *n.* **1.** circular building or hall, esp. one having a dome. **2.** large, high-ceilinged room or hall, as a main room of a hotel. [Latin *rotunda,* feminine of *rotundus* circular.]

ro·tun·di·ty (rō tun′də tē) *pl.,* -**ties.** *n.* **1.** state or condition of being rotund; roundness; fullness. **2.** that which is round, as a part or protuberance.

Rou·ault, Georges (rōō ō′; zhôrzh) 1871–1958, French painter.

rou·ble (rōō′bəl) ruble.

rou·é (rōō ā′, rōō′ā) *n.* dissipated, lecherous man; rake; profligate. [French *roué,* from *rouer* to break on the wheel, from *roue* wheel, from Latin *rota;* originally applied to a group of eighteenth-century French profligates, with the feeling that they deserved such punishment.]

Rou·en (rōō än′, -än′) *n.* port city in northern France, on the Seine, site of Joan of Arc's execution. Pop. (1968), 120, 471.

rouge (rōōzh) *n.* **1.** any of various red or pink cosmetics used to color the cheeks. **2.** red, powdery pigment, composed chiefly of ferric oxide, used as an abrasive and polishing agent for metal, gems, and other materials. —*v.t.* **rouged, roug·ing.** to color with rouge. —*v.i.* to use cosmetic rouge. [French *rouge* red, from Latin *rubeus.*]

rouge et noir (rōōzh′ ā nwär′) gambling game in which the players bet on which color of cards will win. [French *rouge et noir* literally, red and black, from Latin *rubeus* red + *et* and + *niger* black.]

rough (ruf) *adj.* **1.** having an uneven surface; not smooth or level: *rough wood, a rough road, rough stucco walls.* **2.** characterized by or showing force, violence, or boisterousness: *Ice hockey is a rough game. A rough bunch of rowdies interrupted the speech.* **3.** having or showing harshness of temperament; brutal: *a rough way of dealing with people.* **4.** stormy; tempestuous; turbulent: *rough seas.* **5.** partially, inexactly, or hastily done: *a rough estimate, a rough sketch.* **6.** in a natural or crude state: *rough, unpolished gems.* **7.** lacking grace, culture, or refinement; uncouth: *a rough manner of talking.* **8.** characterized by strain or hardship; difficult: *a rough day on the job. The pioneers led a rough life.* **9.** having a shaggy or uneven texture; coarse: *rough wool, rough, tangled hair.* **10.** (of sound) harsh; discordant: *the rough and woeful music that we have* (Shakespeare, *Pericles, Prince of Tyre*). **11.** *Phonetics.* pronounced with the sound of *h,* as in *heaven.* —*v.t.* **1.a.** to deal with or treat violently (with *up*): *The gang roughed up their hostage before releasing him.* **b.** in football, to treat (an opponent) with unnecessary violence. **2.** to plan, shape, or sketch in an incomplete form (usually with *in* or *out*): *to rough out the layout of a house.* **3.** to make rough; roughen. **4. to rough it.** to live without the usual comforts or conveniences: *to rough it on a canoe trip.* —*adv.* in a rough manner; roughly. —*n.* **1.** rough, uneven, or difficult object, state, or condition: *to take the rough along with the smooth in life.* **2.** unmowed part of a golf course surrounding the fairways and greens. **3.** crude, rough person; ruffian; rowdy. **4. in the rough.** in a crude or unfinished condition. [Old English *rūh* not smooth, shaggy.] —**rough′ly,** *adv.* —**rough′ness,** *n.*

Syn. *adj.* **1. Rough, uneven, irregular** indicate a surface or edge that lacks smoothness or uniformity. **Rough** is the general term: *His beard was rough to the touch.* **Uneven** suggests a jagged line or a broken surface: *It was difficult moving over the uneven ground.* **Irregular** implies a fault due to the absence of smoothness, straightness, or order: *His smile showed a mouth of irregular teeth.* **7.** see **uncouth.**

rough·age (ruf′ij) *n.* **1.** coarse food material, as bran or lettuce, that has a relatively high percentage of cellulose and other indigestible constituents, and serves to stimulate peristalsis in the digestive tract. **2.** any rough or coarse material.

rough-and-read·y (ruf′ən red′ē) *adj.* rough and crude, but effective in use or action.

rough-and-tum·ble (ruf′ən tum′bəl) *adj.* characterized by roughness, violence, and disregard for rules: *a rough-and-tumble fight.* —*n.* rough fight or struggle.

rough·cast (ruf′kast′) *n.* **1.** coarse plaster for covering an outside surface, as a wall. **2.** rough or preliminary model or form. —*v.t.* -**cast,** -**cast·ing. 1.** to cover with roughcast. **2.** to make or shape in a rough or preliminary form.

rough·dry (ruf′drī′) -**dried,** -**dry·ing.** *v.t.* to dry (laundry) without smoothing or ironing. —*v.t., v.i.* to make or become rough.

rough·en (ruf′ən) *v.t., v.i.* to make or become rough.

rough·hew (ruf′hū′) -**hewed,** -**hewed** or -**hewn, hew·ing.** *v.t.* **1.** to hew (something, as timber or stone) without smoothing or finishing. **2.** to shape in rough or preliminary form; roughcast: *There is a divinity that shapes our ends, roughhew them how we will* (Shakespeare, *Hamlet*). —**rough′hewn′,** *adj.*

rough·house (ruf′hous′) *n.* rough, boisterous play or conduct. —*v.i.,* -**housed,** -**hous·ing.** to behave or play in a rough, boisterous way. —*v.t.* to handle or treat in a rough, unrestrained manner, esp. in fun.

rough·neck (ruf′nek′) *n. Informal.* rough, belligerent person; rowdy.

rough·rid·er (ruf′rī′dər) *n.* **1.** one who breaks in or rides wild, untrained horses. **2. Roughrider.** member of the First U.S. Cavalry Volunteers, a regiment recruited in 1898 by Theodore Roosevelt and Leonard Wood to fight in the Spanish–American War.

rough·shod (ruf′shod′) *adj.* **1.** having horseshoes with calks or other projections to prevent slipping. **2. to ride roughshod over.** to treat roughly and with arrogance; be inconsiderate to.

rou·lade (rōō läd′) *n.* **1.** musical embellishment consisting of a rapid succession of notes sung to one syllable. **2.** thin slice of meat rolled around a filling and cooked. [French *roulade,* from *rouler* to roll, revolve, from Old French *rouler.* See ROLL.]

rou·lette (rōō let′) *n.* **1.** gambling game in which the players bet on which compartment of a wheel a ball will come to rest in after the wheel has been spun. **2.** small wheel with a raised pattern used to make repeating marks or holes when rolled over a surface. [French *roulette* gambling game, small wheel, going back to *roue* wheel, from Latin *rota.*]

Rou·ma·ni·a (rōō mā′nē ə, -mān′yə) Romania.

Rou·ma·ni·an (rōō mā′nē ən, -mān′yən) Romanian.

round (round) *adj.* **1.** shaped like a sphere or part of a sphere; spherical, as a globe or ball. **2.** shaped like a circle or part of a circle; circular, as a tire: *a table with round edges.* **3.** having circular cross sections; cylindrical: *a round tower.* **4.** having a curved surface; not angular or flat: *round shoulders, a plump, round body.* **5.** full; complete; entire: *a round dozen.* **6.** liberal, as in amount or volume; ample; large: *a round sum of money.* **7.** expressed to the nearest whole number or to a convenient multiple of five or ten. In round numbers, 498 would be 500. **6.** is the round figure for 5%. **8.** quick and vigorous; brisk: *The horses proceeded at a good, round pace.* **9.** full and mellow; sonorous: *The piano had a rich, round tone.* **10.** candid; outspoken; blunt: *a round assertion.* **11.** *Phonetics.* pronounced with the lips assuming a nearly oval shape: *a round vowel.* —*n.* **1.** something round in shape; that which is spherical, circular, or cylindrical. **2. rounds.** fixed or customary course, action, or duty: *the postman's rounds, a doctor's rounds.* **3.** recurring or successive series, as of actions or events: *a round of duties, a round of parties.* **4.** single outburst, as of applause or cheering. **5.** any of various periods or sections into which certain sports and games are divided: *a round of golf, a boxing match of ten rounds.* **6.** *Music.* short song in which each section is the same length as, and can be harmonized with, any other section. It is sung by three or more voices, each voice beginning in turn at equal intervals. "Row, Row, Row Your Boat" is a round. **7.a.** single discharge of a firearm. **b.** ammunition for a single shot. **8.** one service of an alcoholic drink to each of the members of a group. **9.** cut of beef just above the hind shank, between the leg and the rump. **10.** round dance. **11.** movement in a circle or about an axis; revolution. **12. in the round. a.** performed on or having a central stage surrounded by seats. **b.** in full sculptured form, standing free from any background. **13. to go** (or **make) the rounds.** to be passed continually from one person or place to another; be in circulation. —*v.t.* **1.** to make round in shape: *The sculptor rounded the clay into a sphere.* **2.** to pass or travel to the other side of; go around: *to round a corner. They rounded the tip of the peninsula.* **3.** to make complete; finish or perfect (usually with *off* or *out*): *We are such stuff as dreams are made on; and our little life is rounded with a sleep* (Shakespeare, *The Tempest*). *He rounded out the concert with an encore.* **4.** to express as a round number (usually with *off*): *Round off 1457 to the nearest hundred.* **5.** *Phonetics.* to pronounce with the lips nearly oval. **6. to round up.** to gather or drive together; assemble: *to round up cattle, to round up all the children at a party.* —*v.i.* **1.** to become round in shape. **2.** to turn or spin around. **3.** to become complete, full, or finished (usually with *into* or *out*): *The child rounded out into a lovely young woman.* **4.** to take a circular or curved course. —*adv.* **1.** around: *The top went round and round.* **2.** through a recurring or complete period of time; from beginning to end: *He now lives in Florida the whole year*

round. —*prep.* **1.** around: *The crowd gathered round the speaker.* **2.** all during; throughout: *round the year.* ▲ **Round** and **around** may be used interchangeably in their adverbial and prepositional senses. *Around* is more common in American usage: *They hunted around until they found the still* (Faulkner, 1931). In British use, *round* is generally preferred: *He gripped my wrist and twisted it round* (Orwell, 1950). [Old French *ront* circular, from Latin *rotundus*. Doublet of RO-TUND.] —**round′ness,** *n.*

round·a·bout (round′ə bout′) *adj.* circuitous; indirect: *a roundabout route, a roundabout way of saying something.* —*n.* **1.** formerly, a short, tight-fitting jacket for men or boys. **2.** *British.* **a.** merry-go-round. **b.** traffic circle.

round dance **1.** any of several ballroom dances characterized by circular or revolving movements, as the waltz or the polka. **2.** folk dance in which the dancers move in a circle.

roun·del (round′əl) *n.* **1.** round form or figure, as a window or panel. **2.** rondeau. **3.** roundelay *(def. 2).* [Old French *roundel* form of lyric poetry. See RONDEAU.]

roun·de·lay (round′əl ā′) *n.* **1.** song in which a section, phrase, or line, esp. the first verse, is continually repeated. **2.** dance performed in a circle. [Old French *rondelet,* diminutive of *rondel* form of lyric poetry; confused with *lay*[1] song. See RONDEAU.]

round·er (roun′dər) *n.* **1.** habitual drunkard or petty criminal; dissolute drifter. **2. rounders.** English game similar to baseball. ▲ construed as singular. **3.** one who or that which rounds, esp. a tool for rounding the edges or surface of something.

Round·head (round′hed′) *n.* member of the Puritan or Parliamentary party during the English civil war from 1642 to 1652. [From the short-cropped hair of the members of this party, as distinguished from the long hair of their opponents, the Cavaliers.]

round·house (round′hous′) *n.* **1.** circular building with a turntable in the center, used for housing, repairing, and switching locomotives. **2.** cabin on the rear part of the quarterdeck of a ship. **3.** blow delivered with a wide swing of the arm. **4.** pitch in baseball in which the ball makes a slow, wide curve.

round·ish (roun′dish) *adj.* somewhat round.

round·ly (round′lē) *adv.* **1.** in a frank, straightforward manner; bluntly; candidly: *He denounced the proposal roundly.* **2.** fully; thoroughly: *to be beaten roundly.* **3.** in a round form.

round robin **1.** tournament, as in tennis, in which each player or team plays every other player or team. **2.** document, as a petition, circulated for signature or comment, esp. one in which the signatures are arranged in a circle so as to disguise the order of signing.

round·shoul·dered (round′shōl′dərd) *adj.* having the shoulders bent forward so that the shoulders and upper back appear rounded.

round steak steak cut from the round section of beef.

Round Table **1.** *Arthurian Legend.* table around which King Arthur and his knights sat. It was round to prevent quarrels about the order of seating. **2.** King Arthur and his knights. **3. round table. a.** group of persons gathered for a conference or discussion. **b.** such a conference or discussion. —**round′ta′ble,** *adj.*

round-the-clock (round′thə klok′) *adj., adv.* throughout the twenty-four hours of the day: *round-the-clock negotiations.*

round trip trip to a place and back to the starting point. —**round′-trip′,** *adj.*

round·up (round′up′) *n.* **1.** act of bringing scattered cattle together, as for counting, branding, or selling. **2.** men and horses engaged in this. **3.** any gathering together, as of people, objects, or data: *a news roundup, a roundup of criminal suspects.*

round·worm (round′wurm′) *n.* any nematode worm, esp. a species, *Ascaris lumbricoides,* that lives as a parasite in the intestines of man and other animals.

rouse (rouz) *roused, rous·ing. v.t.* **1.** to cause to awaken from sleep, unconsciousness, or a similar resting condition: *Sounds of gunfire roused us at daybreak.* **2.** to stir up, as to action or strong emotion; excite: *His tirade roused the crowd to a frenzy.* —*v.i.* **1.** to awaken from sleep, unconsciousness, or a similar resting position. **2.** to become active or excited. [Of uncertain origin.] —**rous′er,** *n.*

rous·ing (rou′zing) *adj.* **1.** able to inspire enthusiasm or excitement; stirring: *a rousing cheer.* **2.** brisk; active; lively: *to do a rousing business.* **3.** *Informal.* extraordinary; astonishing.

Rous·seau (rōō sō′) **1.** Hen·ri (äN rē′). 1844–1910, French painter. **2.** Jean Jacques (zhän zhäk). 1712–78, French philosopher and writer, born in Switzerland.

roust·a·bout (roust′ə bout′) *n.* **1.** unskilled, often transient laborer, esp. one who works on a ranch or at an oil-drilling site. **2.** laborer on a dock or ship. **3.** laborer at a circus who sets up and dismantles the tents. [Dialectal *roust* to rout out (possibly modification of ROUSE) + ABOUT.]

rout[1] (rout) *n.* **1.** overwhelming defeat. **2.** disorderly flight or retreat after a defeat. —*v.t.* **1.** to defeat overwhelmingly: *to rout a team in*

football. **2.** to put to disorderly flight. [Old French *route* defeat, going back to Latin *rupta,* feminine past participle of *rumpere* to break; because a defeat implies the breaking up of an army.]

rout[2] (rout) *v.t.* **1.** to uncover by searching; bring to view; discover (with *out*): *to rout out the traitors in an organization.* **2.** to drive or force out; expel: *The storm routed us from our homes.* **3.** to dig up with the snout. —*v.i.* **1.** to dig with the snout. **2.** to search; rummage. [Form of ROOT[1].]

route (rōōt) *n.* **1.** course, road, or way for travel: *a trade route, an overland route, to take the most direct route.* **2.a.** territory covered by a salesman or deliveryman: *a milk route, a newspaper route.* **b.** job of servicing or the right to service such a route. —*v.t.,* **rout·ed, rout·ing. 1.** to arrange the route or itinerary for: *Our travel agent routed us through Europe. The new subway line was routed through the financial district.* **2.** to send by a certain route; dispatch. [Old French *route* way, path, going back to Latin *rupta,* feminine past participle of *rumpere* to break; because a route was originally a path broken through a forest.]

Syn. *n.* **1.** Route, passage, course mean a path along which a person or thing moves or travels to reach a place. Route suggests a planned and established way followed regularly: *Which is the best route to Chicago?* Passage is a way for traveling toward a desired destination, esp. a narrow channel that affords transit: *The river is our only passage in the rainy season.* Course is often restricted to a route followed by a natural moving object and determined by natural rather than human influence: *This stream has changed its course since last summer.*

rou·tine (rōō tēn′) *n.* **1.** fixed method of doing something; regular procedure: *a person's daily routine. The children had established an elaborate bedtime routine.* **2.** habitual repetition of actions or procedures: *We were bored with the routine of camp life.* **3.** theatrical act or part of an act, as a funny story or a dance number. —*adj.* **1.** in accordance with or using routine; regular; habitual: *routine chores, routine complaints.* **2.** not creative or original; commonplace: *a routine performance.* [French *routine* regular procedure, diminutive of *route* way, path. See ROUTE.]

rove[1] (rōv) *roved, rov·ing. v.i.* to move aimlessly from place to place; wander about. —*v.t.* to wander over or through. [Probably of Scandinavian origin.] —**Syn.** *v.i.* see ROAM.

rove[2] (rōv) *v.* past tense and a past participle of REEVE[2].

rov·er[1] (rō′vər) *n.* one who roves; wanderer. [ROVE[1] + -ER[1].]

rov·er[2] (rō′vər) *n. Archaic.* **1.** pirate. **2.** pirate ship. [Middle Dutch *rover* robber.]

row[1] (rō) *n.* **1.** series of people or things arranged in a line; line: *a row of trees. The children stood in rows.* **2.** line of seats, as in a theater or classroom: *We were seated in the last row.* **3.a.** line of houses on a street. **b.** street lined with buildings on both sides. **4. hard** (or **long**) **row to hoe.** tiresome, difficult task. [Old English *rāw, rǣw* line[1].]

row[2] (rō) *v.i.* to use oars to propel a boat. —*v.t.* **1.** to propel, as a boat, by the use of oars. **2.** to transport in a boat by rowing: *to row a person to shore.* **3.** to engage in (a race or contest) by using oars. **4.** (of a boat) to have or be propelled by (a specified number of oars). **5.** to use (oars, rowers, or a certain stroke) in rowing a race. **6.** to row against in a race. —*n.* act or instance of using oars. [Old English *rōwan* to use oars to propel a boat.] —**row′er,** *n.*

row[3] (rou) *n.* **1.** a noisy quarrel or fight. **2.** disturbance; commotion; clamor. —*v.i.* to engage in a noisy quarrel or disturbance. [Of uncertain origin.]

row·an (rō′an, rou′-) *n.* **1.** reddish, berrylike fruit of a Eurasian mountain ash, *Sorbus aucuparia,* belonging to the rose family. Also, **row′-an·ber′ry. 2.** the tree itself, raised for its hard wood. [Of Scandinavian origin.]

row·boat (rō′bōt′) *n.* boat propelled by oars.

row·dy (rou′dē) *pl.,* **-dies.** *n.* rude, boisterous, disorderly person. —*adj.* **-di·er, -di·est.** rude; boisterous; disorderly. [Probably from ROW[3].] —**row′di·ish,** *adj.* —**row′di·ness, row′-di·ism,** *n.*

row·el (rou′əl) *n.* **1.** wheel with sharp radiating points, as on the end of a rider's spur. —*v.t.,* **-eled, -el·ing;** *also, British,* **-elled, -el·ling.** to urge on (a horse) with a rowel; spur. [Old French *roel(e)* small wheel, diminutive of *roue* wheel, from Latin *rota.*]

Rowel on a spur
Rowel

row·en (rou′ən) *n.* second crop or mowing of grass or hay in a season.

row·lock (rō′lok′) *n.* oarlock.

roy·al (roi′əl) *adj.* **1.** of or relating to a king, queen, or other sovereign: *a royal command, royal blood, the royal palace.* **2.** belonging to or serving the government of a king, queen, or other sovereign: *the royal navy.* **3.** established or authorized by a king, queen, or other sovereign.

at; āpe; cär; end; mē; it; īce; hot; ōld; fôrk; wood; fōōl; oil; out; up; ūse; turn; sing; thin; this; zh in treasure; ə in ago, taken, pencil, lemon, circus.

4. suitable for or characteristic of a king, queen, or other sovereign; magnificent; majestic; stately. **5.** first-rate; excellent: *We were in royal spirits.* —*n.* small sail or mast above the topgallant. [Old French *roial* regal, kingly, from Latin *rēgālis,* from *rēx* king.] —**roy′al·ly,** *adv.*
Syn. *adj.* **4. Royal, regal, kingly** mean suitable for or characteristic of a king, queen, or other sovereign. **Royal** suggests the magnificence and splendor associated with a sovereign: *The astronauts received a royal welcome.* **Regal** implies the stateliness and dignity characteristic of the sovereign himself: *She wore the dress with a regal elegance.* **Kingly** emphasizes the personal qualities a king should have: *He has a kingly tolerance of the faults of others.*
Royal Academy, association of English artists and scholars dedicated to promoting the fine arts, founded in 1768 by King George III. Also, **Royal Academy of Arts.**
royal blue, vivid reddish blue.
Royal Horse Guards, regiment of cavalry, which, with the Life Guards, form the Household Cavalry of the British sovereign.
roy·al·ism (roi′ə liz′əm) *n.* adherence to a monarch or to the principles of a monarchy.
roy·al·ist (roi′ə list) *n.* **1.** one who supports a king in power or wishes to restore or establish a royal government. **2. Royalist.** supporter of King Charles I in his struggle with Parliament; Cavalier. **3. Royalist.** American colonist who supported the British in the American Revolution; Tory.
royal jelly, white jellylike substance that is rich in proteins and vitamins, secreted by worker honeybees. It is fed to all young larvae of bees, and fed continuously to those larvae chosen to be queen bees.
Royal Oak, city in southeastern Michigan. Pop. (1970), 85,499.
royal palm, any of a group of tall ornamental palm trees, genus *Roystonea.* native to the West Indies and Florida, widely cultivated in tropical regions.
roy·al·ty (roi′əl tē) *pl.,* **-ties.** *n.* **1.** king, queen, or other sovereign; royal families collectively. **2.** position or power of a king, queen, or other sovereign. **3.** royal quality or nature; kingliness. **4.** right or privilege enjoyed by or as by one of royal blood. **5.a.** share of the proceeds from the sale or performance of a work paid to the author, composer, or originator of the work, as by a publisher or producer. **b.** payment made to the owner of a patent, property, or other right for the use made of that right. [Old French *roialte* kingship, from *roial* regal, kingly. See ROYAL.]
r.p.m., revolutions per minute.
R.R. 1. Railroad. **2.** Right Reverend. **3.** rural route.
R.S.F.S.R., Russian Soviet Federated Socialist Republic.
R.S.V.P., please reply. [Abbreviation of French *répondez s'il vous plaît.*]
rte., route.
Rt. Hon., Right Honorable.
Ru, ruthenium.
rub (rub) **rubbed, rub·bing.** *v.t.* **1.** to apply friction or pressure over the surface of: *The swimmer rubbed his leg to ease the cramp.* **2.** to apply or spread (something) by means of friction or pressure: *He rubbed the ointment on his arm.* **3.** to move (an object or objects) against another or each other: *to rub two sticks together, to rub a cloth back and forth over a stain.* **4.** to subject (something) to pressure and friction in order to clean, polish, or make smooth: *She rubbed the silverware until it gleamed.* **5.** to irritate or wear down by friction: *The elastic on this cuff is rubbing my wrist.* **6.** to remove or erase by friction or pressure (with *off* or *out*): *to rub off tarnish, to rub out ink stains.* **7. to rub down.** to massage: *to rub down an athlete after a game.* **8. to rub it in.** *Slang.* to repeat or emphasize something unpleasant. **9. to rub out.** *Slang.* to kill. **10. to rub the wrong way.** *Slang.* to irritate; annoy; irk. —*v.i.* **1.** to exert friction or pressure; press: *The cat rubbed gently against his leg.* **2.** to be able to be removed or erased by friction (with *out* or *off*): *This ink rubs out easily.* **3. to rub off on.** *Informal.* to be transmitted to by close or frequent contact or association: *His love of sailing rubbed off on his son.* —*n.* **1.** application of friction or pressure; rubbing: *an alcohol rub.* **2.** irritating or sarcastic remark. **3.** difficulty; conflict; hindrance: *Aye, there's the rub* (Shakespeare, *Hamlet*). **4.** uneven or rough spot caused by irritation or friction. [Of uncertain origin.]
rub·ber¹ (rub′ər) *n.* **1.** tough, elastic, waterproof substance obtained from the milky liquid or latex in any of several tropical trees. Various kinds of materials with the same properties as natural rubber have been chemically synthesized. **2.** overshoe made of this substance. **3.** any of various other articles made of this substance, as a rubber band or a pencil eraser. **4.** flat piece of rubber on which a baseball pitcher must place one foot while in the act of pitching. **5.** one who or that which rubs. —*adj.* made of rubber. [RUB + -ER¹; because originally often used to rub out or erase pencil marks.]
rub·ber² (rub′ər) *n.* **1.** in bridge and other games and sports, a series of an odd number of games, usually three, in which the final winner is the side that takes the majority of games. **2.** game that breaks a tie

and determines the outcome of such a series. [Of uncertain origin.]
rubber band, elastic loop of rubber, used to hold things together.
rubber cement, adhesive substance that hardens quickly when exposed to air, consisting of a solution of latex in a chemical solvent.
rub·ber·ize (rub′ə rīz′) **-ized, -iz·ing.** *v.t.* to coat or treat with rubber or a rubber preparation.
rub·ber·neck (rub′ər nek′) *Slang. n.* one who gazes about with curiosity and strains his neck to see everything around him. —*v.i.* to gaze about with curiosity; gawk; stare.
rubber plant 1. tropical evergreen plant, *Ficus elastica,* of the mulberry family, found growing wild as a tree in India and Malaya and widely raised as a houseplant, having a single woody stem, and thick leathery leaves. **2.** any of various plants yielding rubber.
rub·ber-stamp (rub′ər stamp′) *v.t.* **1.** to print or mark with a rubber stamp. **2.** *Informal.* to give approval or endorsement to as a matter of routine: *a legislature that rubber-stamps all the bills proposed by the state's governor.*
rubber stamp 1. hand stamp with a raised message or design made of rubber which can be inked and applied to desired articles. **2.** *Informal.* person or group that gives approval or endorsement as a matter of routine.
rub·ber·y (rub′ər ē) *adj.* resembling rubber, as in elasticity or appearance.
rubbing alcohol, denatured alcohol used esp. for rubbing on the skin and as an antiseptic.
rub·bish (rub′ish) *n.* **1.** useless waste material; refuse; trash. **2.** worthless talk or thoughts; nonsense. [Of uncertain origin.]
rub·ble (rub′əl) *n.* **1.** rough fragments of solid material, as stone or rock. **2.** masonry made of rough, irregular stones. [Of uncertain origin.]
rub·down (rub′doun′) *n.* massage.
rube (rōōb) *n. Slang.* naive, unsophisticated rural person; hick.
ru·bel·la (rōō bel′ə) *n.* German measles. [Modern Latin *rubella,* from Latin *rubellus* reddish, from *ruber* red.]
Ru·bens, Peter Paul (rōō′bənz) 1577–1640, Flemish painter.
ru·be·o·la (rōō bē′ə lə) *n.* measles. [Modern Latin *rubeola,* from Latin *rubeus* red.]
Ru·bi·con (rōō′bi kon′) *n.* **1.** small stream in north-central Italy that formed the northern boundary of the ancient Roman republic. Julius Caesar's crossing of the Rubicon in 49 B.C. began a civil war in Rome that led to his dictatorship. **2. to cross the Rubicon.** to take an irrevocable step; make an unchangeable decision.
ru·bi·cund (rōō′bi kənd) *adj.* reddish; ruddy: *a rubicund complexion.* [Latin *rubicundus.*] —**ru′bi·cun′di·ty,** *n.*
ru·bid·i·um (rōō bid′ē əm) *n.* soft, light, silver-white metallic element with properties similar to potassium and sodium, used esp. in photoelectric cells and electron tubes. Symbol: Rb See **element** for table. [Modern Latin *rubidium,* from Latin *rubidus* reddish, red; from the red lines in its spectrum.]
Ru·bin·stein (rōō′bən stīn′) **1. An·ton** (än tôn′). 1829–94, Russian pianist and composer. **2. Ar·tur** (är′tər). 1886—, U.S. pianist, born in Poland.
ru·ble (rōō′bəl) *also,* **rou·ble.** *n.* **1.** standard monetary unit of the Soviet Union. **2.** coin or paper money equivalent to one ruble. [Russian *rubl'.*]
ru·bric (rōō′brik) *n.* **1.** title, chapter heading, or other division in an early book or manuscript, printed in red or in a special color or design to distinguish it from the rest of the text. **2.** direction or rule for the conduct of a religious ceremony, inserted in a prayer book, missal, or similar book. **3.** any established rule, guide, or custom. [Latin *rubrica* red earth for coloring, title of law written in red, from *ruber* red.]
ru·bri·cal (rōō′bri kəl) *adj.* of, relating to, or conducted according to religious rubrics.
ru·by (rōō′bē) *n.* **1.** highly prized gemstone, a transparent red variety of corundum, also used to make bearings for watches and scientific instruments. **2.** deep-red color. **3.** something made of or resembling a ruby. [Old French *rubi(s)* the gem, going back to Latin *rubeus* red.]
ruck (ruk) *n.* mass of ordinary undistinguished persons or things. [Possibly of Scandinavian origin.]
ruck·sack (ruk′sak′, rook′-) *n.* knapsack. [German *Rucksack* literally, back sack.]
ruck·us (ruk′əs) *n. Slang.* loud commotion. [Possibly blend of RUCTION and RUMPUS.]
ruc·tion (ruk′shən) *n. Informal.* noisy disturbance; uproar. [Possibly modification and shortening of INSURRECTION.]
rud·der (rud′ər) *n.* **1.** broad, flat, movable piece of wood, metal, or similar material, usually attached vertically at the stern of a boat or ship, and used in steering. **2.** similar piece at the tail of an aircraft. [Old English *rōther* paddle.]

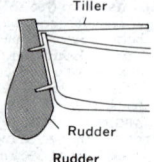

Tiller

Rudder

Rudder

at; āpe; cär; end; mē; it; īce; hot; ōld; fôrk; wood; fōōl; oil; out; up; ūse; turn; sing; thin; this; zh in treasure; ə in ago, taken, pencil, lemon, circus.

rud·dy (rud′ē) -di·er, -di·est. *adj.* **1.** of or having a healthy redness: *a ruddy complexion.* **2.** tinged with red; reddish. [Old English *rudig* reddish.] —**rud′di·ness,** *n.*

rude (rood) rud·er, rud·est. *adj.* **1.** offensive in manner or actions; not polite or courteous; ill-mannered; uncivil: *a rude reply, a rude child.* **2.** roughly made or formed; showing a lack of skill or polish; crude: *People of the Stone Age used rude tools.* **3.** rough; violent; forceful: *a rude awakening.* **4.** primitive; undeveloped: *a rude culture, to follow a plan from its rude beginning all the way through to its completion.* [Latin *rudis* rough, wild, unskilled.] —**rude′ly,** *adv.* —**rude′ness,** *n.* —**Syn. 1.** see **uncouth.**

ru·di·ment (roo′də mənt) *n.* **1.** fact, rule, or element; first principle. ▲ usually used in the plural: *to learn the rudiments of baseball.* **2.** beginning or early stage of something. ▲ usually used in the plural: *the rudiments of civilization.* **3.** *Biology.* organ or part that is not completely developed, esp. one that has no function in the adult individual, as the appendix. [Latin *rudimentum.*]

ru·di·men·ta·ry (roo′də men′tər ē, -trē) *adj.* **1.** of or having the nature of a first principle; elementary: *rudimentary instruction.* **2.** in a beginning or early stage of development. **3.** *Biology.* incompletely or imperfectly developed: *A penguin has rudimentary wings.* —**Syn. 1.** see **elementary.**

rue[1] (roo) rued, ru·ing. *v.t.* to feel sorrow or remorse for; regret: *to rue one's folly. He rued the day he left home.* [Old English *hrēowan* to cause regret or sorrow.]

rue[2] (roo) *n.* any of a large family, Rutacae, of aromatic plants, including citrus trees, often raised for their edible fruits, handsome wood, or attractive flowers and foliage, esp. the **common rue,** *Ruta graveolens,* an herb bearing dull-yellow flowers once widely used in medicine. [Old French *rue,* from Latin *ruta,* from Greek *rhytē.*]

rue anemone, American herb, *Anemonella thalictroides,* of the crowfoot family, having a slender stem and showy white or pink flowers.

rue·ful (roo′fəl) *adj.* **1.** expressing or showing sorrow or regret: *a rueful cry.* **2.** worthy of causing sorrow or grief; pitiable: *a rueful situation.* —**rue′ful·ly,** *adv.* —**rue′ful·ness,** *n.*

ruff[1] (ruf) *n.* **1.** collar of distinctively marked or projecting feathers or hairs along or around the neck of a bird or mammal. **2.** stiff, circular ruff, worn as a collar by men and women in the fifteenth, sixteenth, and seventeenth centuries. [Probably from **RUFFLE**[1].] —**ruffed,** *adj.*

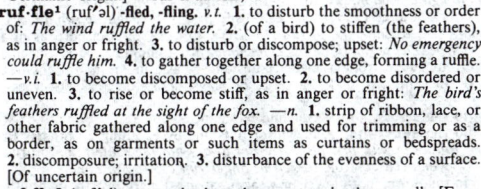

Ruff[1] *(def. 2)*

ruff[2] (ruf) *v.t.* to trump (a card) in bridge and certain other card games. —*v.i.* to trump. —*n.* act of trumping. [Old French *roffle, ronfle* a card game, possibly modification of *triomphe* trump[1], card game, from Latin *triumphus* victory. See **TRIUMPH.**]

ruffed grouse, North American game bird, *Bonasa umbellus,* having predominantly brownish plumage and a fan-shaped tail, the male of which has a tuft of black feathers on each side of the neck. Length: 16–19 inches.

ruf·fi·an (ruf′ē ən, ruf′yən) *n.* rough, brutal, or violent person. —*adj.* rough, brutal, and violent: *ruffian behavior.* [Middle French *rufien* pander, from Italian *ruffiano,* from *roffia* dirt, filth; of Germanic origin.] —**ruf′fi·an·ism,** *n.*

Ruffed grouse

ruf·fle[1] (ruf′əl) -fled, -fling. *v.t.* **1.** to disturb the smoothness or order of: *The wind ruffled the water.* **2.** (of a bird) to stiffen (the feathers), as in anger or fright. **3.** to disturb or discompose; upset: *No emergency could ruffle him.* **4.** to gather together along one edge, forming a ruffle. —*v.i.* **1.** to become discomposed or upset. **2.** to become disordered or uneven. **3.** to rise or become stiff, as in anger or fright: *The bird's feathers ruffled at the sight of the fox.* —*n.* **1.** strip of ribbon, lace, or other fabric gathered along one edge and used for trimming or as a border, as on garments or such items as curtains or bedspreads. **2.** discomposure; irritation. **3.** disturbance of the evenness of a surface. [Of uncertain origin.]

ruf·fle[2] (ruf′əl) *n.* steady drum beat, not as loud as a roll. [From earlier *ruff* drum beat; imitative.]

ru·fous (roo′fəs) *adj.* brownish-red. [Latin *rufus* reddish.]

rug (rug) *n.* **1.** piece of heavy, often woven fabric, used to cover part of a floor: *an Oriental rug.* **2.** animal hide used as a covering: *bearskin rug.* **3.** lap robe. [Of Scandinavian origin.]

Rug·by (rug′bē) *n.* **1.** *also,* **rugby.** form of football played with an oval ball by two fifteen-man teams, in which the ball may be passed laterally or backward, carried, and kicked. The American form of football devel-

oped from this game. **2.** city in central England. Pop. (1961) 51,651. **3.** school for boys at Rugby, where this game was first played.

rug·ged (rug′id) *adj.* **1.** having a sharply irregular outline or surface; rough and uneven: *rugged mountain peaks, a rugged coastline.* **2.** capable of enduring physical hardship; sturdy; robust: *a rugged football team.* **3.** (of the face or its features) strong, lined, and irregular. **4.** difficult to do or endure; harsh; hard: *the rugged life of a seaman, a rugged test.* **5.** stormy; tempestuous: *We had a rugged crossing.* [Of Scandinavian origin.] —**rug′ged·ly,** *adv.* —**rug′ged·ness,** *n.* —**Syn. 2.** see **tough.**

Ruhr (roor) *n.* **1.** river in northwestern Germany, a tributary of the Rhine. **2.** coal mining and industrial region along this river.

ru·in (roo′in) *n.* **1.** total destruction or decay; complete collapse: *the ruin of an empire.* **2.** condition of destruction or decay: *The boat had gone to ruin through years of neglect.* **3. ruins.** remains of something destroyed or decayed: *to visit the ruins of the Aztecs, to stand among the ruins of a bombed building.* **4.** loss of position, power, honor, means, or health: *financial ruin.* **5.** something that causes destruction, decay, or collapse: *Fame will be the ruin of him.* —*v.t.* **1.** to bring to ruin; devastate. **2.** to spoil or harm irrevocably: *His sprained ankle ruined his chances of winning the tournament.* **3.** to bring to moral or financial ruin. [Old French *ruine* downfall, remains of a building that has fallen down, from Latin *ruina.*] —**Syn. n. 1.** see **destruction.**

ru·in·a·tion (roo′i nā′shən) *n.* **1.** act of ruining; being ruined. **2.** something that causes ruin: *His dishonesty was his ruination.*

ru·in·ous (roo′i nəs) *adj.* **1.** bringing or tending to bring ruin; disastrous; destructive: *a ruinous war.* **2.** fallen to ruin; decayed; destroyed: *a building in a ruinous condition.* —**ru′in·ous·ly,** *adv.* —**ru′in·ous·ness,** *n.*

rule (rool) *n.* **1.** fixed principle or direction regulating behavior, procedure, or action: *the rules of baseball, the rules of etiquette, the rules of logic.* **2.a.** controlling power or authority; government: *The rule of the many is better than the rule of the few. Our household lived under our father's rule.* **b.** period of having control; reign: *The tyrant's rule was marked by violence and strife.* **3.** code or body of regulations, esp. that observed by a religious order. **4.** *Law.* **a.** regulation regarding the procedures of a court of law. **b.** order made by a court of law with specific rather than general application. **5.** ruler *(def. 2).* **6.** *Printing.* thin strip of metal, as brass or steel, that is used to print a line or lines. **7.** something that usually or normally occurs or is done; that which is often the case: *Long hair is the rule among the boys in our town.* **8. as a rule.** generally; usually. —*v.t.* **ruled, rul·ing. 1.** to exercise authority over; govern; control: *to rule a country.* **2.** to have influence over; guide: *Fear ruled his actions.* **3.** to declare or determine with authority: *to rule someone out of order, to rule a law unconstitutional.* **4.** to keep in check; restrain: *to rule one's temper.* **5.** to mark with lines, esp. by using a ruler: *He ruled the test paper carefully.* **6.** to form or mark (a line or lines) with or as with a ruler: *He ruled boxes on the page for a graph.* **7. to rule out.** to decide to reject or exclude. —*v.i.* **1.** to have authority or power; govern: *to rule with justice and mercy.* **2.** to make an authoritative decision or determination: *The club ruled against accepting new members.* **3.** to be current or prevalent. [Old French *riule* regulation, ruler, order, precept, from Latin *regula* bar, model. Doublet of **RAIL**[1].] —**rul′a·ble,** *adj.*

Syn. *v.i.* **1. Rule, govern, reign** mean to exercise power or authority over others. **Rule** means to exercise supreme political power: *The king ruled with an iron rod.* **Govern** means to manage the affairs of state by controlling, directing, and guiding others: *The president governs with the help of his cabinet.* **Reign** means to hold the power or status of a sovereign, without necessarily exercising supreme authority: *The British monarchs reign but do not rule.* —**Syn. n. 1.** see **law.**

rule of thumb 1. general principle or guide that is widely useful although it is not derived scientifically. **2.** rough measurement or procedure.

rul·er (roo′lər) *n.* **1.** one who rules or governs. **2.** straight-edged strip of wood or metal marked off into measuring units, used for drawing straight lines or measuring.

rul·ing (roo′ling) *n.* **1.** authoritative decision, as of a judge or regulatory commission. **2.** ruled lines. —*adj.* **1.** having authority; governing: *the ruling class.* **2.** predominating; prevalent: *the ruling opinion in the community.*

rum[1] (rum) *n.* **1.** alcoholic liquor distilled from fermented derivatives of sugar cane such as juice, syrup, or molasses, or a combination of these derivatives. **2.** any alcoholic beverage. [Short for earlier *rumbullion;* of uncertain origin.]

rum[2] (rum) *adj.* **1.** bad; difficult. **2.** *British. Slang.* odd; queer. [Earlier *rome* good, possibly from Romany *rom* man, Gypsy; of Sanskrit origin.]

Ru·ma·ni·a (roo mā′nē ə, -mān′yə) Romania.

Ru·ma·ni·an (roo mā′nē ən, -mān′yən) Romanian.

rum·ba (rum′bə, room′-) *also,* **rhum·ba.** *n.* **1.** Cuban dance of African

at; āpe; cär; end; mē; it; īce; hot; ōld; fôrk; wood; fōōl; oil; out; up; ūse; turn; sing; thin; this; zh in treasure; ə in ago, taken, pencil, lemon, circus.

869

origin. **2.** modern ballroom adaptation of this dance. **3.** music for this dance. —*v.i.* to dance the rumba. [Spanish *rumba* the dance, the music for this dance; of uncertain origin.]

rum·ble (rum′bəl) **-bled, -bling.** *v.i.* **1.** to make a heavy, deep, rolling sound, as thunder. **2.** to move or proceed with such a sound: *The tank rumbled along the road.* —*v.t.* to utter with such a sound. —*n.* **1.** heavy, deep, rolling sound. **2.** indication or expression of discontent or uneasiness: *A rumble went through the crowd at the mention of the dictator's name.* **3.** *Slang.* fight between gangs of youths. **4.** area in the back of a carriage used for seating or as a luggage compartment. [Possibly of Low German origin.]

Rumble seat

rumble seat, open, folding seat in the back of an automobile, as in a coupé or roadster.

ru·men (rōō′min) *pl.*, **ru·mi·na** (rōō′mi nə). *n.* **1.** first stomach of a ruminant, or cud-chewing animal. **2.** cud of a ruminant. [Latin *rūmen* gullet.]

Rum·ford, Count (rum′fərd) 1753–1814, British scientist, born in America. His given name was Benjamin Thompson.

ru·mi·nant (rōō′mə nənt) *n.* any of numerous cud-chewing, even-toed, hoofed mammals, constituting the suborder Ruminantia, that have a stomach consisting of four chambers. Cows, sheep, deer, antelope, giraffes, and camels are ruminants. —*adj.* **1.** of, relating to, or designating a ruminant. **2.** meditative; contemplative. [Latin *rūmināns,* present participle of *rūminārī* to chew the cud, from *rūmen* gullet.]

ru·mi·nate (rōō′mə nāt′) **-nat·ed, -nat·ing.** *v.i.* **1.** to meditate or muse; ponder: *to ruminate on misfortunes.* **2.** to chew the cud. —*v.t.* **1.** to chew (food) again. **2.** to meditate upon; muse about. [Latin *rūminātus,* past participle of *rūminārī* to chew the cud. See RUMINANT.]

ru·mi·na·tion (rōō′mə nā′shən) *n.* **1.** meditation; contemplation. **2.** act or process of chewing the cud. —**ru′mi·na′tive,** *adj.*

rum·mage (rum′ij) **-maged, -mag·ing.** *v.t.* **1.** to search through (something) thoroughly, esp. by handling, moving about, and disarranging its contents: *He rummaged the entire attic for his old scrapbook.* **2.** to find or bring forth by searching (with *out, up,* or *from*): *to rummage an old suit out of a trunk.* —*v.i.* to search thoroughly and, usually, haphazardly: *The child rummaged in the toy box.* —*n.* **1.** thorough search made by handling, and usually disarranging, things. **2.** miscellaneous items, esp. those on sale at a rummage sale. [Short for Middle French *arrumage* stowing cargo in a ship's hold, going back to Old French *a* to (from Latin *ad*) + *run* ship's hold (of Germanic origin); with reference to the disorder connected with disposing of a ship's cargo.]

rummage sale 1. sale of miscellaneous donated items, as furniture or old clothing, usually held to raise money for some charitable purpose. **2.** sale of merchandise for clearance, or of unclaimed items, as at a warehouse or dock.

rum·my¹ (rum′ē) *n.* card game in which the players try to lay down all the cards in their hands by melding them in sets of three or four cards of the same rank, or in sets of three or more cards of the same suit in sequence. [Of uncertain origin.]

rum·my² (rum′ē) *n. Slang.* drunkard. [RUM¹ + -Y¹.]

ru·mor (rōō′mər) *n.* **1.** report or statement circulating as truth without any evidence to support it; unverified story: *vicious rumors.* **2.** general talk; hearsay: *Rumor has it that the star will leave the show next week.* —*v.t.* to circulate or tell by rumor. [Old French *rumor* noise, quarrel, from Latin *rūmor* noise, report.]

ru·mor·mon·ger (rōō′mər mung′gər, -mong′-) *n.* one who spreads rumors, esp. with the knowledge that they are untrue.

rump (rump) *n.* **1.** that part of an animal's body where the trunk and legs are joined. **2.** cut of beef from this part. **3.** in man, the buttocks. **4.** last, least important, or inferior part; remnant. **5.** legislative body having, through expulsion or resignation, only a small part of its former membership and therefore regarded as unrepresentative and lacking authority. [Probably of Scandinavian origin.]

rum·ple (rum′pəl) **-pled, -pling.** *v.t.,v.i.* to disarrange or become disarranged by wrinkling or creasing. —*n.* irregular crease; wrinkle. [Middle Dutch *rompelen* to wrinkle.]

rum·pus (rum′pəs) *n. Informal.* noisy disturbance; uproar. [Of uncertain origin.]

rumpus room, room for play and informal parties.

rum·run·ner (rum′run′ər) *n.* person or ship engaged in smuggling alcoholic liquor.

run (run) **ran, run, run·ning.** *v.i.* **1.** to move quickly by alternately springing the legs off the ground so that both feet are in the air for an instant during each step; proceed at a pace faster than walking: *He ran to catch the bus.* **2.** to go rapidly; rush; hasten. **3.** to leave or retreat rapidly; flee: *The dog broke loose and ran.* **4.** to make a short or quick trip: *to run to the store for a loaf of bread.* **5.** to go or travel regularly; ply: *The express runs hourly between Boston and New York.* **6.** to move about freely; go without restraint: *We always let our cats run loose in the house.* **7.** to move, pass, or slide easily: *A rope runs in a pulley. The drawer runs on gliders.* **8.** to pass or move quickly or lightly: *A wind ran through the tall grass. The days ran by.* **9.** to participate in a race: *Seven horses ran in the derby.* **10.** to compete for election: *to run for mayor.* **11.** to finish (in a specified position or condition) in a race, contest, or election: *Our candidate ran a poor second.* **12.** to extend in space; lie in direction: *The road runs due north. The street runs through the town.* **13.** (of plants) to grow (in a specified direction or area); creep; climb: *The ivy runs up the wall.* **14.** to be in operation; work; function: *The clock runs on batteries. The mills run night and day.* **15.** to be in effect; continue in time; last: *a contract that will run for ten months. Our sale will run for one week.* **16.** to proceed, as in a certain course or direction: *Feelings ran high against him.* **17.** to become current; circulate among the public: *An epidemic ran through the city. Gossip was running rampant.* **18.** to pass (into a specified state or condition): *to run into trouble.* **19.** to be, occur, or range in a specified character, size, quality, or price: *These shirts run small. Prices are running high.* **20.** to occur to the mind repeatedly: *The melody ran through his head.* **21.** to be persistent or common; recur: *Blonde hair runs in her family.* **22.** to tend or incline: *Her tastes run to the ornate.* **23.** to flow in a stream: *The water stopped running through the pipes.* **24.** to spread or mingle, esp. when exposed to water: *The colors ran after the first washing.* **25.** to be wet: *The lost child's cheeks ran with tears.* **26.** to discharge serum, mucus, or pus: *The sore on his leg ran for three days.* **27.** to become liquid; melt. **28.** to have the stitches break at some point and unravel, esp. along the length of a line of stitches. **29.** to be expressed (in a certain form or arrangement): *The refrain runs like this.* **30.** (of fish) to migrate, as upstream or from the sea, for spawning, esp. in a school: *Salmon are running.* **31.** to perform or be performed continually: *The musical ran for a year on Broadway.* **32.** *Law.* **a.** to have legal validity or force, as in a certain area or for a specified period of time. **b.** to accompany, go along with, or be attached to: *Swimming rights run with the land.* **33.** to continue to accrue or remain unpaid, as a debt. —*v.t.* **1.** to go along by running, as a path or route: *to run the length of the yard.* **2.** to pass rapidly over or through: *He ran the rapids in a canoe.* **3.** to make or perform: *to run a race, to run an errand.* **4.** to cause (an animal) to run or move rapidly: *to run a horse until it is exhausted.* **5.** to bring to (a specified place, state, or condition) by or as by running: *to run a car off the road. He ran himself ragged.* **6.** to enter (a contestant, as a horse or dog) in a race. **7.** to enter as a candidate for election: *The party will run Edwards for mayor.* **8.** to keep functioning; operate: *to run an engine.* **9.** to expose oneself to; incur: *to run a risk.* **10.** to cause to move, pass, or slide easily: *to run a flag up a pole.* **11.** to direct; conduct; manage: *The chairman ran the meeting well. He runs the store alone.* **12.** to cause (a conveyance) to go from place to place regularly: *to run a train from Boston to Washington.* **13.** to cause to flow or move in a stream: *to run water into a bathtub.* **14.** to cause to extend in a certain direction; lead: *to run a pipe underneath a building.* **15.** to cause to move quickly, as the eye or hand: *to run one's eyes down a page.* **16.** to publish, as in a newspaper or magazine: *to run an advertisement. They ran the story in three issues.* **17.** to cause to be presented or shown: *to run a movie.* **18.** to perform or execute: *to run tests for allergies.* **19.** to mark or trace, as a boundary line. **20.** to drive, force, or thrust: *to run one's hand through a window.* **21.** to suffer from; have: *to run a fever.* **22.** to flow with: *The streets ran blood.* **23.** to slip past or through: *to run a blockade.* **24.** to smuggle: *to run rifles.* **25.** to carry or transport, as in a vehicle: *Please run this dress to the tailor.* **26.** to hunt or chase, as game. **27.** to shape from a melted substance; cast; mold: *to run bullets.* **28.** in games, to make (a series of plays, shots, or strokes) successfully.

to run across, to meet or find by chance.

to run away with. a. to win or outshine all others by excelling: *He ran away with first prize. He ran away with the contest.* **b.** to drive beyond self-control: *He let his anger run away with him.*

to run down. a. to lower or weaken, as in strength, worth, or health: *Office tensions ran him down.* **b.** to pursue until caught or killed: *to run down a stag, to run down a criminal.* **c.** to cease operating; stop functioning: *The clock ran down last week.* **d.** to knock down by colliding with. **e.** to disparage. **f.** to find or trace by searching: *to run down the source of the trouble.*

to run for, to run in order to escape.

to run in. a. *Slang.* to arrest: *The police ran him in for disturbing the peace.* **b.** to insert or include. **c.** *Printing.* to cause to be without breaks or paragraphs; make continuous.

to run into. a. to meet or find by chance: *to run into an old friend.* **b.** to collide with: *The car ran into a telephone pole.*
to run off. a. to print or make copies of. **b.** to cause to be played or performed again to decide the outcome, as of a contest.
to run on. to talk or write without stopping.
to run out. to come to an end; be used up; expire: *The time ran out. His strength ran out.*
to run out of. to exhaust a supply of; use up: *to run out of sugar.*
to run over. a. to ride or drive over: *He ran over the cat in the road.* **b.** to review or examine quickly: *The speaker ran over his notes before the lecture.*
to run through. a. to use up or spend rapidly or wantonly: *to run through a fortune.* **b.** to drive into; pierce. **c.** to review or examine quickly.
to run up. a. to construct or produce quickly, as on a sewing machine. **b.** to allow to accumulate or mount up: *to run up a bill at the drugstore.*
—*n.* **1.** act of running or moving rapidly: *to take a run around the block.* **2.** pace faster than a walk: *to break into a run.* **3.** distance covered or time taken by moving at such a pace: *a mile run, a few minute's run from the station.* **4.** short, quick trip or visit: *to make a run into the city.* **5.a.** distance regularly traveled between two places, as by a train: *The conductor worked on the run from Boston to New York.* **b.** journey or trip over this distance: *The train made four runs daily.* **6.** regularly traveled route or course: *The delivery man finished his run early.* **7.** freedom to move about; right to use: *the run of the hotel facilities. The dogs were given the run of the farm.* **8.** continuous spell or unbroken series: *a run of rainy days.* **9.** period of continuing performance or exhibition: *a three-week run. The movie had a long run.* **10.** general type or class: *the usual run of applicants.* **11.** general direction or tendency; trend: *the run of events.* **12.a.** period of operation or functioning, as of a factory or machine. **b.** amount produced during such a period; output. **13.** continuous stretch or extent: *a run of iron pipe.* **14.** series of demands for money: *a run on a bank.* **15.** any extensive demand: *There was a run on milk because of rumors of a strike.* **16.** place where stitches have broken and unraveled, esp. along the length of a row of stitches: *a run in a stocking.* **17.** flowing movement, as of a liquid. **18.** amount or period of time of such a flow. **19.** small swift stream or rush of water. **20.** track or path made or frequented by animals. **21.** number of animals, esp. a school of fish moving together. **22.** enclosed area where animals can exercise: *The kennel had a large run for the dogs.* **23.** course, slope, or other area over which something can travel, as for skiing or bobsledding. **24.** series of successful plays, shots, or strokes in any of various games. **25.** in card games, a number of consecutive cards in one suit: *a run in spades.* **26.** *Baseball.* **a.** score made by touching home plate after touching the three bases. **b.** point so scored. **27.** *Football.* attempt to advance the ball by carrying it around or through the opponent's line. **28.** *Cricket.* **a.** score made when both batsmen run to the opposite wicket successfully. **b.** point so scored. **29.** *Music.* rapid succession of tones, as a roulade. **30.** approach of a bombing plane to its target. **31. a run for (one's) money. a.** heavy competition: *He really gave his competitors a run for their money.* **b.** return or satisfaction for one's expenditure of effort. **32. in the long run,** in the end; ultimately. **33. on the run. a.** hurrying, as from one place to another: *He was on the run all day long.* **b.** in rapid retreat or flight. [Old English *rinnan* to move the legs quickly so as to proceed at a pace faster than walking, hasten, flow.]
run·a·bout (run'ə bout') *n.* **1.** small motorboat. **2.** roadster. **3.** light, open carriage or wagon. **4.** one who wanders about from place to place.
run·a·round (run'ə round') *n. Slang.* evasion or deception, esp. in the form of evasive answers or excuses in response to a request.
run·a·way (run'ə wā') *n.* **1.** one who or that which runs away, as a fugitive, or a horse that has broken out of the driver's control. **2.** act of running away. **3.** complete or easy victory. —*adj.* **1.** escaping from control; running away; fleeing: *a runaway horse, runaway slaves.* **2.** easily won, as a race. **3.** brought about by running away or eloping: *a runaway marriage.* **4.** rising or expanding rapidly: *runaway prices, runaway inflation.*
run·back (run'bak') *n.* **1.** football play in which a player catches a punt or kickoff, or intercepts a pass, and carries it back toward the opposing team's goal. **2.** distance covered by such a play.
run·ci·nate (run'sə nit, -nāt') *adj.* (of a leaf) saw-toothed, usually with the lobes or notches pointing backward, as the leaves of some dandelions. [Latin *runcinātus,* past participle of *runcināre* to plane off, from *runcīna* plane² (formerly also understood to mean "saw"), from Greek *rhykanē.*]
run·down (run'doun') *n.* summary; résumé.
run·down (run'doun') *adj.* **1.** in poor health; tired out; exhausted. **2.** in disrepair; dilapidated: *a run-down old mansion.* **3.** not wound and not working, as a clock or watch.

rune¹ (rōōn) *n.* **1.** letter or character used in an ancient Germanic system of writing found mainly in Scandinavia and England. **2.** similar letter or character that is supposed to have mysterious or magical power or meaning. [Old English *rūn* mystery, letter of an ancient Germanic system of writing; because writing was regarded as a mystery in earlier times when few could read and write.] —**ru'nic,** *adj.*

Rune¹

rune² (rōōn) *n.* ancient Scandinavian poem or song. [Finnish *runo,* from Old Norse *rūn* runic character.] —**ru'nic,** *adj.*
rung¹ (rung) past participle and a past tense of **ring².**
rung² (rung) *n.* **1.** crosspiece forming a step of a ladder. **2.** supporting crosspiece placed between the legs or within the framework of the back of a chair. [Old English *hrung* pole¹, staff.]
run-in (run'in') *n. Informal.* disagreement; quarrel: *a run-in with the law.*
run·let (run'lit) *n.* small stream or brook; runnel.
run·nel (run'əl) *n.* small stream or brook; rivulet. [Old English *rynel,* from *rinnan* to run, flow.]
run·ner (run'ər) *n.* **1.** person or animal that runs, as a contestant in a race. **2.a.** *Baseball.* base runner. **b.** *Football.* player attempting to advance the ball by running. **3.a.** any of various devices that aid movement, as the

Runner

Runner

support on which a sliding drawer moves. **b.** one of the long narrow parts on which a sled or ice skate glides. **4.** one who runs errands or delivers messages. **5.** one who solicits business, as for a store. **6.** long, narrow rug or carpet, used for hallways and staircases. **7.** narrow strip of cloth used to cover table-tops, dressers, and other furniture. **8.** person or ship engaged in smuggling. **9.** *Botany.* **a.** slender trailing stem of certain plants that gives rise to roots that produce new plants. **b.** plant having such a stem, as the strawberry.
run·ner-up (run'ər up') *n.* contestant or team that finishes in second place.
run·ning (run'ing) *n.* **1.** act of one who or that which runs. **2. in the running,** having a good chance for success. **3. out of the running,** unlikely to win. —*adj.* **1.** moving rapidly; proceeding at a run. **2.** flowing: *running water.* **3.** going on continuously; proceeding without interruption: *a running battle.* **4.** started with, performed during, or accompanied by a run: *a running broad jump. The outfielder made a running catch.* **5.** in operation, as a machine; working: *We can't replace any of the running parts.* **6.** discharging matter: *a running sore.* **7.** (of measurements) in a straight line: *the cost per running foot.* **8.** in progress; current: *a running account in a store.* **9.** of duration, operation, or performance: *the running time of a movie.* —*adv.* in close succession; consecutively: *I had the same incredible dream for six nights running.*
running board, footboard, esp. along the side of an automobile.
running gear, working parts of an automobile or other vehicle, as the wheels, axle, and motor, excluding the body.
running head, title or heading placed at the top of each page or every other page, as in a book or magazine. Also, **running title.**
running knot, knot made so as to form a noose that tightens as the line is pulled.
running light, one of the lights displayed at night by a ship or aircraft.
running mate, one who campaigns for office in association with another on the same ticket, esp. the candidate for the lesser of the two offices.
running stitch, series of small, even stitches made by hand or machine.
Run·ny·mede (run'e mēd') *n.* meadow on the Thames, near London, where King John signed the Magna Carta on June 15, 1215.
run-off (run'ôf') *n.* **1.** something that runs off. **2.** rain or snow not absorbed by the soil, which forms surface streams. **3.** final contest or election held to break a tie or to determine the outcome of a previous competition in which there was no decisive winner.
run-of-the-mill (run'əv thə mil') *adj.* not special or outstanding in any way; ordinary; average.
run-on (run'ôn', -on') *n.* added or appended without a break.
run-on entry, undefined dictionary entry added at the end of a defined entry. It is formed by the addition of a suffix to the defined word, and its meaning can be derived from the meaning of the defined word and the meaning of the suffix. *Ruggedness* is a run-on entry under the word *rugged.*

---

at; āpe; cär; end; mē; it; īce; hot; ōld; fôrk; wood; fōōl; oil; out; up; ūse; turn; sing; thin; this; zh in treasure; ə in ago, taken, pencil, lemon, circus.

runt (runt) *n.* stunted or undersized animal or person. [Of uncertain origin.]

run-through (run′thrōō′) *n.* quick rehearsal, review, or examination.

runt·y (run′tē) **runt·i·er, runt·i·est.** *adj.* stunted; undersized.

run·way (run′wā′) *n.* **1.** long, narrow area where an airplane can take off and land. Runways on land are often surfaced with concrete. **2.** ramp extending from a stage into the theater. **3.** way, track, or path along, through, or over which something moves. **4.** beaten track of deer or other animals.

ru·pee (rōō pē′) *n.* monetary unit and coin of India, Pakistan, Ceylon, and various other countries. [Hindustani *rūpiyah*, from Sanskrit *rūpya* silver.]

Ru·pert, Prince (rōō′pərt) 1619–82, German prince who was a nephew and supporter of Charles I of England.

ru·pi·ah (rōō pē′ə) *n.* monetary unit of Indonesia. [Indonesian *rupiah*, from Hindustani *rūpiyah*. See RUPEE.]

rup·ture (rup′chər) *n.* **1.** act or instance of breaking open or bursting: *a rupture of the aorta.* **2.** hernia, esp. one in or near the groin. **3.** a break in friendly relations between people or countries. —*v.t.,* **-tured, -tur·ing. 1.** to break open or apart; burst: *to rupture a blood vessel, to rupture a tire.* **2.** to sever (diplomatic or friendly relations): *The naval incident ruptured relations between the two countries.* **3.** to affect with a hernia, esp. one in or near the groin. —*v.i.* **1.** to suffer a break; burst: *His appendix ruptured.* **2.** to suffer a hernia, esp. one in or near the groin. **3.** to be severed. [Latin *ruptūra* fracture, breach.]

ru·ral (roor′əl) *adj.* **1.** of, relating to, or characteristic of the country, as distinguished from the city: *rural areas, a rural landscape, the rural population.* **2.** of or relating to agriculture: *a rural economy.* [Latin *rūrālis* relating to the country, from *rūs* the country.] —**ru′ral·ly,** *adv.* **Syn. 1. Rural, rustic, bucolic** mean relating to or typical of the country as contrasted with city life. **Rural** suggests the simple, quiet way of living in the country or a small town: *She vacationed for a month in rural Vermont.* **Rustic** suggests the primitive crudeness and lack of refinement of country life: *Rustic conditions made camping an adventure. The rustic woodsman's homespun wisdom impressed us all.* **Bucolic** suggests boorish coarseness: *He disliked the hillbilly's bucolic humor.*

rural free delivery, delivery of mail in rural or farm areas by carriers employed by the government.

ruse (rōōz) *n.* action or plan intended to deceive; trick. [Middle French *ruse*, from *ruser* to use tricks, from Old French *reüser* to refuse, escape (as by using tricks), going back to Latin *recūsāre* to refuse.]

rush¹ (rush) *v.i.* **1.** to move, go, or come with speed or haste: *He had to rush to catch the bus. Blood rushed to her head.* **2.** to act quickly and often rashly (with *into*): *He rushed into the campaign without any political experience.* —*v.t.* **1.** to cause to move with speed or haste: *to rush a bill through Congress. Stop rushing me.* **2.** to perform or complete quickly and hastily: *I can't rush this work without making errors.* **3.** to attack or overcome swiftly and forcefully: *They planned to rush the fortress in the morning.* **4.** *Informal.* to lavish attention on, as when courting or seeking (someone's) membership: *He has been rushing her for a month. My sorority is rushing twenty girls this semester.* **5.** in football, to move (the ball) forward by carrying it. —*n.* **1.** act of rushing; sudden swift movement: *a rush of wind.* **2.** sudden and hasty movement of many people to get to a place: *the Monday morning rush of commuters to the city.* **3.** bustling activity; being busy; haste: *the rush of a crowded department store.* **4.** sudden, eager demand (with *for* or *on*): *a rush on a new stock, a rush for tickets to the championship game.* **5.** sudden outpouring or onset of activity: *a rush of questions, a rush of orders.* **6.** hurried state: *to be in a rush.* **7.** in football, an attempt to advance the ball by running with it. **8. rushes.** in motion pictures, the first film prints of a scene, before they have been cut or edited. **9.** *Informal.* lavishing of attention, as on someone being courted. **10.** *Informal.* social gathering held by a fraternity or sorority to entertain and select new members. —*adj.* **1.** requiring haste; urgent: *a rush job.* **2.** characterized by great activity: *the rush season.* [Old French *reüser* to push back, refuse, retreat, escape. See RUSE.] —**rush′er,** *n.*

rush² (rush) *n.* **1.** any of several reedy or grasslike plants, genus *Juncus* or *Butomus,* found in marshy areas, having slender, often hollow stems, and clusters of small green or brown flowers. **2.** stem of such a plant, often woven into mats, baskets, chair seats, and other products. [Old English *risc.*] —**rush′y,** *adj.*

rush hour, period during a workday when traffic is heaviest and public transportation facilities are most crowded.

Rush·more, Mount (rush′môr) mountain in the Black Hills of western South Dakota, on the side of which are carved huge heads of Washington, Jefferson, Lincoln, and Theodore Roosevelt.

rusk (rusk) *n.* **1.** sweet or plain bread or cake baked in the oven, sliced, and baked again to make it brown, dry, and crisp. **2.** light, soft, sweetened biscuit. [Spanish *rosca* twist, roll (as of bread); of uncertain origin.]

Rus·kin, John (rus′kin) 1819–1900, English author, art critic, and social reformer.

Russ. 1. Russia. **2.** Russian.

Rus·sell (rus′əl) **1. Bertrand.** 1872–1970, English philosopher and mathematician. **2. George William.** 1867–1935, Irish poet and author who used the pen name Æ.

rus·set (rus′it) *n.* **1.** yellowish-brown or reddish-brown color. **2.** any of various kinds of apples having russet-colored skin. **3.** coarse, homespun, russet-colored woolen fabric formerly used for clothing, esp. in England. [Old French *rousset,* diminutive of *rous* reddish-brown, reddish, going back to Latin *russus* red.]

Rus·sia (rush′ə) *n.* **1.** Soviet Union. **2.** former empire in eastern Europe and northern Asia ruled by the czars, terminated in 1917. Its capital was St. Petersburg. **3.** Russian Soviet Federated Socialist Republic.

Rus·sian (rush′ən) *adj.* of or relating to Russia, its people, their language, or their culture. —*n.* **1.** native or inhabitant of Russia. **2.** language belonging to the eastern division of the Slavic branch of the Indo-European language family, spoken predominantly in Russia.

Russian Church, largest branch of the Orthodox Church, governed by a patriarch and a number of other prelates. It was the official church of imperial Russia. Also, **Russian Orthodox Church.**

Russian dressing, dressing made of mayonnaise mixed with chili sauce or ketchup, and other ingredients, as chopped pickles or olives.

Russian Republic, Russian Soviet Federated Socialist Republic.

Russian Revolution, revolution in Russia in 1917 that ended the czarist form of government and established the soviets, councils of workers and soldiers, as the Russian government under the leadership of the Bolsheviks and Lenin.

Russian roulette 1. deadly game of chance in which a person spins the cylinder of a revolver loaded with only one bullet, aims the gun at his or someone else's head, and pulls the trigger. **2.** any situation involving the risk of total destruction.

Russian Soviet Federated Socialist Republic, largest republic of the Soviet Union, comprising more than three-quarters of the country's area. Area, approx. 6,592,658 sq. mi. Pop. (1963 est.), 123,441,000. Also, **Russia, Soviet Russia.**

Russian thistle, bushy weed, *Salsola kali,* having threadlike prickly leaves and branches that break away in a tangled mass.

Russian wolfhound, borzoi.

rust (rust) *n.* **1.** reddish-brown or orange brittle mixture of iron compounds that forms on the surface of iron when it is exposed to moisture and oxygen. **2.** similar mixture of compounds, mainly metallic oxides, formed on other metals by oxidation or corrosion. **3.** any of various plant diseases caused by parasitic fungi, characterized by the appearance of reddish-brown or orange blisterlike spots and streaks on the plants. **4.** any of several parasitic fungi causing such a disease, composed of tiny threadlike structures that obtain nourishment from the tissues of the host plant. **5.** reddish-brown or orange color. **6.** any harmful or deteriorating effect or influence, esp. one that is the result of inactivity: *Sunday clears away the rust of the whole week* (Addison, 1711). —*v.i.* **1.** to corrode by becoming covered with rust. **2.** to deteriorate or lose usefulness, as through inactivity: *Without practice his pitching will rust.* **3.** (of a plant) to become infected with a rust. —*v.t.* **1.** to cause to corrode by becoming covered with rust. **2.** to cause deterioration through lack of use. **3.** to cause (a plant) to become infected with rust. [Old English *rūst* the reddish-brown coating that forms on certain metals, corruption.]

rus·tic (rus′tik) *adj.* **1.** of, relating to, or characteristic of the country: *a quaint, rustic setting.* **2.** characteristic of country people or life; simple; plain: *his rustic innocence, rustic manners.* **3.** made of undressed wood: *rustic furniture.* —*n.* one who lives in the country, esp. one who is unsophisticated, simple, or awkward. [Latin *rūsticus* relating to the country, from *rūs* the country.] —**rus′ti·cal·ly,** *adv.* —**rus·tic·i·ty** (rus tis′ə tē), *n.* —**Syn.** *adj.* **1, 2.** see rural.

rus·ti·cate (rus′ti kāt′) **-cat·ed, -cat·ing.** *v.i.* to go or retire to the country; stay in the country. —*v.t.* **1.** to send to the country. **2.** *British.* to suspend (a student) from a school or college. [Latin *rūsticātus,* past participle of *rūsticārī* to live in the country.] —**rus′ti·ca′tion,** *n.*

rus·tle (rus′əl) **-tled, -tling.** *v.i.* **1.** to make a series of soft sounds, as that of papers, silk, or leaves being stirred about. **2.** *Informal.* to steal cattle. —*v.t.* **1.** to cause to make a series of soft, fluttering sounds: *The wind rustled the leaves.* **2.** *Informal.* to make, get, or collect with much activity or energy (often with *up*). **3.** *Informal.* to steal (cattle). —*n.* succession of soft, fluttering sounds. [Imitative.]

rus·tler (rus′lər) *n.* cattle thief.

rust·proof (rust′prōōf′) *adj.* not subject to rusting.

rust·y (rus′tē) **rust·i·er, rust·i·est.** *adj.* **1.** covered or affected with rust: *a rusty nail.* **2.** consisting of or made by rust: *rusty spots on the gate.* **3.** of the color of rust. **4.** weakened or deteriorated through neglect or

at; āpe; cär; end; mē; it; īce; hot; ōld; fôrk; wood; fōōl; oil; out; up; ūse; turn; sing; thin; this; zh in treasure; ə in ago, taken, pencil, lemon, circus.

lack of practice: *My French is a bit rusty.* **5.** less skilled through disuse; out of practice: *He's gotten rusty in math.* **6.** shabby, worn, or faded. —**rust′i·ly,** *adv.* —**rust′i·ness,** *n.*

rut¹ (rut) *n.* **1.** groove or other depression made in the ground by a wheel or by continuous wear. **2.** rigid way of living, thinking, or acting; boring routine. —*v.t.,* **rut·ted, rut·ting.** to make a rut in. [Middle French *route* way, track. See ROUTE.]

rut² (rut) *n.* **1.** periodically recurring sexual excitement of various male animals, as deer, goats, and sheep. **2.** period during which this lasts. —*v.i.,* **rut·ted, rut·ting.** to be in such a state. [Old French *rut* the sexual excitement, its period, going back to Latin *rūgītus* roar (from the noise made by deer in rut).]

ru·ta·ba·ga (rōō′tə bā′gə) *n.* plant, *Brassica napobrassica,* of the mustard family, bearing thick yellow or white tubers that are used as food and livestock feed. [Dialectal Swedish *rotabagge.*]

ruth (rōōth) *n. Archaic.* **1.** pity; compassion. **2.** sorrow; remorse. [Old Norse *hrygth* affliction, sorrow.]

Ruth (rōōth) *n.* **1.** in the Old Testament, daughter-in-law of Naomi, to whom she was devoted, and the wife of Boaz. **2.** book of the Old Testament relating her story.

Ruth, Babe (rōōth; bāb) 1895–1948, U.S. baseball player; born George Herman Ruth.

Ru·the·ni·a (rōō thē′nē ə) *n.* former province of eastern Czechoslovakia, ceded to the Soviet Union in 1945. —**Ru·the′ni·an,** *adj., n.*

ru·the·ni·um (rōō thē′nē əm) *n.* hard, silvery metallic element used as a hardener for platinum, for jewelry, and in alloys for electrical contacts. Symbol: **Ru** See **element** for table. [Modern Latin *ruthenium,* from Medieval Latin *Ruthenia* Russia; because it was discovered in Russia.]

Ruth·er·ford, Lord Ernest (ruth′ər fərd) 1871–1937, English physicist.

ruth·less (rōōth′lis) *adj.* merciless and unrelenting in the pursuit of one's own ends: *a ruthless politician.* —**ruth′less·ly,** *adv.* —**ruth′less·ness,** *n.*

rut·ty (rut′ē) **-ti·er, -ti·est.** *adj.* full of ruts. —**rut′ti·ness,** *n.*

R.V., Revised Version (of the Bible).

Rwan·da (rōō än′də) *n.* country in east-central Africa. Capital: Kigali. Area, 10,169 sq. mi. Pop. (1967 est.), 3,306,000.

-ry, form of **-ery,** as in *baptistry, revelry, jewelry, ministry.* [Short for -ERY.]

Ry., railway.

rye (rī) *n.* **1.** grain of a hardy slender-stemmed plant, *Secale cereale,* of the grass family, used chiefly as feed for animals, and in the manufacture of flour, whiskey, gin, and grain alcohol. **2.** the plant, widely cultivated for its edible grain, and also raised as a winter cover crop to prevent soil erosion. **3.** whiskey distilled from fermented mash of rye grains or a mixture of rye and malt. [Old English *ryge* the grain.]

Grain head   Plant
Rye

rye grass, any of a group of grasses, genus *Lolium,* having long, narrow, flat leaves and terminal flower spikes, widely cultivated as forage grasses.

Ryu·kyu Islands (rē ōō′kū′) island chain in the western Pacific extending in an arc from Kyushu, Japan to Taiwan. Land area, 1800 sq. mi. Pop. (1969 est.), 982,000.

---

at; āpe; cär; end; mē; it; īce; hot; ōld; fôrk; wood; fōōl; oil; out; up; ūse; turn; sing; thin; **th**is; zh in treasure; ə in ago, taken, pencil, lemon, circus.

S

s, S (es) *pl.* **s's, S's.** *n.* **1.** nineteenth letter of the English alphabet. **2.** shape of this letter or something having such a shape.

-s¹, inflectional ending used to form the plural of most nouns: *horses.*

-s², inflectional ending used to form the third person singular of the present indicative of most verbs: *talks, runs, eats.*

-s³ *suffix* used to form certain adverbs: *always, sometimes.*

's¹, inflectional ending used to form the possessive case of singular nouns, of plural nouns not ending in *s,* and of some pronouns: *a girl's dress, children's toys, anyone's hat.*

's² **1.** is: *She's three years old. She's away. She's left.* **2.** has: *He's already been there.* **3.** us: *Let's go now.*

s. **1.** second. **2.** shilling. **3.** singular.

S, sulfur.

S **1.** South. **2.** Southern.

S. **1.** Saturday. **2.** Sunday. **3.** September. **4.** Saint. **5.** School.

S.A. **1.** South America. **2.** South Africa. **3.** Salvation Army.

Saar (sär, zär) *n.* **1.** river flowing from northeastern France into West Germany, joining the Moselle. **2.** Saarland.

Saar·brück·en (zär′brook′ən, sär′-) *n.* city in western West Germany, on the Saar. Pop. (1968 est.), 132,622.

Saar·land (sär′land′, zär′-) *n.* political subdivision of West Germany, in the western part of the country. Area, 991 sq. mi. Pop. (1968 est.), 1,128,900. Also, **Saar.**

Sa·bah (sä′bə) *n.* political subdivision of Malaysia, on the northeastern coast of Borneo. Area, 29,388 sq. mi. Pop. (1965 est.), 526,000.

Sab·ba·tar·i·an (sab′ə tär′ē ən) *n.* **1.** one who observes Saturday as the Sabbath. **2.** one who adheres to a strict observance of the Sabbath. —*adj.* of or relating to the Sabbath or to Sabbatarians. —**Sab′ba·tar′i·an·ism,** *n.*

Sab·bath (sab′əth) *n.* day of the week reserved for rest and religious worship. Sunday is the Sabbath to most Christians; Saturday is observed as the Sabbath by the Jews and by some Christian denominations; Friday is the Muslim Sabbath. [Latin *sabbatum* the Sabbath, from Greek *sabbaton,* from Hebrew *shabbāth* rest, the Jewish Sabbath.]

sab·bat·i·cal (sə bat′i kəl) *n.* **1.** period of leave from instructional duties, usually consisting of a year, granted at intervals to a professor or other teacher for travel, study, or rest. **2.** any similar period of leave from one's regular employment. Also, **sabbatical leave, sabbatical year.** —*adj.* also, **Sabbatical,** of, relating to, or appropriate for the Sabbath. Also, **sab·bat′ic.** [Greek *sabbatikos* relating to the Sabbath (from *sabbaton* the Jewish Sabbath) + -AL¹; referring to the ancient Hebrew practice of resting the fields every seventh year by not cultivating them. See SABBATH.]

sa·ber (sā′bər) *also, British,* **sa·bre.** *n.* **1.** heavy single-edged sword designed for cutting, having a long, usually slightly curved blade. **2.** light, double-edged fencing sword, used for slashing and thrusting. —*v.t.* to strike, wound, or kill with a saber. [French *sabre* the heavy sword, through German, from Magyar *szablya,* from *szabni* to cut.]

sa·ber-toothed tiger (sā′bər tōōtht′) any of various extinct, tigerlike mammals, family Felidae, that had long, curved, daggerlike canine teeth in the upper jaw.

Saber-toothed tiger

Sa·bin, Albert Bruce (sā′bin) 1906—, Polish-born U.S. physician and microbiologist, developer of an oral vaccine against polio.

Sa·bine (sā′bīn) *n.* **1.** member of a tribe that lived in hills northeast of ancient Rome and waged war against the Romans until 290 B.C.

2. extinct language of the Sabines, belonging to the Italic branch of the Indo-European language family. —*adj.* of or relating to the Sabines or their language.

sa·ble (sā′bəl) *n.* **1.** any of various martens, family Mustelidae, esp. the **Russian sable,** *Martes zibellina,* which is native to the northern pine forests of Siberia and Europe and has a bushy, foxlike tail, round ears, and fur which is usually grayish-brown in color. **2.** the expensive fur itself, used for making coats, stoles, and trimmings. **3.** the color black. **4. sables.** black mourning clothes. —*adj.* **1.** of the color black. **2.** dark. [Old French *sable* the animal and the fur, through German, from Russian *sobol'.*]

sab·ot (sab′ō, sa bō′) *n.* **1.** shoe carved from a single piece of wood, worn esp. in the Netherlands, Belgium, and France. **2.** heavy leather sandal or shoe having a thick wooden sole. [French *sabot* wooden shoe; of uncertain origin.]

Sabots

sab·o·tage (sab′ə tazh′) *n.* **1.** deliberate damage or destruction of property or interference with operational activities for the purpose of obstructing normal functioning or production, as that done by enemy agents to hinder a nation's war or defense effort. **2.** any deliberate, treacherous attempt to harm, destroy, or obstruct some activity or effort. —*v.t.,* **-taged, -tag·ing.** to commit sabotage against. [French *sabotage* deliberate destruction of property, from *saboter* to damage, bungle, from *sabot* wooden shoe; supposedly referring to the former practice of damaging an employer's machinery by throwing wooden shoes into it. See SABOT.]

sab·o·teur (sab′ə tur′, -toor′) *n.* one who commits or engages in sabotage.

sa·bra (sä′brə) *n.* native-born Israeli. [Hebrew *sābrāh.*]

sa·bre (sā′bər) *British.* saber. —*v.t.,* **-bred, -bring.** to saber.

sac (sak) *n.* pouch or pouchlike structure or part in a plant or animal often containing a liquid. [Latin *saccus* bag. See SACK¹.]

Sac (sak, sôk) *pl.* **Sacs** or **Sac.** *n.* Sauk.

SAC, Strategic Air Command.

sac·cha·rin (sak′ər in) *n.* white crystalline powder that has a sweetening power several hundred times that of cane sugar, chiefly used as a calorie-free substitute for sugar.

sac·cha·rine (sak′ər in, -ə rīn′) *adj.* **1.** sweet to an excessive or cloying degree: *a saccharine smile.* **2.** of, relating to, or of the nature of sugar. —*n.* saccharin. [Medieval Latin *saccharum* sugar (from Greek *sakcharon,* going back to Sanskrit *sharkarā* gravel, sugar) + -INE¹.] —**sac′cha·rine·ly,** *adv.*

sac·cule (sak′ūl) *n.* **1.** small sac. **2.** smaller of the two sacs in the membranous labyrinth of the inner ear. Also, **sac·cu·lus** (sak′yə ləs). [Latin *sacculus* little bag, diminutive of *saccus* bag. See SACK¹.]

sac·er·do·tal (sas′ər dōt′əl) *adj.* of or relating to a priest or the priesthood; priestly. [Latin *sacerdōtālis,* from *sacerdōs* priest.]

sac·er·do·tal·ism (sas′ər dōt′əl iz′əm) *n.* beliefs, practices, or character of the priesthood. —**sac′er·do′tal·ist,** *n.*

sa·chem (sā′chəm) *n.* among certain North American Indians, the hereditary ruler or chief of a confederation of tribes. [Algonquian *sachem.*]

sa·chet (sa shā′) *n.* **1.** small bag or pad containing a fragrant substance, as perfumed powder, used esp. to scent articles of clothing. **2.** perfumed powder used in such a bag or pad. [French *sachet* small bag, diminutive of *sac* bag, from Latin *saccus.* See SACK¹.]

sack¹ (sak) *n.* **1.** large bag made of coarse, strong material: *to put mail in sacks, a sack of potatoes.* **2.** any bag. **3.a.** sack and that which it contains. **b.** quantity of material contained in a sack. **4.** *also,* **sacque,** short, loose-fitting jacket for women and children. **5. the sack.** *Slang.* **a.** a dismissal from employment. **b.** bed. **6. to hit the sack.** *Slang.* to

at; āpe; cär; end; mē; it; īce; hot; ōld; fôrk; wood; fōōl; oil; out; up; ūse; turn; sing; thin; this; zh in treasure; ə in ago, taken, pencil, lemon, circus.

go to bed; go to sleep. —*v.t.* **1.** to put into a sack or sacks. **2.** *Slang.* to dismiss from employment; fire. —*v.i.* **to sack out.** *Slang.* to go to bed; go to sleep. [Old English *sacc* bag, sackcloth, from Latin *saccus,* from Greek *sakkos,* from Hebrew *saq.*]

sack² (sak) *v.t.* to break into or in upon and strip of possessions or goods by open force; plunder, as a captured city. —*n.* act of sacking, esp. of sacking a captured city. [French *sac* plunder, from Italian *sacco,* going back to Latin *saccus* bag; referring to carrying off booty in a bag when plundering. See SACK¹.]

sack³ (sak) *n.* **1.** dry, light-colored sherry. **2.** any of several strong, dry white wines from southern Europe. [French *(vin) sec* dry (wine), from Latin *siccus* dry.]

sack·but (sak′but′) *n.* musical instrument of medieval times, forerunner of the trombone. [French *saquebute* trombone, from Old French *saquer* to pull (of uncertain origin) + *bouter* to push (of Germanic origin); because it is played by pushing and pulling its sliding piece.]

sack·cloth (sak′klôth′) *n.* **1.** coarse cloth for making sacks; sacking. **2.** garment made of this or any similar coarse, rough cloth, worn as a sign of mourning, humility, or penitence.

sack coat, man's loose-fitting jacket having a straight back.

sack·ful (sak′fool′) *pl.,* **-fuls.** *n.* amount that a sack holds; quantity sufficient to fill a sack.

sack·ing (sak′ing) *n.* any of various coarse, woven cloths, as burlap, used for making such items as bags and sacks.

sacque (sak) *n.* sack¹ (def. 4).

sac·ra·ment (sak′rə mənt) *n.* **1.** any of several Christian rites considered to be outward visible signs of inner spiritual grace. The Roman Catholic, Orthodox, and some Anglican churches recognize seven sacraments: baptism, penance, Holy Communion, confirmation, matrimony, holy orders, and anointing of the sick. **2.** *also,* the **Sacrament. a.** Holy Communion. **b.** consecrated bread and wine used in Holy Communion, or the bread alone. **3.** something considered to have a sacred or mysterious character or significance. [Late Latin *sacrāmentum* religious rite, from Latin *sacrāmentum* oath, solemn obligation, going back to *sacer* holy.]

sac·ra·men·tal (sak′rə ment′əl) *adj.* **1.** of, relating to, or used in a sacrament. **2.** constituting, of the nature of, or having the force of a sacrament. —*n.* in the Roman Catholic, Orthodox, and some Anglican churches, any object or ceremony instituted to aid in devotion and in obtaining grace, as the use of holy water. —**sac′ra·men′tal·ly,** *adv.*

Sac·ra·men·to (sak′rə men′tō) *n.* **1.** capital of California, in the central part of the state, on the Sacramento River. Pop. (1970), 254,413. **2.** river flowing from northern California into San Francisco Bay.

sa·cred (sā′krid) *adj.* **1.** set apart for, belonging to, or dedicated to a deity or religious use or purpose; commanding religious veneration or respect: *sacred ground, the sacred name of God.* **2.** of or relating to religion; not secular; religious: *sacred music.* **3.** exclusively devoted, dedicated, or consecrated to someone or something: *a temple sacred to Venus.* **4.** regarded with or entitled to respect or reverence similar to that shown holy things: *a philosopher whose memory is still sacred to his disciples.* **5.** secured, as by religious feeling or respect, against violation; not to be violated, profaned, or treated thoughtlessly: *a sacred duty.* [Middle English *sacred,* past participle of *sacren* to consecrate, from Latin *sacrāre.*] —**sa′cred·ly,** *adv.* —**sa′cred·ness,** *n.* —**Syn. 1.** see **holy.**

Sacred College, College of Cardinals. Also, **Sacred College of Cardinals.**

sacred cow, something or someone supposedly above reproach and not to be criticized.

sac·ri·fice (sak′rə fīs′) *n.* **1.** act of making an offering, as of an animal or of a human life, to a deity, in propitiation or worship. **2.** person, animal, or thing so offered. **3.a.** act of giving up, foregoing, or destroying something, esp. something valued or desired, usually for the sake of something else. **b.** that which is so given up. **4.** loss of profit incurred in selling something below its supposed value. **5.** *Baseball.* sacrifice hit. —*v.t.,* **-ficed, -fic·ing. 1.** to offer as a sacrifice to a deity. **2.** to give up, forego, or suffer to be lost or destroyed for the sake of something else. **3.** to sell or part with at a loss. **4.** *Baseball.* to advance (a runner or runners) by making a sacrifice hit. —*v.i.* **1.** to offer or make a sacrifice. **2.** *Baseball.* to make a sacrifice hit. [Old French *sacrifice* offering to a god, from Latin *sacrificium,* from *sacer* holy + *facere* to make.] —**sac′ri·fic′er,** *n.*

sacrifice fly *Baseball.* fly ball that enables a runner on third base to score after the ball is caught by an opposing player.

sacrifice hit *Baseball.* bunt that advances the runner or runners on base but results in the batter being put out.

sac·ri·fi·cial (sak′rə fish′əl) *adj.* of, relating to, used in, or of the nature of a sacrifice. —**sac′ri·fi′cial·ly,** *adv.*

sac·ri·lege (sak′rə lij) *n.* **1.** violation or desecration of anything sacred. **2.** outrageous disrespect toward or disregard for a cherished or revered person or thing. [Old French *sacrilege* desecration of a sacred

thing, from Latin *sacrilegium* robbing of a temple, going back to *sacer* holy + *legere* to gather.]

sac·ri·le·gious (sak′rə lij′əs, -lē′jəs) *adj.* **1.** constituting, relating to, or involving sacrilege. **2.** guilty of sacrilege. —**sac′ri·le′gious·ly,** *adv.* —**sac′ri·le′gious·ness,** *n.*

sac·ris·tan (sak′ris tən) *n.* one who is in charge of a sacristy.

sac·ris·ty (sak′ris tē) *pl.,* **-ties.** *n.* room or rooms in a church where the sacred vessels, robes, and other objects used in ceremonies are kept. [Medieval Latin *sacristia,* going back to Latin *sacer* holy.]

sac·ro·il·i·ac (sak′rō il′ē ak′) *n.* fibrous joint in the lower part of the back, formed by the two hipbones and the sacrum. —*adj.* of or relating to this joint or the ligaments joining the sacrum and the ilium. [SACR(UM) + ILIAC.]

sac·ro·sanct (sak′rō sangkt′) *adj.* very sacred; inviolable. [Latin *sacrōsānctus,* from *sacer* holy + *sānctus* holy.] —**sac′ro·sanc′ti·ty,** *n.*

sa·crum (sak′rəm, sāk′-) *pl.,* **-ra** (-rə) or **-rums.** *n.* triangular bone composed of five fused vertebrae, located near the base of the spine and forming the back of the pelvis. [Late Latin *(os) sacrum*

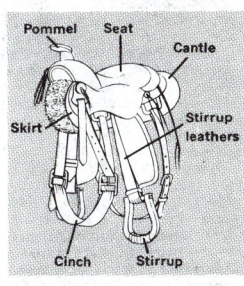

holy (bone), going back to Latin *sacer* holy; referring to its use in sacrifice to the gods in ancient times.]

sad (sad) **sad·der, sad·dest.** *adj.* **1.** feeling or expressing low spirits, unhappiness, or sorrow. **2.** causing or marked by unhappiness, sorrow, or gloom. **3.** extremely or pitifully bad; deplorable; pathetic: *a sad state of affairs.* **4.** (of color) dark; dull; drab. [Old English *sæd* sated, weary.] —**sad′ly,** *adv.* —**sad′ness,** *n.*

sad·den (sad′ən) *v.t., v.i.* to make or become sad.

sad·dle (sad′əl) *n.* **1.** seat for a rider, to be used on the back of a horse or similar animal, usually made of heavy leather over a well-padded frame and held to the animal's back by one or more girths that pass around the body. **2.** similar padded seat, as on a motorcycle. **3.** something resembling a saddle in shape, position, or function. **4.** padded part of a harness that fits over an animal's back and supports the shafts. **5.** depression in a ridge joining two peaks or higher elevations, or the ridge itself. **6.** cut of meat, esp. of mutton, veal, or lamb, consisting of the undivided back of an animal including the two loins. **7. in the saddle.** in a position of power or control. —*v.t.,* **-dled, -dling. 1.** to put a saddle on: *to saddle a horse.* **2.** to encumber or load, as with a burden; burden: *to be saddled with debts.* **3.** to place or impose on, as a burden or responsibility (with *on* or *upon*): *The boy saddled the blame for his behavior on his sister.* —*v.i.* to put a saddle on a horse or similar animal and get into the saddle (often with *up*). [Old English *sadol* seat for a rider put on the back of a horse or similar animal.]

sad·dle·bag (sad′əl bag′) *n.* bag or pouch of leather or other material, usually one of a pair hung from a saddle.

saddle blanket, blanket or pad put on an animal's back beneath the saddle to prevent chafing or irritation.

sad·dle·bow (sad′əl bō′) *n.* arched front part of a saddle.

sad·dle·cloth (sad′əl klôth′) *n.* **1.** cloth bearing the number of a racehorse placed either under or over the saddle. **2.** saddle blanket.

saddle horse, horse trained or suitable for riding.

sad·dler (sad′lər) *n.* one who makes, repairs, or sells saddlery.

sad·dler·y (sad′lər ē) *pl.,* **-dler·ies.** *n.* **1.** saddles, harnesses, and other equipment, collectively, for horses, esp. equipment made of leather. **2.** shop of a saddler. **3.** craft, business, or work of a saddler.

saddle shoe, oxford shoe, usually white in color, having a band of contrasting color or texture across the instep.

saddle soap, mild soap, usually containing neat's-foot oil, used to clean, soften, and preserve leather and leather articles.

sad·dle·tree (sad′əl trē′) *n.* frame of a saddle.

Sad·du·cee (saj′ə sē′, sad′yə-) *n.* member of a Jewish political and religious sect that believed in strict, literal interpretation of written Mosaic Law, rejected oral law, and denied belief in fate, life after death, and resurrection.

sad·i·ron (sad′ī′ərn) *n.* flatiron having two pointed ends and a removable handle. [SAD (in the dialectal sense of "heavy") + IRON.]

Caption (saddle figure): Pommel, Seat, Cantle, Skirt, Stirrup leathers, Cinch, Stirrup — **Saddle**

sa·dism (sā'diz'əm, sad'iz'-) n. abnormal tendency to derive pleasure from the infliction of physical or mental pain or punishment on others. Distinguished from **masochism**. [French *sadisme*, from Marquis de *Sade*, 1740–1814, whose writings described and advocated behavior arising from such a tendency.] —**sa'dist**, n.

sa·dis·tic (sə dis'tik) adj. relating to or characterized by sadism. —**sa·dis'ti·cal·ly**, adv.

sa·fa·ri (sə fär'ē) pl., -ries. n. 1. hunting expedition, esp. in Africa. 2. any long or arduous trip, esp. one in search of something. [Swahili *safari* journey, from Arabic *safarī* relating to a journey, from *safar* journey.]

safe (sāf) saf·er, saf·est. adj. 1. free from harm or danger: *It's not safe to walk there alone at night.* 2. free from or having escaped hurt or injury; unharmed: *The messenger arrived safe at headquarters after crossing enemy lines.* 3. affording security, protection, or freedom from harm, danger, or injury: *Find a safe place in which to put the papers.* 4. involving no risk, uncertainty, or danger of failure, mishap, or error: *a safe bet, a safe investment.* 5. unable or unlikely to cause or do harm or injury: *The lion is safe in its cage.* 6. avoiding risk, danger, or uncertainty; prudent; cautious: *a safe player.* 7. *Baseball.* having succeeded in reaching a base without being put out. —n. 1. strong container of metal or other material, capable of being locked, used for the safekeeping of valuables. 2. any place used for storage and protection, as a cooled box in which to keep perishable foods. [Old French *salf, sauf* free from danger or death, from Latin *salvus* unharmed, well¹.] —**safe'ly**, adv. —**safe'ness**, n.

Syn. adj. 1. **Safe, secure** mean free from danger or peril. **Safe** may be applied to a person or thing that has passed beyond or is out of the reach of actual danger: *A harbor is a safe place for a ship in a storm.* **Secure** emphasizes freedom from anxiety and reliance on the strength of something that affords unassailable protection or shields one from harm, injury, or loss: *A child feels secure when it is near its mother.*

safe-con·duct (sāf'kon'dukt) n. 1. privilege of protected passage through a hazardous region, as enemy or occupied territory. 2. official document or escort assuring this privilege.

safe-crack·er (sāf'krak'ər) n. thief who breaks into safes for the valuables they contain.

safe-de·pos·it (sāf'di poz'it) adj. relating to or designating a metal drawer or other container, esp. in a bank, for the safekeeping of valuables. Also, **safe'ty-de·pos'it.**

safe·guard (sāf'gärd') n. 1. something that serves as a guard, protection, or defense, or that promotes or ensures safety. 2. mechanical device or technical procedure designed to prevent accident and injury. —v.t. to safeguard; protect; defend.

safe·keep·ing (sāf'kē'ping) n. 1. act of keeping safe. 2. protection; custody.

safe·ty (sāf'tē) pl., -ties. n. 1. quality or state of being safe; freedom from harm, danger, injury, or risk. 2. device designed to prevent accident or injury or to reduce hazard, as the catch on a firearm that prevents it from firing. 3. *Football.* **a.** score of two points for the defensive team, resulting from the ball being downed by the offensive team on or behind its own goal line, after that team caused the ball to pass the line. **b.** play in which this occurs. **c.** defensive player who takes the position nearest to his team's goal line. —adj. contributing to or giving safety.

safety belt 1. belt, strap, or harness used to fasten a person working at great heights to a fixed object to prevent falling or injury. 2. seat belt.

safety glass, laminated glass formed by inserting a layer of transparent plastic material between two sheets of glass in order to prevent shattering.

safety lamp, lamp designed for use in mines, constructed to avoid explosion where flammable gases are present, usually by having its flame enclosed in a metal gauze screen.

safety match, match that will ignite only when struck against a friction surface coated with red phosphorus.

safety pin, pin bent back on itself so as to form a spring, having a sheath at one end to cover and hold the point.

safety razor, razor with a guard or guards around the blade to reduce the instance and seriousness of skin cuts.

safety valve 1. device on a container, as on a steam boiler, that opens automatically to allow gases or fluids to escape when the pressure in the container reaches a danger point. 2. anything serving as an outlet for the release of an excess, as of energy or emotion.

saf·flow·er (saf'lou'ər) n. 1. tall thistlelike plant, *Carthamus tinctorius*, bearing yellowish-orange flower heads and cultivated for an edible oil extracted from its seeds. 2. bright-red dye made from the flower heads of this plant, used in cosmetics. [Middle French *saffleur*, through Italian, from Arabic *asfar* yellow, yellow plant; influenced by SAFFRON, FLOWER.]

saf·fron (saf'rən) n. 1. yellow coloring and flavoring agent made from the dried styles of a crocus, *Crocus sativus*, of the iris family. 2. the plant itself, having fragrant purple or white flowers. 3. orange-yellow color. Also, *(def. 3)* **saffron yellow**. [Old French *safran*, going back to Arabic *za'farān* the plant.]

S. Afr., South Africa; South African.

sag (sag) sagged, sag·ging. v.i. 1. to hang down or curve or incline downwards, from or as if from weight, pressure, or loss of firmness, resilience, or original shape: *This mattress sags so much that I get backaches when I sleep on it.* 2. to bend or hang unevenly or loosely: *The rusty gate sagged on its hinges.* 3. to lose firmness, strength, or elasticity; sink; weaken: *Their spirits sagged when they realized help wasn't on the way.* 4. to slow up, decrease, or move unsteadily; decline: *Production has sagged during the recession.* 5. (of a boat or ship) to drift, esp. to leeward. —n. 1. act, state, or extent of sagging. 2. place where something sags. [Probably of Scandinavian origin.] —**Syn.** v.i. 1. see **droop.**

sa·ga (sä'gə) n. 1. prose narrative composed in Iceland during the Middle Ages, usually dealing with heroic figures and incidents from Scandinavian legend and history. 2. any long, involved story or narrative, often one dealing with colorful or adventurous deeds. [Old Norse *saga* story.]

sa·ga·cious (sə gā'shəs) adj. having or showing wisdom, sound judgment, and keen perception or discernment: *a sagacious ruler.* [Latin *sagāci-*, stem of *sagāx* keen + -OUS.] —**sa·ga'cious·ly**, adv. —**sa·ga'cious·ness**, n.

sa·gac·i·ty (sə gas'ə tē) n. quality of being sagacious.

sag·a·more (sag'ə môr') n. among certain North American Indian tribes, an elective ruler or chief, esp. one subordinate to a sachem. [Algonquian *sagimo* literally, he prevails.]

sage¹ (sāj) n. man of profound wisdom, esp. an elderly man who is widely revered for his wisdom, judgment, or experience. —adj. sag·er, sag·est. having, proceeding from, or showing far-seeing wisdom and sound, calm judgment; prudent; wise. [Old French *sage* wise, going back to Latin *sapere* to be wise.] —**sage'ly**, adv. —**sage'ness**, n.

sage² (sāj) n. 1. fragrant leaves of a small plant, *Salvia officinalis*, of the mint family, widely used to flavor food. 2. the plant itself, having fragrant, bell-shaped blue, purple, or white flowers. 3. any plant of the genus *Salvia*. 4. sagebrush. [Old French *sau(l)ge* the plant, from Latin *salvia* literally, the healing plant, from *salvus* unharmed, well¹; because it was thought to have healing qualities.]

sage·brush (sāj'brush') n. any of several hardy shrubs, genus *Artemisia*, that grow on the dry plains of western North America, often in the form of dense bushes with silvery leaves and small yellow or whitish flower heads.

Sage leaves

sage grouse, grouse, *Centrocercus urophasianus*, native to the plains of western North America. It is the largest North American grouse.

sage hen, sage grouse, esp. a female sage grouse.

Sag·i·naw (sag'ə nô') n. city in east-central Michigan. Pop. (1970), 91,849.

Sag·it·tar·i·us (saj'ə tār'ē əs) n. 1. constellation located near the horizon in the northern sky, conventionally depicted as a centaur drawing a bow. 2. ninth sign of the zodiac. See **zodiac** for illustration. [Latin *sagittārius* archer.]

sag·it·tate (saj'ə tāt') adj. shaped like an arrowhead, as certain leaves. [Modern Latin *sagittatus*, from Latin *sagitta* arrow.]

sa·go (sā'gō) pl., -gos. n. 1. grainy or powdered starch extracted from the trunk and stems of various tropical palm trees and palmlike plants. 2. sago palm. [Malay *sāgū* the starch.]

Sagittate leaf

sago palm, either of two trees, *Metroxlyn sagu* or *M. rumphi*, found in marshy areas of the East Indies, having long leaves made up of lance-shaped leaflets. They are the major source of sago.

sa·gua·ro (sə gwär'ō, -wär'ō) pl., -ros. also, **sa·hua·ro** (sä wär'ō). n. giant cactus, *Carnegiea gigantea*, found in southern Arizona and neighboring regions, having sparse branches covered with heavy spines, and bearing white flowers and edible fruit. [Spanish *saguaro*; of Mexican Indian origin.]

Sa·ha·ra (sə har'ə, -här'ə, -hâr'ə) n. desert in northern Africa, the largest in the world. Area, approx. 3,000,000 sq. mi.

sa·hib (sä'ib, -hib, -ēb, -hēb) n. sir; master. ▲ formerly used as a title of respect in India and Pakistan, esp. for Europeans. [Urdu *sāhib* lord, companion, from Arabic *sāhib*.]

said (sed) v. past tense and past participle of **say.** —adj. named or

mentioned before; aforesaid. ▲ usually used only in legal or business contexts.

Sai·gon (sī gon′) *n.* capital and chief port of South Vietnam, in the southern part of the country. Pop. (1968 est.), 1,682,000.

sail (sāl) *pl.,* **sails** or *(def. 4)* **sail.** *n.* **1.** piece of canvas or other material attached to a vessel so as to spread to the wind and cause the vessel to move through the water. **2.** such pieces collectively. **3.** something resembling a sail in shape, position, or function, as an arm of a windmill. **4.** trip or ride in a vessel, esp. in a sailboat. **5. to make sail.** **a.** to spread out the sail or sails of a vessel. **b.** to begin a voyage by water. **6. to set sail.** to begin a voyage by water. **7. under sail.** moving under the power of a sail or sails. —*v.i.* **1.** (of a vessel) to move or be propelled over water by means of a sail or sails or by mechanical power. **2.** to travel over water in a vessel. **3.** to begin a voyage by water: *The ship will sail for Hawaii in two weeks.* **4.** to manage or operate a sailboat, esp. for sport. **5.** to move or proceed smoothly and effortlessly: *The volleyball sailed over the net.* **6. to sail into. a.** to attack or criticize violently. **b.** to begin or enter into with vigor and energy. —*v.t.* **1.** to move or travel over or across (a body of water): *This ship sailed the Mediterranean last year.* **2.** to steer, manage, or navigate (a vessel). [Old English *seg(e)l* piece of cloth attached to a vessel so as to catch the wind and cause the vessel to move through the water.] —**Syn.** *v.i.* **5.** see **fly²**.

sail·boat (sāl′bōt′) *n.* boat equipped with a sail or sails, by means of which it is propelled.

sail·cloth (sāl′klôth′) *n.* canvas or other strong material suitable or used for making sails, tents, or the like.

sail·er (sā′lər) *n.* boat or ship, esp. a sailing vessel, with reference to its sailing capability or power: *a fast sailer.*

sail·fish (sāl′fish′) *pl.,* **-fish** or **-fish·es.** *n.* any of several saltwater game fish, family Istiophoridae, found in warm coastal waters, having a large, sail-like dorsal fin and a long, spearlike snout. Length: up to 12 feet.

Sailfish

sail·ing (sā′ling) *n.* **1.** art or sport of managing, operating, or riding in sailboats. **2.** art or skill of steering, managing, or navigating a vessel. **3.** act of one who or that which sails.

sail·or (sā′lər) *n.* **1.** one whose trade or occupation is handling, sailing, or navigating boats and ships. **2.** seaman below the rank of an officer. **3.** member of a country's navy, esp. an enlisted man. **4.** person traveling by water, with reference to his susceptibility to seasickness. **5.** sailor hat.

sailor hat, straw hat with a low, flat crown and a flat brim.

sail·plane (sāl′plān′) *n.* light glider having a streamlined fuselage and slender wings and tail.

saint (sānt) *n.* **1.** *Religion.* **a.** person honored after his death for exceptional piety and holiness, and, esp. in the Roman Catholic and Orthodox churches, one who has been formally declared to be in heaven and worthy of veneration on earth. **b.** one who has died and whose spirit has gone to heaven. **2.** one who is noted for holiness, godliness, or virtue. **3.** person who is exceptionally kind, patient, or unselfish. —*v.t.* to proclaim or venerate as a saint; canonize. [Old French *saint* holy, holy person, person canonized by the Roman Catholic Church, from Latin *sānctus* holy.]

Saint (sānt) Biographical entries for Saints appear at the name of the individual. For other entries not found here, see also **St.** and **Ste.**

Saint Agnes's Eve, the night of January 20, on which, according to traditional superstition, a girl would see a vision of her future husband.

Saint Ber·nard (bər närd′) large, reddish-brown and white dog having a massive head, a long bushy tail, and a dense, usually coarse, coat, noted for its use in rescuing people lost in the snow of the Swiss Alps. Height: to 30 inches at the shoulder. [From its use by monks of the hospice of *Saint Bernard* in the Swiss Alps.]

Saint Bernard

saint·ed (sān′tid) *adj.* **1.** proclaimed or venerated as a saint; canonized. **2.** relating to or befitting a saint. **3.** pious; saintly. **4.** regarded as being among the saints in heaven; deceased.

Saint El·mo's fire (el′mōz) luminous, often audible, electrical discharge from pointed objects, such as spires, ships' masts, or airplane wings, that occurs during storms when the atmosphere has a strong electrical charge. Also, **Saint Elmo's light.** [From *St. Elmo,* patron saint of sailors; supposedly because sailors in the Mediterranean, upon seeing the discharge, thought it to be a manifestation of him.]

saint·hood (sānt′hood′) *n.* **1.** character or condition of being a saint. **2.** saints collectively.

saint·ly (sānt′lē) **-li·er, -li·est.** *adj.* relating to, resembling, or befitting a saint. —**saint′li·ness,** *n.*

Saint Patrick's Day, day set aside to honor Saint Patrick, observed annually on March 17.

Saint-Saëns, Charles Ca·mille (saN säns′; shärl kä mē′yə) 1835–1921, French composer.

saint·ship (sānt′ship′) *n.* sainthood *(def. 1).*

Saint Val·en·tine's Day (val′ən tīnz′) Valentine's Day.

Saint Vi·tus' dance (vī′tə siz) nervous disorder characterized by involuntary twitching of the muscles in the face, arms, and legs. Also, **cho·re′a.** [Because prayers for a cure of this disorder were addressed to *Saint Vitus,* the patron saint of actors and dancers.]

Sai·pan (sī pan′, -pän′) *n.* one of the Mariana Islands, in the western Pacific, east of the Philippines, administered by the United States. Area, 47 sq. mi. Pop. (1962), 7830.

saith (seth, sā′ith) *Archaic.* third person singular present indicative of **say.**

sake¹ (sāk) *n.* **1.** good or advantage; benefit; welfare: *You may not want to hear this, but I'm saying it for your own sake.* **2.** purpose; reason: *For the sake of argument, let's assume he's innocent.* [Old English *sacu* strife, lawsuit.]

sa·ke² (sä′kē) *also,* **sa·ki.** *n.* fermented alcoholic beverage of Japanese origin, made from rice. [Japanese *sake.*]

Sak·ha·lin (sak′ə lēn) *n.* large island of the Soviet Union, in the western Pacific, just off the eastern coast of Siberia. Area, 29,344 sq. mi. Pop. (1967 est.), 640,000.

sal (sal) *n.* salt. ▲ used chiefly in pharmaceutical and chemical contexts. [Latin *sāl.*]

sa·laam (sə läm′) *n.* **1.** in certain Asian countries, salutation or obeisance performed by bowing low, and usually clasping the hands together or touching the right hand to the forehead. **2.** verbal greeting meaning "peace", used esp. among Muslims. —*v.i.* to make a salaam. —*v.t.* to greet with a salaam. [Arabic *salām* peace, salutation.]

sal·a·ble (sā′lə bəl) *also,* **sale·a·ble.** *adj.* that can be sold; marketable. —**sal′a·bil′i·ty, sal′a·ble·ness,** *n.*

sa·la·cious (sə lā′shəs) *adj.* **1.** stimulating or appealing to the sexual imagination; obscene. **2.** lustful; lecherous. [Latin *salāci-,* stem of *salāx* lustful (from *salīre* to leap) + -OUS.] —**sa·la′cious·ly,** *adv.* —**sa·la′cious·ness, sa·lac·i·ty** (sə las′ə tē), *n.*

sal·ad (sal′əd) *n.* **1.** cold dish consisting chiefly of raw, or sometimes cooked, chopped or sliced vegetables, as lettuce, tomato, and cucumber, usually served with a dressing. **2.** course consisting of such a dish. **3.** cold dish consisting of chopped fruit, eggs, fish, or other food, often mixed with raw, chopped vegetables, usually prepared with mayonnaise or other dressing. **4.** any vegetable or herb used in or grown for salad. [Old French *salade* cold dish of seasoned vegetables, from Old Provençal *salada,* from *salar* to salt, from *sal* salt, from Latin *sāl.*]

salad days, time of youthful innocence and inexperience. [From "my salad days, when I was green in judgment" (Shakespeare, *Antony and Cleopatra*).]

Sal·a·din (sal′ə din) *n.* c.1138–93, Muslim conquerer and sultan of Egypt and Syria.

sal·a·man·der (sal′ə man′dər) *n.* **1.** any of a group of lizardlike amphibians, order Caudata, found in and near fresh water, having scaleless, usually smooth, moist skin. **2.** mythical lizard or

Salamander

other creature supposedly able to endure or live in fire. **3.** object used in fire or capable of withstanding heat, as a poker. [Old French *salamandre* the mythical creature, through Latin, from Greek *salamandrā.*]

sa·la·mi (sə lä′mē) *n.* sausage of seasoned pork or beef. [Italian *salami,* plural of *salame,* from *salar* to salt, going back to Latin *sāl* salt.]

Sal·a·mis (sal′ə mis) *n.* island in eastern Greece, west of Athens, site of a decisive Greek naval victory over the Persians in 480 B.C. Area, 39 sq. mi. Pop. (1961), 2645.

sal ammoniac, ammonium chloride. [Latin *sāl ammoniacus* literally, salt of Ammon; because this salt supposedly was first prepared from camel dung near a temple of Ammon in Africa.]

sal·a·ried (sal′ə rēd) *adj.* receiving or yielding a salary: *a salaried clerk, a salaried position.*

sal·a·ry (sal′ə rē) *pl.,* **-ries.** *n.* fixed sum of money paid at regular intervals to someone employed, in return for work or service. [Latin

salārium pay, allowance; originally, money given soldiers to buy salt, going back to *sāl* salt.] —**Syn.** see **pay**[1].
sale (sāl) *n.* **1.** transfer of ownership of something from one party to another in exchange for money or its equivalent: *the sale of a house.* **2.** act or instance of offering or selling off goods at reduced price: *an end-of-the-season sale.* **3.** for sale. available for purchase. **4.** on sale. offered at reduced price: *to buy sheets on sale.* **5.** public disposal of goods or property to the highest bidder; auction. **6.** sales. **a.** quantity sold; gross receipt: *Sales are up at that store.* **b.** activities, work, or department related to selling goods or services: *He's interested in a job in sales.* [Old English *sala* act of selling.]
sale·a·ble (sā′lə bəl) *adj.* salable. —**sale′a·bil′i·ty, sale′a·ble·ness,** *n.*
Sa·lem (sā′ləm) *n.* capital of Oregon, in the northwestern part of the state. Pop. (1970), 68,296.
Sa·ler·no (sə lur′nō, -lâr′-) *n.* port city in southwestern Italy. Pop. (1968 est.), 146,554.
sales·clerk (sālz′klurk′) *n.* one employed to sell merchandise in a store.
sales·girl (sālz′gurl′) *n.* girl or woman employed to sell merchandise in a store.
sales·la·dy (sālz′lā′dē) *pl.,* -dies. *n.* saleswoman.
sales·man (sālz′mən) *pl.,* -men. *n.* **1.** man who is employed to sell merchandise in a store. **2.** one who is employed to sell merchandise or services within a given area, as a traveling representative of a company.
sales·man·ship (sālz′mən ship′) *n.* ability, skill, or technique in selling.
sales·peo·ple (sālz′pē′pəl) *n.,pl.* salespersons.
sales·per·son (sālz′pur′sən) *n.* one employed to sell merchandise, esp. in a store.
sales talk, persuasive argument or talk, sometimes accompanied by a demonstration, intended to convince others to buy a product or service or to accept an idea or proposal. Also, **sales pitch.**
sales tax, general tax placed on the sale of goods, usually levied as a flat percentage of the selling price of an item.
sales·wom·an (sālz′woom′ən) *pl.,* -wom·en. *n.* woman or girl employed to sell merchandise, esp. in a store. Also, **sales′la′dy.**
Sa·li·an (sā′lē ən, sāl′yən) *adj.* of, relating to, or designating a tribe of Franks who settled in a region near the Zuider Zee in the fourth century A.D. —*n.* Salian Frank.
Sal·ic (sal′ik, sā′lik) *also,* **Sa·lique.** *adj.* of, relating to, or designating the Salian Franks.
sal·i·cin (sal′ə sin) *n.* crystalline alcohol compound of glucose, chiefly obtained from the bark of willow and poplar trees, and used in medicine. Formula: C₁₁H₁₈O₇. [French *salicine,* from Latin *salix* willow.]
Salic law, law that excluded women from the right of succession to the throne, effective in France, Spain, and certain other European kingdoms and states. [Because the French established this law by broadly interpreting one provision of the old law code of the Salian Franks, which prohibited women from inheriting land.]
sa·lic·y·late (sə lis′ə lāt′, -lit) *n.* salt or ester of salicylic acid.
sal·i·cyl·ic acid (sal′ə sil′ik) white, crystalline, organic compound used esp. in the manufacture of aspirin. Formula: C₆H₄(OH)(COOH).
sa·lience (sāl′yəns, sā′lē əns) *n.* **1.** state or quality of being salient. **2.** salient object, part, or feature. Also, **sa′lien·cy.**
sa·lient (sāl′yənt, sā′lē ənt) *adj.* **1.** standing out prominently from the rest; readily, strikingly, or conspicuously noticeable: *the salient traits of a personality, the salient contention in his theory.* **2.** projecting or extending beyond a line or surface; jutting or protruding outward. **3.** leaping; bounding; jumping. —*n.* part of a bastion, fortification, or line of defense that most projects towards the enemy. [Latin *saliēns,* present participle of *salīre* to leap.] —**sa′lient·ly,** *adv.*
sa·li·en·tian (sā′lē en′chən) *n.* any of a group of tail-less amphibians, order Salientia, including frogs and toads, having a broad body in which the head and trunk are fused and long, powerful hind legs. —*adj.* of, relating to, or belonging to this order. [Modern Latin *Salientia* literally, leaping ones (from Latin *saliēns*) + -AN. See SALIENT.]
sa·line (sā′lēn, -līn) *adj.* **1.** of, relating to, or resembling salt. **2.** consisting of or containing salt. **3.** relating to or containing any of the salts of the alkali metals or of magnesium. —*n.* **1.** saline solution, esp. as used in medicine, surgery, or biological experimentation. **2.** metallic salt, esp. a salt of an alkali metal or of magnesium, often used in medicine as a cathartic. [French *salin* containing salt, salty, going back to Latin *sāl* salt.] —**sa·lin·i·ty** (sə lin′ə tē), *n.*
Sa·lique (sə lēk′, sal′ik, sā′lik) *adj.* Salic.
Salis·bur·y (sôlz′ber′ē, salz′-) *n.* capital and largest city of Rhodesia, in the northeastern part of the country. Pop. (1968 est.), 180,000.
Salis·bur·y steak (sôlz′ber′ē, salz′-) ground beef, usually mixed with eggs or bread crumbs, formed into patties and either fried or broiled. [From J. H. *Salisbury,* nineteenth-century English physician interested in nutrition.]

Sa·lish (sā′lish) *n.* **1.** member of a tribe of North American Indians living in northwestern Montana. **2.** family of languages spoken by these and certain other North America Indians in the northwestern United States and in British Columbia. Also *(def. 2),* **Sa′lish·an.**
sa·li·va (sə lī′və) *n.* colorless fluid that contains the enzyme ptyalin and is secreted by the parotids and other glands of the mouth. Saliva keeps the mouth moist, lubricates the food during chewing, and starts the digestion of starches. [Latin *salīva.*]
sal·i·var·y (sal′ə ver′ē) *adj.* of, relating to, or secreting saliva: *salivary gland.*
sal·i·vate (sal′ə vāt′) -vat·ed, -vat·ing. *v.i.* to secrete saliva; undergo a secretion of saliva. [Latin *salīvātus,* past participle of *salīvāre* to spit.] —**sal′i·va′tion,** *n.*
Salk, Jonas Edward (sôlk, sôk) 1914—, U.S. physician and microbiologist, noted for developing the first successful vaccine for injection against polio.
sal·low[1] (sal′ō) *adj.* of a sickly, yellowish color or complexion. [Old English *salo.*] —**sal′low·ness,** *n.*
sal·low[2] (sal′ō) *n.* any of various trees of the willow family, esp. *Salix caprea,* the wood of which is used as a source of charcoal. [Old English *sealh.*]
Sal·lust (sal′əst) *n.* 86–c.34 B.C., Roman historian and politician.
sal·ly (sal′ē) -lied, -ly·ing. *v.i.* **1.** to set, start, or go out briskly or energetically (usually with *forth*). **2.** to rush out suddenly (usually with *forth*). —*n. pl.,* -lies. **1.** charge at an enemy made from a besieged position. **2.** quick, witty, bold retort or quip. **3.** a sudden rushing forth. **4.** setting or going forth, as on a short excursion. [French *saillie* an issuing forth, from *saillir* to issue forth, gush; earlier, leap, from *salīre* to leap.]
sal·ma·gun·di (sal′mə gun′dē) *n.* **1.** dish consisting of chopped ingredients, as meat, anchovies, eggs, and onions, usually arranged in rows and served with a dressing. **2.** any mixture or medley; hodgepodge. [French *salmigondis,* possibly from Middle French *salemine* viands (going back to Latin *sāl* salt) + *condir* to season (from Latin *condīre*).]
sal·mi (sal′mē) *also,* **sal·mis** (sal′mē). *n.* highly spiced dish consisting of fowl or game partially roasted and stewed in wine. [French *salmis,* short for *salmigondis.* See SALMAGUNDI.]
salm·on (sam′ən) *pl.,* -on or -ons. *n.* **1.** any of a group of food and game fish, family Salmonidae, usually having a silver

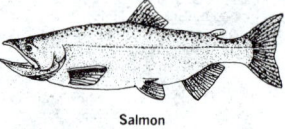

Salmon

body with a dark back. Each salmon returns to spawn in the stream where it was hatched. Although some live and spawn in fresh water, most live in salt water and migrate to fresh water in order to spawn. **2.** yellowish-pink color. Also *(def. 2),* **salmon pink.** [Old French *saumon* the fish, from Latin *salmō.*]
salmon trout, any of several trout that resemble salmon.
Sa·lo·me (sə lō′mē) *n.* in the New Testament, the daughter of Herodias. Herod granted Salome the head of John the Baptist as a reward for her dancing.
sa·lon (sə lon′) *pl.,* -lons. *n.* **1.** reception hall or room, often elegantly furnished and large in size, for receiving or entertaining guests. **2.** gathering of guests in such a room, esp. a periodic gathering of renowned or fashionable people, as literary figures, artists, or intellectuals. **3.** stylish shop or business establishment, esp. one specially equipped to provide a particular service or product: *a beauty salon, a beautiful gown that came from the town's best dress salon.* **4.** place used for the exhibition of works of art. **5.** exhibition of works of art. [French *salon* drawing room, from Italian *salone* hall, drawing room, from *sala* hall; of Germanic origin.]
Sa·lo·ni·ka (sal′ə nē′kə, sə lon′i kə) *n.* port city in northern Greece, known in ancient times as Thessalonica. Pop. (1961), 250,920. Also, *Greek,* **Thes′sa·lo·ni′ka.**
sa·loon (sə lōōn′) *n.* **1.** place where alcoholic drinks are served; bar; tavern. **2.** large room or hall for public gatherings or use, as for receptions, esp. the main social lounge on a passenger ship. [French *salon* drawing room. See SALON.]
sa·loon·keep·er (sə lōōn′kē′pər) *n.* one who owns or operates a saloon where alcoholic drinks are served.
sal·si·fy (sal′sə fī′) *pl.,* -fies. *n.* **1.** edible, carrot-shaped root of a plant, *Tragopogon porrifolius,* having white skin, grayish-white flesh, and an oysterlike flavor, eaten as a vegetable. **2.** the plant itself, having narrow, tapering leaves and bearing showy purple flower heads. Also, **oyster plant.** [French *salsifis* the plant, from obsolete Italian *salsifica;* of uncertain origin.]
sal soda, sodium carbonate *(def. 2).*

at; āpe; cär; end; mē; it; īce; hot; ōld; fôrk; wood; fōōl; oil; out; up; ūse; turn; sing; thin; this; zh in treasure; ə in ago, taken, pencil, lemon, circus.

salt (sôlt) *n.* **1.** white crystalline compound found in abundant amounts in mineral deposits in the earth and dissolved in sea water, used as a food seasoning and preservative and as a source of sodium and chlorine in industry. Formula: NaCl Also, **sodium chloride. 2.** any compound formed, along with water, by the reaction of an acid with a base and composed of the positive ion of the base and the negative ion of the acid. **3. salts. a.** any of various salts used as a laxative, as Epsom salts. **b.** smelling salts. **c.** bath salts. **4.** element that gives flavor, liveliness, or piquancy. **5.** sharp, pungent humor; wit. **6.** *Informal.* sailor, esp. an experienced one. **7. to be worth one's salt.** to be so dependable or capable as to be deserving of wages or support. **8. with a grain of salt.** with some reservation or skepticism concerning accuracy, sincerity, or truthfulness. —*adj.* **1.** tasting of or containing salt: *salt tears.* **2.** treated or preserved with salt: *salt butter.* **3.** flooded with or growing in or near salt water: *a salt meadow, a salt plant.* —*v.t.* **1.** to sprinkle or season with salt. **2.** to cure or preserve with salt or a salt solution (often with *down* or *away*). **3.** to enrich artificially and fraudulently, esp. to place material, as gold or oil, at the site of a mine or well, to make it appear that large quantities of the material are present. **4.** to give (an animal) salt. **5.** to add flavor or zest to; make lively or piquant; season. **6. to salt away.** *Informal.* to store away; save. **7. to salt out.** to cause (materials in solution or suspension) to precipitate by adding salt. [Old English *sealt* the food seasoning.]

salt-and-pep·per (sôlt′ən pep′ər) *adj.* pepper-and-salt.

salt·cel·lar (sôlt′sel′ər) *n.* shaker or dish used at the table for holding and dispensing salt. [SALT + obsolete *saler* saltcellar (from Old French *salier(e)* salt box, going back to Latin *sāl* salt).]

Saltcellar

salt·er (sôl′tər) *n.* **1.** one who manufactures or sells salt. **2.** one who treats or cures something, as meat or fish, with salt.

salt·ine (sôl tēn′) *n.* thin, crisp, flat cracker sprinkled with salt.

Salt Lake City, capital and largest city of Utah, in the northern part of the state. Pop. (1970), 175,885.

salt lick 1. exposed natural salt deposit that animals can lick to obtain salt needed in their diet. **2.** preparation of salt with other mineral additives, set out, usually in the form of blocks, as a nutritive supplement for livestock and other animals.

salt of the earth, any person or persons of good, sturdy character; extremely admirable individual or group. [From Matthew 5:13.]

salt·pe·ter (sôlt′pē′tər) *also,* **salt·pe·tre.** *n.* potassium nitrate. [Old French *salpetre,* going back to Latin *sāl* salt + *petra* rock (from Greek *petra*); perhaps from the saltlike crust it forms on rocks.]

salt·shak·er (sôlt′shā′kər) *n.* container with a perforated top for sprinkling salt.

salt·wa·ter (sôlt′wô′tər, -wot′ər) *adj.* of, consisting of, or living in salt water or the sea.

salt·y (sôl′tē) **salt·i·er, salt·i·est.** *adj.* **1.** relating to, containing, or tasting of salt. **2.** of or suggesting the sea or life at sea. **3.** piquant; witty. —**salt′i·ly,** *adv.* —**salt′i·ness,** *n.*

sa·lu·bri·ous (sə lōō′brē əs) *adj.* promoting or favorable to health or well-being; wholesome. [Latin *salūbris* (from *salūs* health) + -OUS.] —**sa·lu′bri·ous·ly,** *adv.* —**sa·lu′bri·ous·ness, sa·lu·bri·ty** (sə lōō′brə tē), *n.*

sal·u·tar·y (sal′yə ter′ē) *adj.* promoting or favorable to health; healthful. **2.** producing an improvement or beneficial effect. [Latin *salūtāris* healthful, from *salūs* health.]

sal·u·ta·tion (sal′yə tā′shən) *n.* **1.** act of greeting, welcoming, or saluting by gestures or words. **2.** gesture or expression used in greeting, welcoming, or saluting. **3.** word or phrase of greeting, as "Dear Sir," opening a letter and usually immediately preceding the body of the letter.

sa·lu·ta·to·ri·an (sə lōō′tə tôr′ē ən) *n.* the student, usually ranking second in his class, who delivers the salutatory at a commencement exercise.

sa·lu·ta·to·ry (sə lōō′tə tôr′ē) *adj.* of, relating to, or expressing a greeting or salutation. —*n. pl.,* **-ries.** opening address, esp. one given at a commencement exercise.

sa·lute (sə lōōt′) **-lut·ed, -lut·ing.** *v.t.* **1.** to recognize formally or pay respect to (a superior officer) in a prescribed manner, esp. by raising the right hand to the forehead. **2.** to honor or recognize ceremonially (someone or something): *They saluted the visiting ambassador by firing off guns on board ship.* **3.** to greet or address with words or gestures of welcome, good wishes, or respect. **4.** to strike, as the senses. —*v.i.* to make a gesture of respect or formal or ceremonious recognition, esp. by raising the right hand to the forehead. —*n.* **1.** act, gesture, or ceremony of saluting. **2.** position or attitude assumed in saluting: *to stand at salute.* [Latin *salūtāre* to greet, wish health to, from *salūs* health.]

Salv., Salvador.

sal·va·ble (sal′və bəl) *adj.* capable of being saved or salvaged. [Late Latin *salvāre* to save (from *salvus* unharmed, well[1]) + -ABLE.]

Sal·va·dor (sal′və dôr′) *n.* **1.** El Salvador. **2.** port city on the eastern coast of Brazil, north of Rio de Janeiro. Pop. (1968), 892,392.

Sal·va·do·ran (sal′və dôr′ən) *n.* native or inhabitant of El Salvador. —*adj.* of or relating to El Salvador or its people. Also, **Sal′va·do′ri·an.**

sal·vage (sal′vij) **-vaged, -vag·ing.** *v.t.* to save or rescue from loss or destruction: *They managed to salvage the cargo of the sinking ship.* —*n.* **1.** act of saving a ship or its crew or cargo from loss or destruction, as from wreck or capture. **2.** ship, crew, or cargo so saved. **3.** compensation given to those who aid in saving a ship or its crew or cargo from loss or destruction. **4.** act of saving any endangered property from damage, loss, or destruction. **5.** property so saved. [Middle French *salvage* compensation to those who aid in saving a ship or its cargo, going back to Latin *salvus* unharmed, well[1].] —**sal′vage·a·ble,** *adj.* —**sal′vag·er,** *n.*

sal·va·tion (sal vā′shən) *n.* **1.** preservation or deliverance from difficulty, danger, destruction, or evil. **2.** source, cause, or means of such preservation or deliverance. **3.** *Religion.* deliverance of the soul from sin and from punishment for sin; redemption. [Late Latin *salvātiō* a saving, going back to Latin *salvus* unharmed, well[1].]

Salvation Army, international Protestant evangelical and charitable organization founded in 1865 by William Booth and operated on a semimilitary pattern.

salve[1] (sav, säv) *n.* **1.** semisolid preparation, usually medicated, for application to the surface of the body, used esp. in the treatment of external injuries and skin disorders; ointment. **2.** anything that soothes, remedies, or assuages: *a salve for one's conscience.* —*v.t.,* **salved, salv·ing. 1.** to soothe; assuage: *Kind words salved his hurt feelings.* **2.** to put salve on, as a burn. [Old English *sealf* the ointment.]

salve[2] (salv) **salved, salv·ing.** *v.t.* to salvage. [From SALVAGE.]

sal·ver (sal′vər) *n.* tray, usually made of metal, used esp. for serving food or drink. [Spanish *salva* tray, from *salvar* to taste food (placed on a tray) in order to detect poison, to save, from Late Latin *salvāre* to save. See SALVABLE.]

sal·vi·a (sal′vē ə) *n.* any of a large group of plants, genus *Salvia,* of the mint family, found in temperate and warm regions throughout the world. [Modern Latin *Salvia,* from Latin *salvia* the plant sage; literally, the healing plant. See SAGE[2].]

sal·vo (sal′vō) *pl.,* **-vos** or **-voes.** *n.* **1.** a simultaneous firing of several guns, often as a salute. **2.** simultaneous release of all the bombs or missiles carried by an aircraft. **3.** bombs or missiles so released. **4.** sudden outburst, as of cheers or applause. [Italian *salva* firing of guns as a salute, from Latin *salvē* hail, be well, imperative of *salvēre* to be well.]

sal vo·la·ti·le (sal′ və lat′əl ē) aromatic solution of ammonium carbonate, used as smelling salts. [Modern Latin *sal volatile* literally, volatile salt; referring to the fact that it evaporates into SAL, VOLATILE.]

Salz·burg (sôlz′burg′; German zälts′-boork′) *n.* city in western Austria. Pop. (1968), 120,204.

Sam., Samuel.

S. Am., South America; South American.

sam·a·ra (sam′ər ə, sə mar′ə) *n.* dry fruit, as of the maple or elm, whose seed or seeds are covered by a winglike structure that helps the wind convey them. Also, **key fruit.** [Latin *samara* seed of the elm; possibly of Celtic origin.]

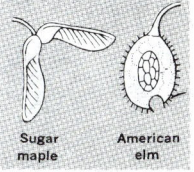

Sugar maple   American elm

Samaras

Sa·ma·ra (sə mär′ə) *n.* see **Kuibyshev.**

Sa·mar·i·a (sə mar′ē ə) *n.* **1.** in the Bible, an ancient region west of the Jordan. **2.** main city of this region.

Sa·mar·i·tan (sə mar′ət ən) *n.* **1.** member of the people that inhabited Samaria. **2.** Good Samaritan. —*adj.* of or relating to Samaria or its people.

sa·mar·i·um (sə mar′ē əm) *n.* silvery metallic element used in the production of certain lasers and in nuclear reactors. Symbol: **Sm** See **element** for table. [Modern Latin *samarium,* from earlier *samarskite* a mineral in which it was discovered, from Col. von *Samarski,* a nineteenth-century Russian mine inspector.]

Sam·ar·kand (sam′ər kand′) *n.* city in Soviet Central Asia, in the Uzbekistan republic. Pop. (1970 est.), 267,000.

sam·ba (sam′bə, säm′-) *n.* **1.** dance of Brazilian origin characterized by a dipping movement of the knees. **2.** music for this dance. —*v.i.* to dance the samba. [Portuguese *samba;* of African origin.]

Sam Browne belt (sam′ broun′) belt for a military or similar uniform, with a supporting strap running diagonally from the left of

the waist and passing over the right shoulder, designed to carry the weight of a pistol or sword. [From Sir Samuel J. *Browne*, 1824–1901, British general who designed it.]

same (sām) *adj.* **1.** resembling or corresponding to another in every respect; exactly alike: *They wore the same dress to the dance.* **2.** having a single or particular identity; being the very one; not another: *She's the same girl I sat next to in class last year.* **3.** unchanged, as in character: *She's the same generous person now as she was years ago.* **4.** just mentioned or indicated; aforesaid. —*n.* **1.** one who or that which is the same. **2. all the same. a.** in spite of everything; notwithstanding; nevertheless: *You may think she's trustworthy, but I'd check out her story all the same.* **b.** not a matter for concern; equally acceptable: *It's all the same to me whether you stay or go.* **3. just the same.** nevertheless. **4. the same.** in the same manner: *I feel the same as you about it.* [Old English *same* similarly.]
Syn. *adj.* **1. Same, identical** mean not different when compared with each other. **Same** sometimes stresses complete identity but more often implies only that the things compared resemble each other so closely as to be essentially indistinguishable: *Although these two drugs have different names they are made from the same chemical substance.* **Identical** stresses agreement in every respect: *The cadets wore identical uniforms for the parade.*
same·ness (sām′nis) *n.* **1.** state or quality of being the same. **2.** absence of variety; monotony.
S. Amer., South America; South American.
sam·i·sen (sam′i sen′) *n.* musical instrument of Japanese origin, resembling a banjo but having three strings. [Japanese *samisen*, from Chinese (Mandarin) *san hsien* three strings.]
sam·ite (sam′īt, sā′mīt) *n.* heavy, rich silk fabric, usually interwoven with gold or silver threads. [Old French *samit*, from Medieval Latin *examitum*, from Late Greek *hexamiton* fabric woven with six threads, from Greek *hex* six + *mitos* thread.]
Sam·nite (sam′nīt) *n.* **1.** member of an ancient Italic tribe conquered by the Romans in the third century B.C. **2.** their extinct language, belonging to the Italic branch of the Indo-European language family.
Sa·mo·a (sə mō′ə) *n.* island group in the South Pacific, divided into Western Samoa and American Samoa. Land area, 1209 sq. mi. Pop. (1963 est.), 140,000.
Sa·mo·an (sə mō′ən) *n.* **1.** member or close descendant of the people of Samoa. **2.** language spoken by these people, belonging to the Polynesian branch of the Malayo-Polynesian family of languages. —*adj.* of or relating to Samoa, its people, or their language or culture.
Sa·mos (sā′mos, sä′mōs) *n.* mountainous Greek island off the western coast of Turkey. Area, 192 sq. mi. Pop. (1961), 41,124. —**Sa·mi·an** (sā′mē ən, sam′ē-), *adj.*, *n.*
sam·o·var (sam′ə vär′, sam′ə vär′) *n.* metal urn having a spigot and an internal heating tube, used esp. in Russia for boiling water for tea. [Russian *samovar* literally, self-boiler.]
Sam·o·yed (sam′ə yed′) *n.* **1.** member of a nomadic people speaking a Ural-Altaic language and living in northwestern Siberia and northeastern Russia. **2.** dog of a breed originally developed in Siberia for pulling sleds and herding reindeer, having a thick, white coat that forms a ruff around the shoulders. Height: 24 inches at the shoulder.

Samoyed

samp (samp) *n.* **1.** coarsely ground hominy or Indian corn. **2.** porridge made of this. [Algonquian *(na)-saump* mush.]
sam·pan (sam′pan′) *n.* small flat-bottomed boat, as used in China and Japan, usually propelled by a scull at the stern and often having a single sail and a rounded shelter made of mats. [Chinese (Mandarin) *san pan* literally, three boards.]
sam·phire (sam′fīr) *n.* glasswort. [Earlier *sampire*, modification of French *(herbe de) Saint Pierre* St. Peter's (herb).]

Sampan

sam·ple (sam′pəl) *n.* **1.** small part or piece of anything, or an individual item, from which the quality or nature of the whole may be inferred: *a sample of her work.* **2.** number of individuals or items selected or drawn from a group for examination or analysis, usually in order to determine the characteristics or nature of the group. Also *(def. 2),* **sam′pling.** —*v.t.,* **-pled, -pling.** to test, examine, or judge the

quality of by taking a sample: *I sampled the soup and it needs salt.* [Short for Old French *essample* illustration, pattern. See EXAMPLE.] —**Syn.** *n.* **1.** see **example.**
sam·pler[1] (sam′plər) *n.* decorative piece of needlework consisting of cloth embroidered with designs or letters. [Short for Old French *essemplaire* pattern, sample, going back to Latin *exemplum*.]
sam·pler[2] (sam′plər) *n.* one who samples. [SAMPLE + -ER[1].]
sam·pling (sam′pling) *n.* **1.** sample *(def. 2).* **2.** act or process of taking such a sample.
Sam·son (sam′sən) *n.* **1.** in the Old Testament, judge or ruler of the ancient Hebrews, renowned for his extraordinary strength, betrayed to the Philistines by Delilah. **2.** any man of great strength.
Sam·u·el (sam′ū əl) *n.* **1.** Hebrew judge and prophet who anointed both Saul and David as kings of Israel. **2.** either of two books in the Old Testament, containing Hebrew history from the birth of Samuel to the death of David.
sam·u·rai (sam′oo rī′) *pl., n.* **1.** in feudal Japan, a member of the warrior class, who were vassals of the daimios. **2.** warrior class itself. [Japanese *samurai* warrior.]
Sa·na (sä nä′) *n.* capital and largest city of Yemen, in the central part of the country. Pop. (1960 est.), 89,000.
San An·ge·lo (san an′jə lō′) city in central Texas. Pop. (1970), 63,884.
San An·to·ni·o (san′ an tō′nē ō′) city in south-central Texas. Pop. (1970), 654,153.
san·a·tive (san′ə tiv) *adj.* having the power to heal or cure. [Medieval Latin *sanativus*, going back to Latin *sānus* healthy.]
san·a·to·ri·um (san′ə tôr′ē əm) *pl.,* **-to·ri·ums** or **-to·ri·a** (-tôr′ē ə). *n.* **1.** institution or establishment for the care and treatment of patients affected with chronic diseases, as tuberculosis, that require long-term care. **2.** sanitarium. [Modern Latin *sanatorium*, from Late Latin *sānātōrius* giving health, going back to Latin *sānus* healthy.]
San Ber·nar·di·no (san′ bur′nər dē′nō) city in southern California, east of Los Angeles. Pop. (1970), 104,251.
San·cho Pan·za (san′chō pan′zə; *Spanish* sän′chō pän′thä) peasant squire of Don Quixote, noted for his simple, practical nature.
sanc·ti·fy (sangk′tə fī′) **-fied, -fy·ing.** *v.t.* **1.** to set apart as sacred or holy; reserve for religious use; consecrate. **2.** to make free from sin; purify. **3.** to give religious sanction to, so as to render legitimate or binding. **4.** to impart social or moral acceptability to. [Church Latin *sānctificāre* to make holy, from Latin *sānctus* holy + *facere* to make.] —**sanc′ti·fi·ca′tion, sanc′ti·fi′er,** *n.*
sanc·ti·mo·ni·ous (sangk′tə mō′nē əs) *adj.* making a hypocritical, exaggerated, or smug show of piety or righteousness. —**sanc′ti·mo′ni·ous·ly,** *adv.* —**sanc′ti·mo′ni·ous·ness,** *n.*
sanc·ti·mo·ny (sangk′tə mō′nē) *n.* affected piety or righteousness. [Latin *sānctimōnia* piety.]
sanc·tion (sangk′shən) *v.t.* **1.** to give approval, support, or encouragement to; countenance: *You're sanctioning such corrupt practices by failing to take measures against them.* **2.** to permit, accept, or approve officially or authoritatively. —*n.* **1.** official or authoritative permission, acceptance, or approval. **2.** approval, support, or encouragement, as that of public opinion, which serves to render something acceptable or permissible. **3.** *usually,* **sanctions.** in international law, action instituted by one or more states to bring pressure on another state to force it to comply with legal obligations. **4.a.** provision annexed to a law requiring a penalty for disobedience to or violation of it. **b.** penalty so provided. **5.** binding force, or something that gives binding force. [Latin *sānctiō* decreeing of something as inviolable, ordinance.] —**Syn.** *v.t.* **1.** see **approve.**
sanc·ti·ty (sangk′tə tē) *pl.,* **-ties.** *n.* **1.** piety, as of life or character; saintliness; godliness. **2.** quality or state of being hallowed; sacredness. **3.** quality or state of being regarded with solemn respect or reverence; inviolability: *the sanctity of individual rights.* **4.** *usually,* **sanctities.** something considered sacred. [Latin *sānctitās* holiness.]
sanc·tu·ar·y (sangk′chōo er′ē) *pl.,* **-ar·ies.** *n.* **1.** any place of refuge or protection. **2.** refuge, protection, or immunity from arrest, punishment, or prosecution provided by such a place: *The ambassador who defected sought sanctuary in our country.* **3.a.** holy or sacred place, as a church, temple, or mosque. **b.** most holy part of such a place. **4.** area in a church around the main altar, including the area occupied by the clergy; chancel. **5.** any of the Temples in ancient Jerusalem, or its holy of holies. **6.** wildlife preserve where animals are protected from hunters and can live unmolested. [Latin *sānctuārium* shrine.] —**Syn. 1.** see **shelter.**
sanc·tum (sangk′təm) *pl.,* **-tums** or **-ta** (-tə) *n.* **1.** holy or sacred place. **2.** private retreat or room where one is not to be disturbed. [Latin *sānctum* holy place.]
sanc·tum sanc·to·rum (sangk′təm sangk tôr′əm) **1.** holy of holies *(def. 1).* **2.** place of inviolable privacy. [Latin *sānctum sānctōrum* holy of holies.]

Sanc·tus (sangk′təs) *n.* hymn immediately preceding the canon in the Mass and other Eucharistic services. [Latin *sānctus* holy; the first word of this hymn.]

sand (sand) *n.* **1.** loose, gritty material consisting of tiny, fragmental grains derived from rocks and minerals by the erosive action of water or ice. **2.** *usually,* **sands.** tract or region covered with or composed mainly of this material, as a desert or beach. **3. sands.** moments or portions of life or time, as if measured by an hourglass. —*v.t.* **1.** to scrape, smooth, or polish with sand or sandpaper: *to sand a floor.* **2.** to sprinkle or cover with or as with sand. **3.** to add sand to. **4.** to fill up with sand. [Old English *sand* the loose, gritty material.]

Sand, George (sand, säNd; zhôrzh) 1804–76, French novelist; born Amandine Aurore Lucie Dupin.

san·dal (sand′əl) *n.* **1.** shoe consisting of a sole that is held to the foot by one or more straps or thongs. **2.** shoe having a top cut out with openwork and usually fastened with a strap or straps, worn esp. by children. [Latin *sandalium* sole held to the foot by straps, going back to Greek *sandalon.*]

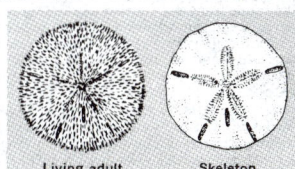
Sandal

san·dal·wood (sand′əl wood′) *n.* **1.** hard, yellowish, fine-grained wood of an evergreen tree, *Santalum album,* used as for making ornamental boxes, chests, and fans and yielding a fragrant oil used in perfumes and soaps. **2.** tree yielding this wood, widely cultivated throughout most of Asia, and bearing leathery oval leaves and trumpet-shaped flowers. **3.** any of several unrelated trees whose wood is similar to sandalwood.

sand·bag (sand′bag′) *n.* **1.** bag filled with or designed to hold sand, used for such purposes as ballast, in military fortifications, and in strengthening levees during floods. **2.** small, narrow bag filled with sand and used as a clublike weapon. —*v.t.,* **-bagged, -bag·ging. 1.** to place sandbags in or around; furnish with sandbags: *to sandbag the banks of a river.* **2.** to hit or stun with or as with a sandbag. **3.** *Informal.* to impel or force to do something.

sand·bank (sand′bangk′) *n.* ridge or mass of sand, as on a hillside or shoal.

sand·bar (sand′bär′) *also,* **sand bar.** *n.* mass or ridge of sand, gravel, or other alluvial material deposited in a river or bay or along the shore, built up by the action of waves and currents and often obstructing navigation.

sand·blast (sand′blast′) *v.t.* to clean, grind, or decorate a hard surface, as glass, metal, or the exterior of a building, by subjecting it to a high-speed stream of sand or other abrasive material. —*n.* high-speed stream of such abrasive material.

sand·box (sand′boks′) *n.* low, boxlike structure, as in a playground, filled with sand for children to play in.

sand·bur (sand′bur′) *also,* **sand·burr.** *n.* any of several weedy plants, genus *Cenchrus,* found in tropical and temperate regions, whose seeds are covered with spiny burrs.

Sand·burg, Carl (sand′burg′) 1878–1967, U.S. poet and writer.

sand dollar, any of a group of round, flat, spiny, marine animals, class Echinoidea, living in shallow ocean waters throughout the world.

Living adult   Skeleton
Sand dollar

sand·er (san′dər) *n.* **1.** machine that sands, usually electric-powered and used esp. for floors or woodwork. **2.** one who sands.

sand flea 1. flea found in sandy places, as the chigoe. **2.** any of various small crustaceans that are found on sandy beaches and that leap or hop like fleas.

sand fly, any of a group of tiny, mosquitolike, blood-sucking flies, genus *Culicoides,* found near the seashore and in damp areas.

sand·glass (sand′glas′) *n.* hourglass.

sand·hog (sand′hôg′, -hog′) *n.* laborer who works on underground or underwater construction projects, as in a caisson.

San Di·e·go (san′ dē ā′gō) port city in southern California, at the Mexican border. Pop. (1970), 696,769.

sand·lot (sand′lot′) *also,* **sand·lot.** *adj.* of, relating to, or designating games played by amateurs, often in organized leagues and usually in a vacant lot: *sandlot baseball.*

sand·man (sand′man′) *pl.,* **-men.** *n.* in folklore, man who supposedly makes children sleepy by sprinkling sand on their eyes at bedtime.

sand·pa·per (sand′pā′pər) *n.* strong, heavy paper with a coating of sand or other abrasive material bonded to it, used for smoothing, polish-

ing, or cleaning surfaces. —*v.t.* to smooth, polish, or clean by rubbing with sandpaper.

sand·pip·er (sand′pī′pər) *n.* any of various shore birds, family Scolopacidae, having a long, slender bill, long legs, and brown or grayish plumage. Length: 5–12 inches.

sand·stone (sand′stōn′) *n.* sedimentary rock composed of sand grains, usually of the mineral quartz, that are cemented together, varying widely in color and texture, widely used as a building material.

Sandpiper

sand·storm (sand′stôrm′) *n.* storm of high winds that carry sand through the air, commonly occurring in desert areas.

sand trap, hazard on a golf course consisting of a pit or other depression in the ground filled with sand.

sand·wich (sand′wich) *n.* **1.** two or more slices of bread with a filling of meat, cheese, or other food. **2.** something resembling a sandwich: *an ice-cream sandwich.* —*v.t.* to place, fit, or insert tightly: *The folder was sandwiched in between the two bulging files in the drawer.* [From the fourth Earl of *Sandwich,* 1718–92, who supposedly devised the sandwich so that he would not have to interrupt his card game and leave the gambling table to eat.]

sandwich board, pair of signboards, each of which bears an advertisement or public notice, connected at the top by straps so as to hang from the wearer's shoulders.

Sandwich Islands, see Hawaiian Islands.

sandwich man, one who is hired to advertise by wearing a sandwich board.

sand·wort (sand′wurt′) *n.* any of a group of low-growing plants, genus *Arenaria,* found in temperate regions of the Northern Hemisphere, whose white flowers usually form mosslike tufts.

sand·y (san′dē) *adj.* **sand·i·er, sand·i·est.** *adj.* **1.** consisting of, covered with, or like sand. **2.** yellowish-red in color: *a sandy moustache.* —**sand′i·ness,** *n.*

sane (sān) **san·er, san·est.** *adj.* **1.** free from mental derangement; sound and healthy in mind. **2.** having, showing, or proceeding from reason or sound, clear judgment; sensible; rational: *sane advice, a sane approach to the problem.* [Latin *sānus* sound², healthy.] —**sane′ly,** *adv.* —**sane′ness,** *n.*

San·for·ize (san′fə rīz′) **-ized, -iz·ing.** *v.t.* to process (fabric) so as to be Sanforized.

San·for·ized (san′fə rīzd′) *adj.* *Trademark.* (of fabric) having been preshrunk by a patented process before being made into clothing. [From *Sanford* L. Cluett, 1874–1968, American inventor of the process.]

San Fran·cis·co (san′ fran sis′kō) port city in western California, on the Pacific. Pop. (1970), 715,674.

San Francisco Bay, inlet of the Pacific, on the central coast of California.

sang (sang) past tense of **sing.**

sang-froid (säN frwä′) *n.* calmness or imperturbability, esp. in trying circumstances; cool composure. [French *sang froid* literally, cold blood, from Latin *sanguis* blood + *frīgidus* cold.]

san·gri·a (sang grē′ə, sän-) *n.* drink usually consisting of red wine and citrus fruit.

san·gui·nar·y (sang′gwə ner′ē) *adj.* **1.** characterized by or attended with much bloodshed; bloody. **2.** eager to shed blood; bloodthirsty. **3.** consisting of or stained with blood. [Latin *sanguinārius* relating to blood, from *sanguis* blood.] —**san′gui·nar·i·ly,** *adv.* —**san′gui·nar′i·ness,** *n.*

san·guine (sang′gwin) *adj.* **1.** cheerful and confident; hopeful; optimistic: *a sanguine personality, a sanguine outlook.* **2.** of a red color; ruddy: *a sanguine complexion.* [Latin *sanguineus* bloody, of blood, from *sanguis* blood, the humor thought to cause cheerfulness. See HUMOR.] —**san′guine·ly,** *adv.* —**san′guine·ness, san·guin′i·ty,** *n.*

san·guin·e·ous (sang gwin′ē əs) *adj.* **1.** of, relating to, or containing blood. **2.** of the color of blood; red. **3.** of or involving bloodshed. **4.** hopeful; confident; sanguine.

San·he·drin (san′hi drin′) *also,* **San·he·drim.** *n.* highest religious and judicial tribunal of ancient Palestine during the first century B.C. and several centuries thereafter.

san·i·tar·i·an (san′ə tār′ē ən) *n.* one who works or is an expert in the area of public health or sanitation. —*adj.* of or relating to sanitation or health; sanitary.

san·i·tar·i·um (san′ə tār′ē əm) *pl.,* **-i·ums** or **-i·a** (-ē ə). *n.* **1.** health resort. **2.** sanatorium. [Modern Latin *sanitarium,* from Latin *sānitās* health.]

san·i·tar·y (san′ə ter′ē) *adj.* **1.** of or relating to health or to the preservation of health. **2.** free from dirt, bacteria, or conditions condu-

cive to infection or disease. [French *sanitaire* relating to the preservation of health, from Latin *sānitās* health.] —**san·i·tar·i·ly** (san′ə tār′ə lē), *adv.* —**san′i·tar′i·ness,** *n.*

sanitary belt, belt, usually of elastic, for holding a sanitary napkin in place.

sanitary napkin, absorbent pad, as of gauze and cotton, worn to absorb menstrual flow.

san·i·ta·tion (san′ə tā′shən) *n.* **1.** formulation and application of measures for the preservation and protection of public health by maintaining sanitary conditions, as by disposing of sewage and refuse, ensuring the purity of food, and controlling the growth of insects, rodents, and environmental pollution. **2.** removal and disposal of sewage and refuse. [From SANITARY.]

san·i·tize (san′ə tīz′) **-tized, -tiz·ing.** *v.t.* to make sanitary, as by sterilizing.

san·i·ty (san′ə tē) *n.* **1.** sound and healthy mental state or condition; state of being sane. **2.** soundness and clarity of judgment; sensibleness; reasonableness. [Latin *sānitās* health.]

San Joa·quin (san′ wä kēn′) river in central California flowing westward to the mouth of the Sacramento.

San Jo·se (san′ hō zā′) city in western California. Pop. (1970), 445,-779.

San Jo·sé (san′ hō zā′, -sā′) capital, largest city, and commercial and cultural center of Costa Rica, in the central part of the country. Pop. (1966 est.), 182,961.

San Jose scale, tiny scale insect, *Aspidiotus perniciosus,* found throughout North America, that is destructive to fruit, trees, and shrubs. [Because it first appeared in the United States in *San Jose, California.*]

San Juan (san hwän′) capital and port city of Puerto Rico, in the northeastern part of the island. Pop. (1970), 445,000.

sank (sangk) past tense of **sink.**

San Le·an·dro (san′ lē an′drō) city in central California, southeast of Oakland. Pop. (1970), 68,698.

San Ma·ri·no (sän′ mə rē′nō) **1.** tiny country in southern Europe, near the Adriatic, completely surrounded by Italy. Capital, San Marino. Area, 23 sq. mi. Pop. (1970 est.), 19,000. **2.** capital of this country.

San Ma·te·o (san′ mə tā′ō) city in western California, south of San Francisco. Pop. (1970), 78,991.

sans (sanz; *French* sän) *prep.* without. [French *sans,* going back to Latin *sine;* influenced by Latin *absentīa* in the absence of.]

San Sal·va·dor (san sal′və dôr′) **1.** capital, largest city, and commercial and cultural center of El Salvador, in the central part of the country. Pop. (1968), 340,544. **2.** island of the central Bahamas, southeast of Miami, Florida, believed to be the first landing place of Columbus in the New World. Area, 60 sq. mi. Pop. (1963), 986.

sans-cu·lotte (sanz′kyoo lot′) *n.* **1.** revolutionary in the French Revolution of 1789; Jacobin. **2.** any radical or revolutionary. [French *sans-culotte* literally, without knee breeches, from *sans* (see SANS) + *culotte* breeches, from *cul* (see CULOTTE); referring to lower-class Frenchmen, who wore trousers rather than the knee breeches associated with the upper classes at the time of the French Revolution.]

San Se·bas·tián (san′tə säs′chän) port city on the northern coast of Spain. Pop. (1968), 152,872.

San·sei (sän sā′, sän′sā′) *pl.* **-sei** or **-seis.** *also,* **san·sei.** *n.* third-generation Japanese-American. [Japanese *sansei,* from *san* third + *sei* generation.]

San·skrit (san′skrit) *also,* **San·scrit.** *n.* literary and religious language of ancient India, belonging to the Indo-Iranian branch of the Indo-European language family. —**San·skrit′ic,** *adj.*

sans ser·if (san ser′if) *also,* **sans-ser·if.** letter or typeface without serifs. [SANS + SERIF.]

San·ta An·a (san′tə an′ə) city in southern California, southeast of Los Angeles. Pop. (1970), 156,601.

San·ta Bar·ba·ra (san′tə bär′bər ə) city in southern California, on the Pacific, north of Los Angeles. Pop. (1970), 70,215.

Santa Barbara Islands, island group off the southern coast of California.

San·ta Cat·a·li·na (san′tə kat′ə lē′nə) one of the Santa Barbara Islands, a resort area noted for its fine beaches and sports fishing. Area, approx. 100 sq. mi. Also, **Cat′a·li′na, Catalina Island.**

San·ta Clar·a (san′tə klar′ə) city in western California. Pop. (1970), 87,717.

San·ta Claus (san′tə klôz′) in American folklore, legendary figure who brings presents to children at Christmas, usually represented as a fat, jolly, white-bearded old man in a red suit. [Dialectal Dutch *Sante Klaas.*]

San·ta Cruz de Te·ne·ri·fe (san′tə krōōz′ də ten′ə rē′fä) chief city and port in the Canary Islands. Pop. (1968 est.), 159,852.

San·ta Fe (san′tə fā′) capital of New Mexico, in the north-central part of the state. Pop. (1970), 41,167.

San·ta Fé (san′tə fä′) city in eastern Argentina, north of Buenos Aires. Pop. (1960 est.), 208,900.

Santa Fe Trail, overland trade route between Independence, Missouri and Santa Fe, New Mexico, widely used from approximately 1821 to 1880.

San·ta Is·a·bel (san′tə iz′ə bel′) capital and largest city of Equatorial Guinea. Pop. (1968 est.), 25,000.

San·ta Ma·ri·a (san′tə mə rē′ə) flagship of Columbus on his first voyage to the New World in 1492.

San·ta Mon·i·ca (san′tə mon′i kə) city in southern California, on the Pacific, near Los Angeles. Pop. (1970), 88,289.

San·ti·a·go (san′tē ä′gō, sän tyä′-) *n.* capital and largest city of Chile, in the central part of the country. Pop. (1970), 510,246.

Santiago de Cu·ba (dä kōō′vä) port city in southeastern Cuba. Pop. (1966), 249,600.

San·to Do·min·go (san′tō də ming′gō) capital, largest city, and chief port of the Dominican Republic, on the southern coast of the country, formerly known as Ciudad Trujillo. Pop. (1969), 654,757.

San·tos (sän′tōs) *n.* port city in southeastern Brazil, on the Atlantic. Pop. (1968), 313,771.

São Lu·is (souɴ′ loo ēs′) city in northern Brazil. Pop. (1968), 218,-783.

São Pau·lo (souɴ pou′loo) largest city in Brazil, in the southeastern part of the country. Pop. (1970), 5,684,706.

São To·mé and Prín·ci·pe (souɴ tə mä′; prin′sə pə) island country located off the west coast of Africa in the Gulf of Guinea. Land area, 370 sq. mi. Pop. (1970), 73,800.

sap[1] (sap) *n.* **1.** watery solution that circulates through a plant, carrying minerals, gases, and food materials from one part of the plant to another. **2.** any bodily fluid essential to life, health, or vitality. **3.** energy; vitality; vigor. **4.** *Slang.* one who is foolish or easily deceived or manipulated. [Old English *sæp* the watery solution in plants.]

sap[2] (sap) **sapped, sap·ping.** *v.t.* **1.** to weaken, exhaust, or destroy gradually and stealthily; undermine: *to sap someone's strength.* **2.** to weaken by removing the underlying support of (a structure), as by digging under or wearing away the foundation. **3.** to approach (an enemy position under siege) by the use of one or more protected trenches dug for that purpose. —*v.i.* to dig such a trench or trenches. —*n.* protected trench dug for the purpose of approaching an enemy's position. [Middle French *sapper* to undermine, dig into, from Italian *zappare* to till the soil, from *zappa* spade[1], hoe; of uncertain origin.]

sa·pi·ence (sā′pē əns) *n.* wisdom. Also, **sa′pi·en·cy.**

sa·pi·ent (sā′pē ənt) *adj.* wise; sage. [Latin *sapiēns,* present participle of *sapere* to be wise.] —**sa′pi·ent·ly,** *adv.*

sap·less (sap′lis) *adj.* **1.** without sap; withered; dry. **2.** without energy, vitality, or vigor; dull; insipid.

sap·ling (sap′ling) *n.* **1.** young tree. **2.** young person; a youth.

sap·o·dil·la (sap′ə dil′ə) *n.* **1.** tall evergreen tree, *Achras zapota,* found in tropical America, having a heavy, fine-grained wood, bearing an edible fruit, and yielding chicle. **2.** sweet, apple-shaped fruit of this tree, having brownish-yellow flesh and rough brown skin. [Spanish *zapotillo,* diminutive of *zapote,* from Nahuatl *tzapotl* this tree.]

sap·o·na·ceous (sap′ə nā′shəs) *adj.* resembling soap; soapy. [Modern Latin *saponaceus,* from Latin *sāpō* soap; of Germanic origin.]

sa·pon·i·fy (sə pon′ə fī′) **-fied, -fy·ing.** *v.t.* to make (an ester of an acid) react with an alkali to form an alcohol and an acid salt, esp. to make (a fat) react with an alkali to form glycerol and soap. —*v.i.* to become converted into soap. [French *saponifier,* from Latin *sāpō* + *facere* to make.] —**sa·pon′i·fi·ca′tion, sa·pon′i·fi′er,** *n.*

sap·per (sap′ər) *n.* **1.** soldier, often a member of an engineering corps, chiefly employed in laying, locating, and disarming mines or in constructing fortifications and trenches. **2.** one who or that which saps. [SAP[2] + -ER[1].]

Sap·phic (saf′ik) *adj.* **1.** of or relating to Sappho. **2.** of or relating to poetic forms used by Sappho. —*n.* Sapphic line or stanza.

Sap·phi·ra (sə fī′rə) *n.* in the New Testament, the wife of Ananias, who, with her husband, was struck dead after being rebuked by Peter for lying.

sap·phire (saf′īr) *n.* **1.** highly prized precious stone, a transparent to translucent blue variety of corundum. **2.** any other colored variety of corundum other than the red, that is used as a gem. **3.** deep-blue color. [Old French *safir* the precious stone, from Latin *sapphīrus,* from Greek *sappheiros,* probably from Hebrew *sappīr,* possibly from Sanskrit *shanipriya* literally, dear to the planet Saturn (because gems were often associated with planets).]

Sap·pho (saf′ō) *n.* born c.612 B.C., Greek poetess.

sap·py (sap′ē) **-pi·er, -pi·est.** *adj.* **1.** full of sap; juicy. **2.** *Slang.* **a.** overly or foolishly sentimental; mawkish; maudlin. **b.** silly; foolish.

sap·ro·phyte (sap′rə fīt′) *n.* nongreen plant that obtains its food materials from dead or decaying plant or animal matter, as the mushroom. [Greek *sapros* rotten, putrid + -PHYTE.]

sap·suck·er (sap′suk′ər) n. any of several North American wood-peckers having predominantly black or brownish plumage and a yellow belly, that feed on the sap of trees. Length: 8–9 inches.

sap·wood (sap′wood′) n. youngest portion of the wood of a tree or woody plant, that contains living cells and is active in the flow of sap. Also, **al·bur′num**.

Sar·a·cen (sar′ə sən) n. **1.** any Muslim, esp. of the time of the Crusades or during the Middle Ages. **2.** any Arab. **3.** member of a nomadic desert tribe that lived between Egypt and Arabia as early as the fourth century A.D. —**Sar·a·cen·ic** (sar′ə sen′ik), adj.

Sar·a·gos·sa (sar′ə gos′ə) n. city in northeastern Spain. Pop. (1968), 379,893.

Sar·ah (sâr′ə) n. in the Old Testament, the wife of Abraham and mother of Isaac.

Sa·ra·je·vo (sar′ə yâ′vō) also, **Sa·ra·ye·vo**, **Se·ra·je·vo**. n. city in central Yugoslavia, where the assassination of the Austrian Archduke Francis Ferdinand took place in 1914, leading to the outbreak of World War I.

Sapsucker

sa·ran (sə ran′) n. any of various thermoplastic resins used to make transparent wrappings and acid-resistant pipes.

sa·ra·pe (sə rä′pē, -pä) serape.

Sa·ra·tov (sä rä′tôf) n. city in the southwestern Soviet Union, on the Volga River, in the Russian Republic. Pop. (1970 est.), 758,000.

Sa·ra·wak (sə rä′wäk, -wä) n. political subdivision of Malaysia, in northwest Borneo, formerly a British colony. Area, approx. 48,250 sq. mi. Pop. (1965 est.), 838,000.

Sa·ra·ye·vo (sar′ə yâ′vō) Sarajevo.

sar·casm (sär′kaz′əm) n. **1.** use of sharp, cutting remarks or language intended to mock, wound, or subject to contempt or ridicule: *He feels sarcasm is effective in intimidating people he finds obnoxious.* **2.** sharp, cutting remark or language. **3.** characteristic quality of such remarks or language: *The sarcasm in her voice was unmistakable.* [Late Latin *sarcasmos* taunt, bitter jest, from Late Greek *sarkasmos* sneer, mockery, from Greek *sarkazein* to tear flesh like dogs, speak sharply, sneer.]

sar·cas·tic (sär kas′tik) adj. **1.** characterized by or having the nature of sarcasm: *sarcastic comments.* **2.** given to the use of sarcasm. —**sar·cas′ti·cal·ly**, adv.

sar·co·ma (sär kō′mə) pl., **-mas** or **-ma·ta** (-mə tə). n. any of various highly malignant tumors originating mainly in connective tissue. [Modern Latin *sarcoma*, from Greek *sarkōma* fleshy growth.]

sar·coph·a·gus (sär kof′ə gəs) pl., **-gi** (-jī′) or **-gus·es**. n. ceremonial coffin or burial casket placed above ground, usually of stone and often ornamented with sculpture or painting. [Latin *sarcophagus*, from Greek *sarkophagos* literally, flesh-eating, from *sarx* flesh + *phagein* to eat; referring to the making of coffins by the ancient Greeks from a kind of limestone thought to consume the flesh of corpses.]

sard (särd) n. reddish-brown chalcedony quartz, used esp. in jewelry. [Latin *sarda* a precious stone, probably carnelian, possibly from Greek *sardion* literally, stone from *Sardis*.]

sar·dine (sär dēn′) pl., **-dines** or **-dine**. n. **1.** pilchard, esp. a young, small one, used for food and usually packed tightly in oil, in small, flat cans. **2.** any young herring or herringlike fish of the family Clupeidae similarly preserved for eating in tightly packed cans. [French *sardine* pilchard, from Latin *sardīna*.]

Sardine

Sar·din·i·a (sär din′ē ə) n. **1.** Italian island in the Mediterranean, west of Italy. Area, 9196 sq. mi. Pop. (1964 est.), 1,448,100. **2.** former kingdom that included this island and Savoy, Piedmont, and Nice. —**Sar·din′i·an**, adj., n.

Sar·dis (sär′dis) n. ancient city in western Asia Minor, the capital of Lydia, thought to have been destroyed by Tamerlane.

sar·don·ic (sär don′ik) adj. sarcastically mocking or sneering, often in a nasty or bitter way. [French *sardonique*, from Latin *Sardonicus (rīsus)*, translation of Greek *Sardonios (gelōs)* Sardinian or bitter (laughter); referring to the fact that a certain poisonous plant of Sardinia, when eaten, was supposed to distort the face and cause convulsions resembling laughter.] —**sar·don′i·cal·ly**, adv. —**sar·don′i·cism**, n.

sar·don·yx (sär don′iks) n. chalcedony quartz of a variety having layers of white or black alternating with red or reddish-brown, used esp. in the making of cameos. [Latin *sardonyx*, from Greek *sardonyx* literally, onyx of Sardis, from *Sardeis* Sardis + *onyx* fingernail, onyx.]

sar·gas·so (sär gas′ō) n. gulfweed. Also, **sargasso weed**, **sar·gas·sum**

(sär gas′əm). [Portuguese *sargaço*, possibly from *sarga* grape; with reference to the resemblance of its sacs to grapes.]

Sar·gas·so Sea (sär gas′ō) oval-shaped part of the central North Atlantic, between the West Indies and the Azores, noted for its abundance of floating seaweed.

Sar·gent, John Singer (sär′jənt) 1856–1925, U.S. painter.

Sar·gon II (sär′gon) died 705 B.C., king of Assyria, from 722 to 705 B.C.

sa·ri (sär′ē) pl., **-ris**. n. outer garment worn chiefly by women in India and Pakistan, consisting of a long piece of fabric, usually cotton or silk, that is wrapped around the waist with the free end brought up in front and thrown over the left shoulder. [Hindi *sārī*.]

Sari

Sar·ma·ti·a (sär mä′shē ə, -shə) n. ancient region in eastern Europe, in present-day Poland and the Soviet Union.

sa·rong (sə rông′, -rong′) n. skirtlike outer garment consisting of a long, rectangular piece of fabric, usually printed cotton, that is draped around the waist, worn chiefly in the Malay Archipelago and other islands of the Pacific by both men and women. [Malay *sărong* sheath, covering.]

sar·sa·pa·ril·la (sas′pə ril′ə, sär′sə pə-) n. **1.** any of several climbing or trailing vines, genus *Smilax*, of the lily family, found in Mexico, Central America, and South America, having prickly stems and large heart-shaped leaves with toothed edges. **2.** dried, aromatic roots of such a plant, used to flavor syrups and soft drinks. **3.** flavoring extract obtained from these roots. **4.** soft drink flavored with sarsaparilla. [Spanish *zarzaparrilla* the plant, from *zarza* bramble (from Arabic *sharas* thorny plant) + *parrilla*, diminutive of *parra* vine (of uncertain origin).]

Sar·to, Andrea del (sär′tō) see **Andrea del Sarto**.

sar·to·ri·al (sär tôr′ē əl) adj. **1.** of or relating to tailors or their work. **2.** of or relating to clothing or dress, esp. men's. [Latin *sartor* tailor + -IAL.] —**sar·to′ri·al·ly**, adv.

sar·to·ri·us (sär tôr′ē əs) n. flat, narrow muscle of the thigh, the longest muscle in the human body, extending obliquely from the hip across the front of the thigh. [Modern Latin *sartorius*, from Latin *sartor* tailor; because it makes it possible to sit in the cross-legged position of a tailor at work.]

Sar·tre, Jean Paul (sär′trə, särt; zhän pôl) 1905—, French philosopher.

sash¹ (sash) n. ornamental, usually broad, band of cloth or ribbon, often worn around the waist or over one shoulder. [Earlier *shash*, from Arabic *shāsh* turban.]

sash² (sash) n. frame, esp. a sliding one, in which the panes of glass are set in a window or door. —*v.t.* to furnish with a sash or sashes. [Modification of CHASSIS.]

sa·shay (sa shā′) *v.i.* **1.** *Informal.* to walk, move, or go in a pronouncedly nonchalant or swaggering manner. **2.** to execute a chassé. [Modification of CHASSÉ.]

Sask., Saskatchewan.

Sas·katch·e·wan (sas kach′ə wən) n. province of Canada, in the western part of the country. Area, 251,700 sq. mi. Pop. (1966), 955,344.

Sas·ka·toon (sas′kə tōōn′) n. city in south-central Saskatchewan, Canada. Pop. (1968), 125,000.

sass (sas) *Informal.* n. back talk; impudence. —*v.t.* to talk back to; talk impudently or disrespectfully to: *Bobby was punished for sassing his mother.* [From SASSY.]

sas·sa·fras (sas′ə fras′) n. **1.** any of a small group of aromatic trees, genus *Sassafras*, found in North America and Asia, esp. *S. albidum* of the eastern United States, the bark of whose roots is used as a flavoring. **2.** the bark itself, used to make a tea and to flavor various products, as root beer, tobacco, and chewing gum. [Spanish *sasafrás* the tree; of uncertain origin.]

sas·sy (sas′ē) **-si·er**, **-si·est**. adj. *Informal.* impudent; saucy. [Dialectal form of SAUCY.]

sat (sat) a past tense and past participle of **sit**.

Sat., Saturday.

Sa·tan (sāt′ən) n. the Devil. [Late Latin *Satan*, from Greek *Satan*, from Hebrew *sātān* enemy, adversary.]

sa·tan·ic (sə tan′ik, sā-) adj. **1.** of or relating to Satan. **2.** characteristic of or befitting Satan; extremely or fiendishly evil or cruel. Also, **sa·tan′i·cal**. —**sa·tan′i·cal·ly**, adv.

satch·el (sach′əl) n. bag or valise for carrying clothing, instruments, books, or other articles, sometimes having a shoulder strap. [Old French *sachel* little bag, from Latin *sacellus*, diminutive of *saccus* bag. See SACK¹.]

sate¹ (sāt) **sat·ed**, **sat·ing**. *v.t.* **1.** to fill or satisfy completely, as an appetite or desire. **2.** to furnish with more than enough, so as to weary,

bore, or disgust; glut. [Probably blend of obsolete *sade* to satiate (from Old English *sadian*) and Latin *sat* enough.] —**Syn.** 2. see *satiate.*

sate² (sāt, săt) *Archaic.* a past tense and past participle of **sit.**

sa·teen (sa tēn′) *n.* strong, usually cotton, fabric woven with a smooth, lustrous finish so as to resemble satin, used for such items as linings and theatrical costumes. [Modification (influenced by VELVETEEN) of SATIN.]

sat·el·lite (sat′əl īt′) *n.* **1.** celestial body that revolves in an orbit around another body larger than itself; moon. **2.** man-made object designed to revolve in a particular orbit around a body in space, as the earth or the moon. **3.** separate country dominated or controlled by or thoroughly cooperating with another more powerful country: *the Soviet Union and its Communist satellites.* **4.** follower or attendant of a person of importance. **5.** any subservient or obsequious follower. **6.** something or someone subordinate to, dependent on, or dominated by another. [Latin *satellit*-, stem of *satelles* attendant; possibly of Etruscan origin.]

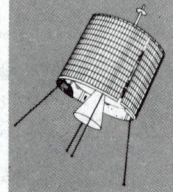

Satellite *(def. 2)*

sa·ti·a·ble (sā′shə bəl, sā′shē ə-) *adj.* that can be satiated. —**sa′tia·bil′i·ty, sa′tia·ble·ness,** *n.*

sa·ti·ate (sā′shē āt′) *-at·ed, -at·ing. v.t.* **1.** to furnish with more than enough, so as to weary, bore, or disgust; cloy; glut. **2.** to satisfy completely, as an appetite or desire. [Latin *satiātus,* past participle of *satiāre* to fill, satisfy, from *satis* enough.] —**sa′ti·a′tion,** *n.*

Syn. 1. Satiate, Sate¹, surfeit mean to fill to the point of excess. **Satiate** suggests the disparity between fulfilling a physical requirement and gratifying desire: *All that starchy food satiated without satisfying him.* **Sate** suggests that one's unending desires, esp. of a sensual nature, can be met by an equally inexhaustible supply: *The prince was continually sated by wine, women, and song.* **Surfeit,** like *sate,* suggests gratification which is initially pleasurable, but when taken to excess causes revulsion: *We were so surfeited by the acts of violence that we left before the end of the film.*

sa·ti·e·ty (sə tī′ə tē) *n.* state or condition of being satiated. [Latin *satietās* sufficiency.]

sat·in (sat′in) *n.* fabric having a smooth, lustrous, glossy face and dull back, made of silk or various synthetic fibers, used for such items as evening clothes. —*adj.* resembling satin; smooth; glossy: *satin skin.* [Old French *satin* the fabric, from Arabic *zaitūnī* relating to Zaitūn, from *Zaitūn* Tzu-t'ing (now Chuanchow), a port in southeastern China where satin was made.]

sat·in·wood (sat′in wood′) *n.* **1.** any of several woods having a satiny luster, esp. the wood of a small West Indian tree, *Zanthoxylum flavum,* or of a medium-sized tree, *Chloroxylon swietenia,* of India and Ceylon, used for veneers and furniture. **2.** any of the trees yielding such wood.

sat·in·y (sat′in ē) *adj.* resembling satin in softness, smoothness, or glossiness.

sat·ire (sat′īr) *n.* **1.** literary work that exposes or holds up to ridicule human vices or follies, usually in a witty or ironic way. **2.** branch of literature composed of such works, or the art of writing them. **3.** any work, production, or presentation similar to such literary works in purpose, content, or technique: *That movie's a clever satire on the advertising industry.* **4.** use of wit or irony, often in such forms as burlesque, caricature, or parody, to expose, attack, or ridicule human vices, follies, or abuses or evils of any kind. [Latin *satira,* form of *satura* medley, dish, from *satur* full, didactic poem on miscellaneous subjects.]

sa·tir·i·cal (sə tir′i kəl) *adj.* **1.** of, characterized by, or of the nature of satire. **2.** given to the use of satire. Also, **sa·tir′ic.** —**sa·tir′i·cal·ly,** *adv.*

sat·i·rist (sat′ər ist) *n.* one who creates satirical works, esp. a writer of satires.

sat·i·rize (sat′ə rīz′) *-rized, -riz·ing. v.t.* to criticize, attack, or ridicule by means of satire; subject to satire. [Latin *satira* satire.]

sat·is·fac·tion (sat′is fak′shən) *n.* **1.** state or feeling of being satisfied, fulfilled, or contented. **2.** act of satisfying or fulfilling. **3.** release from doubt or anxiety; certainty; conviction. **4.** reparation or compensation, as for a wrong or injury. **5.** opportunity to repair a wrong, injury, or insult, as by fighting a duel. **6.** cause or means of being satisfied; source of contentment or gratification. [Latin *satisfactiō* amends, explanation.]

Syn. 1. Satisfaction, contentment mean the happy state that follows the fulfillment of a need. **Satisfaction** stresses full appeasement of all needs and longings and the attainment of all desired ends: *Ben derives considerable satisfaction from doing his work well.* **Contentment** falls short of the full gratification suggested by satisfaction and implies a state of being satisfied with what one immediately has rather than yearning

for other or further gratifications: *The cat purred with contentment when Maria stroked her.*

sat·is·fac·to·ry (sat′is fak′tər ē) *adj.* good enough to meet a need, expectation, requirement, or demand. —**sat′is·fac′to·ri·ly,** *adv.*

sat·is·fy (sat′is fī′) *-fied, fy·ing. v.t.* **1.** to come up to or fulfill the desires, needs, expectations, or demands of; make contented: *The team's performance didn't satisfy the coach.* **2.** to supply, indulge, or appease fully with what is desired or needed: *to satisfy one's curiosity, to satisfy one's thirst with water.* **3.** to release or set free from doubt or anxiety; assure; convince. **4.** to fulfill or answer the conditions or requirements of: *to satisfy the requirements of a course.* **5.** to pay off or discharge fully, as a debt. **6.** to make reparation for; redress. **7.** to answer sufficiently or convincingly; dispel. **8.** to give what is due to: *to satisfy a creditor.* —*v.i.* to give satisfaction. [Old French *satisfier* to make amends, content, going back to Latin *satisfacere.*] —**sat′is·fi′er,** *n.*

sa·trap (sā′trap, sat′rap) *n.* **1.** governor of a province in the ancient Persian empire. **2.** any subordinate official or ruler, esp. a despotic one. [Latin *satrapēs* the Persian governor, from Greek *satrapēs,* from Old Persian *xshathrapāvān* protector of a province.]

sa·trap·y (sā′trə pē, sat′rə-) *pl.,* **-trap·ies.** *n.* territory or jurisdiction of a satrap.

sat·u·ra·ble (sach′ər ə bəl) *adj.* capable of being saturated.

sat·u·rate (sach′ə rāt′) *-rat·ed, -rat·ing. v.t.* **1.** to fill, supply, or treat with something to the point where no more can be absorbed, esp., to soak thoroughly. **2.** to fill full or to excess; cause to be thoroughly pervaded: *The candidate saturated radio time with political announcements.* **3.** to weary or cause to become indifferent or unresponsive by supplying with an excess; surfeit. **4.** *Chemistry.* to supply (a solvent or solution) with as much of a particular solute as can be dissolved in it at a given temperature and pressure. [Latin *saturātus,* past participle of *saturāre* to fill.] —**Syn. 1.** see *soak.*

sat·u·rat·ed (sach′ə rā′tid) *adj.* *Chemistry.* **a.** (of solutions) containing the maximum amount of solute capable of being dissolved at a given temperature and pressure. **b.** (of organic compounds) having all the valence bonds of its atoms, esp. carbon atoms, attached to other atoms. **2.** (of colors) of the highest intensity of hue; not diluted with white.

sat·u·ra·tion (sach′ə rā′shən) *n.* **1.** act or process of saturating. **2.** state or condition of being saturated. **3.** degree of intensity or vividness of a color.

Sat·ur·day (sat′ər dē, -dā′) *n.* seventh day of the week. [Old English *Saeterdaeg,* translation of Latin *Saturnī diēs* day of Saturn.]

Saturday night special, *Slang.* kind of inexpensive handgun that is widely sold.

Sat·urn (sat′ərn) *n.* **1.** Roman god of agriculture. His Greek counterpart is Cronus. **2.** second largest planet of the solar system and sixth in order of distance from the sun, having ten satellites. It is the only celestial body known to be surrounded by a system of rings that are thought to be composed of millions of minute ice particles.

Sat·ur·na·li·a (sat′ər nā′lē ə, -nāl′yə) *pl.,* **-lia** or **-lias.** *n.* **1.** principal ancient Roman festival of Saturn, that began on December 17 and continued for seven days, characterized by great public celebration, feasting, and merrymaking. **2.** saturnalia. any period or occasion of unrestrained, often orgiastic, merrymaking and revelry. [Latin *Sāturnālia* the ancient Roman festival.]

sat·ur·na·li·an (sat′ər nā′lē ən, -nāl′yən) *adj.* **1.** characterized by or of the nature of unrestrained or orgiastic merrymaking and revelry. **2. Saturnalian.** of or relating to the Saturnalia.

Sa·tur·ni·an (sə tur′nē ən) *adj.* **1.** of or relating to the god Saturn. **2.** of or relating to the planet Saturn.

sat·ur·nine (sat′ər nīn′) *adj.* having or showing a gloomy, morose, or taciturn nature. [SATURN + -INE¹; referring to the supposedly gloomy disposition of those born under the sign of the planet Saturn.] —**sat′ur·nine′ly,** *adv.*

sat·yr (sat′ər, sā′tər) *n.* **1.** *Greek Mythology.* minor deity of the woods and mountains, usually represented as a man having the horns, tail, and legs of a goat. **2.** lecherous or lustful man. [Latin *satyrus* the woodland deity, from Greek *satyros.*]

sauce (sôs) *n.* **1.** any fluid or semisolid preparation, usually consisting of several ingredients, used in the making of or eaten as an appetizing accompaniment to food. **2.** fruit that has been stewed into a pulp and sweetened. **3.** something that adds zest, piquancy, or flavor to something else. **4.** *Informal.* impertinence. **5.** *Slang.* alcoholic liquor. —*v.t.* **sauced, sauc·ing. 1.** to prepare or flavor with sauce. **2.** to add zest or flavor to. **3.** *Informal.* to be impertinent to. [Old French *sauce* the fluid preparation, from Latin *salsa,* feminine of *salsus* salted, going back to Latin *sāl* salt.]

Satyr

sauce·pan (sôs′pan′) n. small enamel or metal pot with a projecting handle, used for cooking food.

sau·cer (sô′sər) n. 1. small, usually slightly concave dish, esp. one for holding a cup. 2. something resembling a saucer in shape. [Old French *saussier* dish for holding sauces, from *sausse* sauce. See SAUCE.]

sau·cy (sô′sē) -ci·er, -ci·est. adj. 1. bold or disrespectful in a flippant, brazen, or spirited way. 2. piquant; roguish; sprightly. [SAUCE + -Yˡ.] —**sau′ci·ly**, adv. —**sau′ci·ness**, n.

Sa·u·di Arabia (sä ōo′dē, sou′-, sô′-) country in southwestern Asia, occupying most of the Arabian peninsula. Capital, Riyadh. Area, 830,-000 sq. mi. Pop. (1966 est.), 6,870,000.

sauer·bra·ten (sour′brä′tən, sou′ər-) n. beef marinated in vinegar, water, wine, onions, and spices, and then cooked like a pot roast. [German *Sauerbraten*, from *sauer* sour + *Braten* roast meat.]

sauer·kraut (sour′krout′, sou′ər-) n. finely shredded cabbage that has been salted and fermented in its own juice. [German *Sauerkraut*, from *sauer* sour + *Kraut* cabbage.]

Sauk (sôk) pl. **Sauks** or **Sauk**. also, **Sac**. n. member of an Algonquian tribe of North American Indians who formerly lived in what is now Michigan and Wisconsin, now living in Oklahoma, Iowa, and Kansas.

Saul (sôl) n. 1. in the Old Testament, the first king of Israel. 2. in the New Testament, the Apostle Paul before his conversion to Christianity. Also (def. 2), **Saul of Tarsus**.

Sault Ste. Ma·rie Canals (sōo′ sänt mə rē′) two canals linking Lake Superior and Lake Huron, and forming part of the U.S.-Canadian border. Also, **Soo Canals**.

sau·na (sou′nə, sô′-) n. 1. bath of a kind developed in Finland and resembling a steam bath, in which the bather is exposed to hot, relatively dry air that is usually produced by water being thrown over hot stones. 2. room or other enclosure in which to take such a bath. [Finnish *sauna* literally, bathroom.]

saun·ter (sôn′tər, sän′-) v.i. to walk in a leisurely, relaxed, or nonchalant way; stroll. —n. 1. leisurely, relaxed, or nonchalant way of walking: *to walk with a saunter*. 2. leisurely walk; idle stroll: *to take a saunter around the city*. [Of uncertain origin.] —**Syn.** v.i. see **walk**.

sau·ri·an (sôr′ē ən) n. lizard or lizardlike reptile, as the crocodile or dinosaur. —adj. of or relating to lizards or lizardlike reptiles. [Modern Latin *Sauria* (from Greek *sauros* lizard) + -AN.]

sau·sage (sô′sij) n. finely chopped seasoned meat, as pork, beef, or veal, made into patties or enclosed in the prepared intestine of an animal or other casing. [Dialectal Old French *saussiche*, from Late Latin *salsīcia* literally, seasoned with salt, from Latin *salsus* salted.]

sau·té (sō tā′) -téed, -té·ing. v.t. to cook or brown quickly in an open pan using a small amount of very hot fat. —n. food cooked in this manner. —adj. cooked or browned quickly in a small amount of very hot fat. [French *sauté* fried, tossed in a pan, from *sauter* to toss something occasionally while cooking it in a pan to prevent its sticking, leap, from Latin *saltāre* to dance.]

sau·terne (sō turn′) also. **Sau·ternes**. n. a sweet, white table wine. [From *Sauternes*. area in France producing this wine.]

sav·age (sav′ij) adj. 1. mercilessly brutal; cruel; vicious: *savage fighting*. 2. of a primitive or early stage of human social development; uncivilized: *a savage tribe*. 3. not domesticated or tamed; wild; ferocious: *savage beasts*. 4. not affected by man or human settlement; uncultivated; rugged: *a savage jungle*. —n. 1. one who belongs to an uncivilized people, group, or tribe, esp. one belonging to a people in the most primitive stage of development or civilization. 2. brutal, cruel, or vicious person. 3. rude, ill-mannered, boorish person. [Old French *sauvage* wild, going back to Latin *silvāticus* relating to a forest, wild, from *silva* forest.] —**sav′age·ly**, adv. —**sav′age·ness**, n. —**Syn.** adj. 1. see **fierce**. 2. see **barbarian**.

sav·age·ry (sav′ij rē) pl., -ries. n. 1. state or quality of being savage. 2. savage disposition, behavior, or act.

sa·van·na (sə van′ə) also. **sa·van·nah**. n. 1. broad, treeless plain with grass or other low vegetation. 2. tropical region of grassland with some trees and shrubs. [Earlier Spanish *zavana* large, treeless plain; of Taino origin.]

Sa·van·nah (sə van′ə) n. 1. port city in southeastern Georgia. Pop. (1960), 149,245. 2. river in the southeastern United States, flowing into the Atlantic, forming most of the border between South Carolina and Georgia.

sa·vant (sa vänt′, sə-, sav′ənt) n. man of great learning. [French *savant*, from *savoir* to know, going back to Latin *sapere* to be wise.]

save¹ (sāv) saved, sav·ing. v.t. 1. to deliver or free from harm, danger, or destruction; rescue: *to save someone's life*. 2. to set apart or aside for or as for future use (often with *up*): *She saves part of her salary each week*. 3. to keep from being lost, spent, or expended: *We omitted the last step to save time*. 4. to prevent the need, use, or occurrence of: *to save wear and tear*. 5. to keep intact or unhurt; safeguard; preserve: *to save one's reputation*. 6. to treat carefully so as to avoid or lessen damage, wear, or fatigue: *Save your eyes by reading in good*

light. 7. to deliver from sin and its consequences. —v.i. 1. to set aside or accumulate money by way of economy. 2. to avoid expense or waste; economize: *It's difficult to save on groceries*. [Old French *sauver*, *salver* to deliver from harm, danger, or destruction, from Late Latin *salvāre* to make safe, from Latin *salvus* unharmed, well¹.] —**sav′er**, n.

Syn. v.t. 1. **Save, rescue** mean to free a person from danger. **Save** may be used when one delivers a person or thing from a present danger or wards off an impending threat of harm in order to preserve him or it for further life, use, and service: *The operation saved the old man's life*. **Rescue** may be preferred when one saves a person from an imminent danger, capture, confinement, or death by prompt and forceful action: *The firemen rescued the child from the burning building*.

save² (sāv) prep. with the exception of; except; but: *No one save the immediate family attended the wedding*. —conj. 1. except; but (often with *that*): *I would have come, save that I had no car*. 2. Archaic. unless. [Form of SAFE with the obsolete meaning of reserving, excepting.]

sav·in (sav′in) also. **sav·ine**. n. 1. spreading shrub, *Juniperus sabina*, of the cypress family, whose tops yield a volatile oil used in medicine. 2. the oil itself, or a solution prepared from it. [Old French *safine*, *savine* the shrub, going back to Latin *Sabina (herba)* literally, Sabine herb.]

sav·ing (sā′ving) adj. 1. compensating; redeeming: *Her only saving grace is her sense of humor*. 2. thrifty; economical; frugal. 3. making or containing a reservation; qualifying: *a saving clause*. —n. 1. act of one who or that which saves something. 2. that which is saved. 3. reduction in expenditure or cost. 4. savings. money saved, esp. in a bank account. —prep. 1. with the exception of; save. 2. with respect to or for. —conj. except; save.

savings account, bank account maintained for the purpose of saving money and on which interest is paid.

savings bank, bank whose principal function is to accept deposits, invest its funds, and pay interest on the deposits.

sav·ior (sāv′yər) also, British, **sav·iour**. n. 1. one who saves from harm, danger, or destruction, or one who brings salvation. 2. **Savior**, Jesus. ▲ often used with *the*. [Old French *sauveor*, from Late Latin *salvātor*, going back to Latin *salvus* unharmed, well¹.]

sa·voir-faire (sav′wär fār′) n. faculty of knowing exactly what to do and the right or most charming way to do it; social tact. [French *savoir-faire* tact; literally, to know what to do, going back to Latin *sapere* to be wise + *facere* to do.]

Sav·o·na·ro·la, Gi·ro·la·mo (sav′ə nə rō′lə; ji rol′ə mō′) 1452-98, Italian friar, political and religious reformer, and martyr.

sa·vor (sā′vər) also, British, **sa·vour**. n. 1. particular flavor or aroma. 2. quality of a thing that affects the sense of taste or smell. 3. distinctive or characteristic quality. 4. power to arouse interest or excitement. —v.t. 1. to taste or smell with pleasure or zest: *to savor a meal*. 2. to take great delight in: *She savored the news that her chief rival had lost also*. 3. to give flavor to; season. —v.i. 1. to have a particular flavor or aroma (with *of*): *The room savors of garlic*. 2. to have or show a particular quality or trace; smack (with *of*): *The explosion savors of sabotage*. [Old French *savour* flavor, seasoning, from Latin *sapor* taste, flavor.] —**sa′vor·er**, n. —**sa′vor·ous**, adj.

sa·vor·y¹ (sā′vər ē) also, British, **sa·vour·y**. adj. 1. agreeable to the taste or smell; appetizing or fragrant. 2. morally acceptable or respectable: *a savory reputation*. 3. stimulating or sharp to the taste; pungent. [Old French *savoure* tasty, fragrant, from *savour*. See SAVOR.]

sa·vor·y² (sā′vər ē) pl., -vor·ies. n. any of several aromatic plants and small shrubs, genus *Satureja*, having narrow leaves and bearing clusters of white, pink, or purple flowers, esp. *S. hortensis* and *S. montana*, whose leaves are used to flavor food. [Old English *sætherīe*, from Latin *satureīa*.]

sa·vour·y (sā′vər ē) pl., -vour·ies. British. n. small portion of highly seasoned food, usually resembling a canapé, served at the end of a meal or as an appetizer. —adj. savory¹.

sa·voy (sə voi′) n. cabbage of a variety having a compact head and wrinkled leaves. [From *Savoy*, France, where it originated.]

Sa·voy (sə voi′) n. historic region in southeastern France, formerly part of the kingdom of Sardinia.

Sa·voy·ard¹ (sə voi′ərd, sav′oi ärd′) n. native or inhabitant of Savoy. —adj. of or relating to Savoy or its people. [French *Savoyard*, from *Savoie* Savoy.]

Sa·voy·ard² (sə voi′ərd, sav′oi ärd′) n. performer in, producer of, or admirer of Gilbert and Sullivan operas. [From the *Savoy Theatre* in London, England, where many Gilbert and Sullivan operas were first performed.]

sav·vy (sav′ē) -vied, -vy·ing. Slang. v.i. to know; understand; comprehend. —n. understanding, esp. of a practical or shrewd nature; good sense. [Modification of Spanish ¿ *sabe (Usted)?* do (you) know?, from *saber* to know, going back to Latin *sapere* to be wise.]

saw¹ (sô) n. 1. any of various hand or power tools having a metal blade or plate whose edge is notched with pointed teeth, used for cutting

wood, metal, or other hard materials. **2.** machine having such a tool or tools. —*v.t.,* **sawed, sawed** or **sawn, saw·ing. 1.** to cut with or as with a saw: *to saw a log in half.* **2.** to shape or form by cutting with a saw: *The boys sawed a hole in the ice so that they could fish.* **3.** to cleave or cut through as if using a saw: *As he talked, the teacher sawed the air with his ruler.* **4.** to cause to move with a to-and-fro motion, as if using a saw: *to saw a knife through meat.* —*v.i.* **1.** to use a saw; cut with a saw: *to saw along the grain of wood.* **2.** to admit of being cut with a saw: *This stone saws more easily than hardwood.* **3.** (of a saw) to cut. **4.** to make motions as if using a saw: *The fiddler sawed at the strings.* [Old English *saga* cutting tool with a toothed edge.] —**saw′er,** *n.*

saw² (sô) past tense of **see¹.**

saw³ (sô) *n.* traditional and familiar saying, esp. one hackneyed from frequent use or repetition: *He ended his essay with that old saw "Too many cooks spoil the broth."* [Old English *sagu* a saying.]

saw·buck¹ (sô′buk′) *n.* sawhorse, esp. one having X-shaped ends that extend above the crossbar. [Translation of Dutch *zaagbok.*]

saw·buck² (sô′buk′) *n. Slang.* ten-dollar bill. [From SAWBUCK¹ (supposedly from the resemblance of X, the Roman numeral ten, to the ends of a sawbuck); possibly influenced by BUCK².]

saw·dust (sô′dust′) *n.* fine particles that fall from wood or other material as it is being sawed.

sawed-off (sôd′ôf′) *adj.* **1.** having one end sawed off: *a sawed-off shotgun.* **2.** *Slang.* of less than average height; short.

Sawfish

saw·fish (sô′fish′) *pl.,* **-fish** or **-fish·es.** *n.* any of a group of large fish, family Pristidae, having a long, flat snout with sharp teeth along both edges. Length: to 35 feet.

saw·fly (sô′flī′) *pl.,* **-flies.** *n.* any of a group of bluish-black, flylike insects, suborder Tenthredinoidea, whose larvae feed on the leaves of fruit and shade trees and on the stems of wheat plants. The female has a sawlike organ which she uses to cut holes into plants and insert her eggs.

saw·horse (sô′hôrs′) *n.* frame on which to rest boards or other objects while they are being sawed, usually consisting of a crossbar supported by a pair of legs at each end. Also, **buck.**

saw·mill (sô′mil′) *n.* place where logs are sawed into lumber by machinery.

sawn (sôn) a past participle of **saw¹.**

saw·yer (sô′yər) *n.* one whose work is sawing wood, as in a sawmill. [Middle English *sawier,* from SAW¹ + -IER.]

sax (saks) *n. Informal.* saxophone.

sax·horn (saks′hôrn′) *n.* any of various valved brass wind instruments resembling a trumpet, having a full, mellow tone and a wide range of notes. It is most frequently used in marching bands. [From Antoine Joseph Sax, 1814–94, Belgian instrument maker who invented it + HORN.]

sax·i·frage (sak′sə frij) *n.* any of a large group of low-growing or trailing plants, genus *Saxifraga,* native to cool and temperate regions, bearing clusters of white, pink, purple, or yellow flowers, and often cultivated in rock gardens. [Late Latin *saxifraga (herba)* literally, rock-breaking (plant), from Latin *saxum* rock + *frangere* to break; probably because it grows among rocks.]

Sax·on (sak′sən) *n.* **1.** member or descendant of a Germanic tribe that inhabited parts of northwestern Germany. A portion of this tribe, along with the Angles and Jutes, conquered Britain in the fifth and sixth centuries and founded the kingdoms of Essex, Sussex, and Wessex. **2.** an Anglo-Saxon *(def. 1).* **3.** language of the Saxons. **4.** person of English nationality or descent. **5.** native or inhabitant of Saxony. —*adj.* **1.** of or relating to the early Saxons or Anglo-Saxons or to their languages. **2.** English. **3.** of or relating to Saxony.

Sax·o·ny (sak′sə nē) *n.* any of several former regions and political divisions of northwestern and central Germany.

sax·o·phone (sak′sə fōn′) *n.* single-reed wind instrument having a curving conical body made of metal and a series of keys for regulating the pitch of the tones. [From Antoine Joseph *Sax,* its inventor (see SAXHORN) + Greek *phōnē* sound, voice.] —**sax′o·phon′ist,** *n.*

sax·tu·ba (saks′tōō′bə, -tū′-) *n.* large bass or contrabass saxhorn. [SAX(HORN) + TUBA.]

Saxophone

say (sā) **said, say·ing.** *v.t.* **1.** to utter or pronounce the sound or sounds of; speak aloud: *I can't hear a word you're saying.* **2.** to make known or express in words; verbalize; state: *John said he'd call you soon.* **3.** to state as an opinion or with assurance: *No one can say how much longer the strike will last.* **4.** to take for or suppose as a fact; estimate; assume: *Let's say that we'll need two hundred dollars to make the purchase.* **5.** to repeat, as from memory; recite: *to say one's prayers.* **6.** to communicate, as by signs or symbols; indicate; show: *Her actions said more than a thousand words.* **7.** to report or allege; maintain: *Rugby is said to be the roughest of all sports.* —*v.i.* **1.** to express oneself; speak; declare: *He saw her an hour ago, or so he says.* **2. that is to say.** in other words. —*n.* **1.** right or chance to express an opinion: *Give him his say before you condemn him.* **2.** right or power to influence or decide; voice; authority: *to have the final say.* **3.** what one says or has to say: *He said his say and then sat down.* —*adv.* **1.** as an estimate; approximately: *an industrialist who's worth, say, four million dollars.* **2.** for example: *Let's take a trip, say, along the coast.* —*interj.* used to attract attention or to express surprise, pleasure, annoyance, or the like. Also, *British,* **I say.** [Old English *secgan* to tell, speak.] —**say′er,** *n.*

Syn. *v.t.* **Say, utter¹, state** mean to put into words. **Say** often suggests merely the expression of a thought, feeling, or idea in speech or writing but may sometimes refer to the exact words articulated: *What did John say when he saw you?* **Utter** stresses the act rather than the content of speech, esp. when it serves to give vent to a sudden emotion: *He uttered an oath when he heard the news.* **State** suggests a sense of clarity and formality in speech and stresses the setting forth of such particulars as reasons, facts, or conditions: *State your name, age, and occupation.*

say·ing (sā′ing) *n.* **1.** pithy, familiar, commonly repeated statement believed to contain truth, wisdom, or common sense. "A stitch in time saves nine" is a saying. **2.** any commonly repeated phrase, expression, or statement: *He's mad as a hatter, as the saying goes.* **3.** something said; statement: *She collected sayings of her favorite authors in a small notebook.*

says (sez) third person singular present indicative of **say.**

say-so (sā′sō′) *n. Informal.* **1.** authoritative judgment or assertion; authority: *The architect went ahead with the building plans on the owner's say-so.* **2.** unsupported assurance or assertion: *No one's going to blame him on just your say-so.*

sb., substantive.

Sb, antimony. [Latin *stibium.*]

S.B., Bachelor of Science.

sc. 1. scale. **2.** scene. **3.** science; scientific. **4.** namely. **5.** *Sculpture.* he carved or engraved it.

s.c. *Printing.* small capitals.

Sc, scandium.

Sc. 1. Scotch. **2.** Scottish. **3.** Scotland.

SC 1. Security Council (of the United Nations). **2.** Supreme Court. **3.** Signal Corps.

S.C., South Carolina.

scab (skab) *n.* **1.** crust of dried blood and fluids that forms a protective cover over a wound or sore during healing. **2.** *Informal.* worker who refuses to join a labor union or who works under conditions contrary to those established by a labor union, esp. one who works when the union workers are on strike. **3.** scabies *(def. 2).* **4.** any of several plant diseases caused by bacteria and fungi in which crusty or scablike spots form on the fruits, stems, and roots. —*v.i.* **scabbed, scab·bing. 1.** to become covered with or form a scab. **2.** *Informal.* to act as a scab.

scab·bard (skab′ərd) *n.* case or sheath for the blade of a sword, bayonet, or other similar weapon. [Short for Anglo-Norman *escaubers* sheaths; of Germanic origin.]

Scabbard with cavalry sword

scab·by (skab′ē) **-bi·er, -bi·est.** *adj.* **1.** consisting of, covered with, or resembling a scab or scabs. **2.** afflicted with scab. **3.** *Informal.* contemptible; low; mean. —**scab′bi·ly,** *adv.* —**scab′bi·ness,** *n.*

sca·bies (skā′bēz, -bē ēz′) *n.,pl.* **1.** contagious skin disease in human beings characterized by intense itching, caused by parasitic mites that burrow under the skin and deposit eggs and irritating wastes. Also, **the itch.** **2.** similar disease in animals, esp. sheep. ♦ both meanings are construed as singular. [Latin *scabiēs* roughness, itch.]

sca·bi·ous¹ (skā′bē əs) *adj.* **1.** of, relating to, or resembling scabies. **2.** having or resembling a scab or scabs. [Latin *scabiōsus* scabby, scurfy, from *scabiēs.* See SCABIES.]

sca·bi·ous² (skā′bē əs) *n.* any of a group of plants, genus *Scabiosa,* bearing showy blue, rose, yellowish, or white flower heads. [Medieval Latin *scabiosa (herba)* plant believed to heal some skin diseases, going back to Latin *scabiēs.* See SCABIES.]

at; āpe; cär; end; mē; it; īce; hot; ōld; fôrk; wood; fōōl; oil; out; up; ūse; turn; sing; thin; this; zh in treasure; ə in ago, taken, pencil, lemon, circus.

scab·rous (skab′rəs, skā′brəs) *adj.* **1.** having a prickly or scabby surface; rough to the touch. **2.** difficult to solve or handle; knotty: *a scabrous problem.* **3.** off-color; risqué. [Late Latin *scabrōsus* rough, from Latin *scaber.*]

scads (skadz) *n.,pl. Informal.* large quantities or amounts: *There are scads of fish in that lake.* [Of uncertain origin.]

scaf·fold (skaf′əld) *n.* **1.** temporary wooden or metal platform, often suspended from a roof, used to support workmen and materials, as in the repairing or cleaning of a building. **2.** elevated platform on which criminals are executed. **3.** any raised framework, as for drying tobacco or fish. **4.** raised stage or stand, as for exhibition purposes. —*v.t.* to furnish or support with a scaffold or scaffolding. [Old French *eschafaud* (earlier *escadafaut*) pieces of wood supporting a platform, possibly going back to Latin *ex* out of + *cata* by (from Greek *kata* down) + *fala* scaffolding (of Etruscan origin).]

scaf·fold·ing (skaf′əl ding) *n.* **1.** scaffold or a connected series of scaffolds. **2.** materials used to construct a scaffolding.

scal·a·wag (skal′ə wag′) *also,* **scal·la·wag, scal·ly·wag.** *n.* **1.** in American history, any white Southerner who aided in carrying out the Republican program of Reconstruction following the Civil War. **2.** worthless person; rascal. [Of uncertain origin.]

scald[1] (skôld) *v.t.* **1.** to burn with or as with hot liquid or steam: *The coffee spilled and scalded his hand.* **2.** to clean or treat with steam or boiling liquid: *to scald medical instruments.* **3.** to heat to a temperature just below the boiling point: *to scald milk.* —*v.i.* to be or become scalded. —*n.* burn caused by hot liquid or by a hot moist vapor, as steam. [Dialectal Old French *escalder* to burn with hot water, heat, from Late Latin *excaldāre* to wash in hot water, from *ex* out, very + *calidus* hot.] —**Syn.** *v.t.* **1.** see **scorch.**

scald[2] (skôld, skäld) skald.

scale[1] (skāl) *n.* **1.** any device or machine for determining the weight of an object by balancing it against another weight or against the force of a spring. **2. scales.** balance *(def. 7).* **3.** dish, pan, or platform of a balance. **4. Scales.** Libra. **5. to tip the scales** (or **scale**). to have a decisive influence or effect: *The lawyer's brilliant defense tipped the scales in his client's favor.* **6. to tip the scales** (or **scale**) **at.** to have a specified weight of; weigh: *The boxer tipped the scales at 200 pounds.* —*v.i.* **scaled, scal·ing.** to amount to in weight; weigh. —*v.t.* to weigh (something) in a scale or scales. [Old Norse *skál* bowl, dish of a balance.]

scale[2] (skāl) *n.* **1.a.** one of the horny, flattened, platelike structures forming part or all of the external covering of certain animals, as many snakes, lizards, and fish. **b.** any structure resembling this, as on the wings of some insects or the legs of most birds. **2.** thin, flat, flaky piece or plate, as of skin. **3.** flattened, platelike structure or modified leaf, as a bud scale, on certain plants. **4.** scale insect. **5.** crust of metallic oxide that forms on hot metals as they cool. **6.** crust formed on the inside of steam boilers by the evaporation of water containing minerals. —*v.t.,* **scaled, scal·ing.** **1.** to remove the scales or scale from, esp. by scraping: *to scale a fish.* **2.** to remove in thin layers or scales: *to scale the bark off a branch.* —*v.i.* **1.** to peel or come off in scales, flakes, or thin layers; flake. **2.** to become covered with a scale or scales. [Old French *escale* shell, husk; of Germanic origin.]

scale[3] (skāl) *n.* **1.** graduated or progressive classification, grouping, or order; series or scheme of steps or degrees: *the social scale.* **2.a.** proportion that a plan, map, model, or other representation bears to what it represents; ratio of the dimensions represented to the actual dimensions: *The scale of this map is one inch to 200 miles.* **b.** divided line, as on a map, representing or indicating this proportion. **3.** series of marks made along a line at regularly spaced distances or graduated intervals, used in measuring or calculating: *the scale on a slide rule, the scale on a protractor.* **4.** any instrument marked in this way, used esp. for measuring. **5.** relative extent or size: *The project was undertaken on a grand scale.* **6.** *Music.* series of tones ascending or descending in pitch according to fixed intervals, esp. such a series contained within an octave. **7.** *Mathematics.* numbers of a particular numeration system, collectively: *the decimal scale.* —*v.t.,* **scaled, scal·ing.** **1.** to climb up or ascend: *to scale a mountain.* **2.** to adjust or regulate by or as by a fixed proportion or scale: *to scale down the level of fighting.* **3.** to make according to a scale: *to scale a drawing.* —*v.i.* **1.** to climb; ascend. **2.** to rise, as in steps or stages. [Latin *scāla* ladder.] —**Syn.** *v.t.* **1.** see **climb.**

scale insect, any of various tiny insects, superfamily Coccoidea, the

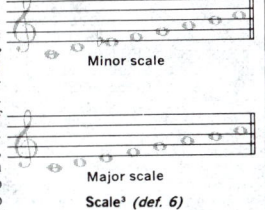

Minor scale

Major scale

Scale[3] *(def. 6)*

females of which secrete tough, waxy scales that form a protective shield for the body.

sca·lene (skā lēn′, skā′lēn) *adj.* (of a triangle) having three unequal sides. [Late Latin *scalēnus* of unequal sides, from Greek *skalēnos* uneven, unequal.]

scal·la·wag (skal′ə wag′) scalawag.

scal·lion (skal′yən) *n.* **1.** young green onion whose bulb is just beginning to form. Also, **green onion. 2.** shallot. **3.** leek. [Anglo-Norman *scal(o)un,* going back to Latin *(caepa) Ascalōnia* (onion) of Ascalon, a city in Palestine.]

scal·lop (skol′əp, skal′-) *also,* **scol·lop, es·cal·lop.** *n.* **1.** any of a group of bivalve mollusks, family Pectinidae, found on the ocean floor, having circular hinged shells, often ridged and with wavy edges. **2.** edible muscle of certain

Scallop *(def. 1)*

species of this mollusk, used as food. **3.** one of a series of semicircles or curves resembling the edge of a scallop shell, made as an ornamental border on clothing and other articles. **4.** thin, boneless slice of meat, esp. of veal. **5.** shell of a scallop, or a similarly shaped fish, in which food, esp. seafood, is baked or served. **6.** shell of a scallop worn in the Middle Ages by pilgrims returning from the Holy Land as a sign of their pilgrimage. —*v.t.* **1.** to shape or ornament with scallops, esp. by cutting: *The edges of the tablecloth were scalloped.* **2.** to bake in a casserole with a sauce, often with a topping of bread crumbs; escallop: *to scallop potatoes.* [Old French *escalope* shell; of Germanic origin.]

scal·ly·wag (skal′i wag′) scalawag.

sca·lop·pi·ne (skä′lə pē′nē, skal′ə-) *also,* **scal·lo·pi·ni, sca·lop·pi·ni.** *n.* dish consisting of small, thin slices of meat, esp. veal, that are sautéed or cooked and served in a wine or tomato sauce. [Modification of Italian *scaloppine,* plural of *scaloppina* thin, boneless slice of meat, going back to Old French *escalope* shell; because often served curled like a shell. See SCALLOP.]

scalp (skalp) *n.* **1.** skin that covers the human skull, usually covered with hair. **2.** part of this skin and attached hair, as that formerly cut or torn from the head of an enemy as a trophy or symbol of victory. **3.** skin covering the skull of certain animals, esp. a wolf. **4.** any trophy or symbol of victory. —*v.t.* **1.** to cut or tear the scalp from. **2.** *Informal.* to buy and resell (tickets) at an excessive profit. **3.** *Informal.* to swindle or defraud; cheat: *confidence men who scalp the public.* [Probably of Scandinavian origin.] —**scalp′er,** *n.*

scal·pel (skal′pəl) *n.* small, pointed knife with a straight handle and curved cutting edge, used in surgery and dissections. [Latin *scalpellum,* diminutive of *scalprum* knife.]

scalp lock, long lock or tuft of hair left on the crown of the shaven head by certain North American Indians as a challenge to their enemies.

scal·y (skā′lē) *adj.* **scal·i·er, scal·i·est.** **1.** covered with or consisting of scales. **2.** resembling scales. **3.** peeling or coming off in scales or flakes; flaking. —**scal′i·ness,** *n.*

scaly anteater, pangolin.

scamp[1] (skamp) *n.* **1.** worthless, dishonest, or unprincipled person; rogue. **2.** mischievous or playful person, esp. a youngster. [From obsolete *scamp* to roam, from Middle Dutch *schampen* to run away, from Old French *escamper,* going back to Latin *ex* out of + *campus* field.]

scamp[2] (skamp) *v.t.* to do or perform carelessly or hastily. [Probably a blend of SCANT and SKIMP.]

scam·per (skam′pər) *v.i.* **1.** to run or flee quickly or hastily: *The rabbit scampered off into the woods.* **2.** to move about playfully or nimbly: *children scampering about.* —*n.* act of scampering. [Obsolete *scamp* to roam + -ER[4]. See SCAMP[1].]

scan (skan) scanned, scan·ning. *v.t.* **1.** to look at closely and carefully; examine intensively: *She scanned his face for some sign of recognition.* **2.** to search, pass, or look over (a wide area) thoroughly, esp. by a slow, sweeping movement: *to scan the horizon for a ship.* **3.** to glance over or go through quickly or hastily; skim: *to scan a manuscript for errors.* **4.** to mark off or analyze (verse) according to a metrical pattern. **5.** to sweep or cover (an area) with an electronic detecting device, as radar. **6.** to trace out closely spaced parallel lines on a cathode-ray tube or other target). —*v.i.* **1.** to scan verse. **2.** (of verse) to conform to the form of a metrical pattern. **3.** (of a beam from an electron gun) to trace out closely spaced parallel lines that cover a target, as the viewing screen of a radar set or some other cathode-ray tube. —*n.* **1.** act of scanning. **2.** scope of vision or knowledge; perception. [Late Latin *scandere* to measure verses, from Latin *scandere* to climb, rise.] —**scan′ner,** *n.*

Scand., Scandinavia; Scandinavian.

scan·dal (skand′əl) *n.* **1.** any action, circumstance, or occurrence that shocks or offends public morality and disgraces those associated with it: *Housing conditions in the slums of this city are a scandal.* **2.** reaction of indignation, outrage, or strong disapproval produced by such an action, circumstance, or occurrence: *Disclosure of the senator's under-*

at; āpe; cär; end; mē; it; īce; hot; ōld; fôrk; wood; fōol; oil; out; up; ūse; turn; sing; thin; this; zh in treasure; ə in ago, taken, pencil, lemon, circus.

887

world ties gave rise to a nationwide scandal. **3.** defamatory talk; malicious gossip: *a family whose name has never been touched by scandal.* **4.** one whose conduct is a cause of disgrace or dishonor: *The doctor's unorthodox methods made him a scandal to his profession.* **5.** damage to reputation; disgrace; dishonor: *One traitor brought scandal to the whole battalion.* [Late Latin *scandalum* cause of offense, stumbling block, from Greek *skandalon* originally, trap. Doublet of SLANDER.]

scan·dal·ize (skand′əl īz′) **-ized, -iz·ing.** *v.t.* to shock or offend by something considered immoral or improper; outrage.

scan·dal·mon·ger (skand′əl mung′gər, -mong′-) *n.* one who spreads scandal or malicious gossip.

scan·dal·ous (skand′əl əs) *adj.* **1.** causing scandal; disgraceful; shocking. **2.** consisting of or spreading scandal; defamatory. —**scan′dal·ous·ly,** *adv.* —**scan′dal·ous·ness,** *n.*

scandal sheet, newspaper or periodical that deals primarily in news of a scandalous or sensational nature.

Scan·di·na·vi·a (skan′də nā′vē ə) *n.* **1.** region in northern Europe consisting of Norway, Sweden, and Denmark and sometimes Iceland or Finland. **2.** large peninsula of northern Europe occupied by Norway and Sweden.

Scan·di·na·vi·an (skan′də nā′vē ən) *adj.* of or relating to Scandinavia, its people, their language, or culture. —*n.* **1.** member or close descendant of the people of Scandinavia. **2.** languages of Scandinavia and Iceland collectively, a division of the Germanic branch of the Indo-European language family.

scan·di·um (skan′dē əm) *n.* rare, very light, silver-white metallic element. Symbol: Sc See **element** for table. [Modern Latin *scandium,* from Medieval Latin *Scandia* Scandinavia; because it was discovered there.]

scan·sion (skan′shən) *n.* analysis of verse according to one of several metrical patterns, using either long or short syllables, as in Latin poetry, or accented and unaccented syllables, as in English poetry. [Late Latin *scānsiō,* from Latin *scānsiō* a climbing.]

scant (skant) *adj.* **1.** lacking or inadequate in amount or quantity; scarcely enough; meager: *scant provisions for our journey.* **2.** not quite amounting to a specified measure. ▲ often used with the indefinite article, even with a plural noun: *a scant six miles, a scant half-hour.* **3.** having an insufficient supply (with *of*): *to be scant of breath.* —*v.t.* **1.** to furnish a scant amount of; skimp on. **2.** to treat in an inadequate or careless manner. [Old Norse *skamt,* neuter of *skammr* short, brief.] —**scant′ly,** *adv.* —**scant′ness,** *n.*

scant·ling (skant′ling) *n.* **1.** small piece of lumber, used esp. as a vertical member in the frame of a building. **2.** such lumber collectively. **3.** size of building materials, as of pieces of lumber or stone. **4.** small amount, quantity, or portion. [Modification of Old French *escantillon* sample, standard (of weights and measures), going back to Latin *scandere* to climb (probably referring to gradations on a scale).]

scant·y (skant′ē) *scant·i·er, scant·i·est. adj.* **1.** scarcely sufficient or adequate in amount or quantity; meager. **2.** limited or insufficient in extent or size: *a scanty bathrobe.* [SCANT + -Y¹.] —**scant′i·ly,** *adv.* —**scant′i·ness,** *n.* —**Syn. 1.** see **meager.**

Scap·a Flow (skap′ə flō′) sheltered expanse of sea north of Scotland, a major British naval anchorage during World Wars I and II.

scape¹ (skāp) *n.* **1.** leafless flower stalk rising from the ground, as that of the dandelion. **2.** something similar to a stalk, as the shaft of a feather or the shaft of a column. [Latin *scāpus* shaft, stalk¹.]

scape² (skāp) *also,* **'scape.** *Archaic.* escape.

-scape *combining form* view; scene: *seascape, moonscape.* [From LANDSCAPE.]

scape·goat (skāp′gōt′) *n.* person or thing made to suffer for or bear the blame for the shortcomings, misfortunes, or mistakes of another or others or against which the irrational hostility or aggression of another or others is directed. [SCAPE² + GOAT; referring to the goat upon whose head Aaron symbolically placed the sins of the people and which was then allowed to escape into the wilderness (Leviticus 16:8,10).]

scape·grace (skāp′grās′) *n.* incorrigible, mischievous, or unprincipled person; scamp; rascal. [Short for *escape grace* (suggesting one who has escaped divine grace).]

scap·u·la (skap′yə lə) *pl.* **-lae** (-lē) *or* **-las.** *n.* shoulder blade. [Latin *scapula* shoulder, shoulder blade.]

scap·u·lar (skap′yə lər) *n.* **1.** in the Roman Catholic Church, outer garment consisting of two long, narrow pieces of cloth hanging from the shoulders in front and behind and reaching almost to the feet, worn by certain religious orders. **2.** two small squares of cloth joined by string, worn under the clothing about the shoulders by Roman Catholics as a mark of religious devotion. **3.** one of the shoulder feathers of a bird. —*adj. also,* **scap·u·lar·y** (skap′yə ler′ē). of or relating to the shoulder or shoulder blade. [Medieval Latin *scapulare* garment covering the shoulders, from Latin *scapula* shoulder, shoulder blade.]

scar (skär) *n.* **1.** any mark, discolored area, or similar trace left, esp. on the skin, by the replacement of tissue that has been destroyed by

injury or disease. **2.** any mark or blemish resembling this. **3.** lasting impression or injurious effect of a distressing or traumatic experience. **4.** *Botany.* mark indicating a former point of attachment, as where a leaf has fallen from a stem. —*v.t.* **scarred, scar·ring.** to mark with a scar or scars; leave a scar or scars upon. —*v.i.* to form or become marked with a scar. [Old French *escare* scab, from Late Latin *eschara* scab, mark left by a burn, from Greek *eschará* scab, hearth.]

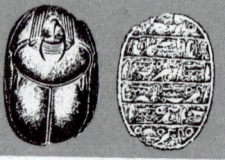

Scarab *(def. 2)*

scar·ab (skar′əb) *n.* **1.** any of a large group of beetles, family Scarabaeidae, having stocky, oval bodies, esp. one of a species regarded as sacred by the ancient Egyptians. **2.** representation of this beetle, as a gem cut in its shape or a piece of jewelry bearing its image. [Latin *scarabaeus* beetle.]

scarce (skârs) **scarc·er, scarc·est.** *adj.* **1.** insufficient for a need, demand, or requirement: *Provisions were growing scarce aboard ship.* **2.** difficult to acquire or find; rare: *Corn on the cob is scarce at this time of year.* **3. to make (oneself) scarce.** *Informal.* to go or stay away. —*adv.* scarcely. [Dialectal Old French *escars* scanty, going back to Latin *excerptus,* past participle of *excerpere* to select, pick out.] —**scarce′ness,** *n.* —**Syn. 2.** see **uncommon.**

scarce·ly (skârs′lē) *adv.* **1.** by a narrow margin; just; barely: *I had scarcely come in when the phone rang.* **2.** almost not: *There was scarcely a person on the street.* **3.** certainly or most probably not: *A better carpenter was scarcely to be found.*

scar·ci·ty (skâr′sə tē) *pl.* **-ties.** *n.* **1.** that which is scarce; insufficient amount or supply. **2.** quality or state of being scarce.

Syn. 1. Scarcity, dearth mean a shortage of something. **Scarcity** may be preferred when referring to a supply inadequate to a demand: *The scarcity of jobs is characteristic of a recession.* **Dearth** suggests the mere absence or lack of something: *The dearth of good restaurants is surprising in such a large city.*

scare (skâr) **scared, scar·ing.** *v.t.* **1.** to cause to be afraid or alarmed, esp. to strike with sudden fear; frighten: *The thunder scared the children.* **2.a.** to drive or force by frightening: *to scare away a child.* **b.** to cause to be in a specified condition by frightening: *to scare someone speechless.* —*v.i.* **1.** to become scared: *I don't scare easily.* **2. to scare up.** *Informal.* to find, gather together, or prepare hastily: *I'll scare up some lunch for our visitors.* —*n.* **1.** sudden fear or alarm, often with little or no ground; fright: *The sound of the explosion gave the girl quite a scare.* **2.** state of widespread or public fear or alarm; panic: *a bomb scare.* [Old Norse *skirra* to frighten.]

scare·crow (skâr′krō′) *n.* **1.** crude representation of a human figure, esp. of a man dressed in old clothes, set in a field to frighten crows and other birds away from crops. **2.** person resembling a scarecrow, esp. a skinny or ragged person. **3.** something frightening but not really harmful.

scarf¹ (skärf) *pl.,* **scarfs** *or* **scarves.** *n.* **1.** piece of cloth, usually rectangular, oblong, or triangular, worn for warmth, protection, or adornment, as about the neck or head. **2.** strip of cloth used to cover the top of a piece of furniture, as a dresser or table. [Probably from dialectal Old French *escarpe* sash, sling; of Germanic origin.]

scarf² (skärf) *pl.,* **scarfs.** *n.* **1.** joint in which the ends of two timbers are notched or cut so that they lap over and interlock to form one continuous piece, often secured by bolts or straps. Also, **scarf joint.** **2.** notched or cut end of a timber, used to make such a joint. —*v.t.* **1.** to join by means of a scarf joint. **2.** to cut or notch the end of (a timber). [Probably of Scandinavian origin.]

scarf·skin (skärf′skin′) *n.* outermost layer of skin; epidermis.

scar·i·fi·ca·tion (skar′ə fi kā′shən) *n.* **1.** act or process of scarifying. **2.** mark or marks made by scarifying; superficial incision or scratch.

scar·i·fy (skar′ə fī′) **-fied, -fy·ing.** *v.t.* **1.** to make a number of superficial incisions or scratches in, as in the skin during surgery. **2.** to criticize harshly or severely; wound with cutting remarks. **3.** to loosen, as topsoil, by scratching or breaking up the surface. **4.** to slit or soften the coating (of a seed) to hasten sprouting. [Late Latin *scarīficāre* to scratch open, going back to Greek *skariphâsthai* to sketch, scratch an outline.] —**scar′i·fi′er,** *n.*

scar·la·ti·na (skär′lə tē′nə) *n.* **1.** scarlet fever. **2.** *Informal.* mild form of scarlet fever. [Modern Latin *scarlatina,* from Italian *scarlattina,* from *scarlatto* scarlet, probably from Persian *saqalāt.* See SCARLET.]

Scar·lat·ti (skär lä′tē) **1. A·les·san·dro** (ä′le sän′drō). 1660–1725, Italian composer. **2. Do·me·ni·co** (dō men′i kō′). 1685–1757, his son; Italian composer and harpsichord virtuoso.

scar·let (skär′lit) *n.* bright-red color, tending toward orange. —*adj.* **1.** having the color scarlet. **2.** sinful or unchaste. [Modification

of Old French *escarlate* rich cloth, usually red in color, probably from Persian *saqalāt*, through Arabic and Greek, from Latin *sigillātus* decorated with little figures.]

scarlet fever, highly contagious disease occurring most often in children, caused by a streptococcus and characterized by a scarlet rash, high fever, and a sore throat.

scarlet runner, tall climbing bean plant, *Phaseolus coccineus,* found in the American tropics, bearing clusters of bright-red flowers and cultivated as an ornamental.

scarlet tanager, North American tanager, *Piranga olivacea,* the male of which is bright red with black wings and tail, and the female greenish above and yellow below.

scarp (skärp) *n.* **1.** cliff or steep slope. **2.** wall or steep slope at the outer part of a fortification. —*v.t.* to cut or make into a steep slope; form into a scarp. [Italian *scarpa* slope (of land); of Germanic origin.]

scar tissue, tough, fibrous connective tissue that replaces any body tissue damaged or destroyed by disease or injury.

scarves (skärvz) a plural of **scarf¹.**

scar·y (skâr′ē) **scar·i·er, scar·i·est.** *adj. Informal.* **1.** causing fear, alarm, or uneasiness; frightening: *a scary movie.* **2.** characterized by fear: *a scary feeling.* **3.** easily scared; timid.

scat¹ (skat) **scat·ted, scat·ting.** *v.i. Informal.* to go away quickly. ▲ usually used in the imperative. [Possibly short for SCATTER.]

scat² (skat) *n.* jazz singing consisting of the improvisation of nonsense syllables. Also, **scat singing.** —*v.i.,* **scat·ted, scat·ting.** *Informal.* to sing scat. [Possibly imitative.]

scathe (skā_th_) **scathed, scath·ing.** *Archaic. v.t.* **1.** to injure or hurt, esp. by burning. **2.** to criticize severely. [Of Scandinavian origin.]

scath·ing (skā′_th_ing) *adj.* **1.** bitterly severe; unsparingly harsh: *scathing sarcasm, a scathing rebuke.* **2.** severely injurious or painful. —**scath′ing·ly,** *adv.*

scat·o·log·i·cal (skat′ə loj′i kəl) *adj.* of, relating to, or characterized by scatology. Also, **scat·o·log′ic.**

sca·tol·o·gy (skə tol′ə jē) *n.* **1.** preoccupation or concern with excrement or excretory functions, in literature. **2.** study of excrement, as in paleontology or medicine. [Greek *skat-,* stem of *skōr* dung + -LOGY.]

scat·ter (skat′ər) *v.t.* **1.** to spread or throw about randomly or in various places; strew: *A gust of wind scattered leaves all over the yard.* **2.** to cause to separate and go off in various directions; disperse: *The gunshot scattered the herd.* **3.** to drive away or cause to vanish; dispel: *This final setback scattered all hopes for victory.* **4.** *Physics.* to deflect (particles or waves) by collisions or other interactions. —*v.i.* to separate and go off in various directions: *The crowd scattered when the police arrived.* —*n.* small, scattered amount: *a scatter of raindrops on the windshield.* [Probably a form of SHATTER.] —**scat′ter·er,** *n.*

Syn. v.t. **2.** *Scatter, disperse* mean to cause a group of persons or animals to separate and break up. *Scatter* suggests that the group is broken up as a result of a random, casual, or disorganized effort: *The thundershower had temporarily scattered the swimmers.* In contrast, *disperse* suggests the group is broken up permanently or more completely as a result of a disciplined and organized effort: *The private guards were hired to disperse the fans before the singers arrived at the theater.*

scat·ter·brain (skat′ər brān′) *n.* one lacking in powers of mental concentration; flighty, forgetful, or unthinking person.

scat·ter·brained (skat′ər brānd′) *adj.* **1.** flighty, forgetful, or unthinking. **2.** contrary to reason or common sense; ridiculous: *a scatter-brained idea.*

scat·ter·ing (skat′ər ing) *n.* **1.** small, scattered number or amount: *Only a scattering of celebrities was in the audience.* **2.** act of scattering. **3.** *Physics.* deflection of particles or waves, produced by collisions or other interactions.

scatter rug, small rug used to cover part of a floor. Also, **throw rug.**

scaup (skôp) *n.* broad-billed diving duck, genus *Aythya,* native to cold and temperate regions of the Northern Hemisphere. Also, **scaup duck.** [From Scottish *scaup,* form of dialectal English *scalp* bank of sand serving as a bed for shellfish (on which these ducks feed); of uncertain origin.]

Scaup

scav·enge (skav′inj) **-enged, -eng·ing.** *v.i.* to search, as for food or something salvageable: *Divers scavenged through the ship's wreckage.* —*v.t.* **1.** to find or collect (something) by searching: *They scavenged what food they could to keep alive.* **2.** to search (something) for salvageable material. **3.** to remove dirt or refuse from; clean up. [From SCAVENGER.]

scav·en·ger (skav′in jər) *n.* **1.** animal, as the hyena or vulture, that feeds on decaying plant or animal matter. **2.** one who or that which

scavenges, esp. one who searches through refuse or discarded material for salvageable or useful things. [Modification of obsolete *scavager* officer who supervised street cleaning and, in earlier times, collected a toll on foreign merchants, going back to Anglo-Norman *scawage* the toll itself, inspection, going back to dialectal Old French *escauwer* to inspect; of Germanic origin.]

sce·nar·i·o (si när′ē ō′, -när′-) *pl.,* **-nar·i·os.** *n.* **1.a.** rough script of a planned motion picture, giving an outline of the plot, short sketches of the characters, and other information. **b.** finished script used during the actual filming of the picture; screenplay. **2.** plot outline or synopsis of any dramatic work. [Italian *scenario* scenery, outline of a play, from Late Latin *scēnārius* relating to the stage, dramatic, from Latin *scēna* stage. See SCENE.]

sce·nar·ist (si när′ist, -när′-) *n.* one who writes scenarios, esp. for motion pictures.

scene (sēn) *n.* **1.** place where an event or action occurs or has occurred: *the scene of a robbery.* **2.** place and time in which the action or part of the action of a dramatic, theatrical, or literary work is supposed to occur; setting: *The scene of this story is Germany during World War I.* **3.** subdivision of an act of a dramatic or theatrical work: *The first scene in the second act contains a lengthy soliloquy.* **4.** episode, situation, or sequence in a dramatic, theatrical, or literary work, as containing a particular feature: *a murder scene.* **5.** set (*def.* 5). **6.** something presented to the eye; view; picture: *Taxis and buses were part of the street scene.* **7.** real or imaginary incident, event, or set of circumstances, esp. when described: *The parting of the lovers was a very moving scene.* **8.** display of strong or excited feeling or unseemly behavior, often resulting in embarrassment or public disturbance. **9.** particular area or field of activity or interest: *the political scene.* **10. behind the scenes.** in private; secretly. [Latin *scēna* stage, background of a stage, from Greek *skēnē* stage; originally, booth or tent in which actors dressed.]

Syn. **1. Scene, site, spot** mean a place where something is located or happens. *Scene* implies a place where an actual event has occurred, esp. when considered as a broad area: *This is the scene of the battle.* *Site* suggests an area set apart for a particular activity or on which something is or was built: *This is the site of the new factory.* *Spot* is applied to a very restricted place or plot of ground, indoors or outdoors, that is considered suitable for a given purpose: *Mother chose an ideal spot for the picnic.*

scen·er·y (sē′nər ē) *pl.,* **-er·ies.** *n.* **1.** general appearance or visible features of a locality, esp. the striking or picturesque natural features of a place. **2.** backdrops, hangings, or other structures used to create the setting of a dramatic or theatrical production.

sce·nic (sē′nik, sen′ik) *adj.* **1.** of, relating to, or abounding in natural scenery; picturesque: *a scenic route through the mountains.* **2.** of or relating to the stage or to stage scenery or effects. **3.** representing an action, event, or situation, as in a painting.

scent (sent) *n.* **1.** distinctive smell, esp. an agreeable or delicate one: *the scent of lilacs, the scent of spices.* **2.** characteristic smell left behind by an animal or man, used as a means of tracking. **3.** trail or track by which someone or something can be traced or pursued: *Some deceptive clues threw the detectives off the scent of the gang.* **4.** sense of smell. **5.** perfume (*def.* 1). **6.** inkling; suggestion; trace: *a scent of danger.* —*v.t.* **1.** to perceive, recognize, or identify by the sense of smell. **2.** to perceive as if by smell; get an inkling or hint of: *to scent trouble.* **3.** to make fragrant; perfume: *She put sachet in the drawers to scent her clothes.* —*v.i.* (of a hound or other animal) to hunt by the sense of smell. [Old French *sentir* to feel, smell, from Latin *sentīre* to feel, perceive.] —*Syn. v.* see SMELL.

scep·ter (sep′tər) *also, British.* **scep·tre.** *n.* **1.** rod or staff serving as a symbol of royal office or power, carried by a sovereign, esp. on ceremonial occasions. **2.** royal office or power. [Old French *sceptre* royal staff, from Latin *scēptrum,* from Greek *skēptron* staff, royal staff.]

scep·tic (skep′tik) *n.* skeptic. —**scep′ti·cal,** *adj.* —**scep′ti·cism,** *n.*

sched·ule (skej′ool, -oo əl; *British* shed′yool, shej′ool) *n.* **1.** list of the times at which certain events are to take place: *a television schedule, a schedule of train departures.* **2.** plan or group of items to be handled or of events to occur at or during a particular time: *a busy social schedule.* **3.** detailed plan or program of action, as for a proposed objective, esp. with regard to the time allotted for each item or phase included: *The factory was put on a new production schedule.* **4.** time planned, indicated, or agreed upon, as in a schedule: *The planes are running behind schedule because of the strike.* **5.** written or printed table or list, as of rates or prices: *a schedule of postal rates.* —*v.t.,* **-uled, -ul·ing. 1.** to place in or on a schedule: *The airline scheduled additional flights because of the holidays.* **2.** to plan or arrange for a specified time: *I scheduled an appointment with my dentist for Friday.* [Late Latin *schedula* small sheet of paper, diminutive of Latin *scheda* strip of papyrus.]

Sche·her·a·za·de (shə her′ə zä′də, -zäd′, -hēr′-) *n.* in Arabian mythology, the bride of a sultan who resolved to kill each of his wives

on the morning after their marriage. She tricked him into sparing her life by relating tales to him nightly for 1001 nights, in such a clever way that he remained interested in hearing them.

Schel·ling, Frie·drich Wil·helm Joseph von (shel′ing; frē′drikʜ vil′helm) 1775–1854, German philosopher.

sche·ma (skē′mə) *pl.* **-ma·ta** (-mə tə). *n.* diagrammatic or generalized representation, outline, or plan. [Greek *schēma* form.]

sche·mat·ic (skē mat′ik) *adj.* of, relating to, or in the form of a schema or scheme; diagrammatic: *a schematic drawing.* —*n.* structural or generalized diagram or plan, esp. of an electrical or mechanical system.

scheme (skēm) *n.* **1.** program or course of action for accomplishing some objective; plan: *a scheme for building a new community center.* **2.** underhanded, devious, or secret plan; plot: *That so-called sale is a scheme to swindle the consumer.* **3.** connected and orderly arrangement of related parts or pieces; system; design: *a striking color scheme for a room.* **4.** chart, diagram, or outline; sketch: *a scheme of a rocket's control system.* —*v.t., v.i.,* **schemed, schem·ing.** to plan or contrive, esp. in a devious manner; plot. [Latin *schēma* shape, figure, form, from Greek *schēma*.] —**schem′er,** *n.* —**Syn.** *n.* **1.** see **plan.**

Sche·nec·ta·dy (skə nek′tə dē) *n.* city in eastern New York. Pop. (1970), 77,859.

scher·zan·do (sker tsän′dō, -tsan′-) *adj. Music.* playful; sportive. [Italian *scherzando,* gerund of *scherzare* to play, sport, from *scherzo.* See **SCHERZO.**]

scher·zo (sker′tsō) *pl.,* **-zos** or **-zi** (-tsē). *n.* playful, lively, or humorous movement or passage, esp. in a sonata or symphony. [Italian *scherzo* play, sport, lively movement (in music), from German *Scherz* fun, jest.]

Schick test (shik) test used to determine immunity to diphtheria, consisting of the injection of a dilute diphtheria toxin just beneath the skin. Reddening of the area indicates susceptibility to the disease. [From Béla *Schick,* 1877–1967, U.S. pediatrician born in Hungary, who developed the test.]

Schil·ler, Jo·hann Frie·drich von (shil′ər; yō′hän frē′drikʜ) 1759–1805, German dramatist, poet, and historian.

schil·ling (shil′ing) *n.* monetary unit and coin of Austria. [German *Schilling.*]

schism (siz′əm, skiz′-) *n.* **1.a.** division within a church or other religious body, usually over matters of discipline or jurisdiction. **b.** offense of causing or contributing to such a division. **c.** sect or group formed by such a division. **2.** any separation or breach of unity, esp. a division into mutually opposed factions or groups. [Late Latin *schisma* split, separation, from Greek *schisma* split, division.]

schis·mat·ic (siz mat′ik, skiz-) *adj.* relating to, promoting, or guilty of schism. Also, **schis·mat′i·cal.** —*n.* one who promotes or takes part in a schism.

schist (shist) *n.* metamorphic rock that is easily split because of its layered structure. It has a high mica content. [French *schiste,* through Latin, from Greek *schistos* easily split.]

schis·tose (shis′tōs) *also,* **schis·tous** (shis′təs). *adj.* relating to, resembling, or characteristic of schist.

schiz·o (skit′sō) *n. Slang.* a schizophrenic.

schiz·o- *combining form* split; cleft; divided: *schizophrenia.* [Greek *schizein* to split.]

schiz·o·carp (skiz′ə kärp′) *n. Botany.* dry fruit, separating at maturity into two or more usually one-seeded vessels that remain closed. [SCHIZO- + Greek *karpos* fruit.]

schiz·oid (skit′soid, skiz′oid) *adj.* relating to, characterized by, resembling, or showing a tendency toward schizophrenia. —*n.* one who shows a tendency toward schizophrenia.

schiz·o·phre·ni·a (skit′sə frē′nē ə, skiz′ə-) *n.* **1.** any of a group of psychoses characterized by a severe withdrawal from reality, illogical thought, inappropriate moods, hallucinations, and delusions. **2.** split personality *(def. 1).* [Modern Latin *schizophrenia,* from SCHIZO- + Greek *phrēn* mind.]

schiz·o·phren·ic (skit′sə fren′ik, skiz′ə-) *adj.* of, relating to, or characteristic of schizophrenia. —*n.* one who suffers from schizophrenia.

schle·miel (shlə mēl′) *n. Slang.* one who is clumsy, dull, and easily duped by others; bungler. [Yiddish *shlumiel,* possibly from Hebrew *Shelūmiel,* Biblical figure (Numbers) who, according to the Jewish tradition, lost battles constantly and thus became a symbol of bad luck.]

schlep (shlep) **schlepped, schlep·ping.** *also,* **schlepp.** *Slang. v.t.* to carry, esp. clumsily or with difficulty; drag; lug. —*n.* **1.** long and tiresome distance or journey: *It's quite a schlep from here to the movie theater.* **2.** dull, insignificant, or stupid person. [Yiddish *shleppen* to drag, from Middle Low German *slēpen.*]

Schles·wig-Hol·stein (shles′wig hōl′stīn) *n.* political subdivision in northern West Germany, south of Denmark. Pop. (1967 est.), 2,499,700.

Schlie·mann, Hein·rich (shlē′män′; hīn′rikʜ) 1822–90, German

archaeologist noted for his discovery of the ruins of ancient Troy and Mycenae.

schmaltz (shmôlts, shmälts) *also,* **schmalz.** *n.* **1.** *Informal.* extreme or maudlin sentimentality, as in music or drama. **2.** fat or grease used in cooking, esp. chicken fat. [German *Schmalz* melted fat, lard.] —**schmaltz′y,** *adj.*

schmo (shmō) *pl.* **schmoes.** *also,* **schmoe.** *n. Slang.* one who is foolish, dull, or naive. [Probably modification of Yiddish *shmok,* from Slovene *šmok.*]

schmuck (shmuk) *n. Slang.* stupid or despicable person. [Yiddish *schmuck* penis, from German *Schmuck* ornament.]

schnapps (shnäps) *pl.,* **schnapps.** *also,* **schnaps.** *n.* any strong liquor. [German *Schnapps,* from Dutch *snaps* dram, mouthful.]

schnau·zer (shnou′zər) *n.* wire-haired dog having a rectangular head, small pointed ears and bearded muzzle. There are three distinct breeds, which differ only in size: the **miniature schnauzer,** to 14 inches at the shoulder; the **standard schnauzer,** to 20 inches; and the **giant schnauzer,** to 25 inches. [German *Schnauzer,* from *Schnauze* snout.]

Schnauzer

schnook (shnook) *n. Slang.* one who is easily fooled or taken advantage of by others. [Yiddish *shnok,* form of *shmok* fool. See SCHMO.]

schol·ar (skol′ər) *n.* **1.** one who has thorough knowledge of, and is considered to be an authority in, a particular field, esp. in one of the humanities: *a noted Shakespearean scholar.* **2.** person having much knowledge and a serious interest in learning and study; learned or erudite person: *a judge who is both a gentleman and a scholar.* **3.** one holding a scholarship. **4.** one who learns from a teacher or attends school; pupil: *an apt scholar.* [Late Latin *scholāris* relating to a school, from Latin *schola.* See SCHOOL[1].]

schol·ar·ly (skol′ər lē) *adj.* **1.** of, characteristic of, or befitting a scholar: *a scholarly life.* **2.** of, characteristic of, or based on scholarship: *a scholarly and illuminating book on the economics of the Depression.* **3.** having the qualities of a scholar: *a scholarly young man.* —**schol′ar·li·ness,** *n.*

schol·ar·ship (skol′ər ship′) *n.* **1.** grant of financial aid awarded to a student, as by a private foundation or an educational institution and usually in recognition of both need and academic merit, to help him pursue his studies. **2.** academic or scholarly achievement: *to excel in scholarship in school.* **3.** knowledge acquired by study; learning; erudition: *a book that displays the considerable scholarship of its author.* **4.** body of existing knowledge or study and research contributing to it: *the advanced state of scholarship in classical studies.*

scho·las·tic (skə las′tik) *adj.* **1.** of or relating to schools, scholars, or education: *scholastic standing, a scholastic meet.* **2.** usually, **Scholastic.** of or relating to scholasticism or its teachings and methods. **3.** overly refined and restrictive; pedantic. Also, **scho·las′ti·cal.** —*n.* **1.** usually, **Scholastic.** theologian or philosopher in the Middle Ages who adhered to or taught the doctrines of scholasticism. **2.** student; pupil. **3.** pedant. [Latin *scholasticus* relating to a school, from Greek *scholastikos* learned, having leisure, going back to *scholē.* See SCHOOL[1].] —**scho·las′ti·cal·ly,** *adv.*

scho·las·ti·cism (skə las′tə siz′əm) *also,* **Scho·las·ti·cism.** *n.* dominant philosophical and theological system in western Europe during the Middle Ages that sought to reconcile faith and reason by harmonizing the teachings of the Fathers of the Church with Greek philosophy, esp. that of Aristotle.

scho·li·ast (skō′lē ast′) *n.* commentator, esp. an ancient grammarian who annotated the Greek or Latin classics. [Late Greek *scholiastēs,* going back to Greek *scholion* comment, note.]

scho·li·um (skō′lē əm) *pl.,* **-li·a** (-lē ə) or **-li·ums.** *n.* **1.** explanatory marginal note or comment, esp. one made by a scholiast in Greek or Latin classical texts. **2.** note that illustrates or develops a point, as in a mathematical or scientific text. [Modern Latin *scholium,* from Greek *scholion.*]

school[1] (skool) *n.* **1.** institution for academic instruction: *He got his bachelor's degree at one of the finest schools in the country.* **2.** institution for instruction in a particular field or skill: *a dancing school.* **3.** department or division of a college or university for instruction in a specialized field: *the school of medicine.* **4.** classrooms, offices, building, or group of buildings of an educational institution: *The students helped build the new school.* **5.** session, period, or set time of instruction at an educational institution: *There's no school today because of the snowstorm.* **6.** process of being educated, esp. in a formal program of studies; attendance at school: *He finished school at sixteen and went to work.* **7.** student body or the students, faculty, and other staff members of an

at; āpe; cär; end; mē; it; īce; hot; ōld; fôrk; wood; fōōl; oil; out; up; ūse; turn; sing; thin; this; zh in treasure; ə in ago, taken, pencil, lemon, circus.

educational institution: *The whole school was talking about the new library.* **8.a.** group of people adhering to or influenced by the same teacher, beliefs, method, or style: *the Epicurean school of Greek philosophy.* **b.** beliefs, method, or style of such a group: *a painting of the impressionist school.* **9.** group of people sharing common traditions, opinions, or a general style of life: *She's of the school that believes in doing as little work as possible.* **10.** any means or source of learning or instruction: *the school of experience.* —*v.t.* **1.** to teach in or as in a school; educate. **2.** to bring under control; train; discipline: *Doctors must school themselves to be calm during emergencies.* [Old English *scōl* place of learning, from Latin *schola* place of learning, leisure devoted to learning, sect, from Greek *scholē* leisure, esp. that devoted to learning, place of learning.]

school² (skōōl) *n.* large group of fish or water animals of the same kind swimming together: *a school of tuna.* —*v.i.* to swim together in a school. [Dutch *school* troop, crowd.]

school board, local board of education, usually elected by a district or community, responsible for budgeting funds, determining policy and curriculum, hiring personnel, and regulating operations in the public schools of the area.

school·book (skōōl′bŏŏk′) *n.* book used for study in schools; textbook.

school·boy (skōōl′boi′) *n.* boy attending school.

school·girl (skōōl′gurl′) *n.* girl attending school.

school·house (skōōl′hous′) *n.* building used as a school.

school·ing (skōōl′ing) *n.* process of being educated, esp. in a formal program of studies. —**Syn.** see **education.**

school·man (skōōl′mən) *pl.,* **-men.** *also,* **School·man.** *n.* a scholastic of the Middle Ages.

school·marm (skōōl′märm) *also,* **school·ma'am** (skōōl′mam′). *n. Informal.* female schoolteacher, esp. one in a rural or country school or one considered to be strict, old-fashioned, or prudish.

school·mas·ter (skōōl′mas′tər) *n.* **1.** male schoolteacher. **2.** headmaster of a school. —**school′mis′tress,** *n.*

school·mate (skōōl′māt′) *n.* companion at school.

school·room (skōōl′rōōm′, -rŏŏm′) *n.* classroom.

school·teach·er (skōōl′tē′chər) *n.* one who teaches in a school below the college level.

school·work (skōōl′wurk′) *n.* lessons or assignments given to a student.

school·yard (skōōl′yärd′) *n.* yard or playground of a school.

school year, that part of the year during which school is in session, usually from September to June.

schoon·er (skōō′nər) *n.* **1.** fore-and-aft-rigged ship having two or more masts. **2.** large beer glass. **3.** prairie schooner. [Possibly from dialectal English *scoon* to skim along, from Scottish *scon* to make a stone skip across water; probably of Scandinavian origin.]

Schooner (def. 1)

Scho·pen·hau·er, Arthur (shō′pən hou′ər) 1788–1860, German philosopher.

schot·tische (shŏt′ish) *n.* **1.** round dance resembling the polka, marked by hopping and gliding steps. **2.** music for this dance. [German *schottische (Tanz)* Scottish (dance), going back to Late Latin *Scottus* Scot; of Celtic origin.]

Schu·bert, Franz Peter (shōō′bərt; fränts) 1797–1828, Austrian composer.

Schu·mann, Robert Alexander (shōō′män) 1810–56, German composer.

schuss (shoos, shōōs) *v.i.* to ski down a straight, steep course without decreasing speed. —*v.t.* to ski down (a course) in this manner. —*n.* **1.** straight downhill run on skis, made without decreasing speed. **2.** straight, steep course on which such a run is made. [German *Schuss* shot¹, swoop.]

schwa (shwä, shvä) *n.* unstressed vowel sound occurring in many unstressed syllables in English, as the *a* in *ago* or the *o* in *lemon,* represented phonetically by the symbol ə. [Hebrew *sh'wā* sign indicating a faint vowel sound or the absence of a vowel sound.]

Schwei·tzer, Albert (shwīt′sər, shvīt′-) 1875–1965, Alsatian doctor, philosopher, Protestant missionary, and theologian, noted esp. for his extensive humanitarian work in Africa.

sci., science; scientific.

sci·at·ic (sī at′ik) *adj.* **1.** of, relating to, or affecting the ischium. **2.** affecting the hip or the sciatic nerve. [Late Latin *sciaticus* relating to pains in the hip, modification of Latin *ischiadicus,* from Greek *ischiadikos,* going back to *ischion* hip joint.]

sci·at·i·ca (sī at′i kə) *n.* neuralgia affecting the sciatic nerve and its branches, usually caused by injury or infection, characterized by severe pain in the hips, thighs, and legs. [Medieval Latin *sciatica,* from Late Latin *sciaticus.* See SCIATIC.]

sciatic nerve, largest nerve of the body, extending along the back part of the thigh and leg.

sci·ence (sī′əns) *n.* **1.** body of knowledge and theory on the nature and operation of natural phenomena and of the universe and all things in it, in which facts are organized into a systematic and meaningful pattern developed as a result of experimentation, observation, and insight. **2.** any branch of such knowledge, as physics, chemistry, or biology. **3.** any branch of systematized knowledge, esp. one in which the techniques and principles of the scientific method are followed: *the science of philology.* **4.** any activity, skill, or field of interest that may be studied like a science and to which systematic methods or principles may be applied: *an essay maintaining that chess is a science, not just a game.* [Old French *science* knowledge, from Latin *scientia.*]

science fiction, fiction based on actual or imaginary developments or discoveries in science, often futuristic or fantastic.

sci·en·tif·ic (sī′ən tif′ik) *adj.* **1.** of, relating to, derived from, or used in science: *a scientific theory.* **2.** based on, using, or conforming to the principles and methods of science; systematic; exact: *to take a scientific approach to a problem.*

sci·en·tif·i·cal·ly (sī′ən tif′ik lē) *adv.* in a scientific manner.

scientific method, method for obtaining knowledge, involving the gathering and objective observation of data relevant to a problem and the formulation of a hypothesis that must be tested and validated through experimentation.

sci·en·tist (sī′ən tist) *n.* one who is highly skilled or knowledgeable in science, esp. in the area of natural science, and is engaged in it as a profession.

scil·i·cet (sil′ə set′) *adv.* that is to say; namely. [Latin *scilicet* it is evident, from *scīre* to know + *licet* it is permitted.]

scim·i·tar (sim′ə tər) *also,* **scim·i·ter, sim·i·tar.** *n.* curved, single-edged sword of Oriental and Asian origin. [Italian *scimitarra,* from Persian *shimshīr.*]

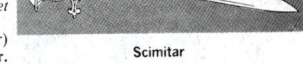

Scimitar

scin·til·la (sin til′ə) *n.* very small amount; trace: *There was only a scintilla of truth in his statement.* [Latin *scintilla* spark.]

scin·til·late (sint′əl āt′) -lat·ed, -lat·ing. *v.i.* **1.** to be vibrant, animated, or brilliant: *an author whose short stories scintillate with wit.* **2.** to give off sparks or flashes of light; sparkle: *a rushing stream that scintillated in the morning sun.* **3.** to twinkle, as a star. —*v.t.* to give off as a flash or flashes. [Latin *scintillātus,* past participle of *scintillāre* to sparkle.]

scin·til·lat·ing (sint′əl ā′ting) *adj.* vibrant; animated; brilliant: *a scintillating conversation.*

scin·til·la·tion (sint′əl ā′shən) *n.* **1.** act of scintillating. **2.** spark or flash of light. **3.** the twinkling of the stars.

scintillation counter, instrument that detects radiation, consisting of a fluorescent material that gives off flashes of light when struck by radiation and an electron tube that converts this light into electric pulses.

sci·o·lism (sī′ə liz′əm) *n.* superficial or pretended knowledge; charlatanism. [Late Latin *sciolus* one who knows little (diminutive of Latin *scius* knowing) + -ISM.] —**sci′o·list,** *n.* —**sci′o·lis′tic,** *adj.*

sci·on (sī′ən) *n.* **1.** *also,* **ci·on.** bud, or a branch having one or more buds, cut from a plant and used for grafting onto the stock of another plant. **2.** descendant; heir: *the wealthy scion of a noble family.* [Old French *scion;* of Germanic origin.]

Scip·i·o Af·ri·ca·nus (sip′ē ō′ af′rə kā′nəs, skip′ē ō′) **1.** the Elder, c.234–c.183 B.C., Roman general who defeated Hannibal in 202 B.C. **2.** the Younger, c.185–129 B.C., Roman statesman and general who destroyed Carthage in 146 B.C.

scis·sion (sizh′ən, sish′-) *n.* act of cutting or dividing; division; separation. [Late Latin *scissiō* a dividing, from Latin *scindere* to cut, split.]

scis·sor (siz′ər) *v.t.* to cut with scissors. —*n.* scissors.

scis·sors (siz′ərz) *n.,pl.* cutting implement having two blades that are fastened together by a bolt and form a double cutting edge when they are closed over each other. ▲ construed as singular or plural: *The scissors is in the left hand drawer of my desk. The scissors are in the drawer.* However, the phrase *pair of scissors* is construed only as singular: *This pair of scissors isn't very sharp.* **2.** wrestling hold in which the legs are placed around a part of the opponent's body and locked in place by crossing the ankles. **3.** gymnastic exercise in which the movement of the legs suggests the opening and closing of scissors. ▲ defs. 2 and 3 are construed as singular. [Old French *cisoires* shears, going back to

Late Latin *cīsōrium* cutting implement, going back to Latin *caedere* to cut; Modern English spelling due to confusion with Latin *scissor* carver.]

scissors kick, swimming kick, used chiefly with the sidestroke, in which the legs are moved apart, one forward and one backward with the knees bent, and then snapped sharply together.

scle·ra (sklēr′ə) *n.* tough white fibrous membrane covering the surface of the eye, except for the surface of the cornea. [Modern Latin *sclera,* from Greek *sklēros* hard.]

scle·rom·e·ter (sklə rom′ə tər) *n.* instrument for determining the degree of hardness of a substance, esp. of a mineral. [Greek *sklēros* hard + -METER.]

scle·ro·sis (sklə rō′sis) *pl.,* **-ses** (-sēz). *n.* **1.** abnormal hardening of a tissue or part of the body, as the wall of an artery. **2.** hardening of a cell wall or tissue of a plant, as by the formation of wood. [Medieval Latin *sclerosis* callosity, from Greek *sklērōsis* hardening.]

scle·rot·ic (sklə rot′ik) *adj.* **1.** of or relating to the sclera. **2.** of, relating to, or affected by sclerosis. [Modern Latin *scleroticus* hard, going back to Greek *sklēros.*]

scoff (skof, skôf) *v.i.* to express ridicule or contempt; mock; jeer (often with *at*). —*n.* expression of ridicule, contempt, or mockery. [Probably of Scandinavian origin.] —**Syn.** *v.i.* see **jeer.**

scoff·law (skof′lô′, skôf′-) *n. Informal.* person who flouts the law, esp. one who habitually fails to pay fines incurred for traffic violations.

scold (skōld) *v.t.* to find fault with; speak sharply to; reprimand. —*v.i.* to find fault or express dissatisfaction sharply or continuously. —*n.* one who scolds, esp. a shrewish woman. [Probably from Old Norse *skāld* poet (probably with reference to satirical poems).]

Syn. *v.t.* **Scold, upbraid, berate** mean to find fault with someone sharply and harshly. **Scold,** the common term, suggests a noisy verbal reproach in an angry or irritated mood: *The mother scolded the boy for not cleaning up his room.* **Upbraid** suggests a vehement rebuke meted out usually by a superior for a definite offense and on justifiable grounds: *The coach upbraided the team for their bad play.* **Berate** suggests heaping reproaches on a person in a lengthy, heated, and abusive browbeating that censures a whole performance rather than a single instance of misbehavior: *The shareholders berated the management for mismanaging the company.*

scol·lop (skol′əp) scallop.

sconce[1] (skons) *n.* projecting wall bracket or fixture used esp. for holding a candle or other light. [Old French *esconse* hiding place, screened lantern, going back to Latin *absconsa,* feminine past participle of *abscondere* to hide.]

sconce[2] (skons) *n.* head; skull. [Of uncertain origin.]

scone (skōn, skon) *n.* **1.** small biscuit, often round, usually served with butter. **2.** originally, in Scotland, a thin oatmeal cake baked on a griddle. [Possibly short for Middle Dutch *schoonbrot* fine bread.]

Sconce

scoop (skōop) *n.* **1.** any of various implements resembling a ladle or shovel, consisting of a usually deep-sided, often curved, container attached to a handle, used chiefly for taking up loose material or powdery substances, as flour or sugar. **2.** utensil usually consisting of a deep circular bowl attached to a handle, used for forming and dispensing ball-shaped portions of food, as ice cream. **3.** large bucket of a dredge or steam shovel, used for taking up and depositing a load, as of dirt. **4.** amount taken up in a scoop, esp. a ball-shaped portion: *a scoop of ice cream.* **5.** dipping or sweeping movement: *The baby picked up the pebbles with a scoop of his hand.* **6.** place hollowed out; bowl-shaped hole or cavity. **7.** *Informal.* news story reported first or exclusively, as by a newspaper or television network. —*v.t.* **1.** to take up or out with or as with a scoop (often with *out*): *Scoop out the center of the melon before you serve it.* **2.** to form by or as by scooping: *The glacier scooped a canyon out of the rocks.* **3.** to gather or put quickly or with a sweeping motion: *I scooped up my books and left the house.* **4.** *Informal.* to get the better of (a competitor) by reporting a news story first or exclusively. [Partly from Middle Dutch *schōpe* bucket; partly from Middle Dutch *schoppe* shovel.]

scoop·ful (skōop′fool′) *pl.,* **-fuls.** *n.* amount that a scoop holds: *to eat three scoopfuls of ice cream.*

scoot (skōot) *v.i. Informal.* to go hurriedly; dart: *The rabbit scooted off into the woods.* [Probably of Scandinavian origin.]

scoot·er (skōo′tər) *n.* **1.** toy vehicle consisting of a narrow footboard mounted on two aligned wheels and having a long upright steering post, propelled by pushing one foot against the ground while resting the other foot on the board. **2.** motor scooter. **3.** wide, flat-bottomed sailboat with runners, capable of sailing on water or on ice. [From SCOOT.]

scope (skōp) *n.* **1.** range within which something operates or applies;

area dealt with or taken in: *Relocating tenants falls within the scope of this agency.* **2.** extent of perception, outlook, or ability; grasp: *an intellect rather limited in its scope.* **3.** opportunity or room for expression, development, or action: *to give someone full scope to air his views.* **4.** *Nautical.* length of cable between a boat and its anchor when the boat is moored. [Italian *scopo* target, aim, from Greek *skopos.*]

Syn. **1. Scope, compass, range** indicate how much can be covered or comprehended. **Scope** suggests inclusion of everything within defined or understood limits: *A landing on Mars is within the scope of current physical theory.* **Compass** implies a wide sweep within certain limits: *Foreign affairs is outside the compass of the course's syllabus.* **Range** suggests the entire sweep of the senses or abilities: *His talk covered the whole range of contemporary politics.*

-scope combining form instrument for viewing or examining: *kaleidoscope, fluoroscope.* [Modern Latin *-scopium,* from Greek *-skopion,* from *skopein* to view, examine.]

Scopes, John Thomas (skōps) 1901–70, American high school biology teacher tried in Tennessee in 1925 and found guilty of teaching the Darwinian theory of evolution, contrary to a state law.

sco·pol·a·mine (skō pol′ə mēn′, -min) *n.* drug used as a sedative and painkiller, esp. during childbirth, as a dilator of the pupils of the eyes, and as a truth serum. Also, **hy′os·cine.** [Modern Latin *Scopolia* a genus of plants from which the drug is obtained (from G. A. *Scopoli,* 1723–88, Italian naturalist) + AMINE.]

scor·bu·tic (skôr bū′tik) *adj.* relating to, characteristic of, or affected with scurvy. Also, **scor·bu′ti·cal.** [Modern Latin *scorbuticus,* from *scorbutus* scurvy; probably of Germanic origin.]

scorch (skôrch) *v.t.* **1.** to burn so as to change in appearance, taste, or texture: *The hot iron scorched the tablecloth.* **2.** to dry up or wither with or as with heat; parch: *The grass was scorched by the summer sun.* **3.** to criticize sharply or severely. —*v.i.* to become scorched. —*n.* slight burn. [Possibly from Old Norse *skorpna* to shrivel.]

Syn. *v.t.* **1. Scorch, sear, singe, scald** mean to injure or damage by burning. **Scorch** means to burn an exposed surface so that it changes color, texture, or flavor without being consumed: *The laundress scorched the shirt while ironing it.* **Sear** means to burn human and animal tissues by the application of intense heat: *The branding iron seared the flesh of the horse.* **Singe** means to burn lightly or superficially so that the ends curl and shrivel: *Dan accidentally singed his beard with his cigarette.* **Scald** means to burn with or as if with boiling liquid: *He scalded his hand with the boiling water.*

scorched-earth (skôrch′urth′) *adj.* of, relating to, or involving scorched-earth policy: *a scorched-earth campaign.*

scorched-earth policy, policy or strategy of destroying whatever lies in the path of an advancing or retreating army, as crops or industrial equipment, so that it is not useful to the enemy.

scorch·er (skôr′chər) *n.* **1.** very hot day. **2.** one who or that which scorches. **3.** *Informal.* sharp or severe criticism.

score (skôr) *n.* **1.a.** record of points made in a game or contest: *The score after six innings was 5 to 4.* **b.** number of points made by one side or individual in such a competition: *The skier's brilliant performance earned him the highest score of the day.* **c.** act or instance of making a point or points: *The score came on a last-minute touchdown.* **2.** grade or rating on a test or examination. **3.** set or group of twenty; twenty: *a score of years.* **4. scores.** indefinitely large number; very many: *Scores of people flock to the beach every summer.* **5.** account; ground; basis: *He had no right to brag on that score.* **6.** account or reckoning, as of grievances, kept as if by a tally: *to even up the score.* **7.** notch, line, or other mark. **8.** amount due; debt. **9.** musical composition written as an accompaniment, as for a motion picture or theatrical production. **10.** complete written or printed notation for a musical composition, having all the instrumental and vocal parts arranged on two or more staffs aligned vertically. **11.** *Informal.* reality of a situation; truth: *to learn the score.* —*v.t.,* **scored, scor·ing. 1.** to make or gain (points) in a game or contest. **2.** to keep a record of points made in (a game or contest). **3.** to count for or be worth (a specified number of points): *A touchdown scores six points.* **4.** to record or set down, with or as if with a notch or line: *Score three points on your list for our side.* **5.** to evaluate and give a grade or rating to: *to score an examination.* **6.** to make a specified grade or rating of: *Several students scored 100% on the spelling test.* **7.** to achieve; win: *to score a victory.* **8.** to cancel, eliminate, or strike out by or as if by drawing a line through (often with *out*): *Several passages in the manuscript had been scored out.* **9.** to make a mark or marks in or upon: *to score a horse's back with a whip.* **10.** to criticize or denounce severely: *Union leaders scored the mayor for his decision.* **11.** to make superficial cuts in (meat or other food). **12.a.** to arrange or adapt (music) for a particular instrument or voice. **b.** to orchestrate. **13.** *Baseball.* to cause or enable (a runner) to make a run: *Ed's hit scored the runner from first base.* —*v.i.* **1.** to make or gain a point or points in a game or contest. **2.** to keep the score in a game or contest. **3.** to make a specified grade or rating: *to score in*

the top third of the class. **4.** to achieve a success or advantage: *to score in an argument.* [Old Norse *skor* notch, tally, twenty.] **—scor′er,** *n.*

score·board (skôr′bôrd′) *n.* large board or other surface on which the score of a game or contest, and often other pertinent information, is shown.

score·card (skôr′kärd′) *n.* card on which the scores of participants in a game or contest are recorded.

score·keep·er (skôr′kē′pər) *n.* one who keeps the score during a game or contest.

sco·ri·a (skôr′ē ə) *pl.,* **sco·ri·ae** (skôr′ē ē′). *n.* **1.** rough, irregular, cinderlike lava. **2.** refuse remaining after metal has been smelted; slag. [Latin *scōria* dross, from Greek *skōriā,* from *skōr* dung.]

scorn (skôrn) *n.* feeling of contempt and repugnance for someone or something considered vile or inferior: *to regard political deception with scorn.* —*v.t.* **1.** to treat or regard as contemptible, low, or vile; despise: *to scorn insincerity in one's friends.* **2.** to refuse or reject with contempt: *to scorn an offer.* [Modification of Old French *esc(h)arnir* to deride; of Germanic origin.]

scorn·ful (skôrn′fəl) *adj.* showing or feeling scorn; contemptuous. **—scorn′ful·ly,** *adv.* **—scorn′ful·ness,** *n.*

Scor·pi·o (skôr′pē ō′) *also,* **Scor·pi·us** (skôr′pē əs). *n.* **1.** constellation in the southern sky, conventionally depicted as a scorpion. **2.** eighth sign of the zodiac. See **zodiac** for illustration. [Latin *scorpiō.* See SCORPION.]

scor·pi·on (skôr′pē ən) *n.* any of a group of arachnids, order Scorpionida, found in temperate and tropical regions, having a long, segmented tail which ends in a venomous stinger. Length: to 8 inches. [Latin *scorpiō,* going back to Greek *skorpios.*]

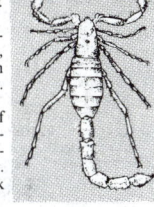

Scorpion

Scot (skot) *n.* **1.** member or close descendant of the people of Scotland. ▲ See usage note under **Scottish. 2.** member of an ancient Celtic people who migrated from northern Ireland to the northwestern part of Great Britain in the sixth century.

Scot. 1. Scottish. **2.** Scotland. **3.** Scotch.

scotch (skoch) *v.t.* **1.** to put an end to; crush; suppress: *to scotch a rebellion.* **2.** to injure so as to make harmless: *to scotch a snake.* [Of uncertain origin.]

Scotch (skoch) *n.* **1.** the Scottish. **2.** *also,* **scotch.** whiskey distilled in Scotland from malted barley and having a smoky flavor. Also, **Scotch whisky.** ▲ See usage note under **whiskey. —***adj.* Scottish. ▲ See usage note under **Scottish.**

Scotch-I·rish (skoch′ī′rish) *n.* member or close descendant of the people of Northern Ireland who are descended from Scottish settlers. —*adj.* of or relating to these people.

Scotch plaid 1. plaid pattern, esp. one that is predominantly bright red or blue combined with yellow, black, and white. **2.** fabric woven into such a pattern.

scotch tape, cellulose tape, usually transparent and with adhesive on only one side. Trademark: Scotch Tape.

Scotch terrier, Scottish terrier.

sco·ter (skō′tər) *n.* any of various large diving ducks, genera *Oidemia* and *Melanitta,* native to northern regions of Europe and North America. Also, **coot.** [Of uncertain origin.]

scot-free (skot′frē′) *adj.* free from injury, loss, punishment, or other penalty: *The defendant got off scot-free.* [Middle English *scot* payment, tax (from Old Norse *skot* contribution) + FREE.]

Scot·land (skot′lənd) *n.* division of the United Kingdom, north of England. Capital, Edinburgh. Area, 30,411 sq. mi. Pop. (1969 est.), 5,195,000.

Scotland Yard 1. metropolitan police of London, esp. the branch engaged in crime detection. **2.** its headquarters. [From *Scotland Yard,* an area off Whitehall in which its original headquarters were located, where, during the Middle Ages, kings of Scotland stayed when visiting London.]

Scots (skots) *adj.* Scottish. ▲ See usage note under **Scottish. —***n.* Scottish (*def.* 2).

Scots·man (skots′mən) *pl.,* **-men.** *also,* **Scotch·man.** *n.* Scot. ▲ See usage note under **Scottish.**

Scott (skot) **1. Dred** (dred). c.1795–1858, black American slave whose suit for freedom led to a Supreme Court decision in 1857 that involved the extension of slavery into all U.S. territories. **2. Robert Falcon.** 1868–1912, English naval officer and Antarctic explorer. **3. Sir Walter.** 1771–1832, Scottish author.

Scot·ti·cism (skot′ə siz′əm) *n.* word, phrase, or usage originating in Scotland or peculiar to Scotland.

Scot·tish (skot′ish) *adj.* of, relating to, or characteristic of Scotland, its people, or their language. **—***n.* **1. the Scottish.** the people histori-

cally inhabiting Scotland and those who have descended from them. **2.** any of the dialects of English spoken in Scotland. ▲ Of the adjectives *Scotch, Scots,* and *Scottish, Scottish* and *Scots* are generally preferred to *Scotch* both in Scotland and in formal usage in America. However, *Scotch* has become a standard form in certain combinations, as in *Scotch plaid* and *Scotch whisky.* Of the corresponding nouns, *Scot* and *Scotsman* are preferred to *Scotchman,* and the plural forms *Scots* and *(the) Scottish* are preferred to *(the) Scotch.*

Scottish Gaelic, Gaelic as spoken by the inhabitants of the Scottish Highlands. Also, **Erse.**

Scottish terrier, small, short-legged terrier, believed to be the oldest breed native to Scotland, having a large head, pointed ears, and a rough coat of black, gray, or light tan hair. Height: 10 inches at the shoulder. Also, **Scotch terrier, Scot·tie** (skot′ē).

Scottish terrier

scoun·drel (skoun′drəl) *n.* unprincipled, base, or dishonest person; villain; rogue. [Of uncertain origin.] **—scoun′drel·ly,** *adj.* **—Syn.** see **rogue.**

scour¹ (skour) *v.t.* **1.** to rub (something) vigorously, often with an abrasive, in order to clean, wash, or brighten it: *to scour a pot.* **2.** to remove by rubbing in this manner: *to scour the rust off an old stove.* **3.** to remove dirt and grease from, as by washing with a detergent: *to scour wool.* **4.** to clear, as a channel, by flushing with water. **5.** *Archaic.* to clear or rid (an area) of something undesirable: *to scour the sea of pirates.* —*v.i.* to rub something vigorously in order to clean, wash, or brighten. —*n.* act of rubbing vigorously in order to clean, wash, or brighten. [Middle Dutch *schūren* to clean, from Old French *escurer,* going back to Latin *ex* utterly + *cūrāre* to take care of.]

scour² (skour) *v.t.* to move over or through, esp. in making a thorough search: *Police scoured the countryside for the fugitive.* —*v.i.* to move swiftly, as in making a search. [Possibly of Scandinavian origin.]

scourge (skurj) *n.* **1.** whip; lash. **2.** any means of inflicting punishment, vengeance, or suffering: *such was God's scourge for disobedient sons* (Shelley, 1819). **3.** cause of great, usually widespread, affliction or destruction: *War has always been a scourge of mankind.* —*v.t.,* **scourged, scourg·ing. 1.** to whip; lash; flog. **2.** to punish or criticize severely. **3.** to afflict; ravage; devastate: *the numerous wars that have scourged Europe.* [Old French *escorge* leather strap of a whip, from *escorgier* to whip, going back to Latin *ex* out of + *corrigia* strap.]

scout¹ (skout) *n.* **1.a.** one sent out to gather and bring back information, esp. one sent out from a main body, as of troops, to observe and obtain information about the terrain or enemy ahead. **b.** ship or aircraft sent out to reconnoiter. **2.** one employed in finding or recruiting new talent, esp. in sports or entertainment. **3.** *also,* **Scout.** member of the Boy Scouts or Girl Scouts. **4.** *Sports.* one employed in observing opposing teams and obtaining information about their players and techniques. **5.** *Informal.* fellow; guy: *a good old scout.* —*v.i.* **1.** to make a search; hunt: *Scout around and see what you can find.* **2.** to gather and bring back information as a scout; be employed for reconnaissance: *an Indian who scouts for the cavalry.* **3.** to search for new talent, esp. in sports or entertainment. —*v.t.* to observe, examine, or survey in order to obtain information: *Two men rode ahead and scouted the pass.* [Old French *escoute* spy, listener, from *escouter* to listen, going back to Latin *auscultāre* to listen to.]

scout² (skout) *v.t.* to reject with scorn or derision: *to scout a suggestion.* —*v.i.* to scoff: *to scout at a notion as foolish and impractical.* [Of Scandinavian origin.]

scout·ing (skou′ting) *also,* **Scout·ing.** *n.* activities of the Boy Scouts or Girl Scouts, collectively.

scout·mas·ter (skout′mas′tər) *n.* adult leader of a troop of Boy Scouts.

scow (skou) *n.* large, flat-bottomed boat with square ends that is usually towed, used chiefly for transporting freight. [Dutch *schouw* ferryboat.]

Scow

scowl (skoul) *n.* facial expression of anger, sullenness, or disapproval; angry frown. —*v.i.* to wrinkle the forehead and contract the eyebrows in anger, sullenness, or disapproval; frown angrily. —*v.t.* to express with a scowl: *He scowled his objection to the idea.* [Probably of Scandinavian origin.] **—Syn.** *v.i.* see **frown.**

scrab·ble (skrab′əl) **-bled, -bling.** *v.i.* **1.a.** to scratch, scrape, or paw about with hands, feet, or claws. **b.** to scramble; climb; crawl;

at; āpe; cär; end; mē; it; īce; hot; ōld; fôrk; wood; fōōl; oil; out; up; ūse; turn; sing; thin; this; zh in treasure; ə in ago, taken, pencil, lemon, circus.

893

2. to struggle; strive: *to scrabble for a living.* 3. to scribble, as on a wall. [Dutch *schrabbelen* to scratch, from *schrabben* to scrape.]

scrag (skrag) *n.* 1. thin, scrawny person or animal. 2. lean, bony piece of meat, esp. of mutton or veal. [Possibly modification of obsolete *crag* throat, neck, from Middle Dutch *crāghe* neck, collar.]

scrag·gly (skrag′lē) -gli·er, -gli·est. *adj.* having a ragged, sparse, or untended appearance: *a scraggly beard, a scraggly lawn.*

scrag·gy (skrag′ē) -gi·er, -gi·est. *adj.* 1. scrawny. 2. scraggly. —**scrag′gi·ness,** *n.*

scram (skram) **scrammed, scram·ming.** *v.i. Slang.* to leave quickly or immediately. ▲ usually used in the imperative. [Short for SCRAMBLE.]

scram·ble (skram′bəl) -bled, -bling. *v.t.* 1. to mix together haphazardly; mix up: *to scramble the pieces of a puzzle.* 2. to fry (eggs) with the whites and yolks mixed together. 3. to gather or collect quickly and haphazardly: *The lawyer scrambled his papers together and raced out of the courtroom.* 4. to alter (a message-carrying wave) so that only a receiver which reverses the alterations can reproduce the message. —*v.i.* 1. to make one's way quickly by using the hands or feet to gain a hold; climb: *The hikers scrambled down the rocks along the stream.* 2. to move or act hurriedly or frantically; rush: *She scrambled into her clothes.* 3. to struggle or compete with others: *Many countries were scrambling for control of the territory.* 4. to get airplanes into the air on short notice to intercept enemy aircraft. —*n.* 1. confused, disorderly struggle or competition: *a scramble for the best seats in the arena.* 2. act of moving or climbing quickly or frantically: *He broke his leg in his scramble down the mountainside.* 3. difficult climb or walk, as over rough or rocky ground: *It's quite a scramble to reach the top of the cliff.* [Form of SCRABBLE.] —**scram′bler,** *n.*

Scran·ton (skran′tən) *n.* city in northeastern Pennsylvania. Pop. (1970), 103,564.

scrap¹ (skrap) *n.* 1. small piece or fragment; bit: *a scrap of paper, not a scrap of evidence.* 2. **scraps.** leftover or discarded bits of food. 3. used or discarded metal that may be reclaimed by melting and refining: *to sell an old car for scrap.* 4. any material that is left over or discarded as refuse or can be reprocessed for reuse. 5. **scraps.** cracklings. —*v.t.,* **scrapped, scrap·ping.** 1. to discard or abandon as useless, worthless, or ineffective: *to scrap an idea.* 2. to break up into parts for reprocessing or disposal; make scrap of: *to scrap an old battleship.* [Old Norse *skrap* trifles, gossips.]

scrap² (skrap) *Informal. n.* quarrel or disagreement, often involving a fist fight or scuffle. —*v.i.,* **scrapped, scrap·ping.** to take part in a scrap; fight. [Possibly from SCRAPE.] —**scrap′per,** *n.*

scrap·book (skrap′book′) *n.* book with blank pages in which pictures, clippings, or other items may be mounted or inserted for preservation.

scrape (skrāp) **scraped, scrap·ing.** *v.t.* 1. to injure or damage the surface of by rubbing against something sharp or rough: *to scrape one's knee, to scrape the fender of a car.* 2. to draw, move, or rub (something) roughly or forcefully or with a harsh, grating sound: *The speaker scraped his chair on the floor as he stood up.* 3. to move or rub roughly or with a harsh, grating sound on or across (something): *The boat's keel scraped the bottom of the lake.* 4. to rub (a surface), as with something sharp or abrasive, in order to remove an outer layer or make smooth or clean: *Scrape the dinner plates before you put them in the sink.* 5. to remove by or as if by rubbing in this manner (often with *off*): *to scrape old paint off a wall.* 6. to make or form by digging or rubbing, as with a sharp object: *to scrape one's name on a rock.* 7. to collect, gather, or produce, esp. with difficulty or serious effort (with *up* or *together*): *to scrape up some money for a trip.* —*v.i.* 1. to rub or rub roughly or with a harsh, grating sound: *The broken tail pipe scraped along the ground.* 2. to manage or make one's way barely or with difficulty (with *through, along,* or *by*): *The couple scraped by on their small income.* 3. to draw the foot back along the ground in making a bow. —*n.* 1. mark or abrasion made on a surface by scraping. 2. harsh, grating sound produced by scraping. 3. act of moving or rubbing roughly or with a harsh, grating sound. 4.a. difficult, troublesome, or unpleasant situation. b. fight or quarrel; scrap. [Old Norse *skrapa* to scratch.]

scrap·er (skrā′pər) *n.* 1. any of various tools or devices for cleaning or smoothing a surface or removing paint or other matter. 2. one who or that which scrapes.

scrap·ing (skrā′ping) *n.* 1. act of one who or that which scrapes. 2. sound produced by scraping. 3. *also,* **scrapings.** that which is removed or collected by scraping.

scrap·ple (skrap′əl) *n.* boiled mixture of ground pork, corn meal or flour, and seasonings, which is chilled until firm and then sliced and fried. [Diminutive of SCRAP¹.]

scrap·py¹ (skrap′ē) -pi·er, -pi·est. *adj.* composed of scraps or fragments; fragmentary: *scrappy evidence.* [SCRAP¹ + -Y¹.] —**scrap′pi·ness,** *n.*

scrap·py² (skrap′ē) -pi·er, -pi·est. *adj. Informal.* 1. full of fighting

spirit; vigorous and aggressive. 2. given to fighting; quarrelsome. [SCRAP² + -Y¹.] —**scrap′pi·ly,** *adv.* —**scrap′pi·ness,** *n.*

scratch (skrach) *v.t.* 1.a. to cut, mark, or mar the surface of with something rough, sharp, or pointed. b. to scrape, tear, or wound with or as with the nails or claws: *The brambles scratched my legs.* 2. to rub or scrape (a part of the body), esp. to relieve itching: *Please scratch my back where I can't reach.* 3. to cause to feel itchy or irritated: *The starched collar scratched my neck.* 4. to strike out, withdraw, or cancel by or as if by drawing a line through (often with *out* or *off*): *The laboratory scratched that experiment for this year. The last sentence was scratched out.* 5. to write or draw by or as if by scraping or cutting into a surface: *He scratched his initials on the freshly painted wall.* 6. to write or draw hurriedly or carelessly. 7. to drag or rub (something) over a surface with a harsh, grating sound. 8. to amass or acquire with effort or difficulty (with *up* or *together*). 9. *Sports.* to withdraw (an entry) from a race or other competition. —*v.i.* 1. to dig, scrape, or wound, as with the nails or claws: *The chickens scratched in the dirt for corn.* 2. to rub or scrape a part of the body to relieve itching: *My dog's been scratching so much I think he's got fleas.* 3. to rub with a harsh, grating sound: *We could hear the puppy whimpering and scratching at the door.* 4. to become cut, marked, or scraped: *a plastic that scratches easily.* 5. to itch or irritate: *This sweater scratches.* —*n.* 1. slight flesh wound or cut. 2. any mark made by scratching: *a scratch on a finished surface.* 3. harsh, grating sound: *the scratch of the branch against the windowpane.* 4. hasty or rough mark or scribble, as made by a pencil. 5. shot in billiards and pool that results in a penalty. 6. *Archaic.* line or mark indicating the starting place of a race or contest. 7. **from scratch.** from the beginning; from nothing. 8. **up to scratch.** *Informal.* meeting a certain level or standard; in proper or fit condition: *Her performance just wasn't up to scratch.* —*adj.* used for quick, rough, or informal writing or sketching: *scratch paper.* [Blend of obsolete *scrat* to tear or scrape with the nails, and obsolete *cratch* to tear or scrape with the nails; both of uncertain origin.]

scratch test, one of various tests to determine immunity or susceptibility, as to disease or allergy, made by rubbing a particular substance into small scratches made in the skin.

scratch·y (skrach′ē) **scratch·i·er, scratch·i·est.** *adj.* 1. that chafes or causes itching: *scratchy wool.* 2. making a harsh, grating sound: *a scratchy recording.* 3. rough; irregular; uneven: *scratchy handwriting.* —**scratch′i·ly,** *adv.* —**scratch′i·ness,** *n.*

scrawl (skrôl) *v.t., v.i.* to write or draw (something) hastily or carelessly in a sprawling, irregular manner. —*n.* irregular, sprawling, almost illegible handwriting. [Of uncertain origin.]

scraw·ny (skrô′nē) -ni·er, -ni·est. *adj.* thin, bony, or undersized; skinny: *a scrawny old nag.* [Possibly of Scandinavian origin.] —**scraw′ni·ness,** *n.*

scream (skrēm) *v.i.* 1.a. to utter a loud, shrill, piercing cry, esp. from fright or pain. b. to move with or make a loud, shrill, piercing sound. 2. to shout or speak loudly or shrilly, esp. to express anger or displeasure: *Don't scream, I can hear what you're saying.* 3. to laugh loudly and wildly: *The clown's antics left us screaming.* 4. to have a startling or arresting effect, as if by making a shout: *The headlines about the earthquake screamed from the front page.* 5. to make an urgent demand or request: *The schools are screaming for federal aid.* —*v.t.* to utter or express with or as if with a loud, shrill, piercing cry: *The foreman screamed his instructions above the noise.* —*n.* 1. loud, shrill, piercing cry or sound: *a scream of terror, the scream of a train whistle.* 2. *Informal.* hilariously funny person or thing. [Of uncertain origin.] —**Syn.** *v.* 2. see SHOUT.

scream·er (skrē′mər) *n.* 1. one who or that which screams. 2. any of various long-toed birds, family Anhimidae, native to South and Central America, having a loud, shrill cry.

scream·ing (skrē′ming) *adj.* 1. startling in effect; boldly striking. 2. uttering screams. 3. hilariously funny. 4. *Informal.* extreme; absolute; unmitigated: *He's a screaming lunatic.*

scream·ing·ly (skrē′ming lē) *adv. Informal.* extremely: *a screamingly funny joke.*

screech (skrēch) *v.i.* 1.a. to utter a shrill, high-pitched cry. b. to move with or make a shrill, piercing, or grating sound: *Metal screeched against metal. The car screeched to a halt.* 2. to speak in shrill, high-pitched tones: *As they argued they screeched at each other.* —*v.t.* to utter or express with or as with a shrill, high-pitched cry. —*n.* shrill, high-pitched cry or sound: *the screech of brakes.* [Modification of earlier *scritch;* of imitative origin.]

screech owl, brown or gray North American owl, *Otus asio,* having earlike tufts of feathers on its forehead and a melodious, whistling call. Length: 10 inches.

screech·y (skrē′chē) **screech·i·er, screech·i·est.** *adj.* resembling a screech; shrill: *a screechy voice.*

screed (skrēd) *n.* 1. long, tiresome harangue or piece of writing. 2. strip of plaster, metal, or other material placed on a wall or other

surface as a guide to indicate the desired thickness of material to be laid or applied, as plaster or concrete. [Form of SHRED.]

screen (skrēn) *n.* **1.** tough mesh or netting, usually of wire and enclosed in a frame: *a window screen, a screen in front of a fireplace.* **2.** portable device or structure consisting of a frame or a series of frames hinged together, often used as a room divider or as an ornament. **3.** anything that serves to separate, conceal, or protect: *The sun set beyond . . . the screen of western hills* (Sir Walter Scott, 1818). **4.** surface, usually of light-reflecting material, on which motion pictures or slides may be projected. **5.** surface on which the image is displayed in a cathode-ray tube, as that of a television or radar set. **6.** the motion picture medium or industry; motion pictures collectively: *star of stage, screen, and television. His play was adapted for the screen.* **7.** sieve, perforated plate, or similar device used for sifting or grading. —*v.t.* **1.** to shield, conceal, or protect with or as if with a screen: *to screen a porch. The dense forest screened the enemy's movements. We screened our eyes from the sun with our hands.* **2.** to sift or grade by passing through a screen. **3.** to block, remove, or filter as if by a screen (with *out*): *The earth's atmosphere screens out much of the sun's radiation.* **4.** to examine carefully or systematically, esp. so as to determine suitability or to make a selection: *to screen job applicants.* **5.** to show (a motion picture) on a screen. [Old French *escren* device used to protect from the heat of a fire, from Middle Dutch *scherm* shield, protection.]

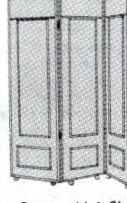

Screen (def. 2)

screen·play (skrēn′plā′) *n.* script for a motion picture.

screen test, short sequence filmed to appraise a person's ability as a motion-picture actor.

screen·writ·er (skrēn′rī′tər) *n.* writer of screenplays.

screw (skrōō) *n.* **1.** any of various fastening devices, consisting of a tapering rod ridged with a spiraling thread and having a head, usually slotted, at one end. It is driven in place by being twisted or turned, as with a screwdriver. **2.a.** similar device, consisting of a threaded cylinder, to be driven into a hole or socket cut with a matching thread. **b.** threaded cylindrical socket into which such a device fits. **3.** something resembling a screw in shape or function. **4.** twist or turn of or as of a screw. **5.** propeller. **6. to have a screw loose** (or **missing**). *Informal.* to be odd, eccentric, or crazy. **7. to put the screws on.** *Informal.* to exert pressure or force on: *The gang put the screws on him to find the stolen loot.* —*v.t.* **1.** to attach or fasten with a screw or screws. **2.** to insert, attach, or fix (a screw or other threaded or grooved object) in place by a twisting or turning motion: *to screw a bulb into a socket. Screw the cap back on the tube of toothpaste.* **3.** to twist out of shape; contort (often with *up*): *She screwed up her mouth with displeasure.* **4.** to twist or turn: *He screwed his head around to see if they had arrived.* **5.** to call forth or summon with difficulty; muster (with *up*): *to screw up the courage to speak.* **6.** *Slang.* to make a mess of; botch (with *up*): *to screw up one's life. I really screwed up that question on the exam.* **7.** *Slang.* to take advantage of or cheat: *That company really screwed you on this deal. That guy screwed me out of a job.* —*v.i.* **1.** to become attached or fastened by means of a screw or screws: *The towel rack screws to the wall.* **2.** to become inserted, attached, or fixed in place by a twisting or turning motion: *The fuse screws into the socket.* **3.** to twist or turn as or like a screw: *The lid screws to the left to be closed.* [Old French *escroue* the hole in which a screw turns, nut for a bolt¹, going back to Latin *scrōfa* sow²; possibly because the threads of a screw resemble the coiling of a sow's tail.]

screw·ball (skrōō′bôl′) *n.* **1.** *Informal.* odd, eccentric, or crazy person. **2.** *Baseball.* ball that is pitched by snapping the wrist in a backward direction so that the ball curves as it passes the batter. —*adj. Informal.* contrary to reason or common sense; ludicrous: *a screwball notion.*

screw·driv·er (skrōō′drī′vər) *n.* **1.** tool for turning screws, consisting of a handle attached to a rod, usually of metal, having a beveled or grooved end that fits into the corresponding slot or slots of a screw. **2.** cocktail consisting of vodka and orange juice.

screw propeller, propeller.

screw thread, thread (def. 4).

screw·y (skrōō′ē) *adj.* **screw·i·er, screw·i·est.** *Informal.* **1.** odd; eccentric; crazy: *He's one of the screwiest people I ever met.* **2.** markedly absurd, strange, or unlikely: *a screwy idea. There's something screwy going on here.* —**screw′i·ness,** *n.*

scrib·ble (skrib′əl) **-bled, -bling.** *v.t.* **1.** to write or draw (something)

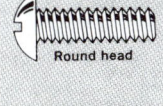

Round head

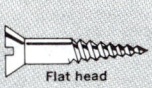

Flat head

Screws

carelessly or hastily: *He scribbled down the names of all who volunteered.* **2.** to cover with careless, illegible, or meaningless writing or marks. —*v.i.* to write or draw in a careless or hasty manner; make random or meaningless marks: *to scribble on a pad.* —*n.* writing, drawing, or mark made by scribbling: *margins covered with messy scribbles.* [Medieval Latin *scribillare* to write hastily, from Latin *scribere* to write.]

scrib·bler (skrib′lər) *n.* **1.** one who scribbles. **2.** inferior or unimportant writer; author of little or no reputation.

scribe (skrīb) *n.* **1.** one whose profession is writing down or copying letters, manuscripts, contracts, or other documents. **2.** public clerk or secretary. **3.** writer; author. **4.** teacher who interpreted the Mosaic law among the ancient Hebrews. **5.** scriber. —*v.t.* **scribed, scrib·ing.** to mark with a scriber or other pointed instrument. [Latin *scriba* public writer, clerk, secretary.]

scrib·er (skrī′bər) *n.* pointed steel tool for incising a mark on material, as wood or metal, that is to be cut.

scrim (skrim) *n.* loosely woven cotton or linen fabric used for such items as curtains or bunting. [Of uncertain origin.]

scrim·mage (skrim′ij) *n.* **1.** rough and confused struggle or fight; tussle; scuffle. **2.** *Football.* **a.** play that occurs from the time the ball is snapped back until it is called dead. **b.** practice session, often taking the form of a full game. —*v.i.*, **-maged, -mag·ing.** *Football.* to participate in a scrimmage. [Modification of obsolete *scrimish,* form of SKIRMISH.]

scrimp (skrimp) *v.i.* to be very sparing or frugal, esp. with money; economize (often with *on*): *to scrimp and save for a new dress to wear to the Christmas dance, to scrimp on movies and other expenses in order to pay for a vacation.* —*v.t.* to be excessively sparing of or with. [Of uncertain origin.]

scrimp·y (skrim′pē) *adj.* **scrimp·i·er, scrimp·i·est.** *adj.* scarcely adequate in amount or quantity; skimpy; meager. —**scrimp′i·ly,** *adv.* —**scrimp·i·ness,** *n.*

scrim·shaw (skrim′shô′) *n.* **1.** carved or engraved article made of bone, ivory, shell, or the like, often decorated with nautical scenes or motifs. **2.** such articles collectively, esp. as made by sailors during long whaling or other voyages. —*v.t.* to carve or engrave into scrimshaw. —*v.i.* to make or produce scrimshaw. [Of uncertain origin.]

scrip¹ (skrip) *n.* **1.** any temporary money equivalent or substitute, as a certificate or token, usually issued by a government or business concern, to be exchanged for goods or services. **2.** paper money issued for temporary use in times of emergency, as that in amounts of less than a dollar issued in the United States during the Civil War. **3.** temporary certificate representing a fractional share of stock; such certificates collectively. [Short for obsolete *(sub)scrip(tion) (receipt)* receipt for part of a loan.]

scrip² (skrip) *n. Archaic.* small scrap of paper, esp. with something written on it, as a list or schedule. [Form of SCRIPT.]

scrip³ (skrip) *n. Archaic.* small bag or satchel. [Possibly from Old Norse *skreppa* bag.]

script (skript) *n.* **1.** cursive handwriting. **2.** any of various styles of type resembling this. **3.** writing system or style: *Babylonian script, Gothic script.* **4.** typed or written text of a theatrical presentation, motion picture, or radio or television program, that is used by the performers, director, and other members of the production staff. [Latin *scriptum* something written.]

scrip·to·ri·um (skrip tôr′ē əm) *pl.* **-to·ri·a** (-tôr′ē ə) or **-to·ri·ums.** *n.* room, esp. one in a monastery, set apart for writing, copying, or illuminating manuscripts. [Medieval Latin *scriptorium,* going back to Latin *scriptus,* past participle of *scribere* to write.]

Scrip·tur·al (skrip′chər əl) *adj.* of, based on, or according to Scripture or any sacred writings.

Scrip·ture (skrip′chər) *n.* **1.** *also,* **the Scriptures.** books of the Old and New Testaments, and often the Apocrypha, collectively; the Bible. **2.** *also,* **scripture.** book or writings sacred to a religion. **3. scripture.** writing or body of writings regarded as authoritative or absolutely true. [Latin *scriptūra* a writing.]

script·writ·er (skript′rī′tər) *n.* one who writes scripts, as for a motion picture or radio or television program.

scriv·ner (skriv′nər) *n. Archaic.* one whose work is copying, preparing, or certifying documents or other writings; scribe. [From obsolete *scrivein,* from Old French *escrivein,* from Late Late *scrībānus* notary, from Latin *scriba* public writer.]

scrod (skrod) *n.* young cod. [Probably of Dutch origin.]

scrof·u·la (skrof′yə lə) *n.* rare disorder primarily characterized by swelling and inflammation of the lymph glands, esp. those in the neck, resulting from infection with tuberculosis. Also, **stru′ma.** [Late Latin *scrōfulae* swellings of the neck glands, diminutive of Latin *scrōfa* sow²; possibly because the swellings were thought to resemble small pigs.]

scrof·u·lous (skrof′yə ləs) *adj.* **1.** relating to, affected with, or resembling scrofula. **2.** morally corrupt; degenerate.

---

at; āpe; cär; end; mē; it; īce; hot; ōld; fôrk; wood; fōol; oil; out; up; ūse; turn; sing; thin; this; zh in treasure; ə in ago, taken, pencil, lemon, circus.

scroll (skrōl) *n.* **1.** roll of parchment, paper, silk, or other material containing or used for writings or paintings, often wound around one or a pair of rods so as to be conveniently used or stored. **2.** figure or ornamental device resembling a partly unrolled scroll, as the curved head on a violin. [Modification (influenced by ROLL) of obsolete *scrow* roll of parchment or paper, from Anglo-Norman *escrowe* scrap¹, strip² (as of parchment); of Germanic origin.]

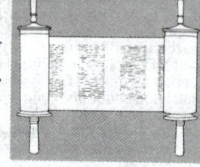

Scroll *(def. 1)*

scroll saw, hand or power saw having a narrow blade with fine teeth, used to cut curved or intricate patterns in thin wood.

scroll·work (skrōl′wurk′) *n.* ornamental work consisting chiefly of scroll-like patterns, esp. such work cut with a scroll saw.

Scrooge (skrōōj) *also.* **scrooge.** *n.* nasty, mean-tempered miser. [From Ebenezer *Scrooge,* a mean-tempered, miserly old man in *A Christmas Carol,* a story by Charles Dickens.]

scro·tum (skrō′təm) *pl.* **-ta** (-tə) *or* **-tums.** *n.* external sac of skin and muscle that in most male mammals contains the testicles. [Latin *scrōtum.*] **—scro′tal,** *adj.*

scrounge (skrounj) **scrounged, scroung·ing.** *Slang. v.t.* **1.** to obtain, collect, or gather with effort or difficulty or as by foraging (often with *up*): *We scrounged some rusty tools out of that decrepit shack. He managed to scrounge up enough money for the rent.* **2.** to borrow (something) without intending to return or repay; grub: *to scrounge a meal.* —*v.i.* **1.** to search; forage (often with *around*): *Can you scrounge around in that mess and dig up my book?* **2.** to grub; mooch. [Form of dialectal English *scrunge* to steal; of uncertain origin.]

scrub¹ (skrub) **scrubbed, scrub·bing.** *v.t.* **1.** to rub vigorously in order to wash or clean. **2.** to remove by such rubbing: *She scrubbed the ink stains off her hands.* **3.** to cleanse (a gas or vapor) of impurities. **4.** *Informal.* to postpone or cancel (a planned event or activity): *NASA scrubbed the missile launch.* —*v.i.* to wash or clean something by hard rubbing. —*n.* act of rubbing hard in order to wash or clean. [Middle Dutch *schrobben* to scrape, rub.]

scrub² (skrub) *n.* **1.** vegetation consisting chiefly of low, stunted trees or shrubs. **2.** land, tract, or region that can support only such vegetation. **3.** animal of undersized growth or inferior or mixed stock. **4.** undersized or insignificant person. **5.** player who is not a member of the first or regular team. —*adj.* **1.** undersized, stunted, or inferior: *a scrub tree, scrub cows.* **2.** of, composed of, or played by players not on the first or regular team: *a scrub team, a scrub game.* [Form of SHRUB¹.]

scrub·ber (skrub′ər) *n.* **1.** device used for scrubbing, esp. an apparatus for cleansing gas of impurities. **2.** one who scrubs.

scrub·by (skrub′ē) **-bi·er, -bi·est.** *adj.* **1.** of inferior growth or stock; undersized; stunted: *a scrubby bush.* **2.** covered with or consisting of scrub. **3.** shabby; mean; paltry. **—scrub′bi·ness,** *n.*

scrub·wom·an (skrub′woom′ən) *pl.* **-wom·en.** *n.* woman hired to clean; charwoman.

scruff (skruf) *n.* back of the neck or the skin covering it. [Modification of obsolete *scuff;* of uncertain origin.]

scruff·y (skruf′ē) **scruff·i·er, scruff·i·est.** *adj.* worn or dirty; shabby. **—scruff′i·ness,** *n.*

scrump·tious (skrump′shəs) *adj. Informal.* delectable; splendid.

scrunch (skrunch) *v.t.* **1.a.** to press or squeeze into irregular folds or creases; crumple. **b.** to twist out of shape or draw into a more compact mass; squeeze, as if crumpling (often with *up*): *The child scrunched up her face in distaste. He scrunched himself up in the chair.* **2.** to crunch; crush: *The bear scrunched the ants beneath its paws.* —*v.i.* **1.** to make or move with a crunching sound: *The gravel scrunched under our feet. The car scrunched over the snow.* **2.** to assume or draw into a more compact shape; crouch: *He scrunched down in his seat so that she wouldn't see him.* —*n.* crunching sound. [Modification of CRUNCH.]

scru·ple (skrōō′pəl) *n.* **1.** moral or ethical principle, consideration, or objection that restrains action or gives rise to doubt, hesitancy, or uneasiness of mind: *He has no scruples about telling people exactly what he thinks of them.* **2.** very small amount or portion. **3.** apothecaries' weight equal to 20 grains, or ¹⁄₂₄ of an ounce. Three scruples are equal to one dram. See **weights and measures** for table. —*v.i.* **-pled, -pling.** to hesitate because of scruples; have scruples: *She doesn't scruple about lying when it serves her purpose.* [Latin *scrūpulus* small sharp stone, uneasiness (as that felt when having a stone in one's shoe), small weight, diminutive of *scrūpus* sharp stone, uneasiness.]

scru·pu·lous (skrōō′pyə ləs) *adj.* **1.** having or showing a strict regard for what is right; unswervingly attentive to moral or ethical standards. **2.** thoroughly attentive to or careful of even the smallest details; pains-

taking: *scrupulous neatness. We copied the letters with scrupulous care.* **—scru·pu·los·i·ty** (skrōō′pyə los′ə tē), **scru′pu·lous·ness,** *n.* **—scru′pu·lous·ly,** *adv.*

scru·ti·nize (skrōōt′ən īz′) **-nized, -niz·ing.** *v.t.* to look at or examine closely or critically; inspect carefully or minutely: *He scrutinized her face for a sign of recognition.*

Syn. Scrutinize, inspect, examine mean to look at or over carefully. **Scrutinize** commonly stresses close attention to minute details: *The officer scrutinized our passports and travel papers and detained us because our vaccination certificates were missing.* **Inspect** adds to *scrutinize* the sense of an official review, esp. when compared with a standard of excellence: *Each article is inspected and tested before it leaves the factory.* **Examine** suggests a probing inquiry to determine the validity, truth, or legality of something: *The lawyer examined the title deeds and found that they were in order.*

scru·ti·ny (skrōōt′ən ē) *pl.* **-nies.** *n.* **1.** close, critical study, examination, or inquiry; careful inspection. **2.** close observation or watch; surveillance: *The suspect's movements were under the scrutiny of the police.* [Late Latin *scrūtinium* search, inquiry, from Latin *scrūtārī* to search, examine.]

scu·ba (skōō′bə) *n.* portable, underwater breathing device consisting of one or more cylinders of compressed air which are fastened on a diver's back and a hose or hoses for transmitting the oxygen to a mouthpiece. —*adj.* of or relating to scuba or to scuba diving: *a scuba tank, scuba equipment.* [Abbreviation of *s(elf)-c(ontained) u(nderwater) b(reathing) a(pparatus).*]

scuba diver, one who engages in scuba diving.

scuba diving, swimming underwater for extended periods of time with a scuba.

scud (skud) **scud·ded, scud·ding.** *v.i.* **1.** to run or move swiftly: *The clouds scudded across the sky.* **2.** *Nautical.* to run before a gale with little or no sail set. —*n.* **1.** act of scudding or moving swiftly. **2.** light clouds, spray, or rain driven swiftly before the wind. [Probably of Scandinavian origin.]

scuff (skuf) *v.t.* **1.** to scratch, mar, or roughen the surface of by scraping or wear. **2.** to move (the feet) with a scraping or dragging movement. —*v.i.* **1.** to walk by dragging the feet; shuffle. **2.** to become scratched, marred, or roughened by scraping or wear: *This linoleum scuffs easily.* —*n.* **1.** act or sound of scuffing. **2.** light, flat-heeled house slipper, esp. one having no covering for the heel. [Of Scandinavian origin.]

scuf·fle (skuf′əl) *n.* **1.** confused, often rough, struggle or fight: *A crowd gathered, and a scuffle ensued.* **2.** sound of feet shuffling. —*v.i.,* **-fled, -fling. 1.** to struggle or fight at close quarters in a rough, confused manner. **2.** to drag the feet; shuffle. [Probably of Scandinavian origin.]

scull (skul) *n.* **1.** oar used to propel a boat by working it from side to side over the stern. **2.** one of a pair of light oars used together, one on each side of a boat, by a single rower. **3.** small boat propelled by sculls, esp. a light racing boat propelled by one or more rowers. —*v.t., v.i.* to propel (a boat) by a scull or sculls, esp. by a single oar worked from side to side over the stern. [Of uncertain origin.] **—scull′er,** *n.*

Scull *(def. 2)*

scul·ler·y (skul′ər ē) *pl.* **-ler·ies.** *n.* place, often a small room adjoining a kitchen, where cooking utensils are cleaned and stored and other rough, messy kitchen chores are done. [Old French *escuelerie,* from *escuelle* dish, going back to Latin *scutella* salver, diminutive of *scutra* tray, dish.]

scul·lion (skul′yən) *n. Archaic.* **1.** servant employed to wash cooking utensils and do dirty, messy, menial work in a kitchen. **2.** low, contemptible person; wretch. [Of uncertain origin.]

scul·pin (skul′pin) *pl.* **-pins** *or* **-pin.** *n.* any of a group of inedible, spiny-finned fish, family Cottidae, found in fresh and salt waters of North

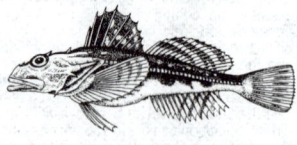

Sculpin

America, Europe, and Asia, having a large head, broad mouth, and sharp spines in front of the gills. Also, **mill′er's-thumb′.** [Of uncertain origin.]

sculpt (skulpt) *v.t.* to carve or otherwise form (a figure or design) by means of sculpture: *to sculpt a statue.* —*v.i.* to produce sculpture; work as a sculptor: *to sculpt in marble.*

at; āpe; cär; end; mē; it; īce; hot; ōld; fôrk; wood; fōōl; oil; out; up; ūse; turn; sing; thin; this; zh in treasure; ə in ago, taken, pencil, lemon, circus.

sculp·tor (skulp′tər) *n.* one who produces sculpture. [Latin *sculptor.*] —**sculp′tress**, *n.*

sculp·ture (skulp′chər) *n.* 1. art or process of producing three-dimensional figures or designs, as by carving or chiseling stone or marble, modeling in clay or wax, or casting in bronze or a similar metal. 2. figure or design so produced; such figures or designs collectively. —*v.t.*, **-tured, -tur·ing.** 1. to produce sculpture; sculpt. 2. to ornament or cover with sculpture. 3. to form or shape, as in the manner of sculpture. —*v.i.* to sculpt. [Latin *sculptūra* a carving.] —**sculp′tur·al**, *adj.*

scum (skum) *n.* 1. filmy layer, as of foul or extraneous matter, that forms on or rises to the surface of a liquid or body of water. 2. low, vile, despicable person, or such people collectively: *the scum of the earth. The entire regiment regarded the traitor as scum.* —*v.i.*, **scummed, scum·ming.** to become covered with or form scum. [Middle Dutch *schüm(e)* foam.]

scum·my (skum′ē) **-mi·er, -mi·est.** *adj.* 1. covered with, containing, or resembling scum. 2. low; vile; despicable.

scup (skup) *pl.,* **scups** or **scup.** *n.* commercially important food fish, *Stenotomus chrysops,* found along the eastern coast of the United States. [Short for Algonquian *mishcup,* from *mishe* large + *kuppe* close together; referring to its scales.]

scup·per (skup′ər) *n.* hole in the side of a ship that allows water to drain off the deck. [Of uncertain origin.]

scup·per·nong (skup′ər nông′, -nong′) *n.* 1. pale-green muscadine grape with a plumlike taste, cultivated in the southeastern United States. 2. sweet white wine made from this grape. [From *Scuppernong,* a river and lake in North Carolina, where this grape was found in the eighteenth century.]

scurf (skurf) *n.* 1. dead, flaky skin, esp. dandruff. 2. any scaly or flaky matter sticking to a surface. [Of Scandinavian origin.]

scurf·y (skur′fē) **scurf·i·er, scurf·i·est.** *adj.* covered with, resembling, or consisting of scurf. —**scurf′i·ness**, *n.*

scur·ril·i·ty (skə ril′ə tē) *pl.,* **-ties.** *n.* 1. quality of being scurrilous. 2. that which is scurrilous.

scur·ri·lous (skur′ə ləs) *adj.* 1. marked by obscenities and coarse abuse; offensively gross: *scurrilous language, a scurrilous attack on his character.* 2. given to using coarse, obscene, or abusive language: *a scurrilous writer.* [Latin *scurrilis* like a buffoon, jeering (from *scurra* buffoon) + -OUS.] —**scur′ri·lous·ly**, *adv.* —**scur′ri·lous·ness**, *n.*

scur·ry (skur′ē) **-ried, -ry·ing.** *v.i.* to go or move hurriedly: *The deer scurried off into the woods. She scurried from store to store.* —*n.* *pl.,* **-ries.** act or sound of scurrying: *the scurry of mice in the eaves.* [Short for HURRY-SCURRY.]

scur·vy (skur′vē) *n.* disease caused by lack of vitamin C in the diet, characterized by spongy and bleeding gums, bleeding under the skin from hemorrhaging blood vessels, and extreme weakness. —*adj.*, **-vi·er, -vi·est.** mangy and vile; contemptible; base: *a scurvy crew of thieves.* [SCURF + -Y¹.] —**scur′vi·ly**, *adv.* —**scur′vi·ness**, *n.*

scut (skut) *n.* short tail, as of a rabbit or deer. [Possibly of Scandinavian origin.]

scu·tage (skū′tij) *n.* money payment given to a feudal lord by his vassal in lieu of military service. [Medieval Latin *scutagium* literally, shield money, from Latin *scūtum* shield.]

Scu·ta·ri (skoo′tär ē) *n.* Usküdar.

scu·tate (skū′tāt) *adj.* 1. *Botany.* shaped like a small shield, as a nasturtium leaf. 2. *Zoology.* covered with bony or horny plates or large scales. [Latin *scūtātus* armed with a shield, from *scūtum* shield.]

scutch (skuch) *v.t.* to separate (flax or other plant fibers) from woody tissue or foreign particles. —*n.* also, **scutch′er.** device or machine for scutching. [Obsolete French *escoucher* to beat flax, going back to Latin *excutere* to shake out.]

scutch·eon (skuch′ən) *n.* escutcheon.

scu·tel·late (skū tel′it, skūt′əl āt′) *adj. Zoology.* covered with a scutellum.

scu·tel·lum (skū tel′əm) *pl.,* **-tel·la.** *n.* small plate, scale, or other shieldlike part, found esp. on insects and birds. [Modern Latin *scutellum,* diminutive of Latin *scūtum* shield.]

scut·tle¹ (skut′əl) **-tled, -tling.** *v.t.* 1. to cause (a boat or ship) to sink by cutting, boring, or uncovering an opening in the bottom, deck, or sides. 2. to abandon or destroy, as hopes or plans. —*n.* 1. opening, esp. in the deck, side, or compartment of a ship, usually having a movable cover. 2. lid or cover for such an opening. [Possibly from obsolete French *escoutille* hatch², from Spanish *escotilla,* diminutive of *escote* opening for the neck in a garment; of Germanic origin.]

scut·tle² (skut′əl) *n.* coal scuttle. [Latin *scutella* salver, diminutive of *scutra* dish.]

scut·tle³ (skut′əl) **-tled, -tling.** *v.i.* to go or move with short, rapid steps: *crabs scuttling across the ocean bottom.* —*n.* rapid pace; short, hurried run. [Form of dialectal English *scuddle* to run away, from SCUD.]

scut·tle·butt (skut′əl but′) *n.* rumor; gossip. [SCUTTLE¹ + BUTT².]

scu·tum (skū′təm) *pl.,* **-ta** (-tə). *n.* one of the bony, shieldlike scales or plates forming the covering of certain fish and reptiles. [Latin *scūtum* shield.]

Scyl·la (sil′ə) *n.* 1. *Greek Mythology.* monster having six heads and twelve feet, who lived in a cave on the Strait of Messina, opposite the monster Charybdis. Sailors who weren't drowned by Scylla were snatched from their ships and devoured by Scylla. 2. **between Scylla and Charybdis.** caught between two dangers, neither of which can be avoided without confronting the other.

scythe (sīth) *n.* hand implement consisting of a long curved blade attached at an angle to a long bent handle, used for mowing, cutting, or reaping. —*v.t.*, **scythed, scyth·ing.** to mow or cut with or as with a scythe. [Old English *sīthe* the implement; Modern English spelling influenced by Latin *scindere* to cut.]

Scyth·i·a (sith′ē ə) *n.* ancient region that extended over parts of Asia and southern Europe.

Scyth·i·an (sith′ē ən) *n.* member of the people that inhabited Scythia. —*adj.* of or relating to Scythia, its people, or their language or culture.

S. Dak., South Dakota. Also, **S.D.**

Se, selenium.

SE, southeast; southeastern.

sea (sē) *n.* 1. the continuous body of salt water that covers nearly three-fourths of the earth's surface; the ocean. 2. large portion of this, partly or almost entirely enclosed by land, as the Caribbean Sea or the Aegean Sea. 3. large inland body of water, salt or fresh, as the Sea of Galilee or the Dead Sea. 4. condition of the ocean's surface, esp. with regard to the motion of the waves: *a calm sea, a stormy sea.* 5. large, heavy swell or wave: *The ship floundered in rough seas.* 6. anything suggesting the sea in vastness or extent; overwhelming quantity or mass: *the sea of time, a sea of troubles, a sea of faces.* 7. the sea considered as affording an occupation or way of life: *The sea has been my life for many years.* 8. mare². 9. **at sea. a.** out on the ocean. **b.** at a loss; bewildered. 10. **to go to sea. a.** to become a sailor. **b.** to set out on an ocean voyage. 11. **to put (out) to sea.** to embark on an ocean voyage; sail from land. [Old English *sǣ.*]

sea anchor, conical canvas-covered frame or other anchor that is dragged along behind a vessel in order to reduce drift or help keep the vessel heading into the wind. Also, **drogue.**

sea anemone, any of a group of marine animals, class Anthozoa, that attach themselves to rocks, wharves, and other objects, having numerous tentacles that bear stinging cells used to stun prey.

Sea anemone

sea bass (bas) any of a group of saltwater bass that have spiny fins and are important food and game fish.

Sea·bee (sē′bē′) *n.* member of a U.S. Navy construction battalion that is composed of skilled workers of all trades who build and maintain various installations, as shipyards and ammunition depots. [Modification of *C.B.,* abbreviation of *C(onstruction) B(attalion).*]

sea bird, any water bird frequenting the sea or seacoast.

sea biscuit, hardtack. Also, **sea bread.**

sea·board (sē′bôrd′) *n.* land near or bordering on the sea; seacoast.

sea·borne (sē′bôrn′) *adj.* carried on or by the sea.

sea bream, any of several food and game fish, family Sparidae, found chiefly along the Atlantic coast of North America.

sea breeze, breeze blowing inland from the sea.

sea·coast (sē′kōst′) *n.* land near or bordering on the sea.

sea cow 1. dugong, manatee, or similar animal. 2. walrus.

sea cucumber, any of a group of cucumber-shaped marine animals, class Holothuroidea, found in coastal waters and having a flexible body with several tentacles around the mouth. Length: ¼ inch–20 inches.

Sea cucumber

sea dog, sailor, esp. an old or experienced one.

sea duck, any of various diving ducks, as the scoter.

sea eagle, any of various eagles that feed chiefly on fish.

sea·far·er (sē′fâr′ər) *n.* one engaged in seafaring, esp. a sailor.

sea·far·ing (sē′fâr′ing) *adj.* 1. following the sea as a business or calling: *a seafaring merchant.* 2. of or relating to the sea or to life or work as a sailor: *The old man fondly recalled his seafaring days.* 3. traveling on the sea: *a seafaring ship.* —*n.* 1. business or calling of a sailor. 2. travel by sea.

sea·food (sē′food′) *also,* **sea food.** *n.* edible saltwater fish or shellfish.

sea·fowl (sē′foul′) *n.* sea bird or sea birds collectively.

at; āpe; cär; end; mē; it; īce; hot; ōld; fôrk; wood; fōōl; oil; out; up; ūse; turn; sing; thin; this; zh in treasure; ə in ago, taken, pencil, lemon, circus.

897

sea front, land bordering on the sea.

sea·girt (sē′gûrt′) *adj.* surrounded by the sea.

sea·go·ing (sē′gō′ing) *adj.* **1.** designed, suitable, or used for sea travel. **2.** seafaring.

sea green, medium bluish-green.

sea gull, gull¹.

sea horse 1. any of various slender fish, genus *Hippocampus*, found in warm and temperate seas, having a horselike head and neck and a prehensile tail. Length: 2–8 inches. **2.** walrus. **3.** mythical sea creature, half fish and half horse.

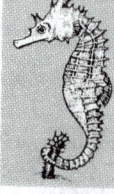

Sea horse

Sea Islands, island chain in the southeastern United States, along the Atlantic coast of South Carolina, Georgia, and northern Florida.

seal¹ (sēl) *pl.* **seals** or **seal.** *n.* **1.** any of several marine mammals, families Otariidae and Phocidae, having a streamlined body, a muscular neck, and limbs that are modified to form flippers. Some seals, **fur seals,** are hunted for their valuable pelt. Length: to 22 feet. **2.** pelt or fur of such an animal, esp. sealskin. **3.** leather made from the hide of such an animal. —*v.i.* to hunt seals. [Old English *seolh* the marine mammal.]

seal² (sēl) *n.* **1.** impression in relief of a device, as a design, figure, or word, stamped on wax, paper, or other soft material to show ownership or authenticity and intended to represent officially a person, institution, or governing body. **2.** representation of such an impression, or a disk or wafer of wax, paper, or other material bearing such an impression, affixed to a document to prove authenticity or to seal it shut. **3.** stamp, die, ring, or other object engraved with a device, used to impart such impressions. **4.** something that fastens firmly, closes completely, or makes airtight or watertight: *to lick the seal on an envelope, to break the seal on a jar.* **5.** decorative gummed stamp or sticker. **6.** something that serves to authenticate, confirm, or secure; pledge; assurance. **7.** *Archaic.* mark or sign indicating ownership or serving as visible evidence of something. —*v.t.* **1.** to fasten or shut firmly or make airtight or watertight: *to seal an envelope, to seal a tomb. My lips are sealed.* **2.** to fill or obstruct; stop up (often with *up*): *to seal the cracks in a wall. An avalanche of rocks sealed up the cave.* **3.** to shut in or confine; enclose tightly: *They sealed the documents in a strongbox.* **4.** to prevent or restrict access to (often with *off*): *Police sealed off the area and questioned everyone closely.* **5.** to confirm, conclude, or assure as if by affixing a seal: *to seal a bargain with a handshake.* **6.** to put beyond question, doubt, or reversal; decide finally or irrevocably: *The arrival of reinforcements sealed our victory.* **7.** to place a seal on, as to prove authenticity, signify authorization, or prevent tampering. **8.** to mark or stamp with a seal in order to certify or attest to the size, weight, accuracy, or quality of: *to seal a scale.* [Old French *seel* engraved signet for stamping documents in order to authenticate them, going back to Latin *sigillum* little mark, small figure, diminutive of *signum* sign, mark¹.]

sea lavender, any of a group of plants, genus *Limonium*, found in seaside regions of the Northern Hemisphere, bearing small, usually blue or purple flowers.

sea legs *Informal.* ability to walk steadily aboard ship, esp. on rough seas.

seal·er¹ (sē′lər) *n.* **1.** one who or that which fastens, closes, or makes airtight or watertight. **2.** substance applied to a porous or unfinished surface in preparation for painting or varnishing. **3.** official who inspects and tests weights, measures, or materials and certifies that they have met certain standards. [SEAL² + -ER¹.]

seal·er² (sē′lər) *n.* person or ship engaged in seal hunting. [SEAL¹ + -ER¹.]

seal·er·y (sē′lər ē) *pl.* **-er·ies.** *n.* **1.** occupation of hunting for seals; seal hunting. **2.** place where seals are hunted.

sea level, mean level of the surface of the sea, esp. halfway between mean high and low water, used as a standard above and below which land elevations and sea depths are measured.

sea lily, crinoid.

sealing wax, mixture usually consisting of shellac and turpentine, which is fluid when heated but quickly solidifies as it cools, used for sealing letters, packages, jars, and other items.

sea lion, any of various large seals found chiefly in the Pacific Ocean, esp. the **California sea lion,** *Zalophus californianus.*

seal ring, signet ring.

seal·skin (sēl′skin′) *n.* **1.** pelt or fur of a fur seal.

Sea lion

Sea·ly·ham terrier (sē′lē ham′, -lē əm) small, short-legged terrier having a long head, round-tipped ears, and a rough, wiry coat of white hair. Height: 10 inches at the shoulder.

Sealyham terrier

seam (sēm) *n.* **1.** line formed by sewing together the edges of two or more pieces of cloth, leather, or similar material. **2.** similar line, groove, or ridge formed by adjoining edges, as of planks or layers of bricks. **3.** any mark resembling a seam, as a scar or crack. **4.** stratum or thin layer, as of coal or rock. —*v.t.* **1.** to join together by or as by sewing. **2.** to mark (a surface) with a seam or seams; furrow: *Years of living in the open air had seamed the old sailor's face.* —*v.i.* to become furrowed; crack open. [Old English *sēam* line formed by sewing or joining two edges.]

sea·man (sē′mən) *pl.* **-men.** *n.* **1.** sailor; mariner. **2.** person having or excelling in seamanship. **3.** in the U. S. Navy and Coast Guard, an enlisted man of any of the three lowest grades.

sea·man·ship (sē′mən ship′) *n.* skill in and knowledge of all that relates to working, managing, or maneuvering a boat or ship.

sea·mark (sē′märk′) *n.* any landmark visible from the sea, as a lighthouse or beacon, that serves as a navigational aid.

sea mew, mew².

seam·stress (sēm′stris) *n.* woman who is skilled at sewing, esp. one whose occupation is sewing. Also, **semp′stress.**

seam·y (sē′mē) **seam·i·er, seam·i·est.** *adj.* **1.** dismal, squalid, or degraded; sordid: *the seamy side of life.* **2.** having or showing seams. —**seam′i·ness,** *n.*

sé·ance (sā′äns) *n.* meeting in which a group of people attempt to communicate with the spirits of the dead through the help of a medium. [French *séance* session, from Old French *seoir* to sit, from Latin *sedēre.*]

sea otter, dark-brown otter, *Enhydra lutris,* found along the western coast of North America and around offshore islands of the Pacific, having broad, flipperlike hind feet. It is the largest of all otters and the only one that lives in salt water. Length: 50–64 inches, including the tail.

sea·plane (sē′plān′) *n.* airplane, esp. one equipped with floats, that is designed to take off from and land on water. Also, **hy′dro·plane′.**

Seaplane

sea·port (sē′pôrt′) *n.* **1.** port or harbor for seagoing vessels. **2.** city or town having such a port or harbor.

sea power 1. nation that possesses formidable naval strength. **2.** naval strength.

sea purse, tough, protective case or pouch encasing the eggs of skates and certain other fish.

sear (sēr) *v.t.* **1.** to burn the surface of; char; scorch. **2.** to dry up or wither: *The prairie sun seared the fall grass.* **3.** to have a lasting and injurious effect on, esp. to harden or make callous: *To give firmness to sensibility . . . without searing its feelings* (Mackenzie, 1772). —*n.* mark made by searing or burning. —*adj. Archaic.* sere. [Old English *sēar* dry, withered.] —**Syn.** *v.t.* **1.** see **scorch.**

search (sûrch) *v.t.* **1.** to look through, inspect, or explore carefully and thoroughly in order to find something: *I've searched all my drawers, but my notebook is still missing.* **2.** to look into or examine carefully and closely; probe: *to search one's soul.* **3.** to find, uncover, or come to know by exploration or investigation (with *out*): *to search out the truth.* —*v.i.* to look carefully and thoroughly; make an examination or investigation: *He searched through his pockets and still can't find his keys. Philosophers have been searching for that answer for centuries.* —*n.* act of searching. [Old French *cerchier* to seek, from Late Latin *circāre* to go round, explore, from Latin *circum* around, about.] —**search′er,** *n.*

search·ing (sûr′ching) *adj.* **1.** keenly observant and penetrating: *a searching glance.* **2.** investigating and probing carefully and in every detail: *a searching inquiry, searching questions.* —**search′ing·ly,** *adv.*

search·light (sûrch′līt′) *n.* **1.** device that projects a strong beam of light in any direction by means of a concave reflector or a lens that focuses the light in a concentrated stream of rays. **2.** beam of light so projected. **3.** flashlight (*def. 1*). **4.** something that probes, reveals, or sheds light on what is hidden or obscure: *Each . . . turned on some miscarriage of civil justice the searchlight of truth* (Tallentyre, 1904).

search warrant, court order authorizing the search of a house or other specified premises for wanted persons or stolen or unlawfully held property believed to be on the premises.

at; āpe; cär; end; mē; it; īce; hot; ōld; fôrk; wood; fool; oil; out; up; ūse; turn; sing; thin; this; zh in treasure; ə in ago, taken, pencil, lemon, circus.

sea robin, any of a group of reddish-brown fish, family Triglidae, found in shallow tropical and temperate seas, having a bony, often spiny head, winglike side fins, and several slender, fingerlike feelers under the fins. Length: to 3 feet.

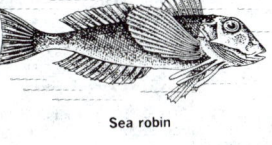

sea room, sufficient unobstructed space at sea in which a boat or ship can be maneuvered easily and safely.

Sea robin

sea rover 1. buccaneer; pirate. **2.** pirate ship.

sea·scape (sē′skāp′) *n.* **1.** picture depicting a sea scene. Also, **ma·rine′**. **2.** view of the sea. [SEA + (LAND)SCAPE.]

sea serpent, any of various legendary marine monsters, usually represented as a snakelike or dragonlike creature of enormous size and strength.

sea·shell (sē′shel′) *n.* shell of any marine mollusk, as an oyster or clam.

sea·shore (sē′shôr′) *n.* land near or bordering on the sea.

sea·sick (sē′sik′) *adj.* nauseated and dizzy as a result of the rolling motion of a vessel at sea. **—sea′sick′ness,** *n.*

sea·side (sē′sīd′) *n.* land near or bordering on the sea; seashore.

sea snake 1. any of a group of venomous snakes, family Hydrophidae, found in the warm inshore seas of Asia. **2.** *Archaic.* sea serpent.

sea·son (sē′zən) *n.* **1.** one of the divisions of the year, as determined by the position of the earth in its orbit around the sun. The four seasons, spring, summer, autumn, and winter, are characterized chiefly by differences in weather, average temperature, and number of hours of daylight. **2.** period or time of the year with reference to the weather conditions that characterize it: *the rainy season, the monsoon season.* **3.** period or time of the year associated with, allotted to, or marked by a particular activity or thing: *the holiday season, the football season, the opera season.* **4.** period or time of the year during which something flourishes or is best or available: *the peach season, the oyster season.* **5.** period or time of the year during which a particular place is most frequented for social activities, amusement, or recreation: *the Newport season. Plane reservations for Bermuda are cheaper when you go out of season.* **6.** appropriate, natural, or appointed time: *This is the season for sleeveless dresses. To every thing there is a season, and a time to every purpose under the heaven* (Ecclesiastes 3:1). **7.** period of time. **8. in season. a.** available or in the best condition for eating: *Peaches are now in season.* **b.** legally permitted to be hunted or caught: *Deer are now in season.* **c.** (of animals) ready to mate or breed; in heat. **9. out of season.** not in season. *—v.t.* **1.** to add seasoning to (food) in order to heighten or improve flavor. **2.** to add zest, interest, or relish to: *to season a dull lecture with anecdotes.* **3.** to cure or render more suitable for use, as by drying or aging: *Knowledge and timber shouldn't be much used till they are seasoned* (O. W. Holmes, 1858). **4.a.** to mature, condition, discipline, or make fit through experience: *to season an athlete.* **b.** to make accustomed or inured; harden; acclimate: *to season troops to battle.* **5.** *Archaic.* to make less severe; moderate; temper: *When mercy seasons justice* (Shakespeare, *The Merchant of Venice*). *—v.i.* to become more suitable for use. *—adj.* valid for a specified period of time and often sold at a reduced rate: *a season pass to football games, a season subscription to the ballet.* [Old French *saison, seson* period of the year, from Medieval Latin *satio* time of sowing, from Latin *satiō* a sowing, planting.]

sea·son·a·ble (sē′zə nə bəl) *adj.* **1.** usual for or in keeping with the time of year: *Seasonable temperatures are expected through Friday.* **2.** occurring or coming at the right or proper time; opportune; timely. **—sea′son·a·ble·ness,** *n.* **—sea′son·a·bly,** *adv.*

sea·son·al (sē′zə nəl) *adj.* affected by, characteristic of, or occurring at a certain season or seasons: *seasonal storms, seasonal unemployment.* **—sea′son·al·ly,** *adv.*

sea·son·ing (sē′zə ning) *n.* **1.** something used to bring out, heighten, or improve the flavor of food, as a spice, herb, or condiment. **2.** something that adds zest, interest, or relish.

sea squirt, any of a small group of saclike marine animals, phylum Chordata, that live attached to the ocean bottom as adults and that, when disturbed, contract their bodies to shoot out streams of water. Also, **tu′ni·cate.**

seat (sēt) *n.* **1.a.** something to sit on: *The front seat holds fewer people than the back one.* **b.** place to sit: *You'll have to find seats on the floor.* **2.** that part of an object on which one sits: *the seat of a chair.* **3.a.** that part of the body on which one sits; buttocks. **b.** that part of a garment which covers the buttocks. **4.a.** membership or official position, as in a legal, commercial, or legislative body: *a seat in the Senate, a seat on the stock exchange.*

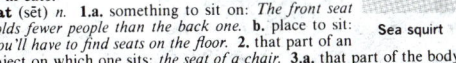

Mouth

Sea squirt

b. reserved accommodation for sitting: *We have two seats for the afternoon performance.* **5.** part on which something rests; base. **6.** center or source: *a seat of learning, the seat of the emotions.* **7.** manner of sitting, as on horseback. **8.** place of residence, esp. a country estate. *—v.t.* **1.** to place on or conduct to a seat; assign a seat to: *to seat a child on a stool.* **2.** to have capacity for: *a room that seats 400.* **3.** to establish in a particular place; settle; locate. **4.** to put a seat in or on. **5. to be seated.** to sit down. [Old Norse *sæti* chair, position.]

seat belt, strap or straps that may be buckled to hold a person in the seat of a vehicle. Also, **safety belt.**

seat·ing (sē′ting) *n.* **1.** pattern or system by which seats have been arranged or assigned. **2.** act of conducting to or providing with a seat or seats. **3.** material used for upholstering seats.

SEATO (sē′tō) Southeast Asia Treaty Organization, mutual defense agreement between the United States, the United Kingdom, France, Pakistan, Thailand, the Philippines, Australia, and New Zealand, established in 1954.

sea trout 1. any of various trout that migrate to salt water and later return to fresh water to spawn. **2.** any of various weakfish.

Se·at·tle (sē at′əl) *n.* port city in western Washington, on Puget Sound. Pop. (1970), 530,831.

sea urchin, any of a group of marine animals, class Echinoidea, having a thin skeleton of limy plates under the skin and, usually, bearing hard, movable spines.

sea wall, strong wall or embankment made to prevent erosion of a shoreline or to act as a breakwater.

sea·ward (sē′wərd) *adj.* toward the sea: *a seaward course.* *—adv. also,* **sea·wards. 1.** in the direction of the sea: *The explorers walked seaward.* **2. to seaward.** away from the land.

sea·way (sē′wā′) *n.* **1.** route over the sea; shipping lane. **2.** inland waterway deep and wide enough for ocean shipping. **3.** headway of a ship or boat. **4.** moderately rough sea.

sea·weed (sē′wēd′) *n.* any of various plants or algae living in the sea, esp. as found floating along the shore.

sea·wor·thy (sē′wur′thē) *adj.* (of a ship or boat) fit or safe to sail under all conditions. **—sea′wor′thi·ness,** *n.*

se·ba·ceous (si bā′shəs) *adj.* **1.** of or relating to oil or fat; oily; greasy. **2.** secreting oil or fat. [Latin *sēbāceus* made of tallow, from *sēbum* tallow, grease.]

sebaceous gland, any of the glands of the skin that secrete an oily lubricating fluid to the skin and hair.

Se·bas·to·pol (si bas′tə pōl′) Sevastopol.

sec, secant.

sec. 1. second. **2.** secretary. **3.** section.

SEC, Securities and Exchange Commission.

se·cant (sē′kant, -kənt) *n.* **1.** *Trigonometry.* **a.** (of either acute angle of a right triangle) ratio of the length of the hypotenuse to the length of the side adjacent to the angle. **b.** straight line drawn from the center of a circle through one end point of an arc to the tangent drawn from the other end point of the same arc. **2.** *Geometry.* line intersecting a curve at two or more points. *—adj.* intersecting. [Latin *secāns,* present participle of *secāre* to cut; because the line intersects or *cuts* the curve.]

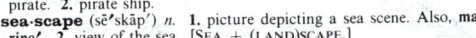

Secant of angle A = AC/AB

se·cede (si sēd′) *-ced·ed, -ced·ing. v.i.* to withdraw formally, esp. as a group, from a larger organization, usually to form an alternative organization. [Latin *sēcēdere* to go away, withdraw.]

se·ces·sion (si sesh′ən) *n.* **1.** act or instance of seceding. **2.** *also,* **Secession.** withdrawal from the Union by the eleven Southern states that formed the Confederacy. [Latin *sēcessiō* withdrawal, separation.]

se·ces·sion·ism (si sesh′ə niz′əm) *n.* theory or principles of those who advocate secession.

se·ces·sion·ist (si sesh′ə nist) *n.* **1.** one who favors or advocates secession. **2.** member of a group that secedes. *—adj.* relating to or advocating secession or secessionism.

Seck·el (sek′əl, sik′-) *n.* pear of a small, yellowish-brown variety. [From *Seckel,* the surname of the Pennsylvania farmer who first grew it.]

se·clude (si klōōd′) *-clud·ed, -clud·ing. v.t.* to keep apart or remove from the company of others; isolate. [Latin *sēclūdere* to shut off.] **—Syn.** see segregate.

se·clud·ed (si klōō′did) *adj.* **1.** shut off or screened from view: *The yard was secluded from the road.* **2.** removed from others; solitary: *a secluded life.* **—se·clud′ed·ness,** *n.*

se·clu·sion (si klōō′zhən) *n.* act of secluding; being secluded. [Medieval Latin *seclusio* a setting aside, from Latin *sēclūsus,* past participle of *sēclūdere* to shut off.] **—Syn.** see solitude.

se·clu·sive (si klōō′siv) *adj.* fond of or inclined toward seclusion. **—se·clu′sive·ness,** *n.*

at; āpe; cär; end; mē; it; īce; hot; ōld; fôrk; wood; fōōl; oil; out; up; ūse; turn; sing; thin; this; zh in treasure; ə in ago, taken, pencil, lemon, circus.

899

sec·ond¹ (sek′ənd) *adj.* **1.** (the ordinal of two) coming next after the first, as in order of time: *the second house from the corner.* **2.** that repeats or duplicates another; new or different; another: *a second visit to the dentist, a second helping of potatoes.* **3.** alternate: *to receive a magazine every second month.* **4.** subordinate; inferior. **5.** *Music.* of, relating to, or designating a part lower in pitch than or subordinate to another part written for or sounded by a like instrument or voice: *second violin, second soprano.* **6.** *Mechanics.* relating to or designating the forward gear next above first or low. —*adv.* in the group or position next after the first: *to finish second in a race.* —*n.* **1.** one who or that which is second. **2.** endorsement of an initial proposal or motion: *The chairman asked for a second.* **3.** one who or that which assists and supports another, esp. one who aids or advises a dueler or fighter. **4.** *also,* **seconds.** inferior or defective merchandise. **5.** *Mechanics.* forward gear next above first or low in a motor vehicle. **6.** *Music.* **a.** interval between two notes or tones separated by one degree on the diatonic scale. **b.** note or tone separated by this interval from another. **c.** harmonic combination of two such notes or tones. —*v.t.* **1.** to formally approve or support; endorse: *to second a motion.* **2.** to give support, encouragement, or assistance to. [Old French *second* the next to the first, from Latin *secundus* following, the next to the first, from *sequi* to follow; because it *follows* what is first.]

sec·ond² (sek′ənd) *n.* **1.** ¹⁄₆₀ of a minute or ¹⁄₃₆₀₀ of an hour of time. **2.** any very short interval of time: *It will take me only a second to put on my coat.* **3.** ¹⁄₆₀ of a minute or ¹⁄₃₆₀₀ of a degree of angular measurement. [Medieval Latin *secunda (minuta)* second (minute) (referring to the *second* division of the hour, resulting in 60 seconds, as distinguished from the first division into 60 minutes), from Latin *secunda,* feminine of *secundus* the next to the first.]

Second Advent, Second Coming.

sec·ond·ar·y (sek′ən der′ē) *adj.* **1.** not principal or chief; subordinate. **2.** coming from or based on that which is original or primary; derived: *He got all his information from secondary sources.* **3.** coming below or after the first as in order, place, or time. **4.** of or relating to an electrical coil or winding in which a current is produced by induction when the current in another, primary, coil or winding changes. —**sec′ond·ar′i·ly,** *adv.*

secondary accent **1.** the weaker of the two stresses in any word that has two syllables accented or stressed. The third syllable of *sec′ond·ar′y* has a secondary accent. **2.** mark (′) indicating this accent. Also, **secondary stress.**

secondary emission, emission of electrons from a substance bombarded by electrons or other charged particles.

secondary school, school providing instruction after elementary or grade school, comprising grades 7, 8, or 9 through 12.

secondary sex characteristic, any of the physical features that are characteristic of each sex and usually appear at puberty, as breast development or beard growth.

second base *Baseball.* **1.** base that must be touched second by a base runner. **2.** position of the player stationed near this base.

sec·ond-best (sek′ənd best′) *adj.* next or inferior to the best.

second childhood, condition of old age marked by feebleness or childishness; senility.

sec·ond-class (sek′ənd klas′) *adj.* **1.** less than the highest or best; inferior. **2.** of or relating to a class of mail consisting primarily of newspapers and magazines. **3.** of or relating to a class of travel ranking next in price or luxury below first class. —*adv.* by or in second class.

second class **1.** second-class travel accommodations. **2.** second-class mail.

Second Coming *Religion.* return of Christ on Judgment Day to judge the living and the dead. Also, **Second Advent.**

second fiddle, any subordinate or less prominent position or role: *to play second fiddle to an older brother.*

sec·ond-guess (sek′ənd ges′) *v.t., v.i.* **1.** to make judgments about (someone or some decision) after the results of a course of action are known. **2.** to outguess or anticipate.

sec·ond-hand (sek′ənd hand′) *also,* **sec·ond-hand.** *adj.* **1.** that has already been owned, used, or worn by someone else: *a secondhand car.* **2.** not obtained from the original source; derivative; borrowed: *secondhand knowledge of a subject.* **3.** dealing in previously used merchandise. —*adv.* in a secondhand manner; indirectly.

second hand, hand or pointer of a clock or watch that indicates seconds as it moves in a circle.

second lieutenant, in the U.S. Army, Air Force, and Marine Corps, an officer of the lowest rank, ranking below a first lieutenant.

sec·ond·ly (sek′ənd lē) *adv.* in the second place.

second nature, acquired tendency or quality that is so deeply fixed in one's character as to appear innate.

second person, form of a pronoun or verb that indicates the person or thing addressed. In the sentence *You left the room, you* and *left* are in the second person.

sec·ond-rate (sek′ənd rāt′) *adj.* not best in some quality or degree; mediocre or inferior.

second sight, supposed power of seeing things that are not physically present, as distant or future events; clairvoyance.

second-story man *Informal.* burglar who enters a building through an upstairs window.

sec·ond-string (sek′ənd string′) *adj.* **1.** *Sports.* belonging to a less able group or team that does not play at the start of a game but may be substituted in later. **2.** not preferred or best; mediocre. —**sec′ond-string′er,** *n.*

second thought **1.** *also,* **second thoughts.** reservation or doubt about an earlier decision, idea, or course of action. **2. on second thought,** after reconsideration.

second wind, renewed energy after a brief rest.

se·cre·cy (sē′krə sē) *n.* **1.** state of being kept secret. **2.** ability or practice of keeping secrets.

se·cret (sē′krit) *adj.* **1.** known only to oneself or a few; kept from general knowledge: *a secret password.* **2.** having goals, methods, or ceremonies known only to the initiated: *a secret organization.* **3.** built or made to escape notice: *a secret panel.* **4.** beyond ordinary understanding; not readily apparent; mysterious. **5.** dependable in keeping confidence; close-mouthed; discreet. **6.** providing privacy; secluded. —*n.* **1.** that which is known only to oneself or a few and is kept from general knowledge: *to keep a secret.* **2.** short, often hidden reason or explanation: *the secret of one's success.* **3.** true method or way of attaining something; key: *the secret of happiness.* **4.** cause or process not readily understood or explained; mystery: *the secrets of nature.* **5. in secret.** not openly or in public; in private. [Old French *secret* hidden, discreet, from Latin *sēcrētus* hidden, past participle of *sēcernere* to put apart, separate.] —**se′cret·ly,** *adv.*

Syn. *adj.* **1. Secret, covert, stealthy** mean hidden. **Secret** is the broad term to imply being purposely kept from knowledge or view so as to escape detection: *The field commanders made secret plans to attack the enemy at night.* **Covert** suggests what is concealed or disguised, but does not imply the same fear of discovery as secret: *The couple exchanged covert signals at the auction.* **Stealthy** throws emphasis on an attempt to avoid notice in a manner characterized by slyness, quietness, and wariness: *The thief crept in a stealthy manner toward the door.*

secret agent, spy or other agent whose identity or operations are known only to a few, esp. one in the employ of a government.

se·cre·tar·i·al (sek′rə târ′ē əl) *adj.* of or relating to a secretary or a secretary's duties.

se·cre·tar·i·at (sek′rə târ′ē it, -at′) *n.* **1.** administrative department of an organization: *the secretariat of the United Nations.* **2.** officials who keep records or perform secretarial duties. **3.** office or position of a secretary, esp. of a government department. [French *secrétariat,* from Medieval Latin *secretariatus* office of a secretary, from Late Latin *sēcrētārius.* See SECRETARY.]

sec·re·tar·y (sek′rə târ′ē) *pl.,* **-tar·ies.** *n.* **1.** person employed to handle correspondence, do routine work, and keep records for an individual or company. **2.** officer of an organization or company responsible for important records and correspondence. **3.** one who heads an executive department of a government. **4.** piece of furniture having a fold-up writing surface, enclosed bookshelves, and drawers or compartments below. [Late Latin *sēcrētārius* confidential officer, going back to Latin *sēcrētus.* See SECRET.]

secretary bird, long-legged bird, *Sagittarius serpentarius,* native to the plains of southern Africa, having gray plumage. Height: to 4 feet.

Secretary bird

sec·re·tar·y-gen·er·al (sek′rə ter′ē jen′ər əl) *pl.,* **sec·re·tar·ies-gen·er·al.** *n.* chief administrative officer of a secretariat.

se·crete¹ (si krēt′) **-cret·ed, -cret·ing.** *v.t.* to produce by means of secretion: *Some glands secrete hormones.* [From SECRETION.]

se·crete² (si krēt′) **-cret·ed, -cret·ing.** *v.t.* to put in a hiding place; hide away. [Modification of obsolete *secret* to hide, from SECRET.]

se·cre·tion (si krē′shən) *n.* **1.** the process by which a particular substance is produced in an organism through some specialized cellular or glandular activity. **2.** the substance so produced. [Latin *sēcrētiō* separation.]

se·cre·tive (sē′kri tiv, si krē′-) *adj.* **1.** of, characterized by, or indicating secrecy or concealment: *a secretive smile.* **2.** secretory. —**se′cre·tive·ly,** *adv.* —**se′cre·tive·ness,** *n.*

se·cre·to·ry (si krē′tər ē) *adj.* relating to or causing secretion.

at; āpe; cär; end; mē; it; īce; hot; ōld; fôrk; wood; fōōl; oil; out; up; ūse; turn; sing; thin; this; zh in treasure; ə in ago, taken, pencil, lemon, circus.

Secret Service 1. division of the U.S. Treasury Department that protects the president and enforces federal laws against counterfeiting U.S. currency and bonds. **2.** *also,* **secret service.** government department or bureau that engages in such secret operations as espionage and counterespionage: *Her Majesty's secret service.*

secs. 1. seconds. **2.** sections.

sect (sekt) *n.* **1.** religious body, esp. a small group separated from a larger, established denomination. **2.** any relatively small group having the same philosophical or political principles, beliefs, or opinions. [Latin *secta* following, faction, school (of philosophy).]

Syn. 1. Sect, denomination, cult mean a system of organized religion. **Sect** is more frequently applied to a group that has differed with and broken away from an established church over matters of doctrine: *Buddhism has two main sects.* **Denomination** applies to a community of believers within a larger body, having common beliefs: *Baptists form one denomination of Protestants.* **Cult** is commonly used in reference to a system of unorthodox belief and worship carried on by a small group and often focusing on a single idea or personality: *The cult of Aphrodite was popular in ancient Greece.*

sect., section.

sec·tar·i·an (sek tār′ ən) *adj.* **1.** limited to one small and narrow group; not applying to all. **2.** of or relating to a religious sect: *a sectarian college.* —*n.* one who belongs to a religious sect.

sec·tar·i·an·ism (sek tār′ē ə niz′ əm) *n.* practice of being sectarian.

sec·ta·ry (sek′tər ē) *pl.,* **-ries.** *n.* **1.** dissenter from an established church, esp. a Protestant nonconformist. **2.** one who is sectarian. [Medieval Latin *sectarius* adherent, partisan, from Latin *secta.* See SECT.]

sec·tile (sek′til) *adj.* that can be cut or severed smoothly with a knife.

sec·tion (sek′shən) *n.* **1.** part of something separated or distinct from the rest; portion. **2.** subdivision of something written, as a book or document: *the sports section of the paper.* **3.** part, piece, or unit that fits together with others: *to replace several sections of pipe.* **4.** group of musicians who all play the same instrument or kind of instrument: *the violin section of the orchestra.* **5.** piece or segment within certain kinds of fruit, as grapefruit. **6.** region or area, as of a nation or other unit, having characteristics that distinguish it from the rest. **7.** drawing or other representation of something as it would appear if cut through to show its internal structure. **8.** thin slice of matter used for study with a microscope. **9.** act of cutting. **10.** special office or division, as of a bureau: *The message was sent to the decoding section.* **11.** measure of public land equal to one square mile or 640 acres and making up ¹⁄₃₆ of a township. **12.** portion of a railroad track maintained by one crew of workmen. —*v.t.* to divide, as by cutting into parts (often with *off*): *We sectioned off the pasture from the rest of the farm.* [Latin *sectiō* a cutting, from Latin *secāre* to cut.]

Syn. n. 1. Section, segment mean a portion or part considered apart from the whole. **Section** implies a conspicuously distinct and detached subdivision formed by or as if by cutting and dividing and set apart from other parts by certain characteristics: *She planted one section of the garden in herbs.* **Segment** suggests a constituent part set off from the whole by natural dividing lines: *She separated the orange into segments.*

sec·tion·al (sek′shən əl) *adj.* **1.** of, arising from, or characteristic of different regions or areas: *sectional interests.* **2.** made up of several sections or parts fitting into one another: *a sectional cabinet.* —**sec′tion·al·ly,** *adv.*

sec·tion·al·ism (sek′shən əl iz′əm) *n.* excessive concern for or emphasis on a particular region or area.

sec·tor (sek′tər) *n.* **1.** particular division or part, as of a population or economy: *the industrial sector of a country.* **2.** area; zone: *the American sector of Berlin.* **3.** *Geometry.* plane figure bounded by two radii of a circle and the intercepted arc. **4.** *Military.* distinct defense area within which a unit operates and for which it is responsible. [Late Latin *sector* the geometric figure, going back to Latin *secāre* to cut.]

sec·u·lar (sek′yə lər) *adj.* **1.** of or relating to the actual world or the prevailing order of events outside the church, rather than to the spiritual world. **2.** not concerned with or devoted to religion: *secular art.* **3.** existing or operating separately from or independently of any particular church or religious institution: *a secular system of public education.* **4.** (of clergy) living in an outside community, as a parish, rather than in a monastery or other purely religious community. **5.** occurring or observed once in a century or more: *the secular games of ancient Rome.* **6.** continuing through long ages: *secular changes of the earth's surface.* —*n.* priest who does not belong to a religious order. [Late Latin *saeculāris* worldly, profane, from Latin *saeculāris* relating to an age, from Latin *saeculum* age, generation.] —**sec′u·lar·ly,** *adv.*

sec·u·lar·ism (sek′yə lə riz′əm) *n.* indifference to or rejection of religion or religious control, as in civil matters or public education. —**sec′u·lar·ist,** *n., adj.* —**sec′u·lar·is′tic,** *adj.*

sec·u·lar·i·ty (sek′yə lar′ə tē) *n.* quality or condition of being secular.

sec·u·lar·ize (sek′yə lə rīz′) **-ized, -iz·ing.** *v.t.* **1.** to separate from religion or religious institutions; make secular. **2.** to transfer (church property) to secular ownership. —**sec′u·lar·i·za′tion,** *n.*

se·cure (si kyoor′) *adj.* **1.** not likely to be taken away; certain or guaranteed: *a secure job.* **2.** not exposed to danger, as of loss or attack; safe. **3.** free from worry, care, or fear: *Having insurance made him feel secure.* **4.** not likely to give way; stable: *The house stands on a secure foundation.* —*v.t.* **-cured, -cur·ing. 1.** to obtain; acquire; get: *to secure a hall for a meeting.* **2.** to put or fasten firmly in place: *to secure the hatches of a ship.* **3.** to bring about; effect: *to secure a desired result.* **4.** to make safe; guard; protect: *The gold shipments were secured against robbers.* **5.** to make sure or certain; guarantee. **6.** to pledge property for repayment of (a loan) or fulfillment of (a contract). [Latin *secūrus* free from care. Doublet of SURE.] —**se·cure′ly,** *adv.* —**se·cure′ment,** *n.* —**Syn.** *adj.* **2.** see **safe.** *v.t.* **1.** see **gain.**

se·cu·ri·ty (si kyoor′ə tē) *pl.,* **-ties.** *n.* **1.** protection from danger, as of loss or attack. **2.** freedom from worry, care, or fear. **3.** state of being certain or guaranteed: *The workers have job security and cannot be fired.* **4.a.** measures taken to guard, as against espionage or crime: *The building's security is good.* **b.** those assigned to carry out such measures. **5.** document representing some form of ownership or indebtedness, as a stock or bond: *He sold his securities to finance his son's education.* **6.** property given as a pledge, as for repayment of a loan or fulfillment of a contract. **7.** one who agrees to be financially responsible for another; surety. [Latin *securitās* freedom from care or danger.]

Security Council, body of the United Nations responsible for maintaining international peace, composed of five permanent members and ten rotating members elected by the General Assembly.

secy., secretary. Also, **sec'y.**

se·dan (si dan′) *n.* automobile with two or four doors, a solid roof, and a full-length seat in front and in back. [Of uncertain origin.]

sedan chair, conveyance for one person, consisting of an enclosed chair suspended on two poles carried by servants.

se·date (si dāt′) *adj.* quiet and restrained in style or manner; not excited or disturbed; calm. —*v.t.* **-dat·ed, -dat·ing.** to calm down or make sedate, with or as if with a sedative: *to sedate a patient.* [Latin *sēdātus* quiet, calm, past participle of *sēdāre* to settle, assuage.] —**se·date′ly,** *adv.* —**se·date′ness,** *n.*

se·da·tion (si dā′shən) *n.* **1.** state of being sedated: *The patient is under sedation.* **2.** act or process of sedating.

sed·a·tive (sed′ə tiv) *n.* **1.** drug or other agent that lessens nervous excitement. **2.** anything that lessens excitement, distress, or awareness. —*adj.* that lessens excitement; soothing; calming.

sed·en·tar·y (sed′ən ter′ē) *adj.* **1.** involving or engaging in little or no physical exercise, activity, or movement: *a sedentary life.* **2.** (of certain water animals, as barnacles) attached to one place or surface; not free-swimming. **3.** remaining in one area; not migratory: *sedentary birds.* [Latin *sedentārius* relating to sitting, going back to *sedēre* to sit.] —**sed′en·tar′i·ness,** *n.*

Se·der (sā′dər) *n.* in Judaism, religious service and ceremonial feast commemorating the Exodus from Egypt on Passover. [Hebrew *sēdher* order, arrangement, division.]

sedge (sej) *n.* any of a large group of grassy plants, genus *Carex,* growing in marshes and other wet areas, bearing spikelike clusters of tiny greenish flowers. [Old English *secg.*]

sed·i·ment (sed′ə mənt) *n.* **1.** matter that settles to the bottom of a liquid. **2.** *Geology.* solid matter carried in suspension from its original site and deposited by water, ice, or wind. **3.** anything left behind or deposited. [Latin *sedimentum* a settling.] —**sed·i·men·tal** (sed′ə ment′əl), *adj.*

sed·i·men·tar·y (sed′ə men′tər ē) *adj.* **1.** of or relating to sediment. **2.** formed from or by the deposit of sediment: *sedimentary rock.*

sed·i·men·ta·tion (sed′ə mən tā′shən) *n.* act or process of depositing or accumulating sediment.

se·di·tion (si dish′ən) *n.* speech or action inciting rebellion against the existing government. [Latin *sēditiō* dissension, insurrection.]

se·di·tious (si dish′əs) *adj.* **1.** taking part in, promoting, or advocating sedition. **2.** of, relating to, or containing sedition. —**se·di′tious·ly,** *adv.*

se·duce (si dōōs′, -dūs′) **-duced, -duc·ing.** *v.t.* **1.** to persuade to engage in sexual intercourse. **2.** to tempt or persuade, as with trickery or enticement: *The candidate seduced us with his false promise to reduce taxes.* [Late Latin *sēdūcere* to lead astray, from Latin *sēdūcere* to lead apart.] —**se·duc′a·ble;** *also,* **se·duc′i·ble,** *adj.* —**se·duc′er,** *n.*

se·duc·tion (si duk′shən) *n.* **1.** act of seducing; being seduced. **2.** that which seduces. Also, **se·duce′ment** (si dōōs′mənt).

se·duc·tive (si duk′tiv) *adj.* that seduces or aids in seducing; alluring; enticing. —**se·duc′tive·ly,** *adv.* —**se·duc′tive·ness,** *n.*

sed·u·lous (sej′ə ləs) *adj.* constant in application; diligent; industrious. [Latin *sēdulus* diligent, zealous, going back to *sē dolō* without deception.] —**se·du·li·ty** (si dōō′lə tē, -dū′-), **sed′u·lous·ness,** *n.* —**sed′u·lous·ly,** *adv.*

---

at; āpe; cär; end; mē; it; īce; hot; ōld; fôrk; wood; fōōl; oil; out; up; ūse; turn; sing; thin; this; zh in treasure; ə in ago, taken, pencil, lemon, circus.

se·dum (sē′dəm) *n.* stonecrop. [Latin *sedum* houseleek.]

see[1] (sē) saw, seen, see·ing. *v.t.* **1.** to perceive with the eyes; succeed in getting a view of: *Can you see the sign?* **2.** to perceive with the mind; understand: *I don't see why you have to leave so soon.* **3.** to attend as a spectator: *to see a movie.* **4.** to regard; judge; view: *My friend and I see things the same way.* **5.** to find out; ascertain: *I'll see what he wants.* **6.** to make sure: *See that she leaves on time.* **7.** to accompany; escort: *to see someone to the door.* **8.** to visit, encounter, or meet: *to see friends, to see a doctor.* **9.** to receive or admit, as for a visit, interview, or examination: *to see a patient.* **10.** to experience or undergo: *to see service in the Army.* **11.** to be marked or characterized by: *a corner that has seen many car accidents.* **12.** to predict or foresee: *I see many years of trouble ahead.* **13.** to prefer to have: *He'd see us fail rather than change his mind.* **14.** *Cards.* **a.** to match the bet of (a player). **b.** to match (a bet). **15. to see off.** to go with (someone leaving, as on a trip) to the departure point. **16. to see out.** to continue with to the end; finish. **17. to see things.** to seem to see something, although it isn't really there: *I thought I saw a ghost, but I must have been seeing things.* **18. to see through. a.** to continue with to the end. **b.** to aid or watch over in time of difficulty. —*v.i.* **1.** to have or use the power of sight. **2.** to understand; comprehend: *I see.* **3.** to judge or discover: *See for yourself.* **4. to see fit.** to judge or consider to be right: *Do it as you see fit.* **5. to see through.** to penetrate the true meaning or nature of. **6. to see to.** to attend to; take care of. [Old English *sēon* to perceive with the eyes, to perceive mentally.] —**Syn.** *v.t.* **1.** see *look*.

see[2] (sē) *n.* office or jurisdiction of a bishop. [Old French *sed, sied* seat, throne, from Latin *sēdēs* seat, abode.]

seed (sēd) *pl.*, **seeds** or **seed.** *n.* **1.** reproductive body that contains the developing embryo of a new plant. **2.** seeds collectively. **3.** any small roundish grainlike part or fruit, as a kernel of corn or a grain of wheat. **4.** any part of a plant that serves to reproduce it, as a tuber, bulb, or spore. **5.** sperm; semen. **6.** origin or beginning from which something larger will grow or develop: *seeds of dissent.* **7.** *Archaic.* children, descendants, or offspring collectively. ▲ construed as singular or plural. **8.a. to go to seed.** to become useless or run down; deteriorate. **b.** to reach the stage of developing and shedding seeds. —*v.t.* **1.** to sow (land) with seed. **2.** to sow seed. **3.** to remove the seeds from: *to seed a tomato.* **4.** *Sports.* **a.** to place (tournament contestants) so that stronger competitors will not meet each other in the early rounds. **b.** to arrange (a tournament) in this way. **5.** to spray (clouds) with dry ice, silver iodide crystals, or other substances in order to produce rain. —*v.i.* to produce seed. [Old English *sǣd* that which is sown, offspring.]

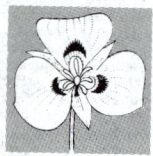

Seed coat
Epicotyl of embryo
Hypocotyl of embryo
Cotyledon
Hilum

Seed

seed·case (sēd′kās′) *n.* part of a flowering plant, as a pod or capsule, that contains the seeds; pericarp.

seed coat, protective covering of a seed. See **seed** for illustration.

seed·er (sē′dər) *n.* **1.** one who sows or plants seeds. **2.** device for sowing seeds. **3.** device for removing seeds, as from fruit.

seed leaf *Botany.* leaf forming part of the embryo in a seed; cotyledon.

seed·ling (sēd′ling) *n.* **1.** any young plant grown from a seed. **2.** young tree less than three feet high.

seed pearl, a very small pearl.

seeds·man (sēdz′mən) *pl.*, **-men.** *n.* **1.** one who scatters seed; sower of seed. **2.** dealer in seed.

seed·y (sē′dē) seed·i·er, seed·i·est. *adj.* **1.** no longer looking fresh, new, or prosperous; shabby; run down; gone to seed. **2.** having many seeds. —**seed′i·ness,** *n.*

see·ing (sē′ing) *conj.* considering the fact.

Seeing Eye dog, dog specially trained to be a guide and companion for a blind person. [From the *Seeing Eye,* Inc., a philanthropic organization founded near Morristown, New Jersey, in 1929, to breed and train such dogs.]

seek (sēk) sought, seek·ing. *v.t.* **1.** to go in search of; try to find; look for: *to seek a stolen car.* **2.** to try; attempt: *Every candidate seeks to win.* **3.** to desire or try to obtain; ask for: *to seek aid.* —*v.i.* to search; make inquiry: *Seek and ye shall find* (Matthew 7:7). [Old English *sēcan* to look for, ask for.] —**seek′er,** *n.*

seem (sēm) *v.i.* **1.** to give the feeling of being; present the outward appearance of being; appear to be: *The prisoner seemed much older than he really was.* **2.** to be or be true, so far as one can tell: *The child seems happy in his new home.* [Old Norse *sǣma* to honor, conform to.]

Syn. 1. Seem, appear mean to be so as far as one can tell, but not necessarily so in reality. **Seem** emphasizes an opinion or impression based on the outward aspect of something, and usually suggests some uncertainty: *He seems friendly but I will know for sure when I get to*

know him better. **Appear** stresses a visual impression that may be superficial, illusory, or distorted: *He appears well but he is really sick.*

seem·ing (sē′ming) *adj.* that is true, so far as one can tell: *seeming improvements in garbage collection.* —*n.* outward appearance. —**seem′ing·ly,** *adv.*

seem·ly (sēm′lē) -li·er, -li·est. *adj.* **1.** suitable, as to a purpose or occasion; decorous; proper: *It is not seemly to speak loudly in a church.* **2.** *Archaic.* pleasant to look at; handsome. [Old Norse *sǣmiligr* becoming.] —**seem′li·ness,** *n.*

seen (sēn) past participle of **see**[1].

seep (sēp) *v.i.* to spread or flow slowly, through or as through small pores: *Water seeped from the cracked pipe.* [Possibly form of dialectal English *sipe* to ooze, drip, from Old English *sipian.*]

seep·age (sē′pij) *n.* **1.** act or process of seeping. **2.** that which seeps.

seer (sēr) *n.* one who is believed to have a special power of foreseeing future events or of knowing hidden or profound things. —**seer′ess,** *n.*

seer·suck·er (sēr′suk′ər) *n.* lightweight fabric with a creped effect, usually woven with alternating plain and crinkled stripes, used chiefly for summer clothing and children's wear. [Hindi *sīrsakar,* from Persian *shīr o shakkar* striped linen garment; literally, milk and sugar (phrase used to describe the alternating stripes of the fabric).]

see·saw (sē′sô′) *n.* **1.** playground device consisting of a plank supported at the middle so that as one of its ends goes up the other goes down. Also, **tee′ter-tot′ter, teeter board.** **2.** any up-and-down or back-and-forth action or movement: *the seesaw of political power.* —*v.i.* **1.** to move up and down on a seesaw. **2.** to move, act, or proceed in a way similar to the action of a seesaw: *The battle seesawed back and forth, with neither side gaining an overwhelming advantage.* [Repetition of SAW[1], with vowel change in the first syllable; from the motion of persons sawing wood or stone.]

seethe (sēth) seethed, seeth·ing. *v.i.* **1.** to be in a state of intense, inward agitation, as from anger or frustration. **2.** to rise, surge, or form bubbles as if boiling: *The waves seethed around the rocks.* —*v.t. Archaic.* **1.** to soak or steep. **2.** to boil. [Old English *sēothan* to boil.]

seg·ment (seg′mənt) *n.* **1.** each of the parts into which a thing is or may be divided; division; section. **2.** *Geometry.* **a.** part of a plane figure cut off by a line, as a part of a circle bounded by an arc and a chord. **b.** part of a sphere cut off by a plane or by parallel planes. —*v.t., v.i.* to divide into segments. [Latin *segmentum* a piece cut off, from *secāre* to cut.] —**Syn.** *n.* **1.** see **section.**

seg·men·tal (seg men′təl) *adj.* of, relating to, or composed of segments. Also, **seg·men·tar·y** (seg′mən ter′ē). —**seg·men′tal·ly,** *adv.*

seg·men·ta·tion (seg′mən tā′shən) *n.* **1.** act or process of dividing into segments; state of being divided into segments. **2.** *Biology.* division of a cell into many others, as in a fertilized egg; cleavage.

segmentation cavity, blastocoele.

se·go (sē′gō) *pl.*, **se·gos.** *n.* **1.** lilylike, bell-shaped flower of the deserts of the western United States, usually white with pink, purple, or greenish-yellow markings. **2.** plant, *Calochortus nuttallii,* of the lily family, that bears this flower, having edible underground roots. Also, **sego lily.** [Of Paiute origin.]

Sego

seg·re·gate (seg′rə gāt′) -gat·ed, -gat·ing. *v.t.* **1.** to set apart from others or the rest; isolate: *to segregate a patient with a contagious disease.* **2.** to impose racial segregation upon (a group of people or an institution). —*v.i.* **1.** to become separate or separated; go apart. **2.** to have or practice racial segregation. [Latin *sēgregātus,* past participle of *sēgregāre* to set apart, set apart from the flock, from *sē* apart + *grex* flock.] —**seg′re·ga′tive,** *adj.*

Syn. *v.t.* **Segregate, isolate, seclude** mean to separate from others. **Segregate** is usually used in reference to a group that is separated from the main body and confined, often unwillingly, to a place or area: *In former times lepers were segregated in colonies.* **Isolate** suggests being cut off completely from the outside world, whether by choice, compulsion, or circumstances: *The flood waters isolated the town.* **Seclude** emphasizes a shielding from outside influences and a keeping apart from the company of others in an inaccessible place: *The millionaire secluded himself in his mountain retreat.*

seg·re·ga·tion (seg′rə gā′shən) *n.* **1.** practice of separating groups of people, esp. Negroes, from other people by making them live in certain areas and use different schools and social facilities. **2.** act or process of segregating; being segregated.

seg·re·ga·tion·ist (seg′rə gā′shə nist) *n.* one who practices or supports racial segregation.

Seid·litz powders (sed′lits) mild, effervescent laxative. [From *Seidlitz,* village in Czechoslovakia having a spring whose water has a similar laxative effect.]

sei·gneur (sēn yur′) *n.* seignior. [Middle French *seigneur* lord, sir,

at; āpe; cär; end; mē; it; īce; hot; ōld; fôrk; wood; fōōl; out; up; ūse; turn; sing; thin; this; zh in treasure; ə in ago, taken, pencil, lemon, circus.

going back to Latin *senior* elder, older person. Doublet of SEIGNIOR, SIEUR.]

seign·ior (sēn′yər) *n.* feudal nobleman, esp. the lord of a manor. [Old French *seignor* lord, sir, from Latin *senior* elder, older person. Doublet of SEIGNEUR, SIEUR.]

sei·gnio·ri·al (sēn yôr′ē əl) *adj.* of or relating to a seignior.

seign·ior·y (sēn′yər ē) *pl.*, -**ior·ies.** *n.* **1.** authority or jurisdiction of a seignior. **2.** domain of a seignior. **3.** group of lords, esp. such a group as the governing council of a medieval Italian republic. [Old French *seignorie* dominion, exalted position, power, from *seignor* lord. See SEIGNIOR.]

seine (sān) *n.* fishing net, esp. a long one that hangs vertically in the water, supported by floats on its upper edge and kept taut by weights on the bottom edge. —*v.t.*, *v.i.*, **seined, sein·ing.** to catch (fish) with a seine. [Old English *segne* fishing net that hangs vertically, from Latin *sagēna* large fishing net, from Greek *sagēnē*.] —**sein′er,** *n.*

Seine (sān) *n.* river flowing from eastern France northwestward into the English Channel.

seis·mic (sīz′mik, sīs′-) *adj.* of, relating to, caused by, or subject to earthquakes. [Greek *seismos* earthquake + -IC.]

seismo- *combining form* of earthquakes: *seismology.* [Greek *seismos* earthquake.]

seis·mo·gram (sīz′mə gram′, sīs′-) *n.* record made by a seismograph.

seis·mo·graph (sīz′mə graf′, sīs′-) *n.* instrument that records the direction, intensity, and duration of earthquakes and other earth vibrations. Also, **seis·mom′e·ter.** [SEISMO- + -GRAPH.]

seis·mog·ra·phy (sīz mog′rə fē, sīs-) *n.* art or science of using the seismograph in recording earthquakes or other earth vibrations. —**seis·mo·graph·ic** (sīz′mə graf′ik, sīs′-), *adj.*

seis·mol·o·gy (sīz mol′ə jē, sīs-) *n.* study of earthquakes and related phenomena. [SEISMO- + -LOGY.] —**seis·mo·log·i·cal** (sīz′mə loj′i kəl, sīs′-), *adj.* —**seis·mol′o·gist,** *n.*

seis·mom·e·ter (sīz mom′ə tər, sīs-) *n.* seismograph.

seize (sēz) *seized, seiz·ing. v.t.* **1.** to take hold of suddenly and forcibly; grab on to: *The dog greedily seized the bone.* **2.** to take away or gain control or possession of: *The health authorities seized the whole shipment of tainted food.* **3.** to take advantage of aggressively; make immediate use of: *to seize an opportunity.* **4.** to have a sudden and powerful effect on; possess; afflict: *Panic seized the crowd.* **5.** to bind or lash (ropes) together. **6.** *Law.* to put in possession of. —*v.i.* **to seize on** (or **upon**). to take hold of suddenly: *to seize on an idea.* [Old French *seisir* to take possession of, from Medieval Latin *sacire*; of Germanic origin.] —**Syn.** *v.t.* **1.** see **take. 2.** see **catch.**

seiz·ing (sē′zing) *n.* **1.** act of fastening together two ropes or the like with turns of small rope, cord, or a similar material. **2.** small rope, cord, or a similar material used for such a fastening. **3.** fastening made in such a way.

sei·zure (sē′zhər) *n.* **1.** act of seizing. **2.** sudden onset of a disease or of a symptom; attack.

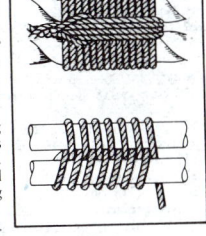

Seizing

Sek·on·di-Ta·ko·ra·di (sek′ən dē tä′kə rä′dē) *n.* port city in southern Ghana. Pop. (1960 est.), 123,300.

se·lah (sē′lə) *n.* word of unknown meaning frequently occurring at the end of a verse in the Psalms, believed to be a musical direction or an indication to the reader. [Hebrew *selāh.*]

se·lam·lik (si läm′lik) *n.* portion of a Muslim house reserved for men. [Turkish *selämliq,* from Arabic *salām* peace.]

sel·dom (sel′dəm) *adv.* on few occasions; rarely: *We seldom see him.* [Old English *seldan, seldum.*]

se·lect (si lekt′) *v.t.* **1.** to take or pick out from among many; choose: *to select a partner.* **2.** to be responsive to; accept: *The eye selects certain wavelengths of light.* —*v.i.* to make a selection; choose: *Don't select until you have seen what is available.* —*adj.* **1.** selected because of special excellence or fitness: *to coach a select group of athletes.* **2.** of high quality; choice: *select apples.* **3.** careful or fastidious in selecting; exclusive; discriminating. [Latin *sēlectus* chosen, past participle of *sēligere* to choose, pick out.] —**se·lect′ness,** *n.* —**Syn.** *v.t.* **1.** see **choose.**

se·lect·ee (si lek′tē′) *n.* one who is selected, esp. a draftee.

se·lec·tion (si lek′shən) *n.* **1.** act or process of selecting; being selected. **2.** one thing or that which is selected: *to read selections from a long novel.* **3.a.** one who or that which may be selected: *the selections on a menu.* **b.** group or variety of such selections. **4.** *Biology.* natural selection.

se·lec·tive (si lek′tiv) *adj.* **1.** that selects or is fastidious in selecting. **2.** that responds to or admits electromagnetic radiations of a certain frequency only.

selective service, compulsory military service according to age and physical fitness.

se·lec·tiv·i·ty (si lek′tiv′ə tē) *n.* **1.** state or quality of being selective. **2.** ability of a circuit or receiver to respond to electromagnetic waves of a particular frequency and exclude others.

se·lect·man (si lekt′mən) *pl.*, -**men.** *n.* member of a board that governs a town in most New England states.

se·lec·tor (si lek′tər) *n.* one who or that which selects.

Se·le·ne (si lē′nē) *n.* Greek goddess of the moon, often identified with Artemis.

sel·e·nite (sel′ə nīt′) *n.* clear, colorless variety of gypsum that often splits into large, thin plates. [Latin *selēnītēs,* from Greek *selēnītēs (lithos)* (stone) of the moon, from *selēnē* moon; because its brightness supposedly was affected by the phases of the moon.]

se·le·ni·um (si lē′nē əm) *n.* poisonous, nonmetallic element resembling sulfur in chemical properties and in having several allotropic forms. Its electrical conductivity increases with bright light, and it is used to make photoelectric cells and is found in the retina of the eye. Symbol: **Se** See **element** for table. [Modern Latin *selenium,* from Greek *selēnē* moon; by analogy with *tellurium,* similar element named after earth (Latin *tellūs*).]

Se·leu·cus I (si lōō′kəs) c.358–281 B.C., ruler of ancient Syria and most of Asia Minor from 312 to 281 B.C.

self (self) *pl.* **selves.** *n.* **1.** one's own person as distinguished from all others. **2.** qualities or characteristics which constitute a person or thing: *to appeal to one's better self.* **3.** personal interests, welfare, advantage, or the like. —*adj.* **1.** being the same throughout. **2.** of the same material as a garment or article itself: *a self belt.* [Old English *self* own, very, same.]

self- *prefix* **1.** of oneself or itself: *self-confidence, self-expression, self-contradiction.* **2.** by oneself or itself: *self-educated, self-contained, self-sustaining.* [From SELF.]

self-a·base·ment (self′ə bās′mənt) *n.* humiliation and degradation of oneself.

self-ab·ne·ga·tion (self′ab nə gā′shən) *n.* self-denial; selflessness.

self-ab·sorbed (self′ab sôrbd′, -zôrbd′) *adj.* preoccupied with one's own thoughts, interests, or activities. —**self-ab·sorp·tion** (self′ab-sôrp′shən, -zôrp′-), *n.*

self-act·ing (self′ak′ting) *adj.* working or moving independently without external influence or manipulation; automatic.

self-ad·dressed (self′ə drest′) *adj.* addressed to oneself: *I enclose a self-addressed envelope for returning the pictures to me.*

self-ad·vance·ment (self′əd vans′mənt) *n.* act of promoting oneself or one's own interests.

self-ap·point·ed (self′ə poin′tid) *adj.* appointed by oneself alone without the consent or support of others: *a self-appointed spokesman.*

self-as·ser·tion (self′ə sur′shən) *n.* act of insisting upon one's own ideas, claims, or superiority. —**self′-as·ser′tive,** *adj.*

self-as·sured (self′ə shoord′) *adj.* having confidence in oneself or being sure of one's ability, position, or worth. —**self′-as·sur′ance,** *n.*

self-cen·tered (self′sen′tərd) *also, British,* **self-cen·tred.** *adj.* preoccupied or engrossed in one's own thoughts, interests, or activities to the point of selfishness; egocentric.

self-clos·ing (self′klō′zing) *adj.* closing automatically: *a self-closing refrigerator door.*

self-com·mand (self′kə mand′) *n.* control of one's own actions or feelings; self-control; composure.

self-com·pla·cent (self′kəm plā′sənt) *adj.* overly pleased or satisfied with oneself or itself; complacent about itself: *a self-complacent bureaucracy.* —**self′-com·pla′cence,** *n.* —**self′-com·pla′cen·cy,** *n.* —**self′-com·pla′cent·ly,** *adv.*

self-com·posed (self′kəm pōzd′) *adj.* having or showing composure. —**self-com·pos·ed·ly** (self′kəm pō′zid lē), *adv.*

self-con·ceit (self′kən sēt′) *n.* too high an opinion of oneself or one's worth. —**self′-con·ceit′ed,** *adj.*

self-con·cept (self′kon′sept) *n.* self-image. Also, **self-con·cep·tion** (self′kən sep′shən).

self-con·fessed (self′kən fest′) *adj.* that has admitted oneself to be so: *a self-confessed liar.*

self-con·fi·dent (self′kon′fə dənt) *adj.* that has confidence or faith in one's own ability or worth. —**self′-con′fi·dence,** *n.* —**self′-con′fi·dent·ly,** *adv.*

self-con·scious (self′kon′shəs) *adj.* **1.** uncomfortably aware of one's own actions, words, or thoughts, esp. in the presence of others; highly sensitive to the attitudes and opinions of others toward oneself. **2.** showing such awareness or sensitivity: *a self-conscious laugh.* **3.** having consciousness of oneself as a separate, existing being. —**self′-con′scious·ly,** *adv.* —**self′-con′scious·ness,** *n.*

self·con·sist·ent (self'kən sis'tənt) *adj.* in agreement with oneself or itself. —**self'-con·sist'en·cy,** *n.*

self·con·tained (self'kən tānd') *adj.* **1.** reserved or restrained in behavior. **2.** having all that is necessary in oneself or itself; complete: *a self-contained machine.* **3.** having or showing self-control.

self·con·tra·dic·tion (self'kon'trə dik'shən) *n.* **1.** fact of contradicting or being inconsistent with oneself or itself. **2.** something, as a statement or concept, which contains elements that contradict one another.

self·con·tra·dic·to·ry (self'kon'trə dik'tər ē) *adj.* inconsistent with or contradicting oneself or itself.

self·con·trol (self'kən trōl') *n.* effective command or control over one's own actions or emotions.

self·crit·i·cal (self'krit'i kəl) *adj.* critical of oneself. —**self-crit·i·cism** (self'krit'ə siz'əm), *n.*

self·de·cep·tion (self'di sep'shən) *n.* act of deceiving or deluding oneself. Also, **self·de·ceit** (self'di sēt'). —**self'-de·cep'tive,** *adj.*

self·de·feat·ing (self'di fē'ting) *adj.* that has consequences which defeat or go against the original purpose.

self·de·fense (self'di fens') *also, British,* **self·de·fence.** *n.* act, practice, or right of defending and protecting oneself, as from attacks or threats.

self·de·ni·al (self'di nī'əl) *n.* practice of refusing to satisfy one's own immediate desires and interests, esp. from a moral, religious, or economic motive. —**self'-de·ny'ing,** *adj.*

self·de·struct (self'di strukt') *v.i.* to destruct.

self·de·struc·tion (self'di struk'shən) *n.* destruction of oneself, esp. suicide.

self·de·ter·mi·na·tion (self'di tur'mə nā'shən) *n.* **1.** deciding one's own actions or opinions without external influence. **2.** right of a people to determine the form of government they shall have. —**self'-de·ter'min·ing,** *adj.*

self·dis·ci·pline (self'dis ə plin) *n.* stern control or disciplining of one's own actions, responses, or emotions.

self·ed·u·cat·ed (self'ej'ə kā'tid) *adj.* educated by reading books or studying on one's own, without any formal classroom schooling or teachers. —**self'-ed'u·ca'tion,** *n.*

self·ef·fac·ing (self'i fā'sing) *adj.* tending to stay in the background; modest or shy. —**self'-ef·face'ment,** *n.* —**self'-ef·fac'ing·ly,** *adv.*

self·em·ployed (self'im ploid') *adj.* earning income from one's own business or profession rather than being paid by an employer. —**self'-em·ploy'ment,** *n.*

self·es·teem (self'es tēm') *n.* high opinion of oneself or one's abilities.

self·ev·i·dent (self'ev'ə dənt) *adj.* that requires no extra proof or reasoning to establish; evident in itself; obviously so.

self·ex·am·i·na·tion (self'ig zam'ə nā'shən) *n.* examination into or reconsideration of one's own physical condition, beliefs, motives, or interests.

self·ex·ist·ent (self'ig zis'tənt) *adj.* having an existence that does not depend on anything else.

self·ex·plan·a·to·ry (self'iks plan'ə tôr'ē) *adj.* needing no extra explanation or details; containing or being its own explanation: *The instructions are self-explanatory.*

self·ex·pres·sion (self'iks presh'ən) *n.* act or process of showing or making known one's thoughts, feelings, or true personality, as by means of art. —**self'-ex·pres'sive,** *adj.*

self·fer·ti·li·za·tion (self'furt'l i zā'shən) *n.* fertilization of a flower by its own pollen or of an animal by its own sperm.

self·gov·ern·ing (self'guv'ər ning) *adj.* **1.** that has or exercises self-government. **2.** that controls or regulates itself.

self·gov·ern·ment (self'guv'ərn mənt, -guv'ər-) *n.* government or rule of a political unit by its own citizens rather than by an external authority: *Many former colonies have achieved self-government.*

self·heal (self'hēl') *n.* low-growing weed, *Prunella vulgaris,* found widely distributed in temperate regions, bearing clusters of small, purple flowers. It was once used as a medicine.

self·help (self'help') *n.* act or condition of caring or providing for oneself or itself, rather than depending upon assistance from others: *The community needs more self-help and less patronizing aid.*

self·hyp·no·sis (self'hip nō'sis) *n.* act of hypnotizing oneself, as with special mental exercises.

self·i·den·ti·cal (self'ī den'ti kəl) *adj.* that is or remains the same as itself; identical. —**self'-i·den'ti·ty,** *n.*

self·im·age (self'im'ij) *n.* one's mental concept or picture of oneself, including esp. an opinion of one's own abilities and of the kind of person one is or wants to be.

self·im·mo·la·tion (self'im'ə lā'shən) *n.* intentional sacrificing of one's own body by burning, esp. as a protest against a social or political wrong.

self·im·por·tant (self'im pôrt'ənt) *adj.* having an exaggerated opinion of one's own importance; pompous and conceited. —**self'-im·por'tance,** *n.*

self·im·posed (self'im pōzd') *adj.* imposed by oneself: *a self-imposed restriction on eating sweet foods.*

self·im·prove·ment (self'im prōov'mənt) *n.* improvement of oneself through one's own efforts.

self·in·crim·i·na·tion (self'in krim'ə nā'shən) *n.* giving evidence against oneself that would make one liable to criminal prosecution.

self·in·duced (self'in dōōst', -dūst') *adj.* **1.** brought about or produced through one's own efforts: *self-induced hypnosis, self-induced illness.* **2.** produced by self-induction.

self·in·duc·tion (self'in duk'shən) *n.* ability of an electric circuit to produce an electromotive force when the current in the circuit changes.

self·in·dul·gence (self'in dul'jəns) *n.* indulgence of one's own weaknesses or desires. —**self'-in·dul'gent,** *adj.* —**self'-in·dul'gent·ly,** *adv.*

self·in·flict·ed (self'in flik'tid) *adj.* inflicted by oneself on oneself: *a self-inflicted cut.*

self·in·ter·est (self'in'trist, -tər ist) *n.* **1.** individual interest or advantage: *Preventing a war is in the self-interest of both countries.* **2.** principle or practice of regarding one's own welfare as more important than the welfare of others.

self·ish (sel'fish) *adj.* concerned for or serving one's own desires and interests above all others: *a selfish person, a selfish outlook.* [SELF + -ISH.] —**self'ish·ly,** *adv.* —**self'ish·ness,** *n.*

self·knowl·edge (self'nol'ij) *n.* awareness of one's own abilities and shortcomings.

self·less (self'lis) *adj.* having little thought for oneself; unselfish. —**self'less·ly,** *adv.* —**self'less·ness,** *n.*

self·load·ing (self'lō'ding) *adj.* (of firearms) automatic or semi-automatic.

self·love (self'luv') *n.* high regard for or love of oneself; pride or conceit.

self·made (self'mād') *adj.* **1.** made by oneself or itself. **2.** rising to wealth or success through one's own efforts: *a self-made man.*

self·mov·ing (self'mōō'ving) *adj.* capable of moving under its own power.

self·o·pin·ion·at·ed (self'ə pin'yə nā'tid) *adj.* **1.** conceited. **2.** holding stubbornly to one's own opinions.

self·per·pet·u·at·ing (self'pər pech'ōō ā'ting) *adj.* that continues as it is regardless of efforts or demands to change.

self·pit·y (self'pit'ē) *n.* feeling of pity for oneself.

self·pol·li·na·tion (self'pol'ə nā'shən) *n.* transfer of pollen from the anthers to the stigmas of the same flower or another flower on the same plant.

self·por·trait (self'pôr'trit, -trāt) *n.* portrait of oneself made by oneself.

self·pos·sessed (self'pə zest') *adj.* in control of oneself; composed; restrained. —**self·pos·ses·sion** (self'pə zesh'ən), *n.*

self·praise (self'prāz') *n.* praise of oneself.

self·pres·er·va·tion (self'prez'ər vā'shən) *n.* drive or desire to keep itself or oneself from injury, death, or danger.

self·pro·claimed (self'prō klāmd') *adj.* said or announced to be so by oneself, without proof or corroboration from others: *a self-proclaimed prophet.*

self·pro·pelled (self'prə peld') *adj.* containing its own means of propulsion, as an automobile.

self·pro·tec·tion (self'prə tek'shən) *n.* self-defense.

self·re·cord·ing (self'ri kôr'ding) *adj.* recording automatically.

self·reg·u·lat·ing (self'reg'yə lā'ting) *adj.* regulating oneself or itself without need for further external control. —**self'-reg'u·la'tion,** *n.*

self·re·li·ance (self'ri lī'əns) *n.* reliance on one's own resources or abilities. —**self'-re·li'ant,** *adj.*

self·re·proach (self'ri prōch') *n.* condemnation or censure of oneself by one's own conscience. —**self'-re·proach'ful,** *adj.*

self·re·spect (self'ri spekt') *n.* proper regard for or awareness of one's own worth and capabilities as a person. —**self'-re·spect'ing,** *adj.*

self·re·straint (self'ri strānt') *n.* restraint imposed by oneself upon one's own actions or behavior.

self·re·veal·ing (self'ri vē'ling) *adj.* revealing one's inner thoughts or feelings, esp. when not intentional. —**self'-rev'e·la'tion,** *n.*

self·right·eous (self'rī'chəs) *adj.* characterized by thinking that one's own actions and beliefs are more moral or right than those of others. —**self'-right'eous·ly,** *adv.* —**self'-right'eous·ness,** *n.*

self·ris·ing (self'rī'zing) *adj.* rising by itself, esp. without the addition of leaven, as flour.

self·sac·ri·fice (self'sak'rə fīs') *n.* the giving up or ignoring of one's own interests and desires for the sake of duty or the welfare of another. —**self'-sac'ri·fic'ing,** *adj.*

self·same (self'sām') *adj.* identical; same.

at; āpe; cär; end; mē; it; īce; hot; ōld; fôrk; wood; fōōl; oil; out; up; ūse; turn; sing; thin; <u>th</u>is; zh in treasure; ə in ago, taken, pencil, lemon, circus.

self·sat·is·fied (self′sat′is fīd′) *adj.* feeling or showing satisfaction with oneself or one's achievements. —**self′-sat′is·fac′tion,** *n.*

self·seal·ing (self′sē′ling) *adj.* able to seal itself: *a self-sealing tire.*

self·seek·ing (self′sē′king) *adj.* overly occupied in furthering one's own selfish interests; selfish. —*n.* selfishness.· —**self′-seek′er,** *n.*

self·ser·vice (self′sur′vis) *adj.* that requires or allows the users to serve themselves or operate the machines by themselves: *a self-service delicatessen; a self-service elevator.*

self·start·er (self′stär′tər) *n.* device that starts an internal-combustion engine automatically.

self·styled (self′stīld′) *adj.* called or designated so by oneself alone, without the agreement of others: *a self-styled judge of people's characters.*

self·suf·fi·cient (self′sə fish′ənt) *adj.* capable of fulfilling one's own needs; independent. —**self′-suf·fi′cien·cy,** *n.*

self·sup·port (self′sə pôrt′) *n.* support or provision for oneself without outside assistance. —**self′-sup·port′ing,** *adj.*

self·sus·tain·ing (self′səs tā′ning) *adj.* that sustains or keeps oneself or itself in existence without outside aid: *The program is self-sustaining because the trainees eventually become teachers.*

self·taught (self′tôt′) *adj.* taught by oneself without aid from others: *a self-taught bricklayer.*

self·willed (self′wild′) *adj.* obstinately adhering to one's own methods or aims, unmindful of the commands or wishes of others.

self·wind·ing (self′wīn′ding) *adj.* (of a clock or watch) not needing to be wound by hand; wound automatically.

Sel·juk (sel′jōōk, sel jōōk′) *n.* any member of a Turkish family who established several dynasties in western Asia during the eleventh and twelfth centuries. The Seljuks were Muslims and fought the Crusaders. —*adj.* of or relating to the Seljuks: *Seljuk Turks.* Also, **Sel·juk′i·an.**

sell (sel) **sold, sell·ing.** *v.t.* **1.** to transfer the possession or use of to someone else in return for money; accept money in payment for: *to sell a car, to sell time on a radio station.* **2.** to offer for sale; deal in: *Does this store sell shoes?* **3.** to bring about or promote the sale of: *Advertising sells soap.* **4.** to convince (someone) by vigorous, persuasive methods to do, approve, or accept something (with *on*): *to sell the bank on giving me a loan to open a new store.* **5.** to convince someone to do, approve, or accept (something) by such methods: *to sell a political candidate to the public.* **6. to sell out. a.** to betray: *Their leader sold them out by talking to the police.* **b.** to dispose of the whole of by selling: *to sell out one's stock of shoes.* —*v.i.* **1.** to sell goods, property, or the like, esp., to engage in selling things for a living. **2.** to be offered for sale or be sold: *an unwanted item that won't sell, fur coats that sell for $1000. All the items that were marked down sold quickly.* **3.** to gain acceptance: *The war program won't sell with the public.* **4. to sell out. a.** to dispose of the whole of a stock of goods, tickets, or the like: *Her size sold out.* **b.** to betray or give up on something, esp. for personal or material gain: *to sell out to your enemies.* [Old English *sellan* to hand over (for money), give.]

sell·er (sel′ər) *n.* **1.** one who sells or desires to sell. **2.** that which is sold, esp. that which is in great demand: *This new model car is the best seller we've ever had.*

sell·out (sel′out′) *also,* **sell-out.** *n.* **1.** act of selling out. **2.** performance or event for which all tickets have sold: *Friday night's championship fight was a sellout.*

selt·zer (selt′sər) *n.* **1.** soda water. **2.** *Seltzer.* naturally effervescent water containing various minerals and having a slightly salty taste. [Modification of German *Selterser* (water) of *Nieder selters,* West German village (near Wiesbaden) where this kind of mineral water was found.]

sel·vage (sel′vij) *also,* **sel·vedge.** *n.* narrow, tightly woven edge on a fabric that prevents unraveling. [SELF + EDGE.]

selves (selvz) plural of **self.**

se·man·tic (si man′tik) *adj.* **1.** of, based on, or concerned with the various meanings of words. **2.** of or having to do with the study of semantics.

se·man·tics (si man′tiks) *n.,pl.* branch of linguistics that deals with word meanings, esp. with regard to their historical development and change. ▲ construed as singular. [French *sémantique,* from Greek *sēmantikos* significant, going back to *sēma* sign.]

sem·a·phore (sem′ə fôr′) *n.* **1.** method of visual signaling using two flags, one held in each hand, the different positions of the arms representing the letters of the alphabet. **2.** any apparatus for signaling, as by a post with movable arms or an arrangement of lights or flags. —*v.i., v.t.,* **-phored, -phor·ing.** to signal by semaphore. [Greek *sēma* sign, signal + *-phoros* carrying.]

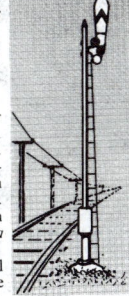

Semaphore

Se·ma·rang (sə mär′ang) *n.* port city in Indonesia, on the northern coast of Java. Pop. (1961), 487,006.

sem·blance (sem′bləns) *n.* **1.** outward show, similarity, or appearance, esp. one that is suspicious or false: *The shoplifter's face had a semblance of innocence.* **2.** likeness, image, or copy. [Old French *semblance* resemblance, appearance, from *sembler* to seem, resemble, from Latin *simulāre* to make like, represent.]

Sem·e·le (sem′ə lē) *n. Greek Mythology.* beautiful young woman who was stricken dead by thunderbolts when Zeus, at her request, dropped his disguise as a mortal and appeared as a god. Zeus rescued their unborn son Dionysus from her ashes.

se·men (sē′mən) *n.* fluid secreted by the testes, containing the male reproductive cells. [Latin *sēmen* seed.]

se·mes·ter (si mes′tər) *n.* division of an academic year, usually about eighteen weeks. [German *Semester,* from Latin *sēmēstris* relating to six months, semiannual, from *sex* six + *mēnsis* month.]

semi- *prefix* **1.** half: *semitone.* **2.** in part; partly; not completely: *semiconscious.* **3.** next to; just before: *semifinals.* [Latin *sēmi-* half.]

sem·i·an·nu·al (sem′ē an′ū əl) *adj.* occurring twice a year, esp. at six-month intervals. —**sem′i·an′nu·al·ly,** *adv.*

sem·i·a·quat·ic (sem′ē ə kwä′tic, -kwat′ik) *adj.* living near and often entering water, but not inhabiting it: *A beaver is a semiaquatic animal.*

sem·i·ar·id (sem′ē ar′id) *adj.* of or relating to an area having an annual average of less than twenty inches of precipitation, and characterized by grasslands, as the Great Plains of the United States.

sem·i·au·to·mat·ic (sem′ē ô′tə mat′ik) *adj.* **1.** partly automatic. **2.** (of firearms) firing one shot each time the trigger is pulled, without reloading or cocking.

sem·i·breve (sem′ē brēv′) *n. Music.* whole note.

sem·i·cir·cle (sem′ē sur′kəl) *n.* half a circle or something arranged in or resembling half a circle. —**sem′i·cir′cu·lar,** *adj.*

semicircular canal, any of three curved tubes of membrane opening into the vestibule of the inner ear that help the body maintain equilibrium.

sem·i·civ·i·lized (sem′ē siv′ə līzd′) *adj.* partly civilized.

sem·i·clas·si·cal (sem′ē klas′i·kəl) *adj.* partly classical, as in form.

sem·i·co·lon (sem′ē kō′lən) *n.* mark of punctuation (;) that indicates a grammatical separation stronger than that indicated by a comma, but not as strong as that indicated by a period.

sem·i·con·duc·tor (sem′ē kən duk′tər) *n.* material, as germanium or silicon, whose ability to conduct an electric current is greater than that of an insulator but less than that of a conductor, having a crystalline structure to which impurities, as arsenic or boron, are added to improve conductivity. Semiconductors are used in transistors.

sem·i·con·scious (sem′ē kon′shəs) *adj.* not completely conscious. —**sem′i·con′scious·ly,** *adv.* —**sem′i·con′scious·ness,** *n.*

sem·i·des·ert (sem′ē dez′ərt) *n.* arid region or area with very sparse vegetation.

sem·i·de·tached (sem′ē di tacht′) *adj.* **1.** (of a building) sharing one side wall with another building. **2.** partially detached or separate.

sem·i·di·vine (sem′ē di vīn′) *adj.* half ordinary or mortal and half divine.

sem·i·fi·nal (sem′ē fīn′əl) *adj.* immediately preceding the final match, as in a tournament. —*n.* semifinal match.

sem·i·fi·nal·ist (sem′ē fīn′əl ist) *n.* one who takes part in a semifinal match.

sem·i·lit·er·ate (sem′ē lit′ər it) *adj.* **1.** able to read and write only a little. **2.** able to read but not write.

sem·i·lu·nar (sem′ē lōō′nər) *adj.* shaped like a half moon.

semilunar valve, either of two heart valves consisting of three crescent-shaped flaps located at the opening of the aorta and at the opening of the pulmonary artery, that allow blood to flow out of the ventricles and keep it from flowing back into the heart.

sem·i·met·al (sem′ē met′əl) *n.* metalloid. —**sem′i·me·tal′lic,** *adj.*

sem·i·month·ly (sem′ē munth′lē) *adj.* appearing or occurring two times a month. —*n. pl.,* **-lies.** anything which takes place two times a month, as a periodical. —*adv.* twice a month.

sem·i·nal (sem′in əl) *adj.* **1.** of, relating to, or containing semen or seed. **2.** of, belonging to, or promoting early growth or development. [Latin *sēminālis* relating to seed, from *sēmen* seed.]

sem·i·nar (sem′ə när′) *n.* **1.** group of scholars, esp. advanced college or university students, selected to do supervised study or research. **2.** meeting or course of study where such a group reports and discusses

Semicircular canals
Stapes Cochlea
Semicircular canals

its findings. [German *Seminar* class for advanced, supervised research, from Latin *sēminārium* nursery garden, seed plot, from *sēmen* seed. Doublet of SEMINARY.]

sem·i·nar·y (sem'ə ner'ē) *pl.,* **-nar·ies.** *n.* **1.** institution for the education of men for the priesthood, ministry, or rabbinate. **2.** school or academy at or beyond the high school level, esp. a boarding school for young women. [Latin *sēminārium* nursery garden, seed plot, from *sēmen* seed. Doublet of SEMINAR.] **—sem·i·nar·i·an** (sem'ə nār'-ē ən), *n.*

sem·i·na·tion (sem'ə nā'shən) *n.* act of sowing or disseminating.

sem·i·nif·er·ous (sem'i nif'ər əs) *adj.* **1.** *Botany.* bearing or producing seed. **2.** containing or conveying semen. [Latin *sēmen* seed + -FEROUS.]

sem·i·niv·o·rous (sem'i niv'ər əs) *adj.* feeding on seeds. [Latin *sēmin-,* stem of *sēmen* seed + *-vorus* devouring.]

Sem·i·nole (sem'ə nōl') *pl.,* **-noles** or **-nole.** *n.* member of a tribe of Muskogean North American Indians closely related to the Creeks, who originally lived in Florida. Most of this tribe now lives in Oklahoma but a small number remain in the Florida Everglades.

sem·i·of·fi·cial (sem'ē ə fish'əl) *adj.* having some degree of authority; partly official.

sem·i·per·me·a·ble (sem'ē pur'mē ə bəl) *adj.* (of a membrane) that permits the passage of solvent molecules but not solute molecules, or the passage of liquids but not the colloidal particles dispersed in them.

sem·i·pre·cious (sem'ē presh'əs) *adj.* (of gems and minerals) having some commercial value, but less than that of precious stones.

sem·i·pri·vate (sem'ē prī'vit) *adj.* partly private, as a hospital room shared by two to four patients.

sem·i·pro (sem'ē prō') *n.* semiprofessional.

sem·i·pro·fes·sion·al (sem'ē pro fesh'ən əl) *n.* one who engages in an activity, as a sport, on a part-time basis, receiving some form of remuneration, as a salary or expenses. **—adj. 1.** engaged in an activity, as a sport, for some form of remuneration, but on a part-time basis. **2.** of, having to do with, or engaged in by semiprofessionals: *semiprofessional football.*

sem·i·qua·ver (sem'ē kwā'vər) *n. Music.* sixteenth note.

Se·mir·a·mis (sə mir'ə mis) *n.* legendary queen of Assyria who ruled the city of Nineveh after her husband's death and founded Babylon.

sem·i·skilled (sem'ē skild') *adj.* possessing or requiring limited skill, training, or ability.

sem·i·sweet (sem'ē swēt') *adj.* slightly sweetened, as chocolate.

Sem·ite (sem'īt) *n.* **1.** member of a group of peoples speaking related languages, living predominantly in the Middle East and parts of Africa, and including in modern times, Hebrews, Arabs, Syrians, and a number of Ethiopians. **2.** a Jew.

Se·mit·ic (sə mit'ik) *adj.* of or relating to Semites. *—n.* subdivision of the Semito-Hamitic language family, including Hebrew, Arabic, Syrian, and such ancient languages as Aramaic, Phoenician, and Assyrian.

Sem·i·tism (sem'ə tiz'əm) *n.* **1.** Semitic traits or characteristics. **2.** word or idiom of the Semitic language. **3.** inclination or tendency in favor of Jews.

Sem·i·to·Ha·mit·ic (sem'ə tō ha mit'ik) *adj.* of or belonging to a family of languages of various parts of Africa and in the Middle East, including Arabic, Hebrew, and Berber.

sem·i·tone (sem'ē tōn') *n. Music.* half step *(def. 1).*

sem·i·trail·er (sem'ē trā'lər) *n.* **1.** trailer with no front wheels, designed to be attached to a tractor. **2.** truck consisting of a tractor and a semitrailer.

sem·i·trans·par·ent (sem'ē trans par'ənt) *adj.* partly or imperfectly transparent.

sem·i·trop·i·cal (sem'ē trop'i kəl) *adj.* subtropical.

sem·i·vow·el (sem'ē vou'əl) *n.* letter or sound that has the vocal quality of a vowel but is used as a consonant. In English, *w* and *y* are often considered semivowels.

sem·i·week·ly (sem'ē wēk'lē) *adj.* issued or occurring twice a week: *a semiweekly newspaper.* *—adv.* twice a week. *—n. pl.,* **-lies.** semiweekly publication.

sem·i·year·ly (sem'ē yēr'lē) *adj.* issued or occurring twice a year or once every six months. *—adv.* two times a year. *—n. pl.,* **-lies.** that which is issued or occurs twice a year.

sem·o·li·na (sem'ə lē'nə) *n.* hard, coarsely ground kernels of wheat that are left when fine-ground flour is sifted out, used in making soup, pudding, and pasta. [Italian *semolino,* diminutive of *semola* bran, fine flour, from Latin *simila* fine flour.]

sem·pi·ter·nal (sem'pi tur'nəl) *adj.* having no end; lasting forever; eternal. [Late Latin *sempiternālis,* going back to Latin *semper* always + *aeternus* everlasting.] **—sem'pi·ter'nal·ly,** *adv.*

semp·stress (semp'stris, sem'-) *n.* seamstress.

sen (sen) *pl.,* **sen.** *n.* one-hundredth of a yen in Japanese currency. [Japanese *sen,* from Chinese (Mandarin) *ch'ien* coin, money.]

Sen. 1. Senate. **2.** Senator. **3. sen.** senior.

sen·ate (sen'it) *n.* **1.** governing or lawmaking council or assembly. **2. Senate. a.** upper chamber of the legislature of the United States or of most states of the United States. **b.** similar chamber in other countries. **c.** in ancient Rome, ruling body of citizens selected from the patricians and wealthy plebeians. [Latin *senātus* the council of elders of ancient Rome, from *senex* old, old man.]

sen·a·tor (sen'ə tər) *also,* **Sen·a·tor.** *n.* member of a senate. **—sen'a·tor·ship',** *n.*

sen·a·to·ri·al (sen'ə tôr'ē əl) *also,* **Sen·a·to·ri·al.** *adj.* of, relating to, electing, consisting of, or befitting a senator or a senate: *a senatorial debate.*

send (send) **sent, send·ing.** *v.t.* **1.** to cause to go to a certain place or from one place to another: *to send the news by telegraph, to send a spacecraft into orbit.* **2.** to cause to go into a certain state: *to send one's mind reeling.* **3.** to cause to occur: *The music sent thrills up and down my back.* *—v.i.* **1.** to send messages or a signal, as on a radio. **2.** to ask someone to get or bring someone or something: *to send out for a pizza.* [Old English *sendan* to dispatch, cause to go, cause to happen.] **—send'er,** *n.*

Syn. *v.t.* **1. Send, dispatch, transmit** mean to cause to go from one place to another. **Send** is the general term and stresses what or who initiates or impels action: *Every Christmas Jack sends gifts to all his friends.* **Dispatch** stresses the act of sending and suggests urgency and efficiency as an important element: *The police dispatched an ambulance to the scene of the accident.* **Transmit** emphasizes the means of sending and is more appropriately used in relation to immaterial things: *The news was transmitted by radio.*

Sen·dai (sen'dī') *n.* city in Japan, on the northeastern coast of Honshu. Pop. (1960), 425,250.

send-off (send'ôf') *n. Informal.* demonstration of good will in honor of the start of a journey, new career, or the like.

Sen·e·ca (sen'ə kə) *n.* member of the largest tribe of the Iroquois Confederacy of North American Indians, formerly living in western New York State. [Dutch *Sennecaas* name for a confederation of Iroquois tribes (including the Seneca tribe); probably of Algonquian origin.]

Sen·e·ca, Lucius An·nae·us (sen'ə kə; ə nē'əs) 4 B.C.–65 A.D., Roman philosopher and dramatist.

Sen·e·gal (sen'ə gôl') *n.* **1.** country in western Africa, on the Atlantic. Capital, Dakar. Area, 76,124 sq. mi. Pop. (1967 est.), 3,670,000. **2.** river in western Africa, on the southern border of the Sahara, flowing into the Atlantic.

Sen·e·gal·ese (sen'ə gô lēz', -lēs') *pl.,* **-ese.** *n.* native or inhabitant of Senegal. *—adj.* of, relating to, or characteristic of Senegal, its people, or their language.

se·nes·cent (si nes'ənt) *adj.* growing old; aging. [Latin *senēscēns,* present participle of *senēscere* to grow old, going back to *senex* old, old man.] **—se·nes'cence,** *n.*

sen·es·chal (sen'ə shəl) *n.* official in charge of a royal or noble household, esp. in medieval times. [Old French *seneschal;* of Germanic origin.]

se·nile (sē'nīl) *adj.* **1.** suffering loss or weakness of bodily health and strength and mental powers, as often occurs in old age. **2.** of, having to do with, or caused by old age. [Latin *senīlis* relating to old people, aged, from *senex* old man.] **—se'nile·ly,** *adv.*

se·nil·i·ty (si nil'ə tē) *n.* **1.** physical and, sometimes, mental infirmities of old age. **2.** state of being old.

sen·ior (sēn'yər) *adj.* **1.** older of two. Distinguished from **junior.** ▲ used after the name of a father whose son has the same name: *John Smith, Senior.* **2.** of relatively old age or long experience or service: *a senior member of the legal profession.* **3.** of higher position or rank, esp. after long service: *senior officers of the army.* **4.** (of a U.S. senator) that has occupied his or her seat longer than the other senator from the same state. **5.** relating to, enrolled in, or designating the final year of high school or college. *—n.* **1.** one who is older than another. **2.** student in the final year of high school or college. **3.** old person. [Latin *senior* older, comparative of *senex* old. Doublet of SIRE.]

senior high school, school attended after junior high school, usually including grades nine or ten through twelve.

sen·ior·i·ty (sēn yôr'ə tē, -yor'-) *n.* state of being more advanced than another or others in age, position, or period of service, sometimes qualifying one for special power or consideration, pay raises, promotions, and the like.

sen·na (sen'ə) *n.* **1.** laxative made from the dried leaves of any of various tropical plants, genus *Cassia.* **2.** dried leaves themselves. [Modern Latin, from Arabic *sanā.*]

Sen·nach·er·ib (sə nak'ər ib) *n.* died 681 B.C., king of Assyria, from 705 to 681 B.C.

sen·nit (sen′it) *n.* **1.** flat, plaited cordage made by braiding strands of rope yarn or similar fiber. **2.** plaited grass or a similar material used esp. for making hats. [Of uncertain origin.]

se·ñor (sen yôr′) *pl.*, **se·ño·res** (sen yôr′ās). *n.* sir; mister. ▲ Spanish form of polite or respectful address for a man. [Spanish *señor*, from Latin *senior* older, comparative of *senex* old, old man.]

se·ño·ra (sen yôr′ə) *n.* mistress; madame. ▲ Spanish form of respectful or polite address for a married woman. [Spanish *señora*, feminine of *señor*. See SEÑOR.]

se·ño·ri·ta (sen′yə rē′tə) *n.* miss. ▲ Spanish form of respectful or polite address for an unmarried girl or woman. [Spanish *señorita*, diminutive of *señora*. See SEÑORA.]

Sennit

sen·sate (sen′sāt) *adj.* capable of feeling and perceiving; having consciousness or sensibility. [Late Latin *sēnsātus* gifted with sense, from Latin *sēnsus*. See SENSE.]

sen·sa·tion (sen sā′shən) *n.* **1.** conscious impression resulting from the effect of a stimulus on a sense organ: *the sensation of touch.* **2.** action or power of the senses collectively. **3.** vague feeling arising from some particular circumstance: *a sensation of something wrong.* **4.** state of excitement or intense interest: *The new book caused a sensation in literary circles.* **b.** that which causes such excitement or interest.

sen·sa·tion·al (sen sā′shən əl) *adj.* **1.** arousing or intended to arouse intense excitement or interest: *sensational newspaper exposés.* **2.** of or having to do with the senses. **3.** *Informal.* exceptionally good; spectacular; great: *Susan looked sensational in her new dress.* **—sen′sa′tion·al·ly**, *adv.*

sen·sa·tion·al·ism (sen sā′shən əl iz′əm) *n.* **1.** practice or effect of presenting sensational things in order to excite or stimulate an audience or public: *the sensationalism of a scandal magazine.* **2.** *Philosophy.* extreme form of empiricism, holding that knowledge is derived only from sensation. **—sen′sa′tion·al·ist**, *n., adj.*

sense (sens) *n.* **1.** any of the special modes or types of sensation, as sight, hearing, smell, taste, and touch. **2.** that which is reasonable or logical: *Talk sense.* **3.** wisdom or usefulness: *What is the sense of merely protesting if nothing ever comes of it?* **4.** meaning or signification: *a word with many senses.* **5.** vague consciousness or feeling: *a sense of well-being.* **6.** mental or emotional capacity to perceive or appreciate (with *of*): *a sense of humor.* **7.** *also*, **senses.** normal, sound mental faculties: *a person of good sense.* **8.** final, briefly summarized opinion or judgment: *The sense of the meeting was that we need a new chairman.* **9.** sensation (def. 4). **—v.t.**, **sensed**, **sens·ing.** to be conscious of; feel: *We sensed the tension in the conference room.* [Latin *sēnsus* perception, feeling, understanding.] **—Syn.** *n.* **see meaning.**

sense·less (sens′lis) *adj.* **1.** lacking wisdom, usefulness, or logic; foolish; stupid: *a senseless action.* **2.** unconscious: *The blow knocked him senseless.* **3.** not conveying anything; having no meaning; lacking signification: *senseless slogans.* **—sense′less·ly**, *adv.* **—sense′less·ness**, *n.*

sense organ, any of the organs that receive stimuli, including the eyes, ears, nose, taste buds, and the like.

sen·si·bil·i·ty (sen′sə bil′ə tē) *pl.*, **-ties.** *n.* **1.** refined or delicate feeling or feeling of what is decent and right. **2.** capacity to receive and respond to sensory stimuli.

sen·si·ble (sen′sə bəl) *adj.* **1.** having, exhibiting, or characterized by good sense or judgment; logical; judicious: *a sensible man, a sensible decision.* **2.** that can be easily perceived, noticed, or detected by the mind or senses; marked: *a sensible error in a calculation.* **3.** taking notice; conscious; aware (with *of*): *to be sensible of another's feelings.* [Late Latin *sēnsibilis* able to perceive, that can be perceived, from Latin *sēnsus*, past participle of *sentīre* to perceive, feel.] **—sen′si·ble·ness**, *n.* **—sen′si·bly**, *adv.*

sen·si·tive (sen′sə tiv) *adj.* **1.** easily or readily affected by (with *to*): *sensitive to cold.* **2.** easily damaged, hurt, or irritated: *A baby's skin is very sensitive.* **3.** capable of receiving, discriminating, or registering outward processes or stimuli: *a very sensitive seismograph for recording the slightest tremors.* **4.** likely to be painful or cause pain with any slight contact: *My sprained toe is very tender and sensitive.* **5.** quick to take offense; having a sore spot; touchy: *He is very sensitive on the subject of religion.* **6.** keenly attuned to or sensible of what goes on, esp. of the feelings of others. **7.** that is under great pressure or is the focus of many oppositions or conflicts; precarious; ticklish: *a sensitive post in the defense department.* **8.** of, having to do with, or affecting the senses of sensation. **—n.** one who is unusually receptive to occult or psychic powers. [Medieval Latin *sensitivus* relating to sensation, from Latin *sēnsus*, past participle of *sentīre* to perceive, feel.] **—sen′si·tive·ly**, *adv.* **—sen′si·tive·ness**, *n.*

sensitive plant. 1. shrubby, tropical American plant, *Mimosa pudica*, whose leaflets fold up when touched. **2.** any of various other plants sensitive to touch.

sen·si·tiv·i·ty (sen′sə tiv′ə tē) *n.* **1.** state, condition, or degree of being sensitive. **2.** degree to which a radio or television receiver responds to incoming signals.

sen·si·tize (sen′sə tīz′) **-tized**, **-tiz·ing.** *v.t.* to make sensitive. **—sen′si·ti·za′tion**, *n.*

sen·sor (sen′sər, -sôr) *n.* any of various devices used to measure or detect light, radiation, heat, or other stimuli and to transmit a resulting electrical impulse, as for operating a control.

sen·so·ri·um (sen sôr′ē əm) *pl.*, **-so·ri·a** or **-so·ri·a** (-sor′ē ə). *n.* *Archaic.* seat or locale of receiving sensations; part of the brain that receives impressions of sensation. [Late Latin *sēnsōrium* the seat or organ of sensation, from Latin *sēnsus*, past participle of *sentīre* to perceive, feel.]

sen·so·ry (sen′sər ē) *adj.* of, relating to, consisting of, or conveying sensation: *sensory stimulation, a sensory nerve.*

sen·su·al (sen′shō̅̅ al) *adj.* **1.** that enjoys and seeks bodily, esp. sexual, pleasure and gratification. **2.** physically pleasing or alluring: *full, sensual, red lips.* **3.** of or relating to stimulation of the body or senses rather than the spirit or intellect: *sensual delights.* [Late Latin *sensuālis* endowed with feeling, from Latin *sēnsus* perception, feeling.] **—sen′su·al·ly**, *adv.*

sen·su·al·ist (sen′shō̅̅ ə list) *n.* one who is given to or has sensuality. **—sen′su·al·ism**, *n.*

sen·su·al·i·ty (sen′shō̅̅ al′ə tē) *n.* **1.** state or quality of being sensual. **2.** lewdness.

sen·su·al·ize (sen′shō̅̅ ə līz′) **-ized**, **-iz·ing.** *v.t.* to make sensual.

sen·su·ous (sen′shō̅̅ əs) *adj.* **1.** of, relating to, or affecting the senses. **2.** sensual. **—sen′su·ous·ly**, *adv.* **—sen′su·ous·ness**, *n.*

sent (sent) past tense and past participle of **send.**

sen·tence (sen′təns) *n.* **1.** formal unit of spoken or written language that consists of a word or words expressing a complete thought. It usually contains a subject and predicate. **2.** *Law.* **a.** judgment by a court or judge setting the punishment of a defendant after conviction. **b.** the punishment itself. **3.** *Archaic.* saying; maxim. **4.** *Mathematics.* any statement that expresses a relationship between numbers. A sentence may be true, as 5 + 3 = 8, false, as 6 − 2 = 3, or neither true nor false, as X + 4 > 7. A **closed sentence** has no unknown quantities, as 3 + 2 = 5; an **open sentence** contains at least one variable, as X + 6 = 15. **—v.t.**, **-tenced**, **-tenc·ing.** to set the punishment of: *The judge sentenced her to three months in jail for stealing.* [Old French *sentence* opinion, decision given by judges, punishment, from Latin *sententia* opinion, way of thinking.] **—sen·ten′tial** (sen ten′shəl), *adj.*

sen·ten·tious (sen ten′shəs) *adj.* **1.** inclined to sermonize; moralistic; affected; pompous. **2.** tending to use trite phrases or maxims. [Latin *sententiōsus* full of meaning, pithy, from *sententia* opinion, way of thinking.] **—sen·ten′tious·ly**, *adv.* **—sen·ten′tious·ness**, *n.*

sen·tience (sen′shəns) *n.* ability to receive sense impressions or sensory stimuli; capacity for feeling.

sen·tient (sen′shənt) *adj.* capable of experiencing sensation; having the power of feeling. [Latin *sentiēns*, present participle of *sentīre* to preceive, feel.]

sen·ti·ment (sen′tə mənt) *n.* **1.** mental attitude or point of view, esp. one arrived at after deliberation; opinion: *Popular sentiment is against the war.* **2.** expression of feeling or emotion or the feeling or emotion expressed: *I appreciate the sentiment, but you didn't have to buy me a gift.* **3.** refined or tender emotion. **4.** emotion that is exaggerated and mawkish. **5.** thought or attitude based on or reflecting an emotion. [Medieval Latin *sentimentum* opinion, feeling, from Latin *sentīre* to preceive, feel.]

sen·ti·men·tal (sen′tə ment′əl) *adj.* **1.** characterized by or showing emotion or feeling: *a sentimental song.* **2.** influenced by or apt to be swayed by feeling. **3.** appealing to the emotions rather than to reason: *The candidate made a sentimental plea for support.* **4.** having to do with, or based on sentiment: *sentimental reasons.* **5.** characterized by exaggerated and mawkish emotion. **—sen′ti·men′tal·ly**, *adv.*

sen·ti·men·tal·ism (sen′tə ment′əl iz′əm) *n.* **1.** quality or state of being sentimental. **2.** instance of this. **—sen′ti·men′tal·ist**, *n.*

sen·ti·men·tal·i·ty (sen′tə men tal′ə tē, -mən-) *pl.*, **-ties.** *n.* **1.** quality or state of being sentimental. **2.** instance of this.

sen·ti·men·tal·ize (sen′tə ment′əl īz′) **-ized**, **-iz·ing.** *v.i.* to be sentimental; indulge in sentiment. **—v.t.** **1.** to make (someone or something) an object of sentiment. **2.** to make sentimental. **—sen′ti·men′tal·i·za′tion**, *n.*

sen·ti·nel (sent′ən əl) *n.* person or animal that is stationed to keep watch and alert others of danger; guard; sentry. **—v.t.** **-neled**, **-nel·ing**; *also, British,* **-nelled**, **-nel·ling.** to watch over as a sentinel. [French *sentinelle* sentry, from Italian *sentinella* sentry, probably going back to Latin *sentīre* to perceive, feel.]

sen·try (sen′trē) *pl.*, **-tries.** *n.* **1.** sentinel, esp. a soldier stationed to keep watch and alert others of danger. **2.** watch kept by a sentry. [Possibly abbreviation of obsolete *centrinel*, form of SENTINEL.]

---

at; āpe; cär; end; mē; it; īce; hot; ōld; fôrk; wood; fo͞ol; oil; out; up; ūse; turn; sing; thin; this; zh in treasure; ə in ago, taken, pencil, lemon, circus.

sentry box. small building or booth intended to shelter a sentry at his post.

Seoul (sōl, sä ōōl′) *n.* capital and largest city of South Korea, in the northwestern part of the country. Pop. (1965 est.), 3,470,-900. Also, **Kei′jo.**

Sep. 1. September. **2.** Septuagint.

se·pal (sē′pəl) *n.* one of the leaflike divisions of the calyx of a flower, usually green but sometimes, as in the tulip, the same color as the petals. [Modern Latin *sepalum,* from modification of Greek *skepē* covering + Modern Latin *petalum.* See PETAL.]

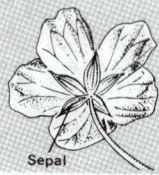
Sepal

Sepals of a geranium

sep·a·ra·ble (sep′ər ə bal, sep′rə-) *adj.* that can be separated. —**sep′a·ra·bil′i·ty,** *n.* —**sep′a·ra·bly,** *adv.*

sep·a·rate (*v.,* sep′ə rāt′; *adj., n.,* sep′ər it) **-rat·ed, -rat·ing.** *v.t.* **1.** to keep apart, esp. by acting as or placing a barrier between; divide: *A fence separates the garden from the sidewalk.* **2.** to set apart; disconnect: *to separate reason from emotion.* **3.** to divide or sort into individual parts or elements: *to separate a tangle of threads.* **4.** *Law.* to cause (a married couple) to live apart by court order. —*v.i.* **1.** to come apart; withdraw; part: *At the bell, the fighters separated and returned to their corners.* **2.** (of a married couple) to live apart but without a divorce. —*adj.* **1.** set apart or divided from others: *two separate rooms.* **2.** different; distinct: *Those are separate problems and cannot be handled in the same manner.* **3.** single; individual: *each separate item on a list.* —*n.* **separates.** coordinated articles of clothing designed to be worn in various combinations. [Latin *sēparātus,* past participle of *sēparāre* to part, divide.] —**sep′a·rate·ly,** *adv.*

sep·a·ra·tion (sep′ə rā′shən) *n.* **1.** act or process of separating; being separated. **2.** point at which two or more objects or parts are divided from each other; division. **3.** condition in which a husband and wife live apart by agreement or by a court order. **4.** removal of a person from an organization, as a serviceman from the armed forces.

sep·a·ra·tism (sep′ər ə tiz′əm, sep′rə-) *n.* principle of advocating or wanting separation, esp. political or religious separation. —**sep′a·ra·tist,** *n.*

sep·a·ra·tive (sep′ə rā′tiv, sep′ər ə-, sep′rə-) *adj.* tending or causing to separate.

sep·a·ra·tor (sep′ə rā′tər) *n.* **1.** one who or that which separates. **2.** apparatus for separating liquids, as cream from milk.

Se·phar·di (sə fär′dē) *pl.,* **-dim** (-dim). *n.* member or descendant of the group of Jewish people who settled in Spain and Portugal. Distinguished from **Ashkenazi.** —**Se·phar′dic,** *adj.*

se·pi·a (sē′pē ə) *n.* **1.** dark brown pigment made from the inky fluid secreted by the cuttlefish. **2.** dark brown color. [Latin *sēpia* cuttlefish, ink of the cuttlefish, from Greek *sēpiā.*]

se·poy (sē′poi) *n.* native of India serving as a soldier in a European army, esp. in the British army. [Portuguese *sipai(a)* native soldier of India in the service of the British, from Hindustani *sipāhī* soldier, from Persian *sipāhī,* from *sipāh* army.]

sep·sis (sep′sis) *n.* poisonous condition caused by the absorption of certain bacteria and their toxins into the bloodstream from a point of infection. [Modern Latin *sepsis,* from Greek *sēpsis* putrefaction.]

Sept. 1. September. **2.** Septuagint.

Sep·tem·ber (sep tem′bər) *n.* the ninth month of the year, containing thirty days. [Latin *September,* name of the seventh month in the early Roman calendar, in which March was the first month, from *septem* seven.]

sep·te·nar·y (sep′tə ner′ē) *adj.* **1.** of, forming into, or containing the number seven or seven things. **2.** of seven years; septennial. [Latin *septēnārius* consisting of seven, going back to *septem* seven.]

sep·ten·ni·al (sep ten′ē əl) *adj.* **1.** consisting of or lasting seven years. **2.** occurring once in every seven years. [Latin *septennium* period of seven years (going back to *septem* seven + *annus* year) + -AL¹.] —**sep·ten′ni·al·ly,** *adv.*

sep·tet (sep tet′) *also,* **sep·tette.** *n.* **1.a.** a musical composition for seven voices or instruments. **b.** musical ensemble of seven performers. **2.** group or set of seven persons or things. [German *Septett* musical composition for seven instruments or voices, from Latin *septem* seven.]

sep·tic (sep′tik) *adj.* **1.** causing sepsis or infection. **2.** caused by sepsis or infection. [Latin *sēpticus* causing putrefaction, from Greek *sēptikos,* from *sēpein* to make rotten.]

sep·ti·ce·mi·a (sep′tə sē′mē ə) *also,* **sep·ti·cae·mi·a.** *n.* disease caused by the absorption of certain bacteria and their toxins into the bloodstream; blood poisoning. [Modern Latin *septicaemia,* from Greek *sēptikos* causing putrefaction + *haima* blood.]

septic tank, underground tank in which solid waste matter is decomposed by the action of bacteria.

sep·til·lion (sep til′yən) *n.* **1.** in the United States and France, the

cardinal number that is represented by 1 followed by 24 zeros. **2.** in Great Britain and Germany, the cardinal number that is represented by 1 followed by 42 zeros. —*adj.* numbering one septillion. [French *septillion* one followed by 24 zeros, from Latin *septem* seven, on the model of *million.* See MILLION.] —**sep·til′lionth,** *adj., n.*

sep·tu·a·ge·nar·i·an (sep′tōō ə jə när′ē ən, -tū ə-, -chōō ə-) *n.* one who is seventy or between seventy and eighty years old. —*adj.* being seventy or between seventy and eighty years old. [Latin *septuāgēnārius* containing seventy (going back to *septuāgintā* seventy) + -AN.]

Sep·tu·a·ges·i·ma (sep′tōō ə jes′ə mə, -tū-, -chōō-) *n.* third Sunday before Lent. [Latin *septuāgesima (diēs)* literally, seventieth (day); day that was reckoned approximately as the seventieth day before Easter.]

Sep·tu·a·gint (sep′tōō ə jint, -tū-, -chōō-) *n.* Greek translation of the Old Testament compiled by Jewish scholars before the time of Christ. [Latin *septuāgintā* seventy; because this translation was supposedly done by seventy Jewish scholars.]

Septum

Septum of a pepper

sep·tum (sep′təm) *pl.,* **-ta** (-tə). *n.* dividing wall, membrane, or partition in an animal or plant structure. [Latin *saeptum* fence.]

sep·tu·ple (sep′tə pəl, sep′tōō′pəl, -tū′-) *adj.* **1.** consisting of seven parts or members. **2.** seven times as great as many. —*v.t., v.i.,* **-pled, -pling.** to make or become seven times as great or as many; multiply by seven. —*n.* number or amount seven times as great as another. [Late Latin *septuplus* sevenfold, from Latin *septem* seven + -plus -fold.]

sep·ul·cher (sep′əl kər) *also, British,* **sep·ul·chre.** *n.* **1.** burial place, esp. a vault or tomb. **2.** receptacle for relics, esp. in an altar. —*v.t.* to bury, in or as in a sepulcher; entomb; inter. [Old French *sepulcre* tomb, from Latin *sepulcrum,* from *sepelīre* to bury.]

se·pul·chral (si pul′krəl) *adj.* **1.** of or relating to a sepulcher or tomb. **2.** of or having to do with burial or the dead. **3.** deep, dark, and dismal; funereal.

sep·ul·ture (sep′əl chər) *n.* burial; interment. [Old French *sepulture* a burying, from Latin *sepultūra* burial.]

seq., the following. [Latin *sequēns,* present participle of *sequī* to follow.]

se·quel (sē′kwəl) *n.* **1.** literary work, complete in itself, that continues or completes a previous work. **2.** something that follows. **3.** result; consequence. [Latin *sequēla* result, that which follows, from *sequī* to follow.]

se·que·la (si kwē′lə) *pl.,* **-lae** (-lē). *n.* **1.** abnormal condition resulting directly or indirectly from a previous disease. **2.** sequel. [Latin *sequēla* result, that which follows. See SEQUEL.]

se·quence (sē′kwəns) *n.* **1.** fixed condition or order of one thing following directly after another. **2.** section of a film, confined to one time and place without any break or interruption, or edited to appear this way: *It took a week to film the fight sequence.* **3.** *Mathematics.* ordered set of numbers such that there is a first term, second term, and so on. 1, ⅓, ⅕, ⅐ . . . is a sequence. **4.** group or collection of connected things: *a sonnet sequence.* **5.** consequence: *a movement which was a small sequence of her energetic resolution* (G. Eliot, 1863). [Late Latin *sequentia* that which follows, from Latin *sequēns,* present participle of *sequī* to follow.]

Syn. 1. Sequence, series mean a number of things connected or ordered in a definite manner. In a **sequence** there is a recurrent pattern or a logical connection in the way one follows another in a regular alphabetical or numerical order: *The words in this dictionary are arranged in alphabetical sequence.* In a **series** a number of similar things need have no necessary progression or climax, but stress the individuality of each rather than the fact that they follow in a certain order: *The professor gave a series of talks on Alaska.*

se·quent (sē′kwənt) *adj.* that follows in sequence or is ordered in a sequence. Also, **se·quen·tial** (si kwen′chəl). [Latin *sequēns,* present participle of *sequī* to follow.]

se·ques·ter (si kwes′tər) *v.t.* **1.** to withdraw from or take out of the world at large; hide safely away: *money sequestered in a safe.* **2.** *Law.* to take and hold, as property, until a debt or claim is settled. **3.** to confiscate (enemy property). [Late Latin *sequestrāre* to separate, give up for safekeeping, from Latin *sequester* mediator, trustee.]

se·ques·trate (si kwes′trāt) **-trat·ed, -trat·ing.** *v.t.* **1.** to confiscate. **2.** *Archaic.* to sequester.

se·ques·tra·tion (sē′kwis trā′shən, si kwes′trā′-) *n.* **1.** act of sequestering; being sequestered. **2.** process of taking property into custody until a debt or claim is settled. **3.** confiscation of the property of an enemy national.

at; āpe; cär; end; mē; it; īce; hot; ōld; fôrk; wood; fōōl; oil; out; up; ūse; turn; sing; thin; this; zh in treasure; ə in ago, taken, pencil, lemon, circus.

se·quin (sē′kwin) *n.* **1.** small, thin, usually disk-shaped ornament of metal or glass, esp. one sewn in large numbers onto a fabric. **2.** former gold coin of Turkey and Italy. [French *sequin* small Italian coin, from Italian *zecchino* gold coin, from *zecca* mint², from Arabic *sikkah* die¹ (for coining).]

se·quined (sē′kwind) *adj.* ornamented with or as with sequins.

se·quoi·a (si kwoi′ə) *n.* **1.** giant evergreen tree, *Sequoia-dendron giganteum,* that is native to central California and Oregon and has thick, spongy reddish-brown bark and sharply pointed leaves. Sequoias are among the oldest and largest of trees. **2.** redwood *(def. 1).* [Modern Latin *sequoia,* from *Sequoya* (died 1843), Cherokee Indian who devised a system of writing for the Cherokee language.]

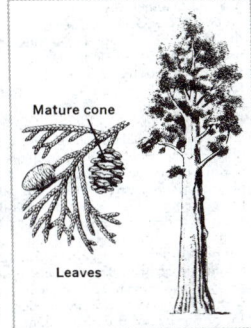

Mature cone

Leaves

Sequoia

se·ra (sēr′ə) a plural of **serum.**

se·ragl·io (si ral′yō, -räl′-) *pl.,* **-ragl·ios.** *n.* **1.** portion of a Muslim house reserved for women; harem. **2.** Turkish palace, esp. of a sultan. [Italian *serraglio* enclosure, harem, palace, from *serrare* to enclose, lock, going back to Latin *sera* bolt¹, bar; influenced by Turkish *serāī* palace.]

Se·ra·je·vo (ser′ə yä′vō) Sarajevo.

se·ra·pe (sə rä′pē) *also,* **sa·ra·pe.** *n.* blanketlike outer garment resembling a cloak or poncho, often made with bright colors and patterns, worn chiefly by men in Mexico and other Latin-American countries. [Spanish *serape;* of uncertain origin.]

ser·aph (ser′əf) *pl.,* **-aphs** *or* **-a·phim** (-ə fim′). *n.* member of the highest order of angels who are said to stand before the throne of God and burn with love for Him. [Hebrew *serāphīm,* plural of *sārāph,* celestial being described in Isaiah 6:2; literally, the burning one.] —**se·raph·ic** (si raf′ik) *adj.* —**se·raph′i·cal·ly,** *adv.*

Se·ra·pis (sə rä′pis) *n.* god of the dead, first worshiped in Egypt, later identified by the Greeks with their gods of the underworld, the heavens, and medicine.

Serb (surb) *n.* **1.** native or inhabitant of Serbia. **2.** language of the Serbs; Serbo-Croatian. —*adj.* Serbian.

Ser·bia (sur′bē ə) *n.* largest political subdivision of Yugoslavia, in the eastern part of the country, formerly independent. Area, 34,116 sq. mi. Pop. (1961), 7,642,227.

Ser·bi·an (sur′bē ən) *adj.* of or relating to Serbia, the Serbs, or their language. —*n.* Serb.

Ser·bo-Cro·a·tian (sur′bō krō ā′shən) *adj.* both Serbian and Croatian. —*n.* language belonging to the southern branch of the Slavic languages, spoken predominantly by Serbs and Croats in parts of Yugoslavia. Serbo-Croatian is written in the Cyrillic alphabet by the Serbs and in the Roman alphabet by the Croats.

sere (sēr) *adj.* withered; dry. [Form of SEAR.]

ser·e·nade (ser′ə nād′) *n.* **1.** pleasant, melodious song or other musical performance played and sung personally for someone, to express one's love or admiration for them. **2.** instrumental composition, usually written for a small orchestra or ensemble, typically consisting of a series of varied movements. —*v.t.,* **-nad·ed, -nad·ing.** to perform a serenade to or for. —*v.i.* to perform a serenade. —**ser′e·nad′er,** *n.*

ser·en·dip·i·ty (ser′ən dip′ə tē) *n.* ability or gift of making fortunate discoveries by accident. [From characters who had this ability in a fairy tale by Horace Walpole, *The Three Princes of Serendip.*] —**ser′en·dip′i·tous,** *adj.*

se·rene (sə rēn′) *adj.* **1.** peaceful; calm; tranquil: *serene old age.* **2.** clear: *rising through the serene air.* [Latin *serēnus.*] —**se·rene′ly,** *adv.* —**Syn. 1.** see **calm.**

se·ren·i·ty (sə ren′ə tē) *n.* state or quality of being serene.

serf (surf) *n.* peasant bound legally or by custom to the land or to the service of the landlord. A serf could neither leave at will nor be forced off the land, and was sold only along with the land. [French *serf* servant, thrall, from Latin *servus* slave.]

serf·dom (surf′dəm) *n.* **1.** state or condition of being a serf. **2.** practice or institution of working the land with serfs, esp. as it prevailed during the feudal periods of the Muslims, Chinese, Japanese, western Europeans, and Russians.

serge (surj) *n.* any of a group of fabrics characterized by a flat twill weave, esp. a durable worsted used for suits. [French *serge,* going back to Latin *sērica,* feminine of *sēricus* silken, from Greek *sērikos,* from *Sēres* the Chinese, who were famous for their silken fabrics.]

ser·geant (sär′jənt) *n.* **1.** in the U.S. Army, Air Force, and Marine Corps, a noncommissioned officer ranking above either a corporal or an airman first class. **2.** police officer ranking above patrolman and below a captain or lieutenant. [Old French *sergent* officer, going back to Latin *serviēns,* present participle of *servīre* to be a servant, be of service to.] —**ser′gean·cy,** *n.*

sergeant at arms *pl.,* **sergeants at arms.** *n.* official charged with preserving order at meetings, as of a legislative assembly or court of law.

sergeant first class, in the U.S. Army, a noncommissioned officer ranking below a master sergeant and above a staff sergeant.

sergeant major 1. in the U.S. Army, Air Force, and Marine Corps, a sergeant, usually a master sergeant, who acts as an assistant to a headquarters commander, esp. on a regimental level. **2.** in the U.S. Army and Marine Corps, a noncommissioned officer of the highest grade. **3.** in the U.S. Army, a master sergeant appointed to serve as a personal assistant to the Chief of Staff for matters relating to enlisted personnel.

se·ri·al (sēr′ē əl) *n.* long story broken up into segments that are shown or printed every so often, usually with the end of each segment leading on to the next so that the audience or reader is eager to see what will happen. —*adj.* **1.** of or relating to a serial: *The novel appeared in serial form.* **2.** of, relating to, or arranged in a series. **3.** *Music.* of, relating to, or composed in the twelve-tone scale. [SERIES + -AL¹.] —**se′ri·al·ly,** *adv.*

se·ri·al·ize (sēr′ē ə līz′) **-ized, -iz·ing.** *v.t.* to publish or arrange as a serial.

serial number, number assigned to a person or thing, as to a member of the armed forces or an automobile engine, for the purpose of identification.

se·ri·a·tim (sēr′ē ā′tim, ser′-) *adv.* one after the other; in a series. [Medieval Latin *seriatim* in order, in succession, from Latin *seriēs* row¹, succession.]

ser·i·cul·ture (ser′ə kul′chər) *n.* breeding of silkworms for the production of raw silk. [French *sériculture,* going back to Latin *sēricus* silken + *cultūra* cultivation. See SERGE.]

se·ries (sēr′ēz) *pl.,* **-ries.** *n.* **1.** group of similar or related things coming one after another: *a whole series of mistakes leading to the present dilemma, a series of rose bushes along the path.* **2.** set of things that go together to make a whole, often in a certain order: *a series of exercises.* **3.** television program, esp. a dramatic one, seen each day or each week, rather than only once, and usually having a fixed set of characters but a different story from program to program. **4.** *Mathematics.* indicated sum of the numbers of a sequence. $1 + \frac{1}{3} + \frac{1}{5} + \frac{1}{7} + \ldots$ is a series. **5. in series.** (of electrical devices or circuits) arranged with the positive electrode of one connected to the negative electrode of the next, so that the same current flows through all devices or circuits. Opposed to **in parallel.** [Latin *seriēs* row¹, succession.] —**Syn. 1.** see **sequence.**

ser·if (ser′if) *n. Printing.* any of the extra crosswise lines or triangles on the main strokes of certain type faces, as Roman. [Possibly from Dutch *schreef* dash, line¹.]

ser·i·graph (ser′ə graf′) *n.* print made by the silk-screen process.

se·ri·o-com·ic (sēr′ē ō kom′ik) *adj.* combining serious and comic elements.

se·ri·ous (sēr′ē əs) *adj.* **1.** of, characterized by, or showing deep and earnest thought; grave; solemn: *a serious manner, a serious man.* **2.** not joking; in earnest; sincere: *to be serious about one's work.* **3.** requiring thought or consideration; weighty; important: *a serious literary work. The overuse of insecticides has become a serious problem.* **4.** causing concern or anxiety; dangerous: *a serious illness.* [Late Latin *seriōsus* weighty, earnest, from Latin *sērius* earnest.] —**se′ri·ous·ly,** *adv.* —**se′ri·ous·ness,** *n.*

se·ri·ous-mind·ed (sēr′ē əs mīn′did) *adj.* characterized by or having a serious disposition or intention.

ser·mon (sur′mən) *n.* **1.** discourse delivered in public by a clergyman for the purpose of giving religious or moral instruction. **2.** any long moralizing speech. [Latin *sermō* speech, discourse.]

ser·mon·ize (sur′mə nīz′) **-ized, -iz·ing.** *v.i.* **1.** to deliver a sermon, as in a church. **2.** to go on at great length in a righteous tone about morals or religion.

Sermon on the Mount, Christ's discourse to His disciples, containing important principles of Christianity, including the Beatitudes.

se·rol·o·gy (si rol′ə jē) *n.* branch of science that deals with serums, esp. their use in curing or preventing disease.

se·rous (sēr′əs) *adj.* **1.** of, relating to, or secreting serum. **2.** having a thin consistency. [Modern Latin *serosus,* from Latin *serum* whey.]

serous membrane, thin membrane that lines certain cavities of the

at; āpe; cär; end; mē; it; īce; hot; ōld; fôrk; wood; fōōl; out; up; ūse; turn; sing; thin; this; zh in treasure; ə in **ago, taken, pencil, lemon, circus.**

909

body not open to the outside, as the peritoneum, and secretes a serous fluid.

ser·pent (sur′pənt) *n.* **1.** snake, esp. an extremely large or venomous one. **2.** snakelike monster or creature, esp. a sea serpent. **3.** one who is thought of as sly and wicked. [Latin *serpēns* snake; literally, creeping thing, from *serpere* to creep.]

ser·pen·tine (sur′pən tēn′, -tīn′) *adj.* **1.** winding about like a snake's body: *a serpentine path through a garden.* **2.** sly and wicked. **3.** of or resembling a snake or serpent. —*n.* hydrated silicate mineral, usually green with a greasy texture, used as a source of magnesium compounds. Its fibrous form, chrysotile, is the most important source of asbestos. Formula: $3MgO·2SiO_2·2H_2O$ [Late Latin *serpentīnus* relating to snakes, from Latin *serpēns* snake. See SERPENT.]

ser·rat·ed (ser′ā tid) *adj.* jagged or saw-toothed, as the edges of certain leaves. Also, **ser′rate.** [Latin *serrātus* notched like a saw, from *serra* saw¹.]

ser·ra·tion (se rā′shən) *n.* **1.** act of making serrated; being serrated. **2.** notch or jagged point on a serrated edge. **3.** series of such notches.

ser·ried (ser′ēd) *adj.* **1.** packed closely together like ranks of marching soldiers. **2.** serrated: *a serried edge of fabric.*

ser·ru·late (ser′ə lit, -lāt′, ser′ə-) *adj.* having very small serrations. [Modern Latin *serrulatus*, from Latin *serrula* little saw, diminutive of *serra* saw¹.]

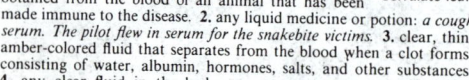

Serrulate leaf

se·rum (sēr′əm) *pl.* **se·rums** or **se·ra** (sēr′ə). *n.* **1.** antitoxin used to prevent or cure a disease, esp. one obtained from the blood of an animal that has been made immune to the disease. **2.** any liquid medicine or potion: *a cough serum. The pilot flew in serum for the snakebite victims.* **3.** clear, thin, amber-colored fluid that separates from the blood when a clot forms, consisting of water, albumin, hormones, salts, and other substances. **4.** any clear fluid in the body, as lymph. [Latin *serum* whey, watery part of something.]

ser·val (sur′vəl) *n.* large wild cat, *Felis serval*, native to Africa, having large erect ears, a short tail, and usually yellowish fur with black markings. Height: 20 inches at the shoulder. [French *serval*, from Spanish *(gato) cerval* lynx; literally, deerlike (cat), going back to Latin *cervus* deer.]

Serval

serv·ant (sur′vənt) *n.* **1.** one who is employed in a household to perform certain duties, as cooking or cleaning. **2.** one who is dedicated to the service of someone or something, as a religion or cause: *a servant of God.* [Old French *servant*, noun use of present participle of *servir* to wait upon, be useful, serve (God), from Latin *servīre.* See SERVE.]

serve (surv) **served, serv·ing.** *v.t.* **1.a.** to prepare and set (food or drink) on a table or before a person or persons: *to serve dinner.* **b.** to set food or drink before (a person or persons): *The waiter served his customer tea.* **2.a.** to supply (customers) regularly or continuously, as with a service or product: *The bakery serves us with fresh bread daily.* **b.** to supply (a service or product) regularly or continuously. **3.** to act as a servant to; attend or wait upon; work for: *The maid served the same family for years.* **4.** to come to the aid of; give assistance to: *The clerk asked if he could serve us.* **5.** to give homage or obedience to: *to serve God.* **6.** to pass (a specified period of time), as in military service, public office, or imprisonment: *He served two terms in the state legislature.* **7.** to be of use or service to; meet the requirements of: *The agreement no longer serves our needs.* **8.** to treat in a specified manner: *The reporter served the mayor fairly in the news story.* **9.** in tennis, badminton, and other racket games, to put (the ball or shuttlecock) in play. **11.** *Law.* **a.** to present (a court order or writ) to a person. **b.** to present with a court order or writ: *to serve a person with a subpoena.* **12.** to serve one **right.** to be just what one deserves, esp. as punishment for doing something wrong or dishonest. —*v.i.* **1.** to set food or drink before a person or persons. **2.** to perform a duty or duties, as of an office: *to serve on a jury. He served as mayor.* **3.** to act; be; suffice: *The sofa served as a bed.* **4.** to be a servant. **5.** to be favorable or suitable. **6.** in tennis, badminton, and other racket games, to put the ball or shuttlecock in play. **7.** to be a server for a priest during Mass. —*n.* **1.** act, instance, or manner of serving a ball or shuttlecock. **2.** a turn at serving. [Latin *servīre* to be a servant, be of use or service to, be fit for.]

serv·er (sur′vər) *n.* **1.** one who serves. **2.** that which is used in serving, as a tray. **3.** player who puts a ball or shuttlecock in play in tennis, badminton, or other racket games. **4.** attendant who helps the priest during Mass.

serv·ice (sur′vis) *n.* **1.** act, process, or means of serving or helping; conduct that contributes to the welfare or advantage of another or others: *She did us a great service.* **2.** system or means of supplying or providing something useful or necessary, esp. for the general public: *postal service.* **3.** *usually,* **services.** useful economic activity other than the production of goods. **4.** enterprise or establishment that supplies useful work, esp. one not engaged in the production of goods: *a research service.* **5.** activity of or arrangement for serving special needs of customers, esp. by repairing, maintaining, or replacing goods that have been sold. **6.** manner of waiting at a table or serving food: *The service is very poor in that restaurant.* **7.** public worship, esp. that which follows a prescribed ritual: *A burial service was held for the deceased.* **8.a.** one of the branches of the armed forces: *He spent three years in the service.* **b.** duty in any such branch. **9.a.** branch or department of public employment: *the foreign service.* **b.** persons employed in this. **10.** set of things required for table use, as silver or dishes: *a service for eight.* **11.** state of being employed, esp. as a domestic servant. **12.** act, instance, or manner of putting the ball or shuttlecock in play in tennis, badminton, and other racket games. **13.** *Law.* the presentation or delivery of a court order or writ to the person named therein. **14. at one's service.** ready or available to serve or help one; at one's disposal: *My entire staff is at your service.* **15. in service.** in use or operation; functioning. **16. of service.** of use or assistance; useful; helpful: *Can I be of service to you?* —*v.t.* **-viced, -vic·ing.** **1.** to make fit for use; keep conditioned or repaired: *to service an automobile.* **2.** to supply service to. —*adj.* **1.** of, relating to, or used by those in service: *a service entrance.* **2.** of or relating to the armed forces. **3.** of or relating to useful economic activity other than the production of goods. [Latin *servitium* slavery, servitude.]

serv·ice·a·ble (sur′vi sə bəl) *adj.* **1.** capable of giving useful service; helpful; beneficial. **2.** wearing well in long or hard use; durable. —**serv′ice·a·bil′i·ty, serv′ice·a·ble·ness,** *n.* —**serv′ice·a·bly,** *adv.*

serv·ice·ber·ry (sur′vis ber′ē) *n.* **1.** fruit of a service tree. **2.** the shadbush or its fruit.

service club **1.** organization dedicated to working for the good of the community while serving certain needs of its members. **2.** recreational facility for members of the armed forces.

serv·ice·man (sur′vis man′) *pl.* **-men.** *n.* **1.** member of one of the branches of the armed forces. **2.** one whose work is maintaining or repairing something.

service mark, symbol, word, or device used to identify a firm that supplies a service to the public, as an airline, laundry, or insurance company.

service station **1.** gas station. **2.** place where repairs and adjustments can be made and parts are supplied for any of various mechanical or electrical devices.

service stripe, stripe worn on the left sleeve of the uniform by a member of the armed forces to indicate a certain period of active service.

service tree, tree of either of two European species, genus *Sorbus,* related to the mountain ash and having edible berries. [Earlier *serves* (thought incorrectly to be a singular), plural of obsolete *serve* this tree, from Old English *syrfe,* going back to Latin *sorbus.*]

ser·vi·ette (sur′vē et′) *n. British.* table napkin. [French *serviette,* from *servir* to wait upon. See SERVANT.]

ser·vile (sur′vil, -vīl) *adj.* **1.** having or showing the character of a slave; lacking self-respect or independence; slavish; obsequious: *servile behavior.* **2.** of, relating to, or appropriate for a slave: *servile duties.* [Latin *servīlis,* from *servus* slave.] —**ser′vile·ly,** *adv.* —**ser′vile·ness, ser·vil·i·ty** (sər vil′ə tē), *n.*

serv·ing (sur′ving) *n.* **1.** portion of food; helping. **2.** act of a person or thing that serves. —*adj.* used in serving food.

ser·vi·tor (sur′və tər) *n.* one who serves another; servant; attendant. [Old French *servitor,* from Late Latin *servītor,* from Latin *servīre* to be a servant.]

ser·vi·tude (sur′və tood′, -tūd′) *n.* **1.** condition of being a slave; slavery; bondage. **2.** compulsory labor as a punishment. [Latin *servitūdō* slavery.]

ser·vo·mech·a·nism (sur′vō mek′ə niz′əm) *n.* automatic feedback control system in which one or more of the operations involves mechanical motion, used for various assembly line processes and for automatic pilot systems.

ses·a·me (ses′ə mē) *n.* **1.** small oval, aromatic seed of a tropical plant, *Sesamum indicum,* native to India, used mainly in baked goods and candies. **2.** the plant itself. **3.** see **open sesame.** [Greek *sēsamē* this plant; of Semitic origin.]

ses·qui·cen·ten·ni·al (ses′kwi sen ten′ē əl) *n.* one hundred and fiftieth anniversary or its celebration. —*adj.* of or relating to a period of a century and a half. [Latin *sesqui-* one and a half + CENTENNIAL.]

ses·qui·pe·da·li·an (ses′kwi pi dā′lē ən) *adj.* **1.** measuring a foot and a half. **2.** having many syllables; very long. **3.** given to using long

at; āpe; cär; end; mē; it; īce; hot; ōld; fôrk; wood; fōol; oil; out; up; ūse; turn; sing; thin; this; zh in treasure; ə in ago, taken, pencil, lemon, circus.

words. —*n.* a very long word. [Latin *sesquipedālis* one foot and a half in length (from *sesqui-* one and a half + *pedālis* relating to the foot) + -AN.]

ses·sile (ses′il, -īl) *adj.* **1.** attached directly at the base rather than by a stem or stalk: *sessile leaves.* **2.** permanently attached; not moving or swimming about; fixed; sedentary: *Sea anemones are sessile organisms.* [Latin *sessilis* relating to sitting, from *sessus,* past participle of *sedēre* to sit.]

ses·sion (sesh′ən) *n.* **1.a.** meeting, as of a court, council, or legislature, for the transaction of business. **b.** series of such meetings. **c.** term of such a meeting or meetings. **2.a.** period into which a school year is divided; term: *John will attend the summer session.* **b.** time during which classes are conducted in a school or college: *The evening session begins at six o'clock.* **3.** meeting held for any purpose or activity: *a recording session.* **4. in session.** in the process of meeting or being conducted: *Court is now in session.* [Latin *sessiō* a sitting, a meeting, from *sedēre* to sit.] —**ses′sion·al,** *adj.*

ses·terce (ses′turs) *n.* ancient Roman coin, originally of silver, but later of copper or bronze. [Latin *sestertius.*]

ses·tet (ses tet′) *n.* **1.a.** last six lines of a Petrarchan sonnet. Distinguished from **octet. b.** any six-line unit of verse. **2.** *Music.* sextet. [Italian *sestetto* sextet in music, from *sesto* sixth, from Latin *sextus.*]

set (set) *set,* **set·ting.** *v.t.* **1.** to place in some location or position; put; place: *She set the lamp on the table.* **2.a.** to put in the correct, proper, or desired place, position, or condition: *to set a broken bone.* **b.** to arrange (the hair), as with rollers or clips, so as to assume a desired style. **c.** to prepare or arrange for use: *to set a trap, to set the table for a meal.* **d.** to arrange scenery and properties on (a stage) for a presentation. **3.** to adjust or regulate, esp. in accordance with a standard: *to set one's watch.* **4.** to cause to be in a certain condition: *to set a prisoner free, to set a log on fire, to set a boat adrift. The scream set his nerves on edge.* **5.** to cause to be in a firm, settled, or fixed position or condition: *to set cement, to set one's jaw, to set one's mind on doing something.* **6.** to determine or fix firmly; establish or appoint: *to set a date for a wedding.* **7.** to fix or determine (a price, value, or rate): *to set a mortgage rate of 7½%.* **8.** to place in a certain category or rank: *Most critics set Shakespeare above all other English writers.* **9.** to establish as the highest or greatest level or achievement: *He set a record in the high jump.* **10.** to assign or allot: *to set a guard at the gate.* **11.** to present or provide for others to follow: *to set the pace, to set a poor example for others.* **12.** to cause to take a particular direction; direct: *to set one's course toward land.* **13.** to cause to sit. **14.** to place in a frame or mounting: *to set a diamond.* **15.** to adorn or ornament: *to set a crown with jewels.* **16.** *Printing.* **a.** to arrange (type) for printing. **b.** to put into type: *to set a manuscript.* **17.** *Music.* **a.** to write, adapt, or fit (words) to music. **b.** to compose or arrange (music) for words. **c.** to compose or arrange (music) for certain voices or instruments. **18.a.** to put (a hen) on eggs in order to hatch them. **b.** to put (eggs) under a hen or in an incubator in order to hatch them. **19.** (of a hunting dog) to point (game). **20.** *Bridge.* to defeat (one's opponents or their contract). —*v.i.* **1.a.** to go down below the horizon: *At what time will the sun set today?* **b.** to decline; wane: *The power of the British Empire began to set after World War I.* **2.a.** to become firm or hard: *The cement set after a few hours.* **b.** (of a broken bone) to mend properly. **c.** to become fast or permanent, as a dye or color. **3.** to hang or fit: *That jacket sets well on you.* **4.** to make a beginning, as in a task; apply oneself: *to set to work.* **5.** (of a hen) to sit on eggs. **6.** (of a hunting dog) to point game. **7.** to have a specified direction; tend. **8.** (of a young plant) to begin to develop, esp. as a result of pollination. **9.** to sit.
to set about. to begin to do; start.
to set against. a. to cause to be hostile or unfriendly toward. **b.** to balance or compare.
to set aside. a. to place apart or to one side, as for later use; reserve; save. **b.** to discard, dismiss, or reject. **c.** to declare null and void; overrule; annul: *to set aside a verdict.*
to set back. a. to reverse, hinder, or check. **b.** *Informal.* to cost (a person) a certain sum of money: *That coat set me back ninety dollars.*
to set down. a. to place on a surface. **b.** to record, esp. in writing or printing. **c.** to ascribe; attribute: *Set his behavior down to youthful indiscretion.* **d.** to consider; regard.
to set forth. a. to make known; state; declare. **b.** to start out on a journey. **c.** to publish.
to set in. a. to begin to take place or prevail: *Pneumonia set in. Winter set in early this year.* **b.** (of wind or water) to blow or flow toward shore.
to set off. a. to make prominent by contrast; show to best advantage: *Dark hair sets off a fair complexion.* **b.** to start out or begin, as on a course or journey. **c.** to cause to explode; discharge: *to set off fireworks.* **d.** to cause to begin; touch off: *The senator's statement set off a lively debate.* **e.** to place apart from others; put by itself.
to set on (or **upon**). to attack or urge to attack.

to set out. a. to start out on a journey or course. **b.** to begin with a certain intention; undertake; attempt: *The detective set out to establish a motive for the crime.* **c.** to arrange or display: *to set out items for sale.* **d.** to plan or lay out, as a room, garden, or town. **e.** to establish the limits or boundaries of. **f.** to plant.
to set to. a. to make a beginning; start working. **b.** to start fighting.
to set up. a. to put in an upright position. **b.** to raise or elevate. **c.** to raise to a position of authority or power. **d.** to assemble, erect, or prepare for use: *to set up a tent.* **e.** to establish; found: *to set up an organization.* **f.** to provide (a person) with the means for something: *He set up his son in business.* **g.** to put forward; propose, as a theory. **h.** to lay claim for (oneself) as being something: *He sets himself up as an expert on politics.* **i.** to plan (something, esp. a crime) carefully. **j.** to pay for (drinks) for another or others; treat (someone) to a drink or drinks.
—*adj.* **1.** appointed or prescribed beforehand; specified; established: *a set procedure, a set fee.* **2.** fixed; rigid; immovable: *a set smile.* **3.** stubbornly fixed, as in opinion or disposition; obstinate: *That old man is set in his ways.* **4.** determined; resolute; intent: *She is set on going.* **5.** customary; conventional; stereotyped: *a set phrase.* **6.** deliberately composed, arranged, or conceived; intentional: *a set purpose.* **7.** formed, built, or made in a certain way. ▲ used with a specifying adverb: *deep-set eyes, a heavy-set man.* **8.** ready; prepared: *to get set to run. We are all set to leave on our trip.* —*n.* **1.** act or manner of setting; being set. **2.a.** number or group of persons associated in some way, as through status, interests, habits, or occupation: *a set of clients, the sporting set.* **b.** select or exclusive social group: *the fashionable set.* **3.a.** group or collection of things which belong and are usually used together: *a set of furniture, a chess set.* **b.** group or collection of printed works, as books or magazines, written by the same author or dealing with the same subject. **4.** *Mathematics.* collection of numbers, points, objects, or other things grouped together or having a certain property in common that distinguishes them from all other things not within the collection. The set of positive integers less than 5 is {1, 2, 3, 4}. **5.** complete unit of scenery, props, and structures used for a scene in a play, motion picture, or television program. **6.** sending or receiving apparatus assembled as a unit for radio, television, telephone, or other communication. **7.** group of six or more games comprising a unit of a match in tennis. One player or side must win at least two more games than the other. **8.** position or attitude of the body, or a part of it; form: *the set of his shoulders.* **9.** way something fits or hangs, as an article of clothing: *the set of a dress.* **10.** general movement in a certain direction; inclination; tendency. **11.** direction or course of a current or wind. **12.** the sinking of a heavenly body below the horizon. **13.** permanent change of form, as of a metal, caused esp. by strain, pressure, or chemical action. **14.** young plant or a plant part, as a slip or shoot, suitable for planting. **15.a.** number of couples required to perform a square dance. **b.** series of movements or figures that compose a square dance. [Old English *settan* to cause to sit, place, plant, establish, found, subside.] —**Syn.** *v.t.* **6.** see **fix.**

Set (set) *also,* **Seth.** *n.* Egyptian god of evil, often portrayed with a doglike head and associated with darkness and drought.

se·ta (sē′tə) *pl.,* **-tae** (-tē). *n.* any stiff hairlike structure or organ, as on certain plants, earthworms, or insects. [Latin *saeta* bristle.]

se·ta·ceous (si tā′shəs) *adj.* having or resembling bristles or setae.

set·back (set′bak′) *n.* **1.** defeat or other check to progress, esp. one that is temporary or unexpected; reversal. **2.** any recessed upper section of a tall building, as to allow maximum light and ventilation in the street below. **3.** offset *(def. 5).*

Seth (seth) *n.* **1.** in the Old Testament, a son of Adam and Eve. **2.** Set.

set·off (set′ôf′) *n.* **1.** thing used to adorn; decoration; ornament. **2.** anything that counterbalances or compensates for something else. **3.** act of setting off on a journey; start. **4.** rightful claim of a defendant against a plaintiff. **5.** offset *(def. 5).*

se·tose (sē′tōs) *adj.* bristly; setaceous.

set·screw (set′skrōō′) *n.* screw used to fasten parts of a machine together, as gears to a shaft.

set·tee (se tē′) *n.* upholstered seat for two people, with a high back and, usually, arms. [Possibly form of SET-TLE².]

set·ter (set′ər) *n.* **1.** any of several long-haired bird dogs having drooping ears and a soft, silky coat, originally trained to crouch, or set, when finding game but now trained to point. Height: to 26 inches at the shoulder. **2.** person or thing that sets.

Setter

set theory, branch of mathematics dealing with sets and their properties and relationships.

set·ting (set'ing) *n.* **1.** that in which something, as a jewel, is set. **2.** place and time of a dramatic or literary work: *The setting of the novel is London during World War II.* **3.** scenery and other properties for a theatrical performance. **4.** that which surrounds a person or thing; background; environment. **5.** china, silverware, and other articles for setting a place at a table. **6.** music composed for a specific text: *a setting for the twenty-third Psalm.* **7.** number of eggs that a hen sets on or that are placed in an incubator for hatching at one time. **8.** act of one who or that which sets.

set·tle¹ (set'əl) **-tled, -tling.** *v.t.* **1.** to determine or decide, as something in doubt or debate; come to agreement concerning; resolve: *to settle an argument.* **2.** to arrange (something) in an orderly manner, esp. permanently: *I must settle all my affairs before leaving.* **3.** to make final disposition of by or as by paying: *to settle an account.* **4.a.** to establish inhabitants in; colonize. **b.** to cause to take up residence: *He settled his family in their new home.* **4.** to establish or fix, as in a profession or way of life. **5.** to place (someone or something) in a proper or desired position; adjust: *James settled his feet in the stirrups.* **7.** to make tranquil or calm; compose: *He took a pill to settle his stomach.* **8.** to cause (a liquid) to change from an agitated or muddy condition to one of clearness; clarify. **9.** to make compact, firm, or solid: *The dry, cool weather settled the fresh tar on the road.* **10.** *Law.* to give (property or the income from it) to a person or persons by legal means (with *on* or *upon*). —*v.i.* **1.** to decide, select, or agree, esp. beforehand: *Laura finally settled on the red dress.* **2.** to establish a residence, esp. permanently: *He settled in the country after his retirement.* **3.** to come to rest; assume a stationary position; alight: *The butterfly settled on the flower.* **4.** to sink gradually, as the foundations of a building. **5.** to sink to the bottom, as sediment. **6.** to become compact, firm, or solid: *The fresh plaster settled in one hour.* **7.** to be established in a serene, orderly way of life, esp. as a result of marriage (often with *down*).
8. to settle down. a. to become calm or composed. **b.** to exert direct steady effort and attention: *to settle down to work.* [Old English *setlan* to fix, place, from *setl* seat.] —**Syn.** *v.t.* **1.** see **decide.**

set·tle² (set'əl) *n.* long bench or seat for two or more people, with a high back, arms, and, sometimes, drawers under the seat. [Old English *setl* seat.]

High-backed settle

set·tle·ment (set'əl mənt) *n.* **1.** act of settling; being settled. **2.** deciding or determining, as of something in doubt or debate. **3.** orderly arrangement of affairs. **4.** small village or group of houses. **5.a.** establishment of inhabitants in a new country; colonization. **b.** colony, esp. in its earlier stages. **6.** establishment of a person in life, marriage, a profession, or business. **7.** adjustment or payment, as of claims. **8.** *Law.* **a.** act of settling property upon a person or persons. **b.** property so given. **9.** settlement house. **10.** a sinking down of all or part of a structure.

settlement house, neighborhood institution with a staff of social workers that provides counseling, recreation, food, and other services to poor residents of the area.

set·tler (set'lər) *n.* **1.** one who settles in a new country or territory. **2.** any person or thing that settles.

set·tlings (set'lingz) *n.,pl.* sediment; dregs.

set·to (set'too') *pl.,* **-tos.** *n. Informal.* fight; conflict.

set·up (set'up') *n.* **1.** way in which a thing is arranged, assembled, or organized; structure or plan of something. **2.** contest or task deliberately made easy. **3.** ice, soda water, or other mixer for use in alcoholic drinks.

Seu·rat, Georges (sœ rä'; zhôrzh) 1859–91, French painter.

Se·vas·to·pol (si vas'tə pōl') *also* **Se·bas·to·pol.** *n.* port city in the Soviet Union, on the Black Sea, near the southwestern tip of the Crimean peninsula. Pop. (1970 est.), 229,000.

sev·en (sev'ən) *n.* **1.** the cardinal number that is one more than six. **2.** symbol representing this number, as 7 or VII. **3.** something having this many units or members, as a playing card. —*adj.* numbering one more than six. [Old English *seofon.*]

seven deadly sins, the sins of anger, avarice (or covetousness), envy, gluttony, lust, pride, and sloth, regarded as the source of all other sins. Also, **cardinal sins, deadly sins.**

sev·en·fold (sev'ən fōld') *adv.* **1.** seven times as great or as numerous. **2.** having or consisting of seven parts. —*adj.* so as to be seven times greater or more numerous.

Seven Hills, seven low hills upon and around which Rome was built.

seven seas, all the oceans and seas of the world, now considered to be the North Atlantic, South Atlantic, North Pacific, South Pacific, Arctic, Antarctic, and Indian oceans.

Seven Sisters, Pleiades.

sev·en·teen (sev'ən tēn') *n.* **1.** the cardinal number that is seven more than ten. **2.** symbol representing this number, as 17 or XVII. **3.** something having this many units or members. —*adj.* numbering seven more than ten. [Old English *seofontiene.*]

sev·en·teenth (sev'ən tēnth') *adj.* **1.** (the ordinal of seventeen) next after the sixteenth. **2.** being one of seventeen equal parts. —*n.* **1.** that which is next after the sixteenth. **2.** one of seventeen equal parts; ¹⁄₁₇.

seventeen-year locust (sev'ən tēn'yēr') North American cicada, *Magicicada septendecim,* that has an underground larval stage lasting seventeen years or, esp. in the South, thirteen years. It then emerges from the soil to live a short time as an adult.

sev·enth (sev'ənth) *adj.* **1.** (the ordinal of seven) next after the sixth. **2.** being one of seven equal parts. —*n.* **1.** that which is next after the sixth. **2.** one of seven equal parts; ¹⁄₇. **3.** *Music.* **a.** tone, esp. the subdominant, seven diatonic degrees from a given tone. **b.** interval of seven degrees between two tones of the diatonic scale. **c.** harmonic combination of two tones separated by this interval. —*adv.* in the seventh place.

Sev·enth-Day Adventist (sev'ənth dā') member of an Adventist sect that observes the Sabbath on Saturday, the seventh day of the week.

seventh heaven 1. condition of great joy and happiness. **2.** according to certain theologies, the highest and most exalted part of heaven.

sev·en·ti·eth (sev'ən tē ith) *adj.* **1.** (the ordinal of seventy) next after the sixty-ninth. **2.** being one of seventy equal parts. —*n.* **1.** that which is next after the sixty-ninth. **2.** one of seventy equal parts; ¹⁄₇₀.

sev·en·ty (sev'ən tē) *n.* the cardinal number that is seven times ten. **2.** symbol representing this number, as 70 or LXX. **3. the seventies.** number series from seventy through seventy-nine. ▲ used esp. in reference to the seventh decade of a century or of a person's life. —*adj.* numbering seven times ten. [Old English *seofontig.*]

Seven Wonders of the World, the seven most remarkable man-made structures of ancient times, usually listed as the Pyramids of Egypt, the hanging gardens of Babylon, the Colossus of Rhodes, the Mausoleum at Halicarnassus, the temple of Diana (Artemis) at Ephesus, the statue of Zeus by Phidias at Olympia, and the Pharos (lighthouse) of Alexandria.

sev·er (sev'ər) *v.t.* **1.** to separate by violence; cut apart or off: *The strain severed the rope.* **2.** to break off; divide; dissolve: *to sever diplomatic relations with another country.* **3.** to put or keep distinct or apart; separate. —*v.i.* to become separated; be divided into parts; part. [Old French *sevrer* to separate, going back to Latin *sēparāre.*] —**sev'·er·a·ble,** *adj.*

sev·er·al (sev'ər əl, sev'rəl) *adj.* **1.** more than two but not many: *to stay for several hours.* **2.** individual; different: *They went their several ways.* **3.** considered individually; single; separate: *the several degrees on a scale.* —*n.* more than two but not many; a few: *We managed to recover several of the missing articles.* [Anglo-Norman *several* separate, distinct, going back to Latin *sēpar* different.]
Syn. *adj.* **1. Several, various, sundry** mean consisting of an indefinite number of things. **Several** suggests a small number that all fall within the same group, class, or type: *My friend speaks several languages.* **Various** implies a wider range or representation within the same general category: *I placed the advertisement in various local and trade papers.* **Sundry** suggests a greater number and stresses the difference and dissimilarity of the collected items: *The attic was full of sundry books, toys, and other childhood mementos.*

sev·er·al·ly (sev'ər ə lē, sev'rə-) *adv.* **1.** separately; individually. **2.** respectively.

sev·er·al·ty (sev'ər əl tē, sev'rəl-) *pl.,* **-ties.** *n.* **1.** a being separate. **2.** estate that a person holds in his own right, without being joined by any other person. **3.** condition of an estate so held.

sev·er·ance (sev'ər əns, sev'rəns) *n.* act of severing; being severed; separation.

severance pay, sum of money paid in addition to salary to an employee upon termination of employment.

se·vere (sə vēr') -**ver·er,** -**ver·est.** *adj.* **1.** very exacting; harsh: *severe punishment.* **2.** stern, austere, or grim in manner or appearance: *a severe face.* **3.** serious; dangerous; grave: *a severe illness, a severe wound.* **4.** austerely plain or simple; without ornament: *a severe dress.* **5.** causing great discomfort; extremely harsh: *a severe winter, severe cold.* **6.** difficult; rigorous: *a severe test.* **7.** exact, accurate, or methodical: *severe conformity to rules.* [Latin *sevērus* serious, strict.] —**se·vere'·ly,** *adv.* —**se·vere'·ness,** *n.*
Syn. 2. Severe, stern¹, austere mean grim in manner or appearance. **Severe** emphasizes an unpleasantly harsh seriousness that reflects firm purpose and rigorous standards: *The officer's severe look discouraged personal discussion.* **Stern** adds the idea of a dour and forbidding appearance that may indicate a lack of compassion: *The criminal trembled before the stern judge.* **Austere** suggests a manner that reflects self-restraint and an absence of passion: *The monk had an austere face.*

at; āpe; cär; end; mē; it; īce; hot; ōld; fôrk; wood; fōōl; oil; out; up; ūse; turn; sing; thin; this; zh in treasure; ə in ago, taken, pencil, lemon, circus.

se·ver·i·ty (sə ver′ə tē) *pl.* **-ties.** *n.* **1.** sternness; harshness. **2.** austere simplicity of style or taste. **3.** extreme harshness or sharpness: *the severity of a storm.* **4.** sternness of manner or appearance. **5.** rigid accuracy or exactness.

Sev·ern (sev′ərn) *n.* river flowing from central Wales eastward, through part of England, into the Bristol Channel.

Se·ve·rus, Lucius Sep·tim·i·us (sə vēr′əs; sep tim′ē əs) A.D. 146–211, Roman emperor from 193 to 211.

Se·ville (sə vil′) *n.* city in southwestern Spain. Pop. (1968), 496,035. Also, *Spanish,* **Se·vil·la** (se vēl′yä).

Sè·vres (sev′rə) *n.* French porcelain of a kind originally made in the French city of Sèvres, distinguished by its excellent workmanship and fine design. Also, **Sèvres ware.**

sew (sō) **sewed, sewed** or **sewn, sew·ing.** *v.i.* to work with needle and thread or with a sewing machine. —*v.t.* **1.** to fasten, join, or attach with stitches: *to sew a button on a jacket.* **2.** to make or mend by means of a needle and thread or a sewing machine: *to sew a dress.* **3.** to close with stitches (usually with *up*): *to sew up a cut in a person's arm.* **4. to sew up.** *Informal.* **a.** to get or have complete control of. **b.** to bring to a successful conclusion; make certain of success in: *to sew up a business deal.* [Old English *siw(i)an* to fasten together with thread.]

sew·age (sōō′ij) *n.* waste matter carried off by sewers and drains.

Sew·ard, William Henry (sōō′ərd) 1801–72, U.S. statesman.

sew·er[1] (sōō′ər) *n.* underground pipe or conduit used for carrying off waste water and refuse. [Old French *sewiere* channel to drain a pond, going back to Latin *ex* out of + *aqua* water.]

sew·er[2] (sō′ər) *n.* one who or that which sews. [SEW + -ER[1].]

sew·er·age (sōō′ər ij) *n.* **1.** removal of waste matter by means of sewers. **2.** system of sewers. **3.** sewage.

sew·ing (sō′ing) *n.* **1.** work done with a needle and thread or with a sewing machine. **2.** something to be sewed. **3.** act of one who sews.

sewing circle, group of women who meet regularly to sew, usually for charitable purposes.

sewing machine, mechanical device for sewing fabric and other materials, usually powered by a small electric motor.

sewn (sōn) a past participle of **sew.**

sex (seks) *n.* **1.** either of the two divisions, male or female, into which human beings and most other organisms are divided according to their functions in the process of reproduction. **2.a.** the sum of the characteristics that determine whether an organism is male or female. **b.** character or condition of being male or female. **3.** the instincts and urges attracting one sex to another, esp. as manifested in behavior. **4.** sexual activity, esp. sexual intercourse. [Latin *sexus* either of the divisions male or female.]

sex·a·ge·nar·i·an (sek′sə jə när′ē ən) *n.* one who is sixty or between sixty and seventy years old. —*adj.* being sixty or between sixty and seventy years old. [Latin *sexāgēnārius* containing sixty (going back to *sexāgintā* sixty) + -AN.]

Sex·a·ges·i·ma (sek′sə jes′ə mə) *n.* second Sunday before Lent. [Latin *sexāgēsima (dies)* literally, sixtieth (day); reckoned approximately as the sixtieth day before Easter.]

sex·a·ges·i·mal (sek′sə jes′ə məl) *adj.* relating to or based upon the number sixty.

sex appeal, quality, as physical attractiveness, that arouses sexual interest in members of the opposite sex.

sex chromosome, either of the two types of chromosomes that determine the sex of an offspring; X chromosome or Y chromosome. A female germ cell always has an X chromosome; a male germ cell may have either an X chromosome or a Y chromosome. A fusion of germ cells resulting in a fertilized cell with two X chromosomes produces a female organism; a male results from an XY chromosome combination.

sex hormone, any of several hormones that affect the growth and functioning of the reproductive system, the development of secondary sex characteristics, or the secretion of milk.

sex·less (seks′lis) *adj.* **1.** lacking sexual characteristics; neuter. **2.** lacking sexual desire or sex appeal. —**sex′less·ness,** *n.*

sex linkage, condition in which the inheritance of certain traits is determined or influenced by the genetic structure of the sex chromosomes.

sex-linked (seks′lingkt′) *adj.* **1.** (of an inherited trait) determined by a gene carried by a sex chromosome, esp. one present in an X chromosome but not in a Y chromosome. **2.** (of a gene) carried by a sex chromosome.

sext (sekst) *n.* fourth of the seven canonical hours. [Latin *sexta (hōra)*

sixth (hour); because it was originally the sixth or noon hour of the day.]

sex·tant (seks′tənt) *n.* instrument, used mainly in navigation, for measuring the altitude of the sun or a star as an aid in determining the position of the observer. [Latin *sextant-,* stem of *sextāns* sixth part; because it has the shape of a sixth of a circle.]

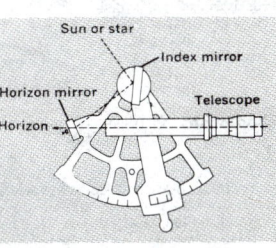

Sextant

sex·tet (seks tet′) *also,* **sex·tette.** *n.* **1.a.** musical composition for six voices or instruments. **b.** musical ensemble of six performers. **2.** group of six persons or things. [Modification (influenced by Latin *sex* six) of SESTET.]

sex·til·lion (seks til′yən) *n.* **1.** in the United States and France, the cardinal number that is represented by 1 followed by 21 zeros. **2.** in Great Britain and Germany, the cardinal number that is represented by 1 followed by 36 zeros. —*adj.* numbering one sextillion. [French *sextillion* 1 followed by 21 zeros (from Latin *sextus* sixth), on the model of *million.* See MILLION.] —**sex·til′lionth,** *adj., n.*

sex·ton (seks′tən) *n.* man employed by a parish to take care of church property. His duties sometimes include ringing the church bell and formerly included digging graves for churchyard burials. [Old French *secrestein,* from Medieval Latin *sacristanus* keeper of sacred objects, going back to Latin *sacer* holy.]

sex·tu·ple (seks tōō′pəl, -tū′-, -tup′əl) *adj.* **1.** consisting of six parts or members. **2.** six times as great or as many. —*v.t., v.i.* **-pled, -pling.** to make or become six times as great or as many; multiply by six. —*n.* number or amount six times as great as another. [Latin *sextus* sixth, on the model of QUADRUPLE.]

sex·tu·plet (seks tup′lit, -tōō′plit, -tū′-) *n.* **1.a.** one of six offspring born at one birth. **b.** sextuplets, six offspring born at one birth. **2.** any set or combination of six. [SEXTUPLE + -ET.]

sex·u·al (sek′shōō əl) *adj.* **1.** of or relating to sex or the sexes: *sexual instincts, sexual relations, sexual behavior.* **2.** Biology. **a.** having the distinction of sex. **b.** involving the union of male and female germ cells: *sexual reproduction.* [Late Latin *sexuālis* relating to sex, from Latin *sexus.* See SEX.] —**sex′u·al·ly,** *adv.*

sexual intercourse, sexual union, esp. between humans; coitus.

sex·u·al·i·ty (sek′shōō al′ə tē) *n.* **1.** condition of being distinguished by sex; sexual quality. **2.** sexual desire or interest.

sex·y (sek′sē) **sex·i·er, sex·i·est.** *adj.* *Informal.* arousing or intended to arouse sexual desire. —**sex′i·ly,** *adv.* —**sex′i·ness,** *n.*

sf., sforzando.

SF, science fiction.

sfer·ics (sfer′iks) *n.,pl.* atmospherics. ▲ construed as singular.

Sfor·za (sfôrt′sə) *n.* powerful family that ruled the city-state of Milan from 1450 to 1500 and from 1521 to 1535.

sfor·zan·do (sfôrt sän′dō) *Music. adj.* heavily accented, as a single note or chord. —*adv.* in a sforzando manner. [Italian *sforzando* forcing, gerund of *sforzare* to force, going back to Latin *ex* out of + *fortis* strong.]

sfz., sforzando.

s.g., specific gravity.

Sgt., Sergeant.

shab·by (shab′ē) **-bi·er, -bi·est.** *adj.* **1.** faded and dingy from wear or exposure: *a shabby coat, a shabby house.* **2.** wearing worn and faded clothes; seedy. **3.** contemptibly mean, ungenerous, or dishonorable: *a shabby act, shabby treatment.* [From obsolete *shab* scab, low fellow, from Old English *sceabb* scab, itch.] —**shab′bi·ly,** *adv.* —**shab′bi·ness,** *n.*

Sha·bu·oth (shə vōō′ōt, -ōs) Shavuoth.

shack (shak) *n.* small, roughly built hut or cabin; shanty. [Of uncertain origin.]

shack·le (shak′əl) *n.* **1.** metal band fastened around the ankle or wrist of a prisoner, usually one of a pair connected by a chain; fetter. **2.** *usually,* **shackles,** anything that hinders or restrains freedom of action or thought. **3.** hobble for a horse. **4.** any of various devices for fastening or coupling. —*v.t.* **1.** to put a shackle or shackles on; fetter. **2.** to hinder or restrain (someone or something), as from freedom of thought or action. **3.** to fasten or couple with a shackle. [Old English *sceacul* fetter.] —**shack′ler,** *n.*

Shack·le·ton, Sir Ernest Henry (shak′əl tən) 1874–1922, British antarctic explorer, born in Ireland.

shad (shad) *pl.* **shad** or **shads.** *n.* any of several commercially important food and game fish of the herring family, found in the coastal waters

of Europe and North America, esp. *Alosa sapidissima,* the **American shad,** which swims up coastal rivers in the spring to spawn, and whose roe is considered a delicacy. Weight: 1–8 pounds. [Old English *sceadd.*]

shad·ber·ry (shad′-ber′ē) *pl.* **-ries.** *n.* **1.** berry of the shadbush. **2.** shadbush.

shad·bush (shad′-boosh′) *n.* any of a group of shrubs and small trees, genus *Amelanchier,* of the

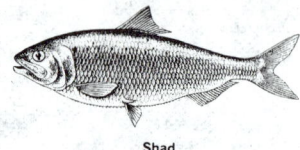

Shad

rose family, bearing clusters of showy white flowers and round, juicy berries of dark purple, mainly found growing wild in North America. Also, **shad·blow** (shad′blō′), **ser′vice·ber′ry.** [Because it blooms about the same time in the spring that *shad* appear in the rivers.]

shad·dock (shad′ək) *n.* **1.** large, pale-yellow, usually pear-shaped citrus fruit of a tropical tree, *Citrus grandis.* It resembles the closely related grapefruit, but is larger, coarser, and drier. **2.** tree that bears this fruit, native to southern Asia. [From a Captain *Shaddock,* who introduced this tree to the West Indies in the late seventeenth century.]

shade (shād) *n.* **1.** relative or partial darkness caused by something intercepting rays of light, as from the sun. **2.** place or spot sheltered from light, esp. from the rays of the sun: *He could find no shade to stand in while waiting.* **3.** window shade. **4.** device fitted over a lamp to reduce or deflect the flow of light. **5.** anything that shuts out or reduces light or heat: *The clerk wore a green shade over his eyes.* **6.** gradation or intensity of color; degree of darkness or lightness in color: *a deep shade of green.* **7.** representation of a dark or unilluminated surface, as in a painting. **8.** small degree or amount; trifle; trace; nuance: *a shade of doubt.* **7.** comparative obscurity or insignificance. **8.** disembodied spirit; ghost. **9. (the) shades. a.** growing darkness, as after sunset. **b.** the abode of the dead; Hades. **10. shades.** *Slang.* sunglasses. —*v.t.,* **shad·ed, shad·ing. 1.** to shelter, screen, or protect from glare, heat, or light. **2.** to mark (a drawing, painting, or the like) with gradations of darkness or color: *He shaded the border with a contrasting color.* **3.** to cover with shadow or make gloomy. **4.** to lower or reduce slightly, as a price. **5.** to cause to change or vary by slight degrees. —*v.i.* to change or vary slightly or by degrees. [Old English *sceadu* shadow.] —**shad′er,** *n.* —**Syn.** *n.* 6. see tint.

shad·ing (shā′ding) *n.* **1.** the representing of different degrees of light and dark in a painting, drawing, or the like, as by using lines, dots, or varying tones of color. **2.** small degree of change or variation; slight gradation. **3.** shelter or screening, as from light or heat.

sha·doof (shä dōōf′) *n.* device used in Egypt and adjacent regions since ancient times, consisting of a long pole on a pivot with a bucket on one end and a weight on the other, used for lifting buckets of water from a stream to an irrigation ditch. [Arabic *shādūf.*]

shad·ow (shad′ō) *n.* **1.** relatively dark region produced when rays from a source of light are blocked by an opaque object. **2.** dark image or figure that approximates the person or thing

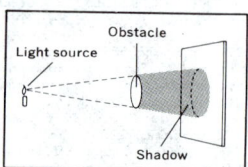

Shadow

blocking these light rays. **3.** partial darkness; shade. **4.** darker or shaded portion of a picture. **5.** reflected image, as in a mirror or in water. **6.** ghost; phantom. **7.** something delusive, unsubstantial, or unreal; product of the imagination. **8.** faint or obscure image or representation: *The event was a shadow of things to come.* **9.** slight indication of something previous; remnant; vestige. *He existed in the shadow of past greatness.* **10.** slight degree or suggestion; faintest trace: *The shadow of a smile played over Cathy's face.* **11.a.** constant companion; close friend; follower. **b.** person who follows another closely and usually secretly, as a spy. **12.** sadness; gloom; unhappiness. **13.** *Archaic.* protection; shelter. **14. the shadows.** darkness or deep shade. —*v.t.* **1.** to cast a shadow on or over; cover or obscure with a shadow. **2.** to represent or indicate faintly or vaguely. **3.** to follow closely, esp. to watch secretly. **4.** to make gloomy; sadden. **5.** *Archaic.* to protect or shelter from light; shade. [Old English *sceaduwe,* dative of *sceadu* shade.] —**shad′ow·er,** *n.*

shad·ow·box (shad′ō boks′) *v.i.* to make the motions of boxing with an imaginary opponent, esp. for practice or exercise. —**shad′ow·box′ing,** *n.*

shad·ow·graph (shad′ō graf′) *n.* **1.** image produced by throwing a shadow, usually made by the hands, on a lighted surface. **2.** X-ray photograph.

shadow play, theatrical presentation performed by projecting the shadows of actors or puppets onto a lighted screen.

shad·ow·y (shad′ō ē′) *adj.* **1.** full of shadow or shade; shady. **2.** like a shadow; dim; indistinct: *a shadowy figure.* **3.** without reality; imaginary; unsubstantial.

shad·y (shā′dē) *adj.* **shad·i·er, shad·i·est.** *adj.* **1.a.** sheltered from the sun; full of shade; shaded. **b.** shadowy or dark like shade. **2.** providing shade. **3.** *Informal.* of doubtful legality or honesty; disreputable: *a shady business deal.* —**shad′i·ly,** *adv.* —**shad′i·ness,** *n.*

shaft (shaft) *n.* **1.** long, slender body connected to the head of an arrow or spear. **2.** arrow or spear. **3.** something like an arrow or missile in effect: *barbed shafts of wit.* **4.** ray or beam: *bright shafts of morning light.* **5.** either of the two wooden poles between which a horse or other draft animal is harnessed to pull a vehicle. **6.** long, straight handle of an of various tools or implements, as a hammer or hockey stick. **7.** any long, straight cylindrical object or part, as a pole. **8.** bar in a machine that serves to support a rotating part or to convey motion to other parts. **9.a.** deep passage, usually vertical, from ground level to an underground excavation, as in a mine. **b.** any well-like passage, as for an elevator or ventilation. **10.a.** portion of a column between the base and capital. **b.** slender column, such as those used to support vaulting. **c.** obelisk, column, or the like serving as a memorial. **11.** the rodlike, stiff, central part of a feather from which the vane extends to either side. [Old English *sceaft* long, slender part of a spear or arrow.]

shag¹ (shag) *n.* **1.** rough, matted hair, wool, or the like. **2.** mass of this. **3.** long, coarse nap, esp. of wool, cotton, or man-made fabrics used for rugs. **4.** fabric or article, as a rug, having such a nap. **5.** strong pipe tobacco cut into fine shreds. [Old English *sceacga* rough hair or wool.]

shag² (shag) **shagged, shag·ging.** *v.t.* to chase after and retrieve (a baseball or golf ball) during practice. [Of uncertain origin.]

shag·bark (shag′bärk′) *n.* **1.** a hickory tree, *Carya ovata,* native to Canada and the eastern United States, having shaggy gray bark that peels off in long strips, grown for its timber and edible nuts. **2.** wood of

Leaves
Fruit **Bark**

Shagbark

this tree, the most widely used hickory timber. **3.** nut of this tree. Also, **shell′bark′.**

shag·gy (shag′ē) **-gi·er, -gi·est.** *adj.* **1.** covered with or having long, rough hair or wool. **2.** long, bushy, and rough, as eyebrows. **3.** poorly groomed; unkempt: *a shaggy tramp.* **4.** having a long, coarse nap, as a rug. **5.** covered with rough, tangled growth: *a shaggy hillside.* [SHAG¹ + -Y¹.] —**shag′gi·ly,** *adv.* —**shag′gi·ness,** *n.*

sha·green (shə grēn′) *n.* **1.** untanned leather having a rough, granular surface, often dyed green, and used esp. for ornamental objects. It is made from the skins of various animals, as the horse, camel, seal, and shark. **2.** the rough skin of certain sharks. [French *chagrin,* from Turkish *sagry* the back of a horse, skin of the back of a horse (from which such leather was originally made).]

shah (shä) *n.* hereditary sovereign of Iran or Persia. [Persian *shāh.*]

shake (shāk) **shook, shak·en, shak·ing.** *v.t.* **1.** to cause to move quickly and irregularly to and fro, up and down, or from side to side: *Shake the bottle to mix the ingredients.* **2.** to cause to tremble, vibrate, or quiver: *The earthquake shook the building.* **3.** to dislodge by or as if by such movement: *The dog shook the snow from his back.* **4.** to cause to totter or waver; make unsteady: *The currency crisis shook the economy.* **5.** to weaken or impair; make less firm: *Cross-examination shook the witness's testimony.* **6.** to move or stir the feelings of; upset; disturb: *Clara was greatly shaken by the bad news.* **7.** *Informal.* to get rid of: *to shake one's pursuers.* **8.** *Music.* to trill. **9. to shake a leg.** *Informal.* to move or go quickly; hurry. **10. to shake down. a.** to bring or cast from a higher place by shaking: *to shake down apples from a tree.* **b.** to cause to settle or become compact: *to shake down flour.* **c.** *Slang.* to extort money from. **11. to shake hands.** to grasp (another's hand), esp. as a salutation or an expression of confirmation or friendship. **12. to shake off.** to rid oneself of: *to shake off a habit.* **13. to shake up. a.** to shake with force. **b.** to jar mentally or physically; shock. —*v.i.* **1.** to move quickly and irregularly to and fro, up and down, or from side to side; vibrate: *The house shakes when the trains go by.* **2.** to tremble; quiver: *to shake with fright.* **3.** to admit of being shaken: *Loose dirt will shake off.* **4.** to shake hands. **5.** *Music.* to trill. —*n.* **1.** act of shaking: *One shake of the stick scared the dog away. He gives his harness bells a shake* (Frost, 1923). **2.** something, esp. a beverage, made by shaking ingredients together. **3.** crack or fissure produced during formation or growth, as in timber or the earth. **4.** *Informal.* earthquake. **5.** *Informal.* brief time; moment; instant: *I'll be done in*

at; āpe; cär; end; mē; it; īce; hot; ōld; fôrk; wood; fōōl; oil; out; up; ūse; turn; sing; thin; **th**is; zh in treasure; ə in ago, taken, pencil, lemon, circus.

three shakes. **6.** *Music.* trill. **7. a fair shake.** *Informal.* just or fair treatment. **8. (the) shakes.** *Informal.* physical state or condition characterized by trembling or shivering, esp. one involving fever and chills. **9. no great shakes.** *Informal.* not unusual or outstanding; average. [Old English *sceacan* to move quickly, vibrate, cause to vibrate.] —**shak′a·ble;** *also,* **shake′a·ble,** *adj.*
Syn. *v.i.* **2. Shake, quake, tremble** mean to make quick and agitated involuntary movements. **Shake** suggests a broad, sweeping motion, often as a result of a physical or external source: *He shook with cold.* **Quake** suggests a convulsive motion, often conveying a grotesque or comic quality of exaggerated reaction: *He lay in bed quaking with terror at the sound of the creaking stairs.* **Tremble** suggests a slight but continuous motion on the surface, that often conveys a vulnerable attitude: *Her lips trembled and the tears streamed down her face as she tried to apologize.*

shake·down (shāk′doun′) *n.* **1.** act or process of shaking down. **2.** *Slang.* extortion. **3.** makeshift bed, as of straw or blankets on the floor. —*adj.* designed to test the performance of a ship or aircraft under actual operating conditions: *a shakedown cruise.*

shak·er (shā′kər) *n.* **1.** container having a perforated top, as for salt or pepper. **2.** any of various other devices or machines used for shaking: *a cocktail shaker.* **3.** one who shakes.

Shak·er (shā′kər) *n.* member of an American religious sect practicing celibacy and communal living and holding all property in common. [Because they used to sing and dance with *shaking* movements at their prayer meetings.]

Shake·speare, William (shāks′pēr) 1564–1616, English poet and dramatist.

Shake·spear·e·an (shāk spēr′ē ən) *also,* **Shake·spear·i·an.** *adj.* of, relating to, or like Shakespeare or his works. —*n.* scholar of Shakespeare or his works.

Shakespearean sonnet, sonnet form made famous by Shakespeare, consisting of three quatrains and a concluding couplet. The rhyme scheme is usually *abab cdcd efef gg.* Also, **Elizabethan sonnet, English sonnet.**

shake·up (shāk′up′) *n.* sudden and radical change in organization, as of a government.

shak·o (shak′ō) *pl.,* **shak·os.** *n.* high, stiff military hat with a visor and, usually, a plume attached in front. [French *s(c)hako,* from Magyar *csákó (süveg)* peaked (cap), going back to German *Zacke* point, peak.]

shak·y (shā′kē) shak·i·er, shak·i·est. *adj.* **1.** trembling; shaking. **2.** liable to break down or give way; unsound: *a shaky bridge.* **3.** not to be depended on. —**shak′i·ly,** *adv.* —**shak′i·ness,** *n.*

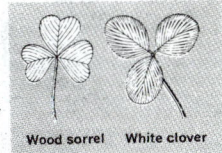
Shako

shale (shāl) *n.* fine-grained sedimentary rock, composed predominantly of hardened clay in very thin layers that separate easily. [Probably from Old English *scealu* shell.]

shall (shal) Present: *sing.,* first person, **shall;** second, **shall** or *(archaic)* **shalt;** third, **shall;** *pl.,* **shall.** Past: **should** or *(archaic second person sing.)* **shouldest** or **shouldst.** *auxiliary verb* (followed by an infinitive) **1.** in the first person, used to express simple futurity: *I shall be glad to help you.* **2.** in the second and third persons, used to express determination, obligation, or compulsion: *She shall do as she is told.* **3.** in all persons, used in direct questions when *shall* is expected in the answer: *Shall he leave tomorrow? Yes, he shall.* **4.** in all persons, used in conditional clauses to express future time: *If he shall die, his nephew shall succeed him.* [Old English *sceal,* first and third person singular of *sculan* to owe, be under obligation.] ▲ **shall, will.** Grammarians have traditionally drawn a distinction between *shall* and *will,* holding that in simple future statements *shall* is the correct usage with the first person, as *When shall we three meet again* (Shakespeare, *Macbeth*), and *will* is correct with the second and third persons, as *Some say the world will end in fire* (Frost, 1923). For statements expressing determination or obligation, *will* is used with the first person, as *All the world over, I will back the masses against the classes* (Gladstone, 1886) and *shall* with the second or third, as *We here highly resolve . . . that this nation . . . shall have a new birth of freedom* (Lincoln, 1863). However, this distinction has never been faithfully observed, even by the best speakers and writers, as *We shall never surrender* (Churchill, 1940) to express determination, or *Show me a hero and I will write you a tragedy* (Fitzgerald, 1937) to express simple futurity. In current American usage, *shall* and *will* are considered interchangeable, with *will* greatly predominating in frequency of use. Though *shall* is common in British English, most American speakers feel that it carries a tone of artificiality or excessive formality.

shal·loon (sha lōōn′) *n.* lightweight woolen fabric woven with a twill, used esp. for linings. [From *Châlons,* French town where it was first made.]

shal·lop (shal′əp) *n.* small open boat propelled by sails or oars. [French *chaloupe,* from Dutch *sloep* sloop. Doublet of SLOOP.]

shal·lot (sha lot′) *n.* **1.** small bulb or clove of a plant, *Allium ascalonicum,* closely related to the onion, used to flavor foods. **2.** the small plant that grows from this bulb. [Shortened from Middle French *eschalote* an onionlike plant, modification of Old French *eschaloigne,* from Latin *Ascalōnia (caepa)* (onion) of *Ascalon,* a city in Palestine.]

shal·low (shal′ō) *adj.* **1.** of little depth; not deep: *a shallow pond.* **2.** lacking depth of thought, reasoning, knowledge, or feeling. —*n.* shallow area in a body of water. —*v.t., v.i.* to make or become shallow. [Probably from an unrecorded Old English word.] —**shal′low·ly,** *adv.* —**shal′low·ness,** *n.* —**Syn.** *adj.* **2.** see **superficial.**

sha·lom (sha lōm′) *interj.* used as a Jewish salutation or farewell. [Hebrew *shālōm* peace.]

shalt (shalt) *Archaic.* second person singular, present tense, of **shall.** ▲ used with *thou.*

shal·y (shā′lē) *adj.* of, like, or containing shale.

sham (sham) *n.* **1.** something false intended to appear genuine or true; deceptive imitation; fraud; counterfeit. **2.** one who falsely assumes a certain character for the purpose of deception. **3.** decorative cover made to simulate an article of household linen and used in its place or over it: *a pillow sham.* —*adj.* **1.** pretended; feigned: *a sham battle.* **2.** intended to deceive; false: *sham friendship.* **3.** imitation: *sham diamonds.* —*v.t.,* **shammed, sham·ming. 1.** to assume the appearance of; feign. **2.** to produce a deceptive imitation of. —*v.i.* to make false pretenses; pretend. [Possibly dialectal form of SHAME.] —**sham′mer,** *n.*

sha·man (shä′mən, shā′-) *n.* in certain religions, a priest believed to have magical powers, esp. to cure illness, through communication during trances with supernatural beings. [Russian *shaman,* from Tungus *saman,* possibly going back to Sanskrit *shramana* Buddhist monk, ascetic.] —**sha′man·ism, sha′man·ist,** *n.* —**sha′man·is′tic,** *adj.*

sham·ble (sham′bəl) **-bled, -bling.** *v.i.* to walk awkwardly or unsteadily; shuffle. —*n.* shambling walk or gait. [From earlier *shamble* ungainly, from *shamble* table for the sale of meat (with reference to its straddling trestles). See SHAMBLES.]

sham·bles (sham′bəlz) *n.,pl.* **1.** scene of wholesale slaughter or of great bloodshed. **2.** slaughterhouse. **3.** place or condition of great disorder. ▲ construed as singular or plural. [Plural of earlier *shamble* table for the sale of meat (associated with the blood of the slaughtered animals), from Old English *scamel* table, bench, from Latin *scamellum* little bench, stool.]

shame (shām) *n.* **1.** painful feeling of guilt or embarrassment caused by consciousness of something wrong, indecent, or foolish. **2.** perception of what is improper or disgraceful: *Have you no shame?* **3.** dishonor; ignominy; disgrace: *Ted's actions brought shame to his entire family.* **4.** one who or that which brings or causes disgrace: *Widespread corruption was the shame of his administration.* **5.** thing to be sorry about: *What a shame that Frank didn't win.* **6. for shame.** shame on you; how shameful. **7. to put to shame. a.** to inflict disgrace or dishonor upon; cause to feel ashamed. **b.** to surpass another or others in accomplishment or ability; outdo. —*v.t.,* **shamed, sham·ing. 1.** to cause to feel shame; make ashamed; embarrass. **2.** to bring disgrace upon; be a cause of disgrace to; dishonor. **3.** to force or drive through shame or fear of shame: *They shamed him into volunteering to help.* [Old English *sceamu* feeling of being disgraced, disgrace.]

shame·faced (shām′fāst′) *adj.* **1.** bashful; shy. **2.** showing shame; ashamed. [Modification (influenced by FACE) of archaic *shamefast,* from Old English *sc(e)amfæst* literally, restrained by shame, from *sceamu* shame + *fæst* firm.]

shame·ful (shām′fəl) *adj.* **1.** causing shame; disgraceful. **2.** indecent; offensive: *a shameful display of vulgarity.* —**shame′ful·ly,** *adv.* —**shame′ful·ness,** *n.*

shame·less (shām′lis) *adj.* **1.** having no sense of shame; immodest; brazen. **2.** done without shame: *a shameless disregard for honesty.* —**shame′less·ly,** *adv.* —**shame′less·ness,** *n.*

sham·my (sham′ē) *pl.,* **-mies.** *n.* chamois *(def. 2).*

sham·poo (sham pōō′) **-pooed, -poo·ing.** *v.t.* **1.** to wash (the hair or scalp) with soap and water or a special preparation. **2.** to wash the hair and scalp of. **3.** to clean (upholstery or rugs) with any of various cleaning preparations. **4.** to massage. —*n.* **1.** act of washing the hair or scalp. **2.** any of various preparations for use in shampooing. [Hindi *chāmpo,* imperative of *chāmpnā* to press, massage.] —**sham·poo′er,** *n.*

sham·rock (sham′rok′) *n.* **1.** leaf consisting of three oval leaflets, as the three-leaf clover. The shamrock is the national emblem of Ireland. **2.** any of several plants having such leaves, esp. the clover. [Irish *seamróg* trefoil, clover, diminutive of *seamar.*]

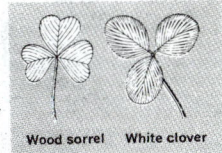
Wood sorrel   White clover

Shamrocks

sha·mus (shä′məs, shā′-) *n.* *Slang.* **1.** policeman. **2.** private detec-

at; āpe; cär; end; mē; it; īce; hot; ōld; fôrk; wood; fōōl; oil; out; up; ūse; turn; sing; thin; this; zh in treasure; ə in ago, taken, pencil, lemon, circus.

915

tive. [Possibly blend of Irish *Séamus* James, and Yiddish *shames* sexton in a synagogue (from Hebrew *shammāsh* servant).]

shan·dy·gaff (shan′dē gaf′) *n.* drink made of ale or beer mixed usually with ginger beer, ginger ale, or lemonade. Also, **shan′dy.** [Of uncertain origin.]

shang·hai (shang′hī, shang hī′) **-haied, -hai·ing.** *v.t.* **1.** to render (someone) insensible by drugs, liquor, or violence in order to secure him as a sailor on a ship against his will. **2.** to compel (someone) to do something against his will, esp. by fraud or force. [From the earlier practice of acquiring sailors against their will for voyages to *Shanghai.*]

Shang·hai (shang hī′) *n.* chief port and largest city of China, in the eastern part of the country. Pop. (1957 est.), 6,900,000.

Shan·gri-La (shang′gri lä′) *n.* imaginary earthly paradise. [From *Shangri-La*, an imaginary ideal land described in the novel *Lost Horizon* by James Hilton, 1900–54, English writer.]

shank (shangk) *n.* **1.** the part of the leg in man that extends from the knee to the ankle. **2.** a corresponding part in certain animals and birds. **3.** the entire leg. **4.** cut of meat from the leg of an animal. **5.** part of an instrument, tool, or the like, that connects the acting part with a handle or the part by which it is held or moved, as the straight part of a nail. **6.** *Printing.* the body of a piece of type. **7.** the narrow part of a shoe under the arch of the foot, connecting the sole and the heel. **8.a.** the latter end or part of anything. **b.** the early or best part of a period of time: *the shank of the evening.* **9.** the part of an anchor between the stock and the flukes. See **anchor** for illustration. **10. on shank's mare.** on foot. **11. to ride shank's mare.** to walk. —*v.t.* to hit (a golf ball) with the heel of the club. [Old English *sceanca* shinbone, leg.]

Shan·non (shan′ən) *n.* river flowing from north-central Ireland into the Atlantic.

shan't (shant, shänt) shall not.

Shan·tung (shan′tung′; *def. 3 also* shan′tung′) *n.* **1.** province in northeast China. Area, 55,560 sq. mi. Pop. (1957 est.), 54,030,000. **2.** peninsula in this province, extending into the Yellow Sea. **3. shantung.** medium-weight soft fabric, esp. one of silk, having a textured surface resulting from the interspersion of extra-thick threads here and there throughout the weave.

shan·ty¹ (shan′tē) *pl.,* **-ties.** *n.* crude, flimsily built hut or cabin. [Possibly from Irish *sean toigh* literally, old house.]

shan·ty² (shan′tē) *pl.,* **-ties.** *also,* **shan·tey.** *n.* chantey.

shan·ty·town (shan′tē toun′) *n.* poor section of a town where people live mainly in shanties.

shape (shāp) *n.* **1.** overall or external outline or configuration; form; figure: *All circles have the same shape. Melted glass can be molded into many shapes.* **2.** one of the forms or variations in which a thing may exist or be represented; kind; sort. **3.** something that has or gives form; mold; pattern. **4.** assumed or external appearance; guise. **5.** imaginary or supernatural form; phantom. **6.a.** condition: *He was in bad shape after the accident. That company is in good shape financially.* **b.** good physical condition: *He exercises regularly to keep from getting out of shape.* **7.** contour of a person's body; figure. **8.** definite, regular, or proper form or arrangement; order: *Let's get things in shape before the others arrive.* **9.** to take shape. to have or assume a definite form, order, or plan. —*v.t.,* **shaped, shap·ing. 1.** to give form to; fashion; mold: *to shape dough into loaves.* **2.** to adapt in form; adjust; modify. **3.** to give definite direction or character to. **4.** to form mentally; plan; devise. **5.** to express verbally. —*v.i.* to take shape; develop (usually with *up*): *Things are shaping up nicely.* [Old English *(ge)sceap* a form, creation.]

Syn. *n.* **1. Shape, figure, form** mean the aspect of some thing. **Shape** suggests the three-dimensional qualities of bulk or mass: *The sculptor worked the clay into the shape of a woman.* **Figure** suggests the abstract or conventional representations of objects: *He drew the figure of a circle on the board.* **Form** is the most general term, suggesting the unity of an object when viewed as a whole: *The scarecrow's arms were outstretched in the form of a cross.*

shape·less (shāp′lis) *adj.* **1.** without definite or regular shape. **2.** having no beauty or elegance of form; unshapely. —**shape′less·ly,** *adv.* —**shape′less·ness,** *n.*

shape·ly (shāp′lē) **-li·er, -li·est.** *adj.* having a beautiful or elegant shape; well-formed. —**shape′li·ness,** *n.*

shape-up (shāp′up′) *n.* system of selecting work crews, esp. of longshoremen, by having the workers assemble at a certain place, with the foreman choosing among them.

shard (shärd) *n.* **1.a.** fragment of some brittle material, as of glass. **b.** potsherd. **2.** elytron. [Old English *sceard* fragment.]

share¹ (shâr) *n.* **1.** part which is allotted to or belongs to one individual. **2.** part of anything jointly owned by several parties. **3.** one of the equal portions into which the capital of a company or corporation is divided. **4. to go shares.** to participate in or contribute toward; an enterprise.

—*v.t.,* **shared, shar·ing. 1.** to use, bear, enjoy, or participate in jointly or in common: *to share an apartment, to share someone's happiness.* **2.** to divide into portions and give to others as well as oneself: *to share one's dinner with friends.* —*v.i.* to have a share; take part: *to share in the profits of a company.* [Old English *scearu* division, cutting.] —**shar′er,** *n.*

Syn. *v.i.* **Share, participate** mean to do or use something together with others. **Share** stresses the group as the basis of an effort or experience: *We shared in the fun.* **Participate** stresses the individual contribution in making up the whole or accomplishing a goal: *I participated in the street fair, selling tickets and setting up booths.*

share² (shâr) *n.* plowshare. [Old English *scear.*]

share·crop·per (shâr′krop′ər) *n.* tenant farmer who farms land for the owner in return for a share of the crops.

share·hold·er (shâr′-hōl′dər) *n.* stockholder.

shark¹ (shärk) *n.* any of numerous medium to large, mostly saltwater predatory fish, order Squaliformes, having skeletons of cartilage rather than bone, with usually gray rough skin, a

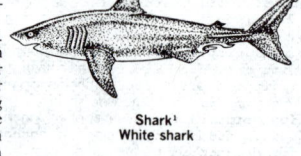

Shark¹
White shark

deeply forked tail, and a large mouth on the underside of the head with several rows of sharp teeth. [Of uncertain origin.]

shark² (shärk) *n.* **1.** dishonest person who preys on others; swindler. **2.** *Slang.* one who has exceptional ability in some special area: *a card shark.* [German *Schurke* rogue.]

shark·skin (shärk′skin′) *n.* **1.** durable, tightly woven, crisp fabric of worsted or synthetic fibers, characterized by a color effect produced by two different threads being used in both the warp and filling. **2.** the skin of a shark, esp. as used for making leather.

sharp (shärp) *adj.* **1.** hiving a fine cutting edge or point; well-suited for cutting or piercing: *a sharp blade.* **2.** having a pointed end; not rounded or blunt: *a sharp peak.* **3.** abrupt, esp. with regard to angle or direction: *a sharp turn.* **4.** harsh; severe; biting: *a sharp rebuke.* **5.** keenly affecting the senses or emotions: *sharp pangs of hunger.* **6.** (of food) having an acrid or penetrating taste: *sharp cheese.* **7.** high-pitched; shrill. **8.** clear or distinct, as in outline or contour. **9.** having a keen awareness or ability to discern quickly: *a sharp sense of smell.* **10.** shrewd or clever in pursuing one's own gain: *to play at cards.* **11.** watchful; alert; vigilant: *Keep a sharp lookout.* **12.** rapid; brisk; energetic: *He walked off at a sharp pace.* **14.** *Slang.* strikingly attractive; stylish; classy: *You really look sharp in that new outfit.* **15.** *Music.* **a.** raised a half step in pitch. **b.** above the true or proper pitch; too high. **c.** (of a key) having sharps in the signature. **16.** (of a consonant) articulated with the breath only; voiceless. —*adv.* **1.** at the moment specified; promptly; exactly: *to leave at 1:30 sharp.* **2.** in a sharp manner. —*n.* **1.** *Music.* **a.** note or tone one half step above a given note or tone. **b.** symbol (♯) which, when placed before a note or on a degree of the staff, indicates that the pitch will be raised by a half step. **2.** sharper. **3.** *Informal.* an expert. [Old English *scearp* having a fine cutting edge or point, keen, severe.] —**sharp′ly,** *adv.* —**sharp′ness,** *n.*

sharp·en (shär′pən) *v.t., v.i.* to make or become sharp or sharper. —**sharp′en·er,** *n.*

sharp·er (shär′pər) *n.* **1.** swindler; cheat. **2.** dishonest gambler.

sharp·ie (shär′pē) *n.* **1.** long, narrow, flat-bottomed sailboat having one or two masts. **2.** *Slang.* shrewd, quick-witted person.

Sharpie

sharp·shoot·er (shärp′shōō′tər) *n.* **1.** anyone skilled in shooting, esp. with a rifle. **2.a.** the second category of proficiency in target shooting. **b.** one who has qualified in this category. —**sharp′shoot′ing,** *n.*

sharp·sight·ed (shärp′sī′təd) *adj.* **1.** having acute eyesight. **2.** having or showing mental acuteness.

sharp·tongued (shärp′tungd′) *adj.* using or tending to use harsh, biting, critical, or sarcastic language.

sharp·wit·ted (shärp′wit′id) *adj.* having or showing a quick, acute mind.

Shas·ta, Mount (shas′tə) volcanic mountain in northern California, in the Cascade Range.

Shasta daisy 1. showy white daisylike flower of any of several varieties of a plant, *Chrysanthemum maximum,* of the composite family. **2.** plant bearing this flower head. [From Mount *Shasta.*]

at; āpe; cär; end; mē; it; īce; hot; ōld; fôrk; wood; fōōl; oil; out; up; ūse; turn; sing; thin; this; zh in treasure; ə in ago, taken, pencil, lemon, circus.

shat·ter (shat'ər) *v.t.* **1.** to break (something, esp. a hard or brittle thing) into pieces, as by a sudden blow. **2.** to destroy completely or damage greatly: *Their lives were shattered by the horrible experience of war.* —*v.i.* to break suddenly into pieces; go to pieces. —*n.* **1.** act of shattering. **2. shatters.** *Archaic.* fragments: *a sea which dashed the ship to shatters against the rock* (Dorrington, 1727). [Of uncertain origin.] —**Syn.** *v.t.* **1.** see **break.**

shat·ter·proof (shat'ər prōōf') *adj.* made so as not to shatter, esp. so that fragments will not fly off: *The window was made of shatterproof glass.*

shave (shāv) **shaved, shaved** or **shav·en, shav·ing.** *v.t.* **1.** to remove hair from (a part of the body) with a razor: *to shave one's legs.* **2.** to cut (hair, esp. the beard) down close to the skin with a razor. **3.** to cut down the surface of by removing thin shavings or parings: *to shave the edge of a board.* **4.** to cut off in thin slices or parings, as ice. **5.** to cut very closely, as a lawn. **6.** to touch slightly, as in passing, or come very near touching; graze. **7.** to reduce or lower by a slight margin: *to shave prices.* —*v.i.* to remove hair with a razor. —*n.* **1.** act of cutting off hair with a razor. **2.** thin slice; shaving; paring. **3.** tool for shaving. **4.** *Informal.* situation in which danger was barely avoided. [Old English *scafan* to scrape, scrape away.]

shave·ling (shāv'ling) *n.* **1.** tonsured monk or priest. ▲ usually considered offensive. **2.** youth.

shav·en (shā'vən) *v.* a past participle of **shave.** —*adj.* **1.** shaved. **2.** closely cut or trimmed, as grass. **3.** tonsured.

shav·er (shā'vər) *n.* **1.** one who shaves. **2.** any device for shaving. **3.** *Informal.* youngster; boy.

shave·tail (shāv'tāl') *n.* *Slang.* second lieutenant, esp. a recently commissioned one.

Sha·vi·an (shā'vē ən) *adj.* of, relating to, or characteristic of George Bernard Shaw or his works. —*n.* scholar or admirer of Shaw or his works.

shav·ing (shā'ving) *n.* **1.** very thin piece or slice, esp. a thin slice of wood cut off by a plane. **2.** act or process of removing hair or trimming a surface with as with a razor.

shaving cream, soapy cream or foam for softening the beard before shaving.

Sha·vu·oth (shə vōō'əs) *also,* **Sha·bu·oth, Sha·vu·ot.** *n.* Jewish holiday, originally a harvest festival, observed fifty days after the first day of Passover and commemorating the giving of the law to Moses. Also, **Pen'te·cost'.** [Hebrew *shābhū'oth,* plural of *shabhūa'* week.]

Shaw, George Bernard (shô) 1856–1950, British playwright, critic, and social theorist, born in Ireland.

shawl (shôl) *n.* large scarf or wrap consisting of a square or oblong piece of fabric, often embroidered, usually worn over the shoulders. [Persian *shāl* shawl made of a superior wool, probably from *Shaliat,* a town in India where supposedly it was first made.]

shawm (shôm) *n.* medieval double-reed wind instrument, the forerunner of the oboe. [Old French *chalemie,* form of *chalemel* reed pipe, going back to Latin *calamus* reed, from Greek *kalamos.*]

Shaw·nee (shô nē') *pl.* **-nees** or **-nee.** *n.* member of a tribe of Algonquian Indians, formerly living at various times in the East, South, and Midwest, now living mainly in Oklahoma.

shay (shā) *n.* chaise. [Old French CHAISE, mistaken for a plural.]

Shays' Rebellion (shāz) series of tax revolts by western Massachusetts farmers against the Massachusetts legislature in 1786–87.

she (shē) *sing.* nominative, **she;** possessive, **her, hers;** objective, **her;** *pl.* nominative, **they;** possessive, **their, theirs;** objective, **them.** *pron.* **1.** female person or animal, or an object personified as female, that has been previously mentioned. **2.** the woman or girl: *She who listens learns.* —*n. pl.,* **shes.** female person or animal. [Old English *sēo, sīo,* feminine of *se;* originally, that.]

sheaf (shēf) *pl.,* **sheaves.** *n.* **1.** one of the bundles in which stalks of cereal plants, such as wheat, are bound after reaping. **2.** any bundle of things all of a kind put or tied together: *a sheaf of papers, a sheaf of arrows.* —*v.t.* to bind into a sheaf; sheave. [Old English *scēaf* bundle of stalks, esp. of grain.]

shear (shēr) **sheared** or *(archaic)* **shore, sheared** or **shorn, shear·ing.** *v.t.* **1.** to clip or cut with shears, scissors, or a similar sharp instrument. **2.** to cut the wool or hair from: *to shear sheep.* **3.** to cut off; remove by clipping: *to shear fleece.* **4.a.** to subject (a solid body) to shearing stress. **b.** to cause to break by shearing stress (usually with *off*): *to shear off a bolt.* —*v.i.* to come apart or break because of shearing stress. —*n.* **1.** act or process of shearing. **2.** one blade of a pair of shears. **3.** pair of shears. **4.a.** shearing stress. **b.** deformation of a solid body by shearing stress, such that two parts or pieces of it slide on each other in opposite directions. [Old English *sceran* to cut, shave.] —**shear'er,** *n.*

shearing stress, force acting on a solid body in such a way as to cause adjacent parts of the solid to slide past one another parallel to the plane of contact.

shears (shērz) *n.,pl.* **1.** any of various, usually large, scissorlike instruments. **2.** large scissors. **3.** device for lifting heavy loads, having two legs spread at the bottom and fastened together at the top to support a block and tackle. [Old English *scēara* (plural) scissors.]

shear·wa·ter (shēr'wô'tər, -wot'ər) *n.* any of several web-footed seabirds, esp. of the genus *Puffinus,* having slender, hooked bills, long wings, and plumage that is gray, black, or brown above and often whitish below. Length: 12–25 inches. [From its habit of skimming the water as it flies, appearing to cut the crests of the waves.]

sheath (shēth) *pl.,* **sheaths** (shēthz). *n.* **1.** case for the blade of a cutting weapon, as a sword or knife. **2.** any similar covering, as a membrane covering a muscle. **3.** tight, close-fitting dress. —*v.t.* to sheathe. [Old English *scæth* case for a blade.]

sheathe (shēth) **sheathed, sheath·ing.** *v.t.* **1.** to put into a sheath or scabbard: *to sheathe a sword.* **2.** to enclose or protect in a case or covering: *to sheathe a roof with metal.* **3.** to retract or draw in (claws).

Shears (def. 3)

sheath·ing (shē'thing) *n.* **1.** something that covers or protects, as the first covering of boards on a house or one of the metal plates on the bottom of a ship. **2.** act of one who sheathes.

sheath knife, knife made to be carried in a sheath, usually having a fixed blade.

sheave[1] (shēv) **sheaved, sheav·ing.** *v.t.* to gather and bind into a sheaf or sheaves. [From SHEAF.]

sheave[2] (shēv) *n.* grooved wheel, as the wheel of a pulley. [Form of dialectal English *shive* slice, probably from an unrecorded Old English word.]

sheaves (shēvz) **1.** plural of **sheaf. 2.** plural of **sheave**[2].

She·ba (shē'bə) *n.* **1.** ancient country in southwestern Arabia. **2. Queen of.** in the Old Testament, a beautiful and wealthy queen who visited Solomon to learn for herself if he was really as wise as he was reputed to be.

she·bang (shi bang') *n.* *Slang.* thing; affair; business. [Of uncertain origin.]

She·boy·gan (shi boi'gən) *n.* city in eastern Wisconsin, on Lake Michigan. Pop. (1970), 48,484.

shed[1] (shed) *n.* **1.** slight structure used for shelter or storage. **2.** large, strongly built structure, often with open ends or sides, used for storage. [Old English *sced, scead* shade, shelter.]

shed[2] (shed) **shed, shed·ding.** *v.t.* **1.** to cause to flow; let fall; let pour, as blood or tears. **2.a.** to throw off or lose by natural process, as skin or antlers. **b.** to cast off; remove. **3.** to emit or send forth; radiate; emanate; exude: *The lilacs had shed their gentle fragrance throughout the room.* **4.** to cause to flow off without penetrating: *a coat that sheds rain.* **5. to shed blood.** to cause death or severe injury. —*v.i.* **1.** to throw off or lose a covering, esp. hair, by natural process. **2.** to fall off or drop, as leaves or seed. [Old English *scēadan* to separate, divide, scatter.]

she'd (shēd) **1.** she had. **2.** she would.

shed·der (shed'ər) *n.* **1.** one who or that which sheds. **2.** animal, as a crab, lobster, or snake, that is about to shed its shell or skin; or has just done so.

sheen (shēn) *n.* lustrous brightness; shininess. [From earlier *sheen* beautiful, from Old English *scēne.*] —**sheen'y,** *adj.* —**Syn.** see **luster.**

sheep (shēp) *pl.,* **sheep.** *n.* **1.** cud-chewing, cloven-hooved mammal, genus *Ovis,* akin to the goat, esp. any of numerous domesticated breeds of the species *O. aries,* widely raised for their fleece, and for meat, milk, and leather. Height: 1½–4 feet at the shoulder. **2.** timid, stupid, or submissive person. **3.** sheepskin (defs. 1, 2). [Old English *scēap* this animal.]

Sheep

sheep·cote (shēp'kōt') *n.* shed or similar shelter for sheep.

sheep dog *also,* **sheep·dog** (shēp'dôg'). **1.** Old English sheep dog. **2.** dog trained to guard, drive, or tend sheep, as a collie.

sheep·fold (shēp'fōld') *n.* enclosure for sheep, as a pen.

sheep·herd·er (shēp'hur'dər) *n.* person who raises or tends a large number of sheep, esp. on the open range. —**sheep'herd'ing,** *n.*

sheep·ish (shē'pish) *adj.* **1.** awkwardly bashful or embarrassed. **2.** like a sheep; timid, stupid, or submissive. —**sheep'ish·ly,** *adv.* —**sheep'ish·ness,** *n.*

sheeps·head (shēps′hed′) *n.* large, gray or yellow saltwater food fish, *Archosargus probatocephalus,* related to the porgy, found along the Atlantic and Gulf coasts of the United States. Length: to 30 inches.

sheep·skin (shēp′skin′) *n.*
1. skin of a sheep, esp. one prepared with the wool on it, used for such items as gloves and coats. **2.** leather or parchment made from this skin. **3.** *Informal.* diploma.

Sheepshead

sheep sorrel, a common weed, *Rumex acetosella,* having sourtasting leaves. It is found growing chiefly in dry or sandy soil.
sheep·walk (shēp′wôk′) *n. British.* pasture or range for sheep.
sheer[1] (shēr) *adj.* **1.** very thin and fine; nearly transparent: *sheer fabric.* **2.** unmixed with anything else: *He grew despondent from the sheer loneliness of his way of living.* **3.** utter; downright: *sheer nonsense, sheer stupidity.* **4.** straight up or straight down; steep: *a sheer drop.* —*adv.* **1.** completely; quite; altogether. **2.** very steeply up or down. [Possibly modification of dialectal English *shire* bright, thin, complete, clear, from Old English *scīr* bright, pure.] —**sheer′ly,** *adv.* —**sheer′ness,** *n.*
sheer[2] (shēr) *v.i.* to deviate from a course; turn aside or away; swerve: *The ship sheered off from the rocks.* —*v.t.* to cause to sheer. —*n.* **1.** a moving away of a ship or boat from its course. **2.** the upward curve from the middle of a boat or ship to the bow or stern. **3.** position in which a boat or ship, held by a single anchor, is placed to keep it clear of the anchor. [Dutch *scheren* to cut, go away, move aside.]
sheet[1] (shēt) *n.* **1.** large piece of fabric, usually cotton, used as a bed covering. **2.** any broad, usually flat and thin piece or object: *a sheet of clear plastic.* **3.** oblong or square piece of paper or parchment, esp. for writing or printing on. **4.** newspaper. **5.** broad expanse or surface: *sheets of flame, a sheet of water.* **6.** sail. —*v.t.* **1.** to furnish with a sheet or sheets. **2.** to cover with a sheet: *Snow sheeted the ground.* [Old English *scēte* large piece of cloth.]
sheet[2] (shēt) *n.* **1.** rope or chain attached to one or both of the lower ends of a sail, used to adjust or control the sail. **2. sheets.** space at both the bow and stern of an open boat, esp. in front of and behind the cross seats of a rowboat. [Old English *scēata* piece of cloth, lower corner of a sail.]
sheet anchor 1. large anchor usually carried in the middle of a ship and used only in emergencies. **2.** final reliance or resort when everything else has failed. [Of uncertain origin.]
sheet·ing (shē′ting) *n.* **1.** fabric used for bed sheets. **2.** lining or covering of timber or metal, used on a surface for protection.
sheet lightning, lightning appearing as bright, broad flashes, as from within a cloud or beyond the horizon.
sheet metal, metal in thin, flat-rolled pieces.
sheet music, music printed on unbound sheets of paper.
Shef·field (shef′ēld′) *n.* city in northern England. Pop. (1968), 531,-800.
sheik (shēk) *also.* **sheikh.** *n.* **1.** leader of an Arab clan, tribe, or, other large group. **2.** Muslim religious leader, or similar head of a religious community. [Arabic *shaikh* elder, chief.] —**sheik′dom;** *also,* **sheikh′dom,** *n.*
shek·el (shek′əl) *n.* **1.** any of various ancient units of weight, esp. one of the Babylonians, Phoenicians, Hebrews, and Assyrians, equal to about half an ounce. **2.** ancient silver coin of the Hebrews weighing one shekel. **3. shekels.** *Slang.* coins; money. [Hebrew *sheqel* ancient Hebrew coin and unit of weight.]
shel·drake (shel′drāk′) *pl.,* **-drakes** or **-drake.** *n.* **1.** any of several large, gooselike ducks, family Anatidae, of Europe, North Africa, and Asia, esp. the **common sheldrake,** *Tadorna tadorna,* the male of which has a red bill with a prominent knob on top.

Sheldrake

Length: to 25 inches. **2.** any of various similar ducks, esp. the mergansers. [Probably from dialectal English *sheld* pied (from Middle Dutch *schillede* variegated) + DRAKE.]
shelf (shelf) *pl.,* **shelves.** *n.* **1.** thin, flat piece of wood, metal, stone, or other material, fastened horizontally to a wall or frame to hold things, as books or dishes. **2.** contents of a shelf. **3.** anything like a shelf, as a projecting ledge of rock. **4.** sandbar or reef. **5. on the shelf.** in a state of inactivity or uselessness. [Old English *scylfe* plank, ledge.]
shell (shel) *n.* **1.a.** hard or tough outer covering of any of various animals, as the turtle, lobster, or snail. **b.** material of which such a covering is composed. **2.** any similar outer covering, as of a seed, fruit,

or egg. **3.** something like a shell; empty or frail surrounding structure: *He was mere shell of his former self.* **4.** reluctance, refusal, or inability to communicate with others; air of reserve: *to bring a shy person out of his shell.* **5.a.** framework or outer walls and roof of a building. **b.** rounded or dome-shaped structure, as a band shell. **6.** hollow, rounded piece of pastry for holding filling. **7.a.** artillery projectile that is designed to explode at or in a target or in the air. **b.** piece of small-arms ammunition, esp. for a shotgun. **c.** that part of a cartridge or similar piece of ammunition that encases the charge and remains after the projectile has been fired off. **8.** long, light racing boat propelled by oarsmen. **9.** *Physics.* one of the energy levels surrounding an atom, analogous to a planetary orbit, in which an electron may be said to function. —*v.t.* **1.** to remove the shell, husk, or pod of: *to shell peanuts.* **2.** to remove grains from the ear or cob of: *to shell corn.* **3.** to subject to artillery fire; bombard with explosive shells. **4. to shell out.** *Informal.* to pay out, esp. to pay a considerable amount with reluctance or under pressure. —*v.i.* to undergo separation between the shell or covering and the contents: *These peas shell easily.* [Old English *sciell* hard outer covering of an animal, fruit, or egg.]
she'll (shēl) **1.** she shall. **2.** she will.
shel·lac (shə lak′) *n.* **1.** solution of purified lac in alcohol, used as a varnish on floors, furniture, or similar surfaces. **2.** the lac itself when not dissolved, used in making certain insulating materials and phonograph records. —*v.t.,* **-lacked, -lack·ing. 1.** to coat or treat with shellac. **2.** *Informal.* **a.** to defeat decisively. **b.** to beat; batter. [SHELL + LAC[1].]
shell·bark (shel′bärk′) *n.* shagbark.
Shel·ley (shel′ē) **1. Mary Woll·stone·craft** (wool′stən kraft′). 1797-1851, English novelist; wife of Percy Bysshe. **2. Percy Bysshe** (bish). 1792-1822, English poet.
shell·fire (shel′fīr′) *n.* the bursting of artillery shells.
shell·fish (shel′fish′) *pl.,* **-fish** or **-fish·es.** *n.* any invertebrate having a shell and living in water, esp. a mollusk or crustacean. [Old English *scilfisc.*]
shell game, game of chance, usually a swindle, in which the player bets on the location of a small object, as a pea, that supposedly has been placed under one of three walnut shells or small cups that have been shifted around quickly by the operator, who can change the object's location by sleight of hand.
shell·proof (shel′prōof′) *adj.* able to resist shells or bombs.
shell shock, any nervous or mental disorder resulting from combat in war.
shell·shocked (shel′shokt′) *adj.* suffering from shell shock.
shell·y (shel′ē) **shell·i·er, shell·i·est.** *adj.* **1.** abounding in or covered with shells, esp. seashells. **2.** consisting of a shell or shells. **3.** forming or resembling a shell.
shel·ter (shel′tər) *n.* **1.** something that covers or protects, as from weather or attack. **2.** protection; refuge. —*v.t.* **1.** to provide cover or protection for; shield. **2.** to take under one's protection. —*v.i.* to find or take shelter. [Possibly modification of obsolete *sheltron* phalanx, from Old English *scildtruma* literally, shield troop.] —**shel′ter·er,** *n.*
Syn. 1. Shelter, sanctuary, refuge mean a place of safety. **Shelter** suggests a relatively small and enclosed area that affords temporary cover, esp. from natural elements or catastrophe: *The Red Cross turned the school into a shelter for victims of the earthquake.* **Sanctuary** implies a larger but still limited area permanently set apart for the protection and preservation of a person or a group, suggesting an environment that is isolated, even sacred, and not to be tampered with: *The poet found the island an ideal sanctuary in a world that was overly civilized and commercialized.* **Refuge** suggests an entity rather than a limited area that affords freedom and security, esp. to those escaping from political or religious persecution: *America was a refuge for those who fled Hitler's Germany.*
shelter tent, pup tent.
shel·tie (shel′tē) *pl.,* **-ties.** *also,* **shel·ty.** *n.* **1.** Shetland sheepdog. **2.** Shetland pony. [Probably from Old Norse *hjalti* inhabitant of the Shetland Islands.]
shelve[1] (shelv) **shelved, shelv·ing.** *v.t.* **1.** to place on a shelf: *to shelve books.* **2.** to put away or aside as done with or not needed: *to shelve a plan.* **3.** to remove from active service. **4.** to furnish with shelves. [From SHELVES.]
shelve[2] (shelv) **shelved, shelv·ing.** *v.t.* to slope gradually. [Of uncertain origin.]
shelves (shelvz) plural of **shelf.**
shelv·ing (shel′ving) *n.* **1.** material for shelves, as wood or metal. **2.** shelves collectively.
Shem (shem) *n.* in the Old Testament, the eldest of the three sons of Noah, traditionally considered to be the ancestor of the Semitic peoples.
Shem·ite (shem′īt) *n.* Semite.
Shen·an·do·ah (shen′ən dō′ə) *n.* river flowing from northern Virginia into the Potomac.

at; āpe; cär; end; mē; it; īce; hot; ōld; fôrk; wood; fōōl; oil; out; up; ūse; turn; sing; thin; this; zh in treasure; ə in ago, taken, pencil, lemon, circus.

she·nan·i·gan (shi nan′i gən) *usually,* **shenanigans.** *n. Informal.* nonsense or trickery. [Of uncertain origin.]

Shen·yang (shun′yäng′) *n.* Mukden.

She·ol (shē′ol) *n.* **1.** in the Old Testament, the abode of the spirits of the dead; the underworld. **2.** *also,* **sheol.** hell. [Hebrew *she'ōl* the underworld.]

Shep·ard, Alan Bart·lett (shep′ərd; bärt′lit) 1923—, U.S. astronaut, the first American to fly in outer space.

shep·herd (shep′ərd) *n.* **1.** one who guards and otherwise takes care of a flock of sheep. **2.** spiritual leader; pastor. —*v.t.* **1.** to tend as a shepherd. **2.** to watch over or guide like a shepherd. [Old English *scēaphyrde* one who herds sheep, from *scēap* sheep + *hyrde* herdsman.] —**shep′herd·ess,** *n.*

shepherd dog, sheep dog.

shepherd's pie, casserole consisting of cubed meat, as beef or lamb, cooked in gravy, with a top crust or ring of mashed potatoes.

shepherd's purse, common weedy plant, *Capsella bursa-pastoris,* of the mustard family, having small triangular seedpods resembling purses or pouches.

Sher·a·ton (sher′ə tən) *adj.* in, of, or relating to a style of furniture characterized by overall simplicity of line, gracefulness, and the use of inlaid and applied decoration, esp. with porcelain plaques. [From Thomas *Sheraton,* 1751–1806, English furniture designer.]

sher·bet (shur′bit) *n.* **1.** frozen dessert made of fruit juice, water, sweeteners, and small amounts of egg whites or milk. **2.** *British.* beverage of sweetened fruit juice diluted with water, originally from the Middle East. [Turkish and Persian *sherbet* drink made of sweetened fruit juice, from Arabic *sharbah* a drink.]

sherd (shurd) shard.

Sher·i·dan (sher′əd ən) **1. Philip Henry.** 1831–88, Union general in the Civil War. **2. Richard Brins·ley** (brinz′lē). 1751–1816, British dramatist and statesman, born in Ireland.

she·rif (she rēf′) *n.* **1.** descendant of Muhammad through his daughter and only child, Fatima. **2.** Arab ruler, esp. the chief magistrate of Mecca or, formerly, the sovereign of Morocco. [Arabic *sharīf* noble.]

sher·iff (sher′if) *n.* chief law enforcement officer of a county, who is in charge of keeping the peace, serving court orders, maintaining the jails, and other administrative functions. [Old English *scīrgerēfa* high officer representing the king in a shire, from *scīr* shire + *gerēfa* officer.]

Sher·lock Holmes (shur′lok) **1.** fictional British detective. noted for his remarkable powers of observation, analysis, and deduction, the main character in mystery stories by Sir Arthur Conan Doyle. **2.** any remarkably shrewd, observant, or gifted detective or investigator.

Sher·man (shur′mən) **1. Roger.** 1721–93, U.S. statesman and signer of the Declaration of Independence. **2. William Te·cum·seh** (tə kum′sə). 1820–91, Union general in the Civil War.

Sher·pa (shur′pə) *n.* member of a people of Tibetan origin living in the Himalaya Mountains of Nepal, best known as guides or porters for mountain-climbing expeditions.

sher·ry (sher′ē) *pl.* **-ries.** *n.* strong, relatively sweet wine of a kind that originated in Spain, having a characteristic nutlike flavor and varying in color and taste from pale amber and somewhat dry to dark brown and quite sweet. [From earlier *sherris* (mistaken for a plural), a modification of *Xeres* (now *Jerez*), the town that is the center of the sherry-producing region of southern Spain.]

Sher·wood Forest (shur′wood) ancient royal forest of England, known as the legendary home of Robin Hood.

she's (shēz) **1.** she is. **2.** she has.

Shet·land (shet′land) *n.* **1.** Shetland pony. **2.** Shetland wool. **3.** Shetland Islands.

Shetland Islands, island group off northern Scotland, in the Atlantic. Land area, 550 sq. mi. Pop. (1967 est.), 17,231.

Shetland pony, small, hardy, rough-coated pony of a breed that originated in the Shetland Islands, having a long mane and tail. Height: 36–46 inches at the shoulder. Also, **shet′land.**

Shetland sheepdog, thick-coated dog closely resembling the collie but approximately 10 inches shorter. Height: 10 to 16 inches at the shoulder. Also, **shet′land.**

Shetland wool, soft, lustrous wool obtained from the undercoats of sheep of a breed that originated in the Shetland Islands.

Shetland pony

Shetland sheepdog

shew (shō) **shewed, shewn, shew·ing.** *Archaic. v.t., v.i.* to show. —*n.* show.

shew·bread (shō′bred′) *also,* **show·bread.** *n.* in the ancient Jewish religion, unleavened bread placed near the altar by the priest on the Sabbath as an offering to God.

shib·bo·leth (shib′ə lith, -leth′) *n.* **1.** catchword or slogan of a group or party, esp. one frequently repeated or adhered to unthinkingly. **2.** any characteristic, as of speech or usage, that distinguishes a group. [Hebrew *shibbōleth* stream. According to the story in Judges 12:6, this word was used to identify members of an enemy tribe, who were unable to pronounce the *sh,* saying *sibbōleth* instead.]

shied (shīd) past tense and past participle of **shy.**

shield (shēld) *n.* **1.** piece of defensive armor carried on the arm. **2.** one who or that which serves as a defense against danger, injury, or distress. **3.** something shaped like a shield, as a policeman's badge. **4.** escutcheon. **5.** piece of some moisture-repellent fabric worn inside a garment, usually under the arms, as a protection from soiling by perspiration. —*v.t.* to act as a shield to; protect; defend. —*v.i.* to serve as a shield. [Old English *sceld* the piece of armor.] —**Syn.** *v.t.* see **defend.**

shi·er (shī′ər) comparative of **shy¹.**

shi·est (shī′ist) superlative of **shy¹.**

shift (shift) *v.t.* **1.** to move or transfer from one person, place, or position to another: *to shift furniture around.* **2.** to switch or change: *The candidate was constantly shifting his position on the issues.* **3.** to change (gears) from one arrangement to another, as in an automobile. —*v.i.* **1.** to move or change, as from one place or position to another: *She shifted in her chair.* **2.** to change gears from one arrangement to another, as in driving an automobile. **3. to shift for oneself.** to provide for one's own needs; get along by oneself: *As a stranger in the city, the girl learned to shift for herself.* —*n.* **1.** switch or change: *a shift in policy.* **2.** movement or transference, as from one place or position to another: *The shift in weight caused the rowboat to capsize.* **3.a.** group of workers who alternate with another group or groups in carrying on some work or operation: *The day shift begins work at eight A.M.* **b.** working time of such a group. **4.** gearshift, esp. in an automobile. **5.** loosely fitting dress designed to fall with straight lines from the shoulders to the hips. **6.** ingenious, evasive, or fraudulent means for effecting some purpose; expedient. **7.** chemise *(def. 1).* [Old English *sciftan* to divide, arrange.] —**shift′er,** *n.* —**Syn.** *v.t.* **1.** see **transfer.**

shift·less (shift′lis) *adj.* **1.** lacking in ambition; good-for-nothing; lazy. **2.** showing a lack of energy, efficiency, or resourcefulness. —**shift′less·ly,** *adv.* —**shift′less·ness,** *n.*

shift·y (shif′tē) **shift·i·er, shift·i·est.** *adj.* **1.** not to be trusted or believed; dishonest; tricky. **2.** expressing deception, trickery, or dishonesty: *shifty eyes.* **3.** capable of shifting for oneself; resourceful. **4.** capable of quick, elusive movements: *a shifty halfback.* —**shift′i·ly,** *adv.* —**shift′i·ness,** *n.*

Shi·ko·ku (shi kō′kōō) *n.* smallest of the four main islands of Japan, in the southern part of the country. Area, 7247 sq. mi. Pop. (1967 est.), 3,942,000.

shill (shil) *n. Slang.* one who acts as a decoy, as for a peddler or gambler, by pretending to buy or bet on something. [Of uncertain origin.]

shil·le·lagh (shə lā′lē, -lə) *also,* **shil·la·lah.** *n.* cudgel, usually of oak or blackthorn. [From *Shillelagh,* village in Ireland noted for its oak trees and blackthorns.]

shil·ling (shil′ing) *n.* **1.** coin of the United Kingdom equal to five pence or one-twentieth of a pound, formerly equal to twelve pence. **2.** any of various coins used in several other countries, esp. those that were or are members of the Commonwealth of Nations. [Old English *scilling* the British coin.]

shil·ly-shal·ly (shil′ē shal′ē) **-lied, -ly·ing.** *v.i.* **1.** to be undecided or hesitant. **2.** to waste time; dawdle. [Repetition, with modifications, of *shall I?*]

shi·ly (shī′lē) shyly.

shim (shim) *n.* thin, often wedge-shaped piece of metal or wood used to fill in a gap, as in a machine, or to align or secure adjoining sections in a construction. —*v.t.* **shimmed, shim·ming.** to fit with a shim or shims. [Of uncertain origin.]

shim·mer (shim′ər) *v.i.* to shine with a faint, wavering light; glimmer. —*n.* faint, wavering light; glimmer; gleam. [Old English *scimrian* to shine faintly.] —**shim′mer·y,** *adj.* —**Syn.** *n.* see **glimmer.**

shim·my (shim′ē) *pl.* **-mies.** *n.* **1.** unusual shaking or vibration. **2.** dance characterized by much shaking of the body, popular in the 1920s. **3.** *Informal.* chemise *(def. 1).* —*v.i.,* **-mied, -my·ing. 1.** to shake; vibrate. **2.** to shake the body in or as in dancing the shimmy. [Modification of CHEMISE (mistaken for a plural).]

shin (shin) *n.* **1.** front part of the leg, extending from the knee to the ankle. **2.** corresponding part in certain animals and birds. —*v.t., v.i.,*

at; āpe; cär; end; mē; it; īce; hot; ōld; fôrk; wood; fōōl; oil; out; up; ūse; turn; sing; thin; this; zh in treasure; ə in ago, taken, pencil, lemon, circus.

shinned, shin·ning. to climb (something) by shinnying. [Old English *scinu* this part of the leg.]

Shi·nar (shī'när) *n.* in the Old Testament, Babylonia.

shin·bone (shin'bōn') *n.* tibia. (*def. 1*).

shin·dig (shin'dig') *n.* Slang. festive or noisy social gathering, as a dance or party. [Possibly SHIN + DIG.]

shine (shīn) (*v.i.*) shone or (*v.t.*) shined, shin·ing. *v.i.* **1.** to give or send out light or brightness, as the sun. **2.** to be bright or gleam with reflected light; glow. **3.** to be eminent or distinguished; excel. —*v.t.* **1.** to put a gloss or polish on: *to shine shoes.* **2.** to cause to shine: *to shine a flashlight.* **3. to shine up to,** Slang. to try to make oneself pleasing to. —*n.* **1.** light; brightness; radiance. **2.** luster or sheen, as of an object reflecting light. **3.** fair weather; sunshine: *Let's go on a hike, come rain or shine.* **4.** polish given to shoes. **5.** Slang. fancy; liking: *to take a shine to someone.* **6.** Slang. trick; prank. [Old English *scinan* to give out light, gleam, to excel.] —**Syn.** see **flash.**

shin·er (shī'nər) *n.* **1.** one who or that which shines. **2.a.** any of various small, silvery freshwater fish, genus *Notropis*, related to the minnows. **b.** any of various other silvery fish. **3.** Informal. black eye.

shin·gle¹ (shing'gəl) *n.* **1.** thin piece of wood or other material, as asphalt, applied to roofs and outside walls in overlapping rows. **2.** Informal. small signboard, esp. that of a doctor or lawyer. **3.** woman's close-cropped haircut. —*v.t.*, **-gled, -gling. 1.** to cover with shingles. **2.** to cut the (hair) very close. [Latin *scindula* split piece of wood.] —**shin'gler,** *n.*

shin·gle² (shing'gəl) *n.* loose, water-worn beach gravel composed of flattened pebbles and stones. [Of uncertain origin.]

shin·gles (shing'gəlz) *n.pl.* virus infection characterized by painful irritation of a group of nerves and the eruption of blisters. Also, **herpes zoster.** ▲ construed as singular. [Medieval Latin *cingulus*, from Latin *cingulum* belt; because the eruption is often like a belt around the body.]

shin·ing (shī'ning) *adj.* **1.** sending out or reflecting light; bright. **2.** brilliant; distinguished. —**shin'ing·ly,** *adv.*

shin·ny¹ (shin'ē) **-nied, -ny·ing.** *v.i.* to climb by alternating the use of the hands or arms and the feet or legs in grasping or pulling (often with *up*): *to shinny up a tree.* [From SHIN.]

shin·ny² (shin'ē) *n.* game resembling hockey, esp. as played by schoolboys with a curved stick and a ball or block of wood. [Possibly from *shin ye,* a cry used in the game.]

shin·plas·ter (shin'plas'tər) *n.* **1.** medicated plaster applied to a sore leg. **2.** Informal. currency of little value, as that of a very small denomination or that rendered almost worthless by inadequate security or inflation.

Shin·to (shin'tō) *n.* **1.** ancient native religion of Japan, emphasizing worship of nature, reverence of ancestors and ancient heroes, and the divinity of the emperor. **2.** adherent of or believer in this religion. [Japanese *shintō* the religion, from Chinese (Mandarin) *shĕn tao* way of the gods.] —**Shin'to·ism, Shin'to·ist',** *n.*

shin·y (shī'nē) **shin·i·er, shin·i·est.** *adj.* **1.** shining; bright. **2.** worn to a glossy smoothness. —**shin'i·ness,** *n.*

ship (ship) *n.* **1.a.** any large seagoing vessel. **b.** crew of such a vessel. **2.** airplane, airship, or spacecraft. **3.** sailing vessel having three or more masts. **4. when one's ship comes home (or in).** when one's fortune has been made. —*v.t.*, **shipped, ship·ping. 1.** to send or transport, as by ship, rail, or truck. **2.** (of a boat or ship) to take in (water) over the side. **3.** to engage for service on a ship. **4.** to put (an object) in its proper place for use on a boat or ship: *to ship a mast.* —*v.i.* **1.** to go on board a ship; embark. **2.** to depart on a ship, esp. as a member of the crew (often with *out*). **3.** (of certain perishable foods) to withstand shipment: *Some fruit doesn't ship well.* [Old English *scip* seagoing vessel.]

-ship *suffix* (used to form nouns.) **1.** quality, state, or condition of being: *relationship, friendship.* **2.** office, status, or rank of: *ambassadorship.* **3.** art or skill of being: *horsemanship.* [Old English *-scipe,* suffix denoting state or condition.]

ship biscuit, hardtack.

ship·board (ship'bôrd') *n.* **on shipboard.** aboard a ship.

ship·build·er (ship'bil'dər) *n.* one who builds or designs ships. —**ship'build'ing,** *n.*

ship canal, canal large enough to allow the passage of ships.

ship·load (ship'lōd') *n.* all that a ship can hold or carry.

ship·man (ship'mən) *pl.*, **-men.** *n.* Archaic. **1.** sailor. **2.** master of a ship.

ship·mas·ter (ship'mas'tər) *n.* one in command of a ship.

ship·mate (ship'māt') *n.* fellow sailor on the same ship.

ship·ment (ship'mənt) *n.* **1.** act of shipping goods. **2.** that which is shipped.

ship money, English tax, abolished in 1640, that required coastal towns to provide ships, or money for ships.

ship of the line, formerly, a warship large enough to take a position in the line of battle.

ship·own·er (ship'ō'nər) *n.* one who owns a ship or ships.

ship·per (ship'ər) *n.* person or company that ships goods.

ship·ping (ship'ing) *n.* **1.** act or business of sending or transporting goods, as by ship. **2.** ships collectively, esp. those belonging to a particular port, country, or company. **3.** total tonnage of such ships.

shipping clerk, one whose job is the shipping and receiving of goods.

shipping room, room or area in a business establishment from which goods are shipped.

ship-rigged (ship'rigd') *adj.* having three or more square-rigged masts.

ship·shape (ship'shāp') *adj.* in good or proper order; neat. —*adv.* in a shipshape manner.

ship·worm (ship'wurm') *n.* any of a group of wormlike marine mollusks, genus *Teredo,* having long slender bodies and two limy shells which are used to burrow into wharves, ship bottoms, or other waterlogged wood in the sea.

ship·wreck (ship'rek') *n.* **1.** destruction or loss of a ship. **2.** remains of a wrecked ship; wreckage. **3.** total failure, destruction, or loss. —*v.t.* **1.** to cause (a ship or its passengers) to undergo shipwreck. **2.** to ruin; destroy. —*v.i.* to suffer shipwreck.

ship·wright (ship'rīt') *n.* one whose work is building or repairing ships.

ship·yard (ship'yärd') *n.* place containing docks, workshops, and warehouses where ships can be built, equipped, and repaired.

Shi·raz (shi räz') *n.* city in southwestern Iran. Pop. (1966 est.), 269,-865.

shire (shīr) *n.* in Great Britain, a county. [Old English *scīr.*]

shirk (shurk) *v.t.* to avoid or neglect doing (something that should be done): *to shirk one's duties.* —*v.i.* to avoid or neglect doing something that should be done. [Possibly from German *Schurke* rogue.] —**shirk'er,** *n.*

shirr (shur) *v.t.* **1.** to gather (fabric) by means of a series of parallel threads. **2.** to bake (eggs) in a shallow dish with butter. [Of uncertain origin.]

shirr·ing (shur'ing) *n.* shirred arrangement of fabric.

shirt (shurt) *n.* **1.** any of various garments for the upper part of the body, esp. one having a collar, sleeves, and buttons down the front. **2.** undershirt. **3. to give (someone) the shirt off one's back.** to give (someone) everything one owns or possesses. **4. to keep one's shirt on.** Slang. to remain calm or patient. **5. to lose one's shirt.** Slang. to lose everything one owns or possesses. [Old English *scyrte* tunic, short garment.]

Shirring

shirt·ing (shur'ting) *n.* fabric used for making shirts or blouses.

shirt sleeve, 1. sleeve of a shirt. **2. in one's shirt sleeves.** without a coat or jacket over one's shirt.

shirt·tail (shurt'tāl') *n.* part of the shirt extending below the waist, esp. in the back.

shirt·waist (shurt'wāst') *n.* **1.** tailored dress having a bodice that resembles a shirt. Also, **shirtwaist dress. 2.** tailored blouse.

shish ke·bab (shish' kə bob') *also,* **shish ka·bob, shish ke·bob.** cubes of meat, as lamb or beef, and usually vegetables, as onions, tomatoes, or green peppers, threaded on skewers and broiled. [Of Turkish origin.]

shist (shist) *n.* schist.

Shi·va (shē'və) *n.* Hindu god who personifies the destructive forces of the universe and, with Brahma and Vishnu, forms the Hindu trinity. [Hindi *Shiva,* from Sanskrit *Siva* literally, the auspicious (one).]

shiv·a·ree (shiv'ə rē', shiv'ə rē') *n.* charivari.

shiv·er¹ (shiv'ər) *v.i.* to shake, as with cold or fear; tremble. —*n.* **1.** act of shivering. **2.** shivering sensation: *His tale of horror sent shivers up my spine.* [Of uncertain origin.]

shiv·er² (shiv'ər) *v.t., v.i.* to break into fragments or splinters; shatter. —*n.* small broken bit; fragment. [Of uncertain origin.]

shiv·er·y (shiv'ər ē) *adj.* **1.** shivering, as from cold or fear; trembling. **2.** causing shivers. **3.** inclined to shiver, as from cold.

shoal¹ (shōl) *n.* **1.** sandbank or sandbar visible at low tide. **2.** any area, as in a river or the ocean, where the water is shallow. —*v.i.* to become shallow. —*v.t.* to make shallow. —*adj.* of little depth; shallow. [Old English *sceald* shallow.]

shoal² (shōl) *n.* school of fish. —*v.i.* to collect in a shoal. [Old English *scolu* crowd, multitude.]

shoal·y (shō'lē) *adj.* full of shoals or shallows.

shoat (shōt) *also,* **shote.** *n.* young pig that has been weaned. [Of uncertain origin.]

shock¹ (shok) *n.* **1.a.** sudden, violent disturbance of the mind or emotions: *He never recovered from the shock of his son's death.* **b.** cause of this: *The news came as a shock to us.* **2.** physical sensation, sometimes accompanied by muscular convulsions, produced by the passage of an electric current through the body. **3.** sudden, violent

at; āpe; cär; end; mē; it; īce; hot; ōld; fôrk; wood; fōol; oil; out; up; ūse; turn; sing; thin; **this**; zh in treasure; ə in ago, taken, pencil, lemon, circus.

shake, blow, or impact, as of an explosion or earthquake. **4.** serious weakening of the body or mind caused by a severe physical or emotional injury, and characterized by a weak pulse, cold skin, an ashen complexion, and a great drop in blood pressure. —*v.t.* **1.** to disturb the mind or emotions of, as by surprising, horrifying, or disgusting. **2.** to give an electric shock to. [French *choc* collision, clash, from Old French *choquer* to strike against, clash; probably of Germanic origin.] —**shock′er,** *n.*

shock² (shok) *n.* bundle, as of wheat or corn, set upright in a field. —*v.t., v.i.* to gather into a shock or shocks. [Possibly from Middle Dutch *schocke* heap, shock of grain.]

shock³ (shok) *n.* thick, bushy mass, as of hair. [Possibly from SHOCK² (from its resemblance to a shock of wheat).]

shock absorber, any of various devices, as in automobiles, airplanes, or machines, that reduce the jarring or shaking effect on an object when it comes into sudden contact with another object.

shock·head·ed (shok′hed′id) *adj.* having a thick, bushy mass of hair.

shock·ing (shok′ing) *adj.* **1.** offensive, distasteful, or revolting: *His behavior was a shocking display of vulgarity.* **2.** causing horror or surprise. —**shock′ing·ly,** *adv.*

shock·proof (shok′prōōf′) *adj.* protected against damage from a sudden, violent blow or impact: *The watch is shockproof.* —*v.t.* to provide with protection against damage from a sudden, violent blow or impact.

shock therapy, form of psychotherapy in which convulsions are produced by electric current or chemicals, used esp. with severely depressed psychotic patients. Also, **shock treatment.**

shock troops, troops specially chosen and trained to make sudden devastating or paralyzing attacks.

shock wave, disturbance created by a body, as an airplane or rocket, traveling at supersonic speed, causing an abrupt increase in the pressure, density, and temperature of the medium through which it passes.

shod (shod) past tense and past participle of **shoe.**

shod·dy (shod′ē) **-di·er, -di·est.** *adj.* **1.** inferior, as in quality; poorly made or done: *a shoddy piece of work.* **2.** lacking attentiveness and courtesy: *We resented his shoddy treatment of us.* **3.** worn out; shabby; seedy: *The old carpet looks pretty shoddy.* **4.** made of or consisting of wool fibers reclaimed from woolen waste or other remnants. **5.** made of shoddy cloth. —*n. pl.,* **-dies. 1.** wool fibers reclaimed from woolen waste or other remnants. **2.** cloth made of such fibers. [Of uncertain origin.] —**shod′di·ly,** *adv.* —**shod′di·ness,** *n.*

shoe (shōō) *n.* **1.** any of various outer coverings, usually of leather, that serve to protect and support the human foot. **2.** something resembling a shoe in shape, position, or function. **3.** horseshoe. **4.** protective metal covering, as on the end of a shaft or post. **5.** curved metal piece in a brake that presses against the wheel, creating the friction that slows or stops the wheel. **6.** outer casing of an automobile tire. **7.** sliding contact plate by which an electric car receives current from the third rail. **8. in another's shoes.** in another person's position or place. **9. to fill someone's shoes.** to take another person's place and assume his responsibilities. **10. the shoe is on the other foot.** the situation is completely the opposite. —*v.t.,* **shod, shoe·ing. 1.** to provide with a shoe or shoes. **2.** to provide or protect the end or edge of something with a metal covering. [Old English *scōh* the outer covering for the foot.]

shoe·horn (shōō′hôrn′) *n.* curved device inserted at the back of a shoe to aid the foot in slipping into the shoe.

shoe·lace (shōō′lās′) *n.* cord, usually of cloth or leather, for fastening a shoe.

shoe·mak·er (shōō′mā′kər) *n.* one who makes or repairs shoes and other footwear. —**shoe′mak′ing,** *n.*

shoe·shine (shōō′shīn′) *n.* **1.** act of cleaning and polishing a pair of shoes. **2.** shine resulting from this.

shoe·string (shōō′string′) *n.* **1.** shoelace. **2. on a shoestring.** with very little money or resources: *The young artist was living on a shoestring.*

shoe tree, device inserted in a shoe to maintain its shape when it is not being worn.

sho·gun (shō′gun′, -gōōn′) *n.* any of the hereditary administrative and political rulers of Japan from 1192 to 1867. [Japanese *shōgun* general (short for *Sei-i-tai-Shogun* literally, great general who subdues barbarians), from Chinese (Mandarin) *chiang chün* general.] —**sho′gun·ate,** *n.*

shone (shōn) past tense and past participle of **shine.**

shoo (shōō) *interj.* exclamation used to frighten or drive away a person or animal. —*v.t.,* **shooed, shoo·ing.** to frighten or drive away by or as by crying or calling "shoo." —*v.i.* to cry or call "shoo."

shook (shook) past tense of **shake.**

shoot (shōōt) **shot, shoot·ing.** *v.t.* **1.** to wound or kill (a person or animal) with a bullet, arrow, or other missile discharged from a weapon. **2.a.** to propel or discharge (a missile) from a weapon, as a gun or bow.

b. to make or remove in this way (often with *off*): *to shoot holes in a bucket.* **3.** to cause to discharge or explode (often with *off*): *to shoot a gun, to shoot off fireworks.* **4.** to send forth or direct rapidly or suddenly: *He shot a nasty look at her.* **5.** to pass rapidly down, through, or over: *to shoot the rapids of a river.* **6.a.** to propel (a ball, puck, or other object) toward an objective, as a goal. **b.** to score, as points or a goal, in this way. **7.** to measure the altitude of (a heavenly body), as with a sextant: *to shoot the sun.* **8.** to film (something) for television or a motion picture. **9.** to variegate, esp. with streaks of color: *His stiff, black hair a little shot with gray* (Sala, 1860). **10.** to take a picture of (someone or something). **11.** to empty out or discharge down or as down a chute; dump. **12.** to slide into or out of a fastening, as the bolt of a door. **13.** to play, as pool or craps. —*v.i.* **1.** to propel or discharge a bullet, arrow, or other missile from a weapon: *Don't shoot until the target shows.* **2.** (of a weapon) to propel a missile, as a bullet or arrow, in a certain way: *The rifle shoots high.* **3.** to go or move suddenly or rapidly; dart: *His feet shot out from under him.* **4.** to propel a ball, puck, or other object toward a goal or in a certain manner. **5.** to extend in a particular direction; project. **6.** to film something for television or a motion picture. **7.** to take a picture; photograph. **8. to shoot at** (or **for**). *Informal.* to try very hard to attain; strive for. **9. to shoot up.** *Informal.* to grow or rise suddenly or rapidly. —*n.* **1.** new or young growth, as from a bud; sprout. **2.** that part of a plant that bears leaves and buds. **3.** trip, expedition, or contest for shooting. **4.** chute. [Old English *scēotan* to dart, rush, send forth, let fly.] —**shoot′er,** *n.*

shooting gallery, place, usually with an enclosed area, for shooting at targets.

shooting star 1. meteor. **2.** any of a group of North American plants, genus *Dodecatheon,* of the primrose family, having showy pink and white flowers.

shop (shop) *n.* **1.** small retail store: *a dress shop.* **2.** department in a large store that specializes in a particular type of merchandise. **3.** place where a specified type of work is done or where a specified service is provided: *a beauty shop.* **4.** place where things are produced or repaired. **5. to set up shop.** to begin work or start a business. **6. to close shop.** to stop work. **7. to talk shop.** to talk about matters relating to one's work. —*v.i.,* **shopped, shop·ping. 1.** to visit stores to look at, price, or purchase merchandise. **2.** to be a regular customer: *I always shop in that grocery store.* **3.** to look; search (often with *around*): *She's shopping around for a husband.* [Old English *sceoppa* stall¹, booth.]

shop·keep·er (shop′kē′pər) *n.* one who owns or operates a shop.

shop·lift·er (shop′lif′tər) *n.* one who steals merchandise from a store while pretending to be a customer. —**shop′lift′ing,** *n.*

shoppe (shop) shop (*defs. 1, 2*).

shop·per (shop′ər) *n.* one who visits stores to look at, price, or purchase merchandise; customer.

shopping center, place or area, esp. in the suburbs, consisting of a complex of buildings that house various kinds of stores, shops, and other facilities.

shop steward, worker in a factory or other business establishment, elected by his union to represent its members in dealing with management and to enforce union rules.

shop·talk (shop′tôk′) *n.* **1.** discussion of matters relating to one's work, esp. after working hours. **2.** jargon of an occupation.

shop·worn (shop′wôrn′) *adj.* **1.** soiled, frayed, or otherwise defective from being displayed or handled in a store. **2.** worn out, as from overuse; no longer fresh or new.

shor·an (shôr′an) *n.* short-range navigation system using radar that enables a ship or airplane to determine its position relative to two ground stations of known location. [Abbreviation of *sh(ort) ra(nge) n(avigation)*.]

shore¹ (shôr) *n.* **1.** land along the edge of a body of water, as an ocean or lake. **2.** land: *The sailors are stationed on shore.* **3.** also, **shores.** country: *one's native shore.* **4.** *Law.* land lying between high-water and low-water marks. [Middle Dutch *schōre* coast, strand, beach.] —**Syn. 1.** see **beach.**

shore² (shôr) **shored, shor·ing.** *v.t.* to support with or as with a timber or beam (often with *up*). —*n.* prop, esp. a timber or beam, placed against the side of a structure as a temporary support. [Middle Dutch *schoor* prop.]

shore³ (shôr) *Archaic.* past tense of **shear.**

shore dinner, meal consisting of several different types of seafood.

shore leave, leave to go ashore granted to a crew on board a ship.

shore·line (shôr′līn′) *n.* outline or contour of a shore.

Shore Patrol, detail of the U.S. Navy, Coast Guard, or Marine Corps, assigned to military police duties on shore.

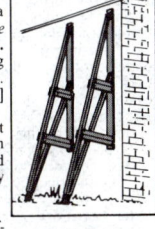

Shores

at; āpe; cär; end; mē; it; īce; hot; ōld; fôrk; wood; fōōl; oil; out; up; ūse; turn; sing; thin; this; zh in treasure; ə in ago, taken, pencil, lemon, circus.

921

shore·ward (shôr′wərd) *adv., adj.* toward the shore.
shor·ing (shôr′ing) *n.* **1.** act of supporting with or as with shores. **2.** system of shores used as a support.
shorn (shôrn) a past participle of **shear.**
short (shôrt) *adj.* **1.** having little linear extension; not long: *John has short hair. This dress has a short jacket that matches it.* **2.** having relatively little height; not tall: *Harry is shorter than his brothers.* **3.** not long in time; of brief duration: *You will have a short wait.* *We took a short trip to the mountains.* **4.** using few words; concise; brief: *She gave a short explanation of what was to be done.* **5.** having an insufficient amount or supply of; lacking (often with *of* or *on*): *We were short of funds. My laundry was short a pair of socks.* **6.** inadequate in amount or quantity: *We had a short supply of towels.* **7.** rudely brief or abrupt; curt: *Mary was very short with me when I spoke to her.* **8.** not retentive: *Joan has a short memory.* **9.** (of dough or pastry) brief and flaky due to the addition of shortening. **10.** (of vowels) relatively brief in duration, as the *i* in *bit.* **11.** *Finance.* **a.** not owning the securities or commodities one is selling. The short seller borrows the securities through his broker and contracts to repurchase and return them at a later date. **b.** of or relating to the sale of securities or commodities that the seller does not own at the time of sale. **12. short of.** less than: *Nothing short of a disaster will prevent our accomplishing this.* —*adv.* **1.** abruptly; suddenly: *We almost hit the car ahead of us when it stopped short.* **2.** not quite up to; on the near side of: *The player kicked the ball short of the goal line.* **3.** curtly; rudely. **4. to sell short. a.** to sell securities or commodities without owning them at the time of their sale. **b.** to underestimate the ability, determination, power, or chances of success of (someone or something). —*n.* **1.** something short. **2.** short circuit. **3.** short subject. **4. shorts. a.** short pants that extend to the knee or above. **b.** men's underpants. **5.** *Baseball.* shortstop. **6. for short.** by way of abbreviation: *Jonathan·is called Jon for short.* **7. in short.** in summary; briefly. —*v.i., v.t.* to short-circuit (an electrical circuit). [Old English *sceort* having little linear extension, brief.] —**short′ness,** *n.*
Syn. *adj.* **4. Short, brief** mean using few words. **Short** suggests incomplete or interrupted expression, sometimes causing or conveying anger or annoyance by its abruptness: *His short speech left many questions unanswered.* **Brief,** often used in official or public contexts, suggests that the expression is complete and even gains in clarity and distinctness as a result of such a limitation: *The brief introduction was remarkable for its thoroughness.*
short·age (shôr′tij) *n.* **1.** deficiency in quantity: *a shortage of funds.* **2.** amount by which anything is deficient: *a shortage of twenty dollars.*
short·bread (shôrt′bred′) *n.* crumbly, rich cookie made of flour, sugar, and shortening.
short·cake (shôrt′kāk′) *n.* dessert consisting of a rich biscuit or cake covered or filled with fruit, as strawberries, and usually topped with whipped cream.
short·change (shôrt′chānj′) -changed, -chang·ing. *also,* **short-change.** *v.t.* **1.** to give less than the proper change to. **2.** to swindle; cheat. —**short′chang′er,** *n.*
short·cir·cuit (shôrt′sur′kit) *v.t.* to bring about a short circuit in. —*v.i.* to be affected with a short circuit.
short circuit, condition that occurs in an electrical circuit when two points are connected, usually accidentally, by a path of abnormally low resistance, thus shortening the distance the current must travel. A short circuit results in an excessive flow of current and may blow a fuse or cause a fire. Also, **short.**
short·com·ing (shôrt′kum′ing) *n.* deficiency; fault.
short·cut (shôrt′kut′) *also,* **short cut.** *n.* **1.** way that is shorter than the ordinary way. **2.** any way or means that saves time or effort.
short·en (shôrt′ən) *v.t.* **1.** to make short or shorter. **2.** to make rich or flaky by adding shortening. **3.** *Nautical.* to reef (*def. 1*). —*v.i.* to become short or shorter. —**short′en·er,** *n.*
short·en·ing (shôrt′ən ing, shôrt′ning) *n.* **1.** any of various fats, as butter, lard, or solidified vegetable oils, used in cooking. **2.** act of making or becoming short or shorter.
short·hand (shôrt′hand′) *n.* method of rapid handwriting in which the words are replaced by symbols, characters, or letters. Opposed to **longhand.** —*adj.* **1.** using shorthand. **2.** written in shorthand.

Shorthand for *As we have not heard from you*

short·hand·ed (shôrt′han′did) *adj.* lacking the necessary or usual number of workmen or assistants.
short·horn (shôrt′hôrn′) *n.* one of a breed of beef cattle with short horns, originally bred in northern England. Weight: to 2500 pounds.
short·ish (shôr′tish) *adj.* somewhat short.
short·lived (shôrt′līvd′, -livd′) *adj.* living or lasting only a short time.

short·ly (shôrt′lē) *adv.* **1.** in a short time; presently; soon. **2.** in a few words; briefly. **3.** abruptly; curtly; sharply.
Syn. **1. Shortly, presently, soon** refer to something happening in the future. **Shortly** suggests that a brief but definite time elapses, often relating to a fixed schedule or other ordered series: *The doctor is with another patient now but will see you shortly.* **Presently** implies that a brief but less definite time elapses, suggesting more flexible, even leisurely circumstances: *Father said he'd be home presently; he had a few stops he wanted to make first.* **Soon** extends further in time but is still within the scope of the near future, suggesting that planning and preparedness precede an event or occurrence: *We'll be ready to leave for our vacation soon.*
short-or·der (shôrt′ôr′dər) *adj.* of or relating to food requiring a short time to prepare.
short order, food requiring a short time to prepare, usually served at a lunch counter or diner.
short-range (shôrt′rānj′) *adj.* **1.** not reaching far into the future: *short-range plans.* **2.** capable of firing only a short distance: *short-range guns.*
short rib, cut of beef consisting of the ends of the ribs.
short shrift **1.** confession and absolution given in a short period of time, as to a condemned person before execution. **2.** abrupt treatment, as of a person, showing little interest, concern, or mercy: *Christopher gave short shrift to the panhandler.* **3. to make short shrift of.** to dispose of quickly.
short-sight·ed (shôrt′sī′tid) *adj.* **1.** not having foresight: *a short-sighted plan.* **2.** nearsighted; myopic. —**short′sight′ed·ly,** *adv.* —**short′sight′ed·ness,** *n.*
short·stop (shôrt′stop′) *n.* *Baseball.* **1.** infield position between second and third base. **2.** player playing this position.
short story, fictional prose work with a single theme, full plot, limited number of characters, and shorter in length than a novel.
short subject, short film, as a documentary or cartoon, usually shown with a main feature. Also, **short.**
short-tem·pered (shôrt′tem′pərd) *adj.* easily or quickly angered; quick-tempered; irascible.
short-term (shôrt′turm′) *adj.* **1.** planned for or involving a short period of time. **2.** requiring repayment within a short period of time, as a loan.
short ton, ton (*def. 1a*).
short·wave (shôrt′wāv′) *n.* radio wave of sixty meters or less.
short-wind·ed (shôrt′wind′did) *adj.* **1.** suffering from shortness of breath. **2.** concise, brief, or uneven: *a short-winded speech.*
Sho·sho·ne (shə shō′nē, shō-) *pl.* -nes. *also,* **Sho·sho·ni.** *n.* **1.** member of a tribe of North American Indians living in Montana, Nevada, Oregon, Wyoming, and Utah. **2.** language of this tribe, belonging to the Shoshonean group of the Uto-Aztecan language family.
Sho·sho·ne·an (shə shō′nē ən, shō-) *adj.* of or relating to a group of North American Indian languages of the Uto-Aztecan language family.
Sho·sta·ko·vich, Dmi·tri (shos′tə kō′vich; də mē′trē) 1906–75, Russian composer.
shot¹ (shot) *pl.,* **shots** or (*def. 4.*) **shot.** *n.* **1.** discharge of a firearm or other weapon. **2.** act of shooting: *That was a poor shot.* **3.** one who shoots; marksman: *John is a good shot.* **4.** tiny ball of lead or steel, a quantity of which are contained in a cartridge and discharged by a shotgun. **5.** single ball of lead used as ammunition for a gun or cannon. **6.** launching of a rocket or missile toward a particular target: *moon shot.* **7.** injection given with a needle or syringe; hypodermic. **8.** distance over which something, as a missile or sound, can travel; reach; range: *We are out of cannon shot.* **9.** aim or stroke, esp. in a game: *Jim took a practice shot at the basket.* **10.** attempt or guess. **11.a.** photograph. **b.** act or process of taking a photograph. **c.** single piece of motion picture film or magnetic tape recording a continuous action, taken by one camera from one angle. **12.** *Sports.* heavy metal ball used in the shot put. **13.** blast, as in mining. **14.** *Informal.* small amount of liquor, often consumed in one gulp; nip. [Old English *sceot* a shooting, missile, rapid movement, contribution.]
shot² (shot) *v.* past tense and past participle of **shoot.** —*adj.* **1.** streaked, mixed, or woven so as to have variegated color: *She wore a scarf of red silk shot with blue.* **2.** completely worn out or ruined: *These shoes are shot.*
shote (shōt) *n.* shoat.
shot·gun (shot′gun′) *n.* smoothbore gun designed to fire cartridges that release a quantity of shot when discharged.
shot put, (poot) field event in which a shot is thrown for distance. Also, **shot′-put′ting.** —**shot′-put′ter,** *n.*
should (shood) past tense of **shall.** *auxiliary verb* **1.** used to express an obligation or duty: *Mary should write a letter to her mother.* **2.** used to express a condition: *I should have come if you had invited me.* **3.** used to express doubt or uncertainty: *If I should go to Europe*

at; āpe; cär; end; mē; it; īce; hot; ōld; fôrk; wood; fōōl; oil; out; up; ūse; turn; sing; thin; this; zh in treasure; ə in ago, taken, pencil, lemon, circus.

this summer, I would probably go by ship. **4.** used to lessen the b untness or directness of a statement: *I should not do that if I were you.* —**Syn. 1.** see **must¹.**

shoul·der (shōl′dər) *n.* **1.** part on either side of the body extending from the base of the neck to the upper arm or forelimb. **2. shoulders.** both shoulders and the part of the back connecting them. **3.** portion of a garment covering the shoulders. **4.** front quarter of an animal. **5.** edge or border on either side of a road or highway. **6.** any projecting part or slope: *the shoulder of a hill.* **7.** *Printing.* flat upper surface on a type body that extends beyond the base of the letter. **8. to put one's shoulder to the wheel.** to exert great effort. **9. straight from the shoulder.** without evasion or deceit; honestly; frankly. —*v.t.* **1.** to force by pushing with the shoulder or shoulders: *to shoulder one's way through a crowd.* **2.** to take upon oneself, as a burden; assume: *to shoulder the blame, to shoulder responsibility.* **3.** to place on and support or carry with the shoulder or shoulders. **4. to shoulder arms.** to bring a rifle to an upright position with the barrel resting against the shoulder and the butt resting in the hand on the same side. —*v.i.* to push forward or force one's way with the shoulder or shoulders. [Old English *sculder* the part of the body.]

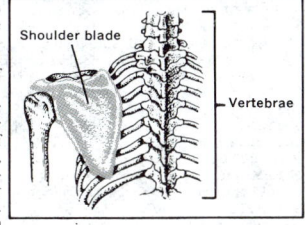
Shoulder blade — Vertebrae

shoulder blade, either of two flat, triangular bones in the upper part of the back. Also, **scap′u·la.**
shoulder knot, ornamental knot of ribbon or lace worn on the shoulder.
shoulder patch, cloth insignia indicating one's branch or unit in the armed forces, worn on the upper part of the sleeve of a uniform.

shoulder strap 1. strap worn over the shoulder to support a garment or attached item, as a purse. **2.** ornamental cloth strip fastened on the shoulder of a uniform, often holding an insignia to indicate rank.

should·n't (shood′ənt) should not.
shouldst (shoodst) *also,* **should·est** (shood′ist). *Archaic.* past second person singular of **shall.** ▲ used with *thou.*

shout (shout) *v.i.* to cry out loudly; yell. —*v.t.* to utter with a shout; express by a shout: *Shout the alarm!* —*n.* loud cry made to express emotion or attract attention. [Of uncertain origin.] —**shout′er,** *n.*
Syn. *v.i.* **Shout, yell, scream** mean to speak loudly. **Shout** suggests speaking in a raised voice so as to be heard above other voices, at a distance, or by someone deaf: *He shouted into his grandmother's good ear.* **Yell** is a hoarse or harsh shout used esp. when urgency is required, as in a warning or appeal for help: *He yelled for her to move out of the way, but it was too late and the car hit her.* **Scream** suggests a hysterical loss of control, as from anger or other violent emotions that result in a louder and more shrill tone than that of *yell* or *shout: Mother screamed at me to get back up to my room.*

shove (shuv) **shoved, shov·ing.** *v.t.* **1.** to move along by the application of strength from behind; push: *Shove the chair closer to the table.* **2.** to push or press roughly: *The two boys shoved each other off the sidewalk.* —*v.i.* **1.** to push or press roughly. **2.a. to shove off.** to push a boat away from the shore. **b.** *Informal.* to leave. —*n.* strong push. [Old English *scūfan* to thrust, push.] —**shov′er,** *n.*

shov·el (shuv′əl) *n.* **1.** tool with a broad blade attached to a long handle, used for taking up and moving loose material, as soil, snow, or gravel. **2.** any large power-driven machine for taking up and moving loose material. **3.** shovelful. —*v.t.,* **-eled, -el·ing;** *also, British,* **-elled, -el·ling. 1.** to take up and move with a shovel. **2.** to dig or clear with a shovel, as a path. **3.** to move or throw in large quantities as if with a shovel: *to shovel food into one's mouth.* —*v.i.* to use a shovel. [Old English *scofl* spadelike tool.]
shov·el·er (shuv′ə lər) *also, British,* **shov·el·ler.** *n.* **1.** one who or that which shovels. **2.** any of several freshwater ducks, esp. *Spatula clypeata,* having a broad, flat bill.
shov·el·ful (shuv′əl fool′) *pl.,* **-fuls.** *n.* quantity that a shovel can hold.
shovel hat, hat with a stiff, broad brim turned up at the sides and projecting in front, worn by some clergymen of the Church of England.
show (shō) **showed, shown** *or* **showed, show·ing.** *v.t.* **1.** to expose to view; display: *Please show your tickets at the door.* **2.** to bring to public view; present; exhibit: *The theater showed the movie last week. The artist showed his works at the gallery.* **3.** to make known or manifest, esp. by one's behavior; reveal: *She showed her anger by throwing a book.* **4.** to point out or lead: *Show him the way to the bus station.* **5.** to act as an escort to; conduct; guide: *Mary showed the prospective buyers through the house.* **6.** to register, as on a scale: *The thermometer shows*

his temperature to be quite high. **7.a.** to demonstrate, prove, or explain to: *He showed his brother how to change a tire. I'll show you that I'm right.* **b.** to demonstrate, prove, or explain: *She showed what he did wrong. I'll show that it can be done.* **8.** to give; bestow: *The judge showed little mercy in his decision.* **9. to show off.** to display in a proud or ostentatious manner: *He showed off his new suit.* **10. to show up. a.** to expose; reveal: *You showed him up for what he really was.* **b.** *Informal.* to be superior to; outdo: *He showed up his competitors.* —*v.i.* **1.** to become exposed to view; be displayed; appear. **2.** to be exhibited. **3.** to finish third in a horse race. Distinguished from **place** and **win. 4.** *Informal.* to make one's appearance; be present: *Do you think he'll show?* **5. to show off.** to behave in such a way as to call attention to oneself; be an exhibitionist. **6. to show up. a.** to be conspicuous or prominent; stand out: *Do her wrinkles show up in the photograph?* **b.** *Informal.* to make one's appearance. —*n.* **1.** that which is shown; exhibition or demonstration. **2.** any entertainment, esp. a theatrical, radio, or television presentation. **3.** any public presentation: *a dog show, an art show.* **4.** elaborate or ostentatious display: *He wears a jeweled stickpin just for show.* **5.** appearance; sign: *There was little show of recognition when we met.* **6.** feigned or misleading appearance; pretense: *He denied the accusation with a great show of anger.* **7.** act of showing. **8.** third position in a horse race. **9.** indication; trace. [Old English *scēawian* to look at, see, display.]
Syn. *n.* **3. Show, display, exhibition** mean an arrangement or presentation of something for public viewing. **Show** is designed to arouse public interest in a particular field of activity, as art, fashion, or gardening, esp. by dramatizing the event, as by the awarding of prizes or other theatrical elements: *Diana is modeling for a fashion show.* **Display** is a show primarily designed to stimulate sales, esp. by a beautiful and lavish arrangement: *The bookstore has an attractive display of new books for Christmas gift giving.* **Exhibition** is usually a large, highly organized and wide-ranging show designed as much to inform and entertain as to promote sales, esp. by demonstrating new products or machines: *Our town holds an annual industrial exhibition.*

show bill, poster advertising an entertainment.
show·boat (shō′bōt′) *n.* boat having a theater and troupe of performers on board for providing entertainment.
show·bread (shō′bred′) shewbread.
show·case (shō′kās′) *n.* glass case for displaying and protecting articles, as in a store or museum.
show·down (shō′doun′) *n.* confrontation that brings a matter to a climax or conclusion.
show·er (shou′ər) *n.* **1.a.** fall of rain of brief duration. **b.** fall of hail, sleet, or snow of brief duration. **2.** fall of anything in large number, as of tears, sparks, or meteors. **3.a.** bath in which water is sprayed on a person from an overhead nozzle. **b.** room or apparatus for such a bath. Also, **shower bath. 4.** abundant quantity or supply: *a shower of criticism.* **5.** party for someone, as a future bride, to which gifts are brought. —*v.i.* **1.** to rain or fall in a shower. **2.** to take a shower. —*v.t.* **1.** to wet with water or other liquid; sprinkle; spray. **2.** to cause or appear to cause to fall in a shower: *to shower hail, to shower meteors.* **3.** to bestow lavishly: *to shower compliments on a person.* [Old English *scūr* a fall of rain of brief duration.] —**show′er·y,** *adj.*
show·ing (shō′ing) *n.* **1.** act or instance of bringing to public view; presentation: *She was invited to a special showing of paintings.* **2.** that which is presented; exhibition; display. **3.** performance, as in a contest or test: *John made a poor showing.*
show·man (shō′mən) *pl.,* **-men.** *n.* **1.** one who produces, presents, or manages a theatrical presentation. **2.** one who acts or presents something in a dramatic or theatrical manner. —**show′man·ship′,** *n.*
shown (shōn) a past participle of **show.**
show·off (shō′ôf′) *n.* **1.** one who shows off; exhibitionist. **2.** act of showing off.
show·piece (shō′pēs′) *n.* something displayed, esp. as a fine example of its kind.
show·place (shō′plās′) *n.* **1.** place exhibited to the public because of its beauty, fame, or historical interest. **2.** any place that is beautifully and tastefully decorated.
show·room (shō′room′, -room′) *n.* room used for the display of merchandise.
show·y (shō′ē) **show·i·er, show·i·est.** *adj.* **1.** making a striking display: *showy flowers.* **2.** ostentatious or gaudy. —**show′i·ly,** *adv.* —**show′i·ness,** *n.*
shrank (shrangk) past tense of **shrink.**
shrap·nel (shrap′nəl) *n.* **1.** thin-walled shell filled with small lead fragments or balls that are scattered over a large area when the shell explodes. **2.** fragments from an exploding shell or bomb. [From General Henry *Shrapnel,* 1761–1842, its British inventor.]

Shrapnel

shred (shred) *n.* **1.** very small piece or narrow strip torn or cut off.

2. particle; scrap; bit: *There is not a shred of truth in his story.* —*v.t.* **shred·ded** or **shred, shred·ding.** to tear or cut into shreds. [Old English *scrēade* fragment, strip, scrap.]

Shreve·port (shrēv′pôrt′) *n.* city in northwestern Louisiana. Pop. (1970), 182,064.

shrew (shrōō) *n.* **1.** bad-tempered, nagging woman. **2.** any of numerous very small mammals, family Soricidae, related to the mole, found in nearly all parts of the world, having a long, pointed snout, short, rounded ears, and usually brownish fur. [Old English *scrēawa* this animal (because it is quarrelsome and was once supposed to be poisonous).]

Shrew (def. 2)

shrewd (shrōōd) *adj.* **1.** clever or keen in practical matters; astute: *a shrewd businessman.* **2.** *Archaic.* sharp: *a sting of shrewdest pain* (Tennyson, 1842). [From SHREW.] —**shrewd′ly,** *adv.* —**shrewd′ness,** *n.*

shrew·ish (shrōō′ish) *adj.* like a shrew; bad-tempered. —**shrew′ish·ly,** *adv.* —**shrew′ish·ness,** *n.*

shrew·mouse (shrōō′mous′) *pl.,* -**mice.** *n.* shrew *(def. 2).*

shriek (shrēk) *n.* loud, shrill cry or sound: *shrieks of laughter, the shriek of a whistle.* —*v.i.* to make a loud, shrill cry or sound. —*v.t.* to utter with a shriek. [Possibly from Old Norse *skrækja* to screech.] —**shriek′er,** *n.*

shrift (shrift) *n. Archaic.* **1.** confession to a priest or the absolution given by a priest. **2.** act of shriving. [Old English *scrift* penance, from *scrīfan* to impose penance, shrive. See SHRIVE.]

shrike (shrīk) *n.* any of various predatory birds, family Laniidae, having a large head, a strong, hooked beak, and a long tail. Length: 7–10 inches. Also, **butch′er·bird′.** [Old English *scrīc* thrush.]

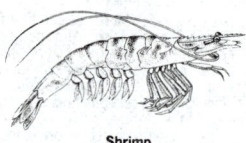
Shrike

shrill (shril) *adj.* **1.** sharp and high-pitched in sound. **2.** emitting or producing such a sound: *a shrill whistle.* —*v.i.* to make or emit a shrill sound: *The bagpipes shrilled.* —*v.t.* to utter shrilly: *The crowd shrilled its protests.* —*n.* shrill sound. [Imitative.] —**shrill′ness,** *n.* —**shrill′ly,** *adv.*

shrimp (shrimp) *pl.,* **shrimps** or **shrimp.** *n.* **1.** any of numerous long-tailed aquatic crustaceans, orders Decapoda, Stomatopoda, and Anostraca. **2.** *Slang.* person who is of small stature or size. [Of uncertain origin.]

Shrimp

shrine (shrīn) *n.* **1.** case or other receptacle for sacred relics; reliquary. **2.** tomb of a saint. **3.** place consecrated to a deity, saint, or other sacred being. **4.** place or thing hallowed by its history or past association. —*v.t.* to enshrine. [Old English *scrīn* Ark of the Covenant, box containing a saint's relics, from Latin *scrīnium* case, chest.]

shrink (shringk) **shrank** or **shrunk, shrunk** or **shrunk·en, shrink·ing.** *v.i.* **1.** to contract with heat, cold, or moisture: *Woolen cloth shrinks in hot water.* **2.** to draw back, as in fear, horror, or disgust. **3.** to become reduced; diminish: *The population of the town has shrunk in recent years.* —*v.t.* to cause to contract or be reduced: *The laundry shrank my new blouse.* —*n.* act or instance of shrinking. [Old English *scrincan* to contract, shrivel up.] —**shrink′a·ble,** *adj.* —**shrink′er,** *n.* —**Syn.** *v.i.* **1.** see contract.

shrink·age (shring′kij) *n.* **1.** act or process of shrinking. **2.** amount of shrinking. **3.** reduction, as in quantity or value; depreciation: *the shrinkage of the dollar in times of inflation.*

shrive (shrīv) **shrove** or **shrived, shriv·en** or **shrived, shriv·ing.** *v.t.* **1.** to hear the confession of and grant absolution to. **2.** to rid (oneself) of sin by confessing and doing penance. —*v.i.* to make confession, as to a priest. **2.** to hear confessions. [Old English *scrīfan* to hear the confession of, impose penance, going back to Latin *scrībere* to write.]

shriv·el (shriv′əl) -**eled, -el·ing;** *also, British,* -**elled, -el·ling.** *v.i.* **1.** to shrink and become wrinkled or curled up: *The flowers shriveled and died after a week.* **2.** to become useless, helpless, or ineffectual. —*v.t.* to cause to shrivel. [Possibly of Scandinavian origin.] —**Syn.** *v.i.* see wither.

shriv·en (shriv′ən) a past participle of **shrive.**

shroud (shroud) *n.* **1.** cloth or garment used to wrap a dead body for burial. **2.** something that covers, conceals, or obscures. **3.** rope or wire giving lateral support to a mast on a boat or ship. —*v.t.* **1.** to clothe

for burial. **2.** to cover so as to conceal; obscure; veil: *The whole affair was shrouded in secrecy.* [Old English *scrūd* garment, clothing.]

shrove (shrōv) a past tense of **shrive.**

Shrove·tide (shrōv′tīd′) *n.* the three days preceding Ash Wednesday.

Shrove Tuesday, day preceding Ash Wednesday.

shrub[1] (shrub) *n.* woody plant smaller than a tree and having many stems that branch at or near the ground rather than a distinct trunk. [Old English *scrybb.*]

shrub[2] (shrub) *n.* beverage made from fruit juice, sugar, and often liquor. [Arabic *shurb* beverage.]

shrub·ber·y (shrub′ər ē) *pl.,* -**ber·ies.** *n.* **1.** shrubs collectively. **2.** plot planted with shrubs, as in a garden.

shrub·by (shrub′ē) -**bi·er, -bi·est.** *adj.* **1.** of or resembling a shrub. **2.** consisting of or covered with shrubs. —**shrub′bi·ness,** *n.*

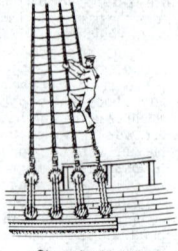
Shrouds (def. 3)

shrug (shrug) **shrugged, shrug·ging.** *v.t.* **1.** to raise or draw up (the shoulders) to express doubt, indifference, or displeasure. **2. to shrug off,** to dismiss as being unimportant. —*v.i.* to raise or draw up the shoulders to express doubt, indifference, or displeasure. —*n.* act of shrugging. [Of uncertain origin.]

shrunk (shrungk) a past participle and past tense of **shrink.**

shrunk·en (shrung′kən) *v.* a past participle of **shrink.** —*adj.* shriveled up; contracted; reduced.

shuck (shuk) *n.* **1.** outer covering of corn or certain nuts. **2.** shell of an oyster or clam. —*v.t.* **1.** to remove the shucks from. **2.** to take off; remove (often with *off*): *to shuck off one's clothes.* [Of uncertain origin.] —**shuck′er,** *n.*

shucks (shuks) *interj.* exclamation of disappointment or annoyance.

shud·der (shud′ər) *v.i.* to tremble suddenly, as from horror, fear, disgust, or cold. —*n.* act or instance of shuddering. [Middle English *shoddren* to tremble with fear, going back to Old English *scūdan* to shake, tremble.] —**shud′der·ing·ly,** *adv.*

shuf·fle (shuf′əl) -**fled, -fling.** *v.t.* **1.** to drag (the feet) along the ground or floor. **2.** to mix (playing cards) so as to rearrange them. **3.** to move (something) from one place to another: *to shuffle papers.* **4. to shuffle off,** to get rid of or evade; thrust aside. —*v.i.* **1.** to walk by dragging the feet: *to shuffle down the street.* **2.** to mix playing cards so as to rearrange them. **3.** to move things about from one place to another. **4.** to move, act, or do something in a clumsy, haphazard, or hasty manner. **5.** to perform a dance in which one shuffles the feet. —*n.* **1.** act or instance of shuffling the feet. **2.a.** act or instance of shuffling playing cards. **b.** right or turn to shuffle playing cards. **3.** underhanded or evasive behavior; subterfuge; trick. **4.** dance characterized by a series of shuffling steps. [Probably from Low German *schuffeln* to walk awkwardly.] —**shuf′fler,** *n.*

shuf·fle·board (shuf′əl bōrd′) *n.* **1.** game played by pushing disks with a cue on a smooth level surface marked off in scoring areas. **2.** marked surface on which this game is played. [Modification of obsolete *shove-board* this game, from SHOVE + BOARD.]

shun (shun) **shunned, shun·ning.** *v.t.* to keep away from, esp. persistently or habitually; avoid. [Old English *scunian.*] —**shun′ner,** *n.* —**Syn.** see avoid.

shunt (shunt) *v.t.* **1.** to move or turn aside or away. **2.** to switch (a train) from one track to another. **3.** to carry or divert (part of an electric current) by means of a shunt. —*v.i.* to move or turn aside or away. —*n.* **1.** act of shunting. **2.** railroad switch. **3.** conductor joining two points in an electric circuit that provides an electrical bypath for part of the current. [Possibly from SHUN.] —**shunt′er,** *n.*

shush (shush) *interj.* be quiet; hush. —*v.t.* to quiet or silence.

shut (shut) **shut, shut·ting.** *v.t.* **1.** to move (something) into a closed position so as to obstruct or eliminate an entrance, passageway, or opening: *to shut a window.* **2.** to bring together the parts of so as to form a whole or eliminate openings: *to shut an umbrella, to shut a book.* **3.** to prevent access to (often with *off* or *up*): *to shut off several rooms of a house, to shut up a house.* **4.** to confine or enclose (often with *up*): *to shut an animal into a cage, to shut someone up in a room.* **5.** to prevent from entering; keep out (with *out*): *to shut someone out of the house.* **6.** to suspend or stop the operation or operations of (often with *down*): *to shut a store, to shut down a mine.* **7.** to prevent the passage or flow of (with *off*): *to shut off water.* **8. to shut out.** to prevent (the opposing team) from scoring in a contest, as a baseball game. **9. to shut up.** *Informal.* to quiet or silence (someone). —*v.i.* **1.** to become shut. **2. to shut up.** *Informal.* to become silent. [Old English *scyttan* to bolt[1], as a door.]

shut·down (shut′doun′) *n.* stopping of work, as in a factory.

shut-eye (shut′ī′) *n. Slang.* sleep.

at; āpe; cär; end; mē; it; īce; hot; ōld; fôrk; wood; fōōl; oil; out; up; ūse; turn; sing; thin; **this**; zh in treasure; ə in ago, taken, pencil, lemon, circus.

shut-in (shut′in′) *adj.* confined to the house or a hospital. —*n.* person who is confined to the house or a hospital, as by illness.

shut-out (shut′out′) *n.* **1.** *Sports.* **a.** the preventing of the opposing team from scoring. **b.** game in which one team does not score. **2.** lockout.

shut-ter (shut′ər) *n.* **1.** movable panel or screen for a door or window, used to shut out light or to provide protection or privacy. **2.** device that opens and closes the lens aperture of a camera. **3.** one who or that which shuts. —*v.t.* to provide or cover with shutters. [SHUT + -ER¹.]

shut-ter-bug (shut′ər bug′) *n.* *Slang.* amateur photographer.

shut-tle (shut′əl) *n.* **1.** device on a loom that carries the weft yarn back and forth across or through the warp yarn. **2.** any of various devices that hold and carry thread, as in a sewing machine. **3.** vehicle in a public transportation system that makes frequent trips back and forth between two points. —*v.t., v.i.* to move back and forth in or as a shuttle. [Old English *scytel* dart, arrow.]

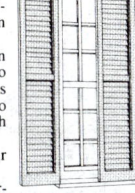

Shutters

shut-tle-cock (shut′əl kok′) *n.* cone-shaped object with feathers inserted into a rounded cork base, used in the game of badminton. Also, **bird.**

shy¹ (shī) **shy-er** or **shi-er, shy-est** or **shi-est.** *adj.* **1.** uncomfortable in the presence of others; bashful; retiring. **2.** exhibiting a lack of courage; easily frightened; timid. **3.** cautious or distrustful; wary. **4.** *Informal.* lacking; short: *shy of money, a few dollars shy.* —*v.i.* **shied, shy-ing. 1.** to move suddenly back or aside, as in fear; start: *The horse shied at the loud noise.* **2.** to draw back, as from caution, distaste, or doubt (often with *away*). —*n. pl.* **shies.** sudden movement back or aside, as in fear. [Old English *scēoh* timid.] —**shy′ly,** *adv.* —**shy′ness,** *n.*

Syn. *adj.* **1. Shy, bashful** mean awkward in the presence of others. **Shy** suggests a person whose quiet and reserved nature makes conversation or other social involvement, esp. with strangers and persons of the opposite sex, difficult: *The man was too shy to ask her to dance.* **Bashful** suggests an unwillingness to call attention to oneself or one's achievements that may result from shyness: *She was bashful about discussing her rescue of the little boy from the flaming house.*

shy² (shī) **shied, shy-ing.** *v.t., v.i.* to throw (something), esp. with a jerk; fling; toss. —*n. pl.* **shies.** quick, jerking throw. [Possibly from the former sport of *shying* or throwing sticks at cocks that had been taught to be *shy* or wary of missiles hurled at them.]

Shy-lock (shī′lok′) *n.* **1.** exacting and merciless moneylender in Shakespeare's play *The Merchant of Venice.* **2.** any exacting creditor.

shy-ster (shī′stər) *n.* *Slang.* lawyer or other person who is professionally unethical. [Of uncertain origin.]

si (sē) *n. Music.* ti. [See GAMUT.]

Si, silicon.

Si-am (sī am′) see **Thailand.**

Si-a-mese (sī′ə mēz′, -mēs′) *pl.,* **-mese.** *n.* Thai. —*adj.* Thai.

Siamese cat, cat of a breed having a long, slender body, wedge-shaped head, and short hair.

Siamese twins, identical twins who are born joined together in some manner. [From the twins Eng and Chang, 1811–74, who were born in Siam joined together.]

Si-an (sē′än′) *n.* city in central China. Pop. (1957 est.), 1,310,000.

sib (sib) *adj.* related by blood; akin. —*n.* **1.** kinsman; relative. **2.** kinsmen; kindred. [Old English *sibb.*]

Si-be-ri-a (sī bēr′ē ə) *n.* region of the Soviet Union, extending from the Ural Mountains to the Pacific. Area, approx. 5,000,000 sq. mi. Pop. (1959), 21,466,800. —**Si-be′ri-an,** *adj., n.*

Siberian husky, sturdy dog of a breed having a brushlike tail and a soft coat that may be gray, tan, white, black, or a combination of these. Height: 20–23 inches at the shoulder.

sib-i-lant (sib′ə lənt) *adj.* having a hissing sound. —*n.* consonant pronounced with a hissing sound, as *s* or *sh.* [Latin *sībīlāns,* present participle of *sībīlāre* to hiss.] —**sib′i-lance, sib′i-lan-cy,** *n.* —**sib′i-lant-ly,** *adv.*

sib-ling (sib′ling) *n.* brother or sister. [Old English *sibling* kinsman.]

sib-yl (sib′əl) *n.* **1.** *Greek and Roman Mythology.* any of various women who had powers of prophecy. **2.** prophetess, fortuneteller, or witch.

Shuttlecock

Siamese cat

sib-yl-line (sib′ə lēn′, -līn′, -lin) *adj.* **1.** of, like, or coming from a sibyl. **2.** prophetic or mysterious. Also, **si-byl-ic, si-byl-lic** (si bil′ik).

sic¹ (sik) *adv. Latin.* thus; so. ▲ used to indicate that an erroneous word or phrase in a quotation is an exact reproduction of the original.

sic² (sik) **sicked** or **sicced, sick-ing** or **sic-cing.** *also,* **sick.** *v.t.* **1.** to set upon; attack. ▲ used in the imperative: *Sic him!* **2.** to incite to make an attack: *He sicked his dog on me.* [Form of SEEK.]

sic-ca-tive (sik′ə tiv) *adj.* causing to dry; drying. —*n.* siccative substance, esp. one used in painting. [Late Latin *siccātīvus* drying, from Latin *siccāre* to dry.]

Si-cil-ian (si sil′yən) *adj.* of or relating to Sicily, its people, or their dialect. —*n.* **1.** member or recent descendant of the people of Sicily. **2.** dialect of Italian spoken predominantly in Sicily.

Sic-i-ly (sis′ə lē) *n.* island in the Mediterranean, off the southwestern tip of Italy. Area, 9831 sq. mi. Pop. (1968 est.), 4,867,700.

sick¹ (sik) *adj.* **1.** suffering from some disease; having poor health; ill. **2.** affected with nausea; nauseated. **3.** of or for sick people: *The company has very good sick benefits.* **4.** indicating sickness: *He has a sick look.* **5.** thoroughly weary: *John is sick of his job.* **6.** disgusted; chagrined: *Petty gossip makes her sick.* **7.** deeply affected with some strong feeling: *John is sick with envy.* **8.** emotionally or mentally disturbed. **9.** spiritually ailing; corrupt: *a sick society.* **10.** unsound; impaired: *That old car of his looks sick.* **11.** sadistic or unwholesome in some way; morbid: *a sick joke.* —*n.* **the sick.** sick persons collectively. [Old English *sēoc* ill.]

sick² (sik) *sic².*

sick bay, hospital or dispensary, esp. on a ship.

sick-bed (sik′bed′) *n.* bed on which a sick person lies.

sick-en (sik′ən) *v.t., v.i.* to make or become sick.

sick-en-ing (sik′ə ning) *adj.* affecting with or causing nausea or disgust. —**sick′en-ing-ly,** *adv.*

sick headache, migraine.

sick-ish (sik′ish) *adj.* **1.** somewhat sick. **2.** sickening. —**sick′ish-ly,** *adv.* —**sick′ish-ness,** *n.*

sick-le (sik′əl) *n.* hand implement consisting of a sharp crescent-shaped blade attached to a short handle, used for cutting grass, grain, or weeds. [Old English *sicol,* going back to Latin *secula.*]

sick-ly (sik′lē) *-li-er, -li-est. adj.* **1.** habitually sick; in poor health. **2.** of or characteristic of sickness: *a sickly complexion.* **3.** characterized by the presence of sickness. **4.** affecting with nausea; sickening: *sickly smells.* **5.** faint; feeble: *a sickly winter sun.* **6.** insipid or weakly sentimental: *a sickly smile.* —*adv.* in a sick manner. —**sick′li-ness,** *n.*

sick-ness (sik′nis) *n.* **1.** state of being sick. **2.** particular disease or malady. **3.** nausea.

sic tran-sit glo-ri-a mun-di (sik tran′sit glôr′ē ə moon′dī) *Latin.* thus passes away the glory of the world.

side (sīd) *n.* **1.** one of the surfaces or lines bounding an object or figure. **2.** either of the two surfaces or lines of an object or figure, as distinguished from the ends, the front or back, or the top or bottom: *The chair fell on its side. John repainted the sides of his car. Mary drew a rectangle having sides twice as long as the ends.* **3.** either of two surfaces of a flat object, such as a piece of cloth, paper, or wood: *One side of the cloth is rough.* **4.a.** either of two parts of a place lying to the right or left of a central line or point: *Put the chairs on the left side of the room.* **b.** any of various parts of a region or place lying beyond a particular, usually central, line or point: *Helen lives on the west side of town.* **5.** either the right or left part of the body of a person or animal. **6.** area or space next to one's person: *Come stand at my side.* **7.** region or area separated from another region or area by an object, space, or line: *He has lived on both sides of the Atlantic.* **8.** slope of a hill or bank. **9.** either of two opposing groups or persons: *There were losses on both sides. Neither side scored in the game.* **10.** position, attitude, or point of view: *There are always two sides to an argument.* **11.** aspect of a person or thing: *Get on his good side. Look at all sides of the question.* **12.** line of descent: *He is my second cousin on my father's side.* **13. on the side.** *Informal.* **a.** in addition to the usual or principal job or duties: *She takes in laundry on the side.* **b.** in addition to the main part or course: *Mary ordered turnips on the side.* **14. side by side.** next to one another. **15. to take sides.** to support the position of one of two opposing groups or persons. —*adj.* **1.** situated at or lying near one side. **2.** coming from or directed toward one side. **3.** secondary; subordinate: *There were too many distracting side issues.* **4.** in addition to the main part. —*v.t., v.i.* **sid-ed, sid-ing.** to provide with sides or siding. —*v.i.* **to side with.** to support. [Old English *sīde* lateral surface, place with reference to a central point.]

side-arm (sīd′ärm′) *adj.* of or designating a motion of the arm almost parallel to the ground, as in throwing a ball: *a sidearm pitch.* —*adv.* with a sidearm motion: *to throw sidearm.*

Sickle

at; āpe; cär; end; mē; it; īce; hot; ōld; fôrk; wood; fōōl; oil; out; up; ūse; turn; sing; thin; *this*; zh in treasure; ə in ago, taken, pencil, lemon, circus.

925

side arm, weapon carried at the side, as a sword or revolver.

side·board (sīd′bôrd′) *n.* piece of dining-room furniture, used for storing tableware and linen.

side·burns (sīd′burnz′) *n.,pl.* hair growing below the hairline on the sides of a man's face, esp. when worn as short whiskers with the rest of the beard shaved off. [Modification of BURNSIDES.]

side·car (sīd′kär′) *n.* small one-wheeled car attached to the side of a motorcycle for carrying a passenger.

sid·ed (sī′dĭd) *adj.* having a side or sides. ▲ used in combination: *one-sided.*

side dish, portion of food served in addition to the main course, usually in a separate dish.

side effect, secondary and often harmful effect, as of a medication or drug.

Sideburns

side·kick (sīd′kĭk′) *n. Informal.* close friend; companion; pal.

side·light (sīd′līt′) *n.* **1.** light coming from the side. **2.** incidental information. **3.** one of two lights, a red one on the port side and a green one on the starboard side, carried by a ship sailing at night.

side·line (sīd′līn′) *n.* **1.** either of two lines that mark the limits of a playing area in certain sports, as football or basketball. **2.** sidelines. area just beyond these lines. **3.** work additional to one's usual job or duties. **4.** line of goods additional to that regularly sold. —*v.t.,* **-lined, -lin·ing.** to keep from participating, as in a sport.

side·ling (sīd′lĭng) *adj.* **1.** directed to the side; oblique: *a sideling motion.* **2.** inclined; sloping. —*adv.* sideways; sidelong.

side·long (sīd′lông′) *adj.* **1.** directed to the side: *He gave a sidelong glance.* **2.** not straightforward; devious; indirect. —*adv.* toward the side.

side·piece (sīd′pēs′) *n.* piece forming the side or a portion of the side of something.

si·de·re·al (sī dēr′ē əl) *adj.* **1.** of or relating to the stars. **2.** determined or measured by means of the stars. [Latin *sidereus* relating to the stars (from *sidus* star, group of stars) + -AL¹.]

sidereal day, day *(def. 3b).*

sidereal month, month *(def. 4).*

sidereal year, year *(def. 2b).*

sid·er·ite (sĭd′ə rīt′) *n.* **1.** iron mineral of iron carbonate. Formula: $FeCO_3$. **2.** meteorite consisting mainly of iron. [Latin *siderites* from Greek *siderites,* from *sideros* iron.]

side·sad·dle (sīd′săd′əl) *n.* woman's saddle so constructed that the rider sits with both legs on the same side of the horse. —*adv.* on a sidesaddle.

side·show (sīd′shō′) *n.* **1.** minor show connected to or forming part of a larger entertainment or exhibition. **2.** minor incident or issue; subordinate matter or affair.

side·slip (sīd′slĭp′) *n.* **1.** act or instance of slipping or skidding to one side. **2.** (of an airplane) act or instance of sliding sideward, esp. downward toward the center of the curve made while turning. —*v.i.* **-slipped, -slip·ping.** to slip or skid to one side.

side·split·ting (sīd′splĭt′ĭng) *adj.* **1.** boisterous or unrestrained: *sidesplitting laughter.* **2.** causing boisterous or unrestrained laughter: *a sidesplitting farce.*

side·step (sīd′stĕp′) **-stepped, -step·ping.** *v.t.* to avoid by or as by stepping aside: *to sidestep a decision.* —*v.i.* **1.** to step to one side. **2.** to avoid a responsibility, decision, or difficulty. —**side′step′per,** *n.*

side step, step or movement to one side, as in boxing.

side·stroke (sīd′strōk′) *n.* swimming stroke performed while the swimmer is on his side and in which the forward arm reaches ahead while the rear arm pushes back, the arms then returning to meet in front of the chest, accompanied by a scissors kick with the feet.

side·swipe (sīd′swīp′) **-swiped, -swip·ing.** *v.t.* to strike with a blow along the side, as in passing. —*n.* blow made on or along the side.

side·track (sīd′trăk′) *v.t.* **1.** to turn aside from the main concern, purpose, or course: *She is easily sidetracked.* **2.** to shift (a train) to a siding. —*v.i.* to shift a train to a siding. —*n.* railroad siding.

side·walk (sīd′wôk′) *n.* walk along the side of a street or road for pedestrians.

side·ward (sīd′wərd) *adj.* moving or directed toward one side. —*adv.* also, **side·wards.** toward one side.

side·ways (sīd′wāz′) also, **side·way, side·wise** (sīd′wīz′). *adv.* **1.** toward or from one side. **2.** with one side foremost. —*adj.* moving or directed toward one side.

side·wheel (sīd′hwēl′, -wēl′) *adj.* (of a steamboat) having a paddle wheel on each side. —**side′-wheel′er,** *n.*

side whiskers, whiskers on the side of the face.

sid·ing (sī′dĭng) *n.* **1.** short railroad track connected by a switch to a main track. **2.** wood, metal, or other material forming the outside covering of a frame building.

si·dle (sīd′əl) **-dled, -dling.** *v.i.* to move sideways, esp. in a furtive or unobtrusive manner. —*n.* sideways movement. [From SIDELING.]

Sid·ney, Sir Philip (sĭd′nē) 1554–86, English soldier and poet.

Si·don (sīd′ən) *n.* ancient Mediterranean port city of the Phoenician empire, on the southwestern coast of present-day Lebanon. —**Si·do·ni·an** (sī dō′nē ən), *adj., n.*

siege (sēj) *n.* **1.** act or process of surrounding an enemy position in order to capture it by constant attack and by cutting off its supplies over a long period of time. **2.** any long or persistent attempt to overcome resistance. **3.** long, distressing or tiring period, as of illness. **4. to lay siege to. a.** to subject to a siege; besiege. **b.** to try to capture or gain by long and persistent effort. —*v.t.,* **sieged, sieg·ing.** to lay siege to; besiege. [Old French *s(i)ege* seat, act of sitting, act of settling, going back to Latin *sedere* to sit.]

Siege Perilous, place at King Arthur's Round Table, reserved for the knight destined to find the Holy Grail and fatal to any other knight. [See SIEGE, PERILOUS.]

Sieg·fried (sĕg′frēd) *n. Germanic Legend.* a hero who killed a dragon and gained the treasure of the Nibelungs. His adventures are described in the *Nibelungenlied.*

Si·en·a (sē en′ə) *n.* city in central Italy, northwest of Rome, noted for its medieval buildings and numerous works of art. Pop. (1964 est.), 52,600.

si·en·na (sē en′ə) *n.* **1.** brown earth containing ferric oxide and manganese, used as a yellowish-brown pigment in its natural state (raw sienna) or, after being roasted, as a reddish-brown pigment (burnt sienna). **2.** yellowish-brown or reddish-brown color. [Short for Italian *terra di Sienna* literally, earth of Siena, where it was first obtained.]

si·er·ra (sē er′ə) *n.* chain of rugged hills or mountains with sharp, jagged peaks that suggest the teeth of a saw. [Spanish *sierra* saw¹, chain of hills, from Latin *serra* saw¹.]

Si·er·ra Le·o·ne (sē er′ə lē ō′nē, lē ōn′) country on the western coast of Africa. Capital, Freetown. Area, 27,925 sq. mi. Pop. (1969 est.), 2,512,000.

Si·er·ra Ma·dre (sē er′ə mä′drā) mountain system in eastern and western Mexico.

Si·er·ra Ne·vad·a (sē er′ə nə vad′ə, -vä′də) mountain range in eastern California.

si·es·ta (sē es′tə) *n.* afternoon nap or rest, esp. that taken during the hottest part of day in Spain and certain other hot countries. [Spanish *siesta,* from Latin *sexta (hōra)* sixth (hour), noon.]

sieve (siv) *n.* utensil or instrument having a perforated or meshed bottom, used for sifting or draining substances. —*v.t., v.i.,* **sieved, siev·ing.** to pass through a sieve. [Old English *sife* strainer.]

sift (sĭft) *v.t.* **1.a.** to separate by passing through a sieve: *to sift sand from gravel.* **b.** to remove lumps from or make lighter by passing through a sieve: *to sift flour.* **2.** to sprinkle by shaking through a sieve: *to sift sugar over doughnuts.* **3.** to separate as if with a sieve; select: *to sift the truth from fiction.* **4.** to examine with close scrutiny: *to sift evidence.* —*v.i.* **1.** to sift something. **2.** to fall loosely as if through a sieve: *Dust sifted through the cracks.* [Old English *siftan* to strain.] —**sift′er,** *n.*

sigh (sī) *v.i.* **1.** to emit a very long, deep audible breath, as from grief, relief, or weariness. **2.** to make a sound suggestive of a sigh. **3.** to wish earnestly; yearn; long: *The old man sighed for the good old days.* —*v.t.* to express with a sigh: *He sighed his relief.* —*n.* act or sound of sighing. [Middle English *sighen* to emit a deep breath, going back to Old English *sīcan.*] —**sigh′er,** *n.*

sight (sīt) *n.* **1.** faculty or power of seeing; vision. **2.** act or instance of seeing. **3.** range of one's vision: *Keep it out of sight.* **4.** something seen; view: *The sunset was a beautiful sight.* **5.** usually, **sights.** something striking or worth seeing: *John enjoyed seeing the sights in New York.* **6.** personal estimation; judgment; mental regard: *In my sight, he can do nothing wrong.* **7.** any of various devices used as an aid in observing or aiming, as on a surveying instrument or firearm. **8.** observation or aim taken with such a device. **9.** *Informal.* something messy or unpleasant to look at: *The room was a sight after the party.* **10. at** (or **on**) **sight. a.** as soon as seen; immediately. **b.** on presentation. —*v.t.* **1.** to perceive with the eyes; see: *After hiking for hours, we finally sighted a clearing in the forest.* **2.** to take sight of with an instrument. **3.** to aim by means of a sight or sights. **4.** to adjust the sight or sights of. [Old English *(ge)siht* a thing seen.]

sight draft, draft payable on presentation.

sight·less (sīt′lĭs) *adj.* **1.** unable to see; blind. **2.** invisible. —**sight′less·ness,** *n.*

sight·ly (sīt′lē) **-li·er, -li·est.** *adj.* **1.** pleasing to the eye; comely. **2.** affording a fine view. —**sight′li·ness,** *n.*

sight·see·ing (sīt′sē′ĭng) *n.* act or instance of visiting places of interest. —*adj.* used for or engaged in visiting places of interest. —**sight′see′er,** *n.*

sig·ma (sĭg′mə) *n.* **1.** eighteenth letter of the Greek alphabet (Σ, σ, ς), corresponding to the English letter S, s. **2.** *Physics.* any of three

at; āpe; cär; end; mē; it; īce; hot; ōld; fôrk; wood; fōōl; oil; out; up; ūse; turn; sing; thin; this; zh in treasure; ə in ago, taken, pencil, lemon, circus.

subatomic particles of the baryon group. See **subatomic particle** for table.

sig·moid (sig′moid) *adj.* **1.** shaped like the letter *S*. **2.** of, relating to, or affecting the sigmoid flexure of the colon. Also, **sig·moi′dal.** [Greek *sigmoeidēs* shaped like a sigma, from *sigma* sigma + *eidos* form, shape.]

sigmoid flexure, last curving portion of the colon before the rectum.

sign (sīn) *n.* **1.** something that serves to represent, indicate, or suggest some state, quality, condition, or feeling: *There were signs of wear on the carpet. His failure to write is no sign that he has forgotten you.* **2.** motion, gesture, or action that expresses an idea or issues a command or warning: *The referee gave the sign to start the game.* **3.** inscribed plate or board that serves to convey information or issue a command or warning: *The sign on the door said they were closed for the day.* **4.** conventional device or symbol that serves to represent an object, process, relationship, idea, or the like. **5.** warning or indication of what is to come; portent; omen: *Except ye see signs and wonders, ye will not believe* (John 4:48). **6.** trace: *There is no sign of him anywhere.* **7.** one of the twelve divisions of the zodiac. —*v.t.* **1.a.** to affix one's signature to: *John signed the receipt.* **b.** to attest or confirm by affixing one's signature to: *If the artist signed the painting, it must be genuine.* **2.** to inscribe as a signature: *She signed her name to the document.* **3.** to engage or hire by means of a contract or other written agreement: *The team signed him for the year.* **4.** to communicate or express by a sign. **5. to sign away** (or **over**). to dispose of or transfer by or as by affixing one's signature to a document. —*v.i.* **1.** to write one's signature. **2.** to accept employment or be hired by means of a contract or other written agreement. **3. to sign in.** to sign a register upon arrival. **4. to sign off.** to cease television or radio transmission for the day. **5. to sign out.** to sign a register upon departure. **6. to sign up.** to enlist in or join an organization or group, esp. a branch of military service. **7. to sign up for.** to enroll, as in a course of study. [Old French *signe* mark, token, from Latin *signum.*] —**sign′er,** *n.*

Syn. *n.* **2. Sign, signal** mean a gesture that serves as a means of conveying information. **Sign** is more frequently used to convey an idea through a physical gesture alone: *The man nodded as a sign of approval.* **Signal** implies a generally accepted symbol that serves to warn, direct, or command: *The whistle was the signal to start the game.*

sig·nal (sig′nəl) *n.* **1.** something, as a gesture, sound, or light, that serves to warn, direct, inform, or instruct: *The flashing light was a signal that a train was coming.* **2.** action or occurrence that serves to incite: *The tyrannous act was a signal for insurrection.* **3.** electric current that transmits sounds or pictures to receiving equipment. —*v.t.,* -**naled,** -**nal·ing;** *also, British,* -**nalled,** -**nal·ling.** **1.** to make a signal or signals to: *We signaled a passing ship for help.* **2.** to communicate or make known by a signal or signals: *The bugler signaled a retreat.* —*v.i.* to make a signal or signals. —*adj.* **1.** used as a signal: *a signal light.* **2.** remarkable; striking; notable: *a signal event.* [Medieval Latin *signale* something intended as a sign, going back to Latin *signum* mark, token.] —**sig′nal·er;** *also, British,* **sig′nal·ler,** *n.* —**Syn.** **1.** see **sign.**

Signal Corps, part of the U.S. Army in charge of communications.

sig·nal·ize (sig′nə līz′) -**ized,** -**iz·ing.** *v.t.* **1.** to make notable or striking. **2.** to point out distinctly.

sig·nal·ly (sig′nə lē) *adv.* in a signal manner; remarkably; notably.

sig·nal·man (sig′nəl mən, -man′) *pl.* -**men.** *n.* one whose job is sending signals, as on a railroad, ship, or in the armed forces.

sig·na·to·ry (sig′nə tôr′ē) *pl.* -**ries.** *n.* person or country that signs a document, as a treaty. —*adj.* that has signed a document.

sig·na·ture (sig′nə chər) *n.* **1.** name of a person, or a mark representing his name, written in his own hand. **2.** melody, sound effect, or visual effect that identifies a radio or television program. **3.** *Printing.* **a.** folded sheet ready for binding on which thirty-two pages, or any multiple of four, have been printed, forming one section of a book. **b.** letter or number printed at the foot of the first page of such a sheet, serving as a guide for collating. **4.** that part of a medical prescription giving the amount and frequency of dosage. **5.** *Music.* symbol or group of symbols at the beginning of a staff to indicate pitch or meter. [Medieval Latin *signatura* a signing, going back to Latin *signum* mark, token.]

sign·board (sīn′bôrd′) *n.* board bearing a notice or advertisement.

sig·net (sig′nit) *n.* **1.** small seal, esp. one used to give authority to a document. **2.** impression made by or as by a signet. —*v.t.* to stamp or mark with a signet. [Old French *signet* seal², stamp, diminutive of *signe* mark, token. See SIGN.]

signet ring, finger ring containing a signet.

sig·nif·i·cance (sig nif′i kəns) *n.* **1.** state or quality of having special value or relevance; importance: *This fact has little significance for us.* **2.** that which is intended to be or actually is signified; meaning; import: *What is the significance of her actions?* **3.** expressiveness; suggestiveness. Also, **sig·nif′i·can·cy.** —**Syn.** **2.** see **meaning.**

sig·nif·i·cant (sig nif′i kənt) *adj.* **1.** having special value or relevance; important; weighty: *a significant event.* **2.** signifying something; having a meaning. **3.** having or expressing a special covert meaning; suggestive: *a significant look.* [Latin *significāns* full of meaning, present participle of *significāre* to show by signs.] —**sig·nif′i·cant·ly,** *adv.* —**Syn.** **2.** see **expressive.**

sig·ni·fi·ca·tion (sig′nə fi kā′shən) *n.* **1.** meaning; import: *the signification of a word.* **2.** act of signifying; communication.

sig·nif·i·ca·tive (sig nif′ə kā′tiv) *adj.* **1.** signifying something; having a meaning. **2.** significant; suggestive.

sig·ni·fy (sig′nə fī′) -**fied,** -**fy·ing.** *v.t.* **1.** to be a sign, symbol, or indication of; represent; mean: *Her smile signified her happiness.* **2.** to convey by signs, speech, or actions: *He signified his disapproval by bowing his head.* —*v.i.* to be of importance; matter. [Latin *significāre* to show by signs, from *signum* mark, token + *facere* to do, make.] —**sig·ni·fi′a·ble,** *adj.* —**sig′ni·fi′er,** *n.*

sign language, system of communication in which gestures are substituted for speech, used esp. by the deaf.

sign manual *pl.,* **signs manual.** person's signature, esp. that of a sovereign serving to authenticate a document.

sign of the cross, sign made in the outline of a cross by touching one's forehead, chest, and shoulders with the fingers of the right hand as an act of religious devotion.

si·gnor (sēn′yôr, sēn yôr′, sin-) *pl.* **si·gnors** or **si·gno·ri** (sēn yôr′ē, sin-). *also,* **si·gnior.** *n.* mister; sir. ▲ Italian form of respectful or polite address for a man, usually used before the name. [Italian *signor,* form of *signore.* See SIGNORE.]

si·gno·ra (sēn yôr′ə, sin-) *pl.,* **si·gno·re** (sēn yôr′ā, sin-). *n.* mistress; lady. ▲ Italian form of respectful or polite address for a married woman. [Italian *signora,* feminine of *signore.* See SIGNORE.]

si·gno·re (sēn yôr′ā, sin-) *pl.,* **si·gno·re** (sēn yôr′ē, sin-). *n.* mister; sir. ▲ Italian form of respectful or polite address for a man, used in direct address without the name. [Italian *signore,* from Latin *senior* older, comparative of *senex* old, old man.]

si·gno·ri·na (sēn′yô rē′nə) *pl.,* -**ne** (-nā). *n.* miss. ▲ Italian form of respectful or polite address for an unmarried girl or woman. [Italian *signorina,* diminutive of *signora.* See SIGNORA.]

sign·post (sīn′pōst′) *n.* **1.** post bearing a sign. **2.** indication or clue.

Sig·urd (sig′ərd) *n.* *Norse Legend.* the warrior who slew the dragon Fafnir and captured the treasure it was guarding.

Sikh (sēk) *n.* follower of a monotheistic religion developed about A.D. 1500 that combines elements of both Hinduism and Islam. [Hindi *sikh* disciple, from Sanskrit *sishya.*]

Sik·kim (sik′im, si kēm′) *n.* kingdom and protectorate of India in the Himalayas of south-central Asia. Capital, Gangtok. Area, 2745 sq. mi. Pop. (1969 est.), 191,000.

si·lage (sī′lij) *n.* ensilage *(def. 2).*

si·lence (sī′ləns) *n.* **1.** absence of sound; complete quiet; stillness. **2.** state of being or keeping silent: *to listen in silence.* **3.** absence or omission of mention or notice: *to pass over a fact in silence.* —*v.t.,* -**lenced,** -**lenc·ing.** **1.** to cause to be or keep silent; bring to silence: *to silence a noisy classroom.* **2.** to put a stop to; suppress: *Oppressive measures were used to silence the critics of the government.* **3.** to put to rest: *to silence a child's fears.* **4.** to disable (enemy guns) by superior fire. —*interj.* be silent.

si·lenc·er (sī′lən sər) *n.* **1.** one who or that which silences. **2.** tubelike device attached to the front of a gun barrel to deaden its sound.

si·lent (sī′lənt) *adj.* **1.** characterized by the absence of sound; completely quiet; still: *We went into the silent forest. The old theater was empty and silent.* **2.** refraining from noise or speech: *The spectators at the trial were silent during her testimony.* **3.** not given to speaking; taciturn; reticent: *He was the most silent of men.* **4.** not uttered or expressed; unspoken: *There was much silent opposition to our proposal.* **5.** free from activity or disturbance; inactive: *A silent volcano was located in the center of the island.* **6.** characterized by the absence or omission of mention or notice; omitting all reference: *The book was silent on that subject.* **7.** (of motion pictures) having no sound track. **8.** *Linguistics.* not pronounced, as the *b* in *debtor.* —**si′lent·ly,** *adv.* —**si′lent·ness,** *n.*

silent partner, partner who has a financial investment in a business but does not participate actively in its management.

Si·le·nus (sī lē′nəs) *pl. (def. 2).* -**ni** (-nī). *n.* **1.** *Greek Mythology.* nature spirit who was foster father, tutor, and companion of Dionysus. **2.** **silenus.** any of the older satyrs.

si·le·sia (si lē′zhə, -shə, sī-) *n.* cotton fabric having a glossy finish used for linings. [From *Silesia,* where it was first made.]

Si·le·sia (si lē′zhə, -shə, sī-) *n.* historic region in southwestern Poland and northern Czechoslovakia. —**Si·le′sian,** *adj., n.*

Si·lex (sī′leks) *n.* **1.** *Trademark.* vacuum coffee maker made of heat-resistant glass. [Latin *silex* flint.]

at; āpe; cär; end; mē; it; īce; hot; ōld; fôrk; wood; fōōl; oil; out; up; ūse; turn; sing; thin; this; zh in treasure; ə in ago, taken, pencil, lemon, circus.

927

sil·hou·ette (sil´ōō et´) *n.* **1.** outline of a figure or object filled in with a solid color, usually black. **2.** dark outline seen against a lighter background. —*v.t.*, **-et·ted, -et·ting.** to cause to appear in or as in a silhouette. [From Étienne de *Silhouette*, 1709–67, French minister of finance noted for his petty economic policies; probably because silhouettes were far less expensive than painted portraits.] —**Syn.** *n.* **1.** see **profile.**

sil·i·ca (sil´i kə) *n.* hard, glasslike, transparent mineral occurring naturally as quartz, used in the manufacture of glass and ceramics. Also, **silicon dioxide.** Formula: SiO₂ [Modern Latin *silica*, from Latin *silex* flint.]

silica gel, porous, absorbent form of silica, used as a drying agent and for deodorizing and cleaning air.

sil·i·cate (sil´ə kit, -kāt´) *n.* any of various compounds containing silicon, oxygen, any of various metals, and sometimes hydrogen. Window glass and building bricks consist of silicates.

si·li·ceous (si lish´əs) *adj.* of, resembling, or containing silica. [Latin *siliceus* relating to flint, from *silex* flint.]

si·lic·ic (si lis´ik) *adj.* of or relating to silica or silicon.

sil·i·con (sil´i kən, -kon´) *n.* nonmetallic element that exists in its pure state as either brown powder or as dark-grey or black crystals. Silicon is the second most abundant element in the earth's crust. Symbol: Si See **element** for table. [From SILICA.]

silicon carbide, extremely hard, bluish-black, crystalline substance, used as an abrasive.

silicon dioxide, silica.

sil·i·cone (sil´i kōn´) *n.* any of a class of polymeric compounds composed of chains of silicon and oxygen atoms to which organic radicals are attached. Silicones are used as oils, plastics, and synthetic rubbers and in various industrial processes because they are unaffected by extremes of temperature.

sil·i·co·sis (sil´i kō´sis) *n.* chronic disease of the lungs caused by the continuous inhalation of air containing particles of certain silicon compounds. [Modern Latin *silicosis*, from SILICA + -OSIS.]

silk (silk) *n.* **1.** soft, lustrous, resilient fiber spun by silkworms. **2.** strong, lustrous fabric made from these fibers, woven in various weights and used for such items as scarves, ties, and blouses. **3.** filament or material resembling silk. **4. silks.** cap and blouse having distinctive colors, worn by a jockey or harness driver to identify the owner of the horse he rides or drives. —*adj.* of, resembling, or relating to silk. [Old English *seolc* the fiber, the fabric, going back to Greek *sērikon* the fabric, from *Sēres* the Chinese (who were famous for their silken fabrics).]

silk cotton, light fiber obtained from the seed pods of the silk-cotton tree. Also, **ka´pok.**

silk-cot·ton tree (silk´kot´ən) any of various tropical trees found in South America, Java, Ceylon, and the Philippines, esp. *Ceiba pentandra*, from which kapok is derived.

silk·en (sil´kən) *adj.* **1.** made of silk. **2.** like silk in appearance or texture; silky. **3.** dressed in silk. **4.** luxurious or elegant.

silk-screen process (silk´skrēn´) method or process of printing in which pigment or ink is forced through a screen of silk or other fine fabric on which a design, usually in the form of a cut stencil, has been imposed.

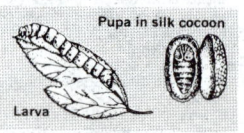

Pupa in silk cocoon

Larva

Silkworm

silk-stock·ing (silk´stok´ing) *adj.* aristocratic or wealthy: *a silk-stocking district of a city.* —*n.* aristocratic or wealthy person.

silk·worm (silk´wurm´) *n.* larva, or caterpillar, of a moth, *Bombyx mori*, originally domesticated in China. The cocoon it spins is processed to make silk thread and fabric.

silk·y (sil´kē) **silk·i·er, silk·i·est.** *adj.* **1.** like silk in appearance or texture; smooth, soft, and lustrous. **2.** made of silk. **3.** *Botany.* covered with fine soft hairs, as a leaf. —**silk´i·ly,** *adv.* —**silk´i·ness,** *n.*

sill (sil) *n.* **1.** horizontal member across the bottom of a door or window. **2.** horizontal beam which either rests on or forms the foundation of a structure. [Old English *syll* base¹, support.]

sil·la·bub (sil´ə bub´) syllabub.

sil·ly (sil´ē) **-li·er, -li·est.** *adj.* **1.a.** lacking in judgment or common sense; stupid: *a silly person.* **b.** absurd; ridiculous: *a silly notion.* **2.** *Informal.* stunned; dazed, as by a blow. [Old English *(ge)sælig* happy, fortunate.] —**sil´li·ness,** *n.*

si·lo (sī´lō) *pl.* **-los.** *n.* **1.** structure, usually a tall, cylindrical tower of metal, concrete, or other mate-

Sill *(def. 1)*

rial, for the storage and fermentation of green fodder. **2.** deep hole in the ground for storing and launching missiles. [Spanish *silo* underground granary, from Latin *sīrus*, from Greek *siros*.]

silt (silt) *n.* fine sand, clay, or other similar matter carried by water and deposited as sediment. —*v.t.*, *v.i.* to fill or choke with silt (with *up*). [Possibly of Scandinavian origin.] —**silt´y,** *adj.*

Si·lu·ri·an (si loor´ē ən, sī-) *n.* third geological period of the Paleozoic era, during which the first land plants appeared. See **geology** for table. —*adj.* of, relating to, or characteristic of this period. [Latin *Silures* ancient people who once lived in Wales + -IAN; because rocks of this period were mainly studied in Wales.]

Silo

sil·van (sil´vən) sylvan.

sil·ver (sil´vər) *n.* **1.** lustrous, white metallic element that is soft and easily shaped and is the best conductor of heat and electricity of any metal, used esp. in the manufacture of mirrors and as a catalyst in certain chemical processes. Symbol: Ag See **element** for table. **2.** silver used as a commodity or as a standard of currency. **3.** coins, esp. those made from silver; change. **3.** articles, as tableware, made of or coated with a thin layer of silver. **4.** color of silver. —*adj.* **1.** made of or coated with a thin layer of silver. **2.** of or relating to silver: *silver mining.* **3.** resembling silver, as in color or luster. **4.** having a clear, bell-like tone; melodious: *silver laughter.* **5.** smooth and convincing; eloquent: *a silver tongue.* **6.** of or advocating the use or adoption of silver as a standard of currency. **7.** of or marking the twenty-fifth year or event in a series: *a silver wedding anniversary.* —*v.t.* **1.** to coat with a thin layer of silver or anything resembling silver. **2.** to give (something) the color or luster of silver: *Age had silvered her hair.* —*v.i.* to become silver or silvery in color. [Old English *siolfor, seolfor* white precious metal, money.]

silver bell, North American tree, *Halesia carolina*, bearing showy clusters of white bell-shaped flowers.

silver certificate, certificate issued by the U.S. government, formerly circulated as money, stating that a certain amount of silver has been deposited in the Treasury for redemption on demand.

sil·ver·fish (sil´vər fish´) *pl.*, **-fish** or **-fish·es.** *n.* small white or gray wingless insect, *Lepisma saccharina*, a common household pest that feeds on wallpaper, bookbindings, and other starchy materials. Length: to ½ inch.

Silver bells

silver fox 1. red fox whose fur is black, tipped with gray or white. **2.** fur of this animal.

sil·vern (sil´vərn) *adj. Archaic.* of or resembling silver.

silver nitrate, white, crystalline compound used in preparing photographic emulsions, in silver-plating, and in making hair dyes. It is produced by the reaction of silver and nitric acid. Formula: AgNO₃

sil·ver·plate (sil´vər plāt´) **-plat·ed, -plat·ing.** *v.t.* to coat with a thin layer of silver, as by electroplating.

silver plate, articles made of or coated with a thin layer of silver, as table utensils.

sil·ver·smith (sil´vər smith´) *n.* one who makes or repairs articles of silver.

sil·ver·tongued (sil´vər tungd´) *adj.* having smooth, agreeable, and convincing speech; eloquent.

sil·ver·ware (sil´vər wâr´) *n.* **1.** articles, esp. tableware, made of or coated with a thin layer of silver. **2.** any metal table utensils.

sil·ver·y (sil´vər ē) *adj.* **1.** having the lustrous whiteness of silver. **2.** having a soft and clear musical sound. **3.** made of or coated with a thin layer of silver. —**sil´ver·i·ness,** *n.*

Sim·e·on (sim´ē ən) *n.* **1.** in the Old Testament, a son of Jacob and Leah. **2.** one of the twelve tribes of Israel descended from him.

sim·i·an (sim´ē ən) *adj.* of, relating to, or resembling an ape or monkey. —*n.* ape or monkey. [Latin *sīmia* ape (probably from *sīmus* snub-nosed, from Greek *sīmos*) + -AN.]

sim·i·lar (sim´ə lər) *adj.* **1.** having or bearing a marked resemblance; alike: *The general features of the two landscapes were similar.* **2.** *Geometry.* having corresponding angles equal and corresponding sides proportional: *similar triangles.* [French *similaire* like, from Latin *similis*.] —**sim´i·lar·ly,** *adv.* —**Syn. 1.** see **like¹.**

sim·i·lar·i·ty (sim´ə lar´ə tē) *pl.* **-ties.** *n.* **1.** quality or state of being similar; likeness. **2.** instance or point of likeness.

at; āpe; cär; end; mē; it; īce; hot; ōld; fôrk; wood; fōōl; oil; out; up; ūse; turn; sing; thin; this; zh in treasure; ə in ago, taken, pencil, lemon, circus.

sim·i·le (sim′ə lē) n. figure of speech in which one object or idea is compared with another in order to suggest a similarity between the two; for example: *His face shone like the sun. She was as cold as ice.* [Latin *simile* comparison, likeness.]

si·mil·i·tude (si mil′ə tōōd′, -tūd′) n. **1.** similarity; likeness. **2.** one who or that which is similar to another. [Latin *similitūdō* likeness.]

sim·i·tar (sim′ə tər) n. scimitar.

sim·mer (sim′ər) v.i. **1.** (of a liquid or something in a liquid) to cook at, or just below, the boiling point. **2.** to make a murmuring sound, as a liquid when just beginning to boil. **3.** to be on the verge of breaking forth: *to simmer with anger.* **4. to simmer down.** *Informal.* to become calm. —v.t. **1.** to cook at, or just below, the boiling point. **2. to simmer down.** to reduce (a liquid) in volume by simmering. —n. state or process of simmering. [Earlier *simper;* possibly imitative.]

si·mo·ni·ac (si mō′nē ak′) n. one who practices simony. —**si·mo·ni·a·cal** (sī′mə nī′ə kəl, sim′ə-), adj.

Si·mon Peter (sī′mən) see Peter (def. 1).

si·mon-pure (sī′mən pyoor′) adj. genuine; authentic. [From *Simon Pure,* a Quaker in Susanna Centlivre's comedy *A Bold Stroke for a Wife* (1718), who is impersonated and must prove he is the real Simon Pure.]

si·mo·ny (sī′mə nē, sim′ə-) n. act or practice of buying or selling ecclesiastical preferments or benefices. [Late Latin *sīmōnia* sale of sacred things, from *Simon Magus,* who tried to buy the gift of the Holy Ghost (Acts 8:18–19).]

si·moom (si mōōm′) also, **si·moon** (si mōōn′). n. hot, dry, sand-laden wind of the Arabian and African deserts. [Arabic *samūm,* from *samm* to poison; because of its effect on people.]

simp (simp) n. *Slang.* simpleton; fool. [Short for SIMPLETON.]

sim·per (sim′pər) v.i. **1.** to smile in a silly, self-conscious, affected way. —v.t. to say with a simper. —n. silly, self-conscious smile. [Possibly of Scandinavian origin.]

sim·ple (sim′pəl) -pler, -plest. adj. **1.** easily done, used, or understood: *a simple task, a simple math problem.* **2.** consisting of only one part or one unit; uncompounded; unmixed: *a simple substance.* **3.** with nothing added; mere; pure: *the simple truth.* **4.** without elaboration or ornament; unadorned; plain: *a simple style of writing, a simple interior.* **5.a.** without sophistication, vanity, or pretense; unsophisticated or unpretentious; artless: *a simple and unaffected person.* **b.** without duplicity or guile; straightforward; honest; sincere: *a simple heart, simple motives.* **6.** without rank; humble or common: *a simple laborer, a simple citizen.* **7.** lacking in judgment or common sense; foolish. —n. **1.** that which is uncompounded; simple substance or element. **2.** one who lacks judgment or common sense. **3.** *Archaic.* person of humble birth or position; rustic. **4.** *Archaic.* herb or other plant from which a medicine is made. [Old French *simple* plain¹, going back to Latin *simplex.*] —**sim′ple·ness,** n. —**Syn.** adj. 1. see easy.

simple fraction, common fraction.

sim·ple-heart·ed (sim′pəl här′tid) adj. straightforward; sincere.

simple machine, machine (def. 2).

sim·ple-mind·ed (sim′pəl mīn′did) adj. **1.** unsophisticated; artless. **2.** uneducated, foolish, or stupid. **3.** weak-minded.

simple sentence, sentence that consists of one independent clause without a dependent clause; for example: *He walks quickly.*

sim·ple·ton (sim′pəl tən) n. unwise or silly person; fool. [From SIMPLE.]

sim·plic·i·ty (sim plis′ə tē) pl., -ties. n. **1.** state or quality of being simple; freedom from difficulty or complexity. **2.** freedom from elaboration or ornament; plainness: *Her clothes were characterized by their simplicity and good taste.* **3.** freedom from duplicity or guile; sincerity. **4.** lack of common sense; foolishness or stupidity. [Latin *simplicitās* plainness, frankness.]

sim·pli·fi·ca·tion (sim′plə fi kā′shən) n. **1.** act of simplifying; being simplified. **2.** result of this.

sim·pli·fy (sim′plə fī′) -fied, -fy·ing. v.t. to make less difficult, complex, or elaborate; make simple. [French *simplifier,* from Medieval Latin *simplificare,* from Latin *simplus* not complex, plain¹ + *facere* to make.] —**sim′pli·fi′er,** n.

sim·plis·tic (sim plis′tik) adj. characterized by a tendency to oversimplify a problem or issue. —**sim·plis′ti·cal·ly,** adv.

Sim·plon (sim′plon) n. **1.** mountain pass across the Alps of southern Switzerland and northern Italy. **2.** railroad tunnel near this pass.

sim·ply (sim′plē) adv. **1.** in a clear, unpretentious, or straightforward manner. **2.** without elaboration or ornament; plainly: *The room was decorated simply.* **3.** merely; only: *It is simply a question of convenience.* **4.** to the fullest or highest degree: *She is simply lovely.*

sim·u·la·crum (sim′yə lā′krəm) pl., -cra (-krə) or -crums. n. **1.** shadowy or unreal likeness of something. **2.** representation of something; image. [Latin *simulacrum.*]

sim·u·late (sim′yə lāt′) -lat·ed, -lat·ing. v.t. **1.** to make a pretense of; pretend: *to simulate grief.* **2.** to have or take on the appearance or form

of; imitate: *That painted panel simulates marble.* —adj. pretended; feigned. [Latin *simulātus,* past participle of *simulāre* to pretend, make like.] —**sim′u·la′tive,** sim·u·la·to·ry (sim′ye lə tôr′ē), adj. —**sim′u·la′tor,** n. —**Syn.** v.t. 1. see pretend.

sim·u·la·tion (sim′yə lā′shən) n. **1.** act or process of simulating. **2.** that which simulates; imitation: *His art collection included both genuine ivory carvings and simulations.*

si·mul·cast (sī′məl kast′, sim′əl-) -cast or -cast·ed, -cast·ing. v.t. to broadcast (a program) over radio and television simultaneously. —n. program broadcast in this way. [SIMUL(TANEOUS) + (BROAD)CAST.]

si·mul·ta·ne·ous (sī′məl tā′nē əs, sim′əl-) adj. existing, occurring, or accomplished at the same time: *Their replies were simultaneous.* [Latin *simul,* on the model of INSTANTANEOUS.] —**si′mul·ta·ne·ous·ly,** adv. —**si·mul·ta·ne·i·ty** (sī′məl tə nē′ə tē, sim′əl-), **si′mul·ta′ne·ous·ness,** n.

simultaneous equations, two or more equations having variables that are satisfied by the same set of values. The equations $x + 2y = 10$ and $x + y = 4$ are simultaneous equations.

sin (sin) n. **1.** willful violation of divine law or some religious principle. **2.** instance of this. **3.** any violation of a standard, as of taste or propriety. —v.i. sinned, sin·ning. **1.** to violate a divine law or religious principle; commit sin. **2.** to commit an offense or wrong of any kind. [Old English *synn* violation of divine law, wrongdoing.]

sin, sine¹.

Si·nai (sī′nī) n. **1.** triangular desert area between Israel and Egypt, extending southward from the Mediterranean to the northern end of the Red Sea. Also, **Sinai Peninsula. 2. Mount.** in the Old Testament, the mountain on which Moses received the Ten Commandments.

since (sins) adv. **1.** from then till now: *He left last week and has been away ever since.* **2.** at some time between then and now: *My son was sick last month but has since recovered.* **3.** before now: *He's been long since gone.* —prep. **1.** continuously after the time of: *He has been gone since five o'clock.* **2.** during the time following: *There have been many changes since his boyhood.* —conj. **1.** during the period following the time when: *I haven't seen him since he graduated.* **2.** continuously from the time when: *She has lived abroad since she was a young girl.* **3.** in view of the fact that: *Since he can't do the job, I'll do it.* [Middle English *sinnes,* contraction of *sithenes* then, from *that time,* going back to Old English *siththan* after that, later.]

sin·cere (sin sēr′) -cer·er, -cer·est. adj. without affectation, hypocrisy, or pretense: *a sincere wish, a sincere friend.* [Latin *sincērus* pure, genuine.] —**sin·cere′ly,** adv.

sin·cer·i·ty (sin ser′ə tē) n. state or quality of being sincere.

Sin·clair, Up·ton Beall (sin·klâr′; up′tən bel) 1878–1968, U.S. writer and social reformer.

sine¹ (sīn) n. (of either acute angle of a right triangle) ratio of the length of the side opposite the angle to the length of the hypotenuse. [Medieval Latin *sinus* (translation of Arabic *jaib* sine), from Latin *sinus* fold¹, bosom.]

Sine of angle $A = BC/AB$

si·ne² (sī′nē, sē′nā) prep. *Latin.* without.

si·ne·cure (sī′nə kyoor′, sin′ə-) n. office or position that demands little or no work or responsibility, esp. one with a good salary. [Church Latin (*beneficium*) *sine cūrā* (benefice) without care (of souls).]

si·ne di·e (sī′nē dī′ē) without fixing a day for a future meeting: *to adjourn sine die.* [Latin *sine diē* without a day (being set).]

si·ne qua non (sī′nē kwä non′) something absolutely necessary or essential. [Latin *sine quā nōn* literally, without which not.]

sin·ew (sin′ū) n. **1.** tendon. **2.** muscular power or strength. **3.** *also,* **sinews.** source of power or strength: *The sinews of a nation are its youth.* [Old English *sinu* tendon.]

sin·ew·y (sin′ū ē) adj. **1.** characteristic of or containing sinews; tough; stringy: *a sinewy cut of meat.* **2.** physically strong or powerful; muscular. **3.** vigorous; robust.

sin·ful (sin′fəl) adj. full of or marked by sin; wicked; corrupt. —**sin′ful·ly,** adv. —**sin′ful·ness,** n.

sing (sing) sang or sung, sung, sing·ing. v.i. **1.** to utter words or sounds in musical succession or with a musical tone; perform a song. **2.** to produce melodious sounds, as a musical instrument or bird. **3.** to relate or praise something in song or verse (with *of*): *The poet sang of victory.* **4.** to make a whistling, ringing, or humming sound: *The steam sang as it escaped from the pipe.* **5.** to have a whistling, ringing, or humming sensation, as in the ears. **6.** to be adaptable for singing: *His poetry sings easily.* **7.** *Slang.* to confess to or give information about a crime: *to sing to the authorities.* **8. to sing out.** *Informal.* to call or cry out loudly. —v.t. **1.** to render by singing: *to sing a song. The tenor sang the high notes with ease.* **2.** to bring to a particular state or condition

by or with singing: *to sing a child to sleep.* **3.** to recite in a singing voice; intone. **4.** to proclaim enthusiastically: *He has sung your praises ever since he met you.* —*n.* group gathering for the purpose of singing together: *We went to the community sing.* [Old English *singan* to make vocal sounds musically, chant, recount in song or verse.] —**sing'a·ble,** *adj.*

sing., singular.

Sin·ga·pore (sing'gə pôr', sing'ə-) *n.* **1.** island country off the southern tip of the Malay Peninsula. Capital, Singapore. Area, 224 sq. mi. Pop. (1969 est.), 2,034,000. **2.** capital and largest city of this country. Pop. (1968), 1,987,900.

singe (sinj) *singed, singe·ing. v.t.* **1.** to burn superficially or lightly; scorch: *The hot iron singed her dress.* **2.** to burn the ends or tips of (hair). **3.** to remove feathers or bristles from by subjecting briefly to a flame. —*n.* **1.** act of singeing. **2.** superficial burn. [Old English *sengan* to burn superficially.] —**Syn.** *v.t.* **1.** see **scorch.**

sing·er (sing'ər) *n.* **1.** one who sings, esp. a trained or professional vocalist. **2.** bird that sings.

Sin·gha·lese (sing'gə lēz', -lēs') *also,* **Sin·ha·lese.** *adj.* of or relating to Ceylon, its people, or their language. —*n. pl.,* **-lese.** **1.** member or close descendant of the people of Ceylon. **2.** language belonging to the Indo-Iranian language family, spoken predominantly in Ceylon.

sin·gle (sing'gəl) *adj.* **1.** being a solitary object, unit, or individual. **2.** consisting of only one part or unit. **3.** of or designed for the use of one person only: *I requested a single room at the hotel.* **4.a.** single-minded. **b.** of, relating to, or characteristic of the unmarried state or unmarried persons. **5.** without another or others; unaccompanied. **6.** involving only two persons; man-to-man: *The two kings decided the matter by single combat.* **7.** honest; sincere: *nothing but a pure and single heart* (Dickens, 1848). **8.** (of a flower) having only one row or set of petals. —*n.* **1.** solitary person or thing; individual. **2.** that which is for one person only, as a hotel room or a ticket: *I've reserved a single for you.* **3.** golf game for two people only. **4.** *Baseball.* hit that allows the batter to go no further than first base. **5. singles.** match between two persons, as in tennis. ▲ construed as singular. **6.** *Informal.* one-dollar bill. —*v.t.* **-gled, -gling. 1.** to select or separate from others (with *out*): *Mary singled him out as her favorite.* **2.** *Baseball.* **a.** to cause (a base runner) to advance by making a single. **b.** to cause (a run) to score by making a single (often with *in*). —*v.i. Baseball.* to make a hit that allows the batter to advance to first base. [Old French *single* each, alone, not multiple, from Late Latin *singulus* separate, one only, from Latin *singulī* one to each, separate.] —**sin'gle·ness,** *n.*

Syn. *adj.* **1. Single, solitary** mean one only. **Single** suggests the idea of being unique and therefore special or significant: *He's the single person that can help us.* **Solitary** suggests separation and isolation from others of its kind: *A solitary tree shaded the lawn.*

sin·gle-breast·ed (sing'gəl bres'tid) *adj.* (of garments, esp. coats or jackets) having a row of buttons or other fastenings on one side only.

single file, line of persons or things one behind another.

sin·gle-foot (sing'gəl foot') *n.* gait of a horse in which each foot is put down separately. —*v.i.* to go at such a gait.

sin·gle-hand·ed (sing'gəl han'did) *adj.* **1.** without the aid or support of another or others; unassisted: *a single-handed victory.* **2.** having, using, or needing only one hand. —**sin'gle-hand'ed·ly,** *adv.* —**sin'gle-hand'ed·ness,** *n.*

sin·gle-heart·ed (sing'gəl här'tid) *adj.* straightforward; sincere.

sin·gle-mind·ed (sing'gəl mīn'did) *adj.* **1.** having only one aim or purpose. **2.** honest; sincere. —**sin'gle-mind'ed·ly,** *adv.* —**sin'gle-mind'ed·ness,** *n.*

sin·gle·stick (sing'gəl stik') *n.* **1.** fencing with a wooden stick requiring one hand. **2.** stick used in this type of fencing.

single tax, tax levied on land as the sole source of public revenue.

sin·gle·ton (sing'gəl tən) *n.* **1.** playing card that is the only one of a particular suit held in the hand. **2.** single thing, as distinct from a pair.

sin·gle-track (sing'gəl trak') *adj.* having a limited range; narrow: *a single-track mind.*

sin·gle·tree (sing'gəl trē') *n.* whiffletree. [Modification of SWINGLE-TREE.]

sin·gly (sing'glē) *adv.* **1.** one at a time; individually; separately: *to consider each item singly.* **2.** without the aid of another or others; single-handedly.

Sing Sing (sing' sing') state prison in southeastern New York.

sing·song (sing'sông') *n.* **1.** montonous, rhythmical cadence or tone, as in speaking. **2.** verse, song, or speech characterized by this. —*adj.* having a monotonous, rhythmical cadence or tone.

sin·gu·lar (sing'gyə lər) *adj.* **1.** out of the ordinary; unusual or remarkable; extraordinary. **2.** strange; peculiar; odd: *singular behavior.* **3.** being the only one of its kind; unique: *a singular example of courage.* **4.** of or relating to a grammatical form that denotes a single person or thing. —*n.* form of a word denoting a single person or thing. [Latin

singulāris single, separate, extraordinary, from *singulī* one to each, separate.] —**sin'gu·lar·ly,** *adv.*

sin·gu·lar·i·ty (sing'gyə lar'ə tē) *pl.,* **-ties.** *n.* **1.** state or quality of being singular. **2.** that which is singular.

Sin·ha·lese (sin'hə lēz', -lēs') Singhalese.

sin·is·ter (sin'is tər) *adj.* **1.** threatening or suggesting evil; ominous: *a sinister expression.* **2.** malicious or evil: *a sinister plot.* **3.** *Heraldry.* situated on the bearer's left and thus to the right of the viewer. Distinguished from **dexter. 4.** *Archaic.* of, relating to, or on the left. [Latin *sinister* left; referring to the belief of augurs in ancient times that the *left* side was unlucky.]

sin·is·tral (sin'is trəl) *adj.* **1.** on the left side. **2.** left-handed. —**sin'is·tral·ly,** *adv.*

sink (singk) *sank* or *sunk, sunk* or *sunk·en, sink·ing. v.i.* **1.** to become partly or completely submerged in or as in water: *The wheels sank into the mud. The ship sank after the collision.* **2.** to descend or appear to descend to a lower level, esp. gradually: *The water in the pond sank three feet last summer. The sun sank behind the mountain.* **3.** to slope downward: *The road sinks into a ditch.* **4.** to diminish or decrease, as in volume, force, degree, or intensity: *The sick man's voice sank to a whisper.* **5.** to become less in value or estimation; decline: *The value of money sank during the inflationary period. His reputation has sunk in our opinion.* **6.** to pass or fall gradually into a certain state or condition: *He sank into a deep sleep.* **7.** to decline or fail rapidly in health; come near death. **8.** to penetrate deeply: *The stain sank into the cloth.* **9.** to become or seem hollow, as the eyes. —*v.t.* **1.** to cause to become partly or completely submerged in or as in water. **2.** to cause to descend to a lower level. **3.** to reduce, as in volume, force, degree, or intensity. **4.** to excavate or dig: *We sank a well behind the house.* **5.** to force, lay, or bury in the ground: *The workmen sank a pipeline.* **6.a.** to invest (money). **b.** to lose (money) by investing unwisely. **7.** to pass over silently; conceal; suppress. **8.** *Basketball.* to toss (the ball) into a basket. **9.** *Golf.* to putt (the ball) into a hole. —*n.* **1.** basin of metal or porcelain usually connected to a water supply, used for washing. **2.** depression in a land surface where water collects. **3.** place where vice or corruption prevail. [Old English *sincan* to become submerged in water, descend to a lower level.] —**sink'a·ble,** *adj.*

sink·er (sing'kər) *n.* **1.** one who or that which sinks. **2.** weight used esp. to sink a fishing line. **3.** *Slang.* doughnut.

sink·hole (singk'hōl') *n.* vertical cavity worn in rock, esp. limestone, by water dripping downward.

sinking fund, fund set aside in order to pay off a debt.

sin·less (sin'lis) *adj.* free from or without sin. —**sin'less·ly,** *adv.* —**sin'less·ness,** *n.*

sin·ner (sin'ər) *n.* one who sins.

Sinn Fein (shin' fān') Irish political party, founded about 1905, that demanded Irish independence from Great Britain. [Irish *sinn féin* we ourselves.]

Sino- *combining form* Chinese: Sinology. [Late Latin *Sinae* the Chinese, from Greek *Sinai,* going back to Chinese (Mandarin) *Ch'in* name of a Chinese dynasty of the third century B.C.]

Si·nol·o·gy (sī nol'ə jē, si-) *n.* study of the Chinese people, their history, language, literature, or culture. [SINO- + -LOGY.] —**Si·nol·og·i·cal** (sī'nə loj'i kəl), *adj.* —**Si·nol'o·gist,** *n.*

Si·no-Ti·bet·an (sī'nō ti bet'ən) *n.* language family including Burmese, Chinese, and Thai, and other languages spoken predominantly in Burma, China, Thailand, Tibet, and certain other Far Eastern countries. —*adj.* of or relating to this language family.

sin·u·ate (sin'ū āt') *adj.* **1.** irregularly turning or curving; sinuous. **2.** (of a leaf) having a wavy margin. [Latin *sinuātus,* past participle of *sinuāre* to wind[2], bend.]

sin·u·os·i·ty (sin'ū os'ə tē) *pl.,* **-ties.** *n.* **1.** state or quality of being sinuous. **2.** curve or bend.

sin·u·ous (sin'ū əs) *adj.* full of bends, curves, or winds. [Latin *sinuōsus* full of folds or curves, from *sinus* fold[1], curve.] —**sin'u·ous·ly,** *adv.* —**sin'u·ous·ness,** *n.*

si·nus (sī'nəs) *pl.,* **-nus·es.** *n.* **1.a.** any of the air-filled cavities connected with the nostrils in the bones of the face. **b.** channel for the passage of venous blood. **2.** narrow passage leading to an abscess. **3.** curving part or hollow. **4.** rounded indentation between two projecting lobes, as of a leaf. [Latin *sinus* fold[1], bay, curve.]

Frontal
Sphenoid
Ethmoid
Maxillary

Sinuses

si·nus·i·tis (sī'nə sī'tis) *n.* inflammation of a sinus or sinuses.

at; āpe; cär; end; mē; it; īce; hot; ōld; fôrk; wood; fōōl; oil; out; up; ūse; turn; sing; thin; this; zh in treasure; ə in ago, taken, pencil, lemon, circus.

Si·on (sī′ən) Zion.

Siou·an (sōō′ən) *n.* **1.** family of North American Indian languages, including the Sioux, Osage, and Crow. **2.** Sioux *(def. 1).* —*adj.* of or relating to the Siouan language family.

Sioux (sōō) *pl.,* **Sioux** (sōō, sōōz). *n.* **1.** member of various tribes of North American Indians speaking a Siouan language, formerly living in Minnesota, North and South Dakota, and Wyoming. **2.** Dakota *(def. 3).* **3.** Siouan language spoken by these tribes.

Sioux City, city in western Iowa, on the Missouri. Pop. (1970), 85,-925.

Sioux Falls, city in southeastern South Dakota. Pop. (1970), 72,488.

sip (sip) **sipped, sip·ping.** *v.t.* to drink a very small quantity of (a liquid) at a time; drink little by little: *He sipped the hot coffee.* —*v.i.* to drink a very small quantity of a liquid at a time. —*n.* **1.** quantity of liquid drunk at one time. **2.** act of sipping. [Old English *sypian* to absorb moisture.]

si·phon (sī′fən) *also,* **sy·phon.** *n.* **1.** bent tube with legs of unequal length, used to transfer a liquid from one container to another one at a lower level by atmospheric pressure. **2.** tubelike organ of certain aquatic animals, as the clam, used for drawing in and expelling liquids. —*v.t.* to draw off through or as through a siphon. —*v.i.* to pass through a siphon. [Latin *sīphō* pipe, tube, from Greek *si-phōn*.] —**si′phon·al,** *adj.*

Siphon

sir (sur) *n.* **1.** mister. ▲ form of respectful or polite address for a man, used in direct address without the name. **2. Sir.** title and form of address for a knight or baronet. **3.** *Archaic.* title of respect used before a noun indicating a man's rank or profession: *sir Knight.* [Form of SIRE.]

sir·dar (sur′där, sər där′) *n.* dignitary or other man of high rank or importance in India, Pakistan, or Afghanistan. [Hindi *sardār* chief, from Persian *sardār*.]

sire (sīr) *n.* **1.** male parent of an animal, as a horse. **2.** father or forefather. **3. Sire.** used as a form of address in speaking to a king. —*v.t.,* **sired, sir·ing.** to be the male parent of. [Old French *sire* sir, master, lord, going back to Latin *senior* older, comparative of *senex* old. Doublet of SENIOR.]

si·ren (sī′rən) *n.* **1.** device that produces a loud, shrill sound by the periodic escape of compressed air through a rotating shutter. **2. Siren.** *Greek Mythology.* one of several sea nymphs, part bird and part woman, whose singing lured sailors to their destruction. **3.** charming, dangerously alluring, or enticing woman. —*adj.* of or like a Siren; charming, dangerously alluring, or enticing. [Latin *Sīrēn* this sea nymph, from Greek *Seirēn.*]

si·re·ni·an (sī rē′nē ən) *n.* any herbivorous, aquatic mammal of the order Sirenia, including the manatee and dugong. [Modern Latin *Sirenia* from Latin *Sīrēn* siren) + -AN. See SIREN.]

Sir·i·us (sir′ē əs) *n.* double star, the brightest star in the heavens, located in the constellation Canis Major. [Latin *Sīrius,* from Greek *Seirios;* named after *Sirius,* the hunting dog of the Greek hero Orion.]

sir·loin (sur′loin) *n.* cut of beef from the upper part of the loin. [Earlier *surloyn,* from Old French *surlonge,* from *sur* above (from Latin *super* over, above) + *longe* loin (going back to Latin *lumbus*).]

si·roc·co (si rok′ō) *pl.,* **-cos.** *n.* **1.** hot, dry wind blowing northward from North Africa across the Mediterranean Sea and into southern Europe, where it becomes warm and humid. **2.** any hot, oppressive wind. [Italian *s(c)irocco* the southeast wind, from Arabic *sharq* east.]

sir·rah (sir′ə) *n.* *Archaic.* fellow. ▲ a contemptuous form of address used to men or boys. [Modification of SIR.]

sir·up (sir′əp, sur′-) syrup.

sis (sis) *n. Informal.* sister.

sis·al (sī′səl, sis′əl) *n.* **1.** coarse, strong fiber obtained from the leaves of any of several tropical American plants, genus *Agave,* esp. *Agave sisalana,* used to make rope and bags. Also, **sisal hemp. 2.** plant yielding this fiber. [From *Sisal,* Mexican town.]

sis·sy (sis′ē) *pl.,* **-sies.** *n.* **1.** boy or man whose behavior is effeminate. **2.** coward. [SIS + -Y².]

sis·ter (sis′tər) *n.* **1.** female person having the same parents as another person of either sex. **2.** female person having one parent in common with another person of either sex; half sister. **3.** stepsister. **4.** female fellow member, as of a church, club, or sorority. **5.** member of a religious order for women; nun. **6.** that which is related by resemblance or corresponds in some way to another and is thought of as feminine: *Those two ships are sisters.* **7.** *British.* nurse, esp. a head nurse in charge of a hospital ward. [Of Scandinavian origin.]

sis·ter·hood (sis′tər hood′) *n.* **1.** state or quality of being a sister or sisters; relationship between sisters. **2.** group of women united by some common aim or who are bound by vows to a religious organization.

sis·ter-in-law (sis′tər in lô′) *pl.,* **sis·ters-in-law.** *n.* **1.** sister of one's

husband or wife. **2.** wife of one's brother. **3.** wife of one's husband's or wife's brother.

sis·ter·ly (sis′tər lē) *adj.* relating to, characteristic of, or befitting a sister; kind; affectionate. —*adv.* in the manner of a sister. —**sis′ter·li·ness,** *n.*

Sis·tine Chapel (sis′tēn, -tin) chapel in the Vatican in Rome, noted for its frescoes by Michelangelo.

sis·trum (sis′trəm) *pl.,* **-trums** or **-tra** (-trə). *n.* musical instrument consisting of a metal frame fitted with metal bars, used esp. in ancient Egypt in the worship of Isis. [Latin *sīstrum,* from Greek *seistron,* from *seiein* to shake.]

Sis·y·phe·an (sis′ə fē′ən) *adj.* **1.** of or relating to Sisyphus. **2.** endless and futile: *a Sisyphean task.*

Sis·y·phus (sis′ə fəs) *n. Greek Mythology.* king of Corinth, noted for his craftiness, punished in the Underworld by having to push a huge rock to the top of a hill, from which it would roll back down, thus forcing him to begin again.

Sistrum

sit (sit) **sat** or *(archaic)* **sate, sit·ting.** *v.i.* **1.** to be in a position in which the weight of the body rests on the buttocks, while the rest of the body bends at the hips and knees. **2.** to rest on a perch; roost. **3.** (of a chicken) to cover eggs in order to hatch them; brood. **4.** to be situated, placed, or positioned: *The hut sits in the middle of a forest. He left his car sitting alongside the road.* **5.** to assume or hold a particular position or attitude for an artist or photographer; pose. **6.** to be or remain unused or inactive: *The store sat empty for a year.* **7.** to be a member of a council, jury, assembly, or legislative body. **8.** to hold a session; be convened: *The legislature sits in the fall.* **9.** to bear down as a burden; weigh: *Old age sits lightly upon him.* **10.** to fit: *The dress sits well on her hips.* **11.** to take care of a person or persons too young or too infirm to care for themselves. **12. to sit in on.** to attend or take part in. **13. to sit out. a.** to endure to the end of: *to sit out a bad performance.* **b.** to remain seated and take no part in: *to sit out a dance.* **14. to sit up. a.** to delay retiring until after one's usual bedtime. **b.** to become attentive or alert: *to sit up in surprise.* —*v.t.* **1.** to cause to sit; seat (often with *down*). **2.** to ride (a horse). [Old English *sittan* to be seated, perch, be situated, take a seat.]

si·tar (si tär′) *n.* stringed musical instrument of India, having a long, fretted neck and a rounded body, made from a gourd or hollowed-out wood, played with a plectrum. [Hindi *sitār.*]

sit-down strike (sit′doun′) strike in which the strikers remain at their place of employment until an agreement is reached.

site (sīt) *n.* **1.** position, as of a town, city, or building, esp. with reference to the surrounding region: *The village occupied a mountain site.* **2.** ground on which anything is, has been, or is to be located: *the site of an ancient city.* —*v.t.,* **sit·ed, sit·ing.** to place; locate. [Latin *situs* position, situation.] —**Syn. 2.** see scene.

Sitar

sith (sith) *adv., prep., conj. Archaic.* since. [Old English *siththa* then, after.]

sit-in (sit′in′) *n.* protest demonstration in which persons sit in a public place and remain until forcibly removed. —*v.i.* **sat-in, sit·ting-in.** to participate in a sit-in.

si·tol·o·gy (sī tol′ə jē) *n.* science of nutrition and diet; dietetics. [Greek *sitos* food, grain + -LOGY.]

sit·ter (sit′ər) *n.* **1.** one who sits. **2.** one who takes care of a young child or young children during the temporary absence of their parents; baby-sitter. **3.** brooding hen.

sit·ting (sit′ing) *n.* **1.** act of sitting or one who or that which sits. **2.** period of time that one sits for a particular purpose. **3.** session or term of a court or meeting. **4.** number of eggs on which a hen sits at one time.

Sit·ting Bull (sit′ing) c.1834–90, chief of the Sioux Indians and a leader in the Battle of the Little Bighorn.

sitting duck *Informal.* easy target.

sitting room, room used for sitting, as in a home, hotel, or club.

sit·u·ate (sich′ōō āt′; *adj. also* sich′ōō it) **-at·ed, -at·ing.** *v.t.* to give a position to; place. —*adj. Archaic.* situated. [Late Latin *situā-tus,* past participle of *situāre* to locate, place, from Latin *situs* position.]

sit·u·at·ed (sich′ōō ā′tid) *adj.* **1.** placed in relation to surroundings: *The house is poorly situated.* **2.** placed in relation to circumstances: *He is well situated with his new job.*

sit·u·a·tion (sich′ōō ā′shən) *n.* **1.** condition or state of affairs: *Tom found himself in a difficult situation financially. What is the political situation in that country?* **2.** place in relation to surroundings; location;

at; āpe; cär; end; mē; it; īce; hot; ōld; fôrk; wood; fōōl; oil; out; up; ūse; turn; sing; thin; this; zh in treasure; ə in ago, taken, pencil, lemon, circus.

931

position: *The situation of the barn is at the left of the house.* **3.** work in which one engages or is employed; post of employment. —**sit′u·a′tion·al,** *adj.* —**Syn. 1.** see **circumstance. 2.** see **place.**

si·tus (sī′təs) *pl.,* **-tus.** *n.* position, esp. the proper or usual position, as of a part or organ. [Latin *situs.*]

Si·va (sē′və, shē′və) Shiva.

six (siks) *n.* **1.** the cardinal number that is one more than five. **2.** symbol representing this number, as 6 or VI. **3.** something having this many units or members, as a playing card. **4. at sixes and sevens. a.** in confusion. **b.** at odds; in disagreement. —*adj.* numbering one more than five. [Old English *six.*]

six·fold (siks′fōld′) *adj.* **1.** six times as great or as numerous. **2.** having or consisting of six parts. —*adv.* so as to be six times greater or more numerous.

six·gun (siks′gun′) *n.* six-shooter.

Six Nations, the Iroquois.

six·pence (siks′pəns) *n.* coin of the United Kingdom equal to six pennies.

six·pen·ny (siks′pen′ē, -pə nē) *adj.* **1.** worth or costing six British pennies. **2.** of little value or worth; cheap. **3.** designating a nail two inches in length.

six-shoot·er (siks′shōō′tər) *n. Informal.* revolver that can be fired six times without being reloaded.

six·teen (siks′tēn′) *n.* **1.** the cardinal number that is six more than ten. **2.** symbol representing this number, as 16 or XVI. **3.** something having this many units or members. —*adj.* numbering six more than ten. [Old English *sixtýne.*]

six·teenth (siks′tēnth′) *adj.* **1.** (the ordinal of sixteen) next after the fifteenth. **2.** being one of sixteen equal parts. —*n.* **1.** that which is next after the fifteenth. **2.** one of sixteen equal parts; ¹⁄₁₆.

sixteenth note *Music.* note having one-sixteenth the time value of a whole note. See **note** for illustration.

sixth (siksth) *adj.* **1.** (the ordinal of six) next after the fifth. **2.** being one of six equal parts. —*n.* **1.** that which is next after the fifth. **2.** one of six equal parts; ¹⁄₆. **3.** *Music.* **a.** tone, esp. the subdominant, six diatonic degrees from a given tone. **b.** interval of six degrees between two tones of the diatonic scale. **c.** harmonic combination of two tones separated by this interval. —*adv.* in the sixth place.

sixth sense, power of perception, seemingly over and above the five senses; intuition.

six·ti·eth (siks′tē ith) *adj.* **1.** (the ordinal of sixty) next after the fifty-ninth. **2.** being one of sixty equal parts. —*n.* **1.** that which is next after the fifty-ninth. **2.** one of sixty equal parts; ¹⁄₆₀.

six·ty (siks′tē) *pl.,* **-ties.** *n.* **1.** the cardinal number that is six times ten. **2.** symbol representing this number, as 60 or LX. **3. the sixties.** number series from sixty through sixty-nine. ▲ used esp. in reference to the sixth decade of a century or of a person's life. —*adj.* numbering six times ten. [Old English *sixtig.*]

six·ty-fourth note (siks′tē fôrth′) *Music.* note having one sixty-fourth the time value of a whole note.

siz·a·ble (sī′zə bəl) *also,* **size·a·ble.** *adj.* somewhat large. —**siz′a·bly;** *also,* **size′a·bly,** *adv.*

size¹ (sīz) *n.* **1.** degree of length, breadth, or height to which something extends in space: *the size of a room, the size of a tree.* **2.** greatness of extent; bigness: *There is no house of any size in that neighborhood.* **3.** amount or number: *the size of an inheritance, the size of a town.* **4.** measurement by which manufactured articles are classified, arranged, or sorted: *the size of a hat.* **5.** (of persons) mental or moral qualities or rank or position with reference to the ability to meet requirements: *The position needs a man of larger size.* **6.** *Informal.* true state of affairs; actual circumstances: *That's the size of it.* —*v.t.,* **sized, siz·ing. 1.** to classify, arrange, or sort according to size. **2.** to make of a certain or required size. **3. to size up.** *Informal.* to make an estimate or evaluation of; form an opinion of: *to size up a situation.* —*v.i.* **to size up.** to meet some standard or grade. [Short for ASSIZE (mistaken for *a size*) in the earlier sense of "a fixed quantity."]

size² (sīz) *n.* any of various glues or pastes used to coat or glaze a porous surface, as of fabric or paper. —*v.t.,* **sized, siz·ing.** to treat or coat with size. [Of uncertain origin.]

sized (sīzd) *adj.* having a specified size. ▲ used in combination: *small-sized, full-sized.*

siz·ing (sī′zing) *n.* **1.** size². **2.** act or process of treating with or applying size.

siz·zle (siz′əl) **-zled, -zling.** *v.i.* **1.** to make a hissing sound, esp. while burning or frying. **2.** to be very hot, as a summer day: *It's sizzling outside.* —*n.* hissing sound. [Imitative.]

S.J., Society of Jesus.

Skag·er·rak (skag′ə rak′) strait between Norway and Denmark, an arm of the North Sea.

skald (skôld, skäld) *also,* **scald.** *n.* ancient Scandinavian poet; bard. [Old Norse *skald.*] —**skald′ic,** *adj.*

skat (skät, skat) *n.* card game for three players, played with thirty-two cards. [German *Skat,* from Italian *scarto* discard (of a card), going back to Latin *ex* out of, from + *charta* paper. See CARD¹.]

skate¹ (skāt) *n.* **1.** ice skate. **2.** roller skate. —*v.i.,* **skat·ed, skat·ing.** to glide or move along on or as on skates. [Dutch *schaats* an ice skate, from Old French *eschace* stilt; of Germanic origin.] —**skat′er,** *n.*

skate² (skāt) *pl.,* **skates** or **skate.** *n.* any of a group of cartilaginous fish, family Rajidae, related to sharks and rays, found in warm and temperate seas, having two broad, winglike side fins. [Old Norse *skata.*]

Skate

skate³ (skāt) *n. Slang.* fellow; guy. [Of uncertain origin.]

skate·board (skāt′bôrd′) *n.* short, flat, oblong board having wheels attached to the bottom, ridden usually with the rider balancing himself in a standing position.

skat·ing (skā′ting) *n.* act or sport of moving over a surface on ice skates or roller skates.

ske·dad·dle (ski dad′əl) **-dled, -dling.** *v.i. Informal.* to run away; flee in haste. [Of uncertain origin.]

skeet shooting (skēt) trapshooting in which clay pigeons are launched to simulate the flight of birds and are fired at from various positions along the range. Also, **skeet.**

skein (skān) *n.* **1.** continuous strand of yarn or thread coiled in a bundle. **2.** something like or resembling this: *a skein of hair.* [Old French *escaigne* hank of yarn; of uncertain origin.]

skel·e·tal (skel′ət əl) *adj.* of, relating to, forming, or resembling a skeleton.

skel·e·ton (skel′ət ən) *n.* **1.** framework of bones supporting the muscles, organs, and other soft parts of the body of a vertebrate. **2.** supporting framework or structure, as of a building. **3.** outline, as of a literary work; sketch. **4.** *Informal.* very thin or emaciated person or animal. **5. skeleton in the closet.** secret, as about one's past, kept hidden because of fear, shame, or possible dishonor. —*adj.* **1.** of, relating to, or resembling a skeleton. **2.** consisting of or reduced to the mere outline or essential number required for something: *a skeleton staff.* [Modern Latin *skeleton,* from Greek *skeleton* mummy, from *skeletos* dried up.]

Human skeleton

Skull
Collarbone
Breastbone
Rib
Vertebra
Pelvis
Femur
Kneecap
Tibia
Fibula

skel·e·ton·ize (skel′ət ən īz′) **-ized, -iz·ing.** *v.t.* to reduce to or construct in skeleton form.

skeleton key, key with a large part of the bit filed away to enable it to open a number of different locks.

skep·tic (skep′tik) *also,* **scep·tic.** *n.* **1.** one who habitually doubts or questions the truth of generally accepted beliefs or conclusions. **2.** one who tends to be doubtful or suspicious, esp. concerning the assertions of others. **3.** one who doubts religious principles or doctrines. **4.** *also,* **Skeptic.** adherent of any philosophical school of skepticism. [Greek *skeptikos* thoughtful.]

skep·ti·cal (skep′ti kəl) *also,* **scep·ti·cal.** *adj.* **1.** characterized by or showing doubt or suspicion; questioning; disbelieving. **2.** of, relating to, or characteristic of skeptics or skepticism. —**skep′ti·cal·ly,** *adv.*

skep·ti·cism (skep′tə siz′əm) *also,* **scep·ti·cism.** *n.* **1.** doubting, questioning, or suspicious attitude, disposition, or state of mind. **2.** doubt concerning religious principles or doctrines. **3.** *also,* **Skepticism.** philosophical view that man cannot attain any certain knowledge.

sketch (skech) *n.* **1.** rough, unfinished, or rapidly executed drawing or study, esp. one intended to serve as the basis of a more finished work. **2.** short description, presentation, or plan giving the essential features of something; outline. **3.** brief, informal literary composition. **4.** short scene or play, as in a revue, musical comedy, or other theatrical program. —*v.t.* to make a sketch, rough drawing, or outline of. —*v.i.* to make a sketch or sketches. [Dutch *schets* model, draft, through Italian, from Latin *schedium* extemporaneous poem, going back to Greek *schedios* offhand, extemporaneous.] —**sketch′er,** *n.*

sketch·book (skech′book′) *n.* **1.** pad or book used for sketching or drawing. **2.** book of literary sketches.

sketch·y (skech′ē) **sketch·i·er, sketch·i·est.** *adj.* **1.** not detailed or

finished. **2.** incomplete or fragmentary; imperfect; slight: *The dazed driver could give only a sketchy account of the accident.* —**sketch′i·ly,** *adv.* —**sketch′i·ness,** *n.*

skew (skū) *v.i.* **1.** to take an oblique course or direction; swerve; twist. **2.** to look obliquely; squint. —*v.t.* **1.** to give an oblique position or direction to; set at an angle. **2.** to slant or twist the meaning or significance of; distort. —*adj.* **1.** having an oblique position or direction; turned to one side. **2.** having a part that deviates from a straight line, right angle, or the like. **3.** not symmetrical. —*n.* oblique movement, position, or direction; deviation from a straight line. [Dialectal Old French *eskiuwer,* form of *eschiver* to shun; of Germanic origin.]

skew·back (skū′bak′) *n.* **1.** slanting surface topping the end of an arch. **2.** stone, course of masonry, or other supporting member having such a surface.

skew·er (skū′ər) *n.* **1.** long pin of wood or metal used to hold meat together while cooking. **2.** any of various items having a similar shape or use. —*v.t.* to fasten or pierce with or as with a skewer or skewers. [Form of dialectal English *skiver;* of uncertain origin.]

ski (skē; *British* shē) *pl.,* **skis** or **ski.** *n.* **1.** one of a pair of long, narrow runners, usually of wood or metal, curving upward at the front and designed to be fastened to a boot for gliding over snow. **2.** water ski. —*v.i.,* **skied, ski·ing.** to glide or travel on skis, esp. as a sport. —*v.t.* to glide or travel over on skis. [Norwegian *ski* billet of wood, ski for traveling over snow, from Old Norse *skīth* snowshoe.] —**ski′er,** *n.*

ski boot, heavy, leather shoe for skiing that covers the ankle and has a groove around the heel to hold the ski bindings.

skid (skid) *n.* **1.** act of sliding or slipping, usually sideways, as over an icy surface. **2.** device, as a wedge of wood or metal, placed against the wheel of a vehicle to prevent the vehicle from moving. **3.** plank or frame used as a track on which something heavy may be slid or pushed along. **4.** runner that is part of the landing gear of certain aircraft. **5. on the skids.** *Slang.* rapidly declining in prestige, power, value, or quality: *an actor whose career is on the skids.* —*v.i.* **skid·ded, skid·ding. 1.** to slide or slip, usually sideways, esp. because of loss of traction: *The airplane skidded on the wet runway.* **2.** (of a wheel of a moving vehicle) to slide without rotating. —*v.t.* **1.** to prevent (a wheel) from moving by applying a skid. **2.** to haul, slide, move, or place on a skid or skids. [Possibly of Scandinavian origin.]

skid row *Slang.* section of a city inhabited and frequented by vagrants and derelicts, and consisting chiefly of cheap rooming houses and bars.

skies (skīz) plural of **sky.**

skiff (skif) *n.* small, light boat propelled by motor, sail, or oars. [French *esquif* little boat, from Italian *scifo;* of Germanic origin.]

ski·ing (skē′ing) *n.* act or sport of gliding or traveling on skis.

ski jump 1. steep snow-covered ramp, track, or course ending abruptly above a long, gentle slope, designed for long-distance jumping by skiers. **2.** jump made by a skier.

ski lift, apparatus for transporting skiers up a slope, usually consisting of a motor-operated cable to which seats are attached.

skill (skil) *n.* **1.** competence resulting from knowledge, training, practice, or experience; proficiency: *to show great skill in playing the violin.* **2.** particular power or ability: *reading skills.* [Old Norse *skil* distinction, knowledge.] —**Syn. 2.** see **ability.**

skilled (skild) *adj.* **1.** having or showing skill or competence; proficient. **2.** having or requiring specialized ability or training: *skilled labor.* —**Syn. 1.** see **expert.**

skil·let (skil′it) *n.* **1.** frying pan. **2.** *British.* saucepan with a long handle. [Possibly from Old French *escuellette* small dish, diminutive of *escuelle* dish, going back to Latin *scutella* salver.]

skill·ful (skil′fəl) *also, British.* **skil·ful.** *adj.* having, showing, or involving skill: *a skillful chess player, a skillful maneuver.* —**skill′ful·ly,** *adv.* —**skill′ful·ness,** *n.*

skim (skim) *v.t.* **skimmed, skim·ming. 1.** to clear (a liquid) of floating matter. **2.** to remove (floating matter) from a liquid. **3.** to glance over or read hastily or superficially. **4.** to move or glide lightly and swiftly over or across. **5.** to throw so as to glide or pass lightly or bouncingly over, across, or along a surface: *to skim a stone across a lake.* **6.** to cover with a thin film or layer, as of ice. —*v.i.* **1.** to move or glide lightly and swiftly over or across a surface. **2.** to make a hasty or superficial examination of something (with *over* or *through*): *to skim through a newspaper.* **3.** to become covered with a thin film or layer. —*n.* **1.** act of skimming. **2.** something that has been skimmed. **3.** thin film or layer. —*adj.* skimmed. [Probably from Old French *escumer* to clear (a liquid) of floating matter, from *escume* foam, scum; of Germanic origin.]

skim·mer (skim′ər) *n.* **1.** one who or that which skims. **2.** utensil, esp. a shallow ladle having a flat, perforated bowl, used to skim liquids. **3.** any

Skimmer *(def. 3)*

of various gull-like sea birds, family Rynchopidae, having predominantly black or brown plumage. Length: 16–19 inches. **4.** wide-brimmed hat, usually of straw, with a flat crown.

skim milk *also,* **skimmed milk.** milk from which the cream has been removed.

skimp (skimp) *v.i.* to be very or overly sparing or thrifty. —*v.t.* **1.** to perform (a task) carelessly, hastily, or with poor material. **2.** to be very or overly sparing or thrifty with. [Of uncertain origin.]

skimp·y (skim′pē) **skimp·i·er, skimp·i·est.** *adj.* **1.** scanty; insufficient; meager. **2.** overly sparing or thrifty. —**skimp′i·ly,** *adv.* —**skimp′i·ness,** *n.* —**Syn. 1.** see **meager.**

skin (skin) *n.* **1.** outer body covering of an animal. **2.** such an outer covering removed from the body of an animal; pelt or hide. **3.** anything resembling skin in appearance, nature, or function: *the skin of an apple.* **4.** vessel or container made of animal skin, used for holding liquids, esp. wine. **5.** one's life or personal safety: *to save one's skin.* **6. by the skin of one's teeth.** by a very narrow margin; barely. **7. to get under one's skin.** to be or become annoying or irritating. **8. to have a thick skin.** to be insensitive, esp. to criticism or insult. **9. to have a thin skin.** to be very sensitive, esp. to criticism. —*v.t.,* **skinned, skin·ning. 1.** to remove the skin of or from: *to skin a rabbit.* **2.** to injure the surface of or remove a portion of skin from, esp. by scraping: *to skin one's knee.* **3.** to cover with or as with skin. **4.** *Slang.* to swindle; cheat. —*v.i.* **1.** to become covered with skin. **2.** to climb: *to skin up a rope.* [Old Norse *skinn* hide[2].]

skin-deep (skin′dēp′) *adj.* superficial; shallow: *Beauty is only skin-deep.*

skin-dive (skin′dīv′) **-dived** or **-dove, -dived, -div·ing.** *v.i.* to engage in skin diving.

skin diver, one who engages in skin diving.

skin diving, underwater swimming for extended periods of time, usually with a face mask and flippers, and sometimes with oxygen tanks or a snorkel to enable the swimmer to remain submerged longer.

skin·flint (skin′flint′) *n.* extremely stingy person; miser.

skin·ful (skin′fool′) *pl.,* **-fuls.** *n.* **1.** amount of liquid that a skin container can hold. **2.** *Informal.* as much as one can contain, esp. the amount of liquor that one can drink.

skin game *Informal.* dishonest or fraudulent game or trick.

skin·ner (skin′ər) *n.* **1.** one who deals in animal skins, esp. one who removes and processes animal skins and furs. **2.** driver of draft animals, esp. a mule driver.

skin·ny (skin′ē) **-ni·er, -ni·est.** *adj.* very thin; lean; emaciated. —**skin′ni·ness,** *n.*

skin test, any test made on the skin, as a patch test, to detect susceptibility to or the presence of a disease or allergy.

skin-tight (skin′tīt′) *adj.* fitting tightly: *skintight pants.*

skip (skip) *v.i.* **skipped, skip·ping. 1.** to spring or bound along, hopping lightly on one foot and then the other. **2.** to pass from one point to another omitting or paying little or no attention to what lies between: *to skip over a chapter.* **3.** to bounce along or across a surface; skim. **4.** to be promoted in school beyond the next regular grade. **5.** *Informal.* to leave hurriedly or in secret: *The cashier skipped with the day's profits.* —*v.t.* **1.** to jump or spring lightly over: *to skip rope.* **2.** to omit or pass over or by: *Rick skipped the problems he couldn't do.* **3.** to cause to bounce along or across a surface; skim. **4.** to be promoted in school beyond (the next regular grade). **5.** *Informal.* to leave (a place) hurriedly or in secret: *The embezzler skipped town.* —*n.* **1.** light springing, bounding, or jumping step. **2.** gait consisting of such steps. **3.** act of passing over or omitting. [Probably of Scandinavian origin.]

skip·jack (skip′jak′) *pl.,* **-jacks** or **-jack.** *n.* any of various fish that often leaps above the surface of the water.

ski pole, long, slender pole with a metal point on the bottom and an encircling disk just above the point, used as an aid by skiers.

skip·per[1] (skip′ər) *n.* **1.** captain of a ship, esp. of a small trading, fishing, or pleasure boat. **2.** one who is in a position of leadership, as the captain of a sports team. [Middle Dutch *schipper* sailor, from *schip* ship.]

skip·per[2] (skip′ər) *n.* **1.** one who or that which skips. **2.** any of a group of butterflies, family Hesperiidae, that fly with quick, darting movements. [SKIP + -ER[1].]

skirl (skurl) *v.i.* (of a bagpipe) to sound loudly and shrilly. —*v.t.* to

play (music) on a bagpipe. —n. loud, shrill sound of a bagpipe. [Of Scandinavian origin.]

skir·mish (skur′mish) n. 1. minor engagement or conflict between small forces, esp. between detached portions of the main forces. 2. any brief or minor encounter or conflict. —v.i. to take part in a skirmish. [Old French eskirmiss-, a stem of eskirmir to fight with a sword; of Germanic origin.] —**skir′mish·er**, n.

skirt (skurt) n. 1. woman's or girl's garment that is fastened around the waist or hips and hangs down to varying lengths. 2. that part of a dress or similar garment that hangs from the waist down. 3. **skirts.** outlying or bordering parts, esp. of a town or city; outskirts. 4. rim, edge, or outer margin. 5. one of the flaps hanging from the side of a saddle. 6. Slang. girl or woman. —v.t. 1. to lie along or form the border or edge of: Trees skirted the country estate. 2. to move along the border or edge of; pass around rather than go through. 3. to avoid, as by refusing to discuss or deal with: to skirt the issue. 4. to border or edge with. —v.i. to move along or be near the border or edge of something. [Old Norse skyrta shirt.]

ski run, slope or course used for skiing.

skit (skit) n. brief, often humorous dramatic presentation or literary piece. [Probably of Scandinavian origin.]

ski tow, continuous, motor-operated moving rope or cable for pulling skiers up a slope.

skit·ter (skit′ər) v.i. to glide or skim lightly and quickly over a surface. —v.t. to cause to skitter. [Dialectal English skite to dart swiftly (probably of Scandinavian origin) + -ER¹.]

skit·tish (skit′ish) adj. 1. easily frightened or excited; jumpy. ▲ used esp. of horses. 2. not dependable; fickle; capricious. 3. bashful; coy. [Dialectal English skit to move rapidly (probably of Scandinavian origin) + -ISH.] —**skit′tish·ly**, adv. —**skit′tish·ness**, n.

skit·tle (skit′əl) n. 1. **skittles.** ninepins in which a wooden disk or ball is used to knock down the pins. ▲ construed as singular. 2. pin used in this game. [Possibly of Scandinavian origin.]

skiv·vy (skiv′ē) pl., **-vies.** n. Slang. 1. man's undershirt. 2. **skivvies.** man's underwear. [Of uncertain origin.]

skoal (skōl) interj. to your health. ▲ used as a toast. [Danish and Norwegian skaal cup, from Old Norse skāl bowl¹.]

Skt., Sanskrit.

sku·a (skū′ə) n. gull-like sea bird, Catharacta skua, found in the cold waters of the Pacific and Atlantic oceans, having dark-brown plumage. Length: 20–23 inches. [Of Scandinavian origin.]

skul·dug·ger·y (skul′dug′ər ē) also, **skull·dug·ger·y.** n. underhanded or deceitful actions; trickery. [Of uncertain origin.]

skulk (skulk) v.i. 1. to move in a furtive or stealthy manner. 2. to hide or conceal oneself; stay out of sight. —n. one who skulks. [Of Scandinavian origin.] —**skulk′er**, n.

skull (skul) n. 1. framework of bones of the head of a vertebrate, consisting of the bones that enclose the brain and support the face. 2. the head, esp. regarded as the seat of thought, intelligence, or understanding: He couldn't get it through his skull that he was wrong. 3. death's-head. [Of Scandinavian origin.]

Front view   Side view

Human skull

skull and crossbones, representation of a human skull above two crossed bones, a symbol of death once used on the flags of pirate ships, now used chiefly as a warning sign, as on poisons.

skull·cap (skul′kap′) n. close-fitting, brimless cap covering only a small portion of the crown of the head, often worn indoors, and usually having religious significance.

skunk (skungk) n. 1. any of several black-and-white mammals, family Mustelidae, native to North, Central, and South America, discharging a rank-smelling liquid when frightened or attacked. The most common species in North America is the striped skunk, Mephitis mephitis, having two white bands extending down its back. Length: 2½ feet including tail. 2. Informal. despicable or contemptible person. —v.t. Slang. to defeat decisively or overwhelmingly in a game or contest, esp. without allowing an opponent to score. [Of Algonquian origin.]

skunk cabbage, weedy marsh plant, Symplocarpus foetidus, found in eastern North America, noted for its foul-smelling leaves.

sky (skī) pl., **skies.** n. 1. the upper atmosphere, appearing as a great hemisphere over the earth and having a light-blue color on clear days. 2. area or expanse of the heavens; firmament: one of the brightest stars in the sky. 3. also, **skies.** condition or appearance of the upper atmosphere: a cloudy sky, sunny skies. 4. climate. 5. the celestial heaven. 6. highest point or level. 7. **out of a clear (blue) sky.** without warning;

suddenly; unexpectedly. —v.t. **skyed, sky·ing.** to throw or hit into the air. [Old Norse skȳ cloud.]

sky blue, warm, light blue, like the color of the clear sky.

sky·cap (skī′kap′) n. porter at an airport or air terminal. [SKY + (RED)CAP.]

sky·dive (skī′dīv′) **-dived** or **-dove, -dived, -div·ing.** v.i. to engage in skydiving. —**sky′div·er**, n.

sky·div·ing (skī′dī′ving) n. act or sport of parachuting from an airplane and falling as far as safely possible before opening the parachute, sometimes including the execution of certain intricate maneuvers during free fall.

Skye, Isle of (skī) island off the coast of Scotland. Area, 670 sq. mi. Pop. (1965 est.), 7250.

Skye terrier, small terrier of a breed originally developed on the Isle of Skye, having a long body, short legs, and a coat of long, straight hair. Height: 10 inches at the shoulders.

Skye terrier

sky·ey (skī′ē) adj. 1. of, relating to, from, or resembling the sky. 2. of great height; lofty.

sky-high (skī′hī′) adv. 1. to an extremely high point, level, or degree: The cost of living rose sky-high. 2. into pieces; to bits; apart: The explosion blew the building sky-high. —adj. extremely high.

sky·jack (skī′jak′) v.t. Informal. to hijack (an airplane), esp. a commercial airliner. [SKY + (HI)JACK.] —**sky′jack·er**, n.

sky·lark (skī′lärk′) n. lark, Alauda arvensis, native to Europe, Asia, and northern Africa, having dull-brown plumage with black and whitish markings, noted for the rippling, flutelike song produced by the male during the breeding season. —v.i. to frolic about; play.

sky·light (skī′līt′) n. window in a roof or ceiling for admitting daylight.

sky·line (skī′līn′) n. 1. outline of buildings, mountains, or other objects seen against the sky. 2. line at which the earth and sky appear to come together; horizon.

sky pilot Slang. clergyman, esp. a military chaplain.

sky·rock·et (skī′rok′it) n. small rocket used chiefly in fireworks displays, designed to explode high in the air giving off a shower of colored sparks and lights. —v.i. to rise rapidly, suddenly, or greatly: Rents in the city were skyrocketing. —v.t. to cause to rise rapidly, suddenly, or greatly: Higher wages skyrocketed construction costs.

sky·sail (skī′sāl′, -səl) n. light sail above the royal in a square-rigged ship.

sky·scrap·er (skī′skrā′pər) n. very tall building.

sky·ward (skī′wərd) adv. also, **sky·wards.** toward or in the direction of the sky. —adj. directed toward the sky: a skyward glance.

sky·way (skī′wā′) n. 1. route used by airplanes. 2. elevated highway.

sky·writ·ing (skī′rī′ting) n. 1. act or process of forming words, symbols, or the like in the sky by releasing a trail of smoke or other visible substance from an airplane. 2. words or symbols so formed. —**sky′writ′er**, n.

slab (slab) n. 1. broad, flat, and usually thick piece of some material: a slab of stone. 2. rough outside piece cut from a log. [Of uncertain origin.]

slack¹ (slak) adj. 1. not tight, taut, or firm; loose: a slack rope, a slack grip. 2. slow in motion; unhurried; sluggish: a slack pace. 3. lacking in activity; not busy or lively: a slack season during which unemployment rose sharply. 4. negligent, careless, or inefficient. 5. (of the wind or tide) moving with little force or speed. —n. 1. part, as of a rope, that is slack or hangs loose. 2. looseness. 3. period of little or no activity; lull. 4. cessation of movement, as in a current of water. 5. **slacks.** trousers, esp. for casual wear. —v.t. 1. to slacken. 2. to slake (lime). —v.i. 1. to be or become slack. 2. to be or become less diligent, careful, or efficient (often with off): to slack off in one's duties. 3. **to slack off.** to decrease in activity or intensity. —adv. in a slack or loose manner. [Old English slæc slow, lazy, careless.] —**slack′ly**, adv. —**slack′ness**, n.

slack² (slak) n. small bits of coal remaining after coal is screened. [Probably from Middle Dutch slacke slag, dross.]

slack·en (slak′ən) v.t. 1. to make slower: to slacken one's pace. 2. to make less tight, taut, or firm: to slacken a tense wire. 3. to reduce the intensity, forcefulness, or severity of: As time passed, the people slackened their opposition to the proposal. —v.i. 1. to become slower. 2. to become less tight, taut, or firm. 3. to become less active, intense, forceful, or severe.

slack·er (slak′ər) n. one who avoids or attempts to avoid work or an obligation or responsibility.

slack water, period at the turn of the tide when there is no visible tidal current. Also, **slack tide.**

slag (slag) n. 1. fused waste material remaining after metallic ore is

smelted. **2.** volcanic scoria. [Middle Low German *slagge* metal dross.] —**slag′gy,** *adv.*

slain (slān) past participle of **slay.**

slake (slāk) **slaked, slak·ing.** *v.t.* **1.** to relieve or satisfy; quench: *The cool water slaked the workman's thirst.* **2.** to make less active or intense. **3.** to cause a chemical change in (lime) by treatment with water. —*v.i.* **1.** (of lime) to undergo a chemical change through treatment with water. **2.** *Archaic.* to become less active or intense. [Old English *slacian* to grow slack.]

slaked lime, white compound formed by treating lime with water, used in mortar and cement; calcium hydroxide.

sla·lom (slä′ləm) *n.* **1.** downhill skiing race over a zigzag course marked by flag-topped poles. **2.** water skiing, esp. on one ski, often through a zigzag course marked by buoys. —*v.i.* **1.** to ski in a slalom. **2.** water-ski a slalom course. [Norwegian *slalom* ski course having an even slope, from *slad* sloping + *lom* path.]

slam[1] (slam) **slammed, slam·ming.** *v.t.* **1.** to close forcefully and with a loud noise: *to slam a car door.* **2.** to strike, throw, put, or move (something) with force and a loud noise: *He slammed his fist on the table to get everyone's attention.* **3.** *Informal.* to criticize harshly or severely. —*v.i.* **1.** to close with force and a loud noise. **2.** to strike or move forcefully and noisily: *The automobile slammed against a tree.* —*n.* **1.a.** forceful and noisy closing or striking. **b.** noise made by this. **2.** *Informal.* harsh or severe criticism. [Probably of Scandinavian origin.]

slam[2] (slam) *n.* the winning of twelve or all thirteen tricks in a round of bridge; grand slam or little slam. [Of uncertain origin.]

slan·der (slan′dər) *n.* **1.** *Law.* act or crime of uttering a false and malicious statement about another person that is damaging to his reputation or well-being. Distinguished from **libel.** **2.** such a statement. —*v.t.* to utter false and malicious statements about; injure by spreading slander against. —*v.i.* to utter or spread slander. [Old French *esclandre* offense, disgrace, noise, from Late Latin *scandalum* cause of offense, from Greek *skandalon;* originally, trap. Doublet of SCANDAL.] —**slan′der·er,** *n.*

slan·der·ous (slan′dər əs) *adj.* **1.** containing or constituting slander. **2.** uttering or spreading slander. —**slan′der·ous·ly,** *adv.*

slang (slang) *n.* **1.** colloquial, nonstandard speech that expresses ideas in an unconventional, often striking manner. Much slang is popular for only a short time, but many words that were originally considered slang are now in standard usage. **2.** vocabulary peculiar to a particular group, class, or profession; jargon: *military slang.* [Of uncertain origin.] —**Syn.** see lingo.

slang·y (slang′ē) **slang·i·er, slang·i·est.** *adj.* **1.** of the nature of, characterized by, or containing slang. **2.** given to the use of slang: *a slangy writer.* —**slang′i·ly,** *adv.* —**slang′i·ness,** *n.*

slank (slangk) *Archaic.* past tense of **slink.**

slant (slant) *v.i.* to have or take a direction that deviates from the horizontal or vertical, or from a straight line or course: *The barn roof slants toward the ground. The road slants to the left.* —*v.t.* **1.** to cause to slant; give an oblique direction to. **2.** to present so as to express or support a particular opinion or bias, or appeal to a particular interest: *to slant a magazine toward the young.* —*n.* **1.** slanting or oblique direction, line, surface, or plane; inclination; angle: *The picture hung on a slant.* **2.** point of view; attitude; opinion: *The senator's speech offered a new slant on an old problem.* —*adj.* having or being on a slant; oblique. [Of Scandinavian origin.]

Syn. *v.i.* **Slant, slope, incline** mean to lean or diverge from a straight line or level surface. **Slant** carries the clearest implication of such an oblique divergence from a vertical or horizontal line: *Italic letters slant to the right.* **Slope** emphasizes a gradual and downward change of direction or level: *The hill slopes gently to the river bank.* **Incline** may imply deviation from a straight line in an upward direction: *The road inclines upward toward the summit of the mountain.*

slant·wise (slant′wīz′) *adv. also,* **slant·ways** (slant′wāz′). in a slanting direction or position; at a slant. —*adj.* slanting; oblique.

slap (slap) *n.* **1.a.** sharp, quick blow, esp. with the open hand or with something flat. **b.** sound made by or as by such a blow. **2.** sharp or insulting reproof or remark. —*v.t.* **slapped, slap·ping. 1.** to strike with a sharp, quick blow, esp. with the open hand or with something flat. **2.** to put, place, or throw forcefully, noisily, or carelessly. **3.** *Informal.* to impose; administer (often with *on*): *The judge slapped a fifty-dollar fine on the defendant for contempt of court.* **4. to slap down.** *Informal.* to restrain or reprove sharply. —*v.i.* to strike or beat with or as with a slap: *The waves slapped against the side of the boat.* —*adv. Informal.* **1.** straight; directly. **2.** suddenly; abruptly. [Low German *slapp* sound made by a blow; of imitative origin.]

slap·dash (slap′dash′) *adv.* in a hasty and careless manner. —*adj.* hasty and careless. —*n.* hasty and careless work or action.

slap·hap·py (slap′hap′ē) *adj. Informal.* dazed or silly from or as from repeated blows to the head; punch-drunk.

slap·jack (slap′jak′) *n.* **1.** pancake; griddlecake; flapjack. **2.** card game played chiefly by children.

slap·stick (slap′stik′) *n.* **1.** comedy characterized by loud, exaggerated, and boisterous action. **2.** paddle usually consisting of two long, narrow, flat pieces of wood fastened together so as to slap against each other loudly when struck against something, used as by clowns or comedians. —*adj.* resembling, characterized by, or relating to slapstick: *slapstick humor.*

slash (slash) *v.t.* **1.** to cut or wound with a forceful, sweeping stroke or strokes, as with a knife or other sharp instrument. **2.** to strike with a whip; lash. **3.** to cut slits in (a garment), as to show underlying material of a different color. **4.** to reduce sharply or drastically: *to slash production costs.* **5.** to criticize severely. —*v.i.* to make a forceful, sweeping stroke or strokes with or as with a knife or other sharp instrument. —*n.* **1.** forceful, sweeping stroke made with a sharp instrument or whip. **2.** cut or wound made by or as by such a stroke. **3.** ornamental slit in a garment. **4.** sharp or drastic reduction: *a slash in prices.* **5.a.** clearing in a forest, produced as by logging operations, usually littered with wood chips, broken branches, and other debris. **b.** debris found in such a clearing. **6.** low, swampy area, usually overgrown with bushes or trees. **7.** virgule. [Possibly from Old French *esclachier* to break; of imitative origin.] —**slash′er,** *n.*

slat (slat) *n.* thin, narrow, flat strip of wood, metal, or other material, as in a Venetian blind. —*v.t.* **slat·ted, slat·ting.** to provide or make with slats. [Short for Old French *esclat* splinter, from *esclater* to split; of Germanic origin.]

slate (slāt) *n.* **1.** fine-grained, usually bluish-gray metamorphic rock that splits easily into thin sheets or layers. **2.** thin piece of this rock used esp. to make roofing tiles and blackboards. **3.** small blackboard. **4.** record of a person's past actions or performance. ▲ used chiefly in the phrase *a clean slate.* **5.** list of candidates proposed for nomination or election. **6.** dull, dark, bluish-gray color, like slate. —*v.t.* **slat·ed, slat·ing. 1.** to cover with slate or a substance like slate. **2.** to put on a list of candidates. **3.** to schedule or designate: *The conference was slated for early June.* [Old French *esclate,* form of *esclat* splinter, from *esclater* to split. See SLAT.]

slat·er (slā′tər) *n.* one employed to lay slates, as for roofing.

slath·er (slath′ər) *v.t. Informal.* to spread thickly: *to slather jam on bread.* [Of uncertain origin.]

slat·tern (slat′ərn) *n.* untidy, slovenly woman or girl. [Possibly from dialectal English *slatter* to spill, slop, from *slat* to flap, dash; possibly of Scandinavian origin.]

slat·tern·ly (slat′ərn lē) *adj.* relating to or characteristic of a slattern; slovenly; untidy. —*adv.* in a slovenly manner. —**slat′tern·li·ness,** *n.*

slat·y (slā′tē) **slat·i·er, slat·i·est.** *adj.* **1.** of, relating to, containing, or resembling slate. **2.** having the color of slate; bluish-gray.

slaugh·ter (slô′tər) *n.* **1.** act of killing an animal or animals for food. **2.** brutal or violent killing of a person; massacre. **3.** indiscriminate killing of a large number of persons; massacre. **4.** *Informal.* complete or overwhelming defeat, esp. in an athletic contest. —*v.t.* **1.** to kill (an animal or animals) for food; butcher. **2.** to kill in a brutal or violent manner. **3.** to kill (persons) indiscriminately or in large numbers; massacre. **4.** *Informal.* to defeat completely or overwhelmingly, esp. in an athletic contest. [Old Norse *slātr* butcher's meat.] —**slaugh′ter·er,** *n.*

slaugh·ter·house (slô′tər hous′) *n.* place where animals are butchered for food.

slaugh·ter·ous (slô′tər əs) *adj.* murderous; brutally destructive. —**slaugh′ter·ous·ly,** *adv.*

Slav (släv, slav) *n.* member or close descendant of a group of culturally and linguistically related peoples living predominantly in eastern, southeastern, and central Europe, usually divided into **Western Slavs,** composed chiefly of Poles, Czechs, and Slovaks, **Southern Slavs,** composed chiefly of Serbs, Slovenes, and Bulgarians, and **Eastern Slavs,** composed of Russians, Ukrainians, and Byelorussians.

slave (slāv) *n.* **1.** person who is the property of another and is under his complete domination. **2.** one who is under the control of some influence or person: *an unwilling slave to heroin.* **3.** one who works or is compelled to work hard and long: *a housewife who felt like a slave to her own home.* —*v.i.* **slaved, slav·ing.** to work hard and long: *The editor had been slaving away at his desk for hours.* [Medieval Latin *Sclavus* one of the Slavic people, bond servant of Slavic descent, bond servant, from Late Greek *Sklabos,* going back to *(hoi) Sklabēnoi* (the) Slavic people (of Slavic origin); referring to the enslavement of many Slavs by the Germans in the early Middle Ages.]

Slave Coast, region on the western coast of Africa, between Ghana and Nigeria. It was a center of the slave trade from the sixteenth to nineteenth centuries.

slave driver 1. person charged with overseeing slaves at work. **2.** harsh or exacting employer or taskmaster.

slave·hold·er (slāv′hōl′dər) *n.* one who owns slaves. —**slave′hold′ing,** *adj., n.*

---

slav·er¹ (slā′vər) *n.* **1.** one who deals in slaves. **2.** ship used to transport slaves. [SLAVE + -ER¹.]

slav·er² (slav′ər) *v.i.* to let saliva run out from the mouth; drool; slobber. —*v.t. Archaic.* to wet or cover with saliva. —*n.* saliva running out from the mouth. [Of Scandinavian origin.]

slav·er·y (slā′vər ē) *n.* **1.** institution or practice of owning slaves. **2.** state or condition of being a slave. **3.** condition of being under the control of some influence or person. **4.** hard or exhausting work; drudgery.

Slave State, any state of the United States in which slavery was legal before the Civil War.

slave trade, traffic in slaves, esp. the former transportation of black Africans to America for sale as slaves.

slav·ey (slā′vē) *pl.,* **-eys** *n. British. Informal.* female domestic servant, esp. one who does all kinds of housework.

Slav·ic (slä′vik, slav′ik) *adj.* of or relating to the Slavs or their languages. —*n.* group of languages spoken by the Slavs, belonging to the Indo-European language family.

slav·ish (slā′vish) *adj.* **1.** of, like, characteristic of, or befitting a slave or slaves. **2.** not original or independent; imitative: *a slavish copy of a great painting.* —**slav′ish·ly,** *adv.* —**slav′ish·ness,** *n.*

Sla·vo·ni·a (slə vō′nē ə) *n.* region in northern Yugoslavia. —**Sla·vo′ni·an,** *adj., n.*

Sla·von·ic (slə von′ik) *adj.* Slavic. —*n.* any Slavic language, or the Slavic language group.

slaw (slô) *n.* coleslaw. [Dutch *sla,* short for *salade* salad, from French *salade.* See SALAD.]

slay (slā) **slew** or *(def. 2)* **slayed, slain, slay·ing** *v.t.* **1.** to kill by violent means. **2.** *Slang.* to overcome completely, as with laughter; overwhelm: *The comedian slayed his audience with his repertoire of jokes and imitations of actors.* [Old English *slēan* to strike, kill.] —**slay′er,** *n.* —**Syn.** 1. see **kill¹.**

slea·zy (slē′zē) **-zi·er, -zi·est.** *adj.* **1.** (of fabric) thin or flimsy in texture or substance. **2.** of poor quality; shoddy; cheap: *a sleazy hotel.* [Of uncertain origin.] —**slea′·zi·ly,** *adv.* —**slea′zi·ness,** *n.*

sled (sled) *n.* **1.** vehicle on runners that is used to carry people or loads over snow and ice; sledge. **2.** small, similarly constructed vehicle having a wooden frame, used for sliding down snow-covered slopes, as by children. —*v.i.,* **sled·ded, sled·ding.** to ride or be carried on a sled. —*v.t.* to carry on a sled. [Middle Dutch *sledde* sledge¹.]

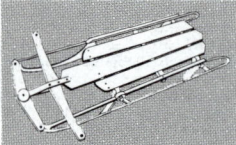

Sled

sled·ding (sled′ing) *n.* **1.** act of riding on or using a sled. **2.** condition of the ground for the use of sleds: *The heavy snow made for good sledding.* **3.** conditions affecting the course or progress of any action.

sledge¹ (slej) *n.* sled or sleigh. —*v.i.,* **sledged, sledg·ing.** to ride or be carried on a sled or sleigh. —*v.t.* to carry on a sled or sleigh. [Middle Dutch *sleedse* sled.]

sledge² (slej) *n.* sledgehammer. —*v.t.,* **sledged, sledg·ing.** to sledgehammer. [Old English *slecg* heavy hammer.]

sledge·ham·mer (slej′ham′ər) *n.* heavy hammer with a long handle, usually held with both hands. —*v.t.* to strike with or as if with such a hammer. —*adj.* like a sledgehammer; powerful; smashing.

sleek (slēk) *adj.* **1.** smooth and glossy, as if polished: *the cat's sleek black fur.* **2.** having a healthy, well-groomed, or well-fed appearance. **3.** polished in manner or speech, esp. in a specious or insincere way. —*v.t.* to make smooth and glossy; polish. [Form of SLICK.] —**sleek′ly,** *adv.* —**sleek′ness,** *n.*

sleep (slēp) *n.* **1.** naturally recurring state of relatively suspended sensory and motor activity, characterized by total or partial unconsciousness and the inactivity of nearly all voluntary muscles. **2.** period of sleep: *a restless sleep.* **3.** any condition of inactivity or reduced consciousness that resembles sleep, as death or a hypnotic trance. —*v.i.,* **slept, sleep·ing.** **1.** to be or fall asleep. **2.** to be in a condition resembling or likened to sleep. **3. to sleep in.** (of domestic help) to sleep at the place of one's employment. **4. to sleep on.** to postpone a decision on, esp. overnight, to allow more time for consideration. **5. to sleep over.** to spend the night. —*v.t.* **1.** to repose in (a particular kind of sleep): *to sleep the peaceful sleep of the young.* **2.** to provide or be able to provide with accommodations for sleeping: *This cabin sleeps six people.* **3. to sleep away.** to spend in sleeping: *to sleep away the afternoon.* **4. to sleep off** (or **away**). to get rid of by sleeping: *to sleep off a hangover.* [Old English *slǣpan* to slumber, be dead, be numb, be inert.]

Syn. *v.i.* **1.** Sleep, slumber, drowse mean to cease being awake. **Sleep** is the general term to imply the natural and periodical repose of mind

and body characterized by total or partial unconsciousness: *Did you sleep well last night?* **Slumber** is more specific in suggesting a sleep that is light, quiet, and easy: *The baby slumbered peacefully.* **Drowse** suggests the state in which one drifts off to sleep involuntarily often on account of listless inactivity or a dull and sluggish feeling: *Grandpa drowsed over his newspaper and woke up with a start.*

sleep·er (slē′pər) *n.* **1.** one who or that which sleeps, esp. in a particular manner: *a light sleeper.* **2.** someone or something previously unknown or unimportant that unexpectedly or suddenly attains success, fame, or importance, as a motion picture, book, or racehorse. **3.** Pullman. **4.** strong horizontal beam used as a support, esp. a railroad tie.

sleeping bag, long, warmly filled or padded bag, often waterproof, used to sleep in, esp. out-of-doors.

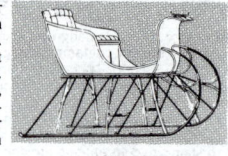

Sleeping bag

sleeping car, railroad car having sleeping accommodations for passengers; Pullman.

sleeping pill, pill or capsule containing a sleep-inducing drug, esp. a barbiturate.

sleeping sickness, infectious disease, often fatal, characterized by headaches, high fever, convulsions, and coma.

sleep·less (slēp′lis) *adj.* **1.** unable to sleep. **2.** marked by the absence of sleep; affording no sleep: *a sleepless night.* **3.** constantly in motion or action. **4.** always alert and watchful; vigilant. —**sleep′less·ly,** *adv.* —**sleep′less·ness,** *n.*

sleep·walk·ing (slēp′wô′king) *n.* act or practice of walking about while asleep; somnambulism. —**sleep′walk′er,** *n.*

sleep·y (slē′pē) **sleep·i·er, sleep·i·est.** *adj.* **1.** ready for, in need of, or inclined to sleep; drowsy. **2.** of, showing, or characterized by drowsiness: *sleepy eyes.* **3.** characterized by lack of activity; dull; quiet: *a sleepy little village.* —**sleep′i·ly,** *adv.* —**sleep′i·ness,** *n.*

sleep·y·head (slē′pē hed′) *n. Informal.* sleepy person.

sleet (slēt) *n.* **1.** precipitation consisting of ice pellets, smaller than hail, formed by the freezing or partial freezing of rain. **2.** mixture of rain and snow or hail. —*v.i.* to shower sleet. [From an unrecorded Old English word.] —**sleet′y,** *adj.*

sleeve (slēv) *n.* **1.** part of a garment that covers and usually encloses all or part of the arm. **2.** *Machinery.* tubelike part that fits over another part. **3. up one's sleeve.** secretly in reserve for later use; hidden. [Old English *slīef* part of a garment that covers the arm.] —**sleeved,** *adj.*

sleigh (slā) *n.* vehicle on runners, usually horse-drawn, used for traveling over snow or ice. —*v.i.* to ride or travel in a sleigh. [Dutch *slee,* form of *slede* sled.]

Sleigh

sleight (slīt) *n.* **1.** skill or dexterity in doing or making something. **2.** craftiness; cunning. **3.** clever trick or deception. [Old Norse *slœgth* slyness.]

sleight of hand **1.** skill and dexterity in using the hands, esp. in performing tricks or feats with the hands. **2.a.** tricks or feats requiring such skill, as those performed by a magician or juggler. **b.** performance of such tricks or feats.

slen·der (slen′dər) *adj.* **1.** thin, esp. in an attractive or graceful way: *slender fingers.* **2.** having a small circumference in proportion to height or length: *a slender pole.* **3.** small in size, amount, extent, or degree: *The candidate was elected governor of the state by a slender margin.* [Of uncertain origin.] —**slen′der·ly,** *adv.* —**slen′der·ness,** *n.* —**Syn.** 1. see **lean².**

slen·der·ize (slen′də rīz′) **-ized, -iz·ing** *v.t.* **1.** to make slender. **2.** to cause to appear slender. —*v.i.* to become slender.

slept (slept) past tense and past participle of **sleep.**

sleuth (slooth) *n.* **1.** *Informal.* detective. **2.** sleuthhound. —*v.i. Informal.* to act as a detective. [Old Norse *slōth* track.]

sleuth·hound (slooth′hound′) *n.* bloodhound.

slew¹ (sloo) past tense of **slay.**

slew² (sloo) slue¹.

slew³ (sloo) *n.* slough¹ *(def. 2).*

slew⁴ (sloo) *n. Informal.* large number or group; great amount: *a whole slew of people.* [Irish Gaelic *sluagh* multitude.]

slice (slīs) *n.* **1.** thin, flat piece cut from a larger object: *a slice of bread.* **2.** part, portion, or share. **3.** any of various implements having a thin, broad blade, as a spatula. **4.** *Sports.* **a.** stroke that causes a ball to curve off to the side. **b.** course followed by such a ball. —*v.t.,* **sliced, slic·ing.** **1.** to cut into slices or pieces: *to slice a cake.* **2.** to remove in the form of a slice or slices (often with *off*). **3.** to divide into parts, portions,

or shares. **4.** to move through or across like a knife. **5.** *Sports.* to hit (a ball) so that it curves off to the side. —*v.i.* **1.** to move or cut like a knife: *The speeding boat sliced through the waves.* **2.** *Sports.* **a.** to hit a ball with a slice. **b.** (of a ball) to curve in a slice. [Old French *esclice* splinter, from *esclicier* to split; of Germanic origin.] —*slic′er, n.*

slick (slik) *adj.* **1.** smooth and glossy; sleek: *slick wet hair.* **2.** slippery. **3.** cleverly or skillfully devised, done, or said. **4.** shrewd or sly in thought, action, or speech: *a slick confidence man.* **5.** having or showing skill that is only superficial or that lacks any real significance, as a style of writing. **6.** *Slang.* excellent; great. —*n.* **1.** smooth or slippery area on a surface. **2.** oily film, esp. on the surface of water. **3.** *Informal.* magazine printed on glazed or coated paper. —*v.t.* **1.** *Informal.* to make sleek, smooth, or glossy. **2.** to make neat, trim, or tidy (often with *up*). [Old English *slician* to make smooth.] —**slick′ly,** *adv.* —**slick′ness,** *n.*

slick·er (slik′ər) *n.* **1.** raincoat made of oilskin, plastic, or a similar material. **2.** *Informal.* clever, sly, or deceptive person.

slide (slīd) *slid* (slid), *slid,* or *slid·den* (slid′ən), *slid·ing. v.i.* **1.** to pass or move along a surface with a smooth, continuous movement: *The wet bar of soap slid across the floor.* **2.** to shift, fall, or move suddenly from a position, as by a loss of balance or traction: *As I crossed the icy walk, my feet slid out from under me.* **3.** to pass or move smoothly, quietly, or gradually: *Ken slid into the seat next to me and we drove off.* **4.** to continue or go by without intervention or interference: *We let the matter slide for the moment.* **5.** to pass or fall into a specified state or condition. **6.** *Baseball.* to throw oneself along the ground toward a base, usually feet first, in order to avoid being tagged by the baseman. —*v.t.* **1.** to cause to move along a surface with a smooth, continuous movement: *to slide a heavy box along the floor.* **2.** to put or move smoothly, quietly, or imperceptibly: *to slide a note under a door.* —*n.* **1.** act or instance of sliding. **2.** smooth, usually inclined track, channel, or surface for sliding, esp. a playground apparatus consisting of an inclined chute for sliding down upon. **3.** small plate of glass on which an object is placed for examination under a microscope. **4.** small, transparent photograph to be magnified and projected on a screen. **5.a.** fall of a mass of rock, snow, or other matter down a slope. **b.** such a mass of matter. **6.** part that operates by sliding, esp. the U-shaped section of tubing of a trombone that is pushed in or out to alter the pitch of the tones. [Old English *slīdan* to glide.] **Syn.** *v.i.* **1.** Slide, slip', glide mean to move along smoothly. Slide emphasizes rapid and effortless motion as well as continuous contact with a smooth surface: *The boy slid down the banister.* Slip implies a swift and easy motion over a slippery surface but unlike *slide* is involuntary or accidental and of shorter duration: *The girl slipped on the icy road and fell.* Glide is closer in meaning to *slide* than to *slip* in stressing an even, flowing, and, often, quiet motion that meets with no resistance but does not necessarily imply continuous contact with a surface: *The boat glided through the still water like a phantom.*

slid·er (slī′dər) *n.*
1. one who or that which slides. **2.** *Baseball.* fast pitch that curves sharply for a short distance.

slide rule, instrument consisting of a ruler and a central sliding piece that

Slide rule

are both marked with logarithmic scales, used to perform arithmetic calculations.

sliding scale, scale of wages, prices, tariffs, or the like that varies or can be adjusted in accordance with certain conditions or factors, as the cost of living or the selling price of goods.

sli·er (slī′ər) a comparative of **sly.**

sli·est (slī′ist) a superlative of **sly.**

slight (slīt) *adj.* **1.** small in quantity, degree, or intensity: *a slight possibility of success.* **2.** of small importance: *a slight problem.* **3.** slender or thin in build or form; delicate. **4.** lacking in substance or strength; flimsy. —*v.t.* **1.** to treat with disrespect or indifference or with a marked lack of consideration. **2.** to do or perform carelessly or negligently: *to slight one's duty.* **3.** to treat as unimportant: *to slight someone's advice.* —*n.* show of disrespect or indifference, esp. when contemptuous and deliberate. [Middle Dutch *slicht, slecht* even[1], simple.] —**slight′ly,** *adv.* —**slight′ness,** *n.*

slight·ing (slī′ting) *adj.* constituting or conveying a slight; disparaging. —**slight′ing·ly,** *adv.*

sli·ly (slī′lē) *adv.* sly or slyly.

slim (slim) *slim·mer, slim·mest. adj.* **1.** small in thickness in proportion to height or length; slender; thin: *The human body had a very slim figure.* **2.** small in amount, degree, or extent: *a slim chance of victory.* —*v.t., v.i.* *slimmed, slim·ming.* to make or become slim or slender (often with *down*). [Dutch *slim* awry, bad.] —**slim′ly,** *adv.* —**slim′ness,** *n.*

slime (slīm) *n.* **1.** wet, soft, often sticky mud. **2.** any substance resembling this, esp. when regarded as disgusting or filthy. **3.** thin, sticky mucuslike substance given off by certain animals, as snails. [Old English *slīm* sticky mud.]

slime mold, any of a group of fungi, class Myxomycetes, having both plant and animal characteristics, that live on dead wood and other decaying matter.

slim·y (slī′mē) *slim·i·er, slim·i·est. adj.* **1.** covered with slime. **2.** of or like slime. **3.** disgusting; vile; foul. —**slim′i·ly,** *adv.* —**slim′i·ness,** *n.*

sling (sling) *n.* **1.** device for hurling stones, usually consisting of a piece of leather with a string fastened to each end. **2.** slingshot. **3.** loop of cloth suspended from the neck to support an injured arm or hand. **4.** strap for carrying a rifle or other object over the shoulder. **5.** device, as a chain or rope formed into a loop, used for raising, lowering, carrying, or suspending heavy objects. **6.** act of slinging or hurling; throw. —*v.t.* **slung, sling·ing. 1.** to hurl with or as with a sling; throw; fling: *to sling a rock.* **2.** to suspend with a sling or strap: *A rifle was slung over the hunter's shoulder.* **3.** to hang or throw loosely: *to sling a hammock between two trees.* **4.** to raise, lower, carry, or suspend by means of a sling. [Probably from Old Norse *slyngva* to fling, throw.] —**sling′er,** *n.*

sling chair, any of various lightweight chairs having a seat and back made of a single piece of canvas, leather, or similar material that is attached loosely to a frame.

sling·shot (sling′shot′) *n.* Y-shaped piece of wood or metal, with an elastic band fastened to the prongs, used to shoot small stones or similar missiles.

slink (slingk) *slunk* or *(archaic)* slank, slunk, slink·ing. *v.i.* to move in a quiet, stealthy, or sneaking manner. [Old English *slincan* to creep, crawl.]

slink·y (sling′kē) *slink·i·er, slink·i·est. adj.* **1.** stealthy; sneaking. **2.** *Informal.* sleek and sinuous in form, appearance, or movement: *a slinky evening dress.*

slip[1] (slip) *slipped* or *(archaic)* slipt, slip·ping. *v.i.* **1.** to lose one's balance or footing; slide suddenly or accidentally: *to slip on a banana peel.* **2.** to move or slide out of place or out of control; shift or fall from a position: *The bottle slipped out of my hands.* **3.** to move or pass smoothly, or with an easy, gliding motion: *The boy slipped into bed and went right to sleep.* **4.** to move or go quietly, stealthily, or unnoticed: *The thief slipped out of the apartment without a sound.* **5.** (of time) to pass imperceptibly: *Another month slipped by.* **6.** to escape (often with *by* or *away*): *You let the chance of a lifetime slip by!* **7.** to be lost from memory: *The appointment had completely slipped from my mind.* **8.** to be said, divulged, or made known unintentionally (often with *out*): *Don't let the truth slip out.* **9.** to decline or fall, as from an accustomed or desired level: *Sales slipped sharply last year.* **10.** to decline or deteriorate in physical or mental condition or ability: *The old man feared his health was slipping.* **11.** to put on or take off clothing, esp. quickly or easily (with *into* or *out of*). **12.** to pass or fall into a specified state, condition, or activity: *to slip into unconsciousness.* **13.** to make a mistake; fall into error (often with *up*): *Dan often slips up when he's under pressure.* —*v.t.* **1.** to cause to move with a smooth, sliding motion: *to slip a ring off one's finger.* **2.** to put, give, or insert, esp. stealthily, quietly, or quickly: *to slip a pill into someone's drink.* **3.** to fail to be remembered or noticed by: *Her name had slipped my mind.* **4.** to put on or take off (clothing), esp. quickly or easily (with *on* or *off*): *She slipped the sweater on and dashed out the door.* **5.** to free oneself or itself from: *The horse slipped its bridle.* **6.** to release or free, as a dog from a leash; let loose. **7.** to dislocate, as a bone. **8.** to transfer (a stitch) from one needle to another without knitting it. **9. to slip one** (or **something**) **over on.** *Informal.* to take advantage of by deception; trick. —*n.* **1.** act of slipping or sliding. **2.** mistake or error, as in speech, judgment, or conduct. **3.** mishap; accident. **4.** decline or fall, as from an accustomed level: *a slip in prices.* **5.** woman's undergarment, usually of a light material, as nylon. **6.** pillowcase. **7.** space between wharves or piers where ships can dock. **8.** sloping pier leading into the water and serving as a landing place. **9.** inclined plane leading down to the water, on which ships are built or repaired. **10. to give (someone) the slip.** to escape from; elude. [Middle Dutch *slippen* to glide, slide.] —**Syn.** *v.i.* **1.** see **slide.**

slip[2] (slip) *n.* **1.** small shoot or twig cut from a plant, used for grafting or planting. **2.** long, thin piece or strip of some material, as cloth. **3.** small piece of paper, esp. one designed or used for a specific purpose: *a bank deposit slip.* **4.** slender or slight person, esp. a young one: *a mere slip of a girl.* —*v.t.* **slipped, slip·ping.** to cut a shoot or twig from (a plant) for grafting or planting. [Middle Dutch *slippe* strip, slit.]

slip·case (slip′kās′) *n.* protective box for a book or set of books, open at one end.

slip·cov·er (slip′kuv′ər) *n.* removable cover, usually of cloth, for a piece of furniture, as a sofa.

at; āpe; cär; end; mē; it; īce; hot; ōld; fôrk; wood; fōōl; oil; out; up; ūse; turn; sing; thin; this; zh in treasure; ə in ago, taken, pencil, lemon, circus.

slip·knot (slip′not′) *n.* **1.** knot made so that it will slip along the rope or line around which it is tied. **2.** knot made so that it can be easily undone by pulling on either of the free ends.

slip noose, noose made with a slipknot.

slip-on (slip′ôn′, -on′) *adj.* (of an article of clothing) easily put on or removed. —*n.* slip-on article of clothing.

slip·o·ver (slip′ō′vər) *adj.* (of a garment) designed to be put on or removed by drawing over the head. —*n.* slipover garment.

slip·page (slip′ij) *n.* **1.** act of slipping. **2.** amount or extent of slipping.

Slipknot *(def. 1)*

slipped disk, disorder caused by the protrusion of one of the spongy plates of tissue that serve as cushions between the vertebrae of the spine, characterized by severe back pain.

slip·per (slip′ər) *n.* light, low shoe that is easily slipped on or off the foot, worn chiefly indoors. —**slip′pered,** *adj.*

slip·per·y (slip′ər ē) -**per·i·er, -per·i·est.** *adj.* **1.** causing or likely to cause slipping or sliding: *Freezing rain made the roads slippery.* **2.** tending to slip or slide, as from the grasp: *The wet fish was too slippery to hold.* **3.** not to be relied or depended on; tricky. **4.** able to slip away or escape easily; elusive. [Middle English *sliper* (from Old English *slipor*) + -Y¹.] —**slip′per·i·ness,** *n.*

slippery elm, **1.** North American elm tree, *Ulmus fulva,* having gray or dark, reddish-brown outer bark and white, sticky inner bark. **2.** dried, powdered inner bark of this tree.

slip ring, one of two or more metal rings in an electric motor or machine that serves to conduct a current through contact with stationary brushes.

slip·shod (slip′shod′) *adj.* careless or slovenly, as in appearance or workmanship.

slip·stream (slip′strēm′) *n.* current of air driven back by the revolving propeller of an aircraft.

slipt (slipt) *Archaic.* past tense of **slip¹.**

slip-up (slip′up′) *n.* *Informal.* mistake; error; oversight.

slit (slit) *n.* long, narrow, usually straight cut or opening. —*v.t.,* **slit, slit·ting.** to cut or make a slit or slits in. [Middle English *slitten* to cut, divide, possibly going back to Old English *slītan* to tear, divide.]

slith·er (slith′ər) *v.i.* **1.** to move along with a sliding or gliding motion. **2.** to slip or slide, as on a loose or slippery surface. —*v.t.* to cause to slither or slide. [Old English *sliderian* to slip.]

slith·er·y (slith′ər ē) *adj.* slippery; slick.

sliv·er (sliv′ər) *n.* **1.** slender, often pointed piece that has been broken, cut, or torn off; splinter. **2.** continuous strand of loose, untwisted textile fiber after it has been carded. —*v.t., v.i.* to cut or break into slivers. [From dialectal English *slive* to cleave, slice off, from Old English *slīfan* to cleave.]

slob (slob) *n.* *Informal.* sloppy, dirty, or crude person. [Irish *slab* mud; probably of Scandinavian origin.]

slob·ber (slob′ər) *v.i.* **1.** to let saliva, food, or liquid run or spill from the mouth; slaver. **2.** to express oneself in an overly sentimental manner; speak or write effusively; gush. —*v.t.* to wet or smear with saliva, food, or liquid running from the mouth. **2.** overly sentimental speech or writing. [Probably imitative.] —**slob′ber·y,** *adj.*

sloe (slō) *n.* **1.** blackthorn *(def. 1).* **2.** tart, plumlike fruit of the blackthorn. [Old English *slāh* fruit of the blackthorn.]

slog (slog) **slogged, slog·ging.** *v.i.* **1.** to work with great effort; plod: *The weary soldiers slogged through the mud for hours.* **2.** to hit hard. —*v.t.* to make (one's way) with great effort. [Form of SLUG².]

slo·gan (slō′gən) *n.* **1.** distinctive phrase, statement, or motto used by a particular group, as a club or political party, or by a particular individual, as a candidate for political office. **2.** catch phrase used in advertising or in promoting a particular product, business, or service. **3.** formerly, rallying or battle cry used by the Highland clans. [Gaelic *sluagh-ghairm* the signal for battle among the Highland clans, from *sluagh* army + *gairm* outcry.]

sloop (slōōp) *n.* fore-and-aft-rigged sailboat with a single mast, a mainsail, and a jib. [Dutch *sloep.* Doublet of SHALLOP.]

sloop of war, formerly, small warship having guns mounted on only one deck.

slop (slop) *n.* **1.** liquid spilled or splashed. **2.** soft, watery mud or snow; slush. **3.** unappetizing or dis-

Sloop

tasteful food or liquid. **4.** *also,* **slops.** refuse food used to feed pigs or other animals; swill. **5.** any liquid or semiliquid waste. —*v.i.,* **slopped, slop·ping.** **1.** (of liquid) to spill or splash (often with *over*). **2.** to walk or move with splashes through mud, slush, or water. **3.** *Informal.* to talk or act with excessive sentiment or emotion (with *over*). —*v.t.* **1.** to cause (a liquid) to spill or splash. **2.** to spill or splash liquid upon. **3.** to feed slop to animals. [Old English *-sloppe* dung (in *cūsloppe* cowslip; literally, cow dung).]

slope (slōp) **sloped, slop·ing.** *v.i.* to lie or move at an angle from the horizontal or vertical; take a slanting direction. —*v.t.* to cause to slope. —*n.* **1.** stretch of ground that is not flat or level; natural or artificial incline. **2.** any slanting line, surface, position, or direction. **3.a.** any deviation from the horizontal. **b.** degree or amount of such deviation. **4.a.** degree of inclination measured by the tangent of an angle formed by a line and the x-axis. **b.** (of a point of a plane curve) slope of the line that is tangent to a curve at a point. [Short for earlier *aslope* sloping, possibly from Old English *āslōpen,* past participle of *āslūpan* to slip away.] —**Syn.** *v.i.* see **slant.**

slop·py (slop′ē) -**pi·er, -pi·est.** *adj.* **1.** very wet, muddy, or slushy: *The streets were wet and sloppy* (Dickens, 1837). **2.** spotted or splashed with liquid or slop: *a sloppy floor.* **3.** *Informal.* careless; slipshod. **4.** *Informal.* very untidy; messy: *a sloppy room.* **5.** *Informal.* excessively sentimental; maudlin. —**slop′pi·ly,** *adv.* —**slop′pi·ness,** *n.*

slosh (slosh) *v.i.* to move clumsily or splash about, as in water or mud: *to slosh through a bog.* —*v.t.* to stir or splash about (a liquid or something in a liquid). —*n.* **1.** slush. **2.** sound of splashing liquid. [Form of SLUSH.]

slot¹ (slot) *n.* **1.** narrow, usually straight opening or groove. **2.** *Informal.* place or position, as in a schedule or sequence: *That television program will appear in the ten o'clock time slot next season.* —*v.t.,* **slot·ted, slot·ting.** to make or cut a slot in. [Old French *esclot* the depression between the breasts; of uncertain origin.]

slot² (slot) *n.* track or trail of an animal, esp. a deer. [Old French *esclot* print of a horse's hoof, from Old Norse *slōth* track, trail.]

sloth (slôth, slōth, sloth) *n.* **1.** disinclination to work or exertion; laziness. **2.** any of several slow-moving, tree-dwelling mammals, family Brachypodidae, native to the tropical forests of Central and South America, having long limbs with curved claws, and coarse, shaggy hair. Length: 2 feet. [From SLOW.]

Sloth *(def. 2)*

sloth bear, long-haired black bear, *Melursus ursinus,* native to India and Ceylon. Height: 2½ feet at the shoulder.

sloth·ful (slôth′fəl, slōth′-, sloth′-) *adj.* characterized by sloth; lazy; indolent. —**sloth′ful·ly,** *adv.* —**sloth′ful·ness,** *n.*

slot machine, gambling or vending machine that is operated by the insertion of a coin through a slot.

slouch (slouch) *v.i.* **1.** to sit, stand, or walk with an awkward, drooping posture, or in an overly loose or relaxed manner. **2.** to hang down, as the brim of a hat; droop. —*n.* **1.** drooping of the head and shoulders in sitting, standing, or walking; awkward, drooping posture. **2.** a hanging down, as of the brim of a hat. **2.** *Informal.* awkward, lazy, or incompetent person. ▲ used chiefly in the phrase *no slouch at: Herb's no slouch at tennis.* [Of uncertain origin.]

slouch hat, soft, usually felt hat, with a broad, flexible brim.

slouch·y (slou′chē) **slouch·i·er, slouch·i·est.** *adj.* slouching, esp. in posture. —**slouch′i·ly,** *adv.* —**slouch′i·ness,** *n.*

slough¹ (*defs. 1, 3* slou; *def. 2* slōō) *n.* **1.** place full of soft, deep mud. **2.** *also,* **slue, slue.** swamp, marsh, or bog, esp. one that is part of a backwater. **3.** state of dejection, discouragement, or degradation. [Old English *slōh* piece of muddy ground.] —**slough′y,** *adj.*

slough² (sluf) *n.* **1.** outer skin shed by a snake. **2.** layer of dead skin or tissue that separates from the surrounding tissue, as of a healing wound. **3.** anything that has been shed or cast off: *The mountain .. has cast his cloudy slough* (Tennyson, 1868). —*v.t.* **1.** to shed or cast off (often with *off*). **2.** to get rid of; discard (often with *off*): *She could slough off a sadness and replace it by a hope* (Hardy, 1873). —*v.i.* **1.** to be shed or cast off. **2.** to shed an outer skin. **3.** to separate from the surrounding tissue (often with *off*). [Of uncertain origin.] —**slough′y,** *adj.*

Slo·vak (slō′vak) *n.* **1.** member or close descendant of a Slavic people living predominantly in Slovakia and closely related to the Czechs and the Moravians. **2.** language of these people, belonging to the western branch of the Slavic languages and closely related to Czech. —*adj.* of or relating to Slovakia, its people, or their language or culture. Also, **Slo·va′ki·an.**

at; āpe; cär; end; mē; it; īce; hot; ōld; fôrk; wood; fōōl; oil; out; up; ūse; turn; sing; thin; this; zh in treasure; ə in ago, taken, pencil, lemon, circus.

Slo·va·ki·a (slō vä′kē ə, -vak′ē ə) n. historic region in eastern Czechoslovakia. Area, 18,902 sq. mi. Pop. (1963 est.), 4,283,000.

slov·en (sluv′ən) n. one who is untidy or careless, esp. in appearance or dress. [Possibly from Middle Dutch *slof* careless, lax.]

Slo·vene (slō′vēn) n. **1.** member or close descendant of a Slavic people living in Slovenia and closely related to the Serbs and Croats. **2.** language of these people, belonging to the southern branch of the Slavic languages and closely related to Serb and Croatian. —*adj.* or or relating to Slovenia, its people, or their language or culture. Also, **Slo·ve′ni·an.**

Slo·ve·ni·a (slō vē′nē ə, -vēn′yə) n. political subdivision of Yugoslavia, in the northwestern part of the country. Area, 7708 sq. mi. Pop. (1963 est.), 1,619,000.

slov·en·ly (sluv′ən lē) -li·er, -li·est. *adj.* **1.** untidy or careless, esp. in appearance or dress. **2.** characteristic of a sloven; slipshod. —*adv.* in a slovenly manner. —**slov′en·li·ness,** n.

slow (slō) *adj.* **1.** acting, moving, or occurring with little speed; not fast or quick: *a slow reader, a slow pace, slow progress.* **2.** taking or requiring a relatively long time to be completed or performed: *a slow trip, a slow game.* **3.** (of a timepiece) indicating a time behind the true time: *My watch is always slow.* **4.** not quick to learn or understand; mentally dull: *a slow student.* **5.** unsuitable for or not conducive to rapid movement: *a slow track.* **6.** not active; sluggish: *Business is slow this season.* **7.** not prompt, hasty, or easily moved: *slow to answer letters, slow to anger.* **8.** lacking in liveliness; uninteresting; dull; boring: *Shy guests make for a slow party.* **9.** burning at moderate intensity; low: *a slow fire.* **10.** *Photography.* allowing for a long exposure time: *slow film.* —*adv.* in a slow manner; slowly. —*v.t.* to make slow or slower, or cause to proceed at a slow or slower speed (often with *up* or *down*): *to slow down the rate of production.* —*v.i.* to become slow or slower, or proceed at a slow or slower speed (often with *up* or *down*). [Old English *slāw* dull, sluggish.] —**slow′ly,** adv. —**slow′ness,** n.

slow·down (slō′doun′) n. reduction in pace, esp. a deliberate slowing down of the rate of production by workers or management.

slow·ish (slō′ish) *adj.* somewhat slow.

slow·mo·tion (slō′mō′shən) *adj.* **1.** of or relating to a motion picture in which the action appears to be taking place at a much slower than normal speed. **2.** moving or operating at less than normal speed.

slow·poke (slō′pōk′) n. *Informal.* one who moves, works, or acts at a very slow pace.

slow·wit·ted (slō′wit′id) *adj.* slow to understand; mentally dull.

slow·worm (slō′wurm′) n. blindworm.

sludge (sluj) n. **1.** mud or mire, esp. a muddy deposit at the bottom of a body of water. **2.** any mudlike or slushy mass or mixture, as the deposit formed in a boiler or the sediment produced in the treatment of sewage. **3.** broken or half-formed ice, as on the sea. [Of uncertain origin.] —**sludg′y,** *adj.*

slue¹ (slōō) slued, slu·ing. also, **slew.** *v.t.* to cause to turn or twist about, esp. on a pivot or fixed point. —*v.i.* to turn or twist about; swing around. —*n.* **1.** act of sluing. **2.** position attained by sluing. [Of uncertain origin.]

slue² (slōō) n. slough¹ *(def. 2).*

slug¹ (slug) n. **1.** any of several mollusks, class Gastropoda, closely resembling a snail, but either lacking a shell or having only a rudimentary shell. **2.** larva of a moth or certain other insects that resembles a slug. **3.** sluggard. **4.a.** small piece or lump of metal, esp. a piece of lead or other metal for firing from a gun. **b.** *Slang.* bullet. **5.** piece of metal shaped like and used in place of a coin, esp. one used illegally, as in a vending machine. **6.** *Printing.* **a.** strip of metal, thicker than a lead, used to space lines of type. **b.** line of type cast in one piece, as by a linotype machine. **7.** *Physics.* unit of mass that acquires an acceleration of one foot per second when acted upon by a force of one pound. It is equal to about 32.2 pounds. **8.** *Slang.* single drink of alcoholic liquor; shot. [Probably of Scandinavian origin.]

Slug¹ *(def. 1)*

slug² (slug) slugged, slug·ging. *Informal. v.t.* to strike heavily, as with the fist or a blunt instrument. —*n.* heavy blow, as with the fist. [Possibly from SLUG¹.]

slug·fest (slug′fest′) n. *Informal.* **1.** fight or boxing match in which many hard blows are exchanged. **2.** baseball game in which many hits and runs are made.

slug·gard (slug′ərd) n. one who is habitually lazy or idle. —*adj.* also, **slug′gard·ly.** lazy or idle; slothful. [Possibly from obsolete *sluggy* lazy (probably of Scandinavian origin) + -ARD.]

slug·ger (slug′ər) n. one who slugs, esp. a prizefighter able to throw hard punches or a hard-hitting baseball player.

slug·gish (slug′ish) *adj.* **1.** having or marked by little motion, speed, or activity: *Trading was sluggish on the stock market today.* **2.** characterized by or showing a lack of vigor, energy, or alertness. **3.** disinclined to action or exertion; slothful; lazy. **4.** not acting or functioning with full or usual energy or efficiency: *My car engine is sluggish on cold mornings.* [SLUG¹ + -ISH.] —**slug′gish·ly,** adv. —**slug′gish·ness,** n.

sluice (slōōs) n. **1.** artificial channel for conducting water, equipped with a gate or valve for controlling the flow. **2.** gate or valve of such a channel, usually a sliding vertical plate. Also, **sluice gate.** **3.** water controlled by such a gate. **4.** any artificial channel, esp. one for draining off excess water. **5.** long, sloping trough through which water is run, as for separating gold ore or floating logs. —*v.t.,* **sluiced, sluic·ing. 1.** to draw off by or through a sluice. **2.a.** to wash with water running through or from a sluice. **b.** to wash with a rush of water; drench. **3.** to float (logs) in a sluice. —*v.i.* to flow out from or as from a sluice. [Old French *escluse* floodgate, going back to Latin *exclūsa* feminine past participle of *exclūdere* to shut out.]

Sluice *(def. 5)*

sluice·way (slōōs′wā′) n. artificial channel for the passage of water; sluice.

slum (slum) n. *also,* **slums.** heavily populated section of a city, characterized by poverty, deteriorated housing, and squalid living conditions. —*v.i.,* **slummed, slum·ming. 1.** to visit a slum out of curiosity or for amusement. ▲ used chiefly in the phrase *to go slumming.* **2.** to visit a place regarded as socially inferior or disreputable, as for amusement. [Of uncertain origin.]

slum·ber (slum′bər) *v.i.* **1.** to sleep. **2.** to be quiet, calm, or inactive. —*v.t.* to pass or spend in sleeping (often used with *away*): *to slumber away the day.* —*n.* **1.** sleep. **2.** quiet, calm, or inactive state. [Middle English *slumeren* to doze, be inactive, going back to Old English *slūma* light sleep.] —**slum′ber·er,** n. —**Syn.** *v.i.* **1.** see **sleep.**

slum·ber·ous (slum′bər əs) also, **slum·brous** (slum′brəs) *adj.* **1.** sleepy; drowsy. **2.** causing sleep; soporific. **3.** like or characteristic of sleep. **4.** calm; quiet; peaceful.

slum·lord (slum′lôrd′) n. landlord of slum housing, esp. one who charges high rents and is negligent in caring for his property.

slump (slump) *v.i.* **1.** to fall or sink suddenly or heavily: *The dazed boxer staggered, then slumped to the floor.* **2.** to decline, drop off, or deteriorate sharply, as in activity, performance, or value: *The football team slumped badly after its star quarterback was injured.* **3.** to assume a drooping posture; slouch. —*n.* **1.** decline, dropping off, or deterioration, usually sharp or prolonged, as in business activity or performing ability: *a slump in sales.* **2.** act or instance of slumping. [Imitative.]

slung (slung) past tense and past participle of **sling.**

slunk (slungk) past tense and past participle of **slink.**

slur (slur) slurred, slur·ring. *v.t.* **1.** to pass over hurriedly or carelessly, as without giving due attention or consideration (often with *over*): *In his haste to complete the report, the author slurred over many facts.* **2.** to speak slightingly of; disparage. **3.** to pronounce indistinctly, as by running sounds together. **4.** *Music.* **a.** to play or sing (two or more tones of different pitch) in a smooth, connected manner. **b.** to mark with a slur. —*n.* **1.** disparaging statement or remark; aspersion: *His accusation was a slur on my reputation.* **2.** indistinct pronunciation. **3.** *Music.* **a.** combination of two or more slurred tones. **b.** curved mark indicating this. [Possibly from Middle Dutch *sleuren* to trail in mud.]

Slur *(def. 3b)*

slurp (slurp) *Slang. v.t., v.i.* to drink, sip, or eat noisily. —*n.* noise made by slurping. [Dutch *slurpen* to lap¹.]

slur·ry (slur′ē) pl. **-ries.** n. thin mixture of water or other liquid and some fine, insoluble substance, as cement or plaster of Paris.

slush (slush) n. **1.** partially melted snow or ice. **2.** soft mud; mire. **3.** any of various greasy materials used as lubricants. **4.** maudlin or silly, sentimental speech or writing; drivel. [Of uncertain origin.] —**slush′i·ness,** n. —**slush′y,** *adj.*

slush fund 1. money set aside for bribery, graft, or other corrupt political practices. **2.** any sum of money set aside for some purpose.

slut (slut) n. **1.** immoral or disreputable woman. **2.** dirty, slovenly woman. [Of uncertain origin.] —**slut′tish,** adj. —**slut′tish·ly,** adv. —**slut′tish·ness,** n.

sly (slī) sli·er or sly·er, sli·est or sly·est. *adj.* **1.** displaying or characterized by cleverness, shrewdness, or craftiness: *a sly trick.* **2.** clever or skillful in avoiding notice or detection; skilled in acting stealthily: *The sly thief had eluded the police for months.* **3.** mischievous in a playful way: *a sly glance.* —*n.* **on the sly.** in a stealthy way; secretly; furtively. [Old Norse *slǣgr* cunning.] —**sly′ly,** adv. —**sly′ness,** n.

Syn. *adj.* **1. Sly, cunning, crafty, wily** characterize indirect and devious dealings. Sly suggests a secretiveness and slippery evasiveness in accom-

plishing a malicious goal: *He made sly efforts to undermine the leader's authority.* **Cunning** suggests an instinctive response, esp. in reaction to danger: *With the cunning of an animal, the fugitive made his way to the border.* **Crafty,** in contrast, suggests a process involving a more complex level of reasoning as well as a wary and practiced expertness in deceiving others or promoting one's own interest: *His crafty scheme to embezzle the bank took all the loopholes into account.* **Wily,** like *crafty,* suggests a calculated effort, but one based on influencing others by an uncanny knowledge of their weaknesses: *The wily servant played on his master's love of luxury to gain power over him.*

Sm, samarium.

S.M. 1. Master of Science. **2.** Soldier's Medal.

smack¹ (smak) *v.t.* **1.** to press together and open (the lips) rapidly so as to make a sharp sound. **2.** to strike or slap sharply, as with the open hand: *to smack someone's face.* **3.** to kiss noisily. —*v.i.* **1.** to smack the lips. **2.** to strike something forcibly and noisily: *The car skidded and smacked into the side of the barn.* —*n.* **1.** sharp sound made by smacking the lips. **2.** sharp blow or slap, as with the open hand. **3.** noisy kiss. —*adv.* *Informal.* **1.** in a sudden, violent manner: *The boy rode his bicycle smack into a tree.* **2.** precisely; directly: *Judy ran smack into the very person she was trying to avoid.* [Imitative.]

smack² (smak) *n.* **1.a.** distinctive or characteristic taste or flavor, esp. one that is only slightly perceptible: *The pudding had a smack of cinnamon.* **b.** suggestion; trace. **2.** small quantity or amount. —*v.i.* **1.** to have a taste or flavor (with *of*): *The meat smacks of garlic.* **2.** to have a suggestion or trace (with *of*): *That statement smacks of treason.* [Old English *smæc* taste.]

smack³ (smak) *n.* small sailboat, usually fore-and-aft-rigged, used chiefly for fishing. [Dutch *smak.*]

smack·er (smak′ər) *n.* **1.** one who or that which smacks. **2.** *Slang.* dollar.

smack·ing (smak′ing) *adj.* brisk or vigorous; lively: *a smacking breeze.*

small (smôl) *adj.* **1.** not large or great in size, amount, or numbers, esp. in comparison to others of the same kind: *a small car, a small waist, a small crowd.* **2.** limited in degree, extent, duration, intensity, or value: *a small possibility.* **3.** of limited importance; not very significant; trivial: *a small problem.* **4.** carrying on business or some financial activity on a limited scale: *a small businessman, a small investor.* **5.** of low or inferior social position or rank. **6.** modest; humble: *Everyone contributed in his own small way.* **7.** young: *When I was a small boy, I loved to visit the zoo.* **8.** soft or weak; not loud; low: *a small voice.* **9.** mean, petty, or selfish; small-minded. **10.** to feel small. to feel humiliated or ashamed: *Her kindness made me feel small after my rash accusations.* —*adv.* **1.** in or into small pieces. **2.** in low tones; softly. **3.** in a small manner. —*n.* small or narrow part, esp. of the back. [Old English *smæl* thin, narrow, of limited size.] —**small′ness,** *n.*

small arms, firearms, as pistols or rifles, that can be carried easily and can be held in the hands when fired. Distinguished from **artillery.**

small capital, capital letter of slightly smaller size than the regular letter of the same font. The word TODAY is in small capitals.

small change 1. coins of small denomination. **2.** something of little value or importance.

small-clothes (smôl′klōz′, -klōthz′) *n.,pl.* close-fitting knee breeches worn in the eighteenth century.

small fry 1. young or small child or children. **2.** people or things of little or no importance.

small game, small wild animals and birds sought by hunters for sport.

small hours, hours between midnight and dawn.

small intestine, that part of the alimentary canal extending from the stomach to the large intestine, consisting of the duodenum, the jejunum, and the ileum, about twenty feet long in the adult human.

small·ish (smô′lish) *adj.* somewhat small.

small letter, letter that is not a capital letter.

small-mind·ed (smôl′mīn′did) *adj.* having or showing a narrow, selfish, or petty outlook or nature; prejudiced. —**small′-mind′ed·ly,** *adv.* —**small′-mind′ed·ness,** *n.*

small potatoes *Informal.* unimportant or insignificant persons or things.

small·pox (smôl′poks′) *n.* acute, highly contagious disease caused by a virus and characterized by fever and pustular skin eruptions that often leave small, pit-shaped permanent scars. Also, **va·ri·o·la.**

small-scale (smôl′skāl′) *adj.* **1.** of small or limited scope; not extensive: *a small-scale undertaking, to launch a small-scale attack.* **2.** drawn or made on a small scale and permitting little detail to be shown, as a map.

small talk, light conversation about common or unimportant matters.

small-time (smôl′tīm′) *adj.* *Informal.* of no real importance; minor; petty: *a small-time crook.*

smart (smärt) *adj.* **1.** clever; intelligent; shrewd: *You made a very smart investment.* **2.** *Informal.* flippantly or disrespectfully witty: *Don't give me any smart answers!* **3.** neat and trim; spruce; sharp: *to look smart in a uniform.* **4.** fashionable; stylish: *She bought a smart new outfit to wear to the wedding.* **5.** brisk; vigorous. **6.** causing sharp or stinging pain. **7.** *Informal.* considerable; large. —*v.i.* **1.** to cause or be the source of sharp or stinging pain: *The antiseptic smarted as it was applied to the wound.* **2.** to feel or experience such pain: *My face smarted from the blast of hot air.* **3.** to feel or undergo mental pain, suffering, or distress: *The man smarted when his wife's caustic reproach.* **4.** to suffer the penalty (with *for*): *to smart for a wrongdoing.* —*v.t.* to cause to smart or feel pain. —*n.* sharp or stinging physical or mental pain. —*adv.* in a smart manner; smartly. [Old English *smeortan* to be painful.] —**smart′ly,** *adv.* —**smart′ness,** *n.*

smart al·eck (al′ik) *Informal.* one who is obnoxiously or arrogantly conceited and assertive. —**smart′-al′eck·y,** *adj.*

smart·en (smärt′ən) *v.t.* **1.** to improve in appearance; spruce up (often with *up*): *The soldiers smartened up the barracks before the colonel arrived.* **2.** to make more brisk or lively. **3.** to make more aware, clever, or knowing (often with *up*): *Smarten up your brother before he gets into trouble.* —*v.i.* to become more aware, clever, or knowing (often with *up*).

smart set, fashionable, sophisticated people considered as a social group.

smart-weed (smärt′wēd′) *n.* **1.** any of several weedy plants of the genus *Polygonum,* having a strong bitter-tasting juice. **2.** any of various plants, as nettles, that cause a stinging sensation when touched.

smash (smash) *v.t.* **1.** to break (something), esp. into pieces, suddenly and often with noise and violence: *The little boy smashed the plate with a hammer.* **2.** to propel, throw, or otherwise cause to move forcefully and noisily: *The angry lawyer smashed his fist against the desk.* **3.** to strike with a hard blow: *The man smashed the would-be thief in the head with an umbrella.* **4.** to accomplish or produce by striking forcefully: *Firemen smashed the door down.* **5.** to destroy, crush, or defeat completely or decisively: *to smash a crime organization, to smash a theory. This final setback smashed all hope of victory.* **6.** to hit with a racket, as a tennis ball, with a hard, swift overhand stroke. —*v.i.* **1.** to break into pieces, esp. as the result of impact: *The plate slipped out of my hand and smashed on the floor.* **2.** to move or be propelled with force or violence (often with *against, into,* or *through*): *The speeding motorcyclist smashed into the side of a building.* —*n.* **1.** act or instance of smashing; being smashed. **2.** noise produced by smashing. **3.** hard blow. **4.** collision; crash; smashup. **5.** complete or crushing defeat or disaster; total ruin. **6.** hard, swift overhand stroke made with a racket, as in tennis. **7.** beverage made of water, sugar, mint, and an alcoholic liquor, as brandy. **8.** *Informal.* tremendous success: *The show was an immediate smash.* —*adj. Informal.* tremendously successful: *The new play is a smash hit.* [Probably blend of SMACK¹ and MASH.] —**smash′er,** *n.* —**Syn.** *v.t.* **1.** see **break.**

smash·ing (smash′ing) *adj. Informal.* extremely good or impressive; outstanding; tremendous: *Her debut as an actress was a smashing success.* —**smash′ing·ly,** *adv.*

smash-up (smash′up′) *n.* **1.** violent collision, as of automobiles; crash. **2.** complete collapse, failure, or defeat.

smat·ter (smat′ər) *v.t.* **1.** to speak with little knowledge or with very limited understanding, as a foreign language. **2.** to study or learn superficially; dabble in. —*n.* smattering. [Possibly of Scandinavian origin.]

smat·ter·ing (smat′ər ing) *n.* superficial or very limited knowledge.

smear (smēr) *v.t.* **1.** to cover, spread, or stain with paint, grease, dirt, or other substance: *The child smeared his face with mud.* **2.** to spread or apply (paint, grease, dirt, or other substance): *The boy smeared dirt all over his clothes.* **3.** to cause to become indistinct, untidy, or disordered, as by rubbing with the hand: *to smear a signature.* **4.** to damage the reputation of, as by making slanderous statements: *The candidate smeared his opponent's political record by accusing him of past misdeeds.* **5.** *Slang.* to defeat completely or overwhelmingly, as in an athletic contest. —*v.i.* to be or become smeared or spread. —*n.* **1.** mark or stain made by smearing: *There was a lipstick smear on his cheek.* **2.** small quantity of a substance, as blood, placed on a slide for microscopic examination. **3.** substance to be smeared on a surface. **4.** attack on a person's reputation, as with slanderous statements: *The politician was subjected to vicious smears by his opponent's supporters.* [Old English *smerian* to annoint or rub with a greasy substance.]

smear·y (smēr′ē) *smear·i·er, smear·i·est. adj.* **1.** marked or characterized by smears; smeared. **2.** tending or likely to smear or smudge. —**smear′i·ness,** *n.*

smell (smel) *smelled* or *smelt, smell·ing. v.t.* **1.** to perceive by means of the nose and its olfactory nerves; detect the odor of: *Do you smell something burning?* **2.** to test or sample by smelling: *to smell food to see if it's fresh.* **3.** to sense the presence or existence of: *to smell danger.* **4.** to seek or find by or as by smelling (with *out*): *to smell out a bargain,*

to smell out a secret. **5. to smell up.** to cause to have an unpleasant or offensive odor: *That awful cheese is smelling up the refrigerator.* —*v.i.* **1.** to have or give off an odor: *The kitchen smells of onions.* **2.** to have or give off an unpleasant or offensive odor: *Rotten meat smells.* **3.** to use the sense of smell; sniff: *The dog smelled at the meat and then gulped it down.* **4.** to give or exhibit an indication; be suggestive (with *of*): *Your actions smell of cowardice.* —*n.* **1.** sense by means of which odors are perceived. **2.** that property of a thing or substance that makes it perceptible to the sense of smell; odor: *the smell of the sea.* **3.** act of smelling: *He took one smell of the awful brew and became quite ill.* **4.** suggestion, hint, or feeling of something: *The smell of victory was in the air long before the game was over.* [Of uncertain origin.] —**smell′er,** *n.*
Syn. *n.* **2. Smell, odor, aroma, scent** mean the quality of a thing that is perceived by the nose. **Smell** is the general term to suggest the quality of one thing as distinguished from another: *What is that smell?* **Odor** is common as a scientific term, implying a heavier and more recognizable smell, esp. one coming from a single source: *The odor of chloroform overpowered him.* **Aroma,** like *odor,* suggests a pervasive and pungent quality, but one that is pleasing or stimulating, esp. to the appetite: *The aroma of food cooking made me hungry.* **Scent,** like *aroma,* suggests an agreeable smell but one that is piercing and penetrating yet delicate: *The scent of roses lingered in the air after the rain.*
smelling salts, ammonium salt in an aromatic liquid solution that evaporates on contact with air, emitting an odor that acts as a stimulant or restorative, as in a case of fainting.
smell·y (smel′ē) smell·i·er, smell·i·est. *adj.* having or giving off an unpleasant or offensive smell.
smelt¹ (smelt) *v.t.* **1.** to melt (ore) to separate the metal from it. **2.** to obtain or refine (metal) in this manner. [Middle Dutch *smelten* to melt, make liquid, found.]
smelt² (smelt) *pl.,* **smelts** or **smelt.** *n.* any of a group of slender, silvery food fish, family Osmeridae, found in cold and temperate waters of the Northern Hemisphere. [Old English *smelt.*]
smelt³ (smelt) a past tense and past participle of smell.
smelt·er (smel′tər) *n.* **1.** one whose work or business is smelting. **2.** establishment for smelting. **3.** furnace for smelting.
smid·gen (smij′ən) *also,* **smid·geon, smid·gin.** *n. Informal.* very small amount; bit. [Of uncertain origin.]
smi·lax (smī′laks) *n.* **1.** a climbing African vine, *Asparagus asparagoides,* having stiff, shiny branches and tiny greenish-white flowers that ripen into small purple berries, often grown indoors as an ornamental. **2.** greenbrier. [Latin *smīlax* bindweed, from Greek *smílax.*]

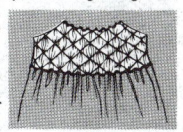
Smilax *(def. 1)*

smile (smīl) *n.* **1.** facial expression characterized by an upward turning of the corners of the mouth, showing any of a wide range of feelings or attitudes, as happiness, amusement, friendliness, sympathy, or contempt. **2.** favorable or pleasant appearance, aspect, or disposition. —*v.i.,* **smiled, smil·ing.** **1.** to have, show, or give a smile. **2.** to show or seem to show approval or favor (often with *on, upon,* or *at*): *Fortune smiled upon our plans.* —*v.t.* **1.** to express with a smile: *The old man smiled his gratitude.* **2.** to affect, change, or accomplish by or as by smiling: *to smile away one's fears.* [Possibly of Scandinavian origin.] —**smil′er,** *n.* —**smil′ing·ly,** *adv.*
Syn. *n.* **1. Smile, grin** indicate a facial expression or response used to convey feeling by an upward curve of the lips. While **smile** is the general term indicating the way in which the eyes light up and the face is animated, it is often used to suggest the effort or strain involved, esp. when such expression is false or insincere: *The saleswoman managed a wan smile before lapsing back into blank indifference.* **Grin** implies a broad and toothy smile and may suggest that an impulsive and sometimes embarrassing revelation has occurred: *With a sheepish grin, he admitted that he'd eaten the rest of the cake.*
smirch (smurch) *v.t.* **1.** to stain, soil, or discolor with dirt, grime, or similar substance. **2.** to bring dishonor or disgrace upon. —*n.* **1.** dirty spot or stain; smudge. **2.** blot or stain on reputation or honor. [Of uncertain origin.]
smirk (smurk) *v.i.* to smile in an affected, self-satisfied, or silly manner. —*n.* affected, self-satisfied, or silly smile. [Old English *smearcian* to smile.]
smite (smīt) smote, smit·ten or smit (smit) or smote, smit·ing. *v.t.* **1.** to strike hard, esp. with the hand or with a weapon. **2.** to destroy, kill, or defeat by or as by striking in this manner. **3.** to afflict or attack, esp. suddenly and with a disastrous effect: *to be smitten by disease.* **4.** to affect suddenly or strongly with some powerful or distressing feeling, as love, fear, or remorse. —*v.i.* to strike with or as by a hard blow. [Old English *smītan* to smear, pollute.] —**smit′er,** *n.*
smith (smith) *n.* **1.** one who makes or repairs metal objects. ▲ usually

used in combination, as in *gunsmith.* **2.** blacksmith. [Old English *smith.*]
Smith (smith) **1. Adam.** 1723–90, Scottish economist. **2. Alfred Emanuel.** 1873–1944, U.S. politician. **3. Captain John.** 1580–1631, English adventurer, explorer, and writer. **4. Joseph.** 1805–44, U.S. religious leader and founder of the Mormon Church.
smith·er·eens (smith′ə rēnz′) *n.,pl. Informal.* little pieces or fragments; bits: *The explosion blew the old shack to smithereens.* [Irish Gaelic *smidirīn,* diminutive of *smiodar* fragment.]
smith·er·y (smith′ər ē) *pl.,* **-er·ies.** *n.* **1.** work or craft of a smith. **2.** smithy (*def. 1*).
smith·y (smith′ē, smith′ē) *pl.,* **smith·ies.** *n.* **1.** workshop of a smith, esp. a blacksmith's shop; forge. **2.** blacksmith. [Old Norse *smithja* forge, from *smithr* smith.]
smit·ten (smit′ən) a past participle of smite.
smock (smok) *n.* **1.** loose outer garment, usually resembling a long shirt, worn to protect clothing. —*v.t.* to ornament with smocking. [Old English *smoc* woman's undergarment.]
smock·ing (smok′ing) *n.* decorative pattern formed by gathering fabric with rows of stitches, often with a honeycomb design.
smog (smog, smôg) *n.* combination of smoke and fog, found esp. over industrial and manufacturing areas. [Blend of SMOKE and FOG.] —**smog′gy,** *adj.*

Smocking

smoke (smōk) *n.* **1.** suspension of solid matter in a gas, esp. the vaporous mixture produced by combustion of organic matter, as wood or coal, and made visible by the carbon particles suspended in it. **2.** anything resembling this, as steam or mist. **3.** something lacking substance, value, or permanence. **4.** act or period of smoking tobacco: *to take time out for a smoke.* **5.** cigarette, cigar, or the like. **6.** pale bluish-gray color. —*v.i.* **1.** to emit or produce smoke: *We could see a chimney smoking in the distance.* **2.** to emit smoke excessively or improperly: *The fireplace is smoking.* **3.a.** to draw the smoke of a cigarette, cigar, or the like into the mouth, and often the lungs, and exhale it. **b.** to smoke habitually. —*v.t.* **1.** to draw in and exhale the smoke of (a cigarette, cigar, or the like). **2.** to cure or preserve, as meat, by exposure to smoke. **3.** to subject or expose to smoke. **4.** to fumigate. **5. to smoke out.** to force into the open with or as with smoke; drive or bring out of hiding or secrecy. [Old English *smoca* visible vapor given off by burning substances.]
smoke·house (smōk′hous′) *n.* building where meat or fish is exposed to smoke to preserve and flavor it.
smoke jumper *also,* **smoke·jump·er** (smōk′jum′pər). firefighter who parachutes into an area near or in a forest fire.
smoke·less (smōk′lis) *adj.* having or giving off little or no smoke.
smokeless powder, propellant that consists chiefly of nitrocellulose and gives off little or no smoke.
smok·er (smō′kər) *n.* **1.** one who or that which smokes, esp. a person who habitually smokes tobacco. **2.** railroad car or compartment where smoking is permitted. Also, **smoking car. 3.** informal social gathering for men.
smoke screen 1. thick cloud of smoke used to hinder or prevent observation, as of a military force or movement. **2.** anything used or intended to conceal or deceive.
smoke·stack (smōk′stak′) *n.* pipe or funnel for the escape of smoke or gases, as on a factory, ship, or locomotive.
smoke tree, any of several shrubs and small trees, genus *Cotinus,* of the cashew family, having flower clusters resembling puffs of smoke.
smoking jacket, man's loose jacket for wear at home.
smok·y (smō′kē) smok·i·er, smok·i·est. *adj.* **1.** giving off smoke, esp. an excessive or undesirable amount of smoke: *a smoky fire, a smoky chimney.* **2.** filled with or containing smoke: *a smoky room, smoky air.* **3.** resembling or like smoke, as in color or taste. **4.** darkened or discolored by smoke. —**smok′i·ly,** *adv.* —**smok′i·ness,** *n.*
Smoky Mountains, Great Smoky Mountains.
smol·der (smōl′dər) *also,* **smoul·der.** *v.i.* **1.** to burn and smoke with little or no flame. **2.** to exist or continue in a suppressed state: *All seemed calm, but resentment smoldered among the people.* **3.** to display repressed emotion: *Her eyes smoldered with rage at his accusation.* —*n.* smoldering fire or the smoke produced by or as by such a fire. [Of uncertain origin.]
Smo·lensk (smo lensk′) *n.* city in the western Soviet Union, on the Dnieper. Pop. (1970 est.), 211,000.
Smol·lett, To·bi·as George (smol′it; tō bī′əs) 1721–71, British novelist, born in Scotland.
smolt (smōlt) *n.* young salmon, bright silver in color, when it first descends to the sea. [Of uncertain origin.]
smooch (smōoch) *Slang. v.i.* to kiss; pet. —*n.* kiss. [Possibly imitative.]

at; āpe; cär; end; mē; it; īce; hot; ōld; fôrk; wood; fōol; oil; out; up; ūse; turn; sing; thin; this; zh in treasure; ə in ago, taken, pencil, lemon, circus.

smooth (smŏŏth) *adj.* **1.a.** having a surface that is free or relatively free from perceptible projections or irregularities: *a smooth road, smooth skin.* **b.** having projections worn down or away by use: *a smooth tire.* **2.** even, easy, or gentle in movement: *a smooth ride, smooth sailing. Despite the bad weather, the pilot made a smooth landing.* **3.** having an even consistency; free from lumps: *a smooth pancake batter.* **4.** free from difficulties or obstacles: *a smooth transition, smooth progress.* **5.** emotionally calm or even; serene: *a smooth disposition.* **6.** able, skillful, or polished: *a smooth dancer, a smooth talker.* **7.** flowing easily: *a smooth style of writing.* **8.** pleasing to the taste; not harsh or biting: *a smooth liquor.* —*v.t.* **1.** to make smooth, even, or level: *to smooth a wrinkled tablecloth.* **2.** to remove or eliminate (often with *away* or *out*): *to smooth out wrinkles. Do you think we can smooth out our differences?* **3.** to free from difficulties or obstacles; make easy: *to smooth the way.* **4.** to calm; soothe: *to smooth someone's temper.* **5.** to make more polished or flowing, as a writing style; refine. **6.** to minimize (often with *over*). —*v.i.* to become smooth. —*adv.* in a smooth manner; smoothly. —*n.* **1.** smooth part or surface. **2.** act of smoothing. [Old English *smōth* not uneven or rough.] —**smooth′er, smooth′ness,** *n.* —**smooth′ly,** *adv.*

smooth·bore (smŏŏth′bôr′) *adj.* (of a firearm) not rifled. —*n.* firearm having a bore that is not rifled.

smooth·en (smŏŏ′thən) *v.t., v.i.* to make or become smooth.

smooth muscle, muscle that forms the walls of such internal organs as the esophagus, stomach, and bladder, controlled by the autonomic nervous system.

smooth·tongued (smŏŏth′tungd′) *adj.* able to speak smoothly, convincingly, or ingratiatingly.

smor·gas·bord (smôr′gəs bôrd′) *also,* **smör·gås·bord.** *n.* **1.** large assortment of food, as hors d'oeuvres, meats, fish, and cheese, usually arranged on a table for each person to serve himself. **2.** meal consisting of such an assortment. **3.** restaurant offering a smorgasbord. [Swedish *smörgåsbord* assortment of hors d'oeuvres served before a meal, from *smörgås* sandwich + *bord* table.]

smote (smōt) past tense and a past participle of **smite.**

smoth·er (smuth′ər) *v.t.* **1.a.** to prevent from breathing in air. **b.** to kill in this way. **2.** to cause (a fire) to go out or die down by covering it so as to cut off oxygen: *He smothered the flames with a blanket.* **3.** to cover thickly: *to smother a steak with onions.* **4.** to conceal or suppress: *to smother a yawn, to smother feelings of resentment.* **5.** to provide (someone) with an excessive or stifling amount of something: *Some parents smother their children with love.* —*v.i.* **1.a.** to be prevented from breathing in air. **b.** to die in this way. **2.** to be concealed or suppressed. —*n.* that which smothers, as a dense cloud of smoke or dust. [Middle English *smorther* dense stifling smoke, going back to Old English *smorian* to suffocate.] —**smoth′er·y,** *adj.*

smoul·der (smōl′dər) smolder.

smudge (smuj) **smudged, smudg·ing.** *v.t.* **1.** to soil or smear; make dirty: *to smudge a white shirt with grimy hands.* **2.** to fill (a planted area) with dense smoke to repel insects or protect against frost. —*v.i.* to be or become smudged or smeared: *A charcoal drawing smudges easily.* —*n.* **1.** mark or stain made by smearing or smudging: *The child's dirty hand left a smudge on the wall.* **2.a.** smoky fire built to repel insects or protect against frost. **b.** dense smoke produced by such a fire. [Of uncertain origin.] —**smudg′i·ly,** *adv.* —**smudg′i·ness,** *n.*

smudge pot, pot or similar vessel for burning a fuel to produce smudge.

smug (smug) **smug·ger, smug·gest.** *adj.* having, showing, or characterized by great or excessive self-satisfaction; overly pleased with oneself; complacent. [Probably from Low German *smuck* neat, trim.] —**smug′ly,** *adv.* —**smug′ness,** *n.*

smug·gle (smug′əl) **-gled, -gling.** *v.t.* **1.** to take into or out of a country secretly and unlawfully, as goods on which the required duties have not been paid, or whose importation or exportation is prohibited by law: *to smuggle heroin into a country.* **2.** to bring, take, or transport secretly or stealthily: *to smuggle a weapon to a prisoner in jail.* —*v.i.* to engage in smuggling. [Low German *smuggeln.*] —**smug′gler,** *n.*

smut (smut) *n.* **1.a.** sooty matter; soot; dirt. **b.** particle of such matter. **2.** spot or stain made by soot or dirt; smudge. **3.a.** obscene material or writing; pornography. **b.** indecent or obscene language. **4.a.** any of several fungus diseases of plants, commonly affecting cereal grains, as corn and wheat, and characterized by the appearance of black, powdery masses or spores. **b.** any of several parasitic fungi that cause such a disease. —*v.t.* **smut·ted, smut·ting.** to mark, stain, or affect with smut. —*v.i.* to become affected by smut. [Possibly of Low German origin.]

smutch (smuch) *v.t.* to make dirty; soil; smudge. —*n.* smudge; stain. [Possibly from Middle High German *smutzen* to smear.]

Smuts, Jan Chris·ti·aan (smuts; yän kris′tē än′) 1870–1950, South African soldier and statesman.

smut·ty (smut′ē) **-ti·er, -ti·est.** *adj.* **1.** soiled with smut; dirty. **2.** obscene, indecent, or pornographic: *smutty language, a smutty film.* **3.** (of plants) affected with smut. —**smut′ti·ly,** *adv.* —**smut′ti·ness,** *n.*

Smyr·na (smur′nə) see **Izmir.**

Sn, tin. [Latin *stannum.*]

snack (snak) *n.* small quantity of food or drink, esp. a light meal eaten between regular meals. —*v.i.* to eat a snack. [Probably from Middle Dutch *snacken* to snap at, bite, snatch.]

snack bar, eating place where snacks are served, esp. at a counter.

snaf·fle (snaf′əl) *n.* slender, jointed horse's bit. Also, **snaf·fle·bit** (snaf′əl bit′). —*v.t.,* **-fled, -fling.** to provide or control with a snaffle. [Probably from Dutch *snavel* beak, horse's muzzle.]

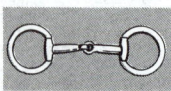

Snaffle

sna·fu (sna fŏŏ′) *Slang. adj.* in a state of great or total confusion or disorder. —*v.t.,* **-fued, -fu·ing.** to throw into confusion or disorder. —*n.* confused or chaotic situation. [Abbreviation of *s(ituation) n(or-mal) a(ll) f(ouled) u(p).*]

snag (snag) *n.* **1.** sharp, jagged, or rough projecting part, as one of the points on barbed wire. **2.** branch, stump, or trunk of a tree embedded in the bottom of a body of water and constituting a hazard to navigation. **3.** tear or hole made by or as by a sharp projection. **4.** unexpected or concealed obstacle or difficulty. —*v.t.,* **snagged, snag·ging. 1.** to catch, tear, or damage on or as on a snag. **2.** to impede; hinder; block. **3.** to clear (a body of water) of snags. **4.** *Informal.* to catch or obtain, esp. by quick action: *The outfielder leaped and snagged the fly ball.* —*v.i.* to be or become caught on or impeded by a snag. [Probably of Scandinavian origin.] —**snag′gy,** *adj.*

snag·gle·tooth (snag′əl tŏŏth′) *pl.,* **-teeth.** *n.* tooth that projects or is broken or irregular. —**snag·gle·toothed** (snag′əl tŏŏtht′, -tŏŏthd′) *adj.*

snail (snāl) *n.* **1.** any of a large group of soft-bodied mollusks, class Gastropoda, found in water and on land and having a spirally coiled shell. **2.** slow-moving or lazy person: *Susan is such a snail that she never gets anywhere on time.* [Old English *snegel* the mollusk.]

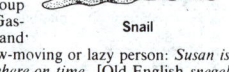

Snail

snake (snāk) *n.* **1.** any of a group of limbless reptiles, suborder Serpentes, having long, scaly bodies. Many snakes have a venomous bite. **2.** treacherous, deceitful, or despicable person. **3.** plumbing tool used to clear clogged drains, consisting of a long, very flexible metal wire or rod. —*v.i.* **snaked, snak·ing. 1.** to move or crawl like a snake. **2.** to follow a winding or curving course. —*v.t.* to drag or pull along the ground, esp. with a chain or rope, as a log. [Old English *snaca* the reptile.]

snake·bird (snāk′burd′) *n.* any of various large, fish-eating birds, family Anhingidae, having a snakelike neck, a small head, and a sharp-pointed bill. Also, **dart·er.**

snake·bite (snāk′bīt′) *n.* **1.** bite of a snake, esp. a venomous snake. **2.** poisoning caused by such a bite.

snake charmer, entertainer who appears to charm or control snakes by means of music and rhythmic body movements.

snake dance 1. ceremonial dance in which snakes are handled or imitated by the dancers, esp. a Hopi Indian dance in which live rattlesnakes are held in the mouths of the participants. **2.** informal parade or procession of persons moving single file in a winding or zigzag course.

snake fence, worm fence.

snake oil, any of various preparations supposedly able to cure a wide variety of ailments, sold esp. by peddlers at a carnival.

Snake River, river in the northwestern United States, the principal tributary of the Columbia River.

snake·root (snāk′rŏŏt′, -root′) *n.* **1.** any of several plants whose roots were once believed to be a cure for snakebite. **2.** root of such a plant.

snake·skin (snāk′skin′) *n.* skin of a snake, or leather made from such a skin.

snak·y (snā′kē) **snak·i·er, snak·i·est.** *adj.* **1.** of or relating to a snake or snakes. **2.** having a form or movement like that of a snake; winding; twisting. **3.** treacherous; deceitful. **4.** infested with snakes: *a snaky swamp.* —**snak′i·ly,** *adv.* —**snak′i·ness,** *n.*

snap (snap) **snapped, snap·ping.** *v.i.* **1.** to make or emit a sudden, sharp sound: *The dry wood snapped and crackled as it burned.* **2.** to break or be released suddenly, usually with a sharp sound: *The twig snapped when I stepped on it.* **3.** to give way suddenly, esp. under mental strain or tension: *This final misfortune caused the man's mind to snap.* **4.** to close or move into place with a swift movement and often with a sharp sound: *The lid snapped shut.* **5.** to attempt to bite or seize something by closing the jaws with a sudden, swift motion (often with

at): *The fish snapped at the bait.* **6.** to seize or snatch suddenly or eagerly (often with *at*): *to snap at an opportunity.* **7.** to speak harshly, abruptly, or angrily (often with *at*). **8.** to move or act quickly and smartly: *to snap to attention.* **9. to snap out of.** *Informal.* to recover or change from a specified state: *to snap out of a hypnotic trance.* —*v.t.* **1.** to seize or snatch with or as with a swift biting motion (often with *up*): *The puppy snapped the cookie out of the child's hand.* **2.** to break or sever suddenly, usually with a sharp sound: *The enormous fish snapped the line.* **3.** to utter harshly, abruptly, or angrily: *The witness snapped a furious reply to the attorney's question.* **4.** to cause to make or emit a sudden, sharp sound: *to snap one's fingers.* **5.** to close, fasten, or move into place, often with a sharp sound: *to snap a padlock close.* **6.a.** to take (a photograph): *The reporter snapped two pictures without anyone knowing it.* **b.** to take a snapshot of (someone or something): *Father snapped the passing scenery as we drove along.* **7.** to move quickly, suddenly, or smartly. **8.** *Football.* to put (the ball) into play by sending it back from the line of scrimmage to a member of the backfield: *The center snapped the ball to the quarterback.* **9. to snap (someone) out of.** *Informal.* to cause to recover or change from a specified state: *The loud noise snapped Eve out of her daydream.* —*n.* **1.** sharp sound made by or as by snapping or breaking. **2.** act of snapping or breaking. **3.** any of several fastening devices that operate with a snapping or clicking sound. **4.** sudden attempt to seize or snatch with or as with a swift biting motion. **5.** brief spell or period, esp. of cold weather. **6.** thin, crisp cookie. **7.** snapshot. **8.** *Informal.* something of little or no difficulty; task requiring little effort: *That spelling test was a snap.* **9.** *Informal.* vigor; energy; liveliness: *Put some snap in your step!* **10.** *Football.* act of snapping the ball. —*adj.* **1.** made or done hastily or without due deliberation: *a snap decision.* **2.** fastening with a snap. **3.** *Informal.* of little or no difficulty; requiring little work or effort: *Astronomy is no snap course.* [Middle Dutch *snappen* to seize, speak quickly.]

snap·back (snap′bak′) *n.* snap (def. 10).

snap bean, stringbean.

snap·dra·gon (snap′drag′ən) *n.* **1.** sac-shaped flower of any of a group of erect or climbing plants, genus *Antirrhinum,* esp. *A. majus,* the common snapdragon, usually red, purple, or white, widely cultivated as a garden flower. **2.** plant bearing these flowers. [Because the flower is thought to resemble a dragon's mouth.]

Red snapper

snap·per (snap′ər) *n.* **1.** one who or that which snaps. **2.** snapping turtle. **3.** any of a large group of brightly colored food and game fish, family Lutjanidae, found in warm seas, esp. the **red snapper,** *Lutjanus blackfordi.*

snapping beetle, click beetle.

snapping turtle, any of several freshwater turtles, family Chelydridae, found in North and Central America, having powerful jaws.

snap·pish (snap′ish) *adj.* **1.** abrupt and sharp in speech or manner; irritable. **2.** inclined to snap or bite, as a dog. —**snap′pish·ly,** *adv.* —**snap′pish·ness,** *n.*

Snapping turtle

snap·py (snap′ē) -pi·er, -pi·est. *adj.* **1.** *Informal.* lively; brisk: *to walk at a snappy pace.* **2.** *Informal.* smart in appearance; stylish: *a snappy dresser.* **3.** *Informal.* briskly cool or chilly: *a snappy breeze.* **4.** snappish. —**snap′pi·ly,** *adv.* —**snap′pi·ness,** *n.*

snap·shot (snap′shot′) *n.* informal photograph taken with a small hand-held camera.

snare[1] (snâr) *n.* **1.** trap for catching small animals, usually consisting of a noose set up to close suddenly when triggered. **2.** anything by which one is entangled or entrapped. —*v.t.,* **snared, snar·ing. 1.** to catch with a snare or similar device. **2.** to catch, acquire, or accomplish, esp. by means of skill, cleverness, or trickery: *Detectives snared the jewel thief.* [Old English *snearu* noose, from Old Norse *snara.*]

snare[2] (snâr) *n.* one of the wires or strings of gut or rawhide stretched across the bottom of a snare drum. [Probably from Middle Low German *snāre* cord, string.]

snare drum, small double-headed drum

Snare drum

having wires or strings of gut or rawhide stretched across the lower head which produce a rattling sound when the drum is struck.

snarl[1] (snärl) *v.i.* **1.** to growl viciously or angrily while baring the teeth, as a dog or wolf. **2.** to speak angrily or harshly. —*v.t.* to utter or express with a snarl. —*n.* **1.** vicious or angry growl. **2.** angry or harsh utterance. [Modification of obsolete *snar* to growl, from Middle Low German *snarren* to rattle.] —**snarl′er,** *n.* —**snarl′ing·ly,** *adv.*

snarl[2] (snärl) *n.* **1.** tangled or knotted mass, as of hair. **2.** confused, tangled, or chaotic state or situation: *The bankrupt company's records were in a complete snarl.* —*v.t.* **1.** to make tangled or knotted: *The wind and rain had snarled Lisa's hair.* **2.** to make confused, disordered, or chaotic: *The fierce storm snarled traffic for hours.* —*v.i.* to become snarled: *Traffic snarled when an accident blocked one lane of the highway.* [From SNARL[1].]

snarl·y[1] (snär′lē) snarl·i·er, snarl·i·est. *adj.* inclined to snarl; irritable; cross. [SNARL[1] + -Y[1].]

snarl·y[2] (snär′lē) snarl·i·er, snarl·i·est. *adj.* full of snarls or tangles. [SNARL[2] + -Y[1].]

snatch (snach) *v.t.* **1.** to seize or grasp suddenly, quickly, or eagerly. **2.** to take, remove, or get suddenly or hastily. **3.** *Slang.* to kidnap. —*v.i.* **1.** to attempt to seize or grasp something suddenly or quickly (with *at*). **2.** to accept or take advantage of something eagerly (with *at*): *to snatch at an opportunity.* —*n.* **1.** act of snatching. **2.** brief period of time: *to sleep in snatches.* **3.** small amount, part, or portion; bit: *The spy overheard snatches of the general's conversation.* **4.** *Slang.* a kidnaping. [Of uncertain origin.] —**snatch′er,** *n.*

snatch·y (snach′ē) *adj.* done in snatches; not continuous; irregular.

snath (snath) *also,* **snathe** (snāth). *n.* long handle of a scythe. [Form of dialectal English *snead,* from Old English *snǣd.*]

snaz·zy (snaz′ē) -zi·er, -zi·est. *adj. Slang.* attractive or stylish, esp. in a showy way; smart; flashy. [Possibly a blend of SN(APPY) and (J)AZZY.]

sneak (snēk) *v.i.* **1.** to move or go in a stealthy or furtive manner to avoid being detected: *to sneak into a theater without paying.* **2.** to behave in a furtive, cowardly, or servile manner. —*v.t.* to move, take, get, or put in a stealthy or secret manner: *The shoplifter sneaked a watch into her purse.* —*n.* **1.** one who sneaks, esp. a despicably underhanded or cowardly person. **2.** act of sneaking. **3.** *Informal.* sneaker (def. 1). —*adj.* done, planned, or acting in a stealthy or secret manner: *a sneak attack.* [Possibly form of Middle English *sniken* to creep, crawl, from Old English *snican.*]

sneak·er (snē′kər) *n.* **1.** canvas shoe with a soft rubber sole, worn chiefly for sports. **2.** one who sneaks; sneak.

sneak·ing (snē′king) *adj.* **1.** furtive; stealthy; underhanded. **2.a.** not admitted or made known; secret. **b.** nagging; persistent: *I have a sneaking suspicion that Ted stole the letter from my desk.* —**sneak′ing·ly,** *adv.*

sneak preview, advance, single showing of a motion picture before its release to the general public, as to observe audience reaction.

sneak thief, one who steals without employing violent or forceful means, as by sneaking into buildings through unlocked doors or windows rather than breaking into them.

sneak·y (snē′kē) sneak·i·er, sneak·i·est. *adj.* **1.** like or having the characteristics of a sneak: *a politician too sneaky to be trusted.* **2.** characteristic of a sneak: *That was a pretty sneaky trick you pulled!* —**sneak′i·ly,** *adv.* —**sneak′i·ness,** *n.*

sneer (snēr) *n.* **1.** facial expression showing contempt or derision, usually characterized by a slight curling of the upper lip. **2.** contemptuous, derisive, or disparaging speech or writing. —*v.i.* **1.** to have or show a sneer. **2.** to speak or write in a contemptuous, derisive, or disparaging manner. —*v.t.* to utter or express with a sneer or in a sneering manner. [Possibly of Low German origin.] —**sneer′er,** *n.* —**sneer′ing·ly,** *adv.* —**Syn.** *v.i.* **2.** see jeer.

sneeze (snēz) sneezed, sneez·ing. *v.i.* **1.** to expel air suddenly and violently through the nose and mouth by an involuntary spasm, as a result of irritation of the nasal mucous membrane. **2. to sneeze at.** *Informal.* to show insufficient regard, consideration, or respect for. ▲ used chiefly in the phrase *not to be sneezed at: Such a large sum of money is not to be sneezed at.* —*n.* act or instance of sneezing. [Modification of Middle English *fnesen* to sneeze, from Old English *fnēosan.*] —**sneez′er,** *n.* —**sneez′y,** *adj.*

sneeze·weed (snēz′wēd′) *n.* any of several coarse North American plants, genus *Helenium,* esp. the **common sneezeweed,** *H. autumnale,* having toothed leaves and showy yellow flowers. [Because its odor is thought to cause sneezing.]

snell (snel) *n.* short piece of material, as nylon or gut, by which a fishhook is fastened to a longer line. [Of uncertain origin.]

snick (snik) *v.t.* **1.** to cut; to cut slightly. —*n.* small or slight cut; nick. [From obsolete *snick and snee* to thrust and cut (with knives), modification of *stick and snee,* from Dutch *steken en snijen.*]

snick·er (snik′ər) *n.* sly or partly suppressed laugh, usually expressing

derision or disrespect. —*v.i.* to laugh in such a manner. Also, **snig′ger.** [Imitative.]

snide (snīd) **snid·er, snid·est.** *adj.* malicious or disparaging, esp. in a sly or sarcastic way: *a snide remark.* [Of uncertain origin.]

sniff (snif) *v.i.* **1.** to inhale through the nose in short, quick, audible breaths, as in smelling something. **2.** to express disdain or contempt by or as by sniffing (often with *at*). —*v.t.* **1.** to inhale (something) through the nose. **2.** to smell by sniffing. **3.** to detect or discover by or as if by sniffing (often with *out*): *to sniff out danger.* —*n.* **1.** act or sound of sniffing. **2.** something sniffed; scent; smell. [Imitative.]

snif·fle (snif′əl) **-fled, -fling.** *v.i.* to breathe noisily through the nose, as when crying, or when the nose is congested; sniff repeatedly. —*n.* **1.** act or sound of sniffling. **2. the sniffles,** condition accompanied by sniffling, as a head cold. Also *(def. 2.),* **the snuffles.** [SNIFF + -LE.]

sniff·y (snif′ē) **sniff·i·er, sniff·i·est.** *adj. Informal.* inclined to sniff, as in contempt; disdainful.

snift·er (snif′tər) *n.* pear-shaped glass that narrows at the top to concentrate the aroma of its contents, as of brandy.

snig·ger (snig′ər) *n., v.i.* snicker.

snip (snip) **snipped, snip·ping.** *v.t.* **1.** to cut or clip with scissors or shears in a short, quick stroke or strokes. **2.** to remove (something) by or as by cutting in this way (often with *off*). —*v.i.* to cut or clip with short, quick strokes. —*n.* **1.** act or sound of snipping. **2.** small cut made by snipping. **3.** small piece that is snipped off. **4.** any small amount, piece, or portion; bit. **5.** *Informal.* **a.** young, small, or insignificant person. **b.** rude or impertinent person. [Dutch *snippen* to clip, snap.]

snipe (snīp) *pl.,* **snipes** or **snipe.** *n.* any of several long-billed wading birds, family Scolopacidae, native to marshes and bogs in most parts of the world, usually having brownish plumage mottled with black and white. Length: 10–16 inches. —*v.i.,* **sniped, snip·ing.** **1.** to

Snipe

shoot at a person or persons from a concealed place. **2.** to attack with criticism, esp. in a snide manner (often with *at*). **3.** to hunt or shoot snipe. [Probably of Scandinavian origin.]

snip·er (snī′pər) *n.* one who shoots at a person or persons from a concealed place.

snip·pet (snip′it) *n.* small piece or part; bit; scrap.

snip·py (snip′ē) **-pi·er, -pi·est.** *adj.* **1.** *Informal.* curt or sharp, esp. in an impertinent or insolent way. **2.** composed of bits or scraps; fragmentary. Also, **snip·pet·y** (snip′i tē). —**snip′pi·ness,** *n.*

snit (snit) *n. Informal.* state of irritation, anger, or agitation. ▲ used chiefly in the phrase *in a snit.* [Of uncertain origin.]

snitch (snich) *Slang. v.i.* **1.** to be an informer; tattle (often with *on*). —*v.t.* to steal; swipe; pilfer. —*n. also,* **snitch′er.** one who snitches; informer. [Of uncertain origin.]

sniv·el (sniv′əl) **-eled, -el·ing;** *also, British,* **-elled, -el·ling.** *v.i.* **1.** to cry with sniffling. **2.** to have mucus running from the nose. **3.** to draw mucus up through the nose noisily; sniffle. **4.** to complain in a whining or tearful manner. —*n.* **1.** act of sniveling. **2.** nasal mucus. [Possibly from an unrecorded Old English word.] —**sniv′el·er;** *also, British,* **sniv′el·ler,** *n.*

snob (snob) *n.* **1.** one who places great value on wealth and social position, and looks with contempt on those he considers inferior to him in social status. **2.** one who has an offensively superior attitude or manner, as for some assumed personal excellence: *an intellectual snob.* [Of uncertain origin.]

snob·ber·y (snob′ər ē) *pl.,* **-ber·ies.** *n.* snobbish character or conduct.

snob·bish (snob′ish) *adj.* of, relating to, or characteristic of a snob. —**snob′bish·ly,** *adv.* —**snob′bish·ness,** *n.*

snood (snōod) *n.* **1.** small net or netlike bag, sometimes forming part of a hat, worn by women to keep the hair in place. **2.** band or ribbon for a woman's hair; fillet. —*v.t.* to bind or secure (the hair) with a snood. [Old English *snōd* band for the hair.]

snook (snook, snŏok) *pl.,* **snooks** or **snook.** *n.* any of a group of food and game fish, family Centropomidae, that inhabits warm waters of the Atlantic and Pacific oceans, esp. the common snook, *Centropomus undecimalis,* of the southern Atlantic. [Dutch *snoek* pike.]

snook·er (snook′ər) *n.* variety of pool in which fifteen red balls and six other balls are used. [Of uncertain origin.]

snoop (snōop) *Informal. v.i.* to look or go about in a sneaking, sly way; prowl or pry: *The thief was snooping around the warehouse.* —*n. also,* **snoop′er.** one who snoops. [Dutch *snoepen* to eat secretly.]

snoop·y (snōo′pē) **snoop·i·er, snoop·i·est.** *adj. Informal.* given or inclined to snooping.

snoot (snōot) *n. Slang.* **1.** nose. **2.** face. [Form of SNOUT.]

snoot·y (snōo′tē) **snoot·i·er, snoot·i·est.** *adj. Informal.* snobbish. —**snoot′i·ly,** *adv.* —**snoot′i·ness,** *n.*

snooze (snōoz) **snoozed, snooz·ing.** *Informal. v.i.* to take a short nap; doze. —*n.* nap; doze.

snore (snôr) **snored, snor·ing.** *v.i.* to make harsh or noisy sounds in sleep by breathing through the open mouth or through the mouth and nose. —*n.* act or noise of snoring. [Possibly imitative.] —**snor′er,** *n.*

snor·kel (snôr′kəl) *n.* **1.** device in a submarine that permits it to remain submerged for long periods, consisting of retractable tubes that extend above the surface of the water to take in fresh air and discharge foul air and exhaust gases. **2.** J-shaped tube permitting a person to breathe while swimming on or just below the surface with the face held underwater. —*v.i.* to swim using a snorkel. [German *Schnorchel* snorkel of a submarine, air inlet.]

snort (snôrt) *v.i.* **1.** to force air violently and noisily through the nostrils. **2.** to make any similar sound. **3.** to express contempt, indignation, or anger by snorting. **4.** *Informal.* to laugh loudly or boisterously. —*v.t.* **1.** to utter or express with a snort. **2.** to expel or discharge by or as by a snort: *The elephant snorted water over his back.* —*n.* **1.** act or sound of snorting. **2.** *Slang.* small drink of alcoholic liquor taken quickly. [Possibly imitative.] —**snort′er,** *n.*

snout (snout) *n.* **1.** part of an animal's head that projects forward, including the nose, mouth, and jaws, as in a pig. **2.** similar extension of the anterior part of the head in certain insects, as weevils. **3.** something similar to an animal's snout in shape or use. **4.** *Informal.* the human nose, esp. when large. [Probably of Low German origin.]

snout beetle, weevil *(def. 1).*

snow (snō) *n.* **1.** solid precipitation in the form of soft, white, crystalline flakes of widely varying shape, formed by the freezing of water vapor in the atmosphere. **2.** fall of snow; snowstorm. **3.** accumulation or expanse of snow. **4.** something that resembles snow, as in color. **5.** small white spots on a television screen as a result of weak reception. —*v.i.* to fall as snow. ▲ used with *it: It snowed all night.* —*v.t.* **1.** to cause to fall or scatter as or like snow. **2.** to cover, obstruct, or shut in with or as with snow (often with *in* or *under*). ▲ usually used in the passive: *The hunters were snowed in at the lodge for three days. The post office was snowed under with Christmas mail.* **3.** *Slang.* to overpower with insincere flattery, esp. in order to deceive. [Old English *snāw* the frozen vapor of the atmosphere that falls in flakes, snowstorm.]

snow·ball (snō′bôl′) *n.* **1.** roundish mass of snow pressed or rolled together, as for throwing. **2.** any of several shrubs, genus *Viburnum,* having large clusters of white, sterile flowers resembling snowballs. —*v.t.* to throw snowballs at. —*v.i.* to grow rapidly in importance, size, or number as a snowball rolling over snow: *That small business has snowballed into a huge industry.*

snow·bank (snō′bangk′) *n.* large mound or drift of snow.

snow·ber·ry (snō′ber′ē) *pl.,* **-ries.** *n.* small, bushy North American shrub, *Symphoricarpos albus,* of the honeysuckle family, bearing clusters of pink flowers and small white berries. Also, **wax′ber′ry.**

snow·bird (snō′burd′) *n.* **1.** grayish North American junco, *Junco hyemalis,* which breeds in cold northern regions and winters throughout the United States, having white plumage on its underside. Length: 6 inches. **2.** snow bunting.

snow·blind (snō′blīnd′) *adj.* affected with snow blindness.

snow blindness, temporary or partial blindness caused by the reflection of ultraviolet rays from snow.

snow·bound (snō′bound′) *adj.* shut in or confined to a place by a heavy fall of snow.

snow bunting, small finch, *Plectrophenax nivalis,* of cold northern regions, having predominantly white plumage with brown or black patches. Length: 6 inches.

snow·cap (snō′kap′) *n.* cap or crest of snow, as on a mountain peak. —**snow′-capped′,** *adj.*

snow·drift (snō′drift′) *n.* heap or mass of snow piled up by the wind.

snow·drop (snō′drop′) *n.* any of a small group of Eurasian plants, genus *Galanthus,* that bloom in the early spring, esp. a common garden species, *G. nivalis,* bearing a single white drooping flower.

snow·fall (snō′fôl′) *n.* **1.** fall of snow. **2.** amount of snow that falls during a given period or in a particular area.

snow·flake (snō′flāk′) *n.* one of the small, feathery masses or crystals in which snow falls.

snow leopard, large cat, *Panthera uncia,* of the mountains of Central Asia, having gray or buff fur marked with black broken rings. Length: 6½ feet including tail. Also, **ounce.**

Snow leopard

snow line, line on a mountain slope above which it is always covered with snow.

snow·man (snō′man′) *pl.,* **-men.** *n.* figure roughly resembling that of a person, made by shaping a mass of snow.
snow·mo·bile (snō′mō bēl′) *n.* vehicle adapted for travel on snow, usually equipped with runners or skis.
snow·plow (snō′plou′) *n.* **1.** any of various devices or vehicles for clearing away snow, as from a road or sidewalk. **2.** *Skiing.* maneuver used for stopping or slowing down in which the heels of both skis are forced outward.
snow·shed (snō′shed′) *n.* long shed or shelter for protection against snow, as over a railroad track on a mountain slope.
snow·shoe (snō′shōō′) *n.* light, racket-shaped wooden frame strung with a webbing of rawhide, attached to the foot to enable a person to walk over deep snow without sinking in. —*v.i.,* **-shoed, -shoe·ing.** to walk or travel by means of snowshoes. —**snow′-sho′er,** *n.*

Snowshoe

snowshoe rabbit, North American hare, *Lepus americanus,* having white fur in winter and brown fur in summer and large hind feet covered with long hairs that enable it to travel over deep snow. Also, **snowshoe hare.**
snow·slide (snō′slīd′) *n.* avalanche of snow.
snow·storm (snō′stôrm′) *n.* heavy fall of snow accompanied by strong winds.
snow·suit (snō′sōōt′) *n.* child's one-piece or two-piece heavily lined outer garment for cold weather.
snow tire, tire with a deeply grooved tread designed to provide added traction on snow or ice.
snow train, special train that carries passengers to and from a place for winter sports, esp. skiing.
snow-white (snō′hwīt′, -wīt′) *adj.* white as snow.
snow·y (snō′ē) **snow·i·er, snow·i·est.** *adj.* **1.** abounding in snow; covered with snow: *snowy peaks.* **2.** characterized by the presence of snow: *snowy weather.* **3.** resembling snow; white or unblemished. —**snow′i·ly,** *adv.* —**snow′i·ness,** *n.*
snub (snub) **snubbed, snub·bing.** *v.t.* **1.** to treat with contempt and deliberate neglect. **2.** to check or rebuke in a sharp or sarcastic manner. **3.** to check or stop suddenly by means of a rope or line, as a boat or unbroken horse. **4.** to stop or check (a rope or cable that is running out) suddenly. —*n.* **1.** scornful treatment; deliberate slight. **2.** sharp or sarcastic rebuke. **3.** sudden check or stop, as of a rope or cable that is running out. —*adj.* (of the nose) short and slightly turned up. [Old Norse *snubba* to rebuke.] —**snub′ber,** *n.*
snub·by (snub′ē) **-bi·er, -bi·est.** *adj.* somewhat snub.
snub-nosed (snub′nōzed′) *adj.* having a snub nose.
snuff[1] (snuf) *v.t.* **1.** to inhale through the nose. **2.** to detect or perceive by smelling. **3.** (of an animal) to examine by smelling; sniff at. —*v.i.* **1.** to sniff, esp. curiously. **2.** to inhale pulverized tobacco into the nose. —*n.* **1.** preparation of pulverized tobacco taken into the nose by inhalation. **2. up to snuff.** *Informal.* in good or usual order or conditon. ▲ usually used negatively: *His work has not been up to snuff lately.* [Middle Dutch *snuffen* to snuffle, sniff.]
snuff[2] (snuf) *v.t.* **1.** to cut or pinch off the charred end of (a candlewick). **2.** to put out or extinguish (often with *out*): *to snuff out a candle.* **3.** to put an end to suddenly and completely (often with *out*): *The defeat snuffed out the rebels' hope of overthrowing the government.* —*n.* charred part of a candlewick. [Of uncertain origin.]
snuff·box (snuf′boks′) *n.* box for holding snuff, esp. one small enough to be carried in the pocket.
snuff·ers (snuf′ərz) *n.,pl.* instrument resembling scissors, used for removing the burnt wick or putting out the flame of a candle.
snuf·fle (snuf′əl) **-fled, -fling.** *v.i.* **1.** to breathe noisily because of partly obstructed nasal passages. **2.** to snuff or smell. **3.** to speak through the nose; talk in a nasal tone. —*v.t.* to utter or say in a nasal tone. —*n.* **1.** act of snuffling or the sound made by it. **2.** nasal tone of voice. **3. the snuffles.** the sniffles. [Dutch *snuffelen* to smell out.] —**snuf′fler,** *n.*
snuff·y (snuf′ē) **snuff·i·er, snuff·i·est.** *adj.* **1.** resembling snuff, as in color or smell. **2.** soiled with or smelling of snuff.
snug (snug) **snug·ger, snug·gest.** *adj.* **1.** comfortable and warm; cozy. **2.** fitting closely or tightly, as a garment. **3.** enabling one to live comfortably: *a snug income.* **4.** out of sight; hidden; concealed. **5.** (of a ship or its parts). **a.** neat; trim; compact. **b.** seaworthy. —*v.t.,* **snugged, snug·ging.** to make snug. —*v.i.* to lie or nestle closely; snuggle. —*adv.* in a snug manner. [Probably of Scandinavian origin.] —**snug′ly,** *adv.* —**snug′ness,** *n.*
snug·ger·y (snug′ər ē) *pl.,* **-ger·ies.** *n.* cozy or comfortable place, as a room.
snug·gle (snug′əl) **-gled, -gling.** *v.i.* to lie closely and comfortably, as for warmth or to show affection; cuddle (often with *up*

or *together*). —*v.t.* to draw close, as for warmth or comfort, or to show affection. [SNUG + -LE:]
so[1] (sō) *adv.* **1.** in the way or manner described, shown, or suggested; in such manner: *Write the words so.* **2.** in this or that way; as follows; thus: *So the story goes.* **3.** of or in that condition, state, or description: *The lock was worn and had been so for three months.* **4.** to this or that extent or degree: *He wasn't so brave.* **5.** to such an extent or degree; to the same degree: *He wasn't so rich as his brother.* **6.** very; extremely: *I am so tired.* **7.** very much: *He loved her so.* **8.** for this or that reason; accordingly; therefore: *Tom was tired, so he went home early.* **9.** too; also: *He wanted to play football; so did his younger brother.* **10.** *Informal.* such being the case; as it seems: *So, you don't like the cake I baked.* —*adj.* in accordance with fact; true: *Is it so you're thinking of leaving the club?* —*conj.* **1.** with the reason or purpose that; in order that: *Please turn out the light so I can sleep.* **2.** with the result that. —*pron.* **1.** that which is as mentioned before; the same: *He's a lazy boy and will always be so.* **2. or so.** more or less: *a month or so.* —*interj.* used to express surprise, awareness, or displeasure. [Old English *swā* in such a manner, to that extent, thus.]
so[2] (sō) *n.* sol[1]. [See GAMUT.]
So. 1. South. **2.** Southern.
soak (sōk) *v.t.* **1.** to make very wet; wet thoroughly; drench: *The rain soaked him to the skin.* **2.** to take in by or as by absorption; absorb (with *in* or *up*): *The ground soaked up the heavy rainfall.* **3.** to cause (something) to remain immersed in water or another liquid, as for cleansing: *He soaked his sprained ankle to reduce the swelling.* **4.** *Informal.* to make pay too heavily; overcharge: *a new tax that soaks the middle class.* —*v.i.* **1.** to become thoroughly wet. **2.** to remain immersed in a liquid. **3.** to penetrate into or through something, as a liquid does. **4.** to become absorbed in the mind, as an idea. —*n.* **1.** act of soaking; being soaked. **2.** *Slang.* heavy drinker; drunkard. [Old English *socian* to remain in liquid until saturated.] —**soak′er,** *n.*
Syn. *v.t.* **2. Soak, steep**[2]**, saturate** mean to keep in liquid until some process is complete. **Soak** is the general term: *Soak the shirt in water until the stain comes out.* **Steep** implies a process in with something is released into the liquid: *To make tea, steep the tea leaves in boiling water.* **Saturate** implies a process in which something is absorbed from the liquid: *Let the dye saturate the blouse before taking it out.*
soak·age (sō′kij) *n.* **1.** act of soaking; being soaked. **2.** amount of liquid that soaks into or seeps out of something.
so-and-so (sō′an sō′) *pl.,* **-sos.** *n.* **1.** someone or something not named or specified. **2.** *Informal.* offensive or disagreeable person. ▲ used as a euphemism for more offensive terms.
soap (sōp) *n.* **1.** any of various substances used for washing and cleansing, usually consisting of a mixture of the sodium or potassium salts of various fats, and made by treating such a fat with alkali. **2.** any metallic salt of a fatty acid. **3. no soap.** *Slang.* **a.** not acceptable or permissible: *We asked him for help, but he told us no soap.* **b.** having no effect; unsuccessful; futile. —*v.t.* to rub, cover, or treat with soap. [Old English *sāpe* substance used for washing and cleansing.]
soap·bark (sōp′bärk′) *n.* **1.** Chilean tree, *Quillaja saponaria,* having shiny leaves and white flowers. **2.** bark of this tree, used as a substitute for soap. **3.** any of several other trees or shrubs having similar bark.
soap·ber·ry (sōp′ber′ē) *pl.,* **-ries.** *n.* **1.** pulpy fruit of any of various chiefly tropical trees, genus *Sapindus,* used as a substitute for soap. **2.** any of these trees.
soap·box (sōp′boks′) *n.* **1.** container in which soap is packed, as a box or crate. **2.** empty box or other improvised platform for making an informal, impromptu, or unofficial speech, esp. on a public street. —*adj.* speaking or spoken in an impassioned, eccentric, or demagogic manner: *soapbox oratory.*
soapbox derby, race in which homemade children's racing cars without power coast down a hill.
soap bubble 1. bubble formed from soapy water. **2.** anything unsubstantial or impermanent.
soap opera, television or such serial drama, usually presented in the daytime. [Because many such programs were originally sponsored by soap manufacturers.]
soap plant, plant having a part which may be used as a substitute for soap, esp. *Chlorogalum pomeridianum,* a California herb having small white flowers and a bulb formerly used as soap.
soap·stone (sōp′stōn′) *n.* soft stone having a soapy feel, used for hearths, laboratory tabletops, and carvings. Also, **ste′a·tite′.**
soap·suds (sōp′sudz′) *n.,pl.* suds from soapy water.
soap·wort (sōp′wurt′) *n.* herb, *Saponaria officinalis,* native to Europe and having clusters of pink or white flowers and leaves that yield a soapy substance.
soap·y (sō′pē) **soap·i·er, soap·i·est.** *adj.* **1.** containing or combined with soap: *soapy water.* **2.** covered with soap: *soapy dishes.* **3.a.** resembling soap; smooth or greasy. **b.** *Informal.* unctuous; suave; oily: *soapy manners.* —**soap′i·ly,** *adv.* —**soap′i·ness,** *n.*

at; āpe; cär; end; mē; it; īce; hot; ōld; fôrk; wood; fōōl; oil; out; up; ūse; turn; sing; thin; this; zh in treasure; ə in ago, taken, pencil, lemon, circus.

soar (sôr) *v.i.* **1.** to fly upward or rise high into the air. **2.** (of a bird) to fly or glide high in the air without visibly moving the wings. **3.** (of an aircraft) to glide along without losing altitude. **4.** to rise to a great height, as a mountain or building. **5.a.** to go or move upward in position or status; rise sharply: *Prices soared because of the change in economic policy.* **b.** to rise or aspire to a more lofty or exalted level: *Her imagination soared above the boredom of her daily life.* —*n.* **1.** act of soaring. **2.** height attained in soaring. [Middle French *essorer* to throw up in the air, fly up, going back to Latin *ex* out of + *aura* breeze (from Greek *aura*).] —**soar′er,** *n.* —**Syn.** *v.i.* **1.** see **fly²**.

sob (sob) **sobbed, sob·bing.** *v.i.* **1.** to cry audibly while catching the breath in short, irregular gasps. **2.** to make a sound resembling this. —*v.t.* **1.** to utter with a sob or sobs (often with *out*): *She sobbed out the story of the tragic accident.* **2.** to put, bring, or send by sobbing: *to sob oneself to sleep.* —*n.* **1.** act or sound of sobbing. **2.** sound resembling a sob: *the sob of the wind on a cold, wintry night.* [Probably imitative.]

so·ber (sō′bər) *adj.* **1.** not drunk. **2.** habitually moderate or temperate, esp. in the use of alcoholic drink. **3.** grave or sedate in character or nature; serious; solemn. **4.** not bold or gaudy, as colors or clothes; somber; subdued. **5.** showing no exaggeration or excess: *sober facts.* **6.** rational; sensible: *sober judgment.* —*v.t., v.i.* to make or become sober (often with *up*). [Old French *sobre* temperate, moderate, from Latin *sōbrius* not drunk, temperate.] —**so′ber·ly,** *adv.* —**so′ber·ness,** *n.*

so·bri·e·ty (sə brī′ə tē) *pl.,* **-ties.** *n.* **1.** state or quality of being sober. **2.** temperance or moderation, esp. in the use of alcoholic drink. **3.** seriousness; gravity; solemnity. [Latin *sōbrietās* temperance, moderation.]

so·bri·quet (sō′brə kā′) *also,* **sou·bri·quet.** *n.* nickname. [French *sobriquet;* of uncertain origin.]

sob sister, journalist, esp. a woman, who writes overly sentimental stories about human misfortune.

sob story, overly sentimental story of personal hardship or misfortune told to gain sympathy.

soc., society.

so-called (sō′kôld′) *adj.* called thus, esp. incorrectly or improperly: *a so-called expert.*

soc·cer (sok′ər) *n.* game in which two teams of eleven players each attempt to move a round ball into a goal by kicking it or by striking it with any part of the body except the hands and arms. Also, **associa·tion football.** [Abbreviation of *(as)soc(ciation football)* + -ER¹.]

so·cia·bil·i·ty (sō′shə bil′ə tē) *pl.,* **-ties.** *n.* quality, state, or instance of being sociable.

so·cia·ble (sō′shə bəl) *adj.* **1.** liking to associate with others; fond of company; friendly; affable. **2.** characterized by or giving opportunity for companionship and friendly conversation: *a sociable atmosphere.* —*n.* social. [Latin *sociābilis* easily united, going back to *socius* companion, ally.] —**so′cia·bly,** *adv.*

Syn. *adj.* **1. Sociable, social** mean one who is at ease associating with others. **Sociable** implies one whose genuine and sincere interest in others makes them feel comfortable: *Such a sociable bachelor is a wonderful asset at any gathering.* **Social** implies one who meets or brings together many different people to maintain one's social position or to fulfill social obligations and stresses a reliance on etiquette and social graces in making others comfortable: *Mrs. Bennet is a social person who usually entertains once a week.*

so·cial (sō′shəl) *adj.* **1.** pertaining to human beings as a group; having to do with society: *The family is a social unit.* **2.** relating to the life, welfare, and relations of human beings: *social behavior, a country plagued by social unrest.* **3.** relating to or based on rank or status within a particular society: *one's social set.* **4.** of or relating to fashionable or polite society: *Her debut was the biggest social event of the season.* **5.** relating to or characterized by companionship or friendly relations: *a social engagement.* **6.** enjoying the company of others; friendly; sociable. **7.** living or inclined to live in company with others, rather than in isolation. **8.a.** (of animals) habitually living in organized communities, as ants or bees. **b.** (of plants) growing in clumps or patches. —*n.* informal social gathering, as for members of a church. [Latin *sociālis* allied, companionable, from *socius* companion, ally.] —**Syn.** *adj.* **6.** see **sociable.**

social climber, one who attempts to gain acceptance in fashionable society.

social contract, theory that society came into being from the voluntary association of individuals for mutual protection and that government therefore rests on the consent of the governed.

social democracy, principles of a social democrat.

social democrat, member of a political party advocating a gradual, peaceful, and democratic change from capitalism to socialism.

social democratic, relating to a social democrat or social democracy.

social disease, venereal disease.

so·cial·ism (sō′shə liz′əm) *n.* **1.** theory or system of social organization based on collective or government ownership and control of the basic means of production, distribution, and exchange. **2.** policies or practices of those who advocate such a system. **3.** in Marxist theory, the stage of society following capitalism in the transition to communism.

so·cial·ist (sō′shə list) *n.* **1.** advocate or supporter of socialism. **2.** *also,* **Socialist.** member of a Socialist Party. —*adj.* socialistic.

so·cial·is·tic (sō′shə lis′tik) *adj.* **1.** of, relating to, or resembling socialism. **2.** advocating or supporting socialism. —**so′cial·is′ti·cal·ly,** *adv.*

Socialist Party, political party advocating socialism, as the U.S. party founded in 1901 under the leadership of Eugene V. Debs.

so·cial·ite (sō′shə līt′) *n.* member of fashionable society; socially prominent person.

so·ci·al·i·ty (sō′shē al′ə tē) *n.* **1.** state or quality of being social; sociability. **2.** tendency of individuals to form social groups or communities.

so·cial·ize (sō′shə līz′) **-ized, -iz·ing.** *v.t.* **1.** to establish or regulate according to the theories of socialism; make socialistic. **2.** to make fit for companionship with others; cause to become sociable. **3.** to adapt or make conform to the needs of a social group. —*v.i.* to take part in social activities; associate with others. —**so′cial·i·za′tion,** *n.*

socialized medicine, system for providing complete medical care for the entire population at nominal cost by means of government regulation and subsidization of medical and health services.

so·cial·ly (sō′shə lē) *adv.* **1.** in a social manner: *Are you acquainted with him professionally or socially?* **2.** as a part of society; with regard to society: *socially prominent.* **3.** by or from society: *socially imposed standards of behavior.*

social register, directory listing people who are socially prominent.

social science 1. study of society and the activities and relationship of individuals and groups within society. **2.** particular field of study dealing with society or social behavior, as sociology, psychology, history, political science, or economics.

social security 1. any system that provides economic or other assistance for an individual or his family through government programs financed by public taxation. **2.** *also,* **Social Security.** system of old-age, unemployment, or disability insurance maintained by the U.S. government through compulsory payments by employers and employees.

social service, social work.

social studies, course of instruction in an elementary or secondary school, encompassing social sciences such as geography, history, and political science.

social work, any activity or service designed to improve the social conditions of a community, as aid to the needy, aged, or handicapped, health and recreation facilities, and the like.

social worker, one who does social work, esp. as a profession.

so·ci·e·ty (sə sī′ə tē) *pl.,* **-ties.** *n.* **1.** human beings as a group; all people collectively: *to act for the good of society.* **2.** system or condition of individuals living together as members of a community for their mutual benefit and protection. **3.** group of people forming a community and having common interests, traditions, and culture: *an agricultural society.* **4.** portion of a community regarded as forming a class with certain distinguishing standards or characteristics: *middle-class society.* **5.** group of persons associated for a common purpose or interest, as a club or fraternity: *a literary society.* **6.** wealthy or aristocratic members of a community; fashionable people as a group. **7.** companionship; company. **8.** group of plants or animals, esp. of the same species, living together under the same conditions and influences. —*adj.* of or relating to fashionable society: *a society column.* [Latin *societās* fellowship, alliance, community, association.]

Society Islands, French island group in the east-central Pacific, northeast of New Zealand. Land area, 636 sq. mi. Pop. (1962), 74,883.

Society of Friends, Christian religious group founded by George Fox in England in about 1650, having no ritual, ordained clergy, or formal sacraments, and opposed to all forms of violence, including war. Its members are commonly called Quakers.

Society of Jesus, religious order of the Jesuits.

so·ci·o·ec·o·nom·ic (sō′sē ō ek′ə nom′ik, -ē′kə-, sō′shē ō-) *adj.* of, relating to, or involving both social and economic factors.

so·ci·ol·o·gy (sō′sē ol′ə jē, sō′shē-) *n.* science or study of human society, including its origin, history, organization, and institutions; study of social behavior and relationships. [French *sociologie,* from Latin *socius* companion, sharing + Greek *-logía.* See -LOGY.] —**so·ci·o·log·i·cal** (sō′sē ə loj′i kəl, sō′shē-), *adj.* —**so′ci·o·log′i·cal·ly,** *adv.* —**so′ci·ol′o·gist,** *n.*

so·ci·o·po·lit·i·cal (sō′sē ō pə lit′i kəl, sō′shē-) *adj.* of, relating to, or involving both social and political factors.

sock¹ (sok) *n.* **1.** short stocking, esp. one reaching above the ankle but below the knee. **2.** light, low shoe worn by comic actors in ancient

Greek and Roman plays. **3.** comic drama; comedy. [Old English *socc* slipper, from Latin *soccus* low-heeled light shoe.]

sock² (sok) *Slang. v.t.* to hit or strike hard, esp. with the fist. —*n.* hard blow or punch. [Of uncertain origin.]

sock·et (sok′it) *n.* **1.** hollow part or place into which something fits. **2.** opening that forms a holder for an electric bulb or plug. **3.** hollow part of the body into which another part fits. [Anglo-Norman *soket* spearhead shaped like a small plowshare, diminutive of Old French *soc* plowshare; probably of Celtic origin.]

sock·eye (sok′ī′) *n.* salmon, *Onorhynchus nerka*, of northern Pacific coastal waters, that ascends rivers to spawn in spring and is a commercial food fish. [Modification of Salish *suk-kegh.*]

Soc·ra·tes (sok′rə tēz) *n.* 469–399 B.C., Greek philosopher and teacher.

So·crat·ic (sə krat′ik, sō-) *adj.* of or relating to Socrates, his philosophy, or his followers.

Socratic method, dialectic method of teaching used by Socrates, in which the instructor, by means of a successive series of questions, guides the one who answers to a foreseen conclusion.

sod (sod) *n.* **1.** surface of the ground, esp. when covered with grass. **2.** layer or piece of soil covered with grass and held together by roots. —*v.t.,* **sod·ded, sod·ding.** to cover with sod. [Middle Low German or Middle Dutch *sode* turf.]

so·da (sō′də) *n.* **1.** any of a group of compounds that contain sodium, esp. sodium carbonate, sodium bicarbonate, sodium hydroxide, or sodium oxide. **2.a.** soda water. **b.** soft drink made with soda water and flavoring. **c.** beverage containing soda water, flavoring, and often ice cream. [Medieval Latin *soda* a plant from which the chemical soda is produced; of uncertain origin.]

soda ash, impure form of anhydrous sodium carbonate, used commercially.

soda biscuit **1.** biscuit made with sodium bicarbonate and sour milk or buttermilk. **2.** soda cracker.

soda cracker, light, crisp cracker made from yeast dough containing sodium bicarbonate.

soda fountain **1.** counter having equipment for preparing and serving soft drinks, sodas, sundaes, ice cream, and the like. **2.** apparatus for drawing off soda water through faucets.

soda jerk *Slang.* one who works at a soda fountain.

soda lime, mixture of sodium hydroxide and slaked lime, used as a reagent and to absorb moisture and gases.

so·dal·i·ty (sō dal′ə tē) *pl.,* **-ties.** *n.* **1.** fellowship; companionship; brotherhood. **2.** society of the Roman Catholic Church having religious or charitable aims. **3.** any association or society. [Latin *sodālitās* companionship; association.]

soda pop *Informal.* soft drink containing soda water and flavoring.

soda water, bubbling liquid consisting of water charged under pressure with carbon dioxide gas. Also, **selt′zer.**

sod·den (sod′ən) *adj.* **1.** filled with water or moisture; soaked through; saturated. **2.** (of food) heavy and moist because of improper cooking. **3.** expressionless, dull, or stupid, as from drunkenness. —*v.t., v.i.* to make or become sodden. [Obsolete past participle of SEETHE.] —**sod′den·ly,** *adv.* —**sod′den·ness,** *n.*

so·di·um (sō′dē əm) *n.* very light, soft, silver-white metallic element similar to potassium. Symbol: **Na** See **element** for table. [Modern Latin *sodium,* from SODA; because first obtained from caustic soda.]

sodium benzoate, white, odorless powder, the sodium salt of benzoic acid, used chiefly as a food preservative. Formula: C_6H_5COONa

sodium bicarbonate, white, crystalline compound with a slightly salty taste, used esp. in baking powder and fire extinguishers and in medicine as an antacid. Formula: $NaHCO_3$ Also, **baking soda, bicarbonate of soda.**

sodium carbonate **1.** white, powdery, anhydrous compound used as in the manufacture of glass, soap, and paper. Formula: Na_2CO_3 **2.** crystalline, hydrated form of this compound. Formula: $Na_2CO_3H_2O$ Also *(def. 2),* **sal soda, washing soda.**

sodium chloride, salt *(def. 1).*

sodium cyanide, extremely poisonous, white, powdery compound used in electroplating metals, extracting gold and silver from ores, and as an insecticide. Formula: $NaCN$

sodium fluoride, poisonous solid compound, chiefly used in the fluoridation of water, as an insecticide, and in rat poisons. Formula: NaF

sodium hydroxide, white, solid compound that is a strong, caustic base, used in making rayon, soap, and detergents. Formula: $NaOH$ Also, **caustic soda.**

sodium hyposulfite **1.** colorless, crystalline salt used as a bleaching agent. Formula: $Na_2S_2O_4$ **2.** sodium thiosulfate.

sodium nitrate, colorless, crystalline compound used as an oxidizer in solid rocket propellants and in making explosives and fertilizer. Formula: $NaNO_3$ Also, **Chile saltpeter.**

sodium oxide, white powder that reacts with water to produce sodium hydroxide. Formula: Na_2O

sodium pentothal, drug derived from barbituric acid, used as an anesthetic and truth serum. Trademark: Pentothal Sodium.

sodium silicate, water glass *(def. 2).*

sodium thi·o·sul·fate (thī′ō sul′fāt) colorless or white crystalline salt, used in dyeing and as a fixing agent in photography. Formula: $Na_2S_2O_3 \cdot 5H_2O$ Also, **hy′po, hy′po·sul′fite.**

so·di·um-va·por lamp (sō′dē əm vā′pər) electric lamp in which a current passing between two electrodes causes the sodium vapor in the lamp to glow with a yellow, glareless light, used on streets and highways.

Sod·om (sod′əm) *n.* in the Old Testament, a city near the Dead Sea which, along with the nearby city of Gomorrah, was destroyed by fire from heaven because of the wickedness of the inhabitants.

so·ev·er (sō ev′ər) *adv.* **1.** in any way; to any extent or degree. ▲ usually used with an adjective preceded by *how* or a superlative preceded by *the: how hard soever the task may be.* **2.** of any or every kind. ▲ usually used with a noun modified by *any, no,* or *what: all who wish to help in any way soever.*

-soever *combining form* soever: *whatsoever, howsoever, whosoever.*

so·fa (sō′fə) *n.* long, upholstered seat with a back and arms. [Arabic *suffah.*]

sofa bed, sofa having a concealed section that pulls out to form a bed.

sof·fit (sof′it) *n.* underside of a structural part, as a beam or arch. [Italian *soffitto* ceiling, going back to Latin *suffixus,* past participle of *suffigere* to fasten below.]

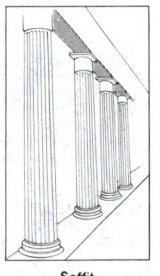

Soffit

So·fi·a (sō′fē ə, sō fē′ə) *n.* capital of Bulgaria, in the western part of the country. Pop. (1968 est.), 840,113.

soft (sôft) *adj.* **1.** easily yielding to touch or pressure; readily shaped or worked; not hard: *a soft bed.* **2.** not hard for its kind; not as hard as normal or desirable: *soft wood.* **3.** smooth or fine to the touch; having a delicate texture; not rough or coarse: *soft skin.* **4.** not loud or harsh; quiet or melodious; gentle: *a soft tone of voice.* **5.** not glaring, sharp, or harsh to the sight; subdued: *soft lighting.* **6.** mild and agreeable; gentle; temperate: *a soft breeze.* **7.a.** showing or expressing sympathy or kindness; tender: *soft words.* **b.** yielding easily or too easily to emotion; sympathetic; compassionate: *a soft heart.* **8.a.** lacking strength; not robust; flabby; weak: *Lack of exercise had made him soft.* **b.** of weak character; unmanly; effeminate. **c.** *Informal.* stupid or silly. ▲ usually used in the phrase *soft in the head.* **d.** easily influenced, imposed upon, or impressed; compliant. **9.** not harsh or severe; lenient. **10.** *Informal.* requiring little work or effort; easy: *a soft job.* **11.** (of water) comparatively free from mineral salts that interfere with the lathering and cleansing action of soap. **12.** *Phonetics.* **a.** (of *c* and *g*) pronounced with the sound of *s,* as in *city,* and *j,* as in *gem.* **b.** (of consonants) pronounced with vibration of the vocal cords; voiced. —*adv.* in a soft manner; softly. —*n.* anything that is soft. [Old English *sōfte* gentle.] —**soft′ly,** *adv.* —**soft′ness,** *n.*

soft·ball (sôft′bôl′) *n.* **1.** game very similar to baseball but played on a smaller field with a larger and softer ball that must be pitched underhand. **2.** ball used in this game.

soft-boiled (sôft′boild′) *adj.* (of eggs) boiled for only a short time, so that the yolk is still soft.

soft coal, bituminous coal.

soft drink, beverage that contains no alcohol, esp. one that is carbonated.

soft·en (sô′fən) *v.t.* **1.** to make soft or softer. **2. to soften up.** to weaken the resistance or opposition of. —*v.i.* to become soft or softer. —**soft′en·er,** *n.*

soft-finned (sôft′find′) *adj.* (of fish) having fins supported by soft or flexible rays rather than by spines.

soft-head·ed (sôft′hed′id) *adj.* having a weak mind; stupid; foolish; silly. —**soft′-head′ed·ness,** *n.*

soft-heart·ed (sôft′här′tid) *adj.* sympathetic; kind; tender. —**soft′-heart′ed·ness,** *n.*

soft·ies (sôf′tēz) plural of **softy.**

soft landing, landing, as of a spacecraft on the moon or another body, at a slow speed in order to avoid damaging the vehicle or its contents.

soft palate, soft tissue at the back of the roof of the mouth, partially dividing the mouth and the pharynx; velum.

soft-ped·al (sôft′ped′əl) **-aled, -al·ing;** *also,* **British, -alled, -al·ling.** *v.t.* **1.** to soften the tone of by means of the soft pedal. **2.** to make less conspicuous or emphatic: *to soft-pedal criticism.*

soft pedal, pedal of a piano that is pressed with the foot to soften the tone.

soft sell, subtle, indirect, quietly persuasive method of selling or advertising a product. Distinguished from **hard sell.**

soft-shell (sôft′shel′) *also,* **soft-shelled.** *adj.* (of certain shellfish) having a soft shell, as a crab that has recently molted.

soft-shell clam, common edible clam, *Mya arenaria,* of the eastern coast of North America, having a soft, thin, elongated shell.

soft-shoe (sôft′shōō′) *adj.* of or relating to a kind of tap dancing done without metal taps on the shoes.

soft shoulder, soft earth along the edge of a paved road.

soft-soap (sôft′sōp′) *v.t. Informal.* to flatter, esp. in order to deceive. —**soft′-soap′er,** *n.*

soft soap 1. fluid or semifluid soap. **2.** *Informal.* flattery.

soft-spo·ken (sôft′spō′kən) *adj.* **1.** (of persons) speaking with a soft, low voice. **2.** (of words) spoken softly or mildly.

soft·ware (sôft′wâr′) *n.* written programs used in the operation of a computer, as distinguished from its physical equipment.

soft·wood (sôft′wŏŏd′) *n.* **1.** any of a large group of trees bearing cones and having needlelike leaves, as pines, firs, and spruces. **2.** wood of such a tree, used chiefly for construction purposes. **3.** any soft, light, easily cut wood.

soft·y (sôf′tē) *pl.,* **soft·ies.** *n. Informal.* **1.** one who is easily imposed upon or moved to emotion; sentimental or susceptible person. **2.** weak or effeminate person.

sog·gy (sog′ē) **-gi·er, -gi·est.** *adj.* **1.** saturated with water or moisture; soaked. **2.** damp and heavy, as poorly baked bread or cake. **3.** lacking life or spirit; dull. [Dialectal English *sog* bog (of uncertain origin) + -Y¹.] —**sog′gi·ness,** *n.*

So·ho (sō′hō, sō hō′) *n.* district in London noted for its foreign restaurants and cafés.

soi-di-sant (swä dē zäN′) *adj. French.* so-called; self-styled. ▲ usually used disparagingly: *a soi-disant intellectual.*

soil¹ (soil) *n.* **1.** part of the earth's surface in which plants grow, a loose material made up of small rock particles, decayed organic matter, and living organisms. **2.** particular kind of soil: *sandy soil.* **3.** land, country, or region: *foreign soil.* **4.** any place or condition favorable to growth or development. [Anglo-Norman *soil* land, possibly going back to Latin *solium* seat; influenced in meaning by Latin *solum* ground.]

soil² (soil) *v.t.* **1.** to make dirty, esp. on the surface. **2.** to bring disgrace or dishonor to; sully: *Malicious gossip can soil a person's reputation.* —*v.i.* to become soiled or dirty. —*n.* **1.** dirty mark or place; spot; stain. **2.** filthy matter, as refuse or sewage. **3.** manure that is used as fertilizer. **4.** act of soiling; state of being soiled. [Old French *soillier* to dirty, going back to Latin *suculus* little boar, diminutive of *sūs* pig, boar.]

soil·age (soi′lij) *n.* green crops cut for feeding to penned livestock.

soi·ree (swä rā′) *also,* **soi·rée.** *n.* party, reception, or other social gathering taking place in the evening. [French *soirée,* from *soir* evening, going back to Latin *sērus* late.]

so·journ (sō′jûrn, sō jûrn′) *v.i.* to live in a place temporarily, as on a visit. —*n.* temporary stay. [Old French *sojorner* to rest, stay, going back to Latin *sub* under + *diurnus* relating to the day, daily.] —**so′journ·er,** *n.*

sol¹ (sōl) *n. Music.* fifth of the series of syllables used to name the eight tones of the diatonic scale. Also, **so.** See **do²** for illustration. [See GAMUT.]

sol² (sol, sôl) *n.* standard monetary unit of Peru. [Spanish *sol* sun, from Latin *sōl;* because of the design of the sun on the coin.]

sol³ (sol, sôl) *n.* colloidal system in a liquid state. [From SOLUTION.]

Sol (sol) *n.* **1.** Roman god of the sun. His Greek counterpart is Helios. **2.** the sun. [Latin *sōl.*]

sol. 1. solution. **2.** soluble.

Sol. 1. Solomon. **2.** Solicitor.

sol·ace (sol′is) *n.* **1.** relief from sorrow or disappointment; comfort; consolation: *The widow found solace in the companionship of her friends.* **2.** that which gives comfort or consolation: *Her friends were a solace to her during her grief.* —*v.t.,* **-aced, -ac·ing. 1.** to relieve from sorrow or disappointment; comfort; console. **2.** to amuse or soothe, as sorrow. [Old French *solaz* consolation, from Latin *sōlācium.*] —**Syn.** *v.t.* **1.** see **comfort.**

so·la·num (sə lā′nəm) *n.* any of a large group of herbs and shrubs, genus *Solanum,* of the nightshade family, including the potato and eggplant. [Latin *sōlānum* nightshade; literally, sunflower, from *sōl* sun.]

so·lar (sō′lər) *adj.* **1.** of or relating to the sun: *solar phenomena.* **2.** produced by or proceeding from the sun: *solar energy.* **3.** measured by the earth's course in relation to the sun: *solar time.* **4.** (of a mechanism) operating by means of or with the aid of the light or heat of the sun: *a solar furnace, a solar telegraph.* [Latin *sōlāris* relating to the sun, from *sōl* sun.]

solar battery, device that converts the radiant energy of the sun into electricity.

solar day, day (*def. 3a*).

solar eclipse, see **eclipse** (*def. 1*).

solar flare, sudden eruption of gases from the surface of the sun.

so·lar·i·um (sə lâr′ē əm) *pl.,* **-lar·i·a** (-lâr′ē ə). *n.* glass-enclosed room, porch, or balcony exposed to the rays of the sun, as in a hospital or sanitarium.

so·lar·ize (sō′lə rīz′) **-ized, -iz·ing.** *v.t.* **1.** to affect by exposure to the sun's rays. **2.** (in photography) to overexpose (a film or plate) to light. —**so′lar·i·za′tion,** *n.*

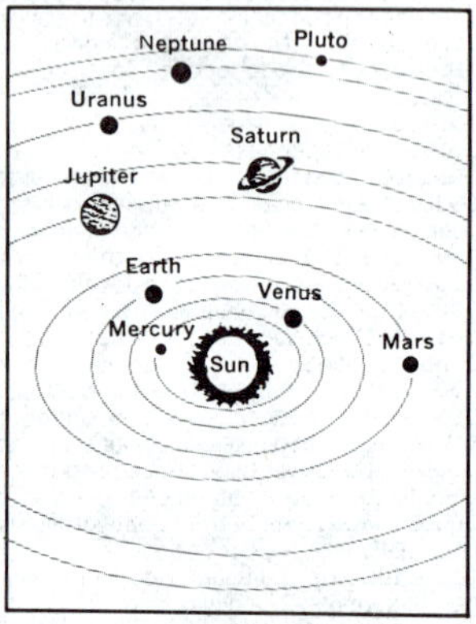

solar month, month (*def. 5*).

solar plex·us (plek′səs) **1.** large network of nerves located in the upper part of the abdomen, just behind the stomach. **2.** *Informal.* pit of the stomach.

solar system, sun and all the heavenly bodies that revolve around it, including the planets, their satellites, asteroids, comets, and meteors.

solar year, year (*def. 2a*).

sold (sōld) past tense and past participle of **sell.**

sol·der (sod′ər) *n.* **1.** any metal or metallic alloy used when melted for joining metal surfaces or parts. **2.** anything that joins or unites. —*v.t.* **1.** to join, fasten, or repair with solder. **2.** to unite firmly or closely. —*v.i.* **1.** to work with solder. **2.** to become joined or united with or as with solder. [Old French *soldure* this metal, from *sou(l)der* to fasten together, going back to Latin *solidus* firm.] —**sol′der·er,** *n.*

sol·dier (sōl′jər) *n.* **1.** one who serves in an army. **2.** enlisted man in an army, as distinguished from a commissioned officer. **3.** brave, skilled, or experienced warrior. **4.** one who works for any cause: *a soldier of Christ.* **5.** ant or termite having a large head and large, powerful jaws adapted for fighting in defense of the colony. —*v.i.* to be a soldier; serve in an army. [Old French *soldier* one who fights for pay, from *soulde* pay, from Late Latin *solidus* a Roman gold coin. See SOLIDUS.]

sol·dier·ly (sōl′jər lē) *adj.* relating to or characteristic of a soldier.

soldier of fortune 1. one who will serve in any army for money, adventure, or pleasure; exclusive. **2.** any restless, adventurous person.

Soldier's Medal, U.S. military decoration awarded for heroic action not involving combat with an enemy.

sol·dier·y (sōl′jər ē) *pl.,* **-dier·ies.** *n.* **1.** soldiers as a group. **2.** body of soldiers. **3.** military knowledge or training; military science.

sol·do (sōl′dō) *pl.,* **-di** (-dē). *n.* former copper coin of Italy, equal to ¹⁄₂₀ of a lira. [Italian *soldo,* from Late Latin *solidus* a Roman gold coin. See SOLIDUS.]

sole¹ (sōl) *n.* **1.** bottom surface of the foot. **2.** corresponding part of a shoe, boot, sock, or other article of footwear. **3.** lower part or bottom surface of anything, as the bottom of the head of a golf club. —*v.t.,* **soled, sol·ing.** to furnish with a sole. [Old English *sole* sandal, going back to Latin *solea* sole of a sandal, sandal, from *solum* ground, bottom.]

sole² (sōl) *adj.* **1.** being the only one; without another or others; only; individual; single: *the sole heir to a fortune.* **2.** limited or belonging to a single person or group; exclusive: *The film company bought sole rights to two popular novels.* **3.** *Archaic.* having no companion; alone; solitary. [Latin *sōlus* alone.] —**Syn. 1.** see **only.**

sole³ (sōl) *pl.,* **soles** or **sole.** *n.* **1.** any of a group of flatfish, family Soleidae, found in warm and temperate seas. The **European sole,** *Solea solea,* is highly valued as a food fish. **2.** any of various other edible flatfish. [Old French *sole,* from Latin *solea* sandal, sole¹; with reference to its being as flat as a sandal.]

sol·e·cism (sol′ə siz′əm, sō′lə-) *n.* **1.** violation of grammatical values or accepted usage of a language, esp. by use of substandard words. **2.** error in social behavior; violation of etiquette. **3.** any error, impropriety, or incongruity. [Latin *soloecismus* grammatical error, from Greek *soloikismos,* going back to *Soloi,* a Greek colony in Asia Minor, where Greek was spoken incorrectly.]

sole·ly (sōl′lē) *adv.* **1.** without any other; by oneself or itself; singly;

Solar system

[Diagram labels: Neptune, Pluto, Uranus, Saturn, Jupiter, Earth, Venus, Mercury, Sun, Mars]

at; āpe; cär; end; mē; it; īce; hot; ōld; fôrk; wood; fōōl; oil; out; up; ūse; turn; sing; thin; this; zh in treasure; ə in ago, taken, pencil, lemon, circus.

alone: *He is solely to blame for the accident.* **2.** entirely; exclusively; merely: *That company is in business solely for profit.*

sol·emn (sol′əm) *adj.* **1.** having a grave, serious, or earnest character; sober. **2.** inspiring serious thoughts or reflections; causing awe: *a solemn occasion.* **3.** having to do with religion or religious observances; sacred. **4.** performed with or accompanied by formality or ceremony. [Latin *sōllemnis* established, religious, from *sollus* whole + *annus* year.] —**sol′emn·ly,** *adv.* —**sol′emn·ness,** *n.* —**Syn. 1.** see **grave¹.**

so·lem·ni·ty (sə lem′nə tē) *pl.,* **-ties.** *n.* **1.** state or quality of being solemn; seriousness; gravity; impressiveness. **2.** *also,* **solemnities.** a solemn ceremony, proceeding, or observance.

sol·em·nize (sol′əm nīz′) *-nized, -niz·ing.* *v.t.* **1.** to celebrate with formal ceremony or by a ritual, as a religious holiday. **2.** to perform (a ceremony): *to solemnize a marriage.* **3.** to cause to have a solemn character; make serious. —**sol·em·ni·za′tion,** *n.*

so·le·noid (sō′lə noid′) *n.* cylindrical coil of wire that produces a magnetic field through the center when an electric current is passed through it. The solenoid is the basis for all electromagnets. [French *solénoïde,* from Greek *sōlēnoeidēs* shaped like a pipe, from *sōlēn* pipe, channel.] —**so′le·noi′dal,** *adj.*

sol-fa (sōl′fä′) *Music. n.* **1.** sol-fa syllables. **2.** system or practice of singing tones to the sol-fa syllables. —*v.i.* **-faed, -fa·ing.** to use the sol-fa syllables in singing. —*v.t.* to sing (a melody or exercise) to the sol-fa syllables. [SOL¹ + FA. See GAMUT.]

sol-fa syllables *Music.* syllables *do, re, mi, fa, sol, la,* and *ti,* used in singing or naming the tones of the scale.

sol·feg·gio (sol fej′ō, -fej′ē ō′) *pl., -gios. n. Music.* **1.** singing exercise in which scales, arpeggios, or similar runs are sung to the sol-fa syllables. **2.** solmization. [Italian *solfeggio* sol-fa, from *solfa* gamut, scale¹, from *sol* SOL¹ + *fa* FA. See GAMUT.]

so·lic·it (sə lis′it) *v.t.* **1.** to seek to obtain; ask for earnestly: *to solicit business.* **2.** to entreat or petition (a person) to do something; urge; importune. **3.** to tempt or entice to do wrong. **4.** to accost or lure for an immoral purpose. —*v.i.* to solicit someone or something. [Latin *sollicitāre* to incite, urge to wrongdoing.]

so·lic·i·ta·tion (sə lis′ə tā′shən) *n.* **1.** act of soliciting; earnest plea or request; entreaty. **2.** temptation or enticement to do wrong.

so·lic·i·tor (sə lis′ə tər) *n.* **1.** one who solicits, esp. a person who seeks business or trade. **2.** British lawyer who advises clients and prepares cases for presentation in court but who may plead cases only in the lower court. Distinguished from **barrister.** **3.** lawyer for a city, county, or other division of government.

solicitor general *pl.,* **solicitors general.** **1.** law officer ranking next below an attorney general. **2.** chief law officer in some states of the United States.

so·lic·i·tous (sə lis′ə təs) *adj.* **1.** full of concern or anxiety; concerned: *to be solicitous about a person's health.* **2.** eager; desirous; anxious. [Latin *sollicitus* anxious, agitated.] —**so·lic′i·tous·ly,** *adv.* —**so·lic′i·tous·ness,** *n.*

so·lic·i·tude (sə lis′ə tōōd′, -tūd′) *n.* **1.** state of being solicitous; care; concern; anxiety. **2.** excessive concern. **3.** *usually,* **solicitudes.** that which causes care or concern. —**Syn. 1.** see **care.**

sol·id (sol′id) *adj.* **1.** having a definite shape and volume; not liquid or gaseous. **2.** free from empty spaces; completely filled with matter; not hollow. **3.** not loose; compact; firm: *solid ground.* **4.a.** of one material; unmixed throughout: *solid gold.* **b.** having the same character throughout; unvaried; uniform: *a solid color.* **5.** without breaks or openings; continuous: *a solid line of people.* **6.** having strength or firmness; not weak or flimsy; firm; sound: *a solid foundation.* **7.** of sound character; dependable; reliable: *a solid citizen.* **8.** financially sound: *a solid investment.* **9.** exhibiting soundness of mind; sensible; intelligent: *a solid argument.* **10.** genuine; real: *solid comfort.* **11.** marked by or involving seriousness; not light, frivolous, or amusing: *solid instruction.* **12.** united, as in opinion; unanimous: *The candidate got solid backing.* **13.** whole; complete: *He slept for twelve solid hours.* **14.** having the three dimensions of length, breadth, and thickness. **15.** (of compound words) written without a hyphen, as *sunroom* and *mailbox.* **16.** *Printing.* having no added space, or leading, between the lines. —*n.* **1.** form of matter having a definite shape and volume and whose atoms or molecules are strongly bound to each other. Distinguished from **gas** and **liquid.** **2.** figure having length, breadth, and thickness, as a sphere, cube, or pyramid. [Latin *solidus* firm¹, dense.] —**sol′id·ly,** *adv.* —**sol′id·ness,** *n.* —**Syn.** *adj.* **1.** see **firm¹.**

sol·i·dar·i·ty (sol′ə dar′ə tē) *pl.,* **-ties.** *n.* agreement or unity of interests, standards, purposes, or opinions among members of a group; fel-

lowship. [French *solidarité,* from *solidaire* interdependent, from Latin *(in) solidum* (for) the whole.] —**Syn.** see **union.**

solid geometry, branch of geometry dealing with three-dimensional figures.

so·lid·i·fy (sə lid′ə fī′) *-fied, -fy·ing.* *v.t.* **1.** to make solid, firm, or compact. **2.** to cause to be firmly united. —*v.i.* to become solid, firm, or compact: *The water solidified into ice.* —**so·lid′i·fi·ca′tion,** *n.*

so·lid·i·ty (sə lid′ə tē) *n.* **1.** state or quality of being solid. **2.** soundness or stability of mind, moral character, or finances.

sol·id-state (sol′id stāt′) *adj.* **1.** of or relating to the branch of physics that deals with the structure and properties of solids, esp. crystals. **2.** of or relating to electronic devices made with semiconductors, as transistors.

sol·i·dus (sol′i dəs) *pl.,* **-di** (-dī′). *n.* **1.** Roman gold coin introduced by Constantine and used until the fall of the Byzantine Empire, commonly called a bezant during medieval times. **2.** sign (/) used to separate shillings from pence and in writing fractions or dates. [Late Latin *solidus* a Roman gold coin, from Latin *solidus* firm¹.]

so·lil·o·quize (sə lil′ə kwīz′) *-quized, -quiz·ing.* *v.i.* **1.** to talk to oneself; utter a soliloquy.

so·lil·o·quy (sə lil′ə kwē) *pl.,* **-quies.** *n.* **1.** act or instance of talking to oneself. **2.** dramatic speech in which a character reveals his thoughts to the audience but not to the other characters by speaking as if to himself. [Late Latin *sōliloquim* talking to oneself, from Latin *sōlus* alone + *loqui* to speak.]

So·ling·en (zō′ling ən, sō′-) *n.* city in western West Germany. Pop. (1968), 173,922.

sol·ip·sism (sol′ip siz′əm) *n. Philosophy.* theory that the self cannot know anything but its own experiences or that nothing but the self exists. [Latin *sōlus* alone + *ipse* self + -ISM.]

sol·i·taire (sol′ə tār′) *n.* **1.** any of a number of card games for one person. Also, **pa′tience.** **2.** single gem, esp. a diamond set by itself in a ring. [Old French *solitaire* alone, lonely, from Latin *sōlitārius.* Doublet of SOLITARY.]

sol·i·tar·y (sol′ə ter′ē) *adj.* **1.** living, being, or going alone: *a solitary traveler.* **2.** made, done, or spent alone: *a solitary life.* **3.** not frequented; secluded; desolate; lonely: *a solitary cabin high in the mountains.* **4.** having no companions; lonesome; lonely. **5.** being the only one; only; sole. —*n. pl.,* **-tar·ies.** **1.** one who lives alone, away from others; hermit; recluse. **2.** *Informal.* solitary confinement. [Latin *sōlitārius* alone, lonely. Doublet of SOLITAIRE.] —**sol′i·tar′i·ly,** *adv.* —**sol′i·tar′i·ness,** *n.* —**Syn.** *adj.* **2.** see **alone. 5.** see **single.**

solitary confinement, confinement of a prisoner in a cell or other place completely isolated from all other prisoners.

sol·i·tude (sol′ə tōōd′, -tūd′) *n.* **1.** state of being or living alone; isolation; remoteness; seclusion. **2.** lonely, secluded, or unfrequented place. [Latin *sōlitūdō,* from *sōlus* alone.]

Syn. 1. Solitude, seclusion, privacy mean the state of being alone and suggest the absence of distractions or intrusions. **Solitude** emphasizes the quiet and tranquillity of such an existence, and the opportunity to think or meditate on or to test one's character: *The monk sought the solitude of the desert.* **Seclusion** emphasizes making oneself inaccessible to others, esp. as a shield against outside influences regarded as negative or corrupt: *Francesca grew up in the seclusion of the convent. The actress was forced into seclusion after all the publicity.* **Privacy** emphasizes what is by nature personal and individual and not to be known or seen by others: *In the privacy of his own thoughts he could review the events of the afternoon.*

sol·ler·et (sol′ə ret′) *n.* flexible steel shoe made of overlapping plates, forming part of a medieval suit of armor.

sol·mi·za·tion (sol′mə zā′shən) *n. Music.* act, practice, or system of using certain syllables, esp. the sol-fa syllables, in naming the tones of the scale. [French *solmisation,* going back to *sol* (see SOL¹) + *mi* (see MI). See GAMUT.]

so·lo (sō′lō) *pl.,* **-los.** *n.* **1.** musical composition or passage for a single voice or instrument, with or without accompaniment. **2.** any performance or action done by one person alone, as an airplane flight. —*adj.* **1.** composed or arranged for or performed by a single voice or instrument. **2.** playing a solo, as a musician or instrument: *solo trumpet.* **3.** made or done by one person alone: *a solo flight.* —*v.i.* **-loed, -lo·ing.** **1.** to make a flight alone in an airplane, esp. for the first time. **2.** to perform alone. [Italian *solo* alone, from Latin *sōlus.*]

So·lo (sō′lō) *n.* Surakarta.

so·lo·ist (sō′lō ist) *n.* one who performs a solo.

Sol·o·mon (sol′ə mən) *n.* **1.** king of Israel in the tenth century B.C., the son of David. He built the first Temple at Jerusalem and was noted for his wisdom. **2.** very wise man.

Solomon Islands, island group in the southwestern Pacific, east of New Guinea. Some of these islands form part of the Territory of New Guinea; the rest are a protectorate of Great Britain. Land area, 15,820 sq. mi. Pop. (1962 est.), 185,000.

---

at; āpe; cär; end; mē; it; īce; hot; ōld; fôrk; wood; fōol; oil; out; up; ūse; turn; sing; thin; this; zh in treasure; ə in ago, taken, pencil, lemon, circus.   949

Sol·o·mon's-seal (sol′ə mənz sēl′) *n.* any of a small group of erect leafy plants of the lily family, genus *Polygonatum,* having greenish drooping flowers and scarred rhizomes.

Solomon's seal, figure consisting of two triangles placed one upon the other to form a six-pointed star, formerly believed to possess magical powers and used as an amulet.

So·lon (sō′lən, -lon) *n.* **1.** c.638–c.559 B.C., Athenian lawgiver. **2.** *also,* **solon,** wise man, esp. a wise lawmaker.

so long *Informal.* good-by.

sol·stice (sol′stis) *n.* **1.** either of the two times during the year when the sun appears farthest from the equator. In the Northern Hemisphere, the sun reaches the northernmost point on its path, the **summer solstice,** on or about June 21. The sun reaches its southernmost point, the **winter solstice,** on or about December 22. The summer solstice is the longest period of daylight during the year, and the winter solstice is the shortest.

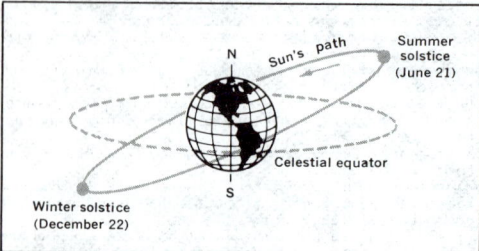

N Sun's path Summer solstice (June 21)

Celestial equator

S

Winter solstice (December 22)

Solstice

2. either of the two diametrically opposite points on the apparent annual path of the sun that is farthest from the celestial equator. [Old French *solstice,* from Latin *sōlstitium,* going back to *sōl* sun + *sistere* to cause to stand.]

sol·sti·tial (sol stish′əl) *adj.* of or relating to a solstice.

sol·u·bil·i·ty (sol′yə bil′ə tē) *pl.,* **-ties.** *n.* **1.** quality or condition of being soluble; ability of a substance to be dissolved in another substance. **2.** amount of a substance that can be dissolved in a given solvent at a given temperature.

sol·u·ble (sol′yə bəl) *adj.* **1.** capable of being dissolved in another substance. **2.** capable of being solved. [Late Latin *solūbilis* dissolvable, from Latin *solvere* to loosen, dissolve.] —**sol′u·bly,** *adv.*

soluble glass, water glass *(def. 2).*

sol·ute (sol′ūt, sō′lōōt) *n.* substance in a solution that is dissolved by another substance. Distinguished from **solvent.** [Latin *solūtus,* past participle of *solvere* to loosen, dissolve.]

so·lu·tion (sə lōō′shən) *n.* **1.** act, process, or method of solving a problem. **2.** answer to a problem; explanation. **3.a.** homogeneous mixture of atoms, molecules, or ions of two or more substances. Solutions are usually formed by solids, liquids, or gases dissolved in liquids but can also consist of gases dissolved in gases or solids dissolved in solids. **b.** act or process of forming such a mixture: *the solution of sugar in water.* **c.** state of being dissolved: *Sea water contains salts in solution.* **4.** a separation or breaking up. [Latin *solūtiō* a loosening, explanation.]

solution set *Mathematics.* set of all the values that satisfy an equation. Also, **truth set.**

solv·a·ble (sol′və bəl) *adj.* capable of being solved: *a solvable problem.* —**solv′a·bil′i·ty,** *n.*

Sol·vay process (sol′vā) process for making sodium carbonate from common salt. Carbon dioxide is passed through a solution of salt and ammonia to produce sodium bicarbonate, which is then heated to produce sodium carbonate. [From Ernest *Solvay,* 1838–1922, Belgian chemist who invented it.]

solve (solv) **solved, solv·ing.** *v.t.* to find the solution to; provide an answer for: *to solve a problem.* [Latin *solvere* to loosen, explain, dissolve.] —**solv′er,** *n.*

Syn. Solve, resolve mean to find an answer to a problem or question. **Solve** implies that there is a single right answer that can be determined easily or routinely once the mechanism or formula is known or the necessary clues provided: *We solved the math problem.* **Resolve** implies that there is no one correct answer but rather a number of satisfactory solutions, one of which is chosen as the best compromise or the most suitable under the circumstances: *We resolved the problem of where to meet by deciding that each of us would go to the theater separately.*

sol·ven·cy (sol′vən sē) *n.* quality or state of being solvent.

sol·vent (sol′vənt) *adj.* **1.** able to pay all debts, as a business establishment whose assets exceed its liabilities. **2.** having the power to dissolve;

causing solution. —*n.* **1.** substance in a solution that dissolves another substance or substances. Solvents are usually liquids but can be solids or gases. Distinguished from **solute.** **2.** something that solves. [Latin *solvēns,* present participle of *solvere* to loosen, pay, dissolve.]

Sol·way Firth (sol′wā) arm of the Irish Sea between England and Scotland.

Sol·y·man (sol′ē mən) Suleiman I.

so·ma (sō′mə) *pl.,* **so·ma·ta** (sō′mə tə). *n.* an entire living organism, excluding the germ cells. [Greek *sōma* body.]

So·ma·li (sə mä′lē) *pl.,* **-li** or **-lis.** *n.* **1.** member of a group of Hamitic people living in parts of Somalia, Kenya, and Ethiopia. **2.** Hamitic language of these people.

So·ma·lia (sə mäl′yə) *n.* country in eastern Africa, on the Indian Ocean and Gulf of Aden. Capital, Mogadishu. Area, 246,201 sq. mi. Pop. (1975 est.), 3,200,000.

Somali Republic, Somalia.

so·mat·ic (sō mat′ik, sə-) *adj.* **1.** of or relating to the body, as distinguished from the mind, soul, or psyche; physical; corporeal. **2.** of or relating to the walls of the body cavity. **3.** of or relating to the soma. [Greek *sōmatikos* relating to the body, from *sōma* body.]

somatic cell, any cell of the body other than a germ cell.

so·ma·to·plasm (sō′mə tə plaz′əm, sə mat′ə-) *n.* protoplasm of a somatic cell, as distinguished from that of a germ cell. [Greek *sōmat-,* stem of *sōma* body + -PLASM.]

so·ma·to·type (sō′mə tə tīp′, sō mat′ə-) *n.* classification that describes a person's body build. [Greek *sōmat-,* stem of *sōma* + TYPE.]

som·ber (som′bər) *also,* **som·bre.** *adj.* **1.** dark and gloomy; dark and dull: *a somber sky, a somber shade of gray.* **2.** melancholy, dismal, or depressing: *a somber mood.* [French *sombre* dark, gloomy, going back to Latin *sub* under + *umbra* shade.] —**som′ber·ly;** *also,* **som′bre·ly,** *adv.* —**som′ber·ness;** *also,* **som′bre·ness,** *n.* —**Syn. 2.** see **grave[1].**

som·brer·o (səm brâr′ō, som-) *pl.,* **-brer·os.** *n.* hat with a broad brim and high crown, worn esp. in Mexico and the southwestern United States. [Spanish *sombrero* hat, from *sombra* shade, going back to Latin *sub* under + *umbra* shade.]

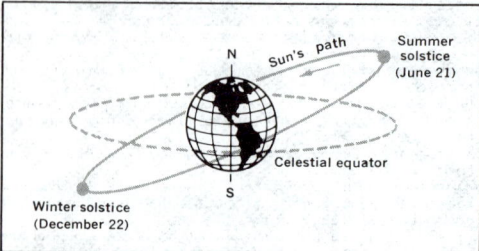

Sombrero

some (sum; *unstressed* səm) *adj.* **1.** being a certain one or ones not specified or known: *Some people are offended by his sarcasm. Some birds cannot fly.* **2.** being of a certain unspecified number, quantity, or amount: *It happened some weeks ago. Please have some potatoes.* **3.** *Informal.* worthy of consideration; remarkable; striking; unusual: *That was some game yesterday.* —*pron.* **1.** certain ones not specified or known: *Some still believe he was innocent of the crime.* **2.** a certain unspecified number, quantity, or amount: *He kept some and gave the rest away.* —*adv.* **1.** approximately; about: *The club has some forty members.* **2.** *Informal.* somewhat: *The patient's condition has improved some.* [Old English *sum.*]

-some[1] *suffix* (used to form adjectives) characterized by, tending to, or tending to be (what is indicated by the stem): *handsome, wholesome, gruesome.* [Old English -*sum.*]

-some[2] *suffix* used to form nouns indicating a group of a specified number: *threesome, foursome.* [Old English *sum* some.]

-some[3] *combining form* body: *chromosome.* [Greek *sōma* body.]

some·bod·y (sum′bod′ē, -bə dē) *pron.* unknown or unspecified person; someone: *Somebody has taken my raincoat.* —*n. pl.,* **-bod·ies.** one who is important or famous.

some·day (sum′dā′) *adv.* at some future time: *That species may someday become extinct.*

some·how (sum′hou′) *adv.* in a way or by a method not known, stated, or understood: *We must get this fixed somehow.*

some·one (sum′wun′, -wən) *pron.* somebody: *Someone will have to mail these letters.*

some·place (sum′plās′) *adv.* *Informal.* somewhere: *We'll have dinner someplace near the theater.*

som·er·sault (sum′ər sôlt′) *also,* **sum·mer·sault.** *n.* **1.** acrobatic leap, roll, or dive in which the body turns heels over head, making a complete revolution. —*v.i.* to perform a somersault. [Old French *sombresau(l)t* leap, through Provençal, from Latin *suprā* above + *saltus* leap.]

som·er·set (sum′ər set′) *n.* somersault. —*v.i.* **-set·ted, -set·ting.** to somersault.

Som·er·ville (sum′ər vil′) *n.* city in eastern Massachusetts, suburb of Boston. Pop. (1970), 88,779.

some·thing (sum′thing) *pron.* certain thing not specified or known; some thing: *Something is wrong with the car.* —*n.* important person or thing: *She thinks she's something since she won the beauty contest.* —*adv.* to some extent; somewhat. ▲ used in the phrase *something like: Your house is something like ours.*

some·time (sum′tīm′) *adv.* **1.** at some time not specified or known: *I bought this sometime last spring.* **2.** at some unspecified time in the future: *I'll finish this work sometime.* —*adj.* having been formerly; former: *a sometime movie actress.*

some·times (sum′tīmz′) *adv.* now and then; at times; occasionally: *Sometimes we spend the weekend in the country.*

some·way (sum′wā′) *also,* **some·ways.** *adv.* in some way; somehow.

some·what (sum′hwät′, -wät′, -hwot, -wot, sum′hwät′, -wät′) *adv.* in some measure or degree; to some extent; rather: *somewhat upset. His work is somewhat better than it was last year.* —*n.* some part, portion, amount, or degree: *She is somewhat of an artist.*

some·where (sum′hwâr′, -wâr′) *adv.* **1.** in, at, or to some place not specified or known: *I left my jacket somewhere.* **2.** at some time, amount, degree, age, or figure: *somewhere about five o'clock. It costs somewhere around ten dollars.* —*n.* place that is not known or specified.

som·me·lier (sum′əl yā′) *n.* a wine steward in a restaurant. [French *sommelier,* from Old French *sommelier* person in charge of supplies, driver of pack animals, going back to Late Latin *sagma* pack-saddle, from Greek *sagma.*]

som·nam·bu·lant (som nam′byə lənt) *adj.* walking while asleep or having the habit of walking while asleep.

som·nam·bu·late (som nam′byə lāt′) -**lat·ed, -lat·ing.** *v.i.* to walk while asleep. [Latin *somnus* sleep + AMBULATE.] —**som·nam′bu·la′tion, som·nam·bu·la′tor,** *n.*

som·nam·bu·lism (som nam′byə liz′əm) *n.* sleepwalking. —**som·nam′bu·list,** *n.* —**som·nam′bu·lis′tic,** *adj.*

som·nif·er·ous (som nif′ər əs) *adj.* causing or inducing sleep; soporific. [Latin *somnifer* + -OUS.]

som·no·lence (som′nə ləns) *n.* sleepiness; drowsiness.

som·no·lent (som′nə lənt) *adj.* **1.** sleepy; drowsy. **2.** tending to cause sleep. [Latin *somnolentus* sleepy, from *somnus* sleep.] —**som′no·lent·ly,** *adv.*

Som·nus (som′nəs) *n.* Roman god of sleep. His Greek counterpart is Hypnos.

son (sun) *n.* **1.** male child considered in relation to one or both of his parents. **2.** male child adopted as a son. **3.** male descendant: *the sons of Adam.* **4.** person regarded as the product or offspring of a certain country or place: *a son of the soil.* **5.** someone or something considered as a son in relation to source or origin: *sons of the Depression.* **6.** familiar term of address to a boy or man from an older person. **7. the Son.** Jesus Christ. [Old English *sunu.*]

so·nance (sō′nəns) *n.* condition or quality of being sonant.

so·nant (sō′nənt) *adj.* **1.** having sound; sounding. **2.** *Phonetics.* voiced. —*n. Phonetics.* voiced sound. [Latin *sonāns,* present participle of *sonāre* to make a noise.]

so·nar (sō′när) *n.* device that detects the presence and determines the location of submerged objects, as submarines, by means of sound waves reflected from or produced by the objects. [Short for *so(und) na(viga-tion) r(anging).*]

so·na·ta (sə nä′tə) *n.* instrumental composition, often written for the piano, typically having three or four movements in contrasting forms and rhythms but related keys. [Italian *sonata* literally, a sounding, from *sonare* to sound, from Latin *sonāre* to make a noise.]

son·a·ti·na (son′ə tē′nə) *n.* short or simplified sonata. [Italian *sonatina,* diminutive of *sonata.* See SONATA.]

song (sông) *n.* **1.** musical composition for one or more voices. **2a.** poem that can be set to music. **b.** poetry; verse. **3.** act or art of singing. **4.** any melodious sound or series of sounds, as the call of a bird. **5. for a song.** at a very low price; very cheaply: *I bought this painting for a song.* [Old English *sang.*]

song and dance *Informal.* detailed, complicated, or evasive statement, esp. one offered as an excuse.

song·bird (sông′burd′) *n.* bird that utters a musical call.

song·fest (sông′fest′) *n.* informal gathering at which there is group singing.

song·ful (sông′fəl) *adj.* **1.** full of song; melodious; tuneful.

song·less (sông′lis) *adj.* devoid of song; unable to sing: *a songless bird.*

Song of Solomon, book of the Old Testament, formerly attributed to Solomon, containing lyric and mystical hymns of love. Also, **Song of Songs, Can·ti·cles.**

song sparrow, common North American sparrow, *Melospiza melodia,* having predominantly brownish plumage marked with dark-brown streaks, noted for its song.

song·ster (sông′stər) *n.* **1.** one who sings. **2.** writer of songs or poems. **3.** songbird. [Old English *sangestre* singer.]

song·stress (sông′stris) *n.* female singer, esp. of popular songs.

song thrush, European thrush, *Turdus philomelos,* having predominantly brown plumage with a yellow-and-white breast marked with brown spots. Length: 9 inches. Also, **ma′vis.**

song·writ·er (sông′rī′tər) *n.* one who composes lyrics or music for both for songs, esp. popular songs.

son·ic (son′ik) *adj.* **1.** of, relating to, or utilizing sound: *sonic vibrations.* **2.** relating to or denoting the speed at which sound travels through the air at sea level, about 1088 feet per second. [Latin *sonus* noise + -IC.]

sonic barrier, sound barrier.

sonic boom, loud, explosive noise caused by the shock wave that emanates from an aircraft traveling at or above the speed of sound.

son-in-law (sun′in lô′) *pl.,* **sons-in-law.** *n.* husband of one's daughter.

son·net (son′it) *n.* poem containing fourteen lines, usually in iambic pentameter, having a fixed pattern of rhyme and usually dealing with a single theme, idea, or sentiment. The two basic forms are the Shakespearean sonnet and the Petrarchan sonnet. [Italian *sonetto,* diminutive of *suono*[1], from Latin *sonus* noise.]

son·net·eer (son′ə tēr′) *n.* one who writes sonnets.

sonnet sequence, series of sonnets written by one poet and usually having a single theme or subject.

son·ny (sun′ē) *pl.,* **-nies.** *n.* young boy. ▲ used as a familiar form of address.

So·no·ra (sə nôr′ə) *n.* state in northwestern Mexico. Pop. (1968 est.), 1,249,000.

so·nor·i·ty (sə nôr′ə tē, -nor′-) *n.* quality or state of being sonorous.

so·no·rous (sə nôr′əs, son′ər əs) *adj.* **1.** producing or capable of producing sound, esp. deep, full, or rich sound. **2.** (of sound) loud, deep, or resonant. **3.** rich and full in sound, as language or the voice. **4.** having an imposing or impressive quality, effect, or style. [Latin *sonōrus* resounding, noisy, from *sonor* noise.] —**so·no′rous·ly,** *adv.* —**so·no′rous·ness,** *n.*

son·ship (sun′ship′) *n.* fact, condition, or relation of being a son.

Soo Canals (sōō) Sault Sainte Marie Canals.

Soo·chow (sōō′chou′) *n.* city in eastern China, west of Shanghai. Pop. (1957 est.), 633,000.

soon (sōōn) *adv.* **1.** in the near future; before long; shortly: *Visit us again soon.* **2.** ahead of the normal or appointed time; early. **3.** without delay; promptly; quickly: *I'll come as soon as I can.* **4.** readily; willingly: *I would as soon do it now as later.* [Old English *sōna* within a short time.] —**Syn. 1.** see **shortly.**

soot (soot, sŏŏt) *n.* black, powdery substance, composed mostly of particles of carbon, produced during the incomplete burning of such fuels as wood, coal, or oil. —*v.t.* to soil or cover with soot. [Old English *sōt* the black, powdery substance.]

sooth (sōōth) *Archaic.* *n.* truth; reality. —*adj.* **1.** true; real. **2.** soft; soothing; sweet. [Old English *sōth.*]

soothe (sōōth) **soothed, sooth·ing.** *v.t.* **1.** to bring to a quiet or composed condition; give solace to; calm; comfort: *The soft music soothed his nerves.* **2.** to make less painful or severe; relieve; alleviate: *The medicine soothed his headache.* —*v.i.* to have a soothing effect. [Old English *sōthian* to prove to be true.] —**sooth′er,** *n.* —**Syn. v.t. 1.** see **appease.**

sooth·ing (sōō′thing) *adj.* that soothes; calming; quieting: *soothing words, a soothing medicine.* —**sooth′ing·ly,** *adv.*

sooth·ly (sōōth′lē) *adv.* Archaic. in truth; truly.

sooth·say·er (sōōth′sā′ər) *n.* one who claims to be able to foretell future events. [SOOTH + SAY + -ER[1]]

sooth·say·ing (sōōth′sā′ing) *n.* **1.** act or practice of foretelling future events. **2.** thing foretold; prediction; prophecy.

soot·y (soot′ē, sōō′tē) **soot·i·er, soot·i·est.** *adj.* **1.** covered or soiled with soot: *sooty buildings.* **2.** relating to, consisting of, or producing soot: *sooty deposits.* **3.** having the color of soot. —**soot′i·ly,** *adv.* —**soot′i·ness,** *n.*

sop (sop) *n.* **1.** piece of food soaked or dipped in a liquid, as bread in milk or gravy. **2.** anything that is thoroughly soaked. **3.** anything given to pacify or quiet, as a bribe: *That law is merely a sop to those who have been calling for reform.* —*v.t.* **sopped, sop·ping. 1.** to soak or dip in a liquid: *to sop bread in milk.* **2.** to take up (water or other liquid) by absorption (usually with *up*). **3.** to wet thoroughly; drench. —*v.i.* **1.** to be or become thoroughly wet. **2.** (of a liquid) to be absorbed; soak in. [Old English *sopp* piece of bread soaked in liquid.]

sop., soprano.

soph., sophomore.

soph·ism (sof′iz′əm) *n.* argument having an appearance of truth or reason, but actually false, esp. one used in order to deceive or to display ingenuity. [Latin *sophisma* fallacy, from Greek *sophisma* clever device, captious argument, going back to *sophos* wise, clever.]

soph·ist (sof′ist) *n.* **1.** *usually,* **Sophist.** one of a class of teachers of philosophy, rhetoric, and ethics in Greece in the fifth century B.C., some of whom were criticized for relying on eloquence, subtlety, or ingenuity rather than on sound reasoning in their arguments. **2.** learned person. **3.** one who argues in a clever but fallacious manner; misleading reasoner.

---

at; āpe; cär; end; mē; it; īce; hot; ōld; fôrk; wood; fōōl; oil; out; up; ūse; turn; sing; thin; this; zh in treasure; ə in ago, taken, pencil, lemon, circus.   951

so·phis·tic (sə fis′tik) *adj.* **1.** relating to or characteristic of sophists or sophistry: *sophistic tricks, sophistic subtlety.* **2.** clever and subtle but unsound: *a sophistic argument.* Also, **so·phis′ti·cal.** **—so·phis′ti·cal·ly,** *adv.*

so·phis·ti·cate (*v.,* sə fis′tə kāt′; *n.,* sə fis′tə kit, -kāt′) **-cat·ed, -cat·ing.** *v.t.* **1.** to make less natural, simple, or artless; cause to become artificial, urbane, or worldly wise. **2.** to make complex, intricate, or refined. **3.** to make impure; adulterate. **4.** to mislead or corrupt (a person). **—v.i.** to use sophistry. **—n.** sophisticated person. [Medieval Latin *sophisticatus,* past participle of *sophisticare* to adulterate, tamper with, disguise, going back to Greek *sophistikos* sophistical, from *sophistēs* sophist.]

so·phis·ti·cat·ed (sə fis′tə kā′tid) *adj.* **1.a.** having worldly knowledge and experience; lacking natural simplicity; not naive; worldly wise. **b.** able to make subtle distinctions; perceptive; knowledgeable; cultured: *a sophisticated novelist.* **2.** suitable for or appealing to sophisticated people: *sophisticated entertainment.* **3.** developed to a highly complex, refined, or intricate level; characterized by advanced form or technique: *The company has spent millions of dollars developing this sophisticated electronic equipment.*

so·phis·ti·ca·tion (sə fis′tə kā′shən) *n.* **1.** quality or character of being sophisticated; sophisticated ideas, tastes, or ways. **2.** act of sophisticating.

soph·ist·ry (sof′is trē) *pl.,* **-ries.** *n.* **1.** method of reasoning that is clever, subtle, and superficially plausible but fundamentally unsound. **2.** clever but false argument; sophism. **3.** methods or teachings of the sophists.

Soph·o·cles (sof′ə klēz′) *n.* c.496–c.406 B.C., Greek dramatist.

soph·o·more (sof′ə môr′) *n.* **1.** student in the second year of a four-year high school or college. **2.** one who is in the second year of any endeavor. [Earlier *sophumer,* from *sophom,* obsolete form of SOPH-ISM; with reference to the earlier use of sophistical arguments for intellectual training.]

soph·o·mor·ic (sof′ə môr′ik, -mor′-) *adj.* **1.** of or relating to a sophomore or sophomores. **2.** overconfident of knowledge and intelligence though immature, shallow, and uninformed.

so·po·rif·er·ous (sop′ə rif′ər əs, sō′pə-) *adj.* bringing sleep; soporific. [Latin *soporifer* + -OUS.] **—sop′o·rif′er·ous·ly,** *adv.* **—sop′o·rif′er·ous·ness,** *n.*

so·po·rif·ic (sop′ə rif′ik, sō′pə-) *adj.* **1.** causing or tending to cause sleep. **2.** sleepy; drowsy. **—n.** something that causes sleep, esp. a drug. [Latin *sopor* deep sleep + -FIC.]

sop·ping (sop′ing) *adj.* thoroughly wet; soaked; drenched.

sop·py (sop′ē) **-pi·er, -pi·est.** *adj.* **1.** soaked through with water or other liquid; saturated: *soppy land.* **2.** rainy: *soppy weather.*

so·pran·o (sə pran′ō, -prä′nō) *pl.,* **-pran·os.** *n.* **1.** highest singing voice of women and boys. **2.** singer having such a voice. **3.** instrument having the highest range in a family of musical instruments. **4.** part composed for a soprano voice or instrument. **—adj.** **1.** able to sing soprano: *a soprano voice.* **2.** for a soprano: *a soprano score.* **3.** having the highest range in a family of musical instruments: *a soprano recorder.* [Italian *soprano* highest, treble in music, from *sopra* above, from Latin *suprā.*]

so·ra (sôr′ə) *n.* small, short-billed wading bird, *Porzana carolina,* of the rail family, common in the marshes of North America. [Probably of American Indian origin.]

sorb¹ (sôrb) *n.* **1.** any of several trees of the apple family, as the service tree or rowan tree. **2.** fruit of any of these trees. [Latin *sorbum* the fruit of this tree, *sorbus* this tree.]

sorb² (sôrb) *v.t.* to absorb or adsorb. [From ABSORB and ADSORB.]

Sor·bonne (sôr bon′) *n.* seat of the faculties of literature and science of the University of Paris.

sor·cer·er (sôr′sər ər) *n.* one who practices sorcery. **—sor′cer·ess,** *n.*

sor·cer·y (sôr′sər ē) *pl.,* **-cer·ies.** *n.* supposed use of supernatural powers gained through the aid of evil spirits, esp. to do harm to another person; witchcraft. [Old French *sorcerie* casting of lots, magic, going back to Latin *sors* lot.] **—sor′cer·ous,** *adj.* **—Syn.** see magic.

sor·did (sôr′did) *adj.* **1.** dirty or filthy; squalid; foul: *a sordid tenement, sordid surroundings.* **2.** having a base or degraded character; low; mean; vile: *the sordid details of the crime.* **3.** meanly selfish; mercenary; avaricious. [Latin *sordidus* dirty, vile.] **—sor′did·ly,** *adv.* **—sor′did·ness,** *n.*

sore (sôr) **sor·er, sor·est.** *adj.* **1.** painful or sensitive to the touch; causing physical pain, as an injured or diseased part of the body: *sore muscles.* **2.** feeling physical pain, as from wounds or bruises: *He was sore after the rough game.* **3.** filled with sadness, grief, or misery; distressed: *a sore heart, a sore conscience.* **4.** causing sadness, grief, or misery; distressing: *to be in sore need.* **5.** causing irritation or anger; annoying; vexing: *His failure on the test is a sore point with him.* **6.** *Informal.* annoyed; angry; offended: *Are you still sore at him for not*

inviting you to his party? **—n.** **1.** area of the body where the skin or tissue is broken, bruised, or inflamed, causing pain. **2.** any source of pain, anger, sorrow, or distress. **—adv.** *Archaic.* sorely. [Old English *sār* painful.] **—sore′ness,** *n.*

sore·head (sôr′hed′) *n.* *Informal.* one who is easily angered, annoyed, or offended.

sore·ly (sôr′lē) *adv.* **1.** painfully; grievously; severely: *sorely troubled.* **2.** to a great extent; extremely.

sore throat, painful throat due to an inflammation of the tissues that line the pharynx, usually caused by a bacterial or viral infection.

sor·ghum (sôr′gəm) *n.* **1.** any of a group of tall, tropical grasses, *Sorghum vulgare,* widely cultivated for grain, fodder, syrup, and broom fiber. **2.** syrup made from the juices of a sweet variety of sorghum. [Modern Latin *sorghum,* from Italian *sorgo* this grass, possibly going back to Latin *Syricum (grāmen)* (grass) of Syria.]

sor·go (sôr′gō) *pl.,* **-gos.** *n.* any of several varieties of sorghum cultivated chiefly for their sweet, watery juice, from which syrup is made, and also used for fodder. [Italian *sorgo.* See SORGHUM.]

Sorghum (def. 1)

so·ri (sôr′ī) plural of **sorus.**

so·ror·i·cide¹ (sə rôr′ə sīd′, -ror′-) *n.* act of killing one's sister. [Late Latin *sorōricīdium,* from Latin *soror* sister + *-cīdium.* See -CIDE¹.]

so·ror·i·cide² (sə rôr′ə sīd′, -ror′-) *n.* one who kills his sister. [Latin *sorōricīda,* from *soror* sister + *-cīda.* See -CIDE².]

so·ror·i·ty (sə rôr′ə tē, -ror′-) *pl.,* **-ties.** *n.* club of girls or women, esp. a society of female students in a college. [Medieval Latin *sororitas* sisterhood, from Latin *soror* sister.]

sorp·tion (sôrp′shən) *n.* absorption or adsorption. [From ABSORP-TION and ADSORPTION.]

sor·rel¹ (sôr′əl, sor′-) *n.* any of several weedy plants, genus *Rumex,* bearing long branching clusters of small, usually greenish flowers and sour, heart-shaped leaves. The leaves of certain species are sometimes used as salad greens. [Old French *surele,* from *sur* sour; of Germanic origin.]

sor·rel² (sôr′əl, sor′) *n.* **1.** reddish-brown color. **2.** horse of this color. [Old French *sorel* reddish-brown horse, from *sor;* of Germanic origin.]

sorrel tree, small North American tree, *Oxydendrum arboreum,* of the heath family, having large drooping clusters of white flowers and sour leaves. Also, **sour′wood′.**

sor·row (sor′ō, sôr′ō) *n.* **1.** mental suffering or distress caused by loss, injury, disappointment, or affliction. **2.** cause of grief or regret: *Her illness is a sorrow to her family.* **3.** expression of grief, regret, sadness, or disappointment. **—v.i.** to feel or express sorrow; be sad. [Old English *sorg* grief, anxiety.] **—sor′row·er,** *n.*

sor·row·ful (sor′ō fəl, sôr′ə-, sôr′-) *adj.* **1.** feeling sorrow; sad: *A sorrowful crowd watched the funeral cortege pass by.* **2.** expressing sorrow: *a sorrowful lament.* **3.** causing sorrow: *a sorrowful occasion.* **—sor′row·ful·ly,** *adv.* **—sor′row·ful·ness,** *n.*

sor·ry (sor′ē, sôr′ē) **-ri·er, -ri·est.** *adj.* **1.** full of or feeling sorrow, pity, sympathy, or remorse: *He was sorry to hear of her illness.* **2.** inferior in value or quality; poor; worthless: *a sorry attempt.* **3.** causing or inspiring sadness or pity; wretched; miserable: *The once beautiful village was a sorry sight after the war.* [Old English *sārig* sad.] **—sor′ri·ly,** *adv.* **—sor′ri·ness,** *n.*

sort (sôrt) *n.* **1.** group of persons or things distinguished by common characteristics; class; kind; type: *This sort of plant usually grows in swampy soil.* **2.** quality; character; nature: *Sarcastic remarks of that sort will only make him more angry.* **3.** particular kind of person: *He's not a bad sort.* **4.** particular method of action or procedure; way; manner. **5. sorts.** one of the characters in a font of type. **6. of sorts. a.** of a poor or mediocre kind or quality: *a musician of sorts.* **b.** of different or various kinds. **7. out of sorts. a.** ill-tempered; cross. **b.** slightly ill. **8. sort of.** *Informal.* to some extent; somewhat: *He's been acting sort of strange lately.* **—v.t.** to place, arrange, or separate according to class, kind, or nature (often with *out*): *to sort mail, to sort socks by color.* **—v.i.** *Archaic.* to be alike; agree; harmonize. [Old French *sorte* manner, kind, from Medieval Latin *sors* kind, from Latin *sors* lot, condition, destiny.] **—sort′er,** *n.* **—Syn.** *n.* **1.** see kind².

sor·tie (sôr′tē, sôr tē′) *n.* **1.** sudden attack by troops in a besieged position upon the besiegers; sally. **2.** single round trip of an aircraft on a combat mission. [French *sortie* a going out, departure, from *sortir* to go out; of uncertain origin.]

so·rus (sôr′əs) *pl.,* **so·ri.** *n.* dotlike cluster of sporangia on the underside of the frond of a fern. [Modern Latin *sorus,* from Greek *sōros* heap.]

SOS (es′ō′es′) **1.** coded signal of distress, used esp. by ships and airplanes. In the international code used in telegraphy, it is represented by (· · · — — — · · ·). **2.** any call or signal for help.

at; āpe; cär; end; mē; it; īce; hot; ōld; fôrk; wood; fōͤl; oil; out; up; ūse; turn; sing; thin; **th**is; zh in treasure; ə in ago, taken, pencil, lemon, circus.

so·so (sō′sō′) *adj.* not very good or bad; mediocre: *His performance was so-so.* —*adv.* in a mediocre manner; passably.

sos·te·nu·to (sos′tə nōō′tō) *Music. adj.* sustained or prolonged in the time value of the tones. —*n. pl.,* **-tos** or **-ti** (-tē). movement or passage performed in this manner. —*adv.* in a sostenuto manner. [Italian *sostenuto,* past participle of *sostenere* to maintain, uphold, from Latin *sustinēre.*]

sot (sot) *n.* one who habitually drinks to excess; chronic drunkard. [Old English *sott* fool, from Medieval Latin *sottus* stupid; of uncertain origin.]

sot·tish (sot′ish) *adj.* **1.** stupefied from or as from excessive drinking; stupid. **2.** given to excessive drinking; drunken. —**sot′tish·ly,** *adv.* —**sot′tish·ness,** *n.*

sot·to vo·ce (sot′ō vō′chē) in a low tone of voice, esp. so as not to be overheard. [Italian *sotto voce* literally, under the voice, from Latin *subtus* below + *vōx* sound¹, tone, voice.]

sou (sōō) *n.* former French coin of varying value. [French *sou,* going back to Late Latin *solidus* ancient Roman gold coin. See SOLIDUS.]

sou·bise (sōō bēz′) *n.* white or brown sauce containing onions. [From Prince Charles *Soubise,* 1715–87, French general.]

sou·brette (sōō bret′) *n.* **1.** in light opera or comedy, the role of a pert, scheming lady's maid or of any coquettish young woman. **2.** singer or actress playing such a part. [French *soubrette,* from Provençal *soubreto,* feminine of *soubret* affected, from *soubra* to pass over, exceed, from Latin *superāre* to surpass.]

sou·bri·quet (sō′brə kā′, sō′brə kā′) sobriquet.

sou·chong (sōō′shong′, -chong′) *n.* variety of black tea, originally from China. [Chinese (Mandarin) *hsiao chung* small kind.]

souf·flé (sōō flā′) *n.* baked dish made with egg yolks, white sauce, and other ingredients, as cheese or chocolate, made light and fluffy by adding beaten egg whites before baking. —*adj.* made light and fluffy in cooking. [French *soufflé,* from *souffler* to blow, from Latin *sufflāre* to blow up, puff out.]

sough (sou, suf) *v.i.* to make a rushing, rustling, or sighing sound: *The wind soughed through the branches overhead.* —*n.* rushing, rustling, or sighing sound. [Old English *swōgan* to sound¹.]

sought (sôt) past tense and past participle of **seek.**

soul (sōl) *n.* **1.** principle of life in man, consisting of the faculties of thought, emotion, and action and regarded as being a separate entity distinct from the body; spiritual part of man as distinguished from the physical. **2.** moral or spiritual part of man considered in relation to God, believed to be immortal and to separate from the body at death. **3.** spirit of a dead person, thought of as having an existence of its own. **4.** emotional part of man's nature, as distinguished from his intellect. **5.** spiritual or emotional warmth, force, or energy: *His novels are clever, but they lack soul.* **6.** essential, fundamental, or animating part; vital element: *Discipline is the soul of an army.* **7.** one who leads or inspires: *Churchill was the soul of British resistance to Germany in World War II.* **8.** one who is considered to embody a certain quality; personification: *He is the soul of integrity.* **9.** person: *Not a soul was about.* —*adj. Slang.* relating to, characteristic of, or derived from Negroes or Negro culture: *soul food, soul music.* [Old English *sāwol* principle of life in man, spiritual part of man, disembodied spirit of a dead person.]

soul·ful (sōl′fəl) *adj.* full of or expressing deep feeling: *a soulful gaze, soulful poetry.* —**soul′ful·ly,** *adv.* —**soul′ful·ness,** *n.*

soul·less (sōl′lis) *adj.* having no soul; lacking deep feelings; insensitive. —**soul′less·ly,** *adv.*

soul-search·ing (sōl′sur′ching) *n.* deep and serious examination of one's own beliefs, motives, and values.

sound¹ (sound) *n.* **1.** vibrations transmitted through air, water, or another medium that are capable of being perceived by the ear. **2.** sensation produced in the organs of hearing by such vibrations. **3.** particular instance of this sensation; something that is heard: *the sound of music.* **4.** distance over which a sound may be heard: *We were within sound of the cannon.* **5.** one of the noises made by the vocal organs that make up human speech. **6.** mental effect produced or caused by what is heard; implication: *That sounds reasonable.* **7.** meaningless noise. —*v.i.* **1.** to make or give forth a sound: *The bell sounded from the tower.* **2.** to convey a certain impression; seem: *That sounds reasonable.* **3. to sound off.** *Informal.* **a.** to call out one's name or serial number in a military formation. **b.** to speak in a loud, offensive, or complaining way: *He is always sounding off about the mayor's policies.* —*v.t.* **1.** to cause to make a sound: *The driver sounded his horn.* **2.** to give an order or signal for by a sound; announce by a sound: *to sound a warning.* **3.** to make known; proclaim: *Each speaker sounded the praises of the party's candidate.* **4.** to utter audibly; pronounce: *to sound a syllable.* **5.** to examine or test by causing to give forth sounds: *The doctor sounded his chest for signs of pneumonia.* [Old French *son* sensation produced on the organ of hearing by vibrations, from Latin *sonus* noise.]

sound² (sound) *adj.* **1.** free from damage, defect, or decay: *sound*

timbers. **2.** free from injury or illness; healthy: *a sound mind in a sound body.* **3.a.** having a firm basis; solid: *a sound foundation.* **b.** stable or safe; secure; reliable: *a sound investment.* **4.** in accordance with truth, fact, or reason; sensible: *sound reasoning.* **5.** legally valid. **6.** morally good; honest; upright: *a man of sound character.* **7.** compatible with a conventional point of view; conservative; orthodox. **8.** thorough; complete: *a sound thrashing.* **9.** (of sleep) deep and unbroken. —*adv.* in a sound manner; soundly: *sound asleep.* [Old English (ge)*sund* healthy, unhurt.] —**sound′ly,** *adv.* —**sound′ness,** *n.*

sound³ (sound) *v.t.* **1.** to measure the depth of (water), as by letting down a calibrated line with a weight on the end or by echoing sound off the bottom. **2.** to measure (depth) in this way, esp. at sea. **3.** to explore or examine (the bottom of the sea or another body of water) by means of a line adapted to bring up adhering particles of matter. **4.** to seek to determine or ascertain; investigate; examine: *to sound a person's opinions on an issue.* **5.** to try to learn the opinions and attitudes of (usually with *out*): *He sounded out the other members of the club about the proposal.* **6.** to probe or examine (a cavity in the body) with a sound: *to sound the bladder.* —*v.i.* **1.** to measure the depth of water or a body of water. **2.** (of a whale or fish) to go deep under water; dive swiftly downward. **3.** to make an inquiry or investigation. —*n.* long, slender instrument, usually of metal, with which doctors examine the esophagus, bladder, uterus, and other cavities in the body. [Old French *sonder* to try, test, search the depth of, going back to Latin *sub* under + *unda* wave.]

sound⁴ (sound) *n.* **1.** relatively long, narrow passage of water between larger bodies of water or between the mainland and an island. **2.** long inlet or arm of the sea. **3.** air bladder of a fish. [Old English *sund* swimming, strait (that one can swim across).]

sound barrier, sudden sharp increase in resistance which the air presents to an aircraft as its speed nears the speed of sound. Also, **sonic barrier.**

sound·board (sound′bôrd′) *n.* sounding board *(def. 1).*

sound box, hollow chamber in a stringed musical instrument for increasing the fullness and richness of its tone.

sound effects, artificially produced sounds, as of rain or hoofbeats, used to simulate the sounds called for in a play, motion picture, or radio or television program.

sound·er¹ (soun′dər) *n.* **1.** one who or that which makes a sound. **2.** device in a telegraph that converts electromagnetic code impulses into sound. [SOUND¹ + -ER¹.]

sound·er² (soun′dər) *n.* one who or that which measures the depth of water. [SOUND³ + -ER¹.]

sound·ing¹ (soun′ding) *adj.* **1.** causing or making a sound. **2.** giving forth a deep, full sound; resounding; resonant. **3.** having an imposing sound but little significance; high-sounding. [SOUND¹ + -ING².]

sound·ing² (soun′ding) *n.* **1.** act or process of measuring the depth of water, as by letting down a weighted line. **2.** *also,* **soundings.** depth of water so measured. **3. soundings.** place where the water is shallow enough to allow a sounding line to reach bottom. **4.** investigation of conditions in space or in the atmosphere at a given altitude, esp. with a rocket. **5.** examination, investigation, or sampling, as of public opinion. [SOUND³ + -ING².]

sounding board 1. thin, resonant board of wood in a musical instrument, as a piano or violin, for increasing the fullness of its tone. Also, **sound′board′. 2.** structure suspended behind or over a stage, platform, rostrum, or pulpit to reflect the sound of a speaker's voice toward the audience. **3.** means of spreading or popularizing an idea or opinion. **4.** person or group on whom one tests one's opinions, ideas, or plans: *The executive used his secretary as a sounding board.*

sounding lead (led) lead or other weight at the end of a sounding line.

sounding line, line weighted at one end and marked at intervals of a fathom, used in determining the depth of water.

sound·less¹ (sound′lis) *adj.* having or making no sound; silent. [SOUND¹ + -LESS.] —**sound′less·ly,** *adv.*

sound·less² (sound′lis) *adj.* so deep that it cannot be sounded; unfathomable: *the soundless depths of the ocean.* [SOUND³ + -LESS.]

sound·proof (sound′prōōf′) *adj.* not letting sound pass in or out; deadening or absorbing sound: *a soundproof room.* —*v.t.* to make soundproof of *a building.*

sound track 1. narrow strip along one edge of a motion-picture film that carries the sound recording. **2.** recording of the musical score of a motion picture.

sound truck, truck carrying one or more loudspeakers, used for broadcasting public announcements, as political speeches.

sound wave, longitudinal pressure wave in a material medium, as air or water, esp. one that is audible to the human ear.

soup (sōōp) *n.* **1.** liquid food made by boiling meat, vegetables, or fish in a fluid, esp. water, often with rice or other ingredients added.

2. *Slang.* thick fog. **3.** *Slang.* nitroglycerine. **4. in the soup.** *Slang.* in trouble or difficulty. —*v.t.* **to soup up.** *Slang.* to increase the power or capacity for speed of (a motor, engine, or motor vehicle). [French *soupe* sop, broth; of Germanic origin.]

soup·çon (sŏŏp sôN′, sŏŏp′sôN′) *n.* slight trace or flavor; minute quantity: *Add a soupçon of salt to the meat.* [French *soupçon* suspicion, hint, going back to Late Latin *suspectiō* awe, suspicion, from Latin *suspicere* to regard with awe, mistrust.]

soup kitchen, place that serves food free or at very low cost to needy people.

soup·spoon (sŏŏp′spŏŏn′) *n.* spoon used in eating soup, somewhat larger than a teaspoon.

soup·y (sŏŏ′pē) **soup·i·er, soup·i·est.** *adj.* having the consistency or appearance of soup; like soup.

sour (sour, sou′ər) *adj.* **1.** having the taste produced chiefly by acids; tasting sharp, tart, or tangy, as lemon or lime juice, green fruits, or vinegar. **2.** having an acid or rancid taste because of fermentation; fermented. **3.** having a rank or rancid odor: *sour breath.* **4.a.** distasteful or disagreeable; unpleasant. **b.** having or showing an irritable, sullen, or morose nature; bad-tempered; cross; peevish: *a sour expression.* **5.** below the desired or usual standard or quality; poor: *The inexperienced bugler played several sour notes.* **6.** (of soil) containing excessive acid and damaging to crops. **7.** (of gasoline) containing excessive sulfur; contaminated by sulfur compounds. —*n.* **1.** something sour. **2.** cocktail made with lemon or lime juice: *a whiskey sour, a scotch sour.* —*v.i., v.t.* to become or make sour: *The milk soured when it was left in the hot sun.* [Old English *sūr* having a tart or acid taste, fermented.] —**sour′ly,** *adv.* —**sour′ness,** *n.*

sour·ball (sour′bôl′, sou′ər-) *n.* hard, round piece of candy with a sour taste.

source (sôrs) *n.* **1.** spring, lake, or other body of water that is the point of origin of a river or stream. **2.** place or thing from which something comes, develops, or derives: *The dam is a source of electrical power.* **3.** one who or that which supplies information or evidence, as a book, document, or article: *That almanac is a reliable source.* [Old French *sourse* point of origin of a river or stream, from *sourdre* to rise, going back to Latin *surgere.*] —**Syn. 2.** see **origin.**

sour cherry. 1. small cherry tree, *Prunus cerasus,* having gray bark, stiff, pointed leaves, and clusters of small white flowers. 2. tart, red fruit of this tree, used as in baking.

sour cream, thick cream made sour either by the action of lactic acid bacteria or by artificial processes, used in cooking and in certain dishes.

sour·dough (sour′dō′, sou′ər-) *n.* **1.** fermented dough used as leaven in making bread. **2.** prospector or pioneer in western Canada or Alaska, esp. in the Yukon.

sour grapes, attitude of scorn or disparagement toward something because one cannot have it. [From Aesop's fable about a fox that calls some grapes sour because he is unable to reach them.]

sour gum, North American tree, *Nyssa sylvatica,* having close-grained wood and blue-black fruit.

sour·ish (sour′ish, sou′ər-) *adj.* somewhat sour.

sour mash, grain mash used in distilling some whiskeys, consisting of a mixture of new mash with some mash from a previous distillation.

sour·puss (sour′poos′, sou′ər-) *n.* *Slang.* one who has a gloomy or disagreeable expression or disposition; grouch.

sour·sop (sour′sop′, sou′ər-) *n.* **1.** small evergreen tree, *Annona muricata,* of tropical America, belonging to the same family as the custard apple. **2.** juicy, edible fruit of this tree, having a greenish skin and a slightly acid pulp.

sour·wood (sour′wood′, sou′ər-) *n.* sorrel tree.

Sou·sa, John Philip (sŏŏ′zə) 1854–1932, U.S. musical composer and bandmaster.

sou·sa·phone (sŏŏ′zə fōn′) *n.* large circular tuba with a wide flaring bell that faces forward, used chiefly in brass bands. [From John Philip *Sousa.*]

souse (sous) **soused, sous·ing.** *v.t.* **1.** to plunge into water or other liquid; immerse. **2.** to make soaking wet; drench. **3.** to steep or soak in vinegar or brine; pickle. **4.** *Slang.* to make drunk; intoxicate. —*v.i.* **1.** to be or become immersed or soaked in water or other liquid. **2.** to become drunk. —*n.* **1.a.** pickled food, esp. the feet, ears, and head of a pig. **b.** liquid used in pickling; brine. **2.** act of plunging into water or another liquid. **3.** *Slang.* drunkard. [Old French *sous* something pickled; of Germanic origin.]

sou·tache (sŏŏ tash′) *n.* narrow flat braid in a herringbone effect, used for trimming and decoration. [French *soutache* galloon, from Magyar *sujtás.*]

sou·tane (sŏŏ tän′, -tan′) *n.* cassock worn by priests of the Roman Catholic Church. [French *soutane,* from Italian *sottana* literally, undergarment (because worn under vestments), from *sotto* under, from Latin *subtus* beneath.]

south (south) *n.* **1.** general direction to one's left as one faces the sunset. **2.** one of the four cardinal points of the compass, lying directly opposite north and at 180 degrees. **3.** *also,* **South.** any region situated toward this direction in relation to a specified point of reference. **4. the South.** region of the United States south of Pennsylvania, the Ohio River, and Missouri, esp. the states that fought for the Confederacy in the Civil War. —*adj.* **1.** toward or in the south; southern. **2.** coming from the south: *a south wind.* —*adv.* toward the south: *Many birds fly south in the winter.* [Old English *sūth* in the direction opposite to the north.]

South Africa, Republic of, country in southern Africa, on the Atlantic and Indian oceans, formerly the Union of South Africa. Administrative capital, Pretoria; judicial, Bloemfontein; legislative, Cape Town. Area, 472,359 sq. mi. Pop. (1969 est.), 19,618,000.

South African 1. relating to southern Africa. **2.** relating to the Republic of South Africa. **3.** one who was born or lives in the Republic of South Africa, esp. one of European descent.

South African Dutch, Afrikaans.

South America, fourth-largest continent, in the Western Hemisphere. Area, approx. 6,881,000 sq. mi. Pop. (1966 est.), 171,000,000. —**South American.**

South·amp·ton (south amp′tən, -hamp′-) *n.* port city on the southern coast of England. Pop. (1968), 210,100.

South Bend, city in northern Indiana. Pop. (1970), 125,580.

south·bound (south′bound′) *adj.* going southward: *a southbound train.*

South Carolina, state in the southeastern United States, on the Atlantic. Capital, Columbia. Area, 31,055 sq. mi. Pop. (1970), 2,590,-516. Abbreviation, S.C. —**South Carolinian.**

South China Sea, part of the Pacific, bounded by southeastern China, Vietnam, the Malay Peninsula, Borneo, and the Philippines.

South Da·ko·ta (də kō′tə) state in the north-central United States. Capital, Pierre. Area, 77,047 sq. mi. Pop. (1970), 665,507. Abbreviations, S. Dak., S.D. —**South Dakotan.**

South·down (south′doun′) *n.* one of a breed of small, hornless sheep of English origin, having short wool and raised esp. for food.

south·east (south′ēst′) *n.* **1.** point on the compass halfway between south and east. **2.** region or place in this direction. **3. the Southeast.** southeastern part of the United States. —*adj.* **1.** toward or in the southeast; southeastern. **2.** from the southeast: *a southeast wind.* —*adv.* toward the southeast.

Southeast Asia, region of Asia comprising the countries of Burma, Cambodia, Indonesia, Laos, Malaysia, Philippines, Singapore, Thailand, North Vietnam, and South Vietnam. Area, 1,734,000 sq. mi.

south·east·er (south′ēs′tər) *n.* strong wind or storm from the southeast.

south·east·er·ly (south′ēs′tər lē) *adj., adv.* toward or from the southeast.

south·east·ern (south′ēs′tərn) *adj.* toward or in the southeast.

south·east·ward (south′ēst′wərd) *adv. also,* **south·east·wards.** toward the southeast. —*adj.* toward or in the southeast. —*n.* region or place in the southeast.

south·east·ward·ly (south′ēst′wərd lē) *adj., adv.* toward the southeast.

south·er (sou′thər) *n.* strong wind or storm from the south.

south·er·ly (suth′ər lē) *adj., adv.* **1.** toward the south: *a southerly direction, to travel southerly.* **2.** from the south.

south·ern (suth′ərn) *adj.* **1.** toward or in the south: *a room with a southern exposure.* **2.** of, relating to, or characteristic of the south or South. **3.** from the south: *a southern wind.* [Old English *sūtherne* from the south, relating to the south.]

Southern Alps, mountain range in New Zealand, on South Island.

Southern Cross, southern constellation having four bright stars in the form of a cross. Also, **Crux.**

south·ern·er (suth′ər nər) *n.* **1.** one who was born or lives in the south. **2.** *usually,* **Southerner.** one who was born or lives in the South of the United States.

Southern Hemisphere, half of the earth south of the equator.

Southern lights, aurora australis.

south·ern·most (suth′ərn mōst′) *adj.* farthest south.

Southern Rhodesia, see **Rhodesia.**

Southern Yemen, country on the southern coast of the Arabian peninsula, bordered on the north by Saudi Arabia and Yemen. Capital, Aden. Area, approx. 111,000 sq. mi. Pop. (1975 est.), 1,700,000. Also, **People's Democratic Republic of Yemen.**

South·ey, Robert (sou′thē, suth′ē) 1774–1843, English poet.

South·field (south′fēld′) *n.* city in southeastern Michigan. Pop. (1970), 69,285.

South Gate, city in southern California. Pop. (1970), 56,909.

South Island, larger of the two main islands of New Zealand. Area, 58,093 sq. mi. Pop. (1968), 798,681.

South Korea, country occupying the southern part of the Korean

at; āpe; cär; end; mē; it; īce; hot; ōld; fôrk; wood; fŏŏl; oil; out; up; ūse; turn; sing; thin; this; zh in treasure; ə in ago, taken, pencil, lemon, circus.

peninsula. Capital, Seoul. Area, 38,004 sq. mi. Pop. (1969 est.), 31,-139,000.

south·land (south′lənd, -land′) *n.* land in the south, as the southern region of a country.

south·paw (south′pô′) *Informal. n.* **1.** player who is left-handed, esp. a left-handed baseball pitcher. **2.** any left-handed person. —*adj.* left-handed.

South Pole **1.** southernmost point on the earth; the southern end of the earth's axis. **2. south pole.** pole of a magnet that points to the south when the magnet swings freely.

South Sea Islands, islands of the South Pacific; Oceania.

South Seas, seas south of the equator, esp. the South Pacific.

south·south·east (south′south′ēst′) *n.* point on the compass halfway between south and southeast. —*adj., adv.* toward the south-southeast.

south·south·west (south′south′west′) *n.* point on the compass halfway between south and southwest. —*adj., adv.* toward the south-southwest.

South Vietnam, country in southeastern Asia, bordering North Vietnam on the north, Laos and Cambodia on the west, and the South China Sea on the east. Capital, Saigon. Area, 65,987 sq. mi. Pop. (1969 est.), 17,867,000.

south·ward (south′wərd) *adv.* also, **south·wards.** toward the south: *to travel southward.* —*adj.* toward the south. —*n.* southern part or direction; south: *The river flows to the southward.*

south·west (south′west′) *n.* **1.** point on the compass halfway between south and west. **2.** region or place in this direction. **3. the Southwest.** southwestern part of the United States, esp. Oklahoma, Texas, New Mexico, Arizona, and southern California. —*adj.* **1.** lying toward or situated in the southwest; southwestern. **2.** coming from the southwest: *a southwest wind.* —*adv.* toward the southwest: *to sail southwest.*

South-West Africa, territory on the southwestern coast of Africa, administered by the Republic of South Africa. Area, 318,262 sq. mi. Pop. (1969 est.), 615,000.

south·west·er (south′wes′tər, sou′wes′-) *also,* **sou'west·er.** *n.* **1.** heavy wind or storm from the southwest. **2.** waterproof hat with a broad brim that widens in the back to protect the neck in stormy weather, worn esp. by sailors.

Southwester (def. 2)

south·west·er·ly (south′wes′tər lē) *adj., adv.* toward or from the southwest.

south·west·ern (south′wes′tərn) *adj.* toward or in the southwest.

south·west·ward (south′west′wərd) *adv.* also, **south·west·wards.** toward the southwest. —*adj.* toward or in the southwest. —*n.* region or place in the southwest.

south·west·ward·ly (south′west′wərd lē) *adj., adv.* toward or from the southwest.

sou·ve·nir (sōō′və nēr′, sōō′və nēr′) *n.* thing serving as a reminder of a person, place, or event; keepsake; memento: *souvenirs of a trip.* [French *souvenir,* from *souvenir* to remember, from Latin *subvenīre* to come up, come to mind.] —**Syn.** see **keepsake.**

sou'west·er (sou′wes′tər) *n.* southwester.

sov·er·eign (sov′rən, sov′ər ən) *n.* **1.** supreme ruler of a monarchy, as a king or queen. **2.** individual or group having supreme authority. **3.** former British gold coin worth one pound. —*adj.* **1.** having supreme power, rank, or authority: *a sovereign ruler.* **2.** not controlled by others; having independent authority: *a sovereign state.* **3.** superior to all others; supreme; highest. **4.** effective or powerful, as a cure or remedy. [Old French *soverain* supreme ruler, supreme, going back to Latin *super* above.] —**sov′er·eign·ly,** *adv.* —**Syn.** *n.* **1.** see **monarch.**

sov·er·eign·ty (sov′rən tē, sov′ər ən-) *pl.,* **-ties.** *n.* **1.** supreme authority: *The king holds sovereignty in a monarchy.* **2.** independence of the political control of other states; power of self-government. **3.** state, community, or other political unit that is sovereign. **4.** rank, dominion, or authority of a sovereign.

so·vi·et (sō′vē et′, -it, sov′ē-) *n.* **1.** fundamental legislative and executive unit of government in the Soviet Union, existing at village, city, county, province, and national levels. Members of soviets are popularly elected. **2. Soviets.** government officials or people of the Soviet Union. —*adj.* **1.** relating to a soviet or government by soviets. **2. Soviet.** relating to the Soviet Union. [Russian *sovet* council.]

so·vi·et·ism (sō′vē ə tiz′əm, sov′ē-) *n.* system of government by soviets.

so·vi·et·ize (sō′vē ə tīz′, sov′ē-) *-ized, -iz·ing. v.t.* **1.** to change to a soviet system of government. **2.** *usually,* **Sovietize.** to bring under the control or influence of the Soviet Union. —**so′vi·et·i·za′tion,** *n.*

Soviet Russia **1.** Soviet Union. **2.** Russian Soviet Federated Socialist Republic.

Soviet Union, largest country in the world in area, extending from eastern Europe to the northeastern coast of Asia, divided into fifteen constituent republics. Capital, Moscow. Area, 8,599,300 sq. mi. Pop. (1969 est.), 240,571,000. Also, **Union of Soviet Socialist Republics, Rus′sia, Soviet Russia.**

sov·ran (sov′rən) *n., adj.* *Archaic.* sovereign.

sow¹ (sō) *sowed, sown* or *sowed, sow·ing. v.t.* **1.** to spread or scatter (seed) over the ground for growth: *to sow corn.* **2.** to spread or scatter seed on or upon (land): *to sow a field with corn.* **3.** to spread, disseminate, or propagate: *to sow dissension, to sow suspicion.* **4.** to spread or cover with anything. —*v.i.* to spread or scatter seed over the ground for growth. [Old English *sāwan* to scatter seed over the ground for growth.] —**sow′er,** *n.*

sow² (sou) *n.* adult female pig. [Old English *sugu.*]

sow bug (sou) wood louse (*def. 1*).

sow thistle (sou) any plant of the genus *Sonchus,* esp. *S. oleraceus,* a coarse, spiny weed with yellow flowers that is a common garden pest.

sox (soks) *n.,pl. Informal.* socks.

soy (soi) *n.* **1.** salty, dark-brown sauce made from soybeans fermented and steeped in brine, used esp. in Chinese and Japanese cooking. Also, **soy sauce. 2.** soybean. [Japanese *shōyu* the sauce, from Chinese (Mandarin) *chiang yu.*]

soy·bean (soi′bēn′) *n.* **1.** seed of a bushy Asian plant, *Glycine max,* of the pea family, widely cultivated esp. in the United States, which is rich in oil and protein, and is used for fodder and soil improvement. Oil and meal from the seeds are also used in making many food and chemical products. **2.** the plant itself.

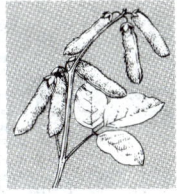

Soybean pods

sp. **1.** special. **2.** species. **3.** specific. **4.** specimen **5.** spelling.

Sp. **1.** Spain. **2.** Spanish.

SP, Shore Patrol.

spa (spä) *n.* **1.** a mineral spring. **2.** locality where such springs exist, esp. a resort. [From *Spa,* Belgian town famous as a resort with mineral springs.]

space (spās) *n.* **1.a.** unlimited distance extending in all directions; infinite expanse within which all material objects are contained and all events take place. **b.** region beyond the earth's atmosphere; outer space: *to launch a rocket into space.* ▲ often used attributively: *space travel.* **2.** distance, expanse, or area between or within points or objects: *a space between buildings.* **3.** area or extent set apart or available for some purpose: *a parking space.* **4.a.** particular extent of time: *a space of an hour.* **b.** interval or period of time; while: *The hikers rested for a space.* **5.** reserved or available accommodations on a train, bus, airplane, or other means of transportation. **6.** area or time available for or used by advertising, as in a magazine or newspaper or on a television or radio program. **7.** *Printing.* small blank piece of type metal used to separate words or characters. **8.** *Music.* one of the degrees or intervals between the lines of the staff. **9.** interval during the transmission of a telegraph message when the key is open or not in contact. **10.** *Mathematics.* set of abstract objects among which a metrical or other relationship exists. —*v.t.,* **spaced, spac·ing. 1.** to separate by spaces: *The builder spaced the houses far apart.* **2.** to divide into spaces. [Old French *espace* extent of place or time, from Latin *spatium* room, extent, interval.]

space capsule, capsule (*def. 2*).

space·craft (spās′kraft′) *pl.,* **-craft.** *n.* any vehicle, manned or unmanned, designed to be orbited around the earth or launched into outer space. Also, **space′ship′.**

space flight, flight into or in outer space.

space heater, small heating unit, often portable, for warming an enclosed area, as a room or tent.

space·less (spās′lis) *adj.* **1.** having no limits in space; infinite; boundless. **2.** occupying no space.

space·man (spās′man′, -mən) *pl.,* **-men.** *n.* astronaut.

space medicine, branch of medicine that deals with the medical, physiological, and psychological problems encountered in space flight.

space·port (spās′pôrt′) *n.* installation at which spacecraft are tested, launched, or maintained.

space probe, artificial satellite or other spacecraft equipped with instruments designed to obtain and record information about outer space.

space·ship (spās′ship′) *n.* spacecraft.

space shuttle, space vehicle used to carry men and equipment between the earth and an orbiting space station.

space station, manned artificial satellite designed to orbit the earth and to be used for observation and as a launching site for further space travel. Also, **space platform.**

space suit, protective pressurized suit capable of withstanding low pressure and temperatures, for use in space flights.

---

space-time (spās′tīm′) *n.* four-dimensional frame of reference within which any event may be precisely located. Three of these dimensions are the ordinary space coordinates, length, breadth, and thickness, and the fourth is time. Also, **space-time continuum.**

space writer, journalist or other writer who is paid according to the amount of space in print filled by his writing.

spac·ing (spā′sing) *n.* **1.** act of one who or that which spaces. **2.** arrangement of spaces, as in printing: *open spacing, wide spacing.* **3.** space or spaces, as between printed words.

spa·cious (spā′shəs) *adj.* **1.** having or providing much space; roomy: *a house with spacious rooms.* **2.** having a broad scope or range; of great extent; vast: *spacious skies.* [Latin *spatiōsus* roomy, of great extent, from *spatium* room, extent, interval.] —**spa′cious·ly,** *adv.* —**spa′cious·ness,** *n.*

Spack·le (spak′əl) *n. Trademark.* substance, either in paste or powder form, that hardens upon drying, used to fill in holes or cracks in plaster, esp. before painting or papering. —*v.t.* **-led, -ling.** to apply Spackle to (holes or cracks).

spade[1] (spād) *n.* **1.** tool used for digging, having a heavy, flat iron blade which can be pressed into the ground with the foot, and a long handle with a grip at the top. **2.** any of various tools or implements resembling a spade. **3. to call a spade a spade.** to call something by its right name; speak frankly and truly. —*v.t.* to dig or cut with a spade: *to spade a garden.* [Old English *spadu* tool for digging.] —**spad′er,** *n.*

spade[2] (spād) *n.* **1.** playing card bearing one or more black figures shaped like this: ♠ **2. spades.** suit of such playing cards. [Italian *spada* sword, figure on a playing card, from Latin *spatha* broadsword, from Greek *spathē* broad blade.]

spade·work (spād′wûrk′) *n.* **1.** work done with a spade. **2.** preliminary work necessary to a project or activity.

spa·dix (spā′diks) *pl.,* **spa·dix·es** or **spa·di·ces** (spā dī′sēz). *n.* thick or fleshy spike of tiny flowers, usually enclosed in a spathe, as in the calla. [Latin *spādīx* palm branch broken off, from Greek *spādīx.*]

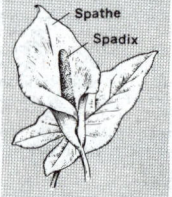

Spathe
Spadix

Spadix

spa·ghet·ti (spə get′ē) *n.* food consisting of a mixture of wheat flour and water shaped into long strings, thinner than macaroni and not hollow. It is cooked by boiling. [Italian *spaghetti,* plural of *spaghetto* string, diminutive of *spago* string, cord; of uncertain origin.]

Spain (spān) *n.* country in southwestern Europe, on the Iberian Peninsula. Capital, Madrid. Area, 194,884 sq. mi. Pop. (1969 est.), 32,949,-000. Also, *Spanish.* **Es·pa′ña.**

spake (spāk) *Archaic.* a past tense of **speak.**

span[1] (span) *n.* **1.** distance from the tip of the thumb to the tip of the little finger when the hand is fully spread out, considered as nine inches when used as a unit of measure. **2.** full extent, amount, or reach of anything: *the span of a person's life, a short span of attention.* **3.a.** distance between two supports, as of an arch, beam, or bridge. **b.** part or section between two supports. **4.** distance between the wing tips of an airplane. **5.** short space of time. —*v.t.,* **spanned, span·ning. 1.** to measure by or as by the hand with the thumb and little finger extended. **2.** to encircle or encompass with a hand or hands, as the waist or wrist. **3.** to extend over or across: *That highway spans the state.* **4.** to provide with something that extends over or across: *to span a river with a bridge.* [Old English *span(n)* such a distance measured from the thumb.]

span[2] (span) *n.* pair of mules or other draft animals driven together in harness. [Dutch *span.*]

span[3] (span) *Archaic.* a past tense of **spin. Span.,** Spanish.

span·drel (span′drəl) *n.* **1.** triangular space between the outer curve of an arch and the rectangular framework surrounding it. **2.** space between two adjoining arches and the horizontal molding or cornice running above them. [Diminutive of Anglo-Norman *spaundre,* from Old French *espandre* to spread out, expand, from Latin *expandere.*]

Spandrels

span·gle (spang′gəl) *n.* **1.** small, thin, often circular piece of glittering metal or plastic used for decoration, esp. one sewn on a garment. **2.** any small glittering object. —*v.t.,* **-gled, -gling.** to decorate with or as with spangles; cause to glitter. —*v.i.* to sparkle with or as with spangles; glitter. [Diminutive of obsolete *spang* small glittering ornament, from Middle Dutch *spange* clasp, buckle.]

Span·iard (span′yərd) *n.* member or close descendant of the people of Spain.

span·iel (span′yəl) *n.* small or medium-sized dog of any of various breeds, usually having short legs, long drooping ears, and a silky, wavy coat. [Old French *espaignol* literally, Spanish, from Spanish *español* Spanish, from *España* Spain, from Latin *Hispānia.*]

Span·ish (span′ish) *adj.* relating to or characteristic of Spain, its people, or their language or culture. —*n.* **1.** people of Spain collectively. **2.** Romance language spoken in Spain and Spanish America.

Spanish America, countries south of the United States in which the chief language is Spanish, including Mexico, Central America except British Honduras, South America except Brazil and the Guianas, and most of the West Indies.

Span·ish-A·mer·i·can (span′ish ə mer′i kən) *adj.* **1.** relating to Spain and America or to Spain and the United States. **2.** relating to Spanish America or its people. —*n.* **1.** member or close descendant of the people of Spanish America. **2.** resident of the United States who is of Spanish or Spanish-American descent.

Spanish-American War, war between the Unites States and Spain in 1898.

Spanish Armada, fleet sent against England in 1588 by Philip II of Spain. It was defeated by the English and later almost destroyed by storms. Also, **the Armada.**

Spanish bayonet, tall treelike plant, *Yucca aloifolia,* found in the southern United States, Mexico, and the West Indies, bearing stiff, sword-shaped leaves and large showy flowers.

Spanish fly 1. bright-green blister beetle, *Lytta vesicatoria,* native to southern Europe. **2.** poisonous substance prepared from these beetles, formerly used to treat a variety of diseases and as an aphrodisiac.

Spanish Inquisition, form of the Inquisition practiced in Spain from 1478 to 1820, notorious for its cruel treatment of those accused of heresy.

Spanish mackerel, any of several edible sea fish of the genus *Scomberomorus,* esp. *S. maculatus,* a commercially important species found in warm Atlantic waters.

Spanish Main 1. formerly, the mainland of Spanish America, esp. the northern coast of South America, from the mouth of the Orinoco River to the Isthmus of Panama. **2.** part of the Caribbean Sea through which Spanish merchant ships traveled in colonial times, a former haunt of pirates.

Spanish moss, grayish-green flowering plant, *Tillandsia usneoides,* that grows in long, slender, hanging strands on the branches of certain trees in the southern United States and tropical America.

Spanish onion, large onion with a yellowish skin and a mild flavor.

Spanish moss

Spanish Sahara, overseas possession of Spain, on the northwestern coast of Africa. Area, 102,703 sq. mi. Pop. (1969 est.), 63,000.

spank (spangk) *v.t.* to strike with the open hand or a flat object, esp. on the buttocks, as punishment. —*n.* blow with the open hand or with something flat. [Possibly imitative.]

spank·er (spang′kər) *n.* **1.** fore-and-aft sail, attached to a gaff and boom, on the mast nearest the stern of a square-rigged ship. **2.** mast nearest the stern in a ship having four or more masts.

spank·ing (spang′king) *adj.* **1.** exceptional of its kind; very large, great, or fine. **2.** (of a breeze) brisk and fresh. **3.** moving with a quick, vigorous pace: *a spanking trot.* [Of uncertain origin.]

span·ner (span′ər) *n.* **1.** one who or that which spans. **2.** *British.* wrench.

span·worm (span′wurm′) *n.* inch worm.

spar[1] (spär) *n.* **1.** pole, as a yard, gaff, or boom, supporting or extending a sail of a ship. **2.** one of the principal lateral members of the framework of an airplane wing. —*v.t.,* **sparred, spar·ring.** to furnish (a ship) with spars. [Possibly from Old Norse *sperra* beam, rafter.]

Spar[1]

spar[2] (spär) *v.i.,* **sparred, spar·ring. v.i. 1.** to engage in boxing, esp. for practice. **2.** to argue or dispute cautiously or in a restrained way, as if to test one's opponent. **3.** (of a gamecock) to fight or strike with the feet or spurs. [Old English *sperran* to strike.]

spar[3] (spär) *n.* any of various crystalline, lustrous minerals that split easily into flakes or layers. [Middle Low German *spar* gypsum.]

SPAR (spär) *also,* **Spar.** *n.* member of the women's reserve of the U.S.

Coast Guard. [From Latin *s(emper) par(ātus)* always ready (motto of the U.S. Coast Guard).]

spare (spâr) *spared, spar·ing. v.t.* **1.** to refrain from inflicting harm on; leave unhurt or uninjured: *The emperor gave a sign to spare the fallen gladiator.* **2.** to deal with gently or leniently; show consideration for: *to spare a person's feelings.* **3.** to save or free (someone) from pain, sorrow, shame, or trouble: *to spare oneself trouble. Please spare me the gory details of the accident.* **4.** to manage or do without; part with, esp. without inconvenience: *Can you spare a cup of sugar? Could you spare a few minutes to help me with this problem?* **5.** to have left over or in reserve. ▲ used chiefly in the phrase *to spare: We caught the train with only a minute to spare.* **6.** to refrain from employing or dispensing freely. ▲ used chiefly in negative phrases: *Give me some more meat, and don't spare the gravy.* —*v.i.* **1.** to refrain from inflicting harm or punishment; be merciful or forbearing. **2.** to use or practice economy; be frugal. —*adj.* **spar·er, spar·est. 1.** in excess of what is needed or held in reserve: *a spare tire, a spare room, spare cash.* **2.** (of time) not taken up by usual or ordinary duties; free: *a few spare minutes.* **3.** not fat; thin; lean: *a man with a spare figure.* **4.** scanty; meager: *a spare meal, a spare diet.* —*n.* **1.** something extra or held in reserve, as a spare tire. **2.** Bowling. **a.** act or instance of knocking down all the pins with two rolls of the ball in one frame. **b.** score so made. [Old English *sparian* to leave unhurt, abstain from.] —**spare′ly,** *adv.* —**spare′ness, spar′er,** *n.*

spare·ribs (spâr′ribz′) *n.pl.* cut of pork consisting of the thin end of the ribs with most of the meat trimmed off. [Inverted form of earlier *ribspare,* from Middle Low German *ribbespēr* rib cut, from *ribbe* rib + *spēr* spit[2].]

spar·ing (spâr′ing) *adj.* **1.** merciful or forbearing. **2.** careful in spending or using; frugal. **3.** small in amount, quantity, or extent; scanty; meager. —**spar′ing·ly,** *adv.* —**spar′ing·ness,** *n.*

spark¹ (spärk) *n.* **1.** small, hot, glowing particle, esp. one thrown off from something burning or produced by the striking of one hard body against another. **2.a.** short, brilliant flash of light produced by a discharge of electricity through air or another insulating material. **b.** the discharge itself. **c.** electrical discharge in a spark plug. **d.** mechanism controlling such a discharge. **3.** any sparkle or flash of light. **4.** vital or animating factor: *The assassination of the king was the spark that touched off the war.* **5.** small amount; trace: *a spark of interest.* **6.** trace of life or vitality. —*v.i.* **1.** to throw off or produce sparks. **2.** to flash or fall as or like sparks. —*v.t.* to stir to activity; activate; incite: *to spark a revolt. The young pitcher's display of skill sparked his team to victory.* [Old English *spearca* small particle of fire, small amount.]

spark² (spärk) *n.* **1.** dashing, foppish young man. **2.** beau, lover, or suitor. —*v.t., v.i. Informal.* to court; woo. [Possibly from Old Norse *sparkr* lively.]

spark arrester, device that prevents sparks from escaping, as a piece of mesh on top of a chimney.

spark coil, induction coil used to produce an electric spark, as in an internal-combustion engine.

spark gap, open space between two electrodes through which a discharge of electricity may pass.

spar·kle (spär′kəl) *-kled, -kling. v.i.* **1.** to shine, as if giving off sparks; reflect or emit flashes of light: *The jewels sparkled. Her eyes sparkled with merriment.* **2.** to give off sparks. **3.** to be brilliant, lively, or vivacious: *His conversation sparkled with wit.* **4.** to effervesce, as champagne or soda water; bubble. —*v.t.* to cause to sparkle. —*n.* **1.** sparkling appearance or quality: *the sparkle of clear blue ocean waters.* **2.** brilliance, liveliness, or vivacity. **3.** small spark or glowing particle. [SPARK¹ + -LE.] —**Syn.** *v.i.* **2.** see *flash.*

spar·kler (spär′klər) *n.* **1.** one who or that which sparkles. **2.** firework that burns slowly and throws off a brilliant shower of sparks. **3.** *Informal.* gem that sparkles, esp. a diamond.

sparkling wine, wine that is naturally carbonated by a second fermentation within the bottle, as champagne.

spark plug 1. device that is fitted into the cylinder of an internal-combustion engine and ignites the mixture of fuel and air by means of an electric spark. **2.** *Informal.* one who activates, inspires, or leads some activity or undertaking: *He is the spark plug of the team.*

sparring partner, one with whom a boxer spars for practice.

spar·row (spar′ō) *n.* any of numerous small, seed-eating birds, families Fringillidae and Ploceidae, having a stout, conical bill, medium-length tail, and predominantly brown plumage with a white, gray, or buff underside, as the house sparrow or song sparrow. Length: 5–7 inches. [Old English *spearwa.*]

sparrow hawk 1. reddish-brown hawk, *Falco sparverius,* native to North and Central America, the male of which has blue wings. Length: 9–12 inches. **2.** bird-eating hawk, *Accipiter nisus,* native to Europe and Asia. Length: 11–15 inches.

sparse (spärs) *spars·er, spars·est. adj.* thinly spread or distributed; not crowded or dense: *a sparse population.* [Latin *sparsus,* past participle of *spargere* to scatter.] —**sparse′ly,** *adv.* —**sparse′ness, spar′si·ty,** *n.* —**Syn.** see *meager.*

Spar·ta (spär′tə) *n.* ancient Greek city-state in the southeastern part of the Peloponnesus, noted for the austerity of its life and the stern discipline and military effectiveness of its soldiers.

Spar·ta·cus (spär′tə kəs) *n.* died 71 B.C., Thracian slave and gladiator, leader of a slave rebellion against Rome from 73 to 71 B.C.

Spar·tan (spär′tən) *adj.* **1.** relating to Sparta, its people, or their culture. **2.** resembling or characteristic of the Spartans; stoical, highly disciplined, courageous, or austere. —*n.* **1.** native or citizen of Sparta. **2.** one who has Spartan characteristics. —**Spar′tan·ism,** *n.*

spasm (spaz′əm) *n.* **1.** sudden, involuntary, often convulsive, contraction of a muscle or group of muscles. **2.** any sudden, brief burst of energy, activity, or feeling: *a spasm of anguish, a spasm of fear.* [Latin *spasmus* convulsion, from Greek *spasmos,* from *spaein* to draw, tear.]

spas·mod·ic (spaz mod′ik) *adj.* **1.** relating to or characterized by a spasm or spasms. **2.a.** resembling a spasm; sudden, violent, and temporary. **b.** happening irregularly; intermittent; fitful: *spasmodic interest. His spasmodic attempts to improve his grades were unsuccessful.* **3.** highly emotional or excitable. [Modern Latin *spasmodicus,* from Greek *spasmōdēs* convulsive, from *spasmos* convulsion.] —**spas·mod′i·cal·ly,** *adv.*

spas·tic (spas′tik) *adj.* **1.** relating to, characterized by, or suffering from a spasm or spasms. **2.** suffering from spastic paralysis. —*n.* one who is suffering from spastic paralysis. [Latin *spasticus* afflicted with spasms, from Greek *spastikos* drawing in, from *spān* to draw, pull.] —**spas′ti·cal·ly,** *adv.*

spastic paralysis, form of paralysis, caused by brain damage, in which the affected muscles are tense and somewhat rigid, and the reflexes are abnormally active.

spat¹ (spat) *n.* **1.** petty quarrel; slight argument. **2.** *Informal.* a slap. **3.** slapping or splashing sound. —*v.i.* **1.** to engage in a petty quarrel. **2.** to strike with a slapping or splashing sound. —*v.t. Informal.* to slap. [Possibly imitative.]

spat² (spat) a past tense and a past participle of *spit¹.*

spat³ (spat) *usually,* **spats.** *n.* short covering of cloth or leather worn over the instep of a shoe and the ankle, usually fastened under the shoe with a strap. [From earlier *spatterdash* a long legging, from SPATTER + DASH.]

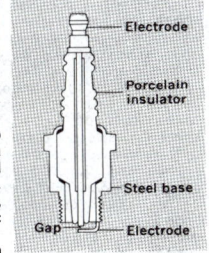

Spat³

spat⁴ (spat) *n.* **1.** spawn of an oyster or similar shellfish. **2.a.** young oyster. **b.** young oysters collectively. —*v.i.* **spat·ted, spat·ting.** (of oysters) to spawn. [Of uncertain origin.]

spate (spāt) *n.* **1.** sudden or strong outpouring, as of words or emotion: *a spate of hostile feeling.* **2.** *British.* **a.** sudden flood. **b.** sudden heavy fall of rain. [Of uncertain origin.]

spathe (spāth) *n.* leaf or leaflike part, often large, enclosing a flower cluster or spadix, as in the calla. [Latin *spatha* broad, flat, wooden instrument, from Greek *spathē* broad blade.]

spa·tial (spā′shəl) *adj.* **1.** relating to space. **2.** existing or occurring in space. [Latin *spatium* room, extent + -AL¹.] —**spa·ti·al·i·ty** (spā′shē al′ə tē), *n.* —**spa′tial·ly,** *adv.*

spa·ti·o·tem·po·ral (spā′shē ō tem′pər əl) *adj.* of, relating to, or existing in both space and time.

spat·ter (spat′ər) *v.t.* **1.** to scatter in drops or small particles: *to spatter paint on a canvas.* **2.** to splash with drops or small particles, esp. so as to soil or stain: *The mud spattered their shoes.* **3.** to stain with slander or disgrace; defame. —*v.i.* **1.** to send out or throw off drops or small particles. **2.** to fall or strike in or as in a shower: *Bullets spattered around the target.* —*n.* **1.a.** act or instance of spattering. **b.** sound made by this: *the spatter of raindrops on a roof.* **2.** splash or spot of something spattered: *There were spatters of grease on the stove.* [Possibly imitative.]

spat·ter·dock (spat′ər dok′) *n.* any of a group of water plants, genus *Nuphar,* of the water lily family, found in stagnant waters of eastern North America and having yellowish flowers that grow above the water.

spat·u·la (spach′ə lə) *n.* small implement with a flat, flexible blade, used for spreading, stirring, or mixing thick, soft substances, as paint, plaster, and foods, and for lifting or scraping, as in cooking. [Latin

Electrode
Porcelain insulator
Steel base
Gap — *Electrode*
Spark plug

spatula broad piece, diminutive of *spatha* broad, flat, wooden instrument for stirring, broadsword, from Greek *spathē* broad blade.]

spat·u·late (spach′ə lit) *adj.* shaped like a spatula: *a spatulate leaf.*

spav·in (spav′in) *n.* disease of horses in which a bony growth forms below the hock, causing stiffness and lameness. [Shortened from Old French *espavin;* of uncertain origin.] —**spav′ined,** *adj.*

spawn (spôn) *n.* **1.** eggs of certain aquatic animals, as fish, shellfish, or amphibians, deposited in masses. **2.** numerous offspring. **3.** product; outcome; result. **4.** mycelium of fungi. —*v.i.* to lay eggs. —*v.t.* **1.** to produce (eggs or offspring). **2.** to give birth to; bring forth; engender. [Anglo-Norman *espaundre* to shed roe, going back to Latin *expandere* to spread out. Doublet of EXPAND.]

spay (spā) *v.t.* to remove the ovaries of (an animal). [Anglo-Norman *espeier* to pierce with a sword, from Old French *espee* sword, from Latin *spatha.* See SPADE².]

Spatulate leaf

S.P.C.A., Society for the Prevention of Cruelty to Animals.

S.P.C.C., Society for the Prevention of Cruelty to Children.

speak (spēk) **spoke** or *(archaic)* **spake, spo·ken** or *(archaic)* **spoke, speak·ing.** *v.i.* **1.** to utter words with the voice: *The baby hasn't learned to speak yet. She speaks with a slight French accent.* **2.** to make known or convey an idea, fact, or feeling: *Will you speak to John about his behavior? Actions speak louder than words.* **3.** to converse: *They spoke to each other for several hours.* **4.** to deliver a speech: *The author spoke before a large audience.* **5.** to emit a sound. **6.** (of dogs) to bark when ordered. **7. so to speak.** speaking figuratively; as if it were so. **8. to speak for. a.** to serve as a representative or spokesman for. **b.** to request. **9. to speak of.** deserving mention: *He didn't receive anything to speak of.* **10. to speak out** (or **up**). **a.** to speak loud enough to be understood. **b.** to speak freely. —*v.t.* **1.** to give voice to; utter: *She spoke words of sympathy.* **2.** to use or be able to use in speaking: *Michael speaks Gaelic fluently.* **3.** to make known or convey; reveal; express: *She always speaks the truth.* [Old English *specan* to utter words.] —**Syn.** *v.i.* **3.** see **talk.**

speak·eas·y (spēk′ē′zē) *pl.* **-eas·ies.** *n. Slang.* place where alcoholic beverages are sold illegally, as during Prohibition.

speak·er (spē′kər) *n.* **1.** one who speaks, esp. one who engages in or practices public speaking. **2.** *usually,* **Speaker.** presiding officer of a legislative assembly: *Speaker of the House.* **3.** loudspeaker.

speak·er·ship (spē′kər ship′) *n.* position of presiding officer in a legislative assembly.

speak·ing (spē′king) *adj.* **1.** that uses, allows, or involves speech: *a speaking voice, a speaking distance, a speaking engagement.* **2.** expressive, suggestive, or striking: *a speaking gesture, a speaking likeness.* —*n.* act or utterance of one who speaks.

speaking in tongues, glossolalia (*def.* 1).

spear (spēr) *n.* **1.** weapon consisting of a sharp-pointed head attached to a long shaft, used for thrusting or throwing. **2.** shoot or slender stalk, as of grass: *asparagus spears.* —*v.t.* to stab, penetrate, or take hold with or as with a spear. —*v.i.* (of a plant) to send forth shoots or stems; sprout. [Old English *spere* this weapon.] —**spear′er,** *n.*

spear·head (spēr′hed′) *n.* **1.** sharp-pointed head of a spear. **2.** person or group that leads in an action or endeavor: *the spearhead of a fund-raising drive. The paratroopers were the spearhead of the invasion.* —*v.t.* to be in the forefront of; lead: *to spearhead an attack.*

spear·man (spēr′mən) *pl.,* **-men.** *n.* one who is armed with a spear, esp. a soldier.

spear·mint (spēr′mint′) *n.* fragrant plant, *Mentha spicata,* of the mint family, bearing sharply toothed, lance-shaped leaves. **2.** aromatic oil obtained from this plant, used as a flavoring.

spear side, paternal branch or male side of a family. Opposed to **distaff side.**

spec., special.

spe·cial (spesh′əl) *adj.* **1.** out of the ordinary; unusual; exceptional: *a special talent.* **2.** marked off from others by some distinguishing quality or character: *a special day.* **3.** made, arranged, or designed for a particular occasion, purpose, or person: *a special broadcast. You must have special permission to photograph these paintings.* —*n.* **1.** something made, designed, or used for a particular occasion or purpose. **2.** special offer or price reduction, as on food. [Latin *speciālis* individual, particular, from *speciēs* appearance, kind².] —**spe′cial·ly,** *adv.*

Spearmint

special delivery, delivery of mail in advance of regular delivery for an additional fee.

spe·cial·ist (spesh′ə list) *n.* one who devotes or restricts himself to a particular branch of a profession or field of study, esp. a doctor who restricts his practice to one branch of medicine.

spe·cial·ize (spesh′ə līz′) **-ized, -iz·ing.** *v.i.* **1.** to concentrate on a particular product, activity, branch of a profession, or field of study. **2.** *Biology.* to become adapted to a special function or environment. —*v.t.* **1.** to adapt or limit to a specific purpose, use, or function. **2.** to mention specifically; itemize. —**spe′cial·i·za′tion,** *n.*

spe·cial·ty (spesh′əl tē) *pl.,* **-ties.** *n.* **1.** particular branch of a profession or field of study that a person devotes or restricts himself to. **2.** particular product or service that a store or similar establishment excels or deals in. **3.** state of being special or of having a special character or quality. Also, *British.* **spe·ci·al·i·ty** (spesh′ē al′ə tē).

spe·cie (spē′shē) *n.* coined money; coin. [Latin *(in) speciē* (in) kind (ablative singular of *speciēs* kind²).]

spe·cies (spē′shēz) *pl.,* **-cies.** *n.* **1.a.** subdivision of a genus in plant and animal classification, containing members having certain permanent characteristics in common. **b.** plant or animal belonging to such a subdivision. **2.** distinct kind or type; sort. **3.** consecrated bread or wine used in the Mass. **4. the species.** the human race. [Latin *speciēs* appearance, kind². Doublet of SPICE.]

specif., specifically.

spe·cif·ic (spi sif′ik) *adj.* **1.** distinctly or explicitly named or defined: *a specific offer, a specific amount.* **2.** belonging exclusively to; peculiar to: *the specific characteristics of a region.* **3.** (of a remedy) effective in the prevention or treatment of a particular disease. **4.** (of a disease) produced by a particular condition or microorganism. —*n.* **1.** something adapted to or intended for a specific effect or result, as a medicine used to prevent or treat a particular disease. **2.** *usually,* **specifics.** *Informal.* particulars; details. [Late Latin *specificus* constituting a species, particular, from Latin *speciēs* kind, appearance + *facere* to make.] —**Syn.** *adj.* **1.** see **explicit.** **2.** see **particular.**

spe·cif·i·cal·ly (spi sif′ik lē) *adv.* in a specific manner; definitely; explicitly: *Mother specifically said to come right home.* —**spec·i·fic·i·ty** (spes′ə fis′ə tē), *n.* —**Syn.** see **especially.**

spec·i·fi·ca·tion (spes′ə fi kā′shən) *n.* **1.** act of specifying. **2.** item or article specified, as in a plan or contract. **3.** *usually,* **specifications.** detailed description of the particulars of a projected work, as a building.

specific gravity, ratio of the density of a given substance to the density of a substance used as a standard. Water is used as the standard for solids and liquids and air is used for gases.

specific heat, amount of heat necessary to raise the temperature of one gram of a given substance by one degree centigrade.

spec·i·fy (spes′ə fī′) **-fied, -fy·ing.** *v.t.* **1.** to mention specifically; state or describe in detail: *John forgot to specify the place where we should meet.* **2.** to set down as a specification: *The architect specified oak for the wood trim.* [Old French *specifer* to particularize, from Late Latin *specificare* to endow with form, from *specificus* particular. See SPECIFIC.]

spec·i·men (spes′ə mən) *n.* **1.** single person or thing considered to be representative or typical of its class or group; example. **2.** sample, as of tissue or urine, for medical analysis and diagnosis. **3.** *Informal.* peculiar person; sort. [Latin *specimen* example, indication.] —**Syn.** **1.** see **example.**

spe·cious (spē′shəs) *adj.* **1.** seemingly true, probable, or reasonable, but actually false; plausible: *He used specious arguments to justify his position.* **2.** outwardly and deceptively attractive or worthy of confidence. [Latin *speciōsus* beautiful, from *speciēs* appearance, form.] —**spe′cious·ly,** *adv.* —**spe′cious·ness,** *n.*

speck (spek) *n.* **1.** very small bit; particle: *There was not a speck of dirt anywhere after we finished cleaning.* **2.** small spot, stain, or mark. —*v.t.* to mark with specks; speckle. [Old English *specca* spot, mark.] —**Syn.** *n.* see **bit².**

speck·le (spek′əl) *n.* spot or mark, as on fur or skin. —*v.t.,* **-led, -ling.** to mark or cover with speckles.

speckled trout, brook trout.

specs (speks) *n.,pl. Informal.* **1.** spectacles. **2.** specifications.

spec·ta·cle (spek′tə kəl) *n.* **1.** something seen, esp. an impressive or unusual sight. **2.** public display, exhibition, or performance, esp. on a grand scale. **3.** spectacles. eyeglasses. **4. to make a spectacle of oneself.** to behave badly or improperly in public. [Latin *spectāculum* show, sight.]

spec·ta·cled (spek′tə kəld) *adj.* **1.** wearing spectacles. **2.** (of an animal) having a marking or markings that suggest spectacles.

spec·tac·u·lar (spek tak′yə lər) *adj.* of, relating to, or resembling a spectacle. —*n.* something lavish, imposing, or magnificent, as a lengthy and elaborately produced television presentation. —**spec·tac′u·lar·ly,** *adv.*

spec·ta·tor (spek′tā′tər, spek tā′-) *n.* one who looks on without participating; observer. [Latin *spectātor.*]
Syn. *n.* **Spectator, onlooker, observer** mean one who watches without participating in an activity, event, or occurrence. **Spectator** implies one who is formally part of an audience, esp. as a viewer of some organized activity, as a sports event or contest, and suggests a certain excitement and partisan interest in viewing the outcome: *Twenty thousand spectators were at the arena to see the Olympic games.* **Onlooker** implies one who takes a casual, more fleeting, and detached view, esp. as a result of some sudden or unusual activity: *Several onlookers gathered in the street to watch the fight.* **Observer** implies one who is impartial and objective while taking great interest in careful notice of detail, esp. with the intention of recording impressions and learning something from them: *That poet is a keen observer of nature.*
spec·ter (spek′tər) *also, British,* **spec·tre.** *n.* **1.** visible spirit of a dead person; ghost. **2.** something that haunts or disturbs the mind: *the specter of inflation.* [Latin *spectrum* appearance, apparition.] —**Syn. 1.** see **ghost.**
spec·tra (spek′trə) a plural of **spectrum.**
spec·tral (spek′trəl) *adj.* **1.** of or resembling a specter; ghostly: *Somber, spectral trees, their trunks pale as cigar ash* (Miller, 1934). **2.** of, relating to, or produced by a spectrum.
spectro- *combining form* of or concerning a spectrum: *spectroscope.* [From SPECTRUM.]
spec·tro·gram (spek′trə gram′) *n.* photograph of a spectrum.
spec·tro·graph (spek′trə graf′) *n.* instrument used for photographing a spectrum, esp. the spectrum of a celestial object.
spec·tro·he·li·o·graph (spek′trō hē′lē ə graf′) *n.* instrument used for studying and photographing the spectrum of the sun.
spec·trom·e·ter (spek trom′ə tər) *n.* instrument for measuring the spectral wavelengths or indexes of refraction.
spec·tro·scope (spek′trə skōp′) *n.* instrument that separates white light into a spectrum by causing the light to pass through a series of lenses and a prism or diffraction grating. [SPECTRO- + -SCOPE.] —**spec·tro·scop·ic** (spek′trə skop′ik) *also,* **spec′tro·scop′i·cal,** *adj.* —**spec′tro·scop′i·cal·ly,** *adv.*
spec·tros·co·py (spek tros′kə pē) *n.* study of spectra with a spectroscope. —**spec·tros′co·pist,** *n.*
spec·trum (spek′trəm) *pl.* **-tra** (-trə) or **-trums.** *n.* **1.** band of colors into which white light is separated according to wavelength by being passed through a prism or diffraction grating. The colors of the spectrum are red, orange, yellow, green, blue, indigo, and violet. **2.** range of electromagnetic radiation, from the shortest to the longest waves. **3.** range or scope of related ideas, activities, or qualities: *the political spectrum.* [Latin *spectrum* appearance.]
spec·u·lar (spek′yə lər) *adj.* of, relating to, or resembling a mirror. [Latin *speculāris,* from *speculum* mirror.]
spec·u·late (spek′yə lāt′) *-lat·ed, -lat·ing. v.i.* **1.** to think carefully or seriously in order to form a tentative conclusion; conjecture: *She speculated about her friend's motives.* **2.** to engage in a risky business venture with the hope of making large gains. **3.** to buy or sell securities, commodities, land, or the like in order to profit by the rise or fall of prices. [Latin *speculātus,* past participle of *speculārī* to watch, examine, from *specula* watchtower.]
spec·u·la·tion (spek′yə lā′shən) *n.* **1.** act or instance of speculating; conjecture. **2.** conclusion or opinion reached by or based on conjecture. **3.** act or practice of speculating in securities, commodities, land, or the like.
spec·u·la·tive (spek′yə lā′tiv, -lə tiv) *adj.* **1.** given to serious thinking or inquiry; reflective; thoughtful: *He has a speculative mind.* **2.** of, characterized by, or based upon speculation; theoretical rather than practical: *His ideas are very speculative.* **3.** involving financial risk on the chance of great profit: *These stocks are very speculative.* **4.** of, relating to, or involved in financial speculation: *The speculative investor bought shares of stock on margin.* —**spec′u·la′tive·ly,** *adv.* —**spec′u·la′tive·ness,** *n.*
spec·u·la·tor (spek′yə lā′tər) *n.* one who speculates, esp. in business. [Latin *speculātor* explorer, spy.]
spec·u·lum (spek′yə ləm) *pl.* **-la** (-lə) or **-lums.** *n.* **1.** mirror, esp. of polished metal, used as a reflector in telescopes. **2.** surgical instrument used to enlarge an opening for the purpose of examination. [Latin *speculum* mirror.]
sped (sped) a past tense and past participle of **speed.**
speech (spēch) *n.* **1.** faculty of expressing an idea, fact, or feeling by the use of distinct and meaningful combinations of words. **2.** act of speaking. **3.** something spoken, esp. before an audience on a formal occasion: *The candidate gave his acceptance speech on television.* **4.** characteristic or habitual manner of speaking. **5.** particular idiom, dialect, or language. **6.** study of public speaking and the techniques of effective oral communication. [Old English *spæc* act of speaking, talk, language.]

speech·i·fy (spē′chə fī′) **-fied, -fy·ing.** *v.i.* to make a speech, esp. a long, wordy, or pompous speech; harangue. —**speech′i·fi′er,** *n.*
speech·less (spēch′lis) *adj.* **1.** temporarily unable to speak or respond, esp. because of extreme emotion or shock: *We sat speechless with anger listening to his insults.* **2.** that cannot be or is not expressed in words: *She was filled with speechless anxiety.* **3.** lacking the faculty or power of speech; mute; dumb. —**speech′less·ly,** *adv.* —**speech′less·ness,** *n.*
speed (spēd) *n.* **1.** rapidity or quickness of motion; swiftness: *He ran with all the speed he could muster.* **2.** rate of motion; velocity: *Drive at a safe speed.* **3.** gear or combination of gears, as in the transmission of a motor vehicle. **4.a.** sensitivity of a photographic film, paper, or plate to light, expressed in any of several number systems. **b.** amount of light that a fully open lens permits to pass through, indicated by its *f* number. **5.** *Archaic.* prosperity; success. **6.** *Slang.* amphetamine. —*v.i.* **sped** or **speed·ed, speed·ing.** **1.** to move or act rapidly or quickly; hasten: *He sped through his chores.* **2.** to drive a motor vehicle faster than is safe or legally permitted. **3.** *Archaic.* to prosper or succeed. —*v.t.* **1.** to cause to move rapidly or quickly; give speed to: *He sped the car through the streets.* **2.** to hasten the progress or process of; expedite: *The post office sped the letter on its way.* **3.** to advance toward a conclusion; further: *The lawyer helped speed the processing of the will.* **4.** *Archaic.* to cause or help to prosper or succeed. [Old English *spēd* quickness, swiftness, success.]
speed·boat (spēd′bōt′) *n.* motorboat built to travel at high speeds.
speed·er (spē′dər) *n.* one who or that which speeds, esp. one who drives a motor vehicle faster than is safe or legally permitted.
speed limit, maximum or minimum speed that is legally permitted on a given road.
speed·om·e·ter (spē dom′ə tər, spi-) *n.* device for measuring the speed of a vehicle in miles per hour.
speed·ster (spēd′stər) *n.* one who speeds, esp. one who drives a motor vehicle at very high speeds.
speed trap, town or section of a road that is closely watched by police or checked by radar and where traffic laws are strictly enforced.
speed·up (spēd′up′) *n.* increase in speed, output, or work.
speed·way (spēd′wā′) *n.* **1.** road prepared or reserved for driving at high speeds. **2.** track for motorcycle or automobile races.
speed·well (spēd′wel′) *n.* any of various herbs, genus *Veronica,* found in cool and temperate regions, having small pink, blue, or white flowers. Also **ve·ron′i·ca.**
speed·y (spē′dē) **speed·i·er, speed·i·est.** *adj.* **1.** characterized by rapid motion; swift: *speedy runners.* **2.** without delay; prompt: *a speedy reply.* —**speed′i·ly,** *adv.* —**speed′i·ness,** *n.*
spe·le·ol·o·gy (spē′lē ol′ə jē) *n.* exploration and scientific study of caves. —**spe·le·o·log·i·cal** (spē′lē ə loj′i kəl), *adj.* —**spe·le·ol′o·gist,** *n.*
spell¹ (spel) **spelled** or **spelt, spell·ing.** *v.t.* **1.** to write or name the letters of (a word), esp. in their proper or correct order. **2.** (of letters) to form (a word): *D-o-g spells dog.* **3.** to amount to; signify: *Hesitation spelled ruin for him.* **4.** to spell out. **a.** to explain clearly or in detail; make explicit. **b.** to read slowly or with difficulty. —*v.i.* to form a word or words by letters. [Old French *espeller* to explain; of Germanic origin.]
spell² (spel) *n.* **1.** word or word formula having occult or magic power. **2.** state of enchantment. **3.** irresistible influence or attraction; fascination; charm. [Old English *spell* story, saying.]
spell³ (spel) *n.* **1.** brief, indefinite period of time: *We sat outside for a spell.* **2.** period of weather of a specified sort: *a hot spell, a dry spell.* **3.** attack, bout, or fit of something, as an illness: *a dizzy spell.* **4.** period or term of work or other activity: *a three-year spell as a writer.* **5.** turn of work taken to relieve another: *a spell at the oars* —*v.t.* **spelled, spell·ing.** to relieve by taking a turn: *John and his friend spelled each other at the wheel during the trip.* [Old English *spelian* to take the place of.]
spell·bind (spel′bīnd′) **-bound, -bind·ing.** *v.t.* to hold under or as if under a spell; enchant.
spell·bind·er (spel′bīn′dər) *n.* speaker who holds another or others spellbound, esp. a political speaker.
spell·bound (spel′bound′) *adj.* held as by a spell; entranced; rapt.
spell·er (spel′ər) *n.* **1.** one who spells words. **2.** textbook used to teach spelling to students. Also (*def. 2*), **spelling book.**
spell·ing (spel′ing) *n.* **1.** manner in which a word is spelled; orthography. **2.** act of one who spells.
spelling bee, competition that is won by the person or team spelling the most words correctly.
spelt¹ (spelt) a past tense and past participle of **spell**¹.
spelt² (spelt) *n.* variety of wheat, *Triticum spelta,* cultivated in southern Europe, used mainly for livestock feed. [Old English *spelt,* from Late Latin *spelta;* of Germanic origin.]
spel·ter (spel′tər) *n.* zinc, esp. in the form of slabs, plates, or ingots.

at; āpe; cär; end; mē; it; īce; hot; ōld; fôrk; wood; fool; oil; out; up; ūse; turn; sing; thin; this; zh in treasure; ə in ago, taken, pencil, lemon, circus.

[Possibly a modification (influenced by Italian *peltro* pewter) of Dutch *spiauter* pewter.]

spe·lunk·er (spi lung′kər) *n.* one who explores caves. [Obsolete *spelunk* cave (from Latin *spēlunca*, from Greek *spēlynx*) + -ER[1].]

spe·lunk·ing (spi lung′king) *n.* act or process of exploring caves.

spen·cer (spen′sər) *n.* short, tailless jacket worn by men and women in the late eighteenth and early nineteenth centuries, usually having a collar that turned down and long, tight sleeves. [From the 2nd Earl *Spencer*, 1758–1834.]

Spen·cer, Herbert (spen′sər) 1820–1903, English philosopher.

Spen·ce·ri·an[1] (spen sēr′ē ən) *adj.* of or relating to Herbert Spencer or his philosophy. —*n.* follower of Herbert Spencer or his philosophy.

Spen·ce·ri·an[2] (spen sēr′ē ən) *adj.* of or relating to a system of penmanship characterized by clearly formed, rounded, and slanted letters. [From Platt Rogers *Spencer*, 1800–64, U.S. teacher who developed the Spencerian system of penmanship.]

spend (spend) *spent, spend·ing. v.t.* **1.** to pay out (money); disburse: *Helen spent ten dollars on a scarf.* **2.** to pass (time) in a specified manner or place: *Charlotte spent a weekend in Vermont. Tom spent two years traveling through Europe.* **3.** to use up or wear out; exhaust: *Hank spent his energy organizing the rally.* —*v.i.* to pay out or use up money or other possessions. [Old English *spendan* to pay out, from Latin *expendere* to weigh out (money), pay. Doublet of EXPEND.] —**spend′er,** *n.*

Syn. *v.t.* **1. Spend, expend, disburse** mean to use a specified amount of money for some purpose. **Spend** is the most general term, frequently applied to an individual's use of his own money, esp. to buy or pay for something: *I am willing to spend up to ten dollars to have the television fixed.* **Expend** implies large sums of money allotted, as by a business or government, to meet various needs: *Only ten percent of the school's budget was expended on hiring new teachers.* **Disburse**, like *expend*, emphasizes the allocation of large sums by an organization, but is often applied to one that is a central source for the authorization or distribution of funds for various groups which will then actually utilize the money: *The foundation disbursed twenty million dollars to medical schools around the country.*

spending money, money reserved or used for personal expenses.

spend·thrift (spend′thrift′) *n.* one who spends money foolishly, lavishly, or wastefully; extravagant person. —*adj.* lavish or wasteful; extravagant.

Spen·ser, Edmund (spen′sər) 1552–99, English poet.

Spen·se·ri·an (spen sēr′ē ən) *adj.* of, relating to, or characteristic of Edmund Spenser or his poetry.

Spenserian stanza, stanza consisting of eight lines in iambic pentameter followed by a final Alexandrine, and rhyming *ababbcbcc.* [From Edmund *Spenser*, who used it in his allegorical poem *The Faerie Queene.*]

spent (spent) *v.* past tense and past participle of **spend.** —*adj.* deprived of strength or energy; worn out; exhausted: *a spent athlete, a spent volcano.*

sperm[1] (spurm) *n.* **1.** fluid secreted by the testes, containing the male reproductive cells; semen. **2.** male reproductive cell; spermatozoon. [Late Latin *sperma* seed, from Greek *sperma.*]

sperm[2] (spurm) *n.* **1.** spermaceti. **2.** sperm whale. [Short for SPERMACETI, SPERM OIL, and SPERM WHALE.]

sper·ma·cet·i (spur′mə set′ē, -sē′tē) *n.* white, waxy substance derived from sperm oil, used to make cosmetics and to waterproof paper and fabrics. [Medieval Latin *sperma cetī* sperm of a whale, from Late Latin *sperma* seed (see SPERM[1]) + Latin *cētī,* genitive of *cētus* whale[1] (from Greek *kētos.*)]

sper·ma·ry (spur′mər ē) *pl.,* -**ries.** *n.* organ or gland in which male reproductive cells are generated.

sper·mat·ic (spur mat′ik) *adj.* of or relating to sperm or to a spermary.

sper·ma·to·phyte (spur mat′ə fīt′, spur′mə tə-) *n.* any of the seed-producing plants of the division Spermatophyta, including the angiosperms and gymnosperms. [Greek *spermat-*, stem of *sperma* seed + -PHYTE.]

sper·ma·to·zo·id (spur′mə tə zō′id) *n.* ciliated, motile male gamete of a plant, usually produced in an antheridium. [From SPERMATOZOON.]

sper·ma·to·zo·on (spur′mə tə zō′ən) *pl.,* -**zo·a** (-zō′ə). *n.* male reproductive cell; male gamete. Also, **sperm.** [Greek *spermat-*, stem of *sperma* seed + *zōion* animal.]

sperm oil, yellow oil derived from the sperm whale, used as a lubricant.

sperm whale, large toothed whale, *Physeter catodon,* having a massive, barrel-shaped head. Length: 60 feet.

Sperm whale

spew (spū) *also,* **spue.** *v.t.* to cast up, throw out, or discharge; eject; vomit: *The chimney spewed smoke.* —*v.i.* to vomit. —*n.* that which is spewed. [Old English *spīwan,* *spēowan* to cast out, vomit.]

Spe·zia (spet′syä, spāt′sē ə) *n.* La Spezia.

sp gr, specific gravity.

sphag·num (sfag′nəm) *n.* any of a group of pale-green mosses found growing in bogs and marshes, often used by florists as a packing material for plants. [Modern Latin *sphagnum,* from Greek *sphagnos.*]

sphal·er·ite (sfal′ə rīt′, sfā′lə-) *n.* ore of zinc, usually containing iron and cadmium. Formula: ZnS Also, **zinc blende.** [Greek *sphaleros* slippery, deceptive + -ITE[1]; because commonly mistaken for lead ore.]

sphen·o·don (sfē′nə don′, sfen′ə-) *n.* tuatara.

sphe·noid (sfē′noid) *adj.* **1.** wedge-shaped. **2.** of, relating to, or designating a wedge-shaped compound bone of the skull located below the frontal bone and to the front of the temporal bone. Also, **sphe·noid′al.** —*n.* the sphenoid bone. [Modern Latin *sphenoides,* from Greek *sphēnoeidēs* wedge-shaped, from *sphēn* wedge + *eidos* form, shape.]

sphere (sfēr) *n.* **1.** three-dimensional figure having all the points of its surface equidistant from the center. **2.** body having this shape; ball; globe. **3.** range, field, or extent of interest, influence, knowledge, or activity. **4.** social class, rank, or position. **5.** any of various celestial bodies, as stars or planets. **6.** celestial sphere. **7.** any of a series of ten concentric globes believed by ancient astronomers to revolve around the earth and to carry the planets and stars. [Late Latin *sphēra* ball, globe, going back to Greek *sphaira.*] —**Syn.** **2.** see ball[1].

spher·i·cal (sfer′i kəl) *adj.* **1.** shaped like a sphere; globular. **2.** of or relating to a sphere or spheres. Also, **spher′ic.** —**spher′i·cal·ly,** *adv.*

sphe·ric·i·ty (sfi ris′ə tē) *n.* state of being spherical; roundness.

sphe·roid (sfēr′oid) *n.* round three-dimensional figure that approaches a sphere in shape. —**sphe·roi′dal,** *adj.* —**sphe·roi′dal·ly,** *adv.*

spher·ule (sfer′ōōl, -ūl, sfēr′-) *n.* little sphere or spherical body; globule.

sphinc·ter (sfingk′tər) *n.* circular band of muscle that surrounds a passage or opening in the body and contracts or expands to close or open it. [Late Latin *sphinctēr,* from Greek *sphinktēr* band[2], muscle closing an opening.]

sphinx (sfingks) *pl.,* **sphinx·es** or **sphin·ges** (sfin′jēz). *n.* **1.** ancient Egyptian mythological creature depicted with the head of a human or animal and the body of a lion. **2.** the Sphinx. large statue of this mythological creature at Giza. **3.** Sphinx. *Greek Mythology.* winged monster having the head and breasts of a woman and the body of a lion, who proposed a riddle to passersby and strangled all who could not guess it. **4.** someone or something enigmatic. [Latin *Sphinx* Sphinx of Greek mythology, from Greek *Sphinx,* from *sphingein* to bind tight, strangle.]

sphyg·mo·graph (sfig′mə graf′) *n.* instrument that records the rate, strength, and variations of the pulse. [Greek *sphygmos* pulse + -GRAPH.]

sphyg·mo·ma·nom·e·ter (sfig′mō mə nom′ə tər) *n.* instrument that measures blood pressure. [Greek *sphygmos* pulse + MANOMETER.]

spi·ca (spī′kə) *pl.,* **spi·cae** (spī′sē) or **spi·cas.** *n.* **1.** spiral bandage with reversed turns. **2.** Spica. bright bluish-white star in the constellation Virgo. **3.** *Botany.* spike[2]. [Latin *spīca* point, ear of grain.]

spi·cate (spī′kāt) *adj.* *Botany.* having or forming a spike or spikes; arranged in spikes. [Latin *spīcātus,* past participle of *spīcāre* to furnish with ears of grain, from *spīca* point, ear of grain.]

spice (spīs) *n.* **1.** any of various aromatic or pungent vegetable substances used to season food. **2.** such substances collectively. **3.** that which adds zest or interest: *Variety is the spice of life.* **4.** pungent or fragrant odor, as of perfume. —*v.t.,* **spiced, spic·ing.** **1.** to season with a spice or spices. **2.** to add zest or interest to: *He spiced his conversation with anecdotes.* [Old French *espice* substance used to season food, from Late Latin *speciēs,* from Latin *speciēs* kind[2], appearance. Doublet of SPECIES.]

sperm[1]
Sperm cells

Sperm[1]
Sperm cells

Roundworm

Front and side views / Salamander

Man

at; āpe; cär; end; mē; it; īce; hot; ōld; fôrk; wood; fōōl; oil; out; up; ūse; turn; sing; thin; this; zh in treasure; ə in ago, taken, pencil, lemon, circus.

spice·ber·ry (spīs'ber'ē) *pl.,* **-ries.** *n.* wintergreen *(def. 1).*
spice·bush (spīs'boosh') *n.* **1.** aromatic shrub, *Lindera benzoin,* found in swamps in eastern North America, bearing clusters of small yellow flowers. **2.** shrub, *Calycanthus occidentalis,* found in California, sometimes cultivated for its fragrant pale-brown flowers.

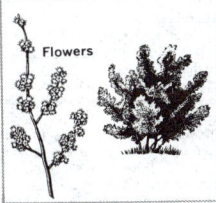
Flowers
Spicebush

Spice Islands, see Moluccas.
spic·er·y (spī'sər ē) *n.* **1.** spices. **2.** spicy quality, flavor, or fragrance.
spick-and-span (spik'ən span') *also,* **spic-and-span.** *adj.* fresh, neat, and clean: *a spick-and-span house.* [Short for obsolete *spick-and-span-new: spick,* form of SPIKE[1] (referring to a newly made nail) + AND + *span-new* entirely new, from Old Norse *spânnÿr* new as a chip just shaved off (from *spânn* chip + *-nÿr* new).]
spic·u·late (spik'yə lāt', -lit) *adj.* **1.** having or forming a spicule or spicules. **2.** resembling a spicule; needlelike. Also, **spic'u·lar.**
spic·ule (spik'ūl) *n.* small, needlelike part, esp. one of the siliceous or crystalline projections that form the skeleton of a sponge. [Latin *spīculum* small, sharp point, arrow, diminutive of *spīca* point, ear of grain.]
spic·y (spī'sē) **spic·i·er, spic·i·est.** *adj.* **1.** seasoned with spice; containing spice: *spicy food.* **2.** resembling spice; pungent or fragrant. **3.** zesty; keen: *a spicy debate.* **4.** slightly improper; risqué; racy. —**spic'i·ly,** *adv.* —**spic'i·ness,** *n.*
spi·der (spī'dər) *n.* **1.** any of a group of widely distributed invertebrates, order Araneida, characterized by a body divided into two parts, four pairs of legs, and several pairs of spinnerets that spin silken threads for making cocoons and webs. **2.** one who or that which resembles or suggests a spider. **3.** frying pan having a long handle and legs. [Old English *spīthra* invertebrate of the order Araneida; literally, spinner, going back to *spinnan* to spin.]

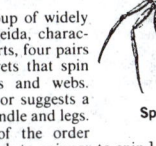
Spider

spider crab, any of various crabs characterized by long, slender legs and a relatively small, triangular body.
spider monkey, any of a group of monkeys of tropical America, genus *Ateles,* having long slender limbs and a long prehensile tail.
spi·der·wort (spī'dər wurt') *n.* any of a group of trailing plants, genus *Tradescantia,* bearing small white, blue, or purple flowers.
spi·der·y (spī'dər ē) *adj.* **1.** resembling or suggesting a spider or a spider's web. **2.** infested with spiders.
spiel (spēl, shpēl) *n. Slang.* lengthy speech, esp. one intended to persuade; harangue. [Dialectal German *spiel* talk.] —**spiel'er,** *n.*
spiff·y (spif'ē) **spiff·i·er, spiff·i·est.** *adj. Slang.* smart in dress or appearance; dapper; neat. [Of uncertain origin.]
spig·ot (spig'ət) *n.* **1.** faucet. **2.** plug or valve in a faucet for regulating the flow of liquid. **3.** small wooden plug or peg for stopping the vent of a barrel or cask. [Of uncertain origin.]
spike[1] (spīk) *n.* **1.** large, heavy nail. **2.** sharp-pointed, usually metal object or projection, as along the top of a wall or fence. **3.a.** one of several sharp-pointed metal projections attached to the sole and heel of a shoe, worn in certain sports, as football, golf, or baseball. **b. spikes.** pair of shoes having such projections. **c.** long, narrow high heel attached to a woman's shoe. —*v.t.,* **spiked, spik·ing. 1.** to fasten or provide with spikes. **2.** to cut or pierce with a sharp-pointed object. **3.** to stand in the way of or put an end to; block; thwart: *to spike a plan.* **4.** *Slang.* to add an alcoholic beverage to: *to spike the punch.* [Possibly from Middle Dutch *spike* nail.]
spike[2] (spīk) *n.* **1.** ear of grain. **2.** flower cluster in which the flowers arise directly from an elongated, unbranched stalk. [Latin *spīca* point, ear of grain.]

Spike[2]
Spike of wheat

spike·let (spīk'lit) *n.* small spike, esp. a small cluster of flowers that make up part of the spike of a grass.
spike·nard (spīk'nərd, -närd) *n.* **1.** aromatic ointment made in ancient times from the fragrant roots and stems of an East Indian plant, *Nardostachys jatamansi.* **2.** the plant itself, having spoon-shaped leaves and bearing clusters of reddish-purple flowers. **3.** woodland herb, *Aralia racemosa,* of eastern North America,

having spicy, aromatic roots and bearing clusters of small greenish flowers. [Medieval Latin *spica nardi* ear of nard, from Latin *spīca* (see SPIKE[2]) + *nardus* (see NARD).]
spik·y (spī'kē) *adj.* **1.** having or provided with a spike or spikes: *a spiky helmet.* **2.** resembling a spike: *spiky thorns.*
spile (spīl) *n.* **1.** wooden plug for stopping the vent of a barrel or cask. **2.** small wood or metal spout for conducting sap from a sugar maple. **3.** strong beam or post driven vertically into the ground as a support; pile. —*v.t.,* **spiled, spil·ing.** to furnish, support, or stop up with a spile. [Middle Low German *spile* splinter, peg.]
spil·ing (spī'ling) *n.* spiles collectively; piling.
spill[1] (spil) **spilled** or **spilt, spill·ing.** *v.t.* **1.** to cause or allow (a substance) to fall, flow, or run out of a container. **2.** to shed (blood). **3.** to empty (a sail) of wind. **4.** *Informal.* to reveal; divulge: *to spill a secret.* —*v.i.* to flow or run out: *The water spilled all over the floor. The crowd spilled into the street.* —*n.* **1.** act or instance of spilling. **2.** amount spilled. **3.** *Informal.* tumble or fall, as from a horse. [Old English *spillan* to destroy, waste.]
spill[2] (spil) *n.* thin strip of wood or folded piece of paper, used to light a fire. [Probably from Middle Low German *spil(l)e* splinter, peg.]
spil·li·kin (spil'i kin) *n.* jackstraw. [SPILL[2] + -KIN.]
spill·way (spil'wā') *n.* channel that allows the escape of surplus water, as from a reservoir.
spilt (spilt) past tense and past participle of **spill**[1].
spin (spin) **spun** or *(archaic)* **span, spun, spin·ning.** *v.t.* **1.** to draw out and twist (fibers) into thread. **2.** to form or make (thread) in this way. **3.** to form (a silken thread, web, or cocoon) from a liquid gumlike substance that is extruded from the body and hardens when exposed to air, as spiders or silkworms. **4.** to cause to turn or revolve quickly or rapidly; twirl: *The child was spinning a top.* **5.** to extend in length or duration; prolong; draw out (often with *out*): *They spun out the debate.* **6.** to tell: *The old man enjoyed spinning ghost stories.* —*v.i.* **1.** to turn or revolve quickly or rapidly; whirl. **2.** to make by spinning, as thread. **3.** to have a sensation of revolving rapidly; feel dazed or dizzy: *All that noise made my head spin.* **4.** to go or move rapidly: *The racing car spun over the track.* —*n.* **1.** act of spinning; being spun. **2.** short ride in a motor vehicle, esp. for pleasure. **3.** tailspin *(def. 1).* [Old English *spinnan* to draw out and twist into thread.]
spin·ach (spin'ich) *n.* **1.** dark-green oblong leaves of a plant, *Spinacia oleracea,* eaten as a vegetable either cooked or raw. **2.** the plant itself, native to Asia, cultivated in many temperate regions of the world. [Old French *espinache,* from Spanish *espinaca,* from Arabic *isfinâj,* from Persian *aspanâkh.*]
spi·nal (spī'nəl) *adj.* of, relating to, or affecting the spinal column or the spinal cord. —*n.* spinal anesthetic. [Late Latin *spīnālis* relating to the spine, from Latin *spīna* backbone.]
spinal column, series of vertebrae joined in a column that encloses the

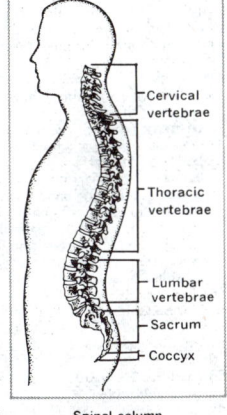
Cervical vertebrae
Thoracic vertebrae
Lumbar vertebrae
Sacrum
Coccyx
Spinal column

spinal cord and forms the central supporting structure of the body in all vertebrates. Also, **spine, back'bone', vertebral column.**
spinal cord, thick, tubular mass of nerve tissue extending down from the brain through the spinal column. The spinal cord conducts impulses to and from the brain and acts as a center for simple reflexes.
spin·dle (spind'əl) *n.* **1.** round, tapered stick weighted at one end and revolved by hand, used to twist fibers into thread. **2.** pin or rod on a spinning machine, used

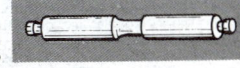
Spindle *(def. 2)*

to hold a bobbin. **3.** any rod that turns or serves as an axis by which something turns, as a shaft or axle. **4.** spike set upright in a base, on which papers are impaled. **5.** *Biology.* mass of nuclear fibers formed between the centrioles during cell division. —*v.i.,* **-dled, -dling.** to grow into a long, slender stalk, shape, or body. —*v.t.* **1.** to form into a spindle. **2.** to impale (paper) on a spindle. [Old English *spinel* rod used in spinning thread.]
spin·dle·leg·ged (spind'əl leg'id, -legd') *adj.* having spindlelegs. Also, **spin'dle-shanked'.**
spin·dle·legs (spind'əl legz') *n.,pl.* **1.** long, slim legs. **2.** *Informal.*

person with long, thin legs. ▲ construed as singular in def. 2. Also, **spin·dle·shanks** (spind′əl shangks′).

spin·dling (spind′ling) *adj.* tall and slender, esp. disproportionately thin in relation to height: *spindling pines.*

spin·dly (spind′lē) **-dli·er, -dli·est.** *adj.* having a tall slender shape; spindling.

spin·drift (spin′drift′) *n.* spray blown from the sea by heavy winds. Also, **spoon′drift′.** [Form of SPOONDRIFT.]

spine (spin) *n.* **1.** spinal column. **2.** anything resembling or functioning as a backbone, as the back of a book. **3.** any stiff, pointed, thornlike projection on an animal or plant. [Latin *spina* thorn, prickle (of certain animals), backbone.]

spi·nel (spi nel′, spin′əl) *n.* crystalline mineral most commonly composed of oxides of magnesium and aluminum, sometimes used as a gem. [French *spinella,* from Italian *spinella,* going back to Latin *spina* thorn; referring to its pointed crystals.]

spine·less (spin′lis) *adj.* **1.** lacking a spinal column; invertebrate. **2.** lacking stiff, pointed, thornlike projections. **3.** lacking moral courage or will power. **—spine′less·ly,** *adv.* **—spine′·less·ness,** *n.*

spin·et (spin′it) *n.* **1.** stringed keyboard instrument resembling a small harpsichord, having one keyboard and one string for each musical tone. **2.** small upright piano. [Middle French *espinette* small harpsichord, from Italian *spinetta;* possibly from its Italian inventor, Giovanni Spinetti.]

spin·na·ker (spin′ə kər) *n.* large sail that swells or billows out when filled, used on a yacht or other racing boat when sailing before the wind. [Possibly a modification of *Sphinx,* name of the first yacht to use this sail regularly.]

Spinnaker

spin·ner (spin′ər) *n.* one who or that which spins.

spin·ner·et (spin′ə ret′) *n.* **1.** organ by which various invertebrates, as spiders and certain caterpillars, spin silken threads. **2.** plate with numerous small openings through which man-made fibers are spun. [SPINNER + -ET.]

spin·ney (spin′ē) *pl.,* **-neys.** *n.* *British.* small wood or thicket; grove. [Old French *espinei* place full of thorny shrubs, from Latin *spinētum,* from *spina* thorn.]

spin·ning (spin′ing) *n.* act or process of twisting fibers into thread. **—adj.** that spins or is used for spinning.

spinning jenny, hand-operated spinning machine having more than one spindle so that a number of threads can be spun at once.

spinning wheel, hand-operated spinning machine consisting of a large wheel and single spindle, used to spin fibers into thread.

spin·off (spin′ôf′) *also,* **spin·off.** *n.* **1.** distribution of the stock that is held by a parent corporation in a subsidiary among the shareholders of the parent corporation. **2.** secondary product or enterprise, as a television series based on characters or situations that originated in an earlier, usually successful series.

spi·nose (spi′nōs) *adj.* full of or covered with sharp, thornlike projections; thorny. [Latin *spinōsus,* from *spina* thorn.]

spi·nous (spi′nəs) *adj.* **1.** resembling a thorn; sharp. **2.** spinose; thorny.

Spi·no·za, Ba·ruch (or **Benedict**) (spi nō′zə; bə rook′) 1632–77, Dutch philosopher.

spin·ster (spin′stər) *n.* **1.** unmarried woman, esp. a woman who remains single beyond the ordinary marrying age; old maid. **2.** woman who spins fibers into thread. [SPIN + -STER; referring to the fact that unmarried women formerly spent much of their time spinning.] **—spin′ster·hood′,** *n.* **—spin′ster·ish,** *adj.*

spi·nule (spi′nūl, spin′ūl) *n.* small, sharp, thornlike projection.

spin·y (spi′nē) **spin·i·er, spin·i·est.** *adj.* **1.** having or covered with sharp, thornlike projections; thorny. **2.** resembling a thorn; sharp. **3.** perplexing; troublesome; difficult. **—spin′i·ness,** *n.*

spiny anteater, echidna.

spiny lobster, any of several edible crustaceans, genus *Panulirus,* having sharp spines on the body and lacking the large pincer claws of the true lobster. Also, **rock lobster.**

spi·ra·cle (spi′rə kəl, spir′ə-) *n.* opening for breathing, as one of the paired openings in the abdomen of an insect or spider or the opening behind the eye of a shark. [Latin *spirāculum,* from *spirāre* to breathe.]

spi·rae·a (spi rē′ə) *n.* spirea.

spi·ral (spi′rəl) *n.* **1.** plane curve traced by a point moving around a fixed point while continuously increasing or diminishing its distance from it. **2.** three-dimensional curve that winds around the surface of a cylinder or cone; helix. **3.** something having the shape or form of a spiral. **4.** continuous, accelerating increase or decrease: *the inflationary spiral.* **—adj.** having the shape or form of a spiral; circling; winding:

a spiral staircase. **—v.i.** *v.t.* **-raled, -ral·ing;** *also, British,* **-ralled, -ral·ling.** to take or cause to take a spiral form or course; wind in a spiral. [Medieval Latin *spiralis* winding, Latin *spira* coil, from Greek *speira.*] **—spi′ral·ly,** *adv.*

spiral galaxy, galaxy having a central nucleus of closely packed stars and two or more arms consisting of stars and interstellar material spiraling out from it. Also, **spiral nebula.**

spi·rant (spi′rənt) *n.* fricative. [Latin *spirāns,* present participle of *spirāre* to breathe.]

spire¹ (spir) *n.* **1.** tall, tapering structure on the top of a tower. **2.** any tapering and pointed object or formation; pinnacle. **—v.i.** **spired, spir·ing.** to rise up in the form of a spire. [Old English *spir* stalk of a plant.]

spire² (spir) *n.* **1.** spiral or single twist of a spiral. **2.** upper portion of a spiral shell. [Latin *spira* coil, from Greek *speira.*]

spi·re·a (spi rē′ə) *also,* **spi·rae·a.** *n.* any of a group of shrubs, genus *Spiraea,* of the rose family, bearing loose clusters of small white or pink flowers, found throughout the Northern Hemisphere, often cultivated as an ornamental. [Latin *spiraea,* from Greek *speiraiā.*]

spi·ril·lum (spi ril′əm) *pl.,* **-ril·la** (-ril′ə). *n.* any of a genus of coiled, rod-shaped, flagellate bacteria. [Modern Latin *spirillum* little coil, from Latin *spira* coil. See SPIRE².]

Spire¹
(def. 1)

spir·it (spir′it) *n.* **1.** moral or spiritual part of man, believed to be immortal and to separate from the body at death; soul. **2.** animating, fundamental, or vital principle: *that pure breath of life, the spirit of man* (Milton, 1667). **3.** religious, mental, or emotional part of man's nature: *to be concerned with the things of the spirit.* **4.a.** supernatural, disembodied being, often thought to haunt the living; specter; ghost. **b.** small, often mischievous supernatural being having magical powers; fairy: *elf: woodland spirits.* **5. the Spirit,** third person of the Trinity; Holy Ghost. **6.** person considered to have a certain specified character or temperament: *a noble spirit, a brave spirit.* **7.** pervading quality, mood, or tendency: *the spirit of the age.* **8.** essence, real meaning, or intent: *the spirit of the law.* **9.** liveliness; vivacity; animation: *She danced with spirit and grace.* **10.** enthusiasm, devotion, and loyalty: *school spirit.* **11. spirits.** mental state or attitude; disposition: *to be in high spirits.* **12.** *usually,* **spirits. a.** any of various solutions produced by distillation. **b.** distilled alcoholic beverage. **—v.t. 1.** to remove or carry off secretly or mysteriously (with *off* or *away*): *Someone spirited her away during the night.* **2.** to enliven; animate; stimulate (usually with *up*). [Latin *spiritus* breath, life, soul. Doublet of ESPRIT, SPRITE.]

spir·it·ed (spir′i tid) *adj.* **1.** full of animation; lively; vigorous: *a spirited person.* **2.** having (a specified kind of) character or temperament. ▲ used in combination: *a mean-spirited man, a high-spirited horse.* **—spir′it·ed·ly,** *adv.* **—spir′it·ed·ness,** *n.*

spir·it·ism (spir′i tiz′əm) *n.* spiritualism.

spir·it·less (spir′it lis) *adj.* lacking animation, enthusiasm, or energy; dejected; listless.

spirit level, level consisting of a glass tube that is filled with alcohol and in which an air bubble floats. The air bubble rests in the center when the tube is exactly horizontal.

spir·i·to·so (spir′i tō′sō) *adj.* *Music.* spirited; animated. [Italian *spiritoso* jocular, witty, from *spirito* spirit, soul, wit, from Latin *spiritus* breath, life, soul.]

spirits of turpentine, turpentine *(def.* 2).

spir·i·tu·al (spir′i choo əl) *adj.* **1.** of, relating to, or consisting of spirit; immaterial. **2.** of, relating to, or concerned with things of the spirit. **3.** of, relating to, or concerned with religious or ecclesiastical matters; sacred. **—n.** religious folk song originated by Negroes in the southern United States. **—spir′i·tu·al·ly,** *adv.* **—spir′it·u·al·ness,** *n.*

spir·i·tu·al·ism (spir′i choo ə liz′əm) *n.* **1.** belief that the dead communicate with the living, esp. through mediums. **2.** any of various philosophical or religious theories that reality is essentially spiritual rather than material. **—spir′i·tu·al·ist,** *n.* **—spir′i·tu·al·is′tic,** *adj.*

spir·i·tu·al·i·ty (spir′i choo al′ə tē) *pl.,* **-ties.** *n.* devotion to or concern with things of the spirit; state or quality of being spiritual.

spir·i·tu·al·ize (spir′i choo ə liz′) **-ized, -iz·ing.** *v.t.* **1.** to make spiritual. **2.** to invest with a spiritual sense or meaning. **—spir′i·tu·al·i·za′tion,** *n.*

spir·i·tu·el (spir′i choo el′) *also,* **spir·i·tu·elle.** *adj.* marked by or demonstrating grace, refinement, or wit. [French *spirituel,* going back to Latin *spiritus* breath, mind, soul.]

spir·i·tu·ous (spir′i choo əs) *adj.* containing alcohol produced by distillation: *spirituous liquors.* **—spir′i·tu·os·i·ty** (spir′i choo os′ə tē), *n.*

spi·ro·chete (spi′rə kēt′) *n.* any of a large group of bacteria, order

at; āpe; cär; end; mē; it; īce; hot; ōld; fôrk; wood; fōol; oil; out; up; ūse; turn; sing; thin; this; zh in treasure; ə in ago, taken, pencil, lemon, circus.

Spirochaetales, having a slender, spiral shape. [Modern Latin *Spirochaeta,* from Latin *spīra* coil + Greek *chaitē* long hair. See SPIRE².]

spi·ro·gy·ra (spī′rə jī′rə) *n.* any of a genus of freshwater green algae having spiral chloroplasts. [Modern Latin *spirogyra,* from Latin *spīra* coil + Greek *gȳros* circle. See SPIRE².]

spi·rom·e·ter (spī rom′ə tər) *n.* instrument for measuring the volume of air inhaled and exhaled by the lungs. [Latin *spīrāre* to breathe + -METER.]

spirt (spurt) spurt.

spir·y (spīr′ē) *adj.* having the form of a spire.

spit¹ (spit) **spit** or **spat, spit·ting.** *v.i.* **1.** to eject saliva from the mouth. **2.** to express scorn or contempt by or as by spitting. **3.** to make a hissing noise; sputter. —*v.t.* **1.** to eject from the mouth: *to spit blood.* **2.** to eject or utter in a violent, noisy, or explosive manner: *to spit insults.* —*n.* **1.** saliva. **2.** act of spitting. **3.** frothy mass secreted by certain insects. Also *(def. 3),* **spit′tle.** [Old English *spittan* to eject saliva from the mouth.] —**spit′ter,** *n.*

spit² (spit) *n.* **1.** slender, pointed rod on which meat is roasted over a fire. **2.** narrow point of land extending into the sea. —*v.t.,* **spit·ted, spit·ting.** to thrust through with or as with a spit. [Old English *spitu* the pointed rod.]

spit·ball (spit′bôl′) *n.* **1.** wad of folded and chewed paper used as a missile. **2.** illegal pitch in baseball delivered after the ball has been moistened, as with saliva.

spite (spit) *n.* **1.** rankling feeling of ill will toward another; malice. **2. in spite of.** regardless of; despite. —*v.t.,* **spit·ed, spit·ing.** to irritate, hurt, or humiliate. [Short for DESPITE.]

spite·ful (spīt′fəl) *adj.* filled with spite; malicious. —**spite′ful·ly,** *adv.* —**spite′ful·ness,** *n.*

spit·fire (spit′fīr′) *n.* quick-tempered, fiery person.

Spits·ber·gen (spits′bûr′gən) *n.* Norwegian island group in the Arctic Ocean, north of Norway. Pop. (1962 est.), 4000.

spitting image, exact likeness.

spit·tle (spit′əl) *n.* **1.** saliva. **2.** spit¹ *(def. 3).* [Old English *spǣtl* saliva; influenced by SPIT¹.]

spit·toon (spi tōōn′) *n.* receptacle for spit; cuspidor.

spitz (spits) *n.* small, stocky dog having a pointed muzzle, small, erect ears, a fluffy tail that curls over the back, and a white or spotted thick coat. Height: 18 inches at the shoulder. [German *Spitz,* from *spitz* pointed; referring to its pointed muzzle.]

splash (splash) *v.t.* **1.** to scatter or throw (a liquid) about: *She accidentally splashed paint on the floor.* **2.** to wet, soil, or stain with a liquid or other substance by scattering or throwing: *He splashed his face with water. A passing car splashed her dress with mud.* **3.** to mark or decorate by or as by splashing: *The wallpaper was splashed with bright colors.* **4.** to make (one's way) by splashing. —*v.i.* **1.** to cause a liquid to scatter about. **2.** to fall, strike, or move with a splash or splashes: *The car splashed through the flooded streets.* **3.** (of spacecraft) to land on a body of water (with *down*). —*n.* **1.** act or sound of splashing. **2.** spot or patch, as of color: *The horse had a splash of white on its forehead.* **3.** something that creates a sensation or stir: *The playwright made quite a splash on Broadway with his comedy.* [Modification of PLASH.] —**splash′er,** *n.*

splash·down (splash′doun′) *n.* landing of a spacecraft on a body of water.

splash·y (splash′ē) **splash·i·er, splash·i·est.** *adj.* **1.** making a splash or splashes. **2.** full of irregular spots or patches; blotchy; spotty. **3.** creating a sensation or stir; ostentatious; showy.

splat (splat) *n.* flat piece of wood, used esp. to form the central part of a chair back. [Of uncertain origin.]

splat·ter (splat′ər) *v.i., v.t.* to spatter. —*n.* spatter. [Blend of SPATTER and SPLASH.]

splay (splā) *adj.* **1.** spread or spreading out; broad. **2.** awkward or awkwardly formed; clumsy. —*n.* sloping surface, esp. in the opening of a window or door. —*v.t.* **1.** to spread out; extend. **2.** to make slanting; bevel. —*v.i.* **1.** to be spread out. **2.** to slant. [Short for DISPLAY.]

Splay

splay·foot (splā′fŏŏt′) *pl.,* **-feet.** *n.* **1.** broad flat foot. **2.** abnormal condition in which the foot is flat and turns outward. —**splay′foot′ed,** *adj.*

spleen (splēn) *n.* **1.** large, oval, ductless organ near the stomach, that serves to produce white blood cells and filter the blood. **2.** ill temper; malice; spite: *to vent one's spleen.* **3.** *Archaic.* low spirits; melancholy. [Latin *splēn* the organ, from Greek *splēn.*]

splen·dent (splen′dənt) *adj.* **1.** gleaming; lustrous. **2.** impressive; illustrious. [Latin *splendēns,* present participle of *splendēre* to shine.]

splen·did (splen′did) *adj.* **1.** having or marked by brilliance or magnificence: *a splendid array of colors, a splendid interior.* **2.** impressive; illustrious; glorious: *a splendid reputation.* **3.** very good; excellent: *a splendid shot, a perfectly splendid dinner.* [Latin *splendidus* bright, magnificent.] —**splen′did·ly,** *adv.* —**splen′did·ness,** *n.* —**Syn. 1.** see magnificent.

splen·dif·er·ous (splen dif′ər əs) *adj. Informal.* splendid; magnificent.

splen·dor (splen′dər) *also, British,* **splen·dour.** *n.* **1.** great or stately display, as of riches or beautiful objects; magnificence; pomp: *the splendor of a palace.* **2.** impressive or commanding quality or character; illustriousness; glory. **3.** great brightness; brilliance; luster: *the splendor of the sun, the splendor of polished silver.* [Latin *splendor* brightness, brilliance.]

sple·net·ic (spli net′ik) *adj.* **1.** of or relating to the spleen. **2.** ill-tempered; malicious; spiteful. Also, **sple·net′i·cal.** —**sple·net′i·cal·ly,** *adv.*

splen·ic (splē′nik, splen′ik) *adj.* of, relating to, or contained within the spleen. [Latin *splēnicus,* from Greek *splēnikos,* from *splēn.* See SPLEEN.]

splice (splīs) **spliced, splic·ing.** *v.t.* **1.** to unite or join together, as ropes, by interweaving the strands of the ends. **2.** to join together (film or magnetic tape) at the ends. **3.** to join together (timber) by overlapping. —*n.* joint or union made by splicing. [Middle Dutch *splissen* to join ropes together by interweaving the strands of the ends.] —**splic′er,** *n.*

spline (splīn) *n.* **1.** narrow, thin strip of wood, metal, or other material; slat. **2.** flexible strip of wood, metal, or other material used in drawing curves. **3.** rectangular key projecting from a mechanical part, as a shaft, that fits into a groove or slot in another mechanical part. —*v.t.,* **splined, splin·ing.** to fit or provide with a spline. [Of uncertain origin.]

splint (splint) *n.* **1.** device made of wood, metal, or other material, used to immobilize and protect a fractured, dislocated, or broken bone. **2.** thin, flexible strip of wood used in weaving baskets or caning chairs. **3.** splinter. **4.** bony growth on the splint bone of a horse. [Middle Low German *splinte* metal plate or pin.]

splint bone, one of the two small bones on either side of the cannon bone between the hock or knee and the fetlock in hoofed animals, esp. horses.

splin·ter (splin′tər) *n.* long, sharp, usually small piece chipped or broken off from a main body, as of wood, glass, or metal. —*v.t., v.i.* to break or split (something) into splinters. [Middle Dutch *splinter* shaving, chip.] —**splin′ter·y,** *adj.*

split (split) **split, split·ting.** *v.t.* **1.** to break apart or divide lengthwise or in layers: *Jack split logs all afternoon.* **2.** to divide or break up into separate parts or portions (often with *up*): *We split the check three ways. The family agreed to split up the estate.* **3.** to burst or tear open or apart: *When Tom fell off his bicycle, he split his pants at the seams.* **4.** to divide or separate into sides or factions: *The issue will split the Democratic Party.* **5.** to divide (the stock of a company) into a larger number of shares. **6.** *Physics.* to divide (a heavy atomic nucleus) into two nuclei of approximately equal mass by bombarding it with neutrons. **6. to split hairs.** to make overly subtle or petty distinctions. —*v.i.* **1.** to break apart lengthwise or in layers: *The timber splits easily.* **2.** to become divided; separate: *The two friends split over differences in opinion.* **3.** (of stock) to be or become split. **4.** *Slang.* to leave: *Let's split!* —*n.* **1.** act of splitting; being split. **2.** division or rupture in a group. **3.** sweet dish of sliced bananas or other fruit, ice cream, whipped cream, and a topping of syrup and nuts. **4.** *Informal.* bottle of an alcoholic or carbonated drink that is half the usual size, or about six ounces. **5.** *also,* **splits.** movement or exercise in dancing or calisthenics in which the body slides to the floor with the legs spread apart and parallel to the floor. **6.** stock split. —*adj.* **1.** divided lengthwise or in layers. **2.** broken up; separated. [Middle Dutch *splitten* to cleave.] —**split′ter,** *n.*

split infinitive, infinitive having a word or phrase, as an adverb, placed between *to* and the verb: *to really love, to hardly know.*

split-lev·el (split′lev′əl) *adj.* designed so as to have two or more levels separated from each other by half flights of stairs: *a split-level house.*

split personality 1. condition in which a person intermittently displays two or more distinct patterns of behavior that are inconsistent with or contradictory to each other. **2.** schizophrenia *(def. 1).*

split second, extremely brief period of time; instant; flash.

split ticket, ballot cast for candidates of more than one political party.

split·ting (split′ing) *adj.* **1.** (of the head) aching severely. **2.** acute; severe: *a splitting headache.*

splotch (sploch) *n.* large, irregular spot; blot; stain. —*v.t.* to soil or cover with splotches. [Possibly blend of SPOT and BLOTCH.] —**splotch′y,** *adj.*

splurge (splurj) **splurged, splurg·ing.** *v.i.* **1.** to spend money without

at; āpe; cär; end; mē; it; īce; hot; ōld; fôrk; wood; fōŏl; oil; out; up; ūse; turn; sing; thin; this; zh in treasure; ə in ago, taken, pencil, lemon, circus.

963

attention to cost; indulge oneself in excessive spending: *to splurge on clothes.* **2.** to make an ostentatious display; show off. —*n.* period or spell of excessive spending: *to go on a splurge.* [Possibly blend of SPLASH and SURGE.]

splut·ter (splut′ər) *v.i.* **1.** to speak incoherently, as when confused, angry, or excited. **2.** to make popping, spitting, or hissing sounds, as food being fried; sputter. —*v.t.* to utter or express incoherently: *to splutter an apology.* —*n.* spluttering noise or disturbance. [Modification (influenced by SPLASH) of SPUTTER.] —**splut′ter·er,** *n.*

spoil (spoil) **spoiled** or **spoilt, spoil·ing.** *v.t.* **1.** to cause damage or harm to (something), esp. with regard to its excellence, quality, value, or efficacy. **2.** to weaken or damage the character of, as by excessive praise or indulgence. **3.** to put an end to; destroy: *The scandal spoiled his chances for reelection.* —*v.i.* **1.** to become unfit for use: *The meat spoiled when we left it out overnight.* **2.** to be eager or anxious: *Hank is spoiling for a fight.* —*n. usually,* **spoils. 1.** goods or property seized by force, esp. in time of war; booty; plunder. **2.** appointive public offices or other favors given to supporters of a victorious political party. [Old French *espoillier* to strip, plunder, from Latin *spoliāre,* from *spolium* booty.]

spoil·age (spoi′lij) *n.* **1.** act or process of spoiling; being spoiled. **2.** something that has spoiled. **3.** amount that has spoiled.

spoil·er (spoi′lər) *n.* **1.** one who or that which causes spoilage. **2.** device on the upper surface of an airplane wing that can be raised to increase drag and decrease lift.

spoils·man (spoilz′mən) *pl.,* **-men.** *n.* one who supports a political party or candidate for a share of political spoils.

spoil·sport (spoil′spôrt′) *n.* one who spoils the pleasure of others by his behavior or attitude.

spoils system, system or practice of distributing appointive public offices or other favors to supporters of a victorious political party.

spoilt (spoilt) *a* past tense and past participle of **spoil.**

Spo·kane (spō kan′) *n.* city in eastern Washington. Pop. (1970), 170,516.

spoke¹ (spōk) past tense and archaic past participle of **speak.**

spoke² (spōk) *n.* **1.** one of the bars or rods radiating from the hub to the rim of a wheel. **2.** rung of a ladder. —*v.t.,* **spoked, spok·ing.** to fit or provide with a spoke or spokes. [Old English *spāca* bar or rod of a wheel.]

spo·ken (spō′kən) *v.* past participle of **speak.** —*adj.* **1.** uttered or expressed in speech; oral. **2.** speaking or using a (specified kind of) speech. ▲ used in combination: *a plain-spoken woman.*

spoke·shave (spōk′shāv′) *n.* carpenter's tool having a blade between two handles, used to plane wood.

spokes·man (spōks′mən) *pl.,* **-men.** *n.* one who speaks on behalf of another or others.

spo·li·a·tion (spō′lē ā′shən) *n.* act or instance of plundering, esp. in time of war. [Latin *spoliātiō.*]

spon·da·ic (spon dā′ik) *adj.* of, relating to, or consisting of spondees.

spon·dee (spon′dē) *n.* in poetry, a metrical foot consisting of two accented syllables. [Latin *spondēus,* from Greek *spondeios,* from *spondē* libation; because solemn songs were sung in this meter at libations.]

sponge (spunj) *n.* **1.** any of a large group of aquatic, chiefly marine, animals, phylum Porifera, that live attached to rocks or other solid objects and have porous bodies supported by a fibrous skeleton. Sponges are of various sizes, shapes, and colors. **2.** light, fibrous, absorbent network forming the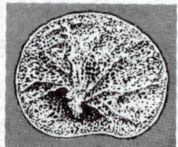

Sponge

skeleton of certain sponges, used for washing or other purposes. **3.** article made from any of various substances, as cellulose or rubber, resembling this skeleton in structure or use. **4.** absorbent pad, as of gauze or absorbent cotton, used in surgery. **5.** soft, light-textured, raised dough. **6.** *Informal.* one who makes a practice of living at the expense of another or others. **7. to throw** (or **toss**) **in the sponge.** *Informal.* to admit defeat. —*v.t.,* **sponged, spong·ing. 1.** to cleanse or rub with or as with a wet sponge (often with *down*). **2.** to remove with a sponge (with *out* or *off*): *The mother sponged crayon marks off the wall.* **3.** to absorb (often with *up*). **4.** *Informal.* to get without paying: *to sponge a cigarette.* —*v.i.* **1.** to absorb liquid, as a sponge. **2.** to gather sponges from the sea. **3.** *Informal.* to live at the expense of another or others (with *on* or *off*).

sponge bath, bath taken by washing with a wet sponge or damp cloth without the use of a shower or bathtub.

sponge cake, light cake made without shortening, and containing eggs, sugar, flour, and flavoring.

spong·er (spun′jər) *n.* **1.** *Informal.* one who makes a practice of living at the expense of another or others. **2.** person or boat that gathers sponges.

spon·gy (spun′jē) **-gi·er, -gi·est.** *adj.* of or resembling a sponge; elastic, porous, or absorbent. —**spon′gi·ness,** *n.*

spon·son (spon′sən) *n.* **1.** structure projecting from the side of a boat or ship, used to support or protect something, as a gun or searchlight. **2.** air-filled structure attached to either side of a canoe or seaplane to increase stability and prevent sinking. [Possibly form of EXPANSION.]

Sponson

spon·sor (spon′sər) *n.* **1.** one who assumes responsibility or support for a person or thing. **2.** individual or organization, as a business firm, that finances some event or entertainment, as a benefit or radio or television program. **3.** one who answers for an infant at baptism, making the required promises and professions of faith; godfather or godmother. —*v.t.* to act as sponsor for. [Latin *spōnsor* surety.] —**spon·so·ri·al** (spon sôr′ē əl), *adj.* —**spon′sor·ship′,** *n.* —**Syn. 1.** see **patron.**

spon·ta·ne·i·ty (spon′tə nē′ə tē, -nā′-) *pl.,* **-ties.** *n.* **1.** fact, quality, or condition of being spontaneous. **2.** spontaneous action, impulse, or behavior.

spon·ta·ne·ous (spon tā′nē əs) *adj.* **1.** prompted entirely by natural impulse or desire; unpremeditated: *spontaneous laughter.* **2.** arising or occurring without external cause; having an internal cause or origin: *spontaneous motion.* **3.** (of plants) growing naturally without cultivation. [Late Latin *spontāneus* voluntary, from Latin *sponte* voluntarily.] —**spon·ta′ne·ous·ly,** *adv.* —**spon·ta′ne·ous·ness,** *n.* —**Syn.** see **automatic.**

spontaneous combustion, the catching fire of a substance, as oily rags, because of an accumulation of heat from slow oxidation.

spoof (spōof) *Informal. n.* **1.** light parody. **2.** trick or deception; hoax. —*v.t.* **1.** to make a parody of; satirize lightly. **2.** to trick or deceive. [From *Spoof* (probably blend of SPORT and GOOF), a card game involving trickery and tomfoolery devised by Arthur Roberts, 1852–1933, English comedian.]

spook (spōok) *Informal. n.* ghost; specter. —*v.t.* to haunt (a person or place). **2.** to frighten; scare. [Dutch *spook* ghost.]

spook·y (spōo′kē) **spook·i·er, spook·i·est.** *adj. Informal.* causing fear, alarm, or uneasiness; scary: *a spooky old house, a spooky visitor.*

spool (spōol) *n.* **1.** small, cylindrical piece of wood, plastic, or other material around which thread, wire, or tape may be wound. **2.** amount of thread, wire, or tape wound on a spool. —*v.t.* to wind on a spool. [Middle Dutch *spoele* bobbin.]

spoon (spōon) *n.* **1.** utensil of wood, metal, or plastic, consisting of a handle with a small, shallow bowl at the end, used in preparing, serving, or eating food. **2.** something resembling this in shape or function. **3.** golf club having a wooden head, used for long shots; number three wood. —*v.t.* to lift up or transfer with a spoon: *He spooned the soup into his mouth.* —*v.i. Informal.* to make love, as by kissing or caressing. [Old English *spōn* chip, splinter.]

spoon·bill (spōon′bil′) *n.* **1.** any of several long-legged wading birds, family Threskiornithidae, native to most temperate and tropical regions of the world, having a long, flat bill with a tip shaped like a spoon. Length: 3 feet. **2.** various birds having a similar bill, as the shoveler.

Spoonbill

spoon bread, moist bread made of cornmeal, milk, and shortening, baked to a consistency that is soft enough to be served with a spoon.

spoon·drift (spōon′drift′) *n.* spindrift. [Obsolete *spoon* to scud (of uncertain origin) + DRIFT.]

spoon·er·ism (spōo′nə riz′əm) *n.* unintentional transposition of initial or other sounds of two or more words, as in *seeping slickness* for *sleeping sickness.* [From W. A. *Spooner,* 1844–1930, English clergyman, who was famous for such expressions.]

spoon·fed (spōon′fed′) *adj.* **1.** fed with a spoon. **2.** spoiled by overindulgence or coddling; pampered. **3.** not given the opportunity to act or think for oneself.

spoon·feed (spōon′fēd′) **-fed, -feed·ing.** *v.t.* to cause (someone) to be spoon-fed.

spoon·ful (spōon′fool′) *pl.,* **-fuls.** *n.* amount that a spoon can or does hold.

spoor (spoor, spôr) *n.* track or trail, esp. of a wild animal. —*v.t., v.i.* to trace by or follow a spoor. [Dutch *spoor* trail, track.]

spo·rad·ic (spə rad′ik) *adj.* **1.** occurring at irregular intervals; occa-

at; āpe; cär; end; mē; it; īce; hot; ōld; fôrk; wood; fōol; oil; out; up; ūse; turn; sing; thin; this; zh in treasure; ə in ago, taken, pencil, lemon, circus.

sional: *sporadic visits to the city.* **2.** occurring or appearing singly or in widely separate localities. **3.** (of a disease) occurring in isolated instances or cases; not epidemic. Also, **spo·rad'i·cal.** [Medieval Latin *sporadicus* scattered, from Greek *sporadikos* scattered, going back to *spora* seed, a sowing.] **—spo·rad'i·cal·ly,** *adv.* **—Syn. 1.** see **periodic.**

spo·ran·gi·um (spə ran'jē əm) *pl.,* **-gi·a** (-jē ə). *n.* sac in certain plants, as ferns, in which spores are produced; spore case. [Modern Latin *sporangium,* from Greek *sporā* seed + *angeion* receptacle.]

spore (spôr) *n.* **1.** tiny reproductive body formed by a plant or microscopic animal and distributed by air or water currents to a place suitable for germination. **2.** hard-covered body that is highly resistant to chemical and physical conditions, formed by a microorganism, as a bacterium. [Modern Latin *spora,* from Greek *sporā* seed.]

spo·ro·phyll (spôr'ə fil') *also,* **spo·ro·phyl.** *n.* leaf that bears spores or sporangia. [Greek *sporā* seed + *phyllon* leaf.]

spo·ro·phyte (spôr'ə fīt') *n.* stage in the life cycle of plants that undergo alternation of generations, during which spores are produced. Distinguished from **gametophyte.** [Greek *sporā* seed + -PHYTE.]

spo·ro·zo·an (spôr'ə zō'ən) *n.* any of a group of parasitic one-celled animals having a complex life cycle, as the parasite that causes malaria. **—adj.** of, relating to, or designating this group. [Modern Latin *Sporozoa,* from *spora* (see SPORE) + Greek *zōia,* plural of *zōion* animal + -AN.]

spor·ran (spôr'ən, spor'-) *n.* large pouch or purse worn from the belt in front of the kilt. [Scottish Gaelic *sporan.*]

Sporran

sport (spôrt) *n.* **1.** any game that requires physical activity and involves a degree of competition, as baseball, soccer, bowling, or basketball. **2.** any pastime or activity that provides pleasure or recreation; amusement; diversion. **3.** playfulness; jest; fun: *He did that in sport.* **4.** *Informal.* **a.** one who is a fair or obliging companion. **b.** person with regard to his ability to accept teasing, criticism, or defeat: *Joe is a good sport.* **5.** *Informal.* one who is interested in sports for purposes of gambling. **6.** *Biology.* plant or animal that exhibits a sudden or marked variation from the normal type. **7. to make sport of.** to ridicule. **—v.i. 1.** to engage in physical exercise or activity for pleasure or recreation; play. **2.** to make fun; treat lightly; joke; trifle. **3.** *Biology.* to mutate. **—v.t.** to display ostentatiously: *Harry sported a loud tie.* **—adj. also, sports. 1.** of or relating to sports. **2.** fitted or suitable for informal wear: *sport clothes.* [Short for DISPORT.] **—sport'ful,** *adj.* **—sport'ful·ly,** *adv.* **—sport'ful·ness,** *n.* **—Syn. 1.** see **play.**

sport·ing (spôr'ting) *adj.* **1.** of, relating to, suitable for, in, or engaged in sports: *a sporting event, sporting goods, sporting dogs.* **2.** characteristic of a sportsman; fair or obliging: *That was very sporting of him.* **3.** of or relating to gambling, esp. on sports. **—sport'ing·ly,** *adv.*

sporting chance *Informal.* even or fair chance for a successful outcome.

spor·tive (spôr'tiv) *adj.* **1.** frolicsome; playful; lively. **2.** of, relating to, or characterized by sport. **—sport'tive·ly,** *adv.* **—sport'tive·ness,** *n.*

sports car *also,* **sport car.** small, low automobile designed to maneuver easily and achieve high speeds, usually seating two passengers.

sports·cast (spôrts'kast') *n.* radio or television broadcast of a sports event or of sports commentary. **—sports'cast'er,** *n.*

sports·man (spôrts'mən) *pl.,* **-men.** *n.* **1.** one who is interested or engages in sports, esp. outdoor sports, as hunting or fishing. **2.** one who plays fair and accepts defeat graciously. **—sports'man·like', sports'man·ly,** *adj.*

sports·man·ship (spôrts'mən ship') *n.* **1.** conduct characteristic or worthy of a sportsman, as fair play or the ability to accept defeat graciously. **2.** skill in sports.

sports·wear (spôrts'wâr') *n.* clothing designed for informal wear.

sports·wom·an (spôrts'woom'ən) *pl.,* **-wom·en.** *n.* woman who is interested or engages in sports, esp. as a professional.

sports·writ·er (spôrts'rī'tər) *n.* one who writes about sports events, esp. for a newspaper.

sport·y (spôr'tē) **sport·i·er, sport·i·est.** *adj. Informal.* **1.** characteristic of a sportsman; sporting. **2.** loud or flashy, esp. in dress. **—sport'i·ly,** *adv.* **—sport'i·ness,** *n.*

spor·u·late (spôr'yə lāt') **-lat·ed, -lat·ing.** *v.i.* to form spores. [Modern Latin *sporula* little spore, from *spora* (see SPORE) + -ATE¹.] **—spor'u·la'tion,** *n.*

spot (spot) *n.* **1.** discoloration produced by foreign matter: *a spot of grease.* **2.** flaw or blemish: *a spot on one's reputation.* **3.** small mark or part differing from the surrounding area, as in color or material: *a*

dog with brown spots. **4.** site; location: *an interesting spot for a picnic.* **5.** position or situation: *a good spot in line.* **6.a.** one of the marks on dominoes, dice, or playing cards. **b.** playing card having a (specified number of) such marks. **7.** *British. Informal.* small quantity; little bit: *a spot of tea.* **8.** *Slang.* spotlight. **9.** *Slang.* piece of paper currency having a specified value: *a ten spot.* **10. in a spot.** in a difficult, disagreeable, or embarrassing situation. **11. on the spot. a.** at the place already mentioned. **b.** immediately; at once. **c.** *Slang.* in an awkward or difficult position. **12. to hit the spot.** *Informal.* to be exactly right or exactly what is needed. **—v.t. spot·ted, spot·ting. 1.** to mark with a spot or spots: *The mud spotted the rug.* **2.** to locate or pick out with the eyes; recognize: *We spotted her easily in the crowd.* **3.** to blemish; disgrace. **4.** to place or scatter in various locations: *Guards were spotted throughout the store.* **5.** to place in a specific position. **—v.i. 1.** to become spotted: *The fabric will spot easily.* **2.** to cause a stain; make a spot: *The ink spots permanently.* **—adj.** paid or requiring payment on delivery: *spot cash, spot transaction.* [Possibly from Middle Dutch *spotte* stain, speck.] **—Syn. n. 4.** see **scene.**

spot-check (spot'chek') *v.t.* to make a quick examination by selecting samples at random.

spot check, quick examination made by selecting samples at random.

spot·less (spot'lis) *adj.* **1.** absolutely clean; immaculate: *a spotless kitchen.* **2.** having no flaws or blemishes: *a spotless reputation.* **—spot'less·ly,** *adv.* **—spot'less·ness,** *n.*

spot·light (spot'līt') *n.* **1.** strong beam of light projected on a particular person, place, or object, esp. for dramatic or theatrical effect. **2.** lamp projecting such a light. **3.** public attention or notoriety: *The scientist drew the spotlight away from his colleagues by his surprise discovery.*

spot·ted (spot'id) *adj.* **1.** marked or covered with spots: *a spotted pony.* **2.** blemished; sullied.

spotted fever, any of several fevers characterized by spots on the skin, as typhus.

spot·ter (spot'ər) *n.* **1.** one who removes spots from garments in dry cleaning. **2.** one who watches for enemy planes, usually over a populated area. **3.** *Informal.* detective who keeps watch for dishonesty among employees, as in a store.

spot·ty (spot'ē) *adj.* **1.** marked or covered with spots; spotted. **2.** not consistent or uniform; uneven: *spotty attendance.* **—spot'ti·ly,** *adv.* **—spot'ti·ness,** *n.*

spous·al (spou'zəl) *adj.* of or relating to marriage.

spouse (spous, spouz) *n.* married person; husband or wife. [Old French *espous* bridegroom, husband, and *espouse* bride, wife; respectively from Latin *spōnsus* bethrothed man, and *spōnsa* betrothed woman.]

spout (spout) *v.t.* **1.** to pour out (a liquid or other substance) forcibly in a stream or spray; spurt: *An elephant spouts water from his trunk.* **2.** *Informal.* to speak in a wordy, pompous manner: *The old man swaggered about the house spouting his philosophy of life.* **—v.i. 1.** to pour out forcibly: *Blood spouted from the torn artery.* **2.** to discharge a liquid or other substance continuously or in spurts. **3.** *Informal.* to make a wordy pompous speech (often with *off*). **—n. 1.** tube or lip projecting from a vessel that channels the liquid being poured. **2.** pipe or other channel, as a faucet or spigot, through which liquid flows or is discharged. **3.** jet or column, as of water. [Possibly from Middle Dutch *spouten* to spurt.] **—spout'er,** *n.*

S.P.Q.R., Roman Senate and People. [Abbreviation of Latin *S(enatus) P(opulus)que R(omanus).*]

sprag (sprag) *n.* piece of wood or bar of metal used to prevent a wheeled vehicle from rolling. [Possibly of Scandinavian origin.]

sprain (sprān) *n.* injury caused by a violent or sudden wrenching or twisting of the ligaments or tendons around a joint. **—v.t.** to subject to a sprain. [Old French *espreindre* to press, wring, from Latin *exprimere* to press out.]

sprang (sprang) a past tense of **spring.**

sprat (sprat) *n.* **·1.** bluish-green, saltwater fish, *Clupea sprattus,* found off the Atlantic coast of Europe, used for food. **2.** any of various related fish, as a young herring. [Old English *sprott.*]

sprawl (sprôl) *v.i.* **1.** to lie or sit with the body and limbs stretched out in an awkward or careless manner: *The boy sprawled on the sofa.* **2.** to spread out in an irregular or straggling manner: *The housing development sprawled across the countryside.* **—v.t.** to cause to spread out in an awkward, careless, or straggling manner. **—n.** act, instance, or position of sprawling. [Old English *sprēawlian* to move the limbs convulsively.]

spray¹ (sprā) *n.* **1.** water or other liquid in the form of fine particles or droplets: *the spray from a waterfall.* **2.** anything resembling this: *a spray of glass.* **3.** any of various liquids emitted in a stream of fine particles by a device, as an atomizer or pressurized can: *a spray for bugs.* **4.** the device itself. **—v.t. 1.** to apply spray to (a surface): *to spray a bookcase with paint.* **2.** to apply a spray of: *to spray perfume on her arm.*

---

at; āpe; cär; end; mē; it; īce; hot; ōld; fôrk; wood; fōōl; oil; out; up; ūse; turn; sing; thin; this; zh in treasure; ə in ago, taken, pencil, lemon, circus.

3. to discharge a spray in: *to spray a room with disinfectant.* —*v.i.* to scatter or emit spray. [Possibly from Middle Dutch *spra(e)yen* to sprinkle.] —**spray′er,** *n.*

spray² (sprā) *n.* **1.** slender twig or branch of a plant with its leaves, flowers, or fruit; sprig. **2.** ornament, pattern, or design resembling this. [Probably from an unrecorded Old English word.]

spray gun, device that emits a spray under pressure applied by a pump.

spread (spred) *spread, spread·ing. v.t.* **1.** to unfold or open up so as to cover a larger area: *to spread a map on the table.* **2.** to push or move further apart: *to spread one's legs.* **3.** to cover with a thin layer of something: *to spread a canvas with paint, to spread a roll with jam.* **4.** to put as a thin covering: *to spread butter on toast.* **5.** to distribute or disperse over an area: *to spread fertilizer on the ground, to spread furniture about the room.* **6.** to extend over a period of time: *to spread the work over three days, to spread the payment over a year.* **7.** to cause to become more widely known: *to spread rumors.* **8.a.** to set (a table) for a meal; place food on. **b.** to set (food) on a table. —*v.i.* **1.** to be situated, distributed, or dispersed over an area: *The forest spread out across the landscape. The rash spread on her arm. The fire spread through the house.* **2.** to be put as a thin covering: *The butter spreads easily.* **3.** to become more widely known; circulate: *Word spread quickly about the accident.* **4.** to be pushed apart; become more separated. —*n.* **1.** act of spreading. **2.** amount of spreading or capacity for spreading. **3.** that which is spread out: *the spread of gravel in the driveway, the spread of branches overhead.* **4.** cloth covering, esp. for a bed. **5.** printed material, as an advertisement, that covers two facing pages or several columns in a periodical or newspaper. **6.** soft food that can be spread, as butter or cheese. **7.** *Informal.* lavish display of food; feast. **8.** *Informal.* ranch or farm. [Old English *sprēdan* to extend.]

Syn. *v.t.* **7. Spread, circulate, disseminate** mean to make more widely known. **Spread** emphasizes something that is easily given out or easily taken up by an increasing number of persons, esp. by word-of-mouth, without necessarily returning to the original source: *Spread the good word.* **Circulate** implies a more highly organized activity that occurs within a specific or limited circle: *Circulate the petition among your friends and neighbors and then mail it to the governor.* **Disseminate** also implies organized distribution, but usually from a central source that is able to reach a larger or more widespread group without appealing to or contacting persons individually: *All the mass media were used to disseminate propaganda during the war.*

spread-ea·gle (spred′ē′gəl) *adj.* **1.** having or suggesting the form or appearance of an eagle with legs and wings spread out. **2.** *Informal.* boastful or extravagant, esp. in patriotic expression or display. —*v.t., v.i.,* **-gled, -gling.** to stretch out or cause to stretch out in a spread-eagle position.

spread eagle, representation of an eagle with legs and wings spread out, used as an emblem of the United States.

spread·er (spred′ər) *n.* **1.** one who or that which spreads. **2.** small knife used to spread butter, cheese, or other soft food. **3.** device or machine used to spread seed, hay, or fertilizer.

spree (sprē) *n.* **1.** unrestrained or excessive indulgence in an activity: *a shopping spree, a drinking spree.* **2.** lively frolic. [Of uncertain origin.]

spri·er (sprī′ər) a comparative of **spry.**

spri·est (sprī′ist) a superlative of **spry.**

sprig (sprig) *n.* **1.** shoot, twig, or branch of a plant with its leaves, flowers, or fruit: *a sprig of parsley.* **2.** pattern or ornament resembling this. **3.** small brad without a head. **4.** young man; youth. —*v.t.,* **sprigged, sprig·ging.** to fasten with brads. [Of uncertain origin.]

spright·ly (sprīt′lē) **-li·er, -li·est.** *adj.* full of animation and light-heartedness; merry; gay: *a sprightly air.* [*Spright,* form of SPRITE + -LY².] —**spright′li·ness,** *n.*

spring (spring) **sprang** or **sprung, sprung, spring·ing.** *v.i.* **1.** to move quickly or with a sudden propelling effort: *John sprang from his seat. The gazelle sprang gracefully into the air.* **2.** to appear or arise suddenly: *The words sprang to her lips.* **3.** to shift or move by or as by elastic force: *The door sprang shut.* **4.** to come into existence or grow suddenly or rapidly: *Towns sprang up overnight. The weeds sprang up everywhere.* **5.** to be descended: *Harry springs from an illustrious, old family.* **6.** to become warped, cracked, or split: *The window sprang from the humidity.* —*v.t.* **1.** to cause to spring. **2.** to cause (a mechanism) to work suddenly: *to spring a trap.* **3.** to produce hastily or unexpectedly: *to spring a surprise.* **4.** to leap over; clear: *to spring a fence.* **5.** to cause

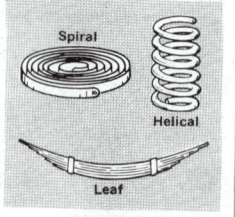

Springs

to warp, crack, or split: *The wind sprang the tree.* **6.** to be afflicted with; develop: *The radiator sprang a leak.* **7.** *Slang.* to obtain the release of or free (someone), as from prison. —*n.* **1.** act of springing; leap. **2.** elastic device, as a spiral-shaped piece of metal, that recovers its original shape when released after being bent, compressed, or stretched, used to transmit motion, check motion, or maintain a separation between two objects. **3.** elasticity or buoyancy: *There was little spring in his muscles. There was no spring in his walk.* **4.** place where underground water flows out of the earth. **5.** season of the year coming between winter and summer. In the Northern Hemisphere it extends from the vernal equinox, about March 21, to the summer solstice, about June 21. **6.** first or early stage: *He was in the spring of his life.* **7.** source or origin: *the springs of thought.* —*adj.* **1.** of, relating to, characteristic of, or suitable for the season of spring: *spring wheat, spring rain, a spring outfit.* **2.** of, acting like, or suspended on a spring or springs: *a spring mattress, a spring watch, a spring valve.* [Old English *springan* to grow, come forth, move with a sudden jerk.] —**Syn.** *v.i.* **1.** see **jump.**

spring beauty 1. delicate pink or white flower of any of a group of plants, genus *Claytonia,* found in meadows and fields of North America. **2.** plant bearing this flower, having fleshy leaves.

spring·board (spring′bôrd′) *n.* **1.** flexible board used for tumbling or diving. **2.** starting point, as for a discussion.

spring·bok (spring′bok′) *pl.,* **-bok** or **-boks.** *also,* **spring·buck** (spring′-buk′). *n.* small antelope, *Antidorcas marsupialis,* native to the plains of southern Africa, having horns and a predominantly tan-and-white coat. Height: 30 inches at the shoulder. [Afrikaans *springbok,* from Dutch *springen* to spring + *bok* buck¹; because it springs into the air when startled.]

Springbok

spring chicken 1. young chicken, esp. a broiler or fryer. **2.** *Slang.* young woman.

spring-clean·ing (spring′klē′ning) *n.* thorough cleaning, as of a house, usually in the spring.

springe (sprinj) *n.* snare consisting of a noose attached to a branch, used to catch small game. —*v.t.,* **springed, spring·ing.** to capture in a springe. [Probably from an unrecorded Old English word.]

spring·er (spring′ər) *n.* **1.** one who or that which springs. **2.** first or lowest wedge-shaped block of an arch.

springer spaniel, sporting dog having a predominantly white coat, often used for flushing and retrieving game, as the **English springer spaniel.** Height: to 18 inches at the shoulder.

English springer spaniel

spring fever, feeling of laziness or listlessness that is commonly associated with the coming of spring.

Spring·field (spring′fēld′) *n.* **1.** capital of Illinois, in the central part of the state. Pop. (1970), 91,753. **2.** city in southwestern Massachusetts, on the Connecticut River. Pop. (1970), 163,905. **3.** city in southwestern Missouri. Pop. (1970), 120,096.

spring·halt (spring′hôlt′) stringhalt.

spring·house (spring′hous′) *n.* small building constructed over a spring, used to keep perishable foods cool.

spring·let (spring′lit) *n.* small spring or stream.

spring·tail (spring′tāl′) *n.* any of a group of small, wingless insects, order Collembola, having a powerful appendage on the abdomen that enables the insect to make a springlike jump.

spring·tide (spring′tīd′) *n.* springtime.

spring tide 1. tide that has the greatest rise and ebb, occurring at or soon after the new or full moon. **2.** any great rush, flood, or swell: *in the spring tide of prosperity.*

spring·time (spring′tīm′) *n.* spring season.

spring·y (spring′ē) **spring·i·er, spring·i·est.** *adj.* characterized by elasticity; resilient; flexible: *a springy step, a springy mattress.* —**spring′·i·ly,** *adv.* —**spring′i·ness,** *n.*

sprin·kle (spring′kəl) **-kled, -kling.** *v.t.* **1.** to scatter (a liquid or other substance) in small drops or particles: *to sprinkle powdered sugar on cake.* **2.** to scatter small drops or particles of a liquid or other substance on: *to sprinkle clothes with water.* —*v.i.* **1.** to rain lightly: *It sprinkled*

this morning. **2.** to scatter a liquid or other substance in drops or small particles. —*n.* **1.** light rain. **2.** small quantity of something; sprinkling. **3.** act of sprinkling. [Possibly from Dutch *sprenkelen* to sprinkle (with water), from Middle Dutch *sprenkel* small spot.]

sprin·kler (spring′klər) *n.* **1.** any of various devices for sprinkling a lawn, as a perforated nozzle attached to a hose. **2.** outlet of a sprinkler system.

sprinkler system 1. automatic system for extinguishing fires in buildings. **2.** system of pipes or hoses, usually underground, for sprinkling a lawn, garden, or other area.

sprin·kling (spring′kling) *n.* small or limited quantity falling or scattered at random.

sprint (sprint) *n.* short race at full speed. —*v.i.* to run at full speed, esp. for a short distance. [Of Scandinavian origin.] —**sprint′er,** *n.*

sprit (sprit) *n.* small spar extending diagonally from the mast to the upper corner of a fore-and-aft-sail. [Old English *sprēot* pole¹.]

sprite (sprīt) *n.* small, often mischievous supernatual being; elf. [Old French *esprit* soul, mind, from Latin *spiritus* breath, mind, soul. Doublet of ESPRIT, SPIRIT.]

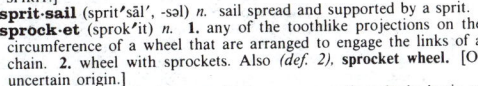

Sprit / Mast / Spritsail / Sprit

sprit·sail (sprit′sāl′, -səl) *n.* sail spread and supported by a sprit.

sprock·et (sprok′it) *n.* **1.** any of the toothlike projections on the circumference of a wheel that are arranged to engage the links of a chain. **2.** wheel with sprockets. Also *(def. 2).* **sprocket wheel.** [Of uncertain origin.]

sprout (sprout) *v.i.* **1.** to put forth young growth or buds; begin to grow: *The seeds we planted finally sprouted.* **2.** to develop or grow suddenly or rapidly: *Stores have sprouted up near the new factories.* —*v.t.* to cause to sprout. —*n.* **1.** new or young growth on a plant developed from a seed, bud, or root. **2. sprouts.** Brussels sprouts. [Old English *sprūtan* to shoot forth, grow.]

spruce¹ (sprōōs) *n.* **1.** any of a group of cone-bearing evergreen trees, genus *Picea,* of the pine family, having short, needlelike leaves and drooping cones, found in cold and temperate regions of the Northern Hemisphere. **2.** its wood, used for construction and paper pulp. [From obsolete *Spruce* Prussia, modification of *Pruce,* from Medieval Latin *Prussia;* probably because the tree came from Prussia.]

spruce² (sprōōs) *spruced,* *spruc·ing.* *v.t.* **1.** to make or become neat or trim (usually with *up*). —*adj.* spruc·er, spruc·est. having a neat or trim appearance; dapper. [Possibly from obsolete *Spruce* Prussia, brought from Prussia (hence, considered neat or smart). See SPRUCE¹.] —**spruce′ly,** *adv.* —**spruce′ness,** *n.*

sprung (sprung) *a* past tense and past participle of **spring.**

spry (sprī) *spry·er* or *spri·er,* *spry·est* or *spri·est.* *adj.* lively and nimble: *a spry old gentleman.* [Of uncertain origin.] —**spry′ly,** *adv.* —**spry′ness,** *n.*

spt., seaport.

spud (spud) *n.* **1.** narrow, sharp, spadelike tool for digging up weeds or removing bark from trees. **2.** *Informal.* potato. —*v.t.* **spud·ded, spud·ding.** to dig or remove with a spud. [Of uncertain origin.]

spue (spū) *spued,* *spu·ing.* *v.t., v.i.* to spew.

spume (spūm) *n.* foam; froth. —*v.i.,* spumed, spum·ing. to foam; froth. [Latin *spūma* foam.]

spu·mo·ne (spə mō′nē) *also,* **spu·mo·ni.** *n.* Italian ice cream having various layers of different flavors and colors, sometimes containing fruit or nuts. [Italian *spumone,* from *spuma* foam, from Latin *spūma.*]

spun (spun) past tense and past participle of **spin.**

spunk (spungk) *n. Informal.* courage, spirit, and determination; pluck: *He has a lot of spunk.* [Of uncertain origin.]

spunk·y (spung′kē) *spunk·i·er, spunk·i·est. adj. Informal.* characterized by or having courage, spirit, and determination; plucky. —**spunk′i·ly,** *adv.* —**spunk′i·ness,** *n.*

spun silk, silk made from the short fibers of silk waste.

spun sugar, cotton candy.

spur (spur) *n.* **1.** device worn on the heel of a horseman's boot, used to urge a horse forward. **2.** that which goads, impels, or urges to action: *His wife's encouragement was the spur he needed to succeed.* **3.** something that resembles a spur, as the sharp, hard projection on the leg of certain birds, as the domestic rooster. **4.** short, stunted branch, as of a fruit tree. **5.** ridge or mountain projecting from the main mountain range. **6.** spur track. **7.** *Botany.* hollow tubular projection from some part of a flower, as from the calyx of a columbine. **8. on the spur of the moment.** without premeditation or planning; on an impulse; suddenly. —*v.t., v.i.* **spurred, spur·ring.**

Spur

1. to urge forward with a spur or spurs. **2.** to move or urge on; stimulate; incite: *The cheers spurred the team to victory.* —*v.i.* to ride quickly by urging one's horse with spurs. [Old English *spura* the device on a horseman's heel.]

spurge (spurj) *n.* any of a large family of plants, genus *Euphorbia,* that have a milky, acrid sap. [Old French *espurge,* from *espurgier* to purge, from Latin *expurgāre* to purge; some of these plants were once used as laxatives.]

spur gear 1. cogwheel with the teeth on its rim parallel to its axis. **2.** gear mechanism having such cogwheels, used to connect two parallel shafts.

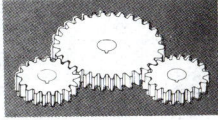

Spur gears

spu·ri·ous (spoor′ē əs) *adj.* not being what it appears or is claimed to be; not genuine or authentic; false: *a spurious argument, a spurious passport.* [Latin *spurius.*] —**spu′ri·ous·ly,** *adv.* —**spu′ri·ous·ness,** *n.*

spurn (spurn) *v.t.* **1.** to reject with contempt or disdain; scorn. **2.** to strike or push away with the foot. —*v.i.* to exhibit contempt or disdain. —*n.* **1.** contemptuous or disdainful rejection. **2.** kick. [Old English *spurnan* to reject with disdain.]

spurred (spurd) *adj.* fitted with or having spurs.

spurt (spurt) *also,* **spirt.** *v.i.* **1.** to gush or pour out suddenly or forcibly in a stream; spout: *The water spurted from the broken pipe.* **2.** to make or show a sudden brief effort: *The car spurted ahead.* —*v.t.* to throw or force out suddenly or forcibly in a stream. —*n.* **1.** sudden gush, esp. of liquid. **2.** sudden, brief spell, as of activity, effort, or emotion: *She works in spurts.* [Of uncertain origin.]

spur track, short side track of a railroad connected with the main track.

sput·nik (sput′nik, spoot′-) *n.* any of several man-made earth satellites launched by the Soviet Union. The first was Sputnik I, launched on October 4, 1957. [Russian *sputnik* companion, satellite.]

sput·ter (sput′ər) *v.i.* **1.** to make popping, spitting, or hissing noises: *The motor sputtered and stopped.* **2.** to utter words or sounds in a confused or hasty manner: *He sputtered incoherently in his anger.* **3.** to throw out or spit small particles of food or saliva, as when speaking excitedly. —*v.t.* **1.** to throw out or spit small particles (food or saliva), as when speaking excitedly. **2.** to utter (words or sounds) in a confused or hasty manner. —*n.* **1.** act or noise of sputtering. **2.** confused or hasty speech. [Probably imitative.] —**sput′ter·er,** *n.*

spu·tum (spū′təm) *pl.,* -ta (-tə). *n.* saliva; spittle; spit. [Latin *spūtum.*]

spy (spī) *pl.,* **spies.** *n.* **1.** undercover agent who is employed by a government to discover the military, political, or other secrets about another government. **2.** one who watches others secretly or who gathers secret information about others. —*v.i.,* spied, spy·ing. **1.** to act as a spy (often with *on* or *upon*). **2.** to make a search or investigation; pry (usually with *into*). —*v.t.* **1.** to catch sight of; observe; notice: *to spy a ship at the horizon.* **2.** to discover or observe secretly (with *out*): *The detective spied out the suspected thief.* [Old French *espier* to watch attentively; of Germanic origin.]

spy·glass (spī′glas) *n.* small telescope.

sq. 1. square. **2.** the following.

sq. ft., square foot; square feet.

sq. in., square inch; square inches.

sq. mi., square mile; square miles.

squab (skwob) *pl.,* **squabs** or **squab.** *n.* young pigeon, esp. while still an unfledged nestling. —*adj.* (of birds) unfledged or newly hatched. [Probably of Scandinavian origin.]

squab·ble (skwob′əl) *-bled,* -bling. *v.t.* to argue noisily, esp. over something of little importance; bicker; wrangle: *The children squabbled over who would ride the bicycle first.* —*n.* petty argument or dispute. [Probably imitative.] —**squab′bler,** *n.*

squad (skwod) *n.* **1.** military unit usually composed of ten men and forming part of a platoon, usually commanded by a noncommissioned officer. **2.** small group of persons organized for a common purpose or specific function: *a patrol squad, a baseball squad.* [Obsolete French *esquade* small party (of soldiers), from Italian *squadra* group, square, going back to Latin *ex-* (see EX-¹) + *quadra* square; with reference to the arranging of soldiers into square formations.]

squad car, police car assigned to a particular area and equipped with a radiotelephone for communication with headquarters.

squad·ron (skwod′rən) *n.* **1.** U.S. Air Force. basic combat unit consisting of twelve or more planes divided into three or more flights of three to five planes each. **2.** U.S. Navy. unit of a fleet, including eight amphibious ships of varying types and four minesweepers. **3.** formerly, a unit of cavalry usually having from 120 to 200 men. **4.** any large organized body or group. [Italian *squadrone* troop of men, from *squadra* group, square. See SQUAD.]

squal·id (skwol´id) *adj.* **1.** having a gloomy, wretched, poverty-stricken appearance; *a squalid beggar, squalid tenements.* **2.** morally objectionable; sordid: *the squalid details of the scandal.* [Latin *squālidus* filthy.] —**squa·lid´i·ty, squal´id·ness,** *n.* —**squal´id·ly,** *adv.*

squall[1] (skwôl) *n.* **1.** sudden, violent storm or wind, often accompanied by rain, snow, or sleet. **2.** *Informal.* sudden, short disturbance or commotion. —*v.i.* to blow a squall. [Probably of Scandinavian origin.]

squall[2] (skwôl) *v.i.* to cry or scream loudly or harshly: *The child squalled when he was spanked.* —*n.* loud, harsh cry or scream. [Possibly imitative.] —**squall´er,** *n.*

squall·y (skwô´lē) **squall·i·er, squall·i·est.** *adj.* **1.** marked by squalls; stormy; gusty: *squally seas, squally winds.* **2.** *Informal.* marked by or threatening trouble.

squal·or (skwol´ər) *n.* state or condition of being squalid. [Latin *squālor* filth.]

squa·ma (skwā´mə) *pl.,* **-mae** (-mē). *n.* scale or scalelike structure. [Latin *squāma* scale[2].]

squa·mate (skwā´māt) *adj.* having or covered with scales.

squa·mous (skwā´məs) *also,* **squa·mose** (skwā´mōs). *adj.* like, covered with, or formed of scales. [Latin *squāmōsus,* from *squāma* scale[2].]

squan·der (skwon´dər) *v.t.* to spend, use, or expend in a wasteful or extravagant manner: *to squander an inheritance, to squander one's affections.* [Of uncertain origin.] —**squan´der·er,** *n.*

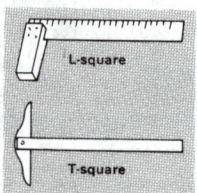

Squares

square (skwâr) *n.* **1.** plane figure having four sides of equal length and four right angles. **2.** object, part, or the like having this shape: *I moved the piece to the next square on the checkerboard.* **3.** open space in a city or town bounded by streets on all sides, often planted with grass, trees, or flowers, and usually used as a park. **4.** any similar open space, esp. one formed by the intersection of several streets. **5.a.** space or section in a city or town, bounded by streets on four sides: *The shopping area took up ten squares in the center of town.* **b.** distance between one of these streets and the next, block. **6.** an L-shaped or T-shaped instrument for laying out or testing right angles. **7.** product of a number or algebraic expression multiplied by itself: *Twenty-five is the square of five.* **8.** one who is conventional and conservative and does not know or follow the latest trends, fashions, or facts. **9. on the square. a.** at right angles. **b.** *Informal.* in a just or fair way; honestly. **10. out of square. a.** not at right angles. **b.** not in order; incorrect; at variance. —*adj.* **squar·er, squar·est. 1.a.** having four sides of equal length and four right angles. **2.** resembling a square in form: *a square suitcase, a square jaw.* **3.** designating a unit of measure expressing area in the form of a square having sides of a specified length: *a square yard.* **4.** of a specified length on each of four sides of a square: *a piece of land one hundred feet square.* **5.** forming a right angle. **6.** just; equitable; honest: *a businessman who was always square with his customers.* **7.** on equal terms; even: *The teams were square going into the fifth inning. When he pays me back we'll be square.* **8.** straightforward; absolute; unequivocal: *a square denial.* **9.** being the square of an integer. 1, 4, 9, and 16 are square numbers. **10.** solid and strong, esp. having a broad, stocky build. **11.** *Informal.* having or characterized by a lack of knowledge of or interest in the latest trends, fashions, or fads; conventional or conservative: *Dad's old-fashioned, and his taste in music is really square.* —*v.t.,* **squared, squar·ing. 1.** to form with four equal sides and four right angles; make or form like a square. **2.** to bring to or as to the form of a right angle or a straight line: *to square one's shoulders.* **3.** to mark out or divide into squares. **4.** to arrange to fit some given measure or standard; regulate; adjust: *to square facts with his story, to square one's opinion with that of the majority.* **5.** to adjust so as to leave no balance; settle: *to square accounts.* **6.** to make equal, level, or even, as a score. **7.** *Mathematics.* **a.** to multiply (a number or algebraic expression) times itself. **b.** to find the square measure of (an area). —*v.i.* **1.** to agree; conform; fit: *Patrick's opinions don't square with mine.* **2. to square away. a.** to place the yards at right angles to the keel, so the ship sails before the wind. **b.** *Informal.* to get ready. **3. to square off.** *Informal.* to prepare to fight; assume a defensive or offensive position. —*adv.* **1.** so as to be at or form right angles. **2.** firmly. **3.** directly. **4.** *Informal.* fairly or honestly. [Old French *esquarre,* past participle of *esquarrer* to make quadrangular, going back to Latin *ex-* (see EX-[1]) + *quadrāre* to make quadrangular, put in proper order, agree.] —**square´ly,** *adv.* —**square´ness,** *n.*

square dance, folk or social dance, developed in America and performed by groups of four or more couples who are arranged in a square at the beginning of the dance.

square deal *Informal.* fair and honest treatment or transaction.

square knot, knot formed by two interlaced loops going in opposite directions. See **knot** for illustration.

square meal, complete or substantial meal: *to eat three square meals a day.*

square measure, unit or system of units for measuring area.

square-rigged (skwâr´rigd´) *adj.* having square sails as the principal sails.

square-rig·ger (skwâr´rig´ər) *n.* square-rigged ship.

Square-rigged ship

square root, number that when squared produces a given number. Three is the square root of nine.

square sail, four-sided sail, as used on a schooner when sailing before the wind.

square shooter *Informal.* one who is honest and straightforward in dealing with others.

squar·ish (skwâr´ish) *adj.* almost or somewhat square.

squash[1] (skwosh) *v.t.* **1.** to beat or press into a soft or flat mass; crush: *to squash berries for a sauce, to accidentally squash flowers by stepping on them.* **2.** to force or squeeze into a small area; cram; crowd: *to squash three people into a phone booth.* **3.** to put down or suppress completely and forcibly: *to squash a revolt.* —*v.i.* **1.** to be crushed or crowded. **2.** to make or move with a squashing sound. —*n.* **1.** crushed or crowded mass, esp. of people. **2.** act of squashing; being squashed. **3.** sound of squashing. **4.** either of two games, **squash racquets** or **squash tennis,** in which a rubber ball is hit with a racket against a wall in a concrete court. **5.** *British.* soft drink, usually containing fruit juice and soda water. [Old French *esquasser* to break in pieces, going back to Latin *ex-* (see EX-[1]) + *quassāre* to shake, shatter.] —**squash´er,** *n.*

squash[2] (skwosh) *n.* **1.** round or oblong fruit of any of a group of plants, genus *Cucurbita,* of the gourd family, cooked and eaten as a vegetable, or used as food for livestock. **2.** plant bearing this fruit, having broad leaves and threadlike tendrils, cultivated in most parts of the world. [Shortened from Algonquian *askutasquash* literally, vegetables eaten green.]

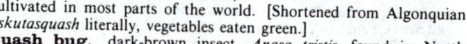

Squash[2]

squash bug, dark-brown insect, *Anasa tristis,* found in North America, destructive to squash plants.

squash·y (skwosh´ē) **squash·i·er, squash·i·est.** *adj.* soft and wet; easily squashed: *squashy tomatoes, squashy mud.* —**squash´i·ly,** *adv.* —**squash´i·ness,** *n.*

squat (skwot) **squat·ted** or **squat, squat·ting.** *v.i.* **1.** to set or crouch with the knees bent and drawn close to or under the body: *Keith squatted down to pet the cat.* **2.** to settle on land before gaining title or right to it, often in order to gain title or right. —*v.t.* to put (oneself) in a squatting position. —*adj.* **1.** short and thick; low and broad: *a squat man waddling down the street.* **2.** sitting or being in a crouching position. [Old French *esquatir* to crush, going back to Latin *ex-* (see EX-[1]) + *coāctus* forced, past participle of *cogere* to drive together, force.] —**squat´ly,** *adv.* —**squat´ness,** *n.*

squat·ter (skwot´ər) *n.* one who or that which squats, esp. one who settles on land to which he has no right or title. Squatters are sometimes given title to land after having lived on it for a certain period of time.

squat·ty (skwot´ē) **-ti·er, -ti·est.** *adj.* squat.

squaw (skwô) *n.* **1.** North American Indian woman or wife. **2.** *Slang.* woman or wife. [Algonquian *squaws* woman.]

squawk (skwôk) *v.i.* **1.** to utter a shrill, harsh cry, as a gull or parrot. **2.** to complain or protest loudly or raucously: *The secretary squawked at having to make the boss's coffee.* —*n.* **1.** shrill, harsh cry. **2.** *Informal.* loud complaint or protest. [Imitative.] —**squawk´er,** *n.*

squeak (skwēk) *n.* short, thin high-pitched cry or sound. —*v.i.* **1.** to make or utter a squeak: *a woman squeaking at the sight of a mouse. The rusty gate squeaked when it opened.* **2.** *Informal.* to accomplish, get, or earn something by a narrow margin (with *through* or *by*). —*v.t.* to utter or produce with a squeak. [Probably imitative.] —**squeak´er,** *n.*

squeak·y (skwē´kē) **squeak·i·er, squeak·i·est.** *adj.* tending to squeak; squeaking: *squeaky floorboards.* —**squeak´i·ly,** *adv.* —**squeak´i·ness,** *n.*

 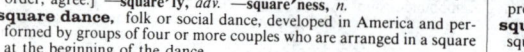 at; āpe; cär; end; mē; it; īce; hot; ōld; fôrk; wood; fōōl; oil; out; up; ūse; turn; sing; thin; this; zh in treasure; ə in ago, taken, pencil, lemon, circus.

squeal (skwēl) *v.i.* **1.** to make or utter a loud, shrill cry or sound: *Judy squealed with delight when she saw the gift.* **2.** *Slang.* to betray a confidence; turn informer: *The accomplice squealed to the cops.* —*v.t.* to utter or produce with a squeal. —*n.* loud, shrill cry or sound. [Imitative.] —**squeal′er,** *n.*

squeam·ish (skwē′mish) *adj.* **1.** easily sickened or nauseated: *to be squeamish about the sight of blood.* **2.** sickish; nauseated: *The boat trip made Kate squeamish.* **3.** readily offended or shocked; overly modest; prudish: *a squeamish attitude toward sex.* **4.** overly scrupulous, fastidious, or sensitive, as in standards of action or belief: *trifles magnified into importance by a squeamish conscience* (Macaulay, 1855). [Modification of earlier *squeymous, scoymus* from Anglo-Norman *escoymous* fastidious; of uncertain origin.] —**squeam′ish·ly,** *adv.* —**squeam′ish·ness,** *n.*

squee·gee (skwē′jē) *n.* **1.** T-shaped implement with a rubber or leather edge, used in wiping off or spreading liquid on flat, smooth surfaces, as in washing windows. **2.** device with a rubber roller or brush, used in photography for pressing excess water from a negative or print. —*v.t.,* **-geed, -gee·ing.** to wipe, spread, or press with a squeegee. [From *squeege,* form of SQUEEZE.]

squeeze (skwēz) *squeezed, squeez·ing. v.t.* **1.** to subject to strong pressure from opposing sides, as in a vise. **2.** to obtain (something) by the application of pressure; extract: *to squeeze juice from an orange.* **3.** to extort, esp. money: *He tried to squeeze a contribution from the millionaire.* **4.** to press or hug, as in sympathy or affection: *to squeeze someone's hand.* **5.** to force by pressure; thrust forcibly: *to squeeze a book into a crowded shelf.* **6.** to oppress. —*v.i.* **1.** to apply or exert pressure. **2.** to be capable of being squeezed; yield to pressure. **3.** to pass or force one's way by squeezing: *to squeeze into a seat, to squeeze between parked cars.* —*n.* **1.** act of squeezing; application of pressure. **2.** close embrace; hug. **3.** pressure of a crowd of people; crush: *There is always a squeeze in the subway during rush hours.* **4.** impression of some object, as a coin, made by pressing a substance around or over it. **5.** *Informal.* uncomfortable or inescapable pressure or position, as that caused by financial difficulty: *to be in a tight squeeze.* [Possibly modification of obsolete *quease* to press, from Old English *cwȳsan* to bruise, crush.] —**squeez′a·ble,** *adj.* —**squeez′er,** *n.*

squeeze play, play in baseball in which a runner on third base runs toward home plate as the ball is pitched and the batter attempts to bunt the ball so that the runner can score.

squelch (skwelch) *v.t.* **1.** to stamp out or eliminate forcibly and completely; crush; squash: *to squelch political opposition, to squelch ambition with constant criticism.* **2.** to put down or subdue, as with a crushing or sarcastic remark. —*v.i.* to make or move with a sucking or splashing sound, as when walking on wet ground. —*n.* **1.** *Informal.* crushing remark or response. **2.** sucking or splashing sound. [Imitative.] —**squelch′er,** *n.*

squib (skwib) *n.* short, written or spoken attack of a witty or satiric nature. **2.** a small firework that burns with a hissing noise and then explodes. **3.** broken firecracker that burns but does not explode. [Of uncertain origin.]

squid (skwid) *pl.* **squids** *or* **squid.** *n.* any of a group of saltwater invertebrates, order Dibranchia, having a cylindrical body, a pair of fins which aid it in swimming, and ten arms with suckers, used for catching prey. Length: 2 inches to 50 feet. [Of uncertain origin.]

Squid

squill (skwil) *n.* any of several plants of the lily family, native to Europe, Asia, and Africa, having a fleshy underground bulb and long, straplike leaves and bearing clusters of small flowers. [Latin *squilla, scilla,* from Greek *skilla.*]

squint (skwint) *v.i.* **1.** to look with partially closed eyes: *The sailor squinted in the bright sunlight.* **2.** to look questioningly or doubtfully; look askance. **3.** to incline or tend: *a remark that squinted toward an insult.* —*v.t.* **1.** to hold (the eyes) partly closed: *Smoke made Lilly squint her eyes.* **2.** to cause to squint. —*n.* **1.** act or habit of squinting. **2.** inclination; tendency. —*adj.* looking obliquely or askance; indirect. [Shortened from earlier *asquint* obliquely, askance; of uncertain origin.] —**squint′er,** *n.*

squire (skwīr) *n.* **1.** English country gentleman or landowner. Used as a title and form of address. **2.** in feudal society, young nobleman who, in preparation for his own knighthood, attended a knight. **3.** man who escorts a woman. **4.** local U.S. judicial official, as a justice of the peace or magistrate. —*v.t.* **squired, squir·ing.** to attend (someone) as a squire or escort. [Short for ESQUIRE.]

squirm (skwurm) *v.i.* **1.** to turn or twist the body with a snakelike motion; wriggle; writhe: *Oscar was bored and began to squirm in his seat.* **2.** to show or feel discomfort, uneasiness, or mental distress: *to blush and squirm with embarrassment.* —*n.* act or motion of squirming.

squir·rel (skwur′əl) *n.* **1.** any of various tree-dwelling rodents, family Sciuridae, native to most regions of the world, usually having a slender body and a long, bushy tail, and feeding chiefly on nuts. Length: to 3 feet including tail. **2.** its short, soft gray, reddish, or dark-brown fur. **3.** any of various burrowing or ground-dwelling members of the squirrel family, as the flying squirrel, chipmunk, gopher, and prairie dog. [Old French *escurel* the tree-dwelling rodent, going back to Latin *sciūrus,* from Greek *skiouros* literally, shadow-tail, from *skiā* shade + *ourā* tail; with reference to its bushy tail.]

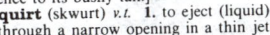

Squirrel

squirt (skwurt) *v.t.* **1.** to eject (liquid) through a narrow opening in a thin jet or stream. **2.** to wet or bespatter with liquid so ejected: *to squirt a fire with a hose.* —*v.i.* **1.** to come out in a thin jet or stream: *The ink squirted from the fountain pen.* **2.** to eject a thin jetlike stream of liquid. —*n.* **1.** act of squirting. **2.** thin, usually short, jet or stream. **3.** something used for squirting liquid, as a syringe or small pump. **4.** *Informal.* insignificant but presumptuous person, esp. one who is young or small. [Form of dialectal English *swirt,* possibly from Low German *swirtjen* to eject liquid in a stream.] —**squirt′er,** *n.*

squirting cucumber, trailing vine, *Ecballium elaterium,* of the gourd family, native to the Mediterranean region, bearing small, prickly, oblong fruits that squirt their seeds and juicy pulp when ripe.

squish (skwish) *v.i.* to make a splashing or gushing sound when pressed or walked on. —**squish′y,** *adj.*

sq. yd., square yard; square yards.

Sr, strontium.

Sr. 1. senior. **2.** sister. **3.** senor.

Sra., senora.

Sri Lan·ka (srē län kə) island country off southern Asia, in the Indian Ocean, east of the southern tip of India, formerly called Ceylon. Capital, Colombo. Area, 25,332 sq. mi. Pop. (1975 est.), 14,000,000.

Sri·na·gar (srē nug′ər) *n.* largest city of Kashmir, in the western part of the region. Pop. (1961), 285,257.

SRO, standing room only. Also, **S.R.O.**

SS, corps of black-uniformed German troops organized by Hitler in the 1920s as his personal bodyguard and later put in charge of extermination and massacres in conquered countries, such as Poland. [Abbreviation of German *Schutzstaffel* literally, protection staff.]

SS 1. steamship. Also, **S/S. 2.** Sunday school. Also, **S. S.**

SSE, south-southeast. Also, **sse, s.s.e.**

SSW, south-southwest. Also, **ssw, s.s.w.**

st. 1. street. **2.** stanza. **3.** stone (weight).

St. 1. Saint. **2.** Street. **3.** Strait.

stab (stab) **stabbed, stab·bing.** *v.t.* **1.** to pierce with or as with a pointed weapon: *to stab one's finger on a thorn.* **2.** to thrust or drive (a pointed instrument or weapon) into something: *to stab a fork into meat.* **3. to stab (someone) in the back,** to do harm or injury to (someone) in a treacherous manner; betray. —*v.i.* to thrust with or as with a pointed weapon. —*n.* **1.** thrust made with or as with a pointed weapon. **2.** wound or puncture made by stabbing. **3.** sharp but momentary sensation or feeling; pang: *a stab of pain, a stab of regret.* **4.** *Informal.* effort; try: *to make a stab at a hard job.* [Possibly form of dialectal English *stob* to pierce, from *stob* nail, stick, form of STUB.] —**stab′ber,** *n.*

sta·bil·i·ty (stə bil′ə tē) *pl.,* **-ties.** *n.* **1.** condition of being stable. **2.** reliability or consistency of character, purpose, or the like. **3.** immunity from essential change or destruction; permanence. **4.** *Aeronautics.* ability of an aircraft to return to equilibrium after displacement.

sta·bi·lize (stā′bə līz′) **-lized, -liz·ing.** *v.t.* **1.** to make stable, firm, or steady. **2.** to prevent from fluctuating: *to stabilize stock prices.* **3.** *Aeronautics.* to secure or maintain the equilibrium of (a craft), as by special construction or by using special control devices. —**sta′bi·li·za′tion,** *n.*

sta·bi·liz·er (stā′bə lī′zər) *n.* **1.** one who or that which makes something stable. **2.** gyroscopic device in a ship, airplane, or the like that keeps it steady in rough water or turbulent air. **3.** the vertical fin on either of the horizontal surfaces of the tail of an airplane.

sta·ble¹ (stā′bəl) *n.* **1.** building, esp. one with stalls, where horses or cattle are kept and fed. **2.** animals housed in such a building. **3.** *also,* **stables.** **a.** race horses belonging to a particular establishment or owner. **b.** personnel, grounds, and equipment collectively of such an establishment. **4.** group of persons engaged in the same activity and under the same management: *a publisher's stable of authors, a manager's stable*

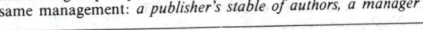

at; āpe; cär; end; mē; it; īce; hot; ōld; fôrk; wood; fōōl; out; up; ūse; turn; sing; thin; this; zh in treasure; ə in ago, taken, pencil, lemon, circus.

969

of boxers. —*v.t., v.i.* **-bled, -bling.** to put or keep in or as in a stable. [Old French *estable* covered place where one lodges animals, from Latin *stabulum* abode, stall.]

sta·ble² (stā′bəl) *adj.* **1.** not easily moved, shaken, or overthrown; fixed in position; firm: *a stable platform, a stable government.* **2.** reliable, consistent, or predictable, as in character or purpose. **3.** persisting without essential change; permanent; enduring: *a stable language.* **4.** *Chemistry.* (of chemical compounds) resistant to chemical change; not easily decomposed. **5.** *Physics.* **a.** (of a substance) not radioactive. **b.** resistant to forces that disturb the position or form of a body. [Old French *(e)stable* firm, upright, from Latin *stabilis* firm, steady, from *stāre* to stand.] —**sta′bly,** *adv.*

sta·ble-boy (stā′bəl boi′) *n.* man or boy who works in a stable.

stab·lish (stab′lish) *v.t., v.i. Archaic.* to establish.

stacc., staccato.

stac·ca·to (stə kä′tō) *adj.* **1.** *Music.* produced with or having breaks between the successive tones; disconnected; abrupt. **2.** composed of or characterized by abrupt, sharp emphasis, sound, or movement: *staccato gunfire.* —*adv.* in a staccato manner. [Italian *staccato* literally, detached, past participle of *staccare,* short for *distaccare* to detach, separate, going back to Latin *dis-* apart + Low German *takk* pointed thing.]

stack (stak) *n.* **1.** large, rectangular or cone-shaped pile of hay, straw, or unthreshed grain left in the field, often thatched or otherwise arranged to protect it from the weather. **2.** orderly or systematically arranged pile: *a stack of plates, Christmas cards arranged in small stacks on the table.* **3.** number of rifles standing muzzle upward against each other and forming a cone. **4.** a pipe or series of pipes carrying off smoke, waste, or poisonous flames. **5.a.** *also,* **stacks.** rack in which books are arranged above one another on shelves. **b. stacks.** library area in which most of the books are shelved. **6.** *British.* measure, used esp. for firewood or coal, equal to 108 cubic feet. **7.** *Informal.* large quantity. —*v.t.* **1.** to gather or arrange in a stack: *to stack papers, to stack corn up in the barn.* **2.** to load with stacks of material. **3. to stack the cards** (or **a deck**). **a.** to arrange (playing cards) beforehand so that they will come up in a certain order. **b.** to prearrange circumstances, esp. to someone's disadvantage: *The cards were stacked against him.* —*v.i.* **stack up.** to measure up or equal (often with *against*): *How does your new car stack up against that old jalopy you had?* [Old Norse *stakkr* haystack.]

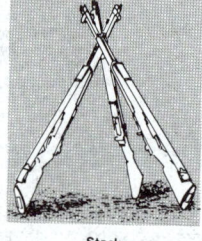

Stack

sta·di·a¹ (stā′dē ə) *n.* surveying method using a long graduated rod, the number of whose divisions when sighted through a telescope between two horizontal wires is multiplied by a constant to give the distance between the observer and the rod. [Of uncertain origin.]

sta·di·a² (stā′dē ə) a plural of **stadium.**

sta·di·um (stā′dē əm) *pl.* **-di·ums** or **-di·a,** *n.* **1.** large, usually roofless, oval or U-shaped structure surrounding an open area, used for athletic events and other purposes, as rallies or concerts, and equipped with rows of seats for spectators. **2.** U-shaped ancient Greek track for foot races and other athletic events, about 607 feet long with rows of seats for spectators except at the open end. [Latin *stadium* measure of length of about 607 feet, course for racing, from Greek *stadion.*]

Staël, Madame de (stäl) 1766–1817, French author.

staff (staf) *pl.* **staffs** or *(defs. 1, 4)* **staves.** *n.* **1.a.** stick, rod, or pole, often used as an aid in walking and as a weapon or symbol of authority. **b.** flagpole. **2.** body of permanent employees comprising an institution or business or any specialized group within that body: *advisory staff, a nursing staff, the hospital staff.* **3.** military personnel whose duties are planning and administration and who do not usually take part in combat. **4.** *Music.* the five horizontal lines and four spaces on which musical notation is made, used to represent the pitches of tones. —*v.t.* to provide (an office, establishment, military unit, or the like) with officers or employees: *to staff the new store.* [Old English *stæf* stick, pole.]

Staff (def. 4)

staff officer, officer who is a member of a staff. Distinguished from **line officer.**

staff of life, any staple food, esp. bread, regarded as the mainstay of a diet.

staff sergeant *U.S. Military.* a noncommissioned officer ranking in the Army below a sergeant first class, in the Air Force below a technical sergeant, and in the Marine Corps below a gunnery sergeant.

stag (stag) *n.* **1.** full-grown male of various deer, esp. of the red deer. **2.** male of various other animals, esp. when castrated after reaching maturity. **3.** man who goes to a social gathering unaccompanied by a woman. **4.** social gathering attended by men only. —*adj.* for or attended by men only: *a stag party.* —*adv.* (of a man) not accompanied by a woman: *to go to a dance stag.* [From an unrecorded Old English word.]

stage (stāj) *n.* **1.** raised platform or similar structure in a theater or hall, on which a performance takes place. **2.** the theater as a profession: *to write for the stage.* **3.** place where some important event takes place; scene of action: *Europe was the stage for war.* **4.** step, period, or degree in a process, progression, development, or the like: *an early stage of childhood, in the last stage of the disease.* **5.** distance traveled between two places of rest on a road or journey; definite portion of a journey: *to proceed in short stages.* **6.** regular stopping place on a journey. **7.** stagecoach. **8.** one of the self-propelling sections of a rocket vehicle which can be separated from the rest of the vehicle. **9.** raised floor or platform. **10.** platform or scaffold, as for workmen. **11. by easy stages.** gradually; slowly. —*v.t.,* **staged, stag·ing. 1.** to put, arrange, or exhibit on or as on a stage: *to stage a play.* **2.** to effect; do; conduct: *to stage a victorious campaign.* [Old French *estage* dwelling, story², floor, condition, going back to Latin *stāre* to stand.]

stage-coach (stāj′kōch′) *n.* horse-drawn coach traveling on a regular schedule over a fixed route, carrying passengers, mail, and baggage.

stage-craft (stāj′kraft′) *n.* skill in any of the arts associated with

Stagecoach

the production of a theatrical presentation, as writing, directing, and lighting.

stage fright, nervousness experienced by an actor or speaker before an audience.

stage-hand (stāj′hand′) *n.* in the theater, a person who moves scenery, sets props, controls lighting, and performs certain other duties.

stag·er (stā′jər) *n.* person experienced in a profession or way of life; veteran. [Possibly from Old French *estagier* resident, from *estage.* See STAGE.]

stage-struck (stāj′struk′) *adj.* fascinated by the theater, esp. with the hopes of becoming an actor or actress.

stage whisper 1. in the theater, a whisper meant to be heard by the audience and supposedly unheard by some or all of the other players on the stage. **2.** whisper intended to be overheard by persons other than the person addressed.

stag·ey (stā′jē) stag·i·er, stag·i·est. *adj.* stagy.

stag·ger (stag′ər) *v.i.* **1.** to move unsteadily or with a swaying motion; totter; reel: *to stagger under a heavy load.* **2.** to become confused or overwhelmed; falter in purpose or action; waver; hesitate: *to stagger at a seemingly impossible task.* —*v.t.* **1.** to cause to totter or reel: *The punch staggered the fighter.* **2.** to confuse or overwhelm, as with grief or surprise; cause to falter or waver; shock: *a feat that staggers the imagination.* **3.** to schedule, arrange, or distribute in a continuous or overlapping order, as to relieve congestion: *to stagger traffic lights, to stagger work shifts.* —*n.* **1.** act or motion of staggering. **2.** staggered pattern or arrangement. **3. staggers.** disease of the central nervous system in cattle and other domestic animals, causing sudden falls and a staggering gait. [Old Norse *stakra* to push, cause to reel.] —**stag′ger·er,** *n.* —**stag′ger·ing·ly,** *adv.*

stag·ing (stā′jing) *n.* **1.** scaffolding or similar temporary platform. **2.** directing and presentation of a theatrical production or similar entertainment.

staging area, area where military personnel or supplies are assembled prior to embarkation or movement to another zone, usually in preparation for a battle.

stag·nant (stag′nənt) *adj.* **1.** motionless; still, as air or water. **2.** foul from standing still: *stagnant water in a swamp.* **3.** not growing, changing, or developing; inactive; dull: *stagnant trade, a stagnant life.* [Latin *stāgnāns,* present participle of *stāgnāre* to form a pool of standing water, from *stāgnum* pool.] —**stag′nan·cy,** *n.* —**stag′nant·ly,** *adv.*

stag·nate (stag′nāt) -nat·ed, -nat·ing. *v.i.* **1.** to stop growing, changing, or developing; to be or become inactive or dull: *to allow the mind to stagnate.* **2.** to be or become stagnant: *water stagnating in a gutter.* [Latin *stāgnātus,* past participle of *stāgnāre.* See STAGNANT.] —**stag·na′tion,** *n.*

stag·y (stā′jē) stag·i·er, stag·i·est. *also,* stag·ey. *adj.* of, suited to, or suggestive of the stage; having or characterized by a theatrical or affected manner. —**stag′i·ly,** *adv.* —**stag′i·ness,** *n.*

staid (stād) *v. Archaic.* a past tense and past participle of **stay¹.**

at; āpe; cär; end; mē; it; īce; hot; ōld; fôrk; wood; fōol; out; up; ūse; turn; sing; thin; this; zh in treasure; ə in ago, taken, pencil, lemon, circus.

—*adj.* conservative or sober in character or style; sedate. —**staid′ly,** *adv.* —**staid′ness,** *n.*

stain (stān) *n.* **1.** discoloration produced by foreign matter; spot; streak: *an ink stain, grass stains.* **2.** liquid dye or thin pigment used esp. in coloring wood, the surface of which absorbs the liquid. **3.** colored solution used to treat a microscopic specimen so as to render structures visible. **4.** moral taint or blemish. —*v. t.* **1.** to spot, streak, or discolor with foreign matter: *Spilled coffee had stained the carpet.* **2.** to color or treat with a dye, pigment, or other colored solution: *to stain a bookcase, to stain a slide.* **3.** to bring reproach upon; taint; blemish. —*v. i.* **1.** to become or admit of being stained: *This synthetic material stains easily.* **2.** to cause a stain. [Short for DISTAIN.] —**stain′a·ble,** *adj.* —**stain′er,** *n.*

stained glass, glass that has been colored by fusing metal oxides or by having pigments burned into the surface, widely used in church windows where pieces are held together by strips of lead.

stain·less steel (stān′lis) alloy of steel with large amounts of chromium, and often of nickel, that is highly resistant to corrosion and heat and is strong, durable, and easy to shape. It is used for cutlery, instruments, appliances, and structural parts.

stair (stâr) *n.* **1.** *usually,* **stairs.** series or flight of steps for passing from one level or floor to another: *The stairs to the attic have been closed off.* **2.** step or one of a series of steps. [Old English *stæger* flight of steps.]

stair·case (stâr′kās′) *n.* flight or a series of flights of stairs with its supporting framework.

stair·way (stâr′wā′) *n.* staircase.

stair·well (stâr′wel′) *n.* vertical shaft enclosing a staircase.

stake (stāk) *n.* **1.** stick or post sharpened at one end for driving into the ground, esp. one used as a support or boundary. **2.a.** post to which a person was bound for execution by burning: *Joan of Arc was burned at the stake.* **b.** execution performed in this manner. **3.** *also,* **stakes.** that which is risked in a wager or gambling game, as money. **4.** interest, share, or involvement in a project, esp. a financial interest: *As the star of the play, she has a stake in its success.* **5.** *also,* **stakes.** sum of money offered the winner of a contest or race; prize; purse. **6.** **at stake.** in question or jeopardy; at issue: *The firemen acted quickly because lives were at stake.* **7.** **to pull up stakes.** to move on or away; leave. —*v. t.,* **staked, stak·ing.** **1.** to mark the boundaries of with or as with stakes; claim or reserve (often with *off* and *out*): *to stake out a campsite.* **2.** to fasten or tie to a stake; support with a stake. **3.** to gamble or risk: *He staked all his savings on an impractical invention.* **4.** to provide with resources or funds; support financially: *Sam staked Owen to dinner.* [Old English *staca* strong stick, post¹.]

Sta·kha·no·vism (stə kä′nə viz′əm) *n.* in the Soviet Union, a system of speeding up industrial production by increasing single tasks for more productive workers. [From Alexei *Stakhanov,* Russian miner who developed such a system in 1935.] —**Sta·kha′no·vite′,** *n.*

sta·lac·tite (stə lak′tīt, stal′ək tīt′) *n.* iciclelike formation on the ceiling of a cave, usually composed of calcium carbonate deposited by water seeping through the rock above. Distinguished from **stalagmite.** [Modern Latin *stalactites,* from Greek *stalaktos* trickling, dripping; because it results from the dripping of water.] —**stal·ac·tit·ic** (stal′ək tit′ik), *adj.*

sta·lag·mite (stə lag′mīt, stal′əg-mīt′) *n.* formation resembling a cone, built up on the floor of a cave by calcium carbonate dripping from the ceiling. Distinguished from **stalactite.** [Modern Latin *stalagmites,* from Greek *stalagmos* a dripping.] —**stal·ag·mit·ic** (stal′əg-mit′ik), *adj.*

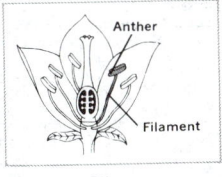

Stalactites

Stalagmites

stale (stāl) *stal·er,* *stal·est.* *adj.* **1.** having lost freshness, esp. tasteless or unpalatable from age: *The cake had become stale and dry.* **2.** having lost its novelty or interest; hackneyed: *stale news.* **3.** out of condition: *The athlete was stale from lack of exercise.* —*v. t.,* **staled, stal·ing.** to lessen the novelty or interest of: *Age cannot wither her, nor custom stale her infinite variety* (Shakespeare, *Antony and Cleopatra*). —*v. i.* to grow stale. [Of uncertain origin.] —**stale′ly,** *adv.* —**stale′ness,** *n.*

stale·mate (stāl′māt′) *n.* **1.** situation in chess in which the player whose turn it is to move cannot move without putting his king in check. Such a move is against the rules, therefore the game is counted as a draw. **2.** any position or situation in which no further action is possible; impasse; standstill. —*v. t.,* **-mat·ed, -mat·ing.** **1.** to subject to a stalemate. **2.** to place in an impasse. [Middle English *stale* stalemate (in chess), probably from Anglo-Norman *estale* position (from *estaler* to stop, set in place; of Germanic origin) + MATE².]

Sta·lin, Joseph (stä′lin) 1879–1953, Soviet revolutionary and from 1924 to 1953 leader of the Soviet Union.

Sta·lin·grad (stä′lin grad′) *n.* see **Volgograd.**

stalk¹ (stôk) *n.* **1.** main stem or axis of a plant. **2.** stem of any plant part, as the petiole of a leaf, or the peduncle of a flower cluster. **3.** part supporting part of an animal or the whole animal. [Middle English *stalke* main stem of a plant, possibly diminutive of *stale* handle, from Old English *stalu* side of a ladder.]

stalk² (stôk) *v. t.* **1.** to hunt, track, or pursue, as game: *The lion stalked his prey. The detective stalked down the real facts.* **2.** to move or walk menacingly or stealthily through; haunt: *The fugitive stalked the streets. Pestilence and famine stalk the countryside.* —*v. i.* **1.** to walk or stride in a stiff, determined, or angry manner: *George stalked out of the room, slamming the door behind him.* **2.** to hunt or track game. [Old English *bestealcian* to go stealthily.] —**stalk′er,** *n.*

stalk·ing-horse (stô′king hôrs′) *n.* **1.** anything used to conceal real motives or actual plans; pretext. **2.** horse or figure of a horse, behind which a hunter conceals himself in stalking game.

stall (stôl) *n.* **1.** compartment in a barn or stable for one horse, cow, or other animal. **2.** booth or counter for setting up wares for sale. **3.** enclosed seat in the chancel of a church, usually reserved for the clergy. **4.** *British.* orchestra seat in the front of a theater. **5.** *Informal.* evasion, pretense, or other delaying tactic. —*v. t.* **1.** to keep from taking action by evasion, pretense, or other delaying tactics (sometimes with *off*): *to stall off creditors. The store owner stalled the robber until the police arrived.* **2.** to obstruct or block the motion or progress of; bring to a standstill: *We were stalled in the train for an hour.* **3.** to cause (an engine, automobile, or the like) to stop running, as because of mechanical failure. **4.** to put or lodge (an animal) in a stall. —*v. i.* **1.** to make delays; be evasive: *to stall for time.* **2.** to come to a standstill. **3.** to stop running: *The train stalled in the tunnel. The car stalled in the ditch.* **4.** *Aeronautics.* to lose the amount of speed necessary to control an aircraft. [Old English *steall* place, station, division in a stable.]

stal·lion (stal′yən) *n.* male horse, esp. one used as a stud horse. [Old French *estalon;* of Germanic origin.]

stal·wart (stôl′wərt) *adj.* **1.** morally or physically strong; valiant. **2.** unwavering, as in support of a cause; resolute: *the stalwart opposition.* —*n.* **1.** one who is stalwart. **2.** unwavering supporter, as of a political party or cause; partisan. [Old English *stælwierthe* serviceable, from *stathol* foundation + *wierthe* worth.] —**stal′wart·ly,** *adv.* —**stal′wart·ness,** *n.*

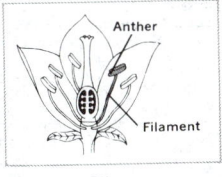

Anther

Filament

Stamen

sta·men (stā′mən) *pl.,* **stamens** or **sta·mi·na.** *n.* pollen-bearing organ of a flowering plant, consisting of a slender stalk, the filament, and the anther, two sacs containing the pollen grains. [Latin *stāmen* thread.]

Stam·ford (stam′fərd) *n.* city in southwestern Connecticut. Pop. (1970), 108,798.

stam·i·na¹ (stam′ə nə) *n.* moral or physical capacity to withstand fatigue, disease, deprivation, or hardship; endurance. [Latin *stāmina,* plural of *stāmen* thread; with reference to the thread supposedly spun by the Fates at birth that determined by its length the duration of one's life.] —**Syn.** see **endurance.**

stam·i·na² (stam′ə nə) a plural of **stamen.**

stam·i·nate (stam′ə nit, -nāt′) *adj.* **1.** having a stamen or stamens. **2.** having stamens but no pistils.

stam·mer (stam′ər) *v.i.* to speak haltingly, esp. with repetitions of a letter, sound, syllable, or the like. —*v. t.* to say or utter with a stammer (sometimes with *out*): *to stammer a refusal.* —*n.* habit or instance of stammering. [Old English *stamerian* to stutter.] —**stam′mer·er,** *n.*

stamp (stamp) *v. t.* **1.** to bring down the foot (or feet) forcefully and heavily: *The spoiled child stamped his foot with rage.* **2.** to strike forcefully with the sole of the foot. **3.** to bring into a desired condition by or as by stamping with the foot or feet: *to stamp out burning embers, to stamp out political opposition.* **4.** to mark (with an impression, design, or the like): *to stamp an initial on stationery, to stamp a pattern on a fabric.* **5.** to mark (an object, surface, or the like) with a device that cuts or imprints a design: *to stamp butter.* **6.** to impress deeply; fix: *an event stamped on one's memory.* **7.** to show to be of a certain quality or nature; characterize: *He stamped himself as an expert on the subject. His words stamped him to be a bigot.* **8.** to affix a postage stamp or other official mark on: *to stamp a letter.* **9.** to pound, crush, or pulverize (something, as ore). —*v. i.* to strike the foot forcefully downward upon the ground, as in walking: *She stamped out of the room.* —*n.* **1.** device or tool for cutting or impressing a design, as words or a pattern, on paper, wax, metal, or other surface. **2.** impression or design made with such a device. **3.a.** postage stamp. **b.** any similar stamped or printed

at; āpe; cär; end; mē; it; īce; hot; ōld; fôrk; wood; fōōl; oil; out; up; ūse; turn; sing; thin; this; zh in treasure; ə in ago, taken, pencil, lemon, circus.

971

paper, usually issued by a government and affixed to some article to indicate the prepayment of a tax or other charge. **4.** impressed mark or seal used to certify or assure validity: *a royal stamp.* **5.** distinguishing imprint or impression; mark: *His work bears the stamp of a vivid imagination.* **6.** type; sort; kind: *He is of the same stamp as his father.* **7.** heavy metal block used to crush rock, ore, or the like. **8.** act of stamping. [Probably from an unrecorded Old English word.]

stam·pede (stam pēd′) *n.* **1.** sudden scattering or headlong flight of frightened animals, as a herd of cattle or horses. **2.** sudden scattering or headlong flight of a mob or crowd. **3.** mass movement set off by a common impulse: *a stampede of resignations.* —*v.i.,* **-ped·ed, -ped·ing.** to be part of a stampede. —*v.t.* to cause to stampede: *The rustlers stampeded the cattle.* [Spanish *estampida* uproar, rush, from *estampar* to stamp; of Germanic origin.]

stamp·er (stam′pər) *n.* **1.** one who stamps or operates a machine that stamps. **2.** machine or instrument used for stamping.

stamping ground *Informal.* one's favorite or frequent gathering place or haunt.

stance (stans) *n.* **1.** manner or mode of standing, esp. the particular position assumed by an athlete while playing. **2.** moral or intellectual attitude; viewpoint. [French *stance* stay¹ (obsolete), stanza, from Italian *stanza* station, dwelling, stanza. See STANZA.]

stanch¹ (stônch, stänch) *also,* **staunch.** *v.t.* **1.** to stop or check the flow of (blood or other fluid). **2.** to stop or check the flow of blood or other liquid from (a wound or other opening). [Old French *estanchier* to stop the flow of blood, slake thirst; of uncertain origin.] —**stanch′er,** *n.*

stanch² (stônch, stänch) *adj.* staunch¹. —**stanch′ly,** *adv.* —**stanch′ness,** *n.*

stan·chion (stan′shən) *n.* **1.** an upright pillar or bar used as a support. **2.** device for restricting the movements of animals, as cattle, usually consisting of a pair of bars loosely fitting around the neck. —*v.t.* **1.** to provide with or support by stanchions. **2.** to fasten (cattle) to or enclose with stanchions. [Old French *estanchon* prop, diminutive of *estance,* going back to Latin *stāre* to stand.]

stand (stand) stood, stand·ing. *v.i.* **1.** to be in an upright position supported by one's feet: *We had to stand because there were no seats available.* **2.** to assume such a position; rise: *The congregation was asked to stand for the singing of a hymn.* **3.** to be of a specified height when upright or vertical, as on one's feet or on a base: *David stands six feet three inches. The skyscraper stands 500 feet.* **4.** to be or remain upright: *A ladder stood against the side of the barn.* **5.** to have location or position; be situated: *The village stands at the foot of the hill.* **6.** to hold a particular place, as of degree, rank, or class: *to stand first in total scoring in the contest.* **7.** to be in a specified state or condition: *to stand prepared. I stand corrected.* **8.** to remain valid, unchanged, or in force; hold good: *The judge's decision stands and cannot be appealed.* **9.** to endure; last: *The building stood for many years.* **10.** to assume or maintain a specific position: *to stand aside, to stand at attention.* **11.** to assume a particular attitude; adopt a certain course: *to stand and fight for one's rights.* **12.** to collect and remain: *Water stood in the gutter.* **13.** to come to a stop; halt: *The traffic laws prohibit standing from here to the corner.* **14.** to be a candidate, esp. for election to public office. **15.** (of a dog) to point. **16.** *Nautical.* to hold a specified course; take a direction: *The ship stood into the gale.* —*v.t.* **1.** to set in an upright position: *Stand the barrel on its end.* **2.** to put up with; endure; tolerate: *I can't stand all this noise.* **3.** to undergo without damage; withstand: *to stand the test of time.* **4.** to be subjected to; undergo: *to stand trial.* **5.** *Informal.* to bear the expense of: *to stand a round of drinks.*

to stand a chance. to have a chance or likelihood.

to stand by. **a.** to be present without interfering, as a spectator: *Keith refused to stand by and watch the dog be mistreated.* **b.** to take the side of; support; defend: *Natalie stood by her friend during the crisis.* **c.** to abide by; maintain: *to stand by one's promise.* **d.** to be or become ready, as for use or action: *Please stand by and wait for further instructions.*

to stand for. **a.** to represent; symbolize; mean. **b.** *Informal.* to put up with; tolerate: *The teacher wouldn't stand for such behavior.*

to stand in for. to be a substitute for.

to stand off. to repel or keep at a distance: *A small troop of brave soldiers stood the enemy off.*

to stand on. **a.** to be based or grounded on. **b.** to insist upon; make much of; demand: *to stand on ceremony.*

to stand out. **a.** to jut out; project; protrude. **b.** to be prominent or conspicuous: *Robert's red hair made him stand out in a crowd.* **c.** to refuse to yield or comply.

to stand pat. **a.** in poker, to play one's hand as dealt, without drawing new cards. **b.** to resist or oppose change or reform.

to stand to reason. to be consistent with or conform to reason; be logical: *It stands to reason that with that much popular support he can't lose the election.*

to stand up. **a.** to rise to or be on one's feet. **b.** to withstand wear, hardship, pressure, or the like; endure; last. **c.** *Informal.* to fail to keep an appointment with.

to stand up for. to take the part of; defend; support.

to stand up to. to confront fearlessly; encounter boldly.

—*n.* **1.** position, attitude, or opinion, as in a controversial issue: *What is the president's stand on disarmament?* **2.** determined effort for or against something: *to take a stand against segregation.* **3.** stop or halt, esp. for defense or resistance: *Custer's last stand.* **4.** place where or in which someone or something stands: *The guards' stand was at the gate.* **5.** device, as a rack or similar structure, on or in which articles may be placed, as for support or display: *an umbrella stand.* **6.** structure, as a booth, counter, or stall, from which business is conducted: *newspaper stand.* **7.** raised platform or similar structure, usually consisting of several tiers on which one can sit or stand: *We watched the baseball game from the stands. The marchers passed the reviewing stand.* **8.** witness stand. **9.** place or station from which vehicles may be hired: *a taxi stand.* **10.** one of a series of performances made on a theatrical tour. **11.** group of trees or plants, growing in a particular area. [Old English *standan* to be in or assume an upright position.] —**Syn.** *v.t.* **2.** see **bear¹.**

stand·ard (stan′dərd) *n.* **1.** anything recognized or accepted as correct or perfect and used as a basis of comparison; model: *standards of taste, moral standards.* **2.** commodity, as gold, used to define the basic currency unit of a monetary system. **3.** established unit of weight or measure. **4.** flag, figure, or other object used as an emblem: *the standard of a regiment.* **5.** upright support or part: *the standard of a lamp.* **6.** tree or shrub with one tall stem, that stands without support. **7.** large, upper petal of a flower. —*adj.* **1.** serving or fitted to serve as a standard or model. **2.** having recognized and lasting excellence or authority: *a standard book on English literature.* **3.** widely and customarily used; usual: *standard practices.* **4.** conforming to usage in speech or writing that is generally accepted as correct or preferred: *standard spelling, standard English.* [Old French *estandart, estandard* flag, banner; probably of Germanic origin.]

Syn. *n.* **1. Standard, criterion, gauge** are means of judgment, evaluation, and comparison. **Standard** implies that a set of rules, established by authority or custom and applied objectively and consistently, may be used to obtain uniformity or to maintain certain desirable levels, as of performance or appearance: *The army enforces strict standards of dress and conduct.* **Criterion** is not so much a clearly formulated rule as an ideal by which to judge value or excellence: *Money is not a criterion of success.* **Gauge** suggests a scale can be used to measure something that varies or changes, without referring to a fixed standard or ideal: *The polls will give us a gauge of the candidate's popularity.*

stand·ard·bear·er (stan′dərd bâr′ər) *n.* **1.** one who is assigned to carry the flag or standard of a unit or group. **2.** one who is the leader or representative of a movement, organization, or the like.

stand·ard·bred (stan′dərd bred′) *n.* horse of a breed developed in America for harness racing.

stand·ard·ize (stan′dər dīz′) **-ized, iz·ing.** *v.t.* to cause to conform to or regulate by a standard. —**stand′ard·i·za′tion,** *n.*

standard of living. average level of goods, services, luxuries, and the like available to and enjoyed by a person, group, or country.

standard time. civil time for any region based on its longitudinal distance from the meridian of Greenwich, England. The earth is divided into twenty-four time zones. In the continental United States the four standard time zones are Eastern, Central, Mountain, and Pacific.

stand·by (stand′bī′) *pl.,* **-bys.** *n.* one who or that which can be depended upon, as for use as a substitute or in an emergency.

stand·ee (stan dē′) *n. Informal.* one who stands, esp. when there are no vacant seats, as in a theater, train, or the like.

stand-in (stand′in′) *n.* **1.** one who takes the place of a motion-picture or television actor or actress while lights, cameras, and other technical equipment are being set up and adjusted. **2.** any substitute.

stand·ing (stan′ding) *adj.* **1.** remaining upright or on end; straight; erect: *standing corn, a standing collar, a standing screen.* **2.** done from or in an upright position: *a standing start, a standing ovation.* **3.** continuing in existence, operation, or effect; permanently established or maintained: *a standing rule, a standing joke, a standing committee.* **4.** (of water) stagnant; still. —*n.* **1.** status, grade, or rank, as in a profession or society; repute: *amateur standing, scholastic standing.* **2.** good reputation, credit, or position: *A man of his standing has no need to keep up appearances.* **3.** length or period of time for which something goes on; duration: *a friendship of long standing.* **4.** act or condition of standing; erectness. —**Syn.** *n.* **1.** see **rank¹.**

at; āpe; cär; end; mē; it; īce; hot; ōld; fôrk; wood; fŏŏl; oil; out; up; ūse; turn; sing; thin; this; zh in treasure; ə in ago, taken, pencil, lemon, circus.

Stanchion

standing rigging *Nautical.* ropes or wires of a ship's rigging which are fastened down. Stays and shrouds are part of the standing rigging.

standing room, space in which to stand, as in a theater, when there are no vacant seats.

Stan·dish, Miles (stan'dish; mīlz) c.1584–1656, U.S. colonist.

stand·off (stand'ôf') *n.* **1.** tie or draw, as in a game or contest. **2.** reserve; aloofness.

stand·off·ish (stand'ôf'ish) *adj.* lacking warmth or cordiality; reserved; aloof.

stand·out (stand'out') *n.* one who or that which is noticeable or prominent, as for its excellence or superiority.

stand·pipe (stand'pīp') *n.* large vertical pipe or tower used to store water, usually standing on high ground so as to provide pressure to make the water flow readily through mains.

stand·point (stand'point') *n.* position from which things are viewed and judged; point of view.

stand·still (stand'stil') *n.* state in which there is no movement or progress, as through fatigue, obstruction, or other difficulty; halt; stop: *The strike brought the steel industry to a standstill.*

stand·up (stand'up') *adj.* **1.** in a standing or erect position: *a stand-up collar.* **2.** performed or accomplished in a standing position: *a stand-up meal.*

stan·hope (stan'hōp, stan'əp) *n.* light, open, two-wheeled or four-wheeled carriage, usually seating one or two passengers. [From Fitzroy *Stanhope*, 1787–1864, English clergyman, for whom the first one was made.]

Stan·i·slav·sky, Kon·stan·tin (stan'i släv'skē, -släf'-; kon stän tēn') 1863–1938, Russian stage director and actor.

stank (stangk) a past tense of **stink.**

Stan·ley, Sir Henry Mor·ton (stan'lē; môr'tən) 1841–1904, British journalist and explorer in Africa.

stan·nic (stan'ik) *adj.* of, relating to, or containing tin, esp. in its higher oxidation state of +4. [Latin *stannum* tin + -IC.]

stan·nous (stan'əs) *adj.* of, relating to, or containing tin, esp. in its lower oxidation state of +2.

St. Anthony's fire, erysipelas.

stan·za (stan'zə) *n.* in poetry, group of lines, usually four or more, arranged in any of various patterns according to meter, rhyme, and the like. [Italian *stanza* dwelling, room, stanza, going back to Latin *stāre* to stand.]

sta·pes (stā'pēz) *pl.* **sta·pes** or **sta·pe·des** (stə pē'dēz, stā'pə-). *n.* innermost of the three small bones in the middle ear; stirrup. [Medieval Latin *stapes* stirrup, probably going back to Latin *stāre* to stand + *pēs* foot.]

staph (staf) *n.* staphylococcus.

staph·y·lo·coc·cus (staf'ə lə kok'əs) *pl.* **-coc·ci** (-kok'sī). *n.* **1.** any of various bacteria, genus *Staphylococcus*, occurring in irregular clusters and including a number of pathogenic organisms. **2.** infection caused by these bacteria. [Modern Latin *Staphylococcus*, from Greek *staphylos* bunch of grapes + COCCUS.]

sta·ple¹ (stā'pəl) *n.* **1.** small bent piece of thin wire used for fastening together papers, fabrics, or other thin materials. **2.** a U-shaped piece of metal with pointed ends, driven into something for fastening, as to support a hook or solid wire fencing to a post. —*v.t.* **-pled, -pling.** to secure, fasten, or attach with or as with a staple or staples. [Old English *stapol* post¹; pillar.]

sta·ple² (stā'pəl) *n.* **1.** basic commodity or other ordinary item in widespread use or demand, as flour, salt, or cotton. **2.** major product grown or manufactured in a country or region: *Wine is a staple of France.* **3.** basic or major element; substance; bulk. **4.** raw material. **5.a.** textile fiber of a given average length and quality for spinning in the manufacture of yarn. **b.** length of such a fiber. —*adj.* **1.** major; basic; substantial: *staple industries, a staple reference book found in every library.* **2.** regularly produced, used, or sold in large quantities for the market: *a staple crop.* —*v.t.* **-pled, -pling.** to sort according to fiber or fiber length. [Old French *estaple* mart, from Middle Dutch *stapel* pillar, mart.]

sta·pler¹ (stā'plər) *n.* any of various small devices for fastening paper and other thin materials together with wire staples. [STAPLE¹ + -ER¹.]

sta·pler² (stā'plər) *n.* person who sorts and grades fibers according to staple. [STAPLE² + -ER¹.]

star (stär) *n.* **1.** any celestial body that appears as a bright point of light in the night sky. **2.** *Astronomy.* large, roughly spherical celestial body

Stapes
Bones of the middle ear

(labels on illustration: Incus (anvil); Malleus (hammer); Stapes (stirrup))

that produces its own light, as distinguished from planets with their satellites and comets and meteors. **3.a.** geometric figure usually having five or more points radiating from a center. **b.** something resembling or suggesting this shape: *The horse had a white star on his forehead.* **4.** asterisk. **5.** person who is outstanding in some field: *a baseball star.* **6.** actor, actress, or other performer who plays the lead in a performance. **7.** heavenly body regarded as influencing human destiny. **8.** *also,* **stars.** fate; destiny. **9. to see stars.** *Informal.* to have the sensation of seeing flashes of light, as from a hard blow on the head. **10. to thank one's (lucky) stars.** to be thankful for one's good fortune. —*v.t.* **starred, star·ring. 1.** to set or ornament with stars or spangles. **2.** to mark with an asterisk: *to star a favorite passage.* **3.** to present (a performer) in a leading role: *The movie starred my favorite actor.* —*v.i.* **1.** to perform a leading part: *to star in a play.* **2.** to be excellent or prominent; perform outstandingly. —*adj.* **1.** most prominent; best; leading: *a star performer, a star baseball player.* **2.** of or relating to a star or stars. [Old English *steorra* celestial body.]

star·board (stär'bərd) *n.* right side of a boat or ship, as one faces forward. —*v.t., v.i.* to turn (the helm or rudder) of a boat or ship to the right so that the vessel will move to the right. —*adj.* of, relating to, or on the right side of a boat or ship. [Old English *steorbord* side on which a ship was steered, from *steor* steering paddle + *bord* board, side of a ship; because early Teutonic ships were steered by a paddle on the *right* side.]

starch (stärch) *n.* **1.** white, granular carbohydrate manufactured and stored in all green plants. Starch is used in the food, paper, and textile industries. **2.** any food rich in starch, as rice, corn, and wheat products. **3.** any of various substances, including natural starch, used for stiffening or finishing linen and for industrial purposes. **4.** stiffness, pomposity, or formality, as in manner or conduct: *Armed with statistics, the debater took the starch out of his opponent.* **5.** *Informal.* boldness; spirit. —*v.t.* to stiffen with or as with starch: *The laundry starched all my shirts.* [From Middle English *sterchen* to stiffen, going back to Old English *stearc* stiff.]

Star Chamber 1. formerly, a secret English court that heard many kinds of criminal cases without a jury, often using torture, and was able to impose any punishment except death. It was abolished by Parliament in 1641. **2.** *also,* **star chamber.** any court or group that proceeds by secret or unfair methods. [Probably with reference to the ceiling of the room of the original Star Chamber, which was supposedly decorated with gilt *stars.*]

starch·y (stär'chē) starch·i·er, starch·i·est. *adj.* **1.** of, resembling, or containing starch: *a starchy liquid, a starchy diet.* **2.** stiffened with starch. **3.** stiff; formal; pompous. —**starch'i·ness,** *n.*

star·dom (stär'dəm) *n.* status of a star performer: *to achieve stardom after a long career.*

stare (stâr) stared, star·ing. *v.i.* **1.** to look intently with eyes wide open, as in surprise, admiration, or fear. —*v.t.* **1.** to stare at. **2.** to affect by staring in a particular way (often with *down*): *to stare a heckler into silence.* **3. to stare one in the face.** to be obvious or imminent to: *with ruin and bankruptcy staring him in the face.* —*n.* act or instance of staring: *the stares of the audience, a vacant stare.* [Old English *starian* to look intently.] —**star'er,** *n.*

star·fish (stär'fish') *pl.* **-fish** or **-fish·es.** *n.* any of a group of flattened, star-shaped echinoderms, found on or near the sea bottom, usually having five tapering arms.

Starfish

star·gaze (stär'gāz') -gazed, -gaz·ing. *v.i.* **1.** to gaze at or study the stars. **2.** to daydream. —**star'gaz·er,** *n.*

stark (stärk) *adj.* **1.** absolute or unqualified; complete: *stark tyranny, stark misery.* **2.** strictly and distinctly expressed; plain: *the stark truth.* **3.** harsh, grim, or severe: *stark weather, a stark countenance.* **4.** barren or desolate; bare: *a stark room, a stark landscape.* —*adv.* **1.** absolutely; completely: *to go stark raving mad, stark naked.* **2.** in a stark manner. [Old English *stearc* hard, stiff, severe.] —**stark'ly,** *adv.* —**stark'ness,** *n.*

star·let (stär'lit) *n.* in motion pictures, an inexperienced actress or singer who is considered to have potential and is being given training and publicity by her studio.

star·light (stär'līt') *n.* light from a star or stars. —*adj.* starlit.

star·ling (stär'ling) *n.* any of various birds, family Sturnidae, found in most parts of the world, usually having a stout body, pointed wings, and a short tail, as the common starling, *Sturnus vulgaris,* having black plumage with purplish markings. Length: 7–13 inches. [Old English *stærlinc.*]

Starling

at; āpe; cär; end; mē; it; īce; hot; ōld; fôrk; wood; fŏŏl; oil; out; up; ūse; turn; sing; thin; this; zh in treasure; ə in ago, taken, pencil, lemon, circus.

973

star·lit (stär′lit′) *adj.* lighted by the stars: *the starlit sky.* Also, **star′light′.**

star-of-Beth·le·hem (stär′əv beth′lē əm, -beth′lə hem′) *n.* low plant, *Ornithogalum umbellatum,* of the lily family, bearing small green and white star-shaped flowers, growing wild in eastern North America and the Mediterranean area.

Star of Bethlehem, in the New Testament, the star that heralded Christ's birth and guided the Magi to Bethlehem.

Star of David, six-pointed star formed by superimposing one equilateral triangle over another, a symbol of Judaism and now of Israel. Also, **Magen David, Mogen David.**

Star of David

star·ry (stär′ē) **-ri·er, -ri·est.** *adj.* **1.** studded with or lighted by stars. **2.** shining like or as a star; bright. **3.** shaped or arranged in the form of a star. **4.** of, relating to, or proceeding from the stars.

star·ry-eyed (stär′ē īd′) *adj.* given to wishful, impractical, or naive thinking.

Stars and Bars, first official flag of the Confederacy.

Stars and Stripes, flag of the United States, consisting of alternating red and white stripes representing the thirteen original colonies and, in the upper left corner, a blue field with fifty stars representing the states.

star-span·gled (stär′spang′gəld) *adj.* spangled or studded with stars.

Star-Spangled Banner 1. U.S. national anthem, the words of which were written by Francis Scott Key during the War of 1812. **2.** flag of the United States.

start (stärt) *v.i.* **1.** to make a beginning; set out: *We started on our trip Monday.* **2.** to begin; commence: *The movie starts at ten o'clock.* **3.** to make a sudden, involuntary movement, as from fear or surprise: *She started when I walked up behind her.* **4.** to move suddenly, as with a springing, jumping, or flinching movement: *The horse started and threw its rider.* **5.** to issue forth suddenly or violently. **6.** to appear to burst or protrude. **7.** to break away; become loose. **8.** to be among the entrants, as in a race or contest. **9. to start in.** to begin: *Start in eating before the food gets cold.* **10. to start out.** to begin, as an enterprise or a journey. —*v.t.* **1.** to begin (something): *to start a sermon with a biblical quote.* **2.** to cause to move; set in action or motion: *to start an engine.* **3.** to put in operation; establish; initiate: *to start a business, to start a controversy.* **4.** to cause or enable to begin or enter upon some course, as a business: *to start them on a journey.* **5.** to rouse: *to start the birds from the bush.* **6.** to cause to loosen: *The water started a crack in the molding.* **7.** to cause to be one of the entrants in a race or contest. **8. to start up.** to begin operating, as a machine: *to start up an engine.* —*n.* **1.** beginning, as of a course of action, movement, or journey. **2.** sudden involuntary movement, as a jerk: *He gave a start when I tapped him on the shoulder.* **3.** opportunity for beginning something, as a career: *to give someone a good start.* **4.** initial movement in some course or direction; impetus: *to get a running start.* **5.** sudden burst of activity. **6.** advantage gained by beginning first, as in a race: *to give someone a twenty-foot start.* **7.a.** point or line at which a race begins. **b.** signal to start something, as a race. [Probably from an unrecorded Old English word.] —**Syn.** *v.i.* see **begin.**

start·er (stär′tər) *n.* **1.** one who begins or initiates something. **2.** first element or beginning of a process, activity, or series: *You might try to be helpful, as a starter.* **3.** culture used to start fermentation of a substance. **4.** self-starter. **5.** one whose work is supervising the departure of public conveyances: *a bus starter.* **6.** one who gives the signal for starting a race. **7.** any of the competitors starting in a race.

star·tle (stärt′əl) **-tled, -tling.** *v.t.* to arouse or excite suddenly, as with surprise, fear, or astonishment; shock. —*v.i.* to become startled. —*n.* sudden surprise, fright, or astonishment; shock. [Old English *steartlian* to struggle.]

star·tling (stärt′ling) *adj.* causing sudden surprise, fear, or astonishment: *startling news.* —**star′tling·ly,** *adv.*

star·va·tion (stär vā′shən) *n.* act or instance of starving; being starved.

starve (stärv) **starved, starv·ing.** *v.i.* **1.** to suffer or die of hunger. **2.** to need or desire greatly; feel deprived of (with *for*): *a child who starved for affection.* **3.** *Informal.* to feel hungry. —*v.t.* **1.** to deprive of adequate food or nourishment; cause to suffer or die because of hunger: *to starve a plant, to starve the enemy.* **2.** to bring to a specified condition by starving: *to starve a prisoner into confessing to a crime.* [Old English *steorfan* to die.]

starve·ling (stärv′ling) *n.* starving person or animal. —*adj.* **1.** starving; hungry: *starveling pines.* **2.** insufficient for needs; meager; inadequate.

stash (stash) *Informal. v.t.* to store or conceal for safekeeping or future use (often with *away*). —*n.* that which is stored or concealed. [Of uncertain origin.]

stat. 1. statute. **2.** stationary. **3.** statistics. **4.** statuary.

state (stāt) *n.* **1.** mental, emotional, or physical mode of existence; condition: *a state of anxiety, a state of disrepair.* **2.** position, rank, or standing, as in the world or community; station: *What is his state in life?* **3.** *also,* **State. a.** sovereign political community that has authority over its own members: *The continent of Africa has many new, independent states.* **b.** one of the subdivisions, usually the largest, of a nation that has a federal system. The United States and West Germany are divided into states. **4.** *also,* **State.** civil or secular government, authority, or organization: *a diplomat involved in important matters of state, to maintain the separation of Church and State.* **5.** one of the three conditions, solid, liquid, or gaseous, of matter. **6.** *Informal.* condition of disarray, confusion, or agitation: *Susan ran out, leaving her room in a state.* **7.** *Archaic.* dignity and pomp. **8. the States.** United States. **9. to lie in state.** (of a dead person) to lie with certain honor and ceremony in some public place prior to burial. —*v.t.* **stat·ed, stat·ing. 1.** to express or explain fully in words; declare; represent: *to state an opinion. Please state your problem.* **2.** to establish; set; fix: *to state a time for the meeting.* —*adj.* **1.** *also,* **State.** of or relating to a state: *a state tax, a state highway.* **2.** of or relating to national or state government: *state policy, state affairs.* **3.** of, relating to, or for ceremonious or official occasions; formal: *a state reception, a state dinner.* [Latin *status* condition, position, from *stāre* to stand.] —**Syn.** *v.t.* see **say.**

state bank, bank operating under a state charter.

state·craft (stāt′kraft′) *n.* art of conducting state affairs; statesmanship.

stat·ed (stā′tid) *adj.* **1.** explicitly set forth; announced; declared: *The stated facts conflict with what actually happened.* **2.** fixed; established; regular: *at the stated salary of $10,000.*

state·hood (stāt′hood′) *n.* condition or status of a state, esp. one of the states of the United States.

state·house (stāt′hous′) *also,* **state house, State House.** *n.* building in which the legislature of a state of the United States meets.

state·ly (stāt′lē) **-li·er, -li·est.** *adj.* imposing; majestic; dignified: *a stately mansion, a stately procession.* —**state′li·ness,** *n.* —**Syn.** see **grand.**

state·ment (stāt′mənt) *n.* **1.** act, process, or manner of stating something: *an accurate statement of the facts.* **2.** something stated; declaration; assertion: *a false statement.* **3.** written or oral communication setting forth facts, arguments, or the like: *The president issued a statement on tax reform.* **4.** report or summary of the financial condition of a business establishment or of an account maintained with a business establishment: *a bank statement, a corporation's statement of profit and loss.*

Stat·en Island (stat′ən) island southwest of Manhattan, coextensive with the borough of Richmond in New York City.

state prison, prison maintained by a state for the confinement of prisoners, esp. those convicted of felonies.

state·room (stāt′room′, -room′) *n.* private, often luxurious, room or compartment on a ship or railroad train.

state's attorney, attorney elected or appointed to represent the state in court.

state's evidence 1. testimony given by an accomplice to a crime against his associates. **2. to turn state's evidence.** to testify against one's accomplices in a crime, usually in return for some consideration, as a lesser sentence or immunity from prosecution.

States-Gen·er·al (stāts′jen′ər əl) *n.* **1.** in France before the revolution of 1789, national assembly divided into three groups, the Church, the nobles, and the common people, each representing one of the social classes of the realm. It had the power to petition the king. Also, **Estates′-Gen′er·al. 2.** parliament of the Netherlands, made up of an upper and a lower chamber.

state·side (stāt′sīd′) *also,* **State·side.** *adj.* of or in the United States. —*adv.* to, toward, or in the United States.

states·man (stāts′mən) *pl.,* **-men.** *n.* one engaged in public or national affairs, esp. a political leader who shows wisdom and distinction in promoting the public good. —**states′man·ly,** *adj.* —**states′man·ship′,** *n.*

Syn. Statesman, politician mean one engaged in political affairs. **Statesman** suggests one who has benefited from age and long experience and attained a status that places him above narrow partisanship, giving him the opportunity to articulate the theories and principles of government, to offer counsel, and to exercise leadership on a national or international level: *Churchill was one of the great elder statesmen of the century.* **Politician** usually has derogatory overtones in referring to one who pursues a career in party politics and manipulates the party system to advance his own or the interests of a limited constituency: *The politicians of that county successfully blocked the reformer's nomination.*

States of the Church, Papal States.

at; āpe; cär; end; mē; it; īce; hot; ōld; fôrk; wood; fōōl; oil; out; up; ūse; turn; sing; thin; this; zh in treasure; ə in ago, taken, pencil, lemon, circus.

states' rights *also,* **state rights.** **1.** rights or powers not delegated to the federal government nor prohibited to the states under the Constitution. **2.** doctrine that the powers of the U.S. federal government should be shared to a greater degree with the various state governments.

state·wide (stāt'wīd') *also,* **state-wide.** *adj.* extending throughout a state: *a statewide alarm, statewide elections.*

stat·ic (stat'ik) *adj.* **1.** characterized by or showing little or no growth, change, or progress; that remains the same: *a static population.* **2.** showing no movement; stationary. **3.** of or relating to bodies at rest or to forces in equilibrium. **4.** acting by weight without producing motion: *static pressure.* **5.** of or relating to charges of electricity that have accumulated on a body and do not move about. Static electricity can be produced by combing dry hair with a dry comb. —*n.* **1.** random electrical charges in the atmosphere, as produced by lightning, power stations, or cosmic radiation, that may be picked up by a radio receiver and heard as crackling or hissing sounds. **2.** *Slang.* any interference, esp. verbal, with the expression or accomplishment of something. [Modern Latin *staticus,* from Greek *statikos* causing to stand.] —**stat'i·cal·ly,** *adv.*

stat·ics (stat'iks) *n.,pl.* branch of mechanics that deals with bodies at rest or in equilibrium under the action of several forces. ▲ construed as singular.

sta·tion (stā'shən) *n.* **1.** place, building, or establishment set up as a headquarters for a business, public service, or the like: *first-aid station.* **2.** regular stopping place along a route, as of a bus or train line, for the transfer of freight or passengers; terminal; depot. **3.** place or position in which one stands or is assigned to stand in the performance of some duty; assigned post: *sentry station.* **4.** social position of an individual; standing; rank. **5.a.** place where radio or television programs are recorded and transmitted. **b.** specific channel or frequency recording and transmitting scheduled or special broadcasts. —*v.t.* to assign to a station; place in a post or position: *sailors stationed at Pearl Harbor.* [Latin *statiō* a standing still, place, position.]

sta·tion·ar·y (stā'shə ner'ē) *adj.* **1.** having a fixed place or position; permanent. **2.** unchanging in character, condition, or quantity. [Latin *statiōnārius* relating to a post² or station, from *statiō* a standing still, place, position.]

station break, interruption or pause in a television or radio program to identify a network or station or to make an announcement.

sta·tion·er (stā'shə nər) *n.* one who sells stationery. [Medieval Latin *stationarius* shopkeeper (with reference to having a fixed, as opposed to a traveling, shop), from *statio* shop, from Latin *statiō* a standing still, place, position.]

sta·tion·er·y (stā'shə ner'ē) *n.* **1.** writing paper and envelopes. **2.** materials used in writing, as pens, pencils, or paper and office supplies.

station house, **1.** police station. **2.** firehouse.

sta·tion·mas·ter (stā'shən mas'tər) *n.* one in charge of a railroad station or bus station.

Stations of the Cross, in the Roman Catholic Church, series of fourteen representations of the last events of Christ's life from His condemnation to His Crucifixion and burial, before which devotions are performed.

Station wagon

station wagon, automobile having one or more folding or removable rear seats and a door across the back that can be used as for loading and unloading passengers or luggage.

stat·ism (stā'tiz'əm) *n.* advocacy of and tendency toward the centralization of all forms of control, planning, authority, and power in the government or state. —**stat'ist,** *n.*

sta·tis·tic (stə tis'tik) *n.* single numerical fact or element that is part of statistical data.

sta·tis·ti·cal (stə tis'ti kəl) *adj.* of, relating to, consisting of, or based on statistics: *a statistical problem, a statistical analysis.* —**sta·tis·ti·cal·ly,** *adv.*

stat·is·ti·cian (stat'is tish'ən) *n.* one who is expert in compiling and interpreting statistics.

sta·tis·tics (stə tis'tiks) *n.,pl.* **1.** science of collecting, classifying, and using numerical data as it is related to a particular subject. **2.** numerical data itself. ▲ construed as singular in def. 1, as plural in def. 2. [German *Statistik* science of collecting, classifying, and using numerical data, from Modern Latin *statisticus* relating to state affairs, from Latin *status* condition, position, state.]

sta·tor (stā'tər) *n.* stationary part of a motor, dynamo, or similar machine about which a rotor revolves. [Modern Latin *stator,* from Latin *stator* one that stands.]

stat·o·scope (stat'ə skōp') *n.* **1.** highly sensitive aneroid barometer. **2.** instrument that detects small variations in the altitude of an aircraft. [Greek *statos* standing + -SCOPE.]

stat·u·ar·y (stach'ōō er'ē) *pl.,* **-ar·ies.** *n.* **1.** statues collectively. **2.** art of carving statues. —*adj.* of, relating to, or suitable for a statue or statues.

stat·ue (stach'ōō) *n.* representation in the round, often life size or larger, of a human or animal figure, carved, cast, or modeled in stone, bronze, clay, or a similar material. [Old French *statue,* from Latin *statua* image, statue, going back to *stāre* to stand.]

Statue of Liberty, monumental statue of a crowned woman, personifying liberty, holding a torch aloft, located on an island in New York harbor. It was given to the United States by France.

stat·u·esque (stach'ōō esk') *adj.* resembling or suggestive of a statue, as in proportion, grace, or dignity; stately.

stat·u·ette (stach'ōō et') *n.* small statue. [French *statuette,* diminutive of *statue.*]

stat·ure (stach'ər) *n.* **1.** height of a body, esp. a person, in a normal standing position: *a woman of average stature.* **2.** level, development, or growth attained; standing: *moral stature. The position calls for a man of his stature.* [Old French *stature* height or position of a body, from Latin *statūra* upright posture, height.]

sta·tus (stā'təs, stat'əs) *n.* **1.** state; condition: *the status of the repertory theater in America.* **2.** relative place or rank, esp. social or professional standing: *student status. He was stripped of his status as a party member.* **3.** character or condition of a person or thing as determined by law: *marital status.* [Latin *status* condition, position.]

status quo (kwō) existing or present state of affairs. [Latin *status quō* the condition in which (things are).]

stat·ute (stach'ōōt) *n.* **1.** law enacted by a legislative body. **2.** written rule or law regulating an organization, as a university or corporation. [Old French *statut* decree, law, from Late Latin *statūtum,* from Latin *statuere* to establish.]

statute law, law as established by statutes; written law.

statute mile, mile.

statute of limitations, law limiting the time in which legal action may be taken in certain cases.

stat·u·to·ry (stach'ə tôr'ē) *adj.* of, relating to, set by, or punishable under statute: *a statutory fine, a statutory offense.*

statutory rape, sexual intercourse with a girl who is under the legal age of consent, with or without her actual consent.

St. Au·gus·tine (ô'gəs tēn') historic city in northeastern Florida, the oldest continuously occupied city in the United States. Pop. (1970), 12,352.

staunch¹ (stônch, stänch) *also,* **stanch.** *adj.* **1.** loyal and dependable; steadfast: *a staunch ally.* **2.** soundly built or constructed: *a staunch ship, a staunch argument.* [Old French *estanche* reliable, watertight, from *estancher.* See STANCH¹.] —**staunch'ly,** *adv.* —**staunch'ness,** *n.*

staunch² (stônch) stanch¹.

Staves of a barrel

stave (stāv) *n.* **1.** any long, narrow, flexible strip of wood, as that which forms the sides of a barrel, cask, or bucket. **2.** rod, pole, or staff. **3.** rung, as of a ladder or chair. **4.** verse or stanza of a poem, song, or the like. **5.** *Music.* staff. —*v.t.,* **staved** or **stove,** **stav·ing.** **1.** to smash or break in, as the staves of a cask or barrel. **2.** to puncture a hole in: *A rock stove the hull of the ship.* **3.** to furnish with a stave or staves. **4.** **to stave off.** to ward off or prevent: *to stave off a blow, to stave off an unpleasant discussion.* —*v.i.* to be punctured or smashed in. [From *staves,* plural of STAFF.]

staves (stāvz) a plural of **staff.**

stay¹ (stā) **stayed** or (*archaic*) **staid, stay·ing.** *v.i.* **1.** to continue in a specified place or condition: *to stay seated, to stay young.* **2.** to reside in a place, esp. for a short or indefinite period of time: *They stayed at a hotel. Tom is staying with friends for the weekend.* **3.** to cease movement or activity; stop; halt: *I can only stay for a minute.* **4.** to linger; wait: *We could not stay for the ball.* **5.** *Informal.* to last or persevere, as in a race or contest. —*v.t.* **1.** to check or stop, esp. temporarily; abate: *This accident stayed for the time further developments* (James, 1903). **2.** to put off; keep back; defer: *The judge stayed the sentence until the following day.* **3.** to remain for the duration of: *to stay the night in a motel.* **4.** *Archaic.* to wait for; await. —*n.* **1.** act of staying or remaining; continuance in a place: *a short stay in town. Aunt Jane's stay was cut short after two days.* **2.** break or delay of action, motion, or progression; stop; halt: *The governor requested a stay on raises for all state employees.* **3.** *Law.* temporary delay in the execution of an order of a court of law. **4.** *Informal.* power of endurance or resistance. [Probably from Old French *estai-,* a stem of *ester* to stand, from Latin *stāre.*]

Syn. *v.i.* **1. Stay, remain** mean to maintain the same state or condition. **Stay** stresses accomplishing one's goal or purpose: *We're going to stay awake to see the eclipse.* **Remain** stresses that obstacles or difficulties have been or must be overcome, allowing a particular state or condition to last or endure: *Despite heavy criticism, the minister remained in power for another six years.*

stay² (stā) *n.* **1.** something used to support, strengthen, or sustain; prop; brace. **2.** piece of plastic, metal, or other stiff material, inserted in corsets, bathing suits, shirt collars, and other garments to give shape and support. **3. stays.** corset. —*v.t.*, **stayed, stay·ing.** to support, strengthen, or sustain. [Old French *estayer* to prop, support, from *estaye* a prop, support; of Germanic origin.]

stay³ (stā) *n.* **1.** strong rope, usually of wire, used to support a mast on a boat or ship. **2.** any rope or chain used for a similar purpose. **3. in stays,** (of a boat or ship) heading toward the wind in the process of changing from one tack to another. —*v.t.* **stayed, stay·ing. 1.** to secure or steady with a stay or stays. **2.** to cause (a boat or ship) to change from one tack to another. —*v.i.* (of a boat or ship) to change from one tack to another. [Old English *stæg* large rope used to support a mast.]

staying power, ability to endure; stamina.

stay·sail (stā′sāl′, -sɔl) *n.* sail, usually triangular, that is attached to a stay.

St. Ber·nard Pass (bər närd′) **1. Great.** historic mountain pass in the Alps on the Swiss-Italian border. **2. Little.** historic mountain pass in the Alps in southeastern France near the Italian border.

St. Cath·a·rines (kath′ər inz) city in southeastern Canada, in Ontario. Pop. (1966), 97,101.

St. Clair (klār) **1. Lake.** shallow body of water on the boundary line between southeastern Michigan and southwestern Ontario, Canada. **2.** river between Michigan and Ontario, Canada, connecting Lake Huron with Lake St. Clair.

St. Clair Shores, city in southeastern Michigan, a residential suburb of Detroit. Pop. (1970), 88,093.

St. Croix (kroi′) largest and southernmost of the Virgin Islands. It belongs to the United States. Area, 82 sq. mi. Pop. (1970), 31,892.

S.T.D., Doctor of Sacred Theology.

Ste., Sainte.

stead (sted) *n.* **1.** place or position usually or previously occupied by another: *I sent my brother off to the party in my stead.* **2. to stand in good stead,** to be of use or service to; be advantageous to: *Peter's honesty always stood him in good stead.* —*v.t.* *Archaic.* to be of use or service to; benefit; help. [Old English *stede* place.]

stead·fast (sted′fast′, -fəst) *also,* **sted·fast. 1.** consistent in adhering to a principle or action; unwavering; faithful: *steadfast loyalty to a cause.* **2.** firmly fixed; direct; steady: *a steadfast gaze.* [Old English *stedefæst* firmly fixed, from *stede* place + *fæst* firm.] —**stead′fast′ly,** *adv.* —**stead′fast′ness,** *n.* —**Syn. 1.** see **faithful.**

stead·y (sted′ē) **stead·i·er, stead·i·est.** *adj.* **1.** that is maintained at an even rate; regular or uniform in operation or intensity: *a steady pace, a steady diet of starch, a steady rise in unemployment.* **2.** firm or sure in movement or position; not tottering, shaking, or faltering: *a steady hand, to take steady aim.* **3.** regular; permanent: *a steady customer, a steady job.* **4.** reliable; sober; dependable. **5.** not easily upset; calm. **6.** constant or unwavering in principle or action; steadfast. **7.** (of a boat or ship) remaining upright, as in a turbulent sea. **8. to go steady.** to date (someone) regularly and exclusively. —*v.t.,* **stead·ied, stead·y·ing.** to make or keep steady. —*v.i.* to become steady. —*interj.* **1.** take it easy; keep calm. **2.** *Nautical.* keep the ship headed in the same direction. ▲ used as a command to the helmsman. —*adv.* in a steady manner; steadily. —*n. pl.,* **stead·ies.** *Slang.* person one dates regularly and exclusively. [STEAD + -Y¹.] —**stead′i·ly,** *adv.* —**stead′i·ness,** *n.*

stead·y-state theory (sted′ē stāt′) theory that the average properties of the universe as a whole do not change with time. Although the universe is constantly expanding, new matter is being created continuously at a rate that balances the thinning-out effect of the expansion.

steak (stāk) *n.* **1.a.** piece of meat, esp. beef, cut for cooking by broiling or frying. **b.** boneless slice of large fish, as salmon or swordfish. **2.** chopped or ground beef, usually formed into patties for cooking. [Old Norse *steik* slice of meat roasted on a spit.]

steal (stēl) **stole, sto·len, steal·ing.** *v.t.* **1.** to take from another secretly and without right, permission, or authority: *Several paintings were stolen from the exhibition.* **2.** to take or obtain by surprise, stealth, or contrivance: *to steal a kiss, to steal an hour off from work. She stole his heart away.* **3.** to move, carry, or place secretly or unobserved: *to steal noiselessly down the stairs, to steal a note into someone's hand.* **4.** *Baseball.* to gain (the next base) without the assistance of a hit or error. —*v.i.* **1.** to commit or practice theft. **2.** to move or pass secretly, gradually, or imperceptibly: *A look of contentment stole over his face. We stole off to be alone.* **3.** *Baseball.* to steal a base. —*n.* **1.** act or instance of stealing; a theft. **2.** *Baseball.* act of stealing a base.

3. *Informal.* bargain: *A dress for only seven dollars is a real steal.* [Old English *stelan* to take dishonestly or secretly.] —**steal′er,** *n.*

Syn. *v.t.* **1. Steal, pilfer, filch** mean to take what rightfully or legally belongs to another. **Steal,** the most common word generally applied to the theft of money, objects, or goods, implies that what is stolen is so important or significant that its absence immediately calls attention to itself or is easily discovered: *Help! That man just stole my purse!* **Pilfer** stresses the accumulation of small but not necessarily unimportant items that can be easily concealed and go unnoticed and suggests a recurrent series, rather than a single act, that finally brings the theft to light: *The owner accused the clerks of pilfering merchandise.* **Filch** is more usually used of things of little value and stresses the defenseless victim taken unawares or by surprise: *The boy filched the pencil case from her as she walked home from school.*

stealth (stelth) *n.* secret action, procedure, or manner of behavior: *The store obtained the information about its competitors by stealth.* [From STEAL.]

stealth·y (stel′thē) **stealth·i·er, stealth·i·est.** *adj.* moving, proceeding, or acting in a secret manner; characterized by stealth. —**stealth′i·ly,** *adv.* —**stealth′i·ness,** *n.* —**Syn.** see **secret.**

steam (stēm) *n.* **1.** water in the form of a gas. It is used to provide heat for buildings and for industrial processes, and to power engines and other mechanical devices. **2.** mechanical power, heat, or other energy generated by steam: *to turn the steam up.* **3.** mist formed by condensed vapor. **4.** any vapor or fume given off by a heated substance. **5.** *Informal.* driving power; energy; initiative: *He built the bookcase under his own steam.* **6. to let (or blow) off steam.** *Informal.* to release pent-up emotions, energy, or tensions. —*v.t.* **1.** to treat with or expose to the action of steam: *to steam clams, to steam out the wrinkles in a dress.* —*v.i.* **1.** to give off steam or vapor: *The shirt steamed from the heat of the iron.* **2.** to become or rise in the form of steam. **3.** to be covered by condensed vapor or mist (often with *up*): *My glasses steamed up in the warm room.* **4.** to move or travel by steam: *The vessel steamed into port.* **5.** *Informal.* to be angry; seethe. **6.** *Informal.* to be uncomfortably warm. [Old English *stēam* vapor, smoke.]

steam bath 1. act of bathing by exposing oneself to steam, so as to produce perspiration. **2.** building equipped with a special room or rooms for bathing in steam.

steam·boat (stēm′bōt′) *n.* any of various steam-driven boats, used esp. in lake and river navigation.

steam boiler, closed vessel in which water is boiled in order to generate steam.

steam chest, in a steam engine, the chamber from which steam is admitted to the cylinder from the boiler by the action of a valve. Also, **steam box.**

steam engine, engine using the energy of steam to do mechanical work, as by the expansion of the steam within a cylinder to drive a piston in a back and forth motion.

steam·er (stē′mər) *n.* **1.** boat driven by steam; steamship. **2.** soft-shell clam, usually cooked by steaming. **3.** vessel in which something is steamed, esp. a cooking utensil for steaming clams.

steamer trunk, trunk designed to fit under the berth in a ship.

steam fitter, one who installs and repairs steam pipes, fittings, and other steam heating equipment.

steam heat, heat given off by a steam heating system.

steam heating, system of heating large buildings and other facilities with steam produced by a boiler and piped through radiators.

steam iron, electric iron with a compartment for water, the steam of which is given off from the bottom onto the fabric being pressed to aid in ironing.

steam·roll (stēm′rōl′) *v.i., v.t.* to steamroller.

steam·roll·er (stēm′rō′lər) *also,* **steam roller.** *n.* **1.** vehicle moving on heavy rollers, used in road work, as for leveling freshly laid pavement or smoothing earth. **2.** any force or power for overwhelming, suppressing, or defeating opposition. —*v.i. Informal.* to move or proceed with overwhelming force or organization: *The campaign steamrollered through the South.* —*v.t.* **1.** to overwhelm or suppress ruthlessly; defeat: *to steamroller opposition.* **2.** to level or smooth with a steamroller.

steam·ship (stēm′ship′) *n.* large, ocean-going vessel propelled by steam power.

steam shovel, power-driven digging machine having a single large bucket or scoop at the end of a long beam.

Steam shovel

steam table, table or counter, used in restaurants, fitted with trays for cooked food that are kept heated by warm water or steam circulating beneath them.

at; āpe; cär; end; mē; it; īce; hot; ōld; fôrk; wood; fo͞ol; oil; out; up; ūse; turn; sing; thin; this; zh in treasure; ə in ago, taken, pencil, lemon, circus.

steam turbine, turbine using steam as a source of energy.
steam·y (stē′mē) **steam·i·er, steam·i·est.** *adj.* **1.** giving off, covered by, or filled with steam. **2.** uncomfortably warm; humid. —**steam′i·ly,** *adv.* —**steam′i·ness,** *n.*
ste·ap·sin (stē ap′sin) *n.* the lipase of pancreatic juice. [Greek *steār* fat + (PE)PSIN.]
ste·a·rate (stē′ə rāt′, stēr′āt) *n.* salt of stearic acid. Soaps are stearates.
ste·ar·ic (stē ar′ik, stēr′ik) *adj.* of or relating to stearin. [Greek *steār* fat + -IC.]
stearic acid, colorless, waxy compound found in animal and vegetable fats and used to make lubricants, soaps, and shoe polish. It is the most common fatty acid. Formula: $CH_3(CH_2)_{16}CO_2H$
ste·a·rin (stē′ər in, stēr′in) *n.* colorless, crystalline or powdery compound found in most fats and used to make candles, synthetic ivory and stone, and soap. Formula: $C_3H_5(C_{18}H_{35}O_2)_3$. [French *stéarine*, from Greek *steār* fat.]
ste·a·tite (stē′ə tīt′) *n.* soapstone. [Latin *steātītis*, from Greek *steat-,* stem of *steār* fat.] —**ste·a·tit·ic** (stē′ə tit′ik), *adj.*
sted·fast (sted′fast′, -fəst) *adj.* steadfast. —**sted′fast′ly,** *adv.* —**sted′fast′ness,** *n.*
steed (stēd) *n.* horse, esp. a high-spirited riding horse. [Old English *stēda* stallion.]
steel (stēl) *n.* **1.** any alloy of iron mixed with a small amount of carbon. There are many steel alloys which contain specified amounts of other elements added to improve certain properties, as strength or malleability. **2.** something made from steel, as a sword. **3.** quality characteristic of steel, esp. hardness, strength, or durability. —*adj.* **1.** made or consisting of steel. **2.** of or relating to the production of steel: *a steel mill.* **3.** resembling steel. —*v.t.* **1.** to cover with steel, as by edging or plating. **2.** to cause to be unflinching or unyielding; strengthen; harden: *He steeled himself for the blow.* [Old English *stēli, stýle* artificially produced variety of iron.]
steel band, musical band of a type which originated in Trinidad, using tuned steel oil drums played with drumsticks.
steel blue, dark grayish-blue, as of tempered steel.
Steele, Sir Richard (stēl) 1672–1729, English essayist.
steel wool, fine threads of steel matted together, used for polishing or cleaning surfaces, as of wood or metal.
steel·work·er (stēl′wur′kər) *n.* one who works in a steel mill.
steel·works (stēl′wurks′) *n.,pl.* plant or facilities where steel is made. ▲ construed as singular or plural.
steel·y (stē′lē) **steel·i·er, steel·i·est.** *adj.* **1.** made or consisting of steel. **2.** resembling or suggestive of steel: *steely eyes.* —**steel′i·ness,** *n.*
steel·yard (stēl′yärd′, stil′yərd) *n.* weighing device consisting of a horizontal bar with the object to be weighed at one end and a movable weight at the other. The weight is slid along the bar until a balance is reached and the correct weight is registered on a scale marked off on the bar. [STEEL + YARD¹, owing to the incorrect translation of Middle Low German *stålhof* sample courtyard (Middle Low German *stāl* sample, confused with Middle Low German *stāl* steel); so called because a scale was hung in the *Stalhof* of the Hanseatic merchants in London in the thirteenth century.]

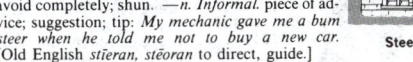

Steelyard

steen·bok (stēn′bok′, stän′-) *pl.* **-boks** or **-bok.** *also,* **stein·bok.** *n.* small, light-brown or gray antelope, *Raphicerus campestris,* native to southeastern Africa. Height: 22 inches at the shoulder. [Dutch *steenbok,* from *steen* stone + *bok* buck¹; because it is found in rocky places.]
steep¹ (stēp) *adj.* **1.** having an almost perpendicular face or slope: *a steep stairway.* *to climb the steeper side of the mountain.* **2.** *Informal.* excessive; extreme; unreasonable: *The lawyer exacted a steep fee from his client.* —*n.* steep slope or place. [Old English *stēap* high.] —**steep′ly,** *adv.* —**steep′ness,** *n.*

Steenbok

steep² (stēp) *v.t.* **1.** to soak in liquid, so as to soften, cleanse, or extract some element. **2.** to imbue or permeate thoroughly; saturate: *a mind steeped in classical literature, a house steeped in mystery.* —*v.i.* to undergo soaking in liquid. —*n.* **1.** act or process of soaking; being soaked. **2.** liquid used for soaking. [Possibly from Old Norse *steypa* to pour out liquids, cast metals.] —*Syn.* **v.t. 1.** see soak.
steep·en (stē′pən) *v.t.,v.i.* to make or become steeper: *The path steepened as we climbed higher.*

stee·ple (stē′pəl) *n.* **1.** lofty tower with a spire or similar superstructure at the top, esp. on a church. **2.** spire on the top of the tower of a church or similar building. [Old English *stēpel, stýpel* high tower.]
stee·ple·bush (stē′pəl boosh′) *n.* hardhack.
stee·ple·chase (stē′pəl chās′) *n.* horse race on a course furnished with hedges, ditches, and other obstacles over which the horses must jump. [STEEPLE + CHASE; supposedly from the eighteenth-century English sport of selecting a church steeple as the goal of a race.]
stee·ple·jack (stē′pəl jak′) *n.* man whose work is climbing steeples, towers, and other tall structures to paint them or to make repairs.
steer¹ (stēr) *v.t.* **1.** to guide the course of (a vessel or vehicle) as with a wheel, handle, or the like. **2.** to set and follow (a course): *to steer a course for the West Indies.* **3.** to direct; guide; channel: *to steer a child through a crowd, to steer a complaint to the proper authorities.* —*v.i.* **1.** to guide a vessel or vehicle. **2.** to follow or direct one's course. **3.** to admit of being guided. **4. to steer clear of.** to avoid completely; shun. —*n. Informal.* piece of advice; suggestion; tip: *My mechanic gave me a bum steer when he told me not to buy a new car.* [Old English *stīeran, stēoran* to direct, guide.]

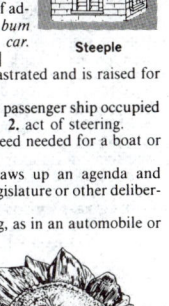

Steeple

steer² (stēr) *n.* bull, esp. one that has been castrated and is raised for beef. [Old English *stēor* young ox.]
steer·age (stēr′ij) *n.* **1.** formerly, portion of a passenger ship occupied by those passengers paying the cheapest fare. **2.** act of steering.
steer·age·way (stēr′ij wā′) *n.* sufficient speed needed for a boat or ship to be steered successfully.
steering committee, committee that draws up an agenda and recommends proposals to be considered by a legislature or other deliberative body.
steering gear, mechanism used for steering, as in an automobile or a ship.
steering wheel, wheel turned by the driver or pilot on a vehicle or vessel in order to operate the steering gear.
steers·man (stērz′mən) *pl.* **-men.** *n.* helmsman.
steg·o·sau·rus (steg′ə sôr′əs) *pl.* **-sau·ri** (-sôr′ī). *n.* any of a group of plant-eating dinosaurs, genus *Stegosaurus,* found in North America during the Jurassic period, having a spiked tail and two rows of bony plates along its back. Length: to 20 feet. [Modern Latin *Stegosaurus,* from Greek *stegos* roof + *sauros* lizard; with reference to the earlier belief that certain bones of this creature were arranged like a roof's slates.]

Stegosaurus

stein (stīn) *n.* beer mug, usually holding about a pint. [Possibly from German *Steingut* earthenware, pottery.]
Stein·beck, John (stīn′bek′) 1902–68, U.S. novelist.
stein·bok (stīn′bok′) *n.* steenbok.
Stein·metz, Charles P. (stīn′mets) 1865–1923, U.S. scientist and electrical engineer.
ste·le (stē′lē, stēl) *pl.* **-lae** (-lē) *or* **-les.** *n.* **1.** vertical stone slab or pillar, engraved as with an inscription or sculptural design, usually serving as a memorial. **2.** prepared surface, as on the face of a building, engraved as with an inscription or sculptural design. [Greek *stēlē* gravestone.]
stel·lar (stel′ər) *adj.* **1.** of, relating to, or resembling a star or stars. **2.** of or relating to a star performer. **3.** chief; principal. [Late Latin *stēllāris* starry, from Latin *stēlla* star.]
stel·late (stel′āt, -it) *adj.* radiating from a center like the points of a star; star-shaped: *a stellate leaf.* Also, **stel′lat·ed.** [Latin *stēllātus* starry, set with stars, from *stēlla* star.]
stem¹ (stem) *n.* **1.** main axis of a plant, that supports leaves or flowers and may bear buds. **2.** stalk supporting a leaf, flower, or fruit, as a petiole, peduncle, or pedicel. **3.** something resembling this in shape or function: *the stem of a wine glass, the winding stem of a watch, the stem of a pipe.* **4.** main line of descent in a family. **5.** that part of a word to which affixes and inflectional endings are added to change the meaning of the word. *Swim* is the stem of *swimming, swims,* and *swimmer.* **6.** upright member extending from the keel of a boat or ship, to which the sides are joined at the bow. **7.** bow of a boat or ship. **8. from stem to stern.** from one end to the other; thoroughly: *The house had to be cleaned from stem to stern.* —*v.t.,* **stemmed, stem·ming. 1.** to remove

the stem of or from:. *to stem tobacco, to stem a cluster of grapes.* **2.** to fit with a stem or stems. —*v.i.* to originate or develop: *to stem from royalty, a controversy stemming from philosophical differences.* [Old English *stemn* trunk of a tree, stalk of a plant, prow of a ship.] —**stem'mer,** *n.*

stem² (stem) **stemmed, stem·ming.** *v.t.* **1.** to stop, check, or restrain by or as if by damming; stanch: *to stem the tide of rebellion.* **2.** to make progress or headway against (something, as an opposing force): *to stem the gale, to stem a crowd.* —*v.i.* to point the skis inward and shift one's weight in order to turn, stop, or slow down. —*n.* act or instance of stemming on skis. [Old Norse *stemma* to dam up, restrain.]

stemmed (stemd) *adj.* **1.** having a stem. ▲ used chiefly in combination, as in *long-stemmed roses.* **2.** having the stem removed.

stem·ware (stem'wâr') *n.* drinking vessels, usually of glass, that have stems.

stem-wind·ing (stem'wīn'ding) *adj.* (of a watch) wound by turning a ridged knob attached to a stem.

stench (stench) *n.* disagreeable or offensive odor. [Old English *stenc* odor.]

sten·cil (sten'səl) *n.* **1.** thin sheet, as of metal or paper, in which a pattern is cut so that when paint or ink is applied it passes through the sheet to form a design on the surface against which the sheet has been pressed. **2.** printing or design produced by using a stencil. —*v.t.,* **-ciled, -cil·ing;** *also, British,* **-cilled, -cil·ling.** to mark or paint with a stencil. [Old French *estenceler* to sparkle, cover with stars, adorn with colors, from *estencelle* spark, going back to Latin *scintilla.*]

Sten·dhal (sten däl', stän-) *n.* 1783–1842, French novelist and critic; born Marie-Henri Beyle.

sten·o·graph (sten'ə graf') *n.* **1.** writing in shorthand. **2.** keyboard machine for writing in shorthand. —*v.t.* to write in shorthand.

ste·nog·ra·pher (stə nog'rə fər) *n.* one who is skilled at recording and transcribing dictated material in shorthand.

sten·o·graph·ic (sten'ə graf'ik) *adj.* of, relating to, or using stenography. Also, **sten'o·graph'i·cal.** —**sten'o·graph'i·cal·ly,** *adv.*

ste·nog·ra·phy (stə nog'rə fē) *n.* art or method of taking shorthand, esp. when recorded from another's spoken words. [Greek *stenos* narrow + -GRAPHY.]

sten·o·type (sten'ə tīp') *n.* **1.** keyboard machine used in stenotypy. Trademark: Stenotype. **2.** letter or group of letters representing a sound, word, or phrase in stenotypy. [Greek *stenos* narrow + TYPE.]

sten·o·typ·y (sten'ə tī'pē) *n.* method of shorthand in which letters of the alphabet represent sounds, words, and phrases.

Sten·tor (sten'tôr) *n.* *Greek Legend.* herald who had a voice as loud as fifty men.

sten·to·ri·an (sten tôr'ē ən) *adj.* extremely loud: *in stentorian tones.* [From STENTOR (from Greek *stenein* to moan, groan) + -IAN.]

step (step) *n.* **1.** single complete movement of raising the foot and putting it down in a new position in walking, climbing, dancing, or the like. **2.** distance covered in one such movement: *Larry was two steps from the door when it swung open.* **3.** any short distance; little way: *The store is only a few steps from our house.* **4.** place or rest for the foot in going up or coming down, as a stair or rung of a ladder. **5. steps.** flight of stairs: *to trip and fall down the steps.* **6.** action or one of a series of actions leading to a particular goal or result: *to take steps to ensure that a similar accident could not happen.* **7.** degree, grade, or stage in a progression or series: *to bring a project one step nearer to completion, a bright child who was a step ahead of her classmates.* **8.** sound made by putting the foot down; footfall. **9.** footprint: *The new snow covered our steps.* **10.** *also,* **steps.** course; path; example: *Dan followed in his father's steps and became a professor.* **11.** manner of walking or otherwise taking steps: *a light, graceful step.* **12.** combination of foot and body movements in dancing which form a basic pattern: *Pam said that the waltz step is the hardest to learn.* **13.** rhythm or pace of another or others, esp. in marching: *to be out of step. Billy was too tired to keep step with the other Boy Scouts.* **14.** something resembling a step, as the socket or supporting frame holding the lower end of a ship's mast. **15.** *Music.* interval corresponding to one degree on the staff or in a scale. **16. step by step.** little by little; by degrees; gradually. **17. to watch one's step.** to act or proceed carefully and cautiously. —*v.i.* **stepped, step·ping. 1.** to move by taking a step or steps: *to step to the rear of the bus.* **2.** to walk a short distance. **3.** to put or press the foot: *to step on a piece of broken glass.* **4.** to move into a new situation, condition, or the like as if in a single leap: *The new employee stepped into the job without sufficient preparation.* **5.** *Informal.* to move or act quickly. **6. to step down.** to resign from or abdicate a position or office. **7. to step in.** to begin to participate, as in an affair or dispute, usually without right or welcome; intervene: *Certain Bishops and other chief men stepped in to preserve peace* (Freeman, 1867). **8. to step on it.** *Informal.* to go faster; hurry up: *We'll stop here and try to make the train in time.* **9. to step out. a.** to go outside briefly. **b.** *Informal.* to go out for fun or entertainment. **c.** to step with brisk, long strides. —*v.t.* **1.** to put or move (the

foot) in taking a step: *the first man who stepped foot on the moon.* **2.** to measure by taking steps: *to step off twenty paces.* **3.** to cut steps in; furnish with steps. **4.** *Nautical.* to fix or place (a mast) in a socket or supporting framework. **5. to step down.** to decrease gradually or in stages: *The factory stepped production down during the recession.* **6. to step up.** to increase or accelerate gradually or in stages. [Old English *steppan* to tread, go on foot, advance.]

step- *prefix* related by the remarriage of a parent rather than by blood: *stepchild, stepbrother.* [Old English *stéop-* originally, orphaned.]

step·broth·er (step'bruth'ər) *n.* stepparent's son by a former marriage.

step·child (step'chīld') *pl.,* **-chil·dren.** *n.* child of one's spouse by a former marriage; stepdaughter or stepson.

step·daugh·ter (step'dô'tər) *n.* daughter of one's husband or wife by a former marriage.

step-down (step'doun') *adj.* that decreases or reduces by degrees or stages.

step·fa·ther (step'fä'thər) *n.* husband of one's mother after the death or divorce of one's father.

Ste·phen (stē'vən) **1.** Saint. died A.D. c.35, the first Christian martyr, stoned to death by a mob. **2.** c.1097–1154, king of England from 1135 to 1154.

step-in (step'in') *adj.* (of a garment or shoes) put on by being stepped into. —*n.* step-in garment or shoe.

step·lad·der (step'lad'ər) *n.* ladder that stands by itself on four legs and has flat steps instead of rungs.

step·moth·er (step'muth'ər) *n.* wife of one's father after the death or divorce of one's mother.

step·par·ent (step'pâr'ənt) *n.* stepfather or stepmother.

steppe (step) *n.* **1.** any of the vast, grassy plains extending from southeastern Europe into central Siberia. **2.** any extensive plain. [Russian *step'* wasteland.]

step·per (step'ər) *n.* one who or that which steps, esp. in a lively manner, as a horse or a dancer.

step·ping-stone (step'ing stōn') *also,* **stepping stone.** *n.* **1.** stone or one of a series of stones on which to step, as in crossing a stream. **2.** opportunity, as for social, political, or economic advancement; means of progressing toward some goal or aim: *The Senate has traditionally been considered a steppingstone to the Presidency.*

step·sis·ter (step'sis'tər) *n.* stepparent's daughter by a former marriage.

step·son (step'sun') *n.* son of one's spouse by a former marriage.

step-up (step'up') *n.* increase or escalation in intensity, amount, or activity: *a step-up in the war, a step-up in sales.* —*adj.* that increases by degrees or stages.

step·wise (step'wīz') *adv.* in the manner or arrangement of a series of steps; gradually.

-ster *suffix* (used to form nouns) **1.** one who makes, uses, or is occupied with: *punster, prankster.* **2.** one who is: *youngster.* **3.** one who is related or belongs to: *gangster.* [Old English *-estre, -istre.*]

stere (stēr) *n.* metric measure of capacity equal to one cubic meter. [French *stère,* from Greek *stereos* solid, firm¹.]

ster·e·o (ster'ē ō', stēr'-) *pl.,* **-os.** *n.* **1.** stereophonic system of sound reproduction. **2.** stereophonic sound. —*adj.* stereophonic.

stereo- *combining form* three-dimensional; solid: *stereoscope.* [Greek *stereos* solid, firm¹.]

ster·e·o·chem·is·try (ster'ē ō kem'is trē, stēr'-) *n.* study of the spatial arrangement of atoms and molecules in chemical compounds.

ster·e·o·phon·ic (ster'ē ə fon'ik, stēr'-) *adj.* **1.** of or relating to a system of sound reproduction in which the sound is heard from two or more sources. In stereophonic recording, sounds are picked up by two or more microphones in different locations and reproduced through two or more separate loudspeaker systems, thus giving the effect of natural sound. Distinguished from **monaural. 2.** of, relating to, characterized by, or designating sound as it is heard naturally by both ears.

ster·e·op·ti·con (ster'ē op'ti kən, stēr'-) *n.* compound slide projector, which can project two overlapping pictures simultaneously, or in quick succession so as to produce a fading of one into the other. [STEREO- + Greek *optikon,* neuter of *optikos* relating to vision.]

ster·e·o·scope (ster'ē ə skōp', stēr'-) *n.* optical instrument consisting of two lenses through which each eye views a given scene from a different angle, giving the illusion of a realistic three-dimensional quality to pictures so viewed. [STEREO- + -SCOPE.]

Stereoscope

ster·e·o·scop·ic (ster'ē ə skop'ik, stēr'-) *adj.* **1.** designating or adapted for three-dimensional viewing; marked by a three-dimensional

appearance. **2.** of or relating to a stereoscope. Also, **ster′e·o·scop′i·cal.** —**ster′e·o·scop′i·cal·ly,** *adv.*

stereoscopic microscope, binocular microscope having two parallel systems of compound lenses, which produces a three-dimensional image.

ster·e·o·type (ster′ē ə tīp′, stēr′-) *n.* **1.** method or process of making metal plates by taking a mold of composed type, in or as in papier-mâché, and making a cast in type metal from the mold. **2.** printing plate of type metal cast by this process. **3.** oversimplified or conventional image of a certain person, group, issue, or the like, usually held in common by some segment of society. **4.** one who embodies an oversimplified or conventional pattern of behavior considered typical of his group: *The main character in the play was a stereotype of a miserly businessman.* —*v.t.,* **-typed, -typ·ing. 1.** to make a stereotype of. **2.** to develop a fixed, conventional view of. —**ster′e·o·typ′er,** *n.* —**ster·e·o·typ·ic** (ster′ē ə tip′ik, stēr′-); *also,* **ster′e·o·typ′i·cal,** *adj.*

ster·e·o·typed (ster′ē ə tīpt′, stēr′-) *adj.* **1.** characterized by a lack of originality or individuality; conventional. **2.** printed from stereotype plates.

ster·e·o·typ·y (ster′ē ə tī′pē, stēr′-) *n.* **1.** process or art of making stereotype plates. **2.** act of printing from such plates.

ster·ile (ster′əl) *adj.* **1.** incapable of reproducing; not producing offspring; barren. **2.** producing little or no vegetation; not fertile; arid: *a dry and sterile region.* **3.** free from bacteria or microorganisms: *sterile surgical instruments, sterile milk bottles.* **4.** lacking imagination or vitality; conventional; stale: *sterile writing.* [Latin *sterilis* barren.] —**Syn. 1.** see **barren.**

ste·ril·i·ty (stə ril′ə tē) *n.* condition or quality of being sterile.

ster·i·li·za·tion (ster′ə li zā′shən) *n.* act or process of sterilizing; being sterilized.

ster·i·lize (ster′ə līz′) *-lized, -liz·ing. v.t.* to make sterile. —**ster′i·liz′er,** *n.*

ster·ling (stur′ling) *adj.* **1.** containing 92.5 percent pure silver. **2.** made of sterling silver. **3.** consisting of, relating to, or payable in British money. **4.** of accepted or proven worth; excellent: *a sterling reputation.* —*n.* **1.a.** sterling silver. **b.** article or articles made of sterling silver, as flatware. **2.** British money. **3.** British standard of fineness for gold and silver coinage. [Middle English *sterling* English silver penny of the medieval period, going back to Old English *steorra* star + -LING (with reference to the star on early coins).]

stern¹ (sturn) *adj.* **1.** severe in disposition or conduct; strict; inflexible; uncompromising: *a stern moralist, to adopt a stern policy toward criminals.* **2.** characterized by or expressing extreme displeasure; harsh: *a stern rebuke, to speak in one's sternest voice.* **3.** grim or forbidding in manner or appearance; austere; gloomy: *a stern look.* **4.** not easily shaken or swayed; resolute; unwavering: *a stern resolve. He is made of sterner stuff than that.* **5.** impossible to escape or avoid; compelling; relentless: *stern reality.* [Old English *stirne* severe, hard.] —**stern′ly,** *adv.* —**stern′ness,** *n.* —**Syn. 3.** see **severe.**

stern² (sturn) *n.* rear part of a boat or ship. [Probably from Old Norse *stjörn* a steering.]

ster·nal (sturn′əl) *adj.* of, near, or relating to the breastbone.

stern chaser, gun mounted in the stern of a ship, to be fired against a pursuing ship.

stern·most (sturn′mōst′) *adj.* nearest astern.

stern·post (sturn′pōst′) *n.* principal upright member, extending from the keel of a boat or ship, usually supporting the rudder.

stern sheets, area at the rear of an open boat.

ster·num (stur′nəm) *pl.* **-nums** or **-na** (-nə). *n.* flat, narrow bone in the center of the chest to which the ribs are joined; breastbone. [Modern Latin *sternum,* from Greek *sternon* chest.]

ster·nu·ta·tion (sturn′yə tā′shən) *n.* act or instance of sneezing. [Latin *sternutātio.*]

ster·nu·ta·to·ry (stər nōō′tə tôr′ē, -nū′-) *adj.* causing or tending to cause sneezing. Also, **ster·nu′ta·tive.**

stern·ward (sturn′wərd) *adj.* toward or at the stern. —*adv.* also, **stern·wards.** toward the stern.

stern·way (sturn′wā′) *n.* backward movement of a boat or ship.

stern·wheel·er (sturn′hwē′lər, -wē′-) *n.* steamboat propelled by a single paddle wheel at the stern.

ster·oid (ster′oid, stēr′-) *n.* any of a group of organic compounds made of rings containing seventeen carbon atoms. Hormones, digitalis, and sterols are steroids. New steroids have been synthesized for use in medicine. [STER(OL) + -OID.]

ster·ol (ster′ôl, stēr′-) *n.* steroid with an alcohol group attached. Cholesterol is a sterol. [From CHOLESTEROL.]

ster·to·rous (stur′tər əs) *adj.* characterized or accompanied by a deep snoring or rasping sound: *stertorous sleep.* [Modern Latin *stertor* snoring (from Latin *stertere* to snore) + -OUS.] —**ster′to·rous·ly,** *adv.* —**ster′to·rous·ness,** *n.*

stet (stet) *n.* proofreading mark indicating that canceled or corrected matter should be printed as it appeared originally. —*v.t.,* **stet·ted, stet·ting.** to cancel a correction or deletion by writing *stet* in the margin and underlining the correction or deletion with a row of dots. [Latin *stet* let it stand.]

steth·o·scope (steth′ə skōp′) *n.* instrument used to listen to sounds made by the internal organs of the body, esp. the lungs and heart. [Greek *stēthos* chest + -SCOPE.]

steth·o·scop·ic (steth′ə skop′ik) *adj.* **1.** observed or obtained by means of a stethoscope: *a stethoscopic examination.* **2.** of or relating to a stethoscope or its use. Also, **steth′o·scop′i·cal.** —**steth′o·scop′i·cal·ly,** *adv.*

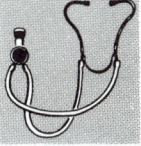
Stethoscope

St. É·tienne (saN tā tyen′) city in southeastern France. Pop. (1968), 213,468.

Stet·tin (shte tēn′) *n.* see **Szczecin.**

Steu·ben, Baron Frederick William von (stōō′bən, stū′-; *German* shtoi′bən) 1730–94, Prussian general who aided in the American Revolution.

ste·ve·dore (stē′və dôr′) *n.* man whose work is loading and unloading cargo from ships. —*v.t.,* **-dored, -dor·ing.** to load or unload the cargo of. —*v.i.* to load or unload a ship. [Spanish *estivador,* from *estivar* to stow cargo, from Latin *stīpāre* to press together.]

Ste·ven·son, Robert Louis (stē′vən sən) 1850–94, Scottish novelist and poet.

stew (stōō, stū) *v.t.* to cook (food) slowly by simmering. —*v.i.* **1.** to be cooked by slow simmering; undergo stewing: *She let the pears stew for half an hour.* **2.** *Informal.* to be angry, disturbed, or agitated; fret. **3.** to stew in one's own juice, to remain disturbed or suffer, esp. from one's own actions. —*n.* **1.** food cooked by stewing, esp. a mixture of meats and vegetables cooked together. **2.** *Informal.* state of anxiety, anger, or agitation. [Old French *estuver* to bathe in hot water, going back to Latin *ex-* out + Greek *typhos* smoke, vapor.]

stew·ard (stōō′ərd, stū′-) *n.* **1.** one who manages or supervises another's property, finances, or affairs. **2.** man in charge of the food and other passenger services, as on a ship, airplane, or train. **3.** any male member of a staff or crew who waits on the passengers of a ship, airplane, or train. **4.** person employed in an institution or resort as the manager of household affairs. **5.** shop steward. [Old English *stigweard* official directing a household, from *stig* house, hall + *weard* keeper.] —**stew′ard·ship′,** *n.*

stew·ard·ess (stōō′ər dis, stū′-) *n.* female steward, esp. one employed to provide passenger service on an airplane.

stew·pan (stōō′pan′, stū′-) *n.* utensil, esp. a saucepan, used for stewing.

St. Got·thard (got′ərd) **1.** Alpine mountain group in south-central Switzerland. **2.** mountain pass located there. **3.** railroad tunnel near this pass.

St. He·le·na (hə lē′nə) small British island in the South Atlantic, site of Napoleon Bonaparte's exile from 1815 until his death in 1821. Area, 47 sq. mi. Pop. (1969), 4829.

sthen·ic (sthen′ik) *adj.* accompanied by or exhibiting abnormal increase in heartbeat, respiration, and the like: *a sthenic fever.* [Modern Latin *sthenicus,* from Greek *sthenos* strength.]

stib·i·um (stib′ē əm) *n.* antimony. [Latin *stibium,* from Greek *stibi;* of Egyptian origin.]

stick¹ (stik) *n.* **1.** long, slender piece of wood. **2.** anything resembling a stick, esp. in shape: *a stick of dynamite.* **3.** implement used to propel a ball or puck in any of various games: *a hockey stick.* **4.** lever that controls the up-and-down and side-to-side movement of an airplane. **5.a.** composing stick. **b.** amount of type that a composing stick can hold. **6.** *Informal.* dull, stiff, unresponsive person. **7. the sticks.** *Informal.* area that is far from a city or town, esp. one regarded as being provincial or culturally backward. —*v.t.* to provide a stick or sticks for support. [Old English *sticca* short piece of wood, slender branch of a tree or shrub.]

stick² (stik) stuck, stick·ing. *v.t.* **1.** to stab, pierce, or puncture (something) with a pointed object: *The child stuck the balloon with a pin.* **2.** to push, thrust, or drive the point or end of (something) into or through something else: *to stick a tack in a bulletin board.* **3.** to fasten or attach with or as with a pin, nail, or other pointed object: *to stick a notice on a bulletin board.* **4.** to fasten or attach by means of an adhesive substance or material: *to stick a stamp on an envelope.* **5.** to put or thrust into a specified place or position: *The little boy stuck his tongue out at us.* **6.** to keep from proceeding; detain; delay: *Our car was stuck in traffic for an hour.* **7.** to kill by piercing. **8.** *Informal.* to puzzle; confuse: *You stuck me on that question.* **9.** *Informal.* to cause to bear the responsibility or blame for (with *with*): *They stuck him with the bill.* **10.** *Slang.* to cheat or take advantage of. **11. to stick up.** *Slang.* to rob, esp. at gunpoint. —*v.i.* **1.** to be or become fixed in place by having the end or point embedded in something: *The piece of glass stuck*

in his foot. **2.** to extend; protrude: *His handkerchief stuck out from his pocket.* **3.** to continue in the performance or pursuit of something, as a course of action: *to stick to a job until it's finished.* **4.** to remain faithful or loyal: *to stick to a bargain.* **5.** to become or remain closely attached or associated: *If we don't stick together, we'll get lost in this crowd.* **6.** to be or become unworkable or immovable: *The drawer stuck when I tried to open it.* **7.** to hold fast, as if glued; cling: *The wet shirt stuck to his back.* **8.** to follow closely (with *to*): *We should stick to the main road since we're not sure of the way.* **9.** to be puzzled. **10. to be stuck on.** *Informal.* to be in love or infatuated with. **11. to stick around.** *Informal.* to remain or wait nearby. **12. to stick out.** *Informal.* to be obvious or conspicuous. **13. to stick up for.** to support or defend; speak or act in defense of. —*n.* **1.** a poke, thrust, or stab with or as with a pointed object: *a stick in the ribs.* **2.** state or power of adhering. [Old English *stician* to stab, pierce, remain fixed.]

stick·ball (stik′bôl′) *n.* form of baseball played with a rubber ball and a broomstick or similar object for a bat.

stick·er (stik′ər) *n.* **1.** slip of printed material with an adhesive surface, used esp. as a label, promotional device, or decoration. **2.** burr, bramble, or the like. **3.** one who or that which sticks.

sticking plaster, adhesive tape.

stick-in-the-mud (stik′in thə mud′) *n.* *Informal.* one who is too dull or staid to take part in any progressive or entertaining activity.

stick·le (stik′əl) -led, -ling. *v.i.* **1.** to argue or insist stubbornly, esp. about trifles. **2.** to hesitate or raise objections over trifles; scruple. [Modification of obsolete *stightle* to arrange, control, strive, going back to Old English *stihtan* to arrange.]

stick·le·back (stik′əl-bak′) *pl.*, **-back** or **-backs.** *n.* any of a group of fish, family Gasterosteidae,

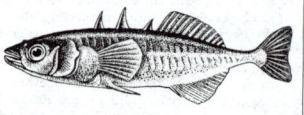

Stickleback

having sharp bony spines on the back and bony plates on the sides in place of scales. [Middle English *stykylbak*, from Old English *sticel* prickle, sting + *bæc* back¹; referring to the prickles on its back.]

stick·ler (stik′lər) *n.* **1.** one who stubbornly insists on adhering to or observing something completely and exactly (often with *for*). **2.** *Informal.* something puzzling or difficult.

stick·pin (stik′pin′) *n.* long ornamental pin, usually with a jeweled head, worn esp. in a necktie or ascot.

stick·tight (stik′tīt′) *n.* any of several weedy plants, genus *Bidens*, of the composite family, usually having yellow flower heads, bearing small barbed fruits that stick to clothing and animal fur.

stick-to-it·ive (stik′tōō′i tiv) *adj.* *Informal.* persistent; persevering. —**stick′·to′-it·ive·ness,** *n.*

stick·up (stik′up′) *n.* *Slang.* robbery, esp. at gunpoint.

stick·y (stik′ē) **stick·i·er, stick·i·est.** *adj.* **1.** tending to stick or hold fast. **2.** coated or covered with adhesive matter. **3.** hot and humid; muggy. **4.** difficult to deal with tactfully; touchy. —**stick′i·ly,** *adv.* —**stick′i·ness,** *n.*

stiff (stif) *adj.* **1.** not easily bent; not pliant. **2.** unable to move easily without pain or difficulty: *My back was stiff after sitting for so many hours.* **3.** not natural, easy, or graceful in manner or movement; formal: *a stiff bow.* **4.** harsh; severe: *The judge gave him a stiff sentence.* **5.** unusually high, as in amount or degree; excessive: *a stiff price.* **6.** that requires considerable effort; difficult: *a stiff examination in mathematics.* **7.** not liquid or fluid; thick: *Beat the egg whites until they are stiff.* **8.** not working or moving smoothly or easily, as parts of machinery. **9.** having a strong, steady movement or force: *a stiff breeze.* **10.** tightly drawn; taut. **11.** strong or potent, as an alcoholic drink. —*n. Slang.* **1.** dead body; corpse. **2.** very dull, staid, and unresponsive person. **3.** rough, awkward person. **4.** fellow; man: *a couple of working stiffs.* —*adv.* completely or extremely: *to be bored stiff.* [Old English *stif* rigid.] —**stiff′ly,** *adv.* —**stiff′ness,** *n.*

Syn. *adj.* **1. Stiff, inflexible, rigid** mean difficult to bend. **Stiff** describes something that can be bent under pressure and may return to its original shape when that pressure is removed: *The bristles of a toothbrush are stiff.* **Inflexible** implies that something cannot be bent in its present state without permanently damaging it: *The glass rod remained inflexible until it was heated.* **Rigid** refers to something that is so hard and strong that it cannot be bent without breaking it: *A steel girder is rigid.*

stiff·en (stif′ən) *v.t.*, *v.i.* to make or become stiff or stiffer. —**stiff′en·er,** *n.*

stiff-necked (stif′nekt′) *adj.* unyielding; stubborn.

sti·fle (stī′fəl) **-fled, -fling.** *v.t.* **1.** to prevent or inhibit the growth, development, progress, or functioning of: *to stifle someone's creativity.* **2.** to prevent the emission of; hold back: *to stifle a yawn.* **3.** to kill by depriving of air. —*v.i.* **1.** to feel smothered because of a lack of air, as in a stuffy room. **2.** to die of suffocation. [Possibly modification of

Old French *estouffer* to suffocate; of uncertain origin.] —**Syn.** *v.t.* **3.** see **suffocate.**

stig·ma (stig′mə) *pl.*, **stig·ma·ta** (stig mä′tə, stig′mə tə) or **stig·mas.** *n.* **1.** mark or token of shame, infamy, or disgrace: *branded with the stigma of illegitimacy* (Blunt, 1882). **2.** distinguishing mark or characteristic, esp. one indicating a defect or abnormality. **3.** mark or spot on the skin that bleeds, usually as a result of nervous tension. **4.** part of the pistil of a plant on which pollen is deposited from the anther in pollination. See **flower** for illustration. **5. stigmata.** marks or wounds corresponding to and resembling the five wounds on the crucified body of Jesus, often appearing on the bodies of certain mystics. **6.** *Archaic.* mark burned into the skin of a slave or criminal; brand. [Latin *stigma* mark¹, brand, from Greek *stigma.*]

stig·mat·ic (stig mat′ik) *adj.* of, relating to, or marked by a stigma or stigmata. Also, **stig·mat′i·cal.** —*n.* one who is marked with religious stigmata.

stig·ma·tize (stig′mə tīz′) **-tized, -tiz·ing.** *v.t.* **1.** to characterize or brand as shameful, infamous, or disgraceful. **2.** to mark with stigmata; brand. **3.** to cause stigmata to appear on. —**stig′ma·ti·za′tion,** *n.*

stile¹ (stīl) *n.* **1.** step or series of steps permitting passage over a wall or fence. **2.** turnstile. [Old English *stigel* the series of steps.]

stile² (stīl) *n.* one of the vertical members of a frame or panel, as in a door or window. [Dutch *stijl* doorpost, probably going back to Latin *stilus* post¹, stake.]

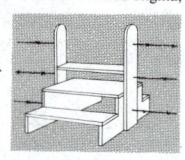

Stile *(def. 1)*

sti·let·to (stə let′ō) *pl.*, **-tos** or **-toes.** *n.* **1.** dagger with a very narrow tapering blade. **2.** small, pointed instrument used for making eyelets in embroidery. [Italian *stiletto,* diminutive of *stilo* dagger, from Latin *stīlus* pointed instrument.]

still¹ (stil) *adj.* **1.** without movement; motionless: *The water was still after the storm.* **2.** without sound; noiseless; silent; quiet: *Be still and listen.* **3.** free from agitation or excitement; tranquil; peaceful: *The night is still.* **4.** not loud; subdued; soft: *a still voice.* **5.** having little or no effervescence; not carbonated or sparkling: *still wine.* **6.** of, relating to, or being a single photograph, as distinguished from a motion picture. —*v.t.* **1.** to make silent; quiet. **2.** to allay, as fears. **3.** to make peaceful or tranquil. —*v.i.* to become still or calm. —*n.* **1.** quiet; silence; calm: *in the still of the night.* **2.** single photograph, esp. one made from a single frame of a motion picture and used for publicity purposes. —*adv.* **1.** without movement; motionless: *Sit still.* **2.** at or up to the time indicated; as before: *She still lives here. Years from now this problem will still exist.* **3.** in increasing amount or degree; beyond this: *Still greater things were expected.* **4.** even then; all the same; nevertheless: *Though he labored, he still could not lose weight.* **5.** *Archaic.* constantly; always. —*conj.* despite that; yet: *It's raining; still I'd like to go.* [Old English *stille* motionless, silent.] —**still′ness,** *n.* —**Syn.** *adj.* **2.** see **quiet¹.**

still² (stil) *n.* **1.** apparatus for distilling liquids, esp. alcoholic liquors, in which a mixture of liquid substances is heated until the most volatile liquid vaporizes. **2.** distillery. [From obsolete *still* to distill, short for DISTILL.]

still alarm, fire alarm given by telephone or other means without sounding the regular signal apparatus.

still·birth (stil′bûrth′) *n.* **1.** birth of a stillborn fetus. **2.** stillborn fetus.

still·born (stil′bôrn′) *adj.* dead at birth.

still-life (stil′līf′) *adj.* of or relating to still life.

still life *pl.*, **still lifes.** **1.** representation of inanimate objects, as bottles, vases, fruit, or flowers, in painting or photography. **2.** painting or photograph containing such subject matter.

still·ly (*adj.*, stil′lē; *adv.*, stil′lē) **-li·er, -li·est.** *adj.* quiet; still; calm. —*adv.* calmly; quietly.

stilt (stilt) *pl.*, **stilts** or *(def. 3)* **stilt.** *n.* **1.** one of a pair of long poles, each having a footrest attached at some distance from the bottom end, used to enable a person to walk with his feet above the ground. **2.** one of the posts used to support a building, pier, or other structure, above ground or water. **3.** any of several water birds, family Recurvirostridae, native to most temperate and tropical regions of the world, having a slender bill, long, thin legs, and usually predominantly white plumage. Length: 13–16 inches. [Possibly of Low German origin.]

stilt·ed (stil′tid) *adj.* **1.** artificially or stiffly dignified or formal: *an old-fashioned, stilted style of writing.* **2.** elevated or supported by or as by stilts so as to be above ground or water. **3.** (of an arch) having its arc heightened by an extended vertical support. —**stilt′ed·ly,** *adv.* —**stilt′ed·ness,** *n.*

Stil·ton cheese (stilt′ən) rich white cheese, resembling Roquefort, made of whole milk and cream and marbled with blue-green mold. [From *Stilton,* a village in England where it supposedly was first sold.]

stim·u·lant (stim′yə lənt) *n.* **1.** drug or other substance that increases, heightens, or arouses the activity of an organism or bodily function or part. **2.** anything that rouses or incites to action; stimulus. **3.** alcoholic beverage. —*adj.* stimulating. [Latin *stimulāns,* present participle of *stimulāre* to prick with a goad, urge on, from *stimulus* goad, incentive.]

stim·u·late (stim′yə lāt′) -lat·ed, -lat·ing. *v.t.* **1.** to rouse to increased action or effort; have an animating effect on. **2.** to act as a stimulus or stimulant to (an organism or bodily function or part). **3.** to affect with an alcoholic beverage. —*v.i.* to act as a stimulus or stimulant to an organism or bodily function or part. [Latin *stimulātus,* past participle of *stimulāre* to prick with a goad, urge on. See STIMULANT.] —**stim′u·la′tion, stim′u·la′tor;** *also,* **stim′u·lat′er,** *n.*

stim·u·la·tive (stim′yə lā′tiv) *adj.* tending or serving to stimulate. —*n.* that which stimulates; stimulus.

stim·u·lus (stim′yə ləs) *pl.,* -li (-lī′). *n.* **1.** something that rouses or incites to action or effort: *Reduced tariffs were a stimulus to foreign trade.* **2.** anything that produces a response in or influences the activity of an organism or bodily function or part. [Latin *stimulus* goad, incentive.] —**Syn. 1.** see incentive.

sti·my (stī′mē) *pl.,* -mies. *n.* stymie. —*v.t.,* -mied, -my·ing. to stymie.

sting (sting) stung, sting·ing. *v.t.* **1.** to prick painfully with a sharp, usually pointed, organ or object: *The bee stung me on the foot.* **2.** to cause to feel a sharp, smarting pain by or as by pricking with a sharp, usually pointed, organ or object: *The iodine stung his cut finger.* **3.** to cause to suffer sharp mental or emotional pain: *I was stung by his harsh criticism.* **4.** to goad or incite suddenly and sharply. **5.** *Slang.* to take advantage of, esp. by overcharging. —*v.i.* **1.** to have, use, or wound with a stinger, as certain insects. **2.** to cause or feel sharp physical or mental pain: *The soap will sting if it gets in your eyes.* —*n.* **1.** act or instance of stinging. **2.** wound or smarting, burning sensation resulting from this. **3.** that which causes sharp mental or physical pain; stinging quality or capacity. **4.** stinger *(def. 1).* **5.** goad; spur. [Old English *stingan* to pierce with a pointed organ or object.]

sting·a·ree (sting′ə rē′) *n.* stingray.

sting·er (sting′ər) *n.* **1.** sharp, usually pointed organ with which an insect or animal inflicts a sting. **2.** one who or that which stings.

sting·ray (sting′rā′) *n.* any of a group of rays, family Dasyatidae, having a whiplike tail with a poisonous spine near the end. Length: to 14 feet the tail.

Stingray

stin·gy (stin′jē) -gi·er, -gi·est. *adj.* **1.** giving or sharing something, esp. money, grudgingly or sparingly; not generous. **2.** scarcely sufficient in amount or quantity; scanty; meager: *a stingy portion of food.* [Possibly from *stinge,* dialectal form of STING + -Y¹.] —**stin′gi·ly,** *adv.* —**stin′gi·ness,** *n.*

stink (stingk) *n.* **1.** strong, offensive smell; disgusting odor; stench. **2.** *Slang.* great fuss, disturbance, or outcry: *There was quite a stink over the incident.* —*v.i.* **stank** or **stunk, stunk, stink·ing. 1.** to give off or be permeated by a strong, offensive smell. **2.** to be extremely offensive or abhorrent. **3.** *Slang.* to have or possess something to an extreme or offensive degree (often with *of* or *with*). **4.** *Slang.* to be of an extremely low or inferior character or quality: *That play stinks.* —*v.t.* **1.** to cause to stink (often with *up*). **2. to stink out.** to drive or force out with a strong, offensive, or suffocating odor or fumes. [Old English *stincan* to have an odor.]

stink·bug (stingk′bug′) *n.* any of a group of bugs, family Pentatomidae, that emit a foul-smelling liquid when disturbed.

stink·er (stingk′kər) *n.* **1.** one who or that which stinks. **2.** *Informal.* offensive, untrustworthy, or disagreeable person.

stink·weed (stingk′wēd′) *n.* any of various plants having a strong, offensive odor, as the jimsonweed.

stint (stint) *v.t.* **1.** to limit or restrict, as in amount or degree; be stingy or sparing with: *to stint one's praise.* **2.** *Archaic.* to cease; stop. —*v.i.* to be stingy or sparing. —*n.* **1.** fixed or allotted amount or share of work or duty to be carried on or served within a specified period of time: *to serve a two-year stint in the army.* **2.** limitation; restriction: *to lavish money on someone without stint.* [Old English *styntan* to make dull, blunt.]

stipe (stīp) *n. Botany.* stalk or stemlike support, as that supporting the cap of a mushroom. [French *stipe,* from Latin *stīpes* tree trunk, log.]

sti·pel (stī′pəl) *n.* stipule. [Modern Latin *stipella,* diminutive of Latin *stipula* stem.]

sti·pend (stī′pend, -pənd) *n.* fixed or regular pay or allowance, esp. one given to a student on a scholarship or fellowship. [Latin *stīpendium*

tax, tribute, pay, from *stips* contribution, wages + *pendere* to weigh out, pay.]

sti·pen·di·ar·y (stī pen′dē er′ē) *adj.* **1.** receiving or performing services for a stipend. **2.** paid for by a stipend, as services. **3.** of or having the nature of a stipend. —*n. pl.,* -ar·ies. one who receives a stipend, as a clergyman.

stip·ple (stip′əl) -pled, -pling. *v.t.* **1.** to paint, draw, or engrave by using dots or light, short touches instead of strokes or lines. **2.** to produce gradations in shade or color in by painting, drawing, or engraving in this way. —*n. also,* **stip′pling. 1.** art or technique of producing a painting, drawing, or engraving by using dots or light, short touches. **2.** effect produced by this technique. **3.** painting, drawing, or engraving produced by this technique. [Dutch *stippelen* to speckle, going back to *stip* point.] —**stip′pler,** *n.*

stip·u·lar (stip′yə lər) *adj.* **1.** of, relating to, or resembling a stipule or stipules. **2.** growing on a stipule or stipules.

stip·u·late¹ (stip′yə lāt′) -lat·ed, -lat·ing. *v.t.* **1.** to demand or specify as an essential condition of agreement: *The actor stipulated that he be allowed to have final approval of the film's script.* **2.** to guarantee, as in a contract or agreement. —*v.i.* **1.** to make an express demand for something as a condition of agreement (with *for*). **2.** to make an agreement or contract. [Latin *stipulātus,* past participle of *stipulārī* to bargain.] —**stip′u·la′tor,** *n.*

stip·u·late² (stip′yə lit, -lāt′) *adj.* having stipules. [Latin *stipula* stem + -ATE¹.]

stip·u·la·tion (stip′yə lā′shən) *n.* **1.** act of stipulating. **2.** something stipulated; term or condition of an agreement or contract.

stip·ule (stip′ūl) *also,* **sti·pel.** *n.* one of a pair of small leaflike structures occurring at the base of certain leaves. [Latin *stipula* stem.]

Stipules

stir¹ (stur) stirred, stir·ring. *v.t.* **1.** to agitate (something, as a liquid) in order to change the relative position of its parts, esp. by a continuous circular movement: *to stir paint.* **2.** to urge on, incite, or instigate (often with *up*): *to stir someone to action.* **3.** to excite to deep feeling or emotion; affect strongly; move: *His impassioned plea for mercy stirred the jury.* **4.** to call forth; work (often with *up*): *That song stirs up old memories.* **5.** to rouse, as from sleep. **6.** to cause to move, esp. slightly: *The breeze stirred the fallen leaves.* —*v.i.* **1.** to make a slight movement: *The sleeping child didn't stir all night.* **2.** to be active; move about: *When no one in the house was stirring, and the lights were all extinguished* (Dickens, 1848). **3.** to begin to show signs of activity. **4.** to be roused or excited. **5.** to be capable of being stirred. **6.** to be in circulation; be current: *Rumors were stirring through the town.* —*n.* **1.** commotion; disturbance; tumult: *His appearance created quite a stir.* **2.** slight or momentary movement. **3.** act of stirring, as with a spoon. [Old English *styrian* to move, agitate.] —**stir′rer,** *n.* —**Syn.** *v.t.* **1.** see mix.

stir² (stur) *n. Slang.* prison: *The convict had been in stir for nine years.* [Of uncertain origin.]

stir crazy *Slang.* extremely restless or irritable as a result of confinement.

stirps (sturps) *pl.,* stir·pes (stur′pēz). *n.* family or branch of a family; line of descendants. [Latin *stirps* stock, stem.]

stir·ring (stur′ing) *adj.* **1.** inspiring or exciting; thrilling. **2.** active; lively. —**stir·ring·ly,** *adv.*

stir·rup (stur′əp, stir′-) *n.* **1.** one of a pair of metal, wooden, or leather loops or rings, flattened at the bottom and suspended from a saddle, used to support a rider's foot in mounting and riding. **2.** any of various similarly shaped devices, used esp. as a support. **3.** innermost of the three bones in the middle ear, shaped somewhat like a stirrup; stapes. Also *(def. 3),* **stirrup bone.** [Old English *stigrāp* loop suspended from a saddle to support a rider's foot, from *stīgan* to climb + *rāp* rope.]

Stirrups

stirrup cup, farewell drink, esp. a cup of liquor given to a rider mounted for departure.

stitch (stich) *n.* **1.** one complete movement of a threaded needle in and out of fabric, as in sewing, or through skin and flesh, as in surgery. **2.** similar complete movement made with a needle and yarn or thread, as in knitting. **3.** single loop or knot of thread made by a stitch. **4.** particular method of arranging the thread, as in sewing or knitting. **5.** sudden, sharp pain, esp. in the side or back. **6.** *Informal.* article or piece of clothing. **7.** *Informal.* slightest bit: *I didn't do a stitch of work all day.* **8. in stitches.** *Informal.* laughing hilariously: *His imitation of a seal had us in stitches.* —*v.t.* **1.** to make, fasten, join, or mend with stitches (often with *up*): *to stitch up a hole.* **2.** to fasten by means of

staples. —*v.i.* to make stitches; sew. [Old English *stice* sudden, sharp pain, puncture.]

stith·y (stith′ē, stith′ē) *pl.* **stith·ies.** *n.* 1. anvil. 2. smithy or forge. [Old Norse *stethi* anvil.]

sti·ver (stī′vər) *n.* 1. coin of the Netherlands, equal to ¹⁄₂₀ of a guilder. 2. anything of little or no value. [Dutch *stuiver* the coin.]

St. John's, capital of Newfoundland, a port on the southeastern coast. Pop. (1966), 79,884.

St. John's bread, flat leathery pod of the carob tree, containing many seeds and surrounded by an edible pulp.

St.-John's-wort (sānt jonz′wurt′) *n.* any of a large group of plants and shrubs, genus *Hypericum,* having abundant yellow flowers.

St. Joseph, city in northwestern Missouri, on the Missouri River. Pop. (1970), 72,691.

St. Lawrence 1. river in North America flowing from Lake Ontario northeast into the Gulf of St. Lawrence. It is the chief outlet of the Great Lakes. 2. Gulf of. arm of the Atlantic, on the eastern coast of Canada, at the mouth of the St. Lawrence River.

St. Lawrence Seaway, inland waterway in east-central North America connecting the Atlantic Ocean with the Great Lakes.

St. Lou·is (lōō′is, lōō′ē) city in eastern Missouri, on the Mississippi. Pop. (1970), 622,236.

St. Marys, river flowing from Lake Superior to Lake Huron, forming the border between northeastern Michigan and Ontario, Canada.

St. Mo·ritz (sānt′ mə rits′; *French,* saN mō rēts′) resort town in southeastern Switzerland, in the Alps. Pop. (1960), 3751.

sto·a (stō′ə) *pl.*, **sto·ae** (stō′ē) or **sto·as.** *n.* 1. portico or covered colonnade, often detached, having columns on one side and a wall on the other. 2. Stoa. colonnaded hall in ancient Athens. [Greek *stoā.*]

stoat (stōt) *n.* the ermine, esp. when in its brown summer coat. [Of uncertain origin.]

stock (stok) *n.* 1. total amount of goods that a merchant or commercial establishment keeps on hand for sale. 2. quantity of something accumulated or held in reserve, esp. for future use; store: *The squirrel was putting away a stock of nuts for the winter.* 3. domestic animals raised or kept on a farm or ranch, as cattle, sheep, or pigs; livestock 4. ancestry or descent: *a person of Scandinavian stock.* 5. source of a line of descent; original progenitor, as of a family. 6. group of related languages; family. 7. original type from which a group of plants or animals has descended. 8. family or other related group of plants or animals. 9. ethnic group; race. 10. liquid in which meat, poultry, or fish has been boiled, used as a base for gravies, soups, or sauces. 11.a. total number of shares that a company or corporation is authorized to issue. b. number of shares held by an individual stockholder. c. stock certificate. 12. raw material from which something is made. 13. stocks. wooden frame with holes for confining a person's ankles and sometimes his wrists, formerly used as a punishment for minor crimes. 14. wooden or metal support or handle of a gun, to which the barrel and mechanism are attached. 15.a. stem of a plant onto which a graft is made. b. tree, plant, or plant part that furnishes cuttings for grafting. 16. trunk or main stem of a tree or other plant. 17. underground stem; rhizome. 18. crosspiece below the ring of an anchor. 19. stocks. timber framework that is used to support a boat or ship during construction. 20.a. stock company *(def. 2).* b. repertoire of a stock company. 21. close-fitting, stiff neckcloth worn in the eighteenth and nineteenth centuries. 22. any of a group of downy plants, genus *Matthiola,* of the mustard family, bearing stiff showy spikes of broad, petaled flowers, as the gillyflower. 23. in stock. available for sale or use. 24. out of stock. not available for sale or use. 25. to put (or take) stock in. to have faith, trust, or confidence in. 26. to take stock. a. to make an inventory of the goods one has on hand. b. to make an estimate or appraisal. —*v.t.* 1. to supply or furnish with stock or a stock: *They stocked the cabin with enough food for the weekend.* 2. to have or keep a supply of, esp. for future use or sale: *That hardware store stocks all kinds of tools.* 3. to supply with livestock: *to stock a farm.* 4. to provide with wild animals, fish, or other game, esp. for private or restricted hunting or fishing: *to stock a lake.* 5. to lay in a stock or supply. —*v.i.* 1. to lay in a stock or supply (often with *up*): *to stock up for a party.* 2. (of a plant) to send out new shoots. —*adj.* 1. regularly kept in stock: *a stock size.* 2. commonly or constantly used or brought forward; commonplace: *a stock phrase.* 3. employed in handling or caring for goods or merchandise: *a stock clerk.* [Old English *stocc* log, post¹, trunk of a tree.]

Syn. —*n.* 2. Stock, store, reserve mean a quantity of something set aside for use. Stock stresses a permanent collection of related or similar items maintained for occasional use: *I have a stock of hunting rifles and guns.* Store stresses the gradual accumulation of basic necessities that would be unobtainable at the time needed, as during an emergency: *Our family has a store of dried and canned foods that can be used until the snow-storm is over.* Reserve implies something conserved from a regular supply or else set aside all at once to meet some special demand or

emergency: *We have a cash reserve in case one of us gets sick and can't work.*

stock·ade (sto kād′) *n.* 1. defensive barrier made of strong, usually tall, posts set upright in the ground, usually forming an enclosure. 2. any similar barrier or enclosure. 3. military prison. —*v.t.* -**ad·ed,** -**ad·ing.** to surround or fortify with a stockade. [French *estacade* bulwark made with stakes, from Spanish *estacada,* from *estaca* stake; of Germanic origin.]

stock·bro·ker (stok′brō′kər) *n.* one who buys and sells stocks or other securities for others.

stock·bro·ker·age (stok′brō′kər ij) *n.* work or business of a stockbroker.

stock car 1. standard automobile modified for racing. 2. railroad car used for transporting livestock.

stock certificate, certificate issued by a company or corporation to a stockholder as evidence of his ownership of a particular number of shares.

stock company 1. company or corporation whose capital is divided into shares. 2. theatrical troupe playing regularly at a particular theater in a variety of productions.

stock exchange 1. place where stocks and bonds are bought and sold. 2. association of stockbrokers who engage in the business of buying and selling stocks and bonds.

stock·fish (stok′fish′) *pl.* -**fish** or -**fish·es.** *n.* fish, as cod, that is split and dried in the open air without salt.

stock·hold·er (stok′hōl′dər) *n.* one who owns stock in a company or corporation; shareholder.

Stock·holm (stok′hōm, -hōlm) *n.* capital and largest city of Sweden, on the eastern coast of the country. Pop. (1968), 756,697.

stock·i·net (stok′ə net′) *also,* **stock·i·nette.** *n.* elastic knitted fabric, often of wool or cotton, used for making such items as underwear or stockings.

stock·ing (stok′ing) *n.* 1. close-fitting, knitted covering for the foot and leg, esp. one made of nylon or other man-made fiber and worn by women. 2. anything resembling this. 3. in one's stocking feet. wearing socks or stockings but no shoes. [Obsolete *stock* this covering for the leg (from Old English *stocc* log, tree trunk) + -ING¹.]

stocking cap, knitted cap, usually having a pointed end that is worn flopped over toward the back.

Stocking cap

stock in trade 1. goods in which a store or shop deals. 2. quality or ability that is characteristic of or peculiar to a particular person or group: *Smooth talk is the stock in trade of that salesman.*

stock·job·ber (stok′job′ər) *n.* 1. stockbroker. ▲ often used disparagingly. 2. *British.* member of the stock exchange who buys and sells stocks and bonds for stockbrokers, but not for the public.

stock·man (stok′mən) *pl.* -**men.** *n.* man who raises livestock.

stock market 1. place where stocks and bonds are bought and sold. 2. business carried on in such a place.

stock·pile (stok′pīl′) *n.* supply of foodstuffs, raw materials, or other items accumulated and held in reserve for future use, as during an emergency or shortage: *a stockpile of nuclear weapons.* —*v.t.* -**piled,** -**pil·ing.** to accumulate a stockpile. —*v.i.* to accumulate a stockpile.

stock·room (stok′rōōm′, -room′) *n.* room in which stocks of goods are stored.

stock split, division of the shares of stock of a corporation into a larger number of shares, usually without any increase in their total value.

stock-still (stok′stil′) *adj.* motionless: *to stand stock-still.*

Stock·ton (stok′tən) *n.* city in central California. Pop. (1970), 107,-644.

stock·y (stok′ē) **stock·i·er, stock·i·est.** *adj.* having a solid, sturdy, and compact build, and usually short; thickset. —**stock′i·ly,** *adv.* —**stock′i·ness,** *n.*

stock·yard (stok′yärd′) *n.* enclosure consisting of pens and sheds where livestock is kept before being slaughtered or shipped to market.

stodg·y (stoj′ē) **stodg·i·er, stodg·i·est.** *adj.* 1. extremely old-fashioned and stuffy: *Jane thought her father was stodgy because he disapproved of miniskirts.* 2. lacking freshness or interest; commonplace; dull: *a stodgy speech.* 3. (of food) heavy and thick; indigestible. 4. thickset; stocky. [Earlier *stodge* to fill full (of uncertain origin) + -Y¹.] —**stodg′i·ly,** *adv.* —**stodg′i·ness,** *n.*

sto·gy (stō′gē) *pl.* -**gies.** *also,* **sto·gey, sto·gie.** *n.* long, slender, inexpensive cigar. [From *(Cone)stoga(a),* town in Pennsylvania.]

Sto·ic (stō′ik) *n.* 1. adherent of a school of philosophy founded by Zeno of Citium in about 300 B.C., that stressed calm, dignified acceptance of fate. Stoics believed that everything happened according to a universal, rational order and that all men were brothers. 2. stoic. one

who is apparently indifferent to or unaffected by pain or pleasure. —*adj.* **1.** of or relating to the Stoics or Stoicism. **2.** stoic. indifferent to or unaffected by pain or pleasure, esp. accepting or resigned to suffering. Also *(def. 2),* **sto′i·cal.** [Latin *Stōicus* relating to the Stoics, from Greek *Stōikos* literally, relating to a *stoa* stoa (because Zeno taught at a stoa in Athens).] —**sto′i·cal·ly,** *adv.*

Sto·i·cism (stō′ə siz′əm) *n.* **1.** philosophy of the Stoics. **2.** stoicism. indifference to pleasure or pain; impassivity.

stoke (stōk) stoked, stok·ing. *v.t., v.i.* **1.** to stir up and feed fuel to (a fire or a furnace). **2.** to tend (a fire or furnace). [From STOKER.]

stoke·hold (stōk′hōld′) *n.* room or compartment on a ship containing the furnaces or boilers.

stoke·hole (stōk′hōl′) *n.* **1.** hole through which fuel is fed into a furnace. **2.** stokehold.

Stoke-on-Trent (stōk′ŏn trent′, -on-) *n.* city in west-central England. Pop. (1968), 273,000.

stok·er (stō′kər) *n.* **1.** man who tends and supplies fuel to a furnace or boiler, as on a steamship or locomotive. **2.** mechanical device that supplies fuel to a furnace. [Dutch *stoker* one who kindles a fire, from *stoken* to make a fire, stir up.]

STOL (stōl) airplane that needs only a short distance to take off and land. [Abbreviation of *s(hort) t(ake) o(ff and) l(anding).*]

stole¹ (stōl) past tense of **steal.**

stole² (stōl) *n.* **1.** woman's long scarf, usually of fur, worn around the shoulders with the ends hanging down in front. **2.** vestment consisting of a long narrow strip of silk or other material, worn around the neck by a clergyman during certain religious services. **3.** long outer garment or robe worn by matrons in ancient Rome. [Old English *stole* long robe, from Latin *stola* robe, garment, from Greek *stolē*.]

sto·len (stō′lən) past participle of **steal.**

stol·id (stŏl′id) *adj.* having or showing little or no emotion; not easily moved or stirred; impassive. [Latin *stolidus* firm¹, dull.] —**sto·lid·i·ty** (stə lid′ə tē) *n.* —**stol′id·ly,** *adv.*

sto·lon (stō′lən) *n.* **1.** *Botany.* stem that trails along the ground and takes root at the tip to form a new plant; runner. **2.** *Zoology.* stemlike growth on the body of certain animals, as the coral, that gives rise to buds from which new organisms develop. [Latin *stolon-,* stem of *stolō* shoot, branch, sucker of a plant.]

sto·ma (stō′mə) *pl.,* **sto·ma·ta** or **sto·mas.** *n.* small opening or pore, esp. on a plant leaf, through which gases and water vapor pass in or out. [Modern Latin *stoma,* from Greek *stoma* mouth.]

stom·ach (stum′ək) *n.* **1.** in man and other vertebrates, the muscular saclike organ of the alimentary canal that receives ingested food from the esophagus, lubricates it, mixes it, and begins the digestion of proteins and fats. **2.** the corresponding part in certain invertebrates, as lobsters and insects. **3.** part of the body containing the stomach; abdomen; belly. **4.** inclination or liking; desire: *to have no stomach for blood or violence.* **5.** desire for food; appetite. —*v.t.* **1.** to put up with; tolerate; endure: *I can't stomach his constantly inconsiderate behavior.* **2.** to take into and retain in the stomach. [Old French *estomac* this organ, from Latin *stomachus,* from Greek *stomachos.*]

stom·ach·ache (stum′ək āk′) *n.* pain in or near the region of the stomach.

stom·ach·er (stum′ə kər) *n.* former ornamental garment covering the stomach and chest, often extending in a V-shape to below the waistline, worn esp. by women in the sixteenth and seventeenth centuries.

sto·mach·ic (stō mak′ik) *adj.* **1.** of or relating to the stomach; gastric. **2.** beneficial to or stimulating digestion in the stomach. Also, **stom·ach·al** (stum′ə kal), **stom·ach′i·cal.** —*n.* medicine that stimulates the functioning of the stomach.

stomach pump, suction pump with a long flexible tube, used to empty the contents of the stomach, as in a case of poisoning.

sto·ma·ta (stō′mə tə, stom′ə-) plural of **stoma.**

sto·ma·tal (stom′ət əl, stō′mət-) *adj.* of, relating to, or having a stoma or stomata.

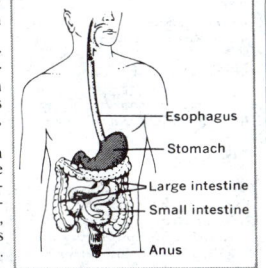

Esophagus
Stomach
Large intestine
Small intestine
Anus

Stomach

stomp (stomp) *v.t.* **1.** to tread heavily or violently on or upon. **2.** to bring down (the foot or feet) forcefully and heavily; stamp. —*v.i.* to tread heavily or violently. [Form of STAMP.]

stone (stōn) *pl.,* **stones** or *(def. 8)* **stone.** *n.* **1.** hard, naturally formed mass of mineral matter; rock. **2.** small fragment or piece of this. **3.** piece of stone that has been shaped or cut for a particular purpose, as for building, marking a grave, or paving a road. **4.** precious stone; gem. **5.** anything resembling a stone, as in shape or hardness. **6.** hardened mass of matter found in certain organs of the body, as the gall bladder or kidney. **7.** hard inner layer enclosing the seed of a drupe, as the cherry, peach, or avocado. **8.** unit of weight of varying amount. In Great Britain it is equal to fourteen pounds avoirdupois. **9. to cast the first stone.** to be the first to attack, accuse, or criticize. —*adj.* **1.** made or built of stone: *a stone house, a stone wall.* **2.** made of stoneware. —*v.t.,* **stoned, ston·ing. 1.** to pelt or kill with stones. **2.** to furnish, fit, pave, or line with stones: *to stone a road.* **3.** to remove the stones from (fruit). [Old English *stān* rock, hard mineral matter, piece of rock, piece of hard mineral matter.]

Stone, Lucy (stōn) 1818–93, U.S. leader in the woman's rights movement.

Stone Age, earliest known stage in the development of human culture, characterized by the use of stone tools and weapons.

stone-blind (stōn′blīnd′) *adj.* completely blind.

stone-broke (stōn′brōk′) *adj. Informal.* without funds; penniless.

stone-chat (stōn′chat′) *n.* small, thrushlike bird, *Saxicola torquata,* native to Europe, Africa, and Asia, having predominantly brown plumage and a reddish breast. Length: 5 inches.

stone·crop (stōn′krop′) *n.* any of a large group of fleshy low-growing plants, genus *Sedum,* found in cool regions of the Northern Hemisphere, bearing clusters of white, yellow, pink, or blue flowers. Also, **se′dum.** [Old English *stāncrop.*]

stone·cut·ter (stōn′kut′ər) *n.* one who or that which cuts or carves stone.

stoned (stōnd) *adj. Slang.* intoxicated, as by drugs or liquor.

stone-deaf (stōn′def′) *adj.* completely deaf.

stone fruit, fleshy fruit in which the seed is enclosed in a hard endocarp; drupe.

Stone·henge (stōn′henj′) *n.* structure in southern England erected by a prehistoric people, consisting mainly of a circular arrangement of giant stone blocks, now in ruins.

stone marten 1. marten, *Martes foina,* native to Europe and Asia, having gray-brown fur with a patch of white on the throat and breast. **2.** fur of this animal.

stone·ma·son (stōn′mā′sən) *n.* person who cuts stone or builds structures in stone.

stone's throw, a short distance.

stone·ware (stōn′wâr′) *n.* nonporous pottery made of clay and stone that have been ground into a fine powder and baked at a very high temperature.

stone·work (stōn′wurk′) *n.* **1.** work made of stone. **2.** art, process, or technique of working in stone. **3. stoneworks.** place where stone is cut and prepared. —**stone′work′er,** *n.*

ston·y (stō′nē) **ston·i·er, ston·i·est.** *adj.* **1.** fixed; motionless: *the stony stare of a preoccupied man.* **2.** having or feeling no emotion: *a stony heart.* **3.** abounding in or covered with stones. **4.** hard as stone. —**ston′i·ly,** *adv.* —**ston′i·ness,** *n.*

stood (stood) past tense and past participle of **stand.**

stooge (stōōj) *n. Informal.* **1.** entertainer who assists a comedian, as by feeding him lines, heckling him from the audience, or serving as the butt of his jokes. **2.** anyone who is used or taken advantage of by another; dupe. [Of uncertain origin.]

stool (stōōl) *n.* **1.** individual seat supported on legs or a pedestal, usually having no back or arms. **2.** low backless and armless bench, used as a support for the feet or by one when sitting or for the knees when kneeling. **3.** toilet *(def. 2).* **4.** waste matter evacuated from the bowels at each movement. **5.a.** stump from which sprouts shoot up. **b.** shoots growing from such a stump. —*v.i.* to send out shoots; sprout. [Old English *stōl* seat.]

stool pigeon 1. pigeon used as a decoy to trap other pigeons. **2.** *Slang.* any person acting as an informer or decoy, esp. for the police. Also *(def. 2),* **stool′ie.**

stoop¹ (stōōp) *v.i.* **1.** to bend the body forward and downward, often with the knees bent: *She stooped to pick up the paper she had dropped.* **2.** to stand or walk with the head and shoulders bent forward. **3.** to lower or degrade oneself to do or employ something: *to stoop to cheating in order to pass an examination.* **4.** to pounce or swoop down, as a bird on prey. —*v.t.* to bend (one's head or other part of the body) forward. —*n.* **1.** a forward bending of the head and shoulders, esp. habitually: *The old man walked with a stoop.* **2.** act of bending forward and downward. **3.** act of swooping down, as a bird on prey. [Old English *stūpian* to bend down, bow down.]

at; āpe; cär; end; mē; it; īce; hot; ōld; fôrk; wood; fōōl; oil; out; up; ūse; turn; sing; thin; this; zh in treasure; ə in ago, taken, pencil, lemon, circus.

983

stoop² (stŌŌp) *n.* structure at the entrance of a building or house, consisting of a number of steps leading up to a raised platform. [Dutch *stoep* flight of steps.]

stop (stop) **stopped, stop·ping.** *v.t.* **1.** to check or arrest the movement, action, or progress of: *to stop a car, to stop a clock, to stop traffic.* **2.** to put an end to; prevent the continuance of: *to stop the spread of a fire, to stop an enemy's advance.* **3.** to prevent (a person) from carrying out a contemplated action; restrain: *We couldn't stop him from causing a scene.* **4.** to obstruct or close up (a hole, passage, or cavity) by or as by stuffing something into it or placing something over it (often with *up*): *to stop up a drain.* **5.** to close (a receptacle or ves-

Stoop²

sel) by blocking its mouth with a plug or other stopper (often with *up*): *to stop up a bottle.* **6.** to prevent the passage or flow of: *to stop a leak.* **7.** to desist from: *Please stop making so much noise.* **8.** to keep back or withhold: *to stop payment on a check.* **9.** to instruct a bank to withhold payment on: *to stop a check.* **10.** *Music.* to close (a finger hole) or press down on (a string) in order to produce a desired tone. **11.** *Sports.* to defeat. —*v.i.* **1.** to come to an end; discontinue: *The music stopped at midnight.* **2.** to come to a standstill or halt, as in walking, talking, or any other action or procedure: *She stopped in the middle of her speech and asked if there were any questions.* **3.** to halt during one's course or journey. **4. to stop off** (or **over**). *Informal.* to stop for a brief visit or stay, esp. during the course of a journey. —*n.* **1.** act of stopping; being stopped. **2.** place at which a stop is made: *a bus stop.* **3.** that which stops or hinders, as an obstacle or impediment. **4.** device or part of a device that serves to check or control movement or action in a mechanism. **5.** punctuation mark. **6.** *Photography.* aperture of a camera lens. **7.** *Music.* **a.** graduated set of organ pipes operated by one lever. **b.** lever operating such a set of pipes. **c.** any mechanical part or aid used to stop a string or finger hole. **8.** *Phonetics.* **a.** complete stopping of the outgoing breath stream, followed by its sudden release. **b.** consonant formed by such a stopping, as *p, t, k, b,* or *d;* plosive. **9. to put a stop to.** to cause to stop; end. [Old English *-stoppian* (found only in the compound *forstoppian* to stop up, close), from Late Latin *stuppāre* to stop up with tow, cram, from Latin *stūppa* tow', from Greek *styppē.*]
Syn. *v.i.* **1. Stop, cease, desist** mean to come to an end. **Stop** is the most general word, suggesting an abrupt or complete conclusion: *I hope the rain stops soon.* **Cease** is the more formal word, often used in an official or military context: *Custom officials announced that illegal drug traffic across the border had ceased.* **Desist** is also a formal word that implies a temporary end or suspension, esp. of some repeated action or effort, often as a result of restraint or futility: *He desisted from making any more requests for the time being.*

stop·cock (stop'kok') *n.* valve for controlling the flow of a liquid or gas.

stope (stŌp) *n.* excavation from which ore has been removed in a series of steps after shafts have been sunk. [Possibly from Low German *stope* literally, step of a building.]

stop·gap (stop'gap') *n.* something devised or used to supply a need temporarily; makeshift.

stop·light (stop'līt') *n.* **1.** traffic light. **2.** light on the rear end of a vehicle that lights up when the brakes are applied.

stop·o·ver (stop'ō'vər) *n.* brief visit or stay, esp. overnight, at a place during the course of a journey. Also, **stop'off'.**

stop·page (stop'ij) *n.* act or instance of stopping; being stopped.

stop·per (stop'ər) *n.* **1.** something, as a cork or plug, used to close or stop up an opening in a receptacle or vessel. **2.** one who or that which stops or arrests the movement, action, or progress of something. —*v.t.* to close up with a stopper.

stop·ple (stop'əl) *n.* stopper. —*v.t.,* **-pled, -pling.** to close with a stopper. [Probably from STOP.]

stop·watch (stop'woch') *n.* watch having a button that can be pressed to stop the hand or hands instantly, used for making very precise timings of races and contests.

stor·age (stor'ij) *n.* **1.** act of storing goods or other items, as in a warehouse. **2.** state of being stored. **3.** place for storing goods or other items. **4.** charge for storing, as in a warehouse. **5.** component in an electronic computer in which information is stored.

storage battery, battery that produces an electric current by a chemical reaction and can be recharged by an electric current.

sto·rax (stor'aks) *n.* **1.** any of several trees or shrubs, genus *Styrax,* that produce a fragrant resin used in perfume. **2.** fragrant resin obtained from any of those trees. [Late Latin *storax,* form of Latin *styrax.* See STYRENE.]

store (stor) *n.* **1.** place or establishment in which a variety of goods are kept for sale: *a grocery store, a hardware store, a clothing store.* **2.** quantity of something laid up or held in reserve for future use: *a store of weapons, a store of energy.* **3. stores.** supplies, as of food or equipment. **4.** place where things are put for future use or safekeeping; storehouse. **5. in store.** in reserve; forthcoming: *There's a surprise in store for you when you get home.* **6. to set store by.** to regard; value; esteem: *The doctor sets little store by those quack cures.* —*v.t.,* **stored, stor·ing. 1.** to put away or hold in reserve for future use: *The squirrel is storing nuts for the winter.* **2.** to put in a warehouse or other place for safekeeping. **3.** to provide or furnish; supply. [Old French *estor* provision, from *estorer* to establish, restore, going back to Latin *instaurāre* to construct, restore.] —**Syn.** *n.* **2.** see **stock.**

store·house (stor'hous') *n.* **1.** place or building where things are stored. **2.** abundant supply or source: *My history teacher was a storehouse of information.*

store·keep·er (stor'kē'pər) *n.* **1.** one who owns or runs a retail store. **2.** one who is in charge of receiving and distributing stores or supplies, as on a ship.

store·room (stor'rŌŌm', -room') *n.* room in which stores are kept.

sto·rey (stor'ē) *pl.,* **-reys.** *n.* story².

sto·ried¹ (stor'ēd) *adj.* **1.** celebrated or recorded in story, history, or legend. **2.** ornamented with designs representing scenes from history or legend. [STORY¹ + -ED².]

sto·ried² (stor'ēd) *adj.* having or divided into stories or floors. ▲ usually used in combination: *a six-storied building.* [STORY² + -ED².]

stork (stork) *pl.,* **storks** or **stork.** *n.* any of various long-legged wading birds, family Ciconiidae, having a long neck, a large, strong bill, and, typically, black, white, and gray plumage. Height: 3–6 feet. [Old English *storc.*]

storm (storm) *n.* **1.** any disturbed state of the atmosphere, usually accompanied by strong winds and some form of precipitation, as rain or snow. **2.** any wind whose speed is from sixty-four to seventy-two miles per hour on the Beaufort scale. **3.** sudden or violent outburst, as of emotion or excitement: *a storm of tears.* **4.** violent disturbance or upheaval, as in political, civil, or domestic affairs: *The scandal caused a storm in parliament, resulting in the prime minister's resignation.* **5.** sudden, violent attack, esp. on a fortified position: *The enemy took the hill by storm.* **6.** heavy discharge or shower of objects, as missiles. —*v.i.* **1.** to blow with great force; rain, snow, sleet, hail, or otherwise precipitate heavily: *It stormed all day Friday.* **2.** to move or rush violently or angrily: *He stormed into the house.* **3.** to be extremely angry; rage. —*v.t.* **1.** to make a sudden, violent attack on; take or attempt to take by storm: *The rebels stormed the gates of the palace.* [Old English *storm* tempest, disturbance, tumult, violent attack.]

Stork

storm·bound (storm'bound') *adj.* isolated, delayed, or confined by the effects of a storm.

storm cellar, underground shelter for use during cyclones, tornadoes, or the like.

storm center 1. center of a cyclonic storm, an area of low atmospheric pressure and relative calm. **2.** focal point or center of trouble, commotion, or controversy.

storm door, additional door outside of an ordinary door, used for protection against storms or other severe weather.

storm petrel, any of various small petrels, family Hydrobatidae, usually having black or brownish plumage and white markings, whose presence, according to superstition, indicates an approaching storm. Also, **stormy petrel, Mother Carey's chicken.**

storm trooper, member of a military organization in Nazi Germany noted for terrorism and brutality. Also, **brown shirt.**

storm window, additional window outside of an ordinary window, used for protection against storms or other severe weather.

storm·y (stor'mē) **storm·i·er, storm·i·est.** *adj.* **1.** affected by, characterized by, or subject to storms: *stormy weather, stormy seas.* **2.** characterized by violent or intense emotion or activity: *a stormy life, a stormy session of Congress.* —**storm'i·ly,** *adv.* —**storm'i·ness,** *n.*

sto·ry¹ (stor'ē) *pl.,* **-ries.** *n.* **1.** narrative or recital of an event or series of events that have happened or are alleged to have happened. **2.** narrative, often fictional, intended to entertain the reader or hearer. **3.** account, allegation, or statement of the facts of a matter or case: *According to his story, you started the argument.* **4.** short story. **5.** joke; anecdote. **6.** *U.S.* news article, as in a newspaper. **8.** material for such an article. **7.** succession or order of events and incidents in a play, novel, or the like. **8.** romantic or traditional legend or history: *The king lives on in song and story.* **9.** *Informal.* falsehood; lie. [Anglo-Norman *storie* history, tale, from Latin *historia* narrative of past events, tale,

at; āpe; cär; end; mē; it; īce; hot; ōld; fôrk; wood; fŌŌl; oil; out; up; ūse; turn; sing; thin; **this**; zh in treasure; ə in ago, taken, pencil, lemon, circus.

from Greek *historia* inquiry, information, account. Doublet of HIS-TORY.] —**Syn.** 3. see **account.**

sto·ry² (stôr′ē) *pl.,* -**ries.** *also,* **sto·rey.** *n.* 1. one of the horizontal structural divisions of a building, comprising the area between two successive floors. 2. set of rooms on the same floor level of a building. 3. any of a series of horizontal divisions, stages, or levels. [Possibly from Medieval Latin *historia* picture, section of a building decorated with pictures, story of a building, from Latin *historia* narrative of past events. See STORY.] —**Syn.** 1. see **floor.**

sto·ry·book (stôr′ē book′) *n.* book containing a story or stories, esp. for children. —*adj.* occurring in or resembling the style of a storybook; romantic: *a storybook marriage.*

sto·ry·tell·er (stôr′ē tel′ər) *n.* 1. one who tells or writes stories. 2. *Informal.* liar; fibber. —**sto′ry·tell′ing,** *adj., n.*

stoup (stoop) *n.* 1. basin containing holy water at or near the entrance of a church. 2. *Archaic.* drinking vessel, as a cup, flagon, or tankard. [Old Norse *staup* cup.]

stout (stout) *adj.* 1. having a thick, bulky figure; thickset; fat. 2. valiant; brave; courageous. 3. having strength and vigor; physically strong; robust: *stout laborers.* 4. solid in structure, substance, or material: *a stout ship, a stout meal.* —*n.* strong, very dark, heavy ale. [Old French *estout* bold, fierce, insolent; of Germanic origin.] —**stout′ly,** *adv.* —**stout′ness,** *n.* —**Syn.** *adj.* 1. see **fat.**

stout-heart·ed (stout′här′tid) *adj.* valiant; brave; courageous. —**stout′-heart′ed·ly,** *adv.* —**stout′-heart′ed·ness,** *n.*

stove¹ (stōv) *n.* 1. kitchen appliance that uses gas or electricity and consists of burners, an oven, and sometimes a storage compartment, used for cooking. 2. any of various heating or cooking devices that uses wood, coal, gas, oil, or electricity. 3. heated room or box used for some special purpose, as a hothouse or kiln. [Middle Dutch *stove* heated chamber.]

stove² (stōv) past tense and past participle of **stave.**

stove·pipe (stōv′pīp′) *n.* 1. pipe, usually of sheet metal, used to convey smoke, fumes, and noxious gases from a stove. 2. *Informal.* tall silk hat.

stow (stō) *v.t.* 1. to put or pack away, esp. in a neat, compact manner. 2. to fill by packing; load. 3. (of a space or receptacle) to have room or space for; accommodate; hold. 4. *Slang.* to stop; cease. —*v.i.* **to stow away,** to be a stowaway. [Middle English *stowen* to place, from *stowe* a place, from Old English *stōw.*]

stow·age (stō′ij) *n.* 1. act or manner of stowing; being stowed. 2. room or space for stowing goods or other items. 3. that which is stowed or to be stowed. 4. charge for stowing goods.

stow·a·way (stō′ə wā′) *n.* one who conceals himself on a ship or airplane, esp. in order to obtain free passage.

Stowe, Harriet Bee·cher (stō; bē′chər) 1811–96, U.S. author.

St. Paul, capital of Minnesota, in the southeastern part of the state, on the Mississippi opposite Minneapolis. Pop. (1970), 309,980.

St. Pe·ters·burg (pē′tərz burg′) 1. see **Leningrad.** 2. city in west-central Florida on the Gulf of Mexico. Pop. (1970), 216,232.

str. 1. steamer. 2. strait.

stra·bis·mus (strə biz′məs) *n.* abnormality of vision in which both eyes cannot be focused on the same point at the same time. [Modern Latin *strabismus,* from Greek *strabismos* squinting.] —**stra·bis′mal, stra·bis′mic,** *adj.*

Stra·bo (strā′bō) c.63 B.C.–A.D. c.21, Greek geographer and historian.

strad·dle (strad′əl) -**dled, -dling.** *v.t.* 1. to sit, stand, or walk with one leg on each side of: *to straddle a fence, to straddle a horse.* 2. to appear to favor both sides of (an issue). 3. to spread (the legs) wide apart. —*v.i.* 1. to sit, stand, or walk with the legs wide apart. 2. to appear to favor both sides of an issue. 3. (of the legs) to be wide apart. —*n.* 1. act of straddling. 2. distance between the two legs of one who straddles. [STRIDE + -LE.] —**strad′dler,** *n.*

Strad·i·var·i, An·to·nio (strad′ə vär′ē, -vär′ē; än tō′nyō) c.1644–1737, Italian violin maker.

Strad·i·var·i·us (strad′ə vär′ē əs) *n.* violin, viola, or cello made by Stradivari.

strafe (strāf) **strafed, straf·ing** *v.t.* to attack (troops, ships, or the like) with machine-gun or rocket fire from low-flying aircraft. —*v.i.* to attack with machine-gun or rocket fire from low-flying aircraft. [From the German expression (used in World War I) *Gott strafe England* God punish England.] —**straf′er,** *n.*

strag·gle (strag′əl) -**gled, -gling.** *v.i.* 1. to wander or move about in an irregular, rambling manner. 2. to stray from or lag behind the main course or body. [Of uncertain origin.] —**strag′gler,** *n.*

strag·gly (strag′lē) -**gli·er, -gli·est.** *adj.* spread out or scattered in an irregular, rambling manner.

straight (strāt) *adj.* 1. proceeding in the same direction without curve, bend, or angularity: *a straight line.* 2. not curly, wavy, or kinky: *straight hair.* 3. not crooked or stooping; erect: *to stand with a straight back.*

4. in proper arrangement, order, or condition: *She tried to keep her room straight. I couldn't keep the twins' names straight.* 5. frank; candid: *a straight answer.* 6. without interruption; unbroken; continuous: *She spoke for three hours straight.* 7. marked by adherence to truth, fairness, and honesty; upright. 8. strictly adhering to or supporting the platform, policy, and candidates of a particular political party: *He voted a straight Democratic ticket.* 9. not mixed, altered, or diluted, as an alcoholic liquor. —*adv.* 1. in a straight line or course: *Go straight down Main Street.* 2. all the way to the end; continuously. 3. without delay; immediately: *I went straight home after the movie.* 4. **straight off** (or **away**). without delay; immediately. 5. **to go straight.** to reform after having engaged in criminal activities. —*n.* 1. something straight, as a line or part. 2. straight part of a race course between the last turn and the finish line. 3. *Poker.* hand consisting of five cards in sequence. [Middle English *streiht* not crooked, direct, past participle of *strecchen* to extend, from Old English *streccan.*] —**straight′ly,** *adv.* —**straight′ness,** *n.*

straight angle, angle of 180 degrees.

straight-arm (strāt′ärm′) *v.t. Football.* to ward off (a potential tackler) by holding one's arm out straight.

straight·a·way (strāt′ə wā′) *adv.* at once; immediately. —*adj.* extending in a straight line or course. —*n.* straight course or part, esp. of a race course.

straight·edge (strāt′ej′) *n.* ruler (def. 2).

straight·en (strāt′ən) *v.t., v.i.* 1. to make or become straight (often with *up* or *out*). 2. to restore or be restored to the proper order, arrangement, or condition (usually with *up* or *out*). 3. to make or become honest or respectable (usually with *out*). —**straight′en·er,** *n.*

straight face, face that shows or betrays no emotion.

straight-faced (strāt′fāst′) *adj.* showing no emotion.

straight flush, hand in poker consisting of a sequence of five cards in the same suit.

straight·for·ward (strāt′fôr′wərd) *adj.* 1. honest; frank; sincere. 2. proceeding or directed straight ahead. —*adv. also,* **straight′-for′wards.** in a straightforward manner or course. —**straight′for′-ward·ly,** *adv.* —**straight′for′ward·ness,** *n.*

straight jacket, strait jacket.

straight man, entertainer who assists a comedian, as by feeding him lines or serving as the butt of his jokes.

straight·way (strāt′wā′) *adv.* at once; immediately.

strain¹ (strān) *v.t.* 1. to draw or pull tight; stretch: *The weight of the cargo strained the ropes.* 2. to injure, weaken, or impair by excessive stretching or overexertion: *to strain a muscle.* 3. to exert to the utmost: *She strained her voice to be heard above the noise of the engine.* 4. to stretch beyond proper, normal, or legitimate limits: *The judge strained the law when passing sentence.* 5.a. to press or pour through a strainer, sieve, or other filtering device. b. to separate or remove by filtration. 6. to change (a material body) in size or shape by the application of stress. —*v.i.* 1. to make continuous and violent effort to do or achieve something; exert oneself to the utmost: *She strained to reach her goal.* 2. to pull forcibly (with *at*): *The horse strained at the rope.* 3. to be subjected to great pressure or force: *The awning strained under the heavy snow.* 4. to admit of being strained, as a liquid. —*n.* 1. extreme physical force or pressure. 2. injury or impairment caused by excessive stretching or overexertion. 3. extreme mental or emotional pressure or tension: *He broke under the strain of combat.* 4. act of straining; being strained. 5. change in the size and shape of a material body resulting from the application of stress. [Old French *estraindre* to grip, wring, press tightly, from Latin *stringere* to draw tight.] —**Syn.** 3. see **stress.**

strain² (strān) *n.* 1.a. line of descent; ancestry; stock. b. descendants of a common ancestor collectively. 2. group of animals or plants having distinguishing characteristics and forming a small part or subdivision of a larger group. 3. inherited or characteristic quality or tendency: *a strain of nobility.* 4. manner, style, or tone of expression. 5. *also,* **strains.** musical passage; tune. [Old English *strēon* gain, product.]

strain·er (strā′nər) *n.* 1. any of various utensils or devices, as a colander or sieve, through which liquids are passed to separate them from solids. 2. one who or that which strains.

strait (strāt) *n.* 1. narrow waterway or channel connecting two larger bodies of water. 2. *also,* **straits.** position or circumstance of difficulty, distress, or need: *to be in desperate financial straits.* —*adj. Archaic.* 1. narrow or confining. 2. righteous or strict. [Anglo-Norman *estreit* narrow, strict, from Latin *strictus* tight, severe, past participle of *stringere* to draw tight. Doublet of STRICT.]

strait·en (strāt′ən) *v.t.* 1. to cause to be in need or difficulty, esp. financially. 2. to make narrow or confining.

strait jacket *also,* **straight jacket.** jacketlike canvas garment with elongated sleeves that wrap around the body, used to confine the arms of a violent patient or prisoner.

strait-laced (strāt′lāst′) *adj.* excessively strict or rigid in morals or manners; prudish.

strake (strāk) *n.* continuous line of planking or plating extending along the side of a ship from the bow to the stern.

stra·mo·ni·um (strə mō′nē əm) *n.* drug prepared from the dried leaves and seed of the jimsonweed, used as a sedative. [Modern Latin *stramonium;* of uncertain origin.]

strand[1] (strand) *v.t., v.i.* **1.** to drive or run (a boat or ship) aground. **2.** to leave or be left in a difficult or helpless position, esp. in a strange or isolated place. —*n.* land bordering a body of water; shore or beach. [Old English *strand* land bordering a body of water.]

strand[2] (strand) *n.* **1.** one of the threads, wires, or fibers twisted together to form a rope, cord, or other line. **2.** any single thread, hair, or other stringlike structure: *a strand of spaghetti, strands of hair.* **3.** string of things joined together by twisting, twining, or threading: *a strand of pearls.* [Of uncertain origin.]

strange (strānj) **strang·er, strang·est.** *adj.* **1.** differing from the usual or ordinary; remarkable or odd: *That was a strange thing for her to do.* **2.** not previously known, seen, or experienced; unfamiliar: *That part of town is strange to me.* **3.** ill at ease; uncomfortable: *I would feel strange asking him such a favor.* **4.** unaccustomed to or inexperienced in (with *to*): *I'm strange to this work.* [Old French *estrange* foreign, from Latin *extrāneus* external, foreign, from *extrā* outside. Doublet of EXTRANEOUS.] —**strange′ly,** *adv.* —**strange′ness,** *n.*
Syn. 1. Strange, odd, peculiar mean varying markedly from what is ordinary, usual, or expected. **Strange** is applied to what is new, novel, or foreign and implies fear or curiosity: *The strange object seen last night has not yet been identified.* **Odd** is applied to what stands out as inconsistent, irregular, or otherwise unrelated to others of the same group or type, often arousing amusement or interest: *That's an odd question—I just don't know how to answer it.* **Peculiar** is applied to what is distinctive about something and therefore may not be easily categorized: *She has a peculiar way of talking.*

stran·ger (strān′jər) *n.* **1.** person with whom one is not acquainted or familiar. **2.** foreigner, outsider, or newcomer. **3.** one who is ignorant of, unacquainted with, or unaccustomed to something specified (with *to*): *He's no stranger to political intrigue.*

stran·gle (strang′gəl) **-gled, -gling.** *v.t.* **1.a.** to kill or attempt to kill by squeezing the throat to stop the breath; throttle. **b.** to suffocate or choke in any manner. **2.** to hold back; stifle: *to strangle a laugh.* **3.** to prevent or inhibit the growth, development, or functioning of: *a bill intended to strangle foreign trade.* —*v.i.* to become strangled. [Old French *estrangler* to choke, from Latin *strangulāre,* from Greek *strangalān.*] —**stran′gler,** *n.*

stran·gle·hold (strang′gəl hōld′) *n.* **1.** illegal wrestling hold that chokes an opponent. **2.** any force or influence that hinders, restricts, or stifles freedom or progress.

stran·gu·late (strang′gyə lāt′) **-lat·ed, -lat·ing.** *v.t.* **1.** to strangle. **2.** to obstruct, compress, or constrict (a bodily part) so as to prevent circulation or the passage of fluid. [Latin *strangulātus,* past participle of *strangulāre* to choke. See STRANGLE.]

stran·gu·la·tion (strang′gyə lā′shən) *n.* **1.** act of strangling; being strangled. **2.** obstruction, compression, or constriction of a bodily part so as to prevent circulation or the passage of fluid.

strap (strap) *n.* **1.** long, narrow, flexible strip of leather, cloth, or other material, often having a buckle or other fastener, for securing or holding things together or in position. **2.** loop of metal, leather, or other material, grasped by the hand and used to steady oneself in a moving vehicle. **3.** shoulder strap. **4.** narrow metal band used to fasten or hold things together or in position. **5.** strop. —*v.t.,* **strapped, strap·ping. 1.** to fasten, secure, or support with a strap. **2.** to beat with a strap. **3.** to sharpen on a strop. [Form of STROP.]

strap·hang·er (strap′hang′ər) *n.* Informal. standing passenger on a bus or subway who holds onto an overhead strap or other support.

strapped (strapt) *adj.* Informal. having little or no money; broke.

strap·ping (strap′ing) *adj.* Informal. tall and sturdy; robust: *a strapping young man.*

Stras·bourg (stras′bûrg′, sträz′boorg′) *n.* city in northeastern France, on the Rhine. Pop. (1968), 249,396.

stra·ta (strā′tə, strat′ə, strä′tə) a plural of *stratum.*

strat·a·gem (strat′ə jəm) *n.* **1.** scheme or maneuver designed to outwit, deceive, or surprise an enemy. **2.** scheme or trick used to achieve a goal or obtain an advantage. [French *stratagème,* from Latin *stratēgēma,* from Greek *stratēgēma,* from *stratēgos* general. See STRATEGY.]

stra·te·gic (strə tē′jik) *adj.* **1.** of or relating to strategy. **2.** important or essential to strategy, esp. military strategy. **3.** trained or intended to destroy the communications, industry, and transportation of an enemy in order to lessen his ability to fight. Also, **stra·te′gi·cal.** —**stra·te′gi·cal·ly,** *adv.*

strat·e·gist (strat′ə jist) *n.* one who is trained or skilled in strategy, esp. military strategy.

strat·e·gy (strat′ə jē) *pl.* **-gies.** *n.* **1.** art or science of planning and directing large-scale military operations and campaigns. Distinguished

from **tactics. 2.** skillful use of planning, as in business, politics, or social relations. **3.** plan or device designed to achieve a specific goal or advantage. [Greek *strategia* generalship, command, from *stratēgos* general, from *stratos* army + *agein* to lead.]

Strat·ford-on-A·von (strat′fərd ôn ā′vən, -av′ən, -on-) *n.* town in central England, on the Avon River, noted as the birthplace, home, and burial place of William Shakespeare. Pop. (1963 est.), 17,000. Also, **Strat′ford.**

strat·i·fi·ca·tion (strat′ə fi kā′shən) *n.* **1.** act or process of stratifying; being stratified. **2.** stratified structure or formation, as of rock.

strat·i·fy (strat′ə fī′) **-fied, -fy·ing.** *v.t.* **1.** to form or arrange in layers or strata. **2.** to divide into social groups or classes, as according to common social or economic characteristics. —*v.i.* to form strata. [French *stratifier* to arrange in layers or strata, from Medieval Latin *stratificāre* to form strata, from Latin *strātum* covering + *facere* to make.]

stra·tig·ra·phy (strə tig′rə fē) *n.* branch of earth science dealing with the formation, composition, and age of rock strata. [STRATUM + -GRAPHY.] —**strat·i·graph·ic** (strat′ə graf′ik) *adj.; also,* **strat′i·graph′i·cal,** *adj.*

stra·to·cu·mu·lus (strā′tō kū′myə ləs, strat′ō-) *pl.* **-li** (-lī′) *or* **-lus.** *n.* mass of low-lying, watery clouds spread out against the sky in a layer of puffy rolls. [STRAT(US) + CUMULUS.]

strat·o·sphere (strat′ə sfēr′) *n.* layer of the atmosphere, above the troposphere and below the mesosphere, extending from about twelve to about thirty-five miles above the earth's surface. Ozone formed in the upper part of this region protects the earth from ultraviolet radiation from the sun. [STRAT(UM) + (ATM)OSPHERE.] —**strat·o·spher·ic** (strat′ə sfer′ik) *adj.; also,* **strat′o·spher′i·cal,** *adj.*

stra·tum (strā′təm, strat′əm, strä′təm) *pl.* **stra·ta** *or* **stra·tums.** *n.* **1.** horizontal layer of material, esp. one of several parallel layers placed or lying one on top of the other. **2.** social group or class distinguished by certain common social or economic characteristics. **3.** *Geology.* **a.** rock formation consisting of a number of layers of rock of approximately the same material. **b.** single layer of sedimentary rock. [Modern Latin *stratum,* from Latin *strātum* covering; literally, something spread out, from *sternere* to spread out.]

stra·tus (strā′təs, strat′əs) *pl.* **stra·ti** (strā′tī, strat′ī) *or* **stra·tus.** *n.* low-lying, grayish, watery cloud having a uniform horizontal base and a foglike appearance. [Modern Latin *stratus,* from Latin *strātus,* past participle of *sternere* to spread out.]

Strauss (strous, shtrous) **1.** Jo·hann (yō′hän). 1804–49, Austrian composer. **2.** Johann. 1825–99, his son; Austrian composer. **3.** Rich·ard (riKH′ärt, riKH′ärt). 1864–1949, German composer.

Stra·vin·sky, I·gor Feo·do·ro·vich (strə vin′skē; ē′gôr fyô′də rō′vich) 1882–1971, Russian composer.

straw (strô) *n.* **1.** long slender tube, as of paper or plastic, used for sucking up a liquid. **2.** dry stalks or stems of any of various grains, as rye, oats, wheat, or barley, after they have been threshed. Straw is used esp. as bedding for livestock and for making hats, baskets, and other woven products. **3.** a single one of such stalks or stems. **4.** something of little value or significance; trifle. **5. to clutch** (or **catch** or **grasp**) **at a straw** (or **straws**). to use any means that offers even the slightest possibility of being helpful. —*adj.* **1.** made of straw: *a straw hat.* **2.** of or resembling straw. **3.** of little value or significance; trifling. **4.** yellowish in color. [Old English *strēaw* stalks of certain grains.]

straw·ber·ry (strô′ber′ē) *pl.* **-ries.** *n.* **1.** edible, sweet, juicy red fruit of any of a group of plants, genus *Fragaria,* of the rose family. **2.** low-growing plant bearing this fruit, having many slender stalks and grown in temperate regions of the world.

Strawberries

strawberry blond *also,* **strawberry blonde.** person having reddish-blond hair.

straw·board (strô′bôrd′) *n.* coarse cardboard made of straw, used for boxes, book covers, and the like.

straw boss *Informal.* assistant foreman, esp. of a work crew.

straw man 1. bundle of straw made to resemble the figure of a man. **2.** weak argument deliberately set up by a person so that he may easily refute it. **3.** one who is weak or unimportant. **4.** person who disguises the activities of another, esp. one who serves as a front in a fraudulent activity.

straw poll, unofficial poll taken to determine the trend of public opinion, as on a particular issue or political candidate. Also, **straw vote.**

stray (strā) *v.i.* **1.** to wander from a given course or group or beyond proper limits. **2.** to wander or move about idly or without direction; rove. **3.** to turn from a course that is considered morally right or good; err. **4.** to digress or become easily distracted from the matter at hand: *His thoughts strayed.* —*adj.* **1.** wandering, lost, or homeless: *a stray*

at; āpe; cär; end; mē; it; īce; hot; ōld; fôrk; wood; fōōl; oil; out; up; ūse; turn; sing; thin; this; zh in treasure; ə in ago, taken, pencil, lemon, circus.

sheep. **2.** found or occurring randomly or occasionally; scattered or isolated: *There were a few stray hairs on her coat.* **3.** deviating from the proper or intended course: *An innocent bystander was hit by a stray bullet.* —*n.* lost or homeless animal or person. [Old French *estraier* to rove, go astray, going back to Latin *extrā* beyond + *vagārī* to wander.]

streak (strēk) *n.* **1.** long, thin irregularly shaped mark, line, or band differing in color or texture from the material or surface of which it forms a part: *to have streaks of gray in one's hair.* **2.** slight trace or tendency: *a streak of genius, a streak of madness.* **3.** temporary run; brief period: *a streak of bad luck.* **4.** unbroken series: *a winning streak of ten consecutive games.* —*v.t.* to mark with a streak or streaks; form streaks on or in. —*v.i.* **1.** to form a streak or streaks. **2.** to become streaked. **3.** to move, run, or go at great speed. [Old English *strica* mark, line[1].]

streak·y (strē'kē) **streak·i·er, streak·i·est.** *adj.* **1.** marked with, characterized by, or occurring in streaks. **2.** of variable quality or character; inconsistent: *a streaky hockey player.* —**streak'i·ly,** *adv.* —**streak'i·ness,** *n.*

stream (strēm) *n.* **1.** body of running water, esp. a small river. **2.** force, volume, or direction of the current in a body of water. **3.** steady flow or current of any fluid: *a stream of air.* **4.** any continuous, uninterrupted movement, emission, or succession: *a stream of people, a stream of words.* **5.** ray or beam of light. —*v.i.* **1.** to flow or issue in a stream: *Tears streamed down her face. Light streamed into the room when I parted the curtains.* **2.** to pour forth or emit a stream (often with *with*): *The runner came off the track streaming with sweat.* **3.** to move along steadily or smoothly; flow: *The audience streamed out of the auditorium.* **4.** to wave, float, or extend outward: *The banners streamed in the wind.* **5.** to hang or fall loosely: *Her hair streamed over her shoulders.* —*v.t.* to pour out, discharge, or emit in a stream. [Old English *strēam* current, flowing water, river.]

stream·er (strē'mər) *n.* **1.** long, narrow flag or banner. **2.** any long, narrow strip of material. **3.** newspaper headline that extends across the entire page.

stream·let (strēm'lit) *n.* little stream.

stream·line (strēm'līn') **-lined, -lin·ing.** *v.t.* **1.** to design or construct so that there is the least possible resistance to air or water: *to streamline an automobile.* **2.** to make more modern or efficient: *to streamline the administration of government.* —*adj.* streamlined.

stream·lined (strēm'līnd') *adj.* **1.** designed or constructed so as to offer the least possible resistance to air or water. **2.** efficient and modern. **3.** neat, trim, and having few curves.

stream of consciousness 1. the conscious experience of an individual regarded as a series of events or experiences flowing continuously onward, rather than as separate, disconnected occurrences. **2.** literary device that presents the dramatic action of a novel through the spontaneous flow of the thoughts, feelings, and emotions of a character.

street (strēt) *n.* **1.** public way in a city or town, usually with sidewalks and buildings on one or both sides: *a tree-lined street, a street of shops.* **2.** that part of such a roadway for vehicles, excluding the sidewalks and buildings: *Be careful crossing the street.* **3.** people who live, work or gather in a street: *The whole street went to the meeting.* [Old English *strēt* paved way, road, from Late Latin *strāta (via)* paved (way), from Latin *sternere* to spread out, pave.]

street Arab, homeless child that wanders about the streets.

street·car (strēt'kär') *n.* public passenger vehicle that operates on rails in city streets by electricity. Also, **trol'ley, trolley car.**

strength (strengkth, strength) *n.* **1.** state or quality of being strong; physical power or energy: *He lifted heavy weights to build up his strength.* **2.** power to sustain or resist attack, force, strain, or stress without breaking or yielding: *to test the strength of a rope.* **3.** power or ability to act, command, enforce obedience, or make decisions: *His strength as a general lay in his ability to gain the respect of his men.* **4.** firmness of mind, character, will, or purpose; moral courage: *It took great strength to resist the pressure of the authorities.* **5.** legal, moral, or intellectual power, influence, or effectiveness: *the strength of an argument.* **6.** vigor or vehemence, as of feeling or conviction: *the strength of his devotion.* **7.** degree of intensity, as of light, sound, or color: *the strength of an electric current.* **8.** degree of concentration or effectiveness: *the strength of a wine, the differing strengths of a drug.* **9.** concentration of available force or backing: *The strength of the party is among the liberal and urban elements of the nation.* **10.** military power derived as from numbers, equipment, or resources. **11.** one who or that which strengthens; source of power or force. **12. on the strength of.** based on or depending on: *He was convicted on the strength of the witness's evidence.* [Old English *strengthu* quality of being strong, power.]

strength·en (strengk'thən, streng'-) *v.t., v.i.* to make or become strong or stronger. —**strength'en·er,** *n.*

stren·u·ous (stren'ū əs) *adj.* **1.** requiring or characterized by great

effort or exertion: *a strenuous task.* **2.** very active or ardent; vigorous; energetic: *strenuous opposition.* [Latin *strēnuus* vigorous, active.] —**stren'u·ous·ly,** *adv.* —**stren'u·ous·ness,** *n.*

strep throat (strep) serious infection of the throat caused by a streptococcus and characterized by fever and the presence of pus in the throat.

strep·to·coc·cal (strep'tə kok'əl) *adj.* of, relating to, or caused by streptococci. Also, **strep·to·coc·cic** (strep'tə kok'sik).

strep·to·coc·cus (strep'tə kok'əs) *pl.* **-coc·ci** (-kok'sī). *n.* any of a genus of spherical bacteria that multiply by dividing in one direction only, forming chains. Such diseases as scarlet fever, rheumatic fever, and strep throat are caused by various species of streptococcus. [Modern Latin *streptococcus,* from Greek *streptos* twisted chain + *kokkos* berry, seed.]

strep·to·my·cin (strep'tō mī'sin) *n.* powerful antibiotic prepared from a type of fungus, effective against tuberculosis, typhoid fever, certain types of meningitis, and other bacterial infections. [Greek *streptos* twisted + *mykēs* fungus + -IN[1].]

stress (stres) *n.* **1.a.** mental or emotional tension or pressure. **b.** problem or situation causing this; constraining influence. **2.** special significance, emphasis, or importance attached to something (with *on* or *upon*): *Father always put a lot of stress on good table manners.* **3.** relative emphasis given to a particular sound, syllable, or word in speech. In the word *employ,* the stress is on the second syllable. **4.** relative emphasis given to a particular word or syllable marking the rhythm of verse, usually occurring at fixed intervals. **5.** *Music.* emphasis given to certain notes or chords. **6.** *Physics.* **a.** externally applied force or pressure that tends to strain or deform a material body. **b.** internal resistance of a material body to such force or pressure. **c.** intensity of such force or pressure, usually measured in pounds per square inch. —*v.t.* **1.** to place special significance, emphasis, or importance on: *The magazine article stressed the need for conservation of natural resources.* **2.** to pronounce (a syllable, word, or words) with a particular stress. **3.** to subject (a material body) to stress. [Partly shortened from DISTRESS; partly from Old French *estrece* narrowness, oppression, going back to Latin *strictus.* past participle of *stringere* to draw tight.]

Syn. *n.* **1.b. Stress, pressure, strain[1]** refer to the factor producing a condition of unrest or disturbance. **Stress** suggests a specific or clearly defined problem or adverse circumstance: *He was under great financial stress.* **Pressure** implies a less vague and more pervasive influence that cannot be easily resolved or withstood: *The pressure to conform was evident in everything the group did.* **Strain** suggests that the intense effort and exertion required in dealing with a problem is itself damaging and destructive: *The strain of working overtime every night sent him to bed.* **2.** see **emphasis.**

stretch (strech) *v.t.* **1.** to straighten or spread out to full length or width (often with *out*): *He stretched his legs out into the aisle.* **2.** to hold out; put forth (often with *out*): *He stretched his hand out to shake mine.* **3.** to cause to extend from one place to another or across a given area: *to stretch a clothesline across a yard.* **4.** to draw or pull tight: *to stretch a canvas over a frame.* **5.** to strain; pull: *to stretch a muscle.* **6.** to extend beyond proper, natural, or legitimate limits: *to stretch a point in an argument, to stretch the rules.* **7.** to widen, lengthen, or pull out of shape by force: *to stretch a sweater.* **8.** to extend in time; prolong (often with *out*): *to stretch a visit out for two weeks.* **9.** to use or exert to the utmost. —*v.i.* **1.** to lie down and extend the body to full length (often with *out*): *He stretched out on the couch.* **2.** to straighten or spread out one's body or limbs to full length. **3.** to extend from one place to another or across a given area: *The road stretches for another thirty miles.* **4.** to become widened, lengthened, or pulled out of shape. **5.** to extend over a period of time: *The experiment stretched over a period of two years.* —*n.* **1.** unbroken space or area: *We flew over a stretch of desert.* **2.** unbroken period of time: *She was out of the country for a stretch of two years.* **3.** act of stretching; being stretched. **4.** straight part of a race course, esp. the part between the last turn and the finish line. **5.** *Informal.* last part of any contest or activity: *The election campaign is now coming into the stretch.* **6.** *Informal.* period or term of imprisonment. —*adj.* made of material having elastic qualities: *stretch gloves, stretch pants.* [Old English *streccan* to extend.]

stretch·er (strech'ər) *n.* **1.** bedlike structure consisting of a piece of canvas or similar material stretched across a frame, used for carrying a sick, injured, or dead person. **2.** any of various devices used to widen, lengthen, or shape a material or garment, as the wooden frame on which an artist's canvas is spread. **3.** one who or that which stretches.

strew (strōō) **strewed, strewed** *or* **strewn, strew·ing.** *v.t.* **1.** to spread or throw about at random or in various places: *to strew hay on a barn floor.* **2.** to cover with something spread or thrown about in this way: *The floor was strewed with scraps of paper and other litter.* **3.** to be scattered over (a surface): *Confetti strewed the floor.* [Old English *strēowian* to scatter.]

at; āpe; cär; end; mē; it; īce; hot; ōld; fôrk; wood; fōōl; oil; out; up; ūse; turn; sing; thin; this; zh in treasure; ə in ago, taken, pencil, lemon, circus.

987

stri·a (strī′ə) pl., **stri·ae** (strī′ē). n. narrow groove, band, streak, or stripe of distinctive color, texture, or structure, esp. one of a number that are parallel in arrangement. [Latin *stria* furrow, channel, groove.]

stri·at·ed (strī′ā′tid) adj. marked or characterized by striae. Also, **stri′ate.**

striated muscle. muscle that has fibers consisting of alternate light and dark bands, and that can be controlled at will. All the muscles attached to the skeleton are striated muscles.

stri·a·tion (strī ā′shən) n. 1. state or condition of being striated: *the striation of muscle.* 2. one of a set or system of striae; stria.

strick·en (strik′ən) v. a past participle of **strike.** —adj. 1. strongly affected or overwhelmed, as by sorrow, disease, or catastrophe. 2. struck or wounded: *a stricken deer.*

Striae of a column

strict (strikt) adj. 1. demanding or observing rigid conformity to rules or regulations: *a strict disciplinarian.* 2. rigorously or closely maintained, enforced, or adhered to: *strict visiting hours, to keep a strict watch on the supplies.* 3. based on or following exactly; literal: *a strict interpretation of the rules.* 4. complete; absolute: *He told me the plan in strict confidence.* [Latin *strictus* tight, severe, past participle of *stringere* to draw tight. Doublet of STRAIT.] —**strict′ly,** adv. —**strict′ness,** n.

stric·ture (strik′chər) n. 1. unfavorable or severe criticism; censure. 2. that which limits, confines, or restrains. 3. abnormal contraction or narrowing of some duct or tube of the body. [Latin *strictūra* contraction, pressure.]

stride (strīd) **strode, strid·den** (strid′ən), **strid·ing.** v.i. 1. to walk with long, sweeping steps, esp. in a vigorous or imposing manner. 2. to take a single long step, as in passing over or across an obstacle. —v.t. 1. to straddle; bestride. 2. to move over, along, or through with long, sweeping steps. —n. 1. long sweeping step or steps. 2. distance covered by such a step or steps. 3. forward progressive movement of an animal, esp. a horse, completed when all the feet are returned to the same relative positions that they occupied at the beginning. 4. *usually,* **strides.** advancement, progress, or improvement. 5. **to take in (one's) stride.** to adjust to, accept, or deal with without undue difficulty, effort, or hesitation. 6. **to hit one's stride.** to reach one's normal speed or level of activity. [Old English *strīdan* to straddle.]

stri·dent (strīd′ənt) adj. making or having a harsh, shrill, grating sound. [Latin *strīdēns,* present participle of *strīdēre* to make a harsh sound.] —**stri′dence, stri′den·cy,** n. —**stri′dent·ly,** adv.

strid·u·late (strij′ə lāt′) **-lat·ed, -lat·ing.** v.i. to make a harsh, shrill, grating sound, as a cricket or grasshopper does by rubbing certain parts of the body together. [Latin *strīdulus* creaking, rattling + -ATE¹.] —**strid′u·la′tion,** n.

strife (strīf) n. 1. bitter dissension, discord, or conflict. 2. contest or struggle between rivals to gain superiority: *armed strife.* [Old French *estrif* debate, contention; of uncertain origin.]

strike (strīk) **struck, struck** or **strick·en, strik·ing.** v.t. 1. to give a physical blow to: *The soldier was court-martialed for striking an officer.* 2. to deal; inflict: *to strike a blow.* 3. to come against forcibly; meet with physical impact: *The car skidded and struck a tree.* 4. to cause to make forceful contact with; hit: *She struck her head against the shelf when she fell.* 5.a. to cause to ignite by friction: *to strike a match.* b. to produce (a fire, spark, or light) by friction. 6. to erase, cancel, or otherwise remove (often with *off, from,* or *out*): *His testimony was struck from the record.* 7. to attack; assault: *Our troops struck the enemy camp at dawn.* 8. to give the impression of being; appear to: *She struck me as being very spoiled.* 9. to come into the mind of; occur to: *The solution struck me immediately.* 10. to assume; to strike a pose. 11. to give or announce by ringing or otherwise sounding: *The clock struck the hour.* 12. to come upon suddenly or unexpectedly; discover; find: *to strike oil.* 13. to cause to be overwhelmed or seized with (with *with*): *Rebecca's appearance struck Amelia with terror* (Thackeray, 1848). 14. to cause (a feeling or emotion) to penetrate deeply: *His sudden appearance struck terror into their hearts.* 15. to impress strongly or appeal to: *The idea struck my fancy.* 16. to participate in a work stoppage against (an industry, employer, factory, or other source of employment) in order to receive certain demands, as higher pay or better working conditions. 17. to arrive at or determine, esp. by computation: *to strike a balance.* 18. to make or conclude: *to strike a bargain.* 19. to come to; reach: *The strains of music struck his ears.* 20. to fall upon: *Sunlight struck the leaves.* 21. to bring suddenly and completely into some specified state: *to be struck dumb.* 22. to make or form by pressing or stamping: *to strike coins.* 23. to lower or take down, as a sail or flag: *The ship struck its colors.* 24. **to strike it rich.** to come into sudden wealth or success. 25. **to strike out.** *Baseball.* to put out (a batter) by a strikeout. —v.i. 1. to deal or aim a blow or blows. 2. to come into forcible contact; hit. 3. to make an attack: *We will strike at dawn.* 4. to participate in a work stoppage in order to receive certain demands: *There is no right*

to strike against the public safety (Coolidge, 1919). 5. to make a sound, as by ringing: *The chimes struck at midnight.* 6. to be announced, as by ringing: *The hour struck.* 7. (of fish) to seize the bait. 8. **to strike out. a.** to begin, as an undertaking or journey: *We struck out for California.* **b.** *Baseball.* to be put out by a strikeout. **c.** *Informal.* to be a failure in some undertaking. 9. **to strike up.** to start; begin: *to strike up a conversation.* —n. 1. act or instance of striking; blow. 2. work stoppage in order to receive certain demands, as higher pay or better working conditions. 3. sudden or unexpected discovery, as of a rich vein of ore: *a gold strike.* 4. unexpected or sudden stroke of success or good luck. 5. *Baseball.* **a.** pitched ball that a batter swings at and misses. **b.** pitched ball that is not swung at but is judged by the umpire to be within the strike zone. **c.** foul bunt, or a foul tip that is not caught by the catcher. **d.** any other foul ball not caught by a fielder, unless the batter already has two strikes against him. 6. *Bowling.* **a.** act or instance of knocking down all the pins with the first ball. **b.** score made in this way. 7. a seizing of the bait by a fish. 8. **to have two strikes against one.** *Informal.* to be at a great disadvantage because of an existing handicap or liability. [Old English *strīcan* to go, move, rub, stroke, smooth.]

strike·break·er (strīk′brā′kər) n. one who continues to work during a strike, takes the place of a worker on strike, or supplies workers to take the place of strikers. —**strike′break′ing,** n.

strike·out (strīk′out′) n. *Baseball.* out resulting from three strikes charged against a batter.

strik·er (strī′kər) n. 1. worker who participates in a strike. 2. one who or that which strikes. 3. enlisted man in the U.S. Navy training for a petty officer's rating.

strike zone *Baseball.* area directly over home plate and between the batter's knees and armpits, through which a pitched ball must pass in order to be judged a strike if it is not swung at.

strik·ing (strī′king) adj. making a vivid impression on the mind or senses; impressive: *There was a striking contrast between the two paintings.* —**strik′ing·ly,** adv. —**strik′ing·ness,** n.

Strind·berg, Jo·han Au·gust (strind′burg, strin′-; ü′hän ou′goost) 1849–1912, Swedish playwright and novelist.

string (string) n. 1. slender line consisting of twisted or intertwined strands of fiber, wire, or similar material. 2. anything resembling this, as a strip of cloth used for tying parts together: *the strings of an apron.* 3. set or number of things joined together by twisting, twining, or arranging on a string: *a string of pearls, a string of daisies.* 4. series or succession, as of persons, things, or events: *a string of lights, a string of robberies.* 5. *usually,* **strings.** *Informal.* limitation or condition connected with something: *There were no strings attached to his offer.* 6. thin strand of wire, gut, nylon, or other material used to produce tones in certain musical instruments. 7. **strings.** musical instruments played on such strings, as the violin, viola, and cello, esp. these instruments collectively in an orchestra or ensemble. 8. group of players on an athletic team who are ranked together as a unit, esp. according to ability: *The injured player was replaced by a member of the third string.* 9. stringlike organ, part, or formation, as the fiber or fibers of certain vegetables. 10. **to pull strings.** to use one's power or influence in order to obtain what one wants. —v.t., **strung, string·ing.** 1. to put on or as on a string: *to string beads.* 2. to furnish with a string or strings: *to string a bow, to string a tennis racket.* 3. to extend from one place to another or across a given area: *to string a clothesline across a yard.* 4. to arrange in or as in a row: *We strung the lights on the Christmas tree.* 5. to remove fibers or strings from: *to string beans.* 6. **to string (someone) along.** *Informal.* to fool or deceive (someone). 7. **to string out.** *Informal.* to extend beyond the usual or proper limits; prolong. 8. **to string up.** *Slang.* to kill by hanging. —v.i. 1. to form into or proceed in a string or series. 2. **to string along.** *Informal.* to agree or cooperate: *We'll string along with you if you keep your part of the bargain.* [Old English *streng* line¹, cord, thread.]

string bean, long, green bean, related to the kidney bean, the pod of which is eaten as a vegetable. Also, **green bean, snap bean.**

string·course (string′kôrs′) n. horizontal band, as of stone or brick, often ornamented, projecting from or flush with a building.

strin·gen·cy (strin′jən sē) pl., **-cies.** n. quality or condition of being stringent.

strin·gent (strin′jənt) adj. 1. rigorously maintained, enforced, or adhered to; rigid: *stringent requirements.* 2. persuasive; convincing: *a stringent argument.* 3. characterized by or proceeding from a scarcity or lack of available funds: *a stringent market.* [Latin *stringēns,* present participle of *stringere* to draw tight.] —**strin′gent·ly,** adv.

String beans

string·er (string′ər) n. 1. one who or that which strings. 2. long

at; āpe; cär; end; mē; it; īce; hot; ōld; fôrk; wood; fool; oil; out; up; ūse; turn; sing; thin; this; zh in treasure; ə in ago, taken, pencil, lemon, circus.

horizontal member supporting the vertical members or crosspieces of a framework or structure. **3.** member of a particular string on an athletic team. ▲ usually used in combination: *second-stringer.* **4.** part-time or local correspondent for a news publication or news service.

string·halt (string′hôlt′) *n.* disease of horses causing involuntary spasms of the hind legs when walking or trotting. Also, **spring′halt′.** [Probably STRING + HALT².]

string·piece (string′pēs′) *n.* long horizontal beam used for strengthening, supporting, or connecting parts of a framework.

string tie, narrow necktie, usually worn tied in a bow.

string·y (string′ē) **string·i·er, string·i·est.** *adj.* **1.** having or consisting of tough fibers or strings: *stringy celery.* **2.** resembling string; thin: *stringy hair.* **3.** forming strings: *stringy glue.* —**string′i·ness,** *n.*

strip¹ (strip) **stripped** or **stript, strip·ping.** *v.t.* **1.** to remove or pull off the clothing or other covering from. **2.** to remove or pull off, as clothing (often with *off*): *to strip bark from a tree, to strip off one's clothes.* **3.** to remove all the details, accessories, working parts, or essentials from; make bare or empty: *to strip an automobile.* **4.** to deprive, as of rights, honors, or possessions; divest: *The soldier was court-martialed and stripped of his rank.* **5.** to rob or plunder: *The burglars stripped the museum of all its ancient art treasures.* **6.** to damage or break the threads or teeth of (a bolt, gear, screw, or the like). **7.** to extract milk thoroughly from (a cow's udder). —*v.i.* to undress. [Old English -*strīepan* (in the compound *bestrīepan* to rob, plunder).] —**strip′per,** *n.*

strip² (strip) *n.* **1.** long, narrow piece of something: *a strip of paper, a strip of land.* **2.** airstrip. **3.** comic strip. [Possibly from Middle Low German *strippe* strap.]

stripe¹ (strīp) *n.* **1.** long, narrow band differing, as in color or texture, from the material or surface of which it forms a part: *The material had white stripes on a red background.* **2.** any of various strips of cloth worn on the sleeve of a military uniform to indicate rank, length of service, or some other distinction. **3.** particular kind or character; sort: *The religious faiths of the immigrants were various, not all of one stripe* (Hosmer, 1890). —*v.t.*, **striped, strip·ing.** to mark with a stripe or stripes. [Possibly from Middle Dutch *strīpe* strip², streak.]

stripe² (strīp) *n.* stroke or lash, as with a rod or whip. [Of uncertain origin.]

striped (strīpt, strī′pid) *adj.* having or marked with a stripe or stripes.

strip·ling (strip′ling) *n.* youth; lad. [STRIP² + -LING¹; in the sense of "slender as a strip."]

strive (strīv) **strove** or **strived, striv·en** (striv′ən), **striv·ing.** *v.i.* to make a strenuous effort: *to strive to succeed, to strive for accuracy in one's work.* [Old French *estriver* to contend, from *estrif* contention. See STRIFE.]

strobe light (strōb) electric device that emits a very brief and intense flash of light, used esp. in photography. [From STROBOSCOPE.]

stro·bi·lus (strō bī′ləs) *pl.*, **-li** (-lī). *n.* **1.** cone, as of a pine tree. **2.** cone-shaped structure consisting of a mass of compactly arranged scalelike leaves that produce spores. Also, **stro′bile.** [Late Latin *strobilus* cone of a pine tree, from Greek *strobīlos* round ball, whirlwind, from *strobos* a whirling around.]

stro·bo·scope (strō′bə skōp′) *n.* instrument that allows moving objects to be seen as if they were standing still, esp. by flashing an intense light at regular intervals. [Greek *strobos* a whirling around + -SCOPE.] —**stro·bo·scop·ic** (strō′bə skop′ik); *also,* **strob′o·scop′i·cal,** *adj.*

strode (strōd) past tense of **stride.**

stroke¹ (strōk) *n.* **1.** act or instance of striking, as with the hand. **2.** action or event having a specified effect: *a stroke of misfortune.* **3.** brilliant or inspired act, achievement, or idea: *a stroke of genius.* **4.** sound produced by striking. **5.** time indicated by striking, as of a clock: *They left at the stroke of three.* **6.** single unbroken or complete movement, as of the hand, an instrument, or something held in the hand. **7.** mark made by a pen, pencil, brush, or other implement. **8.** apoplexy. **9.** combination of repeated arm and leg movements for propelling the body through water in swimming. **10.a.** act or instance of striking the ball in certain sports, as golf or tennis. **b.** manner in which this is done. **11.** pulsation, as of the heart. **12.** stroke oar (*def.* 2). —*v.t.*, **stroked, strok·ing.** to act as stroke oar for. [Probably from an unrecorded Old English word.] —**Syn.** *n.* **6.** see **blow¹.**

stroke² (strōk) **stroked, strok·ing.** *v.t.* to rub gently or caressingly with the hand, usually in the same direction and repeatedly. —*n.* light, caressing movement of the hand. [Old English *strācian* to rub gently with the hand.]

stroke oar 1. oar at the stern of the boat. **2.** rower that pulls this oar and sets the rhythm for the other oarsmen.

stroll (strōl) *v.i.* to walk in a leisurely or idle manner. —*v.t.* to walk along or through in a leisurely or idle manner. —*n.* leisurely walk. [Possibly from dialectal German *strollen* to rove about.] —**Syn.** *v.i.* see **walk.**

stroll·er (strō′lər) *n.* **1.** small, chairlike, wheeled vehicle in which a small child sits and is wheeled about. **2.** one who strolls.

Strom·bo·li (strom′bə lē, -bō-) *n.* small Italian island north of Sicily, site of an active volcano. Area, approx. 5 sq. mi.

strong (strông) *adj.* **1.** having great muscular power; physically powerful: *strong arms, a strong athlete.* **2.** having good health: *I don't think she's strong enough to undergo the operation.* **3.** exerting or having great influence, power, or authority: *a strong ruler, a strong government.* **4.** capable of resisting or sustaining attack, strain, stress, or force; not easily broken, destroyed, or injured: *a strong chain, a strong piece of furniture.* **5.** firm in mind, character, will, or purpose; morally powerful or courageous: *He's not strong enough to resist the temptation.* **6.** having the power to be persuasive; cogent; convincing: *a strong argument.* **7.** exceeding that which is usual, moderate, or reasonable; extreme: *strong measures.* **8.** having a sharp, bitter, or offensive taste or odor: *a strong cheese, a strong tobacco.* **9.** clearly perceptible; marked; distinct: *He bears a strong resemblance to his father.* **10.** marked or characterized by forcefulness or vehemence: *The senator took a strong stand on the issue.* **11.** critical, abusive, or harsh in nature: *He used strong words to describe his opponent.* **12.** moving with or having great force or speed: *strong winds, a strong undertow.* **13.** having a great degree of intensity, force, or power: *a strong smell, a strong heartbeat, a strong light.* **14.** securely fixed; firm: *He took a strong hold on the rope.* **15.** having great competence or ability in a specified field or subject: *He is strong in science.* **16.** containing much alcohol. **17.** having a large amount of the proper or essential ingredients: *strong tea.* **18.** having a specified numerical force: *an army 10,000 strong.* **19.** *Phonetics.* stressed; accented. **20.** *Grammar.* (of a verb) forming the past tense and past participle by changing a vowel within the stem of the word, as in *ring, rang, rung.* —*adv.* in a strong manner; vigorously; powerfully. [Old English *strang* physically powerful, resolute, forceful, able, severe, rigorous.] —**strong′ly,** *adv.* —**Syn.** *adj.* **1.** see **tough.**

strong-arm (strông′ärm′) *Informal. adj.* using or depending on physical power, force, or coercion: *strong-arm tactics.* —*v.t.* to use physical power, force, or coercion against.

strong·box (strông′boks′) *n.* strongly made chest or safe for storing money, documents, and other valuables.

strong·hold (strông′hōld′) *n.* **1.** place fortified against attack or danger. **2.** place of predominance or concentration: *The area is a stronghold of political conservatism.*

Syn. 1. Stronghold, citadel, fortress mean a structure capable of defense against an enemy. **Stronghold** is the general term, and unlike the others, may be applied to a natural structure that is often remote and perfect as a hideaway: *The gang occupied a mountain stronghold.* In contrast, **citadel** and **fortress** are man-made structures occupying central positions of defense. **Citadel,** like **stronghold,** takes advantage of the terrain and is set up on a commanding height to overlook and protect a city while itself remaining difficult to attack, and that is why it is always the final point of defense during a siege: *The citadel held out after the entire country was overrun.* **Fortress** is applied to a large and permanent fort or series of forts that often includes a town, surrounded by trenches and a stockade, compensating in this way for its poor geographical position: *The emperor built a fortress at the hostile border.*

strong-mind·ed (strông′mīn′did) *adj.* having or showing firmness or determination of mind, will, or purpose. —**strong′-mind′ed·ly,** *adv.* —**strong′-mind′ed·ness,** *n.*

stron·ti·um (stron′shē əm, -tē-) *n.* soft, silvery metallic element, sometimes used in alloys and in the manufacture of vacuum tubes. Symbol: Sr See **element** for table. [Modern Latin *strontium,* from *Strontian,* village in Scotland, where it was discovered.]

strontium 90 *also,* **strontium-90.** radioactive isotope of strontium with a half-life of twenty-eight years, used in radio therapy and nuclear batteries. It is found in dangerous amounts in fallout from nuclear bombs.

strop (strop) *n.* flexible strip of material, as leather or canvas, used to sharpen razors. —*v.t.,* **stropped, strop·ping.** to sharpen on a strop. [Old English *stropp* thong, from Latin *stroppus* thong, strap, from Greek *strophos* twisted cord.]

stro·phe (strō′fē) *n.* **1.** in ancient Greek drama, that part of an ode sung by the chorus while moving from right to left. **2.** *Poetry.* stanza. [Greek *strophē* stanza of a choral ode; literally, a turning (referring to the turning of the chorus after singing such a stanza).] —**stroph·ic** (strof′ik, strō′fik), *adj.*

strove (strōv) a past tense of **strive.**

struck (struk) *v.* past tense and past participle of **strike.** —*adj.* closed or affected by a labor strike.

struc·tur·al (struk′chər əl) *adj.* **1.** of, relating to, having, or characterized by structure: *a structural fault in a building, the structural unity of a novel.* **2.** used in or necessary to building or construction: *a structural beam.* **3.** of or relating to the organic structure of animals or plants; morphological. **4.** relating to the structure of rocks and other parts of the earth's crust. —**struc′tur·al·ly,** *adv.*

structural formula, see **formula** (*def.* 3).

struc·ture (struk′chər) n. 1. anything that is built or constructed, as a building. 2. way in which something is constructed, arranged, or organized: *the structure of a society, the structure of a language.* 3. arrangement or interrelation of the constituent parts or elements of a whole: *to study the structure of a cell.* 4. organized body or combination of mutually connected and dependent parts or elements. —v.t., **-tured, -tur·ing.** to arrange in an orderly, systematic manner: *to structure a teaching program so as to emphasize class participation.* [Latin *structūra* a fitting together, construction.]

stru·del (strōōd′əl, shtrōōd′-) n. pastry consisting of a filling, as of fruit, wrapped in a very thin sheet of dough and baked. [German *Strudel* literally, whirlpool.]

strug·gle (strug′əl) **-gled, -gling.** v.i. 1. to make strenuous effort; strive: *John struggled to pass his final examinations.* 2. to progress or make one's way with great effort: *The children struggled through the heavy snow drifts.* 3. to engage in physical combat, as with an adversary: *I struggled with him for the knife.* —n. 1. very great or strenuous effort: *It was a struggle for her to make him understand.* 2. physical effort to resist force or to free oneself from constraint: *The suspected murderer gave up without a struggle.* [Of uncertain origin.] —**strug′gler,** n. —Syn. n. 1. see **fight.**

strum (strum) **strummed, strum·ming.** v.t. to play, esp. in an idle, monotonous, or unskillful manner: *to strum a banjo, to strum a tune.* —v.i. to play a stringed musical instrument, esp. in an idle, monotonous, or unskillful manner. —n. act or sound of strumming. [Possibly blend of STRING and THRUM¹.] —**strum′mer,** n.

stru·ma (strōō′mə) pl., **-mae** (-mē). n. 1. scrofula. 2. goiter. 3. *Botany.* cushionlike swelling on an organ, as at the base of certain moss capsules. [Latin *strūma* scrofulous tumor.]

strum·pet (strum′pit) n. prostitute; whore. [Of uncertain origin.]

strung (strung) past tense and past participle of **string.**

strut¹ (strut) **strut·ted, strut·ting.** v.i. to walk in a vain, pompous, or arrogant manner. —n. vain, pompous, or arrogant manner of walking. [Old English *strūtian* to stand out stiffly.] —**strut′ter,** n.

strut² (strut) n. bar, brace, or other supporting piece designed to resist pressure or thrust, as in a structural framework. —v.t. **strut·ted, strut·ting.** to brace or support with or as with a strut or struts. [Probably from STRUT¹ (referring to a stiff piece of wood).]

Strut

King post

Strut²

strych·nine (strik′nīn, -nēn, -nīn) *also,* **strych·nin.** n. very bitter poisonous drug obtained from nux vomica and related plants, commonly used as a poison. [French *strychnine,* from Latin *strychnos* nightshade, from Greek *strychnos.*]

St. Thomas 1. westernmost of the Virgin Islands, belonging to the United States. Area, 32 sq. mi. 2. see **Charlotte Amalie.**

Stu·art (stōō′ərt, stū′-) n. 1. royal family that ruled Scotland from 1371 to 1603 and Scotland and England from 1603 until 1714. 2. member of this family. 3. **Mary.** see **Mary, Queen of Scots.** 4. **Gilbert.** 1755–1828, U.S. painter. 5. **James Ew·ell Brown** (ū′əl). 1833–64, Confederate general, known as Jeb Stuart.

stub (stub) n. 1. short piece that remains after something has been worn away, used, cut, or broken off: *a cigar stub, the stub of a pencil.* 2. remaining or detachable portion, as of a check, ticket, or bill, that provides a record or receipt of payment. 3. short, thick, projecting piece or part. 4. stump of a tree trunk or plant stem. —v.t., **stubbed, stub·bing.** 1. to strike (one's toe or foot) accidentally against something. 2. to dig up by the roots. 3. to clear (land) of stumps. [Old English *stub(b)* stump of a tree or shrub.]

stub·ble (stub′əl) n. 1. short stalks of grain and certain other plants left standing in the ground after the crop has been harvested. 2. anything resembling this, as a short, bristly beard. [Old French *estouble* straw, from Late Latin *stupula,* form of Latin *stipula* stem, straw.] —**stub′bly,** adj.

stub·born (stub′ərn) adj. 1. not yielding or receptive to argument, persuasion, or reason; obstinate. 2. done, carried on, or maintained in an unyielding, obstinate manner: *His stubborn refusal to answer questions exasperated the interrogator.* 3. difficult to overcome, treat, or cure: *a stubborn illness.* [Middle English *stiborne* obstinate, possibly from Old English *stubb* stub or stump of a tree or shrub (as if meaning "unyielding like a stub").] —**stub′born·ly,** adv. —**stub′born·ness,** n.

stub·by (stub′ē) **-bi·er, -bi·est.** adj. 1. short and thick: *a stubby tail, stubby toes.* 2. short, thick, and bristly: *a stubby beard.* 3. covered with or consisting of stubs or stubble: *a stubby field.* —**stub′bi·ness,** n.

stuc·co (stuk′ō) pl., **-cos** or **-coes.** n. 1. plaster or cement, of varying degrees of fineness, used for coating walls or for making ornamental reliefs and other decorations. 2. ornamental work made of stucco. —v.t. **-coed, -co·ing.** to cover or ornament with stucco. [Italian *stucco* plaster; of Germanic origin.]

stuc·co·work (stuk′ō wurk′) n. work done in stucco.

stuck (stuk) past tense and past participle of **stick².**

stuck-up (stuk′up′) adj. *Informal.* conceited; snobbish.

stud¹ (stud) n. 1. nail head, knob, or similar object, usually of metal, fixed to and protruding from a surface, used, esp. as an ornament. 2. ornamental buttonlike fastener used on men's formal shirts. 3. vertical post, as in the framework of a wall, to which horizontal boards, laths, and the like are nailed. 4. any of various short, projecting pins, as on a machine. —v.t., **stud·ded, stud·ding.** 1. to set or ornament with or as with studs: *to stud a bracelet with diamonds.* 2. to lie scattered over or be spread about in: *Stars studded the sky.* 3. to furnish with or support by a vertical post or posts. [Old English *studu* post¹, support.]

stud² (stud) n. 1. male animal, esp. a horse, kept for breeding. 2. group of animals, esp. horses, selected and raised for breeding. 3. place where horses are kept for breeding. 4. collection of horses kept for hunting, riding, or racing. [Old English *stōd* place where horses are kept for breeding, group of such horses.]

stud·book (stud′book′) n. official registry of the pedigrees of thoroughbred animals, esp. horses or dogs.

stud·ding (stud′ing) n. 1. studs collectively, as those in the framework of a wall. 2. material from which such studs are made.

stu·dent (stōōd′ənt, stūd′-) n. 1. person enrolled in or attending a school, college, or university. 2. one devoted to study or investigation of a particular subject: *a student of language.* [Latin *studēns,* present participle of *studēre* to be eager or diligent, apply oneself to learning.]

student teacher, person studying to be a teacher who practices teaching in an elementary or secondary school under professional supervision.

student union, organization and building at a college or university, providing social, recreational, cultural, and, often, dining facilities.

stud·horse (stud′hôrs′) n. male horse used for breeding; stallion.

stud·ied (stud′ēd) adj. characterized by or showing deliberate effort or intention: *a government's studied neglect of its poor citizens.* —**stud′ied·ly,** adv. —**stud′ied·ness,** n.

stu·di·o (stōō′dē ō′, stū′-) pl., **-di·os.** n. 1. place where an artist or photographer works. 2. place for instruction in and practice of one of the performing arts: *The new dance studio offers classes in ballet and modern dance.* 3.a. place where motion pictures are filmed. b. place where radio or television programs are performed or recorded. [Italian *studio* workroom, office, study, from Latin *studium* zeal, application to learning.]

studio apartment, one-room apartment with kitchen and bathroom facilities.

studio couch, couch that can be used as a bed.

stu·di·ous (stōō′dē əs, stū′-) adj. 1. given to or fond of study or learning. 2. showing or characterized by careful or earnest consideration or attention: *a studious effort, to be studious of one's health.* —**stu′di·ous·ly,** adv. —**stu′di·ous·ness,** n.

stud·y (stud′ē) **stud·ied, stud·y·ing.** v.t. 1. to apply the mind in order to acquire a knowledge of (something): *to study medicine, to study history.* 2. to look at closely or critically; examine; scrutinize: *The expert studied the painting and decided it was a forgery.* 3. to look or inquire into; investigate: *to study the geology of a region.* 4. to give careful thought and consideration to: *I will study the matter and give you my opinion.* 5. to seek to learn by memorizing: *The actor studied the part before the audition.* —v.i. 1. to apply the mind in order to acquire knowledge: *to study for a test.* 2. to pursue a regular course of instruction; be a student: *to study for the ministry. He is studying at the state university.* —n. pl., **stud·ies.** 1. act or process of studying: *His years of study were useful in his job.* 2. act or process of acquiring knowledge of something specified: *the study of medicine, the study of human nature.* 3. careful or critical examination or investigation. 4. product of such examination or investigation: *The crime commission's study will be published next week.* 5. that which is studied or to be studied; branch of learning. 6. room in a house used or set apart for study, reading, writing, or meditation. 7. preliminary sketch, design, or plan for an artistic work or for some detail or portion of it. 8. artistic work, esp. a painting, devoted to the detailed consideration of a particular aspect or subject: *a study in black and white.* 9. state of being absorbed in deep thought or meditation. 10. *Informal.* perfect example: *The look on his face was a study of disappointment.* 11. person, esp. an actor, with reference to his ability to memorize: *a quick study.* [Latin *studium* zeal, application to learning.] —Syn. v.t. 4. see **consider.**

study hall 1. room in a school reserved for studying. 2. period of a school day set aside for studying.

stuff (stuf) n. 1. substance or material of which a thing is made or of which a thing can be made: *What kind of stuff is in this pillow?* 2. indefinite, vague substance or matter: *The druggist gave him some stuff for his cough.* 3. inward character or capabilities: *They thought*

he too would surrender, but being made of sterner stuff, he fought on. **4.** personal belongings; possessions: *He packed all his stuff in the back of the car.* **5.** fabric, esp. one made of wool. **6.** worthless or useless matter or things; rubbish; junk. **7.** foolish, irrational, and worthless ideas, speech, or writing; nonsense. —*v.t.* **1.** to fill by loading to excess; cram full: *to stuff a closet with dresses.* **2.** to force or thrust (something) tightly, as into a container: *to stuff papers into an envelope.* **3.** to fill with suitable material, as for padding: *to stuff a pillow with foam rubber.* **4.** to block or stop up (an aperture or cavity) by thrusting something tightly in; plug: *He stuffed his ears with cotton.* **5.** to fill with too much food: *Stop stuffing yourself.* **6.** *Cooking.* to fill (poultry or other food) with stuffing. **7.** to fill the skin of (a dead animal) to restore and preserve its natural appearance. **8.** to put fraudulent votes into (a ballot box). [Old French *estoffe* material, matter, going back to Latin *stuppa* tow², from Greek *styppē*.]

stuffed shirt *Informal.* one who is extremely pompous or formal and has an inflated concept of his own importance.

stuff·ing (stuf′ing) *n.* **1.** act of one who or that which stuffs. **2.** something used for filling, packing, enlarging, or stuffing something. **3.** food mixture, as of seasoned bread crumbs or rice, used to fill poultry or other food.

stuff·y (stuf′ē) **stuff·i·er, stuff·i·est.** *adj.* **1.** having inadequate ventilation; close: *a stuffy room.* **2.** lacking freshness; uninteresting; boring. **3.** extremely strait-laced; formal; pompous: *a stuffy old man with no sense of humor.* **4.** affected with the sensation of obstruction in the respiratory passages: *The cold made her nose stuffy.* —**stuff′i·ly,** *adv.* —**stuff′i·ness,** *n.*

stul·ti·fy (stul′tə fī′) **-fied, -fy·ing.** *v.t.* **1.** to make ineffectual, futile, or worthless: *to stultify ambition.* **2.** to cause to be or appear foolish, dull-witted, or illogical. [Late Latin *stultificāre* to render foolish, from Latin *stultus* foolish + *facere* to make.] —**stul′ti·fi·ca′tion,** *n.*

stum·ble (stum′bəl) **-bled, -bling.** *v.i.* **1.** to lose one's balance, as by missing one's footing, stubbing one's toe, or tripping over an obstacle. **2.** to move or walk unsteadily or awkwardly: *He stumbled around the dark room until he found the light switch.* **3.** to behave, act, or speak in a clumsy, awkward manner, as from confusion or nervousness: *to stumble over a difficult word, to stumble through a performance.* **4.** to make a mistake or blunder. **5.** to discover accidentally or unexpectedly (with *on* or *across*): *He stumbled on the solution to the crime while interrogating the witness.* —*v.t.* **1.** to cause to stumble or fall; trip. —*n.* **1.** act or instance of stumbling. **2.** mistake; blunder; slip. [Probably of Scandinavian origin.] —**stum′bler,** *n.* —**stum′bling·ly,** *adv.*

stum·ble·bum (stum′bəl bum′) *n. Slang.* blundering or incompetent person.

stumbling block, that which causes someone or something to stumble or err; hindrance; obstruction.

stump (stump) *n.* **1.** the part of a tree trunk or plant stem remaining in the ground after the main part is cut or breaks off. **2.** that part of anything which remains after the main or more important part has been removed, esp. the remaining part of an amputated portion of the body. **3.** place or occasion for a political speech. **4.** wooden leg. **5.a.** heavy step or gait, as that of a person with a wooden leg. **b.** heavy, blunted sound made by such a step or gait; thud; clomp. **6. stumps.** *Slang.* legs. **7.** small pointed roll of paper or leather or piece of soft rubber, used to shade the tones in pencil or charcoal drawings. **8. up a stump.** *Informal.* in a difficult or perplexing situation; baffled. —*v.t.* **1.** to cause to be at a loss; perplex; baffle: *They tried to stump the panel of experts. This problem has really got me stumped.* **2.** to reduce to a stump; truncate; lop off. **3.** to remove stumps from (land). **4.** *Informal.* to travel through, as a state or section, making political speeches. —*v.i.* **1.** to walk stiffly, heavily, or noisily, as if with a wooden or lame leg: *The old sailor stumped down the street.* **2.** *Informal.* to travel about making political speeches. [Middle Dutch *stomp* stub, stem.] —**stump′er,** *n.*

stump·y (stump′ē) **stump·i·er, stump·i·est.** *adj.* **1.** short and thick like a stump. **2.** (of land) abounding with tree stumps. —**stump′i·ness,** *n.*

stun (stun) **stunned, stun·ning.** *v.t.* **1.** to make unconscious or semiconscious, as by a blow. **2.** to overwhelm with some strong emotion or impression: *The country was stunned by the president's announcement.* **3.** to daze or bewilder, as with some loud noise: *He was stunned by the explosion.* [Old French *estoner* to astonish, resound, going back to Latin *ex-* out + *tonāre* to thunder.]

stung (stung) a past tense and past participle of **sting.**

stunk (stungk) a past tense and past participle of **stink.**

stun·ner (stun′ər) *n.* **1.** one who or that which stuns. **2.** *Informal.* extraordinarily attractive person.

stun·ning (stun′ing) *adj.* **1.** *Informal.* extremely attractive or good-looking: *a stunning figure, a stunning complexion.* **2.** that stuns, as a blow. —**stun′ning·ly,** *adv.*

stunt¹ (stunt) *v.t.* **1.** to check the growth or development of: *You will*

stunt that tree if you try to direct its growth. **2.** to check or hinder (growth, development, or progress). —*n.* act or instance of stunting. [From dialectal English *stunt* dwarfed in growth, going back to Old English *stunt* foolish.]

stunt² (stunt) *Informal. n.* any act which is done to attract attention, esp. one requiring or exhibiting extraordinary strength, skill, or daring: *She performed death-defying stunts on the high trapeze.* —*v.i.* to perform a stunt or stunts. [Of uncertain origin.]

stunt man, man skilled in performing physical feats or stunts, who substitutes for an actor in scenes requiring such skill, esp. in dangerous scenes involving aerial acrobatics, crashes, leaps, falls, or high-speed riding or driving.

stu·pa (stōō′pə) *n.* Buddhist shrine consisting of a dome-shaped mound of masonry or the like, often containing a sacred relic. [Sanskrit *stūpa* dome.]

stupe (stōōp, stūp) *n.* cloth wrung out of hot water and applied to a part of the body, used as a compress. [Latin *stup(p)a* tow², from Greek *styppē*.]

stu·pe·fa·cient (stōō′pə fā′shənt, stū′-) *adj.* producing stupor; stupefying. —*n.* narcotic drug. [Latin *stupefaciēns,* present participle of *stupefacere* to benumb, stun. See STUPEFY.]

stu·pe·fac·tion (stōō′pə fak′shən, stū′-) *n.* **1.** act of stupefying; being stupefied. **2.** overwhelming astonishment; amazement.

stu·pe·fy (stōō′pə fī′, stū′-) **-fied, -fy·ing.** *v.t.* **1.** to cause to become stupid, senseless, or torpid; blunt the faculties or senses of. **2.** to amaze; astound: *The daring stunt stupefied the audience.* [Latin *stupefacere* to benumb, stun, from *stupēre* to be amazed + *facere* to make.] —**stu′pe·fi′er,** *n.*

stu·pen·dous (stōō pen′dəs, stū-) *adj.* causing astonishment; overwhelming; astounding. [Latin *stupendus* to be wondered at, gerundive of *stupēre* to be amazed.] —**stu·pen′dous·ly,** *adv.* —**stu·pen′dous·ness,** *n.*

stu·pid (stōō′pid, stū′-) *adj.* **1.** lacking ordinary intelligence; slow-witted; dumb. **2.** dull in ideas or expression; inane; uninteresting; boring: *I'm tired of this stupid game.* **3.** having one's faculties deadened or blunted; in a stupor; stunned; dazed. **4.** of, resulting from, or characterized by a lack of intelligence: *a stupid answer, a stupid attempt.* —*n. Informal.* stupid person. [Latin *stupidus* senseless, dull.] —**stu′pid·ly,** *adv.* —**stu′pid·ness,** *n.*

stu·pid·i·ty (stōō pid′ə tē, stū-) *pl.,* **-ties.** *n.* **1.** lack of intelligence, comprehension, or common sense; slowness of perception or understanding; ignorance: *His answer revealed his stupidity. The stupidity of their plan was obvious.* **2.** statement, act, or the like which reveals a lack of intelligence or understanding.

stu·por (stōō′pər, stū′-) *n.* **1.** partly conscious condition; lessening of the power to feel. **2.** mental or moral numbness; apathy. [Latin *stupor* numbness, stupidity.]

stur·dy (stur′dē) **-di·er, -di·est.** *adj.* **1.** having a strong, hardy constitution: *sturdy pioneers.* **2.** solidly built or constructed: *a sturdy fortress.* **3.** hard to overcome; unyielding; resolute: *They put up a sturdy defense.* [Old French *estourdi* reckless, dazed, past participle of *estourdir* to daze, possibly going back to Latin *ex-* (see EX-¹) + *turdus* thrush (thought of as drunk or foolish).] —**stur′di·ly,** *adv.* —**stur′di·ness,** *n.*

stur·geon (stur′jən) *pl.,* **-geons** or **-geon.** *n.* any of a group of fish, family Acipenseridae, found in fresh and salt waters in temperate regions, having rows of bony, pointed scales, and valued as food and as a source of caviar and isinglass. Length: 7–10 feet. [Anglo-Norman *sturgeon;* of Germanic origin.]

Sturgeon

stut·ter (stut′ər) *v.t., v.i.* to utter (a word or the like) or speak with frequent, involuntary repetition of sounds or syllables, often caused by a nervous defect, fear, or excitement: *He stuttered some ridiculous excuse for being late. She has stuttered ever since the shock of the accident.* —*n.* act, instance, or habit of stuttering. [Dialectal English *stut* to stutter (of Germanic origin) + -ER⁴.] —**stut′ter·er,** *n.* —**stut′ter·ing·ly,** *adv.*

Stutt·gart (stut′gärt, stoot′-) *n.* city in southwestern West Germany. Pop. (1968 est.), 614,994.

Stuy·ve·sant, Peter (stī′və sənt) 1592–1672, Dutch colonial administrator in America.

St. Vi·tus' dance (vī′təs) see **Saint Vitus' dance.**

sty¹ (stī) *pl.,* **sties.** *n.* **1.** pen or enclosure where pigs are kept; pigpen; pigsty. **2.** any filthy place; hovel. [Old English *stig* hall, pen².]

sty² (stī) *pl.,* **sties.** *also,* **stye.** *n.* a small, inflamed swelling, similar to a small boil, on the edge of the eyelid. [From earlier *styany* (thought to mean "sty on the eye"), going back to Old English *stīgend* literally, rising (in the sense of "swelling") + *ēage* eye.]

Styg·i·an (stij′ē ən) *adj.* **1.** of, relating to, or characteristic of the mythological river Styx or the lower world in which it flows. **2.** resembling the river Styx or its atmosphere; black; gloomy.

style (stīl) *n.* **1.** particular mode of dress; fashion: *to dress in the style of the nineteenth century.* **2.** condition that accords with fashionable standards; elegance; tastefulness: *to live in style.* **3.** distinctive mode of doing or making something; way: *His style of speaking annoyed her.* **4.** mode of expression in the arts: *the style of New Orleans jazzmen, poetry in the style of Wordsworth.* **5.** *also,* **sty·lus. a.** a pointed instrument used by the ancients to write on wax tablets. **b.** something pointed or used like a stylus, as the pointer on a compass. **6.** *Botany.* stalklike structure of the pistil of a flower, extending from the ovary to the stigma. See **flower** for illustration. **7.** *Printing.* special rules or system, as of spelling, punctuation, or capitalization, followed by a particular author, publisher, or printer. **8.** *Archaic.* formal or official name or title. — *v.t.*, **styled, styl·ing. 1.** to design in accordance with a particular mode; fashion: *She commissioned him to style her entire fall wardrobe.* **2.** to change in order to conform to a particular style of printing or writing: *She had to style the entire manuscript.* **3.** to name; call: *He styled himself "World Champion."* [Old French *style* pointed writing instrument, manner of expressing oneself, from Latin *stilus.*] —**Syn.** *n.* **1.** see **fashion.**

style·book (stīl′book′) *n.* **1.** book containing printing rules, as of punctuation, capitalization, or spelling, observed or employed by a particular author, printer, or publisher. **2.** book showing the styles in dress and when they were in fashion.

styl·ish (stī′lish) *adj.* conforming to current or approved style; fashionable. —**styl′ish·ly,** *adv.* —**styl′ish·ness,** *n.*

styl·ist (stī′list) *n.* **1.** writer or speaker who is distinguished for the excellence or individuality of his style. **2.** one who designs or advises on styles, as in clothing or furnishings.

sty·lis·tic (stī lis′tik) *adj.* of or relating to style; characteristic of a particular style or current styles.

sty·lis·ti·cal·ly (stī lis′tik lē) *adv.* with respect to style, esp. a specific style: *Stylistically speaking, this artist can be classified as an impressionist.*

styl·ize (stī′līz) *-ized, -iz·ing, v.t.* to make (an artistic representation) conform to the rules of a particular style or convention, rather than to nature or reality.

sty·lo·bate (stī′lə bāt′) *n. Architecture.* continuous base or substructure supporting a colonnade.

sty·lus (stī′ləs) *pl.,* **-li** (-lī) *or* **-lus·es.** *n.* **1.** instrument with a pointed or rounded head used to make stencils or impressions on soft materials or for similar purposes. **2.a.** phonograph needle that follows the grooves on a record, its vibrations being transformed into an electric current that is amplified and turned into sound. **b.** needle used to make a phonograph

Stylus

record. **3.** pen that records impulses on a graph or chart, as in a seismograph or chronograph. **4.** style *(def. 5).* [Incorrect spelling of Latin *stilus* pointed writing instrument.]

sty·mie (stī′mē) *-mied, -mie·ing, also,* **sti·my.** *v.t.* **1.** to bring to or keep at a standstill or in a state of inaction; frustrate; block: *He was stymied at every turn.* **2.** to hinder by a stymie in golf. —*n.* situation in golf in which one player's ball lies on the putting green in a direct line between another player's ball and the cup. [Of uncertain origin.]

styp·tic (stip′tik) *adj.* able to stop bleeding by contracting the tissues; astringent. —*n.* styptic agent or substance. [Latin *stypticus* astringent, from Greek *styptikos,* from *styphein* to contract.]

styptic pencil, small stick of alum or other styptic agent used to stop bleeding from small cuts, as in shaving.

sty·rene (stī′rēn, stēr′ēn) *n.* colorless, aromatic liquid hydrocarbon, used esp. in making plastics and the most widely used type of synthetic rubber. Formula: $C_6H_5CHCH_2$ [Latin *styrax* storax (from Greek *styrax*) + *-ENE*; because obtained from storax.]

Sty·ro·foam (stī′rə fōm′) *n. Trademark.* lightweight, buoyant, rigid material made from plastic foam, used esp. as packing or insulating material. [STYR(ENE) + FOAM.]

Styx (stiks) *n. Greek Mythology.* the chief river surrounding Hades, the land of the dead. Its waters are sacred to the gods.

su·a·ble (sōō′ə bəl) *adj.* capable of being or liable to be sued.

sua·sion (swā′zhən) *n.* act or instance of exhorting or urging; persuasion. [Latin *suāsio,* from *suādēre* to persuade.]

sua·sive (swā′siv) *adj. Archaic.* having the ability to influence or persuade; persuasive.

suave (swäv) *adj.* having a smooth, urbane manner. [Latin *suāvis* sweet, agreeable.] —**suave′ly,** *adv.* —**suave′ness, suav′i·ty,** *n.*

sub (sub) *Informal. n., adj.* **1.** substitute. **2.** submarine. —*v.i.,* **subbed, sub′bing.** to act as a substitute.

sub- *prefix* **1.** under; below; beneath: *substrata, substandard.* **2.** used to express a further division or distinction: *subcontract, subdivide.* **3.** partially; slightly: *subhuman.* **4.** used to designate one who is in a lower position: *subdeacon.* **5.** of minor importance or size: *subcommittee, subhead.* [Latin *sub* under.]

sub. 1. substitute. **2.** subscription. **3.** suburban.

sub·ac·id (sub as′id) *adj.* **1.** slightly acid. **2.** slightly tart or biting: *subacid comment.*

sub·a·gent (sub ā′jənt) *n.* one who is employed to work for or under an agent; agent of an agent. —**sub·a′gen·cy,** *n.*

sub·al·tern (sub ôl′tərn, sub′əl tərn) *n.* **1.** person of subordinate rank or position; aide. **2.** officer in the British army, ranking below a captain. —*adj.* **1.** having a subordinate rank or position. **2.** of or relating to a subaltern. [Late Latin *subalternus* subordinate, going back to Latin *sub* under + *alter* other.]

sub·a·quat·ic (sub′ə kwat′ik, -ə kwot′-) *adj.* partly aquatic and partly terrestrial.

sub·a·que·ous (sub ā′kwē əs, -ak′wē-) *adj.* existing, performed, constructed, or used underwater.

sub·arc·tic (sub ärk′tik, -är′tik) *adj.* of or relating to those regions just outside the Arctic Circle.

sub·ar·id (sub ar′id) *adj.* moderately dry; partially arid.

sub·a·tom·ic (sub′ə tom′ik) *adj.* of or relating to an entity smaller than an atom or a phenomenon occurring within an atom.

subatomic particle, any of a number of particles smaller than an atom that are the most fundamental constituents of nature as yet known. For each particle there exists a corresponding particle called an antiparticle. Also, **elementary particle.**

SUBATOMIC PARTICLES

CLASSIFICATION	PARTICLE NAME	PARTICLE SYMBOL	ANTIPARTICLE SYMBOL	MASS[1]	ELECTRIC CHARGE[2]
	photon	γ	(γ)	0	0
LEPTON	electron's neutrino	ν_e	$\bar{\nu}_e$	0	0
	muon's neutrino	ν_μ	$\bar{\nu}_\mu$	0	0
	electron	e^-	e^+	1	—1
	muon	μ^-	μ^+	207	—1
MESON	pion (pi meson)	π^o	$\bar{\pi}^o$	264	0
		π^+	π^-	273	+1
	kaon (kappa meson)	K^+	K^-	966	+1
		K^o	$\bar{K}^o$	975	0
	eta meson	η^o	$\bar{\eta}^o$	1074	0
BARYON					
NUCLEON	proton	p	$\bar{p}$	1836	+1
	neutron	n	$\bar{n}$	1839	0
HYPERON	lambda	Λ	$\bar{\Lambda}$	2183	0
	sigma	Σ^+	$\bar{\Sigma}^-$	2328	+1
		Σ^o	$\bar{\Sigma}^o$	2333	0
		Σ^-	$\bar{\Sigma}^+$	2343	—1
	xi	Ξ^o	$\bar{\Xi}^o$	2572	0
		Ξ^-	$\bar{\Xi}^-$	2585	—1
	omega	Ω^-	Ω^+	3276	—1

[1] approximate masses based on the mass of an electron.
[2] antiparticles have a charge opposite to particles and have a neutral charge when the particle's charge is neutral.

sub·base·ment (sub′bās′mənt) *n.* basement that is below a main basement.

sub·cel·lar (sub′sel′ər) *n.* cellar below another or main cellar.

sub·chas·er (sub′chā′sər) *n.* a small, fast patrol boat designed for antisubmarine operations.

sub·class (sub′klas′) *n.* major subdivision of a class, esp. a taxonomic category ranking below a class but above an order.

sub·com·mit·tee (sub′kə mit′ē) *n.* committee formed from and acting under a main committee for some special purpose.

sub·con·scious (sub kon′shəs) *adj.* **1.** existing in the mind but not in consciousness. **2.** not completely conscious; involving feeble or vague

at; āpe; cär; end; mē; it; īce; hot; ōld; fôrk; wood; fōōl; oil; out; up; ūse; turn; sing; thin; **this**; zh in treasure; ə in ago, taken, pencil, lemon, circus.

perception. —*n. Psychoanalysis.* portion of the mind that retains experiences and feelings that are difficult to bring back to awareness, often because awareness of them would be painful or produce anxiety. —**sub·con′scious·ly,** *adv.* —**sub·con′scious·ness,** *n.*

sub·con·ti·nent (sub kont′ən ənt) *n.* large land mass that is smaller than a continent, esp. a large section of a continent regarded as a distinct geographical or political unit: *the Indian subcontinent.*

sub·con·tract (*n.,* sub kon′trakt; *v.,* sub′kən trakt′) *n.* contract made subordinate to another contract, carrying out all or part of the original contract: *The lumber company had a subcontract to provide all of the lumber needed for the building.* —*v.i., v.t.* to contract to carry out (all or part of a previous contract).

sub·con·trac·tor (sub kon′trak tər, sub′kən trak′-) *n.* person or company that contracts to carry out all or part of a previous contract.

sub·cul·ture (sub′kul′chər) *n.* 1. bacteria culture made from another culture. 2. group within a larger culture having distinctive elements distinguishing it from others in the same society.

sub·cu·ta·ne·ous (sub′kū tā′nē əs) *adj.* 1. situated under the skin. 2. (of certain parasites) living under the skin of the host. 3. injected or performed beneath the skin; hypodermic. —**sub′cu·ta′ne·ous·ly,** *adv.*

sub·dea·con (sub dē′kən) *n.* in the Roman Catholic and Orthodox churches, a cleric next below a deacon in rank.

sub·deb (sub′deb′) *n. Informal.* subdebutante.

sub·deb·u·tante (sub deb′yoo tänt′, -yə-) *n.* young woman soon to become a debutante.

sub·di·vide (sub′di vīd′, sub′di vīd′) **-vid·ed, -vid·ing.** *v.t.* to redivide or separate (a part of a whole) after a previous division: *to subdivide a tract of land into building lots.* —*v.i.* to become redivided.

sub·di·vi·sion (sub′di vizh′ən, sub′di vizh′ən) *n.* 1. act or instance of redividing (a part of a whole) into still smaller parts; being subdivided. 2. one of the parts into which a larger part has been divided; part of a part. 3. area of land divided into lots for building homes.

sub·dom·i·nant (sub dom′ə nənt) *Music. n.* fourth tone of the diatonic scale; tone next below the dominant. —*adj.* of, based on, or related to the subdominant.

sub·due (səb dōō′, -dū′) **-dued, -du·ing.** *v.t.* 1. to bring under control; overcome; to bring into subjection by persuasion: *The police subdued the angry crowd.* 2. to bring into subjection; conquer; vanquish: *to subdue an enemy.* 3. to reduce the intensity, strength, or force of; tone down; soften: *to subdue the light in a room. The laughter in the room was subdued.* [Old French *suduire* to seduce, from Latin *subdūcere* to draw away; influenced in meaning by Latin *subdere* to subjugate, bring under.] —**sub·du′a·ble,** *adj.* —**sub·du′er,** *n.*

su·be·re·ous (soo bēr′ē əs) *adj.* composed of, resembling, or characteristic of cork; corky. Also, **su·ber·ous** (soo′bər əs), **su·ber·ose** (soo′bə rōs′). [Latin *sūbereus* relating to cork, from *sūber* cork.]

su·ber·in (soo ber′in) *n.* hard, waxy substance present in the walls of cork cells.

su·ber·ize (soo′bə rīz′) **-ized, -iz·ing.** *v.i., v.t.* to become, or cause to become, impregnated with suberin. —**su′ber·i·za′tion,** *n.*

sub·fam·i·ly (sub fam′ə lē, sub′fam′-) *pl.,* **-lies.** *n.* major subdivision of a family, esp. a taxonomic category ranking below a family but above a genus.

sub·freez·ing (sub′frē′zing) *adj.* below freezing: *subfreezing weather.*

sub·ge·nus (sub jē′nəs) *pl.,* **-gen·er·a** (-jen′ər ə) or **-ge·nus·es.** *n.* major subdivision of a genus, esp. a taxonomic category ranking below a genus but above a species.

sub·group (sub′grōōp′) *n.* group composed from and subordinate to a larger group.

sub·head (sub′hed′) *n.* 1. subordinate heading or title, as in a book, chapter, or article. 2. one of the subdivisions into which a main head or title is broken up.

sub·head·ing (sub′hed′ing) *n.* subhead.

sub·hu·man (sub hū′mən, sub ū′-) *adj.* 1. belonging to or characteristic of any species considered to be lower than the human species. 2. having some characteristics of human beings, but not quite human.

subj. 1. subject. 2. subjective. 3. subjunctive.

sub·ja·cent (sub jā′sənt) *adj.* 1. situated underneath; underlying. 2. situated at a lower level, but not directly beneath. [Latin *subjacēns,* present participle of *subjacēre* to lie under.]

sub·ject (*n., adj.,* sub′jikt; *v.,* səb jekt′) *n.* **1.a.** something that is the basis of thought, discussion, or investigation; topic: *The subject under discussion today is politics.* **b.** material or field for study, as in a course: *English was my best subject in school.* **2.** theme of a work of art or literary composition. **3.** *Music.* theme (*def. 3a*). **4.** word, phrase, or clause that performs the action of the verb or, if the verb is in the passive voice, receives the action of the verb. In the sentence *He ran fast, He* is the subject. **5.** one who or that which is under the authority, control, or influence of another: *The people were loyal subjects of the king.*

6. one who or that which is the recipient of certain treatment: *They used mice as subjects in the experiments. He was the subject of much criticism.* **7.** term of a proposition in logic which another term either affirms or denies. In the proposition *Aristotle is a man, Aristotle* is the subject. **8.** *Philosophy.* mind; self; ego. —*adj.* **1.** under the control, rule, or influence of; obligated (with *to*): *The employees are subject to the rules and regulations of the company.* **2.** liable; prone; susceptible (with *to*): *subject to all kinds of allergies.* **3.** dependent or conditional upon (with *to*): *subject to my approval.* —*v.t.* **1.** to bring under domination, influence, or control; subjugate. **2.** to cause to undergo or experience; expose (with *to*): *to subject someone to ridicule, to subject clay to great heat in a kiln.* [Latin *subjectus,* past participle of *subicere* to place under, throw under.] —**Syn.** *n.* 5. see **citizen.**

sub·jec·tion (səb jek′shən) *n.* **1.** act of bringing under the control or domination of another; subjugation. **2.** state or condition of being under the control or domination of another.

sub·jec·tive (səb jek′tiv) *adj.* **1.** of, existing in, or proceeding from the individual who is thinking, based on his own thoughts, experiences, and the like: *His decision was completely subjective and did not take the wishes of the other members into consideration.* **2.** in literature and art, based on or expressing the feelings, thoughts, and experiences of the artist or author. **3.** designating the case of the subject of a verb. —**sub·jec′tive·ly,** *adv.* —**sub·jec′tive·ness,** *n.*

sub·jec·tiv·i·ty (sub′jek tiv′ə tē) *n.* quality, condition, or tendency of viewing things solely in relation to one's own feelings, thoughts, or experiences.

subject matter 1. the main body of facts or ideas with which something is concerned; that with which a discussion, project, or the like is concerned. 2. body of ideas presented in a book, speech, or the like, as distinguished from form or style.

sub·join (səb join′) *v.t.* to add at the end; append. [Middle French *subjoindre* to add (to), from Latin *subjungere* to join.]

sub·ju·gate (sub′jə gāt′) **-gat·ed, -gat·ing.** *v.t.* to bring under or have under one's control or dominance; subdue. [Late Latin *subjugātus,* past participle of *subjugāre* to bring under the yoke, subject, from Latin *sub* under + *jugum* yoke; with reference to the Roman custom of forcing defeated soldiers to crawl under a yoke to symbolize their defeat.] —**sub′ju·ga′tion, sub′ju·ga′tor,** *n.*

sub·junc·tive (səb jungk′tiv) *n.* **1.** the mood of a verb that indicates action or state of being as possible, conditional, contrary to fact, or dependent, rather than as actual. In the sentence *If I were you, I wouldn't go,* were is in the subjunctive. **2.** verb form in this mood. —*adj.* of, relating to, or constituting this mood. [Late Latin *subjūnctīvus* subordinate, connecting, from Latin *subjūnctus,* past participle of *subjungere* to join to.]

sub·king·dom (sub king′dəm, sub′king′-) *n.* major subdivision of a kingdom, esp. a taxonomic category ranking next below a kingdom but above a phylum of animals or a division of plants.

sub·lease (*n.,* sub′lēs′; *v.,* sub lēs′) *n.* lease granted by a tenant transferring all or part of his rights under a lease to another person. —*v.t.* **-leased, -leas·ing.** to grant or obtain a sublease for.

sub·let (sub let′, sub′let′) **-let, -let·ting.** *v.t.* **1.** to grant or obtain a sublease for (some property or business); sublease. **2.** to give to another a part of (a contract held by oneself); subcontract: *His company sublet the contract for the electrical work.*

sub·li·mate (*v.,* sub′lə māt′; *n., adj.,* sub′lə mit, -māt′) **-mat·ed, -mat·ing.** *v.t.* **1.** to act upon (something) so as to produce a refined product; refine; purify. **2.** to subject (thoughts or impulses) to sublimation. **3.** to sublime (a substance). —*n.* any solid, crystalline material resulting when a substance is converted directly into a gas and then back into a solid. Mercuric chloride is a poisonous sublimate of mercuric sulfate and salt. —*adj.* purified; refined; sublimated. [Latin *sublīmātus,* past participle of *sublīmāre* to lift up, from *sublīmis* lofty.]

sub·li·ma·tion (sub′lə mā′shən) *n.* **1.** act of sublimating or subliming; being sublimated. **2.** that which has been sublimated or sublimed. **3.** process by which painful or socially unacceptable thoughts and impulses that have been repressed in the subconscious emerge in a new, socially acceptable form.

sub·lime (səb līm′) *adj.* elevated or exalted in manner, expression, or appearance; grand; lofty; noble: *sublime scenery, a sublime countenance.* —*n.* that which is elevated or exalted in manner, expression, or appearance. —*v.t.,* **-limed, -lim·ing.** to cause (a substance) to pass directly from a solid to a gaseous state, or from a gaseous to a solid state, without passing through a liquid state. —*v.i.* to change directly from a solid to a vapor, or from a vapor to a solid, without first becoming a liquid. Mothballs and dry ice sublime. [Latin *sublīmis* lofty.] —**sub·lim′er,** *n.*

sub·lim·i·nal (sub lim′ən əl, -lī′mən-) *adj.* existing below the threshold of sensation or consciousness; too low or slight to be consciously recognized: *a subliminal impression, subliminal motivation.* [SUB- + Latin *līmin-,* stem of *līmen* threshold + -AL¹.]

sub·lim·i·ty (səb lim′ə tē) *pl.*, **-ties.** *n.* **1.** state or quality of excellence; loftiness; grandeur. **2.** one who or that which is sublime.

sub·lu·nar·y (sub′loo ner′ē, sub-loo′nər ē) *adj.* of, existing, or situated beneath the moon, either between the moon and the earth or on the earth. Also, **sub·lu·nar** (sub-loo′nər). [Late Latin *sublūnāris* under the moon, from Latin *sub* under + *lūna* moon.]

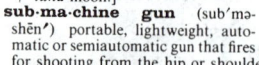

sub·ma·chine gun (sub′mə-shēn′) portable, lightweight, automatic or semiautomatic gun that fires pistol ammunition and is designed for shooting from the hip or shoulder.

Submachine gun

sub·mar·gin·al (sub mär′jin əl) *adj.* **1.** near the margin. **2.** below the margin. **3.** not productive enough to be profitable: *submarginal farmland, submarginal ore deposits.*

sub·ma·rine (*n.,* sub′-mə rēn′, sub′mə rēn′; *adj.,* sub′mə rēn′) *n.* vessel that can operate underwater as well as on the surface, used as an attack or reconnaissance vessel or for oceanographic research. —*adj.* situated, existing, occurring, relating to, or used below the surface of the sea.

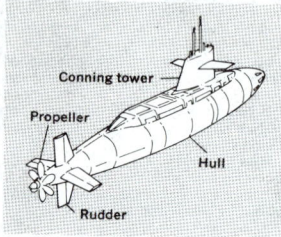

Submarine

sub·max·il·lar·y (sub-mak′sə ler′ē) *pl.*, **-lar·ies.** *n.* **1.** lower jawbone. **2.** submaxillary gland. —*adj.* **1.** of or relating to the lower jaw or jawbone. **2.** of or relating to the submaxillary glands.

submaxillary gland, one of a pair of salivary glands that lie on either side of the mouth beneath the mandible.

sub·merge (səb murj′) **-merged, -merg·ing.** *v.t.* **1.** to place under or cover with some liquid, esp. water. **2.** to overshadow so as to make unnoticeable; cover; hide; obscure. —*v.i.* to sink out of sight by or as by passing beneath the surface of a liquid. [Latin *submergere* to plunge under.] —**sub·mer′gence,** *n.* —**Syn.** *v.t.* **1.** see **dip.**

sub·merse (səb murs′) **-mersed, -mers·ing.** *v.t.* to submerge. [Latin *submersus,* past participle of *submergere* to plunge under.] —**sub·mer·sion** (səb mur′zhən, -shən), *n.*

sub·mers·i·ble (səb mur′sə bəl) *adj.* that can be submerged. —*n.* any of certain vessels that can operate underwater, as for research or exploration.

sub·mis·sion (səb mish′ən) *n.* **1.** act of yielding to some power or authority. **2.** state or quality of being submissive or deferential; acquiescence; humility. **3.** referral of a dispute to the decision or judgment of a third party or parties. [Latin *submissiō* a lowering.] —**Syn.** see **surrender.**

sub·mis·sive (səb mis′iv) *adj.* inclined to yield to power or authority; exhibiting ready compliance; meek; humble. —**sub·mis′-sive·ly,** *adv.* —**sub·mis′sive·ness,** *n.* —**Syn.** see **obedient.**

sub·mit (səb mit′) **-mit·ted, -mit·ting.** *v.i.* **1.** to yield oneself to some power or authority; give up; surrender: *The rebels swore never to submit.* **2. to submit to.** to subject oneself to; undergo: *The old woman refused to submit to surgery. How can he submit to her nagging?* —*v.t.* **1.** to present for the consideration or decision of another or others: *She submitted her term paper three weeks late.* **2.** to put forward as an opinion or proposition; urge in a respectful manner; propose: *I submit that the defendant is not guilty.* [Latin *submittere* to let down, lower, put below.] —**Syn.** *v.i.* **1.** see **defer².**

sub·nor·mal (sub nôr′məl) *adj.* **1.** less than usual, average, or normal, esp. in intelligence. **2.** deficient; defective. —*n.* person of less than normal intelligence. —**sub′nor·mal′i·ty,** *n.* —**sub·nor′mal·ly,** *adv.*

sub·or·bit·al (sub ôr′bit əl) *adj.* **1.** (of a missile, spacecraft, space flight, or the like) not attaining an orbit; not orbiting the earth or a celestial body for one complete turn. **2.** below or under the eye or its orbit.

sub·or·der (sub′ôr′dər) *n.* major subdivision of an order, esp. a taxonomic category ranking below an order but above a family.

sub·or·di·nate (*adj.,n.,* sə bôr′də nit; *v.,* sə bôr′də nāt′) *adj.* **1.** belonging to a lower rank, grade, class, or the like: *a subordinate officer.* **2.** having less importance; not principal or predominant; minor. **3.** dependent upon the main or principal thing; secondary. —*n.* one who or that which is lower than, subordinate to, or dependent on another. —*v.t.*, **-nat·ed, -nat·ing.** to cause to be, or treat as, secondary or inferior; render dependent, subservient, or of less importance. [Medie-

val Latin *subordinatus,* past participle of *subordinare* to place in a lower order, going back to Latin *sub* under + *ordō* row¹, rank¹.] —**sub·or′di·na′tion,** *n.*

subordinate clause, dependent clause.

subordinating conjunction, conjunction that introduces dependent clauses, as *if* or *when.*

sub·orn (sə bôrn′) *v.t.* **1.a.** to cause (a witness) to give false testimony in a court of law. **b.** to obtain (perjured testimony). **2.** to influence (a person) to commit a misdeed, esp. by bribery. [Latin *subōrnāre* to provide, incite secretly.] —**sub·or·na·tion** (sub′ôr nā′shən), **sub·orn′er,** *n.*

sub·phy·lum (sub fī′ləm) *pl.*, **-la** (-lə). *n.* major subdivision of a phylum, esp. a taxonomic category below a phylum but above a class.

sub·plot (sub′plot′) *n.* minor or secondary story line in a literary work, as a play or novel.

sub·poe·na (sə pē′nə) *also*, **sub·pe·na.** *n.* official document ordering a person to appear in a court of law; summons. —*v.t.*, **-naed, -na·ing.** to summon (someone or something) to a court of law by presenting with a subpoena. [Latin *sub poenā* under a penalty (the first words of this writ).]

sub ro·sa (sub rō′zə) confidentially; privately. [Latin *sub rosā* under the rose; the rose was associated with the ancient Greek god of silence.]

sub·scribe (səb skrīb′) **-scribed, -scrib·ing.** *v.i.* **1.** to pay a specified amount in order to receive a newspaper, magazine, or other periodical or similar material for a specified period of time (with *to*). **2.** to promise to pay or contribute a definite amount of money for some special purpose or service (with *to*): *Mr. Morgan subscribes to the same charities every year.* **3.a.** to sign one's name at the end of something to signify one's assent or concurrence (with *to*). **b.** to express agreement, concurrence, or acquiescence; give one's assent or approval: *I heartily subscribe to that sentiment.* —*v.t.* **1.** to promise to give or pay, esp. by writing one's name under an agreement: *Each member subscribed ten dollars for the charity.* **2.** to sign (one's name) beneath, as if to signify assent or concurrence. **3.** to sign one's name to (something) to express agreement or consent: *to subscribe an appeal for support.* [Latin *subscrībere* to write under, sign, agree to.] —**sub·scrib′er,** *n.*

sub·script (sub′skript) *n.* character, as a number, letter, or symbol, usually of relatively small size, printed or written beneath or on the lower half of a line. —*adj.* printed or written beneath or on the lower half of the line. [Latin *subscrīptus,* past participle of *subscrībere* to write under, sign.]

sub·scrip·tion (səb skrip′shən) *n.* **1.** right to receive a newspaper, magazine, or other periodical or similar material for a certain period of time in return for a specified payment. **2.** sum of money pledged, as to a charity; donation; contribution. **3.** fund raised through the contributions of a number of persons. **4.** something added at the end of a piece of writing, as a document, esp. a signature. **5.** act of subscribing.

sub·sec·tion (sub′sek′shən) *n.* part or division of a section.

sub·se·quence (sub′sə kwəns) *n.* **1.** state or condition of being subsequent. **2.** that which is subsequent; sequel; result.

sub·se·quent (sub′sə kwənt) *adj.* coming or occurring later or after, or as a result (often with *to*): *subsequent circumstances. Subsequent to his phone call, I received a confirmation in the mail.* [Latin *subsequēns,* present participle of *subsequī* to follow.] —**sub′se·quent·ly,** *adv.*

sub·serve (səb surv′) **-served, -serv·ing.** *v.t.* to be instrumental in promoting or furthering (someone or something); assist; aid. [Latin *subservīre* to serve, comply with.]

sub·ser·vi·ence (səb sur′vē əns) *n.* **1.** obsequious, servile behavior or attitude; fawning servility; slavish obedience. Also, **sub·ser′vi·en·cy.** **2.** state or instance of being useful.

sub·ser·vi·ent (səb sur′vē ənt) *adj.* **1.** slavishly submissive in behavior or attitude; obsequious. **2.** useful as an instrument or means to further an end; instrumental; serviceable. [Latin *subserviēns,* present participle of *subservīre* to serve, comply with.] —**sub·ser′vi·ent·ly,** *adv.*

sub·set (sub′set′) *n.* set whose members are all contained within another given set. The subsets of the set {a,b} are {a,b}, {a}, {b}, and {o}.

sub·side (səb sīd′) **-sid·ed, -sid·ing.** *v.i.* **1.** to sink to a low or lower level, esp. to the normal or usual level: *The flood waters subsided.* **2.** to decrease in volume, activity, or intensity; be calmed; abate: *The fury of the storm subsided.* **3.** to sink down or fall to the bottom; settle; precipitate. [Latin *subsīdere* to settle down.] —**sub·sid·ence** (səb-sīd′əns, sub′səd əns), *n.*

sub·sid·i·ar·y (səb sid′ē er′ē) *adj.* **1.** serving to help, assist, or supplement; auxiliary; supplementary. **2.** subordinate; secondary. **3.** of, relating to, consisting of, or depending on a subsidy or subsidies. —*n. pl.*, **-ar·ies.** **1.** company owed or controlled by another company, usually resulting from the parent company's ownership of all or a majority of the other company's stock. Also, **subsidiary company.** **2.** any subsidiary person or thing. [Latin *subsidiārius* relating to a reserve, from *subsidium* reserve troops, aid.]

at; āpe; cär; end; mē; it; īce; hot; ōld; fôrk; wood; fōol; oil; out; up; ūse; turn; sing; thin; this; zh in treasure; ə in ago, taken, pencil, lemon, circus.

sub·si·dize (sub′sə dīz′) -dized, -diz·ing. *v.t.* **1.** to aid or support with a subsidy: *The government subsidizes farmers when they agree not to produce certain crops.* **2.** to purchase the aid or assistance of by the payment of a subsidy. **3.** to secure the cooperation of by bribery. —sub′si·di·za′tion, sub′si·diz′er, *n.*

sub·si·dy (sub′sə dē) *pl.*, **-dies.** *n.* contribution, esp. of money, given as a supplement or assistance. [Latin *subsīdium* reserve troops, aid.]

sub·sist (səb sist′) *v.i.* **1.** to maintain existence; support life; exist (usually with *on*): *The lost explorers barely managed to subsist on the fruits and berries they could find.* **2.** to have existence or continue to exist; remain; abide: *traditions that have subsisted through the ages.* [Latin *subsistere* to stand still, stay¹.]

sub·sist·ence (səb sis′təns) *n.* **1.a.** state or condition of maintaining life; continued existence. **b.** means of supporting life; support; livelihood. **2.** actual existence; real being. —sub·sist′ent, *adj.*

sub·soil (sub′soil′) *n.* layer of soil lying immediately beneath the surface soil.

sub·son·ic (sub son′ik) *adj.* of, relating to, or characterized by a speed, or a body moving at a speed, less than that of sound.

sub·spe·cies (sub′spē′shēz, sub spē′-) *pl.*, **-cies.** *n.* subdivision of a species, esp. a taxonomic grouping of plants or animals within a species, usually distinguished by geographical distribution and physical type, as a race or variety.

subst. **1.** substitute. **2.** substantive.

sub·stance (sub′stəns) *n.* **1.a.** that which a physical thing consists of; underlying matter; basic material. **b.** material or matter of a particular type: *A grayish substance covered the entire surface.* **2.** real or essential thing or part; essence, esp. of something written or spoken. **3.a.** ample or solid quality; density; body: *These cheap, light plastics have no substance to them.* **b.** quality of being real and substantial, rather than apparent: *There is substance to his accusation; he did not just invent it.* **4.** wealth; means: *a man of substance.* **5.** in substance. **a.** for the most part; in the main. **b.** actually; really. [Latin *substantia* essence, material; literally, that which stands beneath, going back to *sub* beneath + *stāre* to stand.] —Syn. **1.** see material.

sub·stand·ard (sub stan′dərd, sub′stan′-) *adj.* deviating from or below the established or normal standard.

sub·stan·tial (səb stan′shəl) *adj.* **1.** of considerable amount or importance; ample: *to show a substantial profit, to enjoy substantial success.* **2.** having a solid base or basis; firmly or strongly established or constructed. **3.** possessing abundant wealth; well-to-do; wealthy. **4.** having actual existence or corporeal form; not imaginary or visionary; real. [Late Latin *substantiālis* relating to the essence, from Latin *substantia* essence. See SUBSTANCE.] —sub·stan·ti·al·i·ty (səb stan′shē al′ə tē), *n.*

sub·stan·tial·ly (səb stan′shə lē) *adv.* **1.** in the main; essentially. **2.** actually; really. **3.** strongly; solidly.

sub·stan·ti·ate (səb stan′shē āt′) -at·ed, -at·ing. *v.t.* **1.** to furnish factual evidence in order to prove; verify: *Can you substantiate his alibi?* **2.** to give actual form to; embody. —sub·stan′ti·a′tion, *n.* —Syn. **1.** see confirm.

sub·stan·ti·val (sub′stən tī′vəl) *adj.* of, relating to, or characteristic of a substantive or substantives.

sub·stan·tive (sub′stən tiv) *n.* noun or pronoun, or an adjective, phrase, or clause used as a noun substitute. —*adj.* **1.a.** used as a noun or noun substitute. **b.** denoting the verb of existence, *to be.* **2.** standing of or by itself; independent. **3.** substantial; solid; real. [Late Latin *substantīvus* self-existent, from Latin *substantia* essence. See SUBSTANCE.] —sub′stan·tive·ly, *adv.*

sub·sta·tion (sub′stā′shən) *n.* subsidiary station, as of a post office.

sub·sti·tute (sub′stə tōōt′, -tūt′) *n.* one who or that which acts or is used in place of another. —*v.t.* **-tut·ed, -tut·ing.** to put (someone or something) in place of another: *We substituted John for Bill at first base.* —*v.i.* to act as a substitute. —*adj.* taking the place of or performing the function of another: *a substitute teacher.* [Latin *substitūtus*, past participle of *substituere* to put instead of.]

Syn. *n.* **Substitute, proxy** mean a person who takes the place or performs the duties of another in his absence. **Substitute** is usually applied to one who stands by to serve when needed: *A substitute was sent out to bat in place of the injured player.* **Proxy** is usually applied to one who is empowered to act for another at a ceremony or election without further obligations: *The groom was represented at the wedding by a proxy.*

sub·sti·tu·tion (sub′stə tōō′shən, -tū′-) *n.* act of substituting; being substituted. —sub′sti·tu′tion·al, sub′sti·tu′tion·ar′y, *adj.*

sub·sti·tu·tive (sub′stə tōō′tiv, -tū′-) *adj.* of, relating to, or tending to carry out substitution. **2.** being a substitute or capable of being one.

sub·strate (sub′strāt′) *n.* **1.** substratum. **2.** substance activated by an enzyme or one on which an enzyme acts.

sub·stra·tum (sub strā′təm, -strat′əm) *pl.*, **-stra·ta** (-strā′tə,

-strat′ə) or **-stra·tums.** *n.* **1.** substance that lies under another, esp. a layer of earth beneath the surface layer. **2.** basis or foundation. [Modern Latin *substrātum* spread underneath, from Latin *substrātum,* neuter past participle of *substernere* to spread under.]

sub·struc·ture (sub′struk′chər) *n.* underlying part which supports a main structure; foundation.

sub·sume (səb sōōm′) -sumed, -sum·ing. *v.t.* to include in some larger, higher, or more general classification or category (with *under*). [Modern Latin *subsūmere* to take under, from Latin *sub* under + *sūmere* to take.]

sub·tem·per·ate (sub tem′pər it) *adj.* of or relating to colder parts or areas of a temperate zone; barely temperate in climate.

sub·ten·an·cy (sub ten′ən sē) *pl.*, **-cies.** *n.* status, right, or holding of a subtenant.

sub·ten·ant (sub ten′ənt) *n.* one who occupies a place by renting or subleasing from a tenant.

sub·tend (səb tend′) *v.t.* **1.** to extend under or be positioned opposite to or across from so as to mark the extent of. A chord subtends its arc. **2.** *Botany.* (of a leaf or bract) to extend so as to enclose or enfold, as a bud. [Latin *subtendere* to stretch beneath.]

sub·ter·fuge (sub′tər fūj′) *n.* device or expedient used for escape or concealment; evasion; ruse. [Late Latin *subterfugium,* going back to Latin *subter* secretly, underneath + *fugere* to flee.]

sub·ter·ra·ne·an (sub′tə rā′nē ən) *adj.* **1.** existing, situated, or taking place below the surface of the earth; underground: *a subterranean tunnel, subterranean life.* **2.** existing or occurring out of sight; done secretly. Also, **sub′ter·ra′ne·ous.** [Latin *subterrāneus* underground (from *sub* under + *terra* earth) + -AN.]

sub·tile (sut′əl, sub′til) *adj.* *Archaic.* subtle. —sub′tile·ly, *adv.*

sub·til·i·ty (sub til′ə tē) *pl.*, **-ties.** *n.* *Archaic.* subtlety.

sub·til·ty (sut′əl tē, sub′til-) *pl.*, **-ties.** *n.* *Archaic.* subtlety.

sub·ti·tle (sub′tī′təl) *n.* **1.** secondary or additional title, as of a book or article, usually of an explanatory nature. **2.** translation of foreign-language dialogue in a motion picture, superimposed on the screen, usually near the bottom.

sub·tle (sut′əl) *adj.* **1.** having a faint, delicate quality, so as to be nearly imperceptible; elusive; tenuous: *a subtle odor.* **2.** secret; provocative; mysterious: *The subject in the painting is famous for her subtle smile.* **3.** capable of discerning or understanding fine distinctions in meaning; perceptive: *a subtle mind.* **4.** treacherously or deceitfully cunning; crafty; sly: *a subtle plan to cheat someone.* **5.** characterized by cleverness or ingenuity; artful; ingenious. **6.** difficult to solve or understand; ambiguous; abstruse: *a subtle problem.* [Old French *soutil* thin, keen, crafty, from Latin *subtīlis* thin, keen, precise; originally, finely woven, from *sub* under + *tēla* web.] —sub′tly, *adv.* —sub′tle·ness, *n.*

sub·tle·ty (sut′əl tē) *pl.*, **-ties.** *n.* **1.** quality or instance of being subtle. **2.** that which is subtle, esp. a fine distinction.

sub·ton·ic (sub ton′ik) *n.* *Music.* seventh tone of the diatonic scale; tone next below the upper tonic.

sub·top·ic (sub′top′ik) *n.* secondary topic that is a subdivision of the main topic, as of an article or lecture.

sub·to·tal (sub′tōt′əl, sub tōt′-) *n.* sum of part of a group of numbers or quantities being added, esp. such a sum arrived at in the process of determining the final, complete total for the whole group. —*v.t., v.i.* **-taled, -tal·ing;** *also, British,* **-talled, -tal·ling.** to determine the sum of part of a group of numbers or quantities being added.

sub·tract (səb trakt′) *v.t.* **1.** to take away or deduct (a number) from a given number in order to determine the number remaining: *If you subtract 3 from 7, that leaves 4.* **2.** to withdraw or take away (any element) from a whole; deduct. —*v.i.* to perform the operation or process of subtraction: *Do you know how to subtract with negative numbers?* [Latin *subtractus,* past participle of *subtrahere* to draw off, remove.] —sub·tract′er, *n.*

sub·trac·tion (səb trak′shən) *n.* **1.** operation or process of determining the difference between two numbers. **2.** act or instance of subtracting.

sub·trac·tive (səb trak′tiv) *adj.* **1.** inclined to or having the ability to subtract; detracting. **2.** that is to be subtracted; having the minus sign (−).

sub·tra·hend (sub′trə hend′) *n.* number or quantity that is to be subtracted from another. In the equation 11 − 4 = 7, 4 is the subtrahend. Distinguished from **minuend.** [Latin *subtrahendus* to be subtracted, gerundive of *subtrahere* to draw off, remove.]

sub·treas·ur·y (sub trezh′ər ē, sub′trezh′-) *pl.*, **-ur·ies.** *n.* subordinate or branch treasury.

sub·trop·i·cal (sub trop′i kəl) *adj.* of or relating to regions bordering on the tropics; having a nearly tropical climate.

sub·trop·ics (sub trop′iks) *n.,pl.* subtropical regions.

sub·urb (sub′urb) *n.* **1.** residential district close to or on the outer edge of a city. **2. the suburbs.** area consisting of such districts. [Latin *suburbium,* from *sub* under + *urbs* city.]

at; āpe; cär; end; mē; it; īce; hot; ōld; fôrk; wood; fōōl; oil; out; up; ūse; turn; sing; thin; this; zh in treasure; ə in ago, taken, pencil, lemon, circus.

995

sub·ur·ban (sə bur'bən) *adj.* of, relating to, or characteristic of a suburb.

sub·ur·ban·ite (sə bur'bə nīt') *n.* one who lives in the suburbs.

sub·ur·bi·a (sə bur'bē ə) *n.* **1.** the suburbs or suburbanites collectively. **2.** interests, activities, or viewpoints regarded as characteristic of the suburbs or suburbanites.

sub·ven·tion (səb ven'shən) *n.* **1.** grant of money for aid or support, esp. a government subsidy. **2.** act or instance of giving such aid. [Late Latin *subventiō* assistance, from Latin *subvenīre* to assist, come to one's aid.]

sub·ver·sion (səb vur'zhən, -shən) *n.* **1.** act of undermining or bringing about the destruction of a government or other established institution. **2.** that which causes such undermining or destruction. [Late Latin *subversiō* an overthrow, from Latin *subvertere* to turn upside down, overthrow.]

sub·ver·sive (səb vur'siv) *adj.* attempting, advocating, or tending to overthrow, undermine, or destroy: *a subversive speech, subversive activities.* —*n.* one who advocates or attempts the overthrow or undermining of a government or other established institution.

sub·vert (səb vurt') *v.t.* **1.** to bring about the destruction of; overthrow; destroy: *to subvert a dictatorship.* **2.** to undermine, as the loyalty, faith, or principles of; corrupt. [Latin *subvertere* to turn upside down, overthrow.] —**sub·vert'er,** *n.*

sub·way (sub'wā') *n.* **1.** railway that runs wholly or partly underground, esp. one in a large urban area providing passenger and commuting service. **2.** *British.* underground passage, esp. for conveying pipes or wires, or for pedestrians to travel from one point to another.

suc·ceed (sək sēd') *v.i.* **1.** to have the desired result or conclusion; turn out successfully: *The venture succeeded even better than they had expected.* **2.** to accomplish what is attempted or intended; obtain the desired object or outcome: *He succeeded in discovering a new vaccine.* **3.** to come next in the place of another or that which has preceded, esp. to ascend to a position after the removal or death of the occupant (with *to*): *After the death of the king, his son succeeded to the throne.* —*v.t.* to take the place of; be heir or successor to, as in some occupation or position: *John succeeded Harry as treasurer of the club.* [Latin *succēdere* to go beneath, follow.] —**suc·ceed'er,** *n.* —**Syn.** *v.i.* 3. see **follow.**

suc·cess (sək ses') *n.* **1.** favorable result or conclusion; attainment of a desired end. **2.** attainment or acquisition of wealth, status, or other desirable condition. **3.** one who or that which succeeds or is successful: *The young actor was an overnight success.* [Latin *successus* good result, from *succēdere* to follow.]

suc·cess·ful (sək ses'fəl) *adj.* having, attaining, or resulting in success; fortunate. —**suc·cess'ful·ly,** *adv.* —**suc·cess'ful·ness,** *n.*

suc·ces·sion (sək sesh'ən) *n.* **1.** group of people or things following one another in time or place; sequence; series: *The poor man had a succession of misfortunes. A succession of children followed the Pied Piper.* **2.** act of one person or thing following another in time or place. **3.a.** right of being next in line for an office, rank, or the like held by another: *His succession to the vice-presidency was unchallenged.* **b.** order or line of persons having such a right. **4. in succession.** one after another; in orderly sequence.

suc·ces·sive (sək ses'iv) *adj.* coming one after another in an uninterrupted sequence. —**suc·ces'sive·ly,** *adv.* —**suc·ces'sive·ness,** *n.*
Syn. **Successive, consecutive** mean to follow one after another in sequence. **Successive** refers to events that follow in sequence but may be separated by a time interval: *The football team celebrated its fourth successive victory.* **Consecutive** implies that one thing follows another without interruption: *May, June, and July are consecutive months.*

suc·ces·sor (sək ses'ər) *n.* one who or that which follows or takes the place of another, esp. a person who succeeds or is in line to succeed another in some office, rank, or the like. [Latin *successor* follower.]

suc·cinct (sək singkt') *adj.* **1.** written or spoken in few words; brief and concise; terse. **2.** characterized by verbal brevity and conciseness: *a succinct style of writing.* [Latin *succinctus* prepared, short, past participle of *succingere* to tuck up, gird below.] —**suc·cinct'ly,** *adv.* —**suc·cinct'ness,** *n.* —**Syn.** 1. see **concise.**

suc·cor (suk'ər) *also, British,* **suc·cour.** *n.* help; assistance; relief. —*v.t.* to give help, assistance, or relief to. [Old French *sucurre* to aid, assist, from Latin *succurrere* to run up to, aid.]

suc·co·ry (suk'ər ē) *pl.,* **-ries.** *n.* chicory.

suc·co·tash (suk'ə tash') *n.* corn kernels and beans, usually lima beans, cooked together. [Modification of Algonquian *msiquatash* ear of corn; literally, the grains are unbroken.]

suc·cu·bus (suk'yə bəs) *pl.,* **-bi** (-bī') *n.* female demon or evil spirit, esp. in medieval legend, that supposedly appeared to men while they were sleeping and sought sexual intercourse with them. [Medieval Latin *succubus* strumpet, from Late Latin *succuba,* from Latin *succubāre* to lie under.]

suc·cu·lence (suk'yə ləns) *n.* state or quality of being succulent. Also, **suc'cu·len·cy.**

suc·cu·lent (suk'yə lənt) *adj.* **1.** full of juice; juicy. **2.** rich and delicious: *a succulent morsel.* **3.** providing mental stimulation; provoking interest. **4.** having thick, fleshy leaves and stems that can store large quantities of water. —*n.* succulent plant, as a cactus. [Latin *succulentus* full of juice, from *succus* juice.]

suc·cumb (sə kum') *v.i.* **1.** to give way, as under pressure or force; submit; yield (often with *to*). **2.** to yield to a disease, wound, or the like; die (often with *to*): *to succumb to a bullet wound.* [Latin *succumbere* to lie under, surrender.]

such (such) *adj.* **1.** of the same kind or degree: *Have you ever heard such a story?* **2.** of that particular kind or degree: *Such meager assistance was next to useless.* **3.** of a similar kind or degree; like: *She bought lettuce, tomatoes, and such items for a salad.* **4.** of an extreme degree, quantity, or kind: *It was such a surprise.* **5.** *also,* **such and such.** of indefinite name, location, or the like; some: *He went to such and such a movie.* —*pron.* **1.** one who or that which has previously been mentioned or indicated. **2. as such. a.** being of the same or similar kind as previously mentioned or indicated: *He is not really a scholar, as such.* **b.** in itself; intrinsically: *Success, as such, does not always bring happiness.* **3. such as. a.** of the same or particular kind or degree: *A man such as he will surely succeed.* **b.** for example: *dogs, such as dachshunds and poodles.* [Old English *swylc, swelc, swilc* of the kind mentioned or implied.]

such·like (such'līk') *adj.* of the same or a similar kind. —*pron.* persons or things of such a kind.

suck (suk) *v.t.* **1.** to draw (something) into the mouth by creating a partial vacuum with the lips and tongue: *She liked to suck milk through a straw.* **2.** to draw, esp. a liquid, from (something) by applying the mouth: *to suck an orange.* **3.** to hold in the mouth and absorb by the action of the tongue and the muscles of the cheeks: *She sucked a lozenge for her sore throat.* **4.** to draw in or absorb by the use of suction: *The vacuum cleaner sucked the dust up out of the crevices.* **5.** to swallow up; engulf. —*v.i.* **1.** to draw by sucking or suction. **2.** to draw milk from a breast or a bottle; suckle. **3.** (of a pump) to draw air instead of water. —*n.* **1.** act or instance of sucking. **2.** sound made when sucking. [Old English *sūcan* to draw liquid with the mouth.]

suck·er (suk'ər) *n.* **1.** one who or that which sucks. **2.** any of a group of toothless freshwater fish, family Catostomidae, native to North America and Asia, having fleshy, sucking lips on the underside of the head. Length: from 2 inches to 3 feet. **3.** organ of any of certain animals, as squid, barnacles, or certain parasites, used for sucking or for attaching to something by suction. **4.** shoot growing from the underground stem or root of a plant. **5.** *Slang.* one who can easily be cheated, deceived, or imposed upon. **6.** *Informal.* piece of candy which is licked or held in the mouth and absorbed, as a lollipop. —*v.i.* (of a plant) to produce suckers. —*v.t.* to remove suckers or young shoots from (corn, tobacco, or other plants).

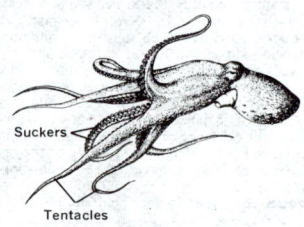

Suckers

Tentacles

Sucker *(def. 3)*

suck·le (suk'əl) **-led, -ling.** *v.t.* **1.** to give milk to (someone or something) from a breast, udder, or the like. **2.** to bring up; nurture. —*v.i.* to drink milk from a breast, udder, or the like. [SUCK + -LE.]

suck·ling (suk'ling) *n.* infant or young animal that is not yet weaned. —*adj.* **1.** young and inexperienced. **2.** not yet weaned.

su·cre (sōō'krā) *n.* monetary unit of Ecuador. [From Antonio José de Sucre, 1795–1830, South American military leader and liberator.]

Su·cre (sōō'krā) *n.* official capital of Bolivia, in the southern part of the country. Pop. (1965 est.), 58,359.

su·crose (sōō'krōs) *n.* common sugar, a crystalline, organic compound with a sweet taste, used for sweetening foods and also in the manufacture of plastics and explosives. Formula: $C_{12}H_{22}O_{11}$. [French *sucre* (see SUGAR) + -OSE[2].]

suc·tion (suk'shən) *n.* **1.** force created by a complete or partial vacuum that draws a gas or liquid into a space from which all or part of the air or liquid has been removed. **2.** act or instance of drawing a liquid or gas into a space where a partial vacuum has been created. —*adj.* causing, relating to, or done by suction. [Late Latin *sūctiō* a sucking, from Latin *sūctus,* past participle of *sūgere* to suck.]

suction stop, click (*n., def.* 3).

suc·to·ri·al (suk tôr'ē əl) *adj.* relating to, adapted for, or characterized by sucking or suction.

Su·dan (sōō dan') *n.* **1.** country in northwestern Africa, on the southern border of Egypt, formerly known as the Anglo-Egyptian Sudan.

at; āpe; cär; end; mē; it; īce; hot; ōld; fôrk; wood; fōōl; oil; out; up; ūse; turn; sing; thin; this; zh in treasure; ə ago, taken, pencil, lemon, circus.

Capital, Khartoum. Area, 967,500 sq. mi. Pop. (1969 est.), 15,186,000. **2.** region extending across Africa from the Atlantic to Ethiopia and south from the Sahara to the central and western tropical forests. Much of the Sudan is semiarid grassland.

Su·da·nese (sōō′də nēz′, -nēs′) *adj.* of, relating to, or characteristic of the country or region of Sudan, its inhabitants, or their culture. —*n. pl.,* **-nese.** native or inhabitant of the country or region of Sudan.

Sudan grass, sorghum of a variety native to the Sudan, suited to semiarid conditions and cultivated as hay and fodder for livestock.

su·da·to·ri·um (sōō′də tôr′ē əm) *pl.,* **-to·ri·a** (-tôr′ē ə). *n.* room in which a steam bath or hot-air bath is taken to produce sweating. [Latin *sūdātōrium* a sweating bath, going back to *sūdor* sweat.]

sud·den (sud′ən) *adj.* **1.** done or occurring without warning; unexpected: *The sudden arrival of guests forced her to change her plans.* **2.** swift; abrupt; hasty: *a sudden decision. The sudden stop caused many passengers to lurch.* —*n.* **all of a sudden.** without notice; all at once; unexpectedly. [Middle French *soudain* immediate, quick, going back to Latin *subitāneus* unexpected, hasty.] —**sud′den·ness,** *n.*

sudden death *Sports.* extra play undertaken to break a tie, the winner being the first side to go ahead, as by scoring in football or by winning a hole in golf.

sud·den·ly (sud′ən lē) *adv.* without warning, preparation, or premeditation.

Su·de·ten·land (sōō dāt′ən land′) *n.* mountainous border region in northern and western Czechoslovakia.

su·dor·if·er·ous (sōō′də rif′ər əs) *adj.* secreting or producing sweat.

su·dor·if·ic (sōō′də rif′ik) *adj.* of, relating to, or causing sweat. [Modern Latin *sudorificus,* going back to Latin *sūdor* sweat + *facere* to make.]

suds (sudz) *n.,pl.* **1.** frothy mass of bubbles that forms on the top of water containing soap or detergent. **2.** such a frothy mass together with its water. **3.** any foam or froth. **4.** *Slang.* beer. —*v.i.* (of a soap or detergent) to produce suds. —*v.t.* to wash (something) with water containing suds. [Probably from Middle Dutch *sudse* marsh, bog.] —**suds′y,** *adj.*

sue (sōō) sued, su·ing. *v.t.* **1.** to start a suit against in a court of law, esp. to obtain a certain amount in damages. —*v.i.* **1.** to take legal action. **2.** to appeal or plead (with *for*): *In vain he sued for forgiveness.* **3.** *Archaic.* to pay court to; woo. [Old French *suir,* form of *sivre* to follow, going back to Latin *sequī* to follow.] —**su′er,** *n.* —**Syn.** *v.i.* **2.** see **appeal.**

suede (swād) *also,* **suède.** *n.* **1.** soft leather that has a velvety nap, usually on the flesh side of the skin. **2.** fabric made with a short nap on one side to resemble this leather. —*adj.* of, resembling, or characteristic of suede. [French *Suède* Sweden, as in the phrase *gants de Suède* (leather) gloves of Sweden.]

su·et (sōō′it) *n.* the hard fat from around the kidneys and loins of cattle and sheep. [From an unrecorded diminutive of Anglo-Norman *sue, seu* suet, from Latin *sēbum.*] —**su′et·y,** *adj.*

Sue·to·ni·us (swi tō′nē əs) *n.* A.D. c.69–c.140, Roman historian.

Su·ez (sōō ez′, sōō′ez) *n.* **1.** port city in northeastern Egypt, at the southern entrance of the Suez Canal. Pop. (1966), 264,500. **2.** Suez Canal.

Suez Canal, canal in northeastern Egypt connecting the Mediterranean and Red seas.

suf-, form of **sub-** before *f,* as in *suffix, suffuse.*

suf·fer (suf′ər) *v.i.* **1.** to experience or be subject to intense physical, emotional, or mental discomfort or stress: *She suffers from various allergies. The child suffered under the cruel tyrant.* **2.** to undergo loss or damage; be hurt: *His schoolwork suffered from all his social activities.* —*v.t.* **1.** to feel or be subject to; undergo: *She suffered acute embarrassment when speaking before a group.* **2.** to allow; permit: *Suffer the little children to come unto me* (Mark 10:14). **3.** to bear up under; put up with; tolerate. [Latin *sufferre* to undergo, endure.] —**suf′fer·y,** *adj.*

suf·fer·a·ble (suf′ər ə bəl, suf′rə-) *adj.* capable of being endured, tolerated, or permitted.

suf·fer·ance (suf′ər əns, suf′rəns) *n.* **1.** sanction, consent, or acquiescence given or implied by the absence of intervention or prevention. ▲ usually used in the phrase *on sufferance,* and implying bare tolerance. **2.** *Archaic.* capacity to undergo suffering; patient endurance; submission.

suf·fer·ing (suf′ər ing, suf′ring) *n.* act, instance, or condition of undergoing extreme pain, distress, or hardship. —**Syn.** see **distress.**

suf·fice (sə fīs′) -ficed, -fic·ing. *v.i.* **1.** to be sufficient or adequate; be enough: *One suit will suffice for the weekend. A simple answer will suffice.* —*v.t.* to meet the desires, needs, or requirements of; be enough for; satisfy. [Latin *sufficere* to provide, be enough.]

suf·fi·cien·cy (sə fish′ən sē) *pl.,* **-cies.** *n.* **1.** adequate amount or quantity. **2.** state or quality of being adequate or sufficient; adequacy. **3.** self-sufficiency; self-confidence.

suf·fi·cient (sə fish′ənt) *adj.* **1.** as much as is necessary or needed;

adequate; enough: *One blanket will provide sufficient warmth.* **2.** *Archaic.* competent; capable. [Latin *sufficiēns,* present participle of *sufficere* to provide, be enough.] —**suf·fi′cient·ly,** *adv.* —**Syn. 1.** see **enough.**

suf·fix (*n.,* suf′iks; *v.,* suf′iks, sə fiks′) *n.* word element added as an inflection at the end of a word to form another word of different meaning or function, as in *bad*ness, *good*ly, *boy*ish. —*v.t.* to add or attach at the end, esp. as a suffix. [Modern Latin *suffixum,* from Latin *suffixum,* neuter past participle of *suffīgere* to fasten to or beneath.]

suf·fix·al (suf′ik səl) *adj.* of, relating to, or characteristic of a suffix or suffixes.

suf·fo·cate (suf′ə kāt′) -cat·ed, -cat·ing. *v.t.* **1.** to kill by preventing breathing. **2.** to interrupt or impede the breathing of: *The small room was suffocating him.* **3.** to smother; stifle; extinguish. —*v.i.* **1.** to die from an interrupted or insufficient supply of air: *The children soon suffocated when they couldn't get out of the old icebox.* **2.** to be or become stifled or smothered: choke: *She was suffocating in the crowded train.* [Latin *suffocātus,* past participle of *suffocāre* to choke.] —**suf′fo·cat′ing·ly,** *adv.* —**suf′fo·ca′tion,** *n.* —**suf′fo·ca′tive,** *adj.*

Suf·folk (suf′ək) *n.* former county in eastern England.

suf·fra·gan (suf′rə gən) *n.* **1.** in the Anglican Church, a bishop who assists another bishop but who does not have the right of succession. **2.** any bishop in relation to his archbishop or metropolitan. —*adj.* assisting; assistant. [Old French *suffragant* subordinate, bishop subordinate to an archbishop, going back to Latin *suffrāgārī* to vote for, support.]

suf·frage (suf′rij) *n.* **1.** right or privilege of voting, esp. the exercise of voting power in political affairs; franchise. **2.** act of casting a vote; voting. **3.** a vote, esp. in favor of a person to occupy an office or trust. **4.** short prayer or petition. [Latin *suffrāgium* a vote, the right of voting.]

suf·fra·gette (suf′rə jet′) *n.* woman who militantly advocates that women have the right to vote and hold office.

suf·fra·gist (suf′rə jist) *n.* one who favors extending the right to vote, esp. to women.

suf·fuse (sə fūz′) -fused, -fus·ing. *v.t.* to spread through or over, as with a light, color, or emotion: *a room suffused with sunshine, eyes suffused with tears. His face was suffused with happiness.* ▲ usually construed in the passive. [Latin *suffūsus,* past participle of *suffundere* to pour beneath, fill, tinge.] —**suf·fu′sion,** *n.*

Su·fi (sōō′fē) *n.* member of a mystical Islamic sect. [Arabic *sūfī* literally, man of wool (probably a reference to the woolen garments of the Sufis), from *sūf* wool.] —**Su·fism** (sōō′fiz′əm), *n.*

sug-, form of **sub-** before *g,* as in *suggest.*

sug·ar (shoog′ər) *n.* **1.** any of several white or brown crystalline forms of the organic compound sucrose, obtained mainly from sugarcane and sugar beets and used esp. for sweetening foods. Formula: $C_{12}H_{22}O_{11}$ **2.** any of a class of carbohydrates having a relatively simple molecular structure, including sucrose, glucose, fructose, maltose, and lactose. —*v.t.* **1.** to mix, cover, sprinkle, or sweeten with sugar: *The child liked to sugar her grapefruit.* **2.** to sugar-coat: *He tried to sugar the bad news.* **3. to sugar off.** to boil down maple syrup to make maple sugar. —*v.i.* to form sugar. [Old French *sucre* sweet substance extracted from various plants, through Italian, Arabic, and Persian, from Sanskrit *sharkarā* gravel, grit, granule, candied sugar.]

sugar beet, leafy plant, *Beta vulgaris,* whose long, thick, yellow or white roots are a major source of sugar.

sugar bush, grove of sugar maples.

sug·ar·cane (shoog′ər kān′) *n.* high-growing plant, *Saccharum officinarum,* of the grass family, containing sweet dark-gray juice that is a major source of sugar, having jointed stems, or canes, and downy white flowers.

sug·ar·coat (shoog′ər kōt′) *v.t.* **1.** to cover with sugar: *to sugar-coat a cookie.* **2.** to disguise or soften (something unpleasant) in order to make it more pleasant or acceptable.

sugar corn, sweet corn.

sugar daddy *Slang.* well-to-do, usually older, man who gives expensive gifts or money to a young woman in return for her sexual favors and companionship.

sug·ar·loaf (shoog′ər lōf′) *n.* **1.** conical hard mass of refined sugar. **2.** something having the shape of a sugarloaf, as a conical hill. **3.** high, cone-shaped hat worn esp. by European men during the sixteenth and seventeenth centuries. —*adj.* having the high conical shape of a sugarloaf.

sugar maple, a maple tree, *Acer saccharum,* whose sap is the major source of maple syrup.

sugar pine, tall pine trees, *Pinus lambertiana,* found from Oregon

Sugarcane

to lower California, having deep-green leaves with white lines on the back and large cones.

sug·ar·plum (shoog′ər plum′) *n.* small, usually round piece of candy; bonbon.

sug·ar·y (shoog′ər ē) *adj.* **1.** of, consisting of, containing, or characteristic of sugar. **2.** excessively sweet or honeyed, esp. in order to disguise deceit; cloying: *a sugary smile. She didn't like the sugary tone of his voice.* —**sug′ar·i·ness,** *n.*

sug·gest (səg jest′, sə jest′) *v.t.* **1.** to offer or mention for consideration or action: *I suggest we meet again at a later date.* **2.** to bring or call to mind, as through association or connection: *Her perfume suggests roses.* **3.** to express or indicate indirectly; intimate; hint: *His work suggests that he's ready for more responsibility.* **4.** to provide a motive for; prompt: *His report would suggest a further investigation.* [Latin *suggestus,* past participle of *suggerere* to carry under, supply, advise.]

sug·gest·i·ble (səg jes′tə bəl, sə jes′-) *adj.* **1.** highly susceptible to suggestion; easily influenced or manipulated. **2.** able to be suggested. —**sug·ges′ti·bil′i·ty,** *n.*

sug·ges·tion (səg jes′chən, sə jes′-) *n.* **1.** act or instance of suggesting: *We left at his suggestion.* **2.** that which is suggested: *The suggestion was acceptable to everyone.* **3.** process by which something is brought to mind through an association or connection with something else. **4.** very small indication; trace; hint: *the slightest suggestion of garlic in the sauce.*

sug·ges·tive (səg jes′tiv, sə jes′-) *adj.* **1.** giving a suggestion or hint (with *of*): *The decor is suggestive of another era.* **2.** tending to bring to mind ideas or courses of action; full of suggestions. **3.** tending to suggest something improper or indecent; provocative. —**sug·ges′tive·ly,** *adv.* —**sug·ges′tive·ness,** *n.*

su·i·cid·al (sōō′ə sīd′əl) *adj.* **1.** of, relating to, or causing suicide: *suicidal tendencies.* **2.** dangerously rash; apt to cause disaster to oneself; ruinous: *a suicidal business policy. The suicidal vote put the committee out of existence.* **3.** having a definite inclination to suicide: *a suicidal youth.* —**su′i·cid′al·ly,** *adv.*

su·i·cide[1] (sōō′ə sīd′) *n.* **1.** act or instance of intentionally taking one's own life. ▲ usually used in the phrase *to commit suicide.* **2.** destruction of one's own interests or aims, as in business or politics. [Modern Latin *suicidium,* from Latin *suī* of oneself + *-cidium.* See -CIDE[1].]

su·i·cide[2] (sōō′ə sīd′) *n.* one who has intentionally taken his own life. [Modern Latin *suicidium,* from Latin *suī* of oneself + *-cīda.* See -CIDE[2].]

su·i ge·ne·ris (sōō′ī jen′ər is) *Latin.* of his, her, its, or their own kind; singular; unique.

suit (sōōt) *n.* **1.** set of garments designed to be worn together, esp. a jacket with a matching pair of trousers or skirt. **2.** act, process, or proceeding in a court of law for the redress of a wrong or the enforcement of a claim. **3.** any of the four sets of playing cards in a deck, as spades, hearts, diamonds, or clubs. **4.** act or instance of suing or petitioning, esp. for a woman's hand in marriage. **5.** set of similar or matched things used or intended to be used together. **6. to follow suit. a.** to play a card of the same suit as the card led. **b.** to do the same thing as someone or something else. —*v.t.* **1.** to meet the requirements of; be correct or adapted to: *a house that suits our needs.* **2.** to make right for; adapt: *to suit comedy material to a particular audience.* **3.** to be flattering to: *That color suits you well.* **4.** to please; satisfy: *to suit one's tastes.* **5.** *Archaic.* to furnish with clothes; dress. **6. to suit oneself.** to act in the manner one wishes. —*v.i.* to be suitable, fitting, or convenient. [Old French *siute* pursuit, retinue, going back to Latin *sequī* to follow.]

suit·a·ble (sōō′tə bəl) *adj.* that suits a particular purpose, object, or occasion. —**suit′a·bil′i·ty, suit′a·ble·ness,** *n.* —**suit′a·bly,** *adv.* —Syn. see fit[1].

suit·case (sōōt′kās′) *n.* flat, usually rectangular bag used for carrying clothes and other articles when traveling; valise.

suite (swēt; *def. 2, also* sōōt) *n.* **1.** group of connected rooms considered as a unit, as in a hotel. **2.** set of matching furniture: *a living room suite.* **3.** any set of similar or matched things, used or intended to be used together. **4.** group of attendants or followers; retinue. **5.** *Music.* **a.** early form of instrumental composition consisting of a series of dance tunes in the same or related key. **b.** instrumental composition consisting of a series of short movements, often adapted from a longer work. [French *suite* retinue, set, modification of Old French *siute* pursuit, retinue. See SUIT.]

suit·ing (sōō′ting) *n.* fabric used chiefly for making suits.

suit·or (sōō′tər) *n.* **1.** man who courts or woos a woman. **2.** party to a lawsuit who institutes the suit. **3.** one who pleads or petitions; suppliant.

su·ki·ya·ki (sōō′kē yä′kē, skē yä′kē) *n.* Japanese dish consisting chiefly of thin strips of meat and vegetables sauteed quickly, usually at the dining table. [Japanese *sukiyaki* slices of beef.]

Suk·koth (sook′əs; *Hebrew* sōō kôt′) *also,* **Suk·kot.** *n.* Jewish holiday in the early fall, giving thanks for the harvest and commemorating the wandering of the Hebrews in the wilderness after the Exodus from Egypt. [Hebrew *sukkōth* booths, tabernacles; referring to the temporary shelters used by the Hebrews while wandering in the wilderness.]

Su·lei·man I (sōō′lā män′) *also,* **Sol·y·man.** c.1495–1566, sultan of the Ottoman Empire from 1520 to 1566.

sul·fa·di·a·zine (sul′fə dī′ə zēn′, -zin) *also,* **sul·pha·di·a·zine.** *n.* sulfa drug derived from sulfanilamide, used in treating various infections, esp. pneumonia and meningitis.

sul·fa drug (sul′fə) *also,* **sulpha drug.** any of a group of synthetic drugs used, often with antibiotics, to treat many infectious diseases such as pneumonia, meningitis, and cholera.

sul·fa·nil·a·mide (sul′fə nil′ə mīd′, -mid) *also,* **sul·pha·nil·a·mide.** *n.* early sulfa drug, now used esp. in the manufacture of other, less toxic sulfa drugs.

sul·fa·pyr·i·dine (sul′fə pēr′ə dēn′, -din) *also,* **sul·pha·pyr·i·dine.** *n.* sulfa drug now used chiefly to treat certain skin inflammations.

sul·fate (sul′fāt) *also,* **sul·phate.** *n.* salt of sulfuric acid. [Modern Latin *sulphatum,* from Latin *sulphur, sulfur* sulfur.]

sul·fa·thi·a·zole (sul′fə thī′ə zōl′) *also,* **sul·pha·thi·a·zole.** *n.* sulfa drug, formerly used esp. in treating pneumonia.

sul·fide (sul′fīd) *also,* **sul·phide.** *n.* compound resulting when sulfur is heated with another element. [SULFUR + -IDE.]

sul·fite (sul′fīt) *also,* **sul·phite.** *n.* salt of sulfurous acid. [SULFUR + -ITE[2].]

sul·fon·a·mide (sul fon′ə mīd′) *also,* **sul·phon·a·mide.** *n.* any of the sulfa drugs.

sul·fur (sul′fər) *also,* **sul·phur.** *n.* yellow, nonmetallic element with three common allotropic forms, two crystalline and one amorphous. Sulfur is very abundant in nature and is used to make sulfuric acid, in the vulcanization of rubber, and as a fungicide. Symbol: **S** See element for table. [Latin *sulphur, sulfur.*]

sul·fu·rate (sul′fə rāt′, -fyə-) **-rat·ed, -rat·ing.** *v.t.* to combine or treat (something) with sulfur or a sulfur compound.

sulfur dioxide, colorless gas with a sharp, irritating odor, used to make sulfuric acid and as a bleaching agent, refrigerant, and food preservative. Formula: SO_2

sul·fu·re·ous (sul fyoor′ē əs) *also,* **sul·phu·re·ous.** *adj.* **1.** of, relating to, or containing sulfur. **2.** like sulfur, esp. in odor or color.

sul·fu·ric (sul fyoor′ik) *also,* **sul·phu·ric.** *adj.* **1.** of or relating to sulfur. **2.** containing sulfur in its higher valence.

sulfuric acid, colorless, oily, very reactive liquid compound containing sulfur, hydrogen, and oxygen, used in the manufacture of nearly all chemical products. Also, **oil of vitriol.** Formula: H_2SO_4

sul·fur·ous (sul′fər əs, sul fyoor′əs) *also,* **sul·phur·ous.** *adj.* **1.** of or relating to sulfur. **2.** containing sulfur in its lower valence. **3.** like burning sulfur, as in odor. **4.** of or resembling the fires of hell; infernal.

sulfurous acid, colorless, unstable solution of sulfur dioxide in water, used esp. in synthesizing organic compounds and as a food preservative. Formula: H_2SO_3

sul·fur·y (sul′fər ē) *also,* **sul·phur·y** *adj.* of or resembling sulfur.

sulk (sulk) *v.i.* to be silent or withdrawn as a sign of bad humor or resentfulness. —*n.* **1.** state of sulking: *to be in a sulk.* **2. the sulks.** display or mood of sulking. [Possibly from SULKY.]

sulk·y (sul′kē) **sulk·i·er, sulk·i·est** *adj.* obstinately silent or withdrawn as a display of bad humor or resentfulness. —*n. pl.,* **sulk·ies.** light two-wheeled, one-horse carriage seating one passenger, used esp. for racing. [Possibly from obsolete *sulke* slow (possibly going back to Old English *āsolcen* slothful) + -Y[1].] —**sulk′i·ly,** *adv.* —**sulk′i·ness,** *n.*

Sulky

Sul·la, Lu·cius Cor·nel·ius (sul′ə; lōō′shəs, kôr nēl′yəs) 138–78 B.C., dictator of Rome from 82 to 79 B.C.

sul·len (sul′ən) *adj.* **1.** obstinately withdrawn or gloomy because of bad humor; sulky; morose. **2.** dismal or depressing: *a sullen morning.* [Old French *solain* solitary, going back to Latin *sōlus* alone.] —**sul′len·ly,** *adv.* —**sul′len·ness,** *n.*

Sul·li·van, Sir Arthur Seymour (sul′ə vən) 1842–1900, English composer who collaborated with the librettist Sir William S. Gilbert.

sul·ly (sul′ē) **-lied, -ly·ing.** *v.t.* **1.** to stain the honor or purity of; defile or disgrace: *The scandal sullied the family name.* **2.** to stain the cleanness of; soil. —*n. pl.,* **-lies.** *Archaic.* that which sullies; stain; blemish. [French *souiller* to soil, dirty. See SOIL[2].]

sul·pha·di·a·zine (sul′fə dī′ə zēn′, -zin) sulfadiazine.

at; āpe; cär; end; mē; it; īce; hot; ōld; fôrk; wood; fōōl; oil; out; up; ūse; turn; sing; thin; **this**; zh in treasure; ə in ago, taken, pencil, lemon, circus.

sulpha drug, sulfa drug.
sul·pha·nil·a·mide (sul'fə nil'ə mīd', -mid) sulfanilamide.
sul·pha·pyr·i·dine (sul'fə pēr'ə dēn', -din) sulfapyridine.
sul·phate (sul'fāt) sulfate.
sul·pha·thi·a·zole (sul'fə thī'ə zōl') sulfathiazole.
sul·phide (sul'fīd) sulfide.
sul·phite (sul'fīt) sulfite.
sul·phon·a·mide (sul fon'ə mīd') sulfonamide.
sul·phur (sul'fər) n. 1. sulfur. 2. any of several yellow or orange butterflies, family Pieridae.
sul·phu·re·ous (sul fyoor'ē əs) sulfureous.
sul·phu·ric (sul fyoor'ik) sulfuric.
sul·phur·ous (sul'fər əs, sul fyoor'əs) sulfurous.
sul·phur·y (sul'fər ē) sulfury.
sul·tan (sult'ən) n. in a Muslim country, sovereign or ruling monarch. Turkey and Morocco were formerly ruled by sultans. [French *sultan,* from Arabic *sultān* power, ruler, from Aramaic *shultānā* power.]
sul·tan·a (sul tan'ə, -tä'nə) n. 1. female member of a sultan's court, as a wife, mother, or sister of a sultan. 2. Thompson seedless grape, used for raisins. [Italian *sultana,* feminine of *sultano* sultan, from Arabic *sultān.* See SULTAN.]
sul·tan·ate (sult'ən āt') n. 1. country or area under a sultan's rule. 2. office or reign of a sultan.
sul·try (sul'trē) -tri·er, -tri·est. adj. 1. oppressively hot and humid; sweltering: *the sultry tropics.* 2. producing or emitting excessive heat. 3. suggesting, expressing, or eliciting the heat of passion; sensual. [From obsolete *sulter* to be very hot, form of SWELTER.] —**sul'tri·ness,** n.
Su·lu (soo'loo) n. 1. member of the chief tribe of Moros, living in the Sulu Archipelago. 2. language of the Malay Moro tribes of the Sulu Archipelago, belonging to the Malayo-Polynesian language family.
Sulu Archipelago, group of several hundred islands in the southern Philippines. Area 1,086 sq. mi. Pop. (1960), 326,898.
sum (sum) n. 1. result obtained from addition. 2. the whole quantity; entirety: *the sum of all our efforts.* 3. amount of money: *Untold sums were spent on repairs.* 4. *Informal.* arithmetic problem, esp. a list of numbers to be added. 5. summary; substance; gist: *That's the sum of it.* —v.t., **summed, sum·ming.** 1. to find the numerical sum of (with up). 2. to give a summary of (with up). —v.i. to summarize (with up). [Latin *summa* top, summit, amount, total; originally, feminine of *summus* highest; referring to the Roman practice of reckoning upward and placing the sum at the top.]
sum-, form of **sub-** before *m,* as in *summon.*
su·mac (shoo'mak, soo'-) *also,* **su·mach.** n. 1. any of a large group of trees and shrubs, genus *Rhus,* of the cashew family, having milky or resinous juice that is sometimes poisonous. Poison sumac and poison ivy are sumacs. 2. dried leaves of some of these trees or shrubs, esp. *R. coriaria,* which yield tannin, used in processing leather. [Old French *sumac* sumac tree, from Arabic *summāq,* probably from Syriac *summāq* red.]
Su·ma·tra (soo mä'trə) n. westernmost island of the Malay Archipelago, in Indonesia. Area, 182,860 sq. mi. Pop. (1967), 18,300,000. —**Su·ma'tran,** adj., n.
Su·mer (soo'mər) n. ancient country in southern Mesopotamia.
Su·me·ri·an (soo mēr'ē ən, -mer'-) adj. of, relating to, or characteristic of the inhabitants of Sumer, their language, or their culture. —n. 1. member of an ancient people whose civilization existed in Sumer from about 4000 B.C. to 2000 B.C. 2. extinct language of these people, of unknown origin, preserved in cuneiform inscriptions.
sum·ma cum lau·de (soom'ə koom lou'dē, sum'ə kum lô'də) with highest praise. Distinguished from **cum laude** and **magna cum laude.** ▲ used to signify graduation with highest honors from a college or university. [Modern Latin *summa cum laude.*]
sum·ma·rize (sum'ə rīz') -rized, -riz·ing. v.t. to state briefly or succinctly; make a summary of; sum up. —**sum'ma·rist, sum'ma·ri·za'tion, sum'ma·riz'er,** n.
sum·ma·ry (sum'ər ē) n. pl., -ries. n. condensed statement or brief account containing the main points: *The theater program had a summary of the play.* —adj. 1. containing the main points; concise; brief: *John gave a summary statement of his beliefs.* 2. performed rapidly without hesitation or formality: *Harold ended the dispute by the summary process of turning and walking away.* [Latin *summārium* abstract, epitome, from *summa* amount, principal part, total.] —**sum·mar·i·ly** (sə mar'ə lē, sum'ər ə-), adv.

Syn. n. **Summary, synopsis, précis** are all condensations of a larger work. **Summary** often implies a rather complete and detailed statement sometimes divided under headings for clarity in discussing a large and varied subject: *The newspaper printed only a summary of the speech for lack of space.* **Synopsis** suggests a short statement, esp. in written form, giving a general idea of the subject: *The book contained synopses of the plots of Shakespeare's plays.* **Précis** suggests extreme concentration of

something that has been reduced to the bare essentials and is very precise: *I would like a précis of your career in the foreign service.*
sum·ma·tion (sə mā'shən) n. 1. act or process of finding the total; addition. 2. result of addition; total. 3. final part of an argument in which the facts are reviewed and a conclusion presented.
sum·mer (sum'ər) n. season of the year coming between spring and autumn. In the Northern Hemisphere it extends from about June 21 to about September 22. —adj. of, like, characteristic of, or occurring in summer: *summer vacation.* —v.i. to pass the summer: *We summered in the south of France.* —v.t. to keep or maintain during the summer: *to summer livestock.* [Old English *sumor* this season.]
sum·mer·house (sum'ər hous') n. small, roofed, often rustic structure situated in a garden or park, used as a shady retreat in summer.
sum·mer·sault (sum'ər sôlt') n. somersault.
summer solstice, see solstice *(def. 1).*
summer squash, any of a group of squashes having relatively thin skins and light-colored flesh that are grown in the summer and eaten before ripening.
sum·mer·time (sum'ər tīm') n. summer season.
sum·mer·y (sum'ər ē) adj. characteristic of or suitable for summer.
sum·mit (sum'it) n. 1. highest part or degree; acme. 2. highest level, as of government or political authority: *to have a meeting at the summit.* [Old French *somete* the top, highest point, diminutive of *som* the top (esp. of a hill), from Latin *summum* the top, highest place.] —**Syn.** 1. see peak.
sum·mon (sum'ən) v.t. 1. to send for or request the presence of, esp. with authority: *to summon the police.* 2. to order to appear in court by means of a summons; issue a summons to. 3. to cause to assemble; convene, convoke: *to summon a council.* 4. to request or command to do some specified act: *to summon someone to wait, to summon a garrison to surrender.* 5. to bring or urge to action; rouse (often with *up*): *to summon up one's courage, to summon all one's strength.* [Latin *summonēre* to remind, suggest, warn.] —**sum'mon·er,** n. —**Syn.** v.t. 1. see call.
sum·mons (sum'ənz) pl., -mons·es. n. 1. notice, signal, or command to appear somewhere or to do something. 2. *Law.* document notifying someone that he is required to appear in court. [Old French *somonse* act of calling together, warning, from *somondre* to remind, warn, bid, going back to Latin *summonēre* to remind, warn, suggest.]
sum·mum bo·num (sum'əm bō'nəm) *Latin.* the highest or supreme good.
sump (sump) n. 1. pit or reservoir for collecting liquid, as water, oil, or sewage. 2. pit or well at the bottom of a mining shaft to collect water and from which it can be pumped. [Middle Dutch *sump* pool, swamp.]
sump·ter (sump'tər) n. a horse or mule, for carrying loads; pack animal. [Old French *sommetier* driver of a pack animal, going back to Late Latin *sagmatus,* from Greek *sagma.*]
sump·tu·ar·y (sump'choo er'ē) adj. regulating expenditure: *sumptuary laws.* [Latin *sūmptuārius* relating to expenses, from *sūmptus* expense.]
sump·tu·ous (sump'choo əs) adj. involving or produced at great expense; costly and magnificent; lavish: *a sumptuous apartment, a sumptuous dinner.* [Latin *sūmptuōsus,* from *sūmptus* expense.] —**sump'tu·ous·ly,** adv. —**sump'tu·ous·ness,** n. —**Syn.** see magnificent.
Sum·ter, Fort (sum'tər) fort in the harbor of Charleston, South Carolina. On April 12, 1861, the Civil War began when Confederate forces attacked this fort.
sun (sun) n. 1. star that is the central body of the solar system, around which the earth and other planets revolve and from which they receive light and heat. The sun has a mean distance from earth of about 93,-000,000 miles, a diameter of about 864,000 miles, and a mass of about 300,000 times that of the earth. 2. light and heat from the sun; sunshine: *Too much sun at one time can produce a painful burn.* 3. any star that is the center of a planetary system. 4. **a place in the sun.** prominent position or condition. —v.t., **sunned, sun·ning.** 1. to expose to the rays of the sun. 2. to warm or dry in the sun. —v.i. to expose oneself to the rays of the sun: *Charlotte sunned on the terrace.* [Old English *sunne* the brightest of the heavenly bodies as seen from earth.]
Sun., Sunday.
sun bath, exposure of the body to the rays of the sun or a sunlamp.
sun·bathe (sun'bāth') -bathed, -bath·ing. v.i. to bask in the sun; take a sun bath. —**sun'bath'er,** n.
sun·beam (sun'bēm') n. beam of sunlight.
sun·bird (sun'burd') n. any of several small songbirds, family Nectariniidae, found in tropical regions of Africa, Asia, and Australia and having brightly colored, iridescent plumage. Length: to 8 inches.
sun·bon·net (sun'bon'it) n. woman's bonnet with a broad brim that protects the face and a flap that protects the neck.
sun·burn (sun'burn') n. inflammation of the skin caused by overexposure to the sun or a sunlamp. —v.t., -burned or -burnt, -burn·ing. to overexpose to the sun or a sunlamp; affect with sunburn: *At the beach,*

---

at; āpe; cär; end; mē; it; īce; hot; ōld; fôrk; wood; fōōl; oil; out; up; ūse; turn; sing; thin; this; zh in treasure; ə in ago, taken, pencil, lemon, circus.   999

he sunburned his back. —*v.i.* to become affected with sunburn: *She sunburns easily.*

sun·burst (sun′bûrst′) *n.* **1.** sudden burst of sunlight, as through a break in the clouds. **2.** ornamental pin with a central disk and rays emanating from it.

sun·dae (sun′dē, -dā) *n.* ice cream served with a topping, as syrup, nuts, or fruit. [Possibly modification of SUNDAY; supposedly because it was originally sold only on Sunday as a special treat since it was more expensive than plain ice cream.]

Sun·day (sun′dē, -dā) *n.* first day of the week and the Sabbath for most Christians. [Old English *sunnandæg* literally, sun's day, translation of Latin *diēs sōlis.*]

Sunday best *Informal.* one's best clothes.

Sunday school **1.** school usually affiliated with a church and held on Sunday for religious instruction. **2.** pupils and teachers of such a school.

sun deck roof or terrace used for sunbathing.

sun·der (sun′dər) *v.t., v.i.* to make or become divided; divide; separate. [Old English *sundrian.*] —**sun′der·a·ble,** *adj.* —**sun′der·ance,** *n.*

Sun·der·land (sun′dər lənd) *n.* port city in northeastern England, on the North Sea. Pop. (1968), 219,700.

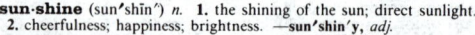

Sundew

sun·dew (sun′dōō′, -dū′) *n.* any of a group of plants, genus *Drosera,* having leaves covered with sticky hairlike structures that trap and digest insects.

sun·di·al (sun′dī′əl, -dīl′) *n.* device that indicates the time of the day by the position and length of a shadow cast on a surface, usually a round, flat surface marked with numerals.

sun·dog (sun′dôg′) *n.* parhelion.

sun·down (sun′doun′) *n.* sunset.

sun·dries (sun′drēz) *n.,pl.* numerous, miscellaneous small items.

sun·dry (sun′drē) *adj.* more than one; indefinite in number; several; various. [Old English *syndrig* separate.] —**Syn.** see **several.**

sun·fast (sun′fast′) *adj.* that will not fade when exposed to sunlight.

Sunfish

sun·fish (sun′fish′) *pl.* **-fish** or **-fish·es.** *n.* **1.** any of several freshwater fish, family Centrarchidae, found in North America. Length: 1–15 inches. **2.** ocean sunfish.

sun·flow·er (sun′flou′ər) *n.* **1.** large flower of any of several tall plants, genus *Helianthus,* of the composite family, having petal-like rays surrounding a yellowish or purplish-brown disk. **2.** plant bearing such a flower.

sung (sung) a past tense and the past participle of **sing.**

Sung (soong) *n.* Chinese dynasty that ruled from A.D. 960 to 1279, a period noted for high artistic achievement, esp. in painting and ceramics.

sun·glass·es (sun′glas′iz) *n.,pl.* eyeglasses having shaded or tinted lenses to protect the eyes from the sun's glare.

sun god god identified with the sun.

sunk (sungk) a past tense and the past participle of **sink.**

sunk·en (sung′kən) *v.* a past participle of **sink.** —*adj.* **1.** having sunk below the surface of the water or ground: *sunken treasure, sunken rock.* **2.** situated below the surrounding area: *a sunken living room.* **3.** abnormally depressed; hollow: *sunken cheeks.*

Sunflower

sun·lamp (sun′lamp′) *n.* lamp that gives off ultraviolet radiation, used for tanning the skin.

sun·less (sun′lis) *adj.* without sunlight; dark or gloomy.

sun·light (sun′līt′) *n.* light of the sun.

sun·lit (sun′lit′) *adj.* lighted by the sun: *a cheery, sunlit room.*

sun·ny (sun′ē) **-ni·er, -ni·est.** *adj.* **1.** full of or warmed by sunlight: *a sunny room.* **2.** cheerful; happy; bright: *a sunny disposition, a sunny smile.* —**sun′ni·ly,** *adv.* —**sun′ni·ness,** *n.*

sun parlor room or porch with glass walls or large windows for admitting sunlight. Also, **sun porch, sun′room′.**

sun·rise (sun′rīz′) *n.* **1.** apparent rising of the sun above the horizon at the beginning of the day. **2.** time when the sun rises: *The farmer began his chores before sunrise.*

sun·set (sun′set′) *n.* **1.** apparent descent of the sun below the horizon at the end of the day. **2.** time when the sun sets.

sun·shade (sun′shād′) *n.* something used to provide protection from the sun, as an awning or parasol.

sun·shine (sun′shīn′) *n.* **1.** the shining of the sun; direct sunlight. **2.** cheerfulness; happiness; brightness. —**sun′shin′y,** *adj.*

sun·spot (sun′spot′) *n.* one of the dark spots that occur in groups at regular intervals on the surface of the sun.

sun·stroke (sun′strōk′) *n.* illness caused by overexposure to the rays of the sun and characterized by prostration and sometimes unconsciousness.

sun·up (sun′up′) *n.* sunrise.

sun·ward (sun′wərd) *adv.* also, **sun·wards.** toward the sun. —*adj.* directed toward the sun.

Sun Yat-sen (soon′ yät′sen′) 1866–1925, Chinese revolutionary leader and statesman.

sup[1] (sup) **supped, sup·ping.** *v.i.* to eat the evening meal. [Old French *super;* of Germanic origin.]

sup[2] (sup) **supped, sup·ping.** *v.t.* to take (liquid) in small quantities; sip. —*n.* sip of a liquid. [Old English *sūpan* to take liquid in small quantities.]

sup. **1.** above; supra. **2.** superior. **3.** superlative. **4.** supine. **5.** supplement.

su·per (sōō′pər) *n.* *Informal.* **1.** superintendent in an apartment house. **2.** performer having a minor, nonspeaking part; supernumerary; extra. —*adj. Slang.* first-rate; excellent; very good.

super- *prefix* **1.** over; above: *superstructure; supersede.* **2.** higher or greater; superior: *superhighway, superpower.* **3.** to an excessive extent or degree: *superfine.* [Latin *super* over, above, beyond.]

su·per·a·ble (sōō′pər ə bəl) *adj.* able to be overcome or conquered; surmountable. [Latin *superābilis,* from *superāre* to overcome, from *super* over.] —**su′per·a·bly,** *adv.*

su·per·a·bound (sōō′pər ə bound′) *v.i.* to abound greatly or excessively. [Late Latin *superabundāre.* See SUPERABUNDANT.]

su·per·a·bun·dant (sōō′pər ə bun′dənt) *adj.* more than is necessary or desirable: too abundant; excessive. [Late Latin *superabundāns,* present participle of *superabundāre* to be very abundant, from Latin *super* over, above + *abundāre* to overflow. See ABOUND.] —**su′per·a·bun′dance,** *n.* —**su′per·a·bun′dant·ly,** *adv.*

su·per·add (sōō′pər ad′) *v.t.* to add over and above. [Latin *superaddere.*] —**su′per·ad·di′tion,** *n.*

su·per·an·nu·ate (sōō′pər an′ū āt′) **-at·ed, -at·ing.** *v.t.* **1.** to retire with a pension because of age or infirmity. **2.** to set aside as too old or obsolete. —*v.i.* to become too old or obsolete. [From SUPERANNUATED.]

su·per·an·nu·at·ed (sōō′pər an′ū ā′tid) *adj.* **1.** retired from service with a pension because of age or infirmity. **2.** too old for use or work. **3.** out-of-date; obsolete. [Modification (influenced by ANNUAL) of Medieval Latin *superannuatus* more than a year old (from Latin *super* above, beyond + *annus* year) + -ED[2].] —**su′per·an′nu·a′tion,** *n.*

su·perb (sōō pûrb′) *adj.* **1.** having nobility or grandeur; magnificent; splendid: *a superb building.* **2.** sumptuous; elegant; rich: *a superb wardrobe.* **3.** of superior quality; very fine; first-rate: *a superb example.* [Latin *superbus* proud, superior.] —**su·perb′ly,** *adv.* —**su·perb′ness,** *n.*

su·per·car·go (sōō′pər kär′gō) *pl.* **-goes** or **-gos.** *n.* officer on board a merchant ship who is in charge of the cargo and the commercial transactions of the voyage. [Modification of earlier *supracargo,* from Spanish *sobrecargo,* from *sobre* over, above (from Latin *super*) + *cargo* load. See CARGO.]

su·per·charge (sōō′pər chärj′) **-charged, -charg·ing.** *v.t.* to increase the power of (an engine) with or as with a supercharger.

su·per·charg·er (sōō′pər chär′jər) *n.* device for increasing the power of an internal-combustion engine by compressing air or a mixture of fuel and air and forcing it into the cylinder at a pressure greater than that of the surrounding atmosphere.

su·per·cil·i·ar·y (sōō′pər sil′ē er′ē) *adj.* of, relating to, or situated near the eyebrow. [Modern Latin *superciliaris,* from Latin *supercilium* eyebrow.]

su·per·cil·i·ous (sōō′pər sil′ē əs) *adj.* having or showing excessive pride or scorn; haughty; disdainful; arrogant. [Latin *superciliōsus,* from *supercilium* eyebrow, pride (with reference to showing pride by raising the eyebrows) from *super* above, over + *cilium* eyelid.] —**su′per·cil′i·ous·ly,** *adv.* —**su′per·cil′i·ous·ness,** *n.*

su·per·con·duc·tiv·i·ty (sōō′pər kon′dək tiv′ə tē) *n. Physics.* apparent complete loss of all resistance to the passage of an electrical current in certain metals and alloys at temperatures near absolute zero. —**su′per·con·duc′tive,** *adj.* —**su′per·con·duc′tor,** *n.*

su·per·cool (sōō′pər kōōl′) *v.t.* to cool (a liquid) below its freezing point without causing solidification.

su·per·dom·i·nant (sōō′pər dom′ə nənt) *n. Music.* sixth tone of the diatonic scale; tone next above the dominant.

su·per·e·go (sōō′pər ē′gō, eg′ō) *pl.* **-gos.** *n. Psychoanalysis.* part of the psyche that acts as a moral censor and creates guilt and anxiety when its instructions are ignored.

su·per·em·i·nent (sōō′pər em′ə nənt) *adj.* supremely eminent. —**su′per·em′i·nence,** *n.* —**su′per·em′i·nent·ly,** *adv.*

su·per·e·ro·gate (sōō′pər er′ə gāt′) **-gat·ed, -gat·ing.** *v.i.* to do more than is requested or required. [Late Latin *superērogātus,* past participle of *superērogāre* to pay out more, from′ Latin *super* over, above + *ērogāre* to pay out.]

su·per·e·ro·ga·tion (sōō′pər er′ə gā′shən) *n.* act or instance of doing more than is requested or required.

su·per·e·rog·a·to·ry (sōō′pər i rog′ə tôr′ē) *adj.* **1.** going beyond what is requested or required. **2.** superfluous.

su·per·fam·i·ly (sōō′pər fam′ə lē, -fam′lē) *pl.,* **-lies.** *n. Biology.* category in the classification of plants and animals ranking below an order and above a family.

su·per·fi·cial (sōō′pər fish′əl) *adj.* **1.** of, relating to, or located on the surface: *a superficial resemblance, a superficial wound.* **2.** lacking depth or thoroughness; shallow: *a superficial person, superficial research.* [Late Latin *superficiālis* relating to the surface, from Latin *superficiēs* surface.] —**su·per·fi·ci·al·i·ty** (sōō′pər fish′ē al′ə tē), **su′per·fi′cial·ness,** *n.* —**su′per·fi′cial·ly,** *adv.*

Syn. 2. Superficial, shallow mean having little depth. **Superficial** suggests that everything is visible and on the surface and implies treatment or expression that fails to take into account the complexity of a problem or situation: *Jones has only a superficial knowledge of subjects outside his field.* **Shallow** suggests limited perceptions which make a comprehensive treatment or expression impossible: *The critic's comments were shallow because he failed to understand the playwright's objective.*

su·per·fi·ci·es (sōō′pər fish′ē ēz′, -fish′ēz) *pl.,* **-ci·es.** *n.* **1.** surface of a body or area. **2.** outward appearance or aspect. [Latin *superficiēs* surface.]

su·per·fine (sōō′pər fīn′) *adj.* **1.** extremely fine in quality; of the best kind: *superfine cloth.* **2.** excessively refined or subtle; fastidious: *superfine distinctions.* **3.** consisting of extremely fine particles or parts: *superfine sugar.*

su·per·flu·i·ty (sōō′pər flōō′ə tē) *pl.,* **-ties.** *n.* **1.** state of being superfluous. **2.** greater quantity than is needed or desired; excess: *a superfluity of inhabitants* (Malthus, 1803). **3.** that which is superfluous: *He wasted his money on expensive superfluities.*

su·per·flu·ous (sōō pur′flōō əs) *adj.* **1.** more than is needed or desired. **2.** needless; unnecessary: *a superfluous warning.* [Latin *superfluus* overflowing, unnecessary.] —**su·per′flu·ous·ly,** *adv.* —**su·per′flu·ous·ness,** *n.* —**Syn. 1.** see **surplus.**

su·per·gi·ant star (sōō′pər jī′ənt) extremely large, bright star.

su·per·heat (sōō′pər hēt′) *v.t.* **1.** to heat to an extremely high temperature; overheat. **2.** to raise the temperature of (a liquid) above its normal boiling point without causing vaporization. **3.** to raise the temperature of (vapor or steam) to increase its pressure. —*n.* **1.** state of being superheated. **2.** amount by which a vapor is superheated. —**su′per·heat′er,** *n.*

su·per·het·er·o·dyne (sōō′pər het′ər ə dīn′) *adj.* of or relating to a method of radio reception in which the received carrier wave is changed by the heterodyne process into a new, lower frequency, which is amplified and rectified to reproduce sound. —*n.* superheterodyne radio receiver. [SUPER(SONIC) + HETERODYNE.]

su·per·high·way (sōō′pər hī′wā′) *n.* high-speed highway, usually having four or more lanes with opposing lanes of traffic separated by a median strip.

su·per·hu·man (sōō′pər hū′mən, -ū′mən) *adj.* **1.** beyond what is human; divine: *of superhuman origin.* **2.** beyond the ordinary human capacity or power: *a superhuman effort, superhuman strength.* —**su′per·hu′man·ly,** *adv.*

su·per·im·pose (sōō′pər im pōz′) **-posed, -pos·ing.** *v.t.* to place (something) over or on top of something else. —**su′per·im′po·si′tion,** *n.*

su·per·in·cum·bent (sōō′pər in kum′bənt) *adj.* **1.** lying or resting on or above something else. **2.** exerted from above: *superincumbent atmospheric pressure.* —**su′per·in·cum′bence, su′per·in·cum′ben·cy,** *n.* —**su′per·in·cum′bent·ly,** *adv.*

su·per·in·duce (sōō′pər in dōōs′, -dūs′) **-duced, -duc·ing.** *v.t.* to bring in over and above something else; introduce in addition. —**su′per·in·duc′tion,** *n.*

su·per·in·tend (sōō′pər in tend′, sōō′pər in-) *v.t.* to direct or control the work or operation of; oversee; manage. [Late Latin *superintendere,* from Latin *super* over, above + *intendere* to direct.] —**su′per·in·tend′ence,** *n.*

su·per·in·tend·en·cy (sōō′prin ten′dən sē, sōō′pər in-) *pl.,* **-cies.** *n.* **1.** position, duty, or authority of a superintendent.

su·per·in·tend·ent (sōō′prin ten′dənt, sōō′pər in-) *n.* **1.** one who directs the work or operation of something, as a group of workers, an institution, or a business: *a superintendent of the police, a superintendent of a school.* **2.** one who manages and is responsible for the maintenance of an apartment or office building.

Syn. 1. Superintendent, supervisor mean a person in charge of a piece of work. A **superintendent** is usually in charge of a place, institution, or operation with wide powers of direction and management: *Our town has a new superintendent of public works.* A **supervisor** is one who coordinates, directs, and inspects an operation personally: *A research team of ten scientists worked under a supervisor.*

su·pe·ri·or (sə pēr′ē ər, sōō-) *adj.* **1.** higher or greater than the ordinary or average in degree or quality; surpassing others; exceptional: *superior talent, a superior individual, a superior piece of writing.* **2.** higher in status, rank, or office: *a superior officer.* **3.** greater in amount or quantity: *a superior force.* **4.** supercilious; haughty; disdainful: *a superior attitude.* **5.** not influenced or affected by; indifferent to (with *to*): *to be superior to one's surroundings.* **6.** (of an organ or part) higher in place or position; above in relation to another structure. **7.** having an orbit outside that of the earth: *a superior planet.* —*n.* **1.** one who is higher than others, as in status, rank, or office: *John's superior at work reprimanded him.* **2.** head of an abbey, monastery, or other religious community. [Latin *superior* higher, comparative of *superus* upper, that is above, from *super* over, above.] —**su·pe·ri·or·i·ty** (sə pēr′ē ôr′ə tē, -or′-, soo-), *n.* —**su·pe′ri·or·ly,** *adv.*

Su·pe·ri·or, Lake (sə pēr′ē ər, soo-) largest and northernmost of the Great Lakes, on the U.S.-Canadian border.

superl., superlative.

su·per·la·tive (sə pur′lə tiv, soo-) *adj.* **1.** of the highest degree or quality; surpassing all others; supreme. **2.** denoting the third or highest degree of quality, quantity, or relation that can be expressed by an adjective or adverb. **Fastest** is the superlative degree of the adjective **fast.** Distinguished from **positive** and **comparative.** —*n.* **1.** one who or that which surpasses all others; highest example. **2.a.** superlative degree. **b.** word or group of words that expresses this degree. [Late Latin *superlātīvus* exaggerated, in the superlative degree, going back to Latin *super* above, beyond + *lātus,* past participle of *ferre* to carry, bear′.] —**su·per′la·tive·ly,** *adv.* —**su·per′la·tive·ness,** *n.*

su·per·man (sōō′pər man′) *pl.,* **-men.** *n.* man possessing more than human strength or intelligence.

su·per·mar·ket (sōō′pər mär′kit) *n.* self-service retail store, usually large, carrying food and other household items.

su·per·nal (soo purn′əl) *adj.* **1.** relating to a higher world; celestial; heavenly. **2.** of, relating to, or existing in the sky. [Old French *supernal* higher, supreme, from Latin *supernus* upper, celestial, from *super* over, above.] —**su·per′nal·ly,** *adv.*

su·per·na·tant (sōō′pər nāt′ənt) *adj.* floating on the surface.

su·per·nat·u·ral (sōō′pər nach′ər əl) *adj.* **1.** of or relating to a realm or existence beyond or exceeding the power of the natural world: *supernatural forces.* **2.** of or relating to ghosts or spirits. **3.** one who or that which exists beyond the natural world. —**su′per·nat′u·ral·ly,** *adv.* —**su′per·nat′u·ral·ness,** *n.*

su·per·nat·u·ral·ism (sōō′pər nach′ər ə liz′əm) *n.* **1.** quality or state of being supernatural. **2.** belief in supernatural forces or beings. —**su′per·nat′u·ral·ist,** *n., adj.* —**su′per·nat′u·ral·is′tic,** *adj.*

su·per·no·va (sōō′pər nō′və) *pl.,* **-vae** (-vē) or **-vas.** *n.* extremely bright nova.

su·per·nu·mer·ar·y (sōō′pər nōō′mə rer′ē, -nū′-) *adj.* exceeding in number what is usual, expected, or needed; additional; extra. —*n. pl.,* **-ar·ies. 1.** one who or that which is extra. **2.** performer in a theatrical or film production having a minor, nonspeaking part. [Late Latin *supernumerārius* excessive in number, from Latin *super* beyond + *numerus* unit (in counting), quantity.]

su·per·phos·phate (sōō′pər fos′fāt) *n.* widely used fertilizer made by the action of sulfuric acid on rock that contains insoluble phosphates.

su·per·pose (sōō′pər pōz′) **-posed, -pos·ing.** *v.t.* **1.** to place on, above, or over something else. **2.** to place (a geometric figure) on top of another so that all parts coincide. [French *superposer* to place above something else, modification (influenced by French *poser* to place) of Latin *superpōnere* to place over.] —**su·per·po·si·tion** (sōō′pər pə zish′ən), *n.*

su·per·pow·er (sōō′pər pou′ər) *n.* one of the powerful nations dominating world affairs, esp. through the possession of nuclear weapons.

su·per·sat·u·rate (sōō′pər sach′ə rāt′) **-rat·ed, -rat·ing.** *v.t.* to add to or concentrate in (a solution) more solute than it can normally hold at a given pressure and temperature. If a solution is supersaturated it becomes very unstable, and the excess solute readily forms a precipitate. —**su′per·sat′u·ra′tion,** *n.*

su·per·scribe (sōō′pər skrīb′, sōō′pər skrīb′) **-scribed, -scrib·ing.** *v.t.* **1.** to write or engrave on the top or outside of something, esp. to write (a name or address) on a letter or package. **2.** to write or engrave on the top or outside of. [Latin *superscrībere* to write over.]

su·per·script (sōō′pər skript′) *adj.* written above. —*n.* character or symbol written, printed, or set above and to one side of another. In *a*², the symbol ² is the superscript. [Latin *superscrīptus,* past participle of *superscrībere* to write over.]

su·per·scrip·tion (sōō′pər skrip′shən) *n.* writing or inscription on the top or outside of something, esp. an address on a letter or package.

su·per·sede (sōō′pər sēd′) *-sed·ed, -sed·ing. v.t.* **1.** to force out of use as inferior; make obsolete, void, or useless: *This rule supersedes all previous policy statements. Jets have superseded prop planes on most transatlantic flights.* **2.** to take the position, function, or office of; succeed: *His new assistant was rapidly superseding him as manager of the project.* **3.** to remove or cause to be removed in favor of another; displace: *The town council voted to have him superseded immediately.* [Latin *supersedēre* to be superior to, refrain; literally, to sit above.] —**su′per·sed′er,** *n.*

su·per·sen·si·tive (sōō′pər sen′sə tiv) *adj.* excessively sensitive. —**su′per·sen′si·tive·ly,** *adv.* —**su′per·sen′si·tive·ness,** *n.*

su·per·son·ic (sōō′pər son′ik) *adj.* **1.** relating to, designating, or characterized by a speed, or a body moving at a speed, greater than that of sound in air (762 m.p.h. at sea level). **2.** capable of traveling at a speed greater than the speed of sound: *a supersonic aircraft.* **3.** ultrasonic.

su·per·sti·tion (sōō′pər stish′ən) *n.* **1.** irrational belief or set of beliefs based on assumptions that are inconsistent with scientific fact or religious doctrine, often resulting from fear of the unknown combined with a trust in the power of magical forces. **2.** particular rite or practice based on such a belief or set of beliefs. [Latin *superstitiō* wonder, unreasonable religious belief; literally, a standing over.]

su·per·sti·tious (sōō′pər stish′əs) *adj.* **1.** given to believe in superstitions: *a superstitious nature.* **2.** of, relating to, or characterized by superstition: *a superstitious belief.* —**su′per·sti′tious·ly,** *adv.* —**su′·per·sti′tious·ness,** *n.*

su·per·struc·ture (sōō′pər struk′chər) *n.* **1.** that part of a building above the foundation. **2.** that part of a ship, esp. a warship, above the main deck. **3.** any structure perceived in relation to a more basic foundation: *the symbolic superstructure of a novel.*

su·per·tax (sōō′pər taks′) *n.* surtax.

su·per·ton·ic (sōō′pər ton′ik) *n.* second tone of the diatonic scale; tone next above the tonic.

su·per·vene (sōō′pər vēn′) *-vened, -ven·ing. v.i.* to take place as something additional, and often as an interruption or a cause of change. [Latin *supervenīre* to come upon, be added to.] —**su·per·ven·tion** (sōō′pər ven′shən), *n.*

su·per·vise (sōō′pər vīz′) *-vised, -vis·ing. v.t.* to control and watch over the execution, work, or use of; oversee: *to supervise the cleaning staff, to supervise a fund-raising campaign.* [Medieval Latin *supervisus,* past participle of *supervidere* to look over, oversee, from Latin *super* over + *vidēre* to see.] —**su·per·vi·sion** (sōō′pər vizh′ən), *n.*

su·per·vi·sor (sōō′pər vī′zər) *n.* one who supervises, esp. an administrator in charge of a business, government, or educational department or project. —**Syn.** see **superintendent.**

su·per·vi·so·ry (sōō′pər vī′zər ē) *adj.* of, relating to, designating, or characteristic of a supervisor or supervision: *supervisory personnel, supervisory decisions.*

su·pine (*adj.,* sōō pīn′; *n.,* sōō′pīn) *adj.* **1.** lying on the back or with the face turned upward. **2.** having or showing moral or mental indifference; apathetic: *supine neglect, supine slaves of authority.* —*n.* in Latin, a verbal noun formed from the stem of the past participle and occurring only in the accusative and ablative cases. [Latin *supīnus* lying on the back, indolent.] —**su·pine′ly,** *adv.* —**su·pine′ness,** *n.*

supp. 1. supplement. **2.** supplementary. Also, **suppl.**

sup·per (sup′ər) *n.* **1.** last meal of the day, eaten in the evening. **2.** social or community event where such a meal is served: *a church supper.* [Old French *soper* evening meal, from *soper* to eat one's supper; of Germanic origin.]

sup·plant (sə plant′) *v.t.* **1.** to displace and take the place of: *Supermarkets have supplanted the old corner grocery store.* **2.** to take the place of (someone) by scheming, treachery, or other devious means. **3.** to remove or get rid of in order to replace with something else. [Latin *supplantāre* to overthrow, trip up one's heels, from *sub* under + *planta* sole of the foot, plant.]

sup·ple (sup′əl) *-pler, -plest. adj.* **1.** easily bent or folded without breaking or cracking; flexible: *a soft, supple collar, a supple fishing rod.* **2.** exhibiting or characterized by agility, as in bending, twisting, or other movement: *a supple grace, the supple limbs of a dancer.* **3.** readily yielding to persuasion or influence, esp. to the point of being compliant or servile. **4.** showing or having a mental subtlety and quickness: *a supple intellect.* [Old French *souple* agile, flexible, from Latin *supplex* submissive; literally, bending under.] —**sup′ple·ly,** *adv.* —**sup′·ple·ness,** *n.* —**Syn.** see **flexible.**

sup·ple·ment (*n.,* sup′lə mənt; *v.,* sup′lə ment′) *n.* **1.** something added to make up for a deficiency or to extend or improve the whole, esp. an addition to a publication. **2.** measure of an angle or arc that must be added to the measure of a given angle or arc to produce a sum equal to 180°. —*v.t.* to add or form a supplement to: *to supplement a*

diet with vitamins, two books that supplement one another.* [Latin *supplēmentum* a filling up, supply.] —**Syn. n. 1.** see **complement.**

sup·ple·men·ta·ry (sup′lə men′tər ē) *adj.* serving as a supplement; additional. Also, **sup′ple·men′tal.**

supplementary angle, angle that is added to a given angle to make the sum of the two angles 180°.

sup·pli·ant (sup′lē ənt) *n.* one who supplicates. —*adj.* **1.** asking or entreating humbly and earnestly; imploring; beseeching. **2.** expressing supplication: *to bow and sue for grace with suppliant knee* (John Milton, 1667). [French *suppliant,* present participle of *supplier* to supplicate, from Latin *supplicāre.*] —**sup′pli·ance,** *n.* —**sup′pli·ant·ly,** *adv.*

Angle A 135° Angle B 45°

Supplementary angles

sup·pli·cant (sup′lə kənt) *n.* one who supplicates. —*adj.* asking or entreating humbly and earnestly; beseeching. [Latin *supplicāns,* present participle of *supplicāre* to supplicate.]

sup·pli·cate (sup′lə kāt′) *-cat·ed, -cat·ing. v.t.* **1.** to make a humble and earnest request for: *to supplicate a blessing.* **2.** to ask humbly and earnestly of; beseech: *to supplicate a king for mercy.* —*v.i.* to make a humble and earnest request, as by prayer. [Latin *supplicātus,* past participle of *supplicāre* to beg humbly, implore.] —**sup′pli·ca′tor,** *n.*

sup·pli·ca·tion (sup′lə kā′shən) *n.* **1.** act of supplicating. **2.** earnest request or humble prayer.

sup·pli·ca·to·ry (sup′lə kə tôr′ē) *adj.* making or expressing supplication.

sup·pli·er (sə plī′ər) *n.* one who or that which supplies.

sup·ply[1] (sə plī′) *-plied, -ply·ing. v.t.* **1.** to make (what is wanted, needed, or desirable) available for use: *to supply information, a reservoir that supplies water to the community.* **2.** to provide with what is wanted, needed, or desired: *He supplied me with the answer. Our company supplies wholesalers.* **3.** to meet or comply with (a need or want): *Too few shares were issued to supply the demand for the stock.* **4.** to make good or compensate for (a loss or deficiency). —*n., pl.,* **-plies. 1.** amount necessary or available for a given use; stock; store: *a new supply of wine, a week's supply of linen and towels.* **2.** usually, **supplies.** necessary items, as food, clothing, or equipment, that are set aside and held for distribution and use: *The army was cut off from its supplies.* **3.** quantity of a commodity available for sale at a certain price at a given time. **4.** act of supplying. [Old French *soupleier* to fill up, make up, from Latin *supplēre* to fill up.] —**Syn. v.t. 2.** see **furnish.**

sup·ply[2] (sup′lē) *adv.* in a supple manner. [SUPPLE + -LY[1].]

sup·port (sə pôrt′) *v.t.* **1.** to bear or hold up; keep from falling: *Aluminum brackets supported the shelves. That chair won't support your weight.* **2.** to provide for or maintain, as with money or the necessary means of living: *He's not in a position to support a family. We doubt that the planet can support life.* **3.** to strengthen the cause or position of by one's assistance or approval; back; uphold: *The senator did not support the new tax reform. I can't support either of the candidates.* **4.** to comfort or strengthen, as in time of need: *Her religion supported her after his death.* **5.** to make valid or true; verify; substantiate: *There is no evidence to support your theory.* **6.** to put up with; endure; tolerate: *His weakened body could never support another attack.* **7.** to act in a lesser part or as an added attraction with (a leading actor). —*n.* **1.** act of supporting; being supported: *to undertake the support of a foster child.* **2.** one who or that which supports. [Old French *supporter* to endure, from Late Latin *supportāre,* from Latin *supportāre* to bring to.]

sup·port·a·ble (sə pôr′tə bəl) *adj.* bearable; endurable. —**sup·port′a·bly,** *adv.*

sup·port·er (sə pôr′tər) *n.* **1.** one who supports, esp. one who aids or approves: *an ardent supporter of home rule.* **2.** that which supports, as a garter or a device used to bind some part of the body.

sup·por·tive (sə pôr′tiv) *adj.* providing approval, aid, or support.

sup·pose (sə pōz′) *-posed, -pos·ing. v.t.* **1.** to consider as true or real, esp. for the sake of argument: *If we suppose that it will rain, we can make alternate plans.* **2.** to hold as an opinion; believe probable: *I suppose my mother will let me go. I suppose we will expand in the near future, but that depends on the economy.* **3.** to consider as a possibility or suggestion: *Suppose you let me finish.* ▲ used in the imperative. **4.** to expect; require; obligate: *The plane is supposed to arrive at nine o'clock.* ▲ used in the passive. **5.** to require as a condition; imply; presuppose: *His plan supposes a universal desire for peace.* [Old French *supposer* to set under, imagine, modification (influenced by French *poser* to place, put) of Latin *supponere* to put under.]

sup·posed (sə pōzd′) *adj.* considered to be true, real, or possible, esp. wrongly. —**sup·pos·ed·ly** (sə pōz′zid lē), *adv.*

sup·po·si·tion (sup′ə zish′ən) *n.* **1.** that which is supposed; hypothesis: *On the supposition that he had eaten, we went on without him.* **2.** act of supposing. [Medieval Latin *suppositiō* hypothesis, from Latin *suppositiō* substitution.] —**sup′po·si′tion·al,** *adj.*

at; āpe; cär; end; mē; it; īce; hot; ōld; fôrk; wood; fōōl; oil; out; up; ūse; turn; sing; thin; this; zh in treasure; ə in ago, taken, pencil, lemon, circus.

sup·pos·i·ti·tious (sə poz′ə tish′əs) *adj.* **1.** substituted in order to deceive or defraud; spurious; counterfeit. **2.** supposed; hypothetical. [Late Latin *supposīcius* substituted, false.] —**sup·pos′i·ti′tious·ly**, *adv.*

sup·pos·i·to·ry (sə poz′ə tôr′ē) *pl.*, **-ries.** *n.* solid medicinal substance, usually in the form of a cone or cylinder, made to be inserted into the rectum or other body cavity. [Late Latin *suppositōrium* (something) placed underneath, going back to Latin *suppōnere* to put under.]

sup·press (sə pres′) *v.t.* **1.** to put an end to or to put down forcibly; crush: *to suppress a revolt.* **2.** to hold or keep in; restrain: *to suppress a laugh.* **3.** to prevent or prohibit the publication, circulation, or expression of; keep secret; censor: *to suppress evidence, to suppress a story.* **4.** to stop or arrest the flow or course of, as a hemorrhage. [Latin *suppressus*, past participle of *supprimere* to press under, restrain.] —**sup·press′i·ble,** *adj.* —**sup·pres′sor;** *also,* **sup·press′er,** *n.* —**Syn. 1.** see **oppress.**

sup·pres·sion (sə presh′ən) *n.* **1.** act of suppressing; being suppressed. **2.** psychological process by which a memory, thought, or action is deliberately excluded from consciousness. Distinguished from **repression.**

sup·pres·sive (sə pres′iv) *adj.* tending to suppress.

sup·pu·rate (sup′yə rāt′) **-rat·ed, -rat·ing.** *v.i.* to form or discharge pus. [Latin *suppūrātus*, past participle of *suppūrāre* to form pus.]

sup·pu·ra·tion (sup′yə rā′shən) *n.* **1.** formation or discharge of pus. **2.** pus.

sup·pu·ra·tive (sup′yə rā′tiv) *adj.* **1.** causing suppuration. **2.** discharging pus. —*n.* medicine, salve, or other agent that causes or induces suppuration.

su·pra (sōō′prə) *adv.* above. ▲ used esp. as a reference to an earlier part of a text. [Latin *suprā.*]

supra- *prefix* **1.** above; over; beyond: *suprarenal, supranational.* [Latin *suprā.*]

su·pra·na·tion·al (sōō′prə nash′ən əl) *adj.* extending beyond the boundaries or limitations of a state or nation: *supranational ethics of war.* [**SUPRA- + NATIONAL.**]

su·pra·re·nal (sōō′prə rēn′əl) *adj.* situated on or above the kidneys; adrenal. —*n.* a suprarenal gland or other bodily part. [**SUPRA- + RENAL.**]

su·prem·a·cist (sə prem′ə sist, soo-) *n.* one who believes in or advocates the supremacy of a particular group, esp. a racial group.

su·prem·a·cy (sə prem′ə sē, soo-) *n.* **1.** quality or condition of being supreme. **2.** supreme power or authority: *naval supremacy.*

su·preme (sə prēm′, soo-) *adj.* **1.** greatest in rank, authority, or power. **2.** highest in significance, degree, or quality; utmost: *supreme artistry, supreme wisdom.* **3.** ultimate; final; last: *the supreme goal.* [Latin *suprēmus* highest, superlative of *superus* upper, that is above, from *super* above.] —**su·preme′ly,** *adv.*

Supreme Being, God.

Supreme Court 1. highest federal court in the United States, with the power to hear appeals from lower courts and to declare laws unconstitutional. The chief justice presides over the Supreme Court. **2.** highest court in some states of the United States. **3.** highest court in some other countries, as the German Democratic Republic and Denmark.

supreme sacrifice, sacrifice of one's own life.

Supreme Soviet, legislature of the Soviet Union, consisting of two equal houses, one of which is elected according to population and the other elected by the various national groups.

Supt., Superintendent.

sur-[1] *prefix* over; above; beyond: *surcharge, surpass.* [Old French *s(o)ur* on, over, above, from Latin *super.*]

sur-[2], form of **sub-** before *r,* as in **surrogate.**

Su·ra·ba·ja (sōōr′ə bä′yə) *also,* **Su·ra·ba·ya.** *n.* port city, principal naval base, and commercial and industrial center of Indonesia, in eastern Java. Pop. (1961 est.), 1,007,945.

su·rah (sōōr′ə) *n.* soft twilled fabric made of silk or man-made fibers. [From *Surat,* India, where it was first made.]

Su·ra·kar·ta (sōōr′ə kär′tə) *n.* city in central Java, Indonesia. Pop. (1961 est.), 367,626. Also, **So′lo.**

Su·rat (soo rat′, sōōr′ət) *n.* city in western India, north of Bombay. Pop. (1969), 368,917.

sur·cease (sur sēs′) *Archaic. n.* cessation; end. —*v.t., v.i.,* **-ceased, -ceas·ing.** to cease; stop. [Old French *sursis,* past participle of *surseoir* to refrain, from Latin *supersedēre* literally, to sit above.]

sur·charge (*n.,* sur′chärj′; *v.,* sur chärj′, sur′chärj′) *n.* **1.** addition to the usual amount, fare, or fee: *a tax surcharge.* **2.** additional mark officially printed over a postage stamp to raise its value. —*v.t.,* **-charged, -charg·ing. 1.** to charge an extra amount, fee, or fare. **2.** to overcharge. **3.** to weigh down; overburden; overload: *Till his spirit sank, surcharged, within him* (Wordsworth, 1804). **4.** to print an additional mark on (postage stamps) to raise their value, instead of issuing new stamps.

[French *surcharger* to overload, from *sur* (see **SUR-[1]**) + *charger* to load. See **CHARGE.**]

sur·cin·gle (sur′sing′gəl) *n.* belt or band around the body of a horse or pack animal to hold down a saddle, blanket, or pack. [Old French *surcengle,* from *sur* (see **SUR-[1]**) + *cengle* a girth (from Latin *cingula* belt).]

sur·coat (sur′kōt′) *n.* outer coat, esp. a short garment worn during the Middle Ages over armor. [Old French *surcote,* from *sur* (see **SUR-[1]**) + *cote* (see **COAT.**)]

Surcoat

surd (surd) *n.* **1.** consonant sound articulated without vibration of the vocal cords, as *f, k, p,* and *t.* **2.** irrational number that is a root of a positive integer or quotient of positive integers. The numbers $\sqrt{3}$ and $\sqrt{3/5}$ are surds. —*adj.* **1.** articulated without vibration of the vocal cords; voiceless. **2.** *Mathematics.* irrational. [Latin *surdus* deaf, silent.]

sure (shoor) **sur·er, sur·est.** *adj.* **1.** firmly believing in the existence, inevitability, or truth of something; having or showing no doubt; confident: *to be sure of someone's approval. I'm sure my answer is correct.* **2.** incapable of being doubted or questioned; completely true; indisputable: *I have sure knowledge of his promotion.* **3.** bound to be happen; destined; inevitable: *a sure winner, a problem sure to be worked out.* **4.** not liable to miss or fail; unerring; infallible: *a sure sign of a storm, the surest way to get there on time.* **5.** not liable to give way; steady; firm: *a sure hand, on sure ground.* **6.** worthy of being relied upon or trusted; dependable: *a sure friend.* **7. for sure.** without doubt; unquestionably. **8. to be sure,** undoubtedly; indeed. **9. to make sure,** to be or cause to be absolutely sure: *We must make sure our facts are right.* —*adv. Informal.* surely. [Old French *sur* certain, safe, from Latin *secūrus* free from care. Doublet of **SECURE.**] —**sure′ness,** *n.*

Syn. *adj.* **1. Sure, certain, positive** mean free from doubt. **Sure** implies an inner confidence, as in the importance, value, or correctness of what is involved: *Are you sure about what you're doing?* **Certain** implies a sense of confidence but also suggests a more factual basis for one's belief: *I am certain that he left—I saw him go out the door.* **Positive** implies a settled and unshakable conviction in the truth of an opinion or assertion: *I am positive I've seen his face somewhere before, but I can't remember where.*

sure·fire (shoor′fīr′) *adj. Informal.* bound to be successful; that cannot fail: *a sure-fire scheme.*

sure·foot·ed (shoor′foot′id) *adj.* not liable to stumble or fall. —**sure′-foot′ed·ness,** *n.*

sure·ly (shoor′lē) *adv.* **1.** without doubt; truly; positively: *Surely I can't have been sleeping for two hours.* **2.** without hesitation; firmly; steadily: *The driver guided the car surely around the curves.* **3.** without fail; inevitably; infallibly.

sure·ty (shoor′ə tē) *pl.,* **-ties.** *n.* **1.** security, as against loss or damage, or for the fulfillment of an obligation. **2.** *Law.* one who agrees to be responsible for the obligations of another, as for debts or for the failure to perform a duty. **3.** state of being sure, esp. of oneself; assurance; certainty. **4.** basis for confidence or certainty: *the surety of one's faith.* **5.** *Archaic.* that which is beyond doubt.

surf (surf) *n.* swell of the sea or the splash or foam of its waves breaking on the shore or upon a reef. —*v.i.* to engage in surfing. [Of uncertain origin.] —**surf′er,** *n.*

sur·face (sur′fis) *n.* **1.** outer face or exterior extent of a thing: *the earth's surface.* **2.** external appearance or aspect; appearance: *He's pleasant enough on the surface but rather nasty the closer you get to know him.* **3.** straight or curved set of points that has length and width but no thickness. —*adj.* **1.** of, on, or relating to a surface. **2.** superficial; apparent: *a surface explanation.* —*v.i.,* **-faced, -fac·ing.** to come or rise to the surface: *The submarine surfaced. His anger finally surfaced during that last argument.* —*v.t.* to cover or finish the surface of, esp. to make smooth or level: *to surface tennis courts with clay.* [French *surface* exterior of something, from *sur* (see **SUR-[1]**) + *face* (see **FACE.**)]

surface mail, mail that is sent by land or sea.

surface tension, property of liquids, due to the tendency of their molecules at the surface to draw together, causing the surface to behave like a thin elastic film.

surf·board (surf′bôrd′) *n.* flat, wide buoyant board used for surfing. —*v.i.* to engage in surfing.

surf·boat (surf′bōt′) *n.* strong, buoyant boat used esp. in heavy surf.

Surfboard

surf·cast·ing (surf′kas′ting) *n.* act or sport of fishing by casting one's line into the surf from the shore. —**surf′cast′er,** *n.*

sur·feit (sur′fit) *v.t.* to feed or supply to excess; sate; satiate. —*v.i. Archaic.* to indulge to excess; overindulge. —*n.* **1.** excessive amount or supply; excess: *a surfeit of biographies of a man who was an unimportant figure.* **2.** act or instance of overindulging oneself, esp. with food or drink. **3.** disgust or discomfort caused by overindulgence. [Old French *sorfait* excess; originally, past participle of *sorfaire* to overdo, going back to Latin *super* above + *facere* to do, make.] —**Syn.** *v.t.* see **satiate.**

surf·fish (surf′fish′) *pl.*, **-fish** or **-fish·es.** *n.* any of a group of saltwater fish, family Embiotocidae, found in temperate coastal waters of the Pacific Ocean, having oval bodies and spiny fins. Length: 5–18 inches.

surf·ing (surf′ing) *n.* sport in which a person rides the crest of a breaking wave into the shore, usually on some floating apparatus, as a surfboard.

surge (surj) surged, surg·ing. *v.i.* **1.** to move with a violent, heaving, swelling motion, as waves: *The crowd surged forward to catch a glimpse of the assassin. The lava surged over the volcano.* **2.** to increase or rise suddenly: *The stock market surged today.* —*n.* **1.** heaving or swelling motion like that of waves: *the surge of angry citizens storming the barricades.* **2.** sudden increase or onset: *a surge of electric current, a surge of public opinion.* **3.** rolling swell, wave, or billow of water. [Old French *sorgir* to rise, going back to Latin *surgere.*]

sur·geon (sur′jən) *n.* doctor of medicine who specializes in surgery. [Anglo-Norman *surgien,* short for Old French *cirurgien,* from *cirurgie* surgery, through Latin, going back to Greek *cheirourgiā.* See SUR-GERY.]

Surgeon General *pl.,* **Surgeons General. 1.** chief medical officer of one of the armed services of the United States. **2.** chief medical officer of the U.S. Public Health Service.

sur·ger·y (sur′jər ē) *pl.,* **-ger·ies.** *n.* **1.** branch of medicine that deals with the treatment of diseases, injuries, and the like by the removal or repair of the affected parts of the body. **2.** room or suite of rooms, esp. in a hospital, where such treatment is performed. **3.** the treatment itself: *to undergo surgery.* [Old French *surgerie, cirurgerie* the art of performing surgical operations, through Latin, going back to Greek *cheirourgiā,* from *cheir* hand + *ergon* work.]

sur·gi·cal (sur′ji kəl) *adj.* of, relating to, used in, or done by means of surgery: *surgical procedures, surgical instruments, surgical complications.* —**sur′gi·cal·ly,** *adv.*

Su·ri·nam (soor′ə nam′) *n.* territory of the Netherlands on the northeastern coast of South America, formerly known as Dutch or Netherlands Guiana. Area, approx. 55,144 sq. mi. Pop. (1968 est.), 375,000.

sur·ly (sur′lē) -li·er, -li·est. *adj.* expressing or characterized by bad-tempered rudeness or hostility; gruff: *a surly beggar, a surly demand.* [Earlier *sirly* literally, like a "sir" or lord in arrogance, from SIR + -LY².] —**sur′li·ness,** *n.*

sur·mise (*v.,* sur′mīz′; *n.,* sər mīz′, sur′mīz) -mised, -mis·ing. *v.t., v.i.* to infer (something) from little or no evidence; guess. —*n.* **1.** idea or opinion based on little or no evidence; guess. **2.** act or process of surmising. [Old French *surmise* accusation, from *surmettre* to accuse, from Medieval Latin *supermittere,* from Latin *super* above + *mittere* to send.] —**Syn.** *v.t.* see **guess.**

sur·mount (sər mount′) *v.t.* **1.** to prevail over; conquer; overcome: *to surmount financial difficulties.* **2.** to climb up or get over physically: *to surmount a wall.* **3.** to stand, lie, or be above; top; crown: *A dome surmounts the whole structure.* [Old French *surmonter* to surpass, rise above, going back to Latin *super* above + *mōns* mountain.] —**sur·mount′a·ble,** *adj.*

sur·name (*n.,* sur′nām′; *v.,* sur′nām′, sur nām′) *n.* last name or family name. —*v.t.,* -named, -nam·ing. to give a surname to; call by a surname. [Partial translation of Old French *surnom* epithet or additional name, from *sur* (see SUR-¹) + *nom* name (from Latin *nōmen*).]

sur·pass (sər pas′) *v.t.* **1.** to go beyond, as in degree, amount, or quality; excel: *The young skater from the Soviet Union far surpassed the other contestants.* **2.** to be beyond the range, reach, or capacity of; exceed: *Love surpasses understanding.* [French *surpasser* to exceed, from *sur* (see SUR-¹) + *passer.* See PASS.] —**sur·pass′a·ble,** *adj.* —**Syn. 1.** see **excel.**

sur·pass·ing (sər pas′ing) *adj.* excelling others in degree, amount, or quality; excellent: *a horse of surpassing beauty and speed.* —**sur·pass′ing·ly,** *adv.*

sur·plice (sur′plis) *n.* white vestment with wide sleeves, reaching to the knees, worn by clergymen, choir singers, and those assisting at the altar in

Surplice

the Roman Catholic and certain other churches. [Anglo-Norman *surplis,* from Medieval Latin *superpelliceum,* going back to Latin *super* above + *pellis* pelt², skin; because it was originally worn over a garment of fur.]

sur·plus (sur′plus′, -pləs) *n.* **1.** amount or quantity over and above what is used or needed; excess: *a crop surplus, a surplus of dishes.* **2.a.** assets remaining after all costs, expenses, and debts have been paid. **b.** excess of the net worth of a business establishment over the stated value of its stock. —*adj.* that is over and above what is used or needed: *surplus army goods.* [Anglo-Norman *surplus* overplus, going back to Latin *super* over + *plūs* more.]

Syn. *adj.* **Surplus, superfluous** mean an excess. **Surplus** is more often applied to goods, objects, or money to suggest that more than what is needed is available and may be kept as a reserve to be drawn upon for use as needed: *The government often sells surplus machinery to the public.* **Superfluous** is usually applied to writings or statements to suggest that the excess is useless or irrelevant: *There's a great deal of superfluous material in that essay.* —*n.* **1.** see **balance.**

sur·plus·age (sur′plus′ij) *n.* **1.** surplus; excess. **2.** unnecessary or irrelevant words; verbiage.

sur·prise (sər prīz′) -prised, -pris·ing. *v.t.* **1.** to cause to feel sudden wonder or astonishment: *My daughter sometimes surprises me when she's so cheerful in the morning.* **2.** to come upon suddenly or unexpectedly; take or catch unawares: *to surprise a thief.* **3.** to attack or capture suddenly and without warning: *We surprised the enemy with a pre-dawn attack.* **4.a.** to cause (someone) to do or say something unintended (with *into*): *to surprise the suspect into a confession.* **b.** to bring out (something) in such a manner: *to surprise an admission of guilt out of someone.* —*n.* **1.** state or feeling of being surprised; sudden feeling of wonder: *I could hardly contain my surprise when he called.* **2.** that which causes this feeling: *The news came as a surprise. The gift was a delightful surprise.* **3.** act of surprising; taking or catching unawares. **4. to take by surprise. a.** to come upon suddenly and unexpectedly; take or catch unawares. **b.** to astound or amaze. [Middle French *surprise* a taking unawares, from *surprendre* to take unawares, overtake, going back to Latin *super* over + *prehendere* to seize.]

sur·pris·ing (sər prī′zing) *adj.* causing surprise or wonder, unexpected: *a surprising defeat.* —**sur·pris′ing·ly,** *adv.*

sur·re·al·ism (sə rē′ə liz′əm) *n.* movement in twentieth-century art and literature characterized by dreamlike distortions and unexpected arrangements of subject matter, often intended to reflect the workings of the subconscious. [French *surréalisme,* from *sur* (see SUR-¹) + *réalisme* realism (going back to Latin *rēs* thing).] —**sur·re′al·ist,** *adj., n.*

sur·re·al·is·tic (sə rē′ə lis′tik) *adj.* of, relating to, or characteristic of surrealism. Also, **sur·re′al.** —**sur·re·al′is·ti·cal·ly,** *adv.*

sur·ren·der (sə ren′dər) *v.t.* **1.** to give over possession or control of because of force or demand: *to surrender a fort, to surrender a car to a bank.* **2.** to yield in favor of another: *The incumbent senator will surrender his seat at the beginning of the year.* **3.** to put aside as hopeless or useless; abandon: *to surrender all thought of winning.* **4.** to yield (oneself), as to an emotion, influence, or course of action. —*v.i.* to give oneself up, as to an enemy. —*n.* act or instance of surrendering. [Old French *surrendre* to hand over, from *sur* (see SUR-¹) + *rendre* to yield. See RENDER.]

Syn. *n.* **Surrender, submission, capitulation** mean the act of giving in to someone else. **Surrender,** the most general term, implies giving up the possession of, or power over, something to the victor in a war: *The surrender of Japan brought World War II to a close.* **Submission** implies the mental or emotional willingness or desire to yield to another's control or care, esp. as a result of feelings of futility and extreme fatigue: *Even though their army was defeated, the people could not be brought to submission.* **Capitulation,** in contrast, stresses merely the formal or official agreement arranged by the parties at war: *Capitulation was the only way to save the besieged city.*

sur·rep·ti·tious (sur′əp tish′əs) *adj.* **1.** done or accomplished by stealthy means: *a surreptitious encounter, a surreptitious spy.* **2.** acting in a secret, sly manner: *a surreptitious spy.* [Latin *surreptītius* stolen, concealed, going back to *sub* under, secretly + *rapere* to seize.] —**sur′rep·ti′tious·ly,** *adv.* —**sur′rep·ti′tious·ness,** *n.*

sur·rey (sur′ē) *pl.,* **-reys.** *n.* light, four-wheeled carriage with two seats, usually with a top. [From *Surrey,* England, where it was first made.]

Surrey

Sur·rey (sur′ē) *n.* **1.** county in southeastern England. **2. Earl of.** c.1515–47, English poet; born Henry Howard.

sur·ro·gate (sur′ə gāt′, -git) *n.* **1.** one who or that which is sub-

stituted for another; substitute. **2.** in some states, a judge or judicial officer having charge of certain matters, as the administration of estates, guardianships, and the probate of wills. [Latin *surrogātus*, past participle of *surrogāre* to substitute.]

sur·round (sə round′) *v.t.* **1.** to stand, lie, or be situated on all sides of; form a circle around: *A crowd surrounded his car.* **2.** to cause to be encircled: *to surround a pool with a fence.* **3.** to enclose or confine, as a place or body of troops, so as to prevent escape or communication. [Old French *s(o)uronder* to overflow, surpass, going back to Latin *super* above + *unda* wave; influenced in form and meaning by association with ROUND.]

sur·round·ings (sə roun′dingz) *n.,pl.* objects, circumstances, or conditions characteristic of a place or way of life: *to grow up in fashionable surroundings.*

sur·tax (sur′taks′) *n.* additional or extra tax, esp. one added to the normal income tax. Also, **su′per·tax**. [French *surtaxe*, from *sur* (see SUR-¹) + *taxe* tax (going back to Latin *taxāre* to rate¹, value).]

sur·tout (sər tōō′, -tōōt′) *n.* man's long, close-fitting overcoat, as worn in the eighteenth century. [French *surtout*, from *sur* (see SUR-¹) + *tout* all (from Latin *tōtus*).]

sur·veil·lance (sər vā′ləns, -vāl′yəns) *n.* **1.** close watch kept over a person, group, or place, as to discover information: *We have the suspect under constant surveillance.* **2.** observation for the purpose of supervision and control: *The group worked under my surveillance.* [French *surveillance* supervision, from *surveiller* to watch, going back to Latin *super* above, over + *vigilāre* to watch.]

sur·vey (*v.* sər vā′; *n.* sur′vā, sər vā′) *v.t.* **1.** to view or consider comprehensively; examine as a whole: *to survey the panorama of the city below. The course surveys English literature from 1800 to 1900.* **2.** to examine or inspect in detail, esp. for a specific purpose: *We surveyed the prospects for building in the area. The cats surveyed each other from a distance.* **3.** to determine the shape, area, and boundaries of (a region or tract of land) by taking measurements of lines and angles with various instruments and applying the principles of geometry and trigonometry. —*v.i.* to survey land. —*n. pl.*, **-veys. 1.** detailed study or examination, as one made by taking a sampling of opinions: *a telephone survey, a statistical survey.* **2.** general or comprehensive view: *The exhibition is a survey of modern art.* **3.a.** act or process of surveying land. **b.** plan, map, or written statement of the results of this. [Anglo-Norman *surveier* to look over, going back to Latin *super* above, over + *vidēre* to see.]

sur·vey·ing (sər vā′ing) *n.* act, science, or occupation of making land surveys.

sur·vey·or (sər vā′ər) *n.* one who or that which surveys, esp. one whose work is surveying land.

surveyor's measure, system of linear measurement used by surveyors, having the chain as its unit.

sur·viv·al (sər vī′vəl) *n.* **1.** act of surviving; state of having survived. **2.** one who or that which survives, as a custom or ritual from the past.

survival of the fittest, natural selection.

sur·vive (sər vīv′) **-vived, -viv·ing.** *v.t.* **1.** to live longer than; remain alive after the death of; outlive: *He survived his brothers.* **2.** to live, exist, or be active through and after: *to survive an automobile accident. He survived the official purges and continued in power for many years.* —*v.i.* to continue to live, exist, or remain active; endure: *These plants won't survive without sun. The music of Bach has survived through the years.* [Middle French *survivre* to outlive, from Latin *supervīvere.*]

sur·vi·vor (sər vī′vər) *n.* one who or that which survives.

sus-, form of sub- before *c, p, t,* as in *susceptible, suspect, sustain.*

Su·sa (sōō′sə) *n.* ancient capital of Elam, in what is now southwestern Iran.

Su·san·na (sōō zan′ə) *n.* **1.** book of the Protestant and Catholic Apocrypha. **2.** heroine of this book, saved by the prophet Daniel.

sus·cep·ti·bil·i·ty (sə sep′tə bil′ə tē) *pl.*, **-ties. 1.** quality or condition of being susceptible. **2.** susceptibilities. strong or sensitive feelings.

sus·cep·ti·ble (sə sep′tə bəl) *adj.* **1.** easily affected or influenced by; readily yielding; open (often with *to*): *a child susceptible to colds, an argument susceptible to criticism.* **2.** capable of undergoing or experiencing; admitting (with *of*): *a good paper susceptible of improvements.* **3.** highly emotional or sensitive; impressionable. [Late Latin *susceptibilis* capable of receiving, from Latin *suscipere* to receive.] —**sus·cep′ti·ble·ness,** *n.* —**sus·cep′ti·bly,** *adv.*

sus·cep·tive (sə sep′tiv) *adj.* **1.** receptive. **2.** susceptible. —**sus·cep′tive·ness, sus·cep·tiv·i·ty** (sus′ep tiv′ə tē), *n.*

sus·pect (*v.*, sə spekt′; *n.*, sus′pekt; *adj.*, sus′pekt′, sə spekt′) *v.t.* **1.** to consider true, likely, or possible; have an inkling of: *I suspect she's already left for the day. I suspect trouble.* **2.** to think (someone) guilty with little or no proof: *The police suspected him of arson.* **3.** to have doubts about; lack confidence in; distrust: *to suspect the evidence. I suspect all fast-talking salesmen.* —*v.i.* to have suspicions. —*n.* one

who is suspected, esp. of having committed a crime. —*adj.* open to or viewed with suspicion; suspected: *His motives are suspect.* [Latin *suspectus,* past participle of *suspicere* to look up to, mistrust.]

sus·pend (sə spend′) *v.t.* **1.** to attach from above so as to allow free movement; hang: *We suspended the swing from a tree branch.* **2.** to keep from falling or sinking with no apparent support: *to suspend particles in a liquid.* **3.** to make ineffective, invalid, or inoperative, esp. on a temporary basis: *to suspend a sentence, to suspend a driver's license.* **4.** to cause to stop for a time; interrupt: *to suspend payments, to suspend service during a strike, to suspend a hearing to a later date.* **5.** to exclude for a time from some privilege, function, or rank, usually as a punishment: *to suspend a student from school.* **6.** to refrain from forming or concluding definitely; hold in abeyance: *I'll suspend judgment for a while.* —*v.i.* **1.** to stop for a time: *The rain suspended long enough for us to walk home.* **2.** to fail to meet one's financial obligations; stop payment. [Latin *suspendere* to hang up.]

suspended animation, state of unconsciousness with no apparent signs of life.

sus·pend·ers (sə spen′dərz) *n.,pl.* pair of straps worn over the shoulders and attached to the waistband of a garment, such as trousers or a skirt, usually worn instead of a belt to hold up the garment.

sus·pense (sə spens′) *n.* **1.** state of being anxiously uncertain or excited, resulting from an undecided situation: *The children can't be kept in suspense any longer; we must announce the winner.* **2.** state of being undecided or in doubt: *The outcome of the trial was still in suspense.* [Old French *suspens* abeyance, delay, going back to Latin *suspēnsus,* past participle of *suspendere* to hang up.] —**sus·pense′ful,** *adj.*

sus·pen·sion (sə spen′shən) *n.* **1.** act of suspending; being suspended. **2.** mixture consisting of small solid particles or liquid droplets, dispersed in a liquid. The particles will separate out if the suspension is allowed to stand. **3.** condition of the particles or droplets in such a mixture: *Earth particles are held in suspension in muddy water.* **4.** device from which something is suspended. **5.** system of springs, torsion bars, absorbers, and other parts, used to support the body of a vehicle in order to maintain a smooth ride. **6.** a stopping of payment of one's financial obligations.

suspension bridge, bridge suspended from cables or chains that are hung between towers firmly anchored at each end.

Suspension bridge

sus·pen·sive (sə spen′siv) *adj.* **1.** having the power or serving to suspend operation or activity: *suspensive conditions.* **2.** of, relating to, or characterized by suspense or indecision.

sus·pen·so·ry (sə spen′sər ē) *adj.* **1.** serving to hold up or support: *a suspensory bandage.* **2.** causing a delay in the completion of something: *a suspensory proposal.* —*n. pl.*, **-ries.** *also,* **sus·pen′sor.** device that supports a part of the body, as a truss, bandage, or athletic support.

suspensory ligament, muscle or ligament that supports an organ or bodily part, esp. the ligament supporting the lens of the eye.

sus·pi·cion (sə spish′ən) *n.* **1.** act or instance of suspecting something wrong or bad with little or no proof; feeling of mistrust or uncertainty. **2.** any feeling or impression that is based on little or no proof: *I have a suspicion that you're right.* **3.** state or condition of being suspected: *A man of such integrity is above suspicion.* **4.** slight trace or suggestion. **5.** condition. suspected of being wrong, bad, or guilty. [Latin *suspiciō* mistrust.]

sus·pi·cious (sə spish′əs) *adj.* **1.** tending to arouse suspicion; questionable: *the suspicious circumstances of his arrest.* **2.** inclined to suspect; distrustful: *to be suspicious of change.* **3.** expressing or indicating suspicion: *a suspicious query.* —**sus·pi′cious·ly,** *adv.* —**sus·pi′cious·ness,** *n.*

sus·pire (sə spīr′) **-pired, -pir·ing.** *v.i. Archaic.* **1.** to sigh. **2.** to take a breath; breathe. [Latin *suspīrāre* to draw a deep breath, sigh.] —**sus′pi·ra′tion,** *n.*

Sus·que·han·na (sus′kwə han′ə) *n.* river flowing through New York, Pennsylvania, and Maryland into Chesapeake Bay.

sus·tain (sə stān′) *v.t.* **1.** to keep in effect or in existence, as an action or process; keep going: *We were too tired to sustain an interesting conversation. Local support is needed to sustain the program.* **2.** to keep up the spirits or courage of; keep from despair; comfort: *His faith sustained him in his hour of need.* **3.** to supply with food, clothing, or other necessities of life; support: *These provisions will sustain us for a week.* **4.** to keep from sinking or falling; support from below: *More poles were needed to sustain the weight of the roof.* **5.** to bear up under or against; be able to endure: *a metal that can sustain the pressure of supersonic speed. This book can sustain comparison with the classics.* **6.** to undergo

or experience, as loss or injury: *The boxer sustained a blow to his jaw.*
7. to accept or uphold as valid, true, or just: *The judge sustained the objection, overruling the prosecution.* **8.** to bear out the truth or validity of; prove; confirm: *New data sustains our earlier findings.* [Old French *so(u)stein-,* a stem of *so(u)stenir* to hold up, going back to Latin *sustinēre.*] —**sus·tain′a·ble,** *adj.* —**sus·tain′er,** *n.*

sustaining program, radio or television program without a sponsor, presented by a station or network at its own expense.

sus·te·nance (sus′tə nəns) *n.* **1.** that which sustains or supports life, esp. food. **2.** means of support; livelihood. **3.** act or process of sustaining; being sustained. [Old French *so(u)stenance* maintenance, support, from *so(u)stenir* to hold up. See SUSTAIN.]

sut·ler (sut′lər) *n.* formerly, one who followed an army or established a store on an army post to sell food and provisions to the army and soldiers. [Obsolete Dutch *soeteler* one who does menial work.]

sut·tee (su tē′, sut′ē) *n.* former funeral practice or custom in which the surviving wife of a deceased man burned herself to death on the man's funeral pyre. Suttee was practiced in India until the British prohibited it in 1829. [Sanskrit *satī* faithful wife.]

su·ture (sōō′chər) *n.* **1.** act or method of joining together the edges of a cut or wound by or as if by stitching. **2.** one of the stitches or fastenings of thread, wire, or other material so used. **3.** line or seam formed in joining two surfaces, as that of a wound sewed together. **4.** act of sewing together or joining together as if by sewing. **5.** line where two bones join, found esp. in the skull. **6.** line along which plant parts meet, as that between the parts that can be split in a pea pod. —*v.t.,* **-tured, -tur·ing.** to secure or join together with or as with a suture. [Latin *sūtūra* a sewing together, seam.]

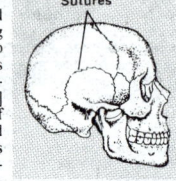

Sutures

Sutures of a human skull

Su·wan·nee (sə won′ē, -wô′nē, swon′ē, swô′nē) *n.* river in Florida and Georgia flowing into the Gulf of Mexico. Also, **Swa′nee.**

su·ze·rain (sōō′zər in, -zə rān′) *n.* **1.** feudal lord. **2.** state or government having supremacy over another state which has its own ruler or government. [French *suzerain* feudal lord, from *sus* above (from Latin *sursum*); influenced by French *souverain* sovereign.]

su·ze·rain·ty (sōō′zər in tē, -zə rān′tē) *pl.,* **-ties.** *n.* position or power of a suzerain.

svelte (svelt, sfelt) **svelt·er, svelt·est.** *adj.* slender; graceful; willowy. [French *svelte,* from Italian *svelto,* from *svellere* to pluck or pull out, back to Latin *ex* out + *vellere* to pluck, pull.]

Sverd·lovsk (sverd lôfsk′) *n.* city in the west-central Soviet Union. Pop. (1970 est.), 1,026,000.

SW, southwest.

swab (swob) *also,* **swob.** *n.* **1.** small piece of cotton, sponge, or other material, usually wound on a small stick, used esp. to apply medication or cosmetics and to clean certain parts of the body. **2.** mop used esp. on ships to clean floors or other surfaces. **3.** long brush for cleaning the bore of a firearm. **4.** *Slang.* clumsy, awkward fellow; lout. —*v.t.,* **swabbed, swab·bing.** to clean, treat, or apply with or as with a swab: *to swab the decks, to swab an open cut with ointment.* [From SWABBER.]

swab·ber (swob′ər) *n.* **1.** one who uses a swab, esp. on a ship. **2.** swab (*def. 2*). [Dutch *zwabber.*]

swad·dle (swod′əl) **-dled, -dling.** *v.t.* **1.** to wrap or bind with or as with bandages. **2.** to wrap (an infant) in swaddling clothes. —*n.* band of cloth or bandage used for swaddling, bandage.] [Old English *swæthel* band used for swaddling, bandage.]

swaddling clothes 1. long, narrow bands of cloth formerly wrapped around newborn infants to prevent free movement of the limbs. **2.** rigid controls or restrictions, as those placed on the young or inexperienced. Also, **swaddling bands.**

swag (swag) *n.* **1.** ornamental drapery, fabric, or garland hung in a loop between two points. **2.** *Slang.* stolen or illegally obtained goods or profits; booty: *The burglar escaped with the swag.* [Probably of Scandinavian origin.]

swage (swāj) *n.* tool, die, or stamp, often one of a pair, for bending metal or for shaping or impressing it by hammering. —*v.t.,* **swaged, swag·ing.** to bend, shape, or impress (metal) by using a swage. [French *suage* decorative molding; of uncertain origin.]

swag·ger (swag′ər) *v.i.* **1.** to walk or behave in a bold, rude, or superior manner: *The young cadet swaggered about like a general reviewing his troops.* **2.** to boast; brag. —*n.* swaggering movement, expression, or behavior. [SWAG + -ER′.] —**swag′ger·er,** *n.*

swagger stick, short, light cane with metal at each end, carried esp. by army officers.

Swa·hi·li (swä hē′lē) *n.* Bantu language containing words borrowed

from Arabic, spoken predominantly in eastern Africa and the Congo.

swain (swān) *n.* **1.** lover; suitor. **2.** country youth, esp. a shepherd. [Old Norse *sveinn* lad, servant.]

swale (swāl) *n.* wet or marshy lowland. [Probably of Scandinavian origin.]

swal·low¹ (swol′ō) *v.t.* **1.** to cause (a food or other substance) to pass through the mouth and the esophagus into the stomach. **2.** to take in or engulf by or as if by swallowing; devour; envelop (often with *up*): *The earthquake swallowed up the whole city.* **3.** to utter indistinctly; mumble: *It is hard to understand what Don says because he swallows his words.* **4.** to keep from expressing or giving vent to; suppress: *to swallow one's pride and ask for a favor.* **5.** to put up with; accept without protest; tolerate: *to swallow an insult.* **6.** to take back; retract. **7.** *Informal.* to accept too readily or without question: *Mother swallowed that lie I told her.* —*v.i.* to perform the act or motion of swallowing: *The speaker swallowed nervously and went on with his lecture.* —*n.* **1.** act or instance of swallowing: *to drink the water in one swallow.* **2.** quantity swallowed at one time: *to take a swallow of soup just to taste it.* [Old English *swelgan* to take into the stomach through the throat.] —**swal′low·er,** *n.*

swal·low² (swol′ō) *n.* any of various perching birds, family Hirundinidae, having a slender body and, often, a deeply forked tail. It is noted for the extent and regularity of its migrations. Length: 4–9 inches. [Old English *swealwe.*]

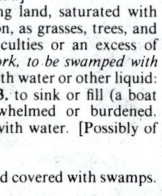

Swallow²

swal·low·tail (swol′ō tāl′) *n.* **1.** deeply forked tail, as that of a kite or certain butterflies, resembling the tail of a swallow. **2.** swallow-tailed coat.

swal·low-tailed (swol′ō tāld′) *adj.* having a deeply forked tail resembling that of a swallow.

swallow-tailed coat, man's coat with tails, used for formal wear.

swam (swam) *a past tense of* **swim.**

swa·mi (swä′mē) *pl.,* **-mis.** *n.* Hindu mystic or religious teacher. [Hindi *swāmī* master, lord, from Sanskrit *svāmin.*]

swamp (swomp, swômp) *n.* area of low-lying land, saturated with water and usually covered with dense vegetation, as grasses, trees, and shrubs. —*v.t.* **1.** to overwhelm, as with difficulties or an excess of something; burden: *to swamp someone with work, to be swamped with requests for autographs.* **2.** to drench or cover with water or other liquid: *The spring floods swamped the coastal areas.* **3.** to sink or fill (a boat or ship) with water. —*v.i.* **1.** to be overwhelmed or burdened. **2.** (of a boat or ship) to sink or become filled with water. [Possibly of Low German origin.]

swamp fever *Informal.* malaria.

swamp·land (swomp′land′, swômp′-) *n.* land covered with swamps.

swamp·y (swom′pē, swôm′-) **swamp·i·er, swamp·i·est.** *adj.* of, consisting of, or resembling a swamp or swamps.

swan (swon) *n.* any of several graceful, long-necked water birds, family Anatidae, having a broad, flat bill, a plump body, webbed feet, and the adult of which has, in most species, white plumage. Length: 3½–6 feet. [Old English *swan.*]

Swan

swan dive, dive in which the arms are extended straight out to the side, with the back arched, the arms being brought together in front of the head just before entering the water.

Swa·nee (swä′nē) Suwannee.

swank·y (swang′kē) **swank·i·er, swank·i·est.** *adj. Slang.* having or characterized by elegance, luxury, or pretension; stylish; posh: *a swanky outfit, a swanky hotel.* Also, **swank.** —**swank′i·ly,** *adv.* —**swank′i·ness,** *n.*

swan's-down (swonz′doun′) *n.* **1.** soft down of a swan, used for such purposes as trimming women's dresses. **2.** fine, thick, soft fabric made from wool or cotton, used for such items as infants' wear and underwear.

Swan·sea (swon′sē, -zē) *n.* port city and industrial center in southern Wales. Pop. (1968 est.), 171,200.

swan song 1. song which, according to legend, a swan sings just before it dies. **2.** final work, appearance, or expression, as at the end of a career, life, or period of time.

swap (swop) **swapped, swap·ping.** *also,* **swop.** *Informal. v.t.,v.i.* to exchange (one thing for another); trade. —*n.* exchange; trade. [Middle English *swappen* to strike (referring to the custom of striking the hands to signify a bargain has been made); probably imitative.] —**swap′per,** *n.*

at; āpe; cär; end; mē; it; īce; hot; ōld; fôrk; wood; fōōl; oil; out; up; ūse; turn; sing; thin; this; zh in treasure; ə in ago, taken, pencil, lemon, circus.

sward (swôrd) *also,* **swarth** (swôrth). *n.* land covered with grass; lawn; meadow. [Old English *sweard* skin.]

swarm[1] (swôrm) *n.* **1.** large group of insects or other small animals flying or moving about together. **2.a.** group of bees, led by the queen of a hive, that flies off together to start a new colony. **b.** such a group of bees newly settled together in a hive. **3.** great number of people, animals, or the like, esp. when in motion: *Swarms of shoppers filled the stores at Christmas time.* **4.** cluster of free-swimming or free-floating cells or unicellular organisms moving together. —*v.i.* **1.** (of bees) to fly off together to start a new colony. **2.** to come together, occur, or move in a large mass or group: *an audience swarming out of the theater.* **3.** to be filled, crowded, or overrun; teem: *a river swarming with alligators.* —*v.t.* to fill with a throng or multitude; crowd. [Old English *swearm* group of bees that leaves the old hive to start a new one.]

swarm[2] (swôrm) *v.t., v.i.* to climb (a pole, tree, or the like) by grasping with the arms and legs. [Of uncertain origin.]

swarth·y (swôr´thē, -thē) **swarth·i·er, swarth·i·est.** *adj.* having a dark or sunburned color or complexion: *swarthy skin.* Also *(archaic),* **swart, swarth.** [Modification of obsolete *swarty,* going back to Old English *sweart* black, dark + -Y[1].] —**swarth´i·ly,** *adv.* —**swarth´i·ness,** *n.*

swash (swosh, swôsh) *v.t.* **1.** to dash (water or other liquid) about; splash. **2.** to splash water or other liquid upon or against. —*v.i.* **1.** to strike, move, or wash noisily or with a splash, as waves do. **2.** to swagger. —*n.* **1.** swashing action or sound, esp. of water. **2.** swagger. **3.** channel running through or behind a sandbank. [Imitative.]

swash·buck·ler (swosh´buk´lər, swôsh´-) *n.* flamboyant or boastful adventurer, soldier, ruffian, or the like. Also, **swash´er.** [SWASH + BUCKLER; referring to the swaggering behavior of a swordsman who showed off by repeatedly hitting his adversary's buckler with a sword.]

swash·buck·ling (swosh´buk´ling, swôsh´-) *adj.* acting like or characteristic of a swashbuckler; flamboyant; boastful.

swas·ti·ka (swos´ti kə) *n.* **1.** symbol or ornament, used widely in both ancient and modern times, in the shape of an equal-armed cross, the spars bent in the center at right angles. **2.** this symbol having the spars bent clockwise, used as an emblem by the Nazi party. [Sanskrit *svastika* a good luck sign, from *svasti* good luck, well-being.]

swat (swot) **swat·ted, swat·ting.** *v.t., v.i.* to hit (someone or something) with a short, sharp blow: *to swat a mosquito, to swat at somebody with a damp towel.* —*n.* short, sharp blow. [Form of SQUAT.] —**swat´ter,** *n.*

swatch (swoch) *n.* small sample of a particular cloth or other material. [Of uncertain origin.]

swath (swoth, swôth) *also,* **swathe.** *n.* **1.** area covered by a single sweep of a scythe or other mowing implement or machine. **2.** width or strip of grass or other grain cut in one such sweep. **3.** long broad belt, strip, or path: *a swath of color encircling the hem of a dress.* **4.** area or extent destroyed as if by a scythe. **5. to cut a wide swath.** to make a big impression or display; have a great influence. [Old English *swæth* track, trace[1].]

swathe (swoth, swāth) **swathed, swath·ing.** *v.t.* **1.** to bind or wrap: *to swathe an· arm with bandages. to swathe one's hair in a turban.* **2.** to surround; enclose. —*n.* a wrapping or binding; bandage. [Old English *swathian* to wrap.]

sway (swā) *v.i.* **1.** to move or swing back and forth or from side to side: *to sway in time to music, branches swaying in the wind.* **2.** to bend, lean, or turn to one side, as from excess weight or pressure: *The car swayed off the road after taking a sharp turn.* —*v.t.* **1.** to cause to move back and forth or from side to side. **2.** to cause to bend, lean, or turn to one side. **3.** to turn aside or divert, as from a course of action; deter: *Nothing could sway the soldier from his duty.* **4.** to cause to be directed or biased in a particular way; have or exert pressure, power, or control over: *The lawyer's reasonable argument visibly swayed the jurors.* —*n.* **1.** act or instance of swaying; back-and-forth or side-to-side motion: *the sway of a ladder, to walk with a sway.* **2.** prevailing or overpowering pressure, power, or control; domination: *Her father has too great a sway in Sue's life.* **3.** sovereign power or authority; dominion; rule: *Although he had officially retired, the general still held sway over his country.* [Old Norse *sveigja* to bend.]

sway·back (swā´bak´) *n.* extreme concave or sagging condition of the back, as of a horse, usually resulting from overwork.

sway·backed (swā´bakt´) *adj.* having the back concave or sagging to an unusual degree.

Swa·zi·land (swä´zē land´) *n.* small country in southeastern Africa, formerly a British colony. Capital, Mbabane. Area, 6705 sq. mi. Pop. (1966 est.), 375,000.

swear (swâr) **swore, sworn, swear·ing.** *v.t.* **1.** to make a solemn declaration with an appeal to God or to some other sacred being or object. **2.** to make a solemn promise. **3.** to use profane language. **4. to swear by.** **a.** to appeal to or name (someone or something) as when taking an oath. **b.** to place great confidence in; consider infallible: *I'll swear by anything he says.* **5. to swear off.** *Informal.* to promise to give up; vow to abstain from: *to swear off smoking.* —*v.t.* **1.** to declare (something) solemnly with an appeal to God or some other sacred being or object: *He swore her accusation was untrue.* **2.** to promise (something) in a solemn manner: *Jim swore the error would never happen again.* **3.** to cause to take an oath; bind by an oath: *The soldier was sworn to defend his country.* **4.** to take or utter (an oath). **5. to swear in.** to induct into office by administering an oath: *A judge swore the mayor in.* **6. to swear out.** to get (a warrant for arrest) by making a charge on oath. [Old English *swerian* to take an oath, make a solemn promise.]

swear·word (swâr´wurd´) *n.* profane or obscene word used in cursing or swearing.

sweat (swet) *n.* **1.** clear fluid produced by glands beneath the skin and secreted through the pores. **2.** similar moisture either exuded by something or gathered on its surface. **3.** act or state of emitting sweat through the pores of the skin, esp. as a result of heat, exertion, or emotion. **4.** *Informal.* emotional state, as impatience, irritation, or anxiety, which may induce sweat: *Don't get into a sweat over the problem.* —*v.i.,* **sweat** or **sweat·ed, sweat·ing.** **1.** to secrete sweat through the pores of the skin. **2.** to exude moisture. **3.** to gather moisture from the surrounding air by condensation. **4.** to be soaked in drops; ooze. **5.** *Informal.* to work hard; drudge; toil. —*v.t.* **1.** to emit (moisture) in drops, as from the pores. **2.** to wet, soak, or stain with sweat. **3.** to cause to sweat. **4.** to cause to exude moisture; force moisture out of, esp. in the process of curing or preparing for use: *to sweat hides.* **5.** to get rid of or eliminate by or as by sweating: *to sweat a cold out, to sweat excess weight off.* **6.** to join (metal parts) by heating another substance to which they both adhere. **7.** to heat (metal) in order to extract an easily fusible constituent. **8.** to cause to work hard; overwork. **9.** *Informal.* to force (someone, as an employee) to work under bad conditions, for low wages, or the like. **10.** *Slang.* **a.** to extract (information or the like) from a person, as by intense interrogation: *The policeman sweated a confession out of the prisoner.* **b.** to extract information from, as by intense interrogation. **11. to sweat out.** *Slang.* to wait anxiously or impatiently for: *The defendant sweated out the jury's verdict.* [Old English *swætan* to perspire, work hard.]

sweat·band (swet´band´) *n.* **1.** narrow band of leather or other material, sewn into the edge of the crown of a hat to absorb sweat. **2.** narrow band of terry or similar material worn around the forehead or wrists to absorb sweat.

sweat·er (swet´ər) *n.* knitted garment, often of wool, for the upper part of the body.

sweat gland, small gland beneath the skin, that secretes sweat.

sweat pants, loose-fitting cotton jersey pants elasticized or drawn in at the ankles and waist, used when exercising to prevent chill and to induce sweating.

sweat shirt, loose-fitting cotton jersey shirt, worn esp. during athletic exercise.

sweat·shop (swet´shop´) *n.* business establishment where workers are employed for long hours, at low wages, or under unfavorable conditions.

sweat·y (swet´ē) **sweat·i·er, sweat·i·est.** *adj.* **1.** covered with, stained with, or smelling of sweat: *sweaty hands, sweaty shoes.* **2.** causing sweat; laborious. —**sweat´i·ly,** *adv.* —**sweat´i·ness,** *n.*

Swed. 1. Sweden. **2.** Swedish.

Swede (swēd) *n.* member or close descendant of the people of Sweden.

Swe·den (swēd´ən) *n.* country in northern Europe, on the eastern part of the Scandinavian peninsula. Capital, Stockholm. Area, 173,666 sq. mi. Pop. (1969 est.), 7,978,000.

Swe·den·borg, E·ma·nu·el (swēd´ən bôrg´; i mä´nōō el´) 1688–1772, Swedish scientist, mystic, and theologian; born Emanuel Svedberg.

Swe·den·bor·gi·an (swēd´ən bôr´jē ən, -gē-) *n.* one who believes in or practices the religious doctrines of Swedenborg. —*adj.* of or relating to Swedenborg, his doctrines, or his followers.

Swed·ish (swē´dish) *adj.* of or relating to Sweden, its people, their language, or their culture. —*n.* **1.** people of Sweden, collectively. **2.** language of Sweden, belonging to the northern group of the Germanic branch of the Indo-European language family.

sweep (swēp) **swept, sweep·ing.** *v.t.* **1.** to clear or cleanse with or as with a broom, brush, or the like: *to sweep a floor.* **2.** to remove, collect, or clear away with or as with a broom, brush, or the like: *to sweep the dust that collected under the sofa.* **3.** to touch or pass over the surface of with a sweeping motion: *The train of her gown swept the floor.* **4.** to pass over or through with a swift, continuous movement: *His eyes swept the newspaper for reports of the incident.* **5.** to move, bring, or carry with a swift, surging movement: *Wind swept the leaves from the sidewalk. The river swept away everything in its path.* —*v.i.* **1.** to clear or cleanse a surface with or as with a broom, brush, or the like. **2.** to move or pass along with a swift, surging movement: *The wind swept through the trees. Cars swept past the house.* **3.** to move with dignity

or stateliness: *The lady swept up to the platform.* **4.** to extend continuously for a long distance: *The highway sweeps along the coast.* —*n.* **1.** act of sweeping. **2.** any swift, surging, or continuous force, movement, or process: *the sweep of the tides, to point out the scenery with a sweep of the hand.* **3.** turn, bend, or curve: *the sweep of her hair as it fell over her eye.* **4.** reach or range of a continuous motion: *the sweep of an ax, the sweep of a telescope as it scans the sky.* **5.** extent, range, stretch, or expanse: *a sweep of desert.* **6.** one who sweeps, esp. a chimney sweep. **7.** long oar used to steer or propel a boat or ship. **8.** sweeps. [Of uncertain origin.]

sweep·er (swē′pər) *n.* person or thing that sweeps floors or other surfaces, esp. a mechanical device used to sweep carpets.

sweep·ing (swē′ping) *adj.* **1.** moving, passing, or curving continuously over a surface or wide area: *a sweeping arc.* **2.** extending over or affecting a wide area; comprehensive; complete: *sweeping reforms, a sweeping generalization.* —*n.* **1.** sweepings, things swept out or up; trash; rubbish. **2.** act of one who or that which sweeps. —**sweep′-ing·ly,** *adv.*

sweep·stakes (swēp′stāks′) *also,* **sweep-stake.** *n.,pl.* **1.** lottery in which the winners are determined by the running of a horse race. **2.** horse race run for this purpose. **3.** any of the prizes awarded on the results of such a race.

sweet (swēt) *adj.* **1.** having a pleasant taste or flavor, esp. one like that of sugar or honey. **2.** pleasing to the mind or senses: *a sweet fragrance, a sweet melody.* **3.** not sour or salted: *sweet cream, sweet butter.* **4.** having or marked by pleasing, agreeable, or kindly characteristics: *a sweet disposition, a sweet and thoughtful gesture.* **5.** dear; beloved: *My own sweet Alice, we must die* (Tennyson, 1833). **6.** (of soil) free from acid and thus good for farming. **7. to be sweet on.** *Informal.* to have a special fondness for; be enamored of. —*n.* **1.** one who or that which is sweet. **2.** *British.* sweet dish, esp. a dessert. **3.** sweets. sweet edible things, as cake or candy. **4.** one who is dear or beloved; darling. ▲ usually used as a term of endearment. **5.** that which is pleasing or agreeable. —*adv.* in a sweet manner; sweetly. [Old English *swēte* pleasing to the senses of taste, smell, and hearing.] —**sweet′ly,** *adv.* —**sweet′ness,** *n.*

sweet alyssum, low-growing European plant, *Lobularia maritima,* widely cultivated for its clusters of tiny, fragrant white flowers.

sweet bay 1. North American tree or shrub, *Magnolia virginiana,* raised for its fragrant white flowers. **2.** laurel *(def. 1).*

Sweet bay

sweet·breads (swēt′bredz′) *n.,pl.* pancreas or thymus gland of an animal, esp. a calf or lamb, when used as food.

sweet·bri·er (swēt′brī′ar) *also,* **sweet·bri·ar.** *n.* rosebush, *Rosa eglantaria,* bearing pink flowers and small scarlet fruit. Also, **eg′lan-tine′.**

sweet cider, freshly made, unfermented cider.

sweet corn, variety of corn with kernels having a high sugar content that are shriveled when fully mature, grown chiefly in the central United States.

sweet·en (swēt′ən) *v.t.* **1.** to make sweet with or as with sugar: *to sweeten coffee.* **2.** to make less painful or trying; lighten: *They sweetened his task with their good humor.* **3.** *Informal.* to increase the value or attractiveness of by adding to, as a pot in poker. —*v.i.* to become sweet or sweeter.

sweet·en·er (swēt′ən ər) *n.* one who or that which sweetens, esp. a noncaloric or low-calorie sugar substitute, as saccharin.

sweet·en·ing (swēt′ən ing, swēt′ning) *n.* **1.** one who or that which sweetens; sweetener. **2.** act or process of making something sweet.

sweet fern, aromatic shrub, *Comptonia peregrina,* found in North America, having fernlike leaves and grown as an ornamental.

sweet flag, fragrant marsh plant, *Acorus calamus,* whose root yields an aromatic oil used in liqueurs and perfumes. Also, **cal′a·mus.**

sweet gale, aromatic shrub, *Myrica gale,* growing along streams in cool regions of the Northern Hemisphere, bearing brown male flowers in catkins and female flowers in small conelike clusters.

sweet gum, tall North American tree, *Liquidambar styraciflua,* bearing glossy starshaped leaves, and having a reddish-brown bark that yields a fragrant yellow resin used in medicine to treat scabies.

sweet·heart (swēt′härt′) *n.* one who is loved by and loves another: *They've been sweethearts for years.*

Sweet gum

sweet·ie (swē′tē) *n. Informal.* sweetheart. Also, **sweetie pie.**

sweet·ing (swē′ting) *n.* **1.** sweet apple. **2.** *Archaic.* darling; sweetheart.

sweet·ish (swē′tish) *adj.* somewhat or rather sweet.

sweet marjoram, marjoram.

sweet·meat (swēt′mēt′) *n.* any sweet food, esp. candy, cake, or candied or preserved fruit.

sweet pea 1. fragrant pealike flower of a plant, *Lathyrus odoratus,* growing singly or in short-stalked clusters in a variety of colors. **2.** the plant itself, having a rough hairy stem, and bearing pairs of short oval or oblong leaflets.

sweet pepper 1. mild-flavored, podlike, edible fruit of a pepper plant, esp. *Capsicum frutescens.* variety *grossum,* usually having a bell shape and eaten in its ripe (red) or unripe (green) state. **2.** plant bearing this fruit.

sweet potato 1. fleshy edible root of a long trailing vine, *Ipomoea batatas,* of the morning glory family, having yellow, brown, or reddish skin and soft orange flesh, cooked and eaten as a vegetable. **2.** the vine itself, widely cultivated in warm areas throughout the world, bearing violet or pink funnel-shaped flowers.

sweet·sop (swēt′sop′) *n.* **1.** tropical American tree, *Annona squamosa,* bearing sweet yellowish-green fruits and thin bluish-gray leaves. **2.** fruit of this tree, sometimes used for making sherbets, jams, and jellies.

sweet tooth, fondness or craving for sweets.

sweet william *also,* **sweet William.** Eurasian plant, *Dianthus barbatus,* widely cultivated for its dense, rounded clusters of red and white flowers with fringed petals.

swell (swel) *swelled,* **swelled** or **swol·len,** **swell·ing.** *v.i.* **1.** to increase in size or extent, esp. by absorption of moisture or inflation with air: *The sponge swelled as it absorbed the water. Her foot swelled in the heat.* **2.** to be distended; bulge out; protrude: *The sails swelled in the breeze.* **3.** to increase in amount, degree, intensity, or force: *The popularity of the party continues to swell.* **4.** to rise above the ordinary or surrounding level: *The heavy rains made the river swell. The mountain swelled in the distance.* **5.** to become greater in volume; grow louder: *The baby's whimper soon swelled to a howl.* **6.** *Informal.* **a.** to become filled with pride, arrogance, or other emotion. **b.** to arise and increase; well up: *Hope swelled in his breast.* —*v.t.* **1.** to cause to increase in size; enlarge: *The infection swelled his hand.* **2.** to cause to distend: *The wind swelled the sails.* **3.** to cause to increase in amount, degree, intensity, or force: *Volunteers swelled the ranks of the marchers.* **4.** *Informal.* to be filled with (pride, arrogance, or other emotion): *Happiness swelled his heart.* —*n.* **1.** act of swelling; being swollen. **2.** part that is swollen or distended; protuberance; swelling: *The ice reduced the swell on his head.* **3.** piece of land which rises gradually and evenly above the surrounding level; rounded elevation. **4.a.** tall, unbroken wave or waves; billows; surge. **b.** waves coming from a direction other than that from which the wind is blowing. **c.** ground swell *(def. 1).* **5.** (of sound) gradual increase in loudness or force. **6.** *Music.* **a.** gradual crescendo immediately followed by a gradual diminuendo. **b.** sign (<>) indicating this. **c.** device, as in a pipe organ, by which the volume of a tone may be varied. **7.** *Informal.* person of high social position, esp. one who is fashionably or stylishly dressed. —*adj. Slang.* **1.** excellent; fine. **2.** elegant; stylish. [Old English *swellan* to increase in size, become distended.] —**Syn.** *v.i.* **1.** see **expand.**

swelled head, excessively high opinion of oneself.

swell·head (swel′hed′) *n.* one who thinks too highly of himself. —**swell′head·ed,** *adj.*

swell·ing (swel′ing) *n.* **1.** act or process of increasing, as in size or extent. **2.** abnormal enlargement of some part of the body.

swel·ter (swel′tər) *v.i.* to suffer or sweat from heat. —*v.t.* to oppress with heat. —*n.* sweltering condition. [From dialectal *swelt* to be overcome (by heat), from Old English *sweltan* to die.]

swel·ter·ing (swel′tər ing) *adj.* suffering from or characterized by excessive heat; very hot: *a sweltering day.* —**swel′ter·ing·ly,** *adv.*

swept (swept) past tense and past participle of **sweep.**

swept·back (swept′bak′) *adj.* (of the wing of an airplane) having the leading edge extending backward to form an acute angle with the fuselage.

swerve (swurv) *swerved,* **swerv·ing.** *v.t.,v.i.* to turn aside from a straight course or aim. —*n.* act or process of swerving. [Old English *sweorfan* to rub, polish.]

swift (swift) *adj.* **1.** moving or capable of moving with great speed; fleet: *a swift runner.* **2.** happening, passing, or accomplished quickly or without delay: *a swift rebuttal, a swift kick.* **3.** acting or responding readily; prompt: *swift to make excuses.* —*adv.* fast. —*n.* any of various swallowlike birds, family Apopidae, having narrow, crescent-shaped wings and predominantly dark-gray, brown, or bluish plumage. Length: 3½–9 inches. [Old English *swift* rapid, prompt.] —**swift′ly,** *adv.* —**swift′ness,** *n.*

---

at; āpe; cär; end; mē; it; īce; hot; ōld; fôrk; wood; fōōl; oil; out; up; ūse; turn; sing; thin; this; zh in treasure; ə in ago, taken, pencil, lemon, circus.

Swift, Jonathan (swift) 1667–1745, English author and satirist.

swig (swig) *Informal. n.* large swallow or gulp, as of liquor. —*v.t.,* **swigged, swig·ging.** to drink heartily or eagerly. [Of uncertain origin.] —**swig′ger,** *n.*

swill (swil) *n.* **1.a.** liquid or semiliquid mixture used to feed animals, esp. slops fed to swine. **b.** kitchen refuse; garbage. **c.** any dirty liquid or semiliquid mess. **2.** large swallow of liquor; swig. —*v.t.* **1.** to drink freely, thirstily, or to excess; guzzle. **2.** to feed or supply (hogs or the like) with swill. —*v.i.* to guzzle liquor. [Old English *swilian* to wash.]

swim (swim) swam or *(archaic)* **swum, swim·ming.** *v.i.* **1.** to move along on or in the water by means of movements of the body or parts of the body. **2.** to move with a gliding, flowing motion, as if swimming through water: *small clouds swimming across the sky.* **3.** to float on water or other liquid. **4.** to be covered or flooded with or immersed in water or other liquid: *The child's eyes swam with tears.* **5.** to have a dizzy or giddy sensation; reel; whirl: *All this confusion makes my head swim.* —*v.t.* **1.** to swim across or through: *to swim the English Channel.* **2.** to cause to swim. —*n.* **1.** action, instance, period, or distance of swimming: *a quick swim before lunch.* **2. in the swim.** in the current trend of affairs, esp. aware of or participating in what is fashionable. [Old English *swimman* to move in water by movements of parts of the body, float.] —**swim′mer,** *n.*

swim bladder, air bladder. Also, **swimming bladder.**

swim·mer·et (swim′ə ret′) *n.* one of the abdominal appendages of many crustaceans, adapted for swimming and, in the female, serving as a place for attaching fertilized eggs. [SWIM + -ER¹ + -ET.]

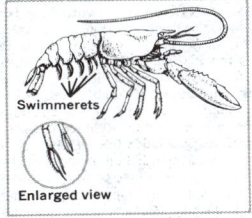
Swimmerets
Enlarged view
Swimmerets

swim·ming (swim′ing) *n.* act of one who or that which swims. —*adj.* of, relating to, or used for swimming or swimmers.

swim·ming·ly (swim′ing lē) *adv.* very well; successfully; smoothly: *Those two people get on swimmingly.*

swimming pool, pool¹ (def. 2).

swim·suit (swim′sōōt′) *n.* bathing suit.

Swin·burne, Al·ger·non Charles (swin′bərn; al′jər nən) 1837–1909, English poet, dramatist, critic, and novelist.

swin·dle (swind′əl) **-dled, -dling.** *v.t.* **1.** to deprive by fraud of money or property rightfully due. **2.** to obtain (something, as money or property) by this means. —*v.i.* to practice fraud; cheat. —*n.* act or instance of swindling; fraud. —**swin′dler,** *n.* —**Syn.** *v.t.* **2.** see **cheat.**

swine (swīn) *pl.* **swine.** *n.* **1.** any of various stout-bodied mammals, family Suidae, as the pig or boar, having a long, mobile snout, cloven hoofs, and thick, bristly skin. **2.** vicious, brutal, or contemptible person. [Old English *swīn* this animal.]

swine·herd (swīn′hurd′) *n.* one who tends swine.

swing (swing) swung, swing·ing. *v.t.* **1.** to cause to move backward and forward, esp. with a steady movement, as below or about a fixed point. **2.** to cause to turn or make a circular movement, as about a pivot; move in an arc: *Richard swung his arms around as he talked.* **3.** to suspend so as to hang freely: *The children swung the strings of popcorn from the branches of the Christmas tree.* **4.** *Informal.* to influence or control to one's advantage; bring about successfully: *to swing an election, to swing a contract.* —*v.i.* **1.** to move backward and forward, esp. with a steady movement, as below or about a fixed point: *The gate swung on one rusty hinge.* **2.** to ride on a swing: *The little girl swung higher and higher when her brother pushed her.* **3.** to strike or attempt to strike with a swinging motion: *The batter swung at the ball and missed.* **4.** to act or move freely, smoothly, and easily: *The car swung into the driveway.* **5.** *Informal.* to be hanged: *He'll swing for his crime.* **6.** *Slang.* to be lively; move at a fast pace: *This town swings in the summer.* —*n.* **1.** act of swinging: *the swing of a pendulum, the swing of public opinion.* **2.** distance covered by the arc or curve made by swinging. **3.** recreational device consisting of some form of seat suspended by ropes, chains, or the like, on which one may move back and forth. **4.** free, swinging, rhythmic movement or gait: *There is a swing in her step this morning.* **5.** sweeping blow or stroke: *One swing of the ax was enough to fell the tree.* **6.** freedom of action; license. **7.** continuous, vigorous, and forceful movement or progress. **8.** form of jazz developed in the 1930s, characterized by the use of a large band, written arrangements, and a steady, pulselike rhythm. **9. in full swing.** operating to the greatest extent: *Ten weeks before the election the campaign was in full swing.* —*adj.* of, relating to, or characteristic of swing music: *a swing arrangement, a swing band.* [Old English *swingan* to scourge, rush.] —**swing′er,** *n.*

swin·gle (swing′gəl) *n.* large, knifelike, wooden instrument used for beating flax or hemp to remove the woody or coarse portions. —*v.t.,* **-gled, -gling.** to clean (flax or hemp) with such an instrument. [Middle Dutch *swinghel* instrument for beating flax.]

swin·gle·tree (swing′gəl trē′) *n.* whiffletree.

swing shift, work shift between the day and night shifts, usually between 3 P.M. and 11 P.M.

swin·ish (swī′nish) *adj.* like or befitting swine; brutish; beastly: *trodden down under the hoofs of a swinish multitude* (Burke, 1790). —**swin′ish·ly,** *adv.* —**swin′ish·ness,** *n.*

swipe (swīp) *n. Informal.* hard, sweeping stroke, glancing blow, or punch: *The cat took a swipe at the ball of yarn.* —*v.t.,* **swiped, swip·ing.** **1.** *Informal.* to hit with a sweeping or glancing blow. **2.** *Slang.* to steal; pilfer; snatch: *to swipe a pocketbook.* [Possibly modification of SWEEP.]

swirl (swurl) *v.i.* to move with a twisting or eddying motion; whirl: *A gust of wind made the leaves swirl.* —*v.t.* to cause to whirl; twist; curl. —*n.* **1.** whirling motion; eddy. **2.** something having a twisted shape; curl; spiral: *We decorated the cake with chocolate swirls.* [Possibly imitative.]

swish (swish) *v.i.* **1.** to move with or make a soft, muffled sound; rustle: *Her satin skirt swished as she came through the narrow hallway.* **2.** to move with or make a thin, hissing or whistling sound, as a slender rod or scythe cutting through the air. —*v.t.* to cause to swish: *The cow stood silently swishing her tail.* —*n.* swishing movement or sound. [Imitative.]

Swiss (swis) *adj.* of or relating to Switzerland, its people, or their culture. —*n. pl.,* **Swiss.** member or close descendant of the people of Switzerland.

Swiss chard, beet, *Beta vulgaris,* often cultivated for its yellowish-green leaves and long, thick, whitish leafstalks, both of which are cooked and eaten as a vegetable. Also, **chard.**

Swiss cheese, firm, pale-yellow or whitish cheese having many large holes.

Swiss Guards, corps of soldiers, recruited from Switzerland, employed as bodyguards of the pope since the sixteenth century.

Swiss chard

switch (swich) *n.* **1.** slender, flexible rod, twig, or stick used for whipping. **2.** stroke, lash, or other sudden, whisking movement. **3.** act or instance of changing; shift, as of opinion or approach. **4.** device used to open or close an electric circuit or to transfer current from one conductor to another. **5.** electric apparatus for transferring trains or train cars from one track to another. **6.** woman's hairpiece consisting of a thick bunch or braid of real or synthetic hair. **7.** bushy end of the tail of certain animals, as cows. —*v.t.* **1.** to turn aside, divert, or change: *to switch the conversation to a less controversial topic.* **2.** to exchange: *to switch plates.* **3.** to connect or disconnect by means of a switch (with *on* or *off*): *to switch the lights on, to switch off the furnace.* **4.** to move (a train or train cars) from one track to another; shunt. **5.** to beat, strike, or whip with or as with a switch: *to switch a horse.* **6.** to move or swing sharply or suddenly; whisk: *The cat switched his tail in anger.* —*v.i.* **1.** to turn aside; change: *The senator switched to another political party.* **2.** to be turned aside or changed. [Possibly from Middle Dutch *swijch* twig, branch, whip.] —**switch′er,** *n.*

switch·back (swich′bak′) *n.* railroad, road, path, or the like that ascends a steep incline in a zigzag arrangement.

switch·blade (swich′blād′) *n.* pocketknife with a blade operated by a spring and released by a catch. Also, **switchblade knife.**

switch·board (swich′bōrd′) *n.* control panel with switches, dials, buttons, or receptacles for plugs, that connects, disconnects, combines, or adjusts electric circuits, as for telephone lines.

switch hitter, baseball player who can bat both left-handed and right-handed.

switch·man (swich′mən) *pl.,* **-men.** *n.* man in charge of one or more switches on a railroad.

switch·yard (swich′yärd′) *n.* railroad yard where trains are assembled and switched from one track to another.

Switz·er·land (swit′sər lənd) *n.* small, mountainous country in central Europe. Capital, Bern. Area, 15,940 sq. mi. Pop. (1969 est.), 6,184,000.

swiv·el (swiv′əl) *n.* **1.** link or other fastening device that allows attached parts of a chain to turn freely. **2.** pivoted support on which something, as a gun, may be turned in a horizontal plane. **3.** cannon that turns on such a support or pivot. (def. 3.) **swivel gun.** —*v.i.,* **-eled, -el·ing;** *also, British,* **-elled, -el·ling.** **1.** to turn on or as on a swivel: *Lily swiveled around when she heard her name called.*

at; āpe; cär; end; mē; it; īce; hot; ōld; fôrk; wood; fōōl; oil; out; up; ūse; turn; sing; thin; this; zh in treasure; ə in ago, taken, pencil, lemon, circus.

1009

—*v.t.* **1.** to turn (something) on or as on a swivel. **2.** to secure with or fasten by means of a swivel. [Middle English *swyvel* the fastening device, from Old English *swīfan* to revolve.]

swivel chair, chair whose seat turns horizontally on a swivel.

swiz·zle stick (swiz′əl) short rod or stick, as of wood or plastic, used to stir drinks, esp. alcoholic beverages.

swob (swob) swab.

swol·len (swō′lən) *v.* a past participle of **swell.** —*adj.* enlarged by or as by swelling: *swollen eyes, the swollen tide.*

swoon (swoōn) *v.i.* to faint. —*n.* act of swooning; fainting fit. [Middle English *swownen* to faint, going back to Old English *geswōgen* in a faint.]

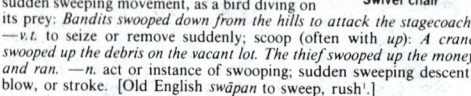

Swivel chair

swoop (swoōp) *v.i.* to rush or descend with a sudden sweeping movement, as a bird diving on its prey: *Bandits swooped down from the hills to attack the stagecoach.* —*v.t.* to seize or remove suddenly; scoop (often with *up*): *A crane swooped up the debris on the vacant lot. The thief swooped up the money and ran.* —*n.* act or instance of swooping; sudden sweeping descent, blow, or stroke. [Old English *swāpan* to sweep, rush¹.]

swop (swop) swap.

sword (sôrd) *n.* **1.** weapon, as a saber, scimitar, or broadsword, usually of metal, consisting of a hilt and a straight or curved pointed blade, used for thrusting or cutting. **2.** sovereign power or authority. **3.** force or the use of force, as in war: *The pen is mightier than the sword. Those who live by the sword shall die by the sword.* **4.** any instrument or cause of death, destruction, or ruin. **5. at swords' points.** ready to fight; mutually antagonistic; hostile. **6. to cross swords. a.** to fight. **b.** to disagree or argue violently. **7. to put to the sword.** to kill or slay with a sword, esp. in battle. [Old English *sweord* this weapon, military force, a destroying agency.]

Swordfish

sword·fish (sôrd′fish′) *pl.,* **-fish** or **-fish·es.** *n.* large saltwater food and game fish, *Xiphias gladius,* found in temperate and tropical seas, having a scaleless, streamlined body and a long, flattened, swordlike snout. Length: to 15 feet.

sword grass, any of various grasses or plants with swordlike leaves.

sword knot, ribbon or tassel attached to the hilt of a sword for ornament.

Sword of Damocles, threat of disaster; impending crisis. [From the sword suspended over Damocles' head. See DAMOCLES.]

sword·play (sôrd′plā′) *n.* action, art, or technique of using a sword, esp. in fencing.

swords·man (sôrdz′mən) *pl.,* **-men.** *also,* **sword·man,** *n.* **1.** one who is armed with a sword, as a soldier or fencer. **2.** one who is skilled in the use of a sword. —**swords′man·ship′,** *n.*

swore (swōr) past tense of **swear.**

sworn (swôrn) past participle of **swear.**

'swounds (zwoundz, zoundz) zounds.

swum (swum) past participle and archaic past tense of **swim.**

swung (swung) past tense and past participle of **swing.**

sy-, form of **syn-** before *s* plus a consonant, as in *systole.*

syb·a·rite (sib′ə rīt′) *n.* one who is devoted to luxury and pleasure; epicure. [Latin *Sybarīta* inhabitant of Sybaris, from Greek *Sybarītēs,* from *Sybaris,* an ancient city in southern Italy notorious for luxurious living.] —**syb·a·rit·ic** (sib′ə rit′ik); *also,* **syb′a·rit′i·cal,** *adj.*

syc·a·more (sik′ə môr′) *n.* **1.** American plane tree, *Platanus occidentalis,* found in eastern North America, sometimes planted as an ornamental. Also, **but′ton·wood′.** **2.** a fig tree, *Ficus sycamorus,* found in Egypt and Asia Minor, bearing sweet edible fruit. [Late Latin *sȳcomorus* mulberry tree, from Greek *sȳkomoros* fig tree; probably of Semitic origin.]

syc·o·phan·cy (sik′ə fən sē) *pl.,* **-cies.** *n.* practice or character of a sycophant; fawning or self-seeking servility.

syc·o·phant (sik′ə fənt) *n.* one who fawns over or flatters powerful or important people as a means of gaining favor or influence. [Latin *sȳcophanta* informer, flatterer, from Greek *sȳkophantēs* informer.] —**syc·o·phan·tic** (sik′ə fan′tik); *also,* **syc′o·phan′ti·cal,** *adj.*

Syd·ney (sid′nē) *n.* chief port and largest city of Australia, on the eastern coast of the country. It is the capital of New South Wales. Pop., metropolitan area (1968), 2,444,735.

sy·e·nite (sī′ə nīt′) *n.* any igneous rock composed essentially of feld-

spar and hornblende or biotite. [Latin *Syēnītēs (lapis)* (stone) of Syene, syenite, from *Syene,* a town in ancient Egypt where this stone was once quarried.]

syl-, form of **syn-** before *l,* as in *syllable.*

syl·lab·ic (si lab′ik) *adj.* **1.** of, relating to, or consisting of a syllable or syllables. **2.** relating to a consonant sound that forms a separate syllable by itself without the help of a vowel sound, as the *l* in *rattle.* **3.** pronounced with each syllable distinctly enunciated. **4.** designating a type of poetry based on the number of syllables in a line rather than on stress or rhythm. —*n.* syllabic sound. —**syl·lab′i·cal·ly,** *adv.*

syl·lab·i·cate (si lab′ə kāt′) **-cat·ed, -cat·ing.** *v.t.* to form or divide into syllables. —**syl·lab′i·ca′tion,** *n.*

syl·lab·i·fy (si lab′ə fī′) **-fied, -fy·ing.** *v.t.* to syllabicate. —**syl·lab′i·fi·ca′tion,** *n.*

syl·la·ble (sil′ə bəl) *n.* **1.** unit of spoken language pronounced with a single uninterrupted sounding of the voice, consisting of a single vowel sound or of a vowel sound grouped with one or more consonants or of a single consonant pronounced alone. The words *bit* and *break* have one syllable; the word *amazement* has three. **2.** letter or group of letters used in writing and printing to represent such a spoken unit, serving to indicate where a word may be hyphenated at the end of a line. **3.** slightest bit, mention, or expression: *There was not a syllable of doubt as to his guilt.* —*v.t.,* **-bled, -bling.** to pronounce in syllables. [Old French *sillabe* part of a word forming only one sound, through Latin, from Greek *syllabē* literally, that which holds together.]

syl·la·bub (sil′ə bub′) *also,* **sil·la·bub.** *n.* whipped drink or topping, usually made with cream and liquor and sometimes thickened with gelatin for use as a chilled dessert.

syl·la·bus (sil′ə bəs) *pl.,* **-bi** (-bī′) or **-bus·es.** *n.* brief statement, summary, or plan listing main points to be covered and requirements to be met, as in a course of study. [Modern Latin *syllabus,* from a printer's mistaken rendering of Latin *sittybas,* accusative plural of *sittyba* label from Greek *sittybā*.]

syl·lo·gism (sil′ə jiz′əm) *n.* **1.** form of argument or reasoning consisting of a major premise, a minor premise, and a conclusion that is logically drawn from them. If the premises are accepted as true, it must follow that the conclusion is true. For example: All men are mortal (major premise). Socrates is a man (minor premise). Therefore, Socrates is mortal (conclusion). **2.** deductive reasoning. [Latin *syllogismus,* from Greek *syllogismos* calculation, reasoning, deductive argument.]

syl·lo·gis·tic (sil′ə jis′tik) *adj.* of, relating to, or consisting of a syllogism or syllogisms. Also, **syl′lo·gis′ti·cal.** —**syl′lo·gis′ti·cal·ly,** *adv.*

syl·lo·gize (sil′ə jīz′) **-gized, -giz·ing.** *v.t.,v.i.* to argue, reason, or deduce by means of syllogisms.

sylph (silf) *n.* **1.** slender, graceful girl or young woman. **2.** one of a race of imaginary beings supposed to inhabit the air. [Modern Latin *sylphes* (plural), possibly coined by Paracelsus from Latin *sylva* (form of *silva* a wood, forest) and *nympha.* See NYMPH.]

syl·van (sil′vən) *also,* **sil·van.** *adj.* **1.** of, situated in, or inhabiting a wood or woods: *a sylvan deity.* **2.** formed by or abounding in trees; wooded; woody: *a sylvan grove, a sylvan region.* **3.** relating to or characteristic of a wood or woods; rustic. [Latin *silvānus* relating to a wood, from *silva* a wood, forest.]

sym-, form of **syn-** before *b, m,* and *p,* as in *symbiosis, symmetry, symptom.*

sym·bi·ont (sim′bī ont′, -bē-) *n.* organism that lives in a state of symbiosis.

sym·bi·o·sis (sim′bī ō′sis, -bē-) *pl.,* **-ses** (-sēz). *n.* **1.** the living together in close association of two unlike organisms, esp. in a relationship that is mutually beneficial. The association between termites and the protozoans living in their stomachs and intestines is an example of symbiosis. The protozoans break down the cellulose eaten by the termite so that it can be digested, and in turn all the protozoans' nourishment is provided by the termite. **2.** any association of mutual interdependence, as between persons or groups. [Modern Latin *symbiosis,* from Greek *symbiōsis* a living together.]

sym·bi·ot·ic (sim′bī ot′ik, -bē-) *adj.* relating to, living in, or characterized by symbiosis. Also, **sym′bi·ot′i·cal.** —**sym′bi·ot′i·cal·ly,** *adv.*

sym·bol (sim′bəl) *n.* **1.** something that stands for or represents something else, esp. a material object considered to typify some abstract or invisible quality, condition, or idea: *The robin is a symbol of spring. A gold band is a symbol of marriage.* **2.** letter, figure, or other printed or written device used to express or represent an object, quantity, process, relation, or the like, as in mathematics, music, or chemistry: *C is a symbol for carbon.* —*v.t.,* **-boled, -bol·ing;** *also, British,* **-bolled, -bol·ling.** to symbolize. [Latin *symbolum* token, sign, from Greek *symbolon*.]

sym·bol·ic (sim bol′ik) *adj.* **1.** serving as a symbol: *a symbolic handshake. The owl is symbolic of wisdom and learning.* **2.** relating to or expressed by a symbol or symbols. **3.** characterized by or involving the

use of symbols, esp. in art or literature. Also, **sym·bol′i·cal.** —**sym·bol′i·cal·ly,** *adv.*

sym·bol·ism (sim′bə liz′əm) *n.* **1.** practice or convention of representing things by symbols or of investing objects, acts, or relations with symbolic meaning or significance, esp. in art or literature. **2.** category or system of symbols: *pictorial symbolism, pagan symbolism.* **3.** symbolic quality, character, or meaning. **4.** theories and practices of symbolists in art or literature.

sym·bol·ist (sim′bə list) *n.* **1.** one who uses symbols. **2.** one who is skilled in the interpretation of symbols. **3.** one who uses or is skilled in the use of symbolism, esp. an artist or writer. **4.** any of a group of chiefly French artists and writers of the late nineteenth century who rejected realism and attempted to express ideas and emotions through the use of symbolic sounds, words, and objects. —**sym′bol·is′tic;** *also,* **sym′bol·is′ti·cal,** *adj.*

sym·bol·ize (sim′bə līz′) **-ized, -iz·ing.** *v.t.* **1.** to be or serve as a symbol of; represent or stand for: *A lily symbolizes purity.* **2.** to represent by a symbol or symbols: *Writing symbolizes the sounds that we make in speaking.* —*v.i.* to use symbols. —**sym′bol·i·za′tion,** *n.*

sym·bol·o·gy (sim bol′ə jē) *n.* study of symbols or symbolism.

sym·met·ri·cal (si met′ri kəl) *adj.* having or exhibiting symmetry. Also, **sym·met′ric.** —**sym·met′ri·cal·ly,** *adv.*

sym·me·trize (sim′ə trīz′) **-trized, -triz·ing.** *v.t.* to make symmetrical.

sym·me·try (sim′ə trē) *pl.,* **-tries.** *n.* **1.** exact correspondence in size, form, and arrangement of the parts of something, either on opposite sides of a median line or plane, or around a central point or axis. Leaves, starfish, and human beings all have symmetry. **2.** properly proportioned shape, structure, or arrangement of parts; beauty or harmony of form. [Latin *symmetria* proportion, from Greek *symmetriā.*]

sym·pa·thet·ic (sim′pə thet′ik) *adj.* **1.** expressing, feeling, or resulting from sympathy: *a sympathetic friend, a sympathetic statement.* **2.** favorably inclined toward; in agreement with (with *to*): *He is sympathetic to our plans.* **3.** being in accord or harmony; congenial. **4.** of or relating to that part of the autonomic nervous system associated with the involuntary responses of the body to changes in the external environment, such as increasing the rate and strength of the heartbeat and producing adrenalin in times of stress. Distinguished from **parasympathetic. 5.** produced by responsive vibrations caused by the transmission of vibrations from one body to another: *sympathetic sound, sympathetic tone.* —**sym′pa·thet′i·cal·ly,** *adv.*

sym·pa·thize (sim′pə thīz′) **-thized, -thiz·ing.** *v.i.* **1.** to feel or express compassion. **2.** to share in or agree with the feelings or ideas of; be in accord: *I sympathize with his efforts for reform.* [French *sympathiser* to feel alike, from *sympathie* feeling in common, from Latin *sympathīa.* See SYMPATHY.] —**sym′pa·thiz′ing·ly,** *adv.*

sym·pa·thiz·er (sim′pə thī′zər) *n.* one who sympathizes, esp. a person who is favorably inclined toward a particular party or cause without being fully committed to it: *a Communist sympathizer.*

sym·pa·thy (sim′pə thē) *pl.,* **-thies.** *n.* **1.** act or capacity of entering into or sharing the feelings of another or others. **2.** feeling or expression of pity or compassion; commiseration: *We sent our sympathies to the bereaved family. The newspaper article aroused a great deal of sympathy for the victims of the hurricane.* **3.** relationship between two things whereby whatever affects one one affects the other in the same way. **4.** agreement in personality, disposition, or point of view; affinity: *It was impossible for much sympathy to exist between two such different people.* **5.** favorable attitude or leaning toward some cause or party; accord, allegiance, or commitment: *I am in sympathy with the aims of that union.* [Latin *sympathīa* feeling in common, from Greek *sympatheia,* going back to *syn* together + *pathos* feeling.] —**Syn. 2.** see **pity.**

sympathy strike, strike by a body of workers to give support to a strike by another group.

sym·pet·al·ous (sim pet′əl əs) *adj.* gamopetalous.

sym·phon·ic (sim fon′ik) *adj.* **1.** of, relating to, or having the character of a symphony or symphony orchestra. **2.** agreeing in sound; harmonious. —**sym·phon′i·cal·ly,** *adv.*

sym·pho·ni·ous (sim fō′nē əs) *adj.* in harmony; harmonious.

sym·pho·ny (sim′fə nē) *pl.,* **-nies.** *n.* **1.** extended orchestral composition usually having three or four movements written in varied forms, tempos, and keys. **2.** symphony orchestra. **3.** harmony, esp. of sounds. **4.** anything characterized by an agreeable or harmonious blending of elements. [Latin *symphōnia* harmony, concord, agreement of sounds, from Greek *symphōnia,* going back to *syn* together + *phōnē* sound.]

symphony orchestra, large orchestra for playing symphonies and other similar compositions, usually consisting of string, brass, woodwind, and percussion sections.

sym·po·si·um (sim pō′zē əm) *pl.,* **-si·ums** or **-si·a** (-zē ə). *n.* **1.** meeting or conference for the discussion of a particular subject, esp. a meeting at which several speakers give short addresses before an

audience on a single topic. **2.** collection of comments or opinions on a particular subject, esp. a published group of essays or articles. [Latin *symposium* banquet, from Greek *symposion* banquet, drinking party, from *syn* together + *posis* drinking; referring to the ancient Greek custom of having intellectual discussions at a drinking party.]

symp·tom (simp′təm, sim′-) *n.* **1.** noticeable change in the normal condition or functions of the body or any of its parts, that indicates or accompanies a disease or other disorder: *Vomiting and muscular cramps are symptoms of cholera.* **2.** anything serving as a sign or indication of something: *Civil unrest may be a symptom of the decline of a society.* [Late Latin *symptōma* indication of disease, from Greek *symptōma* happening, accident.]

symp·to·mat·ic (simp′tə mat′ik, sim′-) *adj.* **1.** indicating or accompanying a disease or other abnormal condition of the body: *Fever, chills, and repeated coughing may be symptomatic of pneumonia.* **2.** of or relating to the symptoms of a disease: *symptomatic treatment.* **3.** serving as a sign or indication: *The spontaneous demonstration of protest was symptomatic of the discontent of the people.* —**symp′to·mat′i·cal·ly,** *adv.*

syn- *prefix* occurring at the same time or in conjunction; together; with: *synod.* [Greek *syn* together, with.]

syn. 1. synonym. **2.** synonymous.

syn·a·gogue (sin′ə gog′) *n.* **1.** congregation of Jews assembled for religious instruction and worship. **2.** building used for such instruction and worship. [Late Latin *synagōga,* from Greek *synagōgē* a bringing together, assembly.]

syn·apse (sin′aps, si naps′) *n.* point at which a nerve impulse is transmitted between two nerve cells. [Greek *synapsis* contact, junction.]

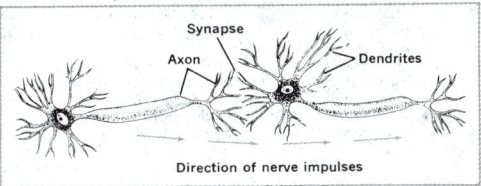

Direction of nerve impulses

Synapse

syn·chro·mesh (sing′krə mesh′, -krō-) *n.* device in an automobile transmission that synchronizes the speeds of the gears so that they will mesh smoothly when shifted. —*adj.* relating to or using such a device: *a synchromesh transmission, synchromesh shifting.*

syn·chro·nism (sing′krə niz′əm) *n.* **1.** condition or quality of being synchronous; simultaneous occurrence; coincidence. **2.** chronological listing or arrangement of historical events or persons to indicate their simultaneous occurrence or existence.

syn·chro·nize (sing′krə nīz′) **-nized, -niz·ing.** *v.i.* **1.** to happen at the same time; agree in time; coincide: *The closing of the old store synchronized with the opening of the new shopping plaza.* **2.** to move or operate at the same rate and exactly together. —*v.t.* **1.** to cause to happen or operate at the same rate and exactly together: *to synchronize the marchers in a parade, to synchronize the sound and the action of a motion picture.* **2.** to make (timepieces) agree in keeping or indicating time. **3.** to list or arrange (historical events or persons) to indicate simultaneous occurrence or existence. [Greek *synchronizein* to be contemporary with, going back to *syn* together + *chronos* time.] —**syn′chro·ni·za′tion, syn′chro·niz′er,** *n.*

syn·chro·nous (sing′krə nəs) *adj.* **1.** occurring at the same time; simultaneous; coincident. **2.** happening or operating at the same rate. **3.** *Physics.* having the same period and phase, as vibrations. [Late Latin *synchronus* contemporary, from Greek *synchronos,* from *syn* together + *chronos* time.] —**syn′chro·nous·ly,** *adv.* —**syn′chro·nous·ness,** *n.*

syn·chro·tron (sing′krə tron′) *n.* device for accelerating subatomic particles to very high speeds by means of a magnetic field and an alternating electric field of high frequency. The intensity of the magnetic field is increased as the speed of the particles increases, so as to hold them in a stable orbit.

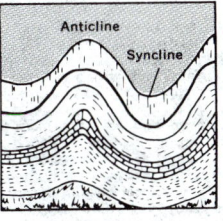

Anticline

Syncline

Syncline

syn·cline (sing′klīn′, sin′-) *n.* fold of rocks in which the strata dip inward from both sides toward the axis. [Greek *synklīnein* to lean.] —**syn·cli′nal,** *adj.*

syn·co·pate (sing′kə pāt′, sin′-) -pat·ed, -pat·ing. *v.t.* **1.** *Music.* to treat or modify (a tone or passage) by syncopation. **2.** to shorten (a word) by omitting one or more sounds or letters, as *sou'wester* for *southwester.* [Late Latin *syncopātus,* past participle of *syncopāre* to swoon, shorten by syncope, from *syncopē* a swooning, contraction. See SYNCOPE.]

syn·co·pa·tion (sing′kə pā′shən, sin′-) *n.* **1.a.** *Music.* metric pattern created by stressing one or more normally unaccented beats in a measure, used esp. in jazz or ragtime music. **b.** syncopated music, rhythm, dance step, or the like. **2.** syncope (*def. 1*).

syn·co·pe (sing′kə pē, sin′-) *n.* **1.** contraction of a word by the omission of one or more sounds or letters from the middle, as *Lester* for *Leicester.* **2.** loss of consciousness caused by a temporary inadequate supply of blood to the brain. [Latin Latin *syncopē* a swooning, contraction, from Greek *synkopē* a cutting short.]

syn·dic (sin′dik) *n.* **1.** one who represents and manages the affairs of a community or corporation, esp. a university. **2.** civil magistrate or other government official. [Late Latin *syndicus* delegate, advocate, from Greek *syndikos* advocate, from *syn* with + *dikē* lawsuit, judgment.]

syn·di·cal·ism (sin′di kə liz′əm) *n.* political and economic theory advocating that all means of production and distribution be brought under the control of groups of workers by means of direct action, as industrial sabotage, boycotts, demonstrations, and esp. a general strike. —**syn′di·cal·ist,** *n.*

syn·di·cate (*n.,* sin′di kit; *v.,* sin′di kāt′) *n.* **1.a.** association of individuals or companies formed to carry out a business enterprise, esp. one requiring a large amount of capital. **b.** group of persons combined to carry out any enterprise. **2.** organization that sells material, as special articles and photographs, for simultaneous publication in a number of newspapers or periodicals. **3.** council or body of syndics. **4.** *Informal.* association of racketeers or gangsters controlling organized crime. —*v.t.,* -cat·ed, -cat·ing. **1.** to manage as or combine into a syndicate. **2.** to sell (an article, column, comic strip, or the like) for simultaneous publication in a number of newspapers or periodicals. —*v.i.* to form a syndicate. [French *syndicat* trusteeship, from *syndic* trustee, from Late Latin *syndicus* delegate, advocate. See SYNDIC.] —**syn′di·ca′tion,** *n.*

syn·drome (sin′drōm) *n.* **1.** group of symptoms that together are characteristic of a particular disease or condition. **2.** any group of characteristics that indicate or identify a particular condition or quality, esp. an undesirable social condition. [Modern Latin *syndrome,* from Greek *syndromē* a running together, combination.]

syn·ec·do·che (si nek′də kē) *n.* figure of speech in which a part is substituted for the whole, or the whole for a part, as, many *mouths* (people) to feed; starting a *car* (the car's engine). [Late Latin *synecdoche,* from Greek *synekdoche* literally, a receiving together.]

syn·er·gism (sin′ər jiz′əm) *n.* action of separate substances, agents, or organs that produces a greater effect than the sum of their individual actions, as in a medicine composed of several different drugs. —**syn′er·gist,** *n.* —**syn′er·gis′tic,** *adj.*

syn·es·the·sia (sin′is thē′zhə, -zhē ə, -zē ə) *n.* phenomenon in which the stimulation of one of the senses produces a secondary, subjective sensation associated with a different sense, as when the hearing of a particular sound gives someone a mental impression of a certain color.

syn·od (sin′əd) *n.* **1.** council or assembly of ecclesiastical officials. **2.** any council or assembly. **3.** in the Presbyterian Church, a governing body ranking next above the presbytery. [Late Latin *synodus* ecclesiastical council, from Greek *synodos* meeting, assembly, from *syn* together + *hodos* away.] —**syn′od·al,** *adj.*

syn·od·i·cal (si nod′i kəl) *adj.* **1.** of or relating to the conjunctions of celestial bodies, esp. the period between two successive conjunctions of a planet with the sun. **2.** relating to or of the nature of a synod. Also, **syn·od′ic.**

syn·o·nym (sin′ə nim) *n.* **1.** word that has the same or nearly the same meaning as another word in the same language. *Large* is a synonym of *big; leap* is a synonym of *jump.* Opposed to **antonym. 2.** word or phrase accepted as a substitute for another; symbolic or figurative name; metonym: *Broadway has become a synonym for the American commercial theater.* **3.** *Biology.* scientific name that has been rejected as incorrect or out-of-date. [Latin *synōnymum* word having the same meaning as another word, from Greek *synōnymon.*]

syn·on·y·mize (si non′ə mīz′) -mized, -miz·ing. *v.t.* to give a synonym or synonyms for (a word).

syn·on·y·mous (si non′ə məs) *adj.* **1.** equivalent or very similar in meaning; being a synonym or synonyms: *The words "puma" and "cougar" are synonymous.* **2.** expressing or implying the same idea; having the same significance: *Lack of education is not synonymous with lack of intelligence.* —**syn·on′y·mous·ly,** *adv.*

syn·on·y·my (si non′ə mē) *pl.* -mies. *n.* **1.** state or quality of being synonymous. **2.** study or classification of synonyms. **3.** list or collection of synonyms, esp. one in which synonyms are discriminated from one another according to their implications, connotations, and uses.

syn·op·sis (si nop′sis) *pl.* -ses (-sēz). *n.* brief statement giving a review, outline, or condensation of a book, speech, play, or similar work; summary: *a synopsis of the plot of a novel.* [Late Latin *synopsis* general view, plan, from Greek *synopsis* general view.] —**Syn.** see **summary.**

syn·op·tic (si nop′tik) *adj.* **1.** of, relating to, or forming a synopsis; providing a general view. **2.** presented from or taking a common point of view. **3.** *usually.* **Synoptic.** relating to or designating the first three Gospels of the New Testament. Also, **syn·op′ti·cal.** —**syn·op′ti·cal·ly,** *adv.*

syn·o·vi·a (si nō′vē ə) *n.* clear, viscid lubricating fluid secreted by certain membranes, as those lining the joints. [Modern Latin *synovia;* coined by Paracelsus.] —**syn·o′vi·al,** *adj.*

syn·tac·tic (sin tak′tik) *adj.* of, relating to, or according to the rules of syntax. Also, **syn·tac′ti·cal.** —**syn·tac′ti·cal·ly,** *adv.*

syn·tax (sin′taks) *n.* **1.** the way in which words are put together to form sentences and phrases; relationship and arrangement of words in a sentence. **2.** branch of grammar that deals with this. [Late Latin *syntaxis* the connection of words, from Greek *syntaxis* arrangement, a putting together of words.]

syn·the·sis (sin′thə sis) *pl.* -ses (-sēz′). *n.* **1.** the assembling or combining of separate elements or subordinate elements into a complex or systematic whole. Opposed to **analysis. 2.** complex whole or entity formed in this manner. **3.** act or process of producing a complex chemical compound by combining two or more simpler compounds, elements, or radicals. [Latin *synthesis* mixture, compound, from Greek *synthesis* a putting together.]

syn·the·size (sin′thə sīz′) -sized, -siz·ing. *v.t.* **1.** to combine so as to form a complex or systematic whole: *an effort to synthesize Oriental and Western philosophies.* **2.** to produce by chemical synthesis: *to synthesize rubber.*

syn·the·siz·er (sin′thə sī′zər) *n.* **1.** one who or that which synthesizes. **2.** electronic device having a keyboard and solid-state circuitry, that can simulate the sounds made by a wide variety of musical instruments and also produce sounds not obtainable from ordinary instruments.

syn·thet·ic (sin thet′ik) *adj.* **1.** produced artificially by chemical synthesis; not occurring naturally; man-made: *Nylon is a synthetic fiber.* **2.** lacking genuine emotion or sincerity; artificial: *a synthetic smile.* **3.** relating to, of the nature of, or proceeding by synthesis. Also, **syn·thet′i·cal.** —**syn·thet′i·cal·ly,** *adv.* —**Syn.** *adj.* **1.** see **artificial.**

syph·i·lis (sif′ə lis) *n.* infectious, chronic venereal disease caused by a spirochete, usually transmitted by sexual intercourse or acquired congenitally. If untreated, the disease progresses by three stages of increasing severity, the first being characterized by a hard sore at the site of initial infection and the second by a skin rash and ulcerous sores. The third stage, which may develop in one to twenty years after infection, can damage the heart, blood vessels, spinal cord, eyes, or brain. [Modern Latin *syphilis,* from *Syphilus,* the hero of a poem about the disease by Girolamo Fracastoro, 1483–1553, Italian physician and poet.]

syph·i·lit·ic (sif′ə lit′ik) *adj.* of, relating to, or affected with syphilis. —*n.* one who is affected with syphilis.

sy·phon (sī′fən) siphon.

Syr·a·cuse (sir′ə kūs′) *n.* **1.** city in central New York. Pop. (1970), 197,208. **2.** port city in southeastern Sicily, in ancient times a leading Greek city. Pop. (1968), 101,098.

Syr·i·a (sir′ē ə) *n.* **1.** country in southwestern Asia. Capital, Damascus. Area, 71,498 sq. mi. Pop. (1969 est.), 5,866,000. **2.** ancient country at the eastern end of the Mediterranean, comprising roughly what is now Syria, Lebanon, Israel, and adjacent areas.

Syr·i·ac (sir′ē ak′) *n.* Semitic language based on ancient Aramaic, spoken in Syria from the third to the thirteenth century A.D., surviving chiefly as the liturgical and literary language of several Eastern Christian churches.

Syr·i·an (sir′ē ən) *adj.* of or relating to Syria or its people. —*n.* member or close descendant of the people of Syria.

Syrian Desert, desert in southwestern Asia, in northern Saudi Arabia, southern Syria, eastern Jordan, and western Iraq. Area, approx. 200,000 sq. mi.

sy·rin·ga (sə ring′gə) *n.* mock orange.

Syringe

sy·ringe (sə rinj′, sir′inj) *n.* **1.** device consisting of a nozzle and a rubber bulb or piston, by means of which a liquid may be drawn in and then forced out in a thin

at; āpe; cär; end; mē; it; īce; hot; ōld; fôrk; wood; fōol; oil; out; up; ūse; turn; sing; thin; this; zh in treasure; ə in ago, taken, pencil, lemon, circus.

stream. It is used esp. for injecting fluids into the body and cleansing wounds. **2.** hypodermic syringe. —*v.t.,* **-ringed, -ring·ing.** to cleanse, inject, or the like, with or as with a syringe. [Medieval Latin *syringa* the device, going back to Greek *syrinx* pipe, tube.]

syr·inx (sir′ingks) *pl.,* **sy·rin·ges** (sə rin′ jēz, -gēz) or **syr·inx·es.** *n.* **1.** panpipe. **2.** Eustachian tube. **3.** vocal organ of birds, located at the lower end of the trachea at its junction with the bronchi. [Greek *syrinx* shepherd's pipe, tube.]

syr·up (sir′əp, sur′-) *also,* **sir·up.** *n.* sweet, thick liquid, esp. one obtained by boiling sugar with water or fruit juice, often with the addition of flavoring or medication: *cough syrup.* [Old French *sirop,* going back to Arabic *sharāb* beverage.]

syr·up·y (sir′ə pē, sur′-) *also,* **sir·up·y.** *adj.* **1.** of or like syrup, esp. in appearance or consistency. **2.** excessively sentimental; mawkish: *syrupy dialogue.*

sys·tem (sis′təm) *n.* **1.** group of things or parts related or combined in such a way as to form a unified or complex whole: *a heating system, a system of roads, a public school system, a loudspeaker system.* **2.a.** set of organs or parts of the body that have a similar structure and act together to perform a specific function: *the digestive system.* **b.** the entire body considered as a functioning organism: *His system was greatly weakened by his long illness.* **3.** related group or series of natural objects, as rivers or mountains. **4.** organized and comprehensive set of facts, rules, laws, doctrines, or principles: *a system of philosophy, a system of government.* **5.a.** any particular form of political, economic, or social organization or practice: *the capitalist system, the communist system.* **b.** *usually,* **the system.** the established structure of society or government, esp. when regarded as hindering, restrictive, or repressive. **6.** method or form of classification, arrangement, or notation: *a taxo-* *nomic system.* **7.** plan or method of operation or procedure: *to have a system for studying for an examination, to bet on horse races according to a system.* **8.** condition of orderliness or regularity. **9.** group of bodies moving or existing in relation to one another in accordance with certain natural laws, as the solar system. **10.** *Geology.* a major division of rocks, composed of all the rocks formed during a geological period. [Late Latin *systēma* a whole consisting of several parts, from Greek *systēma.*]

sys·tem·at·ic (sis′tə mat′ik) *adj.* **1.** of, constituting, or relating to a system: *a systematic statement of foreign policy, a systematic philosophy of life.* **2.** carried out or done by or as by a system: *a systematic course of study, a systematic attack on a person's reputation.* **3.** characterized by system or method; methodical: *a systematic person.* Also, **sys′·tem·at′i·cal.** —**sys′tem·at′i·cal·ly,** *adv.* —**Syn. 2.** see orderly.

sys·tem·a·tize (sis′tə mə tīz′) **-tized, -tiz·ing.** *v.t.* to form into or arrange according to a system. —**sys′tem·a·ti·za′tion, sys′tem·a·tiz′er,** *n.*

sys·tem·ic (sis tem′ik) *adj.* **1.** of or relating to a system or systems. **2.** of, relating to, or affecting the body as a whole.

sys·tem·ize (sis′tə mīz′) **-ized, -iz·ing.** *v.t.* to systematize. —**sys′·tem·i·za′tion, sys′tem·iz′er,** *n.*

sys·to·le (sis′tə lē) *n.* normal contraction of the heart, alternating rhythmically with the period of dilation, or diastole. During systole the blood is forced outward from the heart. [Greek *systolē* contraction.] —**sys·tol·ic** (sis tol′ik), *adj.*

Szcze·cin (shche tsēn′) *n.* port city in northwestern Poland, formerly known as Stettin. Pop. (1968 est.), 331,700.

Sze·chuan (se′chwan′, su′-) *also,* **Sze·chwan.** *n.* province in southwestern China. Area, 219,700 sq. mi. Pop. (1957 est.), 72,160,000.

---

at; āpe; cär; end; mē; it; īce; hot; ōld; fôrk; wood; fōōl; oil; out; up; ūse; turn; sing; thin; this; zh in treasure; ə in ago, taken, pencil, lemon, circus.

t, T (tē) *pl.,* **t's, T's.** *n.* **1.** twentieth letter of the English alphabet. **2.** shape of this letter or something having such a shape. **3. to a T.** to perfection; exactly.

t. **1.** teaspoon. **2.** temperature. **3.** tense. **4.** transitive. **5.** time. **6.** tenor. **7.** ton; tons.

T. **1.** Tuesday. **2.** Territory. **3.** Testament. **4.** tablespoon.

Ta, tantalum.

tab (tab) *n.* **1.** small flap, strip, or other attachment projecting from an object, used esp. to facilitate opening, fastening, or handling. **2.** small extension on a card or the edge of a paper, used as an aid in filing or indexing. **3.** small ornamental flap or loop on a garment, as a man's shirt. **4.** auxiliary airfoil attached or set into a larger control surface of an airplane. **5.** *Informal.* bill to be paid; check: *to pick up the tab for a meal.* **6. to keep tabs** (or **a tab**) **on.** *Informal.* to watch closely; check up on: *The police kept tabs on the gangster's activities.* —*v.t.,* **tabbed, tab·bing. 1.** to provide with a tab. **2.** to pick out or designate: *That player has been tabbed as a future star by fans of the team.* [Of uncertain origin.]

tab·ard (tab′ərd) *n.* any of various short, loose coats or coatlike outer garments, as those worn by knights over their armor. [Old French *tabart;* of uncertain origin.]

Ta·bas·co (tə bas′kō) *n. Trademark.* pungent sauce made from the fruit of a variety of capsicum. [From *Tabasco,* a Mexican state and river.]

tab·by (tab′ē) *pl.,* **-bies.** *n.* **1.** domestic cat having a tawny or gray coat with darker stripes. **2.** any domestic cat, esp. a female. **3.** fabric with a plain weave, as silk or taffeta with a moiré or watered finish. —*adj.* tawny or gray with darker stripes. [Old French *tabis* striped taffeta, from Arabic *'attābīy* watered silk, a district of Baghdad where this silk was first made.]

Tabby

tab·er·na·cle (tab′ər nak′əl) *n.* **1.** place of worship, esp. one for a large body of worshipers. **2. Tabernacle. a.** portable tent containing the Ark of the Covenant, which served as a place of worship for the Jews during their wanderings from Egypt to Palestine. **b.** Jewish temple. **3.** in the Roman Catholic and some Anglican churches, a container for the consecrated host, usually placed in the center of the altar. **4.** canopied niche or recess, esp. one containing a tomb or shrine. [Latin *tabernāculum* tent, diminutive of *taberna* hut.]

ta·ble (tā′bəl) *n.* **1.** piece of furniture consisting of a flat, horizontal surface supported by one or more vertical legs: *a coffee table, a billiard table.* **2.** such a table upon which food is served: *He left the table before the meal was over.* **3.** food served at a table or a particular place. **4.** people seated at a table: *The table in the rear was very noisy.* **5.** very concise, ordered list or guide; synopsis: *a table of contents.* **6.** orderly arrangement of facts or information, usually in a series of columns to facilitate comparison of the given data: *a table of measurements, a statistical table.* **7.** information given in such a table: *to learn the multiplication tables.* **8.** gambling table, as for poker or roulette. **9.** tableland; plateau. **10.** any flat, horizontal surface. **11.** *Architecture.* **a.** vertical member, usually rectangular and often ornamented, set into or projecting from a wall. **b.** horizontal projecting course or molding, as a cornice. **12.** thin, flat slab, as of stone or metal, used esp. for writing; tablet. **13. on the table.** postponed for discussion or decision for an indefinite period of time. **14. to turn the tables.** to reverse the situation, as between two opponents. **15. under the table.** secretly and illegally: *to pay money under the table in return for special favors.* —*v.t.,* **-bled, -bling. 1.** to postpone discussion or decision of indefinitely: *to table a motion.* **2.** to put on a table. **3.** to form into a list or catalogue; tabulate. [Old English *tabule* board, tablet, from Latin *tabula.*]

tab·leau (tab lō′) *pl.,* **-leaux** (-lōz′) or **-leaus.** *n.* **1.** vivid and pic-turesque description or representation: *The movie was a tableau of life in Russia.* **2.** group of persons or objects forming a picturesque scene. **3.** silent and motionless representation of a scene, painting, or incident, executed by a person or persons appropriately costumed and posed: *a tableau of Washington crossing the Delaware.* [French *tableau* picture, scene, diminutive of *table* table, slab, from Latin *tabula* board, tablet, picture.]

ta·ble·cloth (tā′bəl klôth′) *n.* cloth for covering a dining table, esp. at meals.

ta·ble d'hôte (tab′əl dōt′, tä′bəl) meal consisting of several specified courses served at a fixed price. Distinguished from **à la carte.** [French *table d'hôte* literally, table of the host, going back to Latin *tabula* board + *dē* from + *hospes* host¹, guest.]

ta·ble·land (tā′bəl land′) *n.* elevated, relatively flat, land area; plateau.

table linen, items made of linen or similar material, used in setting a table.

ta·ble·spoon (tā′bəl spoon′) *n.* **1.** spoon larger than a teaspoon or dessert spoon, used esp. for serving and measuring. **2.** amount one tablespoon will hold, a standard cooking measurement equivalent to three teaspoons or one-half fluid ounce.

ta·ble·spoon·ful (tā′bəl spoon fool′) *pl.,* **-fuls.** *n.* amount one tablespoon holds; tablespoon.

tab·let (tab′lit) *n.* **1.** number of sheets of paper glued, sewn, or otherwise fastened together at one edge, used esp. for writing; pad. **2.** small, compressed piece of material, as medicine, soap, or candy. **3.** thin, flat slab, as of wood or stone, used for writing or drawing. **4.** slab of stone or metal bearing an inscription, esp. a commemorative or explanatory one; plaque. [Old French *tablete* something flat used for writing, small table, diminutive of *table* table, from Latin *tabula* board, tablet, picture.]

table talk, informal conversation at or as if at meals.

table tennis, game similar to tennis played on a table with a small plastic ball and wooden paddles. Also, **ping′-pong′.**

ta·ble·ware (tā′bəl wâr′) *n.* articles placed on a table for use at meals, as dishes, glasses, and silverware.

table wine, still wine that contains less than fourteen percent alcohol, usually served with meals.

tab·loid (tab′loid) *n.* **1.** newspaper with pages half the size of an ordinary newspaper page, having brief news articles and many pictures, esp. one having items of a sensational nature. **2.** compressed tablet of medicine. *Trademark:* Tabloid. —*adj.* condensed; shortened. [TABL-(ET) + -OID.]

ta·boo (tə boo′, ta-) *pl.,* **-boos.** *also,* **ta·bu.** *n.* **1.** prohibition or restriction observed, as by Polynesians, out of fear that grave danger, misfortune, or death will come directly to anyone who breaks it. **2.** any prohibition or ban, esp. one imposed by social custom or convention. —*adj.* **1.** prohibited or restricted under a taboo. **2.** prohibited or forbidden for any reason: *During Prohibition the sale of alcoholic beverages was taboo.* —*v.t.,* **-booed, -boo·ing.** to put under a taboo; ban; prohibit. [Polynesian *tabu,* sacred, set apart.]

ta·bor (tā′bər) *n.* small drum, esp. one formerly used to accompany a pipe or fife played by the same person. [Old French *tabour* drum, possibly going back to Persian *tabīr.*]

tab·o·ret (tab′ə ret′, -rā′) *also,* **tab·ou·ret.** *n.* **1.** small, low seat or stool. **2.** frame for embroidery. **3.** small tabor. [French *tabouret* stool, diminutive of Old French *tabour* drum. See TABOR.]

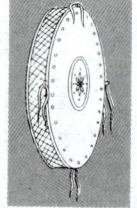

Tabor

Ta·briz (tä brēz′) *n.* city in northwestern Iran. Pop. (1966 est.) 403,413.

tab·u·lar (tab′yə lər) *adj.* **1.** having a broad, flat surface. **2.** of or arranged in lists or tables. **3.** computed or calculated by means of tables. [Latin *tabulāris* relating to a board, from *tabula* board, tablet.]

ta·bu·la ra·sa (tab′yə lə rä′sə, rä′zə) **1.** slate that is blank or has been erased; clean slate. **2.** the mind before it has received any impressions from experience. [Latin *tabula rāsa* erased tablet, clean slate.]

tab·u·late (*v.*, tab′yə lāt′; *adj.* tab′yə lit, -lāt′) **-lat·ed, -lat·ing.** *v.t.* to arrange in lists or columns; put into a table: *to tabulate statistics.* —*adj.* having a broad, flat surface; tabular. —**tab′u·la′tion,** *n.*

tab·u·la·tor (tab′yə lā′tər) *n.* **1.** device on a typewriter used for arranging material in columns. **2.** machine that tabulates. **3.** one who tabulates.

tac·a·ma·hac (tak′ə mə hak′) *n.* **1.** a gum resin with a strong odor, used in incenses, ointments, and formerly in medicines. **2.** any of various trees yielding this resin, esp. a North American poplar. [Obsolete Spanish *tacamahaca* the tree; of Nahuatl origin.]

ta·chom·e·ter (ta kom′ə tər, tə-) *n.* **1.** instrument that indicates the revolutions per minute of a revolving shaft, as of an engine. **2.** any of various devices for measuring speed. [Greek *tachos* speed + -METER.]

tac·it (tas′it) *adj.* **1.** not openly expressed but understood or implied: *Her smile was a tacit approval.* **2.** without words; unspoken; silent: *a tacit prayer.* [Latin *tacitus,* past participle of *tacēre* to be silent.] —**tac′it·ly,** *adv.* —**tac′it·ness,** *n.*

tac·i·turn (tas′ə turn′) *adj.* not inclined to speak very much; silent or extremely reserved. [Latin *taciturnus* quiet.] —**tac′i·tur′ni·ty,** *n.* —**tac′i·turn′ly,** *adv.*

Tac·i·tus (tas′ə təs) *n.* A.D. c.55–117, Roman historian.

tack (tak) *n.* **1.** small nail with a sharp point and a broad, flat head: *a carpet tack.* **2.** stitch that can be easily removed, used as a fastening. **3.** course or line of action or method: *His argument went off on a different tack.* **4.a.** direction of a boat or ship's fore-and-aft line with respect to the wind. When the wind is on a ship's starboard or right side, the ship is on a starboard tack. **b.** change of a boat or ship's direction to take advantage of side winds. **c.** zigzag course against the wind. **d.** one of a series of movements of a boat or ship to starboard and port alternately in a zigzag against the wind. **5.** *Nautical.* **a.** rope holding in place a corner of some sails, as the lower forward corner of a fore-and-aft sail. **b.** corner thus held in place. —*v.t.* **1.** to fasten with or as with a tack or tacks. **2.** to sew or fasten with temporary stitches: *to tack a bow on a dress.* **3.** to attach as a supplement; add: *to tack an amendment on to a bill.* **4.** *Nautical.* **a.** to change the course (of a boat or ship) by turning its head to the wind. **b.** to navigate (a boat or ship) against the wind by a series of tacks. —*v.i.* **1.** to tack a boat or ship. **2.** to go on an opposite tack or change course by going on opposite tacks. [Dialectal Old French *taque* nail; of Germanic origin.] —**tack′er,** *n.*

tack·le (tak′əl) *n.* **1.** equipment or gear used for an activity, as fishing. **2.** system of ropes and pulleys for hoisting, lowering, or pulling heavy loads, as those used on a ship to raise, lower, and move the sails. **3.** *Football.* **a.** either of the two players who line up between the guard and the end. **b.** position played by either of these players. **c.** act of tackling. **4.** act of seizing, stopping, and bringing to the ground. —*v.t.,* **-led, -ling.** **1.** to deal with; work on: *to tackle a problem.* **2.** to seize and jump on in order to stop. **3.** *Football.* to bring (a ball carrier) to the ground by seizing him or by using one's weight against him. **4.** to harness (a horse). —*v.i.* to make a football tackle. [Middle Low German *takel* equipment, ship's rigging, from *taken* to lay hold of.] —**tack′ler,** *n.* —**Syn.** *n.* **1.** see *gear.*

tack·y¹ (tak′ē) *adj.* sticky, as partially dried paint or glue. [TACK + -Y¹; with reference to a tack's use in attaching things.] —**tack′i·ness,** *n.*

tack·y² (tak′ē) **tack·i·er, tack·i·est.** *Informal. adj.* lacking taste or style; cheap, dowdy, or shabby: *a tacky dress.* [Of uncertain origin.] —**tack′i·ness,** *n.*

ta·co (tä′kō) *pl.* **-cos.** *n.* Mexican dish consisting of a fried tortilla wrapped around a filling, as of cheese, ground beef, or chicken. [Spanish *taco* wad, light meal; probably of Germanic origin.]

Ta·co·ma (tə kō′mə) *n.* city in western Washington, on Puget Sound. Pop. (1970), 154,581.

tac·o·nite (tak′ə nīt′) *n.* low-grade iron ore, consisting of a flintlike rock containing silica and iron minerals, occurring esp. in the areas of Michigan, Wisconsin, and Minnesota around Lake Superior. [From the *Taconic* mountain range in New England + -ITE¹.]

tact (takt) *n.* ability to handle people or situations without giving offense: *You need more tact in the dangerous art of giving presents than in any other social action* (Bolitho, 1929). [Latin *tāctus* touch.]

tact·ful (takt′fəl) *adj.* having or showing tact: *a tactful person, tactful criticism.* —**tact′ful·ly,** *adv.* —**tact′ful·ness,** *n.*

tac·tic (tak′tik) *n.* **1.** plan of action or device used to achieve a goal.

2. method of arranging and using military forces in action. [Modern Latin *tacticus,* from Greek *taktikos* fit for arranging, from *tassein* to arrange.]

tac·ti·cal (tak′ti kəl) *adj.* **1.** of or relating to tactics, esp. combat tactics. **2.** showing skill in tactics; characterized by clever planning and maneuvering. —**tac′ti·cal·ly,** *adv.*

tactical unit, unit of troops, aircraft, or ships that can operate independently, usually including support elements, as artillery.

tac·ti·cian (tak tish′ən) *n.* **1.** one who is skilled in military tactics. **2.** anyone who is skilled in planning and executing the means to an end; clever maneuverer: *a political tactician.*

tac·tics (tak′tiks) *n.,pl.* **1.** art or science of using and moving military forces and equipment in actual combat. Distinguished from **strategy.** ▲ construed as singular. **2.** such arrangement and use of military forces. **3.** any methods or devices employed to achieve a goal: *campaign tactics.* [Plural of TACTIC.]

tac·tile (tak′til, -tīl) *adj.* **1.** of or relating to touch: *The skin receives tactile sensations.* **2.** endowed with the sense of touch: *The whiskers of a cat are tactile organs.* **3.** perceptible to the touch; tangible. [Latin *tāctilis* tangible, from *tāctus,* past participle of *tangere* to touch.] —**tac·til·i·ty** (tak til′ə tē), *n.*

tact·less (takt′lis) *adj.* having or showing no tact; lacking diplomacy: *a tactless comment.* —**tact′less·ly,** *adv.* —**tact′less·ness,** *n.*

tac·tu·al (tak′chōō əl) *adj.* **1.** of or relating to touch. **2.** caused by the touch; producing a feeling of touch. [Latin *tāctus* touch + -AL¹.] —**tac′tu·al·ly,** *adv.*

tad·pole (tad′pōl′) *n.* aquatic larva of a frog or toad, having external gills, an egg-shaped body, and a tadpole's tail. Also, **pol′li·wog′.** [Middle English *tad-depol* literally, toad (that is all) head, from *tadde* toad + *pol* head. See TOAD, POLL.]

Tadpole

Ta·dzhik·i·stan (tä jik′i stan′) *n.* republic of the Soviet Union, in the south-central part of the country, bordering Afghanistan and China. Area, approx., 55,000 sq. mi. Pop. (1967 est.), 2,579,000.

Tae·gu (tī′gōō, tī-) *n.* city in southeastern South Korea. Pop. (1966 est.), 845,073.

ta′en (tān) *Archaic.* taken.

taf·fe·ta (taf′ə tə) *n.* shiny, somewhat stiff fabric, usually made of silk or rayon. [Old French *taffetas* smooth, shiny cloth of silk, going back to Persia *tāftah* silken or linen cloth.]

taff·rail (taf′rāl′) *n.* **1.** rail around the stern of a ship. **2.** upper part of the stern of a ship. Also, **taf·fe·rel, taf·fe·rel** (taf′ər əl). [Dutch *taffereel* panel, diminutive of *tafel* table, going back to Latin *tabula* board, tablet.]

taf·fy (taf′ē) *n.* chewy candy made of brown sugar or molasses mixed with butter that is boiled down and then pulled until it holds its shape. [Form of TOFFEE.]

Taft, William Howard (taft) 1857–1930, twenty-seventh president of the United States, from 1909 to 1913, and chief justice of the U.S. Supreme Court, from 1921 to 1930.

tag¹ (tag) *n.* **1.** piece of paper, plastic, or other material attached to or hanging loosely from something for the purpose of labeling or identifying it: *a name tag, a luggage tag.* **2.** part or piece hanging from or loosely attached to something else. **3.** hard tip or binding on a string, as at the end of a shoelace. **4.** *Informal.* automobile license plate. **5.** identifying epithet; verbal label. **6.** saying or quotation used in speech or writing, for emphasis, ornament, or effect. —*v.t.,* **tagged, tag·ging.** **1.** to fasten an identifying or labeling tag to. **2.** to label or designate with an epithet: *They tagged him as a poor sport.* **3.** to add as an appendage: *to tag superfluous comments on to a report.* **4.** to follow closely. **5.** to make (a substance used in the body) combine with another, easily detectable substance, as a dye or a radioisotope, so that it can be traced or followed on its path through the body. —*v.i.* to follow closely; trail: *The dog tagged along wherever they went.* [Probably of Scandinavian origin.]

tag² (tag) *n.* **1.** game in which one player (usually called "it") chases the other players until he touches one who then, in turn, becomes "it." **2.** in baseball and similar games, act of putting out a runner by touching him with the ball or with the hand holding the ball. —*v.t.,* **tagged, tag·ging.** **1.** to touch or tap, as in the game of tag. **2.** in baseball and similar games, to put out (a base runner) by touching him with the ball or with the hand holding the ball. **3.** to hit with great force or strength: *to tag a ball into the outfield. He tagged his opponent with an uppercut.* —*v.i.* **1.** in baseball and similar games, to make a tag. **2.** to tag up, *Baseball.* to return to and touch a base before running to the next base after a fly ball has been caught. [Of uncertain origin.]

Ta·ga·log (tä gä′lòg, -lóg) *pl.* **-logs** or **-log.** *n.* **1.** member of a people of Malayan stock who make up part of the native population of the Philippines. **2.** their language, belonging to the Indonesian branch of

the Malayo-Polynesian language family, now the official national language of the Philippines.

tag end, last part of anything; remnant.

tag line, last line of a joke, phrase, speech, play, or the like.

Ta·gore, Sir Ra·bin·dra·nath (tə gôr′; rə bin′drə nät′) 1861–1941, Hindu philosopher and poet.

Ta·hi·ti (tə hē′tē) n. largest of the Society Islands, midway between Australia and South America. Area, 402 sq. mi. Pop. (1967), 61,519.

Ta·hi·tian (tə hē′shən, -hē′tē ən) adj. of or relating to Tahiti, its people, or their language. —n. 1. native or inhabitant of Tahiti. 2. language of Tahiti, belonging to the Polynesian branch of the Malayo-Polynesian language family.

Ta·hoe, Lake (tä′hō) mountain lake in eastern California and western Nevada.

tail (tāl) n. 1. hindmost part of an animal's body, which in vertebrates consists of a number of vertebrae forming a flexible attachment at the end of the spine. 2. anything resembling a tail in shape. 3. stream of luminous gases and solid matter trailing from a comet. 4. rear portion of an aircraft. 5. rear, bottom, or last part of anything: *the tail of a bicycle.* 6. long lock of hair banded or braided together. 7. **tails.** side of a coin not bearing a figure or inscription; reverse side of a coin. 8. one of the two panels in the back of a man's formal coat. 9. **tails.** a. swallow-tailed coat. b. man's full-dress evening wear. 10. *Informal.* one who or that which follows closely, as a spy or detective: *The police put a tail on the suspect.* 11. **to turn tail.** to flee from danger, trouble, or something unpleasant. —v.t. 1. to furnish with or as with a tail. 2. to cut the tail from. 3. to be the end or tail of. 4. to join end to end: *to tail two ropes together.* 5. to fasten the end of (a beam, brick, or similar part) into a wall or other support. 6. *Informal.* to follow closely, esp. secretly and for the purpose of observing: *The secret agent tailed the spy.* —v.i. 1. to form or move in a line suggesting a tail. 2. to lessen gradually; diminish (usually with *off*): *Protests tailed off after the new policies were put in effect.* —adj. located at or coming from the rear: *a tail gunner in a bomber.* [Old English *tægel* hindmost part of an animal's body.]

tail·gate (tāl′gāt′) n. board at the rear of a station wagon or other vehicle that can be let down or removed for loading or unloading. Also, **tail′board′.** —v.i., v.t., **-gat·ed, -gat·ing.** *Informal.* to drive too closely behind another vehicle.

tail·ing (tā′ling) n. 1. part of a projecting stone or brick fastened into a wall. 2. **tailings.** part of a material separated as refuse, as in mining or grain milling.

tail·light (tāl′līt′) n. light, usually red, at the rear of a vehicle.

tai·lor (tā′lər) n. one who makes, alters, or mends clothing, esp. outer garments. —v.t. 1. to make or fashion as a tailor: *He tailored the dress to fit the woman.* 2. to make, alter, or adapt to meet a special requirement or need: *The program was tailored to the needs of young children.* 3. to fit or furnish with clothing. —v.i. to do a tailor's work. [Old French *tailleur* cutter, from *taillier* to cut, from Late Latin *tāliāre,* from Latin *tālea* rod, cutting.]

tai·lor·bird (tā′lər burd′) n. any of several warblers, family Sylviidae, native to Asia and Africa, that sew their nests by stabbing the edges of broad leaves with their needlelike bills to draw vegetable fibers through the holes. Length: 5 inches.

tai·lored (tā′lərd) adj. 1. (of woman's clothing) well-finished with neat, simple lines and a trim fit. 2. made by a tailor.

tai·lor·ing (tā′lər ing) n. 1. workmanship or skill of a tailor. 2. business or occupation of a tailor.

tai·lor-made (tā′lər mād′) adj. 1. made by a tailor or with the workmanship characteristic of a tailor. 2. meeting specific needs or requirements; well-suited: *That role was tailor-made for him.*

tail·piece (tāl′pēs′) n. 1. part that is the end or that is added on at the end. 2. *Printing.* a small ornamental mark placed at the bottom of a page, esp. at the end of a chapter. 3. triangular piece of wood at the lower end of violins and similar instruments to which the strings are attached. 4. short beam or rafter inserted in a wall and supported by a header.

tail pipe, pipe that carries exhaust gases from an engine to the rear of a vehicle.

tail·race (tāl′rās′) n. 1. channel that carries water away from a waterwheel. 2. channel or trough for carrying water away from a hydraulically operated machine.

tail·spin (tāl′spin′) n. 1. rapid descent of an airplane in a spiral path, with the nose pointing downward and moving in a smaller circle than the tail. 2. sudden or worsening state of confusion, anxiety, or depression.

tail wind, wind blowing in the same direction that something is moving, as on an aircraft or ship.

Taine, Hip·po·lyte A·dolphe (tān; ē pô lēt′ a dôlf′) 1828–93, French historian, critic, and philosopher.

Tai·no (tī′nō) pl. **-nos.** n. 1. member of a tribe of South American

Indians formerly inhabiting parts of the West Indies, now extinct. 2. their language, distantly related to the Tupi-Guarani languages.

taint (tānt) v.t. 1. to touch or affect with something that blemishes, spoils, or sullies: *His reputation was tainted by scandal.* 2. to corrupt or weaken morally: *He was tainted by association with criminals.* —v.i. to become tainted. —n. touch or hint of something undesirable, as a blemish or a mark of decay; corruption. [Partly from French *teint,* past participle of *teindre* to dye, stain, from Latin *tingere* to moisten, dye; partly short for ATTAINT.]

Tai·pei (tī′pā′) also, **Tai·peh.** n. capital of Taiwan, in the northern part of the island. Pop. (1969 est.), 1,604,543.

Tai·wan (tī′wän′) n. island country in the western Pacific, east of mainland China, seat of the Nationalist government of China since 1949. Capital, Taipei. Area, 13,885 sq. mi. Pop. (1969 est.), 13,800,000. Also, **For·mo′sa.**

Taj Ma·hal (täzh′ mə häl′, täj′) mausoleum of white marble in Agra, India, considered to be one of the most beautiful examples of Islamic architecture.

take (tāk) took, tak·en, tak·ing. v.t. 1. to lay hold of, as with the hand; grasp: *He took his books and left.* 2. to get possession of: *to take control of a business.* 3. to bring into one's possession by force; catch; capture: *to take a prisoner.* 4. to win or earn, as in a contest: *to take first prize.* 5. to rent or hire: *to take an apartment.* 6. to buy: *I'll take both suits.* 7. to receive regularly for payment: *to take a newspaper.* 8. to choose; select: *to take sides. He took the road on the left.* 9. to proceed to occupy: *to take a seat.* 10. to carry with one; bring: *We took two suitcases on the trip.* 11. to move away; remove: *He couldn't take his eyes from her face.* 12. to remove by death: *The harsh winter took many of the settlers.* 13. to subtract; deduct. 14. to conduct; lead: *This staircase will take you to an exit.* 15. to use as a means of transportation: *We took the train home.* 16. to escort: *He took her to the party.* 17. to resort to; make use of: *to take sanctuary.* 18. to come down with; be infected with: *to take cold.* 19. to receive into the body, as by swallowing or inhaling: *to take a breath of fresh air, to take medicine.* 20. to avail oneself of, esp. as an indulgence: *to take a bath, to take a coffee break.* 21. to do, perform, or accomplish: *to take a walk.* 22. to undertake or participate in: *to take a test, to take dramatic lessons.* 23. to assume, as an office, duty, or task: *He took credit for the entire project.* 24. to receive; accept: *He wouldn't take money from his friends.* 25. to endure; withstand: *He couldn't take criticism.* 26. to be subjected to; undergo; suffer: *to take a beating.* 27. to react to: *to take bad news calmly.* 28. to have a sense of; feel: *to take offense, to take pride in one's home.* 29. to be guided by; follow: *to take a hint, to take directions.* 30. to need; require: *It takes strength to lift this box. I usually take a size seven shoe.* 31. to please or charm; captivate: *to take one's fancy.* 32. to record by writing: *to take notes at a meeting.* 33. to make (an image or likeness): *to take a picture of a group.* 34. to determine by some special procedure or method: *to take inventory, to take a person's temperature.* 35. to be able to acquire or absorb: *This material takes dye easily.* 36. *Baseball.* (of a batter) to let (a pitched ball) pass without swinging at it. 37. *Grammar.* to be used with in a construction: *A transitive verb takes a direct object.* 38. *Slang.* to swindle; cheat. —v.i. 1. to be effective; work: *The dye took immediately.* 2. to detract (with *from*): *The smokestacks take from the beauty of the city.* 3. to become: *to take sick.* 4. (of a seed or plant) to begin to grow.

to take after. to resemble in appearance, character, or actions: *He takes after his father.*

to take back. to retract: *I take back what I just said.*

to take down. a. to remove from a high place. b. to disassemble; dismantle. c. to record in writing. d. to lower the pride or position of; humble.

to take for. to suppose to be, esp. mistakenly: *He was always taken for his older brother.*

to take in. a. to receive; admit: *to take in boarders.* b. to reduce in size; make smaller: *She had to take in all her clothes after she lost weight.* c. to comprehend; understand. d. *Informal.* to deceive; cheat; dupe. e. to include; comprise: *The article takes in all aspects of the problem.* f. *Informal.* to go to see; view or attend: *to take in a movie.*

to take it. a. to assume; believe: *I take it you're ready.* b. to withstand or endure hardship or adversity.

to take it out on. *Informal.* to use (another person or object) to relieve one's anger or frustration.

to take off. a. to remove, as a garment. b. to deduct; subtract. c. *Informal.* to imitate, esp. in ridicule; mimic. d. to rise up in flight. e. *Informal.* to depart; leave.

to take on. a. to hire; employ: *to take on extra help at Christmas time.* b. to begin to deal with or handle; undertake: *to take on a responsibility.* c. to face as an opponent.

to take out. a. to remove. b. to obtain from the proper agency or authority: *to take out a loan.* c. *Informal.* to escort.

to take over. a. to assume ownership, control, or management of: *to*

at; āpe; cär; end; mē; it; īce; hot; ōld; fôrk; wood; fōōl; oil; out; up; ūse; turn; sing; thin; this; zh in treasure; ə in ago, taken, pencil, lemon, circus.

take over the leadership of a group. **b.** to assume responsibility or control. **to take to. a.** to go to, as for escape: *to take to the hills.* **b.** to form a liking for: *We took to each other immediately.* **to take up. a.** to fold or pull up so as to make shorter or smaller: *to take up a hem.* **b.** to begin to engage in; undertake: *She has taken up knitting in her spare time.* **c.** to occupy or consume, as space or time: *This chair takes up too much room.* **d.** to accept or agree to. **e.** to pick up; raise; lift. **to take up with.** *Informal.* to begin to be friendly with. —*n.* **1.** act of taking. **2.** that which is taken. **3.** amount or quantity of fish or game caught at one time. **4.** *Informal.* profit or receipts, as from a show or sporting event. **5.a.** portion of a movie, television program, or recording that is photographed or recorded without interruption. **b.** act or instance of photographing or recording such a portion. **6. to be on the take.** *Slang.* to be looking for or receiving graft or illegal money. [Old Norse *taka* to seize, grasp.] —**tak′er,** *n.*
Syn. *v.t.* **1.** Take, grasp, seize mean to lay hold of, as with the hand. Take is the most general term, simply describing the action, and often suggests preparation for removing the object once it is held: *Take a cigar from the box.* Grasp emphasizes the idea of holding something firmly with a clasping action as by tightening the fingers around it: *Rachel grasped the fleeing child's arm and would not let go of it.* Seize refers to a quick action and the application of strength or force and is usually used with an object that is difficult to get or keep hold of: *The policeman seized the gun before the assailant could shoot.*
take-home pay (tāk′hōm′) money that is left after deductions, as for taxes or insurance, have been made from one's wages or salary.
tak·en (tā′kən) past participle of **take.**
take-off (tāk′ôf′) *n.* **1.** act of leaving the ground, esp. in the beginning of an airplane flight: *The airport was foggy, but we had a smooth takeoff.* **2.** spot from which one takes off. **3.** *Informal.* imitation, esp. in a satirical manner.
take-o·ver (tāk′ō′vər) *n.* assumption or seizure of ownership, control, responsibility, or authority: *The new management executed a smooth take-over.*
tak·ing (tā′king) *adj.* attractive; captivating. —*n.* **1.** act of gaining possession; being possessed: *The candy is there for the taking.* **2.** *also,* **takings.** that which is taken, esp. receipts, as money.
talc (talk) *n.* soft, translucent, magnesium silicate mineral, green, white, or dark gray in color, used in making powders and other cosmetic preparations and as an ingredient in ceramics, electrical insulators, paints, and rubber. Formula: $Mg_3Si_4O_{10}(OH)_2$ [French *talc,* from Arabic *talq.*]
tal·cum powder (tal′kəm) fine powder made of white talc, often perfumed or medicated, used esp. on the face and body.
tale (tāl) *n.* **1.** story or account of an event or series of events; narrative: *a tale of woe, tales of the seven seas.* **2.** a malicious or scandalous story; piece of gossip: *to spread tales all over town.* **3.** story that is untrue; falsehood; lie: *No one believes his tales of success.* **4.** *Archaic.* count; tally. [Old English *talu* narrative.]
tale·bear·er (tāl′bâr′ər) *n.* one who deliberately spreads secrets or rumors. —**tale′bear′ing,** *n.*
tal·ent (tal′ənt) *n.* **1.** special aptitude or ability: *an actress with talent. Writing poetry is one of his many talents.* **2.** person or persons having talent: *a search for new acting talent.* **3.** *Informal.* tendency or knack: *a talent for saying the right thing.* **4.** any of various ancient units of weight and money. [Old French *talent* will, desire, sum of money, from Latin *talentum* weight, sum of money, from Greek *talanton.*] —**Syn.** 1. see ability.
tal·ent·ed (tal′ən tid) *adj.* having, exhibiting, or characterized by talent: *a talented performer.*
talent scout, one whose business is to discover unknown talented people for motion pictures, professional sports, or other fields of activity.
ta·ler (tä′lər) *n. also,* **tha·ler.** any of several former coins of Germany. [German *Taler,* earlier *Thaler.* See DOLLAR.]
tales·man (tālz′mən, tā′lēz-) *pl.,* **-men.** *n.* person chosen from the onlookers in a court to act as a juror when there are not enough of those summoned to fill the jury. [Medieval Latin *tales (de circumstantibus)* such (of the bystanders), plural of Latin *tālis* such + MAN.]
tale·tell·er (tāl′tel′ər) *n.* **1.** one who relates stories; narrator; storyteller. **2.** talebearer. —**tale′tell′ing,** *n.*
tal·is·man (tal′is mən, -iz-) *pl.,* **-mans.** *n.* **1.** engraved stone, ring, or other object believed to have power to keep away evils and bring good fortune. **2.** anything regarded as having magical or supernatural power. [French *talisman,* from Arabic *tilsam, tilasm* magical image, from Late Greek *telesma* consecrated object, mystery, from Greek *telesma* payment, from *telein* to pay, initiate into the mysteries.] —**Syn.** 1. charm.
tal·is·man·ic (tal′is man′ik, -iz-) *adj.* of, relating to, or like a talisman; magical.

talk (tôk) *v.i.* **1.** to express ideas or information by means of speech; speak; converse. **2.** to express ideas or information by some other means: *to talk in sign language.* **3.** to make sounds suggestive of speech, as some birds. **4.** to consult or confer, esp. for the purpose of negotiating: *Labor refused to talk with management.* **5.** to speak trivially; chatter; prate. **6.** to spread rumors; gossip. **7.** *Informal.* to reveal information, esp. under duress: *The prisoner refused to talk.* **8. to talk back,** to give a rude reply. **9. to talk down to,** to speak to in a condescending or patronizing manner. —*v.t.* **1.** to express in words: *You're talking nonsense.* **2.** to make the subject of one's speech; discuss: *to talk politics.* **3.** to use in speaking; express oneself orally in: *to talk Spanish.* **4.** to bring to, persuade, or cause by speech: *to talk someone out of leaving.* **5. to talk down.** to silence by speaking longer, louder, or more effectively; outtalk. **6. to talk over.** to go over in conversation; discuss. **7. to talk up.** to speak in favor of; advocate. —*n.* **1.** expression of ideas in speech; conversation: *The talk at our table centered on politics.* **2.** speech or lecture, esp. one that is informal or impromptu: *They asked him to give a short talk on the subject.* **3.** oral interchange of views, opinions, or information; conference: *peace talks.* **4.** rumor; gossip. **5.** subject of conversation or gossip: *The new show is the talk of New York.* **6.** empty or meaningless speech: *That's just talk.* **7.** *Informal.* way of speaking peculiar to a specified group; argot. [Middle English *talken* to converse, speak, possibly based on Old English *talian* to reckon, account.]
Syn. *n.* **1.** Talk, speech, discourse mean verbal exchange between people. Talk may involve several speakers but frequently suggests only one speaker with an audience: *The talk following the dinner was about the space program.* Speech may be formal or informal, among several people, or directed by one person at an audience: *We thought he would just say a few words, but he gave an entire speech.* Discourse implies formality and may suggest an exchange of ideas among several people or a presentation of ideas by one person: *His discourse on the lives of the Romantic poets was the highlight of the session.*
talk·a·tive (tô′kə tiv) *adj.* given to talking a great deal. —**talk′a·tive·ly,** *adv.* —**talk′a·tive·ness,** *n.*
Syn. Talkative, loquacious, garrulous mean inclined to talk a great deal. Talkative simply suggests the strong inclination toward verbal expression, often implying an outgoing disposition as much as a bothersome habit: *Jane is a friendly and talkative child.* Loquacious is a mildly disapproving term which emphasizes incessant, excessive, and compulsive talking, often without regard to one's listeners: *After a sip of brandy he became as loquacious as ever.* Garrulous is a term of disapproval suggesting wordy, boring, and seemingly unending chatter characteristic of a person disposed to monopolize conversation and unable to be concise: *Liz fled at the approach of the garrulous old gossip.*
talk·ie (tô′kē) *n. Informal.* talking picture.
talking picture, motion picture with sound synchronized to the action.
talk·ing-to (tô′king tōō′) *pl.,* **-tos.** *n. Informal.* scolding; reprimand: *That child needs a good talking-to.*
talk·y (tô′kē) **talk·i·er, talk·i·est.** *adj.* **1.** talkative. **2.** containing too much talk: *The first speech on the program was so talky that the audience became irritated and restless.*
tall (tôl) *adj.* **1.** of more than average height; not low or short: *a tall man, a tall tree.* **2.** having a specified height: *She is only five feet tall.* **3.** *Informal.* unusually large in amount or degree; formidable: *a tall price, a tall order.* **4.** *Informal.* exaggerated so as to be improbable; unbelievable: *a tall story.* [Old English *(ge)tæl* swift, prompt.] —**tall′ness,** *n.* —**Syn.** 1. see high.
Tal·la·has·see (tal′ə has′ē) *n.* capital of Florida, in the northwestern part of the state. Pop. (1970), 71,897.
Tal·ley·rand (tal′ē rand′) *n.* 1754–1838, French statesman and diplomat; full name, Charles Maurice de Talleyrand-Périgord.
Tal·linn (täl′lin) *n.* city in the Soviet Union, on the Gulf of Finland, capital of Estonia. Pop. (1970), 363,000.
tal·low (tal′ō) *n.* fat extracted from the suet of cattle and sheep, used chiefly for making candles, soap, and margarine. —*v.t.* to smear with tallow. [Probably of Low German origin.] —**tal′low·y,** *adj.*
tal·ly (tal′ē) *pl.,* **-lies.** *n.* **1.** account; reckoning: *The first tally of the vote was incorrect.* **2.** piece of wood with notches that indicate an amount, as of a debt or payment. **3.** anything on which a record or account is kept. **4.** mark representing a certain number or quantity, used in keeping a record. **5.** thing that corresponds exactly with another; counterpart. **6.** agreement; correspondence. —*v.t.,* **-lied, -ly·ing.** **1.** to count or make a count or record (often with *up*): *The grocer tallied up our bill.* **2.** to cause to correspond or agree; match. —*v.i.* **1.** to correspond; agree: *His story does not tally with the facts.* **2.** to make a point or points in a game; score. [Anglo-Norman *tallie* notch, score kept on a piece of wood, going back to Latin *tālea* rod, cutting.]
tal·ly·ho (*interj.,* tal′ē hō′; *n.,* tal′ē hō′) *interj.* huntsman's shout signifying his sighting of a fox. —*n. pl.,* **-hos.** **1.** act of shouting "tal-

lyho." **2.** coach drawn by four horses. [Probably modification of French *taïaut*, an interjection used in deer hunting; of imitative origin.]

Tal·mud (tăl′mood, tal′məd) *n.* collection of Jewish civil and canonical law, consisting of a compilation of oral tradition based on the Old Testament, the Mishna, and a group of interpretations on the Mishna. [Hebrew *talmūd* instruction.]

Tal·mud·ic (tal mōō′dik, -mū′-) *adj.* of, relating to, or characteristic of the Talmud: *a Talmudic scholar.*

Tal·mud·ist (tăl′moo dist, tal′mə-) *n.* **1.** one of the authors of the Talmud. **2.** student of the Talmud; Talmudic scholar. **3.** one who accepts or follows the doctrines of the Talmud.

tal·on (tal′ən) *n.* **1.** claw of a bird or other animal, esp. of a bird of prey. **2.** anything that resembles a claw in appearance or action. [Old French *talon* heel, going back to Latin *tālus* heel, ankle.]

ta·lus¹ (tā′ləs) *pl.*, **-li** (-lī). *n.* anklebone. [Latin *tālus* ankle, anklebone, heel.]

ta·lus² (tā′ləs) *n.* **1.** slope. **2.** sloping heap of coarse rock at the base of a cliff or on top of a slope below a cliff. [French *talus* slope, probably from Latin *talūtium* slope that gives evidence of the existence of gold under the earth; of Celtic origin.]

tam (tam) *n.* tam-o'-shanter.

ta·ma·le (tə mä′lē) *n.* Mexican dish made of corn meal, minced meat, and red peppers, rolled up and tied in cornhusks, and cooked by steaming or roasting. [Spanish *tamales*, plural of *tamal* tamale, from Nahuatl *tamalli.*]

tam·a·rack (tam′ə rak′) *n.* **1.** larch tree, *Larix laricina*, of the pine family, found in swampy regions of northern North America and valued for its wood. Also, **American larch.** **2.** wood of this tree, used esp. for fence posts, telephone poles, and railroad ties. [Of Algonquian origin.]

tam·a·rind (tam′ə rind) *n.* **1.** tropical evergreen tree, *Tamarindus indica*, of the pea family, bearing clusters of small yellow flowers and edible fruit. **2.** the acid-flavored fruit itself, that is eaten raw, cooked with rice, or used to make cold drinks. [Spanish *tamarindo*, from Arabic *tamr hindī* date of India.]

tam·a·risk (tam′ə risk′) *n.* any of a group of shrubs and small trees, genus *Tamarix*, of western Europe and Asia, having pink or white flowers borne in clusters and branches covered with tiny scalelike leaves. [Late Latin *tamariscus*, form of Latin *tamarīx*.]

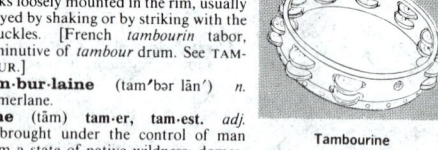

Tamarisk

tam·bour (tam′boor) *n.* **1.** drum. **2.** pair of embroidery hoops that fit together to form a frame that holds the fabric to be embroidered. **3.** embroidery done on such a frame. [French *tambour* drum, from Old French *tabour*. See TABOR.]

tam·bou·rine (tam′bə rēn′) *n.* shallow, one-headed drum having metal disks loosely mounted in the rim, usually played by shaking or by striking with the knuckles. [French *tambourin* tabor, diminutive of *tambour* drum. See TAMBOUR.]

Tam·bur·laine (tam′bər lān′) *n.* Tamerlane.

Tambourine

tame (tām) **tam·er, tam·est.** *adj.* **1.** brought under the control of man from a state of native wildness; domesticated. **2.** showing no ferocity, fear, or shyness, as if domesticated; accustomed to man; gentle: *The deer was tame enough to let us photograph it.* **3.** made submissive or meek; docile: *a person with a tame spirit.* **4.** without force or effect; dull; insipid: *a tame reprimand, a tame description.* —*v.t.,* **tamed, tam·ing. 1.** to remove from a wild state and make domestic: *to tame a wild stallion.* **2.** to take the spirit or courage from; make submissive or subdued: *to tame a wild throng of rioters.* **3.** to tone down; soften. —*v.i.* to become tame. [Old English *tam* domesticated, docile.] —**tame′ly,** *adv.* —**tame′ness, tam′er,** *n.*

tame·less (tām′lis) *adj.* not tamed or able to be tamed.

Tam·er·lane (tam′ər lān′) *n.* c.1336–1405, Mongol conqueror of central Asia and eastern Europe. Also, **Tam′bur·laine′.**

Tam·il (tam′əl) *n.* **1.** member of a Dravidian people living in parts of southern India, northern Ceylon, and Malaysia. **2.** their language, belonging to the Dravidian language family. —*adj.* of, relating to, or characteristic of the Tamils or their language.

Tam·ma·ny Hall (tam′ən ē) political organization affiliated with the Democratic Party, once a powerful influence in New York City politics. Also, **Tam′ma·ny.** [From *Tammany Hall*, the headquarters of this organization, from *Tammany*, the name of a seventeenth-century Indian chief who was friendly to white men.]

tam-o'-shan·ter (tam′ə shan′tər) *n.* soft, woolen cap of Scottish origin, with a wide, flat, circular crown and a fitted headband, often having a pompom in the center. Also, **tam.** [From the hero of Robert Burns's poem *Tam o' Shanter.*]

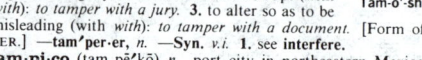

Tam-o'-shanter

tamp (tamp) *v.t.* **1.** to force or pound down by a series of light blows or taps; pack down: *to tamp tobacco into a pipe.* **2.** to pack (a drilled hole) with sand or dirt after an explosive charge has been placed in the hole. —*n.* implement for tamping. [From TAMPION.]

Tam·pa (tam′pə) *n.* port city in western Florida. Pop. (1970), 277,767.

tam·per (tam′pər) *v.i.* **1.** to interfere or meddle, usually with a harmful effect (with *with*): *Someone has been tampering with the radio.* **2.** to plot or negotiate illegally, as to influence or corrupt (with *with*): *to tamper with a jury.* **3.** to alter so as to be misleading (with *with*): *to tamper with a document.* [Form of TEMPER.] —**tam′per·er,** *n.* —Syn. *v.i.* see **interfere.**

Tam·pi·co (tam pē′kō) *n.* port city in northeastern Mexico. Pop. (1969), 155,292.

tam·pi·on (tam′pē ən) *n.* plug or cover put in the muzzle of a gun or cannon when not in use to keep out dust and moisture. [French *tampon* stopper, plug, form of *tapon;* of Germanic origin.]

tam·pon (tam′pon) *n.* cylinder of cotton or other absorbent material inserted in a wound or cavity of the body to stop bleeding or absorb secretions. —*v.t.* to fill or stop with or as with a tampon. [French *tampon* stopper. See TAMPION.]

tan (tan) **tanned, tan·ning.** *v.t.* **1.** to make (a hide or skin) into leather by soaking it in tannin or a similar solution. **2.** to make brown or tawny, esp. by exposure to sun. **3.** *Informal.* to beat; thrash. —*v.i.* to become brown or tawny, as by exposure to the sun: *My skin tans slowly.* —*n.* **1.** yellowish-brown color. **2.** brown or tawny tint imparted to a person's skin, as by exposure to the sun. **3.** tannin or a similar tanning agent. **4.** tanbark. [Medieval Latin *tannare* to make a hide into leather, from *tannum* oak bark (used for tanning hides); possibly of Celtic origin.]

tan, tangent.

tan·a·ger (tan′ə jər) *n.* any of various brightly colored birds, family Thraupidae, found chiefly in Central and South America, having a compact body, a cone-shaped bill, and typically short, rounded wings. Length: 4–8 inches. [Modern Latin *tanagra;* of Tupi-Guarani origin.]

Tanager

Ta·na·na·rive (tə nan′ə rēv′) *n.* capital and largest city of the Malagasy Republic, on the island of Madagascar. Pop. (1968 est.), 332,885.

tan·bark (tan′bärk′) *n.* bark, as of oak or hemlock, yielding tannin. It is used as a covering after the tannin has been removed, as for circus rings.

tan·dem (tan′dəm) *adv.* one behind the other; in single file: *to march tandem.* —*adj.* arranged or having parts or participants arranged one behind the other: *a tandem bicycle, tandem seats.* —*n.* **1.** bicycle having two or more seats, one behind the other. **2.** team, esp. of horses, harnessed one behind the other. **3.** two-wheeled carriage drawn by two or more horses so harnessed. **4. in tandem. a.** one behind the other: *They rode their bicycles in tandem.* **b.** in close association: *The federal project works in tandem with local programs.* [Latin *tandem* at length; the modern meanings are a pun on the Latin, which actually meant "at length in time."]

Tandem bicycle

Ta·ney, Roger Brooke (tô′nē; brook) 1774–1864, U.S. jurist and statesman, chief justice of the Supreme Court from 1836 to 1864.

tang¹ (tang) *n.* **1.** sharp taste, flavor, or odor: *the tang of burning leaves, the tang of crisp apples.* **2.** slight trace or suggestion; hint: *His words had a tang of remorse in them.* **3.** distinctive characteristic or quality: *The food lacked the tang that a good cook could have added.* **4.** pronglike extension of a blade, as of a chisel, file, or sword, to which the handle is fitted. [Of Scandinavian origin.]

tang² (tang) *n.* loud, ringing sound; ring; clang. —*v.i., v.t.* to make or cause to make such a sound. [Imitative.]

Tan·gan·yi·ka (tang′gən yē′kə) *n.* **1.** former country in eastern Africa, now part of Tanzania. **2. Lake.** lake in east-central Africa, lying between Congo, Tanzania, and Zambia. It is the longest freshwater lake in the world.

tan·ge·lo (tan′jə lō′) *n.* any of a variety of hybrid citrus fruits produced by crossing a tangerine with a grapefruit, usually resembling an orange in appearance and flavor. [Modification of TANGERINE.]

tan·gen·cy (tan′jən sē) *n.* state of being tangent.

tan·gent (tan′jənt) *adj.* **1.** touching. **2.** *Geometry.* touching a geometric figure at only one point but not passing through the figure. —*n.* **1.** *Geometry.* line, curve, or surface that touches but does not pass through another line, curve, or surface. **2.** *Trigonometry.* (of an acute angle of a right triangle) the ratio of the length of the side opposite the acute angle to the length of the side adjacent to the angle. **3.** abrupt and often irrelevant change in thought, discussion, or course of action; digression: *to go off on a tangent.* [Latin *tangēns* touching, present participle of *tangere* to touch.]

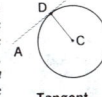

Tangent
AB is tangent
at *D*

tan·gen·tial (tan jen′chəl) *adj.* **1.** of, relating to, or in the direction of a tangent. **2.** divergent; digressive: *His talk was filled with tangential but interesting comments.* **3.** slightly connected.

tan·ge·rine (tan′jə rēn′) *n.* **1.** sweet juicy orange or reddish-orange citrus fruit of a small Asiatic evergreen tree, *Citrus reticulata,* containing small pointed seeds and having a skin that is easily peeled. **2.** tree bearing this fruit, closely related to the mandarin orange, widely cultivated in warm regions of the United States and in southern Africa. **3.** deep orange color. [From *Tangier,* from which this fruit was originally obtained.]

tan·gi·ble (tan′jə bəl) *adj.* **1.** capable of being touched; perceptible by touch; substantial; material: *The medals were tangible reminders of his heroic feats.* **2.** capable of being measured or appraised for value: *tangible assets.* **3.** capable of being grasped by the mind; definite; real: *tangible proof.* —*n. pl.,* **tangibles.** those things that can be measured or appraised, esp. material assets. [Late Latin *tangibilis* touchable, from Latin *tangere* to touch.] —**tan′gi·bil′i·ty,** *n.* —**tan′gi·bly,** *adv.*

Tan·gier (tan jēr′) *n.* port city in northern Morocco, on the Strait of Gibraltar. Pop. (1969), 160,000.

tan·gle (tang′gəl) -**gled,** -**gling.** *v.t.* **1.** to intertwine or unite in a disordered mass; snarl: *The wind had tangled her hair.* **2.** to catch or involve in surroundings or situations that hamper, obstruct, or confuse: *The fly was tangled in the spider's web. The power failure had tangled traffic in the city.* —*v.i.* **1.** to be or become entangled: *The branches tangled as they grew.* **2.** *Informal.* to fight, quarrel, or argue: *We were warned not to tangle with the guards.* —*n.* **1.** jumbled, knotted, or twisted mass: *a tangle of yarn.* **2.** confused or jumbled condition. **3.** *Informal.* dispute; argument: *The boys got into a tangle over the rules of the game.* [Of Scandinavian origin.]

tan·gly (tang′glē) *adj.* full of or consisting of tangles; knotted; snarled.

tan·go (tang′gō) *pl.* -**gos.** *n.* **1.** ballroom dance of Latin-American origin, performed by couples and characterized by long gliding steps. **2.** music for such a dance. —*v.i.,* -**goed,** -**go·ing.** to dance the tango. [Spanish *tango* the dance; of uncertain origin.]

tan·gram (tang′grəm) *n.* Chinese puzzle consisting of a square cut into five triangles, a square, and a rhomboid, which can be assembled to form a large number of different shapes. [Possibly Chinese (Cantonese) *t'ang* Chinese + -GRAM, on the model of words like *cryptogram.*]

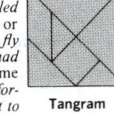

Tangram

tang·y (tang′ē) -**gi·er,** -**gi·est.** *adj.* having a tang.

tank (tangk) *n.* **1.** large container for holding a liquid or gas: *an oxygen tank.* **2.** amount that a tank can hold; tankful. **3.** *Military.* armored combat vehicle armed with machine guns, cannon, and often rocket launchers and moving on caterpillar tracks. —*v.t.* to place or store in a tank. [Gujarati *tānkh* cistern, reservoir, possibly from Sanskrit *tadāga* pond.]

tank·age (tang′kij) *n.* **1.** amount that a tank can hold. **2.a.** act or process of putting or storing in tanks. **b.** amount charged or paid for storage in tanks. **3.** rendered waste matter from a slaughterhouse, used as fertilizer or animal feed.

tank·ard (tang′kərd) *n.* large, one-handled drinking cup, often having a hinged lid and made of pewter or silver. [Of uncertain origin.]

tank·er (tang′kər) *n.* **1.** cargo ship equipped

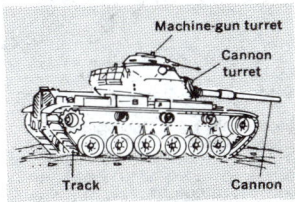

Machine-gun turret

Cannon turret

Track

Cannon

Tank

Tankard

with tanks for carrying oil or other liquids. **2.** airplane, truck, or other vehicle similarly equipped for carrying liquids.

tank farming, hydroponics.

tank·ful (tangk′fool′) *n.* amount that a tank can hold.

tan·nate (tan′āt) *n.* salt of tannic acid.

tan·ner (tan′ər) *n.* one whose work or business is the tanning of hides.

tan·ner·y (tan′ər ē) *pl.,* -**ner·ies.** *n.* place where hides and skins are tanned and finished as leather.

Tann·häu·ser (tän′hoi′zər) *n.* in medieval German legend, a knight and poet who, after leaving the earth to live a life of pleasure with Venus, returns and seeks absolution.

tan·nic acid (tan′ik) yellowish or brownish mixture of chemical compounds found in the bark and wood of many trees and in nutgalls, used esp. in tanning hides and in the preparation of ink, rubber, and medicine.

tan·nin (tan′in) *n.* **1.** tannic acid. **2.** any of various other substances used to tan hides. [French *tanin,* from *tan* tanbark; possibly of Celtic origin.]

tan·ning (tan′ing) *n.* **1.** art or process of converting hide or skins into leather. **2.** act or process of making the skin brown or tawny, as by exposure to the sun. **3.** *Informal.* severe beating; whipping.

tan·sy (tan′zē) *pl.,* -**sies.** *n.* any of a group of strong-smelling plants, genus *Tanacetum,* of the composite family, growing throughout the Northern Hemisphere, esp. *T. vulgare,* having yellow flower heads and feathery leaves that are sometimes used as a flavoring in cooking. [Old French *tanesie,* possibly short for Medieval Latin *athanasia,* from Greek *athanasia* immortality.]

tan·ta·lite (tan′tə līt′) *n.* heavy, black, crystalline mineral that is the principal ore of tantalum, used for filaments of electric lamps. Formula: Fe (TaO,.)₂

tan·ta·lize (tan′tə līz′) -**lized,** -**liz·ing.** *v.t.* to torment or tease by or as if by tempting with something that is not attainable. [TANTALUS + -IZE; from the teasing nature of the punishment of Tantalus.] —**tan′ta·li·za′tion, tan′ta·liz′er,** *n.* —**tan′ta·liz′ing·ly,** *adv.*

tan·ta·lum (tan′tə ləm) *n.* heavy, very hard, metallic element with a very high melting point, used in alloys for missile and aircraft parts and surgical instruments. Symbol: Ta See **element** for table. [From TANTALUS.]

Tan·ta·lus (tan′tə ləs) *n.* Greek Mythology. a son of Zeus who served up his own son as a meal to the gods. He was punished by being immersed in water that receded as he bent down to drink it, and being surrounded by delicious fruit that rose up beyond his grasp as he reached to eat it.

tan·ta·mount (tan′tə mount′) *adj.* having as much importance, value, force, or effect; equivalent (with *to*): *Those comments are tantamount to treason.* [Anglo-Norman *tant amunter* to amount to as much, from Old French *tant* so much (from Latin *tantus*) + *amonter* to amount to. See AMOUNT.]

tan·tar·a (tan tar′ə, tan′tär ə) *n.* flourish blown on a trumpet or horn; fanfare. [Imitative.]

tan·trum (tan′trəm) *n.* outburst of bad temper or anger; violent fit of rage. [Of uncertain origin.]

Tan·za·ni·a (tan′zə nē′ə) *n.* country in east-central Africa, formed in 1964 by the merger of the former countries of Tanganyika and Zanzibar. Capital, Dar es Salaam. Area, 362,820 sq. mi. Pop. (1967 est.), 12,173,000.

Tao·ism (tou′iz′əm) *n.* one of the principal religions of China, based on the doctrines of its founder, the ancient philosopher Lao-tse, and characterized by a belief in a harmony with nature and one's fellow man. [Chinese (Mandarin) *tao* way, truth, reason + -ISM.] —**Tao′ist,** *adj., n.*

tap¹ (tap) tapped, tap·ping. *v.t.* **1.** to strike (something) lightly: *The blind man tapped the sidewalk with his cane.* **2.** to strike lightly and usually repeatedly with: *The conductor tapped his baton for attention.* **3.** to make, do, or produce by striking lightly and repeatedly: *to tap out a beat, to tap a hole.* **4.** to attach a piece of metal or leather to (the bottom of a shoe or boot). **5.** to select or designate, as for membership in a club. —*v.i.* to strike with a light blow or blows: *to tap on a desk with a ruler.* —*n.* **1.a.** light or gentle blow. **b.** sound of such a blow. **2.** piece of metal or leather placed on the bottom of a shoe or boot. [Old French *taper* to strike; of imitative origin.]

tap² (tap) *n.* **1.** device consisting of a valve and a hand part that opens or closes it, used to turn on or off a flow of liquid, as from a pipe or keg. **2.** long peg or plug used to close a hole in a cask or other vessel containing liquid. **3.** liquor of a particular quality, brew, or cask. **4.** removal of fluid from a body cavity: *a spinal tap.* **5.** place for connecting electrical devices or additional wires to a flow of current. **6.** plug screwed into a hole to cut internal screw threads. **7.** wiretap. **8. on tap. a.** (of beer or liquor) ready to be drawn and served. **b.** *Informal.* ready for immediate action or use; available. —*v.t.* tapped, tap·ping. **1.** to pierce (something) in order to draw liquid from: *to tap the trunk*

of a maple tree for sap. **2.** to pull out the tap from (a barrel, cask, or other container). **3.** to draw off (liquid) from a source: *to tap the beer in a keg.* **4.** to furnish with a tap or spigot. **5.** to draw fluid from (a cavity of the body) by using a long hollow needle. **6.** to draw upon or begin to use: *to tap the vast resources of the oceans.* **7.** to make a connection on in order to draw from (a water, gas, or electric line). **8.** to cut into and connect with secretly, so as to obtain information: *to tap a telephone.* **9.** to cut an internal screw thread. [Old English *tæppa* stopper, plug, faucet.]

ta·pa (tä′pə) *n.* unwoven cloth made in the Pacific islands by steeping and beating the fibrous inner bark of any of several native trees, esp. the mulberry. [Of Polynesian origin.]

tap-dance (tap′dans′) **-danced, -danc·ing.** *v.i.* to perform a tap dance. **—tap′danc′er,** *n.*

tap dance, dance in which the steps and the rhythm are emphasized by audible taps made by the dancer's foot, toe, or heel.

tape (tāp) *n.* **1.** long, narrow strip of woven fabric, as that used to bind books or seams. **2.** any long, narrow strip of metal, plastic, paper, or other material. **3.** magnetic tape on which sound, light, or information has been recorded: *The producers saw a tape of the show before it was actually broadcast.* **4.** thin strip of string, cloth, or other material stretched across the finishing line of a foot race. **—v.t.,** **taped, tap·ing.** **1.** to fasten, bind, or decorate with tape. **2.** to record on magnetic tape: *to tape an interview, to tape a television program.* **3.** to measure with a tape measure. [Old English *tæppe* strip of cloth.]

tape deck, tape recording machine made for use with other components, lacking its own speakers and power amplifier.

tape measure, long, flexible strip of cloth or steel marked with a scale for measuring, often coiled up in a case.

ta·per (tā′pər) *v.t., v.i.* **1.** to make or become gradually narrower toward one end: *to taper a pair of trousers, a collar that tapers to a point.* **2.** to decrease gradually, as in volume or intensity; diminish (usually with *off*): *Sales tapered off after the holiday rush.* **—n.** **1.** small candle or wax-coated wick, as used in religious services or to light lamps or fires. **2.** gradual decrease of thickness or width: *the taper of a spire.* [Old English *tapor* wax candle; with reference to the fact that a candle is often narrower at one end than the other.]

tape-re·cord (tāp′ri kôrd′) *v.t.* to record (as music or a television program) on magnetic tape.

tape recorder, device for recording sound, light patterns, or data on a tape coated with magnetically sensitive material. Most tape recorders also have a reproduction system for playing back the sound recorded.

tape recording 1. act or process of recording sound, light patterns, or data on magnetic tape. **2.** tape on which sound, light patterns, or data have been recorded.

tap·es·try (tap′is trē) *pl.* **-tries.** *n.* **1.** heavy fabric, traditionally handwoven, decorated with designs or pictures often depicting historical or mythological events. Tapestries are used as wall hangings, floor coverings, and on furniture. **2.** any of various fabrics made to resemble tapestry, used for such items as upholstery and garments. **—v.t.,** **-tried, -try·ing.** to cover with or as with tapestry: *The garden walls were tapestried with ivy.* [French *tapisserie* the heavy decorated fabric, going back to *tapis* carpet, going back to Greek *tapētion*, diminutive of *tapēs* carpet.]

tape-worm (tāp′wurm′) *n.* any of a group of flatworms, class Cestoda, which in the adult stage are parasites in the intestines of man and other vertebrates. Length: to 20 feet.

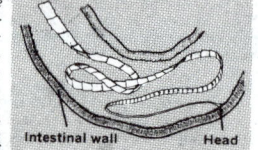
Tapeworm in human intestine
Intestinal wall   Head

tap·i·o·ca (tap′ē ō′kə) *n.* granular starch obtained from the root of the cassava plant, used in cooking to make pudding and as a thickening agent. [Portuguese *tapioca*, from Tupi-Guarani *tipioca* juice obtained from the cassava plant, from *tipi* dregs + *ok* to squeeze out.]

ta·pir (tā′pər) *n.* any of several hooved, piglike mammals, genus *Tapirus*, native to the tropical regions of Latin America and southeastern Asia, having a heavy, rounded body and a short, flexible snout. Height: to 4 feet at the shoulder. [Tupi-Guarani *tapíra.*]

tap·pet (tap′it) *n.* an arm, cam, or other projection attached to a movable part so that it can receive intermittent motion and transmit it to another part of the machine. [TAP[1] + -ET.]

Tapir

tap·room (tap′rōōm′, -room′) *n.* barroom; tavern.

tap·root (tap′rōōt′, -root′) *n.* primary downward-growing root of a plant from which lateral roots may develop.

taps (taps) *n.,pl.* military signal, usually on a bugle, regularly played at the end of the day to indicate that all lights must be turned off, and also sounded at military funerals and memorial services. ▲ construed as singular.

tap·ster (tap′stər) *n.* bartender or barmaid. [Old English *tæppestre* woman who taps liquors, from *tæppa* tap[2].]

tar[1] (tär) *n.* dark, sticky, semifluid substance obtained chiefly by the destructive distillation of soft coal and pinewood, used widely as road-paving and waterproofing material. **—v.t.,** **tarred, tar·ring. 1.** to smear, coat, or cover with or as with tar: *to tar a highway.* **2. to tar and feather.** to pour heated tar over (someone) and then cover with feathers as a punishment. **—adj.** of, containing, or covered with tar. [Old English *teoru* that is dark, sticky, semifluid substance.]

tar[2] (tär) *n. Informal.* sailor. [Short for TARPAULIN; from the tarpaulin hats formerly worn by sailors in the British Navy.]

tar·an·tel·la (tar′ən tel′ə) *n.* **1.** lively southern Italian dance done in 6/8 time, usually performed by a single couple. **2.** music for such a dance. [Italian *tarantella* the dance, from *Taranto;* also influenced by the belief that this dance was a cure for a disease that was supposedly caused by a *tarantula* bite.]

Ta·ran·to (tär′ən tō′, tə rän′tō) *n.* port city in southeastern Italy, on the Ionian Sea. Pop. (1968), 215,635.

ta·ran·tu·la (tə ran′chə lə) *pl.,* **-las** or **-lae** (-lē). *n.* any of a group of hairy spiders, suborder Orthognatha, found chiefly in tropical and semitropical regions. Tarantulas can inflict a bite that is painful but usually not dangerous to man. [Medieval Latin *tarantula*, from Italian *tarantola*, from *Taranto*, where it is frequently found.]

Tarantula

tar·boosh (tär bōōsh′) *n.* brimless cap of cloth or felt, worn by Muslim men. It is similar to a fez and is usually red with a blue silk tassel. [Arabic *tarbūsh*.]

tar·dy (tär′dē) **-di·er, -di·est.** *adj.* **1.** coming or happening after the specified or appropriate time; late: *The student was punished for being tardy so frequently.* **2.** moving or happening slowly: *We were tardy in making preparations for the trip.* [Old English *tardif*, going back to Latin *tardus.*] **—tar′di·ly,** *adv.* **—tar′di·ness,** *n.* **—Syn. 1.** see late.

tare[1] (tär) *n.* **1.** widely distributed vetch, *Vicia sativa,* cultivated in the United States as a forage or cover crop. **2.** seed of this plant. **3.** in the New Testament, a weed harmful to crops, possibly the darnel. [Of uncertain origin.]

tare[2] (tär) *n.* deduction made from gross weight to allow for the weight of the container. [French *tare* waste, loss, going back to Arabic *tarhah* deduction; literally, that which is thrown away.]

targe (tärj) *n. Archaic.* light shield or buckler. [Old French *targe;* of Germanic origin.]

tar·get (tär′git) *n.* **1.** object that is aimed at in shooting practice and competitions, as a padded disk marked with concentric circles, used in archery. **2.** anything that is shot at or that is the object of a military attack: *a bombing target.* **3.** one who or that which is the object of ridicule, criticism, or abuse: *His outspoken remarks made him an easy target for the opposition.* **4.** that which one hopes to reach or accomplish: *The target of this advertising campaign is the young housewife.* [Old French *targuete,* form of *targete* small shield, diminutive of *targe* shield. See TARGE.]

target date, date designated for the undertaking or completion of a project.

tar·iff (tar′if) *n.* **1.** list or system of duties imposed by a government on imports or exports. **2.** duty or rate of duty so imposed: *a low tariff on cameras.* **3.** any list of rates or prices, as at a railroad or hotel. [French *tarif* rate, list of prices, through Spanish, from Arabic *ta′rīf* information.]

Tar·king·ton, Booth (tär′king tən) 1869–1946, U.S. novelist.

tar·la·tan (tär′lət ən) *n.* thin, transparent muslin with an open weave and a stiff finish, used chiefly for theater costumes, drapes, and millinery. [French *tarlatane,* earlier *tarnatane;* of uncertain origin.]

tarn (tärn) *n.* small mountain lake or pool. [Old Norse *tjörn.*]

tar·nish (tär′nish) *v.t.* **1.** to dull the luster of or discolor, as a metallic surface by oxidation. **2.** to mar the purity of, disgrace; sully: *The scandal tarnished the family name.* **—v.i.** to become dull or discolored, as by oxidation: *The silver will tarnish if left uncovered.* **—n.** **1.** coating or surface resulting from tarnishing. **2.** loss of luster; discoloration. [French *terniss-,* a stem of *ternir* to dull, stain; probably of Germanic origin.]

ta·ro (tär′ō, tar′ō) *pl.* **-ros.** *n.* **1.** tropical plant, *Colocasia esculenta,*

of the arum family, widely grown in Hawaii and other Pacific islands for its edible tuber. **2.** the fleshy round tuber itself, used to make poi or cooked and eaten like a potato. [Of Polynesian origin.]

tar·pau·lin (tär pô′lin, tär′pə lin) *n.* waterproofed canvas or other material, as nylon, used as a protective cover for boats, athletic fields, or other objects exposed to the weather. [Earlier *tarpauling,* from TAR[1] + PALL[1] + -ING[1].]

Tarpon

tar·pon (tär′pən) *pl.,* **-pons** or **-pon.** *n.* large, silvery game fish, *Megalops cyprinoides,* found in coastal waters of the Atlantic and sometimes in fresh water, weighing up to 350 pounds. Length: to more than 8 feet. [Of uncertain origin.]

tar·ra·gon (tar′ə gon′, -gən) *n.* **1.** fragrant leaves of a plant, *Artemisia dracunculus,* of the composite family, used as a seasoning. **2.** bushy European plant bearing these leaves and having small, greenish-white flower heads.

tar·ry[1] (tar′ē) **-ried, -ry·ing.** *v.i.* **1.** to delay in doing something, esp. in coming or going: *We can't tarry if we are to arrive on time.* **2.** to remain in a place; stay, esp. longer than one expected: *The tourists tarried a while in Rome before going on to their next stop.* [Of uncertain origin.] —**tar′ri·er,** *n.*

tar·ry[2] (tär′ē) **-ri·er, -ri·est.** *adj.* of, like, or covered with tar. [TAR[1] + -Y[1].]

tar·sal (tär′səl) *adj.* of or relating to a tarsus. —*n.* any bone or cartilage in the ankle.

Tar·shish (tär′shish) *n.* in the Old Testament, a country rich in metals, thought to have been in Spain.

tar·si·er (tär′sē ā′, -sē ər) *n.* any of various tree-dwelling mammals, family Tarsiidae, native to the East Indies, having large eyes and ears, long fingers and toes, and a long, thin tail. Length: 16 inches, including tail. [French *tarsier,* from *tarse* ankle, from Modern Latin *tarsus;* because it has long ankles. See TARSUS.]

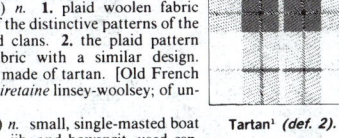

Tarsier

tar·sus (tär′səs) *pl.* **-si** (-sī). *n.* **1.** the ankle, consisting of seven small bones in man. **2.** shank of a bird's leg. **3.** terminal segment of the leg in insects and certain other arthropods, corresponding to the foot. **4.** small plate of connective tissue that supports the edge of the eyelid. [Modern Latin *tarsus,* from Greek *tarsos* ankle, sole of the foot, flat basket.]

Tar·sus (tär′səs) *n.* city in south-central Turkey, the birthplace of Saint Paul. Pop. (1965), 57,000.

tart[1] (tärt) *adj.* **1.** sharp in taste; not sweet; sour. **2.** sharp in tone or meaning; caustic: *a tart remark.* [Old English *teart* sharp, severe.] —**tart′ly,** *adv.* —**tart′ness,** *n.*

tart[2] (tärt) *n.* **1.** individual piece of pastry having a filling, as custard or fruit, with or without a top crust. **2.** *British.* any fruit pie. **3.** *Slang.* loose woman; prostitute. [Old French *tarte;* of uncertain origin.]

tar·tan[1] (tär′tən) *n.* **1.** plaid woolen fabric woven with one of the distinctive patterns of the Scottish Highland clans. **2.** the plaid pattern itself. **3.** any fabric with a similar design. —*adj.* of, like, or made of tartan. [Old French *tertaine,* form of *tiretaine* linsey-woolsey; of uncertain origin.]

tar·tan[2] (tär′tən) *n.* small, single-masted boat with a lateen sail, jib, and bowsprit, used esp. in the Mediterranean. [French *tartane,* from Italian *tartana,* possibly from Arabic *tarīdah* small boat.]

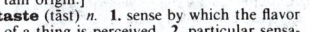

Tartan[1] **(def. 2).**

tar·tar (tär′tər) *n.* **1.** sediment or residue that collects in wine casks, consisting mainly of cream of tartar and calcium tartrate, used to make tartaric acid. **2.** brownish deposit on the teeth caused by a combination of food particles and various salts. [Medieval Latin *tartarum* the sediment, from Middle Greek *tartaron;* of uncertain origin.]

Tar·tar (tär′tər) *also,* **Ta·tar.** *n.* **1.** member of the tribes of Mongols and Turks who overran parts of Asia and Europe during the Middle Ages. **2.** member of a Turkish people descended from them, now living chiefly in parts of the Soviet Union in central and western Asia. **3.** language of these people, belonging to the Turkic branch of the Ural-Altaic language family. **4. tartar.** one who has a violent temper

or savage disposition. —*adj.* of, relating to, or characteristic of the Tartars, their language, or their customs.

tar·tar emetic (tär′tər) poisonous white compound with a sweet taste, containing antimony, used in medicine to cause vomiting and as a mordant for cloth and leather.

tar·tar·ic acid (tär tar′ik) colorless crystalline compound with an acid taste, used in baking powder, plastics, and effervescent drinks, in photography, and in several industrial processes, including dyeing and tanning. It occurs in fruits and vegetables, esp. grapes. Formula: $HOOC(CH_2OH)_2COOH$

tar·tar·ous (tär′tər əs) *adj.* of, like, containing, or derived from tartar.

tartar sauce *also,* **tar·tare sauce.** sauce made of mayonnaise and chopped condiments, as pickles, capers, onions, and olives, served esp. with seafood.

Tar·ta·rus (tär′tər əs) *n. Greek Mythology.* **1.** a region deep in the underworld where wicked people were punished for their crimes after death. **2.** the land of the dead; underworld.

Tar·ta·ry (tär′tər ē) *also,* **Ta·ta·ry.** *n.* region in Asia and eastern Europe ruled by the Tartars in the thirteenth and fourteenth centuries.

tart·let (tärt′lit) *n.* small pastry tart.

tar·trate (tär′trāt) *n.* salt of tartaric acid.

tar·trat·ed (tär′trā tid) *adj.* **1.** containing or derived from tartar. **2.** combined with tartaric acid.

Tash·kent (täsh kent′) *n.* city in the south-central Soviet Union, capital of Uzbekistan. Pop. (1970 est.), 1,385,000.

task (task) *n.* **1.** piece of work to be done, esp. one assigned by one person to another. **2.** tiring or burdensome job or duty. **3. to take to task.** to call to account; reprimand. —*v.t.* **1.** to assign a task to. **2.** to burden with excessive work; put a strain on. [Medieval Latin *tasca,* form of *taxa* a taxation, rating, from *taxare* to impose a tax. See TAX.] —**Syn. 1.** see **job.**

task force 1. number of military units, esp. naval units, brought together under one commander for a specific mission. **2.** any group that is formed or brought together to deal with a specific problem: *an urban task force.*

task·mas·ter (task′mas′tər) *n.* one who assigns and closely supervises the performance of tasks; severe or burdensome ones.

Tas·ma·ni·a (taz mā′nē ə) *n.* island south of Australia, a political subdivision of the country. Area, 26,215 sq. mi. Pop. (1966), 371,217. —**Tas·ma′ni·an,** *adj., n.*

Tasmanian devil, bearlike marsupial, *Sarcophilus ursinus,* native to Tasmania, having a coarse brown or black coat and a foot-long tail. Length: 3 feet without tail.

Tass (tas, täs) *n.* government-run news agency in the Soviet Union.

tas·sel (tas′əl) *n.* **1.** hanging ornament on umbrellas, hats, shade pulls and other items, consisting of a group of threads, cords, or similar materials bound together at one end. **2.** anything resembling this in shape, as the branched male flower at the top of a stalk of corn. —*v.t.,* **-seled, -sel·ing;** *also,* **British, -selled, -sel·ling.** to attach a tassel or tassels to. —*v.i.* (of corn) to put forth a tassel. [Old French *tassel* fastening, clasp; of uncertain origin.]

Tassels on a corn plant

taste (tāst) *n.* **1.** sense by which the flavor of a thing is perceived. **2.** particular sensation as perceived by this sense. The four basic tastes are sweet, bitter, sour, and salty. **3.** small amount to be eaten or sampled by the sense of taste: *I'll take a taste of your dessert.* **4.** slight experience of anything; sample: *a taste of the excitement of the theater.* **5.** preference; liking: *That house is not to my taste.* **6.** ability to recognize and appreciate that which is excellent, beautiful, or appropriate, as in art or decorum: *She has no taste in men's clothes.* **7.** manner in which the quality of such ability is reflected: *She was always dressed in impeccable taste. Your remarks are in poor taste.* —*v.t.,* **tast·ed, tast·ing. 1.** to perceive or distinguish the flavor of through the sense of taste: *I can taste the garlic in this meal.* **2.** to take (something) into the mouth in order to test or try the flavor: *to taste soup for salt. He got a job tasting tea.* **3.** to take a small quantity of (a food or drink) into the mouth. **4.** to experience, esp. briefly or for the first time: *to taste power.* —*v.i.* **1.** to have a particular flavor: *The sauce tastes too sweet.* **2.** to have the sense of taste; perceive flavor. **3.** to take a small quantity of something into the mouth, as in testing the flavor. **4.** to have experience or knowledge; partake (usually with *of*): *to taste of freedom.* [Old French *taster* to feel, try, handle, possibly going back to a blend of Latin *tangere* to touch, and *gustāre* to eat a little, partake of.]

taste bud, any of a cluster of cells located in the lining of the tongue or mouth that contains receptors which are sensitive to taste.

taste·ful (tāst′fəl) *adj.* having or exhibiting a good sense of what is beautiful, excellent, or appropriate. —**taste′ful·ly,** *adv.* —**taste′ful·ness,** *n.*

taste·less (tāst′lis) *adj.* 1. without flavor; bland: *a tasteless meal.* 2. having or exhibiting poor judgment as to what is excellent, beautiful, or appropriate: *a tasteless exhibition of furniture.* —**taste′less·ly,** *adv.* —**taste′less·ness,** *n.*

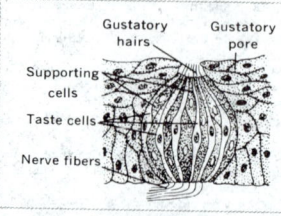

Gustatory hairs   Gustatory pore
Supporting cells
Taste cells
Nerve fibers

Taste bud

tast·er (tās′tər) *n.* one who tastes, esp. one who is employed to judge quality, as of tea or wine, by tasting.

tast·y (tās′tē) **tast·i·er, tast·i·est.** *adj.* 1. pleasing to the sense of taste; flavorful; savory. 2. tasteful. —**tast′i·ly,** *adv.* —**tast′i·ness,** *n.*

tat (tat) **tat·ted, tat·ting.** *v.i.,v.t.* to make by tatting; make tatting. [From TATTING.]

Ta·tar (tä′tər) *n.* Tartar.

Ta·ta·ry (tä′tər ē) Tartary.

tat·ter (tat′ər) *n.* 1. irregularly torn, often hanging piece or shred. 2. tatters. worn or ragged clothing; rags. —*v.i.,v.t.* to be or tear in shreds; make or become ragged. [Of Scandinavian origin.]

tat·ter·de·mal·ion (tat′ər di māl′yən, -mal′-) *n.* person in worn or ragged clothing; ragamuffin. [TATTER + *-demalion* (word element of uncertain meaning and origin).]

tat·tered (tat′ərd) *adj.* 1. hanging or torn in shreds: *a tattered shirt.* 2. dressed in worn or ragged clothes: *a tattered waif.*

tat·ting (tat′ing) *n.* 1. art or process of making a knotted lace by looping and pulling knots into cotton or linen thread with a special shuttle. 2. lace made in this way, used for such items as doilies, collars, and trimmings. [Of uncertain origin.]

tat·tle (tat′əl) **-tled, -tling.** *v.i.* 1. to reveal the secrets, activities, or private affairs of another: *to tattle to the teacher.* 2. to talk idly; prate; chatter. —*v.t.* to tell or reveal by gossiping: *to tattle a secret all over town.* —*n.* idle talk or chatter; gossip. [Middle Dutch *tatelen* to stutter; of imitative origin.] —**tat′tler,** *n.*

tat·tle·tale (tat′əl tāl′) *n. Informal.* one who deliberately reveals secrets; talebearer; telltale.

tat·too¹ (ta tōō′) *pl.* **-toos.** *n.* 1. military signal, as on a bugle, given at night to call soldiers or sailors to return to their quarters. 2. military exercises given as entertainment. 3. rapid, continuous beating or tapping: *the tattoo of rain on a roof.* [Dutch *taptoe* this signal, from *tap* tap¹ + *toe* to shut; possibly referring to the earlier custom of giving a signal in the evening to shut off the taps of casks in bars.]

tat·too² (ta tōō′) **-tooed, -too·ing.** *v.t.* 1. to mark (the skin) permanently with colored figures or designs, usually by pricking it with a pointed instrument that has been dipped in pigment. 2. to mark (figures or designs) on the skin in this way. —*n. pl.,* **-toos.** pattern, figure, or design made by tattooing. [Polynesian *tatau* a tattoo mark.] —**tat·too′er,** *n.*

tau (tou, tô) *n.* the nineteenth letter (T, τ,) of the Greek alphabet, corresponding to the English letter *T. t.*

taught (tôt) past tense and past participle of **teach.**

taunt (tônt, tänt) *v.t.* 1. to reproach with insults or scornful language: *The crowd taunted the athlete for his poor performance.* 2. to goad or provoke by taunting: *The children taunted him into diving off the high board.* —*n.* insulting, often provocative remark. [Of uncertain origin.]

taupe (tōp) *n.* dark gray color, tinged with brown, purple, or yellow.

Tau·rus (tôr′əs) *n.* 1. constellation in the northern sky containing Aldebaran, the Hyades, and the Pleiades, conventionally depicted as a bull. 2. second sign of the zodiac. See **zodiac** for illustration. [Latin *taurus* bull.]

taut (tôt) *adj.* 1. tightly drawn or stretched; not slack or loose: *a taut wire.* 2. tense; tight: *My nerves are taut.* 3. in good condition; orderly; tidy: *to keep a taut ship.* [Middle English *toght* tense; of uncertain origin.] —**taut′ly,** *adv.* —**taut′ness,** *n.*

tau·tog (tô tog′, -tôg′) *n.* food fish, *Tautoga onitis,* found in Atlantic coastal waters of the United States. Also, **black′fish′.** [Algonquian *tautauog,* plural of *tautau* sheepshead.]

tau·tol·o·gy (tô tol′ə jē) *pl.* **-gies.** *n.* 1. useless repetition of an idea in different words. 2. instance of such repetition. The sentence *We left simultaneously at the same time* is a tautology. 3. statement that is necessarily true because it includes all possibilities, for example: *Either it will rain tomorrow or it will not.* [Late Latin *tautologia,* from Greek

tautologiā going back to *to auto* the same (thing) + *legein* to speak.] —**tau·to·log·i·cal** (tôt′əl oj′i kəl), *adj.* —**tau′to·log′i·cal·ly,** *adv.*

tav·ern (tav′ərn) *n.* 1. place where alcohol or alcoholic beverages are sold to be drunk on the premises; saloon; bar. 2. public place providing food and lodging, esp. for travelers. [Old French *taverne,* from Latin *taberna* hut.]

taw (tô) *n.* 1. fancy marble with which a player shoots in a game of marbles. 2. line from which the players shoot in this game. [Of uncertain origin.]

taw·dry (tôd′rē) **-dri·er, -dri·est.** *adj.* tasteless; showy; gaudy. [Modification of *St. Audrey* (referring to the gaudy laces sold at St. Audrey's annual fair, formerly held in Ely, England).] —**taw′dri·ly,** *adv.* —**taw′dri·ness,** *n.*

taw·ny (tô′nē) **-ni·er, -ni·est.** *adj.* brownish yellow: *a tawny complexion.* [Old French *tan(n)e,* past participle of *tan(n)er* to tan hides, from Medieval Latin *tannare.* See TAN.] —**taw′ni·ness,** *n.*

tax (taks) *n.* 1. compulsory contribution paid for the support of a government. 2. oppressive burden or heavy demand; strain. —*v.t.* 1. to place or impose a financial tax on: *A government can tax its citizens directly, and it can tax the property they own.* 2. to make a heavy demand on; burden; strain: *to tax one's brain for a solution, to tax one's strength.* 3. to take to task; accuse; reprove: *The chairman taxed him for his constant lateness.* [Medieval Latin *taxare* to impose a financial tax, from Latin *taxāre* to rate¹, value, handle.] —**tax′er,** *n.*

tax·a·ble (tak′sə bəl) *adj.* subject or liable to taxation: *Certain portions of his income were not taxable.* —**tax′a·bil′i·ty,** *n.*

tax·a·tion (tak sā′shən) *n.* 1. act or system of imposing and collecting financial taxes: *Taxation without representation is tyranny* (Otis, 1761). 2. tax or assessment imposed; revenue raised by taxes.

tax-ex·empt (taks′ig zempt′) *adj.* not subject to taxes.

tax·i (tak′sē) *pl.* **tax·is** or **tax·ies.** *n.* taxicab. —*v.i.* **tax·ied, tax·i·ing** or **tax·y·ing.** 1. to ride in a taxicab: *We taxied to the theater.* 2. (of an aircraft) to move slowly along the ground or over the surface of water. —*v.t.* to cause (an airplane) to taxi.

tax·i·cab (tak′sē kab′) *n.* automobile for public hire having a meter that records the fare to be paid. [TAXI(METER) + CAB.]

tax·i·der·mist (tak′si dur′mist) *n.* one whose work or business is taxidermy.

tax·i·der·my (tak′si dur′mē) *n.* art of preparing and stuffing the skins of dead animals and mounting them in lifelike positions for study or display. [Greek *taxis* arrangement + *derma* skin.]

tax·i·me·ter (tak′sē mē′tər, tak sim′ə tər) *n.* meter in a taxicab for automatically computing and registering the fare due. [French *taximètre,* from *taxe* rate¹, charge (going back to Medieval Latin *taxare* to impose a tax) + *-mètre* -meter. See TAX, -METER.]

tax·is (tak′sis) *pl.,* **tax·es** (tak′sēz). *n.* involuntary movement made by an animal in response to a specific stimulus. [Greek *taxis* arrangement.]

tax·o·nom·ic (tak′sə nom′ik) *adj.* of, relating to, or according to taxonomy. Also, **tax′o·nom′i·cal.** —**tax′o·nom′i·cal·ly,** *adv.*

tax·on·o·my (tak son′ə mē) *n.* 1. the grouping of animals and plants into categories, as genus and species, on the basis of their structural and evolutionary relationships. 2. study of the general principles of classification. [French *taxonomie* science of the laws of classification, from Greek *taxis* arrangement + *-nomiā* arrangement, law.] —**tax·on·o′mist,** *n.*

tax·pay·er (taks′pā′ər) *n.* one who pays or is subject to a tax.

tax shelter, way (such as an investment or a depreciation allowance) for a person or a corporation to reduce income taxes.

Tay·lor, Zach·a·ry (tā′lər; zak′ər ē) 1784–1850, U.S. general, twelfth president of the United States, from 1849 to 1850.

Tb, terbium.

TB, tuberculosis.

Tbi·li·si (tbi lē′sē) *n.* city in the southwestern Soviet Union, capital of Georgia, formerly known as Tiflis. Pop. (1970), 889,000.

T-bone steak (tē′bōn′) loin steak containing some tenderloin and a T-shaped bone. Also, **T-bone.**

tbs., tablespoon; tablespoons. Also, **tbsp.**

Tc, technetium.

Tchai·kov·sky, Peter Il·yich (chī kôf′skē; il′yich) 1840–93, Russian composer.

Te, tellurium.

tea (tē) *n.* 1. beverage made from the dried and prepared leaves of a shrub or small tree, *Thea sinensis,* of Asia. 2. dried leaves used to make this beverage. 3. plant bearing these leaves, having mildly fragrant, drooping white flowers. 4. any of various beverages made by soaking the leaves or other parts of certain other plants or from beef or other extracts: *camomile tea, sage tea.* 5. *British.* late afternoon refreshment usually consisting of bread and butter, cakes, and similar light food served with tea. 6. reception or other social gathering, usually small in size and occurring in the afternoon, at which tea and other refresh-

ments are served. [Dialectal Chinese *t'e* the tea plant, beverage made from its leaves.]

tea bag, small, porous bag of thin paper or cloth containing tea leaves, usually shredded or ground, for immersing in hot water to make tea.

tea ball 1. small, perforated metal ball for immersing tea leaves in hot water to make tea. **2.** tea bag.

tea·cart (tē′kärt′) *n.* tray or small table set on wheels, used in serving tea and other refreshments or food; serving cart. Also, **tea wagon.**

teach (tēch) *taught, teach·ing. v.t.* **1.** to impart knowledge to, esp. by way of formal schooling, study, or lessons; give instruction to: *She's interested in a career in teaching the handicapped.* **2.** to give instruction or lessons in; impart a knowledge of: *to teach English literature, to teach violin playing.* **3.** to cause or help to learn: *My father taught me to drive. The accident taught her to be more careful.* —*v.i.* to act or be employed as a teacher; give instruction: *Gladly would he learn, and gladly teach* (Chaucer, c. 1387). [Old English *tǣcan* to show, instruct.]
Syn. *v.t.* **1. Teach, instruct, educate, train** mean to provide with knowledge or skill. **Teach,** when used in an academic context, suggests a guided process of assigned classroom work and directed study: *Each instructor teaches five classes a day.* **Instruct** suggests the imparting of highly specialized knowledge in a rather detailed or elaborate manner: *The rabbi instructed the boy in Hebrew.* **Educate** stresses the object rather than the content of teaching and often implies a course of formal study that results in a comprehensive understanding of the subject: *He was educated in the field of electronics.* **Train** usually refers to a particular skill or specialty and implies its sharpening and development to a high point by drill, exercise, precept, and discipline: *The military academy trains cadets to be leaders.*

teach·a·ble (tē′chə bəl) *adj.* **1.** capable of learning by being taught, as a person. **2.** capable of being taught, as a lesson. —**teach′a·bil′i·ty, teach′a·ble·ness,** *n.*

teach·er (tē′chər) *n.* one who teaches, esp. as an occupation.

teachers college *also,* **teachers' college.** college specializing in the training of teachers.

teach-in (tēch′in′) *pl.,* **teach-ins.** *n.* extended, informal gathering, as at a college or university, for the purpose of discussion and debate of a particular public issue, often held as an expression of social protest.

teach·ing (tē′ching) *n.* **1.** act, work, or occupation of a teacher. **2.** *also,* **teachings.** that which is taught, esp. a doctrine or precept: *the teachings of Plato.*

teaching machine, any of various devices that present a course of programmed instruction and that are operated by the student, allowing him to learn at his own rate of speed.

tea·cup (tē′kup′) *n.* **1.** cup in which tea is served. **2.** teacupful.

tea·cup·ful (tē′kup fool′) *pl.,* **-fuls.** *n.* amount that a teacup will hold, usually four fluid ounces.

tea dance, dance held in the late afternoon.

tea·house (tē′hous′) *n.* public place, esp. in China and Japan, where tea and other light refreshments are served.

teak (tēk) *n.* **1.** hard, fragrant, yellowish-brown wood of a tree, *Tectona grandis,* used in shipbuilding and in the manufacture of furniture and flooring. Also, **teak′wood′. 2.** tree bearing this wood, cultivated in Asia, western Africa, and tropical America, having large, oval leaves, and small white or bluish flowers. [Portuguese *teca,* from Malayalam *tēkka.*]

tea·ket·tle (tē′ket′əl) *n.* pot, usually with a lid, spout, and handle, in which water is boiled, esp. for making tea.

teal (tēl) *pl.,* **teals** *or* **teal.** *n.* **1.** any of several short-necked small river ducks, family Anatidae, having predominantly gray, brown, green, and white plumage. Length: 14–17 inches. **2.** dark dull-blue or blue-green color. [Of uncertain origin.]

Teal

team (tēm) *n.* **1.** group making up one side in an athletic contest or other competition: *a debating team, a hockey team. The class was split up into teams for the softball game.* **2.** any group working together in some joint action: *a comedy team, a team of engineers, a research team in a laboratory.* **3.** two or more horses or other animals harnessed together, as to pull a wagon or plow. **4.** vehicle together with the animal or animals harnessed to it. —*v.t.* **1.** to bring or join together in a team: *to team horses.* **2.** to haul or transport by means of a team: *to team logs.* —*v.i.* **1.** to work together; form a team (often with *up*): *The children teamed up to collect the money.* **2.** to drive a team. [Old English *tēam* brood, two or more animals harnessed together for work.]

team·mate (tēm′māt′) *n.* fellow member of a team.

team·ster (tēm′stər) *n.* **1.** one whose work or occupation is driving a truck. **2.** *Archaic.* one whose work or occupation is driving a team of horses or other animals.

team·work (tēm′wurk′) *n.* cooperative and coordinated effort or

action on the part of a number of people working together, as to achieve a common goal: *They have no star players, but they rarely lose a game because of their great teamwork.*

tea·pot (tē′pot′) *n.* pot with a lid, spout, and handle, for making and serving tea.

tear¹ (târ) *tore, torn, tear·ing. v.t.* **1.** to pull, split, or separate into pieces, as by force or with a sharp edge, usually so as to leave ragged or irregular edges: *to tear a paper in half. She tore the letter up after reading it.* **2.** to make by tearing: *to tear a hole in one's coat.* **3.** to wound by tearing; lacerate: *The thorns tore her skin.* **4.** to pull, pluck, or remove forcibly or rudely, as from an attachment or fixed place: *to tear a poster off a wall. The tornado tore the tree stump from the ground.* **5.** to distress by pulling: *We couldn't tear our eyes away from the movie screen.* **6.** to disrupt, divide, or split into sides or factions; feel the effect of opposing or conflicting forces: *a country torn by civil war. He was torn between the two alternatives.* **7.** to distress violently or painfully; torment: *Grief tore her heart.* **8.** to disarrange or damage by or as by doing violence to (often with *apart* or *up*): *We tore the place apart looking for the missing papers.* —*v.i.* **1.** to become torn. **2.** to move with great haste or energy; rush headlong: *He tore out of the house.* **3.** to make pulling, snatching, or tearing motions (with *at*). **4.** to move, touch, or distress (with *at*): *a sad movie that tears at your heartstrings.* **5. to tear into.** *Informal.* to set upon or attack vigorously: *They tore into her for being disloyal.* —*n.* **1.** torn part or place, as a split or hole: *Let me sew the tear in your sleeve.* **2.** act or process of tearing. **3.** headlong rush. **4.** *Informal.* spree: *to go on a tear.* [Old English *teran* to rend, lacerate.]
Syn. *v.t.* **1. Tear, rip¹, rend** mean to pull or split apart by force. **Tear** suggests roughness in the action of pulling apart, with the result that what is torn is left shredded or uneven: *Hastily she tore the letter to bits.* **Rip** suggests a stronger force, having a more drastic result, often leaving a clean or even break or split: *She ripped the gift paper off the box in no time.* **Rend,** a more literary term, suggests even greater damage, as from deep cuts or from being wrenched apart: *The lion, in its fury, rent the lamb.*

tear² (tēr) *n.* **1.** drop of the clear, slightly salty fluid secreted by the lacrimal gland in the eye, which lubricates the eyeballs and keeps them free from foreign bodies, and which in weeping or crying flows from the eye. **2.** something resembling a tear. **3. tears.** act of weeping or crying: *to burst into tears. She left the party in tears.* —*v.i.* to shed tears. [Old English *tēar* drop of fluid secreted by the eye.]

tear·drop (tēr′drop′) *n.* **1.** a tear. **2.** something resembling a tear in shape, as a pendant gem.

tear·ful (tēr′fəl) *adj.* **1.** full of or covered with tears; weeping: *tearful eyes.* **2.** causing tears; woeful; sad: *a tearful story.* —**tear′ful·ly,** *adv.* —**tear′ful·ness,** *n.*

tear gas (tēr) any of various gases that irritate the eyes, causing a flow of tears and temporary blindness, used chiefly in dispersing riotous crowds and in driving persons from fortified positions.

tear-jerk·er (tēr′jur′kər) *n. Slang.* extremely sad or poignant film, play, or other presentation, often one intended to arouse sympathetic feeling by being maudlin or mawkish.

tea·room (tē′rōōm′, -room′) *n.* small room or restaurant where beverages and light meals are served, often catering chiefly to women and having a sedate or subdued atmosphere.

tea rose 1. any of various large, pale roses descended chiefly from a rose of Chinese origin, *Rosa odorata,* having a delicate scent thought to resemble that of tea. **2.** spreading shrub bearing such a rose, cultivated esp. in warmer regions of the United States.

tear·y (tēr′ē) *tear·i·er, tear·i·est. adj.* full of or wet with tears; marked by weeping. —**tear′i·ly,** *adv.* —**tear′i·ness,** *n.*

tease (tēz) *teased, teas·ing. v.t.* **1.** to say something provoking to in jest; playfully make fun of. **2.** to provoke, vex, or harass, as with mischievous or malicious gibes or taunts. **3.** to fluff (hair) by combing or brushing in strokes from the end of a strand toward the scalp. **4.** to raise a nap on (cloth), esp. by means of a teasel. **6.** to separate the fibers of; card or comb, as wool, in preparation for spinning. —*v.i.* to engage in teasing; provoke, harass, or playfully make fun of someone. —*n.* **1.** one given to teasing others. **2.** flirtatious, coquettish girl or woman. **3.** act of teasing; being teased. [Old English *tǣsan* to pluck, pull, card (as wool).]

tea·sel (tē′zəl) *also,* **tea·zel, tea·zle.** *n.* **1.** any of a group of coarse thistlelike plants, genus *Dipsacus,* esp. the **fuller's teasel,** *D. fullonum,* raised for its dense, bristly flower heads, which are dried and used for brushing wool fabrics to raise a nap on them and make them soft and fuzzy. **2.** such a flower head. **3.** any device used for raising a nap on cloth. —*v.t.* **-seled, -sel·ing;** *also, British,* **-selled, -sel·ling.** to raise a nap on (cloth) with a teasel or teasels. [Old English *tǣsel* the plant.]

teas·er (tē′zər) *n.* **1.** one who or that which teases. **2.** *Informal.* something difficult, perplexing, or annoying; puzzler.

tea service, set of articles, as of silver or china, used in serving tea

or other hot beverages, consisting of such items as a matching teapot, sugar bowl, and creamer.

tea·spoon (tē'spoon') *n.* **1.** spoon, smaller than a tablespoon or soup spoon, used esp. to stir beverages in a cup and to eat desserts. **2.** amount one teaspoon will hold, a standard cooking measurement equivalent to ⅓ of a tablespoon, or 1⅓ fluid drams.

tea·spoon·ful (tē'spoon fool') *pl.,* **-fuls.** *n.* teaspoon (*def. 2*).

teat (tēt, tit) *n.* small projection on the breast or udder in most female mammals, through which milk is drawn; nipple. [Old French *tete;* of Germanic origin.]

tea wagon, teacart.

tea·zel (tē'zǝl) *also,* **tea·zle.** *n.* teasel. —*v.t.,* **-zeled, -zel·ing;** *also, British,* **-zelled, -zel·ling.** to teasel.

tech. 1. technical. **2.** technology.

tech·ne·ti·um (tek nē'shē ǝm) *n.* silver-gray, radioactive metallic element, the first chemical element to be produced artificially. It has never been found to occur naturally on earth. Symbol: **Tc** See **element** for table. [Modern Latin *technetium,* from Greek *technētos* artificial.]

tech·nic (tek'nik, tek nēk') *n.* technique. [Greek *technikos* relating to art, skillful. See TECHNIQUE.]

tech·ni·cal (tek'ni kǝl) *adj.* **1.** relating to, involving, or characteristic of some science, art, profession, or other field, or the particulars peculiar to it: *technical experts, technical training, technical language.* **2.** of or relating to engineering, applied science, or the mechanical or industrial arts: *a technical school that offers few courses in liberal arts.* **3.** of, relating to, or showing technique: *a musician with technical virtuosity but little imagination.* **4.** according to strict interpretation or application of specific rules and principles: *If you really want to be technical, he should've been disqualified altogether, not just penalized.* [Greek *technikos* relating to art, skillful (from *technē* art, skill, craft) + -AL¹.] —**tech'ni·cal·ly,** *adv.* —**tech'ni·cal·ness,** *n.*

tech·ni·cal·i·ty (tek'ni kal'ǝ tē) *pl.,* **-ties.** *n.* **1.** something peculiar to a particular science, art, profession, or other field, esp. a point or detail so minute or specialized as to seem petty or a matter of form only: *He won his case by tripping up his opponent on a legal technicality.* **2.** state or quality of being technical.

technical knockout *Boxing.* decision determined in favor of a fighter when his opponent, although not actually knocked out, is unable to continue fighting, as because of injuries, or has been beaten so severely that the referee stops the fight.

technical sergeant, noncommissioned officer in the U.S. Air Force ranking next above a staff sergeant and next below a master sergeant.

tech·ni·cian (tek nish'ǝn) *n.* **1.** one who is skilled in the technicalities of some science, art, profession, or other field, esp. a person trained to deal with specialized equipment or processes: *a medical technician, a lighting technician.* **2.** one who is skilled in technique, as a writer, artist, or musician: *a film director who is a good technician but who lacks originality.*

Tech·ni·col·or (tek'ni kul'ǝr) *n.* **1.** *Trademark.* process of making color motion pictures, in which three single-color films, one in red, one in yellow, and one in blue, are exposed and then processed and combined into a single developed film that reproduces the filmed sequence in the colors of the original scene. **2.** *also,* **technicolor.** bright, vivid color, as that resulting from or reproduced by this process.

tech·nique (tek nēk') *n.* **1.** manner of attending to, performing, or accomplishing the particulars and specialized procedures of a science, art, profession, or other field: *teaching techniques, a novelist skilled in the techniques of creating realistic characters.* **2.** method or manner used to perform any operation or achieve a goal: *They used various techniques to get their prisoners to cooperate.* [French *technique* procedures and methods of an art or profession, from Greek *technikos* relating to art, skillful, from *technē* art, skill, craft.]

tech·noc·ra·cy (tek nok'rǝ sē) *pl.,* **-cies.** *n.* theory that government and society should be controlled by a selected group especially trained to solve technical problems, as scientists, engineers, and other technicians. [Greek *technē* art, skill, craft + *-kratiā* power, rule.] —**tech·no·crat** (tek'nǝ krat'), *n.* —**tech'no·crat'ic,** *adj.*

tech·no·log·i·cal (tek'nǝ loj'i kǝl) *adj.* **1.** of, relating to, or involving technology: *technological advances, technological era.* **2.** resulting from technical progress: *technological unemployment.* Also, **tech'no·log'ic,** —**tech·no·log·i·cal·ly,** *adv.*

tech·nol·o·gy (tek nol'ǝ jē) *n.* **1.** application of scientific knowledge and advances to practical purposes, esp. in the field of industry. **2.** body of methods, processes, and devices derived or resulting from such application. **3.** terminology characteristically used in a particular field, science, art, or profession. **4.** any use of materials or objects, as tools, to serve human needs. [Greek *technologia* systematic treatment, from *technē* art, skill, craft + *-logia.* See -LOGY.] —**tech·nol'o·gist,** *n.*

tech·y (tech'ē) *adj.* **tech·i·er, tech·i·est.** *adj.* tetchy.

ted (ted) **ted·ded, ted·ding.** *v.t.* to spread out or scatter for drying, as newly mown hay. [Old Norse *tethja* to spread manure.] —**ted'der,** *n.*

ted·dy bear (ted'ē) *also,* **Ted·dy bear.** toy resembling a small bear, usually stuffed with soft material and covered with plush to imitate fur. [From *Teddy,* nickname of President Theodore Roosevelt; because of a cartoon in which he was represented as having spared the life of a bear cub while hunting.]

Te De·um (tā dā'ǝm, tē dē'ǝm) **1.** in the Roman Catholic and Anglican churches, a hymn of praise sung at morning service, and also, on special occasions, as a thanksgiving service. **2.** musical setting for this hymn. [Latin *Tē Deum (laudāmus)* Thee, God (we praise), the opening words of this hymn.]

te·di·ous (tē'dē ǝs, tē'jǝs) *adj.* causing weariness and boredom, as because of length or dullness; boring: *a tedious lesson, a tedious conversation.* [Late Latin *taediōsus,* wearisome, irksome, from Latin *taedium* weariness, disgust.] —**te'di·ous·ly,** *adv.* —**te'di·ous·ness,** *n.*

te·di·um (tē'dē ǝm) *n.* state or quality of being tedious.

tee¹ (tē) *n.* **1.a.** small peg of wood, plastic, or other material, having a concave head on which a golf ball is placed to be driven at the beginning of each hole. **b.** small mound of earth or sand used for the same purpose. **2.** area, usually raised, from which a player starts each hole on a golf course. —*v.t., v.i.,* **teed, tee·ing. 1.** to place (a golf ball) on a tee (often with *up*). **2.** to tee off. **a.** to drive a golf ball from a tee in starting play. [Of uncertain origin.]

tee² (tē) *n.* **1.** target aimed at in certain games, as curling. **2.** to a tee. perfectly; exactly. [Possibly because such targets were once shaped like the letter *T.*]

teem¹ (tēm) *v.i.* to be at or as if at the point of overflowing; be full; abound; swarm (with *with*): *The creek teemed with trout. By noon the beach was teeming with people.* [Old English *tēman* to bring forth.]

teem² (tēm) *v.i.* to rain very hard; pour. [Of Scandinavian origin.]

teen (tēn) *adj.* teenage. —*n.* teenager.

-teen *suffix* (used to form cardinal numbers from thirteen to nineteen) ten: *sixteen.* [Old English *-tēne, -tȳne,* inflected form of ten.]

teen·age (tēn'āj') *also,* **teen-age, teen-aged, teen-aged.** *adj.* relating to, characteristic of, or designating people in their teens.

teen·ag·er (tēn'ā'jǝr) *also,* **teen-ag·er.** *n.* one who is older than twelve and younger than twenty years of age.

teens (tēnz) *n.,pl.* **1.** the years of one's life from thirteen to nineteen inclusive: *to be barely out of one's teens.* **2.** the numbers thirteen to nineteen inclusive. [See -TEEN.]

tee·ny (tē'nē) *also,* **-ni·er, -ni·est.** *adj. Informal.* extremely small; tiny. Also, **teen·sy** (tēn'sē).

tee·pee (tē'pē) *also,* tepee.

tee shirt, T-shirt.

tee·ter (tē'tǝr) *v.i.* **1.** to walk or move unsteadily and uncertainly, often with a swaying motion, as if about to fall: *The acrobat teetered on the tightrope.* **2.** to move back and forth in an uncertain, unpredictable way; waver: *The continent teetered on the brink of war.* —*n.* **1.** a teetering movement. **2.** seesaw (*def. 1*). [Form of earlier *titter* to totter, sway, possibly from Old Norse *titra* to tremble.]

tee·ter-tot·ter (tē'tǝr tot'ǝr) *n.* seesaw (*def. 1*). Also, **teeter board.**

teeth (tēth) plural of **tooth.**

teethe (tēth) **teethed, teeth·ing.** *v.i.* to grow or develop teeth; cut one's teeth.

teething ring, ring of plastic, rubber, or other material upon which a teething infant may bite.

tee·to·tal (tē'tōt'ǝl) **-taled, -tal·ing;** *also British,* **-talled, -tal·ling.** *v.i.* to abstain totally from alcoholic liquor. —*adj.* **1.** of or relating to total abstinence from alcoholic liquor. **2.** *Informal.* total; complete. [From TOTAL, with repetition of the first letter *t* for emphasis.]

tee·to·tal·er (tē'tōt'ǝl ǝr) *also, British,* **tee·to·tal·ler.** *n.* one who totally abstains from drinking alcoholic liquor.

tee·to·tal·ism (tē'tōt'ǝl iz'ǝm) *n.* principle or practice of totally abstaining from alcoholic liquor. —**tee'to'tal·ist,** *n.*

Te·gu·ci·gal·pa (tē goo'sē gäl'pä) *n.* capital of Honduras, in the south-central part of the country. Pop. (1969), 253,283.

teg·u·lar (teg'yǝ lǝr) *adj.* **1.** relating to, resembling, or consisting of a tile or tiles. **2.** arranged like tiles. [Latin *tēgula* tile + -AR¹.]

teg·u·ment (teg'yǝ mǝnt) *n.* outer covering, as a husk, shell, or rind; integument. [Latin *tegumentum* covering.]

Te·hran (te'hǝ rän', -rän', tā'ǝ-) *also,* **Te·he·ran.** *n.* capital and largest city of Iran, in the north-central part of the country. Pop. (1966), 2,719,730.

tek·tite (tek'tīt') *n.* any of numerous small glassy objects of various shapes found strewn over large areas of the earth's surface, as in Australia, Indonesia, and the southwestern United States, thought to have originated in outer space. [Greek *tēktos* molten + -ITE¹.]

tel. 1. telephone. **2.** telegram. **3.** telegraph.

Tel·Au·to·graph (tel ô'tǝ graf') *n. Trademark.* telegraphic device that transmits electrical signals corresponding to the motions of a pen, used to reproduce handwriting, diagrams, sketches, and other material over a distance.

at; āpe; cär; end; mē; it; īce; hot; ōld; fôrk; wood; fōōl; oil; out; up; ūse; turn; sing; thin; this; zh in treasure; ǝ in ago, taken, pencil, lemon, circus.

Tel A·viv (tel´ ə vēv´) city in west-central Israel, on the Mediterranean, combined with Jaffa in 1950. Official name: **Tel Aviv-Jaffa.** Pop. (1968), 384,700.

tele- *combining form* **1.** at a distance; far: *telepathy.* **2.** of or relating to television: *telethon.* [Greek *tēle* far off, afar.]

tel·e·cast (tel´ə kast´) -cast or -cast·ed, -cast·ing. *v.t., v.i.* to broadcast (a program) by television; televise. —*n.* program broadcast over television. [TELE(VISION) + (BROAD)CAST.]

tel·e·com·mu·ni·ca·tion (tel´ə kə mū´nə kā´shən) *also,* **tel·e·com·mu·ni·ca·tions.** *n.* science or study of communicating or sending messages over long distances by electronic means, as by telegraph, television, or telephone.

tel·e·gen·ic (tel´ə jen´ik) *adj.* having or likely to have an attractive appearance on television. [TELE- + (PHOTO)GENIC.]

tel·e·gram (tel´ə gram´) *n.* message sent by telegraph.

tel·e·graph (tel´ə graf´) *n.* system, process, and equipment used for sending messages over a distance by means of coded electrical impulses. —*v.t.* **1.** to send (a message) by telegraph. **2.** to send a message to by telegraph. **3.** to reveal or indicate unintentionally to another, as by a look or gesture. —*v.i.* to send a message by telegraph. [TELE- + -GRAPH.]

te·leg·ra·pher (tə leg´rə fər) *n.* one whose work is sending and receiving messages by telegraph; telegraph operator.

tel·e·graph·ic (tel´ə graf´ik) *adj.* relating to, resembling, or sent by telegraph. Also, **tel´e·graph´i·cal.** —**tel´e·graph´i·cal·ly,** *adv.*

te·leg·ra·phy (tə leg´rə fē) *n.* operation or use of telegraphs to send messages; communications by means of a telegraph.

tel·e·ki·ne·sis (tel´ə ki nē´sis) *n.* production of motion in an object, as by a spiritualist medium, seemingly without physical contact, application of force, or other perceivable or explicable means. [TELE- + Greek *kinēsis* movement.]

Te·lem·a·chus (tə lem´ə kəs) *n. Classical Legend.* son of Ulysses and Penelope, who after many years is reunited with his father and helps him slay Penelope's suitors.

te·lem·e·ter (tə lem´ə tər, tel´ə mē´tər) *n.* electronic instrument, as in a rocket, for measuring a quantity, as speed, temperature, pressure, or radiation, and transmitting the data to a distant receiving station. —*v.t., v.i.* to measure or transmit by telemeter.

te·lem·e·try (tə lem´ə trē) *n.* branch of engineering, esp. relating to space studies, dealing with the measurement at a distance of various physical quantities, as temperature, pressure, or radiation. [TELE- + -METRY.] —**tel·e·met·ric** (tel´ə met´rik) *also,* **tel´e·met´ri·cal,** *adj.*

te·le·ol·o·gy (tel´ē ol´ə jē, tē´lē-) *pl.,* **-gies.** *n.* **1.** fact or quality of having or being directed toward a definite end or purpose. **2.** doctrine that natural processes or events are not entirely determined by mechanical forces, but are directed onward toward an ultimate goal. **3.** explanation or evaluation of a thing according to its purpose, aim, or end. [Modern Latin *teleologia,* from Greek *telos* end + -LOGY.]

te·lep·a·thy (tə lep´ə thē) *n.* apparent communication of one mind with another by means other than ordinary speaking, writing, or gesturing. [TELE- + -PATHY.] —**tel·e·path·ic** (tel´ə path´ik), *adj.* —**tel´e·path´i·cal·ly,** *adv.* —**te·lep´a·thist,** *n.*

tel·e·phone (tel´ə fōn´) *n.* **1.** system for sending messages over distances, esp. by converting sound into electrical impulses that are transmitted, often over wires, and turned back into sound by a receiver. **2.** instrument in such a system equipped

Telephones

with a transmitter, a receiver, and often a dial or buttons for directing calls. —*v.t.,* **-phoned, -phon·ing. 1.** to communicate with by telephone. **2.** to send by telephone. —*v.i.* to communicate by telephone: *Did you telephone ahead for reservations?* [TELE- + Greek *phōnē* voice, sound.] —**tel´e·phon´er,** *n.*

tel·e·phon·ic (tel´ə fon´ik) *adj.* of, relating to, or transmitted by or as by a telephone.

te·leph·o·ny (tə lef´ə nē) *n.* study of the construction and operation of telephone systems.

tel·e·pho·to·graph (tel´ə fō´tə graf´) *n.* **1.** photograph taken with a camera equipped with a telephoto lens. **2.** photograph or picture sent by telephotography.

tel·e·pho·to·graph·ic (tel´ə fō´tə graf´ik) *adj.* of, relating to, or characteristic of telephotography. Also, **tel´e·pho´to.**

tel·e·pho·tog·ra·phy (tel´ə fə tog´rə fē) *n.* **1.** photography employing a camera with a lens that can focus on distant objects and enlarge their size on the negative. **2.** production of facsimiles of photographs or pictures by radio or telegraph.

tel·e·pho·to lens (tel´ə fō´tō) camera lens that magnifies the image of a distant object.

tel·e·print·er (tel´ə print´ər) *n.* teletypewriter.

Tel·e·promp·ter (tel´ə promp´tər) *n. Trademark.* television set placed before a speaker or performer on which a magnified script is unrolled line by line.

tel·e·ran (tel´ə ran´) *n.* navigation system in which radar information and maps are transmitted to airplanes over television. [Short for *tele(vision) r(adar) a(ir) n(avigation).*]

tel·e·scope (tel´ə skōp´) *n.* optical instrument for making distant objects, as heavenly bodies, appear nearer and larger, consisting of one or more tubes. A refracting telescope has at the objective, or far end, a concave lens that refracts light toward the eyepiece; a reflecting telescope

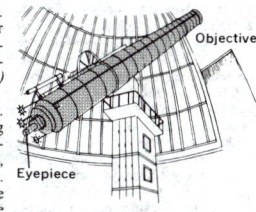

Telescope

has a concave mirror that reflects light toward it. The eyepiece, through which the observer looks, is a magnifying lens or system of lenses. —*v.t.,* **-scoped, -scop·ing. 1.** to compress or drive together or into one another, as the sliding tubes of certain telescopes: *The impact of the collision telescoped the car.* **2.** to condense; abridge. [Modern Latin *telescopium,* going back to Greek *tēle* afar + *-skopion.* See -SCOPE.]

tel·e·scop·ic (tel´ə skop´ik) *adj.* **1.** of, relating to, or characteristic of a telescope. **2.** seen or obtained by means of a telescope. **3.** visible only through a telescope. **4.** able to see at a great distance; far-seeing. **5.** consisting of parts capable of sliding into one another like the tubes of certain telescopes. —**tel´e·scop´i·cal·ly,** *adv.*

tel·e·thon (tel´ə thon´) *n.* long television program during which callers make pledges to a charity. [TELE(VISION) + (MARA)THON.]

Tel·e·type (tel´ə tīp´) *n. Trademark.* communications equipment by which a message typed on one teletypewriter is transmitted over an electrical circuit to another teletypewriter, which types out the message. —*v.t., v.i.,* **-typed, -typ·ing.** to transmit (a message) by teletypewriter.

tel·e·type·writ·er (tel´ə tīp´rī´tər) *n.* keyboard machine that looks like an electric typewriter, used for receiving and sending messages over an electrical circuit. Also, **tel´e·print´er.**

tel·e·view (tel´ə vū´) *v.t., v.i.* to watch or observe by means of television. —**tel´e·view´er,** *n.*

tel·e·vise (tel´ə vīz´) **-vised, -vis·ing.** *v.t., v.i.* to transmit or receive by television.

tel·e·vi·sion (tel´ə vizh´ən) *n.* **1.** system of sending and receiving images and accompanying sounds by transforming them into variations in electric currents, then into waves, then back into electric currents, which are turned back into picture and sound by the receiving set. **2.** set in which such images are received and reproduced. **3.** industry, medium, or art of television broadcasting. [TELE- + VISION.]

tell (tel) told, tell·ing. *v.t.* **1.** to give a detailed account of; narrate: *to tell a fairy tale to a child.* **2.** to put or express in written or spoken words: *to promise not to tell a lie.* **3.** to give information to; let know: *Tell us about your vacation.* **4.** to make known, esp. that which is confidential; reveal; disclose: *to tell a secret.* **5.** to give an order, command, or direction to: *I told you to be quiet.* **6.** to distinguish, as one thing from another; discern; determine: *to tell a real diamond from an imitation. Barbara couldn't tell the twins apart.* **7.** to assure emphatically: *It won't work, I tell you!* **8.** to name or count one by one, as the beads of a rosary. **9. to tell off. a.** to count off and detach, as for some special duty. **b.** *Informal.* to reprimand severely. —*v.i.* **1.** to give an account: *The sailor told of his many great adventures.* **2.** to disclose something secret; report; inform: *If you misbehave, I'll tell.* **3.** to serve as evidence; indicate: *Only time will tell if we have been successful.* **4.** to have or produce an effect: *William's age is beginning to tell on him.* [Old English *tellan* to reckon, narrate.]

Tell, William (tel) legendary hero of Swiss independence who was forced to shoot an apple off his son's head with a bow and arrow.

tell·a·ble (tel´ə bəl) *adj.* capable of or suitable for being told.

tell·er (tel´ər) *n.* **1.** one who relates, narrates, or informs: *a teller of tall stories.* **2.** one who counts or enumerates. **3.** one who is employed in a bank and receives or gives out money over a counter.

tell·ing (tel´ing) *adj.* having the intended effect; striking; forceful: *a telling blow that sent his opponent reeling.* —**tell´ing·ly,** *adv.*

tell·tale (tel´tāl´) *n.* **1.** tattletale. **2.** something that reveals information. —*adj.* that which reveals what is not intended to be known or seen: *There was a telltale blood-stain on the suspect's coat.*

tel·lu·ride (tel´yə rīd´) *n.* compound of tellurium with a metallic element. Lead telluride is used as a semiconductor.

tel·lu·ri·um (te loor′ē əm) *n.* lustrous, silver-white, semimetallic element that is a semiconductor and is also used in steel and lead alloys. Symbol: Te See **element** for table. [Modern Latin *tellurium*, from Latin *tellūr-*, stem of *tellūs* earth.]

Tel·u·gu (tel′ə gōō′) *pl.*, **-gu** or **-gus.** *n.* **1.** member or close descendant of a Dravidian people living predominantly in southern India. **2.** their language, belonging to the Dravidian language family.

tem·blor (tem′blər, -blôr; *Spanish* tem blôr′) *pl.*, **-blors** or *(Spanish)* **-blo·res** (-blôr′ās). *n.* earthquake. [Spanish *temblor* a trembling, going back to Latin *tremulus* trembling.]

te·mer·i·ty (tə mer′ə tē) *n.* excessive or reckless boldness; rashness. [Latin *temeritās.*]

temp. **1.** temperature. **2.** temporary.

tem·per (tem′pər) *n.* **1.a.** inclination to give way to anger or irritation: *He has quite a temper.* **b.** anger; rage. **2.** habitual or usual frame of mind; temperament: *an even temper. Steve has a mean temper when he is angry.* **3.** command over the emotions; self-control; composure; equanimity: *to lose one's temper.* **4.** hardness, elasticity, or other quality of a material, esp. a metal, imparted by mixing it with another substance or by treating it in a specific way. **5.** substance added to another to modify, neutralize, or subdue its properties. —*v.t.* **1.** to restrain the severity or harshness of; moderate; soften: *to temper justice with mercy.* **2.** to bring (a substance) to a proper or desired condition by mixing it with another substance or by treating it in a specific way: *to temper steel with heat.* **3.** to adjust the pitch of (a note or instrument) by temperament; tune. [Old English *temprian* to mingle, regulate, from Latin *temperāre.*] —**Syn.** *v.* **2.** see **disposition.**

tem·per·a (tem′pər ə) *n.* **1.** painting medium usually consisting of egg yolk, ground pigment, and water. **2.** art or technique of painting with such a medium. [Italian *tempera,* from *temperare* to mix colors, moderate, from Latin *temperāre* to mingle, regulate.]

tem·per·a·ment (tem′prə mənt, -pər ə mənt) *n.* **1.** combination of qualities which constitute the natural disposition of an individual and affect actions, thinking, and emotions. **2.** natural inclination to assert one's individuality, esp. a tendency to be extremely moody, sensitive, or irritable. **3.** *Music.* **a.** tuning of an instrument, esp. a keyboard instrument, so that the intervals of all twelve half tones are equal, making it possible to play all keys. **b.** system according to which this is done. [Latin *temperāmentum* mixing in due proportion, disposition; with reference to the earlier belief that one's temperament resulted from the relative proportions of the four humors in one's system. See HUMOR.] —**Syn.** **1.** see **disposition.**

tem·per·a·men·tal (tem′prə ment′əl, -pər ə ment′əl) *adj.* **1.** having or exhibiting extreme moodiness, sensitivity, or irritability. **2.** relating to or caused by temperament. —**tem′per·a·men′tal·ly,** *adv.* —**Syn.** **1.** see **moody.**

tem·per·ance (tem′pər əns, tem′prəns) *n.* **1.** observance of moderation or self-restraint in behavior of any kind, esp. in regard to the drinking of alcoholic beverages. **2.** total abstinence from alcoholic beverages. [Latin *temperantia* moderation.]

tem·per·ate (tem′pər it, -prit) *adj.* **1.** characterized by temperance. **2.** free from extremes of temperature: *a temperate climate.* [Latin *temperātus* moderate, past participle of *temperāre* to mingle, moderate, regulate.] —**tem′per·ate·ly,** *adv.* —**tem′per·ate·ness,** *n.*

Temperate Zone, either of the two climatic zones of the earth characterized by a temperate climate with four distinct seasons. One zone lies north of the equator between the Arctic Circle and the Tropic of Cancer, the other south of the equator between the Tropic of Capricorn and the Antarctic Circle. See **zone** for illustration.

tem·per·a·ture (tem′pər chər, tem′prə ə-) *n.* **1.** degree of heat or coldness of a body or substance as measured by a thermometer or other graduated scale. **2.** *Informal.* abnormally high body temperature; fever. [Latin *temperātūra* due measure, proportion.]

tem·per·a·ture-hu·mid·i·ty index (tem′prə chər hū mid′ə tē, -ū mid′-, tem′pər ə-) measurement of a combination of temperature and humidity, on a scale from seventy to eighty, used by the United States Weather Bureau to express the relative comfort or discomfort caused by both the heat and humidity factors of the weather.

tem·pered (tem′pərd) *adj.* **1.** having a specified disposition. ▲ used in combination: *an even-tempered man.* **2.** modified or moderated by the addition of some other substance or quality; lessened; softened. **3.** treated so as to have the desired degree of hardness and elasticity: *tempered steel.* **4.** *Music.* adjusted or tuned to a temperament.

tem·pest (tem′pist) *n.* **1.** violent windstorm, usually accompanied by rain, hail, snow, or thunder. **2.** any violent commotion or disturbance; tumult. [Old French *tempest(e)* storm, going back to Latin *tempestās* season, weather, storm, from *tempus* time, season.]

tem·pes·tu·ous (tem pes′chōō əs) *adj.* **1.** characteristic of a tempest; turbulent; stormy: *a tempestuous airplane flight.* **2.** subject to or characterized by strong or violent emotion: *a tempestuous mob.* —**tem·pes′tu·ous·ly,** *adv.* —**tem·pes′tu·ous·ness,** *n.*

Tem·plar (tem′plər) *n.* **1.** member of a medieval religious and military order of knights that protected the pilgrims on their crusades to the Holy Land. Also, **Knight Templar. 2.** Knight Templar *(def. 2).* [Medieval Latin *templarius* member of a religious and military order of knights in the Middle Ages, from Latin *templum* sanctuary, consecrated place.]

tem·ple[1] (tem′pəl) *n.* **1.** building dedicated to the worship of a god or gods. **2. Temple.** any of three buildings erected successively in Jerusalem as the center of Jewish worship. **3.** synagogue. **4.** Christian church. **5.** place or object in which God is considered to dwell, as in the body of one who is sanctified. **6.** any Mormon house of worship. **7. Temple.** either of two buildings in London, the **Inner Temple** and the **Middle Temple,** formerly the dwelling place of the Knights Templar, now belonging to English legal societies. [Old English *temp(e)l* building dedicated to divine worship, from Latin *templum* sanctuary, consecrated place.]

tem·ple[2] (tem′pəl) *n.* flattened part on either side of the forehead, above the cheekbone and in front of the ear. [Old French *temple,* going back to Latin *tempus.*]

tem·po (tem′pō) *pl.*, **-pos** or **-pi** (-pē). *n.* **1.** *Music.* relative speed at which a musical composition, movement, or passage is or should be rendered. **2.** characteristic pace or speed: *the tempo of life in a modern city.* [Italian *tempo* time, from Latin *tempus.* Doublet of TENSE[2].]

tem·po·ral[1] (tem′pər əl, -prəl) *adj.* **1.** of or relating to time. **2.** of short duration; temporary. **3.** of or relating to this life on earth; material; worldly: *temporal pleasures.* **4.** not religious; secular; civil; lay: *a religious leader with temporal powers.* [Late Latin *temporālis* worldly, from Latin *tempus,* stem *tempor-* relating to time, from *tempus* time, season.] —**tem′po·ral·ly,** *adv.* —**tem′po·ral·ness,** *n.*

tem·po·ral[2] (tem′pər əl, -prəl) *adj.* of, relating to, or situated near the temples. —*n.* either of two bones of the head, located above and in front of the ear. [Late Latin *temporālis* relating to the temples (of the head), from Latin *tempus* temple[2].]

tem·po·ral·i·ty (tem′pə ral′ə tē) *pl.*, **-ties.** *n.* **1.** state or quality of being temporal; temporariness. **2.** *also,* **temporalities.** that which is temporal or secular, esp. material possessions of a church.

tem·po·rar·y (tem′pə rer′ē) *adj.* lasting, existing, or occuring for a limited time only; not permanent. [Latin *temporārius,* from *tempus* time.] —**tem′po·rar′i·ly,** *adv.* —**tem′po·rar′i·ness,** *n.*

tem·po·rize (tem′pə rīz′) **-rized, -riz·ing.** *v.t.* **1.** to delay or postpone immediate action or decision, so as to avoid arguments, disapproval, or other difficulty. **2.** to adapt one's acts or opinions in order to conform to the time or circumstances; comply. **3.** to effect a settlement, esp. through compromise; negotiate. [French *temporiser* to delay, through Medieval Latin *temporizāre,* from Latin *tempus* time.] —**tem′po·ri·za′tion, tem′-po·riz′er,** *n.*

tempt (tempt) *v.t.* **1.** to attempt to persuade (someone) to act, esp. to do something that is sinful, illegal, or foolish. **2.** to attract strongly; lure: *The unappetizing food didn't tempt her.* **3.** to act presumptuously or recklessly toward; provoke; defy: *to tempt fate.* [Latin *temptāre* to handle, test, try.] —**tempt′a·ble,** *adj.*

temp·ta·tion (temp tā′shən) *n.* **1.** act of tempting; being tempted. **2.** one who or that which tempts.

tempt·er (temp′tər) *n.* one who or that which tempts or entices.

tempt·ing (temp′ting) *adj.* that entices or allures; attractive; seductive: *a tempting offer.* —**tempt′ing·ly,** *adv.*

tempt·ress (temp′tris) *n.* woman who tempts, esp. a seductive, alluring woman.

tem·pus fu·git (tem′pəs fū′jit) *Latin.* time flies.

ten (ten) *n.* **1.** the cardinal number that is one more than nine. **2.** symbol representing this number, as 10 or X. **3.** something having this many units or members, as a playing card. —*adj.* numbering one more than nine. [Old English *tēn, tien.*]

ten·a·ble (ten′ə bəl) *adj.* capable of being held, maintained, or defended: *a tenable fortress, a tenable statement, a tenable theory.* [Old French *tenable* holdable, from *tenir* to hold, from Latin *tenēre.*] —**ten′a·bil′i·ty, ten′a·ble·ness,** *n.* —**ten′a·bly,** *adv.*

te·na·cious (ti nā′shəs) *adj.* **1.** holding or inclined to hold firmly: *a tenacious grasp.* **2.** tending to adhere to another substance; adhesive; sticky: *Tar is a tenacious substance.* **3.** not easily pulled or broken apart; tough: *a tenacious alloy.* **4.** persistent; resolute; obstinate: *a tenacious will, a tenacious resistance to change.* **5.** tending to retain; retentive: *a tenacious memory.* [Latin *tenāci-,* stem of *tenāx* holding fast + -OUS.] —**te·na′cious·ly,** *adv.* —**te·na′cious·ness,** *n.*

te·nac·i·ty (ti nas′ə tē) *n.* quality or state of being tenacious.

ten·an·cy (ten′ən sē) *pl.*, **-cies.** *n.* **1.** occupancy of property for which rent is paid; state of being a tenant. **2.** period of time during which a tenant occupies property. **3.** habitation or property occupied by a tenant.

ten·ant (ten′ənt) *n.* **1.** one who pays rent to occupy or use the property of another, as land, a house, apartment, or office. **2.** occupant or inhab-

itant of any place: *the present tenant of the White House.* **3.** one who possesses land or property by any kind of title. —*v.t.* to hold or occupy as a tenant; inhabit. [Old French *tenant* one who holds or possesses, from *tenir* to hold, from Latin *tenēre.*]

tenant farmer, farmer who works land owned by another and pays rent either in cash or a share of the crops.

ten·ant·ry (ten'ən trē) *pl.,* **-ries.** *n.* **1.** tenants collectively. as of an estate. **2.** state of being a tenant; tenancy.

tench (tench) *pl.,* **tench·es** or **tench.** *n.* freshwater fish, *Tinca tinca,* of the carp family, found in Europe and Asia. It is capable of living out of water for fairly long periods. [Old French *tench,* from Late Latin *tinca;* possibly of Celtic origin.]

Ten Commandments, the ten rules for living and for worship that, according to the Old Testament, God presented to Moses on Mount Sinai, engraved on tablets of stone.

tend[1] (tend) *v.i.* **1.** to be disposed in action or thought; be likely or apt: *He tends to be overweight. His novels tend to be pessimistic.* **2.** to lead to some state or condition; have a specified result: *Unsanitary living conditions tend to produce disease.* **3.** to move, extend, or be directed in a particular direction: *The path tends toward the left at the river.* [Old French *tendre* to stretch, bend, aspire to, offer, from Latin *tendere* to stretch, direct, aim.]

tend[2] (tend) *v.t.* **1.** to attend to the needs or requirements of; care for; watch over; minister to: *to tend a sick person, to tend a plant, to tend a child.* **2.** to serve or wait (with *on* or *upon*). —*v.i.* **1.** *Informal.* to take care of; pay attention (with *to*): *Tend to your own affairs.* **2.** to be in charge of or watch at; manage or operate: *to tend a machine, to tend a store.* [Short for ATTEND.]

tend·ance (ten'dəns) *n.* attention or care, as to the sick.

tend·en·cy (ten'dən sē) *pl.,* **-cies.** *n.* natural or habitual disposition to move or act in a particular manner: *He has a tendency to sulk if he is criticized. My car's engine has a tendency to stall in cold weather.* [Medieval Latin *tendentia* direction, going back to Latin *tendere* to stretch, direct, aim.] —**Syn.** see **direction.**

ten·den·tious (ten den'shəs) *adj.* written or spoken in behalf of some particular cause or point of view; biased: *a tendentious account of the rebellion.* [Medieval Latin *tendentia* direction. See TENDENCY.] —**ten·den'tious·ly,** *adv.* —**ten·den'tious·ness,** *n.*

ten·der[1] (ten'dər) *adj.* **1.** soft or delicate in substance; not tough or hard: *tender beef.* **2.** easily injured or bruised; not hardy, robust, or strong; fragile: *the tender petals of a flower.* **3.** having the delicacy of youth; fresh; immature: *a tender age, tender years.* **4.** not forcible or rough; light; gentle: *a tender touch.* **5.** expressing or characterized by warmth of feeling; kind or loving; affectionate: *a tender look, a tender tone of voice, tender memories.* **6.** acutely or painfully sensitive; easily hurt; sore: *a tender bruise. His arm was still tender after the cut healed.* **7.** sensitive to the feelings of others; sympathetic; compassionate: *a tender heart.* **8.** requiring cautious, delicate, or tactful handling or treatment; ticklish: *a tender subject.* **9.** easily injured, distressed, or offended: *a tender conscience, a woman of tender sensibilities.* **10.** delicate or soft in quality or effect, as light or a color. [Old French *tendre* delicate, gentle, from Latin *tener* delicate, soft.] —**ten'der·ly,** *adv.* —**ten'der·ness,** *n.* —**Syn. 4.** see **gentle.**

ten·der[2] (ten'dər) *v.t.* **1.** to present for acceptance, esp. in a formal manner; offer: *to tender one's resignation.* **2.** *Law.* to offer in payment of a debt, claim, demand, or other obligation. —*n.* **1.** act of making an offer; offer presented for acceptance. **2.** that which is tendered, esp. money offered in payment. **3.** *Law.* an offer of money, goods, or services in payment of a debt or other obligation. [Old French *tendre* to offer, from Latin *tendere* to stretch, direct, aim.] —**ten'der·er,** *n.*

tend·er[3] (ten'dər) *n.* **1.** one who cares for, attends to, or manages someone or something. **2.** small boat or ship used to attend a large vessel, as by carrying supplies or passengers between the vessel and the shore. **3.** railroad car attached to the rear of a steam locomotive, used to carry fuel and water. [TEND[2] + -ER[1].]

Tender[3] (def. 3)

ten·der·foot (ten'dər foot') *pl.,* **-foots** or **-feet.** *n.* **1.** newcomer to ranch or mining life of the West, who is unused to the hardships or rough conditions of such life. **2.** any inexperienced person; novice. **3.** boy who is in the lowest rank of the Boy Scouts.

ten·der-heart·ed (ten'dər här'tid) *adj.* easily moved to pity, love, or sorrow; compassionate; sympathetic. —**ten'der-heart'ed·ly,** *adv.* —**ten'der-heart'ed·ness,** *n.*

ten·der·ize (ten'də rīz') **-ized, -iz·ing.** *v.t.* to make (meat) tender, as by pounding, marinating, or applying a tenderizer.

ten·der·iz·er (ten'də rī'zər) *n.* any substance applied to meat to

make it tender, esp. one containing an enzyme from papaya juice.

ten·der·loin (ten'dər loin') *n.* **1.** tenderest part of the loin of beef or pork, located under the short ribs and running parallel to the backbone. **2.a. Tenderloin.** formerly, a district of New York City below 42nd Street west of Broadway, in which there was much vice and graft, and which was regarded as a choice assignment for a corrupt policeman. **b.** any district of a city notorious for vice and graft.

ten·di·nous (ten'də nəs) *adj.* **1.** of, relating to, or resembling a tendon. **2.** consisting of tendons.

ten·don (ten'dən) *n.* strong cord or band of fibrous connective tissue that attaches a muscle to a bone or other part of the body; sinew. [French *tendon,* from Latin *tendere* to stretch.]

ten·dril (ten'drəl) *n.* **1.** threadlike, leafless, often spirally coiling part of a climbing plant, as the grape, that serves to support itself by twining around or clinging to a tree trunk, wall, or other object. **2.** something resembling this, as a wispy curl of hair. [Modification of obsolete French *tendrillon* tender shoot, diminutive of Old French *tendron,* going back to Latin *tener* delicate, soft.]

Achilles' tendon

Toes

Heel

Tendon

ten·e·brous (ten'ə brəs) *adj.* dark; gloomy. [Latin *tenebrōsus,* from *tenebrae* darkness.]

ten·e·ment (ten'ə mənt) *n.* **1.** apartment building or rooming house that is poorly built or maintained and usually overcrowded, esp. one that is located in a slum and inhabited by poor people. Also, **tenement house. 2.** any house or building to live in, esp. one that is rented or intended for rent. **3.** room or set of rooms occupied by a tenant as a separate dwelling. **4.** *Law.* any permanent property that one person may hold for another, as land or buildings. **5.** any residence or dwelling place; abode. [Medieval Latin *tenementum* a holding, fief, house, from Latin *tenēre* to hold.]

ten·et (ten'it, tē'nit) *n.* doctrine, principle, or belief held to be true by an individual or group. [Latin *tenet* he holds.] —**Syn.** see **doctrine.**

ten·fold (ten'fōld') *adj.* **1.** ten times as great or numerous. **2.** having or consisting of ten parts. —*adv.* so as to be ten times greater or more numerous.

ten-gal·lon hat (ten'gal'ən) man's wide-brimmed felt hat with a high crown, worn esp. in the southwestern United States.

Tenn., Tennessee.

Ten·nes·see (ten'ə sē') *n.* **1.** state in the southeastern United States. Capital, Nashville. Area, 42,244 sq. mi. Pop. (1970), 3,219,311. Abbreviation, **Tenn. 2.** river in the southeastern United States, flowing through Tennessee, Alabama, and Kentucky into the Ohio River. —**Ten'nes·se'an,** *adj.*

Tennessee Valley Authority, see TVA.

ten·nis (ten'is) *n.* **1.** racket game in which two or four players hit a light, fabric-covered rubber ball back and forth over a low net stretched across the center of a level, rectangular court of grass, clay, concrete, or other material. Also, **lawn tennis. 2.** any of several similar and related games, as court tennis. [Old French *tenez* hold (supposedly referring to the call of the player serving the ball), imperative of *tenir* to hold, from Latin *tenēre.*]

tennis shoe, low sneaker worn in playing tennis.

Ten·ny·son, Alfred, Lord (ten'ə-sən) 1809–92, English poet.

Te·noch·ti·tlán (te nōch'tēt län') *n.* capital of the ancient Aztec empire, on the site of present-day Mexico City.

ten·on (ten'ən) *n.* projecting part cut on the end of a timber or other piece of wood for insertion into a corresponding hole, or mortise, in another piece to form a joint. —*v.t.* **1.** to cut such a projecting part in (a piece of wood). **2.** to join (two pieces of wood) with a tenon and mortise joint. [Old French *tenon* the end of a piece of wood put into a mortise, from *tenir* to hold, from Latin *tenēre.*]

Tenon

Mortise

Tenon

ten·or (ten'ər) *n.* **1.** general or usual tendency, course, or direction: *the quiet tenor of his life.* **2.** general meaning or effect of something spoken or written; drift: *The sad tenor of her letter worried him.* **3.** *Music.* **a.** highest natural adult male voice, intermediate between baritone and countertenor. **b.** singer who has a tenor voice. **c.** instrument corresponding in range to this voice. **d.** part composed for a tenor voice or instrument. —*adj. Music.* **1.a.** able to sing tenor: *a tenor voice.* **2.** for the tenor: *the tenor score.* **3.** having a range corresponding to that of a tenor voice: *a tenor saxophone.* [Latin *tenor* a holding on, course, sense of a law, tone.]

ten pence, coin of the United Kingdom equal to ten pennies or 1/10 of a pound.

ten·pen·ny (ten′pen′ē, -pə nē) *adj.* **1.** worth or costing ten pennies, esp. ten British pennies. **2.** designating a nail three inches in length.

ten·pin (ten′pin′) *n.* **1. tenpins,** bowling game using ten bottle-shaped wooden pins and a large ball, and allowing a player to bowl two balls in each frame. ▲ construed as singular. **2.** one of the pins used in this game.

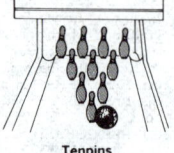

Tenpins

tense[1] (tens) **tens·er, tens·est.** *adj.* **1.** stretched or drawn tight; strained; taut: *tense muscles.* **2.** undergoing or showing mental or emotional strain: *a tense person, a tense expression.* **3.** characterized by or causing strain or suspense: *a tense moment, a tense situation, a tense drama.* —*v.t., v.i.,* **tensed, tens·ing.** to make or become tense. [Latin *tensus,* past participle of *tendere* to stretch.] —**tense′ly,** *adv.* —**tense′ness,** *n.*

tense[2] (tens) *n.* **1.** form of a verb that shows the time of its action or state of being. **2.** set of such forms indicating a particular time: *the future tense, the past tense.* [Old French *tens* time, from Latin *tempus.* Doublet of TEMPO.]

ten·sile (ten′sil, -sīl) *adj.* **1.** of or relating to tension: *tensile strain.* **2.** capable of being elongated or stretched; ductile: *a tensile metal.* [Modern Latin *tensilis,* from Latin *tendere* to stretch.] —**ten·sil·i·ty** (ten sil′ə tē), *n.*

tensile strength, resistance to lengthwise stress, measured by the greatest amount of stretching force that can be applied to a material without tearing it apart. It is usually expressed in pounds per square inch.

ten·sion (ten′shən) *n.* **1.** act of stretching or making taut; being stretched. **2.** mental or emotional strain; feeling of anxiety, fear, excitement, or suspense. **3.** any strained state or relationship: *tension between rival nations that lasted for many years.* **4.** *Physics.* **a.** force or combination of forces tending to cause extension or elongation of the parts of a material, as a line or cord; stress caused by pulling. **b.** condition of a body when acted upon by such a force or forces. **5.** voltage. **6.** device for regulating tautness, as of thread in a sewing machine. [Latin *tensiō* a stretching.]

ten·sion·al (ten′shən əl) *adj.* relating to tension.

ten·si·ty (ten′sə tē) *n.* state of being tense; tension.

ten·sive (ten′siv) *adj.* relating to or causing tension.

ten·sor (ten′sər, -sôr) *n.* any muscle that stretches or tenses a part of the body. [Modern Latin *tensor,* from Latin *tensus,* past participle of *tendere* to stretch.]

ten·strike (ten′strīk′) *n.* **1.** strike in the game of tenpins. **2.** *Informal.* any entirely successful action or undertaking.

tent (tent) *n.* **1.** collapsible, portable shelter, usually of canvas, supported by one or more poles and fastened by cords attached to pegs in the ground. **2.** anything that resembles this in form or use, as an oxygen tent. —*v.i.* **1.** to live or camp in a tent; encamp: *We tented by the stream for the night.* **2.** to provide with or lodge in tents. —*v.t.* to cover with or as with a tent. [Old French *tente* pavilion, going back to Latin *tendere* to stretch.]

ten·ta·cle (ten′tə kəl) *n.* **1.** any of various long, slender, flexible processes or appendages of animals, esp. invertebrates, usually growing on the head or about the mouth, and used esp. for feeling, grasping, and moving. **2.** anything resembling this, as a grasping, far-reaching power or influence: *a city held in the tentacles of organized crime.* **3.** sensitive, hairlike growth on the leaves of some plants, as sundews. [Modern Latin *tentaculum,* from Latin *tentāre* to feel, try.] —**ten·tac·u·lar** (ten tak′yə lər), *adj.*

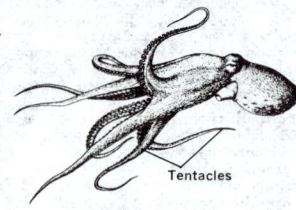

Tentacles

Tentacles of an octopus

ten·ta·tive (ten′tə tiv) *adj.* **1.** made, done, or proposed as a trial or experiment; not definite or final; provisional: *tentative plans, a tentative agreement, a tentative outline for a novel.* **2.** showing hesitancy or uncertainty: *The shy girl gave us a tentative smile.* [Medieval Latin *tentativus* trying, from Latin *tentāre* to feel, try.] —**ten′ta·tive·ly,** *adv.* —**ten′ta·tive·ness,** *n.*

tent caterpillar, any of a group of destructive caterpillars, family Lasiocampidae, that spins large, tentlike, silken webs on the branches of trees.

ten·ter (ten′tər) *n.* framework or machine on which cloth is stretched so as to dry evenly without shrinkage. —*v.t.* to stretch (cloth) on a tenter. [Middle English *tentour,* from Latin *tentus,* past participle of *tendere* to stretch.]

ten·ter·hook (ten′tər hook′) *n.* **1.** sharp hooked nail used for fastening cloth on a tenter. **2. on tenterhooks,** in a state of suspense or anxiety: *The candidate's followers were on tenterhooks as they awaited the results of the election.*

tenth (tenth) *adj.* **1.** (the ordinal of ten) next after the ninth. **2.** being one of ten equal parts. —*n.* **1.** that which is next after the ninth. **2.** one of ten equal parts; 1/10. —*adv.* in the tenth place.

ten·u·i·ty (ti nōō′ə tē, -nū′-, te-) *n.* state of being thin, insubstantial, or rarefied; tenuous condition.

ten·u·ous (ten′ū əs) *adj.* **1.** having a thin, slender, or delicate form, as a thread. **2.** having little strength, substance, or significance; weak; flimsy: *a tenuous argument, a tenuous claim to the inheritance.* **3.** not dense, as air at high altitudes; rare. [Latin *tenuis* thin, fine + -OUS.] —**ten′u·ous·ly,** *adv.* —**ten′u·ous·ness,** *n.*

ten·ure (ten′yər) *n.* **1.** act or right of holding or possessing something, as property, a title, or office. **2.** length of time during which something is held: *The tenure of the presidency is four years.* **b.** conditions or terms under which something is held. **3.** status assuring an employee, as a teacher or civil servant, of holding his position permanently, acquired after specified requirements are fulfilled. [Old French *tenure* a holding, possession, condition under which one holds a fief, going back to Latin *tenēre* to hold.]

te·nu·to (tā nōō′tō, tə-) *adj. Music.* held or sustained for its full time value. [Italian *tenuto* held, past participle of *tenere* to hold, from Latin *tenēre.*]

te·pee (tē′pē) *also,* **tee·pee.** *n.* cone-shaped tent, usually of animal skins, used by North American Indians, esp. the Plains Indians. [Dakota *tipi,* from *ti* to dwell + *pi* for use.]

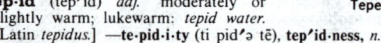
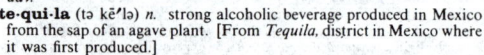

Tepee

tep·id (tep′id) *adj.* moderately or slightly warm; lukewarm: *tepid water.* [Latin *tepidus.*] —**te·pid·i·ty** (ti pid′ə tē), **tep′id·ness,** *n.* —**tep′id·ly,** *adv.*

te·qui·la (tə kē′lə) *n.* strong alcoholic beverage produced in Mexico from the sap of an agave plant. [From *Tequila,* district in Mexico where it was first produced.]

ter. **1.** terrace. **2.** territory.

tera- combining form one trillion: *teravolt.* [Greek *teras* marvel, monster.]

ter·a·tol·o·gy (ter′ə tol′ə jē) *n.* scientific study of monstrosities or abnormal formations in animals or plants. [Greek *terat-,* stem of *teras* marvel, monster + -LOGY.]

ter·bi·um (tur′bē əm) *n.* very soft, silver-gray, metallic rare-earth element, used as a laser material. Symbol: **Tb** See **element** for table. [From *(Yt)terb(y),* Swedish town where it was discovered.]

ter·cel (tur′səl) *n.* male falcon, esp. the male of the peregrine falcon. [Old French *tercel,* going back to Latin *tertius* third; with reference to the belief that every third egg laid by a hawk produced a male.]

ter·cen·te·nar·y (tur′sen ten′ər ē, tər sent′ən er′ē) *pl.,* **-nar·ies.** *n.* a 300th anniversary or its celebration. —*adj.* of or relating to a period of 300 years. [Latin *ter* three times + CENTENARY.]

ter·cet (tur′sit) *n.* group of three lines of verse that rhyme together or are connected by rhyme with the adjacent group or groups of lines. [French *tercet,* from Italian *terzetto,* diminutive of *terzo* third, from Latin *tertius.*]

te·re·do (tə rē′dō) *pl.,* **-dos.** *n.* shipworm.

Ter·ence (ter′əns) *n.* c.190–c.159 B.C., Roman playwright.

Te·re·sa (tə rē′sə, -zə, tə rā′-) see **Theresa, Saint.**

ter·gal (tur′gəl) *adj.* of or relating to the tergum; dorsal.

ter·gi·ver·sate (tur′jə vər sāt′) **-sat·ed, -sat·ing.** *v.i.* **1.** to change one's beliefs about or become a renegade to a cause or political party. **2.** to be evasive; use subterfuge; equivocate. [Latin *tergiversātus,* past participle of *tergiversārī* to turn one's back, shift, evade, going back to *tergum* back + *vertere* to turn.] —**ter′gi·ver·sa′tion, ter′gi·ver·sa′tor,** *n.*

ter·gum (tur′gəm) *pl.,* **-ga** (-gə). *n.* back of an animal, esp. the dorsal surface of the body of an arthropod. [Latin *tergum* the back.]

ter·i·ya·ki (ter′ē yä′kē) *n.* Japanese dish consisting of cubes of meat or fish marinated or dipped in soy sauce and then broiled, grilled, or barbecued, usually on skewers. [Japanese *teriyaki,* from *teri* sunshine + *yaki* broiling.]

term (turm) *n.* **1.** word or phrase having a precise meaning in some particular field: *legal terms, scientific terms.* **2.** any word or phrase used in a precise sense: *"Darling" is a term of endearment.* **3. terms.** particu-

lar manner of speaking or type of language used: *He answered the question in vague terms.* **4.** definite or limited period of time; time during which a thing lasts: *the term of a lease, a term of office.* **5.** division of a school year: *the spring term.* **6.** *Law.* period of time during which a court of law is in session. **7. terms.** relationship between or among people: *to be on good terms with someone.* **8. terms.** conditions or stipulations according to which something is to be done: *terms of surrender, the terms of a treaty.* **9.** *Mathematics.* **a.** each of the quantities that composes a fraction or ratio or forms a series or progression. **b.** each of the quantities connected by plus or minus signs in an algebraic expression. **10.** *Logic.* **a.** either the subject or predicate of a proposition. **b.** one of the three elements of a syllogism, each of which appears twice. **11.** *Archaic.* boundary; limit; end. **12. to bring to terms.** to cause to agree, esp. by force. **13. to come to terms.** to reach an agreement: *The two sides came to terms and the strike was ended.* **14. in terms of.** with regard to; in relation to; considering: *Applicants for the typist's job will be judged in terms of accuracy as well as speed.* —*v.t.* to apply a particular term to; name; designate: *The governor can be termed a conservative in economic matters.* [Old French *terme* limit, date, word, going back to Latin *terminus* boundary line, end. Doublet of TERMINUS.]

ter·ma·gant (tur′mə gənt) *n.* boisterous, quarrelsome, scolding woman; shrew. —*adj.* having the characteristics of a termagant; quarrelsome; shrewish. [From Old French *Tervagan* a supposed Muslim divinity who was represented in medieval plays as violent; of uncertain origin.]

ter·mi·na·ble (tur′mə nə bəl) *adj.* **1.** that can be terminated; not perpetual: *a terminable contract.* **2.** terminating after a certain time: *a terminable annuity.* —**ter′mi·na·bil′i·ty, ter′mi·na·ble·ness,** *n.* —**ter′mi·na·bly,** *adv.*

ter·mi·nal (tur′mən əl) *adj.* **1.** situated at or forming the end, end part, or boundary of something. **2.** *Botany.* growing at the end of a stem or branch: *a terminal bud.* **3.** coming or occurring at the end of a series; concluding; closing: *the terminal payment on a loan.* **4.** of or relating to a term; occurring in each term: *terminal examinations.* **5.** relating to or in the final state of a fatal disease: *terminal cancer, a terminal patient.* **6.** relating to, situated at, or forming the end of a railroad or other transportation line. —*n.* **1.** that which terminates; terminal part or structure; extremity; end. **2.a.** point on an electric circuit where a connection can be made. **b.** device making such a connection. **3.a.** either end of a railroad, bus, air, or other transportation line. **b.** city or station located at such a point. **c.** any station on a transportation line, esp. one that is centrally located or serves as a junction with other lines. **4.** ornamental figure or object, as a carving, situated at the end of a structure. [Latin *terminālis* relating to a boundary or end, from *terminus* boundary line, end.] —**ter′mi·nal·ly,** *adv.*

terminal leave, leave of absence granted to a member of the armed forces immediately before his discharge, equal to the amount of unused leave time he has accumulated.

ter·mi·nate (tur′mə nāt′) -nat·ed, -nat·ing. *v.t.* **1.** to bring to end; put an end to: *to terminate a marriage by divorce.* **2.** to come at the end; form the conclusion of: *A prayer terminated the services.* **3.** to form or be situated at the boundary of; bound; limit. —*v.i.* **1.** to come to an end: *The show terminated at eleven o'clock.* **2.** to have a specified end or result (usually with *in*): *The game terminated in a victory for the home team.* [Latin *terminātus,* past participle of *termināre* to limit.] —**Syn.** *v.t.* **2.** see **end.**

ter·mi·na·tion (tur′mə nā′shən) *n.* **1.** act of terminating; being terminated. **2.** end of something in space or time; limit or conclusion. **3.** outcome; result. **4.** end of a word, as a suffix or inflectional ending.

ter·mi·na·tor (tur′mə nā′tər) *n.* **1.** one who or that which terminates. **2.** line separating the illuminated and dark portions of the disk of a planet or the moon.

ter·mi·nol·o·gy (tur′mə nol′ə jē) *pl.,* **-gies.** *n.* terms or system of terms used in an art, science, trade, or other specialized subject: *legal terminology, the terminology of chemistry.* [German *Terminologie,* from Medieval Latin *terminus* definition, expression (from Latin *terminus* end) + Greek *-logiā* (see -LOGY). See TERM.] —**ter′mi·no·log′i·cal** (tur′mə nə loj′i kəl), *adj.* —**ter′mi·no·log′i·cal·ly,** *adv.*

term insurance, life insurance that expires at the end of a specified period of time.

ter·mi·nus (tur′mə nəs) *pl.,* **-ni** (-nī′) or **-nus·es.** *n.* **1.** point or place at which something comes to an end; end or goal. **2.a.** either end of a railroad, bus, air, or other transportation line. **b.** city or station at such a point. **3.a.** boundary, border, or limit. **b.** stone, post, or other object used to indicate a boundary or limit. [Latin *terminus* boundary line, end. Doublet of TERM.]

Ter·mi·nus (tur′mə nəs) *n.* Roman god who presided over boundaries and landmarks.

ter·mite (tur′mīt′) *n.* any of a group of social insects, order Isoptera, found in temperate and tropical regions, having a whitish body and dark

head. Termites feed on wood, paper, and other organic material, causing great damage to buildings, furniture, and some crops. Also, **white ant.** [Modern Latin *termit-,* stem of *termes,* from Latin *termes* woodworm.]

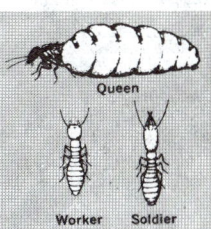

Queen

Worker Soldier

Termites

term paper, long report, essay, or other written assignment required of a student during a school or college term.

tern (turn) *n.* any of various web-footed sea birds, family Laridae, closely related to gulls, having a slender body, narrow wings, a deeply forked tail, and, usually, white and gray plumage with a black patch on the head. Length: 8–23 inches. [Of Scandinavian origin.]

ter·na·ry (tur′nər ē) *adj.* **1.** consisting of or relating to three; grouped in threes. **2.** *Chemistry.* relating to or containing three different elements, atoms, radicals, or groups: *a ternary acid.* **3.** third in rank, order, or position. [Latin *ternārius* consisting of three, going back to *ter* three times.]

ter·nate (tur′nāt, -nit) *adj.* consisting of or arranged in groups of three, as a compound leaf composed of three leaflets. [Modern Latin *ternatus,* going back to Latin *ter* three times.]

Terp·sich·o·re (turp sik′ər ē) *n. Greek Mythology.* Muse of dancing and choral song.

terp·si·cho·re·an (turp′si kə rē′ən, -si kôr′ē ən) *adj.* relating to dancing.

Tern

terr. **1.** terrace. **2.** territory.

ter·race (ter′is) *n.* **1.** open platform extending from a floor of a house or apartment building; balcony. **2.** open, usually paved or tiled area adjacent to a house, used esp. for lounging, outdoor cooking or dining, and parties. **3.** raised, level platform of earth with a vertical or sloping front or side, usually covered with masonry, turf, or the like, esp. one of a series of such levels placed one above the other. **4.** relatively level strip of land extending along the margin of a sea, lake, or river and descending abruptly on the side toward the water. **5.a.** group of houses or apartments built on a raised or sloping area of land. **b.** street on which such a row of houses or apartments faces. ▲ often used in the names of streets. **6.** parklike strip of land in the middle of a street. **7.** flat roof of a house, esp. an Oriental or Spanish house. —*v.t.,* **-raced, -rac·ing.** to form into or provide with a terrace or terraces: *to terrace a hillside.* [Middle French *terrace* platform, pile of earth, going back to Latin *terra* earth.]

ter·ra cot·ta (ter′ə kot′ə) **1.** hard, durable, brownish-orange earthenware used esp. for vases, statuettes, or as a facing for buildings. **2.** object made of this substance: *an exhibition of terra cottas.* **3.** brownish-orange color. [Italian *terra cotta* earthenware; literally, baked earth, from Latin *terra* earth + *cocta,* feminine past participle of *coquere* to cook.]

ter·ra fir·ma (ter′ə fur′mə) solid ground; dry land. [Latin *terra firma* solid land.]

ter·rain (tə rān′, te-) *n.* **1.** region or tract of land, esp. with regard to its natural features or suitability for some special purpose, as use in warfare: *hilly terrain, rocky terrain.* **2.** *Geology.* terrane. [French *terrain* ground, earth, site, going back to Latin *terrēnum* land, from *terra* land, earth.]

ter·ra in·cog·ni·ta (ter′ə in′kog nē′tə, in kog′ni tə) unknown or unexplored region or field of knowledge. [Latin *terra incognita* unknown land.]

Ter·ra·my·cin (ter′ə mī′sin) *n. Trademark.* antibiotic derived from a microorganism found in the soil, effective against a large number of disease-causing bacteria and some viruses. [Latin *terra* earth + Greek *mykēs* fungus + -IN¹.]

ter·rane (tə rān′, te-) *n. Geology.* rock formation or series of related formations. [Form of TERRAIN.]

ter·ra·pin (ter′ə pin′) *n.* any of a group of edible North American turtles, family Emydidae, found in fresh and brackish waters, esp. the diamondback. [Modification of Algonquian *torope* little turtle.]

ter·rar·i·um (tə râr′ē əm) *pl.,* **-i·ums** or **-i·a** (-ē ə). *n.* small enclosure or container, esp. a glass case, for growing plants or raising small land-dwelling animals, as snakes, turtles, or lizards. [Modern Latin *terrarium,* from Latin *terra* land (on the model of AQUARIUM).]

ter·raz·zo (te raz′ō, -rät′sō) *n.* mosaic flooring usually consisting of small chips of marble or colored stone set in plain or colored cement. [Italian *terrazzo* mosaic floor, balcony, going back to Latin *terra* earth.]

at; āpe; cär; end; mē; it; īce; hot; ōld; fôrk; wood; fōōl; oil; out; up; ūse; turn; sing; thin; <u>th</u>is; zh in treasure; ə in ago, taken, pencil, lemon, circus.   1029

Ter·re Haute (terʹə hōtʹ) city in western Indiana. Pop. (1970), 70,286.

ter·res·tri·al (tə resʹtrē əl) *adj.* **1.** of, relating to, or representing the earth: *a terrestrial globe, terrestrial magnetism.* **2.** relating to or consisting of land, as distinct from water or air. **3.** growing in the ground or land: *a terrestrial plant.* **4.** living on land, rather than in the air, water, or trees: *The deer is a terrestrial animal.* **5.** of or relating to this world; worldly; earthly; mundane. —*n.* inhabitant of the earth. [Latin *terrestris* earthly, relating to the earth (from *terra* earth) + -AL¹.] —**ter·resʹtri·al·ly,** *adv.*

ter·ret (terʹit) *n.* one of the rings on a harness through which the reins pass. [Old French *toret* small wheel, diminutive of *tour* a turn, circuit, lathe, from Latin *tornus* lathe. See TOUR.]

ter·ri·ble (terʹə bəl) *adj.* **1.** causing terror or awe; dreadful; awful: *The volcano erupted with a terrible roar.* **2.** extremely violent or severe; causing great distress or pain: *a terrible automobile accident, the terrible effects of the bombing.* **3.** *Informal.* inferior or poor in quality; very bad or unpleasant: *a terrible performance, terrible food.* **4.** *Informal.* very great; excessive: *a terrible bore.* [Latin *terribilis* frightful, from *terrēre* to frighten.] —**terʹri·bly,** *adv.* —**terʹri·ble·ness,** *n.*

ter·ri·er (terʹē ər) *n.* any of various lively, rugged, usually small dogs with a coat that ranges from smooth and short to wiry and fairly long, as the fox terrier or Scottish terrier. Terriers were originally used to hunt animals that burrow in the ground, but are now kept chiefly as pets. Height: 9–23 inches at the shoulder. [French *terrier,* from *terrier* burrow, from *terre* earth, from Latin *terra*.]

Terrier (fox terrier)

ter·rif·ic (tə rifʹik) *adj.* **1.** causing great fear or dread; terrifying; dreadful. **2.** *Informal.* unusually great, intense, or severe: *a terrific pain, a terrific hardship.* **3.** *Slang.* extremely good; excellent; wonderful: *a terrific singer. I have a terrific idea.* [Latin *terrificus* frightful, from *terrēre* to frighten + *ficus.* See -FIC.] —**ter·rifʹi·cal·ly,** *adv.*

ter·ri·fy (terʹə fīʹ) -**fied,** -**fy·ing.** *v.t.* to fill with terror; frighten or alarm greatly. [Latin *terrificāre* to frighten.] —**terʹri·fyʹing·ly,** *adv.*

ter·ri·to·ri·al (terʹə tôrʹē əl) *adj.* **1.** of, relating to, or belonging to land or territory: *territorial acquisitions, territorial laws.* **2.** relating to or restricted to a particular district or region: *He has territorial rights to drill for oil in this county.* **3.** relating to a territory of the United States. **4.** *also,* **Territorial.** organized in regional groups for home defense: *the British Territorial Army.* —*n. also,* **Territorial.** member of a territorial military force. —**terʹri·toʹri·al·ly,** *adv.*

ter·ri·to·ri·al·ism (terʹə tôrʹē ə lizʹəm) *n.* social system giving predominance in a state to the landowners. —**terʹri·toʹri·al·ist,** *n.*

ter·ri·to·ri·al·i·ty (terʹə tôrʹē alʹə tē) *n.* quality, condition, or status of being a territory.

ter·ri·to·ri·al·ize (terʹə tôrʹē ə līzʹ) -**ized,** -**iz·ing.** *v.t.* **1.** to reduce to the status of a territory; establish as a territory; make territorial. **2.** to enlarge by adding territory to. —**terʹri·toʹri·al·i·zaʹtion,** *n.*

territorial waters, coastal and inland waters under the jurisdiction of a state or nation, esp. ocean waters within three miles of shore.

ter·ri·to·ry (terʹə tôrʹē) *pl.,* -**ries.** *n.* **1.** any large tract of land of unspecified boundaries; region; area: *unexplored territory, territory held by the enemy.* **2.** land and waters under the jurisdiction of a state, nation, or ruler: *The Yukon is a territory of Canada.* **3.a.** formerly, part of the United States not having the status of a state and usually administered by an appointed governor, but having its own legislature. **b.** any region with a similar status, as in Canada or Australia. **4.** assigned district or area, as of a salesman or agent. **5.** field or sphere of action, thought, or interest: *His scientific investigations cover a wide territory.* **6.** particular area inhabited by an animal or pair or group of animals, usually used for nesting, breeding, and foraging, and defended against intruders of the same species. [Latin *territōrium* domain, district, from *terra* land.]

ter·ror (terʹər) *n.* **1.** overpowering or intense fear. **2.** one who or that which causes intense fear: *The cruel dictator was a terror to the oppressed citizens.* **3.** party, group, or program employing terrorism. **4.** *Informal.* annoying or troublesome person or thing, esp. a mischievous child. ▲ used esp. in the phrase *a holy terror.* [Latin *terror* dread, great fear, from *terrēre* to frighten.]

Syn. 1. Terror, panic mean extreme fear. **Terror** is caused by the awareness of imminent great danger and is so stark and intense that it may paralyze the body and mind: *The villagers stared in helpless terror as the tornado approached.* **Panic** is a sudden and overwhelming wave of fear that may lead to hysterical confusion or irrational activity: *Abandoning his post, the soldier fled in panic down the rough hillside.*

ter·ror·ism (terʹə rizʹəm) *n.* **1.** act of terrorizing; use of terror, violence, or intimidation. **2.** state of fear and subjugation produced by this. **3.** use of violent and terrifying actions for political purposes, as by a government to intimidate the population or by an insurgent group to oppose the government in power.

ter·ror·ist (terʹər ist) *n.* one who advocates or uses terrorism. —*adj.* relating to or characteristic of terrorism or terrorists: *terrorist methods.* Also, **terʹror·isʹtic.**

ter·ror·ize (terʹə rīzʹ) -**ized,** -**iz·ing.** *v.t.* **1.** to fill with extreme fear; overcome with terror: *The brutal outlaw gang terrorized the countryside.* **2.** to control, dominate, or coerce through the use of terror. —**terʹror·i·zaʹtion,** *n.*

ter·ry (terʹē) *pl.,* -**ries.** *n.* **1.** uncut loop forming the pile of a fabric. **2.** pile fabric having uncut loops on both sides, esp. a highly absorbent cotton cloth used chiefly for towels and robes. Also *(def. 2),* **terry cloth.** [Of uncertain origin.]

terse (turs) **ters·er, ters·est.** *adj.* having no superfluous words; brief and effective; concise; succinct: *a terse summary, a terse editorial.* [Latin *tersus* clean, neat, past participle of *tergēre* to wipe, polish.] —**terseʹly,** *adv.* —**terseʹness,** *n.* —**Syn.** see **concise.**

ter·tial (turʹshəl) *adj.* relating to or designating the flight feathers on the basal part of a bird's wing. —*n.* tertial feather. [Latin *tertius* third + -AL¹; because these feathers form the *third* row of a bird's flight feathers.]

ter·tian (turʹshən) *adj.* recurring every other day, or every three days when counting from each day of occurrence. A tertian fever occurs once in 48 hours. —*n.* tertian fever or ague, esp. a tertian malaria. [Latin *tertiāna* the fever, from *tertius* third.]

ter·ti·ar·y (turʹshē erʹē) *pl.,* -**ar·ies.** *n.* **1. Tertiary.** first geological period of the Cenozoic era, during which high mountain systems, as the Alps, Rockies, and Himalayas, were formed and modern mammals and plants appeared. See geology for table. **2.** tertial feather. **3.** member of the third order of a religious body. —*adj.* **1.** third in rank, order, degree, importance, or value. **2. Tertiary.** of, relating to, or characteristic of the Tertiary period. **3.** tertial. **4.** relating to the Third Order of a religious body. **5.** relating to or designating an accent that is weaker than a secondary accent. **6.** *Chemistry.* **a.** resulting from the substitution of three atoms or groups. **b.** relating to a carbon atom joined to three other carbon atoms in a chain or ring. [Latin *tertiārius* containing a third part, from *tertius* third.]

ter·za ri·ma (terʹtsə rēʹmə) form of iambic verse in which each line has ten or eleven syllables. The lines are arranged in tercets and the middle line of each tercet rhymes with the first and third lines of the following tercet. The form was first used by medieval Italian poets. [Italian *terza rima,* from *terza,* feminine of *terzo* third (from Latin *tertius*) + *rima* verse, rhyme (of Germanic origin).]

Tes·la, Ni·ko·la (tesʹlə; nikʹō lə) 1856–1943, U.S. electrical engineer and inventor, born in Croatia.

tes·sel·late (*v.,* tesʹə lātʹ; *adj.,* tesʹə lit, -lātʹ) -**lat·ed, -lat·ing.** *v.t.* **1.** to form of small squares or cubes; form or arrange in a mosaic or checkered pattern, as a floor. —*adj.* arranged in a mosaic or checkered pattern; tessellated. [Latin *tessellātus* of small square stones, checkered, going back to *tessera* square piece of stone or wood. See TESSERA.] —**tesʹsel·laʹtion,** *n.*

Tessellate table top

tes·ser·a (tesʹər ə) *pl.,* **tes·ser·ae** (tesʹər ē). *n.* **1.** small, usually square piece of marble, stone, glass, or similar material, used in mosaic work. **2.** small tablet, esp. of bone, wood, or ivory, used in ancient Rome as a token, tally, label, or ticket. [Latin *tessera* square piece of stone or wood, possibly from dialectal Greek *tessera,* neuter of *tesseres* four.]

test¹ (test) *n.* **1.** set of questions, problems, or exercises intended to determine a person's knowledge, aptitude, skill, or intelligence: *a spelling test, a history test.* **2.** any method, process, or means of determining the nature or quality of something: *a hearing test, a blood test, a swimming test.* **3.** that by which the quality or genuineness of something is tried: *Their friendship has withstood the test of time.* **4.** particular means of evaluation or judgment; standard; criterion. **5.** *Chemistry.* **a.** procedure for detecting the presence of an ingredient in a substance or determining the nature of a substance: *a test for carbon dioxide.* **b.** substance employed in such a procedure: *Litmus is the test for the presence of acid.* **6.** vessel formerly used in assaying or refining precious metals. —*v.t.* **1.** to subject to a test of any kind; administer a test to; try: *to test a class, to test a car, to test a person's loyalty.* **2.** to subject to a chemical test. —*v.i.* **1.** to undergo or give a test (usually with *for*): *to test for a job, to test for acidity.* **2.** to exhibit specified tendencies or qualities under testing (often with *out*): *That boy tests out as almost a genius.* [Middle English *test* vessel used to assay metals, from Old French *test* pot, from Latin *testum* pot, earthen vessel.] —**testʹa·ble,** *adj.*

at; āpe; cär; end; mē; it; īce; hot; ōld; fôrk; wood; fōōl; oil; out; up; ūse; turn; sing; thin; this; zh in treasure; ə in ago, taken, pencil, lemon, circus.

test² (test) *n.* hard outer covering of certain invertebrate animals, as the shell of certain mollusks. [Latin *testa* shell.]

Test., Testament.

tes·ta (tes′tə) *pl.,* **-tae** (-tē). *n.* hard outer covering of a seed. [Latin *testa* covering, shell.]

tes·ta·ceous (tes tā′shəs) *adj.* **1.** of the nature or substance of a shell or shells. **2.** having a shell, esp. a hard shell: *a testaceous animal.* **3.** having a dull reddish-brown or yellowish-brown color. [Latin *testāceus* covered with a shell, from *testa* shell.]

tes·ta·cy (tes′tə sē) *n.* condition of being testate.

tes·ta·ment (tes′tə mənt) *n.* **1.** will, esp. one disposing of personal property. ▲ now used chiefly in the phrase *last will and testament.* **2.** in the Bible, a covenant between God and man. **3. Testament. a.** either of the two main divisions of the Bible; Old Testament or New Testament. **b.** New Testament or a volume containing it. **4.** statement of beliefs or principles; creed. **5.** evidence or proof of the existence, validity, or quality of something: *That magnificent cathedral is a testament to Christopher Wren's greatness as an architect.* [Church Latin *testāmentum* Scripture, from Latin *testāmentum* last will, from *testārī* to be a witness, make a will.]

tes·ta·men·ta·ry (tes′tə men′tər ē, -men′trē) *adj.* **1.** relating to a will or the administration or settlement of a will. **2.** given by or contained in a will: *in compliance with his testamentary directions* (Hawthorne, 1851). **3.** done in accordance with a will.

tes·tate (tes′tāt) *adj.* having made a legally valid will before death. [Latin *testātus,* past participle of *testārī* to make a will, be a witness.]

tes·ta·tor (tes′tā′tər, tes tā′-) *n.* one who has died and left a legally valid will.

tes·ta·trix (tes tā′triks) *pl.,* **tes·ta·tri·ces** (tes tā′tri sēz, tes′tə-trī′sēz). *n.* woman testator.

test ban, agreement among nations not to engage in the testing of nuclear weapons, esp. in the atmosphere.

test case **1.** legal case whose outcome is likely to be used as a precedent. **2.** case entered into for the purpose of testing the constitutionality of a particular law.

test·er¹ (tes′tər) *n.* one who or that which tests. [TEST + -ER¹.]

tes·ter² (tes′tər) *n.* canopy, esp. one over a bed or pulpit. [Medieval Latin *testrum* canopy of a bed, going back to Latin *testa* shell, covering.]

tes·tes (tes′tēz) plural of **testis.**

tes·ti·cle (tes′ti kəl) *n.* one of the pair of male reproductive glands in man and most other mammals, producing sperm and male sex hormones and usually enclosed in the scrotum. [Latin *testiculus,* diminutive of *testis* testicle, from *testa* shell (of virility).]

tes·ti·fy (tes′tə fī′) **-fied, -fy·ing.** *v.i.* **1.** to give evidence under oath in a court of law: *He testified for the defense.* **2.** to serve as evidence; be proof: *The stolen goods in his home testified to his guilt.* **3.** to bear witness, esp. for the purpose of establishing some truth or fact: *I can testify to that.* —*v.t.* **1.** to declare under oath in a court of law: *He testified that the defendant was innocent.* **2.** to affirm as fact or truth; declare solemnly. **3.** to give evidence of; demonstrate; show: *His pallor testifies his poor health.* **4.** to make known publicly; declare openly. [Latin *testificārī* to bear witness, from *testis* witness + *facere* to make.] —**tes′ti·fi′er,** *n.*

tes·ti·mo·ni·al (tes′tə mō′nē əl) *n.* **1.** affirmation of the superior character or quality of someone or something; letter or statement of recommendation: *Many actors are now giving testimonials for various products.* **2.** something given or done to express respect, admiration, or appreciation: *The retiring employee was given a watch as a testimonial for his years of service.* —*adj.* relating to or constituting a testimonial: *a testimonial dinner, a testimonial gift.*

tes·ti·mo·ny (tes′tə mō′nē) *pl.,* **-nies.** *n.* **1.** oral statement or declaration made under oath by a witness in a court of law, usually in response to questioning by a lawyer. **2.** proof or demonstration; evidence: *Her trembling hands were testimony of her nervousness.* **3.** open declaration or attestation, esp. of one's faith or of a religious experience. **4.** in the Bible, the Ten Commandments, esp. in their original form on two stone tablets. **5. testimonies.** precepts or laws of God, esp. the Scriptures. [Latin *testimōnium* evidence, from *testis* witness.] —**Syn. 1.** see **evidence.**

tes·tis (tes′tis) *pl.,* **-tes.** *n.* testicle. [Latin *testis* testicle, witness (as of virility).]

tes·tos·ter·one (tes tos′tə rōn′) *n.* **1.** sex hormone produced by the testes, that controls the growth of the male reproductive system and stimulates the development of the male secondary sexual characteristics, as the growth of the beard. **2.** this hormone obtained from bulls' testicles or produced synthetically, used in medicine to treat certain deficiencies and diseases.

test paper **1.** paper on which a person taking a test has written his answers. **2.** paper saturated with a reagent, esp. litmus, and used in making chemical tests.

test pattern, fixed picture, usually a special design of lines and circles

broadcast by a television station for testing purposes or for a set time before regular programming begins.

test pilot, pilot who tests new or experimental aircraft.

test tube, thin transparent glass tube closed and rounded at the bottom, used esp. in chemical and biological experiments.

tes·tu·do (tes tōō′dō, -tū′-) *pl.,* **-di·nes** (-di nēz′). *n.* **1.** portable shelter with a strong, arched roof, used by the ancient Romans to protect a force besieging a stronghold. **2.** shelter formed by a body of troops locking their shields together above their heads. [Latin *testūdō* tortoise, tortoise shell, ancient Roman military shelter.]

tes·ty (tes′tē) **-ti·er, -ti·est.** *adj.* showing or characterized by irritability, impatience, or crossness; peevish; touchy: *a testy answer, a testy old man.* [Anglo-Norman *testif* headstrong, from Old French *teste* head, from Late Latin *testa* skull, from Latin *testa* shell.] —**tes′ti·ly,** *adv.* —**tes′ti·ness,** *n.*

Tet (tet) *n.* lunar new year as celebrated in southeastern Asia, esp. Vietnam. [Vietnamese *tet;* of Chinese origin.]

te·tan·ic (te tan′ik) *adj.* relating to or characterized by tetanus.

tet·a·nize (tet′ən īz′) **-nized, -niz·ing.** *v.t.* to cause (a muscle) to have tetanic spasms; produce tetanus in.

tet·a·nus (tet′ən əs) *n.* acute, often fatal infectious disease caused by the toxin of a certain bacillus that usually enters the body through a wound, as a nail puncture. Tetanus is characterized by violent spasms and stiffness of the voluntary muscles, esp. those of the neck and jaw. Also, **lock′jaw′.** [Latin *tetanus* spasm of the neck, from Greek *tetanos* convulsive spasm.]

tet·a·ny (tet′ən ē) *n.* disorder characterized by periodic painful spasms of the muscles, usually caused by a deficiency in calcium salts. [From TETANUS.]

tetch·y (tech′ē) **tetch·i·er, tetch·i·est.** *also,* **tech·y.** *adj.* irritable; peevish; touchy. [Possibly from obsolete *teche* blemish, fault (from Old French *teche;* probably of Germanic origin) + -Y¹.] —**tetch′i·ly,** *adv.* —**tetch′i·ness,** *n.*

tête-à-tête (tāt′ə tāt′, -ə tāt′) *n.* **1.** private or intimate conversation between two people. **2.** S-shaped sofa or seat on which two people can sit facing each other. —*adv.* (of two people) face to face; together in private: *to dine tête-à-tête.* —*adj.* for or between two people only; private; intimate. [French *tête-à-tête* private conversation between two people; literally, head to head, from *tête* head, from Old French *teste.* See TESTY.]

teth·er (teth′ər) *n.* **1.** rope or chain used to fasten a horse, donkey, or other animal so that it is confined within certain limits. **2.** range of one's strength, ability, or resources. **3. at the end of one's tether.** at the extreme end or limit of one's resources, patience, or endurance. —*v.t.* to fasten or confine with or as with a tether. [Probably from Old Norse *tjóthr* fetter for a animal.]

teth·er·ball (teth′ər bôl′) *n.* game played by two people with a ball hanging from a cord fastened to the top of a pole. The object of each player is to strike the ball so as to wind the cord completely around the pole.

tet·ra (tet′rə) *pl.,* **-ras** or **-ra.** *n.* any of several small, brightly colored tropical fish of the family Characidae, often kept in aquariums.

tetra- *combining form* four: *tetrachord.* [Greek *tetra-,* combining form of *tettares* four.]

tet·ra·chlo·ride (tet′rə klôr′īd) *n.* chloride containing four atoms of chlorine in each molecule.

tet·ra·chord (tet′rə kôrd′) *n.* *Music.* series of four consecutive tones of the diatonic scale, having an interval of a fourth between the first and the last. [Greek *tetrachordon* scale of four notes, from *tetra-* (see TETRA-) + *chordē* string.]

tet·ra·cy·cline (tet′rə sī′klēn) *n.* yellow crystalline antibiotic used in treating a wide variety of diseases. Formula: $C_{22}H_{24}N_2O_8$

tet·rad (tet′rad) *n.* **1.** group or set of four. **2.** *Chemistry.* atom, element, or radical having a valence of four. [Greek *tetrad-,* stem of *tetras* group of four.]

tet·ra·eth·yl lead (tet′rə eth′əl led′) heavy, colorless, poisonous flammable liquid added to gasoline to reduce engine knock. Formula: $Pb(C_2H_5)_4$

tet·ra·he·dral (tet′rə hē′drəl) *adj.* relating to or having the form of a tetrahedron; having four sides.

tet·ra·he·dron (tet′rə hē′drən) *pl.,* **-drons** or **-dra** (-drə). *n.* solid figure with four faces, esp. one with four plane triangular faces. [TETRA- + Greek *hedra* seat, base; on the model of Late Greek *tetraedron,* neuter of *tetraedros* having four sides.]

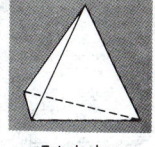

Tetrahedron

te·tral·o·gy (te trol′ə jē, -tral′-) *pl.,* **-gies.** *n.* series of four related artistic works, as plays, operas, or novels. [Greek *tetralogiā* group of four dramas, from *tetra-* (see TETRA-) + *-logiā.* See -LOGY.]

te·tram·e·ter (te tram′ə tər) *n.* **1.** line of verse containing four metrical feet. **2.** verse consisting of such lines. —*adj.* consisting of four metrical feet. [Latin *tetrametrus*, from Greek *tetrametros* having four measures.]

tet·rarch (tet′rärk′, tēt′-) *n.* **1.** governor of a part, esp. a fourth part, of a province in the ancient Roman Empire. **2.** subordinate ruler, esp. a ruler of a fourth part. [Late Latin *tetrarcha*, from Greek *tetrarchēs*, from *tetra-* (see TETRA-) + *archos* ruler.]

tet·rar·chy (tet′rär′kē, tēt′-) *pl.,* **-chies.** *n.* **1.** government, territory, or jurisdiction of a tetrarch. **2.** government by a group of four. **3.** group of four rulers.

tet·ra·va·lent (tet′rə vā′lənt) *adj.* having a valence of four.

tet·rode (tet′rōd) *n.* electron tube containing four electrodes.

te·trox·ide (te trok′sīd, -sid) *n.* oxide containing four atoms of oxygen in each molecule.

tet·ter (tet′ər) *n.* any of several skin diseases characterized by itching and eruptions, as eczema, psoriasis, and shingles. [Old English *teter.*]

Te·tuan (tā twän′) *n.* port city on the northern coast of Morocco. Pop. (1969), 120,000.

Teu·ton (tōōt′ən, tūt′-) *n.* **1.** member of an ancient tribe, probably of Germanic stock, that inhabited parts of what is now northern Germany. **2.** member of any of several groups of northern European peoples, including the Germans, Dutch, Scandinavians, and English. **3.** native of Germany or person of German descent; German.

Teu·ton·ic (tōō ton′ik, tū-) *adj.* **1.** of or relating to the ancient Teutons. **2.** of or relating to any of the Teutons, their languages, or their cultures. **3.** German or Germanic. —*n.* Germanic.

Tex., Texas.

Tex·ar·kan·a (tek′sär kan′ə) *n.* twin cities with separate municipal governments, one in northeastern Texas, the other in southwestern Arkansas. Pop. (1970), Texas, 30,497; Arkansas, 21,682.

tex·as (tek′səs) *n.* structure on the upper deck of a river steamboat, where the pilothouse and officers' cabins are located. [From TEXAS; because the cabins on Mississippi steamboats were named after the different states, and the officers' cabins were the largest.]

Tex·as (tek′səs) *n.* state in the south-central United States, bordering Mexico and the Gulf of Mexico. Capital, Austin. Area, 267,339 sq. mi. Pop. (1970), 11,196,730. Abbreviation, Tex. —Tex′an, *adj., n.*

Texas fever, infectious disease of cattle caused by a protozoan parasite in the red blood cells and transmitted by ticks.

Texas leaguer *Baseball.* short fly ball that falls beyond the infielders and in front of the outfielders for a base hit. [From *Texas League,* a minor baseball league.]

Texas Ranger, member of a mounted police force of the state of Texas, originally a small band of mounted riflemen organized to fight Indians and maintain order on the frontier.

Texas tower, offshore platform supported by pilings sunk into the ocean floor, used esp. as a radar station. [From its resemblance to structures used for drilling oil off the coast of *Texas.*]

text (tekst) *n.* **1.** main body of matter on a written or printed page, as distinguished from headings, illustrations, notes, or appendixes. **2.** any of the various forms or versions in which a written work exists. **3.** original or actual words of a writer or speaker, as opposed to a revision, condensation, or translation. **4.** short passage or verse of Scripture, quoted in support of a doctrine or used as the subject of a sermon. **5.** any subject on which one writes or speaks; theme; topic. **6.** textbook. [Medieval Latin *textus* Gospel, passage, wording, from Latin *textus* texture, style (of an author), context, from *texere* to weave.]

text·book (tekst′book′) *n.* book used in the study of a particular subject, esp. one used as a basis of instruction in an academic course: *a history textbook, an algebra textbook.*

tex·tile (teks′tīl, -til) *n.* **1.** fabric made by weaving, knitting, or otherwise arranging yarn, thread, or other fibers. **2.** any material that can be made into such a fabric, as cotton, wool, or nylon. —*adj.* relating to textiles or their manufacture. [Latin *textilis* woven, from *texere* to weave.]

tex·tu·al (teks′chōō əl) *adj.* relating to, based on, or contained in a text: *textual inaccuracies.* —**tex′tu·al·ly,** *adv.*

tex·ture (teks′chər) *n.* **1.** character of a woven fabric resulting from the arrangement, feel, quality, or size of its threads: *loose texture. Silk has a smooth texture.* **2.** characteristic arrangement of the parts or particles of any body or material; composition; structure: *the loose texture of snow. Sandpaper has a rough texture.* **3.** essential or distinctive nature or quality of anything: *the texture of modern life, a long novel of uneven texture.* **4.** character of the surface of a painting or other work of art, or the surface structure of an object or part in such a work. **5.** anything produced by weaving; woven fabric. —*v.t.* **-tured, -tur·ing.** to cause to have a particular texture. [Latin *textūra* web, fabric, structure, from *texere* to weave.] —**tex′tur·al,** *adj.* —**tex′-tur·al·ly,** *adv.*

-th *suffix* used to form ordinal numbers: *fifth, seventeenth, hundredth.* [Old English *-(o)tha, -(o)the.*]

Th, thorium.

Th., Thursday.

Thack·er·ay, William Make·peace (thak′ər ē; māk′pēs′) 1811–63, English novelist.

Thai (tī) *n.* **1.** member or close descendant of the people of Thailand. **2.** official language of Thailand. **3.** group of languages spoken in parts of southeastern Asia, a branch of the Sino-Tibetan language family. —*adj.* of or relating to Thailand, its people, or their language. Also, Si′a·mese′.

Thai·land (tī′land′) *n.* country in southeastern Asia, formerly known as Siam. Capital, Bangkok. Area, 198,500 sq.mi. Pop. (1967 est.), 32,680,000.

thal·a·mus (thal′ə məs) *pl.,* **-mi** (mī′). *n.* **1.** large oblong mass in the diencephalon of the forebrain, composed largely of gray matter, from which nerve fibers extend to the cerebellum, spinal cord, cranial nerves, and cerebral cortex. The major function of the thalamus is to relay nerve impulses from one part of the brain to another. **2.** *Botany.* receptacle of a flower. [Latin *thalamus* inner chamber, from Greek *thalamos.*]

tha·ler (tä′lər) *pl.,* **-ler.** *n.* taler.

Tha·les (thā′lēz) *n.* c.640–c.546 B.C., Greek philosopher.

Tha·li·a (thə lī′ə, thal′yə) *n. Greek Mythology.* **1.** the Muse of comedy and pastoral poetry. **2.** one of the three Graces.

tha·lid·o·mide (thə lid′ə mīd′) *n.* crystalline solid formerly used as a sedative and hypnotic drug. Its use during the early stages of pregnancy may cause abnormalities of the fetus, esp. malformed limbs. Formula: $C_{13}H_9N_2O_4$

thal·li·um (thal′ē əm) *n.* soft, bluish-gray, poisonous metallic element that looks like lead, used in ant and rat poisons and in the manufacture of artificial gems, optical glass, and infrared equipment. Symbol: Tl See element for table. [Modern Latin *thallium* from Greek *thallos* green shoot; because there is a green line in its spectrum.]

thal·lo·phyte (thal′ə fīt′) *n.* any of a large group of primitive plants lacking roots, stems, or leaves, including algae, fungi, slime molds, and bacteria. [Modern Latin *Thallophyta,* from Greek *thallos* green shoot + -PHYTE.] —**thal·lo·phyt·ic** (thal′ə fit′ik) *adj.*

thal·lus (thal′əs) *pl.,* **thal·li** (thal′ī) or **thal·lus·es.** *n.* plant body not differentiated into distinct roots, stems, and leaves and not having vascular tissue. [Modern Latin *thallus,* from Greek *thallos* green shoot.]

Thames (temz) *n.* river in southern England, flowing east through London to the North Sea.

than (<u>th</u>an; *unstressed* <u>th</u>ən) *conj.* **1.** used after an adjective or adverb to introduce the second part of a comparison: *A cow is bigger than a rabbit. This stamp is worth more than fifty dollars. She would rather listen to music than study.* **2.** used after an adjective or adverb such as *other* or *else* to express exception or difference: *He respects no opinion other than his own.* —*prep.* used in such phrases as *than whom* and *than which* to express comparison: *a city than which there is none more beautiful.* ▲ In formal writing, *than* is construed as a conjunction in sentences involving comparison. The word introduced by *than* may be in either the nominative or objective case, depending on its function in the clause following *than: He is taller than she (is). The movie amused me more than (it amused) her.* In informal writing and speech, *than* is sometimes considered to be a preposition, in which case the word following *than* is in the objective: *He is older than her. He spent more money than me.* This construction is often regarded as substandard. [Old English *thanne, thonne.*]

thane (thān) *also,* **thegn.** *n.* **1.** in English history, man who held lands from the king in return for military service, esp. a member of a class ranking above ordinary freemen but below the nobility. **2.** in Scottish history, a lord or baron, esp. the chief of a clan. [Old English *theg(e)n* man who held lands from the king in return for military service.]

thank (thangk) *v.t.* **1.** to express gratitude or appreciation to, as for something given or done; give thanks to: *to thank a person for a gift. She thanked her hostess for a lovely evening.* ▲ often used in the conventional polite phrase *thank you,* with the suplet *I* understood: *Thank you for the flowers.* **2.** to consider or hold responsible; credit or blame: *He has only himself to thank for failing the test.* [Old English *thancian* to give thanks.]

thank·ful (thangk′fəl) *adj.* feeling or expressing thanks; grateful. —**thank′ful·ly,** *adv.* —**thank′ful·ness,** *n.* —Syn. see **grateful.**

thank·less (thangk′lis) *adj.* **1.** not likely to be rewarded or appreciated: *a thankless task.* **2.** not feeling or showing gratitude; ungrateful. —**thank′less·ly,** *adv.* —**thank′less·ness,** *n.*

thanks (thangks) *interj.* I thank you: *Thanks for the ride.* —*n. pl.* **1.a.** expression of gratitude: *to give thanks. I return it to you with my sincere thanks.* **b.** feeling of gratitude: *He expressed his thanks for their kindness.* **2. thanks to.** as a result or consequence of; owing to; because of: *Thanks to her efforts, the project will be a success.*

thanks·giv·ing (thangks′giv′ing) *n.* **1.** act of giving thanks. **2.** expression of thanks, esp. a prayer of thanks to God. **3.** day set apart to give thanks for God's favor, esp. in a public celebration. **4. Thanksgiving.** Thanksgiving Day.

Thanksgiving Day 1. legal holiday in the United States, observed on the fourth Thursday in November as a day of thanksgiving and feasting. It commemorates the harvest feast celebrated by the Pilgrims in 1621. **2.** similar holiday celebrated in Canada on the second Monday of October.

Thant, U (thänt, tänt; ōō) 1909–75, Burmese diplomat, secretary-general of the United Nations from 1961 to 1971.

that (that) *pl.,* **those.** *adj.* **1.** used to indicate a person or thing previously mentioned, pointed out, or understood: *That girl won the prize. Who wrote that book?* **2.** used to indicate something more distant than or contrasted with another thing: *I prefer this coat to that one. This problem is more difficult than that one.* Distinguished from **this.** —*pron. pl.,* **those.** **1.** used to indicate a person or thing previously mentioned, pointed out, or understood: *That is the man who did it. That was the best movie I've seen this year.* **2.** used to indicate something more distant than or contrasted with another thing: *I prefer this dress to that.* Distinguished from **this.** **3.** used in restrictive clauses in place of *who, whom,* or *which: the boy that lives next door, the man that I saw, the animals that are native to Africa.* ▲ *That* may be used of people, animals, or things; *which* may refer to either animals or things; *who* and *whom* are used only of people. **4.** used to designate a point in time: *the year that they were married.* —*conj.* **1.** used to introduce a subordinate clause, esp. one serving as the subject or object of the main verb: *I am sure that he will accept the job.* **2.** used to show reason or cause: *I'm sorry that you can't come to the party.* **3.** used to show result: *She ate so much that she was ill the next day.* **4.** used to show purpose: *He died that others might live.* ▲ often used with *so. Open the door so that the dog can come in.* **5.** used to introduce an expression of desire: *Oh, that he were with us today!* **6.** used to introduce an expression of surprise or indignation: *That he should act so rudely toward you!* —*adv.* to such an extent or degree; to that extent; so: *He's not that rich. How could she sing that well after only one lesson?* ▲ In current usage a distinction is often made between *that* and *which* in relative clauses. *That* is preferred when introducing a restrictive clause: *New York is the only American city that has more than seven million people. Which* is preferred when introducing a nonrestrictive clause: *New York, which has more than seven million people, is America's largest city.* However, many speakers and writers use *that* and *which* interchangeably in restrictive clauses, and the distinction between them is now usually limited to formal language. [Old English *that.*]

thatch (thach) *n.* **1.** straw, reeds, rushes, or similar material used to cover a roof. **2.** roof or roofing of such material. **3.** anything resembling such a covering, esp. the hair of the head. —*v.t.* to cover with or as with thatch. [Old English *theccan* to cover.]

Thatched roof

thau·ma·tur·gy (thô′mə tur′jē) *n.* working of miracles or wonders; magic. [Greek *thaumatourgiā* literally, wonder working, going back to *thauma* wonder + *ergon* work.]

thaw (thô) *v.i.* **1.** to pass from a frozen state to a liquid or unfrozen state; become free of frost or ice; melt: *The ice on the road thawed from the heat of the sun.* **2.** to become free of the physical effects of cold (often with *out*): *The ice skaters thawed out before a large fire.* **3.** (of the weather or temperature) to become warm enough to melt ice or snow; rise above the freezing point. **4.** to grow less stiff and reserved in manner; become more friendly: *His aloof manner thawed under her hospitality.* —*v.t.* to cause to thaw: *The sun thawed the snow on the roof.* —*n.* **1.** act of thawing. **2.** period of weather warm enough to melt ice and snow: *the spring thaw.* **3.** becoming less cold, formal, or reserved; lessening of tension or hostility: *The meeting of the heads of state marked a thaw in relations between the two countries.* [Old English *thāwian* to cause to melt.]

the[1] (*before a consonant,* thə; *before a vowel,* thē) *definite article* The refers to a particular person, thing, or group. Some specific uses of *the* are: **1.** to indicate a particular one or ones previously mentioned, pointed out, or understood: *Close the door. Give me the book.* **2.** to show that a noun designates something unique: *the sun, the wind, the past, the Amazon.* **3.** to indicate a particular one regarded as best known, most important, or greatest: *the place to go for a winter vacation.* ▲ usually emphasized by italics in writing or by stress in speech. **4.** to make a singular noun general: *The lion is found in Africa. He plays the bugle well.* **5.** in place of a possessive pronoun: *A stone struck him on the arm.* **6.** before an adjective to make it function as a noun: *a home for the aged.* **7.** before part of a title: *the Duke of Edinburgh; The Honorable John Marshall.* **8.** to refer to each individual of a group separately,

equivalent in meaning to "per," "each," or "every": *50 cents the dozen.* [Old English *thē, the.*]

the[2] (thə, thē) *adv.* used to modify comparative adjectives and adverbs: *The sooner you finish it the better.* [Old English *thē, thȳ, thon.*]

the·a·ter, the·a·tre (thē′ə tər) *n.* **1.** building, part of a building, or outdoor structure for the presentation of plays, operas, motion pictures, ballets, or other similar performances. **2.** place resembling a theater, esp. a room or hall having tiers of seats rising like steps, used esp. for lectures and surgical demonstrations. **3.** the writing and performing of plays; dramatic art or literature; the drama: *French theater, modern theater.* **4.** world of the theater and those involved in theatrical productions. **5.** quality or effectiveness of a dramatic presentation: *That new play is excellent theater.* **6.** place where some action takes place; field of operations: *a theater of war.* [Latin *theātrum* playhouse, stage, from Greek *theātron* place for seeing (esp. plays).]

the·a·ter·go·er, the·a·tre·go·er (thē′ə tər gō′ər) *n.* one who attends the theater, esp. a person who goes frequently or regularly.

the·a·ter·in·the·round (thē′ə tər in thə round′) *n.* theater in which the stage is at the center of the auditorium, surrounded by seats on all sides. Also, **arena theater.**

theater of the absurd, twentieth-century dramatic movement based on a belief in the irrationality of man and the absurdity of life. Theater of the absurd uses incongruous or meaningless dialogue and unconventional plot structure and characterization to express a feeling of alienation and futility.

the·at·ri·cal (thē at′ri kal) *adj.* **1.** relating to or characteristic of the theater, actors, or dramatic presentations: *a theatrical performance.* **2.** suggestive of a dramatic performance; artificial or affected; showy; overdone: *a theatrical display of grief.* —*n.* **theatricals.** theatrical performances, esp. by amateurs. —**the·at′ri·cal·i·ty** (thē at′ri kal′ə tē), *n.* —**the·at′ri·cal·ly,** *adv.*

the·at·rics (thē at′riks) *n.,pl.* **1.** art of staging plays. ▲ construed as singular. **2.** dramatic or artificial effects or behavior; histrionics.

Thebes (thēbz) *n.* **1.** ancient Egyptian city on the Nile, a former capital of Egypt. The site, now occupied in part by Luxor and Karnak, is renowned for its tombs and ruins. **2.** one of the leading city-states of ancient Greece, northwest of Athens. —**The′ban,** *adj.*

the·ca (thē′ka) *n.* **-cae** (-sē). *n.* case, sac, sheath, or capsule covering an organism or one of its parts. [Latin *thēca* case[2], cover, from Greek *thēkē.*]

thé dan·sant (tā′ dän sän′) *pl.,* **thés dan·sants** (tā′ dän sän′). *French.* tea dance.

thee (thē) *pron.* objective case of **thou.** ▲ *Thee* was formerly used in place of *thou* by members of the Society of Friends: *Thee speaks the truth.* [Old English *thē.*]

theft (theft) *n.* act or instance of stealing; larceny. [Old English *thēofth.*]

thegn (thān) *n.* thane.

the·ine (thē′ēn, -in) *n.* caffeine, esp. as found in tea. [Modern Latin *thea* tea (from dialectal Chinese *t'e*) + -INE[2].]

their (thâr) *adj.* possessive form of **they:** *their house, their class, their efforts.* [Old Norse *their(r)a.*]

theirs (thârz) *pron.* **1.** of, relating to, or belonging to them: *The money is theirs.* ▲ often used with *of: He is a friend of theirs.* **2.** thing or things relating to or belonging to them: *Our car is new; theirs is old.* ▲ *Theirs* is the absolute form of the possessive adjective **their,** used when no noun follows: *The land is theirs.*

the·ism (thē′iz′əm) *n.* **1.** belief in one personal God as creator and ruler of the universe. **2.** belief in the existence of a god or gods. [Greek *theos* god + ISM.] —**the·ist,** *n.* —**the·is′tic,** *adj.*

them (them; *unstressed* thəm) *pron.* objective case of **they:** *He met them at the station.* [Old Norse *theim.*]

the·mat·ic (thē mat′ik) *adj.* of or relating to a theme or themes.

theme (thēm) *n.* **1.** main subject or train of thought, as in a speech, conversation, or written composition; topic: *The theme of the departmental meeting was "Methods of Increasing Sales."* **2.** brief essay or written composition: *We were assigned a few themes in our English literature course.* **3.** *Music.* **a.** principal melody in a composition, movement, or passage; subject. **b.** melody on which variations are constructed. **4.** theme song (def. 2). [Latin *thema* subject, topic, from Greek *thema* proposition, subject; literally, something laid down.]

theme song 1. melody recurring throughout a film, musical, or dramatic presentation, often intended to convey a mood, that becomes identified with the production. **2.** melody used to identify or identified with a particular performer, group, or radio or television program.

The·mis·to·cles (thə mis′tə klēz′) *n.* c.527–c.460 B.C., Athenian statesman and general.

them·selves (them selvz′, thəm-) *pron.* **1.** emphatic form of **they** or **them:** *They had to do the job themselves.* **2.** reflexive form of **them:** *They blamed themselves for the tragedy.* **3.** their normal or average selves: *The players on the losing team were certainly not themselves today.*

---

at; āpe; cär; end; mē; it; īce; hot; ōld; fôrk; wood; fōōl; oil; out; up; ūse; turn; sing; thin; this; zh in treasure; ə in ago, taken, pencil, lemon, circus.　　　**1033**

then (then) *adv.* **1.** at that time: *He was much thinner then.* **2.** immediately or soon afterward; next in time, order, or space: *The overture ended and then the curtain went up.* **3.** at another time: *Sometimes the car will run smoothly; then it will stall at every corner.* **4.** in that case; if that is so; consequently; therefore: *If the part is faulty, then replace it.* **5.** in addition; besides: *The rent is reasonable, and then the location is highly desirable.* —*adj.* being or acting as such at that time; of that time: *the then ruler, the then ambassador.* —*n.* that time: *I hope to have it finished before then.* [Old English *thaenne* at that time, in that case.]

thence (thens) *adv.* **1.** from that place; from there: *The bank is two blocks thence.* **2.** from that time; after that: *a few weeks thence.* **3.** from that fact, circumstance, or reason; consequently; therefore. [Middle English *thannes* from that place, going back to Old English *thanon.*]

thence·forth (thens′fôrth′) *adv.* from that time on; after that; thereafter.

the·oc·ra·cy (thē ok′rə sē) *pl.*, **-cies.** *n.* **1.** government in which God or a god is considered the supreme ruling power. **2.** government by a priesthood or other religious authority claiming to rule by divine sanction. **3.** country or group ruled in such a way. [Greek *theokratiā* rule of God, from *theos* a god + *-kratiā* rule.]

the·o·crat (thē′ə krat′) *n.* **1.** one who rules or is a member of the ruling group in a theocracy. **2.** one who advocates or supports theocracy.

the·o·crat·ic (thē′ə krat′ik) *adj.* of or relating to a theocracy.

The·oc·ri·tus (thē ok′ri təs) *n.* Greek poet of the third century B.C.

the·od·o·lite (thē od′əl īt′) *n.* instrument used in surveying for measuring horizontal and vertical angles. [Of uncertain origin.]

The·od·o·ric (thē od′ər ik) *n.* A.D. c.454–526, king of the Ostrogoths.

The·o·do·si·us I (thē′ə dō′shē əs, -shəs) A.D. 346–395, emperor of Rome from A.D. 379 to 395.

the·o·lo·gian (thē′ə lō′jən, -jē ən) *n.* one who is versed or trained in theology.

the·o·log·i·cal (thē′ə loj′i kəl) *adj.* of, relating to, or concerned with theology: *a theological seminary.* Also, **the′o·log′ic.** —**the′o·log′i·cal·ly,** *adv.*

theological virtues, faith, hope, and charity, considered by St. Paul and other early Christian moralists to be necessary for a good Christian life. Often distinguished from **cardinal virtues.**

the·ol·o·gize (thē ol′ə jīz′) **-gized, -giz·ing.** *v.i.* **1.** to theorize or speculate on theological subjects; reason theologically. **2.** to make theological; treat theologically.

the·ol·o·gy (thē ol′ə jē) *pl.*, **-gies.** *n.* **1.** study of the nature and being of God and His relations to man and the universe, esp. in connection with an organized system of religion. **2.** particular system of religion or religious beliefs, esp. of a Christian church. [Latin *theologia* science of divine things, from Greek *theologiā,* going back to *theos* a god + *-logiā.* See -LOGY.]

the·o·rem (thē′ər əm) *n.* **1.** any statement or proposition that is not self-evident but can be proved to be true or is accepted as such. **2.** statement in mathematics that has been proved or can be proved from certain assumptions and definitions. **3.** rule or statement of relations expressed in an equation or formula. [Late Latin *theōrēma* proposition to be proved, from Greek *theōrēma* spectacle, principle, speculation, from *theōrein* to look at.]

the·o·ret·i·cal (thē′ə ret′i kəl) *adj.* **1.** of, relating to, or consisting of theory. **2.** limited to or derived from theory; not based on fact or experience; not practical or applied; hypothetical: *theoretical physics.* **3.** given to theorizing; speculative. Also, **the′o·ret′ic.** —**the′o·ret′i·cal·ly,** *adv.*

the·o·re·ti·cian (thē′ər ə tish′ən) *n.* one who theorizes, esp. one who specializes in the theory of a particular subject rather than in its practical application.

the·o·rist (thē′ər ist) *n.* one who theorizes.

the·o·rize (thē′ə rīz′) **-rized, -riz·ing.** *v.i.* to form a theory or theories; speculate: *to theorize about life after death.* —**the′o·ri·za′tion, the′o·riz′er,** *n.*

the·o·ry (thē′ər ē) *pl.*, **-ries.** *n.* **1.** idea or ideas that explain a group of facts or phenomena; hypothesis that has been confirmed or proved by observation, experiment, or reasoning: *the theory of relativity.* **2.** formulation assumed to be true but based on certain principles not completely verified. **3.** that branch of a science or art which deals with its principles, methods, or abstract applications rather than its practice. **4.** abstract reasoning; speculation. **5.** assumption or guess based on some evidence: *Have you any theories as to what caused the explosion?* [Late Latin *theōria* philosophical speculation, from Greek *theōriā* a beholding, consideration, speculation.]

the·os·o·phy (thē os′ə fē) *n.* **1.** any of several philosophical or religious systems that claims to have a special knowledge of the nature of God and the world through mystical insight. **2.** *often,* **Theosophy.**

doctrines and beliefs of a modern sect founded in the United States in 1875, incorporating aspects of Buddhism and Brahmanism, esp. a belief in reincarnation. [Medieval Latin *theosophia* knowledge of divine things, from Late Greek *theosophiā,* going back to Greek *theos* a god + *sophiā* wisdom.] —**the·o·soph·ic** (thē′ə sof′ik); *also,* **the′o·soph′i·cal,** *adj.* —**the′o·soph′i·cal·ly,** *adv.* —**the·os′o·phist,** *n.*

ther·a·peu·tic (ther′ə pū′tik) *adj.* of or relating to the treatment or curing of diseases or disorders; curative: *therapeutic medicine, the therapeutic effects of a warm, dry climate.* Also, **ther′a·peu′ti·cal.** [Greek *therapeutikos* inclined to serve, inclined to take care of (medically), from *therapeuein* to serve, treat medically.] —**ther′a·peu′ti·cal·ly,** *adv.*

ther·a·peu·tics (ther′ə pū′tiks) *n.,pl.* branch of medical science dealing with the treatment of disease. ▲ construed as singular.

ther·a·peu·tist (ther′ə pū′tist) *n.* therapist.

ther·a·pist (ther′ə pist) *n.* one who gives therapy, esp. a doctor or other person who specializes in a particular kind of therapy: *a physical therapist.*

ther·a·py (ther′ə pē) *pl.*, **-pies.** *n.* treatment of a disease or physical or mental disorder by any of various methods: *speech therapy.* ▲ often used in combination: *psychotherapy, hydrotherapy.* [Modern Latin *therapia,* from Greek *therapeiā* service, medical treatment.]

there (thār) *adv.* **1.** at or in that place: *Stay there. Put the box down there.* ▲ also used to indicate or emphasize a specific person or thing being referred to: *Helen, there, is our best singer.* **2.** to, toward, or into that place: *We walked there after lunch.* **3.** at that point, as in time, action, or thought: *There the speaker paused. He stopped working there and waited for further instructions.* **4.** on or concerning that matter or issue: *I agree with you there.* **5.** *there* is also used: **a.** to introduce a sentence or clause in which the verb precedes the real subject: *There is no more milk.* ▲ In such constructions the number of the verb is determined by the number of the real subject: *There is a man at the door. There are thirty-one days in March.* **b.** as the equivalent of a pronoun in expressions of encouragement or approval: *There's a good girl.* **c.** as a vague substitute for a name in addressing a person: *Hey, there! Well, hello there.* **d.** to call attention to someone or something: *There is the noon whistle.* —*n.* that place: *Do you know the way home from there?* —*interj.* used to express various emotions, as triumph, satisfaction, encouragement, or sympathy: *There! I can do it! There, there! Don't worry.* [Old English *thǣr.*]

there·a·bouts (thār′ə bouts′) *also,* **there·a·bout.** *adv.* near that place, time, number, amount, or degree: *ten dollars or thereabouts, twenty years old or thereabouts. He lives in Chicago or thereabouts.*

there·af·ter (thār af′tər) *adv.* **1.** from then on; after that; afterward. **2.** *Archaic.* according to that; accordingly.

there·at (thār at′) *adv.* **1.** at that place or time; there. **2.** because of that; on that account.

there·by (thār bī′, thār′-) *adv.* **1.** by that means: *He finished first in the race, thereby winning the championship for his school.* **2.** in that connection: *Thereby hangs a tale* (Shakespeare, *Merry Wives of Windsor*).

there·for (thār fôr′) *adv.* for or in return for this, that, or it: *He agreed to lend me the money and wrote a check therefor.*

there·fore (thār′fôr′) *adv.* for this or that reason; as a result; consequently: *He injured his leg and therefore could not play in the game.* ▲ often used as a conjunction: *It rained; therefore the game was called off.*

there·from (thār frum′, -from′) *adv.* from this, that, or it.

there·in (thār in′) *adv.* **1.** in or into that place, time, or thing: *The fire destroyed the warehouse and all the property therein.* **2.** in that particular point or respect; in that matter.

there·in·af·ter (thār′in af′tər) *adv.* in a later or subsequent part, as of a legal document, speech, or book.

there·in·to (thār in′tōō) *adv. Archaic.* into that place; into that.

there·of (thār uv′, -ov′) *adv.* **1.** of that or it. **2.** from that or it; therefrom.

there·on (thār ôn′, -on′) *adv.* **1.** on or upon that or it. **2.** immediately after that; thereupon.

there's (thārz) there is.

The·re·sa, Saint (tə rē′sə, -zə, -rā′-) *also,* **Te·re·sa.** 1515–82, Spanish Carmelite nun, mystic, and writer. Also, **Theresa of A·vi·la** (ä′və lä′).

there·to (thār tōō′) *adv.* **1.** to that place or thing. **2.** *Archaic.* in addition to that; besides; also.

there·to·fore (thār′tə fôr′) *adv.* before or until that time; up to then.

there·un·der (thār un′dər) *adv.* under or beneath this, that, or it.

there·un·to (thār un′tōō, thār′un tōō′) *adv.* thereto.

there·up·on (thār′ə pôn′, -pon′) *adv.* **1.** immediately after that; at once. **2.** as a consequence of that; therefore. **3.** with reference to that; upon that.

there·with (thār with′, -with′) *adv.* **1.** with this, that, or it. **2.** immediately after that; thereupon.

at; āpe; cär; end; mē; it; īce; hot; ōld; fôrk; wood; fōōl; oil; out; up; ūse; turn; sing; thin; this; zh in treasure; ə in ago, taken, pencil, lemon, circus.

there·with·al (thâr′with ôl′) *adv.* **1.** in addition to that; besides. **2.** *Archaic.* with that; therewith.

therm-, form of thermo- before vowels, as in *thermion.*

ther·mal (thur′məl) *adj.* of, relating to, or causing heat or warmth: *a thermal unit, thermal baths.* —*n.* rising current of warm air. [Greek *thermē* heat + -AL¹.] —**ther′mal·ly,** *adv.*

thermal barrier, limit to the speed of a rocket, spacecraft, or other vehicle in the atmosphere, imposed by the effect of aerodynamic heat. Also, **heat barrier.**

thermal spring, spring having waters of a higher temperature than the mean temperature of the area in which it is located.

ther·mic (thur′mik) *adj.* thermal.

therm·i·on (thurm′ī′ən, thur′mē ən) *n.* electrically charged particle given off by a heated body. [THERM(O)- + ION.]

therm·i·on·ic (thurm′ī on′ik, thur′mē-) *adj.* relating to thermions: *thermionic current, thermionic emissions.*

ther·mis·tor (thər mis′tər) *n.* component of an electrical circuit whose resistance decreases as its temperature increases, usually made of a semiconductor and used to regulate temperature and voltage. [THERM(AL) + (RES)ISTOR.]

Ther·mit (thur′mit) *n. Trademark.* mixture of powdered oxide of iron and aluminum that yields an intense heat when ignited, used in incendiary bombs and welding.

thermo- *combining form* heat: *thermoelectricity.* [Greek *thermē* heat.]

ther·mo·chem·is·try (thur′mō kem′is trē) *n.* branch of chemistry dealing with the relationship between chemical action and heat.

ther·mo·cou·ple (thur′mə kup′əl) *n.* device for measuring temperature, consisting of two dissimilar metallic conductors joined together at their ends. When one of these junctions is heated to a higher temperature than the other, an electric current flows around the circuit. The difference in temperature of the two junctions can be determined by measuring the voltage of the current. Also, **thermoelectric couple.**

ther·mo·dy·nam·ics (thur′mō dī nam′iks) *n.,pl.* branch of physics that deals with the relationship between heat and other forms of energy, esp. mechanical energy, and the conversion of one of these forms into another. ▲ construed as singular. —**ther′mo·dy·nam′ic,** *adj.*

ther·mo·e·lec·tric (thur′mō i lek′trik) *adj.* of or having to do with the direct relationship between heat and electricity. Also, **ther′mo·e·lec′tri·cal.**

ther·mo·e·lec·tric·i·ty (thur′mō i lek tris′ə tē, -ē′lek-) *n.* electricity produced by the direct action of heat, esp. that produced in a circuit composed of two wires of dissimilar materials when one of the junctions of the wires is kept at a higher temperature than the other.

ther·mo·graph (thur′mə graf′) *n.* instrument that automatically makes a continuous recording of temperature readings on a graph.

ther·mom·e·ter (thər mom′ə tər) *n.* device for measuring temperature, usually by the expansion or contraction of a substance according to changes in temperature. The most common type is a thin glass tube containing mercury or colored alcohol and marked with a numbered scale, in which the height of the liquid in the tube indicates the temperature. [French *thermomètre,* from Greek *thermē* heat + *metron* measure.]

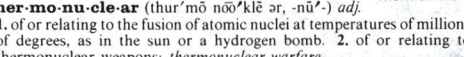
Thermometer

ther·mo·nu·cle·ar (thur′mō nōō′klē ər, -nū′-) *adj.* **1.** of or relating to the fusion of atomic nuclei at temperatures of millions of degrees, as in the sun or a hydrogen bomb. **2.** of or relating to thermonuclear weapons: *thermonuclear warfare.*

ther·mo·plas·tic (thur′mə plas′tik) *adj.* that becomes soft and pliable when subjected to heat, without any change in its original properties, as certain plastics or resins. —*n.* thermoplastic substance.

Ther·mop·y·lae (thər mop′ə lē) *n.* mountain pass in central Greece, site of a battle in 480 B.C. between the Greeks and Persians.

ther·mos bottle (thur′məs) bottle in which liquids can be kept hot or cold for many hours, usually consisting of an outer container of metal enclosing a glass bottle within another, with a vacuum between the bottles to inhibit the passage of heat. Trademark: Thermos. [Greek *thermos* hot + BOTTLE.]

ther·mo·set·ting (thur′mō set′ing) *adj.* that hardens into a permanent shape when subjected to heat, as certain plastics or resins.

ther·mo·stat (thur′mə stat′) *n.* instrument that automatically regulates a temperature-controlling system, as in a furnace, oven, or refrigerator. [THERMO- + Greek *statos* standing.] —**ther′mo·stat′ic,** *adj.* —**ther′mo·stat′i·cal·ly,** *adv.*

the·sau·rus (thə sôr′əs) *pl.,* **-sau·ri** (-sôr′ī). *n.* **1.** book containing a store of words or information, esp. a book of synonyms and antonyms arranged in categories. **2.** treasury or storehouse. [Latin *thēsaurus* treasure, storehouse, from Greek *thēsauros.* Doublet of TREASURE.]

these (thēz) plural of **this.**

The·se·us (thē′sē əs, -sōōs) *n. Greek Legend.* hero and king of Athens, who killed the Minotaur and escaped from the Labyrinth with the help of Ariadne.

the·sis (thē′sis) *pl.,* **-ses** (-sēz) *n.* **1.** statement or proposition advanced or proclaimed and defended or maintained, esp. in argument or debate. **2.** essay or dissertation on a specific topic or theme, esp. one presented by a candidate for an academic degree: *a doctoral thesis.* [Latin *thesis* proposition, from Greek *thesis* a placing, position, a setting down.]

thes·pi·an (thes′pē ən) *adj.* **1.** of or relating to drama; dramatic. **2.** *also,* **Thespian.** of or relating to Thespis. —*n.* actor or actress. [*Thespis,* supposed founder of ancient Greek tragedy + -AN.]

Thes·pis (thes′pis) *n.* Greek dramatist of the sixth century B.C.

Thess., Thessalonians.

Thes·sa·lo·ni·an (thes′ə lō′nē ən) *adj.* of, relating to, or characteristic of Thessalonica or its people. —*n.* **1.** native or inhabitant of Thessalonica. **2. Thessalonians.** either of two books of the New Testament consisting of epistles written by Saint Paul to the people of Thessalonica.

Thes·sa·lon·i·ca (thes′ə lon′i kə) see **Salonika.**

Thes·sa·lo·ni·ki (thes′ə lə nē′kē) *n. Greek.* Salonika.

Thes·sa·ly (thes′ə lē) *n.* region in northern Greece, bordering the Aegean. —**Thes·sa·li·an** (the sā′lē ən), *adj., n.*

the·ta (thā′tə, thē′-) *n.* eighth letter of the Greek alphabet (Θ, θ), corresponding to the English *th.*

The·tis (thē′tis) *n. Greek Legend.* mother of Achilles who made him invulnerable, except for his heel, by dipping him in the river Styx when he was a baby.

thews (thōōz) *n.,pl.* muscles; sinews. [Old English *thēaw* habit, custom.]

they (thā) *pl.,* nominative, **they;** possessive, **their, theirs;** objective, **them.** *pron.* **1.** persons or things previously or last mentioned or implied. **2.** people in general; any persons. [Old Norse *their* those.]

they'd (thād) **1.** they had. **2.** they would.

they'll (thāl) **1.** they will. **2.** they shall.

they're (thâr) they are.

they've (thāv) they have.

T.H.I., temperature-humidity index.

thi·a·mine (thī′ə min, -mēn′) *also,* **thi·a·min** (thī′ə min). *n.* vitamin necessary for normal carbohydrate metabolism, found in lean pork, dry beans, peas, and liver. Also, **vitamin B₁.**

thick (thik) *adj.* **1.** having relatively great extent or depth from one surface or side to its opposite; not thin: *a thick piece of wood.* **2.** having a specified measurement between opposite surfaces or sides: *a stone wall three-feet thick.* **3.** having relatively great density or consistency; not fluid: *thick soup.* **4.** having its constituent parts closely packed together: *thick underbrush, a thick beard.* **5.** abounding, filled, or covered (with *with*): *a field thick with wheat.* **6.** considerable or pronounced: *He spoke with a thick German accent.* **7.** mentally dull; stupid. **8.** indistinct and husky in sound. **9.** existing or occurring in large numbers; numerous; plentiful: *His legions . . . thick as autumnal leaves that strow the brooks in Vallombrosa* (Milton, 1667). **10.** humid and oppressive: *The air is thick today.* **11.** broad or fat: *She's pretty thick through the midriff.* **12.** *Informal.* very close or friendly; intimate. —*adv.* **1.** so as to be thick; thickly. **2. to lay it on thick.** *Informal.* to exaggerate or be excessive, as in one's praise or flattery. —*n.* **1.** thickest part of anything. **2.** part, place, or stage of greatest intensity or activity. **3. through thick and thin.** through the good times and the bad; under any circumstances. [Old English *thicce* not thin, plentiful, dense.] —**thick′ish,** *adj.* —**thick′ly,** *adv.*

thick·en (thik′ən) *v.t., v.i.* **1.** to make or become thick or thicker. **2.** to make or become more intense, intricate, or complex, as the plot of a story. —**thick′en·er,** *n.*

thick·en·ing (thik′ə ning) *n.* **1.** something added to a liquid to thicken it. **2.** act or process of making or becoming thick. **3.** thickened place or part.

thick·et (thik′it) *n.* dense growth, as of shrubs or bushes. [Old English *thiccet.*]

thick·head·ed (thik′hed′id) *adj.* slow to learn or understand; stupid; dull. —**thick′-head′ed·ness,** *n.*

thick·ness (thik′nis) *n.* **1.** state or quality of being thick. **2.** dimension of a solid between its two opposite surfaces, as distinguished from its length or width. **3.** layer or sheet, as of paper.

thick·set (thik′set′) *adj.* **1.** having a short, stocky build. **2.** planted, placed, or growing close together: *thickset trees.*

thick·skinned (thik′skind′) *adj.* **1.** having a thick skin, as certain fruit. **2.** insensitive or oblivious, esp. to criticism, ridicule, or reproach: *Some politicians have to become thick-skinned.*

thick·wit·ted (thik′wit′id) *adj.* dull; stupid.

thief (thēf) *pl.,* **thieves.** *n.* one who steals, esp. secretly and without the use of force. [Old English *thēof.*]

thieve (thēv) **thieved, thiev·ing.** *v.t., v.i.* to steal. [Old English *thēofian*.]

thiev·er·y (thē′vər ē) *pl.,* **-er·ies.** *n.* act, instance, or practice of stealing.

thieves (thēvz) plural of **thief.**

thiev·ish (thē′vish) *adj.* **1.** inclined or addicted to stealing. **2.** characteristic of or resembling a thief; stealthy; furtive; sly: *a thievish manner.* —**thiev′ish·ly,** *adv.* —**thiev′ish·ness,** *n.*

thigh (thī) *n.* part of the leg that extends from the hip to the knee. [Old English *thēoh.*]

thigh·bone (thī′bōn′) *n.* long bone of the upper leg, extending from the pelvis to the knee; femur.

thill (thil) *n.* either of the shafts between which an animal is hitched to the vehicle it is drawing. [Possibly from Old English *thille* plank.]

Thill

thim·ble (thim′bəl) *n.* **1.** small metal cap designed to be worn on the finger tip to protect it when pushing the needle through material in sewing. **2.** metal ring in a rope or in the rope hole of a sail to prevent wear. **3.** short length of pipe used in forming a joint. [Old English *thȳmel* covering worn to protect a finger, from *thūma* thumb.]

thim·ble·ber·ry (thim′bəl ber′ē) *pl.,* **-ries.** *n.* any of various raspberries with a thimble-shaped fruit, as *Rubus odoratus,* of the rose family, found in North America.

thim·ble·ful (thim′bəl fool′) *pl.,* **-fuls.** *n.* as much as a thimble can hold; very small quantity.

thim·ble·rig (thim′bəl rig′) *n.* type of shell game using thimblelike cups rather than shells. —**thim′ble·rig′ger,** *n.*

Thim·bu (tim′boo) *n.* capital of Bhutan, in the western part of the country.

thin (thin) **thin·ner, thin·nest.** *adj.* **1.** having relatively little distance from one surface or side to its opposite; having little thickness or depth: *a thin piece of wood, thin paper.* **2.** not plump or fat; lean: *a long, thin face.* **3.** having little density, substance, or consistency; watery: *a thin gravy.* **4.** easily seen through; not convincing or adequate; flimsy: *a thin excuse.* **5.** not dense: *thin air.* **6.** having a faint, often shrill sound; lacking fullness, volume, or depth; weak: *She answered in a small thin voice.* **7.** few in number; scanty: *There was a thin showing of hands when volunteers were called for.* **8.** having little or no depth or intensity of color; pale: *a thin shade of blue.* —*adv.* so as to be thin; thinly. —*v.t., v.i.,* **thinned, thin·ning.** to make or become thin or thinner (often with *out* or *down*): *It took her two months to thin down.* [Old English *thynne* not thick or dense, lean², scanty, of little worth.] —**thin′ly,** *adv.* —**thin′ness,** *n.* —**Syn.** *adj.* **2.** see **lean².**

thine (thīn) *Archaic. pron.* possessive case of **thou. 1.** belonging to thee: *Thine is the kingdom.* **2.** the one or ones belonging to thee. —*adj.* thy. ▲ used before a vowel or *h: Drink to me only with thine eyes* (Jonson, 1616). [Old English *thīn* of thee.]

thing (thing) *n.* **1.** that which has a separate existence or is conceived, perceived, or imagined as having a separate existence: *A thing of beauty is a joy forever* (Keats, 1818). **2.** something that is the subject of discussion, concern, feeling, or action: *We have to go over these things before we make a final decision.* **3.** inanimate object, as distinguished from a living organism: *A book is a thing. She cares more for things than for people.* **4.** organic being: *I wish no living thing to suffer pain* (Shelley, 1819). **5.** act; deed: *That was a terrible thing to do! He will do great things.* **6.** detail; item: *She didn't overlook a thing in planning the party.* **7.** idea; notion: *Say the first thing that comes into your mind.* **8.** statement; utterance: *Don't say things like that.* **9.** article of clothing: *We must change our things before dinner. I haven't got a thing to wear.* **10. things.** general state of affairs: *Things have changed since you've been gone.* **11.** piece of information: *He wouldn't tell us a thing about the party.* **12. things. a.** possessions; belongings: *I put all my things in a box.* **b.** equipment or implements needed for some special activity or purpose: *I can't find my tennis things.* **13.** person or animal regarded as an object of pity, affection, or contempt: *She certainly is a silly little thing.* **14.** desired end or result: *The thing is to get ahead.* **15.** *Informal.* idea, desire, or fear that obsesses: *She has a thing about heights. He has a thing for girls with blond hair and blue eyes.* **16. the thing.** latest style or fashion. **17.** work of art, music, or literature: *I've seen a few things that he's painted.* **18.** *Informal.* object that is not or cannot be described, particularized, or named: *What in the world is that thing?* **19. sure thing.** *Informal.* **a.** something certain; certainty. **b.** certainly; surely. **20. to do one's (own) thing.** *Slang.* to act, speak, or think according to one's beliefs or inclinations. **21. to make a good thing of.** *Informal.* to derive profit or gain from. **22. to see (or hear) things.** to have hallucinations. [Old English *thing* being, entity, matter, act, meeting.]

thing·a·ma·bob (thing′ə mə bob′) *also,* **thing·u·ma·bob.** *n. Informal.* something whose name is not known or has been forgotten.

thing·a·ma·jig (thing′ə mə jig′) *also,* **thing·u·ma·jig.** *n. Informal.* thingamabob.

thing·um·bob (thing′əm bob′) *Informal.* thingamabob.

think (thingk) **thought, think·ing.** *v.i.* **1.** to exercise the mind, as in forming opinions, drawing inferences, or using judgment: *Those who think must go join those that toil* (Goldsmith, 1764). **2.** to have in the mind as an impression, opinion, belief, or attitude (with *of*): *She always thought of him as a very young man.* **3.** to occupy one's thoughts with something or someone; reflect (often with *of* or *on*): *I'll have to think on it before I decide. He's always thinking of her.* **4.** to conceive or entertain the idea or notion of doing something: *We're thinking of going to Europe this summer.* **5.** to call to mind or remember (with *of*): *Can you think of anything we've forgotten? She could not think of the incident without smiling.* **6.** to have care or consideration (with *of*): *He always thinks of himself first.* **7.** to form an image or idea in the mind (with *of*): *Who thought of the first alphabet?* **8.** to be of a particular opinion: *If you think so, don't come.* —*v.t.* **1.** to form or have in the mind, as an impression, opinion, belief, or attitude: *She thought we were sisters.* **2.** to hold the opinion that: *I don't think you are right.* **3.** to examine by reasoning in order to arrive at a decision, conclusion, or answer (with *over, out,* or *through*): *Think it through carefully before you give me your final decision.* **4.** to regard as certain or probable; anticipate; expect: *We did not think to meet him there.* **5.** to have in mind as a purpose; intend; mean: *They think to influence the voters.* **6.** to devise or conceive of (with *up*): *to think up a plan.* **7.** to regard as; consider: *I think it only proper that you escort her home.* **8.** to recall (something) to the mind or memory; remember: *I can't think what he looks like.* **9.** to have one's mind full of or focused on: *Think happy thoughts and you'll feel better.* **10. to think better of.** to change one's mind after reconsidering. **11. to think twice.** to consider very carefully before acting. —*n.* **1.** *Informal.* act of thinking: *She has another think coming if she expects me to go.* **2.** product of this; thought: *A thing must be a think before it be a thing* (MacDonald, 1887). [Old English *thencan* to exercise the mind, form an opinion, consider, meditate.]

think·a·ble (thing′kə bəl) *adj.* that can be thought; conceivable; possible.

think·er (thing′kər) *n.* **1.** one who thinks. **2.** one who has developed and exercised his mental powers to an exceptional degree.

think·ing (thing′king) *adj.* having the ability to think or reason: *Man is a thinking animal.* —*n.* **1.** act of one who thinks. **2.** product of this.

thin·ner (thin′ər) *n.* liquid, as turpentine, used to thin a substance, esp. paint.

thin-skinned (thin′skind′) *adj.* **1.** having a thin skin: *a thin-skinned fruit.* **2.** acutely and unduly sensitive to criticism, ridicule, or reproach; easily hurt or offended.

third (thurd) *adj.* **1.** (the ordinal of three) next after the second. **2.** being one of three equal parts. —*n.* **1.** that which is next after the second. **2.** one of three equal parts; ⅓. **3.** third forward gear, as of an automobile. **4.** *Music.* **a.** interval of three degrees between two tones of the diatonic scale. **b.** tone separated from another tone by this interval, esp. the third tone of the diatonic scale. **c.** harmonic combination of two tones separated by this interval. —*adv.* in the third place. [Old English *thridda* (the ordinal of three) next after the second.]

third base *Baseball.* **1.** third base that a player must try to reach. **2.** position played by the player stationed in this area of the field.

third-class (thurd′klas′) *adj.* **1.** of, relating to, or belonging to a class next after the second. **2.** designating a class of mail that includes all printed matter except newspapers and magazines and meets certain governmental limits, as of weight. **3.** designating a class of travel accommodations on a ship or other conveyance, usually the least expensive and luxurious, ranking next below second class. —*adv.* by third-class mail or conveyance.

third class 1. third-class travel accommodations. **2.** third-class mail.

third degree *Informal.* intensive and often brutal interrogation of a prisoner, esp. by the police, to obtain information or a confession.

third estate third and lowest organized political group of a kingdom, esp. in France before the revolution of 1789, comprising the common people, as distinguished from the nobility or clergy.

third·ly (thurd′lē) *adv.* in the third place.

Third Order, organization of lay members affiliated with a certain religious order.

third person, form of a pronoun or verb that indicates the person or thing spoken of. In the sentence *He sees his mistakes, he, sees,* and *his* are in the third person.

third rail, rail that runs parallel to the tracks of an electric railroad and carries the current.

third-rate (thurd′rāt′) *adj.* **1.** third in class, order, quality, or importance: *That country is a third-rate power today.* **2.** distinctly inferior; very poor: *a third-rate movie.*

Third Reich, Germany under the Nazis, from 1933 to 1945.

Third World, nations that are not aligned with either the Communist or the non-Communist bloc of nations.

thirst (thurst) *n.* **1.a.** uncomfortable feeling of dryness in the mouth and throat caused by a desire or need to drink fluids. **b.** desire or need to drink: *He has an insatiable thirst.* **2.** strong or powerful desire; craving: *a thirst for power.* —*v.i.* **1.** to want something to drink; be thirsty. **2.** to have a strong desire; yearn: *He thirsted for recognition as a cellist.* [Old English *thurst* uncomfortable feeling caused by lack of drink.]

thirst·y (thurs'tē) thirst·i·er, thirst·i·est. *adj.* **1.** feeling or having the sensation of wanting something to drink. **2.** lacking water or moisture; parched; arid. **3.** having a strong desire; craving (with *for*): *The dictator was still thirsty for power.* —**thirst'i·ly,** *adv.* —**thirst'i·ness,** *n.*

thir·teen (thur'tēn') *n.* **1.** the cardinal number that is three more than ten. **2.** symbol representing this number, as 13 or XIII. **3.** something having this many units or members. —*adj.* numbering three more than ten. [Old English *thrēotēne.*]

thir·teenth (thur'tēnth') *adj.* **1.** (the ordinal of thirteen) next after the twelfth. **2.** being one of thirteen equal parts. —*n.* **1.** that which is next after twelve. **2.** one of thirteen equal parts; 1/13.

thir·ti·eth (thur'tē ith) *adj.* **1.** (the ordinal of thirty) next after the twenty-ninth. **2.** being one of thirty equal parts. —*n.* **1.** that which is next after twenty-nine. **2.** one of thirty equal parts; 1/30.

thir·ty (thur'tē) *pl.,* **-ties.** *n.* **1.** the cardinal number that is three times ten. **2.** symbol representing this number, as 30 or XXX. **3. the thirties.** number series from thirty to thirty-nine. ▲ used esp. in reference to the third decade of a century or of a person's life. —*adj.* numbering three times ten. [Old English *thrītig.*]

thir·ty-sec·ond note (thur'tē sek'ənd) *Music.* note having a time value equal to one thirty-second of a whole note. Also, **dem'i·sem'i·qua'ver.**

Thirty Years' War, series of religious and territorial wars among various European countries between 1618 and 1648.

this (this) *pl.,* **these.** *adj.* **1.** used to indicate a person or thing that is present or near at hand: *this book, this man.* **2.** used to indicate a person or thing that is understood or has just been mentioned or pointed out: *This news is most distressing.* **3.** indicating a person or thing that is nearer than or contrasted with another: *This dress is nicer than that one.* Distinguished from *that.* —*pron. pl.,* **these. 1.** used to indicate a person or thing that is present or near at hand: *Is this your coat? Who is this?* **2.** used to indicate a person or thing that is understood or has just been mentioned or pointed out: *This man just arrived.* **3.** person or thing that is nearer than or contrasted with another: *This is mine; that is hers.* Distinguished from *that.* **4.** that which is about to be said or explained: *This is what I mean.* —*adv.* to this extent or degree; so: *Is it this hot every day?* [Old English *thes* (masculine), *thēos* (feminine), *this* (neuter).]

This·be (thiz'bē) *n.* see Pyramus and Thisbe.

this·tle (this'əl) *n.* any of several prickly leaved plants of the composite family, as the common thistle, *Cirsium vulgare,* that bears reddish or purplish flower heads. [Old English *thistel.*]

this·tle·down (this'əl doun') *n.* silky down on the flower head of a thistle.

this·tly (this'lē) *adj.* resembling a thistle or thistles; prickly.

thith·er (thith'ər) *Archaic. adv.* to or toward that place. —*adj.* located on the farthest side. [Old English *thider* to that place.]

thith·er·ward (thith'ər wərd) also, **thith·er·wards.** *adv. Archaic.* to or toward that place; thither.

tho (thō) also, **tho'.** *conj. adv.* though.

thole (thōl) *n.* peg or pair of pegs, as of wood or metal, on the upper edge of either side of a boat, serving as fulcrum for an oar in rowing. Also, **thole'pin'.** [Old English *thol.*]

Thom·as (tom'əs) *n.* one of Christ's Apostles, who refused to believe in the Resurrection unless he could touch Christ's wounds.

Thom·as, Dyl·an (tom'əs; dil'ən) 1914–53, Welsh poet.

Tho·mism (tō'miz'əm, thō'-) *n.* philosophy of Saint Thomas Aquinas and his followers, that emphasized application of the powers of both faith and reason to phenomena of the natural world to attain knowledge of the universe. —**Tho'mist,** *adj., n.*

Thomp·son seedless (tomp'sən) *n.* a pale-green, oval-shaped grape that is the major source of seedless raisins. Also, **sul·tan'a.**

Thompson submachine gun *Trademark.* .45-caliber, air-cooled, gas-operated automatic weapon designed to be carried and operated by one man. [From John T. *Thompson,* 1860–1940, U.S. army officer who was one of its inventors.]

thong (thông, thong) *n.* **1.** narrow strip of leather or similar material,

used esp. as a fastening. **2.** sandal that is held to the foot by a pair of thongs that fits between the first two toes. **3.** lash of a whip. [Old English *thwang* narrow strip of leather.]

Thor (thôr) *n. Norse Mythology.* god of thunder.

tho·rac·ic (thô ras'ik) *adj.* of, relating to, or situated in or near the thorax.

tho·rax (thôr'aks) *pl.,* **tho·rax·es** or **tho·ra·ces** (thôr'ə sēz'). *n.* **1.** in man and certain other vertebrates, that part of the body extending from the base of the neck to the diaphragm, containing the heart, lungs, and ribs. **2.** section of an insect's body, extending from the head to the abdomen, that contains the wings and legs. [Latin *thōrax* chest, breastplate, from Greek *thōrax.*]

Tho·reau, Henry David (thə rō', thôr'ō) 1817–62, U.S. writer, philosopher, and naturalist.

tho·rite (thôr'īt) *n.* rare, highly radioactive mineral of variable color, consisting essentially of a silicate of thorium. Formula: ThSiO₄

tho·ri·um (thôr'ē əm) *n.* heavy, silver-white, radioactive metallic element used in the manufacture of electronic devices. Symbol: **Th** See **element** for table. [Modern Latin *thorium,* from THOR.]

thorn (thôrn) *n.* **1.** short, sharp-pointed growth on a stem or branch. **2.** any of various trees or shrubs bearing thorns. [Old English *thorn.*]

thorn apple, fruit of the hawthorn; haw.

thorn·y (thôr'nē) thorn·i·er, thorn·i·est. *adj.* **1.** full of thorns; spiny; prickly. **2.** difficult or irritating: *a thorny problem.*

thor·ough (thur'ō) *adj.* **1.** done or carried out to the fullest extent; omitting nothing: *a thorough search, a thorough cleaning.* **2.** painstakingly accurate and conscientious, esp. with regard to details: *She is very thorough in her research.* **3.** utter; absolute; unqualified: *He is a thorough bore.* [Old English *thuruh,* form of *thurh.* See THROUGH.] —**thor'ough·ly,** *adv.* —**thor'ough·ness,** *n.*

thor·ough·bred (thur'ō bred') *n.* **1.** animal, as a horse or dog, that is of pure or unmixed breed or stock. **2. Thoroughbred.** horse descended from a breed originally developed at the end of the eighteenth century by crossing English mares with any one of three specific Arabian stallions. Thoroughbreds are bred and trained chiefly for horse racing. **3.** person of good breeding and education. —*adj.* **1.** of pure or unmixed breed or stock. **2. Thoroughbred.** relating to, designating, or being a Thoroughbred. **3.** having good breeding and education.

thor·ough·fare (thur'ə fâr') *n.* **1.** public road or street that is open at both ends, esp. one that is a major route of travel. **2.** strait, waterway, or similar passage that is open at both ends and is a major route of travel. —**Syn. 1.** see **road.**

thor·ough·go·ing (thur'ə gō'ing) *adj.* **1.** characterized by thoroughness, esp. with regard to details. **2.** utter; unqualified; thorough: *a thoroughgoing liar.*

those (thōz) plural of **that.**

thou (thou) *sing.* nominative, **thou;** possessive, **thy, thine;** objective, **thee;** *pl.* nominative, **you, ye;** possessive, **your, yours;** objective, **you, ye.** *pron. Archaic.* the one spoken to; you. [Old English *thū.*]

though (thō) *conj.* **1.** in spite of the fact that: *I was late for work, though I got up early.* **2.** but; yet; nevertheless; however: *The speech is good, though it could be better.* **3.** granting or supposing that; even if: *Though we be poor, we will still be happy.* —*adv.* nevertheless; however: *You can count on him, though.* [Of Scandinavian origin.]

thought (thôt) *v.* past tense and past participle of **think.** —*n.* **1.** act or process of thinking: *lost in thought.* **2.** product of thinking; idea: *What are your thoughts on the subject?* **3.** intellectual activity or mental product characteristic of a particular group, time, or place: *modern thought, scientific thought.* **4.** careful notice, attention, or consideration; heed: *Please give some thought to the problem.* **5.** that which is intended; aim: *His thought was to become a candidate for state senator.* **6.** expectation; anticipation: *I had no thought of meeting him.* [Old English *thōht* act of thinking, idea.] —**Syn. 2.** see **idea.**

thought·ful (thôt'fəl) *adj.* **1.** expressing, showing, or characterized by a regard for others and their feelings; considerate: *a thoughtful person, a thoughtful gift.* **2.** engaged in or full of thought; meditative. **3.** showing or characterized by thought: *a thoughtful question.* —**thought'ful·ly,** *adv.* —**thought'ful·ness,** *n.*

thought·less (thôt'lis) *adj.* **1.** having, showing, or characterized by little or no regard for others and their feelings; inconsiderate: *His thoughtless remark hurt her feelings.* **2.** showing or characterized by a lack of thought; careless; heedless. —**thought'less·ly,** *adv.* —**thought'less·ness,** *n.*

thou·sand (thou'zənd) *n.* **1.** the cardinal number that is ten times a hundred. **2.** symbol representing this number, as 1000 or M. —*adj.* numbering ten times a hundred. [Old English *thūsend.*]

thou·sand·fold (thou'zənd fōld') *adj.* **1.** one thousand times as great or as numerous. **2.** having or consisting of one thousand parts. —*adv.* so as to be one thousand times greater or more numerous.

Thousand Islands, group of about 1700 small islands in the United States and Canada, in the St. Lawrence River.

Thistle

thou·sandth (thou′zəndth, -tənth) *adj.* **1.** (the ordinal of thousand) next after the 999th. **2.** being one of a thousand equal parts. —*n.* **1.** that which is next after the 999th. **2.** one of a thousand equal parts; ¹/₁₀₀₀.

Thrace (thrās) *n.* ancient and historic region in southeastern Europe, comprising the eastern part of the Balkan Peninsula. Once a Roman province, it is now divided among Greece, Bulgaria, and Turkey.

Thra·cian (thrā′shən) *adj.* of, relating to, or characteristic of Thrace or its people. —*n.* native or inhabitant of Thrace.

thrall (thrôl) *n.* **1.** one who is in bondage; slave; serf. **2.** one who is enslaved by some power or influence. **3.** condition of being in bondage; slavery. [Old Norse *thrǽll* serf, slave.]

thrall·dom (thrôl′dəm) *also,* **thral·dom.** *n.* state of being a thrall.

thrash (thrash) *v.t.* **1.** to administer repeated, forceful blows to; give a beating to. **2.** to defeat completely; overwhelm. **3.** to thresh. **4. to thrash out.** to discuss thoroughly and bring to a conclusion. **5. to thrash over.** to go over repeatedly, as in one's mind. —*v.i.* to make wild, flailing movements; toss violently: *The animal thrashed about trying to get free from the trap.* [Form of THRESH.]

Thrasher

thrash·er (thrash′ər) *n.* **1.** one who or that which thrashes. **2.** thresher *(def. 3).* **3.** any of various North American songbirds, family Mimidae, closely related to the mockingbird, having a curved bill, a long tail, short wings, and predominantly brownish plumage. Length: 8–13 inches.

thread (thred) *n.* **1.a.** very fine thin cord made of two or more fibers, as of cotton, wool, or silk, twisted together, used in sewing and in weaving cloth. **b.** piece of this. **2.** anything resembling thread, as in slenderness, length, or composition. **3.** anything that runs through the whole course of something and connects its successive parts: *the thread of a story.* **4.** spiral ridge running continuously around a screw or nut. Also *(def. 4),* **screw thread.** —*v.t.* **1.** to pass a thread through, esp. in order to sew: *to thread a needle.* **2.** to string together on or as on a thread: *to thread beads.* **3.** to pass or proceed through in a winding or twisting manner: *I threaded all the windings of this new labyrinth* (Malkin, 1809). **4.** to make (one's way) in this manner: *He threaded his way through the crowd.* **5.** to cut a thread on, in, or around (a screw or nut). —*v.i.* **1.** to pass or proceed in a winding or twisting manner: *The river threads between the mountains.* **2.** to form a fine thread when dropped from a spoon, as boiling syrup that has reached a certain consistency. [Old English *thrǽd* fine long cord.]

thread·bare (thred′bâr′) *adj.* **1.** having the nap worn off so as to expose the threads; worn; shabby: *threadbare upholstery.* **2.** wearing threadbare clothes; seedy. **3.** hackneyed; stale: *a threadbare joke.*

thread·worm (thred′wûrm′) *n.* any of various threadlike roundworms.

thread·y (thred′ē) **thread·i·er, thread·i·est.** *adj.* **1.** composed of, covered with, or resembling thread. **2.** weak and thin: *a thready voice.* —**thread′i·ness,** *n.*

threat (thret) *n.* **1.** expression of the intention to inflict punishment, harm, or pain. **2.** one who or that which is a source of misfortune, danger, or harm: *The murderer was a threat to society.* **3.** indication or possibility, as of impending misfortune, danger, or harm: *We lived under the threat of war.* [Old English *thréat* danger, menace.]

threat·en (thret′ən) *v.t.* **1.** to utter or make a threat against. **2.** to be a threat to; endanger: *The drought threatened the whole crop.* **3.** to be an indication of: *The dark clouds threaten rain.* **4.** to make a threat of: *He threatened to go to the police if we didn't agree to his plan.* —*v.i.* **1.** to use or utter threats. **2.** to pose a threat; menace. [Old English *thréatnian* to force.] —**threat′en·er,** *n.,* —**threat′en·ing·ly,** *adv.*

three (thrē) *n.* **1.** the cardinal number that is one more than two. **2.** symbol representing this number, as 3 or III. **3.** something having this many units or members, as a playing card. —*adj.* numbering one more than two. [Old English *thréo.*]

three-D (thrē′dē′) *also,* **3-D.** *n.* three-dimensional motion picture, representation, or the like. —*adj.* three-dimensional.

three-deck·er (thrē′dek′ər) *n.* **1.** ship having three decks or gun decks. **2.** anything having three stories, layers, or levels, esp. a sandwich made with three slices of bread.

three-di·men·sion·al (thrē′di men′shən əl) *adj.* **1.** of, relating to, or having three dimensions. **2.** having or giving the illusion of depth.

three·fold (thrē′fōld′) *adj.* **1.** three times as great or numerous. **2.** having or consisting of three parts. —*adv.* so as to be three times greater or more numerous.

three-mile limit (thrē′mīl′) area of water extending three miles out

from the shore of a nation and regarded, under international law, as the outer bound of that nation's jurisdiction.

three·pence (thrip′əns, threp′-, thrup′-) *n.* **1.** sum of three British pennies; three pence. **2.** coin having this value.

three·pen·ny (thrip′ən ē, threp′-, thrup′-, thrē′pen′ē) *adj.* **1.** having the value of or costing threepence. **2.** of little worth; cheap; worthless.

three-ply (thrē′plī′) *adj.* consisting of or having three thicknesses, layers, or folds.

three R's, reading, writing, and arithmetic, considered as the three basic elements of elementary education. [From the jocular spelling *r(eading), 'r(iting),* and *'r(ithmetic).*]

three·score (thrē′skôr′) *adj., n.* three times twenty; sixty.

three·some (thrē′səm) *n.* group of three persons.

Three Wise Men, in the New Testament, the Magi.

thren·o·dy (thren′ə dē) *pl.,* **-dies.** *n.* song or poem of lamentation, esp. one composed for the funeral of an important person. [Greek *thrēnōidía* lamentation, from *thrēnos* lament + *ōidē* song.]

thresh (thresh) *v.t.* **1.a.** to separate the grain from (a cereal grass) with a threshing machine or by beating with a flail. **b.** to separate (grain) from straw or chaff in this manner. **2.** to give a beating to; thrash. **3. to thresh out.** to thrash out. **4. to thresh over.** to thrash over. —*v.i.* **1.** to thresh grain. **2.** to toss violently; thrash. [Old English *therscan* to separate the grains of a cereal from the husks, esp. by beating with a flail, flog.]

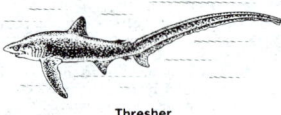

Thresher

thresh·er (thresh′ər) *n.* **1.** one who or that, which threshes. **2.** threshing machine. **3.** large shark, genus *Alopias,* having a very long tail that it thrashes about in the water in order to drive together schools of small fish on which to feed. Also *(def. 3),* **thrash′er.**

threshing machine, machine that separates grain from the stalk, straw, or chaff.

thresh·old (thresh′ōld, -hōld′) *n.* **1.** piece of wood, stone, metal, or the like forming the lower horizontal member of a door frame. **2.** point of entering or beginning: *on the threshold of a new job.* **3.** limit or point below which a stimulus cannot produce a response or be perceived: *to have a high threshold for pain.* [Old English *therscold* piece of stone or wood beneath a doorway, line crossed in entering.]

threw (thrōō) past tense of **throw.**

thrice (thrīs) *adv.* **1.** three times. **2.** greatly; extremely: *Thrice blest whose lives are faithful prayers* (Tennyson, 1850). [Old English *thríga, thríwa* three times.]

thrift (thrift) *n.* **1.** careful or frugal management of money and other material resources; frugality. **2.** any of a group of summer-flowering plants, genus *Armeria,* usually having white or pink flowers, often used in rock gardens. [Old Norse *thrift* prosperity.]

thrift·less (thrift′lis) *adj.* not exercising frugality; wasteful; extravagant. —**thrift′less·ly,** *adv.,* —**thrift′less·ness,** *n.*

thrift·y (thrif′tē) **thrift·i·er, thrift·i·est.** *adj.* **1.** prudent in the use and management of resources; avoiding waste or extravagance; frugal. **2.** thriving; flourishing. —**thrift′i·ly,** *adv.,* —**thrift′i·ness,** *n.*

Syn. 1. Thrifty, frugal, economical mean prudent in the use of resources. Thrifty implies the use of care and judgment to avoid unnecessary expense, often for the purpose of building up one's savings: *David was so thrifty that he managed to save fifty dollars a month out of his meager salary.* **Frugal** suggests a simplicity and sparseness of life associated with the limited spending of resources, esp. spending restricted to bare necessities: *In the country, away from the city's temptations, they lived in a frugal manner.* **Economical** stresses efficiency in the tailoring of spending to actual needs, with maximum results from the limited use of resources: *During the drought, citizens were asked to be economical in their use of water.*

thrill (thril) *n.* **1.** pleasurable or exciting feeling or sensation: *the thrill of seeing a baby take it's first steps.* **2.** something that produces such a feeling or sensation: *His first train trip was a thrill for him.* —*v.t.* to fill with a sudden wave of pleasure or excitement: *The speech thrilled the crowd.* —*v.i.* **1.** to experience a sudden wave of pleasure or excitement. **2.** to move tremulously; quiver. [Earlier *thirl* to pierce, from Old English *thŷrlian.*] —**thrill′ing·ly,** *adv.*

thrill·er (thril′ər) *n.* **1.** play, story, book, or the like that arouses feelings of excitement or suspense. **2.** one who or that which thrills.

thrips (thrips) *n.* any of a group of destructive insects, order Thysanoptera, that feeds on fruit, vegetables, cotton, and other crop plants. [Latin *thrips* woodworm, from Greek *thríps.*]

thrive (thrīv) **throve** or **thrived, thrived** or **thriv·en** (thriv′ən), **thriv·ing.** *v.i.* **1.** to be successful or fortunate. **2.** to grow vigorously: *The plant*

thrived in the sunlight. [Old Norse *thrífask* to prosper; literally, to grasp for oneself, from *thrífa* to grasp.] —**thriv′ing·ly,** *adv.* —**Syn. 2.** see **prosper.**

throat (thrōt) *n.* **1.** area behind and below the mouth containing the pharynx, upper part of the esophagus, larynx, and upper part of the trachea. **2.** front surface of the neck, extending from below the chin to the collarbones. **3.** any narrow opening or passage resembling the throat: *the throat of a bottle.* [Old English *throte.*]

throat·ed (thrō′tid) *adj.* having or marked by a (specified kind of) throat. ▲ used in combination: *a white-throated bird.*

throat·y (thrō′tē) **throat·i·er, throat·i·est.** *adj.* produced or modified deep in the throat; husky; guttural: *a throaty laugh.* —**throat′i·ness,** *n.*

throb (throb) **throbbed, throb·bing.** *v.i.* **1.** to pulsate or pound heavily and with increasing rapidity, esp. as the result of fear or excitement, as the heart. **2.** to have or experience a throbbing sensation: *The noise made her head throb.* **3.** to vibrate or sound with a strong, steady rhythm: *the throb of drums.* —*n.* **1.** act of throbbing. **2.** beat or vibration; pulsation. [Probably imitative.] —**throb′bing·ly,** *adv.*

throe (thrō) *n.* **1. throes.** condition of extreme pain, anguish, or struggle accompanying or preceding an action or event: *in the throes of creating a masterpiece, in the throes of death.* **2.** *also,* **throes.** violent spasm or pang, esp. of pain. [Earlier *throwe,* possibly going back to Old English *thrawu* threat, affliction, pang.]

throm·bo·cyte (throm′bə sīt′) *n.* blood platelet. [Greek *thrombos* clot + *kytos* hollow vessel.]

throm·bo·sis (throm bō′sis) *n.* formation of a clot of blood in a blood vessel or chamber of the heart, causing a complete or partial obstruction to the flow of blood. [Modern Latin *thrombosis,* from Greek *thrombōsis* blocked vein, going back to *thrombos* clot.]

throne (thrōn) *n.* **1.** chair occupied by a sovereign, pope, bishop, or other dignitary during state or ceremonial occasions. **2.** royal power or authority; sovereignty. **3.** member of the third highest of the nine orders of angels. —*v.t.,* **throned, thron·ing.** to place on or as on a throne; enthrone. [Latin *thronus* elevated seat, from Greek *thronos* chair, chair of state.]

throng (thrông, throng) *n.* **1.** large number of people assembled or crowded together. **2.** any large number of things assembled or crowded together. —*v.i.* to move or assemble in a group or large numbers; crowd: *The people thronged to the county fair.* —*v.t.* **1.** to fill (a place) to capacity; crowd into: *Spectators thronged the courtroom.* **2.** to crowd around; press in on: *Fans thronged the singer wherever he went.* [Old English *(ge)thrang* crowd.] —**Syn.** *n.* see **crowd.**

throt·tle (throt′əl) *n.* **1.** valve that controls or regulates the supply of steam in a steam engine or turbine or the supply of fuel vapor in an internal-combustion machine. Also, **throttle valve.** **2.** lever or pedal that operates such a valve. —*v.t.,* **-tled, -tling.** **1.** to prevent the breathing of by squeezing the throat; kill by choking. **2.** to check the expression or action of; suppress. **3.a.** to reduce or shut off the flow of (steam or fuel vapor) in an engine. **b.** to reduce the speed of (an engine) in this way (often with *down).* [Possibly THROAT + -LE.]

through (thrōō) *prep.* **1.** from the beginning to the end of: *She read through the book in one day.* **2.** in one side or end and out the opposite or other side or end: *to drive a nail through a board.* **3.** in or to various parts or places in: *We plan to travel through Europe this summer.* **4.** in the midst of; among: *to wander through the trees.* **5.** by reason of; on account of: *He lost his job through tardiness.* **6.** by means of: *We got the news through our friend.* **7.** having finished, completed, or done with: *Is he through college yet?* —*adv.* **1.** from one side or end to the opposite or other side or end. **2.** from beginning to end: *to read a letter through.* **3.** to a conclusion or termination: *to carry a project through.* **4.** along the whole distance; all the way: *The river runs through to the mill.* **5.** throughout; entirely; completely: *to be soaked through.* ▲ often used emphatically in the phrase *through and through.* —*adj.* **1.** that goes the whole distance with few or no stops and no changes: *a through train.* **2.** relating to or allowing travel to the end of the line with few or no stops and no changes: *a through ticket.* **3.** that allows free or unobstructed passage: *a through street.* **4.** having arrived at a point of completion, conclusion, or termination; finished: *Are you through with your homework?* **5.** no longer having relations, dealings, or connections: *I'm through with that club forever!* [Old English *thurh* from one side to the other, from end to end, everywhere in, by means of, because of.]

through·out (thrōō out′) *prep.* **1.** in every part of; everywhere in: *He is famous throughout Europe.* **2.** during the whole time or course of: *She visited me throughout my illness.* —*adv.* **1.** in or to every place or part; everywhere: *He was soaked throughout.* **2.** from beginning to end.

throve (thrōv) a past tense of **thrive.**

throw (thrō) **threw, thrown, throw·ing.** *v.t.* **1.** to propel up into or through the air with or as with the hand or hands: *Please throw me a towel.* **2.** to cause to fall to the ground: *The horse threw its rider.*

3. to put on or take off carelessly or hurriedly, as an article of clothing. **4.** to put or place in a specified position, state, or condition: *to throw a crowd into confusion, to throw a coat over a chair.* **5.** to direct, turn, or project; cast: *He threw me a nasty look when I mentioned the incident.* **6.** to move (a lever or switch) so as to connect or disconnect parts of a mechanism. **7.** to lose or shed: *The horse threw a shoe.* **8.** to play or put aside (a card or cards). **9.** to shape on a potter's wheel. **10.a.** to roll (dice). **b.** to roll (a specified number) with dice: *to throw a ten.* **11.** (of certain domestic animals) to bring forth (young). **12.** to twist (silk or other filaments) into threads or yarn. **13.** *Informal.* to lose (a game, race, or other contest) intentionally and often for profit. **14.** *Informal.* **a.** to surprise, confuse, or disconcert: *The reporter's question threw him.* **b.** to mislead; deceive: *Don't let his smile throw you; he's really very angry.* **15.** *Slang.* to give (a party, dance, or the like).

to throw away. a. to dispose of; discard. **b.** to spend or use in a wasteful or extravagant manner; squander: *He threw away his fortune by gambling.* **c.** to neglect to take advantage of: *to throw away an opportunity.*

to throw cold water on. to discourage by being indifferent, pessimistic, or disparaging.

to throw in. to add or include as a bonus.

to throw off. a. to rid or free oneself of. **b.** to give off; emit. **c.** to do or say in a rapid, haphazard manner.

to throw oneself at. to strive to win the attention, love, or friendship of.

to throw oneself into. to enter into or engage in rigorously or completely: *He threw himself into his work.*

to throw open. a. to open suddenly or widely, as a door or window. **b.** to remove all restrictions or barriers from.

to throw out. a. to reject; discard: *They threw out all his suggestions.* **b.** to utter or offer, as a hint or suggestion. **c.** *Baseball.* to put out (a runner) by throwing the ball to the player on the base toward which he is running.

to throw over. to forsake; jilt.

to throw the book at. *Slang.* to penalize or punish severely.

to throw together. to make, put together, or assemble hurriedly or haphazardly: *to throw together a meal.*

to throw up. a. *Informal.* to vomit. **b.** to erect or build rapidly. **c.** to give up; abandon.

—*v.i.* to propel something up into or through the air, esp. with the hand or hands. —*n.* **1.** act of throwing; toss. **2.** distance that something is or may be thrown. **3.** scarf, shawl, or similar covering worn draped over the shoulders. **4.** spread, coverlet, or similar covering draped over something, as a sofa or bed. **5.** roll of dice; number rolled. [Old English *thrāwan* to twist, turn, hurl.] —**throw′er,** *n.*

Syn. *v.t.* **1. Throw, hurl, pitch¹** mean to propel an object through the air by releasing it from the hand after a swing of the arm. **Throw** is the most widely applied of these words: *The infielder threw the ball to home plate.* **Hurl** implies considerable force or strength in the propelling: *The soldiers hurled grenades at the enemy tanks.* **Pitch** suggests careful aim at a definite target: *On her very first day, Mary was pitching horseshoes like an expert.*

throw·a·way (thrō′ə wā′) *n.* leaflet or handbill distributed free, as on the streets.

throw·back (thrō′bak′) *n.* **1.** reversion to an earlier or ancestral type or character. **2.** instance of this.

thrown (thrōn) past participle of **throw.**

throw rug. scatter rug.

thru (thrōō) through.

thrum¹ (thrum) **thrum·med, thrum·ming.** *v.t.* to play (a stringed instrument), esp. in an idle, monotonous, or unskillful manner; strum. —*v.i.* **1.** to drum or tap idly or repeatedly with the fingers: *He thrummed on his notebook.* **2.** to thrum a stringed instrument. —*n.* monotonous sound produced by thrumming. [Imitative.]

thrum² (thrum) *n.* **1.a.** fringe of warp threads left on a loom after the fabric has been cut off. **b.** one of these threads. **2.** any short tuft or fringe of threads or fibers. [Old English *-thrum* ligament (found in *tungethrum* ligament of the tongue).]

thrush (thrush) *n.* any of numerous songbirds, family Turdidae, including the robin, bluebird, wood thrush, and nightingale, usually having a chunky body, long legs, a slender bill, and solid or mottled black, brown, or gray plumage. Length: 4–13 inches. [Old English *thrysce.*]

Thrush (wood thrush)

thrust (thrust) **thrust, thrust·ing.** *v.t.* **1.** to push or shove forcibly or suddenly: *He thrust the money into his pocket.* **2.** to drive or force (a pointed instrument or weapon) into something or someone: *He thrust the fork into the meat.* **3.** to put forcibly into some condition, position,

or situation: *He was thrust into the limelight by all the publicity.* —*v.i.* **1.** to make a stab or lunge with or with a pointed instrument or weapon: *to thrust with a knife.* **2.** to make or force one's way, as through a crowd. —*n.* **1.** sudden, forceful push, shove, or drive made with or as with a pointed instrument. **2.** *Architecture.* outward and downward pressure exerted by one part on another, as the pressure exerted by one stone on another in an arch. **3.** driving force exerted by a propeller as it rotates. **4.** force pushing a rocket or jet engine forward, created when hot gases, formed by the combustion of propellants, rush out through a rear nozzle. [Old Norse *thrȳsta* to press, force.]

thru·way (thrōō′wā′) *n.* wide, usually divided, toll highway with limited points of access or exit, providing rapid and direct transit between distant points.

Thu·cyd·i·des (thōō sid′ə dēz′) *n.* c.460–c.400 B.C., Greek historian.

thud (thud) *n.* **1.** dull, heavy sound. **2.** heavy stroke or blow producing such a sound. —*v.i.* **thud·ded, thud·ding.** to make a thud when falling or striking against something. [Probably from Old English *thyddan* to strike, push.]

thug (thug) *n.* **1.** rough, brutal, and often violent person; ruffian. **2. Thug.** member of a secret and violent religious society in northern India that robbed and strangled its victims, suppressed by the British in the 1830s. [Hindi *thag* cheat, robber who strangles travelers, from Sanskrit *sthaga* rogue.]

Thu·le (thōō′lē) *n.* ultima Thule (*def.* 1).

thu·li·um (thōō′lē əm) *n.* soft, lustrous metallic element, least abundant of the rare earths. Symbol: Tm See **element** for table. [Modern Latin *thulium,* from THULE.]

thumb (thum) *n.* **1.** short, thick finger of the human hand, next to the index finger. **2.** corresponding digit in other primates. **3.** that part of a glove or mitten that covers the thumb. **4. all thumbs.** clumsy with regard to the hands. **5. thumbs down.** sign or gesture expressing disapproval or rejection. **6. thumbs up.** sign or gesture expressing approval or acceptance. **7. under the thumb of.** completely under the power, control, or influence of. —*v.t.* **1.** to turn and glance at the pages of; leaf (with *through*): *to thumb through a magazine.* **2.** to soil or wear out by handling carelessly or frequently with or as with the thumb. **3.** to perform, manipulate, or handle awkwardly with or as with the thumbs. **4.** *Informal.* to obtain or make by hitchhiking: *to thumb a ride, to thumb one's way to New York.* —*v.i. Informal.* to hitchhike. [Old English *thūma* the short, thick finger of the human hand.]

thumb-in·dex (thum′in′deks) *v.t.* to provide with a thumb index.

thumb index, series of labeled, graduated indentations cut into the outside edges of the pages of a book, providing easy access to specific parts of the book.

thumb·nail (thum′nāl′) *n.* nail of the thumb. —*adj.* very brief, but complete: *a thumbnail sketch.*

thumb·screw (thum′skrōō′) *n.* **1.** screw, often having a flat, upright head, designed to be turned by the thumb and a finger. **2.** formerly, instrument of torture used to crush or squeeze the thumbs.

thumb·tack (thum′tak′) *n.* tack designed to be pressed into a wall, board, or the like by the thumb.

thump (thump) *n.* **1.** heavy blow, as with a blunt object. **2.** heavy, hollow sound made by such a blow. —*v.t.* to strike, beat, or hit so as to produce a heavy, hollow sound: *He thumped his head on the floor when he fell.* —*v.i.* **1.** to produce a thump when falling or striking against something. **2.** to pulsate or pound heavily and with increasing rapidity; throb. [Imitative.] —**thump′er,** *n.*

Thumbscrew

thun·der (thun′dər) *n.* **1.** loud, rumbling sound produced by a lightning discharge as the result of rapid heating and expansion of the air along the path of the lightning. **2.** any noise resembling thunder: *the thunder of applause, the thunder of cannons.* **3.** threatening, terrifying, or vehement utterance: *He directed the thunders of the church against heresy* (Gibbon, 1781). **4. to steal someone's thunder.** to anticipate and use another's idea or methods without permission and without giving credit. —*v.i.* **1.** to give forth or produce thunder. **2.** to make a noise resembling thunder: *The train thundered into the station.* **3.** to utter loud denunciations or threats. —*v.t.* to utter loudly, esp. in a threatening manner; shout. [Old English *thunor* the sound accompanying lightning.]

thun·der·bolt (thun′dər bōlt′) *n.* **1.** flash of lightning accompanied by a clap of thunder. **2.** something that is sudden, unexpected, and terrible. **3.** one who acts with furious and restless energy.

thun·der·clap (thun′dər klap′) *n.* **1.** loud crash or burst of thunder. **2.** anything acting with the suddenness and violence of a thunderclap.

thun·der·cloud (thun′dər kloud′) *n.* dark, billowing, electrically charged cloud that produces thunder and lightning.

thun·der·head (thun′dər hed′) *n.* one of the round, swelling cloud masses that often develops into a thundercloud.

thun·der·ous (thun′dər əs) *adj.* producing a noise like thunder.

thun·der·show·er (thun′dər shou′ər) *n.* shower accompanied by thunder and lightning.

thun·der·storm (thun′dər stôrm′) *n.* storm accompanied by thunder and lightning, and usually rain.

thun·der·struck (thun′dər struk′) *adj.* astonished; amazed. Also, **thun·der·strick·en** (thun′dər strik′ən).

thu·ri·ble (thur′ə bəl) *n.* censer. [Latin *t(h)ūribulum,* from *t(h)ūs* incense, from Greek *thyos* burnt sacrifice.]

Thu·rin·gi·a (thoo rin′jē ə) *n.* historic region and former state in central Germany, now part of East Germany. —**Thu·rin′gi·an,** *adj., n.*

Thurs., Thursday. Also, **Thur.**

Thurs·day (thurz′dē, -dā′) *n.* fifth day of the week. [Old English *Thūres dæg* literally, Thor's day; influenced by Old Norse *Thōrsdagr* literally, Thor's day. See THOR.]

thus (thus) *adv.* **1.** in this, that, or the following way. **2.** as a result; consequently; therefore: *He didn't study and thus failed his test.* **3.** to this extent or degree: *thus far.* [Old English *thus* in this way, to this extent.]

thwack (thwak) *v.t.* to strike vigorously with something flat; whack. —*n.* sharp, vigorous blow with something flat. [Probably imitative.]

thwart (thwôrt) *v.t.* **1.** to prevent from doing or achieving something; act in opposition to: *Nothing will thwart him in his quest for success.* **2.** to prevent (something) from being accomplished or achieved. —*n.* transverse seat in a boat, on which a rower or passenger sits. —*adj.* lying or extending across something; transverse. —*adv., prep. Archaic.* across. [Old Norse *thvert* across, originally neuter of *thverr* transverse.] —**Syn.** *v.t.* **1.** see frustrate.

thy (thī) *pron.* possessive case of **thou.** *Archaic.* of or belonging to you; your. [Short for THINE.]

thyme (tīm) *n.* any of a group of erect or trailing plants, genus *Thymus,* of the mint family, whose leaves have a strong mintlike odor and are often used as a seasoning. [Latin *thymum,* from Greek *thymon.*]

thy·mine (thī′mēn, -min) *n.* pyrimidine base that is an essential constituent of DNA. Formula: $C_5H_6N_2$

thy·mol (thī′môl) *n.* crystalline compound made synthetically or obtained from an oil found in thyme and certain other plants, used esp. as an antiseptic. Formula: $C_{10}H_{13}OH$

thy·mus (thī′məs) *n.* endocrine gland, usually located in the neck or chest, that produces hormones that influence growth and play a role in immunity. It grows from childhood to adolescence and then shrinks to a very small size in adulthood. Also, **thymus gland.** [Modern Latin *thymus,* from Greek *thymos.*]

Trachea — Larynx — Thyroid
Lung — Heart
Thymus

Thymus at adolescence

thy·roid (thī′roid) *n.* **1.** thyroid gland. **2.** thyroid cartilage. **3.** medicine obtained from the dried and powdered thyroid glands of certain domestic animals, used in the treatment of disorders that result from the malfunctioning of the thyroid gland. —*adj.* of, relating to, or characteristic of the thyroid gland or thyroid cartilage. [Modern Latin *thyroides,* from Greek *thyreoeidēs* shield-shaped, from *thyreos* oblong shield (from *thyrā* door) + *eidos* form, shape.]

thyroid cartilage, largest cartilage of the larynx, which covers and protects the thyroid gland and forms the Adam's apple.

thyroid gland, endocrine gland that secretes thyroxin, located in front of and on either side of the trachea.

thy·rox·in (thī rok′sin) *also,* **thy·rox·ine.** *n.* hormone obtained from the thyroid gland or made synthetically, important in the regulation of growth and the rate of metabolism of the body cells, used in the treatment of thyroid disorders, as goiter and cretinism.

thyr·sus (thur′səs) *pl.,* **-si** (-sī). *n.* staff topped with a pine cone and ringed with leaves and branches, carried by Dionysus and his attendants. [Latin *thyrsus,* from Greek *thyrsos.*]

thy·self (thī self′) *pron. Archaic.* yourself. ▲ used as the reflexive or emphatic form of *thee* or *thou.*

ti (tē) *n. Music.* seventh of the series of syllables used to name the eight tones of the diatonic scale. See *do²* for illustration. [Modification of SI.]

Ti, titanium.

ti·ar·a (tē ar′ə, -är′ə) *n.* **1.** crownlike ornament, often made with jewels or precious metals, worn by women. **2.** triple crown worn by the pope, symbolic of the papal office. **3.** raised headdress or high cap worn by the ancient Persians. [Latin *tiāra* ancient Oriental headdress, from Greek *tiārā* ancient Persian headdress.]

Tiara

at; āpe; cär; end; mē; it; īce; hot; ōld; fôrk; wood; fōōl; oil; out; up; ūse; turn; sing; thin; this; zh in treasure; ə in ago, taken, pencil, lemon, circus.

Ti·ber (tī′bər) *n.* river flowing southward from north-central Italy, through Rome, into the Tyrrhenian Sea.

Ti·be·ri·as, Lake (tī bēr′ē əs) see **Galilee, Sea of.**

Ti·be·ri·us (tī bēr′ē əs) *n.* 42 B.C.–A.D. 37, Roman emperor from A.D. 14 to 37.

Ti·bet (ti bĕt′) *n.* remote region of southwestern China, famed as the center of Lamaism, since 1951 under Chinese Communist control. Area, approx. 470,-000 sq. mi. Pop. (1965), 1,321,500.

Ti·bet·an (ti bĕt′ən) *also,* **Thi·bet·an.** *adj.* of, relating to, or characteristic of Tibet, its people, their language, or their culture. —*n.* **1.** member or recent descendant of the Mongoloid people of Tibet. **2.** language of Tibet, belonging to the Sino-Tibetan language family.

tib·i·a (tĭb′ē ə) *pl.,* **-i·ae** (-ē ē′) or **-i·as.** *n.* **1.** inner and thicker of the two bones of the leg, extending from the knee to the ankle; shinbone. **2.** corresponding bone in the legs of birds and certain other animals. **3.** in insects, fourth joint of the leg, between the femur and the tarsus. **4.** ancient flute, originally made from an animal's legbone. [Latin *tībia* shinbone, flute.]

tib·i·al (tĭb′ē əl) *adj.* of or relating to the tibia.

tic (tĭk) *n.* habitual, involuntary twitching of a muscle, esp. in the face or the extremities. [French *tic;* probably of imitative origin.]

tick[1] (tĭk) *n.* **1.** light, rhythmic, recurring sound, as that made by a watch or a clock. **2.** dot, slash, or other mark, often used in checking off items in a series. **3.** *Informal.* very short period of time, as between two ticks of a clock; instant. —*v.i.* **1.** to make a light, rhythmic, recurring sound, as that of a clock. **2.** (of time) to pass: *The minutes ticked away as he waited.* **3.** *Slang.* **what makes someone tick.** what is the source or cause of someone's behavior or feelings. —*v.t.* **1.** to indicate with or as with a tick (with *off*). **2.** *Slang.* **to tick off.** to cause to become angry, annoyed, or irritated. [Probably imitative.]

tick[2] (tĭk) *n.* **1.** any of a group of wingless insectlike arachnids, order Acarina, that are parasites of mammals, birds, and reptiles, attaching themselves to the skin of the host and sucking its blood. Ticks transmit various diseases to both animals and humans. Length: to ½ inch. **2.** any of various insects, family Hippoboscidae, that are parasites of horses, sheep, and birds. [Old English *ticia.*]

tick[3] (tĭk) *n.* **1.** cloth covering or case of a mattress or pillow. **2.** ticking. [Middle Dutch *tīke* case[2], cover, going back to Latin *t(h)ēca,* from Greek *thēkē.*]

tick·er (tĭk′ər) *n.* **1.** one who or that which ticks. **2.** telegraphic receiving instrument that prints stock market reports or news on a paper tape. **3.** *Slang.* the heart. **4.** *Slang.* watch.

ticker tape, paper tape or ribbon on which a ticker prints.

tick·et (tĭk′ĭt) *n.* **1.** card or piece of paper indicating that the bearer is entitled to specified rights, privileges, or services: *We have to buy our tickets before boarding the train. You must present your ticket when picking up your laundry.* **2.** card, tag, or other piece of paper attached to something, esp. to indicate its contents, price, or owner. **3.** list or group of candidates belonging to a particular political party, to be voted on in an election. **4.** *Informal.* summons ordering a person to appear in court, esp. for a traffic violation. **5. to write one's own ticket.** to state and obtain one's own terms in an arrangement or agreement, esp. with respect to a fee or a salary. —*v.t.* **1.** to attach a ticket to: *They ticketed our baggage at the airport.* **2.** to give a legal summons to, esp. for a traffic violation. [Middle French *etiquet* a little note or label[1], from Old French *estiquier* to attach. See ETIQUETTE.]

tick·ing (tĭk′ĭng) *n.* strong, durable fabric of closely woven cotton or linen twill, used esp. to make covers for mattresses and pillows.

tick·le (tĭk′əl) **-led, -ling.** *v.t.* **1.** to touch (a person or a part of the body) so as to produce a chilling or tingling sensation, usually resulting in laughter. **2.** to affect or excite agreeably; please: *The aroma from the kitchen tickled his taste buds.* **3.** to give great pleasure or joy to; delight: *The children were tickled by the clown's antics.* —*v.i.* **1.** to feel or produce a chilling or tingling sensation. **2. to be tickled pink.** *Informal.* to be extremely pleased or delighted. —*n.* **1.** act of tickling; being tickled. **2.** tickling sensation: *A tickle in his throat made him cough.* [Of uncertain origin.]

tick·ler (tĭk′lər) *n.* **1.** one who or that which tickles. **2.** memorandum book, card index, or other device used to aid the memory.

tick·lish (tĭk′lĭsh) *adj.* **1.** sensitive to tickling. **2.** requiring caution, tact, and careful handling; delicate: *a ticklish situation.* **3.** easily offended; sensitive; touchy. —**tick′lish·ly,** *adv.* —**tick′lish·ness,** *n.*

Tibia illustration labels: Femur, Fibula, Tibia, Foot, Tibia

Tick[2] illustration caption: Tick[2]

tick·seed (tĭk′sēd′) *n.* **1.** coreopsis. **2.** tick trefoil.

tick·tock (tĭk′tŏk′) *n.* sound made by a clock or watch. —*v.i.* to make this sound.

tick trefoil, any of a group of mostly weedy tropical plants, genus *Desmodium,* of the pea family, having clusters of blue or purple flowers.

Ti·con·der·o·ga (tī′kŏn də rō′gə) *n.* village and historic fort on Lake Champlain, in northeastern New York. Pop. (1970), 3268.

tic-tac-toe (tĭk′tăk tō′) *also,* **tick-tack-toe.** *n.* game played with a diagram having nine squares, in which two players alternately put x's or o's in the squares, the winner being the first to complete a row of three x's or o's.

Tic-tac-toe illustration caption: Tic-tac-toe

tid·al (tīd′əl) *adj.* **1.** of, relating to, or affected by tides: *tidal basin, tidal action.* **2.** dependent on the state of the tide, as a ship whose time of arrival and departure is regulated by the time of the tides: *a tidal steamer.*

tidal bore, high wave or wall of tidal water that forms in a funnel-shaped, shallow bay or estuary and moves upstream at high tide with great force. Also, **bore.**

tidal wave 1. swift, powerful ocean wave caused by an underwater earthquake. **2.** any great movement or manifestation of strong feeling, opinion, or sentiment.

tid·bit (tĭd′bĭt′) *also,* **tit·bit,** *n.* small, choice piece, as of food or gossip. [Dialectal English *tid* nice (of uncertain origin) + BIT[2].]

tid·dly·winks (tĭd′lē wĭngks′) *n.* game in which the players attempt to propel small colored disks into a little cup by snapping them on the edge with a larger disk. Also, **tid·dle·dy·winks** (tĭd′l dē wĭngks′).

tide[1] (tīd) *n.* **1.** alternate rise and fall of the oceans and other large bodies of water, caused by the gravitational pull of the moon and the sun. High tide occurs at a given spot about every twelve hours and twenty-five minutes, with low tide occurring halfway between. **2.** general or dominant trend, tendency, or direction: *The tide of the battle turned against us.* **3.** anything that tends to rise and fall or increase and decrease. **4.** time or season. **5.** usually used in combination: *High over all the yellowing Autumn-tide* (Tennyson, 1872). **5. to turn the tide.** to reverse a condition or situation, esp. to a more favorable one. —*v.t.,* **tid·ed, tid·ing. to tide (someone) over.** to aid in getting along during a difficult period or until a specific time: *This money should tide you over until payday.* [Old English *tīd* time, season, opportunity.]

tide[2] (tīd) **tid·ed, tid·ing.** *v.i.* *Archaic.* to betide; befall; happen. [Old English *tīdan* to happen, from *tīd* time.]

tide·land (tīd′land′) *n.* **1.** land alternately covered and uncovered by tides. **2. tidelands.** area of submerged land, often yielding oil, within the historical boundaries of a coastal state of the United States and regarded as belonging to it.

tide·wa·ter (tīd′wô′tər, -wŏt′ər) *n.* **1.** body of water affected by tides. **2.** low-lying coastal land whose waters are affected by tides. **3.** water that inundates land at high tide. —*adj.* of, relating to, or situated along a tidewater.

tide·way (tīd′wā′) *n.* channel in which a tidal current runs.

ti·dings (tī′dĭngz) *n.,pl.* news; information: *The messenger brought good tidings.* [Old English *tīdung,* probably from Old Norse (plural) *tīthendi.*]

ti·dy (tī′dē) **-di·er, -di·est.** *adj.* **1.** arranged in a clean and orderly manner; well-organized: *Her closet was not very tidy.* **2.** inclined to keep oneself or one's things in a clean and orderly manner. **3.** *Informal.* relatively large; considerable: *We managed to save a tidy sum of money.* —*v.t.,* **-died, -dy·ing.** to arrange in a clean and orderly manner; make tidy (often with *up*): *to tidy up a room, to tidy the drawers in a desk.* —*v.i.* to arrange (things or oneself) in a clean and orderly manner (with *up*): *Would you like to tidy up before dinner?* —*n. pl.,* **-dies.** small decorative covering placed over the back or arms of a chair or sofa to keep it from becoming soiled or worn. [Middle English *tidy* timely, in good condition, from *tid* time (from Old English *tīd*) + -Y[1].] —**ti′di·ly,** *adv.* —**ti′di·ness,** *n.*

tie (tī) **tied, ty·ing.** *v.t.* **1.** to secure with a rope, string, or similar material, esp. by knotting the ends together: *to tie a price tag to a suit. She tied her hair with a ribbon.* **2.** to bring the parts of together by securing with a knotted or otherwise intertwined rope or string: *to tie a shoe.* **3.** to make a knot or bow in: *to tie one's shoelaces.* **4.** to make (a knot or bow). **5.** to draw together or join closely or firmly: *Mutual interests tied us together.* **6.** to restrain or restrict; confine: *Family obligations tied him to his home town.* **7.a.** to equal the record, score, or achievement of (an opponent). **b.** to equal (a record, score, or achievement). **8.** *Music.* to unite (notes) by a tie. **9. to tie down.** to hinder from action or movement; restrain;

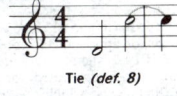

Tie (def. 8)

confine: *The new baby tied her down.* **10. to tie in.** to connect, esp. so as to make relevant or consistent. **11. to tie up. a.** to secure with a rope, string, or similar material. **b.** to hinder from movement or action; block: *The accident tied up traffic for hours.* **c.** to be in use, committed, or busy in such a way as to be unavailable for anything else: *We've tied up our cash in the stock market. The campaign had our staff tied up for weeks.* **d.** to bring to an end; finish, esp. successfully: *to tie up a business deal.* **e.** to make interrelated. —*v.i.* **1.** to be secured with a rope, string, or similar material: *This gown ties in the front.* **2.** to make the same record, score, or achievement; be equal: *The candidates tied in the straw poll.* **3. to tie in.** to be related or connected in some way; be linked: *His research ties in with mine.* **4. to tie up.** to interrelate. —*n.* **1.** cord, string, or similar material used to tie things. **2.** anything that unites or joins together: *ties of friendship.* **3.** necktie. **4.a.** equality between opponents or competitors, as in scores, records, or achievement. **b.** competition where such equality occurs; draw. **5.** structural member, as a beam or rod, that holds together or strengthens other members. **6.** one of the transverse pieces, usually of wood, to which railroad rails are fastened. **7. ties.** low shoes fastened with laces. **8.** *Music.* curved line written above or below notes of the same pitch, indicating that the tone is to be held for the combined time values of the two notes. [Old English *tīgan* to secure, as with a rope, from *tēag* rope.] —**Syn.** *n.* **2. see bond.**

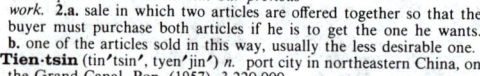

King post

Tie beam

Tie beam

tie beam, timber or piece serving as a tie, esp. the lowest horizontal member of a roof truss connecting the lower ends of the two principal rafters.

tie-in (tī'in') *n.* **1.** relation or connection: *This report has no tie-in with our previous work.* **2.a.** sale in which two articles are offered together so that the buyer must purchase both articles if he is to get the one he wants. **b.** one of the articles sold in this way, usually the less desirable one.

Tien-tsin (tin'tsin', tyen'jin') *n.* port city in northeastern China, on the Grand Canal. Pop. (1957), 3,220,000.

tier[1] (tēr) *n.* one of a series of rows, as of seats, arranged one above another. —*v.t.* to arrange in tiers. [Old French *tire* rank[1], row[1], series, order; possibly of Germanic origin.]

ti-er[2] (tī'ər) *n.* one who or that which ties. [TIE + -ER[1].]

tierce (tērs) *n.* **1.a.** formerly, liquid measure equal to forty-two gallons. **b.** cask holding this amount. **2.** sequence of three playing cards of the same suit. **3.** *Fencing.* third guard position. **4.** *Music.* interval of a third. **5.** third of the seven canonical hours, or the service for it. [Old French *tierce,* feminine of *tiers* third, from Latin *tertius.*]

Tier-ra del Fue-go (tyer'ə del fwā'gō) archipelago at the southern tip of South America, divided between Chile and Argentina. Land area, approx. 27,500 sq. mi.

tie-up (tī'up') *n.* **1.** stoppage or slowdown of work, action, or progress: *The accident caused a tie-up at the intersection.* **2.** *Informal.* connection; association: *I don't see the tie-up between those two events.*

tiff (tif) *n.* **1.** slight, usually petty quarrel; spat. **2.** slight fit of bad temper or peevishness; huff. —*v.i.* to be in or have a tiff. [Of uncertain origin.]

Tif-lis (tif'lis) see **Tbilisi.**

ti-ger (tī'gər) *n.* carnivorous Asian mammal, *Panthera tigris,* having a yellowish coat marked with black or brownish stripes. Length: to 13 feet, including tail. [Old French *tigre,* from Latin *tigris,* from Greek *tigris.*]

Tiger

tiger beetle, any of a group of brightly colored beetles, family Cicindelidae, whose larvae live in burrows in sandy soil.

tiger cat, any of several tigerlike wildcats, as the ocelot and serval. **2.** domestic cat having striped markings, esp. a tabby.

ti-ger-ish (tī'gər ish) *adj.* resembling a tiger in manner or appearance; fierce. Also, **ti'grish.**

tiger lily, slender Oriental plant, *Lilium tigrinum,* often cultivated for its showy, trumpet-shaped flowers, which are reddish-orange spotted with black.

tiger moth, any of a large group of moths, family Arctiidae, found in temperate and tropical regions. [Because the wings of certain species are banded in black and orange or yellow.]

ti-ger's-eye (tī'gərz ī') *also,* **ti-ger-eye.** *n.* semiprecious stone, usually yellowish-brown and containing iron oxide. It is a variety of quartz.

Tiger lily

tight (tīt) *adj.* **1.** fastened or held firmly; secure: *These windows are too tight to open.* **2.** closely arranged or packed; compactly put together: *a tight weave, a small, tight handwriting.* **3.** of such close construction as to be impervious or impermeable to liquid or gas: *a tight boat.* **4.** pulled or drawn to the fullest extent: *as tight as a drum.* **5.** fitting the body closely, esp. too closely: *a tight belt.* **6.** difficult to deal with or manage: *to be in a tight spot.* **7.** strict; severe: *We have to keep tight controls on public utilities.* **8.** concisely worded, reasoned, or otherwise put together: *a tight argument. The prosecution had built a tight case around the evidence.* **9.** constricted, as from tension: *a tight feeling in the pit of the stomach.* **10.** *Informal.* close-fisted; stingy. **11.** *Informal.* evenly matched; close: *a tight pennant race.* **12.** *Slang.* intoxicated; drunk. **13.a.** difficult to obtain: *Jobs are tight right now.* **b.** characterized by a scarcity, as of goods or money: *a tight market.* **14.** *Archaic.* well-made; trim; tidy. —*adv.* **1.** in a tight manner; firmly; securely: *to close a jar tight.* **2. to sit tight.** to hold onto one's position or opinion; take no action. **3. to sleep tight.** to sleep soundly. [Old Norse *thēttr* watertight, close.] —**tight'ly,** *adv.* —**tight'ness,** *n.*

tight-en (tīt'ən) *v.t., v.i.* to make or become tight or tighter.

tight-fist-ed (tīt'fis'tid) *adj.* stingy; miserly.

tight-lipped (tīt'lipt') *adj.* **1.** having the lips closed tightly. **2.** disinclined or reluctant to speak; quiet or secretive.

tight-rope (tīt'rōp') *n.* wire, cable, or rope tautly stretched between two poles or other objects, on which acrobats perform.

tights (tīts) *n.,pl.* skin-tight garment covering the lower part of the body and the feet or extending from the waist to the ankles.

tight-wad (tīt'wod') *n.* *Slang.* stingy person; miser.

ti-gress (tī'gris) *n.* female tiger.

Ti-gris (tī'gris) *n.* river in southwestern Asia, flowing from eastern Turkey through Iraq, where it joins the Euphrates to empty into the Persian Gulf.

ti-grish (tī'grish) tigerish.

Ti-jua-na (tē wä'nə) *n.* resort city in northwestern Mexico, at the U.S. border. Pop. (1969), 354,805.

tike (tīk) tyke.

til-bu-ry (til'ber'ē) *pl.,* **-ries.** *n.* light, open, two-wheeled carriage. [From *Tilbury,* the Englishman who designed it in the nineteenth century.]

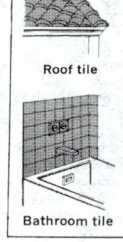

Roof tile

Bathroom tile

Tile

til-de (til'də) *n.* **1.** in Spanish, diacritical mark (˜) used over *n* to indicate the pronunciation *ny,* as in *señor* (se nyôr'). **2.** in Portuguese, the same mark, used over the vowels *a* and *o* to indicate nasal pronunciation, as in *João* (zhouN). [Spanish *tilde,* diacritical mark, from Latin *titulus* superscription, label.]

tile (tīl) *n.* **1.** thin, often decorated slab, as of baked clay, cement, porcelain, or linoleum, used for covering roofs, floors, or walls. **2.** tiles collectively; tiling. **3.** piece used in playing various games, as dominoes, mah jongg, or anagrams. **4.** short pipe, as of clay or concrete, used as a drain. —*v.t.* **tiled, til-ing.** to cover with tiles. [Old English *tigele* tile used for covering roofs, from Latin *tēgula* literally, that which covers, from *tegere* to cover.]

til-er (tī'lər) *n.* one who makes or lays tile.

til-ing (tī'ling) *n.* **1.** tiles collectively. **2.** act of covering with tiles. **3.** something covered with or consisting of tiles.

till[1] (til) *prep.* **1.** up to the time of: *Wait till tomorrow before calling.* **2.** before (a specified time): *They won't arrive till Sunday.* —*conj.* **1.** up to the time when or that: *Wait till you hear from me before writing.* **2.** before: *We didn't see the president till after the meeting.* [Old English *til* to.]

till[2] (til) *v.t.* to prepare and use (land) for raising crops. [Old English *tilian* to labor, cultivate.] —**till'a-ble,** *adj.*

till[3] (til) *n.* drawer or other receptacle in which money is kept, as in a store. [Of uncertain origin.]

till-age (til'ij) *n.* **1.** cultivation of land. **2.** land that is under cultivation. Also, **tilth.**

till-er[1] (til'ər) *n.* lever used to turn the rudder of a boat. [Old French *telier* weaver's beam, going back to Latin *tēla* web.]

till-er[2] (til'ər) *n.* one who or that which tills land. [TILL[2] + -ER[1].]

Tiller

Rudder

Tiller[1]

tilt (tilt) *v.t.* **1.** to raise one end or side of; put or place at an angle; tip: *Tilt the skillet so the eggs will slide onto the plate. Don't tilt your chair or you will fall.* **2.a.** to point or thrust (a lance) in a joust. **b.** to charge (an opponent) in or as in a joust. **3.** to forge or hammer with a tilt hammer. —*v.i.* **1.** to be in or assume a sloping position or direction; incline. **2.** to engage in a joust. **3.** to charge or attack in or as in a joust (with *at*): *Satire's my weapon,*

but I'm too discreet to run amuck, and tilt at all I meet (Pope, 1733). **4. to tilt at windmills.** to attack imaginary enemies or injustices. —*n.* **1.** tilting position; inclination: *the tilt of her head.* **2.** formal combat between two mounted knights or other individuals armed with lances and other weapons; joust. **3.** any combat, confrontation, or struggle resembling this. **4.** tilt hammer. **5. at full tilt.** at full speed. [Middle English *tilten* to totter, fall, cause to fall, probably going back to Old English *tealt* unsteady.]

tilth (tilth) *n.* **1.** tillage. **2.** texture or composition of soil under cultivation. [Old English *tilth* tillage, crop.]

tilt hammer, heavy hammer having a pivoted lever with a heavy head, used in forging.

Tim., Timothy.

tim·bal (tim′bəl) *also,* **tym·bal.** *n.* kettledrum. [French *timbale,* through Spanish, going back to Arabic *attabl* the drum.]

tim·bale (tim′bəl) *n.* **1.a.** dish made of finely minced meat, fish, vegetables, or cheese, cooked in a mold. **b.** mold, usually drum-shaped, in which such a dish is cooked. **2.** small cup-shaped mold made of fried pastry and often filled, as with a minced meat mixture. [French *timbale* dish, as of meat or fish, prepared in a mold, kettledrum; referring to the resemblance of the mold to a drum. See TIMBAL.]

tim·ber (tim′bər) *n.* **1.** wood suitable for building, carpentry, or similar forms of construction. **2.** single piece of wood used in construction; beam. **3.** one of the curved pieces leading from the keel and forming part of the framework of a ship. **4.** trees collectively. **5.** timberland; forest. —*v.t.* to cover, support, or provide with timber. [Old English *timbre* building, material for building.]

tim·bered (tim′bərd) *adj.* **1.** covered with growing trees; wooded: *a heavily timbered region.* **2.** built or made of timber.

timber hitch, knot used to fasten a line around a spar, post, or the like. See hitch for illustration.

tim·ber·ing (tim′bər ing) *n.* **1.** timbers collectively. **2.** work made of timbers.

tim·ber·land (tim′bər land′) *n.* land covered with trees to be used commercially, esp. for lumber.

timber line, imaginary line on mountains and in arctic regions above which trees do not grow.

timber wolf, gray wolf, *Canis lupus,* native to forest regions of Canada and the northern United States.

tim·bre (tim′bər, tam′-) *n.* characteristic property of sound, independent of pitch and volume, that distinguishes one voice or musical instrument from another. [French *timbre,* from Old French *timbre* bell that is struck by a hammer, drum, timbrel, going back to Greek *tympanon* kettledrum.]

Timber wolf

tim·brel (tim′brəl) *n.* tambourine or similar instrument. [Diminutive of Middle English *timbre,* from Old French *timbre.* See TIMBRE.]

Tim·buk·tu (tim′buk tōō′, tim buk′tōō) *n.* town in western Africa, in Mali, a great trade and cultural center in the twelfth through fifteenth centuries, now a small market center. Also, *French,* **Tom·bouc·tou′.**

time (tīm) *n.* **1.** indefinite extent during which events, conditions, and actions occur, exist, or continue in uninterrupted succession: *History is the witness that testifies to the passing of time* (Cicero, 55 B.C.). **2.** finite duration as distinguished from infinity or eternity: *the dawn of time.* **3.** exact point in time as shown by a clock or calendar: *What time is it?* **4.** definite or specific point in time: *The senator has no comment at this time.* **5.** favorable, appropriate, customary, or appointed point in time: *This is not the right time to ask for a raise. It's time for lunch.* **6.** particular point in time or portion of time in which something has occurred, is occurring, or will occur: *At the time of their marriage, they were living in New York.* **7.** definite or specific part or portion of time: *Summer is the warmest time of the year.* **8.** portion of time available or necessary for some purpose: *I have no time to argue with you. Give him time to think it over.* **9.** amount of time: *There's very little time left before she gets here. How much time has elapsed since he last called?* **10.** specific amount of time taken or needed for the completion of a given action or process: *The runner's time for the mile was four minutes.* **11.** system of measuring or computing time: *solar time.* **12.** *also,* **times. a.** particular or extent of time in history: *the time of Julius Caesar, medieval times.* **b.** the present time: *the leading dramatist of our time.* **c.** portion or extent of time considered with reference to prevailing conditions: *These are the times that try men's souls* (Paine, 1776). **13.** portion or extent of time considered with reference to someone's personal experience: *I had the dullest time of my life last night.* **14.** lifetime: *One man in his time plays many parts* (Shakespeare, *As You Like It*). **15.** one of a number of repeated or recurring actions or instances: *Cowards die many times before their deaths* (Shakespeare,

Julius Caesar. **16. times.** instances of being multiplied: *After the experiment, the rabbit was three times larger in size.* **17.** period worked or to be worked by an employee, or the pay received for this period. **18.** moment of death: *The old man felt his time drawing near.* **19.** *Informal.* period of imprisonment: *to serve time for robbery.* **20.** rate of speed or movement, as in marching. **21.** *Music.* **a.** rhythm; meter. **b.** tempo. **c.** characteristic rhythm and tempo of a particular kind of musical composition: *waltz time.* **d.** duration of a note or rest. **against time.** in an effort to finish within or before a certain time: *Police were working against time in their search for the hidden bomb.* **ahead of time.** before the time due or expected; early: *She arrived at the appointed place ahead of time.* **at the same time.** however; nevertheless. **at times.** sometimes; occasionally. **behind the times.** old-fashioned. **for the time being.** for the present; temporarily. **from time to time.** now and then; occasionally. **in good time. a.** at the proper time; within reasonable time. **b.** when or sooner than expected; quickly. **in no time.** almost instantly; very rapidly. **in time. a.** before it is too late: *Do you think we can get there in time for the first act?* **b.** in the course of time; eventually: *In time, all this will be forgotten.* **c.** in the correct or corresponding rhythm or tempo: *to clap in time to music.* **on time. a.** at the correct or appointed time; punctual or punctually. **b.** payable in installments over a period of time. **time after time.** repeatedly. Also, **time and again.** **time out of mind.** longer than can be remembered. **to keep time.** to record time, as a clock. **to make time. a.** to move rapidly, as in attempting to recover lost time. **b.** *Slang.* to progress in gaining favor or acceptance, as in carrying on a flirtation. —*v.t.,* **timed, tim·ing. 1.** to regulate, adjust, or arrange according to time: *to time one's footsteps to music. The bomb was timed to go off at midnight.* **2.** to measure or ascertain the time, duration, or rate of: *to time a race, to time a runner, to time a cake while it is baking.* **3.** to choose the time or occasion for: *The senator timed his speech to maximize its effect on the coming election.* —*adj.* **1.** of or relating to time. **2.** regulated, adjusted, or devised to operate at a certain time, as a bomb or lock. **3.** payable at a future date or in installments over a period of time. [Old English *tīma* period of existence or duration, point in such a period, era, age, opportunity.]

time and a half, payment equal to one and one half times the regular rate of pay, as for overtime.

time bomb, bomb that can be set to explode at a specific time.

time capsule, receptacle containing records and objects of current culture, deposited in a secure place for discovery by some future age.

time-card (tīm′kärd′) *n.* card for recording the number of hours that an employee has worked.

time clock, clock with a mechanism for automatically recording the arrival and departure times of an employee on a timecard.

time-con·sum·ing (tīm′kən sōō′ming) *adj.* taking up or wasting a great deal of time.

time deposit, bank deposit that cannot be withdrawn without advance notice or until a specified future date.

time draft, draft payable after a specified number of days stated in the draft.

time exposure 1. exposure of a photographic film for a relatively long period of time, often for more than one or two seconds. **2.** photograph made by such an exposure.

time fuse, fuse set to detonate an explosive device at a specific time.

time-hon·ored (tīm′on′ərd) *adj.* revered, respected, or observed because of age or long usage: *a time-honored custom.*

time immemorial, time so long past as to be beyond memory or record.

time-keep·er (tīm′kē′pər) *n.* one who or that which keeps, measures, or records time.

time-less (tīm′lis) *adj.* **1.** unaffected by the passage of time; eternal. **2.** referring to or characteristic of no particular time.

time lock, lock having a mechanism that can be set to open at a specific time.

time-ly (tīm′lē) -li·er, -li·est. *adj.* occurring at a suitable or appropriate time; well-timed. —**time′li·ness,** *n.*

time-out (tīm′out′) *n.* **1.** in sports, short period of time requested by a team, during which play is stopped, as for rest or substitutions. **2.** any brief cessation of work or activity; break.

time-piece (tīm′pēs′) *n.* any apparatus that records, measures, or keeps time, esp. a watch or clock.

tim·er (tī′mər) *n.* **1.** one who or that which measures, records, or keeps time; timekeeper. **2.** device for measuring intervals of time, as a stopwatch. **3.** device that indicates, as by a buzzer or bell, the lapse of a

preset interval of time, or automatically starts or stops, at preset times, another mechanism, as a light. **4.** device in an internal-combustion engine that causes the spark to be produced in the cylinder at the right instant.

times (tīmz) *prep.* multiplied by: *Two times two equals four.*

time-sav-ing (tīm′sā′ving) *adj.* lessening the amount of time spent on or needed for doing something. —**time′sav′er,** *n.*

time-serv-er (tīm′sur′vər) *n.* one who conforms to the current or popular standards of conduct or thinking in order to achieve personal gain or win approval. —**time′serv′ing,** *adj., n.*

time signature, sign, usually expressed as a fraction, placed on a staff to indicate the meter of the music which follows.

Time signature for three-quarter time

Times Square, area in downtown Manhattan, a noted entertainment center of New York City.

time-ta-ble (tīm′tā′bəl) *n.* schedule showing the times at which successive events are to be done or happen, esp. a schedule showing the arrival and departure times of trains, buses, boats, or airplanes.

time-worn (tīm′wôrn′) *adj.* **1.** showing the effects of time or long use. **2.** used too frequently; trite.

time zone, any of the twenty-four longitudinal regions, of fifteen degrees each, into which the earth is divided for measuring standard time from the prime meridian at Greenwich, England.

tim-id (tim′id) *adj.* characterized by or exhibiting a lack of courage, boldness, or self-confidence; shy. [Latin *timidus.*] —**ti-mid′i-ty, tim′id-ness,** *n.* —**tim′id-ly,** *adv.*

tim-ing (tī′ming) *n.* regulation or ascertainment of the opportune moment or appropriate speed for some action or occurrence in order to produce the desired effect: *The aerialist's timing was off, and he fell into the net.*

Ti-mor (tē′môr) *n.* island southeast of Celebes and north of Australia, divided between Portugal and Indonesia. Area, 13,094 sq. mi. Pop. (1961 est.), 1,100,000.

tim-or-ous (tim′ər əs) *adj.* characterized by or exhibiting a lack of courage, boldness, or self-confidence; timid. [Medieval Latin *timorosus,* from Latin *timor* fear.] —**tim′or-ous-ly,** *adv.* —**tim′-or-ous-ness,** *n.*

tim-o-thy (tim′ə thē) *n.* tall stout grass, *Phleum pratense,* having smooth, hollow stems with narrow spikelike clusters of tiny flowers at the tips, cultivated for hay and sometimes for grazing. [From *Timothy* Hanson, U.S. farmer who supposedly brought it from New York to the Carolinas about 1720.]

Tim-o-thy (tim′ə thē) *n.* **1.** disciple of Saint Paul. **2.** either of two books of the New Testament consisting of epistles written to Timothy by Paul.

Timothy

tim-pa-ni (tim′pə nē) *sing.,* -**no** (-nō′). *also,* **tym-pa-ni.** *n.,pl.* kettledrums. [Italian *timpani,* plural of *timpano* kettledrum, from Latin *tympanum* drum. See TYMPANUM.] —**tim′pa-nist,** *n.*

tin (tin) *n.* **1.** lustrous, silver-white, metallic element that resists corrosion, used esp. as a coating on sheet steel for cans. Symbol: **Sn** See **element** for table. **2.** tin plate. **3.** any receptacle made of tin, as a baking sheet. **4.** *British.* can² *(def. 2).* —*adj.* made or consisting of tin. —*v.t.,* **tinned, tin-ning. 1.** to cover, coat, or plate with tin. **2.** to preserve or pack in tin cans; can. [Old English *tin* the metal.]

tin-a-mou (tin′ə mōō′) *n.* any of various game birds, family Tinamidae, native to Central and South America, resembling the partridge. Length: 15 inches. [French *tinamou,* from Carib *tinamu.*]

tinct (tingkt) *Archaic. adj.* tinged. —*n.* tint. [Latin *tinctus,* past participle of *tingere* to moisten, dye.]

tinc-ture (tingk′chər) *n.* **1.** solution, usually in alcohol, containing a drug or other medicinal agent. **2.** small amount; trace; hint. **3.** tinge of color; tint. —*v.t.,* **-tured, -tur-ing. 1.** to give a tinge of a peculiar quality or character to. **2.** to tint; stain. [Latin *tinctūra* a dyeing.]

tin-der (tin′dər) *n.* any substance that burns easily, esp. something used to kindle a fire from a spark, as dry twigs. [Old English *tynder.*]

tin-der-box (tin′dər boks′) *n.* **1.** box used for holding the materials necessary for kindling a fire, as flint or coal. **2.** any place or situation that is a potential source of strife or trouble.

tine (tīn) *n.* sharp projecting point or prong, as of a fork. [Old English *tind.*]

tin-foil (tin′foil′) *n.* very thin sheet of tin or other metal, as aluminum, used as a wrapping.

ting (ting) *n.* clear, high-pitched, metallic sound, as that made by a

small bell. —*v.t., v.i.* to emit or cause to emit a ting. [Imitative.]

tinge (tinj) **tinged, tinge-ing** *or* **ting-ing.** *v.t.* **1.** to color slightly; tint; stain. **2.** to affect with a slight trace, touch, or flavor of some other quality or characteristic: *This grief tinged the whole of Mr. Croker's subsequent life* (Jennings, 1884). —*n.* **1.** faint trace of color. **2.** small amount; touch; trace: *She felt a tinge of autumn in the air.* [Latin *tingere* to moisten, dye.]

tin-gle (ting′gəl) **-gled, -gling.** *v.i.* **1.** to have a slight vibrating or stinging sensation, as from sudden excitement, cold, or a sharp blow. **2.** to cause such a sensation. —*v.t.* to cause to tingle. —*n.* tingling sensation. [Probably form of TINKLE.]

tink-er (ting′kər) *n.* **1.** craftsman, usually itinerant, who mends pots, pans, and other metal household utensils. **2.** person who can do many different kinds of repair work. **3.** unskillful or clumsy workman; bungler. —*v.i.* **1.** to busy oneself in a trifling or aimless way; putter. **2.** to work in an unskilled or clumsy manner. **3.** to work as a tinker; mend household utensils. [Possibly from obsolete *tink* to tinkle, ring (of imitative origin) + -ER¹; referring to the tinkling sound made in working on pots and pans.]

tinker's damn *also,* **tinker's dam.** *Slang.* slightest bit: *His opinion isn't worth a tinker's damn.*

tin-kle (ting′kəl) **-kled, -kling.** *v.i.* to produce or emit clear, light, ringing sounds. —*v.t.* **1.** to cause to tinkle. **2.** to summon or call by tinkling. —*n.* clear, light, ringing sound. [Obsolete *tink* to ring (of imitative origin) + -LE.]

tin-ner (tin′ər) *n.* **1.** one who works in a tin mine. **2.** one who works with or deals in tin; tinsmith.

tin-ny (tin′ē) **-ni-er, -ni-est.** *adj.* **1.** of, relating to, or containing tin. **2.** having a metallic flavor, sound, or quality. —**tin′ni-ness,** *n.*

tin-pan alley (tin′pan′) **1.** composers, performers, and publishers of popular music collectively. **2.** popular music industry.

tin plate, thin sheets of metal, esp. iron or steel, coated with tin.

tin-sel (tin′səl) *n.* **1.** very thin strips of glittering metallic material, used for ornamentation, esp. on Christmas trees. **2.** anything showy or attractive but having little or no intrinsic worth. **3.** fabric woven with metallic threads, as of silver or gold. —*v.t.,* **-seled, -sel-ing;** *also, British,* **-selled, -sel-ling.** to trim with or as with tinsel. —*adj.* **1.** made of, resembling, or decorated with tinsel. **2.** showy or attractive but having little or no intrinsic worth. [Shortened from Middle French *estincelle* spark, flash, going back to Latin *scintilla* spark.]

tin-smith (tin′smith′) *n.* one who works with or deals in tin or tinware.

tint (tint) *n.* **1.** shade or variety of a color: *There were tints of gold in her hair.* **2.** delicate, pale color, esp. one that has been softened by the addition of light or white pigment. —*v.t., v.i.* to add or give a slight color to: *She tinted the Easter eggs with vegetable dye.* [Earlier *tinct,* from Latin *tinctus* a dyeing, from *tingere* to moisten, dye.]

Syn. *n.* **1.** Tint, shade, hue¹ mean some particular color. **Tint** is often applied to a faint or slight trace of color, esp. artificial color, as that of oil paint, hair dye, or nail polish, and is used to suggest delicacy and subtlety or to set a mood, esp. one of a romantic nature: *The blue tint of those sunglasses makes you look very glamorous.* **Shade** is applied to slight differences among a group of a single color, esp. those that are deeper or darker, and suggests a keen attention to subtle variations: *I'd like a suit in a softer shade of gray.* **Hue** is applied to varieties of the basic colors or red, yellow, and blue and often is used to suggest brightness and clarity: *The bird's plumage has a reddish hue.*

tin-tin-nab-u-la-tion (tin′tə nab′yə lā′shən) *n.* **1.** tinkling, ringing, or pealing of bells. **2.** sound produced by or as by bells. [Latin *tintin-nābulum* bell + -ATION.]

Tin-to-ret-to (tin′tə ret′ō) *n.* 1518–94, Venetian painter.

tin-type (tin′tīp′) *n.* photograph made on a tin-coated iron plate treated with a light-sensitive substance.

tin-ware (tin′wâr′) *n.* articles made of tin plate.

ti-ny (tī′nē) **-ni-er, -ni-est.** *adj.* very small or slight; wee. [Obsolete *tine* (of uncertain origin) + -Y¹.]

-tion *suffix* (used to form nouns) **1.** action or process of: *adoption.* **2.** state or condition of being: *relaxation.* **3.** result of: *contamination.* [Latin *-tiō,* often through French *-tion.*]

tip¹ (tip) *n.* **1.** extreme or outermost point or end of anything: *He scuffed the tip of his shoe.* **2.** small piece or part attached to or forming the end of something. —*v.t.,* **tipped, tip-ping. 1.** to furnish with a tip. **2.** to cover, decorate, or serve as the tip of. [Of uncertain origin.]

tip² (tip) **tipped, tip-ping.** *v.t.* **1.** to raise one end or side of. **2.** to cause to fall or tumble; overturn (often with *over*): *He accidentally tipped over the chair.* **3.** to raise or touch (one's hat) in greeting. —*v.i.* **1.** to be in or assume a sloping position or direction; tilt. **2.** to fall or topple (with *over*): *The ashtray tipped over.* —*n.* inclined position; tilt. [Of uncertain origin.]

tip³ (tip) *n.* **1.** gift of money given in return for services rendered; gratuity: *He gave the doorman a tip for helping him with his packages.*

at; āpe; cär; end; mē; it; īce; hot; ōld; fôrk; wood; fōōl; oil; out; up; ūse; turn; sing; thin; this; zh in treasure; ə in ago, taken, pencil, lemon, circus.

2.a. piece of useful information, given privately or secretly, esp. by an expert: *I invested $300 on a tip from my broker.* **b.** any useful or helpful hint or suggestion: *He gave her some tips about the care of her new car.* —*v.t.,* **tipped, tip·ping. 1.** to give a gratuity to. **2.** to give private or secret information to (often with *off*): *The informer tipped off the police about the plan to rob the bank.* —*v.i.* to give a tip or tips. [Of uncertain origin.] —**tip′per,** *n.*

tip⁴ (tip) **tipped, tip·ping.** *v.t.* **1.** to strike or hit lightly; tap. **2.** *Baseball.* to hit (the ball) with a glancing blow. —*n.* light, sharp blow; tap. [Possibly from Low German origin.]

tip-off (tip′ôf′) *n. Informal.* hint or warning.

Tip·pe·ca·noe (tip′ē kə nōō′) *n.* river in northwestern Indiana.

Tip·per·ar·y (tip′ə rär′ē) *n.* county in the southern part of the Republic of Ireland. Area, approx. 1643 sq. mi. Pop. (1966), 122,812.

tip·pet (tip′it) *n.* **1.** scarflike covering worn about the neck and shoulders with loose ends hanging down in front. **2.** in the Anglican Church, long black scarf worn over the robe of a clergyman. **3.** formerly, long, narrow hanging part, as of a hood or sleeve. [Of uncertain origin.]

tip·ple (tip′əl) **-pled, -pling.** *v.t., v.i.* to drink (alcoholic beverages) habitually and continuously in small quantities. —*n.* alcoholic liquor. [Of uncertain origin.] —**tip′pler,** *n.*

tip·ster (tip′stər) *n. Informal.* one who gives or sells private or secret information, esp. to bettors or speculators. [TIP³ + -STER.]

tip·sy (tip′sē) **-si·er, -si·est.** *adj.* **1.** slightly intoxicated. **2.** inclined to tip; unsteady. [From TIP².] —**tip′si·ly,** *adv.* —**tip′si·ness,** *n.*

tip·toe (tip′tō′, -tō′) **-toed, -toe·ing.** *v.i.* to move or walk on or as if on the tips of one's toes; walk quietly or stealthily. —*n.* on tiptoe. **a.** standing or walking on the tips of one's toes. **b.** full of expectation or eagerness. **c.** quietly; stealthily.

tip·top (tip′top′) *Informal. n.* highest point or part. —*adj.* **1.** situated at the highest point. **2.** of the highest quality; first-rate; excellent.

ti·rade (tī rād′, tī′rād′) *n.* prolonged, vehement speech, esp. one containing abuse, criticism, or censure. [French *tirade* long speech, from Italian *tirata* literally, a pulling, from *tirare* to pull; of uncertain origin.]

Ti·ra·na (ti rä′nə) *also,* **Ti·ra·ne.** *n.* capital and largest city of Albania, in the central part of the country. Pop. (1967), 169,300.

tire¹ (tīr) **tired, tir·ing.** *v.t.* **1.** to weaken or exhaust the strength or energy of; make weary; fatigue: *Reading in the dim light soon tired his eyes.* **2.** to exhaust the attention, interest, or patience of; bore: *The speaker's monotonous voice soon tired his listeners.* **3.** to tire out. —*v.i.* **1.** to become fatigued or weary. **2.** to become bored with (with *of*): *The children tired of the new game quickly.* [Old English *tēorian* to become weary, weary.] —**Syn.** *v.t.* **1.** see **fatigue.**

tire² (tīr) *also, British.* **tyre.** *n.* covering of fabric and rubber, either solid or filled with air under pressure, mounted on the rim of a wheel and usually having a tread. Tires serve as a cushion and a gripping surface on road vehicles, tractors, aircraft landing gear, baby carriages, and other mobile machinery. [Possibly from TIRE³; because thought of as the wheel's *attire.*]

tire³ (tīr) *Archaic. n.* **1.** attire. **2.** headdress. —*v.t.,* **tired, tir·ing.** to dress. [Short for ATTIRE.]

tired (tīrd) *adj.* fatigued; weary; exhausted. [TIRE¹ + -ED².] —**tired′ly,** *adv.* —**tired′ness,** *n.*

tire·less (tīr′lis) *adj.* never wearying; untiring. —**tire′less·ly,** *adv.* —**tire′less·ness,** *n.*

tire·some (tīr′səm) *adj.* tedious; boring; tiring. —**tire′some·ly,** *adv.* —**tire′some·ness,** *n.*

ti·ro (tī′rō) *pl., -ros. n.* tyro.

Ti·rol (ti rōl′, tī′rōl) Tyrol.

Tir·o·lese (tir′ə lēz′, -lēs′) Tyrolese.

'tis (tiz) it is.

tis·sue (tish′ōō) *n.* **1.** in animals and plants, a group of similar cells performing the same function. In the human body there are four basic types of tissue: epithelium, connective tissue, muscle, and the tissue that makes up the nervous system. **2.** soft, thin, absorbent piece of paper, usually consisting of two layers, used esp. as a handkerchief. **3.** tissue paper. **4.** woven fabric, usually having a light, gauzy texture. **5.** interwoven series or sequence; web: *a tissue of lies.* [Old French *tissue* woven, woven cloth, from *tistre* to weave, from Latin *texere.*]

tissue paper, very thin, nearly transparent paper, used esp. as a wrapping or packing material.

tit¹ (tit) *n.* **1.** titmouse. **2.** any of various small birds, as the pipit. [From TITMOUSE.]

Tippet (def. 3)

tit² (tit) *n.* teat or breast. [Old English *tit.*]

Ti·tan (tīt′ən) *n.* **1.** *Greek Mythology.* any of a race of giants who were the offspring or descendants of Uranus and Gaea and who ruled the world until overthrown by the Olympian gods. **2. titan.** one who has extraordinary size, strength, or power. —*adj.* Titanic.

Ti·ta·ni·a (ti tā′nē ə) *n. Medieval Legend and Literature.* wife of Oberon and queen of the fairies.

Ti·tan·ic (tī tan′ik) *adj.* **1.** of, relating to, or characteristic of the Titans. **2. titanic.** having great size, strength, or power.

ti·ta·ni·um (tī tā′nē əm, ti-) *n.* light, strong, silver-white metallic element found in the earth's crust and on the moon, used esp. to make structural parts of aircraft and spacecraft. Symbol: Ti See **element** for table. [From TITAN.]

tit·bit (tit′bit′) *n.* tidbit.

tit for tat, retaliation in kind; blow for blow.

tithe (tīth) *n.* **1.** one-tenth of a person's annual income from his land or labor, paid either in kind or money, esp. for the support of the church and the clergy. **2.** one-tenth of anything. **3.** any small tax, tribute, or levy. **4.** very small part. —*v.t.,* **tithed, tith·ing. 1.** to impose a tax of a tenth on. **2.** to give one-tenth of (one's annual income), esp. for the support of the church and the clergy. [Old English *tēotha,* contraction of *teogotha* tenth.]

Ti·tho·nus (ti thō′nəs) *n. Greek Mythology.* beloved of Eos, who secured immortality for him but not eternal youth, so that he became old and shriveled and was finally changed into a grasshopper.

ti·tian (tish′ən) *n.* reddish or golden-brown color. [From *Titian,* who often used this color in painting hair.]

Ti·tian (tish′ən) *n.* c.1477–1576, Venetian painter.

Ti·ti·ca·ca, Lake (tē′tē kä′kə) largest lake in South America, in the Andes, in southeastern Peru and western Bolivia.

tit·il·late (tit′əl āt′) **-lat·ed, -lat·ing.** *v.t.* **1.** to excite or stimulate agreeably. **2.** to produce a tickling sensation in. [Latin *titillātus,* past participle of *titillāre* to tickle.] —**tit′il·la′tion,** *n.*

tit·i·vate (tit′ə vāt′) **-vat·ed, -vat·ing.** *v.t., v.i. Informal.* to add finishing touches to; dress up. [Possibly from TIDY, on the model of CULTIVATE.] —**tit′i·va′tion,** *n.*

tit·lark (tit′lärk′) *n.* pipit. [TIT¹ + LARK¹.]

ti·tle (tīt′əl) *n.* **1.a.** name by which a particular thing, as a book, painting, or other work of art, is identified, known, or referred to. **b.** general or descriptive heading, as of a chapter or section of a book. **2.** word or group of words attached to the proper name of a person or family, used as an expression or mark of respect, courtesy, or distinction, or to indicate office, rank, occupation, status, or condition in life. **3.** in certain sports, championship. **4.** *Law.* **a.** right that a person has to the ownership of property. **b.** that which serves as evidence of such a right, as a deed. **c.** means by which one acquires such a right. **5.** section of a bill or law, usually given a roman numeral. **6.** established or recognized right; just claim. —*v.t.,* **-tled, -tling.** to give the title of; call; entitle. [Old French *title* name indicating rank, designation of a subject treated in a book, from Latin *titulus* label, superscription. Doublet of TITTLE.]

ti·tled (tīt′əld) *adj.* having a title, esp. of nobility.

title deed, deed that constitutes or is evidence of title to property.

title page, page at the beginning of a book, usually containing the title of the book and the names of the author and publisher.

title role, role or character in a play, motion picture, or other theatrical presentation for which the presentation is named.

tit·mouse (tit′mous′) *pl., -mice. n.* any of various plump songbirds, family Paridae, having soft, thick, predominantly gray and brown plumage. Length: 3–8 inches. Also, **tit.** [Middle English *titmose,* from *tit* something small (of imitative origin) + Old English *māse* titmouse.]

Titmouse

Ti·to, Marshal (tē′tō) 1892—, Yugoslav president and premier; born Josip Broz.

Ti·to·ism (tē′tō iz′əm) *n.* system of national Communism based on independence from the Soviet Union, nonalignment in foreign policy, and decentralized economic development, first established by Tito in Yugoslavia in the late 1940s.

ti·trate (tī′trāt) **-trat·ed, -trat·ing.** *v.t., v.i.* to determine the concentration of (a solution) by titration. [French *titrer* (from *titre* standard, qualification, heading, going back to Latin *titulus* label) + -ATE¹.]

ti·tra·tion (tī trā′shən) *n.* method of determining the concentration of a solute in a solution by noting the amount of a solution of known strength that must be added to produce a completed chemical reaction, as shown by a certain effect, such as a change in the color of the solution.

tit·ter (tit′ər) *v.i.* to laugh in a restrained or nervous manner. —*n.* restrained or nervous laugh. —**tit′ter·er,** *n.*

tit·tle (tit′əl) *n.* **1.** very small part or amount; minute quantity.

2. small diacritical mark, as over a letter, in writing or printing. The dot over a *j* is a tittle. [Medieval Latin *titulus* mark over a letter, accent, from Latin *titulus* label, superscription. Doublet of TITLE.]

tit·tle-tat·tle (tit′əl tat′əl) -**tled**, -**tling**. *v.i.* to talk idly or foolishly; prate. —*n.* idle or foolish talk. [Repetition of TATTLE, with a change of vowel in the first syllable.]

tit·u·lar (tich′ə lər) *adj.* **1.** having the title or name of an office without having or exercising the powers or duties implied by it; nominal: *The former president was the titular leader of the political party.* **2.** having a title, esp. of nobility; titled. **3.** of or designating a title role: *the titular character in a play.* [Latin *titulus* label, superscription + -AR¹.]

Ti·tus (tī′təs) *n.* **1.** A.D. c.39–81, Roman emperor from A.D. 79 to 81. **2.** convert and disciple of Saint Paul. **3.** book of the New Testament consisting of an epistle written to Titus by Saint Paul.

tiz·zy (tiz′ē) *pl.*, -**zies.** *n. Slang.* state of extreme excitement, agitation, or confusion; dither. ▲ used chiefly in the phrase *to be in a tizzy.* [Of uncertain origin.]

Tl, thallium.

Tm, thulium.

TM, transcendental meditation.

tme·sis (tə mē′sis, mē′sis) *n.* separation of a compound word by the insertion of another word or words, as in *what might be soever* for *whatsoever might be.* [Greek *tmēsis* a cutting.]

tn., ton.

TNT, yellow organic compound, widely used as a high explosive. [Abbreviation of T(RI)N(INTRO)T(OLUENE).]

to (tōō; *unstressed* too, tə) *prep.* **1.a.** in the direction of; toward: *Turn to the left. His back was to the audience. She pointed to a clump of trees.* **b.** in the direction of and reaching: *the train to London. The tree fell to the ground.* **2.** as far as: *wet to the skin, generous to a fault.* **3.** near or in contact with; on, upon, or against: *Nail it to the floor. She applied polish to her nails.* **4.** toward or into a condition of: *The glass was smashed to bits. They worked to exhaustion.* **5.** so as to cause or result in: *sentenced to life imprisonment. To our surprise, he agreed with the plan.* **6.** for the purpose of; for: *The coast guard came to our aid.* **7.a.** until: *The store is open from nine to six.* **b.** before: *It's five minutes to three.* **8.** as compared with: *We won by a score of three to one.* **9.** comprising; constituting. **10.** accompanied by; along with; with: *to dance to music.* **11.** belonging with or used with: *the key to a door. Where is the vest to this suit?* **12.** in agreement or accord with: *a plan drawn to scale.* **13.** in honor of: *They drank a toast to the queen.* **14.** regarding; about; concerning: *That's all there was to it.* **15.** To is also used: **a.** for indicating the application of an adjective: *hostile to strangers, unknown to us, a portrait that is true to life.* **b.** for indicating the application of a noun: *a newcomer to the city, a pretender to the throne. The flood brought suffering to the population.* **c.** for indicating the recipient of an action: *She gave the letter to him.* **d.** for introducing the infinitive form of a verb: *She began to cry. I learned to swim last summer.* ▲ in this sense *to* is often used alone when the verb is understood from the context: *You may go home whenever you want to.* —*adv.* **1.** forward: *The boat turned to.* **2.** into a shut or closed position: *He slammed the door to.* **3.** to the matter at hand; to action or work. **4. to and fro,** alternately in opposite directions; backwards and forwards. [Old English *tō* toward, until, in order to, so as to result in.]

to·ad (tōd) *n.* **1.** any of a group of stout, squat frogs, family Bufonidae, inhabiting most regions of the world, having rough, dry, bumpy skin and relatively short legs. **2.** any of various similar amphibians. [Old English *tāde*, short for *tādige.*]

Toad

toad·fish (tōd′fish′) *pl.*, -**fish** or -**fish·es.** *n.* any of a group of stout-bodied, scaleless fish, family Batrachoididae, found in temperate and tropical waters along the Atlantic coast of the Americas, having a large, sharp-toothed mouth and often poisonous spines on the back. Length: to 18 inches.

Toadfish

toad·stool (tōd′stōōl′) *n.* **1.** any of various mushrooms. **2.** *Informal.* poisonous mushroom.

toad·y (tō′dē) *pl.*, -**toad·ies.** *n.* one who flatters another for personal gain; obsequious, fawning person. —*v.i.*, -**toad·ied,** -**toad·y·ing.** to be or behave like a toady (with *to*): *to toady to one's superiors.* —*v.t.* to fawn upon in an obsequious manner. [From earlier *toadeater* assistant of a charlatan who pretended to eat a *toad* (once considered poisonous) so that the charlatan might appear to save the assistant's life with his quack medicines.] —**toad′y·ism,** *n.*

to-and-fro (tōō′ən frō′) *adj.* moving forward and backward. —*adv.* fro (def. 1).

toast¹ (tōst) *n.* sliced bread browned by heat. —*v.t.* **1.** to brown by heating, as in a toaster or over a fire. **2.** to warm thoroughly, as before a fire or heater: *to toast one's feet.* —*v.i.* to become toasted. [Old French *toster* to roast, going back to Latin *tostus,* past participle of *torrēre* to parch.]

toast² (tōst) *n.* **1.** act of drinking in honor of or to the health of a person or thing: *There were several toasts before dinner.* **2.** one who or that which is the subject of such drinking. —*v.t.* to drink in honor of or to the health of: *We toasted the bride and groom.* —*v.i.* to propose or drink a toast or toasts. [From TOAST¹; supposedly from the former practice of flavoring liquor by putting spiced *toast* in it.]

toast·er (tōs′tər) *n.* device, usually electrical, for toasting bread. [TOAST¹ + -ER¹.]

toast·er² (tōs′tər) *n.* one who proposes a toast. [TOAST² + -ER¹.]

toast·mas·ter (tōst′mas′tər) *n.* one who proposes the toasts and introduces the guests and speakers at a formal dinner or other gathering.

Tob., Tobit.

to·bac·co (tə bak′ō) *pl.*, -**cos** or -**coes.** *n.* **1.** prepared leaves of any of various plants, genus *Nicotiana,* of the nightshade family, used for smoking, chewing, and as a snuff. **2.** any of these plants, esp. *N. tabacum,* having large, lance-shaped leaves covered with hairs and pink, white, or red funnel-shaped flowers. **3.** products prepared from the leaves of these plants, as cigars, cigarettes, or snuff. [Spanish *tabaco* the plant, its leaves, from Taino *tabaco* pipe in which the plant was smoked, roll of tobacco leaves for smoking.]

Tobacco leaves

to·bac·co·nist (tə bak′ə nist) *n.* dealer in tobacco.

To·ba·go (tə bā′gō) *n.* island of the Lesser Antilles, near Venezuela, forming part of the country of Trinidad and Tobago. Area, 116 sq. mi. Pop. (1960), 33,200.

To·bi·as (tə bī′əs) *n.* in the Douay Bible, Tobit.

To·bit (tō′bit) *n.* book of the Protestant Apocrypha.

to·bog·gan (tə bog′ən) *n.* long, flat-bottomed, sledlike vehicle without runners and having a curled-up front end, used for coasting on snow or for transporting goods. —*v.i.* **1.** to coast or ride on a toboggan. **2.** to decline or decrease rapidly, as in value. [Micmac *tobâgun* type of Algonquian Indian sled.]

to·by (tō′bē) *pl.*, -**bies.** *n.* small jug or mug, usually in the form of a fat man wearing a long coat and a three-cornered hat. Also, **toby jug.** [From *Toby,* familiar form of *Tobias,* masculine proper name.]

toc·ca·ta (tə kä′tə) *n.* musical composition for a keyboard instrument, written in the style of an improvisation, intended to exhibit the performer's technique. [Italian *toccata,* from *toccare* to touch, play (a keyboard instrument), from an assumed Vulgar Latin word based on an imitation of the sound of striking.]

to·coph·er·ol (tō kof′ə rōl′) *n.* any of a group of oily, fat-soluble vitamin compounds, necessary in the diet of certain mammals, including man, that may affect the reproductive system, found chiefly in leafy green vegetables, cereal, grains, and corn oil. Also, **vitamin E.** [Greek *tokos* childbirth + *pherein* to bear + -OL.]

Tocque·ville, A·le·xis de (tōk′vil′; ä lek sē′ də) 1805–59, French political theorist.

toc·sin (tok′sin) *n.* **1.** signal or alarm sounded on a bell. **2.** bell or other signal used to sound an alarm. [French *tocsin* alarm bell, going back to Provençal *tocar* to strike, touch (from an assumed Vulgar Latin word based on an imitation of the sound of striking) + *senh* bell, mark (from Latin *signum* mark).]

to·day (tə dā′) *also,* **to-day.** *n.* the present day, time, or age. —*adv.* **1.** on or during the present day. **2.** at the present time; nowadays; currently: *Fashions today are different from what they were ten years ago.* [Old English *tōdæg(e)* on this day.]

tod·dle (tod′əl) -**dled,** -**dling.** *v.i.* to walk or move with short, unsteady steps, as a child who is just learning to walk. —*n.* act of toddling. [Of uncertain origin.]

tod·dler (tod′lər) *n.* small child, esp. one who is just learning to walk.

tod·dy (tod′ē) *pl.*, -**dies.** *n.* **1.** drink made with liquor, as brandy or whiskey, hot water, spices, sugar, and a slice of lemon. **2.a.** drink made from the fermented sap of certain East Indian palm trees. **b.** sap of such trees. [Hindi *tārī* sap of the palm tree, from *tār* palm tree, from Sanskrit *tāla;* probably of Dravidian origin.]

to-do (tə dōō′) *pl.*, -**dos.** *n. Informal.* bustle or fuss.

toe (tō) *n.* **1.** any of the five end parts of the foot. **2.** part of a stocking, shoe, or other piece of footwear that covers the toes. **3.** forward part of a foot or hoof. **4.** anything resembling a toe in shape, position, or function. **5. on one's toes.** prepared for any eventuality; mentally or

at; āpe; cär; end; mē; it; īce; hot; ōld; fôrk; wood; fōōl; oil; out; up; ūse; turn; sing; thin; this; zh in treasure; ə in ago, taken, pencil, lemon, circus.

physically alert. —*v.t.* **toed, toe·ing. 1.** to furnish with a toe or toes.
2.a. to drive (a nail) obliquely. **b.** to fasten or attach by nails driven
in this way. **3. to toe the line** (or **mark**). **a.** to act in accordance with
an established rule, standard, or code of behavior; conform. **b.** to stand
with the tips of one's toes touching a starting line or mark, as in a race.
—*v.i.* to turn the toes in a specific direction: *to toe out.* [Old English
tā any of the five digits of the human foot.]
toed (tōd) *adj.* having toes, esp. a specific number or kind of toes.
⏶ usually used in combination: *a three-toed sloth, square-toed shoes.*
toe·nail (tō′nāl′) *n.* **1.** nail that grows on a toe. **2.** nail driven
obliquely. —*v.t.* to fasten or attach with obliquely
driven nails.
tof·fee (tô′fē, tof′ē) *pl.,* **-fees.** *also.* **tof·fy.** *n.*
hard, chewy candy made of butter, sugar, and often
nuts. [Of uncertain origin.]
tof·fy (tô′fē, tof′ē) *pl.,* **-fies.** *n.* toffee.
tog (tog) *n.* **togs.** clothes. —*v.t.,* **togged, tog·ging.**
to dress or array (often with *out* or *up*). [Possibly
short for obsolete *togemans* cloak, from Latin *toga*
man's outer garment in ancient Rome.]
to·ga (tō′gə) *pl.,* **-gas** or **-gae** (-jē) *n.* **1.** loose outer
garment draped over the entire body, covering the
left arm and leaving the right arm exposed, worn
by male citizens of ancient Rome. The approximate
social position of a person could be determined by
the color and ornamentation of the toga he wore.
2. robe or similar garment characteristic of an office
or profession. [Latin *toga* man's outer garment in
ancient Rome.] —**to′gaed,** *adj.*

Toga

to·geth·er (tə geth′ər) *adv.* **1.** one with the other;
with one another; in company: *The bride and her father walked down
the aisle together.* **2.** in or into one gathering, company, mass, or body:
The staff will meet together next week. **3.** in or into union, contact,
combination, or association with each other: *The streets come together
at the intersection. Mix the flour and water together.* **4.** in or into
agreement, harmony, or cooperation: *Let's try to get together on this
problem.* **5.** considered as a whole: *He knows more than all of us
together.* **6.** at the same time; simultaneously. **7.** without intermission;
continuously. [Old English *tōgædere* into one company or gathering,
into union.]
tog·ger·y (tog′ər ē) *pl.,* **-ger·ies.** *n. Informal.* clothes; togs.
tog·gle (tog′əl) *n.* **1.** pin, bolt, or rod put through the eye of a rope
or the link of a chain to prevent slipping, to tighten, or to secure an
attachment. **2.** ornamental, oblong button sewn to clothing or other
items and serving as a fastening when inserted through a loop or similar
opening. **3.** toggle joint, or a device having
one. —*v.t.,* **-gled, -gling.** to fasten or furnish
with a toggle or toggles. [Of uncertain origin.]
toggle joint, joint consisting of two bars
pivoted together end to end and bent at an
angle so that when a force is applied to the
joint to straighten it, pressure is transmitted
to the outer ends.

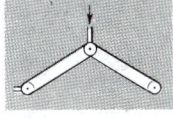

Toggle joint

toggle switch, switch consisting of a
projecting lever whose movement through a small arc opens or closes an
electric circuit.
To·go (tō′gō) *n.* country in western Africa, on the Gulf of Guinea,
between Ghana and Dahomey. Capital, Lomé. Area, 21,580 sq. mi.
Pop. (1970 est.), 1,857,000.
To·go·land (tō′gō land′) *n.* former German colony in western
Africa, on the Gulf of Guinea, later divided between Great Britain and
France. The British section is now a part of Ghana, the French is now
the country of Togo.
toil[1] (toil) *n.* hard and exhausting work or effort. —*v.i.* **1.** to engage
in hard and exhausting work, esp. for a considerable length of time.
2. to move with difficulty, weariness, or pain. [Anglo-Norman *toiller*
to dispute, strive, from Old French *toeillier* to make dirty, drag about,
stir, from Latin *tudiculāre* to stir up, from *tudicula* machine for bruising
olives, from *tundere* to beat.] —**toil′er,** *n.*
toil[2] (toil) *n.* **1.** **toils.** something that ensnares or entangles as a net:
While in the Toils of Hell I lie (Wesley, 1738). **2.** *Archaic.* net for
trapping game. [French *toile* cloth, web, from Latin *tēla* web.]
toi·let (toi′lit) *n.* **1.** bathroom. **2.** fixture consisting of a water-filled
basin usually having a lid, a hinged seat, and a flushing device connected
to a water tank, used for the elimination and disposal of human waste
products. **3.** act or process of washing, dressing, and grooming oneself.
4. *Archaic.* dressing table. **5.** person's dress; attire. **6. to make one's
toilet.** to wash, dress, and groom oneself. —*adj.* of, relating to, or for
the toilet. [French *toilette* doily, dressing table, lavatory, dress, diminutive of *toile* cloth. See TOIL².]

toilet paper, thin, absorbent paper, usually in a roll, used for cleaning
oneself after urination or defecation.
toi·let·ry (toi′lit rē) *pl.,* **-ries.** *n.* any of various articles for use in
making one's toilet.
toi·lette (toi let′, twä-) *n.* **1.** act or process of washing, dressing, and
grooming oneself; toilet. **2.** person's dress or manner of dress.
[French *toilette.* See TOILET.]
toilet water, scented liquid serving as a light perfume, as for use after
a bath; cologne.
toil·some (toil′səm) *adj.* tiresome; laborious.
toil·worn (toil′wôrn′) *adj.* exhausted or worn out by toil.
To·kay (tō kā′) *n.* **1.** rich, golden wine varying from dry to very sweet.
2. any similar wine. **3.** whitish or purplish grape from which this wine
is made. [From *Tokay,* a town in Hungary, where this wine was first
made.]
to·ken (tō′kən) *n.* **1.** something that serves to indicate or represent
some fact, event, object, or feeling; sign; symbol: *This gift is a token
of our appreciation.* **2.** something given as an expression of affection or
to be kept as a memento. **3.** something that serves to indicate authenticity, authority, or identity. **4.** piece of metal resembling a coin, used
as a substitute for money, as in paying for transportation fares or in
operating a telephone. **5.** in various board games, a playing piece.
6. by the same token. in an equivalent manner; likewise; similarly.
7. in token of. as evidence, proof, or indication of. —*adj.* having little
or no value, force, or effect: *a token fee, token resistance.* [Old English
tāc(e)n sign, symbol.]
To·ky·o (tō′kē ō′) *n.* capital and largest city of Japan, in the east-
central part of Honshu.
told (tōld) *v.* past tense and past participle of **tell.** —*adj.* **all told.**
counting all; in all.
To·le·do (tə lē′dō) *pl.* (*def.* 3). **-dos.** *n.* **1.** port city in northwestern
Ohio, on Lake Erie. Pop. (1970), 383,818. **2.** historic city in central
Spain. Pop. (1965 est.), 40,700. **3.** fine-tempered sword blade or sword,
as formerly made in Toledo, Spain.
tol·er·a·ble (tol′ər ə bəl) *adj.* **1.** that can be endured; bearable.
2. moderately good; passable: *a tolerable performance.* [Latin *tolerābilis*
bearable, endurable, from *tolerāre* to bear¹, endure.] —**tol′er·a·ble-
ness,** *n.* —**tol′er·a·bly,** *adv.*
tol·er·ance (tol′ər əns) *n.* **1.** ability or willingness to accept or respect
the behavior, customs, opinions, or beliefs of others. **2.a.** act of tolerating. **b.** state or quality of being tolerant. **3.** ability to take or endure
increasing amounts of something, as a drug or poison, without being
affected, esp. in an adverse way. **4.** power or ability to endure something, as pain. **5.** permissible deviation from a specified standard, as
in the weight of coins or in the size of a machine part.
Syn. 1. Tolerance, toleration mean a permissive attitude toward beliefs
and practices different from or conflicting with one's own. **Tolerance**
suggests a personal acceptance of difference but one that is limited in
degree and passive in nature: *He has little tolerance of those who oppose
the war.* **Toleration** suggests that a public, official, or legal policy rather
than personal conviction serves as the basis for allowing individuals,
esp. those of a minority, to practice their beliefs: *Religious toleration
has marked the governmental policy of the United States.*
tol·er·ant (tol′ər ənt) *adj.* **1.** inclined to accept or respect the behavior, opinions, customs, or beliefs of others. **2.** capable of resisting or
enduring the effects of something, as a drug or poison. —**tol′er·ant·ly,**
adv.
tol·er·ate (tol′ə rāt′) **-at·ed, -at·ing.** *v.t.* **1.** to allow to exist or be done
without prohibition or interference. **2.** to suffer or endure; put up with;
bear: *How can you tolerate all that noise while you're working?*
3. to develop or have tolerance for (a drug, poison, or the like).
[Latin *tolerātus,* past participle of *tolerāre* to bear¹, endure.]
tol·er·a·tion (tol′ə rā′shən) *n.* **1.** act or practice of tolerating.
2. recognition of an individual's right to enjoy certain freedoms and
privileges, esp. freedom of worship. —**Syn. 2.** see **tolerance.**
toll[1] (tōl) *v.i.* (of a bell) to sound with slow, regular strokes; peal.
—*v.t.* **1.** to cause (a bell) to sound with slow, regular strokes. **2.** to
announce or summon by tolling: *The bells tolled the beginning of the
service.* —*n.* **1.** act of tolling a bell. **2.** sound made by a bell being tolled.
[Middle English *tollen* to pull, draw (referring to pulling a bell to make
a sound); of uncertain origin.]
toll[2] (tōl) *n.* **1.** tax or fixed fee paid for the right or privilege to use
something, as a bridge, highway, or tunnel. **2.** charge for a particular
service rendered, as the transmission of a long-distance telephone call.
3. number of people or things lost, destroyed, or damaged: *The earthquake took a heavy toll of lives.* [Old English *toll* payment, tax, duty,
going back to Late Latin *telōnium* custom house, from Greek *telōnion,*
from *telos* tax.]
toll bar, gate or other barrier, as across a road, used to obstruct
passage until a toll is paid.
toll booth, booth, as at a toll bridge, where a toll is collected.

toll bridge, bridge at which a toll is charged for passage.

toll call, telephone call, the charge for which is higher than for a local call.

toll collector, person employed to collect tolls at a tollgate. Also, **toll′keep′er.**

toll·gate (tōl′gāt′) *n.* gate or other barrier used to obstruct passage until a toll is paid.

Tol·stoy, Leo (tōl′stoi) 1828–1910, Russian novelist and philosopher; born Count Lev Nikolayevich Tolstoy.

Tol·tec (tol′tek) *n.* member of a group of Nahuatl-speaking Indian tribes dominant in central and southern Mexico from the eleventh to the thirteenth centuries. —*adj.* of or relating to the Toltecs, their culture, or their civilization.

to·lu (tə lōō′) *n.* fragrant balsam obtained from a tropical tree, genus *Myroxylon,* of the pea family, used in cough drops, candies, and chewing gum and in making perfumes. [From Santiago de *Tolú,* city in Colombia where it is found.]

tol·u·ene (tol′yōō ēn′) *n.* flammable, aromatic hydrocarbon compound made from petroleum, used in airplane fuel and as a solvent. Formula: $C_6H_5CH_3$ [TOLU (from which it was first obtained) + -ENE.]

tom (tom) *n.* male of certain animals, esp. cats. —*adj.* male: *a tom turkey.* [From *Tom,* familiar form of the masculine proper name *Thomas.*]

tom·a·hawk (tom′ə hôk′) *n.* any of various axlike weapons or tools used by Indians of North America. —*v.t.* to attack, strike, or kill with a tomahawk. [Algonquian *tämähäk,* short for *tämähäkan* cutting implement.]

to·ma·to (tə mā′tō, -mä′-) *pl.,* **-toes.** *n.* **1.** juicy red, green, or yellow smooth-skinned fruit of a plant, *Lycopersicon esculentum,* of the nightshade family, eaten as a vegetable either raw or cooked. **2.** the plant itself, bearing yellow, bell-shaped flowers. [Spanish *tomate,* from Nahuatl *tomatl.*]

tomb (tōōm) *n.* **1.** vault or chamber in which a dead body is placed. **2.** any place of burial. **3.** death. [Old French *tombe* grave, from Late Latin *tumba,* from Greek *tymbos.*]

Tom·bouc·tou (tōm bōōk tōō′) *French.* Timbuktu.

tom·boy (tom′boi′) *n.* girl who enjoys those activities and interests that are usually considered to be preferred by boys. —**tom′boy′ish,** *adj.* —**tom′boy′ish·ly,** *adv.* —**tom′boy′ish·ness,** *n.*

tomb·stone (tōōm′stōn′) *n.* stone placed at the head of a grave, usually inscribed with the dead person's name and dates of birth and death.

tom·cat (tom′kat′) *n.* male cat.

tom·cod (tom′kod′) *n.* small saltwater fish, *Microgadus tomcod,* of the cod family, found in waters along the eastern coast of North America. Length: to 14 inches.

Tom, Dick, and Harry, any people taken at random. ▲ often used disparagingly and preceded by *every: We invited every Tom, Dick, and Harry.*

tome (tōm) *n.* **1.** book, esp. a large, heavy, scholarly one. **2.** one of a set of books containing several volumes. [French *tome* volume, from Latin *tomus,* from Greek *tomos.*]

tom·fool (tom′fōōl′) *adj.* extremely stupid or foolish: *a tomfool thing to do.* —*n.* one who acts in a stupid or foolish manner.

tom·fool·er·y (tom′fōō′lər ē) *pl.,* **-er·ies.** *n.* foolish or absurd behavior; nonsense.

Tom·my gun (tom′ē) *Informal.* Thompson submachine gun.

tom·my·rot (tom′ē rot′) *n. Informal.* utter nonsense.

to·mor·row (tə môr′ō, -mor′ō) *also,* **to·mor·row.** *n.* **1.** the day after today: *Tomorrow is my birthday.* **2.** some indefinite time in the future: *The world of tomorrow will be very different.* —*adv.* on the day after today: *We are going to play tomorrow.* [Middle English *to morwe,* going back to Old English *tō* to + *morgen* morning, morrow.]

Tomsk (tômsk) *n.* city in the south-central Soviet Union, in the Russian Republic. Pop. (1970 est.), 339,000.

Tom Thumb 1. in folklore, tiny boy who was no bigger than his father's thumb. **2.** any diminutive person.

tom·tit (tom′tit′) *n.* any of various small birds, as the titmouse and wren.

tom-tom (tom′tom′) *n.* any of various primitive, small drums, usually beaten with the hands. [Hindi *tam-tam* drum; of imitative origin.]

ton (tun) *n.* **1.a.** unit of weight equal to 2000 pounds avoirdupois in the United States and Canada. Also, **short ton. b.** unit of weight equal to 2240 pounds avoirdupois in Great Britain. Also, **long ton. 2.** unit for measuring the carrying capacity of a ship, equal to one hundred cubic feet. **3.** unit for measuring the freight-carrying capacity of a ship, equal to forty cubic feet. **4.** unit for measuring the weight of water displaced by a ship, equal to thirty-five cubic feet of sea water weighing approximately one long ton. **5.** metric ton. **6.** *Informal.* extremely large quantity of anything: *I have a ton of work to do before I leave.*

[Old English *tunne* barrel, large cask (referring to its weight when full). See TUN.]

ton·al (tōn′əl) *adj.* of or relating to tone or tonality. —**ton′al·ly,** *adv.*

to·nal·i·ty (tō nal′ə tē) *pl.,* **-ties.** *n.* **1.** *Music.* **a.** relation or sum of relations, both melodic and harmonic, existing between the tones of a scale or musical system. **b.** particular scale or system of tones; key. **2.** arrangement of tones or colors in a painting.

tone (tōn) *n.* **1.** any sound considered with reference to its pitch, quality, duration, or volume. **2.** quality of sound. **3.** *Music.* **a.** sound having definite pitch and character. **b.** whole step. **4.** particular style or manner of speaking or writing: *I knew he was angry by his tone of voice.* **5.** general or prevailing character, style, or tendency, as of thought or behavior: *The tone of the meeting was serious.* **6.** degree of tension or firmness, as of muscle. **7.** effect of the combination of light, shade, and color in a picture: *a silvery tone.* **8.** tint or shade of a particular color: *The painter used various tones of blue.* —*v.t.,* **toned, ton·ing. 1.** to give particular tone or quality to, as in sound or color. **2.** to alter or correct the color of. **3. to tone down.** to soften or lessen, as in volume, intensity, or severity. **4. to tone up.** to increase or gain, as in strength, intensity, or vitality. —*v.i.* **1.** to harmonize in color. **2.** to assume a particular color or tint. [Latin *tonus* sound, a stretching, from Greek *tonos* musical note, a stretching, thing stretched.]

tone arm, arm of a phonograph, which holds the cartridge.

tone-deaf (tōn′def′) *adj.* unable to distinguish differences in musical pitch. —**tone′-deaf′ness,** *n.*

tong (tong, tông) *v.t.* to grasp, hold, or handle with tongs. [From TONGS.]

Ton·ga (tong′gə) *n.* island country under British protection, in the southwestern Pacific, comprised of about 160 small islands. Capital, Nukualofa. Land area, 270 sq. mi. Pop. (1969 est.), 83,000. Also, **Tonga Islands, Friendly Islands.**

tongs (tongz, tôngz) *n.,pl.* any of various devices for grasping objects, usually having two curved arms pivoted together. [Old English *tange.*]

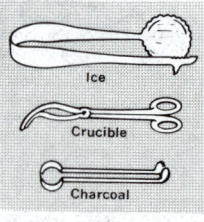

Tongs

tongue (tung) *n.* **1.** the movable organ attached to the floor of the mouth, used in tasting, swallowing, and, in man, for talking. **2.** animal's tongue prepared and used as food. **3.** spoken language or dialect: *His native tongue is French.* **4.** manner of speaking, esp. in regard to meaning or intent: *a biting tongue.* **5.** ability to speak; power of speech: *The child couldn't find his tongue.* **6.** anything resembling the human tongue in shape, position, or function, as a tapering jet of flame or a narrow strip of land projecting into a body of water. **7.** strip of leather or other material lying under the laces or fastenings of a shoe or boot. **8.** clapper of a bell. **9.** pole of a wagon, carriage, or similar vehicle to which horses are yoked. **10.** free or vibrating end of a reed in a musical wind instrument. **11.** *Carpentry.* projecting strip on the edge of a board that fits into a groove on the edge of another board. **12. on the tip of one's tongue.** on the verge of being remembered or spoken. **13. to hold one's tongue.** to refrain from speech; be silent. **14. (with) tongue in cheek.** with sarcasm or irony. —*v.t.,* **tongued, tongu·ing. 1.** to modify or interrupt the tones of (a flute or certain other wind instruments) with the tongue. **2.** to touch or lick with the tongue. **3.** *Carpentry.* **a.** to cut a tongue on (a board). **b.** to fit (boards) together by means of a joint formed by the tongue of one board and the groove of the other. **4.** *Archaic.* to scold or reprimand. —*v.i.* to use the tongue in playing the flute and certain other wind instruments. [Old English *tunge* the movable organ in the mouth, power of speech, language.]

tongue-in-cheek (tung′in chēk′) *adj.* sarcastic; insincere: *a tongue-in-cheek remark.*

tongue-tied (tung′tīd′) *adj.* **1.** unable to speak or express oneself, as from fear, shyness, or embarrassment. **2.** unable to speak distinctly because of an abnormally short frenum.

ton·ic (ton′ik) *n.* **1.** anything that refreshes, invigorates, or strengthens. **2.** medicine or drug that invigorates or strengthens. **3.** *Music.* note on which a scale or system of tones is based. **4.** carbonated beverage containing quinine, used for mixing with liquor, as gin or vodka. **5.** liquid preparation for the hair or scalp. —*adj.* **1.** refreshing; bracing; invigorating. **2.** denoting or characterized by continuous contraction, esp. of the muscles: *tonic spasm.* **3.** of or relating to tone or tones. **4.** *Music.* of, relating to, or based on a tonic. **5.** of, relating to, or characterized by tone or pitch, as certain languages: *the tonic changes of the Chinese language.* [Greek *tonikos* relating to stretching, relating to tones, from *tonos* musical note, a stretching.]

to·nic·i·ty (tō nis′ə tē) *n.* **1.** normal elastic tension or tone of living muscles, arteries, and other parts of the body.

to·night (tə nīt′) *also,* **to-night.** *n.* **1.** the night of this day. **2.** the present night; this night. —*adv.* on or during the present or coming night. [Old English *tōniht* on the night of this day. See TO, NIGHT.]

Ton·kin, Gulf of (ton′kin′, tong′-) gulf in southeastern Asia, bordered by North Vietnam and China.

ton·nage (tun′ij) *n.* **1.** carrying capacity of a ship, expressed in tons. **2.** total amount of shipping, as of a port or nation, with reference to carrying capacity. **3.** duty, tax, or similar charge levied on ships at so much per ton of cargo. **4.** weight, as of goods shipped or produced, measured in tons.

ton·neau (tə nō′, to-) *pl.* **-neaus** or **-neaux** (-nōz′.) *n.* **1.** rear compartment in an early type of automobile, containing seats for passengers. **2.** whole body of an automobile having such a compartment. [French *tonneau* cask, diminutive of *tonne* cask. See TUNNEL.]

ton·sil (ton′səl) *n.* **1.** either of a pair of oval masses of spongy tissue located on each side of the tongue at the back of the mouth in man. **2.** any of several similar masses of tissue located in the mouth or throat of amphibians, birds, reptiles, and mammals. [Latin *tōnsillae* (plural) tonsils, diminutive of *tōlēs* (plural) goiter.] —**ton′sil·lar;** *also,* **ton′·sil·ar,** *adj.*

ton·sil·lec·to·my (ton′sə lek′tə mē) *pl.* **-mies.** *n.* surgical removal of a tonsil or tonsils. [Latin *tonsillae* tonsils + Greek *ektomē* a cutting out.]

ton·sil·li·tis (ton′sə lī′tis) *n.* inflammation of a tonsil or tonsils. [Latin *tōnsillae* tonsils + -ITIS.]

ton·so·ri·al (ton sôr′ē əl) *adj.* of or relating to a barber or his work. ▲ often used humorously. [Latin *tōnsōrius* relating to shaving (from *tōnsor* barber) + -AL[1].]

ton·sure (ton′shər) *n.* **1.** in the Roman Catholic and Orthodox churches, a shaving of a part or all of the head of a man entering the priesthood of a monastic order. **2.** that part of the head so shaven. —*v.t.,* **-sured, -sur·ing.** to shave the head of. [Latin *tōnsūra* a shearing, clipping.]

ton·tine (ton′tēn, ton tēn′) *n.* **1.** annuity shared by a group of subscribers, with the share of the survivors increasing as various subscribers die until the last survivor receives the total amount that is left. **2.** share that each subscriber receives. **3.** subscribers to such an annuity, collectively. **4.** any of various similar insurance plans. [French *tontine* the annuity, the share, from Lorenzo *Tonti,* seventeenth-century Italian banker who devised the system.]

too (tōō) *adv.* **1.** in addition; besides; also: *He is very bright and a good worker too.* **2.** more than enough: *There were too many people in the room.* **3.** exceedingly; very: *I was not too sorry to see them go.* **4.** *Informal.* indeed. ▲ used as an intensifier: *You will too come!* [Form of TO.]

took (tŏŏk) past tense of **take.**

tool (tōōl) *n.* **1.** any of various devices held in the hand and used in doing work, as a hammer, wrench, or saw. **2.a.** power-driven instrument or machine used to cut and shape machinery parts. **b.** cutting or shaping part of such an instrument or machine. **3.** person who is manipulated and used by another; dupe. **4.** anything used in or necessary to the carrying out of an action, operation, profession, or trade: *Mechanical knowledge is a great and glorious tool in the hands of man* (Hunt, 1847). —*v.t.* **1.** to work, shape, or mark with a tool. **2.** to provide (a factory or plant) with machinery or tools for production (often with *up*). **3.** to drive (a vehicle). —*v.i.* **1.** to work with a tool or tools. **2.** to drive a vehicle: *They tooled along the country road.* [Old English *tōl* implement for manual work, means.] —**Syn.** **1.** see **implement.**

tool·ing (tōō′ling) *n.* work or ornamentation done with tools, esp. stamped or gilded designs on leather.

toot (tōōt) *v.t.* **1.** to cause (a horn, whistle, or the like) to sound with a short, quick blast or blasts. —*v.i.* to produce a short, quick blast or blasts: *The factory whistle tooted every day at noon.* —*n.* **1.** short, quick blast, as that produced by a horn. **2.** act of producing such a sound. [Imitative.]

tooth (tōōth) *pl.* **teeth.** *n.* **1.** in man and certain other vertebrates, one of the hard calcified structures set in the jaws and supported by the gums, used for biting and chewing. A human adult has thirty-two permanent teeth. **2.** similar structure in certain invertebrates. **3.** something resembling a tooth in shape, position, or function, as one of the projecting pieces on a comb. **4.** to **fight tooth and nail.** to fight with all one's strength or power. **5. to get** (or **sink**) **one's teeth into.** to become completely involved in; get a firm grasp of. **6. armed to the teeth.** completely or fully armed. —*v.t.* **1.** to furnish or supply with teeth or toothlike projections: *to tooth a*

saw. **2.** to make jagged, as an edge. [Old English *tōth* one of the bonelike structures set in the jaws.]

tooth·ache (tōōth′āk′) *n.* pain in a tooth, the teeth, or the surrounding area.

tooth·brush (tōōth′brush′) *n.* small, narrow brush with a long handle, used for cleaning the teeth.

tooth·ed (tōōtht) *adj.* **1.** having teeth, esp. of a specific kind or number. ▲ usually used in combination: *a saber-toothed tiger.* **2.** having notches; serrated; jagged: *a toothed leaf.*

tooth·less (tōōth′lis) *adj.* **1.** having no teeth. **2.** without force or effect; ineffectual.

tooth·paste (tōōth′pāst′) *n.* paste dentifrice used for cleaning the teeth.

tooth·pick (tōōth′pik′) *n.* small, narrow sliver of wood, plastic, or similar material, used to remove food or other matter from between the teeth.

tooth·some (tōōth′səm) *adj.* **1.** pleasing to the taste; palatable; tasty. **2.** attractive; pleasant.

top[1] (top) *n.* **1.** highest or uppermost point, part, surface, or end of something: *the top of a flagpole, the top of a page, the top of the stairs, the top of a hill.* **2.** cover or lid of something, or a part forming a cover: *a box top.* **3.** garment for the upper half of the body, usually part of a two-piece outfit: *a pajama top.* **4.** head, esp. the crown of the head. **5.** part of certain plants that grows above ground. **6.a.** highest or leading position or rank: *to graduate at the top of one's class.* **b.** one who or that which occupies this position or rank. **7.** highest pitch or degree: *The child was screaming at the top of his voice.* **8.** best or choicest part. **9.** beginning or first part. **10.** platform around the head of a lower mast of a ship, used as a place to stand on for extending the rigging of the topmast. **11. off the top of one's head.** without careful thought or advance preparation. **12. on top.** **a.** at the highest point or level. **b.** in a dominant or successful position. **13. on top of.** **a.** on or at the top of. **b.** resting or lying upon. **c.** in addition to: *On top of everything else, he also lost his wallet.* **d.** closely or immediately following: *one problem on top of another.* **e.** *Informal.* in control of: *to be on top of a situation.* **14. over the top.** **a.** over the front of a trench, as in attacking. **b.** beyond the goal or quota. —*adj.* **1.** of or at the top, or comprising the top part or position: *the top drawer, the top floor of a building.* **2.** first or highest in rank, position, or quality; foremost: *the top man in his field.* **3.** greatest or maximum in degree or amount: *to drive at top speed.* —*v.t.,* **topped, top·ping.** **1.** to provide with a top or cover; put a top on. **2.** to serve as, be at, or form the top of. **3.** to reach the top of. **4.** to go above or beyond the top of. **5.** to surpass; exceed. **6.** to cut off or remove the top of. **7.** to hit (a ball) above center, as in golf or tennis. **8. to top off.** to complete, esp. by adding a finishing touch. —*v.i.* to top someone or something. [Old English *top* highest point or part.]

top[2] (top) *n.* toy usually having a rounded body that tapers to a point on which it is spun. [Old English *top.*]

Top[2]

to·paz (tō′paz) *n.* lustrous crystalline mineral, occurring in a variety of colors, used as a gem, esp. in the yellow variety. [Latin *topazus,* from Greek *topazos.*]

top boot, high boot, usually having the upper part trimmed with a different material or color.

top·coat (top′kōt′) *n.* lightweight overcoat.

top dog *Informal.* person or group holding a position of power or authority, esp. as a result of winning in a competition.

top-drawer (top′drôr′) *adj.* of the highest quality, rank, importance, or merit.

tope (tōp) *toped, top·ing. v.t., v.i.* to drink (alcoholic liquor) often and to excess. [Of uncertain origin.]

To·pe·ka (tə pē′kə) *n.* capital of Kansas, in the northeastern part of the state. Pop. (1970), 127,011.

top·er (tō′pər) *n.* one who topes; drunkard.

top·flight (top′flīt′) *adj.* excellent; superior.

top·gal·lant (top′gal′ənt, tə gal′-) *n.* mast, sail, rigging, or the like above the topmast. —*adj.* of or relating to the topgallant.

top hat, man's hat, usually made of silk, having a high, cylindrical crown and a small brim, worn on formal occasions.

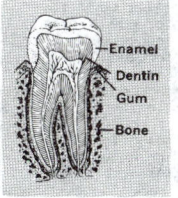

top-heav·y (top′hev′ē) *adj.* disproportionately heavy at the top and often unstable and liable to topple.

Top hat

top·ic (top′ik) *n.* subject, as of a speech, discussion, or written composition. [Latin *Topica* title of a rhetorical treatise by Aristotle, from Greek *(Ta) Topika* literally, things relating to commonplaces, from Greek *topos* place.]

top·i·cal (top′i kəl) *adj.* **1.** relating to or dealing with matters of

Enamel — Dentin — Gum — Bone

Tooth

current or local interest: *a topical speech, a topical book.* **2.** of, relating to, or belonging to a specific area or place; local. **3.** of or relating to a topic or topics. **4.** *Medicine.* relating to, applied to, or affecting a particular part or organ of the body.

top·knot (top′not′) *n.* **1.** knot, tuft, or crest of hair or feathers on the top of the head. **2.** bow or other ornament worn on the top of the head.

top·loft·y (top′lôf′tē) *adj. Informal.* haughty or pompous in manner or character.

top·mast (top′mast′) *n.* second section of a mast above the lower mast.

top·most (top′mōst′) *adj.* at the very top; uppermost; highest.

top·notch (top′noch′) *adj. Informal.* first-rate; superior.

to·pog·ra·pher (tə pog′rə fər) *n.* one who is skilled at or expert in topography.

top·o·graph·i·cal (top′ə graf′i kəl) *adj.* of, relating to, or involving topography: *a topographical map, a topographical survey.* Also, **top′o·graph′ic.** —**top′o·graph′i·cal·ly,** *adv.*

to·pog·ra·phy (tə pog′rə fē) *n., pl.* **-phies.** *n.* **1.** detailed description or drawing of the natural and artificial surface features of a place or area. **2.** all the natural and artificial surface features of a place or area, as hills, depressions, lakes, roads, and bridges. [Late Latin *topographia* description of a place, from Greek *topographiā.*]

to·pol·o·gy (tə pol′ə jē) *n.* **1.** branch of mathematics dealing with properties of figures that are not changed when the figures are stretched, twisted, or otherwise distorted. **2.** anatomy of regions or specific parts of the body. [Greek *topos* place + -LOGY.]

top·per (top′ər) *n.* **1.** *Informal.* one who or that which is exceptionally good or excellent, esp. in relation to that which has come before. **2.** short, lightweight overcoat for a woman. **3.** *Informal.* top hat.

top·ping (top′ing) *n.* sauce, frosting, or other garnish put on food: *a dessert topping.*

top·ple (top′əl) **-pled, -pling.** *v.i.* **1.** to fall forward; tumble (often with *over*): *The bookcase toppled over.* **2.** to lean or hang over, as if about to fall. —*v.t.* to cause to fall or tumble; overturn. [TOP¹ + -LE.]

tops (tops) *adj. Informal.* the very best; first-rate.

top·sail (top′sāl′, -səl) *n.* **1.** on a square-rigged ship, square sail next above the lowest sail on a mast. **2.** on a fore-and-aft-rigged ship, square or triangular sail above the gaff of a lower sail.

top·se·cret (top′sē′krit) *adj.* of, relating to, or containing highly confidential information.

top sergeant *Informal.* first sergeant.

top·side (top′sīd′) *n.* upper part of a ship's side, esp. above the water line. —*adv. also,* **top·sides.** to or on the upper portions of a ship; on deck.

top·soil (top′soil′) *n.* top or upper part of the soil that contains most of the materials, including minerals and humus, essential to plant growth.

top·sy·tur·vy (top′sē tur′vē) *adv.* **1.** in reverse of the usual or natural order; upside down. **2.** in or into a state of utter confusion or disorder. —*adj.* **1.** utterly confused or disorderly. **2.** turned upside down. —*n.* state of utter confusion or disorder. [Possibly from TOP¹ + modification of so¹ (in the sense of "as") + obsolete *tirve* to turn, overturn (of uncertain origin); literally, top as if overturned.]

toque (tōk) *n.* **1.** small, close-fitting woman's hat with a soft crown and either a small, rolled brim or no brim at all. **2.** small plumed hat with a brim, worn by men and women in the sixteenth century. [French *toque,* from Spanish *toca;* of uncertain origin.]

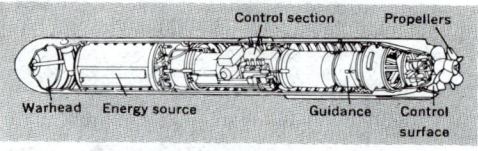

Toque

tor (tôr) *n.* high, rocky hill.

To·rah (tôr′ə) *also,* **To·ra.** *n. Judaism.* **1.** the Pentateuch. **2.** handwritten scrolls containing the Pentateuch, used in a synagogue during services. **3.** *also,* **torah.** whole body of Jewish teaching, thought, and literature. **4.** torah. instruction, doctrine, or law. [Hebrew *tōrāh* instruction, doctrine, law.]

torch (tôrch) *n.* **1.** flaming light consisting of a stick of resinous wood or some inflammable substance wound around the end of a stick. **2.** any of various hand-held devices producing a very hot flame, used esp. in welding. **3.** something considered to be a source or symbol of enlightenment, inspiration, or guidance: *The torch of Greek learning and civilization was to be extinguished* (Smith, 1878). **4.** *British.* flashlight. **5. to carry a (or the) torch for.** *Slang.* to be in love with someone, esp. when it is unrequited. [Old French *torche* light made of a bundle of twisted straw covered with wax, link², going back to Latin *torquēs* twisted neck chain, wreath.]

torch·bear·er (tôrch′bâr′ər) *n.* **1.** one who carries a torch. **2.** one who is a source of enlightenment, truth, or inspiration.

torch·light (tôrch′līt′) *n.* light given off by a torch or torches.

tor·chon lace (tôr′shon) **1.** handmade bobbin lace made of loosely twisted cotton or linen threads in simple open patterns. **2.** machine-

made imitation of this. [French *torchon* dishcloth (from *torche* torch) + LACE. See TORCH.]

torch singer, one who sings torch songs.

torch song, sentimental popular song of unrequited love and yearning. [From the phrase *to carry a torch for.* See TORCH.]

tore (tôr) past tense of **tear¹.**

tor·e·a·dor (tôr′ē ə dôr′) *n.* matador. [Spanish *toreador,* going back to *toro* bull, from Latin *taurus.*]

to·re·ro (tə rãr′ō) *pl.* **-ros.** *n.* matador, esp. one who fights on foot.

to·ri (tôr′ī) plural of **torus.**

to·ri·i (tôr′ē ē′) *pl.* **-ri·i.** *n.* gateway at the entrance of a Shinto temple, consisting of two uprights supporting a concave lintel with a straight crosspiece below it. [Japanese *torii.*]

To·ri·no (tô rē′nō) *n.* Turin.

tor·ment (*v.,* tôr ment′; *n.,* tôr′ment) *v.t.* **1.** to afflict with extreme mental or physical pain or suffering. **2.** to worry, annoy, or aggravate excessively. —*n.* **1.** extreme mental or physical pain or suffering; agony. **2.** source of such pain or suffering. [Old French *torment* torture, from Latin *tormentum.*]

Torii

tor·men·tor (tôr ment′tər) *also,* **tor·ment·er.** *n.* one who or that which torments.

torn (tôrn) past participle of **tear¹.**

tor·na·do (tôr nā′dō) *pl.* **-does** or **-dos.** *n.* dark, funnel-shaped column of air, suspended from dark, black clouds and rotating around a low-pressure center at speeds of up to 500 miles per hour. Because of the powerful suction of the relative vacuum at its center, objects are drawn up into the storm and almost everything along its narrow path is destroyed. [Modification of Spanish *tronada* thunderstorm, going back to Latin *tornāre* to thunder.]

To·ron·to (tə ron′tō) *n.* port city and capital of Ontario, a major industrial, commercial, and financial center of Canada, in the southeastern part of the country, on Lake Ontario. Pop. (1968), 664,584.

tor·pe·do (tôr pē′dō) *pl.* **-does.** *n.* **1.** large, self-propelled, cigar-shaped underwater missile that can be launched from ships, submarines, or airplanes, used for underwater attack against enemy vessels or installations.

Control section / Propellers

Warhead / Energy source / Guidance / Control surface

Torpedo

2. small explosive charge placed on a railroad track, serving as a signal when detonated by the weight of the train passing over it. **3.** type of firework that explodes when thrown against a hard surface. **4.** any of several electric rays, genus *Torpedo.* —*v.t.* **-doed, -do·ing.** to damage, destroy, or sink with or as with a torpedo. [Latin *torpēdō* electric ray (whose electrical discharges stun its victims), numbness, from *torpēre* to be numb.]

torpedo boat, PT boat.

tor·pid (tôr′pid) *adj.* **1.** lethargic; sluggish; dull. **2.** dormant, as an animal in hibernation. **3.** devoid of the power of motion or feeling; numb. [Latin *torpidus* benumbed.] —**tor·pid′i·ty, tor′pid·ness,** *n.* —**tor′pid·ly,** *adv.*

tor·por (tôr′pər) *n.* state or quality of being torpid. [Latin *torpor* numbness.]

torque (tôrk) *n.* **1.** turning effect of a force about a pivot point, measured as the product of the force and the distance between the point where the force is applied and the pivot point. **2.** ornamental necklace, bracelet, or armband, usually made of twisted metal, worn esp. by the ancient Gauls and Britons. [Latin *torquēs* twisted neck chain, wreath.]

tor·re·fy (tôr′ə fī′, tor′-) **-fied, -fy·ing.** *v.t.* to dry or parch by exposing to heat. [Latin *torrefacere.*]

tor·rent (tôr′ənt, tor′-) *n.* **1.** violent, swiftly flowing stream, esp. of water. **2.** violent, overwhelming flow of anything: *a torrent of insults.* [Latin *torrēns* a rushing stream (of water), boiling, impetuous.]

tor·ren·tial (tô ren′chəl, tə-) *adj.* of, resembling, or caused by a torrent: *a torrential rainfall.*

Tor·re·ón (tôr′ē ōn′) *n.* city in northern Mexico, northwest of Mexico City. Pop. (1969), 243,234.

Tor·ri·cel·li, E·van·ge·lis·ta (tôr′ə chel′ē; i van′jə lis′tə)

1608–47, Italian physicist and the inventor of the barometer.

tor·rid (tôr'id, tor'-) *adj.* **1.** subjected to or parched by the intense heat of the sun: *the torrid regions of the world.* **2.** intensely hot or burning; scorching: *a torrid climate.* **3.** passionate; ardent: *a torrid love story.* [Latin *torridus* parched.] —**tor·rid'i·ty,** *n.*

Torrid Zone, warm region between the Tropic of Cancer and the Tropic of Capricorn.

tor·sion (tôr'shən) *n.* **1.** act of twisting; being twisted. **2.** strain exerted on a body when one end is twisted in one direction while the other end is held firm or twisted in the opposite direction. [Late Latin *torsiō* torture, a wringing, from Latin *torquēre* to twist.] —**tor'sion·al,** *adj.* —**tor'sion·al·ly,** *adv.*

tor·so (tôr'sō) *pl.,* **-sos.** *n.* **1.** trunk of the human body. **2.** any artistic representation of this. [Italian *torso* stalk[1], stump, trunk of a statue, through Latin, from Greek *thyrsos* stalk[1], rod, thyrsus.]

tort (tôrt) *n.* *Law.* any private or civil wrong or injury not involving breach of contract, for which the wronged party may bring civil suit. [Old French *tort* wrong, offense, from Medieval Latin *tortum* wrong, going back to Latin *torquēre* to twist.]

torte (tôrt) *n.* rich cake made of eggs, sugar, breadcrumbs or a little flour, and usually ground nuts. [German *Torte* flat cake, tart[2], probably going back to Late Latin *tōrta.* See **TORTILLA.**]

tor·ti·col·lis (tôr'tə kol'is) *n.* wryneck *(def. 1).* [Modern Latin *torticollis,* from Latin *tortus,* past participle of *torquēre* to twist + *collum* neck.]

tor·til·la (tôr tē'yə) *n.* thin, round, unleavened bread made from water and corn meal and baked on a griddle. [Spanish *tortilla* little cake, diminutive of *torta* round cake, from Late Latin *tōrta* round loaf of bread; of uncertain origin.]

tor·toise (tôr'təs) *pl.,* **-tois·es** or **-toise.** *n.* slow-moving land turtle, family Testudinidae, found on every continent except Australia. [Earlier *tortuce,* from Late Latin *tortūca* tortoise, turtle, possibly from Latin *tortus,* past participle of *torquēre* to twist; supposedly with reference to its crooked feet.]

tortoise beetle, small, turtle-shaped beetle destructive to crops.

tor·toise·shell (tôr'təs shel') *adj.* **1.** made of tortoise shell. **2.** having the variegated yellow-and-brown colors of tortoise shell.

tor·toise shell 1. hard, mottled, yellow-and-brown material making up the outer shell of certain turtles, used esp. to make combs, small decorative objects, and furniture inlay. **2.** any of a group of butterflies with mottled yellow, brown, and black coloration.

tor·tu·ous (tôr'chŏō əs) *adj.* **1.** having many twists, turns, or bends; winding: *a tortuous road.* **2.** not direct, straightforward, or frank; devious: *a narrow and tortuous criticism* (Sears, 1858). [Latin *tortuōsus* full of turns, entangled, from *tortus,* past participle of *torquēre* to twist.] —**tor'tu·ous·ly,** *adv.* —**tor'tu·ous·ness,** *n.*

tor·ture (tôr'chər) —*tured,* **-tur·ing.** *v.t.* **1.** to subject to severe physical abuse or cruelty: *The enemy tortured the prisoners.* **2.** to cause to suffer extreme mental or physical pain or suffering: *He was tortured by the knowledge of what he had done.* **3.** to distort, as in shape or meaning; twist. —*n.* **1.** extreme mental or physical pain or suffering; agony. **2.** act of inflicting or subjecting to extreme physical abuse or cruelty. **3.** source or cause of mental or physical pain or suffering: *The traffic today will be torture.* [Late Latin *tortūra* twisting, torment, from Latin *tortus,* past participle of *torquēre* to twist.] —**tor'tur·er,** *n.*

tor·tur·ous (tôr'chər əs) *adj.* relating to, characterized by, or causing torture: *a torturous toothache.*

to·rus (tôr'əs) *pl.,* **to·ri** (tôr'ī). *n.* **1.** large convex molding, usually forming part of the base of a column. **2.** *Anatomy.* any rounded ridge or protruding part. **3.** receptacle of a flower. **4.** *Geometry.* doughnut-shaped figure. [Latin *torus* bulge, cushion, round molding.]

Torus

To·ry (tôr'ē) *pl.,* **-ries.** *n.* **1.** member of a political party in Great Britain that favored royal power and the preservation of existing institutions. **2.** any colonial American who remained loyal to England at the time of the American Revolution. **3.** *also,* **tory.** any person or group that is conservative in politics. —*adj.* of, relating to, or characteristic of a Tory or Tories. [Irish *tōraidhe* pursued person, robber; originally referring to Irishmen who, persecuted by the English in the seventeenth century, became outlaws.] —**To'ry·ism,** *n.*

Tos·ca·ni·ni, Ar·tu·ro (tos'kə nē'nē; är toor'ō) 1867–1957, Italian conductor.

toss (tôs, tos) *v.t.* **1.** to propel lightly up into or through the air, esp. with the hand or hands: *Please toss me a towel.* **2.** to fling or move back and forth: *The waves tossed the little boat.* **3.** to lift quickly or suddenly: *The horse tossed its head.* **4.** to mix (a salad) lightly, esp. so as to coat with a dressing. **5.** to cause to fall to the ground: *The horse tossed its rider.* **6.a.** to throw (a coin) into the air so as to decide something by the side that lands upward. **b.** to toss a coin with (someone): *I'll toss*

you to see who goes first. **7.** *Informal.* to discuss (something) freely or casually, as in a group. **8. to toss off. a.** to do quickly, casually, and easily. **b.** to drink the whole of: *He tossed off three glasses of wine.* —*v.i.* **1.** to move about restlessly, esp. in one's sleep: *He tossed and turned all night.* **2.** to be flung or moved back and forth. **3.** to throw a coin into the air so as to decide something by the side that lands upward. —*n.* **1.** act of tossing. **2.** distance over which something is or can be tossed. [Possibly of Scandinavian origin.]

Syn. *v.t.* **1. Toss, fling, cast** mean to throw an object up or down or back and forth with a swing of the arm. **Toss** suggests a leisurely yet deft throw that implies playful or casual activity: *Daddy tossed the baby into the air. Alan tossed the dog a bone.* **Fling** implies a forceful or violent throw that is often used to indicate strong or intense feeling: *He flung down the book in disgust.* **Cast** is frequently used in literary context and suggests a definite or purposeful aim, esp. in throwing a light object: *Neither cast ye pearls before swine* (St. Matthew 7:6).

toss·up (tôs'up', tos'-) *n.* **1.** even chance or possibility. **2.** act of tossing a coin in order to decide something.

tot[1] (tot) *n.* **1.** small child. **2.** small amount of something, as an alcoholic beverage. [Of uncertain origin.]

tot[2] (tot) **tot·ted, tot·ting.** *v.i., v.t.* to total (usually with *up*).

to·tal (tōt'əl) *adj.* **1.** being, relating to, or comprising a whole; full; entire: *I paid the total amount.* **2.** absolute; complete; utter: *a total disaster, a total absence of respect.* —*n.* whole amount; sum. —*v.t.,* **-taled, -tal·ing;** *also, British.* **-talled, -tal·ling. 1.** to compute or find the sum of; add up: *to total a bill.* **2.** to reach to the sum of. —*v.i.* to amount (often with *to*): *The bill totals to ten dollars.* [Medieval Latin *totalis* whole, entire, from Latin *tōtus.*] —**Syn.** *adj.* **2.** see **complete.**

to·tal·i·tar·i·an (tō tal'ə târ'ē ən) *adj.* characteristic of or tending toward totalitarianism. —*n.* one who favors or supports totalitarianism.

to·tal·i·tar·i·an·ism (tō tal'ə târ'ē ə niz'əm) *n.* system of government in which one political party aims at total control over the lives of people, as by employing a powerful secret police, restricting meetings and assemblies, and censoring publications.

Syn. Totalitarianism, dictatorship mean a form of government maintained without the consent of the governed. **Totalitarianism** is a centralized and authoritarian regime of the modern state based on any political philosophy advocating total regimentation of all aspects of life and effective in suppressing civil liberties and gaining the obedience of its citizens: *Nazi Germany was an example of totalitarianism.* **Dictatorship** is based solely on the exercise of absolute power by a single individual who is neither sanctioned by hereditary right nor limited by a constitutional framework. Unlike *totalitarianism,* *dictatorship* usually has no philosophical or governmental basis for continuing its rule beyond the death or retirement of its leader: *Dictatorship is the most common form of government in Latin America.*

to·tal·i·ty (tō tal'ə tē) *pl.,* **-ties.** *n.* **1.** total amount; whole; sum. **2.** state of being whole or complete.

to·tal·i·za·tor (tōt'əl ə zā'tər) *n.* pari-mutuel *(def. 2).*

to·tal·iz·er (tōt'əl ī'zər) *n.* **1.** totalizator. **2.** adding machine.

to·tal·ly (tōt'əl ē) *adv.* completely; entirely; wholly.

tote (tōt) **tot·ed, tot·ing.** *v.t. Informal.* **1.** to haul or carry, esp. on one's back or in one's arms. **2.** to have on one's person habitually: *He totes a gun.* [Of uncertain origin.] —**tot'er,** *n.*

tote bag, large handbag used by women, esp. to carry small packages and other items.

to·tem (tō'təm) *n.* **1.** among North American Indians and certain other peoples, animal, plant, or other natural object taken as the ancestral emblem of a clan or other family group related by blood. **2.** representation of this, esp. one carved and painted on poles. [Ojibwa *ototeman* his brother-sister kin.] —**to·tem·ic** (tō tem'ik), *adj.*

to·tem·ism (tō'tə miz'əm) *n.* **1.** belief in totems and the customs and practices associated with them. **2.** social system in which tribes are divided into clans or families according to their totems.

totem pole, pole consisting of carved and painted representations of totems, erected in front of a dwelling, esp. by the American Indians of the northwestern Pacific coast.

toth·er (tuth'ər) *also,* **t'oth·er.** *Informal.* *pron., adj.* the other. [Middle English *the tother,* incorrect division of *thet other* the other, from Old English *thæt* that + **OTHER.**]

Totem pole

tot·ter (tot'ər) *v.i.* **1.** to walk or move with weak, unsteady steps. **2.** to shake or sway as if about to fall; be unbalanced or unsteady: *The glass tottered on the edge*

---

of the table. **3.** to be unstable and about to collapse: *The government tottered after the insurrection.* —*n.* act or condition of tottering. [Possibly from Middle Dutch *touteren* to swing.]

tot·ter·y (tot′ər ē) *adj.* unsteady; shaky.

tou·can (tōō′kan, tōō kan′) *n.* any of various tropical American birds, family Ramphastidae, having a heavy body, a very large beak, and, typically, brightly colored plumage. Length: 7–25 inches. [Tupi-Guarani *tucana, tucã;* referring to the sound of its cry.]

Toucan

touch (tuch) *v.t.* **1.** to bring a hand, finger, or other part of the body in contact with: *She accidentally touched the stove and burned her hand.* **2.** to bring (something) into contact with something else: *He touched his nose to the window.* **3.** to be in or come into contact with: *His hand was touching mine.* **4.** to affect the emotions or feelings of; move, as to pity, kindness, or compassion. **5.** to modify or improve by making slight changes or additions (with *up*): *to touch up one's make-up.* **6.** to have an effect or bearing on: *The new taxes will not touch the very rich.* **7.** to use or partake of: *She didn't touch any of her food.* **8.** to color slightly; tinge: *His hair was touched with gray.* **9.** to compare with; equal: *No one can touch him in his field.* **10.** to lay a hand or hands on, esp. so as to harm or molest: *If you touch me, I'll scream!* **11.** to be next to; border on. **12.** to arrive at or visit in passing: *I'm going to go ashore when we touch port.* **13.** to affect through contact; make a physical impression on: *No file or cutting tool will touch it* (Young, 1881). **14.** to impair slightly; blemish: *The plants were touched by the frost.* **15.** *Slang.* to succeed in getting or borrowing money from: *to touch the bank for a loan.* **16. to touch off. a.** to cause to explode; ignite. **b.** to cause to occur; initiate: *to touch off an argument.* —*v.i.* **1.** to come into or be in contact. **2.** to make a brief stop in passing (often with *at*): *They touched at every port in Europe.* **3. to touch down,** (of an aircraft) to land. **4. to touch on.** to deal with or mention, esp. in passing: *He tried not to touch on any controversial topic in his speeches.* —*n.* **1.** sense by which external objects are perceived through direct contact with a part of the body. **2.** quality of an object as perceived by touching or coming into contact with it. **3.** act or instance of touching or coming into contact. **4.** subtle sign or indication, as of a quality or attribute: *a touch of genius.* **5.** small amount; little bit: *a touch of salt.* **6.** slight attack; twinge: *a touch of rheumatism.* **7.** slight change or addition made to modify or improve, as a painting or literary work. **8.** state of being in close communication or contact: *Have you kept in touch with him?* **9.** distinctive manner or way of doing something: *The room showed the touch of a decorator.* **10.** light stroke or dab, as with a pen, pencil, or brush. **11.a.** manner of striking or touching the keys of a keyboard instrument, as a piano or typewriter. **b.** manner in which the keys of a keyboard instrument respond to the pressure exerted on them by the fingers. **12.** official stamp on gold, silver, or other metal indicating that it has been tested and testifying to its fineness. **13.** *Slang.* person from whom money is obtained. **14. to put the touch on.** *Slang.* to obtain or attempt to obtain money from. [Old French *touchier* to strike, affect, from an assumed Vulgar Latin word based on an imitation of the sound of striking.]

touch-and-go (tuch′ən gō′) *adj.* of uncertain outcome: *The ball game was touch-and-go up to the last few seconds.*

touch and go, uncertain, precarious, or risky situation or state of affairs.

touch·back (tuch′bak′) *n. Football.* play in which the ball is declared dead beyond a team's goal line after it has been impelled there by the opposing team. No points are awarded for a touchback.

touch·down (tuch′doun′) *n.* **1.** *Football.* **a.** scoring play worth six points, made by being in possession of the ball on or beyond the opponent's goal line. **b.** score so made. **2.** act or moment of landing an aircraft.

touched (tucht) *adj.* **1.** moved, as to feelings of pity, tenderness, or compassion; emotionally stirred: *She was touched by the child's tears.* **2.** *Informal.* slightly mentally unbalanced.

touch football, form of football in which a ball carrier is stopped by being touched with one or both hands rather than tackled.

touch·ing (tuch′ing) *adj.* stirring or appealing to the emotions or feelings. —*prep.* with respect to; as to; concerning. —**touch′ing·ly,** *adv.* **Syn.** *adj.* **Touching, moving, poignant** mean appealing to or affecting the emotions. **Touching** is usually associated with circumstances that do or should affect one slightly or momentarily, or is used otherwise in an ironic manner to suggest excessive sentimentality: *The dog's touching devotion to his master made us smile.* **Moving,** in contrast, is associated with circumstances that do and should affect one deeply, influencing or expressing a change of heart or course of action: *As a*

result of the president's moving appeal, legislation for the poverty-stricken areas was finally enacted.* **Poignant** is characterized by a sharp, piercing, and bittersweet quality and is often associated with circumstances of regret or nostalgia: *The faded photograph stirred poignant memories of her childhood.*

touch-me-not (tuch′mē not′) *n.* **1.** wildflower native to North America, having trumpet-shaped flowers and seed pods that burst open when ripe. There are two species: *Impatiens pallida,* bearing pale-yellow flowers, and *I. biflora,* bearing orange-yellow flowers spotted with red. **2.** any of several other plants whose fruit burst open when ripe, esp. the squirting cucumber.

touch·stone (tuch′stōn′) *n.* **1.** hard, black stone, as basalt or jasper, used to test the fineness of an alloy of gold or silver by comparing the color of the streak made on the stone by the alloy with the streak made by an alloy of known fineness. **2.** anything by which the quality, value, or genuineness of something is tested; test.

touch system, method of typewriting without looking at the keyboard, each finger being trained to a particular key or keys.

touch-type (tuch′tīp′) **-typed, -typ·ing.** *v.t., v.i.* to type using the touch system.

touch·wood (tuch′wood′) *n.* dry, decayed wood used as tinder; punk.

touch·y (tuch′ē) **touch·i·er, touch·i·est.** *adj.* **1.** easily offended; very sensitive. **2.** requiring caution, tact, and careful handling: *a touchy situation.* —**touch′i·ly,** *adv.* —**touch′i·ness,** *n.*

tough (tuf) *adj.* **1.** able to withstand great pressure or strain without breaking; strong but pliable. **2.** difficult to cut, sever, or chew: *a tough piece of meat.* **3.** capable of enduring great strain, hardship, or adversity; having strength and resilience: *a tough constitution.* **4.** characterized by or showing harshness or inflexibility of temperament; stern: *The laws are tough on offenders.* **5.** difficult to do, deal with, or accomplish; requiring a great deal of effort: *a tough job, a tough question.* **6.** difficult to manage, influence, or intimidate: *a tough customer.* **7.** having or characterized by a rough, brutal, and often violent atmosphere: *a tough neighborhood.* **8.** *Informal.* unhappy or unfortunate: *He's had a tough life.* —*n.* rough, brutal, and often violent person; ruffian; thug. [Old English *tōh* not easily broken, not tender, sticky.] —**tough′ly,** *adv.* —**tough′ness,** *n.*

Syn. *adj.* **3. Tough, strong, rugged** mean physically powerful. **Tough** implies that one has been physically and mentally hardened by experience, acquiring a stamina that resists weakening and fatigue: *Only the toughest soldiers were chosen for the mission into enemy territory.* **Strong** shifts the emphasis to inherent bodily power, muscular force, and soundness of constitution that allow one to accomplish any physical labor with relative ease: *A strong woman could lift that table.* **Rugged** comes closer to *tough* than to *strong,* but is used in a somewhat more complimentary manner to suggest the vigor and robustness of one who lives an active outdoor life: *Legends have grown up around the figure of the rugged lumberjack.*

tough·en (tuf′ən) *v.t., v.i.* to make or become tough or tougher.

Tou·lon (tōō lôn′) *n.* port city in southeastern France, on the Mediterranean. Pop. (1968), 174,746.

Tou·louse (tōō lōōz′) *n.* city in southern France. Pop. (1968), 370,796.

Tou·louse-Lau·trec, Hen·ri de (tōō lōōs′lō trek′, -lōōz′; äɴ rē′) 1864–1901, French painter and illustrator.

tou·pee (tōō pā′) *n.* quantity of real or artificial hair worn by men to cover baldness. [French *toupet* tuft of hair, from Old French *to(u)p;* of Germanic origin.]

tour (toor) *n.* **1.** journey in which many places are visited, usually for short periods of time: *They took a tour of the Greek isles.* **2.a.** brief journey, often organized for a group of people, to or through a place for the purpose of seeing or inspecting it: *Joan took us on a tour of the house.* **b.** group of people organized for or making such a journey: *I joined the tour in Paris.* **3.** circuit or journey, as of a theatrical or musical company, made to a number of places in order to give performances. **4.** period of time in which some obligatory or assigned task or service is fulfilled in one place, esp. in the military service. —*v.t.* to make a tour of or through. —*v.i.* to go on a tour. [Old French *to(u)r* a turn, circuit, lathe, from Latin *tornus* lathe, from Greek *tornos.*] —**Syn.** *n.* **1.** see **journey.**

tour de force (toor′də fôrs′) feat of extraordinary strength, skill, or ingenuity, esp. one that is not likely to be repeated or equaled. [French *tour de force* feat of strength or skill. See **TOUR, FORCE.**]

touring car, large, open automobile seating five or more passengers.

tour·ism (toor′iz′əm) *n.* **1.** business of providing services for tourists: *Tourism is the basis of that country's economy.* **2.** travel for pleasure.

tour·ist (toor′ist) *n.* one who travels for pleasure. —*adj.* of or for tourists.

tourist class 1. on a passenger ship, class of accommodations next below cabin class. **2.** on an airplane, class of accommodations below first class.

at; āpe; cär; end; mē; it; īce; hot; ōld; fôrk; wood; fōōl; oil; out; up; ūse; turn; sing; thin; this; zh in treasure; ə in ago, taken, pencil, lemon, circus.

tour·ma·line (toor′mə lin, -lēn′) *also,* **tour·ma·lin** (toor′mə lin). *n.* glassy or lustrous silicate of boron and aluminum, occurring in a variety of colors, esp. black, often used as a gem, esp. in the red or green variety. [French *tourmaline,* going back to Singhalese *tōramalli* carnelian.]

tour·na·ment (toor′nə mənt, tur′-) *n.* **1.** series of contests involving two or more persons or teams: *a bridge tournament.* **2.a.** formal combat between two or more mounted knights or other individuals armed with lances and other weapons. **b.** series of such combats. [Old French *torneiement,* from *torneier* to joust, turn round. See TOURNEY.]

tour·ney (toor′nē, tur′-) *pl.,* **-neys.** *n.* tournament. —*v.i.* **-neyed, -ney·ing.** to take part in a tournament. [Old French *tornei* tournament, from *torneier* to joust, turn round, going back to Latin *tornāre* to turn in a lathe. See TURN.]

tour·ni·quet (tur′nə kit, toor′-) *n.* device used to stop the flow of blood to a particular part of the body or to control severe bleeding, usually consisting of a strip of cloth or bandage that is tightened by twisting with a stick or other apparatus. [French *tourniquet,* from *tourner* to turn, from Latin *tornāre* to turn in a lathe. See TURN.]

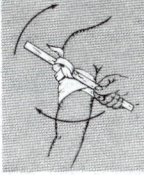

Tourniquet

Tours (toor) *n.* city in west-central France. In A.D. 732 Charles Martel defeated the Moors in a battle near here. Pop. (1968), 128,120.

tou·sle (tou′zəl) **-sled, -sling.** *v.t.* to put into disorder; dishevel: *The wind tousled her hair.* —*n.* untidy, disheveled mass, esp. of hair. [Dialectal *touse* to pull roughly, tear (of uncertain origin) + -LE.]

tout (tout) *Informal.* *v.i.* to solicit customers, employment, patronage, or the like, esp. in a persistent or brazen way: *The campaign manager touted for votes.* —*v.t.* **1.** to solicit; importune. **2.** to praise or publicize in an exaggerated manner: *The actor was touted as the next great movie star.* **3.** to give or sell information about (a race horse) to a bettor. —*n.* one who touts. [Probably from an unrecorded Old English word.] —**tout′er,** *n.*

tout à fait (tōō tä fā′) *French.* completely; entirely; quite.

tout de suite (tōōt swēt′) *French.* at once; immediately.

tout en·sem·ble (tōō tän sän′blə) *French.* all the parts considered as or forming a whole; general effect.

tow¹ (tō) *v.t.* to pull, drag, or draw behind, esp. by means of a rope, chain, or the like: *The truck towed the car to the service station.* —*n.* **1.** act of towing. **2.** that which is being towed. **3.** towline. **4. in tow.** **a.** being towed or pulled along: *a small boy with a red wagon in tow.* **b.** under one's protection, guidance, or influence: *Richard took his little brother in tow and taught him to play football.* [Old English *togian* to draw, pull.]

tow² (tō) *n.* coarse, shorter fibers of flax or hemp used to make yarn and twine. [Old English *tow-* a spinning.]

tow·age (tō′ij) *n.* **1.** act of towing; being towed. **2.** service or charge made for towing.

toward (tôrd, tō′ərd, tə wôrd′) *also,* **towards.** *prep.* **1.** in the direction of: *The puppy ran toward the car.* **2.** with respect to; concerning; regarding: *What are his feelings toward her?* **3.** near in time; shortly before: *The snow stopped toward morning.* **4.** as a contribution or an aid to; in order to obtain: *She saved her lunch money toward a new dress. He's taking courses toward a master's degree.* [Old English *tōweard* in the direction of, from *tō* to + *-weard* -ward.]

tow·boat (tō′bōt′) *n.* tugboat.

tow·el (tou′əl) *n.* **1.** piece of absorbent material, esp. paper or terry cloth, used for wiping or drying. **2. to throw in the towel.** *Informal.* to give up; admit defeat; quit. —*v.t.,* **-eled, -el·ing;** *also, British,* **-elled, -el·ling.** to wipe or dry with a towel: *to towel oneself after swimming. Steve toweled his baby after his bath.* [Old French *toaille* cloth for wiping or drying; of Germanic origin.]

tow·el·ing (tou′ə ling) *also, British,* **tow·el·ling.** *n.* any of various absorbent, relatively coarse fabrics, as cotton or linen, used for making towels.

tow·er (tou′ər) *n.* tall but relatively narrow structure, often forming a part of and rising from a building or other structure. —*v.i.* to rise or extend to a great height: *The skyscraper towered above the other buildings. Steve towered over all the other members of his family.* [Old French *tour* tall structure, from Latin *turris* citadel, high structure, from Greek *tyrsis*.] —**tow′er·y,** *adj.*

tow·er·ing (tou′ə ring) *adj.* **1.** very tall; lofty: *Towering palm trees*

Tower

lined the beach. **2.** very great; outstanding: *the towering musical genius of Beethoven.* **3.** very violent or intense: *a towering rage.*

Tower of London, historic fortress and prison on the north bank of the Thames, in London, England.

tow·head (tō′hed′) *n.* person having very pale blond hair. —**tow′-head′ed,** *adj.*

tow·hee (tou′hē′, tō′-) *n.* any of several North American finches, family Fringillidae, resembling a sparrow. Length: 6–10 inches. Also, **che·wink′.** [Imitative of its cry.]

tow·line (tō′līn′) *n.* rope, chain, or the like used for towing.

town (toun) *n.* **1.** geographical and political division, smaller than a county, that governs itself under a broad grant of power from a state legislature. **2.** in New England, basic governmental unit that may include both rural and compactly settled areas. Several villages may be within the limits of one town. **3.** any densely populated area, esp. an urban district. **4.** inhabitants of a town collectively. **5.** commercial or industrial section of a specific locality, esp. in a rural area: *Mother went into town for groceries.* **6. to go to town.** *Informal.* to do or act with exceptional speed, ability, and efficiency. **7. to paint the town (red).** *Informal.* to go on a spree; celebrate wildly. [Old English *tūn* enclosure, village; referring to the protection of settlements in earlier times by enclosures.]

town clerk, official in charge of the records and correspondence of a town.

town crier, formerly, person employed to make public proclamations or announcements in the streets of a town.

town hall, building that houses the offices of officials of a town or is used for town meetings.

town house, one of a row of houses, usually connected by common side walls and located in a city.

town meeting **1.** meeting of all the voters of a town, esp. in New England, to express their opinions and decide directly on matters of local jurisdiction. **2.** any general meeting of the inhabitants of a town.

towns·folk (tounz′fōk′) *n.,pl.* townspeople.

town·ship (toun′ship′) *n.* **1.** geographical and political division of a county, having certain powers of municipal government. **2.** in surveys of public land, an area containing thirty-six sections of one square mile each. [Old English *tūnscipe* village community, from *tūn* village + *-scipe* -ship.]

towns·man (tounz′mən) *pl.,* **-men.** *n.* **1.** inhabitant of a town. **2.** fellow inhabitant of one's town.

towns·peo·ple (tounz′pē′pəl) *n.,pl.* inhabitants of a town collectively.

tow·path (tō′path′) *n.* path along the bank of a canal or river used, as by draft animals, in towing boats.

tow·rope (tō′rōp′) *n.* rope used in towing, esp. a hawser or cable used for towing boats.

tox·e·mi·a (tok sē′mē ə) *also,* **tox·ae·mi·a.** *n.* blood poisoning. [Modern Latin *toxaemia,* going back to Greek *toxikon (pharmakon)* (poison) for arrows + *haima* blood. See TOXIC.]

tox·e·mic (tok sē′mik) *also,* **tox·ae·mic.** *adj.* **1.** of, relating to, or caused by toxemia. **2.** affected with or having toxemia.

tox·ic (tok′sik) *adj.* **1.** of, relating to, or caused by poison. **2.** affected with poison; poisoned. [Medieval Latin *toxicus* poisonous, from Latin *toxicum* poison, from Greek *toxikon (pharmakon)* (poison) for arrows, from *toxon* bow².]

tox·ic·i·ty (tok sis′ə tē) *pl.,* **-ties.** *n.* **1.** state or quality of being toxic. **2.** degree to which something is toxic.

tox·i·col·o·gy (tok′sə kol′ə jē) *n.* branch of medical science that deals with the nature and effects of poisons and the treatment of poisoning. [TOXIC + -LOGY.] —**tox′i·co·log′i·cal,** *adj.* —**tox′i·col′o·gist,** *n.*

tox·in (tok′sin) *n.* any poisonous product of animal or vegetable cells. The toxins produced by harmful bacteria cause the symptoms of many diseases. [TOX(IC) + -IN¹.]

toy (toi) *n.* **1.** object constructed or intended to be played with by a child. **2.** something of little or no value or importance. —*v.i.* to consider, handle, or deal with someone or something in an idle or capricious manner; trifle without any serious intention: *to toy with someone's feelings, to toy with an idea.* —*adj.* **1.** of, like, or used as a toy. **2.** smaller than is usual or standard, as certain breeds of dog. [Of uncertain origin.]

to·yon (tō′yən) *n.* tall evergreen shrub, *Photinia arbutifolia,* of the rose family, native to California, bearing red or yellow fruits and shiny deep-green leaves which are often used as Christmas decorations. [Spanish *tollon;* probably of Nahuatl origin.]

tp., township.

tr. **1.** transitive. **2.** translation; translator. **3.** transpose. **4.** treasurer.

trace¹ (trās) *n.* **1.** something left behind as evidence of the existence of some person, place, thing, or event: *The earthquake left its traces on the village.* **2.** track made by the passage of someone or something, as

a footprint or tire mark. **3.** small, almost indiscernible amount or indication: *a trace of mint in the drink. There was a trace of sarcasm in his tone.* **4.** line drawn, esp. one made by a self-recording instrument, as an electrocardiograph. —*v.t.,* **traced, trac·ing. 1.** to follow the track, trail, or path of; pursue: *to trace a missing person. They traced the thieves to their hideout.* **2.** to follow the course, development, or history of: *to trace a system of government back to the ancient Romans.* **3.** to discover or ascertain by research or investigation: *to trace the origins of a word, to trace the connection between poverty and crime.* **4.** to mark out; delineate: *to trace a figure in the sand, to trace an outline of a plan, to trace a route on a map.* **5.** to copy, as a drawing, by following lines as seen through a transparent sheet placed over it. **6.** to ornament with tracery. **7.** to record by means of a curved or broken line: *A machine traced the patient's respiration rate.* —*v.i.* to have its origin; go back in time: *Our feud traces back to our childhood.* [Old French *tracier* to follow a trail, going back to Latin *tractus,* past participle of *trahere* to draw, drag.] —**trace′a·bil′i·ty,** *n.* —**trace′a·ble,** *adj.* —**trace′a·bly,** *adv.*

Syn. *n.* **1. Trace, vestige** mean a mark remaining of some previous presence or occurrence. **Trace** is usually regarded as a clue or as providing evidence: *Detectives found traces of a struggle in the room.* **Vestige** is usually applied to a remnant or remains, esp. of something no longer clearly understood, useful, or functional: *These instruments are the vestiges of an outmoded method of handicraft.*

trace² (trās) *n.* **1.** either of the two straps, ropes, or chains by which the harness of a draft animal is attached to the vehicle it pulls. **2. to kick over the traces,** to free oneself from control or influence; show independence; rebel. [Old French *trais,* plural of *trait* a pulling, harness strap, from Latin *tractus* a pulling, dragging.]

trace element, element present in very small amounts that are detectable but not measurable.

trac·er (trā′sər) *n.* **1.** one who or that which traces. **2.** any of various devices for making tracings of drawings. **3.** inquiry sent from place to place to locate someone or something that is missing, esp. mail lost in transit. **4.** easily detected and located substance, usually a radioisotope, that is introduced internally in some system, as a gas pipeline or a human body, to keep track of the movements and changes inside. —*n.* projectile, as a bullet or shell, treated with a chemical compound so that its trajectory may be visible.

trac·er·y (trā′sər ē) *pl.,* **-er·ies.** *n.* **1.** ornamental stonework forming geometric or curved patterns, used esp. in Gothic windows and arches. **2.** any similar ornamentation, as in a screen, paneling, or embroidery.

Tracery

tra·che·a (trā′kē ə) *pl.,* **-che·ae** (-kē ē′). *n.* tube extending from the larynx to the bronchi. Also, **wind′pipe′.** [Medieval Latin *trachea,* going back to Greek *trācheia (artēría)* literally, rough (windpipe); because of its roughness.] —**tra′che·al,** *adj.*

tra·che·ot·o·my (trā′kē ot′ə mē) *pl.,* **-mies.** *n.* surgical operation in which an opening is made through the neck into the trachea, usually to remove an obstruction.

tra·cho·ma (trə kō′mə) *n.* contagious disease caused by a virus, characterized by inflammation and granulation of the eyelids. If untreated, it may lead to blindness. [Modern Latin *trachoma,* from Greek *trāchōma* roughness; because of the symptomatic roughness of the eyelids.]

trac·ing (trā′sing) *n.* **1.** act of one who or that which traces. **2.** copy of something, made by tracing its lines through transparent paper. **3.** line or similar record made by a self-registering instrument.

track (trak) *n.* **1.** mark or set of marks made by a person, animal, or object in passage: *tire tracks in the snow. The deer's tracks were easy to follow.* **2.** course along which anything moves; path; route: *the track of a comet, the track of a storm, a track through the woods.* **3.** course of action or way of proceeding: *to go off on another track. His younger brother followed in the same track.* **4.** bar or set of parallel bars on which a vehicle, as a railroad car, travels. **5.** course laid out for racing. **6.a.** sport consisting of running events, as high hurdles or relay races. **b.** track and field. **7.** one of the two continuous metal belts on which a crawler tractor or similar vehicle runs. **8. in one's tracks.** *Informal.* exactly where one is at the moment; then and there: *The sight made him stop in his tracks.* **9. to keep track of.** to maintain contact with or keep informed about. **10. to lose track of.** to fail to maintain contact with or keep informed about. **11. to make tracks.** to depart or move rapidly; go quickly. —*v.t.* **1.** to follow the tracks or scent of: *to track wild game through the jungle.* **2.** to discover, pursue, or ascertain by following tracks or investigating evidence (often with *down*): *to track down the address of an old friend, to track down the instigators of a riot.*

3. to observe and record the path of: *to track a hurricane, to track a space vehicle.* **4.** to make a track of footprints or other marks on: *to track a freshly waxed floor.* **5.** to make marks with (something) carried on one's feet: *to track snow on a carpet.* [Old French *trac* trace¹, beaten path, course; probably of Germanic origin.] —**track′er,** *n.*

track·age (trak′ij) *n.* **1.** tracks of a railway system collectively. **2.a.** right of one railroad company to use the tracks of another. **b.** charge for this right.

track and field, group of sports events involving the basic physical activities of walking, running, jumping, and throwing.

track·less (trak′lis) *adj.* **1.** without or unmarked by paths or trails: *a trackless wilderness.* **2.** not running on tracks or rails.

track meet, athletic contest consisting of track and field events.

tract¹ (trakt) *n.* **1.** stretch or expanse of land; area; region: *a tract of woodland.* **2.** group of parts or organs in the body that together have a specific function: *the digestive tract, the urinary tract.* **3.** *Archaic.* period or lapse of time. [Latin *tractus* region, course, a drawing out. Doublet of TRAIT.]

tract² (trakt) *n.* booklet or pamphlet, esp. one on a religious or moral subject. [Modification of Latin *tractātus* handling, treatise.]

trac·ta·ble (trak′tə bəl) *adj.* **1.** easily controlled, dominated, or influenced; compliant; docile. **2.** easily worked or handled; malleable: *a tractable metal.* [Latin *tractābilis* manageable, from *tractāre* to handle. See TREAT.] —**trac′ta·bil′i·ty, trac′ta·ble·ness,** *n.* —**trac′ta·bly,** *adv.*

trac·tile (trak′til) *adj.* capable of being drawn out in length.

trac·tion (trak′shən) *n.* **1.** act of drawing or pulling something, as a vehicle or load, along a road or other surface. **2.** state or condition of being drawn or pulled. **3.** power used for drawing or pulling: *steam traction.* **4.** adhesive friction of a body on a surface. A deep tread in tires provides better traction on snow-covered roads. **5.** act of pulling a muscle, as of the leg, by means of some apparatus, as to relieve pressure or bring fractured or dislocated bones into place. [Medieval Latin *tractiō* act of drawing, from Latin *tractus,* past participle of *trahere* to draw, drag.]

traction engine, locomotive for pulling heavy loads on roads or fields rather than on tracks.

trac·tive (trak′tiv) *adj.* capable of or used in drawing or pulling.

trac·tor (trak′tər) *n.* **1.** motor vehicle having rubber tire wheels or treads, used esp. on farms for hauling heavy loads over rough terrain. **2.** truck consisting of a motor and a driver's cab, used in combination

Tractor

with a trailer for transporting freight. **3.** airplane with the propeller forward of the wings. [Modern Latin *tractor* literally, that which drags, from Latin *tractus,* past participle of *trahere* to drag, draw.]

trade (trād) *n.* **1.** business of buying and selling; exchange of goods; commerce: *foreign trade, domestic trade.* **2.** level of activity of such business: *to do a brisk trade in men's wear.* **3.** exchange of one thing for another; swap: *The little boy is trying to make a trade for his new pair of skates.* **4.** transaction, esp. one that is a bargain. **5.** that which one does to earn a living, esp. an occupation requiring manual or mechanical skill: *the tools of one's trade. He is an electrician by trade.* **6.** people or firms engaged in the same business or occupation: *Discounts are available to the trade only.* **7.** regular customers; clientele: *a restaurant that caters to the theater trade.* **8. trades.** trade winds. —*v.i.,* **trad·ed, trad·ing. 1.** to engage in buying and selling; be in commerce. **2.** to exchange one thing for another. **3.** to do business; shop: *I refuse to trade with that company again. We trade at the local shops.* —*v.t.* **1.** to exchange or swap: *to trade places, to trade blows.* **2.** to buy and sell. **3. to trade in.** to give in exchange as payment or part payment for something else: *to trade in an old car for a new one.* **4. to trade off.** to dispose of by sale or exchange. **5. to trade on.** to take advantage of or profit from: *to trade on someone's good will.* [Middle Low German *trade* track, course.]

trade-in (trād′in′) *n.* something given or received as payment or partial payment for something else, esp. a used item given to a dealer as partial payment for a similar, new item.

trade·mark (trād′märk′) *n.* **1.** distinctive mark, as a word, symbol, or device, adopted and usually registered officially by a specific merchant or manufacturer to identify and distinguish his goods or services from those of his competitors. **2.** any distinctive sign, characteristic, or the like by which a person or thing comes to be known: *That tune has become the singer's trademark.* —*v.t.* **1.** to place a trademark on. **2.** to register as a trademark.

trade name 1. name, often registered as a trademark, used by a specific merchant or manufacturer to distinguish his goods or services from those of his competitors. **2.** name by which an article, service, or

at; āpe; cär; end; mē; it; īce; hot; ōld; fôrk; wood; fo͞od; oil; out; up; ūse; turn; sing; thin; **this;** zh in treasure; ə in ago, taken, pencil, lemon, circus.

the like is commonly referred to in trade. **3.** name under which a firm carries on business.

trad·er (trā′dər) *n.* **1.** one whose business is buying and selling. **2.** ship used in trading.

trade school, vocational school.

trades·man (trādz′mən) *pl.*, **-men.** *n.* shopkeeper.

trade union *also, British,* **trades union. 1.** labor union in which the members are made up of workers engaged in a particular trade or craft. **2.** any labor union.

trade unionism, unionism (*def. I*).

trade unionist 1. member of a trade union. **2.** one who favors or supports trade unionism.

trade wind, prevailing winds blowing toward the equator from about 30 degrees north latitude to about 30 degrees south latitude, coming from the northeast north of the equator and from the southeast south of the equator.

trading post, store or station established by a trader or trading company in a sparsely inhabited region for the purpose of supplying the inhabitants with necessary commodities, often in exchange for local products.

trading stamp, stamp given as a premium to a customer, esp. in a retail establishment, to be exchanged in specified quantities for merchandise.

tra·di·tion (trə dish′ən) *n.* **1.** handing down of knowledge, beliefs, customs, or the like from one generation to another. **2.** knowledge, beliefs, customs, or the like handed down in this manner. **3.** long-established and generally accepted custom, practice, or the like: *It is a tradition that the men in his family serve in the Navy.* **4.a.** among the Jews, the body of unwritten laws and doctrines said to have been handed down by Moses. **b.** among certain Christians, the unwritten precepts and doctrines handed down by Christ and the Apostles to the Church and preserved by its theologians. [Latin *trāditiō* surrender, delivery. Doublet of TREASON.]

tra·di·tion·al (trə dish′ən əl) *adj.* of, derived from, or in accordance with tradition. Also, **tra·di·tion·ar·y** (trə dish′ən ner′ē). —**tra·di′tion·al·ly,** *adv.*

tra·duce (trə dōōs′, -dūs′) **-duced, -duc·ing.** *v.t.* to speak falsely or maliciously of; slander. [Latin *trādūcere* to lead across, dishonor.] —**tra·duc′er,** *n.*

Tra·fal·gar, Cape (trə fal′gər) cape in southwestern Spain on the Atlantic, the site of a naval battle on October 21, 1805, in which the fleets of France and Spain were defeated by a British fleet led by Horatio Nelson.

traf·fic (traf′ik) *n.* **1.** vehicles, vessels, people, or the like moving along or through an area or route: *There was little traffic on the highway in the early morning hours.* **2.** passage or flow of vehicles, vessels, people, or the like along or through an area or route: *The stop sign actually made traffic safer and faster.* **3.** exchange of goods, esp. for profit; buying and selling; trade. **4.** dealing or bargaining in something illegal or improper: *The police attempted to stop narcotics traffic in the city.* **5.a.** business done by a railroad, steamship, or other transportation line. **b.** passengers or freight transported by such a line. **6.** dealings; business; connection: *The so-called witches were accused of having traffic with the devil.* —*v.i.,* **-ficked, -fick·ing. 1.** to carry on commerce, esp. illegally; deal (with *in*): *to traffic in stolen goods.* **2.** to have dealings or trade (with *with*): *He was known to traffic with criminals.* [Middle French *trafique* commerce, from Italian *traffico*; of uncertain origin.] —**traf′fick·er,** *n.*

traffic circle, circular intersection around which traffic moves in one direction, allowing vehicles to enter or leave any of the converging roads without disturbing the flow of traffic. Also, **ro′ta·ry.**

traffic island, marked or raised area, as a median strip, used to separate opposing lanes of traffic or to provide pedestrians with protection from the flow of traffic.

traffic light, signal, usually with red and green and sometimes amber or yellow lights, that by changing color or blinking on or off controls the flow of traffic, esp. at an intersection. Also, **traffic signal, stop′light′.**

trag′a·canth (trag′ə kanth′) *n.* dull-white gum obtained from any of several western Asian plants, esp. a shrub, *Astragalus gummifer,* used as a thickening and emulsifying agent in ice cream and candy, and in the making of printing inks and cosmetics. [Latin *tragacantha* plant from which this gum is obtained, from Greek *tragakantha,* from *tragos* goat + *akantha* thorn.]

tra·ge·di·an (trə jē′dē ən) *n.* actor who specializes in playing tragic roles.

tra·ge·di·enne (trə jē′dē en′) *n.* actress who specializes in playing tragic roles.

trag·e·dy (traj′ə dē) *pl.*, **-dies.** *n.* **1.** drama in which life is viewed or treated seriously, usually having a sad ending that is brought about by a flaw in the protagonist's character or by some other circumstance. **2.** branch of drama composed of such plays. Distinguished from

comedy. **3.** any work of literature having the characteristics of a dramatic tragedy. **4.** art of writing, acting, or producing a tragedy or tragedies: *Shakespeare was a master of tragedy.* **5.** sad, dreadful, or disastrous event or set of circumstances: *The tragedy in the mine claimed seventeen lives.* **6.** sad, dreadful, or disastrous state, quality, or effect: *The inability to love was the tragedy of his life.* [Old French *tragedie* serious play that usually has an unhappy ending, from Latin *tragoedia,* from Greek *tragōidiā* literally, goat song, from *tragos* goat + *ōidē* song; the reason for the name "goat song" is still disputed.]

trag·ic (traj′ik) *adj.* **1.** of, relating to, or characteristic of tragedy, esp. dramatic tragedy: *The play had a tragic ending.* **2.** very sad, unfortunate, or disastrous: *a tragic accident, a tragic decision.* Also, **trag′i·cal.** [Latin *tragicus,* from Greek *tragikos* relating to tragedy, relating to a goat, from *tragos* goat. See TRAGEDY.] —**trag′i·cal·ly,** *adv.*

tragic flaw, flaw in the character of the hero of a tragedy that brings about his downfall.

trag·i·com·e·dy (traj′i kom′ə dē) *pl.*, **-dies.** *n.* **1.** drama containing both tragic and comic elements, usually having a happy ending. **2.** event or set of circumstances combining tragic and comic elements. [French *tragicomédie,* going back to Latin *tragicocōmoedia* drama containing both tragic and comic elements, from *tragicus* (see TRAGIC) + *cōmoedia* (see COMEDY).] —**trag′i·com′ic;** *also,* **trag′i·com′i·cal,** *adj.*

trail (trāl) *n.* **1.** passage through a wild or uninhabited region. **2.** mark, scent, or path made by an animal or person in passage: *The snail left a slimy trail on the glass of the tank. The hounds lost the escaped convict's trail at the river edge.* **3.** that which follows or is drawn along behind: *a trail of smoke. The soldiers left a trail of destruction behind them.* —*v.t.* **1.** to follow behind, esp. in a haphazard or lagging manner: *The children trailed the parade down the street.* **2.** to drag or draw along or behind: *The children trailed their kites on the ground.* **3.** to follow the track or scent of: *to trail one's prey. They trailed the thieves to their hideout.* **4.** to be behind or losing, as in a competition: *Our product trailed the others in sales.* —*v.i.* **1.** to hang down or be drawn behind, as the train of a dress. **2.** to move or flow slowly; stream: *The audience trailed in after the intermission. Smoke trailed through the trees.* **3.** to extend or grow over or along the ground or other surface: *The vines trailed down the side of the building.* **4.** to be losing, as in a contest or game; lag: *Our team trailed in the fifth inning, but went on to win.* **5.** to diminish gradually (with *off* or *away*): *Conversation trailed off as the evening wore on.* [Old French *trailler* to tow a boat; going back to Latin *trāgula* drag-net.]

trail·blaz·er (trāl′blā′zər) *n.* **1.** pathfinder. **2.** pioneer in any field: *a painter who was a real trailblazer in abstract art.*

trail·er (trā′lər) *n.* **1.** one who or that which trails. **2.** vehicle without its own motive power, designed to be pulled by a car, truck, or similar vehicle, used as for transporting goods or the like.

Trailer *(def. 3)*

3. similar vehicle, used esp. as a dwelling place. **4.** plant or vine that extends or grows over or along the ground or other surface. **5.** short film or video tape used to advertise a motion picture or program that will be shown in the future.

trailer court, large area, usually equipped with plumbing and electrical facilities, where trailers can be parked and lived in. Also, **trailer camp, trailer park.**

trailing arbutus, evergreen vine, *Epigaea repens,* of the heath family, growing along the ground in shady areas, bearing clusters of small, very fragrant pink or white blossoms.

train (trān) *n.* **1.** connected line of railroad cars. **2.** group of people, animals, or vehicles traveling together, esp. in a long line or procession: *a wagon train, a mule train.* **3.** connected series or succession, as of events or ideas: *to follow a train of thought.* **4.** series of events, circumstances, or conditions resulting from or following something. **5.** part of a dress or robe that hangs down from the skirt and trails behind the wearer. **6.** that which is drawn along behind, as the tailfeathers of a peacock or the tail of a comet. **7.** group of attendants; following; retinue: *a train of courtiers.* **8.** group of vehicles and men following and attending an army, esp. to carry its supplies. **9.** a series of interconnected mechanical parts for transmitting motion, as the wheels and pinions of a watch. —*v.t.* **1.** to develop or mold the character, thoughts, and behavior of; bring up; rear: *to train a child to respect the rights of others.* **2.** to make proficient by instruction and practice, as in a particular skill or profession: *to train a new salesman.* **3.** to prepare physically, as with a regular drill, diet, and exercise: *to train a fighter.* **4.** to instruct (an animal) so as to make it obedient or capable of performing certain tasks or tricks. **5.** to cause to grow or lie in a desired form or direction: *to train one's hair to curl under, to train ivy to grow up a wall.*

6. to focus or direct; aim: *She trained her eyes on the screen.* —*v.i.* to undergo and follow a course of instruction and discipline: *to train for a big race, to train for the ministry.* [Old French *trainer* to drag, draw, going back to Latin *trahere.*] —**Syn.** *v.t.* 2. see **teach.**

train·ee (trā nē′) *n.* one who is undergoing training, esp. vocational or military training.

train·er (trā′nər) *n.* **1.** one who trains, esp. one responsible for the physical training and conditioning of an athlete, race horse, or the like. **2.** device used in training.

train·ing (trā′ning) *n.* **1.** act, process, or method of one who trains. **2.** state or process of being trained. —**Syn.** 1. see **education.**

train·load (trān′lōd′) *n.* amount that a freight train or passenger train can carry.

train·man (trān′mən) *pl.,* -**men.** *n.* one who is employed on a railroad, as a brakeman.

traipse (trāps) **traipsed, traips·ing.** *v.i. Informal.* to walk about idly or aimlessly.

trait (trāt) *n.* distinguishing aspect or quality, as of character: *bravery, honesty, and other noble traits.* [French *trait,* from Latin *tractus* a drawing out, region, course. Doublet of TRACT¹.] —**Syn.** see **characteristic, quality.**

trai·tor (trā′tər) *n.* **1.** one who commits treason. **2.** one who betrays any trust. [Old French *traitor,* from Latin *trāditor.*] —**trai′tress,** *n.*

trai·tor·ous (trā′tər əs) *adj.* **1.** of, relating to, or characteristic of a traitor. **2.** of, relating to, or of the nature of treason. —**trai′tor·ous·ly,** *adv.*

Tra·jan (trā′jən) *n.* A.D. c.53–117, Roman emperor from A.D. 98 to 117.

tra·jec·to·ry (trə jek′tər ē) *pl.,* -**ries.** *n.* curved path described by a vehicle or projectile body, as a bullet, ballistic missile, or meteor, moving through space or the atmosphere. [Medieval Latin *trajectorius* throwing across, from Latin *trājectus,* past participle of *trāicere* to throw across.]

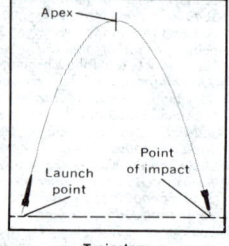

Apex

Launch point

Point of impact

Trajectory

tram (tram) *n.* **1.** *British.* streetcar. Also, **tram′car.** **2.** *British.* tramway (*def.* 1). **3.** four-wheeled vehicle that runs on tracks, used to convey coal in a mine. [Middle Low German *trame* beam.]

tram·mel (tram′əl) *also,* **tram·el, tram·ell.** **1.** *also,* **trammels.** anything that confines, restrains, or hinders freedom, action, or progress: *to shake off the trammels of the world and of public opinion* (Hazlitt, 1821). **2.** shackle for hobbling a horse and training him to amble. **3.** hook in a fireplace for suspending pots over the fire. **4.** net for catching fish, consisting of two taut outside nets with large mesh and a slack middle net with a fine mesh. Also (*def.* 4), **trammel net.** —*v.t.,* -**meled, -mel·ing;** *also, British,* -**melled, -mel·ling.** **1.** to hinder the freedom, action, or progress of; impede. **2.** to entangle in or as in a net; ensnare. [Middle French *tremail* dragnet, from Late Latin *trēmāculum* net with meshes for catching fish, possibly from Latin *trēs* three + *macula* mesh.] —**tram′mel·er;** *also, British,* **tram′mel·ler,** *n.*

tramp (tramp) *v.i.* **1.** to walk with a firm, heavy step. **2.** to travel on foot; walk. **3.** to travel or wander as a tramp or vagabond. —*v.t.* **1.** to press or compress by stepping heavily upon; trample: *to tramp the grass.* **2.** to travel over or through on foot: *The hikers tramped the countryside.* —*n.* **1.** one who wanders or travels from place to place, has no permanent residence or means of support, and usually begs for food, money, or temporary employment. **2.** heavy, regular footstep or succession of footsteps. **3.** sound made by such a step or steps: *We could hear the tramp of the marching soldiers.* **4.** long walk; hike. **5.** cargo ship, esp. a steamship, that does not trade regularly between fixed ports, but takes cargo wherever obtainable and for any port. [Probably of Germanic origin.] —**tramp′er,** *n.*

tram·ple (tram′pəl) -**pled, -pling.** *v.t.* **1.** to tread on so heavily as to injure, crush, or destroy: *Don't trample the flowers. She was trampled by the panicking mob.* **2.** to treat cruelly, harshly, or contemptuously (often with *down*): *When his opponents gained power, the dictator trampled them down.* —*v.i.* to tread heavily. —*n.* act of trampling.

[TRAMP + -LE.] —**tram′pler,** *n.*

tram·po·line (tram′pə lēn′, tram′pə lēn′) *n.* piece of gymnastic equipment consisting of elastic or net anchored by springs to a metal frame on legs, used for acrobatic tumbling. [Italian *trampolino* springboard, from *trampoli* stilts; of Germanic origin.] —**tram′po·lin′er, tram′po·lin′ist,** *n.*

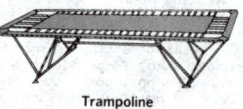

Trampoline

tram road, railway in a coal mine.

tram·way (tram′wā′) *n. British.* **1.** streetcar track. **2.** tramroad.

trance (trans) *n.* **1.** semiconscious state resembling sleep, as that produced by hypnotism. **2.** dazed or stunned state; stupor. **3.** state of deep mental absorption or abstraction. **4.** state of intense rapture, esp. one induced through a religious or spiritual experience. —*v.t.,* **tranced, tranc·ing.** *Archaic.* to put into or as into a trance. [Old French *transe* great fear, swoon, going back to Latin *trānsīre* to go across, die.]

tran·quil (trang′kwəl) -**quil·er, -quil·est;** *also, British,* -**quil·ler, -quil·lest.** *adj.* **1.** free from agitation or disturbance: *Grandfather recalled his tranquil childhood spent on a farm.* **2.** quiet and motionless: *a blue and tranquil ocean lake* (Bennett, 1875). [Latin *tranquillus.*] —**tran′quil·ly,** *adv.* —**Syn.** 1. see **calm.**

tran·quil·ize (trang′kwə līz′) -**ized, -iz·ing.** *v.t., v.i.* to make or become tranquil, esp. by the use of tranquilizers.

tran·quil·iz·er (trang′kwə lī′zər) *also,* **tran·quil·liz·er.** *n.* any of certain drugs, other than barbiturates, that produce a calming effect by reducing tension, nervous strain, and the like.

tran·quil·li·ty (trang kwil′ə tē) *also,* **tran·quil·i·ty.** *n.* state or quality of being tranquil.

trans- *prefix.* **1.** across; through; over: *transatlantic, transept.* **2.** so as to change completely: *transmute.* [Latin *trāns* across, beyond, over, through.]

trans. **1.** transitive. **2.** transportation. **3.** transactions.

trans·act (tran sakt′, -zakt′) *v.t.* to conduct and carry through, esp. business affairs. —*v.i.* to conduct negotiations; do business. [Latin *trānsāctus,* past participle of *trānsigere* to drive through, accomplish.] —**trans·ac′tor,** *n.*

trans·ac·tion (tran sak′shən, -zak′-) *n.* **1.** act of transacting; being transacted. **2.** that which is or has been transacted, esp. a business dealing.

trans·al·pine (trans al′pīn, -pin, tranz-) *adj.* being or situated beyond the Alps, esp. in relation to Rome.

trans·at·lan·tic (trans′ət lan′tik, tranz′-) *adj.* **1.** that extends across or crosses the Atlantic: *a transatlantic telephone call.* **2.** being or situated on the opposite side of the Atlantic.

Trans·cau·ca·sia (trans′kô kā′zhə, -shə) *n.* region in the southwestern Soviet Union, between the Black and Caspian seas.

tran·scend (tran send′) *v.t.* **1.** to pass or extend beyond the limits or powers of; exceed: *The concept of infinity transcends human understanding. Her love was an emotion that transcended mere affection.* **2.** to go beyond or better than in some respect, quality or attribute; surpass: *The beauty of this painting transcends that of the artist's earlier works.* **3.** in theology and philosophy, to exist above, beyond, or independent of (the universe, material existence, experience, or the like). [Latin *trānscendere* to climb over, surpass.]

tran·scend·ence (tran sen′dəns) *n.* act of transcending; being transcendent.

tran·scend·ent (tran sen′dənt) *adj.* **1.** surpassing or excelling others; superior; preeminent. **2.** *Theology.* (of God) existing above and independently of the universe. —**tran·scend′ent·ly,** *adv.*

tran·scen·den·tal (tran′sen den′təl) *adj.* **1.** superior; transcendent. **2.** beyond or contrary to human experience or to what is natural; supernatural. **3.** in Kantian philosophy, not derived from experience but based on the a priori elements of experience; transcending experience but not knowledge. **4.** *Mathematics.* not capable of being a solution of a rational algebraic equation. π is a transcendental number. —**tran′scen·den′tal·ly,** *adv.*

tran·scen·den·tal·ism (tran′sen den′təl iz′əm) *n.* **1.** state or quality of being transcendental. **2.** religious and philosophical ideas of a group of New England thinkers, including Emerson and Thoreau, active from about 1835 to 1860, who held that God is inherent in Nature and in man and that each individual must use his own conscience and intuition to discover moral and spiritual truths. **3.** doctrine, as in the philosophy of Kant, that reality transcends human experience, and that knowledge of it can be obtained by a priori or intuitive, rather than empirical, principles. —**tran′scen·den′tal·ist,** *adj., n.*

transcendental meditation. Hindu system of meditation that is supposed to lead to a state of consciousness somewhere between sleep and wakefulness.

trans·con·ti·nen·tal (trans′kon tə nent′əl) *adj.* **1.** that extends across or crosses a continent: *a transcontinental communication network.* **2.** of, being, or situated on the opposite side of a continent.

tran·scribe (tran skrīb′) -**scribed, -scrib·ing.** *v.t.* **1.** to make a written or typewritten copy of; rewrite or type: *to transcribe the minutes of the meeting.* **2.** to write out or type out, esp. from one written form to another, as from shorthand to script. **3.** to translate or transliterate. **4.** to arrange or adapt (a musical composition) for a different voice or instrument. **5.** to make a recording of (a radio program or the like) to be broadcast later. [Latin *trānscrībere* to copy off, transfer in writing.] —**tran·scrib′er,** *n.*

tran·script (tran'skript') *n.* **1.** written copy: *The judge reviewed the transcript of the trial.* **2.** any reproduction. [Latin *tránscriptum,* neuter past participle of *tránscríbere* to copy off, transfer in writing.]

tran·scrip·tion (tran skrip'shən) *n.* **1.** act of transcribing. **2.** transcript; copy. **3.** adaption or arrangement of a musical composition for another voice or instrument. **4.** recording, as on magnetic tape, of a radio program or the like to be broadcast later.

tran·sept (tran'sept) *n.* **1.** transverse portion of a cruciform church. **2.** one of the two parts of this transverse portion, on either side of the main section of the church. [Modern Latin *transeptum,* going back to Latin *tráns* across + *septum* fence, enclosure.]

Transept *(def. 1)*

trans·fer (*v.,* trans fur', trans'fər; *n.,* trans'fər) **-ferred, -fer·ring.** *v.t.* **1.** to convey or remove or cause to be conveyed or removed from one person, place, or the like to another: *She transferred the bracelet from her right wrist to her left.* **2.** to make over title or possession of to another: *to transfer land.* **3.** to convey (a drawing, design, pattern, or the like) from one surface to another. —*v.i.* **1.** to transfer oneself: *Elizabeth transferred to a new school.* **2.** to be transferred: *The office will transfer to new quarters.* **3.** to switch from one vehicle or transportation line to another, usually with little or no extra charge. —*n.* **1.** act of transferring; being transferred. Also, **trans·fer'al, trans·fer'ral. 2.** that which is transferred, esp. a drawing, design, pattern, or the like conveyed from one surface to another. **3.** ticket entitling a passenger to continue his journey on another vehicle or transportation line, usually with little or no extra charge. **4.** place or means of transferring. [Latin *tránsferre* to carry over, .transport.] —**trans·fer·a·bil·i·ty,** *n.* —**trans·fer'a·ble,** *adj.*

Syn. *v.t.* **1. Transfer, shift** mean to move from one person, place, or position to another. **Transfer** is more often used to suggest movement involving a considerable change or distance, esp. one of a permanent nature: *The company has transferred its main office from New York to Chicago.* **Shift,** in contrast, is more often used to indicate a redistribution or relatively small rearrangement, esp. one that is somewhat less sure or stable: *He shifted his weight after a few moments.*

trans·fer·ence (trans fur'əns, trans'fər əns) *n.* **1.** act of transferring; being transferred. **2.** *Psychology.* reproduction of emotions relating to forgotten or repressed experiences, esp. of childhood, by transferring them to another object, usually the psychoanalyst.

trans·fig·u·ra·tion (trans fig'yə rā'shən) *n.* **1.** act of transfiguring; being transfigured. **2. the Transfiguration. a.** in the New Testament, the miraculous change in the appearance of Christ that took place on a mountain in the presence of the Apostles Peter, James, and John. **b.** church festival commemorating this event. August 6.

trans·fig·ure (trans fig'yər) **-ured, -ur·ing.** *v.t.* **1.** to change the outward appearance of; alter in form or figure. **2.** to give an idealized or glorified appearance to; glorify. [Latin *tránsfigūrāre* to change in shape, transform.]

trans·fix (trans fiks') *v.t.* **1.** to make motionless, as from awe or fear. **2.** to pierce through with or as with a sharpened instrument; impale: *to transfix a butterfly with a pin.* **3.** to fix or fasten by piercing: *The nail transfixed the sign to the wall.* [Latin *tránsfíxus,* past participle of *tránsfígere* to pierce through.]

trans·form (trans fôrm') *v.t.* **1.** to alter in shape, form, or appearance: *A little paint will soon transform this old car.* **2.** to change the character, condition, nature, or the like of: *to transform a solid to a liquid. Fatherhood transformed him into a more responsible person.* **3.** to change (one form of energy) into another, as mechanical energy into electricity, or electric energy into light or heat. **4.** to change (an electric current) to a higher or lower voltage or to direct or alternating current. **5.** *Mathematics.* to change the form but not the value of. [Latin *tránsfōrmāre* to change the form of.]

trans·for·ma·tion (trans'fər mā'shən) *n.* act of transforming; being transformed.

trans·form·er (trans fôr'mər) *n.* **1.** one who or that which transforms. **2.** device for transferring electric energy from one alternating current circuit to another, usually with a change in voltage and current.

trans·fuse (trans fūz') **-fused, -fus·ing.** *v.t.* **1.** to pour (a liquid) from one receptacle into another; transfer by pouring . **2.** to transfer (blood) from one individual to another, either directly or by removing the blood from one individual into a container and then transferring the blood to the second individual. **3.** to inject (a saline solution or the like) into a blood vessel. **4.** to cause to be imparted or instilled: *His words trans-*

fused his hysteria into the crowd. [Latin *tránsfūsus,* past participle of *tránsfundere* to pour from one receptacle into another, transfer.]

trans·fu·sion (trans fū'zhən) *n.* act of transfusing, esp. the transfer of blood.

trans·gress (trans gres', tranz-) *v.i.* **1.** to break or violate a law, commandment, or the like; sin. —*v.t.* **1.** to break or violate (a law, commandment, or the like). **2.** to exceed or go beyond (any limit or bound): *a restriction that transgresses the rights of the individual.* [Latin *tránsgressus,* past participle of *tránsgredí* to step across.] —**trans·gres'sor,** *n.*

trans·gres·sion (trans gresh'ən, tranz-) *n.* act or instance of transgressing, esp. the breaking of a law or commandment.

tran·ship (tran ship') *v.t., v.i.* to transship. —**tran·ship'ment,** *n.*

tran·sience (tran'shəns) *n.* state or quality of being transient. Also, **tran'sien·cy.**

tran·sient (tran'shənt) *adj.* **1.** of temporary or brief duration; not lasting or durable; transitory: *transient fame, transient beauty.* **2.** stopping only for a short time; passing through: *a transient house guest.* —*n.* one who or that which is transient, esp. a person who passes through a place or stays in it only for a short time: *This boarding house caters mainly to transients.* [Latin *tránsiēns,* present participle of *tránsíre* to go across, pass over.] —**tran'sient·ly,** *adv.*

tran·sis·tor (tran zis'tər) *n.* **1.** miniature electronic device made of crystals of semiconductors, used instead of vacuum tubes to control and amplify electric current in television sets, computers, and other electronic equipment. **2.** transistorized radio. [TRANS(FER) + (RE)SISTOR; because it transfers an electronic signal across a resistor.]

tran·sis·tor·ize (tran zis'tə rīz') **-ized, -iz·ing.** *v.t.* to equip with transistors.

trans·it (tran'sit, -zit) *n.* **1.** act or instance of passing across or through; movement from one place or point to another: *We were delayed in transit by traffic.* **2.** act or instance of carrying from one place or point to another; being carried; conveyance: *The transit of fresh fruit to markets must be done quickly.* **3.** transition or change. **4.** telescope used in surveying to measure horizontal and vertical angles. **5.** *Astronomy.* **a.** passage of a planet directly between the earth and the sun so that it can be seen as a black dot moving across the disk of the sun. **b.** passage of a celestial body across the celestial meridian. —*v.t.* to pass across or through. [Latin *tránsitus* a going over.]

tran·si·tion (tran zish'ən) *n.* **1.** passage from one state, position, condition, or activity to another. **2.** period or location of such a passage. **3.** *Music.* a. change of key. **b.** passage connecting two parts, themes, or the like. [Latin *tránsitiō* a going across.] —**tran·si'tion·al,** *adj.* —**tran·si'tion·al·ly,** *adv.*

tran·si·tive (tran'sə tiv, -zə-) *adj.* (of verbs) taking a direct object to complete the action of the sentence. —*n.* transitive verb. [Late Latin *tránsitīvus* passing over, from Latin *tránsitus,* past participle of *tránsíre* to go across.]

tran·si·to·ry (tran'sə tôr'ē) *adj.* of brief duration; momentary. —**tran'si·to·ri·ly,** *adv.* —**tran'si·to·ri·ness,** *n.*

Trans·jor·dan (trans jôrd'ən, tranz-) see **Jordan.**

trans·late (trans lāt', tranz-) **-lat·ed, -lat·ing.** *v.t.* **1.** to express in or change into another language: *to translate Shakespeare's plays into German.* **2.** to explain by using other words, terms, or signs: *His theorem cannot be translated into simpler terms.* **3.** to change from one place, form, or condition to another: *to translate dreams into reality.* **4.** to remove bodily to heaven before death: *The prophet Elijah was translated in a fiery chariot by angels.* —*v.i.* **1.** to act as translator: *A guide translated for the tourists.* **2.** to admit of translation: *an idiomatic style that doesn't translate well.* [Latin *tránslātus,* past participle of *tránsferre* to carry over, transfer.] —**trans·lat'a·ble,** *adj.*

trans·la·tion (trans lā'shən, tranz-) *n.* **1.** act of translating; being translated. **2.** that which is produced as a result of translating, esp. a literary work in a different language from the original.

trans·la·tor (trans lā'tər, tranz-) *n.* one who translates from one language into another.

trans·lit·er·ate (trans lit'ə rāt', tranz-) **-at·ed, -at·ing.** *v.t.* to change (letters or words of one alphabet) into characters of another alphabet that have corresponding sounds. [TRANS- + Latin *littera* letter + -ATE.] —**trans·lit·er·a'tion,** *n.*

trans·lu·cence (trans lōō'səns, tranz-) *n.* state or quality of being translucent. Also, **trans·lu'cen·cy.**

trans·lu·cent (trans lōō'sənt, tranz-) *adj.* allowing light to pass, but diffusing it so that objects on the other side can be clearly distinguished, as frosted glass. [Latin *tránslūcēns,* present participle of *tránslūcēre* to shine through.] —**trans·lu'cent·ly,** *adv.* —**Syn.** see **clear.**

trans·ma·rine (trans'mə rēn', tranz-) *adj.* **1.** that extends across or crosses a sea. **2.** being or situated on the opposite side of a sea.

trans·mi·grate (trans mī'grāt, tranz-) **-grat·ed, -grat·ing.** *v.i.* **1.** (of a soul) to pass to another body at death. **2.** to migrate from one place of abode to another, esp. from one country to another. [Latin

trānsmigrātus, past participle of *trānsmigrāre* to migrate from one place to another.] —**trans′mi·gra′tion,** *n.*

trans·mis·si·ble (trans mis′ə bəl, tranz-) *adj.* capable of being transmitted.

trans·mis·sion (trans mish′ən, tranz-) *n.* **1.** act of transmitting; being transmitted. Also, **trans·mit′tal. 2.** that which is transmitted, as a television picture or telegraphic message. **3.** in an automobile, a series of gears and mechanical devices for transmitting power from the engine to the driving wheels. **4.** sending out of signals, as in radio and television communication. [Latin *trānsmissiō* a sending across.]

trans·mit (trans mit′, tranz-) **-mit·ted, -mit·ting.** *v.t.* **1.** to send or cause to go from one person or place to another: *to transmit freight, to transmit a virus.* **2.** to communicate or convey: *to transmit greetings. The frown on father's face transmitted his anger to us.* **3.** to pass on by or as by inheritance or heredity; hand down: *cultural traditions transmitted from father to son. Genes are transmitted from one generation to another by the chromosomes.* **4.a.** to cause (something, as light, heat, or sound) to pass through a medium: *A tuning fork transmits sound waves through the air.* **b.** (of a medium) to allow (something, as light, heat, or sound) to pass through: *Water transmits sound.* **5.** to send out (signals, a radio or television program, or the like) on electromagnetic waves. [Latin *trānsmittere* to send across, dispatch.] —**Syn. 1.** see **send.**

trans·mit·tal (trans mit′əl, tranz-) *n.* transmission *(def. 1).*

trans·mit·ter (trans mit′ər, tranz-) *n.* **1.** one who or that which transmits. **2.** apparatus that produces radio or television frequency current for sending from an antenna. **3.** device in a telegraph or telephone which changes the message into electrical impulses that can be carried over wires.

trans·mog·ri·fy (trans mog′rə fī′, tranz-) **-fied, -fy·ing.** *v.t.* to change into another form or shape, esp. one that is fantastic or grotesque. [Of uncertain origin.]

trans·mu·ta·tion (trans′mū tā′shən, tranz′-) *n.* **1.** act of transmuting; being transmuted. **2.** *Physics.* conversion of one element into another by a natural or artificially produced change in its nuclear structure. —**trans′mu·ta′tion·al, trans·mu′ta·tive** (trans mū′tə tiv, tranz-), *adj.*

trans·mute (trans mūt′, tranz-) **-mut·ed, -mut·ing.** *v.t.* to change in form, nature, or quality: *Alchemists tried to transmute metal into gold.* [Latin *trānsmūtāre* to change, from *trans-* (see TRANS-) + *mūtāre* to change.] —**trans·mut′a·bil′i·ty, trans·mut′a·ble·ness, trans·mut′er,** *n.* —**trans·mut′a·ble,** *adj.*

trans·o·ce·an·ic (trans′ō shē an′ik, tranz′-) *adj.* **1.** that extends across or crosses an ocean. **2.** being or situated on the opposite side of the ocean.

tran·som (tran′səm) *n.* **1.** window above a door or other window, usually hinged to a horizontal bar. **2.** horizontal bar that divides a window or separates a door or window from a window above. [Probably a modification of Latin *trānstrum* crossbeam, from *trāns* across.]

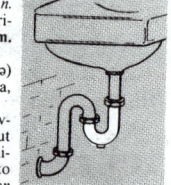
Transom

trans·pa·cif·ic (trans′pə sif′ik) *adj.* **1.** that extends across or crosses the Pacific. **2.** being or situated on the opposite side of the Pacific.

trans·par·en·cy (trans pār′ən sē, -par′-) *pl.,* **-cies.** *n.* **1.** state or quality of being transparent. Also, **trans·par′ence. 2.** something transparent, esp. a photographic slide.

trans·par·ent (trans pār′ənt, -par′-) *adj.* **1.** transmitting light so that objects on the other side can be seen distinctly, as the lenses in a pair of glasses or the panes of a window. **2.** easily perceived or seen through; evident; obvious: *a transparent lie.* **3.** frank; open; candid. [Medieval Latin *transparens,* present participle of *transparere* to show through, from Latin *trāns* through, across + *pārēre* to appear.] —**trans·par′ent·ly,** *adv.* —**trans·par′ent·ness,** *n.* —**Syn. 1.** see **clear.**

tran·spi·ra·tion (tran′spə rā′shən) *n.* act or process of transpiring, esp. the giving off of vaporous waste products by a living organism.

tran·spire (tran spīr′) **-spired, -spir·ing.** *v.i.* **1.** to happen; occur: *It was impossible to predict what would transpire once positive action was taken.* **2.** to become known; come to light: *The conditions of the contract were not allowed to transpire* (Froude, 1856). **3.** to give off waste products in the form of vapor, as through the pores of the skin. —*v.t.* to give off (waste products) in the form of vapor. [French *transpirer* to exhale, perspire, become known, from Latin *trāns* through, across + *spīrāre* to breathe.]

trans·plant (trans plant′) *v.t.* **1.** to remove (a plant) from one site and plant it again in another. **2.** to convey from one place to another; transport: *They transplanted the entire herd to a new pasture.* **3.** to transfer (skin, an organ, or the like) from one person or animal to another or from one part of the body to another. —*v.i.* to admit of or withstand transplanting. —*n.* **1.** that which is transplanted: *The trans-*

plant flourished in new soil. The patient received a kidney transplant. **2.** act or process of transplanting. [Late Latin *trānsplantāre* to remove, transport, from Latin *trāns* across + *plantāre* to plant, fix in place.] —**trans·plant′a·ble,** *adj.* —**trans·plan·ta·tion** (trans′plan tā′shən, tranz′-), **trans·plant′er,** *n.*

trans·port (*v.,* trans pôrt′; *n.,* trans′pôrt′) *v.t.* **1.** to bring or convey from one place or person to another: *to transport freight by rail.* **2.** to carry away by strong emotion; enrapture: *The beautiful music transported her.* **3.** to punish (a criminal) by deporting him from his own country. **4.** *Archaic.* to kill. —*n.* **1.** act of transporting. **2.** ship used to carry military personnel. **3.** airplane used to transport passengers, mail, or freight. **4.** state or condition of being transported by emotion; rapture. **5.** convict who is sentenced to exile. [Latin *trānsportāre* to carry across.] —**trans·port′a·bil′i·ty, trans·port′er,** *n.* —**trans·port′a·ble,** *adj.* —**Syn.** *v.t.* **1.** see **carry.**

trans·por·ta·tion (trans′pər tā′shən) *n.* **1.** act of transporting; being transported. **2.** means of transporting, as a vehicle. **3.** cost of transporting, esp. for traveling by a public conveyance: *Transportation to and from work was sixty cents per day.*

trans·pose (trans pōz′, tranz-) **-posed, -pos·ing.** *v.t.* **1.** to put each of (two or more things) in the place of the other or others; reverse the order of; interchange: *The typesetter accidentally transposed the President's initials from JFK to KFJ.* **2.** to move (something) from one place or time to another: *a medieval story transposed by the author to the twentieth century.* **3.** to write or perform (music) in other than the original or given key. **4.** to transfer (an algebraic term) from one side of an equation to the other, changing the plus or minus sign to maintain equality. [Middle French *transposer* to transfer, move from one place to another, modification (influenced by French *poser* to place, put) of Latin *trānspōnere* to place across, remove, transfer.] —**trans·pos′er,** *n.*

trans·po·si·tion (trans′pə zish′ən) *n.* **1.** act of transposing; being transposed. **2.** that which has been transposed. Also, **trans·po·sal** (trans pō′zəl, tranz-). —**trans′po·si′tion·al,** *adj.*

trans·ship (trans ship′) **-shipped, -ship·ping.** *also,* **tran·ship.** *v.t., v.i.* to transfer (cargo) from one ship, train, truck, or other conveyance to another for further transit. —**trans·ship′ment,** *n.*

trans·son·ic (trans son′ik) *adj.* of, relating to, or moving at a speed just above or just below the speed of sound.

tran·sub·stan·ti·a·tion (tran′səb stan′shē ā′shən) *n.* **1.** transformation of one substance into another. **2.** doctrine that the substance of the bread and wine of the Eucharist becomes, after consecration by a priest, the substance of the body and blood of Christ, with only the appearance of the bread and wine remaining. Distinguished from **con·substantiation.** [Medieval Latin *transubstantiatio* transmutation, going back to Latin *trāns* across, over + *substantia* essence, material.]

Trans·vaal (trans väl′, tranz-) *n.* province of the Republic of South Africa, in the northeastern part of the country. Area, 110,450 sq. mi. Pop. (1960), 6,273,477.

trans·ver·sal (trans vur′səl, tranz-) *adj.* transverse. —*n.* line that intersects two or more lines.

trans·verse (trans vurs′, tranz-) *adj.* situated or lying across or in a crosswise direction. —*n.* **1.** that which is transverse. **2.** axis of a conic section that passes through its foci. [Latin *trānsversus* turned across, athwart.] —**trans·verse′ly,** *adv.*

trans·ves·ti·tism (trans ves′tə tiz′əm) *n.* compulsive need to dress in clothing appropriate for the opposite sex. Also, **trans·ves′tism.** —**trans·ves·tite** (trans ves′tīt), *n.*

Tran·syl·va·ni·a (tran′sil vā′nē ə, -vān′yə) *n.* historic region in central Romania. Area, approx. 24,000 sq. mi.

trap¹ (trap) *n.* **1.** contrivance, as a falsely covered pit or mechanical device that springs shut suddenly, used for catching game or other animals. **2.** any artifice, trick, or strategem used to catch a person unawares: *The lawyer's question was a trap that caused the defendant to admit his guilt.* **3.** bend in a pipe, usually U-shaped or S-shaped, that fills with liquid to form a seal, as to keep air in the pipe or to prevent the return flow of a gas. **4.** device used to hurl clay pigeons or the like into the air for target shooting. **5.** light, two-wheeled carriage with springs. **6.** in certain games, an obstacle or hazard, esp. a sand trap in a golf course. **7.** trap door. **8.** *Slang.* mouth: *Shut your trap!* —*v.t.,* **trapped, trap·ping. 1.** to catch in a trap; entrap; ensnare: *Hunters trapped the bear. The reporters trapped the official into declaring his candidacy.* **2.** to furnish or provide with a trap or traps. **3.** to stop and hold (gas, liquid, or the like) as with a trap. —*v.i.* **1.** to set traps for game: *The poacher was arrested for trapping in the game preserve.* **2.** to be a trapper. [Old English *træppe* device for catching animals.]

Trap *(def. 3)*

trap² (trap) **trapped, trap·ping.** *v.t.* to furnish or adorn with trappings.

---

at; āpe; cär; end; mē; it; īce; hot; ōld; fôrk; wood; fōōl; oil; out; up; ūse; turn; sing; thin; this; zh in treasure; ə in ago, taken, pencil, lemon, circus.

—*n.,pl.* **traps.** *Informal.* personal belongings, esp. luggage or baggage. [Probably from Old French *drap* cloth. See DRAPE.]

trap door, hinged or sliding door in a floor, ceiling, or roof.

tra·peze (tra pēz´, trə-) *n.* short, swinging horizontal bar suspended from two ropes, used in gymnastics and acrobatics. [French *trapèze,* from Late Latin *trapezium* trapezium, from Greek *trapezion* small table, trapezium.]

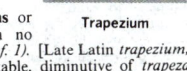

Trapezium

tra·pe·zi·um (trə pē´zē əm) *pl.,* **-zi·ums** or **-zi·a** (-zē ə). *n.* **1.** quadrilateral with no two sides parallel. **2.** *British.* trapezoid *(def. 1).* [Late Latin *trapezium,* from Greek *trapezion* trapezium, small table, diminutive of *trapeza* table.]

trap·e·zoid (trap´ə zoid´) *n.* **1.** quadrilateral with only two sides parallel. **2.** *British.* trapezium *(def. 1).* [Modern Latin *trapezoides,* from Greek *trapezoeidēs* shaped like a table or trapezium, from *trapeza* table + *eidos* form.]

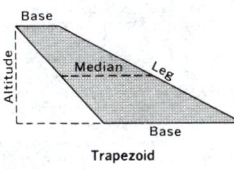

Trapezoid

trap·per (trap´ər) *n.* one who traps wild animals, esp. one who traps fur-bearing animals for their pelts.

trap·pings (trap´ingz) *n.,pl.* **1.** ornamented cloth or covering spread over the harness or saddle of a horse. **2.** external or superficial adornments: *the stately trappings of some prince* (Cowper, 1791), *to strip a man of all his trappings of birth, rank, and education* (Helps, 1859). [TRAP² + -ING¹ + -S¹.]

Trap·pist (trap´ist) *n.* member of a Roman Catholic order of monks established in 1664 as a branch of the Cistercians, noted for observing strict silence and other austere rules. —*adj.* of or relating to the Trappists. [French *Trappiste,* from *La Trappe,* a monastery of this order in Normandy, France.]

trap·shoot·ing (trap´shōō´ting) *n.* recreational and competitive sport in which shooters fire 12-gauge shotguns at clay pigeons hurled into the air singly or in pairs at an angle like that of a game bird taking flight. —**trap´shoot´er,** *n.*

trash (trash) *n.* **1.** worthless or discarded objects or matter. **2.** worthless, inferior, or foolish talk, writing, ideas, or the like: *How can a book that's such trash be so popular?* **3.** low, contemptible, or worthless person or persons. **4.** that which is broken or cut off, esp. trimmings from a plant or tree. [Of uncertain origin.]

trash·y (trash´ē) *adj.* **trash·i·er, trash·i·est.** *adj.* of, like, or containing trash; worthless; inferior: *a trashy movie.* —**trash´i·ly,** *adv.* —**trash´i·ness,** *n.*

trau·ma (trô´mə, trou´-) *pl.,* **-ma·ta** (-mə tə) *or* **-mas.** *n.* **1.** severe and painful emotional shock, usually having a lasting effect on the personality. **2.** bodily wound or injury. [Greek *trauma* wound.]

trau·mat·ic (trô mat´ik, trou-) *adj.* of, relating to, of the nature of, or caused by a trauma. —**trau·mat´i·cal·ly,** *adv.*

trau·ma·tize (trô´mə tīz´, trou´-) **-tized, -tiz·ing.** *v.t.* **1.** to wound or injure. **2.** to subject (an individual) to a severe and painful emotional shock.

trav·ail (trə vāl´, trav´āl) *n.* **1.** arduous, exhausting mental or physical labor. **2.** intense anguish or suffering, esp. when caused by extreme hardship. **3.** *Archaic.* pains of childbirth; labor. —*v.i.* **1.** to exert oneself; toil. **2.** *Archaic.* to suffer the pains of childbirth; be in labor. [Old French *travail* toil, labor, torment, going back to Medieval Latin *trepalium* instrument of torture (possibly made of three stakes), from Latin *trēs* three + *pālus* stake.]

trav·el (trav´əl) **-eled, -el·ing;** *also, British,* **-elled, -el·ling.** *v.i.* **1.** to move from one place to another; make a journey: *to travel through Ireland.* **2.** to go from place to place as a traveling salesman. **3.** to pass or be transmitted from one point to another: *Sound waves travel through water.* **4.** to be habitually in the company of; associate with (with *with*): *to travel with a bad crowd.* **5.** *Basketball.* to walk or run illegally while holding the ball. **6.** *Informal.* to move with speed: *We'll have to travel in order to make the train in time.* —*v.t.* to move or journey over or through; make a tour of: *to travel the country making speeches.* —*n.* **1.** act of traveling from one place to another. **2.** movement or progress in general; advancement. **3.a.** motion of a mechanical part, esp. a reciprocating one. **b.** length of stroke, as of a piston. **4. travels. a.** extended trip to many different places; journeys: *He met many interesting people in his travels.* **b.** written account of one's experiences and observations while traveling. [Form of TRAVAIL; probably originally referring to the discomforts and dangers of travel in earlier times.]

travel agency, business establishment that makes travel arrangements for travelers, as by arranging transportation or securing hotel reservations.

trav·eled (trav´əld) *also, British,* **trav·elled.** *adj.* **1.** having done extensive traveling, esp. to foreign countries. **2.** (of a road, route, or the like) frequented by many travelers.

trav·el·er (trav´ə lər, trav´lər) *also, British,* **trav·el·ler.** *n.* **1.** one who travels. **2.** *British.* traveling salesman.

traveler's check, check or draft, usually one of a set, sold in various denominations, as by a bank. It is payable when countersigned by the bearer in the presence of the person cashing it.

traveling salesman, salesman, usually working for a firm, who travels from place to place selling or taking orders for goods.

trav·e·logue (trav´ə lôg´, -log´) *also,* **trav·e·log.** *n.* **1.** lecture, usually illustrated with films, describing travel. **2.** motion picture about a particular country or region. [TRAVEL + -*logue,* as in MONOLOGUE or DIALOGUE.]

trav·erse (trav´ərs, trə vurs´) **-ersed, -ers·ing.** *v.t.* **1.** to pass across, over, or through: *The climbers traversed the mountain range.* **2.** to go back and forth over or along; cross and recross. **3.** to turn (something, as a cannon or lathe) to the right or left; swivel. **4.** to oppose; hinder; thwart: *to watch their motions and traverse their designs* (Macaulay, 1855). **5.** to examine carefully; scrutinize: *to traverse a book for a particular passage.* —*v.i.* **1.** to move or go along, across, or back and forth: *The skier traversed down the slope.* **2.** to go or turn from side to side; pivot. —*n.* **1.a.** act of traversing or crossing. **b.** distance traversed or crossed. **2.** something, as a part or structure, put or lying across. **3.** bank or wall of earth protecting a trench or an exposed place in a fortification. **4.** gallery or loft going from one side of a building, esp. a church, to the other. **5.** transversal. **6.** sideways motion, as that of a ship, piece of artillery, part in a machine, or skier. **7.** *Nautical.* zigzag line taken by a ship because of contrary winds or currents. **8.** something that hinders or opposes; obstacle. —*adj.* lying or being across. —*adv.* *Archaic.* across; crosswise. [Old French *traverser* to cross, thwart, from Late Latin *trānsversāre* to cross, from Latin *trānsversus* turned across, athwart.] —**trav´ers·a·ble,** *adj.* —**trav´ers·er,** *n.*

trav·er·tine (trav´ər tēn´, -tin) *also,* **trav·er·tin.** *n.* variety of calcium carbonate deposited by water from springs, a compact form of which is cut and polished for use as a decorative building stone. [Italian *travertino,* modification of earlier *tivertino,* from Latin *(lapis) Tīburtīnus* (stone) from Tibur, an ancient town in Latium.]

trav·es·ty (trav´is tē) *pl.,* **-ties.** *n.* **1.** grotesque or absurd imitation: *The jury's biased verdict was a travesty of justice.* **2.** in literature, grotesque or burlesque treatment of a serious work or a serious subject. —*v.t.,* **-tied, -ty·ing.** to ridicule by grotesque parody or imitation. [French *travesti,* past participle of *travestir* to disguise, burlesque, going back to Latin *trāns* across + *vestīre* to dress.]

tra·vois (trə voi´, trav´oi) *pl.,* **-vois.** *n.* V-shaped sled, used esp. by Indians of the Great Plains, consisting of a platform or net supported by two long poles, the front ends of the poles harnessed to a horse, dog, or other draft animal, the rear ends dragging along the ground.

trawl (trôl) *n.* **1.** strong, usually bag-shaped, net towed over the ocean bottom to catch fish. Also, **trawl net. 2.** long line usually resting near the ocean floor and supported by buoys, having short lines with baited hooks every few feet along its length, used to catch fish. Also, **trawl line.** —*v.i.* to fish with a trawl. —*v.t.* to catch (fish) with a trawl. [Middle Dutch *traghelen* to drag, probably going back to Latin *trāgula* dragnet.]

trawl·er (trô´lər) *n.* **1.** fishing boat used for trawling. **2.** one who fishes with a trawl.

tray (trā) *n.* flat, shallow vessel with a slightly raised rim, used for carrying, storing, or exhibiting objects. [Old English *trēg, trīg.*]

treach·er·ous (trech´ər əs) *adj.* **1.** likely to betray a trust; traitorous; disloyal. **2.** dangerous; hazardous: *Many ships have capsized on that treacherous reef.* —**treach´er·ous·ly,** *adv.* —**treach´er·ous·ness,** *n.*

treach·er·y (trech´ər ē) *pl.,* **-er·ies.** *n.* willful betrayal or violation of a trust. [Old French *trecherie* deceit, cheating, from *trechier* to deceive, cheat; of uncertain origin.]

trea·cle (trē´kəl) *n.* *British.* molasses. [Old French *triacle* antidote against venom made with honey or syrup, going back to Latin *thēriaca* antidote against venom, from Greek *thēriakē,* from *thērion* wild or venomous animal.]

tread (tred) *v.t.* or *(archaic)* **trode,** *or* **trod,** **tread·ing.** *v.t.* **1.** to walk on, along, or over; step upon: *Where'er you tread, the blushing flow'rs shall rise* (Pope, 1704). **2.** to press with the feet; trample. **3.** to form, do, or follow by or as by walking. **4.** to put down or oppress; subdue; crush. **5. to tread water.** to keep the head above water while maintaining an upright position, usually by moving the feet up and down in a walking motion. —*v.i.* **1.** to move on or as if on foot; walk or step: *Tread softly because you tread on my dreams* (Yeats, 1899). **2.** to trample (with *on* or *upon*). —*n.* **1.** act, manner, or sound of treading. **2.** outer, grooved surface of an automobile tire: *Most of the tread had been worn off the old tire.* **3.** the horizontal part of a step in a staircase. **4.** the part of a wheel that touches the ground or rails. **5.** the part of the sole of a shoe that touches the ground. [Old English *tredan* to step upon, walk on, go, trample on.] —**tread´er,** *n.*

---

trea·dle (tred′əl) *n.* lever or pedal worked by the foot to impart motion to operate a machine, as a potter's wheel. —*v.i.* **-dled, -dling.** to work a treadle. [Old English *tredel* step, stair.]

tread·mill (tred′mil) *n.* **1.** apparatus rotated by animals or persons walking on the moving steps of a wheel or treading an endless sloping belt, used to impart rotary motion for doing work. **2.** any monotonous, wearisome routine or activity.

treas. 1. treasurer. **2.** treasury.

trea·son (trē′zən) *n.* betrayal of one's country, esp. by giving aid and comfort to the enemy in wartime. [Anglo-Norman *tres(o)un*, from Latin *trāditiō* a handing over, surrender, betrayal. Doublet of TRADITION.]

trea·son·a·ble (trē′zə nə bəl) *adj.* of, relating to, involving, or characteristic of treason. Also, **trea′son·ous.** —**trea′son·a·bly,** *adv.* —**trea′son·a·ble·ness,** *n.*

treas·ure (trezh′ər) *n.* **1.** store of valuables, as money or jewels; accumulated riches. **2.** one who or that which is greatly valued or considered precious: *His grandchildren are his greatest treasure.* —*v.t.* **-ured, -ur·ing. 1.** to consider or regard as being of great value; hold or keep as precious; cherish: *to treasure one's family heirlooms. She treasured every moment with him.* **2.** to put away or lay aside for preservation, security, or future use; store up; hoard. [Old French *tresor* store of precious objects, anything considered precious, going back to Latin *thēsaurus* store, storehouse, from Greek *thēsauros.* Doublet of THESAURUS.] —**Syn.** *v.t.* **1.** see cherish.

treas·ur·er (trezh′ər ər) *n.* one who is officially entrusted with the receipt, care, and disbursement of funds, as of a corporation, club, or the like.

treas·ure-trove (trezh′ər trōv′) *n.* **1.** *Law.* money, jewels, or other valuables, found hidden and whose owner is not known. **2.** any discovery which proves to be valuable. [Anglo-Norman *tresor trove* literally, treasure found, from *tresor* (see TREASURE) + *trove,* past participle of *trover* to find (of uncertain origin).]

treas·ur·y (trezh′ər ē) *n. pl.* **-ur·ies. 1.** place where funds, esp. public revenue, are deposited and stored. **2.** funds or revenues, as of a corporation or government. **3.** *Treasury.* governmental department that is in charge of the collection of taxes and the management of a country's finances. **4.** place or receptacle where treasure is kept. **5.** one who or that which is considered to be a repository of things considered to be precious or of great value: *He was a treasury of information about the Civil War. The book is a treasury of medieval poetry.*

treasury note, note or bill issued by the U.S. Treasury, used as legal tender for all debts.

treat (trēt) *v.t.* **1.** to act or behave toward in a specified manner: *to treat children with kindness. The judge treated each defendant fairly.* **2.** to regard, consider, or deal with in a specified manner: *to treat a minor accident as a catastrophe.* **3.** to give medical or surgical attention to: *to treat a patient with a broken leg, to treat a cut with iodine.* **4.** to subject to a chemical or physical process or application, as for altering or improving: *to treat cloth with a chemical to make it waterproof.* **5.** to deal with in speech or writing; discuss: *The article treated various aspects of the political scene.* **6.** to deal with, develop, or represent (a subject in art or literature), esp. in a specified manner or style: *The exploits of Robin Hood have been treated in poems and stories.* **7.** to pay for or provide the entertainment, food, drink, or the like of (someone): *to treat a friend to a good meal.* —*v.i.* **1.** to deal with a subject in speech or writing (often with *of*): *a book that treats of military history.* **2.** to pay for another's entertainment, food, drink, or the like. **3.** to carry on negotiations; discuss or arrange terms. —*n.* **1.** entertainment, food, drink, or the like given or paid for by another. **2.** something that gives unexpected or unusual pleasure: *Going to the circus was a treat for Jimmy.* **3.** act of treating or entertaining or one's turn to treat. [Old French *traitier* to handle, conduct, drag, from Latin *trahere* to draw, draw.] —**treat′a·ble,** *adj.* —**treat′er,** *n.*

trea·tise (trē′tis) *n.* book or other piece of writing dealing in a formal and systematic method with some subject: *a treatise on the nature of democratic government.* [Anglo-Norman *tretiz,* from Old French *traitier* to conduct, handle. See TREAT.]

treat·ment (trēt′mənt) *n.* **1.** act, process, or manner of treating. **2.** course of action or means used to treat something, esp. the care and medication provided to treat an illness.

trea·ty (trē′tē) *n. pl.* **-ties. 1.** formal agreement, esp. one between nations, signed and approved by each party: *a peace treaty signed by all nations involved in the conflict.* [Old French *trait(i)e,* from Latin *tractātus* handling, treatment, discussion.]

tre·ble (treb′əl) *adj.* **1.** three times as much or as many; triple. **2.** of, relating to, or for the highest musical instrument or voice; soprano. —*n.* soprano voice, part, or instrument. —*v.t., v.i.* **-bled, -bling.** to make or become three times as much or as many. [Old French *treble* triple, from Latin *triplus* threefold, from Greek *triplous.* Doublet of TRIPLE.] —**tre′bly,** *adv.*

treble clef, clef placed on the second line of the staff, indicating that that line corresponds to the note G above middle C. Also, **G clef.** See **clef** for illustration.

tree (trē) *n.* **1.** perennial plant, often of considerable height, having a single, self-supporting stem or trunk which develops a solid, permanent, woody tissue, as distinguished from herbs, and which develops branches and leaves at some distance above the ground. **2.** any of various bushes, shrubs, or perennial herbaceous plants, such as the banana, which resemble a tree in size or shape. **3.** any structure or device resembling a tree in shape or outline: *a shoe tree.* **4.** diagram resembling a tree with its branches, esp. a diagram of a family, having the original ancestor as the root, and the various descendants as the branches. **5.** *Archaic.* gallows. **6.** *Archaic.* cross on which Jesus Christ was crucified. **7. up a tree.** *Informal.* in an awkward, embarrassing, or difficult position, esp. one from which there is no escape. —*v.t.* **treed, tree·ing. 1.** to chase or force into or up a tree; cause to take refuge in a tree: *The hounds treed a raccoon.* **2.** to stretch or shape on a tree, as a shoe or glove. **3.** *Informal.* to put into an awkward, embarrassing, or difficult position. [Old English *trēo(w)* large, perennial woody plant, wood, beam, stick[1].]

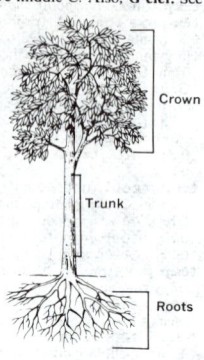

Crown

Trunk

Roots

Tree

tree fern, any of various treelike ferns, having large fronds and, usually, thick stems growing upright.

tree frog, any of a group of small frogs, family Hylidae, usually living in trees in temperate and tropical regions. Length: 3–5½ inches. Also, **tree toad.**

tree heath, shrub or small tree, *Erica arborea,* found in the Mediterranean region, bearing fragrant, ball-shaped, white flowers. Also, **bri′ar.**

tree·lined (trē′līnd′) *adj.* having a row of trees on both sides: *a treelined avenue.*

tree·nail (trē′nāl′, tren′əl, trun′-) *also,* **tre·nail, trun·nel.** *n.* hardwood pin used to secure a joint or fasten timbers together.

tree of heaven, fast-growing tree, *Ailanthus altissima,* planted as a shade tree in Europe and eastern North America, esp. in cities because it is hardy and resistant to smog and fumes.

tree of knowledge, in the Bible, a tree in the Garden of Eden, whose fruit conferred knowledge of good and evil. Adam and Eve were cast out of Eden for eating its fruit.

tree toad, tree frog.

tree·top (trē′top′) *n.* top or uppermost branches of a tree.

tre·foil (trē′foil′) *n.* **1.** any of several plants of the pea family, having leaves that usually consist of three oval leaflets. **2.** any of various clovers. **3.** ornament, used esp. in architecture, consisting of three foils or arcs joined by pointed projections. [Anglo-Norman *trifoil* three-leaved plant, from Latin *trifolium,* from *tri-* three + *folium* leaf.]

trek (trek) *v.i.* **trekked, trek·king. 1.** to travel or journey, esp. in a slow, arduous manner. **2.** in South Africa, to travel by ox wagon. —*n.* journey or migration, esp. one that is slow or arduous. [Afrikaans *trekken* to pull, travel, from Middle Dutch *trecken.*]

trel·lis (trel′is) *n.* **1.** lattice, esp. one used as a support for growing vines. **2.** to interlace or cross so as to form a trellis. [Middle French *treliz* coarsely woven fabric, going back to Latin *trilīx* woven with three threads, from *tri-* three + *licium* thread.]

trel·lis-work (trel′is wurk′) *n.* openwork made from, consisting of, or resembling a trellis.

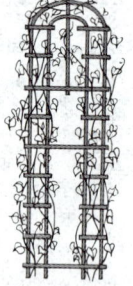

Trellis

trem·a·tode (trem′ə tōd′) *n.* fluke[1] *(def. 2).* [Modern Latin *Trematoda* (neuter plural) from Greek *trēmatōdēs* having holes, from *trēma* hole.]

trem·ble (trem′bəl) **-bled, -bling.** *v.i.* **1.** to shake involuntarily, as with cold, weakness, fear, or anger. **2.** to have a slight, continued, vibratory motion, as from a jarring external force: *The ground trembled as the volcano erupted.* **3.** to be filled with apprehension or anxiety: *I tremble to think of the consequences.* —*n.* act or instance of trembling. [Old French *trembler* to shiver, shake, going back to Latin *tremulus* quaking, quivering.] —**trem′bler,** *n.* —**trem′bling·ly,** *adv.* —**trem′bly,** *adj.* —**Syn.** *v.i.* **1.** see shake.

at; āpe; cär; end; mē; it; īce; hot; ōld; fôrk; wood; fōōl; oil; out; up; ūse; turn; sing; thin; this; zh in treasure; ə in ago, taken, pencil, lemon, circus.

tre·men·dous (tri men′dəs) *adj.* **1.** of extraordinarily great size, amount, or intensity: *a tremendous appetite. A tremendous wave capsized the boat.* **2.** *Informal.* extraordinary or wonderful; astounding: *The landing of men on the moon was a tremendous scientific achievement.* **3.** terrible; dreadful: *tremendous crimes committed in a war.* [Latin *tremendus* fearful, dreadful, gerundive of *tremere* to quake, shake.] —**tre·men′dous·ly,** *adv.* —**tre·men′dous·ness,** *n.*

trem·o·lo (trem′ə lō′) *pl.,* **-los.** *n. Music.* **1.** a trembling or vibrating effect produced by the rapid repetition of a single tone or by the rapid alternation of two tones. **2.** device or stop in an organ used to produce such an effect. [Italian *tremolo* trembling, shaking, from Latin *tremulus.* Doublet of TREMULOUS.]

trem·or (trem′ər) *n.* **1.** rapid shaking or vibrating movement: *a tremor caused by an earthquake.* **2.** involuntary, continued shaking or trembling, esp. of the body or a limb. **3.** nervous thrill caused by emotion or excitement: *A tremor of delight went through the audience.* [Latin *tremor* trembling, quaking.]

trem·u·lous (trem′yə ləs) *adj.* **1.** characterized or affected by trembling; shaking: *The old man spoke in a tremulous voice.* **2.** lacking firmness, resolution, or courage; timid; wavering. [Latin *tremulus* trembling, shaking. Doublet of TREMOLO.] —**trem′u·lous·ly,** *adv.* —**trem′u·lous·ness,** *n.*

tre·nail (trē′nāl′, tren′əl, trun′-) treenail.

trench (trench) *n.* **1.** long, narrow excavation in the earth; deep furrow: *A trench was dug in the field to help irrigate it.* **2.** long, narrow ditch with the excavated earth piled up in front, used esp. for the protection of soldiers in combat. —*v.t.* **1.** to dig a trench or trenches in. **2.** to surround or fortify with a trench or trenches. —*v.i.* **1.** to dig a trench or trenches. **2. to trench on** (or **upon**). **a.** to encroach; infringe. **b.** to come close to infringing on. [Old French *trenchier* to cut, hack[1], dig, going back to Latin *truncāre* to cut off, mutilate.]

trench·ant (trench′ənt) *adj.* **1.** cutting; sarcastic: *trenchant repartee that cuts off the poor answer's head like a razor* (Mitford, 1824). **2.** forceful or effective: *The debater supported his view with a trenchant argument.* **3.** sharply defined or outlined; distinct: *The line of demarcation is seemingly most sharp and trenchant.* [Old French *trenchant,* present participle of *trenchier* to cut. See TRENCH.] —**trench′an·cy,** *n.* —**trench′ant·ly,** *adv.*

trench·er (tren′chər) *n. Archaic.* wooden platter or board on which food, esp. meat, was carved and served. [Old French *trencheor* platter, cutting instrument, from *trenchier* to cut; referring to carving meat on a platter. See TRENCH.]

trench·er·man (tren′chər mən) *pl.,* **-men.** *n.* **1.** one who eats, esp. one who eats with a hearty appetite. **2.** *Archaic.* hanger-on; sponger; parasite.

trench fever, acute infectious fever caused by a microorganism that is transmitted by lice. It was first observed among soldiers serving in the trenches in World War I.

trench mouth, acute inflammation of the mouth and gums, caused by certain bacteria, and characterized by painful, bleeding gums.

trend (trend) *n.* general direction, tendency, or course: *The trend of the river was to the South. They predicted a national trend toward conservatism. She didn't like the trend the discussion was taking.* —*v.i.* to have or proceed in a specified direction or course; be inclined; tend. [Old English *trendan* to revolve, roll.] —**Syn.** *n.* see **direction.**

Trent (trent) *n.* **1.** city in northern Italy. Pop. (1965 est.), 84,000. Also, Italian, **Tren·to** (tren′tō). **2. Council of,** Roman Catholic Church council held intermittently from 1545 to 1563 at Trent. It settled important points of church doctrine and established the ideals of the Counter Reformation.

Tren·ton (trent′ən) *n.* capital of New Jersey, in the western part of the state, on the Delaware River. Pop. (1970), 104,638.

tre·pan (tri pan′) *n.* **1.** surgical instrument similar to and now largely replaced by a trephine. —*v.t.* **-panned, -pan·ning.** to operate on with a trepan. [Medieval Latin *trepanum* surgical instrument, from Greek *trypānon* surgical instrument, auger, from *trypān* to bore.]

tre·pang (tri pang′) *n.* any of various sea cucumbers whose dried flesh is used in the Orient for making soup. [Malay *trīpang.*]

tre·phine (tri fīn′, -fēn′) *n.* surgical instrument consisting of a cylindrical saw, used for cutting out a disk of bone, esp. from the skull. —*v.t.,* **-phined, -phin·ing.** to operate on with a trephine. [Modification (influenced by TREPAN) of Latin *trēs fīnēs* three ends; referring to its shape.]

trep·i·da·tion (trep′ə dā′shən) *n.* **1.** nervous anticipation; fearful apprehension; anxiety: *She faced her stage debut with trepidation.* **2.** involuntary vibrating motion; trembling; tremor. [Latin *trepidātio* alarm, agitation.]

tres·pass (tres′pəs, -pas′) *v.i.* **1.** *Law.* to commit an illegal act that does injury to the rights, property, or person of another, esp. to enter unlawfully on the land of another: *The hunter was arrested for trespassing on private property.* **2.** to go beyond the limits of rectitude or propriety, esp. to make an improper inroad on (a person's time, patience, or the like). **3.** to commit a transgression; sin. —*n.* **1.** voluntary breach of law, duty, or the like; wrong; sin. **2.** *Law.* **a.** illegal act causing injury to the person, property, or rights of another. **b.** legal action brought to recover damages for injury caused by such an illegal act. [Old French *trespasser* to pass over, go across, going back to Latin *trāns* across + *passus* step.] —**tres′pass·er,** *n.* —**Syn.** *v.i.* **2.** see **intrude.**

tress (tres) *n.* **1.** curl, tuft, or strand of human hair. **2. tresses.** woman's or girl's hair, esp. when worn long and loose. [Old French *trece* lock or braid of hair; of uncertain origin.]

tres·tle (tres′əl) *n.* **1.** short beam or bar supported by four diverging legs, used as a support. **2.** framework consisting of vertical or inclined pieces with horizontal or diagonal braces, used to support a railroad bridge or other elevated structure. [Old French *trestel* beam, going back to Latin *trānstrum* crossbeam.]

Trestle (def. 2)

tres·tle·tree (tres′əl trē′) *n.* one of two strong bars, as of timber or steel, attached horizontally, fore-and-aft on opposite sides of a masthead to support the crosstrees.

tres·tle·work (tres′əl wurk′) *n.* **1.** trestle or a series of trestles. **2.** bridge composed of trestles.

trey (trā) *n.* playing card, die, or domino having three marks, or pips. [Old French *trei* three, from Latin *trēs.*]

tri- *combining form* **1.** having or consisting of three elements or parts: *triangle, tricycle.* **2.** *Chemistry.* containing three specified atoms, elements, radicals, or the like: *trioxide.* **3.** occurring three times in a specified period or once in three specified periods: *triennial, triweekly.* [Latin *trēs, tria* three, or Greek *treis, tria* three, often through French *tri-*].

tri·ad (trī′ad, -əd) *n.* **1.** group of three persons or things. **2.** *Music.* chord of three tones, esp. one consisting of a given tone with its third and fifth. [Late Latin *triad-,* stem of *trias* the number three, from Greek *trias.*]

tri·al (trī′əl) *n.* **1.** judicial examination of a case in a court of law. **2.** process or procedure used to ascertain a result. **3.** state of being tried or tested. **4.** difficult test of one's endurance, patience, or faith; hardship; affliction: *a comfort in time of trial.* **5.** source or cause of pain or trouble: *That boy has been a constant trial to his parents.* **6.** act of making an effort; attempt; try. —*adj.* of, for, relating to, done as, or used in a trial: *a trial run, a trial lawyer.* [Anglo-Norman *trial* act of judging in court, sentence, from *trier* to choose, pick out, sift; of uncertain origin.]

trial balance, in double entry bookkeeping, the addition of the total entries on each side of the ledger in which the sum of the debits should be equal to the sum of the credits.

trial jury, group, usually consisting of twelve persons, chosen to hear a case in a court of law and render a verdict.

tri·an·gle (trī′ang′gəl) *n.* **1.** polygon with three sides and three angles. **2.** something shaped like a triangle. **3.** musical instrument consisting of a metal bar bent into the shape of a triangle, producing a high, bell-like tone when struck. **4.** group of three persons or things. [Latin *triangulum* this polygon, from *tri-* three + *angulus* corner, angle[1].]

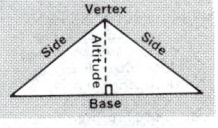

Triangle

tri·an·gu·lar (trī ang′gyə lər) *adj.* **1.** of, relating to, or resembling a triangle. **2.** of, relating to, or consisting of three persons or things.

tri·an·gu·late (*v.,* trī ang′gyə lāt′; *adj.,* trī ang′gyə lit, -lāt′) **-lat·ed, -lat·ing.** *v.t.* **1.** to divide into triangles. **2.** to survey by triangulation. **3.** to make triangular. —*adj.* composed of or marked with triangles.

tri·an·gu·la·tion (trī ang′gyə lā′shən) *n.* **1.** method used in surveying to determine the relative position of three points on the earth's surface, by using the known distance between two of the points and the measured angles of sight to the third to calculate the remaining sides and angle of the triangle formed by the points. **2.** network of such triangles used to survey large areas of land.

Tri·as·sic (trī as′ik) *n.* earliest geological period of the Mesozoic era, during which time there was much volcanic activity, widespread movements of the earth's crust, and dinosaurs became dominant. See **geology** for table. —*adj.* of, relating to, or characteristic of this period. [German *Trias* the earliest geological period of the Mesozoic era (from Greek *trias* the number three) + -IC; referring to the three stratigraphic divisions of this period.]

---

at; āpe; cär; end; mē; it; īce; hot; ōld; fôrk; wood; fo̅o̅l; oil; out; up; ūse; turn; sing; thin; this; zh in treasure; ə in ago, taken, pencil, lemon, circus.

trib·al (trī′bəl) *adj.* of, relating to, or characteristic of a tribe or tribes: *a tribal society, tribal customs.* —**trib′al·ly,** *adv.*

tribe (trīb) *n.* **1.** group of people connected by a common ancestry, culture, social customs, and, usually, the same political system: *The ancient Jewish nation was composed of twelve tribes.* **2.** any group or class of people, usually distinguished by a common characteristic, interest, or the like: *a tribe of ruffians, the whole tribe of newspaper reporters.* **3.** generic classification of a group of animals or plants, usually forming a subdivision of an order. [Latin *tribus* a division of the ancient Roman people.]

tribes·man (trībz′mən) *pl.,* **-men.** *n.* member of a tribe.

trib·u·la·tion (trib′yə lā′shən) *n.* state or condition of severe affliction or misery; suffering: *The Depression brought much trial and tribulation to the people.* [Church Latin *trībulātiō,* from *trībulāre* to oppress, from Latin *trībulāre* to press¹.]

tri·bu·nal (trī bōō′nəl, tri-) *n.* **1.** court of justice. **2.** any place of judgment. [Latin *tribūnal* raised platform on which magistrates sat.]

tri·bu·nate (trib′yə nāt′, trī bū′nit) *n.* office, rank, or term of the tribune in ancient Rome.

trib·une¹ (trib′ūn) *n.* **1.** official in ancient Rome appointed to protect the rights and interests of the plebeians against the patricians in the Senate. **2.** protector or defender of the rights of the public; champion of the people. [Latin *tribūnus* the ancient Roman official, chieftain, from *tribus* a division of the Roman people.] —**trib′une·ship,** *n.*

trib·une² (trib′ūn) *n.* raised platform, stand, or seat, as a pulpit for the throne of a bishop. [French *tribune* rostrum, through Italian and Medieval Latin, from Latin *tribūnal* raised platform on which magistrates sat.]

trib·u·tar·y (trib′yə ter′ē) *pl.,* **-tar·ies.** *n.* **1.** river or stream that flows into a larger body of water: *The Tennessee River is a major tributary of the Ohio River.* **2.** one who or that which pays tribute. —*adj.* **1.** flowing into a larger body of water. **2.** subject to paying tribute; taxed. **3.** paid or offered as tribute: *a tributary gift to the conquerer.* **4.** bringing auxiliary supplies or aid; supporting; contributory.

trib·ute (trib′ūt) *n.* **1.** anything done, given, or observed as an acknowledgment of devotion, gratitude, or respect: *The dinner was a tribute to the president.* **2.** money paid by one ruler or nation to another in acknowledgment of submission or to ensure peace or protection. **3.** any payment given under force or coercion. [Latin *tribūtum* payment, contribution.] —**Syn. 1.** see **eulogy.**

trice¹ (trīs) **triced,** **tric·ing.** *v.t.* to pull up and secure, as a sail, with a rope (often with *up*). [Middle Dutch *trīsen* to hoist, from *trīse* pulley.]

trice² (trīs) *n.* very short time; instant; moment: *I'll have that fixed in a trice.* [From TRICE¹, as in the phrase *at a trice* at a pull.]

tri·ceps (trī′seps) *n.* any of several muscles in the body, esp. the large muscle at the back of the upper arm, that, when contracted, straightens the forearm. [Latin *triceps* having three heads, from *tri-* three + *caput* head.]

tri·cer·a·tops (trī ser′ə tops′) *n.* plant-eating dinosaur, order Ornithischia, that lived in North America in the late Cretaceous period, having one long horn over each

Triceratops

eye, a shorter horn on the snout, and a bony shield projecting from the skull over the back of the neck. Length: to more than 25 feet.

tri·chi·na (tri kī′nə) *pl.,* **-nae** (-nē). *n.* parasitic roundworm, *Trichinella spiralis,* which infests mammals, including man. Trichinae enter the host in infected pork, and the adult worms lodge in the intestines, while the larvae form cysts in the involuntary muscles. [Modern Latin *trichina,* from Greek *trichinos* relating to hair, from *trich-,* stem of *trix* hair.]

trich·i·no·sis (trik′ə nō′sis) *n.* disease caused by trichinae that invade the intestines and muscular tissues and characterized by nausea, diarrhea, and stiff and swollen muscles. [Modern Latin *trichinosis,* from TRICHINA + -OSIS.]

trich·i·nous (trik′ə nəs) *adj.* **1.** of, relating to, or characteristic of trichinae or trichinosis. **2.** infected with trichinae or affected with trichinosis.

trick (trik) *n.* **1.** something intended to deceive or cheat; crafty or fraudulent device: *The misleading advertisement was a trick to draw customers.* **2.** feat of dexterity or skill, esp. one meant to amuse: *The boy taught his dog many tricks.* **3.** particular art or skill of doing something easily and successfully; knack: *She knows the trick of putting others at ease.* **4.** mischievous act; practical joke; prank: *He was always playing tricks on others.* **5.** characteristic habit, trait, or practice; man-

nerism: *He has this annoying trick of looking over your shoulder when he is talking to you.* **6.a.** group of cards made up of one card played from each hand. **b.** such a group considered as a unit of score. **c.** card which can take a trick. **7.** turn of duty allotted to one to stand at the helm of a ship. **8. to do (or turn) the trick.** to perform or accomplish what is needed or wanted. —*v.t.* **1.** to cheat or deceive with a trick: *The swindler tricked the old lady into giving him her life savings.* **2.** to arrange, dress, or decorate; adorn (with *up*). —*v.i.* to practice trickery or deception. —*adj.* **1.** relating to or involving a trick or deception: *a trick deck of cards, a hidden, trick drawer.* **2.** inclined to give way or collapse: *The accident left him with a trick knee.* [Dialectal Old French *trique,* form of Old French *triche* deceit, cheating, from *trichier* to deceive, cheat; of uncertain origin.]

trick·er·y (trik′ər ē) *pl.,* **-er·ies.** *n.* act or instance of intentionally deceiving; deceitful behavior or stratagem.

trick·le (trik′əl) **-led, -ling.** *v.i.* **1.** to flow or fall drop by drop or in a thin stream: *The rain trickled down the window. Blood trickled from the cut in his arm.* **2.** to move or proceed in a very slow, irregular manner: *Rumors of the army's defeat trickled into the city. The children trickled into the classroom after recess.* —*v.t.* to cause to trickle: *The engine was trickling oil.* —*n.* **1.** act or instance of trickling. **2.** slow or irregular stream or movement: *a slow day in the store with only a trickle of customers.* [Probably imitative.] —**Syn.** *v.i.* **1.** see **drip.**

trick·ster (trik′stər) *n.* one who plays tricks or practices trickery.

trick·sy (trik′sē) *adj.* **1.** mischievous; prankish; playful. **2.** cunning; crafty; wily. —**trick′si·ness,** *n.*

trick·y (trik′ē) **trick·i·er, trick·i·est.** *adj.* **1.** given to or characterized by tricks or trickery; crafty; wily: *a tricky sales pitch.* **2.** having unseen or unexpected difficulties; requiring cautious action or handling; deceptive: *a tricky situation.* —**trick′i·ly,** *adv.* —**trick′i·ness,** *n.*

tri·col·or (trī′kul′ər) *adj. also,* **tri·col·ored.** having three colors. —*n.* **1.** flag having three colors, esp. in large, equal masses. **2.** *also,* **Tricolor.** national flag of France, having three equal vertical bands of red, white, and blue. [French *tricolore* having three colors, going back to Latin *tri-* three + *color* hue.]

tri·cot (trē′kō) *n.* **1.** lightweight, knitted fabric made by hand or machine, from wool, nylon, or rayon. **2.** fine-woven worsted fabric made of wool. [French *tricot* knitting, jersey, from *tricoter* to knit; of uncertain origin.]

tri·cus·pid (trī kus′pid) *adj.* having three cusps or points. —*n.* any tooth that has three cusps or points. [Latin *tricuspid-,* stem of *tricuspis* having three points, from *tri-* three + *cuspis* point.]

tricuspid valve, heart valve consisting of three flaps, located between the right atrium and the right ventricle.

tri·cy·cle (trī′si kəl, -sik′əl) *n.* three-wheeled vehicle, usually used by children, having two wheels in the back and one in the front, driven by pedals and steered with handlebars. [TRI- + CYCLE.]

tri·dent (trīd′ənt) *n.* three-pronged spear. —*adj. also,* **tri·den·tate** (trī den′tāt). having three prongs, teeth, or tines. [Latin *tridēns,* from *tri-* three + *dēns* tooth.]

Tricycle

tried (trīd) *v.* past tense and past participle of **try.** —*adj.* proven, as by experience or examination; tested.

tried-and-true (trīd′ən trōō′) *adj.* tested and proven trustworthy or useful: *a tried-and-true friend, a tried-and-true method.*

tri·en·ni·al (trī en′ē əl) *adj.* **1.** lasting or continuing for three years. **2.** done or occurring every three years. —*n.* **1.** event that occurs every three years. **2.** a third anniversary. [Latin *triennium* period of three years (from *tri-* three + *annus* year) + -AL.] —**tri·en′ni·al·ly,** *adv.*

tri·er (trī′ər) *n.* one who or that which tries.

Tri·este (trē est′) *n.* port city in northeastern Italy, at the head of the Adriatic Sea. Pop. (1968), 280,017.

tri·fle (trī′fəl) *n.* **1.** something of little or no intrinsic value or importance; insignificant matter or thing: *There's no sense arguing over trifles.* **2.** somewhat; bit. ▲ commonly used adverbially in the phrase *a trifle,* as in *He is a trifle annoyed with their careless work.* **3.** small sum of money. **4.** dessert made of sponge cake and macaroons, having a layer of custard, fruit, or jam, and topped with whipped cream or meringue. —*v.i.,* **-fled, -fling. 1.** to treat something as having little value or importance; treat lightly (with *with*): *He has been known to trifle with important business affairs.* **2.** to handle or treat in an idle, careless manner (with *with*): *He is always trifling with his cigarette lighter.* —*v.t.* to pass or spend (time, money, or the like) in an idle, frivolous manner; waste (with *away*): *He trifled away his entire inheritance.* [Old French *trufle* mockery, trickery; of uncertain origin.] —**tri′fler,** *n.*

tri·fling (trī′fling) *adj.* **1.** having little or no value or significance; unimportant; small. **2.** lacking depth or seriousness; shallow; frivolous. —tri′fling·ly, *adv.* —**Syn. 1.** see paltry.]

tri·fo·li·ate (trī fō′lē it, -āt′) *adj. Botany.* having three leaves, leaflets, or three leaflike parts. [TRI- + Latin *foliātus* leaved (from *folium* leaf).]

tri·fo·ri·um (trī fôr′ē əm) *pl.* **-fo·ri·a** (-fôr′-ē ə). *n.* gallery or arcade in the wall of a church, above the arches at the sides of the nave, choir, or transept. [Medieval Latin *triforium,* possibly from Latin *tri-* three + *foris* door, opening.]

trig (trig) *adj.* tidy; neat; trim. [Old Norse *tryggr* faithful, trusty.]

trig. **1.** trigonometry. **2.** trigonometric. Also, **trigon.**

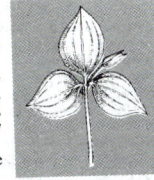

Trifoliate branch

trig·ger (trig′ər) *n.* **1.** small lever on a gun or other firearm which, when pulled back or pressed, as with the finger, causes the firearm to discharge. **2.** any similar device, as a lever that is pressed or pulled to initiate a process or mechanism. **3.** something, as an act or event, that precipitates an event or series of events: *Prayer is the trigger which liberates the Divine Power* (Tyndall, 1871). **4.** quick on the trigger. **a.** able to quickly draw and fire a gun. **b.** *Informal.* acting or responding quickly; alert. —*v.t.,* **-gered, -ger·ing.** to initiate or precipitate, as an event or series of events: *Jealousy triggered her angry outburst.* [Earlier *tricker,* from Dutch *trekker* lever on a gun; literally, thing that pulls, from *trekken* to pull.]

trig·ger·hap·py (trig′ər hap′ē) *adj. Informal.* inclined to resort to or react with violent, often irresponsible, actions, esp. readily resorting to the use of firearms or weaponry.

tri·glyph (trī′glif′) *n.* member of a Doric frieze, usually consisting of a projecting block or tablet with two vertical grooves and a half groove at each side, alternating with metopes. [Latin *triglyphus,* from Greek *triglyphos,* from *tri-* three + *glyphein* to carve.]

trig·o·nom·e·try (trig′ə nom′ə trē) *n.* branch of mathematics dealing with the relations between the sides and angles of triangles and the properties of these relations. [Modern Latin *trigonometria,* from Greek *trigōnon* triangle + -METRY.] —**trig·o·no·met·ric** (trig′ə nə met′rik); *also,* **trig′o·no·met′ri·cal,** *adj.* —**trig′o·no·met′ri·cal·ly,** *adv.*

tri·graph (trī′graf′) *n.* three successive letters pronounced as a single sound, as the *eau* in *beau.*

tri·he·dron (trī hē′drən) *pl.* **-drons** or **-dra** (-drə). *n.* geometric figure formed by three planes meeting in a point. [TRI- + Greek *hedrā* seat, base.] —**tri·he′dral,** *adj.*

tri·lat·er·al (trī lat′ər əl) *adj.* having three sides. [Latin *trilaterus* (from *tri-* three + *latus* side) + -AL.]

tri·lin·gual (trī lin′gwəl) *adj.* having, consisting of, expressed in, or speaking three languages.

trill (tril) *n.* **1.** tremulous, usually high-pitched sound or succession of notes: *the chirping trill of a bird.* **2.** *Music.* rapid alternation of two notes either a whole step or a half step apart. **3.** *Phonetics.* **a.** rapid vibration of the tip of the tongue. **b.** speech sound, as a consonant, produced in such a way, esp. the sound of *r.* —*v.t.* to sing, play, produce, or articulate (something) with a trill. —*v.i.* to sing, play, produce, or articulate a trill. [Italian *trillare* to quaver, warble; probably of Germanic origin.]

tril·lion (tril′yən) *adj.* **1.** in the United States and France, the cardinal number that is represented by one followed by 12 zeros. **2.** in Great Britain and Germany, the cardinal number that is represented by one followed by 18 zeros. —*adj.* numbering one trillion. [French *trillion* one followed by 12 zeros, (from Latin *tri-* three), on the model of *million.* See MILLION.] —**tril′lionth,** *adj., n.*

tril·li·um (tril′ē əm) *n.* any of a group of low plants, genus *Trillium,* of the lily family, having a whorl of three smooth, oval leaves, and bearing flowers composed of three oval petals. [Modern Latin *Trillium,* from Latin *tri-* three; referring to its whorl of three leaves.]

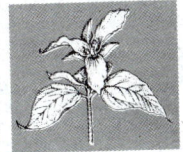

Trillium

tri·lo·bate (trī lō′bāt, trī′lə bāt′) *adj.* having three lobes, as certain leaves. Also, **tri·lo′bat·ed.**

tri·lo·bite (trī′lə bīt′) *n.* any of a group of extinct arthropods, class Trilobita, common in the oceans during the middle of the Paleozoic era, having a segmented body divided into three longitudinal lobes. [Modern Latin *Trilobites,* from Greek *trilobos* having three lobes.]

tril·o·gy (tril′ə jē) *pl.* **-gies.** *n.* group of three complete plays, operas, novels, or the like, that together make a related series. [Greek *trilogiā* group of three tragic dramas, from *tri-* three + *logos* speech, story.]

trim (trim) *trimmed, trim·ming. v.t.* **1.** to make neat and orderly by removing excess parts, as by cutting: *to trim one's hair, to trim a rose*

bush. **2.** to remove (an excess or irregular part or object) in order to make neat or orderly (often with *off* or *away*): *to trim the thorns on a rose, to trim frivolous items off a budget.* **3.** to add ornaments or decorations to; decorate: *to trim a cake, to trim a dress with lace.* **4.** to balance (a boat or ship) as by arranging the cargo or ballast. **5.** to adjust (yards or sails) for sailing. **6.** to keep (an aircraft) in a level position while in flight by adjusting various controls. **7.** *Informal.* to defeat: *The challenger is sure to trim the champ in three rounds.* **8.** *Informal.* to rebuke sharply; scold. —*v.i.* **1.** to maintain a neutral course or position, as in a contest or controversy between others. **2.** *Nautical.* **a.** to be or remain in balance. **b.** to adjust yards or sails for sailing. —*n.* **1.** ornamentation; decoration: *The dress had a sequined trim. The chrome trim on the car door was scratched in the collision.* **2.** act of trimming, as by clipping or cutting; being trimmed. **3.** state of adjustment, fitness, order, or preparedness. **4.** condition of a ship with reference to her fitness for sailing, esp. when properly balanced. **5.** position of a boat or ship in the water, esp. with reference to the difference between the amount of the boat or ship that is in the water at the bow and at the stern. **6.** woodwork used ornamentally in the interior or exterior of a building, esp. moldings around windows or doors. **7.** *Archaic.* equipment; outfit; dress. —*adj.,* **trim·mer, trim·mest.** in good order or condition: *Her clothes were always neat and trim.* —*adv. also,* **trim′ly.** in a trim manner. [Old English *trymman* to strengthen, array.] —**trim′-ness,** *n.*

tri·mes·ter (trī mes′tər) *n.* period or term consisting of three months, esp. one of the three terms into which the academic year is sometimes divided. [French *trimestre,* going back to Latin *tri-* three + *mēnsis* month.]

trim·e·ter (trim′ə tər) *n.* line of verse consisting of three metrical feet to each line. —*adj.* consisting of three metrical feet or of lines having three metrical feet. [Latin *trimetrus* consisting of three metrical feet, from Greek *trimetros,* from *tri-* three + *metron* measure, meter.]

trim·mer (trim′ər) *n.* **1.** one who or that which trims. **2.** beam that receives the end of a header in floor framing.

trim·ming (trim′ing) *n.* **1.** anything used as a decoration or ornament: *The dress had sequin trimming on the sleeves. There was very little chrome trimming on the car.* **2.** trimmings. **a.** pieces or parts cut off in trimming something, as parings or scraps. **b.** *Informal.* traditional or usual accessories or accompaniments, esp. the side dishes or garnishes of an entree: *a birthday party with ice cream, cake, and all the trimmings.* **3.** *Informal.* beating; defeat: *The home team took a trimming.* **4.** *Informal.* sharp rebuke; scolding.

tri·month·ly (trī munth′lē) *adj.* occurring or done every three months.

tri·nal (trīn′əl) *adj.* having or composed of three parts.

trine (trīn) *adj.* threefold; triple. —*n.* **1. Trine.** the Trinity. **2.** *Astrology.* of or relating to the aspect of two planets 120 degrees apart from each other. [Latin *trīnus* threefold.]

Trin·i·dad (trin′ə dad′) *n.* one of the Lesser Antilles, off the coast of Venezuela, part of the country of Trinidad and Tobago. Area, 1864 sq. mi. Pop. (1960), 794,624.

Trinidad and Tobago, country comprising the West Indian islands of Trinidad and Tobago. Capital, Port-of-Spain. Land area, 1980 sq. mi. Pop. (1968 est.), 1,021,000.

Trin·i·tar·i·an (trin′ə tār′ē ən) *adj.* **1.** professing belief in the doctrine of the Trinity. **2.** of or relating to the Trinity or the doctrine of the Trinity. —*n.* one who professes belief in the Trinity.

tri·ni·tro·tol·u·ene (trī nī′trō tol′ū ēn′) *n.* TNT. Also, **tri·ni·tro·tol·u·ol** (trī nī′trō tol′ū ōl′).

Trin·i·ty (trin′ə tē) *pl.* **-ties.** *n.* **1.** *Theology.* the union of the Father, the Son, and the Holy Ghost as three divine persons in one Godhead. **2.** *Informal.* Trinity Sunday. **3. trinity.** any combination or group of three persons or things. **4. trinity.** state or condition of being three or threefold. [Old French *trinite* the Trinity, from Late Latin *trīnitās,* from Latin *trīnitās* a triad.]

Trinity Sunday, feast day in honor of the Trinity, celebrated on the eighth Sunday after Easter.

trin·ket (tring′kit) *n.* **1.** any small ornament or fancy article, esp. a piece of costume jewelry. **2.** anything of little value or significance; trifle. [Of uncertain origin.]

tri·no·mi·al (trī nō′mē əl) *adj.* **1.** consisting of three terms: *a trinomial equation.* **2.** having or consisting of three names. Trinomial nomenclature is used to classify certain plants and animals. The genus name is given first and is followed by the species and then the subspecies or variety. —*n.* mathematical expression consisting of three terms joined by plus or minus signs. The expression $4x + 7y - 1$ is a trinomial. [TRI- + (BI)NOMIAL.]

tri·o (trē′ō) *pl.* **tri·os.** *n.* **1.** musical composition for three voices or instruments. **2.** three musicians performing such a composition. **3.** any group of three persons or things. [Italian *trio* set of three, from Latin *trēs, tria* three.]

at; āpe; cär; end; mē; it; īce; hot; ōld; fôrk; wood; foŏl; oil; out; up; ūse; turn; sing; thin; this; zh in treasure; ə in ago, taken, pencil, lemon, circus.

1063

tri·ode (trī′ōd) *n.* electron tube consisting of an anode, a cathode, and a grid which controls the flow of electrons between them. [TRI- + -ODE.]

tri·o·let (trī′ə lit) *n.* poem having eight lines and only two rhymes, with the first line used also as the fourth and seventh lines, and the second line used also as the eighth line. The rhyme scheme is *abaaabab.* [French *triolet,* probably diminutive of Italian *trio* set of three. See TRIO.]

tri·ox·ide (trī ok′sīd, -sid) *n.* oxide having three atoms of oxygen in each molecule.

trip (trip) *n.* **1.a.** act or instance of traveling from one place to another, esp. over a relatively long distance: *a trip through southern Europe. His last trip lasted two months.* **b.** act or instance of going from one place to another: *Will you please bring back some butter on your next trip to the kitchen?* **2.** fall or stumble caused by striking one's foot against an object or by losing one's foothold. **3.** light, quick, lively movement, esp. of the feet. **4.** catch or other device that releases a part, as in setting a mechanism in operation. Also, **trip′per. 5.** act of catching or entangling a person's foot within one's own, so as to cause him to lose his balance and fall. **6.** error; blunder; slip: *The witness made a trip in that last statement.* —*v.i.* **tripped, trip·ping. 1.** to strike the foot against something so as to stumble or fall: *to trip over the edge of a rug.* **2.** to make a mistake; commit an error; blunder: *The speaker tripped when he made that statement.* **3.** to falter in articulation or pronunciation: *to trip over a difficult word.* **4.** to move with quick, light steps; prance: *The lambs tripped across the meadow.* **5.** *Machinery.* to be released, triggered, or set in operation, as a spring, catch, or mechanism. —*v.t.* **1.** to cause to fall or stumble (often with *up*). **2.** to cause to make a mistake or commit a blunder (often with *up*): *The reporters tried to trip him up with their questions.* **3.** to catch in a fault, offense, or error: *They couldn't trip him in his alibi.* **4.** *Machinery.* **a.** to operate (a mechanism) by releasing a spring, catch, or other device. **b.** to release (a spring, catch, or other device) in order to set a mechanism in operation. [Old French *trip(p)er* to dance, from Middle Dutch *trippen* to skip.] —**Syn.** *n.* **1.** see *journey.*

tri·par·tite (trī pär′tīt) *adj.* **1.** divided into three parts. **2.** having three corresponding parts or copies. **3.** of, relating to, or made by three parties: *an international tripartite agreement.* [Latin *tripartītus* divided into three parts, from *trī-* three + *partītus,* past participle of *partīrī* to divide.]

tripe (trīp) *n.* **1.** walls of the first and second stomachs of a ruminant, esp. the ox, used as food. **2.** *Informal.* anything of such poor quality as to be useless or worthless. [Old French *tripe* entrails of an animal; of uncertain origin.]

trip·ham·mer (trip′ham′ər) *n.* power-driven hammer that is operated by a cam or other device that trips a lever and allows the hammer to fall.

triph·thong (trif′thông′, -thong′, trip′-) *n.* vowel sound produced by the combining, during pronunciation, of three vowel sounds within one syllable. The *ayo* in *mayor* is a triphthong. [TRI- + (DI)PH-THONG.]

tri·plane (trī′plān′) *n.* airplane with three wings, arranged one above the other.

tri·ple (trip′əl) *adj.* **1.** consisting of three parts. **2.** three times as much or as many; multiplied by three. —*n.* **1.** number or amount that is three times as much as another. **2.** *Baseball.* hit which enables a batter to reach third base. —*v.t.* **-pled, -pling. 1.** to make three times as much or as many: *He tripled his income in five years.* **2.** *Baseball.* to advance (a runner) by hitting a triple. —*v.i.* **1.** to become three times as much or as many: *The company's profits tripled in three years.* **2.** *Baseball.* to hit a triple. [Latin *triplus* threefold, from Greek *triplous.* Doublet of TREBLE.]

Triple Entente alliance between Great Britain, France, and Russia prior to World War I.

triple play *Baseball.* a play during which three men are put out.

tri·plet (trip′lit) *n.* **1.a.** one of three offspring born at one birth. **b.** triplets, three offspring born at one birth. **2.** any set or combination of three. **3.** *Music.* group of three notes of equal time value to be performed in the time of two. **4.** three successive lines of rhyming verse, usually of equal length. [TRIPLE + -ET.]

triple time, musical time or rhythm having three beats to the measure, the accent falling on the first beat.

tri·plex (trip′leks, trī′pleks) *adj.* triple; threefold. —*n.* something which has three parts, esp. an apartment with three floors. [Latin *triplex* threefold, triple.]

trip·li·cate (*adj., n.,* trip′lə kit, -kāt′; *v.,* trip′lə kāt′) *adj.* three times as much or as many; triple. —*v.t.* **-cat·ed, -cat·ing.** to multiply by three; triple. —*n.* **1.** one of three identical things, esp. copies of printed matter. **2. in triplicate.** in three exactly corresponding copies. [Latin *triplicātus,* past participle of *triplicāre* to triple.] —**trip′li·ca′tion,** *n.*

tri·ply (trip′lē) *adv.* in a triple degree, amount, or manner.

tri·pod (trī′pod′) *n.* **1.** three-legged stand for supporting a camera or a surveying instrument. **2.** pot, stool, table, or similar structure resting on three legs. [Latin *tripūs* three-legged seat, from Greek *tripous* three-legged table or cauldron, having three feet.]

Trip·o·li (trip′ə lē) *n.* **1.** region on the northern coast of Africa, now in western Libya, once a major base for the Barbary pirates. **2.** largest city, commercial center, and one of the two capitals of Libya, a port in the northeastern part of the country, on the Mediterranean Sea. Pop. (1968), 247,365. **3.** port city in northern Lebanon, on the Mediterranean Sea. Pop. (1964), 127,611. —**Tri·pol·i·tan** (tri pol′ə tən), *adj., n.*

trip·per (trip′ər) *n.* **1.** one who trips or causes another to trip. **2.** trip *(def. 4).* **3.** *British. Informal.* one who goes on a trip, esp. as a tourist.

trip·ping (trip′ing) *adj.* moving quickly and lightly: *A quick, tripping footstep sounds in the deserted street* (Jerrold, 1851). —**trip′ping·ly,** *adv.*

Tripod

trip·tych (trip′tik) *n.* **1.** triple painting or carving consisting of three panels hinged together, esp. one depicting a religious subject and used as an altarpiece. **2.** set of three writing tablets tied or hinged together, used in ancient times. [Greek *triptychos* consisting of three layers, threefold, from *tri-* three + *ptyché* fold.]

tri·reme (trī′rēm) *n.* ancient galley, esp. a warship, with three horizontal rows of oars, one above the other, on each side. [Latin *trirēmis,* from *tri-* three + *rēmus* oar.]

tri·sect (trī sekt′) *v.t.* **1.** to divide into three parts. **2.** *Geometry.* to divide into three equal parts: *to trisect an angle.* [TRI- + Latin *sectus,* past participle of *secāre* to cut.] —**tri·sec′tion,** *n.*

Tris·tan (tris′tən) *n.* *Medieval Legend.* knight who falls in love with Isolde. Also, **Tris·tram** (tris′trəm).

tri·syl·la·ble (trī sil′ə bəl, trī-) *n.* word that has three syllables. —**tri·syl·lab·ic** (trī′si lab′ik, tris′i-), *adj.* —**tri·syl·lab′i·cal·ly,** *adv.*

Trireme
Position of oars

trite (trīt) trit·er, trit·est. *adj.* lacking originality or freshness due to constant repetition. [Latin *trītus,* past participle of *terere* to rub, wear away.] —**trite′ly,** *adv.* —**trite′ness,** *n.*

trit·i·um (trit′ē əm, trish′-) *n.* radioactive isotope of hydrogen having an atomic weight of 3, containing one proton and two neutrons. It is the fusion of tritium with deuterium that releases the explosive force of the hydrogen bomb. [Modern Latin *tritium,* from Greek *tritos* third.]

tri·ton (trīt′ton) *n.* nucleus of a tritium atom. [Greek *triton,* neuter of *tritos* third.]

Tri·ton (trīt′ən) *n.* *Greek Mythology.* son of Poseidon who was half man and half fish and lived at the bottom of the sea.

trit·u·rate (trich′ə rāt′) -rat·ed, -rat·ing. *v.t.* to reduce to very fine particles or powder, as by crushing or grinding. —*n.* any triturated substance. [Late Latin *trītūrātus,* past participle of *trītūrāre* to thresh, from Latin *trītūra* threshing, rubbing.]

trit·u·ra·tion (trich′ə rā′shən) *n.* **1.** act of triturating. **2.** any medicine so prepared.

tri·umph (trī′umf) *n.* **1.** outstanding success, achievement, or victory: *It was the triumph of civilization over brute force* (Newman, 1853). **2.** great joy or exultation caused by victory or success: *We could see his triumph on his face. Great triumph and rejoicing was in heaven* (Milton, 1667). **3.** in ancient Rome, procession and public celebration honoring a victorious commander or other leader. —*v.i.* **1.** to achieve a victory; be successful; win: *to triumph over the enemy.* **2.** to rejoice or celebrate over a victory or success. [Latin *triumphus* triumphal procession, victory, possibly from Greek *thriambos* hymn to Bacchus sung in processions in his honor.] —**Syn.** *n.* **1.** see *victory.*

tri·um·phal (trī um′fəl) *adj.* of, relating to, characteristic of, or celebrating a triumph or victory: *a triumphal procession honoring the victor.*

tri·um·phant (trī um′fənt) *adj.* **1.** victorious or successful. **2.** celebrating for or as for victory or success; rejoicing; exultant. —**tri·um′phant·ly,** *adv.*

tri·um·vir (trī um′vər) *pl.* **-virs** or **-vi·ri** (-ə rī′). *n.* in ancient Rome, one of the members of a triumvirate. [Latin *triumvir,* from the phrase *trium virōrum* (one) of three men.]

tri·um·vi·rate (trī um′vər it) *n.* **1.** political institution, esp. during periods in ancient Rome, under which three men divided the authority

of the highest public office. **2.** position or term of office of a triumvir. **3.** any group or association of three persons, esp. three who jointly hold some power, authority, or distinction.

tri·une (trī′ŭn) *adj.* (of the Godhead) three in one: *the triune deity.* [TRI- + Latin *ūnus* one.]

tri·u·ni·ty (trī ū′nə tē) *pl.,* **-ties.** *n.* trinity (*defs.* 3, 4).

tri·va·lent (trī vā′lənt) *adj.* having a valence of three. [TRI- + Latin *valēns,* present participle of *valēre* to be strong.] **—tri·va′lence,** tri·va′len·cy, *n.*

triv·et (triv′it) *n.* **1.** three-legged stand or support used for holding pots over a fire. **2.** metal or ceramic plate, often having three short legs, placed under hot plates or dishes on a table. [Old English *trefet,* from Latin *tripēs* having three feet.]

triv·i·a (triv′ē ə) *n.,pl.* unimportant or insignificant facts, matters, or information; trifles. ▲ construed as singular or plural. [Possibly from TRIVIAL.]

triv·i·al (triv′ē əl) *adj.* **1.** having little or no importance, significance, or consequence; trifling. **2.** *Archaic.* having no freshness or novelty; commonplace; everyday. [Latin *triviālis* that may be found anywhere, commonplace; literally, that belongs to crossroads, from *trivium* place where three roads meet, crossroad, from *tri-* three + *via* way.] **—triv′i·al·ly,** *adv.* **—Syn. 1.** see **petty**

triv·i·al·i·ty (triv′ē al′ə tē) *pl.,* **-ties.** *n.* **1.** quality or state of being trivial. **2.** thing or matter of little importance, significance, or consequence; something trivial.

triv·i·um (triv′ē əm) *n.* in medieval universities, three subjects, grammar, rhetoric, and logic, that composed the less advanced group of the seven liberal arts. Distinguished from **quadrivium.** [Medieval Latin *trivium,* from Latin *trivium* place where three roads meet. See TRIVIAL.]

tri·week·ly (trī wĕk′lē) *adv.* **1.** every three weeks. **2.** three times a week. **—adj. 1.** occurring or done every three weeks. **2.** occurring or done three times a week. **—n.** *pl.,* **-lies.** newspaper, magazine, or the like issued three times a week or once every three weeks.

tro·cha·ic (trō kā′ik) *adj.* of, relating to, or consisting of trochees. **—n.** line of verse or poem written in trochees.

tro·che (trō′kē) *n.* disk containing medicine to be dissolved in the mouth; lozenge; pastille. [From obsolete *trochisk,* from Late Latin *trochiscus* small ball[1], from Greek *trochiskos* small wheel, pill, diminutive of *trochos* wheel.]

tro·chee (trō′kē) *n.* metrical foot consisting of two syllables, the first accented or long and the second unaccented or short, for example: Pe′ter Pe′ter pump′kin eat′er. [Latin *trochaeus,* from Greek *trochaios (pous)* running (foot); because this meter produces the effect of running.]

trod (trod) a past tense and past participle of **tread.**

trod·den (trod′ən) a past participle of **tread.**

trode (trōd) *Archaic.* a past tense of **tread.**

trog·lo·dyte (trog′lə dīt′) *n.* **1.** low, despised person, esp. one who lives under primitive or hermitlike conditions, as in a cave in the earth. **2.** anthropoid ape, as a gorilla or chimpanzee. [Latin *Trōglodytae* (plural) a people of Ethiopia who lived in caves, from Greek *trōglodytēs* cave man, one who creeps into holes, from *trōglē* hole + *dyein* to enter.]

troi·ka (troi′kə) *n.* **1.** Russian vehicle, as a carriage, drawn by three horses abreast. **2.** team of three such horses. **3.** group or association of three persons, esp. three persons jointly holding power or authority.

Troi·lus (troi′ləs, trō′i ləs) *n.* *Greek Legend.* Trojan prince, son of King Priam, who, in medieval legend, is portrayed as the lover and betrayer of Cressida.

Tro·jan (trō′jən) *adj.* of, relating to, or characteristic of Troy, its people, or their culture. **—n. 1.** inhabitant of Troy. **2.** one who exhibits great courage, energy, or forbearance: *She took the bad news like a Trojan.*

Trojan horse 1. *Greek Legend.* large, hollow wooden horse, given by the Greeks to the Trojans apparently as a gift, but containing soldiers who crept out and opened the city gates to the Greek army. **2.** one who or that which is designed or intended to undermine or destroy something, as an organization, from within.

Trojan War, war between the Greeks and the Trojans that lasted ten years and ended in the destruction of Troy, and, according to Greek legend, was started by the abduction of Helen by Paris, a Trojan.

troll[1] (trōl) *v.i.* **1.** to fish with a moving line, usually by trailing the line behind the boat. **2.** to sing, as a tune, in a full, rich voice. **3.** to be uttered in such a voice. **—v.t. 1.** (of several singers) to sing the parts of (a song) in succession, as in a round. **2.** to sing or utter in a full, rich voice. [Middle French *troller* to wander, ramble; possibly from Middle High German *trollen* to run with short steps.]

troll[2] (trōl) *n.* *Scandinavian Folklore.* dwarf or, sometimes, a giant, who lives underground or in a mountain cave. [Old Norse *troll* monster, demon.]

trol·ley (trol′ē) *pl.,* **-leys.** *n.* **1.** small grooved wheel or pulley that moves along an overhead wire to pick up electricity for an electric streetcar, train, or bus. **2.** trolley car. **3.** *British.* low cart or truck; handcart. [Probably from TROLL[1] (in the obsolete senses of "to move about," "ramble").]

trolley car, electric streetcar that gets its current from an overhead wire by means of a trolley.

trol·lop (trol′əp) *n.* cheap, low, or vulgar woman.

trom·bone (trom bōn′, trom′bōn) *n.* brass musical instrument consisting of two long, U-shaped tubes, one of which ends in a bell and the other of which may be slid back and forth to vary the pitch of the tones. [Italian *trombone* trombone, trumpet, from *tromba* trumpet, from Old High German *trumpa.*] **—trom·bon′ist,** *n.*

Trolley car

Trond·heim (trŏn′hām) *n.* historic city, commercial center, and port in central Norway. Pop. (1968 est.), 122,323.

troop (trōōp) *n.* **1.** organized body of soldiers, police, or the like. **2.** formerly, a cavalry unit of the U.S. Army corresponding to an infantry company. **3.** **troops.**

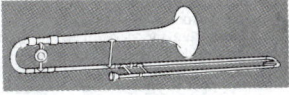

Trombone

members of the armed forces collectively. **4.a.** large group working or congregating together: *A whole troop of sign painters went to work on the blank walls.* **b.** *usually,* **troops.** great number; flock; swarm. **5.** unit, usually consisting of several patrols, of Boy or Girl Scouts, usually with from sixteen to thirty-two members. **6.** troupe. **—v.i.** to walk or march in a group, esp. in a forceful or orderly fashion: *The game was over and the players trooped home. The delegation of angry citizens trooped into the mayor's office.* [French *troupe* group of persons, herd, possibly from *troupeau* herd, from Late Latin *troppus;* of Germanic origin.]

troop·er (trōō′pər) *n.* **1.** member of a military or police troop, as a state policeman or a member of the National Guard. **2.** trouper.

troop·ship (trōōp′ship′) *n.* ship used to transport military personnel.

trope (trōp) *n.* **1.** use of a word or phrase in a figurative sense. **2.** figure of speech. **3.** figurative language in general. [Latin *tropus* figure of speech, from Greek *tropos* figure of speech, turn.]

tro·phy (trō′fē) *pl.,* **-phies.** *n.* **1.** loving cup, bowl, statuette on a pedestal, or other object for display, usually awarded for some achievement, as winning a sports contest or other competition. **2.** something taken and kept as a reminder or proof of victory or achievement or of participation in a conflict, as a weapon captured from an enemy or a lion's head. **3.** *Archaic.* arrangement or display of weapons, flags, or other objects. [French *trophée* sign of victory, through Latin, from Greek *tropaion* monument of an enemy's defeat, from *tropē* defeat, turning.]

trop·ic (trop′ik) *n.* **the tropics.** *also,* **the Tropics.** region of the earth lying between the Tropic of Cancer and the Tropic of Capricorn; the Torrid Zone. **—adj.** of or relating to the tropics; tropical. [Late Latin *tropicus* relating to a turning (of the sun), from Greek *tropikos,* from *tropē* a turning.]

trop·i·cal (trop′i kəl) *adj.* of, relating to, found in, suitable to, or characteristic of the tropics: *tropical clothing, tropical plants.*

tropic bird, any of various long-winged, tropical seabirds, family Phaëthontidae, having webbed feet, two very long tail feathers, a red or yellow bill, and white plumage with black markings on the head and wings. Length: 16–19 inches.

Tropic of Cancer 1. imaginary line parallel to the equator at latitude 23° 27′ north, that marks the northernmost distance from the equator at which the sun appears to be overhead at noon. **2.** circle of the celestial sphere corresponding to this, parallel to the celestial equator.

Tropic of Capricorn 1. imaginary line parallel to the equator at latitude 23° 27′ south, that marks the southernmost distance from the equator at which the suns appears to be overhead at noon. **2.** circle of the celestial sphere corresponding to this, parallel to the celestial equator.

tro·pism (trō′piz əm) *n.* response of a plant or some of its parts to a specific stimulus, esp. a response of turning toward the light. [Greek *tropos* a turning + -ISM.] **—tro·pis·tic** (trō pis′tik), *adj.*

trop·o·sphere (trop′ə sfēr′) *n.* layer of the atmosphere nearest the earth's surface, extending to an altitude of about twelve miles, in which most of the earth's weather phenomena occur. [Greek *tropos* turning + SPHERE.]

at; āpe; cär; end; mē; it; īce; hot; ōld; fôrk; wood; fōōl; oil; out; up; ūse; turn; sing; thin; <u>th</u>is; zh in treasure; ə in ago, taken, pencil, lemon, circus.

trot (trot) *n.* **1.a.** gait of a horse or other quadruped, between a walk and a gallop, in which the left hind foot and the right forefoot are lifted together and then the left forefoot and right hind foot are lifted. **b.** sound of this. **2.** jogging gait of a human being, between a walk and a run. **3.** any quick but easy pace. **4.** *Informal.* pony *(def. 3).* —*v.i.,* **trot·ted, trot·ting. 1.** to ride or move at a trot: *The horse trotted around the corral.* **2.** to move quickly; hurry; bustle: *He trotted to the post office to get the letter out before noon.* —*v.t.* **1.** to cause to trot. **2.** *Informal.* to take or carry at a brisk pace: *Trot this package down to the mail room.* **3. to trot out.** *Informal.* to bring out and show for exhibition, consideration, approval, or the like: *The designer trotted out his latest creations.* [Old French *troter* to go at a trot, walk fast; of Germanic origin.]

troth (trôth, trŏth) *n. Archaic.* promise of fidelity, as in marriage or betrothal. [Old English *trēowth* fidelity, promise.]

trot·line (trot′līn′) *n.* fishing line supported by buoys or suspended across a stream, with many baited hooks at intervals along it.

Trot·sky, Leon (trot′skē) 1879–1940, Russian revolutionary leader; born Lev Davidovich Bronstein.

trot·ter (trot′ər) *n.* **1.** horse that trots, esp. one bred and trained for trotting races. **2.** foot, as of a calf, sheep, or pig, used as food.

trou·ba·dour (trōō′bə dôr′, -dōōr′) *n.* any of many lyric poets who flourished from the eleventh to the thirteenth centuries in southern Europe, esp. in Provence, and were famous for songs about love and chivalry. [French *troubadour,* from Provençal *trobador,* from *trobar* to compose poetry, find; of uncertain origin.]

trou·ble (trŭb′əl) *n.* **1.** state or condition of difficulty, danger, harm, or distress: *The people in the valley will be in trouble if the dam gives way.* **2.** that which causes a problem, is wrong, or makes someone or something unsatisfactory: *The trouble with you is you won't listen. The only trouble is the plan won't work.* **3.** extra exertion or effort; pains: *The hostess went to a lot of trouble to make her guests comfortable.* **4.** disease or illness; ailment: *kidney trouble.* **5.** disturbance; disorder; turmoil: *The sheriff expected a lot of trouble at the demonstration.* —*v.t.,* **-bled, -bling. 1.** to put into a state of mental agitation or distress; worry; disturb: *to trouble someone with your problems.* **2.** to put (someone) to extra effort; inconvenience: *May I trouble you for a glass of water?* **3.** to cause physical pain or inconvenience; hurt; afflict: *to be troubled by ulcers.* —*v.i.* to take pains; bother: *Don't trouble to see me out.* [Old French *trubler, turbler* to disturb, going back to Latin *turba* disturbance, crowd.]

Syn. *v.t.* **1. Trouble, distress** mean to cause pain and agitation. **Trouble** is the more general word, and is used to suggest some unease or question about a problem or situation: *I'm troubled by your unnecessary rudeness.* **Distress** is a somewhat more formal and polite word used esp. to suggest a disturbance that continues for a long period of time, adding the anxiety of suspense to the emotional pressure generated by the problem: *We are distressed not to have heard from you for six months and hope you are well.*

trou·ble·mak·er (trŭb′əl mā′kər) *n.* one who or that which is a source of trouble.

trou·ble·shoot·er (trŭb′əl shōō′tər) *n.* one who specializes in locating and solving troubles, problems, and difficulties.

trou·ble·some (trŭb′əl səm) *adj.* that causes distress, inconvenience, or annoyance: *a troublesome injury, a troublesome situation.*

trou·blous (trŭb′ləs) *adj.* **1.** full of troubles: *troublous times.* **2.** troublesome.

trough (trôf) *n.* **1.** long, deep, narrow receptacle resembling a bin, used esp. for holding water. **2.** channel or conduit, as under or along the eaves of a roof, used for conveying water. **3.** low point, as on a graph. **4.** long, narrow hollow or depression, as between two mountain ridges or two ocean waves. [Old English *trog* narrow and hollow vessel, vat.]

trounce (trouns) *v.t.,* **trounced, trounc·ing.** to beat soundly, in or as in a contest. [Of uncertain origin.]

troupe (trōōp) *also,* **troop.** *n.* theatrical group or company, as of actors, singers, or circus performers, esp. such a company that travels about from place to place. —*v.i.,* **trouped, troup·ing.** to go on a tour with such a group. [French *troupe.* See TROOP.]

troup·er (trōō′pər) *also,* **troop·er.** *n.* **1.** one who faces up to problems or difficulties or persists despite pain or obstacles. **2.** veteran actor or performer. **3.** member of a troupe.

trou·sers (trou′zərz) *n.,pl.* garment for the lower part of the body, extending from the waist or hips to the ankles and divided so as to cover each leg separately. [Modification of archaic *trouse,* from Irish and Scottish Gaelic *triubhas,* possibly from Old French *trebus* breeches; of uncertain origin.]

trous·seau (trōō′sō, trōō sō′) *n.,pl.* **-seaux** (-sōz, -sōz′) *or* **-seaus.** *n.* all the items brought by a bride to her new home, as clothing, linen, and silver. [French *trousseau,* diminutive of *trousse* bundle, possibly from Old French *trusser* to pack[1], bind; of uncertain origin.]

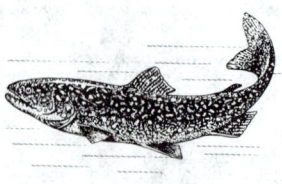
Trout

trout (trout) *pl.,* **trouts** *or* **trout.** *n.* any of a group of food and game fish, family Salmonidae, related to the salmon, found in lakes and streams, including the lake trout and brook trout. [Old English *trūht,* from Late Latin *tructa,* probably from Greek *trōktēs* gnawer, a saltwater fish with sharp teeth.]

trow (trō) *v.i.,v.t. Archaic.* to be of the opinion; suppose; think. [Partly from Old English *trūwian* to trust; partly from Old English *trēowian* to believe.]

trow·el (trou′əl) *n.* **1.** hand tool with a flat, rectangular or triangular blade, used for spreading and smoothing plaster or mortar, as in brick-laying. **2.** scooplike digging tool with a narrow, curved, pointed blade, often used for planting flowers. [Old French *truele* the tool used for spreading plaster and mortar, going back to Late Latin *truella,* diminutive of *trua* ladle.]

Troy (troi) *n.* ancient city and stronghold in northwestern Asia Minor, near the mouth of the Dardanelles. Excavations and archaeological research have shown that it was actually settled nine times. The seventh of these cities was the scene of the Trojan War. Also, **Il′i·um.**

troy weight (troi) standard system of weights used for gems and precious metals. [From *Troyes,* a city in France where this weight was probably first employed for gems and precious metals at the city's famous fairs in the Middle Ages.]

tru·an·cy (trōō′ən sē) *pl.,* **-cies.** *n.* act, instance, or practice of being truant.

tru·ant (trōō′ənt) *n.* **1.** student who is absent from school without permission or a legitimate excuse. **2.** one who shirks or neglects work or responsibilities; idle or lazy person. —*adj.* **1.** of, relating to, or characteristic of truants: *truant behavior.* **2.** (of a student) being truant. [Old French *truant* beggar, vagabond; probably of Celtic origin.]

truant officer, school official who investigates and deals with cases of truancy.

truce (trōōs) *n.* temporary halt to fighting by mutual agreement of combatants, often in order to reach a final settlement. [Middle English *trewes,* plural of *trewe* temporary peace, from Old English *treow* faith, promise, compact.]

Tru·cial O·man (trōō′shəl ō män′) formerly, a group of seven British-protected sheikdoms on the east-central coast of the Arabian peninsula. See **United Arab Emirates.** Also, **Trucial Coast, Trucial States.**

truck¹ (trŭk) *n.* **1.** automotive vehicle designed to carry heavy loads, esp. one with a cab in front for the driver and a trailer or open area behind for the cargo. **2.** low rectangular frame on four wheels, often motorized, used for moving heavy loads, as boxes in a warehouse or railroad station; dolly. **3.** two-wheeled handbarrow used for lifting and carrying trunks, boxes, or similar loads. **4.** set of two or more pairs of wheels mounted closely together in a swiveling frame, as on a railroad car or locomotive. **5.** small disk, pulley, or wheel. —*v.t.* to convey on a truck or trucks. —*v.i.* to drive a truck or engage in trucking. [Probably from Latin *trochus* iron hoop, from Greek *trochos* wheel.]

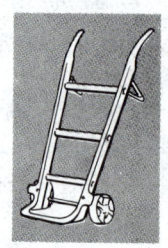
Truck *(def. 2)*

truck² (trŭk) *n.* **1.** vegetables raised for market. **2.** *Informal.* dealings: *Aunt Sarah will have no truck with her neighbors.* **3.** *Informal.* trash; rubbish. **4.** payment of wages in goods or the like, instead of money. [Old French *troquer* to barter; of uncertain origin.]

truck·age (trŭk′ij) *n.* **1.** charge for conveyance by truck. **2.** conveyance by truck.

truck·er (trŭk′ər) *n.* **1.** person or firm who owns or operates a trucking business. **2.** one whose job is driving a truck.

truck farm, farm on which vegetables are raised for market.

truck·ing (trŭk′ing) *n.* business or process of transporting goods by truck.

truck·le (trŭk′əl) *v.i.,* **-led, -ling. 1.** to be subservient or obsequious (with *to*): *to truckle to those in authority.* **2.** *Archaic.* to move on rollers or casters. —*v.t. Archaic.* to cause to move on rollers or casters. —*n.* **1.** truckle bed. **2.** small wheel or caster. [Latin *trochlea* pulley, system of pulleys, from Greek *trochileiā*.]

truckle bed, trundle bed.

tru·cu·lence (trŭk′yə ləns, trōō′kyə-) *n.* truculent behavior, actions, or appearance. Also, **truc′u·len·cy.**

truc·u·lent (truk′yə lənt, trōō′kyə-) *adj.* **1.** savage; fierce; ferocious. **2.** harsh or scathing: *a truculent speech.* **3.** hostile; threatening. [Latin *truculentus* cruel, harsh.] **—truc′u·lent·ly,** *adv.*

trudge (truj) **trudged, trudg·ing.** *v.i.* to make one's way on foot in a steady, laborious manner; drag oneself; plod: *to trudge up a hill.* **—***v.t.* to travel over (a place or distance) in a steady, laborious manner: *They trudged the last mile in the rain.* **—***n.* laborious, tiring walk: *The hunters made the two-mile trudge back to camp.* [Of uncertain origin.]

trudg·en stroke (truj′ən) swimming stroke like a crawl, but usually accompanied by a scissors kick. [From John *Trudgen,* 1852–1902, English swimmer who popularized it.]

true (trōō) **tru·er, tru·est.** *adj.* **1.** that conforms with or correctly represents reality or fact; not false, fictitious, or wrong: *a true story.* **2.** having the proper qualities, attributes, or characteristics of: *a true gentleman.* **3.** actually being what it seems or is claimed to be; real: *true gold.* **4.** firm or steady in adhering to someone or something; loyal; faithful: *He is true to his old friends.* **5.** conforming closely to an original, standard, or type: *a true copy.* **6.** legitimate; rightful: *the true heirs to the estate.* **7.** unerring; sure: *a true sign of insanity.* **8.** accurately aligned or placed. **9.** determined with reference to the earth's axis rather than the magnetic poles: *true south.* **10. to come true.** to be realized in actual experience; be fulfilled. **—***adv.* **1.** in a true manner. **2.** without change from the previous generation: *to breed true.* **—***n.* **1. the true.** that which is true or real. **2.** condition of accurate alignment or placement: *to be in true.* **—***v.t.,* **trued** (trōōd) or **tru·ing** or **true·ing.** to make, adjust, or align accurately (often with *up*). [Old English *trēowe, trywe* trustworthy, faithful.] **—true′ness,** *n.* **—Syn.** *adj.* **1.** see **real**[1].

true bill, bill of indictment endorsed by a grand jury as having sufficient evidence to justify a trial.

true-blue (trōō′blōō′) *adj.* unwavering in loyalty or faith; staunch: *a true-blue patriot.*

true·love (trōō′luv′) *n.* one's beloved; sweetheart.

truf·fle (truf′əl, trōō′fəl) *n.* any of a group of edible potato-shaped mushrooms, genus *Tuber,* that grows underground. [Middle French *trufle,* from *truffe,* possibly going back to Latin *tūber* swelling, truffle.]

tru·ism (trōō′iz′əm) *n.* statement that is so obviously true that no one would argue with it.
Syn. Truism, platitude, cliché mean a commonplace idea or expression. **Truism** applies to an uncontroversial and self-evident statement and is used to suggest a lack of complexity or subtlety in thought: *That the poor live in poverty is a truism.* **Platitude** is a stale, stereotyped idea expressed with an air of profundity, suggesting the self-inflated pomposity of the speaker: *The banker spouted platitudes about "individualism" and "progress" to an audience markedly bored by his complacency.* **Cliché** is applied to an originally interesting, even colorful idea or expression which has lost its power through overuse and suggests the speaker's limited ability or willingness to experiment with language: *He speaks in clichés, you know, always drawing "red herrings" into conversations which reveal that heroes have "feet of clay."*

Tru·jil·lo (trōō hē′ō, -hē′yō) *n.* city in northwestern Peru. Pop. (1969), 149,000.

tru·ly (trōō′lē) *adv.* **1.** sincerely; genuinely: *I'm truly sorry.* **2.** in accordance with fact or reality; truthfully. **3.** accurately; correctly.

Tru·man, Harry S (trōō′mən) 1884–1972, thirty-third president of the United States, from 1945 to 1953.

trump[1] (trump) *n.* **1.** suit of playing cards that temporarily outranks the other suits, as for a single hand. **2.** any card of this suit. **—***v.t.* **1.** to play a trump card on (another card or a trick). **2.** to go (someone) one better; outdo; beat. **—***v.i.* to play a trump card. [Modification of TRIUMPH.]

trump[2] (trump) *n. Archaic.* trumpet. [Old French *trompe,* from Old High German *trumpa;* of imitative origin.]

trump[3] (trump) *v.t.* to devise in order to deceive; fabricate (with *up*): *to trump up a story.* [Possibly from TRUMP[1].]

trump·er·y (trump′pər ē) *pl.,* **-er·ies.** *n.* something that appears to be valuable but is really worthless. [Old French *tromperie* deceit, fraud, from *tromper* to deceive; of uncertain origin.]

trum·pet (trump′pit) *n.* **1.** brass musical instrument consisting of a cylindrical metal tube coiled into a long loop and ending in a bell, the tones of which are varied by the pressure of the player's lips and by the use of three valves. **2.** something resembling a trumpet in shape. **3.** sound like that of a trumpet, as the cry of an elephant. **4.** trumpeter *(def. 1).* **—***v.i.* **1.** to blow a trumpet. **2.** to produce or emit a sound like that of a trumpet, as does an elephant. **—***v.t.* **1.** to sound or produce on a trumpet. **2.** to announce or proclaim widely and loudly

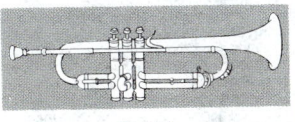

Trumpet

as if with a trumpet; herald: *The team trumpeted their victory through the streets.* [Old French *trompette* this musical instrument, diminutive of *trompe.* See TRUMP[2].]

trumpet creeper, woody climbing vine, *Campsis radicans,* bearing clusters of orange and scarlet funnel-shaped flowers. Also, **trumpet vine.**

trum·pet·er (trump′pi tər) *n.* **1.** one who sounds or plays on a trumpet. **2.** North American swan, *Olor buccinator,* having a deep, resonant, buglelike call. **3.** South American bird, genus *Psophia,* native to humid jungle regions, related to and resembling the crane, having thick, generally dark-colored plumage, and noted for its loud, resonant cry. Length: 20 inches. **4.** one of a breed of domestic pigeons having a crest and feathered feet.

trumpet flower 1. climbing vine, *Bignonia capreolata,* found in North America, having funnel-shaped, orange-red flowers. **2.** trumpet creeper.

trun·cate (trung′kāt) **-cat·ed, -cat·ing.** *v.t.* to reduce in size or diminish by cutting off a part of. **—***adj.* truncated. [Latin *truncātus,* past participle of *truncāre* to cut off, maim.] **—trun·ca′tion,** *n.*

trun·cat·ed (trung′kā tid) *adj.* having or seeming to have a part or section missing or cut off.

trun·cheon (trun′chən) *n.* **1.** club, esp. a long, slender, sturdy one, as used by police. **2.** staff carried as a symbol of office. **—***v.t.* to beat with a truncheon; club. [Old French *tronchon* stump, piece cut off, going back to Latin *truncus* trunk of a tree or human being.]

trun·dle (trun′dl) **-dled, -dling.** *v.t.* to cause to roll along by pushing: *to trundle a bicycle rather than ride it.* **—***v.i.* to move or go on or as if on rollers or wheels. **—***n.* **1.** small wheel or caster. **2.** trundle bed. [Form of earlier *trendle* circle, wheel, from Old English *trendel* circle, ring[1]; influenced by Old French *trondeler* to roll (of Germanic origin).]

trundle bed 1. low movable bed that may be pushed under another bed for storage. **2.** bed including a second low, movable bed that is pushed under it for storage. Also, **truckle bed.**

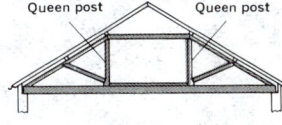

Trundle bed

trunk (trungk) *n.* **1.** the main stem of a tree, as distinguished from its branches. **2.** large, rectangular receptacle with a hinged lid, used for transporting and storing things. **3.** baggage compartment of an automobile. **4.** long flexible snout, esp. of an elephant. **5. trunks.** short men's pants, as those worn by swimmers, that reach from the waist to the upper thigh. **6.** main body of a human being or animal, considered apart from any appendages as the head, limbs, or tail. **7.** thorax of an insect. **8.** main part or stem of something, esp. of a nerve, blood vessel, or the like. **9.** trunk line. [Latin *truncus* trunk of a human being or tree.]

trunk·fish (trungk′fish′) *pl.,* **-fish** or **-fish·es.** *n.* any of various brightly colored, mostly tropical, saltwater fish, family Ostraciidae, having an outer shell of bony, angular plates. Length: 9–16 inches.

trunk hose, full, baggy men's breeches, usually reaching from the waist to the upper thigh, worn in the early sixteenth and early seventeenth centuries.

trunk line 1. main line of a transportation system, as of a railroad. **2.** line that connects telephone exchanges and carries many calls at once.

Trunk hose

trun·nel (trun′əl) treenail.

trun·nion (trun′yən) *n.* either of two projections, on each side of a cannon, that supports it on its carriage. [Old French *trognon* stump, core; of uncertain origin.]

truss (trus) *n.* **1.** device, usually consisting of a pad attached to a belt, used for support in cases of hernia. **2.** framework of wood or metal, usually consisting of triangular units, used to span an opening or support a heavy load, as of a bridge or roof. **3.** bundle of hay or straw. **4.** *Nautical.* rope or iron fitting by which a lower yard is secured to a mast. **—***v.t.* **1.** to bind; tie; fasten (often with *up*). **2.** to support or strengthen, as a roof or bridge, with a truss or trusses. **3.** *Archaic.* to adjust (clothing) by drawing it closely together. [Old French *trusse* bundle, possibly from *trusser* to pack[1], bind; of uncertain origin.]

Truss of a roof

trust (trust) *v.t.* **1.** to have faith or confidence in the integrity, honesty,

ability, reliability, or justice of: *Many doctors do not trust these new techniques. Emily is open and truthful with us because she trusts us.* **2.** to accept the truth or validity of or act on the basis of; rely upon or believe: *to trust your intuitions. to trust the weather reports for next weekend.* **3.** to commit to someone's care; entrust: *to trust a child to a baby sitter.* **4.** to give business credit to: *My neighborhood grocer trusted me for this week's food.* **5.** to assume or feel sure; expect with confidence: *I trust that you will get here on time.* —*v. i.* **1.** to have faith or confidence (often with *in*): *to trust in one's good judgment.* **2.** to assume or feel sure: *You found it, I trust.* —*n.* **1.** firm belief in or reliance on the integrity, honesty, ability, reliability, or justice of someone or something. **2.** keeping; custody; care: *My niece was left in my trust for the weekend.* **3.** fact or state of being trusted: *a position of great power and trust.* **4.** that which is believed, believed in, or assumed; confident expectation: *It is their trust that hunger will eventually be eliminated from the world.* **5.** business combination, as of many companies or corporations, that exercises monopolistic power over the production or distribution of a commodity or service, and can fix prices and eliminate competition. **6.** trust fund. **7.** one who or that which is believed in or relied upon. **8.** one who or that which is committed or entrusted to someone's care. **9.** confidence in the ability or intention of a person to pay, as for goods, at some future time; credit. **10. in trust. a.** in a condition of safekeeping or careful protection: *woodlands held in trust for future generations.* **b.** in a trust fund. [Old Norse *traust* help, confidence.]
Syn. *n.* **2. Trust, confidence, reliance** are characterized by a certainty that something will meet one's expectations. **Trust** implies an absolute emotional security based on intuition or personal relationship rather than rational considerations: *The two brothers had implicit trust in each other.* **Confidence** is more formal and less emotional, implying that standards, esp. of consistency and quality, are applied to determine another's merit and that past performance and proven ability form the basis of one's certainty: *The man has enjoyed the confidence of many important officials.* **Reliance** stresses the active expression of one's trust or confidence, even to excess: *He places too great a reliance on what he reads.*
trust·bust·er (trust′bus′tər) *n.* one who seeks to weaken or break up large business combinations or trusts, as by rigorous enforcement of antitrust laws or by agitation for new or stronger laws.
trust company, company, as a bank, whose main function is the management of property, as money, securities, or real estate, entrusted to it by others.
trus·tee (trus tē′) *n.* individual or organization that holds and manages the property of another person, company, or institution.
trus·tee·ship (trus tē′ship′) *n.* **1.** office or function of a trustee. **2.a.** administration of a trust territory by a country commissioned by the United Nations. **b.** the territory so administered.
trust·ful (trust′fəl) *adj.* full of or disposed to trust; trusting. —**trust′ful·ly,** *adv.* —**trust′ful·ness,** *n.*
trust fund, money, securities, property, or the like held by a trustee, usually a bank.
trust·ing (trus′ting) *adj.* full of or disposed to trust; that trusts.
trust territory, territory, as a former colony, that is administered by another nation under UN supervision, with the aim of becoming independent.
trust·wor·thy (trust′wur′thē) *adj.* that can be trusted or is worthy of trust. —**trust′wor′thi·ness,** *n.*
trust·y (trus′tē) **trust·i·er, trust·i·est.** *adj.* that can be trusted or relied on: *The trapper always carried his trusty knife.* —*n. pl.,* **trust·ies.** well-behaved, cooperative convict who is given certain duties and privileges because he can be trusted. —**trust′i·ly,** *adv.* —**trust′i·ness,** *n.*
truth (trooth) *pl.* **truths** (troothz, trooths). *n.* **1.** that which is true: *the pursuit of truth, to speak the truth.* **2.** state or quality of being true or of accurately reflecting reality or fact: *to doubt the truth of a statement.* **3.** accepted or verified fact, principle, or the like. **4. in truth.** really; actually: *The ugly frog was in truth a handsome prince.* [Old English *trīewth, trēowth* honor, fidelity, covenant.]
truth·ful (trooth′fəl) *adj.* **1.** that usually or habitually tells the truth: *a truthful newspaper, a truthful person.* **2.** conforming to truth, fact, or reality: *The letters give a truthful picture of prison life.* —**truth′ful·ly,** *adv.* —**truth′ful·ness,** *n.*
truth serum, sodium pentothal, scopolamine, or any similar drug used as a sedative, as in psychiatry, to induce someone to reveal suppressed thoughts.
truth set, solution set.
try (trī) **tried, try·ing.** *v. t.* **1.** to make an effort to do or accomplish; attempt; undertake: *They tried moving the sofa themselves.* **2.** to use or apply tentatively; test the effect, efficiency, or operation of: *to try a new remedy. The commuter tried the new route home and saved twenty minutes.* **3.** to subject to a test or tests in order to determine quality, accuracy, or the like (often with *out*): *Try out the brakes before you drive*

down a hill. **4.** to put on (an article of clothing) in order to test its fit or appearance (often with *on*). **5.** (of a court or judge) to investigate or look into the guilt or innocence of an accused person or the truthfulness of allegations in a case. **6.** to attempt to open: *The visitor tried the door, but it was locked.* **7.a.** to subject to trials or suffering; afflict: *His son's scandalous behavior sorely tried the old man.* **b.** to subject to strain; tax: *to try someone's patience.* **8.** *Archaic.* to separate or extract by steaming or melting (often with *out*). —*v. i.* **1.** to make an effort; attempt. **2. to try out for.** to demonstrate one's skill or ability in order to qualify as a member of: *James tried out for the track team.* —*n. pl.,* **tries.** act of trying: *The mountain climbers made one more try to reach the top.* [Old French *trier* to pick¹, choose; of uncertain origin.]
Syn. *v. t.* **1. Try, attempt, endeavor** mean to make an effort to do or accomplish something. **Try** is the most general word, often used to stress a willingness to be flexible even to the point of being uncertain: *I'll try to get downtown this afternoon but I don't know if I can make it.* **Attempt** is often used to stress an effort, esp. a successful one, made in the face of opposition or other great obstacles: *They attempted the impossible and succeeded.* **Endeavor** is the most formal word of the three and therefore is used to suggest a commitment or public dedication to some noble goal: *I shall endeavor to raise this school to a level of prestige worthy of its former reputation.*
try·ing (trī′ing) *adj.* hard to bear or endure; difficulty: *trying circumstances.*
try·out (trī′out′) *n.* **1.** *also,* **tryouts.** period or session during which those who are trying out, as for parts in a play or positions on a team, are checked for skill or ability. **2.** trial or probationary period during which someone or something is evaluated: *to give the new reporter a tryout on some business stories.*
tryp·sin (trip′sin) *n.* enzyme that changes proteins into peptones to aid digestion, secreted by the pancreas and also prepared artificially. [Greek *tripsis* rubbing + -IN¹; because first obtained by *rubbing* the pancreas with glycerin.]
try·sail (trī′sāl′, -səl) *n.* small fore-and-aft sail, usually extended with a gaff from the foremast or mainmast of a boat or ship, used esp. in stormy weather.
try square, L-shaped instrument used in carpentry for laying out and testing right angles.
tryst (trist) *n.* **1.** prearranged meeting, esp. between lovers; rendezvous. **2.** arrangement to meet at a specified time and place. **3.** prearranged place of meeting. [Old French *triste* place for watching, ambush; probably of Scandinavian origin.]
tsar (zär, tsär) czar.
tsar·e·vitch (zär′ə vich′, tsär′-) czarevitch.
tsa·rev·na (zär′ev′nə, tsä-) czarevna.
tsa·ri·na (zä rē′nə, tsä-) czarina.
tsar·ism (zär′iz′əm, tsär′-) czarism.
tsar·ist (zär′ist, tsär′-) czarist.
tset·se fly (tset′sē, tsē′tsē) *also,* **tzet·ze fly.** any of a group of bloodsucking flies, family Glossinidae, found in Africa. Certain species transmit sleeping sickness to man and other fatal diseases to animals. Also, **tset′se, tzet′ze.** [Of Bantu origin.]

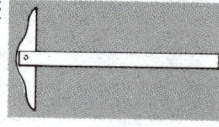
Tsetse fly

T-shirt (tē′shurt′) *also,* **t-shirt, tee shirt.** *n.* **1.** light, close-fitting undershirt of cotton knit, with short sleeves. **2.** outer shirt resembling this, worn for casual wear or for sports.
Tsi·nan (jē′nän′) *n.* city in eastern China. Pop. (1957 est.), 862,000.
Tsing·tao (ching′dou′, tsing′tou′) *n.* port city in northeastern China, on the Yellow Sea. Pop. (1957 est.), 1,121,000.
tsp., teaspoon.

T square

T square, tool used by architects and engineers to draw parallel straight lines, consisting of a long straightedge attached at one end to a short crosspiece that slides up and down the edge of a drawing board.
tsu·na·mi (tsoo nä′mē) *n.* swift, powerful ocean wave caused by an underwater earthquake and causing great destruction to any land area it strikes. [Japanese *tsunami* tidal wave, from *tsu* harbor + *nami* wave.]
Tu., Tuesday.
tu·a·ta·ra (too′ə tär′ə) *n.* reptile, *Sphenodon punctatus*, found on the offshore islands of New Zealand,

Tuatara

at; āpe; cär; end; mē; it; īce; hot; ōld; fôrk; wood; fōōl; oil; out; up; ūse; turn; sing; thin; this; zh in treasure; ə in ago, taken, pencil, lemon, circus.

having olive brown or dull yellowish skin. It is the sole survivor of the order Rhynchocephalia and is distinguished by a third eye on the top of its head. [Of Maori origin.]

tub (tub) *n.* **1.** bathtub. **2.** large, open, circular receptacle, used as for washing clothes. **3.** round container, often of wood or metal, used for holding butter, honey, fat, or other products. **4.** as much as a tub will hold. **5.** something that resembles a tub, esp. an old, clumsy-looking boat or ship. **6.** *Informal.* bath. [Probably of Low German origin.]

tu·ba (tōō′bə, tū′-) *n.* **1.** any of several very large brass musical instruments that produce a deep, mellow tone, consisting of a coiled metal tube whose diameter increases from a narrow mouthpiece at one end to a wide bell at the other. **2.** organ stop producing powerful tones. [Latin *tuba* trumpet.]

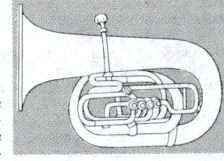
Tuba

Tu·bal-cain (tōō′bəl kān′, tū′-) *n.* in the Old Testament, a descendant of Cain and an early craftsman in iron and brass.

tub·by (tub′ē) **-bi·er, -bi·est.** *adj.* **1.** short and broad in shape, like a tub. **2.** having a dull, wooden sound, like that of an empty tub when struck. **—tub′bi·ness,** *n.*

tube (tōōb, tūb) *n.* **1.** hollow cylindrical structure, as of glass, rubber, or metal, usually used to hold or convey liquids or gases. **2.** anything resembling a tube, as in shape or function. **3.** soft, squeezable container having a screw cap, used for packaging and dispensing toothpaste, shampoo, paint, and other products. **4.** electron tube. **5.** underground or underwater tunnel, or a train or subway that uses such a tunnel. [Latin *tubus* pipe.]

tu·ber (tōō′bər, tū′-) *n.* **1.** *Botany.* enlarged fleshy portion of an underground stem, such as a potato, serving to store food and give rise to new plants. **2.** tubercle *(def. 1).* [Latin *tūber* swelling, tumor.]

tu·ber·cle (tōō′bər kəl, tū′-) *n.* **1.** small, rounded swelling, as on a bone or plant. **2.** swelling caused by the tubercle bacillus. [Latin *tuberculum* small swelling, diminutive of *tūber* swelling, tumor.]

tubercle bacillus, bacterium that causes tuberculosis.

tu·ber·cu·lar (too bur′kyə lər, tyoo-) *adj.* **1.** tuberculous. **2.** of, relating to, or having tubercles; nodular.

tu·ber·cu·lin (too bur′kyə lin, tyoo-) *n.* liquid prepared from cultures of the tubercle bacillus, used in the diagnosis and treatment of tuberculosis.

tu·ber·cu·lo·sis (too bur′kyə lō′sis, tyoo-) *n.* **1.** infectious disease caused by a bacterium, that may affect any organ of the body, esp. the lungs or joints, and is characterized by the formation of tubercles on the affected parts. **2.** tuberculosis of the lungs. Also *(def. 2),* **con·sump′tion.** [Moden Latin *tuberculosis,* from Latin *tūberculum* small swelling + -OSIS.]

tu·ber·cu·lous (too bur′kyə ləs, tyoo-) *adj.* of, relating to, or affected with tuberculosis.

tube·rose (tōōb′rōz′, tūb′-) *n.* Mexican plant, *Polianthes tuberosa,* widely cultivated for its fragrant, waxy, white flowers that are used to make perfumes. [Latin *tūberōsa,* feminine of *tūberōsus* full of swellings; mistakenly thought to be from TUBE + ROSE¹. See TUBEROUS.]

tu·ber·os·i·ty (tōō′bə ros′ə tē, tū′-) *n., pl.* **-ties.** **1.** state or quality of being tuberous. **2.** rounded swelling, esp. on a bone.

tu·ber·ous (tōō′bər əs, tū′-) *adj.* **1.** *Botany.* bearing tubers. **2.** of or resembling a tuber. **3.** covered with many tuberosities. [Latin *tūberōsus* full of swellings, from *tūber* swelling, tumor.]

tub·ing (tōō′bing, tū′-) *n.* **1.** object or material in the form of a tube: *glass tubing bent into shape for neon lights, steel tubing.* **2.** tubes collectively. **3.** length or piece of tube.

tu·bu·lar (tōō′byə lər, tū′-) *adj.* **1.** consisting of tubes: *the tubular frame-work of a lawn chair.* **2.** of, relating to, or shaped like a tube: *a tubular pathway made by a worm.* [Latin *tubulus* small pipe, diminutive of *tubus* pipe + -AR¹.]

tu·bule (tōō′byoōl, tū′-) *n.* small tube or tubelike structure. [Latin *tubulus* small pipe, diminutive of *tubus* pipe.]

tuck (tuk) *v.t.* **1.** to push or fold the edge or ends of (something), esp. so as to hold snugly in place: *to tuck one's shirt in. She tucked her hair behind her ears.* **2.** to put into a tight or narrow place: *The wasps' nest was tucked up underneath the rafters.* **3.** to hide from view or knowledge; store away or conceal (with *away*): *Grandfather had many old bottles tucked away in the cellar.* **4.** to cover snugly, esp. by folding the edges of a blanket or cover snugly under a mattress (with *in* or *into*). **5.** to sew a tuck or tucks in (a garment). **6.** to gather up into a fold or folds. **—***v.i.* to sew a tuck or tucks in a garment. **—***n.* fold sewed in a garment, as to shape, shorten, tighten, or create fullness in it. [Middle Low German *tucken* to tug, pull up.]

tuck·er¹ (tuk′ər) *n.* **1.** covering of lace, linen, or other light material worn around the neck and shoulders. **2.** one who or that which tucks. **3.** sewing machine attachment for making tucks. [TUCK + -ER¹.]

tuck·er² (tuk′ər) *v.t. Informal.* to make tired or weary (often with *out*). [TUCK + -ER¹.]

Tuc·son (tōō′son, tōō son′) *n.* city in southeastern Arizona, noted as a health and tourist resort. Pop. (1960), 262,933.

Tu·cu·man (tōō′kōō män′) *n.* city in northwestern Argentina. Pop. (1960), 280,000.

Tu·dor (tōō′dər, tū′-) *n.* **1.** royal family that ruled England from 1485 to 1603, including Henry VII, Henry VIII, Edward VI, Mary I, and Elizabeth I. **2.** member of this family. **—***adj.* of, relating to, or designating a style of architecture and interior design that flourished in England during the reign of the Tudor monarchs from 1485 to 1558, characterized by flattened arches, gabled roofs, parapets, large bay windows, ornamental chimneys, and interior paneling.

Tues., Tuesday.

Tues·day (tōōz′dē, -dā, tūz′-) *n.* third day of the week. [Old English *Tiwesdæg* literally, day of Tiw (a Teutonic god of war identified with Mars), translation of Latin *diēs Martis* day of Mars.]

tu·fa (tōō′fə, tū′-) *n.* sedimentary calcium carbonate or silica rock formed from material deposited by springs, lakes, or ground water. [Italian *tufo,* from Latin *tōfus.* Doublet of TUFF.]

tuff (tuf) *n.* rock composed of compressed, fine-grained volcanic fragments. [French *tuf*tufa, tuff, from Italian *tufo,* from Latin *tōfus.* Doublet of TUFA.]

tuf·fet (tuf′it) *n.* hassock or footstool.

tuft (tuft) *n.* **1.** dense cluster of flexible fibers, as feathers or hair, bound together or attached at one end and loose and bushy at the other. **2.** small group or clump, as of trees or bushes. **—***v.t.* **1.** to adorn or furnish with a tuft or tufts. **2.** to sew (a mattress, pillow, or quilt) with tufts to keep the padding in place. **—***v.i.* to grow or form in tufts. [Earlier *toft,* probably from Old French *tof(f)e* tuft of hair; of Germanic origin.]

tuft·ed (tuf′tid) *adj.* **1.** having or adorned with a tuft or tufts. **2.** formed into or growing in a tuft or tufts.

tug (tug) **tugged, tug·ging.** *v.i.* **1.** to give a pull on something (with *at* or *on*): *The child tugged at the man's coat to get his attention.* **2.** to strain to pull or haul: *The horse tugged harder, and finally the log began to move.* **—***v.t.* **1.** to give a pull on: *to tug someone's ear.* **2.** to pull or haul with force: *to tug the heavy stones across the field.* **3.** to tow with a tugboat. **—***n.* **1.** act or instance of tugging: *The fisherman felt a tug on the line.* **2.** tugboat. **3.** one of the traces of a harness. [Middle English *toggen* to pull, going back to Old English *tēo(ha)n* to pull, draw, drag.]

tug·boat (tug′bōt′) *n.* small, powerful boat used to push or tow other boats or ships. Also, **tow′boat′.**

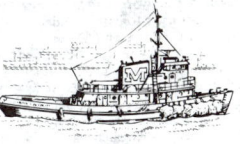
Tug boat

tug of war 1. game in which two players or teams pull at opposite ends of something, as a rope, with each trying to force the other either to let go or to be dragged out of place. **2.** any struggle or contest between opposite forces.

tu·i·tion (tōō ish′ən, tū-) *n.* **1.** amount of money paid by a student for instruction, esp. at a college or university. **2.** *Archaic.* act or business of teaching or being taught. [Latin *tuitiō* a taking care of, protection.]

tu·i·tion·al (tōō ish′ən əl, tū-) *adj.* of, relating to, or charging tuition.

Tu·la (tōō′lä, -lə) *n.* city in the Soviet Union, in the Russian Republic. Pop. (1970 est.), 462,000.

tu·la·re·mi·a (tōō′lə rē′mē ə) *n.* infectious disease of rabbits and other rodents, caused by a bacterium and transmitted to humans by the handling of an infected animal or the bite of certain insects. [Modern Latin *tularemia,* from *Tulare,* a county in California where this disease was first encountered + Greek *haima* blood.]

tu·lip (tōō′lip, tū′-) *n.* **1.** bell-shaped or saucer-shaped flower of any of a group of hardy plants, genus *Tulipa,* of the lily family, native to Asia and the Mediterranean area. **2.** plant bearing these flowers, widely cultivated as an ornamental, having thick, bluish-green leaves which rise directly from an underground bulb. [Modern Latin *Tulipa,* from Turkish *tülbend* turban, from Persian *dulband;* from the resemblance of the flower to a turban. Doublet of TURBAN.]

Tulips

tulip tree, large North American tree, *Liriodendron tulipifera,* having yellowish-green flowers that resemble tulips, and soft wood used to make furniture and other products. Also, **tulip poplar.**

tu·lip·wood (tōō′lip wood′, tū′-) *n.* colorful, striped wood of the tulip tree, used esp. in cabinetwork.

tulle (tōōl) *n.* fine, stiff net fabric of silk or rayon, used in making veils and in dressmaking. [From *Tulle,* French town where it was first produced.]

Tul·sa (tul′sə) *n.* city in northeastern Oklahoma, on the Arkansas River. Pop. (1970), 331,638.

tum·ble (tum′bəl) *-bled, -bling. v.i.* **1.** to fall, esp. in an awkward, rolling manner: *The fruit tumbled from the overturned cart.* **2.** to roll or toss about: *The clothes tumbled in the dryer. The children loved to tumble over and over in the piles of leaves.* **3.** to engage in tumbling. **4.** to go or proceed in a hurried, disorderly manner: *The children tumbled out the door.* **5.** to understand or become aware of something (with *to*). —*v.t.* to cause to tumble or fall. —*n.* **1.** act of tumbling; fall. **2.** state of disorder or confusion; tangle. **3. to give (someone) a tumble.** *Slang.* to indicate slight notice or recognition. [Middle English *tumblen* to perform as an acrobat, fall, from *tumben* to dance, jump, from Old English *tumbian.*]

tum·ble·bug (tum′bəl bug′) *n.* dung beetle.

tum·ble·down (tum′bəl doun′) *adj.* that is in a dilapidated condition.

tum·bler (tum′blər) *n.* **1.** one who engages in tumbling. **2.** drinking vessel, often of glass, having a flat bottom and no handle. **3.** rotating drum, esp. in an automatic clothes dryer, in which objects are tumbled. **4.** lever in a lock that must be moved to the correct height by the key in order to release the bolt. **5.** mechanism in a gun that forces the hammer to move forward when the trigger releases the mainspring. **6.** any of a breed of domestic pigeons that turn over backward repeatedly in flight.

tum·ble·weed (tum′bəl wēd′) *n.* any of several bushy prairie plants that break off from their roots, usually in autumn, and are blown about by the wind, as an amaranth, *Amaranthus albus.*

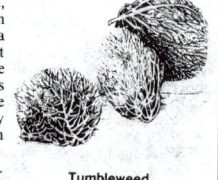

Tumbleweed

tum·bling (tum′bling) *n.* gymnastic or acrobatic activity done on mats or on the ground, as handstands and somersaults, rather than on a trampoline or other devices above floor level.

tum·brel (tum′bril) *also,* **tum·bril.** *n.* **1.** farmer's cart with a body that can be tilted backward to empty out the load. **2.** cart used to carry condemned prisoners to be executed, esp. during the French Revolution. **3.** covered two-wheeled military cart, used as for carrying ammunition or tools. [Old French *tumberel* dumpcart, from *tumber* to fall; of Germanic origin.]

Tumbrel

tu·me·fac·tion (tōō′mə fak′shən, tū′) *n.* **1.** act or state of being swollen. **2.** swollen part, as a tumor.

tu·me·fy (tōō′mə fī′, tū′-) *-fied, -fy·ing. v.t., v.i.* to swell or cause to swell. [Latin *tumefacere* to cause to swell.]

tu·mes·cence (tōō mes′əns, tū-) *n.* **1.** act or process of swelling. **2.** swollen condition. **3.** swollen part or organ.

tu·mes·cent (tōō mes′ənt, tū-) *adj.* swollen or becoming swollen. [Latin *tumēscēns,* present participle of *tumēscere* to begin to swell.]

tu·mid (tōō′mid, tū′-) *adj.* **1.** abnormally enlarged; swollen. **2.** (of language) inflated; pompous. [Latin *tumidus* swollen.]

tum·my (tum′ē) *pl., -mies. n. Informal.* stomach.

tu·mor (tōō′mər, tū′-) *also, British,* **tu·mour.** *n.* **1.** abnormal growth that may be malignant, formed in the body from normal tissue that grows at an abnormally fast rate. **2.** any swollen part. [Latin *tumor* swelling.] —**tu′mor·ous;** *also, British,* **tu′mour·ous,** *adj.*

tu·mult (tōō′məlt, tū′-) *n.* din; commotion; uproar. [Latin *tumultus.*]

tu·mul·tu·ous (tōō mul′chōō əs, tyōō-) *adj.* agitated; clamorous; turbulent. —**tu·mul′tu·ous·ly,** *adv.* —**tu·mul′tu·ous·ness,** *n.*

tu·mu·lus (tōō′myə ləs, tū′-) *-li* (-lī′) *or* **-lus·es.** *n.* mound of earth, esp. an ancient burial mound. [Latin *tumulus.*]

tun (tun) *n.* **1.** large cask or barrel used for holding liquids, esp. wine, ale, or beer. **2.** *Archaic.* amount of liquid equal to 252 gallons. [Old English *tunne* large cask, from Late Latin *tunna* cask; probably of Celtic origin.]

tu·na (tōō′nə) *pl.,* **tu·nas** *or* **tu·na.** *n.* **1.** any of several food and game fish, family Scombridae, related to the mackerel,

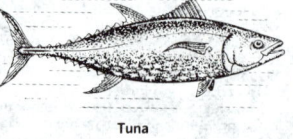

Tuna

found in tropical and temperate seas throughout the world, including the albacore. Length: to 14 feet. Weight: to 1600 pounds. Also, **tun′ny.** **2.** tuna fish *(def. 1).* [Spanish *tuna,* form of *atún* tunny, through Arabic, from Latin *thunnus.* See TUNNY.]

tun·a·ble (tōō′nə bəl, tū′-) *also,* **tune·a·ble.** *adj.* **1.** that can be tuned: *The kettledrum is a tunable drum.* **2.** *Archaic.* in tune; harmonious. **3.** *Archaic.* melodious; tuneful.

tuna fish 1. flesh of the tuna, used for food. **2.** tuna *(def. 1).*

tun·dra (tun′drə, toon′-) *n.* vast, treeless plain in the northernmost parts of Asia, Europe, and North America, having an arctic or subarctic climate and a layer of permanently frozen soil several inches below the surface. [Russian *tundra,* from Lapp *tun-tur* literally, marsh plain.]

tune (tōōn, tūn) *n.* **1.** *Music.* succession of single tones constituting a complete phrase or idea. **2.** short musical piece, esp. a recorded popular song: *Play a tune on the jukebox.* **3.a.** quality or condition of being properly adjusted, tightened, or the like for producing sounds in harmony with itself: *The old piano is badly out of tune.* **b.** quality or condition of being at the proper pitch or in the proper key: *The violinist was playing out of tune.* **c.** quality or condition of being in the same pitch or key as (with *with*): *The orchestra was in tune with the singer.* **4.** stand, approach, outlook, or manner: *Jenny was cheerful and sincere and we liked her tune. The desk manager finally changed his tune and gave us a room.* **5.** quality or condition of harmonious agreement or accord: *in tune with what others are saying, out of tune with the times.* **6. to call the tune.** to decide for everyone; be in command. **7. to sing a different** (or **another**) **tune.** to adopt a different stand, approach, outlook, or manner. **8. to the tune of.** in or around the amount or sum of. —*v.t.,* **tuned, tun·ing. 1.** to adjust to a standard of pitch; put in tune (often with *up*): *to tune a guitar, to tune up a piano.* **2.** to put (a vehicle or machine) into the proper or most efficient working order, as by lubrication or adjustment of parts (often with *up*). **3.** *Archaic.* to express musically; sing. **4. to tune in.** to adjust (a radio or television receiving set) so as to receive a particular station, program, or signal. **5. to tune out.** to adjust a radio or television receiver so as to exclude (interference or a particular station or signal). **6. to tune up.** to bring musical instruments to a standard pitch (with *up*): *The orchestra was tuning up before the concert.* [Form of TONE.]

tune·ful (tōōn′fəl, tūn′-) *adj.* melodious; musical. —**tune′ful·ly,** *adv.* —**tune′ful·ness,** *n.*

tune·less (tōōn′lis, tūn′-) *adj.* having no musical quality.

tun·er (tōō′nər, tū′-) *n.* **1.** one who or that which tunes, esp. one employed to properly tune musical instruments: *a piano tuner.* **2.** part of a radio receiver that selects desired radio signals and directs them to an amplifier where they are converted into sound.

tune-up (tōōn′up′, tūn′-) *n.* adjustment, as of an engine, to the proper or most efficient working condition.

tung·sten (tung′stin) *n.* grayish, very hard, metallic element, most commonly used in making filaments for electric lamps and electron tubes. Symbol: **W** See **element** for table. [Swedish *tungsten,* from *tung* heavy + *sten* stone.]

Tun·gus (toon gōōz′) *pl.,* **-gus·es** *or* **-gus.** *n.* **1.** member of a people who live in central and eastern Siberia and in Manchuria. **2.** language of this people, belonging to the Ural-Altaic language family.

tu·nic (tōō′nik, tū′-) *n.* **1.** garment resembling a long shirt reaching to the knee or below, worn in ancient times by the Greeks and Romans. **2.** woman's garment resembling a blouse extending to the hips or below, often sleeveless and gathered at the waist. **3.** short, close-fitting jacket, often worn as part of a military or police uniform. **4.** loose membranous outer skin or covering, as of a plant or organ. [Latin *tunica* Roman shirtlike garment worn by both sexes; probably of Semitic origin.]

tu·ni·cate (tōō′nə kit, -kāt′, tū′-) *n.* seasquirt. —*adj.* **1.** of, relating, or belonging to the tunicates. **2.** having a tough outer covering, as a tunicate. **3.** *Botany.* having concentric coats or layers, as the bulb of an onion. [Latin *tunicātus,* past participle of *tunicāre* to clothe with a tunic, from *tunica.* See TUNIC.]

Tunic (def. 3)

tuning fork, two-pronged steel instrument that vibrates at a constant rate when struck, producing a tone of definite pitch. It is used in tuning certain musical instruments.

Tu·nis (tōō′nis, tū′-) *n.* **1.** capital, largest city, and chief port of Tunisia, in the northern part of the country. Pop. (1966 est.), 468,997. **2.** see **Tunisia.**

Tu·ni·sia (tōō nē′zhə, -nizh′ə, tū-) *n.* small country on the northern coast of Africa, on the Mediterranean, formerly known as Tunis. Capital, Tunis. Area, 63,379 sq. mi. Pop. (1969 est.), 5,027,000. —**Tu·ni′sian,** *adj.*

tun·nel (tun′əl) *n.* long, narrow, tubular passageway beneath the ground or under the main part of a structure: *a subway tunnel, a tunnel*

at; āpe; cär; end; mē; it; īce; hot; ōld; fôrk; wood; fōōl; oil; out; up; ūse; turn; sing; thin; this; zh in treasure; ə in ago, taken, pencil, lemon, circus.

through the side of a mountain. —*v.i.* -**neled, -nel·ing;** *also, British,* -**nelled, -nel·ling.** to make a passageway under or through something, as by digging: *to tunnel under a wall.* —*v.t.* **1.** to make by tunneling: *The prisoners tunneled an escape route.* **2.** to make a tunnel under, through, or in. [Old French *tonel* cask, diminutive of *tonne,* from Late Latin *tunna.* See TUN.] —**tun′nel·er;** *also, British,* **tun′nel·ler,** *n.*

tun·ny (tun′ē) *pl.* -**nies** or -**ny,** *n.* tuna. [French *thon,* through Provençal, from Latin *thunnus,* from Greek *thynnos.*]

tu·pe·lo (tōō′pə lō′, tū′-) *pl.* -**los.** *n.* any of a group of Asian and North American trees, genus *Nyssa,* bearing tiny greenish flowers that ripen into small fruits and having hard yellow or light-brown wood used to make flooring and crates. [Creek *ito opilwa* swamp tree.]

Tu·pi (tōō′pē, tōō′pē) *pl.* -**pis** or -**pi,** *n.* any of several South American Indian tribes living principally along the Amazon, the Brazilian coast, and in parts of Paraguay.

Tu·pi-Gua·ra·ni (tōō pē′gwär′ə nē′, tōō′pē-) *n.* South American Indian language family consisting of a number of languages that are spoken predominantly in Brazil, Paraguay, and parts of Argentina.

tup·pence (tup′əns) *n.* twopence.

tuque (tōōk, tük) *n.* knitted cap worn esp. in Canada. [French *tuque,* form of *toque* cap. See TOQUE.]

Tu·ra·ni·an (tōō rā′nē ən, tyōō-) *n.* **1.** Ural-Altaic language family that includes Finnish, Hungarian, and Turkish. **2.** one who speaks a language belonging to this language family.

tur·ban (tur′bən) *n.* **1.** head covering, worn esp. in Arab countries and India, consisting of a long scarf that is wound around the head or around a cap. **2.** any similar headdress, as a bandanna worn wound around the head by women. **3.** small, round hat having a little turned-up brim, or no brim at all, worn by women and children. [Middle French *turbant* an Oriental headdress, going back to Turkish *tülbend,* from Persian *dulband.* Doublet of TULIP.]

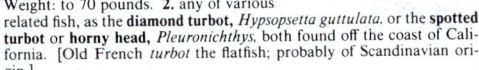

Turban *(def. 1)*

tur·baned (tur′bənd) *adj.* wearing a turban.

tur·bid (tur′bid) *adj.* **1.** thick with suspended matter; not clear; muddy. **2.** characterized by confusion or obscurity; muddled; disordered: *turbid emotions.* [Latin *turbidus,* from *turba* disturbance, crowd.] —**tur·bid′i·ty, tur′bid·ness,** *n.* —**tur′bid·ly,** *adv.*

tur·bi·nate (tur′bi nit, -nāt′) *adj.* **1.** shaped like an inverted cone. **2.** having a spiral shape, as certain shells; whorled. **3.** of or relating to certain scroll-shaped bones located in the nasal passages. —*n.* turbinate bone or shell. [Latin *turbinātus* shaped like a cone, from *turbō* whirling motion, top².]

tur·bine (tur′bin, -bīn) *n.* any of various motors and engines that uses the force of a steadily moving stream of gas, vapor, or liquid against slanted blades to turn a rotor. [French *turbine,* from Latin *turbō* whirling motion, top².]

turbo- *combining form* of, relating to, or operated by a turbine: *turbo-charger.* [From TURBINE.]

tur·bo·charg·er (tur′bō chär′jər) *n.* device that compresses the air entering an engine, as of a racing car, for the combustion of more fuel and production of more horsepower. It is often driven by the exhaust gases of the engine itself.

tur·bo·fan (tur′bō fan′) *n.* engine equipped with a fan that takes in large amounts of cold air and mixes it with hot exhaust gases from the combustion chamber, thus increasing the thrust.

tur·bo·jet (tur′bō jet′) *n.* **1.** jet propulsion engine in which air is taken in, compressed, mixed with fuel, and then ignited, producing hot, high-pressure gases that turn the turbine that drives the compressor. The hot exhaust provides thrust. **2.** airplane propelled by such an engine.

tur·bo·prop (tur′bō prop′) *n.* **1.** turbojet in which the power of the exhaust gases is used to drive a propeller. **2.** airplane propelled by such an engine. [TURBO- + PROP(ELLER).]

tur·bot (tur′bət) *pl.* -**bots** or -**bot.** *n.* **1.** large flatfish, *Rhombus maximus,* found along the European coast of the Atlantic and in the Black and Mediterranean seas, popular as a food fish. Weight: to 70 pounds. **2.** any of various related fish, as the **diamond turbot,** *Hypsopsetta guttulata,* or the **spotted turbot** or **horny head,** *Pleuronichthys,* both found off the coast of California. [Old French *turbot* the flatfish; probably of Scandinavian origin.]

Turbot

tur·bu·lence (tur′byə ləns) *n.* turbulent state or quality. Also, **tur′-bu·len·cy.**

tur·bu·lent (tur′byə lənt) *adj.* **1.** of, causing, or characterized by commotion, disorder, or violence; not calm or smooth; agitated: *a turbulent period of history. turbulent waters.* **2.** *Hydraulics.* characterized by small irregular disturbances or eddies; not moving in a steady, regular pattern. Opposed to **laminar.** [Latin *turbulentus* disturbed, from *turba* disturbance, crowd.]

tu·reen (tōō rēn′, tyōō-) *n.* deep dish with a cover, used for serving food, esp. soup, at the table. [French *terrine* earthen dish or pan, from Old French *terrin* earthen, going back to Latin *terra* earth.]

turf (turf) *pl.* **turfs.** *n.* **1.** grassy area; grassland. **2.** separate clump or clumps of grass and the earth around its roots, as for replanting. **3.** peat, esp. a piece used for fuel. **4.** *Informal.* anything, as a special status or position or a certain territory, that is jealously guarded and controlled by one person or group with challenges to any intrusions by outsiders. **5. the turf.** the sport of horse racing. [Old English *turf* sod, greensward.]

Tur·ge·nev, Ivan Ser·ge·e·vich (toor gā′nyəf; ser gā′yə vich) 1818–83, Russian novelist, short-story writer, and playwright.

tur·ges·cence (tur jes′əns) *n.* swollen or bloated condition.

tur·ges·cent (tur jes′ənt) *adj.* swollen; bloated. **2.** separate clump or present participle of *turgēscere* to begin to swell.]

tur·gid (tur′jid) *adj.* **1.** swollen or distended. **2.** pompous, as for serving language; grandiloquent. [Latin *turgidus.*] —**tur·gid′i·ty, tur′gid·ness,** *n.* —**tur′gid·ly,** *adv.*

Tu·rin (toor′ən, tyoor′-) *n.* city in northwestern Italy, on the Po River. Pop. (1968 est.), 1,142, 210. Also, **To·ri′no.**

Turk (turk) *n.* **1.** member or close descendant of the people of Turkey. **2.** one who speaks a Turkic language.

Turk. 1. Turkey. **2.** Turkish.

Tur·ke·stan (tur′ki stan′, -stän′) *n.* historic region of central Asia divided between the Soviet Union, China, and Afghanistan. It extends from the Caspian Sea to the Gobi desert, and is inhabited mainly by Turkic-speaking Muslims.

tur·key (tur′kē) *pl.* -**keys** or -**key.** *n.* **1.** any of various long-necked birds, family Meleagrididae, related to the pheasant, having a squarish tail and predominantly brown plumage, widely domesticated and raised for meat. Length: 4 feet including tail. **2.** flesh of a turkey used as food. **3.** *Slang.* unsuccessful artistic or dramatic production; flop. **4. to quit** (or **go) cold turkey.** to stop something abruptly, as the taking of an addicting drug. **5. to talk turkey.** *Informal.* to discuss practical matters in a direct, blunt manner. [From TURKEY; originally used as a name for the guinea fowl, probably because it was first brought to Europe through *Turkish* territory by merchants; later applied to an American bird that the early settlers mistakenly thought was the guinea fowl.]

Turkey

Tur·key (tur′kē) *n.* country in western Asia and southeastern Europe. Capital, Ankara. Area, 301,382 sq. mi. Pop. (1969 est.), 34,375,000.

turkey buzzard, brownish-black vulture, *Cathartes aura,* native to North, Central, and South America, having a bare, reddish head. Wingspan: to 6 feet.

turkey cock 1. male turkey. **2.** one who behaves in a conceited, strutting manner.

Turkey red 1. bright red. **2.** cotton cloth of this color.

turkey trot, social ragtime dance of the early twentieth century.

Tur·kic (tur′kik) *n.* any of various languages spoken by the Turks of Turkey, the Turkomans, and other Tartar tribes that, collectively, make up a branch of the Ural-Altaic language family.

Turk·ish (tur′kish) *adj.* of, relating to, or characteristic of Turkey, its people, their language, or their culture. —*n.* the language of the Turks, belonging to the Turkic branch of the Ural-Altaic language family.

Turkish bath, steam bath.

Turkish coffee, very strong beverage made with pulverized coffee, water, and sugar.

Turkish delight, gelatin candy, often cube-shaped, flavored with fruit and having nuts and a coating of powdered sugar.

Turkish Empire, Ottoman Empire.

Turkish towel *also,* **turkish towel.** thick towel of terry cloth.

Turk·men Republic *n.* southernmost republic of the Soviet Union, bordering Iran and Afghanistan. Area, approx. 188,450 sq. mi. Pop. (1965 est.), 1,862,000. Also, **Turk·me·nia** (turk mē′nē ə), **Turk·me·ni·stan** (turk′men ə stan′, -stän′).

Tur·ko·man (tur′kə mən) *pl.* -**mans.** *n.* **1.** member of any of several Turkish tribes living predominantly in the Turkmen Republic and in parts of Iran and Afghanistan. **2.** language of this people, belonging to the Turkic branch of the Ural-Altaic language family.

Tur·ku (toor′kōō) *n.* port city in southwestern Finland. Pop. (1967 est.), 146,992.

tur·mer·ic (tur′mər ik) *n.* **1.** yellow powder with a sharp, bitter taste obtained from the root of an Asian plant, *Curcuma longa*, used as a seasoning and as a coloring agent. **2.** the plant itself, bearing pale-yellow flowers. **3.** yellow, carrotlike root of this plant. [Earlier *tarmaret*, from French *terre mérite* the powder, saffron; literally, deserved or deserving earth (reason for the name not known); of uncertain origin.]

tur·moil (tur′moil) *n.* state or condition of confused agitation or commotion. [Possibly TUR(N) + MOIL.]

turn (turn) *v.i.* **1.** to move around on or as on an axis; rotate or revolve: *The earth turns. The chicken turns on a skewer as it roasts.* **2.** to move partly around in this way: *The plant turned toward the light. The key turned in the lock.* **3.** to change direction; go in a different direction: *We turned onto the highway. The river turns south at the bridge.* **4.** to change or reverse to the opposite direction: *Let's turn and go home. Soon our luck will turn.* **5.** to curve or bend: *The corners of the clown's mouth turned down.* **6.** to change in nature or condition: *The leaves turned yellow.* **7.** to become spoiled, rancid, or sour: *The milk turned.* **8.** to be transformed: *The snow turned to rain.* **9.** to change position in order to attack or resist (with *on* or *against*): *The animal turned on his trainer and mauled him.* **10.** to take on an attitude of hostility (with *on* or *against*): *His friends turned against him.* **11.** to direct one's effort or attention: *to turn to the job at hand, to turn away from his former pursuits.* **12.** to appeal or apply for help or support: *to turn to a friend, to turn to a book for information.* **13.** to direct one's affection or loyalty: *to turn away from a cause. You shouldn't turn away from all your old friends.* **14.** to be contingent; depend (with *on* or *upon*): *The senator's victory will turn on the urban vote.* **15.** to be or become dizzy or nauseated: *The ride on the ferris wheel made her head turn. His stomach turned at the sight of blood.* —*v.t.* **1.** to cause to revolve around on or as if on an axis, as a wheel. **2.** to cause to move partly around: *to turn a doorknob.* **3.** to do or perform by rotating or revolving, as a somersault. **4.** to change the course or direction of: *He turned the car to the left.* **5.** to cause to curve, curl, or bend: *Turn the edges down.* **6.** to twist or wrench: *to turn one's ankle. Bill turned up his nose.* **7.** to change the position of by or as by rotating: *to turn one's head toward the sun, to turn soil.* **8.** to reverse; invert: *to turn a record, to turn flapjacks on a griddle.* **9.** to change one's course so as to get to the other side of; go or get around or beyond: *to turn a corner.* **10.** to cause to change; transform: *to turn cream into butter. The frost turned the leaves orange.* **11.** to translate or rephrase: *to turn German into English.* **12.** to make spoiled, rancid, or sour: *The hot weather turned the meat.* **13.** to make sick; cause nausea or disgust in: *The food turned his stomach.* **14.** to direct; aim: *to turn a weapon on someone. He turned his energies to completing the job.* **15.** to send, esp. by force or pressure; drive: *to turn a horse out to pasture, to turn a beggar away.* **16.** to repel or deflect: *to turn a blow, to turn an enemy's charge.* **17.** to give, transfer, or return: *to turn over a business to one's son.* **18.** to use or employ; apply: *He turned their accusations to his advantage.* **19.** (of age, time, or amount) to be or have passed beyond: *He just turned thirty.* **20.** to shape by rotating against a cutting tool, as in a lathe.

to turn away. to refuse admission or entrance to: *Most of the crowd was turned away from the sellout performance.*

to turn down. a. to reject or refuse: *to turn down a request.* **b.** to lessen the volume or intensity: *to turn down a thermostat.* **c.** to fold over.

to turn in. *Informal.* **a.** to go to bed. **b.** to hand over, as to the police or other authority.

to turn on. a. to cause to flow, as water, gas, or electricity: *to turn on the hot water.* **b.** to cause to operate: *to turn on a lamp, to turn on charm.* **c.** *Slang.* to give great pleasure to; elate: *Bach turns me on.*

to turn out. a. to produce: *This machine turns out fifty copies per minute.* **b.** to assemble; show up; appear: *The whole town turned out for the parade.* **c.** to prove to have a certain result; end in a certain way: *How will the movie finally turn out?* **d.** to put out; extinguish: *to turn out a light.* **e.** to dismiss; discharge.

to turn over. a. (of an engine) to begin to operate or go through at least one complete cycle of operation. **b.** to buy and sell (merchandise). **c.** to invest and get back (capital). **d.** to do business to the amount of: *He turns over $5000 a month.*

to turn to. to begin to work: *The campers turned to and cleaned up their camping site.*

to turn up. a. to appear: *The stolen carvings turned up in a shop in Singapore.* **b.** to discover or ferret out: *The prosecutor turned up some new evidence.* **c.** to increase the volum. or intensity of: *to turn down a radio.*

—*n.* **1.** act or instance of turning: *Give the knob a turn.* **2.** change in position or direction: *the turn of the wind.* **3.** place of changing direction: *a turn in the highway.* **4.** time, occasion, or opportunity that follows another or others in due rotation: *It's his turn to bat.* **5.** act or

deed: *He did me a good turn.* **6.** one revolution or coil, as in a rope. **7.** inclination; aptitude; bent: *He has a turn for mathematics.* **8.** short walk or ride which includes a going and returning, esp. one in or around a limited area: *to take a turn through the countryside.* **9.** particular style, character, or quality: *There was a sarcastic turn to his voice.* **10.** change in condition or nature: *The victim took a turn for the worse and was now critically ill.* **11.** *Informal.* sudden shock or fright: *The explosion gave me quite a turn!* **12.** public appearance or performance; act. **13.** *Music.* melodic ornament or grace, usually consisting of a principal tone and the tones one degree above and below it. **14. at every turn,** in every instance; constantly. **15. by turns,** one after another; not all at once: *Grandpa was by turns a cowboy, farmer, and railroad engineer.* **16. in turn,** in proper sequence. **17. out of turn. a.** not in proper sequence; at the wrong time. **b.** *Informal.* improperly or impolitely: *Don't speak out of turn.* **18. to take turns,** to go in proper sequence. **19. to a turn,** perfectly. [Old English *turnian* to cause to revolve, from Latin *tornāre* to turn in a lathe, round off, from *tornus* lathe, from Greek *tornos*.]

turn·a·bout (tur′nə bout′) *n.* **1.** act of going or turning in a different or opposite direction. **2.** shift in opinion, policy, or loyalty.

turn·buck·le (turn′buk′əl) *n.* sleeve with internal threads that holds together the threaded ends of two rods and can be turned to widen or narrow the gap between the rod ends.

turn·coat (turn′kōt′) *n.* one who switches to the other side; traitor or renegade.

turn·down (turn′doun′) *adj.* folded over: *a turn-down collar.* —*n.* refusal or rejection.

turn·er (tur′nər) *n.* **1.** one who or that which turns. **2.** one who turns or fashions things on a lathe.

Tur·ner, Joseph M. W. (tur′nər) 1775–1851, English painter.

Turnbuckle

turning point, point at which a decisive or significant change takes place; critical point; crisis: *His election to the office of mayor was the turning point in his political career.*

tur·nip (tur′nip) *n.* **1.** edible white or yellow tuber of a plant, *Brassica rapa*, of the mustard family, cooked and eaten as a vegetable. **2.** the plant itself, bearing small bright-yellow flowers in clusters and soft prickly leaves. **3.** rutabaga. [Earlier *turnepe*, probably from TURN (from its rounded root) + *neep* turnip (from Old English *nap*, from Latin *nāpus* kind of turnip, probably from Greek *nāpu* mustard; of Egyptian origin).]

turn·key (turn′kē′) *pl.*, **-keys.** *n.* one who has charge of the keys of a prison or jail.

turn·off (turn′ôf′) *n.* **1.** act of turning off. **2.** exit leading off a main road to a side road.

turn·out (turn′out′) *n.* **1.** act of turning out. **2.** people who have assembled or gathered for some specific occasion: *There was a poor turnout for the school play because of the rainy weather.* **3.** production; output. **4.** section of a road that has been widened to enable vehicles to pass or park. **5.** railroad siding. **6.** carriage with its attendants, horse or horses, and harness.

turn·o·ver (turn′ō′vər) *n.* **1.** pie made by folding half the crust over a filling and upon the other half. **2.a.** number of employees who leave their jobs and are replaced by others during a given period. **b.** ratio of this to the total number of employees of a firm. **3.** number of times that the stock of goods of a firm is sold and replaced during a given period. **4.** total amount of business done in a given period: *Out of a turnover of $5000 for a week, his firm had a profit of $350.*

turn·pike (turn′pīk′) *n.* **1.** road, esp. an expressway, that has, or used to have, a toll gate. **2.** any highway, esp. an expressway. [TURN + PIKE², originally referring to a road barrier consisting of spikes attached to a frame that could be rotated to let people pass.]

turn·stile (turn′stīl′) *n.* revolving gate or movable bar at an exit or entrance, that permits persons to pass through one at a time.

turn·stone (turn′stōn′) *n.* any of several shorebirds, genus *Arenaria*, that breeds near the North Pole and winters along the coasts of the Atlantic and Pacific oceans, noted for flipping beach pebbles over with its bill when searching for food. Length: 9 inches.

turn·ta·ble (turn′tā′bəl) *n.* **1.** revolving structure used to turn things around, esp. a circular railroad platform with tracks used to turn locomotives or cars around. **2.** flat platform on a phonograph that revolves to play records rested upon it.

tur·pen·tine (tur′pən tīn′) *n.* **1.** sticky, viscous oleoresin secreted by certain species of pine trees. **2.** colorless, combustible liquid obtained by distilling this, widely used as a thinner for paints and as a solvent for polishes. Also *(def. 2),* oil of turpentine. [Old French *ter(e)bentine* an oleoresin, going back to Latin *terebinthus* a tree yielding an oleoresin, from Greek *terebinthos*.]

at; āpe; cär; end; mē; it; īce; hot; ōld; fôrk; wood; fōōl; oil; out; up; ūse; turn; sing; thin; this; zh in treasure; ə in ago, taken, pencil, lemon, circus.

tur·pi·tude (tur′pə tōōd′, -tūd′) *n.* **1.** shameful wickedness; depravity; baseness: *moral turpitude.* **2.** instance of this. [Latin *turpitūdō* baseness.]

tur·quoise (tur′kwoiz, -koiz) *n.* **1.** opaque mineral, usually greenish-blue, having a waxy luster and prized as a gem. **2.** greenish-blue color. [French *turquoise* the mineral, short for *pierre turquoise* Turkish stone: *turquoise,* from *turc* Turk, Turkish, from Turkish *Türk;* because it was first found in territory ruled by the Turks.]

tur·ret (tur′it) *n.* **1.** small tower, usually forming part of a larger structure. **2.** armored, usually revolving, structure used to house antiaircraft guns or cannons and their gunners, as on a ship or tank. **3.** strong, transparent plastic bubblelike structure on a military aircraft, used to protect the gunner. **4.** formerly, tower on wheels, used for attacking castles, forts, or walled towns. [Old French *t(o)urete* small tower, diminutive of *t(o)ur* tower. See TOWER.]

Turrets

tur·ret·ed (tur′i tid) *adj.* **1.** having a turret or turrets. **2.** having the shape of a turret. **3.** having long spiraled whorls, as certain sea shells.

tur·tle¹ (turt′əl) *n.* **1.** any of a group of reptiles, order Chelonia, found on land and in fresh and salt water, having a squat body enclosed in a hard, protective shell, and a toothless beak with sharp-edged jaws. On the average, turtles have a longer life span than any other vertebrate, some living to an age of 130 years. **2. to turn turtle.** to turn over; capsize. [Modification (influenced by TURTLE²) of French *tortue* turtle (reptile), tortoise, going back to Late Latin *tortūca* turtle, tortoise. See TORTOISE.]

Turtle

tur·tle² (turt′əl) *n. Archaic.* turtledove. [Old English *turtle,* going back to Latin *turtur;* imitative of the cooing of pigeons.]

tur·tle·back (turt′əl bak′) *n.* arched domelike structure built over the deck of a ship, esp. a steamer, at the bow and often at the stern as protection against heavy seas.

tur·tle·dove (turt′əl duv′) *n.* any of several small wild doves, noted for a soft, cooing call. [TURTLE² + DOVE¹.]

tur·tle·head (turt′əl hed′) *n.* any of various perennial North American herbs, genus Chelone, of the figwort family, having large, showy, usually white or purple flowers.

tur·tle·neck (turt′əl nek′) *n.* **1.** high, often turned-down collar that fits snugly around the neck. **2.** garment, esp. a sweater, having such a collar.

Tus·ca·loos·a (tus′kə lōō′sə) *n.* city in west-central Alabama. Pop. (1970), 65,773.

Tus·can (tus′kən) *adj.* **1.** of, relating to, or characteristic of Tuscany or its people. **2.** of, relating to, or designating an order of architecture characterized by columns that are not fluted, continuous friezes without triglyphs or metopes, and no ornamentation. —*n.* **1.** native or inhabitant of Tuscany. **2.** any of several Italian dialects spoken in Tuscany, esp. that spoken in Florence. **3.** standard literary form of the Italian language.

Tus·ca·ny (tus′kə nē) *n.* region in north-central Italy. Area, 8876 sq. mi. Pop. (1961), 3,286,160.

Tus·ca·ro·ra (tus′kə rôr′ə) *pl.,* **-ras** or **-ra.** *n.* member of a tribe of North American Iroquois Indians formerly living in what is now North Carolina, now living in New York.

tush¹ (tush) *interj.* exclamation expressing reproof, contempt, impatience, or disparagement. [Imitative.]

tush² (tush) *n.* tusk. [Old English *tūsc.*]

tusk (tusk) *n.* **1.** long, pointed, projecting tooth, usually one of a pair, of certain animals, as elephants, walruses, or wild boars. **2.** any long, pointed, projecting tooth or toothlike part. —*v.t.* to dig up or gore with the tusks. [Old English *tūx, tūsc* long, pointed, projecting tooth.]

Tusk

Tusks on an elephant

tusk·er (tus′kər) *n.* animal having well-developed tusks, esp. an elephant or wild boar.

tus·sah (tus′ə) *n.* **1.** coarse brownish or yellowish silk, used in making pongee and shantung. **2.** Asiatic silkworm that produces this silk.

[Hindi *tasar* shuttle, from Sanskrit *tasara;* possibly because of the shape of the cocoon.]

tus·sle (tus′əl) *n.* **1.** vigorous, disorderly physical fight or struggle; scuffle. **2.** any vigorous, disorderly conflict or struggle. —*v.i.* **-sled, -sling.** to engage in a vigorous, disorderly physical fight or struggle: *The man tussled with his attacker.* [Probably a form of TOUSLE.]

tus·sock (tus′ək) *n.* clump, tuft, or matted growth, as of hair or grass. [Of uncertain origin.]

tussock moth, any of a group of dull-colored destructive moths, as the gypsy moth, whose larvae are covered with thick tufts of hair.

tut (tut) *interj.* exclamation expressing impatience, contempt, annoyance, or rebuke.

Tut·ankh·a·men (tōō′tängk ä′mən) *n.* pharaoh of Egypt in about the middle of the fourteenth century B.C.

tu·te·lage (tōōt′əl ij, tūt′-) *n.* **1.** office or function of a guardian; guardianship. **2.** act of teaching; instruction. **3.** state of being under a tutor or guardian. [Latin *tūtēla,* protection + -AGE.]

tu·te·lar·y (tōōt′əl er′ē, tūt′-) *adj. also,* **tu·te·lar** (tōōt′əl ər, tūt′-). **1.** having the position of a guardian; protective: *a tutelary goddess.* **2.** of or relating to a guardian: *tutelary powers.* —*n. pl.,* **-lar·ies.** deity, saint, spirit, or person having tutelary powers. [Latin *tūtēlārius* guardian, from *tūtēla* watching, protection.]

tu·tor (tōō′tər, tū′-) *n.* **1.** teacher or other person who gives private instruction to a student. **2.** *British.* college official who supervises and advises undergraduate students assigned to him. —*v.t.* **1.** to act as a tutor to, esp. by giving private instruction: *He is tutoring to pass his final exams.* **2.** to act or work as a private instructor: *For extra money, she tutors on weekends.* —*v.i.* **1.** to be instructed by a tutor: *He is tutoring to pass his final exams.* **2.** to act or work as a private instructor: *For extra money, she tutors on weekends.* [Latin *tūtor* guardian.]

tu·to·ri·al (tōō tôr′ē əl, tū-) *adj.* of, relating to, or involving a private instructor or instruction: *The school had an afternoon tutorial program.* —*n.* class or session instructed by a tutor for one student or a small group of students.

tu·tor·ship (tōō′tər ship′, tū′-) *n.* position or duties of a tutor.

tut·ti-frut·ti (tōō′tē frōō′tē) *adj.* containing or made with various candied fruits or fruit flavorings: *tutti-frutti ice cream.* [Italian *tutti frutti* literally, all fruits, going back to Latin *tōtus* all + *frūctus* produce, fruit.]

Tutu

tu·tu (tōō′tōō) *n.* very short, full skirt consisting of many layers of sheer fabric, worn by ballerinas. [French *tutu,* from *tutu* backside, baby-talk, modification of *cul* backside, bottom, from Latin *cūlus* backside.]

Tu·tu·i·la (tōō′tōō ē′lä) *n.* principal island of American Samoa. Area, 54 sq. mi.

tux (tuks) *n. Informal.* tuxedo.

tux·e·do (tuk sē′dō) *pl.,* **-dos.** *also,* **Tux·e·do.** *n.* man's formal suit, usually dark in color, having a jacket without tails and trousers with a single stripe of satin or similar material along the outer side of each leg. [From *Tuxedo* Park, N.Y., exclusive community of wealthy families in the nineteenth century, where this suit originated.]

tu·yère (twē yer′, tōō-, twēr′) *n.* nozzle through which air is blown into a blast furnace. [French *tuyère,* from *tuyau* pipe; of Germanic origin.]

TV, television.

TVA, Tennessee Valley Authority, an independent agency of the U.S. government established in 1933 for water control and development of resources, esp. electrical power, along the Tennessee River and its major tributaries in several southern states.

TV dinner, prepared meal frozen in an aluminum tray, needing only to be heated before being served.

twad·dle (twod′əl) *n.* silly or idle talk; prattle. —*v.i.* **-dled, -dling.** to talk in a childish or foolish manner. [Probably a modification of earlier *twattle,* possibly a blend of TWIDDLE and TATTLE.] —*twad′dler,* *n.*

Tuxedo

twain (twān) *n., adj. Archaic.* two. [Old English *twēgen.*]

Twain, Mark (twān) 1835–1910, U.S. author and humorist; born Samuel Langhorne Clemens.

twang (twang) *n.* **1.** sharp, reverberating, ringing sound, as that made

by plucking a string on a musical instrument. **2.** sharp, nasal tone of voice. —*v.i.* **1.** to make a sharp, reverberating, ringing sound: *The rubber band twanged when it broke.* **2.** to have a sharp, nasal tone of voice. —*v.t.* **1.** to cause to make a sharp, reverberating sound. **2.** to utter with a sharp, nasal tone of voice. [Imitative of the sound of a plucked string.]

'twas (twuz, twoz; *unstressed* twəz) it was.

tweak (twēk) *v.t.* to pinch and pull sharply with a twisting motion. —*n.* sharp, twisting pinch. [Probably modification of dialectal English *twick* to pull sharply, from Old English *twiccian.*]

tweed (twēd) *n.* **1.** rough fabric, made esp. of wool, woven with yarns of two or more colors. **2. tweeds.** clothes made of this fabric. [Modification (influenced by *Tweed*, a Scottish river passing through a region noted for manufacturing this cloth) of Scottish *tweel*, form of TWILL.]

twee·dle·dum and twee·dle·dee (twēd′əl dum′ ən twēd′əl dē′) two persons or things between which there is only the least possible distinction. [From earlier *tweedle* to play a musical instrument, pipe (of imitative origin) + *-dee, -dum,* syllables suggesting musical sounds; first used to designate two rival musicians.]

'tween (twēn) *prep.* between.

tweet (twēt) *n.* thin, chirping sound, as that made by a bird. —*v.i.* to utter a tweet or tweets: *The birds were tweeting outside the window.* [Imitative.]

tweet·er (twē′tər) *n.* loudspeaker designed to reproduce high-frequency sound. Distinguished from **woofer.** [TWEET + -ER¹.]

tweeze (twēz) **tweezed, tweez·ing.** *v.t.* to pluck with tweezers. [From TWEEZERS.]

tweez·ers (twē′zərz) *n.,pl.* small pincers for plucking out hairs or for picking up tiny objects. [Modification (influenced by words like PLIERS, SCISSORS) of obsolete *tweeze* case for instruments, going back to French *étui* case², from Old French *estuier* to keep, put in, shut up, possibly going back to Latin *studium* zeal, application to learning.]

twelfth (twelfth) *adj.* **1.** (the ordinal of twelve) next after the eleventh. **2.** being one of twelve equal parts. —*n.* **1.** that which is next after the eleventh. **2.** one of twelve equal parts; ¹/₁₂.

Twelfth day, the twelfth day after Christmas, on which the Epiphany is celebrated. January 6. Formerly it marked the end of the Christmas season.

Twelfth night, the evening of, or the night before, Twelfth day.

twelve (twelv) *n.* **1.** the cardinal number that is one more than eleven. **2.** symbol representing this number, as 12 or XII. **3.** something having this many units or members. **4. the Twelve.** the twelve disciples of Jesus chosen by Him to preach His gospel. They were Peter, James the Great, John, Andrew, Thomas, James the Less, Jude, Philip, Bartholomew, Matthew, Simon, and Judas Iscariot. Also, **the Twelve Apostles.** —*adj.* numbering one more than eleven. [Old English *twelf.*]

twelve·fold (twelv′fōld′) *adj.* **1.** twelve times as great or numerous. **2.** having or consisting of twelve parts. —*adv.* so as to be twelve times greater or more numerous.

twelve·mo (twelv′mō) *pl.* **-mos.** *n.* duodecimo. —*adj.* duodecimo.

twelve·month (twelv′munth′) *n.* period of twelve months; year.

Twelve Tables, earliest Roman legal code and the foundation of Roman jurisprudence, drawn up in 451 B.C.

twelve-tone (twelv′tōn′) *adj. Music.* of, relating to, or written according to the technique of composition based on the successive repetition of the twelve tones of the chromatic scale without emphasis on any particular key or tonality.

twen·ti·eth (twen′tē ith) *adj.* **1.** (the ordinal of twenty) next after the nineteenth. **2.** being one of twenty equal parts. —*n.* **1.** that which is next after the nineteenth. **2.** one of twenty equal parts; ¹/₂₀.

twen·ty (twen′tē) *pl.* **-ties.** *n.* **1.** the cardinal number that is two times ten. **2.** symbol representing this number, as 20 or XX. **3.** something having this many units or members. **4. the twenties.** number series from twenty through twenty-nine. ▲ used esp. in reference to the second decade of a century or of a person's life. —*adj.* numbering twice ten. [Old English *twentig.*]

twen·ty·fold (twen′tē fōld′) *adj.* **1.** twenty times as great or numerous. **2.** having or consisting of twenty parts. —*adv.* so as to be twenty times greater or more numerous.

twen·ty-one (twen′tē wun′) *n.* the card game blackjack.

twerp (twurp) *also,* **twirp.** *n. Slang.* small, annoying, self-important person. [Of uncertain origin.]

twice (twīs) *adv.* **1.** on two occasions or in two instances; two times: *He called twice.* **2.** doubly: *twice as many.* [Old English *twiges* two (successive) times, from *twiga* two times.]

twice-told (twīs′tōld′) *adj.* having been told two times: *a twice-told tale.*

twid·dle (twid′əl) **-dled, -dling.** *v.t.* **1.** to turn or twirl (something) idly: *to twiddle a locket on a chain.* **2.** to twiddle one's thumbs. **a.** to twirl one's thumbs idly about each other, esp. to indicate boredom. **b.** to do nothing; be idle and bored. —*v.i.* **1.** to play with something in an idle

manner. **2.** to be busy about trifles. —*n.* light, twirling motion, as of the thumbs. [Of uncertain origin.]

twig (twig) *n.* small branch or shoot of a tree or other woody plant. [Old English *twigge.*]

twi·light (twī′līt′) *n.* **1.** soft, hazy light reflected from the sun just after sunset and, sometimes, just before sunrise. **2.** period during which this light prevails. **3.** any soft, faint light. **4.** period or condition marked by the decline of glory, success, achievement, or the like: *the twilight of one's life.* —*adj.* of, relating to, or occurring at twilight. [Middle English *twilight* the light reflected from the sun after sunset and before sunrise, the period during which this light prevails, from *twi-* two, twice (from Old English *twi-*) + LIGHT¹.]

twilight sleep, semiconscious condition produced by the hypodermic injection of scopolamine and morphine, used to reduce the pains of childbirth.

twill (twil) *n.* **1.** weave characterized by parallel diagonal ridges. **2.** strong, durable fabric having such a weave. [Old English *twilted* twilled cloth, partial translation of Latin *bilix* with a double thread, from *bi-* two + *licium* thread (Old English *twi-* two being substituted for *bi-*); because woven by doubling the warp threads.]

twilled (twild) *adj.* woven with parallel diagonal ridges on the surface.

Twill

twin (twin) *n.* **1.** one of two offspring born at one birth. **2.** either of two persons, animals, or things that are similar or identical; mate. —*adj.* **1.** being two or one of two born at one birth: *She gave birth to twin boys. Her twin brother is five minutes older than she.* **2.** having, forming, or being one of two things that are similar or identical. —*v.i.,* **twinned, twin·ning.** to give birth to twins. [Old English *twinn* twofold, double.]

Twin Cities, Minneapolis and St. Paul.

twine (twīn) *n.* **1.** strong string or cord composed of two or more strands twisted together. **2.** something formed by twisting two or more strands, threads, or the like together. —*v.t.* **twined, twin·ing. 1.** to twist together. **2.** to form by twisting together. **3.** to wind or coil (something) around something else: *We twined the ivy around the trellis.* **4.** to cover or wrap in this way: *to twine a pole with ribbons.* —*v.i.* **1.** to extend, proceed, or grow in a winding manner or course: *Ivy twined over the walls.* [Old English *twīn* linen, twisted thread.]

twinge (twinj) *n.* **1.** sudden, sharp pain: *a twinge of arthritis.* **2.** sudden, sharp feeling of mental or emotional distress: *a twinge of conscience.* —*v.t., v.i.* **twinged, twing·ing.** to feel or cause to feel a twinge. [Old English *twengan* to pinch.]

twi·night (twī′nīt′) *adj. Baseball.* designating a double-header in which the first game is played in the late afternoon and the second game is played in the evening under artificial light. [TWI(LIGHT) + NIGHT.]

twin·kle (twing′kəl) **-kled, -kling.** *v.i.* **1.** to shine with or emit flashes of light: *The stars twinkled in the sky. The lights on the distant boats twinkled in the night.* **2.** (of the eyes) to be bright, as with amusement or pleasure. **3.** to move lightly and quickly. **4.** *Archaic.* to wink; blink. —*n.* **1.** flicker or flash of light. **2.** brightness of the eyes, as in amusement or pleasure. **3.** very brief period of time; twinkling. [Old English *twinclian* to sparkle, glitter.]

twin·kling (twing′kling) *n.* **1.** very brief period of time; moment; instant. **2.** act of shining with or emitting flashes of light. **3.** flicker or flash of light; twinkle.

twin-screw (twin′skrōō′) *adj.* having two screw propellers, esp. ones that revolve in opposite directions, as certain ships.

twirl (twurl) *v.t., v.i.* **1.** to rotate or cause to rotate rapidly on or as on an axis. **2.** *Baseball. Slang.* to pitch. —*n.* **1.** act of twirling; being twirled. **2.** something having a curled or spiral shape. [Possibly a blend of TWIST and WHIRL.] —**twirl′er,** *n.*

twirp (twurp) twerp.

twist (twist) *v.t.* **1.** to wind (two or more strands, threads, or the like) around each other. **2.** to make or form in this way. **3.** to combine closely. **4.** to form into a spiral, as by turning the ends in opposite directions. **5.** to change the natural or usual shape or position of; contort; distort. **6.** to injure a part of the body in this way; sprain: *He fell and twisted his ankle.* **7.** to change or distort the meaning of: *She was always twisting my words.* **8.** to cause (a ball) to spin while moving in a curved direction. —*v.i.* **1.** to turn so as to face in a different direction. **2.** to move in or follow a winding course: *The new highway twists through the mountains.* **3.** to move in a circle or spiral; rotate. **4.** to writhe; squirm. **5.** to become sprained. **6.** to admit of being wound: *This thin wire will twist easily.* —*n.* **1.** curve, bend, or turn: *There is a twist in the road up ahead.* **2.** act of twisting; being twisted; rotation. **3.** something having a curled or spiral shape. **4.** unexpected change in or deviation from the usual or ordinary. **5.** peculiar or eccentric bent, inclination, or attitude: *His mind had a sadistic twist.* **6.** in certain games, spinning motion given

at; āpe; cär; end; mē; it; īce; hot; ōld; fôrk; wood; fōōl; oil; out; up; ūse; turn; sing; thin; this; zh in treasure; ə in ago, taken, pencil, lemon, circus.

to a ball in striking or throwing it in a particular way. **7.** thread, cord, or rope made of two or more strands that are twisted together. [Old English *-twist* rope (as in the compound *mæst-twist* a rope to support a mast[1].] —**Syn.** *v.t.* **5.** see **bend**[1].

twist·er (twis'tər) *n.* **1.** one who or that which twists. **2.** *Informal.* tornado.

twit (twit) *twit·ted, twit·ting. v.t.* to tease or taunt, esp. by reminding of past errors or embarrassments. —*n.* reproach; taunt. [Short for obsolete *atwite* to reproach, from Old English *ætwītan*.]

twitch (twich) *v.i.* to move with a sudden, involuntary jerk. —*v.t.* to pull with an abrupt tug or jerk. —*n.* **1.** sudden, involuntary muscle contraction: *I have a twitch in my left eye.* **2.** sudden, sharp pull or tug; jerk. [Probably from an unrecorded Old English word.]

twit·ter (twit'ər) *n.* **1.** series of short, light, chirping sounds, made by birds. **2.** state or condition of nervous agitation or excitement. ▲ used chiefly in the phrase *in a twitter: She's always in a twitter before a party.* —*v.i.* **1.** to utter a series of light, chirping sounds, as a bird. **2.** to laugh in a nervous or restrained manner; titter. **3.** to be in a state of nervous agitation or excitement. —*v.t.* to utter or express with a twitter. [Imitative.]

twixt (twikst) *also,* **'twixt.** *prep.* between; betwixt.

two (tōō) *pl.,* **twos.** *n.* **1.** the cardinal number that is one more than one. **2.** symbol representing this number, as 2 or II. **3.** something having this many units or members, as a playing card. **4. in two.** in or into two parts or pieces. **5. to put two and two together.** to come to the obvious conclusion after considering the facts. —*adj.* numbering one more than one. [Old English *twā.*]

two-base hit *n.* double *(def. 4).* Also, **two'-bag'ger.**

two-bit (tōō'bit') *adj. Slang.* of little worth or value; cheap.

two bits *Informal.* twenty-five cents; quarter.

two-by-four (tōō'bī fôr', -bə-) *n.* **1.** rough piece of lumber measuring two inches by four inches, used esp. in building. **2.** finished piece of lumber measuring 1⅝ by 3⅝ inches, used esp. in building. —*adj.* **1.** measuring two units by four units, as two inches by four inches. **2.** *Informal.* very small or insignificant.

two-edged (tōō'ejd') *adj.* **1.** having two edges, esp. two cutting edges: *a two-edged sword.* **2.** having two meanings, interpretations, effects, or implications: *a two-edged compliment.*

two-faced (tōō'fāst') *adj.* **1.** having two faces or aspects. **2.** deceitful; hypocritical.

two-fist·ed (tōō'fis'tid) *adj.* powerful; strong.

two-fold (tōō'fōld') *adj.* **1.** two times as great or as numerous. **2.** having or consisting of two parts. —*adv.* so as to be two times greater or more numerous.

two-hand·ed (tōō'han'did) *adj.* **1.** having two hands. **2.** involving or requiring the use of both hands at the same time: *a two-handed sword.* **3.** intended for use by two persons: *a two-handed saw.* **4.** involving or intended for two persons: *a two-handed card game.* **5.** using both hands equally well; ambidextrous.

two-pence (tup'əns) *also,* **tup.pence.** *n.* sum of money and coin equal to two British pennies; two pence.

two-pen·ny (tup'ə nē) *adj.* **1.** having the value of or equal to twopence. **2.** of very little value; trifling; worthless.

two-ply (tōō'plī') *adj.* **1.** composed or consisting of two layers, thicknesses, or strands. **2.** consisting of two webs woven into each other: *a two-ply carpet.*

two-some (tōō'səm) *n.* **1.** two persons together; couple. **2.a.** round of golf played by two people. **b.** the players.

two-step (tōō'step') *n.* **1.** ballroom dance consisting of sliding steps in 2/4 time. **2.** music for such a dance.

two-time (tōō'tīm') *-timed, -tim·ing. v.t. Slang.* to be unfaithful to or deceive, esp. in love. —**two'-tim'er,** *n.*

two-way (tōō'wā') *adj.* **1.** moving or allowing movement in two directions: *two-way traffic, a two-way street.* **2.** allowing communication in two directions, esp. by having the capacity to transmit and receive: *a two-way radio.*

-ty[1] *suffix* multiplied by ten: *twenty, thirty.* [Old English *-tig.*]

-ty[2] *suffix* (used to form nouns) state, condition, or quality of being: *safety.* [Old French *-te, -tet,* from Latin *-tās.*]

ty·coon (tī kōōn') *n.* **1.** wealthy, powerful businessman, industrialist, or financier. **2.** shogun. [Japanese *taikun* shogun, from Chinese (Mandarin) *ta* great + *chün* ruler.]

ty·ing (tī'ing) present participle of **tie.**

tyke (tīk) *also,* **tike.** *n.* **1.** *Informal.* small child, esp. one who is mischievous. **2.** mongrel dog; cur. [Old Norse *tík* bitch.]

Ty·ler (tī'lər) **1. John.** 1790–1862, tenth president of the United States, from 1841 to 1845. **2.** city in eastern Texas. Pop. (1970), 57,770.

tym·bal (tim'bəl) *n.* timbal.

tym·pan (tim'pən) *n.* **1.** frame on which paper is placed in a hand printing press. **2.** membranelike sheet or plate of some thin material, tightly stretched over an apparatus, as a drum. **3.** *Architecture.* tym-

panum. [Latin *tympanum* drum, from Greek *tympanon* kettledrum.]

tym·pa·ni (tim'pə nē) timpani.

tym·pan·ic (tim pan'ik) *adj.* **1.** of or relating to the eardrum or the middle ear. **2.** relating to or resembling a drum.

tympanic membrane, thin membrane that separates the external ear from the middle ear; eardrum.

tym·pa·nist (tim'pə nist) *n.* member of an orchestra who plays a kettledrum and, usually, other percussion instruments.

tym·pa·num (tim'pə nəm) *pl.,* **-nums** or **-na** (-nə). *n.* **1.** eardrum. **2.** middle ear. **3.** *Architecture.* **a.** recessed, often ornamented, triangular space forming the central panel of a pediment. **b.** space enclosed by an arch, as over a doorway or window. Also *(def. 3),* **tym'pan.** [Latin *tympanum* drum, from Greek *tympanon* kettledrum.]

Tyn·dale, William (tind'əl) c.1492–1536, English Protestant reformer and translator of the Bible.

Tyn·dall effect (tind'əl) phenomenon in which a light beam becomes visible when passing through air or solution that contains suspended particles, but is invisible when passing through clean air or pure solution. [From John *Tyndall,* 1820–93, Irish physicist who discovered it.]

type (tīp) *n.* **1.** particular kind, class, or group sharing certain common traits or characteristics. ▲ Although *type* is usually followed by *of,* as in *a new type of automobile engine,* in informal speech and writing, the *of* is sometimes omitted, as in *a new type automobile engine.* **2.** one who or that which exhibits the characteristic qualities of a kind, class, or group; typical or perfect example. **3.** general form, structure, style, or character that distinguishes or characterizes a particular kind, class, or group. **4.a.** rectangular piece or block of metal or wood on one surface of which there is a raised letter, numeral, or other symbol that forms a printing surface. **b.** such pieces or blocks collectively. **5.** printed or typewritten character or characters. **6.** design or other device on either side of a coin or medal. **7.** blood type. **8.** *Informal.* person regarded as embodying all the characteristics of a particular profession, social group, way of life, or the like: *John says one can usually pick out the executive types by the way they dress.* —*v.t.,* **typed, typ·ing. 1.** to write (something) on a typewriter: *to type a letter.* **2.** to identify or determine the type of (a blood sample). **3.** to place in a particular class or group. **4.** to represent; typify. —*v.i.* to write on a typewriter. [Latin *typus* image, figure, form, from Greek *typos* impression, model, image, form, stamp.] —**Syn.** *n.* **1.** see **kind**[2].

type·cast (tīp'kast') *v.t.* **1.** to cast (an actor) in a role that is particularly suited to his own personality, physical appearance, and the like. **2.** to cast (an actor) repeatedly in the same type of role.

type·face (tīp'fās') *n. Printing.* face.

type·script (tīp'skript') *n.* material that has been typewritten.

type·set·ter (tīp'set'ər) *n.* **1.** person who sets type for printing. **2.** machine that sets type for printing.

type·set·ting (tīp'set'ing) *n.* act or process of setting type for printing. —*adj.* used or adapted for setting type: *a typesetting machine.*

type·write (tīp'rīt') *-wrote, -writ·ten, -writ·ing. v.t., v.i.* to write (something) with a typewriter; type.

type·writ·er (tīp'rī'tər) *n.* **1.** machine used to produce clear, printlike writing, consisting of a set of keys that, when struck, impress letters on paper through an ink-soaked ribbon. **2.** typist.

type·writ·ing (tīp'rī'ting) *n.* **1.** act or process of using a typewriter. **2.** that which is done or produced on a typewriter.

Typewriter

ty·phoid (tī'foid) *n.* typhoid fever. —*adj.* of, relating to, resembling, or characteristic of typhoid fever. [TYPH(US) + -OID.]

typhoid bacillus, bacterium that causes typhoid fever, usually found in the intestine of one who carries or is infected with the disease.

typhoid fever, infectious, sometimes fatal fever characterized by intestinal inflammation and rose-colored spots on the skin, caused by a bacillus taken into the body with food or drink. People can be inoculated with a vaccine against typhoid fever.

ty·phoon (tī fōōn') *n.* severe tropical hurricane occurring in the western Pacific Ocean chiefly during the months of July, August, September, and October. [Chinese (Cantonese) *tai fung* literally, great wind; influenced by Greek *typhōn* whirlwind.]

ty·phus (tī'fəs) *n.* any of a group of acute infectious diseases characterized by severe headache, high fever, and a spotted rash, caused by germs carried by fleas or lice. [Modern Latin *typhus,* from Greek *typhos* a fever.]

typ·i·cal (tip'i kəl) *adj.* **1.** conforming to, exhibiting, or indicating the character, qualities, attributes, or nature characteristic or peculiar to a particular type: *a typical small-town high school.* **2.** of the nature of or constituting a type. —**typ'i·cal·ly,** *adv.*

---

at; āpe; cär; end; mē; it; īce; hot; ōld; fôrk; wood; fōōl; oil; out; up; ūse; turn; sing; thin; this; zh in treasure; ə in ago, taken, pencil, lemon, circus.

Syn. 1. Typical, natural, normal mean conforming to some standard or pattern. **Typical** stresses the detail or particular that characterizes, distinguishes, or exemplifies a pattern or group: *That sarcastic remark is typical of his attitude.* **Natural** stresses the harmony of the particular detail with the whole: *It was natural for a man as kind as he to respond with such generosity.* **Normal** suggests that what is common to a group is accepted as a standard of judgment: *If this is her normal manner, I wonder what she's like when she's really angry.*

typ·i·fy (tip′ə fī′) **-fied, -fy·ing.** *v.t.* **1.** to embody or exhibit the common or usual characteristics of; be typical of; exemplify. **2.** to serve as a symbol of; represent; symbolize. [Latin *typus* image + -FY. See TYPE.] —**typ′i·fi·ca′tion,** *n.*

typ·ist (tī′pist) *n.* one who types, esp. one whose occupation is operating a typewriter.

ty·po (tī′pō) *pl.,* **-pos.** *n. Informal.* typographical error.

ty·pog·ra·pher (tī pog′rə fər) *n.* printer *(def. 1).*

ty·po·graph·i·cal (tī′pə graf′i kəl) *adj.* of or relating to typography: *a typographical error.* Also, **ty′po·graph′ic.** —**ty′po·graph′i·cal·ly,** *adv.*

ty·pog·ra·phy (tī pog′rə fē) *n.* **1.** act, art, or process of producing printed matter, esp. by means of a printing press. **2.** arrangement, appearance, or style of printed matter. [Modern Latin *typographia,* from Greek *typos* impression, stamp + -GRAPHY.]

Tyr (tēr) *n.* Norse god of war, a son of Odin.

ty·ran·ni·cal (ti ran′i kəl, tī-) *adj.* of, relating to, or characteristic of a tyrant; cruel and unjust. Also, **ty·ran′nic.** [Latin *tyrannicus* (from Greek *tyrannikos,* from *tyrannos* absolute ruler) + -AL¹.] —**ty·ran′ni·cal·ly,** *adv.*

ty·ran·ni·cide¹ (ti ran′ə sīd′, tī-) *n.* act of killing a tyrant. [Latin *tyrannicīdium,* from *tyrannus* despot + -cīdium. See TYRANT, -CIDE¹.]

ty·ran·ni·cide² (ti ran′ə sīd′, tī-) *n.* one who kills a tyrant. [Latin *tyrannicīda,* from *tyrannus* despot + -cīda. See TYRANT, -CIDE².]

tyr·an·nize (tir′ə nīz′) **-nized, -niz·ing.** *v.i.* **1.** to exercise power in a cruel and unjust way (often with *over*): *The great were not allowed to tyrannize over the poor* (Sharpe, 1846). **2.** to rule as a tyrant. —*v.t.* to treat or govern tyrannically.

ty·ran·no·saur (ti ran′ə sôr′, tī-) *n.* huge carnivorous dinosaur, *Tyrannosaurus rex,* found in North America during the Cretaceous period. Also, **ty·ran′no·sau′rus.** [Modern Latin *Tyrannosaurus,* from Greek *tyrannos* absolute ruler + *sauros* lizard.]

tyr·an·nous (tir′ə nəs) *adj.* cruel and unjust; despotic; tyrannical. —**tyr′an·nous·ly,** *adv.*

tyr·an·ny (tir′ə nē) *pl.,* **-nies.** *n.* **1.** arbitrary or oppressive exercise of power; cruel and unjust use of force or authority. **2.** in ancient Greece, office of or government by a tyrant. **3.** any oppressive or unjustly severe rule or government by one person; despotism. **4.** harshness; severity. **5.** tyrannical act. [Late Latin *tyrannia* tyrannical conduct, despotic rule, from Latin *tyrannus* ruler, despot. See TYRANT.]

ty·rant (tī′rənt) *n.* **1.** one who exercises power or authority in a cruel and unjust manner. **2.** one who has absolute power and rules or governs in a cruel and unjust manner; absolute ruler; despot. **3.** in ancient Greece, an absolute ruler who obtained his authority illegally. [Old French *tyrant, tiran* despot, from Latin *tyrannus* ruler, despot, from Greek *tyrannos* absolute ruler.]

tyre (tīr) *British.* tire².

Tyre (tīr) *n.* principal city of Phoenicia and important commercial center of the ancient world, on the Mediterranean Sea.

Tyr·i·an (tir′ē ən) *adj.* of or relating to ancient Tyre or its people.

Tyrian purple 1. highly valued crimson or purple dye used in ancient times, derived from certain mollusks found in the Mediterranean. **2.** purplish-red color.

ty·ro (tī′rō) *pl.,* **-ros.** *also,* **ti·ro.** *n.* one who is just beginning to learn or do something; beginner; novice. [Latin *tīrō* recruit, beginner.]

Ty·rol (tir′ol, tī′rōl, ti rōl′) *also,* **Ti·rol.** *n.* region in western Austria, in the Alps, bordering Italy, Germany, and Switzerland. Area, 4883 sq. mi. Pop. (1961), 462,899.

Tyr·o·lese (tir′ə lēz′, -lēs′) *also,* **Tir·o·lese.** *adj.* of or relating to the Tyrol or its inhabitants. —*n. pl.,* **-lese.** native or inhabitant of the Tyrol.

Tyr·rhe·ni·an Sea (ti rē′nē ən) part of the Mediterranean between Italy, Sicily, Sardinia, and Corsica.

tzar (zär, tsär) czar.

tzar·e·vitch (zär′ə vich, tsär′-) czarevitch.

tza·rev·na (zä rev′nə, tsä-) czarevna.

tza·ri·na (zä rē′nə, tsä-) czarina.

tzar·ism (zär′iz′əm, tsär′-) czarism.

tzar·ist (zär′ist, tsär′-) czarist.

tzet·ze fly (tset′sē, tsĕt′-) tsetse fly. Also, **tzet′ze.**

at; āpe; cär; end; mē; it; īce; hot; ōld; fôrk; wood; fōōl; oil; out; up; ūse; turn; sing; thin; this; zh in treasure; ə in ago, taken, pencil, lemon, circus.

u, U (ū) *pl.,* **u's, U's.** *n.* **1.** twenty-first letter of the English alphabet. **2.** shape of this letter or something having such a shape.

U, uranium.

U. **1.** University. **2.** Upper.

UAR, United Arab Republic.

UAW, United Automobile Workers (of America).

U·ban·gi (ū bang'gē, ōō bang'-) *pl.,* **-gis** or **-gi.** *n.* **1.** river in central Africa, a major tributary of the Congo River. **2.** member of any of various Negro tribes living near this river in the Central African Republic.

u·biq·ui·tous (ū bik'wə təs) *adj.* being or seeming to be everywhere at once: *a ubiquitous aroma, ubiquitous spies and officials.* [UBIQUITY + -OUS.] —**u·biq'ui·tous·ly,** *adv.* —**u·biq'ui·tous·ness,** *n.*

u·biq·ui·ty (ū bik'wə tē) *n.* state or capacity of being or seeming to be everywhere at once. [French *ubiquité,* from Latin *ubīque* everywhere.]

U-boat (ū'bōt') *n.* German submarine, esp. one used in World War I or II. [German *U-boot,* short for *Unterseeboot* submarine; literally, undersea boat.]

U-bolt (ū'bōlt') *also,* **U bolt.** *n.* U-shaped bolt fitted with threads and a nut at each end.

u.c. *Printing.* upper case.

ud·der (ud'ər) *n.* large sac hanging from the underside of certain female animals, as cows or ewes, and holding one or more milk-producing glands, each with a teat or nipple for suckling offspring. [Old English *ūder.*]

u·dom·e·ter (ū dom'ə tər) *n.* rain gauge. [Latin *ūdus* wet + -METER.]

UFO, unidentified flying object.

U·gan·da (ū gan'də, ōō gan'-) *n.* country in east-central Africa. Capital, Kampala. Area, 91,134 sq. mi. Pop. (1969 est.), 9,526,000.

ugh (ug, ōōкн, ūкн) *interj.* grunt or exclamation expressing such emotions as disgust or horror. [Imitative.]

ug·li (ug'lē) *n.* hybrid citrus fruit produced by crossing a tangerine with a grapefruit, having a thick, yellowish-green rind that peels easily. [Probably from UGLY; because its rind is unsightly.]

ug·ly (ug'lē) **-li·er, -li·est.** *adj.* **1.** very unattractive or displeasing to the eye or the aesthetic sense: *an ugly scar, an ugly painting.* **2.** causing disquiet, discomfort, or disgust; disagreeable; offensive: *an ugly story. His enemies spread ugly rumors about his sudden departure.* **3.** likely to cause trouble or harm; ominous: *There's an ugly storm brewing.* **4.** disposed to quarrel or display hostility; bad-tempered: *an ugly customer. Stay away from her; she's in an ugly mood today.* **5.** morally reprehensible or objectionable: *an ugly prejudice. Torture and other ugly methods were employed to obtain information.* [Old Norse *uggligr* fearful, dreadful.] —**ug'li·ness,** *n.*

ugly duckling, ugly or unpromising child, esp. one who grows into an unexpectedly beautiful or impressive person. [From a story by Hans Christian Andersen, in which a supposed ugly duckling becomes a beautiful swan.]

uhf *also,* **UHF.** ultrahigh frequency.

uh·lan (ōō'län, ū'lən) *n.* formerly, cavalryman or lancer of a type in the armies of various European countries, esp. in the German army. [German *U(h)lan,* through Polish, from Turkish *oghlan* youth.]

U.K., United Kingdom.

u·kase (ū'kās', ū'kāz') *n.* **1.** official or authoritative proclamation or decree; edict. **2.** decree or order having the force of law, issued under the czarist regime in Russia. [Russian *ukaz* edict, order, decree.]

U·kraine (ū krān', ū'krān) *n.* republic of the Soviet Union, in the southwestern part of the country, on the Black Sea. Official name: **Ukrainian Soviet Socialist Republic.** Area, 232,047 sq. mi. Pop. (1970 est.), 47,136,000.

U·krain·i·an (ū krā'nē ən) *n.* **1.** member or close descendant of the people inhabiting the Ukraine. **2.** the Slavic language spoken predominantly in the Ukraine, closely related to Russian. —*adj.* of or relating to the Ukraine, its people, their language, or their culture.

Ukulele

u·ku·le·le (ū'kə lā'lē) *n.* stringed musical instrument closely resembling but smaller than a guitar, having four strings. [Hawaiian *ukulele,* from *uku* flea + *lele* jumping; supposedly referring to the rapid movement of the fingers in playing the instrument.]

u·lan (ōō'län, ū'lən) uhlan.

U·lan Ba·tor (ōō'län bä'tôr) capital and largest city of the Mongolian People's Republic, in the northeastern part of the country. Pop. (1962 est.), 195,300.

ul·cer (ul'sər) *n.* **1.** open sore on the skin or a mucous membrane, as the stomach lining. **2.** corruptive, destructive, or evil influence or condition: *an ulcer on the body politic.* [Latin *ulcer-,* stem of *ulcus* a sore.]

ul·cer·ate (ul'sə rāt') **-at·ed, -at·ing.** *v.t., v.i.* to make or become ulcerous. [Latin *ulcerātus,* past participle of *ulcerāre* to make sore.]

ul·cer·a·tion (ul'sə rā'shən) *n.* **1.** act or process of ulcerating; being ulcerated. **2.** ulcerous condition; an ulcer.

ul·cer·ous (ul'sər əs) *adj.* **1.** relating to, characterized by, or resembling an ulcer or ulcers. **2.** affected with an ulcer or ulcers.

ul·na (ul'nə) *pl.,* **-nae** (-nē) or **-nas.** *n.* **1.** larger of the two bones of the forearm, extending from the elbow to the wrist. **2.** corresponding bone in the forelimb of other vertebrates. [Latin *ulna* elbow, arm.] —**ul'nar,** *adj.*

ul·ster (ul'stər) *n.* very long, heavy overcoat, often belted and having a cape attached. [From *Ulster,* where it was originally made.]

Ul·ster (ul'stər) *n.* historic province of Ireland now comprising all of Northern Ireland and part of the Republic of Ireland.

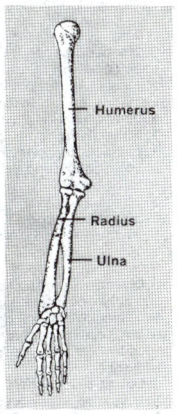
Ulna

ult. **1.** ultimate; ultimately. **2.** ultimo.

▲ used esp. in commercial and business correspondence, as in *in answer to your letter of the fifth ult.*

ul·te·ri·or (ul tēr'ē ər) *adj.* **1.** lying beyond what is shown or expressed; intentionally withheld or concealed; hidden: *ulterior motives.* **2.** more distant or remote; farther off: *ulterior regions.* [Latin *ulterior* farther, beyond.]

ul·ti·ma (ul'tə mə) *n.* last syllable of a word. [Latin *ultima,* feminine of *ultimus* last, farthest.]

ul·ti·mate (ul'tə mit) *adj.* **1.** coming as a climax or at the end; final: *The ultimate cost of the project was greater than the original estimate.* **2.** greatest or maximum possible; unsurpassed; absolute: *Ultimate authority is exercised by the king.* **3.** that cannot be further reduced, analyzed, or traced: *man's ultimate origins.* —*n.* **1.** that which is perfect, complete, or unsurpassed; peak: *the ultimate in fashion, the ultimate in luxury.* **2.** something final, absolute, or fundamental; final stage, degree, or result. [Medieval Latin *ultimatus* last, final, going back to Latin *ultimus* last, farthest.] —**Syn.** *adj.* **1.** see *last*[1].

ul·ti·mate·ly (ul′tə mit lē) *adv.* in the end; finally.
ultima Thule **1.** the land considered by ancient geographers to be the northernmost part of the habitable world. It was situated somewhere in the sea beyond northwestern Europe. Also, **Thu′le.** **2.** any faraway, mysterious region. **3.** utmost limit, point, or degree attainable, as of an ideal. [Latin *ultima Thule* farthest Thule, from *ultima*, feminine of *ultimus* last, farthest + *Thūlē* Thule (from Greek *Thoulē*).]
ul·ti·ma·tum (ul′tə mā′təm) *pl.* **-tums** or **-ta** (-tə). *n.* final, uncompromising demand, proposal, or set of terms issued by one party to another, the rejection of which will result in conflict, a break in relations, or strong or punitive action. [Modern Latin *ultimatum*, from *ultimatum*, neuter of Medieval Latin *ultimatus* last. See ULTIMATE.]
ul·ti·mo (ul′tə mō′) *adv.* *Archaic.* in or of the month that preceded the present one. [Latin *ultimō (mēnse)* in the last (month).]
ul·tra (ul′trə) *adj.* going beyond what is usual or moderate; excessive; extreme. —*n.* extremist. [Latin *ultrā* beyond.]
ultra- *prefix* **1.** beyond what is usual or moderate; excessively; extremely: *ultraconservative, ultracritical.* **2.** on the other side of; beyond in space: *ultraviolet, ultralunar.* **3.** beyond the range or limits of: *ultrasonic.* [Latin *ultrā* beyond.]
ul·tra·con·serv·a·tive (ul′trə kən sur′və tiv) *adj.* extremely or excessively conservative. —*n.* ultraconservative person.
ul·tra·crit·i·cal (ul′trə krit′i kəl) *adj.* extremely, excessively, or unnecessarily critical.
ul·tra·high frequency (ul′trə hī′) frequency range of radio waves from 300 to 3000 megacycles, used esp. for radio and television broadcasting.
ul·tra·lu·nar (ul′trə lōō′nər) *adj.* on the other side of or beyond the moon: *an ultralunar expedition.*
ul·tra·ma·rine (ul′trə mə rēn′) *n.* **1.** deep-blue color. **2.** blue pigment made from powdered lapis lazuli. **3.** any of several pigments that is made artificially and may be blue, green, or violet. —*adj.* **1.** deepblue. **2.** lying beyond the sea. [Medieval Latin *ultramarinus* coming from beyond the sea, going back to Latin *ultrā* beyond + *mare* sea; referring to the earlier importing of lapis lazuli from Asia "beyond the sea."]
ul·tra·mi·cro·scope (ul′trə mī′krə skōp′) *n.* microscope in which light is cast from the side upon the object to be viewed, making its reflection visible against a dark background, used esp. in the study of colloids.
ul·tra·mon·tane (ul′trə mon tān′) *adj.* **1.** situated beyond the mountains: *the ultramontane territory along the west coast.* **2.** of or relating to the regions or people situated beyond or south of the Alps, esp. Italy or the Italians. **3.** supporting or advocating the supreme authority of the pope in ecclesiastical or political matters. —*n.* **1.** person living beyond the mountains, esp. one living south of the Alps. **2.** one who supports or advocates the supreme authority of the pope in ecclesiastical and political matters. [Medieval Latin *ultramontanus* situated beyond the mountains, going back to Latin *ultrā* beyond + *mōns* mountain.]
ul·tra·mun·dane (ul′trə mun′dān, -mun dān′) *adj.* lying beyond the limits of the known universe or physical existence. [Late Latin *ultrāmundānus* beyond the world, going back to Latin *ultrā* beyond + *mundus* world.]
ul·tra·son·ic (ul′trə son′ik) *adj.* of, relating to, or designating sound waves having a frequency beyond the range audible to human beings, usually above 20,000 cycles per second.
ul·tra·son·ics (ul′trə son′iks) *n.,pl.* the science and technology of sound waves above the range audible to human beings. ▲ construed as singular.
ul·tra·vi·o·let (ul′trə vī′ə lit) *adj.* **1.** (of electromagnetic radiation) having a frequency beyond the violet end of the visible spectrum and before X rays, ranging from 40 to 4000 angstroms. **2.** relating to, employing, or producing ultraviolet radiation.
ul·tra vi·res (ul′trə vī′rēz) *Latin.* going beyond the lawful or authorized powers, as of a corporation.
ul·u·lant (ūl′yə lənt) *adj.* ululating.
ul·u·late (ūl′yə lāt′, ul′-) **-lat·ed, -lat·ing.** *v.i.* **1.** to utter a wailing cry; howl. **2.** to lament loudly. [Latin *ululātus*, past participle of *ululāre* to howl.] —**ul′u·la′tion,** *n.*
U·lys·ses (ū lis′ēz) *n.* *Greek and Roman Legend.* king of Ithaca and one of the shrewdest Greek leaders in the Trojan War, who was forced to wander for ten years after the fall of Troy until the gods finally permitted him to return home. Also, **O·dys′se·us.**
um·bel (um′bəl) *n.* flower cluster in which the flower stalks radiate from a common center at the top of the stem, like the ribs of an umbrella. [Latin *umbella* parasol, diminutive of *umbra* shade.]
um·bel·late (um′bə lit, -lāt′) *adj.* having, resembling, or forming an umbel or umbels.
um·bel·lif·er·ous (um′bə lif′ər əs) *adj.* bearing an umbel or umbels, as plants of the carrot or parsley family.

um·ber (um′bər) *n.* **1.** brown earth containing ferric oxide and manganese, used as a brown pigment in its natural state (raw umber) or, after being roasted, as a reddish-brown pigment (burnt umber). **2.** brown or reddish-brown color. —*adj.* brown or reddish-brown. [French *ombre*, short for *terre d'ombre* literally, earth of shadow, from Latin *terra* earth + *dē* from + *umbra* shade, shadow; probably because used by painters for shading.]
um·bil·i·cal (um bil′i kəl) *adj.* of, relating to, or located near the navel or umbilical cord. —*n.* umbilical cord.
umbilical cord **1.** cordlike structure in mammals that connects the navel of the fetus to the placenta of the mother's womb, providing nourishment for and removing wastes from the fetus. **2.** any of various lines that service and connect a spacecraft to the ground or launching site and are detached before launching.
um·bil·i·cus (um bil′i kəs, um′bə lī′kəs) *pl.* **-ci** (-sī). *n.* **1.** the navel. **2.** something resembling a navel in shape, as the hollow at the base of the shell in certain mollusks. [Latin *umbilīcus* navel, center.]
um·bra (um′brə) *pl.* **-brae** (-brē) or **-bras.** *n.* **1.** *Astronomy.* **a.** completely dark, cone-shaped, inner part of the shadow cast by the moon in a solar eclipse or by the earth in a lunar eclipse. See **eclipse** for illustration. **b.** cone of complete shadow cast by a nonradiant body, as a planet, in the direction away from the sun. **c.** the central, darkest portion of a sunspot. **2.** shaded area or shadow, esp. the central part of a shadow from which all direct light is cut off. Distinguished from **penumbra** in all definitions. [Latin *umbra* shade, shadow.]
um·brage (um′brij) *n.* **1.** feeling of displeasure or resentment, esp. at an imagined injury or insult; offense: *to take umbrage at a casual remark.* **2.** *Archaic.* **a.** shade; shadow. **b.** that which gives shade, as foliage. [Old French *umbrage* shade, suspicion, going back to Latin *umbra* shade, shadow.]
um·bra·geous (um brā′jəs) *adj.* **1.** shady. **2.** easily offended.
um·brel·la (um brel′ə) *n.* **1.** device for protection from rain, sun, or the like, consisting of a circular piece of cloth or other material attached to narrow ribs that radiate from a long central rod. **2.** something resembling an umbrella in shape or function, as protective cover given by military aircraft to land or sea forces. —*adj.* applying to or covering related elements; inclusive; general: *an umbrella organization, an umbrella clause.* [Italian *ombrella* device for protection from sun or rain, diminutive of *ombra* shade, from Latin *umbra* shade, shadow.]
umbrella tree **1.** either of two American magnolia trees, *Meliaceae tripetala* or *M. fraseri*, having long leaves and spreading branches and bearing clusters of cup-shaped white flowers. **2.** any of various trees with leaves or flower clusters shaped like open umbrellas.
Um·bri·a (um′brē ə) *n.* historic region in central Italy. Area, 3266 sq. mi. Pop. (1961), 794,745.
Um·bri·an (um′brē ən) *adj.* of, relating to, or characteristic of Umbria, its people, or their culture. —*n.* **1.a.** native or inhabitant of modern Umbria. **b.** member of a people that inhabited Umbria in ancient times. **2.** extinct Italic language of this people, closely related to ancient Latin.
u·mi·ak (ōō′mē ak′) *n.* large, open boat, about thirty feet long, made of skins stretched over a wooden frame, developed and used esp. by Eskimos. [Eskimo *umiak*.]

Umiak

um·laut (oom′lout′) *n.* **1.** in the Germanic languages, a change in a vowel sound caused by absorbing the sound of another vowel that originally occurred in the next syllable. The change from *foot* to *feet* is an umlaut. **2.** vowel so changed. **3.** diacritical mark (¨) placed over such a vowel, esp. in German. —*v.t.* to change or modify by umlaut. [German *Umlaut* modification of a vowel, from *um* about + *Laut* sound.]
um·pire (um′pīr) *n.* **1.** official in certain sports and games, as baseball, who rules on plays, interprets and enforces the rules, and settles disputed points. **2.** person having the authority to settle a dispute or decide an issue, as between opposing persons or groups. —*v.t.,* **-pired, -pir·ing.** to act as umpire in or of. —*v.i.* to act as umpire. [Earlier *numpire*, from Old French *nomper* odd, not equal, going back to Latin *nōn* not + *par* equal; referring to the umpire's position as the *odd* or third man in deciding a dispute between others. The initial *n* was lost by being joined to the preceding indefinite article: *a numpire* became *an umpire*.]
ump·teen (ump′tēn′) *adj. Informal.* of a large but indefinite number; innumerable: *umpteen guests for the weekend.* —**ump′teenth′,** *adj.*
UMW, United Mine Workers.
un-¹ *prefix* (used to form adjectives, adverbs, and nouns) the opposite or negative of (what is indicated by the stem): *uncooked, unbeliever.* [Old English *un-*.] ▲ The meaning of a word in the list at the bottom of the following pages can be understood by combining *un-* with the root word.

un-² *prefix* **1.** (used to form verbs from verbs) **a.** to do the opposite of; reverse the action of: *to unfasten.* **b.** to emphasize or intensify the negative action of: *to unloose.* **2.** (used to form verbs from nouns) **a.** to release, remove, or free from: *to unearth.* **b.** to cause to cease to be; deprive of the qualities of: *to unman.* [Old English *un-, on-, an-*] ▲ The meaning of a word in the following list at the bottom of this and the following pages can be understood by combining *un-* with the root word.

UN, United Nations.

un·a·bashed (un′ə basht′) *adj.* not ashamed, self-conscious, or disconcerted. —**un′a·bash′ed·ly,** *adv.*

un·a·ble (un ā′bəl) *adj.* lacking power, skills, or qualifications (to do something): *I'm unable to type.*

un·a·bridged (un′ə brijd′) *adj.* not shortened or condensed; complete: *an unabridged edition.*

un·ac·com·pa·nied (un′ə kum′pə nēd′) *adj.* **1.** without a companion or escort; unattended; alone. **2.** *Music.* without accompaniment.

un·ac·count·a·ble (un′ə koun′tə bəl) *adj.* **1.** that cannot be accounted for; inexplicable. **2.** not liable to be called to account.

un·ac·count·a·bly (un′ə koun′tə blē) *adv.* inexplicably.

un·ac·count·ed-for (un′ə koun′tid fôr′) *adj.* not accounted for; unexplained.

un·ac·cus·tomed (un′ə kus′təmd) *adj.* **1.** not in the habit of; unused (with *to*). **2.** unfamiliar; unusual; strange: *to act with unaccustomed strength.*

un·ac·knowl·edged (un′ək nol′ijd) *adj.* generally accepted without having formal or official recognition: *He is the unacknowledged leader of our group.*

un·a·dorned (un′ə dornd′) *adj.* not embellished or artificial; simple; plain: *an unadorned style of writing.*

un·a·dul·ter·at·ed (un′ə dul′tə rā′tid) *adj.* not diluted or corrupted by extraneous matter; unmixed; pure: *unadulterated foods.*

un·ad·vised (un′əd vīzd′) *adj.* **1.** without due consideration; ill-advised; imprudent. **2.** not supplied with advice.

un·ad·vis·ed·ly (un′əd vī′zid lē) *adv.* in a rash, thoughtless manner; imprudently.

un·af·fect·ed¹ (un′ə fek′tid) *adj.* not influenced; unmoved: *They were unaffected by his pleas.* [UN-¹ + AFFECTED¹.]

un·af·fect·ed² (un′ə fek′tid) *adj.* not pretentious or artificial; genuine; sincere: *unaffected speech. He regarded them with unaffected dislike.* [UN-¹ + AFFECTED².] —**un′af·fect′ed·ly,** *adv.* —**un′af·fect′ed·ness,** *n.*

un-A·mer·i·can (un′ə mer′i kən) *adj.* alien or opposed to the supposedly true American character, traditions, and institutions.

un·a·neled (un′ə nēld′) *adj. Archaic.* not having been anointed by a priest before death. [UN-¹ + *aneled,* past participle of obsolete *anele* to give extreme unction (going back to Old English *an on* + *ele* oil, from Latin *oleum* oil). See OIL.]

u·na·nim·i·ty (ū′nə nim′ə tē) *n.* state of being unanimous; complete agreement; unity.

u·nan·i·mous (ū nan′ə məs) *adj.* **1.** of one mind or opinion; in complete agreement. **2.** characterized by or resulting from complete agreement: *done with the unanimous consent of the members.* [Latin *ūnanimus* of one mind.] —**u·nan′i·mous·ly,** *adv.* —**u·nan′i·mous·ness,** *n.*

un·ap·peal·ing (un′ə pē′ling) *adj.* not attractive, interesting, or enjoyable.

un·ap·pe·tiz·ing (un ap′ə tī′zing) *adj.* not appealing, esp. to the appetite.

un·ap·proach·a·ble (un′ə prō′chə bəl) *adj.* **1.** difficult to know or deal with; unfriendly; aloof: *an unapproachable person.* **2.** that cannot be approached; inaccessible: *The house is unapproachable in winter.* **3.** unequaled; matchless; unrivaled: *a speech unapproachable in its eloquence.* —**un′ap·proach′a·ble·ness,** *n.* —**un′ap·proach′a·bly,** *adv.*

un·arm (un ärm′) *v.t. Archaic.* to deprive of weapons or armor; disarm.

un·armed (un ärmd′) *adj.* **1.** without arms or weapons; defenseless. **2.** (of animals or plants) not having sharp, pointed projections, as claws, thorns, or scales.

un·as·sail·a·ble (un′ə sā′lə bəl) *adj.* **1.** that cannot be denied, disputed, or questioned: *an unassailable argument, an unassailable reputation.* **2.** that cannot be successfully attacked or seized; impregnable: *an unassailable fortress.*

un·as·sum·ing (un′ə sōō′ming) *adj.* modest in nature or manner; not bold, forward, or boastful. —**un′as·sum′ing·ly,** *adv.*

un·at·tached (un′ə tacht′) *adj.* **1.** not fastened, joined, or connected. **2.** not engaged or married. **3.** not assigned to or associated with a particular body, group, or organization: *an unattached army officer.* **4.** *Law.* (of a person or property) not taken or seized as security.

un·at·tend·ed (un′ə ten′did) *adj.* **1.** not accompanied or escorted; alone. **2.** not done or taken care of; neglected (often with *to*). **3.** without an audience; lacking attendance.

un·a·vail·ing (un′ə vā′ling) *adj.* futile; useless: *unavailing cries for help.* —**un′a·vail′ing·ly,** *adv.*

un·a·void·a·ble (un′ə voi′də bəl) *adj.* that cannot or could not be avoided or prevented; inevitable: *an unavoidable delay, an unavoidable clash of opinions.* —**un′a·void′a·bly,** *adv.*

un·a·ware (un′ə wâr′) *adj.* not conscious, cognizant, or informed (often with *of*): *unaware of her own tactlessness.* —*adv.* unawares.

un·a·wares (un′ə wârs′) *adv.* **1.** without warning; unexpectedly; suddenly: *The storm took the farmers in the area unawares.* **2.** without design or intention; inadvertently; unintentionally: *I let the error slip by unawares.*

un·backed (un bakt′) *adj.* **1.** without financial support or other aid or endorsement. **2.** without a back for support, as a bench or book. **3.** (of a horse) never having been mounted by a rider; unbroken. **4.** not bet on, as a horse.

un·bal·ance (un bal′əns) -anced, -anc·ing. *v.t.* **1.** to disturb the equilibrium, proportion, or stability of. **2.** to disorder or derange, as the mind. —*n.* condition of being unbalanced.

un·bal·anced (un bal′ənst) *adj.* **1.** not in a state of equilibrium; improperly balanced. **2.** mentally disordered; deranged. **3.** not adjusted so that the debit and credit sides are equal: *an unbalanced budget, an unbalanced account.*

un·bar (un bär′) -barred, -bar·ring. *v.t.* to remove a bar or bars from; unbolt; open.

un·bear·a·ble (un bâr′ə bəl) *adj.* that cannot be borne or endured; intolerable: *unbearable pain, unbearable suspense.* —**un·bear′a·ble·ness,** *n.* —**un·bear′a·bly,** *adv.*

un·beat·a·ble (un bē′tə bəl) *adj.* that cannot be defeated or surpassed: *an unbeatable player, an unbeatable combination.*

un·beat·en (un bēt′ən) *adj.* **1.** never defeated or surpassed: *an*

un′a·bat′ed	un′aes·thet′ic	un′a·mused′	un′as·ser′tive
un′ab·bre′vi·at·ed	un′af·fil′i·at·ed	un′a·mus′ing	un′as·sessed′
un′a·bet′ted	un′a·fraid′	un·an′i·mat′ed	un′as·sign′a·ble
un′ab·solved′	un·aged′	un′an·nounced′	un′as·signed′
un′ab·sorbed′	un′ag·gres′sive	un·ans′wer·a·ble	un′as·sim′i·lat·ed
un′ac·a·dem′ic	un·ag′i·tat·ed	un·ans′wer·a·bly	un′as·sist′ed
un·ac′cent·ed	un′a·gree′a·ble	un·ans′wered	un′as·sumed′
un′ac·cen′tu·at·ed	un·aid′ed	un′an·tic′i·pat·ed	un′at·tain′a·ble
un′ac·cept′a·ble	un·aired′	un′a·pol′o·get′ic	un′at·tained′
un′ac·cept′ed	un′a·larmed′	un·ap′par·ent	un′at·tempt′ed
un′ac·cli·mat′ed	un′a·ligned′	un′ap·peal′a·ble	un′at·test′ed
un′ac·cli′ma·tized	un·a·like′	un′ap·peas′a·ble	un′at·tract′ed
un′ac·com′mo·dat·ed	un·al′le·vi·at·ed	un·ap′peased′	un′at·trac′tive
un′ac·com′mo·dat′ing	un·al′lied′	un′ap·pre′ci·at′ed	un′au·then′tic
un′ac·com′plished	un′al·low′a·ble	un′ap·pre′ci·a·tive	un′au·then′ti·cat·ed
un′ac·cred′it·ed	un′al·loyed′	un′ap·pro′pri·ate	un·au′thor·ized′
un′ac·quaint′ed	un·al′pha·bet·ized′	un′ap·pro′pri·at·ed	un′a·vail′a·bil′i·ty
un′a·dapt′a·ble	un·al′ter·a·ble	un·ar′mored	un′a·vail′a·ble
un′a·dapt′ed	un·al′ter·a·bly	un′ar·rest′ed	un·a′venged′
un′ad·just′ed	un·al′tered	un′ar·tic′u·lat·ed	un·awed′
un′ad·van·ta′geous·ly	un·am′big′u·ous	un·a·shamed′	un·baked′
un′ad·ven′tur·ous	un·am′bi′tious	un·asked′	un·ban′dage
un′ad·ver·tised′	un′am·bi′tious	un·asked′-for′	un·bap′tized
un′ad·vis′a·ble	un′am·pli·fied′	un′as·pi·rat′ed	un·based′
un′ad·vis′a·bly		un′a·spir′ing	un·beau′ti·ful

unbeaten team. **2.** not walked over; untrod, as a path. **3.** not shaped or mixed by beating: *unbeaten gold, an unbeaten egg.*

un·be·com·ing (un′bi kum′ing) *adj.* **1.** not flattering or attractive: *The colors are unbecoming to her complexion.* **2.** not suitable or appropriate; indecorous: *unbecoming language.* —**un′be·com′ing·ly,** *adv.* —**un′be·com′ing·ness,** *n.*

un·be·knownst (un′bi nōnst′) *also,* **un·be·known** (un′bi nōn′). *adj., adv.* *Informal.* without the knowledge or awareness of (with *to*): *Unbeknownst to her friends, she had left the city.*

un·be·lief (un′bi lēf′) *n.* absence of belief, esp. in matters of religion. **Syn. Unbelief, disbelief, incredulity** mean the act or state of failing to believe. **Unbelief** is the most absolute word, suggesting a complete, final, and habitual lack of belief: *Unbelief in God marks the atheist.* **Disbelief** is the most common word, expressing an attitude of skepticism or scorn that resists proof of sense experience: *I watched in disbelief as the police towed my car away.* **Incredulity** expresses a wide-eyed amazement and, in contrast to *disbelief,* suggests that one is actually convinced by sense experience notwithstanding previous knowledge or experience to the contrary: *The audience watched with incredulity as the magician pulled rabbits and handkerchiefs out of his hat.*

un·be·liev·a·ble (un′bi lē′və bəl) *adj.* not to be believed; incredible: *unbelievable weather, an unbelievable bore.* —**un′be·liev′a·bly,** *adv.*

un·be·liev·er (un′bi lē′vər) *n.* **1.** one who does not believe in a particular religion. **2.** one who withholds belief, esp. one who has no religious faith.

un·be·liev·ing (un′bi lē′ving) *adj.* **1.** doubting; skeptical; incredulous. **2.** lacking religious belief or beliefs. —**un′be·liev′ing·ly,** *adv.*

un·bend (un bend′) **-bent, -bend·ing.** *v.t.* **1.** to straighten (something curved or crooked). **2.** to free from concentrated effort or strain. **3.** to unfasten, untie, or cast loose (a sail, line, cable, or the like). —*v.i.* **1.** to become free of tension, formality, or strain; relax. **2.** to become straight or almost straight.

un·bend·ing (un ben′ding) *adj.* **1.** that cannot or will not relax, soften, or relent; unyielding; inflexible: *an unbending will.* **2.** not bending or curving; stiff.

un·bi·ased (un bī′əst) *also, British,* **un·bi·assed.** *adj.* free from partiality or prejudice; fair.

un·bid·den (un bid′ən) *adj.* **1.** not asked or invited: *unbidden guests for dinner.* **2.** spontaneous: *unbidden thoughts, unbidden tears.* **3.** not commanded or ordered. Also, **un·bid′.**

un·bind (un bīnd′) **-bound, -bind·ing.** *v.t.* **1.** to release from bonds or restraint; set free: *Unbind my hands.* **2.** to remove or undo (something that binds); unfasten; loose: *to unbind a bandage.*

un·blem·ished (un blem′isht) *adj.* **1.** free from imperfection or flaw: *an unblemished record, an unblemished character.* **2.** not marked or marred: *an unblemished complexion.*

un·blessed (un blest′) *also,* **un·blest.** *adj.* **1.** not consecrated. **2.** cursed; evil; unholy.

un·blink·ing (un bling′king) *adj.* **1.** not blinking. **2.** without displaying an emotional response; unquestioning: *an unblinking acceptance of brutality.* **3.** fearless; forthright: *an unblinking appraisal of necessary reforms.*

un·blush·ing (un blush′ing) *adj.* **1.** without shame or remorse; shameless; brazen. **2.** not blushing or reddening. —**un·blush′ing·ly,** *adv.*

un·bolt (un bōlt′) *v.t.* to open by drawing back a bolt or bolts; unlock.

un·bolt·ed[1] (un bōl′tid) *adj.* not fastened by a bolt or bolts. [UN-¹ + *bolted,* past participle of BOLT¹.]

un·bolt·ed[2] (un bōl′tid) *adj.* not sifted. [UN-¹ + *bolted,* past participle of BOLT².]

un·born (un bôrn′) *adj.* not yet born or existing: *our unborn child, the inheritance of unborn ages.*

un·bos·om (un booz′əm, -boo′zəm) *v.t.* **1.** to disclose or confide, as one's thoughts or feelings: *He unbosomed his sorrows to a perfect stranger.* **2.** to unburden (oneself), as of thoughts, secrets, or feelings.

un·bound·ed (un boun′did) *adj.* having no limits or bounds; boundless; measureless: *unbounded space, unbounded admiration.*

un·bowed (un′boud′) *adj.* **1.** not tamed or subdued, as by defeat. **2.** not bowed or bent.

un·bri·dled (un brīd′əld) *adj.* **1.** absolutely uncontrolled; ungoverned: *unbridled lust.* **2.** not wearing or fitted with a bridle.

un·bro·ken (un brō′kən) *adj.* **1.** not torn, fragmented, or tampered with; whole; intact: *an unbroken seal. He was left with hardly a bone unbroken.* **2.** not interrupted; continuous; uniform: *unbroken ranks, an unbroken chain of events.* **3.** not beaten or surpassed: *an unbroken record.* **4.** (of an animal) unaccustomed to a harness or rider; untamed. **5.** not weakened, subdued, or humbled: *a spirit unbroken by poverty.* **6.** not violated, as a vow. —**un·bro′ken·ly,** *adv.* —**un·bro′ken·ness,** *n.*

un·buck·le (un buk′əl) **-led, -ling.** *v.t.* to undo or unfasten the buckle or buckles of.

un·bur·den (un burd′ən) *v.t.* **1.** to free or relieve by disclosing or discussing something burdensome: *He unburdened himself to his friend.* **2.** to cast off (something burdensome) by disclosing or discussing; reveal: *to unburden one's troubles.* **3.** to rid of a burden or load.

un·but·ton (un but′ən) *v.t.* to open by or as if by unfastening the button or buttons of.

un·called-for (un kôld′fôr′) *adj.* inappropriate and unnecessary; impertinent; unwarranted: *uncalled-for rudeness.*

un·can·ny (un kan′ē) *adj.* **1.** strange and inexplicable, so as to inspire fear or wonder; eerie; weird: *It was uncanny the way the sounds seemed to die away, then return louder than ever.* **2.** so unusually good or acute as to seem superhuman: *an uncanny talent for finding a bargain.* —**un·can′ni·ly,** *adv.* —**un·can′ni·ness,** *n.*

un·ceas·ing (un sē′sing) *adj.* without stop or end; continuous; incessant: *an unceasing barrage of requests.* —**un·ceas′ing·ly,** *adv.*

un·cer·e·mo·ni·ous (un′ser ə mō′nē əs) *adj.* **1.** without courtesy or consideration; abrupt; curt: *an unceremonious rebuke, an unceremonious departure.* **2.** characterized by a lack of ceremony; informal. —**un′cer·e·mo′ni·ous·ly,** *adv.* —**un′cer·e·mo′ni·ous·ness,** *n.*

un·cer·tain (un surt′ən) *adj.* **1.** not surely known, established, or settled: *a manuscript of uncertain origin. The outcome of the battle is still uncertain.* **2.** having, showing, or experiencing doubt, hesitancy, or reservation; lacking confidence or sure knowledge: *I'm uncertain about his motives. He approached the hostile crowd with an uncertain smile on his face.* **3.** that cannot be depended upon to remain in one state or condition; subject to change; unsteady; variable: *uncertain weather.* **4.** not clearly defined; vague; ambiguous: *An uncertain shape loomed ahead in the darkness. She gave him an ultimatum in no uncertain terms.* —**un·cer′tain·ly,** *adv.* —**un·cer′tain·ness,** *n.*

un·cer·tain·ty (un surt′ən tē) *pl.,* **-ties.** *n.* **1.** state or quality of being uncertain, esp. of being in doubt. **2.** something uncertain: *The many uncertainties of the situation made us all uneasy.*

uncertainty principle *Physics.* principle stating that it is impossible to measure simultaneously both the position and the momentum of an elementary particle with absolute accuracy.

un·chain (un chān′) *v.t.* to release from a chain or chains; set free.

un·char·i·ta·ble (un char′ə tə bəl) *adj.* not generous or forgiving, esp. in judging others; severe; harsh. —**un·char′i·ta·ble·ness,** *n.* —**un·char′i·ta·bly,** *adv.*

un·chart·ed (un chär′tid) *adj.* not indicated or included in a map, chart, scheme, or plan; unexplored; unknown: *uncharted islands, the uncharted regions of the unconscious.*

un·checked (un chekt′) *adj.* **1.a.** not sharply or forcefully halted in progress: *the unchecked advance of enemy troops.* **b.** not held in control or restraint: *unchecked anger.* **2.** not tested, investigated, or verified as to accuracy or correctness: *The unchecked copy must be reviewed before publication.*

un·chris·tian (un kris′chən) *adj.* **1.** not in accord with the Christian

---

un′be·fit′ting	un·brib′a·ble	un·cap′	un·changed′
un′be·lov′ed	un·bridge′a·ble	un·cap′i·tal·ized′	un·chang′ing
un′be·seem′ing	un·bridged′	un·cared′-for′	un′chap′er·oned′
un·blam′a·ble	un·bri′dle	un·car′ing	un′char·ac·ter·is′tic
un·blamed′	un·broth′er·ly	un·car′pet·ed	un′char·ac·ter·is′ti·cal·ly
un·bleached′	un·bruised′	un′cat·e·gor′i·cal	un′char′tered
un·block′	un·brushed′	un′cat·e·gor′i·cal·ly	un·chaste′
un·bod′ied	un·bur′ied	un·cel′e·brat′ed	un·chaste′ly
un·bound′	un·bus′i·ness-like′	un·cen′sored	un·chas′tened
un·brace′	un·but′tered	un·cert′ti·fied′	un·cheer′ful
un·braced′	un·but′toned	un·chal′lenge·a·ble	un·chewed′
un·braid′	un·cage′	un·chal′lenged	un·chilled′
un·brand′ed	un·cal′cu·lat′ed	un·chal′leng·ing	un·chiv′al·rous
un·break′a·ble	un·cal′cu·lat′ing	un·change′a·ble	un·cho′sen
un·breath′a·ble	un′ca·non′i·cal	un·change′a·bly	un·chris′tened

---

at; āpe; cär; end; mē; it; īce; hot; ōld; fôrk; wood; foōl; oil; out; up; ūse; turn; sing; thin; this; zh in treasure; ə in ago, taken, pencil, lemon, circus.

spirit; uncharitable: *an unchristian remark*. **2.** not of the Christian religion.

un·church (un church′) *v.t.* **1.** to expel from a church; excommunicate. **2.** to deprive (a sect or congregation) of standing as a church.

un·cial (un′shəl, -shē əl) *adj.* of, relating to, or designating a style of writing having letters similar to but more rounded than modern capitals, found in Greek and Latin manuscripts dating from about the fourth to the ninth centuries. —*n.* **1.** uncial letter or writings. **2.** manuscript written in the uncial writing style. [Latin *unciālis* relating to an inch or an ounce, from *uncia* a twelfth part, inch, ounce; referring to the large size of an uncial letter.]

ABCDEFGHJKL
MNOPQRSTU

Uncial letters

un·ci·form (un′sə fôrm′) *adj.* shaped like a hook; hooklike. [Modern Latin *unciformis*, from Latin *uncus* hook + -FORM.]

un·ci·nate (un′sə nit, -nāt′) *adj.* hooked or bent at the tip. [Latin *uncīnātus* furnished with hooks, from *uncīnus* hook.]

un·cir·cum·cised (un sur′kəm sīzd′) *adj.* **1.** not circumcised. **2.** not Jewish; Gentile. **3.** heathen.

un·civ·il (un siv′əl) *adj.* not polite or courteous; rude: *an uncivil reply*. —**un·civ′il·ly**, *adv.*

un·civ·i·lized (un siv′ə līzd′) *adj.* of a primitive or early stage of human social development; not civilized; savage.

un·clad (un klad′) *adj.* not clothed or dressed; naked; nude.

un·clasp (un klasp′) *v.t.* **1.** to open, unfasten, or loosen the clasp of: *to unclasp the bracelet, to unclasp a handbag*. **2.** to release from a grasp or embrace.

un·cle (ung′kəl) *n.* **1.** brother of one's father or mother. **2.** husband of one's aunt. **3.** *Informal.* elderly man. ▲ used as a term of address. **4. to say** (or **cry**) **uncle.** *Informal.* to give in; surrender: *The gangsters put pressure on the storekeeper until he cried uncle.* —*interj. Informal.* used to express surrender. [Anglo-Norman *uncle* brother of one's father or mother, from Latin *avunculus* a mother's brother, diminutive of *avus* grandfather.]

un·clean (un klēn′) *adj.* **1.** not physically clean; dirty; foul. **2.** impure or unacceptable according to certain standards of morality; *unclean thoughts.* **3.** not fit for ceremonial or lawful religious use; defiled; tainted. [Old English *unclǣne.*] —**un·clean′ness**, *n.*

un·clean·ly[1] (un klēn′lē) *adj.* not cleanly; unclean. [Old English *unclǣnlīc.*] —**un·clean′li·ness**, *n.*

un·clean·ly[2] (un klēn′lē) *adv.* in an unclean manner. [Old English *unclǣnlīce.*]

un·clench (un klench′) *v.t., v.i.* to open or become opened from a clenched position.

Uncle Sam (sam) **1.** figure personifying the government or people of the United States, represented as an old man who is dressed in the national colors. **2.** the government or people of the United States. [From the initials *U.S.* (abbreviation of *United States*), which were stamped on meat supplies for the U.S. Army during the War of 1812 supposedly by Samuel Wilson, American meat inspector, who was nicknamed *Uncle Sam.*]

Uncle Tom, any Negro who is considered servile or unduly respectful to whites. [From the faithful Negro slave in the novel *Uncle Tom's Cabin* by Harriet Beecher Stowe.]

un·cloak (un klōk′) *v.t.* **1.** to remove a cloak or cover from. **2.** to reveal; expose: *to uncloak a plot.* —*v.i.* to remove one's cloak or outer garment.

un·clothe (un klōth′) -**clothed** or -**clad**, -**cloth·ing.** *v.t.* to remove the clothing or cover from; strip.

un·coil (un koil′) *v.t., v.i.* to unwind.

un·com·fort·a·ble (un kumf′tə bəl, -kum′fər tə-) *adj.* **1.** causing physical or mental distress or discomfort: *an uncomfortable mattress, an uncomfortable lecture.* **2.** feeling mental or physical distress; ill at ease: *The diplomat was uncomfortable speaking to reporters.* —**un·com′fort·a·ble·ness**, *n.* —**un·com′fort·a·bly**, *adv.*

un·com·mit·ted (un′kə mit′id) *adj.* not devoted or pledged to a particular course of action, viewpoint, or allegiance.

un·com·mon (un kom′ən) *adj.* **1.** rare; unusual: *It's not uncommon to hear talk of flying saucers.* **2.** unusual in amount, extent, or degree; exceptional: *She dances with uncommon grace. The housekeeper took uncommon care in arranging the flowers.* —**un·com′mon·ly**, *adv.* —**un·com′mon·ness**, *n.*

Syn. 1. Uncommon, rare[1], **scarce** indicate something that seldom occurs or is encountered. **Uncommon** suggests that no particular significance or value is attached to such an instance: *Jones is not an uncommon name.* **Rare** emphasizes the great value or interest of something: *The rare books are kept in a vault.* **Scarce** suggests not only value or interest, but the danger or threat of something being in short supply: *Some scarce species of marine life are internationally protected.*

un·com·mu·ni·ca·tive (un′kə mū′nə kā′tiv, -kə-) *adj.* not inclined to communicate or disclose information readily; reticent; taciturn. —**un′com·mu·ni·ca′tive·ly**, *adv.* —**un′com·mu·ni·ca′tive·ness**, *n.*

un·com·pli·men·ta·ry (un′kom plə men′trē, -tər ē) *adj.* insulting; derogatory: *an uncomplimentary remark.*

un·com·pro·mis·ing (un kom′prə mī′zing) *adj.* not open to change or compromise; unyielding; inflexible: *an uncompromising decision, a man of uncompromising honesty.* —**un·com′pro·mis′ing·ly**, *adv.*

un·con·cern (un′kən surn′) *n.* **1.** lack of interest. **2.** freedom from care or anxiety.

un·con·cerned (un′kən surnd′) *adj.* **1.** not interested, involved, or occupied (with *with*): *He's unconcerned with your problems.* **2.** free from care or anxiety; untroubled (often with *about* and *for*): *unconcerned for one's safety.* —**un′con·cern′ed·ly** (un′kən sur′nid lē), *adv.*

un·con·di·tion·al (un′kən dish′ən əl) *adj.* not limited by or subject to a condition or conditions; absolute; complete: *unconditional obedience, an unconditional guarantee.* —**un′con·di′tion·al·ly**, *adv.*

un·con·di·tioned (un′kən dish′ənd) *adj.* **1.** unconditional. **2.** *Psychology.* not a result of a learning or conditioning process; natural: *an unconditioned response.*

un·con·nec·ted (un′kən nek′tid) *adj.* **1.** not joined or fastened together; separate; distinct: *Two unconnected buildings make up the plant.* **2.** having no order or sequence; incoherent; rambling: *an unconnected speech.* —**un′con·nec′ted·ly**, *adv.* —**un′con·nec′ted·ness**, *n.*

un·con·quer·a·ble (un kong′kər ə bəl) *adj.* **1.** that cannot be vanquished or secured or overcome by force. **2.** that cannot be mastered or brought under control: *He had an unconquerable will.* —**un·con′quer·a·bly**, *adv.*

un·con·scion·a·ble (un kon′shən ə bəl) *adj.* **1.** not influenced, guided, or restrained by conscience; unscrupulous; unprincipled: *an unconscionable landlord.* **2.** beyond what is reasonable or just; excessive; immoderate: *an unconscionable demand, an unconscionable price.* —**un·con′scion·a·bly**, *adv.*

un·con·scious (un kon′shəs) *adj.* **1.** temporarily deprived of consciousness, as in a coma: *The driver was unconscious for three days after the accident.* **2.** not knowing or perceiving; failing to consider or take note of; unaware (with *of*): *unconscious of his sloppy appearance, unconscious of the dangers involved.* **3.** not produced or accompanied by conscious effort or knowledge; not consciously realized, done, or planned: *an unconscious pun, unconscious prejudice. John has an unconscious habit of tapping his fingers on the desk.* **4.** lacking thoughtful awareness of or attention to oneself, others, or one's environment: *She's the most unconscious creature I know.* **5.** not endowed with mind or consciousness: *unconscious stones.* **6.** *Psychology.* of relating to, or involving mental or emotional processes that are not consciously perceived; not perceived at the level of awareness: *unconscious guilt, an unconscious death wish.* —*n. Psychology.* sum of the wishes, memories, and other mental phenomena that is not consciously perceived but that influences conscious thought and behavior. —**un·con′scious·ly**, *adv.* —**un·con′scious·ness**, *n.*

un·con·sti·tu·tion·al (un′kon stə tōō′shən əl, -tū′-) *adj.* violating or not in keeping with the constitution of a nation, state, or group, esp., contrary to the Constitution of the United States. —**un·con·sti·tu-**

un·claimed′	un′co·erced′	un′com·pre·hen′si·ble	un′con·sci·en′tious
un·clar′i·fied′	un·col′lect′ed	un′com·pre·hen′si·bly	un′con·sci·en′tious·ly
un·clas′si·fi′a·ble	un·col′o·nized′	un′com·pro·mised′	un′con·se·crat′ed
un·clas′si·fied′	un·combed′	un′con·ceal′a·ble	un′con·sid′ered
un·cleaned′	un′com·bined′	un′con·cealed′	un′con·soled′
un·clear′	un′com·mend′a·ble	un′con·clud′ed	un′con·sol′i·dat′ed
un·cleared′	un′com·pen·sat′ed	un·con·demned′	un′con·strained′
un·clog′	un′com·pet′i·tive	un′con·densed′	un′con·strict′ed
un·clogged′	un′com·plain′ing	un′con·du′cive	un′con·sumed′
un·clothed′	un′com·plet′ed	un′con·fined′	un′con·sum′mat′ed
un·cloud′ed	un′com·pli·cat′ed	un′con·firmed′	un′con·tam′i·nat′ed
un·clut′tered	un′com·pre·hend′ing	un′con·gen′ial	un′con·test′ed
un·cock′	un′com·pre·hend′ing·ly	un′con·quered′	un′con·tra·dict′ed

at; āpe; cär; end; mē; it; īce; hot; ōld; fôrk; wood; fōōl; oil; out; up; ūse; turn; sing; thin; <u>th</u>is; zh in treasure; ə in ago, taken, pencil, lemon, circus.

tion·al·i·ty (un′kon stə tōō′shə nal′ə tē, -tū′-), *n.* —**un′con·sti·tu′-tion·al·ly,** *adv.*

un·con·trol·la·ble (un kən trō′lə bəl) *adj.* that cannot be held in check or restrained: *uncontrollable laughter.* —**un′con·trol′la·bly,** *adv.*

un·con·ven·tion·al (un′kən ven′shən əl) *adj.* not adhering to convention; out of the ordinary: *unconventional clothing, an unconventional life style, the unconventional way in which the author builds tension in this scene.* —**un·con·ven·tion·al·i·ty** (un′kən ven′shə nal′ə tē), *n.* —**un′con·ven′tion·al·ly,** *adv.*

un·cork (un kôrk′) *v.t.* to draw or remove the cork from.

un·count·ed (un koun′tid) *adj.* **1.** too many to count; innumerable: *medical research that will benefit uncounted millions of people.* **2.** not counted or enumerated: *an uncounted stack of letters.*

un·cou·ple (un kup′əl) -**pled, -pling.** *v.t.* **1.** to disconnect; unfasten; detach: *to uncouple railroad cars.* **2.** to set free; unleash, as hounds.

un·couth (un kōōth′) *adj.* **1.** lacking polish, culture, or refinement; crude. **2.** awkward or clumsy; ungainly. **3.** *Archaic.* not common, familiar, or usual; rare; strange. [Old English *uncūth* unknown, strange, from *un-* not + *cūth* known, familiar, past participle of *cunnan* to know.] —**un·couth′ly,** *adv.* —**un·couth′ness,** *n.*
Syn. 1. Uncouth, rough, rude mean lacking in social polish, civility, or refinement. **Uncouth** suggests an awkward, even crude manner, esp. of someone provincial or otherwise ignorant of manners or customs considered as standard: *Europeans often accuse traveling Americans of being uncouth.* **Rough** suggests crudity or a harshness of manner, esp. as contrasted with an inner gentleness that is awkwardly expressed because of ignorance or lack of experience: *The rough miner, trying to play with his grandchild, frightened the boy with his loud voice and his tight grip.* **Rude** suggests that one's manner results not from ignorance or lack of experience, as in *uncouth* or *rough,* but from a refusal to be considerate of others, to the point of being offensive: *I'm not leaving that rude waiter a tip.*

un·cov·er (un kuv′ər) *v.t.* **1.** to lay bare or make known; bring to light; disclose: *The police investigation uncovered a conspiracy to kidnap the ambassador.* **2.** to remove the cover or covering from: *Uncover the dish before you put it in the oven.* **3.** to expose to view by this means: *We uncovered relics buried by the desert sands. They uncovered the statue at the beginning of the ceremony.* **4.** to remove a hat or the like from (one's head) as a sign of respect. —*v.i.* to bare the head as a sign of respect.

un·cross (un krôs′) *v.t.* to change from a crossed position: *to uncross one's legs.*

unc·tion (ungk′shən) *n.* **1.** act of anointing as part of a religious or ceremonial ritual. **2.** substance used in anointing; oil, ointment, or salve. **3.** that which soothes, comforts, or restores; balm: *Lay not a flattering unction to your soul* (Shakespeare, *Hamlet*). **4.** exaggerated, excessive, or affected emotion, as in language. [Latin *unctiō* an anointing.]

unc·tu·ous (ungk′chōō əs) *adj.* **1.** characterized by exaggerated or affected emotion; excessively suave or ingratiating: *an unctuous dandy, unctuous flattery.* **2.** having the characteristics of oil or ointment; slippery to the touch; greasy. **3.** (of soil or clay) easily worked; rich. [Medieval Latin *unctuosus* oily, greasy, from Latin *unctus* an anointing.] —**unc′tu·ous·ly,** *adv.* —**unc′tu·ous·ness,** *n.*

un·cut (un kut′) *adj.* **1.** not cut or cut down, off, or into: *uncut flowers.* **2.** not shortened or edited; unabridged: *the uncut version of a film.* **3.** not changed or shaped by cutting: *an uncut diamond.* **4.** (of a book) not having the page edges slit open.

un·daunt·ed (un dôn′tid, -dän′-) *adj.* not intimidated or discouraged; fearless; intrepid. —**un·daunt′ed·ly,** *adv.*

un·de·ceive (un′di sēv′) -**ceived, -ceiv·ing.** *v.t.* to free from deception, illusion, or error.

un·de·cid·ed (un′di sī′did) *adj.* **1.** not having the mind made up; not having reached a decision: *I'm still undecided about what to wear to the dance.* **2.** not yet determined or settled: *The outcome of the election is still undecided.* —**un′de·cid′ed·ly,** *adv.* —**un′de·cid′ed·ness,** *n.*

un·de·mon·stra·tive (un′di mon′strə tiv) *adj.* not given to an open

display of affection or feeling; reserved. —**un′de·mon′stra·tive·ly,** *adv.* —**un′de·mon′stra·tive·ness,** *n.*

un·de·ni·a·ble (un′di nī′ə bəl) *adj.* **1.** that cannot be denied; irrefutable: *undeniable evidence, the undeniable truth of the statement.* **2.** unquestionably good; outstanding; excellent: *the undeniable value of good friendship.* —**un′de·ni′a·bly,** *adv.*

un·der (un′dər) *prep.* **1.** in a place or position down from or lower than: *under a pile of books, under the bed.* **2.** below the surface of: *under the skin.* **3.** covered, sheltered, or protected by: *under an umbrella, under one roof.* **4.** smaller or less than in number, degree, or amount: *under eight pounds, under an hour. We drove twenty miles under the speed limit.* **5.** subject to the authority, command, instruction, or guidance of; subordinate to: *to study under a professional, to serve under a general, to be under supervision.* **6.** undergoing the effects of; subject to: *under the influence of drugs. The fire is under control.* **7.** in the process of: *under consideration.* **8.** restrained, confined, or oppressed by: *under a dictatorship, under guard, under great pressure.* **9.** in conformity with; according to: *under the new plan.* **10.** required or bound by the terms, limitations, or conditions of: *under contract, under oath.* **11.** because of; considering: *under the existing circumstances.* **12.** during the reign or administration of: *The drama in England flourished under Elizabeth I.* **13.** beneath the category or heading of: *That book was under medical history. The listing can be found under the author's last name.* **14.** beneath the guise or cover of: *The actor traveled under an alias.* **15.** with the authorization of; attested by: *under the president's seal.* —*adv.* **1.** in or into a position down from or lower than something; below the surface: *The raft was sucked under by the eddy.* **2.** less than a certain standard or amount; downward through a specified range: *selling for $20 and under. The book is for children six years and under.* **3.** so as to be covered, sheltered, or concealed: *We were snowed under.* **4.** in or into a subordinate position or status; in subjection or submission. **5. to go under.** to fail, as a business. [Old English *under* beneath, below.]

under- *combining form* **1.** situated or located in a lower place or position: *underpass.* **2.** located beneath or enveloped by a surface or covering: *underwear, underwater, underground.* **3.** smaller or less than is usual, normal, or required in number, degree, or amount; insufficient; inadequate: *underweight, underage.* **4.** lower or inferior in rank, status, or importance; subordinate: *undergraduate, understudy.* **5.** subdued; restrained: *undertone.* [From UNDER.]

▲ The meaning of a word in the following list can be understood by combining *under-* with the root word.

un′der·clothed′	un′der·pop′u·lat′ed
un′der·cook′	un′der·pow′ered
un′der·dose′	un′der·praise′
un′der·eat′	un′der·priced′
un′der·ed′u·cat′ed	un′der·pro·duce′
un′der·em′pha·size′	un′der·ripe′
un′der·ex′er·cise′	un′der·spend′
un′der·fi·nance′	un′der·stock′
un′der·fur′nished	un′der·stocked′
un′der·lay′er	un′der·sup·ply′
un′der·men′tioned	un′der·sur′face
un′der·named′	un′der·theme′
un′der·of′fi·cer	un′der·trained′
un′der·peo′pled	un′der·worked′

un·der·a·chiev·er (un′dər ə chē′vər) *n.* one whose performance or achievement, esp. in school, is considered to be below his potential.

un·der·age (un′dər āj′) *adj.* not of the usual, required, or legal age.

un·der·arm (un′dər ärm′) *adj.* **1.** used, located, or occurring in the armpit; under the arm: *underarm perspiration.* **2.** underhand *(def. 1).* —*n.* armpit. —*adv.* underhand *(def. 1).*

un·der·bel·ly (un′dər bel′ē) *pl.* **-lies.** *n.* **1.** undersurface of something, esp. the lower abdominal region of an animal. **2.** any sensitive or vulnerable part: *the soft underbelly of the Axis* (Winston Churchill, 1942).

un′con·trolled′	un·cowed′	un·curl′	un′de·fend′ed
un′con·ver′sant	un·crate′	un·curled′	un′de·filed′
un′con·vert′ed	un′cre·a′tive	un′cur·tailed′	un′de·fin′a·ble
un′con·vert′i·ble	un′cre·a′tive·ly	un·cus′tom·ar·y	un′de·fined′
un′con·vinced′	un·cred′it·ed	un·dam′aged	un′de·lin′e·at′ed
un′con·vinc′ing	un·crit′i·cal	un·dat′ed	un′de·liv′er·a·ble
un′con·vinc′ing·ly	un·crowd′ed	un′de·bat′a·ble	un′de·mand′ing
un·cooked′	un·crowned′	un′de·cayed′	un′dem·o·crat′ic
un′co·op′er·a·tive	un·crys′tal·lized′	un′de·ci′pher·a·ble	un′dem·o·crat′i·cal·ly
un′co·or′di·nat′ed	un·cul′ti·va·ble	un′de·ci′phered	un′de·mon′stra·ble
un·cor′dial	un·cul′ti·vat′ed	un′de·clared′	un′de·mon′stra·bly
un′cor·rect′ed	un·cul′tured	un′de·clin′a·ble	un′de·nied′
un′cor·rob′o·rat′ed	un·curbed′	un′de·con′tam·i·na·ble	un′de·nom′i·na′tion·al
un′cor·rupt′ed	un·cured′	un′de·feat′ed	un′de·pend′a·ble

at; āpe; cär; end; mē; it; īce; hot; ōld; fôrk; wood; fōōl; oil; out; up; ūse; turn; sing; thin; this; zh in treasure; ə in ago, taken, pencil, lemon, circus.

un·der·bid (un′dər bid′) **-bid, -bid·ding.** *v.t.* to bid lower than (a competitor).

un·der·bred (un′dər bred′) *adj.* **1.** of mixed stock; not purebred. **2.** ill-mannered; vulgar.

un·der·brush (un′dər brush′) *n.* growth of bushes, shrubs, or similar plants beneath the large trees in a wood or forest.

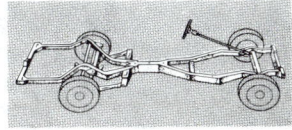

un·der·car·riage (un′dər kar′ij) *n.* **1.** supporting framework, as of an automobile. **2.** landing gear of an airplane.

Undercarriage (def. 1)

un·der·charge (*v.,* un′dər chärj′; *n.,* un′dər chärj′) **-charged, -charg·ing.** *v.t.* **1.** to charge (someone) too small a price. **2.** to supply or load with an insufficient charge, as a gun. —*n.* insufficient or inadequate charge.

un·der·class·man (un′dər klas′mən) *pl.,* **-men.** *n.* freshman or sophomore in secondary school or college.

un·der·clothes (un′dər klōz′, -klōthz′) *n.,pl.* underwear.

un·der·cloth·ing (un′dər klō′thing) *n.* underwear.

un·der·coat (un′dər kōt′) *n.* **1.** protective coat of a tarlike substance applied to the underside of an automobile to prevent rusting. **2.** coat of paint, varnish, or the like applied to a surface before the final coat. Also (*defs. 1, 2*), **un′der·coat′ing. 3.** layer of short hairs or down hidden by the fur on an animal's body.

un·der·cov·er (un′dər kuv′ər, un′dər kuv′ər) *adj.* working or done in secret, esp. spying or secret investigation: *an undercover agent for the CIA.*

un·der·cur·rent (un′dər kur′ənt) *n.* **1.** current, as of water or air, under another current or below a surface. **2.** underlying strain or tendency, esp. one that contradicts what is visible or apparent: *an undercurrent of annoyance that belied her courteous manner.*

un·der·cut (un′dər kut′) **-cut, -cut·ting.** *v.t.* **1.** to sell or work for lower payment than (a competitor). **2.** to weaken, impair, or destroy the effect, strength, or validity of; undermine: *to undercut an argument with wit.* **3.** to cut under or away, as in carving, esp. in order to leave a portion overhanging. **4.** to give a backspin to (a ball), as in baseball, golf, or tennis. —*n.* **1.** act or result of cutting under or away. **2.** notch that is cut in a tree or branch below the level at which it is to be sawed through to determine the direction of its fall or to prevent splitting.

un·der·de·vel·oped (un′dər də vel′əpt) *adj.* **1.** inadequately or insufficiently developed: *underdeveloped muscles.* **2.** not advanced industrially or technologically; economically dependent: *an underdeveloped nation.* **3.** *Photography.* not having the required degree of contrast: *an underdeveloped negative.*

un·der·dog (un′dər dôg′) *n.* **1.** predicted or most probable loser, as in a contest or game. **2.** victim of social, political, or economic injustice.

un·der·done (un′dər dun′) *adj.* insufficiently cooked; raw or rare.

un·der·es·ti·mate (*v.,* un′dər es′tə māt′; *n.,* un′dər es′tə mit, -māt′) **-mat·ed, -mat·ing.** *v.t.* **1.** to estimate at too low an amount, quantity, or rate: *The contractor underestimated the building costs.* **2.** to place too low a value on; underrate: *You underestimate my charm. The power of faith cannot be underestimated.* —*n.* too low an estimate.

un·der·ex·pose (un′dər iks pōz′) **-posed, -pos·ing.** *v.t.* to expose a photographic film or plate) to light for too short a period of time to produce a satisfactory picture. —**un′der·ex·po′sure,** *n.*

un·der·feed (un′dər fēd′) **-fed, -feed·ing.** *v.t.* to feed too little, esp. to feed less than is necessary for adequate nourishment.

un·der·foot (un′dər foot′) *adj., adv.* **1.** in the way. **2.** beneath or lying beneath the foot or feet; on the ground.

un·der·gar·ment (un′dər gär′mənt) *n.* article of underwear.

un·der·go (un′dər gō′) **-went, -gone, -go·ing.** *v.t.* **1.** to pass through; experience: *a building undergoing renovation, a society undergoing change.* **2.** to bear up under; suffer; endure: *to undergo my great-aunt's interminable complaints.* —**Syn. 1.** see experience.

un·der·grad·u·ate (un′dər graj′ŏŏ it) *n.* college or university student who has not yet received a degree, esp. one who has not received his bachelor's degree.

un·der·ground (*adj., adv.,* un′dər ground′; *n.,* un′dər ground′) *adj.* **1.** situated, operating, or done below the surface of the earth: *an underground installation, underground repairs.* **2.** hidden; secret. **3.** radical, subversive, or avant-garde in style, ideas, or activities: *an underground movement, an underground newspaper.* —*n.* **1.** group operating secretly to resist or overthrow an oppressive, esp. foreign-controlled, government. **2.** group or movement spearheading radical activity, esp. in art; the avant-garde. **3.** place or space below the surface of the earth, as a tunnel. **4.** *British.* subway *(def. 1).* —*adv.* **1.** below the surface of

the earth. **2.** in or into hiding; in secret: *After the coup d'état, the press went underground. The movement is operating underground.*

underground railroad 1. subway *(def. 1).* Also, **underground railway. 2. Underground Railroad.** before the abolition of slavery, a clandestine system of helping escaped American Negro slaves to freedom by transporting or escorting them to Canada or to the Free States.

un·der·growth (un′dər grōth′) *n.* **1.** growth of small plants and other vegetation beneath or among the larger trees of a forest. **2.** short fine hair covered by longer outer hair.

un·der·hand (un′dər hand′) *adv.* **1.** with the hand held below shoulder height. **2.** underhanded. —*adj.* **1.** performed with the hand held below shoulder height. **2.** underhanded.

un·der·hand·ed (un′dər han′did) *adj., adv.* done in a secret, treacherous manner; deceitful; sly. —**un′der·hand′ed·ly,** *adv.* —**un′der·hand′ed·ness,** *n.*

un·der·hung (un′dər hung′) *adj.* **1.** protruding from beneath, as a lower jaw. **2.** resting or moving on a track beneath it, as a sliding door.

un·der·lay (*v.,* un′dər lā′; *n.,* un′dər lā′) **-laid, -lay·ing.** *v.t.* **1.** to place under or below. **2.** to provide with a base or lining. **3.** to raise or support by this means. —*n.* something laid beneath, esp. paper placed under type to raise it to the height required for printing. [Old English *underlecgan* to place beneath, support by placing something beneath.]

un·der·lie (un′dər lī′) **-lay, -lain, -ly·ing.** *v.t.* **1.** to be located under or below. **2.** to be the basis, cause, or foundation of. [Old English *underlicgan* to be subject to, submit to.]

un·der·line (*v.,* un′dər līn′; *n.,* un′dər līn′) **-lined, -lin·ing.** *v.t.* **1.** to draw a line or lines under. **2.** to emphasize; stress: *to underline the importance of harmony.* —*n.* line drawn under words or other writing for emphasis or to indicate italics.

un·der·ling (un′dər ling) *n.* person in a subordinate or servile position; a lackey.

un·der·lip (un′dər lip′) *n.* lower lip.

un·der·ly·ing (un′dər lī′ing) *adj.* **1.** lying under or below: *underlying strata.* **2.** basic; fundamental: *the underlying physical similarity, the underlying principles of a theory.* **3.** hidden; obscure; concealed: *the underlying theme of the drama, his underlying motives.*

un·der·mine (un′dər mīn′) **-mined, -min·ing.** *v.t.* **1.** to weaken, impair, or destroy secretly or by degrees; sap: *to undermine a person's confidence. The illness has severely undermined her health.* **2.** to weaken by wearing away at the foundation or base of; erode: *the river undermining the bank.* **3.** to dig a mine or passage under; dig under or below.

un·der·most (un′dər mōst′) *adj., adv.* lowest in place or position; bottom.

un·der·neath (un′dər nēth′) *prep.* **1.** in a lower place or position; on the underside. **2.** under the guise or appearance of: *Underneath all of his pretense, he's a gracious fellow.* **3.** under the authority or control of; subordinate to —*adv.* lower than or under something; on the underside. [Old English *underneothan* beneath, below, from *under* (see UN-DER) + *neothan* below.]

un·der·nour·ish (un′dər nur′ish) *v.t.* to provide with insufficient food and other substances necessary to life and growth. —**un′der·nour′ish·ment,** *n.*

un·der·pants (un′dər pants′) *n.,pl.* undergarment that is designed to cover the loins, sometimes extending to cover the thighs.

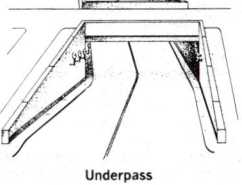

un·der·pass (un′dər pas′) *n.* passage or road that goes underneath, esp. the section that crosses and passes under another road, a bridge, or the like.

un·der·pay (un′dər pā′) **-paid, -pay·ing.** *v.t.* to pay too little or less than deserved.

Underpass

un·der·pin (un′dər pin′) **-pinned, -pin·ning.** *v.t.* **1.** to support or strengthen from below, as by laying or reinforcing the foundation of a building or wall. **2.** to support; substantiate: *to underpin an argument with facts.*

un·der·pin·ning (un′dər pin′ing) *n.* **1.** materials or structure used to support or strengthen a building, wall, or the like from below. **2.** support; prop. **3. underpinnings.** *Informal.* the legs.

un·der·play (un′dər plā′) *v.t.* **1.** to give little or inadequate emphasis or attention to; understate: *The press underplayed the incident. He underplayed the heroism of the chief character.* **2.** to act or play with subtlety and restraint: *The star underplayed the melodramatic scene.*

un·der·priv·i·leged (un′dər priv′ə lijd) *adj.* deprived of certain widely available advantages, such as adequate housing and education, because of poverty or social status.

un·der·pro·duc·tion (un′dər prə duk′shən) n. production that is below capacity or inadequate to meet the demand.

un·der·rate (un′dər rāt′) -rat·ed, -rat·ing. v.t. to rate too low; underestimate.

un·der·score (v., un′dər skôr′; n., un′dər skôr′) -scored, -scor·ing. v.t. to underline. —n. underline.

un·der·sea (un′dər sē′, -sē′) adj. existing, carried on, or designed for use beneath the surface of the sea. —adv. also, **un·der·seas.** beneath the surface of the sea.

un·der·sec·re·tar·y (un′dər sek′rə ter′ē) pl., -tar·ies. n. secretary who ranks directly below the secretary of a government department.

un·der·sell (un′dər sel′) -sold, -sell·ing. v.t. to sell at a lower price than.

un·der·sher·iff (un′dər sher′if) n. sheriff's deputy having the authority to perform all the ordinary duties of a sheriff.

un·der·shirt (un′dər shurt′) n. collarless undergarment usually having short or no sleeves.

un·der·shoot (un′dər shōōt′, un′dər shōōt′) -shot, -shoot·ing. v.t. 1. to shoot or land a missile or aircraft short of (the mark): *He undershot the bull's-eye. The pilot undershot the runway.* 2. (of a missile or aircraft) to land short of (a target or landing area).

un·der·shot (un′dər shot′) adj. 1. (of a water wheel) driven by water passing beneath. 2. having the lower jaw protruding from beneath; underhung.

un·der·side (un′dər sīd′) n. bottom side or surface.

Undershot water wheel

un·der·sign (un′dər sīn′, un′dər sīn′) v.t. to sign one's name at the end of (a document); affix a signature to.

un·der·signed (un′dər sīnd′) adj. having a signature or signatures at the end of a document; signed. —n. the undersigned. the person or persons who have signed a document.

un·der·sized (un′dər sīzd′) also, un·der·size. adj. of a less than normal, usual, or proper size.

un·der·skirt (un′dər skurt′) n. petticoat worn under a skirt.

un·der·sleeve (un′dər slēv′) n. sleeve designed to be worn under an outer sleeve, as one that extends below or can be seen through slashes in the outer sleeve.

un·der·slung (un′dər slung′) adj. attached to and suspended from the axles, as an automobile frame.

un·der·stand (un′dər stand′) -stood, -stand·ing. v.t. 1. to grasp the meaning or significance of; be clear about: *I don't understand what you mean. Do you understand the dream?* 2. to be thoroughly familiar and in sympathy or agreement with: *I don't pretend to understand her. The two sisters understand each other completely.* 3. to have mastery, as of a language or other subject matter: *I don't understand Russian. Do you understand sign language? He understands the business and can take over when I'm away.* 4. to construe; interpret: *We understood the term in its legal sense.* 5. to assume as plausible, factual, or truthful without certain knowledge; conclude: *Am I to understand that you're not going to see her any more?* 6. to be told (something); learn: *I understand that the proposal was vetoed.* 7. to accept or regard as a condition or stipulation; take as agreed or settled: *I understand that I can return the tickets before the performance and still get my money back.* —v.i. 1. to grasp the meaning or significance of (something); master. 2. to be told or assume: *He was going to Colorado, or so I understand.* 3. to be sympathetic. [Old English *understandan* to grasp the meaning, comprehend; literally, to stand under.] —Syn. v.t. 2. see know.

un·der·stand·a·ble (un′dər stan′də bəl) adj. that can be grasped, explained, or sympathized with: *an understandable error.* —un′der·stand′a·bly, adv.

un·der·stand·ing (un′dər stan′ding) n. 1. act of one who or that which understands, or the resulting quality or condition; comprehension: *a limited understanding of Einstein's theory.* 2. individual judgment; specific interpretation: *It was my understanding that he meant the end of the drama to be purposefully vague.* 3. comprehension and settlement of differences, as between friends. 4. informal or secret compact or the subject of such a compact: *The understanding was that someone selling his home would first consult the community. They began negotiations with the understanding that the cease-fire would be in effect for the entire period.* 5. faculty or power by which one understands; the intellect; intelligence: *a person of superior understanding.* —adj. mentally acute, esp. in dealing with people or emotions; sympathetic. —un′der·stand′ing·ly, adv.

un·der·state (un′dər stāt′) -stat·ed, -stat·ing. v.t. 1. to express with restraint, esp. for dramatic impact. 2. to state less than the truth about, as a quantity: *to understate her age.*

un·der·state·ment (un′dər stāt′mənt) n. 1. statement that is inaccurate or incomplete, esp. one that is deliberately restrained for dramatic impact. 2. deliberate restraint in expression.

un·der·stood (un′dər stood′) adj. 1. agreed or settled upon: *It's understood, then, that we'll meet at the corner at four o'clock.* 2. implied though not expressed verbally, as the subject of a sentence; assumed.

un·der·stud·y (un′dər stud′ē) pl., -stud·ies. n. performer who learns another's role in order to substitute, when necessary, for the regular performer. —v.t., -stud·ied, -stud·y·ing. 1. to learn (a role) in order to substitute, when necessary, for the regular performer. 2. to act as an understudy to (a performer). —v.i. to be an understudy.

un·der·take (un′dər tāk′) -took, -tak·en, -tak·ing. v.t. 1. to take upon oneself; set about to do; attempt: *She undertook the journey on horseback. We undertook the task of cleaning up the house.* 2. to accept or commit oneself to the charge or responsibility of: *The nurse undertook the invalid's care and feeding.* 3. *Informal.* to give a promise or pledge that; affirm; assert: *I'll undertake she's never even seen the country, much less lived there.*

un·der·tak·er (def. 1 un′dər tā′kər; def. 2 un′dər tā′kər) n. 1. one whose job or business is supervising burial or cremation and funeral arrangements. 2. one who undertakes something, as a business enterprise.

un·der·tak·ing (defs. 1, 3 un′dər tā′king; def. 2 un′dər tā′king) n. 1. that which is undertaken, as a task or enterprise. 2. business of an undertaker. 3. pledge or promise. —Syn. 1. see project.

un·der·tone (un′dər tōn′) n. 1. low or subdued tone, as of spoken sound. 2. underlying tendency or element; undercurrent: *an undertone of self-reproach.* 3. subdued color, esp. a unifying tone of color seen through various other colors: *The canvas was painted in a blue undertone to emphasize its eerie quality.*

un·der·tow (un′dər tō′) n. strong current flowing in a direction contrary to that of the surface current, esp. the backward pull of water from waves breaking against the shore.

un·der·val·ue (un′dər val′ū) -ued, -u·ing. v.t. to underestimate; underrate. —un′der·val′u·a′tion, n.

un·der·wa·ter (un′dər wô′tər, -wot′ər) adj. lying, used, or performed beneath the surface of the water. —adv. beneath the surface of the water.

un·der·wear (un′dər wâr′) n. clothing designed to be worn under one's outer clothes, usually next to the skin.

un·der·weight (un′dər wāt′) adj. not of the normal, desirable, or required weight; weighing too little. —n. weight below what is normal, desirable, or required.

un·der·went (un′dər went′) past tense of undergo.

un·der·wood (un′dər wood′) n. underbrush; undergrowth.

un·der·world (un′dər wurld′) n. 1. part of society engaged or involved in criminal activities, esp. those people engaged in organized crime. 2. also, **Underworld.** in mythology, as that of the Greeks and Romans, the underground dwelling place of the dead. 3. any region below the surface of the earth or a body of water. 4. *Archaic.* world below the heavens; earth.

un·der·write (un′dər rīt′) -wrote, -writ·ten, -writ·ing. v.t. 1. to provide the money or guarantee financial support for (a business venture or other undertaking): *to underwrite a theatrical production.* 2. to subscribe or agree to, as by signing one's name; concur with: *to underwrite a decision.* 3.a. to sign (an insurance policy), thereby assuming liability in case of specified losses or damage. b. to cover with insurance; insure. c. to assume liability to the amount of (a specified sum) by way of insurance. 4.a. to agree to buy (an issue of stocks or bonds to be sold to the public) on a specified date and at a specified price. b. to agree to buy (those stocks or bonds of a certain issue that are not bought by others before a specified date). 5. to endorse or write underneath (a document or other written matter); subscribe. —v.i. to act as or carry on the business of, an underwriter. [Translation of Latin *subscribere* to write beneath, sign, agree to.]

un·der·writ·er (un′dər rī′tər) n. 1. person or company in the insurance business, esp. one that approves a risk and determines the cost and extent of insurance. 2. person or company that underwrites an issue of stocks or bonds. 3. one who or that which finances or guarantees financial support for something.

un·de·sir·a·ble (un′di zīr′ə bəl) adj. not desirable or pleasing; objectionable; unacceptable: *an undesirable outcome, an undesirable neighborhood.* —n. one considered to be objectionable or unacceptable. —un′de·sir′a·bil′i·ty, un′de·sir′a·ble·ness, n. —un′de·sir′a·bly, adv.

---

un′de·scribed′	un′de·serv′ed·ly	un′des·ig·nat′ed	un′de·sir′ous
un′de·served′	un′de·serv′ing	un′de·sired′	un′de·stroyed′

at; āpe; cär; end; mē; it; īce; hot; ōld; fôrk; wood; fōōl; oil; out; up; ūse; turn; sing; thin; this; zh in treasure; ə in ago, taken, pencil, lemon, circus.

un·did (un did′) past tense of **undo**.

un·dies (un′dēz) *n.,pl. Informal.* underwear, esp. women's or children's underpants.

un·dis·guised (un′dis gīzd′) *adj.* not masked or concealed; open; obvious: *He spoke with undisguised emotion.*

un·dis·posed (un′dis pōzd′) *adj.* **1.** not sold, settled, removed, or concluded. ▲ often used in combination with *of: undisposed garbage, undisposed-of merchandise.* **2.** not having a tendency toward; disinclined (with *to*).

un·do (un dōō′) **-did, -done, -do·ing.** *v.t.* **1.** to release or loosen (a fastening); unfasten; untie: *She undid his tie. My shoelaces were undone.* **2.** to open by releasing a fastening or binding: *to undo a shirt, to undo a package.* **3.** to cause to be as if never done; cancel or reverse (what has been done): *The fire undid the work of six months. She undid her mistake.* **4.** to cause the ruin or downfall of; destroy: *Our folly has undone us.* [Old English *undōn.*] **—un·do′er,** *n.*

un·do·ing (un dōō′ing) *n.* **1.** cancellation or reversal of what has been done. **2.** ruin; downfall; destruction: *He brought on his own undoing.* **3.** cause of ruin or downfall: *Her stubbornness will prove her undoing.* **4.** act of unfastening or opening.

un·done¹ (un dun′) *adj.* not completed or finished; not done. [UN-¹ + DONE.]

un·done² (un dun′) *v.* past participle of **undo.** **—adj.** unfastened; untied; open.

un·doubt·ed (un dou′tid) *adj.* accepted with assurance and certainty as true. **—un·doubt′ed·ly,** *adv.*

un·draw (un drô′) **-drew, -drawn, -draw·ing.** *v.t.* to draw or pull open, back, or aside, as a curtain.

un·dreamt·of (un drèmt′uv′) *also,* **un·dreamed·of** (un drēmd′uv′). *adj.* not thought or considered possible; unimaginable: *undreamt-of riches.*

un·dress (un dres′) *v.t.* **1.** to remove the clothes or covering from; strip: *The child undressed herself and went to bed.* **2.** to remove the dressing or bandages from, as a wound. **—v.i.** to remove one's clothes. **—n. 1.** partial or total nakedness: *in a state of undress.* **2.** casual or informal clothing, as distinguished from formal dress; ordinary clothing.

un·due (un dōō′) *adj.* **1.** going beyond what is necessary, warranted, or appropriate; excessive; immoderate. **2.** not in accordance with what is just, right, or proper.

un·du·lant (un′jə lənt, -dyə-) *adj.* having a wavelike or sinuous form, appearance, or motion; moving in or as in waves.

undulant fever, infectious disease contracted by direct contact with infected animals or by consumption of their products, characterized by intermittent fever, chills, general aches and pains, and extreme fatigue. Also, **bru′cel·lo′sis.**

un·du·late (*v.,* un′jə lāt′, -dyə-; *adj.,* un′jə lit, -lāt′, -dyə-) **-lat·ed, -lat·ing,** *v.i.* **1.** to move in or as in waves; move like a wave or waves: *The snake undulating along the ground. The corn stalks undulate in the wind.* **2.** to have a rippling form or appearance: *The vast plain undulates in hills and valleys* (Ritchie, 1833). **—v.t. 1.** to cause to move in waves or like a wave. **2.** to give a rippling form or appearance to. **—adj.** having a rippling or wavelike form, outline, or appearance, as a leaf. Also, **un′du·lat′ed.** [Latin *undulātus* wavy, going back to *unda* wave.]

un·du·la·tion (un′jə lā′shən, -dyə-) *n.* **1.** movement in or as in waves; wavelike or sinuous motion. **2.** rippling outline, form, or appearance. **3.** one of a series of waves or wavelike curves.

un·du·ly (un dōō′lē, -dū′-) *adv.* **1.** unnecessarily; excessively; immoderately. **2.** without regard for what is just, right, or proper.

un·du·ti·ful (un dōō′ti fəl, -dū′-) *adj.* failing in loyalty, obedience, or a sense of duty: *an undutiful child, an undutiful servant.* **—un·du′ti·ful·ly,** *adv.*

un·dy·ing (un dī′ing) *adj.* without end; eternal; unceasing: *undying devotion.*

un·earned (un urnd′) *adj.* **1.** not gained in exchange for labor or service: *unearned income.* **2.** not merited or deserved: *an unearned scolding.* **3.** not yet earned: *unearned interest.*

unearned increment, increase in the value of property not brought about by any effort or investment made by the owner, as when a growth in population increases the demand for and value of land.

un·earth (un urth′) *v.t.* **1.** to dig up out of the earth; disinter: *to unearth buried treasure.* **2.** to bring to light by or as by searching; discover; reveal: *to unearth evidence damaging to the defendant.*

un·earth·ly (un urth′lē) *adj.* **1.** frighteningly strange or inexplicable; weird: *an unearthly shriek.* **2.** rising above what is characteristic of this world; ideal; sublime: *an unearthly grace.* **3.** *Informal.* inconvenient or uncustomary to an absurd degree; preposterous: *an unearthly hour of the morning.* **—un·earth′li·ness,** *n.*

un·eas·y (un ē′zē) **-eas·i·er, -eas·i·est.** *adj.* **1.** lacking comfort or ease of mind; disturbed; anxious: *I feel uneasy about her being out so late.* **2.** causing or disturbed by unrest, insecurity, or anxiety: *He finally dropped off into an uneasy sleep. An uneasy atmosphere prevailed in the city after the mob was dispersed.* **3.** marked by embarrassment or awkwardness; constrained: *an uneasy laugh, an uneasy silence.* **4.** easily broken or disrupted; unstable; precarious: *an uneasy truce.* **—un·eas′i·ly,** *adv.* **—un·eas′i·ness,** *n.*

un·ed·u·cat·ed (un ej′ə kā′tid) *adj.* lacking enlightenment or education, esp. lacking formal education; not educated: *an uneducated man, an uneducated point of view.*

un·em·ploy·a·ble (un′em ploi′ə bəl) *adj.* not able to hold a job. **—n.** unemployable person.

un·em·ployed (un′em ploid′) *adj.* **1.** without a job; out of work. **2.** not being put to use: *unemployed funds.* **—n. the unemployed.** people out of work, collectively.

un·em·ploy·ment (un′em ploi′mənt) *n.* **1.** state of being unemployed; lack of employment. **2.** number or percentage of people who are out of work: *Unemployment has risen for the second consecutive month.*

un·e·qual (un ēk′wəl) *adj.* **1.** not the same in some measure, as in amount, number, rank, or magnitude: *unequal portions, sleeves of unequal length, unequal opportunities.* **2.** involving two or more persons who are not well or equally matched, as in advantage or strength: *an unequal partnership, an unequal race, an unequal struggle.* **3.** lacking the necessary strength or ability; not fit or qualified; inadequate (with *to*): *His imagination was unequal to the enterprise.* **4.** not regular, uniform, or consistent; variable: *the unequal distribution of heat in the room.* **—un·e′qual·ly,** *adv.*

un·e·qualed (un ēk′wəld) *also,* **British. un·e·qualled.** *adj.* not matched or surpassed; unrivaled: *an unequaled performance.*

un·e·quiv·o·cal (un′i kwiv′ə kəl) *adj.* having a meaning that cannot be misunderstood or doubted; unambiguous: *an unequivocal denial of the charges.* **—un′e·quiv′o·cal·ly,** *adv.*

un′de·tach′a·ble	un′dis·ci′plined′	un·drape′	un·end′ing
un′de·tect′a·ble	un′dis·closed′	un·drink′a·ble	un′en·dorsed′
un′de·tect′ed	un′dis·cour′aged	un·dyed′	un′en·dowed′
un′de·tect′i·ble	un′dis·cov′ered	un·ea′ger	un′en·dur′a·ble
un′de·ter′mi·na·ble	un′dis·crim′i·nat′ing	un·eat′a·ble	un′en·dur′a·bly
un′de·ter′mined	un′dis·crim′i·nat′ing·ly	un·eat′en	un′en·force′a·ble
un′de·terred′	un′dis·mayed′	un′e·clipsed′	un′en·forced′
un′de·vel′oped	un′dis·put′ed	un′e·co·nom′ic	un′en·joy′a·ble
un′de·vi′at·ing	un′dis·solved′	un′e·co·nom′i·cal	un′en·larged′
un′di·ag·nosed′	un′dis·tilled′	un′e·co·nom′i·cal·ly	un′en·light′ened
un′dif·fer·en′ti·at′ed	un′dis·tin′guish·a·ble	un·ed′i·ble	un′en·light′en·ing
un′dif·fused′	un′dis·tin′guished	un′ed·u·ca·ble	un′en·liv′ened
un′di·gest′ed	un′dis·tin′guish·ing	un′e·man′ci·pat′ed	un′en·riched′
un′dig′ni·fied′	un′dis·tort′ed	un′e·mas′cu·lat′ed	un′en·rolled′
un′di·lat′ed	un′dis·trib′ut·ed	un′em·bar′rassed	un′en·sured′
un′di·lut′ed	un′dis·turbed′	un′e·mo′tion·al	un′en·tan′gled
un′di·min′ished	un′di·ver′si·fied′	un′e·mo′tion·al·ly	un′en·ter·pris′ing
un·dimmed′	un′di·vid′ed	un′em·phat′ic	un′en·ter·tain′ing
un′dip·lo·mat′ic	un′di·vulged′	un′em·phat′i·cal·ly	un′en·thu′si·as′tic
un′di·rect′ed	un·doc′u·ment·ed	un′em·ploy′tied	un′en·thu′si·as′ti·cal·ly
un′dis·cerned′	un·do·mes′ti·cat′ed	un′en·closed′	un·en′vi·a·ble
un′dis·cern′i·ble	un·doubt′ing	un′en·cum′bered	un·en′vied′
un′dis·cern′i·bly	un·drai′mat′ic	un′en·dan′gered	un′en·quipped′
un′dis·cern′ing	un·dra·mat′i·cal·ly		

un·er·ring (un ur′ing, -er′-) *adj.* **1.** committing no error or mistake; unfailingly right or appropriate; faultless: *unerring judgment, unerring precision, unerring good taste.* **2.** not going astray or missing the mark; undeviating: *the unerring flight of an arrow.* —**un·err′ing·ly,** *adv.*

UNESCO (ū nes′kō) United Nations Educational, Scientific, and Cultural Organization.

un·es·sen·tial (un′ə sen′shəl) *adj.* not of prime importance; dispensable. —*n.* something dispensable; a nonessential.

un·e·ven (un ē′vən) *adj.* **1.** not in or extending along the same plane; not straight, parallel, or perfectly horizontal: *an uneven hem. The curtains are uneven.* **2.** not smooth or flat; jagged: *the uneven surface of a rock.* **3.** not of uniform or consistent quality throughout: *uneven color. Uneven writing mars this novel.* **4.** subject to variations or sudden changes: *an uneven temper.* **5.** (of a number) odd. **6.** not well-matched or balanced; unfair; one-sided. [Old English *unefen* unequal, unlike.] —**un·e′ven·ly,** *adv.* —**un·e′ven·ness,** *n.* —**Syn. 2.** see **rough.**

un·e·vent·ful (un′i vent′fəl) *adj.* without anything important or noteworthy happening; routine; ordinary: *an uneventful trip.* —**un′e·vent′ful·ly,** *adv.*

un·ex·am·pled (un′ig zam′pəld) *adj.* without precedent; unparalleled; unique: *unexampled cruelty.*

un·ex·cep·tion·a·ble (un′ik sep′shə nə bəl) *adj.* beyond criticism or reproach; wholly admirable: *an unexceptionable statesman.* —**un′·ex·cep′tion·a·bly,** *adv.*

un·ex·cep·tion·al (un′ik sep′shən əl) *adj.* **1.** not different from what is usual or common; ordinary. **2.** admitting of no exception. —**un·ex·cep′tion·al·ly,** *adv.*

un·ex·pect·ed (un′iks pek′tid) *adj.* coming or happening without warning; unforeseen: *an unexpected delay, his unexpected kindness.* —**un′ex·pect′ed·ly,** *adv.* —**un′ex·pect′ed·ness,** *n.*

un·fail·ing (un fā′ling) *adj.* **1.** never weakening or varying; unflagging: *unfailing devotion.* **2.** always accurate; certain; infallible: *an unfailing indication of his mood.* **3.** never running short; inexhaustible: *an unfailing supply of food.* —**un·fail′ing·ly,** *adv.*

un·fair (un fār′) *adj.* **1.** characterized by bias or prejudice; unjust: *an unfair criticism.* **2.** violating accepted rules or standards; fraudulent: *unfair business practices.* [Old English *unfæger* not beautiful, ugly.] —**un·fair′ly,** *adv.* —**un·fair′ness,** *n.*

un·faith·ful (un fāth′fəl) *adj.* **1.** not adhering to a pledge, allegiance, or duty; not truly loyal or devoted; untrustworthy: *an unfaithful servant.* **2.** not true to marriage vows; guilty of adultery: *an unfaithful wife.* **3.** not precisely or truthfully representing an original; not accurate or exact: *an unfaithful translation, an unfaithful account of what happened.* —**un·faith′ful·ly,** *adv.* —**un·faith′ful·ness,** *n.*

un·fa·mil·iar (un′fə mil′yər) *adj.* **1.** not well known or immediately recognizable; strange: *This handwriting is unfamiliar to me.* **2.** lacking knowledge of or experience with (with *with*): *to be unfamiliar with a subject.* —**un′fa·mil′i·ar′i·ty,** *n.* —**un′fa·mil′iar·ly,** *adv.*

un·fas·ten (un fas′ən) *v.t.* to detach or undo the fastening or fastenings of; open: *to unfasten a dress, to unfasten a zipper.* —*v.i.* to become detached, loosened, or opened.

un·fa·vor·a·ble (un fā′vər ə bəl) *also, British* **un·fa·vour·a·ble.** *adj.* **1.** not in one's favor; disadvantageous: *an unfavorable impression, a political climate unfavorable to democracy.* **2.** disapproving; critical: *The play received unfavorable reviews.* **3.** denying something desired or requested; negative: *an unfavorable reply.* **4.** not promising; pessimistic: *an unfavorable diagnosis.* —**un·fa′vor·a·ble·ness;** *also, British,* **un·fa′vour·a·ble·ness,** *n.* —**un·fa′vor·a·bly;** *also, British,* **un·fa′vour·a·bly,** *adv.*

un·feel·ing (un fē′ling) *adj.* **1.** lacking in sympathy or compassion;

callous; cruel: *an unfeeling response to the problems of the migrant workers.* **2.** not able to experience feeling or sensation. —**un·feel′ing·ly,** *adv.* —**un·feel′ing·ness,** *n.*

un·feigned (un fānd′) *adj.* not pretended or hypocritical; genuine; sincere: *unfeigned enthusiasm.* —**un·feign·ed·ly** (un fā′nid lē), *adv.*

un·fet·ter (un fet′ər) *v.t.* to free from chains or other restraints; liberate.

un·fin·ished (un fin′isht) *adj.* **1.** not concluded or completed: *unfinished business.* **2.** not completely treated or processed; rough: *unfinished furniture, unfinished fabric.*

un·fit (un fit′) *adj.* **1.** not adapted, suitable, or appropriate to some end or purpose: *food that is unfit to eat, buildings unfit for human habitation.* **2.** lacking the necessary qualifications; incompetent: *unfit to rule. He was unfit for the position.* **3.** in poor mental or physical condition; unhealthy. —*v.t.,* **-fit·ted** or **-fit, -fit·ting.** to make unfit. —**un·fit′ness,** *n.*

un·flag·ging (un flag′ing) *adj.* not wavering or failing; untiring; sustained: *unflagging energy, unflagging spirits.* —**un·flag′ging·ly,** *adv.*

un·fledged (un flejd′) *adj.* **1.** lacking knowledge of or experience in the world; uninitiated: *an unfledged poet.* **2.** (of a young bird) not yet having developed feathers needed for flight.

un·flinch·ing (un flin′ching) *adj.* not drawing back or away from danger, pain, or other hardship; unshrinking: *unflinching determination.* —**un·flinch′ing·ly,** *adv.*

un·fold (un fōld′) *v.t.* **1.** to open, expand, or spread out (something folded): *to unfold a letter.* **2.** to make known or clear gradually or by degrees; disclose; explain: *to unfold the details of a plan. I could a tale unfold whose lightest word would harrow up thy soul* (Shakespeare, *Hamlet*). **3.** to lay open to view; uncover; display: *When the steep part of the journey is accomplished a lovely prospect is unfolded* (Jenkinson, 1872). —*v.i.* **1.** to become open or spread out, as the petals of a flower. **2.** to be revealed or become clear or known gradually: *The story unfolded suspensefully. New horizons will unfold before your very eyes.* [Old English *unfealdan* to open the folds of, explain.]

un·fore·seen (un′fôr sēn′) *adj.* not anticipated, known, or considered beforehand; unexpected.

un·for·get·ta·ble (un′fər get′ə bəl) *adj.* not to be forgotten; memorable. —**un′for·get′ta·bly,** *adv.*

un·formed (un fôrmd′) *adj.* **1.** having no definite form; shapeless. **2.** not fully developed or organized.

un·for·tu·nate (un fôr′chə nit) *adj.* **1.** having bad luck; unlucky. **2.** causing or attended by misfortune; disastrous. **3.** to be regretted or disapproved of as improper or unsuitable: *his unfortunate choice of words.* —*n.* one who is unfortunate. —**un·for′tu·nate·ly,** *adv.*

un·found·ed (un foun′did) *adj.* having no basis in reality; unwarranted; groundless: *an unfounded accusation.*

Syn. Unfounded, groundless, baseless mean without basis in fact, reason, or reality. **Unfounded** suggests that some evidence exists but is inconclusive or insufficient to support any particular statement or belief: *These old wives' tales are unfounded superstitions.* **Groundless** shifts the emphasis from verifiable proof to inner motivation as a cause: *His suspicion that his friend was lying to him was groundless.* **Baseless** implies no inner or external cause: *The rumors that the minister was ill proved baseless.*

un·fre·quent·ed (un′fri kwen′tid, -frē′kwen tid) *adj.* seldom or never visited: *unfrequented areas of town.*

un·friend·ly (un frend′lē) **-li·er, -li·est.** *adj.* **1.** failing to exhibit the qualities or feelings of a friend; feeling or showing dislike or hostility: *an unfriendly neighbor, an unfriendly act.* **2.** not favorable, pleasant, or propitious: *an unfriendly climate.* —**un·friend′li·ness,** *n.*

un′es·cap′a·ble	un′ex·pend′ed	un′fash′ion·a·ble	un·flat′tered
un′es·cap′a·bly	un′ex·pend′i·ble	un·fath′om·a·ble	un·flat′ter·ing
un′es·cort′ed	un′ex·pe′ri·enced	un·fath′omed	un·fla′vored
un′es·thet′ic	un′ex·pired′	un·fear′ful	un·flexed′
un·es′ti·mat′ed	un′ex·plain′a·ble	un·fea′si·ble	un′for·bid′den
un·eth′i·cal	un′ex·plained′	un·fed′	un′for·bid′ding
un′ex·ag′ger·at′ed	un′ex·plod′ed	un·feign′ing	un·forced′
un·ex·am′ined	un′ex·plored′	un·feign′ing·ly	un′fore·known′
un·ex′ca·vat′ed	un′ex·posed′	un·felt′	un′fore·see′a·ble
un·ex·celled′	un′ex·pressed′	un·fem′i·nine	un′fore·told′
un′ex·change′a·ble	un·ex·pres′sive	un·fenced′	un′for·giv′a·ble
un·ex·cit′ed	un·ex′pur·gat′ed	un′fer·ment′ed	un′for·giv′a·bly
un·ex·cit′ing	un′ex·tin′guish·a·ble	un·fer′ti·lized′	un′for·giv′en
un·ex·cus′a·ble	un′ex·tin′guished	un·filled′	un′for·giv′ing
un·ex·cus′a·bly	un·fad′ed	un·filmed′	un′for·got′ten
un·ex·cused′	un·fad′ing	un·fil′tered	un·for′mu·lat′ed
un·ex′e·cut′ed	un·fal′ter·ing	un·fit′ted	un·for′ti·fied′
un′ex·pec′tant	un·fal′ter·ing·ly	un·fit′ting	un·fought′
un′ex·pend′a·ble	un·fash′ion·a·ble	un·fit′ting·ly	un·framed′

at; āpe; cär; end; mē; it; īce; hot; ōld; fôrk; wood; fo͞ol; oil; out; up; ūse; turn; sing; thin; this; zh in treasure; ə in ago, taken, pencil, lemon, circus.

un·frock (un frok′) *v.t.* to divest (a priest or other cleric) of the right to exercise the functions of office.

un·fruit·ful (un froot′fəl) *adj.* **1.** not producing desired or useful results; unsuccessful; unproductive: *unfruitful peace talks.* **2.** not producing or marked by the production of offspring or vegetation; barren: *an unfruitful season, an unfruitful marriage.* —**un·fruit′ful·ly,** *adv.* —**un·fruit′ful·ness,** *n.*

un·furl (un furl′) *v.t.* to open or spread out, as before the wind; unroll: *to unfurl a flag.* —*v.i.* to become spread out.

un·gain·ly (un gān′lē) **-li·er, -li·est.** *adj.* **1.** lacking grace of movement or form; awkward; clumsy: *ungainly gestures, an ungainly colt.* **2.** difficult to handle or move; unwieldy. [UN-¹ + dialectal English *gainly* graceful, proper (from Old Norse *gegn* straight) + -LY²).] —**un·gain′li·ness,** *n.* —**Syn. 1.** see awkward.

un·gen·er·ous (un jen′ər əs) *adj.* **1.** not liberal; stingy; niggardly: *an ungenerous donor, an ungenerous sum.* **2.** lacking kindness or sympathy; harsh in judgment; uncharitable: *an ungenerous remark, an ungenerous attitude.* —**un·gen′er·ous·ly,** *adv.* —**un·gen′er·ous·ness,** *n.*

un·gird (un gurd′) **-girt** or **-gird·ed, -gird·ing.** *v.t.* **1.** to free from a belt, girdle, or other constraining band. **2.** to loosen or release by or as by unfastening a belt: *to ungird armor, to ungird a sword.*

un·glue (un glōō′) **-glued, -glu·ing.** *v.t.* **1.** to detach or separate by or as if by removing or dissolving glue. **2.** *Informal.* to cause (someone) to become extremely upset or helplessly flustered.

un·god·ly (un god′lē) **-li·er, -li·est.** *adj.* **1.** not feeling or showing a reverence for God or religious laws; impious; sinful. **2.** *Informal.* highly inappropriate or inconvenient; outrageous: *an ungodly hour.* —**un·god′li·ness,** *n.*

un·gov·ern·a·ble (un guv′ər nə bəl) *adj.* impossible to control, rule, or keep in check: *an ungovernable mob, an ungovernable appetite.* —**un·gov′ern·a·bly,** *adv.*

un·gra·cious (un grā′shəs) *adj.* lacking in kindness or courtesy; impolite; rude. —**un·gra′cious·ly,** *adv.* —**un·gra′cious·ness,** *n.*

un·grate·ful (un grāt′fəl) *adj.* **1.** not thankful or appreciative of kindness or benefits received: *an ungrateful wretch.* **2.** disagreeable; unpleasant: *an ungrateful task.* —**un·grate′ful·ly,** *adv.* —**un·grate′ful·ness,** *n.*

un·ground·ed (un groun′did) *adj.* **1.** without justification or basis in reality: *ungrounded hopes, an ungrounded accusation.* **2.** lacking knowledge or instruction; not educated: *to be ungrounded in the sciences.* **3.** (of an electrical circuit) improperly or unsafely connected with the earth.

un·grudg·ing (un gruj′ing) *adj.* without envy or other reservation; wholehearted; unstinting: *ungrudging acceptance.* —**un·grudg′ing·ly,** *adv.*

un·gual (ung′gwəl) *adj.* of, relating to, or resembling a hoof, claw, or nail. [Latin *unguis* hoof, claw, nail + -AL¹.]

un·guard·ed (un gär′did) *adj.* **1.** without guard or protection: *an unguarded entrance.* **2.** characterized by an absence of reserve or caution; unthinking: *in an unguarded moment. He made an unguarded reference to his first romance.* —**un·guard′ed·ly,** *adv.* —**un·guard′ed·ness,** *n.*

un·guent (ung′gwənt) *n.* salve or ointment. [Latin *unguentum.*]

un·guis (ung′gwis) *pl.* **-gues (-gwēz).** *n.* nail, claw, or hoof. [Latin *unguis.*]

un·gu·la (ung′gyə lə) *pl.* **-lae (-lē).** *n.* unguis. [Latin *ungula* claw, hoof.]

un·gu·late (ung′gyə lit, -lāt′) *adj.* **1.** having hoofs. **2.** of or relating to a former order, Ungulata, including all hoofed mammals. **3.** hoof-shaped. —*n.* hoofed mammal. [Late Latin *ungulātus* having claws or hoofs, from Latin *ungula* claw, hoof.]

un·hal·lowed (un hal′ōd) *adj.* **1.** not made holy; unconsecrated. **2.** impious; wicked.

un·hand (un hand′) *v.t.* to release from the hand or hands, or from one's grasp; let go of: *Unhand me, villain!*

un·hap·py (un hap′ē) **-pi·er, -pi·est.** *adj.* **1.** without happiness, joy, or contentment; sad; miserable: *an unhappy child.* **2.** causing, attended by, or resulting from misfortune; unlucky: *unhappy mistake.* **3.** lacking in tact or good taste; inappropriate; ill-chosen: *an unhappy remark.* —**un·hap′pi·ly,** *adv.* —**un·hap′pi·ness,** *n.*

un·har·ness (un här′nis) *v.t.* **1.** to remove a harness from: *to unharness a horse.* **2.** to free from restraint or confinement; release, as energy or emotions.

un·health·ful (un helth′fəl) *adj.* not conducive to good health. —**un·health′ful·ly,** *adv.* —**un·health′ful·ness,** *n.*

un·health·y (un hel′thē) **-health·i·er, -health·i·est.** *adj.* **1.** not in good health; sick; sickly. **2.** causing or conducive to poor health; unwholesome: *a reeking swamp whose presence is unhealthy for the surrounding neighborhood.* **3.** characteristic of or indicating poor health or abnormality: *an unhealthy pulse, an unhealthy fixation.* **4.** harmful to character or morals; corruptive: *an unhealthy influence.* **5.** dangerous; risky; unsafe: *a country where it would be unhealthy to deviate from the official party line.* —**un·health′i·ly,** *adv.* —**un·health′i·ness,** *n.*

un·heard (un hurd′) *adj.* **1.** not perceived by the ear: *cries that went unheard.* **2.** not given a hearing: *an unheard appeal.* **3.** *Archaic.* unheard-of *(def. 2).*

un·heard-of (un hurd′uv′, -ov′) *adj.* **1.** extreme or excessive to an absurd degree; outrageous: *unheard-of demands, unheard-of impudence.* **2.** not previously known or occurring; unknown; unprecedented.

un·heed·ed (un hē′did) *adj.* not paid attention to; disregarded; unnoticed.

un·hes·i·tat·ing (un hez′ə tā′ting) *adj.* **1.** without hesitation or delay; immediate; prompt: *an unhesitating reply.* **2.** steadfast; unfaltering; unwavering: *unhesitating loyalty.* —**un·hes′i·tat′ing·ly,** *adv.*

un·hinge (un hinj′) **-hinged, -hing·ing.** *v.t.* **1.** to remove from hinges, as a door. **2.** to remove the hinges from. **3.** to throw into confusion or disorder; unsettle; unbalance: *The accident unhinged his mind.*

un·hitch (un hich′) *v.t.* to free from being hitched; set loose; unfasten: *to unhitch a mule from a wagon.*

un·ho·ly (un hō′lē) **-li·er, -li·est.** *adj.* **1.** not sanctified or consecrated; unhallowed: *unholy ground.* **2.** sinful; wicked; immoral: *an unholy alliance.* **3.** *Informal.* dreadful; terrible: *He made an unholy racket clambering up the stairs with his suitcase.* [Old English *unhālig* wicked.] —**un·ho′li·ly,** *adv.* —**un·ho′li·ness,** *n.*

un·hook (un hook′) *v.t.* **1.** to release or detach from or as from a hook: *to unhook a latch, to unhook a lantern.* **2.** to unfasten the hook or hooks of: *to unhook a dress.* —*v.i.* to become unhooked.

un·hoped-for (un hōpt′fôr′) *adj.* that is not expected or anticipated: *unhoped-for good news.*

un·horse (un hôrs′) **-horsed, -hors·ing.** *v.t.* **1.** to throw (a rider) from a horse. **2.** to dislodge; overthrow.

un·hur·ried (un hur′ēd) *adj.* without rush or haste; leisurely: *an unhurried exit, an unhurried breakfast.* —**un·hur′ried·ly,** *adv.*

uni- *combining form* of, having, or consisting of only one; single: *unicameral, unicellular.* [Latin *ūnus* one.]

U·ni·ate (ū′nē it, -āt′) *also,* **U·ni·at** (ū′nē ät′). *n.* member of the Uniate Church. —*adj.* of, relating to, or characteristic of the Uniate Church or its members. [Russian *uniyat,* from *uniya* union, unity, going back to Latin *ūnus* one.]

Uniate Church *also,* **Uniat Church.** any of several Christian churches that accepts the doctrines of the Roman Catholic Church and the supremacy of the pope but maintains separate liturgies, customs, and laws.

Unicorn

u·ni·cam·er·al (ū′nə kam′ər əl) *adj.* having or consisting of a single legislative chamber, house, or branch. Distinguished from **bicameral.** [UNI- + Late Latin *camera* chamber + -AL¹. See CHAMBER.]

UNICEF (ū′nə sef′) United Nations International Children's Emergency Fund.

u·ni·cel·lu·lar (ū′nə sel′yə lər) *adj.* having or consisting of a single cell.

u·ni·corn (ū′nə kôrn′) *n.* legendary animal usually represented as

---

at; āpe; cär; end; mē; it; īce; hot; ōld; fôrk; wood; fōōl; oil; out; up; ūse; turn; sing; thin; this; zh in treasure; ə in ago, taken, pencil, lemon, circus. 1087

a white horse with a long pointed horn in the middle of its forehead, regarded as a symbol of innocence and purity. [Latin *únicornus* having one horn, from *ūnus* one + *cornū* horn.]

u·ni·cy·cle (ū′nə sī′kəl) *n.* vehicle consisting of a single wheel and operated by foot pedals, often having a seat or bar mounted on a shaft, used chiefly by acrobats, entertainers, and gymnasts. Also, **mon′o·cy′cle.** [UNI- + CYCLE.]

unidentified flying object, flying or apparently flying object classified by the U.S. Air Force as of unidentified or unknown nature because its appearance cannot be explained after all available information on the sighting has been investigated.

Unicycle

u·ni·fi·ca·tion (ū′nə fi kā′shən) *n.* act or process of unifying; being unified.

u·ni·form (ū′nə fôrm′) *adj.* **1.** without change, fluctuation, or variation; always the same; unvarying: *a uniform rate of acceleration, uniform temperature and pressure. The color is uniform throughout the canvas.* **2.** showing little or no difference in form, design, or size: *All the houses in this development are uniform.* **3.** being the same as another or others: *The townships in this area have uniform building codes.* —*n.* **1.** distinctive or official dress or outfit worn by and identifying the members of a particular group or profession: *policemen in uniform.* **2.** single outfit of this kind: *The orderly brushed off the general's uniform.* —*v.i.* to provide or clothe with a uniform. [Latin *ūniformis* having one form, from *ūnus* one + *forma* shape, form.] —**u′ni·form′ly,** *adv.* —**u′ni·form′ness,** *n.* —**Syn.** *adj.* **1.** see *even*[1].

u·ni·form·i·ty (ū′nə fôr′mə tē) *pl.,* **-ties.** *n.* state, quality, or instance of being uniform.

u·ni·fy (ū′nə fī′) **-fied, -fy·ing.** *v.t.* to combine or make into a unit or coherent whole; cause to be one or as one: *The essay traces the developments that unified the country.* [Medieval Latin *unificare,* from Latin *ūnus* one + *facere* to make.] —**u′ni·fi′er,** *n.*

u·ni·lat·er·al (ū′nə lat′ər əl) *adj.* **1.** of, affecting, or performed or undertaken by one party or person only: *unilateral disarmament, a unilateral withdrawal of troops.* **2.** of, relating to, or affecting only one side. **3.** relating to, concerned with, or considering only one side of a subject. **4.** *Law.* having effect on or obligating only one of two or more parties, as a contract or agreement. —**u′ni·lat′er·al·ly,** *adv.*

u·ni·mag·i·na·tive (un′i maj′ə nə tiv) *adj.* lacking imagination or creativity: *an unimaginative theatrical production, an unimaginative leader.* —**un′i·mag′i·na·tive·ly,** *adv.*

un·im·peach·a·ble (un′im pē′chə bəl) *adj.* not to be called into question; above reproach or blame; faultless. —**un′im·peach′a·bly,** *adv.*

un·im·por·tant (un′im pôrt′ənt) *adj.* lacking any special value, relevance, or meaning; insignificant; trivial: *a relatively unimportant invention.* —**un′im·port′ance,** *n.*

un·in·hib·i·ted (un′in hib′i tid) *adj.* **1.** lacking or having a few social, moral, or psychological inhibitions, as in behavior: *an uninhibited critic of the regime's policies. He's the most uninhibited person I know.* **2.** not held back, checked, or inhibited; unrestrained: *uninhibited laughter.* —**un′in·hib′i·ted·ly,** *adv.*

un·in·spired (un′in spīrd′) *adj.* lacking originality, imagination, or creativity; dull: *an uninspired speech, an uninspired performance of the concerto.*

un·in·tel·li·gent (un′in tel′ə jənt) *adj.* **1.** having or marked by a deficiency in thinking or reasoning. **2.** lacking the faculty or power of thought and reason. —**un′in·tel′li·gent·ly,** *adv.*

un·in·tel·li·gi·ble (un′in tel′ə jə bəl) *adj.* not capable of being made out or understood: *an unintelligible answer. Your handwriting is unintelligible.* —**un′in·tel′li·gi·bil′i·ty,** *n.* —**un′in·tel′li·gi·bly,** *adv.*

un·in·ter·est·ed (un in′tər is tid, -tris tid, -tə res′tid) *adj.* **1.** lacking interest or intellectual or emotional involvement; unconcerned; indifferent. **2.** disinterested *(def. I).*

un·in·ter·rupt·ed (un′in tə rup′tid) *adj.* without interruption; unbroken; continuous: *an uninterrupted flow.* —**un′in·ter·rupt′ed·ly,** *adv.*

un·ion (ūn′yən) *n.* **1.** act of uniting; being united. **2.** something formed by uniting two or more things; whole made up of united parts. **3.** a uniting or joining of various parties, as persons, states, or nations, for a common purpose or for their mutual benefit. **4.** group or body thus formed, esp. a political unit formed by previously independent groups. **5.** accord, agreement, or harmony, as that resulting from such a uniting or joining. **6.** association of laborers or other wage earners organized to advance the mutual interests of its members, esp. with respect to improving wages and working conditions. **7. the Union.** the United States of America regarded as a national whole or unit, esp. those states that remained aligned with the national government, or the national government itself, during the Civil War. **8.** marriage. **9.** *also,* **Union.** student union. **10.** emblem or device on a flag, symbolizing unity among individual political bodies and usually appearing in the upper inner corner near the flagstaff, as the three superimposed crosses on the British flag or the blue rectangle covered with stars on the U.S. flag. **11.** *Mathematics.* set composed of all the elements of two or more given sets, without repetition of any element. Union is represented by the symbol U. For sets {1, 2, 3} and {3, 4, 7}, U = {1, 2, 3, 4, 7}. **12.** coupling device for connecting machinery parts, as pipes or rods. [Late Latin *ūniō* oneness, unity, from Latin *ūnus* one.]

Syn. 3. Union, unity, solidarity mean the state of being together. **Union** stresses a relationship fixed by and operating according to certain rules to attain some common goal: *A federation is a union of states.* **Unity** shifts the emphasis from formal agreement to the spirit or principle of harmony that unites diverse elements into a whole, esp. in the face of opposition or hostility: *National unity is essential in wartime.* **Solidarity** stresses the strength and efficacy of such unity in overcoming opposition and achieving a common goal: *The working-class show of solidarity at the polls carried that prolabor candidate into office.*

union catalog, library card catalog that contains the contents of several catalogs or the contents of more than one library.

Union City, city in northeastern New Jersey. Pop. (1970), 58,537.

un·ion·ism (ūn′yə niz′əm) *n.* **1.** support or advocacy of the formation of a union or unions or membership in a union, esp. with regard to trade unions. **2.** principle of uniting for a common purpose or action or for mutual benefit. **3. Unionism,** loyalty to or support of the U.S. national government during the Civil War. **4. Unionism,** belief in or support of the former political union between Ireland and Britain. —**un′ion·ist,** *n.* —**un′ion·is′tic,** *adj.*

un·ion·ize (ūn′yə nīz′) **-ized, -iz·ing.** *v.t.* **1.** to organize into or cause to join a union: *to unionize workers.* **2.** to put under the rules of a union: *to unionize the aeronautics industry.* —*v.i.* to join or organize a union. —**un′ion·i·za′tion,** *n.*

union jack 1. *usually,* **Union Jack.** flag of the United Kingdom. **2.** any flag that consists of a union only.

Union of South Africa, see South Africa, Republic of.

---

un′i·den′ti·fi′a·ble	un′im·posed′	un′in·dulged′	un′in·struct′ed
un′i·den′ti·fied′	un′im·pos′ing	un′in·dus′tri·al·ized′	un′in·struc′tive
un′ig·nit′a·ble	un′im·pressed′	un′in·dus′tri·ous	un′in·sur′a·ble
un′il·lu′mi·nat′ed	un′im·press′i·ble	un′in·fect′ed	un′in·sured′
un′il·lu′mi·nat′ing	un′im·pres′sion·a·ble	un′in·fest′ed	un′in·te·grat′ed
un′il·lus′trat′ed	un′im·pres′sive	un′in·flat′ed	un′in·tel·lec′tu·al
un′il·lus′tri·ous	un′im·print′ed	un′in·flect′ed	un′in·tend′ed
un′im·ag′i·na·ble	un′im·au′gu·rat′ed	un′in·flu′enced	un′in·ten′tion·al
un′im·ag′i·na·bly	un′in·cin′er·at′ed	un′in·fluen′tial	un′in·ten′tion·al·ly
un′im·ag′i·nar′y	un′in·cit′ed	un′in·formed′	un′in·ter·est·ing
un′im·ag′ined	un′in·cor′po·rat′ed	un′in·hab′it·a·ble	un′in·ter′ro·ga·ble
un′im′i·tat′ed	un′in·crim′i·nat′ed	un′in·hab′it·ed	un′in·ter·rog′a·tive
un′im·mersed′	un′in·crim′i·nat′ing	un′in·i′ti·at′ed	un′in·tim′i·dat′ed
un′im·mu′nized′	un′in·cu′bat′ed	un′in·jured	un′in·ven′tive
un′im·paired′	un′in·cum′bered	un′inked′	un′in·vert′ed
un′im·part′ed	un′in·dexed′	un′in·no·va′tive	un′in·vest′ed
un′im·pas′sioned	un′in·di·cat′ed	un′in·oc′u·lat′ed	un′in·vig′or·at′ing
un′im·ped′ed	un′in·doc′tri·nat′ed	un′in·quis′i·tive	un′in·vit′ed
un′im·pel′led	un′in·dorsed′	un′in·scribed′	un′in·vit′ing
un′im·pe′ri·al·is′tic	un′in·duced′	in′in·sert′ed	un′in·voked′
un′im·plied′	un′in·duct′ed	un′in·spir′ing	un′in·volved′

Union of Soviet Socialist Republics, Soviet Union.

union shop, establishment in which the employees either belong to a union or must join a union within a certain fixed period after they are hired. Distinguished from **closed shop** and **open shop.**

union suit, one-piece undergarment for men and boys, combining shirt and drawers or trousers.

u·nique (ū nēk´) *adj.* **1.** having no like or equal; unmatched or unparalleled, as in quality; singular: *unique talents, his unique contribution to medical science.* **2.** being the only one of its kind; of which there is only one; single; sole: *a unique fossil specimen.* **3.** *Informal.* highly uncommon, rare, or noteworthy; remarkable: *a unique experience.* [French *unique* single, alone of its kind, unparalleled, from Latin *ūnicus.*] **—u·nique´ly,** *adv.* **—u·nique´ness,** *n.*

u·ni·sex·u·al (yōō´nə sek´shōō əl) *adj.* **1.** of or relating to one sex only. **2.** having the sexual organs of only one sex in each individual. **3.** (of flowers) having only stamens or only pistils.

u·ni·son (ū´nə sən, -zən) *n.* **1.** perfect or exact agreement or harmony. **2.** *Music.* identity in pitch, as of two or more tones or voices. **3. in unison. a.** uttering the same words or producing the same sound at the same time; all together: *The congregation answered in unison.* **b.** *Music.* (of voices or instruments) performing the same part at the identical pitch or at the interval of an octave. [Late Latin *ūnisonus* having the same sound, from Latin *ūnus* one + *sonus* sound', noise.]

u·nit (ū´nit) *n.* **1.** person or thing regarded or functioning as a single, distinct entity or whole: *This housing development was designed to be a self-contained living unit.* **2.** person or thing that is a basic organizational component within a large body, regarded or functioning as a separate entity: *an army unit, an essay describing the family as the basic unit of society. Each building contains fifty housing units.* **3.** apparatus, structure, or piece of equipment having a specific function, sometimes part of a larger object: *a refrigeration unit. That wall unit consists of three shelves and two drawers.* **4.** body of personnel, together with such an apparatus,' forming a self-contained, often mobile, entity and performing a specialized function: *The city mobilized its X-ray units as part of the fall health campaign.* **5.** any fixed quantity considered as a standard of measurement, in terms of which the magnitudes of other quantities of the same kind can be stated. An hour is a unit of time. **6.** *Mathematics.* least positive integer; one. [From UNITY.]

U·ni·tar·i·an (ū´nə târ´ē ən) *n.* **1.** *also,* unitarian. one who rejects the doctrines of the Trinity and the divinity of Jesus, holding the belief that God exists as one being. **2.** member of a denomination originating in Protestantism, officially affiliated with the Universalists, who holds these beliefs and stresses personal religious freedom and religious tolerance. **—adj.** of or relating to Unitarians or Unitarianism. [Modern Latin *unitarius* (from Latin *ūnitās* oneness) + -AN.]

U·ni·tar·i·an·ism (ū´nə târ´ē ə niz´əm) *n.* doctrines, beliefs, and practices of Unitarians.

u·ni·tar·y (ū´nə ter´ē) *adj.* **1.** of or relating to a unit or units. **2.** of, characterized by, or based on unity. **3.** resembling a unit.

u·nite (ū nīt´) *v.t.* **-nit·ed, -nit·ing,** *v.t.* **1.** to bring or put together so as to form a unit or whole; make one or as one: *to unite the country, to unite the factions of a party.* **2.** to bring into close association or relationship: *to unite families by marriage.* **3.** to cause to adhere; attach; bond. **4.** to show, have, or embody, as qualities or characteristics, in combination. **—v.i.** **1.** to be brought together so as to form a unit or whole; become one or as one: *The provinces united to form this monarchy twenty years ago.* **2.** to enter into close association or relationship, as for a common purpose; act in concert: *to unite in song, to unite in battle against a common enemy.* **3.** to be or become combined or bound together, as by adhesion or mixture: *Under these conditions oxygen will unite with this element.* [Latin *ūnītus,* past participle of *ūnīre* to join together, from *ūnus* one.] **—Syn.** *v.t.* see **join.**

u·nit·ed (ū nī´tid) *adj.* **1.** put or joined together; made one or as one: *Their united powers still couldn't stop the enemy advance.* **2.** of, formed by, or produced by joint action or association or the union of two or more persons or things: *a united effort, to present a united front.* **3.** in agreement or harmony. **—u·nit´ed·ly,** *adv.*

United Arab Emirates (ə mēr´its) country composed of a group of seven sheikdoms on the east-central coast of the Arabian peninsula. It was formerly known as various times as Trucial States, Trucial Coast, and Trucial Oman. Area, 32,300 sq. mi. Pop. (1975 est.), 200,000.

United Arab Republic, country in northeastern Africa. Capital, Cairo. Area, approx. 386,000 sq. mi. Pop. (1969 est.), 32,501,000. Also, E´gypt.

United Kingdom 1. country in northwestern Europe, composed of England, Scotland, Wales, and Northern Ireland. Capital, London. Area, 94,214 sq. mi. Pop. (1969 est.), 55,534,000. Also, **Great Britain.** **2.** formerly, from 1801 to 1922, country comprising England, Wales, and all of Ireland.

United Nations 1. international organization of sovereign states, founded in 1945, that seeks to maintain world peace, promote coopera-

tion among nations, and encourage respect for treaties and other obligations under international law. **2.** coalition of countries allied against the Axis Powers in World War II.

United States, country mainly in North America, comprising fifty states and the District of Columbia. Capital, Washington, D.C. Area, 3,615,202 sq. mi. Pop. (1969 est.), 203,216,000. Also, **A·mer´i·ca, United States of America.**

u·ni·ty (ū´nə tē) *pl.,* **-ties.** *n.* **1.** state or fact of being one, as one, or united. **2.** state or quality of harmony or agreement; concord; accord: *Citizens of different racial and ethnic origins should live together in unity.* **3.** combination or arrangement of parts or diverse elements to form a whole. **4.** arrangement of the elements or material in a work of art or literature to produce a single, harmonious, and total aesthetic design or effect. **5.** that which is complete in itself and self-contained; unit; entity; whole. **6. the unities.** aesthetic principles of dramatic composition derived from Aristotle, observed esp. by French dramatists of the seventeenth century, that deal with the unity of action, time, and place, requiring a play to have one plot occurring on one day in one place. **7.** *Mathematics.* the number one. [Latin *ūnitās* oneness.] **—Syn. 1.** see **union.**

univ., universal; universally.

Univ. 1. University. **2.** Universalist.

u·ni·va·lent (ū´nə vā´lənt, ū niv´ə lənt) *adj.* *Chemistry.* having a valence of plus or minus one; monovalent. [UNI- + Latin *valēns,* present participle of *valēre* to be strong, have power.] **—u´ni·va´lence,** u´ni·va´len·cy,** *n.*

u·ni·valve (ū´nə valv´) *n.* **1.** mollusk, as a snail, having a single or one-piece shell. **2.** shell of such mollusk. **—adj.** relating to, having, or consisting of a single or one-piece shell.

u·ni·ver·sal (ū´nə vur´səl) *adj.* **1.** including, involving, or shared by all: *universal rejoicing, to replace universal conscription with a volunteer army.* **2.** existing or occurring everywhere or in all places: *a universal shortage of nurses.* **3.** of, relating to, or characteristic of all or the whole: *universal aspects of the human condition.* **4.** operative or effective under all conditions or in all cases: *a universal remedy, a universal solvent.* **5.** embracing or accomplished in a wide range of subjects or activities; comprehensive: *a universal genius.* **6.** adapted or adaptable to a variety of sizes, shapes, or uses: *a universal motor.* **7.** *Logic.* **a.** denoting or including all the members of a given class: *a universal term.* **b.** (of a proposition) asserted or predictable of all members of a given class. "All men are mortal" is a universal proposition. **—n. 1.** that which is universal, as a concept, principle, or pattern of behavior. **2.** *Logic.* universal proposition. [Latin *ūniversālis* relating to the whole, from *ūniversus* whole, general. See UNIVERSE.] **—u´ni·ver´sal·ness,** *n.* **—Syn.** *adj.* **3.** see **general.**

universal donor, person whose blood may be safely transfused into a person of any blood group.

U·ni·ver·sal·ism (ū´nə vur´sə liz´əm) *n.* doctrines, beliefs, and practices of Universalists, esp. the doctrine that because God is good, He will ultimately save all men.

U·ni·ver·sal·ist (ū´nə vur´sə list) *n.* one who believes in the salvation of all mankind, esp. a member of a denomination originating in Protestantism, officially affiliated with the Unitarians, that holds this belief. **—adj.** of or relating to Universalists or Universalism.

u·ni·ver·sal·i·ty (ū´nə vur´ sal´ə tē) *pl.,* **-ties.** *n.* quality, state, or instance of being universal.

u·ni·ver·sal·ize (ū´nə vur´sə līz´) **-ized, -iz·ing,** *v.t.* to make universal.

universal joint, joint or coupling allowing the parts it connects to move in any direction, esp. one used to transmit rotary motion from one shaft to another that is not in line with it. Also, **universal coupling.**

Universal joint

u·ni·ver·sal·ly (ū´nə vur´sə lē) *adv.* in a universal manner; in every instance or place; without exception: *Such a regulation cannot be universally applied. His second novel was universally acclaimed.*

u·ni·verse (ū´nə vurs´) *n.* **1.** all that exists, including the earth, the heavens, the galaxies, and all of space; entire physical world. **2.** earth or its inhabitants. **3.** world, sphere, or domain in which something exists, regarded as a distinct or self-contained totality or whole. [Latin *ūniversum* the whole world, from *ūniversus* whole, general; literally, turned into one, from *ūnus* one + *versus,* past participle of *vertere* to turn.]

u·ni·ver·si·ty (ū´nə vur´sə tē) *pl.,* **-ties.** *n.* **1.** institution of higher education, usually including one or more undergraduate colleges and graduate and professional schools with facilities for teaching and research, authorized to grant bachelor's, master's, and doctoral degrees. **2.** faculty and student body of such an institution. **3.** grounds or buildings occupied by such an institution. [Old French *universite* the institu-

tion of higher learning, from Late Latin *ūniversitās* company, corporation, from *ūniversitās* the whole.]

University City, city in eastern Missouri, a residential suburb of St. Louis. Pop. (1970), 46,309.

un·just (un just′) *adj.* not observing or in accord with the principles of justice or fairness: *an unjust law, an unjust monarch.* —**un·just′ly,** *adv.* —**un·just′ness,** *n.*

un·kempt (un kempt′) *adj.* **1.** not combed or groomed: *shaggy, unkempt hair.* **2.** in a neglected, untidy, or disheveled state; not neat in appearance: *an unkempt lawn.* **3.** lacking refinement; unpolished; crude. [UN- + Middle English *kempt,* past participle of *kemben* to comb (from Old English *cemban*).]

un·kind (un kīnd′) *adj.* lacking in sympathy, consideration, or kindness; harsh; cruel. —**un·kind′ness,** *n.*

un·kind·ly (un kīnd′lē) *adv.* **1.** in an unkind manner: *He spoke unkindly of her.* **2.** as being unkind; with resentment: *The salesgirl took the remark unkindly.* —*adj.,* **-li·er, -li·est.** unkind. —**un·kind′li·ness,** *n.*

un·knit (un nit′) **-knit·ted** or **-knit, -knit·ting.** *v.t.* **1.** to undo (something knit or tied). **2.** to smooth out (something wrinkled): *Unknit that threatening unkind brow* (Shakespeare, *The Taming of the Shrew*). —*v.i.* to become unknit.

un·know·ing (un nō′ing) *adj.* not knowing; ignorant; uninformed; innocent: *an unknowing accomplice.*

un·know·ing·ly (un nō′ing lē) *adv.* without knowledge, design, or deliberate intent; unintentionally: *She unknowingly interrupted the robber when she came into the store.*

un·known (un nōn′) *adj.* **1.** not part of one's knowledge or experience; unfamiliar: *The passage he's quoting is unknown to me.* **2.** not identified, discovered, or ascertained: *to be stranded on an unknown island. The cause of the delay is as yet unknown.* —*n.* one who or that which is unknown: *an actress who was an unknown until recently. Let X be the unknown in this equation.*

Unknown Soldier, unidentified body of a member of the armed forces, interred in a place of honor as a symbol of all the unknown war dead of his country. Also, *British,* **Unknown Warrior.**

un·lace (un lās′) **-laced, -lac·ing.** *v.t.* **1.** to undo the laces of. **2.** to loosen or unfasten the clothing of by or as by undoing laces.

un·latch (un lach′) *v.t.* to unfasten or open by releasing a latch, as a door. —*v.i.* to become unlatched.

un·law·ful (un lô′fəl) *adj.* **1.** against the law; illegal. **2.** contrary to moral standards; immoral; sinful. **3.** born out of wedlock; illegitimate. —**un·law′ful·ly,** *adv.* —**un·law′ful·ness,** *n.*

un·learn (un lurn′) **-learned** or **-learnt, -learn·ing.** *v.t.* to rid the mind of (something learned); forget.

un·learn·ed (*defs. 1, 3* un lur′nid; *def. 2* un lurnd′) *adj.* **1.** uneducated; illiterate; ignorant. **2.** not acquired by learning or study: *an unlearned response.* **3.** characterized by or betraying a lack of knowledge or education: *an unlearned comment.*

un·leash (un lēsh′) *v.t.* **1.** to release or let loose from a leash: *to unleash a puppy.* **2.** to release or let loose as if from a leash: *to unleash a torrent of abuse. The hurricane unleashed its fury.*

un·leav·ened (un lev′ənd) *adj.* not leavened, as bread used during Passover.

un·less (un les′) *conj.* except on the condition that; except under the circumstances that: *Unless you return the book, you can't borrow any more.* [Middle English *onlesse* on a lower condition (than), from *on* (see ON) + *lesse* (see LESS).]

un·let·tered (un let′ərd) *adj.* **1.a.** uneducated; ignorant. **b.** illiterate (*def. 1*). **2.** not marked with letters or lettering.

un·li·censed (un lī′sinst) *adj.* **1.** having no license. **2.** done or undertaken without license or permission; unauthorized. **3.** unbridled; unrestrained.

un·like (un līk′) *prep.* **1.** with little or no resemblance to; dissimilar to; different from: *a reaction unlike fear. Unlike his brother, he has a sense of humor.* **2.** not characteristic or typical of: *It's unlike him to brood.* —*adj.* **1.** having little or no resemblance; different: *unlike situa-*

tions. **2.** not equivalent; unequal: *unlike amounts.* —**un·like′ness,** *n.*

un·like·li·hood (un līk′lē hood′) *n.* improbability.

un·like·ly (un līk′lē) **-li·er, -li·est.** *adj.* **1.** not likely; improbable: *Should such an unlikely situation arise, call me right away. It's unlikely that she overheard you.* **2.** seeming to lack any prospect of success or of a desired result; not likely to succeed; unpromising: *an unlikely way to make money, an unlikely person for such a dangerous job.* —*adv.* improbably. —**un·like′li·ness,** *n.*

un·lim·ber (un lim′bər) *v.t., v.i.* **1.** to detach (a gun or caisson) from its limber. **2.** to prepare (something) for use or action.

un·lim·it·ed (un lim′ə tid) *adj.* without restrictions, qualifications, or other limits.

un·list·ed (un lis′tid) *adj.* **1.** not entered or included on a list, esp. a list made public: *an unlisted phone number.* **2.** of or designating a stock or security not admitted for listing or trading on a regular stock exchange.

un·load (un lōd′) *v.t.* **1.** to take off or discharge (a load): *to unload freight. The plane unloaded the passengers at the terminal.* **2.** to remove a load from: *The dock workers began unloading the ship.* **3.** to withdraw a charge or ammunition from (a firearm). **4.** to give vent or expression to, as grief; pour forth: *to unload one's cares to a friend.* **5.** to relieve, as of something troublesome or oppressive: *If thou cam'st hither to unload thy soul, kneel down* (J. Wilson, 1816). **6.** *Informal.* to dispose or get rid of, esp. by selling in large quantities: *to unload stocks on the market. Don't try to unload the responsibility on me.* —*v.i.* to discharge a cargo or load.

un·lock (un lok′) *v.t.* **1.** to open or undo the lock of, as a door. **2.** to open or release as if by undoing a lock: *He unlocked his grip on her arm.* **3.** to cause to open; give access to: *I know you have a key to unlock hearts* (Eliot, 1859). **4.** to furnish a key or solution to; disclose: *to unlock a mystery.* —*v.i.* to become unlocked.

un·looked-for (un lookt′fôr′) *adj.* not anticipated or expected; unforeseen.

un·loose (un lōōs′) **-loosed, -loos·ing.** *v.t.* **1.** to unbind or let loose; set free; release. **2.** to relax or slacken, as one's grip or hold; loosen. Also, **un·loos′en.**

un·luck·y (un luk′ē) **-luck·i·er, -luck·i·est.** *adj.* **1.** not favored with good luck; unfortunate: *unlucky at cards.* **2.** marked or produced by bad luck; causing harm or misfortune: *an unlucky blow on the head, an unlucky season for the team.* **3.** forecasting or bringing bad luck; ominous: *born under an unlucky star, an unlucky number.* —**un·luck′i·ly,** *adv.* —**un·luck′i·ness,** *n.*

un·make (un māk′) **-made, -mak·ing.** *v.t.* **1.** to reverse or undo the making of (something): *to unmake a bed, to unmake a law.* **2.** to deprive of power, rank, or authority; depose: *a pope who made and unmade kings.* **3.** to ruin; destroy.

un·man (un man′) **-manned, -man·ning.** *v.t.* **1.** to weaken the spirit of; discourage: *Ten years of tyranny have unmanned the people.* **2.** to deprive of virility or strength; emasculate.

un·man·ly (un man′lē) *adj.* **1.** dishonorable; weak; cowardly: *an unmanly attack against the opposition.* **2.** not masculine or virile; effeminate. —**un·man′li·ness,** *n.*

un·manned (un mand′) *adj.* lacking a crew: *an unmanned spacecraft.*

un·man·ner·ly (un man′ər lē) *adj.* having or showing bad manners; rude: *an unmannerly lout, an unmannerly question.* —*adv.* impolitely; rudely. —**un·man′ner·li·ness,** *n.*

un·mask (un mask′) *v.t.* **1.** to remove a mask or disguise from. **2.** to reveal the true nature of; expose: *to unmask a plot.* —*v.i.* to remove one's mask or disguise.

un·mean·ing (un mē′ning) *adj.* **1.** without meaning, purpose, or significance; senseless. **2.** showing no expression, interest, or intelligence; vacant; empty. —**un·mean′ing·ly,** *adv.*

un·meet (un mēt′) *adj.* not fit, proper, or suitable; unseemly.

un·men·tion·a·ble (un men′shə nə bəl) *adj.* not worthy of or fit for notice or discussion; shameful; embarrassing: *an unmentionable topic.*

un·joint′ed	un·life′like′	un·lu′bri·cat′ed	un·mar′ried
un·jus′ti·fi′a·ble	un·light′ed	un·mag′ni·fied′	un·mas′tered
un·jus′ti·fi′a·bly	un·lined′	un·maid′en·ly	un·matched′
un·jus′ti·fied′	un·link′	un·mal′le·a·ble	un·mat′ted
un·kept′	un·liq′ue·fied′	un·man′age·a·ble	un·meant′
un·kin′dled	un·liq′ui·dat′ed	un·man′gled	un·meas′ur·a·ble
un·knot′	un·lit′	un·man′i·fest′ed	un·meas′ur·a·bly
un·la′beled	un·lit′tered	un′man·u·fac′tured	un·meas′ured
un·la′dy·like′	un·liv′a·ble	un·marked′	un′me·chan′i·cal
un′la·ment′ed	un·live′ly	un·mar′ket·a·ble	un·med′i·cat′ed
un·laun′dered	un·loved′	un·mar′ket·ed	un′me·lo′di·ous
un·leased′	un·lov′ing	un·marred′	un·melt′ed
un·lev′el	un·lov′ing·ly	un·mar′riage·a·ble	un·mend′ed

at; āpe; cär; end; mē; it; īce; hot; ōld; fôrk; wood; fōōl; oil; out; up; ūse; turn; sing; thin; this; zh in treasure; ə in ago, taken, pencil, lemon, circus.

un·men·tion·a·bles (un men′shə nə bəlz) *n.,pl.* things that are not to be mentioned or discussed, esp. undergarments.

un·mer·ci·ful (un mur′si fəl) *adj.* **1.** having or showing no mercy; merciless; cruel. **2.** unreasonable; excessive; extreme. —**un·mer′ci·ful·ly,** *adv.* —**un·mer′ci·ful·ness,** *n.*

un·mind·ful (un mīnd′fəl) *adj.* not conscious, aware, or careful; heedless; forgetful (often with *of*). —**un·mind′ful·ly,** *adv.*

un·mis·tak·a·ble (un′mis tā′kə bəl) *adj.* such as cannot be mistaken, misunderstood, or misinterpreted; obvious: *an unmistakable refusal.* —**un′mis·tak′a·bly,** *adv.*

un·mit·i·gat·ed (un mit′ə gā′tid) *adj.* **1.** not softened or lessened in intensity or severity: *unmitigated anger.* **2.** unqualified; complete; absolute: *unmitigated gall, an unmitigated liar.*

un·moor (un moor′) *v.t.* **1.** to release (a boat or ship) from its mooring. **2.** to cast off all but one anchor of (a boat or ship). —*v.i.* to cast off from a mooring.

un·mor·al (un môr′əl, -mor′-) *adj.* not influenced by or involving considerations of right and wrong; amoral. —**un·mor′al·ly,** *adv.* —**Syn.** see immoral.

un·muf·fle (un muf′əl) **-fled, -fling.** *v.t.* to remove a covering from; free from something that muffles.

un·muz·zle (un muz′əl) **-zled, -zling.** *v.t.* **1.** to remove a muzzle from (a dog or other animal). **2.** to free from restraint or censorship.

un·nat·u·ral (un nach′ər əl) *adj.* **1.** contrary to or deviating from the laws or usual course of nature: *an unnatural size for this species.* **2.** characterized by a lack of emotions or behavior regarded as vital, normal, or typically human; shocking to natural feelings; monstrous; inhuman: *an act of unnatural cruelty, an unnatural mother.* **3.** contrary to or deviating from a social, moral, or behavioral standard: *an unnatural disregard for property.* **4.** not genuine or spontaneous; contrived; artificial: *an unnatural smile, an unnatural way of speaking.* —**un·nat′u·ral·ly,** *adv.* —**un·nat′u·ral·ness,** *n.*

un·nec·es·sar·y (un nes′ə ser′ē) *adj.* **1.** not required or essential; needless. —**un·nec′es·sar′i·ly,** *adv.* —**un·nec′es·sar′i·ness,** *n.*

un·nerve (un nurv′) **-nerved, -nerv·ing.** *v.t.* to deprive of firmness, self-control, or composure: *The constant barrage of questions unnerved the witness.*

un·num·bered (un num′bərd) *adj.* **1.** not marked with or identified by a number or numbers: *unnumbered pages.* **2.** innumerable; countless: *unnumbered millions of stars.*

un·ob·tru·sive (un′əb troo′siv) *adj.* that does not cause notice or disturbance; inconspicuous. —**un′ob·tru′sive·ly,** *adv.* —**un′ob·tru′sive·ness,** *n.*

un·oc·cu·pied (un ok′yə pīd′) *adj.* **1.** without an occupant or occupants; vacant: *an unoccupied apartment.* **2.** not held or occupied by troops or enemy forces: *unoccupied territory.* **3.** not busy; unemployed; idle.

un·or·gan·ized (un ôr′gə nīzd′) *adj.* **1.** not formed into an orderly or systematic arrangement or whole; lacking organization: *unorganized thinking, an unorganized group.* **2.** not unionized. **3.** inorganic, as an enzyme.

un·or·tho·dox (un ôr′thə doks′) *adj.* at variance with accepted beliefs, opinions, customs, or doctrines; not orthodox: *unorthodox teachings, unorthodox behavior.*

un·pack (un pak′) *v.t.* **1.** to empty the contents of: *to unpack a suitcase.* **2.** to remove from a container or packaging: *to unpack glassware, to unpack clothes.* **3.** to remove a pack or burden from; unload: *to unpack a mule.* —*v.i.* to unpack something, as luggage.

un·paid (un pād′) *adj.* **1.** not yet paid: *unpaid wages, an unpaid fine, an unpaid creditor.* **2.** serving without pay; unsalaried: *an unpaid volunteer.*

un·par·al·leled (un par′ə leld′) *adj.* without parallel or equal; matchless; unsurpassed: *an unparalleled achievement.*

un·par·lia·men·ta·ry (un′pär lə men′tər ē, -trē) *adj.* at variance with parliamentary rule, procedure, or custom.

un·pin (un pin′) **-pinned, -pin·ning.** *v.t.* **1.** to remove a pin or pins from: *to unpin a hem after it has been sewn.* **2.** to open, loose, or unfasten by or as by removing a pin or pins: *to unpin one's hair.*

un·pleas·ant (un plez′ənt) *adj.* not pleasing; offensive; disagreeable. —**un·pleas′ant·ly,** *adv.*

un·pleas·ant·ness (un plez′ənt nis) *n.* **1.** condition or quality of being unpleasant. **2.** that which is unpleasant, as a quarrel.

un·plug (un plug′) **-plugged, -plug·ging.** *v.t.* **1.** to remove the plug of (an electrical appliance) from an outlet; disconnect: *to unplug a toaster, to unplug a lamp.* **2.** to remove a stopper or plug from. **3.** to clear an obstruction from.

un·plumbed (un plumd′) *adj.* **1.** not fully understood or explored; unfathomed: *the unplumbed depths of the unconscious.* **2.** not measured or sounded with or as with a plumb: *an unplumbed well, unplumbed ocean depths.*

un·pop·u·lar (un pop′yə lər) *adj.* not generally accepted or favorably viewed. —**un′pop·u·lar′i·ty,** *n.* —**un·pop′u·lar·ly,** *adv.*

un·prac·ticed (un prak′tist) *also, British,* **un·prac·tised.** *adj.* **1.** lacking experience, practice, or skill: *an unpracticed lawyer, unpracticed in the art of politics.* **2.** not put into practice.

un·prec·e·dent·ed (un pres′ə den′tid) *adj.* without parallel or precedent: *an unprecedented victory.*

un·pre·dict·a·ble (un′pri dik′tə bəl) *adj.* of a quality or nature impossible to determine in advance; that cannot be foretold, anticipated, or relied upon: *unpredictable weather, an unpredictable personality.* —**un′pre·dict′a·ble·ness,** *n.* —**un′pre·dict′a·bly,** *adv.*

un·prej·u·diced (un prej′ə dist) *adj.* without prejudice or partiality; unbiased.

un·pre·med·i·tat·ed (un′prē med′ə tā′tid) *adj.* not planned or thought out beforehand; impulsive; spontaneous: *an unpremeditated crime.* —**un′pre·med′i·tat·ed·ly,** *adv.*

un·men′tioned	un·note′wor′thy	un·pac′i·fied′	un·pit′y·ing
un·mer′it·ed	un·no′tice·a·ble	un·paired′	un·planned′
un′me·thod′i·cal	un·no′tice·a·bly	un·pal′at·a·ble	un·plant′ed
un·mil′i·tar′y	un·no′ticed	un·pal′at·a·bly	un·played′
un′mis·tak′en	un′ob·jec′tion·a·ble	un·par′don·a·ble	un·pleas′ing
un·mixed′	un′ob·liged′	un·par′don·a·bly	un·pledged′
un·mixt′	un′ob·lig′ing	un·par′doned	un·plowed′
un·mod′i·fied′	un′ob·lig′ing·ly	un′par·ti′tioned	un′po·et′ic
un·mod′u·lat′ed	un′ob·scured′	un·pas′teur·ized′	un′po·et′i·cal
un·mois′tened	un′ob·serv′a·ble	un·pat′ent·ed	un′po·et′i·cal·ly
un·mold′	un′ob·serv′ant	un′pa·tri·ot′ic	un·poised′
un·mold′ed	un′ob·served′	un′pa·tri·ot′i·cal·ly	un·po′lar·ized′
un′mo·lest′ed	un′ob·serv′ing	un·paved′	un·po′liced′
un′mo·ti·vat′ed	un′ob·struct′ed	un·peace′ful	un·pol′ished
un·mount′ed	un′ob·tain′a·ble	un·pen′e·trat′ed	un·polled′
un·mourned′	un′ob·tained′	un·peo′ple	un·pol·lut′ed
un·mov′a·ble	un′ob·trud′ing	un′per·ceived′	un·pol′ym·er·ised′
un·moved′	un′oc·ca′sioned	un′per·ceiv′ing	un·pol′ym·er·ized′
un·mov′ing	un′of·fend′ed	un′per·cep′tive	un·pop′u·lat′ed
un·mown′	un′of·fend′ing	un′per·cep′tive·ly	un·posed′
un·mu′si·cal	un′of·fen′sive	un·per·fect′ed	un·post′ed
un·name′a·ble	un′of·fen′sive·ly	un′per·plexed′	un·prac′ti·ca·ble
un·named′	un′of·fi′cial	un′per·suad′ed	un·prac′ti·cal
mer·ci·less′	un′of·fi′cial·ly	un′per·sua′sive	un′pre·dict·a·bil′i·ty
un·nav′i·ga·ble	un·oiled′	un′per·sua′sive·ly	un′pre·pared′
un·nav′i·gat′ed	un·o′pen	un·per′turb′a·ble	un′pre·par′ed·ness
un·need′ed	un·o′pened	un·per·turbed′	un′pre·pos·sess′ing
un·need′ful	un·op′posed′	un′phil·o·soph′ic	un′pre·pos·sess′ing·ly
un′ne·go′ti·a·ble	un′or·dained′	un′phil·o·soph′i·cal	un′pre·scribed′
un′ne·go′ti·at′ed	un·o·rig′i·nal	un′phil·o·soph′i·cal·ly	un′pre·sent′a·ble
un·neigh′bor·ly	un′os·ten·ta′tious	un·picked′	un·pre·served′
un·not′ed	un·ox′i·dized′	un·pit′ied	un·pressed′

at; āpe; cär; end; mē; it; īce; hot; ōld; fôrk; wood; fōōl; oil; out; up; ūse; turn; sing; thin; this; zh in treasure; ə in ago, taken, pencil, lemon, circus.

un·pre·ten·tious (un′pri ten′shəs) *adj.* not pretentious, affected, or showy; modest; unassuming. —**un′pre·ten′tious·ly,** *adv.* —**un′pre·ten′tious·ness,** *n.*

un·prin·ci·pled (un prin′sə pəld) *adj.* having or showing a lack of moral principles; unscrupulous.

un·print·a·ble (un prin′tə bəl) *adj.* unfit or improper for publication.

un·pro·fes·sion·al (un′prə fesh′ən əl) *adj.* **1.** violating the standards, rules, or traditions of a profession: *unprofessional conduct.* **2.** not relating to, characteristic of, or produced by a profession or a member of a profession: *an unprofessional opinion.* **3.** not belonging to a profession or a professional group. **4.** lacking the skill or polish of professional work; amateurish: *an unprofessional performance.* —**un′pro·fes′sion·al·ly,** *adv.*

un·prof·it·a·ble (un prof′i tə bəl) *adj.* **1.** failing to produce improvement or a desired end; fruitless: *an unprofitable meeting.* **2.** producing no profit or monetary gain: *The investment proved to be unprofitable.* —**un·prof′it·a·bly,** *adv.*

un·qual·i·fied (un kwol′ə fīd′) *adj.* **1.** not having the necessary or proper qualifications; unfit: *an unqualified voter, unqualified to pass judgment.* **2.** not modified, limited, or restricted, as by reservations or conditions; absolute: *an unqualified rejection. His first novel was an unqualified success.* —**un·qual′i·fied′ly,** *adv.*

un·ques·tion·a·ble (un kwes′chə nə bəl) *adj.* beyond doubt, dispute, or criticism: *a person of unquestionable integrity.* —**un·ques′tion·a·bly,** *adv.*

un·ques·tioned (un kwes′chənd) *adj.* **1.** not open to or called into question; not doubted or disputed: *her unquestioned loyalty, the chieftain's unquestioned authority.* **2.** not subjected to questioning; not interrogated.

un·qui·et (un kwī′it) *adj.* **1.** marked by or causing mental or emotional disturbance or apprehension; uneasy; anxious: *unquiet thoughts.* **2.** marked by unrest, disturbance, or disorder; stormy; turbulent: *in these unquiet times.* —**un·qui′et·ly,** *adv.* —**un·qui′et·ness,** *n.*

un·quote (un kwōt′) -**quot·ed,** -**quot·ing.** *v.i.* to close or end a quotation. ▲ used to indicate the conclusion of a quotation, as in *Quote, "To be or not to be," unquote.*

un·rav·el (un rav′əl) -**eled, -el·ing;** *also,* British, **-elled, -el·ling.** *v.t.* **1.** to separate or untangle the threads of: *to unravel a ball of yarn.* **2.** to separate and make clear the elements of; solve; reveal: *to unravel a plot.* —*v.i.* to become unraveled.

un·read (un red′) *adj.* **1.** not yet read or examined: *an unread manuscript.* **2.** having little or no knowledge or education; ignorant.

un·read·a·ble (un rē′də bəl) *adj.* **1.** illegible: *an unreadable signature.* **2.** too dull, distasteful, or obscure to read; not suitable for or worth reading: *an unreadable book.*

un·re·al (un rē′əl, -rēl′) *adj.* **1.** having no substantial or actual existence; imaginary; fictitious. **2.** not based on or corresponding to or true to substantial or actual existence: *an unreal view of the world.* **3.** *Informal.* not to be believed; incredible. —**un·re·al′i·ty** (un′rē al′ə tē), *n.*

un·rea·son·a·ble (un rē′zə nə bəl, -rēz′nə-) *adj.* **1.** not governed by or in accord with reason or good judgment: *You're being unreasonable in demanding that much of his time.* **2.** going beyond what is reasonable or moderate; excessive; exorbitant: *The prices at that restaurant are unreasonable.* —**un·rea′son·a·ble·ness,** *n.* —**un·rea′son·a·bly,** *adv.*
Syn. 1. Unreasonable, irrational mean contrary to good judgment or

reason. **Unreasonable** suggests a lack of moderation that is still within the scope of normal behavior: *Please don't be unreasonable about going shopping; you do need some new clothes.* **Irrational** is much stronger than *unreasonable,* suggesting that such behavior is not subject to reasoned argument nor emotional appeal and has little or no foundation in reality: *When he's in the grip of that irrational prejudice, there's no talking to him.*

un·rea·son·ing (un rē′zə ning, -rēz′ning) *adj.* not accompanied or controlled by reason: *unreasoning anger.* —**un·rea′son·ing·ly,** *adv.*

un·reel (un rēl′) *v.t., v.i.* to unwind (something), as from a reel.

un·re·flec·tive (un′ri flek′tiv) *adj.* not given to or proceeding from thought or reflection. —**un′re·flec′tive·ly,** *adv.*

un·re·gen·er·ate (un′ri jen′ər it) *adj.* **1.** not morally or spiritually renewed. **2.** resistant, as to change or reform; stubborn: *an unregenerate smoker.*

un·re·lent·ing (un′ri len′ting) *adj.* **1.** that does not change, yield, or relent; inflexible; inexorable: *an unrelenting fate.* **2.** not easing, diminishing, or slackening, as in intensity, effort, or speed: *The prosecutor kept up unrelenting pressure on the confused witness.* —**un′re·lent′ing·ly,** *adv.*

un·re·li·a·ble (un′ri lī′ə bəl) *adj.* not to be regarded with trust or confidence; untrustworthy: *an unreliable prediction, an unreliable firm.* —**un′re·li·a·bil′i·ty, un′re·li′a·ble·ness,** *n.* —**un′re·li′a·bly,** *adv.*

un·re·li·gious (un′ri lij′əs) *adj.* **1.** indifferent to or lacking in religion; irreligious. **2.** not connected with religion; nonreligious.

un·re·mit·ting (un′ri mit′ing) *adj.* never ceasing or slackening; incessant; constant: *unremitting jealousy, unremitting labor.* —**un′re·mit′ting·ly,** *adv.*

un·re·quit·ed (un′ri kwī′tid) *adj.* not reciprocated or returned in kind: *unrequited love.*

un·re·served (un′ri zurvd′) *adj.* **1.** done or given without reservation or restriction; unqualified; full: *unreserved approval.* **2.** free from reserve; candid; open: *an unreserved manner.* —**un·re·serv·ed·ly** (un′ri zur′vid lē), *adv.*

un·rest (un rest′) *n.* restlessness; dissatisfaction; discontent: *political unrest.*

un·re·strained (un′ri strānd′) *adj.* **1.** not held in check or under control: *unrestrained laughter.* **2.** free from restraint or reserve; easy; natural: *an unrestrained atmosphere.* —**un·re·strain·ed·ly** (un′ri strā′nid lē), *adv.*

un·ripe (un rīp′) *adj.* **1.** not fully developed; immature: *unripe plums, unripe schemes.* **2.** not ready; unprepared: *to be unripe for taking on such heavy responsibilities.* —**un·ripe′ness,** *n.*

un·ri·valed (un rī′vəld) *also,* British, **un·ri·valled.** *adj.* having no rival or equal; matchless; supreme: *unrivaled eloquence.*

un·roll (un rōl′) *v.t.* **1.** to open, spread out, or expand (something rolled up): *to unroll a blanket.* **2.** to unfold; display; reveal. —*v.i.* to become unrolled.

UNRRA (un′rə) United Nations Relief and Rehabilitation Administration.

un·ruf·fled (un ruf′əld) *adj.* not disturbed or agitated; calm: *unruffled waters, unruffled self-confidence.*

un·ru·ly (un rōō′lē) -**li·er, -li·est.** *adj.* difficult to rule, control, or manage: *unruly hair, an unruly mob.* —**un·ru′li·ness,** *n.*

un·sad·dle (un sad′əl) -**dled, -dling.** *v.t.* to remove the saddle from, as a horse.

un′pre·vent′a·ble	un′pro·voked′	un′re·claim′a·ble	un′re·lat′ed·ness
un′print′ed	un′pruned′	un′re·claimed′	un′re·laxed′
un′proc′essed	un·pub′lished	un·rec′og·niz′a·ble	un′re·lax′ing
un′pro·cur′a·ble	un·pun′ished	un·rec′og·niz′a·bly	un′re·lieved′
un′pro·duc′tive	un·pu′ri·fied′	un·rec′og·nized′	un′re·mark′a·ble
un′pro·duc′tive·ly	un·quench′a·ble	un·rec·on·cil′a·ble	un′re·mark′a·bly
un′pro·duc′tive·ness	un·quenched′	un·rec·on·cil′a·bly	un·rem′e·died′
un′pro·fessed′	un·ques′tion·ing	un·rec′on·ciled′	un′re·mem′bered
un′pro·gres′sive	un·ques′tion·ing·ly	un·rec′ord·ed	un′re·mit′ted
un′pro·hib′it·ed	un·quot′a·ble	un·rec′ti·fied	un′re·mu′ner·at′ed
un·prom′is·ing	un·rat′i·fied′	un′re·deemed′	un′re·mu′ner·a′tive
un·prompt′ed	un·reach′a·ble	un′re·dressed′	un′re·newed′
un′pro·nounce′a·ble	un·read′i·ly	un′re·fined′	un·rent′ed′
un′pro·nounced′	un·read′i·ness	un′re·flect′ed	un′re·paired′
un′pro·pi′ti·at′ed	un·read′y	un′re·flect′ing	un′re·pealed′
un′pro·pi′tious	un′re·al·is′tic	un′re·flect′ing·ly	un′re·pent′ant
un′pros′per·ous	un′re·al·is′ti·cal·ly	un′re·formed′	un′re·pent′ing
un′pro·tect′ed	un′re·al·iz′a·ble	un′re·freshed′	un′re·plen′ished
un′pro·test′ed	un′re·al·ized′	un′re·fresh′ing	un′re·port′ed
un′pro·test′ing	un·rea′soned	un·reg′i·ment′ed	un′rep·re·sen′ta·tive
un′pro·test′ing·ly	un′re·buked′	un·reg′is·tered	un′rep·re·sent′ed
un·proved′	un′re·cep′tive	un·reg′u·lat′ed	un′re·pressed′
un·prov′en	un′re·cep′tive·ly	un′re·hearsed′	un′re·proved′
	un′re·cip′ro·cat′ed	un′re·lat′ed	un′re·quest′ed

′at; āpe; cär; end; mē; it; īce; hot; ōld; fôrk; wood; fōōl; oil; out; up; ūse; turn; sing; thin; **th**is; zh in treasure; ə in ago, taken, pencil, lemon, circus.

un·said (un sed´) v. past tense and past participle of **unsay.** —*adj.* not spoken or expressed: *Some things are better left unsaid.*

un·sat·is·fac·to·ry (un´sat is fak´tər ē) *adj.* not meeting a standard, requirement, or demand; disappointing; inadequate: *an unsatisfactory arrangement.* —**un´sat·is·fac´to·ri·ly,** *adv.*

un·sat·u·rat·ed (un sach´ə rā´tid) *adj.* **1.** (of a solution) capable of dissolving more of a certain substance at a given temperature and pressure. **2.** (of an organic compound) containing double or triple bonds capable of uniting with other elements without giving up original components.

un·sa·vor·y (un sā´vər ē) *also,* British, **un·sa·vour·y.** *adj.* **1.** disagreeable to the taste or smell. **2.** having a sinister, criminal, or morally offensive character or association: *an unsavory reputation. Spare me the unsavory details.* **3.** having no flavor or seasoning; tasteless; bland. —**un·sa´vor·i·ness,** *n.*

un·say (un sā´) **-said, -say·ing.** *v.t.* to take back or cancel (what has been said); retract.

un·scathed (un skāthd´) *adj.* in no way harmed or hurt; uninjured.

un·schooled (un skōold´) *adj.* **1.** not schooled, instructed, or trained: *unschooled in the ways of the world.* **2.** not acquired by schooling or training; natural: *unschooled talent.*

un·sci·en·tif·ic (un´sī ən tif´ik) *adj.* **1.** not in accordance with the principles and methods of science. **2.** showing a lack of scientific knowledge. —**un´sci·en·tif´i·cal·ly,** *adv.*

un·scram·ble (un skram´bəl) **-bled, -bling.** *v.t.* **1.** to make sense out of; put in order. **2.** to make (a scrambled message) intelligible; decode.

un·screw (un skrōō´) *v.t.* **1.** to remove, loosen, or unfasten by withdrawing screws or by turning: *to unscrew a cabinet from the wall. to unscrew the top of a jar.* **2.** to remove the screw or screws from. —*v.i.* to become or admit of being unscrewed.

un·scru·pu·lous (un skrōō´pyə ləs) *adj.* acting without or showing no regard for moral principles or the promptings of conscience. —**un·scru´pu·lous·ly,** *adv.* —**un·scru´pu·lous·ness,** *n.*

un·seal (un sēl´) *v.t.* **1.** to break or remove the seal of: *to unseal an envelope.* **2.** to open (something closed or covered as if with a seal); free from some constraining influence: *The discovery . . . acts . . . to unseal his eyes* (Cowden, 1863).

un·search·a·ble (un sur´chə bəl) *adj.* that cannot be searched or explored; inscrutable; mysterious. —**un·search´a·bly,** *adv.*

un·sea·son·a·ble (un sē´zə nə bəl) *adj.* **1.** not characteristic of or appropriate to the season: *unseasonable weather, unseasonable clothing.* **2.** not occurring or coming at the right or proper time; untimely: inappropriate: *unseasonable interference, an unseasonable hour to pay a visit.* —**un·sea´son·a·ble·ness,** *n.* —**un·sea´son·a·bly,** *adv.*

un·sea·soned (un sē´zənd) *adj.* **1.** not flavored with seasoning: *unseasoned salt.* **2.** not disciplined or acclimated; inexperienced: *unseasoned troops.* **3.** not properly seasoned or aged; unripe; immature: *unseasoned wood.*

un·seat (un sēt´) *v.t.* **1.** to dislodge from a seat, esp. to throw from a saddle. **2.** to deprive of rank, position, or office, esp. an elected office.

un·seem·ly (un sēm´lē) **-li·er, -li·est.** *adj.* inappropriate to the time or place; not proper, becoming, or in good taste; indecorous. —*adv.* in an unseemly manner. —**un·seem´li·ness,** *n.*

un·seen (un sēn´) *adj.* **1.** not noticed or observed: *He came into the room unseen.* **2.** not visible: *an unseen presence.*

un·set·tle (un set´əl) **-tled, -tling.** *v.t.* **1.** to make uneasy or anxious; confuse; disturb. **2.** to change or move from a fixed or stable condition; displace; disrupt.

un·set·tled (un set´əld) *adj.* **1.** not tranquil or orderly; disturbed; disrupted: *during the unsettled times following the Civil War.* **2.** not yet established or stabilized: *My life is still unsettled.* **3.** not determined or decided; unresolved: *an unsettled question.* **4.** not paid, adjusted, or disposed of: *an unsettled debt.* **5.** not occupied, inhabited, or populated: *an unsettled region of the frontier.* **6.** liable to change; variable: *the unsettled state of his health.*

un·sex (un seks´) *v.t.* to deprive of the qualities considered typical of a sex, esp. to make unfeminine or unwomanly.

un·shack·le (un shak´əl) **-led, -ling.** *v.t.* to free from a shackle or other bonds.

un·shak·a·ble (un shā´kə bəl) *also,* **un·shake·a·ble.** *adj.* not easily undermined, swayed, or daunted; firm: *an unshakable conviction.*

un·shaped (un shāpt´) *adj.* **1.** not molded into shape; shapeless. **2.** not completely formed or developed: *unshaped theories.*

un·sheathe (un shēth´) **-sheathed, -sheath·ing.** *v.t.* to draw from or as from a sheath or scabbard; bare.

un·ship (un ship´) **-shipped, -ship·ping.** *v.t.* **1.** to remove (nautical gear) from the proper place or position. **2.** to remove or discharge from a ship, as goods or passengers.

un·sight·ly (un sīt´lē) **-li·er, -li·est.** *adj.* distasteful or offensive to the sight or the aesthetic sense: *unsightly litter strewn about the city parks.* —**un·sight´li·ness,** *n.*

un·skilled (un skild´) *adj.* **1.** lacking skill, training, or competence: *an unskilled actor.* **2.** not involving or requiring skill or special training: *unskilled occupations.* **3.** showing a lack of skill or ability: *unskilled draftsmanship.*

un·skill·ful (un skil´fəl) *also,* British, **un·skil·ful.** *adj.* **1.** lacking in skill; awkward; clumsy. —**un·skill´ful·ly,** *adv.* —**un·skill´ful·ness,** *n.*

un·snap (un snap´) **-snapped, -snap·ping** *v.t.* to undo the snap or snaps of; unfasten.

un·snarl (un snärl´) *v.t.* to free from a snarl or snarls: *to unsnarl a traffic jam. to unsnarl one's hair by brushing it.*

un·so·cia·ble (un sō´shə bəl) *adj.* **1.** not inclined to seek the company of others: *an unsociable neighbor.* **2.** lacking or not conducive to sociability; uncongenial: *an unsociable atmosphere. He maintained an unsociable silence all evening.* —**un´so·cia·bil´i·ty, un·so´cia·ble·ness,** *n.* —**un·so´cia·bly,** *adv.*

un·so·phis·ti·cat·ed (un´sə fis´tə kā´tid) *adj.* **1.** not having knowledge of or experience in the ways of the world; lacking worldliness; naive. **2.** not complex or refined; showing a lack of advanced technical knowledge; simple; artless: *an unsophisticated analysis of the novel.* —**un´so·phis´ti·cat´ed·ly,** *adv.* —**un´so·phis´ti·cat·ed·ness, un´so·phis´ti·ca´tion,** *n.*

un·sound (un sound´) *adj.* **1.** not strong or solid; weak; defective: *an unsound foundation that won't support the weight of the beams.* **2.** not firmly based on truth, fact, or good judgment; not accurate, valid, or sensible: *unsound advice, unsound reasoning.* **3.** physically or mentally unhealthy; diseased: *unsound teeth, of unsound mind.* **4.** not financially judicious or secure: *an unsound investment.* —**un·sound´ly,** *adv.* —**un·sound´ness,** *n.*

un·spar·ing (un spâr´ing) *adj.* **1.** very generous; unstinting; lavish: *his unsparing efforts to make the dance a success.* **2.** unmerciful; harsh; severe: *unsparing criticism.* —**un·spar´ing·ly,** *adv.*

un´re·sist´ant	un·rhyth´mi·cal	un·scratched´	un·shed´
un´re·sist´ed	un·ri´pened	un·screened´	un·shel´tered
un´re·sist´ing	un·ro·man´tic	un·sealed´	un·shod´
un´re·solved´	un·ruled´	un·sea´wor·thy	un·shorn´
un´re·spect´ful	un·safe´	un´se·clud´ed	un·shrink´ing
un´re·spect´ful·ly	un·saint´ly	un·seed´ed	un·sift´ed
un´re·spon´sive	un·sal´a·ried	un·see´ing	un·signed´
un´re·spon´sive·ly	un·salt´ed	un·seg´ment·ed	un·sink´a·ble
un´re·spon´sive·ness	un·sanc´ti·fied´	un´se·lec´tive	un·sis´ter·ly
un·rest´ed	un·sanc´tioned	un´se·lec´tive·ly	un·sized´
un·rest´ful	un·san´i·tar´y	un·self´-con´scious	un·slaked´
un´re·strict´ed	un·sat´ed	un·self´ish	un·sliced´
un´re·ten´tive	un·sa´ti·at´ed	un·self´ish·ness	un·smil´ing
un´re·tract´ed	un·sat´is·fied´	un·sen´si·tive	un·smoked´
un´re·trieved´	un·sat´is·fy´ing	un·sent´	un·so´cial
un´re·turn´a·ble	un·scaled´	un´sen·ti·men´tal	un·soiled´
un´re·vealed´	un·scanned´	un·serv´ice·a·ble	un·sold´
un´re·veal´ing	un·scarred´	un·set´	un·sol´dier·ly
un´re·venged´	un·scent´ed	un·sex´u·al	un·so·lic´it·ed
un´re·vised´	un·scep´ti·cal	un·shad´ed	un·solv´a·ble
un´re·ward´ed	un·sched´uled	un·shak´en	un·solved´
un´re·ward´ing	un·schol´ar·ly	un·shaved´	un·sort´ed
un·rhymed´	un·scorched´	un·shav´en	un·sought´
un·rhyth´mic	un·scoured´		un·sound´ed

at; āpe; cär; end; mē; it; īce; hot; ōld; fôrk; wood; fōol; oil; out; up; ūse; turn; sing; thin; this; zh in treasure; ə in ago, taken, pencil, lemon, circus.

un·speak·a·ble (un spē′kə bəl) *adj.* **1.** incapable of being described or expressed in words: *unspeakable happiness.* **2.** inexpressibly bad, evil, or objectionable: *the unspeakable practices of these cutthroats.* —**un·speak′a·bly,** *adv.*

un·spot·ted (un spot′id) *adj.* **1.** not marked by a spot or spots: *The glassware came out of the dishwasher unspotted.* **2.** without moral taint or blemish: *his unspotted reputation.*

un·sta·ble (un stā′bəl) *adj.* **1.** not firmly fixed in position; easily moved or put off balance: *an unstable scaffolding.* **2.** not settled or steady in character or situation; apt to change or alter: *an unstable government, an unstable relationship.* **3.** emotionally unsettled, troubled, or maladjusted: *an unstable personality.* **4.** *Chemistry.* readily changed into another compound, element, or isotope. —**un·sta′ble·ness,** *n.* —**un·sta′bly,** *adv.*

un·stead·y (un sted′ē) *adj.* **1.** not firm or securely placed; shaky: *an unsteady ladder.* **2.** marked by fluctuation or change; inconstant; variable: *an unsteady flame. Stock prices have been unsteady for months.* **3.** not uniform or consistent; irregular; uneven: *an unsteady gait. He answered the accusation in an unsteady voice.* **4.** irregular or erratic in habits or behavior. —**un·stead′i·ly,** *adv.* —**un·stead′i·ness,** *n.*

un·step (un step′) -**stepped,** -**step·ping.** *v.t. Nautical.* to remove (a mast) from a step or position.

un·stop (un stop′) -**stopped,** -**stop·ping.** *v.t.* **1.** to remove a stop or stopper from: *to unstop a champagne bottle.* **2.** to free from an obstruction: *to unstop a drain, to unstop one's ears.*

un·strap (un strap′) -**strapped,** -**strap·ping.** *v.t.* to remove, unfasten, or loosen the strap or straps of: *to unstrap a trunk.*

un·stressed (un strest′) *adj.* not accented or weakly accented in speech: *an unstressed syllable.*

un·stri·at·ed (un strī′ā tid) *adj.* having no striations; smooth-textured: *unstriated muscle.*

un·string (un string′) -**strung,** -**string·ing** *v.t.* **1.** to remove or loosen the string or strings of: *to unstring a bow, to unstring a violin.* **2.** to remove from a string, as beads or pearls. **3.** to upset emotionally; unnerve: *He was really unstrung by the uncanny resemblance between the two men.*

un·stud·ied (un stud′ēd) *adj.* **1.** not contrived; spontaneous; natural: *her unstudied charm.* **2.** not having been instructed; unversed; unlearned.

un·sub·stan·tial (un′səb stan′shəl) *adj.* **1.** lacking firmness, strength, or solidity. **2.** not based on reason, fact, or good judgment. **3.** without material substance or form; unreal. —**un′sub·stan′tial·ly,** *adv.*

un·suc·cess·ful (un′sək ses′fəl) *adj.* not meeting with or resulting in success: *an unsuccessful suitor, an unsuccessful experiment.* —**un′·suc·cess′ful·ly,** *adv.*

un·suit·a·ble (un sōo′tə bəl) *adj.* not appropriate to or fit for the circumstances: *unsuitable attire.* —**un′suit·a·bil′i·ty,** *n.* —**un·suit′a·bly,** *adv.*

un·sung (un sung′) *adj.* **1.** not honored or celebrated, esp. in song or poetry: *the unsung heroes of the frontier.* **2.** not yet sung.

un·sus·pect·ed (un′səs pek′tid) *adj.* **1.** not under suspicion. **2.** not imagined or known to exist; not considered possible or likely: *an unsuspected source of trouble.*

un·sus·pect·ing (un′səs pek′ting) *adj.* having no suspicion; trusting. —**un′sus·pect′ing·ly,** *adv.*

un·tan·gle (un tang′gəl) -**gled,** -**gling.** *v.t.* **1.** to free from a tangle or tangles. **2.** to clear up; explain; resolve: *to untangle the events that led up to the disaster.*

un·taught (un tôt′) *adj.* **1.** not acquired by learning; natural. **2.** not instructed or educated; ignorant.

un·ten·a·ble (un ten′ə bəl) *adj.* that cannot be held, defended, or maintained: *an untenable thesis, an untenable position.*

un·think·ing (un thing′king) *adj.* **1.** showing or marked by an absence of thoughtfulness, consideration, or careful reflection. **2.** without the ability to think. —**un·think′ing·ly,** *adv.*

un·thread (un thred′) *v.t.* to remove the thread from: *to unthread a needle, to unthread a sewing machine.*

un·ti·dy (un tī′dē) -**di·er,** -**di·est.** *adj.* having an untended or messy appearance; not neat, orderly, or well-organized: *an untidy desk.* —**un·ti′di·ly,** *adv.* —**un·ti′di·ness,** *n.*

un·tie (un tī′) -**tied,** -**ty·ing.** *v.t.* **1.** to loosen or undo (something knotted or tied): *to untie a knot.* **2.** to free from bonds or other restraints: *to untie someone's hands.* —*v.i.* to become untied.

un·til (un til′, un-) *prep.* **1.** up to the time of: *Wait until evening before you call the doctor.* **2.** before (a specified time): *Tickets are not available until Wednesday.* —*conj.* **1.** up to the time when or that: *Wait here until I get back.* **2.** before: *The store couldn't deliver the furniture until the snow had melted.* **3.** to the place, extent, or degree that: *Keep driving straight until you reach the intersection. The salesman talked and talked until I was ready to scream.* [Middle English *untill* to, up to, up to the time of or that, toward, from *un-* unto (from Old Norse *und*) + TILL¹.]

un·time·ly (un tīm′lē) *adj.* **1.** coming or happening before the proper or usual time; premature: *an untimely death.* **2.** coming or happening at the wrong time; inopportune: *an untimely visit.* —*adv.* prematurely; inopportunely. —**un·time′li·ness,** *n.*

un·tir·ing (un tīr′ing) *adj.* not ceasing, faltering, or becoming exhausted; persistent: *untiring patience, untiring efforts.* —**un·tir′ing·ly,** *adv.*

un·to (un′tōo, -tə) *prep. Archaic.* to. [Middle English *unto,* from *un-,* until (from Old Norse *und*) + TO.]

un·told (un tōld′) *adj.* **1.** too great or numerous to be counted or measured: *untold numbers, untold riches, untold suffering.* **2.** not related, revealed, or recounted: *the untold story of the American Indian.*

un·touch·a·ble (un tuch′ə bəl) *adj.* **1.** forbidden to the touch. **2.** beyond criticism or attack; unassailable. **3.** out of reach; inaccessible. **4.** disagreeable or defiling to the touch. —*n. also,* **Untouchable.** in India, a member of the lowest caste, whose touch was formerly considered to defile members of higher castes.

un·to·ward (un tôrd′) *adj.* **1.** marked by or causing trouble or inconvenience; unfortunate; adverse. **2.** difficult to manage or control; unruly; perverse. **3.** not appropriate or proper; unbecoming; unseemly.

un·trav·eled (un trav′əld) *also, British,* **un·trav·elled.** *adj.* **1.** not passed over or through; unfrequented: *an untraveled road.* **2.** not having gained experience by travel; not cosmopolitan.

un·tried (un trīd′) *adj.* **1.** not proved or tested, as by experience or use: *an untried youth.* **2.** not brought before a court for judgment: *untried offenders, an untried case.*

un·true (un trōo′) *adj.* **1.** contrary to fact or to the truth; incorrect; false. **2.** not faithful or loyal. **3.** deviating from a standard or rule; inaccurate; inexact. [Old English *untrēowe* unfaithful.]

un·truss (un trus′) *v.t.* to loose from or as from a truss; unfasten.

un·truth (un trōoth′) *n.* **1.** something untrue; a lie. **2.** character or condition of being untrue. [Old English *untrēowth* unfaithfulness.] —**Syn.** see lie¹.

un·truth·ful (un trōoth′fəl) *adj.* **1.** contrary to fact or to the truth.

---

un·spe′cial·ized′	un′sup·pressed′	un·tal′ent·ed	un·thought′-of′
un′spe·cif′ic	un·sure′	un′tam′a·ble	un·threat′en·ing
un·spe′ci·fied′	un′sur·pass′a·ble	un·tamed′	un·thrift′y
un·spent′	un′sur·passed′	un·tanned′	un·till′a·ble
un·spoiled′	un′sus·cep′ti·ble	un·tapped′	un·tilled′
un·spo′ken	un·sus·tained′	un·tar′nished	un·tinged′
un·sports′man·like′	un·swayed′	un·tast′ed	un·tit′led
un·stamped′	un·sweet′ened	un·taxed′	un·touched′
un·starched′	un·swept′	un·teach′a·ble	un·trace′a·ble
un·stat′ed	un·swerv′ing	un·tech′ni·cal	un·traced′
un·ster′i·lized′	un·sworn′	un·tem′pered	un·trained′
un·stint′ing	un′sym·met′ri·cal	un·tend′ed	un′trans·fer′a·ble
un·strained′	un′sym·pa·thet′ic	un·test′ed	un′trans·lat′a·ble
un·strat′i·fied′	un′sym·pa·thet′i·cal·ly	un·teth′er	un′trans·lat′ed
un·struc′tured	un′sym′pa·thiz′ing	un·thanked′	un′trans·mit′ted
un·sub·dued′	un′sys·tem·at′ic	un·thank′ful	un·trav′ersed
un′sub·stan′ti·at·ed	un′sys·tem·at′i·cal	un·thatched′	un·treat′ed
un·suit′ed	un′sys·tem·at′i·cal·ly	un′the·at′ri·cal	un·trimmed′
un·sul′lied	un·tab′u·lat′ed	un·think′a·ble	un·trod′
un·su′per·vised′	un·tact′ful	un·think′a·bly	un·trou′bled
un·sup·port′ed	un·taint′ed	un·thought′ful	un·trust′wor′thy

---

at; āpe; cär; end; mē; it; īce; hot; ōld; fôrk; wood; fōōl; oil; out; up; ūse; turn; sing; thin; this; zh in treasure; ə in ago, taken, pencil, lemon, circus.

2. given to lying: *an untruthful person.* —**un·truth'ful·ly,** *adv.* —**un·truth'ful·ness,** *n.*

un·tu·tored (un tōō'tərd, -tū'-) *adj.* **1.** lacking formal instruction; uneducated. **2.** not resulting from or improved by instruction: *untutored wisdom.*

un·twine (un twīn') -**twined, -twin·ing.** *v.t.* to undo (something twined or tangled). —*v.i.* to become untwined.

un·used (un ūzd') *adj.* **1.** not in use; not put to use: *an unused expression.* **2.** never having been used; new; fresh: *an unused toothbrush.* **3.** not accustomed or habituated (with *to*): *She's unused to the quiet of the country.*

un·u·su·al (un ū'zhōō əl) *adj.* not usual, common, or ordinary; rare. —**un·u'su·al·ly,** *adv.* —**un·u'su·al·ness,** *n.* —**Syn.** see **extraordinary.**

un·ut·ter·a·ble (un ut'ər ə bəl) *adj.* too deep or great to be put into words; inexpressible: *unutterable joy.* —**un·ut'ter·a·bly,** *adv.*

un·var·nished (un vär'nisht) *adj.* **1.** not covered with or as with varnish. **2.** stated or expressed without disguise or embellishment; plain; unadorned: *the unvarnished truth.*

un·veil (un vāl') *v.t.* **1.** to remove a veil or covering from: *to unveil one's face, to unveil a monument.* **2.** to disclose or open to view as by removing a veil; reveal: *to unveil the meaning of the oracle. The proposed program was unveiled at the committee's hearings.*

un·voiced (un voist') *adj.* **1.** not stated, uttered, or expressed: *an unvoiced objection.* **2.** (of a consonant) spoken without vibration of the vocal cords, as the *t* sound in *toy;* voiceless.

un·war·rant·ed (un wär'ən tid) *adj.* without basis or justification; unjustified: *an unwarranted assumption.*

un·war·y (un wâr'ē) *adj.* not watchful, cautious, or alert, as to the possibility of trouble or deceit; careless; unguarded: *an unwary victim.* —**un·war'i·ly,** *adv.* —**un·war'i·ness,** *n.*

un·wel·come (un wel'kəm) *adj.* not received with pleasure; not welcome or desired: *an unwelcome guest, unwelcome news.*

un·well (un wel') *adj.* ailing; ill; sick.

un·wept (un wept') *adj.* **1.** not mourned or lamented; not wept for. **2.** (of tears) not shed.

un·whole·some (un hōl'səm) *adj.* **1.** injurious to mental, physical, or moral health; unhealthy: *an unwholesome diet, an unwholesome influence.* **2.** suggesting or resulting from disease or decay: *an unwholesome pallor.* **3.** unsound in condition; diseased; decayed. —**un·whole'some·ly,** *adv.* —**un·whole'some·ness,** *n.*

un·wield·y (un wēl'dē) *adj.* difficult to handle, manage, or use, as because of large size or bulky shape; clumsy; cumbersome: *an unwieldy bundle, a poem written in an unwieldy metrical pattern.* —**un·wield'i·ness,** *n.*

un·will·ing (un wil'ing) *adj.* **1.** not prepared or agreeably disposed (to do or be something); reluctant: *an unwilling soldier, to be unwilling to offend.* **2.** not done, said, or given readily or heartily; marked by or showing a lack of eagerness: *unwilling admiration.* —**un·will'ing·ly,** *adv.* —**un·will'ing·ness,** *n.* —**Syn.** see **reluctant.**

un·wind (un wīnd') -**wound, -wind·ing.** *v.t.* **1.** to undo or reverse the winding of; unroll: *to unwind bandages, to unwind yarn.* **2.** to straighten or untangle the twisted parts of. —*v.i.* **1.** to become unrolled or untangled. **2.** to become free from tension or anxiety; relax.

un·wise (un wīz') *adj.* lacking or showing a lack of wisdom or good sense; foolish; imprudent. —**un·wise'ly,** *adv.*

un·wit·ting (un wit'ing) *adj.* **1.** not knowing; unaware; unconscious: *an unwitting accomplice to a crime.* **2.** not intentional; inadvertent: *The joke was an unwitting indication of what he really felt.* —**un·wit'ting·ly,** *adv.*

un·wont·ed (un wôn'tid, -wōn'-) *adj.* not customary or habitual; rare; unusual: *He spoke with unwonted brevity.* —**un·wont'ed·ly,** *adv.*

un·world·ly (un wurld'lē) *adj.* **1.** devoted to or concerned with spiritual matters rather than material interests or gain. **2.** lacking knowledge of or experience in the world; naive. **3.** not of this world; unearthly. —**un·world'li·ness,** *n.*

un·wor·thy (un wur'thē) *adj.* **1.** not deserving or meriting (often with *of*): *an accusation unworthy of notice, to be unworthy of such kindness.* **2.** not befitting or appropriate to the ability, status, or charac-

ter of; not suiting or becoming (often with *of*): *conduct unworthy of a king, writing unworthy of the author. His cruel remarks were unworthy of him.* **3.** lacking value or merit; worthless. **4.** contemptible; base; vile. —**un·wor'thi·ly,** *adv.* —**un·wor'thi·ness,** *n.*

un·wound (un wound') past tense and past participle of **unwind.**

un·wrap (un rap') -**wrapped, -wrap·ping.** *v.t.* to remove a wrapping from; open; undo: *to unwrap a package.* —*v.i.* to become unwrapped.

un·wrin·kle (un ring'kəl) -**kled, -kling.** *v.t.* to remove the wrinkles from; smooth.

un·writ·ten (un rit'ən) *adj.* **1.** not written or put in writing: *unwritten testimony.* **2.** not recorded in writing but accepted and enforced by custom and usage; traditional: *an unwritten code of honor.*

unwritten law, rule, principle, or law basing its authority on custom, tradition, or general usage rather than on legislative action.

un·yoke (un yōk') -**yoked, -yok·ing.** *v.t.* **1.** to release from or as from a yoke. **2.** to separate; part.

up (up) *adv.* **1.** in, to, or toward a higher or more elevated place or position: *to jump up and down. He climbed up to the top of the ladder. The kite is caught up in a tree.* **2.** at, to, or toward a higher point or degree, as of rank, amount, or intensity: *My weight went up over the summer. She turned the sound up on the television.* **3.** at, to, toward, or in a direction, place, or position considered to be more elevated or geographically higher: *We drove up from Richmond to New York. They're spending the summer up in the mountains.* **4.** above the surface or horizon: *The diver came up for air. The sun came up by five o'clock.* **5.** in or to an erect position or posture: *Sit up straight. You can set the easel up by the window.* **6.** out of bed: *I got up at seven o'clock.* **7.** to a state or point of completion, exhaustion, or fulfillment; thoroughly; totally: *He paid up all his debts. We used up all the eggs when we made lunch.* **8.** in or into existence, motion, operation, or action: *The building went up quickly after construction began. Such conditions will always set up a force field.* **9.** in or into a unified, compact, or closed state; together; contracted: *Button up your coat. The bird was shut up in a cage. Fold up the chairs and put them in the closet.* **10.** so as to be even or in line with, as in space or degree; at or to an equal point or position: *Fill the beaker up to the first red line. It wasn't a bad movie, but it didn't come up to our expectations.* **11.** into consideration, attention, or prominence: *His name kept coming up in the conversation.* **12.** at or into a place of storage or concealment, as for safekeeping: *He saved our money for his vacation.* **13.** in or into an excited, agitated, or troubled state: *To be all riled up.* **14.** for each side; apiece: *The score was four up.* **15.** in the lead; ahead: *He finished one up on his opponent.* **16.** *Baseball.* at bat. **17. up against,** facing; confronting: *He is up against tremendous odds.* **18. up on** (or **in**). *Informal.* well-informed or knowledgeable about: *to be up on current events.* **19. up to. a.** *Informal.* on the point of doing; about to do: *What are you up to? b.* as far as: *What chapter are you up to in the book? c.* capable of; equal to: *Is he up to such an important job? She's still sick and isn't up to seeing visitors yet.* **d.** dependent or incumbent upon: *It is up to you to make the change.* —*adj.* **1.** inclining, going, or directed upward: *Take the up escalator.* **2.** at a higher point or degree, as of amount; above a former or usual level: *Unemployment is up again this month.* **3.** risen above the horizon: *The sun is up.* **4.** above the ground: *The alfalfa is up.* **5.** awake or out of bed: *He won't be up this early.* **6.** being presented or considered: *to be up for reelection, to be up for sale.* **7.** at an end; finished; over: *The speaker's time was up.* **8.** being even with, as in space or degree; equal: *His work simply isn't up to standard.* **9.** on trial: *to be up for murder.* **10.** ahead of one's opponent: *to be two games up.* **11.** *Baseball.* at bat. **12.** *Informal.* going on; taking place: *What's up?* —*prep.* **1.** to or toward a higher place or position in or on: *The spider climbed up the wall.* **2.** at, toward, or to a place or position further along: *Their house is up the block.* **3.** to or toward the source or interior or upper part of: *to paddle up a river.* —*n.* **1.** any upward movement or direction; ascent. **2.** spell of prosperity, elation, or good luck: *to have one's ups and downs.* **3. on the up and up.** *Slang.* sincere and aboveboard; honest. —*v.t.,* **upped, up·ping.** *Informal.* **1.** to make higher or larger, as in amount, degree, or intensity; increase: *to up prices, to up production.* **2.** to put, take, or lift up: *to up the hem of a dress.* —*v.i. Informal.* to act abruptly

un·tuft'ed	un·val'ued	un·washed'	un·wished'-for'
un·tuned'	un·van'quished	un·watched'	un·wit'nessed
un·twilled'	un·var'ied	un·wa'tered	un·wom'an·ly
un·twist'	un·var'y·ing	un·wa'ver·ing	un·wood'ed
un·twist'ed	un·veiled'	un·waxed'	un·work'a·ble
un·typ'i·cal	un·ven'ti·lat'ed	un·weaned'	un·worn'
un·urged'	un·ver'i·fi'a·ble	un·wear'a·ble	un·wor'ried
un·us'a·ble	un·ver'i·fied'	un·wea'ry·ing	un·wound'ed
un·u'ti·lized'	un·versed'	un·weed'ed	un·wo'ven
un·ut'tered	un·vi'a·ble	un·weld'ed	un·yield'ing
un·vac'ci·nat'ed	un·vis'it·ed	un·whipped'	un·zip'
un·val'i·dat'ed	un·want'ed	un·wink'ing	un·zoned'

or unexpectedly: *She upped and told everyone the secret. They upped and eloped.* [Partly from Old English *upp* to a higher place or point; partly from Old English *uppe* on high, aloft.]

up·and·com·ing (up'ən kum'ing) *adj.* talented, doing well, and likely to succeed; promising: *an up-and-coming young lawyer.*

up-and-down (up'ən doun') *adj.* **1.** consisting of or marked by an alternate upward and downward movement. **2.** vertical; perpendicular.

U·pan·i·shad (oo pan'ə shad') *n.* in sacred Hindu literature, one of a group of treatises forming a major division of the Veda. [Sanskrit *upanishad* literally, a sitting down near something.]

u·pas (ū'pəs) *n.* **1.** milky, yellowish, poisonous sap of an evergreen tree, *Antiaris toxicaria* of Asia, used to make a deadly arrow poison. **2.** the tree itself. Also *(def. 2),* **upas tree.** [Malay *ūpas* poison; of Javanese origin.]

up·beat (up'bēt') *n. Music.* unaccented beat, esp. the last beat of a measure, indicated by an upward gesture of the conductor's hand. —*adj. Informal.* happy; cheerful; optimistic.

up·braid (up brād') *v.t.* to criticize or scold harshly or vehemently. [Old English *upbregdan* to reproach.] —**Syn.** see **scold.**

up·bring·ing (up'bring'ing) *n.* care and training received during childhood and youth; manner in which a youngster is raised: *a strict upbringing, his religious upbringing.*

up·com·ing (up'kum'ing) *adj.* soon to occur, appear, or be presented; forthcoming: *the upcoming football season, an upcoming Broadway play.*

up·coun·try (up'kun'trē) *also,* **up-coun·try.** *n.* interior or remote part of a region or country; the inland. —*adj.* of, characteristic of, living in, or coming from the upcountry. —*adv.* toward, in, or to the upcountry.

up·date (up dāt') *-dat·ed, -dat·ing. v.t.* to bring up to date with revisions, corrections, and additions: *They updated the textbook.*

up·end (up end') *v.t.* to set, stand, or turn on end. —*v.i.* to become upended.

up·grade (up'grād') *-grad·ed, -grad·ing. v.t.* to raise to a higher grade or standard, as by improving quality or position: *to upgrade a product, to upgrade a worker to the supervisory level, to upgrade livestock.* —*n.* **1.** upward slope or incline, as of a hill or road. **2. on the upgrade.** increasing; improving. —*adv.* up a hill or slope.

up·growth (up'grōth') *n.* **1.** process of growing up; development. **2.** that which grows up or has grown up.

up·heav·al (up hē'vəl) *n.* **1.** act or instance of upheaving; being upheaved: *volcanic upheavals.* **2.** profound or violent disturbance or change: *the social upheavals caused by the outbreak of civil war.*

up·heave (up hēv') *-heaved* or *-hove, -heav·ing. v.t.* to lift or throw up, as by force or pressure from beneath. —*v.i.* to be lifted, thrown, or forced up.

up·hill (up'hil') *adj.* **1.** going up a hill or incline; directed or sloping upward: *an uphill journey, an uphill path.* **2.** presenting difficulties; arduous; hard: *Establishing the newspaper as a going concern was an uphill battle.* —*adv.* **1.** up a hill or incline; upward. **2.** against difficulties.

up·hold (up hōld') *-held, -hold·ing. v.t.* **1.** to support or maintain, as by continuing, defending, or preserving in the face of opposition or challenge: *to uphold the right to dissent, to uphold a tradition.* **2.** to approve or agree with; confirm: *to uphold a lower court's decision.* **3.** to keep from falling or sinking; hold up; raise. —**up·hold'er,** *n.*

up·hol·ster (up hōl'stər) *v.t.* to fit, as furniture, with padding, cushions, or coverings: *to upholster a sofa, to upholster a headboard.* [From UPHOLSTERER.]

up·hol·ster·er (up hōl'stər ər) *n.* one whose work is upholstering furniture. [Earlier *upholdster,* from Middle English *upholden* to repair (from UP + *holden* to keep, hold') + -STER. See HOLD'.]

up·hol·ster·y (up hōl'stər ē, -strē) *pl.,* **-ster·ies.** *n.* **1.** material used in upholstering. **2.** work, business, or craft of upholstering.

UPI, United Press International, a privately owned news-gathering agency that maintains a world-wide communications network for the transmission of news and supplies its clients, which include newspapers, magazines, and radio and television stations, with news reports, photographs, newsreels, and audio services.

up·keep (up'kēp') *n.* **1.** act of keeping in good condition or in a proper state of repair or of supplying what is necessary for support and well-being; maintenance: *Four hundred men are needed for the upkeep of the city parks.* **2.** cost of such maintenance: *The upkeep on the estate is outrageously high. He's always contributed to his parents' upkeep.*

up·land (up'lənd, -land') *n. also,* **uplands.** any area considerably higher than the land surrounding it. —*adj.* of, relating to, or located in an upland.

up·lift (*v.,* up lift'; *n.,* up'lift') *v.t.* **1.** to raise to a higher moral, social, or cultural level or condition. **2.** to elevate emotionally or spiritually; exalt. **3.** to lift up or raise aloft; elevate. —*n.* **1.** act, process, or result of lifting up or raising. **2.** a movement to improve moral, social,

or cultural conditions. **3.** moral, spiritual, or cultural elevation.

up·most (up'mōst') *adj.* uppermost.

up·on (ə pon', ə pon') *prep.* on. [UP + ON.]

up·per (up'ər) *adj.* **1.** higher, as in place, position, or in a scale: *the upper story of the house, the upper register of her voice.* **2.** *also,* **Upper.** constituting the branch of a bicameral legislature that is usually smaller and more restricted in membership and less directly representative of the population, as the House of Lords in the British Parliament. **3.** (of places) lying on higher ground; farther north or farther inland. **4.** *also,* **Upper.** designating a later part of a geological period. —*n.* **1.** any of the parts of a shoe or boot above the sole. **2. on one's uppers.** *Informal.* **a.** wearing shoes with worn-out soles. **b.** in shabby or poor circumstances; poor; destitute.

up·per·case (up'ər kās') *adj.* of, relating to, or printed in capital letters; capital. Distinguished from **lower-case.** —*v.t.* **-cased, -cas·ing.** to set in or print with capital letters.

upper case 1. capital letters. **2.** type case holding capital letters.

up·per·class (up'ər klas') *adj.* of, relating to, or characteristic of the upper class.

upper class, portion of society occupying the highest social and economic position, above the middle class and lower class.

up·per·class·man (up'ər klas'mən) *pl.,* **-men.** *n.* junior or senior in a high school, college, or university.

upper crust *Informal.* that part of the upper class considered to have the greatest wealth or social standing in a society.

up·per·cut (up'ər kut') *n.* blow directed upwards from beneath, as to an opponent's chin. —*v.t.,* **-cut, -cut·ting.** to strike with an uppercut.

upper hand, position of mastery or control; advantage: *Armed with statistics, John easily gained the upper hand in the debate.*

up·per·most (up'ər mōst') *adj.* **1.** highest, as in place or position: *the uppermost floors, the uppermost reaches of the stratosphere.* **2.** having the most importance, prominence, or influence; foremost; predominant: *She's always uppermost in his thoughts. The state of the old man's health is the uppermost concern.* *Also,* **up'most'.** —*adv.* in the highest or foremost place, position, or rank.

Upper Vol·ta (vol'tə) country in western Africa, north of Ghana. Capital, Ouagadougou. Area, 105,869 sq. mi. Pop. (1969 est.), 5,278,-000.

up·pi·ty (up'ə tē) *adj. Informal.* snobbish or impudent; haughty.

up·raise (up rāz') *-raised, -rais·ing. v.t.* to raise or lift up; elevate.

up·right (up'rīt') *adj.* **1.** in a vertical position, posture, or direction; straight up; erect. **2.** having or showing moral integrity; honest; honorable. —*n.* **1.** that which is in a vertical position, as an upright timber or beam. **2.** state of being upright; vertical position: *a column out of upright.* **3.** upright piano. **4.** uprights. *Football.* goal post. —*adv.* in a vertical position. [Old English *upriht* in a vertical position, erect.] —**up'right'ly,** *adv.* —**up'right'ness,** *n.*

upright piano, piano having the strings and mechanism arranged vertically in a rectangular case that is perpendicular to the keyboard. Distinguished from **grand piano.**

up·rise (up rīz') *-rose, -ris·en, -ris·ing. v.i. Archaic.* **1.** to arise or get up, as from a lying or sitting position. **2.** to come into existence or prominence. **3.** to rise to a higher position, as from below the horizon; ascend or rise from view. **4.** to stage an uprising; rebel; revolt.

up·ris·ing (up'rī'zing) *n.* insurrection against a government or other authority; rebellion.

Syn. Uprising, insurrection mean a limited, unsuccessful, and violent effort against a ruling power. **Uprising** is usually applied to a spontaneous local effort to win freedom because of scant equipment, preparation, or support: *The army ruthlessly crushed the uprisings of the slaves.* **Insurrection** is a more formal word to express a quick flaring up and is applied esp. to poorly organized efforts of a military minority to seize political power: *The army general led the insurrection.* See also **revolt.**

up·roar (up'rôr') *n.* **1.** state of noisy or confused excitement, disorder, or agitation: *The jury was in an uproar about the defendant's refusal to leave the witness stand.* **2.** sound of such agitation; confused or tumultuous disturbance or din. [Dutch *oproer* tumult, mutiny; Modern English spelling influenced by ROAR.]

up·roar·i·ous (up rôr'ē əs) *adj.* **1.** making, causing, or marked by an uproar: *an uproarious welcome.* **2.** loud, noisy, and unrestrained; boisterous: *uproarious laughter.* **3.** causing hearty or boisterous laughter; hilarious: *an uproarious comedy.* —**up·roar'i·ous·ly,** *adv.* —**up·roar'i·ous·ness,** *n.*

up·root (up rōt', -root') *v.t.* **1.** to tear or pull up by the roots: *The tractor uprooted the tree.* **2.** to wrench from or deprive of an accustomed location, environment, or way of life; displace: *The outbreak of war uprooted many families.* **3.** to remove or destroy completely; eliminate; eradicate: *to uproot a difficulty at its source.* —**Syn. 3.** see **eradicate.**

up·set (*v., adj.,* up set'; *n.,* up'set') *-set, -set·ting. v.t.* **1.** to turn, tip, or knock over; topple; capsize: *I accidentally upset the pitcher when I*

at; āpe; cär; end; mē; it; īce; hot; ōld; fôrk; wood; fōōl; oil; out; up; ūse; turn; sing; thin; this; zh in treasure; ə in ago, taken, pencil, lemon, circus.

leaned over the table. **2.** to impair, disrupt, or interfere with the functioning, order, or course of; throw into confusion or disorder: *A wildcat strike upset the airline schedule. My grandfather's antics tend to upset people's conceptions of what old people are like.* **3.** to make perturbed, anxious, or uneasy; disturb mentally or emotionally; distress: *News of her accident greatly upset him.* **4.** to cause a physical disturbance or disorder in; make sick: *Eating all that greasy food will upset your stomach.* **5.** to overthrow or defeat unexpectedly. —*adj.* **1.** mentally or emotionally distressed; perturbed: *I was very upset to see how hurt she was.* **2.** suffering from a physical disturbance or disorder: *My stomach was upset for hours after that heavy meal.* —*n.* **1.** unexpected defeat of an opponent or contestant favored to win. **2.** act of throwing into confusion or disorder; disruption. **3.** mental or emotional distress. **4.** physical disturbance or disorder. **5.** act of turning, tipping, or knocking something over. —**Syn.** *v.t.* **3.** see **disturb.**

upset price, minimum price at which something will be offered for sale, as at an auction.

up·shot (up′shot′) *n.* final result; conclusion; outcome. [Up + SHOT'; originally, a final shot in an archery competition.]

upside down *also,* **up·side-down. 1.** so that the upper side or part becomes the under or lower: *You're holding the map upside down.* **2.** in or into complete disorder or confusion: *We turned the house upside down searching for the keys.* [Modification (influenced by obsolete *upside* upper side) of Middle English *up so down,* literally, up as if down.] —**up′side-down′,** *adj.*

upside-down cake, cake baked with the batter covering a layer of fruit, served with the fruit side up.

up·si·lon (ūp′sə lon′, up′-) *n.* twentieth letter of the Greek alphabet (Υ, υ), corresponding to the English letter *U, u* or *Y, y.*

up·stage (up′stāj′) *adv.* at or toward the rear of a stage. —*adj.* **1.** of or relating to the rear of a stage. **2.** *Informal.* snobbish; haughty. —*v.t.* **-staged, -stag·ing. 1.** to draw audience attention away from (another actor) to oneself, as by moving upstage thus forcing him to turn his back to the audience. **2.** to draw attention to oneself at the expense of (another); eclipse: *Every time he tried to tell a joke, his brother upstaged him with some witty remark.* **3.** *Informal.* to treat in a snobbish or haughty manner.

up·stairs (up′stārz′) *adv.* **1.** toward the top of a staircase; up the stairs: *to run upstairs.* **2.** on or to an upper floor or level: *They're watching television upstairs. This passageway leads upstairs.* **3.** *Slang.* in the mind; mentally or emotionally. **4. to kick (someone) upstairs.** *Informal.* to promote (someone) to a position that is higher but actually less responsible or powerful so as to be rid of him. —*adj.* of, relating to, or situated on an upper floor or floors: *an upstairs maid, an upstairs apartment.* —*n.* upper floor or floors. ▲ usually construed as singular: *The upstairs of the house is totally furnished.*

up·stand·ing (up stan′ding, up′stan′-) *adj.* **1.** honest in character and behavior; commanding respect; honorable: *a fine, upstanding member of the community.* **2.** standing up; upright; erect.

up·start (up′stärt′) *n.* **1.** one who has a brash, aggressive, and presumptuous bearing or way of dealing with others. **2.** person of humble origins who attains sudden wealth or importance and usually behaves in an arrogant or vulgar way as a result; parvenu. —*adj.* **1.** characteristic of an upstart. **2.** suddenly risen to a position of wealth or importance.

up·state (up′stāt′) *adj.* of, from, or designating that part of a state lying farther inland or north of a large city: *a vacation in upstate New York.* —*adv.* in, to, or toward such a region. —*n.* upstate region.

up·stream (up′strēm′) *adv.* toward or at the source of a stream; against the current: *to fish upstream, to row upstream.* —*adj.* directed or situated upstream.

up·surge (up′surj′) *n.* sudden, sizable increase or development: *an upsurge of interest in witchcraft.* —*v.i.* **-surged, -surg·ing.** to surge up; increase; rise.

up·sweep (up′swēp′) *n.* **1.** hairdo in which the hair is smoothly combed upward in the back and secured in position on top of the head. **2.** upward sweep or curve.

up·swept (up′swept′) *adj.* **1.** combed upward to the top of the head: *an upswept hairdo.* **2.** swept or curved upward.

up·swing (up′swing′) *n.* **1.** upward swing or movement. **2.** marked increase or improvement, as in activity or movement.

up·take (up′tāk′) *n.* **1.** *Informal.* mental grasp or perception; understanding; comprehension: *to be quick on the uptake.* **2.** flue or shaft for drawing up air or smoke, as from a mine.

up·thrust (up′thrust′) *n.* upward thrust, esp. an upheaval of part of the earth's crust.

up·tight (up′tīt′) *also,* **up tight.** *adj.* *Slang.* **1.** tense; nervous; anxious. **2.** rigidly conforming to social or moral conventions.

up-to-date (up′tə dāt′) *adj.* **1.** extending to the present time, as in coverage of facts or ideas; employing or including the latest information: *an up-to-date telephone listing.* **2.** reflecting the latest in style, ideas, or improvements; fashionable; modern.

up·town (*adv.,* up′toun′; *adj.,* up′toun′) *adv.* to, toward, or in the upper or northern part of a town or city: *We've moved uptown.* —*adj.* of, relating to, or in the upper or northern part of a town or city: *uptown traffic, the uptown bus.* —*n.* upper or northern part of a town or city.

up·turn (*n.,* up′turn′; *v.,* up turn′) *n.* upward turn, curve, or trend, esp. toward improved conditions: *an upturn in stock market prices.* —*v.t.* to turn up or over, as soil with a plow.

up·ward (up′ward) *adv. also,* **up·wards. 1.** from a lower to a higher place or position: *to look upward.* **2.** toward a higher or greater amount, degree, or rank: *Costs have climbed upward.* **3.** toward or into a later time or greater age: *from childhood upward.* **4.** more; over: *Tickets go for five dollars and upward.* **5.** toward a higher or better condition or level; toward something greater or loftier: *minds aspiring upward.* **6.** toward the interior, source, or origin. **7. upward (or upwards) of.** more than: *You'll have to pay upward of fifty dollars in damages.* —*adj.* moving from a lower to a higher place, level, or condition: *an upward trend.* [Old English *upweard* to a higher position.] —**up′ward·ly,** *adv.*

Ur (ur) *n.* city of ancient Sumer in southern Mesopotamia, on the Euphrates.

u·ra·cil (yoor′ə sil) *n.* pyrimidine base that is an essential constituent of RNA. Formula: $C_4H_4N_2O_2$

U·rae·us (yoo rē′əs) *pl.,* **-us·es.** *n.* representation of the sacred serpent of ancient Egypt, depicted upon the headdresses of Egyptian rulers as an emblem of sovereignty. [Modern Latin *uraeus,* from Greek *ouraios* cobra, from Egyptian *uro* cobra, king.]

Uraeus

U·ral-Al·ta·ic (ūr′əl al tā′ik) *n.* family of languages divided into two main branches, the first of which includes Finnish and Hungarian, the second of which includes Turkish and Mongolian. Languages of this family are spoken predominantly in parts of eastern Europe and central Asia.

U·ral Mountains (yoor′əl) mountain system extending north to south in the central Soviet Union, forming part of the traditional boundary between Europe and Asia. Also, **U′rals.**

Ural River, river rising in the southern Ural Mountains, flowing into the Caspian Sea, forming part of the traditional boundary between Europe and Asia. Also, **U′ral.**

U·ra·ni·a (yoo rā′nē ə) *n.* *Greek Mythology.* the Muse of astronomy.

u·ra·nin·ite (yoo ran′ə nīt′) *n.* rare mineral that is the principal ore of uranium. A common variety is pitchblende. Formula: UO_2

u·ra·ni·um (yoo rā′nē əm) *n.* heavy, silvery, radioactive, metallic element with fourteen isotopes, three of which occur naturally. Uranium isotopes are used chiefly as nuclear fuel, in the production of nuclear fuel, and in the manufacture of nuclear weapons. Symbol: U See **element** for table. [Modern Latin *uranium,* from the planet *Uranus,* which had been discovered shortly before the element was named.]

uranium 235 *also,* **uranium-235.** uranium isotope having a mass number of 235, used as fuel for the chain reaction that releases the energy in a nuclear explosion. It is the only naturally occurring material that undergoes nuclear fission. Symbol: U 235

uranium 238 *also,* **uranium-238.** uranium istope having a mass number of 238, the most abundant naturally occurring isotope of uranium. Symbol: U 238

U·ra·nus (yoor′ə nəs, yoo rā′-) *n.* **1.** Greek god who personified the sky and was the earliest ruler of the universe. He was the son and husband of Gaea and father of the Titans. **2.** third largest planet of the solar system and seventh in order of distance from the sun. It has five known satellites. See **solar system** for illustration. [Latin *Ūranus* the god, from Greek *Ouranos,* from *ouranos* sky, heaven.]

ur·ban (ur′ban) *adj.* of, in, relating to, or characteristic of a city or city life: *urban expansion, an urban population.* [Latin *urbānus* relating to a city, refined, from *urbs* city.]

Ur·ban II (ur′bən) c.1042–99, pope from 1088 to 1099 and promoter of the First Crusade.

ur·bane (ur bān′) *adj.* refined or courteous in a smooth, polished way; having or showing elegance, sophistication, or refinement: *urbane manners, an urbane style of writing.* [Latin *urbānus.* See URBAN.] —**ur·bane′ly,** *adv.* —**ur·bane′ness,** *n.*

ur·ban·ite (ur′bə nīt′) *n.* one who lives in a city.

ur·ban·i·ty (ər ban′ə tē) *pl.,* **-ties.** *n.* quality of being urbane.

ur·ban·ize (ur′bə nīz′) **-ized, -iz·ing.** *v.t.* to make urban, in quality, nature, or organization; to urbanize a region. —**ur′ban·i·za′tion,** *n.*

Urban League, voluntary social welfare agency founded in 1910, devoted to eliminating racial discrimination in the United States, esp.

in urban housing and employment. Official name: National Urban League.

urban renewal, planned rehabilitation and reconstruction of deteriorating urban areas, chiefly through the demolition of slums and the building of public housing, usually carried out under a government-subsidized program.

ur·chin (ur′chin) *n.* **1.** small, mischievous or impish boy. **2.** sea urchin. [Dialectal Old French *herichon* hedgehog, going back to Latin *(h)ēricius.*]

Ur·du (oor′dōō, ur′-) *n.* language belonging to the Indo-Iranian branch of the Indo-European language family, a form of Hindustani spoken by Muslims predominantly in Pakistan and parts of India and written in a modified Arabic alphabet. [Hindustani *urdū,* short for *zabān-i-urdū* language of the camp, from Persian *zabān* language + *urdū* army, camp (from Turkish *ordū*).]

-ure *suffix* (used to form nouns) **1.** act, process, state, or result: *exposure, enclosure.* **2.** function or office or a body performing a function: *legislature.* [Old French *-ure,* from Latin *-ūra.*]

u·re·a (yoo rē′ə) *n.* colorless, crystalline, organic compound that is a constituent of almost all body fluids, esp. urine, and is also produced synthetically, used in fertilizers and animal feed and in the manufacture of plastics and explosives. Formula: $(NH_2)_2CO$ [Modern Latin *urea,* going back to Greek *ouron* urine.]

u·re·mi·a (yoo rē′mē ə) *n.* presence in the blood of waste products normally eliminated in the urine, usually caused by improper functioning of the kidneys and characterized, when severe, by headache, nausea, and convulsions. Also, **uremic poisoning.** [Modern Latin *uraemia,* from Greek *ouron* urine + *haima* blood.] —**u·re′mic,** *adj.*

u·re·ter (yoo rē′tər) *n.* either of two tubes that carry urine from the kidneys to the urinary bladder or, in birds, to the cloaca. [Modern Latin *ureter,* from Greek *ourētēr,* going back to *ouron* urine.]

u·re·thra (yoo rē′thrə) *pl.,* **-thrae** (-thrē) or **-thras.** *n.* canal through which urine from the bladder and, in men, semen are discharged from the body. [Late Latin *ūrēthra,* from Greek *ourēthrā,* going back to *ouron* urine.] —**u·re′thral,** *adj.*

urge (urj) *urged, urg·ing. v.t.* **1.** to plead with or request earnestly: *I urge you to examine your motives. We urged the council to approve an amendment to end discrimination.* **2.** to act as a compelling motive, stimulus, or force on; influence, persuade, or otherwise move to some course of action: *The cheers of the crowd urged the team on to victory.* **3.** to press or argue for the doing, making, consideration, or acceptance of: *to urge prison reform.* **4.** to drive or force forward or onward; spur: *The messenger urged his horse on.* —*v.i.* **1.** to press earnestly or make arguments, claims, or the like. **2.** to exert a driving or compelling force, as to a course of action. —*n.* driving or compelling force, influence, or impulse: *the urge to create, to have an urge for strawberries.* [Latin *urgēre* to press[1], drive.]

Syn. *v.t.* **2.** Urge, goad, egg[2] mean to force or move to action. Urge usually suggests an insistent or vigorous influence that sustains the pursuit of some positive or constructive goal: *The man's ambition urged him on to success.* Goad suggests a powerfully distressing force that causes the loss of one's temper or self-control, resulting in negative or violent action that goes against one's natural desire or temperament: *Constant indignities goaded the slaves to revolt.* Egg is less formal than goad, suggesting a more petty and spiteful end that is achieved by deliberately, even maliciously, exploiting another's interests, desires, or self-esteem: *After egging him on to fight, the older boys deserted him.*

ur·gen·cy (ur′jən sē) *n.* quality or condition of being urgent.

ur·gent (ur′jənt) *adj.* **1.** demanding or calling for immediate action or attention; compelling; pressing: *to have urgent business to attend to.* **2.** importunate; insistent: *urgent appeals for funds.* [Latin *urgēns,* present participle of *urgēre* to press[1], drive.] —**ur′gent·ly,** *adv.*

Syn. **1.** Urgent, pressing, imperative mean demanding immediate attention. Urgent implies a critical situation, as an emergency or disaster, that must be taken care of immediately if at all: *Doctor, there's an urgent call for you.* Pressing suggests a situation that is not crucial but which does take priority, suggesting inner or external pressures that spur one to care for or complete something: *Pressing business kept me working nights at the office last week.* Imperative implies a demand based on authority, an ethical code, or other standard of behavior, rather than an urgent or pressing circumstance that compels action: *It is imperative that you be at the meeting to discuss the changes in the plan.*

U·ri·ah (yoo rī′ə) *n.* in the Old Testament, a Hittite officer in King David's army and the husband of Bathsheba. David had him sent to the front ranks of a battle, where he was killed, and then married Bathsheba.

u·ric (yoor′ik) *adj.* of, relating to, found in, or derived from urine.

uric acid, odorless, white, crystalline, organic compound, an end product of protein metabolism, found in the urine of mammals, birds, reptiles, and insects and used in synthesizing other organic compounds. Formula: $C_5H_4N_4O_3$

U·ri·el (yoor′ē əl) *n.* in ancient Jewish writings, one of the archangels.

u·ri·nal (yoor′ən əl) *n.* **1.a.** upright wall fixture used by men for urinating. **b.** room or enclosure, usually public, containing such a fixture or fixtures. **2.** vessel for urine, as one used by a bedridden patient. [Late Latin *ūrīnal* chamber pot, vessel for urine, going back to Latin *ūrīna* urine.]

u·ri·nal·y·sis (yoor′ə nal′ə sis) *pl.,* **-ses** (-sēz). *n.* chemical or microscopic analysis of urine. [URIN(E) + (AN)ALYSIS.]

u·ri·nar·y (yoor′ə ner′ē) *adj.* **1.** of or relating to urine. **2.** of, relating to, or involving the organs that produce and discharge urine.

u·ri·nate (yoor′ə nāt′) *-nat·ed, -nat·ing. v.i.* to discharge urine. [Medieval Latin *urinatus,* past participle of *urinare,* from Latin *ūrīna* urine.] —**u′ri·na′tion,** *n.*

u·rine (yoor′in) *n.* clear amber or yellow fluid containing waste material that is excreted by the kidneys, stored in the urinary bladder, and discharged from the body through the urethra. [Latin *ūrīna.*]

urn (urn) *n.* **1.a.** vase, esp. one with a foot or pedestal, used to hold the ashes of the dead. **b.** vaselike container for the ashes of the dead after cremation. **2.** closed vessel, usually with a spigot, for making, heating, or serving liquids: *a coffee urn.* [Latin *urna* vessel for drawing water, vessel to hold the ashes of the dead.]

Porcelain urn   Coffee urn

Urns

u·ro·gen·i·tal (yoor′ō jen′ət əl) *adj.* of or relating to the urinary and genital organs or their functions. Also, **u′ri·no·gen′i·tal.** [Greek *ouron* urine + GENITAL.]

Ur·sa Major (ur′sə) constellation in the northern sky, containing the stars of the Big Dipper, conventionally depicted as a large bear. [Latin *Ursa Major* the Greater Bear.]

Ursa Minor, constellation in the northern sky, containing the bright star Polaris and the stars of the Little Dipper, conventionally depicted as a small bear. [Latin *Ursa Minor* the Lesser Bear.]

ur·sine (ur′sīn, -sin) *adj.* of, relating to, or having the characteristics of a bear or bears. [Latin *ursīnus* relating to a bear, from *ursus* bear[2].]

Ur·su·la, Saint (ur′sə lə, urs′yə lə) legendary British princess of the Christian faith, said to have been slain with 11,000 other virgins by an army of Huns at Cologne in the fourth or fifth century A.D.

Ur·su·line (ur′sə lin, -līn′) *n.* member of a Roman Catholic religious order of women, founded in Italy in 1535 primarily for the education of girls. —*adj.* of, relating to, or belonging to the Ursulines.

U·ru·guay (yoor′ə gwā′, oor′ə gwī′) *n.* country on the southeastern coast of South America, between Brazil and Argentina. Capital, Montevideo. Area, 72,172 sq. mi. Pop. (1969 est.), 2,852,000. —**U′ru·guay′an,** *adj., n.*

u·rus (yoor′əs) *pl.,* **u·rus·es.** *n.* aurochs *(def. 1).* [Latin *ūrus* wild ox; of Germanic origin.]

us (us; *unstressed* əs) *pron.* objective case of **we.**

U.S., United States.

USA, United States Army.

U.S.A., United States of America.

us·a·ble (ū′zə bəl) *also,* **use·a·ble.** *adj.* capable of being used; fit, available, or convenient for use. —**us·a·bil′i·ty, us′a·ble·ness,** *n.* —**us′a·bly,** *adv.*

USAF, United States Air Force.

us·age (ū′sij, ū′zij) *n.* **1.** act or manner of using, treating, or handling; treatment; use: *My shoes get hard usage. The prisoners taken were subjected to rough usage.* **2.** customary or established way in which the words, sounds, and grammatical forms are used in a language: *standard English usage.* **3.** particular instance of this; particular expression in speech or writing: *an idiomatic usage.* **4.** customary practice, or something established by or done in accordance with custom, habit, or use: *a law established by usage, not legislation. The ceremony is a usage that has persisted in this village for centuries.* [Old French *usage* custom, use, experience, going back to Latin *ūsus.*]

us·ance (ū′zəns) *n.* period of time allowing for the payment of a foreign bill of exchange, established between different countries by commercial usage or custom. [Old French *usance* custom, practice, from *user* to make use of, practice. See USE.]

USCG, United States Coast Guard.

use (v., ūz; n., ūs) *used, us·ing. v.t.* **1.** to employ for a particular purpose or end; avail oneself of; utilize: *May I use your scissors? John used the library to research his term paper.* **2.** to exhaust the whole or entire supply of (often with *up*): *We used up all the bread at breakfast.* **3.** to take advantage of; exploit: *The ambitious young man used his*

friends to further his career. **4.** to take or partake of habitually: *to use tobacco.* **5.** to act or behave toward; treat: *The general used his prisoners cruelly.* **6.** to accustom; habituate (with *to*): ▲ used as a past participle: *I'm used to his curt manner.* —*v.i.* to do formerly or habitually. ▲ used in the past tense with an infinitive expressed or understood: *I used to dislike her. We used to go there regularly.* —*n.* **1.a.** act of using: the *use of a knife for carving.* **b.** state or condition of being used: *The telephone is in use. That textbook is no longer in use.* **2.** inherent quality that makes something suitable for a purpose; usefulness: *My old glasses are of no use to me now. What's the use of worrying about it now?* **3.** need or occasion for using: *Do you have any use for some used tires?* **4.** purpose for which something is used; function: *This gadget has many uses.* **5.** right or privilege to use something: *We have the use of his car for the weekend.* **6.** manner or way of using: *the proper use of a machine.* **7.** power or ability to use something: *to lose the use of one eye.* **8.** continued or repeated practice or procedure; custom; habit. **9.** *Law.* right to take profits or benefits from property that is held in trust for another who has legal title or possession. **10. to make use of.** to use; employ. **11. to have no use for.** *Informal.* to dislike: *He has no use for lazy people.* [Old French *user* to make use of, practice, consume, going back to Latin *ūsus,* past participle of *ūti* to make use of, practice.] **Syn.** *v.t.* **1. Use, utilize, employ** mean turning something to practical account. **Use** is the most general and widely used word, esp. to imply the suitability of means to ends: *You can use the public facilities at the beach to change out of your bathing suit.* **Utilize** is somewhat formal and technical, emphasizing the thorough exploitation of potential: *Scientists have discovered a means for utilizing coal waste.* **Employ** shifts the emphasis from means and ends to the characteristic and habitual manner of working: *We employ this method of dyeing with great success.*

use·a·ble (ū′zə bəl) *adj.* usable. —**use′a·bil′i·ty, use′a·ble·ness,** *n.* —**use′a·bly,** *adv.*

used (ūzd) *adj.* that has undergone use, esp. used or owned previously by another; not new: *used clothing, used textbooks.*

use·ful (ūs′fəl) *adj.* serving a use or purpose, esp. a valuable, practical, or beneficial one: *a useful distinction. How can I make myself useful?* —**use′ful·ly,** *adv.* —**use′ful·ness,** *n.*

use·less (ūs′lis) *adj.* **1.** serving no practical or beneficial purpose; having no use: *Without the right filter, the tank is useless.* **2.** of no avail; ineffectual; vain; futile: *It's useless to tell him to drive more carefully.* —**use′less·ly,** *adv.* —**use′less·ness,** *n.*

ush·er (ush′ər) *n.* **1.** one who is employed to conduct people to their seats, as in a theater or stadium. **2.** male who attends a bridegroom at a wedding, often accompanying a bridesmaid. **3.** one who serves as an official doorkeeper, as in a courtroom or legislative chamber. —*v.t.* **1.** to act as an usher to; conduct; escort: *The headwaiter ushered the group to the front table.* **2.** to mark the beginning or advance of; introduce formally or ceremoniously (usually with *in*): *We ushered the New Year in with great fanfare. The overthrow of the dynasty ushered in a new era.* —*v.i.* to act as an usher. [Anglo-Norman *usser* doorkeeper, going back to Latin *ōstiārius,* from *ōstium* door, entrance, from *ōs* mouth.]

ush·er·ette (ush′ə ret′) *n.* female employed to usher people to their seats, as in a theater or stadium.

USIA, United States Information Agency, a federal organization handling U.S. publicity and information activities abroad, established in 1953 to promote favorable public opinion toward the United States and its foreign policy.

Üs·kü·dar (ōōs′kōō där′) *n.* port city in northeastern Turkey, on the Bosporus. Pop. (1960), 111,831. Also, **Scu′ta·ri.**

USM, United States Mail.

USMA, United States Military Academy.

USMC, United States Marine Corps.

USN, United States Navy.

USNA, United States Naval Academy.

USO, United Service Organizations, a nongovernmental agency founded in 1941 which provides recreational and religious facilities for U.S. military personnel.

USS **1.** United States Ship. **2.** United States Senate.

USSR, Union of Soviet Socialist Republics.

u·su·al (ū′zhōō əl, ū′zhwəl) *adj.* **1.** that ordinarily happens, occurs, or is to be found; frequently or commonly observed, used, or experienced: *Heavy traffic is usual at this hour. The usual symptoms are evident in her case.* **2.** in accordance with custom, practice, or habit: *The dentist charged me the usual fee. She placed her usual order with the grocer.* [Late Latin *ūsuālis* ordinary, general, from Latin *ūsus* use, custom.] —**u′su·al·ly,** *adv.* —**u′su·al·ness,** *n.*

u·su·fruct (ū′zə frukt′) *n.* legal right to use and profit from another's property, provided its substance is not altered or damaged in any way. [Late Latin *ūsūfrūctus,* for Latin *ususfrūctus,* short for *ūsus* et *frūctus* literally, use and fruit or enjoyment.]

u·su·rer (ū′zhər ər) *n.* one who lends money, esp. at an excessive or illegal rate of interest. [Anglo-Norman *usurer,* from Late Latin *ūsurā-rius* moneylender, going back to Latin *ūsūra* use, interest.]

u·su·ri·ous (ū zhoor′ē əs) *adj.* **1.** practicing usury. **2.** of, relating to, or characterized by usury: *a usurious contract.* —**u·su′ri·ous·ly,** *adv.* —**u·su′ri·ous·ness,** *n.*

u·surp (ū surp′, ū zurp′) *v.t.* **1.** to seize and hold, as the power, position, or rights of another, without legal right or authority; take possession of by or as by force: *to usurp a throne.* **2.** to assume or appropriate wrongfully and arrogantly; use without authority or right. [Latin *ūsūrpāre* to acquire, take possession of, going back to *ūsu* by use + *rapere* to seize.] —**u·surp′er,** *n.*

u·sur·pa·tion (ū′sər pā′shən, ū′zər-) *n.* act of usurping, esp. the wrongful or illegal seizure of royal power.

u·su·ry (ū′zhər ē) *pl.* **-ries.** *n.* **1.** act or practice of lending money at an excessive or illegal rate of interest. **2.** excessive or illegal rate of interest. [Old French *usure,* from Latin *ūsūra* use, interest.]

U·tah (ū′tô, ū′tä) *n.* state in the western United States. Capital, Salt Lake City. Area, 84,916 sq. mi. Pop. (1970), 1,059,273. —**U′tah·an,** *adj., n.*

Ute (ūt, ū′tē) *pl.* **Utes** or **Ute.** *n.* **1.** member of a group of North American Indian tribes, formerly living in parts of present-day Utah, Colorado, and New Mexico. **2.** Shoshonean language of these tribes.

u·ten·sil (ū ten′səl) *n.* article or object useful or necessary in doing or making something, esp. an implement or vessel used in a kitchen: *cooking utensils, writing utensils.* [Old French *utensile,* going back to Latin *ūtēnsilis* useful, from *ūti* to make use of.]

u·ter·ine (ū′tər in, -tə rīn′) *adj.* **1.** of or relating to the uterus. **2.** born of the same mother but having a different father: *uterine sisters.* [Late Latin *uterīnus,* from Latin *uterus* womb.]

u·ter·us (ū′tər əs) *pl.* **-ter·i** (-tə rī′). *n.* **1.** hollow muscular organ found in most female mammals, which holds and nourishes the embryo until birth; the womb. **2.** similar or corresponding part in animals other than mammals, that holds and protects the egg or embryo during development. [Latin *uterus* womb.]

U Thant, see **Thant, U.**

U·ther (ū′thər) *n.* legendary king of ancient Britain who was the father of King Arthur. Also, **Uther Pendragon.**

U·ti·ca (ū′ti kə) *n.* city in central New York, on the Mohawk. Pop. (1970), 91,611.

u·til·i·tar·i·an (ū til′ə târ′ē ən) *adj.* **1.** of, relating to, or made for utility. **2.** emphasizing usefulness or practicality over aesthetic or other considerations. **3.** of, relating to, or adhering to utilitarianism. —*n.* adherent or advocate of utilitarianism.

u·til·i·tar·i·an·ism (ū til′ə târ′ē ə niz′əm) *n.* **1.** philosophical theory evaluating human actions or institutions according to their usefulness in increasing human happiness, developed by Jeremy Bentham and John Stuart Mill into the doctrine advocating that social, moral, and political action be directed toward promoting the greatest happiness for the greatest number of people. **2.** philosophical doctrine that usefulness is good and that an act or thing is good insofar as it is useful.

u·til·i·ty (ū til′ə tē) *pl.* **-ties.** *n.* **1.** state or quality of being useful; usefulness. **2.** company that provides an essential service to the public, as by supplying gas, electricity, or water or by operating a telephone or transportation system, and is usually subject to government regulation. Also, **public utility. 3.** service provided by such a company. **4. utilities.** shares of stock in such a company. **5.** something useful or designed to be useful, as a kitchen storage cabinet or a household cleaning implement. **6.** in utilitarianism, the principle of the greatest happiness for the greatest number of people. —*adj.* designed or intended for general use rather than for a specialized function: *a utility table, a utility knife.* [Latin *ūtilitās* usefulness.]

u·ti·lize (ū′tə līz′) **-lized, -liz·ing.** *v.t.* to take full advantage of; employ for some purpose: *to utilize all available extra space, to utilize resources.* —**u′ti·liz′a·ble,** *adj.* —**u′til·i·za′tion, u′ti·liz′er,** *n.* —**Syn.** see **use.**

ut·most (ut′mōst′) *adj.* **1.** of the greatest or highest degree, amount, or number: *to use the utmost confusion, to have the utmost regard for his ability as a scientist.* **2.** being or situated at the farthest limit or point; most remote: *the utmost regions of the north.* —*n.* the most or greatest possible, as in degree, amount, or extent: *the utmost in luxury. The ambassador did his utmost to prevent the outbreak of hostilities.* Also, **ut′ter·most′.** [Old English *ūt(e)mest* outermost, from *ūt(e)* out + *-mest* most.]

U·to-Az·tec·an (ū′tō az tek′ən) *n.* large North and Central American Indian language family, including Shoshone, Pima, Nahuatl, and other languages. —*adj.* of or relating to this language family.

u·to·pi·a (ū tō′pē ə) *also,* **U·to·pi·a.** *n.* **1.** ideal place or society in which men live together in perfect harmony and happiness; state or place of political or social perfection. **2.** any idealistic, usually im-

---

at; āpe; cär; end; mē; it; īce; hot; ōld; fôrk; wood; fōōl; oil; out; up; ūse; turn; sing; thin; this; zh in treasure; ə in ago, taken, pencil, lemon, circus.

practical and unattainable scheme for social improvement or reform. [Modern Latin *utopia* literally, no place, from Greek *ou* not + *topos* place; referring to the imaginary island described as having an ideal political and social life in *Utopia* (1516), a satirical account by Sir Thomas More.]

u·to·pi·an (ū tō′pē ən) *also,* **U·to·pi·an.** *adj.* **1.** excellent or ideal in theory but not possible or practical in reality; extravagantly impractical or idealistic: *utopian schemes.* **2.** involving or founded upon concepts or schemes of political or social perfection: *a utopian community, utopian literature.* —*n.* one who advocates or works for the establishment of a utopia; idealistic but impractical social theorist or reformer.

u·to·pi·an·ism (ū tō′pē ə niz′əm) *also,* **U·to·pi·an·ism.** *n.* beliefs or ideals of a utopian; idealistic and impractical social theory.

U·trecht (ū′trekt) *n.* historic city in the central Netherlands. Pop. (1968 est.), 275,041.

u·tri·cle (ū′tri kəl) *n.* **1.** larger of the two sacs in the vestibule of the inner ear, aiding in maintaining bodily equilibrium and coordination. **2.** small sac or baglike body, as certain small, one-seeded fruits. [Latin *ūtriculus* little leather bag or bottle, diminutive of *ūter* leather bag or bottle.]

U·tril·lo, Maurice (ū tril′ō, ōō trē′yō) 1883–1955, French painter.

ut·ter[1] (ut′ər) *v.t.* **1.** to give voice or expression to; express audibly or aloud: *to utter a sigh, to utter an accusation. He uttered her name*

in his sleep. **2.** *Law.* to put or send (something forged or counterfeit) into circulation. [Middle Dutch *ūteren* to speak, show.] —**Syn. 1.** see **say.**

ut·ter[2] (ut′ər) *adj.* complete; unqualified; total: *utter darkness, an utter refusal to listen to reason.* [Old English *ūter(r)a* outer, comparative of *ūt(e)* out.] —**ut′ter·ly,** *adv.*

ut·ter·ance (ut′ər əns) *n.* **1.** that which is uttered or expressed in words: *The orator's utterances are preserved in various anthologies.* **2.** act of uttering; vocal expression: *to give utterance to a desire.* **3.** manner or power of speaking.

ut·ter·most (ut′ər mōst′) *adj., n.* utmost.

u·vu·la (ū′vyə lə) *pl.,* **-las** or **-lae** (-lē′) *n.* cone-shaped piece of flesh that hangs from the soft palate, above and behind the tongue. [Late Latin *ūvula,* diminutive of Latin *ūva* grape, uvula; referring to its shape.]

u·vu·lar (ū′vyə lər) *adj.* **1.** of or relating to the uvula. **2.** *Phonetics.* articulated with the aid of the uvula or with the back of the tongue close to or against the uvula.

ux·o·ri·ous (uk sôr′ē əs) *adj.* showing or characterized by an excessive, irrational, or foolishly doting devotion to one's wife. [Latin *uxōrius,* from *uxor* wife.] —**ux·o′ri·ous·ly,** *adv.* —**ux·o′ri·ous·ness,** *n.*

Uz·bek·i·stan (ooz bek′i stan′) *n.* republic of the Soviet Union, in Central Asia. Official name: **Uzbek Soviet Socialist Republic.** Area, approx. 173,600 sq. mi. Pop. (1968 est.), 11,270,000.

at; āpe; cär; end; mē; it; īce; hot; ōld; fôrk; wood; fōōl; oil; out; up; ūse; turn; sing; thin; this; zh in treasure; ə in ago, taken, pencil, lemon, circus.

v, V (vē) *pl.,* **v's, V's.** *n.* **1.** twenty-second letter of the English alphabet. **2.** shape of this letter or something having such a shape. **3.** Roman numeral for 5.

V 1. vanadium. **2.** victory. **3.** volt.

v. 1. verb. **2.** verse. **3.** versus. **4.** see. [Latin *vide.*] **5.** voice. **6.** volt. **7.** volume.

V. 1. Venerable. **2.** Viscount.

VA, Veterans' Administration.

Va., Virginia.

va·can·cy (vā′kən sē) *pl.,* **-cies.** *n.* **1.** unoccupied or empty space, esp. an apartment or room for rent: *The landlord said that the building had no vacancies.* **2.** an unfilled post, position, or office: *a vacancy on the board of directors.* **3.** state or condition of being vacant; emptiness. **4.** emptiness of mind; lack of intelligence or awareness. **5.** *Archaic.* inactivity.

va·cant (vā′kənt) *adj.* **1.** containing nothing or no one; empty or unoccupied: *a vacant lot, a vacant apartment, a vacant seat.* **2.** not held or filled, as a post, position, or office. **3.a.** lacking intelligence or awareness: *a vacant mind.* **b.** lacking expressiveness or thoughtfulness: *a vacant stare.* **4.** free from activity; idle: *vacant hours.* [Latin *vacāns* empty, unoccupied, present participle of *vacāre* to be empty.] —**va′cant·ly,** *adv.* —**va′cant·ness,** *n.* —**Syn. 1.** see **empty.**

va·cate (vas′o lāt′) **-cat·ed, -cat·ing.** *v.t.* **1.** to give up occupancy of; leave empty: *to vacate an apartment.* **2.** to give up (a post, position, or office). **3.** *Law.* to make void; annul. —*v.i.* to leave a place or position vacant. [Latin *vacātus,* past participle of *vacāre* to be empty.]

va·ca·tion (vā kā′shən, və-) *n.* **1.** period of rest and freedom from some activity, esp. a period of paid free time granted to an employee. **2.** act or instance of vacating. —*v.i.* to take or spend a vacation: *to vacation in Spain.* [Latin *vacātiō* a being free from a duty, exemption.] —**va·ca′tion·er, va·ca′tion·ist,** *n.*

vac·ci·nate (vak′sə nāt′) **-nat·ed, -nat·ing.** *v.t.* to inoculate as a preventive against smallpox or other disease. —*v.i.* to perform or practice vaccination. [VACCINE + -ATE¹.]

vac·ci·na·tion (vak′sə nā′shən) *n.* **1.** act or practice of vaccinating. **2.** scar left by a vaccination.

vac·cine (vak sēn′, vak′sēn, -sin) *n.* **1.** killed or weakened virus or bacteria of certain diseases, prepared and used for inoculation. **2.** virus that causes cowpox, prepared for inoculation against smallpox. [Latin *vaccīnus* relating to cows, from *vacca* cow; referring to the use of the *cow*pox virus for vaccination.]

vac·il·late (vas′ə lāt′) **-lat·ed, -lat·ing.** *v.i.* **1.** to move to and fro; sway unsteadily; waver. **2.** to fluctuate; oscillate. **3.** to waver in mind or between courses of action; be irresolute or uncertain. [Latin *vacillātus,* past participle of *vacillāre* to totter, waver.] —**vac′il·la′tion,** *n.* —**Syn. 3.** see **hesitate.**

va·cu·i·ty (va kū′ə tē) *pl.,* **-ties.** *n.* **1.** state or quality of being empty; emptiness. **2.** an empty space; vacuum; void. **3.** emptiness of mind; mental dullness. **4.** something foolish or meaningless. **5.** idleness; inactivity. [Latin *vacuitās* empty space, freedom from something.]

vac·u·ole (vak′ū ōl′) *n.* small, usually fluid-filled cavity in a living organism. [French *vacuole* literally, small vacuum, from Latin *vacuus* empty.]

vac·u·ous (vak′ū əs) *adj.* **1.** empty. **2.** lacking or showing a lack of intelligence; foolish. **3.** not meaningfully occupied; idle. [Latin *vacuus* empty.] —**vac′u·ous·ly,** *adv.* —**vac′u·ous·ness,** *n.*

vac·u·um (vak′ū əm, vak′yōom) *pl.,* **vac·u·ums** or *(defs. 1–4)* **vac·u·a** (vak′ū ə). *n.* **1.** space completely devoid of matter. Although theoretically possible, a perfect vacuum has never been produced experimentally. **2.** space from which almost all gas, vapor, and other matter have been removed. **3.** feeling or condition of emptiness; void. **4.** state of isolation from external conditions, influences, or events: *to live in a vacuum.* **5.** vacuum cleaner. —*v.t., v.i. Informal.* to clean with a vacuum cleaner. [Latin *vacuum* empty space.]

vacuum cleaner, apparatus for cleaning, as carpets or floors, that operates by means of suction.

vacuum gauge, gauge for measuring the pressure in a partial vacuum.

vac·u·um-packed (vak′ū əm pakt′, vak′yōom-) *adj.* packed in an airtight container to maintain freshness.

vacuum tube, electron tube.

va·de me·cum (vā′dē mē′kəm, vä′-) *pl.,* **va·de me·cums. 1.** book or manual for ready reference, usually carried on one's person. **2.** something a person carries about with him for regular use. [Latin *vāde mēcum* go with me.]

Va·duz (vä′dōōts) *n.* capital of Liechtenstein. Pop. (1966 est.), approx. 4000.

vag·a·bond (vag′ə bond′) *n.* **1.a.** person who wanders from place to place, having no fixed abode and no visible means of support. **b.** tramp *(def. 1).* **2.** disreputable or worthless person. —*adj.* of, relating to, or characteristic of a vagabond or a vagabond's way of life: *a vagabond existence.* [Latin *vagābundus* strolling about, from *vagārī* to wander.]

vag·a·bond·age (vag′ə bon′dij) *n.* **1.** state of being a vagabond. **2.** vagabonds collectively.

va·gar·y (və gār′ē, vā′gər ē) *pl.,* **-gar·ies.** *n.* unusual, erratic, or capricious act, occurrence, or idea. [Latin *vagārī* to wander.] —**Syn.** see **caprice.**

va·gi·na (və jī′nə) *pl.,* **-nas** or **-nae** (-nē). *n.* **1.** canal extending from the uterus to the external genital opening in female mammals. **2.** sheathlike part. [Latin *vāgīna.*]

vag·i·nal (vaj′ən əl, və jīn′əl) *adj.* **1.** of or relating to the vagina of a female mammal. **2.** of, relating to, or resembling a sheath.

vag·i·nate (vaj′ə nit, -nāt′) *adj.* having or resembling a sheath. Also, **vag·i·nat·ed** (vaj′ə nā′təd).

va·gran·cy (vā′grən sē) *pl.,* **-cies.** *n.* **1.** state or condition of being a vagrant. **2.** conduct of a vagrant. **3.** wandering in mind or thought.

va·grant (vā′grənt) *n.* **1.** person having no regular home or employment who wanders about from place to place; vagabond. **2.** wanderer; rover. **3.** *Law.* idle or disorderly person, as a tramp, having no fixed abode and no visible means of support. —*adj.* **1.** of, relating to, or characteristic of a vagrant or a vagrant's way of life. **2.** wandering; erratic; uncertain. [Anglo-Norman *vagarant* wanderer, vagabond, going back to Latin *vagārī* to wander.] —**va′grant·ly,** *adv.*

vague (vāg) **va·guer, va·guest.** *adj.* **1.** not definitely or precisely expressed: *vague promises.* **2.** not precise or exact in meaning: *vague words.* **3.** not clearly or precisely felt or known: *a vague feeling, a vague idea.* **4.** unable to think with clearness or precision: *a vague old man.* **5.** lacking definiteness of form or outline; obscure: *The skyscraper was a vague shape in the fog.* [Latin *vagus* wandering, uncertain.] —**vague′ly,** *adv.* —**vague′ness,** *n.*

Syn. 1. Vague, obscure, enigmatic mean not clearly expressed. **Vague** implies a lack of precision and detail and is often used of statements that are so broad and general in an effort to cover all possibilities that they are ambiguous: *The law is vague on this point.* It also suggests fuzzy or woolly thinking: *The man could give only a vague description of his assailant.* **Obscure** implies that the meaning of something is hidden by incomplete explanations, esoteric allusions, and unnecessarily difficult language and syntax: *The obscure language of that case history made it boring.* **Enigmatic** implies that something admits of several interpretations and is used of a purposeful effort to create a magical or mysterious air: *The oracle gave an enigmatic reply.*

Labels at right of illustration: Nucleus; Vacuole.

Vacuole

---

at; āpe; cär; end; mē; it; īce; hot; ōld; fôrk; wood; fōōl; oil; out; up; ūse; turn; sing; thin; **th**is; zh in treasure; ə in ago, taken, pencil, lemon, circus.

va·gus (vā′gəs) *pl.,* **va·gi** (vā′jī). *n.* either of a pair of nerves that begins in the medulla oblongata and branches out to the larynx, esophagus, heart, lungs, and stomach. Also, **vagus nerve.** [Latin *vagus* wandering.]

vail (vāl) *v.t. Archaic.* **1.** to cause or allow to descend or sink; lower. **2.** to doff or take off, as a hat, to show respect or submission. [Short for obsolete *avail* to lower, from old French *avaler,* going back to Latin *ad vallem* to the valley.]

vain (vān) *adj.* **1.** overly or excessively preoccupied with or proud of one's appearance, abilities, or accomplishments; conceited. **2.** not successful or effective: *a vain effort.* **3.** of no real significance or worth; empty: *a vain threat.* **4. in vain. a.** without success; ineffective; useless: *All attempts at rescue were in vain.* **b.** without proper respect; lightly; irreverently: *to take God's name in vain.* [Old French *vain* useless, empty, ineffective, from Latin *vānus* empty, fruitless.] —**vain′ly,** *adv.* —**vain′ness,** *n.*

Syn. 2. Vain, fruitless, futile mean useless. Vain stresses failure to achieve the desired result even after effort: *The vain attempt to stop passage of the bill at least served the purpose of uniting the opposition.* Fruitless is more emphatic in suggesting a long and intensive effort that proves totally unproductive: *The police made a fruitless search for the missing girl.* Futile, in contrast, indicates that certain knowledge or circumstances make failure a foregone conclusion, suggesting that any effort is a mere gesture, wasted and misdirected: *The surrounded troops, realizing that opposition was futile, prepared to surrender.*

vain·glo·ri·ous (vān′glôr′ē əs) *adj.* **1.** excessively vain or boastful. **2.** characterized by, displaying, or proceeding from vainglory. —**vain′glo′ri·ous·ly,** *adv.* —**vain′glo′ri·ous·ness,** *n.*

vain·glo·ry (vān′glôr′ē, vān glôr′ē) *n.* **1.** excessive vanity or boastfulness. **2.** vain and ostentatious show or display.

vair (vâr) *n.* **1.** gray and white squirrel fur used in the Middle Ages for lining and trimming garments. **2.** representation of this, consisting of rows of figures resembling small shields, alternately blue and silver. [Old French *vair* squirrel fur, fur of various colors, miniver, from Latin *varius* of various colors, changing.]

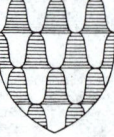

Vair (def. 2)

val·ance (val′əns, vā′ləns) *n.* **1.** short drapery or piece of wood or metal hung across the top of a window, as for decoration or to hide curtain fixtures. **2.** short drapery hanging as from a shelf, table, or frame of a bed, often to the floor. [Probably from *Valence,* city in France noted for making fabrics.]

vale¹ (vāl) *n.* valley. [Old French *val,* from Latin *vallēs.*]

va·le² (vä′lā, vā′lē) *interj., n. Latin.* farewell; good-by.

val·e·dic·tion (val′ə dik′shən) *n.* act or instance of bidding farewell. [Latin *valedictus,* past participle of *valedīcere* to say farewell + -ION.]

val·e·dic·to·ri·an (val′ə dik tôr′ē ən) *n.* student, usually ranking highest in this class, who delivers the valedictory at graduation exercises.

val·e·dic·to·ry (val′ə dik′tər ē) *pl.,* **-ries.** *n.* farewell address, esp. one delivered at graduation exercises. —*adj.* of, relating to, or expressing a farewell. [Latin *valedictus,* past participle of *valedīcere* to say farewell + -ORY.]

va·lence (vā′ləns) *n.* **1.** combining capacity of an element or radical in ionic compounds, expressed as the charge that an atom of the element or that the radical carries as an ion. The sum of the valences of the elements or radicals in the compound must equal zero. For example, sodium has a valence of $+1$ and chlorine has a valence of -1 in sodium chloride (NaCl). **2.** combining capacity of an element or radical in a covalent compound, expressed as the charge that an atom of the element or that the radical would carry if it were regarded as an ion. The sum of the valences of the elements or radicals in the compound must equal zero. For example, carbon has a valence of $+4$ and chlorine has a valence of -1 in carbon tetrachloride (CCl_4). Also, **va′len·cy.** [Late Latin *valentia* power, strength, from Latin *valēre* to be strong, be well.]

Va·len·ci·a (və len′sē ə, -shə) *n.* **1.** port city in eastern Spain. Pop. (1968), 499,131. **2.** city in northern Venezuela, southwest of Caracas. Pop. (1969), 177,199.

Va·len·ci·ennes (və len′sē enz′) *n.* fine bobbin lace, usually having a floral design. Also, **Valenciennes lace.** [From *Valenciennes,* city in France where it was first made.]

val·en·tine (val′ən tīn′) *n.* **1.** greeting card or gift sent on Valentine's Day, usually as an expression of affection for one's sweetheart. **2.** sweetheart, esp. a chosen sweetheart on Valentine's Day.

Val·en·tine, Saint (val′ən tīn′) Christian martyr of the third century A.D.

Valentine's Day, day named in honor of Saint Valentine, traditionally observed by the exchanging of valentines. February 14. Also, **Saint Valentine's Day.**

va·le·ri·an (və lēr′ē ən) *n.* **1.** drug having a pungent odor, obtained from the roots of a plant, *Valeriana officinalis,* and formerly used as a sedative. **2.** the plant itself, native to Europe and Asia, having small white or pink flowers. [Old French *valeriane* the plant, possibly going back to Latin *Valeria,* ancient Roman province where it was supposedly found in abundance.]

Va·le·ri·an (və lēr′ē ən) *n.* A.D. c.193–c.269, Roman emperor from A.D. 253 to 260.

val·et (val′it, val′ā) *n.* **1.** man's male servant who performs various personal services for his employer, as caring for his clothes and helping him dress. **2.** employee, as of a hotel, who performs similar personal services for guests. —*v.t., v.i.* to serve as a valet. [French *valet* servant, from Old French *vaslet* groom, squire, youth; of Celtic origin.]

val·e·tu·di·nar·i·an (val′ə tōōd′ən ār′ē ən, -tūd′-) *n.* invalid, esp. one overly concerned with his health. —*adj.* of, like, or characteristic of such a person; sickly. Also, **val′e·tu′di·nar′y.** [Latin *valētūdinārius* sickly (from *valētūdō* state of health) + -AN.]

Val·hal·la (val hal′ə) *n. Norse Mythology.* great hall to which heroes and warriors slain in battle were taken by the Valkyries to spend their days fighting and their nights feasting at the table of Odin. [Modern Latin *Valhalla,* from Old Norse *Valhöll,* from *valr* those slain in battle + *höll* hall.]

val·ian·cy (val′yən sē) *n.* valor. Also, **val′iance.**

val·iant (val′yənt) *adj.* brave; courageous: *a valiant warrior, to put up a valiant fight.* [Old French *vaillant,* present participle of *valoir* to be worth, avail, from Latin *valēre* to be strong.] —**val′iant·ly,** *adv.* —**val′iant·ness,** *n.* —**Syn.** see **brave.**

val·id (val′id) *adj.* **1.** soundly based on facts or evidence; true: *Subsequent developments proved his accusations valid.* **2.** having the desired result; effective: *valid methods.* **3.** acceptable under the law; legally effective or binding: *a valid will.* **4.** *Logic.* correct: *to derive a valid conclusion from a premise.* [Latin *validus* strong.] —**val′id·ly,** *adv.* —**val′id·ness,** *n.*

val·i·date (val′i dāt′) **-dat·ed, -dat·ing.** *v.t.* **1.** to make or declare legally valid: *to validate election results.* **2.** to prove to be valid, true, or correct; substantiate; confirm: *The scientist could not validate his claims.* —**val′i·da′tion,** *n.*

va·lid·i·ty (və lid′ə tē) *pl.,* **-ties.** *n.* quality, state, or fact of being valid.

va·lise (və lēs′) *n.* small piece of luggage; suitcase. [French *valise,* from Italian *valigia;* of uncertain origin.]

Val·kyr·ie (val kēr′ē, val′kēr ē) *n. Norse Mythology.* any of a group of beautiful warrior maidens, attendants of Odin, who ride through the air on horses and conduct heroes slain in battle to Valhalla. [Old Norse *Valkyrja* literally, chooser of the slain, from *valr* those slain in battle + *kyrja* chooser.]

Val·la·do·lid (väl′yä dō lēd′) *n.* city in north-central Spain. Pop. (1968), 174,579.

val·la·tion (va lā′shən) *n.* rampart; entrenchment. [Late Latin *vallātiō,* going back to Latin *vallum.*]

Val·le·jo (va lā′hō) *n.* port city in western California, north of San Francisco. Pop. (1970), 66,733.

Val·let·ta (vä let′ə) *n.* capital, principal city, and chief port of Malta. Pop. (1968), 15,432.

val·ley (val′ē) *pl.,* **-leys.** *n.* **1.** depression of the earth's surface between hills, mountains, or other high lands, usually having a river or stream flowing through it. **2.** any depression or hollow like or resembling this. **3.** area of land drained by a river system; river basin: *the Nile valley.* **4.** depression or angle formed by two sloping sides of a roof. [Anglo-Norman *valey* the depression between mountains, going back to Latin *vallēs.*]

Valley Forge, village in southeastern Pennsylvania, noted as the site of Washington's encampment during the winter of 1777–78.

Va·lois (val′wä) *n.* dynasty of French kings that ruled from 1328 to 1589.

val·or (val′ər) *also, British,* **val·our.** *n.* outstanding courage, esp. in battle; great bravery. [Late Latin *valor* worth, courage, from Latin *valēre* to be strong, to be worth.]

val·or·i·za·tion (val′ər i zā′shən) *n.* establishment of a certain price or value for a commodity, as by government action or by international business agreement.

val·or·ize (val′ə rīz′) **-ized, -iz·ing.** *v.t.* to set the price or value of (a commodity) by valorization.

val·or·ous (val′ər əs) *adj.* having or showing valor; brave; courageous. —**val′or·ous·ly,** *adv.* —**val′or·ous·ness,** *n.*

Val·pa·rai·so (val′pə rī′zō) *n.* port city in central Chile, the leading Pacific port in South America. Pop. (1968 est.), 286,108.

valse (väls) *pl.,* **valses** (väls). *n. French.* waltz.

val·u·a·ble (val′ū ə bəl, val′yə bəl) *adj.* **1.** having great monetary or material value; worth much money: *a valuable piece of property.* **2.** of great use, worth, or importance: *valuable advice, a valuable friend.*

—*n. usually,* **valuables.** item of personal property having great value, as a piece of jewelry. —**val′u·a·ble·ness,** *n.* —**val′u·a·bly,** *adv.*

Syn. *adj.* **1. Valuable, precious, expensive** mean having great monetary value. **Valuable** suggests a price that is related to the intrinsic worth of something: *David has a valuable art collection.* **Precious** suggests that something's worth is based on its rarity and scarcity as well as the demands of the market: *Rubies are precious gems.* **Expensive** suggests a cost that is beyond one's means or more than something is worth: *Mink coats are expensive.*

val·u·ate (val′ū āt′) **-at·ed, -at·ing.** *v.t.* to set a value on; appraise. —**val′u·a·tor,** *n.*

val·u·a·tion (val′ū ā′shən) *n.* **1.** act or process of estimating the value or price of something. **2.** estimated value or price of something. **3.** estimation or judgment, as of the worth of something.

val·ue (val′ū) *n.* **1.** relative or attributed worth, usefulness, importance, or merit: *We kept the old chair for its sentimental value. My father set great value on family loyalty.* **2.** monetary or material worth; market price: *The value of diamonds has gone up in recent years.* **3.** fair equivalent in money, goods, or services; fair price or return: *to get good value for one's money.* **4. values.** principles or standards of an individual or group; ideals: *The values of today's young people differ from those of their parents.* **5.** exact meaning or significance; import. **6.** numerical quantity, esp. a number represented by a symbol or group of symbols. **7.** *Music.* relative duration of a tone or rest as indicated by a note or other symbol. **8.** quality of sound in speech as represented by letters of the alphabet: *the values of "a" in "hat" and "hate".* **9.** relative lightness or darkness of a color. **10.** relative amount of light and darkness of one portion of a painting or other work of art as compared with another portion. —*v.t.,* **val·ued, val·u·ing. 1.** to estimate the monetary value of; appraise: *The jeweler valued the diamond at one thousand dollars.* **2.** to regard highly; esteem: *to value someone's friendship.* **3.** to rate on the basis of estimated worth, importance, or value: *to value one's honor above one's life.* [Old French *value* worth, price, from *valoir* to be worth, from Latin *valēre* to be strong, to be worth.] —**val′u·er,** *n.*

val·ued (val′ūd) *adj.* highly regarded; esteemed: *a valued friend, a valued possession.*

value judgment, judgment made on the basis of one's own values or opinions.

val·ue·less (val′ū lis) *adj.* having no value; worthless.

val·vate (val′vāt) *adj.* **1.** of, relating to, having, or opening by a valve or valves. **2.** *Botany.* meeting at the edges without overlapping, as the petals of flower buds. [Latin *valvātus* having folding doors, from *valva* folding door.]

valve (valv) *n.* **1.a.** any of various devices used to control the flow of liquids, gases, or loose materials in piping and other closed systems by blocking or partially blocking passages by means of a movable part. **b.** the movable

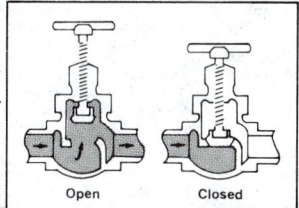

Open   Closed

Valve *(def. 1a)*

part of such a device. **2.** fold in a membrane lining a hollow organ, that allows a fluid, as blood, to flow in one direction and prevents it from flowing in the opposite direction. **3.** device in certain brass instruments, as the trumpet, for altering the pitch of the tone by changing the length of the air column. **4.** one of the pair of hinged shells of an oyster, clam, or other mollusk. **5.** *Botany.* one of the parts into which a seed capsule splits. **6.** *British.* electron tube. [Latin *valva* leaf of a door, folding door.] —**valved,** *adj.*

val·vu·lar (val′vyə lər) *adj.* **1.** of, relating to, or having valves or valvelike parts. **2.** having the form or function of a valve.

va·moose (va mōōs′) **-moosed, -moos·ing.** *v.i.* *Slang.* to leave quickly; go away hastily. [Spanish *vamos* let us go, going back to Latin *vādere* to go.]

vamp¹ (vamp) *n.* upper front part of a shoe or boot, covering the instep and sometimes the toes. —*v.t.* **1.** to provide with a vamp; repair with a new vamp. **2.** to patch up; repair (often with *up*). **3.** to fabricate; invent (often with *up*). [Modification of Old French *avantpie* front part of a foot or shoe, going back to Latin *ab* from + *ante* before + *pēs* foot.] —**vamp′er,** *n.*

vamp² (vamp) *Informal. n.* unscrupulous woman who uses her feminine charms to seduce or take advantage of men. —*v.t.* to seduce or take advantage of (a man) by using feminine charms. [Shortened from VAMPIRE.]

vam·pire (vam′pīr) *n.* **1.** in folklore, a corpse that leaves its grave at

night to suck the blood of sleeping persons. **2.** person who ruthlessly preys on or takes advantage of others, esp. a vamp. **3.** vampire bat. [French *vampire,* through Magyar, possibly going back to Turkish *uber* witch.]

vampire bat 1. any of various bats of tropical America, family Desmodontidae, that feeds on blood. **2.** any of various other bats mistakenly believed to feed on blood.

vam·pir·ism (vam′pīr iz′əm, -pə riz-′) *n.* **1.** belief in vampires. **2.** actions or practices of a vampire.

van¹ (van) *n.* **1.** large, covered truck or other vehicle, used for transporting furniture, goods, or animals. **2.** *British.* closed railroad car, used for carrying baggage or freight. [Short for CARAVAN.]

van² (van) *n.* vanguard.

va·na·di·um (və nā′dē əm) *n.* ductile metallic element used in making corrosion-resistant steel and steel used for springs and high-speed tools. Symbol: V See **element** for table. [Modern Latin *vanadium,* from Old Norse *Vanadīs* a name of the goddess Freya.]

Van Al·len radiation belt (van al′ən) irregular, doughnut-shaped region of intense radiation encircling the earth at varying high altitudes, consisting of electrons and protons trapped by the earth's magnetic field. Also, **Van Allen belt.** [From James A. *Van Allen,* 1914—, U.S. physicist who designed the equipment that first detected the region in 1958.]

Van Bu·ren, Martin (van byoor′ən) 1782–1862, eighth president of the United States, from 1837 to 1841.

Van·cou·ver (van kōō′vər) *n.* **1.** port city in southwestern British Columbia, Canada. Pop. (1966), 410,375. **2.** island of British Columbia, Canada, just off the southwestern coast of the mainland. Area, 12,408 sq. mi. Pop. (1961), 290,835. **3.** port city in southwestern Washington. Pop. (1970), 42,493.

van·dal (vand′əl) *n.* **1.** one who intentionally or maliciously destroys or damages public or private property. **2. Vandal.** member of a Germanic tribe that ravaged Gaul, Spain, and northern Africa in the fourth and fifth centuries A.D., and sacked Rome in A.D. 455. —*adj.* **1.** maliciously or ruthlessly destructive. **2. Vandal.** of or relating to the Vandals. [Latin *Vandalus* member of the Germanic tribe; of Germanic origin.]

van·dal·ism (vand′əl iz′əm) *n.* willful or malicious damage to or destruction of public or private property.

van·dal·ize (vand′əl īz′) **-ized, -iz·ing.** *v.t.* to damage or destroy (property) maliciously.

Van de Graaff generator (van′ də graf′) particle accelerator that consists chiefly of a large, hollow, metal sphere, and uses an electrostatic method to provide the accelerating voltage. [From Robert J. *Van de Graaff,* 1901–67, U.S. physicist who invented it.]

Van Dyck, Sir Anthony (van dīk′) *also,* **Van·dyke.** 1599–1641, Flemish painter.

Van·dyke (van dīk′) *n.* short, pointed beard. [Probably because Van Dyck frequently painted such a beard.]

vane (vān) *n.* **1.** weather vane; weathercock. **2.** blade or flat or curved bladelike part, as of a windmill or propeller. **3.** flat, weblike part of a feather, consisting of the barbs. **4.** projecting, often finlike part attached to the body of a missile to provide stability or guidance. [Old English *fana* flag.]

van Gogh, Vincent (van gō′, GOKH′) 1853–90, Dutch painter.

van·guard (van′gärd′) *n.* **1.** part of an army that moves ahead of the main force. **2.a.** leading or foremost position, as of a movement. **b.** persons occupying such a position. [Old French *avant-garde* vanguard of an army, from *avant* before (going back to Latin *ab* from + *ante* before) + *garde* guard (of Germanic origin).]

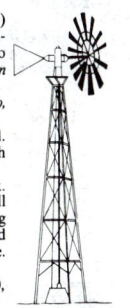

Vanes of a windmill

va·nil·la (və nil′ə) *n.* **1.** flavoring agent extracted from the seed pods of one of a large group of climbing orchids, *Vanilla planifolia,* widely used in candies, ice cream, and cookies. **2.** the seed pod from which this agent is extracted. Also, **vanilla bean. 3.** any of the climbing orchids of the genus *Vanilla,* found in tropical regions throughout the world. [Spanish *vainilla* the orchid, small pod, diminutive of *vaina* sheath, from Latin *vāgīna,* referring to the form of the fruit.]

van·il·lin (və nil′in) *n.* white crystalline substance obtained from the vanilla bean or made synthetically, used for flavoring and in making perfumes. Formula: $C_8H_8O_3$

van·ish (van′ish) *v.i.* **1.** to pass from sight, vanish suddenly or quickly; disappear: *The airplane vanished in the clouds.* **2.** to cease to exist: *All hope of winning the game vanished when our star player was injured.* [Old French *esvaniss-,* a stem of *esvanir* to disappear, going back to Latin *ēvānēscere,* going back to *ex* out of + *vānus* empty.] —**Syn. 1.** see **disappear.**

vanishing point 1. point at which receding parallel lines appear to converge when represented in perspective. 2. point at which something disappears or ceases to exist.

van·i·ty (van'i tē) *pl.*, **-ties.** *n.*
1. excessive preoccupation with or pride in one's appearance, abilities, or accomplishments; conceit. 2. quality of being worthless, ineffective, useless, or meaningless. 3. something that is vain, worthless, or futile. 4. vanity case. 5. dressing table. [Old French *vanite*, from Latin *vānitās* emptiness, worthlessness.]

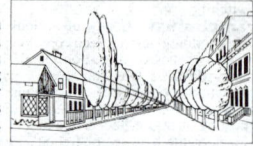
Vanishing point

vanity case, woman's small case for carrying cosmetics, toiletries, and other articles.

vanity fair *also,* **Vanity Fair.** the world or a part of it regarded as a scene of idle amusement, frivolity, or ostentation. [From *Vanity Fair* (the fair in the town of Vanity in John Bunyan's allegory *Pilgrim's Progress*), which symbolizes worldly pomp and vanity.]

van·quish (vang'kwish, van'-) *v.t.* 1. to defeat or conquer, as in battle. 2. to overcome (a feeling): *to vanquish one's fear of heights.* [Modification of Old French *vencus* and *venquis*, past participle and preterit respectively of *veintre* tb conquer, from Latin *vincere*.] —**van'quish·er,** *n.* —**Syn.** 1. see **defeat.**

van·tage (van'tij) *n.* 1. advantageous or superior position. 2. vantage point. 3. *Tennis.* advantage (*def. 4*). [Anglo-Norman *vantage,* short for Old French *advantage* advance, head start. See ADVANTAGE.]

vantage point, position that allows a clear or advantageous view.

van·ward (van'wǝrd) *adj.* situated in the front, or toward the front. —*adv.* to or toward the front.

vap·id (vap'id) *adj.* dull or lifeless; insipid; uninteresting. [Latin *vapidus.*] —**va·pid'i·ty,** *n.* —**vap'id·ness,** *n.* —**vap'id·ly,** *adv.*

va·por (vā'pǝr) *also, British,* **va·pour.** *n.* 1. any visible or cloudy diffused matter suspended in the air, as mist or smoke. 2. gaseous state of a substance that is a liquid or a solid under normal conditions of temperature and pressure. 3. something insubstantial or transitory. 4. **vapors.** *Archaic.* depression, low spirits, or hypochondria. —*v.i.* 1. to rise or pass off in vapor. 2. to give off vapor. 3. to indulge in boastful or idle talk. [Latin *vapor* steam.]

va·por·ish (vā'pǝr ish) *adj.* 1. like or resembling vapor. 2. *Archaic.* inclined to depression, low spirits, or hypochondria.

va·por·ize (vā'pǝ rīz') **-ized, -iz·ing.** *v.t., v.i.* to change or be changed into vapor. —**va'por·iz'a·ble,** *adj.* —**va'por·i·za'tion,** *n.*

va·por·iz·er (vā'pǝ rī'zǝr) *n.* device for converting a liquid into a vapor, esp. such a device for vaporizing a medicinal liquid for inhalation.

vapor lock, blocking of fuel flow in an internal-combustion engine resulting from the formation of air bubbles in the fuel line.

va·por·ous (vā'pǝr ǝs) *adj.* 1. containing, full of, or obscured by vapor; misty. 2. like, resembling, or characteristic of vapor. 3. unsubstantial, vague, or transitory. Also, **va'por·y.**

vapor trail, contrail.

va·que·ro (vä kār'ō) *pl.*, **-ros.** *n.* cowboy, esp. of Mexico, South America, or the southwestern United States. [Spanish *vaquero* cowherd, from *vaca* cow, from Latin *vacca* cow.]

var. 1. variant. 2. variation. 3. variety. 4. various.

Va·ra·na·si (vǝ rä'nǝ sē) *n.* see **Benares.**

var·i·a·ble (vâr'ē ǝ bǝl) *adj.* 1. likely or liable to change; changeable. 2. capable of being changed. 3. *Mathematics.* having no fixed value. 4. *Biology.* liable to deviate from the normal. —*n.* 1. something that varies or is variable. 2. *Mathematics.* **a.** quantity that can assume any of a set of values. **b.** symbol representing such a quantity. —**var'i·a·bil'i·ty, var'i·a·ble·ness,** *n.* —**var'i·a·bly,** *adv.*

variable star, star that varies perceptibly in brightness from time to time.

var·i·ance (vâr'ē ǝns) *n.* 1. act of varying or the quality or state of being variant or variable; difference. 2. discord; dissension; dispute. 3. at variance. in disagreement.

var·i·ant (vâr'ē ǝnt) *adj.* 1. different or varying, often in a slight way, as from another or others of the same kind or from some standard: *Some words have several variant spellings.* 2. liable to vary; changeable. —*n.* something that is variant, as a different spelling, pronunciation, or form of the same word. [Latin *variāns,* present participle of *variāre* to change.]

var·i·a·tion (vâr'ē ā'shǝn) *n.* 1. act, fact, instance, or process of varying. 2. extent or degree to which something varies. 3. something that differs slightly from another of the same kind. 4. *Music.* repetition of a theme or tune with modifications or embellishments, as in melody, harmony, rhythm, or key, esp. one of a series of such repetitions. 5. *Ballet.* a solo dance. 6. *Biology.* deviation of an individual of a species

from others of the species, as in structure. 7. *Astronomy.* deviation of a celestial body from its usual orbit or motion.

var·i·cel·la (var'ǝ sel'ǝ) *n.* chicken pox. [Modern Latin *varicella,* diminutive of *variola.* See VARIOLA.]

var·i·col·ored (ver'i kul'ǝrd, var'-) *adj.* having various colors; variegated.

var·i·cose (var'ǝ kōs') *adj.* 1. swollen and twisted, esp. denoting an abnormal condition affecting the veins of the leg. 2. of, relating to, or affected with varicose veins. [Latin *varicōsus* full of dilated veins, from *varix* dilated vein.]

var·i·cos·i·ty (var'ǝ kos'ǝ tē) *pl.*, **-ties.** *n.* 1. condition of being varicose. 2. part of a vein, esp. in the leg, that is swollen and twisted.

var·ied (vâr'ēd) *adj.* 1. consisting of different or various kinds, items, or parts: *a varied assortment of chocolates, a varied menu.* 2. changed; altered.

var·i·e·gate (vâr'ē ǝ gāt', vâr'ǝ gāt') **-gat·ed, -gat·ing.** *v.t.* 1. to change in appearance, esp. by marking with different colors. 2. to give variety to. [Latin *variēgātus,* past participle of *variēgāre* to make of various colors, from Latin *varius* of various colors, changing + *agere* to drive, do, act.]

var·i·e·gat·ed (vâr'ē ǝ gā'tid, vâr'ǝ gā'-) *adj.* 1. marked or streaked with different colors; varied in color. 2. having or characterized by variety.

var·i·e·ga·tion (vâr'ē ǝ gā'shǝn, vâr'ǝ gā'-) *n.* state or condition of being variegated.

va·ri·e·ty (vǝ rī'ǝ tē) *pl.*, **-ties.** *n.* 1. state or quality of being various or varied; diversity: *A job that lacks variety soon becomes tiresome.* 2. number or collection of different things: *The woman purchased a variety of items at the market.* 3. different kind or form of something: *The writer seemed to have created a new variety of humor.* 4. group of related plants or animals forming a small part or subdivision of a larger group. [Latin *varietās* diversity.]

variety show, show, as on stage or television, consisting of several different entertainment forms, as songs, dances, and comedy sketches.

variety store, store offering a large assortment of merchandise for sale, usually items of low or moderate cost.

var·i·form (vâr'ǝ fôrm') *adj.* varied in form or shape; having various forms.

va·ri·o·la (vǝ rī'ǝ lǝ) *n.* smallpox. [Modern Latin *variola,* from Late Latin *variola* pustule, from Latin *varius* of various colors, changing.]

var·i·om·e·ter (vâr'ē om'ǝ tǝr) *n.* instrument used to measure variations in magnetic force. [Latin *varius* changing + -METER.]

var·i·o·rum (vâr'ē ôr'ǝm) *n.* edition, as of a book, containing notes by various editors or commentators, or containing various versions of a text. —*adj.* of or relating to such an edition. [Shortened from Latin *editiō cum notīs variōrum* edition with the notes of various persons.]

var·i·ous (vâr'ē ǝs) *adj.* 1. different from one another; of different kinds; diversified: *People of various backgrounds applied for the job.* 2. more than one; several; many: *Various senators of both parties objected to the proposal.* 3. many-sided; versatile. 4. *Archaic.* changeable. [Latin *varius* of different colors, changing.] —**var'i·ous·ly,** *adv.* —**Syn.** 2. see **several.**

var·let (vär'lit) *n. Archaic.* 1. scoundrel; knave. 2. attendant; servant. [Old French *varlet,* form of *vaslet,* groom, youth; of Celtic origin.]

var·mint (vär'mǝnt) *n. Informal.* troublesome or objectionable animal or person. [Dialectal form of VERMIN.]

Var·na (vär'nǝ) *n.* port city in eastern Bulgaria, on the Black Sea. Pop. (1968 est.), 200,827.

var·nish (vär'nish) *n.* 1. liquid preparation usually consisting of resinous materials in a volatile solvent, as alcohol, or such materials mixed with an oil, as linseed oil, used to produce a hard, clear or semitransparent coating, as on a wood surface. 2. glossy coating produced by the application of such a preparation when it has dried. 3. outward show or appearance, esp. one that is deceptive; pretense. —*v.t.* 1. to apply varnish to; cover with varnish. 2. to cover or provide with a deceptive appearance. [Old French *vernis* the liquid preparation, from Medieval Latin *veronix* fragrant resin, probably going back to Greek *Berenīkē,* ancient Libyan town where varnish was supposedly first used.] —**var'nish·er,** *n.*

var·si·ty (vär'sǝ tē) *pl.*, **-ties.** *n.* principal team that represents a university, college, or school in an athletic or other competition. [Modification and shortening of UNIVERSITY.]

var·y (vâr'ē) **var·ied, var·y·ing.** *v.t.* 1. to change, as in appearance or nature: *to vary the conditions of an experiment.* 2. to give variety to; diversify: *to vary one's diet.* 3. *Music.* to repeat (a theme or tune) with modifications or embellishments, as in melody, harmony, rhythm, or key. —*v.i.* 1. to become changed, as in appearance or nature; undergo change: *His mood is constantly varying.* 2. to be different; differ: *This author's works vary greatly in quality.* 3. to deviate; depart (with *from*): *to vary from a rule.* 4. *Mathematics.* to be subject to change. [Latin *variāre* to change.]

at; āpe; cär; end; mē; it; īce; hot; ōld; fôrk; wood; fōōl; oil; out; up; ūse; turn; sing; thin; this; zh in treasure; ǝ in ago, taken, pencil, lemon, circus.

vas (vas) *pl.,* **va·sa** (vā′sə). *n.* Biology. duct; vessel. [Latin *vās* dish, utensil.] —**va·sal** (vā′səl), *adj.*

vas·cu·lar (vas′kyə lər) *adj.* of, relating to, composed of, or containing vessels that carry blood, sap, or other animal or plant fluid. [Modern Latin *vascularis,* from Latin *vāsculum* small vessel, diminutive of *vās* dish, vessel, dish.]

vascular bundle Botany. part of the vascular system of a higher plant usually consisting of phloem and xylem.

vascular tissue Botany. tissue in a higher plant consisting of phloem and xylem.

vas·cu·lum (vas′kyə ləm) *pl.,* **-la** (-lə) or **-lums.** *n.* small box or case used to carry plant specimens. [Latin *vāsculum* small vessel. See VASCULAR.]

vas de·fer·ens (vas def′ə renz′) *pl.,* **va·sa de·fer·en·ti·a** (vā′sə-def′ə ren′shē ə). duct that carries sperm from the testicle to the ejaculatory duct of the penis.

vase (vās, vāz, väz) *n.* container that is rounded in shape and usually of greater height than width, used chiefly for holding flowers or for decoration. [French *vase* vessel, from Latin *vās.*]

vas·ec·to·my (va sek′tə mē) *pl.,* **-mies.** *n.* surgical removal of all or a portion of the vas deferens.

Vas·e·line (vas′ə lēn′) *n.* Trademark. ointment made from petroleum; petrolatum. [German *Wasser* water + Greek *elaion* oil + -INE².]

vas·o·mo·tor (vas′ō mō′tər) *adj.* causing dilation or constriction of the blood vessels. [Latin *vās* vessel + MOTOR.]

vas·sal (vas′əl) *n.* **1.** under feudalism, a subject of a lord. Vassals received grants of land and protection from the lord in return for their fealty, support, and homage. **2.** servant; slave. —*adj.* of, relating to, characteristic of, or designating a vassal. [Old French *vassal* subject, tenant, knight, from Medieval Latin *vassallus* servant, retainer, from *vassus* servant; of Celtic origin.]

vas·sal·age (vas′ə lij) *n.* **1.** state or condition of being a vassal. **2.** duties, obligations, or service required of a vassal. **3.** land held by a vassal. **4.** servitude; subjection. **5.** vassals collectively.

vast (vast) *adj.* very great, as in extent, size, or amount: *a vast expanse of land, a vast number of people.* [Latin *vāstus.*] —**vast′ly,** *adv.* —**vast′ness,** *n.* —**Syn.** see huge.

vast·y (vas′tē) vast·i·er, vast·i·est, *adj.* Archaic. vast; immense.

vat (vat) *n.* large container used esp. for holding liquids. —*v.t.,* **vat·ted, vat·ting.** to put into a vat. [Old English *fæt* vessel, cask.]

Vat·i·can (vat′i kən) *n.* **1.** official residence of the pope in Vatican City. **2.** papal government or power, as distinguished from the Quirinal. [Latin *Vāticānus (mōns)* Vatican (hill); of Etruscan origin; referring to the building of the pope's palace on the *Vatican,* a hill of Rome.]

Vatican City, independent state ruled by the pope and located within the city of Rome, Italy, comprising an area of about one-fifth of a square mile. It was established in 1929. Pop. (1965), 1000.

va·tic·i·nate (və tis′ə nāt′) **-nat·ed, -nat·ing.** *v.t.,* to prophesy; foretell. [Latin *vāticinātus,* past participle of *vāticinārī* to prophesy, from *vātēs* seer, prophet.] —**va·tic′i·na′tion, va·tic′i·na′tor,** *n.*

vaude·ville (vôd′vil, vô′də-) *n.* theatrical entertainment popular in the United States in the late nineteenth and early twentieth centuries, consisting of a variety of short performances, as by singers, jugglers, and comedians. [French *vaudeville* light form of comedy, gay country ballad (combined with farces in the eighteenth century), going back to *Vau de Vire* valley of Vire, a region in Normandy noted for gay, satirical songs.]

vaude·vil·lian (vôd-vil′yən, vô′də-) *n.* one who performs in vaudeville. —*adj.* of, relating to, or characteristic of vaudeville.

vault¹ (vôlt) *n.* **1.** arched structure of stone, brick, or concrete serving as a roof or ceiling. **2.** something resembling such a structure; vaultlike covering or structure. **3.** arched space, passage, or chamber, esp. one that is underground. **4.** underground compartment or room used as a cellar or storeroom. **5.** well-protected or fortified room or compartment, as in a bank, used for the safekeeping of valuables or money. **6.** burial chamber. —*v.t.* **1.** to cover, form, or provide with a vault or vaultlike structure. **2.** to build in the shape of a vault. [Middle French *vaute, voute* arched structure, going back to Latin *volvere* to roll, turn.]

vault² (vôlt) *v.i.* to jump over, esp. with the aid of a pole or the hands: *to vault a fence.* —*v.t.* to jump; spring. —*n.* act or instance of vaulting; jump. [Old French *volter* to turn, leap, gambol, going back to Latin *volvere* to turn, roll.] —**vault′er,** *n.*

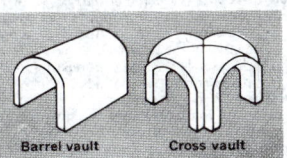

Barrel vault   **Cross vault**

Vault¹ *(def. 1)*

vault·ed (vôl′tid) *adj.* **1.** having the form of a vault; arched. **2.** constructed or covered with a vault.

vault·ing¹ (vôl′ting) *n.* **1.** vaulted or arched structure. **2.** vaults collectively. **3.** art or technique of constructing vaults.

vault·ing² (vôl′ting) *adj.* **1.** leaping upward or over. **2.** overreaching; exaggerated.

vaunt (vônt, vänt) *v.i.* to boast; brag. —*v.t.* to boast of (something); brag about. —*n.* boasting assertion or statement. [Middle French *vanter* to boast, from Late Latin *vānitāre* to flatter, boast, from Latin *vānus* empty, fruitless.] —**vaunt′ing·ly,** *adv.*

vb. **1.** verb. **2.** verbal.

V.C. **1.** Victoria Cross. **2.** Vietcong.

VD, venereal disease.

veal (vēl) *n.* flesh of a calf, used as food. [Old French *veël* calf, from Latin *vitellus* little calf, diminutive of *vitulus* calf.]

Veb·len, Thor·stein (veb′lən; thôr′stīn) 1857–1929, U.S. economist and sociologist.

vec·tor (vek′tər) *n.* **1.** mathematical quantity that has both magnitude and direction. **2.** line representing such a quantity. In physics, vectors are used to represent forces. [Latin *vector* carrier, traveler.] —**vec·to·ri·al** (vek tôr′ē əl), *adj.*

Ve·da (vā′də, vē′-) *n.* **1.** any of the four collections of ancient Hindu sacred writings, including the Rig-Veda and the Upanishads. **2.** these writings collectively. [Sanskrit *veda* knowledge, sacred books.]

V-E Day, May 8, 1945, the day on which the surrender of Germany to the Allied Forces during World War II became effective, marking the end of hostilities in Europe.

ve·dette (vi det′) also, **vi·dette.** *n.* **1.** mounted sentinel positioned in advance of an outpost. **2.** small vessel used for reconnaissance. Also, **vedette boat.** [French *vedette* sentry, through Italian and Spanish, going back to Latin *vigilāre* to keep watch.]

Ve·dic (vā′dik, vē′-) *adj.* of or relating to the Vedas, or to the language in which they were written, an early form of Sanskrit.

veep (vēp) *n.* Informal. **1.** vice-president. **2.** Veep. Vice President of the United States. [From V.P.]

veer (vēr) *v.i.* to change in direction or course; shift; turn: *At the bottom of the hill the road veers sharply to the left.* —*v.t.* to change the direction or course of. —*n.* change in direction or course; swerve. [Middle French *virer* to turn, change direction; of uncertain origin.]

veer·y (vēr′ē) *pl.,* **veer·ies.** *n.* North American thrush, *Hylocichla fuscescens,* having reddish-brown and white plumage. Length: 7 inches. [Possibly imitative.]

Ve·ga (vē′gə, vā′-) *n.* bright white star, one of the twenty brightest, and the brightest star in the constellation Lyra. [Spanish *Vega,* from Arabic *wāqi'* falling, in *al nasr al wāqi'* the falling vulture, the constellation Lyra.]

Veery

Ve·ga, Lo·pe de (vā′gə; lō′pā thā) 1562–1635, Spanish dramatist and poet.

veg·e·ta·ble (vej′tə bəl, vej′ə tə-) *n.* **1.** edible part of any herbaceous plant, eaten cooked or raw. **2.** plant from which such a part comes. **3.** organism classified as a plant. **4.** person leading a dull, inactive, or merely physical existence. —*adj.* **1.** of, relating to, or made or obtained from a plant or plants. **2.** dull or inactive; lifeless: *a vegetable existence.* [Late Latin *vegetābilis* able to grow, animating, from *vegetāre* to animate, from Latin *vegetus* vigorous.]

vegetable marrow, any of various oblong squashes having yellowish-green or cream-colored skin.

veg·e·tal (vej′ət al) *adj.* of, relating to, or characteristic of plants or vegetables.

veg·e·tar·i·an (vej′ə târ′ē ən) *n.* person who will not eat meat, fish, or fowl, usually for health or moral reasons. —*adj.* **1.** of, relating to, advocating, or practicing vegetarianism. **2.** consisting entirely of vegetables.

veg·e·tar·i·an·ism (vej′ə târ′ē ə niz′əm) *n.* practices or principles of vegetarians.

veg·e·tate (vej′ə tāt′) **-tat·ed, -tat·ing.** *v.i.* **1.** to grow or develop in the manner of a plant. **2.** to lead a dull, inactive, or merely physical existence; live a life that lacks mental or physical activity. [Late Latin *vegetātus,* past participle of *vegetāre* to animate. See VEGETABLE.]

veg·e·ta·tion (vej′ə tā′shən) *n.* **1.** plant life; plants collectively: *a region of sparse vegetation.* **2.** act or process of vegetating.

veg·e·ta·tive (vej′ə tā′tiv) *adj.* **1.** of or relating to plants, plant life, or plant growth. **2.** growing or capable of growing, as plants. **3.** characterized by a lack of mental or physical activity; dull or inactive. Also, **veg·e·tive** (vej′ə tiv). —**veg′e·ta′tive·ly,** *adv.* —**veg′e·ta′tive·ness,** *n.*

ve·he·ment (vē′ə mənt) *adj.* **1.** showing or characterized by intensity of feeling; passionate; ardent: *a vehement reply, vehement devotion.*

2. violent; forceful: *vehement wind*. [Latin *vehemēns* eager, violent.] —**ve′he·mence,** *n*. —**ve′he·ment·ly,** *adv*.

ve·hi·cle (vē′ə kəl) *n.* **1.** device designed or used for transporting persons or goods, as an automobile, sled, or carriage. **2.** means by which something is expressed, transmitted, conveyed, or achieved: *Poetry is a vehicle of self-expression.* **3.** medium (*def. 7*). **4.** in the performing arts, a play, dramatic role, musical composition, or the like that is suited to display the particular talents of a performer. [Latin *vehiculum* carriage, conveyance.]

ve·hic·u·lar (vē hik′yə lər) *adj.* **1.** of, relating to, or for vehicles. **2.** serving as a vehicle.

veil (vāl) *n.* **1.** piece of lightweight fabric, as of lace, silk, or net, worn esp. by women over the head and shoulders, or as a covering for the face. **2.** piece of fabric used as a curtain or screen. **3.** anything that obscures or conceals: *a veil of mist, a veil of secrecy.* **4. to take the veil.** to become a nun. —*v.t.* to cover, conceal, obscure, or disguise with or as with a veil. [Anglo-Norman *veil(e)* cloth covering to conceal from view, sail, from Latin *vēlum* cloth, covering, curtain. Doublet of VELUM, VOILE.]

veil·ing (vā′ling) *n.* **1.** any of various lightweight fabrics used for veils. **2.** a veil.

vein (vān) *n.* **1.** one of the vessels that convey blood to the heart from all parts of the body. **2.** one of the bundles of vascular tissue that form the framework of a leaf. **3.** one of the tubular structures that extend in a network through the wing of an insect and serve to stiffen and strengthen the wing. **4.** sheetlike deposit of minerals that forms in the fissure of a rock; lode. **5.** streak or marking of a different color or material, as in marble or wood. **6.** distinctive quality, feeling, or tendency: *There is a vein of bitter sarcasm in . . . the tale* (Freeman, 1867). **7.** mood, attitude, or manner: *We hoped the conversation would not continue in such a pessimistic vein.* **8.** particular form or style of expression: *to write in a poetic vein.* —*v.t.* **1.** to provide, fill, or mark with veins. **2.** to extend through in the manner of a vein or veins: *a dash of genius veining his folly* (Haggard, 1889). [Old French *veine* vessel that carries blood to the heart, from Latin *vēna* blood vessel, mineral deposit, natural tendency.]

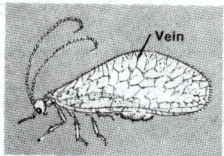

Vein

Vein (def. 3)

veined (vānd) *adj.* having or marked with veins.

vein·ing (vā′ning) *n.* arrangement or pattern of veins.

ve·lar (vē′lər) *adj.* **1.** of or relating to a velum, esp. to the soft palate. **2.** *Phonetics.* articulated with the tongue near or touching the soft palate. —*n. Phonetics.* velar sound. [Latin *vēlāris* relating to a curtain, from *vēlum* curtain, covering, cloth.]

Ve·láz·quez, Die·go Ro·dri·guez de Sil·va y (ve läs′käs; dyā′gō rō drē′gäs thä sēl′vä ē) *also,* **Ve·lás·quez.** 1599–1660, Spanish painter.

veld (velt, felt) *also,* **veldt.** *n.* rolling grassland region in South Africa, having scattered bushes and trees. [Afrikaans *veld(t)* field, from Middle Dutch *veld.*]

vel·le·i·ty (və lē′ə tē) *pl.,* **-ties.** *n.* **1.** act or fact of merely willing, wishing, or desiring without any effort toward action or realization. **2.** mere wish, desire, or inclination without accompanying action or effort. [Modern Latin *velleitas,* from Latin *velle* to wish.]

vel·lum (vel′əm) *n.* **1.** fine parchment prepared from calfskin, lambskin, or kidskin, used esp. for writing or for binding books. **2.** manuscript written on such parchment. **3.** paper made to resemble such parchment. —*adj.* of, relating to, or resembling vellum. [Old French *velin* very fine parchment made from calfskin, from *veël* calf. See VEAL.]

ve·loc·i·pede (vi los′ə pēd) *n.* **1.** early form of a bicycle or tricycle. **2.** child's tricycle. [French *vélocipède,* early form of the bicycle, from Latin *vēlox* swift + *pēs* foot.]

ve·loc·i·ty (vi los′ə tē) *pl.,* **-ties.** *n.* **1.** rapidity of motion; speed. **2.** rate of motion in relation to time; distance covered in a specified time: *Light has a velocity of 186,000 miles per second.* **3.** *Physics.* rate of motion in a particular direction in relation to time. [Latin *vēlocitās* swiftness.]

ve·lour (vi loor′) *pl.,* **-lours** (-loor′, -loorz′). *also,* **ve·lours** (vi loor′). *n.* soft, thick, closely woven fabric having a velvetlike finish, used for clothing, draperies, upholstery, and other items. [French *velours* velvet, going back to Latin *villōsus* shaggy, from *villus* shaggy hair.]

ve·lum (vē′ləm) *pl.,* **-la** (-lə). *n.* **1.** *Biology.* thin, veil-like membranous covering. **2.** *Anatomy.* the soft palate. [Latin *vēlum* cloth, covering, curtain. Doublet of VEIL, VOILE.]

ve·lure (vi loor′) *n.* velvet or a fabric resembling velvet. [Form of VELOUR.]

vel·vet (vel′vit) *n.* **1.** fabric made of silk, rayon, nylon, or other fiber, having a smooth, soft, thick pile. **2.** something resembling velvet, esp.

in smoothness or softness. **3.** soft skin that covers the growing antlers of a deer. —*adj.* **1.** made of or covered with velvet: *a red velvet bedspread.* **2.** resembling velvet, esp. in smoothness or softness. [Middle French *velu* velvety (going back to Latin *villus* shaggy hair) + -ET.]

vel·vet·een (vel′və tēn′) *n.* cotton fabric made with a short, thick pile so as to resemble velvet. [From VELVET.]

vel·vet·y (vel′və tē) *adj.* **1.** smooth and soft like velvet. **2.** smooth to the taste, as some liquors.

Ven., Venerable.

ve·na ca·va (vē′nə kā′və) *pl.,* **ve·nae ca·vae** (vē′nē kā′vē). either of two large veins leading into the right atrium of the heart.

ve·nal (vēn′əl) *adj.* **1.** willing to be bribed; open to bribery; corruptible. **2.** that can be obtained or influenced by bribery, as an office or position. **3.** characterized by corruption. [Latin *vēnālis* for sale, relating to selling, from *vēnum* sale.] —**ve′nal·ly,** *adv.*

ve·nal·i·ty (vē nal′ə tē) *pl.,* **-ties.** *n.* quality, state, or instance of being venal.

ve·na·tion (vē nā′shən, və-) *n.* **1.** arrangement or system of veins, as in a leaf or an insect's wing. **2.** such veins collectively. Also, **ner·va′tion.** [Latin *vēna* vein + -ATION.]

vend (vend) *v.t.* to offer for sale; sell or peddle. —*v.i.* to sell goods. [Latin *vēndere,* going back to *vēnum dāre* to offer for sale.]

vend·ee (ven dē′) *n.* person to whom a thing is sold; buyer.

ven·det·ta (ven det′ə) *n.* **1.** feud in which the relatives of a murdered or injured person seek vengeance on the wrongdoer or members of his family. **2.** any bitter feud or dispute motivated by a desire for vengeance. [Italian *vendetta* revenge, from Latin *vindicta.*]

vend·i·ble (ven′də bəl) *adj.* capable of being sold. —*n.* vendible item. —**vend′i·bil′i·ty,** *n.*

vending machine, coin-operated machine for selling candy, cigarettes, or various other small items.

ven·dor (ven′dər) *also,* **vend·er.** *n.* one who sells goods. [Anglo-Norman *vendo(u)r,* from Latin *venditor.*]

ven·due (ven dōō′, -dū′) *n.* public sale or auction. [Dutch *vendu,* from Old French *vendue* sale, going back to Latin *vendere* to sell.]

ve·neer (vi nēr′) *n.* **1.** thin layer of fine wood or other material used in covering a surface or making plywood. **2.** outward appearance, esp. one that is deceptive or merely superficial: *She tried to hide her ignorance with a veneer of sophistication.* —*v.t.* **1.** to cover (a surface) with a thin layer of fine wood or other material. **2.** to glue together (layers of wood) to make plywood. **3.** to give a superficially attractive appearance to. [Earlier *fineer,* from German *furnieren* to inlay, from French *fournir* to supply; of Germanic origin.]

ven·er·a·ble (ven′ər ə bəl) *adj.* **1.** deserving respect or reverence, as by reason of age, character, or position: *a wise and venerable old gentleman.* **2.** of a building, place, or object) worthy of respect by reason of age or historic or religious association: *the venerable halls of this great university.* **3.** *also,* **Venerable.** deserving reverence. ▲ used as a title of respect in the Anglican and Roman Catholic churches. [Latin *venerābilis* worthy of reverence, from *venerāri* to reverence, worship.] —**ven′er·a·bil′i·ty, ven′er·a·ble·ness,** *n.* —**ven′er·a·bly,** *adv.*

ven·er·ate (ven′ə rāt′) *-at·ed, -at·ing.* *v.t.* to regard with deep respect or reverence. [Latin *venerātus,* past participle of *venerāri* to reverence, worship, from *venus* love.] —**Syn.** see **worship.**

ven·er·a·tion (ven′ə rā′shən) *n.* **1.** feeling of deep respect; reverence. **2.** act of venerating; being venerated.

ve·ne·re·al (və nēr′ē əl) *adj.* **1.** of or relating to sexual intercourse. **2.** (of certain diseases) transmitted by sexual intercourse with an infected person. **3.** of, relating to, or infected with venereal disease. **4.** effective in the treatment or cure of venereal disease. [Latin *venereus* relating to love (from *venus* love) + -AL.]

venereal disease, any of several diseases, as syphilis, usually transmitted by sexual intercourse with an infected person.

ven·er·y¹ (ven′ər ē) *n. Archaic.* gratification of sexual desire. [Latin *vener-,* stem of *venus* love + -Y¹.]

ven·er·y² (ven′ər ē) *n. Archaic.* act, practice, or sport of hunting; the chase. [Old French *venerie* hunting, from *venere* to hunt, from Latin *venāri.*]

Ve·ne·tian (vi nē′shən) *adj.* of or relating to Venice or its people or culture. —*n.* native or inhabitant of Venice.

Venetian blind *also,* **venetian blind.** shade, esp. for a window, having a number of horizontal slats, usually of wood, plastic, or metal, that can be set together at a desired angle or raised or lowered by means of attached cords.

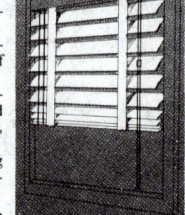

Venetian blind

at; āpe; cär; end; mē; it; īce; hot; ōld; fôrk; wood; fōōl; oil; out; up; ūse; turn; sing; thin; this; zh in treasure; ə in ago, taken, pencil, lemon, circus.

Ve·ne·to (ven′e tō′) *n.* region in northeastern Italy. Area, 7094 sq. mi. Pop. (1964 est.), 3,946,800. Also, **Ve·ne·ti·a** (ve net′syä).

Ven·e·zue·la (ven′ə zwā′lə, -zwē′-) *n.* country in northern South America, on the Caribbean. Capital, Caracas. Area, 352,144 sq. mi. Pop. (1970 est.), 10,399,000. —**Ven′e·zue′lan**, *adj., n.*

venge·ance (ven′jəns) *n.* **1.** act or instance of inflicting injury in return for an injury or offense received: *Such wrongdoing demands swift vengeance.* **2.** desire to inflict such injury: *to swear vengeance against someone.* **3. with a vengeance. a.** with great force or violence. **b.** to an unusual extent; extremely. [Old French *vengeance* revenge, from *venger* to avenge, from Latin *vindicāre*.]
Syn. 1. Vengeance, retribution, retaliation mean like or equal payment in return for injury or harm done. **Vengeance** suggests the vindictive and angry punishment dictated by a primitive and savage code of justice, usually carried out by someone other than the victim: *He exacted vengeance for his father's death.* **Retribution** likewise stresses strict justice meted out by a higher or inhuman power and is usually carried out by some natural force or agency rather than by individual action: *They believed the plague was divine retribution for their sins.* **Retaliation** shifts the emphasis from moral considerations of evil and wrongdoing to tactical considerations in which large-scale destruction is carried out in an impersonal or anonymous manner by one group against another: *Retaliation by the enemy artillery was swift.*

venge·ful (venj′fəl) *adj.* full of or characterized by a desire for vengeance; seeking revenge: *a vengeful mind, a vengeful antagonist.* **2.** showing or arising from a desire for revenge: *a vengeful hatred.* **3.** inflicting or serving to inflict vengeance: *the bold knight's vengeful sword.* —**venge′ful·ly**, *adv.* —**venge′ful·ness**, *n.*

ve·ni·al (vē′nē əl, vēn′yəl) *adj.* **1.** that may be excused or forgiven; pardonable. **2.** (of sin) not very serious; of minor significance. Distinguished from **mortal.** [Late Latin *veniālis* pardonable, from Latin *venia* forgiveness, pardon.] —**ve·ni·al·i·ty** (vē′nē al′ə tē), **ve′ni·al·ness**, *n.* —**ve′ni·al·ly**, *adv.*

Ven·ice (ven′is) *n.* port city in northeastern Italy, situated on 118 islets in the Adriatic. Pop. (1968 est.), 367,323.

ve·ni·re (vi nī′rē) *n.* writ to a sheriff ordering him to summon persons to serve as jurors. Also, **venire fa·ci·as** (fā′shē as′). [Short for Latin *venīre faciās* you are to cause (someone) to come.]

ve·ni·re·man (vi nī′rē mən) *pl.,* -**men.** *n.* person summoned to serve as a juror under a venire.

ven·i·son (ven′ə sən, -zən) *n.* flesh of a deer, used as food. [Old French *veneisun*, from Latin *vēnātiō* hunting.]

ven·om (ven′əm) *n.* **1.** poisonous secretion of some animals, as certain snakes or spiders, usually introduced into the body of a victim by a bite or sting. **2.** malice; spite. [Old French *venin* poison, going back to Latin *venēnum* poison, drug.]

ven·om·ous (ven′ə məs) *adj.* **1.** able to inflict a poisonous wound, esp. by biting or stinging; secreting and transmitting venom: *a venomous snake.* **2.** containing or full of venom: *a venomous bite.* **3.** malicious; spiteful. —**ven′om·ous·ly**, *adv.* —**ven′om·ous·ness**, *n.*

ve·nous (vē′nəs) *adj.* **1.** of, relating to, or characterized by veins. **2.** designating the blood returning to the heart through the veins. Venous blood contains carbon dioxide but no oxygen. [Latin *vēnōsus* full of veins, from *vēna* vein, blood vessel.]

vent¹ (vent) *n.* **1.** hole or other usually small opening for the escape or passage of a gas, liquid, or the like. **2.** means of escape; outlet. **3.** expression. ▲ used chiefly in the phrase *to give vent to: He gave vent to his fury with a string of curses.* **4.** excretory opening of the cloaca in certain animals, as birds and reptiles. **5.** small, usually triangular window in some motor vehicles, used for ventilation. —*v.t.* **1.** to give expression to: *The man vented his rage on the innocent boy.* **2.** to provide with a vent or outlet. **3.** to allow to escape through an opening. [Partly from French *vent* wind, from Latin *ventus*; partly from French *évent* hole, opening, going back to Latin *ex* out + *ventus* wind.]

vent² (vent) *n.* slit in a garment, as at the back of a coat. [Form of dialectal English *fent*, from Old French *fente* slit, from *fendre* to split, from Latin *findere.*]

vent·age (ven′tij) *n.* small opening; vent. [VENT¹ + -AGE.]

ven·ti·late (ven′tl āt′) -**lat·ed, -lat·ing.** *v.t.* **1.** to admit air into, esp. fresh air; circulate fresh air in. **2.** (of air) to circulate through so as to freshen. **3.** to provide with a vent, as for the escape of a gas. **4.** to aerate or oxygenate, esp. blood. **5.** to bring to public notice; submit to examination and discussion. [Latin *ventilātus*, past participle of *ventilāre* to fan, set in motion, from *ventus* wind.]

ven·ti·la·tion (ven′tl ā′shən) *n.* **1.** act or process of ventilating; being ventilated. **2.** system or means of providing or circulating fresh air.

ven·ti·la·tor (ven′tl ā′tər) *n.* apparatus for providing or circulating fresh air, or for expelling foul or stagnant air.

ven·tral (ven′trəl) *adj.* **1.** of or relating to the abdomen or belly; abdominal. **2.** of, relating to, or situated on or near the surface opposite the back. [Late Latin *ventrālis* relating to the belly, from Latin *venter* belly.] —**ven′tral·ly**, *adv.*

ven·tri·cle (ven′tri kəl) *n.* **1.** either of the two lower chambers or cavities of the heart. The right ventricle receives venous blood from the right auricle and pumps it into the artery leading to the lungs. The left ventricle receives oxygenated blood from the left auricle and pumps it into the aorta. See **heart** for illustration. **2.** small cavity in the body, esp. any of a series of four connecting cavities in the brain. [Latin *ventriculus* stomach, ventricle of the heart, diminutive of *venter* belly.]

ven·tri·cose (ven′tri kōs′) *adj.* swollen; distended; inflated. [Modern Latin *ventricosus*, from Latin *venter* belly.] —**ven·tri·cos·i·ty** (ven′trə kos′ə tē), *n.*

ven·tric·u·lar (ven trik′yə lər) *adj.* of, relating to, or of the nature of a ventricle.

ven·tri·lo·qui·al (ven′trə lō′kwē əl) *adj.* of or relating to ventriloquism.

ven·tril·o·quism (ven tril′ə kwiz′əm) *n.* art or practice of speaking or producing sounds without moving the lips so that the sound seems to come from some source other than the speaker. Also, **ven·tril·o·quy** (ven tril′ə kwē). [Late Latin *ventriloquus* ventriloquist; literally, one who speaks from the belly (from Latin *venter* belly + *loquī* to speak) + -ISM; because it was believed that the ventriloquist's voice came from his stomach.]

ven·tril·o·quist (ven tril′ə kwist) *n.* one who practices ventriloquism, esp. an entertainer who holds and apparently carries on a conversation with a dummy.

ven·tril·o·quize (ven tril′ə kwīz′) -**quized, -quiz·ing.** *v.i., v.t.* to speak (words) as a ventriloquist.

ven·ture (ven′chər) *n.* **1.** undertaking, esp. one involving risk or danger: *It was a foolhardy business venture that was sure to fail.* **2.** something that is risked, as in such an undertaking. —*v.t.,* -**tured, -tur·ing.** **1.** to expose to risk or danger: *to venture all one's money on an enterprise.* **2.** to run the risk of; brave: *to venture a storm.* **3.** to express at the risk of criticism, objection, or the like: *to venture a word of advice.* —*v.i.* to do or undertake something despite the risk or danger involved; dare: *to venture out into the darkness in search of help.* [Short for Middle English *aventure*, earlier form of ADVENTURE.]
Syn. *v.t.* **1. Venture, risk** mean to lay open to the possibility of loss, failure, harm, or danger. **Venture** suggests a certain flamboyance and reckless daring in chancing valuables or an extreme action, esp. for gain or profit: *The gambler ventured all his money on the final try.* **Risk** is used more frequently to suggest a chance taken after weighing the advantages and disadvantages and determining that no other options are available, as in an emergency or for a noble cause: *The fireman risked his life to save the children. The reporter risked his job to support the strike.*

ven·ture·some (ven′chər səm) *adj.* **1.** willing or inclined to take risks; bold; daring. **2.** involving risk or danger; hazardous.

ven·tur·ous (ven′chər əs) *adj.* **1.** bold; adventurous. **2.** risky or dangerous; hazardous. —**ven′tur·ous·ly**, *adv.* —**ven′tur·ous·ness**, *n.*

ven·ue (ven′ū, ven′ōō) *n. Law.* **1.** locality where a crime is committed or a cause of action occurs. **2.** county, district, or locality from which a jury must be called and where a trial must be held. **3. change of venue.** change of the place of a trial. [Old French *venue* a coming, from *venir* to come, from Latin *venīre.*]

ven·ule (ven′ūl) *n.* small vein. [Latin *vēnula*, diminutive of *vēna* vein, blood vessel.]

Ve·nus (vē′nəs) *n.* **1.** Roman goddess of love and beauty. Her Greek counterpart is Aphrodite. **2.** statue or other representation of Venus. **3.** very beautiful woman. **4.** sixth largest planet of the solar system and second in order of distance from the sun.

Ve·nu·si·an (vi nōō′sē ən, -shən, -nū′-) *adj.* of or relating to the planet Venus. —*n.* supposed inhabitant of the planet Venus.

Ve·nus's-fly·trap (vē′nə siz flī′trap′) *n.* plant, *Dionaea muscipula*, native to moist sandy regions of North and South Carolina, having two-lobed, hinged leaves that snap shut to trap insects coming into contact with them.

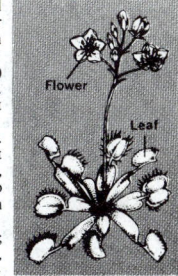
Flower
Leaf
Venus's-flytrap

ve·ra·cious (və rā′shəs) *adj.* **1.** truthful; honest. **2.** accurate; true. [Latin *vērāci-*, stem of *vērāx* truthful (from *vērus* true) + -OUS.] —**ve·ra′cious·ly**, *adv.* —**ve·ra′cious·ness**, *n.*

ve·rac·i·ty (və ras′ə tē) *pl.,* -**ties.** *n.* **1.** truthfulness; honesty. **2.** accuracy; correctness. **3.** that which is true; truth. [Medieval Latin *veracitas* truthfulness, from Latin *vērāx* truthful.]

at; āpe; cär; end; mē; it; īce; hot; ōld; fôrk; wood; fōōl; oil; out; up; ūse; turn; sing; thin; this; zh in treasure; ə in ago, taken, pencil, lemon, circus. 1107

Ver·a·cruz (ver′ə krōōz′) *n.* port city in eastern Mexico, on the Gulf of Mexico. Pop. (1969), 199,546.

ve·ran·da (və ran′də) *also,* **ve·ran·dah.** *n.* open porch, usually roofed, extending along one or more sides of the ground floor of a dwelling. [Hindi *varandā,* from Portuguese *veranda* railing, balcony; of uncertain origin.]

verb (vurb) *n.* word belonging to that part of speech that expresses action, existence, or occurrence, and that usually constitutes the main element in a predicate. [Latin *verbum* word, verb.]

ver·bal (vur′bəl) *adj.* **1.** of, relating to, or consisting of words: *verbal communication.* **2.** concerned with words rather than the ideas they express: *verbal distinctions.* **3.** expressed in speech; not written: *a verbal agreement.* **4.** word for word; literal: *a verbal translation.* **5.** *Grammar.* **a.** of, relating to, or derived from a verb. **b.** used to form verbs: *a verbal suffix.* —*n. Grammar.* noun or adjective that is derived from a verb and retains certain characteristics of a verb, but functions as a noun or adjective. Gerunds, infinitives, and participles are verbals. [Late Latin *verbālis* relating to words or verbs, from Latin *verbum* word, verb.] —**ver′bal·ly,** *adv.* —**Syn.** *adj.* 3. see **oral.**

ver·bal·ism (vur′bə liz′əm) *n.* **1.** verbal expression; a word or phrase. **2.** mere words with little or no meaning; verbiage.

ver·bal·ist (vur′bə list) *n.* **1.** person skilled in the use of words. **2.** person concerned primarily with words rather than ideas or facts.

ver·bal·ize (vur′bə līz′) **-ized, -iz·ing.** *v.t.* **1.** to express in words: *to verbalize one's feelings.* **2.** to transform, as a noun, into a verb. —*v.i.* **1.** to express oneself in words. **2.** to be verbose. —**ver′bal·i·za′tion,** *n.*

ver·ba·tim (vər bā′tim) *adv., adj.* word for word; in exactly the same words. [Medieval Latin *verbatim,* from Latin *verbum* word.]

ver·be·na (vər bē′nə) *n.* any of a large group of trailing or loosely branching plants, genus *Verbena,* having clusters of small flowers of various colors. [Latin *verbēna* foliage, leaf, twig, sacred bough. Doublet of VERVAIN.]

ver·bi·age (vur′bē ij) *n.* use of more words than necessary; wordiness. [French *verbiage,* from Middle French *verbier* to chatter, going back to Latin *verbum* word.]

ver·bose (vər bōs′) *adj.* using or containing an excessive number of words; wordy. [Latin *verbōsus* full of words, from *verbum* word.] —**ver·bose′ly,** *adv.* —**ver·bose′ness, ver·bos·i·ty** (vər bos′ə tē), *n.*

ver·bo·ten (vər bōt′ən) *adj.* German. forbidden; prohibited.

ver·dant (verd′ənt) *adj.* **1.** green with vegetation. **2.** green in color. **3.** lacking experience; unsophisticated. [Possibly from Old French *verdeant,* present participle of *verdoier* to be green, going back to Latin *viridis* green.] —**ver′dan·cy,** *n.* —**ver′dant·ly,** *adv.*

Verde, Cape (vurd) westernmost point of Africa, a peninsula on the coast of Senegal.

Ver·di, Giu·sep·pe (ver′dē; jōō zep′pe) 1813–1901, Italian composer of operas.

ver·dict (vur′dikt) *n.* **1.** decision of a jury on the matter submitted to them in a trial. **2.** decision or conclusion on some matter; judgment. [Anglo-Norman *verdit* testimony given under oath; literally, true saying, going back to Latin *vērus* true + *dictum* saying, speech.]

Syn. 1. Verdict, decision, judgment, decree mean a legal ruling. **Verdict** applies to the formal findings declared by a jury, esp. in a criminal case: *Newspapers reported that the verdict of guilty was unanimous.* **Decision** is restricted to the formal finding of a nonjury case: *The court's decision favored individual rights.* **Judgment** is often applied to a legal decision pronounced in the open court: *A judgment of the U.S. Supreme Court is final.* **Decree** is an order given after a hearing to determine the facts and their legal consequences or to settle a dispute under the sanction of law rather than to determine guilt or innocence: *The firm filed a bankruptcy decree.*

ver·di·gris (vur′də grēs′, -gris) *n.* **1.** poisonous mixture of copper acetates, consisting of blue or green crystals that are formed when copper reacts with acetic acid, used as a paint pigment and insecticide. **2.** greenish coating that forms on copper, brass, or bronze objects, as statues or kitchen utensils, consisting of copper carbonate or a similar copper compound. [Old French *vertegrez,* earlier *vert de Grece* copper acetate; literally, green of Greece, going back to Latin *viridis* green + *dē* from + *Graecia* Greece (from *Graecus* native of Greece). See GREEK.]

Ver·dun (ver dun′, vur-; *French* ver dœn′) *n.* city in northeastern France. Pop. (1962), 21,982.

ver·dure (vur′jər) *n.* **1.** fresh, green color of growing vegetation. **2.** such vegetation itself. **3.** fresh or flourishing condition. [Old French *verdure,* from *verd* green, from Latin *viridis.*] —**ver′dured, ver′dur·ous,** *adj.*

verge[1] (vurj) *n.* **1.** edge or margin of something; brink. **2.** point beyond which something occurs or begins: *The old man had been driven to the verge of despair.* **3.** limiting or enclosing border or boundary. **4.** rod or staff carried as a symbol of authority or office. —*v.i.* **verged,**

verg·ing. to be on the verge, border, or brink (often with *on*): *His speech verges on treason.* [Old French *verge* rod, from Latin *virga.*]

verge[2] (vurj) **verged, verg·ing.** *v.i.* to tend; incline; approach. [Latin *vergere* to bend, incline.]

ver·ger (vur′jər) *n.* **1.** person who carries a verge, or staff, before a bishop, dean, or other dignitary in a procession. **2.** one who cares for the interior of a church; sexton.

Ver·gil (vur′jəl) Virgil.

Ver·gil·i·an (vur jil′ē ən) Virgilian.

ver·i·fi·a·ble (ver′ə fī′ə bəl) *adj.* capable of being verified.

ver·i·fi·ca·tion (ver′ə fi kā′shən) *n.* act of verifying; being verified.

ver·i·fy (ver′ə fī′) **-fied, -fy·ing.** *v.t.* **1.** to prove (something) to be true; confirm: *This photograph verifies my allegation.* **2.** to check or test the accuracy or truth of: *to verify the results of an experiment.* [Old French *verifier* to examine something to make sure it is accurate, going back to Latin *vērus* true + *facere* to make.] —**ver′i·fi′er,** *n.*

ver·i·ly (ver′ə lē) *adv. Archaic.* in truth; really; truly. [VERY + -LY[1].]

ver·i·sim·i·lar (ver′ə sim′ə lər) *adj.* appearing to be true; probable; likely. [Latin *vērisimilis* (going back to *vērus* true + *similis* like) + -AR[1].] —**ver′i·sim′i·lar·ly,** *adv.*

ver·i·si·mil·i·tude (ver′ə si mil′ə tōōd′, -tūd′) *n.* **1.** appearance of being true. **2.** something having the appearance of being true. [Latin *vērisimilitūdō* likelihood, going back to *vērus* true + *similis* like.]

ver·i·ta·ble (ver′i tə bəl) *adj.* true; actual; real. [Old French *veritable,* from *verite* truth, from Latin *vēritās.*] —**ver′i·ta·ble·ness,** *n.* —**ver′i·ta·bly,** *adv.*

ver·i·ty (ver′ə tē) *pl.,* **-ties.** *n.* **1.** quality or state of being true, real, or accurate. **2.** true statement or established fact; a truth. [Latin *vēritās* truth.]

ver·juice (vur′jōōs′) *n.* **1.** sour, acidic juice of unripe fruit, as of crab apples or grapes. **2.** sourness, as of disposition or expression. [Old French *vertjus* sour juice of unripe fruit; literally, green juice, going back to Latin *viridis* green + *jūs* broth, sauce.]

Ver·meer, Jan (vər mēr′; yän) 1632–75, Dutch painter; full name, Jan van der Meer van Delft.

ver·meil (vur′mal) *n.* **1.** the color vermilion. **2.** gilded silver, copper, or bronze. [Old French *vermeil* bright red, from Late Latin *vermiculus* an insect from which a red dye is obtained, from Latin *vermiculus* little worm, diminutive of *vermis* worm.]

ver·mi·cel·li (vur′mə sel′ē, -chel′ē) *n.* pasta made into long, slender threads thinner than spaghetti. [Italian *vermicelli,* plural of *vermicello* little worm, going back to Latin *vermis* worm; because of its shape.]

ver·mi·cide (vur′mə sīd′) *n.* drug or other agent that kills worms, esp. parasitic intestinal worms. [Latin *vermis* worm + -CIDE[2].]

ver·mic·u·lar (vur mik′yə lər) *adj.* **1.** of, relating to, or like a worm or worms, esp. resembling a worm in form or motion. **2.** marked with or characterized by wavy lines resembling the tracks or form of a worm. [Modern Latin *vermicularis,* from Latin *vermiculus* little worm, diminutive of *vermis* worm.]

ver·mi·form (vur′mə fôrm′) *adj.* shaped like a worm. [Modern Latin *vermiformis,* from Latin *vermis* worm + *forma* shape.]

vermiform appendix, appendix.

ver·mi·fuge (vur′mə fūj′) *n.* drug or other agent that expels intestinal worms. [Latin *vermis* worm + *fugāre* to put to flight.]

ver·mil·ion (vər mil′yən) *also,* **ver·mil·lion.** *n.* **1.** bright-red color. **2.** bright-red pigment, usually consisting of mercuric sulfide. [Old French *vermeillon* the color, from *vermeil.* See VERMEIL.]

ver·min (vur′min) *pl.,* **-min.** *n.* **1.** any of various small insects or animals that are harmful, destructive, or troublesome, as lice, fleas, or rats. **2.a.** contemptible or vile person. **b.** such persons collectively. [Old French *vermine* parasitic insects, snakes, worms, going back to Latin *vermis* worm.]

ver·min·ous (vur′mə nəs) *adj.* **1.** of, relating to, or infested with vermin. **2.** caused by vermin. **3.** resembling or of the nature of vermin. —**ver′min·ous·ly,** *adv.*

Ver·mont (vər mont′) *n.* state in the northeastern United States. Capital, Montpelier. Area, 9609 sq. mi. Pop. (1970), 444,330. Abbreviation, **Vt.** —**Ver·mont′er,** *n.*

ver·mouth (vər mōōth′) *n.* white wine flavored with aromatic herbs, used esp. in making cocktails. [French *vermouth(h),* from German *Wermut* vermouth, absinthe, wormwood.]

ver·nac·u·lar (vər nak′yə lər) *n.* **1.** language native to the people of a certain country or locality. **2.** common, everyday language used by the people of a certain country or locality. **3.** vocabulary peculiar to a particular profession or trade. —*adj.* **1.** (of a language or dialect) native to or used by the people of a certain country or locality. **2.** of, in, or using native language, esp. as distinguished from literary language: *a vernacular writer.* [Latin *vernāculus* domestic, native (from *verna* slave born in one's master's house) + -AR[1].] —**ver·nac′u·lar·ly,** *adv.*

ver·nal (vurn′əl) *adj.* **1.** of, relating to, characteristic of, or occurring in spring. **2.** like, resembling, or suggesting spring, as in freshness. **3.** youthful. [Latin *vernālis* relating to spring, going back to *vēr* spring.] —**ver′nal·ly**, *adv.*

vernal equinox, see equinox.

ver·na·tion (vər nā′shən) *n. Botany.* arrangement of leaves in a bud. [Modern Latin *vernatio*, from Latin *vernāre* to bloom.]

Verne, Jules (vurn; jōōlz) 1828–1905, French novelist.

ver·ni·er (vur′nē ər) *n.* **1.** short scale that slides along a longer scale and indicates subdivisions of it, used to make precision measurements. Also, **vernier scale. 2.** auxiliary device used to obtain fine adjustments in precision instruments. [From Pierre *Vernier*, 1580–1637, French mathematician who invented the scale.]

vernier caliper, caliper equipped with a vernier scale.

Ve·ro·na (və rō′nə) *n.* city in northeastern Italy. Pop. (1964 est.), 253,233.

Ver·o·ne·se, Pa·o·lo (ver′ə nā′sē, -zā; pä′ə lō′) 1528–88, Venetian painter.

ve·ron·i·ca (və ron′i kə) *n.* speedwell. [Possibly from *Veronica*, feminine proper name.]

Ver·sailles (vər sī′, ver-) *n.* historic city in north-central France, just southwest of Paris, site of the magnificent palace of Louis XIV. The Treaty of Versailles, the most important of the treaties concluding World War I, was signed there on June 28, 1919. Pop. (1962), 86,759.

ver·sa·tile (vur′sə til) *adj.* **1.** able to do or deal with a variety of things competently: *a versatile actor who could play a clown or a king with equal skill.* **2.** having a variety of uses or functions. **3.** changeable; variable. **4.** *Botany.* turning about freely, as a loosely attached anther. **5.** *Zoology.* **a.** capable of being moved forward or backward, as the toe of a bird. **b.** capable of being moved in any direction, as the antenna of an insect. [Latin *versātilis* that turns round, movable, going back to *vertere* to turn.] —**ver′sa·tile·ly**, *adv.* —**ver′sa·til′i·ty**, *n.*

verse (vurs) *n.* **1.** metrical arrangement of words according to a particular pattern; poetry. **2.** single line of poetry. **3.** poem. **4.** section of a poem or other metrical composition, esp. a stanza. **5.** particular type of metrical structure: *trochaic verse.* **6.** one of the short divisions into which the chapters of the Bible are divided, usually a sentence. [Old English *fers*, *vers* line of poetry, from Latin *versus* furrow, row[1], line of poetry.]

versed (vurst) *adj.* knowledgeable; learned; skilled (with *in*): *to be versed in a subject.* [Latin *versātus*, past participle of *versārī* to busy oneself with + -ED[2].]

ver·si·cle (vur′si kəl) *n.* **1.** short sentence said or sung by the celebrant during religious services, to which the choir or congregation responds. **2.** a little verse. [Latin *versiculus* little line or verse, diminutive of *versus* row[1], line of poetry.]

ver·si·fi·ca·tion (vur′sə fi kā′shən) *n.* **1.** the writing or composing of verses. **2.** art, practice, or theory of writing or composing verses. **3.** poetic form or style; metrical structure.

ver·si·fy (vur′sə fī′) -**fied**, -**fy·ing.** *v.t.* **1.** to change from prose into verse form. **2.** to tell or describe in verse. —*v.i.* to compose verses. [Latin *versificāre* to write in verse, from *versus* line of poetry + *facere* to make.] —**ver′si·fi′er**, *n.*

ver·sion (vur′zhən, -shən) *n.* **1.** account or description as presented from a particular viewpoint: *Let's hear your version of the accident.* **2.a.** translation from one language into another. **b.** *also,* **Version.** translation of the Bible or a part of the Bible. **3.** different or altered form of something: *Congress passed a revised version of the bill.* **4.** adaptation, as of a literary work: *the movie version of a book.* [Medieval Latin *versiō* conversion, translation, a turning, from Latin *vertere* to turn.] —**Syn.** 1. see account.

vers li·bre (ver lē′brə) *French.* free verse.

verst (vurst, verst) *n.* Russian measure of distance, equal to about 3500 feet. [French *verste*, and German *Werst*, both from Russian *versta*.]

ver·sus (vur′səs) *prep.* **1.** against. **2.** in contrast to; as an alternative to. [Latin *versus* turned toward, opposite, past participle of *vertere* to turn.]

ver·te·bra (vur′tə brə) *pl.*, -**brae** (-brē′, -brā′) or -**bras.** *n.* any of the thirty-three small, roughly cylindrical bones that compose the backbone. [Latin *vertebra* joint, joint of the spine.]

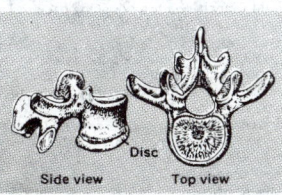

Side view   Top view
Disc

Human vertebra

ver·te·bral (vur′tə brəl) *adj.* **1.** of, relating to, or of the nature of a vertebra or the vertebrae. **2.** composed of or having vertebrae.

vertebral column, spinal column; backbone.

ver·te·brate (vur′tə brāt′, -brit) *adj.* **1.** having a backbone or spinal column. **2.** of, relating to, or characteristic of vertebrates. —*n.* any of a large group of animals, subphylum Vertebrata, consisting of fish, amphibians, reptiles, birds, and mammals, having a backbone or spinal column, a skeleton of bone or cartilage, and a brain enclosed in a skull. [Latin *vertebrātus* jointed, from *vertebra* joint, joint of the spine.]

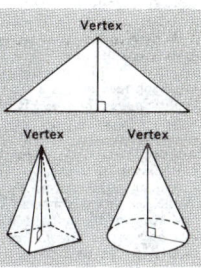

Vertex

Vertex   Vertex

ver·tex (vur′teks) *pl.*, -**tex·es** or -**ti·ces.** *n.* **1.** the highest point of something; summit. **2.** top or crown of the head. **3.** *Geometry.* **a.** point, esp. in a triangle, opposite to and farthest away from the base. **b.** point of intersection of the sides of an angle. [Latin *vertex*, summit, crown of the head.]

ver·ti·cal (vur′ti kəl) *adj.* **1.** perpendicular to the plane of the horizon; upright. Opposed to **horizontal. 2.** of, relating to, or at the vertex or highest point; directly overhead. **3.** *Economics.* of, relating to, or controlling all or most of the stages involved in the production and sale of a commodity. —*n.* something vertical, as a line or plane. [Late Latin *verticālis* perpendicular, from Latin *vertex* summit.] —**ver·ti·cal·i·ty** (vur′tə kal′ə tē), **ver′ti·cal·ness**, *n.* —**ver′ti·cal·ly**, *adv.*

vertical union, industrial union.

ver·ti·ces (vur′tə sēz′) a plural of **vertex.**

ver·ti·cil (vur′tə sil) *n.* circular arrangement, as of leaves or flowers, around a central point. [Latin *verticillus* whirl of a spindle, diminutive of *vertex* whirl, summit.]

ver·tig·i·nous (vər tij′ə nəs) *adj.* **1.** of, relating to, affected with, or causing vertigo. **2.** whirling; rotary. —[Latin *vertīginōsus* one who suffers from dizziness, from *vertīgō* dizziness.]

ver·ti·go (vur′tə gō′) *pl.*, **ver·ti·goes** or **ver·tig·i·nes** (vər tij′ə nēz′). *n.* condition in which a person feels that he or his surroundings are whirling about; dizziness. [Latin *vertīgō* a turning round, dizziness.]

ver·tu (vər tōō′, vur′tōō) virtu.

ver·vain (vur′vān) *n.* any of various plants of the genus *Verbena.* [Old French *verveine*, from Latin *verbēna* foliage, leaf, twig, sacred bough. Doublet of VERBENA.]

verve (vurv) *n.* liveliness or enthusiasm; energy; spirit. [French *verve*, from Old French *verve* caprice, fanciful expression, going back to Latin *verba*, plural of *verbum* word.]

ver·y (ver′ē) *adv.* **1.** in a high degree; to a great extent; extremely; exceedingly: *a very tall building. I'm very sorry about our misunderstanding.* **2.** truly; absolutely; exactly. ▲ used as an intensive: *She's the very worst cook I've ever encountered.* —*adj.*, **ver·i·er**, **ver·i·est. 1.** identical; selfsame: *That's the very textbook we used last term.* **2.** mere: *The very idea of getting up early made him miserable.* **3.** used as an intensive: *The earth grew dark and the very ground trembled.* **4.** actual: *caught in the very act.* **5.** exact; precise: *the very heart of the matter, the very thing I needed.* **6.** absolute; complete; utter: *Expenses had been reduced to the very minimum.* **7.** *Archaic.* true; real; genuine. [Old French *verai* true, going back to Latin *vērus.*]

very high frequency, frequency range of radio waves from 30 to 300 megacycles.

very low frequency, frequency range of radio waves from 10 to 30 kilocycles.

ves·i·cate (ves′i kāt′) -**cat·ed**, -**cat·ing.** *v.t.*, *v.i.* to blister. [Latin *vēsīca* blister + -ATE[1].]

ves·i·cle (ves′i kəl) *n.* any small sac or cyst, esp. one filled with fluid; blister. [Latin *vēsīcula* little bladder or blister, diminutive of *vēsīca* bladder, blister.]

ve·sic·u·lar (vi sik′yə lər) *adj.* **1.** of, relating to, containing, or consisting of vesicles. **2.** resembling a vesicle in form or structure.

ves·per (ves′pər) *n.* **1.** bell that summons to vespers. Also, **vesper bell. 2.** evening prayer, hymn, or religious service. **3.** **Vesper.** the planet Venus as the evening star; Hesperus. **4.** *Archaic.* evening. —*adj.* **1.** of, relating to, or suitable for the evening. **2.** of or relating to vespers. [Latin *vesper* evening, evening star.]

ves·pers (ves′pərz) *also,* **Ves·pers.** *n.,pl.* **1.** sixth of the seven canonical hours or the service for it. **2.** any religious service that is celebrated in the late afternoon or early evening, esp. the Anglican service of evensong. [Old French *vespres* evensong, going back to Latin *vespera* evening.]

ves·per·tine (ves′pər tin, -tīn′) *adj.* **1.** of, relating to, or occurring in the evening. **2.** (of animals or plants) active or blooming in the evening. [Latin *vespertīnus* relating to evening, from *vesper* evening.]

ves·pine (ves′pīn, -pin) *adj.* or, relating to, or resembling wasps. [Latin *vespa* wasp + -INE[1].]

Ves·puc·ci, A·me·ri·go (ve spōō′chē, -spōōt′-; ä′mə rē′gō) 1454–1512, Italian explorer, for whom America was named.

ves·sel (ves′əl) *n.* **1.** conveyance designed for travel on water; a ship or boat. **2.** any of various aircraft or spacecraft. **3.** hollow container or receptacle, as for liquids. **4.** duct or tube that carries a body fluid, as a vein or artery. **5.** tube in plants for conducting water. **6.** person regarded as a receiver or agent of some quality: *a vessel of wrath.* [Old French *vessel, vaissel* vase, container, ship, from Late Latin *vāscellum* small vase or urn, diminutive of Latin *vās* dish.]

Vest *(def. 1)*

vest (vest) *n.* **1.** man's short, sleeveless garment, buttoning in front, usually worn under a suit jacket. **2.** similar garment worn by women. —*v.t.* **1.** to clothe, as with vestments. **2.** to place (authority, power, or the like in (with *with*): *The young prince had been vested with full powers.* **3.** to place (authority, power, or the like) in the control of (with *in*): *All power was vested in an absolute monarch.* —*v.i.* **1.** to clothe oneself, as with vestments. **2.** (of authority, power, or the like) to pass or become vested. [French *veste* short jacket, from Italian *veste* garment, from Latin *vestis.*]

Ves·ta (ves′tə) *n.* **1.** Roman goddess of the hearth and the hearth fire. Her Greek counterpart is Hestia. **2. vesta.** short match of wax or wood.

ves·tal (vest′əl) *n.* **1.** vestal virgin. **2.** chaste woman; virgin. —*adj.* **1.** of or relating to Vesta. **2.** of or relating to the vestal virgins. **3.** chaste; pure.

vestal virgin, any of six virgin priestesses who watched over the sacred fire of Vesta in her temple in ancient Rome.

vest·ed (ves′tid) *adj.* **1.** *Law.* not subject to contingency; fixed; settled: *a vested right.* **2.** clothed, esp. in ecclesiastical vestments.

vested interest 1. strong or special concern for or interest in something because of personal reasons, as the possibility of personal gain. **2.** person or group having a vested interest in something, esp. a person or group that has great power or influence.

vest·ee (ves tē′) *n.* dickey, esp. one designed to resemble a man's vest. [From VEST.]

ves·ti·bule (ves′tə būl′) *n.* **1.** entrance hall or passage between the outer door and the interior of a building; lobby. **2.** enclosed space serving as a passage between one railroad passenger car and another. **3.** any small body cavity that leads to another cavity or canal, esp. the vestibule located in the inner ear, leading to the cochlea. [Latin *vestibulum* entrance, entrance hall.] —**ves·tib·u·lar** (ves tib′yə lər), *adj.*

ves·tige (ves′tij) *n.* **1.** trace, sign, or perceptible evidence of something that once existed but no longer exists: *vestiges of an ancient temple.* **2.** *Biology.* part or organ in an organism, that is not fully developed or useful, but presumably once served a useful purpose in an ancestral form. [French *vestige* footprint, trace[1], from Latin *vestigium.*] —**Syn. 1.** see trace[1].

ves·tig·i·al (ves tij′ē əl) *adj.* of, relating to, or of the nature of a vestige. —**ves·tig′i·al·ly,** *adv.*

vest·ment (vest′mənt) *n.* **1.** any of a group of distinctive garments worn by certain clergymen, esp. in the Roman Catholic, Orthodox, and Anglican churches, in the performance of religious services. **2.** garment, esp. an official or ceremonial robe or gown. [Old French *vestement* garment, from Latin *vestīmentum.*]

vest-pock·et (vest′pok′it) *adj.* small enough to fit into a vest pocket; small: *a vest-pocket dictionary.*

ves·try (ves′trē) *pl.* **-tries.** *n.* **1.** room in a church where the clergy put on their vestments and where the vestments and other articles used in religious services are kept. **2.** room in a church or an attached building, used for Sunday school, prayer meetings, and the like. **3.a.** in parishes of the Anglican churches, a committee composed of the rector and a number of parishioners that manages the financial affairs of the parish. **b.** in Anglican parishes, a meeting of this committee. [Probably modification of Old French *vestiairie* place for keeping vestments, from Latin *vestiārium* wardrobe, going back to *vestis* clothing, garment.]

ves·try·man (ves′trē mən) *pl.* **-men.** *n.* member of a vestry.

ves·ture (ves′chər) *n. Archaic.* **1.** clothing; garments. **2.** something that covers; covering. [Old French *vesture* clothing, going back to Latin *vestīre* to clothe.]

Ve·su·vi·an (vi sōō′vē ən) *adj.* of, relating to, or resembling Mount Vesuvius.

Ve·su·vi·us, Mount (vi sōō′vē əs) active volcano in southern Italy, southeast of Naples. A major eruption occurred in A.D. 79, burying the ancient cities of Pompeii and Herculaneum.

vet[1] (vet) *n. Informal.* veteran.

vet[2] (vet) *n. Informal.* veteran.

vet. 1. veteran. **2.** veterinarian. **3.** veterinary.

vetch (vech) *n.* any of a large group of trailing or climbing plants, genus *Vicia,* of the pea family, grown chiefly for forage and for the purpose of enriching the soil. [Dialectal Old French *veche,* from Latin *vicia.*]

vet·er·an (vet′ər ən, vet′rən) *n.* **1.** one who has had extensive service or experience, as in an occupation, office, or position: *a veteran of stage and screen.* **2.** one who has served in the armed forces. —*adj.* **1.** having extensive service or experience. **2.** having extensive experience in warfare or military matters. [Latin *veterānus* experienced soldier, old, experienced, from *vetus* old.]

Veterans Administration, U.S. Government agency that administers laws benefiting former servicemen.

Veterans Day, legal holiday dedicated to veterans who have fought for the United States, formerly called Armistice Day. November 11. Also, **Armistice Day.**

vet·er·i·nar·i·an (vet′ər ə när′ē ən, vet′rə-) *n.* one who is trained and licensed to practice veterinary surgery or medicine.

vet·er·i·nar·y (vet′ər ə ner′ē, vet′rə-) *adj.* of or relating to the branch of medicine dealing with the prevention and treatment of the diseases of animals, esp. domesticated animals. —*n. pl.* **-nar·ies.** veterinarian. [Latin *veterīnārius* relating to beasts of burden, veterinarian.]

ve·to (vē′tō) *pl.* **-toes.** *n.* **1.** power to prevent the passing or enactment of an act or measure, esp. the power of an executive to reject a bill passed by a legislative body. **2.** use of this power. **3.** any forceful rejection or prohibition. —*v.t.,* **-toed, -to·ing. 1.** to reject (an enactment or measure) by a veto. **2.** to reject or prohibit; refuse to give consent to. [Latin *vetō* I forbid (expression used by the tribunes of ancient Rome to oppose measures of their Senate or magistrates).] —**ve′to·er,** *n.*

vex (veks) *v.t.* **1.** to make impatient or angry, esp. with petty matters. **2.** to trouble; torment. [Latin *vexāre* to shake, annoy.]

vex·a·tion (vek sā′shən) *n.* **1.** act of vexing; being vexed. **2.** one who or that which vexes: *He has been a vexation to his parents.*

vex·a·tious (vek sā′shəs) *adj.* causing or tending to cause vexation; vexing; annoying. —**vex·a′tious·ly,** *adv.*

vex·ed (vekst) *adj.* affected with vexation; annoyed: *She was vexed by his behavior.* —**vex·ed·ly** (vek′sid lē), *adv.*

VFW, Veterans of Foreign Wars, organization formed in 1913 for U.S. servicemen who fought in foreign wars.

vhf, very high frequency. Also, **VHF**

v.i., intransitive verb.

V.I., Virgin Islands.

vi·a (vī′ə, vē′ə) *prep.* by way of: *John went to town via the turnpike.* [Latin *viā,* ablative of *via* way, path, road.]

vi·a·ble (vī′ə bəl) *adj.* **1.** capable of living: *a viable infant.* **2.** capable of growing: *a viable seed.* **3.** capable of being realized or accomplished; workable: *a viable plan, a viable foreign policy.* [French *viable* capable of living, from *vie* life, from Latin *vīta.*] —**vi′a·bil′i·ty,** *n.* —**vi′a·bly,** *adv.*

vi·a·duct (vī′ə dukt′) *n.* bridge for carrying a road or railroad, as over a highway or valley. [Latin *via* way, road + (AQUE)DUCT.]

Viaduct

vi·al (vī′əl) *also,* **phi·al.** *n.* small glass bottle for holding a liquid, esp. perfume or medicine. [Old French *viole, fiole* (later *phiole*), from Latin *phiala* saucer, from Greek *phialē* broad flat bowl.]

vi·and (vī′ənd) *n.* **1.** article of food. **2. viands.** choice food; delicacies. [Old French *viande* food, going back to Latin *vīvenda* things to live on, gerundive of *vīvere* to live.]

vi·at·i·cum (vī at′ə kəm) *pl.* **-ca** (-kə) *or* **-cums.** *n.* **1.** communion given by a Roman Catholic priest to a person in danger of death. **2.** provisions or money for a journey. [Latin *viāticum* provisions or money for a journey, going back to *via* way, road. Doublet of VOYAGE.]

vi·brant (vī′brənt) *adj.* **1.** full of life, energy, and enthusiasm: *a vibrant person.* **2.** vibrating: *a vibrant string.* **3.** resounding; resonant: *vibrant sound.* [Latin *vibrāns,* present participle of *vibrāre* to shake, agitate.] —**vi′bran·cy,** *n.* —**vi′brant·ly,** *adv.*

vi·bra·phone (vī′brə fōn′) *n.* musical instrument resembling and played like a xylophone, having metal bars beneath which are wooden resonators that are opened and closed electronically and give a vibrating quality to the tone. [VIBRA(TE) + Greek *phōnē* sound[1].]

vi·brate (vī′brāt) **-brat·ed, -brat·ing.** *v.i.* **1.** to move back and forth or up and down rapidly. **2.** to respond or react emotionally; thrill: *to*

at; āpe; cär; end; mē; it; īce; hot; ōld; fôrk; wood; fōōl; oil; out; up; ūse; turn; sing; thin; this; zh in treasure; ə in ago, taken, pencil, lemon, circus.

vibrate with anticipation. **3.** (of sounds) to be echoed; resound. —*v.t.* to cause to swing back and forth or up and down rapidly. [Latin *vibrātus,* past participle of *vibrāre* to move rapidly back and forth, agitate.]

vi·bra·tile (vī′brə til, -tīl′) *adj.* **1.** of, relating to, or characterized by vibration. **2.** capable of vibrating: *a vibratile organ on an insect.*

vi·bra·tion (vī brā′shən) *n.* **1.** act of vibrating; being vibrated. **2.** *Physics.* continuing, periodic, usually rapid motion of the particles of an elastic body or medium in alternate directions from a central point of reference, produced by the disturbance of a state of equilibrium. **3.** rapid movement back and forth or up and down; quivering; shaking. **4.** a single complete vibrating motion; oscillation. —**vi·bra′tion·al,** *adj.*

vi·bra·to (vi brä′tō) *pl.,* **-tos.** *n.* *Music.* trembling or pulsating effect caused by a fast, very slight fluctuation of the pitch of a tone as it is produced. [Italian *vibrato,* past participle of *vibrare* to shake, vibrate, from Latin *vibrāre* to shake, agitate.]

vi·bra·tor (vī′brā tər) *n.* **1.** that which vibrates. **2.** electrical instrument used in massage. **3.** *Electricity.* device that converts direct current into alternating current; oscillator.

vi·bra·to·ry (vī′brə tôr′ē) *adj.* **1.** of, relating to, or consisting of vibration. **2.** producing vibration. **3.** capable of vibration.

vi·bur·num (vī bur′nəm) *n.* any of a group of shrubs or trees, genus *Viburnum,* found in temperate and tropical regions, bearing clusters of wheel-shaped or bell-shaped flowers. [Latin *vīburnum.*]

vic·ar (vik′ər) *n.* **1.** in the Church of England, the priest of a parish who receives the smaller tithes or a salary. **2.** in the Protestant Episcopal Church, a clergyman in charge of a chapel in a parish. **3.a.** any of various Roman Catholic prelates who represent the pope or a bishop. **b.** *Vicar.* the Pope considered as the representative of Christ. **4.** one who acts as the representative of another. [Latin *vicārius* substitute, deputy, substituted. Doublet of VICARIOUS.] —**vic′ar·ship,** *n.*

vic·ar·age (vik′ər ij) *n.* **1.** residence of a vicar. **2.** rank, dignity, or duties of a vicar. **3.** benefice of a vicar.

vicar apostolic, in the Roman Catholic Church, titular bishop with ecclesiastical jurisdiction in a region where no diocese has been established.

vic·ar-gen·er·al (vik′ər jen′ər əl) *pl.,* **vic·ars-gen·er·al.** *n.* **1.** in the Roman Catholic Church, a priest who assists a bishop or superior in the administration of a diocese or religious order. **2.** in the Church of England, an official, usually a layman, who assists a bishop, esp. in legal or administrative matters.

vi·car·i·ous (vī kãr′ē əs, vi-) *adj.* **1.** performed, exercised, or endured for another: *vicarious labor, vicarious authority, vicarious punishment.* **2.** substituting for or representing another: *a vicarious agent.* **3.** experienced or enjoyed by imaginary sharing in the experience of another. [Latin *vicārius* substituted, from *vicis* change. Doublet of VICAR.] —**vi·car′i·ous·ly,** *adv.* —**vi·car′i·ous·ness,** *n.*

vice¹ (vīs) *n.* **1.** immoral or harmful habit or practice. **2.** immoral conduct; depravity; wickedness. **3.** fault or flaw; defect: *an intellectual vice.* [Old French *vice* defect, fault, from Latin *vitium.*]

vice² (vīs) *British. n.* vise. —*v.t.,* **viced, vic·ing.** to vise.

vi·ce³ (vī′sē) *prep.* in the place of; instead of. [Latin *vice,* ablative of *vicis* change, stead.]

vice- *prefix* one who acts in place of: *vicegerent.* [Latin *vice.* See VICE³.]

vice admiral, officer in the U.S. Navy ranking below an admiral and above a rear admiral.

vice-chair·man (vīs′chãr′mən) *n.* one who acts as an assistant to or in place of a chairman.

vice-chan·cel·lor (vīs′chan′sə lər, -slər) *n.* deputy, assistant of, or substitute for a chancellor, as in a university.

vice-con·sul (vīs′kon′səl) *n.* official next in rank below a consul.

vice-ge·ren·cy (vīs′jēr′ən sē) *pl.,* **-cies.** *n.* office or function of, or district governed by, a vicegerent.

vice-ge·rent (vīs′jēr′ənt) *n.* one appointed by a king or other ruler to act in his place or exercise his powers; deputy. [Medieval Latin *vicegerens* deputy, from Latin *vice* in place of + *gerēns,* present participle of *gerere* to perform.]

vi·cen·ni·al (vī sen′ē əl) *adj.* occurring once every twenty years. [Late Latin *vīcennium* period of twenty years (from Latin *vīciēs* twenty times + *annus* year) + -AL¹.]

vice-pres·i·dent (vīs′prez′ə dənt) *n.* officer ranking second to a president and acting in his place when necessary. —**vice′-pres′i·den·cy,** *n.* —**vice′-pres′i·den′tial,** *adj.*

vice-re·gal (vīs′rē′gəl) *adj.* of or relating to a viceroy.

vice-re·gent (vīs′rē′jənt) *n.* deputy of a regent.

vice·roy (vīs′roi) *n.* **1.** governor of a province, kingdom, or colony, ruling as the deputy of a sovereign. **2.** orange and black butterfly, *Limenitis archippus,* native to North America and bearing a close resemblance to the monarch butterfly. [French *vice-roi* the governor, going back to Latin *vice* in place of + *rēx* king.]

vice·roy·al·ty (vīs′roi′əl tē) *pl.,* **-ties.** *n.* office or term of office of, or district governed by, a viceroy.

vi·ce ver·sa (vī′sə vur′sə, vīs′ vur′sə) in the opposite or reversed order; conversely. [Latin *vice versā* literally, the position being changed.]

Vich·y (vish′ē) *n.* city in central France, a noted health resort. From 1940 to 1944, Vichy served as the seat of government of unoccupied France. Pop. (1962), 30,614.

vi·chy·ssoise (vish′ē swäz′) *n.* thick, creamy soup containing potatoes and leeks, usually served chilled.

Vichy water **1.** effervescent water from the mineral springs at Vichy, France. **2.** any water resembling this.

vic·i·nage (vis′ə nij) *n.* area near or surrounding a particular place; neighborhood; vicinity. [Old French *voisinage,* going back to Latin *vīcīnus* neighboring. See VICINITY.]

vi·cin·i·ty (vi sin′ə tē) *pl.,* **-ties.** *n.* **1.** area near or surrounding a particular place; neighborhood. **2.** state or quality of being near; proximity. [Latin *vīcīnitās,* from *vīcīnus* neighboring; literally, of the same village or district, from *vīcus* district, village.]

vi·cious (vish′əs) *adj.* **1.** addicted to or having the nature of vice; depraved: *vicious persons, vicious behavior.* **2.** morally corrupt; evil: *a vicious life.* **3.** full of malice; spiteful: *vicious remarks, a vicious attack.* **4.** having an extremely bad disposition; savagely fierce: *a vicious dog.* **5.** intense; severe: *a vicious storm.* [Latin *vitiōsus* full of faults or defects, from *vitium.* See VICE¹.] —**vi′cious·ly,** *adv.* —**vi′cious·ness,** *n.*

vicious circle **1.** situation in which the solving of a problem gives rise to another, often worse problem, which itself cannot be solved without bringing back the original problem. **2.** *Logic.* false reasoning in which a proposition is used to prove a second proposition, but depends on the second proposition for its own proof.

vi·cis·si·tude (vi sis′ə tōōd′, -tūd′) *n.* **1.** *usually,* vicissitudes. irregular, often unexpected change, as in a condition or situation: *the vicissitudes of health, the vicissitudes of fortune.* **2.** regular or alternating change: *the vicissitudes of the tides.* [Latin *vicissitūdō* change.] —**vi·cis·si·tu·di·nar·y** (vi sis′ə tōōd in er′ē, -tūd′-), **vi·cis·si·tu′di·nous,** *adj.*

Vicks·burg (viks′burg′) *n.* port city in western Mississippi, on the Mississippi River. Vicksburg was besieged and captured by Union forces in 1863 during the Civil War. Pop. (1970), 25,478.

vic·tim (vik′təm) *n.* **1.** one who is badly injured, ruined, or killed: *a victim of an automobile accident, a victim of the recession, a murder victim.* **2.** one who is cheated or swindled; dupe: *the victim of a confidence man.* **3.** person or animal sacrificed to a deity. [Latin *victima* animal offered for sacrifice.]
Syn. **1.** Victim, prey, quarry² mean a person who is hurt or killed. **Victim** suggests one who is helpless and vulnerable before any person or thing that ruthlessly exploits this advantage: *They were among the victims of Nazi persecution.* **Prey** is used of one who, like an animal, is pursued and suggests a certain inexorable fate which eventually catches up with its victim: *Mankind is the prey of all the ills of the flesh.* **Quarry,** like *prey,* is influenced by its association with animals that are hunted down for sport or food, but is stronger in suggesting the calculating effort and treachery used to entrap the victim: *The detectives tracked their quarry until they cornered him in an empty warehouse.*

vic·tim·ize (vik′tə mīz′) **-ized, -iz·ing.** *v.t.* **1.** to swindle; cheat. **2.** to make a victim of; inflict harm upon; injure or ruin. —**vic′-tim·i·za′tion,** *n.*

vic·tor (vik′tər) *n.* one who wins or conquers, as in a contest, struggle, or armed conflict. [Latin *victor* conqueror.]

vic·to·ri·a (vik tôr′ē ə) *n.* **1.** low, light, four-wheeled carriage having a folding top, seats for two passengers, and a raised seat in front for the driver. **2.** automobile having a folding top that can be raised to cover the rear seat only. **3.** large water lily, genus *Victoria,* found in South America, having white to rose-red flowers. [From Queen *Victoria.*]

Victoria (def. 1)

Vic·to·ri·a (vik tôr′ē ə) *n.* **1.** Queen. 1819-1901, queen of England from 1837 to 1901, and Empress of India from 1876 to 1901. **2.** political subdivision of Australia, in the southeastern part of the country. Area, 87,884 sq. mi. Pop. (1966), 3,217,832. **3.** Lake. lake in east-central Africa, the largest of the continent. Also, **Victoria Ny·an·za** (nī an′zə, nyän′-) **4.** capital and commercial center of Hong Kong colony. Pop. (1961), 633,138. Also (*def.* 4), **Hong Kong.**

Victoria Cross, British military decoration established by Queen Victoria in 1856, awarded for acts of conspicuous bravery.

Victoria Falls, waterfall in south-central Africa, on the Zambezi River between Rhodesia and Zambia.

Vic·to·ri·an (vik tôr′ē ən) *adj.* **1.** of or relating to Queen Victoria or to the period of her reign. **2.** of, relating to, or having the characteristics generally attributed to Victorian England, esp. prudery, bigotry, and hypocrisy. **3.** of or characteristic of the ornate and massive style of furniture, decoration, and architecture of the Victorian period. —*n.* one who lived during the reign of Queen Victoria, esp. an author or political figure.

Vic·to·ri·an·ism (vik tôr′ē ə niz′əm) *n.* art, taste, customs, or morals characteristic of or associated with the Victorian period.

vic·to·ri·ous (vik tôr′ē əs) *adj.* **1.** having achieved a victory, as in a contest or armed conflict. **2.** of or relating to victory. —**vic·to′ri·ous·ly,** *adv.* —**vic·to′ri·ous·ness,** *n.*

vic·to·ry (vik′tər ē) *pl.* **-ries.** *n.* **1.** act, instance, or condition of having defeated an opponent or enemy, as in a contest or armed conflict. **2.** advantage or superiority gained, as in a contest or struggle. [Latin *victōria*.]
Syn. 1. Victory, triumph mean the successful outcome of any struggle. **Victory** is the general word for the decisive defeat of an enemy or other hostile force: *We gained victory at the cost of demoralizing our nation.* **Triumph** glorifies and acclaims the victor, his brilliance, and supremacy in totally crushing opposition: *They exulted in the triumph of good over evil.*

Vic·tro·la (vik trō′lə) *n. Trademark.* phonograph.

vict·ual (vit′əl) *n. usually*, **victuals.** food for man. —*v.t.*, **-ualed, -ual·ing;** *also, British*, **-ualled, -ual·ling.** to supply with food. —*v.i.* to take on a supply of food. [Old French *vitaille* provisions, from Late Latin *vīctuālia*, going back to Latin *vīctus* nourishment.]

vict·ual·er (vit′əl ər) *also, British*, **vict·ual·ler.** *n.* **1.** one who supplies victuals, esp. to a military force. **2.** *British.* one who keeps an inn or tavern.

vi·cu·ña (vī kōō′nə, -nyə, -kū′-, vi-) *pl.* **-ñas** or **-ña.** *n.* small South American ruminant, *Lama vicugna*, related to the llama, having a slender, graceful body, a long neck, and a woolly coat that is predominantly tawny brown. It is highly valued for its silky fleece. Height: 34 inches at the shoulders. **2.** fabric made from the fleece of this animal, used for scarves, overcoats, or robes. [Spanish *vicuña*, from Quechua *wikuña* this animal.]

vi·de (vī′dē) see; refer to. ▲ used to direct a reader's attention to a particular part of a text. [Latin *vidē*, imperative of *vidēre* to see.]

vi·de·li·cet (vi del′i set′) *adv.* that is to say; namely. [Latin *vidēlicet* clearly, namely, shortened from *vidēre licet* it is easy or permitted to see.]

vid·e·o (vid′ē ō′) *adj.* of or relating to the transmission or reception of television images. —*n.* **1.** visual part of television. Distinguished from **audio.** **2.** television. [Latin *video* I see.]

video tape, magnetic tape used for recording both the picture and sound of a television program.

vi·dette (vi det′) *n.* vedette.

vie (vī) **vied, vy·ing.** *v.i.* to strive for superiority; be rivals; compete: *The teams vied with one another for first place.* [Shortened from Old French *envier* to challenge, invite, from Latin *invītāre* to compete.] —**Syn.** see **compete.**

Vi·en·na (vē en′ə) *n.* capital and largest city of Austria, in the northeastern part of the country, on the Danube River. Pop. (1968) 1,642,072.

Vi·en·nese (vē′ə nēz′, -nēs′) *adj.* of, relating to, or characteristic of the city of Vienna or its people. —*n. pl.*, **-nese.** member or recent descendant of the people of Vienna.

Vien·tiane (vyen tyän′) *n.* capital and largest city of Laos, in the western part of the country. Pop. (1966 est.), 132,253.

Vi·et·cong (vē′et kông′, -kŏng′, vyet′-) *also*, **Viet Cong.** *n.* **1.** Communist insurgent group formed to wage guerrilla warfare in South Vietnam. **2.** member of this group. [Short for Vietnamese *Viet Nam Cong San* Vietnamese Communist.]

Vi·et·minh (vē′et min′, vyet′-) *also*, **Viet Minh.** *n.* Communist-led Vietnamese political league that opposed Japanese occupation and later fought successfully against the French. [Short for Vietnamese *Viet Nam Doc Lap Dong Minh Hoi* Vietnam Independence Federation.]

Vi·et·nam (vē′et näm′, -năm′, vyet′-) *also*, **Viet Nam.** *n.* country in southeastern Asia divided in 1954 into North Vietnam and South Vietnam.

Vi·et·nam·ese (vē et′nä mēz′, -mēs′, -nə-, vyet′-) *adj.* of or relating to Vietnam, its people, culture, or language. —*n. pl.*, **-ese.** **1.** member or close descendant of the people of Vietnam. **2.** language predominantly spoken in Vietnam.

view (vū) *n.* **1.** act or instance of looking or seeing; sight. **2.** range of vision: *In one minute the plane has passed out of view.* **3.** that which is seen or can be seen: *We enjoyed the view from the mountaintop.* **4.** drawing, painting, print, or photograph, esp. of a landscape. **5.** particular manner of considering or regarding a matter; way of thinking; opinion: *I am very interested in his view on that question.*

6. intention; aim: *It was their view to take the short cut home.* **7.** expectation; outlook. **8. in view. a.** capable of being seen; in sight. **b.** under consideration. **9. in view of.** in consideration of. **10. on view.** open for general inspection; on exhibition. **11. with a view to. a.** with the aim or object of. **b.** with anticipation or hope of. —*v.t.* **1.** to look at or see: *The police viewed the scene of the crime.* **2.** to consider: *He viewed her behavior with contempt.* [Anglo-Norman *vewe* seeing, eyes, sight, look, from Old French *veoir* to see, from Latin *vidēre*.] —**Syn.** *n.* **5.** see **opinion.**

view·er (vū′ər) *n.* **1.** one who views something, esp. one who watches television. **2.** any of several optical devices used to look at photographic slides or scientific specimens.

view·find·er (vū′fīn′dər) *n.* finder *(def. 2).*

view·point (vū′point′) *n.* manner of thinking; point of view.

vi·ges·i·mal (vī jes′ə məl) *adj.* **1.** twentieth. **2.** of or relating to twenty; based on twenty. [Latin *vigēsimus* twentieth (going back to *vīginti* twenty) + -AL.]

vig·il (vij′əl) *n.* **1.** act or period of remaining awake, as to guard or observe something. **2.** night spent in prayer, esp. in preparation for a holy day. **3.a.** day and night before a solemn feast day, as before Christmas. **b.** *also*, **vigils.** prayers or religious services held on such a night. [Old French *vigile* watch on the eve of a holy day, from Latin *vigilia* watching.]

vig·i·lance (vij′ə ləns) *n.* quality of being vigilant; alertness; watchfulness.

vigilance committee, formerly, group of citizens banded together to apprehend and punish criminals in areas of the western and southwestern United States, where no law enforcement agency existed.

vig·i·lant (vij′ə lənt) *adj.* attentively or closely observant; alert; watchful: *Disperse then to your posts: be firm and vigilant* (Byron, 1821). [Latin *vigilāns*, present participle of *vigilāre* to watch.] —**vig′i·lant·ly,** *adv.*

vig·i·lan·te (vij′ə lan′tē) *n.* **1.** member of a group of individuals who take the law into their own hands in order to see that their view of justice is carried out. **2.** member of a vigilance committee. [Spanish *vigilante* watchful, watchman, from Latin *vigilāns*. See VIGILANT.]

vi·gnette (vin yet′) *n.* **1.** brief literary description or dramatic sketch. **2.** decorative design or illustration on the title page of a book or at the beginning or end of a chapter. **3.** engraving, drawing, photograph, or the like having no sharply defined border, with the background shading off gradually at the edges. [French *vignette* little vine, ornamental border in which vines and scrolls are used, diminutive of *vigne*. See VINE.]

vig·or (vig′ər) *n.* **1.** active power or force of body or mind. **2.** healthy strength: *the vigor of his youth.* [Old French *vigour* strength, spirit, from Latin *vigor* liveliness, activity.]

vig·or·ous (vig′ər əs) *adj.* full of, characterized by, or performed with vigor. —**vig′or·ous·ly,** *adv.* —**vig′or·ous·ness,** *n.*

vi·king (vī′king) *also*, **Vi·king.** *n.* member of a seafaring race from Scandinavia that attacked and raided the coasts of Europe from the eighth to the eleventh centuries. [Old Norse *vīkingr* pirate.]

vi·la·yet (vē′lä yet′) *n.* administrative division of Turkey. [Turkish *vilâyet* province, region, from Arabic *wilāyah* province, from *wāli* governor.]

vile (vīl) **vil·er, vil·est.** *adj.* **1.** morally base; evil; immoral: *a vile sin.* **2.** foul; loathsome; repulsive: *a vile stench, vile language.* **3.** mean; lowly; degrading. **4.** very bad; unpleasant: *vile weather, a vile, boring job.* [Old French *vil* cheap, base², from Latin *vīlis*.] —**vile′ly,** *adv.* —**vile′ness,** *n.*

vil·i·fy (vil′ə fī′) **-fied, -fy·ing.** *v.t.* to speak or write evil of; slander; revile: *to be vilified in the press.* [Late Latin *vīlificāre* to make of little value, from Latin *vīlis* cheap, base² + *facere* to make.] —**vil′i·fi·ca′tion, vil′i·fi′er,** *n.*

vil·la (vil′ə) *n.* residence, usually large and luxurious, esp. one in the country, on the outskirts of a city, or at the seashore. [Italian *villa* country house, from Latin *villa*.]

vil·lage (vil′ij) *n.* **1.** small community or group of houses, usually smaller than a town. **2.** inhabitants of a village. [Old French *village* small group of houses of peasants that is not enclosed by a wall, going back to Latin *villa* country house, farm.]

vil·lag·er (vil′i jər) *n.* one who lives in a village.

vil·lain (vil′ən) *n.* **1.** wicked, evil, or criminal person. **2.** such a person represented as a character in a dramatic or literary work. **3.** rogue; rascal: *Andrew is a little villain.* **4.** villein. [Old French *vilain* peasant, churl, rustic, base², from Medieval Latin *villanus* serf, farm servant, from Latin *villa* farm.] —**vil′lain·ous,** *adj.* —**vil′lain·ous·ly,** *adv.*

vil·lain·y (vil′ə nē) *pl.*, **-lain·ies.** *n.* **1.** action or conduct characteristic of a villain; extreme wickedness. **2.** villainous act or deed: *the villainies of war.*

vil·la·nelle (vil′ə nel′) *n.* verse form that originated in France, using two rhymes and consisting of five stanzas of three lines each with a final

at; āpe; cär; end; mē; it; īce; hot; ōld; fôrk; wood; fōōl; oil; out; up; ūse; turn; sing; thin; this; zh in treasure; ə in ago, taken, pencil, lemon, circus.

quatrain. [French *villanelle* pastoral poem, from Italian *villanella* rustic song, going back to Latin *villa* farm, country house.]

vil·lein (vil′ən) *n.* in feudalism, peasant attached by rights to his land and owing complete obedience to the lord. [Form of VILLAIN.]

vil·lein·age (vil′ə nij) *n.* **1.** in feudalism, system of rights and duties which bound a villein to his land. **2.** status or condition of a villein.

Vil·lon, Fran·çois (ve yōn′; frän swä′) 1431–c.1463, French poet; born François de Montcorbier.

vil·lous (vil′əs) *adj.* having or covered with villi.

vil·lus (vil′əs) *pl.* **vil·li** (vil′ī). *n.* any of the small hairlike projections from the surface of a mucous membrane, esp. the membrane of the small intestine. These villi absorb certain nutrients. [Latin *villus* shaggy hair, tuft of hair.]

Vil·ni·us (vil′nē oos) *n.* city in the western Soviet Union, capital of Lithuania. Pop. (1970 est.), 372,000. Also, *Russian,* **Vil·na** (vil′nə); *Polish,* **Wil′no.**

vim (vim) *n.* energy; vigor; enthusiasm. [Latin *vim,* accusative of *vīs* strength, force, energy.]

Vi·ña del Mar (vē′nyə del mär′) city in central Chile, on the Pacific. Pop. (1968), 145,658.

vin·ai·grette (vin′ə gret′) *n.* **1.** small ornamental bottle or box for smelling salts or similar aromatic preparation. **2.** vinaigrette sauce. [French *vinaigrette,* diminutive of *vinaigre.* See VINEGAR.]

vinaigrette sauce, sauce made of vinegar and oil, and usually salt, pepper, herbs, mustard, and other seasonings.

Vin·ci, Leonardo da (vin′chē) Leonardo da Vinci.

vin·ci·ble (vin′sə bəl) *adj.* that can be overcome, surmounted, or conquered. [Latin *vincibilis,* from *vincere* to conquer.]

vin·cu·lum (ving′kyə ləm) *pl.,* **-la** (-lə). *n.* **1.** bond of union; tie. **2.** *Mathematics.* line drawn over two or more terms showing that they are to be grouped together and treated as a single term. [Latin *vinculum* bond, fetter.]

vin·di·cate (vin′də kāt′) **-cat·ed, -cat·ing.** *v.t.* **1.** to prove (someone) innocent of suspicion or charges of wrongdoing: *The testimony of witnesses vindicated the defendant.* **2.** to maintain or defend (a right or claim) against opposition. **3.** to justify: *The size of the fish vindicated his choice of bait.* [Latin *vindicātus,* past participle of *vindicāre* to claim, avenge.] **—vin′di·ca′tor,** *n.*

vin·di·ca·tion (vin′də kā′shən) *n.* **1.** act of vindicating; being vindicated. **2.** that which vindicates: *The score was the vindication of the coach's strategy.*

vin·dic·tive (vin dik′tiv) *adj.* **1.** strongly inclined toward revenge; revengeful. **2.** indicating or characterized by a desire for revenge: *vindictive rage.* [Latin *vindicta* revenge + -IVE.] **—vin·dic′tive·ly,** *adv.* **—vin·dic′tive·ness,** *n.*

vine (vīn) *n.* **1.** plant with a long, usually slender stem, that grows along the ground or attaches itself to a tree, wall, or other support and grows upward. **2.** grapevine. [Old French *vi(g)ne* grapevine, from Latin *vīnea* vineyard, vine, from *vīnum* wine.]

vin·e·gar (vin′ə gər) *n.* **1.** sour liquid consisting chiefly of acetic acid, made by fermenting cider, wine, malt, beer, or the like, and used esp. as a condiment or preservative. **2.** disagreeable temperament; sour disposition; bad temper. [Old French *vinaigre* the sour liquid; literally, sour wine, going back to Latin *vīnum* wine + *ācer* sharp.]

vin·e·gar·y (vin′ə gər ē) *adj.* **1.** of or resembling vinegar. **2.** disagreeable in temperament; ill-tempered.

vine·yard (vin′yərd) *n.* **1.** area used to grow grapes. **2.** area of action or field of endeavor, esp. one of a spiritual nature. [VINE + YARD¹.]

vin or·di·naire (vaN ôr dē ner′) *pl.,* **vins or·di·naires** (vaN zôr dē ner′). *n. French.* any cheap wine, usually red.

vi·nous (vī′nəs) *adj.* **1.** of, relating to, characteristic of, or made with wine. **2.** caused or affected by or resulting from drinking wine. [Latin *vīnōsus* full of wine, from *vīnum* wine.]

vin·tage (vin′tij) *n.* **1.** wine produced from a particular crop of grapes: *1964 vintage claret.* **2.** year's crop of grapes. **3.** act or period of gathering grapes and making wine. **4.** wine of exceptional quality or of a particularly good year. **5.** *Informal.* goods, articles, or items of some particular period or time: *a car of 1930 vintage.* **—adj. 1.** of unusually high quality or merit; choice. **2.** of continuing interest or importance; classic: *vintage glassware.* [Modification (influenced by VINTNER) of Middle English *vendage* gathering of grapes, from Old French *vendange* gathering of grapes, wine, from Latin *vindēmia,* from *vīnum* grapes, wine + *dēmere* to take away.]

vint·ner (vint′nər) *n.* one who sells wines and liquors. [Anglo-Norman *vineter,* from Medieval Latin *vinetarius,* going back to Latin *vīnum* wine.]

vi·nyl (vī′nil, vīn′əl) *n.* **1.** organic radical derived from ethylene. Formula: CH_2CH **2.** any of several flexible, shiny plastics formed by polymerization, used in floor tiles, raincoats, phonograph records, and many other products. [Latin *vīnum* wine + -YL.]

vi·ol (vī′əl) *n.* any of various stringed musical instruments similar to the violin, usually having six strings, used chiefly in the sixteenth and seventeenth centuries. [Middle French *viole* viol, viola, from Old Provençal *viola* viol, possibly from *violar* to play the viol; imitative.]

vi·o·la (vē ō′lə, vī-) *n.* stringed musical instrument of the violin family, slightly larger and tuned a fifth lower than the violin. [Italian *viola,* probably from Old Provençal *viola.* See VIOL.]

vi·o·la·ble (vī′ə lə bəl) *adj.* that can be violated: *violable rule of procedure.* **—vi′o·la·bil′i·ty,** *n.* **—vi′o·la·bly,** *adv.*

vi·o·late (vī′ə lāt′) **-lat·ed, -lat·ing.** *v.t.* **1.** to break (a law, rule, regulation, or the like). **2.** to treat irreverently or without proper respect; desecrate; defile: *to violate a sanctuary with profanity.* **3.** to break in upon; interrupt; disturb: *Nightmares violate peaceful sleep.* **4.** to rape (a woman or girl). [Latin *violātus,* past participle of *violāre* to injure, dishonor.] **—vi′o·la′tor,** *n.*

vi·o·la·tion (vī′ə lā′shən) *n.* act or instance of violating; being violated.

vi·o·lence (vī′ə ləns) *n.* **1.** great physical force used so as to injure or harm. **2.** instance of violent or injurious treatment. **3.** harm or injury caused by or as by violent action or treatment. **4.** intensity of emotion or feeling. [Old French *violence* forceful action, abuse of force, from Latin *violentia* vehemence, ferocity.]

Syn. 1. Violence, force mean physical power used against another. **Violence** is applied to brute strength that inflicts pain, injury, or destruction, suggesting cruel and unjust action: *War is an act of violence.* **Force** is applied to suggest coercion or restraint rather than destruction: *Force kept the surging crowd within the boundaries.*

vi·o·lent (vī′ə lənt) *adj.* **1.** acting with or characterized by great or excessive physical force or roughness: *a violent earthquake.* **2.** caused by or exhibiting intense emotion, excitement, or the like; passionate; impetuous. **3.** characterized by great intensity; severe; extreme: *a violent attack of a disease.* **4.** resulting from unusual force, injuries, or circumstances: *a violent death in an airplane crash.* [Latin *violentus* vehement, forcible.] **—vi′o·lent·ly,** *adv.*

vi·o·let (vī′ə lit) *n.* **1.** small purple, white, or rose-colored flower of a plant, *Viola odorata,* native to Europe, Africa, and Asia, having heart-shaped and kidney-shaped leaves, and sometimes used in making perfumes. **2.** plant bearing this flower, related to the pansy. **3.** bluish-purple color. [Old French *violette,* going back to Latin *viola.*]

violet rays, light waves having the shortest wavelength in the range of visible radiation.

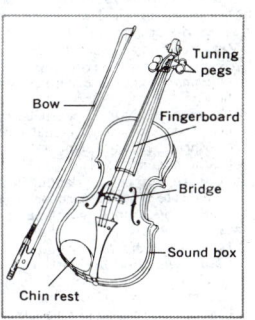

Bow · Tuning pegs · Fingerboard · Bridge · Sound box · Chin rest

Violin

vi·o·lin (vī′ə lin′) *n.* principal member of the family of modern stringed instruments played with a bow, having four strings tuned in fifths. [Italian *violino,* diminutive of *viola.* See VIOLA.]

vi·o·lin·ist (vī′ə lin′ist) *n.* one who plays the violin, esp. professionally.

vi·ol·ist (vī′ə list) *n.* **1.** one who plays the viol. **2.** one who plays the viola, esp. a person who plays professionally.

vi·o·lon·cel·list (vī′ə lən chel′ist, vē′-) *n.* cellist.

vi·o·lon·cel·lo (vī′ə lən chel′ō, vē′-) *pl.,* **-los.** *n.* cello. [Italian *violoncello,* diminutive of *violone* bass viol, from *viola.* See VIOLA.]

vi·os·ter·ol (vī os′tə rôl′) *n.* preparation of vitamin D which, when dissolved in an oil, is used as a medicine to prevent or treat rickets.

VIP *Informal.* very important person. Also, **V.I.P.**

vi·per (vī′pər) *n.* **1.** any of a large group of poisonous snakes, family Viperidae, having a pair of sharp, hollow fangs with which it injects its venom. The group includes the adder, copperhead, cottonmouth, and rattlesnake. **2.** spiteful, treacherous person. [Latin *vīpera* serpent, snake, adder, from *vīvus* living + *parere* to bring forth; because it was once thought that the viper brought forth living young.]

vi·per·ous (vī′pər əs) *adj.* **1.** snakelike. **2.** spiteful; treacherous.

vi·ra·go (vi rä′gō) *pl.,* **-goes** or **-gos.** *n.* bad-tempered, sharp-tongued woman. [Latin *virāgō* female warrior, from *vir* man.]

vi·ral (vī′rəl) *adj.* of, relating to, or caused by a virus.

vir·e·lay (vir′ə lā′) *n.* any of several Old French verse forms using two rhymes to a stanza. [Old French *virelai,* from *vireli* refrain; possibly originally an actual refrain of a song.]

vir·e·o (vir′ē ō′) *pl.,* **-e·os.** *n.* any of various American songbirds, genus *Vireo,* ranging from Canada to Argentina, having green, yellow, brown, or gray plumage mixed with white. Length: 4½–6 inches. [Latin *vireo* greenfinch, from *virēre* to be green.]

---

at; āpe; cär; end; mē; it; īce; hot; ōld; fôrk; wood; fōōl; oil; out; up; ūse; turn; sing; thin; this; zh in treasure; ə in ago, taken, pencil, lemon, circus.　　1113

vi·res·cence (vī res'əns) *n.* state or condition of being or becoming green.

vi·res·cent (vī res'ənt) *adj.* greenish or becoming green. [Latin *virēscēns,* present participle of *virēscere* to become green.]

Vir·gil (vur'jəl) *also,* **Ver·gil.** *n.* 70–19 B.C., Roman poet; born Publius Vergilius Maro.

Vir·gil·i·an (vur jil'ē ən) *also,* **Ver·gil·i·an.** *adj.* relating to or characteristic of Virgil or his poetry.

vir·gin (vur'jin) *n.* 1. person, esp. a woman, who has never had sexual intercourse. 2. **the Virgin.** the Virgin Mary. —*adj.* 1. of, relating to, being, or suitable for a virgin. 2. pure; spotless. 3. not yet used: *virgin timber.* [Old French *virgine* maiden, Virgin Mary, from Latin *virgō* maiden.]

vir·gin·al (vur'jin əl) *adj.* of, relating to, or suitable for a virgin.

virgin birth, doctrine that Jesus was miraculously conceived without a human father by the Virgin Mary and that she retained her virginity after his birth.

Vir·gin·ia (vur jin'yə) *n.* state in the eastern United States. Capital, Richmond. Area, 40,817 sq. mi. Pop. (1970), 4,648,494. Abbreviation, **Va.** —**Vir·gin'ian,** *adj., n.*

Virginia Beach, resort city in southeastern Virginia, on the Atlantic. Pop. (1970), 172,106.

Virginia creeper, hardy, woody, climbing vine, *Porthenocissus quinquefolia,* of the grape family, native to North America, having dull, oval, toothed leaflets and clusters of tiny green flowers. Also, **wood'bine'.**

Virginia deer, white-tailed deer.

Virginia reel, an American folk dance in which partners form two parallel lines facing one another and perform a variety of steps.

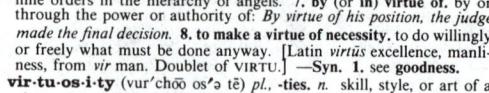

Virginia creeper

Virgin Islands, island group of the Caribbean, the westernmost of the Lesser Antilles, divided politically between the United States and Great Britain. Land area, approx. 192 sq. mi. Pop. (1967 est.), 59,000.

vir·gin·i·ty (vər jin'ə tē) *n.* state or condition of being a virgin.

Virgin Mary, Mary, the mother of Jesus.

vir·gin's-bow·er (vur'jinz bou'ər) *n.* climbing clematis, *Clematis virginiana,* found in eastern North America, having clusters of white flowers.

Vir·go (vur'gō) *n.* 1. constellation in the northern sky containing the bright star Spica, conventionally depicted as a young girl holding a spike of wheat. 2. sixth sign of the zodiac. See **zodiac** for illustration. [Latin *virgō* maiden.]

vir·gule (vur'gūl) *n.* slanting line (/), usually used between two words to indicate that the meaning of either word pertains, as in *and/or.* [Latin *virgula* small rod, diminutive of *virga* rod.]

vir·i·des·cent (vir'ə des'ənt) *adj.* slightly green; greenish. [Late Latin *viridēscēns,* present participle of *viridēscere* to become green, from Latin *viridis* green.] —**vir'i·des'cence,** *n.*

vir·ile (vir'əl) *adj.* 1. manly; masculine. 2. full of masculine vigor or strength. 3. vigorous; forceful. 4. capable of fathering children. [Latin *virīlis* relating to a man, from *vir* man.] —**Syn.** 1. see **masculine.**

vi·ril·i·ty (vi ril'ə tē) *n.* state, quality, or condition of being virile.

vi·rol·o·gy (vī rol'ə jē, vi-) *n.* branch of microbiology that deals with viruses and the diseases caused by them. —**vi·rol'o·gist,** *n.*

vir·tu (vur tōō', vur'tōō) *also,* **ver·tu.** *n.* 1. merit or excellence of an object of art because of some quality, as material, workmanship, or age. 2. knowledge of or taste for objects of art. 3. such objects collectively. [Italian *virtù,* from Latin *virtūs.* Doublet of VIRTUE.]

vir·tu·al (vur'chōō əl) *adj.* being so in essence or effect, though not in fact or name: *One part of it could not be yielded . . . without a virtual surrender of all the rest* (Burke, 1769).

virtual focus, focus *(def. 1b).*

virtual image, image *(def. 7b).*

vir·tu·al·ly (vur'chōō ə lē) *adv.* for all intents and purposes; in effect: *He was virtually a prisoner in his own home.*

Syn. Virtually, practically mean being in essence, force, or effect. **Virtually** is the more precise term for indicating that something is in fact so, even when formally or officially unrecognized: *We were virtually prisoners on the island, although the host spoke of us as his guests.* **Practically** stresses that something is so from a practical rather than an absolute point of view, falling short of completeness by only a slight margin: *They're practically robots.*

vir·tue (vur'chōō) *n.* 1. quality of righteousness, goodness, or moral excellence. 2. particular type of moral excellence: *Humility and charity are virtues.* 3. any good quality or admirable trait of character: *John has the virtue of being a good listener.* 4. chastity, esp. in a woman. 5. inherent power or strength to produce effects; potency; efficacy: *Inoculations have the virtue of preventing disease.* 6. **virtues.** fifth of the

nine orders in the hierarchy of angels. 7. **by** (or **in**) **virtue of.** by or through the power or authority of: *By virtue of his position, the judge made the final decision.* 8. **to make a virtue of necessity.** to do willingly or freely what one must do anyway. [Latin *virtūs* excellence, manliness, from *vir* man. Doublet of VIRTU.] —**Syn.** 1. see **goodness.**

vir·tu·os·i·ty (vur'chōō os'ə tē) *pl.,* **-ties.** *n.* skill, style, or art of a virtuoso.

vir·tu·o·so (vur'chōō ō'sō) *pl.,* **-sos** or **-si** (-sē) *n.* 1. one who is exceptionally skilled in one of the fine arts, esp. in music. 2. one who is exceptionally skilled in any field of endeavor. 3. one who has a cultivated appreciation of artistic merit or excellence. [Italian *virtuoso* one who is exceptionally skilled in an art, skilled, learned, from Late Latin *virtuōsus* skillful, good, from Latin *virtūs* excellence.]

vir·tu·ous (vur'chōō əs) *adj.* 1. characterized by, exhibiting, or of the nature of virtue; righteous; good. 2. chaste. —**vir'tu·ous·ly,** *adv.* —**vir'tu·ous·ness,** *n.*

vir·u·lence (vir'yə ləns, vir'ə-) *n.* quality or state of being virulent. Also, **vir'u·len·cy.**

vir·u·lent (vir'yə lənt, vir'ə-) *adj.* 1. extremely poisonous or harmful: *a virulent infection.* 2. extremely bitter or spiteful; full of hostility and hate: *a virulent speech.* [Latin *vīrulentus* poisonous, from *vīrus* poison.] —**vir'u·lent·ly,** *adv.*

vi·rus (vī'rəs) *n.* 1. any of a group of microorganisms smaller than any known bacteria and dependent upon the living tissue of hosts for their reproduction and growth. Viruses cause many diseases in man, animals, and plants. 2. the poison of any specific infectious disease, present in a person, animal, or plant suffering from that disease. 3. anything that poisons or corrupts the mind or morals; evil influence: *the virus of prejudice.* [Latin *vīrus* poison.]

vi·sa (vē'zə) *also,* **vi·sé.** *n.* official endorsement, usually stamped on a person's passport, giving him permission to enter or leave a country. —*v.t.* **-saed, -sa·ing.** 1. to put a visa on (a passport). 2. to give a visa to. [French *visa* endorsement (as on a passport), from Latin *vīsa* things seen, neuter plural of *vīsus,* past participle of *vidēre* to see.]

vis·age (viz'ij) *n.* 1. face or facial expression of a person. 2. outward aspect or appearance of anything. [Old French *visage* face, from *vis,* from Latin *vīsus* sight, look.]

vis-à-vis (vē'zə vē') *prep.* in regard to; in relation to: *His position vis-à-vis the election was ambiguous.* —*adj.* face to face. —*n., pl.,* **-vis.** one who or that which is opposite or opposing. [French *vis-à-vis* face to face: *vis* face, from Latin *vīsus* look, sight; *à* to, from Latin *ad.*]

Vi·sa·yan (vi sī'ən) *also,* **Bi·sa·yan.** *n.* 1. member of a Malay people in the Philippine Islands, living predominantly on the Visayan Islands and on Mindanao. 2. language of this people, belonging to the Indonesian branch of the Malayo-Polynesian language family.

Visayan Islands, group of islands in the central Philippines. Also, **Bi·sa'yas.**

Visc., Viscount; Viscountess.

vis·cer·a (vis'ər ə) *sing.,* **vis·cus.** *n.,pl.* the soft internal organs of the body, esp. those in the thoracic and abdominal cavities, including the heart, stomach, liver, intestines, and kidneys. [Latin *vīscera,* plural of *vīscus.*]

vis·cer·al (vis'ər əl) *adj.* 1. of or relating to the viscera. 2. arising from or caused by deep emotions, feelings, or the like.

vis·cid (vis'id) *adj.* having a thick, gluey or sticky consistency; viscous. [Late Latin *viscidus,* from Latin *viscum* birdlime.]

vis·cose (vis'kōs) *n.* thick, syrupy solution used for making rayon, formed from wood pulp by adding caustic soda, carbon disulfide, and sodium hydroxide. [Late Latin *viscōsus.* see VISCOUS.]

vis·cos·i·ty (vis kos'ə tē) *pl.,* **-ties.** *n.* 1. quality or state of being viscous. 2. *Physics.* internal friction or resistance to the flow of liquids or gases due to cohesive forces among the constituent molecules.

vis·count (vī'kount') *n.* in Great Britain and certain other countries, nobleman who ranks immediately below an earl or count and immediately above a baron. [Old French *visconte,* going back to Latin *vice* in place of + *comes* companion. See COUNT[2].]

vis·count·cy (vī'kount'sē) *n.* title, rank, or dignity of a viscount. Also, **vis·count·y** (vī'kount'tē).

vis·count·ess (vī'koun'tis) *n.* 1. wife or widow of a viscount. 2. woman who holds a rank equivalent to that of a viscount in her own right.

vis·cous (vis'kəs) *adj.* 1. (of a liquid) having a thick, gluey or sticky consistency. 2. *Physics.* having the property of viscosity. [Late Latin *viscōsus* sticky, from Latin *viscum* birdlime.]

vis·cus (vis'kəs) *n.* singular of **viscera.**

vise (vīs) *also, British,* **vice.** *n.* tool with two jaws moved by a screw mechanism, used to hold an object firmly in place while it is being worked on.

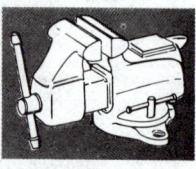

Vise

—*v.t.*, **vised, vis·ing.** to hold by or as by a vise. [Old French *vis* screw, from Latin *vītis* vine (suggesting something winding).]

vi·sé (vē′zā, vē zā′) *n.* visa. —*v.t.*, **-séed, -sé·ing.** [French *visé*, past participle of *viser* to stamp with a visa, endorse, from *visa*. See VISA.]

Vish·nu (vish′nōō) *n.* one of the three chief divinities of Hinduism called "the Preserver" and reincarnated several times, esp. as Krishna. [Sanskrit *Vishnu*.]

vis·i·bil·i·ty (viz′ə bil′ə tē) *pl.,* **-ties.** *n.* **1.** state, condition, or quality of being visible. **2.** distance which the naked eye can see as affected by physical conditions, as light or precipitation: *Visibility is only a quarter of a mile today because of the fog.* **3.** relative degree of being able to see as affected by physical conditions, as light or precipitation: *Visibility is poor tonight.*

vis·i·ble (viz′ə bəl) *adj.* **1.** capable of being seen; perceptible: *The house is visible from the road.* **2.** evident; apparent; obvious: *Her anger at the insult was visible.* [Latin *vīsibilis* that may be seen, from *vidēre* to see.] —**vis′i·bly,** *adv.*

Vis·i·goth (viz′ə goth′) *n.* member of the westernmost branch of the Goths that invaded the Roman Empire in the fourth century A.D. and settled in France and Spain. [Late Latin *Visigothī;* of Germanic origin.] —**Vis′i·goth′ic,** *adj.*

vi·sion (vizh′ən) *n.* **1.** act or power of seeing; sense of sight. **2.** that which is or has been seen. **3.** discernment; foresight: *a ruler of great vision.* **4.** something imagined; mental image: *visions of future triumphs.* **5.** conception; view: *to have an unrealistic vision of the world.* **6.a.** experience of perceiving something of a mystical, religious, or prophetic nature as if with the eyes or in a dream, trance, or similar state. **b.** that which is so perceived. **7.** someone or something of great beauty: *Elaine was a vision of loveliness in the silk gown she had made.* —*v.t.* to see in or as in a vision. [Latin *vīsiō* sight.] —**vi′sion·al,** *adj.* —**vi′sion·al·ly,** *adv.*

vi·sion·ar·y (vizh′ə ner′ē) *adj.* **1.** relating to, resembling, or of the nature of a vision; imaginary. **2.** having or characterized by impractical ideas or plans. **3.** not practical; unrealistic: *a visionary scheme.* **4.** having or capable of having visions: *a strange, solitary, visionary child, to whom an unseen world had revealed itself* (Jameson, 1850). —*n. pl.,* **-ar·ies. 1.** one who has visions. **2.** one whose ideas or plans are impractical or unrealistic; dreamer.

vis·it (viz′it) *v.t.* **1.** to go or come to see (a person or persons) for social, business, or other reasons: *to visit one's relatives, to visit the dentist.* **2.** to go or come to (a place), as for sightseeing: *to visit Quebec.* **3.** to stay with as a guest. **4.** to go or come to see in an official or professional capacity: *The mayor will visit several of the city's jails tomorrow.* **5.** to come upon; afflict; assail: *A plague visited the country.* **6.** to inflict punishment upon or for. **7.** to inflict, as suffering. —*v.i.* **1.** to pay a call or calls; stay with someone as a guest (often with *with*). **2.** *Informal.* to converse; chat. —*n.* **1.** act or instance of visiting a person, place, or thing. **2.** stay or sojourn, usually brief. **3.** act or instance of visiting in an official or professional capacity. [Latin *visitāre* to go to see.]

vis·it·ant (viz′i tənt) *n.* **1.** visitor. **2.** a supernatural being. **3.** migratory bird that stays in a particular place or region for a limited period of time. —*adj.* paying a visit or visits; visiting.

vis·i·ta·tion (viz′i tā′shən) *n.* **1.** act or instance of visiting, esp. an official visit for the purpose of inspection or examination. **2.** an affliction or blessing, esp. considered as a punishment or reward sent by God. **3. Visitation. a.** a visit of the Virgin Mary to the mother of John the Baptist shortly before his birth. **b.** feast day commemorating this event. July 2. —**vis′i·ta′tion·al,** *adj.*

visiting card, calling card.

vis·i·tor (viz′i tər) *n.* one who pays a visit.

vi·sor (vī′zər) *also,* **vi·zor.** *n.* **1.** projecting brim on the front of a cap, designed to shade the eyes from the sun. **2.** in ancient armor, the movable front piece of a helmet, that could be lowered to cover the upper part of the face. **3.** projecting part usually attached above the windshield on the inside of an automobile, designed to shield against glare. [Anglo-Norman *viser* visor of a helmet, from Old French *vis* face. See VISAGE.]

vis·ta (vis′tə) *n.* **1.** view, esp. one seen through an opening or passage, as between rows of trees. **2.** comprehensive mental view of a series of events. [Italian *vista* sight, view, going back to *vedere* to see, from Latin *vidēre*.]

VISTA (vis′tə) U.S. government program that recruits and trains

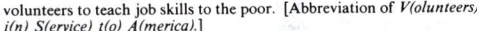

Visor

Visor *(def. 2)*

volunteers to teach job skills to the poor. [Abbreviation of *V(olunteers) i(n) S(ervice) t(o) A(merica).*]

Vis·tu·la (vis′chə lə) *n.* river in Poland flowing into the Baltic Sea.

vis·u·al (vizh′ōō əl) *adj.* **1.** relating to, resulting from, or serving the sense of sight. **2.** capable of being seen; visible. [Late Latin *vīsuālis* relating to sight, from Latin *vīsus* sight.] —**vis′u·al·ly,** *adv.*

visual aid, any of various devices or materials involving the sense of sight, as a chart, motion picture, or slide, used to aid, facilitate, or improve instruction.

vis·u·al·ize (vizh′ōō ə līz′) **-ized, -iz·ing.** *v.t.* to form a mental image of; envision. —*v.i.* to form a mental image. —**vis′u·al·i·za′tion,** *n.*

vi·tal (vīt′əl) *adj.* **1.** of, relating to, or characteristic of life. **2.** necessary to or supporting life: *the vital organs.* **3.** full of life and vigor; energetic. **4.** of prime or critical importance; essential: *Your support is vital to the success of this project.* **5.** deadly; fatal. [Latin *vītālis* relating to life, from *vīta* life.] —**vi′tal·ly,** *adv.* —**vi′tal·ness,** *n.*

vi·tal·ism (vīt′əl iz′əm) *n.* philosophical doctrine that all living beings possess a unique life force, inexplicable in terms of physics and chemistry, which essentially distinguishes them from nonliving entities. —**vi′tal·ist,** *n.* —**vi′tal·is′tic,** *adj.*

vi·tal·i·ty (vī tal′ə tē) *pl.,* **-ties.** *n.* **1.** mental or physical vigor or energy. **2.** power to live or continue living. **3.** power to endure, continue, or survive.

vi·tal·ize (vīt′əl īz′) **-ized, -iz·ing.** *v.t.* **1.** to put vitality or liveliness into. **2.** to give life to. —**vi′tal·i·za′tion,** *n.*

vi·tals (vīt′əlz) *n.,pl.* **1.** parts or organs of the body necessary or vital to life. **2.** parts or features essential to the operation or existence of something.

vital statistics, statistics relating to certain aspects of human life or to factors affecting human life, as births and deaths.

vi·ta·min (vī′tə min) *n.* any of a group of organic compounds needed in very small amounts to maintain the health and normal functioning of the body. Vitamins are obtained from food and in some cases manufactured by the body. [Latin *vīta* life + AMINE; because it was formerly thought to be an amine.]

vitamin A, any of a group of fat-soluble vitamins necessary for good vision at night, normal development of cells, and healthy skin, found in foods of animal origin, as liver, whole milk, and eggs, and manufactured in the body from carotene found in carrots and certain other vegetables.

vitamin B₁, thiamine.

vitamin B₂, riboflavin.

vitamin B₆, pyridoxine.

vitamin B₁₂, complex vitamin containing cobalt, found esp. in liver, necessary for the formation of blood cells and for growth, and used esp. in treating pernicious anemia.

vitamin B complex, group of water-soluble vitamins found in yeast, liver, and other foods, including thiamine, riboflavin, pyridoxine, vitamin B₁₂, biotin, niacin, folic acid, and pantothenic acid.

vitamin C, ascorbic acid.

vitamin D, any of several fat-soluble, antirachitic vitamins necessary for normal bone and tooth formation. Vitamin D is found in fish-liver oils and is manufactured in the body by the action of sunlight on cholesterol.

vitamin E, tocopherol.

vitamin G, riboflavin.

vitamin H, biotin.

vitamin K, any of a group of fat-soluble vitamins necessary for the clotting of blood, found chiefly in leafy green vegetables and tomatoes.

vi·tel·lin (vi tel′ən, vī-) *n.* protein found in the yolk of eggs. [Latin *vitellus* yolk of an egg + -IN¹.]

vi·tel·line (vi tel′in, -ēn, vī-) *adj.* **1.** of or relating to the yolk of an egg. **2.** resembling the color of an egg yolk; yellow. [Latin *vitellus* yolk of an egg + -INE².]

vi·ti·ate (vish′ē āt′) **-at·ed, -at·ing** *v.t.* **1.** to impair the quality of; spoil. **2.** to debase; corrupt. **3.** to make legally ineffective, as a contract; invalidate. [Latin *vitiātus*, past participle of *vitiāre* to spoil, corrupt.] —**vi′ti·a′tion, vi′ti·a′tor,** *n.*

vit·i·cul·ture (vit′ə kul′chər, vī′tə-) *n.* science, art, or practice of cultivating grapes. [Latin *vītis* vine + CULTURE.]

vit·re·ous (vit′rē əs) *adj.* **1.** resembling or of the nature of glass. **2.** of or relating to glass. **3.** made or derived from glass. **4.** of or relating to the vitreous humor. [Latin *vitreus* of glass, glassy, from *vitrum* glass.]

vitreous humor, the transparent, jellylike substance that fills the interior of the eyeball behind the lens.

vit·ri·fi·ca·tion (vit′rə fi kā′shən) *n.* **1.** act or process of vitrifying; being vitrified. **2.** that which is vitrified.

vit·ri·form (vit′rə fôrm′) *adj.* having the form or appearance of glass. [Latin *vitrum* glass + -FORM.]

at; āpe; cär; end; mē; it; īce; hot; ōld; fôrk; wood; fōōl; oil; out; up; ūse; turn; sing; thin; this; zh in treasure; ə in ago, taken, pencil, lemon, circus.

vit·ri·fy (vit′rə fī′) **-fied, -fy·ing.** v.t., v.i. to change into glass or a vitreous substance. [French vitrifier, going back to Latin vitrum glass + facere to make.]

vit·rine (vi trēn′) n. cabinet having a glass door and sometimes a glass top and sides, used esp. to display objects of art. [French vitrine, from vitre window, pane of glass, from Latin vitrum glass.]

vit·ri·ol (vit′rē ol) n. **1.** copper, iron, lead, or zinc sulfate. Copper sulfate is blue; iron sulfate is green; lead sulfate and zinc sulfate are white. **2.** sulfuric acid. Also, **oil of vitriol. 3.** something resembling vitriol in caustic quality, esp. feeling, speech, or writing that is harsh, sharp, or bitter. [Old French vitriol any of various sulfates, going back to Latin vitrum glass; supposedly because of the glassy appearance of these sulfates.]

vit·ri·ol·ic (vit′rē ol′ik) adj. **1.** of, resembling, or derived from a vitriol. **2.** very harsh, sharp, or bitter; caustic.

vit·tle (vit′əl) n. Informal. victual.

vi·tu·per·ate (vī tōō′pə rāt′, -tū′-, vi-) **-at·ed, -at·ing.** v.t. to speak harshly or abusively to or about; berate. [Latin vituperātus, past participle of vituperāre to censure.]

vi·tu·per·a·tion (vī tōō′pə rā′shən, -tū′-, vi-) n. **1.** abusive language; censure. **2.** act of vituperating.

vi·tu·per·a·tive (vī tōō′pə rā′tiv, -pər ə tiv, -tū′-, vi-) adj. characterized by or of the nature of vituperation; abusive. —**vi·tu′per·a·tive·ly,** adv.

vi·va (vē′və, -vä) interj. (long) live (a person or thing specified). ▲ used as an acclamation or salute. [Italian viva, from vivere to live, from Latin vīvere.]

vi·va·ce (vi vä′chā) Music. adv. in a lively or brisk manner. —adj. lively; brisk. [Italian vivace lively, from Latin vīvāx.]

vi·va·cious (vi vā′shəs, vī-) adj. full of life; lively; animated. [Latin vīvāci-, stem of vīvāx lively + -OUS.] —**vi·va′cious·ly,** adv. —**vi·va′cious·ness,** n.

vi·vac·i·ty (vi vas′ə tē, vī-) n. liveliness; animation. [Latin vīvācitās.]

vi·var·i·um (vī vâr′ē əm) pl., **-i·ums** or **-i·a** (-ē ə). n. place where animals or plants are kept or raised in conditions closely resembling their natural environment. [Latin vīvārium enclosure in which animals and fish are kept alive, going back to vīvus alive.]

vi·va vo·ce (vī′və vō′sē) by word of mouth; orally. [Medieval Latin viva voce literally, with the living voice, going back to Latin vīvus living + vōx voice.]

vive (vēv) interj. French. (long) live (a person or thing specified). ▲ used as an acclamation or salute.

viv·id (viv′id) adj. **1.** (of colors) bright; intense; brilliant. **2.** clearly or distinctly perceived: a vivid recollection, a vivid impression. **3.** producing clear or lifelike images in the mind: a vivid description of an accident. **4.** active in forming clear or lifelike mental images: vivid imagination. **5.** full of life; vigorous. [Latin vīvidus full of life, animated, from vīvus living, alive.] —**viv′id·ly,** adv. —**viv′id·ness,** n. —**Syn. 3.** see graphic.

viv·i·fy (viv′ə fī′) **-fied, -fy·ing.** v.t. **1.** to give life to; animate. **2.** to make more lively, vivid, or striking. [Late Latin vīvificāre to make alive, from vīvus alive + facere to make.] —**viv′i·fi·ca′tion,** n.

vi·vip·a·rous (vī vip′ər əs) adj. bringing forth living young, rather than eggs, as most mammals. [Latin vīviparus, from vīvus alive + parere to bring forth.]

viv·i·sect (viv′ə sekt′) v.t. to perform vivisection on (a living animal). —v.i. to practice vivisection. [From VIVISECTION.] —**viv′i·sec′tor,** n.

viv·i·sec·tion (viv′ə sek′shən) n. surgical operation performed on living animals for scientific study. [Latin vīvus alive + SECTION.] —**viv′i·sec′tion·al,** adj.

viv·i·sec·tion·ist (viv′ə sek′shə nist) n. one who practices, advocates, or defends vivisection.

vix·en (vik′sən) n. **1.** female fox. **2.** ill-tempered or quarrelsome woman. [Old English fyxe female fox.] —**vix′en·ish,** adj.

viz., namely. [Latin vidēlicet.]

viz·ard (viz′ərd) n. a mask. [Modification of earlier visar, form of VISOR.]

vi·zier (vi zēr′, viz′yər) also, **vi·zir,** n. in Muslim countries, a high official of the government, esp. a minister of state. [Turkish vezīr, from Arabic wazīr originally, one who bears burdens.] —**vi·zier·ate** (vi-zēr′it, -āt, viz′yər it, -yə rāt′), **vi·zier′ship,** n. —**vi·zier′i·al,** adj.

vi·zor (vī′zər) visor.

V-J Day, August 14, 1945, the day on which Japan acceded to the Allied surrender terms in World War II. The surrender was made official on September 2, 1945.

Vlad·i·vos·tok (vlad′ə vos′tok) n. port city in the southeasternmost Soviet Union, on the Sea of Japan. Pop. (1970 est.), 442,000.

vlf, very low frequency. Also, **VLF**

vocab., vocabulary.

vo·ca·ble (vō′kə bəl) n. word considered as a sequence of letters or sounds, rather than as a unit of meaning. —adj. capable of being spoken. [Latin vocābulum designation, from vocāre to call.]

vo·cab·u·lar·y (vō kab′yə ler′ē) pl., **-lar·ies.** n. **1.** all the words used or understood by a particular person or group, or employed in a particular field of knowledge. **2.** list of words or of words and phrases, usually arranged in alphabetical order and defined or translated. **3.** all the words of a language. [Medieval Latin vocabularium list of words, from Latin vocābulum. See VOCABLE.]

vo·cal (vō′kəl) adj. **1.** of, relating to, or uttered or expressed by the voice. **2.** performed by or intended for the voice. **3.** capable of producing speech or sound; having a voice. **4.** full of voices; resounding. **5.** readily expressing one's views or opinions in speech. **6.** Phonetics. **a.** vocalic. **b.** voiced. —n. **1.** Phonetics. a vocal sound. **2.** that part of a musical composition intended to be sung. [Latin vōcālis sounding, sonorous, from vōx voice, call. Doublet of VOWEL.] —**vo′cal·ly,** adv. —**vo′cal·ness,** n.

vocal cords, either of two pairs of membranes in the throat. The passage of air from the lungs through the lower pair causes them to vibrate, thus producing the sound of the voice.

vo·cal·ic (vō kal′ik) adj. **1.** consisting chiefly or completely of vowel sounds. **2.** of, relating to, or resembling a vowel sound. —**vo·cal′i·cal·ly,** adv.

vo·cal·ist (vō′kə list) n. one who sings, esp. professionally.

vo·cal·ize (vō′kə līz′) **-ized, -iz·ing.** v.t. **1.** to make vocal; utter or express with the voice. **2.** to render articulate; give voice to. **3.** Phonetics. **a.** to change (a consonant) into a vowel sound. **b.** to voice. —v.i. **1.** to produce sound with the voice; sing or speak. **2.** Phonetics. to be changed into a vowel sound. —**vo′cal·i·za′tion, vo′cal·iz′er,** n.

vo·ca·tion (vō kā′shən) n. **1.** occupation or profession; trade. **2.** strong inclination to pursue a certain career or way of life, esp. one of a religious nature; calling. **3.** work or career that one feels called to or especially suited for. [Latin vocātiō a calling, invitation.]

vo·ca·tion·al (vō kā′shən əl) adj. **1.** of or relating to a vocation or occupation. **2.** of, relating to, or providing training or education in a skill, trade, or occupation, or guidance in choosing an occupation: a vocational counselor. —**vo·ca′tion·al·ly,** adv.

vocational school, school that trains young men and women in specific skills or trades, as mechanics, electronics, and stenography.

voc·a·tive (vok′ə tiv) n. **1.** grammatical case in Latin, Greek, and certain other languages that is used to indicate the person or thing addressed by the speaker. **2.** word or construction in this case. —adj. of, relating to, or designating this case. [Late Latin vocātīvus this grammatical case; literally, the calling case, from vocāre to call.]

vo·cif·er·ant (vō sif′ər ənt) adj. vociferous; noisy; clamorous.

vo·cif·er·ate (vō sif′ə rāt′) **-at·ed, -at·ing.** v.i. to cry out loudly; shout. [Latin vōciferātus, past participle of vōciferārī to cry out, from vōx sound¹, voice + ferre to bear¹.] —**vo·cif′er·a′tion, vo·cif′er·a′tor,** n.

vo·cif·er·ous (vō sif′ər əs) adj. making or characterized by loud outcry; clamorous. [VOCIFER(ATE) + -OUS.] —**vo·cif′er·ous·ly,** adv. —**vo·cif′er·ous·ness,** n.

vod·ka (vod′kə) n. colorless alcoholic liquor, originally made in Russia, distilled from fermenting grain or potatoes. [Russian vodka, diminutive of voda water.]

vogue (vōg) n. **1.** accepted fashion at a particular time: This type of literature is currently in vogue. **2.** popular acceptance or favor; popularity. [French vogue fashion; literally, rowing, from voguer to row, move along; probably of Germanic origin.] —**Syn. 1.** see fashion.

voice (vois) n. **1.** sound produced by the vocal organs of a vertebrate, esp. sound so produced by human beings, as in speaking or singing. **2.** ability to produce such sound: to lose one's voice. **3.** quality, condition, or tone of vocal sound: a soft voice, a high-pitched voice, a mournful voice. **4.** sound resembling or suggesting vocal utterance: The voice of thunder shook the wood (Scott, 1801). **5.** something likened to human speech: the voice of conscience. **6.** right or privilege of expressing an opinion, view, or choice: to have a voice in city government. You have no voice in this affair. **7.** expressed opinion, choice, or wish: the voice of the people. **8.** expression: to give voice to one's feelings. **9.** person or agency through which something is expressed: Poetry is the voice of imagination (Reed, 1854). **10.** any of the vocal or instrumental parts in a musical composition. **11.** singer. **12.** Grammar. verb form expressing whether the subject is active or passive. **13.** Phonetics. a sound produced by vibration of the vocal cords. **14. in voice,** in proper condition for singing. **15. with one voice,** unanimously. —v.t., **voiced, voic·ing. 1.** to give utterance to; express: to voice an opinion. **2.** Phonetics. to utter with vibration of the vocal cords. **3.** Music. to regulate the tone of, as the pipes of an organ. [Old French vois sound¹, utterance, word, from Latin vōx.]

voice box, the larynx.

voiced (voist) adj. **1.** having a voice. **2.** expressed by the voice. **3.** Phonetics. spoken with vibration of the vocal cords.

at; āpe; cär; end; mē; it; īce; hot; ōld; fôrk; wood; fōōl; oil; out; up; ūse; turn; sing; thin; this; zh in treasure; ə in ago, taken, pencil, lemon, circus.

voice·less (vois′lis) *adj.* 1. having no voice; mute. 2. *Phonetics.* not voiced; surd. —**voice′less·ly,** *adv.* —**voice′less·ness,** *n.*

void (void) *adj.* 1. having no legal force; not legally valid. 2. not occupied by or containing matter; empty. 3. unoccupied, as an office or position; vacant. 4. lacking; devoid (with *of*): *void of meaning.* 5. ineffective; useless. —*n.* 1. an empty space; vacuum: *No nightmare of hostile objects could be as terrible as this void* (Auden, 1944). 2. feeling of emptiness or loss. 3. gap or space, as in a surface. —*v.t.* 1. to make void or of no effect; invalidate. 2. to empty; discharge. 3. *Archaic.* to make or leave empty; vacate. [Old French *voide* empty, probably going back to Latin *vacāre* to be empty.] —**void′er,** *n.* —**Syn.** *adj.* 2. see **empty.**

void·a·ble (voi′də bəl) *adj.* capable of being voided, esp. capable of being made legally void.

voi·la (vwä lä′) *interj.* French. behold; see; there.

voile (voil) *n.* lightweight, sheer fabric, as of cotton or wool, used for curtains, dresses, and other items. [French *voile* this fabric, veil, from Latin *vēla,* plural of *vēlum* cloth, covering veil. Doublet of VEIL, VELUM.]

vol., volume.

vo·lant (vō′lənt) *adj.* 1. flying or capable of flying. 2. light and quick; nimble: *the volant fingers of a seamstress.* 3. *Heraldry.* (of a bird) represented with the wings extended, as in flying. [Latin *volāns,* present participle of *volāre* to fly.]

vol·a·tile (vol′ə til, -ət əl) *adj.* 1. tending to change readily into vapor, esp. at ordinary temperatures. 2. changeable, unpredictable, or unstable; easily aroused, disturbed, or affected: *a volatile disposition, a volatile political situation.* 3. fleeting; transient. [Latin *volātilis* flying, fleeting, from *volāre* to fly.] —**vol′a·til·i·ty,** *n.*

vol·a·til·ize (vol′ət əl īz′) **-ized, -iz·ing.** *v.t., v.i.* to change or be changed into vapor. —**vol′a·til·i·za′tion,** *n.*

vol·can·ic (vol kan′ik) *adj.* 1. of, relating to, or characteristic of a volcano or volcanoes: *a volcanic eruption.* 2. having or characterized by a volcano or volcanoes: *a volcanic island.* 3. produced by or discharged from a volcano: *volcanic rock.* 4. violently active; explosive: *the volcanic passions . . . in human nature* (Liddon, 1872).

vol·can·ism (vol′kə niz′əm) *n.* volcanic activity or phenomena.

vol·ca·no (vol kā′nō) *pl.* **-noes** or **-nos.** *n.* 1. opening in the surface of the earth from which molten rock, gases, and rock fragments are expelled. 2. cone-shaped hill or mountain built up around such an opening by the material expelled. [Italian *volcano,* from Latin *Vulcānus* Vulcan.]

vole (vōl) *n.* any of various gray or brown mouselike rodents, family Cricetidae, closely related to lemmings and muskrats, having a large head, small round ears, and a short tail. Length: 3½–7 inches. [Earlier *volemouse,* going back to Norwegian *voll* field + *mus* mouse.]

Vole

Vol·ga (vol′gə) *n.* river in the European Soviet Union flowing into the Caspian Sea. It is the longest river in Europe and the chief inland waterway of the Soviet Union.

Vol·go·grad (vol′gə grad′) *n.* port city in the southwestern Soviet Union, on the Volga River. Formerly known as Stalingrad, the city was the scene of a major Soviet victory over the Germans in World War II. Pop. (1970 est.), 818,000.

vo·li·tion (vō lish′ən) *n.* 1. act of willing or deciding. 2. power of willing; will power. [French *volition* act of willing, going back to Latin *volō* I wish.] —**vo·li′tion·al,** *adj.* —**vo·li′tion·al·ly,** *adv.*

vol·ley (vol′ē) *pl.* **-leys.** *n.* 1. discharge of a number of weapons at once. 2. missiles, as stones, arrows, or bullets so discharged. 3. any discharge of a number of things simultaneously or in rapid succession: *a volley of complaints.* 4. *Tennis.* return of a ball before it touches the ground. 5. sequence of hitting a ball back and forth over a net without interruption, as in tennis. —*v.t., v.i.* **-leyed, -ley·ing.** 1. to discharge or be discharged in or as in a volley. 2. to return (a ball) before it touches the ground in tennis and certain other sports. 3. to engage in hitting (the ball) back and forth over the net, as in tennis. [Old French *volee* flight, from *voler* to fly, from Latin *volāre.*]

vol·ley·ball (vol′ē bôl′) *n.* 1. game in which two teams on either side of a high net engage in hitting a large ball back and forth over the net with their hands without letting it touch the ground. 2. ball used in this game.

Vol·sci (vol′sī) *n.,pl.* ancient people of central Italy, conquered by the Romans in the fourth century B.C. Also, **Vol·scians** (vol′shənz). —**vol′scian,** *adj., n.*

volt (vōlt) *n.* 1. unit of electrical potential difference equal to the potential difference between two points in an electric circuit if one joule of work is required to move one coulomb of charge between them.

2. unit of electromotive force supplied by a source of electricity, as a battery. [From Alessandro *Volta.*]

Vol·ta, A·les·san·dro (vōl′tə, -tä; ä′les sän′drō) 1745–1827, Italian physicist and inventor of a device that was a forerunner of the battery.

volt·age (vōl′tij) *n.* electrical potential difference or electromotive force expressed in volts.

vol·ta·ic (vol tā′ik) *adj.* of or relating to an electric current produced by chemical action between plates of dissimilar metals; galvanic. [From Alessandro *Volta* + -IC.]

voltaic battery, battery composed of voltaic cells.

voltaic cell, simple unit that produces electricity through the chemical action of two plates or rods of different metals separated by an electrolytic chemical agent.

voltaic pile, source of electric current consisting of a series of pairs of unlike metal disks, each pair separated by a pad moistened with an electrolyte.

Vol·taire, Fran·çois Ma·rie A·rou·et de (vol tār′, vōl-; fraN swä′ mä rē′ är wä′ də) 1694–1778, French philosopher, poet, historian, and dramatist.

vol·tam·e·ter (vol tam′ə tər) *n.* instrument for measuring an electric current indirectly by measuring the extent or rate of a chemical change that results from producing or conducting the current. [VOLTA(IC) + METER³.]

volt·me·ter (vōlt′mē′tər) *n.* instrument for measuring the potential difference between two points in an electric circuit by passing current through a coil surrounded by a permanent magnet.

vol·u·ble (vol′yə bəl) *adj.* using or characterized by a large, easy, smooth flow of words; fluent; talkative. [Latin *volūbilis,* from *volvere* to roll.] —**vol′u·bil′i·ty,** *n.* —**vol′u·bly,** *adv.*

vol·ume (vol′yōōm, -yəm) *n.* 1. collection of written or printed pages bound together; book. 2. one of a set or series of related books. 3. number of issues of a periodical, usually those published in one year. 4. amount of space occupied or capable of being occupied, as measured in three dimensions: *the volume of a liquid in a container, the volume of the container.* 5. amount or quantity, usually a large one: *volumes of work to be done. The volume of business fell off during the strike.* 6. quantity or intensity of sound; loudness. 7. **to speak volumes.** to be highly expressive or full of significance: *His conduct speaks volumes for his training.* [Old French *volume* book, from Latin *volūmen* roll of writing, scroll, book, from *volvere* to roll.]

vol·u·met·ric (vol′yə met′rik) *adj.* of or relating to measurement by volume. Also, **vol′u·met′ri·cal.** —**vol′u·met′ri·cal·ly,** *adv.*

vo·lu·mi·nous (və lōō′mə nəs) *adj.* 1. of great size or bulk; large: *voluminous sails.* 2. forming or capable of filling a large volume or many volumes: *voluminous praise, voluminous documents on the subject.* 3. writing or speaking at great length: *a voluminous correspondent.* [Late Latin *volūminōsus* full of folds, from Latin *volūmen* roll of writing. See VOLUME.] —**vo·lu′mi·nous·ly,** *adv.*

vol·un·tar·y (vol′ən ter′ē) *adj.* 1. performed, done, or made of one's own free will: *a voluntary admission of guilt, a voluntary decision to retire.* 2. acting in a capacity chosen of one's own free will, and often without pay: *a voluntary search party, voluntary hospital workers.* 3. endowed with the power of willing or free choice: *a voluntary being.* 4. controlled by the will: *voluntary muscles.* 5. done intentionally; not accidental: *voluntary manslaughter.* 6. supported entirely by voluntary contributions: *a voluntary hospital.* —*n. pl.,* **-tar·ies.** organ piece, usually improvised, played before, during, or after a church service. [Latin *voluntārius* willing, from *voluntās* will.] —**vol·un·tar·i·ly** (vol′ən ter′ə lē), *adv.* —**Syn.** 1. see **deliberate.**

vol·un·teer (vol′ən tēr′) *n.* 1. one who serves or offers his services for any undertaking of his own free will, often without expectation of payment: *a campaign staff consisting chiefly of volunteers, volunteers for a dangerous mission.* 2. one who enters military service of his own free will. —*v.i.* to serve or offer one's services of one's own free will: *to volunteer for an unpleasant job.* —*v.t.* 1. to express willingness to give or give readily: *to volunteer the answer to a question. I'll volunteer my car for the trip.* —*adj.* 1. of, relating to, or consisting of volunteers: *volunteer status, a volunteer school board.* 2. serving as a volunteer: *a volunteer scout master.* [French *volontaire* one who offers his services of his own free will, willing, from Latin *voluntārius* willing. See VOLUNTARY.]

vo·lup·tu·ar·y (və lup′chōō er′ē) *pl.,* **-ar·ies.** one who indulges in sensual or luxurious pleasures. —*adj.* of or characterized by sensual or luxurious pleasures. [Late Latin *voluptuārius* sensual, from Latin *voluptās* pleasure.]

vo·lup·tu·ous (və lup′chōō əs) *adj.* 1. having a full and shapely form that is sensually appealing. 2. imparting, arising from, or characterized by sensual pleasure: *a voluptuous painting.* 3. given to indulging in sensual or luxurious pleasures. [Latin *voluptuōsus* full of pleasure, from *voluptās* pleasure.] —**vo·lup′tu·ous·ly,** *adv.* —**vo·lup′tu·ous·ness,** *n.*

vo·lute (və lōōt′) *adj.* spiral in form; rolled up. —*n.* **1.** spiral or twisted form or object. **2.** spiral-shaped ornament resembling a partly unrolled scroll, esp. one found on Ionic or Corinthian capitals. **3.** one of the turns or whorls of a spiral shell. [Latin *volūta* spiral scroll, from *volvere* to roll.]

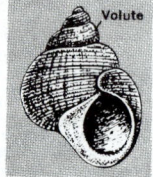

Volute (def. 3)

vom·it (vom′it) *v.i.* **1.** to bring up and eject the contents of the stomach through the mouth. **2.** to be thrown out with force; be ejected violently: *Cinder and ash vomited out of the chimney.* —*v.t.* **1.** to eject from the stomach through the mouth. **2.** to throw out or discharge in large quantities or with force; spew: *The volcano vomited forth lava.* —*n.* that which is vomited from the stomach. [Latin *vomitus*, past participle of *vomere* to throw up.]

von (von; *German* fôn) *prep. German.* from; of. ▲ used in German and Austrian names, esp. of the nobility.

voo·doo (vōō′dōō) *pl.* **-doos.** *n.* **1.** set of mysterious religious rites of West African origin, characterized by a belief in sorcery and the power of charms, practiced in the West Indies. **2.** one who practices these rites. **3.** charm, fetish, or other characteristic of these rites. —*adj.* of or relating to voodoo. —*v.t.*, **-dooed, -doo·ing.** to curse or hex according to voodoo; cast a spell upon. [Of West African origin.]

voo·doo·ism (vōō′dōō iz′əm) *n.* **1.** beliefs and practices of voodoo. **2.** belief in voodoo. —**voo′doo·ist,** *n.* —**voo′doo·is′tic,** *adj.*

vo·ra·cious (vô rā′shəs, və-) *adj.* **1.** eating or desirous of eating large amounts of food; ravenous: *a voracious beast, a voracious appetite.* **2.** eager or immoderate in some activity; insatiable: *a voracious reader.* [Latin *vorāci-,* stem of *vorāx* ravenous + -OUS.] —**vo·ra′cious·ly,** *adv.* —**vo·ra′cious·ness, vo·rac·i·ty** (vô ras′ə tē, və-), *n.*

vor·tex (vôr′teks) *pl.* **-tex·es** or **-ti·ces** (-tə sēz′). *n.* **1.** whirling mass, as of water or air, moving in a circular fashion and having a central depression or hole into which nearby objects are sucked; whirlpool or whirlwind. **2.** state, activity, or situation into which persons or things are irresistibly and steadily drawn: *He was caught in the vortex of company politics.* [Latin *vortex* whirlpool, whirlwind.]

vor·ti·cel·la (vôr′tə sel′ə) *pl.* **-cel·lae** (-sel′ē). *n.* any of a group of bell-shaped protozoa, genus *Vorticella,* having a ring of cilia around the mouth and a stalk with which it attaches itself to objects under water. [Modern Latin *Vorticella,* from Latin *vortex* whirlpool, whirlwind.]

vo·ta·ry (vō′tər ē) *pl.* **-ries.** *n.* **1.** one bound by a vow or vows, esp. a monk, nun, or other person in religious life. **2.** one who is devoted to a particular pastime, study, or activity; devotee. Also, **vo′ta·rist.**

vote (vōt) *n.* **1.** formal expression of a wish, choice, or preference in some matter to be decided: *Each state has two votes in the Senate.* **2.** means by which such a choice is expressed: *a voice vote.* **3.** choice or decision so made: *The vote was against him.* **4.** right or privilege of expressing such a choice; suffrage: *The nineteenth amendment gave women the vote.* **5.** number of votes cast: *a light vote.* **6.** votes collectively: *The vote is in, but has to be tabulated.* **7.** group of people casting similar votes, considered as an entity: *The urban vote won the election for him.* **8.** *Archaic.* voter. —*v.i.*, **vot·ed, vot·ing.** to express one's opinion or choice by a vote; cast a vote: *He has voted in every election since 1900.* —*v.t.* **1.** to support or choose by a vote; cast a vote for: *He always voted a straight party ticket.* **2.** to enact, allow, or establish by a vote: *to vote the necessary funds for a project.* **3.** to declare by general consent: *The critics voted the show a success.* **4. to vote down.** to defeat by voting. **5. to vote in.** to choose by voting for; elect. [Latin *vōtum* vow, wish. Doublet of VOW.] —**vot′er,** *n.*

voting machine, machine that mechanically registers and counts the votes cast on it.

vo·tive (vō′tiv) *adj.* given, offered, or performed because of or in fulfillment of a vow. [Latin *vōtīvus* relating to a vow, from *vōtum* vow.]

vouch (vouch) *v.i.* **1.** to give one's personal assurance; assume responsibility (with *for*): *I'll vouch for her character.* **2.** to serve as evidence or assurance of; assure the truth or validity of (with *for*). —*v.t.* to guarantee or affirm. [Old French *voucher* to summon, claim, from Latin *vocāre* to call.]

vouch·er (vou′chər) *n.* **1.** document serving as proof of payment or as verification of the accuracy of an account, as a canceled check or receipt. **2.** one who vouches.

vouch·safe (vouch sāf′) **-safed, -saf·ing.** *v.t.* to be kind enough to grant; condescend to give. [Originally, *vouch safe* to warrant as safe, guarantee. See VOUCH, SAFE.]

vous·soir (vōō swär′) *n.* one of the wedge-shaped sections that forms part of an arch or vault. [French *voussoir,* going back to *volvere* to roll.]

vow (vou) *n.* **1.** solemn promise or pledge, esp. to behave or live one's life in a specified way: *marriage vows.* **2.** solemn promise made to God or a deity, esp to perform some worthwhile act for a spiritual purpose. **3.** solemn declaration or affirmation: *a vow of appreciation.* **4. to take**

vows. to enter a religious order. —*v.t.* **1.** to promise solemnly. **2.** to pledge or resolve to do, give, or inflict: *to vow fidelity.* **3.** to declare earnestly or solemnly; affirm. **4.** to make a vow. [Old French *veu* solemn promise made to a deity, from Latin *vōtum.* Doublet of VOTE.] —**Syn.** *v.t.* **1.** see **promise.**

vow·el (vou′əl) *n.* **1.** open speech sound produced by the voice and forming a syllable by itself or part of a syllable. Distinguished from **consonant.** **2.** letter of the alphabet that represents such a sound, as *a, e, i, o, u* and sometimes *y.* —*adj.* of or relating to a vowel or vowels. [Old French *voiel(le)* the open speech sound, from Latin *vōcālis (littera)* sounding (letter). Doublet of VOCAL.]

vox po·pu·li (voks′ pop′yə lī′) *Latin.* the voice of the people.

voy·age (voi′ij) *n.* **1.** journey or passage by water, usually one over the sea or other large body of water. **2.** any long journey: *a voyage to the moon.* **3.** *usually,* **voyages.** book or account of one or more sea journeys. [Old French *voiage* way, pilgrimage, military expedition, from Latin *viāticum* provisions or money for a journey. Doublet of VIATICUM.] —**voy′a·ger,** *n.* —**Syn.** **1.** see **journey.**

vo·ya·geur (vwä′yä zhœr′, voi′ə-) *pl.* **-geurs** (-zhœrz′, -zhœr′). *n.* formerly, one employed by fur companies to transport men and goods to and from remote stations in the wilderness of Canada, esp. during the seventeenth century. [French *voyageur* traveler, from: *voyager* to travel, from *voyage* journey, from Old French *voiage.* See VOYAGE.]

vo·yeur (vwä yœr′, voi-) *n.* one who obtains sexual gratification from viewing sexual scenes, acts, or objects. [French *voyeur,* from *voir* to see, from Latin *vidēre.*] —**vo·yeur′ism,** *n.*

V.P., vice-President.

vs. **1.** versus. **2.** verse.

Vt., Vermont.

v.t., transitive verb.

VTOL (vē′tôl) airplane that can take off and land vertically. [Abbreviation of *v(ertical) t(ake)o(ff and) l(anding).*]

Vul·can (vul′kən) *n.* Roman god of fire and later of handicrafts and metalworking. His Greek counterpart is Hephaestus.

vul·can·ite (vul′kə nīt′) *n.* hard, tough rubber that resembles ebony, made by adding a large amount of sulfur to natural rubber, esp. used for combs, toys, and battery cases.

vul·can·ize (vul′kə nīz′) **-ized, -iz·ing.** *v.t.* to treat (natural rubber) with sulfur or other compounds and heat to make it retain its desired properties, as flexibility or hardness, over a wider range of temperatures. [VULCAN + -IZE.] —**vul′can·i·za′tion, vul′can·iz′er,** *n.*

vul·gar (vul′gər) *adj.* **1.** lacking or characterized by a lack of good breeding, refinement, or taste: *a vulgar joke.* **2.** of, relating to, or characteristic of the masses of common people, as distinguished from an educated or privileged elite; common. **3.** expressed in or designating a language used by the common people; vernacular. [Latin *vulgāris* relating to the masses, common, from *vulgus* the masses.] —**vul′-gar·ly,** *adv.* —**vul′gar·ness,** *n.* —**Syn.** **1.** see **coarse.**

vul·gar·i·an (vul gãr′ē ən) *n.* one who is vulgar.

vul·gar·ism (vul′gə riz′əm) *n.* **1.** word, phrase, or expression that is substandard, unrefined, or coarse. **2.** vulgarity.

vul·gar·i·ty (vul gãr′ə tē) *pl.* **-ties.** *n.* **1.** state or quality of being vulgar; lack of good breeding, refinement, or taste. **2.** that which is vulgar, as an offensive action or expression.

vul·gar·ize (vul′gə rīz′) **-ized, -iz·ing.** *v.t.* **1.** to make coarse or crude. **2.** to express (something difficult) in a form that is comprehensible to the common people; popularize.

Vulgar Latin, vernacular form of ancient Latin, the main source of the Romance languages.

Vul·gate (vul′gāt, -git) *n.* the Latin version of the Bible translated by St. Jerome and completed about A.D. 383. The Vulgate is the official Latin text of the Roman Catholic Church and the basis of other translations, esp. the Douay version. [Late Latin *vulgāta (ēditiō)* popular (edition), from Latin *vulgāre* to make common, publish.]

vul·ner·a·ble (vul′nər ə bəl) *adj.* **1.** capable of being physically wounded or damaged: *His knee was his vulnerable spot.* **2.** capable of being wounded emotionally; easily hurt; sensitive. **3.** open to criticism: *a vulnerable argument.* **4.** in contract bridge, having won one game of a rubber and therefore eligible for increased penalties and premiums. [Late Latin *vulnerābilis* wounding, going back to *vulnus* wound.] —**vul′ner·a·bil′i·ty,** *n.* —**vul′ner·a·bly,** *adv.*

vul·pine (vul′pīn′, -pin) *adj.* of, relating to, or resembling a fox. [Latin *vulpīnus,* from *vulpēs* fox.]

vul·ture (vul′chər) *n.* **1.** any of two groups of birds, the family Cathardidae, living in America, and the family Accipitridae, of Africa, Europe, and Asia, having dark, dull plumage and a naked head and neck, and feeding chiefly on dead game. **2.** greedy, predatory, or ruthless person. [Latin *vultur.*]

vul·va (vul′və) *pl.* **-vae** (-vē) or **-vas.** *n.* the external parts of the female genital organs. [Latin *vulva* womb.]

vy·ing (vī′ing) present participle of **vie.**

w, W (dub′əl yōō′) *pl.,* **w's, W's.** *n.* **1.** twenty-third letter of the English alphabet. **2.** shape of this letter or something having such a shape.

w, watt; watts.

W **1.** tungsten. [German *Wolfram.* See WOLFRAM.] **2.** west.

w. **1.** week. **2.** width. **3.** weight. **4.** wife. **5.** wide.

W. **1.** Wednesday. **2.** Wales. **3.** Welsh.

WAAC, Women's Army Auxiliary Corps.

wab·ble (wob′əl) -bled, -bling. *v.t., v.i.* to wobble. —*n.* wobble. —**wab′bler,** *n.*

wab·bly (wob′lē) wobbly.

Wac (wak) *n.* member of the Women's Army Corps.

WAC, Women's Army Corps.

wack·y (wak′ē) wack·i·er, wack·i·est. *also,* **whack·y** *adj. Slang.* absurd, eccentric, or outlandish.

Wa·co (wā′kō) *n.* city in east-central Texas. Pop. (1970), 95,326.

wad (wod) *n.* **1.** small, compact mass or lump of any soft or flexible material: *a wad of cotton, a wad of chewing gum, a wad of paper.* **2.a.** *Informal.* tightly rolled bundle of paper money. **b.** large amount of money. **3.a.** round plug, as of cloth or paper, used to hold a charge of powder in place in a muzzle-loading gun. **b.** disk, as of felt or cardboard, used to hold powder and shot in place in a shotgun cartridge. **4.** wadding (*def. 1*). —*v.t.* **wad·ded, wad·ding. 1.** to roll, press, or pack into a wad. **2.** to stuff, pad, or pack with wadding. **3.** to hold (a shot, powder, or charge) in place with a wad. [Of uncertain origin.]

wad·ding (wod′ing) *n.* **1.** soft, fibrous material used for stuffing, padding, or packing. **2.** soft, flexible material used for making wads, as for guns. **3.** wads collectively.

wad·dle (wod′əl) -dled, -dling. *v.i.* to walk or move with short steps, swaying the body from one side to the other. —*n.* awkward swaying or rocking walk. [WADE + -LE.] —**wad′dler,** *n.*

wade (wād) **wad·ed, wad·ing.** *v.i.* **1.** to walk in or through water, mud, or any other substance that impedes free motion. **2.** to move, proceed, or make one's way slowly and with difficulty: *We had to wade through all the papers on his desk before we found the receipt.* **3. to wade in** (or **into).** *Informal.* to attack, approach, or begin vigorously and energetically. —*v.t.* to walk through or cross by wading: *to wade a brook.* —*n.* act of wading. [Old English *wadan* to go, walk through water.]

wad·er (wā′dər) *n.* **1.** one who wades. **2.** any of various long-legged birds that wade about in shallow water, searching for food, as the crane, heron, or stork. **3. waders.** high, waterproof boots or a pair of pants having such boots for legs, worn esp. by fishermen.

wa·di (wä′dē) *pl.* **-dis.** *n.* **1.** ravine or stream bed in the deserts of Africa or Asia, through which a stream flows after a rainfall. **2.** stream flowing through such a ravine or stream bed. [Arabic *wādī* stream bed.]

wa·dy (wä′dē) *pl.* **-dies.** *n.* wadi.

Waf (waf) *n.* member of the Women's Air Force.

WAF, Women's Air Force.

wa·fer (wā′fər) *n.* **1.** thin, crisp cookie or cracker, often sweetened and flavored. **2.** thin disk of unleavened bread administered as Holy Communion in the Roman Catholic and other churches. **3.** any thin disk, as of chocolate. **4.** small, thin disk, as of dried paste or adhesive paper, used for sealing letters, fastening documents, or the like. [Anglo-Norman *wafre* thin honeycomb, thin small cake; of Germanic origin; referring to the resemblance of such cakes to a honeycomb.]

waf·fle (wof′əl) *n.* crisp batter cake patterned with square-shaped indentations, usually cooked in a waffle iron. [Dutch *wafel* wafer. See WAFER.]

waffle iron, cooking utensil consisting of two hinged metal griddles having square-shaped projections, used to make waffles.

Waffle iron

waft (waft, wäft) *v.i.* to float or be conveyed, as on the wind: *The smell of freshly brewed coffee wafted through the door.* —*v.t.* to carry or convey lightly and gently through the air or over water. —*n.* **1.** light breeze; current of air. **2.** something, as an odor or sound, carried through the air. **3.** act of wafting. [From obsolete *wafter* convoy vessel, from Dutch *wachter* a guard.]

wag[1] (wag) **wagged, wag·ging.** *v.t.* **1.** to cause to move rapidly and repeatedly up and down or from side to side: *Our dog always wags his tail when he sees us.* **2.** to move (the tongue) constantly, esp. in idle chatter or gossip: *excellent persons both, and as thorough gossips as ever wagged a tongue* (Scott, 1820). —*v.i.* **1.** to move rapidly and repeatedly up and down or from side to side. **2.** (of the tongue) to be moving constantly, esp. in idle chatter or gossip. —*n.* act of wagging; wagging motion. [Middle English *waggen* to move, shake, sway, going back to Old English *wagian* to sway, totter.]

wag[2] (wag) *n.* one who is fond of or given to joking or jesting; habitual joker. [Of uncertain origin.]

wage (wāj) *n.* **1.** *usually,* **wages.** payment for work done or services rendered, esp. calculated on an hourly, daily, or piecework basis. **2. wages.** something given in return; reward; recompense: *the wages of war.* ▲ construed as singular or plural in def. 2. —*v.t.,* **waged, wag·ing.** to carry on or engage in, as a war, battle, or contest. [Dialectal Old French *wage* pledge, pay; of Germanic origin.] —**Syn.** *n.* **1.** see **pay**[1].

wage earner, one who works for wages.

wa·ger (wā′jər) *n.* **1.** agreement or pledge that one will pay money or some other specified thing if the outcome of an event is not as one predicts or if something one has said is proved untrue; bet. **2.** something pledged or bet. —*v.t.* to pledge or risk (money or some other specified thing) in a wager; bet. —*v.i.* to make a wager; bet. [Anglo-Norman *wageure* pledge, stake, from dialectal Old French *wagier* to pledge, from *wage.* See WAGE.] —**wa′ger·er,** *n.*

wage scale. 1. scale of wages paid to workers performing related tasks within an industry, factory, or company. **2.** scale of wages paid by a particular employer.

wage-work·er (wāj′wur′kər) *n.* one who works for wages.

wag·ger·y (wag′ər ē) *pl.* **-ger·ies.** *n.* **1.** mischievous merrymaking or jocularity. **2.** jest or joke.

wag·gish (wag′ish) *adj.* **1.** fond of playing jokes; playfully mischievous. **2.** of, relating to, or characteristic of a wag or waggery: *a mischievous young boy with a waggish sense of humor.* —**wag′gish·ly,** *adv.* —**wag′gish·ness,** *n.*

wag·gle (wag′əl) -gled, -gling. *v.t., v.i.* to move or cause to move rapidly and repeatedly up and down or from side to side; wag. —*n.* act of waggling; waggling motion. [WAG + -LE.]

Wag·ner, Richard 1813–83, German composer.

wag·on (wag′ən) *also, British,* **wag·gon.** *n.* **1.** any of various covered or open four-wheeled vehicles, usually drawn by a horse or horses, used esp. for carrying heavy loads. **2.** child's low, rectangular, four-wheeled toy vehicle. **3.** station wagon. **4.** patrol wagon. **5.** *British.* railroad freight car. **6. on the wagon.** no longer drinking alcoholic beverages. **7. to fix (someone's) wagon.** *Slang.* to get revenge on. [Dutch *wagen* wheeled vehicle for carrying heavy loads.]

wag·on·er (wag′ə nər) *n.* one who drives a wagon, esp. as an occupation.

wag·on·ette (wag′ə net′) *n.* four-wheeled carriage with one or two transverse seats in front and two seats running lengthwise and facing each other in the rear.

wag·on·load (wag′ən lōd′) *n.* amount that a wagon carries.

wagon train, line or group of covered wagons traveling together.

wag·tail (wag′tāl′) *n.* any of various small birds, family Motacillidae, usually having a long narrow tail that is habitually wagged up and down.

---

at; āpe; cär; end; mē; it; īce; hot; ōld; fôrk; wood; fōōl; oil; out; up; ūse; turn; sing; thin; this; zh in treasure; ə in ago, taken, pencil, lemon, circus.

wa·hoo (wä'hōō, wä hōō') *pl.*, **-hoos.** *n.* shrub or tree, *Euonymus atropurpureus*, found in eastern North America, having finely toothed leaves that turn a colorful scarlet in the fall. [Dakota *wáhu* arrowwood.]

waif (wāf) *n.* **1.** person having no home, family, or friends, esp. a lost child. **2.** anything that has no apparent owner or home, as a stray animal. [Anglo-Norman *waif* a thing lost and not claimed; probably of Scandinavian origin.]

Wai·ki·ki (wī'kē kē', wī'kē kē') *n.* beach and recreation area in Honolulu, Hawaii.

wail (wāl) *v.i.* **1.** to make a prolonged, mournful sound, esp. as an expression of grief or pain. **2.** to make a sound resembling this, as the wind. —*v.t.* to grieve over; lament; bewail. —*n.* **1.** prolonged, mournful sound, usually expressive of grief or pain. **2.** any sound resembling this. [Of Scandinavian origin.] —**wail'er,** *n.*

Wailing Wall, wall in Jerusalem believed to be the last remaining wall of the temple of Solomon, which was destroyed in A.D. 70. Jews traditionally gather there for prayers and lamentation.

wain (wān) *n. Archaic.* wagon. [Old English *wægen.*]

wain·scot (wān'skət, -skot) *n.* **1.** lining for interior walls, usually paneled and of wood. **2.** lower portion of an interior wall when it is finished differently from the upper portion. —*v.t.,* **-scot·ed, -scot·ing;** *also, British,* **-scot·ted, -scot·ting.** to line or panel with wainscot. [Partial translation of Middle Dutch *wagenschot* lining of wood for walls; possibly, literally, timber for wagons or wains, from *wagen* wagon + *schot* planking.]

wain·scot·ing (wān'skō'ting) *n.* **1.a.** wainscot. **b.** wainscots collectively. **2.** material used for a wainscot.

wain·wright (wān'rīt') *n.* one who makes and repairs wagons.

waist (wāst) *n.* **1.** part of the human body between the ribs and the hips. **2.** waistline *(def. 1).* **3.** garment or part of a garment that covers the body from the shoulders to the waistline. **4.** middle part of anything, esp. when it is narrower than the rest. **5.** section of a ship between the quarter-deck and the forecastle. **6.** middle section of an airplane. [Probably from an unrecorded Old English word.]

waist·band (wāst'band') *n.* band of material that encircles the waist, esp. one that is attached to the top of a skirt or trousers.

waist·cloth (wāst'klôth') *n.* loincloth.

waist·coat (wes'kət, wāst'kōt') *n.* **1.** vest. **2.** close-fitting garment, usually sleeveless, formerly worn by men under a doublet.

waist·line (wāst'līn') *n.* **1.** imaginary line encircling the narrowest part of the waist. **2.** part of a garment that encircles this or falls just above or below it.

wait (wāt) *v.i.* **1.** to remain inactive or in a place in anticipation of something expected (often with *for*): *Wait until you hear from me before leaving. I had to wait for the train this morning.* **2.** to look forward to something (often with *for*): *She waited for the day when he would be well again.* **3.** to remain temporarily undone, neglected, or delayed: *Her trip will have to wait until the job is finished.* **4.** to perform the duties of a waiter, waitress, or the like: *to wait at table.* **5. to wait on** (or **upon**) **a.** to act as a waiter, waitress, or the like to. **b.** to visit or call upon formally. **c.** to be a result or consequence of; depend upon: *Our plans will wait on your decision.* **6. to wait up.** to postpone going to bed in anticipation of the arrival of someone or something (often with *for*): *I'll wait up for you tonight.* —*v.t.* **1.** to remain inactive or in a place in anticipation of (something): *to wait one's turn.* **2.** *Informal.* (of a meal) to put off; delay: *We cannot wait dinner after 8:00.* —*n.* **1.** act of waiting. **2.** period of waiting: *There will be a two-hour wait before the next plane.* **3.** *British.* member of a group of musicians and singers who perform in the streets, esp. at Christmas time. **4. to lie in wait.** to remain in hiding in order to attack. [Dialectal Old French *waitier* to watch; of Germanic origin.]

wait·er (wā'tər) *n.* **1.** man whose job is serving food and drink, as in a restaurant. **2.** person who waits. **3.** small tray, used esp. for carrying dishes.

wait·ing (wā'ting) *n.* **1.** act of one who waits in anticipation of something expected. **2. in waiting.** in attendance on a sovereign or other member of a royal family.

waiting game, stratagem in which action or movement is delayed until a more favorable time.

waiting list, list of the names of people who are waiting for something: *There is a long waiting list for apartments in this building.*

waiting room, room or area provided for the use of people who are waiting, as at an airport or doctor's office.

wait·ress (wā'tris) *n.* woman whose job is serving food and drink, as in a restaurant.

waive (wāv) *v.t.,* **waived, waiv·ing.** **1.** to relinquish or give up voluntarily, as a claim, right, or privilege. **2.** to refrain from insisting upon or taking advantage of. **3.** to put aside for the present; defer: *to waive a question.* [Anglo-Norman *weyver* to abandon; probably of Scandinavian origin.]

waiv·er (wā'vər) *n.* **1.** voluntary relinquishment or giving up of something, as a legal right. **2.** document evidencing such relinquishment. [Anglo-Norman *weyver,* noun use of infinitive *weyver* to abandon. See WAIVE.]

wake¹ (wāk) **waked** or **woke, waked** or *(archaic)* **wo·ken, wak·ing.** *v.i.* **1.** to be roused from sleep; cease to sleep (often with *up*): *He woke up at the sound of the alarm.* **2.** to become aware, alert, or active: *He suddenly woke to the beauty around him.* **3.** to be or remain awake; refrain from sleeping. **4.** *Archaic.* to keep watch or vigil, esp. over a corpse. —*v.t.* **1.** to rouse from sleep: *Be quiet or you'll wake the baby.* **2.** to make active; stir up; arouse: *This woke rivalry and dissension among the other nobles* (Green, 1879). **3.** *Archaic.* to keep watch over something, esp. a corpse. —*n.* watch or vigil over the body of a dead person before burial. [Partly from Old English *wacian* to be awake; partly from Old English *wacan* to be born, arise.]

wake² (wāk) *n.* **1.** track left by a boat, ship, or other object moving through water. **2.** track or path left by anything that has passed: *the wake of a storm.* **3. in the wake of. a.** following close behind. **b.** as a result or consequence of. [Of Scandinavian origin.]

wake·ful (wāk'fəl) *adj.* **1.** unable to sleep. **2.** characterized by absence of sleep: *The sick child spent a wakeful night.* **3.** watchful; vigilant. —**wake'ful·ness,** *n.*

Wake Island (wāk) atoll in the Pacific, west of Hawaii, administered by the United States. Area, 3 sq. mi. Pop. (1969), 1000.

wak·en (wā'kən) *v.t.* **1.** to rouse from sleep; wake. **2.** to stir up; arouse: *His book wakened new interest in the subject.* —*v.i.* to be roused from sleep; cease to sleep: *He awakened when the alarm sounded.* [Old English *waecnan* to arise, be born.]

wake·rob·in (wāk'rob'in) *n.* trillium. [Of uncertain origin.]

Wal·den·ses (wol den'sēz) *n.,pl.* Christian sect founded in the twelfth century in Lyon, France, that joined the Reformation movement in the sixteenth century and exists today primarily in Piedmont, Italy.

wale (wāl) *n.* **1.** one of a series of parallel ridges or ribs on the surface of certain fabrics, as corduroy. **2.** texture or weave of a fabric having such ridges or ribs. **3.** one of several strakes fastened horizontally to the sides of a boat or ship, esp. a wooden ship. **4.** welt *(def. 3).* —*v.t.,* **waled, wal·ing. 1.** to raise a wale or wales on, as by flogging. **2.** to weave with wales. [Old English *walu* ridge, welt.]

Wales (wālz) *n.* division of the United Kingdom, west of and bordering England. Area, 8017 sq. mi. Pop. (1962), 2,645,000.

walk (wôk) *v.i.* **1.a.** to move or proceed by placing one foot on the ground before lifting the other. **b.** (of quadrupeds) to move or proceed by placing two feet on the ground before lifting either or both of the other two. **2.** to move or travel on foot for exercise or for pleasure. **3.** (of inanimate objects) to move in a manner suggestive of walking. **4.** to behave or live in a particular manner: *to walk in peace.* **5.** to appear in visible form and move about, as a ghost. **6.** *Baseball.* (of a batter) to go to first base as a result of having been pitched four balls. **7.** *Basketball.* to move more than two steps while in possession of the ball. **8. to walk away from.** to survive (an accident) with little or no injury. **9. to walk off. a.** to leave unexpectedly, esp. in anger. **b.** to get rid of by walking: *to walk off a headache.* **10. to walk off with. a.** to win, as a prize. **b.** to steal. **11. to walk out.** *Informal.* to go on strike: *The workers threatened to walk out on Monday morning.* **12. to walk out on.** *Informal.* to abandon; desert. —*v.t.* **1.** to move through, over, or across on foot. **2.** to accompany on foot: *I'll walk you to the door.* **3.** to make or help to walk. **4.** to lead, ride, or drive at a slow gait or pace: *to walk a horse uphill.* **5.** to bring to a specified condition by walking: *She walked me to exhaustion.* **6.** to measure or survey by going over on foot; pace (often with *off*): *to walk off three feet.* **7.** to cause to move in a manner suggestive of walking. **8.** *Baseball.* (of a pitcher) to allow (a batter) to advance to first base by pitching four balls. —*n.* **1.** act of walking, esp. for pleasure or exercise. **2.** distance to be walked, often measured in the time required: *It is only a two-minute walk from here.* **3.** manner of walking; characteristic gait. **4.** place specially prepared or set apart for walking: *The walk was covered with leaves.* **5.** particular social position; sphere of activity, profession, or occupation: *People from all walks of life came to hear him speak.* **6.** *Baseball.* act or fact of allowing a batter to advance to first base by pitching four balls. **7.** piece of ground, usually enclosed, that is set aside for the pasture and exercise of domestic animals. [Old English *wealcan* to roll, toss, move about.]
—**Syn.** *v.i.* **2.** Walk, saunter, stroll mean to move on foot. Walk is the general term to suggest moving at a moderate pace, preferred when indicating purpose either in manner or direction: *I walk to my office every day.* Saunter suggests a slow, desultory pace, esp. one characterized by an ambling gait and a leisurely, carefree manner: *She awoke early and sauntered down to the beach.* Stroll is marked by an element of elegant formality as well as a leisurely pace, and is often used in an urban context: *We strolled along the promenade, stopping to window-shop and chat with friends along the way.*

at; āpe; cär; end; mē; it; īce; hot; ōld; fôrk; wood; fōōl; oil; out; up; ūse; turn; sing; thin; this; zh in treasure; ə in ago, taken, pencil, lemon, circus.

walk·a·way (wô′kə wā′) *n. Informal.* contest that is easily won; easy victory. Also, **walk′o′ver.**

walk·er (wô′kər) *n.* **1.** one who walks. **2.** something used as an aid in walking, esp. an enclosed metal framework on wheels.

walk·ie-talk·ie (wô′kē tô′kē) *pl.,* **-talk·ies.** *also,* **walk·y-talk·y.** compact, portable, two-way radio, used esp. to coordinate infantry, police, or firefighting operations.

walking papers *Informal.* official notice of dismissal, esp. from a job.

walking stick **1.** stick carried in the hand, esp. as an aid in walking. **2.** any of a group of brown or green insects, order Phasmida, related to the grasshopper, found in tropical regions, having long legs and a slender body that resembles a stick or twig.

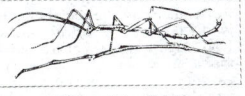
Walking stick (def. 2)

walk-on (wôk′ôn′, -ôn′) *n.* **1.** very small part in a theatrical presentation. **2.** actor or actress playing such a part.

walk-out (wôk′out′) *n. Informal.* strike of workers.

walk-o·ver (wôk′ō′vər) *n. Informal.* walkaway.

walk-up (wôk′up′) *n.* **1.** apartment or office above the first floor in a building having no elevator. **2.** apartment house or building having no elevator.

walk·way (wôk′wā′) *n.* place or passage specially prepared or set apart for walking.

walk·y-talk·y (wô′kē tô′kē) walkie-talkie.

wall (wôl) *n.* **1.** upright structure of stone, plaster, wood, brick, or similar material used to enclose, divide, or protect an area, esp. such a structure serving as the interior surface of a room or building. **2.** interior surface or side of something, as a bodily part; lining: *the wall of the large intestine.* **3.** something resembling a wall in appearance or function: *a wall of people. She sensed a wall of hostility between them.* **4.** *also,* **walls.** fortified barrier; fortification. **5.** **to drive (or push) to the wall.** to place in a desperate condition or position. **6.** **to go to the wall.** to be forced to give way or yield. —*v.t.* to enclose, divide, protect, or obstruct with or as with a wall or walls (often with *up* or *in*). [Old English *weall* rampart, side or vertical division of a building, from Latin *vallum* rampart.]

wal·la·by (wol′ə bē) *pl.,* **-bies** or **-by.** *n.* any of various marsupials, family Macropodidae, native to Australia, New Zealand, and a few nearby islands, closely related to and resembling kangaroos, but usually smaller. Height: 1–4 feet. [Australian native name *wolabā*.]

Wallaby

Wal·lace (wol′is, wô′lis) **1. Alfred R.** 1823–1913, English naturalist. **2. Henry A·gard** (ā′gärd). 1888–1965, U.S. political leader. **3. Lew** (loō). 1827–1905, U.S. author, diplomat, and soldier.

wal·la·roo (wol′ə roō′) *pl.,* **-roos** or **-roo.** *n.* Australian kangaroo, *Macropus robustus,* found chiefly in coastal mountains and rocky inland ranges. [Australian native name *wolarū*.]

wall·board (wôl′bôrd′) *n.* building material made of wood pulp, gypsum, or similar substance pressed into large sheets, used as a substitute for wood or plaster in covering walls or ceilings.

Wal·len·stein, Al·brecht von (wol′ən stīn′; *German* vä′lən-shtīn′; äl′breKHt) 1583–1634, Austrian general during the Thirty Years' War.

wal·let (wol′it, wô′lit) *n.* flat folding case, usually of leather, used for holding paper money, cards, photographs, and the like. [Of uncertain origin.]

wall·eye (wôl′ī′) *n.* **1.** strabismus in which one or both eyes turn outward away from the nose. **2.** eye whose cornea is opaque or whose iris has little or no color. **3.** large staring eye, as of certain fish. **4.** freshwater food and game fish, *Stizostedion vitreum,* found in lakes and streams of eastern North America, having large, staring eyes. Length: to 3 feet. Also (*def. 4*), **walleyed pike.** [From WALLEYED.]

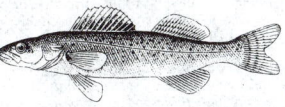
Walleye (def. 4)

wall·eyed (wôl′īd′) *adj.* having or affected with walleyes. [Old Norse *vagleygr* having speckled eyes, from *vagl* wooden beam, blemish in the eye + *auga* eye.]

wall·flow·er (wôl′flou′ər) *n.* **1.** *Informal.* person, esp. a woman, who does not take part in or remains alone at a dance or party, usually because of shyness or lack of a partner. **2.** hardy plant, *Cheiranthus*

cheiri, found in central Europe, bearing dense clusters of fragrant yellow or yellowish-brown flowers.

Wal·loon (wo loōn′) *n.* **1.** member of the French-speaking people who live in central and southern Belgium. **2.** language of this people, a dialect of French. —*adj.* of, relating to, or characteristic of the Walloons, their language, or culture.

wal·lop (wol′əp) *Informal. v.t.* **1.** to give a beating to; thrash. **2.** to hit forcefully; smack; sock. **3.** to overcome, as in a contest; defeat easily: *Our team walloped them.* —*n.* **1.** forceful blow. **2.** power or capacity to deliver such a blow: *The champion has tremendous wallop in his left fist.* [Dialectal Old French *waloper* to gallop; of Germanic origin.]

wal·lop·ing (wol′ə ping) *Informal. n.* thorough beating or defeat. —*adj.* amazingly large or powerful; great.

wal·low (wol′ō) *v.i.* **1.** to toss or roll about in something: *The children wallowed in the pile of leaves.* **2.** to take great pleasure; revel (with *in*): *to wallow in sentimentality.* **3.** to have a great amount of something: *He is wallowing in money.* —*n.* **1.** act of wallowing. **2.** place where an animal, as a pig, goes to wallow. [Old English *wealwian* to roll about.]

wall·pa·per (wôl′pā′pər) *n.* decorative paper used as an interior wall covering. —*v.t.* to put wallpaper on the walls of: *to wallpaper the kitchen.*

wall plug, electric outlet in a wall for a plug.

Wall Street **1.** street in New York City, near the southern tip of Manhattan, that is the financial center of the United States. **2.** banks and financiers who control or influence the economy of the United States.

wal·nut (wôl′nut′, -nət) *n.* **1.** any of the sweet, oily, edible nuts of a group of tall trees, genus *Juglans,* esp. the English walnut. **2.** any of the trees that produce these nuts. **3.** wood of the black walnut. [Old English *walhhnutu* literally, foreign nut.]

Wal·pole, Horace, fourth Earl of Oxford (wôl′pōl′, wol′-) 1717–97, English author.

Wal·pur·gis Night (väl poor′gis) *German Legend.* annual witches' Sabbath, held on the night before May 1. [From St. *Walpurgis,* eighth-century English missionary to Germany, whose feast day in Germany is May 1 and who is regarded as a protectress against magic.]

wal·rus (wôl′rəs, wol′-) *pl.,* **-rus·es** or **-rus.** *n.* large aquatic mammal, *Odobenus rosmarus,* native to the Arctic regions, resembling but larger than a seal, having massive shoulders, a thick neck, a pair of long ivory tusks, and a tough, yellowish-brown hide. Length: to 12 feet. [Dutch *walrus* literally, whale′ horse; of Scandinavian origin.]

Walrus

Wal·ton, I·zaak (wôlt′ən; ī′zäk) 1593–1683, English author.

waltz (wôlts) *n.* **1.** dance in ¾ time having an accent on the first beat, performed by couples who whirl and glide across the dance floor. **2.** music for this dance. —*v.i.* **1.** to dance a waltz. **2.** to move breezily and nimbly, as if dancing: *She waltzed out of the room.* —*v.t.* to lead in a waltz; cause to waltz: *He waltzed her about the dance floor.* [German *Walzer,* from *walzen* to roll, dance the waltz.] —**waltz′er,** *n.*

wam·pum (wom′pəm, wôm′-) *n.* **1.** small, polished beads made from shells and strung together or woven into belts, collars, or necklaces, formerly used by certain tribes of North American Indians as money. **2.** *Slang.* money. [Short for Algonquian *wampompeag* literally, white strings (of shell beads).]

wan[1] (won) **wan·ner, wan·nest.** *adj.* **1.** lacking a natural or healthy color; ashen; pale: *a wan complexion.* **2.** indicating illness or weariness; weak: *a wan smile.* [Old English *wann* dark, livid.] —**wan′ly,** *adv.* —**wan′ness,** *n.* —**Syn. 1.** see **pale**[1].

wan[2] (won) *Archaic.* a past tense of **win.**

wand (wond) *n.* **1.** slender rod, esp. a rod used by a conjurer or magician. **2.** short staff used as a symbol of office, command, or authority. [Old Norse *vöndr* rod, switch.]

wan·der (won′dər) *v.i.* **1.** to move or move about aimlessly or without a fixed destination, direction, or purpose; roam: *We wandered all over the countryside.* **2.** to go at a leisurely pace; stroll: *He wandered home.* **3.** to lose one's way or go astray. **4.** to digress or become easily distracted from the matter at hand (often with *off*): *He wandered off the subject.* —*v.t.* to traverse without a fixed destination, direction, or purpose: *They wandered the streets when they ran out of money.* [Old English *wandrian* to move aimlessly about.] —**wan′der·er,** *n.*

Wandering Jew **1.** *Medieval Legend.* Jew who mocked Jesus on His way to Calvary and was condemned to wander the earth until Judgment Day. **2. wandering Jew,** any of several trailing plants, esp. *Tradescantia fluminensis,* a South American plant having small white flowers and

oval leaves that are purple on the undersides and white and green striped above.

wan·der·lust (wonʹdər lustʹ) *n.* strong urge to travel, esp. in a leisurely manner with no fixed destination. [German *Wanderlust,* from *wandern* to wander + *Lust* desire.]

wane (wān) **waned, wan·ing.** *v.i.* **1.** to decrease gradually, as in size, strength, or intensity: *Her love for him waned.* **2.** to decline, as in power, importance, or influence: *A people are waning to decay and ruin* (Hawthorne, 1860). **3.** to draw to a close; approach an end: *The day wanes.* —*n.* **1.** act of waning; gradual decrease or decline. **2.** period or duration of waning. **3. to be in** (or **on**) **the wane.** to be decreasing or declining. [Old English *wanian* to lessen, fade.]

wan·gle (wangʹgəl) **-gled, -gling.** *Informal.* *v.t.* **1.** to bring about or obtain through cleverness, trickery, or deceit; finagle. **2.** to manipulate or change, esp. in order to deceive or defraud. —*v.i.* to resort to trickery or deceit, esp. to further one's own interests. [Possibly a blend of WAGGLE and dialectal English *wankle* unsteady (from Old English *wancol*).]

want (wont, wônt) *v.t.* **1.** to have a desire for; long for; crave: *Helen wants a new dress. He wants to go to Europe.* **2.** to have too little of or be without; lack: *She wants affection. He was not hired because he wanted experience.* **3.** to need; lack; require: *The stew wants seasoning.* —*v.i.* **1.** to be needy or destitute. **2. to want for.** to have need of. —*n.* **1.** deficiency; lack: *a want of money.* **2.** state or condition of being without the necessities of life; destitution. **3.** that which is needed or desired; need. [Old Norse *vanta* to lack.] —**Syn.** *v.t.* **1.** see **lack.** *n.* **1.** see **lack.**

want ad, small advertisement found esp. in a newspaper, usually offering a job.

want·ing (wonʹting, wônʹ-) *adj.* **1.** missing; lacking: *The pliers were wanting.* **2.** not adequate; deficient: *He was wanting in experience.* —*prep.* **1.** not having; without; lacking: *a pot wanting a handle.* **2.** decreased by; minus: *a month wanting two days.*

wan·ton (wontʹən) *adj.* **1.** characterized by or resulting from extreme recklessness, thoughtlessness, or malice: *wanton cruelty, a wanton attack.* **2.** lacking moral restraint; dissolute; licentious: *a wanton woman.* **3.** luxuriant: *a wanton growth of weeds.* **4.** *Archaic.* playful or frolicsome: *a wanton pony.* —*n.* one who behaves or is inclined to behave in a wanton manner. —*v.i.* to act in a wanton manner. —*v.t.* to spend or waste; squander. [Middle English *wantowen* undisciplined, lewd, sportive, going back to Old English *wan-* lacking + *togen,* past participle of *tēon* to pull, educate.] —**wanʹton·ly,** *adv.* —**wanʹton·ness,** *n.*

wap·i·ti (wopʹi tē) *pl.,* **-tis** or **-ti.** *n.* North American deer, *Cervus canadensis.* Also, **elk.** [Algonquian *wapiti* literally, white rump; referring to its white rump and tail.]

war (wôr) *n.* **1.** armed conflict between countries or factions within a country. **2.** any active hostility or contention; fight; conflict. **3.** profession or science of armed conflict. **4. at war.** in a state of open hostility; engaging in war. **5. to go to war.** to start or enter into a war. —*v.i.* **warred, war·ring.** to engage in war; be in armed conflict; fight. —*adj.* of, relating to, or used in war: *a war dance, war rations.* [Dialectal Old French *werre* hostility; armed conflict, from Old High German *werra* discord.]

War Between the States, U.S. Civil War.

war·ble (wôrʹbəl) **-bled, -bling.** *v.i.* **1.** to sing with quavers, trills, or melodic embellishments, as a bird. **2.** to make a melodic, warbling sound: *The quiet voice of waters warbling near* (Southey, 1814). —*v.t.* to sing with quavers, trills, or melodic embellishments: *to warble a tune.* —*n.* act of warbling. [Dialectal Old French *werbler* to quaver with the voice; of Germanic origin.]

war·bler (wôrʹblər) *n.* **1.** one who warbles. **2.** any of various small songbirds, family Sylviidae, which range throughout Eurasia and Africa, typically having a combination of gray or brown and white plumage. Length: 4–7½ inches. **3.** any of various small songbirds, family

Warbler *(def. 2)*

Parulidae, which range from Alaska to Argentina, often having brightly colored plumage with red, blue, or yellow markings. Length: 4–7½ inches.

war bonnet, ceremonial headdress worn by certain North American Indians, esp. the Plains Indians, usually elaborately constructed of eagle feathers, with each feather representing an act of bravery or other honor earned by the wearer.

war crime, any violation of the international laws and customs governing warfare, as ill-treatment of prisoners or civilians or unnecessary plunder or destruction of property.

war cry, 1. loud call or cry shouted in battle, esp. during an attack. **2.** slogan or motto used to rally support in a contest or conflict.

ward (wôrd) *n.* **1.** division of a town or city organized for purposes of local administration. **2.** division of a hospital containing a number of patients. **3.** division of a jail or prison. **4.** one who is under the care or control of a court or guardian. **5.** act of guarding. **6.** state or condition of being under guard. **7.a.** ridge on the inside of a lock serving as an obstacle to the passing and turning of the wrong key. **b.** notch on a key corresponding to this ridge, enabling the key to turn in the lock and operate the bolt. —*v.t.* **1.** to turn back or repel; avert (usually with *off*): *to ward off an attack.* **2.** *Archaic.* to keep watch over. [Old English *weard* a guarding.]

-ward *suffix* in the direction of: *downward, skyward.* [Old English *-weard.*]

war dance, among certain primitive tribes, a ceremonial dance held before going to war or after a victory.

ward·en (wôrʹən) *n.* **1.** one who is employed to care for or guard someone or something, esp. a person in charge of a prison. **2.** public official who exercises supervision over something, as a market or port, or who enforces certain laws, as in a game preserve. **3.** churchwarden. [Dialectal Old French *wardein* guardian, from *warder* to guard; of Germanic origin.]

ward·er (wôrʹdər) *n.* one who guards; watchman.

ward heeler *Slang.* minor politician who does various jobs for a political boss, esp. one who solicits votes during an election.

ward·robe (wôrʹdrōbʹ) *n.* **1.** articles of clothing collectively, as all the clothes belonging to one person, or clothes used in a theatrical production. **2.** piece of furniture or closet for keeping clothes. [Dialectal Old French *warderobe* to keep clothes, from *warder* to guard + *robe* garment; both of Germanic origin.]

ward·room (wôrʹrōōm, -room) *n.* living, eating, and recreational area on a warship for commissioned officers.

-wards *suffix* **-ward.**

ward·ship (wôrdʹship) *n.* **1.** office or position of a guardian; guardianship. **2.** state or condition of being a ward.

ware¹ (wâr) *n.* **wares.** manufactured articles for sale. **2.** specific kind of manufactured article. ▲ used chiefly in compounds: *glassware, tableware.* **3.** pots, vessels, and other objects made of fired clay; pottery: *ceramic ware.* [Old English *waru* goods, merchandise.]

ware² (wâr) *Archaic. adj.* conscious; aware. —*v.t.,* **wared, war·ing.** to guard against; beware of. [Old English *wær* aware, cautious.]

ware·house (wârʹhousʹ) *n.* building where merchandise is stored.

war·fare (wôrʹfârʹ) *n.* act of carrying on or engaging in war; armed conflict. [Middle English *werrefare* military expedition, from *werre* (see WAR) + *fare* a going (from Old English *faru*).]

war·head (wôrʹhedʹ) *n.* foremost portion of a guided or ballistic missile or torpedo, which contains the explosive charge.

war·horse (wôrʹhôrsʹ) *n.* **1.** horse trained for use in battle; charger. **2.** *Informal.* one who is a veteran, as of many battles, struggles, or conflicts.

war·i·ly (wârʹə lē) *adv.* in a cautious manner; cautiously.

war·i·ness (wârʹē nis) *n.* state or quality of being cautious.

war·like (wôrʹlīkʹ) *adj.* **1.** fond of war; easily provoked to war; martial: *a warlike nation.* **2.** threatening war; hostile: *a warlike atmosphere.* **3.** of, relating to, or characteristic of war: *warlike exploits.*

war·lock (wôrʹlokʹ) *n.* male who practices witchcraft; sorcerer; wizard. [Old English *wærloga* faithless person, devil.]

war·lord (wôrʹlôrdʹ) *n.* strong, often tyrannical military leader who controls a territory, usually in opposition to the national government.

warm (wôrm) *adj.* **1.** having a moderate degree of heat; not cold: *a warm bath, a warm room.* **2.** having the sensation of heat; heated: *to be warm from a fever.* **3.** producing or maintaining body heat: *a warm sweater, warm clothing.* **4.** full of affection or enthusiasm; hearty: *warm thanks.* **5.** having a kind, friendly, or compassionate nature: *a warm person.* **6.** easily stirred up; excitable: *a warm temper.* **7.** animated; heated; lively: *a warm debate.* **8.** newly made; fresh: *a warm trail.* **9.** (of colors) suggesting heat or warmth: *Red and yellow are warm colors.* **10.** *Informal.* close to the person or object sought, as in certain children's games. **11.** *Informal.* uncomfortable or disagreeable: *The gossip made things too warm for her.* —*v.t.* **1.** to make warm or comfortably heated: *She warmed the bottle for the baby.* **2.** to make enthusiastic or ardent. **3.** to inspire with affectionate, kindly feelings: *The sight of home warmed their hearts.* —*v.i.* **1.** to become warm. **2.** to become enthusiastic or ardent: *He warmed to the idea.* **3.** to be inspired with affectionate, kindly feelings. [Old English *wearm* moderately hot.] —**warmʹer, warmʹness,** *n.* —**warmʹly,** *adv.*

warm-blood·ed (wôrmʹbludʹid) *adj.* **1.** having blood, as birds or mammals, that remains relatively constant in temperature despite changes in the temperature of the environment. **2.** characterized by great warmth of feeling; ardent. —**warmʹ-bloodʹed·ness,** *n.*

warm-heart·ed (wôrmʹhärʹtid) *adj.* having a kind, friendly, or compassionate nature. —**warmʹ-heartʹed·ly,** *adv.* —**warmʹ-heartʹed·ness,** *n.*

at; āpe; cär; end; mē; it; īce; hot; ōld; fôrk; wood; fōōl; oil; out; up; ūse; turn; sing; thin; this; zh in treasure; ə in ago, taken, pencil, lemon, circus.

warming pan, large, covered, long-handled pan that holds hot coals, used to warm beds.

war·mon·ger (wôr´mung´gər, -mong´-) *n.* one who favors or tries to bring about war. —**war´mon´ger·ing,** *n., adj.*

warmth (wôrmth) *n.* **1.** state or quality of being warm: *the warmth of the sun.* **2.** enthusiasm; heartiness; fervor: *the warmth of the crowd's applause.* **3.** warm effect produced by certain colors, as reds or yellows.

warn (wôrn) *v.t.* **1.** to put (someone) on guard beforehand, as against approaching danger; urge to be careful; caution. **2.** to advise strongly; admonish: *She warned him about eating too much candy.* **3.** to give notice to; make aware of; signal: *He blinked his lights to warn the driver ahead that he was passing.* **4.** to notify (someone) to keep at a distance (usually with *away* or *off*). —*v.i.* to give a warning. [Old English *warnian* to take heed, admonish.] —**warn´er,** *n.*

warn·ing (wôr´ning) *n.* **1.** act, notice, advice, or admonishment given beforehand, as of an approaching danger or an unpleasant consequence. **2.** something that serves to warn: *The sign was a warning to trespassers.* —*adj.* serving to warn: *a warning signal.* —**warn´ing·ly,** *adv.*

War of 1812, war between the United States and Great Britain lasting from 1812 to 1815.

War of Independence, American Revolution.

warp (wôrp) *v.t.* **1.** to bend, curve, or twist out of shape: *The humidity and dampness had warped the books.* **2.** to turn from what is correct or right; twist: *to warp one's judgment.* **3.** to move (a ship) by pulling on a line or cable secured to a fixed object, as a dock or anchor. —*v.i.* to be or become bent, curved, or twisted, as by shrinkage or contraction. —*n.* **1.** state of being bent, curved, or twisted. **2.** threads running lengthwise in a woven fabric. **3.** line or cable used in moving a ship. [Old English *weorpan* to throw.]

war paint **1.** paint applied to the face and other parts of the body by North American Indians before engaging in war. **2.** *Informal.* woman's cosmetics, as lipstick or rouge.

war·path (wôr´path´) *n.* **1.** route taken by an expedition of North American Indians engaged in war. **2. on the warpath. a.** engaged in or preparing for war. **b.** belligerent; hostile.

war·plane (wôr´plān´) *n.* airplane designed and built for use in war.

war·rant (wôr´ənt, wor´-) *n.* **1.** that which sanctions, authorizes, or justifies: *My word is your warrant. There is no warrant for your accusation.* **2.** written document authorizing an officer to detain or seize a person or property or to execute a judgment. **3.** document authorizing the payment or receipt of money. **4.** official certificate of appointment issued to an officer lower in rank than a commissioned officer. —*v.t.* **1.** to approve officially; authorize. **2.** to provide sufficient grounds for; justify: *The facts do not warrant your conclusion.* **3.** to guarantee: *The gallery director warranted the authenticity of the painting.* **4.** to declare with assurance; assert positively: *I warrant she's the one.* [Dialectal Old French *warant* protection; of Germanic origin.]

war·rant·a·ble (wôr´ən·tə bəl, wor´-) *adj.* that can be warranted. —**war´rant·a·ble·ness,** *n.* —**war´rant·a·bly,** *adv.*

war·ran·tee (wôr´ən tē´, wor´-) *n.* one to whom a warranty is made or given.

warrant officer, officer of the armed forces who receives a certificate of appointment rather than a commission and who ranks between a commissioned officer and an enlisted man.

war·ran·tor (wôr´ən tôr´, wor´-) *n.* one who makes or gives a warranty.

war·ran·ty (wôr´ən tē, wor´-) *n., pl.* **-ties.** *n.* **1.** assurance given by a seller to a buyer that his product is as represented or that it will be repaired or replaced if proven defective within a certain period of time; guarantee. **2.** sanction, authority, or justification; warrant. [Dialectal Old French *warantie* guarantee, from *warantir* to guarantee, from *warant.* See WARRANT.]

war·ren (wôr´ən, wor´-) *n.* **1.** place where rabbits are kept and bred. **2.** place where small game is kept. **3.** densely populated place. [Anglo-Norman *warenne* a preserve; probably of Germanic origin.]

War·ren, Earl (wôr´ən, wor´-) 1891–1974, U.S. political figure and chief justice of the U.S. Supreme Court from 1953 to 1969.

war·ri·or (wôr´ē ər, wôr´yər, wor´-) *n.* one who is engaged or experienced in warfare. [Dialectal Old French *werreieor,* from *werreier* to make war, from *werre* to war. See WAR.]

War·saw (wôr´sô) *n.* capital and largest city of Poland, in the east-central part of the country, on the Vistula River. Pop. (1968), 1,273,600.

war·ship (wôr´ship´) *n.* ship designed and built for use in war.

wart (wôrt) *n.* **1.** small, nonmalignant growth on the skin, caused by a virus. **2.** similar growth on a plant. [Old English *wearte* the small growth on the skin.]

wart hog, African wild hog, *Pha-*

Wart hog

cochoerus aethiopicus, having wartlike growths on the sides of its head, two pairs of curved tusks, and a dark, sparse coat consisting of bristles and long, coarse hairs. Height: 23–28 inches at the shoulder.

war·time (wôr´tīm´) *n.* period of war.

wart·y (wôr´tē) **wart·i·er, wart·i·est.** *adj.* **1.** having or covered with warts. **2.** of or resembling warts.

war whoop, loud call or cry shouted in battle, esp. by North American Indians.

War·wick (wôr´ik, wor´-) *n.* city in eastern Rhode Island, a residential suburb of Providence. Pop. (1970), 83,694.

war·y (wâr´ē) **war·i·er, war·i·est.** *adj.* **1.** habitually on the alert; watchful: *a wary man.* **2.** characterized by caution; guarded: *a wary reply, a wary expression.* [WARE² + -Y¹.] —**war´i·ly,** *adv.* —**war´i·ness,** *n.* —Syn. **1.** see cautious.

was (wuz, woz; *unstressed* wəz) first and third person singular, past indicative of **be.** [Old English *wæs.*]

wash (wôsh, wosh) *v.t.* **1.** to make (something) free of dirt, impurities or stains by applying a liquid, esp. water, often with a cleansing agent, as soap or detergent: *to wash one's face, to wash dishes.* **2.** to remove (dirt, impurities, or stains) by applying a liquid, esp. water, often with a cleansing agent. **3.** to overwhelm and carry away by the action of a liquid, as water: *The sailor was washed overboard.* **4.** to wear away or destroy by the action of water; erode (with *away* or *out*): *Rain gradually washed away the hillside. The flood washed out the highway.* **5.** to cover with moisture; wet: *She looks as clear as morning roses washed with dew* (Shakespeare, *Taming of the Shrew*). **6.** to free from defilement, guilt, sin, or corruption; purify. **7.** to cover with a thin coat of a coloring medium or substance, as paint or metal. —*v.i.* **1.** to wash oneself. **2.** to wash clothes. **3.** to undergo washing without damage, as to color or texture: *This new fabric washes well.* **4.** to be carried away or eroded by the action of a liquid, as water. **5.** to sweep over or beat against with a splashing or slapping sound: *We could hear the waves washing on the rocks.* —*n.* **1.** act of washing; being washed. **2.** quantity of articles, as clothes, washed at one time: *She did the wash this morning.* **3.** motion or onward rush of water or the sound made by this. **4.** liquid preparation used or intended for a particular purpose: *He uses a mouth wash every morning.* **5.** disturbance in the water or air caused by a moving ship or airplane. **6.** thin coat of a coloring medium or substance, as paint or metal. **7.** liquid refuse, esp. that which is used as food for pigs; swill. **8.** tract of land intermittently covered with water. **9.** material carried and deposited by the action of water; alluvium. —*adj.* washable. [Old English *wascan, wæscan* to clean with water.]

Wash., Washington.

wash·a·ble (wô´shə bəl, wosh´ə-) *adj.* that can undergo washing without damage, as to color or texture.

wash-and-wear (wôsh´ən wâr´, wosh´ən-) *adj.* of or designating a fabric or garment that requires little or no ironing after washing.

wash·board (wôsh´bôrd´, wosh´-) *n.* implement with a corrugated surface on which clothes are rubbed during washing.

wash·bowl (wôsh´bōl´, wosh´-) *n.* bowl, basin, or sink used to hold water for washing or shaving. Also, **wash´ba´sin, wash´stand´.**

wash·cloth (wôsh´klôth´, wosh´-) *n.* small cloth used for washing one's body or face. Also, **wash´rag´.**

wash·day (wôsh´dā´, wosh´-) *n.* particular day of the week set aside for doing the washing.

washed-out (wôsht´out´, wosht´-) *adj.* **1.** that has faded, as from age or washing. **2.** *Informal.* deprived of strength or energy; exhausted.

washed-up (wôsht´up´, wosht´-) *adj.* **1.** *Slang.* all through, esp. due to failure; finished. **2.** *Informal.* exhausted.

wash·er (wô´shər, wosh´ər) *n.* **1.** one who or that which washes. **2.** any of various appliances for washing, as a washing machine. **3.** flat, perforated disk of metal, rubber, or other material, used between a nut

Washer (def. 3)

and bolt to prevent friction or leakage or to give a larger supporting surface or tighter fit.

wash·er·wom·an (wô´shər woom´ən, wosh´ər-) *pl.* **-wom·en.** *n.* woman who is employed to wash clothes; laundress. Also, **wash´-wom´an.**

wash·ing (wô´shing, wosh´ing) *n.* **1.** act of cleaning with a liquid, esp. water. **2.** quantity of articles, as clothes, washed at one time.

washing machine, appliance for washing clothes and household linen.

washing soda, sodium carbonate (def. 2).

Wash·ing·ton (wô´shing tən, wosh´ing-) *n.* **1. Book·er T.** (book´ər) 1856–1915, U.S. educator. **2. George.** 1732–99, general in the American Revolutionary War, and first president of the United States, from

1789 to 1797. **3. Martha.** 1731–1802, wife of George Washington. **4.** capital of the United States, lying between Maryland and northern Virginia, and coextensive with the District of Columbia. Pop. (1970), 756,510. Also, **Washington, D.C. 5.** state in the northwestern United States, on the Pacific. Capital, Olympia. Area, 68,192 sq. mi. Pop. (1970), 3,409,169. Abbreviation, **Wash. 6. Mount.** highest mountain in New England, in northern New Hampshire.

Wash·ing·to·ni·an (wŏ′shing tō′nē ən, wosh′ing-) *n.* native or inhabitant of the city or state of Washington. —*adj.* of, relating to, or characteristic of the city or state of Washington.

wash·out (wŏsh′out′, wosh′-) *n.* **1.** the carrying away of something, as a roadbed or topsoil, by the action of water. **2.** channel or hole resulting from this. **3.** *Slang.* failure.

wash·rag (wŏsh′rag′, wosh′-) *n.* washcloth.

wash·room (wŏsh′rōōm′, -room′, wosh′-) *n.* building or room having a toilet and washing facilities; lavatory.

wash·stand (wŏsh′stand′, wosh′-) *n.* **1.** piece of furniture, as a table, for holding a basin and pitcher used for washing. **2.** washbowl.

wash·tub (wŏsh′tub′, wosh′-) *n.* large tub used for soaking or washing clothes or household linen.

wash·wom·an (wŏsh′woom′ən, wosh′-) *pl.,* **-wom·en.** *n.* washerwoman.

wash·y (wŏ′shē, wosh′ē) **wash·i·er, wash·i·est.** *adj.* diluted; watery: *washy tea.*

was·n't (wuz′ənt, woz′-) was not.

wasp (wosp) *n.* any of numerous winged insects, superfamilies Vespoidea and Sphecoidea, that have narrow waists and venomous stings.

Wasp

Most wasps are solitary insects, living and working alone, although a few species are social insects and live in colonies. [Old English *wæsp.*]

Wasp (wosp) *n.* one who is a Protestant Caucasian of English or Northern European descent. [Abbreviation of *w(hite) A(nglo-) S(axon) P(rotestant).*]

wasp·ish (wos′pish) *adj.* **1.** of, resembling, or characteristic of a wasp. **2.** quick to take offense; bad-tempered; irascible. —**wasp′ish·ly,** *adv.* —**wasp′ish·ness,** *n.*

wasp waist, very narrow waist.

wasp-waist·ed (wosp′wās′tid) *adj.* having a very narrow waist.

was·sail (wos′əl, -āl, wos′-) *n.* **1.** salutation used when making a toast, usually when toasting someone's health. **2.** alcoholic beverage prepared for a wassail, esp. ale or wine with sugar, spices, or roasted apples added. **3.** festive party where drinks are served and toasts are made. —*v.i.* **1.** to take part in or drink a wassail. **2.** to go from house to house at Christmas singing carols. —*v.t.* to drink to the health of; toast. [Old Norse *ves heill* be healthy.] —**was′sail·er,** *n.*

Was·ser·mann test (wä′sər man) blood test used in the diagnosis of syphilis. Also, **Was′ser·mann.** [From August von *Wassermann,* 1866–1925, German bacteriologist who developed this test.]

wast (wost; *unstressed* wəst) *Archaic.* second person singular past tense of **be.**

wast·age (wās′tij) *n.* **1.** loss by use, wear, decay, erosion, or the like. **2.** that which is lost in this way.

waste (wāst) **wast·ed, wast·ing.** *v.t.* **1.** to use or spend without adequate return; employ carelessly or extravagantly: *to waste an opportunity, to waste one's time by daydreaming. Jimmy wasted his allowance on candy.* **2.** to consume, wear away, or exhaust, esp. by degrees: *The long illness had wasted the old man's strength.* **3.** to destroy; devastate; ruin: *The advancing army wasted everything in its path.* —*v.i.* to lose energy, strength, health, substance, or the like; become weak or feeble (often with *away*): *to waste away from malnutrition.* —*n.* **1.** act of wasting; being wasted, esp. useless, careless, or unnecessary spending, consumption, or the like: *a waste of time. The waste in the company drove it into bankruptcy.* **2.** wild, uninhabited, or desolate place; wilderness. **3.** gradual wearing away. **4.** useless or superfluous material; refuse. **5.** undigested material eliminated from the body. —*adj.* **1.** rejected, eliminated, or thrown away as worthless; having little or no value; useless. **2.** left over after the completion of a process. **3.** uncultivated; uninhabited; desolate. **4.** in a state of desolation and decay; ruined. **5. to lay waste.** to destroy; devastate. [Dialectal Old French *waster* to devastate, going back to Latin *vāstāre* to make empty, devastate.]

waste·bas·ket (wāst′bas′kit) *n.* receptacle used to deposit useless scraps of paper or other refuse.

waste·ful (wāst′fəl) *adj.* given to or characterized by useless, careless, or unnecessary spending, consumption, or the like. —**waste′ful·ly,** *adv.* —**waste′ful·ness,** *n.* —**Syn.** see **extravagant.**

waste·land (wāst′land′) *n.* barren, uninhabited tract of land.

waste·pa·per (wāst′pā′pər) *n.* paper which is no longer considered useful and has been or is to be thrown away.

waste pipe, pipe for carrying away liquid waste, esp. water.

wast·er (wās′tər) *n.* one who or that which wastes, spends, or consumes uselessly, unnecessarily, or carelessly.

wast·ing (wās′ting) *adj.* that gradually lays waste; devastating; destroying: *a wasting illness, a wasting drought.*

wast·rel (wās′trəl) *n.* **1.** wasteful person; spendthrift. **2.** idle, worthless, disreputable person; good-for-nothing.

watch (woch) *v.t.* **1.** to look at (someone or something) attentively: *The little boy watched television all afternoon.* **2.** to keep under surveillance; guard: *Our neighbors watched our house while we were away.* **3.** to take care of; tend: *The shepherd watched his flock. Can you watch the baby for an hour?* —*v.i.* **1.** to look attentively; be closely observant. **2.** to be on the alert; wait expectantly; be vigilant: *She watched for the right moment to make her request.* **3.** to remain awake at night, esp. in order to keep a vigil. **4.** to do duty as a guard or sentinel. **5.** to be a spectator or onlooker. **6. to watch out.** to be on one's guard; be wary or careful. —*n.* **1.** act of watching; close, careful observation. **2.** one or more persons employed to protect or guard someone or something. **3.** period of time during which a guard is on duty: *John volunteered for the ten-to-midnight watch.* **4.** act of remaining awake, esp. for the purpose of caring for someone or something; vigil: *The mother maintained a watch at her sick child's bedside.* **5.** small apparatus for telling time, usually worn on the wrist or carried on the person. [Old English *wæccan* to be or remain awake, keep vigil.] —**watch′er,** *n.* —**Syn.** *v.t.* **1.** see **look.**

watch·band (woch′band′) *n.* band or strap of leather, metal, or the like, used to fasten a watch to the wrist.

watch·dog (woch′dôg′) *n.* **1.** dog kept to guard a house, property, or the like and to give warning of the approach of intruders. **2.** anyone who serves as a vigilant protector or guardian for another or others: *a watchdog of public morality.*

watch fire, fire kept burning during the night as a signal or warning or as protection.

watch·ful (woch′fəl) *adj.* on the alert; vigilant; wary. —**watch′ful·ly,** *adv.* —**watch′ful·ness,** *n.*

watch·mak·er (woch′mā′kər) *n.* one who makes, cleans, and repairs watches. —**watch′mak′ing,** *n.*

watch·man (woch′mən) *pl.,* **-men.** *n.* man employed to guard a building, property, or the like when the owner or tenant is absent, esp. during the night.

watch meeting, religious service held by certain churches on New Year's Eve.

watch night 1. New Year's Eve, observed by certain churches with religious services that last until the arrival of the new year. **2.** watch meeting.

watch pocket, small pocket, usually in a vest or trousers, for carrying a watch.

watch·tow·er (woch′tou′ər) *n.* tower or tall building from which a guard or sentinel keeps watch.

watch·word (woch′wurd′) *n.* **1.** secret word or phrase that identifies the speaker or allows him to pass a guard. **2.** word or phrase considered as embodying a principle or plan of action, as of a political party or organization; slogan.

wa·ter (wô′tər, wot′ər) *n.* **1.** liquid, solid, or gaseous compound found in abundance on the earth in the form of oceans, seas, lakes, rivers, and the polar caps. It is useful as a catalyst for life processes, as a solvent, and as a carrier of heat. Pure water is clear, tasteless, and a poor conductor of electricity, and has a melting point of zero degrees centigrade (32 degrees Fahrenheit) and a boiling point of 100 degrees centigrade (212 degrees Fahrenheit). Formula: H_2O. **2.** this compound in its liquid state, as distinguished from ice, water vapor, and steam. **3.a.** any body of water, as a sea, lake, or river. **b.** *also,* **waters.** water of a mineral spring or a collection of springs, used medicinally for bathing or drinking. **4.** level of the water of a lake, river, or other body; tide: *The lake is at low water.* **5.** any liquid secretion of the body, as tears, saliva, urine, or the like. **6.** any liquid preparation containing water and a gaseous or volatile substance: *ammonia water.* **7.** transparency and luster of a precious stone or pearl that determines its value. **8.** wavy, lustrous sheen on fabric or metal. **9.** additional shares of stock in a company or corporation issued without a corresponding increase of capital. **10. above water.** out of danger, trouble, or difficulty. **11. by water.** traveling by way of a ship or boat. **12. of the first water.** of the best quality or highest degree. **13. to hold water.** to be logical, consistent, or valid: *The lawyer's argument didn't hold water.* —*v.t.* **1.** to put water into or upon, esp. in order to irrigate; moisten or sprinkle with water: *She watered the plants every day. The valley is continually watered by the melting snow from the mountains.* **2.** to furnish a supply of water to, esp. for feeding: *He had to water the livestock twice a day.* **3.** to dilute or weaken with water: *The bartender watered the drinks.* **4.** to make a wavy, lustrous sheen on (fabric or metal): *to water silk.* **5.** to increase the number of shares of (a stock or company) by issuing

at; āpe; cär; end; mē; it; īce; hot; ōld; fôrk; wood; fōōl; out; up; ūse; turn; sing; thin; **this;** zh in treasure; ə in ago, taken, pencil, lemon, circus.

additional shares without a corresponding increase in capital. —*v.i.*
1. to get or take in water as a supply or in drinking: *The ship put into port to water. The cattle watered at the river.* **2.** to secrete, gather, or emit water from the body, as in the form of tears or saliva: *The smoke made their eyes water. His mouth watered at the thought of dinner.* [Old English *wæter* the liquid forming oceans, seas, rivers, lakes, and rain.] —**wa'ter·er,** *n.*

water beetle, any of several beetles, as the whirligig beetle, adapted for swimming on the surface of the water.

water bird, any bird living on or near the water; swimming or wading bird.

wa·ter-borne (wô'tər bôrn', wot'ər-) *adj.* **1.** supported or conveyed on or by water; floating. **2.** conveyed by ship or by boat.

water bottle, closed container made of glass, rubber, or other similar material, used for holding water.

wa·ter-buck (wô'tər buk', wot'ər-) *n.* any of several antelopes, genus *Kobus,* native to southeastern Africa, that frequent rivers or marshes, having a coat of long, coarse hair that may range from yellowish-brown to nearly black. Height: 4 feet at the shoulder. [Dutch *waterbok.*]

water buffalo, black, Asian buffalo, *Bubalus bubalis,* having long horns that curve backward, widely domesticated for its hide and milk, and often used as a beast of burden. Height: to 6 feet at the shoulder.

water bug 1. common cockroach, *Blatta orientalis,* often found in or near sinks, drains, and other damp places. **2.** any of various insects that live on or near water.

Wa·ter-bur·y (wô'tər ber'ē, wot'ər-) *n.* city in western Connecticut. Pop. (1970), 108,033.

water chestnut 1. edible fruit or corm of any of various aquatic plants, esp. the **Chinese water chestnut,** *Eleocharis dulcis,* the corm of which has a nutlike taste and is widely used in Oriental cooking. **2.** the plant itself.

water clock, device for measuring time by the flow of water from a small opening in a calibrated vessel. Also, **clep'sy·dra.**

water closet, toilet *(defs. 1, 2).*

wa·ter-col·or (wô'tər kul'ər, wot'ər-) *adj.* of, relating to, or made with water colors.

water color 1. paint made by mixing pigment with water. **2.** art or technique of painting with water colors. **3.** picture or design made with water colors.

wa·ter-cool (wô'tər kōōl', wot'ər-) *v.t.* to cool with circulating water, as an engine.

water cooler, device for cooling and dispensing water, often operated by electricity.

wa·ter-course (wô'tər kôrs', wot'ər-) *n.* **1.** any stream of flowing water, as a river or brook. **2.** man-made or natural channel for conveyance of or by water, as a riverbed or canal.

wa·ter-craft (wô'tər kraft', wot'ər-) *n.* **1.** skill in sailing boats or in performing water sports. **2.** boat or ship. **3.** water vessels collectively.

wa·ter-cress (wô'tər kres') *n.* trailing or floating water plant, *Nasturtium officinale,* whose pungent leaves are used as salad greens or as a garnish, bearing long clusters of small white flowers.

water cure, hydrotherapy.

Watercress

wa·ter-fall (wô'tər fôl', wot'ər-) *n.* perpendicular flow of water, usually falling from a high place over a ledge.

water flea, very small crustacean, genus *Daphnia,* found in fresh water, that swims with a jerky, skipping motion.

wa·ter-fowl (wô'tər foul', wot'ər-) *pl.,* -**fowls** or -**fowl.** *n.* water bird, esp. a swimming game bird.

wa·ter-front (wô'tər frunt', wot'ər-) *n.* **1.** that section of an urban or industrial area which is located beside the harbor of a river or ocean, usually being the site of businesses involved in water transportation of people or goods. **2.** land or real estate abutting a lake, river, or the like.

water gap, gorge or valley in a mountain ridge through which a stream flows.

water gas, combustible mixture of gases, mainly carbon monoxide and hydrogen, widely used for heating. It is manufactured by passing steam over very hot coal or coke.

water gate 1. gateway through which water passes or by which access is gained to a body of water. **2.** gate that controls the flow of water.

water glass 1. drinking glass used to hold water or other liquids. **2.** blue-green, glassy compound used in powdered form as an adhesive, abrasive, and pigment. Formula: Na_2SiO_3. Also, **sodium silicate, soluble glass.**

water gun, toy pistol that emits a stream of water. Also, **water pistol.**

water hole, hole or depression in the ground in which water collects, as a pond or pool.

water ice 1. frozen dessert made of sugar, water, and flavoring, esp. fruit flavoring. **2.** ice formed by the direct freezing of water, rather than by the compacting of snow.

watering can, container used for sprinkling water on plants or the like, often having a long spout with a perforated head. Also, **watering pot.**

watering place 1. place where water may be obtained, as for drinking, watering cattle, or for supplying ships. **2.** resort with mineral springs, often offering boating and other water sports.

water jacket, casing containing water, placed about something to keep it cool or to regulate its temperature.

water level 1. level of the surface of any calm body of water. **2.** water table.

water lily, any of a large group of aquatic plants, genus *Nymphaea,* growing in freshwater ponds and lakes throughout temperate and tropical regions. The roots are embedded in the mud, and the leaves and showy flowers float on or stand just above the surface of the water.

Water lily

wa·ter-logged (wô'tər lôgd', -logd', wot'ər-) *also,* **wa·ter·logged.** *adj.* **1.** (of a sailing vessel) being so full of water as to lose buoyancy and become heavy and unmanageable. **2.** thoroughly saturated with or as with water.

Wa·ter-loo (wô'tər lōō', wot'ər-, wô'tər lōō') *n.* **1.** village in central Belgium, scene of the final defeat of Napoleon I on June 18, 1815, by a combined army of English, Dutch, and Prussians. Pop. (1961), 11,846. **2.** any decisive contest, esp. one in which one experiences a crushing defeat. **3.** city in east-central Iowa. Pop. (1970), 75,533.

water main, principal pipe or pipeline used for supplying water to a particular area.

wa·ter-man (wô'tər mən, wot'ər-) *pl.,* -**men.** *n.* man who works on or with boats.

wa·ter-mark (wô'tər märk', wot'ər-) *n.* **1.** line or mark indicating how high the water, as of a river or ocean tide, has risen. **2.** distinctive mark or design impressed on certain kinds of paper and visible when the paper is held up to a light. —*v.t.* **1.** to impress (paper) with a watermark. **2.** to impress (a distinctive mark or design) as a watermark.

wa·ter-mel·on (wô'tər mel'ən, wot'ər-) *n.* **1.** large, juicy fruit of a plant, *Citrullus vulgaris,* having a thick green rind and watery pulp that is pink, red, or yellow. **2.** vine bearing this fruit, having long, hairy stems and large oval leaves that are divided into a number of lobes and bearing funnel-shaped, yellow flowers.

water mill, mill or machine whose source of power is water or a water wheel.

water moccasin, pit viper, *Agkistrodon piscivorus,* found in swamps and other wet, lowland regions of the southeastern United States, having an olive or black body marked with faint crossbars. Length: 3–6 feet. Also, **cot'ton·mouth'.**

water nymph *Classical Mythology.* nymph living in a fountain, brook, stream, or other body of water.

water of hydration, water combined in crystals with another compound so that the water molecules remain intact and can be driven off by heating, with loss of crystalline structure and alteration of the physical but not the chemical properties of the other compound. Also, **water of crystallization.**

water ouzel *also,* **water ousel.** any of various diving birds, genus *Cinclus,* resembling a thrush and having a stocky body, a thin, sharp bill, and a short tail. Also, **dip'per.**

water plantain, any of various aquatic plants, genus *Alisma,* having heart-shaped leaves and bearing branching clusters of small white or pink flowers.

water polo, water sport played with a soccerlike ball by two teams of seven swimmers each, the object being to throw or push the ball through the opponents' goal.

water power 1. power generated by the rush of moving water. **2.** cascade or stream of water used or capable of being used to supply power.

wa·ter-proof (wô'tər prōōf', wot'ər-) *adj.* that will not let water penetrate the surface or pass through, esp. having been treated or coated with a substance that prevents water from entering. —*n. British.* raincoat. —*v.t.* to make waterproof.

water rat 1. any of various aquatic rodents that live on the banks of streams or lakes. **2.** muskrat.

wa·ter·re·pel·lent (wô′tər ri pel′ənt, wot′ər-) *adj.* having a surface or finish that repels water but is not completely waterproof.

water scorpion, any of a small group of bugs, order Hemiptera, that lives underwater and usually has a long breathing tube at the tip of the abdomen.

wa·ter·shed (wô′tər shed′, wot′-ər-) *n.* **1.** ridge or other elevated land area separating two different river basins. **2.** total land area that drains into a single stream or lake and serves as water-storage area for the surrounding countryside. **3.** crucial

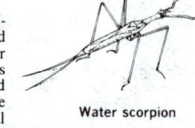

Water scorpion

factor, event, or time; turning point: *The judge's decision marked a watershed in legal history.*

wa·ter·side (wô′tər sīd′, wot′ər-) *n.* land or real property abutting or running along a body of water.

wa·ter·ski (wô′tər skē′, wot′ər-) **-skied, -ski·ing.** *v.i.* to glide over the surface of water on water skis while being pulled by a towline attached to a boat. —**wa′ter·ski′er, wa′ter·ski′ing,** *n.*

water ski, one of a pair of wooden skis wider and shorter than snow skis, used in water-skiing.

water snake, any of various nonpoisonous snakes living in or commonly found in fresh water, esp. those of the genus *Natrix,* found in North America.

wa·ter·soak (wô′tər sōk′, wot′ər-) *v.t.* to fill or saturate thoroughly with water.

water spaniel, curly-haired hunting dog having a solid, liver-colored coat. There are two breeds: the **American water spaniel,** which stands 17 inches at the shoulder and is used to hunt small game, and the **Irish water spaniel,** which stands 23 inches at the shoulder and is used to hunt and retrieve ducks.

wa·ter·spout (wô′tər spout′, wot′ər-) *n.* **1.** pipe or nozzle that carries away unneeded water, esp. one that extends from the roof down the side of a building for the disposing of rainwater. **2.** nozzle end of a pipe running from a vessel or fixture, as a jug or sink, from which water pours when the pipe is opened. **3.** tornado occurring over a body of water, appearing as a long, dark funnel extending from the clouds down toward the surface of the water.

water sprite, sprite or spirit inhabiting an ocean, pool, or stream. Also, **water level.**

water table, upper surface of a water-saturated zone in the ground. Also, **water level.**

wa·ter·tight (wô′tər tīt′, wot′ər-) *adj.* **1.** so closely constructed or fitted as to prevent the passage of water in or out. **2.** perfectly clear and irrefutable; solid; unambiguous: *a watertight argument.*

water tower 1. very large tower used to store a water supply. **2.** formerly, fire-fighting apparatus for throwing water on the upper stories of tall buildings.

Wa·ter·town (wô′tər toun′, wot′ər-) *n.* city in northwestern New York. Pop. (1970), 30,787.

water vapor, water in its gaseous state, but below the boiling point, esp. as dispersed in the atmosphere.

wa·ter·way (wô′tər wā′, wot′ər-) *n.* **1.** water route for the passage of ships. **2.** channel for the passage of water.

water wheel, wheel turned by the weight or pressure of water falling on it, used to provide power.

water wings, waterproof device filled with air, worn under the arms to keep the body afloat while learning to swim.

wa·ter·works (wô′tər wurks′, wot′ər-) *n.,pl.* **1.** entire system for the collection, storage, purification, and distribution of water, including reservoirs, buildings, machinery, pipes, and the like. **2.** building in such a system, housing the machinery for pumping water. **3.** *Slang.* profusion of tears.

wa·ter·worn (wô′tər wôrn′, wot′ər-) *adj.* worn or smoothed by the constant action of running water: *waterworn rocks.*

wa·ter·y (wô′tər ē, wot′ər ē) *adj.* **1.** of, relating to, or consisting of water. **2.** abounding in or saturated with water: *watery soil.* **3.** suffused with tears; tearful: *The head cold made his eyes watery.* **4.** containing too much water: *a watery gravy, watery paint.* **5.** resembling water in appearance or characteristics. **6.** pale, as if diluted by water; weak: *watery colors.*

watt (wot) *n.* unit of electric or mechanical power in the metric system, equal to a rate of one joule of work per second. [From James Watt.]

Watt, James (wot) 1736–1819, Scottish engineer and inventor.

watt·age (wot′ij) *n.* **1.** power, esp. electric power, expressed in watts. **2.** number of watts of electric power needed to run an appliance.

Wat·teau, Jean An·toine (wo tō′; zhän än twän′) 1684–1721, French painter.

watt-hour (wot′our′) *n.* unit of electrical energy, equal to the work done by one watt acting for one hour, or 3600 joules.

wat·tle (wot′əl) *n.* **1.** framework or interlaced structure made of poles,

branches, twigs, or the like woven together, used esp. in building, as for walls, fences, or roofs. **2.** material used to make such a framework or structure. **3.** wattles. poles used to form the framework of a thatched roof. **4.** any of various acacias of Australia that were formerly used to make wattles and the bark of which is now used in tanning. **5.** fleshy, often brightly colored, fold of skin hanging down from the neck or throat of certain fowl and other animals. **6.** barbel of a fish. —*v.t.* **-tled, -tling. 1.** to construct (something) by interlacing twigs, branches, or the like: *to wattle a shelter for the night.* **2.** to form into a network by weaving or interlacing: *to wattle branches to form a roof.* **3.** to bind together with interlaced twigs, branches, or the like. [Old English *watel* interwoven twigs.] —**wat′tled,** *adj.*

watt·me·ter (wot′mē′tər) *n.* instrument for measuring electric power, indicating average power in watts on a graduated scale.

Watts (wots) **1.** George F. 1817–1904, English painter. **2.** **Isaac.** 1674–1748, English clergyman and writer of hymns.

Wau·ke·gan (wô kē′gən) *n.* city in northeastern Illinois, on Lake Michigan. Pop. (1970), 65,269.

Wau·wa·to·sa (wô′wə tō′sə) *n.* city in southeastern Wisconsin, principally a residential suburb of adjoining Milwaukee. Pop. (1970), 58,676.

wave (wāv) **waved, wav·ing.** *v.i.* **1.** to sway freely back and forth or up and down; move with an undulating motion, as a flag or wheat in the wind. **2.** to curve alternately in opposite directions, having an undulating shape: *When Natalie brushes her hair, it waves beautifully.* **3.** to gesture by moving the hand or arm up and down, as in a greeting, farewell, or signal: *He waved until they were out of sight.* —*v.t.* **1.** to cause to move back and forth or up and down: *to wave a flag. The thief waved his gun at the bank teller.* **2.** to signal, indicate, or express by waving something, esp. the hand: *Father waved good-by.* **3.** to give a curving or undulating form, appearance, or pattern to: *to wave hair.* —*n.* **1.** moving or rippling ridge or swell on the surface of a body of liquid, esp. the sea. **2.** anything resembling this in movement or shape. **3.** act of waving, esp. with the hand or something held in the hand, as in a greeting, farewell, or signal: *with a wave of his hand.* **4.** sudden rush or increase of anything, marked by unusual volume, intensity, or extent: *a heat wave. A wave of hysteria swept the city.* **5.** one of a series, as a group of people, animals, events, or the like, occurring or advancing together: *The first wave of tourists arrived in June.* **6.** curve or series of curves, as in the hair. **7.** *Physics.* vibration or disturbance traveling through a solid, liquid, or gaseous medium without any net displacement of that medium. **8.** *also,* **waves.** *Archaic.* body of water, esp. the sea. [Old English *wafian* to make a movement back and forth with the hands.] —**wav′er,** *n.*

Wave (wāv) *n.* member of the WAVES.

wave·length (wāv′lengkth′, -length′) *n. Physics.* the distance between any two corresponding points, as the peaks, of a wave.

wave·let (wāv′lit) *n.* small wave; ripple.

wa·ver (wā′vər) *v.i.* **1.** to move unsteadily up and down or from side to side; sway; totter: *The ladder wavered and fell over.* **2.** to flicker; quiver: *A sign of recognition wavered in his eyes.* **3.** to exhibit doubt or indecision; be irresolute. **4.** to become unsteady; falter. —*n.* act or instance of wavering. [Possibly from Old Norse *vafra* to flicker, move unsteadily.] —**wa′ver·er,** *n.* —**wa′ver·ing·ly,** *adv.* —**Syn.** *v.i.* **3.** see **hesitate.**

WAVES (wāvz) Women's Reserve of the U.S. Navy. [Abbreviation of W(omen) A(ppointed for) V(olunteer) E(mergency) S(ervice).]

wav·y (wā′vē) **wav·i·er, wav·i·est.** *adj.* undulating in movement or shape; full of waves: *a boy with wavy hair, the wavy sea.* —**wav′i·ness,** *n.*

wax¹ (waks) *n.* **1.a.** any of various substances of animal, vegetable, marine, or insect origin that consist of the esters of fatty acids and fatty alcohols. **b.** any of various natural mineral substances that consist of hydrocarbons, as paraffin. **2.** beeswax. **3.** earwax. **4.** sealing wax. —*v.t.* to cover or treat with wax. —*adj.* made of or resembling wax. [Old English *weax* beeswax.]

wax² (waks) **waxed, waxed** or *(archaic)* **wax·en, wax·ing.** *v.i.* **1.** to increase gradually, as in size, strength, or intensity: *The moon waxes and wanes.* **2.** to become something specified: *John waxed eloquent about the beauty of the English countryside.* [Old English *weaxan* to grow, increase.]

wax bean, yellow string bean with a waxy appearance.

wax·ber·ry (waks′ber′ē) *pl.* **-ries.** *n.* **1.** wax myrtle. **2.** snowberry.

wax·en (wak′sən) *adj.* **1.** made of, covered, or treated with wax. **2.** resembling wax, as in consistency or appearance. **3.** pale; wan: *a waxen complexion.*

wax myrtle, any of various tall shrubs or trees, genus *Myrica,* having fragrant, lance-shaped leaves and bearing small grayish berries coated with white wax.

wax paper *also,* **waxed paper.** paper made moisture-proof by being coated with paraffin, used as a protective wrapping.

at; āpe; cär; end; mē; it; īce; hot; ōld; fôrk; wood; fōōl; oil; out; up; ūse; turn; sing; thin; this; zh in treasure; ə in ago, taken, pencil, lemon, circus.

wax·wing (waks'wing') *n.* any of several crested songbirds, genus *Bombycilla*, having a short, thick bill and predominantly brown or gray plumage with black, yellow, white, and red markings. Length: 6–8 inches.

Waxwing

wax·work (waks'wurk') *n.* **1.** work in wax, esp. a figure or ornament made of wax. **2. waxworks.** exhibition or place for exhibiting wax figures representing famous or notorious persons.

wax·y (wak'sē) **wax·i·er, wax·i·est,** *adj.* **1.** resembling wax, as in consistency or appearance. **2.** made of, covered, or treated with wax. —**wax'i·ness,** *n.*

way (wā) *n.* **1.** procedure or agency by which something is done or may be accomplished: *That is the right way to do it.* **2.** course of action to be followed in order to accomplish or attain something: *He thought of a way to solve our problem.* **3.** course leading from one place to another, as a road or path: *The fallen limb blocked the way. That is the quickest way to town.* **4.** direction, as of motion: *The hurricane is heading this way.* **5.** movement or passage along a particular route or in a particular direction: *John saw her on his way back to school.* **6.** distance: *They walked a long way before finding the house.* **7.** *also,* **ways.** habitual or usual style of behaving or speaking: *That's only his way. She has very endearing ways.* **8.** typical or characteristic style of doing something: *Their way of life does not appeal to me.* **9.** that which one desires or resolves upon to have or do: *He has his way in every situation.* **10.** range or scope of one's experience or notice. **11.** path or course of life: *The way of transgressors is hard* (Proverbs 13:15). **12.** particular detail; respect: *In many ways, the plan might succeed.* **13.** *Informal.* condition; state: *Harry is in a bad way financially.* **14. ways.** timbers on which a ship is launched.
by the way. with regard to that; incidentally.
in the way. in such a position or of such a nature as to obstruct or impede.
out of the way. a. so as not to obstruct or hinder. **b.** in a remote or inconvenient place. **c.** extraordinary; unusual. **d.** improper; wrong.
to give way. a. to yield. **b.** to break down or collapse: *The bridge gave way under the heavy load.*
to go out of the (or one's) way. to do something special or unrequested: *They went out of their way to help her.*
to make one's way. a. to proceed; go. **b.** to advance successfully toward one's goal.
to make way. to open a passage or entrance.
under way. in progress; in motion.
[Old English *weg* road, path, course of movement, course of action, manner.]

way·bill (wā'bil') *n.* list of goods being shipped with instructions as to destination and mode of travel. [WAY + BILL¹.]

way·far·er (wā'fâr'ər) *n.* traveler, esp. one who travels on foot.

way·far·ing (wā'fâr'ing) *n., adj.* traveling, esp. on foot.

way·lay (wā'lā', wā'lā') **-laid, -lay·ing.** *v.t.* **1.** to lie in wait for in order to seize or attack: *to waylay a traveler.* **2.** to wait for and accost (a person). [WAY + LAY¹, after Middle Low German *wegelāgen* to lie in wait.] —**way'lay'er,** *n.*

Wayne, Anthony 1745–96, general in the American Revolution, best known as **Mad Anthony.**

-ways *suffix* used to form adverbs denoting direction, position, or manner: *sideways.* [Middle English *wayes*, genitive of WAY.]

way·side (wā'sīd') *n.* land bordering a road or path —*adj.* of, relating to, or located beside a road or path: *a wayside inn.*

way station, small station intermediate between principal stations, as on a railroad.

way·ward (wā'wərd) *adj.* **1.** self-willed, wrongheaded, or disobedient: *a wayward child.* **2.** conforming to no fixed rule, principle, or pattern; irregular; erratic: *wayward fancy.* [Middle English *wayward,* short for *awayward* turned away, from AWAY + -WARD.] —**way'ward·ly,** *adv.* —**way'ward·ness,** *n.*

way·worn (wā'wôrn') *adj.* wearied or worn by traveling.

we (wē) *pl.,* nominative, **we;** possessive, **our, ours;** objective, **us.** *pron.* **1.** persons who are speaking or writing. **2.** single person who is speaking or writing, as an author, sovereign, or judge. [Old English *wē.*]

weak (wēk) *adj.* **1.** liable to fall, fail, or collapse under strain; lacking strength or endurance: *The legs of the chair are weak. The weak bridge swayed under the weight of the trucks.* **2.** lacking in vigor or robustness, as from age, illness, or fatigue: *Harry is too weak to lift the cabinet.* **3.** deficient in ability, power, or authority: *Their team was weaker than ours. He was a weak president.* **4.** unsupported by truth, facts, or reason; unconvincing: *The lawyer gave a weak argument.* **5.** deficient in mental ability or discernment. **6.** deficient in moral strength or firmness; lacking fortitude, will, or character. **7.** lacking forcefulness or effectiveness: *The government employed weak measures to quell the disturbance. The candidate took a weak stand on the issue.* **8.** deficient in intensity or power: *The light was too weak to read by. He spoke with a weak, tremulous voice.* **9.** lacking the full amount of the proper or essential ingredients: *The drink was too weak. She served weak tea.* **10.** deficient or poor in a specified area: *Mary is weak in science.* **11.** *Phonetics.* not stressed or accented. **12.** *Grammar.* (of a verb) forming the past tense and past participle by the addition of a consonant or consonants to the stem, not by the change of a vowel, as in *bake, baked, baked.* [Old Norse *veikr* pliant, feeble.]

weak·en (wē'kən) *v.t., v.i.* to make or become weak or weaker.

weak·fish (wēk'fish') *pl.* **-fish** or **-fish·es.** *n.* any of several saltwater food fish, genus *Cynoscion,* esp. *C. regalis,* found in the coastal waters of eastern North America. [Obsolete Dutch *weekvis,* from *week* soft, weak + *vis* fish; probably referring to its soft and tender flesh.]

weak-kneed (wēk'nēd') *adj.* **1.** having weak knees. **2.** lacking in resolution or determination; yielding easily to intimidation; spineless.

weak·ling (wēk'ling) *n.* one who is physically, mentally, or morally weak. —*adj.* weak; feeble. [WEAK + -LING¹.]

weak·ly (wēk'lē) *adv.* in a weak manner. —*adj.,* **-li·er, -li·est.** not healthy or robust; weak; feeble. —**weak'li·ness,** *n.*

weak-mind·ed (wēk'mīn'did) *adj.* **1.** lacking strength or purpose; irresolute. **2.** feeble-minded.

weak·ness (wēk'nis) *n.* **1.** state or quality of being weak, as in moral or physical strength. **2.** instance of this; weak point. **3.** self-indulgent partiality or liking: *She has a weakness for vanilla ice cream.* **4.** something for which one has such a partiality or liking: *Buying records is his weakness.* —**Syn. 2.** see **fault.**

weal¹ (wēl) *n.* well-being; happiness; prosperity. [Old English *wela.*]

weal² (wēl) *n.* ridge or bump on the skin, as made by a whip or stick; welt. [Form of WALE; influenced by WHEAL.]

wealth (welth) *n.* **1.** abundance of valuable material possessions; riches. **2.** all things having monetary value. **3.** great quantity; profusion; abundance. [From WEAL¹ or WELL¹.]

wealth·y (wel'thē) **wealth·i·er, wealth·i·est.** *adj.* having wealth. —**wealth'i·ly,** *adv.* —**wealth'i·ness,** *n.*

wean (wēn) *v.t.* **1.** to accustom (a child or young animal) to food other than the mother's milk. **2.** to remove (a person) gradually from some accustomed or favored object, practice, or pursuit: *to wean someone from tobacco.* [Old English *wenian* to accustom, to accustom to being without her mother's milk.]

weap·on (wep'ən) *n.* **1.** anything used in combat to attack or defend, as a gun or knife. **2.** any means used in a contest or struggle: *Tears were her only weapon.* [Old English *wǣpn.*]

weap·on·ry (wep'ən rē) *n.,pl.* weapons collectively; arms.

wear (wâr) **wore, worn, wear·ing.** *v.t.* **1.** to carry or bear on the body or a part of the body, as a covering or ornament: *to wear clothes, to wear a bracelet.* **2.** to bear or carry; display: *to wear a frown.* **3.** to damage, erode, or impair, as by rubbing or scraping: *to wear a carpet.* **4.** to cause or produce, as by rubbing or scraping: *to wear a hole in the carpet.* **5.** to bring to a specified state or condition: *to wear a dress to rags.* **6. to wear down.** to overcome by continuous effort: *to wear down someone's resistance.* **7. to wear out. a.** to wear until no longer fit for use. **b.** to tire; exhaust: *The game wore him out.* —*v.i.* **1.** to last or hold out: *These shoes will wear at least a year. The fabric did not wear well.* **2.** to undergo impairment or damage gradually through use or passage of time: *John's clothes have started to wear.* **3.** to arrive at a specified state or condition: *Mary's patience wore thin.* **4.** to pass or advance, esp. slowly or tediously: *The hour wore on.* **5. to wear down.** to lose strength or vitality gradually through use or passage of time; diminish; fade. **6. to wear off.** to diminish gradually. —*n.* **1.** act of wearing; being worn. **2.** article or articles of clothing: *women's wear.* **3.** gradual impairment or damage caused by use or passage of time: *signs of wear.* **4.** capacity for being worn; durability. [Old English *werian* to carry, have on.] —**wear'a·ble,** *adj.* —**wear'er,** *n.*

wear and tear, impairment or damage undergone through use or passage of time.

wear·ing (wâr'ing) *adj.* **1.** of, relating to, or made for wear: *wearing apparel.* **2.** exhausting; tiring: *a wearing experience.*

wea·ri·some (wēr'ē sam) *adj.* causing weariness; tiresome; tedious. —**wea'ri·some·ly,** *adv.* —**wea'ri·some·ness,** *n.*

wea·ry (wēr'ē) **-ri·er, -ri·est.** *adj.* **1.** extremely exhausted, as from mental or physical labor; fatigued. **2.** causing or characterized by fatigue; tedious; tiring: *a weary journey.* **3.** having one's interest, patience, or tolerance exhausted (with *of*): *He grew weary of staying home.* —*v.t.* **-ried, -ry·ing.** to exhaust the strength or endurance of; make weary; fatigue: *The trip wearied her.* —*v.i.* to become weary: *The child wearied quickly.* [Old English *wērig* tired.] —**wea'ri·ly,** *adv.* —**wea'ri·ness,** *n.*

---

at; āpe; cär; end; mē; it; īce; hot; ōld; fôrk; wood; fōōl; oil; out; up; ūse; turn; sing; thin; **this;** zh in treasure; ə in ago, taken, pencil, lemon, circus.

wea·sand (wē′zənd) n. gullet; throat. [Old English wāsend gullet.]

wea·sel (wē′zəl) pl., **-sels** or **-sel.** n. any of various small carnivorous mammals, genus *Mustela,* having a slender body, short legs, a long neck, a long, usually black-tipped tail, and a soft, thick, yellowish-to-dark-brown coat covered with long, shiny outer hairs. In cold climates its coat usually turns white in the winter. Length: 6–31 inches, including tail. —v.i. Informal. **1.** to be under-handed or evasive. **2. to weasel out.** to evade or renege on a duty, responsibility, or obligation. [Old English *wesule.*]

Weasel

weath·er (weth′ər) n. **1.** atmospheric condition at a given time and place. **2.** adverse or unpleasant atmospheric conditions: *We encountered much weather on the flight back.* **under the weather.** *Informal.* **a.** not well; ailing. **b.** slightly drunk. —v.t. **1.** to expose to the weather, esp. in order to dry, bleach, or condition: *to weather lumber.* **2.** to bear up against or overcome; come safely through: *to weather a storm,* to *weather a crisis.* **3.** to pass or sail to the windward of. —v.i. **1.** to become changed through exposure to the weather. **2.** to resist or endure exposure to the weather: *Leather will weather better than wool or cotton.* —adj. windward. [Old English *weder* atmospheric condition, wind¹, storm.]

weath·er-beat·en (weth′ər bēt′ən) adj. **1.** marred, worn, or badly damaged by exposure to the weather: *a weather-beaten old barn.* **2.** seasoned or hardened by exposure to the weather: *a weather-beaten sailor.*

weath·er·board (weth′ər bôrd′) n. clapboard.

weath·er·bound (weth′ər bound′) adj. delayed by bad weather, as an airplane or ship.

Weather Bureau, agency of the U.S. Department of Commerce that observes and forecasts the weather.

weath·er·cock (weth′ər kok′) n. weather vane having the shape of a rooster.

weath·er·glass (weth′ər glas′) n. any of various instruments used to indicate the weather, as a barometer.

weath·er·ing (weth′ər ing) n. action of the weather upon something exposed to it, esp. upon rocks.

weath·er·man (weth′ər man′) pl., **-men.** n. one who studies atmospheric conditions in order to report and forecast the weather.

weather map, map showing atmospheric conditions at a given time, usually over an extensive region.

weath·er·proof (weth′ər prōōf′) adj. capable of resisting successfully the destructive forces of the weather. —v.t. to make weatherproof.

weather ship, ship used in gathering meteorological information.

weather station, station where daily meteorological observations are made and recorded.

weath·er·strip (weth′ər strip′) -stripped, -strip·ping. v.t. to fit or secure with weather stripping.

weather stripping 1. narrow strip of metal, felt, or other material, applied to openings, as of a door or window, to keep out the wind and cold. Also, **weather strip. 2.** such strips collectively.

weather vane, device that is moved by the wind and indicates the direction in which the wind is blowing.

weath·er·wise (weth′ər wīz′) adj. skillful in making predictions about the weather.

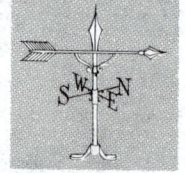

Weather vane

weave (wēv) wove or weaved, wo·ven or wove, weav·ing. v.t. **1.** to lace together (threads, yarn, or strips): *to weave yarn into cloth.* **2.** to form or make by lacing together threads, yarn, or strips of straw or other material: *to weave a basket, to weave cloth.* **3.** to spin (a web or cocoon). **4.** to unite into a connected whole: *to weave the melodies into a single composition.* **5.** to make by turning and twisting: *to weave one's way through a crowd.* —v.i. to form or make by weaving. —n. particular method or pattern of weaving: *an open weave.* [Old English *wefan* to make a fabric by interlacing threads.]

weav·er (wē′vər) n. one who weaves or whose occupation is weaving.

weav·er·bird (wē′vər burd′) n. any of a large number of songbirds, family Ploceidae, native to Africa, Europe, and Asia, which often weave nests of grasses and straw, as the house sparrow.

web (web) n. **1.** something woven, esp. a whole piece of cloth in the process of being woven or just removed from a loom. **2.** network of fine threads spun by a spider; cobweb. **3.** any complex structure or network: *a web of streets.* **4.** any membranous or connective tissue, esp.

the toes of a swimming bird. **5.** vane of a feather. **6.** large, continuous roll of paper used to feed a rotary press. [Old English *webb* woven fabric.]

webbed (webd) adj. having or joined by a web or webs: *Geese have webbed feet.*

web·bing (web′ing) n. **1.** strong, narrow band of woven fabric, made of cotton, hemp, or other fibers, used for various items, as seat belts and harness straps. **2.** anything forming a web or webs.

We·ber (vā′bər) **1. Carl Ma·ri·a von** (mä rē′ä). 1786–1826, German composer. **2. Max.** 1864–1920, German social scientist.

Web·ster (web′stər) **1. Daniel.** 1782–1852, U.S. statesman. **2. John.** c.1580–c.1634, English dramatist. **3. Noah.** 1758–1843, U.S. lexicographer and author.

Web (def. 2)

wed (wed) wed·ded, wed·ded or wed, wed·ding. v.t. **1.** to take as one's husband or wife; marry. **2.** to join as husband and wife; unite in wedlock. **3.** to join closely; unite: *to be wed to one's opinion.* [Old English *weddian* to pledge, marry¹.]

we'd (wēd) **1.** we had. **2.** we would. **3.** we should.

Wed., Wednesday.

wed·ding (wed′ing) n. **1.** marriage ceremony and accompanying festivities. **2.** anniversary of a marriage. [Old English *weddung* espousal, marriage.]

wedge (wej) n. **1.** solid, triangular or tapered object, as of wood or metal, that can be driven in between objects to be separated or into something to be split. **2.** something resembling this in shape: *a wedge of cheese.* **3.** something, as an idea, policy, or procedure, that brings about division or disunity: *The struggle over the inheritance drove a wedge between members of the family.* —v.t., wedged, wedg·ing. **1.** to separate or split by driving a wedge into. **2.** to fasten or fix in place with a wedge or wedges. **3.** to drive, push, or crowd (something), as into a narrow space: *He managed to wedge the book into place on the shelf.* —v.i. to force one's way: *John wedged into the seat on the train.* [Old English *wecg* tapered piece of wood or metal.]

Wedg·wood (wej′wood′) n. earthenware pottery usually characterized by a blue or green tinted ground and white, raised ornament. [From Josiah *Wedgwood,* 1730–95, English potter who created this kind of earthenware pottery.]

Wedgwood

wed·lock (wed′lok′) n. state or condition of being married; matrimony. [Old English *wedlāc* marriage vow, from *wedd* pledge + *-lāc* (suffix indicating activity).]

Wednes·day (wenz′dē, -dā) n. fourth day of the week. [Old English *Wōdnesdæg* literally, Woden's day, translation of Late Latin *Mercuriī diēs* literally, day of Mercury (owing to the identification of Woden with Mercury).]

wee (wē) we·er, we·est. adj. **1.** very small; little. **2.** early: *in the wee hours.* [Middle English *we(i)* a bit, a little, from Old English *wǣge* a weight.]

weed¹ (wēd) n. **1.** useless or harmful plant that grows where it is not wanted or where another plant is desired. **2.** *Informal.* tobacco. **3.** *Informal.* cigar or cigarette. —v.t. **1.** to remove weeds from: *to weed a lawn.* **2. to weed out.** to remove what is useless or harmful: *to weed out the troublemakers from a class.* —v.i. to remove weeds. [Old English *wēod* useless or harmful plant.]

weed² (wēd) n. **1.** weeds. clothes worn by someone in mourning, esp. a widow. **2.** token of mourning, as a black band worn on the arm. [Old English *wǣd* garment.]

weed·er (wē′dər) n. **1.** one who weeds. **2.** tool or device for removing weeds.

weed·y (wē′dē) weed·i·er, weed·i·est. adj. **1.** full of weeds. **2.** of, relating to, or resembling a weed or weeds. **3.** *Informal.* thin and lanky; rangy. —weed′i·ness, n.

week (wēk) n. **1.** period of seven consecutive days, usually considered as beginning with Sunday. **2.** number of days or hours in a seven-day period devoted to a specific activity: *to work a four-day week.* **3.** week commencing on a certain day, containing a specific day, or designated for some specific purpose: *the week of the twelfth, Christmas week.* **4.** one week from a specified day: *I'll see you a week from tomorrow. We haven't spoken since Saturday week.* [Old English *wice* period of seven consecutive days.]

week·day (wēk′dā′) n. any day of the week except Sunday or, often, Saturday and Sunday.

week·end (wēk′end′) n. period extending from Friday night or Satur-

day morning until Sunday night or Monday morning. —*adj.* of, relating to, or occurring during a weekend: *a weekend golf game.* —*v.i.* to spend a weekend: *to weekend in the country.*

week·ly (wēk′lē) *adj.* **1.** of or relating to a week or weekdays: *weekly salary.* **2.** done or occurring once a week: *a weekly telephone call, weekly shopping.* —*n. pl.*, **-lies.** periodical issued once a week. —*adv.* once each week; every week.

ween (wēn) *v.i., v.t. Archaic.* to think; surmise; suppose. [Old English *wēnan.*]

weep (wēp) **wept, weep·ing.** *v.i.* **1.** to show grief, joy, or other strong emotion by shedding tears: *The sad news made Dierdre weep.* **2.** to feel sorrow or grief; mourn; lament (with *for*): *We weep for our dead comrades.* **3.** to drop or flow like tears; ooze. —*v.t.* **1.** to weep for; mourn for: *No poet wept him* (Cowper, 1790). **2.** to shed or let flow in drops: *to weep salty tears.* **3.** to bring to a specified condition by weeping: *the child wept himself to sleep.* [Old English *wēpan.*] to lament, shed tears.]

weep·er (wē′pər) *n.* one who weeps, esp. a person hired to weep at funerals.

weeping willow, wide-spreading tree, *Salix babylonica,* widely cultivated throughout eastern North America, having pale-green leaves and greenish branches that droop almost to the ground.

Weeping willow

wee·vil (wē′vəl) *n.* **1.** any of a group of destructive beetles having a snout or beak. Weevils feed on many cultivated crops, boring into them to deposit their larvae, which also feed on the crops. **2.** any of various other insects that infest and destroy stored grain. [Old English *wifel* any beetle.] —**wee′vil·y;** *also,* **wee′vil·ly,** *adj.*

Snout

Weevil

weft (weft) *n.* woof (*def.* 1). [Old English *weft.*]

weigh (wā) *v.t.* **1.** to determine the weight of, as on a scale or balance: *The doctor weighed the baby every month.* **2.** to measure or apportion (a quantity or quantities of something) according to weight (with *out*): *The chemistry teacher weighed out one ounce of the compound.* **3.** to consider or examine thoughtfully and carefully: *to weigh the advantages and disadvantages of a plan, to weigh one's words before speaking.* **4.** to lie heavily on; oppress or burden (often with *down*): *The heavy snowfall weighed down the branches of the trees. Many taxes weighed the spirits of the peasants.* **5.** to raise or lift (an anchor). —*v.i.* **1.** to have, amount to, or be equal to a specified weight: *The car weighs 3744 pounds. She weighs exactly the same as her sister.* **2.** to be considered important; have influence; matter: *The prisoner's record will certainly weigh heavily with the parole board.* **3.** to be oppressive or burdensome: *His guilt weighed on his conscience.* **4.a.** to raise or lift an anchor. **b.** to start to sail: *to weigh from a port.* **5.** to weigh in. to find out one's weight, as before a boxing match or other contest. [Old English *wegan* to carry, lift, balance on the scales.] —**weigh′er,** *n.* —**Syn.** *v.t.* **3.** see **consider.**

weight (wāt) *n.* **1.** any quantity of heaviness expressed indefinitely or in standard units: *Her weight is only one hundred pounds.* **2.** quality of any mass or body which is the result of gravitational force and centrifugal pressure tending to pull things toward the center of the earth: *The weight of helium is less than the weight of air, causing a helium-filled balloon to rise.* **3.** system of units for expressing weights or mass: *atomic weight.* **4.** unit of weight or mass. **5.** piece of metal or similar material having a particular weight, used as a standard in weighing. **6.** quantity or portion having a definite weight. **7.** heavy mass, esp. one that is used because of its weight to exert gravitational force. **8.** burden; pressure; load: *The weight of his financial problems was ruining his health.* **9.** effective influence; importance; consequence: *a matter of great weight. The senator's vote carried a lot of weight with the other members.* **10.** one of the classes into which athletes competing in certain sports are divided according to body weight. **11. by weight.** as determined by weighing. **12. to pull one's weight.** to do or contribute one's share. **13. to throw one's weight around.** *Informal.* to use one's power, authority, or position, esp. unduly. —*v.t.* **1.** to add weight to; load with additional weight: *They weighted the cartons with rocks.* **2.** to burden heavily, as with a weight: *She was weighted down by her guilty conscience.* **3.** to give heaviness or body to (fabric or yarn) by adding plastic resins or other substances. Silk is sometimes weighted with metallic salts to improve its appearance. [Old English *wiht* measurement of quantity by weighing, a quantity weighing a definite amount.]

weight·less (wāt′lis) *adj.* **1.** having little or no weight. **2.** (of a body) having no apparent weight due to the absence of the pull of gravity, as in space. —**weight′less·ly,** *adv.* —**weight′less·ness,** *n.*

weight lifter, one who engages in weight lifting.

weight lifting, exercise or competitive sport of lifting objects of varying weights.

weight·y (wā′tē) **weight·i·er, weight·i·est.** *adj.* **1.** of great weight; heavy. **2.** effective; convincing: *weighty reasons for taking action.* **3.** very serious; important; grave: *a weighty decision.* —**weight′i·ly,** *adv.* —**weight′i·ness,** *n.* —**Syn.** **1.** see **heavy.**

Wei·mar (vī′mär) *n.* historic town in southern East Germany, southwest of Leipzig. Pop. (1966 est.), 64,300.

weir (wēr) *n.* **1.** dam constructed in a river, as to raise the water. **2.** fence of stakes or wattles put in a stream or channel to catch fish. [Old English *wer.*]

weird (wērd) *adj.* **1.** strange; bizarre; odd: *That was a weird thing for her to say.* **2.** suggestive of or concerned with the supernatural; unearthly; mysterious. **3.** *Archaic.* having supernatural power, esp. having the power of controlling fate or destiny. [Middle English *wyrde* having the power to control fate, from *wyrde* fate, from Old English *wyrd.*] —**weird′ly,** *adv.* —**weird′ness,** *n.*

Weird Sisters, the Fates.

welch (welch, welsh) *also,* **welsh.** *v.i.* to fail or refuse to pay what is owed, esp. a bet. [Of uncertain origin.]

wel·come (wel′kəm) **-comed, -com·ing.** *v.t.* **1.** to greet (someone) gladly and with hospitality: *We welcomed them into our club.* **2.** to receive or accept graciously or with pleasure: *to welcome the news of the event, to welcome advice.* —*n.* **1.** act of making welcome; glad and friendly greeting: *We received a warm welcome.* **2.** kind or hospitable reception: *There was always a welcome waiting.* **3. to wear out one's welcome.** to stay too long or come too frequently. —*adj.* **1.** received kindly and with cordiality: *a welcome visitor.* **2.** giving pleasure or satisfaction: *a welcome compliment.* **3.** free to use, have, or enjoy; willingly permitted: *You are welcome to the telephone.* **4.** under no obligation. ▲ used chiefly in the phrase *you're welcome* as a response to being thanked for something. [Old Norse *velkominn* expression of greeting; literally, well come, from *vel* well¹ + *kominn,* past participle of *koma* to come.] —**wel′com·er,** *n.*

weld (weld) *v.t.* **1.** to join (a substance, as metal or plastic) to another by heating and softening it until it is capable of being hammered and pressed or fused. **2.** to join closely together; unite intimately: *to weld a confederation of states.* —*v.i.* to be capable of being welded. —*n.* **1.** point at which two things are joined by welding. **2.** act or process of welding; being welded. [Modification of obsolete *well* to join by heating and softening, from Old English *wellan* to boil.] —**weld′er,** *n.*

wel·fare (wel′fār′) *n.* **1.** state or condition of being or doing well, as in health or finances. **2.** financial aid or other assistance given to those in need; relief. **3.** governmental agency providing such aid or relief. **4. on welfare.** dependent upon or receiving financial aid or other public assistance. [Middle English *welfare* well-being, good fortune, from the phrase *wel faren* to fare well, from old English *wel faran.*]

Wel·fare Island (wel′fār′) island in the East River in New York City.

welfare state, state that actively ensures the well-being of its population through various programs, as health and unemployment insurance, guaranteed minimum wages, and subsidized housing.

welfare work, work done by government, private agencies, and individuals to provide material aid and special health, education, and social services to people who need assistance.

welfare worker, one who does welfare work, esp. as a profession.

wel·kin (wel′kin) *n. Archaic.* sky; heavens: *making the welkin ring with the music of their deep-toned notes* (Surtees, 1854). [Old English *wolcen* cloud, sky.]

well¹ (wel) **bet·ter, best.** *adv.* **1.** in a satisfactory, good, or favorable manner: *If you're going to do something, do it well.* **2.** thoroughly; completely: *to mix the ingredients well.* **3.** to a considerable extent or degree: *Oscar weighs well over 200 pounds.* **4.** closely; intimately: *Do you know Percy well?* **5.** under the circumstances; reasonably: *I can't very well accept your offer.* **6. as well. a.** in addition; also: *to play the guitar and the drums as well.* **b.** with the same outcome or effect; equally: *You might as well not bother.* **7. as well as. a.** in addition to; besides. **b.** to the same extent or degree as. ▲ *Well* is hyphenated when used in combination with an adjective before a noun: *a well-matched couple.* It is not hyphenated when used with a predicate adjective: *The pictures are well placed on the wall.* —*adj.* **1.** in good health; thriving. **2.** good; fortunate: *It's well that you could.* —*interj.* used to express surprise, doubt, resignation, or to introduce another thought. [Old English *wel* satisfactorily, thoroughly, properly, well, successfully, effectively.]

well² (wel) *n.* **1.** hole or pit made in the ground to obtain a water supply

WEIGHTS AND MEASURES

LINEAR MEASURE

1 foot	=	12 inches
1 yard	=	3 feet
1 rod	=	5½ yards or 16½ feet
1 furlong	=	40 rods
1 mile	=	8 furlongs or 1760 yards or 5280 feet

SQUARE MEASURE

1 square foot	=	144 square inches
1 square yard	=	9 square feet
1 square rod	=	30¼ square yards
1 acre	=	160 square rods or 43,560 square feet
1 square mile	=	640 acres

CUBIC MEASURE

1 board foot	=	144 cubic inches
1 cubic foot	=	1728 cubic inches
1 cubic yard	=	27 cubic feet
1 cord	=	128 cubic feet

LIQUID MEASURE

1 pint	=	4 gills
1 quart	=	2 pints
1 gallon	=	4 quarts
1 barrel	=	31½ gallons
1 hogshead	=	2 barrels

DRY MEASURE

1 quart	=	2 pints
1 peck	=	8 quarts
1 bushel	=	4 pecks

AVOIRDUPOIS WEIGHT

1 dram	=	27.34 grains
1 ounce	=	16 drams
1 pound	=	16 ounces
1 hundredweight	=	100 pounds
1 short ton	=	2000 pounds
1 long ton	=	2240 pounds

TROY WEIGHT

1 pennyweight	=	24 grains
1 ounce	=	20 pennyweights
1 pound	=	12 ounces

APOTHECARIES' WEIGHT

1 scruple	=	20 grains
1 dram	=	3 scruples
1 ounce	=	8 drams
1 pound	=	12 ounces

APOTHECARIES' FLUID MEASURE

1 fluid dram	=	60 minims
1 fluid ounce	=	8 fluid drams
1 pint	=	16 fluid ounces
1 quart	=	2 pints
1 gallon	=	4 quarts

MARINERS' MEASURE

1 fathom	=	6 feet
1 nautical mile	=	1000 fathoms (approx.)
1 league	=	3 nautical miles

CIRCULAR AND ANGULAR MEASURE

1 minute	=	60 seconds
1 degree	=	60 minutes
1 right angle (or 1 quadrant)	=	90 degrees
1 straight angle (or 2 quadrants)	=	180 degrees
1 circle (or 4 quadrants)	=	360 degrees

METRIC SYSTEM

Unit	Metric Equivalent		U.S. Equivalent	
LINEAR MEASURE				
millimeter	0.001	meter	0.03937	inch
centimeter	0.01	meter	0.3937	inch
decimeter	0.1	meter	3.937	inches
meter	1.0	meter	39.37	inches
decameter	10.0	meters	10.93	yards
hectometer	100.0	meters	328.08	feet
kilometer	1000.0	meters	0.6214	mile
WEIGHT OR MASS				
milligram	0.001	gram	0.0154	grain
centigram	0.01	gram	0.1543	grain
decigram	0.1	gram	1.543	grains
gram	1.0	gram	15.43	grains
decagram	10.0	grams	0.3527	ounce avoirdupois
hectogram	100.0	grams	3.527	ounces avoirdupois
kilogram	1000.0	grams	2.2	pounds avoirdupois
CAPACITY				
milliliter	0.001	liter	0.034	fluid ounce
centiliter	0.01	liter	0.338	fluid ounce
deciliter	0.1	liter	3.38	fluid ounces
liter	1.0	liter	1.05	liquid quarts
decaliter	10.0	liters	0.284	bushel
hectoliter	100.0	liters	2.837	bushels
kiloliter	1000.0	liters	264.18	gallons
AREA				
square centimeter	0.0001	centiare	0.155	square inch
square decimeter	0.01	centiare	15.5	square inches
centiare (square meter)	1.0	centiare	10.76	square feet
are	100.0	centiares	0.0247	acre
hectare	10,000.0	centiares	2.47	acres
square kilometer	1,000,000.0	centiares	0.386	square mile
VOLUME				
cubic centimeter	0.001	cubic decimeter	0.061	cubic inch
cubic decimeter	0.001	cubic meter	3.53	cubic feet
stere	1.0	cubic meter	1.308	cubic yards
decastere	10.0	cubic meters	13.10	cubic yards

or tap another substance, as oil. **2.** natural spring or fountain. **3.** something resembling a well in shape or function. **4.** vertical enclosed space in a building, often extending through several floors, as a shaft for stairs, an elevator, or for the admission of air or light. **5.** compartment in a ship's hold that encloses and protects the pumps. —*v.t.* to spring; rise; fill: *Gratitude welled up in his heart. Tears welled in her eyes.* [Old English *wella* spring of water, pit dug to get spring water, source.]

we'll (wēl) we shall; we will.

well·a·day (wel′ə dā′) *interj. Archaic.* alas.

Wel·land Ship Canal (wel′ənd) canal in southeastern Ontario, Canada, which connects lakes Erie and Ontario, part of the St. Lawrence Seaway.

well-ap·point·ed (wel′ə poin′tid) *adj.* properly or excellently furnished or equipped.

well·a·way (wel′ə wā′) *interj. Archaic.* alas.

well-bal·anced (wel′bal′ənst) *adj.* **1.** nicely or evenly balanced; properly adjusted or regulated: *a well-balanced diet.* **2.** sensible; sane.

well-be·haved (wel′bi hāvd′) *adj.* characterized by good conduct or manners.

well-be·ing (wel′bē′ing) *n.* good physical and mental condition.

well-born (wel′bôrn′) *adj.* born of a good family, esp. in regard to lineage, wealth, or social position.

well-bred (wel′bred′) *adj.* **1.** having or characterized by good breeding or training; polite; tasteful. **2.** (of an animal) coming from good stock or pedigree.

well-dis·posed (wel′di spōzd′) *adj.* inclined to favorable action or thought; friendly or favorable: *The staff was well-disposed toward the new boss.*

well-done (wel′dun′) *adj.* (of food) thoroughly cooked.

well-fa·vored (wel′fā′vərd) *adj.* good-looking; handsome.

well-fed (wel′fed′) *adj.* properly or excessively nourished.

well-fixed (wel′fikst′) *adj. Informal.* not lacking in money; financially secure.

well-found (wel′found′) *adj.* well supplied or equipped.

well-found·ed (wel′foun′did) *adj.* based on solid evidence, good judgment, or sound reasoning: *a well-founded argument.*

well-groomed (wel′grōōmd′) *adj.* carefully and attractively dressed and groomed; neat.

well-ground·ed (wel′groun′did) *adj.* **1.** thoroughly familiar with the fundamental principles of a subject: *well-grounded in mathematics.* **2.** well-founded.

well·head (wel′hed′) *n.* **1.** source of a natural spring or well. **2.** chief source of anything: *the wellhead from which every thought and feeling gushed into act* (Hazlitt, 1820).

well-heeled (wel′hēld′) *adj.* having a lot of money; rich.

well-in·formed (wel′in fôrmd′) *adj.* **1.** having substantial information on a wide variety of subjects. **2.** having substantial and correct information on a particular subject.

Wel·ling·ton (wel′ing tən) *n.* **1. Duke of.** 1769–1852, English soldier and statesman who defeated Napoleon I at Waterloo; born Arthur Wellesley. **2.** capital of New Zealand, on the southwestern tip of North Island. Pop. (1969), 134,400.

well-in·ten·tioned (wel′in ten′shənd) *adj.* having or marked by good intentions, usually with unsatisfactory results: *His well-intentioned words only made things worse.*

well-known (wel′nōn′) *adj.* **1.** famous; renowned. **2.** generally, widely, or fully known.

well-man·nered (wel′man′ərd) *adj.* having or marked by good manners; polite.

well-mean·ing (wel′mē′ning) *adj.* **1.** intending good; well-intentioned. **2.** proceeding from good intentions. Also, **well′-meant′.**

well-nigh (wel′nī′) *adv.* very nearly; almost.

well-off (wel′ôf′) *adj.* **1.** fairly wealthy; financially secure. **2.** in a position where things are good or going well.

well-read (wel′red′) *adj.* knowledgeable through having read widely.

well-round·ed (wel′roun′did) *adj.* **1.** having knowledge or interest in a wide variety of fields or subjects. **2.** concerned with or made up of a wide variety of fields or subjects: *a well-rounded curriculum.*

Wells, H(erbert) G(eorge) (welz) 1866–1946, English novelist and social philosopher.

well-spoken (wel′spō′kən) *adj.* **1.** refined in speech. **2.** said or delivered with style and polish: *a well-spoken rebuttal.*

well·spring (wel′spring′) *n.* **1.** fountainhead *(def. 1).* **2.** source of something, esp. an unending source: *a wellspring of knowledge.*

well-timed (wel′tīmd′) *adj.* occurring or done at the correct or suitable time.

well-to-do (wel′tə dōō′) *adj.* having or characterized by more than sufficient means; wealthy; prosperous.

well-wish·er (wel′wish′ər) *n.* one who wishes well, as to another person, a cause, or the like.

well-worn (wel′wôrn′) *adj.* **1.** showing evidence of much wear. **2.** overly used; trite: *a well-worn phrase.*

welsh (welsh, welch) welch.

Welsh (welsh, welch) *adj.* of or relating to Wales, its people, or their language or culture. —*n.* **1.** people of Wales. **2.** their language, belonging to the Celtic branch of the Indo-European language family.

Welsh cor·gi (kôr′gē) short-legged dog having a foxlike face and a coat of stiff, medium-length hair. There are two breeds, the **Cardigan Welsh corgi**, having a long, bushy tail, and the **Pembroke Welsh corgi**, having a short tail. Height: to 12 inches at the shoulder.

Welsh·man (welsh′mən, welch′-) *pl.* **-men.** *n.* male member or recent descendant of the people of Wales.

Welsh rabbit, melted cheese mixed with beer, ale, or milk, seasoned, and served warm over toast or crackers. Also, **Welsh rarebit.** [Apparently of jocular origin.]

welt (welt) *n.* **1.** strip of material, esp. a cord, sewn on an edge or in a seam of a garment or item, as upholstery, usually for strengthening or decorating. **2.** strip of leather or other material between the upper part and the sole of a shoe. **3.** ridge or bump on the skin, as one made by a stick or whip. **4.** blow causing such a ridge or bump. —*v.t.* **1.** to put a welt on or in. **2.** *Informal.* to beat or flog so as to raise welts. [Of uncertain origin.]

wel·ter (wel′tər) *v.i.* **1.** to roll or toss about; wallow. **2.** to be soaked or drenched in some liquid. —*n.* **1.** rolling and tossing motion. **2.** confusion; turmoil. [Possibly from Middle Low German *welteren* to roll.]

well′-ac·cept′ed	well′-cul′ti·vat′ed	well′-man′aged	well′-rep′re·sent′ed
well′-ac·knowl′edged	well′-de·fend′ed	well′-marked′	well′-re·spect′ed
well′-ac·quaint′ed	well′-de·served′	well′-matched′	well′-re·viewed′
well′-a·dapt′ed	well′-de·serv′ing	well′-meas′ured	well′-ri′pened
well′-ad·just′ed	well′-de·vel′oped	well′-mer′it·ed	well′-root′ed
well′-ad·min′is·tered	well′-dis·ci·plined	well′-mixed′	well′-sat′is·fied′
well′-ad′ver·tised′	well′-doc′u·ment′ed	well′-or′dered	well′-se·cured′
well′-aimed′	well′-dressed′	well′-paid′	well′-shaped′
well′-ap·plied′	well′-ed′u·cat′ed	well′-phrased′	well′-sit′u·at′ed
well′-armed′	well′-en·dowed′	well′-planned′	well′-spent′
well′-as·sured′	well′-e·quipped′	well′-played′	well′-stat′ed
well′-at·tend′ed	well′-es·tab′lished	well′-pleased′	well′-stocked′
well′-at·tired′	well′-fi·nanced′	well′-pleas′ing	well′-suit′ed
well′-a·ware′	well′-formed′	well′-prac′ticed	well′-sup·plied′
well′-blessed′	well′-for′ti·fied′	well′-pre·pared′	well′-sus·tained′
well′-built′	well′-fought′	well′-pre·served′	well′-taught′
well′-cho′sen	well′-fur′nished	well′-pro·por′tioned	well′-trained′
well′-clothed′	well′-gov′erned	well′-pro·tect′ed	well′-trav′eled
well′-com′pen·sat′ed	well′-guard′ed	well′-qual′i·fied′	well′-treat′ed
well′-con·cealed′	well′-hid′den	well′-re·ceived′	well′-trimmed′
well′-con·nect′ed	well′-il·lus·trat′ed	well′-rec′og·nized′	well′-un′der·stood′
well′-con·struct′ed	well′-jus′ti·fied′	well′-rec′om·mend′ed	well′-used′
well′-con·tent′	well′-kept′	well′-re·gard′ed	well′-versed′
well′-con·tent′ed	well′-liked′	well′-reg′u·lat′ed	well′-word′ed
well′-con·trolled′	well′-made′	well′-re·mem′bered	well′-writ′ten
well′-cooked′			well′-wrought′

wel·ter·weight (wel′tər wāt′) *n.* athlete who competes in the fifth from the lowest weight class in boxing and wrestling. [Earlier *welter* welterweight (from WELT + -ER[1]) + WEIGHT.]

wen (wen) *n.* benign tumor or cyst on the skin, esp. on the scalp. [Old English *wenn* lump on the body.]

wench (wench) *n.* **1.** girl or young woman. **2.** female servant. **3.** loose or immoral woman. —*v.i.* to associate with loose or immoral women. [Middle English *wenche* girl, female servant, loose woman, from *wenchel* child, from Old English *wencel*.]

Wen·chow (wen′chou′, wun′jō′) *n.* port city in southeastern China, formerly known as Yungkia. Pop. (1953), 201,600.

wend (wend) **wend·ed** or (*archaic*) **went, wend·ing.** *v.t.* to make (one's way); go on (one's way): *We plan to wend our way slowly across the country.* —*v.i.* to go; travel; move: *The boat will wend down the river to New Orleans.* [Old English *wendan* to turn, go.]

Wend (wend) *n.* one of a Slavic people living between the Elbe and Oder rivers in eastern Germany.

went (went) *v.* **1.** past tense of **go.** **2.** archaic past tense and past participle of **wend.**

wept (wept) past tense and past participle of **weep.**

were (wur; *unstressed* wər) *v.* **1.** past indicative plural and second person singular of the verb **to be:** *The athletes were tired and hungry after the game.* **2.** past subjunctive of the verb **to be:** *If I were you, I wouldn't have gone.* [Old English *wǣre* past indicative second person singular, *wǣron* past indicative plural, *wǣre* past subjunctive singular, and *wǣren* past subjunctive plural, all of *wesan* to be.]

we're (wēr) we are.

weren't (wurnt, wur′ənt) were not.

were·wolf (wēr′woolf′, wur′-, wâr′-) *pl.,* **-wolves.** *also,* **wer·wolf.** *n.* in European folklore, a human being who sometimes turns into a wolf or who has the power to transform himself into a wolf. [Old English *werewulf,* from *wer* man + *wulf* wolf.]

wert (wurt; *unstressed* wərt) *Archaic.* were.

We·ser (vā′zər) *n.* major river in northern West Germany flowing into the North Sea.

Wes·ley (wes′lē, wez′-) **1. John.** 1703–91, English religious leader and founder of Methodism. **2. Charles.** 1707–88, his brother; English Protestant reformer.

Wes·ley·an (wes′lē ən, wez′-) *n.* member or disciple of the church founded by John Wesley; Methodist. —*adj.* of or relating to John Wesley or to Methodists or Methodism.

west (west) *n.* **1.** general direction of the sunset in relation to an observer on earth. **2.** one of the four cardinal points of the compass, lying directly opposite east and 90 degrees left of north. **3.** *also,* **West.** any region situated toward this direction in relation to a specified point of reference. **4. the West. a.** western part of the United States, usually considered as that part west of the Mississippi River. **b.** countries of Europe and the Americas, lying to the west of Asia, usually not including those in Africa. **c.** countries aligned with the United States in the cold war. **d.** Western Roman Empire. —*adv.* in or toward the west. —*adj.* **1.** to, toward, facing, or in the west. **2.** coming from the west: *a warm, west wind.* [Old English *west* westward.]

West, Benjamin (west) 1738–1820, U.S. painter.

West Al·lis (al′is) city in southeastern Wisconsin, an industrial suburb of adjoining Milwaukee. Pop. (1970), 71,723.

West Berlin, Allied sector of divided Berlin, part of West Germany, in northeastern Germany. Pop. (1968 est.), 2,149,678.

west·bound (west′bound′) *adj.* going westward: *to ride a westbound train.*

west·er·ly (wes′tər lē) *adj., adv.* **1.** toward the west. **2.** coming from the west: *a westerly wind.*

west·ern (wes′tərn) *adj.* **1.** to, toward, or in the west. **2.** coming from the west. **3.** *also,* **Western.** of, relating to, or characteristic of the west or the West. —*n. Informal.* novel, short story, motion picture, or the like dealing with life in the western frontier region of the United States, esp. with the life of cowboys and the early settlers.

Western Church 1. that part of the Roman Catholic Church which follows the Latin Rite. **2.** the Catholic, Anglican, and Protestant churches of western Europe and the Americas collectively.

Western civilization, civilization derived from Hebrew, Greek, Arabian, and European sources as opposed to Indian and Chinese sources.

Western Empire, Western Roman Empire.

west·ern·er (wes′tər nər) *n.* **1.** one who was born in or lives in the west. **2.** *usually,* **Westerner.** one who was born in or lives in the western part of the United States.

Western Hemisphere, half of the earth west of the Greenwich meridian, including North and South America.

Western Isles, Hebrides.

west·ern·most (wes′tərn mōst′) *adj.* farthest west.

Western Roman Empire, western part of the Roman Empire,

after its division in A.D. 395, including present-day France, Spain, and Britain.

Western Samoa, island country in the South Pacific, east of Australia. Capital, Apia. Land area, 1097 sq. mi. Pop. (1967 est.), 132,000.

West Germany, democratic state in north-central Europe, consisting of the former French, British, and American occupation zones of divided Germany. Capital, Bonn. Area, 95,932 sq. mi. Pop. (1969 est.), 59,061,000. Officially, the **Federal Republic of Germany.**

West Indian 1. of or relating to the West Indies. **2.** native or close descendant of a native of the West Indies.

West Indies, archipelago extending from Florida to the coast of Venezuela, separating the Caribbean from the Atlantic. It comprises the Greater Antilles, the Lesser Antilles, and the Bahamas.

West·ing·house, George (wes′ting hous′) 1846–1914, U.S. inventor.

West I·ri·an (ēr′ē än′) western part of New Guinea and its offshore islands, under Indonesian control, formerly known as Netherlands New Guinea. Land area, 159,375 sq. mi. Pop. (1968 est.), 896,000. Also, **West New Guinea.**

West Malaysia, Malaya.

West·min·ster (west′min′stər) *n.* borough in the central part of Greater London, esp. that part containing the court and government buildings. Pop. (1969 est.), 240,360. Also, **City of Westminster.**

Westminster Abbey, Gothic church of England, in Westminster, London. It is the traditional site of coronations and contains the tombs of many English monarchs, statesmen, and national heroes.

West New Guinea, West Irian.

West Pakistan, one of the two former provinces of Pakistan. In 1971, the other former province, East Pakistan, became the independent country of Bangladesh, and the country of Pakistan now consists of what was the province of West Pakistan.

West·pha·li·a (west fā′lē ə, -fāl′yə) *n.* region in West Germany, formerly a province of Prussia. —**West·pha′li·an,** *adj.*

West Point 1. officially, United States Military Academy, an accredited four-year institution providing college-level instruction and officer training for careers in the U.S. Army. **2.** its site, a military reserve on the Hudson River in southeastern New York.

West Virginia, state in the eastern United States. Capital, Charleston. Area, 24,181 sq. mi. Pop. (1970), 1,744,237. Abbreviation, **W. Va.** —**West Virginian.**

west·ward (west′wərd) *adv. also,* **west·wards.** toward the west. —*adj.* toward the west. —*n.* westward direction, point, or part.

west·ward·ly (west′wərd lē) *adj., adv.* **1.** toward the west. **2.** from the west.

wet (wet) **wet·ter, wet·test.** *adj.* **1.** covered, soaked, or moist with water or other liquid. **2.** not yet dry: *A footprint was made in the wet cement.* **3.** marked by rainfall; rainy. **4.** *Informal.* permitting or in favor of the manufacture and sale of alcoholic beverages. **5. all wet.** *Slang.* completely wrong; entirely mistaken. **6. wet behind the ears.** lacking experience or sophistication. —*v.t.,* **wet** or **wet·ted, wet·ting. 1.** to make wet: *Wet the ground before planting.* **2.** to make wet by urinating: *The baby wet the bed.* —*v.i.* **1.** to become wet. **2. to wet one's whistle.** *Informal.* to take a drink. —*n.* **1.** water; moisture; wetness. **2.** rainy weather; rain. [Old English *wǣt* moist, damp, consisting of moisture, having moisture.] —**wet′ness,** *n.*

wet·back (wet′bak′) *n.* Mexican, esp. an agricultural worker, who enters the United States illegally in order to work. [WET + BACK[1]; referring to the practice of entering the United States illegally by wading or swimming across the Rio Grande at night.]

wet blanket *Informal.* one who or that which has a depressing or dispiriting effect.

wet cell, in electricity, cell having a liquid electrolyte.

weth·er (weth′ər) *n.* castrated male sheep. [Old English *wether* ram.]

wet-nurse (wet′nurs′) **-nursed, -nurs·ing.** *v.t.* **1.** to act as wet nurse to. **2.** to pamper or coddle; be overly protective of.

wet nurse, woman employed to suckle the infant of another.

wet suit, close-fitting, one-piece garment made of neoprene, worn for warmth, esp. by skin divers or scuba divers.

we've (wēv) we have.

Wey·den, Ro·gier van der (vīd′ən; rō gēr′ van dər) c.1399–1464, Flemish painter.

w.f., in printing, wrong font. ▲ used to indicate that a letter or character is the wrong size or style. Also, **wf.**

whack (hwak, wak) *n.* **1.** *Informal.* a sharp, resounding blow. **2.** sound made by such a blow. **3.** *Slang.* chance, attempt, or try at something: *I'll take a whack at fixing the car.* **4. out of whack.** not working properly; broken: *The television set is out of whack.* —*v.t., v.i. Informal.* to hit or slap with a sharp, resounding blow. [Probably imitative.]

whack·ing (hwak′ing, wak′-) *adj. Informal.* extremely large.

whack·y (hwak′ē, wak′ē) **whack·i·er, whack·i·est.** *adj.* wacky.

at; āpe; cär; end; mē; it; īce; hot; ōld; fôrk; wood; fōol; oil; out; up; ūse; turn; sing; thin; this; zh in treasure; ə in ago, taken, pencil, lemon, circus.

whale¹ (hwāl, wāl) *pl.,* **whales** or **whale.** *n.* **1.** any of various large, aquatic mammals, order Cetacea, native to all oceans and certain fresh waters, having a fishlike body, horizontal tail fins, and flippers. There are two groups of whales: **toothed whales,** having small cone-shaped teeth, and **baleen,** or **whalebone, whales,** having a thin plate of horny material instead of teeth. The **blue whale,** *Balaenoptera musculus,* may grow to one hundred feet in length and is the largest animal that has ever lived.

Whale (blue whale)

2. *Informal.* something very large or impressive: *There was a whale of a crowd at the game.* —*v.i.,* **whaled, whal·ing.** to engage in the hunting of whales. [Old English *hwæl* this mammal.]
whale² (hwāl, wāl) **whaled, whal·ing.** *v.t. Informal.* to beat; thrash. [Of uncertain origin.]
whale·back (hwāl′bak′, wāl′-) *n.* freight steamer with a rounded upper deck, used esp. on the Great Lakes.
whale·boat (hwāl′bōt′, wāl′-) *n.* long, narrow rowboat, sharp at both ends, formerly used in whaling and now as a lifeboat, as on large passenger steamers or warships.
whale·bone (hwāl′bōn′, wāl′-) *n.* **1.** elastic, horny material similar to fingernails, forming thin plates which grow in place of teeth in the upper jaw of certain whales. **2.** thin strip of this material, used for stiffening corsets or other items. Also, **ba·leen′.**
whal·er (hwā′lər, wā′-) *n.* **1.** one engaged in whaling. **2.** ship used in whaling. **3.** whaleboat.
whal·ing (hwā′ling, wā′-) *n.* act, industry, or occupation of hunting and killing whales, esp. for their blubber or whalebone.
wham·my (hwam′ē, wam′ē) *pl.,* **-mies.** *n. Slang.* hex; curse; jinx: *to put a whammy on someone.*
whang (hwang, wang) *Informal.* **1.** loud, resounding beating or banging noise: *the whang of the gong.* —*v.t.* to strike with a loud, resounding beating or banging noise. —*v.i.* to make a loud, resounding beating or banging sound. [Imitative.]
wharf (hwôrf, wôrf) *pl.,* **wharves** (hwôrvz, wôrvz) or **wharfs.** *n.* dock¹ (def. 1). [Old English *hwearf.*]
wharf·age (hwôr′fij, wôr′-) *n.* **1.** accommodations at or use of a wharf or wharves, as for mooring a ship, loading or unloading cargo, or storing goods. **2.** charge for using a wharf or wharves. **3.** wharves collectively. [WHARF + -AGE.]
wharf·in·ger (hwôr′fin jər, wôr′-) *n.* one who owns or manages a wharf.
Whar·ton, Edith (hwôr′tən, wôr′-) 1862–1937, U.S. novelist.
what (hwut, hwot, wut, wot; *unstressed* hwət, wət) *pron.* **1.** which specific thing or things, action or actions, or the like: *What do you want to do?* **2.** that which: *They knew what he was thinking.* **3. and what not.** and all kinds of other things; and so forth. **4. what for. a.** why. **b.** beating or scolding: *His father gave him what for for having lied.* **5. what if.** what would happen if; suppose that. **6. what's what.** *Informal.* real state of affairs; actual situation; facts. **7. what with.** taking into consideration: *What with the ice and snow, it's nicer to stay indoors.* —*adj.* **1.** (in interrogative construction) word used in asking for information about the person or thing that will qualify it: *Of what breed is that dog?* **2.** whatever: *What talent he had was quickly developed.* **3.** how surprising, great, absurd, or the like: *What a fool he is!* —*adv.* **1.** in what respect or how much: *What difference will it make?* **2.** which reason; why: *What did you do that for?* —*interj.* exclamation used to show surprise, disbelief, anger, or the like. —*conj. Informal.* **but what.** but that. [Old English *hwæt,* neuter of *hwā.*]
what·ev·er (hwət ev′ər, wət-) *pron.* **1.** no matter what; anything that: *Say whatever you want to say.* **2.** *Informal.* what: *Whatever is that noise?* —*adj.* **1.** any that: *Take whatever books you want to read.* **2.** of any type, sort, or character; at all: *No person whatever could be that cruel.*
what·not (hwut′not′, hwot′-, wut′-, wot′-) *n.* set of open shelves, as for holding ornaments or books.
what's (hwuts, hwots, wuts, wots; *unstressed* hwəts, wəts) what is.
what·so·e'er (hwut′sō âr′, hwot′-, wut′-, wot′-) whatsoever.
what·so·ev·er (hwut′sō ev′ər, hwot′-, wut′-, wot′-) *pron., adj.* whatever.
wheal (hwēl, wēl) *n.* **1.** small swelling on the skin, often caused by insect bites or exposure to sunlight, characterized by itching and burning. **2.** welt (def. 3). [Form of WALE; influenced by obsolete *wheal* to suppurate (from Old English *hwelian*).]
wheat (hwēt, wēt) *n.* **1.** cereal grass, genus *Triticum,* widely cultivated as a major food source for man and animals, having a thin, hollow, jointed stem and long, narrow, grasslike leaves. **2.** tiny grain of this plant, used to make flour and other foods, and having many other commercial uses, as in the manufacture of industrial alcohol, starch, and adhesives. [Old English *hwǣte.*]
wheat·ear (hwēt′ēr′, wēt′-) *n.* thrushlike bird, *Oenanthe oenanthe,* native to the Northern Hemisphere, having buff, gray, and white plumage. Length: 6 inches.
wheat·en (hwēt′ən, wēt′-) *adj.* made of wheat.
whee·dle (hwēd′əl, wēd′-) **-dled, -dling.** *v.t.* **1.** to persuade or try to persuade by cajolery, flattery, or the like: *Steve wheedled his boss into giving him the day off.* **2.** to obtain by wheedling. [Possibly from German *wedeln* to fawn, cringe, wag the tail, from *Wedel* tail.] —**whee′dler,** *n.* —**whee′dling·ly,** *adv.* —Syn. 1. see coax.
wheel (hwēl, wēl) *n.* **1.** circular frame having a hub connected to the rim by spokes, capable of rotating on a central axis, used on vehicles and certain machines. **2.** any of a number of mechanical devices that utilizes a wheel or wheel-like part, as a potter's wheel or spinning wheel. **3.** guiding, controlling, or moving force: *wheels of commerce.* **4. wheels.** *Informal.* automobile, motorcycle, bicycle, or other vehicle: *I'd go to the beach but I don't have any wheels.* **5. at the wheel. a.** doing the steering or driving. **b.** in control. **6. wheels within wheels.** complications within complications. —*v.i.* **1.** to turn on or as on an axis; pivot: *Bill wheeled around when I called his name.* **2.** to move with a circular motion: *Birds wheeled overhead.* **3.** to roll or move along on or as on wheels: *to wheel down the highway.* **4. to wheel and deal.** to engage in a variety of activities, esp. business dealings, designed for one's own advancement. —*v.t.* **1.** to move or convey on wheels: *to wheel the cart around the market.* **2.** to cause to turn on or as on an axis. **3.** to provide with wheels. [Old English *hwēol* circular frame turning on an axle.]
wheel·bar·row (hwēl′bar′ō, wēl′-) *n.* boxlike frame with one or two wheels at the front end and two handles at the back, used to move loads, as of sand or bricks.

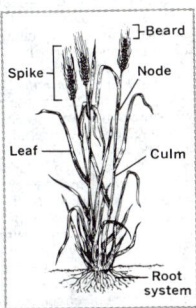

Wheat plant

wheel·base (hwēl′bās′, wēl′-) *n.* distance measured in inches between the center of the front wheel and the corresponding rear wheel of an automobile or similar vehicle.
wheel·chair (hwēl′châr′, wēl′-) *also,* **wheel chair.** *n.* chair mounted on wheels, used esp. by invalids.
wheel·er (hwē′lər, wē′-) *n.* **1.** one who or that which wheels. **2.** that which has a wheel or wheels. **3.** wheel horse or other animal working next to a wheel.

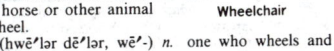

Wheelchair

wheel·er-deal·er (hwē′lər dē′lər, wē′-) *n.* one who wheels and deals.
wheel horse 1. horse harnessed nearest to the front wheels. **2.** *Informal.* one who works harder, longer, or more effectively than others.
wheel·house (hwēl′hous′, wēl′-) *n.* pilothouse.
Wheel·ing (hwē′ling, wē′-) *n.* city in northern West Virginia, on the Ohio. Pop. (1970), 48,188.
wheel·wright (hwēl′rīt′, wēl′-) *n.* man who makes or repairs wheels, or wheeled vehicles, as carriages and wagons.
wheeze (hwēz, wēz) **wheezed, wheez·ing.** *v.t., v.i.* to breathe, say, or utter a hoarse, whistling sound. —*n.* **1.** act or instance of wheezing. **2.** *Informal.* popular saying, story, joke, or the like, esp. a trite one. [Probably from Old Norse *hvæsa* to hiss.]
wheez·y (hwē′zē, wē′-) **wheez·i·er, wheez·i·est.** *adj.* characterized by or affected with wheezing. —**wheez′i·ly,** *adv.* —**wheez′i·ness,** *n.*
whelk (hwelk, welk) *n.* any of various large, saltwater mollusks with spiral shells, as the **common whelk,** *Buchinum undatum,* valued as a food in Europe. [Old English *weoloc.*]
whelm (hwelm, welm) *v.t.* **1.** to cover with water or other liquid; submerge. **2.** overwhelm; overpower. [Probably from an unrecorded Old English word.]
whelp (hwelp, welp) *n.* **1.** young of certain species, as dogs, bears, or lions. **2.** impudent boy or young man. —*v.t., v.i.* to give birth to (whelps). [Old English *hwelp* puppy, cub.]
when (hwen, wen) *adv.* at what or which time: *When did you arrive?* —*conj.* **1.** at the time that: *Come when I call you.* **2.** at any time that: *When he laughs his face gets red.* **3.** at what or which time; and then:

The children played until noon, when they had lunch. **4.** although: *Dan works when he might rest.* **5.** considering that: *How can I go when I haven't been invited?* —*pron.* what time; which time: *Since when have you liked baseball?* —*n.* the time or occasion. [Old English *hwænne* at what time, at the time that.]

whence (hwens, wens) *adv.* from what place or source; from where: *Whence and who is he?* —*conj.* from what place, source, or cause: *We did not know whence the messenger came.* [Middle English *whennes,* going back to Old English *hwanon.*]

whence·so·ev·er (hwens'sō ev'ər, wens'-) *conj. Archaic.* from whatever place, source, or cause.

when·e'er (hwen âr', wen-) *Archaic.* whenever.

when·ev·er (hwen ev'ər, wen-) *conj., adv.* at whatever time. Also, **when·so·ev·er** (hwen'sō ev'ər, wen'-).

where (hwâr, wâr) *adv.* **1.** in or at what place: *Where do you want me to stand? Where do they live?* **2.** to what place: *Where is the train going?* **3.** from what place or source: *Where did you buy that book?* **4.** in or at which: *This is the restaurant where we'll eat.* —*conj.* **1.** in the place in which; at the place at which: *The car is where you parked it.* **2.** in or at which place: *Let's go inside where we can sit down.* **3.** in the case, condition, circumstances, or respect in which: *John was very protective where his sister was concerned.* —*n.* place; locality: *I don't know the when or where of the accident.* [Old English *hwær* in what place, to what place.]

where·a·bouts (hwâr'ə bouts', wâr'-) *adv. also,* **where·a·bout.** near or in what location. —*n., pl.* location of a person or place: *The police established the whereabouts of the suspect.* ▲ construed as singular.

where·as (hwâr az', wâr-) *conj.* **1.** considering that; since: *The document began "whereas the committee has resolved . . ."* **2.** the fact of the matter being that; but; while: *Natalie prefers yellow, whereas I prefer green.* —*n.* phrase or clause, esp. in a legal document, beginning with the word "whereas."

where·at (hwâr at', wâr-) *adv. Archaic.* at what.

where·by (hwâr bī', wâr-) *adv.* **1.** by what or which. **2.** by means of or through which.

wher·e'er (hwâr âr', wâr-) *adv. Archaic.* wherever.

where·fore (hwâr'fôr, wâr'-) *adv.* for what reason; why. —*conj.* for which reason; therefore. —*n.* reason. [WHERE + FOR.]

where·from (hwâr from', -frum', wâr-) *adv. Archaic.* from which; whence.

where·in (hwâr in', wâr-) *adv.* **1.** in which thing, place, or situation. **2.** in what regard; how.

where·in·to (hwâr in'tōō, wâr-, hwâr'in tōō', wâr'-) *adv.* into what or which.

where·of (hwâr ov', -uv', wâr-) *adv.* of what, which, or whom.

where·on (hwâr ôn', -on', wâr-) *adv.* on what or which.

where·so·ev·er (hwâr'sō ev'ər, wâr'-) *adv. Archaic.* wherever.

where·to (hwâr tōō', wâr-) *adv. Archaic. conj.* to which or whom. —*adv.* for what purpose; why.

where·up·on (hwâr'ə pôn', -pon', wâr'-) *conj.* at which time; after which. —*adv. Archaic.* upon what or which.

wher·ev·er (hwâr ev'ər, wâr-) *conj., adv.* in, at, or to whatever place.

where·with (hwâr with', -with', wâr-) *adv. Archaic.* with what or which.

where·with·al (hwâr'with ôl', wâr'-) *n.* necessary means or resources, esp. financial.

wher·ry (hwer'ē, wer'-) *pl.,* **-ries.** *n.* **1.** light rowboat, used esp. to transport passengers and goods on rivers or other sheltered waters. **2.** light rowboat for one person, used esp. for racing. **3.** *British.* any of various large, light boats, as certain fishing boats or barges. [Of uncertain origin.]

whet (hwet, wet) **whet·ted, whet·ting.** *v.t.* **1.** to sharpen by grinding, scraping, or rubbing. **2.** to make keen; stimulate: *The article whetted his interest in the subject.* —*n.* **1.** act of whetting. **2.** that which whets. [Old English *hwettan* to sharpen.]

wheth·er (hweth'ər, weth'-) *conj.* **1.** used to introduce the first of two choices or alternatives: *You must decide whether to fly or take the train.* **2.** if it be the case that: *Write to us whether you'll come next month.* **3.** either: *Whether from bravery or stubbornness, they did not give in.* **4.** whether or not. in any case; regardless. [Old English *hwether.*]

whet·stone (hwet'stōn', wet'-) *n.* stone for sharpening knives or tools.

whew (hwū) *interj.* exclamation used to express relief, surprise, dismay, or the like.

whey (hwā, wā) *n.* watery part of milk that separates from the curd when milk coagulates, as during the process of making cheese. [Old English *hwæg.*]

which (hwich, wich) *pron.* **1.** what or any particular one or ones: *Which is the best?* **2.a.** used as a relative pronoun in a clause providing further information about the antecedent: *This book, which I first read*

as a child, *is still one of my favorites.* **b.** used in place of "that" in a clause providing information that defines or restricts the antecedent: *The team which finishes first will receive the trophy.* See **that** for usage note. **c.** used as a relative pronoun preceded by "that" or as a preposition in defining or restricting the antecedent: *the house in which we live.* **3.** thing, circumstance, event, or the like that: *Jack drove too fast, which was reckless.* **4.** whichever: *Choose which you prefer.* —*adj.* **1.** what or any particular one or ones of a number of persons or things: *Which girl is your sister?* **2.** being the thing or things previously mentioned: *Tom spent four years in college, during which time he learned French.* [Old English *hwilc* what, what one.]

which·ev·er (hwich ev'ər, wich-) *pron., adj.* **1.** any one that: *Buy whichever you like best.* **2.** no matter which: *Whichever road you take, the drive won't be more than an hour.* Also, **which·so·ev·er** (hwich'-sō ev'ər, wich'-).

whiff (hwif, wif) *n.* **1.** sudden, light puff, breath, or gust, as of air. **2.** slight smell or odor. —*v.t.* to drive with a puff or gust. —*v.i.* to blow or be carried in a puff or gust. [Imitative.]

whif·fle (hwif'əl, wif'-) **-fled, -fling.** *v.i.* **1.** to blow in puffs or gusts. **2.** to veer; change; vacillate. —*v.t.* to scatter or blow, as with a light gust or puff. [WHIFF + -LE.] —**whif'fler,** *n.*

whif·fle·tree (hwif'əl trē', wif'-) *n.* crossbar of wood or steel to which the traces of a harness are hitched, as in a horse-drawn carriage or plow. Also, **sin'gle·tree', swing'le·tree', whip'ple·tree'.** [Form of WHIPPLETREE.]

Whig (hwig, wig) *n.* **1.** member of a British political party in the seventeenth through nineteenth centuries that strengthened cabinet government, encouraged foreign trade, and extended suffrage to members of the middle class. **2.** American colonist who supported the Revolution against England. **3.** member of a U.S. political party formed in 1834 in opposition to the Democrats. It split in 1852 over the slavery question. —**Whig'ger·y,** *n.* —**Whig'gish,** *adj.*

while (hwīl, wīl) *n.* **1.** period of time, usually of relatively short duration: *We stopped walking and rested for a while.* **2. between whiles.** between times; at intervals. **3. the while.** during the time. **4. worth (one's) while.** worth time or effort; rewarding. —*conj.* **1.** during or in the time that: *Did you call while I was away?* **2.** at the same time that; although: *While they are my neighbors, I don't know them well.* —*v.t.,* **whiled, whil·ing.** to pass or spend (time or a period of time) in a leisurely or idle manner: *to while away a warm, summer afternoon.* [Old English *hwīl* space of time.]

whiles (hwīlz, wīlz) *Archaic. adv.* **1.** at times; occasionally; sometimes. **2.** in the meantime. —*conj.* during or in the time that; while.

whi·lom (hwī'ləm, wī'-) *Archaic. adj.* former. —*adv.* formerly. [Old English *hwīlum* at times, dative plural of *hwīl* space of time.]

whilst (hwīlst, wīlst) *conj.* while.

whim (hwim, wim) *n.* sudden or unexpected notion or fanciful idea. [Short for earlier *whim-wham;* of uncertain origin.] —**Syn.** see **caprice.**

whim·per (hwim'pər, wim'-) *v.i.* **1.** to cry with weak, broken sounds: *The hungry puppy whimpered.* **2.** to utter with a weak, broken crying sound. —*v.t.* to whimper a cry or sound. [Imitative.] —**whim'per·er,** *n.* —**whim'per·ing·ly,** *adv.*

whim·si·cal (hwim'zi kəl, wim'-) *adj.* full of or characterized by odd or fanciful notions. —**whim'si·cal·ly,** *adv.*

whim·si·cal·i·ty (hwim'zi kal'ə tē, wim'-) *pl.,* **-ties.** *n.* **1.** quality or state of being whimsical. **2.** whimsical idea, notion, or action.

whim·sy (hwim'zē, wim'-) *pl.,* **-sies.** *also,* **whim·sey.** *n.* **1.** capricious, odd, or fanciful notion. **2.** odd, curious, or fanciful humor, as in literature. [Probably from WHIM.]

whin (hwin, win) *n.* furze. [Probably of Scandinavian origin.]

whine (hwīn, wīn) **whined, whin·ing.** *v.i.* **1.** to make a low, plaintive cry or sound, as from pain or peevishness. **2.** to complain in a feeble, petulant, or childish way. —*v.t.* to utter with a low, plaintive cry or sound. —*n.* act or sound of whining. [Old English *hwīnan* to whiz.] —**whin'er,** *n.* —**whin'ing·ly,** *adv.*

whin·ny (hwin'ē, win'ē) **-nied, -ny·ing.** *v.i.* to neigh, esp. in a low, gentle manner. —*v.t.* to express with such a sound. —*n., pl.,* **-nies.** act or sound of whinnying. [Probably from WHINE.]

whin·stone (hwin'stōn', win'-) *n.* any very hard, dark rock, as basalt. [Dialectal *whin* whinstone (of uncertain origin) + STONE.]

whip (hwip, wip) **whipped** or **whipt, whip·ping.** *v.t.* **1.** to strike with a lash, rod, strap, or the like: *to whip a horse.* **2.** to punish by striking thus. **3.** to drive, urge, or force with lashes or blows: *The coachman whipped his horses on.* **4.** to strike in the manner of whipping or lashing: *The cold wind whipped Jane's hair.* **5.** to criticize harshly; castigate. **6.** to beat (a substance, as cream or eggs) so that air is introduced in order to lighten it and increase its volume. **7.** to move, take, throw, or the like suddenly and rapidly: *to whip a gun out of a holster.* **8.** to wind (something) closely in regular, even circles: *Whip the cord around the post.* **9.** to bind or cover (something, as rope) with twine, wire, or the like so as to prevent fraying or wear. **10.** to sew (a hem or other raw

at; āpe; cär; end; mē; it; īce; hot; ōld; fôrk; wood; fōōl; oil; out; up; ūse; turn; sing; thin; this; zh in treasure; ə in ago, taken, pencil, lemon, circus.

edge) with whipstitches. **11.** *Informal.* to defeat, esp. by a large margin. **12. to whip up. a.** to arouse; excite: *The speaker's words whipped up the angry mob.* **b.** to make or prepare quickly: *to whip up a snack.* —*v.i.* **1.** to go, come, move, or turn suddenly and rapidly: *The thief whipped around the corner when he saw the police.* **2.** to move with a flapping or thrashing motion: *The flag whipped in the wind.* —*n.* **1.** instrument consisting of a flexible rod or thong attached to a handle, used esp. for driving animals or inflicting punishment. **2.** whipping or lashing blow, stroke, or motion. **3.** one who handles a whip, as the driver of a coach. **4.** member of a legislative assembly chosen by his party to be assistant to the party leader and to direct its tactics and line up votes for an entire legislative session. **5.** in hunting, person who manages the hounds. **6.** dessert or other dish made with whipped ingredients, esp. cream or eggs. **7.** simple hoisting device consisting of a rope attached to the load and passing through an overhead pulley. [Possibly from Middle Low German *wippen* to swing.] —**whip′per,** *n.*

whip·cord (hwip′kôrd′, wip′-) *n.* **1.** strong, twisted hempen cord, used for the lashes of whips. **2.** durable fabric of worsted, cotton, or other fibers woven with a pronounced diagonal twill, used for such items as suits and sportswear.

whip hand 1. hand in which the whip is held in driving. **2.** position of control or advantage.

whip·lash (hwip′lash′, wip′-) *n.* **1.** lash of a whip. **2.** injury to the neck resulting from a sudden backward or forward movement of the head, as when riding in an automobile that strikes something or is struck.

whip·per·snap·per (hwip′ər snap′-ər, wip′-) *n.* insignificant, impudent person, esp. a young one.

whip·pet (hwip′it, wip′-) *n.* small, slender dog having a short, smooth coat of black, white, or of various colors. The whippet is often used for racing. Height: to 22 inches at the shoulder. [Probably from WHIP + -ET.]

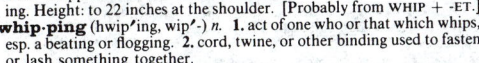

Whippet

whip·ping (hwip′ing, wip′-) *n.* **1.** act of one who or that which whips, esp. a beating or flogging. **2.** cord, twine, or other binding used to fasten or lash something together.

whipping boy, one who is blamed or punished for the misdeeds of another; scapegoat.

whipping post, post to which those sentenced to be flogged are tied.

whip·ple·tree (hwip′əl trē′, wip′-) *n.* whiffletree. [Possibly from WHIP + TREE.]

whip·poor·will (hwip′ər wil′, wip′-) *n.* plump-bodied North American bird, *Caprimulgus vociferus,* having mottled brown, buff, and black plumage. Length: to 10 inches. [Imitative of its cry.]

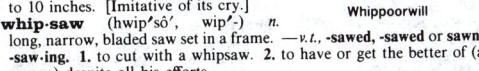

Whippoorwill

whip·saw (hwip′sô′, wip′-) *n.* long, narrow, bladed saw set in a frame. —*v.t.,* **-sawed, -sawed** or **sawn, -saw·ing. 1.** to cut with a whipsaw. **2.** to have or get the better of (a person) despite all his efforts.

whip·stitch (hwip′stich′, wip′-) *n.* slanting stitch made over a hem or other raw edge to prevent raveling or to turn it under to finish the edge. —*v.t.* to sew (a hem or other raw edge) with whipstitches.

whip·stock (hwip′stok′, wip′-) *n.* handle of a whip.

whipt (hwipt, wipt) *a* past tense and past participle of **whip.**

whir (hwur, wur) *v.i.* **whirred, whir·ring.** *also,* **whirr.** *v.i.* to move rapidly with a whizzing or buzzing sound. —*n.* whizzing or buzzing sound, as that made by a rapidly revolving wheel. [Of Scandinavian origin.]

whirl (hwurl, wurl) *v.i.* **1.** to revolve or turn rapidly: *The blades of the propeller whirled around and around.* **2.** to turn around or aside suddenly or quickly: *The sentry whirled about when he heard the noise.* **3.** to move or go swiftly: *The explosion sent fragments of rock whirling through the air.* **4.** to have a sensation of spinning; experience dizziness: *The dazzling lights made my head whirl.* —*v.t.* **1.** to cause to revolve or turn rapidly. **2.** to move, carry, or drive swiftly, esp. in a circular course. —*n.* **1.** act of whirling or spinning; whirling movement or motion. **2.** something undergoing a whirling movement. **3.** confused or highly active state or condition. **4.** rapid succession of activities or events: *a whirl of parties.* **5.** *Informal.* try; attempt: *Rob didn't think he could do it, but he decided to give it a whirl.* [Old Norse *hvirfla* to turn about.] —**whirl′er,** *n.*

whirl·i·gig (hwur′li gig′, wur′-) *n.* **1.** toy designed to whirl or spin about, as a pinwheel. **2.** merry-go-round *(defs. 1, 2).* **3.** something that moves or seems to move in a whirling motion. **4.** whirling motion. [WHIRL + obsolete *gig* top[2] (of uncertain origin).]

whirligig beetle, any of a group of water beetles, family Gyrinidae, that whirls about in curves on the surface of water.

whirl·pool (hwurl′pool′, wurl′-) *n.* **1.** current of water having a swift or violent circular motion, usually occurring in rapidly moving bodies of water. **2.** anything resembling the whirling motion of a whirlpool.

whirl·wind (hwurl′wind′, wurl′-) *n.* **1.** rapidly or violently rotating column of air. **2.** anything resembling a whirlwind, as in swiftness of motion. —*adj.* very swift; hasty: *a whirlwind courtship.* [Possibly of Scandinavian origin.]

whirl·y·bird (hwur′lē burd′, wur′-) *n.* *Informal.* helicopter.

whirr (hwur, wur) whir.

whish (hwish, wish) *n.* soft, rushing sound; swish. —*v.i.* to move with such a sound. [Imitative.]

whisk (hwisk, wisk) *v.t.* **1.** to sweep or brush with swift, light strokes. **2.** to move, cause to move, or convey swiftly or abruptly. **3.** to whip or beat, as eggs. —*v.i.* to move swiftly or lightly. —*n.* **1.** quick, light sweeping motion or movement. **2.** whisk broom. **3.** small bunch, as of straw or feathers, used esp. for brushing. **4.** wire kitchen utensil used esp. for whipping cream or eggs. [Of Scandinavian origin.]

Whisk *(def. 4)*

whisk broom, small, short-handled broom used esp. for brushing clothes.

whisk·er (hwis′kər, wis′-) *n.* **1. whiskers.** hair growing on a man's face; the beard or a part of the beard. **2.** single hair of a beard. **3.** one of the long, stiff hairs growing near the mouth of certain animals, as dogs, cats, and rodents. **4.** *Informal.* very small margin. [WHISK + -ER[1].] —**whisk′ered,** *adj.*

whis·key (hwis′kē, wis′-) *pl.,* **-keys.** *also,* **whis·ky.** *n.* **1.** strong alcoholic liquor distilled from fermenting grain, as rye, corn, barley, or wheat. **2.** a drink of such liquor. ◢ *Whiskey* is often spelled *whisky* when used in combination, as in *Scotch whisky.* [Short for earlier *usquebaugh* this liquor, from Gaelic *uisgebeatha* literally, water of life, from *uisge* water + *beatha* life.]

whis·per (hwis′pər, wis′-) *v.i.* **1.** to speak very softly with little or no vibration of the vocal cords. **2.** to speak quietly or cautiously, as in gossiping or conspiring. **3.** to make a soft, rustling sound, as leaves blown by a breeze. —*v.t.* **1.** to utter very softly: *She whispered the word in my ear.* **2.** to say or tell secretly or confidentially, as a rumor. —*n.* **1.** very soft speech with little or no vibration of the vocal cords. **2.** something whispered, as a rumor or secret. **3.** soft, rustling sound. **4.** small amount; hint: *a whisper of garlic in the sauce.* [Old English *hwisprian* to whisper very softly.] —**whis′per·er,** *n.*

whist[1] (hwist, wist) *n.* card game for two pairs of players, played with a full deck of fifty-two cards. It is the forerunner of bridge. [Earlier *whisk,* possibly from WHISK; supposedly referring to the whisking or sweeping up of cards from the table; influenced in spelling by WHIST[2] (from the silence expected of the players).]

whist[2] (hwist, wist) *interj.* hush; quiet. [Imitative.]

whis·tle (hwis′əl, wis′-) *-tled, -tling.* *v.i.* **1.** to make a clear, shrill sound by forcing breath through contracted lips or through the teeth. **2.** to produce or emit a sound resembling this. **3.** to make or cause a shrill sound by swift movement: *A bullet whistled past the soldier's head.* **4. to whistle for.** to expect or attempt to get in vain. —*v.t.* **1.** to produce by whistling: *to whistle a melody.* **2.** to call, signal, or direct by whistling. —*n.* **1.** device designed or used to produce a whistling sound. **2.** whistling sound. **3. to blow the whistle (on).** *Informal.* to call attention to, as someone's wrongdoing, esp. in order to stop; expose. **4. to wet one's whistle.** *Informal.* to take a drink. [Old English *hwistlian* to make a hissing sound.]

whis·tler (hwis′lər, wis′-) *n.* **1.** one who or that which whistles. **2.** large marmot, *Marmota caligata,* native to northwestern North America. Length: 30 inches.

Whis·tler, James Ab·bott Mc·Neill (hwis′lər, wis′-; ab′ət mək nēl′) 1834–1903, U.S. painter and etcher.

whis·tle-stop (hwis′əl stop′, wis′-) *-stopped, -stop·ping.* *v.i.* to make brief personal appearances in small towns, esp. in campaigning for political office.

whistle stop 1.a. small town at which trains stop only when signaled. **b.** any small or insignificant town. **2.** brief personal appearance in a small town, esp. by a political candidate.

whit (hwit, wit) *n.* tiny amount; bit: *All this sudden wealth made him not a whit happier.* [Old English *wiht* thing, creature.]

white (hwīt, wīt) **whit·er, whit·est.** *adj.* **1.** reflecting all the visible rays of the spectrum. Opposed to **black. 2.** of very light or comparatively light in color. **3.** pale; pallid; ashen: *His face was white with fear.* **4.** silvery or pale gray, as with age. **5.a.** of, relating to, or belonging to the Caucasoid race. **b.** consisting of, restricted to, or controlled by white people: *a*

white neighborhood, a white school. **c.** light-skinned. **6.** free from malice or evil intent; not harmful: a white lie, white magic. **7.** covered with or characterized by the presence of snow; snowy: a white Christmas. **8.** not written or printed upon; blank. **9.** morally or spiritually pure; innocent. **10.** clothed or habited in white. **11.** also, **White.** politically conservative or reactionary, as opposed to radical or revolutionary. **12.** Slang. honorable; fair; decent. —n. **1.** color that is the reflection of all the visible rays of the spectrum. Opposed to black. **2.** white or light-colored part of something, as the albumen of an egg or the white part of an eyeball. **3.** something that imparts white, as a paint or pigment. **4.** light-skinned person; Caucasoid. **5.** also, **whites.** white clothing or a white uniform. **6.** blank space, as in printing. **7.** also, **White.** member of a politically conservative or reactionary group as opposed to a radical or revolutionary. —v.t., **whit·ed, whit·ing.** Archaic. to whiten. [Old English hwīt of the color of snow or milk, fair', of a light color.]

white ant, termite.
white·bait (hwīt'bāt', wīt'-) pl., **-bait.** n. any of various small fish of the herring family, eaten as a delicacy.
white blood cell, one of the cells found in the blood of man and other vertebrates, that protects the body against foreign substances and infection. Also, **leu'ko·cyte'.**
white·cap (hwīt'cap', wīt'-) n. wave with a crest of white foam.
white cedar 1. evergreen tree, Chamaecyparis thyoides, found in the eastern United States. **2.** soft, durable wood of this tree.
white clover, creeping clover, Trifolium repens, bearing white flowers sometimes tinged with pink.
white-col·lar (hwīt'col'ər, wīt'-) adj. of, relating to, or designating workers employed in professional, clerical, or other fields that usually do not involve manual labor. [From the white shirts worn by many such workers.]
white elephant 1. something that is expensive or burdensome to keep and, although often rare or unique, is of little value or use to the owner: Their large old house was a white elephant. **2.** item no longer wanted by its owner, but possibly of value to others. [Referring to the veneration in parts of Asia of light-colored elephants, which are not allowed to work because they are considered sacred.]
white-faced (hwīt'fāst', wīt'-) adj. **1.** having a pale face; pallid. **2.** marked with white on the face or front of the head, as a horse.
white feather 1. sign or symbol of cowardice. **2. to show the white feather,** to act like a coward. [From the belief that a white feather in a gamecock's tail is a sign of cowardice.]
White·field, George (hwīt'fēld', wīt'-) 1714– 70, English clergyman and early leader of Methodism.

Whitefish

white·fish (hwīt'fish', wīt'-) pl. **-fish** or **-fish·es.** n. any of several silvery-white, commercially important food fish of the salmon family, found in freshwater lakes and streams of North America, Europe, and Asia. Length: to 2 feet.
white flag, white flag or piece of cloth, used to indicate surrender or truce.
White Friar, Carmelite. [Referring to the white color of his cloak.]
white gold, alloy of gold and usually nickel, having a platinumlike appearance, used for jewelry.
White·hall (hwīt'hôl', wīt'-) n. **1.** street in London where many government offices are located. **2.** the British government.
White·head, Alfred North (hwīt'hed', wīt'-) 1861–1947, English mathematician and philosopher.
white heat 1. extreme degree of heat, beyond red heat, at which a substance, as a metal, glows white. **2.** state or condition of extreme emotion, excitement, or activity.
White·horse (hwīt'hôrs', wīt'-) n. city in northwestern Canada, capital of the Yukon. Pop. (1966), 4771.
white-hot (hwīt'hot', wīt'-) adj. **1.** glowing white with heat. **2.** extremely angry or excited.
White House 1. official residence of the president of the United States, a white mansion in Washington, D.C. Also, **Executive Mansion. 2.** the executive branch of the U.S. government.
white lead, white, poisonous lead carbonate, used chiefly as a paint pigment.
white-liv·ered (hwīt'liv'ərd, wīt'-) adj. cowardly.
white man's burden, alleged duty of the white peoples to spread their civilization to other peoples regarded as less developed. [From The White Man's Burden, a poem by Rudyard Kipling.]
white matter, that part of the brain and spinal cord consisting chiefly of nerve fibers covered by myelin and having a white appearance.

White Mountains (hwīt, wīt) scenic range of the Appalachian Mountains chiefly in northern New Hampshire.
whit·en (hwīt'ən, wīt'-) v.t., v.i. to make or become white or whiter.
white·ness (hwīt'nis, wīt'-) n. quality or condition of being white.
White Nile, river in eastern Africa, flowing northward through Uganda to Khartoum where it joins the Blue Nile.
white oak 1. any of various oaks, esp. Quercus alba, a large oak of the eastern United States, noted for its heavy, durable wood. **2.** strong, hard wood of any of these trees.
white paper, official government report on a particular subject.
white pepper, see pepper (def. 1).
white pine 1. tall pine tree, Pinus strobus, of eastern North America, having bluish-green leaves and slender cones. **2.** soft wood of this tree. **3.** any of various similar pines.
white plague, tuberculosis of the lungs.
White Plains, city in southeastern New York, principally a residential suburb of New York City. Pop. (1970), 50,220.
White Russia, Byelorussia.
White Russian, Byelorussian.
white sale, sale of towels, sheets, or similar goods at reduced prices.
white sauce, basic sauce made by combining flour and butter or other fat with seasonings and either milk, cream, or a light-colored stock.
white slave, woman forced into or held in prostitution.
white slavery, business of dealing in white slaves; forced prostitution.
white-tailed deer (hwīt'tāld', wīt'-) tawny North American deer, Odocoileus virginianus, having a bushy tail which is white on the underside. Height: 3–4 feet at the shoulder. Also, **Virginia deer.**
white·throat (hwīt'thrōt', wīt'-) n. **1.** small Eurasian warbler, Sylvia communis, having a whitish throat and belly. **2.** North American sparrow, Zonotrichia albicollis, having a white patch on the throat. Also (def. 2), **white-throated sparrow.**

Whitethroat (def. 2)

white tie 1. white bow tie, worn with men's formal evening wear. **2.** men's formal evening wear. Distinguished from black tie.
white·wall (hwīt'wôl', wīt'-) n. automobile tire with a white band on its outer side.
white·wash (hwīt'wôsh', -wosh', wīt'-) n. **1.** white paintlike substance consisting essentially of a mixture of slaked lime and water containing salt, whiting, and a gluing substance, used to coat surfaces, as masonry walks and wood fences. **2.** act of covering up or glossing over something, as a mistake or wrongdoing. **3.** Sports. defeat in which the loser fails to score any points. —v.t. **1.** to coat or cover with whitewash. **2.** to cover up or gloss over (something), as a mistake or wrongdoing. **3.** Sports. to defeat (an opponent) without allowing him to score any points.
white water, churned up, turbulent water, as in rapids.
white·wood (hwīt'wood', wīt'-) n. **1.** any of several trees with whitish or light-colored wood, as the basswood or cotton wood. **2.** wood of any of these trees.
whith·er (hwith'ər, with'-) Archaic. adv. **1.** to what place; where. **2.** to what end, point, or condition. —conj. to which, what, or whatever place, end, point, or condition. [Old English hwider.]
whith·er·so·ev·er (hwith'ər·sō·ev'ər, with'-) adv., conj. Archaic. to whatever place.
whit·ing[1] (hwīt'ing, wīt'-) pl. **-ings** or **-ing.** n. **1.** silvery food fish, Gadus merlangus, related to the cod, found in Atlantic coastal waters from Norway to Spain. Weight: 3–4 pounds. **2.** any of several similar fish, as the kingfish. [Dutch wijting.]

Whiting[1] **(def. 1)**

whit·ing[2] (hwīt'ing, wīt'-) n. white chalk, powdered and washed, used esp. as a pigment. [WHITE + -ING[1].]
whit·ish (hwīt'tish, wīt'-) adj. somewhat white.
whit·low (hwit'lō, wīt'-) n. felon[2]. [Earlier whitflaw, from WHITE + FLAW[1].]
Whit·man, Walt (hwīt'mən, wīt'-) 1819–92, U.S. poet.
Whit·mon·day (hwīt'mun'dē, -dā, wīt'-) n. Monday immediately following Whitsunday, observed as a holiday in Great Britain.
Whit·ney (hwīt'nē, wīt'-) n. **1.** E·li (ē'lī). 1765–1825, U.S. inventor, noted esp. for inventing the cotton gin. **2. Mount.** mountain of the Sierra Nevada, in eastern California, the highest peak in the United States outside Alaska.

at; āpe; cär; end; mē; it; īce; hot; ōld; fôrk; wood; fōol; oil; out; up; ūse; turn; sing; thin; this; zh in treasure; ə in ago, taken, pencil, lemon, circus.

Whit·sun (hwit′sən, wit′-) *adj.* of, relating to, or observed on Whitsunday or Whitsuntide.

Whit·sun·day (hwit′sun′dē, -dā, wit′-, hwit′sən dā′, wit′-) *n.* Pentecost (*def.* 1). [Old English *Hwīta Sunnandæg* literally, white Sunday; referring to the earlier practice of wearing white garments on Whitsunday by the newly baptized.]

Whit·sun·tide (hwit′sən tīd′, wit′-) *n.* the week beginning with Whitsunday, esp. the first three days of this week.

Whit·ti·er, John Green·leaf (hwit′ē ər, wit′-; grēn′lēf′) 1807–92, U.S. poet.

whit·tle (hwit′əl, wit′-) -tled, -tling. *v.t.* 1. to cut shavings or small bits or pieces from (wood) with a knife. 2. to make or shape (something) in this way. 3. to reduce or diminish gradually, as if by whittling with a knife (often with *down* or *away*): *to whittle down expenses.* —*v.i.* to whittle wood. [From dialectal English *whittle* knife, form of *thwittle,* going back to Old English *thwītan* to cut.] —**whit′tler,** *n.*

whiz (hwiz, wiz) **whizzed, whiz·zing.** *also,* **whizz.** *v.i.* to make a hissing, humming, or buzzing sound, esp. while moving swiftly through the air: *The flying saucer whizzed over the roof tops. The automobile whizzed past us.* —*v.t.* to cause to whiz. —*n. pl.,* **whiz·zes.** 1. whizzing sound or movement. 2. *Slang.* person having great skill or ability in some particular activity or field: *Nancy is a whiz at crossword puzzles.* [Imitative.]

who (hōō) possessive, **whose**; objective, **whom.** *pron.* 1. what or which person or persons: *Who gave you that information?* 2. that. ▲ used to introduce a relative clause when referring to a person or persons: *The woman who wrote this play has an odd sense of humor.* 3. the person or persons that; whoever: *Who steals my purse steals trash* (Shakespeare, *Othello*). [Old English *hwā* what or which person or persons.]

whoa (hwō, wō) *interj.* stop. ▲ used chiefly as a command to a horse.

who·dun·it (hōō dun′it) *n. Informal.* mystery story, esp. one that centers on the gradual discovery of the criminal's identity.

who·ev·er (hōō ev′ər) *pron.* 1. any person who; whatever person: *Whoever wants to come to the party is welcome.* 2. no matter who: *Whoever he is, I don't like him.* 3. what person; who. ▲ used emphatically, as to express disbelief: *Whoever told you such a ridiculous story?*

whole (hōl) *adj.* 1. constituting the entire amount, quantity, number, or extent: *Did you read the whole book? David's been sick the whole week.* 2. having all its parts or elements; complete; entire: *A whole deck consists of fifty-two cards.* 3. all or each of the members of a particular group: *The whole family came down with measles. The whole gang was sent to prison.* 4. not divided into parts or pieces; in one unit: *The whale swallowed the small fish whole.* 5. not damaged, injured, or broken; intact. 6. physically sound; healthy. 7. (of a brother or sister) having the same parents. 8. *Mathematics.* integral; not fractional. —*n.* 1. all the parts or elements that together constitute a thing; the entire amount, quantity, number, or extent. 2. combination of parts or elements forming a complete entity or system. 3. **on the whole.** all things considered; in general. [Old English *hāl* unhurt, undamaged, healthy, not divided into parts.] —**whole′ness,** *n.* —**Syn.** *adj.* 2. see **complete.**

whole blood, blood from which none of the elements has been removed, used for transfusions.

whole-heart·ed (hōl′här′tid) *adj.* complete; sincere; enthusiastic: *I will give you my whole-hearted support, but none more of my money.* —**whole′-heart′ed·ly,** *adv.* —**whole′-heart′ed·ness,** *n.*

whole note, musical note having a time value equal to four quarter notes or two half notes.

whole number, non-negative integer.

whole·sale (hōl′sāl′) *n.* selling of goods in large quantities, usually to retailers for resale. Distinguished from *retail.* —*adj.* 1. of, relating to, or engaged in the selling of goods at wholesale. 2. extensive and indiscriminate: *the wholesale slaughter of war.* —*adv.* in a wholesale quantity or at a wholesale price. —*v.t.,* **-saled, -sal·ing.** to sell (goods) at wholesale. —*v.i.* to be sold at wholesale. [From the earlier phrase *by the whole sale* in large quantities.]

whole·sal·er (hōl′sā′lər) *n.* wholesale merchant or dealer.

whole·some (hōl′səm) *adj.* 1. promoting good health; healthful: *wholesome food.* 2. of value to the mind or character; worthwhile: *wholesome entertainment.* 3. indicating or characteristic of good health. [Probably from an unrecorded Old English word.] —**whole′some·ly,** *adv.* —**whole′some·ness,** *n.*

whole step *Music.* interval consisting of two adjacent half steps. Also, **whole tone.**

whole-wheat (hōl′hwēt′, -wēt′) *adj.* 1. made of the whole wheat kernel: *whole-wheat flour.* 2. made with whole-wheat flour: *whole-wheat bread.*

who'll (hōōl) who will; who shall.

whol·ly (hō′lē, hōl′lē) *adv.* 1. entirely; completely. 2. exclusively; only.

whom (hōōm) *pron.* objective case of **who.**

whom·ev·er (hōōm ev′ər) *pron.* objective case of **whoever.**

whom·so·ev·er (hōōm′sō ev′ər) *pron.* objective case of **whosoever.**

whoop (hōōp, hwōōp, wōōp) *n.* 1. loud cry or shout, as of joy or enthusiasm. 2. cry of an owl or certain other birds. 3. loud, gasping sound that follows a fit of coughing in whooping cough. —*v.i.* to utter a whoop or whoops. —*v.t.* 1. to utter with a whoop or whoops. 2. to urge on, drive, or call with whoops or shouts. 3. **to whoop it up.** *Slang.* **a.** to create a loud or noisy disturbance, as in celebrating. **b.** to arouse enthusiasm. [Imitative.]

whoop·ee (hwōō′pē, wōō′-, hwoop′ē, woop′ē) *interj.* used to express joy, gaiety, or the like. —*n.* 1. shout of joy, gaiety, or the like. 2. **to make whoopee.** to celebrate in a noisy, festive way. [From **whoop.**]

whoop·ing cough (hōō′ping, hōōp′ing) highly contagious, infectious disease caused by a bacillus and characterized by fits of coughing that end with a loud, gasping sound. Whooping cough usually occurs in infants and young children.

whooping crane, nearly extinct crane, *Grus americana,* having a white body, black-tipped wings, and a red face. It is the tallest of all North American birds. Height: 5 feet.

whop (hwop, wop) **whopped, whop·ping.** *Informal. v.t.* 1. to hit or beat. 2. to defeat completely. —*n.* 1. sharp blow. 2. sound resulting from such a blow. [Probably imitative.]

whop·per (hwop′ər, wop′-) *n. Informal.* 1. something very large: *That fish you caught is a whopper!* 2. a big lie. [**WHOP** + -ER[1].]

whop·ping (hwop′ing, wop′-) *Informal. adj.* unusually large or great. —*adv.* exceptionally; unusually: *a whopping good meal.* [**WHOP** + -ING[2].]

whore (hōr) *n.* 1. prostitute. 2. any promiscuous woman. —*v.i.,* **whored, whor·ing.** to consort or have intercourse with whores. [Old English *hōre* prostitute.] —**whor′ish,** *adj.*

whore·house (hōr′hous′) *n.* house of prostitution; brothel.

whorl (hwurl, wurl, hwôrl, wôrl) *n.* 1. *Botany.* arrangement of parts, as leaves, around the same point on a stem. 2. *Zoology.* one of the turns or convolutions of a spiral shell. 3. any of the circular ridges of a fingerprint. 4. anything resembling a coil or spiral in form or appearance. [Possibly a form of **WHIRL**.]

Whorl of a fingerprint

whorled (hwurld, wurld, hwôrld, wôrld) *adj.* having or arranged in a whorl or whorls.

whor·tle·ber·ry (hwurt′əl ber′ē, wurt′-) *pl.,* **-ries.** *n.* 1. sweet, black, edible berry of a shrub, *Vaccinium myrtillus,* native to northern Asia and Europe. 2. shrub bearing this berry. [Form of dialectal *hurtleberry,* going back to Old English *horte* whortleberry + *beri(g)e* berry.]

whose (hōōz) *pron.* possessive case of **who** and **which.** ▲ often used adjectivally: *Whose woods these are I think I know* (Frost, 1923).

whose·so·ev·er (hōōz′sō ev′ər) *pron.* of whomsoever.

who·so (hōō′sō) *pron.* whoever.

who·so·ev·er (hōō′sō ev′ər) *pron.* whoever.

why (hwī, wī) *adv.* for what cause, reason, or purpose: *Why are you laughing?* —*conj.* 1. the cause, reason, or purpose for which: *That is why she came home early.* 2. because of which; for which: *I see no reason why you shouldn't go.* —*n. pl.,* **whys.** cause; reason; purpose. —*interj.* used chiefly to express surprise, hesitation, or other feeling. [Old English *hwȳ* for what cause, reason, or purpose.]

W. I. 1. West Indies. 2. West Indian.

Wich·i·ta (wich′i tô′) *n.* largest city in Kansas, in the south-central part of the state. Pop. (1970), 276,554.

Wichita Falls, city in northern Texas. Pop. (1970), 197,564.

wick (wik) *n.* cord or thin bundle of fibers, as in an oil lamp, candle, or cigarette lighter, that acts by capillary action to draw up the fuel or material to be burned. [Old English *wēoce.*]

wick·ed (wik′id) *adj.* 1. morally bad; evil. 2. mischievous; sly. 3. causing or intended to cause harm, trouble, or discomfort. 4. *Informal.* skillful: *John plays a wicked game of tennis.* [From dialectal English *wick* bad, possibly going back to Old English *wicca* wizard.] —**wick′ed·ly,** *adv.* —**wick′ed·ness,** *n.* —**Syn.** 1. see **bad'.**

wick·er (wik′ər) *n.* 1. slender, flexible twig or osier. 2. wickerwork. —*adj.* made of or covered with wicker. [Of Scandinavian origin.]

wick·er·work (wik′ər wurk′) *n.* something made of twigs, osiers, or the like and woven together.

wick·et (wik′it) *n.* 1. small door or gate, esp. one that is part of or near a larger one. 2. small window or opening. 3. *Cricket.*

Wickerwork

a. either of the two sets of three stakes topped by bails. **b.** playing area between these wickets. **4.** *Croquet.* any of the usually wire arches through which the ball must be hit. [Anglo-French *wiket* small gate or door; of Germanic origin.]

wick·et·keep·er (wik′it kē′pər) *n. Cricket.* player stationed immediately behind the wicket.

wick·i·up (wik′ē up′) *n.* loosely built hut often consisting of a circular frame of poles covered with brush, used by certain Indian tribes of North America. [Algonquian *wikiyapi* house, hut.]

Wick·liffe (wik′lif) *also,* **Wic·lif.** Wycliffe.

wide (wīd) **wid·er, wid·est.** *adj.* **1.** extending over or comprising a very large area; vast in extent: *the whole wide world.* **2.** having a relatively greater extent from side to side than is usual or customary: *Suits of this style have wide lapels.* **3.** having a specified extent from side to side: *a belt two inches wide.* **4.** great in extent or inclusiveness: *This store carries a wide assortment of products.* **5.** fully opened or extended: *The boy's eyes were wide with excitement.* **6.** far or away from a specified point or object (often with *of*): *His arrow was wide of the mark. The senator's statements were wide of the truth.* **7.** loose; full; roomy: *wide pants.* **8.** *Phonetics.* articulated with the tongue and muscles of the jaw relatively relaxed. —*adv.* **1.** over a large area; extensively: *to travel far and wide.* **2.** to a large or the full extent: *to open a window wide.* **3.** far or away from something aimed at. [Old English *wīd* vast in extent, having greater extent from side to side, having a specified extent from side to side.] —**wide′ly,** *adv.* —**wide′ness,** *n.*

wide-a·wake (wīd′ə wāk′) *adj.* **1.** fully awake. **2.** alert.

wide-eyed (wīd′īd′) *adj.* with the eyes wide open, as in wonder, disbelief, or surprise.

wid·en (wīd′ən) *v.t., v.i.* to make or become wide or wider.

wide-o·pen (wīd′ō′pən) *adj.* **1.** opened to a large or the full extent. **2.** having little or no law enforcement: *a wide-open town.*

wide·spread (wīd′spred′) *adj.* **1.** extending over a large area: *a widespread epidemic.* **2.** occurring, distributed, or prevalent over a wide area or among many people: *a widespread misconception.* **3.** widely extended: *widespread arms.*

widg·eon (wij′ən) *pl.,* **-eons** *or* **-eon.** *n.* any of several freshwater ducks, genus *Mareca,* having predominantly brownish or grayish plumage. Length: 16–23 inches. [Of uncertain origin.]

widg·et (wij′it) *n.* any small gadget, object, or part, esp. one whose name is not known. [Modification of GADGET.]

wid·ow (wid′ō) *n.* woman whose husband is dead, esp. one who has not married again. —*v.t.* to cause to become a widow. [Old English *widuwe* a woman whose husband is dead.]

wid·ow·er (wid′ō ər) *n.* man whose wife is dead, esp. one who has not married again. [WIDOW + -ER¹.]

wid·ow·hood (wid′ō hood′) *n.* state or period of being a widow.

widow's mite, small contribution given by a person who can scarcely afford it. [From the reference in Mark 12:41–44 to the poor widow who gave two mites to the treasury of the temple.]

widow's peak, V-shaped point in a hairline formed by hair growing down in the middle of the forehead. [From the belief that it indicated early widowhood.]

width (width, witth) *n.* **1.** measurement of something from side to side; size in terms of wideness; breadth. **2.** fact, quality, or state of being wide. **3.** piece of something, esp. of cloth, having a certain width.

width·wise (width′wīz′, witth′-) *adv.* in the direction of the width; from side to side.

wield (wēld) *v.t.* **1.** to handle or use, as a weapon or tool. **2.** to exercise, as influence or power. [Old English *wieldan* to manage, control.] —**wield′er,** *n.*

wie·ner (wē′nər) *n.* frankfurter. Also, **wie·ner·wurst** (wē′nər-wurst′). [Short for German *Wiener Wurst* literally, Viennese sausage.]

Wie·ner schnit·zel (vē′nər shnit′səl) breaded veal cutlet. [German *Wiener Schnitzel* literally, Viennese cutlet.]

Wies·ba·den (vēs′bäd′ən) *n.* city in west-central West Germany, noted as a health resort. Pop. (1968 est.), 258,596.

wife (wīf) *pl.,* **wives.** *n.* **1.** married woman. **2.** *Archaic.* woman. ▲ now used chiefly in combination: *housewife, fishwife.* **3. to take to wife.** to marry. [Old English *wīf.*] —**wife′ly,** *adj.*

wife·hood (wīf′hood′) *n.* state of being a wife.

wig (wig) *n.* artificial covering for the head made of hair or of a synthetic material resembling hair. [Short for PERIWIG.]

wig·gle (wig′əl) **-gled, -gling.** *v.i.* to move with short, quick, jerky movements, as from side to side. —*v.t.* to cause to wiggle. —*n.* act of wiggling; wiggling movement. [Middle English *wigelen* to move to and fro, possibly from Middle Low German *wiggelen* to totter, reel.] —**wig·gly,** *adj.*

wig·gler (wig′lər) *n.* **1.** one who or that which wiggles. **2.** wriggler *(def. 2).*

wight (wīt) *n. Archaic.* human being; person. [Old English *wiht* creature, thing.]

Wight, Isle of (wīt) island in the English Channel, off the southern coast of England. Area, 147 sq. mi. Pop. (1970 est.), 102,100.

wig·wag (wig′wag′) **-wagged, -wag·ging.** *v.t., v.i.* **1.** to move back and forth. **2.** to send (a message) by waving flags, lights, or the like according to a code. —*n.* **1.** act or practice of sending messages by waving flags, lights, or the like according to a code. **2.** message so sent. [Dialectal *wig* to move, wag (possibly from WIGGLE)+ WAG¹.] —**wig′wag′ger,** *n.*

wig·wam (wig′wom, -wôm) *n.* dwelling used by certain tribes of North American Indians, usually consisting of an arched framework of poles covered with bark or leaves. [Algonquian *wigiwam* literally, their dwelling.]

Wigwam

Wil·ber·force, William (wil′bər fôrs′) 1759–1833, English statesman, abolitionist, and philanthropist.

wild (wīld) *adj.* **1.** not brought under the control of man; in a state of nature: *wild beasts.* **2.** growing without the assistance of man. Distinguished from **cultivated. 3.** not inhabited or cultivated; desolate: *the wild prairie.* **4.** uncivilized; savage. **5.** unrestrained or disorderly; uncontrolled: *the wild flight of a frightened animal.* **6.** undisciplined; unruly: *wild children.* **7.** not orderly in appearance; disheveled: *wild hair.* **8.** characterized by violent or intense activity; turbulent; stormy: *the wild sea.* **9.** characterized by or indicating intense emotion; frenzied: *wild with grief.* **10.** reckless or thoughtless; rash: *a wild idea.* **11.** crazy or fantastic: *a wild look in his eye, a wild story.* **12.** wide of the mark: *a wild shot, a wild throw.* **13.** *Informal.* extremely enthusiastic or excited: *The audience was wild about the new singer.* **14.** (of a card) having any value the player designates. —*n. also,* **wilds.** uninhabited or uncultivated place. —*adv.* **1.** in a wild manner. **2. to run wild.** to be free from any form of control or restraint. [Old English *wilde* untamed, uncultivated, unrestrained.] —**wild′ly,** *adv.* —**wild′ness,** *n.*

wild boar, wild hog, genus *Sus,* native to Europe, Asia, and North America, having a coarse, grayish-brown coat and a pair of short tusks. Height: 3 feet at the shoulder.

wild carrot, weed, *Daucus carota,* of the parsley family, found in Europe, Africa, Asia, and North America, having a coarse hairy stem and yellowish-green leaves, and bearing a flat-topped lacelike cluster of tiny white flowers. Also, **Queen Anne's lace.**

wild·cat (wīld′kat′) *n.* **1.** any of various small, wild members of the cat family, including the bobcat and lynx. **2.** ill-tempered or spiteful person, esp. a woman. **3.** exploratory oil well drilled to determine whether oil is actually present at a given locality. —*adj.* **1.** unsound or reckless: *a wildcat bank, a wildcat scheme.* **2.** unauthorized; illegal: *a wildcat strike without the union's approval.* —*v.t., v.i.* **-cat·ted, -cat·ting.** to drill exploratory oil wells in (a locality). —**wild′cat′ter,** *n.*

Wild carrot

Wilde, Oscar (wīld) 1854–1900, Irish playwright, novelist, and essayist.

wil·de·beest (wil′də bēst′) *pl.,* **-beests** *or* **-beest.** *n.* gnu. [Obsolete Afrikaans *wildebeest* literally, wild beast, from Dutch *wild* wild + *beest* beast.]

Wil·der, Thorn·ton Niv·en (wīl′dər; thornt′ən niv′ən) 1897—, U.S. playwright and novelist.

wil·der·ness (wil′dər nis) *n.* **1.** wild, uninhabited, or desolate place. **2.** confused or bewildering aggregate or collection: *a wilderness of tall buildings.* [Middle English *wildernesse* wild region, from *wildern* wild (going back to Old English *wilddēor* wild animal) + *-nesse* (see -NESS).]

wild-eyed (wīld′īd′) *adj.* staring in an angry or demented manner.

wild·fire (wīld′fīr′) *n.* fire that spreads rapidly and is not easily extinguished.

wild·flow·er (wīld′flou′ər) *also,* **wild flower.** *n.* **1.** any flower of a flowering plant that grows wild, as in a field or woods. **2.** the plant itself.

wild·fowl (wīld′foul′) *pl.,* **-fowl** *or* **-fowls.** *n.* game bird, esp. a wild duck or goose.

wild-goose chase (wīld′gōōs′) foolish or hopeless pursuit or endeavor.

wild·ing (wīl′ding) *n.* plant or fruit of a plant that grows wild, esp. a wild apple tree.

wild·life (wīld′līf′) *n.* living things, esp. wild animals, originating in or characteristic of a particular locality.

at; āpe; cär; end; mē; it; īce; hot; ōld; fôrk; wood; fōol; oil; out; up; ūse; turn; sing; thin; this; zh in treasure; ə in ago, taken, pencil, lemon, circus.

wild oat 1. *also,* **wild oats.** any of various wild grasses, genus *Avena,* that resembles the cultivated oat. **2. to sow one's wild oats.** to indulge in the excesses or foibles characteristic of youth.

wild pitch *Baseball.* pitch thrown beyond the catcher's reach that allows a base runner to advance.

wild rice, tall grass, *Zizania aquatica,* that is native to North America and bears edible grains.

Wild West, western frontier region of the United States, noted for its rough and lawless conditions during the nineteenth century.

wild·wood (wīld'wood') *n.* forest that has not been cut or cultivated and is in its natural state.

wile (wīl) *n.* **1.** trick or stratagem: *She employed her wiles to capture him.* **2.** trickery; craftiness. —*v.t.* **wiled, wil·ing. 1.** to tempt; lure. **2. to wile away.** to pass pleasantly. [Possibly of Scandinavian origin.]

wil·ful (wil'fəl) willful.

wil·i·ness (wī'lē nis) *n.* state or quality of being wily.

Wilkes-Bar·re (wilks'bar'ē) *n.* city in northeastern Pennsylvania. Pop. (1970), 58,856.

will¹ (wil) Present: *sing.,* first person, **will;** second, **will** or *(archaic)* **wilt;** third, **will.** Past: *sing.,* first person, **would;** second, **would** or *(archaic)* **wouldst;** third, **would;** *pl.* **would.** *auxiliary verb* (followed by an infinitive) **1.** to be about to; going to: *I will visit you tonight.* **2.** to be willing to: *I will write you if you promise to reply.* **3.** to be obliged or bound to; must: *He will do as he is told.* **4.** to be able to; can: *This chair will not support your weight.* **5.** to be accustomed to: *Sometimes the cat will lie there all afternoon.* ▲ see usage note under **shall.** —*v.t., v.i.* to wish; desire: *What do you will?* [Old English *willan* to be about to, be willing, wish.]

will² (wil) *n.* **1.** power or capacity of free, conscious choice. **2.** ability to determine or control one's actions, esp. self-control: *Does he have the will to stop?* **3.** fixed resolution; purpose: *She survived because of her will to live.* **4.** preferred course of action; wish: *What is his will in the matter?* **5.** *Law.* document giving the final settlement of a person's property after his death. **6. at will.** at one's own discretion or convenience. —*v.t.* **1.** to determine by free choice; bring about by the exercise of will. **2.** to settle conclusively; decide to do. **3.** to induce (someone) to do something. **4.** to dispose of (property) by a will; bequeath. [Old English *willa* faculty of willing, intention, determination, desire.]

willed (wild) *adj.* having a (specified kind of) will. ▲ used in combination, as in *weak-willed, strong-willed.*

wil·let (wil'it) *pl.,* **-lets** or **-let.** *n.* American wading bird, *Catoptrophorus semipalmatus,* having long wings, a long, narrow bill, and gray and white plumage with black and white bands on the wings. Length: 14–17 inches. [Imitative of its cry.]

Willet

will·ful (wil'fəl) *also,* **wil·ful.** *adj.* **1.** determined to do as one pleases; obstinate; stubborn: *a willful youngster.* **2.** deliberate; intentional: *a willful waste.* —**will'ful·ly,** *adv.* —**will'ful·ness,** *n.* —**Syn. 1.** see **headstrong.**

Wil·liam I (wil'yəm) c.1027–1087, king of England from 1066 to 1087. Also, **William the Conqueror.**

William II, 1859–1941, emperor of Germany from 1888 to 1918.

William III, 1650–1702, king of England from 1689 to 1702.

Wil·liams (wil'yəmz) **1.** Roger. c.1603–84, founder of Rhode Island. **2.** Tennessee. 1914—, U.S. dramatist. **3.** William Car·los (kär'lōs). 1883–1963, U.S. poet and physician.

Wil·liams·burg (wil'yəmz bûrg') *n.* historic town in southeastern Virginia. Pop. (1970), 9069.

wil·lies (wil'ēz) *n.pl.* *Slang.* uneasiness or nervousness; jitters. [Of uncertain origin.]

will·ing (wil'ing) *adj.* **1.** favorably disposed; ready: *willing to work.* **2.** characterized by cheerful readiness: *a willing candidate.* **3.** cheerfully given, accepted, or accomplished: *willing service.* —**will'ing·ly,** *adv.* —**will'ing·ness,** *n.*

will-o'-the-wisp (wil'ə thə wisp') *n.* **1.** faint light seen at night hovering over marshes. Also, **ignis fatuus. 2.** something deceptive, as a hope or goal.

wil·low (wil'ō) *n.* **1.** any of a group of trees and shrubs, genus *Salix,* native to temperate regions of the Northern Hemisphere. Among the best-known species are the **black willow,** *S. nigra,* having flaky, deeply ridged bark and growing to a height of thirty to forty feet, and the **weeping willow. 2.** light, soft wood of such a tree or shrub, used to make paper, boxes, and furniture. [Old English *welig* the tree.]

willow herb, small shrub or herb, genus *Epilobium,* having narrow, lance-shaped leaves and bearing small white to rose-purple flowers.

wil·low·y (wil'ō ē) *adj.* **1.** graceful and slender. **2.** abounding with willows.

will·pow·er (wil'pou'ər) *n.* ability to control one's actions; resoluteness of will.

wil·ly-nil·ly (wil'ē nil'ē) *adj.* indecisive; vacillating: *a willy-nilly person.* —*adv.* whether one is willing or not; willingly or unwillingly. [Modification of *will I, nill I* I am willing, I am unwilling; archaic *nill* to be unwilling, not to will, from Old English *nyllan.* See **WILL¹.**]

Wil·ming·ton (wil'ming tən) *n.* largest city of Delaware, a port in the northeastern part of the state. Pop. (1970), 80,386.

Wil·no (vil'nō) Polish. Vilnius.

Wil·son (wil'sən) *n.* **1.** Harold. 1916—, British political leader, prime minister from 1964 to 1970. **2.** Wood·row (wood'rō). 1856–1924, twenty-eighth president of the United States, from 1913 to 1921. **3.** Mount. peak in southern California, site of an astronomical observatory.

wilt¹ (wilt) *v.i.* **1.** to fade or droop; become limp; wither. **2.** to lose energy, strength, or courage. —*v.t.* to cause to wilt. [Form of dialectal *wilk* to wither, a form of dialectal *welk;* possibly of Low German or Dutch origin.] —**Syn. v.i. 1.** see **droop.**

wilt² (wilt) *Archaic.* second person singular, present indicative of **will¹.** ▲ used with thou.

Wil·ton (wilt'ən) *n.* carpet of a type in which the loops of the pile have been cut to give a velvety surface. [From *Wilton,* English town where it was originally made.]

wil·y (wī'lē) **wil·i·er, wil·i·est.** *adj.* full of wiles; cunning; crafty. —**wil'i·ly,** *adv.* —**Syn.** see **sly.**

wim·ble (wim'bəl) *n.* any of various tools for boring holes. —*v.t.,* **-bled, -bling.** to bore with or as with a wimble. [Middle Dutch *wimmel* auger.]

Wim·ble·don (wim'bəl dən) *n.* city in southeastern England, near London, noted as the site of international tennis matches. Pop. (1963 est.), 57,000.

wim·ple (wim'pəl) *n.* cloth covering for the head and neck, formerly worn by women out-of-doors, still worn by nuns. —*v.t.,* **-pled, -pling. 1.** to cover with or as with a wimple. **2.** to lay in folds. **3.** to cause to ripple. —*v.i.* **1.** to lie in folds. **2.** to ripple. [Old English *wimpel* the cloth covering.]

win (win) **won** or *(archaic)* **wan, won, win·ning.** *v.i.* **1.** to be victorious over others: *a good player who wins often at cards.* **2.** to finish first in a race: *The horse won by a head.* Distinguished from **place** and **show. 3.** to succeed in some effort or endeavor. **4. to win out.** *Informal.* to succeed or be victorious: *The truth will win out in the end.* —*v.t.* **1.** to be victorious in: *to win a battle, to win a court case.* **2.** to receive in or as in competition: *to win a vacation for two, to win ten dollars at the race track.* **3.** to obtain by effort or merit: *to win respect, to win favor among the poor.* **4.** to obtain the good will, favor, or support of; persuade (often with *over*): *The lawyer won over the jury with his moving defense.* **5.** to obtain (someone's love, sympathy, or other favorable emotion). **6.** to persuade (someone) to marry or return one's love. **7.** to attain or reach, esp. after long effort: *to win the shore, to win entry.* —*n.* **1.** *Informal.* victory: *The pitcher had ten wins and no losses.* **2.** first position at the finish of a race. [Old English *winnan* to strive, fight.]

wince (wins) **winced, winc·ing.** *v.i.* to draw back or away slightly, as from something painful, dangerous, or unpleasant; flinch: *to wince at the thought of getting up so early in the morning.* —*n.* act or instance of wincing. [From an unrecorded Anglo-Norman form of Old French *guenchir* to flinch, turn aside; of Germanic origin.]

winch (winch) *n.* **1.** machine for hoisting or pulling, consisting of a drum around which cord or chain is wound, worked manually or by machine power. **2.** crank, handle, or lever by which a revolving machine is turned. [Old English *wince* pulley.]

Win·ches·ter (win'ches'tər, -chi stər) *n.* **1.** city in southern England, a noted religious and educational center and site of a well-known Gothic cathedral. Pop. (1965 est.), 30,500. **2.** *Trademark.* breechloading, repeating rifle, first manufactured in 1866.

wind¹ (wind) *n.* **1.** air in motion over the surface of the earth; natural movement or current of air: *The wind whistled through the canyon.* **2.** strong or destructive natural movement of air; gale. **3.** direction from which a natural current of air blows; a point of the compass. ▲ used chiefly in the phrase *the four winds.* **4.** air set in motion artificially, as by a fan or other moving object. **5.** moving air carrying an odor, esp. of a person or animal being hunted; scent: *The dogs followed the wind of the fox.* **6.** any compelling force or influence: *winds of change.* **7.** ability to breathe; breath: *The blow knocked the wind out of him.* **8.** empty, meaningless talk; chatter. **9. winds. a.** wind instruments. **b.** players of these instruments. **10.** gas in the stomach or intestines.

before the wind. with the wind coming from behind.

down the wind. in the direction in which the wind is blowing.

in the wind. happening or going to happen; astir.

into the wind. into or toward the direction from which the wind is blowing.

off the wind. with the wind coming from behind.

on the wind. as close as possible to the direction from which the wind is blowing.

to bend with the wind. to alter one's actions or opinions according to prevailing popular attitudes.

to get (or have) wind of. to receive (or have) information or hints about: *If the newspapers get wind of this, we're ruined.*

to take the wind out of one's sails. to destroy or deflate one's ego, argument, or advantage.

—*v.t.* wind·ed, wind·ing. 1. to cause to be short of breath, as by physical exertion: *Swimming ten laps had winded him.* 2. to expose to the wind or air; ventilate. 3. to perceive or follow by scent. 4. to allow to rest in order to recover breath, as a horse. [Old English *wind* air in motion, breath.]

wind² (wīnd) wound or *(archaic)* wind·ed, wind·ing. *v.t.* 1. to wrap (something) around on itself or on something else: *to wind the yarn into a ball. Sue wound the scarf around her neck.* 2. to cover or entwine, as by wrapping or coiling: *to wind one's hair with ribbons.* 3. to cause to turn on an axis: *to wind a crank.* 4. to cause to move or proceed first in one direction and then another: *to wind one's car through city traffic.* 5. to make (one's way) by moving first in one direction and then another. 6. to adjust or put (a mechanism, as a clock) into action by turning or coiling some part of it: *to wind a clock, to wind the strings of a guitar.* 7. to introduce or present indirectly or deviously: *to wind facts into an argument.* 8. to haul or hoist by or as by a winch, windlass, or other mechanism operated by winding. 9. to wind up. a. to bring to an end; conclude; finish: *Let's wind up this job today.* b. to bring to a state of readiness or excitement; arouse; incite: *His speech had wound up the crowd.* c. to coil, roll, or twine completely around; form into a ball. —*v.i.* 1. to move in one direction and then another; go in a crooked or bending course: *The new highway winds around the mountain.* 2. to twine, turn, or coil around or about something: *The roses wound around the trellis.* 3. to proceed or achieve something indirectly or deviously; pursue a circuitous course: *He tried to wind around their questions.* 4. (of wood) to become warped; bend; twist. 5. to admit of being turned or coiled: *The strings on this guitar wind easily.* 6. to wind up. a. to come to an end; conclude; finish: *The meeting wound up at six o'clock. He is sure to wind up bankrupt.* b. (of a baseball pitcher) to make the movements preparatory to pitching the ball. —*n.* 1. act of winding; being wound. 2. condition of being wound; turn of something wound. [Old English *windan* to turn, twist, move rapidly or forcefully.] —wind'er, *n.*

wind³ (wīnd, wind) wind·ed or wound, wind·ing. *v.t.* 1. to blow (a wind instrument). 2. to sound (a call or signal) by blowing. [From WIND¹.]

wind·age (win'dij) *n.* 1. influence of the wind in deflecting a missile, as a bullet, from its course. 2. amount of such deflection. 3. amount in degrees by which a gunsight must be adjusted to compensate for such deflection. 4. disturbance in the air caused by a moving object. 5. portion of a ship's surface exposed to the wind.

wind·bag (wind'bag') *n. Informal.* one who talks much but says little of substance or interest.

wind·blown (wind'blōn') *adj.* 1. blown by the wind. 2. of or designating a woman's haircut in which the hair is cut short and brushed forward.

wind·borne (wind'bôrn') *adj.* carried by the wind, as pollen.

wind·break (wind'brāk') *n.* structure, as a fence, or growth of trees or shrubs that serves as a protection from the wind.

Wind·break·er (wind'brā'kər) *n. Trademark.* short sports jacket made of any of various tightly woven fabrics that resist the passage of air.

wind·bro·ken (wind'brō'kən) *adj.* (of a horse) having the heaves or other breathing impairment.

wind·burn (wind'bûrn') *n.* irritation of the skin caused by exposure to the wind. —wind'burned', *adj.*

wind·ed (win'did) *adj.* out of breath; breathless: *A winded athlete stepped up to receive the award.*

Win·der·mere, Lake (win'dər mēr') largest lake in England, in the northwestern part of the country.

wind·fall (wind'fôl') *n.* 1. unexpected advantage, opportunity, or gain, esp. a financial gain. 2. fruit that falls from the tree before it is harvested, esp. that which is blown down by the wind.

wind·flow·er (wind'flou'ər) *n.* anemone *(def. 1).* [Translation of Greek *anemōnē* literally, windflower, from *anemos* wind.]

Wind·hoek (vint'hook') *n.* capital of South-West Africa, in the central part of the territory. Pop. (1960), 36,051.

wind·hov·er (win'huv'ər, -hov'-) *n.* kestrel.

wind·ing (wīn'ding) *n.* 1. act or state of one who or that which winds. 2. bend, turn, or curve or a series of these. 3. that which winds or coils, as a wire. 4. manner in which something is wound, as an electrical wire in an armature. —*adj.* 1. full of bends or turns, as a road or stream; rambling. 2. curving about a central core; spiraling: *a winding staircase.*

winding sheet. cloth in which a corpse is wrapped for burial; shroud.

wind instrument (wind) musical instrument sounded by air being blown into it, as the flute, clarinet, trumpet, or tuba.

wind·jam·mer (wind'jam'ər, win'-) *n. Informal.* 1. merchant sailing ship. 2. member of its crew. [WIND¹ + JAM¹ + -ER¹.]

wind·lass (wind'ləs) *n.* winch, esp. one that is turned by a hand crank, used chiefly to lift anchors and buckets in wells. [Middle English *wyndlas*, modification of *windas*, going back to Old Norse *vindáss* literally, winding pole, from *vinda* to wind² + *áss* pole¹.]

wind·mill (wind'mil') *n.* mechanism that converts wind power to mechanical power, consisting of a number of vanes or slats radiating from a central axis that is rotated by the wind. Windmills are now used chiefly to pump water.

win·dow (win'dō) *n.* 1. opening in the wall or roof of a building, boat, or other structure for admitting light or air, usually fitted with a movable sash and one or more panes. 2. sash: *I can't get this window open.* 3. windowpane: *We broke the window playing ball.* 4. anything resembling a window in shape or function, as the structure behind which a cashier sits or a transparent patch on an envelope that enables the address printed on an enclosure to be read. [Old Norse *vindauga* opening in a building for light and air; literally, wind eye, from *vindr* wind¹ + *auga* eye.]

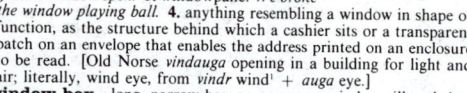

Windmill

window box, long, narrow box on or near a window sill or ledge, used for growing flowering plants.

window dresser, one whose job or occupation is decorating store windows.

window dressing 1.a. act or art of decorating store windows with attractive merchandise displays. b. the displays themselves or the merchandise used to create such displays. 2. anything that is made to seem or is used to make something else seem more attractive, profitable, or acceptable than it really is.

win·dow·pane (win'dō pān') *n.* single pane of glass in a window.

window sash, framework holding the glass in a window.

window seat, seat built under a window or windows, usually in a recess or bay.

Window sash

window shade, piece of material, usually opaque and mounted on a roller that moves by the action of a spring, used to regulate the amount of light entering or the view through a window.

win·dow·shop (win'dō shop') -shopped, -shop·ping. *v.i.* to look at merchandise in store windows or displays without actually buying anything. —win'dow-shop'per, *n.*

window sill, sill of a window.

wind·pipe (wind'pīp') *n.* trachea.

wind·row (wind'rō', win'-) *n.* 1. long row of hay, straw, or grain heaped together to dry. 2. any similar row or ridge of dry leaves, dust, or other material swept together by or as by the wind. —*v.t.* to form into or arrange in a windrow or windrows.

wind·shield (wind'shēld') *n.* transparent screen, often of glass, attached in front of the occupants of an automobile, motorcycle, or other vehicle to protect against wind or precipitation.

wind sock (wind) long, cone-shaped sack hung on a pole or mast, that shows the direction of the wind blowing through it. Also, wind sleeve.

Wind·sor (win'zər) *n.* 1. Duke of. 1894—, son of George V of England, who was King Edward VIII in 1936 before he abdicated the throne. 2. the royal house of Great Britain. The name was adopted by George V in 1917. 3. city in southern England, southwest of London, on the Thames. It is the site of Windsor Castle. Pop. (1964), 29,000. Also, New Windsor. 4. southernmost city in Canada, in the southeastern part of the country. Pop. (1968), 192,544.

Windsor Castle, chief residence of English monarchs since the Norman Conquest, in Windsor, England.

Windsor chair, any of various wooden chairs with a spindle back, slanting legs, and usually a slightly concave seat.

Windsor tie, wide necktie tied in a loose bow.

wind·storm (wind'stôrm') *n.* storm with high winds but little or no precipitation.

wind·swept (wind'swept') *adj.* exposed to or swept by the action of the wind: *a windswept field of grain.*

wind tunnel (wind) chamber in which air is forced over a scale model

at; āpe; cär; end; mē; it; īce; hot; ōld; fôrk; wood; fōōl; out; up; ūse; turn; sing; thin; this; zh in treasure; ə in ago, taken, pencil, lemon, circus.

of an aircraft or some other object, producing the same effect that would occur if the object itself were moving through the air, used in aerodynamic research.

wind·up (wīnd′up′) *n.* **1.** act of winding up; conclusion; finish: *the wind-up of a political campaign.* **2.** movements made by a baseball pitcher before pitching the ball.

wind·ward (wind′wərd) *adj.* located on or moving toward the side toward which the wind is blowing. —*n.* side or direction toward which the wind is blowing. —*adv.* toward the wind. Opposed to **leeward.**

Wind·ward Islands (wind′wərd) Caribbean island group forming the southern part of the Lesser Antilles. Land area, approx. 1412 sq. mi.

wind·y (win′dē) **wind·i·er, wind·i·est.** *adj.* **1.** characterized by or having much wind: *a windy night.* **2.** exposed to or swept by the wind: *a windy beach.* **3.** long-winded and bombastic: *windy rhetoric, a windy demagogue.* **4.** resembling the wind, as in storminess or airiness. —**wind′i·ly,** *adv.* —**wind′i·ness,** *n.*

wine (wīn) *n.* **1.** fermented juice of grapes, used as a beverage, in cooking, and in certain religious ceremonies. **2.** fermented juice of other fruits or plants: *blackberry wine.* **3.** dark purplish-red color, similar to the color of certain wines. —*v.t., v.i.,* **wined, win·ing. 1.** to furnish with or drink wine. **2.** to wine and dine. to entertain or be entertained with lavish food and drink. [Old English *wīn* fermented juice of grapes used as a beverage, going back to Latin *vīnum.*]

wine cellar 1. place for the aging or storage of wine. **2.** stock or store of wine.

wine·glass (wīn′glas′) *n.* small, usually stemmed, glass for drinking wine.

wine·glass·ful (wīn′glas fool′) *pl.,* **-fuls.** *n.* amount that a wineglass holds.

wine·grow·er (wīn′grō′ər) *n.* one whose work or business is cultivating grapes and making wine. —**wine′grow′ing,** *adj., n.*

wine press 1. machine for pressing the juice from grapes. **2.** vat in which juice is pressed from grapes.

win·er·y (wī′nər ē) *pl.,* **-er·ies.** *n.* establishment for making wine.

Wine·sap (wīn′sap′) *n.* bright-red apple with white flesh.

wine·skin (wīn′skin′) *n.* bag made of the skin of a goat or other animal, used for storing and drinking wine.

wing (wing) *n.* **1.** structure that enables a bird, insect, bat, or other flying mammal to fly, corresponding to the forelimb in other animals. **2.** analogous structure in animals not capable of flight, as in the ostrich or penguin. **3.** anything resembling a wing in shape or function. **4.** one of the main lifting and supporting surfaces of an airplane. **5.** foreleg of an animal; human arm. ▲ used humorously. **6.** action, manner, or means of flying. **7.** architectural structure attached to the side of a larger structure or considered as a separate section: *to add a new wing on to a house, an orthopedic wing of a hospital.* **8.** *Theater.* **a.** part on either side of a stage that is not seen by the audience. **b.** scenery projecting on to the side of a stage. **9.** *Sports.* **a.** either of two positions on either side of the center in hockey and certain other goal games. **b.** player in such a position. **10.** division or faction of an organization representing a particular point of view. **11.** *Botany.* leaf-like, membranous extension or appendage of a plant part. **12.** tactical unit of the U.S. Air Force together with its supporting units. **13. wings.** insignia awarded to certain personnel of military aircraft, as pilots or bombardiers, when they have completed their training. **14. on the wing. a.** in flight; flying. **b.** about to take flight; departing. **15. to take wing.** to take flight; depart; flee. **16. under one's wing.** under one's protection or care. —*v.t.* **1.** to effect or accomplish by flight: *The bird winged his way back to the nest.* **2.** to cause to fly as if on wings; give speed to. **3.** to furnish with wings; equip for flight. **4.** to fly through, upon, or across; traverse in flight. **5.** to transport or bear in flight. **6.** to wound (as a bird) in the wing. **7.** *Informal.* to wound superficially: *The bullet winged him in the arm.* **8.** to wing it. to perform with little or no preparation; ad-lib. —*v.i.* to fly; soar: *The plane winged through the sky.* [Old Norse *vængr* bird's wing, aisle.]

wing case, elytron of certain insects, as the beetle. Also, **wing cover.**

wing chair, upholstered armchair with a high back and high sides extending from the back, affording a comfortable support and protection from drafts.

winged (wingd, wing′id) *adj.* **1.** having wings or a winglike part or parts: *a winged bat, a winged seed.* **2.** moving or passing on or as if on wings: *winged hours.* **3.** lofty; elevated; sublime: *winged thoughts.* **4.** wounded in or as in the wing or arm; disabled: *a winged eagle.*

wing nut, nut with winglike projections so that it can be turned easily with the thumb and finger.

wing·span (wing′span′) *n.* distance between the fully extended tips of the wings of a bird, insect, or airplane. Also, **wing·spread** (wing′-spred′).

wink (wingk) *v.i.* **1.** to close and open the eyelid of one eye quickly, esp. as a sign or signal. **2.** to close and open the eyelids of both eyes

quickly. **3.** to pretend not to see; ignore deliberately (with *at*). **4.** to gleam intermittently; twinkle. —*v.t.* **1.** to close and open (an eye or the eyes) quickly. **2.** to signal or express by winking: *She winked her approval.* —*n.* **1.** act of winking. **2.** time required for winking; very short time; instant: *I didn't get a wink of sleep last night.* **3.** sign or signal conveyed by winking. **4.** gleam; twinkle. [Old English *wincian* to close one's eyes.]

win·kle (wing′kəl) *n.* periwinkle².

Win·ne·ba·go (win′ə bā′gō) *pl.,* **-gos** or **-goes** or **-go.** *n.* member of a North American Indian tribe of Siouan stock, now living in parts of Nebraska and Wisconsin.

win·ner (win′ər) *n.* one who or that which wins.

win·ning (win′ing) *adj.* **1.** that wins or results in victory or success: *the winning number in the lottery, the winning home run.* **2.** charming; pleasing; attractive: *a winning smile.* —*n.* **1.** act of one who wins; victory. **2.** that which is won, esp. money. ▲ usually used in the plural: *Al used his winnings to pay the rent.* —**win′ning·ly,** *adv.*

Win·ni·peg (win′ə peg′) *n.* city in southern Canada, the capital, largest, and chief city of Manitoba. Pop. (1968), 257,005.

win·now (win′ō) *v.t.* **1.** to subject (grain) to wind or a current of air to blow away the chaff. **2.** to blow away (chaff) in this way. **3.** to separate or remove (something desirable or undesirable); sort (often with *out*). **4.** to examine closely so as to separate the good from the bad. —*v.i.* to separate grain from chaff. [Old English *windwian* to fan grain in order to blow away the chaff, from *wind.* See WIND¹.] —**win′now·er,** *n.*

win·o (wī′nō) *pl.,* **-os.** *n. Slang.* person habitually drunk on cheap wine.

win·some (win′səm) *adj.* attractive or pleasing; charming: *a winsome smile.* [Old English *wynsum* pleasant, from *wynn* pleasure + *-sum.* See -SOME¹.] —**win′some·ly,** *adv.* —**win′some·ness,** *n.*

Win·ston-Sa·lem (win′stən sā′ləm) *n.* city in north-central North Carolina, the state's leading industrial center and one of the largest tobacco markets in the world. Pop. (1970), 132,913.

win·ter (win′tər) *n.* **1.** season of the year coming between fall and spring. In the Northern Hemisphere it extends from the winter solstice, about December 22, to the vernal equinox, about March 21. **2.** period of time characterized by decline, decay, dreariness, or adversity. —*adj.* **1.** of, like, characteristic of, or occurring in winter: *winter sports.* **2.** (of fruits and vegetables) that may be kept during the winter. **3.** planted in the autumn to be harvested in the spring or summer: *winter wheat.* —*v.i.* to spend or pass the winter. —*v.t.* to keep or maintain during the winter. [Old English *winter* this season, of this season.]

win·ter·green (win′tər grēn′) *n.* **1.** small evergreen plant, *Gaultheria procumbens,* of North America, having bright red berries and aromatic leaves. Also, **check′er·ber′ry, spice′ber′ry. 2.** oil of this plant, used in medicine or for flavoring. **3.** flavor of this oil or something having this flavor.

win·ter·ize (win′tə rīz′) **-ized, -iz·ing.** *v.t.* to prepare or equip for winter weather, as an automobile.

win·ter·kill (win′tər kil′) *v.t., v.i.* (of plants and grains) to kill or die by exposure to winter cold.

winter solstice, see solstice *(def. 1).*

winter squash, any of a group of squashes having hard, inedible rinds, grown in the summer or autumn, and eaten when ripe.

win·ter·time (win′tər tīm′) *n.* winter season.

Win·throp (win′throp) **1. John.** 1588–1649, English colonist in America. **2. John.** 1606–76, his son; English colonist in America, colonial governor of Connecticut.

win·try (win′trē) **-tri·er, -tri·est.** *adj.* **1.** of, like, or characteristic of winter: *wintry weather.* **2.** cold; cheerless. Also, **win·ter·y** (win′tər ē). —**win′tri·ly,** *adv.* —**win′tri·ness,** *n.*

win·y (wī′nē) **win·i·er, win·i·est.** *adj.* having the qualities or taste of wine.

wipe (wīp) **wiped, wip·ing.** *v.t.* **1.** to subject to slight rubbing or friction, usually with a soft or absorbent material, in order to clean or dry. **2.** to remove by or as by rubbing (with *away, off, up,* or *out*): *to wipe up spilled milk. Wipe that smile off your face!* **3.** to rub, move, or apply over a surface: *The boy wiped the ink all over his shirt.* **4.** to wipe out. **a.** to kill or destroy completely; annihilate: *The epidemic wiped out half the town's population.* **b.** to ruin financially: *The stock market crash wiped out many leading businessmen.* —*n.* act or instance of wiping or rubbing. [Old English *wīpian* to clean by rubbing, as with a cloth.]

wip·er (wī′pər) *n.* one who or that which wipes, esp. a device designed or used for wiping.

wire (wīr) *n.* **1.** metal drawn into a thin, usually flexible, strand, thread, or rod. **2.** length of wire, used chiefly as an electrical conductor and structural material. Electrical wires are usually made of copper and surrounded by an insulating or protective covering. **3.** unit consisting of several strands of wire wound together; cable. **4.** telegraph.

5. telegram. **6. to pull wires.** to employ secret or underhanded means to gain a desired end. **7. under the wire.** just within the time allotted; just in time. —*adj.* made of or resembling wire. —*v.t.*, **wired, wir·ing. 1.** to furnish or provide with wiring. **2.** to fasten with a wire or wires. **3.** to send by telegraph: *to wire a message.* **4.** to send a telegram to. —*v.i.* to telegraph: *We'd better wire ahead for reservations.* [Old English *wīr* metal thread.]

wire gauge, gauge for measuring the diameter of wire, usually consisting of a metal disk having slots of various sizes along its outer edge.

wire-haired (wīr′hārd′) *adj.* having coarse, stiff, or wiry hair.

wire·less (wīr′lis) *adj.* **1.** having no wire or wires. **2.** *British.* radio. —*n.* **1.** wireless telegraph or telephone system. **2.** *British.* radio. —*v.t.*, *v.i. British.* to communicate with (someone) by wireless.

wireless telegraphy, telegraphy by means of radio waves. Also, **wireless telegraph.**

wireless telephone. radiotelephone.

wire netting. netting of woven wire.

Wire·pho·to (wīr′fō′tō) *pl.* **-tos.** *n. Trademark.* **1.** method or device for transmitting and receiving photographs by wire. **2.** photograph so transmitted.

wire·pull·er (wīr′pool′ər) *n.* one who uses secret or underhanded means to control others or gain a desired end. —**wire′pull′ing,** *n.*

wire service, news-gathering agency that supplies news, pictures, and the like to subscribing or member newspapers, magazines, and radio and television stations throughout the world.

wire·tap (wīr′tap′) **-tapped, -tap·ping.** *v.i.* to tap a telephone or telegraph wire, esp. to obtain information or evidence. —*v.t.* **1.** to obtain (information or evidence) by wiretapping. **2.** to tap (a telephone or telegraph wire). —*n.* **1.** act or instance of wiretapping. **2.** device used in wiretapping. —**wire′tap′per,** *n.*

wire·worm (wīr′wurm′) *n.* slender, hard-bodied larva of the click beetle, often destructive to the roots and seeds of various crops.

wir·ing (wīr′ing) *n.* network or system of wires, esp. for carrying electric current.

wir·y (wīr′ē) **wir·i·er, wir·i·est.** *adj.* **1.** made of or consisting of wire. **2.** like or resembling wire; stiff. **3.** (of persons or animals) lean, strong, and sinewy. —**wir′i·ly,** *adv.* —**wir′i·ness,** *n.*

Wis., Wisconsin.

Wis·con·sin (wis kon′sən) *n.* state in the north-central United States, bordering Lake Michigan on the east. Capital, Madison. Area, 56,154 sq. mi. Pop. (1970), 4,417,933. Abbreviation, **Wis.**

wis·dom (wiz′dəm) *n.* **1.** ability to perceive or determine what is good, true, or sound. **2.** common sense; sound judgment. **3.** knowledge; learning. [Old English *wīsdōm.*]

Wisdom of Solomon, one of the books of the Old Testament Apocrypha, formerly attributed to Solomon.

wisdom tooth, last molar tooth on either side of the upper and lower jaws in humans, usually appearing between the ages of seventeen and twenty-five.

wise[1] (wīz) **wis·er, wis·est.** *adj.* **1.** having great ability to perceive or determine what is good, true, or sound. **2.** having or showing common sense or sound judgment; sensible. **3.** possessing much knowledge; learned. **4.** shrewd; crafty; clever. **5.** having knowledge or information; informed. **6.** *Slang.* annoyingly arrogant or sarcastic; impudent. **7. to be** (or **get) wise to.** *Informal.* to be or become wise or informed of. **8. to get wise.** *Slang.* **a.** to learn or become aware of the true facts. **b.** to be or become annoyingly or offensively arrogant or sarcastic. **9. to put wise (to).** *Slang.* to make aware (of) or informed (about). —*v.i.*, *v.i.*, **wised, wis·ing.** *Slang.* **wise up (to).** to make or become aware or informed. [Old English *wīs* having sound judgment, learned.] —**wise′ly,** *adv.*

wise[2] (wīz) *n.* way; manner. ▲ used chiefly in the phrases *in no wise, in this wise, in any wise.* [Old English *wīse.*]

-wise *suffix* (used to form adverbs from nouns or adjectives) **1.** in a (specified) manner, direction, or position: *likewise, clockwise.* **2.** with regard or reference to. ▲ generally considered unacceptable in any formal context: *We are in trouble moneywise.* [From WISE[2].]

wise·a·cre (wīz′ā′kər) *n.* person who thinks he knows more than he really does. [Middle Dutch *wijssegger* soothsayer, probably from Old High German *wīssago, wizzago* prophet.]

wise·crack (wīz′krak′) *n.* flippant or sarcastic remark. —*v.i.* to make a wisecrack or wisecracks. [WISE[1] + CRACK.] —**wise′crack′er,** *n.*

wish (wish) *n.* **1.** longing or strong inclination for something; desire: *Alice's own wish in life was to get married.* **2.** expression of such a longing or inclination: *Mark went to California against his mother's wishes.* **3.** that which is wished for: *to get one's wish.* —*v.t.* **1.** to have a wish or longing for; desire: *Herb wished he had more money.* **2.** to desire (a person or thing) to be in a specified state or condition: *I wish this date were over.* **3.** to express or have as a wish or desire concerning (a person or persons): *We wish you the best of luck. They wished us a merry Christmas.* **4.** to bid, as a greeting: *to wish someone good morning.*

5. to order or request: *I wish you to leave.* **6.** to impose; force; foist (with on). —*v.i.* **1.** to have or feel a wish or desire (often with *for*): *to wish for happiness.* **2.** to make a wish: *to wish upon a star.* [Old English *wȳscan* to desire.] —**wish′er,** *n.*

Syn. *v.t.* **1. Wish, desire** mean to long for or crave something one does not have. **Wish** is the more frequently used word, esp. in suggesting yearning for an unrealizable goal: *I wish I were in Florida right now.* **Desire** is a more formal word, stressing the intensity and strength of one's longing and one's determination to achieve a goal that is usually within reach: *Jim desired a new job.*

wish·bone (wish′bōn′) *n.* forked bone in front of the breastbone of most birds. [From the practice of two persons breaking it in two and making wishes because of the belief that the holder of the longer piece of the *bone* will have his *wish* fulfilled.]

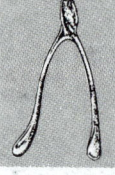

Wishbone

wish·ful (wish′fəl) *adj.* having or expressing a wish or longing. —**wish′ful·ly,** *adv.* —**wish′ful·ness,** *n.*

wishful thinking, the viewing or interpretation of a situation in a way that more closely reflects one's own wishes or desires than the actual circumstances.

wish·y-wash·y (wish′ē wô′shē, -wosh′ē) *adj. Informal.* **1.** lacking in strength, purpose, or decisiveness: *a wishy-washy person who couldn't make up his mind.* **2.** thin; watery.

wisp (wisp) *n.* **1.** small bunch, as of hair or hay. **2.** small or slight bit, piece, or the like: *a wisp of smoke.* **3.** one who or that which is slight, frail, or delicate: *a wisp of a child.* [Of uncertain origin.] —**wisp′y,** *adj.*

wist (wist) *Archaic.* past tense and past participle of **wit**[2].

wis·te·ri·a (wi stēr′ē ə) *also,* **wis·tar·i·a** (wi stēr′ē ə, -stär′-). *n.* any of a group of woody vines, genus *Wisteria,* of the pea family, found in Asia and the United States, that bears long, drooping clusters of white, blue, pink, or purple flowers. [From the U.S. physician Caspar Wistar, 1761–1818.]

wist·ful (wist′fəl) *adj.* pensively or sadly longing; yearning; melancholy. [Possibly from obsolete *wistly* intently (of uncertain origin) + -FUL.] —**wist′ful·ly,** *adv.* —**wist′ful·ness,** *n.*

wit[1] (wit) *n.* **1.a.** ability to make keenly perceptive observations and express such observations in an amusing, ingenious, or unusual way. **b.** person having such ability. **c.** speech or writing characterized by wit. **2.** intelligence or understanding; good sense. **3.** *usually,* **wits. a.** ability to think and reason; ingenuity; resourcefulness: *to live by one's wits.* **b.** mind with regard to mental balance; sanity: *to be scared out of one's wits.* **4. at one's wits' end.** at a loss as to what to do. **5. to have** (or **keep) one's wits about one.** to be or stay calm or alert, as in an emergency. [Old English *wit* understanding, mind.]

wit[2] (wit) *v.* **wist, wit·ting.** *Present:* **1.** first person, **wot;** second, **wost;** third, **wot;** *pl.,* **wite** or **wit·en.** *v.t.*, *v.i.* **1.** *Archaic.* to be or become aware; know; learn. **2. to wit.** that is to say; namely. [Old English *witan* to know.]

wit·an (wit′ən) *n.,pl.* **1.** members of the witenagemot. **2.** witenagemot. ▲ construed as singular in def. 2.

witch (wich) *n.* **1.** person, usually a woman, who practices sorcery or is believed to have a pact with the devil; sorceress. **2.** an ugly, ill-natured old woman; hag. —*v.t.* to affect by or as by witchcraft; bewitch. [Old English *wicce* sorceress.]

witch·craft (wich′kraft′) *n.* **1.** practices or power of a witch; black magic; sorcery. **2.** magical or compelling influence. —**Syn. 1.** see **magic.**

witch doctor, in certain primitive tribes, a shaman or medicine man.

witch·er·y (wich′ər ē) *pl.* **-er·ies.** *n.* **1.** witchcraft; sorcery. **2.** power to charm; fascination.

witch hazel 1. any of a small group of trees and shrubs, genus *Hamamelis,* found in North America, China, and Japan, having a scaly bark and bearing small clusters of yellow flowers in the fall. **2.** lotion made from the leaves and bark of one species of witch hazel, *H. virginiana,* used as a mild astringent.

witch hunt *Informal.* investigation of persons undertaken ostensibly to uncover subversion or disloyalty, but actually to weaken political opposition.

witch·hunt·ing (wich′hun′ting) *n. Informal.* act of engaging in a witch hunt. —**witch′-hunt′er,** *n.*

witch·ing (wich′ing) *adj.* **1.** of, relating to, or suitable for witchcraft: *Midnight is the witching hour.* **2.** bewitching; enchanting. —*n.* witchcraft; sorcery.

wite (wīt) *Archaic.* a present plural of **wit**[2].

wit·en (wit′ən) *Archaic.* a present plural of **wit**[2].

wit·e·na·ge·mot (wit′ən ə gə mōt′) *n.* in Anglo-Saxon England, council of leaders consulted by the king on important questions. Also, **wit′an.** [Old English *witena gemōt* literally, assembly of wise men, from *witena,* genitive plural of *wita* wise man + *gemōt* assembly.]

with (with, with) *prep.* **1.** in the company of: *We went with our friends.* **2.** next to; alongside of: *I sat with my mother.* **3.** into: *We mixed syrup with the milk.* **4.** having or bearing as an attribute or possession: *the girl with the umbrella, the man with a limp.* **5.** by means of; by the use of: *to fish with a pole.* **6.** in a manner characterized by: *to dance with grace.* **7.** in addition to; and: *The bat, with two baseballs, was lost.* **8.** in the association, service, or employment of: *He is with a large firm. We work with a panel of experts.* **9.** in regard or relation to: *We are pleased with the results.* **10.** in the charge or possession of: *She left her jewelry with the guard.* **11.** in the opinion of: *Its all right with me.* **12.** in the experience or sphere of: *With many of the poor, hunger is a constant problem.* **13.** on account of; because of: *to tremble with fear.* **14.** so as to be separated from: *to differ with someone. He hates to part with his money.* **15.** in opposition to; against: *He vied with her other suitors.* **16.** in spite of; notwithstanding: *With all his influence, he couldn't get enough votes.* **17.** in proportion to; according to: *His anger grew with each insult.* **18.** of the same opinions as: *I'm with you in your opposition.* **19.** in the support of; on the side of: *We always vote with the party.* **20.** at the same time as: *She rose with the children every morning.* **21.** in the same direction as: *She was drawn along with the crowd.* **22.** to or unto: *This wire is joined with an extension cord.* **23.** in comparison or contrast to: *to judge a painting with others of the same period.* **24.** having received: *With your approval, we'll leave.* **25.** as well or as skillfully as: *He can run with the best of them.* [Old English *with*, against, together with.]

with- *prefix* **1.** in opposition; against: *withstand.* **2.** back; away: *withdraw, withhold.* [Old English *with-.*]

with·al (with ôl', with-) *adv.* **1.** in addition; besides; also: *advice that was interesting and helpful withal.* **2.** notwithstanding; nevertheless. —*prep.* with: *a cane to support himself withal.* ▲ used at the end of a clause. [WITH + ALL.]

with·draw (with drô', with-) -**drew, -drawn, -draw·ing.** *v.t.* **1.** to draw back or take away: *to withdraw troops from a border.* **2.** to remove from circulation, consideration, or use: *to withdraw one's name from nomination, to withdraw a product from the market.* **3.** to take back; retract: *to withdraw an offer of help.* —*v.i.* **1.** to move or go back or away; retire; retreat: *After dinner, the men withdrew to the living room.* **2.** to remove oneself (from consideration or participation in a particular activity or group): *to withdraw from an election, to withdraw from classes at the university.* **3.** to become socially or emotionally unresponsive: *After the accident, she withdrew into her own world.* [WITH- + DRAW.]

with·draw·al (with drô'əl, with-) *n.* **1.** act or process of withdrawing; being withdrawn. **2.a.** process of stopping the administration or use of a habit-forming drug. **b.** process by which one becomes physically and psychologically adjusted to the removal of the drug.

with·drawn (with drôn', with-) *v.* past participle of **withdraw.** —*adj.* socially or emotionally unresponsive: *a withdrawn child.*

withe (with, with, with) *n.* tough, flexible twig, esp. one made of willow, used for binding or tying. [Old English *withthe.*]

with·er (with'ər) *v.i.* **1.** to dry up or shrivel, as from heat or loss of moisture: *The flowers withered very soon after they were cut.* **2.** to lose freshness, force, or vigor; become weakened or wasted (often with *away*): *That poor stray cat is just withering away.* —*v.t.* **1.** to cause to dry up or shrivel: *A fierce heat that summer withered the crops.* **2.** to cause to lose freshness and vigor: *Time cannot wither her beauty.* **3.** to cause to feel ashamed or embarrassed, as by harsh words or a scornful glance. [Middle English *wideren* to shrivel, lose vigor, probably a form of *wederen* to expose to the weather, going back to Old English *weder.* See WEATHER.] **Syn.** *v.t.* **1.** Wither, shrivel, wizen mean to cause to shrink and become wrinkled or curled up. **Wither** is more frequently applied to vegetation to suggest the extreme devastation caused by the intense heat of the sun: *The summer sun has withered the vines.* **Shrivel** is often applied to thin, flat surfaces, as leaves or skin, wrinkled by heat, age, or decay: *The exposure to fire shriveled the parchment.* Like *shrivel,* **wizen** is commonly used of persons, esp. those shrunken as a result of old age or disease: *The long illness wizened the old woman.*

with·ers (with'ərz) *n.,pl.* highest part of the back of a horse or similar animal, between the shoulder blades. [Possibly from obsolete *wither-* against, going back to Old English *wither;* because the withers resist or work against an animal's load.]

with·hold (with hōld', with-) -**held, -hold·ing.** *v.t.* **1.** to refrain from giving, granting, or allowing: *to withhold permission, to withhold judgment, to withhold payment on a check.* **2.** to hold back; check; restrain: *to withhold one's anger.* [WITH- + HOLD¹.] —**Syn.** see keep.

withholding tax, part of an employee's wages or salary deducted by the employer as an installment on the employee's income tax.

with·in (with in', with-) *prep.* **1.** in or into the inner or interior part or parts of; in the space bounded or enclosed by: *within the walls.* **2.** inside the limits of, as in time, space, amount, or degree: *to return within an hour. The farmhouse is within five miles from here.* **3.** in the scope, range, or influence of: *within memory. That's not within my jurisdiction.* **4.** acting or meeting the fixed requirements or standards of: *within the law.* —*adv.* **1.** in or into the inner or interior part or parts; inside; internally: *The building was locked, and all of us within felt safe.* **2.** inside the body, mind, or heart: *Outwardly, he repented, but within, he felt no remorse.* **3.** indoors: *to inquire within.* —*n.* inner or interior part, place, or area: *to work for reform from within.* [Old English *withinnan* on the inside.]

with·out (with out', with-) *prep.* **1.** in the absence or omission of; not having; lacking: *to go without sleep, to be without a cent.* **2.** free or exempt from: *a diamond without flaw, a world without fear.* **3.** so as to neglect or avoid: *to leave without saying good-by.* **4.** unaccompanied by: *He went to the movies without her.* **5.** at, on, or to the outer or exterior part or parts of; outside of; beyond. —*adv.* **1.** with something absent or lacking: *to go without, to do without.* **2.** on the outer or exterior part or parts; outside; externally. **3.** outdoors. —*conj. Slang.* unless. —*n.* outer part or place: *a voice from without.* [Old English *withūtan* on the outside of.]

with·stand (with stand', with-) -**stood, -stand·ing.** *v.t.* to hold out against or oppose successfully: *to withstand temptation. The house withstood the storm.* —*v.i.* to hold out successfully; endure. [Old English *withstandan* to resist, from *with-* against + *standan* to stand. See STAND.] **Syn.** *v.t.* Withstand, resist, oppose mean to stand up against a hostile force. **Withstand** suggests a passive effort characterized by flexibility, adaptability, patience, and fortitude that allows one to bear up under attack, punishment, or temptation without necessarily winning: *The village withstood the bombing.* **Resist** suggests a defensive but active effort, often hidden or secret, that may be successful against threat, violence, or other repression: *We shall continue to resist censorship of the press.* **Oppose** suggests an offensive action and vigorous effort, openly attacking the enemy and usually with success: *A well-organized minority opposed his nomination to the bench.*

with·y (with'ē, with'ē) *pl.* **with·ies.** *n.* **1.** withe. **2.** rope or halter made of withes. [Old English *withig* willow, willow twig.]

wit·less (wit'lis) *adj.* lacking intelligence or sense; foolish. —**wit'-less·ly,** *adv.* —**wit'less·ness,** *n.*

wit·ness (wit'nis) *n.* **1.** one who has personally seen or heard something and can therefore give a first-hand account of it. **2.** one who testifies in a court of law under oath or affirmation, either orally or by deposition. **3.** one who is present at a transaction, as the signing of a contract or will, and can give evidence as to its authenticity. A witness often signs a document to indicate his presence. **4.** attestation of a fact or event; testimony. ▲ used chiefly in the phrase *to bear witness.* **5.** that which serves as evidence or proof. —*v.t.* **1.** to be present to see or hear; observe personally: *to witness an argument.* **2.** to be the time or scene of: *This century has witnessed the steady growth of urban centers.* **3.** to affix one's signature to (a document) as a witness. **4.** to serve as evidence or proof of: *The wounds we bear all too well witness the cruelty we have endured.* **5.** to testify to. [Old English *witnes* knowledge, evidence, from *wit.* See WIT¹.]

witness stand, area in which a witness stands or sits while being questioned in a court of law.

wit·ted (wit'id) *adj.* having or marked by (a specified kind of) wit. ▲ used in combination, as in *quick-witted, dull-witted.*

wit·ti·cism (wit'i siz'əm) *n.* witty saying or remark. [WITTY + *-ism;* influenced by CRITICISM.]

wit·ting (wit'ing) *v. Archaic.* present participle of wit². —*adj.* done or acting consciously or with deliberation: *a witting accomplice.* —**wit'ting·ly,** *adv.*

wit·ty (wit'ē) -**ti·er, -ti·est.** *adj.* having or characterized by wit; cleverly amusing: *a witty journalist, a witty rebuttal.* [Old English *wittig* wise, from *wit.* See WIT¹.] —**wit'ti·ly,** *adv.* —**wit'ti·ness,** *n.*

wive (wīv) *wived, wiv·ing. Archaic. v.t.* **1.** to marry (a woman). **2.** to furnish with a wife. —*v.i.* to marry a woman. [Old English *wīfian* to marry, take a wife, from *wīf* wife.]

wi·vern (wī'vərn) *also,* **wy·vern.** *n.* in heraldry, a mythical beast resembling a two-legged dragon with wings and a barbed tail. [From Middle English *wivere* viper, from Old French *wivre,* from Latin *vīpera.*]

wives (wīvz) plural of **wife.**

wiz·ard (wiz'ərd) *n.* **1.** man who uses supernatural power to control or influence events, people, or phenomena; male witch; sorcerer. **2.** extraordinarily clever or skillful person; expert; genius: *a financial wizard.* —*adj.* magic. [Middle English *wysard* sage, going back to Old English *wīs.* See WISE¹.]

wiz·ard·ry (wiz'ərd rē) *n.* **1.** art or methods of a wizard; witchcraft; sorcery. **2.** great skill or artistry: *With mechanical wizardry, he repaired the radio.*

wiz·en (wiz'ən) *v.t., v.i.* to shrivel up; wither. —*adj.* wizened. [Old English *wisnian* to wither.] —**Syn.** *v.t.* see wither.

wiz·ened (wiz'ənd) *adj.* dried out; shriveled; withered: *a wizened old sailor.*

wk. *pl.* **wks. 1.** week. **2.** work.

wkly., weekly.

wl, wavelength.

WNW, west-northwest.

woad (wōd) *n.* **1.** erect, branching herb, *Isatis tinctoria,* of the mustard family, native to Europe and formerly widely cultivated for the dye made from its leaves. **2.** the dye itself, blue in color and similar to indigo. [Old English *wād.*]

wob·ble (wob′əl) **-bled, -bling.** *also,* **wab·ble.** *v.i.* **1.** to move or sway unsteadily from side to side: *an old chair that wobbles. The tire wobbled after the blowout.* **2.** to shake or quaver; tremble: *Tom's voice wobbled when he tried to thank me.* **3.** to waver between different opinions, feelings, or courses of action; vacillate. —*n.* unsteady, swaying movement: *the wobble of a warped phonograph record.* [Possibly from Low German *wabbeln* to move unsteadily.] —**wob′bler,** *n.*

wob·bly (wob′lē) *also,* **wab·bly.** *adj.* tending to wobble; unsteady; shaky: *The convalescent moved on wobbly legs.*

Wo·burn (wō′bərn, wōō′-) *n.* city in eastern Massachusetts, northwest of Boston. Pop. (1970), 37,406.

Wo·den (wōd′ən) *n.* Teutonic king of the gods. His Norse counterpart is Odin.

woe (wō) *n.* **1.** great sadness or suffering; sorrow; grief: *a tale of woe.* **2.** great trouble or misfortune; disaster: *our present economic woes.* —*interj.* alas. [Old English *wā.*]

woe·be·gone (wō′bi gôn′, -gon′) *also,* **wo·be·gone.** *adj.* showing great sorrow or grief; mournful: *a woebegone look.*

woe·ful (wō′fəl) *adj.* **1.** afflicted with, characterized by, or expressive of woe; sorrowful; sad. **2.** pitiful; deplorable: *woeful inadequacies, woeful merchandise.* —**woe′ful·ly,** *adv.* —**woe′ful·ness,** *n.*

woke (wōk) past tense of **wake**[1].

wo·ken (wō′kən) *Archaic.* past participle of **wake**[1].

wold (wōld) *n.* high, open tract of rolling land; moor. [Old English *wald, weald* forest.]

wolf (woolf) *pl.,* **wolves.** *n.* **1.** any of various wild mammals of the dog family, esp. *Canis lupus,* found chiefly in the cold regions of the Northern Hemisphere, having a pointed muzzle, a bushy tail, and usually gray fur. Height: to 3 feet at the shoulder. **2.** fur of this animal. **3.** one who is cruel, rapacious, or destructive. **4.** *Slang.* man who chases after women. **5. to cry wolf.** to raise a false alarm. **6. to keep the wolf from the door.** to ward off hunger or want. **7. wolf in sheep's clothing.** one who hides evil intentions or cruelty behind an innocent or friendly exterior. —*v.t.* to devour quickly and ravenously: *to wolf down one's food.* [Old English *wulf* this animal, cruel person.]

Wolf *(def. 1)*

Wolfe (woolf) **1. James.** 1727–59, English general who led the capture of Quebec in 1759. **2. Thomas.** 1900–38, U.S. novelist.

wolf·bane (woolf′bān′) wolfsbane.

wolf dog 1. any of various large dogs used for hunting wolves. **2.** cross between a dog and a wolf.

wolf·hound (woolf′hound′) *n.* large dog of any of various breeds, used for hunting wolves, as the Irish wolfhound and borzoi.

wolf·ish (wool′fish) *adj.* characteristic of or resembling a wolf; rapacious; greedy; cruel. —**wolf′ish·ly,** *adv.* —**wolf′ish·ness,** *n.*

Wolfhound

wolf·ram (wool′frəm) *n.* tungsten. [German *Wolfram* literally, wolf's dirt, from Middle High German *wolf* + *rām* dirt; probably because it was considered inferior to tin.]

wolf·ram·ite (wool′frə mīt′) *n.* black to brown, opaque iron or manganese compound that is the principal ore of tungsten.

wolfs·bane (woolfs′bān′) *also,* **wolf·bane, wolf's·bane.** *n.* aconite *(def. 1).*

Wol·sey, Thomas (wool′zē) c.1475–1530, English cardinal and lord chancellor of England.

wol·ver·hamp·ton (wool′vər hamp′tən) *n.* city in west-central England. Pop. (1968), 264,800.

wol·ver·ine (wool′və rēn′) *also,* **wol·ver·ene.** *n.* ferocious carnivorous mammal, *Gulo gulo,* native to

Wolverine

northern regions, having dark-brown fur with pale bands. It is the largest member of the weasel family. Height: to 17 inches at the shoulder. [From **WOLF;** referring to its wolflike nature.]

wolves (woolvz) plural of **wolf.**

wom·an (woom′ən) *pl.,* **wom·en.** *n.* **1.** adult female human being. **2.** adult female human beings collectively; female part of the human race: *Frailty, thy name is woman* (Shakespeare, *Hamlet*). **3.** female human being endowed with the characteristics and qualities considered to be typical of a woman: *The woman in her rebelled against discrimination based on sex.* **4.** female worker or servant. **5.** sweetheart or mistress. **6.** *Informal.* wife. ▲ used chiefly in the phrase *the little woman.* —*adj.* female: *a woman psychiatrist.* [Old English *wīfman* adult female human being, female servant, from *wīf* adult female human being, wife + *man* human being.] —**Syn.** *n.* **1.** see **female.**

wom·an·hood (woom′ən hood′) *n.* **1.** state of being an adult female human being. **2.** character or qualities considered to be womanly. **3.** women collectively.

wom·an·ish (woom′ən ish) *adj.* **1.** of, for, or characteristic of a woman. **2.** resembling a woman; effeminate; unmanly: *womanish fears.*

wom·an·kind (woom′ən kīnd′) *n.* women collectively.

wom·an·like (woom′ən līk′) *adj.* having the qualities of or befitting a woman; womanly.

wom·an·ly (woom′ən lē) *adj.* **1.** having the qualities generally attributed to or characteristic of women. **2.** relating to or appropriate for a woman. —*adv.* in a womanly way. —**wom′an·li·ness,** *n.*

woman of the world, worldly, sophisticated, and cosmopolitan woman.

woman suffrage, the right of women to vote.

wom·an·suf·fra·gist (woom′ən suf′rə jist) *n.* man or woman who advocates woman suffrage.

womb (woom) *n.* **1.** uterus *(def. 1).* **2.** any place where something is nurtured or generated: *Events that are ripening in the womb of the future* (Coleridge, 1810). **3.** any enveloping space: *the deep dark womb of the sea.* [Old English *wamb* uterus, belly, hollow space or cavity.]

wom·bat (wom′bat) *n.* any of several nocturnal burrowing marsupials, family Phascolomidae, native to Australia, having a stocky body and a coarse coat of black or yellowish-brown hair. Length: 40–60 inches. [Australian native name *womback.*]

wom·en (wim′ən) plural of **woman.**

wom·en·folk (wim′ən fōk′) *also,* **wom·en·folks.** *n.,pl.* women collectively, esp. the female members of a group.

Women's Lib (lib) movement of feminists that demands the same social, economic, and political rights as those claimed by men. Also, **Women's Liberation.**

Women's Liberationist (lib′ər rā′shən ist) one who believes in or supports Women's Lib.

women's rights *also,* **woman's rights,** rights claimed for women of equal opportunities and privileges with men, as in employment and suffrage.

won (wun) past tense and past participle of **win.**

won·der (wun′dər) *n.* **1.** that which arouses astonishment, curiosity, or admiration: *the wonders of the universe. It's a wonder you can concentrate amidst all this noise.* **2.** feeling, attitude, or state caused by this: *We watched with wonder as the sea suddenly became calm.* **3. for a wonder,** surprisingly. **4. to do** (or **work**) **wonders,** to produce very good results. —*v.i.* **1.** to want to know or learn; be curious or doubtful: *I often wonder about how we could have saved the project. Betty wondered if she had time for one more phone call.* **2.** to feel or express admiration and astonishment: *to wonder at an athlete's strength and endurance. I shouldn't wonder if Bob got into trouble again.* —*v.t.* to want to know or learn about; be curious or doubtful about: *I wonder what I should serve for dinner.* [Old English *wundor* marvel, miracle.]

won·der·ful (wun′dər fəl) *adj.* causing or exciting wonder; astonishing: *a wonderful gift. a wonderful work of art.* —**won′der·ful·ly,** *adv.*

won·der·land (wun′dər land′) *n.* **1.** wonderful real place, region, or scene: *Colorado is a winter wonderland.* **2.** wonderful imaginary realm or fantasy world.

won·der·ment (wun′dər ment) *n.* **1.** state or emotion of wonder: *The group of tourists stood in wonderment amidst the ancient ruins.* **2.** that which causes wonder.

won·drous (wun′drəs) *adj.* wonderful —*adv. Archaic.* extraordinarily; wonderfully. [Modification (influenced by -OUS) of obsolete *wonders,* genitive of WONDER.] —**won′drous·ly,** *adv.*

wont (wônt, wōnt, wunt) *adj.* accustomed; used: *We are wont to stay at home on Sundays.* —*n.* customary practice; habit: *It was his wont to read the paper after work.* [Middle English *wont, woned* accustomed, past participle of Middle English *wonen* to be accustomed, dwell, from Old English *wunian.*]

won't (wōnt) will not.

won·ed (wôn′tid, wôn′-, wun′-) *adj. Archaic.* accustomed; customary: *to pay our wonted tribute* (Shakespeare, *Cymbeline*).

woo (wōō) *v.t.* **1.** to seek the love or affection of, esp. with the intent to marry; court. **2.** to entreat enticingly; try to win over: *corporations that woo college graduates with promises of high salaries.* **3.** to try to

at; āpe; cär; end; mē; it; īce; hot; ōld; fôrk; wood; fōōl; oil; out; up; ūse; turn; sing; thin; this; zh in treasure; ə in ago, taken, pencil, lemon, circus.

obtain or gain; seek: *to woo public support, to woo one's own destruction.* —*v.i.* to seek the love or affection of a woman, esp. with the intent to marry. [Old English *wōgian* to court.]

wood (wood) *n.* **1.** hard, fibrous material beneath the bark and making up the greater part of the stems and branches of trees and shrubs. **2.** this material, sometimes with the bark still on, cut or prepared for use, as for building, fuel, or paper manufacture; timber; lumber. **3.** *often,* **woods.** dense growth of trees; forest; grove. **4.** golf club with a wooden head. **5.** something made of wood, as a woodwind instrument. **6. out of the woods.** *Informal.* finally clear of danger, hazard, or other difficulty. —*adj.* **1.** made or consisting of wood; wooden. **2.** made or suitable for using, holding, or cutting wood: *a wood saw.* **3.** inhabiting or growing in woods. —*v.t.* **1.** to cover or plant with trees. **2.** to supply with wood for fuel. —*v.i.* to gather or take in supplies of wood for fuel. [Old English *wudu* dense growth of trees, the hard material beneath the bark of trees and shrubs.]

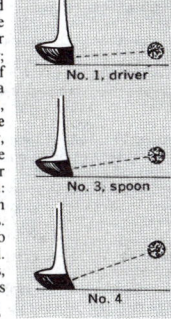

No. 1, driver

No. 3, spoon

No. 4

Wood (def. 4)

Wood, Grant (wood) 1892–1942, U.S. painter.

wood alcohol, methanol.

wood anemone, any of several anemones, esp. *Anemone quinquefolia,* a woodland plant that grows wild in North America, bearing white or purple flowers.

wood·bine (wood′bīn′) *n.* **1.** any of various honeysuckles, esp. *Lonicera periclymenum,* growing in Europe and bearing flowers that are red or purple on the outside. **2.** Virginia creeper. [Old English *wudubind* a climbing plant, as ivy, going back to *wudu* wood + *bindan* to tie fast; referring to its climbing up and winding around trees.]

wood·block (wood′blok′) *n.* woodcut.

wood·carv·ing (wood′kär′ving) *n.* **1.** art or technique of carving wood. **2.** object carved of wood. —**wood′carv′er,** *n.*

wood·chuck (wood′chuk′) *n.* short-legged, North American marmot, *Marmota monax,* having coarse brown or gray fur. Length: to 32 inches including tail. Also, **ground′hog′.** [Probably a modification (influenced by WOOD) of Cree *wuchak* marten, weasel.]

Woodchuck

wood·cock (wood′kok′) *pl.* **-cocks** or **-cock.** *n.* any of several game birds, family Scolopacidae, native to forests of North America, Europe, and Asia, having a plump body, a long slender bill, and buff, brown, and black plumage. Length: 12 inches. [Old English *wuducocc,* from *wudu* wood + *cocc.* See COCK¹.]

wood·craft (wood′kraft′) *n.* **1.** skill and knowledge in things relating to the woods and survival in the woods, as hunting or camping. **2.** art, process, or skill of working with wood.

wood·cut (wood′kut′) *n.* **1.** block of wood engraved so that all the wood is cut away except the design to be printed. **2.** print or impression made from such a block.

wood·cut·ter (wood′kut′ər) *n.* one whose work is cutting trees or chopping wood. —**wood′cut′ting,** *n.*

wood·ed (wood′id) *adj.* having trees or woods: *a wooded area at the edge of town.*

wood·en (wood′ən) *adj.* **1.** made or consisting of wood. **2.** stiff; clumsy; awkward: *to walk with a wooden gait.* **3.** lacking warmth; lifeless; dull: *a wooden expression on one's face.* —**wood′en·ly,** *adv.* —**wood′en·ness,** *n.*

wood engraving 1. block of wood engraved in such a way that the actual carved lines form the design to be printed. **2.** print or impression made from such a block. **3.** art or technique of making such blocks, prints, or impressions.

wood·en·head (wood′ən hed′) *n.* *Informal.* dull or stupid person; blockhead. —**wood′en·head′ed,** *adj.*

wooden horse, Trojan horse.

wooden Indian 1. life-sized figure of a standing American Indian carved of wood and painted, formerly used as an advertisement outside cigar stores. **2.** *Informal.* one who is considered dull, lifeless, or inarticulate.

wood·en·ware (wood′ən wâr′) *n.* articles made of wood for household use, as pails, bowls, or kitchen utensils.

wood·land (*n.,* wood′land′, -lənd; *adj.,* wood′lənd) *n.* land covered with woods or trees. —*adj.* of, relating to, or inhabiting the woods: *a woodland deity.* —**wood′land·er,** *n.*

wood lot, land on which trees are grown for timber.

wood louse 1. any of several small crustaceans, order Isopoda, that have flat, oval bodies and live in dark, damp places, feeding on decaying wood, leaves, and other matter. Also, **sow bug.** **2.** any of various small insects living in dark places, as in the woodwork of houses.

wood·man (wood′mən) *pl.* **-men.** *n.* woodsman.

wood·note (wood′nōt′) *n.* natural song or call, as of a wild bird of the forest.

wood nymph 1. *Greek Mythology.* nymph living in or guarding woods and trees. **2.** destructive butterfly, *Cercyonis pegala,* having brownish wings with yellow markings.

wood·peck·er (wood′pek′ər) *n.* any of various strong-billed birds, subfamily Picinae, inhabiting forests throughout the world, having stiff, pointed tail feathers and curved nails adapted for clinging to trees. It feeds chiefly on insects in trees, which it obtains by drilling holes in bark and wood with its bill. Length: 6–19 inches.

Woodpecker

wood·pile (wood′pīl′) *n.* pile of wood, esp. of wood cut and stacked for use as fuel.

wood pulp, wood reduced to pulp by chemical or mechanical means, used esp. for making paper.

wood pussy *Informal.* skunk.

wood rat, pack rat.

wood·ruff (wood′ruf′) *n.* any of several low-growing herbs, genus *Asperula,* of Europe and Asia, esp. *A. odorata,* whose fragrant leaves are used in sachets and as a wine flavoring. [Old English *wudurōfe.*]

wood·shed (wood′shed′) *n.* shed for storing wood, esp. firewood.

woods·man (woodz′mən) *pl.* **-men.** *also,* **wood·man.** *n.* **1.** man, as a hunter or trapper, who lives or works in the woods and is skilled in woodcraft. **2.** woodcutter; lumberman.

wood sorrel, any of various plants, genus *Oxalis,* found in shaded and temperate climates, having heart-shaped leaves with three leaflets, yellow, white, or pink flowers, and a sour sap.

woods·y (wood′zē) **woods·i·er, woods·i·est.** *adj.* of, relating to, suitable for, or suggestive of the woods: *a woodsy fragrance.*

wood tar, tar obtained from wood by distillation and used in pitch, medicines, and preservatives.

wood thrush, thrush, *Hylocichla mustelina,* found throughout the eastern United States, having brown and white plumage and a reddish head. Length: 7½–8½ inches.

wood·turn·ing (wood′tur′ning) *n.* art or process of shaping pieces of wood on a lathe.

wood·wind (wood′wind′) *n.* **1.** any of various instruments, including the flu*t*e, oboe, clarinet, and saxophone, consisting of a tube through which a column of air passes and having holes in the tube, which are opened and closed to vary the pitch of the tones produced. **2. woodwinds.** section of an orchestra consisting of these instruments. —*adj.* of, for, designating, or composed of these instruments.

wood·work (wood′wurk′) *n.* objects or parts made of wood, esp. the interior wooden parts of a house, as moldings, doors, and window frames.

wood·work·ing (wood′wur′king) *n.* art, process, or occupation of making or shaping things of wood. —**wood′work′er,** *n.*

wood·worm (wood′wurm′) *n.* worm or larva that develops or bores in wood.

wood·y (wood′ē) **wood·i·er, wood·i·est.** *adj.* **1.** consisting of or containing wood: *woody plants.* **2.** covered with or abounding in trees: *a woody island.* **3.** characteristic of or resembling wood: *a plastic with a woody texture.* —**wood′i·ness,** *n.*

woo·er (wōō′ər) *n.* one who woos, esp. a suitor.

woof (woof, wōōf) *n.* **1.** threads running from side to side in a woven fabric, crossing the lengthwise threads of the warp. **2.** texture, as of a fabric. [Old English *ōwef* the weft.]

woof·er (woof′ər) *n.* loudspeaker designed to reproduce low-frequency sound signals. Distinguished from **tweeter.**

wool (wool) *n.* **1.** soft, dense, usually curly, hair of sheep and certain other animals, as the Angora goat, alpaca, or llama, used to make yarn and fabric. **2.** strong, resilient yarn or fabric made from this hair. **3.** any substance resembling the fleece of sheep in texture, as short, kinky human hair or the furry covering on certain plants. **4. to pull the wool over (someone's) eyes,** to deceive or delude (someone). —*adj.* of, relating to, or made of wool. [Old English *wull* the hair of sheep and similar animals.]

wool·en (wool′ən) *also,* **wool·len.** *adj.* **1.** made of wool. **2.** of or relating to wool. —*n., pl.* **woolens.** cloth or garments made of wool.

Woolf, Virginia (woolf) 1882–1941, English novelist and critic.

wool·gath·er·ing (wool'gath'ər ing) *n.* useless or idle thinking or work, esp. daydreaming. —*adj.* given to daydreaming; absent-minded. [Suggested by wandering about to *gather* bits of sheep's *wool* caught on bushes.]

wool·grow·er (wool'grō'ər) *n.* one who raises sheep or other wool-bearing animals for their wool. —**wool'grow'ing,** *adj., n.*

wool·ly (wool'ē) **-li·er, -li·est.** *also,* **wool·y.** *adj.* **1.** consisting of or resembling wool. **2.** covered with wool or something with a similar texture: *a woolly stuffed animal.* **3.** not clear or well-defined; confused; fuzzy: *woolly thinking.* **4.** characteristic of the crude, uncivilized, but exciting atmosphere of the western frontier region of the United States. ▲ used chiefly in the phrase **wild and woolly.** —*n. pl.,* **-lies.** *usually,* **woollies.** garment made of wool, esp. a knitted undergarment. —**wool'li·ness,** *n.*

wool·pack (wool'pak') *n.* **1.** sacking material or sack used to pack raw wool. **2.** cumulus cloud.

wool·y (wool'ē) **wool·i·er, wool·i·est.** *adj.* woolly. —*n. pl.,* **wool·ies.** woolly. —**wool'i·ness,** *n.*

Woon·sock·et (woon sok'it) *n.* city in northern Rhode Island. Pop. (1970), 46,820.

wooz·y (woo'zē, wooz'ē) **wooz·i·er, wooz·i·est.** *adj. Informal.* dizzy or dazed, as from drink or illness. [Possibly modification of OOZY¹.] —**wooz'i·ly,** *adv.* —**wooz'i·ness,** *n.*

Worces·ter (woos'tər) *n.* city in central Massachusetts. Pop. (1970), 176,572.

Worces·ter·shire sauce (woos'tər shēr', -shər) pungent sauce consisting of soy sauce, vinegar, garlic, and other ingredients. [From *Worcester,* England, where it was first made.]

word (wurd) *n.* **1.a.** sound or combination of sounds having meaning and forming an indivisible linguistic unit. **b.** written or printed character or set of characters representing such a unit. **2.** short conversation or discussion: *I'd like a word with you before you leave.* **3.** brief utterance; remark: *She gave him a word of advice.* **4.** assurance; promise: *I gave him my word that I would be there.* **5.** information; news; message: *Have you received any word from him?* **6.** signal or password: *Just give the word and we'll begin.* **7.** command; order: *His word must be obeyed.* **8.** **words. a.** contentious or angry discussion; argument. **b.** text of a musical composition; lyrics. **c.** speech; talk. **9. the Word. a.** the Bible; Scriptures. **b.** divine intelligence incarnate in Christ.

by word of mouth. by means of spoken language; orally.

in a word. in short; briefly.

in so many words. precisely and explicitly.

man of his word. one who keeps his promises.

to be as good as one's word. to abide by one's promise.

to eat one's words. to have to retract something that one has said.

to take someone at his word. to trust the statements of another person and act accordingly.

to take the words out of one's mouth. to say exactly what another person was going to say himself.

word for word. in exactly the same words.

—*v.t.* to express in words: *He worded his reply carefully.* [Old English *word* vocable, speech, utterance, promise, news, command.]

word·age (wur'dij) *n.* words collectively, esp. the quantity of words used in writing something, as an essay.

word·book (wurd'book') *n.* book containing a list of words, with definitions or explanations, as a dictionary.

word class *Grammar.* group or category of words belonging to the same part of speech.

word·ing (wur'ding) *n.* style or manner of expressing something in words; phraseology.

word·less (wurd'lis) *adj.* **1.** that is not expressed in words; silent: *a wordless greeting.* **2.** that cannot be expressed in words: *wordless sorrow.* —**word'less·ly,** *adv.* —**word'less·ness,** *n.*

word of honor. assurance given as a pledge of one's honor.

word order, order of words in a sentence, clause, or phrase.

Words·worth, William (wurdz'wurth') 1770–1850, English poet.

word·y (wur'dē) **word·i·er, word·i·est.** *adj.* using or containing an excessive number of words; verbose: *a wordy author, a wordy play.* —**word'i·ly,** *adv.* —**word'i·ness,** *n.*

wore (wôr) past tense of **wear.**

work (wurk) *n.* **1.** physical or mental exertion directed toward a definite end or purpose; labor. **2.** that which one does to earn a living; occupation; trade: *What work does he do?* **3.** opportunity for earning a living: *He is looking for work.* **4.** something to be done; undertaking; project: *Each man was assigned work.* **5.** that which is being accomplished or produced, esp. as part of one's occupation: *The seamstress took her work with her.* **6.** result of this; something accomplished or produced: *a work of sculpture, works of music.* **7.** manner in which something is accomplished or produced; workmanship: *The vase shows careful work.* **8.** a place of employment: *He can be reached at work.*

She has gone to work. **9.** *usually,* **works.** things accomplished; feats; deeds: *She is known for her good works.* **10. works. a.** establishment for industrial labor, as a factory, plant, or mill. ▲ usually construed as singular. **b.** mechanism of a device, as a watch. **c.** engineering structures, as dams, docks, or bridges. **11.** *Physics.* expenditure of energy in moving mass a given distance, measured by the product of the magnitude of the force and the distance the mass is moved in the direction of the force. **12. to make short work of.** to accomplish quickly. **13. to shoot the works.** *Slang.* to risk all in one supreme effort. —*adj.* of, for, or relating to work: *a work stoppage, a work day, work clothes.* —*v.i.* **worked** or **wrought, work·ing. 1.** to put forth mental or physical exertion in order to accomplish a definite end or purpose; labor. **2.** to be engaged in some business, occupation, or profession; be employed: *He works in a mill.* **3.** to perform a function effectively; operate: *This typewriter works well. His new invention will never work.* **4.** to admit of being shaped, handled, or processed: *This metal does not work easily.* **5.** to move gradually so as to arrive at a specified state: *The ropes worked loose.* **6.** to make progress laboriously and slowly: *The disabled vehicle worked toward the shoulder of the road.* **7.** to be agitated; move restlessly: *His features worked with anger.* **8.** to ferment. **9. to work on** (or **upon**). to attempt to exert an influence upon; try to affect: *She worked on her friends to help her.* **10. to work out. a.** to do exercises or practice: *He worked out at the gym.* **b.** to result; resolve: *How did your meeting work out?* **11. to work up.** to make progress; rise: *He worked up in the business.* —*v.t.* **1.** to cause to perform a function; exert effort upon: *The driver kept working the clutch.* **2.** to carry on one's trade, business, or operation in: *The policeman worked the northern side of town.* **3.** to cause to produce or be productive: *The men worked the mine. The old man still works the farm.* **4.** to do or accomplish; bring about; cause: *The medicine almost works miracles.* **5.** to shape, handle, or process for a particular purpose: *to work copper, to work dough.* **6.** to sew, embroider, weave, or the like. **7.** to attain by effort: *We worked our way upstream.* **8.** to exact labor or service from: *The farmer worked the horses until they were exhausted.* **9.** to give shape or form to; fashion: *The youth worked the wood to make a bowl.* **10.** to solve: *He worked the math problem.* **11.** to act upon the emotions of; excite; rouse: *The orator worked the crowd into a rage.* **12.** *Informal.* to deceive or trick in order to attain something. **13.** to cause fermentation in. **14. to work in.** to put in or insert. **15. to work off.** to get rid of; discharge. **16. to work out. a.** to develop or elaborate on: *Work out all your ideas.* **b.** to solve. **c.** to accomplish. **17. to work over. a.** to develop or plan. **b.** *Slang.* to beat up. **18. to work up.** to develop or plan. **b.** to stir up; excite; rouse. [Old English *weorc* act, deed, task, toil, occupation, handiwork.]

work·a·ble (wur'kə bəl) *adj.* **1.** capable of being carried out or accomplished; feasible: *a workable plan.* **2.** capable of being worked: *workable clay.*

work·a·day (wur'kə dā') *adj.* **1.** commonplace; prosaic: *the workaday world.* **2.** of, relating to, or suitable for workdays.

work·bag (wurk'bag') *n.* bag for holding equipment and materials, esp. those used in needlework.

work·bas·ket (wurk'bas'kit) *n.* basket for holding equipment and materials used in sewing or needlework.

work·bench (wurk'bench') *n.* table used for working, as by a craftsman or mechanic.

work·book (wurk'book') *n.* **1.** book or manual prepared for use by students, containing problems, questions, or exercises based on a particular textbook or relating to a particular course of study. **2.** book containing a record of work planned or completed.

work·box (wurk'boks') *n.* box for holding equipment and materials used in work.

work·day (wurk'dā') *n.* **1.** day on which work is ordinarily done, as distinguished from Sunday or a holiday. **2.** that part of a day in which work is done.

work·er (wur'kər) *n.* **1.** one who works: *a fast worker.* **2.** one who earns a living by working, esp. as a laborer. **3.** one of the undeveloped females in a colony of insects, as bees, ants, or termites, that performs various services for the colony. See **ant** for illustration.

work force, total number of persons available for employment, as in a region or country.

work·horse (wurk'hôrs') *n.* **1.** horse used for heavy labor, as distinguished from a horse for racing or riding. **2.** person who works diligently and tirelessly, esp. on very difficult tasks.

work·house (wurk'hous') *n.* **1.** house of correction for petty offenders, who are made to work in gangs on roads or railways. **2.** in Great Britain, an institution for sheltering and giving work to poor people.

work·ing (wur'king) *adj.* **1.** that works: *a working telephone.* **2.** engaged in work, esp. for a living: *working people.* **3.** that is sufficient for use: *a working hypothesis, a working knowledge of Russian.* **4.** of, relating to, occupied by, or used for working: *working conditions, working hours.* —*n.* **1.** manner in which something works; method of

at; āpe; cär; end; mē; it; īce; hot; ōld; fôrk; wood; fool; oil; out; up; ūse; turn; sing; thin; this; zh in treasure; ə in ago, taken, pencil, lemon, circus.

operation. **2.** *usually,* **workings.** part of a mine where excavation is being done.

working capital 1. assets of a business in excess of current liabilities. **2.** capital in the form of cash or assets easily converted into cash.

working class, class of people completely dependent upon wages for their livelihood.

work·ing·man (wur′king man′) *pl.,* **-men.** *n.* man who works, esp. one who works for a living with his hands or with machines.

working papers, official documents legalizing the employment of aliens or minors.

work·ing·wom·an (wur′king woom′ən) *pl.,* **-wom·en.** *n.* woman who works, esp. one who works for a living with her hands or with machines.

work·load (wurk′lōd′) *also,* **work load.** *n.* amount of work assigned to a worker, department, or machine over a specified period of time.

work·man (wurk′mən) *pl.,* **-men.** *n.* man working for a living, esp. as a craftsman or laborer.

work·man·like (wurk′mən līk′) *adj.* characteristic of or befitting a good workman; well-executed; skillful. Also, **work′man·ly.**

work·man·ship (wurk′mən ship′) *n.* **1.** art or skill of a workman. **2.** manner in which a work is executed: *The workmanship of the table is very fine and painstaking.* **3.** product of a craftsman's work: *That vase is a fine piece of workmanship.*

work·men's compensation (wurk′mənz) insurance payments provided by law for wage earners who are injured at work.

work of art, any work fashioned by a skilled or creative artist and possessing originality and aesthetic merit.

work·out (wurk′out′) *n.* **1.** period of practice, exercise, or other strenuous physical activity. **2.** trial conducted to determine suitability, fitness, or the like: *He gave the bicycle a workout.*

work·room (wurk′rōōm′, -room′) *n.* room in which work is done.

work·shop (wurk′shop′) *n.* **1.** shop or building in which work, esp. manual or mechanical work, is done. **2.** seminar or discussion group devoted to a particular subject or field or study: *a workshop in child guidance, a workshop for poets.*

work·ta·ble (wurk′tā′bəl) *n.* table used for working, as by a craftsman or seamstress.

world (wurld) *n.* **1.a.** earth: *John took a voyage around the world.* **b.** *also,* **World.** particular part of the earth: *the western world.* **2.** all that exists; whole of creation; the universe. **3.** all the human inhabitants of the earth collectively; humanity. **4.** all the inhabitants of a community, state, or country; the public: *Now all the world knows about her.* **5.** particular civilization or period of human history: *the world of the Greeks, the Elizabethan world.* **6.** any sphere or realm of human concern, pursuit, or activity: *the world of art, the world of fashion.* **7.** particular group of people sharing certain interests or activities: *the business world.* **8.** social or secular life and the people devoted to or associated with it: *She chose to live apart from the world and its concerns.* **9.** division of living things: *the plant world.* **10.** any planet or other heavenly body. **11.** any state or condition of existence: *the world of today, the world to come.* **12.** *Informal.* large number or quantity; a great deal: *The rest did him a world of good.* **13. for all the world. a.** for any reason whatsoever. **b.** in every respect; exactly; precisely. **14. in the world.** at all; ever. **15. out of this world.** *Informal.* very fine; extraordinary. **16. world without end.** to all eternity; forever. [Old English *weorold* the earth, mankind, human existence.]

World Court, International Court of Justice.

world·ling (wurld′ling) *n.* one who is devoted to worldly concerns or pleasures. [WORLD + -LING¹.]

world·ly (wurld′lē) **-li·er, -li·est.** *adj.* **1.** devoted to the matters, concerns, interests, or pleasures of this world. **2.** of or relating to this world; earthly; secular: *worldly pursuits.* **3.** wise in the ways or affairs of this world; worldly-wise; sophisticated. —**world′li·ness,** *n.*

world·ly-minded (wurld′lē mīn′did) *adj.* devoted to worldly concerns or pleasures.

world·ly-wise (wurld′lē wīz′) *adj.* wise in the ways or affairs of this world.

world power, country that has considerable influence in or effect upon world affairs.

World Series *also,* **world series.** annual series of baseball games played between the winning teams in the two major professional leagues after the regular season has ended to determine the championship of U.S. professional baseball.

world war, war involving the major powers of the world and extending over a large area.

World War I, war between major European powers lasting from 1914 to 1918. Also, **Great War.**

World War II, war lasting from 1939 to 1945, fought in Europe, Asia, and Africa, and in the Atlantic, Pacific, and Indian oceans.

world-wea·ry (wurld′wēr′ē) *adj.* tired of the world or of living.

world·wide (wurld′wīd′) *adj.* extending over all the world.

worm (wurm) *n.* **1.** any of various elongated, soft-bodied invertebrate animals. True worms include the flatworms, roundworms, and annelids. **2.** anything that resembles a worm, as in appearance or movement. **3.** something that slowly or stealthily eats or works its way inward: *the worm of conscience.* **4.** one who is an object of scorn, disgust, or pity; weak, miserable, or pathetic person. **5.** shaft having a single spiral thread around it, which engages with the teeth of a worm wheel. **6. worms.** any of several diseases caused by the presence of parasitic worms in the body, esp. the intestines. —*v.i.* to move as a worm; wriggle: *He wormed through the window.* —*v.t.* **1.** to move or bring about by moving as a worm. **2.** to bring about by stealth or guile: *He wormed his way into her favor.* **3.** to extract or secure by stealth or guile: *Harry wormed the secret out of her.* **4.** to free from worms. [Old English *wyrm,* this invertebrate animal, serpent, miserable creature.] —**worm′er,** *n.*

worm-eat·en (wurm′ēt′ən) *adj.* **1.** gnawed or bored by worms; wormy: *worm-eaten vegetables.* **2.** old, worn-out, or out-of-date: *worm-eaten ideas.*

worm fence, zigzag fence having rails set so that their ends cross at right angles. Also, **snake fence.**

worm gear 1. worm wheel. **2.** gear that consists of a worm wheel and a revolving shaft with a single spiral thread.

worm·hole (wurm′hōl′) *n.* hole made by a burrowing worm, as in wood or fruit.

Worms (wurmz; German vôrms) *n.* **1.** port city in west-central West Germany, on the Rhine. Pop. (1966 est.), 63,500. **2. Diet of.** council held here in 1521, in which Martin Luther was formally condemned as a heretic.

worm wheel, wheel having teeth that engage with the thread of a worm.

worm·wood (wurm′wood′) *n.* **1.** any of several aromatic plants of the composite family, having small greenish flowers and deeply indented leaves, esp. the **common wormwood,** *Artemisia absinthium.* **2.** something bitter. [Old English *wermōd* the plant; influenced by WORM and WOOD probably because used as a vermifuge.]

worm·y (wur′mē) **worm·i·er, worm·i·est.** *adj.* **1.** containing or infested with worms. **2.** resembling a worm. —**worm′i·ness,** *n.*

worn (wôrn) *v.* past participle of **wear.** —*adj.* **1.** damaged by use or exposure; threadbare: *pants worn at the knees.* **2.** showing the effects of illness, fatigue, or anxiety; exhausted: *He had a worn, weary expression.*

worn-out (wôrn′out′) *adj.* **1.** unfit for use because of extensive or injurious wear. **2.** thoroughly exhausted or fatigued.

wor·ri·ment (wur′ē mənt) *n.* act, instance, or cause of worrying.

wor·ri·some (wur′ē səm) *adj.* **1.** causing worry or anxiety. **2.** given to worry.

wor·ry (wur′ē) **-ried, -ry·ing.** *v.i.* **1.** to experience mental uneasiness or distress; feel anxious or troubled about something. **2.** to pull or tear at something, as with the teeth (with *at*). **3.** to proceed or manage despite hardships or difficulties; struggle (with *along* or *through*). —*v.t.* **1.** to cause to feel anxious or troubled; make uneasy. **2.** to bother; pester; annoy. **3.** to pull, tear at, or touch repeatedly. **4.** to bite at, shake, or mangle with the teeth. —*n. pl.,* **-ries. 1.** act of worrying; being worried; mental uneasiness or distress. **2.** cause of mental uneasiness or distress; source of anxiety. [Old English *wyrgan* to strangle.] —**wor′ri·er,** *n.* —**Syn.** *n.* **1.** see **anxiety.**

wor·ry·wart (wur′ē wôrt′) *n. Informal.* person who tends to worry excessively and unnecessarily.

worse (wurs) comparative of **bad** and **ill.** *adj.* **1.** of more inferior quality, condition, ability, or value: *The food here is worse than at home. You're a worse actor than your brother.* **2.** more unfavorable, distressing, or unpleasant: *Tomorrow's weather will be even worse.* **3.** more harmful, damaging, or severe: *That sort of candy is even worse for your teeth.* **4.** in poorer health; less well: *The patient is worse since he took the medicine.* **5.** bad or evil to a greater degree: *His behavior is worse than ever before.* **6. worse off.** in a worse condition or position. —*adv.* in a worse way or manner: *She sings worse now than before she took lessons.* —*n.* something worse. [Old English *wyrsa.*]

wors·en (wur′sən) *v.t., v.i.* to make or become worse.

wor·ship (wur′ship) *n.* **1.** homage or veneration given to a god or someone or something considered sacred. **2.** expression of such homage or veneration, esp. religious services consisting of prayers and other acts in honor of God. **3.** intense or excessive devotion or regard; adoration. **4.** *British.* title of honor or respect used in addressing magistrates and certain other dignitaries. ▲ usually preceded by *your* or *his.* —*v.t.,* **-shiped** or **-shipped, -ship·ing** or **-ship·ping. 1.** to show religious homage or veneration to. **2.** to have an intense or excessive devotion to or regard for; adore. —*v.i.* to engage in worship, esp. to attend or take part in a religious service. [Old English *weorthscipe* honor, dignity, respect shown, from *weorth* worthy + -*scipe.* See -SHIP.] —**wor′ship·er;** *also,* **wor′ship·per,** *n.*

Syn. *v.t.* **2. Worship, venerate, revere** mean to hold in or regard with deep respect. **Worship** is characterized by the religious ritual and ceremony accorded a divine being. When applied to persons or things, worship suggests an idealized belief that denies the faults, peculiarities, or individuality of another to serve one's own needs and desires: *He worshiped the movie star until he discovered she was married.* In contrast, **venerate** suggests a tempered wisdom and solemnity in raising men or things considered holy above others of their kind: *Saints are venerated in Christian churches.* **Revere** is also considered a proper regard within the secular sphere, suggesting awe of what is considered old, wise, or courageous: *Americans revere Lincoln's memory.*

wor·ship·ful (wur′ship fəl) *adj.* **1.** showing or feeling reverence or adoration; worshiping. **2.** *British.* deserving of homage or respect; honorable. ▲ used as a title in addressing persons of rank.

worst (wurst) superlative of **bad** and **ill.** *adj.* **1.** most inferior in quality, condition, ability, or value: *the worst book ever written.* **2.** most unfavorable, distressing, or unpleasant: *the worst news I've heard all day.* **3.** most harmful, damaging, or severe: *the worst accident he had ever seen.* **4.** most bad or evil: *the worst dictator in history.* **5.** in poorest health; least well. **6. in the worst way.** *Informal.* very much: *That's something I've always wanted in the worst way.* —*adv.* in the worst manner or degree. —*n.* **1.** that which is worst. **2. at worst.** under the most unfavorable circumstances. **3. if (the) worst comes to (the) worst.** if the worst conceivable thing happens. **4. to get the worst of it.** to be defeated or placed at a disadvantage. —*v.t.* to get the better of; defeat. [Old English *wyrresta* most bad, most unpleasant.]

wor·sted (woos′tid, wur′stid) *n.* **1.** smooth, compact yarn made from long wool fibers that are combed parallel and twisted hard, used in making such fabrics as gabardine. **2.** tightly woven wool fabric made from such yarn and having a smooth, hard surface. —*adj.* consisting of or made from worsted. [From *Worsted* (now *Worstead*), English town where it was first made.]

wort (wurt) *n.* **1.** plant or herb. ▲ usually used in combination: *liverwort.* **2.** infusion of malt that becomes beer or ale after fermentation. [Old English *wyrt.*]

worth (wurth) *prep.* **1.** deserving of; meriting: *a film worth seeing.* **2.** equal in value to: *an old coin worth thirty dollars.* **3.** having property or wealth amounting to: *a woman worth sixty thousand dollars.* **4. for all one is worth.** to the utmost of one's powers or ability. —*n.* **1.** quality that makes something useful, desirable, or important; merit or excellence: *a novel of little worth.* **2.** monetary or market value of something: *The painting's worth was estimated at half a million dollars.* **3.** quantity of something that can be had for a specific sum: *fifty cents' worth of apples.* **4.** quality that makes a person deserving of esteem. **5.** wealth; riches. [Old English *weorth* value, of value, worthy.]

worth·less (wurth′lis) *adj.* lacking worth or value: *worthless advice.* —worth′less·ly, *adv.* —worth′less·ness, *n.*

worth·while (wurth′hwīl′, -wīl′) *adj.* sufficiently important or valuable to be worth the time, effort, or money spent.

wor·thy (wur′thē) -thi·er, -thi·est. *adj.* **1.** having worth or value: *to contribute to a worthy cause.* **2.** having sufficient worth or value; deserving: *a leader worthy of our support.* —*n. pl.,* -thies. person of importance, merit, or distinction. —wor′thi·ly, *adv.* —wor′thi·ness, *n.*

wost (wust) *Archaic.* second person singular present indicative of **wit**[2].

wot (wot) *Archaic.* first and third person singular present indicative of **wit**[2].

would (wood; *unstressed* wəd) past tense of **will**[1]. *auxiliary verb* **1.** used to express a condition: *I would help you if I could.* **2.** used to express futurity: *We wondered if Don would be on time.* **3.** used to express strong preference or willingness: *She would rather die than marry you.* **4.** used to express a choice: *Carol would never have taken the job if it weren't for the money.* **5.** used to express intention or determination: *They promised that they would return before dawn.* **6.** used to express longing or desire: *Would that I were with her now!* **7.** used to express probability or possibility: *Legalizing this drug would have disastrous consequences.* **8.** used to express a request: *Would you be kind enough to open the door for me?* **9.** used to express customary or habitual action: *We would sit and talk for hours.* **10.** used to express uncertainty: *The patient's condition would seem to be improving.*

would-be (wood′bē′) *adj.* **1.** desiring or professing to be: *a would-be artist.* **2.** intended to be: *police apprehended the would-be assassin.*

wouldn't (wood′ənt) would not.

wouldst (woodst) *Archaic.* second person singular past tense of **will**[1]. ▲ used with **thou.**

wound[1] (woond) *n.* **1.** injury to any part of the body, esp. an external injury in which the skin is torn, cut, or pierced. **2.** similar external injury to a plant or tree. **3.** injury to the feelings, reputation, or the like. —*v.t., v.i.* to inflict a wound or wounds on or upon (someone). [Old English *wund* external injury.]

wound[2] (wound) a past tense and past participle of **wind**[2] and **wind**[3].

wove (wōv) a past tense and past participle of **weave.**

wo·ven (wō′vən) a past participle of **weave.**

wow (wou) *interj.* used to express surprise, wonder, pleasure, or other feeling. —*v.t. Slang.* to be highly successful with; cause an enthusiastic response in: *The comedian really wowed the audience with his new act.*

WPA, Work Progress Administration.

wpm, words per minute.

wrack (rak) *n.* **1.** destruction. ▲ used chiefly in the phrase *wrack and ruin.* **2.** wreckage, esp. of a ship. **3.** seaweed or other marine vegetation cast ashore. [Partly from Old English *wrǣc* punishment; partly from Middle Dutch *wrak* wreckage.]

wraith (rāth) *n.* **1.** apparition of a person which, when seen while the person is living, is thought to indicate that he will soon die. **2.** ghost; specter. [Of uncertain origin.]

wran·gle (rang′gəl) -gled, -gling. *v.i.* to argue or dispute, esp. in a noisy or angry manner. —*v.t.* **1.** to bring about, obtain, or persuade by argument. **2.** in the western United States, to herd, round up, or tend (horses or other livestock). —*n.* noisy or angry argument; dispute. [Probably of Low German origin.]

wran·gler (rang′glər) *n.* **1.** one who wrangles. **2.** in the western United States, one who herds or tends horses or other livestock; cowboy.

wrap (rap) **wrapped** or **wrapt, wrap·ping.** *v.t.* **1.a.** to fold or place (a covering) around something, as for protection: *to wrap a blanket around a sleeping child.* **b.** to cover in this way: *to wrap a baby in a blanket.* **2.** to cover, esp. with paper, and make secure: *to wrap a package, to wrap a present.* **3.** to cover or surround so as to obscure or conceal: *The skyscraper was wrapped in fog. The transaction was wrapped in mystery.* **4.** to immerse; engross: *to be wrapped in thought.* **5.** to clasp or fold: *He wrapped his arms around her waist.* **6.** *Informal.* to bring to an end; conclude (with *up*): *The detective wrapped up the case in two days.* —*v.i.* **1.** to become wrapped or twined. **2.** to put on warm clothing (with *up*). **3. wrapped up in.** absorbed or involved in: *to be wrapped up in one's work.* —*n.* **1.** an outer covering or garment, as a shawl. **2. under wraps.** in concealment or secrecy: *The plan was kept under wraps.* [Of uncertain origin.]

wrap·a·round (rap′ə round′) *adj.* designating a garment that is wrapped around to fit before being fastened: *a wraparound skirt.*

wrap·per (rap′ər) *n.* **1.** paper or other material in which something is wrapped or enclosed: *a candy wrapper.* **2.** one who or that which wraps packages, parcels, or the like. **3.** long, loose dressing gown, robe, or similar garment.

wrap·ping (rap′ing) *n. usually pl.,* **wrappings.** paper or other material designed or used for wrapping packages or other objects.

wrapt (rapt) a past tense and past participle of **wrap.**

wrap-up (rap′up′) *n. Informal.* brief, summarizing news report.

wrasse (ras) *n.* any of a group of saltwater, often brilliantly colored fish, family Labridae, found chiefly in tropical waters. [Cornish *wrach, gwrach.*]

Wrasse

wrath (rath) *n.* **1.** extreme or violent anger; rage. **2.** act performed in or as an expression of great anger, esp. such an act carried out for punishment or vengeance. [Old English *wrǣththu.*] —**Syn. 1.** see anger.

wrath·ful (rath′fəl) *adj.* full of, resulting from, or expressing wrath. —wrath′ful·ly, *adv.* —wrath′ful·ness, *n.*

wreak (rēk) *v.t.* **1.** to inflict or exact: *to wreak havoc, to wreak vengeance.* **2.** to give free expression to; vent: *The soldier wreaked his anger on the innocent villager.* [Old English *wrecan* to drive, punish, vent, avenge.]

wreath (rēth) *pl.,* **wreaths** (rēthz). *n.* **1.** ring of intertwined flowers or leaves worn on the head as a mark of honor or victory, placed on a grave as a memorial, or used as a decoration. **2.** any ringlike or curving shape or form resembling this: *wreaths of smoke.* [Old English *writha* twisted band[2], fillet.]

wreathe (rēth) **wreathed, wreath·ing.** *v.t.* **1.** to form or shape into a wreath. **2.** to decorate, encircle, or crown with or as with a wreath or wreaths. **3.** to coil, curl, or twist. **4.** to envelop; cover: *Her face was wreathed in smiles.* —*v.i.* **1.** to take the form or shape of a wreath. **2.** to curl; spiral. [Partly from WREATH; partly from Middle English *wrethen,* past participle of *writhen* to writhe, from Old English *writhan* to twist, wrap around.]

wreck (rek) *v.t.* **1.** to cause the physical destruction or ruin of: *to wreck a car in an accident.* **2.** to destroy, ruin, or put an end to: *His drinking wrecked their marriage. The scandal nearly wrecked her career.* **3.** to tear down or dismantle, as an old building. —*v.i.* **1.** to suffer destruction or ruin. **2.** to be employed as a wrecker. —*n.* **1.** act of

at; āpe; cär; end; mē; it; īce; hot; ōld; fôrk; wood; fōol; oil; out; up; ūse; turn; sing; thin; this; zh in treasure; ə in ago, taken, pencil, lemon, circus.

wrecking; being wrecked; destruction. **2.** remains of anything, esp. a ship, automobile, airplane, or other vehicle that has been destroyed, damaged, or disabled. **3.a.** shipwreck. **b.** cargo or wreckage cast ashore after a shipwreck. **4.a.** person in poor physical or mental condition: *The job interview made me a nervous wreck.* **b.** something in poor or broken-down condition or in a state of disorder: *Steve's apartment was a wreck after the party.* [Anglo-Norman *wrec* shipwreck, poverty; of Scandinavian origin.] —**Syn. v.t. 1.** see **demolish.**

wreck·age (rek′ij) *n.* **1.** remains of anything that has been wrecked; debris. **2.** act of wrecking; being wrecked. [WRECK + -AGE.]

wreck·er (rek′ər) *n.* **1.** one who or that which wrecks. **2.** person whose work is tearing down or demolishing buildings. **3.** person, vehicle, or piece of equipment employed in removing, salvaging, or recovering wrecks. **4.** person, boat, or ship employed to recover wrecked or disabled ships or their cargoes. **5.** one who lures ships to destruction by using false lights on shore in order to plunder the wrecks.

wren (ren) *n.* any of various songbirds, family Troglodytidae, having a slender bill, short rounded wings, a short tail, and brownish plumage that is usually marked with brown, black, or white. Length: 4–9 inches. [Old English *wrenna.*]

Wren, Sir Christopher (ren) 1632–1723, English architect.

wrench (rench) *n.* **1.** sharp or violent twist, turn, or pull. **2.** injury or strain, as of the back, caused by a sudden or violent twisting, turning, or jerking motion; sprain. **3.** sharp, usually sudden mental or emotional distress or pain. **4.** change or distortion, as of meaning. **5.** any of various tools having fixed or movable jaws, used esp. for gripping and turning a nut, bolt, or pipe. —*v.t.* **1.** to twist, turn, or pull with a sudden sharp or violent motion. **2.** to injure or strain by twisting or turning suddenly or violently. **3.** to change or distort, as a meaning. **4.** to move or force, as if by great physical effort: *to wrench oneself away from the television set.* **5.** to give sharp mental or emotional distress or pain to. —*v.i.* to give a wrench or twist. [Old English *wrencan* to twist, turn.]

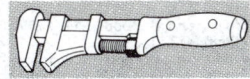

Wrench (def. 5)

wrest (rest) *v.t.* **1.** to pull, twist, or take away forcibly or violently. **2.** to take or seize by force or violence. **3.** to obtain or extract by great effort. **4.** to turn or change from the proper meaning, use, application, or purpose. —*n.* **1.** act of wresting; twist. **2.** wrenchlike key for tuning a stringed instrument, as a harp or piano. [Old English *wrǣsten* to turn, twist.] —*wrest′er, n.*

wres·tle (res′əl) **-tled, -tling.** *v.i.* **1.** to engage in the activity or sport of wrestling; grapple: *Two boys were wrestling around on the ground.* **2.** to struggle or contend, esp. in order to gain mastery: *to wrestle with a problem, to wrestle with one's conscience.* —*v.t.* **1.** to engage in wrestling with: *to wrestle a bear.* **2.** to move or force by or as if by wrestling: *The policeman wrestled the thief to the ground.* —*n.* **1.** act or action of wrestling. **2.** struggle. [Old English *wrǣstlian* to struggle, grapple.] —*wres′tler, n.*

wres·tling (res′ling) *n.* sport or activity in which two opponents struggle hand to hand, esp. in an attempt to throw or force each other to the ground.

wretch (rech) *n.* **1.** unfortunate, unhappy, or pitiable person. **2.** despicable, base, or contemptible person. [Old English *wrecca.*]

wretch·ed (rech′id) *adj.* **1.** very unhappy; deeply distressed: *Ellen sat alone in the corner feeling quite wretched.* **2.** characterized by or causing great unhappiness or discomfort: *to lead a wretched existence.* **3.** so poor, inadequate, or unfortunate as to be pitiful or pathetic: *the wretched living conditions of the slums.* **4.** poor or inferior in quality or ability: *Aaron is a wretched tennis player.* **5.** contemptible; despicable: *a wretched coward.* [WRETCH + -ED[2].] —*wretch′ed·ly, adv.* —*wretch′ed·ness, n.*

wri·er (rī′ər) comparative of **wry.**

wri·est (rī′ist) superlative of **wry.**

wrig·gle (rig′əl) **-gled, -gling.** *v.i.* **1.** to twist or turn from side to side with short, quick movements; squirm. **2.** to move or proceed with a wriggling motion. **3.** to make one's way by evasive or shifty means. —*v.t.* **1.** to cause to wriggle. **2.** to bring, get, or make by wriggling. —*n.* wriggling movement or action. [Middle Low German *wriggeln* to squirm.] —*wrig′gly, adj.*

wrig·gler (rig′lər) *n.* **1.** one who or that which wriggles. **2.** larva of a mosquito. Also *(def. 2),* **wig′gler.**

wright (rīt) *n.* one who makes, constructs, or creates something. ▲ used chiefly in combination: *playwright.* [Old English *wryhta, wyrhta* worker, maker, creator.]

Wright (rīt) **1.** Frank Lloyd. 1869–1959, U.S. architect. **2.** Or·ville (ôr′vil), 1871–1948, and Wil·bur (wil′bər), 1867–1912, U.S. brothers who were the first men to make powered, sustained, and controlled flights in an airplane.

wring (ring) **wrung** or *(archaic)* **wringed, wring·ing.** *v.t.* **1.a.** to

squeeze, twist, or compress, esp. so as to force out liquid (often with *out*): *to wring out wet laundry.* **b.** to force out (liquid) in this way. **2.** to obtain by forceful or persistent effort (often with *out*): *to wring the truth out of someone.* **3.** to clasp and press or twist (the hands) together. **4.** to twist or squeeze forcefully or violently. **5.** to cause emotional or mental pain to; torment: *His misery wrung our hearts.* —*n.* act of wringing; a twist or squeeze. [Old English *wringan* to press, strain, squeeze, twist.]

wring·er (ring′ər) *n.* one who or that which wrings, esp. a device or machine for squeezing water out of wet clothes.

wrin·kle[1] (ring′kəl) *n.* **1.** small fold, ridge, or crease in a normally smooth surface. **2.** small furrow, crease, or line in the skin, as caused by aging. —*v.t.* **-kled, -kling.** to form or make a wrinkle or wrinkles in: *to wrinkle one's brow.* —*v.i.* to become wrinkled: *This fabric won't wrinkle.* [From Middle English *wrinkled* twisted, winding, probably from Old English *gewrinclod* winding, crooked.] —*wrin′kly, adj.*

wrin·kle[2] (ring′kəl) *n. Informal.* clever or original idea, trick, or device. [Diminutive of Old English *wrenc* trick.]

wrist (rist) *n.* **1.** the joint that connects the hand and arm, or the area surrounding this joint. Also, **wrist joint. 2.** eight small bones that constitute this joint; carpus. **3.** corresponding part in certain animals. [Old English *wrist* this joint.]

wrist·band (rist′band′) *n.* band, as of a sleeve, that encircles the wrist.

wrist·let (rist′lit) *n.* **1.** band worn around the wrist, as for warmth. **2.** bracelet *(def. 1).*

wrist pin, pin or stud joining a connecting rod to a piston.

wrist·watch (rist′wach′) *n.* watch worn on a band or strap around the wrist.

writ[1] (rit) *n.* **1.** legal document ordering the person or persons named therein to perform or refrain from performing some act. **2.** something written; writing. [Old English *writ* something written, book, the Bible.]

writ[2] (rit) *Archaic.* past tense and past participle of **write.**

write (rīt) **wrote** or *(archaic)* **writ, writ·ten** or *(archaic)* **writ, writ·ing.** *v.t.* **1.a.** to mark or form (letters, words, symbols, or the like) on a surface, as with a pen or pencil. **b.** to form the letters, words, or symbols of: *to write one's name, to write a formula.* **2.** to express, describe, or communicate in or by writing: *to write one's thoughts in a diary.* **3.** to compose (a musical or literary work); be the author or composer of: *to write short stories.* **4.** to communicate with in writing; send a letter to: *Please write us when you get there.* **5.** to fill in with the required written information: *to write a check, to write an application.* **6.** to draw up in legal form: *to write a will.* **7.** to cover or fill with writing: *You must write at least ten pages.* **8.** to show or indicate plainly: *His guilt was written all over his face.* **9. to write down.** to record in written form. **10. to write in.** to vote for (a person not listed on a ballot) by inserting his name. **11. to write off. a.** to cancel or remove from an account, as a debt. **b.** to regard or acknowledge as a loss or failure. **12. to write out. a.** to put into writing. **b.** to write in full. **13. to write up.** to describe or set down in writing, esp. in a detailed account. —*v.i.* **1.** to form letters, words, or symbols on paper or another surface: *to write in red ink, to write in French.* **2.** to compose or create a book or other literary work; be an author or writer: *to write for a magazine, to write for a living.* **3.** to compose or send a letter: *I'll write as soon as I can.* **4.** to produce writing of a certain quality: *Helene writes quite illegibly. This pen writes beautifully.* **5.** to write script, as opposed to printing. **6. to write down.** to write in a deliberately simplified style, as for readers thought to be less intelligent or sophisticated than the writer. [Old English *writan* to scratch, engrave, delineate with a writing implement, set down in writing, record, compose a literary work in writing.]

write-in (rīt′in′) *n.* vote cast for a person not listed on a ballot by inserting his name. —*adj.* of or relating to such a vote or votes: *a write-in campaign.*

writ·er (rī′tər) *n.* **1.** person who writes. **2.** one whose occupation or profession is writing.

writer's cramp, cramp in the hand or fingers, usually caused by excessive writing.

write-up (rīt′up′) *n.* written account, description, or review: *Most critics gave the new play a terrible write-up.*

writhe (rīth) **writhed, writh·ing.** *v.i.* **1.** to move the body with a twisting or turning motion, as in great pain. **2.** to suffer great mental or emotional distress or discomfort. —*v.t.* to cause to twist or turn. —*n.* writhing movement; contortion. [Old English *wrīthan* to twist, wrap around.]

writ·ing (rī′ting) *n.* **1.** act of one who writes. **2.** penmanship; handwriting: *Her writing is always neat and legible.* **3.** written form: *I'd like this agreement put in writing.* **4.** something written: *There was writing all over the bathroom wall.* **5.** novel, play, or other literary work: *to study the writings of Aristotle.* **6.** occupation or profession of a writer or author. **7.** style, form, or art of literary composition: *journalistic writing.*

writ·ten (rit′ən) a past participle of **write**.

Wroc·law (vrôts′läf) *n.* city in southwestern Poland, formerly known as Breslau. Pop. (1968), 509,400.

wrong (rông) *adj.* **1.** not conforming to truth, fact, or reason; incorrect or inaccurate: *a wrong statement, a wrong impression.* **2.** not in accordance with that which is regarded as moral, just, or good: *John felt it would be wrong to testify against his friend.* **3.** not appropriate, suitable, or proper: *the wrong time to ask for a raise.* **4.** not in proper or normal working order; functioning improperly; amiss: *There is something wrong with my watch.* **5.** not intended, desired, or necessary: *to take a wrong turn.* **6.** with or having the side or surface not meant to be seen: *the wrong side of a fabric.* —*n.* **1.** that which is wrong, as an unjust, damaging, or immoral action. **2. in the wrong.** wrong, mistaken, or at fault. —*adv.* **1.** in a wrong way or manner. **2. to go wrong. a.** to turn out badly or take place incorrectly: *Something must have gone wrong with the experiment.* **b.** to go astray morally. **c.** to make a mistake; err: *Where did you go wrong in baking this cake?* —*v.t.* **1.** to treat in a wrong, unjust, or injurious manner; do wrong to. **2.** to impute evil to unjustly; malign. [Old English *wrang* uneven, injustice, from Old Norse *rangr* crooked, unjust.] —**wrong′ly,** *adv.* —**wrong′ness,** *n.*
  Syn. *adj.* **1. Wrong, false, erroneous** mean not true or correct. **Wrong** assumes that something contradicts or fails to conform to fact: *She gave me the wrong time.* **False** intensifies this sense by suggesting calculation and design meant or used to deceive others: *Janet submitted a false claim to the insurance company.* **Erroneous** is the most formal word, often applied to mistaken ideas or inconsistencies and a lack of logic in thought: *It is erroneous to consider that all of man's scientific advances have been positive.*

wrong·do·er (rông′doō′ər) *n.* one who does wrong. —**wrong′do′ing,** *n.*

wrong·ful (rông′fəl) *adj.* **1.** wrong, unjust, or injurious. **2.** unlawful; illegal. —**wrong′ful·ly,** *adv.* —**wrong′ful·ness,** *n.*

wrong·head·ed (rông′hed′id) *adj.* stubbornly or unreasonably clinging to wrong opinions, judgments, or ideas. —**wrong′head′ed·ly,** *adv.* —**wrong′head′ed·ness,** *n.*

wrote (rōt) a past tense of **write**.

wroth (rôth) *adj.* angry; wrathful. [Old English *wrāth*.]

wrought (rôt) *v.* a past tense and a past participle of **work**. —*adj.* **1.** made; formed. **2.** (of metals) shaped by hammering. **3.** ornamented; embellished. **4.** fashioned with care; not rough or crude. **5. wrought up.** agitated; excited.

wrought iron, extremely pure form of iron that is tough, easily worked and welded, and relatively resistant to corrosion.

wrung (rung) past tense and past participle of **wring**.

wry (rī) **wri·er, wri·est.** *adj.* **1.** made by twisting or distorting the features: *a wry smile.* **2.** humorous in an ironic, bitter, or perverse way: *a wry sense of humor.* **3.** turned, bent, or twisted; contorted. [From Middle English *wrien* to bend, twist, contort, from Old English *wrigian* to turn, move.] —**wry′ly,** *adv.* —**wry′ness,** *n.*

wry·neck (rī′nek′) *n.* **1.** spasm of the muscles of the neck, causing the head to be drawn to one side. **2.** bird, genus *Jynx,* related to and resembling the woodpecker, noted for its habit of twisting its head into odd contortions. Length: 6 inches.

WSW, west-southwest.

wt., weight.

Wu·chang (woō′chäng′) *n.* former city in east-central China, now part of Wuhan.

Wu·han (woō′hän′) *n.* metropolis in east-central China formed by the merger of the cities of Hankow, Hanyang, and Wuchang. Pop. (1957 est.), 2,146,000.

Wundt, Wil·helm (voont; vil′helm) 1832–1920, German psychologist.

Wup·per·tal (voop′ər täl′) *n.* city in western West Germany. Pop. (1968), 412,218.

wurst (wurst, woorst) *n.* sausage. [German *Wurst.*]

Würz·burg (wurts′burg′; *German* voorts′boork′) *n.* city in central West Germany. Pop. (1968), 120,004.

W. Va., West Virginia.

Wy·an·dotte (wī′ən dōt′) *n.* **1.** any of an American breed of domestic fowl raised for its meat and brown-shelled eggs. **2.** city in southeastern Michigan, a residential suburb of Detroit. Pop. (1970), 41,061.

Wy·att, Sir Thomas (wī′ət) 1503–42, English poet and statesman.

Wych·er·ley, William (wich′ər lē) c.1640–1716, English dramatist.

Wyc·liffe, John (wik′lif) *also,* **Wick·liffe, Wic·lif.** c.1320–84, English religious reformer.

Wy·eth, Andrew (wī′əth) 1917—, U.S. painter.

Wyo., Wyoming.

Wy·o·ming (wī ō′ming) *n.* state in the western United States. Capital, Cheyenne. Area, 97,914 sq. mi. Pop. (1970), 332,416. Abbreviation, **Wyo.** —**Wy·o′ming·ite′,** *n.*

wy·vern (wī′vərn) *n.* wivern.

at; āpe; cär; end; mē; it; īce; hot; ōld; fôrk; wood; foōl; oil; out; up; ūse; turn; sing; thin; this; zh in treasure; ə in ago, taken, pencil, lemon, circus.

x, X (eks) *pl.*, **x's, X's.** **1.** twenty-fourth letter of the English alphabet. **2.** shape of this letter or something having such a shape. **3.** Roman numeral for ten. **4.** unknown person, thing, factor, number, or the like. **5.** *Informal.* a ten-dollar bill. **6.** *Mathematics.* **a.** mark used to indicate multiplication: $4 \times 10 = 40$. **b.** unknown quantity or variable. **c.** x-axis. **7.** mark used in place of a signature by an illiterate person. **8.** mark used to indicate a particular point or place on a map or diagram. **9.** mark used to indicate a kiss in a letter or note.

x (eks) **x·ed** or **x'd** (ekst), **x·ing** or **x'ing** (ek'sing). *v.t.* **1.** to delete or mark with an x (often with *out*): *to x a mistake.* **2.** to indicate with or as with an x, as a choice or answer.

Xan·thip·pe (zan tip'ē) *n.* **1.** c.469–399 B.C., wife of Socrates, famous as a shrew. **2.** scolding, nagging woman; shrew.

xan·thous (zan'thəs) *adj.* yellow. [Greek *xanthos.*]

Xa·vi·er, Saint Francis (zā'vē ər, zav'ē-, zāv'yər) 1506–52, Spanish Jesuit missionary.

x-ax·is (eks'ak'sis) *pl.*, **x-ax·es** (eks'ak'sēz). *n.* horizontal axis in the Cartesian coordinate system along which the abscissa is measured.

X chromosome, one of the sex chromosomes.

Xe, xenon.

xe·bec (zē'bek) *also*, **ze·bec, ze·beck.** *n.* small, three-masted ship with square and lateen sails, used esp. in the Mediterranean. [Modification (influenced by obsolete Spanish *xabeque*) of earlier *chebec*, from French *chebec*, from Arabic *shabbāk.*]

xeno- *combining form* stranger or strange; foreigner or foreign: *xenophobia.*

xe·non (zē'non, zen'on) *n.* rare, heavy, gaseous chemical element approximately five times heavier than air, formerly thought to be completely inert, used as a light source in neon lights, lasers, and bubble chambers. Symbol: **Xe** See **element** for table. [Greek *xenon*, neuter of *xenos* strange; because of its rarity.]

xen·o·pho·bi·a (zen'ə fō'bē ə) *n.* abnormal fear of strangers or of anything strange or foreign. [Greek *xenos* stranger + *-phobiā* panic fear.] **—xen'o·pho'bic,** *adj.*

Xen·o·phon (zen'ə fən, -fon') *n.* c.430–355 B.C., Greek historian.

xe·rog·ra·phy (zi rog'rə fē) *n.* process for making positive photographic copies of printed materials, in which a positive image of the

material to be copied is projected onto an electrically charged surface. Light from the white areas of the material to be copied removes the charge, but the dark areas retain it and attract a black plastic powder which forms the print of the copy. [Greek *xēros* dry + -GRAPHY.]

xe·ro·phyte (zēr'ə fīt') *n.* plant that grows in and is adapted to dry conditions of climate and soil. [Greek *xēros* dry + -PHYTE.]

Xe·rox (zēr'oks) *n. Trademark.* process of copying printed or pictorial material by xerography. **—v.t., v.i. *also*, xe·rox.** to reproduce by xerography.

Xerx·es I (zurk'sēz) c.519–465 B.C., king of Persia and Media.

xi (zī, sī, ksē) *n.* **1.** fourteenth letter of the Greek alphabet (Ξ, ξ), corresponding to the English letter, *X, x.* **2.** *Physics.* either of two subatomic particles of the baryon group. See **subatomic particle** for table.

Xmas (kris'məs) Christmas.

X-rat·ed (eks'rā'tid) *adj.* **1.** (of a motion picture) for viewing by adult audiences only. **2.** pornographic or obscene.

X-ray (eks'rā') *v.t.* to examine, photograph, or treat with X rays.

X ray 1. invisible, high-frequency, shortwave, electromagnetic radiation which can pass through substances not permeable by visible light. It is used in medical diagnosis of internal disorders, as broken bones, and in treating certain diseases, as cancer. **2.** photograph made by means of X rays.

xy·lem (zī'ləm, -lem) *n.* the specialized woody plant tissue that serves to carry water and dissolved nutrients from the roots to the leaves and also helps to support the plant. [German *Xylem*, from Greek *xylon* wood.]

xy·lo·phone (zī'lə fōn') *n.* musical instrument consisting of a stand on which a row of wooden bars of graduated length is mounted, sounded by striking the bars with small wooden mallets. [Greek *xylon* wood + *phōnē* voice, sound!.]

Xylophone

at; āpe; cär; end; mē; it; īce; hot; ōld; fôrk; wood; fōol; oil; out; up; ūse; turn; sing; thin; this; zh in treasure; ə in ago, taken, pencil, lemon, circus.

1151

y, Y (wī) *pl.* **y's, Y's.** *n.* **1.** twenty-fifth letter of the English alphabet. **2.** shape of this letter or something having such a shape. **3.a.** *Mathematics.* unknown quantity or variable. **b.** y-axis.

Y, yttrium.

y. 1. yard. **2.** year.

-y[1] *suffix* (used to form adjectives) **1.** characterized by; containing; full of: *rainy, juicy, sooty.* **2.** inclined to: *itchy, thirsty.* **3.** somewhat: *sugary, powdery, chilly.* **4.** resembling: *flowery, icy.* [Old English *-ig.*]

-y[2] *suffix* used to form diminutives and terms of affection: *kitty, aunty, Bobby.* [Middle English *-ie.*]

-y[3] *suffix* (used to form nouns) state or quality: *sincerity, activity, tenacity.* [Latin *-ia,* from Greek *-iā,* often through French *-ie.*]

yacht (yot) *n.* any of various small ships used esp. for pleasure trips or racing. —*v.i.* to cruise or race in a yacht. [Obsolete Dutch *jaghte,* short for *jaghtschip* literally, ship for chasing, from *jagen* to chase + *schip* ship.]

yacht·ing (yot'ing) *n.* art, practice, or sport of sailing a yacht.

yachts·man (yots'mən) *pl.,* **-men.** *n.* one who owns or sails a yacht. —**yachts'man·ship',** *n.*

ya·hoo (yä'hōō) *pl.,* **-hoos.** *n.* rough, coarse, or uncouth person. [From *Yahoo,* a member of a race of brutes who have the shape and appearance of men (in Jonathan Swift's satire *Gulliver's Travels*).]

Yah·weh (yä'we) *also,* **Yah·veh, Jah·veh.** *n.* name of God in ancient Hebrew literature, esp. in the Old Testament. [See JEHOVAH.]

yak[1] (yak) *n.* long-haired ox, *Bos grunniens,* native to Tibet and central Asia, having a large hump at the shoulder and curved horns, used as a beast of burden. Height: 6½ feet at the shoulder. [Tibetan *gyag.*]

Yak

yak[2] (yak; *n. def. 2 also* yok) **yakked, yak·king.** *also,* **yack.** *v.i. Slang.* to talk too much or idly; chatter. —*n.* **1.** idle chatter or talk. **2.** loud, boisterous laugh.

Ya·kut (yä koot') *n.* **1.** member of a people living in northeastern Siberia. **2.** language of the Yakuts, belonging to the Ural-Altaic language family.

Yal·ta (yôl'tə) *n.* resort city on the Black Sea in the Soviet Union, site of a conference held by Roosevelt, Stalin, and Churchill in 1945. Pop. (1966 est.), 55,000.

Ya·lu (yä'lōō') *n.* river in eastern Asia, flowing between Manchuria and Korea into the Yellow Sea.

yam (yam) *n.* **1.** edible tuber of a trailing vine, genus *Dioscorea,* used as food in many tropical and subtropical areas. **2.** the vine itself, having large leaves and bearing spikes of small greenish flowers. **3.** sweet potato. [Portuguese *inhame* the edible tuber; of West African origin.]

yang (yäng, yang) *n.* in Chinese thought and philosophy, the male principle, combining light, warmth, and the creative energy associated with heaven. Distinguished from **yin.** [Chinese (Mandarin) *yang* sun, bright, male element in nature.]

Yang·tze (yäng'tse', yang'sē) *also,* **Yang·tse.** *n.* longest river in China, flowing northeastward from Tibet through central China and into the East China Sea, near Shanghai.

yank (yangk) *Informal. v.t., v.i.* to give a sharp, abrupt pull (to); jerk; tug. —*n.* sharp, abrupt pull. [Of uncertain origin.]

Yank (yangk) *n. Informal.* Yankee.

Yan·kee (yang'kē) *n.* **1.** one who is a native of New England. **2.a.** one who was born or lives in any of the Northern states. **b.** one who fought on the side of the Union in the Civil War. **3.** one who was born or lives in the United States. —*adj.* of or relating to Yankees.

[Possibly from Dutch *Janke,* diminutive of *Jan* John (a name used by the Dutch colonists of New York to designate the English settlers of Connecticut).]

Yankee Doo·dle (dōōd'əl) song popularized by American soldiers during the Revolutionary War.

Yan·kee·ism (yang'kē iz'əm) *n.* **1.** Yankee mannerism or trait. **2.** Yankee idiom or pronunciation.

Ya·oun·dé (ya ōōn dā', youn'dā) *n.* capital of Cameroon, in the south-central part of the country. Pop. (1965 est.), 101,000.

yap (yap) *n.* **1.** brief, sharp, or shrill bark; yelp. **2.** *Slang.* noisy talk. **3.** *Slang.* the mouth. **4.** *Slang.* churlish person. —*v.i.,* **yapped, yap·ping. 1.** to bark sharply or shrilly; yelp. **2.** *Slang.* to talk noisily. [Imitative.]

Yap (yäp) *n.* island group in the western Pacific, part of the Caroline Islands. Land area, 39 sq. mi. Pop. (1959), 3292.

Ya·qui (yä'kē) *pl.,* **-quis** or (*def. 1*) **-qui.** *n.* **1.** member of a tribe of North American Indians living predominantly in northern Mexico. **2.** language spoken by this tribe, belonging to the Uto-Aztecan language family.

yard[1] (yärd) *n.* **1.** area of ground adjoining or surrounding a house or other building. **2.** enclosed area of ground used for a special purpose, as for keeping livestock or for carrying on some work or business. **3.** area adjacent to a railroad station used for storing, switching, or servicing trains. —*v.t.* to put into or enclose in a yard. [Old English *geard* enclosure.]

yard[2] (yärd) *n.* **1.** measure of length equal to thirty-six inches, or three feet. See **weights and measures** for table. **2.** long rod, tapering toward the ends, fastened across a mast, used to support a sail. [Old English *gierd* staff, rod.]

Yard[2] *(def. 2)*

yard·age[1] (yär'dij) *n.* amount or length measured in yards. [YARD[1] + -AGE.]

yard·age[2] (yär'dij) *n.* **1.** the use of a yard or enclosure, as for the loading and unloading of cattle at a railroad yard. **2.** charge made for this use. [YARD[1] + -AGE.]

yard·arm (yärd'ärm') *n.* either end of a yard supporting a square sail.

yard goods, fabric that is sold by the yard.

yard·man (yärd'mən) *pl.,* **-men.** *n.* one who works in a yard, esp. a lumber or railroad yard.

yard·mas·ter (yärd'mas'tər) *n.* one who is in charge of a railroad yard.

yard·stick (yärd'stik') *n.* **1.** flat strip of wood or metal one yard long, used in measuring. **2.** any standard used in making a judgment, evaluation, or comparison.

yar·mul·ke (yär'məl kə, yä'məl-) *n.* skullcap worn by Jewish men and boys, esp. during religious services. [Yiddish *yarmulke,* from Polish and Ukrainian *yarmulka* small hat, possibly from Turkish *yağmurluk* raincoat, from *yağmur* rain.]

yarn (yärn) *n.* **1.** thread spun from natural or man-made fibers, such as cotton, wool, silk, or nylon, used in weaving or knitting. **2.** *Informal.* long, exaggerated, or highly embellished narrative. —*v.i. Informal.* to tell a yarn or yarns. [Old English *gearn* spun thread.]

yar·row (yar'ō) *n.* any of a large group of plants, genus *Achillea,* having lobed, often serrate leaves, and bearing clusters of small yellow, white, or pink flowers, esp. the milfoil, *A. millefolium.* [Old English *gearwe.*]

yaw (yô) *v.i.* **1.** (of a ship) to turn temporarily and unintentionally from a straight course. **2.** (of an aircraft, spacecraft, or projectile) to turn

at; āpe; cär; end; mē; it; īce; hot; ōld; fôrk; wood; fōōl; oil; out; up; ūse; turn; sing; thin; this; zh in treasure; ə in ago, taken, pencil, lemon, circus.

to the right or left on its vertical axis. —*n.* act of turning from a straight course. [Of uncertain origin.]

yawl (yôl) *n.* **1.** sailboat or small yacht with two masts, a large mainmast placed forward and a smaller mast placed astern. **2.** ship's small boat, usually rowed by four or six oarsmen. [Dutch *jol* small sloop, dinghy.]

yawn (yôn) *v.i.* **1.** to open the mouth wide, usually involuntarily and with a deep breath, because of drowsiness, boredom, or fatigue. **2.** to be or draw wide open: *The pit of the crater yawned below.* —*v.t.* to utter or express with a yawn: *to yawn a reply.* —*n.* **1.** act or fact of yawning. **2.** act of opening wide. [Old English *geonian* to open the mouth wide, gape.] —**yawn′er,** *n.*

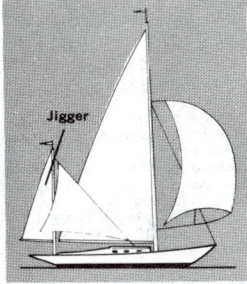
Jigger

Yawl *(def. 1)*

yawp (yôp, yäp) *v.i.* **1.** to utter a loud, sharp cry. **2.** *Slang.* to talk loudly and foolishly. —*n.* **1.** loud, sharp cry. **2.** *Slang.* loud, foolish talk. [Imitative.] —**yawp′er,** *n.*

yaws (yôz) *n.,pl.* infectious disease occurring in the tropics, caused by a spirochete and characterized by growths and raspberrylike sores on the skin. ▲ construed as singular. [Of Carib origin.]

y-ax·is (wī′ak′sis) *pl.,* **y-ax·es** (wī′ak′sēz). *n.* vertical axis in the Cartesian coordinate system along which the ordinate is measured.

Yb, ytterbium.

Y chromosome, one of the sex chromosomes.

y·clept (ē klept′) *also,* **y·cleped.** *adj. Archaic.* called; named. [Old English *gecleopod,* past participle of *cleopian* to call.]

yd, yard; yards.

ye[1] (yē) *pron. Archaic.* the ones spoken to. [Old English *gē.*]

ye[2] (thē) *Archaic.* the. [Archaic transcription of THE[1], because of the resemblance to the letter *y* of a runic letter used for the sound *th* in certain medieval manuscripts.]

yea (yā) *adv.* **1.** yes. ▲ used in affirmation or assent, esp. in voting orally. **2.** *Archaic.* indeed; truly. ▲ used to introduce a sentence or statement. **3.** *Archaic.* not only so, but also; what is more. ▲ used to intensify or amplify. —*n.* affirmative vote or voter. [Old English *gēa* yes.]

yean (yēn) *v.t., v.i.* (of a sheep or goat) to bring forth (young). [Probably from an unrecorded Old English word.]

yean·ling (yēn′ling) *n.* young of a sheep or goat; lamb or kid.

year (yēr) *n.* **1.** period of time consisting of 365 or 366 days, reckoned from January 1 to December 31, and divided into twelve months or fifty-two weeks. Also, **calendar year. 2.a.** interval of time between one vernal equinox and the next, equal to 365 days, 5 hours, 48 minutes, and 46 seconds. Also, **solar year. b.** interval of time required for the earth to complete one revolution around the sun, measured against the relatively fixed background of the stars, equal to 365 days, 6 hours, 9 minutes, and 9.54 seconds. Also, **sidereal year. 4.** any period of twelve months: *Our fiscal year begins June 1. He'll be gone two years in May.* **5.** part of a year devoted to a particular activity: *the academic year.* **6.** period of time in which any planet completes one revolution around the sun. **7.** **years.** age, esp. old age: *a man of years. He's getting on in years.* **8.** **years.** time, esp. a long time: *We've been going there for years.* **9.** **year after year.** every year. **10.** **year by year.** with each succeeding year. **11.** **year in, year out.** every year; continuously. [Old English *gēar* the period of a year.]

year·book (yēr′book′) *n.* **1.** book published every year, usually containing information about or a summary of the events of the previous year. **2.** book issued by a graduating class of a high school or college, containing information and, usually, photographs of the class and its activities and achievements.

year·ling (yēr′ling) *n.* animal that is one year old or in its second year. —*adj.* one-year-old.

year·long (yēr′lông′) *adj.* lasting for a year.

year·ly (yēr′lē) *adj.* **1.** occurring or returning once a year: *my yearly visit to the dentist.* **2.** performed during a year; lasting a year: *a yearly orbit.* **3.** measured by the year: *a yearly income.* —*adv.* once a year; annually. —*n., pl.,* **-lies.** publication issued once a year.

yearn (yurn) *v.i.* **1.** to feel a strong and deep desire: *to yearn for the carefree days of youth.* **2.** to feel pity; be moved with compassion: *It would make anyone's heart yearn to see these homeless children.* [Old English *giernan* to desire.]

yearn·ing (yur′ning) *n.* earnest or deep desire.

year-round (yēr′round′) *adj.* existing, operating, or continuing throughout the year: *a year-round vacation spot.*

yeast (yēst) *n.* **1.** substance consisting of minute cells of any of various fungi, genus *Saccharomyces,* that cause fermentation in liquids containing sugar. Yeast is used commercially in raising bread, making beer and wine, and in other processes. **2.** single plant or cell forming this substance. **3.** yeast cake. **4.** foam; froth; spume. **5.** anything that causes ferment or activity. [Old English *gist* the substance.]

yeast cake, yeast compressed with flour or meal into small cakes, used esp. in baking and brewing.

yeast·y (yēs′tē) **yeast·i·er, yeast·i·est.** *adj.* **1.** of, containing, or resembling yeast. **2.** frothy; foamy: *yeasty sea foam.* **3.** characterized by ferment, agitation, or great activity. **4.** light and superficial.

Yeats, William Butler (yāts) 1865–1939, Irish poet and dramatist.

yegg (yeg) *n. Slang.* thief, esp. a burglar or safecracker. [Supposedly from a U.S. burglar named John *Yegg.*]

yell (yel) *v.i.* **1.** to cry out loudly, as in pain or anger. —*v.t.* to utter or express with a yell. —*n.* **1.** strong, loud cry, as of pain or anger; scream. **2.** rhythmic chant or cheer shouted by a group: *that old college yell.* [Old English *giellan* to cry out loudly.] —**Syn.** *v.i.* see **shout.**

yel·low (yel′ō) *n.* **1.** color occurring between green and orange in the spectrum; color of gold, butter, or ripe lemons. **2.** pigment or dye having or producing this color. **3.** yolk of an egg. —*adj.* **1.** having the color yellow. **2.** having a yellowish complexion. **3.** *Informal.* cowardly. **4.** having turned yellow, as by disease or discoloration. **5.** emphasizing sensationalism and scandal rather than fact: *yellow journalism.* —*v.t., v.i.* to make or become yellow. [Old English *geolu* of this color.]

yel·low·bird (yel′ō burd′) *n.* any of various predominantly yellow birds, as the American goldfinch and the yellow warbler.

yel·low-dog contract (yel′ō dôg′) contract between an employer and employee, no longer legal, in which the employee agrees not to join a union during the time of his employment.

yellow fever, infectious, often fatal disease occurring primarily in the tropics, caused by a virus transmitted by the bite of a mosquito and characterized by high fevers, vomiting, jaundice, and hemorrhaging.

yel·low·ham·mer (yel′ō ham′ər) *n.* **1.** Eurasian finch, *Emberiza citrinella,* having black, brown, and yellow plumage and a short conical bill. Length: 6½ inches. **2.** American flicker, *Colaptes auratus,* of the woodpecker family, having predominantly brown plumage with yellow markings on the wings and tail. [Earlier *yelambre,* possibly going back to Old English *geolu* yellow + *amore,* a bird of uncertain identity.]

yel·low·ish (yel′ō ish) *adj.* somewhat yellow.

yellow jack 1. yellow fever. **2.** yellow flag used as a sign of quarantine, as on a ship.

yellow jacket, any of several wasps that have yellow markings.

yel·low·legs (yel′ō legz′) *n.* either of two American sandpipers, genus *Totanus,* having long, yellow legs.

Yellow jacket

yellow ocher, yellowish-orange color or pigment, usually containing limonite.

yellow peril, alleged threat of the growth and expansion of Oriental peoples as conceived by the nations of the West.

yellow pine 1. yellowish wood of any of several North American pine trees, used esp. as structural timber and in the manufacture of paper. **2.** tree bearing such wood.

Yellow River, Hwang Ho.

Yellow Sea, shallow arm of the Pacific, between northeastern China and Korea.

Yel·low·stone (yel′ō stōn′) *n.* river in the northern United States, mainly in Montana, a major tributary of the Missouri.

Yellowstone National Park, area in northwestern Wyoming and neighboring sections of Montana and Idaho, noted for its scenery, hot springs, and geysers. It was the first national park to be established in the world. Area, 3472 sq. mi.

yellow warbler, American warbler, *Dendroica petechia,* the male of which has yellow plumage with brown streaks.

yelp (yelp) *n.* short shrill cry, as that made by a dog in pain. —*v.i.* to utter or give forth a short shrill cry. —*v.t.* to utter with a yelp. [Old English *gielpan* to boast.] —**Syn.** *v.i.* see **bark**[2].

Yem·en (yem′ən) *n.* **1.** country in the southwestern part of the Arabian peninsula, on the Red Sea, officially known as the **Yemen Arab Republic.** Capital, Sana. Area, 75,300 sq. mi. Pop. (1975 est.), 6,700,-000. **2. People's Democratic Republic of.** See **Southern Yemen.**

yen[1] (yen) *pl.,* **yen.** *n.* monetary unit of Japan, equal to 100 sen. [Japanese *en,* from Chinese (Mandarin) *yüan* dollar, circle.]

yen[2] (yen) *Informal. n.* sharp desire or longing; craving. —*v.i.* **yenned, yen·ning.** to yearn or long; desire sharply. [Chinese (Cantonese) *yan* craving.]

yeo·man (yō′mən) *pl.,* **-men.** *n.* **1.** naval petty officer who performs

clerical or administrative duties. **2.** small farmer, esp. a member of a class of English society who owned and farmed a small amount of land. **3.** *Archaic.* servant or attendant in the household of a sovereign or nobleman. **4.** yeoman of the guard. [Middle English *yoman* servant in a royal or noble household, possibly a contraction of *yongman* young man, from Old English *geong* young + *mann* man.]

yeo·man·ly (yō′mən lē) *adj.* **1.** relating to or having the rank of a yeoman. **2.** befitting a yeoman; brave; staunch. —*adv.* in the manner of a yeoman; bravely.

yeoman of the guard, member of the ceremonial bodyguard for the English monarch and the royal family, instituted in the fifteenth century and consisting of one hundred men and their officers.

yeo·man·ry (yō′mən rē) *n.* yeomen collectively, esp. the class of small farmers.

yeoman's service, faithful, diligent, and useful service or support.

-yer, form of **-ier** after *w,* as in *lawyer.*

Ye·re·van (ye re vän′) *also,* **E·ri·van.** *n.* city in the southwestern Soviet Union, the capital of Armenia. Pop. (1970 est.), 767,000.

yes (yes) *adv.* **1.** as you say or ask; it is so. ◣ used to express acceptance, agreement, consent, or affirmation: *Yes, you are right. Yes, you may borrow my book.* Opposed to **no. 2.** in addition to that; moreover. ◣ used to emphasize a preceding statement by repetition or addition: *Andy is a good athlete, yes, the best on the team.* —*n. pl.* **yes·es.** utterance of the word "yes"; positive response. —*v.t., v.i.,* **yessed, yes·sing.** to say "yes" (to someone or something). [Old English *gēse,* word expressing affirmation, probably from *geā* yea + *sī* be it (third person singular of the present subjunctive of *bēon* to be).]

ye·shi·va (yə shē′və) *pl.,* **-vahs** or **-voth** (-vōt). *also,* **ye·shi·vah.** *n.* **1.** Orthodox Jewish parochial school. **2.** Orthodox Jewish institution of higher learning. [Hebrew *yeshīvāh* a sitting, academy.]

yes man *Informal.* assistant or subordinate who always agrees with his superior.

yes·ter·day (yes′tər dē, -dā′) *n.* **1.** the day before today. **2.** the recent past. —*adv.* **1.** on the day before today. **2.** recently. [Old English *geostran dæg* the day before today, on the day before today.]

yes·ter·eve·ning (yes′tər ēv′ning) *n., adv. Archaic.* yesterday evening. *Also,* **yes·ter·eve′.**

yes·ter·morn·ing (yes′tər môr′ning) *n., adv. Archaic.* yesterday morning. *Also,* **yes·ter·morn′.**

yes·ter·night (yes′tər nīt′) *n., adv. Archaic.* night before today; last night.

yes·ter·year (yes′tər yēr′) *n.* **1.** year before this; last year. **2.** the past; yore.

yes·treen (yes trēn′) *n., adv. Archaic.* yesterday evening.

yet (yet) *adv.* **1.** at the present time; now: *She is not yet old enough to vote.* **2.** up to present time; thus far: *Robert has never yet been late.* **3.** continuously up to this or that time: *Father rose early and is working yet.* **4.** at some future time; eventually: *The mystery will be solved yet.* **5.** after all the time that has or had elapsed: *Aren't you finished eating yet?* **6.** in the time remaining: *There is yet a chance that we will win.* **7.** in addition: *to tell yet another lie. There are three days yet to go until my vacation.* **8.** even; still. ◣ used with a comparative: *to drive at yet a greater speed. It will be colder yet before spring comes.* **9.** nevertheless; however: *The judge was stern, yet completely fair.* **10.** moreover: *Roger wouldn't speak to Peter nor yet to me.* **11.** **as yet.** up to now: *We have not as yet received your letter.* —*conj.* nevertheless; however: *He said he was our friend, yet he wouldn't help us.* [Old English *gīet(a)* still, moreover, in addition, thus far, at length.] —**Syn.** *conj.* see **but.**

yet·i (yet′ē) *n.* abominable snowman. [Of Tibetan origin.]

Yev·tu·shen·ko (yev′tōō sheng′kō; yev gen′ē) **Yev·ge·ny** 1933—, Russian poet.

yew (ū) *n.* **1.** any of a small group of evergreen trees and shrubs, genus *Taxus,* native to the Northern Hemisphere, having scaly reddish-brown bark and flattened needlelike leaves. **2.** wood of this tree, used esp. in making archery bows. [Old English *ēow* this tree.]

Yew branch

Ygg·dra·sill (ig′drə sil) *also,* **Yg·dra·sil, Ygg·dra·sil.** *n. Norse Mythology.* enormous ash tree that grows from the earth and supports the whole universe.

Yid·dish (yid′ish) *n.* language belonging to the western group of the Germanic branch of the Indo-European language family, spoken predominantly by Jews in Europe, Israel, and North and South America. Yiddish, which is written in the Hebrew alphabet, is the descendant of a Middle High German dialect, with the addition of many words from Hebrew, Slavic, and Romance languages. —*adj.* of or relating to this language.

yield (yēld) *v.t.* **1.** to give forth by a natural process or as the result of cultivation or labor: *rich land that yielded a large crop. The combination of elements yielded an acid.* **2.** to give in return, as for an investment: *a bank account yielding 5 percent interest per year.* **3.** to give up, as to superior power: *The outnumbered troops yielded the town to the enemy.* **4.** to concede or grant: *to yield the right of way to pedestrians.* —*v.i.* **1.** to give up; surrender; submit. **2.** to comply, as from coercion or compulsion; consent: *We yielded to their argument.* **3.** to give way, as to force or pressure: *The lock was old and yielded when we pushed the door.* **4.** to give place, as through inferiority: *He yields to no one in devotion to the cause of human rights.* **5.** to provide a return; produce. —*n.* **1.** product, as of cultivation or mining; amount yielded: *a yield of fifty bushels of wheat.* **2.** profit derived from an investment. [Old English *gieldan* to pay[1], repay, render.] —**yield′er,** *n.* —**Syn.** *v.i.* **1.** see **defer[2].**

yield·ing (yēl′ding) *adj.* tending to yield; submissive; obedient.

yin (yin) *n.* in Chinese thought, the female principle, combining the dark, cold, wet, and fertile energy associated with the earth. Distinguished from **yang.** [Chinese (Mandarin) *yin* moon, dark, female principle in nature.]

yip (yip) *n.* yelp, esp. of a dog. —*v.i.* **yipped, yip·ping.** to yelp. [Imitative.]

-yl *suffix* used in chemistry to indicate a radical: *methyl, ethyl.*

YMCA, Young Men's Christian Association.

YMHA, Young Men's Hebrew Association.

Y·mir (ē′mir) *also,* **Y·mir, Y·mer.** *n. Norse Mythology.* giant formed from vapors of melting ice, from whose body Odin and his brothers formed the earth.

yo·del (yōd′əl) **-deled, -del·ing;** *also, British,* **-delled, -del·ling.** *also,* **yo·dle.** *v.t., v.i.* to sing with frequent alternating changes between the natural voice and a falsetto voice. —*n.* act or sound of yodeling. [German *jodeln* to yodel.] —**yo′del·er;** *also, British,* **yo′del·ler,** *n.*

yo·ga (yō′gə) *also,* **Yo·ga.** *n.* system of mental and physical discipline practiced by Hindus in order to become free of the senses and the external world and reach ultimate reality. It is also practiced by non-Hindus to improve mental and physical health and increase powers of concentration. [Sanskrit *yoga* union.]

yo·gi (yō′gē) *pl.,* **-gis.** *n.* **1.** one who practices or is an adherent of yoga. **2.** yoga.

yo·gurt (yō′gərt) *also,* **yo·ghurt, yo·ghourt.** *n.* fermented, semi-solid dairy product made by adding bacteria to milk. [Turkish *yoğhurt.*]

yoicks (yoiks) *interj.* cry formerly used in fox hunting to urge on the hounds.

yoke (yōk) *pl., (defs. 1, 3–7)* **yokes** or *(def. 2)* **yoke.** *n.* **1.** wooden frame consisting of a long, curved bar fitted with two hoops by which two work animals are joined together. **2.** pair of animals, esp. oxen, joined together

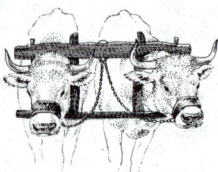

Yoke (def. 1)

by a yoke. **3.** any of various similar devices, as a frame carried on the shoulders and designed to carry a pail or other burden at either end. **4.** oppressive force or influence; burden: *an enslaved people under the yoke of tyranny.* **5.** sign, token, or state of subjection or servitude: *Termagent wives who make wedlock a yoke* (Steele, 1709). **6.** that which joins or unites; bond; tie: *the yoke of friendship.* **7.** top section of a garment, usually consisting of a flat, smooth-fitting piece of fabric, as around the neck and shoulders of a blouse. —*v.t.* **yoked, yok·ing.** **1.** to put a yoke on. **2.** to harness or attach (a work animal) to a yoke. **3.** to join or unite with or as with a yoke. [Old English *geoc* contrivance used to join a pair of draft animals, pair of animals so joined, subjection.]

yoke·fel·low (yōk′fel′ō) *n.* mate or partner in labor.

yo·kel (yō′kəl) *n.* country fellow. ◣ usually used contemptuously. [Possibly from dialectal English *yokel* green woodpecker (used figuratively); probably of imitative origin.]

yoke·mate (yōk′māt′) *n.* yokefellow.

Yo·ko·ha·ma (yō′kə hä′mə) *n.* port city in east-central Japan, on the island of Honshu. Pop. (1968 est.), 2,047,000.

yolk (yōk, yōlk) *n.* **1.** yellow, nutritive substance of an egg, as distinguished from the albumen, or white part, of the egg. **2.** all the substances, as wool grease and perspiration, found in unprocessed sheep's wool. [Old English *geolca* the yellow part of an egg, from *geolu* yellow.]

Yom Kip·pur (yom kip′ər; *Hebrew* yôm kē pōor′) in Judaism, the day of fast and atonement for sins, observed on the tenth day of the first month of the Jewish calendar. *Also,* **Day of Atonement.** [Hebrew *yōm kippūr* day of atonement.]

yon (yon) *adj., adv. Archaic.* yonder. [Old English *geon* that.]

yond (yond) *adj., adv. Archaic.* yonder. [Old English *geond.*]

yon·der (yon′dər) *adv.* in that place; over there. —*adj.* being at a distance indicated: *The cattle are in yonder field.* [Middle English *yonder,* from *yond.* See YOND.]

Yon·kers (yong′kərz) *n.* city in southeastern New York, just north of New York City. Pop. (1970), 204,370.

yore (yôr) *adv.* of yore. of long ago; in the past. [Old English *gēara* formerly, of old; literally, of years, genitive of *gēar* year.]

York (yôrk) *n.* **1.** reigning house of England from 1461 to 1485, a branch of the royal house of Plantagenet. Its emblem was a white rose. **2. Duke of.** 1341–1402, son of Edward III of England; born Edmund Langley. **3.** city in northeastern England. Pop. (1968 est.), 108,600. **4.** city in southeastern Pennsylvania. Pop. (1970), 50,335.

York·ist (yôr′kist) *n.* adherent or member of the house of York. —*adj.* **1.** of or relating to the house of York. **2.** of or relating to the supporters of the house of York against the house of Lancaster.

York·shire pudding (yôrk′shēr, -shər) batter often baked under roasting meat to catch the drippings, served esp. with roast beef.

Yorkshire terrier, small dog having a coat of long, straight, silky hair that is dark steel-blue and tan. Height: 8 inches at the shoulder.

York·town (yôrk′toun′) *n.* historic town in southeastern Virginia, scene in 1781 of the last major encounter of the American Revolution at which Lord Cornwallis surrendered to George Washington.

Yo·sem·i·te Falls (yō sem′i tē) waterfalls in Yosemite National Park, among the world's highest and most magnificent.

Yosemite National Park, large national park in east-central California, noted for the scenic magnificence of its valley, falls, and sequoia trees. Area, 1189 sq. mi.

you (ū; *unstressed* yoo, yə) *sing.,* nominative, **you;** possessive, **your, yours;** objective, **you;** *pl.,* nominative, **you;** possessive, **your, yours;** objective, **you.** *pron.* **1.** the one or ones being addressed: *Do you want to go? I'll meet you at six o'clock.* **2.** a person; one; anyone: *You have to be careful when handling explosives.* ▲ In formal contexts *one* is preferred to *you* as an indefinite pronoun: *One can never be sure what the future will bring.* [Old English *ēow,* dative and accusative of *gē.* See YE[1].]

you-all (ū ôl′, yôl) *pron. Informal.* you. ▲ used chiefly in the Southern states and referring to two or more persons.

you'd (ūd) **1.** you had. **2.** you would.

you'll (ūl; *unstressed* yool) **1.** you will. **2.** you shall.

young (yung) **young·er** (yung′gər), **young·est** (yung′gist) *adj.* **1.** having lived or existed for a short time; in the early part of life or growth; not old. **2.** possessing or exhibiting the characteristics of a young person; fresh; vigorous: *She has a young face for her years.* **3.** of, relating to, or belonging to the early part of life: *He remembered his young years with nostalgia.* **4.** recently begun, formed, or made; in an early stage of progress or development: *a young wine, a young nation.* **5.** of fewer years than. ▲ designating the younger of two people with the same name: *Young Mr. Williams was following in his father's footsteps.* **6.** having little experience, skill, or practice. —*n.* **1.** young people collectively: *That music is popular with the young.* **2.** young offspring, esp. of animals: *an animal's instinct to protect its young.* **3. with young.** pregnant. [Old English *geong* youthful, recent, fresh.] —**young′ness,** *n.*

Young (yung) **1. Brig·ham** (brig′əm). 1801–77, U.S. Mormon leader. **2. Edward.** 1683–1765, English poet.

young blood 1. young people. **2.** youthful ideas, energy, or enthusiasm.

young·ish (yung′ish) *adj.* somewhat young.

young·ling (yung′ling) *n.* **1.** young person, animal, or plant. **2.** one who is inexperienced; novice. —*adj.* young.

young·ster (yung′stər) *n.* young person; child or youth.

Youngs·town (yungz′toun′) *n.* city in northeastern Ohio. Pop. (1970), 139,788.

youn·ker (yung′kər) *n. Archaic.* young man, esp. a young gentleman. [Middle Dutch *jonckher* young nobleman, from *jonc* young + *here* lord.]

your (yoor; *unstressed* yər) *adj.* possessive form of *you: your sister, your house. I agree with your suggestion.* ▲ *Your* is used in some titles, as *Your Majesty, Your Excellency, Your Honor.* It is also used as an indefinite possessive: *The church is on your left as you enter the town. He is not your typical college professor.* [Old English *ēower,* genitive of *gē.* See YE[1].]

you're (yoor, yôr; *unstressed* yər) you are.

yours (yoorz) *pron.* **1.** of, relating to, or belonging to you: *This book is yours.* ▲ used often with *of: He is a great admirer of yours.* **2.** thing or things relating to or belonging to you: *His paper was well-written, but yours was even better.* ▲ *Yours* is the absolute form of the possessive adjective *your,* used when no noun follows: *Yours was my favorite birthday present.*

your·self (yoor self′, yər-) *pl.,* **-selves.** *pron.* **1.** emphatic form of **you:**

You yourself know that she deserves the credit. **2.** reflexive form of **you:** *Be careful of the fire or you will burn yourself.* **3.** your usual, normal, or true self: *You have not been yourself these past few weeks.*

yours truly 1. conventional phrase of politeness before the signature at the close of a letter. **2.** *Informal.* I; me.

youth (ūth) *pl.,* **youths** (ūths, ūthz) or **youth.** *n.* **1.** condition or quality of being young: *He has youth on his side.* **2.** time of life between childhood and adulthood: *the carefree days of his youth.* **3.** early period in the development or existence of anything. **4.** young people collectively: *Our hope lies in the youth of our nation.* **5.** young person, esp. a young man. [Old English *geoguth* quality or state of being young, young people collectively.]

youth·ful (ūth′fəl) *adj.* **1.** having youth; still young in years: *A youthful performer took the stage.* **2.** characteristic of youth: *youthful energy.* **3.** belonging to or suitable for young people: *a youthful dress.* **4.** in an early stage of development or existence. **5.** *Geology.* having undergone only slight erosion: *a youthful mountain.* —**youth′ful·ly,** *adv.* —**youth′ful·ness,** *n.*

you've (ūv; *unstressed* yoov) you have.

yowl (youl) *n.* long, mournful cry, as that of a dog; wail. —*v.i.* to utter a yowl. [Imitative.]

Yo-yo (yō′yō) *pl.,* **-yos.** *n. Trademark.* toy consisting of two disks connected at their center by a pin around which a string is wound, the loose end being attached to the operator's finger. The operator alternately lowers and raises the Yo-yo by unwinding and rewinding the string.

Y·pres (ē′prə) *n.* historic town in western Belgium, noted for the many battles of World War I fought there. Pop. (1964 est.), 18,400.

yr. 1. year; years. **2.** your.

yrs. 1. years. **2.** yours.

yt·ter·bi·a (i tur′bē ə) *n.* compound of ytterbium and oxygen that is colorless when pure, used in making ceramics with very low electrical conductivity. Formula: Yb$_2$O$_3$ Also, **ytterbium oxide.**

yt·ter·bi·um (i tur′bē əm) *n.* soft, silvery, metallic element used in alloys and lasers. Symbol: Yb See **element** for table. [Modern Latin *ytterbium,* from *Ytterby,* Swedish town where it was discovered.] —**yt·ter′bic,** *adj.*

yt·tri·a (it′rē ə) *n.* yellowish-white compound of yttrium and oxygen, used in making color television tubes, special ceramics, and gas mantles. Formula: Y$_2$O$_3$ Also, **yttrium oxide.**

yt·tric (it′rik) *adj.* of or containing yttrium.

yt·tri·um (it′rē əm) *n.* dark-gray metallic element used esp. in iron alloys and in color television tubes, and to make synthetic garnets for lasers. Symbol: Y See **element** for table. [Modern Latin *yttrium,* from *Ytterby,* Swedish town where it was discovered.]

yu·an (ū än′) *pl.,* **yu·an.** *n.* monetary unit of mainland China, equal to 100 fen. [Chinese (Mandarin) *yüan* round, circle.]

Yu·ca·tán (ū′kə tan′; *Spanish* ū′kä tän′). *n.* peninsula in southeastern Mexico and northeastern Central America, between the Gulf of Mexico and the Caribbean. It was the center of Mayan civilization. Area, approx. 70,000 sq. mi.

yuc·ca (yuk′ə) *n.* any of a group of desert plants, genus *Yucca,* of the southwestern United States and Latin America, having a woody stem and bearing clusters of white, bell-shaped, drooping flowers. [Spanish *yuca,* of Carib origin.]

Yucca

Yu·go·slav (ū′gō släv′, -slav′) *also,* **Ju·go·slav.** *n.* member or close descendant of the people of Yugoslavia. —*adj.* of or relating to Yugoslavia or its people.

Yu·go·sla·vi·a (ū′gō slä′vē ə) *also,* **Ju·go·sla·vi·a.** *n.* country in southeastern Europe, on the eastern shore of the Adriatic. Capital, Belgrade. Area, 98,766 sq. mi. Pop. (1966 est.), 19,756,000. —**Yu′go·sla′vi·an,** *adj.*

Yu·go·slav·ic (ū′gō slä′vik, -slav′ik) *also,* **Ju·go·slav·ic.** *adj.* of or relating to Yugoslavia or its people.

Yu·kon (yōo′kon) *n.* **1.** territory in northwestern Canada. Area, 207,076 sq. mi. Pop. (1966), 14,382. **2.** river flowing from this territory through central Alaska into Bering Sea.

Yule (ūl) *n.* **1.** Christmas. **2.** Christmas season. [Old English *geōl* Christmas.]

Yule log, large log burned at Christmas.

Yule·tide (ūl′tīd′) *n.* Christmas time.

Yung·kia (yoong′kyä′) *n.* see Wenchow.

YWCA, Young Women's Christian Association.

YWHA, Young Women's Hebrew Association.

y·wis (i wis′) *also,* **i·wis.** *adv. Archaic.* certainly; indeed.

z, Z (zē) *pl.,* **z's, Z's.** *n.* twenty-sixth and last letter of the English alphabet.

Z, atomic number.

z., zone. Also, **Z.**

Zac·che·us (za kē′əs) *n.* in the New Testament, a tax collector who, because of his short stature, climbed a tree to see Jesus.

Zach·a·ri·ah (zak′ə rī′ə) *n.* **1.** in the New Testament, the father of John the Baptist. **2.** Zechariah.

Za·greb (zä′greb) *n.* city in northwestern Yugoslavia. Pop. (1961), 430,802.

zai·bat·su (zī′bät sōō′) *n.,pl.* the several families that control the industries of Japan. ▲ construed as singular or plural. [Japanese *zaibatsu* plutocracy, from *zai* money, riches + *batsu* clan, family.]

Za·ire (zä ir′) *n.* country in central Africa, formerly known as the **Democratic Republic of the Congo.** Capital, Kinshasa. Area, 905,967 sq. mi. Pop. (1975 est.), 24,500,000.

Zam·be·zi (zam bē′zē) *n.* river in southern Africa flowing eastward through Rhodesia and Mozambique, into the Indian Ocean.

Zam·bi·a (zam′bē ə) *n.* country in south-central Africa, formerly the British protectorate of Northern Rhodesia. Capital, Lusaka. Area, 290,-586 sq. mi. Pop. (1969 est.), 4,054,000.

Zang·will, Israel (zang′wil) 1864–1926, English author.

za·ny (zā′nē) **-ni·er, -ni·est.** *adj.* comically odd or ludicrous. —*n. pl.,* **-nies.** **1.** simpleton; fool. **2.** clown; buffoon. [Italian *zanni* clown, from *Zanni*, dialectal form of *Gianni*, familiar form of *Giovanni* John, from Latin *Jōannēs*, from *zēlos* fervor.] See JOHN.]

Zan·zi·bar (zan′zə bär′) *n.* **1.** large island in the Indian Ocean, off the eastern coast of Africa, part of Tanzania. Area, 640 sq. mi. Pop. (1965 est.), 186,000. **2.** former country consisting of Zanzibar and Pemba, now part of Tanzania.

Za·po·rozh·e (zä′pə rozh′ye) *n.* city in the southwestern Soviet Union, on the Dnieper, in the Ukraine. Pop. (1970 est.), 658,000.

Zar·a·thus·tra (zar′ə thōō′strə) *n.* Zoroaster.

zeal (zēl) *n.* intense desire or devotion; earnest enthusiasm. [Late Latin *zēlus* fervor, jealousy, from Greek *zēlos*.]

Zea·land (zē′lənd) *n.* largest island of Denmark on which Copenhagen is situated. Area, 2709 sq. mi. Pop. (1960), 1,771,557.

zeal·ot (zel′ət) *n.* zealous person, esp. a fanatical partisan. [Late Latin *zēlōtēs*, from Greek *zēlōtēs*, from *zēlos* fervor.] —**Syn.** see **enthusiast.**

zeal·ot·ry (zel′ə trē) *n.* excessive zeal; fanaticism.

zeal·ous (zel′əs) *adj.* filled with, characterized by, or motivated by zeal. —**zeal′ous·ly,** *adv.* —**zeal′-ous·ness,** *n.*

ze·bec (zē′bek) *also,* **ze·beck.** xebec.

Zeb·e·dee (zeb′ə dē′) *n.* in the New Testament, the father of James and John, apostles of Jesus.

ze·bra (zē′brə) *pl.,* **-bras** or **-bra.** *n.* any of several wild horselike mammals, genus *Equus,* native to eastern and southern Africa, having a light-colored coat with black stripes, a short, stiff mane, and a long tail ending in a tuft of hair. Height: to 4½ feet at the shoulder. [Portuguese *zebra,* possibly from a word native to the Congo region.]

Zebra

ze·bu (zē′bū) *n.* Brahma cow or bull. [French *zébu;* of uncertain origin.]

zec·chi·no (ze kē′nō) *pl.,* **-ni** (-nē) or **-nos.** *n.* sequin *(def. 2).*

Zech., Zechariah.

Zech·a·ri·ah (zek′ə rī′ə) *n.* **1.** in the Old Testament, a Hebrew prophet of the sixth century B.C. **2.** book of the Old Testament attributed to him.

zed (zed) *n.* *British.* the letter z. [French *zède,* from Late Latin *zēta,* from Greek *zēta* name of the Greek letter ζ.]

Zed·e·ki·ah (zed′ə kī′ə) *n.* in the Old Testament, the last king of Judah before the Babylonian captivity. He was defeated and blinded by Nebuchadnezzar.

Zeit·geist (tsīt′gīst′) *n.* *German.* characteristic thought or spirit of a period of time; moral and intellectual feeling or tendencies of a time.

Zen (zen) *n.* **1.** Japanese Buddhist sect which differs from other Buddhist sects by stressing enlightenment through intuition and contemplation rather than through the scriptures. **2.** beliefs of this sect. [Japanese *zen* silent meditation, through Chinese, going back to Sanskrit *dhāna*.]

ze·na·na (ze nä′nə) *n.* in Persia and India, the part of the house in which the women of the family are secluded. [Hindi *zenāna,* from Persian *zanāna* belonging to women, from *zan* woman.]

Zend (zend) *n.* the translation and commentary, in a literary form of Persian, of the Zoroastrian Avesta.

Zend-A·ves·ta (zend′ə ves′tə) *n.* the sacred writings of Zoroastrianism collectively, consisting of the original Avesta and its later commentary, the Zend.

ze·nith (zē′nith) *n.* **1.** the point on the celestial sphere directly above the position of the observer. Opposed to **nadir.** **2.** the highest or greatest point: *This performance was the zenith of the musician's career.* [Medieval Latin *cenith* highest point of the sky, going back to Arabic *samt* way, as in *samt ar-rās* way over the head.]

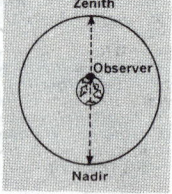

Zenith *(def. 1)*

Ze·no (zē′nō) *n.* c.336–c.262 B.C., Greek philosopher, founder of Stoicism.

Zeph·a·ni·ah (zef′ə nī′ə) *n.* **1.** a Hebrew prophet of the seventh century B.C. **2.** the Old Testament book of prophecies that is attributed to him.

zeph·yr (zef′ər) *n.* **1.** the west wind. **2.** any soft, gentle wind. **3.** any of various lightweight, soft yarns or fabrics. [Latin *zephyrus* west wind, from Greek *zephyros*.]

zep·pe·lin (zep′ə lin) *also,* **Zep·pe·lin.** *n.* large dirigible having a rigid, cigar-shaped body. [From Count Ferdinand von *Zeppelin,* 1838–1917, German airship inventor who designed it.]

ze·ro (zēr′ō) *pl.,* **-ros** or **-roes.** *n.* **1.** number that leaves any number unchanged when it is added to it; number of members in the empty set. **2.** symbol representing this number; 0. **3.** point on a scale, as a thermometer, from which positive or negative measures are reckoned. **4.** temperature corresponding to zero on the scale of a thermometer. **5.** total absence of quantity; nothing: *The business lost no money, but its profit was zero.* **6.** the lowest point; nadir: *The politician's popularity reached zero after the scandal.* **7.** *Slang.* one who or that which is considered to have no value, merit, or the like; failure. —*adj.* **1.** of, relating to, being, or at zero. **2.** none at all; not any. —*v.t.* **-roed, -ro·ing.** **1.** to adjust (something, as an instrument) to an arbitrary point from which positive and negative measures are reckoned. **2. to zero in.** to bring (an aircraft, gun, or the like) into a desired position for aiming and concentrating fire. —*v.i.* **to zero in.** to direct power, attention, or the like toward a specific target or goal: *to zero in on the problems at hand.* [Italian *zero* naught in arithmetic, going back to Arabic *çifr* naught in arithmetic, empty. Doublet of CIPHER.]

zero gravity, condition of a body not subject to any gravitational attraction; weightlessness.

zero hour **1.** designated time, as that set for the beginning of a military operation. **2.** critical turning point.

at; āpe; cär; end; mē; it; īce; hot; ōld; fôrk; wood; fōōl; oil; out; up; ūse; turn; sing; thin; this; zh in treasure; ə in ago, taken, pencil, lemon, circus.

zest (zest) *n.* **1.** keen enjoyment or excitement; relish. **2.** a pleasant or exciting quality, flavor, or the like. —*v.t.* to give a zest to. [Obsolete French *zeste* orange or lemon peel; of uncertain origin.]

zest·ful (zest'fəl) *adj.* characterized by zest. —**zest'ful·ly,** *adv.* —**zest'ful·ness,** *n.*

ze·ta (zā'tə, zē'-) *n.* sixth letter of the Greek alphabet (Z, ζ), corresponding to the English letter Z, z.

Zeus (zōōs) *n. Greek Mythology.* the supreme god, ruler of the heavens and the earth, whose chief weapon was the thunderbolt. His Roman counterpart is Jupiter.

zig·gu·rat (zig'ŏŏ rat') *n.* temple built by the ancient Babylonians, Assyrians, and Sumerians, in the form of a pyramid with a series of receding stages or terraces. [Assyrian *ziqquratu* height, pinnacle.]

zig·zag (zig'zag') *adj.* having or proceeding with a series of short, angular turns in alternating directions. —*adv.* in a zigzag manner. —*n.* **1.** zigzag line, course, or pattern. **2.** one of the short, sharp angles of a zigzag pattern. —*v.t., v.i.,* **-zagged, -zag·ging.** to form or move in a zigzag. [French *zigzag* line having a series of sharp turns in alternating directions, from German *Zickzack*.]

zil·lion (zil'yən) *n. Informal.* very large, indefinite number. [Z + -*illion,* as in MILLION.]

zinc (zingk) *n.* grayish-white metallic element with a blue sheen, used to make alloys, such as brass and bronze, to galvanize iron, and as the anode and casing of dry-cell batteries. Symbol: **Zn** See **element** for table. —*v.t.* **zincked** or **zinced, zinck·ing** or **zinc·ing.** to coat or cover with zinc. [German *Zink* this element.]

zinc blende, sphalerite.

zinc chloride, poisonous, white, crystalline compound, used esp. as a preservative and fireproofing agent for wood and in deodorants. Formula: $ZnCl_2$

zinc ointment, ointment containing zinc oxide in a base of petrolatum, used esp. in treating skin disorders.

zinc oxide, white, powdery compound, used esp. as a pigment in paints and cosmetics and as an antiseptic. Formula: ZnO

zinc sulfide, yellowish-white, fluorescent compound used as a pigment and in the manufacture of television screens and luminous watch dials. Formula: ZnS

zinc white, zinc oxide used as a pigment, or a paint or paste containing this pigment.

zing (zing) *n.* **1.** high-pitched humming or buzzing sound. **2.** *Informal.* vitality; zest; vigor. —*v.i.* to make a high-pitched humming or buzzing sound, esp. in moving rapidly: *A bullet zinged through the air.* [Imitative.]

Zin·jan·thro·pus (zin jan'thrə pəs) *n.* any of a species of hominids thought to have flourished about two million years ago, remains of which were unearthed in Tanzania in 1959. [Modern Latin *Zinjanthropus,* from Arabic *Zīnj* eastern Africa + Greek *anthrōpos* man.]

zin·ni·a (zin'ē ə) *n.* **1.** showy flower head of any of a small group of plants, genus *Zinnia,* of the composite family, growing in all colors except blue and green. **2.** hairy plant bearing this flower head, widely cultivated as a garden plant. [Modern Latin *Zinnia,* from Johann Gottfried *Zinn,* 1727–59, German botanist.]

Zi·on (zī'ən) *also,* **Si·on.** *n.* **1.** hill in Jerusalem on which the royal palace of David and the Temple were built. **2.** the Jewish people or nation; Israel. **3.** the kingdom of heaven. **4.** any place or institution believed to be under God's special protection, such as a national church.

Zi·on·ism (zī'ə niz'əm) *n.* movement to establish a national homeland for Jews in Palestine, resulting in the creation of Israel in 1948 and continuing after that time to support emigration and settlement of Jews in Israel.

Zi·on·ist (zī'ə nist) *n.* one who supports Zionism. —*adj.* of or relating to Zionism or Zionists.

zip (zip) *n.* **1.** sudden, sharp hissing sound, as of a flying bullet. **2.** *Informal.* energy; vitality; vim. —*v.i.* **zipped, zip·ping. 1.** to make or move with a sudden, sharp hissing sound. **2.** *Informal.* to move or act with energy or speed. —*v.t.* to fasten or close with a zipper. [Imitative.]

Zip Code, five-digit number written directly after the address on a letter or other piece of mail, quickly identifying the U.S. postal delivery area to which it is to be sent. [Abbreviation of *z(one) i(mprovement) p(rogram)* + CODE.]

zip·per (zip'ər) *n.* fastener consisting of two rows of interlocking teeth that may be joined or separated by a sliding device, used esp. on clothing and boots.

zip·py (zip'ē) *adj.* **-pi·er, -pi·est.** *Informal.* lively; brisk; energetic.

zir·con (zur'kon) *n.* translucent or transparent silicate of zirconium, used in nuclear reactors and as a semiprecious gem. Formula: $ZrSiO_4$ [German *Zirkon,* from French and Italian *zircone,* from Arabic *zarqūn* cinnabar, from Persian *zargūn* gold-colored, from *zar* gold.]

zir·co·ni·um (zər kō'nē əm) *n.* gray, flammable, scaly or powdery metallic element used in primers for explosives, in nuclear reactor

chambers, and to bond metals to ceramics. It is the ninth most abundant element in the earth's crust. Symbol: **Zr** See **element** for table. [Modern Latin *zirconium,* from ZIRCON; because found in *zircon.*]

zith·er (zith'ər) *n.* musical instrument consisting of a shallow wood sound box over which are stretched thirty to forty-five strings, sounded by plucking the strings with a plectrum and the fingers. [German *Zither,* from Latin *cithara* type of guitar or lute, from Greek *kitharā* type of lyre. Doublet of CITHARA, GUITAR.] —**zith'er·ist,** *n.*

zlo·ty (zlô'tē) *pl.,* **-tys** or **-ty.** *n.* monetary unit of Poland, equal to 100 groszy. [Polish *zloty* literally, golden, from *zloto* gold.]

Zn, zinc.

zo·di·ac (zō'dē ak') *n.* **1.** imaginary belt in the heavens extending approximately 8 degrees on each side of the apparent path of the sun and including the paths of the moon and all the planets except Pluto. The zodiac is divided into twelve parts, called signs, with each part named after a constellation. **2.** figure or diagram representing the zodiac and its signs and symbols, used in astrology. [Latin *zōdiacus* imaginary belt in the heavens containing twelve constellations, from Greek *zōidiakos (kyklos)* literally, (circle) of the figures from *zōidion* figure (of an animal), sign of the zodiac, diminutive of *zōion* animal (with reference to the representation of certain of the twelve constellations of the zodiac by animals).] —**zo·di·a·cal** (zō dī'ə kəl), *adj.*

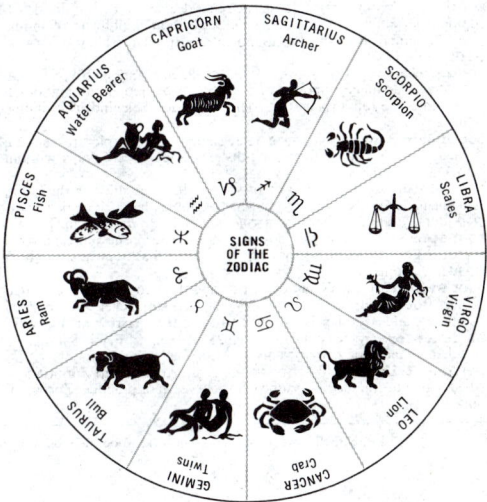

SIGNS OF THE ZODIAC

CAPRICORN Goat / SAGITTARIUS Archer / SCORPIO Scorpion / LIBRA Scales / VIRGO Virgin / LEO Lion / CANCER Crab / GEMINI Twins / TAURUS Bull / ARIES Ram / PISCES Fish / AQUARIUS Water Bearer

Zo·la, É·mile (zō'lə; ā měl') 1840–1902, French novelist and critic.

Zoll·ver·ein (tsôl'fe rīn') *n.* customs union among various states of Germany in the nineteenth century. [German *Zollverein* customs union, from *Zoll* duty, customs, toll[2] + *Verein* union.]

Zom·ba (zom'bə) *n.* capital of Malawi, in the southern part of the country. Pop. (1966), 19,666.

zom·bie (zom'bē) *pl.,* **-bies.** *also,* **zom·bi.** *n.* in voodoo belief, a dead person who has been brought back to life and is completely subject to the will of a sorcerer. [Probably from Bantu *zumbi* fetish.]

zon·al (zōn'əl) *adj.* of, relating to, or marked by a zone or zones.

zone (zōn) *n.* **1.** any of the five climatic regions of the earth, comprising two Frigid Zones, two Temperate Zones, and the Torrid Zone. **2.** any region, area, or section distinguished from surrounding or adjacent areas by some quality, condition, or use. **3.** section of a city regulated by certain restrictions, esp. regarding

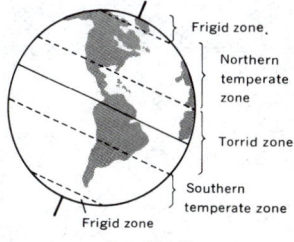

Frigid zone / Northern temperate zone / Torrid zone / Southern temperate zone / Frigid zone

Zone (def. 1)

building: *There were no factories in the residential zone.* **4.a.** in the U.S. postal system, one of a set of circular areas going outward from a mailing point, by which parcel post charges are determined. **b.** local postal district identified by a zip code, usually having a central post office. **5.** belt, band, or stripe having a color or other characteristic distinguishing it from what it encircles. —*v.t.,* **zoned, zon·ing. 1.** to divide into zones. **2.** to be formed into zones. **3.** to surround or encircle with a zone or belt. [Latin *zōna* girdle, belt, one of the imaginary circles that divided the earth into five climates, from Greek *zōnē.*]

zon·ing (zō′ning) *n.* system of districting in cities that regulates by area the construction and use of buildings.

zoo (zōō) *n.* park, garden, or similar place where animals are kept for exhibition. [Short for ZOOLOGICAL GARDEN.]

zoo- *combining form* animal or relating to animals: *zoology, zoogeography.* [Greek *zōion* animal.]

zo·o·ge·og·ra·phy (zō′ə jē og′rə fē) *n.* science dealing with the geographical distribution of animals. —**zo′o·ge·og′ra·pher,** *n.* —**zo′o·ge′o·graph′i·cal;** *also,* **zo′o·ge′o·graph′ic,** *adj.*

zo·o·log·i·cal (zō′ə loj′i kəl) *adj.* **1.** of or relating to zoology. **2.** of or relating to animals. —**zo′o·log′i·cal·ly,** *adv.*

zoological garden, zoo.

zo·ol·o·gist (zō ol′ə jist) *n.* student of or expert in zoology.

zo·ol·o·gy (zō ol′ə jē) *n.* **1.** science that deals with the origin, development, structure, functioning, and classification of all forms of animal life. **2.** animal life, esp. that found in a particular region. [ZOO- + -LOGY.]

zoom (zōōm) *v.i.* **1.** to move or climb suddenly and swiftly, as in an airplane. **2.** to make or move with a low-pitched, loud, humming sound. —*v.t.* to cause (an airplane) to zoom. —*n.* act or sound of zooming. [Imitative.]

zoom lens, single lens on a television or motion-picture camera, which allows a change from long-distance shots to close-ups without moving the camera.

zo·o·phyte (zō′ə fīt′) *n.* any of various invertebrates, as the coral, sea anemone, or sea lily that somewhat resemble plants. [Greek *zōophyton* literally, animal plant, from *zōion* animal + *phyton* plant.]

zo·o·spore (zō′ə spôr′) *n.* any of various waterborne spores, as that produced by certain algae, having cilia or flagella by means of which it swims about.

zoot suit (zōōt) man's suit of an extreme style popular in the United States from about 1935 to 1940, having a long jacket with padded shoulders and wide lapels, and full trousers that narrow at the cuffs.

Zo·ro·as·ter (zôr′ō as′tər) *n.* c.628–551 B.C., Persian religious teacher, founder of Zoroastrianism. Also, **Zar′a·thus′tra.**

Zo·ro·as·tri·an (zôr′ō as′trē ən) *adj.* of or relating to Zoroaster or the religion he founded. —*n.* one who believes in or practices Zoroastrianism.

Zo·ro·as·tri·an·ism (zôr′ō as′trē ə niz′əm) *n.* religious system founded by Zoroaster, which stresses an ethical way of life and the final triumph of good over evil. Also, **Maz′da·ism.**

Zou·ave (zōō äv′, zwäv) *n.* formerly, a member of a body of light infantry of the French army, originally Algerians, later composed of French soldiers. [French *zouave,* from Arabic *Zwāwa* name of a tribe in Algeria from which the first Zouave recruits came.]

zounds (zoundz) *also,* **'swounds.** *interj.* *Archaic.* oath used to express surprise or anger. [Euphemistic contraction of *God's wounds.*]

Zr, zirconium.

zuc·chi·ni (zōō kē′nē) *pl.,* **-ni** or **-nis.** *n.* green, summer squash shaped like a cucumber.

Zui·der Zee (zī′dər zē′) *also,* **Zuy·der Zee.** former inlet of the North Sea, on the northern coast of the Netherlands, now closed off by a dike.

Zu·lu (zōō′lōō) *pl.,* **-lus** or **-lu.** *n.* **1.** member of any of a group of tribes in the Republic of South Africa. **2.** their language, belonging to the Bantu language family.

Zu·ñi (zōō′nyē, -nē) *pl.,* **-ñis** or **-ñi.** *n.* **1.** member of a tribe of North American Indians now living in western New Mexico, who dwell in pueblos. **2.** language of this tribe.

Zu·rich (zoor′ik) *n.* largest city in Switzerland and a principal financial center of Europe, in the northern part of the country. Pop. (1969 est.), 432,400.

zwie·back (swē′bak′, -bäk′, swī′-; zwī′-; *German* tsvē′bäk′) *n.* bread often sweetened and flavored, as with cinnamon, baked and then sliced and toasted until it is crisp and dry. [German *Zwieback* rusk; literally, twice baked, from *zwie-* twice + *backen* to bake.]

Zwing·li, Hul·dreich (zwing′lē, swing′-; *German* tsving′lē; hool′-drīkн) 1484–1531, Swiss Protestant reformer.

Zwing·li·an (zwing′lē ən, swing′-, tsving′-) *adj.* of or relating to Zwingli or his doctrines. —*n.* one who believes in or follows the teachings of Zwingli.

zy·go·spore (zī′gə spôr′, zig′ə-) *n.* spore formed by the sexual union of two gametes, found among certain fungi and algae. [Greek *zygon* yoke + SPORE.]

zy·gote (zī′gōt, zig′ōt) *n.* ovum fertilized by sperm, before the start of embryonic development. [Greek *zygōtos* yoked, from *zygoun* to yoke.]

zy·mase (zī′mās) *n.* enzyme present in yeast, that changes sugar into alcohol and carbon dioxide. [Greek *zȳmē* leaven + -ASE.]

zyme (zīm) *n.* any ferment, virus, or the like formerly thought to cause infectious or contagious diseases. [Greek *zȳme* leaven, ferment.]

zy·mol·o·gy (zī mol′ə jē) *n.* branch of science that deals with fermentation.

zy·mur·gy (zī′mur jē) *n.* branch of chemistry dealing with fermentation, as in brewing and wine making. [Greek *zȳmē* leaven + -*ourgiā* a working (from *ergon* work).]

---

at; āpe; cär; end; mē; it; īce; hot; ōld; fôrk; wood; fōōl; oil; out; up; ūse; turn; sing; thin; this; zh in treasure; ə in ago, taken, pencil, lemon, circus.